A CHRONOLOGY OF AMERICAN MUSICAL THEATER

A CHRONOLOGY OF AMERICAN MUSICAL THEATER

Richard C. Norton

VOLUME 3

OXFORD
UNIVERSITY PRESS
2002

OXFORD
UNIVERSITY PRESS

Oxford New York
Auckland Bangkok Buenos Aires Cape Town Chennai
Dar es Salaam Delhi Hong Kong Istanbul Karachi Kolkata
Kuala Lumpur Madrid Melbourne Mexico City Mumbai Nairobi
São Paulo Shanghai Singapore Taipei Tokyo Toronto
and an associated company in Berlin

Published by Oxford University Press, Inc.
198 Madison Avenue, New York, New York 10016
www.oup.com

Library of Congress Cataloging-in-Publication Data
Norton, Richard C., 1953-
A chronology of American musical theater / Richard C. Norton
Includes indexes
ISBN 0-19-508888-3 (set: cloth : alk. paper) – ISBN 0-19-515565-3 (v. 1: cloth : alk. Paper)
1. Musical theater—New York (State)—New York—Chronology. I. Title.
ML 1711.8.N3 N67 2002
782.1'4'097471—dc21 2001055710

EDITORIAL AND PRODUCTION STAFF

Project Editor: Mark Mones
Production Director: John Sollami
Indexes: Prepared by Magic Fingers
Book Designer: Joan Greenfield
Composition: General Meador, Inc.
Publisher: Karen Day

1 3 5 7 9 8 6 4 2

Printed in the United States of America
on acid-free paper

CONTENTS

A CHRONOLOGY OF
AMERICAN MUSICAL THEATER

VOLUME 1: 1750–1912

VOLUME 2: 1912–1952

VOLUME 3: 1952–2001

INDEXES

Index of Shows
651

Index of Songs
671

Selected Index of Persons
841

A CHRONOLOGY OF AMERICAN MUSICAL THEATER

1952–1953 SEASON

Rosalind Russell and two Brazilian cadets in WONDERFUL TOWN
(Photo: Vandamm Studio)
Billy Rose Theatre Collection, New York Public Library for the Performing Arts

1952–1953 SEASON

1952.10 WISH YOU WERE HERE

A Musical Comedy in Two Acts, 15 Scenes. Book by Arthur Kober and Joshua Logan. Based on Arthur Kober's play "Having Wonderful Time." Music and lyrics by Harold Rome. Direction and dances by Joshua Logan. Settings and lighting by Jo Mielziner. Costumes by Robert Mackintosh. Musical direction, Jay Blackton. Orchestrations by Don Walker. Musical continuity by Trude Rittman. Produced by Leland Hayward and Joshua Logan. Opened 25 June 1952 at the Imperial Theatre and closed 28 November 1953 after 598 performances.

CAST (in order of appearance): *Teddy Stern*: PATRICIA MARAND. *Chick Miller*: JACK CASSIDY. *Fay Fromkin*: SHEILA BOND. *Itchy Flexner*: SIDNEY ARMUS. *Pinky Harris*: PAUL VALENTINE. *Hatty "Muscles" Green*: JOHN PERKINS. *Lou Kandel*: SAMMY SMITH. *Herman Fabricant*: HARRY CLARK. *Marvin*: Fred Sadoff. *Sonja*: Elaine Gordon. *Schmutz*: Larry Blyden. *Eli*: Frank Aletter. *Barney*: Ray Hyson. *Sid*: Robert Dixon. *Lenny*: Richard France. *Sam*: Joe Milan. *Monty*: Tom Ayre. *Henrietta*: Mardi Bayne. *Gussie*: Leila Martin. *Wallflowers (4)*: *Irma*: Roslynd Lowe. *Shirley*: Sybil Lamb. *Lena*: Denise Griffin. *Judy*: Shirley Ann Prior. *Miriam*, who has hay fever: Nancy Franklin. *The New Girl*: Florence Henderson. *The Girl Diver*: Beverly Weston. *The Acrobat*: Steve Wiland. *Eccentric Diver*: Joseph Thomas.

Waiters: *Mel*: Gus Giordano. *Fred*: Stan [Stanley] Grover. *Morrie*: Bill Hogue. *Bill*: Leo Kayeworth. *Butch*: George Lenz. *Joe*: Reid Shelton. *Harry*: Harry Snow. *Phil*: Ray Steele. *Alex*: Tom Tryon. *Mac*: Don Wayne. *Bathing Beauties*: *Billie*: Sue Brin. *Kitty*: Norma Doggett. *Mildred*: Joan Johnston. *Sarah*: Phyllis Newman. *Felice*: Gloria Van Deweel. *Anna*: Jan Stuart. *Wilma*: Rain Winslow. *Athletes, Guests, Staff Members*: Nancy Baker, Joan Berke, Toni Parker, Candi Parsons, Inga Rode, Elliott Feder, Al Lawrence, Don Paterson, Wally Strauss.

The action takes place at Camp Karefree, a summer camp for adults, "where friendships are formed to last a whole lifetime through," located in the heart of Vacationland. It could be the Berkshires, the Adirondacks, the Poconos, the White Mountains—or even the Catskills.

Act 1, Scene 1: Outside Teddy's Cabin. *Scene 2*: Locker Room. *Scene 3*: Porch of the Social Hall. *Scene 4*: Social Hall. *Scene 5*: A Path through the Woods. *Scene 6*: Athletic Field. *Scene 7*: A Path through the Woods. *Scene 8*: Eagle Rock. *Scene 9*: The Boat House. *Scene 10*: The Lake Front.

Act 2, Scene 1: The Campfire. *Scene 2*: A Path through the Woods. *Scene 3*: Pinky's Cabin. *Scene 4*: Porch of the Social Hall. *Scene 5*: Basket Ball Court.

ACT 1

Scene 1

"Camp Karefree"
S. Smith, Waiters, Ensemble

"Goodbye Love"[1]
P. Marand, S. Bond, Girls

"(Ballad of a) Social Director"
S. Armus, Ensemble

"Shopping Around"
S. Bond

Scene 2

"Bright College Days"
Waiters

"Mix and Mingle"
J. Cassidy, Waiters

Scene 3

"Could Be"
P. Marand, Girls

Scene 4

"Tripping the Light Fantastic"
Ensemble

"(Ballad of a) Social Director" (reprise)
S. Armus, Ensemble

Scene 5

"Where Did the Night Go?"
J. Cassidy, P. Marand, Ensemble

Scene 6

"Certain Individuals"
S. Bond, Ensemble

Scene 8

"They Won't Know Me"
J. Cassidy

Scenes 9 and 10

"Summer Afternoon"
P. Valentine, Ensemble

ACT 2

Scene 1

"Where Did the Night Go?" (reprise)
F. Aletter, Ensemble

"Don José (of Far Rockaway)"
S. Armus, Ensemble

"Everybody Love Everybody"
S. Bond, Ensemble

"Wish You Were Here"
J. Cassidy, Waiters

Scene 3

"Relax"
P. Valentine, P. Marand

Scene 4

"Where Did the Night Go?" (Be-Bop Version)
S. Bond, Ensemble

"Flattery"
P. Marand, S. Armus

Scene 5

Finale
Entire Company

[1]During run, replaced with:

"(There's) Nothing Nicer Than People"
P. Marand, S. Bond, Girls

1952.11 AN EVENING WITH BEATRICE LILLIE

A Musical Revue in Two Acts, 13 Scenes. Directed by Edward Duryea Dowling. Settings by Rolf Gerard. At the pianos, Eadie (Griffith) and Rack [Howard Godwin]. Produced by Edward Duryea Dowling. Opened 2 October 1952 at the Booth Theatre and closed 30 May 1953 after 275 performances.

CAST: BEATRICE LILLIE, REGINALD GARDINER, Florence Bray, Xenia Bank, John Philip.

ACT 1[2]

Scene 1

Reginald Gardiner

Scene 2

A Star's First Night (The Girl Friend from WALK A LITTLE FASTER, 1932)
The Star: X. Bank. *The Maid*: F. Bray. *The Star's Friend*: B. Lillie.

[2]During the course of the run and subsequent tour, Beatrice Lillie interpolated other songs and sketches associated with her career including:

"Kiss Me Again" (from MLLE. MODISTE, 1906)
(*Music by* Victor Herbert. *Lyrics by* Henry Blossom.)

Scene 3
One in Three
R. Gardiner
Scene 4
Wind
B. Lillie
Scene 5
Trains (from AT HOME ABROAD, 1935)
R. Gardiner
Scene 6
Father and Son
Father: R. Gardiner. *Son*: B. Lillie.
Scene 7
Anesthesia
R. Gardiner
Scene 8
References (from THE NINE O'CLOCK REVUE, London, 1922; THE CHARLOT REVUE OF 1926, New York, 1925)
Sybil: B. Lillie. *Mrs. Mason*: F. Bray. *Mrs. Barrowdale*: X. Bank.
Scene 9
The Conductor
R. Gardiner

ACT 2

Scene 1
Eadie and Rack at the Pianos
Scene 2
Reginald Gardiner
Scene 3
Beatrice Lillie, accompanied by Rack.
Singer: J. Phillip.
"Come into the Garden, Maud"
J. Phillip
"Rhythm" (from PLEASE!, London, 1933; THE SHOW IS ON, 1936; HAPPY RETURNS, London, 1938)
(*Music by* Richard Rodgers. *Lyrics by* Lorenz Hart.)
"Paree" (from AT HOME ABROAD, 1935; HAPPY RETURNS, London, 1938; BETTER LATE, London, 1946)
(*Music by* Arthur Schwartz. *Lyrics by* Howard Dietz.)
"I've Been to a Marvelous Party" (from SET TO MUSIC, 1939)
(*Music and Lyrics by* Nöel Coward.)
"Nanette" (from THE BANDWAGON)
(*Music by* Arthur Schwartz. *Lyrics by* Howard Dietz.)
"The Lesson With the Fan"
(*Music by* Guy d'Hardelot. *Lyrics by* Frederick E. Weatherly.)
"Please Be Kind"
(*Music by* Saul Chaplin. *Lyrics by* Sammy Cahn.)
"Maud"
(*Music by* Muriel Lillie. *Lyrics by* Nicholas Phipps.)
"Not Wanted on the Voyage"
(*Music by* Beatrice Lillie. *Lyrics by* Nicholas Phipps.)
"Wind 'Round My Heart" (from BIG TOP, London, 1942)
(*Music by* Harry Parr-Davies. *Lyrics by* Barbara Gordon and Basil Thomas.)
"Zither Song"
(*Music by* Beatrice Lillie. *Lyrics by* Bud McCreery.)
"I'm So Weary of It All" (from SET TO MUSIC, 1939; ALL CLEAR, London, 1939)
(*Music and Lyrics by* Noël Coward.)
World War I Medley:
"I Want to Go Back to Michigan" (interpolation, 5064 GERRARD, London, 1915)
(*Music and Lyrics by* Irving Berlin.)
"Lazy"
(*Music and Lyrics by* Irving Berlin.)
"Susannah's Squeaking Shoes" (from THE NINE O'CLOCK REVUE, London, 1922; THE CHARLOT REVUE OF 1926, New York)
(*Music by* Muriel Lillie. *Lyrics by* Arthur Weigall.)
"There Are Fairies at the Bottom of Our Garden" (interpolation, THE THIRD LITTLE SHOW, 1931)
(*Music by* Liza Lehmann. *Lyrics by* Rose Fyleman.)
"The Party's Over Now" (from WORDS AND MUSIC, London, 1932)
(*Music and Lyrics by* Noël Coward.)
Scene 4
Finale
"Rocked in the Cradle of the Deep"
(*Music and Lyrics by* John Philip Knight, Emma Willard.)
"Take My Heart (and Do With It What You Please)"
(*Music by* Fred Ahlert. *Lyrics by* Joe Young.)
"I Got Rhythm" (from GIRL CRAZY, 1930)
(*Music by* George Gershwin. *Lyrics by* Ira Gershwin.)
"Sonny Boy" (from THE SINGING FOOL, film)
(*Music and Lyrics by* Al Jolson, Buddy G. DeSylva, Lew Brown, Ray Henderson.)
"Blue Skies" (from BETSY, 1926; THE JAZZ SINGER, film)
(*Music and Lyrics by* Irving Berlin.)
"On Your Toes" (from ON YOUR TOES, 1936)
(*Music by* Richard Rodgers. *Lyrics by* Lorenz Hart.)
"Rose of Washington Square" (from ZIEGFELD MIDNIGHT FROLIC, 1920)
(*Music by* James Hanley. *Lyrics by* Ballard MacDonald.)
"The Star Spangled Banner" (traditional)
(Bea Lillie version from THE SHOW IS ON, 1936; DOCTOR RHYTHM, film)
"Spinning Song"
(*Music and Lyrics by* Noël Coward.)
"The Irish Song" (Rosie O'Grady)
(*Music and Lyrics by* Noël Coward.)
"A Bar on the Piccola Marina"
(*Music and Lyrics by* Noël Coward.)
"There Are Times" (from A TO Z, London, 1921)
(*Music and Lyrics by* Ivor Novello.)
"Paint"
(*Music by* Norman Hackforth. *Lyrics by* Nicholas Phipps.)
"I Apologize" (Burlesque version introduced in WALK A LITTLE FASTER, 1932; PLEASE!, London, 1933)
(*Music and Lyrics by* Al Hoffman, Al Goodhart, Ed Nelson.)
"Three Little Fishies"
(*Music and Lyrics by* Saxie Dowell.)
"Where the Black-Eyed Susans Grow" (from ROBINSON CRUSOE, 1916; CHEEP, London, 1917)
(*Music by* Richard A. Whiting. *Lyrics by* Dave Radford.)
"He Was a Gentleman"
(*Music by* Jay Gorney. *Lyrics by* E. Y. Harburg.)
The Fan
(*by* Fletcher)

1952.12

THE CONSUL

A Revival of the Opera (Musical Drama) in Three Acts, 6 Scenes[3]. Libretto and music by Gian-Carlo Menotti. Conductor, Thomas Schippers. Settings and costumes by Horace Armistead. Lighting by Jean Rosenthal. Assistant to Mr. Menotti, Bill Butler. Choreography by John Butler. Staged by

[3]Originally produced in New York 15 March 1950 at the Ethel Barrymore Theatre for 269 performances. For Synopsis of Scenes, see original 1950 production. No individual musical numbers given.

Gian-Carlo Menotti. Produced by the New York City Opera Company (Joseph Rosenstock, General director). Opened 8 October 1952 at the New York City Center and closed 29 October 1952 after 3 performances in repertory.

CAST: (in order of appearance): *John Sorel*: RICHARD TORIGI. *Magda Sorel*: PATRICIA NEWAY. *The Mother*: MARY KRESTE. *Secret Police Agent*: EMILE RENAN. *First Plainclothesman*: Charles Kuestner. *Second Plainclothesman*: Thomas Powell. *The Secretary*: GLORIA LANE. *Mr. Kofner*: JON GEYANS [George Gaynes]. *The Foreign Woman*: MARIA MARLO. *Anna Gomez*: Vilma Georgiou. *Vera Boronel*: Edith Evans. *Nika Magadoff*, The Magician: NORMAN KELLEY. *Assan*: Arthur Newman. *Voice on the Record*: Mabel Mercer.

1952.13 BUTTRIO SQUARE

A Musical Play in Two Acts, 6 Scenes. Book by Billy Gilbert and Gen Genovese. Music by Arthur Jones and Fred Stamer. Lyrics by Gen Genovese. Based on a play by Hal Cranton from an original story by Gen Genovese. Settings and lighting by Samuel Leve. Costumes supervised by Sal Anthony. Choral arrangements and direction by Maurice Levine. Dance music composed and arranged by Roger Adams. Orchestrations by Don Walker. Musical director, Maurice Levine. Entire production choreographed and directed by Eugene Loring. Produced by Gen Genovese and Edward Woods. Opened 14 October 1952 at the Century Theatre and closed 18 October 1952 after 7 performances.

CAST (in order of appearance): *Michelino*: David Kurlan. *Padre*: Vincent Barbi. *Angela*: Rina Falcone. *Maria*: Joan Morton. *Elizabetta*: Ann Needham. *Dominic*: Lionel Ames. *Baron D'Alessandro*: Ernest Sarracino. *Rocco*: Ferdinand Hilt. *Vittorio*: James MacCracken. *Cassio*: Orville Sherman. *Pietro*: Ted Thurston. *Emelia*: Jane Harven. *Francesca*: Marie Gibson. *Pappa Mario*: BILLY GILBERT. *Norina*: Charlotte Jones. *Carlo*: Henry Hamilton. *Sgt. McKenzie*: Walter Black. *Capt. Steve Dickson*: LAWRENCE BROOKS. *Pvt. Poole*: James Tarbutton. *Tabulator*: Leon Daniels. *Marisa D'Alessandro*: LOIS HUNT. *Pvt. Burns*: Joe Mantell. *Corporal. Gower*: Al Checco. *Pvt. Whitfield*: George Reeder. *Pvt. Webster*: Don [Donald] Driver. *Terry Patterson*: SUSAN JOHNSON. *Joan Wellington*: Marti Stevens.

Dancing Group: Estelle Aza, Bettina Dearborn, Marcella Dodge, Vera Lee, Zoya Leporsky, Joan Morton, Ann Needham, Ann Olchoff, Sandra Zell, Alvin Bean, James Capp, Don Driver, George Foster, Loren Hightower, Rudy Mattise, Greg O'Brien, George Reeder, Lewis Schaw. *Singing Group*: Sara Bettis, Joyce Carol, Ann DeBella, Rina Falcone, Marie Gibson, Iona Noble, Noella Pelloquin, Jan Scott, Joannne Spiller, Lionel Ames, Vincent Barbi, Robert Gilson, Henry Hamilton, Gene Holman, Mike King, Henry Lawrence, James MacCracken, Ted Thurston, Joseph Tocci. *Children*: Barbara Karen, Babs Wood, Darryl Richards.

The action takes place in a small village in Northeast Italy. The time is the spring and fall, 1946.

Act 1, Scene 1: Road to the Village. Morning. *Scene 2*: Buttrio Square.

Act 2, Scene 1: G.I. Barracks. Several months later. *Scene 2*: Buttrio Square. *Scene 3*: Mario's Bakeshop. *Scene 4*: Buttrio Square.

ACT 1

Opening
D. Kurlan, V. Barbi, E. Sarracino, F. Hilt, Village Dancers, Singers

"Every Day Is a Holiday"
L. Brooks, Villagers

"Let's Make It Forever"
L. Brooks, L. Hunt

"I'll Tell the World"
L. Hunt

"No Place Like This Country"
L. Brooks, GIs

"Take It Away"
GIs, Village Girls
(*Music by* Roger Adams.)

"Get Me Out"
S. Johnson

"I'm Gonna Be a Pop"
B. Gilbert, Villagers

"One Is a Lonely Number"
L. Brooks, Village Dancers

"One Is a Lonely Number" (reprise)
L. Hunt

"Tarantula"
Villagers

ACT 2

"Get Me Out" (reprise)
S. Johnson

"Love Swept Like a Storm"
J. MacCracken, Village Singers, Dancers

"Fraternization Ballet"
A. Checco, V. Barbi, Villagers

"I Keep Telling Myself"
S. Johnson

"More and More"
L. Brooks, L. Hunt

"You're Mine, All Mine"
S. Johnson, O. Sherman

Finale
Entire Company

1952.14 THE MIKADO, or The Town of Titipu

A Revival of the Comic Opera in Two Acts[4]. Libretto by William S. Gilbert. Music by Arthur Sullivan. Staged by S. M. Chartok. Musical director, Lehman Engel. Settings by Ralph Alswang. Costumes by Peggy Morrison. Assistant conductor, Eugene Kusmiak. Production consultant, Martyn Green. Produced by S. M. Chartok. Opened 20 October 1952 at the Mark Hellinger Theatre and closed 25 October 1952 after 8 performances.

CAST: *Nanki-Poo*: ROBERT ROUNSEVILLE. *Noble Lords (2)*: *Go-To*: Radley Flynn. *Pish-Tush*: FRANK ROGIER. *Pooh-Bah*: ROBERT ECKLES. *Ko-Ko*: MARTYN GREEN. *Three Sisters, Wards of Ko-Ko*: *Yum-Yum*: LILLIAN MURPHY. *Pitti-Sing*: MARY ROCHE. *Peep-Bo*: DOROTHY MacNEIL. *Katisha*: ELLA HALMAN. *The Mikado of Japan*: JOSEPH MACAULAY.

School Girls, Nobles, Guards: Mary Louise Beatie, Dolores DePuglia, Helen Dodge, Grace Lang, Stella Matthews, Eileen Moran, Shirley Pringle, Rita Schoen, Catherine Currie, Bonnie Grevatt, Glynn Hill, Jan Newby, Athena Pappas, Gloria Sacks, Jeanne Schlegel, Helen Whitfield, Don Kaplan, Don LaMon, Ray Morrissey, Feodore Tedick, Vincent Henry, Anthony Cerami, Michael Rich, Ken Smith, John Dorrin, Herbert Estrow, Radley Flynn, Roger Franklin, Irl Mowery, Bill Nuss, Stanley Propper, Chase Willard.

1952.15 MY DARLIN' AIDA

A Musical Play in Two Acts, 10 Scenes. Libretto by Charles Friedman, adapted from Giuseppe Verdi's opera 'Aida' (and its libretto by Antonio Ghislanzoni from a scenario by Auguste Mariette). Music by Giuseppe Verdi. Directed by Charles Friedman. Supervised and lighted by Hassard Short. Designed and costumed by Lemuel Ayers. Choreography by Hanya Holm. Musical director, Franz Allers. Choral director, Robert Shaw. New orchestral arrangements by Hans Spialek. Production associate, Shirley Bernstein. Associate producer, Paul Vroom. Produced by Robert L. Joseph. Opened 27 October 1952 at the Winter Garden and closed 10 January 1953 after 89 performances.

CAST (in order of appearance): *Rumford*: WILLIAM WALDERMAN. *Mayor Brad Sourby*: STANLEY CARLSON. *Aida*: ELAINE MALBIN (evenings), EILEEN SCHAULER (matinees). *Raymond Demarest*: WILLIAM OLVIS or HOWARD JARRATT. *Jason*: ALONZO BOSAN. *Morning Star*: Ida Johnson. *Zeporah*: Lavinia Williams. *Lolly*: OLIVE MOOREFIELD. *Wheat*: George Fisher. *Frog*: John Fleming. *Liz*: Fredye Marshall. *Rebecca*: Billie Allen. *Lucy*: Joyce Sellinger. *Yancey Hoyt*: William Sutherland. *Jessica Farrow*: DOROTHY SARNOFF (evenings), BETTE DUBRO (matinees). *General Farrow*: KENNETH SCHON. *Choir Soloist*: Theresa Green. *Sis*: Ruth Ann Fleming. *Dolly*: Ruth McVayne. *Bonnie*: Sue Dorris. *Maggie*: Muriel Birckhead. *Aggie*: Martha Flynn. *Laurie*: Lola Fisher. *Mary*: Ruth Schumacher. *Nellie*: Mary Ann Tomlinson. *Bettie*: Jane Copeland. *Onnie*: Carol Jones. *Maids*: Billie

[4]First presented in New York 20 July, 10-29 August 1885 at the Union Square and People's Theatres for 22 performances. First authorized production presented 19 August 1885 at the Fifth Avenue Theatre by Richard D'Oyly Carte for 250 performances. For Synopsis of Scenes and Musical Numbers, see 19 August 1885 D'Oyly Carte production.

Allen, Jacqueline Hairston, Lavinia Williams. *Magician*: Gordon Hamilton. *Mrs. Sourby*: Jo Anne Taylor. *Howie*: Walter Kelvin. *Bull*: Edward Wellman. *Steve*: Robert Busch. *Hutch*: Thornton Marker. *Adam Brown*: WILLIAM DILLARD. *Flower*: Jacqueline Hairston. *Rebecca*: Billie Allen. *Susie*: Gloria Davy. *Lilly*: Charlotte Holloman. *Liz*: Fredye Marshall. *Morning Star*: Ida Johnson. *Zeporah*: Lavinia Williams. *Pork*: Ned Wright. *Handy*: Calvin Dash. *Wheat*: George Fisher. *Major Stanhope*: William Sutherland. *Children*: Paula Anderson, Gail Culberson, Sharyn Kenney.

Singers: Muriel Birckhead, Dorothy Candee, Jane Copeland, Gloria Davy, Sue Dorris, Lola Fisher, Ruth Anne Fleming, Martha Flynn, Theresa Green, Charlotte Holloman, Ida Johnson, Carol Jones, Fredye Marshall, Ruth McVayne, Joyce Sellinger, Ruth Schumacher, Jo Anne Taylor, Mary Ann Tomlinson, Robert Baird, Gino Baldi, Robert Busch, Benjamin Cassidy, Jack Dabdoub, Calvin Dash, George Fisher, John Fleming, Arthur Hammond, Walter Kelvin, Thornton Marker, William Noble, Michael O'Carolan, Charles O'Neill, Robert Price, Michael Roberts, William Sutherland, Edgar Thompson, Casper Vecchione, Robert Watts, Edward Wellman, Ned Wright, Robert Yeager. *Dancers*: Billie Allen, Betty Buday, Nanci Darken, Bettye Griffin, Dody Goodman, Jacqueline Hairston, Erona Harris, Joan Kruger, Carmelita Lanza, Lavinia Williams, Doris Wright, Paul Gannon, Gordon Hamilton, Eddie Heim, Ed Holleman, Louis Johnson, Joe Nash, Walter Nicks, Paul Olson, Frank Seabolt, Claude Thompson.

The action of the play extends over the first year of the Civil War, on or about General Farrow's plantation, near Memphis, Tennessee.

Act 1, Scene 1: The Terrace of the Big House, May 7, 1861, evening. *Scene 2*: The Giant Oak, immediately afterwards. *Scene 3*: The Cemetery by the Negro Church, the following night. *Scene 4*: Jessica's Boudoir in the Big House, three months later. *Scene 5*: The Square at the Boat Landing, immediately afterwards.

Act 2, Scene 1: The Terrace of the Big House. Three weeks later, night. *Scene 2*: The Path to the Quarter, immediately afterwards. *Scene 3*: The Quarter, immediately afterwards. *Scene 4*: The Hallway in the Big House, toward dawn. *Scene 5*: The Negro Church and the Cemetary, immediately afterwards.

ACT 1

Scene 1

Prelude and Opening

"My Darlin' Aida"
W. Olvis

"Love Is Trouble"
D. Sarnoff, W. Olvis

"Love Is Trouble" (reprise)
E. Malbin, D. Sarnoff, W. Olvis

"Me and Lee"
K. Schon, W. Wilderman, W. Olvis, E. Malbin, D. Sarnoff, Company

Scene 2

"Me and Lee" (reprise)
The Men

"March on for Tennessee"
E. Malbin

Scene 3

"Why We Ain't Free"
T. Green, Women's Choir

"Knights of the White Cross"
W. Wilderman, W. Olvis, the Knights

Scene 4

"A Jamboree"
D. Sarnoff, Girls

Dance
The Maids

"Letter Duet"
E. Malbin, D. Sarnoff

"Me and Lee" (reprise)
The Men

Scene 5

"Homecoming"
Company

"When You Grow Up"
Women, Children

"Soldiers' March"
Men

Ballet
Dancers

"King Called Cotton"
Company

"Gotta Live Free"
W. Dillard

"Master and Slave"—Sextette
W. Dillard, E. Malbin, W. Olvis, D. Sarnoff, W. Wilderman, K. Schon, Company

"Sing! South! Sing!"
Company

ACT 2

Scene 1

Spiritual
The Choir

"I Want to Pray"
D. Sarnoff

"Alone"
E. Malbin

"Three Stones to Stand On"
E. Malbin, W. Dillard

"You're False"
E. Malbin, W. Dillard

"There'll Have To Be Changes Made"
E. Malbin, W. Olvis

"Away"
E. Malbin, W. Olvis

"Land of Mine"
E. Malbin, W. Olvis, W. Dillard

Scene 3

Ballet
Dancers, Singers

Scene 4

"I Don't Want You"
D. Sarnoff, W. Olvis

Scene 5

"The Trial"
D. Sarnoff, W. Wilderman, the Knights

"You Are My Darlin' Bride"
W. Olvis

"Oh, Sky, Goodbye"
E. Malbin

"Why Ain't We Free"
E. Malbin, W. Olvis, D. Sarnoff, the Choir

THE PIRATES OF PENZANCE, or The Slave of Duty

1952.16

A Revival of the Comic Opera in Two Acts[5]. Libretto by William S. Gilbert. Music by Arthur Sullivan. Staged by S. M. Chartok. Musical director, Lehman Engel. Settings by Ralph Alswang. Costumes by Peggy Morrison. Assistant conductor, Eugene Kusmiak. Production consultant, Martyn Green. Produced by S. M. Chartok. Opened 27 October 1952 at the Mark Hellinger Theatre and closed 1 November 1952 after 8 performances.

CAST: *Samuel*: FRANK ROGIER. *Frederick*: ROBERT ROUNSEVILLE. *Ruth*: ELLA HALMAN. *Richard*: JOSEPH MACAULAY. *General Stanley's Daughters (4)*: *Kate*: MARY ROCHE. *Edith*: LILLIAN MURPHY. *Mabel*: SHIRLEY PRINGLE. *Isabel*: Shirley Pringle. *Major-General Stanley*: MARTYN GREEN. *Edward*: Robert Eckles.

General Stanley's Wards: Mary Louise Beatie, Dolores DePuglia, Helen Dodge, Grace Lang, Stella Matthews, Eileen Moran, Shirley Pringle, Rita Schoen, Catherine Currie, Bonnie Grevatt, Glynn Hill, Jan Newby, Athena Pappas, Gloria Sacks, Jeanne Schlegel, Helen Whitfield. *Pirates and Policemen*: Anthony Cerami, Vincent Henry, Don Kaplan, Don La Mon, Ray Morrissey, Michael Rich, Ken Smith, Feodore Tedick, John Dorrin, Herbert Estrow, Radley Flynn, Roger Franklin, Irl Mowery, Bill Nuss, Stanley Propper, Chase Willard.

---

[5]First presented in New York 31 December 1879 at the Fifth Avenue Theatre for a total of 91 performances in two engagements. For Synopsis of Scenes and Musical Numbers, see original 1879 production.

1952.17 TRIAL BY JURY

A Revival of the Comic Opera in One Act[6]. Libretto by William S. Gilbert. Music by Arthur Sullivan. Staged by S. M. Chartok. Musical director, Lehman Engel. Settings by Ralph Alswang. Costumes by Peggy Morrison. Assistant conductor, Eugene Kusmiak. Production consultant, Martyn Green. Produced by S. M. Chartok. Opened 3 November 1952 at the Mark Hellinger Theatre and closed 8 November 1952 after 8 performances.

CAST: *Foreman of the Jury*: ROBERT ECKLES. *Associate*: Robert Franklin. *Usher*: RADLEY FLYNN. *Defendant*: EARL WILLIAM. *The Learned Judge*: MARTYN GREEN. *Counsel for the Plaintiff*: FRANK ROGIER. *The Plaintiff*: AUDREY DEARDEN.

Bridesmaids: Mary Louise Beatie, Helen Dodge, Bonnie Grevatt, Glynn Hill, Grace Lang, Sheila Mathews, Eileen Moran, Shirley Pringle. *Spectators*: Catherine Currie, Dolores de Puglia, Jan Newby, Athena Pappas, Gloria Sacks, Jeanne Schlegel, Rita Schoen, Helen Whitfield, Stanley Propper, Michael Rich, Anthony Cerami. *Jurymen*: Don Kaplan, Don LaMon, Ray Morrissey, Feodore Tedick, Vincent Henry, Ken Smith, John Dorrin, Herbert Estrow, Roger Franklin, Irl Mowery, Bill Nuss, Chase Willard.

1952.18 H.M.S. PINAFORE, or The Lass That Loved a Sailor

A Revival of the Comic Opera in Two Acts[7]. Libretto by William S. Gilbert. Music by Arthur Sullivan. Staged by S. M. Chartok. Musical director, Lehman Engel. Settings by Ralph Alswang. Costumes by Peggy Morrison. Assistant conductor, Eugene Kusmiak. Production consultant, Martyn Green. Produced by S. M. Chartok. Opened 3 November 1952 at the Mark Hellinger Theatre and closed 8 November 1952 after 8 performances.

CAST: *Tommy Tucker*: Bonnie Grevatt. *Bill Bobstay*, Boatswain: Robert Eckles. *Bob Beckett*: Radley Flynn. *Little Buttercup*, Mrs. Cripps, a Portsmouth bum-boat woman: ELLA HALMAN. *Dick Deadeye*, Able Seaman: JOSEPH MACAULAY. *Ralph Rackstraw*, Able Seaman: ROBERT ROUNSEVILLE. *Captain Corcoran*, Commander of the *H.M.S. Pinafore*: FRANK ROGIER. *Josephine*, the Captain's Daughter: LILLIAN MURPHY. *The Rt. Hon. Sir Joseph Porter, K.C.B.*, First Lord of the Admiralty: MARTYN GREEN. *Hebe*: Sir Joseph's First Cousin: Mary Roche.

First Lord's Sisters, His Cousins, His Aunts: Mary Lousie Beatie, Dolores de Puglia, Helen Dodge, Grace Lang, Sheila Mathews, Eileen Moran, Shirley Pringle, Rita Schoen, Glynn Hill, Catherine Currie, Jan Newby, Athena Pappas, Gloria Sacks, Jeanne Schlegel, Helen Whitfield. *Sailors*: Don Kaplan, Don LaMon, Ray Morrissey, Feodore Tedick, Vincent Henry, Anthony Cerami, Michael Rich, Ken Smith, John Dorrin, Herbert Estrow, Roger Franklin, Irl Mowery, Bill Nuss, Stanley Propper, Chase Willard. *Marines*: Edward Marshall, William Briggs, James Maroney, Lynn Allen.

1952.19 IOLANTHE, or The Peer and the Peri

A Revival of the Comic Opera in Two Acts[8]. Libretto by William S. Gilbert. Music by Arthur Sullivan. Staged by S. M. Chartok. Musical director, Lehman Engel. Settings by Ralph Alswang. Costumes by Peggy Morrison. Assistant conductor, Eugene Kusmiak. Production consultant, Martyn Green. Produced by S. M. Chartok. Opened 10 November 1952 at the Mark Hellinger Theatre and closed 15 November 1952 after 8 performances.

CAST: *Leila*: Mary Roche. *Celia*: Audrey Dearden. *Fleta*: Eileen Moran. *The Fairy Queen*: ELLA HALMAN. *Iolanthe*: GLYNN HILL. *Strephon*: FRANK ROGIER. *Phyllis*: LILLIAN MURPHY. *Lord Chancellor*: MARTYN GREEN. *Earl of Tolloller*: EARL WILLIAM. *Earl of Mountararat*: JOSEPH MACAULAY. *Private Willis*: ROBERT ECKLES.

Fairies: Mary Louise Beatie, Dolores DePuglia, Helen Dodge, Grace Lang, Sheila Matthews, Shirley Pringle, Rita Schoen, Catherine Currie, Bonnie Grevatt, Glynn Hill, Jan Newby, Athena Pappas, Gloria Sacks, Jeanne Schlegel, Helen Whitfield. *Peers*: Anthony Cerami, Vincent Henry, Don LaMon, Ray Morrissey, Michael Rich, Ken Smith, Feodore Tedick, John Dorrin, Herbert Estrow, Radley Flynn, Roger Franklin, Irl Mowery, Bill Nuss, Stanley Propper, Chase Willard, Robert Driscoll.

1952.20 TWO'S COMPANY

A Musical Revue in Two Acts, 19 Scenes. Sketches by Charles Sherman, Peter DeVries, (Arnold B. Horwitt, Lee Rogow, Nat Hiken, Billy Friedberg, Mort Green, George Foster, Oliver Wakefield). Music by Vernon Duke, (Sheldon Harnick). Lyrics by Ogden Nash, (Sammy Cahn, Sheldon Harnick). Sketches directed by Jules Dassin. Additional lyrics by Sammy Cahn, (Sheldon Harnick). Musical supervisor and conductor, Milton Rosenstock. Scenery and lighting by Ralph Alswang. Costumes by Miles White. Ballet music by Genevieve Pitot and David Baker. Vocal arrangements by Milton Rosenstock. Associate producer, Clifford Hayman. Dances and musical numbers staged by Jerome Robbins. Entire production under the supervision of John Murray Anderson. Produced by James Russo and Michael Ellis. Opened 15 December 1952 at the Alvin Theatre and closed 8 March 1953 after 90 performances.

CAST: BETTE DAVIS, HIRAM SHERMAN, DAVID BURNS, BILL CALLAHAN, NORA KAYE, STANLEY PRAGER, ELLEN HANLEY, GEORGE S. IRVING, MARIA KARNILOVA, BUZZ MILLER, OLIVER WAKEFIELD, PETER KELLEY.

Singers: Art Carroll, Clifford Fearl, Bill Krach, Robert Neukum, Franklin Neil, Leonore Korman, Tina Louise, May Muth, Basha Regis, Deborah Remsen, (Sue Hight), Teddy Tavenner, Doris Wolin. *Dancers*: William Inglis, John Kelly, Ralph Linn, Job Sanders, Stanley Simmons, Florence Baum, Jeanna Belkin, Eleanor Boleyn, Barbara Heath, Dorothy Hill, Julie Marlowe, Helen Murielle. *ROBERT ORTON'S TEEN ACES*: Robert Orton, Francis Edwards, Henry Mallory, Gilbert Shipley, Armstead Shobey, Norman Shobey.

ACT 1[9]

Scene 1

Opening—"Theatre Is a Lady"
B. Callahan, Boys, Girls
(*Music by* Vernon Duke. *Lyrics by* Ogden Nash. *Orchestrated by* Don Walker.) *Introduced by* H. Sherman.

Scene 2

"Turn Me Loose on Broadway"
B. Davis, B. Miller, R. Pagent, J. Sanders, S. Simmons
(*Music by* Vernon Duke. *Lyrics by* Ogden Nash. *Orchestrated by* Clare Grundman.)

Scene 3

And a Little Child
(*by* Arnold B. Horwitt and Lee Rogow)
Producer: G. S. Irving. *Secretary*: T. Louise. *Dudley Dawson*: D. Burns. *Rollo*: M. Mann. *Butler*: F. Neil. *Mrs. Wilkins*: M. Muth.

Scene 4

"It Just Occurred to Me"
P. Kelley, D. Remsen, Singing Ensemble
(*Music by* Vernon Duke. *Lyrics by* Sammy Cahn. *Orchestrated by* Clare Grundman.)
Danced by F. Baum, B. Heath, H. Murielle, R. Linn, R. Pagent, J. Sanders.

Scene 5

Jealousy
(*by* Nat Hiken and Billy Friedberg)
Helen: B. Davis. *Stanley*: D. Burns.

Scene 6

"Baby Couldn't Dance"
(*Music by* Vernon Duke. *Lyrics by* Ogden Nash. *Orchestrated by* Clare Grundman.)
Girl: N. Kaye. *Boy*: B. Callahan. *Professor*: S. Simmons. *Pupils*: B. Heath, F. Baum.

Scene 7

"A Man's Home"
H. Sherman

---

[6]First presented in New York 15 November 1875 at the Eagle Theatre for 8 performances. For Synopsis of Scenes and Musical Numbers, see original 1875 production.

[7]First produced in New York 15 January 1879 at the Standard Theatre for 175 performances. For Synopsis of Scenes and Musical Numbers, see original 1879 production.

[8]First presented in New York 25 November 1882 at the Standard Theatre for 105 performances. For Synopsis of Scenes and Musical Numbers, see original 1882 production.

[9]Act 1 running order revised after the opening; Hiram Sherman was given a featured specialty in Act 2, following "Esther."

(*Music and Lyrics by* Sheldon Harnick.
Orchestrated by Don Walker.)

Scene 8

One's a Crowd

(*by* Mort Green and George Foster)

That One: B. Davis. *Reggie*: H. Sherman. *J.C.*: G. S. Irving. *Harassed Gentleman*: S. Prager. *Audience*: T. Tavenner, E. Renard, T. Louise, B. Regis, C. Fearl, D. Hill, M. Muth, E. Boleyn, D. Hill, S. Hight, R. Neukum.

Scene 9

"Roundabout"

E. Hanley
(*Music by* Vernon Duke. *Lyrics by* Ogden Nash.
Scenario by Horton Foote and Jerome Robbins. *Orchestrated by* Don Walker.)

Danced by N. Kaye, R. Linn, R. Pagent, W. Inglis, E. Boleyn, B. Heath, Dancing Ensemble.

Scene 10

The Voice of Inexperience

(*by* Oliver Wakefield)
O. Wakefield

Scene 11

"Roll Along, Sadie"

B. Davis, H. Sherman, B. Miller, R. Linn, Company
(*Music by* Vernon Duke. *Lyrics by* Ogden Nash. *Orchestrated by* Phil Lang.)

ACT 2

Scene 1

"(It Came Out of the) Clear Blue Sky"

P. Kelley, S. Hight, Singers
(*Music by* Vernon Duke. *Lyrics by* Ogden Nash. *Orchestrated by* Don Walker.)

Danced by M. Karnilova, R. Pagent, Dancers.

Scene 2

Street Scenes

(*by* Charles Sherman with Peter DeVries)
B. Davis, H. Sherman

Scene 3

"Esther"

(D. Burns)
(*Music by* Vernon Duke. *Lyrics by* Sammy Cahn. *Orchestrated by* Don Walker.)

Melvin: D. Burns. *Esther*: M. Karnilova. *Native*: B. Miller.

Scene 4

When in Rome

(*by* Arnold B. Horwitt and Lee Rogow)

Strombolini: D. Burns. *Nina*: H. Murielle. *Thomaso*: S. Prager. *Porter*: E. Renard. *Jezebela*: B. Davis. *Musician*: G. S. Irving.

Scene 5

"Haunted Hot Spot"

E. Hanley
(*Music by* Vernon Duke. *Lyrics by* Ogden Nash. *Orchestrated by* Don Walker.)

Danced by The Stripper: N. Kaye. *The Drummer*: B. Callahan. *The Pianist*: B. Miller.

Scene 6

"Purple Rose"

(*Sketch by* Charles Sherman with Peter DeVries. *Music by* Vernon Duke. *Lyrics by* Ogden Nash. *Orchestrated by* Phil Lang.)

Sybill: B. Davis. *Peter*: H. Sherman. *Horatio*: E. Renard. *Terrance*: G. S. Irving. *Hilary*: C. Fearl. *Hortense*: M. Muth. *Ginger*: D. Remsen. *Camera Man*: M. Brenner. *Butler*: F. Neil. *Maid*: B. Regis. *Virgil*: R. Neukum. *Cicero*: B. Krach.

Scene 7

"Just Like a Man"

B. Davis
(*Music by* Vernon Duke. *Lyrics by* Ogden Nash.
Orchestrated by Phil Lang.)

Scene 8

Finale

The Company
(*Music by* Vernon Duke. *Lyrics by* Ogden Nash.
Orchestrated by Clare Grundman.)

1953.01 HAZEL FLAGG

A Musical Satire in Two Acts, 15 Scenes. Book by Ben Hecht. Based on the story ("Letter to the Editor") by James Street and the film "Nothing Sacred" by Ben Hecht, (Ring Lardner, Jr.). Music by Jule Styne. Lyrics by Bob Hilliard. Dances and musical numbers staged by Robert Alton. Book directed by David Alexander. Production (settings) designed and lighted by Harry Horner. Costumes by Miles White. Musical director, Pembroke Davenport. Choral arrangements and direction by Hugh Martin. Orchestrations by Don Walker. Ballet arrangements by Oscar Kosarin. Entire production under the supervision of Robert Alton. Produced by Jule Styne in association with Anthony Brady Farrell. Opened 11 February 1953 at the Mark Hellinger Theatre, closing 4 July 1953; re-opened 7 September 1953 and closed 19 September 1953 after 190 performances.

CAST (in order of appearance): *An Editor*: Dean Campbell. *Oleander*: Jonathan Harris. *Laura Carew*: BENAY VENUTA. *Wallace Cook*: JOHN HOWARD. *Vermont Villagers*: Carol Hendricks, B. J. Keating, Joan Morton, Dorothy Love, Laurel Shelby. *Mr. Billings*: Lawrence Weber. *Mr. Jenkins*: Robert Lenn. *Hazel Flagg*: HELEN GALLAGHER. *Dr. Downer*: THOMAS MITCHELL. *Man on the Street*: George Reeder. *Bellboy*: Jerry Craig. *Maximilian Lavian*: John Pelletti. *Fireman*: Bill Heyer. *Miss Winterbottom*: Betsy Holland. *Mayor of New York*: JACK WHITING. *Whitey*: SHEREE NORTH. *Willie*: John Brascia. *Dr. Egelhofer*: Ross Martin. *Chorus Girls*: Lori Jon, Virginia Poe. *Committeemen*: Michael Spaeth, John Bartis. *Policeman*: Eric Schepard.

Dancers: Estelle Aza, Chris Carter, Marcella Dodge, Lillian Donau, Anna Friedland, Ruby Herndon, Lori Jon, Sherry McCutcheon, Betty McMillen, Barbara Michaels, Judy Miller, Joan Morton, Margot Meyers, Virginia Poe, Eva Ralf, Beryl Towbin, Toni Wheelis, Christopher Brown, Ronald Cecill, Don Crichton, Al Craine, Hugh Lambert, Gerard Leavitt, George Reeder, Eric Schepard, Michael Spaeth. *Singers*: Sara Dillon, Mary Harmon, Carol Hendricks, Betsy Holland, Dorsie Hollingsworth, B. J. Keating, Beverly McFadden, Laurel Shelby, John Bartis, Dean Campbell, David Carter, Jerry Craig, Bob Davis, Bill Heyer, Robert Lenn, David Randall.

Act 1, Scene 1: Conference Room of Everywhere Magazine. Late afternoon, 1930s. *Scene 2*: Dr. Downer's House. The next day. *Scene 3*: Railroad Depot, Stonyhead. That evening. *Scene 4*: A New York Street. The next day. *Scene 5*: Hazel's New York Hotel Suite. Later that day. *Scene 6*: Laura Carew's Office. Two weeks later. *Scene 7*: Hazel's Hotel Suite. Evening. A week later. *Scene 8*: (a) A Cross Section of New York City. Later that evening. (b) Roseland Ballroom.

Act 2, Scene 1: A Radio Station in the Hotel. The next morning. *Scene 2*: Hazel's Hotel Bedroom. The same morning. *Scene 3*: The same. Several hours later. *Scene 4*: The Mayor's Luncheon. That afternoon. *Scene 5*: Under the East River Bridge. Later that evening. *Scene 6*: A Barge on the River's edge. A little later. *Scene 7*: Finale.

ACT 1[10]

Scene 1

"A Little More Heart"

B. Venuta, J. Howard, Magazine Staff

Scene 2

"The World Is Beautiful Today"[11]

H. Gallagher

[10]During the first engagement of the show, substantial revisions were made in the book and score. For the September re-opening, the following songs were added:

"Money Burns a Hole in My Pocket" (added to Act 1, Scene 5)
Tony Bavaar (Wallace)

"Something in the Wind" (added to Act 2, Scene 5 before "Laura de Maupassant")
T. Bavaar

[11]During the first engagement replaced by:

"My Wild Imagination" (Act 1, Scene 2)
H. Gallagher

"I'm Glad I'm Leaving"
H. Gallagher
Scene 3
"The Rutland Bounce" (Dance)
J. Morton, G. Reeder, D. Crichton, Villagers
Scene 4
"Hello, Hazel"
B. Venuta, New Yorkers
Scene 5
"Paris Gown" (Ballet)
H. Gallagher, J. Pelletti,
R. Cecill, G. Leavitt, G. Reeder, Models, Attendants
"The World Is Beautiful Today" (reprise)[12]
J. Howard, Editors
Scene 6
"Every Street's a Boulevard in Old New York"
J. Whiting
Scene 7
"How Do You Speak to an Angel?"
J. Howard
Scene 8A
"Autograph Chant"[13]
Autograph Hunters
"I Feel Like I'm Gonna Live Forever"
H. Gallagher
Scene 8B
"You're Gonna Dance With Me, Willie"
H. Gallagher, J. Brascia, Company

ACT 2
Scene 1
"Who Is the Bravest?"
University Glee Club
Scene 2
"Dream Parade" (Ballet)
H. Gallagher, Company
Scene 4
"Salome"
Dancing Girls
Salome: S. North. *Cowboy Singer*: D. Campbell.
Cowboy Dancers: G. Reeder, D. Crichton.
"Everybody Loves To Take a Bow"
B. Venuta, J. Whiting, Men
Scene 5
"Laura De Maupassant"
H. Gallagher
Scene 6
"Autograph Chant" (reprise)
Autograph Hunters
Scene 7
"I Feel Like I'm Gonna Live Forever" (reprise)
Company
followed by "How Do You Speak to an Angel?" (earlier placement)
J. Howard

[12]During the first engagement replaced by:
"Make the People Cry" (Act 1, Scene 5)
B. Venuta, J. Harris, Editors
[13]During the first engagement moved to the end of Scene 7.

1953.02

MAGGIE

A Musical Play in Two Acts, 9 Scenes. Book by Hugh Thomas. Based on James M. Barrie's comedy "What Every Woman Knows." Music and lyrics by William Roy. Directed by Michael Gordon. Sets and costumes by Raoul Pene du Bois. Choreography by June Graham. Lighting by Peggy Clark. Musical direction and choral arrangements by Maurice Levine. Orchestrations by Don Walker. Dance arrangements by Dean Fuller. Production associate, Harry Zevin. Produced by Franklin Gilbert and John Fearnley. Opened 18 February 1953 at the National Theatre and closed 21 February 1953 after 5 performances.

CAST (in order of appearance): *Alick Wylie*: BRAMWELL FLETCHER. *James Wylie*: JAMES BRODERICK. *David Wylie*: FRANK MAXWELL. *Maggie Wylie*: BETTY PAUL. *John Shand*: KETH ANDES. *Prof. Dubois*: Henry Hamilton. *Mrs. MacLaughlin*: Jenny Lou Law. *Madame Marstonne*: ODETTE MYRTIL. *Sybil Tenterdon*: CELIA LIPTON. *Williams*: Gene Holmann. *Venables*: JOHN HOYT. *John Shand (in ballet)*: MARC PLATT. *Maggie Wylie (in ballet)*: ALICIA KRUG. *Sybil Tenterdon (in ballet)*: KATHRYN LEE. *Porters*: Gene Holmann, Henry Hamilton, Oran Osburn. *Conductor*: Paul Ukena.

Singers: Marion Lauer, Jan Scott, Joanne Spiller, Gloria Van Dorpe, Robert Busch, John Ford, Henry Hamilton, Gene Holmann, James E. McCracken, Oran Osburn, Paul Ukena. *Dancers*: Adele Aron, Sura Gesben, Jeanne Jones, Patti Karkalits, Nata Lee, Ruby Ann Saber, J. Corky Geil, John George, Alan Howard, David Nillo, Bob St. Clair, Keith Willis.

Act 1, Scene 1: The Wylie Home in a small town near Glasgow, Scotland. Winter, 1899. *Scene 2*: Covering the years between 1899 and 1905. *Scene 3*: Lobby of the Bright Heather Hotel, Glasgow. Winter, 1905. *Scene 4*: Glasgow. The same night. *Scene 5*: garden of Mme. Marstonne's Country home. A late afternoon in Spring, 1906.

Act 1, Scene 1: Padding Station. Spring, 1906. *Scene 2*: John Shand's Study. The same day. *Scene 3*: Paddington Station. Later that Spring. *Scene 4*: Garden of Mme. Marstonne's Country Home. Summer, 1906.

ACT 1
"I Never Laughed in My Life"
K. Andes
"Long and Weary Wait"
K. Andes, B. Paul
"Thimbleful"
B. Fletcher, F. Maxwell, J. Broderick, K. Andes, B. Paul
"He's the Man"
K. Andes, Singers, Dancers
"What Every Woman Knows"
B. Paul
"Any Afternoon About Five"
O. Myrtil
"Smile For Me"
(*Staged by* Paul Godkin.)B. Paul
"You Become Me"
B. Paul, K. Andes
"He's the Man" (reprise)
Company
"It's Only Thirty Years"
O. Myrtil, J. Hoyt
"What Every Woman Knows" (reprise)
B. Paul
"The New Me" (Ballet)
B. Paul, B. Fletcher, F. Maxwell, J. Broderick, Singers, Dancers

ACT 2
"The Train With the Cushioned Seats"
F. Maxwell, B. Fletcher, J. Broderick
(*Staged by* Paul Godkin.)
"People in Love"
K. Andes, C. Lipton
"Practical"
B. Paul
"Charm"
B. Paul
"Fun in the Country"
O. Myrtil
"What Every Woman Knows" (reprise)
B. Paul

"Smile For Me" (reprise)
B. Paul
"You Become Me" (reprise)
K. Andes

1953.03 WONDERFUL TOWN

A Musical Comedy in Two Acts, 13 Scenes. Book by Joseph Fields and Jerome Chodorov. Based on the play "My Sister Eileen" by Joseph Fields and Jerome Chodorov and the stories of the same name by Ruth McKenney. Music by Leonard Bernstein. Lyrics by Betty Comden and Adolph Green. Dances and musical numbers staged by Donald Saddler. Sets and costumes by Raoul Pene du Bois. Lighting by Peggy Clark. Miss Russell's clothes by Main Bocher. Musical direction and vocal arrangements by Lehman Engel. Orchestrations by Don Walker. Production directed by George Abbott. Produced by Robert Fryer. Opened 25 February 1953 at the Winter Garden and closed 3 July 1954 after 559 performances.

CAST (in order of appearance): *Guide*: Warren Galjour. *Appopolous*: HENRY LASCOE. *Lonigan*: Walter Kelvin. *Helen*: Michele Burke. *Wreck*: JORDAN BENTLEY. *Violet*: Dody Goodman. *Valenti*: Ted Beniades. *Eileen*: EDITH ADAMS. *Ruth*: ROSALIND RUSSELL. *A Strange Man*: Nathaniel Frey. *Drunks*: Lee Papell, Delbert Anderson. *Robert Baker*: GEORGE GAYNES. *Associate Editors*: Warren Galjour, Albert Linville. *Mrs. Wade*: Isabella Hoopes. *Frank Lippencott*: CRIS ALEXANDER. *Chef*: Nathaniel Frey. *Waiter*: Delbert Anderson. *Delivery Boy*: Alvin Bean. *Chick Clark*: DORT CLARK. *Shore Patrolman*: Lee Papell. *First Cadet*: David Lober. *Second Cadet*: Ray Dorian. *Policemen*: Lee Papell, Albert Linville, Delbert Anderson, Chris Robinson, Nathaniel Frey, Warren Galjour, Robert Kole. *Ruth's Escort*: Chris Robinson.

Greenwich Villagers: Jean Eliot, Carol Cole, Marta Becket, Maxine Berke, Helena Seroy, Geraldine Delaney, Margaret Cady, Dody Goodman, Ed Balin, Alvin Bean, Ray Dorian, Edward Heim, Joe Layton, David Lober, Victor Moreno, William Weslow, Pat Johnson, Evelyn Page, Libi Staiger, Patty Wilkes, Helen Rice, Delbert Anderson, Warren Galjour, Robert Kole, Lee Papell, Chris Robinson.

Act 1, Scene 1: Christopher Street, Greenwich Village, New York City, 1935. *Scene 2*: Ruth and Eileen's Studio Apartment. *Scene 3*: Christopher Street. *Scene 4*: Baker's Office at the "Madhatter." *Scene 5*: The Street. *Scene 6*: The Back Yard. *Scene 7*: The Navy Yard. *Scene 8*: The Back Yard.

Act 2, Scene 1: The Christopher Street Station House. *Scene 2*: The Street. *Scene 3*: The Studio Apartment. *Scene 4*: The Street in front of the Village Vortex. *Scene 5*: The Village Vortex.

ACT 1
Scene 1
"Christopher Street"
W. Galjour, Villagers
Scene 2
"Ohio"
R. Russell, E. Adams
"Conquering New York" (Dance)
R. Russell, E. Adams, D. Lober, D. Goodman, Villagers
Scene 3
"One Hundred Easy Ways"
R. Russell
Scene 4
"What a Waste"
G. Gaynes, W. Galjour, A. Linville
"Story Vignettes"
(*by* Betty Comden and Adolph Green)
Rexford: C. Robinson. *Mr. Mallory*: D. Anderson. *Danny*: N. Frey. *Trent*: L. Papell.
Scene 5
"Never Felt This Way Before"
(A Little Bit in Love)
E. Adams
Scene 6
"Pass The Football"
J. Bentley, Villagers
"Conversation Piece" (Nice People, Nice Talk)
R. Russell, E. Adams, C. Alexander, G. Gaynes, D. Clark
"A Quiet Girl"
G. Gaynes
Scene 7
"Conga!"
R. Russell
Danced by the Cadets.
Scene 8
(Finale—Act 1 Conga! reprise)
(R. Russell, Ensemble)

ACT 2
Scene 1
"My Darlin' Eileen"
E. Adams, D. Anderson, Police
Scene 2
"Swing!"
R. Russell, Villagers
Scene 3
"Ohio" (reprise)
R. Russell, E. Adams
Scene 4
"It's Love"
G. Gaynes, (E. Adams), Villagers
Scene 5
("The Village Vortex Blues" dance)
{Let It Come Down}
Villagers
"Wrong Note Rag"
R. Russell, E. Adams, Villagers
(Finale—Act 2 "It's Love" reprise)
Entire Company

1953.04 PORGY AND BESS

A Revival of the Folk Opera in Three Acts, 9 Scenes[14]. Book by DuBose Heyward adapted from the play "Porgy" by DuBose and Dorothy Heyward. Music by George Gershwin. Lyrics by DuBose Heyward and Ira Gershwin. Directed by Robert Breen. Chorus directed by Eva Jessye. Settings by Wolfgang Roth. Costumes by Jed Mace. Musical director, Alexander Smallens. Assistant musical director, Samuel Matlowsky. Produced by Blevins Davis and Robert Breen. Opened 10 March 1953 at the Ziegfeld Theatre and closed 28 November 1953 after 305 performances.

CAST (in order of appearance): *Clara*: HELEN COLBERT. *Mingo*: Jerry Laws. *Sportin' Life*: CAB CALLOWAY. *Serena*: HELEN THIGPEN. *Jake*: JOSEPH JAMES. *Robbins*: Howard Roberts. *Jim*: Hugh Dilworth and Sherman Sneed. *Peter*, the Honey Man: Joseph Crawford. *Lily*, the Strawberry Woman: Helen Dowdy. *Maria*: GEORGIA BURKE. *Porgy*: LeVERN HUTCHERSON, LESLIE SCOTT or

[14]First produced in New York 10 October 1935 at the Alvin Theatre for 124 performances. For Synopsis of Scenes and Musical Numbers, see original 1935 production. Ella Gerbert assisted in the direction of the production. During the summer of 1953, the second intermission was dropped and the Second Act was played in 6 Scenes. Dropped from Act 2, Scene 3 was: "Oh, Doctor Jesus."

Added to this production were the following:
Crap Game Fugue ("Roll Them Bones")
(End of Act 1, Scene 1)
L. Hutcherson, C. Calloway, J. McCurry, Men
"I Ain't Got No Shame" (Opening of Act 2, Scene 1)
C. Calloway, Ensemble
"Buzzard (Song)" (Act 3, Scene 3)
L. Hutcherson

IRVING BARNES. *Crown*: JOHN McCURRY. *Annie*: Catherine Ayers. *Bess*: LEONTYNE PRICE or URYLEE LEONARDOS. *Policeman*: Sam Kasakoff. *Detective*: Walter Riemer. *Undertaker*: William Veasey. *Frazier*: Moses LaMarr. *Ruby*: Elizabeth Foster. *Crab Man*: Ray Yeates. *Coroner*: Sam Kasakoff. *Policeman*: Willis Daily. *Porgy's Goat*: Jebob.

Residents of Catfish Row: Joseph Attles, Irving Barnes, Lawson Bates, James Hawthorne Bey, Rhoda Boggs, Walter P. Brown, Miriam Burton, Sibol Cain, Elsie Clark, Charles Colman, Clarice Crawford, Helen Ferguson, Doris Galiber, Ruby Grene, Kenneth Hibbert, George A. Hill, Joy McLean, Pauline Phelps, Edna Ricks, Anabelle Ross, George A. Royston, Dolores Swan, Clyde Turner, Eloise C. Uggams, Barbara Ann Webb. *Children*: Jacqueline Barnes, George Royston, Jr.

1953.05

REGINA

A Revival of the Musical Drama (Opera) in Three Acts, Prologue and 4 Scenes[15]. Text and music by Marc Blitzstein. Based on the play "The Little Foxes" by Lillian Hellman. Production directed by Robert Lewis. Conductor, Julius Rudel. Settings designed by Horace Armistead. Costumes designed by Aline Bernstein. Choreographer, John Butler. Lighting by Jean Rosenthal. (Orchestrations by Marc Blitzstein.) Produced by the New York City Opera. Opened 2 April 1953 at the New York City Center and closed 29 April 1953 after 3 performances in repertory.

CAST: *Regina Giddens*: BRENDA LEWIS. *Horace Giddens*, her husband: WILLIAM WILDERMAN. *Alexandra Giddens* (Zan), their daughter: PRISCILLA GILLETTE. *Regina's Brothers* (2): *Ben Hubbard*: LEON LISHNER. *Oscar Hubbard*: EMILE RENAN. *Birdie Hubbard*, Oscar's wife: EILEEN FAULL. *Leo Hubbard*, their son: MICHAEL POLLOCK. *Jazz*: WILLIAM DILLARD. *Addie*, cook: LUCRETIA WEST. *Cal*, butler: LAWRENCE WINTERS. *Marshall*: LLOYD THOMAS LEECH. *Belle*, maid: Margaret Tynes. *Bagtry*: Russell Goodwin. *Manders*: Charles Kuestner. *Band*: *Banjo*: Bernard Addison. *Clarinet*: Eddie Barefield. *Trombone*: Theodore Donnelly. *Drums*: Sticks Evans. *Pianist*: Lucy Brown. *Violinist*: Eugene Bergen.

1953.06

DIE FLEDERMAUS

A Revival of the Operetta in Three Acts[16]. (Original libretto by Carl Haffner and Richard Genée. Lyrics by Richard Genée. Based on the comedy "Le Réveillon" by Henri Meilhac and Ludovic Halévy.) English libretto by Ruth and Thomas Martin. Music by Johann Strauss. Staged by William Westerfield. Costume supervisor, Robert Fletcher. Choreography, John Butler. Conducted by Thomas P. Martin. Produced by the New York City Opera. Opened 8 April 1953 at the New York City Center and closed 3 May 1953 after 4 performances in repertory.

CAST: *Eisenstein*: JACK RUSSELL. *Rosalinda*: LAUREL HURLEY. *Adele*: ELAINE MALBIN. *Alfred*: JON CRAIN. *Falke*: WILLIAM SHRINER. *Frank*: RICHARD WENTWORTH. *Blind*: Luigi Vellucci. *Prince Orlofsky*: DONALD GRAMM. *Sally*: Jeanne Beauvais. *Frosch*: Ernest Sarracino. *Ivan*: Michael Arshansky. *Solo Dancers*: Jamie Bauer, Glen Tetley. *Ensemble*: New York City Opera Chorus.

The action takes place in the fashionable suburbs of Vienna in the 1860s.

Act 1: Rosalinda's Boudoir.

Act 2: At the Villa of Orlovsky.

Act 3: The Town Jail.

---

[15]Originally produced in New York 31 October 1949 at the 46th Street Theatre for 56 performances. For Synopsis of Scenes and Musical Numbers, see original 1949 production. An Intermission was added between Act 1, Scenes 1 and 2. Restored to the production:

"Blues"

L. West, B. Lewis

[16]First English language production in New York 16 March 1885 at the Casino Theatre for 42 performances. First New York production of this version 20 December 1950 at the Metropolitan Opera. No list of musical numbers appears in the program for this production. For listing of Musical Numbers, see 19 May 1954 New York City Center Light Opera production.

1953.07

CAN-CAN

A Musical Comedy in Two Acts, 17 Scenes. Music and lyrics by Cole Porter. Book and direction by Abe Burrows. Dances and musical numbers staged by Michael Kidd. Settings and lighting by Jo Mielziner. Costumes by Motley. Musical direction by Milton Rosenstock. Orchestrations by Philip J. Lang. Dance music arranged by Genevieve Pitot. Produced by Cy Feuer and Ernest H. Martin. Opened 7 May 1953 at the Sam S. Shubert Theatre and closed 25 June 1955 after 892 performances.

CAST (in order of appearance): *Bailiff*: David Collyer. *Registrar*: Michael Cavallaro. *Policemen*: Joe Cusanelli, Jon Silo, Arthur Rubin, Ralph Beaumont, Michael DeMarco, Socrates Birsky. *Judge Paul Barriere*: C. K. ALEXANDER. *Court President, Henri Marceaux*: David Thomas. *Judge Aristede Forestier*: PETER COOKSON. *Claudine*: GWEN VERDON. *Gabrielle*: Mary Anne Cohan. *Marie*: Beverly Purvin. *Celestine*: Jean Kraemer. *Hilaire Jussac*: ERIK RHODES. *Boris Adzinidzinadze*: HANS CONREID. *Hercule*: ROBERT PENN. *Theophile*: PHIL LEEDS. *Etienne*: RICHARD PURDY. *Waiter*: Clarence Hoffman. *La Mome Pistache*: LILO. *Second Waiter*: Ferdinand Hilt. *Cafe Waiter*: Jon Silo. *Cafe Customer*: Joe Cusanelli. *Jailer*: Deedee Wood. *Model*: Pat Turner. *Mimi*: Dania Krupska. *Customers*: Sheila Arnold, David Thomas, Ferdinand Hilt. *Doctor*: Michael Cavallaro. *Second*: Arthur Rubin. *Prosecutor*: Ferdinand Hilt.

Dancers: Meredith Baylis, Shelah Hackett, Ina Hahn, Dania Krupska, Vera Lee, Beverly Tassoni, Pat Turner, Ruth Vernon, Deedee Wood, Ralph Beaumont, Socrates Birsky, Michael DeMarco, Al Lanti, Bert May, Tom Panko, Arthur Partington, Eddie Phillips, Michael Scrittorale.

Act 1, Scene 1: Correctional Court. Paris, 1893. *Scene 2*: A Street in Montmartre. *Scene 3*: Bal du Paradis. *Scene 4*: Pistache's Office. *Scene 5*: Bal du Paradis. *Scene 6*: Sidewalk Cafe. *Scene 7*: Jail. *Scene 8*: The Atelier. *Scene 9*: The Street. *Scene 10*: Quatz' Arts Ball.

Act 1, Scene 1: The Atelier. *Scene 2*: The Cafe. *Scene 3*: 'La Blanchisserie.' *Scene 4*: The Street. *Scene 5*: Roof of 'La Blanchisserie.' *Scene 6*: Prison. *Scene 7*: Court of Assizes.

ACT 1

Scene 1

"Maidens Typical of France"
The Laundresses

Scene 3

"Never Give Anything Away"
Lilo

Scene 4

"C'est Magnifique"
Lilo, P. Cookson

Scene 5

"Quadrille"
G. Verdon, B. May, Laundresses, Friends

Scene 6

"Come Along With Me"
E. Rhodes, H. Conried

Scene 7

"Live and Let Live"
Lilo

"I Am in Love"
P. Cookson

Scene 8

"If You Loved Me Truly"
H. Conried, G. Verdon, P. Leeds,
R. Penn, R. Purdy, M. A. Cohan, J. Kraemer, B. Purvin

Scene 10

"Montmart'" (Montmartre)
Singing Ensemble

"The Garden of Eden" Ballet
Eve: G. Verdon. *Inchworms*: I. Hahn, S. Birsky. *Flamingos*: S. Hackett, A. Partington. *Kangaroos*: B. Tassoni, M. Scrittorale. *Penguins*: E. Phillips, D. Wood. *Sea Horses*: R. Vernon, T. Panko. *Frogs*: V. Lee, A. Lanti. *Leopards*: P. Turner, R. Beaumont. *Snake*: B. May.

"Allez-Vous-En" (Go Away)
Lilo

ACT 2

Scene 1

"Never, Never Be an Artist"
H. Conried, P. Leeds, R. Purdy, P. Turner

Scene 2

"It's All Right With Me"
P. Cookson

"Every Man Is a Stupid Man"
Lilo

Scene 3

"The Apaches" (Dance)
G. Verdon, R. Beaumont, Dancers

Scene 5

"I Love Paris"
Lilo

"C'est Magnifique" (reprise)
P. Cookson, Lilo

Scene 7

"Can-Can"
Lilo, G. Verdon, Laundresses

Finale
Entire Company

1953.08 ME AND JULIET

A Musical Comedy in Two Acts, 17 Scenes. Book and lyrics by Oscar Hammerstein II. Music by Richard Rodgers. Scenery and lighting by Jo Mielziner. Costumes by Irene Sharaff. Vocal and orchestral arrangements by Don Walker. Musical director, Salvatore Dell'Isola. Dances and musical numbers staged by Robert Alton. Production directed by George Abbott. Produced by Richard Rodgers and Oscar Hammerstein II. Opened 28 May 1953 at the Majestic Theatre and closed 3 April 1954 after 358 performances.

CAST (in order of appearance): *George*, Second Assistant Stage Manager: Randy Hall. *Sidney*, Electrician: Edwin Phillips. *Jeanie*, Chorus Singer: ISABEL BIGLEY. *Herbie*, Candy Counter Boy: JACKIE KELK. *Trio*: *Chris*, Rehearsal Piano Player: BARBARA CARROLL. *Milton*, Drummer: Herb Wasserman. *Stu*, Bass Fiddle Player: Joe Shulman. *Michael*, A Chorus Boy: Michael King. *Bob*, Electrician: MARK DAWSON. *Larry*, Assistant Stage Manager: BILL HAYES. *Mac*, Stage Manager: RAY WALSTON. *Monica*, Chorus Dancer: Patty Ann Jackson. *Ruby*, Company Manager: Joe Lautner. *Charlie* (Me), Featured Lead: Arthur Maxwell. *Dario*, Conductor: GEORGE S. IRVING. *Lily* (Juliet), Singing Principal: Helena Scott. *Jim* (Don Juan), Principal Dancer: Bob Fortier. *Susie* (Susie), Principal Dancer: Svetlana McLee. *Voice of Mr. Harrison*, Producer: Henry Hamilton. *Voice of Miss Davenport*, Choreographer: Deborah Remsen. *Hilda*, an aspirant for a dancing part: Norma Thornton. *Marcia*, another aspirant for a dancing part: Thelma Tadlock. *Betty*, successor to Susie as Principal Dancer: JOAN McCRACKEN. *Buzz*, Principal Dancer: BUZZ MILLER. *Ralph*, Alley Dancer: Ralph Linn. *Miss Oxford*, a bit player: Gwen Harmon. *Sadie*, an usher: Francine Bond. *Mildred*, Another Usher: Lorraine Havercroft. *A Theatre Patron*: Barbara Lee Smith. *Another Theatre Patron*: Susan Lovell.

Dancing Ensemble: Francine Bond, Betty Buday, Penny Ann Green, Lorraine Havercroft, Patty Ann Jackson, Helene Keller, Lucia Lambert, Harriet Leigh, Sonya Lindgren [Sonja Tyven], Elizabeth Logue, Shirley MacLaine, Cheryl Parker, Dorothy Silverherz, Thelma Tadlock, Norma Thornton, Janyce Ann Wagner, Rosemary Williams, Lance Avant, Grant Delaney, John George, Jack Konzal, Ralph Linn, Eddie Pfeiffer, Augustine Rodriguez, Bob St. Clair, Bill Weber. *Singing Ensemble*: Adele Castle, Gwen Harmon, Susan Lovell, Theresa Mari, Georgia Reed, Deborah Remsen, Thelma Scott, Barbara Lee Smith, Jack Drummond, John Ford, Henry Hamilton, Richard Hermany, Warren Kemmerling, Michael King, Larry Laurence, Jack Rains.

The entire action takes place in and around the theatre in which 'Me and Juliet' is playing.

Act 1, Scene 1: Backstage. *Scene 2*: The Orchestra Pit. *Scene 3*: First Scene of 'Me and Juliet.' *Scene 4*: The Light Bridge. *Scene 5*: During performance of 'Me and Juliet.' *Scene 6*: Backstage. *Scene 7*: The Alley leading to the Stage Door. *Scene 8*: Betty's Dressing Room. *Scene 9*: The Light Bridge. *Scene 10*: Night Club Scene in 'Me and Juliet' and Backstage.

Act 2, Scene 1: Downstairs Lounge in the Theatre. *Scene 2*: The Bar across the Street. *Scene 3*: A Second Act Sequence of 'Me and Juliet.' *Scene 4*: Theatre Manager's Office. *Scene 5*: The Orchestra Pit. *Scene 6*: Last Scene of 'Me and Juliet.' *Scene 7*: Backstage.

ACT 1

Scene 1

"A Very Special Day"
I. Bigley, Trio

"That's the Way It Happens"
I. Bigley, Trio

"That's the Way It Happens" (reprise)
B. Hayes

Dance Impromptu
Chorus, R. Hall, Trio

Scene 2

Overture to 'Me and Juliet'
G. S. Irving, Orchestra

Scene 3

Opening of 'Me and Juliet'
H. Scott, B. Fortier, S. Lee, A. Maxwell

"Marriage Type Love"
A. Maxwell, H. Scott, Singers

Scene 4

"Keep It Gay"
M. Dawson,

Scene 5

"Keep It Gay" (dance reprise)
B. Fortier, Chorus

Scene 6

"Keep It Gay" (dance reprise)
J. McCracken, B. Miller, (Chorus)

"The Big, Black Giant"
B. Hayes

"No Other Love"
I. Bigley, B. Hayes

Scene 7

Dance
R. Linn, F. Bond, E. Logue

"The Big, Black Giant" (reprise)
J. Lautner

Scene 8

"It's Me"
J. McCracken, I. Bigley

Scene 10

("No Other Love") (reprise)
(H. Scott)

First Act Finale of 'Me and Juliet'
H. Scott, J. McCracken, A. Maxwell, B. Fortier, I. Bigley, Chorus

ACT 2

Scene 1

"Intermission Talk"
J. Kelk, Chorus

Scene 2

"It Feels Good"
M. Dawson

Scene 3

Opening Sequence in Second Act of 'Me and Juliet'
A. Maxwell, B. Fortier, H. Scott, Dancers

"The Baby You Love"[17]
H. Scott, Dancers

[17]Dropped after opening.

"We Deserve Each Other"
J. McCracken, B. Fortier, Chorus
Scene 4
"I'm Your Girl"
I. Bigley, B. Hayes
Scene 5
(Change Music of Last Scene of 'Me and Juliet')
(G. S Irving, Orchestra)
Scene 6
Second Act Finale of 'Me and Juliet'
A. Maxwell, H. Scott, J. McCracken, B. Fortier, Chorus
Scene 7
Finale (of Our Play)
Entire Company

1953–1954 SEASON

Carol Haney and Reta Shaw in THE PAJAMA GAME
Billy Rose Theatre Collection, New York Public Library for the Performing Arts

1953–1954 SEASON

1953.09 OKLAHOMA!

A Revival of the Musical Comedy in Two Acts, 6 Scenes[1]. Book and lyrics by Oscar Hammerstein II. Music by Richard Rodgers. Based on the play "Green Grow the Lilacs" by Lynn Riggs. (Originally) Directed by Rouben Mamoulian. Dances by Agnes de Mille, reproduced by Betty Gour. Settings by Lemuel Ayers. Costumes by Miles White. Production reproduced (staged) by Jerome Whyte. Orchestrations by Robert Russell Bennett. Musical director, Peter Laurini. Produced by Richard Rodgers and Oscar Hammerstein II. Opened 31 August 1953 at the New York City Center and closed 3 October 3 1953 after 40 performances.

CAST: *Aunt Eller*: MARY MARLO. *Curly*: RIDGE BOND. *Laurey*: FLORENCE HENDERSON. *Cord Elam*: Charles Hart. *Fred*: Charles Scott. *Slim*: Charles Rule. *Will Parker*: HARRIS HAWKINS. *Jud Fry*: ALFRED CIBELLI, JR. *Ado Annie Carnes*: BARBARA COOK. *Ali Hakim*: DAVID LE GRANT. *Gertie Cummings*: Judy Rawlings. *Ellen*: MAGGI NELSON. *Kate*: Barbara Reisman. *Sylvie*: Patti Parsons. *Armina*: Lynne Broadbent. *Aggie*: Cathy Conklin. *Andrew Carnes*: OWEN MARTIN. *Chalmers*: GEORGE LAWRENCE. *Mike*: Bob Lord.

Singers: Lenore Arnold, Lois Barrodin, Marylin Hardy, Frances Irby, Heidi Palmer, Barbara Reisman, Jeanne Shea, William Ambler, Dino Dante, James Fox, Christopher Golden, Bob Lord, Charles Rule, Charles Scott. *Dancers*: Lynne Broadbent, Bette Burton, Cathy Conklin, Betty Koerber, Gayle Parmelee, Patti Parsons, Cynthia Price, Georganne Shaw, Louellen Sibley, Marguerite Stewart, Payne Converse, Nick Dana, Jack Ketcham, Ronnie Landry, John Pero, Jr., Tom Pickler, Joe Ribeau.

1953.10 ANNA RUSSELL AND HER LITTLE SHOW

An Intimate Revue in Two Acts, 15 Scenes. Music and lyrics by Anna Russell. Staged by Arthur Klein. Lighting by Ralph Alswang. Musical arrangements by Arthur Harris. Choreography by Lorenzo Fuller. Produced by Eastman Boomer and Arthur Klein. Opened 7 September 1953 at the Vanderbilt Theatre and closed 19 September 1953 after 16 performances.

CAST: ANNA RUSSELL, ARTHUR BARNETT, JEAN LEON DESTINÉ, PAUL DUKE, JOSEPH SCANDUR, Doris Haley, Yolande Gaffne. *Duo-Pianists*: JANE ASHLOCK, ARTHUR HARRIS. *Drummers*: Alphonse Cimber, Ti-Marcel.

ACT 1

Scene 1

Jane Ashlock and Arthur Harris: Duo-Pianists

Scene 2

Arthur Barnett

Scene 3

"The Spider and the Lady"
J. L. Destiné, Y. Gaffne, Company
Drummers: A. Cimber, Ti-Marcel.

Scene 4

"A Symphony in Smoke"
P. Duke, D. Haley

Scene 5

Arthur Barnett

Scene 6

Anna Russell:

"Habanera," "O Night! O Day!," "Da Nyet, Da Nyet!," "Anameia's Death Scene," "I Gave My Love a Cherry" or "How to Write Your Own Schubert Operetta" (assisted by J. Scandur),"The Prince of Philadelphia," "Les Cigarettes," "Trink."

ACT 2

Scene 1

Arthur Barnett

Scene 2

Music Appreciation—"The Bagpipes"
A. Russell

Scene 3

"The Witch Doctor"
J. L. Destiné, Company

(Voodoo dance in which the evil spirits are exorcised from the body of the patient.)

Scene 4

"Magic in Rhythm"
P. Duke, D. Haley

Scene 5

Arthur Barnett

Scene 6

Anna Russell:

"Hello! Hello! Oh, A Jolly Good Show" (assisted by J. Scandur), "Guarda La Bella Tomato," "Night and Day."

Scene 7

Anna Russell

"The Decline and Fall of The Popular Song" (as witnessed by Miss Russell), "Feeling Grand," "I'd Be a Red Hot Momma," "Chlorophyll Solly," "Miserable," "Mad."

Scene 8

Jane Ashlock, Arthur Harris (Duo-Pianists)

Scene 9

Finale

1953.11 CARNIVAL IN FLANDERS

A Musical Comedy in Two Acts. Book by Preston Sturges. Based on the film "La Kermesse Héroïque," screenplay by C. Spaak, J. Feyder and B. Zimmer. Music by James Van Heusen. Lyrics by Johnny Burke. Scenery by Oliver Smith. Costumes by Lucinda Ballard. Musical director, Harold Hastings. Vocal arrangements by Elie Siegmeister. Orchestrations by Don Walker. Carnival Ballet and musical numbers staged by Helen Tamiris. Directed by Preston Sturges. Produced by Paula Stone and Mike Sloane in association with Burke and Van Heusen. Opened 8 September 1953 at the New Century Theatre and closed 12 September 1953 after 6 performances.

CAST (in order of appearance): *Siska*: PAT STANLEY. *Jan Breughel*: KEVIN SCOTT. *Tailor*: Paul Reed. *Butcher*: Paul Lipson. *Barber*: Bobby Vail. *Innkeeper*: LEE GOODMAN. *Mayor*: ROY ROBERTS. *Cornelia*: DOLORES GRAY. *Martha*: Dolores Kempner. *Courier*: Matt Mattox. *Mourning Women*: Sandra Devlin, Julie Marlowe, Lorna Del Maestro. *First Officer*: Ray Mason. *Second Officer*: George Martin. *Third Officer*: Jimmy Alex. *The Duke*: JOHN RAITT. *First Citizen*: Wesley Swails. *Second Citizen*: Norman Weise. *Lisa*: Jean Bradley. *Katherine*: Undine Forrest. *Orderly*: William Noble.

Dancers: Lorna Del Maestro, Sandra Devlin, Pat Ferrier, Patti Karkalits, Mary Alice Kubes, Julie Marlowe, Billie Shane, Emy St. Just, Elfrieda Zieger, Jimmy Alex, John Aristedes, Harry Day, Ronnie Field, Skeet Guenther, George Martin, Greg O'Brien, Paul Olson, Richard Reed, Michael Spaeth. *Singers*: Jean Bradley, Jean Cowles, Undine Forrest, Dolores Kempner, Mara Landi, Mary Stanton, Gloria Van Dorpe, Lee Barry, Fred Bryan, Bill Conlon, Stokley Gray, William Noble, Dick Stewart, Wesley Swails, Norman Weise.

The entire action takes place in and around the town of Flacksenburg in Flanders in 1616.

ACT 1

"Ring the Bell"
R. Roberts, P. Lipson, B. Vail, P. Reed, L. Goodman, K. Scott, P. Stanley, Ensemble

"The Very Necessary You"
K. Scott, P. Stanley

"It's a Fine Old Institution"
D. Gray

"I'm One of Your Admirers"
D. Gray

"The Plundering of the Town"
D. Gray, M. Mattox, G. Martin, E. St. Just, J. Aristedes, J. Marlowe, Ensemble

[1]Originally presented in New York 31 March 1943 at the St. James Theatre for 2212 performances. For Synopsis of Scenes and Musical Numbers, see original 1943 production.

"The Stronger Sex"
D. Gray
"The Sudden Thrill"
J. Raitt
"It's an Old Spanish Custom"
D. Gray, J. Raitt
"A Seventeen Gun Salute"
D. Gray, J. Raitt, M. Mattox, R. Mason, G. Martin, Ensemble

ACT 2
"You're Dead!"
R. Roberts, P. Lipson, B. Vail, L. Goodman, P. Reed
"(Here's That) Rainy Day"
D. Gray
"Take the Word of a Gentleman"
J. Raitt
"The Carnival Ballet"
The Virgin: E. St. Just. *The Bats*: G. O'Brien, P. Olson. *The Monk*: J. Aristedes. *The Goat*: H. Day. *The Youngest One*: P. Stanley. *The Plumed Swains*: J. Alex, R. Field, S. Guenther, M. Spaeth, G. Martin, R. Reed. *The Seven Virgins*: S. Devlin, L. Del Maestro, P. Ferrier, J. Marlowe, P. Karkalits, M. A. Kubes, E. Zeiger. *The Spanish Trio*: M. Mattox, G. Martin, J. Alex, Singers of the Town.
"A Moment of Your Love"
D. Gray, J. Raitt
"How Far Can a Lady Go?"
D. Gray
"It's a Fine Old Institution" (reprise)
D. Gray

1953.12 AT HOME WITH ETHEL WATERS

A Musical Revue in Two Acts, 7 Scenes. Staged by Richard Barr. Setting by Oliver Smith. Costumes by Robert Mackintosh. Produced by Charles Bowden and Richard Barr. Opened 22 September 1953 at the 48th Street Theatre and closed 10 October 1953 after 23 performances.

CAST: ETHEL WATERS, REGINALD BEANE (at the piano).

ACT 1
Scene 1
"I Ain't Gonna Sin No More"
(*Music and Lyrics by* Con Conrad and Herb Magidson.)
"(When It's) Sleepy Time Down South"
(*Music and Lyrics by* Clarence Muse, Leon René, Otis René.)
"Throw Dirt"
(*Music and Lyrics by* Shelton Brooks.)
"Am I Blue" (from film ON WITH THE SHOW)
(*Music by* Harry Akst. *Lyrics by* Grant Clarke.)
"Half of Me"
(*Music and Lyrics by* Peter de Rose and Sam Lewis.)
"Washtub Rubsudy" (from RHAPSODY IN BLACK)
(*Music by* Alberta Nichols. *Lyrics by* Mann Holiner.)E. Waters

Scene 2
"Bread and Gravy"
E. Waters, R. Beane
(*Music by* Hoagy Carmichael.)

Scene 3
Moods from his own 'Jazzantasy Suite:'
Blues, Syncopation, Boogie
R. Beane
"Love For Sale"
(*Music by* Cole Porter, arr. R. Beane.)R. Beane

Scene 4
"Dinah" (introduced by Miss Waters in PLANTATION REVUE)
(*Music by* Harry Akst. *Lyrics by* Sam M. Lewis and Joe Young.)
"Go Back Where You Stayed Last Night"
(*Music and Lyrics by* Ethel Waters and Sidney Easton.)
"My Man" (from ZIEGFELD FOLLIES OF 1921)
(*Music by* Maurice Yvain. *French lyrics by* Albert Willemetz, Jacques Charles. *English Lyrics by* Channing Pollock.)
"St. Louis Blues"
(*Music and Lyrics by* W. C. Handy.)
"Suppertime" (from AS THOUSANDS CHEER)
(*Music and Lyrics by* Irving Berlin.)
E. Waters

ACT 2
Scene 1
"Dance Hall Hostess" (from RHAPSODY IN BLACK)
(*Music by* Alberta Nichols. *Lyrics by* Mann Holiner.)
E. Waters

Scene 2
"Odd Moments"
(*by* R Beane)
Jerome Kern Medley
R. Beane

Scene 3
"Takin' a Chance on Love" (from CABIN IN THE SKY)
(*Music by* Vernon Duke. *Lyrics by* John Latouche and Ted Fetter.)
"Somethin' Told Me Not to Trust That Man"
(*Music by* Alberta Nichols. *Lyrics by* Mann Holiner.)
"Happiness is Jes' a Thing Called Joe" (from CABIN IN THE SKY film)
(*Music by* Harold Arlen. *Lyrics by* E. Y. Harburg.)
"Lady Be Good" (from LADY, BE GOOD)
(*Music by* George Gershwin. *Lyrics by* Ira Gershwin.)
"Stormy Weather" (from COTTON CLUB PARADE-1933)
(*Music by* Harold Arlen. *Lyrics by* Ted Koehler.)
"Mammy"
(Original version by the late Will Marion Cook)
"Motherless Chile" (Spiritual)
"Crucifixion" (Spiritual)
"Cabin in the Sky" (from CABIN IN THE SKY)
(*Music by* Vernon Duke. *Lyrics by* John Latouche.)
E. Waters

1953.13 COMEDY IN MUSIC

A Solo Performance in Two Acts. Produced by Harry D. Squires. Opened 2 October 1953 at the John Golden Theatre, vacationed beginning 3 July 1954, resumed 2 August 1954, and closed 21 January 1956 after 849 performances.

CAST: VICTOR BORGE.

MUSICAL NUMBERS[2]

---

[2]Musical Numbers not listed in program. List below prepared from reviews and recordings. Mr. Borge chose from the following material during the course of the New York run and subsequent tour:

1. Variations on a Theme
2. Medley of Popular Songs
3. Warsaw Concerto
   (*Music by* Richard Addinsell.)
4. "Auf Wiedersehn Sweetheart"
   (*Music and Lyrics by* John Sexton, John Turner, Eberhard Storch.)
5. "Tea for Two" (from NO NO NANETTE)
   (*Music and Lyrics by* Vincent Youmans and Irving Caesar.)
6. Malaguena
   (*Music by* Ernesto Lecuona.)
7. "Stardust"
   (*Music by* Hoagy Carmichael and. *Lyrics by* Mitchell Parish.)
8. Nola
   (*Music by* Felix Arndt.)
9. Tales from the Vienna Woods
   (*Music by* Johann Strauss.)
10. Third Man Theme
   (*Music by* Anton Karas.)

(Program read as follows:)

1. Frankly
2. We
3. Don't
4. Know
5. What
6. Mr. Borge
7. Will
8. Do
9. But
10. We're
11. Sure
12. He'll
13. Keep
14. Us
15. Posted
16. From
17. Time
18. To
19. Time

P.S. There is also an intermission . . . but only Mr. Borge knows when.

1953.14

REGINA

A Revival of the Musical Drama (Opera) in Three Acts, a Prologue and 4 Scenes[3]. Text and music by Marc Blitzstein. Based on the play "The Little Foxes" by Lillian Hellman. Production directed by Robert Lewis. Conductor, Julius Rudel. Settings designed by Horace Armistead. Costumes designed by Aline Bernstein. Choreographer, John Butler. Lighting by Jean Rosenthal. (Orchestrations by Marc Blitzstein.) Produced by the New York City Opera. Opened 9 October 1953 at the New York City Center and closed 15 October 1953 after 2 performances in repertory.

CAST: *Regina Giddens*: BRENDA LEWIS. *Horace Giddens*, her husband: WILLIAM WILDERMAN. *Alexandra Giddens* (Zan), their daughter: DOROTHY MacNEIL. *Regina's Brothers (2)*: *Ben Hubbard*: LEON LISHNER. *Oscar Hubbard*: EMILE RENAN. *Birdie Hubbard*, Oscar's wife: WILLABELLE UNDERWOOD. *Leo Hubbard*, their son: MICHAEL POLLOCK. *Jazz*: WILLIAM DILLARD. *Addie*, cook: LUCRETIA WEST. *Cal*, butler: LAWRENCE WINTERS. *Marshall*: LLOYD THOMAS LEECH. *Belle*, maid: Margaret Tynes. *Bagtry*: Russell Goodwin. *Manders*: Charles Kuestner.

---

11. Nocturne
    (*Music by* Frederic Chopin.)
12. Blue Danube Waltz
    (*Music by* Johann Strauss.)
13. "Trees"
    (*Music by* Oscar Rasbach. *Poem by* Joyce Kilmer)
14. "One Fine Day"
    (*Music by* Giacomo Puccini.)
15. "A Mozart Opera" *by* Victor Borge
16. Tango
    (*Music by* Isaac Albeniz.)
17. Minute Waltz
    (*Music by* Frederic Chopin.)
18. Liebestraum
    (*Music by* Franz Lizst.)
19. Family Background
20. Phonetic Punctuation

[3]Originally produced in New York 31 October 1949 at the 46th Street Theatre for 56 performances. For Synopsis of Scenes and Musical Numbers, see original 1949 production. An Intermission was added between Act 1, Scenes 1 and 2. Restored to the production for this revival:

"Blues"
L. West, B. Lewis

1953.15

DIE FLEDERMAUS

A Revival of the Operetta in Three Acts.[4] (Original Viennese libretto by Carl Haffner and Richard Genée. Lyrics by Richard Genée. Based on the comedy "Le Réveillon" by Henri Meilhac and Ludovic Halévy.) English libretto by Ruth and Thomas Martin. Music by Johann Strauss. Staged by Glenn Jordan. Choreography, John Butler. Costume supervisor, Robert Fletcher. Lighting by Hans Sondheimer. Conducted by Thomas P. Martin. Produced by the New York City Opera. Opened 10 October 1953 at the New York City Center and closed 7 November 1953 after 2 performances in repertory; re-opened 27 March 1954 and closed 1 May 1954 after 3 additional performances. Total this season: 5 performances.[5]

CAST: *Eisenstein*: JACK RUSSELL. *Rosalinda*: JEAN FENN. *Adele*: ADELAIDE BISHOP. *Alfred*: LLOYD THOMAS LEECH. *Falke*: EARL REDDING. *Frank*: Richard Wentworth. *Blind*: Luigi Vellucci. *Prince Orlofsky*: DONALD GRAMM. *Sally*: Jennie Andrea. *Frosch*: Coley Worth. *Ivan*: Michael Arshansky. *Solo Dancers*: Felisa Conde, Glen Tetley. *Ensemble*: New York City Opera Chorus.

1953.16

KISMET

A Musical Arabian Night (Musical Comedy) in Two Acts, 14 Scenes. Book by Charles Lederer and Luther Davis. Based on the play of the same name by Edward Knoblock. Music from Alexander Borodin. Musical adaptation and lyrics by Robert Wright and George Forrest. Settings and costumes designed by Lemuel Ayers. Lighting by Peggy Clark. Orchestral and choral arrangements by Arthur Kay. Musical direction by Louis Adrian. Dances and musical numbers staged by Jack Cole. Production directed by Albert Marre. Produced by Charles Lederer in association with Edwin Lester. Opened 3 December 1953 at the Ziegfeld Theatre and closed 23 April 1955 after 583 performances.

CAST (in order appearance): *Imam of The Mosque*: Richard Oneto. *Muezzins*: Gerald Cardoni, Kirby Smith, Ralph Strane, Louis Polacek. *Doorman*: Jack Mei Ling. *First Beggar*: EARLE MACVEIGH. *Second Beggar*: Robert Lamont. *Third Beggar*: Rodolfo Silva. *Dervishes*: Jack Dodds, Marc Wilder. *Omar*: PHILIP COOLIDGE. *Public Poet*, later called *Hajj*: ALFRED DRAKE. *Marsinah*, His Daughter: DORETTA MORROW. *A Merchant*: Kirby Smith. *Hassan-Ben*: HAL HACKETT. *Jawan*: TRUMAN GAIGE. *Street Dancers*: FLORENCE LESSING, Ethel Martin. *Akbar*: Jack Dodds. *Assiz*: Marc Wilder. *Bangle Man*: Richard Oneto. *Chief Policeman*: TOM CHARLESWORTH. *Second Policeman*: HAL HACKETT. *The Wazir of Police*: HENRY CALVIN. *Wazir's Guards*: Stephen Ferry, Steve Reeves. *Lalume*: JOAN DIENER. *Attendants*: Mario Lamm, John Weidemann. *Princesses of Ababu*: Patricia Dunn, Bonnie Evans, Reiko Sato. *The Caliph*: RICHARD KILEY. *Slave Girls*: Carol Ohmart, Joyce Palmer, Sandra Stahl, Lila Jackson. *A Peddler*: EARLE MACVEIGH. *A Servant*: Richard Vine. *Princess Zubbediya of Damascus*: FLORENCE LESSING. *Ayah to Zubbediya*: Lucy Andonian. *Princess Samaris of Bangalore*: BEATRICE KRAFT. *Ayah to Samaris*: Thelma Dare. *Street Women*: Jo Ann O'Connell, Lynne Stuart. *Prosecutor*: EARLE MACVEIGH. *Widow Yussef*: Barbara Slate. *Diwan Dancers*: Neile Adams, Jack Woods, Marc Wilder.

Singers: Gerald Cardoni, Robert Lamont, Richard Oneto, Louis Polacek, Kirby Smith, Ralph Strane, Richard Vine, George Yarick, Anita Coulter, Thelma Dare, Lila Jackson, Jo Ann O'Connell, Barbara Slate, Sandra Stahl, Lynne Stuart, Erica Twiford. *Dancers*: Neile Adams, Patricia Dale, Devra Kline, Ania Romaine, Vida Ann Solomon, Roberta Stevenson.

The action takes place in one day in Bagdad, Act 1 from Dawn to Dusk, Act 2 from Dusk to Dawn.

Act 1, Scene 1: A tent just outside the city. *Scene 2*: On the steps of the Mosque. *Scene 3*: The Bazaar of the Caravans. *Scene 4*: A side street. *Scene 5*; A garden. *Scene 6*: A street near the Bazaar. *Scene 7*: The throne room of His Exalted Excellency, the Wazir of Police.

Act 2, Scene 1: Along the route of the Caliph's Procession. *Scene 2*: The garden. *Scene 3*: Ante-room to the Wazir's harem. *Scene 4*: A rooftop pavilion in the Wazir's palace. *Scene 5*: A corridor in the Wazir's palace. *Scene 6*: Ante-room to the Wazir's harem. *Scene 7*: The ceremonial hall of the Caliph's palace.

---

[4]First English language production in New York 16 March 1885 at the Casino Theatre for 42 performances. First New York production of this adaptation 20 December 1950 at the Metropolitan Opera House. No list of musical numbers appears in the program for this production. For Synopsis of Scenes and Musical Numbers, see May 1954 revival.

[5]Settings uncredited. Settings and costumes were assembled from various sources, a previous Sol Hurok tour of DIE FLEDERMAUS and the Broadway production of MY DARLIN' AIDA.

ACT 1
Scene 1
"Sands of Time"
R. Oneto
"Rhymes Have I"
A. Drake, D. Morrow
"Fate"
A. Drake
Scene 2
"Fate" (reprise)
A. Drake
Scene 3
"Bazaar of the Caravans"
F. Lessing, J. Dodds, M. Wilder, Merchants and Shoppers
"Not Since Ninevah"
J. Diener, H. Calvin, P. Dunn, B. Evans, R. Sato, J. Dodds, M. Wilder, Merchants, Shoppers
"Baubles, Bangles and Beads"
D. Morrow
Scene 5
"Stranger in Paradise"
R. Kiley, D. Morrow
Scene 6
"He's in Love!"
T. Charlesworth, H. Hackett, E. MacVeigh, P. Dunn, B. Evans, R. Sato, J. Dodds, M. Wilder, R. Kiley, P. Coolidge
Scene 7
"Gesticulate"
A. Drake, Wazir's Council
"Fate" (reprise)
A. Drake, Ladies of Wazir's Harem

ACT 2
Scene 1
"Night of My Nights"
R. Kiley, Entourage
Scene 2
"Stranger in Paradise" (reprise)
D. Morrow
"Baubles, Bangles and Beads" (reprise)
R. Kiley
"He's in Love!" (reprise)
Entourage
Scene 3
"Was I Wazir?"
H. Calvin, T. Charlesworth, H. Hackett, Guards
Scene 4
"Rahadlakum"
A. Drake, J. Diener, F. Lessing, B. Kraft, P. Dunn, B. Evans, R. Sato, Ladies of the Wazir's Harem
"And This Is My Beloved"
D. Morrow, R. Kiley, A. Drake, H. Calvin
Scene 5
"The Olive Tree"
A. Drake
Scene 7
"Ceremonial of the Caliph's Diwan"
Diwan Dancers
"Presentation of Princesses"
a. Damascus
F. Lessing, L. Andonian
b. Bangalore
B. Kraft, T. Dare
c. Ababu
P. Dunn, B. Evans, R. Sato
Finale
A. Drake, Ensemble

1953.17

JOHN MURRAY ANDERSON'S ALMANAC

A Musical Revue in Two Acts, Prologue and 25 Scenes. Sketches by Jean Kerr, Sumner Locke-Elliott, Arthur Macrae, Herbert Farjeon, Lauri Wylie, Billy K. Wells, (Leslie Julian Jones, Orson Bean, Phil Green). Music and lyrics by Richard Adler and Jerry Ross, Cy Coleman, Michael Grace, Joseph McCarthy, Henry Sullivan, John Rox, Bart Howard, (Sheldon Harnick, Harry Belafonte, John Murray Anderson, Michael Grace, Carl Tucker, Sammy Gallup, Charles Zwar, Alan Melville). Sketches directed by Cyril Ritchard. Dances and musical numbers staged by Donald Saddler. Scenery by Raoul Pene du Bois. Costumes by Thomas Becher. Musical direction, Buster Davis. Orchestrations by Ted Royal. Vocal arrangements by Buster Davis. Dance music arranged by Gerald Alters. Entire production devised and staged by John Murray Anderson. Produced by Michael Grace, Stanley Gilkey and Harry Rigby. Opened 10 December 1953 at the Imperial Theatre and closed 26 June 1954 after 229 performances.

CAST: HERMIONE GINGOLD, BILLY DE WOLFE, HARRY BELAFONTE, POLLY BERGEN, ORSON BEAN, NANCI CROMPTON, CARLETON CARPENTER, HARRY MIMMO, ELAINE DUNN, CELIA LIPTON, JAMES JEWELL, KAY MEDFORD, Lee Becker, Imelda DeMartin, Dorothy Dushock, Greb Lober, Illona Murai, Margot Myers, Gwen Neilson, Gloria Smith, Jimmy Albright, Hank Brunjes, Ronald Cecill, Dean Crane, Ralph McWilliams, Gerard Leavitt, Jacqueline Mickles, Colleen Hutchins, Monique Van Vooren, Tina Louise, Larry Kert, Bob Kole, George Reeder, Jay Harnick, Kenneth Urmston, Toni Wheelis, Siri, Millard Thomas.

PROLOGUE[6]
"Harlequinade"
(*Music and Lyrics by* Richard Adler and Jerry Ross.)
Harlequin: C. Carpenter. *Puncinello*: H. Mimmo. *Pierrot*: J. Jewell. *Pierrette*: C. Lipton. *Columbine*: N. Crompton. *Pierrettes*: L. Becker, I. DeMartin, D. Dushock, G. Lober, I. Murai, M. Myers, G. Neilson, G. Smith. *Pierrots*: J. Albright, H. Brunjes, R. Cecill, D. Crane, R. McWilliams, G. Leavitt.

ACT 1
Scene 1
The Coronation: "Queen for a Day"
(*Music and Lyrics by* Richard Adler and Jerry Ross.)
The Four Queens: J. Mickles, C. Hutchins, M. Van Vooren, T. Louise. *The Bridegrooms*: L. Kert, B. Kole, G. Reeder, J. Harnick, R. Cecill, R. McWilliams, H. Brunjes, G. Leavitt. *Miss Reingold*: H. Gingold.
Scene 2
My Cousin Who?
(*by* Jean Kerr)
David: B. DeWolfe. *Butlers*: J. Albright, K. Urmston, R. Cecill, R. McWilliams. *Witch Doctor*: D. Crane. *Maids*: T. Wheelis, G. Neilson. *Rebecca*: C. Lipton. *Louise*: I. Murai.
Scene 3
"You're So Much a Part of Me"
(*Music and Lyrics by* Richard Adler and Jerry Ross.)
The Pierrot of 1953: C. Carpenter. *The Pierrette of 1953*: E. Dunn.
Scene 4
"I Dare to Dream"
P. Bergen
(*Music by* Michael Grace and Carl Tucker. *Lyrics by* Sammy Gallup.)
Scene 5
"The Cello"
(*Music by* Charles Zwar. *Lyrics by* Leslie Julian Jones.)
The Cellist: H. Gingold.

---

[6]Added during the run:
Jonathan Winters (Comedian Specialty: Marine Corps sketch)
"Anema e Corre"
Tony Bavaar
(*Music and Lyrics by* Mann Curtis and Harry Akst.)
"With All My Heart and Soul"
(T. Bavaar)
(*Music and Lyrics by* Mann Curtis and Harry Akst.)
The Minstrel: T. Bavaar. *The Countess*: G. Neilson. *Courtiers*: J. Harnick, S. Guenther, H. Brunjes.

Scene 6

Don Brown's Body

(*by* Jean Kerr)

Mike Hammer: O. Bean. *Sally Duprey*: K. Medford. *Man*: C. Carpenter. *Chorus*: J. Harnick, C. Hutchins, J. Mickles, T. Louise, B. Kole, M. Van Vooren, Siri, 5. Reeder, L. 5Kert.

Scene 7

"Mark Twain"[7]

H. Belafonte

(*Music and Lyrics by* Harry Belafonte.)

Guitarist: M. Thomas.

Scene 8

The Nightingale and the Rose (*Adapted* from the story of Oscar Wilde *by* John Murray Anderson.)(from GREENWICH VILLAGE FOLLIES OF 1922)

"Nightingale, Bring Me a Rose"

J. Jewell

(*Music by* Henry Sullivan. *Lyrics by* John Murray Anderson.)

The Story Teller: C. Lipton. *The Student*: D. Crane. *The Prince*: G. Leavitt. *The Coquette*: M. Myers. *The Nightingale*: N. Crompton. *Guests at the Ball*: Siri, M. Van Vooren, T. Louise, C. Hutchins, G. Lober, D. Dushock, G. Smith, G. Neilson, H. Brunjes, R. McWilliams, R. Cecill, G. Reeder, J. Albright.

Note: "The Nightingale and the Rose" was first presented by John Murray Anderson in one of his early "Greenwich Village Follies" (1922). It established a new form of production number which has subsequently become known as a "Ballet Ballad." The music of the present version has been written in its entirety by Henry Sullivan.

Scene 9

European Express

Mrs. A: H. Gingold. *Mrs. B*: B. DeWolfe.

Scene 10

"My Love Is A Wanderer"[8]

P. Bergen

(*Music and Lyrics by* Bart Howard.)

Scene 11

"Tin Pan Alley"

(*Music by* Cy Coleman. *Lyrics by* Joseph McCarthy, Jr.)

The Song Plugger: C. Carpenter. And R. Cecill, J. Harnick, L. Kert, B. Kole.

"Mammy Songs"

R. McWilliams, K. Urmston

"Rhythm Songs"

G. Reeder, I. DeMartin, L. Becker, G. Lober, D. Dushock

"Torch Songs"

G. Smith, I. Murai, M. Myers, H. Brunjes, G. Leavitt, D. Crane

"Patriotic Songs"

E. Dunn

Scene 12

"Merry Little Minuet"[9]

O. Bean

(*Music and Lyrics by* Sheldon Harnick.)

Scene 13

"Hope You Come Back"

(*by* Sumner Locke-Elliot)

(*Music and Lyrics by* Richard Adler and Jerry Ross.)

Meg: P. Bergen. *Beth*: N. Crompton. *Jo*: E. Dunn. *Amy*: H. Gingold. *Marmee*: K. Medford. *Laurie*: B. DeWolfe. *Friends*: J. Jewell, Entire Company.

ACT 2

Scene 1

Ziegfeldiana: "If Every Month Were June"

C. Lipton

(*Music by* Henry Sullivan. *Lyrics by* John Murray Anderson.)

The Spring Bride: C. Hutchins. *The Summer Bride*: Siri. *The Autumn Bride*: J. Mickles. *The Winter Bride*: M. Van Vooren. *The Bouquet*: N. Crompton. *The Train Bearers*: I. DeMartin, L. Becker, D. Dushock, G. Neilson.

[7]Dropped during the run.
[8]Dropped during the run.
[9]Dropped during the run.

Scene 2

"Which Witch?"

H. Gingold

(*Music by* Charles Zwar. *Lyrics by* Alan Melville.)

Scene 3

La Loge (Renoir)

(*by* Herbert Farjeon)

"Fini"

P. Bergen

(*Music and Lyrics by* Richard Adler and Jerry Ross.)

The Man in the Box: J. Harnick.

Scene 4

Cartoon

(*by* Arthur Macrae)

First Secretary: K. Medford. *Second Secretary*: C. Hutchins. *The New Manager*: O. Bean.

Scene 5

"Acorn in the Meadow"

H. Belafonte

(*Music and Lyrics by* Richard Adler and Jerry Ross.)

Scene 6

Harry Mimmo[10]

The Ladies: T. Louise, J. Mickles, M. Van Vooren. *Sedan Chair Bearers*: J. Harnick, L. Kert.

Scene 7

"When Am I Going to Meet Your Mother?"

E. Dunn, C. Carpenter

(*Music and Lyrics by* Richard Adler and Jerry Ross.)

Scene 8

Dinner for One

(*by* Lauri Wylie)

The Lady: H. Gingold. *The Butler*: B. DeWolfe.

Scene 9

(Chinese Monologue) [American Town]

(*by* Orson Bean and Phil Green)

O. Bean

Scene 10

"Hold 'Em Joe"

H. Belafonte

(*Music and Lyrics by* Harry Belafonte.)

Danced by I. Murai, G. Reeder, G. Smith, M. Van Vooren, C. Hutchins, Dancers.

Scene 11

La Pistachio

(*by* Billy K. Wells, *adapted* for the Almanac *by* Sumner Locke-Elliot)

Bobo: H. Gingold. *Cornelius*: B. DeWolfe. *Fifi*: K. Medford.

Scene 12

"The Earth and the Sky"

P. Bergen

(*Music and Lyrics by* John Rox.)

Finale

Entire Company

1954.01 THE GIRL IN PINK TIGHTS

A Musical Extravaganza in Two Acts, 17 Scenes. Book by Jerome Chodorov and Joseph Fields. Music by Sigmund Romberg. Lyrics by Leo Robin. Music developed and orchestrated by Don Walker. Scenery and lighting by Eldon Elder. Costumes by Miles White. Musical direction by Sylvan Levin. Ballet music arranged by Trude Rittman. Dances and musical numbers staged by Agnes de Mille. Entire production directed by Shepard Traube. Produced by Shepard Traube in association with Anthony Brady Farrell. Opened 5 March 1954 at the Mark Hellinger Theatre and closed 12 June 1954 after 115 performances.

CAST (in order of appearance): *Boris*: Joshua Shelley. *Volodya Kuzentsov*: ALEXANDRE KALIOUJNY. *Lisette Gervais*: (Zizi) JEANMAIRE. *Maestro Gallo*: CHARLES GOLDNER. *Lotta Leslie*: BRENDA LEWIS. *Clyde Hallam*: DAVID ATKINSON. *Eddington*: David Aiken. *Hattie Hopkins*: Dania Krupska. *Van Beuren*:

[10]Dropped during the run.

ROBERT SMITH. *British Tars*: Tom Rieder, John Taliaferro. *Policeman*: John Stamford. *Newspaper Boy*: Maurice Hines. *Shoe Shine Boy*: Gregory Hines. *Mike*: Kalem Kermoyan. *Bruce*: John Stamford. *Nellie*: Lydia Fredericks. *Hollister*: Ray Mason. *Simone*: Katia Geleznova. *Mimi*: Eva Rubinstein. *Lucette*: Lynne Marcus. *Odette*: Nancy King. *Gisele*: Lila Popper. *Paulette*: Mickey Gunnersen. *Fire Chiefs*: Ted Thurston, John Taliaferro. *Jenny*: Jenny Workman. *Blanchette*: Beryl Towbin. *Emile*: Ted Thurston. *Sommelier*: John Taliaferro. *Gypsy Violinist*: Douglas Rideout.

Singers: Lydia Fredericks, Jane House, Deedy Irwin, Peggy Kinard, Marni Nixon, Michelle Reiner, Joanne Spiller, Beverly Weston, David Aiken, Herbert Banke, Robert Driscoll, Kalem Kermoyan, Ray Mason, Stas Pajenski, Douglas Rideout, Tom Rieder, James Schlader, John Stamford, John Taliaferro, Ted Thurston. *Dancers*: Meredith Baylis, Joan Bowman, Katia Geleznova, Mickey Gunnerson, Mary Haywood, Rhoda Kerns, Nancy King, Lynne Marcus, Julie Marlowe, Ellen Matthews, Lila Popper, Eva Rubinstein, Dorothy Scott, Beverly Simms, Beryl Towbin, Diana Turner, Jenny Workman, Harry Asmus, Louis Kosman, Paul Olson, Edward Stinnett, William Weslow.

The action of the play takes place immediately following the Civil War in the theatrical district of New York.

Act 1, Scene 1: A Rehearsal Hall, the Academy of Music. *Scene 2*: A Street near the Academy of Music and Niblo's Garden. *Scene 3*: Outside the Academy of Music and Niblo's Garden. *Scene 4*: A Street near the Theatrical District. *Scene 5*: Bowling Green. *Scene 6*: The Stage at Niblo's Garden. *Scene 7*: A Corridor, the Academy of Music. *Scene 8*: The Stage at the Academy of Music. Three days later. *Scene 9*: A Street. *Scene 10*: In front of the Academy of Music.

Act 2, Scene 1: A Pier at Battery park. A week later. *Scene 2*: A Theatrical Costumer's. Two weeks later. *Scene 3*: The Stage at Niblo's Garden. *Scene 4*: A Private Dining Room at the Hotel Brevoort. *Scene 5*: A Corridor Backstage at Niblo's Garden. *Scene 6*: Clyde's Dressing Room. *Scene 7*: The final scene of "The Soul of Dick the Renegade." "The Bill Is Due! It Must Be Paid."

ACT 1[11]

Scene 1

Ballet Class
Danced by the French Ballet Company
Lisette: Jeanmaire. *Volodya*: A. Kalioujny. *Solists*: D. Turner, W. Weslow, L. Marcus, H. Asmus, B. Simms, P. Olson, D. Scott, E. Stinnett.

Scene 2

"That Naughty Show from Gay Paree"
Singing Ensemble

Scene 3

"Lost in Loveliness"
D. Atkinson
Lisette: Jeanmaire. *First Lover*: P. Olson. *Second Lover*: H. Asmus. *Lovers*: E. Stinnett, L. Kosman.

Scene 4

"I Promised Their Mothers"
C. Goldner

Scene 5

"Up in the Elevated Railway"
Jeanmaire, D. Atkinson, A. Kalioujny, D. Krupska, M. Hines, G. Hines, Singing Ensemble

"In Paris and In Love"
D. Atkinson, Jeanmaire

Scene 6

"You've Got To be a Little Crazy"
B. Lewis, L. Fredericks, K. Kermoyan, J. Stamford

Scene 7

"When I Am Free to Love"
Jeanmaire

Scene 8

Pas de Deux
Danced by Jeanmaire, A. Kalioujny

Scene 9

"Out of the Way"/"Roll Out the Hose, Boys"
Singing Ensemble

Scene 10

Finale (Act 1)
Entire Company

ACT 2[12]

Scene 1

"My Heart Won't Say Goodbye"
D. Atkinson, Jeanmaire, Singing Ensemble

"We're All in the Same Boat"
Entire Company

Scene 2

"Lost in Loveliness" (reprise)
D. Atkinson

Scene 3

Bacchanale
Danced by the French Ballet Company
Dionysius: A. Kalioujny. *The Wayward Nymph*: J. Workman. *Nymphs*: M. Baylis, J. Bowman, D. Scott, B. Simms, D. Turner. *Satyrs*: H. Asmus, P. Olson, E. Stinnett, W. Weslow. *Messenger*: B. Towbin. *Attendants*: M. Hines, G. Hines.

"My Heart Won't Say Goodbye" (reprise)
B. Lewis

"Love Is the Funniest Thing"
B. Lewis, C. Goldner

Scene 6

"When I Am Free to Love" (reprise)
Jeanmaire

Scene 7

"The Cardinal's Guard Are We"
B. Lewis, Singing Ensemble

Grand Imperial Ballet
Lucifer: A. Kalioujny. *Hecate*: Jeanmaire. *Devils*: H. Asmus, P. Olson, E. Stinnett, W. Weslow. *Evil Spirits*: K. Geleznova, L. Marcus, D. Scott, B. Simms. *Bats*: M. Hayward, M. Baylis, J. Bowman, J. Marlowe, L. Popper, D. Turner. *Dancing Batlets*: N. King, E. Matthews, E. Rubinstein, J. Workman. *Batlets*: M. Gunnerson, R. Kerns, B. Towbin. *Attendants*: M. Hines, G. Hines.

Finale (Act 2)
Entire Company

1954.02 BY THE BEAUTIFUL SEA

A Musical in Two Acts, 15 Scenes. Book by Herbert and Dorothy Fields. Music by Arthur Schwartz. Lyrics by Dorothy Fields. Settings and lighting by Jo Mielziner. Costumes by Irene Sharaff. Choreography by Helen Tamiris. Directed by Marshall Jamison. Musical direction and vocal arrangements by Jay Blackton. Orchestrations by Robert Russell Bennett. Production associate, Simon P. Herman. Produced by Robert Fryer and Lawrence Carr. Opened 8 April 1954 at the Majestic Theatre, moved 4 October 1954 to the Imperial Theatre and closed 27 November 1954 after 270 performances.

CAST (in order of appearance): *Quartet*: John Dennis, Reid Shelton, Ray Hyson, Larry Laurence. *Acrobats*: Ray Kirchner, Rex Cooper. *Cora Belmont*: Mary Harmon. *Molly Belmont*: Cindy Robbins. *Lillian Belmont*: Gloria Smith. *Ruby Monk*: MAE BARNES. *Mrs. Koch*: Edith True Case. *Carl Gibson*: CAMERON PRUD'HOMME. *Lottie Gibson*: SHIRLEY BOOTH. *Half-Note*: Robert Jennings. *Diabolo*: Thomas Gleason. *Baby Betsy Busch*: CAROL LEIGH. *Mickey Powers*: RICHARD FRANCE. *Dennis Emery*: WILBUR EVANS. *Flora Busch*: ANNE FRANCINE. *Willie Slater*:

[11]Program Note (Warning to the Public!): The characters and events depicted in the extravaganza we are about to present are not altogether fictional and have more than a family resemblance to those characters and events which led to the production of the first American musical comedy.

"... In consequence of the destruction , by fire, of the Academy of Music, this city, Jarrett & Palmer, who were to have produced 'La Biche au Bois' with a ballet troupe from Paris, had on their hands a number of artists. William Wheatley, who was to produce 'The Black Crook,' a melodrama, at Niblo's Garden, was persuaded to utilize the unfortunate ballet company ... Charles M. Barras, the author of 'The Black Crook,' objected to this desecration of his work. But a payment of the sum of \$1500 for the run of the piece, no matter what its duration might be, overcame his objections." From "A History of the New York Stage" by T. Allston Brown

[12]Added during the run to Act 2, Scene 7 after "The Cardinal's Guard Are We," before the Ballet:
"Going to the Devil"
Jeanmaire

Warde Donovan. *Lenny*: Larry Howard. *Sidney*: Eddie Roll. *Mr. Curtis*: Paul Reed. *Burt Mayer*: Larry Laurence. *Viola*: Gaby Monet.

Dancers: Cathryn Damon, Dorothy Donau, Lillian Donau, Pat Ferrier, Sigyn, Mona Tritsch, Rex Cooper, Bob Haddad, Larry Howard, Ray Kirchner, Victor Reilly, Eddie Roll, Arthur Partington. *Singers*: Suzanne Easter, Lola Fisher, Colleen O'Connor, Pat Roe, Jean Sincere, Libi Staiger, John Dennis, Warde Donovan, Thomas Gleason, Ray Hyson, Franklin Kennedy, Larry Laurence, George Lenz, Reid Shelton.

Act 1, Scene 1: Backyard of Lottie Gibson's Boarding House. Coney Island, early 1900s. *Scene 2*: Seaside Street in Coney Island. *Scene 3*: The Midway at Coney Island. *Scene 4*: The Old Mill. *Scene 5*: Backyard of Lottie Gibson's Boarding House. *Scene 6*: Midway at Coney Island. *Scene 7*: Seaside Street in Coney Island. *Scene 8*: Bedroom of Lottie Gibson's Boarding House. *Scene 9*: The Pavillion of Fun.

Act 2, Scene 1: The Backyard of Lottie Gibson's Boarding House. *Scene 2*: Stage of the Brighton Beach Theatre. *Scene 3*: Dreamland Casino. *Scene 4*: Lottie's Bedroom. *Scene 5*: Seaside Street in Coney Island. *Scene 6*: Dreamland Casino.

ACT 1

Scene 1

"Mona from Arizona"
J. Dennis, R. Shelton, R. Hyson, L. Laurence

"The Sea Song"
S. Booth, Boarders, Neighbors

Scene 2

"Old Enough to Love"
R. France

Scene 3

"Coney Island Boat"
S. Booth, R. Jennings, Visitors
(Counter Melody "In the Good Old Summertime" *by* Ben Shields and George Evans.)

Scene 4

"Alone Too Long"
W. Evans

Scene 5

"Happy Habit"
M. Barnes

Scene 6

"Goodtime Charlie"
R. France, L. Howard, E. Roll, M. Harmon, C. Robbins, G. Smith
Sports: Male Dancers. *Spicy Pictures*: *The Vendor*: L. Laurence. *Wicked Women*: Sigyn, L. Donau, C. Damon. *The Iceman*: A. Partington, P. Ferrier. *Serpentina Sal*: G. Monet. *Finale*: Dancing Company.

Scene 7

"Goodtime Charlie" (reprise)
R. France, L. Howard, E. Roll, M. Harmon, C. Robbins, G. Smith

Scene 8

"I'd Rather Wake Up By Myself"
S. Booth

Scene 9

"Hooray for George the Third"
T. Gleason, L. Staiger, Visitors

ACT 2

Scene 1

"Hang Up"
M. Barnes, Boarders, Neighbors

"Alone Too Long" (reprise)
S. Booth

"More Love Than Your Love"
W. Evans

Scene 2

Vaudeville: Acts on the Bill:

1. The Three Clowns. 2. A Lady in Red. 3. Butterfly Wings.

"Lottie Gibson Specialty"
S. Booth

Scene 3

"Throw the Anchor Away"
L. Laurence, A. Partington, M. Harmon

Dance
G. Monet, A. Partington, R. France, R. Cooper, Patrons

"More Love Than Your Love" (reprise)
W. Evans

Scene 4

"Happy Habit" (reprise)
S. Booth

Scene 5

"Old Enough to Love" (reprise)
R. France, C. Leigh

Scene 6

Finale
Entire Company

1954.03 THE GOLDEN APPLE

A Musical in Two Acts, 10 Scenes[13]. Book and lyrics by John Latouche. (A contemporary adaptation of Homer's "The Iliad" and "The Odyssey.") Music by Jerome Moross. Settings by William and Jean Eckart. Costumes by Alvin Colt. Lighting by Klaus Holm. Musical director, Hugh Ross. Orchestral arrangements by Jerome Moross and Hershy Kay. Choreography and musical numbers staged by Hanya Holm. Directed by Norman Lloyd. Produced by Alfred DeLiagre Jr. and Roger L. Stevens in association with T. Edward Hambleton and Norris Houghton. Opened 20 April 1954 at the Alvin Theatre and closed 7 August 1954 after 125 performances. Total including Off-Broadway run: 173 performances.

CAST (in order of appearance): *Helen*, a Farmer's Daughter: KAYE BALLARD. *Lovey Mars*, the Local Matchmaker: BIBI OSTERWALD. *Mrs. Juniper*, the Mayor's Wife: SHANNON BOLIN. *Miss Minerva Oliver*, the Village School Marm: PORTIA NELSON. *Mother Hare*, the Local Mystic: Martha Larrimore. *Penelope*, Ulysses' Wife: PRISCILLA GILLETTE. *Menelaus*, the Old Sheriff: Dean Mitchener. *The Heroes (12)*: *Captain Mars*: Frank Seabolt. *Ajax*: Marten Sameth. *Agamemnon*: Crandall Diehl. *Nestor*: Maurice Edwards. *Bluey*: Murray Gitlin. *Thirsty*: Don Redlich. *Silas*: Peter De Mayo. *Homer*: Barton Mumaw. *Diomede*: Robert Flavelle. *Achilles*: Julian Patrick. *Patroclus*: Martin Keane. *Doc MacCahan*: Gary Gordon. *Ulysses*, a Veteran: STEPHEN DOUGLASS. *Theron*: David Hooks. *Mayor Juniper*: Jerry Stiller. *Paris*, a Travelling Salesman: JONATHAN LUCAS. *Hector Charybdis*, Mayor of Rhododendron: JACK WHITING.

Local Girls: Sara Bettis, Dorothy Etheridge, Nelle Fisher, Dee Harless, Janet Hayes, Lois McCauley, Ann Needham, Joli Roberts, Jere Stevens, Tao Strong, Helen Ahola. *Local Boys*: Santo Anselmo, Bob Gay, Ed Grace, Bill Nuss, Charles Post, Arthur Schoep.

The entire action takes place in the State of Washington between 1900 and 1910.

Act 1: The township of Angel's Roost on the edge of Mt. Olympus. *Scene 1*: In the Orchard. *Scene 2*: The Village Green. *Scene 3*: The Church Social. *Scene 4*: At Helen's House.

Act 2, Scene 1: The Seaport of Rhododendron. *Scene 2*: The Main Street of Rhododendron. *Scene 3*: Back in Angel's Roost. Penelope's Home. *Scene 4*: The Main Street again. *Scene 5*: The Big Spree. (a) Madam Calypso's Parlour. (b) The Brokerage Office of Scylla and Charybdis. (c) A waterfront dive. (d) The Hall of Science. (e) The Wrong Side of the Tracks. *Scene 6*: Angel's Roost. In the back yard.

ACT 1[14]

"Nothing Ever Happens in Angel's Roost"
K. Ballard, B. Osterwald, S. Bolin, P. Nelson

Mother Hare's Seance
(M. Larrimore)

"My Love Is On the Way"
P. Gillette

"The Heroes Come Home"
Entire Company

---

[13]First produced Off-Broadway 11 March-18 April 1954 at the Phoenix Theatre for 48 performances prior to its Broadway transfer. Off-Broadway performers who originated roles but did not play Broadway run: *Mrs. Juniper*, the Mayor's Wife: GERALDINE VITI. *Patroclus*: Larry Chelsi.

[14]Dropped from Off-Broadway for Broadway transfer:

"Wildflowers" (replaced by "When We Were Young")
P. Gillette

"We've Just Begun" (replaced by "The Tirade"/Finale)
S. Douglass, P. Gillette

"It Was a Glad Adventure"
S. Douglass, Heroes
"Come Along Boys"
The Heroes, Ensemble
"It's the Going Home Together"
S. Douglass, P. Gillette
Mother Hare's Prophecy
(M. Larrimore)
"Helen Is Always Willing"
The Heroes
The Church Social
The Heroes, Ensemble
"Introducin' Mr. Paris"
J. Lucas, Ensemble
The Judgement of Paris
B. Osterwald, S. Bolin, P. Nelson, M. Larrimore, J. Lucas
"Lazy Afternoon"
K. Ballard, J. Lucas
The Departure for Rhododendron
Entire Company

ACT 2
"My Picture in the Papers"
P. Gillette, J. Lucas, Male Ensemble
The Taking of Rhododendron
S. Douglass, J. Whiting, J. Lucas
Hector's Song
(J. Whiting)
"Windflowers"
P. Gillette
"Store-bought Suit"
S. Douglass
Calypso
C. Rae
Scylla and Charybdis
D. Michener, J. Whiting
"(By 'Goona-Goona' Lagoon)
(B. Osterwald)
"Doomed, Doomed, Doomed"
P. Nelson
"Circe, Circe"
M. Larrimore, Ensemble
Danced by A. Needham.
The Sewing Bee
P. Gillette, K. Ballard, P. Nelson, S. Bolin,
B. Osterwald, M. Larrimore, S. Douglass, The Suitors
The Tirade
P. Gillette
Finale
Entire Company

1954.04 SHOWBOAT

A Revival of the Musical Play in Two Acts, 14 Scenes[15]. Music by Jerome Kern. Book and lyrics by Oscar Hammerstein II. Based on the novel of the same name by Edna Ferber. Staged by William Hammerstein. Settings by Howard Bay. Costumes by John Boyt. Lighting by Jean Rosenthal. Conductor, Julius Rudel. Orchestrations by Robert Russell Bennett. Produced by The New York City Opera Company. Opened 8 April 1954 at the New York City Center for 3 performances in repertory, closing 2 May 1954; re-opened under the auspices of the New York City Center Light Opera Company 5 May 1954 at the New York City Center and closed 16 May 1954 after 15 additional performances.[16]

CAST[17] (in order of their appearance): *Windy McLain*: Arthur Newman. *Steve*: ROBERT GALLAGHER. *Pete*: Boris Aplon. *Queenie*: HELEN PHILLIPS. *Parthy Ann Hawkes*: MARJORIE GATESON. *Captain Andy*: STANLEY CARLSON. *Ellie*: DIANA DRAKE. *Frank*: JACK ALBERTSON. *Rubberface*: Thomas R. Powell. *Julie*: HELENA BLISS. *Gaylord Ravenal*: ROBERT ROUNSEVILLE. *Vallon*: Lawrence Haynes. *Magnolia*: LAUREL HURLEY. *Joe*: WILLIAM C. SMITH. *Backwoodsman*: Arthur Newman. *Jeb*: Lawrence Haynes. *Barker*: Thomas R. Powell. *Fatima*: Ann Barry. *Second Barker*: Charles Kuestner. *Sport*: Roland Miles. *Strong Woman*: Meri Miller. *Landlady*: SARA FLOYD. *Ethel*: Gloria Wynder. *Jake*: Milton Lyon. *Jim*: Boris Aplon. *Man With Guitar*: Charles Kuestner. *Doorman at Trocadero*: Bill Smith. *Mother Superior*: Ellen Gleason. *Nun*: Barbara Ford. *Kim*, as a child: Adele Newton. *Drunk*: Charles Kuestner. *Lottie*: Marilyn Bladd. *Dolly*: Dorothy Mirr. *Sally*: Gloria Sacks. *Old Lady on Levee*: Sara Floyd. *Kim*, in her Twenties: Greta Thormsen.

Congress of Beauties: Joanne Budill, DeAnn Mears, Peg Shirley, Barbara Sohmers. *Children*: Ginger Brooks, Georgianna Catal, Claudia Crawford, Dale Dennard, Leonard Grinnage, Joan Nickel, Bonnie Sawyer. *Singing Ensemble*: Benjamin Bajorek, Marilyn Bladd, Adelaide Boatner Eugene S. Brice, Doryce Brown, Walter P. Brown, Joseph E. Crawford, Dawin Emanuel, Rina Falcone, John Fleming, Barbara Ford, Mareda Gaither, Ellen Gleason, Russell Goodwin, Louise Hawthorne, Ida Frances Johnson, Charles Kuestner, Sheila Mathews, James Martindale, William McDaniel, Roland Miles, Dorothy Mirr, John Neilsen, Benjamin Plotkin, Madeline Porter, William W. Reynolds, Gloria Sacks, Christine Spencer, William Starling, Joseph Tanner, Frederick L. Thomas, Greta Thormsen, DeLoyd Tibbs, Rodester Timmons, Clyde S. Turner, Rose Virga, Gloria Wynder.

1954.05 THE PAJAMA GAME

A Musical Comedy in Two Acts, 17 Scenes. Book by George Abbott and Richard Bisssell. Based on the novel "7 1/2 Cents" by Richard Bissell. Music and lyrics by Richard Adler and Jerry Ross. Scenery and costumes by Lemuel Ayers. Choreography by Bob Fosse. Musical director, Hal Hastings. Orchestrations by Don Walker. Dance music arrangements by Roger Adams. Production directed by George Abbott and Jerome Robbins. Produced by Frederick Brisson, Robert E. Griffith and Harold S. Prince. Opened 13 May 1954 at the St. James Theatre, moved 12 November 1956 to the Sam S. Shubert Theatre, and closed 24 November 1956 after 1063 performances.

CAST (in order of appearance): *Hines*: EDDIE FOY, JR. *Prez*: STANLEY PRAGER. *Joe*: Ralph Farnsworth. *Hasler*: RALPH DUNN. *Gladys*: CAROL HANEY. *Sid Sorokin*: JOHN RAITT. *Mabel*: RETA SHAW. *First Helper*: Jack Drummond. *Second Helper*: BUZZ MILLER. *Charlie*: Ralph Chambers. *Babe Williams*: JANIS PAIGE. *Mae*: THELMA PELISH. *Brenda*: MARION COLBY. *Poopsie*: Rae Allen. *Salesman*: JACK WALDRON. *Eddie*: Jim Hutchison. *Pop*: William David. *Worker*: PETER GENNARO.

Dancers: Carmen Alvarez, Marilyn Gennaro, Lida Koehring, Shirley MacLaine, Marsha Reynolds, Ann Wallace, Robert Evans, Eric Kristen, Jim Hutchison, Dale Moreda, Augustin Rodriguez, Ben Vargas. *Singers*: Rae Allen, Sara Dillon, Mara Landi, Virginia Martin, Mary Roche, Mary Stanton, Rudy Adamo, Bob Dixon, Jack Drummond, Ralph Farnsworth, John Ford, Gordon Woodburn.

The action takes place in Cedar Rapids, Iowa at the present time.

Act 1, Scene 1: Pajama Game curtain. *Scene 2*: The Sleep-Tite Pajama Factory Shop Floor. *Scene 3*: A Hallway in the Factory. *Scene 4*: The Factory Office. *Scene 5*: A wooded path on the way to the Union picnic. *Scene 6*: The Picnic Grounds. *Scene 7*: The wooded path at twilight. *Scene 8*: The Kitchen of Babe's House. *Scene 9*: The Factory. *Scene 10*: The Factory Shop.

Act 2, Scene 1: Eagle Hall. *Scene 2*: The Kitchen of Babe's House. *Scene 3*: A Hall in the Factory. *Scene 4*: Morning in the Office. *Scene 5*: Hernando's Hideaway. *Scene 6*: The Office. *Scene 7*: A Street near the Park.

ACT 1
Scene 1
"The Pajama Game"
E. Foy, Jr.
Scene 2
"Racing With the Clock"
Girls, Boys
"A New Town Is a Blue Town"
J. Raitt
Scene 3
"I'm Not at All in Love"
J. Paige, Girls

[15]First presented in New York 27 December 1927 at the Ziegfeld Theatre for 572 performances. This revised version first presented 5 January 1946 at the Ziegfeld Theatre for 418 performances. For Synopsis of Scenes and Musical Numbers, see 1946 revival. Act 1, Scenes 2 and 3 combined from 1946 production. Act 2, Scene 8 reset in the Auditorium and Stage of the "Cotton Blossom."
[16]Dances uncredited.

[17]Cast changes for the New York City Opera engagement: *Captain Andy*: BURL IVES. *Frank*: DONN [Donald] DRIVER. *Joe*: LAWRENCE WINTERS.

Scene 4
"I'll Never Be Jealous Again"
E. Foy, Jr., R. Shaw
"Hey There"
J. Raitt
Scene 5
"Her Is"
S. Prager, C. Haney
Scene 6
"Sleep-Tite"
J. Paige, Boys, Girls
"Once a Year Day"
J. Raitt, J. Paige, Company
Danced by C. Haney, B. Miller, P. Gennaro.
Scene 7
("Her Is" reprise)
(S. Prager, T. Pelish)
Scene 8
"Small Talk"
J. Raitt, J. Paige
Scene 9
"There Once Was a Man"
J. Raitt, J. Paige
Scene 10
"Hey There" (reprise)
J. Raitt

ACT 2
Scene 1
"Steam Heat"
C. Haney, B. Miller, P. Gennaro
Scene 2
"Hey There" (reprise)
J. Paige
Scene 3
"Think of the Time I Save"
E. Foy, Jr., Girls
Scene 4
"Hernando's Hideaway"
C. Haney, J. Raitt, Company
Scene 5
"Jealousy Ballet"
E. Foy, Jr., C. Haney, R. Shaw, Boys
Scene 7
"7 1/2 Cents"
J. Paige, S. Prager, Girls, Boys
("There Once Was a Man" reprise)
(J. Raitt, J. Paige)
"The Pajama Game" (Finale)
Entire Company

1954.06 FLEDERMAUS

A Revival of the Comic Opera ("Die Fledermaus") in Three Acts.[18] (Original Viennese libretto by Carl Haffner and Richard Genée. (Based on "Le Réveillon" by Henri Meilhac and Ludovic Halévy.) Music by Johann Strauss. English libretto by Ruth and Thomas Martin. Staged by Glenn Jordan. Conductor, Thomas Martin. Choreography by Robert Pagent. Costumes by John Boyt. Lighting by Jean Rosenthal. Produced by the New York City Center Light Opera Company (William Hammerstein, Director.) Opened 19 May 1954 at the New York City Center and closed 6 June 1954 after 15 performances.[19]

[18]First English language production in New York 16 March 1885 at the Casino Theatre for 42 performances. First New York production of this adaptation 20 December 1950 at the Metropolitan Opera House.
[19]Settings uncredited.

CAST[20] (in order of appearance): *Alfredo*, an operatic tenor: LLOYD THOMAS LEECH, HAROLD R. BROWN. *Adele*, chambermaid: ADELAIDE BISHOP. *Rosalinda*, Eisenstein's wife: GLORIA LIND, GUEN OMERON. *Gabriel Von Eisenstein*, a banker: JACK RUSSELL, LLOYD THOMAS LEECH. *Blind*, Eisenstein's lawyer: CARL NICHOLAS. *Dr. Falke*, a friend of the Eisensteins': JOHN TYERS. *Frank*, prison warden: STANLEY CARLSON. *Sally*, Adele's sister, a ballet dancer: LIDIJA FRANKLIN. *Prince Orlofsky*, a very wealthy Russina Prince: DONALD GRAMM. *Ivan*, servant to Orlofsky: Thomas R. Powell. *Boris*, a dancer: ROBERT PAGENT. *Frosch*, a jailor: COLEY WORTH.

Servants: Stanley Bakis, Hill Eller, Alan James, Don Ratka, James Spicer, George Tucker. *Guests*: Marilyn Bladd, Rina Falcone, Barbara Ford, Ellen Gleason, Sheila Mathews, Dorothy Mirr, Gloria Sacks, Greta Thormsen, Rose Virga, Benjamin Bajorek, Dawin Emanuel, Russell Goodwin, Charles Kuestner, James Martindale, Roland Miles, Benjamin Plotkin, William W. Reynolds, Joseph Tanner.

The action takes place in the fashionable suburbs of Vienna in the 1850s.

Act 1: Rosalinda's Boudoir.

Act 2: At the Villa of Orlofsky.

Act 3: The Town Jail.

ACT 1
Introduction:
a. "Darling Rosalinda"
L. T. Leech
b. "We Are Going to a Party"
A. Bishop
"When These Lawyers Don't Deliver" (Trio)
G. Lind, J. Russell, C. Nicholas
"Come Along to the Ball" (Duet)
J. Tyers, J. Russell
"Oh Dear, It Breaks My Heart" (Trio)
G. Lind, A. Bishop, J. Russell
Finale
G. Lind, L. T. Leech, S. Carlson

ACT 2
"What a Joy to Be Here"
Ensemble
"Chacun à Son Goût"
D. Gramm
"My Friends, Your Kind Attention"
J. Tyers, D. Gramm
"Laughing Song"
A. Bishop, Ensemble
"How Engaging, How Exciting"
G. Lind, J. Russell
"Emperor Waltz" (Ballet)
R. Pagent, L. Franklin
"Voice of My Homeland" (Csardas)
G. Lind
Finale
Principals, Ensemble
a. "The King of Effervescence," b. "Sing to Love," c. "Ah, Happy Day."

ACT 3
"Pantomime"
S. Carlson, C. Worth
"Ever Since I Was a Baby" (Audition Song)
A. Bishop
"Vengeance Is Mine"
G. Lind, L. T. Leech, J. Russell
Finale
Entire Company

[20]Alternates sang roles Saturday and Sunday Matinees, Thursday and Saturday Evenings.

1954–1955 SEASON

Mary Martin in PETER PAN
Billy Rose Theatre Collection, New York Public Library for the Performing Arts

1954–1955 SEASON

1954.07 CAROUSEL

A Revival of the Musical Play in Two Acts, 9 Scenes[1]. Book and lyrics by Oscar Hammerstein II. Based on Ferenc Molnar's play "Liliom" as adapted by Benjamin F. Glazer. Music by Richard Rodgers. Staged by William Hammerstein. Dances by Agnes de Mille, restaged by Robert Pagent. Settings by Oliver Smith. Costumes by John Boyt. Lighting by Jean Rosenthal. Musical director, Julius Rudel. (Orchestrations by Don Walker.) Produced by the New York City Center Light Opera Company (William Hammerstein, Director). Opened 2 June 1954 at the New York City Center and closed 8 August 1954 after 79 performances.

CAST (in order of appearance): *Carrie Pipperidge*: BARBARA COOK. *Julie Jordan*: JO SULLIVAN. *Mrs. Mullin*: WINIFRED HEIDT. *Billy Bigelow*: CHRIS ROBINSON. *First Policeman*: Russell Goodwin. *David Bascombe*: Stanley Carlson. *Nettie Fowler*: JEAN HANDZLIK. *June Girl*: Mavis Ray. *Enoch Snow*: DON BLACKEY. *Jigger Craigin*: JOHN CONTE. *Hannah*: DUSTY WORRALL. *Boatswain*: ROBERT PAGENT. *Arminy*: Marilyn Bladd. *Second Policeman*: William W. Reynolds. *Captain*: Boris Aplon. *Heavenly Friend (Brother Joshua)*: Jay Velie. *Starkeeper*: Daniel Reed. *Louise*: BAMBI LINN. *Carnival Boy*: ROBERT PAGENT. *Enoch Snow, Jr.*: James Martindale. *Principal*: Russell Goodwin.

Townspeople: Marilyn Bladd, Lila Caputo, Rina Falcone, Barbara Ford, Ellen Gleason, Sheila Mathews, Dorothy Mirr, Gloria Sacks, Greta Thormsen, Benjamin Bajorek, Dawin Emanuel, Russell Goodwin, Charles Kuestner, James Martindale, Roland Miles, Benjamin Plotkin, William W. Reynolds, Joseph Tanner. *Dancers*: Ann Barry, Ann Dunbar, Ruby Herndon, Anne Meislik, Meri Miller, Eloise Milton, Mavis Ray, Nadine Revene, Francine Savery, Gini Turner, Rudy Jenkins, Don Little, Don Martin, Dick Rogers, Philip Salem, Mark Ward, Mark West. *Children of the Prelude*: Claudia Crawford, Adele Newton, Chris Snell.

1954.08 HAYRIDE

A Hillbilly Folk Musical (Revue) in Two Acts. (Based on the Old Dominion Barn Dance Show, presented and broadcast weekly from the WRVA Theatre, Richmond, Virginia.) Settings by Art Guild, Jack Woodson, Jack Durrenberger of Richmond, Virginia. Produced by Barron Howard and Jack Stone. Opened 13 September 1954 at the 48th Street Theatre and closed 2 October 1954 after 24 performances.[2]

CAST: SUNSHINE SUE (Femcee), COUSIN JOE MAPHIS (Comedian and Wizard of stringed instruments) & ROSE (Ballads of the prairie country), LESTER FLATT & EARL SCRUGGS (mountain music) FOGGY MOUNTAIN BOYS, Paul Warren, Jake Tulloch, Curly Sechler, The Coon Creek (Kentucky) Girls (songs of the old hill "splinter-kickin" dances and parties), Lilly May, Rosie, Black Eyed Susan, The Trail Blazers, Ray Smith, Roy Horton, Johnny Newton, Eddy (Texas) Smith, Quincy Snodgrass (comedian), Mary Klick (songs of the song and bayou regions), Zeb Robinson, Sonny Day (accordionist from Kentucky), Fiddlin' Irving, Zag the Ozark Mountain Boy (lonesome cabin songs of his native Ozark hills), Gene Jenkins (guitarist), Jody Carver.

Acts 1 and 2: The barn at "Medley Grove" Saturday night.

MUSICAL NUMBERS[3]

"Old MacDonald Had a Farm"

"The Blue Tail Fly"

"Jumbalaya"

Stephen Foster songs

Hank Williams songs

"Little Things Mean a Lot"
Sunshine Sue
(*Music and Lyrics by* Carl Stutz and Edith Lindeman.)

"Vegetable Love"
Zag the Ozark Mountain Boy

1954.09 THE BOY FRIEND

A Musical Comedy of the 1920's in Three Acts. Book, music and lyrics by Sandy Wilson. Directed by Vida Hope. Choreography by John Heawood. Settings and costumes by Reginald Woolley. Supervisor for scenery and lighting, (Abe) Feder. Supervisor for costumes, Robert Mackintosh. Orchestra, Paul McCrane and His Bearcats. Musical director, Anton Coppola. Orchestrations by Ted Royal and Charles L. Cooke. Production by Vida Hope. Produced by Cy Feuer and Ernest Martin. Opened 30 September 1954 at the Royale Theatre and closed 26 November 1955 after 483 performances.

CAST (in order of appearance): *Hortense*: Paulette Girard. *Nancy*: MILLICENT MARTIN. *Maisie*: ANN WAKEFIELD. *Fay*: Stella Claire. *Dulcie*: DILYS LAY. *Polly*: JULIE ANDREWS. *Marcel*: Joe Milan. *Alphonse*: Buddy Schwab. *Pierre*: Jerry Newby. *Madame Dubonnet*: RUTH ALTMAN. *Bobby Van Husen*: BOB SCHEERER. *Percival Browne*: ERIC BERRY. *Tony*: JOHN HEWER. *Phillipe*: Jimmy Alex. *Monica*: Berkley Marsh. *Lord Brockhurst*: GEOFFREY HIBBERT. *Lady Brockhurst*: Moyna MacGill. *Susanne*: Lyn Connorty. *Guests*: Phoebe MacKay, Marge Ellis, Mickey Calin. *Gendarme*: Douglas Deane. *Waiter*: Lyn Robert. *Pepe*: Joe Milan. *Lolita*: Stella Claire.

Act 1: The Drawing-room of the Villa Caprice, Madame Dubonnet's finishing school on the outskirts of Nice. 1926.

Act 2: The Plage. That afternoon.

Act 3: The Terrace of the Cafe Pataplon. That night.

ACT 1

"Perfect Young Ladies"
P. Girard, M. Martin, A. Wakefield, S. Claire, D. Lay

"The Boy Friend"
J. Andrews, A. Wakefield, D. Lay, S. Claire, M. Martin, J. Milan, J. Newby, B. Schwab

"Won't You Charleston With Me?"
A. Wakefield, B. Scheerer

"Fancy Forgetting"
R. Altman, E. Berry

"I Could Be Happy With You"
J. Andrews, J. Hewer

Finale (Act 1), "The Boy Friend" (reprise)
(Ensemble)

ACT 2

"Sur la Plage" (On the Beach)
A. Wakfield, B. Scheerer, S. Claire, J. Milan, D. Lay, B. Schwab, M. Martin, J. Newby, B. Marsh, J. Alex

"A Room in Bloomsbury"
J. Andrews, J. Hewer

"You Don't Want to Play With Me Blues"
R. Altman, E. Berry, S. Claire, D. Lay, M. Martin, B. Marsh

"Safety in Numbers"
A. Wakefield, B. Scheerer, J. Milan, J. Newby, B. Schwab

Finale (Act 2)
Entire Company

ACT 3

"(The) Riviera"
A. Wakefield, B. Scheerer, S. Claire, J. Milan, D. Lay, B. Schwab, M. Martin, J. Newby, B. Marsh, J. Alex

"It's Never Too Late to Fall in Love"
G. Hibbert, D. Lay

"Carnival Tango"
Danced by J. Milan, S. Claire

"Poor Little Pierrette"
R. Altman, J. Andrews

Finale (Act 3)
Entire Company

---

[1]First produced in New York 19 April 1945 at the Majestic Theatre for 890 performances. For Synopsis of Scenes and Musical Numbers, see original 1945 production. For this production, the Prologue became Act 1, Scene 1 (Prelude)

[2]Direction, costumes uncredited.

[3]Neither the program nor extant press materials offer a complete list of songs. The artists listed above performed their specialties, which included those listed.

1954.10

DIE FLEDERMAUS

A Revival of the Operetta in Three Acts[4]. (Original Viennese libretto by Carl Haffner and Richard Genée. Lyrics by Richard Genée. Based on the comedy "Le Réveillon" by Henri Meilhac and Ludovic Halévy). English libretto by Ruth and Thomas Martin. Music by Johann Strauss. Staged by William Westerfield. Costume supervisor, Robert Fletcher. Choreographer, Sophie Maslow. Conductor, Thomas P. Martin. Produced by the New York City Opera. Opened 3 October 1954 at the New York City Center and closed 16 October 1954 after 2 performances in repertory; re-opened 19 March 1955 at the New York City Center and closed 9 April 1955 after 2 additional performances. Total this season: 4 performances.[5]

CAST: *Eisenstein*: ERNEST McCHESNEY. *Rosalinda*: SUSAN JAGER. *Adele*: LAUREL HURLEY. *Alfred*: LLOYD THOMAS LEECH. *Falke*: WILLIAM WILDERMAN. *Frank*: Richard Wentworth. *Blind*: Luigi Vellucci. *Prince Orlofsky*: DONALD GRAMM. *Sally*: Peggy Bonini. *Frosch*: Coley Worth. *Ivan*: Thomas Powell. *Solo Dancers*: Ethel Winter, Donald MacKayle, Alvin Schulman. *Ensemble*: New York City Opera Chorus.

1954.11

BLUES, BALLADS AND SIN SONGS

A One Woman Musical Revue in Two Acts, 4 Scenes. (Concept inspired by Carl Sandburg.) Pianist, Gerald Cook. Musical settings, Gerald Cook. Miss Holman's gowns by Mainbocher (Act 1) and Frank Stanley (Act 2). Opened 4 October 1954 at the Bijou Theatre and closed 16 October 1954 after 12 performances.[6]

CAST: LIBBY HOLMAN.

ACT 1

Scene 1

"Good Morning Blues"
(Gerald Cook)
"Smokey"
"Go 'Way From My Window"
(Gerald Cook)
"In the Evening" (Traditional, arr. Gerald Cook)
"Barbara Allen" (Traditional)
"Rolly Trudum"

Scene 2

"Yandro"
"Cindy"
"Baby, Baby"
"Fare Thee Well" (Traditional, arr. Gerald Cook)

ACT 2

Scene 1

"Careless Love"
(*Music and Lyrics by* W. C. Handy and Spencer Williams.)
"Riddle Song"
"Four Marys"
"The Loathly Bride"
"Johnny Has Gone"

Scene 2

"The Blues"
(*Music by* Duke Ellington.)
"You Can't Go to Heaven"
"Number 12 Train"
"Evil Hearted Me" (Traditional, arr. by Gerald Cook)
"House of the Rising Sun" (Traditional, arr. by Gerald Cook)

Encores:

"Moanin' Low" (from THE LITTLE SHOW)
(*Music by* Ralph Rainger. *Lyrics by* Howard Dietz.)
"Body and Soul" (from THREE'S A CROWD)
(*Music by* Johnny Green. *Lyrics by* Edward Heyman, Robert Sour, Frank Eyton.)
"Something to Remember You By" (from THREE'S A CROWD)
(*Music by* Arthur Schwartz. *Lyrics by* Howard Dietz.)

1954.12

ON YOUR TOES

A Revival of the Musical Comedy in Two Acts, 13 Scenes[7]. Book by Richard Rodgers, Lorenz Hart and George Abbott. Lyrics by Lorenz Hart. Music by Richard Rodgers. Directed by George Abbott. Dances staged by George Balanchine. Settings by Oliver Smith. Costumes by Irene Sharaff. Musical director, Salvatore Dell'Isola. Orchestrations by Don Walker. Produced by George Abbott. Opened 11 October 1954 at the 46th Street Theatre and closed 4 December 1954 after 64 performances.

CAST (in order of appearance): *Phil Dolan II*: Jack Williams. *Lil Dolan*: Eleanor Williams. *Phil Dolan III*: David Winters. *Stage Manager*: George Church. *Lola*: Dorene Kilmer. *Phil Dolan III*, Junior: BOBBY VAN. *Frankie Frayne*: KAY COULTER. *Sidney Cohn*: Joshua Shelley. *Vera Barnova*: VERA ZORINA. *Anushka*: Patricia Wilkes. *Peggy Porterfield*: ELAINE STRITCH. *Sergei Alexandrovitch*: Ben Astar. *Konstantine Morrosine*: Nicolas Orloff. *Snoopy*: John Robb. *Thug*: Nathaniel Frey. *Mischka*: Patrick Welch. *Ivan*: John Nola. *Vassilli*: Edward Pfeiffer. *Dimitri*: Ted Adkins. *Leo*: Robert Lindgren. *Ballet Stage Manager*: Bertram Wood. *Cop*: Arthur Grahl. *On Your Toes Jitterbug Couple*: Dorene Kilmer, Timmy Everett. *Adagio Couple*: Katia Geleznova, Edward Pfeiffer.

Chorus: *Girls*: Phyllis Campbell, Lillian D'Honau, Patricia Drylie, Katia Geneznova, Carolyn George, Marilyn Hale, Dorene Kilmer, Helen Kramer, Sonja Lindgren (Tyven), Paula Lloyd, Sigyn, Barbara Michaels, Lois Platt, Nina Popova, Ruth Sobotka, Mary Stanton, Carol Stevens, Wendy Winn. *Boys*: Ted Adkins, Marvin Arnold, Johnny Bowen, Timmy Everett, Arthur Grahl, Edward Kerrigan, Jack Leigh, Robert Lindgren, John Nola, Edward Pfeiffer.

1954.13

PETER PAN

A Musical in Three Acts, 9 Scenes. Book (adapted from the play) by James M. Barrie[8]. Music by Mark Charlap. Lyrics by Carolyn Leigh. Additional music by Jule Styne; additional lyrics by Betty Comden and Adolph Green. Scenery by Peter Larkin. Costumes by Motley. Lighting by Peggy Clark. Technical direction, Richard Rodda. Music conductor, Louis Adrian. Orchestral arrangements by Albert Sendrey. Incidental music by Trude Rittman and Elmer Bernstein. Assistant to the director, Mary Hunter. Directed and staged by Jerome Robbins. Produced by Richard Halliday. Opened 20 October 1954 at the Winter Garden and closed 26 February 1955 after 152 performances.

CAST (in order of appearance): *Wendy*: KATHY NOLAN. *John*: ROBERT HARRINGTON. *Liza*: HELLER HALLIDAY. *Michael*: Joseph Stafford. *Nana*: Norman Shelly. *Mrs. Darling*: MARGALO GILLMORE. *Mr. Darling*: CYRIL RITCHARD. *Peter Pan*: MARY MARTIN. *Lion*: Richard Wyatt. *Kangaroo*: Don Lurio. *Ostrich*: Joan Tewkesbury. *Slightly*: David Bean. *Tootles*: Ian Tucker. *Curly*: Stanley Stenner. *Nibs*: Paris Theodore. *Crocodile*: Norman Shelly. *First Twin*: Alan Sutherland. *Second Twin*: Darryl Duran. *Captain Hook*: CYRIL RITCHARD. *Smee*: JOE E. MARKS. *Tiger Lily*: SONDRA LEE. *Cecco*: Robert Tucker. *Noodler*: Frank Lindsay.

---

[4]First English language production in New York 16 March 1885 at the Casino Theatre for 42 performances. First New York production of this adaptation 20 December 1950 at the Metropolitan Opera House. For Synopsis of Scenes and Musical Numbers, see May 1954 revival.

[5]Settings uncredited. Settings and costumes were assembled from various sources, a previous Sol Hurok tour of DIE FLEDERMAUS and the Broadway production of MY DARLIN' AIDA.

[6]Producer uncredited.

[7]Originally produced in New York 11 April 1936 at the Imperial Theatre for 315 performances. For Synopsis of Scenes and Musical numbers, see original 1936 production. Same as original production except:

"Two-a-Day for Keith" (Act 1, Scenes 1 and 2 dropped after opening)
"You Took Advantage of Me" (from PRESENT ARMS, added to Act 2, Scene 3)
E. Stritch

[8]Adaptation uncredited.

Starkey: Robert Vanselow. *Mullins*: James White. *Jukes*: Frank Bouley. *Wendy Grown-Up*: Sallie Brophy. *Jane*: KATHY NOLAN. *Tinker Bell's Voice*: Jaye Rubanoff.

Pirates: Robert Tucker, Frank Lindsay, Frank Marasco, James Whyte, William Burke, Chester Fisher, John Newton, Arthur Tookoian, Robert Vanselow, Richard Winter. *Indians*: Robert Banas, Don Lurio, Robert Piper, William Sumner, Richard Wyatt, Linda Dangcil, Lisa Lang, Suzanne Luckey, Joan Tewkesbury.

Act 1, Scene 1: The Nursery of the Darling Residence. *Scene 2*: Flight to Neverland.

Act 2, Scene 1: Neverland. *Scene 2*: Path through the Woods. *Scene 3*: Neverland Home Underground.

Act 3, Scene 1: The Pirate Ship. *Scene 2*: Path through the Woods. *Scene 3*: The Nursery of the Darling Residence. *Scene 4*: The Nursery many years later.

ACT 1

Scene 1

"Tender Shepherd"
M. Gillmore, K. Nolan, R. Harrington, J. Stafford

"I've Got to Crow"
M. Martin

"Neverland"
M. Martin
(*Music by* Jule Styne. *Lyrics by* Betty Comden and Adolph Green.)

"I'm Flying"
M. Martin, K. Nolan, R. Harrington, J. Stafford

ACT 2

Scene 1

"Pirate Song"
C. Ritchard, Pirates

"A Princely Scheme"
C. Ritchard, Pirates

"Indians!"
S. Lee, Indians

"Wendy"
M. Martin, Boys
(*Music by* Jule Styne. *Lyrics by* Betty Comden and Adolph Green.)

"Another Princely Scheme" (Tarantella)
C. Ritchard, Pirates

"Neverland Waltz"
H. Halliday
(*Music by* Jule Styne. *Lyrics by* Betty Comden and Adolph Green.)

Scene 2

"I Won't Grow Up"
M. Martin, Boys

"Mysterious Lady"
M. Martin, C. Ritchard
(*Music by* Jule Styne. *Lyrics by* Betty Comden and Adolph Green.)

Scene 3

"Ugg-aWugg"/"The Pow Wow Polka"
M. Martin, S. Lee, Children, Indians
(*Music by* Jule Styne. *Lyrics by* Betty Comden and Adolph Green.)

"Distant Melody"
M. Martin
(*Music by* Jule Styne. *Lyrics by* Betty Comden and Adolph Green.)

ACT 3

Scene 1

"To the Ship"
M. Martin, Company

"(Captain) Hook's Waltz"
C. Ritchard, Pirates
(*Music by* Jule Styne. *Lyrics by* Betty Comden and Adolph Green.)

"The Battle"
M. Martin, C. Ritchard, Company

Scene 2

"I've Got to Crow" (reprise)
M. Martin, H. Halliday, Company

Scene 3

"Tender Shepherd" (reprise)
K. Nolan, R. Harrington, J. Stafford

"I Won't Grow Up" (reprise)
The Darling Family, Lost Boys

Scene 4

"Neverland" (reprise)
M. Martin

1954.14 SHOWBOAT

A Return Engagement of the Musical Play in Two Acts, 14 Scenes[9]. Music by Jerome Kern. Book and lyrics by Oscar Hammerstein II. Based on the novel of the same name by Edna Ferber. Staged by William Hammerstein. Settings by Howard Bay. Costumes by John Boyt. Lighting by Jean Rosenthal. Conductor, Julius Rudel. Orchestrations by Robert Russell Bennett. Produced by The New York City Opera Company. Opened 28 October 1954 at the New York City Center and closed 31 October 1954 after 2 performances.[10]

CAST: *Captain Andy*: RICHARD WENTWORTH. *Parthy Ann Hawkes*: JEAN HANDZLIK. *Magnolia*: LAUREL HURLEY. *Gaylord Ravenal*: ROBERT ROUNSEVILLE. *Julie*: HELENA BLISS. *Steve*: ROBERT GALLAGHER. *Queenie*: BETTY ALLEN. *Joe*: LAWRENCE WINTERS. *Frank*: JACK BLAIR. *Ellie*: MARIAN NILES. *Jim*: Michael Pollock. *Windy McLain*: Arthur Newman. *Man With Guitar*: Charles Kuestner. *Piano player*: Milton Lyon. *Landlady*: SARA FLOYD. *Pete*: Michael Pollock. *Sheriff Vallon*: Roy Urhausen. *Doorman at Trocadero*: Walter Brown. *Old Lady on Levee*: Sara Floyd. *Ethel*: Gloria Wynder. *Kim*, as a child: Adele Newton. *Backwoodsmen*: Roy Urhausen, Arthur Newman. *Ensemble*: New York City Opera Chorus.

1954.15 FANNY

A Musical Play in Two Acts, 16 Scenes. Book by S. N. Behrman and Joshua Logan. Based on the trilogy of plays "Marius-César-Fanny" by Marcel Pagnol. Music and lyrics by Harold Rome. Directed by Joshua Logan. Scenery and lighting by Jo Mielziner. Costumes by Alvin Colt. Dances by Helen Tamiris. Musical direction and vocal arrangements by Lehman Engel. Orchestral arrangements by Philip J. Lang. Musical continuity by Trude Rittman. Produced by David Merrick and Joshua Logan. Opened 4 November 1954 at the Majestic Theatre, moved 4 December 1956 to the Belasco Theatre, and closed 16 December 1956 after 888 performances.

CAST (in order of appearance): *Arab Rug Seller*: Mohammed el Bakkar. *Marius*, son of Cesar: WILLIAM TABBERT. *Fanny*, daughter of Honorine: FLORENCE HENDERSON. *Maori Vendor*: Katherine Graves. *Lace Vendor*: Betty Carr. *Customers*: Toni Wheelis, Lindsay Kirkpatrick, Dolores Smith, Margaret Baxter. *Twin Sisters*, friends of Fanny: *Claudine*: Tani Seitz. *Claudette*: Dran Seitz. *Charles*: Wally Strauss. *His Friends*: Bill Pope, Dean Crane, Ronald Cecill, Michael de Marco. *Friends of Fanny (4)*: *Nanette*: Norma Doggett. *Mimi*: Carolyn Maye. *Marie*: Ellen Matthews. *Michellette*: Jane House. *Panisse*, wealthy sailmaker: WALTER SLEZAK. *Sailor*: Herb Banke. *The Admiral*, an eccentric waterfront character: GERALD PRICE. *Moroccan Drummer*: Charles Blackwell. *Second Mate*: Henry Michel. *Fisherman*: Steve Wiland. *Sailmaker*: Jack Washburn. *Fish-Stall Woman*: Florence Dunlap. *An Arab*: Michael Scrittorale. *Cesar*, proprietor of cafe on waterfront: EZIO PINZA. *Honorine*, Fanny's

[9]First presented in New York 27 December 1927 at the Ziegfeld Theatre for 572 performances. This revised version first presented 5 January 1946 at the Ziegfeld Theatre for 418 performances; this production presented by the New York City Opera 8 April 1954 at the New York City Center for 3 performances in repertory; re-opened under the auspices of the New York City Center Light Opera Company 5 May 1954 at the New York City Center for 15 additional performances. For Synopsis of Scenes and Musical Numbers, see 1946 revival. Act 1, Scenes 2 and 3 combined from 1946 production. Act 2, Scene 8 reset in the Auditorium and Stage of the "Cotton Blossom."

[10]Dances uncredited.

mother, a fish-stall keeper: EDNA PRESTON. *Escartifique*, a ferryboat captain: ALAN CARNEY. *M. Brun*, customs inspector recently returned from Paris: DON McHENRY. *Arab Dancing Girl*: NEJLA ATES. *Nun*: Ruth Schumacher. *Cesario*: Lloyd Reese. *Butler*: Mike Mason. *Maid*: Pat Finch. *Garage Owner*: Tom Gleason. *Priest*: Ray Dorian. *Acolytes*: Gary Wright, Daniel Labeille.

The action takes place in and around the Old Port of Marseilles over a period of year, not so long ago.

Act 1, Scene 1: The Waterfront of Marseilles. *Scene 2*: Hakim's Cellar. *Scene 3*: César's Bar. *Scene 4*: The Dock. *Scene 5*: César's Bar. *Scene 6*: Honorine's Kiosk. *Scene 7*: Panisse's Sail Shop. *Scene 8*: The Wedding. *Scene 9*: The Waterfront of Marseilles.

Act 2, Scene 1: The Nursery. *Scene 2*: Panisse's Living Room. *Scene 3*: Vignettes, 1, 2 3. *Scene 4*: Cesario's Room. *Scene 5*: The Circus. *Scene 6*: A Garage in Toulon. *Scene 7*: Panisse's Bedroom.

ACT 1[11]

Scene 1

"Never Too Late For Love"
W. Slezak, Ensemble

"Cold-Cream Jar Song"
W. Slezak

"Octopus Song"
G. Price

"Restless Heart"
W. Tabbert, Male Ensemble

"Why Be Afraid to Dance?"
E. Pinza
Danced by E. Pinza, W. Tabbert, F. Henderson, Ensemble.

"Never Too Late For Love" (reprise)
E. Pinza, W. Slezak, E. Preston

Scene 2

"Shika, Shika"
N. Ates, M. el Bakkar, Ensemble

Scene 3

"Welcome Home"
E. Pinza

"I Like You"
W. Tabbert, E. Pinza

"I Have To Tell You"
F. Henderson

"Fanny"
W. Tabbert

Scene 4

Montage: The Lovers; The Sailing
F. Henderson, W. Tabbert, E. Pinza, Ensemble

Scene 6

"Oysters, Cockles and Mussels"
Ensemble

Scene 7

"Panisse and Son"
W. Slezak

Scene 8

Wedding Dance
Danced by C. Blackwell, Ensemble

Scene 9

Finale Act 1
Ensemble

[11]After the opening the order of songs in Act 1 was revised, and the following song was added before "Why Be Afraid to Dance?":
"Does He Know?"
F. Henderson, W. Tabbert
For the West Coast tour, the following song was added:
"Every Night" (early in Act 1)
Doretta Morrow (Fanny)

ACT 2

Scene 1

"Birthday Song"
F. Henderson, E. Preston, Ensemble

Scene 2

"To My Wife"
W. Slezak

"The Thought of You"
W. Tabbert, F. Henderson

"Love Is a Very Light Thing"
E. Pinza

"Other Hands, Other Hearts"
F. Henderson, E. Pinza, W. Tabbert

"Fanny" (reprise)
E. Pinza, F. Henderson, W. Tabbert

Scene 3

Montage
Ensemble

Scene 4

"Be Kind to Your Parents"
F. Henderson, L. Reese

Scene 5

"Cesario's Party" (Cirque Français)
Acrobats: C. Blackwell, M. de Marco, R. Dorian, B. Pope, T. Wheelis. *Pony and Trainer*: W. Strauss, S. Wiland. *Trained Seals*: D. Seitz, T. Seitz. *Living Statues*: B. Carr, R. Cecill, N. Doggett, R. Dorian, E. Matthews, D. Smith. *Clowns*: H. Banke, M. Mason, H. Michel, J. Washburn. *Finale*: Aerialist, D. Crane, Ensemble.

Scene 7

"Welcome Home" (reprise)
E. Pinza, W. Slezak

1954.16 MRS. PATTERSON

A Play with Music in Three Acts. Play by Charles Sebree and Greer Johnson. Songs and incidental music by James Shelton. Settings and costumes by Raoul Pene du Bois. Orchestrations by George Siravo. Musical director, Abba Bogin. Directed by Guthrie McClintic. Produced by Leonard Sillman. Opened 1 December 1954 at the National Theatre and closed 26 February 1955 after 102 performances.

CAST (in order of appearance): *Anna Hicks*: RUTH ATTAWAY. *Selma Mae*: VINIE BURROWS. *Theodora Hicks*, Teddy: EARTHA KITT. *Willie B. Brayboy*: TERRY CARTER. *Aunt Matt Crossy*: Estelle Hemsley. *Mr. D*: AVON LONG. *Bessie Bolt*: HELEN DOWDY. *Sylvanus*: Emory Richardson. *Mrs. Patterson*: ENID MARKEY. *June Embree*: Mary Ann Hoxworth. *Rose Embree*: Mary Harmon. *Fern Embree*: Joan Morgan.

The play takes place in late summer, 1920, at the edge of a small town in Kentucky.

Act 1: Early evening.

Act 2: The following day.

Act 3: The next evening.

MUSICAL NUMBERS

"Mrs. Patterson"
E. Kitt

"If I Was a Boy"
E. Kitt

"I Wish I Was a Boy"
H. Dowdy
(*Lyrics by* Charles Sebree and Greer Johnson.)

"Be Good, Be Good, Be Good" (The Devil Song)
E. Kitt

"Tea in Chicago"
E. Kitt

"My Daddy Is a Dandy"
E. Kitt

Finale
E. Kitt, R. Attaway

1954.17

HIT THE TRAIL

A Musical in Two Acts, 13 Scenes. Book by Frank O'Neill. Music by Frederico Valerio. Lyrics by Elizabeth Miele. Directed by Charles W. Christenberry, Jr. and Byrle Cass. Dances and musical numbers staged by Gene Bayliss. Settings and lighting by Leo Kerz. Costumes by Michi. Orchestrations by Don Walker. Musical director and vocal arranger, Arthur Norris. Produced by Elizabeth Miele. Opened 2 December 1954 at the Mark Hellinger Theatre and closed 4 December 1954 after 4 performances.

CAST: *Jerry*: DONN [Donald] DRIVER. *Joan*: DIANA DRAKE. *Willie*: Fred Lightner. *Clayton Harrison*: PAUL VALENTINE. *Lucy Vernay*: IRRA PETINA. *Murph*: ROBERT WRIGHT. *Aggie July*: TOBY DEANE. *Miller*: Charles G. Martin. *Waiters*: Jack Purcell, Rene Miville.

Dancers: Jeanna Belkin, Lois Bewley, Sandy Bozoki, Diane Consoer, Patty Fitzsimmons, Nancy Hackenberg, Robert Bakanic, Paul Gannon, Jack Purcell, Alton Ruff, Buff Shurr, Fred Zoeter. *Singers*: Josephine Annunciata, Irene Carroll, Peggy Kinard, Dolores Micheline, Michelle Reiner, Martha Rich, Iris Sinding, Flavine Valentine, Lois Van Pelt, Paul Brown, Michael King, Rene Miville, Robert Price, James Schlader.

The action takes place in Virginia City, Nevada, during the late 19th century.

Act 1, Scene 1: Outside Virginia City. *Scene 2*: Lucy Vernay's Dressing Room. *Scene 3*: The Blue Sierra Casino. *Scene 4*: A Street in Virginia City. *Scene 5*: Stage of Piper's Opera House. *Scene 6*: A Park in Virginia City. *Scene 7*: The Blue Sierra Casino.

Act 2, Scene 1: Emporium. *Scene 2*: Gambling Room. *Scene 3*: A Street in Virginia City. *Scene 4*: The Blue Sierra Casino. *Scene 5*: A Street in Virginia City. *Scene 6*: Garden behind Murph's House.

ACT 1

Scene 1

"On With the Show"
D. Driver, D. Drake, Troupers

Scene 2

"Mr. Right"
I. Petina

"Dynamic"
I. Petina, R. Wright

Scene 3

"Blue Sierras"
T. Deane, Patrons

"No! No! No!"
P. Valentine

"The Wide Open Spaces"
P. Valentine, T. Deane, D. Drake, D. Driver

Scene 4

"Gold Cannot Buy"
Townspeople

"Remember the Night"
P. Valentine, I. Petina

"Tell Me How"
R. Wright

Scene 5

"It Was Destiny"
T. Deane, Girls

Scene 6

"Just a Wonderful Time"
D. Driver, D. Drake

Scene 7

"Nevada Hoe Down"
T. Deane, Patrons

ACT 2

Scene 1

"New Look Feeling"
I. Petina, D. Driver, D. Drake, Patrons
(*Staged by* Donn Driver.)

"Set Me Free"
I. Petina

"Somehow I've Always Known"
R. Wright

Scene 2

"Remember the Night" (reprise)
P. Valentine

Scene 3

"My Fatal Charm"
P. Valentine

"Men Are a Pain in the Neck"
T. Deane

Scene 4

"Wherever I May Go"
I. Petina

Scene 5

"Take Your Time"
D. Driver, D. Drake

Scene 6

"Happy Birthday"
Company

"Mr. Right" (reprise)
I. Petina, R. Wright

1954.18

THE SAINT OF BLEECKER STREET

A Musical Drama (Opera) in Three Acts, 5 Scenes. Music and libretto by Gian-Carlo Menotti. Conducted by Thomas Schippers. Staged by Gian-Carlo Menotti. Scenery and costumes by Robert Randolph. Lighting by Jean Rosenthal. Associate musical director, Samuel Krachmalnick. Assistant director, Bill Butler. Production supervisor, Lincoln Kirstein. Produced by Chandler Cowles. Opened 27 December 1954 at the Broadway Theatre and closed 2 April 1955 after 92 performances[12].

CAST (in order of appearance): *Assunta*: Catherine Akos. *Carmela*: Maria Di Gerlando. *Maria Corona*: Maria Marlo. *Her Dumb Son*: Ernesto Gonzales. *Don Marco*: Leon Lishner. *Annina*: VIRGINIA COPELAND or GABRIELLE RUGGIERO. *Michele*: DAVID POLERI or DAVIS CUNNINGHAM. *Desideria*: GLORIA LANE. *Salvatore*: David Aiken. *Concettina*: Lucy Becque. *A Young Man*: Richard Cassilly. *An Old Woman*: Elizabeth Carron. *Bartender*: Russell Goodwin. *First Guest*: Keith Kaldenberg. *Second Guest*: John Reardon. *A Nun*: Dorothy Krebill. *A Young Priest*: Robert Barry.

Neighbors, Friends, Policemen, etc.: Theodora Brandon, Betsy Bridge, Lorraine Bridges, Elizabeth Carron, Doris Davis, Mignon Dunn, Elizabeth Dunning, Joyce Duskin, Elaine Galante, Jeanne Grant, Mary Hensley, Carol Jones, Dorothy Krebill, Leslie MacLennan, Bessie Mijanovich, Doris Okerson, Francesca Roberto, Donna Sanders, Robert Barry, Michael Bulzomi, Richard Cassilly, Rico Froelich, Russell Goodwin, Gary Gordon, Don Grobe, Fred Jones, Keith Kaldenberg, Chester Ludgin, William MacCully, Michael MacLennan, Dan Merriman, John Reardon, Reid Shelton, Alan Smith, Roberts Watts.

Act 1, Scene 1: A cold water flat on Bleecker Street, (New York City). Good Friday afternoon. The present. *Scene 2*: A vacant lot on Mulberry Street. San Gennaro Day.

Act 2: An Italian restaurant, the following May.

Act 3, Scene 1: A subway station, a few months later. *Scene 2*: The cold water flat, several days later.

1954.19

HOUSE OF FLOWERS

A Musical in Two Acts, 13 Scenes. Book by Truman Capote, based on his novela of the same name. Music by Harold Arlen. Lyrics by Truman Capote and Harold Arlen. Directed by Peter Brook. Dances and musical numbers by Herbert Ross. Sets and costumes by Oliver Messel. Lighting by Jean Rosenthal. Musical director, Jerry Arlen. Orchestrations by Ted Royal. Produced by (Arnold) Saint Subber. Opened 30 December 1954 at the Alvin Theatre and closed 21 May 1955 after 165 performances.

CAST (in order of appearance): *Tulip*: DOLORES HARPER. *Gladiola*: ADA MOORE. *Pansy*: ENID MOSIER. *Do*: Winston George Henriques. *Don't*: Solomon Earl Green. *Mother*: Miriam Burton. *Ottilie*, alias Violet: DIAHANN CARROLL. *Madame Fleur*: PEARL BAILEY. *Captain Jonas*: RAY WALSTON. *Madame Tango*:

[12]No individual musical numbers listed.

JUANITA HALL. *Mamselle Ibo-Lele*: Pearl Reynolds. *The Sisters Meringue*: Leu Comacho, Margot Small. *Mamselle Honolulu*: Mary Mon Toy. *Mamselle Cigarette*: Glory Van Scott. *Royal*: RAWN SPEARMAN. *The Champion*: GEOFFREY HOLDER. *Chief of Police*: Don Redman. *Carmen*: Carmen De Lavallade. *Alvin*: Alvin Ailey. *Monsieur Jamison*: Dino DiLuca. *The Houngan*: FREDERICK O'NEAL. *Baron of the Cemetary*: GEOFFREY HOLDER. *Duchess of the Sea*: Miriam Burton. *Steel Band*: Michel Alexander, Roderick Clavery, Alphonso Marshall.

Townspeople: Joseph Comadore, Hubert Dilworth, Phillip Hepburn, Louis Johnson, Mary Louise, Audrey Mason, Arthur Mitchell, Walter Nicks, Albert Popwell, Sabu, Herbert Stubbs.

The action takes place on an island in the West Indies during Mardi Gras weekend.

Act 1, Scene 1: Maison Des Fleurs. *Scene 2*: On the way to the Cockfight. *Scene 3*: At the Cockfight. *Scene 4*: Maison Des Fleurs. *Scene 5*: The Houngan's Hut. *Scene 6*: The harbor of the town.

Act 2, Scene 1: Maison Des Fleurs. *Scene 2*: Madame Fleur's Salon. *Scene 3*: The Houngan's Hut. *Scene 4*: Madame Tango's Salon. *Scene 5*: Madame Fleur's Salon. *Scene 6*: Maison Des Fleurs. (*Scene 7*: Finale.)

ACT 1

Scene 1

"Waitin'"
E. Mosier, D. Harper, A. Moore

"One Man Ain't Quite Enough"
P. Bailey

"Madame Tango's Tango"
J. Hall, Tango Belles

"A Sleepin' Bee"
D. Carroll, E. Mosier, D. Harper, A. Moore

Scene 2

"Bamboo Cage"
G. Holder, The Steel Band, W. G. Henriques, S. E. Green, E. Mosier, D. Harper, A. Moore, J. Hall, D. Redman, Ensemble

Scene 3

"House of Flowers"
R. Spearman, D. Carroll

Scene 4

"Two Ladies in de Shade of de Banana Tree"
E. Mosier, A. Moore
Danced by C. de Lavallade, D. Harper.

"What Is a Friend For?"
P. Bailey

Scene 5

"A Sleepin' Bee" (reprise)
D. Carroll, R. Spearman

Scene 6

"Mardi Gras"
M. Burton
Danced by C. de Lavallade, A. Ailey, Ensemble.

"I Never has Seen Snow"
D. Carroll

ACT 2[13]

Scene 1

"Husband Cage"
E. Mosier, D. Harper, A. Moore, Ensemble

Scene 2

"Has I Let You Down?"
P. Bailey, E. Mosier, D. Harper, A. Moore

Scene 3

Voudou
F. O'Neal, Ensemble
The Drummers: Sabu, J. Comadore, M. Alexander, A. Marshall. *Duchess of the Sea*: M. Burton. *Octopus*: A. Popwell. *Shark*: W. Nicks, A. Mitchell, A. Marshall. *Turtle*: J. Comadore, Ensemble. *Baron of the Cemetary*: G. Holder. (Banda Dance choreographed by Geoffrey Holder.)

[13]Added after opening to Act 2, Scene 1 after "Husband Cage:"
"I'm Gonna Leave Off Wearing My Shoes"
D. Carroll, Ensemble

Scene 4

"Slide, Boy, Slide"
J. Hall, Ensemble
Danced by A. Ailey, Ensemble.

Scene 5

"Don't Like Goodbyes"
P. Bailey

Scene 6

"Turtle Song"
R. Spearman, D. Carroll, Ensemble

Scene 7

Finale: "Bamboo Cage"/"Banana Tree"
Entire Company

1955.01 PLAIN AND FANCY

A Musical Comedy in Two Acts, 17 Scenes. Book by Joseph Stein and Will Glickman. Music by Albert Hague. Lyrics by Arnold B. Horwitt. Production directed by Morton DaCosta. Dances and musical numbers staged by Helen Tamiris. Sets and costumes by Raoul Pene du Bois. Lighting by Peggy Clark. Orchestrations by Philip J. Lang. Vocal arrangements by Crane Calder. Orchestra and chorus directed by Franz Allers. Produced by Richard Kollmar and James W. Gardiner in association with Yvette Schumer. Opened 27 January 1955 at the Mark Hellinger Theatre, moved 28 February 1955 to the Winter Garden, moved 7 November 1955 to the Mark Hellinger Theatre, and closed 3 March 1956 after 461 performances.

CAST (in order of appearance): *Ruth Winters*: SHIRL CONWAY. *Dan King*: RICHARD DERR. *A Man*: John Dennis. *Another Man*: Chris Robinson. *Katie Yoder*: GLORIA MARLOWE. *Papa Yoder*: STEFAN SCHNABEL. *Isaac Miller*: SAMMY SMITH. *Emma Miller*: NANCY ANDREWS. *Ezra Reber*: DOUGLAS FLETCHER RODGERS. *Hilda Miller*: BARBARA COOK. *A Young Miller*: Scotty Engel. *Another Young Miller*: Elaine Lynn. *Peter Reber*: DAVID DANIELS. *Rachel*: Ethel May Cody. *Samuel Zook*: DANIEL NAGRIN. *Levi Stolzfuss*: William Weslow. *Jacob Yoder*: Will Able. *Samuel Lapp*: Chris Robinson. *Abner Zook*: Edgar Thompson. *Ike Pilersheim*: James S. Moore. *Moses Zook*: John Dennis. *Abner Zook*: Tim Worthington. *An Amishman*: Robert Lindgren. *Another Amishman*: Herbert Surface. *Bessie*: Faith Daltry. *Sarah*: Renee Orin. *Esther*: Sybil Lamb. *Rebecca*: Betty McGuire. *Mary*: Muriel Shaw. *State Trooper*: Ray Hyson.

Dancers: Sara Aman, Imelda DeMartin, Ina Hahn, Marcia Howard, Lucia Lambert, Joan Darby, Ann Needham, Tao Strong, Beryl Towbin, Saint Amant, Crandall Diehl, Ronnie Lee, Robert Lindgren, James S. Moore, Philip Nasta, Robert St. Clair, William Weslow, David Wood. *Singers*: Marilyn Bradley, Faith Daltry, Janet Hayes, Sybil Lamb, Renee Orin, Betty McGuire, Muriel Shaw, Betty Zollinger, Ray Hyson, Jack Irwin, Robert Kole, Chris Robinson, John Dennis, Herbert Surface, Edgar F. Thompson, Tim Worthington, Paul Brown, Jim Schlader.

The play takes place in and around Bird-in-Hand, a town in the Amish country of Pennsylvania.

Act 1, Scene 1: A section of road, outside Lancaster. *Scene 2*: Another part of the road. *Scene 3*: The Yoder barnyard. *Scene 4*: The Yoder parlor. *Scene 5*: Side porch of the Yoder house. *Scene 6*: Barnyard on the River Farm. *Scene 7*: A bedroom in the Yoder home. *Scene 8*: The Yoder barnyard. *Scene 9*: In the Yoder barn.

Act 2, Scene 1: The River Farm. *Scene 2*: Kitchen of the Yoder home. *Scene 3*: Back porch of the Yoder home. *Scene 4*: Bedroom of the Yoder home. *Scene 5*: A section of the road. *Scene 6*: A Carnival Grounds. *Scene 7*: Side porch of the Yoder house. *Scene 8*: The Yoder barnyard.

ACT 1

Scene 1

"You Can't Miss It"
R. Derr, S. Conway, Ensemble

"It Wonders Me"
G. Marlowe

Scene 3

"Plenty of Pennsylvania"
N. Andrews, D. F. Rodgers, E. Lynn, Ensemble

"Young and Foolish"
D. Daniels

Scene 4

"Why Not Katie?"
D. F. Rogers, Men

Scene 6

"Young and Foolish" (reprise)
G. Marlowe, D. Daniels

"By Lantern Light"
Danced by D, Nagrin, A. Needham,
S. Aman, L. Lambert, T. Strong, S. Amant, C. Diehl, B. St. Clair

Scene 7

"It's a Helluva Way to Run a Love Affair"
S. Conway

"This Is All Very New to Me"
B. Cook, R. Lindgren, W. Weslow, Ensemble

Scene 8

"Plain We Live"
S. Schnabel, Ensemble

Scene 9

The Shunning
The Company

ACT 2

Scene 1

"How Do You Raise a Barn?"
S. Schnabel, D. F. Rodgers, N. Andrews, D. Nagrin, Ensemble

"Follow Your Heart"
D. Daniels, G. Marlowe, B. Cook

Scene 2

"City Mouse, Country Mouse"
N. Andrews,
with R. Orin, S. Lamb, M. Shaw, E. M. Cody, B. McGuire

Scene 4

"I'll Show Him"
B. Cook

Scene 5

("Young and Foolish" reprise)
G. Marlowe

Scene 6

Carnival Ballet
B. Cook, D. F. Rodgers, Company

On the Midway
Mambo Joe: D. Nagrin. *Scranton Sal*: S. Aman. *Swami*: R. Lindgren. *Sailor*: W. Able. *Barkers*: P. Nasta, C. Robinson, E. F. Thompson.

Dance Hall
The Company

Scene 8

"Take Your Time and Take Your Pick"
B. Cook, R. Derr, S. Conway

Finale
Entire Company

1955.02 SILK STOCKINGS

A Musical Comedy in Two Acts. Book by George S. Kaufman, Leueen MacGrath and Abe Burrows. Suggested by the film "Ninotchka" by Melchior Lengyel. Music and lyrics by Cole Porter. Settings and lighting by Jo Mielziner. Costumes by Lucinda Ballard. Additional costumes by Robert Mackintosh. Musical direction and vocal arrangements by Herbert Greene. Orchestrations by Don Walker. Dance music arranged by Tommy Goodman. Dances and musical numbers staged by Eugene Loring. Directed by Cy Feuer. Produced by Cy Feuer and Ernest H. Martin. Opened 24 February 1955 at the Imperial Theatre and closed 14 April 1956 after 478 performances.

CAST (in order of appearance): *Peter Ilyitch Boroff*: PHILIP STERLING. *Hotel Doorman*: Walter Kelvin. *Hotel Manager*: Stanley Simmonds. *Flower Girl*: Geraldine Delaney. *Ivanov*: HENRY LASCOE. *Brankov*: LEON BELASCO. *Bibinski*: DAVID OPATOSHU. *Steve Canfield*: DON AMECHE. *First Commissar*: Edward Becker. *Guards*: Lee Barry, Dick Humphrey. *Vera*: JULIE NEWMAR. *Commissar Markovitch*: GEORGE TOBIAS. *Choreographer*: Kenneth Chertok. *Ninotchka*: HILDEGARDE NEFF. *Reporters*: Edward Becker, Tony Gardell, Arthur Rubin. *Janice Dayton*: GRETCHEN WYLER. *Pierre Bouchard*: Marcel Hillaire. *Chief Commissar*: Forrest Green. *Minister*: Tony Gardell. *President of Politburo*: Walter Kelvin. *Saleslady*: Ludie Claire. *M. Fabour*: Paul Best. *Bookstall Man*: Louis Polacek. *French Comrades*: Win Mayo, Arthur Ulisse. *Movie Director*: Paul Best. *Assistant Director*: Lee Barry. *Sonia*: Devra Kline. *Grisha*: Forrest Green. *Anna*: Alexandra Moss. *Musicians*: Maurice Kogan, Leon Merian, Mervin Gold. *Guard*: Edward Becker.

Dancers: Estelle Aza, Barbara Bostock, Verna Cain, Geraldine Delaney, Devra Kline, Pat McBride, Carol Risser, Carol Stevens, Onna White, Martin Allen, Tommy [Thomas] Andrew, George Foster, Bruce Hoy, John Ray.

ACT 1

"Too Bad"
H. Lascoe, L. Belasco, D. Opatoshu, Hotel Staff

"Paris Loves Lovers"
D. Ameche, H. Neff

"Stereophonic Sound"
G. Wyler

"It's a Chemical Reaction, That's All"
H. Neff

"All of You"
D. Ameche

"Satin and Silk"
G. Wyler

"Without Love"
H. Neff

"All of You" (reprise)
D. Ameche

ACT 2

"Hail, Bibinski"
H. Lascoe, L. Belasco, D. Opatoshu, French Comrades

"As On Through the Seasons We Sail"
D. Ameche, H. Neff

"Josephine"
G. Wyler, Chorus

"Siberia"
H. Lascoe, L. Belasco, D. Opatoshu

"Silk Stockings"
D. Ameche

"The Red Blues"
The Russians

Finale
Entire Company

1955.03 3 FOR TONIGHT

A Diversion in Song and Dance (Musical Revue) in Two Acts, 12 Scenes. Staged and directed by Gower Champion. Lyrics and special material by Robert Wells. Original music by Walter Schumann. Arrangements by Nathan Scott. Conductor, Richard Pribor. Costumes by Jack's of Hollywood. Production (settings) designed by R. L. Grosh & Sons. Produced by Paul Gregory. Opened 6 April 1955 at the Plymouth Theatre and closed 18 June 1955 after 85 performances.

CAST: MARGE and GOWER CHAMPION, HARRY BELAFONTE, HIRAM SHERMAN, BETTY BENSON, Millard Thomas (guitarist).

THE VOICES OF WALTER SCHUMANN: John Bennett, Robert Brink, Andrew Case, Gina Christen, Diane Doxee, Elaine Drew, Joyce L. Foss, Dorothy Gill, Nancy Harp, Jimmy Harris, Mark Karl, Jerry Madison, Robert Miller, Ned Romero, Jack Steele, Brad Thomas, Robert Trevis, Karen Vonne, Richard Wessler.

ACT 1

Scene 1

Master of Ceremonies
H. Sherman

Scene 2

Impressions

"All You Need Is a Song"
Voices of Walter Schumann

Scene 3

Dance, Dance, Dance; The Clock; By-Play for Drums
Danced by M. Champion, G. Champion

Scene 4

"Jerry" (Traditional)

"Sylvie"

(*Music and Lyrics by* Harry Belafonte.)

"Mark Twain"

(*Music and Lyrics by* Harry Belafonte.)

"When the Saints Go Marching In"

H. Belafonte, *accompanied by* M. Thomas

(*Music and Lyrics by* Huddie Ledbetter and C. C. Carter.)

Scene 5

"The Sunday Picnic Social;" "Summer in Fairview Falls;" "It Couldn't Be a Better Day;" "Here I Stand;" "The Auction;" Finale

Danced by M. Champion, G. Champion

ACT 2

Scene 1

"Fly Bird"

B. Benson, Voices of Walter Schumann

Scene 2

"Noah" (Traditional, arr. by Harry Belafonte and Bill Attaway)

"Take My Mother Home" (Traditional, arr. by Hall Johnson)

"In That Great Gettin' Up Mornin'"

(*Arrangement by* Jester Herston.)

H. Belafonte, *accompanied by* M. Thomas

Scene 3

The Lecture

Read by H. Sherman, *Demonstrated by* M. Champion, G. Champion

Scene 4

"Matilda"

(*Music and Lyrics by* Harry Thomas.)

"Scarlet Ribbons"

(*Music by* Evelyn Danzig. *Lyrics by* Jack Segal.)H. Belafonte

Scene 5

"Yesterday"

"By the Light of the Silvery Moon" (from ZIEGFELD FOLLIES OF 1909)

(*Music by* Gus Edwards. *Lyrics by* Edward Madden.)

"Shine On, Harvest Moon" (from ZIEGFELD FOLLIES OF 1908)

(*Music and Lyrics by* Jack Norworth and Nora Bayes.)

Danced by M. Champion, G. Champion

Scene 6

"Troubles"

H. Belafonte

(*Music and Lyrics by* Harry Belafonte)

Scene 7

Finale

Entire Company

1955.04 ANKLES AWEIGH

A Musical Comedy in Two Act, 9 Scenes. Book by Guy Bolton and Eddie Davis. Music by Sammy Fain. Lyrics by Dan Shapiro. Staged by Fred F. Finklehoffe. Assistant to the director, Edward Clarke Lilley. Choreography by Tony Charmoli. Scenery and lighting by George Jenkins. Costumes by Miles White. Vocal and orchestral arrangements by Don Walker. Musical and choral director, Salvatore Dell'Isola. Dance music devised by Roger Adams. Additional dance music by Donald Pippin. Produced by Howard Hoyt, Reginald Hammerstein and Fred F. Finklehoffe[14]. Opened 18 April 1955 at the Mark Hellinger Theatre and closed 17 September 1955 after 176 performances.

CAST (in order of appearance): *Russ*: Ed Hanley. *Camera Man*: Ray Mason. *Tommy*: Bill Costin. *Pizza Cart Man*: Frank Conville. *Elsey*: BETTY KEAN. *Wynne*: JANE KEAN. *Dinky*: LEW PARKER. *Spud*: GABRIEL DELL. *Lieut. Bill Kelley*: MARK DAWSON. *Native Girl*: Nancy Walters. *Captain Zimmerman*: Mark Allen. *Admiral Pottles*: Will Hussung. *Chipolata*: THELMA CARPENTER. *Joe Mancinni*: MIKE KELLIN. *Tony*: Herb Fields. *Lucia*: Betty George. *The Duchess*: Karen Shepard. *Shore Patrol*: Skeet Guenther.

Dancers: Dick Alderson, Sandi Bonner, Gene Carrons, Patty Fitzsimmons, Marilyn Marsh, Meri Miller, Marianne Olsen, Marsha Rivers, Nina Starkey, Gloria Stevens, Patricia White (Wilde), Ethel Winter, Hank Brunjes, Don Emmons, Skeet Guenther, Jack Purcell, John Smolko, Jack Timmers. *Singers*: Marilynn Bradley, Thelma Dare, Virginia Martin, Ellen McCown, Janet Pavek, Karen Shepard, Nancy Walters, Herb Fields, Henry Hamilton, Warren Kemmerling, Michael King, Ray Mason, Jack Rains, Hobe Streiford.

The action takes place with an American movie company on location in Sicily and French Morocco at the present time.

Act 1, Scene 1: Montefino, The Piazza—afternoon. *Scene 2*: *USS Alamo*, below decks—that night. *Scene 3*: El Dahli Night Spot, Morocco—early the next morning.*Scene 4*: A Bedroom in El Dahli. *Scene 5*: Montefino, the Piazza.

Act 2, Scene 1: Hotel Argento, Montefino—next day. *Scene 2*: A street in Montefino. *Scene 3*: Joe's Room. *Scene 4*: Aboard the *USS Alamo*—the following night.

ACT 1

Scene 1

"Italy"

Boys, Girls

"Old Fashioned Mothers"

B. Kean, J. Kean

"Skip the Build-Up"

B. Kean, L. Parker

"Nothing At All"

J. Kean, M. Dawson

"Walk Like a Sailor"

J. Kean, L. Parker, G. Dell, Girls, B. Kean, H. Brunjes, S. Guenther

Scene 3

"Headin' For the Bottom"

T. Carpenter, Girls, Patrons of Night Spot

"Nothing Can Replace a Man"

J. Kean, Boys

"Here's to Dear Old Us"

B. Kean, L. Parker, G. Dell

Scene 4

"His and Hers"

J. Kean, M. Dawson

Scene 5

"La Festa"

Natives, Boys, Girls

Soloist: R. Mason.

ACT 2

Scene 1

"Ready Cash"

Croupiers, Gamblers

"Kiss Me and Kill Me With Love"

J. Kean, M. Dawson

"Honeymoon"

B. Kean, Girls

"The Villain Always Gets It"

Boys, Girls

Scene 2

"The Code"

Joe's Henchmen

Scene 4

"Walk Like a Sailor" (reprise)

Dancing Boys, Girls

"Eleven O'Clock Song"

B. Kean, J. Kean

Finale

Entire Company

[14]When the three producers withdrew after the opening, Anthony Brady Farrell, the owner of the Mark Hellinger Theatre, took over as producer.

1955.05

ALL IN ONE

A Triple Bill of a One-Act Opera, a Dance Program, and a Drama. Settings and lighting by Eldon Elder. Costumes by Pat Campbell. Produced by Charles Bowden and Richard Barr. Opened 19 April 1955 at the Playhouse and closed 28 May 1955 after 49 performances.

ACT 1

TROUBLE IN TAHITI, an Opera in One Act, 7 Scenes[15]. Libretto and music by Leonard Bernstein. Directed by David Brooks. Pianists, Joseph D. Lewis, Urey Krasnopolsky. Drummer, Max Rich. Bass, Leonard Gaskin.

CAST: *Dinah*: ALICE GHOSTLEY. *Sam*: JOHN TYERS. *Trio*: CONSTANCE BRIGHAM, John Taliaferro, James Tushar.

Scene 1: Sam and Dinah's House. *Scene 2*: Sam's Office. *Scene 3*: The Psychiatrist's Office. *Scene 4*: A Street in the City. *Scene 5*: The Gym. *Scene 6*: The Hat Shop. *Scene 7*: Sam and Dinah's House.

ACT 2

Paul Draper, accompanied by John Colman:

On the Beat

(*Music by* François Couperin.)

Alcina Suite

(*Music by* Georg Friedrich Handel.)

Minuet; Sarabande; Musette; Tambourine

Tea for Two

(*Music by* Vincent Youmans.)

Dance Without Music

In a Dance Hall

(*Music by* Cole Porter.)

Satire on a Political Speech

Improvisation

ACT 3

27 WAGONS FULL OF COTTON, a Drama in One Act, 3 Scenes, by Tennessee Williams. Directed by Vincent J. Donohue.

CAST: *Flora Meighan*: MAUREEN STAPLETON. *Jake Meighan*: MYRON McCORMICK. *Silva Vicarro*: FELICE ORLANDI.

All the action takes place on the front porch of the Meighan's residence near Blue Mountain, Mississippi.

Scene 1: Early evening. *Scene 2*: Noon, the next day. *Scene 3*: Nine o'clock that evening.

1955.06

GUYS AND DOLLS

A Revival of the Musical Fable (Comedy) in Two Acts, 17 Scenes[16]. Book by Jo Swerling and Abe Burrows. Based on a story and characters by Damon Runyon. Music and lyrics by Frank Loesser. Choreography by Onna White (after the original by Michael Kidd). Settings by Jo Mielziner. Costumes by Alvin Colt; Costume supervisor, Franck Spencer. Orchestral arrangements by George Bassman and Ted Royal. Vocal arrangements and direction by Herbert Greene. Musical director, Frederick Dvonch. Directed by Philip Mathias. Produced by the New York City Center Light Opera Company (William Hammerstein, General director). Opened 20 April 1955 at the New York City Center, closing 1 May 1955 after 15 performances; re-opened 31 May 1955 at the New York City Center and closed 12 June 1955 after an additional 16 performances. Total: 31 performances.

CAST (in order of appearance): *Nicely-Nicely Johnson*: OGGIE SMALL. *Benny Southstreet*: AL NESOR. *Rusty Charlie*: Murray Vinces. *Sarah Brown*: LEILA MARTIN. *Arvide Abernathy*: MARTIN WOLFSON. *Mission Band*: Michelle Reiner, Paul Migan, Elaine Spaulding. *Harry the Horse*: TOM PEDI. *Lieut. Brannigan*: TOM AHEARNE. *Nathan Detroit*: WALTER MATTHAU. *Angie the Ox*: Ralph Vucci. *Miss Adelaide*: HELEN GALLAGHER. *Sky Masterson*: RAY SHAW. *Joey Biltmore*: Joe Bernard. *Mimi*: Norma Kaiser. *General Matilda B. Cartwright*: KATE TOMLINSON. *Big Jule*: LOU NOVA. *Drunk*: Robert Karl. *Waiter*: Seth Riggs.

Dancers: Ellen Beach, Sonya Besant, Louise Golden, Diana Hunter, Norma Kaiser, Loys Lozano, Marcia Maier, Kirsten Valbor, Albert Fiorella, Robert Karl, Frank Marasco, Tom Panko, Regis Powers, Victor Reilly, Harry Lee Rogers, Marc West. *Singers*: Ken Emery, Clifford Fearl, Tom Powell, Seth Riggs, Bob Rippy, Evans Thornton, Murray Vines, Ralph Vucci. *Sightseers*: Sheila Hayden, Rosemary Shein, Jane Wagner.

1955.07

SOUTH PACIFIC

A Revival of the Musical Play in Two Acts, 23 Scenes[17]. Book by Oscar Hammerstein II and Joshua Logan. Adapated from James A. Michener's novel "Tales of the South Pacific." Music by Richard Rodgers. Lyrics by Oscar Hammerstein II. Directed by Charles Atkin. Scenery by Jo Mielziner. Costumes by Motley; Costume supervisor, Frank Spencer. Musical director, Frederick Dvonch. Orchestrations by Robert Russell Bennett. Produced by the New York City Center Light Opera Company (William Hammerstein, General director). Opened 4 May 1955 at the New York City Center and closed 15 May 1955 after 15 performances.

CAST (in order of appearance): *Ngana*: Margaret Sokal. *Jerome*: Antonio Obregon. *Henry*: Richard Silvera. *Ensign Nellie Forbush*: SANDRA DEEL. *Emile DeBecque*: RICHARD COLLETT. *Bloody Mary*: SYLVIA SYMS. *Bloody Mary's Assistant*: Julie Winston. *Abner*: J. J. Riley. *Stewpot*: FRANK MAXWELL. *Luther Billis*: HENRY SLATE. *Professor*: GENE SAKS. *Lt. Joseph Cable, U.S.M.C.*: HERB BANKE. *Capt. George Brackett, U.S.N.*: MARTIN WOLFSON. *Cmdr. William Harbison, U.S.N.*: Warren J. Brown. *Yeoman Herbert Quale*: Seth Riggs. *Sgt. Kenneth Johnson*: Howard Lear. *Seabee Richard West*: Evans Thornton. *Seabee Morton Wise*: Murray Vines. *Seaman Tom O'Brien*: Dick Armbrust. *Radio Operator Bob McCaffrey*: Clifford Fearl. *Staff Sgt. Thomas Hassinger*: Ralph Vucci. *Lt. Genevieve Marshall*: Eileen Moran. *Ensign Dinah Murphy*: Edith Lane. *Ensign Janet MacGregor*: Janice Samarie. *Ensign Cora MacRae*: Louise Pearl. *Ensign Bessie Noonan*: Michelle Reiner. *Ensign Connie Walewska*: Helen Baisley. *Ensign Pamela Whitmore*: Elaine Spaulding. *Ensign Sue Yaeger*: Theresa Mari. *Liat*: CAROL LAWRENCE. *Marcel*, Henry's Assistant: Nick Gentile. *Lt. Buzz Adams*: Don Fellows. *Shore Patrol Officer*: Bob Rippy. *Sailors*: Richard Hildebrand, Raymond Wearer. *Islander*: Emy Boselli.

1955.08

DAMN YANKEES

A Musical in Two Acts, 22 Scenes. Book by George Abbott and Douglass Wallop. Based on the novel "The Year the Yankees Lost the Pennant" by Douglass Wallop. Music and lyrics by Richard Adler and Jerry Ross. Dances and musical numbers staged by Bob Fosse. Scenery and costumes designed by William and Jean Eckart. Musical direction by Hal Hastings. Orchestrations by Don Walker. Dance music arrangements by Roger Adams. Production directed by George Abbott. Produced by Frederick Brisson, Robert E. Griffith and Harold S. Prince in association with Albert B. Taylor. Opened 5 May 1955 at the 46th Street Theatre, moved 7 May 1957 to the Adelphi Theatre, and closed 19 October 1957 after 1019 performances.

CAST (in order of appearance): *Meg*: SHANNON BOLIN. *Joe Boyd*: ROBERT SHAFER. *Applegate*: RAY WALSTON. *Sister*: JEAN STAPLETON. *Doris*: Elizabeth Howell. *Joe Hardy*: STEPHEN DOUGLASS. *Henry*: Al Lanti. *Sohovik*: Eddie Phillips. *Smokey*: NATHANIEL FREY. *Vernon*: Albert Linville. *Van Buren*: RUSS BROWN. *Rocky*: JIMMIE KOMACK. *Gloria*: RAE ALLEN. *Teen-Ager*: Cherry Davis. *Lynch*: Del Horstmann. *Welch*: RICHARD BISHOP. *Lola*: GWEN VERDON. *Miss Weston*: Janie Janvier. *Guard*: George Marcy. *Commissioner*: Del Horstmann. *Postmaster*: Albert Linville.

Dancers: Betty Carr, Patricia Ferrier, Marilyn Greer, Marie Kolin, Julia Marlowe, Svetlana McLee, Robert Evans, Timmy Everett, William Joyce, Harvey Jung, Al Lanti, George Marcy, Eddie Phillips, Mark Ward. *Singers*: Cherry Davis, Jeanne Grant, Janet Hayes, Janie Janvier, Joan Keenan, Suzanne Lovell, Frank Bouley, Fred Bryan, Del Horstmann, Ralph Lowe, Albert Linville, Ralph Strane. *Children*: Ronn Cummins, Jackie Scholle.

The action takes place some time in the future—Washington, D.C.

Act 1, Scene 1: Joe and Meg Boyd's Front Porch and Living Room. *Scene 2*: A Corridor under the stands of the Washington Baseball Park. *Scene 3*: The Dugout of the Washington Baseball Park. *Scene 4*: A Billboard near the Ballpark. *Scene 5*: Welch's Office. *Scene 6*: A Bench in front of the Joe hardy Billboard. *Scene 7*: Meg's House.

[15]No individual musical numbers listed; performed as an opera.

[16]First presented in New York 24 November 1950 at the 46th Street Theatre for 1200 performances. For Synopsis of Scenes and Musical Numbers, see original 1950 production. "Travelling Light" omitted for this and all future productions.

[17]First produced in New York 7 April 1949 at the Majestic Theatre for 1925 performances. For Synopsis of Scenes and Musical Numbers, see original 1949 production.

Scene 8: Corridor at the Ball Park. *Scene 9*: The Locker Room. *Scene 10*: In front of black curtain. *Scene 11*: The Stage of the Hotel Ballroom.

Act 2, Scene 1: The Locker Room. *Scene 2*: A Park at dusk. *Scene 3*: Applegate's Apartment. *Scene 4*: The Commissioner's Office. *Scene 5*: A Bench. *Scene 6*: A Night Club. *Scene 7*: The Joe Hardy Billboard. *Scene 8*: The Billboard. *Scene 9*: The Dugout and Stands. *Scene 10*: Corridor at Ballpark. *Scene 11*: Meg's House.

ACT 1

Scene 1

"Six Months Out of Every Year"
S. Bolin, R. Shafer, Baseball Fans, Baseball Widows

"Goodbye, Old Girl"
R. Shafer, S. Douglass

Scene 2

"Heart"
R. Brown, J. Kommack, N. Frey, A. Linville

Scene 3

"Shoeless Joe from Hannibal, Mo."
R. Allen, Baseball Players

Scene 5

"A Man Doesn't Know"
S. Douglass

Scene 6

"A Little Brains—A Little Talent"
G. Verdon

Scene 7

"A Man Doesn't Know" (reprise)
S. Douglass, S. Bolin

Scene 9

"Whatever Lola Wants"
G. Verdon

Scene 10

"Not Meg"[18]
R. Walston, Gossips

Scene 11

"Who's Got the Pain?"
G. Verdon, E. Phillips
(*Dance staged by* Bob Fosse and Gwen Verdon.)

"The American League"[19]
The Downtown Fan Club

ACT 2

Scene 1

"The Game"
J. Kommack, N. Frey, Baseball Players

"Heart" (reprise)[20]
J. Stapleton, R. Cummins, J. Scholle, C. Davis

Scene 2

"Near To You"
S. Douglass, S. Bolin

Scene 3

"Those Were the Good Old Days"
R. Walston

Scene 6

"Two Lost Souls"
G. Verdon, S. Douglass, Guys, Dolls

Scene 11

"A Man Doesn't Know" (reprise)
S. Bolin, R. Shafer

[18]Dropped shortly after opening and replaced by:
"Heart" (reprise)
J. Stapleton, R. Cummins, J. Scholle, C. Davis

[19]Dropped shortly after opening.

[20]Dropped shortly after opening.

1955.09 FINIAN'S RAINBOW

A Revival of the Musical in Two Acts, 10 Scenes[21]. Book by E.Y. Harburg and Fred Saidy. Lyrics by E. Y. Harburg. Music by Burton Lane. Directed by William Hammerstein. Scenery and lighting by Howard Bay. Costume supervision, Frank Spencer. Choreography by Onna White after the original by Michael Kidd. Costumes by Alvin Colt. Orchestrations by Robert Russell Bennett and Don Walker. Conducted by Julius Rudel. Musical director, Frederick Dvonch. Produced by the New York City Center Light Opera Company (William Hammerstein, General director). Opened 18 May 1955 at the New York City Center and closed 29 May 1955 after 15 performances.

CAST (in order of appearance): *Buzz Collins*: Eddie Bruce. *Sheriff*: Jack Bryan. *First Sharecropper*: Evans Thornton. *Second Sharecropper*: Seth Riggs. *Susan Mahoney*: ANITA ALVAREZ. *Henry*: Michael Gilford. *Third Sharecropper*: Rosetta LeNoire. *Finian McLonergan*: WILL MAHONEY. *Sharon McLonergan*: HELEN GALLAGHER. *Woody Mahoney*: MERV GRIFFIN. *Og, A Leprechaun*: DONN [Donald] DRIVER. *Howard*: Terry Carter. *Senator Billboard Rawkins*: Frank Borgman. *First Geologist*: Walter P. Brown. *Second Geologist*: Emory Knight. *Diane*: Lynn-Rose Kohan. *Honey Lou*: Jonelle Allen. *John*, the Preacher: Rodester Timmons. *Mr. Robust*: Oggie Small. *Mr. Shears*: James Elward. *First Passion Pilgrim Gospeller*: John Bouie. *Second Passion Pilgrim Gospeller*: Elwood Smith. *Third Passion Pilgrim Gospeller*: Jay J. Riley. *First Deputy*: Howard Lear. *Second Deputy*: Richard Blofson. *Third Deputy*: Emory Knight.

Dancers: Albert Fiorella, Robert Karl, Tom Panko, Charles Queenan, Jay J. Riley, Harry Lee Rogers, Marc West, Erona Harris, Norma Kaiser, Loys Lozano, Mary Martinet, Vera McNichols, Nadine Revene, Kirsten Valbor, Elizabeth Williamson. *Singers*: John Bouie, Walter P. Brown, Clifford Fearl, Howard Lear, Seth Riggs, Jay J. Riley, Robert Rippy, Elwood Smith, Evans Thornton, Rodester Timmons, Murray Vines, Helen Baisley, Theresa Mari, Rosalie Maxwell, Eileen Moran, Louise Pearl, Michelle Reiner, Janice Samarie, Christine Spencer.

1955.10 SEVENTH HEAVEN

A Musical Play in Two Acts, 16 Scenes. Book by Victor Wolfson and Stella Unger. Based on the play of the same name by Austin Strong. Music by Victor Young. Lyrics by Stella Unger. Scenery and costumes by Vertis. Lighting by Feder. Choreography by Peter Gennaro. Musical director, Max Meth. Orchestral arrangements by David Terry. Choral director, Crane Calder. Entire production staged by John C. Wilson. Produced by Gant Gaither and William Bacher. Opened 26 May 1955 at the ANTA Theatre and closed 2 July 1955 after 44 performances.

CAST (in order of appearance): *Boule*: KURT KASZNAR. *Camille*: GERRIANNE RAPHAEL. *Collette*: PATRICIA HAMMERLEE. *Fifi*: CHITA RIVERA. *Mme. Suze*: BEATRICE ARTHUR. *Father Chevillon*: Malcolm Lee Beggs. *Diane*: GLORIA DE HAVEN. *First Sailor*: Philip Cook. *Second Sailor*: Leo Kayworth. *Policeman*: Walter Brandin. *First Nun*: Nanette Vezina. *Second Nun*: Joy Marlene. *Street Cleaner*: Ralph Quist. *Organ Grinder*: William Carson. *First Senegalese*: Ray Saint Jacques. *Second Senegalese*: James E. Wall. *Dandy*: John Carter. *Baker Boy*: Joseph Flynn. *Housewife*: Jeanne Schegel. *Artist*: Jimmy White. *Streetwalkers*: Lee Becker (Theodore), Bonnie Evans, Helena Seroy. *Midinette*: Nancy Lynch. *Fleegle*: ROBERT CLARY. *Inspector*: Scott Merrill. *Gobin*: David Collyer. *Vulmir*: Ferdi Hoffman. *Chico*: RICARDO MONTALBAN. *Children*: Betty Jane Seagle, Barbara Stabile, Barclay Hodges. *French Official*: George Burles. *Flower Vendor*: Winifred Ainslee. *First French Soldier*: Ray Saint Jacques. *Second French Soldier*: James E. Wall. *First American Soldier*: Ralph Quist. *Second American Soldier*: Joseph Flynn. *Apaches*: Edmund Hall, Ralph Flynn. *Accordionist*: Dominic Cortese.

Dancers: Lee Becker (Theodore), Bonnie Evans, Nancy Lynch, Helena Seroy, Rebecca Vorno, Philip Cook, Victor Duntiere, William Guske, Philip Salem, Jimmy White. *Singers*: Winifred Ainslee, Gwen Harmon, Joy Marlene, Alexandra Moss, Jeanne Schlegel, Nanette Vezina, Walter Brandin, George Burles, William Carson, John Carter, Joseph Flynn, Edmund Hall, Leo Kayworth, Ralph Quist, Ray Saint Jacques, James E. Wall, Ralph Wayne.

The action takes places in and around Paris, 1914-1918.

Act 1, Scene 1: A Cul-de-Sac. *Scene 2*: A Street in Paris. *Scene 3*: Chico's Sewer. *Scene 4*: Rue Notre Dame de Lorette. *Scene 5*: Chico's Attic. *Scene 6*: The Street. *Scene 7*: 'Heaven'—four days later. *Scene 8*: Rue Notre Dame de Lorette. *Scene 9*: Fete Montmartre.

Act 2, Scene 1: Railroad Station. *Scene 2*: The Street. *Scene 3*: In the Trenches. *Scene 4*: No Man's Land. *Scene 5*: Behind the Lines—a Canteen. *Scene 6*: The Search. *Scene 7*: The Cul-de-Sac.

[21]First produced 10 January 1947 at the 46th Street Theatre for 725 performances. For Synopsis of Scenes and Musical Numbers, see original 1947 production.

ACT 1
"C'Est La Vie"
R. Clary, K. Kasznar, B. Arthur, Company
"Where Is That Someone For Me?"
G. DeHaven
"Camille, Collette, Fifi"
C. Rivera, P. Hammerlee, G. Raphael
"Man With a Dream"
R. Montalban
"Remarkable Fellow"
R. Montalban, C. Rivera, S. Merrill, Company
"If It's a Dream"
G. DeHaven
"Happy Little Crook"
R. Clary
"Sun at My Window, Love at My Door"
G. DeHaven, R. Montalban, Company
"Where Is That Someone For Me?" (reprise)
G. DeHaven
"Glove Dance"
B. Evans, N. Lynch, H. Seroy, R. Vorno, P. Cook, V. Duntiere, P. Salem, J. White

ACT 2
"A Miss You Kiss"
R. Montalban, Company
"Camille, Collette, Fifi" (reprise)
C. Rivera, P. Hammerlee, G. Raphael
"Chico's Reverie" (White and Gold Ballet)
Company
"Love, Love, Love"
G. Raphael, P. Hammerlee, C. Rivera, J. White
"If It's A Dream" (reprise)
G. DeHaven
"Love Sneaks Up on You"
R. Clary, P. Hammerlee
Finale
Entire Company

1955–1956 SEASON

Julie Andrews and Rex Harrison in MY FAIR LADY
Museum of the City of New York

1955–1956 SEASON

1955.11 ### ALMOST CRAZY

A Musical Revue in Two Acts, 27 Scenes. Sketches mostly by James Shelton, Hal Hackady and Robert A. Bernstein, (Lester Judson, Kay Medford). Music and lyrics mostly by Portia Nelson, Raymond Taylor and James Shelton, (Lew Kesler, Joyce Geary, Ed Scott, Sam Rosen, Hal Hackady, Lenny Adelson, Jim Kaye, Carley Mills, Bill Russell, Stan Hagler, Helen Bragdon, Gene DePaul, Don Raye). Choreography by William Skipper. Sketches directed by Christopher Hewett. Scenery and lighting by John Robert Lloyd. Costumes by Stanley Simmons. Musical director, Al Rickey. Orchestral arrangements by Ted Royal. Entire production staged by Lew Kesler. Produced by John S. Cobb. Opened 20 June 1955 at the Longacre Theatre and closed 2 July 1955 after 16 performances.

CAST: KAY MEDFORD, JAMES SHELTON, BABE HINES, BETTY COLBY, KAREN ANDERS, KEVIN SCOTT, Alvin Beam, Vincent Beck, Ron Cecill, Nick Dana, Lorna Del Maestro, Phyllis Dorne, Mildred Hughes, Joan Morton, William Skipper, Gloria Smith, Rita Tanno, Richard Towers, Ann York.

ACT 1

Scene 1

"Everything's Gonna Be Much Worse Next Year"
(*Music by* Lew Kesler. *Lyrics by* James Shelton.)
Ladies of the Ensemble: R. Tanno, B. Colby, K. Anders, M. Hughes, J. Morton, L. Del Maestro, A. York, K. Medford. *Quartette*: W. Skipper, A. Beam, K. Scott, N. Dana.

Scene 2

"Mother's Day"
M. Hughes, K. Anders, A. York
(*Music by* Portia Nelson. *Lyrics by* Joyce Geary.)

Scene 3

"Why Not Me?"
P. Dorne, R. Cecill
(*Music by* Ed Scott. *Lyrics by* Sam Rosen.)

Scene 4

Fort Knox, New York
(*by* Lester Judson)

Scene 5

"But It's Love"
G. Smith, A. York, L. Del Maestro,
R. Tanno, J. Morton, W. Skipper, A. Beam, N. Dana, R. Cecill
(*Music by* Ray Taylor. *Lyrics by* Hal Hackady.)

Scene 6

"Don't Bait for Fish You Can't Fry"
B. Hines
(*Music and Lyrics by* Portia Nelson.)

Scene 7

This Is a Living
(*by* Hal Hackady)
Ralph Deadwood: K. Scott. *Mary Smiles Winter*: K. Medford. *A Model*: M. Hughes. *The Husband*: J. Shelton. *Maxine Madison*: K. Anders.

Scene 8

"Where Is the Girl?"
B. Colby, K. Scott
(*Music and Lyrics by* James Shelton.)

Scene 9

"Mother's Day"
M. Hughes, K. Anders, A. York
(*Music by* Portia Nelson. *Lyrics by* Joyce Geary.)

Scene 10

"Goin' to the Moon"
R. Tanno, J. Shelton, V. Beck, K. Medford, R. Towers
(*Music by* Ed Scott. *Lyrics by* Lenny Adelson.)

Scene 11

"Down to Eartha"
B. Colby
(*Music and Lyrics by* Ray Taylor.)

Scene 12

"Chat Noire"
K. Scott
(*Music by* Ray Taylor. *Lyrics by* Jim Kaye.)
Chat Noire: J. Morton. *Bartender*: F. Nay. *Cop*: N. Dana. *Sailor*: R. Cecill. *Street Cleaner*: F. Nay. *The Mouse*: A. Beam.

Scene 13

"I Can Live Without It"
K. Anders
(*Music and Lyrics by* Ray Taylor.)

Scene 14

If I Knew You Were Coming
(*by* Robert A. Bernstein)
Announcer: K. Anders. *Wife*: K. Medford. *Husband*: J. Shelton.

Scene 15

"Come and Get Cozy With Me"
(*Music by* Lew Kesler. *Lyrics by* Carley Mills.)
Lifeguard: K. Scott. *His Girl*: K. Anders. *Kitty's Roommate*: K. Medford. *Kitty's Beau*: J. Shelton. *Lovers*: B. Colby, V. Beck, Company.

ACT 2

Scene 1

"As We Told You"
(*Music by* Lew Kesler. *Lyrics by* James Shelton.)
Ladies of the Ensemble: R. Tanno, B. Colby, K. Anders, M. Hughes, J. Morton, A. York, L. Del Maestro, G. Smith. *Quartette*: W. Skipper, A. Beam, N. Dana, R. Cecill.

Scene 2

"Burlesque"
(*Music by* Bill Russell. *Lyrics by* Stan Hagler.)
Queenie: G. Smith. *Big Queenie*: K. Medford. *Barker*: F. Nay. *The Baritone*: K. Scott.

Scene 3

"Vertigo"
(*Music by* Ray Taylor. *Lyrics by* Helen Bragdon.)
Mistress of the Villa: B. Colby. *Tender of the Grapes*: V. Beck.

Scene 4

I Thought So Too
(*by* James Shelton)
Doctor: R. Towers. *First Woman*: L. Del Maestro. *First Man*: K. Scott. *Second Man*: J. Shelton. *Second Woman*: R. Tanno. *Third Woman*: K. Medford.

Scene 5

"Easy"
B. Hines
(*Music and Lyrics by* James Shelton.)

Scene 6

"Always Tell the Truth"
(*Dialogue by* Hal Hackady. *Music and Lyrics by* Portia Nelson.)
Truth: J. Morton. *Veracity*: K. Medford.

Scene 7

"Mother's Day"
M. Hughes, A. York, K. Anders
(*Music by* Portia Nelson. *Lyrics by* Joyce Geary.)

Scene 8

"Here Come the Blues"
W. Skipper
(*Music by* Gene DePaul. *Lyrics by* Don Raye.)
Danced by W. Skipper, J. Morton, L. Del Maestro, M. Hughes, 'The Leg' P. Dorne.

Scene 9

"More Fish"
K. Anders

Scene 10

"Love in the Barnyard"
B. Hines
(*Music and Lyrics by* Ray Taylor.)
Danced by G. Smith, L. Del Maestro, R. Tanno, P. Dorne, R. Cecill, A. Beam, N. Dana, W Skipper.

Scene 11
Love Me or Leave Me
(*by* Kay Medford and James Shelton)
The Grump: J. Shelton. *Ruth*: K. Medford.
Scene 12
Finale
Entire Company

1955.12 CATCH A STAR

A Musical Revue in Two Acts, 23 Scenes. Sketches by Danny and Neil Simon, (Mike Stewart). Music by Sammy Fain and Phil Charig. Lyrics by Paul (Francis) Webster and Ray Golden. Additional material by Lee Adams. (Additional music by Hal Borne, Sy Kleinman, Jerry Bock, Jay Navarro. Additional lyrics by Dave Ormont, Danny Shapiro, Milton Pascal, Larry Holofcener, Bernie Wayne, Lee Norris, I.A.L. Diamond, Norman Martin.) Sketches directed by Danny Simon. Dances and musical numbers staged by Lee Sherman. Settings devised and designed by Ralph Alswang. Costumes designed by Thomas Becher. Orchestrations and musical direction by Milton Greene. Ballet music composed by Herb Schutz. Revue co-ordinated by Robert Nesbitt. Entire production conceived and supervised by Ray Golden. Produced by Sy Kleinman. Opened 6 September 1955 at the Plymouth Theatre and closed 24 September 1955 after 23 performances.

CAST: PAT CARROLL, DAVID BURNS, ELAINE DUNN, JACK WAKEFIELD, HELEN HALPIN, MARC BREAUX, UNDINE FORREST, SONNY SPARKS, WAYNE SHERWOOD, KAY MALONE, DENNY DESMOND, CALVIN HOLT, TRUDE ADAMS, Lillian D'Honau, Kay Kingston, Mickey Calin, Louise Golden, Carl Jeffrey, Sigyn, Carol Field, Rhoda Kerns.

ACT 1
Scene 1
"Catch a Star!"
W. Sherwood
(*Music by* Sammy Fain. *Lyrics by* Paul Francis Webster.)
Scene 2
"Everybody Wants to Be in Show Business"
(*Music by* Phil Charig. *Lyrics by* Ray Golden, Bud Burtson.)
Producer: D. Burns. *Stage Doorman*: J. Wakefield. *Thief*: C. Jeffrey. *Policeman*: W. Sherwood. *Magician*: C. Holt. *Magician's Assistant*: R. Kerns. *Model*: U. Forrest. *Woman With Baby Carriage*: K. Malone. *Ambulance Attendants*: M. Breaux, D. Desmond. *Patient*: M. Calin. *Chorus Girls*: L. D'Honau, Sigyn. *Waitress*: H. Halpin. *Secretaries*: L. Golden, E. Dunn. *Charity Collector*: K. Kingston.
Scene 3
New Styles in Acting
(*by* Danny Simon)
Producer: D. Burns. *Secretary*: C. Field. *Military Pilot*: J. Wakefield. *Tennis Player*: D. Desmond. *Professor*: S. Sparks. *The Ingenue*: P. Carroll.
Scene 4
"A Little Travelling Music"
(*Music by* Hal Borne. *Lyrics by* Paul Francis Webster and Ray Golden.)
The Traveler: E. Dunn. *Three Improper Bostonians*: L. Golden, Sigyn, L. D'Honau.
Scene 5
Matinee Idles
(*by* Danny and Neil Simon)
Hawker: D. Desmond. *Pete*: W. Sherwood. *Man*: J. Wakefield. *Trixie*: P. Carroll. *Dorothy*: H. Halpin. *Martha*: C. Field. *Lucille*: U. Forrest. *Hazel*: R. Kerns. *Harriett*: K. Malone. *Florence*: K. Kingston. *Actor*: S. Sparks. *Actress*: L. D'Honau.
Scene 6
"One Hour Ahead of the Posse"
(*Music by* Phil Charig. *Lyrics by* Ray Golden and Dave Ormont.)
Killer: W. Sherwood. *Girl*: L. D'Honau. *Sheriff*: M. Breaux. *Posse*: C. Holt, C. Jeffrey, M. Calin, D. Desmond. *Folk Singers*: C. Field, R. Kerns, K. Malone.
Scene 7
And Then I Wrote
(*by* Danny and Neil Simon)
Harry: J. Wakefield. *Kitty*: H. Halpin. *Max Dillingbert*: D. Burns. *Labonza*: S. Sparks. *Gus*: M. Breaux. *Phoebe*: U. Forrest. *Customer*: D. Desmond.
Scene 8
"Las Vegas"
(*Music by* Sy Kleinman. *Lyrics by* Ray Golden and Lee Adams.)
Girl: P. Carroll. *Bellhops*: W. Sherwood, C. Jeffrey, M. Calin, D. Desmond.
Scene 9
"To Be or Not To Be in Love"
(*Music by* Phil Charig. *Lyrics by* Ray Golden, Danny Shapiro, Milton Pascal.)
Girl: T. Adams. *Boy*: M. Breaux.
Scene 10
"The Story of Alice"
(*Music by* Jerry Bock. *Lyrics by* Larry Holofcener.)
Quartet: H. Halpin, W. Sherwood, C. Holt, U. Forrest.
Scene 11
Room for Rent
(*by* Danny and Neil Simon)
Southern Belle: P. Carroll. *First Man*: D. Burns. *First Roomer*: J. Wakfield. *Second Roomer*: S. Sparks. *Third Roomer*: K. Kingston. *Second Man*: W. Sherwood.
Scene 12
"What a Song Can Do"
H. Halpin
(*Music and Lyrics by* Bernie Wayne and Lee Norris.)
Scene 13
"Carnival in Court"
(*Music by* Jay Navarro. *Lyrics by* Ray Golden and I. A. L. Diamond.)
Town Crier: D. Burns. *Bailiff*: C. Holt. *Two Girls*: Sigyn, L. Golden. *Judge*: J. Wakefield. *Plaintiff*: H. Halpin. *Defendant*: S. Sparks. *Private Eye*: M. Breaux. *Private Eye's Wife*: E. Dunn. *Co-respondent*: P. Carroll. *Three Belles*: L. D'Honau, U. Forrest, K. Malone. *Two Sailors*: M. Calin, D. Desmond. *Basketman*: W. Sherwood. *Basketwoman*: C. Field.

ACT 2
Scene 1
Theatre Piece
Three Male Dancers: M. Breaux, M. Calin, C. Holt. *Three Female Dancers*: Sigyn, E. Dunn, L. Golden. *Character*: C. Jeffrey. *Glamour Girls*: U. Forrest, K. Malone, R. Kerns, L. D'Honau (Harlequin).
Scene 2
Arty
(*by* Danny and Neil Simon)
Mom: P. Carroll. *Arty*: J. Wakefield. *First Man*: D. Desmond. *Second Man*: S. Sparks.
Scene 3
"Twist My Arm"
(*Music by* Sammy Fain. *Lyrics by* Paul Francis Webster.)
Girl: E. Dunn. *Boy*: M. Breaux.
Scene 4
"New Hollywood Plots"[1]
D, Burns, D. Desmond, C. Holt
(*Music by* Sammy Fain. *Lyrics by* Paul Francis Webster.)
Scene 5
"Foreign Cars"
T. Adams
(*Music and Lyrics by* Norman Martin)
Scene 6
"Gruntled"
(*Music and Lyrics by* Phil Charig, Ray Golden and Sy Kleinman.)
Girl: H. Halpin. *Boy*: D. Desmond. *Three Couples*: M. Breaux, E. Dunn, C. Holt, L. D'Honau, M. Calin, Sigyn.
Scene 7
Matrimonial Agency
(*by* Danny and Neil Simon)
First Woman: U. Forrest. *Second Woman*: K. Malone. *Adrian*: D. Burns. *First Shopper*: K. Kingston. *First Man*: M. Calin. *Mrs. Ennis*: P. Carroll. *Miss B.*: C. Field. *The Frenchman*: M. Breaux. *The Reject*: J. Wakefield. *The Body*: S. Sparks.

---
[1]Dropped during run.

Scene 8

"Fly Little Heart"
E. Dunn
(*Music by* Jerry Bock. *Lyrics by* Larry Holofcener.)

"Bachelor Hoedown"
E. Dunn, M. Breaux, Sigyn, L. Golden, C. Field, L. D'Honau, R. Kerns, M. Calin, C. Holt, D. Desmond, C. Jeffrey, W. Sherwood
(*Music by* Jerry Bock. *Lyrics by* Larry Holofcener.)

Scene 9

Gift of the Magi
(*by* Mike Stewart)
P. Carroll

Scene 10

"Boffola"
Entire Cast
(*Music by* Phil Charig. *Lyrics by* Danny Shapiro, Milton Pascal, Ray Golden.)

1955.13

HEAR! HEAR!

A Musical Revue in Two Acts, 16 Scenes. Special songs and material, Tom Waring, Charles Henderson, Lumpy Brannum, Jack Dolph, Buddy Bernier, Phyllis Williams. Staged and directed by Fred Waring. Scenery by Sam Leve. Costumes by Jeanne Partington. Stage director, Ray Sax. Choral director, Jack Best. Orchestra director, Fred Culley. Produced by Fred Waring. Opened 27 September 1955 at the Ziegfeld Theatre and closed 23 October 1955 after 38 performances.

CAST: FRED WARING AND ALL THE PENNSYLVANIANS: *Singers*: Dorothy Arms (Soprano), Norma Barnes (Contralto), Patti Beems (Soprano), Ruth Best (Soprano), Jack Best (Bass), Bill Caniff (Tenor), FRANK DAVIS (Bass baritone), Norma Douglas (Alto), EDDIE ERICKSEN (Tenor), George Geyer (Baritone), GORDON GOODMAN (Tenor), Ralph Isbell (Bass), LEONARD KRANENDONK (Baritone), Bob Kranendonk (Baritone), JOE MARINE (Baritone), Preshy Marker (Mezzo-Soprano), T. J. Marker (Bass), George Pilon (Tenor), BOB SANDS (Tenor), Fred Waring, Jr. (Tenor). *Players*: Hawley Ades (Piano), Lamar Alsop (Viola), Lou Bode (Clarient, Saxophone), LUMPY BRANNUM (String Bass), Ward Cole (Trumpet), Fred Culley (Violin, Orchestral Director), Buss Dillon (Drums), Mike Doty (Clarinet), Julius Ehrenworth (Cello), JEAN ELEY (Violin), LOU ELEY (Violin), Charles Evans (Trombone), Ben Feldham (Violin), George Guggisberg (Trumpet), Nelson Keller (Trumpet), Marvin Long (Trombone), POLEY McCLINTOCK (Drums), ROSALIE RANDALL (Harp), Norman Ronemus (Saxophone, Clarinet), RAY SAX (Saxophone, Clarinet).

ACT 1

Scene 1

Thanks for Coming:

"Your Song"
Your Hosts

"Hear! Hear!"
We! We!
(*Music and Lyrics by* Fred Waring.)

Scene 2

Let Freedom Sing:

"America Our Heritage"
The People
(*Music and Lyrics by* Helen Steele.)

"Where in the World But America"
The Same
(*Music and Lyrics by* Glenn Rowell, Fred Waring, Jack Dolph.)

"Paul Revere's Ride"
The Patriots

"Give Me Your Tired, Your Poor" (from MISS LIBERTY)
The People
(*Music by* Irving Berlin. *Lyrics by* Emma Lazarus.)

"Pledge of Allegiance"
US
(*Music by* Fred Waring.)

Scene 3

The Song Is the Thing:

"Say It With Music" (from THE MUSIC BOX REVUE OF 1921)
Singers, Players
(*Music and Lyrics by* Irving Berlin.)

"So Beats My Heart"
P. Beems, Singers, Players
(*Music and Lyrics by* Pat Ballard, Charles Henderson, Tom Waring.)

Scene 4

Long Hair, Horse Hair, Cat Gut and Wire:

"Hora Staccato"
The No-Sing String Section

Scene 5

Rock and Roll:

"I Want You To Be My Baby"
J. Marine, the Beat Boys

Scene 6

Plain and Fancy Folk Songs

"Black Is the Color of My True Love's Hair"
R. Randall, Friends

"Across the Wide Missouri"
B. Kranendonk

"He's Gone Away"
The Girls He Left Behind

"Double Ring Ceremony"
Mountain Lovers
(*Music and Lyrics by* Buddy Bernier and Phyllis Williams.)

"Barefoot"
N. Douglas, J. Best, R. Best, E. Ericksen, P. Marker, F. Waring, Jr.
(*Music and Lyrics by* Buddy Bernier, Charles Naylor, Hugh Brannum.)

Scene 7

Songs of All Faiths:

"No Man Is an Island"
The Men

"Come, Come Ye Saints"
P. Beems, T. J. Marker, N. Barnes, G. Pilon

"I Wonder as I Wander"
D. Arms
(*Music and Lyrics by* John Jacob Niles.)

"Salve Regina"
The Chanters

"Work For the Night Is Coming"
J. Eley, R. Randall, M. Long, N. Keller

"Song of Galilee"
The Folks

"God of Our Fathers"
The People
(*Music and Lyrics by* George William Warren, Daniel Crane Roberts, arranged by Livingston Gearhart.)

Scene 8

Negro Spiritual Inspiration:

"Deep River"
The Congregation

"The Creation" (Sermon from "God's Trombones")
F. Davis
(*Music and Lyrics by* Roy Ringwald and James Weldon Johnson.)

"He's Got the Whole World in His Hands"
The Preacher

Scene 9

Miniature Mammoth Minstrel Show:

"Rampart Street"
Marching Band

"Angels Meet Me at the Crossroads"
The Minstrels

"I'll Be Dar"
L. Kranendonk

"(I Dream of)Jeannie With the Light Brown Hair"
E. Ericksen
(*Music and Lyrics by* Stephen Foster, arranged by Hawley Ades.)

"For Me and My Gal"
G. Geyer
(*Music by* George W. Meyer. *Lyrics by* Edgar Leslie and E. Ray Goetz.)
"Camptown Races"
R. Sax
"My L'ndy Lou"
G. Goodman
"Oh, Susanna"
The Minstrels
(*Music and Lyrics by* Stephen Foster, arranged by Hawley Ades.)
"Dixie"
Marching Band
Take Five (Intermission)
Unsung Dixieland Interlude
Junior's Jumpin' Jivers
(F. Waring, Jr., W. Cole, M. Doty, L. Bode, R. Sax, H. Ades, L. Brannum, B. Dillon.)

ACT 2
Scene 1
Primary Mathematics:
"Inchworm" (from HANS CHRISTIAN ANDERSEN film)
J. Marine, Friends
(*Music and Lyrics by* Frank Loesser.)
Scene 2
Collegiate Conviviality:
"A Toast to Michigan"
Convivial Collegians
(*Music and Lyrics by* Richard Kirk and Louis Elbel.)
"A Toast to All Colleges"
Same later
"Everybody's Alma Mater"
Alumni Association
Scene 3
High-Fidelity:
"My Old High School"
J. Marine, Old Grads
(*Music and Lyrics by* Tom Waring.)
Scene 4
Songs by New Young Pennsylvanians:
"Granada"
B. Sands
"Unchained Melody"
D. Arms
(*Music by* Alex North. *Lyrics by* Hy Zaret.)
"If I Love You" (from CAROUSEL)
P. Beems
(*Music by* Richard Rodgers. *Lyrics by* Oscar Hammerstein II.)
Piano Session (Title to be announced)
N. Douglas
Scene 5
Choral Symphony and Opera
"The Nutcracker Suite"
Choral Symphony Orchestra
(*Music by* Pyotor Tchaikovsky, arranged by Johnson-Cunkle-Simeone-Bernier-Waring.)
"Rigoletto"
Swanee River Quartet (R. Sands, P. Marker, R. Isbell, P. Beems)
Scene 6
The Ever-Shining Old Stars
L. Eley, J. Eley, L. Kranendonk, J. Marine, G. Goodman, L. Brannum, F. Davis
Scene 7
Songs You'd Hope to Hear, Hear and See, See:
"Dry Bones"
The Singers
"Dancing Tambourines"
The Singers, Players
(*Music by* W. C. Polla. *Lyrics by* Phil Ponce.)
"Over the Rainbow" (from THE WIZARD OF OZ film)
Everybody Sings
(*Music by* Harold Arlen. *Lyrics by* E. Y. Harburg.)
"Dear Old Donegal"
"Dark Town Strutters Ball"
(*Music and Lyrics by* Shelton Brooks.)
"Jesus Walked This Lonesome Valley"
"Joshua Fit the Battle of Jericho"
"The Happy Wanderer" (Val-De-Ri, Val-De-Ra)
(*Music by* Friedrich Wilhelm Möller. *Lyrics by* Antonia Ridge.)
"Carry Me Back to Old Virginny"
"Way Back Home"
(*Music and Lyrics by* Al Lewis and Tom Waring.)
"We'll Go a Long, Long Way Together"
(*Music and Lyrics by* Jimmy Kennedy, A. Fragna)
"With a Song in My Heart" (from SPRING IS HERE)
(*Music by* Richard Rodgers. *Lyrics by* Lorenz Hart.)
"You'll Never Walk Alone" (from CAROUSEL)
(*Music by* Richard. Rodgers. *Lyrics by* Oscar Hammerstein II.)
"Battle Hymn of the Republic"
(*Music and Lyrics by* Julia Ward Howe.)
Hear, Hear the People

1955.14 MAURICE CHEVALIER

Songs and Impressions (A Solo Musical Revue) in Two Acts. At the Piano, Fred Freed. Produced by Gilbert Miller. Opened 28 September 1955 at the Lyceum Theatre and closed 6 November 1955 after 47 performances.

ACT 1
Introduction—Fred Freed
"Ca Va, Ca Va"
(*Music by* Fred Freed. *Lyrics by* Maurice Chevalier.)
"Paris Oui Oui"
(*Music by* Henri Betti. *Lyrics by* André Hornez.)
"I Wonder Who's Kissing Her Now" (from THE PRINCE OF TONIGHT)
(*Music by* Joseph E. Howard, Harold Orlob. *Lyrics by* Will M. Hough, Frank R. Adams)
"Les Pas Perdus"
(*Music by* Henri Bourtayre. *Lyrics by* Robert Lamoureux and Maurice Chevalier.)
"L'Orientale"
(*Music by* Henri Betti. *Lyrics by* André Hornez.)
"C'Est Fort la Musique"
(*Music by* Fred Freed. *Lyrics by* Maurice Chevalier.)

ACT 2
Introduction—Fred Freed
"A Boy and a Girl"
(*Music by* Henri Betti. *English Lyrics by* Ben Smith.)
"L'Illusioniste"
(*Music by* Jean Constantin. *Lyrics by* Vittonet.)
"Un Gentleman"
(*Music and Lyrics by* Maurice Chevalier.)
"She and He"
(*Music by* Henri Betti. *English Lyrics by* Ben Smith.
"À Las Vegas"
(*Music by* Louiguy. *English Lyrics by* Maurice Chevalier.)
"Folies-Bergere"
(*Music by* Francis Lopez. *Lyrics by* Maurice Chevalier.)
"À Barcelone"
(*Music by* Henri Betti. *Lyrics by* Maurice Chevalier.)
"Accents Melodiques"
(*Sketch by* Maurice Chevalier.)
"Louise" (from INNOCENTS OF PARIS film)
(*Music by* Richard A. Whiting. *Lyrics by* Leo Robin.)
"Seems Like Old Times"
(*Music by* John Jacob Loeb. *Lyrics by* Carmen Lombardo.)

THE YEOMEN OF THE GUARD,
1955.15 or The Merryman and His Maid

A Revival of the Comic Opera in Two Acts[2]. Libretto by William S. Gilbert. Music by Arthur Sullivan. Scenery and costumes by Peter Goffin. Directed by Robert A. Gibson. Musical director, Isidore Godfrey. Produced by the D'Oyly Carte Opera Company. Opened 3 October 1955 at the Sam S. Shubert Theatre, closing 5 October 1955; re-opened 3 November 1955 and closed 5 November 1955 after 8 performances in repertory.

CAST: *Sir Richard Cholmondeley*, Lieutenant of the Tower: ALAN STYLER. *Colonel Fairfax* under sentence of death: LEONARD OSBORN. *Sergeant Meryll* of the Yeomen of the Guard: DONALD ADAMS. *Leonard Meryll*, his Son: John Fryatt. *Jack Point*, a Strolling Jester: PETER PRATT. *Wilfred Shadbolt*, Head Jailor and Assistant Tormentor: FISHER MORGAN. *First Yeoman*: Frederick Sinden. *Second Yeoman*: John Banks. *First Citizen*: Lawson Johnson. *Second Citizen*: John Reed. *Elsie Maynard*, a Strolling Player: MURIEL HARDING. *Phoebe Meryll*, Sergeant Meryll's Daughter: JOYCE WRIGHT. *Dame Carruthers*, Housekeeper to the Tower: ANN DRUMMOND-GRANT. *Kate*, her Niece: MAUREEN MELVIN. *Chorus of Yeomen of the Guard, Gentlemen, Citizens, etc.*

THE PIRATES OF PENZANCE,
1955.16 or The Slave of Duty

A Revival of the Comic Opera in Two Acts[3]. Libretto by William S. Gilbert. Music by Arthur Sullivan. Costumes designed by George Sheringham. Directed by Robert A. Gibson. Musical director, Isidore Godfrey. Produced by the D'Oyly Carte Opera Company. Opened 6 1955 at the Sam S. Shubert Theatre, closing 8 October 1955; re-opened 27 October 1955, and closed 29 October 1955 after 8 performances in repertory.[4]

CAST: *Major General Stanley*: PETER PRATT. *The Pirate King*: DONALD ADAMS. *Samuel*, his Lieutenant: Trevor Hills. *Frederic*, the Pirate Apprentice: NEVILLE GRIFFITHS. *Sergeant of Police*: FISHER MORGAN. *Mabel, Edith Kate,Isabel*, General Stanley's Daughters: MURIEL HARDING, JOYCE WRIGHT, JOY MORNAY, Margaret Dobson. *Ruth*, Pirate Maid-of-all-work: ANN DRUMMOND-GRANT. *Chorus of Pirates, Police and General Stanley's Daughters.*

1955.17 DIE FLEDERMAUS

A Revival of the Operetta in Three Acts[5]. (Original Viennese libretto by Carl Haffner and Richard Genée. Lyrics by Richard Genée. Based on the comedy "Le Réveillon" by Henri Meilhac and Ludovic Halévy.) English libretto by Ruth and Thomas Martin. Music by Johann Strauss. Staged by William Westerfield. Costume supervisor, Robert Fletcher. Choreographed by Ray Harrison. Conducted by Joseph Rosenstock. Produced by the New York City Opera. Opened 8 October 1955 at the New York City Center and closed 29 October 1955 after 3 performances in repertory; re-opened 31 March 1956 at the New York City Center and closed 7 April 1956 after 2 additional performances. Total this season: 5 performances.[6]

CAST: *Eisenstein*: JACK RUSSELL. *Rosalinda*: PHYLLIS CURTIN. *Adele*: PEGGY BONINI. *Alfred*: LLOYD THOMAS LEECH. *Falke*: JOHN EARDON. *Frank*: Richard Wentworth. *Blind*: Luigi Vellucci. *Prince Orlofsky*: MICHAEL POLLOCK. *Sally*: Jennie Andrea. *Frosch*: COLEY WORTH. *Ivan*: Thomas Powell. *Ensemble*: New York City Opera Chorus.

THE MIKADO,
1955.18 or The Town of Titipu

A Revival of the Comic Opera in Two Acts[7]. Libretto by William S. Gilbert. Music by Arthur Sullivan. Scenery designed by Peter Goffin. Costumes designed by Charles Ricketts. Directed by Robert A. Gibson. Musical director, Isidore Godfrey. Produced by the D'Oyly Carte Opera Company. Opened 10 October 1955 at the Sam S. Shubert Theatre, closing 12 October 1955; re-opened 31 October 1955-2 November 1955, 17 November 1955 and closed 19 November 1955 after 12 performances in repertory.

CAST: *The Mikado of Japan*: DONALD ADAMS. *Nanki-Poo*, his son, disguised as a wandering minstrel in love with Yum-Yum: NEVILLE GRIFFITHS. *Ko-Ko*, Lord High Executioner of Titipu: PETER PRATT. *Pooh-Bah*, Lord High Everything Else: FISHER MORGAN. *Pish-Tush, Go-To*, Noble Lords: Jeffrey Skitch, John Banks. *Yum-Yum, Pitti-Sing, Peep-Bo*, three sisters, wards of Ko-Ko: CYNTHIA MOREY, JOYCE WRIGHT, BERYL DIXON. *Katisha*: ANN DRUMMOND-GRANT. *Chorus of School Girls, Nobles, Guards and Coolies.*

JOYCE GRENFELL
1955.19 REQUESTS THE PLEASURE

A Musical Revue in Two Acts, 26 Scenes. Book and lyrics by Joyce Grenfell. Music by Richard Addinsell. (Additional music by George Bauer, William Blezard, Joan Chorlton, Douglas Gamlin, Terry Stanford, A. Reif, Donald Swann, Malcolm Arnold, Dennis Holloway and Ralph Freed. Additional lyrics by Oliver Bernard.) Directed by Laurier Lister. Musical director, George Bauer. Scenic supervision and lighting by Paul Morrison. Decor by Joan and David de Bethel, Victor Stiebel, Stanley Moore, Peter Rice. Choreography by John Heawood, Wendy Toye, Alfred Rodrigues, Beryl Kaye, Paddy Stone, Irving Davies. Additional arrangements by George Bauer. Additional orchestrations by Clare Grundman. Produced by Producers Theatre (Lyn Austin and Thomas Noyes). Opened 10 October 1955 at the Bijou Theatre and closed 3 December 1955 after 64 performances.

CAST: JOYCE GRENFELL, BERYL KAYE, PADDY STONE, IRVING DAVIES.

ACT 1[8]

Scene 1

"Welcome"
(*by* Joyce Grenfell)J. Grenfell
Proscenium by Joan and David de Bethel. *Decor by* Peter Rice. *Dress by* Victor Stiebel.

Scene 2

"Three's Company"
B. Kaye, P. Stone, I. Davies
(*Music by* George Bauer. *Costumes by* Joan and David de Bethel. *Dance arranged by* John Heawood.)

Scene 3

"The Music's Message"
J. Grenfell
(*Music by* Richard Addinsell. *Lyrics by* Joyce Grenfell.)

Scene 4

"Edinburgh Rock"
B. Kaye, P. Stone, I. Davies
(*Music by* Richard Addinsell. *Decor by* Jack Notman. *Dance arranged by* Alfred Rodrigues.)

---

[2]First presented in New York 17 October 1888 at the Casino Theatre for 100 performances. For Synopsis of Scenes and Musical Numbers, see original 1888 production.
[3]First presented in New York 31 December 1879 at the Fifth Avenue Theatre for a total of 91 performances in two engagements. For Synopsis of Scenes and Musical Numbers, see original 1879 production.
[4]Scenery uncredited.
[5]First English language production presented in New York 16 March 1885 at the Casino Theatre for 42 performances. First New York production of this adaptation 20 December 1950 at the Metropolitan Opera House. For Synopsis of Scenes and Musical Numbers, see May 1954 revival.
[6]Settings uncredited; settings and costumes were assembled from various sources, a previous Sol Hurok tour of DIE FLEDERMAUS and the Broadway production of MY DARLIN' AIDA.
[7]First presented in New York 20 July, 10-29 August 1885 at the Union Square and People's Theatres for 22 performances. First authorized production presented 19 August 1885 at the Fifth Avenue Theatre by Richard D'Oyly Carte for 250 performances. For Synopsis of Scenes and Musical Numbers, see 19 August 1885 D'Oyly Carte production.
[8]The following songs were also included:
"Just the Way You Are"
(Walt Disney music)
"I'll Lend You Everything I've Got Except My Wife" (from ZIEGFELD FOLLIES OF 1910)
(*Music by* Harry Von Tilzer. *Lyrics by* Jean C. Havez.)
"My Little Home in Tennessee"
(*Music by* Carson J. Robison.)

Scene 5
Women at Work: 1. Curiosity Shop, 2. Nursery School
J. Grenfell
(*Written by* Joyce Grenfell. *Dress by* Victor Stiebel.)

Scene 6
"Two Loves"
B. Kaye, P. Stone, I. Davies
(*Music by* Joan Chorlton and Douglas Gamlin. *Dance arranged by* Kaye, Stone and Davies.)

Scene 7
"Basquette"
B. Kaye, P. Stone, I. Davies
(*Music by* William Blezard. *Dance arranged by* Wendy Toye.)

Scene 8
"Period Piece"
J. Grenfell
(*Music by* Richard Addinsell. *Lyrics by* Joyce Grenfell. *Decor by* Joan and David de Bethel. *Dress by* Victor Stiebel.)

Scene 9
"Heart Ride"
I. Davies
(*Music by* Terry Stanford. *Lyrics by* Oliver Bernard. *Dance arranged by* John Heawood. *Decor by* Paul Morrison.)

Scene 10
The Understanding Mother
(*by* Joyce Grenfell)J. Grenfell

Scene 11
"Nothing to Do"
B. Kaye
(*Music by* A. Reif. *Dance arranged by* Peter Hamilton.)

Scene 12
Thought for Today
(*by* Joyce Grenfell)J. Grenfell
(*Decor by* Peter Rice. *Dress by* Victor Stiebel.)

Scene 13
"Favour"
B. Kaye, P. Stone
(*Music by* Donald Swann. *Decor by* Joan and David de Bethel. *Dance arranged by* Wendy Toye.)

Scene 14
"Three Brothers"
J. Grenfell
(*Music by* Richard Addinsell. *Lyrics by* Joyce Grenfell.)

Scene 15
"Palais Dancers"
J. Grenfell, B. Kaye, P. Stone, I. Davies
(*Music by* Richard Addinsell. *Lyrics by* Joyce Grenfell. *Decor by* Stanley Moore. *Dance arranged by* Alfred Rodrigues.)

ACT 2

Scene 1
"Slap Happy"
B. Kaye, P. Stone, I. Davies
("Begin the Beguine" *composed by* Cole Porter. *Dress by* Joan David de Bethel. *Dance arranged by* Wendy Toye.)

Scene 2
Two Young People and a Visitor:
(*by* Joyce Grenfell)J. Grenfell
1. Travel Talk, 2. Musician, 3. Visitor.
(*Dress by* Victor Stiebel.)

Scene 3
"Manana"
P. Stone, I. Davies
(*Music by* William Blezard. *Decor by* Stanley Moore. *Dance arranged by* Alfred Rodrigues.)

Scene 4
"Running Commentary"
J. Grenfell
(*Music by* Richard Addinsell. *Lyrics by* Joyce Grenfell.)

Scene 5
"Ordinary Morning"
B. Kaye, I. Davies
(*Music by* Richard Addinsell. *Lyrics by* Joyce Grenfell. *Decor by* Joan and David de Bethel. *Dance arranged by* John Heawood.)

Scene 6
"Paddy's Nightmare"
P. Stone
(*Music by* Malcolm Arnold. *Costume designed by* Joan and David de Bethel. *Dance devised and arranged by* Paddy Stone.)

Scene 7
"Songs My Mother Taught Me"
J. Grenfell
(*Music arranged by* Viola Tunnard. *Decor by* Paul Morrison. *Dress by* Joan and David de Bethel.)

Scene 8
Life and Literature
(*by* Joyce Grenfell)J. Grenfell

Scene 9
"Three in Time"
B. Kaye, P. Stone, I. Davies
(*Music by* Dennis Holloway. *Dance arranged by* Wendy Toye.)

Scene 10
"Envoi"
B. Kaye, P. Stone, I. Davies
(*Music by* Ralph Freed. *Dance arranged by* Wendy Toye.)

Scene 11
"Farewell"
(*by* Joyce Grenfell. *Dress by* Victor Stiebel.)J. Grenfell

1955.20

PRINCESS IDA, or Castle Adamant

A Revival of the Comic Operetta in Three Acts[9]. Libretto by William S. Gilbert. Music by Arthur Sullivan. Directed by Robert A. Gibson. Scenery and costumes by James Wade. Orchestra directed by Isidore Godfrey. Produced by the D'Oyly Carte Opera Company. Opened 13 October 1955 at the Sam S. Shubert Theatre, closing 15 October 1955; re-opened 7 November 1955 and closed 9 November 1955 after 8 performances in repertory.

CAST: *King Hildebrand*: FISHER MORGAN. *Hilarion*: JOHN FRYATT. *Hilarion's Two Friends*: *Cyril*: LEONARD OSBORN. *Florian*: JEFFREY SKITCH. *King Gama*: PETER PRATT. *His Sons*: *Arac*: DONALD ADAMS. *Guron*: JOHN BANKS. *Scythius*: Trevor Hills. *Princess Ida*, Gama's Daughter: MURIEL HARDING. *Lady Blanche*, Professor of Abstract Science: ANN DRUMMOND-GRANT. *Lady Psyche*, Professor of Humanities: CYNTHIA MOREY. *Melissa*, Lady Blanche's Daughter: BERYL DIXON. *Sacharissa*: MAUREEN MELVIN. *Chloe*: Margaret Dobson. *Ada*: Jennifer Toye. *Soldiers, Courtiers, Girl Graduates, Daughters of the Plough, etc.*

1955.21

TRIAL BY JURY

A Revival of the Comic Opera in One Act[10]. Libretto by William S. Gilbert. Music by Arthur Sullivan. Ladies costumes designed by George Sheringham. Scenery by Joseph and Phil Harker. Directed by Robert A. Gibson. Musical director, Isidore Godfrey. Produced by the D'Oyly Carte Opera Company. Opened 17 October 1955 at the Sam S. Shubert Theatre, closing 19 October 1955; re-opened 10-12 November 1955; re-opened 21 November 1955, and closed 24 November 1955 after 13 performances in repertory.

CAST: *The Learned Judge*: JOHN REED. *Counsel for the Defendant*: ALAN STYLER. *The Defendant*: JOHN FRYATT. *Foreman of the Jury*: John Banks. *Usher*: TREVOR HILLS. *Associate*: GEORGE COOK. *The Plaintiff*: KATHLEEN WEST. *First Bridesmaid*: Margaret Dobson. *Chorus of Jurymen, Bridesmaids and Public.*

9Originally presented in New York City 11 February 1884 at the Fifth Avenue Theatre for 42 performances. For Synopsis of Scenes and Musical Numbers, see original 1884 production.

10First presented in New York 15 November 1875 at the Eagle Theatre for 8 performances. For Synopsis of Scenes and Musical Numbers, see original 1875 production.

H.M.S. PINAFORE,
1955.22 **or The Lass That Loved a Sailor**

A Revival of the Comic Opera in Two Acts[11]. Libretto by William S. Gilbert. Music by Arthur Sullivan. Directed by Robert A. Gibson. Designed and painted by Joseph and Paul Harker. Ladies' costumes designed by George Sheringham. Musical director, Isidore Godfrey. Presented by the D'Oyly Carte Opera Company. Opened 17 October 1955 at the Sam S. Shubert Theatre, closing 19 October 1955; re-opened 10-12 November 1955; re-opened 21 November 1955, and closed 24 November 1955 after 13 performances in repertory.

CAST: *The Rt. Hon. Sir Joseph Porter, K.C.B.*, First Lord of the Admiralty: PETER PRATT. *Captain Corcoran*, Commanding the *H.M.S. Pinafore*: JEFFREY SKITCH. *Ralph Rackstraw*, Able Seaman: NEVILLE GRIFFITHS. *Dick Deadeye*, Able Seaman: DONALD ADAMS. *Bill Bobstay*, Bo'sun's Mate: Trevor Hills. *Bob Beckett*, Carpenter's Mate: George Cook. *Josephine*, the Captain's Daughter: MURIEL HARDING. *Hebe*, Sir Joseph's First Cousin: Joyce Wright. *Little Buttercup*, a Portsmouth Bumboat Woman: ANN DRUMMOND-GRANT. *First Lord's Sisters, his Cousins, his Aunts, Sailors, Marines.*

RUDDIGORE,
1955.23 **or The Witch's Curse**

A Revival of the Comic Opera in Two Acts[12]. Libretto by William S. Gilbert. Music by Arthur Sullivan. Directed by Robert A. Gibson. Costumes and settings by Peter Goffin. Orchestra directed by Isidore Godfrey. Produced by the D'Oyly Carte Opera Company. Opened 20 October 1955 at the Sam S. Shubert Theatre, closing 22 October 1955; re-opened 14 November 1955 and closed 16 November 1955 after 8 performances in repertory.

CAST: *Sir Ruthven Murgatroyd*: PETER PRATT. *Richard Dauntless*: LEONARD OSBORN. *Sir Despard Murgatroyd*: FISHER MORGAN. *Old Adam Goodheart*: John Banks. *Sir Roderic Murgatroyd*: DONALD ADAMS. *Rose Maybud*: CYNTHIA MOREY. *Mad Margaret*: JOYCE WRIGHT. *Dame Hannah*: ANN DRUMMOND-GRANT. *Zorah*: May Sanderson. *Ruth*: Joyce Farrer. *Chorus of Officers, Ancestors, Professional Bridesmaids, etc.*

IOLANTHE,
1955.24 **or The Peer and the Peri**

A Revival of the Comic Opera in Two Acts[13]. Libretto by William S. Gilbert. Music by Arthur Sullivan. Costumes designed by Pat Freeborn. Directed by Robert A. Gibson. Musical director, Isidore Godfrey. Produced by the D'Oyly Carte Opera Company. Opened 24 October 1955 at the Sam S. Shubert Theatre, closing 26 October 1955; re-opened 25 November 1955 and closed 26 November 1955 after 7 performances.[14]

CAST: *The Lord Chancellor*: PETER PRATT. *Earl of Mountararat*: DONALD ADAMS. *Earl Tolloller*: LEONARD OSBORN. *Private Willis* of the Grenadier Guards: FISHER MORGAN. *Strephon*, an Arcadian Shepherd: ALAN STYLER. *Queen of the Fairies*: ANN DRUMMOND-GRANT. *Iolanthe*, a Fairy, Strephon's Mother: JOYCE WRIGHT. *Celia, Leila, Fleta*, Fairies: Maureen Melvin, Beryl Dixon, Margaret Dobson. *Phyllis*, an Arcadian Shepherdess and Ward in Chancery: CYNTHIA MOREY. *Chorus of Dukes, Marquises, Earls, Viscounts, Barons and Fairies.*

1955.25 THE VAMP

A Musical Comedy in Two Acts, 10 Scenes. Book by John Latouche and Sam Locke. Music by James Mundy. Based on a story by John Latouche. Choreography by Robert Alton. Sets and costumes by Raoul Pene du Bois. Musical direction and vocal arrangements by Milton Rosenstock. Incidental music by Jack Pfeiffer. Orchestrations by James Mundy. Directed by David Alexander. Entire production supervised by Robert Alton. Associate producer, Manuel D. Herbert. Produced by Oscar Lerman, Martin Cohen and Alexander Carson. Opened 10 November 1955 at the Winter Garden and closed 31 December 1955 after 60 performances.

CAST (in order of appearance): *Myron H. Hubbard*: JACK WALDRON. *Bessie Bisco*: BIBI OSTERWALD. *Muscle Man*: Steve Reeves. *Barney Ostertag*: Paul Lipson. *Oliver J. Oxheart*: DAVID ATKINSON. *Ticket Girl*: Phyllis Dorne. *Dick Hicks*, ne Stanley Hubermyer: ROBERT RIPPY. *Stark Clayton*: MALCOLM LEE BEGGS. *Elsie Chelsea*: PATRICIA HAMMERLEE. *Bluestone*: Jack Harrold. *Flora Weems*: CAROL CHANNING. *Uncle Garvey*: WILL GEER. *Aunt Hester*: Sandyl Cordell. *Fire Commissioner*: Roger Franklin. *Snake Charmer*: David Neuman. *Samson*: STEVE REEVES. *Whip Man*: David Kashner. *High Priest*: David Neuman. *Charlie*: MATT MATTOX. *Second Cameraman*: Dick Eskeli. *Tyrolean Couples*: Cathryn Damon, Hugh Lambert, Helen Silver, Ron Cecill.

Dancers: Cathryn Damon, Mary Jane Doerr, Phyllis Dorne, Susan Hartman, Barbara Heath, Betty Koerber, Lucia Lambert, Barbara Leigh, Lila Popper, Helen Silver, Pat Wharton, Mark Aldon, Chad Block, Ron Cecill, Robert Daley, Pepe de Chazza, Burnell Dietsch, Rudy Del Campo, Hugh Lambert, Robert Norris, Dom Salinaro, Mike Stevens. *Singers*: Charleen Clark, Joyce Gladmond, Bernice Massi, Donna Sanders, Kelley Stephens, Kay Turner, Dick Eskeli, Roger Franklin, Stokely Gray, William Krach, Vincent McMahon, Ralph Wayne.

Act 1, Scene 1: Hubbard's Coliseum, Fourteenth Street (New York City, 1913). *Scene 2*: A farm in the Bronx. The following morning. *Scene 3*: Hubbard's Movie House. A few weeks later. *Scene 4*: Grand Central Station. Three months later. *Scene 5*: A rooftop in Manhattan. Sometime later.

Act 2, Scene 1: a. The northeast corner of Hollywood and Vine. b. OHO Film Company. One year later. *Scene 2*: Interior of OHO Studios. *Scene 3*: Flora's Dressing Room. *Scene 4*: Executive office, OHO Film Company. The next day. *Scene 5*: Hubbard's Movie Cathedral, Hollywood.

ACT 1
Scene 1
"The Spiel"
J. Waldron, B. Osterwald, Patrons of the Coliseum
"The Flickers"
P. Dorne, Patrons
Scene 2
"Keep Your Nose to the Grindstone"
C. Channing, W. Geer, S. Cordell
"That's Where a Man Fits In"
C. Channing
"I've Always Loved You"[15]
C. Channing, Farm Folk
Scene 3
"You're Colossal"
P. Hammerlee, R. Rippy
"Fan Club Chant"
Movie Fans
Scene 4
"Have You Met Delilah?"
D. Atkinson
"Yeemy Yeemy"
C. Channing, Oriental Entourage
"The Vamps"
M. Mattox, B. Heath, C. Damon, Fans
Scene 5
"Delilah's Dilemma"
C. Channing, Movie Fans

ACT 2
Scene 1
"Four Little Misfits"
P. Hammerlee, B. Osterwald, R. Rippy, M. Mattox
Scene 2
"Samson and Delilah"
C. Channing,
M. Mattox, S. Reevs, D. Kashner, D. Neuman, C. Damon, Movie Company
"Why Does It Have To be You?"
D. Atkinson

[11]Originally presented in New York 15 January 1879 at the Standard Theatre for 175 performances. For Synopsis of Scenes and Musical Numbers, see original 1879 production.
[12]First presented in New York 21 February 1887 at the Standard Theatre for 53 performances. For Synopsis of Scenes and Musical Numbers, see original 1887 production.
[13]First presented in New York 25 November 1882 at the Standard Theatre for 105 performances. For Synopsis of Scenes and Musical Numbers, see original 1882 production.
[14]Scenery uncredited.

[15]Dropped during the run.

"Ragtime Romeo"
B. Osterwald, M. Mattox, Boys

Scene 3

"I'm Everybody's Baby"
C. Channing

Scene 4

"I'm Everybody's Baby" (reprise)
C. Channing, P. Lipson, R. Rippy, J. Waldron, M. L. Beggs

"The Impossible She"[16]
D. Atkinson, OHO Boys

Scene 5

Finale
Company

KATHERINE DUNHAM AND HER COMPANY

1955.26

A Dance Revue in Three Acts, 12 Scenes[17]. Costumes and scenery by John Pratt. Orchestra directed by Gilberto Valdes. Choreography and direction by Katherine Dunham. Produced by Sol Hurok. Opened 22 November 1955 at the Broadway Theatre and closed 17 December 1955 after 32 performances.

CAST: KATHERINE DUNHAM.
Dancers: VANOYE AIKENS, RICARDO AVALOS, Walter Davis, LUCILLE ELLIS, Kupi Fraker, LAVINIA HAMILTON, John Lewis, Marvel Martin, Jewell André, LENWOOD MORRIS, Raimonda Orselli, Madeline Preston, Antonio Rodrigues, Jorge Saenz, Eleanor St. Ann, URAL WILSON, Camille Yarborough.

Singers: ROSALIE KING, Dorothy Speights, Gordon Simpson, URAL WILSON, Robert Wise. *Drummers*: Julito Collazo, Albert Longuerre, Francisco Urrutia, RICARDO AVALOS, Antonio Rodrigues.

ACT 1

Scene 1

Brazilian Suite:

a. Hommage to Dorival Caymmi
(*Music by* Caymmi, arr. Noriega.)
R. King, D. Thompson, G. Simpson, U. Wilson, R. Wise, Company

Dorival Caymmi, Brazilian poet, sings the beauties of his native Bahia. His songs of the sea are full of haunting mystery, his poems of the people are moving and charming. No other Brazilian folkloric writer nor composer has achieved such simplicity of expression.

b. A Preta Do Acaraje
(*Music by* Caymmi, arr. Noriega.)K. Dunham, Company

Late at night, in the deserted streets of Bahia, a street vendor offers her wares to the late passers-by. A few of them stop for a moment and dance.

c. Choros 1 and 4
(*Music by* Vadico Gogliano, Noriega.)
L. Hamilton, R. Orselli, L. Morris, J. Saenz

Variation on a Brazilian Quadrille of the early nineteenth century.

d. Carnevao!

The spirit of Brazil is in its carnivals. From Pernambuco to Rio Grande do Sul excitement and gaiety take over and Carnival is King.

(i) Xaxaado (from the North)
(*Music by* Rodriguez.)
K. Dunham, V. Aikens, Company

(ii) Samba (in Rio the Samba)
(*Music by* Dunham, Rodriguez.)
A. Rodrigues, L. Ellis, L. Hamilton, M. Martin, E. St. Ann

(iii) Frevo (from Recife O Frevo)
(arr. Noreiga)
L. Morris, R. Orselli, M. Martin, C. Yarborough, R. Avalos, J. Lewis

e. Los Indios (Native Air)
W. Davis, K. Fraker, E. St. Ann

In the west of Brazil in the High Andes, two women stop to flirt with a flute player.

Scene 2

Tango (in memory of Pepita Cano)
(*Music by* Osvaldo Pugliese.)
K. Dunham, V. Aikens, L. Ellis, R. Avalos, U. Wilson

In the Argentine there have been many changes in recent years, but the vast city of Buenos Aires still covers the underbeat of the tango. In the cantinas of the street people Katherine Dunham felt the nostalgia of the tango and the restlessness of the times.

Scene 3

Veracruzana
(*Music by* Dorothea Freitag and Foster, adapted by Gogliano-Nardini.)
The Mariachis: R. Orselli, J. Collazo, J. Saenz, F. Urrutia. *The family from Yucatan*: R. King, G. Simpson, K. Fraker. *A 'Tacos' Vendor*: D. Speights. *El Raton*: R. Avalos. *The cuckold*: L. Morris. *The Veracruzana*: K. Dunham. *The favored one*: V. Aikens. *The strong man*: A. Rodrigues. *Bamba dancers of the village*: L. Ellis, L. Hamilton, M. Martin.

ACT 2

Rituals: These rites encompass the transition of an individual or a group of individuals from one important stage of life to another. These rites at the same time sacred and dangerous occur under the supervision of the elders of those already initiated in the community. Their presence is necessary at this critical transition by which the individual who has heretofore occupied a position on a different level in the community should become integrated into complete union with his new level. These rites herein represented do not refer to any one particular society, neither do they pretend to represent the enaction of a realistic ceremony. They have been created in an effort to present, at least partially, the deep emotional interest which every primitive community feels in the individual and to expose the intense personal experience which accompanies every profound change. The primitive community finds itself sensitive to these personal reactions and protective of the individual.

Scene 1

Puberty Ritual
(*Music by* Anderson.)
The Boy: L. Morris. *The Warrior*: V. Aikens.

The ceremony of initiation by which a boy passes from the age of puberty and into manhood. In the first part the boy is isolated and the warrior which he is to become approaches him in a semi-dream state. In the second part the men of his tribe, masked for their own secret society and led by the warrior enter to take the boy, who is filled with both terror and anticipation, to the finalization of his rites of masculinity.

Scene 2

Fertility Ritual
(*Music by* Paquita Anderson.)
The Woman: L. Ellis. *The Man*: W. Davis.

The ceremony of the fertility ritual here concerned with marriage or mating in a primitive society.

Scene 3

Death
(*Music by* Dorothea Freitag, arr. Auric.)
Gede: U. Wilson. *The Queen Widow*: K. Dunham. *The consort*: V. Aikens. *Other widows and warriors*: The Company.

Death is vanquished by life and the newly born takes the place of the dead. In a primitive society orgiastic ceremonies often replace the funeral rites which are the custom in modern societies. In the cult of Rada Dahomey, it is Gede who presides over the ceremony of the dead. God of Death, he struts pompously and by the vulgarity of his gestures he attempts to overcome sorrow, by his obscenity he shows the need to conquer death in order to assure the continuity of life. The community awaits the death of the King, the passage of the royal robe, the widows mourn, the queen accepts the command of Gede and selects a mate to replace her deceased husband.

Scene 4

Shango
(*Music by* [Baldwin] Bergersen.)
Shango priest: J. Collazo. *Shango priestess*: H. Alvarez. *The boy possessed by the snake*: U. Wilson.

The scarifice of the white cock to the Yoruba God Shango takes place in Trinidad, but is known throughout the West Indies.

[16]Dropped during the run.

[17]KATHERINE DUNHAM AND HER COMPANY previously appeared on Broadway 19 April 1950 at the Broadway Theatre for 37 performances.

ACT 3

Americana: Out of the sufferings of slavery came a music rich in rhythms and dances evolved from African origins and overlaid with American forms. The Negroes adopted, interpreted and modified many creative expressions of their masters, and developed dances of strange and extravagant gaiety. In the 'Spirituals,' however, there is the awareness of tragedy but with evidences of hope, one of the most pronounced characteristics of Negro peoples.

Scene 1

Spirituals (Traditional)
R. King, D. Speights, M. Preston, U. Wilson, R. Wise
Dancer: L. Hamilton.

Deepest expression of despair and hope following a direct line from the plaints of the days of slavery.

Scene 2

Barrelhouse: Florida Swamp Shimmy (*Music by* Stacy.)
K. Dunham, Company

A Saturday night encounter during the 1920s.

Scene 3

Flaming Youth
R. King
Kansas City Woman: L. Ellis.

The Charles, the Black Bottom, the Mooch, the Fishtail, Snakehips (Dances)
L. Hamilton, W. Davis, L. Morris, Company

Scene 4

Strutters' Ball
R. King, D. Speights, G. Simpson, U. Wilson, R. Wise

Songs of the turn of the century.

Scene 5

Cakewalk
K. Dunham, V. Aikens, Company

Before the turn of the century the Cakewalk became a dance mania that spread to Europe. Couples competed with exhibitionistic and athletic variations for prizes of elaborately trimmed cakes.

1955.27 PIPE DREAM

A Musical in Two Acts, 18 Scenes. Book and lyrics by Oscar Hammerstein II. Based on the novel "Sweet Thursday" by John Steinbeck. Music by Richard Rodgers. Directed by Harold Clurman. Scenery and lighting by Jo Mielziner. Costumes by Alvin Colt. Orchestrations by Robert Russell Bennett. Musical director, Salvatore Dell'Isola. Dances and musical numbers staged by Boris Runanin. Dance arrangements by John Morris. Produced by Richard Rodgers and Oscar Hammerstein II. Opened 30 November 1955 at the Sam S. Shubert Theatre and closed 30 June 1956 after 246 performances.

CAST (in order of appearance): *Doc*: WILLIAM JOHNSON. *Hazel*: MIKE KELLIN. *Millicent Henderson*: Jayne Heller. *Mac*: G. D. WALLACE. *Suzy*: JUDY TYLER. *Fauna*: HELEN TRAUBEL. *Jim Blaikey*: Rufus Smith. *Ray Busch*: John Call. *George Herman*: Gus Raymond. *Bill*: Steve Roland. *Red*: Keith Kaldenberg. *Whitey*: Hobe Streiford. *Dizzy*: Nicolas Orloff. *Eddie*: Warren Kemmerling. *Alec*: Warren Brown. *Joe*, the Mexican: Kenneth Harvey. *Pancho*, a Wetback: Ruby Braff. *Agnes*: Temple Texas. *Mable*: Jackie McElroy. *Emma*: Marilyn Bradley. *Beulah*: Mildred Slavin. *Marjorie*: Louise Troy. *Cho Cho Sen*: Pat Creighton. *Sumi*: Sandra Devlin. *Sonny Boy*: Joseph Leon. *Esteban*, a Wetback: Jerry LaZarre. *Harriet*: Patricia Wilson. *A Waiter*: Kazimir Kokich. *Hilda*: Ruth Kobart. *Fred*: Marvin Krauter. *Slick*: Gene Kevin. *Slim*: Don Weissmuller. *Basha*: Sigyn. *Bubbles*: Marsha Reynolds. *Sonya*: Annabelle Gold. *Kitty*: Jenny Workman. *Weirde*: Patti Karkalits. *Johnny Garriagra*: Scotty Engel. *Pedro*: Rudolfo Cornejo. *Dr. Ormondy*: Calvin Thomas.

The action takes place in Cannery Row, Monterey County, California at the present time.

Act 1, Scene 1: The Western Biological Laboratory. *Scene 2*: Cannery Row, a few weeks later. *Scene 3*: The Palace Flophouse, immediately following. *Scene 4*: Cannery Row, a few days later, on a Sweet Thursday. *Scene 5*: The Western Biological Laboratory. *Scene 6*: Cannery Row. *Scene 7*: A room in the Bear Flag Cafe. *Scene 8*: Cannery Row. *Scene 9*: Sonny Boy's Pier Restaurant.

Act 2, Scene 1: A room in the Bear Flag Cafe, the following morning. *Scene 2*: Cannery Row. *Scene 3*: The Palace Flophouse, the following night. *Scene 4*: Cannery Row, the next night. *Scene 5*: The Bear Flag Cafe, a few weeks later. *Scene 6*: Cannery Row, the next morning. *Scene 7*: Inside 'The Pipe.' *Scene 8*: Cannery Row, the next morning. *Scene 9*: The Western Biological Laboratory.

ACT 1

Scene 1

"All Kinds of People"
W. Johnson, M. Kellin

"The Tide Pool"
W. Johnson, M. Kellin, G. D. Wallace, J. Tyler

"All Kinds of People" (reprise)
R. Smith

"Everybody's Got a Home But Me"
J. Tyler

Scene 3

"A Lopsided Bus"
G. D. Wallace, M. Kellin, J. Workman, A. Gold, Flophouse Gang

"Bum's Opera"
H. Traubel, K. Harvey, R. Braff, Flophouse Gang

Scene 5

"The Man I Used To Be"
W. Johnson
Danced by D. Weissmuller.

"Sweet Thursday"
H. Traubel

Scene 7

"Suzy Is a Good Thing"
H. Traubel, J. Tyler

Scene 9

"All at Once You Love Her"
W. Johnson, J. Tyler, J. LaZarre

ACT 2

Scene 1

"The Happiest House on the Block"
H. Traubel, Girls

Scene 2

"The Party That We're Gonna Have Tomorrow Night"
G. D. Wallace, Ensemble

Scene 3

Masquerade Brawl at the Flophouse

a) The Party Gets Going
(Company)

b) "I Am a Witch"
H. Traubel, T. Texas, L. Troy, M. Slavin, J. McElroy

c) "Will You Marry Me?"
J. Tyler, H. Traubel, W. Johnson

Scene 4

"Thinkin'"
M. Kellin

Scene 5

"All at Once You Love Her" (reprise)
H. Traubel

Scene 6

"How Long?"
H. Traubel, W. Johnson, Flophouse Boys, Bear Flag Girls

Scene 7

"The Next Time It Happens"
J. Tyler, W. Johnson

Scene 9

"Sweet Thursday" (reprise)
Entire Company

Finale
Entire Company

1956.01 MY FAIR LADY

A Musical in Two Acts, 18 Scenes. Book and lyrics by Alan Jay Lerner. Based on the play "Pygmalion" by George Bernard Shaw, produced on the screen by Gabriel Pascal. Music by Frederick Loewe. Staged by Moss Hart. Choreography and musical numbers staged by Hanya Holm. Production

(settings) designed by Oliver Smith. Costumes by Cecil Beaton. Musical arrangements by Robert Russell Bennett and Philip J. Lang. Lighting by (Abe) Feder. Dance music arranged by Trude Rittman. Musical director, Franz Allers. Produced by Herman Levin. Opened 15 March 1956 at the Mark Hellinger Theatre, moved 28 February 1962 to the Broadhurst Theatre, moved 18 April 1962 to the Broadway Theatre, and closed 29 September 1962 after 2717 performances.

CAST (in order of appearance): *Buskers*: Imelda De Martin, Carl Jeffrey, Joe Rocco. *Mrs. Eynsford-Hill*: Viola Roche. *Eliza Doolittle*: JULIE ANDREWS. *Freddy Eynsford-Hill*: JOHN MICHAEL KING. *Colonel Pickering*: ROBERT COOTE. *A Bystander*: Christopher Hewett. *Henry Higgins*: REX HARRISON. *Selsey Man*: Gordon Dilworth. *Hoxton Man*: David Thomas. *Another Bystander*: Rod McLennan. *First Cockney*: Reid Shelton. *Second Cockney*: Glenn Kezer. *Third Cockney*: James Morris. *Fourth Cockney*: Herb Surface. *Bartender*: David Thomas. *Harry*: Gordon Dilworth. *Jamie*: Rod McLennan. *Alfred P. Doolittle*: STANLEY HOLLOWAY. *Mrs. Pearce*: Philippa Bevans. *Mrs. Hopkins*: Olive Reeves-Smith. *Butler*: Reid Shelton. *Servants*: Rosemary Gaines, Colleen O'Connor, Muriel Shaw, Gloria Van Dorpe, Glenn Kezer. *Mrs. Higgins*: CATHLEEN NESBITT. *Chauffeur*: Barton Mumaw. *Footmen*: Gordon Ewing, William Krach. *Lord Boxington*: Gordon Dilworth. *Lady Boxington*: Olive Reeves-Smith. *Constable*: Barton Mumaw. *Flower Girl*: Cathy Conklin. *Zoltan Karpathy*: Christopher Hewett. *Flunkey*: Paul Brown. *Queen of Transylvania*: Maribel Hammer. *Ambassador*: Rod McLennan. *Bartender*: Paul Brown. *Mrs. Higgins' Maid*: Judith Williams.

Singing Ensemble: Melisande Congdon, Lola Fisher, Rosemary Gaines, Maribel Hammer, Colleen O'Connor, Muriel Shaw, Patti Spangler, Gloria Van Dorpe, Paul Brown, Gordon Ewing, Glenn Kezer, William Krach, James Morris, Reid Shelton, Herb Surface, David Thomas. *Dancing Ensemble*: Estelle Aza, Cathy Conklin, Margaret Cuddy, Imelda De Martin, Pat Diamond, Pat Drylie, Barbara Heath, Vera Lee, Nancy Lynch, Judith Williams, Thatcher Clarke, Crandall Diehl, David Evans, Carl Jeffrey, Barton Mumaw, Gene Nettles, Paul Olson, Joe Rocco, Fernando Schaffenburg, James White.

The place is London, the time 1912.

Act 1, Scene 1: Outside the Opera House, Covent Garden. A cold March night. *Scene 2*: A tenement section—Tottenham Court Road. Immediately following. *Scene 3*: Higgins' Study. The following morning. *Scene 4*: Tenement Section—Tottenham Court Road. Three days later. *Scene 5*: Higgins' study. Later that day. *Scene 6*: Near the race meeting, Ascot. A July afternoon. *Scene 7*: Inside a club tent, Ascot. Immediately following. *Scene 8*: Outside Higgins' house, Wimpole Street. Later that afternoon. *Scene 9*: Higgins' study. Six weeks later. *Scene 10*: The Promenade of the Embassy. Later that night. *Scene 11*: The ballroom of the Embassy. Immediately following.

Act 2, Scene 1: Higgins' study. 3:00 the following morning. *Scene 2*: Outside Higgins' house, Wimpole Street. Immediately following. *Scene 3*: Flower market of Covent Garden. 5:00 that morning. *Scene 4*: Upstairs hall of Higgins' house. 11:00 that morning. *Scene 5*: The conservatory of Mrs. Higgins' house. Later that day. *Scene 6*: Outside Higgins' house, Wimpole Street. Immediately following. *Scene 7*: Higgins' study. Immediately following.

ACT 1

Scene 1

Street Entertainers
I. De Martin, C. Jeffrey, J. Rocco

"Why Can't the English?"
R. Harrison

"Wouldn't It Be Loverly"
J. Andrews, Cockneys

Scene 2

"With a Little Bit of Luck"
S. Holloway, G. Dilworth, R. McLennan

Scene 3

"I'm an Ordinary Man"
R. Harrison

Scene 4

"With a Little Bit of Luck" (reprise)
S. Holloway, Ensemble

Scene 5

"Just You Wait"
J. Andrews

"The Rain in Spain"
R. Harrison, J. Andrews, R. Coote

"I Could Have Danced All Night"
J. Andrews, P. Bevans, R. Gaines, C. O'Connor, M. Shaw, G. Van Dorpe

Scene 7

"Ascot Gavotte"
Full Ensemble

Scene 8

"On the Street Where You Live"
J. M. King

Scene 11

"The Embassy Waltz"
R. Harrison, J. Andrews, C. Hewett, Full Ensemble

ACT 2

Scene 1

"You Did It"
R. Harrison, R. Coote, P. Bevans, Servants

"Just You Wait" (reprise)
J. Andrews

Scene 2

"On the Street Where You Live" (reprise)
J. M. King

"Show Me"
J. Andrews, J. M. King

Scene 3

"Wouldn't It Be Loverly" (reprise)
J. Andrews, Cockneys

"Get Me to the Church on Time"
S. Holloway, G. Dilworth, R. McLennan, Ensemble

Scene 4

"A Hymn to Him"
R. Harrison

Scene 5

"Without You"
J. Andrews, R. Harrison

Scene 6

"I've Grown Accustomed to Her Face"
R. Harrison

1956.02

MR. WONDERFUL

A Musical Comedy in Two Acts, 10 Scenes. Book by Joseph Stein and Will Glickman. Music and lyrics by Jerry Bock, Larry Holofcener and George Weiss. Production (settings) designed by Oliver Smith. Costumes designed by Robert Mackintosh. Lighting by Peggy Clark. Musical director, Morton Stevens. Musical and vocal supervision, Oscar Kosarin. Orchestrations by Ted Royal and Morton Stevens. Entire production staged by Jack Donohue. Production conceived by Jule Styne. Produced by Jule Styne and George Gilbert in association with Lester Osterman, Jr. Opened 22 March 1956 at the Broadway Theatre and closed 23 February 1957 after 383 performances.

CAST (in order of appearance): *Unemployed Actress*: Ann Buckles. *Hal*: HAL LOMAN. *Song Plugger*: Richard Curry. *Soprano*: Rina Falcone. *Rita Romano*: CHITA RIVERA. *Two Comics*: Bob Leslie, Larry B. Leslie. *Audition Annie*: Pat Wilkes. *Johnnie*: John Pelletti. *A Singer*: Karen Shepard. *Dancers*: Tempy Fletcher, Shirley Graser, Susan Hartman, Sally Neal, Patti Ann Rita, Sylvia Shay, Patti Wharton. *Sisters*: Gail Kuhr, Barbara Leigh, Sherry McCutcheon. *Acrobat*: Dorothy D'Honau. *Hoofers*: Marvin Arnold, Bill Reilly, Jimmie Thompson. *Talent Scout*: T. J. Halligan. *Annie's Friend*: Charlotte Foley. *Bop Musicians*: Harold Gordon, Albert Popwell, Claude Thompson. *Fred Campbell*: JACK CARTER. *Lil Campbell*: PAT MARSHALL. *Counterman*: Herb Fields. *Mr. Foster*: MALCOLM LEE BEGGS. *Uncle*: WILL MASTIN. *Dad*: SAMMY DAVIS, SR. *Charlie Welch*: SAMMY DAVIS, JR. *Ethel Pearson*: OLGA JAMES. *Stage Manager*: Bob Kole. *Script Girl*: Ginny Perlowin. *Stagehands*: Frank Marti, Toni Rossi. *Cigarette Girl*: Jerri Gray. *Little Girl*: Marilyn Cooper. *Sophie's Boy*: Ronnie Lee. (THE WILL MASTIN TRIO are Sammy Davis, Jr., Will Mastin, and Sammy Davis, Sr.)

Act 1, Scene 1: 1617 Broadway, New York City, the present. *Scene 2*: The Bandbox in Union City, New Jersey. *Scene 3*: 1617 Broadway. Two weeks later. *Scene 4*: Fred and Lil's Apartment. Several days later. *Scene 5*: An audition hall.

Act 1, Scene 1: The Bandbox, after hours. Several months later. *Scene 2*: An arcade in Miami, Florida. Next day. *Scene 3*: Backstage at the Palm Club, Miami Beach. *Scene 4*: Charlie's Dressing Room. *Scene 5*: The Palm Club.

ACT 1[18]
Scene 1
"1617 Broadway"
C. Rivera, H. Loman, Ensemble
"Without You, I'm Nothing"
J. Carter, P. Marshall
Scene 2
"Jacques D'Iraq"
S. Davis, Jr., Will Mastin, S. Davis, Sr., Ensemble
"Ethel, Baby"
O. James, S. Davis, Jr.
"Mr. Wonderful"
O. James
"Charlie Welch"
J. Carter
Scene 3
"Charlie Welch" (reprise)
J. Carter, Ensemble
"Talk to Him"
P. Marshall, O. James
"Too Close for Comfort"
S. Davis, Jr.
Scene 4
"Without You, I'm Nothing" (reprise)
J. Carter, S. Davis, Jr.
Scene 5
Rita's Audition
C. Rivera
Dance Improvisation: C. Rivera, H. Loman, Ensemble.
The Audition
S. Davis, Jr., W. Mastin, S. Davis, Sr.
"Sing, You Sinners" (from HONEY film)
(*Music by* Sam Coslow. *Lyrics by* W. Frank Harling.)
"Daddy, Uncle and Me"
(*Music and Lyrics by* Sid Kuller and Lyn Murray.)
"Because of You"
(*Music by* Dudley Wilkinson. *Lyrics by* Arthur Hammerstein.)
"That Old Black Magic" (from STAR SPANGLED RHYTHM film)
(*Music by* Harold Arlen. *Lyrics by* Johnny Mercer.)
"Birth of the Blues" (from GEORGE WHITE'S SCANDALS OF 1926)
(*Music by* Ray Henderson. *Lyrics by* Buddy DeSylva and Lew Brown.)
"It's All Right With Me" (from CAN CAN)
(*Music and Lyrics by* Cole Porter.)

ACT 2
Scene 1
"There"
S. Davis, Jr.
Scene 2
"Miami"
P. Marshall, Ensemble
"I've Been Too Busy"
O. James, J. Carter, P. Marshall, S. Davis, Jr.
Scene 3
"Mr. Wonderful" (reprise)
O. James
Scene 5
The Act
S. Davis, Jr., W. Mastin, S. Davis, Sr.
"Sing, You Sinners" (from HONEY film)
(*Music by* Sam Coslow. *Lyrics by* W. Frank Harling.)
"Daddy, Uncle and Me"
(*Music and Lyrics by* Sid Kuller and Lyn Murray.)
"Because of You"
(*Music by* Dudley Wilkinson. *Lyrics by* Arthur Hammerstein.)
"That Old Black Magic" (from STAR SPANGLED RHYTHM film)
(*Music by* Harold Arlen. *Lyrics by* Johnny Mercer.)
"Birth of the Blues" (from GEORGE WHITE'S SCANDALS OF 1926)
(*Music by* Ray Henderson. *Lyrics by* Buddy DeSylva and Lew Brown.)
"It's All Right With Me" (from CAN CAN)
(*Music and Lyrics by* Cole Porter.)
"Dearest (You're the Nearest to My Heart)"
(*Music by* Harry Akst. *Lyrics by* Benny Davis.)
"Liza" (from SHOW GIRL)
(*Music by* George Gershwin. *Lyrics by* Ira Gershwin and Gus Kahn.)
Finale: "Mr. Wonderful" (reprise)
Entire Company

[18]Added after opening to the end of Act 1, Scene 2:
"Big Time"
S. Davis, Jr.

1956.03 THE KING AND I

A Revival of the Musical Play in Two Acts, 17 Scenes[19]. Book and lyrics by Oscar Hammerstein II. Music by Richard Rodgers. Based on the novel "Anna and the King of Siam" by Margaret Landon. Settings by Jo Mielziner. Costumes by Irene Sharaff. Lighting by Jean Rosenthal. Choreography by Jerome Robbins, remounted by June Graham. Orchestrations by Robert Russell Bennett. Musical director, Frederick Dvonch. Directed by John Fearnley. Produced by New York City Center Light Opera Company (William Hammerstein, General director). Opened 18 April 1956 at the New York City Center and closed 6 May 1956 after 23 performances.

CAST (in order of appearance): *Captain Orton*: Leon Shaw. *Louis Leonowens*: Kevin Coughlin. *Anna Leonowens*: JAN CLAYTON. *The Interpreter*: John George. *The Kralahome*: Leonard Graves. *The King*: ZACHARY SCOTT. *Phra Alack*: Hubert Bland. *Lun Tha*: PHILIP WENTWORTH. *Tuptim*: CHRISTINE MATHEWS. *Lady Thiang*: MURIEL SMITH. *Prince Chulalongkorn*: Patrick Adiarte. *Princess Ying Yaowalak*: Lynn Kikuchi. *Sir Edward Ramsay*: Ben Lackland. *Narrator* (The Small House of Uncle Thomas): Christine Mathews. *Uncle Thomas*: Bettina Dearborn. *Little Eva*: Wonci Lui. *Topsy*: Alice Uchida. *Eliza*: Yuriko. *King Simon*: Marion Jim. *Angel*: Dusty Worrall.

Princesses and Princes: Linda Campano, Louis Hernandez, Susan Kikuchi, Barbara Norman, Antonio Obregon, Valentine Obregon, Judith Ramsay, Ronald Harvey, Toby Stevens. *The Royal Dancers*: Olga Bergstrom, Annita Beryll, Hazel Chung, Bettina Dearborn, Dorothy Etheridge, Marion Jim, Norma Kaiser, Wonci Lui, Julie Oser, Nadine Revene, Joan Sandes, Tao Strong, Alice Uchida, Dusty Worrall, Yuriko, Rosemary Zinner, Hubert Bland, John George, James McMillan. *Singers* (Wives, Priests, Amazons, Slaves): Doris Galiber, Jean Maggio, Rose Rosett, Jeanette Scovotti, Rita Shay, Yolanda Vasquez, John Keelin, Robert Reim, Sherman Sneed.

1956.04 THE MOST HAPPY FELLA

A Musical in Three Acts, 11 Scenes. Book, music and lyrics by Frank Loesser. Based on the play "They Knew What They Wanted" by Sidney Howard. Directed by Joseph Anthony. Choreography by Dania Krupska. Scenery and lighting by Jo Mielziner. Costumes by Motley. Orchestrations by Don Walker. Orchestra and choral direction by Herbert Greene. Produced by Kermit Bloomgarden and Lynn Loesser. Opened 3 May 1956 at the Imperial Theatre, moved 21 October 1957 to the Broadway Theatre, and closed 14 December 1957 after 678 performances.

CAST (in order of appearance): *The Cashier*: LEE CASS. *Cleo*: SUSAN JOHNSON. *Rosabella*: JO SULLIVAN. *Waitresses*: Marlyn Greer, Martha Mathes, Myrna Aaron, Meri Miller, Beverly Gaines. *The Postman*: LEE CASS. *Tony*: ROBERT WEEDE, Richard Torigi (alt.). *Marie*: MONA PAULEE. *Max*: Louis Polacek. *Gladys*: Betsy Bridge. *Herman*: SHORTY LONG. *Clem*: Alan Gilbert. *Jake*: JOHN HENSON. *Al*: Roy Lazarus. *Joe*: ART LUND. *Giuseppe*: ARTHUR RUBIN. *Pasquale*: RICO FROEHLICH. *Ciccio*: JOHN HENSON. *Country Girl*: Meri Miller. *City Boy*: John Sharpe. *The Doctor*: KEITH KALDENBERG. *The Priest*: Russell Goodwin. *Tessie*: Zina Bethune. *Gussie*: Christopher Snell. *Neighbors*: Helon Blount, Myrna Aaron, Beverly Gaines, Henry Director, Hunter Ross, Bob Daley. *Neighbor Ladies*: Lillian Shelby, Lois Van Pelt, Marjorie Smith. *Brakeman*: Norris Greer. *Bus Driver*: Ralph Farnworth.

[19]First produced in New York 29 March 1951 at the St. James Theatre for 1246 performances. For Synopsis of Scenes and Musical Numbers, see original 1951 production.

All the Neighbors, and All the Neighbors' Neighbors: Helen Blount, Thelma Dare, Carolyn Maye, Genevieve Owens, Lillian Shelby, Marjorie Smith, Toba Sherwood, Lois Van Pelt, Betsy Bridge, Theodora Brandon, Art Arney, Ken Ayers, Lanier Davis, Henry Director, Ralph Farnworth, Alan Gilbert, Russell Goodwin, Norris Greer, Richard Hermany, Walter Kelvin, Roy Lazarus, Louis Polacek, Evans Thornton, Myrna Aaron, Patti Schmidt, Beverly Gaines, Marlyn Greer, Martha Mathes, Meri Miller, Bob Daley, Athan Karras, Jerry Kurland, Arthur Partington, Hunter Ross, John Sharpe.

Act 1, Scene 1: A Restaurant in San Francisco, January 1927. *Scene 2*: Main Street, Napa, Calaifornia. In April. *Scene 3*: Tony's Barn. A few weeks later. *Scene 4*: Tony's front yard.

Act 2, Scene 1: The Vineyards in May. *Scene 2*: Later in May. *Scene 3*: The Vineyards in June. *Scene 4*: The Barn. *Scene 5*: The Vineyards in July.

Act 3, Scene 1: The Barn an hour later. *Scene 2*: Napa Station. A little later.

ACT 1

Scene 1

"Ooh! My Feet!"
S. Johnson

"I Know How It Is"
J. Sullivan, S. Johnson

"Seven Million Crumbs"
S. Johnson

"I Don't Know" (The Letter)
J. Sullivan

"Maybe He's Kind of Crazy"
S. Johnson

"Somebody, Somewhere"
J. Sullivan

Scene 2

"The Most Happy Fella"
R. Weede, Company

"A Long Time Ago"
M. Paulee, R. Weede

"Standing on the Corner"
S. Long, J. Henson, A. Gilbert, R. Lazarus

"Joey, Joey, Joey"
A. Lund

"Soon You Gonna Leave Me, Joe"
R. Weede

"Rosabella"
R. Weede

Scene 3

"Abbondanza"
R. Froehlich, A. Rubin, J. Henson

"Plenty Bambini"
R. Weede

Scene 4

"Sposalizio"
A. Rubin, J. Henson, R. Froehlich, Ensemble

"Special Delivery!" (I Seen Her at the Station)
L. Cass

"Benvenuta"
R. Froehlich, J. Henson, A. Rubin

"Aren't You Glad?"
J. Sullivan

"No Home, No Job"
J. Sullivan

"Don't Cry"
A. Lund

ACT 2

Scene 1

"Fresno Beauties"/"Cold and Dead"
Ensemble, A. Lund, J. Sullivan

"Love and Kindness"
K. Kaldenberg

"Happy to Make Your Acquaintance"
R. Weede, J. Sullivan, S. Johnson

"I Don't Like This Dame"
M. Paulee, S. Johnson

"Big D"
S. Long, S. Johnson, Ensemble

Scene 2

"How Beautiful the Days"
R. Weede, J. Sullivan, A. Lund

Scene 3

"Young People"
M. Paulee, R. Weede, Ensemble

"Warm All Over"
J. Sullivan

"Old People Gotta"
R. Weede

Scene 4

"I Like Everybody"
S. Long, S. Johnson

Scene 5

"I Love Him"/"I Know How It Is"
J. Sullivan, S. Johnson

"Like a Woman Loves a Man"
J. Sullivan, R. Weede

"My Heart Is So Full of You"
R. Weede, J. Sullivan

"Hoedown"
R. Weede, J. Sullivan, Ensemble

"Mamma, Mamma"
R. Weede

ACT 3

Scene 1

"Abbondanza" (reprise)
R. Froehlich, A. Rubin, J. Hensen

"Goodbye, Darlin'"/"I Like Everybody" (reprise)
S. Johnson, S. Long

"Song of a Summer Night"
K. Kaldenberg, Ensemble

"Please Let Me Tell You"
J. Sullivan

Scene 2

"Tell Tony and Rosabella Goodbye for Me" (Tony's Thoughts)
A. Lund

"She Gonna Come Home Wit' Me"
R. Weede

"Nobody's Ever Gonna Love You"
M. Paulee, R. Weede, S. Johnson

"I Made a Fist"
S. Johnson, S. Long

Finale
R. Weede, J. Sullivan, Ensemble

1956.05 KISS ME, KATE

A Revival of the Musical Comedy in Two Acts, 16 Scenes[20]. Book by Sam [Samuel] and Bella Spewack. (Based on William Shakespeare's "The Taming of the Shrew.") Music and lyrics by Cole Porter. Directed by Burt Shevelove. Choreography by Ray Harrison, based on the original dances by Hanya Holm. Settings by Watson Barratt. Costumes by Alvin Colt. Lighting by Jean Rosenthal. Musical director, Frederick Dvonch. Orchestrations by Robert Russell Bennett. Incidental ballet music arranged by Genevieve Pitot. Produced by the New York City Center Light Opera Company (William Hammerstein, General director). Opened 9 May 1956 at the New York City Center and closed 27 May 1956 after 23 performances.

CAST (in order of appearance): *Fred Graham*: DAVID ATKINSON. *Harry Trevor*: HARRISON DOWD. *Lois Lane*: BARBARA RUICK. *Ralph*, Stage Manager: Vincent

[20]Originally produced in New York 30 December 1948 at the New Century Theatre for 1077 performances. For Synopsis of Scenes and Musical Numbers, see original 1948 production.

McMahon. *Lilli Vanessi*: KITTY CARLISLE. *Hattie*: DELORES MARTIN. *Stage Doorman*: Robert Reim. *Paul*: Bobby Short. *Bill Calhoun*: RICHARD FRANCE. *First Man*: AL NESOR. *Second Man*: TOM PEDI. *Harrison Howell*: Ben Lackland.

"The Taming of the Shrew" Players: *Bianca* (Lois Lane): BARBARA RUICK. *Baptista* (Harry Trevor): HARRISON DOWD. *Gremio* (First Suitor): Philip Wentworth. *Hortensio* (Second Suitor): Ray Weaver. *Lucentio* (Bill Calhoun): RICHARD FRANCE. *Katharine* (Lilli Vanessi): KITTY CARLISLE. *Petruchio* (Fred Graham): DAVID ATKINSON. *Haberdasher*: Arthur Mitchell.

Dancers: Olga Bergstrom, Patricia Birsh (Birch), Dorothy Etheridge, Kate Friedlich, Norma Kaiser, Nadine Revene, Kathleen Stanford, Rosemary Weekly, Gene Gavin, William Inglis, Donald Mahler, Gene Myers, Arthur Mitchell, Robert Norris, Baird Searles, Jon Young. *Singers*: Helen Baisley, Doris Galiber, Nina Greer, Jean Maggio, Louise Pearl, Rose Rosett, Barbara Saxby, Jack Irwin, John Keelin, Vincent McMahon, Robert Reim, Jay Stern, Ray Weaver, Philip Wentworth.

1956.06 CARMEN JONES

A Revival of the Musical Play in Two Acts, 5 Scenes[21]. Book and lyrics by Oscar Hammerstein II. Based on Henri Meilhac and Ludovic Halévy's operatic adaptation of Prosper Merimée's novel "Carmen." Music by Georges Bizet. Directed by William Hammerstein. Musical adaptation by Robert Russell Bennett. Settings and lighting designed by Howard Bay. Costumes for original production by Raoul Pene du Bois, supervised for the City Center by Stanley Simmons. Choreography by Onna White. Choral direction by Leonard Depaur. Musical director, Julius Rudel. Produced by the New York City Center Light Opera Company (William Hammerstein, General director). Opened 31 May 1956 at the New York City Center and closed 17 June 1956 after 22 performances.

CAST (in order* of appearance): *Corporal Morrell*: Sherman Sneed. *Foreman*: Stefan Lind. *Cindy Lou*: RERI GRIST. *Sergeant Brown*: WALTER P. BROWN. *Joe*: WILLIAM DuPREE. *Carmen*: MURIEL SMITH. *Sally*: Glory Van Scott. *T-Bone*: Walter Nicks. *Tough Kid*: Peter Burke. *Drummer*: COZY COLE. *Bartender*: Herbert Stubbs. *Waiter*: James Wamen. *Frankie*: DELORES MARTIN. *Myrt*: AUDREY VANTERPOOL. *Rum*: JOSEPH JAMES. *Dink*: JOHN BUIE. *Husky Miller*: JIMMY RANDOLPH. *Mr. Higgins*: CLYDE TURNER. *Miss Higgins*: Carol Joy. *Photographer*: John Greenwood. *Card Players*: Mary Louise, Carol Joy, Christine Spencer, Louise Parker. *Poncho*: Herbert Stubbs. *Dancing Boxers*: Joseph Nash, James McMillan. *Referee*: Walter Nicks.

Soldiers, Factory Workers, Socialites: Adelaide Boatner, Mareda Gaither, Doris Galiber, John Greenwood, Robert Henson, Addison Hill, Bernice Jackson, Carol Joy, John Keelin, Elzar Levister, Stefan Lind, Mary Louise, Vivan Martin, John Nielsen, Louise Parker, Annabelle Parrish, Sherman Sneed, Christine Spencer, Bill Starling, Herbert Stubbs, Fred Thomas, Rodester Timmons, Clyde Turner, Ruth Tyler, James Wamen, Leontyne Watts, Alexander Yancy. *Dancers*: Georgia Collins, Frank Glass, Lavinia Hamilton, Nathaniel A. Horne, Erona Harris, Jim McMillan, Arthur Mitchell, Joseph Nash, Walter Nicks, Charles Queenan, Kathleen Stanford, Elizabeth Taylor, Ella Thompson, Glory Van Scott, Elizabeth Williamson, Billy Wilson. *Children*: Dennis Butler, Peter Burke, Michael Gilford, Leonard Grinnage, Deborah Jones, Gregory Clinton, Charles Stewart, Jr.

---

[21]Originally produced in New York 2 December 1943 at the Broadway Theatre for 503 performances. For Synopsis of Scenes and Musical Numbers, see original 1943 production.

1956–1957 SEASON

Judy Holliday in BELLS ARE RINGING (Photo: Friedman-Abeles)
Billy Rose Theatre Collection, New York Public Library for the Performing Arts

1956–1957 SEASON

1956.07 SHANGRI-LA

A Musical in Two Acts, 22 Scenes. Book and lyrics by James Hilton, Jerome Lawrence and Robert E. Lee. Based on the novel of the same name by James Hilton. Music by Harry Warren. Production (Settings) designed by Peter Larkin. Costumes by Irene Sharaff. Musical direction, choral arrangements and musical continuity by Lehman Engel. Musical arrangements (orchestrations) by Philip J. Lang. Ballet music composed and arranged by Genevive Pitot. Additional dance arrangements by John Morris. Dances and musical numbers staged by Donald Saddler. Directed by Albert Marre. Produced by Robert Fryer and Lawrence Carr. Opened 13 June 1956 at the Winter Garden and closed 30 June 1956 after 21 performances.

CAST (in order of appearance): *Hugh Conway*: DENNIS KING. *Chao-Li*: Kale Deei. *Robert Henderson*: HAROLD LANG. *Rita Henderson*: JOAN HOLLOWAY. *Charles Mallinson*: JACK CASSIDY. *Miss Brinklow*: ALICE GHOSTLEY. *Chang*: MARTYN GREEN. *Arana*: CAROL LAWRENCE. *Ti*: Edwin Kim Ying. *The Little One*: Leland Mayforth. *Lo-Tsen*: SHIRLEY YAMAGUCHI. *Rimshi*: Ed Kenney. *High Lama*: BARRY KROEGER. *The Dancer Perrault*: ROBERT COHAN.

The People of Shangri-La: *Singers*: Edward Becker, Walter Farrell, George Lenz, Bob McClure, David McDaniel, Jack Rains, Ed Stroll, Ted Wills, Marvin Zeller, Jay Bacon, Sara Bettis, Elizabeth Burgess, Joan Cherof, Sylvia Fabry, Teresa Montes, Eileen Moran, Maggie Worth. *Dancers*: Ralph Beaumont, Michael DeMarco, Ray Dorian, Eddie Heim, Rico Riedl, Ed Stinnett, Dorothy Hill, Greb Lober, Ellen Matthews, Ilona Murai, Mary Ann Niles, Doris Wright.

Act 1, Scene 1: A Patrol Station on the Tibetan border. *Scene 2*: Night on the Mountain. *Scene 3*: The Mountain Pass. *Scene 4*: The Terrace of the Lamasery. *Scene 5*: A Bedchamber in the Lamasery. *Scene 6*: A Music Room. *Scene 7*: The Rope Bridge. *Scene 8*: The Terrace. *Scene 9*: A Corridor. *Scene 10*: The Terrace. *Scene 11*: Outside Conway's Room. *Scene 12*: Chamber of the High Lama.

Act 2, Scene 1: A Prison Camp. *Scene 2*: Chang's Library. *Scene 3*: A Bedchamber in the Lamasery. *Scene 4*: A Corridor. *Scene 5*: Chamber of the High Lama. *Scene 6*: A Corridor. *Scene 7*: A Terrace. *Scene 8*: A Glacier. *Scene 9*: A Prison Camp. *Scene 10*: The Terrace.

ACT 1
Scene 2
"Om Mani Padme Hum"
Male Singers
Scene 4
"Lost Horizon"
Entire Company
Dance of Welcome
R. Cohan, E. K. Ying
Pole Boys: R. Dorian, E. Heim, R. Riedl. *Lotus Girl*: I. Murai. *Tigers*: E. Stinnett, M. DeMarco. *Tiger Tamer*: R. Beaumont.
"The Man I Never Met"
S. Yamaguchi
Scene 5
"Every Time You Danced With Me"
H. Lang, J. Holloway
Scene 6
Dance of Moderate Chastity
A. Ghostley, Dancers
Scene 7
"The World Outside"
S. Yamaguchi, J. Cassidy
Scene 8
Requiem
Singers, Dancers
Scene 9
"I'm Just a Bit Confused"
A. Ghostley
Scene 10
"The Beetle Race"
M. Green, Ensemble
Scene 11
"Somewhere"
J. Cassidy
Scene 12
The Story of Shangri-La (Dance)
R. Cohan, Dancers

ACT 2
Scene 2
"What Every Old Girl Should Know"
A. Ghostley, M. Green
Scene 3
"Second Time in Love"
H. Lang, J. Holloway
"Talkin' With Your Feet"
H. Lang, J. Holloway
Scene 4
"Walk Sweet"
S. Yamaguchi
Scene 6
"Love Is What I Never Knew"
S. Yamaguchi, J. Cassidy
Scene 7
"We've Decided to Stay"
A. Ghostley, H. Lang, J. Holloway
Scene 8
Dance of Time
S. Yamaguchi, Dancers
Scene 10
"Shangri-La"
D. King

1956.08 (LEONARD SILLMAN'S) NEW FACES OF 1956

A Musical Revue in Two Acts, 32 Scenes[1]. Music and lyrics mostly by June Carroll, Arthur Siegel, Marshall Barer, Dean Fuller, Murray Grand, Matt Dubey, Harold Karr, Irvin Graham, Ronny Graham, Paul Nassau, John Rox, Michael Brown, (Leslie Julian-Jones, Elisse Boyd, Richard Maury, Robert Stringer, Sid Silvers.) Sketches mostly by Paul Lynde, Richard Maury, Louis Botto, (Danny and Neil Simon, Terry Ryan, Barry Blitzer, Phil Green, Richard Maury.) Musical numbers staged and directed by David Tihmar, assisted by Peter Conlow. Sketches directed by Paul Lynde. Settings by Peter Larkin. Costumes by Thomas Becher. Lighting by Peggy Clark. Orchestrations by Ted Royal, Albert Sendrey, Joe Glover. Musical direction by Jay Blackton. Entire production conceived and supervised by Leonard Sillman. Produced by Leonard Sillman and John Roberts in association with Yvette Schumer. Opened 14 June 1956 at the Ethel Barrymore Theatre and closed 22 December 1956 after 221 performances.

CAST: Franca Baldwin, Suzanne Bernard, Jane Connell, Billie Hayes, Johnny Haymer, Tiger Haynes, Ann Henry, T. C. [Thomas Craig] Jones, Johnny Laverty, Virginia Martin, Bill McCutcheon, John Reardon, Amru Sani, Bob Shaver, Jimmy Sisco, Maggie Smith, Dana Sosa, Rod Strong, Inga Swenson.

ACT 1
Scene 1
Opening
Entire Company
(*Music and Lyrics by* Ronny Graham.)
Introduction: T. C. Jones.
Scene 2
Madame Interpreter
(*by* Danny and Neil Simon)

[1]The Fifth in the series of revues conceived by Leonard Sillman as a showcase for new talent. The first was produced in 1934.

France: M. Smith. *United States*: B. Shaver. *Italy*: J. Haymer.
Great Britain: B. McCutcheon. *India*: A. Sani. *Brazil*: V. Martin.
U.S.S.R.: J. Reardon. *Mme. Interpreter*: J. Connell.

Scene 3
"What Does That Dream Mean?"
(*Music by* Harold Karr. *Lyrics by* Matt Dubey.)
The Dreamer: J. Haymer. *His Dreams*: F. Baldwin, S. Bernard, D. Sosa, J. Laverty, J. Sisco, R. Strong, J. Haymer, A. Henry, T. Haynes, B. McCutcheon, V. Martin, B. Hayes.

Scene 4
Stars in the Rough
(*by* Paul Lynde)
Announcer: J. Reardon. *Soprano*: I. Swenson. *Helen Hunt*: T. C. Jones.
Patty Potts: D. Sosa. *Old Lady*: J. Connell. *Tony Taps*: J. Laverty.

Scene 5
"One Perfect Moment"
(M. Smith)
(*Music by* Dean Fuller. *Lyrics by* Marshall Barer, Leslie Julian-Jones.)
Woman: M. Smith. *Violinist*: J. Haymer. *Lover*: M. McCutcheon.

Scene 6
"Tell Her"
J. Reardon
(*Music by* Arthur Siegel. *Lyrics by* June Carroll.)
Danced by F. Baldwin, J. Sisco.

Scene 7
"The Washingtons Are Doin' Okay"
T. Haynes
(*Music and Lyrics by* Michael Brown.)

Scene 8
A Canful of Trash
(*by* Louis Botto)
Introduction: M. Smith. *Zelda*: V. Martin. *Manny*: B. McCutcheon.
Moe: J. Haymer. *Junk Man*: B. Shaver. *First Sanitation Man*: R. Strong.
Second Sanitation Man: J. Laverty.

Scene 9
"April in Fairbanks"
J. Connell
(*Music and Lyrics by* Murray Grand.)

Scene 10
"A Doll's House"
(I. Swenson)
(*Music by* Arthur Siegel. *Lyrics by* June Carroll.)
Nurse: M. Smith. *Tina*: I. Swenson. *Urchin*: S. Bernard.
Father Doll: J. Sisco. *Mother Doll*: V. Martin. *Girl Doll*: D. Sosa. *Princess Doll*: F. Baldwin. *Prince Doll*: R. Strong.
Sweeper Doll: B. Hayes.

Scene 11
"And He Flipped"
A. Henry
(*Music and Lyrics by* John Rox. *Staged by* Bob Hamilton.)

Scene 12
"Girls 'n' Girls 'n' Girls"
(J. Reardon, I. Swenson)
(*Music and Lyrics by* Irvin Graham.)
Mother: I. Swenson. *Johnny*: J. Laverty. *Father*: J. Reardon.
Grace: F. Baldwin. *Ava*: S. Bernard. *Marilyn*: V. Martin.

Scene 13
"I Could Love Him"
B. Hayes
(*Music and Lyrics by* Paul Nassau.)

Scene 14
Steady Edna
(*by* Paul Lynde)
Introduction: T. C. Jones. *Eric*: J. Haymer. *Edna*: J. Connell.
Doc: B. McCutcheon. *Steffany*: M. Smith. *Father*: J. Laverty.
Native Chief: R. Strong.

Scene 15
"Hurry"
A. Sani
(*Music by* Murray Grand. *Lyrics by* Murray Grand and Elisse Boyd.)

Scene 16
"Isn't She Lovely"
(T. C. Jones, Company)
(*Music by* Dean Fuller. *Lyrics by* Marshall Barer.)
Introduction: T. C. Jones. *Production Singer*: J. Reardon. *Ponies*: F. Baldwin, S. Bernard, D. Sosa, B. Hayes. *Chorus Boys*: J. Laverty, B. Shaver, J. Sisco, R. Strong. *The Boy Friend*: B. McCutcheon. *Miss Bird Cage*: V. Martin.
Miss Blue Fish: I. Swenson. *Miss Orange*: M. Smith. *Miss Hat*: J. Connell.
Moth of Desire: T. C. Jones.

ACT 2[2]

Scene 1
Entr'acte. *Introduction*: T. C. Jones.
"I Could Love Him"J. Laverty
"Girls 'n Girls"
D. Sosa
"Blues"
J. Sisco
"Don't Wait"
F. Baldwin
"Tell Her"
R. Strong

Scene 2
Twenty Years in the Blackboard Jungle
(*by* Terry Ryan and Barry Blitzer)
Introduction: T. C. Jones. *Teacher*: B. Hayes. *Mahoney*: J. Sisco. *Levine*: T. Haynes. *Kowalski*: B. Shaver. *Roger*: J. Laverty. *Hairy Hilda*: V. Martin.
Girl Monitor: F. Baldwin. *Policeman*: R. Strong. *Principal*: B. McCutcheon.

Scene 3
"Don't Wait 'til It's Too Late to See Paris"
(J. Reardon, S. Bernard)
(*Music by* Arthur Siegel. *Lyrics by* June Carroll.)
Husband: J. Reardon. *Wife*: I. Swenson. *Gamin*: S. Bernard.
Flower Vendor: J. Sisco. *Girl*: D. Sosa. *Boy*: R. Strong.

Scene 4
"Rouge"
J. Connell
(*Music and Lyrics by* Murray Grand.)

Scene 5
Darts
(*by* Phil Green and Paul Lynde)
George: B. McCutcheon. *Harriet*: M. Smith. *Man*: J. Reardon.

Scene 6
"Scratch My Back"
A. Henry, T. Haynes
(*Music by* Dean Fuller. *Lyrics by* Marshall Barer.)

Scene 7
"Boy Most Likely to Succeed"
I. Swenson
(*Music by* Arthur Siegel. *Lyrics by* June Carroll.)
Graduating Class: F. Baldwin, S. Bernard, D. Sosa, J. Laverty, J. Sisco, R. Strong. *Class Valedictorian*: B. Shaver. *Principal*: B. McCutcheon.

Scene 8
"Talent"
V. Martin
(*Music and Lyrics by* Paul Nassau.)

Scene 9
"The Broken Komona"
(T. C. Jones, Entire Company)
(*Sketch and Lyrics by* Richard Maury. *Music by* Robert Stringer.)
Introduction: M. Smith. *Messenger*: J. Laverty. *Bamboo Brothers*: B. McCutcheon, J. Reardon, R. Strong. *Daughter*: T. C. Jones.
Broken Komona: J. Haymer. *Water Color*: T. Haynes. *Pura*: M. Smith.
Caller: B. Shaver. *Townspeople*: F. Baldwin, S. Bernbard, B. Hayes, D. Sosa. *Filly*: A. Henry.

---

[2]Added to Act 2 after opening:
"The Pioneer"
J. Haymer
(*Music and Lyrics by* Bob van Scoyk and Allan Mannings.)

Scene 10

La Ronde: ("This Is Quite a Perfect Night")

(*Music by* Dean Fuller. *Lyrics by* Marshall Barer.)

Introduction: R. Strong. *Roue*: J. Haymer. *Jeune Fille*: I. Swenson. *Adolescent*: B. Shaver. *Femme du Monde*: V. Martin.

Scene 11

"The White Witch of Jamaica"

(J. Reardon)

(*Music by* Arthur Siegel. *Lyrics by* June Carroll.)

Tourists: S. Bernard, M. Smith, J. Lavery, B. Shaver. *Native Man*: J. Reardon. *Native Woman*: D. Sosa. *Lola*: F. Baldwin. *Overseer*: J. Sisco.

Scene 12

"The Greatest Invention"

B. Hayes, J. Haymer

(*Music and Lyrics by* Matt Dubey, Harold Karr and Sid Silvers.)

Scene 13

"Mustapha Abdullah Abu Ben Al Raajid"

(A. Sani)

(*Music by* Dean Fuller. *Lyrics by* Marshall Barer.)

Mrs. Mustapha: A. Sani. *Harem Houris*: M. Smith, I., Swenson, J. Connell, S. Bernard, D. Sosa, F. Baldwin.

Scene 14

Powers Below[3]

(*by* Paul Lynde)

Introduced by T. C. Jones. *Wife*: J. Connell. *Superintendent*: J. Haymer. *Mrs. Carruthers*: V. Martin.

Scene 15

"She's Got Everything"

(T. C. Jones, Company)

(*Music by* Dean Fuller. *Lyrics by* Marshall Barer.)

Four Aristiocrats: J. Laverty, J. Reardon, B. Shaver, J. Sisco. *Hope Diamond*: T. C. Jones.

Scene 16

Finale

Entire Company

1956.09

ORPHEUS IN THE UNDERWORLD

A Revival of the Opera Bouffe in Four Acts[4]. Original French libretto (Orphée Aux Enfers) by Hector Crémieux and Ludovic Halévy. Music by Jacques Offenbach. New English libretto by Eric Bentley. Staged and (settings) designed by Leo Kerz. Costumes designed by Leo Van Witsen. Dances by Anna Sokolow. Choral director, Margaret Hills. Conducted by Erich Leinsdorf. Produced by the New York City Opera (Erich Leinsdorf, Director). Opened 20 September 1956 at the New York City Center and closed 2 November 1956 after 7 performances in repertory.

CAST: *Eurydice*: SYLVIA STAHLMAN. *Orpheus*: JON CRAIN. *Pluto, (Aristeus)*: NORMAN KELLEY. *Miss P. Opinion*: PAULA LAURENCE. *Cupid*: Jacquelynne Moody. *Mars*: Joshua Hecht. *Venus*: Mariquita Moll. *Jupiter*: HIRAM SHERMAN. *Diana*: Beverly Bower. *Juno*: Irene Kramarich. *Mercury*: Michael Pollock. *Minerva*: Mignon Dunn. *John Styx*: Richard Humphrey. *Ensemble*: New York City Opera Chorus.

ACT 1

"On the Parthenon"

Tourists' Chorus

"The House by the Olive Tree"

S. Stahlman

"High Infidelity"

J. Crain, S. Stahlman, Orpheus' Violin

Tourists' Dance

Ballet Ensemble

"Hurrah for the Great Out-of-Doors"

N. Kelley

"To Death: A Valentine"

S. Stahlman

Finale:

"The Power of Negative Thinking"

P. Laurence

Waltz of Orpheus' Music Students

ACT 2

"Goetterdaemmerung"

M. Moll, J. Moody, J. Hecht

"Jupiter's Levee"

H. Sherman, Chorus

"The Man by the Fountain"

B. Bower

"Mercurial"

M. Pollock

"Wish I Were Here, or, La Vie en Prose"

N. Shelley

"The War in Heaven"

Chorus

"The Great Lover"

B. Bower, M. Moll, M. Dunn, J. Moody

Finale: "Tactless Little Troubadour"

ACT 3

"The Underworld: An Expose"

S. Stahlman

"Erewhonia, a Jailer's Song"

R. Humphrey

"In Praise of Police"

Quartet

"Cupid's Biology Book"

J. Moody

"Father's Day"

Quartet

"Buzz, Buzz, or The Life of the Bee"

H. Sherman, S. Stahlman

Dance of the Bees

Ballet Ensemble

ACT 4

"Grand Hotel"

Chorus

"Did You Ever See Your King?"

H. Sherman, Goddesses

Finale:

"Will He Turn?"

"Please Be Good on Sunday"

"Back to the Parthenon"

[3]Dropped after opening.

[4]First presented in New York in English 1 December 1883 at the Bijou Theatre for 107 performances.

1956.10

DIE FLEDERMAUS

A Revival of the Operetta in Three Acts[5]. (Original libretto by Carl Haffner and Richard Genée. Lyrics by Richard Genée. Based on the comedy "Le Réveillon" by Henri Meilhac and Ludovic Halévy.) English libretto by Ruth and Thomas Martin. Music by Johann Strauss. (Settings) Designed by Leo Kerz. Costume supervisor, Robert Fletcher. Staged by David Pressman. Choreography, John Butler. Conducted by Thomas P. Martin. Choreographed by Anna Sokolow. Conducted by Joseph Rosenstock. Produced by the New York City Opera (Erich Leinsdorf, Director). Opened 29 September 1956 at the New York City Center and closed 12 October 1956 after 2 performances in repertory.

CAST: *Rosalinda*: BEVERLY SILLS. *Eisenstein*: ERNEST McCHESNEY. *Adele*: JACQUELYNNE MOODY. *Sally*: Naomi Collier. *Alfred*: JON CRAIN. *Prince Orlofsky*: FRANCES BIBLE. *Falke*: WILLIAM WILDERMAN. *Frank*: Richad Wentworth. *Frosch*: Coley Worth. *Blind*: Michael Pollock.

[5]First English language production in New York 16 March 1885 at the Casino Theatre for 42 performances. First New York production of this adaptation 20 December 1950 at the Metropolitan Opera House. For Synopsis of Scenes and Musical Numbers, see May 1954 revival.

1956.11 THAT GIRL AT THE BIJOU

A One Woman Musical Revue. Composer, pianist, etc., Harvey Brown. Staged by Gene Perlowin. Costumes and choreography by Iva Kitchell. Produced by Luben Vichey. Opened 9 November 1956 at the Bijou Theatre and closed 18 November 1956 after 11 performances.

CAST: IVA KITCHELL.

Dear Audience: Hello! You know, I've been looking forward for years to doing something on Broadway. Now that I'm here, I can't decide what to do. You see, I have accumulated about 50-odd characters and dances through these forward-looking years. Anyway, ever since the Bijou and I came to terms on these dates we have together, I've been trying to pick and choose which dozen numbers I wanted to do. (That's about as many as you or I can manage in one evening.) This didn't work out, however, because I still have 26 left on the list, as you can see by your programs. So tonight, from those remaining 26, I'm just going to pick your dozen as I go along. Must dash now—see you in a few minutes.

Fondly, Iva

P.S. I'll let you know about intermissions and such.

CAST OF CHARACTERS (not in order of their appearance—In fact, all of them won't appear at every performance, but when they do, they will be played by Iva Kitchell.):

Bacchanale (as Seen at the Opera)
(*Music by* Camille Saint-Saëns.)
Chanteuse-Danseuse
(*Music by* Harry Pease, Ed G. Nelson and Gilbert Dodge.)
Dance Espagnole
(*Music by* Georges Bizet, arranged by Harvey Brown.)
Chorus Girl (Vintage 1920)
(*Music by* [Fred] Fisher.)
Coloratura
(*Music by* Harvey Brown.)
Dance & Encore
(*Music by* Frederic Chopin.)
Growing Up
(*Music by* Friedman-Gartner.)
Maisie at the "Moovies"
(arr. by Harvey Brown)
Me-ow
(*Music by* Alda Astori.)
Nocturne
(*Music by* Sergei Rachmaninoff.)
Non-Objective
(No Music)
Obsession
(*Music by* Harvey Brown.)
Oriental Dance (by an Occidental Girl)
(*Music by* [Lily] Strickland.)
Pseudo-Voodoo
(*Music by* Harvey Brown.)
Romance
(*Music by* Friedman-Gartner.)
Salesman (with apologies to the Fuller Brush Man)
(*Music by* Peter Paul Fuchs.)
Something Classic
(*Music by* Ludwig van Beethoven and Franz Schubert)
Scarf Dance—Garland Dance
Fantasy for Body and Piano
(*Music by* Harvey Brown.)
Sonatina Roccoco
(*Music by* Harvey Brown.)
Allegro Artificial—Andante Sentimentale—Rondo con Esprit
Soul in Search (There Isn't Any)
Tale of a Bird
(*Music by* Harvey Brown.)
The Gentleman Friend
(*Music by* Harvey Brown.)
The Vert Bros. (Intro & Extro)
(*Music by* Harvey Brown.)
Valse Triste
(*Music by* Jean Sibelius.)
When I Was Eight
(*Music by* [Théophile] Gautier.)
Ze Ballet
(*Music by* Amilcare Ponchielli.)

1956.12 LI'L ABNER

A Musical Comedy in Two Acts, 20 Scenes. Book by Norman Panama and Melvin Frank. Based on the characters created by Al Capp (from his comic strip of the same name). Music by Gene de Paul. Lyrics by Johnny Mercer. Direction and choreography by Michael Kidd. Scenery and lighting by William and Jean Eckart. Costumes designed by Alvin Colt. Musical direction, continuity and vocal arrangements by Lehman Engel. Orchestrations by Philip J. Lang. Ballet music arranged by Genevieve Pitot. Produced by Norman Panama, Melvin Frank and Michael Kidd. Opened 15 November 1956 at the St. James Theatre and closed 12 July 1958 after 693 performances.

CAST (in order of appearance): *Lonesome Polecat*: Anthony [Tony] Mordente. *Hairless Joe*: Chad Block. *Romeo Scragg*: Marc Breaux. *Clem Scragg*: James Hurst. *Alf Scragg*: Anthony Salverino. *Moonbeam McSwine*: Carmen Alvarez. *Marryin' Sam*: STUBBY KAYE. *Earthquake McGoon*: BERN HOFFMAN. *Daisy Mae*: EDITH ADAMS. *Pappy Yokum*: JOE E. MARKS. *Li'l Abner*: PETER PALMER. *Cronies*: Marc Breaux, Ralph Linn, Jack Matthew, Robert McClure, George Reeder. *Mayor Dawgmeat*: Oran Osburn. *Senator Jack S. Phogbound*: TED THURSTON. *Dr. Rasmussen T. Finsdale*: STANLEY SIMMONDS. *Government Man*: Richard Maitland. *Available Jones*: WILLIAM LANTEAU. *Stupefyin' Jones*: JULIE NEWMAR. *Colonel*: George Reeder. *Radio Commentators*: James Hurst, Robert McClure, Jack Matthew. *President*: Lanier Davis. *General Bullmoose*: HOWARD ST. JOHN. *Secretaries*: Lanier Davis, Robert McClure, Jack Matthew, George Reeder. *Appassionata Von Climax*: TINA LOUISE. *Evil Eye Fleagle*: AL NESOR. *Dr. Smithborn*: George Reeder. *Dr. Krogmeyer*: Ralph Linn. *Dr. Schleifitz*: Marc Breaux. *State Department Man*: Lanier Davis. *Wives*: Carmen Alvarez, Pat Creighton, Lillian D'Honau, Bonnie Evans, Hope Holiday, Deedee Wood. *Butler*: James J. Jeffries. *Colonel*: Lanier Davis.

Singers: Margaret Baxter, Joan Cherof, Pat Creighton, Joyce Gladmond, Hope Holiday, Jane House, Louise Pearl, Jeanette Scovotti, Don Braswell, Lanier Davis, James Hurst, Jack Matthew, Robert McClure, Oran Osburn, George Ritner, Anthony Saverino. *Dancers*: Carmen Alvarez, Lillian D'Honau, Bonnie Evans, Maureen Hopkins, Barbara Klopfer, Christy Peterson, Sharon Shore, Rebecca Vorno, Deedee Wood, Chad Block, Marc Breaux, Grover Dale, Robert Karl, Ralph Linn, Richard Maitland, Anthony Mordente, Tom Panko, George Reeder. *And*: Jan Gunnar, Lucky Kargo, Mario Lamm, Reed Morgan, Aldo Ventura, Robert Wiensko.

Act 1, Scene 1: Dogpatch, U.S.A. *Scene 2*: The Yokum Cabin. *Scene 3*: The Fishing Hole. *Scene 4*: Cornpone Square. *Scene 5*: Dogpatch Road. *Scene 6*: Cornpone Square. *Scene 7*: Washington D. C. Sequence: a. Government Laboratory, b. The President's Office. *Scene 8*: General Bullmoose's Office. *Scene 9*: Dogpatch Road. *Scene 10*: Dogpatch. *Scene 11*: Dogpatch Road. *Scene 12*: Dogpatch.

Act 2, Scene 1: Government Testing Laboratory, Washington. *Scene 2*: The Yokum Cabin. *Scene 3*: General Bullmoose's Cabin. *Scene 4*: Corridor in Bullmoose Mansion. *Scene 5*: Ballroom in Bullmoose Mansion. *Scene 6*: Corridor in Bullmoose Mansion. *Scene 7*: The Government Testing Laboratory. *Scene 8*: Cornpone Square.

ACT 1[6]

"A Typical Day"
Dogpatchers
"If I Had My Druthers"
P. Palmer, Cronies
"If I Had My Druthers" (reprise)
E. Adams
"Jubilation T. Cornpone"
S. Kaye, Dogpatchers
"Rag Offen the Bush"
Dogpatchers
"Namely You"
E. Adams, P. Palmer
"Unnecessary Town"
P. Palmer, E. Adams, Dogpatchers

---

[6]Added during run to Act 1 after "What Good Enough for General Bullmoose":

"There's Room Enough for Us"
Dogpatchers

"What's Good for General Bullmoose"
Secretaries
"The Country's in the Very Best of Hands"
P. Palmer, S. Kaye
"Sadie Hawkins Day" (Ballet)
Dogpatchers

ACT 2
"Oh, Happy Day"
S. Finsdale, G. Reeder, R. Linn, M. Breaux
"I'm Past My Prime"
E. Adams, S. Kaye
"Love in a Home"
P. Palmer, E. Adams
"Progress Is the Root of All Evil"
H. St. John
"Society Party"
Guests, Dogpatchers
"Progress Is the Root of All Evil" (reprise)
H. St. John
"Put 'Em Back"
Wives
"Namely You" (reprise)
E. Adams
"The Matrimonial Stomp"
S. Kaye, Dogpatchers
Finale
Entire Company

1956.13 CRANKS

A Musical Revue in Two Acts, 30 Scenes. (Sketches and lyrics) Written and directed by John Cranko. Music by John Addison. Decor by John Piper. Musical direction by Anthony Bowles. Set supervision and lighting by Paul Morrison. Produced by Richard Charlton and John Krimsky. Opened 26 November 1956 at the Bijou Theatre and closed 29 December 1956 after 40 performances.

CAST: HUGH BRYANT, ANTHONY NEWLEY, ANNIE ROSS, GILBERT VERNON.

ACT 1[7]
"Who's Who"
"Adrift"
"Tra La La"
"Where Has Tom Gone?"
"Cold Comfort"
"Lullaby"
"Broadminded"
"Waiting Room"
"Bats"
"Passacaglia"
"Boo to a Goose"
"Who Is It Always There?"
"Gloves"
"This Is the Sign"
"Chiromancy"
"Valse Anglaise"

ACT 2
"Telephone Tango"
"Don't Let Him Know You"
"Sea Song"
"L'Après-Midi de Gilbert"
"Present for Gilbert"
"Elisabeth"
"Blue"
"I'm the Boy"
"Metamorphosis"
"Would You Let Me Know?"
"Cove in Hove"
"Dirge"
"Arthur, Son of Martha"
"Goodnight"

[7]Program insert details revised song order for opening night.

1956.14 BELLS ARE RINGING

A Musical Comedy in Two Acts, 22 Scenes. Book and lyrics by Betty Comden and Adolph Green. Music by Jule Styne. Entire production directed by Jerome Robbins. Sets and costumes designed by Raoul Pene du Bois. Lighting by Peggy Clark. Orchestrations by Robert Russell Bennett. Musical director, Milton Rosenstock. Vocal arrangements and direction by Herbert Greene and Buster Davis. Dance arrangements and incidental scoring by John Morris. Dances and musical numbers staged by Jerome Robbins and Bob Fosse. Produced by The Theatre Guild. Opened 29 November 1956 at the Sam S. Shubert Theatre, moved 15 December 1958 to the Alvin Theatre, and closed 7 March 1959 after 924 performances.

CAST (in order of appearance): *Sue*: JEAN STAPLETON *Gwynne*: Pat Wilkes. *Ella Peterson*: JUDY HOLLIDAY. *Carl*: PETER GENNARO. *Inspector Barnes*: Dort Clark. *Francis*: Jack Weston. *Sandor*: Eddie Lawrence. *Jeff Moss*: SYDNEY CHAPLIN. *Larry Hastings*: GEORGE S. IRVING. *Telephone Man*: Eddie Heim. *Ludwig Smiley*: Frank Milton. *Charles Bessemer*: Frank Green. *Dr. Kitchell*: Bernie West. *Blake Barton*: Frank Aletter. *Another Actor*: Frank Green. *Joey*: Tom O'Steen. *Olga*: Norma Doggett. *Man from Corvello Mob*: John Perkins. *Other Man*: Kasimir Kokich. *Carol*: Ellen Ray. *Paul Arnold*: Steve Roland. *Michelle*: Michelle Reiner. *Master of Ceremonies*: Eddie Heim. *Singer at Night Club*: Frank Green. *Waiter*: Ed Thompson. *Maitre d'Hotel*: David McDaniel. *Police Officer*: Gordon Woodburn. *Madame Grimaldi*: Donna Sanders. *Mrs. Mallet*: Jeannine Masterson.

Dancers: Norma Doggett, Phyllis Dorne, Patti Karr, Barbara Newman, Nancy Perkins, Marsha Rivers, Beryl Towbin, Anne Wallace, Doria Avila, Frank Derbas, Don Emmons, Eddie Heim, Kasimir Kokich, Tom O'Steen, Willy Sumner, Ben Vargas, Billy Wilson. *Singers*: Pam Abbott, Joanne Birks, Urylee Leonardos, Jeannine Masterson, Michelle Reiner, Donna Sanders, Frank Green, Marc Leon, David McDaniel, Paul Michael, Julian Patrick, Steve Roland, Ed Thompson, Gordon Woodburn.

Act 1, Scene 1: Office of Susanswerphone. Late afternoon. *Scene 2*: Jeff Moss' Living Room. *Scene 3*: An Alley at Night. *Scene 4*: The Office. Early morning. *Scene 5*: A Street in front of the Office. *Scene 6*: Jeff Moss' Living Room. *Scene 7*: A Street. *Scene 8*: A Subway Car. *Scene 9*: A Street. *Scene 10*: Dr. Kitchell's Office. *Scene 11*: A Street. *Scene 12*: A Drug Store. *Scene 13*: A Street. *Scene 14*: The Office. A week later. *Scene 15*: Jeff Moss' Living Room.

Act 2, Scene 1: The Office. The next night. *Scene 2*: The Park. *Scene 3*: Larry Hastings' Penthouse. *Scene 4*" The 'Crying Gypsy' Cafe. *Scene 5*: The 'Pyramid' Night Club. *Scene 6*: Bay Ridge Subway Platform. *Scene 7*: The Office.

ACT 1[8]
"Bells Are Ringing"
Sunsanswerphone Advertisement (Chorus)
Scene 1
"It's a Perfect Relationship"
J. Holliday
Scene 2
"On My Own"
S. Chaplin, Ensemble
"You've Got to Do It"
S. Chaplin
Scene 3
"It's a Simple Little System"
E. Lawrence, Ensemble
Scene 5
"Is It a Crime?"
J. Holliday

[8]Added to Act 1, Scene 6 for National Tour:
"It's Better Than a Dream"
J. Holliday, Hal Linden (Jeff)

Scene 8
"Hello, Hello There!"
J. Holliday, S. Chaplin, Ensemble
Scene 9
"I Met a Girl"
S. Chaplin, Ensemble
Scene 15
"Long Before I Knew You"
J. Holliday, S. Chaplin

ACT 2
Scene 1
"Mu-Cha-Cha"
J. Holliday, P. Gennaro
Dance
E. Ray, P. Gennaro, Dancing Ensemble
Scene 2
"Just in Time"
S. Chaplin, J. Holliday, Ensemble
Scene 3
"Drop That Name"
J. Holliday, Ensemble
"The Party's Over"
J. Holliday
Scene 4
"Salzburg"
J. Stapleton, E. Lawrence
Scene 5
"The Midas Touch"
F. Green, Boys, Girls
Scene 6
"Long Before I Knew You" (reprise)
J. Holliday
Scene 7
"I'm Goin' Back"
J. Holliday
Finale
The Company

1956.15

CANDIDE

A Comic Operetta in Two Acts, 11 Scenes. Book by Lillian Hellman. Based on the satire by Voltaire. Music by Leonard Bernstein. Lyrics by Richard Wilbur. Additional lyrics by John Latouche and Dorothy Parker. Production (settings) designed by Oliver Smith. Costumes by Irene Sharaff. Lighting by Paul Morrison. Musical director, Samuel Krachmalnick. Orchestrations by Leonard Bernstein and Hershy Kay. Directed by Tyrone Guthrie, assisted by Tom Brown. Dance supervisor, Wallace Seibert. Produced by Ethel Linder Reiner in association with Lester Osterman, Jr. Opened 1 December 1956 at the Martin Beck Theatre and closed 2 February 1957 after 73 performances.

CAST (in order of appearance): *Dr. Pangloss*: MAX ADRIAN. *Cunegonde*: BARBARA COOK. *Candide*: ROBERT ROUNSEVILLE. *Baron*: Robert Mesrobian. *Maximilian*: LOUIS EDMONDS. *King of Hesse*: Conrad Bain. *Hesse's General*: Norman Roland. *Man*: BORIS APLON. *Woman*: Doris Okerson. *Dutch Lady*: Margaret Roy. *Dutch Man*: Tony Drake. *Atheist*: Robert Rue. *Arab Conjuror*: Robert Barry. *Infant Casmira*: Maria Novotna. *Lawyer*: WILLIAM CHAPMAN. *Very, Very Old Inquisitor*: Conrad Bain. *Very Old Inquisitor*: Charles Aschman. *Junkman*: Robert Cosden. *Wine-Seller*: Stanley Grover. *Bear*: Charles Morrell. *Bear Man*: Robert Rue. *Alchemist*: Charles Aschman. *Grocery Lady*: Margaret Roy. *Beggars*: Margaret Roy, Robert Cosden, Thomas Pyle. *French Lady*: Maud Scheerer. *Old Lady*: IRRA PETINA. *Marquis Milton*: BORIS APLON. *Sultan Milton*: JOSEPH BERNARD. *Pilgrim Father*: Robert Rue. *Pilgrim Mother*: Dorothy Krebill. *Captain*: Conrad Bain. *Martin*: MAX ADRIAN. *Governor of Buenos Aires*: WILLIAM OLVIS. *Officers*: George Blackwell, Tony Drake, Thomas Pyle. *Ferone*: WILLIAM CHAPMAN. *Madame Sofronia*: IRRA PETINA. *Duchess*: Maud Scheerer. *Prefect of Police* (Bazzini): Norman Roland. *Prince Ivan*: Robert Mesrobian. *Scrub Lady*: BARBARA COOK. *Sultan Milton*: JOSEPH BERNARD. *Marquis Milton*: Boris Aplon. *Duke of Naples*: Charles Aschman. *Croupier*: Robert Barry. *Lady Cutely*: Dori Davis. *Lady Toothly*: George Blackwell. *Lady Soothly*: Fred Jones. *Lady Richmond*: Thomas Pyle. (*Standby for Cunegonde*: MARGOT MOSER.)

Singers: Peggyann Alderman, Charles Aschman, Robert Barry, George Blackwell, Dori Davis, Jack DeLon, Tony Drake, Naomi Farr, Stanley Grover, Fred Jones, Mollie Knight, Dorothy Krebill, Vivian Laurence, Henry Lawrence, Robert Mesrobian, Lois Monroe, Doris Okerson, Thomas Pyle, Margaret Roy, Robert Rue, Mara Schorr, Dorothy White. *Dancers*: Alvin Beam, Charles Czarny, Marvin Gordon, Carmen Gutierrez, Charles Morrell, Frances Noble, Liane Plane, Gloria Stevens.

Act 1, Scene 1: Westphalia. *Scene 1A*: Candide Travels to Lisbon. *Scene 2*: Lisbon. *Scene 2A*: Candide Travels to Paris. *Scene 3*: Paris. *Scene 3A*: They Travel to Buenos Aires. *Scene 4*: Buenos Aires.

Act 2, Scene 1: Buenos Aires. *Scene 1A*: Candide Travels to Venice. *Scene 2*: Venice. *Scene 3*: Westphalia.

ACT 1
Scene 1
"The Best of All Possible Worlds" (Ensemble)
(*Lyrics by* Richard Wilbur.)M. Adrian, (B. Cook, R. Rounseville), Chorus
"Oh, Happy We" (Duet)
R. Rounseville, B. Cook
(*Lyrics by* Richard Wilbur.)
"It Must Be So" (Song)
R. Rounseville
(*Lyrics by* Richard Wilbur.)
Scene 2
Lisbon Sequence
M. Novotna, R. Barry, Chorus
(*Lyrics by* Leonard Bernstein.)
Scene 2A
"It Must Be Me" (Song)
R. Rounseville
Scene 3
Mazurka
(Orchestra)
"Glitter and Be Gay" (Aria)
B. Cook
(*Lyrics by* Richard Wilbur.)
"You Were Dead, You Know" (Duet)
R. Rounseville, B. Cook
(*Lyrics by* Richard Wilbur, John Latouche.)
Scene 3A
"Pilgrims' Procession"
Pilgrims (Chorus)
(*Lyrics by* Richard Wilbur.)
Scene 4
"My Love" (Serenade)
W. Olvis, B. Cook, I. Petina
(*Lyrics by* John Latouche, Richard Wilbur.)
"I Am Easily Assimilated" (Tango)
(*Lyrics by* Leonard Bernstein.)I. Petina, B. Cook, (G. Blackwell, T. Pyle), Chorus
Quartet Finale
B. Cook, R. Rounseville, I. Petina, W. Olvis
(*Lyrics by* Richard Wilbur.)

ACT 2
Scene 1
"Quiet" (Trio)
B. Cook, I. Petina, W. Olvis, (R. Rue)
(*Lyrics by* Richard Wilbur.)
"Eldorado" (Ballad)
R. Rounseville, (Chorus)
(*Lyrics by* Lillian Hellman.)
"Bon Voyage" (Schottische)
W. Olvis, Chorus
(*Lyrics by* Richard Wilbur.)
Scene 2
"What's the Use?" (Waltz)
I. Petina, N. Roland, W. Chapman, R. Mesrobian, Chorus
(*Lyrics by* Richard Wilbur.)
Gavotte
M. Adrian, I. Petina, B. Cook, R. Rounseville
(*Lyrics by* Dorothy Parker.)
Scene 3
Finale: "Make Our Garden Grow"
Entire Company
(*Lyrics by* Richard Wilbur.)

1956.16 HAPPY HUNTING

A Musical Comedy in Two Acts, 16 Scenes. Book by Howard Lindsay and Russel Crouse. Music by Harold Karr. Lyrics by Matt Dubey. Settings and lighting by Jo Mielziner. Costumes by Irene Sharaff. Dances and musical numbers staged by Alex Romero and Bob Herget. Musical direction by Jay Blackton. Orchestrations by Ted Royal. Additional orchestrations by Joe Glover, Don Walker, Seymour Ginzler. Dance music devised by Roger Adams. Directed by Abe Burrows. Produced by Jo Mielziner. Opened 6 December 1956 at the Majestic Theatre and closed 30 November 1957 after 413 performances.

CAST (in order of appearance): *Sanford Stewart, Jr.*: Gordon Polk. *Mrs. Sanford Stewart, Sr.*: Olive Templeton. *Joseph*: Mitchell M. Gregg. *Beth Livingstone*: VIRGINIA GIBSON. *Jack Adams*, reporter: Seth Riggs. *Harry Watson*, reporter: Gene Wesson. *Man who looks like Farouk*: Edward Becker. *Charley*, photographer: Delbert Anderson. *Liz Livingstone*: ETHEL MERMAN. *Photographers (4)*: *Sam*: Clifford Fearl. *Joe*: John Craig. *Freddy*: George Martin. *Wes*: Jim Hutchison. *Reporters* (3): *Mary Mills*: Estelle Parsons. *Dick Davis*: Robert C. Held. *Bob Grayson*: Carl Nicholas. *Maud Foley*: MARY FINNEY. *Police Sergeant*: Mark Zeller. *Arturo*: Leon Belasco. *The Duke of Grenada*: FERNANDO LAMAS. *Count Carlos*: Renato Cibelli. *Waiter*: Don Weissmuller. *Ship's Officer*: John Leslie. *Barman*: Warren J. Brown. *Mrs. B.*: Florence Dunlap. *Mrs. D.*: Madeleine Clive. *Mrs. L.*: Kelley Stephens. *Terence*, a groom: Jim Hutchison. *Tom*, a groom: Eugene Louis. *Daisy*: Moe. *Mr. T.*: a member of the Hunt: John Leslie. *Mr. M.*: a member of the Hunt: Jay Velie. *Albert*, a groom: George Martin. *Margaret*, a maid: Mara Landi.

Singers: Peggy Acheson, Marilynn Bradley, Deedy Irwin, Jane Johnston, Jean Kraemer, Mara Landi, Betty McGuire, Estelle Parsons, Noella Peloquin, Ginny Perlowin, Mary Roche, Kelley Stephens, Helene Whitney, Delbert Anderson, Edward Becker, Warren J. Brown, David Collyer, John Craig, Jack Dabdoub, Clifford Fearl, Robert C. Held, Carl Nicholas, Seth Riggs, Charles Rule, Mark Zeller. *Dancers*: Betty Carr, Alice Clift, Jane Fischer, Roberta Keith, Svetlana McLee, Patti Nestor, Wendy Nickerson, Fleur Raup, Sigyn, Bob Bakanic, John Harmon, Jim Hutchison, Dick Korthaze, Eugene Louis, George Martin, Jim Moore, Lowell Purvis, Don Weissmuller, Roy Wilson.

The time is the present, and the action occurs in Monaco, on ship board and near Philadelphia.

Act 1, Scene 1: Outside the Palace. Monaco. *Scene 2*: Liz Livingstone's Suite, Hotel Riviera. Monaco. *Scene 3*: Terrace of the Hotel. *Scene 4*: Veranda of the Duke's Suite, Hotel Riviera. *Scene 5*: Quai. *Scene 6*: In the ship's bar. *Scene 7*: Afterdeck of the ship. *Scene 8*: In the ship's bar. *Scene 9*: Afterdeck of the ship.

Act 2, Scene 1: Liz Livingstone's estate, near Philadelphia. *Scene 2*: The Livingstone stables. *Scene 3*: Summerhouse. Liz's estate. *Scene 4*: The Philadelphia Hunt Club. *Scene 5*: Another part of the forest. *Scene 6*: Liz's boudoir. *Scene 7*: The Hunt Ball.

ACT 1

Scene 1

"Postage-Stamp Principality"
Tourists, Monegasques

"Don't Tell Me"
G. Polk, V. Gibson

"(Gee, But) It's Good To Be Here"
E. Merman, Reporters

Scene 2

"Mutual Admiration Society"
E. Merman, V. Gibson

Scene 3

"For Love or Money"
Girls

Bikini Dance
V. Gibson

Scene 4

"It's Like a Beautiful Woman"
F. Lamas

Scene 5

"Wedding-of-the-Year Blues"
M. Finney, G. Wesson, S. Riggs, Reporters, Photographers

Scene 6

"Mr. Livingstone"
E. Merman

Scene 7

"If'n"
V. Gibson, G. Polk, Passengers

Scene 9

"This Is What I Call Love"[9]
E. Merman

ACT 2

Scene 1

"A New-Fangled Tango"
E. Merman, V. Gibson, L. Belasco, Guests

"She's Just Another Girl"
G. Polk

Scene 2

"The Game of Love"[10]
E. Merman

Scene 4

"Happy Hunting"
E. Merman, F. Lamas, Members of the Hunt

Scene 6

"I'm a Funny Dame"
E. Merman

"This Much I Know"
F. Lamas

"Just Another Guy"
E. Merman

Scene 7

"Everyone Who's "Who's Who""
S. Riggs, G. Wesson, Footmen

"Mutual Admiration Society" (reprise)
E. Merman, F. Lamas

1957.01 ZIEGFELD FOLLIES (OF 1957)

A Musical Revue in Two Acts, 24 Scenes. Music and lyrics by Jack Lawrence and Richard Myers, Howard Dietz and Sammy Fain, David Rogers and Colin Romoff, Dean Fuller and Marshall Barer, Carolyn Leigh and Philip Springer, (Tony Velone, Larry Spier, Ulpio Minucci.) Sketches by Arnie Rosen and Coleman Jacoby, David Rogers, Alan Jeffreys, Maxwell Grant, (Beatrice Lillie.) Sketch editor, Arnold Auerbach. Dances staged by Frank Wagner. Scenery and costumes by Raoul Pene du Bois. Lighting by Paul Morrison. Musical director, Max Meth. Orchestrations by (Robert) Russell Bennett, Bill Stegmeyer, Joe Glover, Bob Noelneter. Dance composition by Rene Weigert. Vocal arrangements by Earl Rogers. Entire production directed by John Kennedy. Produced by Mark Kroll and Charles Conaway. Opened 1 March 1957 at the Winter Garden and closed 15 June 1957 after 123 performances.

CAST: BEATRICE LILLIE, BILLY DE WOLFE, HAROLD LANG, JANE MORGAN, HELEN WOOD, MICKI MARLO, JOHN PHILIP, BOB and LARRY LESLIE, CAROL LAWRENCE, JAY MARSHALL, TONY FRANCO.

Ziegfeldians: Billie Bensing, Bette Graham, Faith Hilton, Frances Koll, Susan Shaute, Paula Wayne, Chuck Green, Robert Feyti, Tony Franco, Ed Powell, James Stevenson, Gene Varrone. *Dancers*: Vicki Barrett, Ruth Chamberlain, Dorothy D'Honau, Mary Jane Doerr, Wisa D'Orso, Nancy Hachenberg, Marcia Hewitt, Julie Marlowe, Sylvia Shay, Gini Turner, Shirley Vincent, Bob Bernard, James Brooks, Ron Cecill, Alan Conroy, Allan Craine, Hugh Lambert, Jack Leigh, Ted Monson, Lou Richards, Rod Strong, Meritt Thompson. *Ziegfeld Girls*: Roberta Brown, Denise Collette, Ann Drake, Charlotte Foley, Pat Gaston, Nancy Westbrook, Barbara Hall, Gloria Kristy.

ACT 1

Scene 1

"Bring on the Girls"
The Ziegfeldians, Ensemble
(*Music by* Richard Myers. *Lyrics by* Jack Lawrence.)

---

[9]Replaced during the run by :
"Just a Moment Ago"
E. Merman
(*Music and Lyrics by* Kay Thompson.)

[10]Replaced during the run by :
"I'm Old Enough To Know Better and Young Enough Not to Care"
E. Merman
(*Music and Lyrics by* Kay Thompson.)

Scene 2
"Double Indemnity"
(*by* Alan Jeffreys and Maxwell Grant)
Secretary: C. Foley. *Mr. Wedgecliffe*: B. DeWolfe. *Lola La Moundsville*: J. Morgan.

Scene 3
"If You Got Music"
H. Lang, H. Wood, Ensemble
(*Music by* Colin Romoff. *Lyrics by* David Rogers.)

Scene 4
Milady Dines Alone
(*by* Beatrice Lillie)
The Lady: B. Lillie. *Waiter*: B. Laffey.

Scene 5
"The Lover in Me"[11]
M. Marlo
(*Music by* Philip Springer. *Lyrics by* Carolyn Leigh.)

Scene 6
High and Flighty
(*by* Arnie Rosen and Coleman Jacoby)
Hostess: B. Lillie. *Passengers*: J. Philip, B. Leslie, L. Leslie, B. Graham, R. Feyti. *Betty*: J. Doerr.

Scene 7
"I Don't Wanna Rock"
(*Music by* Colin Romoff. *Lyrics by* David Rogers.)
Juvenile Delinquent: B. DeWolfe. *Tenth Street Sheiks*: V. Barrett, J. Brooks, W. D'Orso, C. Green, N. Hachenberg, H. Lambert, J. Marlowe, E. Powell, L. Richards, J. Stevenson, R. Strong, G. Varrone.

Scene 8
Jay Marshall[12] (comedy, prestidigitation, ventriloquism)

Scene 9
"Music for Madame"
(*Music by* Richard Myers. *Lyrics by* Jack Lawrence.)
The Boy: H. Lang. *The Girl*: H. Wood. *Maitre D'*: J. Philip. And Ziegfeldians, Dancers.

Scene 10
"Intoxication"
B. Lillie
(*Music by* Dean Fuller. *Lyrics by* Marshall Barer.)
The Escort: A. Conroy.

Scene 11
Dramatically Speaking
B. DeWolfe

Scene 12
"Song of India"
The Rajah: J. Philip. *His Favorite*: B. Lillie. Assisted by Dancers, The Ziegfeldians.

ACT 2

Scene 1
"Two a Day On the Milky Way"
H. Lang, Ensemble
(*Music by* Dean Fuller. *Lyrics by* Marshall Barer.)
Agent: B. Leslie.

Scene 2
Large Talk
(*by* David Rogers)
First Girl: C. Foley. *Second Girl*: S. Shaute. *Lucille*: B. Lillie. *Harriet*: B. DeWolfe.

Scene 3
"Salesmanship"
J. Morgan, M. Marlo, C. Lawrence, Ziegfeld Girls
(*Music by* Philip Springer. *Lyrics by* Carolyn Leigh.)

Scene 4
Kabuki Lil
(*by* Beatrice Lillie)
B. Lillie

Scene 5
"Honorable Mambo"
C. Lawrence, Ensemble
(*Music by* Dean Fuller. *Lyrics by* Marshall Barer.)

Scene 6
"Miss Follies"
B. DeWolfe, C. Green, E. Powell, J. Stevenson, G. Varrone, Ziegfeld Girls
(*Music by* Colin Romoff. *Lyrics by* David Rogers.)

Scene 7
"Make Me"
J. Morgan, The Ziegfeldians
(*Music and Lyrics by* Tony Velone, Larry Spier, Uhpio Minucci.)

Scene 8
"Miss (All You Don't Catch) Follies of 192—"
B. Lillie
(*Music and Lyrics by* Herman Hupfeld.)
Page Girl: N. Hachenberg.

Scene 9
Jay Marshall[13]

Scene 10
"An Element of Doubt"[14]
H. Lang, M. Marlo
(*Music by* Sammy Fain. *Lyrics by* Howard Dietz.)

Scene 11
"My Late, Late Lady" (parody of 'My Fair Lady')
(*Music by* Dean Fuller. *Lyrics by* Marshall Barer.)
Announcer: E. Powell. *The Original Cast*: B. Lillie, B. DeWolfe, J. Philip.

Scene 12
Finale
Entire Company
(*Music by* Richard Myers. *Lyrics by* Jack Lawrence.)

1957.02 THE BEGGAR'S OPERA

A Revival of the Comic Opera in Two Acts[15]. Original libretto and music by John Gay. New adaptation by Richard Baldridge. Music adapted and arranged by Daniel Pinkham. Musical staging by John Heawood. Setting by Watson Barratt. Costumes by Robert Fletcher. Lighting by Jean Rosenthal. Directed by Richard Baldridge. Musical director and conductor, Miles Morgan. Entire production supervised by Burt Shevelove. Produced by the New York City Center Light Opera Company (Jean Dalrymple, Director), as originally produced at the Cambridge Drama Festival. Opened 13 March 1957 at the New York City Center and closed 24 March 1957 after 15 performances.

CAST (in order of appearance): *Beggar Poet*: PETER TURGEON. *Filch*: Charles Bolender. *Macheath*: JACK CASSIDY. *Matt of the Mint*: Robert Burr. *Jemmy the Twitcher*: Hal England. *Crooked Finger Jack*: Maurice Edwards. *Wat Dreary*: Francis Barnard. *Nimming Ned*: J. C. McCord. *Slippery Sam*: Jack DeLon. *Bob Booty*: DAVID NILLO. *Tom Tizzle*: William Inglis. *Polly Peachum*: SHIRLEY JONES. *Mr. Peachum*: GEORGE S. IRVING. *Mrs. Peachum*: ZAMAH CUNNINGHAM. *Mr. Lockit*: GEORGE GAYNES. *Lucy Lockit*: JEANNE BEAUVAIS. *Mrs. Coaxer*: PAULA LAURENCE. *Jenny Diver*: CONSTANCE BRIGHAM. *Dolly Trull*: MARIA KARNILOVA. *Mrs Vixen*: Anita Cooper. *Betty Doxy*: Jenny Lou Law. *Mrs. Slammekin*: Adnia Rice. *Suky Tawdry*: Shirley Chester. *Molly Brazen*: Charlotte Ray.

Prisoners, Guards and Other Ladies of the Town: William Ashley, Hal Barnet, George Broadhurst, Willie Cooper, Joan DuBrow, Jack Emrek, James Karr, Sara Meade, Louis Saporito, Lee Warren, Hurd Wiese. *Chorus of Prisoners*: Louis Algarra, Jennie Andrea, Evelyn Aring, Robert Atherton, Nicola Barbusci, Don Becker, June Bucknor, Julia Gerace, Peter Held, Maurice Kostroff, Mary Lesawyer, Maria Martell, John Person, Thomas Powell, Robert Ruddy, Mary Thompson, Mara Yavne.

The action takes place at night in Newgate Prison, London. (1728, ca.)

ACT 1
"Let Us Take the Road"
J. Cassidy, the Gang
"My Heart Was So Free"
J. Cassidy

---

[11]Replaced during the run by:
"Mangos"
M. Marlo
(*Music and Lyrics by* Dee Libbey and Sid Wayne.)
Assisted by R. Cecill, A. Craine, M. Davidson, T. Franko, C. Green, H. Lambert, J. Leigh, E. Powell, J. Stevenson, G. Varrone.

[12]Dropped during run.

[13]Dropped during run.

[14]Dropped during run.

[15]First presented in New York 3 December 1750 at the Theatre in Nassau Street for 2 performances.

"Were I Laid on Greenland Coast" (Duet)
J. Cassidy, S. Jones
"Virgins Are Like the Fair Flower"
S. Jones
"Our Polly Is a Sad Slut" (Trio)
G. S. Irving, Z. Cunningham, S. Jones
"The Turtle Thus With Plaintive Crying"
S. Jones
"'Tis Woman That Seduces All Mankind"
G. Gaynes
"Through All the Employments of Life" (Duet)
G. S. Irving, G. Gaynes
"Hanging Is My Only Sport"
G. S. Irving
"Were I Laid on Greenland Coast" (reprise Duet)
S. Jones, J. Cassidy
"O, What a Pain It Is to Part"
S. Jones, J. Cassidy
"No Power on Earth Can E'er Divide"
S. Jones
"Man May Escape from Rope and Gun"
Prisoners
"Why How Now Madam Flirt" (Trio)
J. Beauvais, S. Jones, J. Cassidy
"Is Then His Fate Decreed, Sir?" (Quartet)
S. Jones, J. Beauvais, G. S. Irving, G. Gaynes

ACT 2
"Fill Every Glass"
R. Burr, The Gang, Ladies of the Town
Danced by M. Karnilova, D. Nillo.
"The Ways of the World"
J. Cassidy, The Gang
"Let Us Take the Road" (reprise)
The Gang, Ladies of the Town
"If the Heart of a Man"
P. Laurence
"Youth's a Season Made for Joys"
Ladies of the Town
"When Young at the Bar"
C. Brigham
"In the Days of My Youth" (Trio)
P. Laurence, G. S. Irving, G. Gaynes
"At the Tree I Shall Suffer With Pleasure"
J. Cassidy
"When Young at the Bar" (reprise)
C. Brigham
"I'm Like a Skiff on the Ocean Toss'd"
J. Beauvais
"Come Sweet Lass" (Duet)
J. Beauvais, S. Jones
"The Charge Was Prepar'd"
J. Cassidy, Chorus
"Would I Might Be Hanged"
J. Beauvais, S. Jones, J. Cassidy
"Since Laws Were Made for Every Degree"
Entire Company
"See the Conquering Hero" (Finale)
Entire Company

1957.03 BRIGADOON

A Revival of the Musical Play in Two Acts, a Prologue and 11 Scenes[16]. Book and lyrics by Alan Jay Lerner. Music by Frederick Loewe. Dances and musical numbers by Agnes de Mille, re-staged by James Jamieson. Production directed by George H. Englund. Settings by Oliver Smith. Costumes by Paul duPont. Lighting by Peggy Clark. Musical director, Julius Rudel. Associate conductor, Samuel Matlovsky. (Vocal arrangements by Frederick Loewe. Orchestrations by Ted Royal.) Produced by the New York City Center Light Opera Company (Jean Dalrymple, Director.). Opened 27 March 1957 at the New York City Center, moved 9 April 1957 to the Adelphi Theatre and closed 5 May 1957 after 47 performances.

CAST (in order of appearance): *Tommy Albright*: DAVID ATKINSON. *Jeff Douglas*: SCOTT McKAY. *Archie Beaton*: Elliott Sullivan. *Harry Beaton*: MATT MATTOX. *Angus MacGuffie*: Guy Gordon. *Sandy Dean*: John Dorrin. *Andrew MacLaren*: Russell Gaige. *Fiona MacLaren*: VIRGINIA OSWALD. *Jean MacLaren*: Virginia Bosler. *Meg Brockie*: HELEN GALLAGHER. *Charlie Dalrymple*: ROBERT ROUNSEVILLE. *Maggie Anderson*: Lidija Franklin. *Mr. Lundie*: John C. Becher. *Sword Dancers*: Glenn Olson, Keith Willis. *Frank*: Jack Emrek. *Jane Ashton*: Sloan Simpson. *Bagpiper*: Duncan MacGaskill.

Singers: Jennie Andrea, June Buckner, Marilyn Cooper, Dori Davis, Julia Gerace, Patricia Hall, Jean Maggio, Maria Martell, Sheila Mathews, Mary Thompson, Robert Atherton, Don Becker, Norris Brannstrom, Austin Colyer, Arthur Dilks, John Dorrin, Peter Held, Vincent MacMahon, William Nahr, Stanley Page. *Dancers*: Jeanna Belkin, Pat Birsh (Birch), Anne Boley, Ann Crowell, Geralyn Donald, Dorothy Etheridge, Rosemary Jourdan, Evelyn Taylor, Mona Jo Tritsch, Robert Barnett, Anthony Blum, Jim Brusock, Walter Georgov, Charles McCraw, Glenn Olson, Ray Pointer, Keith Willis, Emmanuel Winston.

1957.04 THE MERRY WIDOW

A Revival of the Operetta in Three Acts and a Prologue[17]. Music by Franz Lehár. (Original Viennese libretto, Die Lustige Witwe by Victor Léon and Leo Stein after "L'Attaché d'Ambassade" by Henri Meilhac. New musical version by Robert Stolz.) New book by Sidney Sheldon and Ben Roberts. New lyrics by Adrian Ross (and Robert Gilbert). Directed by Felix Brentano. Original choreography by George Balanchine. Dances by Edward Brinkman. Settings by George Jenkins. Costumes by Paul duPont. Lighting by Peggy Clark. Produced by the New York City Center Light Opera Company (Jean Dalrymple, Director.). Opened 10 April 1957 at the New York City Center and closed 21 April 1957 after 15 performances.

CAST (in order of appearance): *The King*: Jose Duval. *Popoff*: MELVILLE COOPER. *Cascada*: Alex Alexander. *Natalie*: HELENA SCOTT. *Khadja*: C. K. Alexander. *Olga Bardini*: Lucy Hillary. *General Bardini*: GEORGE LIPTON. *Novakovich*: Lewis Brooks. *Jolidon*: JIM HAWTHORNE. *Guests*: Sonja Savig, Casper Roos. *Nish*: NORMAN BUDD. *Sonia*: MARTA EGGERTH. *St. Brioche*: Warde Donovan. *Prince Danilo*: JAN KIEPURA. *Clo-Clo*: MONIQUE VAN VOOREN. *Gaston*: Jose Duval. *Premiere Danseuse*: MARY ELLEN MOYLAN. *Premier Danseur*: MICHAEL MAULE. *Ballerina*: PAULA LLOYD.

Singers: Jeanne Anderson, Josephine Annunciata, Carol O'Day, June House, Claudine Manson, Sonja Savig, Jan Speers, Barbara Saxby, Yolanda Vasquez, Charles O. Aschmann, Jr., Alan Cole, Wendell Grey, David London, Jack McMinn, Mitchell May, Casper Roos, David Smith, Marvin Solley. *Dancers*: Ann Barry, Marilyn d'Honau, Ruby Herndon, Joan Kruger, Eloise Milton, Charlotte Rae, John Grigas, Scott Hunter, William Inglis, Bill Miller, Richard Monahan, Bob St. Clair. *Lackeys*: Bruce Blaine, James Feeney, Eben Snow.

1957.05 SHINBONE ALLEY

A Musical in Two Acts, 20 Scenes. Book by Joe Darion and Mel Brooks. Based on the 'archy and mehitabel' stories by Don Marquis. Music by George Kleinsinger. Lyrics by Joe Darion. (Direction uncredited[18].) Dances and musical numbers staged by Rod Alexander. Music and choral direction by Maurice Levine. Production (settings) designed by Eldon Elder. Costumes by Motley. Lighting by Tharon Musser. Orchestrations by George Kleinsinger, Irwin Kostal. Additional musical routines by John Morris. Produced by Peter Lawrence. Opened 13 April 1957 at the Broadway Theatre and closed 25 May 1957 after 49 performances.

CAST (in order of appearance): *Voice of Newspaperman*: Julian Barry. *archy*: EDDIE BRACKEN. *mehitabel*: EARTHA KITT. *Phyllis*: Reri Grist. *Mother*: Lillian Hayman.

---

[16]First presented 13 March 1947 at the Ziegfeld Theatre for 581 performances. For Synopsis of Scenes and Musical Numbers, see original 1947 production.

[17]Original New York production first presented 21 October 1907 at the New Amsterdam Theatre for 416 performances; this adaptation first presented in New York 4 August 1943 at the Majestic Theatre for 322 performances. For Synopsis of Scenes and Musical Numbers, see 1943 revival.

[18]During previews, Norman Lloyd withdrew as director.

Ricky: Dorothy Aull. *Jail Cronies*: Buzz Halliday, Elmarie Wendel, Cathryn Damon, Elizabeth Taylor, Carmen Gutierrez, Nora Reho, GWEN HARMON. *'Copper'*: James Marley. *Buzz*: Howard Roberts. *Butch*: Moses LaMarr. *Rusty*: Cathryn Damon. *Big Bill*: GEORGE S. IRVING. *Broadway*: ROSS MARTIN. *Edie*: GWEN HARMON. *Blackie*: Larry Montaigne. *Gladys*: Carmen Gutierrez. *Frankie*: JACQUES D'AMBOISE. *Fighting Dogs*: Don Farnworth, Gene Gavin, Harold E. Gordon, Claude Thompson. *Tyrone T. Tattersal*: ERIK RHODES. *Shorty*: David Winters. *Harry*: Jack Eddleman. *Lady Bugs*: Dorothy Aull, GWEN HARMON, Buzz Halliday. *Bartender*: Bruce MacKay. *Penny*: ALLEGRA KENT. *Tall Cats*: Albert Popwell, James Tarbutton.

Singers: Dorothy Aull, Jack Eddleman, Reri Grist, Buzz Halliday, Gwen Harmon, Lillian Hayman, Moses LaMarr, James Marley, Bruce MacKay, Jack Rains, Howard Roberts, Elmarie Wendel. *Dancers*: Jacques D'Amboise, Cathryn Damon, Don Farnworth, Gene Gavin, Carolyn George, Harold E. Gordon, Carmen Gutierrez, Allegra Kent, Albert Popwell, Nora Reho, Dorothy Scott, James Tarbutton, Eliuzabeth Taylor, Claude Thompson, Myrna White, David Winters.

The entire action takes place in Shinbone Alley and its environs.

Act 1, Scene 1: A Newspaper Office. *Scene 2*: Shinbone Alley. *Scene 3*: The ASPCA Lock-Up. *Scene 4*: Shinbone Alley. *Scene 5*: A Street. *Scene 6*: Shinbone Alley. *Scene 7*: A Street. *Scene 8*: Tyrone's Trunk in Greenwich Village. *Scene 9*: Shinbone Alley.

Act 2, Scene 1: A Street. *Scene 2*: Shinbone Alley. *Scene 3*: A Street Corner. *Scene 4*: Shinbone Alley. *Scene 5*: Another Street. *Scene 6*: Mehitabel's New Home. *Scene 7*: A Bar Beneath the Street. *Scene 8*: A Vacant Lot.*Scene 9*: Mehitabel's New Home. *Scene 10*: A Quiet Street. *Scene 11*: Shinbone Alley.

ACT 1[19]

Scene 2

"What Do We Care?"
E. Kitt, Singing and Dancing Ensemble

Scene 3

"Toujours Gai" (Cheerio My Deerio)
E. Kitt

"Queer Little Insect"
E. Kitt, E. Bracken

Scene 4

"Big Bill"
G. S. Irving, Ladies of Dance Ensemble

"True Romance"
E. Kitt, G. S. Irving
Danced by E. Kitt.

Scene 5

"The Lightning Bug Song"
E. Bracken

"I gotta be"
R. Martin, E. Bracken

Scene 6

Dog and Cat Ballet
Danced by J. D'Amboise, Ensemble

"Flotsam and Jetsam"
E. Bracken, E. Kitt

"Come to Mee-ow"
E. Rhodes

"Suicide Song"
E. Bracken

"Shinbone Alley"
G. S. Irving, Denizens of Shinbone Alley

[19]In late April, Act 1 was shortened, and Act 2 of the show was totally revised. Added credits: Additional Choreography by Arthur Mitchell. Production supervised by Sawyer Falk. Added songs in Act 2:

"The Lullaby"
E. Kitt, Singing Girls

"Mehitabel's a House Cat" (then dropped)
E. Bracken, G. S. Irving, Ensemble

"Flotsam and Jetsam" (reprise)
E. Bracken, E. Kitt

"Shinbone Alley" (Finale)
E. Bracken, E. Kitt, Ensemble

ACT 2

Scene 1

"The Moth Song"
E. Bracken

Scene 2

"A Woman Wouldn't Be a Woman"
E. Kitt, Ensemble

Scene 5

"What the Hell"[20]
E. Kitt

Scene 6

"Pretty Kitty"
Singing Girls, *Danced by* E. Kitt

"Way Down Blues"[21]
E. Kitt

Scene 7

"The Lady Bug Song"
D. Aull, G. Harmon, B. Halliday

Scene 8

Vacant Lot Ballet
Danced by J. D'Amboise, A. Kent, C. Damon, D. Winters, Dancing Ensemble

Scene 9

"Be a Pussycat"
E. Kitt, Dancing Girls

Scene 10

"Quiet Street"[22]
E. Bracken

Scene 11

"Toujours Gai" (reprise)[23]
E. Kitt, E. Bracken, Ensemble

1957.06

SOUTH PACIFIC

A Revival of the Musical Play in Two Acts, 23 Scenes[24]. Book by Oscar Hammerstein II and Joshua Logan. Adapated from James A. Michener's novel "Tales of the South Pacific." Music by Richard Rodgers. Lyrics by Oscar Hammerstein II. Directed by John Fearnley. Scenery by Jo Mielziner. Adaptation and lighting by Peggy Clark. Costumes by Motley, supervised by Florence Klotz Musical director, Frederick Dvonch. (Orchestrations by Robert Russell Bennett.) Produced by the New York City Center Light Opera Company (Jean Dalrymple, Director). Opened 24 April 1957 at the New York City Center and closed 12 May 1957 after 23 performances.

CAST (in order of appearance): *Ngana*: Lynn Kikuchi. *Jerome*: Afredo DeArco. *Henry*: Mark Satow. *Ensign Nellie Forbush*: MINDY CARSON. *Emile DeBecque*: ROBERT WRIGHT. *Bloody Mary*: JUANITA HALL. *Bloody Mary's Assistant*: Julia Gerace. *Abner*: Jim McMillan. *Stewpot*: Lou Wills, Jr. *Luther Billis*: HARVEY LEMBECK. *Professor*: Bill Mullikin. *Lt. Joseph Cable, U.S.M.C.*: ALLEN CASE. *Capt. George Brackett, U.S.N.*: MARTIN WOLFSON. *Cmdr. William Harbison, U.S.N.*: ALAN BAXTER. *Yeoman Herbert Quale*: Ray Weaver. *Sgt. Kenneth Johnson*: Van Stevens. *Marine Cpl. Richard West*: Dan Hannafin *Seabee Morton Wise*: Evans Thornton. *Sgt. Juan Cortez*: Quinto Bagioni. *Seaman Tom O'Brien*: Jack McMinn. *Radio Operator Bob McCaffrey*: Sam Kirkham. *Marine Cpl. Hamilton Steeves*: Lee Warren. *Staff Sgt. Thomas Hassinger*: Charles Aschman. *Seaman James Hayes*: Ralph Vucci. *Lt. Genevieve Marshall*: Miriam Gulager. *Ensign Dinah Murphy*: Christy Palmer. *Ensign Janet MacGregor*: Mildred Slavin. *Ensign Cora MacRae*: Pat Finch. *Ensign Bessie Noonan*: Barbara Saxby. *Ensign Pamella Whitmore*: Betty Graeber. *Ensign Sue Yaeger*: Peggy Hadley. *Ensign Lisa Minelli*: Betty McNamara. *Liat*: IMELDA DE MARTIN. *Lt. Buzz Adams*: Dick Button. *Shore Patrol Officer*: Peter Held. *Islanders*: Vie-Von Thom, Andrea Del Rosario, Claudia Satow.

[20]Dropped during run.
[21]Dropped during run.
[22]Dropped during run.
[23]Dropped during run.
[24]Originally presented in New York 7 April 1949 at the Majestic Theatre for 1925 performances. For Synopsis of Scenes and Musical Numbers, see original 1949 production.

1957.07 NEW GIRL IN TOWN

A Musical in Two Acts, 16 Scenes. Book by George Abbott. Based on the play "Anna Christie" by Eugene O'Neill. Music and lyrics by Bob Merrill. Dances and musical numbers staged by Bob Fosse. Production (settings, costumes) designed by Rouben Ter-Arutunian. Musical direction by Hal Hastings. Dance music devised by Roger Adams. Orchestrations by Robert Russell Bennett and Philip J. Lang. Directed by George Abbott. Produced by Frederick Brisson, Robert E. Griffith and Harold S. Prince. Opened 14 May 1957 at the 46th Street Theatre and closed 24 May 1958 after 432 performances.

CAST (in order of appearance): *Lily*: Lulu Bates. *Moll*: Pat Ferrier. *Katie*: Mara Lynn. *Alderman*: Michael Quinn. *Chris*: CAMERON PRUD'HOMME. *Johnson*: Jeff Killion. *Seaman*: H. F. Green. *Marthy*: THELMA RITTER. *Oscar*: Del Anderson. *Pete*: Eddie Phillips. *Mrs. Dowling*: Ann Willaims. *Smith*: Stokely Gray. *Mrs. Smith*: Dorothy Stinnette. *Bartender*: Mark Dawson. *Ivy*: Rita Noble. *Rose*: Ginny Perlowin. *Anna*: GWEN VERDON. *Flo*: Drusilla Davis. *Pearl*: Mara Landi. *Mat*: GEORGE WALLACE. *Mrs. Hammacher*: Jean Handzlik. *Reporter*: Herb Fields. *Masher*: John Aristedes. *Svenson*: Ray Mason. *Violet*: Deedy Irwin. *Waiter*: Louis Polacek. *Dowling*: Ripple Lewis. *Politician*: H. F. Green. *Krimp*: John Ford. *Henry*: Edgar Daniels.

Dancers: Claiborne Cary, Drusilla Davis, Dorothy Dushock, Pat Ferrier, Marie Kolin, Mara Lynn, Ethel Martin, Joan Petlak, John Aristedes, Robert Bakanic, Harvey Hohnecker, Harvey Jung, Dale Moreda, John Nola, Eddie Phillips, Alton Ruff. *Singers*: Jean Handzlik, Deedy Irwin, Mara Landi, Rita Noble, Ginny Perlowin, Dorothy Stinnette, Ann Williams, Del Anderson, Edgar Daniels, Herb Fields, John Ford, Stokely Gray, H. F. Green, Jeff Killion, Ripple Lewis, Ray Mason, Louis Polacek, Michael Quinn.

The action takes place near the Waterfront, New York City, at the turn of the century.

Act 1, Scene 1: The Waterfront. *Scene 2*: A Street with a mesh fence. *Scene 3*: Johnny-the-Priest's Saloon. *Scene 4*: A Street in the Warehouse District. *Scene 5*: Chris's Barge on a foggy night at sea, off Provincetown. *Scene 6*: A Street near the Waterfront. *Scene 7*: The Waterfront. *Scene 8*: The Street with the fence. *Scene 9*: Chris's Room. *Scene 10*: A Street Scene. *Scene 11*: The Check Apron Ball.

Act 2, Scene 1: The Check Apron Ball. *Scene 2*: In the Street, outside the Brewery. *Scene 3*: A Street in the Warehouse District. *Scene 4*: Chris's Room. *Scene 5*: The Waterfront. One year later.

ACT 1

Scene 1

"Roll Yer Socks Up"
H. F. Green, Dancers, Singers

Scene 2

"Anna Lilla"
C. Prud'Homme

Scene 3

"Sunshine Girl"
D. Anderson, E. Phillips, M. Dawson

"On the Farm"
G. Verdon

Scene 4

"Flings"
T. Ritter, L. Bates, M. Landi

Scene 5

"It's Good To Be Alive"
G. Verdon

Scene 6

"Look at 'Er"
G. Wallace

Scene 7

"It's Good To Be Alive" (reprise)
G. Wallace

Scene 8

"Yer My Friend, Aintcha?"
T. Ritter, C. Prud'Homme

Scene 9

"Did You Close Your Eyes?"
G. Verdon, G. Wallace

Scene 10

"At the Check Apron Ball"
Dancers, Singers

Scene 11

"There Ain't No Flies on Me"
G. Verdon, H. Hohnecker, H. Jung, E. Phillips, D. Moreda, Company

ACT 2

Scene 1

"Ven I Valse"
G. Verdon, C. Prud'Homme, Dancers, Singers

Scene 3

"Sunshine Girl" (reprise)
Dancers, Singers

Scene 4

"If That Was Love"
G. Verdon

Ballet
G. Verdon, J. Aristedes, Dancers

Scene 5

"Chess and Checkers"
T. Ritter, Dancers, Singers

"Look at 'Er" (reprise)
G. Wallace

1957.08 THE PAJAMA GAME

A Revival of the Musical Comedy in Two Acts, 17 Scenes[25]. Book by George Abbott and Richard Bisssell. Based on the novel "7 1/2 Cents" by Richard Bissell. Music and lyrics by Richard Adler and Jerry Ross. Original production directed by George Abbott and Jerome Robbins. Directed by Jean Barrere. Scenery and costumes by Lemuel Ayers. Costume supervisor, Ruth Morley. Dances based on original choreography by Bob Fosse as executed by Erik Kristen. Lighting by Peggy Clark. Musical director, Frederick Dvonch. Orchestrations by Don Walker. Dance music arrangements by Roger Adams. Produced by the New York City Center Light Opera Company (Jean Dalrymple, Director). Opened 15 May 1957 at the New York City Center and closed 2 June 1957 after 23 performances.

CAST (in order of appearance): *Hines*: PAUL HARTMAN. *Prez*: STANLEY PRAGER. *Joe*: Sam Kirkham. *Hasler*: Ralph W. Chambers. *Gladys*: PAT STANLEY. *Sid Sorokin*: LARRY DOUGLASS. *Mabel*: MARGUERITE SHAW. *First Helper*: Richard France. *Second Helper*: Cy Young. *Charlie*: Eugene Wood. *Babe Williams*: JANE KEAN. *Mae*: Thelma Pelish. *Brenda*: Ann Buckles. *Poopsie*: Chele Graham. *Salesman*: Jack Waldron *Pop*: William David.

Dancers: Dorothy Etheridge, Chele Graham, Mickey Gunnerson, Rosemary Jourdan, Vivian Joyce, Barbara Siman, Bonnie West, Jim Brusock, Richard Colacino, Jack Konzal, Richard Monahan, Tom Snow, Keith Willis, Emanuel Winston. *Singers*: Helen Baisley, Julia Gerace, Betty Graeber, Miriam Gulager, Peg Hadley, Sheila Mathews, Barbara Saxby, Mildred Slavin, Don Becker, Norris Branstrom, Arthur Dilks, Peter Held, Sam Kirkham, Vince McMahon, Stanley Page, Ralph Vucci.

---

[25]First presented in New York 13 May 1954 at the St. James Theatre for 1063 performances. For Synopsis of Scenes and Musical Numbers, see original 1954 production.

1957–1958 SEASON

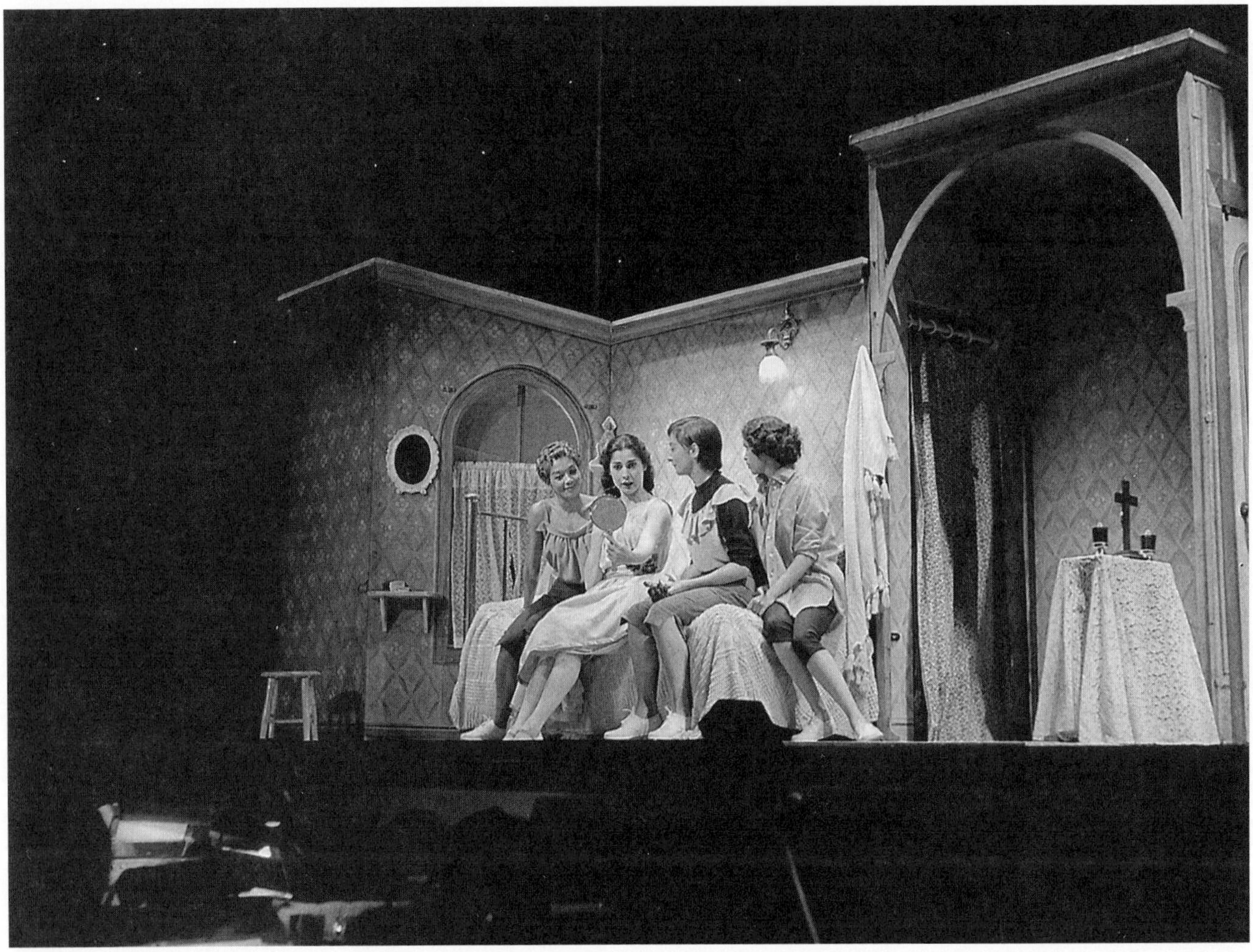

Carol Lawrence (with mirror) in WEST SIDE STORY
Martha Swope/TimePix

1957–1958 SEASON

1957.09 SIMPLY HEAVENLY

A Musical Folk Comedy in Two Acts, 17 Scenes[1]. Book and lyrics by Langston Hughes. (Based on his novel "Simple Takes a Wife" and other "Simple" stories.) Music and orchestrations by David Martin. Directed by Joshua Shelley. Setting and lighting by Raymond Sovey. Musical director, Sticks Evans. (Produced by Vincent Cerow and Abel Enklewitz.) Opened 20 August 1957 at the Playhouse and closed 12 October 1957 after 62 performances. After Broadway run, re-opened Off-Broadway 8 November 1957 at the Renata Theatre, and closed 31 December 1957 after 63 additional performances. Total for all 3 engagements: 169 performances.

CAST[2] (in order of appearance): *Simple*: MELVIN STEWART. *Madam Butler*: Wilhelmina Gray. *Boyd*: Stanley Greene. *Mrs. Caddy*: Dagmar Craig. *Joyce Lane*: MARILYN BERRY. *Hopkins*: Duke Williams. *Bar Pianist*: Willie Pritchett. *Mamie*: CLAUDIA McNEIL. *Bodiddly*: Charles A. McRae. *Character*: Allegro Kane. *Melon*: JOHN BOUIE. *Gitfiddle*: Brownie McGhee. *Zarita*: ANNA ENGLISH. *Arcie*: Josephine Woods. *John Jasper*: Charles Harrigan. *Big Boy, Cop*: Maxwell Glanville. *Nurse, Party Guest*: Dagmar Craig.

Act 1, Scene 1: Simple's Room, Harlem, New York City. An early Spring evening. *Scene 2*: Joyce's Room. Same evening. *Scene 3*: Paddy's Bar. Just before midnight. *Scene 4*: Hospital Room. Next day. *Scene 5*: Paddy's Bar. Saturday night. *Scene 6*: Joyce's Room. Sunday evening. *Scene 7*: Simple's Room. A month later.

Act 2, Scene 1: Paddy's Bar. A week later, evening. *Scene 2*: Joyce's Room. Evening, two weeks later. *Scene 3*: Simple's Room. Evening, a week later. *Scene 4*: Paddy's Bar. Next morning. *Scene 5*: Lenox Avenue. That evening. *Scene 6*: Joyce's Room. Same evening. *Scene 7*: Simple's Room. Same evening. *Scene 8*: Paddy's Bar. A Winter evening. *Scene 9*: A Phone Booth. Christmas Eve. *Scene 10*: Simple's Room. Same evening.

ACT 1

Scene 2

"Love Is Simply Heavenly"
M. Berry

Scene 3

"Let Me Take You for a Ride"
A. English, M. Stewart

"Broken String Blues"
B. McGhee

Scene 5

"Did You Ever Hear the Blues?"
C. McNeil, J. Bouie, Bar Characters

Scene 7

"I'm Gonna Be John Henry"
M. Stewart

ACT 2

Scene 1

"When I'm in a Quiet Mood"
C. McNeil, J. Bouie

"Look For the Morning Star"[3]
A. English

Scene 3

"Let's Ball Awhile"
A. English, Ensemble

Scene 4

"The Men in My Life"
A. English

Scene 8

"I'm a Good Old Girl"
C. McNeil

Scene 10

"Look for the Morning Star" (reprise)
Ensemble

[1]First produced in New York Off-Broadway 21 May 1957 at the 85th Street Playhouse for 44 performances.

[2]Those actors who originated their roles Off-Broadway but did not transfer to Broadway were as follows: *Madam Butler*: Alma Hubbard. *Mrs. Caddy*: Javotte S. Greene. *Hopkins*: Lewison Bates. *Gitfiddle*: Ray Thompson. *Zarita*: ETHEL AYLER. *Big Boy, Cop*: Pierre Rayon. *Nurse, Party Guest*: Javotte S. Greene.

[3]Replaced "Shade and Shadows" (from Off-Broadway run)(E. Ayler).

1957.10 MASK AND GOWN

A Musical Revue in Two Acts, 17 Scenes. Continuity (dialogue) by Ronny Graham and Sidney Carroll. Musical numbers staged and choreographed by Jim Russell. New music and lyrics by Ronny Graham, June Carroll, Arthur Siegel, Dorothea Freitag. Musical direction and arrangements by Dorothea Freitag. Lighting supervision by Lee Watson. Entire production conceived and directed by Leonard Sillman. Produced by Leonard Sillman and Bryant Haliday. Opened 10 September 1957 at the John Golden Theatre and closed 12 October 1957 after 39 performances.

CAST: MR. T. C. [Thomas Craig] JONES , BETTY CARR, GABY MONET, JOHN SMOLKO, ROD STRONG.

ACT 1

Scene 1

"The Circus Is Over"
J. Smolko
(*Music by* Arthur Siegel. *Lyrics by* June Carroll.)
With T. C. Jones, B. Carr, G. Monet, R. Strong.

Scene 2

T. C. on T. C.
(*by* Sidney Carroll) T. C. Jones

Scene 3

T. C. on T. V.
(*by* Ronny Graham) T. C. Jones
With B. Carr, G. Monet, J. Smolko, R. Strong.

Scene 4

"Make Friends"
B. Carr, G. Monet, J. Smolko, R. Strong
(*Music by* Arthur Siegel.)

Scene 5

Catch
T. C. Jones, B. Carr, G. Monet, J. Smolko, R. Strong

Scene 6

"Hesitation Waltz"
B. Carr, R. Strong
(*Music by* Emile Waldteufel.)

Scene 7

"T. C. A. Dance" (from SIMPLE SIMON)
T. C. Jones
(*Music by* Richard Rodgers. *Lyrics by* Lorenz Hart.)

Scene 8

Bolero
(*Music by* Dorothea Freitag.) G. Monet, J. Smolko

Scene 9

T. C. on Hollywood
(*by* Leonard Sillman and Everett Marcy) T. C. Jones, J. Smolko

Scene 10

T. C. on Taps Topside:

"Don't Give Up the Ship" (from film SHIPMATES FOREVER)
T. C. Jones, B. Carr, G. Monet, J. Smolko, R. Strong
(*Music by* Harry Warren. *Lyrics by* Al Dubin.)

Scene 11

On Their Own:

House of Blue Lights
G. Monet

Shangri-La
J. Smolko

"Speedy Gonzales"
B. Carr
(*Music and Lyrics by* Ronny Graham.)

Chopin Waltz in E Minor
R. Strong
Scene 12
T. C. on Certain Singers
T. C. Jones
With B. Carr, G. Monet, J. Smolko, R. Strong.
"Remind Me" (from film ONE NIGHT IN THE TROPICS)
(*Music by* Jerome Kern. *Lyrics by* Dorothy Fields.)
"I Cover the Waterfront" (from film I COVER THE WATERFRONT)
(*Music by* Johnny Green. *Lyrics by* Edward Heyman.)
"How Did he Look?"
(*Music by* Abner Silver. *Lyrics by* Gladys Shelley.)
"New Sounds"
(*Music and Lyrics by* Ronny Graham.)

ACT 2
Scene 1
Setting the Stage
(*Music by* Scarlatti.) R. Strong
Scene 2
T. C. on Avon
(*Idea Conceived by* Mr. Jones.) T. C. Jones
With B. Carr, G. Monet, J. Smolko, R. Strong.
Ethel Merman as Juliet
Marilyn Monroe as Ophelia
Tallulah as Cleopatra
Mae West, Claudette Colbert or Ethel Barrymore as Kate
Bette Davis as Lady Macbeth
Judy Holliday as Portia
Katharine Hepburn as Rosalind
Scene 3
"You Better Go Now" (from NEW FACES OF 1936)
T. C. Jones
With B. Carr, G. Monet, J. Smolko, R. Strong.
(*Music by* Irvin Graham. *Lyrics by* Bickley Reichner.)
Scene 4
"I'll Be Seeing You" (from RIGHT THIS WAY)
T. C. Jones
(*Music by* Sammy Fain. *Lyrics by* Irving Kahal.)
Scene 5
T. C.
Himself

1957.11 CAROUSEL

A Revival of the Musical Play in Two Acts, Prelude and 9 Scenes[4]. Book and lyrics by Oscar Hammerstein II. Based on Ferenc Molnar's "Liliom" as adapted by Benjamin F. Glazer. Music by Richard Rodgers. Directed by John Fearnley. Choreography by Agnes de Mille, restaged by Robert Pagent. Ensemble staging by John Fearnley and Robert Pagent. Scenery by Oliver Smith. Costume supervisor, Florence Klotz. Lighting by Peggy Clark. Musical director, Julius Rudel. Choral director, Charles Smith. (Orchestrations by Don Walker.) Produced by the New York City Center Light Opera Company (Jean Dalrymple, Director). Opened 11 September 1957 at the New York City Center and closed 29 September 1957 after 24 performances.

CAST (in order of appearance): *Carrie Pipperidge*: PAT STANLEY. *Julie Jordan*: BARBARA COOK. *Mrs. Mullin*: KAY MEDFORD. *Billy Bigelow*: HOWARD KEEL. *First Policeman*: Evans Thornton. *David Bascombe*: Robert Eckles. *Girl With Bear*: Elisa Monte. *Nettie Fowler*: MARIE POWERS. *June Girl*: Evelyn Taylor. *Enoch Snow*: RUSSELL NYPE. *Jigger Craigin*: JAMES MITCHELL. *Hannah*: Joan Eheman. *Boatswain*: ROBERT PAGENT. *Second Policeman*: James Gannon. *Captain*: Sam Kirkham. *Heavenly Friend (Brother Joshua)*: Leo Lucker. *Starkeeper*: VICTOR MOORE. *Louise*: BAMBI LINN. *Carnival Boy*: ROBERT PAGENT. *Enoch Snow, Jr.*: Larry Fuller. *Principal*: Bruce Baggett.

Townspeople: Jane Burke, Shirley Chester, Faith Compo, Charry Davis, Elizabeth Edwards, Lindsay McGregor, Beth Parks, Basha Regis, Jeanne Shea, Joy Lynne Sica, Bruce Baggett, Don Becker, Jack Eddleman, James E. Gannon, Sam Kirkham, David London, Vincent B. McMahon, Bob Newkum, Ted Otis, Robert B. Reim. *Dancers*: Patricia Birsh (Birch), Verna Cain, Dorothy Etheridge, Mickey Gunnerson, Sally Gura, Ruby Herndon, Catherine Horn, Reba Howells, Rosemary Jourdan, Eloise Milton, Kiki Minor, Evelyn Taylor, Jim Albright, Charles J. Carow, Gerald Fries, Larry Fuller William T. Inglis, Donald Martin, Glenn Olson, Robert St. Clair, Gerald M. Teijolo, Jr.

1957.12 WEST SIDE STORY

A Musical in Two Acts, 15 Scenes. Book by Arthur Laurents. Based on a conception of Jerome Robbins. Music by Leonard Bernstein. Lyrics by Stephen Sondheim. Entire production directed and choreographed by Jerome Robbins. Scenic production by Oliver Smith. Costumes by Irene Sharaff. Lighting by Jean Rosenthal. Co-choreographer, Peter Gennaro. Musical direction by Max Goberman. Orchestrations by Leonard Bernstein, with Sid Ramin, Irwin Kostal. Produced by Robert E. Griffith and Harold S. Prince by arrangement with Roger L. Stevens. Opened 26 September 1957 at the Winter Garden, moved 2 March 1959 to the Broadway Theatre, and closed 27 June 1959 after 732 performances.[5]

CAST: *THE JETS*: *Riff*, the Leader: MICKEY CALIN. *Tony*, his friend: LARRY KERT. *Action*: Eddie Roll. *A-Rab*: Tony Mordente. *Baby John*: David Winters. *Snowboy*: Grover Dale. *Big Deal*: Martin Charnin. *Diesel*: Hank Brunjes. *Gee-Tar*: Tommy Abbott. *Mouth Piece*: Frank Green. *Tiger*: Lowell Harris. *Their Girls*: *Graziella*: Wilma Curley. *Velma*: Carole D'Andrea. *Minnie*: Nanette Rosen. *Clarice*: Marilyn D'Honau. *Pauline*: Julie Oser. *Anybodys*: Lee Becker.

THE SHARKS: *Bernardo*, the Leader: KEN LeROY. *Maria*, his Sister: CAROL LAWRENCE. *Anita*, his Girl: CHITA RIVERA. *Chino*, his Friend: Jamie Sanchez. *Pepe*: George Marcy. *Indio*: Noel Schwartz. *Luis*: Al De Sio. *Anxious*: Gene Gavin. *Nibbles*: Ronnie Lee. *Juano*: Jay Norman. *Toro*: Erne Castaldo. *Moose*: Jack Murray. *Their Girls*: *Rosalia*: Marilyn Cooper. *Consuelo*: Reri Grist. *Teresita*: Carmen Guiterrez. *Francisca*: Elizabeth Taylor. *Estella*: Lynn Ross. *Marguerita*: Liane Plane.

THE ADULTS: *Doc*: ART SMITH. *Schrank*: Arch Johnson. *Krupke*: William Bramley. *Gladhand*: John Harkins.

The action takes place on the West Side of New York City during the last days of Summer.

Act 1, Scene 1: Prologue: The months before. The Street. 5:00 P.M. *Scene 2*: A Back Yard 5:30 P.M. *Scene 3*: The Bridal Shop. 6:00 P.M. *Scene 4*: The Gym. 10:00 P.M. *Scene 5*: A Back Alley. 11:00 P.M. *Scene 6*: The Drugstore. Midnight. *Scene 7*: The Bridal Shop. The next day, 5:30 P.M. *Scene 8*: The Neighborhood. 6:00 to 9:00 P.M. *Scene 9*: Under the Highway. 9:00 P.M.

Act 2, Scene 1: The Bedroom. 9:15 P.M. *Scene 2*: Another Alley. 10:00 P.M. *Scene 3*: The Bedroom. 11:30 P.M. *Scene 4*: The Drugstore. 11:40 P.M. *Scene 5*: The Cellar. 11:50 P.M. *Scene 6*: The Street. Midnight.

ACT 1
Scene 1
Prologue
Danced by Jets and Sharks
"Jet Song"
M. Calin, D. Winters, G. Dale, Jets
Scene 2
"Something's Coming"
L. Kert
Scene 4
The Dance at the Gym
Jets and Sharks
"Maria"
L. Kert
Scene 5
"Tonight"
L. Kert, C. Lawrence
"America"
C. Rivera, M. Cooper, Shark Girls
Scene 6
"Cool"
M. Calin, Jets

[4]Originally produced in New York 19 April 1945 at the Majestic Theatre for 890 performances. For Synopsis of Scenes and Musical Numbers, see original 1945 production.

[5]Re-opened a return engagement 27 April 1960 at the Winter Garden; see separate entry below.

Scene 7
"One Hand, One Heart"
L. Kert, C. Lawrence
Scene 8
"Tonight" (Quintet and Chorus)
Company
Scene 9
The Rumble
Danced by M. Calin, K. LeRoy, Jets and Sharks

ACT 2
Scene 1
"I Feel Pretty"
C. Lawrence, M. Cooper, C. Guiterrez, E. Taylor
"Somewhere"
R. Grist
Danced by the Company.
Scene 2
"Gee, Officer Krupke"
E. Roll, G. Dale, Jets
Scene 3
"A Boy Like That"
C. Rivera, C. Lawrence
"I Have a Love"
C. Rivera, C. Lawrence
Scene 4
Taunting
C. Rivera, Jets
Scene 6
Finale
The Company

1957.13 DIE FLEDERMAUS

A Revival of the Operetta in Three Acts[6]. (Original Viennese libretto by Carl Haffner and Richard Genée. Lyrics by Richard Genée. Based on the comedy "Le Réveillon" by Henri Meilhac and Ludovic Halévy.) English libretto by Ruth and Thomas Martin. Music by Johann Strauss. Staged by Michael Pollock. Choreographed by Robert Joffrey. (Settings) Designed by Leo Kerz. Conducted by Franz Allers. Produced by the New York City Opera. Opened 13 October 1957 at the New York City Center and closed 17 November 1957 after 3 performances in repertory.

CAST: *Rosalinda*: PHYLLIS CURTIN. *Eisenstein*: ERNEST McCHESNEY. *Adele*: JACQUELYNNE MOODY. *Sally*: Naomi Collier. *Alfred*: DAVID LLOYD. *Prince Orlofsky*: LOREN DRISCOLL. *Falke*: CHESTER LUDGIN. *Frank*: Richard Wentworth. *Frosch*: Coley Worth. *Blind*: David Williams. *Solo Dancers*: Dianne Consoer, Jonathan Watts.

1957.14 COPPER AND BRASS

A Musical Comedy in Two Acts. Book by Ellen Violett and David Craig. Music by David Baker. Lyrics by David Craig. Directed by Marc Daniels. Choreography by Anna Sokolow. Settings and lighting by William and Jean Eckart. Costumes by Alvin Colt. Musical direction and vocal arrangements by Maurice Levine. Orchestrations by Ralph Burns. Dance arrangements by John Morris. Produced by Lyn Austin and Thomas Noyes in association with Anderson Lawlor. Opened 17 October 1957 at the Martin Beck Theatre and closed 16 November 1957 after 36 performances.

CAST (in order of appearance): *First Expert*: Byron Mitchell. *Second Expert*: David Gold. *Third Expert*: Stanley Papich. *Fourth Expert*: Jeff Duncan. *Fifth Expert*: John Dorrin. *Sixth Expert*: Kevin Carlisle. *Seventh Expert*: Bob Roman. *Eighth Expert*: Sam Greene. *Katey O'Shea*: NANCY WALKER. *Commissioner*: Beau Tilden. *Captain*: ALAN BUNCE. *Sergeant*: Bruce Mackay. *Ethel Potts*: Michele Burke. *Mary Potts*: Evelyn Russell. *Estelle O'Shea*: BENAY VENUTA. *Mrs. Zimmer*: Alice Nunn. *Mr. Morphky*: Michael Roberts. *Mrs. Morphky*: Doreen McLean. *Piggy*: Byron Mitchell. *Brawn*: Norma Douglas. *Brains*: Peter Conlow. *Boy*: Stanley Papich. *Principal*: ALICE PEARCE. *Instructor*: Clyde Turner. *George*: DICK WILLIAMS. *Limey*: Hank Jones. *Slam*: Doug Rogers. *Professor*: Ernie Furtado. *Traintime*: Frank Rehak. *Slam's Girl*: Elmarie Wendel. *Limey's Wife*: Elton Warren. *Professor's Girl*: Bette Graham. *Rookie Cops*: Sam Greene, Michael Roberts, John Dorrin, Bob Roman, Nat Wright, Larry Mitchell, Jack Moore. *Roderick*: David Gold. *Policewomen*: Dorothy Aull, Joy Lane, Bette Graham. *Woman in the Window*: Joy Lane. *Guard*: Michael Roberts.

Dancers: Shawneequa Baker, Eve Beck, Judith Coy, Anita Dencks, Kate Friedlich, Ellen Hubel, Coco Ramirez, Tina Ramirez, Ella Thompson, Kevin Carlisle, Jeff Duncan, David Gold, Donald MacKayle, Jack Moore, Stanley Papich, Harold Pierson, Willard Nagel. *Singers*: Dorothy Aull, Laurie Franks, Bette Graham, Buzz Halliday, Joy Lane, Joanne Spiller, Elton Warren, Elmarie Wendel, John Dorrin, Sam Greene, Bruce Mackay, Byron Mitchell, Larry Mitchell, Michael Roberts, Bob Roman, Clyde Turner, Nat Wright.

The action takes place in and around the island of Manhattan.

ACT 1
"Career Guidance"
N. Walker, Eight Experts
"Wearing of the Blue"
N. Walker, Company
"I Need All the Help I Can Get"
N. Walker
"Cool Combo Mambo"
The Kids
"You Walked Out"
D. Williams
"Cool Credo"
D. Williams, N. Walker, Combo, Bandannies, Kids
"Bringing Up Daughter"
B. Venuta
"Don't Look Now"
N. Walker, D. Williams, Dancers
"Baby's Baby"
N. Douglas, P. Conlow, S. Baker, C. Ramirez, T. Ramirez
(*Dance choreographed by* Bob Fosse.)
"You Walked Out" (reprise)
N. Walker

ACT 2
"Call the Police"
N. Walker, Policewomen
"Unmistakable Sign"
N. Walker, B. Venuta
"Why Her?"
D. Williams
"Me and Love"
N. Walker
"Remember the Dancing"
B. Venuta, A. Pearce, A. Bunce,
D. McLean, M. Roberts, A. Nunn, P. Conlow, N. Douglas, Company
"Honk Kong"
B. Venuta, Company
"Argentine Tango"
A. Pearce, A. Bunce
"Sweet William"
B. Venuta, Company
"Don't Look Now" (reprise)
D. Williams
"Little Woman"
N. Walker
"Call the Police" (Finale)
Entire Company

1957.15 THE MERRY WIDOW

A Revival of the Operetta in Three Acts[7]. Music by Franz Lehár. Original Viennese libretto (Die Lustige Witwe) by Victor Léon and Leo Stein after "L'Attaché d'Ambassade." English libretto by Adrian Ross. Staged by Glenn

[6]First English language production in New York 16 March 1885 at the Casino Theatre for 42 performances. First New York production of this adaptation 20 December 1950 at the Metropolitan Opera House. For Synopsis of Scenes and Musical Numbers, see May 1954 revival.

[7]Originally produced in New York 21 October 1907 at the New Amsterdam Theatre for 416 performances. For Synopsis of Scenes and Musical Numbers, see original 1907 production.

Jordan. Choreographed by Robert Joffrey. Scenic design by George Jenkins. Conducted by Franz Allers. Produced by the New York City Opera. Opened 27 October 1957 at the New York City Center and closed 10 November 1957 after 3 performances in repertory.

CAST: *Sonia*: BEVERLY SILLS. *Prince Danilo*: ROBERT ROUNSEVILLE. *Baron Popoff*: HIRAM SHERMAN. *Natalie*: Peggy Bonini. *De Jolidon*: WILLIAM LEWIS. *Marquis de Cascada*: Herbert Beattie. *St. Brioche*: JOHN REARDON. *Admiral Khadja*: Arthur Newman. *Mme. Khadja*: Helen Baisley. *General Novikovich*: Richard Wentworth. *Mme. Novikovich*: Lu Leonard. *Nish*: Coley Worth. *King*: George Del Monte. *Lo-Lo*: Naomi Collier. *Solo Dancers*: Dianne Consoer, Beatrice Tompkins, Gerald Arpino. *Ensemble*: New York City Opera Chorus.

1957.16

JAMAICA

A Musical Comedy in Two Acts, 17 Scenes. Book by E. Y. Harburg and Fred Saidy. Music by Harold Arlen. Lyrics by E. Y. Harburg. Entire production directed by Robert Lewis. Production (Settings) designed by Oliver Smith. Costumes designed by Miles White. Lighting by Jean Rosenthal. Orchestrations by Philip J. Lang. Musical direction, continuity and vocal arrangements by Lehman Engel. Dance music and additional vocal arrangements by Peter Matz. Choreography by Jack Cole. Produced by David Merrick. Opened 31 October 1957 at the Imperial Theatre, closing for vacation 28 June 1958; reopened 11 August 1958 at the Imperial Theatre and closed 11 April 1959 after 558 performances.

CAST (in order of appearance): *Koli*: RICARDO MONTALBAN. *Quico*: Augustine Rios. *Savannah*: LENA HORNE. *Grandma Obeah*: ADELAIDE HALL. *Ginger*: JOSEPHINE PREMICE. *Snodgrass*: Roy Thompson. *Hucklebuck*: Hugh Dilworth. *Island Women*: Ethel Ayler, Adelaide Boatner. *The Governor*: ERIK RHODES. *Cicero*: OSSIE DAVIS. *Lancaster*: James E. Wall. *First Ship's Officer*: Tony Martinez. *Second Ship's Officer*: Michael Wright. *Joe Nashua*: JOE ADAMS. *Dock Worker*: Allen Richards. *Radio Announcer*: Alan Shayne. *Lead Dancers*: Alvin Ailey, Christyne Lawson.

Islanders: Ethel Ayler, Adelaide Boatner, Jayne Craddock, Norma Donaldson, Patricia Dunn, Doris Galiber, Lavinia Hamilton, Sandra Hinton, Chailendra Jones, Audrey Mason, Sally Neal, Pearl Reynolds, Christine Spencer, Carolyn Stanford, Jacqueline Walcott, Barbara Wright, George Boreland, Hugh Bryant, Herb Coleman, Hugh Dilworth, Frank Glass, Harold Gordon, Nat Horne, Albert Johnson, Tony Martinez, Jim McMillan, Charles Moore, Allen Richards, Claude Thompson, Roy Thompson, Billy Wilson, Michael Wright, Ben Vargas.

The action takes place on Pigeon Island, a mythical island off Jamaica at the present time.

Act 1, Scene 1: Grandma Obeah's shack. A day in spring. *Scene 2*: The knoll near Grandma's shack. Next day. *Scene 3*: Ginger's hut. That evening. *Scene 4*: Grandma's shack. Later that evening. *Scene 5*: Koli's boat. the same night. *Scene 6*: Dockside. The next morning. *Scene 7*: The Governor's mansion. A few days later. *Scene 8*: A night club. *Scene 9*: The beach at night. *Scene 10*: Grandma's shack. Early evening. *Scene 11*: Dockside. Next morning.

Act 2, Scene 1: A bluff on the coast. Three days later. *Scene 2*: The Governor's mansion. Next afternoon. *Scene 3*: A room in the Governor's mansion. A few days later. *Scene 4*: Koli's fish market. Next day. *Scene 5*: The Governor's mansion. The same day. *Scene 6*: The knoll. Later afternoon of the same day.

ACT 1[8]

Scene 1
- "Savannah"
  (R. Montalban, Men)

Scene 2
- "Savannah's Wedding Day"
  (A. Hall, R. Thompson, H. Dilworth, A. Rios, Chorus)
- "Pretty to Walk With"
  (L. Horne, Chorus)
- "Push the Button"
  (L. Horne, Chorus)
- "Incompatibility"
  (R. Montalban, Men)

Scene 3
- "Little Biscuit"
  (O. Davis, J. Premice)

Scene 4
- "Cocoanut Sweet"
  (L. Horne)

Scene 5
- "Pity the Sunset"
  (R. Montalban, L. Horne)

Scene 6
- "(Hooray for De) Yankee Dollar"
  (J. Premice, Chorus)
- "What Good Does It Do?"
  (J. Premice, O. Davis, R. Montalban, A. Rios)

Scene 7
- "Monkey in the Mango Tree"
  (R. Montalban, Men)

Scene 8
- "Take It Slow, Joe"
  (L. Horne)

Scene 9
- Beach at Night—Dance

Scene 10
- "Ain't It the Truth"
  (L. Horne)

ACT 2

Scene 1
- "Leave the Atom Alone"
  (J. Premice, Chorus)
- "Cocoanut Sweet" (reprise)
  (L. Horne)

Scene 2
- "For Every Fish (There's a Little Bigger Fish)"
  (A. Hall, Men)
- "I Don't Think I'll End It All Today"
  (L. Horne, R. Montalban, Chorus)

Scene 3
- "Napoleon"
  (L. Horne)

Scene 4
- "Ain't It the Truth" (reprise)
  (L. Horne, Chorus)

Scene 5
- "Savannah" (reprise)
  (L. Horne, R. Montalban, Chorus)

1957.17

RUMPLE

A Musical Comedy in Two Acts, a Prologue and 10 Scenes. Book by Irving Phillips. Music by Ernest G. Schweikert. Lyrics by Frank Reardon. Directed by Jack Donohue. Choreography by Bob Hamilton. Settings and Lighting by George Jenkins. Costumes by Alvin Colt. Orchestrations by Ted Royal. Musical director, Frederick Dvonch. Dance music arranged by Robert Atwood. Original caricatures of Rumple by Mort Drucker. Produced by Paula Stone and Mike Sloan. Opened 6 November 1957 at the Alvin Theatre and closed 14 December 1957 after 45 performances.

CAST (in order of appearance): *The Chief of Oblivia*: Clayton Coots. *Judy Marlowe*: LOIS O'BRIEN. *Ginny*: Ginny Perlowin. *Judy's Friends*: Bonnie West, Janice Wagner, Sally Wile, Sari Clymas. *Nelson Crandal*: STEPHEN DOUGLASS. *Kate Drew*: GRETCHEN WYLER. *Rumple*: EDDIE FOY. *Anna*: BARBARA PERRY. *J. B. Conway*: MILO BOULTON. *The Photographers*: Elliott Gould, Larry Stevens. *Brannigan*: Ken Harvey. *Barney*: Jackie Warner. *Dr. Wellington Winslow*: JEROME COWAN. *Nurse*: Sari Clymas. *The Weird Ones*: Elliott Gould, Doris Lorenz, Pat White, Lila Popper, Gail Kuhr, William Milié. *The Dissenter*: George Martin. *The Match Box*: Claire Gunderman. *He Who Gets Slapped*: Elliott Gould. *Reporter*: Eddie Weston. *The Powder Room*: Pat White. *The Unravelled*: Bonnie West. *Girls on a Bench*: Doris Lorenz, Lila Popper. *Lieutenant Mallory*: Ken Harvey. *The Voice of Oblivia*: Ken Harvey.

Ensemble: Sari Clymas, Claire Gunderman, Gail Kuhr, Doris Lorenz, Lila Popper, Janice Wagner, Bonnie West, Pat White, Sally Wile, Bill Carter, Elliott Gould, Larry Howard, George Martin, William Milié, Roy Palmer, Larry Stevens, Eddie Weston.

Prologue: Somewhere in Oblivia.

[8]Vocalists not identified in the program. List below prepared from production typescript and cast recording.

Act 1, Scene 1: Nelson Crandal's New York Studio Apartment. Evening. *Scene 2*: Barney's Bar. Later that night. *Scene 3*: Nelson's Apartment. Next morning. *Scene 4*: Central Park. Later that morning. *Scene 5*: Nelson's Apartment. That night.

Act 2, Scene 1: Office of Dr. Winslow, Psychiatrist. Afternoon. *Scene 2*: Barney's Bar. Later that afternoon. *Scene 3*: Nelson's Apartment. *Scene 4*: Central Park. That night. *Scene 5*: Nelson's Apartment. Later that night.

ACT 1
Scene 1
"It's You for Me"
S. Douglass, L. O'Brien
"In Times Like These"
E. Foy, B. Perry
Scene 2
"Red Letter Day"
G. Wyler, Ensemble, J. Warner
"The First Time I Spoke of You"
S. Douglass, L. O'Brien
Scene 3
"Oblivia"
E. Foy, B. Perry, Cartoon Characters, Holiday Girls
"Peculiar State of Affairs"
E. Foy, G. Wyler
Scene 4
"How Do You Say Goodbye"
L. O'Brien
Scene 5
"Gentlemen of the Press"
S. Douglass, Cartoon Characters, Holiday Girls

ACT 2
Scene 1
"To Adjust Is a Must"
J. Cowan, Weird Ones
"Coax Me"
G. Wyler
Scene 2
"How Do You Say Goodbye" (reprise)
S. Douglass
"All Dressed Up (and No Place to Go)"
G. Wyler, Ensemble
Scene 3
"In Times Like These" (reprise)
G. Wyler, J. Cowan
"Peculiar State of Affairs" (reprise)
B. Perry
Scene 4
"Wish"
E. Foy
Scene 5
Finale
Entire Company

1957.18 THE MUSIC MAN

A Musical Comedy in Two Acts, 16 Scenes. Book, music and lyrics by Meredith Willson. Story by Meredith Willson and Franklin Lacey. Entire production staged by Morton Da Costa. Choreography by Onna White. Settings and lighting by Howard Bay. Costumes by Raoul Pene du Bois. Orchestrations by Don Walker. Dance arrangements by Laurence Rosenthal. Musical direction and vocal arrangements by Herbert Greene. Produced by Kermit Bloomgarden with Herbert Greene in association with Frank Productions. Inc. Opened 19 December 1957 at the Majestic Theatre, moved 24 October 1960 to the Broadway Theatre, and closed 15 April 1961 after 1375 performances.

CAST (in order of appearance): *Travelling Salesmen*: Russell Goodwin, Hal Norman, Robert Howard, James Gannon, Robert Lenn, Vernon Lusby, Robert Evans. *Charlie Cowell*: PAUL REED. *Conductor*: Carl Nicholas. *Harold Hill*: ROBERT PRESTON. *Mayor Shinn*: DAVID BURNS. THE BUFFALO BILLS (4): *Ewart Dunlop*: Al Shea. *Oliver Hix*: Wayne Ward. *Jacey Squires*: Vern Reed. *Olin Britt*: Bill Spangenberg. *Marcellus Washburn*: IGGIE WOLFINGTON. *Tommy Djilas*: DANNY CARROLL. *Marian Paroo*: BARBARA COOK. *Mrs. Paroo*: PERT KELTON. *Amaryllis*: Marilyn Siegel. *Winthrop Paroo*: EDDIE HODGES. *Eulalie Mackecknie Shinn*: HELEN RAYMOND. *Zaneeta Shinn*: DUSTY WORRALL. *Gracie Shinn*: Barbara Travis. *Alma Hix*: Adnia Rice. *Maud Dunlop*: Elaine Swann. *Ethel Toffelmier*: Peggy Mondo. *Mrs. Squires*: Martha Flynn. *Constable Locke*: Carl Nicholas.

River City Townspeople and Kids: Pamela Abbott, Babs Delmore, Martha Flynn, Janet Hayes, Peggy Mondo, Barbara Williams, Elaine Swann, Marie Santella, Marlys Watters, James Gannon, Russell Goodwin, Robert Howard, Peter Leeds, Robert Lenn, Hal Norman, Carl Nicholas, Joan Bowman, Alice Clift, Nancy Davis, Penny Ann Green, Lynda Lynch, Jacqueline Maria, Marilyn Poudrier, Pat Mariano, Elisabeth Buda, Babs Warden, Tom Panko, Ronn Cummins, Robert Evans, Vernon Lusby, Gary Menteer, John Sharpe, Roy Wilson, Gerald Teijelo, Bob Mariano, Vernon Wendorf.

Act 1, Scene 1: A Railway Coach. Morning, July 4, 1912. *Scene 2*: River City, Iowa. Center of Town. Immediately following. *Scene 3*: The Paroo's House. That evening. *Scene 4*: Madison Gymnasium. Thirty minutes later. *Scene 5*: Exterior of Madison Library. Immediately following. *Scene 6*: Interior of Madison Library. Immediately following. *Scene 7*: A Street. The following Saturday noon. *Scene 8*: The Paroos' Porch. That evening. *Scene 9*: Center of Town. Noon, the following Saturday.

Act 2, Scene 1: Madison Gymnasium. The following Tuesday evening. *Scene 2*: The Hotel Porch. The following Wednesday evening. *Scene 3*: The Paroos' Porch. Immediately following. *Scene 4*: The Footbridge. Fifteen minutes later. *Scene 5*: A Street. Immediately following. *Scene 6*: Madison Park. A few minutes later. *Scene 7*: River City High School Assembly Room. Immediately following.

ACT 1
Scene 1
"Rock Island"
P. Reed, Travelling Salesmen
Scene 2
"Iowa Stubborn"
Townspeople of River City
"(Ya Got) Trouble"
R. Preston, Townspeople
Scene 3
"Piano Lesson"
B. Cook, P. Kelton, M. Siegel
"Goodnight, My Someone"
B. Cook
Scene 4
"Seventy Six Trombones"
R. Preston, Boys, Girls
"Sincere"
The Buffalo Bills
Scene 5
"The Sadder-But-Wiser Girl"
R. Preston, I. Wolfington
"Pickalittle (Talkalittle)"
H. Raymond, E. Swann, P. Mondo, A. Rice, M. Flynn, Ladies of River City
"Goodnight Ladies"
The Buffalo Bills
Scene 6
"Marian the Librarian"
R. Preston, Boys, Girls
Scene 8
"My White Knight"
B. Cook
Scene 9
"Wells Fargo Wagon"
E. Hodges, Townspeople

ACT 2
Scene 1
"It's You"
The Buffalo Bills, H. Raymond, E. Swann, P. Mondo, A. Rice, M. Flynn
"Shipoopi"
I. Wolfington, R. Preston, B. Cook, D. Carroll, D. Worrall, Kids
"Pickalittle" (reprise)
H. Raymond, E. Swann, P. Mondo, A. Rice, M. Flynn, Ladies of River City

Scene 2
"Lida Rose"
The Buffalo Bills
"Will I Ever Tell You"
B. Cook
Scene 3
"Gary, Indiana"
E. Hodges
Scene 4
"It's You" (reprise)
Townspeople, Boys, Girls
"Till There Was You"
B. Cook, R. Preston
Scene 5
"Seventy Six Trombones"/"Goodnight, My Someone" (reprise)
R. Preston, B. Cook
Scene 6
"Till There Was You" (reprise)
R. Preston
Scene 7
Finale
Entire Company

1958.01 THE BODY BEAUTIFUL

A Musical Comedy in Two Acts, 18 Scenes. Book by Joseph Stein and Will Glickman. Music by Jerry Bock. Lyrics by Sheldon Harnick. Musical direction and vocal arrangements by Milton Greene. Ballet music by Genevieve Pitot. Orchestrations by Ted Royal. Costumes by Noel Taylor. Settings and lighting by William and Jean Eckart. Dances and musical numbers by Herbert Ross. Production Staged by George Schaefer. Produced by Richard Kollmar and Albert Selden. Opened 23 January 1958 at the Broadway Theatre and closed 15 March 1958 after 60 performances.

CAST (in order of appearance): *Dave*: JACK WARDEN. *Albert*: William Hickey. *Harry*: LONNIE SATTIN. *Bob*: STEVE FORREST. *Ann*: MINDY CARSON. *Dominic*: Edward Becker. *Eddie*: Tom Raskin. *Richie*: Bob Wiensko. *Florence*: Jane Romano. *Boxer*: Bill Richards. *Handler*: Knute Sullivan. *Frank*: Richard Chitos. *Nicky*: Tony Atkins. *Trainer*: Albert Popwell. *Boxer*: Bob Wiensko. *Marge*: BARBARA McNAIR. *Jane*: Helen Silver. *Kathy*: Kathie Forman. *Danny*: Tommy Halloran. *George*: Armand Bonay. *Artie*: Jeff Roberts. *Josh*: Alan Weeks. *Pete*: Richard DeBella. *Phil*: Edmund Gaynes. *Announcer*: Jack DeLon. *Referee*: Bill Richards. *Reporters*: Mace Barrett, Harry Lee Rogers, Mitchell Nutick, Stanley Papich. *Gloria*: MARA LYNN. *Campbell*: Mark Allen. *Two Men*: Knute Sullivan, Jack DeLon. *Ben*: Joe Ross.

Singers: Dorothy Aull, Mace Barrett, Edward Becker, Jack DeLon, Bette Graham, Buzz Halliday, Mary Louise, Broc Peters, Tom Raskin, Joe Ross, Knute Sullivan, Bob Wiensko. *Dancers*: Bob Daley, Ethelyne Dunfee, Shellie Farrell, Jeanna Belkin, Patti Karr, Patsi King, Louis Kosman, Ralph McWilliams, Mitchell Nutick, Stanley Papich, Albert Popwell, Nora Reho, Bill Richards, Harry Lee Rogers, Yvonne Othon, James McAnany.

The action takes place in and around New York City at the present time.

Act 1, Scene 1: Dave Coleman's Office and the Gym. *Scene 2*: Corridor of the Jersey City Arena. Next night. *Scene 3*: The Gym. The following day. *Scene 4*: The office. *Scene 5*: Community Center Playground and nearby street. *Scene 6*: Several Stadiums. *Scene 7*: Another section of the Gym. A few weeks later. *Scene 8*: The office. *Scene 9*: Dressing rooms in the Hartford Arena. *Scene 10*: The Arena.

Act 2, Scene 1: Summer Training Camp. *Scene 2*: Several Stadiums. *Scene 3*: The office. Three months later. *Scene 4*: A steam bath. *Scene 5*: The street. *Scene 6*: Terrace and Ball Room of the Stockton home. *Scene 7*: Dressing rooms. *Scene 8*: A Stadium corner.

ACT 1
"Where Are They?"
J. Warden, Boy Dancers and Singers
"The Body Beautiful"
M. Carson, B. Daley, L. Kosman, M. Nutick, B. Richards, H. L. Rogers
"Pffft!"[9]
S. Forrest, W. Hickey
"Fair Warning"
B. McNair, L. Sattin, D. Aull, B. Graham, B. Halliday, M. Louise, M. Barrett, J. DeLon, T. Raskin, K. Sullivan
"Leave Well Enough Alone"[10]
M. Carson
"Blonde Blues"
J. Warden
Dance
M. Lynn, J. Warden
"Uh-Huh, Oh-Yeah!"
T. Atkins, A. Bonay, R. Chitos, R. DeBella, E. Gaynes, T. Halloran, J. Roberts, A. Weeks
"All of These and More"
M. Carson, S. Forrest, Ensemble
"Nobility"
E. Becker, B. Daley, J. DeLon, B. Peters, A. Popwell, T. Raskin, K. Sullivan, B. Wiensko
"The Body Beautiful" (reprise)
M. Carson

ACT 2
"Summer Is"
Singers, Dancers, K. Forman
"The Honeymoon Is Over"
M. Lynn, J. Romano, H. Silver
"Just My Luck"
M. Carson, Kids
"All of These and More" (reprise)
B. McNair, L. Sattin
"Art of Conversation"
W. Hickey, Singers, Dancers
"Gloria"
J. Warden, M. Lynn, Dancers
"A Relatively Simple Affair"
M. Carson, B. McNair
Finale
Entire Company
M. Carson, B. McNair

1958.02 OH CAPTAIN!

A Musical Comedy in Two Acts. Book by Al Morgan and Jose Ferrer. Based on an original screenplay ("The Captain's Paradise") by Alec Coppel. Music and lyrics by Jay Livingston and Ray Evans. Scenery and lighting by Jo Mielziner. Costumes by Miles White. Dances and musical numbers created by James Starbuck. Musical direction, vocal and ballet arrangements by Jay Blackton. Orchestrations by Robert Ginzler, Joe Glover, Ray Jaimes, Philip J. Lang, Walter Eiger, Sy Oliver, Cornel Tanassy, Oscar Kosarin. Directed by Jose Ferrer. Produced by Howard Merrill and Theatre Corporation of America. Opened 4 February 1958 at the Alvin Theatre and closed 19 July 1958 after 192 performances.

CAST (in order of appearance): *Captain Henry St. James*: TONY RANDALL. *Mrs. Maud St. James*: JACQUELYN McKEEVER. *Enrico Manzoni*: EDWARD PLATT. *The Crew, S.S.. Paradise*: George Ritner, Bruce MacKay, Louis Polacek, Nolan Van Way. *A Clerk*: Jack Eddleman. *The Neighbors*: Betty McGuire, Dee Harless, Jean Sincere. *Lisa*: ALEXANDRA DANILOVA. *Bobo*: ABBE LANE. *The Guide*: STANLEY CARLSON. *A Spaniard*: PAUL VALENTINE. *Mae*: SUSAN JOHNSON.

English Townspeople, Dockworkers, Tourists, Parisians: Cherie Burgess, Shirley De Burgh, Sally Gura, Birgitta Kiviniemi, Asia Mercoolova, Kiki Minor, Adriane Rogers, Mona Pivar, Sybil Scotford, Mona Tritsch, Joyce Carroll, Dee Harless, Sheila Matthews, Betty McGuire, Alice Nunn, Jean Sincere, Helene Whitney, Bill Atkinson, Alvin Beam, Kevin Carlisle, Allen Conroy, David Lober, Gordon Marsh, Doug Springler, Ken Urmston, Eddie Verso, Jack Eddleman, Bruce MacKay, Louis Polacek, George Ritner, Tony Rossi, Charles Rule, James Stevenson, Nolan Van Way.

The action takes place in suburban London, on board the *S.S. Paradise* , and in Paris.

---

[9]Dropped during the run.

[10]Replaced during the run by:
"A Relatively Simple Affair"
This song also retained its Act 2 position as a reprise.

ACT 1

"A Very Proper Town"
T. Randall, Company

"Life Does a Man a Favor (When It Gives Him Simple Joys)"
J. McKeever, T. Randall

"A Very Proper Week"
English Townspeople

"Life Does a Man a Favor (When It Leads Him Down to the Sea)"
T. Randall, E. Platt, the Crew

"Captain Henry St. James"
Crew of the S.S. *Paradise*

The Dock Dance
Dockworkers

"Three Paradises"
T. Randall

"Surprise"
J. McKeever, Neighbors

"Life Does a Man a Favor (When It Puts Him in Paree)"
T. Randall

"Hey Madame"
T. Randall, A. Danilova

"Femininity"
A. Lane

"It's Never Quite the Same"
E. Platt, Crew

"It's Never Quite the Same" (reprise)
J. McKeever, E. Platt, Crew

"We're Not Children"
J. McKeever, P. Valentine

"Give It All You Got"
S. Johnson, Tourists

"Love Is Hell"
S. Johnson, Ladies of the Ensemble

"Keep It Simple"
A. Lane, Dancing Companions

ACT 2

"The Morning Music of Montmartre"
S. Johnson, People of Montmartre

"You Don't Know Him"
A. Lane, J. McKeever

"I've Been There and I'm Back"
E. Platt, T. Randall

"Double Standard"
A. Lane, J. McKeever

"All the Time"
T. Randall

"You're So Right for Me"
E. Platt, A. Lane

"All the Time" (reprise)
J. McKeever

Finale
Entire Company

1958.03 ANNIE GET YOUR GUN

A Revival of the Musical in Two Acts, 10 Scenes[11]. Book by Herbert and Dorothy Fields. Music and lyrics by Irving Berlin. Production directed by Donald Burr. Scenery by George Jenkins. Lighting by Peggy Clark. Costume supervisor, Florence Klotz. Dances and musical numbers staged by Helen Tamiris. Musical director, Frederick Dvonch. Orchestrations by Philip J. Lang, (Robert) Russell Bennett, Ted Royal. Produced by the New York City Center Light Opera Company (Jean Dalrymple, Director). Opened 19 February 1958 at the New York City Center and closed 2 March 1958 after 15 performances.

[11]First produced in New York 16 May 1946 at the Imperial Theatre for 1147 performances. For Synopsis of Scenes and Musical numbers, see original 1946 production.

CAST (in order of appearance): *Little Boy*: Christopher Shea Trenkle. *Little Girl*: Diane Ramey. *Charlie Davenport*: JACK WHITING. *Iron Tail*: STUART HODES. *Yellow Foot*: Edward Villela. *Mac* (Property Man): Jack Emrek. *Foster Wilson*: Leo Lucker. *Coolie*: Bert Wood. *Dolly Tate*: MARGARET HAMILTON. *Winnie Tate*: RAIN WINSLOW. *Tommy Keeler*: RICHARD FRANCE. *Frank Butler*: DAVID ATKINSON. *Annie Oakley*: BETTY JANE WATSON. *Minnie*, Annie's Sister: Dorleen Thomas. *Jessie*, Another Sister: Elaine Lynn. *Nellie*, Another Sister: Penny Grayam. *Little Jake*, Her Brother: Flip Mark. *Col. Wm.F. Cody (Buffalo Bill)*: JAMES RENNIE. *Mrs. Little Horse*: Hertha Shea. *Mrs. Black Tooth*: Jan Canada. *Trainman*: Laurence Watson. *Porter*: John Buie. *Second Porter*: Walter P. Brown. *Riding Mistress*: RUTHANNA BORIS. *Major Gordon Lillie*, Pawnee Bill: WILLIAM LeMASSENA. *Chief Sitting Bull*: HARRY BELAVER. *The Wild Horse*, Ceremonial Dancer: STUART HODES. *Pawnee's Messenger*: Jack Irwin. *Major Domo*: John Bouie. *First Waiter*: Walter P. Brown. *SecondWaiter*: Laurence Watson. *Mr. Schuyler Adams*: Jack Rains. *Mrs. Schuyler Adams*: Basha Regis. *Dr. Percy Ferguson*: Jack Irwin. *Mrs. Percy Ferguson*: Barbara Saxby. *Sylvia Potter-Porter*: Clare Waring.

Singers: Jane Burke, Janet Canada, Naomi Collier, Patricia Finch, Bonnie Lawrence, Nancy Radcliffe, Basha Regis, Barbara Saxby, Kenneth Ayers, Ralph W. Farnworth, Jack Irwin, Sam Kirkham, Stanley Page, Edgar Powell, Jack Rains, Casper Roos, Van Stevens, Ralph Vucci, Wendell Lynn. *Dancers*: Joan Dubrow, Beverly Gains, Lida Gaschke, Dorothy Hill, Iva March, Miriam Pandor, Fleur Raup, Renee Slade, Carolee Winchester, Doris Wright, Allan Byrns, Marvin Gordon, Charles Jackson, Daniel Jogalsky, Edward Monson, James Moore, Harold Pittard, Parker Wilson, Vic Vallaro.

1958.04 PORTOFINO

A Musical Comedy in Two Acts, a Prologue and 3 Scenes. Book and lyrics by Richard Ney. Music by Louis Bellson and Will Irwin. Additional lyrics by Sheldon Harnick. Choreography by Charles Weidman and Ray Harrison. Scenery by Wolfgang Roth. Costumes by Michael Travis. Lighting by Lee Watson. Orchestrations by Philip J. Lang. Vocal arrangements by Joseph Moon. Musical director, Will Irwin. Underscoring, Will Irwin. Entire production staged by Karl Genus. Produced by Richard Ney. Opened 21 February 1958 at the Adelphi Theatre and closed 22 February 1958 after 3 performances.

CAST: *Nicky*: GEORGES GUETARY. *Kitty*: HELEN GALLAGHER. *Padre, Guido*: ROBERT STRAUSS. *Angela*: Jan Chaney. *Sandro*: Wallace Eley. *Tullio*: Darryl Richard. *Tavern Keeper*: Webb Tilton.

Singers: Patricia Greenwood, Louise Pearl, Joy Marlene, Joy Lynne Sica, Lynne Stuart, Marvin Goodis, Mitchell May, Charles Aschmann, Bill Ryan, Pat Tolson, Jim Fullerton. *Dancers*: Kenley Hammond, Leslie Snow, Sally Wile, Barbara Richman, Gerrie Still, Sari Clymas, Patricia Ann White, Karen Sargent, Roy Palmer, Diki Lerner, Harvey Jung, Jimmy Kirby, Stuart Fleming, John Foster, Hilbert Rapp, Tom Hester.

Act 1: A Piazza in Portofino, a lovely Italian resort town. Early evening, today.

Act 2, Scene 1: Immediately following. *Scene 2*: The next morning.

Prologue
R. Strauss
(*Music by* Will Irwin. *Lyrics by* Sheldon Harnick.)

ACT 1

Opening—"Come Along"
Company
(*Music by* Will Irwin. *Lyrics by* Sheldon Harnick.)

"No Wedding Bells For Me"
G. Guetary
(*Music by* Will Irwin. *Lyrics by* Richard Ney.)

Festa—"Come Along" (reprise)
Company

"Red Collar Job"
R. Strauss
(*Music by* Louis Bellson and Will Irwin. *Lyrics by* Sheldon Harnick.)

"Here I Come"
H. Gallagher
(*Music by* Louis Bellson and Will Irwin. *Lyrics by* Sheldon Harnick.)

"New Dreams for Old"
G. Guetary
(*Music by* Louis Bellson. *Lyrics by* Richard Ney.)

"A Dream for Angela"
J. Chaney
(*Music by* Louis Bellson. *Lyrics by* Richard Ney.)

"Isn't It Wonderful?"
H. Gallagher, G. Guetary, Company
(*Music by* Louis Bellson. *Lyrics by* Richard Ney.)

"Dance of the Whirling Wimpus"
J. Chaney
"Under a Spell"
R. Guetary, Girls
(*Music by* Louis Bellson. *Lyrics by* Richard Ney and Sheldon Harnick.)

ACT 2
Scene 1
"Under a Spell" (reprise)
G. Guetary, Girls
"That's Love"
G. Guetary, Company
(*Music and Lyrics by* Richard Ney.)
"Too Little Time for Love"
W. Tilton
(*Music by* Will Irwin. *Lyrics by* Richard Ney.)
"Guido's Tango"
R. Strauss, H. Gallagher
"It Might Be Love"
G. Guetary
(*Music by* Louis Bellson. *Lyrics by* Richard Ney.)
"Here I Come" (reprise)
H. Gallagher
"Bacchanale"
Company
Scene 2
"Morning Prayer"
Company
(*Music by* Will Irwin. *Lyrics by* Richard Ney.)
"Kitty Car Ballet"
H. Gallagher, Boys
"The Grand Prix of Portofino"
Company
(*Music by* Will Irwin. *Lyrics by* Richard Ney.)
"Portofino"
G. Guetary
(*Music by* Louis Bellson. *Lyrics by* Richard Ney.)
"I'm in League With the Devil"
H. Gallagher
(*Music by* Will Irwin. *Lyrics by* Richard Ney.)
"Why Not For Marriage?"
G. Guetary
(*Music by* Louis Bellson. *Lyrics by* Richard Ney.)
"Portofino" (reprise)
Company

1958.05 WONDERFUL TOWN

A Revival of the Musical Comedy in Two Acts, 13 Scenes[12]. Book by Joseph Fields and Jerome Chodorov. Based on the play "My Sister Eileen" by Joseph Fields and Jerome Chodorov and the stories by Ruth McKinney. Music by Leonard Bernstein. Lyrics by Betty Comden and Adolph Green. Directed by Jerome Chodorov. Choreography by Ralph Beaumont. Entire production supervised by Herbert Ross. Sets and costumes by Raoul Pene du Bois. Costume supervision by Ruth Morley. Lighting by Peggy Clark. Musical direction and vocal arrangements by Lehman Engel. Associate conductor, Gino Smart. Orchestrations by Don Walker. Produced by the New York City Center Light Opera Company (Jean Dalrymple, Director). Opened 5 March 1958 at the New York City Center and closed 16 March 1958 after 15 performances.

CAST (in order of appearance): *Guide*: Wayne Sherwood. *Appopoulos*: GEORGE GIVOT. *Lonigan*: Jack Rains. *Helen*: BETSY VON FURSTENBERG. *Wreck*: JORDAN BENTLEY. *Violet*: Paula Wayne. *Valenti*: Ted Beniades. *Eileen*: JO SULLIVAN. *Ruth*: NANCY WALKER. *A Strange Man*: Don Grusso. *Drunks*: Daniel P. Hannafin, Jack Fletcher. *Robert Baker*: PETER COOKSON. *Associate Editors*: Bill Walker, Mark Zeller. *Mrs. Wade*: Isabella Hoopes. *Frank Lippencott*: CRIS ALEXANDER. *Chef*: Mark Zeller. *Waiter*: Robert Grant. *Delivery Boy*: Alan Johnson. *Chick Clark*: Frank Maxwell. *Shore Patrolman*: Bill Walker. *First Cadet*: Rudy del Campo. *Second Cadet*: Gerald Fries. *Policeman*: Daniel P. Hannafin. *Ruth's Escort*: Jack Fletcher.

Greenwich Villagers: *Singers*: Joan Fagan, Pat Hall, Jane A. Johnston, Barbara A. Lockard, Sadie McCollum, Genevieve Owens, Laine Roberts, Susan Terry, Paula Wayne, Elmarie Wendel, Robert Atherton, Robert Grant, Daniel P. Hannafin, Bob Maxwell, Jack Rains, Wayne Sherwood, Bill Walker, Millard Williams, Mark Zeller. *Dancers*: Nora Bristow, Barbara Giné, Bettye Jenkins, Jeannie Jones, Svetlana McLee, Odette Phillips, Carol-Sue Shaer, Gina Trichonis, Rudy del Campo, Ted Forlow, Jerry Fries, Alan Johnson, John Ira Moore, Eddie Pfeiffer, Marc Scott, Larry Stevens.

1958.06 INTERNATIONAL SOIRÉE

A Musical Revue in Two Acts, 4 Scenes. English Commentary by Arthur Lesser. Orchestra conducted by Jo Basile. Produced by Arthur Lesser. Opened 12 March 1958 at the Bijou Theatre and closed 29 March 1958 after 21 performances.

CAST: PATACHOU, HIRAM SHERMAN, MARCEL CORNELIS, GEORGE LA FAYE and COMPANY (Michele La Faye, Françoise Houlle, René Coquerelle, Loly Pinel), CARACOLILLO and MARIA ROSA, Rogelio Reguera.

ACT 1
Hiram Sherman presents:
Scene 1
Marcel Cornelis (Comic impressionist from Brussels, Belgium)
Scene 2
Georges La Faye and Company (Theatre of Animation from France)
Scene 3
Caracolillo and Maria Rosa (Spanish Dancers), assisted by Rogelio Reguera (Guitarist):
1. "Mezquita", a dance of Andalucia
2. "Soleares de Triana", a flamenco guitar solo
3. "Jota de la Dolores", a peasant dance of Aragon
4. "Allegrias", a flamenco of Cadiz
5. "Farruca con Zapateado", a flamenco of Andalucia
6. "Seguirillas Gitanas"

ACT 2
Hiram Sherman presents Patachou (French singer) whose repertoire was chosen from among the following:
"Ah!"
"Allume Tes Lampions"
"A Paris" (Lemarque)
"Brave Margot"
(*Music and Lyrics by* Georges Brassens.)
"Eh! Bien"
"La Complainte de la Butte" (from the film FRENCH CANCAN)
(*Music and Lyrics by* Jean Renoir, G. Van Parys.)
"La Goualante du Pauvre Jean"
(*Music and Lyrics by* Marguerite Monnot.)
"La Musique"
"Le Piano du Pauvre"
(*Music and Lyrics by* Leo Ferré.)
"Les Jambes Roses"
(*Music and Lyrics by* F. Véran, R. Thoreau.)
"Mon Homme"
(*Music by* Maurice Yvain. *Lyrics by* Albert Willemetz, Jacques Charles.)
"Parce Que"
(*Music and Lyrics by* G. Wagenheim, Charles Aznavour.)
"Paris Se Regarde"
"Pot-Pourri"
"Rue Lepic" (Emer)
"Un Jour Tu Verras"
"Va-Pas T'Imaginer"

[12]Originally produced in New York 25 February 1953 at the Winter Garden for 559 performances. For Synopsis of Scenes and Musical Numbers, see original 1953 production.

1958.07

OKLAHOMA!

A Revival of the Musical Comedy in Two Acts, 6 Scenes[13]. Book and lyrics by Oscar Hammerstein II. Music by Richard Rodgers. Based on the play "Green Grow the Lilacs" by Lynn Riggs. Directed by John Fearnley. (Originally directed by Rouben Mamoulian.) Dances by Agnes de Mille, re-staged by Gemze de Lappe. Musical direction by Frederick Dvonch. Settings by Lemuel Ayers. Costume supervision by Florence Klotz. Lighting by Peggy Clark. Produced by The New York City Center Light Opera Company (Jean Dalrymple, Director). Opened 19 March 1958 at the New York City Center and closed 30 March 1958 after 15 performances.

CAST (in order of appearance): *Aunt Eller*: BETTY GARDE. *Curly*: HERBERT BANKE. *Laurey*: LOIS O'BRIEN. *Will Parker*: GENE NELSON. *Jud Fry*: DOUGLAS FLETCHER RODGERS. *Ado Annie Carnes*: HELEN GALLAGHER. *Ali Hakim*: HARVEY LEMBECK. *Gertie Cummings*: Patricia Finch. *Sylvie*: GENZE DE LAPPE. *Curly* (in ballet): MICHAEL MAULE. *Laurey* (in ballet): GEMZE DE LAPPE. *Jud* (in ballet): GEORGE CHURCH. *The Girl Who Falls Down*: Evelyn Taylor. *Andrew Carnes*: OWEN MARTIN. *Cord Elam*: SHEPPARD KERMAN.

Singers: Jane Burke, Jan Canada, Naomi S. Collier, Patricia Finch, Bonnie Lawrence, Wendy Martin, Nancy Radcliffe, Barbara Saxby, Lois Van Pelt, Lynn Wendell, Kenneth Ayers, Ralph Farnworth, Jack Irwin, Barney Johnston, Sam Kirkham, Stanley Page, Edgar Powell, Casper Roos, Van Stevens, Ralph Vucci. *Dancers*: Patricia Birsh (Birch), Isabelle Farrell, Ruby Herndon, Marilyn Kessler, Naomi Marritt, Ellen Matthews, Elicia Miller, Ilona Murai, Nana Predente, Evelyn Taylor, Toodie Wittmer, Jenny Workman, Richard Colacino, Marvin Gordon, Thomas W. Hasson, James Maher, Gene Neal, David Neuman, William Ross, Eddie Weston.

1958.08

SAY, DARLING

A Comedy about a Musical in Three Acts, 14 Scenes. Book by Richard and Marian Bissell and Abe Burrows. Based on the novel of the same name by Richard Bissell. Music by Jule Styne. Lyrics by Betty Comden and Adolph Green. (Scenery) Designed by Oliver Smith. Costumes by Alvin Colt. Lighting by Peggy Clark. Directed by Abe Burrows. Dances by Matt Mattox. At the pianos, Colin Romoff and Peter Howard. Associate producer, George Gilbert. Produced by Jule Styne and Lester Osterman. Opened 3 April 1958 at the ANTA Theatre, moved 8 December 1958 to the Martin Beck Theatre, and closed 17 January 1959 after 332 performances.

CAST (in order of appearance): *Mr. Schneider*: Gordon B. Clarke. *Frankie Jordan*: CONSTANCE FORD. *Jack Jordan*: DAVID WAYNE. *Photographer*: Jack Naughton. *Pilot Roy Peters*: Jack Manning. *Ted Snow*: ROBERT MORSE. *June*, the Secretary: Eileen Letchworth. *Schatzie Harris*: HORACE McMAHON. *Richard Hackett*: JEROME COWAN. *Irene Lovelle*: VIVIAN BLAINE. *Rudy Lorraine*: JOHNNY DESMOND. *Sidemen*: Wendell Marshall, Peter Howard. *Charlie Williams*: Robert Downing. *Maurice*, a Pianist: Colin Romoff. *Arlene McKee*: Wana Allison. *Jennifer Stevenson*: Jean Mattox. *Earl Jorgeson*: Elliott Gould. *Cheryl Merrill*: Virginia Martin. *Accompanist*: Peter Howard. *Sammy Miles*: Steve Condos. *Rex Dexter*: MITCHELL GREGG. *Boris Reshevsky*: MATT MATTOX. *Waiter*: Jack Naughton. *Morty Krebs*: WALTER KLAVUN. *Tatiana*: Jean Mattox. *Joyce*: Kelly Leigh.

Kids in the Show: Wana Allison, Marcella Dodge, Barbara Hoyt, Kelly Leigh, Julia Marlowe, Jean Mattox, Carolyn Morris, Elliott Gould, Charles Morrell, Richard Tone, Calvin von Reinhold.

Act 1, Scene 1: An Airport in the Corn Country. Time is the present. *Scene 2*: Hackett & Snow's Office in the Big City. *Scene 3*: Stamford . . . The House That Jack Took. *Scene 4*: The Office.

Act 2, Scene 1: The Auditions. *Scene 2*: Stamford. *Scene 3*: Rehearsals. *Scene 4*: Stamford. *Scene 5*: Irene Lovelle's Apartment! *Scene 6*: Stamford[14].

Act 3, Scene 1: That Hotel Room in New Haven. *Scene 2*: Stamford. *Scene 3*: Back to That Hotel Room in New Haven. *Scene 4*: Idlewild Airport in New York.

ACT 1[15]

Scene 2

"Chief of Love"
(recording)

Scene 4

"Try to Love Me"
(V. Blaine)

"It's Doom"
(J. Desmond)

"The Husking Bee"
(J. Desmond, D. Wayne)

ACT 2

Scene 1

"It's the Second Time You Meet That Matters"
(J. Desmond)

("Let the Lower Lights Be Burning")
(D. Wayne, J. Cowan)

"Chief of Love"
(V. Blaine)

Scene 3

"Say, Darling"
(J. Desmond)

"The Carnival Song"
(D. Wayne, V. Blaine, S. Condos)

(Boris' Dance)
(M. Mattox)

ACT 3

Scene 3

"Try to Love Me" (reprise)
(J. Desmond)

"Dance Only With Me"
(V. Blaine, M. Gregg)

"Something's Always Happening on the River"
(D. Wayne, J. Desmond, V. Blaine, M. Gregg, others)

1958.09

TROUBLE IN TAHITI

A Revival of the One Act Opera in 7 Scenes[16]. Libretto and music by Leonard Bernstein. (Presented on a double-bill with the opera "Tale For A Deaf Ear" by Mark Bucci) (Staged by Michael Pollock. Designed by Andreas Nomikos. Conducted by Leonard Bernstein. Produced by the New York City Opera. Opened 6 April 1958 at the New York City Center and closed 18 April 1958 after 3 performances in repertory.

CAST: *Dinah*: BEVERLY WOLFF. *Sam*: DAVID ATKINSON. *Trio*: Naomi Collier, William Metcalf, Stanley Kolk.

1958.10

JOYCE GRENFELL: MONOLOGUES AND SONGS

A Musical Revue[17] in Two Acts, 20 Scenes. (Sketches and lyrics) Written by Joyce Grenfell. Music by Richard Addinsell. Miss Grenfell's Dresses by Victor Stiebel. At the piano, George Bauer. Produced by Roger L. Stevens and Laurier Lister. Opened 7 April 1958 at the Lyceum Theatre and closed 26 April 1958 after 24 performances.

CAST: JOYCE GRENFELL.

ACT 1

Scene 1

"Opening Numbers"

Scene 2

Wibberly

Scene 3

Songs of Many Lands

Scene 4

Writers of Children's Books

[13]Originally produced in New York 31 March 1943 at the St. James Theatre for 2212 performances. For Synopsis of Scenes and Musical Numbers, see original 1943 production.
[14]Act 2, Scene 6 dropped after opening.
[15]Vocalists not identified in program. List below prepared from production typescript and cast recording.

[16]Originally produced in New York as part of a triple bill ALL IN ONE 19 April 1955 at the Playhouse for 49 performances. For Synopsis of Scenes, see original 1955 production.
[17]Billed as an All New Program. Miss Grenfell appeared previously on Broadway in the revue JOYCE GRENFELL REQUESTS THE PLEASURE 10 October 1955 at the Bijou Theatre for 65 performances.

Scene 5

Piano Interlude: "Bess, You Is My Woman Now," and "There's a Boat Dat's Leavin' Soon for New York" (from PORGY AND BESS)
G. Bauer
(*Music by* George Gershwin.)

Scene 6

Artist's Room

Scene 7

"Picture Postcard"

Scene 8

Boat Train

Scene 9

"Joyful Noise"
(*Music by* Donald Swann.)

ACT 2

Scene 1

"The Woman on the Bus"

Scene 2

Friend to Tea

Scene 3

Songs My Mother Taught Me
(*Arranged by* Viola Tunnard) selected from the following: "Hand Me Down My Bonnet," "The Yellow Rose of Texas," "Since Bacon Has Gone Up," "All Night," "Sit Down Sister," "I'll Lend You My Horse," "I'm Gwine Away," "Old Joe Clark," "Step Light Lady," "All the Pretty Little Horses"

Scene 4

"Committee"

Scene 5

"Three Brothers"

Scene 6

Shirl's Girl Friend: The Giant Wheel

Scene 7

Piano Interlude: "Do It Again" and "I've Got Rhythm"
G. Bauer
(*Music by* George Gershwin.)

Scene 8

A Thought for Today

Scene 9

"Time"

Scene 10

Nursery School: Free Activity Period

Scene 11

"It's Almost Tomorrow"

1958.11 LOST IN THE STARS

A Revival of the Musical Tragedy in Two Acts, 20 Scenes[18]. Words (book, lyrics) by Maxwell Anderson. Based on the novel "Cry, the Beloved Country" by Alan Paton. Music by Kurt Weill. Entire production conceived and staged by Jose Quintero. Scenery and costumes by Andreas Nomikos. Lighting by Lee Watson. Conductor, Julius Rudel. Chorus master, Gino Smart. (Musical arrangements and orchestrations by Kurt Weill.) Produced by the New York City Opera Company. Opened 9 April 1958 at the New York City Center and closed 11 May 1958 after 14 performances in repertory.

CAST (in order of appearance): *Leader*: LEE CHARLES. *Answerer*: Robert Atherton. *Nita*: Patti Austin. *Grace Kumalo*: Rosetta LeNoire. *Stephen Kumalo*: LAWRENCE WINTERS. *Station Master*: Robert Ruddy. *The Young Man*: Alexander Yancy, Jr. *The Young Woman*: Mary Louise. *James Jarvis*: NICHOLAS JOY. *Edward Jarvis*: Chris Snell. *Arthur Jarvis*: John Irving. *John Kumalo*: FREDERICK O'NEIL. *Paulus*: Emory Richardson. *William*: Lawson Bates. *Alex*: Frank Riley, Jr. *Foreman*: John Dennison. *Mrs. M'Kize*: Eva Jessye. *Hlabeni*: Garwood Perkins. *Eland*: Conrad Bain. *Linda*: OLGA JAMES. *Johannes Pafuri*: Godfrey Cambridge. *Matthew Kumalo*: DOUGLAS TURNER. *Absalom Kumalo*: LOUIS GOSSETT. *Rose*: Alyce Webb. *The Other Girl*: Claretta Fabray. *Irina*: SHIRLEY CARTER. *Servant*: Laurence Watson. *Policeman*: William Zakariasen. *White Woman*: Naomi Collier. *White Man*: John Dennison. *Burton*: Richard Bowler. *The Judge*: Neil Fitzgerald. *Ensemble*: New York City Opera Chorus.

1958.12 THE NEXT PRESIDENT

A Musical Salmagundi (Revue) in Two Acts, 13 Scenes. Staged by Frank B. Nichols. Entire production designed by Lee Watson. Produced by Frank B. Nichols. Opened 9 April 1958 at the Bijou Theater and closed 19 April 1958 after 13 performances.

CAST: MORT SAHL (Monologuist, Political Satirist), THE JIMMY GIUFFRE 3 (Jimmy Giuffre, Bob Brookmeyer, Jim Hall), THE FOLK SINGERS (David Allen, Erik Darling, Robin Howard, Dylan Todd, Mary Allin Travers, Donald Vogel, Stan Watt, Caroly Wilcox), ANNELIESE WIDMAN.

ACT 1

THE STATUS QUO

Scene 1

"The Chorus of Collective Conscience"
The Folk Singers

Scene 2

"Cry Holy"
The Folk Singers

Scene 3

A Night-to-Night Report of the News with Complete Flexibility as to Foreign Policy
M. Sahl

Scene 4

"The Train and the River"
The Jimmy Giuffre 3
(*Music by* Jimmy Giuffre.)

Scene 5

"Gotta Dance"
A. Widman
(*Music by* Jimmy Giuffre.)

Scene 6

"Deep Blue Sea"
The Folk Singers

Scene 7

Mort Sahl

ACT 2

A BRAND NEW ATTITUDE WITH THE SAME OLD PREJUDICES

Scene 1

"He's Gone Away"
The Folk Singers, featuring R. Howard, D. Todd

Scene 2

"The Green Country"
The Jimmy Giuffre 3
(*Music by* Jimmy Giuffre.)

Scene 3

"Animation"
A. Widman
(*Music by* Marvin Fisher. *Lyrics by* Joe McCarthy, Jr.)

Scene 4

Mort Sahl

Scene 5

"Cloudy Morning"
D. Allen

Scene 6

Press Conference
M. Sahl, The Folk Singers

[18]Originally produced in New York 30 October 1949 at the Music Box Theatre for 281 performances. For Synopsis of Scenes and Musical Numbers, see original 1949 production.

1958.13

REGINA

A Revival of the Musical Drama (Opera) in Three Acts, Prologue and 4 Scenes[19]. Written and composed by Marc Blitzstein. Based on the play "The Little Foxes" by Lillian Hellman. Staged by Herman Shumlin. Conducted by Samuel Krachmalnick. Scenery by Howard Bay. Costumes designed by Aline Bernstein. Choreography by Robert Joffrey. (Orchestrations by Marc Blitzstein.) Produced by the New York City Opera Company. Opened 17 April 1958 at the New York City Center and closed 2 May 1958 after 3 performances in repertory.

CAST (in order of appearance): *Addie*, Cook: CAROL BRICE. *Cal*, Butler: ANDREW FRIERSON. *Alexandra Giddens*, Regina's Daughter: HELEN STRINE. *Birdie Hubbard*, Oscar's Wife: ELISABETH CARRON. *Oscar Hubbard*, Regina's Brother: EMILE RENAN. *Leo Hubbard*, Oscar's Son: LOREN DRISCOLL. *Regina Giddens*: BRENDA LEWIS. *William Marshall*: ERNEST McCHESNEY. *Benjamin Hubbard*, Regina's Brother: GEORGE S. IRVING. *Horace Giddens*, Regina's Husband: JOSHUA HECHT. *Manders*: Robert Ruddy. *Dancers*: Gloria Gustafson, Marie Paquet, Francoise Martinet, Gerald Arpino, Nels Jorgensen, Vicente Nebreda. *Servants, Townspeople, Field Workers*: New York City Opera Chorus.

[19]Originally produced in New York 31 October 1949 at the 46th Street Theatre for 56 performances. For Synopsis of Scenes and Musical Numbers, see original 1949 production. For this revival, an intermission was added between Act 1, Scenes 1 and 2. The Jazz Band was totally eliminated.

1958–1959 SEASON

Gwen Verdon and Richard Kiley in REDHEAD (Photo: Vandamm Studio)
Billy Rose Theatre Collection, New York Public Library for the Performing Arts

1958–1959 SEASON

1958.14
GOLDILOCKS

A Musical Comedy in Two Acts, 11 Scenes. Book by Walter and Jean Kerr. Music by Leroy Anderson. Lyrics by Jean Ford, Walter and Jean Kerr. Dances and musical numbers staged by Agnes de Mille. Directed by Walter Kerr. Settings by Peter Larkin. Costumes by Castillo. Lighting by Feder. Musical director, Lehman Engel. Orchestrations by Leroy Anderson and Philip J. Lang. Dance music arranged by Laurence Rosenthal. Production associate, Joseph I. Levine. Produced by The Producers Theatre and Robert Whitehead. Opened 11 October 1958 at the Lunt-Fontanne Theatre and closed 28 February 1959 after 161 performances.

CAST (in order of appearance): *Maggie Harris*: ELAINE STRITCH. *Clown*: Del Anderson. *George Randolph Brown*: RUSSEL NYPE. *Max Grady*: DON AMECHE. *Lois Lee*: PAT STANLEY. *Pete*: NATHANIEL FREY. *Andy*: Richard Armbruster. *Max's Assistants*: Gene Varrone, Sam Greene. *J.C.*: Martin Wolfson. *Bessie*: MARGARET HAMILTON. *Deputies*: Del Anderson, Beau Tilden. *Chauffeur*: Samye Van.

Singers: Jane Carlyle, Jeanne Grant, Joanne Lavalle, Sadie McCollum, Rita Noble, Suzanne Stahl, Richard Armsbruster, Del Anderson, John Carter, Sam Greene, Ben Parrish, Rufus Smith, Gene Varrone. *Dancers*: Patricia Birsh (Birch), Lynne Broadbent, Judith Chazin, Bunty Kelley, Margaret Lithander, Imelda de Martin, Carolyn Morris, Ilona Murai, Patti Nestor, Evelyn Taylor, Diana Turner, Kelly Brown, Donald Barton, Michael Fesco, Loren Hightower, George Jack, Ronnie Landry, David Nillo, Paul Olson, Peter Saul, Ron Stratton.

Act 1, Scene 1: Onstage, New York City, 1913. (Finale of "Lazy Moon.") *Scene 2*: Maggie's Dressing Room. Immediately following. *Scene 3*: Max's Lot. Next morning. *Scene 4*: Outside Max's Lot. That evening. *Scene 5*: Max's Lot. Four days later. *Scene 6*: The Fat Cat Roof Garden. Later that night. *Scene 7*: Huckleberry Island. Several days later.

Act 2, Scene 1: A Rest Home on the Mainland. Two days later. *Scene 2*: Bessie's Barn, up the Hudson. That afternoon. *Scene 3*: Ballroom, George's Town House. *Scene 4*: Egypt on the Hudson. Next morning.

ACT 1
Scene 1
"Lazy Moon"
Company
Scene 2
"Give the Little Lady"
E. Stritch, Company
"Save a Kiss"
R. Nype, E. Stritch
Scene 4
"No One'll Ever Love You"
E. Stritch, D. Ameche
Scene 5
"Who's Been Sitting in My Chair?"
E. Stritch
Dance
D. Barton, E. Stritch
"There Never Was a Woman"
D. Ameche
Scene 6
"The Pussy Foot"
P. Stanley, Company
Tom Cat: K. Brown. *Brunette*: I. Murai. *Blonde*: L. Broadbent.
Scene 7
Pirate Orgy[1]
Company
ACT 2
Scene 1
"Lady in Waiting"
P. Stanley, R. Nype
Dance
P. Stanley, K. Brown, E. Taylor, Company
"The Beast in You"
E. Stritch
"Shall I Take My Heart and Go?"
R. Nype
Scene 2
"Bad Companions"
N. Frey, M. Hamilton, R. Armbruster, G. Varrone
"I Can't Be in Love"
D. Ameche
Scene 3
"I Never Know When to Say When"
E. Stritch
"The Town House Maxixe" Dance
P. Stanley, D. Nillo, Company
"Two Years in the Making"
N. Frey, M. Hamilton, Singers
Scene 4
"Heart of Stone" (Pyramid Dance)
I. Murai, Company

1958.15
DIE FLEDERMAUS

A Revival of the Operetta in Three Acts[2]. (Original Libretto by Carl Haffner and Richard Genée. Lyrics by Richard Genée. Based on the comedy "Le Réveillon" by Henri Meilhac and Ludovic Halévy). English libretto by Ruth and Thomas Martin. Music by Johann Strauss. Stage director, Barbara Owens. Conducted by Seymour Lipkin. Produced by the New York City Opera. Opened 19 October 1958 at the New York City Center and closed 9 November 1958 after 3 performances in repertory.

CAST: *Rosalinda*: BEVERLY BOWER. *Eisenstein*: ERNEST McCHESNEY. *Adele*: MONTE AMUNDSEN. *Sally*: Jennie Andrea. *Alfred*: JON CRAIN. *Prince Orlofsky*: LOREN DRISCOLL. *Falke*: CHESTER LUDGIN. *Frank*: Paul Ukena. *Frosch*: Coley Worth. *Blind*: Grant Williams. *Solo Dancers*: Dianne Consoer, Jonathan Watts. *Ensemble*: New York City Opera Chorus.

1958.16
THE MERRY WIDOW

A Revival of the Operetta in Three Acts[3]. Music by Franz Lehár. Original German libretto (Die Lustige Witwe) by Victor Léon and Leo Stein after "L'Attaché d'Ambassade." English libretto by Adrian Ross. Staged by Michael Pollock. Conducted by Julius Rudel. Produced by the New York City Opera. Opened 31 October 1958 at the New York City Center and closed 16 November 1958 after 3 performances in repertory.

CAST: *Sonia*: BEVERLY SILLS. *Prince Danilo*: JOHN REARDON. *Baron Popoff*: JACK HARROLD. *Natalie*: Helena Scott. *De Jolidon*: John Alexander. *Marquis de Cascada*: Arnold Voketaitis. *St. Brioche*: Chester Ludgin. *Admiral Khadja*: Arthur Newman. *Mme. Khadja*: Helen Baisley. *General Novikovich*: Keith Kaldenberg. *Mme. Novikovich*: Barbara Lockard. *Nish*: Coley Worth. *Lo-Lo*: Helen Baisley. *Solo Dancers*: Françoise Martinet, Beatrice Tompkins, Gerald Arpino. *Ensemble*: New York City Opera Chorus.

1958.17
MARIA GOLOVIN

A Musical Drama (Opera) in Three Acts, 7 Scenes[4]. Libretto and music by Gian Carlo Menotti. Staged by Gian Carlo Menotti. Supervised by Samuel Chotzinoff. Orchestra conducted by Herbert Grossman. Production co-ordinator, Louis B. Ames. Scenery by Rouben Ter-Arutunian. Lighting by Charles Elson. Costumes supervised by Helene Pons. Produced by David Merrick and the National Broadcasting Company in association with Byron Goldman. Opened 5 November 1958 at the Martin Beck Theatre and closed 8 November 1958 after 5 performances.

CAST: *Donato*: RICHARD CROSS. *Agata*: RUTH KOBART. *The Mother*: PATRICIA NEWAY. *Dr. Zuckertanz*: NORMAN KELLEY. *Maria Golovin*: FRANCA DUVAL. *Trottolo*: Lorenzo Muti. *The Prisoner*: WILLIAM CHAPMAN. *Servant*: John Kuhn.

[1]Programs from the first week of the Broadway run list "Huckleberry Island Ballet" in lieu of Pirate Orgy.

[2]First English language production in New York 16 March 1885 at the Casino Theatre for 42 performances. First New York production of this adaptation 20 December 1950 at the Metropolitan Opera House. For Synopsis of Scenes and Musical Numbers, see May 1954 revival.
[3]Originally produced in New York 21 October 1907 at the New Amsterdam Theatre for 416 performances. For Synopsis of Scenes and Musical Numbers, see original 1907 production.
[4]Produced as an opera; no individual musical numbers listed in program.

The entirze action takes place at Donato's villa near a frontier in a European country. A few years after a recent war.

Act 1, Scene 1: A Living Room in the Villa. Early spring. *Scene 2*: The same. A month later.

Act 2, Scene 1: The Terrace of the Villa. Late afternoon, midsummer. *Scene 2*: The same. That night.

Act 3, Scene 1: The Living Room. Afternoon, early fall. *Scene 2*: The same. In the evening, a week later. *Scene 3*: The same. A few hours later.

1958.18 LA PLUME DE MA TANTE

A Musical (Revue) in Two Acts, 32 Scenes. Written, devised and directed by Robert Dhery. Music and arrangements by Gerard Calvi. English lyrics by Ross Parker. French lyrics by Francis Blanche. Choreography by Colette Brosset. Staged by Alec Shanks. Musical direction by Gershon Kingsley. Scenery supervised and lighted by Charles Elson. Orchestration by Gerard Calvi, Billy Ternent and Ronnie Monro. Overture curtain by Vertes. Produced by David Merrick and Joseph Kipness, by arrangement with Jack Hylton. Opened 11 November 1958 at the Royale Theatre and closed 17 December 1960 1960 after 835 performances.

CAST: ROBERT DHERY, COLETTE BROSSET, PIERRE OLAF, JACQUES LEGRAS, ROGER CACCIA, JEAN LEFEVRE, ROSS PARKER, NICOLE PARENT, PAMELA AUSTIN, HENRI PENNEC, YVONNE CONSTANT, MICHAEL KENT, MICHEL MODO, GENEVIEVE COULOMBEL, Coka Brossecola, Genevieve Zanetti, Francoise Dally, Brigitte Peynaud, Anna Stroppini, Claude Perrin, Mary Reynolds, Jill Hougham, Nadine Gorbatcheff. *Musicians*: Stan Krell (drums), Ernie Mauro (clarinet), Milt Kraus (piano), Aaron Juvelier (bass).

ACT 1

Scene 1
The Company is introduced by Robert Dhery.

Scene 2
Speakerine
C. Brosset

Scene 3
Amsterdam
J. Lefevre

Scene 4
Mobile Squad (Bicycles)
The Pride of the Force: J. Legras, P. Olaf, M. Modo, H. Pennec.

Scene 5
"Rider to the Sea"
M. Kent

Scene 6
"Le Bal Chez Madame Mortemouille"
(*Designed by* Dignimont)
Madame de Mortemouille: P. Austin. *The Major Domo*: M. Kent. *Général Grosfut*: R. Parker. *The Attaché*: H. Pennec. *The Maitre d'Hotel*: R. Caccia. *The Spahi*:. M. Modo. *Johnny Walker*: J. Lefevre. *Master Percy Smith*: P. Olaf. *Mr. Spratts*: J. Legras. *Miss Innocent*: M. Reynolds. *Mademoiselle Colette*: C. Brosset. *Monsieur Robert*: R. Dhery.

Scene 7
Husbands Beware! (includes "Dance of the Wardrobes")
The Wife: Y. Constant. *The Lover*: P. Olaf. *The Elevator Attendant*: H. Pennec. *The Husband*: R. Parker.

Scene 8
Light Soprano ("The Song of the Balloon")
(*Designed by* Erté)P. Austin

Scene 9
In a Small Cafe
(*Designed by* Lilla De Nobili)
The Waiter: R. Dhery. *The Late Diner*: R. Parker.

Scene 10
"Ballet Classique"
(*Designed by* Erté)
The Spirit of the Night: C. Brossecola. *The Prince*: P. Olaf. *The Princess*: G. Coulombel. *The Witch Girl*: N. Parent. With the Entire Corps de Ballet.

Scene 12
"Song of the Swing"
(*Designed by* Alec Shanks.)
Véronique: P. Austin. *Florestan*: M. Kent.

Scene 13
"Precision" (Kickline routine)
The Royal Croquettes

Scene 14
Courting Time
(*Designed by* Erté)
The Father: R. Parker. *The Mother*: R. Caccia. *Their Daughter*: B. Peynaud. *Her Lover*: P. Olaf. *The Explorer*: M. Modo. *The Gendarme*: J. Legras.

Scene 15
"Femmes Fatales" (Dance)
(*Dresses designed by* Jacques Estérel)
Les Femmes: N. Parent, J. Hougham, Y. Constant, M. Reynolds, B. Peynaud, C. Brosset.

Scene 16
On the Beach
R. Caccia, J. Legras, J. Lefevre, R. Parker, G. Zanetti, A. Stroppini

Scene 17
Queen of the Strip-Tease ("Ne Comptez Pas Sur Moi. .Pour Me Montrer Toute Nue")
C. Brosset
("La Plume de Ma Tante")
Girls

Scene 18
Freres Jacques (Bell-ringing Monks)
P. Olaf, J. Legras, R. Caccia, M. Modo, R. Parker

ACT 2

Scene 1
"Hommage Musical"
(*Designed by* Henri Pennec.)R. Dhery, His Festival Ensemble
Guest Artistes: The Ladies Athenian Choir.

Scene 2
Domingo Blazes and his Latin-American Orchestra

Scene 3
In an Indian Temple (Dance)
Temple Girls: The Dugudu Dancers. *The High Priestess*: Y. Constant.

Scene 4
This Other Eden (includes "Like a Little Pussy Cat")
Eve: C. Brosset. *Adam*: R. Dhery. *The Serpent*: J. Legras.

Scene 5
Men at Work
The Workmen: J. Lefevre, H. Pennec.

Scene 6
"Administration"
(*Designed by* Lilla De Nobili.)
Filing Clerks: R. Caccia, J. Legras. *The Secretary*: Y. Constant. *The Boss*: R. Parker.

Scene 7
In the Tuileries Gardens
(*Designed by* Dignimont.)
The Tie Vendor: J. Lefevre. *The Curé*: H. Pennec. *The Bystander*: M. Modo. *The Lovers*: N. Gorbatcheff, Y. Constant. *The Bird Lover*: M. Reynolds. *Agent de Police*: M. Kent. *The Schoolmistress*: P. Austin. *Her Pupils*: G. Coulombel, A. Stroippini, F. Dally, J. Hougham, B. Peynaud, C. Perrin. *Pickpockets*: R. Caccia, J. Legras. *Clowns*: P. Olaf, C. Brosset.

Scene 8
Take-Off
Air Hostess: Y. Constant. *The Passenger*: R. Caccia.

Scene 9
"Ballet Moderne"
The Dancers: G. Coulombel, F. Dally, N. Parent, M. Reynolds. *The Musicians*: S. Krell, E. Mauro, M. Kraus, A. Juvelier.

Scene 10
The Ventriloquist
J. Lefevre

Scene 12
Trapped (Pissotiere)
(*Designed by* Dignimont.)
The Victims: J. Legras, R. Dhery. *A Butcher*: R. Parker. *A Policeman*: H. Pennec. *A Passer-by*: M. Reynolds.

Scene 13
Acrobatie
C. Brosset

Scene 14
Le Finale de Paris
(*Designed by* Erté.)
Entire Company, Entire Corps de Ballet
(Paris is the End!)
("La Plume de Ma Tante"/Striptease/Monks reprise)

1958.19 FLOWER DRUM SONG

A Musical in Two Acts, 14 Scenes. Book by Oscar Hammerstein II and Joseph Fields. Based on the novel "The Flower Drum Song" by C. Y. Lee. Music by Richard Rodgers. Lyrics by Oscar Hammerstein II. Directed by Gene Kelly. Choreography by Carol Haney. Scenic production by Oliver Smith. Costumes by Irene Sharaff. Lighting by Peggy Clark. Orchestrations by Robert Russell Bennett. Musical director, Salvatore Dell'Isola. Dance arrangements by Luther Henderson, Jr. Produced by Richard Rodgers and Oscar Hammerstein II in association with Joseph Fields. Opened 1 December 1958 at the St. James Theatre and closed 7 May 1960 after 600 performances.

CAST (in order of appearance): *Madam Liang*: JUANITA HALL. *Liu Ma*: Rose Quong. *Wang San*: PATRICK ADIARTE. *Wang Ta*: ED KENNEY. *Wang Chi Yang*: KEYE LUKE. *Sammy Fong*: LARRY BLYDEN. *Dr. Li*: Conrad Yama. *Mei Li*: MIYOSHI UMEKI. *Linda Low*: PAT SUZUKI. *Mr. Lung*: Harry Shaw Lowe. *Mr. Huan*: Jon Lee. *Helen Chao*: ARABELLA HONG. *Professor Cheng*: Peter Chan. *Frankie Wing*: Jack Soo. *Head Waiter*: George Yuong. *Night Club Singer*: ANITA ELLIS. *Dr. Lu Fong*: Chao Li. *Madam Fong*: Eileen Nakamura.

Children: Linda Ribuca, Yvonne Ribuca, Susan Lynn Kikuchi, Luis Robert Hernandez. *Dancing Ensemble*: Fumi Akimoto, Paula Chin, Helen Funai, Pat Griffith, Mary Huie, Marion Jim, Betty Kawamura, Baayork Lee, Wonci Lui, Jo Anne Miya, Denise Quan, Vicki Racimo, Shawnee Smith, Maureen Tiongco, Mabel Wing, Yuriko, Jose Ahumada, Victor Duntiere, George Li, David Lober, Robert Lorca, George Minami, David Toguri, George Young.

The action takes place in San Francisco's Chinatown at the present time.

Act 1, Scene 1: The Living Room in the House of Master Wang Chi Yang. *Scene 2*: A Hill overlooking San Francisco Bay. *Scene 3*: The Wang Living Room. *Scene 4*: Wang Chi Yang's Bedroom. *Scene 5*: The Garden of the Wang House. *Scene 6*: Linda's Dressing Room in the Celestial Bar. *Scene 7*: The Celestial Bar.

Act 2, Scene 1: Helen Chao's Room. *Scene 2*: The Wang Living Room. *Scene 3*: Sammy Fong's Penthouse Apartment. *Scene 4*: The Three Family Association. *Scene 5*: Sammy Fong's Penthouse Apartment. *Scene 6*: Grant Avenue, San Francisco's Chinatown. *Scene 7*: The Three Family Association.

ACT 1
Scene 1
"You Are Beautiful"
E. Kenney, J. Hall
"A Hundred Million Miracles"
M. Umeki, C. Yama, K. Luke, J. Hall, R. Quong
Scene 2
"I Enjoy Being a Girl"
P. Suzuki, Dancers
Scene 3
"I Am Going to Like It Here"
M. Umeki
Scene 4
"Like a God"
E. Kenney
Scene 5
"Chop Suey"
J. Hall, P. Adiarte, Ensemble
"Don't Marry Me"
L. Blyden, M. Umeki
"Grant Avenue"
P. Suzuki, Ensemble
Scene 6
"Love Look Away"
A. Hong
Scene 7
"Fan Tan Fannie"
A. Ellis, Girls
"Gliding Through My Memoree"
J. Soo, Girls
Finale: "Grant Avenue" (reprise)
Company

ACT 2
Scene 1
Ballet
Wang Ta: E. Kenney. *Mei Li*: Yuriko. *Linda Low*: J. A. Miya. And Dancers.
"Love Look Away" (reprise)
A. Hong
Scene 2
"The Other Generation"
J. Hall, K. Luke
Scene 3
"Sunday"
P. Suzuki, L. Blyden
Scene 4
"The Other Generation" (reprise)
P. Adiarte, Children
Scene 6
"Wedding Parade"
M. Umeki, Dancers
Scene 7
Finale
Entire Company

1958.20 WHOOP-UP

A Musical Comedy in Two Acts. Book by Cy Feuer, Ernest H. Martin and Dan Cushman. Based on the novel "Stay Away, Joe" by Dan Cushman. Music by Moose Charlap. Lyrics by Norman Gimbel. Settings and lighting by Jo Mielziner. Costumes by Anna Hill Johnstone. Choreography by Onna White. Musical And vocal direction, Stanley Lebowsky. Orchestrations by Philip J. Lang. Dance music arranged by Peter Matz. Directed by Cy Feuer. Produced by Cy Feuer and Ernest H. Martin. Opened 22 December 1958 at the Sam S. Shubert Theatre and closed 7 February 1959 after 56 performances.

CAST (in order of appearance): *Glenda Swenson*: SUSAN JOHNSON. *Jiggs Rock Medicine*: Michael Kermoyan. *Walt Stephenpierre*: Tom Rasking. *Dub Winter Owl*: Jackie Warner. *Bix Winter Owl*: Bobby Shields. *Louis Champlain*: ROMO VINCENT. *Annie Champlain*: SYLVIA SYMS. *Mary Champlain*: JULIENNE MARIE. *Matthew Bearchaser*: Tony Gardell. *Karl Kellenbach*: PAUL FORD. *Clyde Walschmidt*: Wallace Rooney. *George Potter*: DANNY MEEHAN. *Medicine Man*: Tony Gardell. *Joe Champlain*: RALPH YOUNG. *Marlene Standing Rattle*: Ann Barry. *Gran'pere*: P. J. KELLY. *Billie Mae Littlehorse*: ASIA (MERCOOLOVA). *Juke Box Voice*: Bobby Shields. *Mrs. Kellenbach*: Vera Walton. *Baptiste Three Bird*: Paul Michael. *Hotel Proprietor*: Robert Lenn. *Teenager*: Robert Karl. *State Trooper*: Steve Wiland. *Justice of the Peace*: Earl Lippy. *First Stranger*: Edward Becker. *Second Stranger*: Socrates Birsky.

Reservation Residents: Mari Arnell, Ann Barry, Edward Becker, Jeanna Belkin, Socrates Birsky, Tim Brown, Sandra Devlin, Eleanor Dian, Tina Faye, Tony Gardell, Martha Granese, H. F. Green, Salvador Juarez, Robert Karl, Robert Lenn, Earl Lippy, Rae McLean, Michelle Newton, Estelle Parsons, Yolanda Poropat, Tom Raskin, Tony Rosa, Marla Stevens, Ben Vargas, Barbara Webb, Steve Wiland.

The action takes place on or near a United States Indian reservation in northern Montana at the present time.

ACT 1
"Glenda's Place"
S. Johnson, Indinas
"When the Tall Man Talks"
S. Johnson
"Nobody Throw Those Bull"
R. Vincent, Indians
"Rocky Boy Ceremonial" (Chief Rocky Boy)
T. Gardell, Members of the Tribe
"Love Eyes"
R. Young
"Men"
S. Johnson
"Never Before"
J. Marie
"Caress Me, Possess Me Perfume"
B. Shields
"Flattery"
R. Young, S. Johnson

"The Girl in His Arms"
B. Shields
"The Best of What This Country's Got"
D. Meehan

ACT 2
"I Wash My Hands"
R. Young, J. Marie, M. Kermoyan, T. Raskin
"Quarrel-tet"
S. Johnson, R. Young, R. Lenn, T. Raskin
"Sorry for Myself"
S. Syms
"'Til the Big Fat Moon Falls Down"
J. Marie, Asia, Friends
"What I Mean to Say"
D. Meehan
"Montana"
S. Johnson
"She or Her"
R. Young

1958.21 A PARTY WITH BETTY COMDEN AND ADOLPH GREEN

An Intimate Revue in Three Acts, 11 Scenes[5]. Sketches and lyrics by Betty Comden and Adolph Green. (Music by Leonard Bernstein, Morton Gould, Jule Styne, Roger Edens, Andre Previn, Saul Chaplin.) At the Piano, Peter Howard. Decor and lighting by Marvin Ross. Associate producer, Frank Perry. Produced by the Theatre Guild by special arrangement and in association with Town Productions, Inc. as originally presented by JJG Productions under the supervision of Gus Schirmer, Jr. Opened 23 December 1958 at the John Golden Theatre, closing 24 January 1959 after 38 performances; re-opened 16 April 1959 at the John Golden Theatre and closed 23 May 1959 after 44 additional performances. Total performances: 82.

CAST: BETTY COMDEN, ADOLPH GREEN.

ACT 1
THE PERFORMERS
Scene 1
Opening ("I Said Good Morning" from the film IT'S ALWAYS FAIR WEATHER)
(*Music by* Andre Previn.)
Scene 2
The Revuers—Night Club Act
(*Sketches, Music and Lyrics by* The Revuers {Betty Comden, Adolph Green, Judy Holliday, Alvin Hammer, John Frank}.)
1. Movie Ads
2. The Reader's Digest
3. The Screen Writers
4. The Banshee Sisters
5. "The Baroness Bazooka"

ACT 2
THE PERFORMER-WRITERS
Scene 1
ON THE TOWN
(*Music by* Leonard Bernstein.)
1. "New York, New York"
2. "Lonely Town"
3. "Lucky to be Me"
4. "Come Up to My Place"
5. "I Get Carried Away"
Scene 2
BILLION DOLLAR BABY
(*Music by* Morton Gould.)
1. "Bad Timing"
2. "Broadway Blossoms"
Scene 3
GOOD NEWS (Film)
(*Music by* Roger Edens.)
1. "French Lesson"
Scene 4
TWO ON THE AISLE
(*Music by* Jule Styne.)
1. "If You Hadn't But You Did"
2. "Catch Our Act at the Met"
3. "He'll Never Know"

ACT 3
THE WRITER-PERFORMERS
Scene 1
WONDERFUL TOWN
(*Music by* Leonard Bernstein.)
1. "A Hundred Easy Ways to Lose a Man"
2. "Ohio"
3. "Wrong Note Rag"
4. "A Quiet Girl"
5. "It's Love"
Scene 2
PETER PAN
(*Music by* Jule Styne.)
1. "Oh, My Mysterious Lady"
2. "Captain Hook's Waltz"
3. "Never Never Land"
4. "Once Upon a Time and Long Ago"
Scene 3
A Show [BONANZA BOUND]
(*Music by* Saul Chaplin.)
1. "Inspiration"
Scene 4
SAY, DARLING
(*Music by* Jule Styne.)
1. Medley
Scene 5
BELLS ARE RINGING
(*Music by* Jule Styne.)
1. "Just in Time"
2. "The Party's Over"

1959.01 REDHEAD

A Musical Comedy in Two Acts, a Prologue and 16 Scenes. Book by Herbert and Dorothy Fields, Sidney Sheldon and David Shaw. Music by Albert Hague. Lyrics by Dorothy Fields. Production (sets, costumes) designed by Rouben Ter-Arutunian. Lighting by Jean Rosenthal. Orchestrations by Philip J. Lang and Robert Russell Bennett. Musical direction and vocal arrangements by Jay Blackton. Dance music arranged by Roger Adams. Associate choreographer, Donald MacKayle. Directed and choreographed by Bob Fosse. Produced by Robert Fryer and Lawrence Carr. Opened 5 February 1959 at the 46th Street Theatre and closed 19 March 1960 after 455 performances.

CAST (in order of appearance): *Ruth LaRue*: Pat Ferrier. *Maude Simpson*: CYNTHIA LATHAM. *Sarah Simpson*: DORIS RICH. *May*: Joy Nichols. *Tilly*: Pat Ferrier. *Essie Whimple*: GWEN VERDON. *Inspector White*: Ralph Sumpter. *Howard Cavanaugh*: WILLIAM LE MASSENA. *George Poppett*: LEONARD STONE. *Tom Baxter*: RICHARD KILEY. *Alfy*, Stage Doorman: Lee Krieger. *Sir Charles Willingham*: Patrick Horgan. *Tenor*: Bob Dixon. *Inez*, the Blonde: Bette Graham. *Jailer*: Buzz Miller.

Singers: Mame Dennis, Joan Fagan, Lydia Fredericks, Bette Graham, Dee Harless, Janie Janvier, Kelley Stephens, Bob Dixon, Clifford Fearl, John Lankston, Larry Mitchell, Stan Page, Shev Rodgers. *Dancers*: Margery Beddow, Shirley de Burgh, Pat Ferrier, Reby Howells, Patti Karr, Liane Plane, Elaine King, Dean Taliferro, John Aristides, Kevin Carlisle, David Gold, Harvey Hohnecker, Kazimir Kokich, Dale Moreda, Noel Parenti, Alton Ruff.

Prologue: A Theatre Dressing Room.

Act 1, Scene 1: Outside the Simpson Sisters' Waxworks. *Scene 2*: The Interior of the Waxworks. *Scene 3*: Essie's Workshop. *Scene 4*: A Street. *Scene 5*: Stage of the Odeon Theatre. *Scene 6*: Corridor, Backstage. *Scene 7*: Tom's Apartment. *Scene 8*: Outside the

[5]First produced in New York Off-Broadway for a series of Monday night performances 10 November 1958 at the Cherry Lane Theatre.

Museum. *Scene 9*: Backstage of the Odeon Theatre. *Scene 10*: Stage of the Odeon Theatre.

Act 2, Scene 1: Tom's Apartment. *Scene 2*: A Street. *Scene 3*: The Green Dragon Pub. *Scene 4*: The Jail Cell. *Scene 5*: Corridor, Backstage. *Scene 6*: The Museum.

ACT 1
Scene 1
"The Simpson Sisters"
Singers, Dancers
Scene 2
"The Right Finger of My Left Hand"
G. Verdon
Scene 3
"Just For Once"
G. Verdon, R. Kiley, L. Stone
"(I Feel) Merely Marvelous"
G. Verdon
Scene 5
"The Uncle Sam Rag"
L. Stone, Singers, Dancers
"Erbie Fitch's Twitch"
G. Verdon
Scene 6
"Behave Yourself"
G. Verdon, C. Latham, D. Rich, R. Kiley
Scene 7
"Look Who's in Love"
G. Verdon, R. Kiley
Scene 8
"My Girl Is Just Enough Woman for Me"
R. Kiley, Passersby
Scene 9
"Essie's Vision"
G. Verdon, Her Dream People
Scene 10
"Two Faces in the Dark"
G. Verdon, B. Dixon, Singers, Dancers
ACT 2
Scene 1
"I'm Back in Circulation"
R. Kiley
Scene 3
"We Loves Ya, Jimey"
G. Verdon, J. Nichols, P. Ferrier, Ensemble
Scene 4
"Pick-Pocket Tango"
G. Verdon, B. Miller
Scene 5
"Look Who's in Love" (reprise)
R. Kiley
Scene 6
"I'll Try"[6]
G. Verdon, R. Kiley
(The Chase)/Finale
G. Verdon, R. Kiley, Company

1959.02 THE MOST HAPPY FELLA

A Revival of the Musical in Three Acts, 11 Scenes[7]. Book, music and lyrics by Frank Loesser. Based on the play "They Knew What They Wanted" by Sidney Howard. Entire Production directed and supervised by Dania Krupska. Choreography by Dania Krupska, restaged by Arthur Partington. Scenery and lighting by Jo Mielziner. Costumes by Ruth Morley. Art director, Watson Barratt. (Orchestrations by Don Walker.) Musical direction, Abba Bogin. Produced by the New York City Center Light Opera Company (Jean Dalrymple, Director). Opened 10 February 1959 at the New York City Center and closed 22 February 1959 after 16 performances.

CAST (in order of appearance): *The Cashier*: Lee Cass. *Cleo*: LIBI STAIGER. *Rosabella*: PAULA STEWART. *Waitresses*: Jessica Albright, Betty Jenkins, Gloria Kaye, Kitty Malone, Sherry McCutcheon, Sybil Scotford. *The Postman*: Lee Cass. *Tony*: NORMAN ATKINS. *Marie*: MURIEL BIRKHEAD. *Max*: Win Mayo. *Herman*: JACK DE LON. *Clem*: James Schlader. *Jake*: Ken Adams. *Al*: Roy Lazarus. *Joe*: ART LUND. *Giuseppe*: Kenneth Lane. *Pasquale*: Bruce MacKay. *Ciccio*: Michael Davis. *Country Girl*: Jessica Albright. *Country Boy*: Garold Gardner. *Doctor*: Keith Kaldenberg. *Priest*: Fred Conway. *Tessie*: Bernadette Peters. *Gussie*: Johnny Borden. *Train Conductor*: Win Mayo. *Neighbors*: Mary Sue Berry, Gloria Kaye, Barbara Saxby, John Dorrin, Roy Lazarus, George Zima. *Neighbor Ladies*: Thea Bradon, Terry DeLiva, Maggie Task. *Brakeman*: Sheldon Ossosky. *Bus Driver*: Jordan Howard.

All the Neighbors, and All the Neighbors' Neighbors: Lorrie Bentley, Mary Sue Berry, Jan Canada, Terry Deliva, Mary Ann Heitzig, Barbara Saxby, Jeanne Schlegel, Sheila Swenson, Maggie Task, Ken Adams, Fred Conway, Michael Davis, John Dorrin, Jordan Howard, Del Horstmann, Robert Ethridge, Roy Lazarus, Jack McMinn, Win Mayo, Jack McCann, James Schlader, Jessica Albright, Betty Jenkins, Gloria Kaye, Kitty Malone, Sherry McCutcheon, Sybil Scotford, Garold Gardner, Bob LaCrosse, Sheldon Ossosky, Michael Scrittorale, James Senn, George Zima.

1959.03 SAY, DARLING

A Revival of the Comedy about a Musical in Three Acts, 11 Scenes[8]. Book by Richard and Marian Bissell and Abe Burrows. Music by Jule Styne. Lyrics by Betty Comden and Adolph Green. (Scenery) Designed by Oliver Smith. Costumes by Alvin Colt. Lighting by Peggy Clark. Dances by Matt Mattox. Musical director, Colin Romoff. Directed by David Clive. Produced by the New York City Center Light Opera Company (Jean Dalrymple, Director). Opened 25 February 1959 at the New York City Center and closed 8 March 1959 after 16 performances.

CAST (in order of appearance): *Mr. Schneider*: Gordon B. Clarke. *Frankie Jordan*: BETSY VON FURSTENBERG. *Jack Jordan*: ORSON BEAN. *Photographer*: Stephen Franken. *Pilot Roy Peters*: Rober Herrman. *Ted Snow*: ROBERT MORSE. *June*, the Secretary: Kelly Leigh. *Schatzie Harris*: Jack Waldron. *Richard Hackett*: Alexander Clark. *Irene Lovelle*: MINDY CARSON. *Rudy Lorraine*: DAVID ATKINSON. *Charlie Williams*: James Karr. *Maurice*: Brooks Morton. *Arlene McKee*: Janyce Wagner. *Jennifer Stevenson*: Jean Mattox. *Earl Jorgeson*: Elliott Gould. *Cheryl Merrill*: Paula Wayne. *Accompanist*: Joe Richter. *Sammy Miles*: Buddy Ferrard. *Rex Dexter*: Mitchell Gregg. *Boris Reshevsky*: Matt Mattox. *Waiter*: Stephen Franken. *Morty Krebs*: Edward Hunt.

Kids in the Show: Marcella Dodge, Kelly Leigh, Paula Lloyd, Jean Mattox, Janyce Wagner, Elliott Gould, George Martin, Calvin von Reinhold, Eddie Weston. *Sidemen*: Andrew Bagni, Joseph Castka, Tommy Lucas, Ted Flowerman.

1959.04 JUNO

A Musical in Two Acts, a Prologue and 16 Scenes. Book by Joseph Stein. Based on the play "Juno and the Paycock" by Sean O'Casey. Music and lyrics by Marc Blitzstein. Dances and musical numbers staged by Agnes de Mille. Scenery designed by Oliver Smith. Costumes by Irene Sharaff. Lighting by Peggy Clark. Music direction, Robert Emmett Dolan. Orchestrations by Robert Russell Bennett, Marc Blitzstein, Hershy Kay. Associate producer, Lyn Austin. Directed by José Ferrer. Produced by The Playwrights' Company, Oliver Smith and Oliver Rea. Opened 9 March 1959 at the Winter Garden and closed 21 March 1959 after 16 performances.

CAST (in order of appearance): *Mary Boyle*: MONTE AMUNDSEN. *Johnny Boyle*: TOMMY RALL. *Juno Boyle*: SHIRLEY BOOTH. *Jerry Devine*: Loren Driscoll. *Mrs. Madigan*: Jean Stapleton. *Mrs. Brady*: Nancy Andrews. *Mrs. Coyne*: Sada Thompson. *Miss Quinn*: Beulah Garrick. *Charlie Bentham*: Earl Hammond. *Foley*: Arthur Rubin. *Sullivan*: Rico Froehlich. *Michael Brady*: Robert Rue. *Paddy Coyne*: Julian Patrick. *"Captain" Jack Boyle*: MELVYN DOUGLAS. *"Joxer" Daly*: JACK MacGOWRAN. *Molly*: Gemze de Lappe. *"Needle" Nugent*: Liam Lenihan. *I.R.A. Men*: Tom Clancy, Jack Murray. *Mrs. Tancred*: Clarice Blackburn. *Mrs. Dwyer*: Betty Low. *I.R.A. Singer*: Robert Hoyem. *Furniture Removal Men*: George Ritner, Frank Carroll. *Policeman*: Rico Froehlich.

Singers: Anne Fielding, Cleo Fry, Pat Huddleston, Gail Johnston, Barbara Lockard, Pat Ruhl, Diana Sennett, Joanne Spiller, Frank Carroll, Ted Forlow, Rico Froehlich, Robert Hoyem, Jack Murray, Julian Patrick, George Ritner, Robert Rue, James Tushar. *Dancers*: Sharon Enoch, Mickey Gunnersen, Pat Heyes, Rosemary Jourdan, Annabelle Lyon, Marjorie Wittmer, Jenny Workman, Chuck Bennett, Ted Forlow, Curtis Hood, Scott Hunter, Eugene Kelton, James Maher, Enrique Martinez, Howard Parker, Jim Ryan, Glen Tetley.

[6]Dropped during run and for tour.

[7]Originally produced 3 May 1956 at the Imperial Theatre for 678 performances. For Synopsis of Scenes and Musical Numbers, see original 1956 production.

[8]Originally produced 3 April 1958 at the ANTA Theatre for 332 performances. For Synopsis of Scenes and Musical Numbers, see original 1958 production. "My Little Yellow Dress" added to the end of Act 2. Act 3 (formerly 4 Scenes) re-set as one scene in That Hotel Room in New Haven.

The action takes place in Dublin, 1921.

Prologue: The street in front of the Boyle home. Early evening in summer.

Act 1, Scene 1: The Boyle home. *Scene 2*: Another street. *Scene 3*: The street and Foley's bar. *Scene 4*: A park square. *Scene 5*: The Boyle home. *Scene 6*: Another street. *Scene 7*: A square in the city. *Scene 8*: A park square. Evening, a few days later. *Scene 9*: The street.

Act 2, Scene 1: The Boyle home. Evening, a few days later. *Scene 2*: The yard behind the house. *Scene 3*: A street. *Scene 4*: The Boyle home. *Scene 5*: A park square. *Scene 6*: The Boyle home. *Scene 7*: The street and Foley's bar.

ACT 1
Prologue
"We're Alive"
Ensemble
Scene 1
"I Wish It So"
M. Amundsen
"Song of the Ma"
S. Booth
Scene 3
"We Can Be Proud"
A. Rubin, R. Froehlich, R. Rue, J. Patrick
"Daarlin' Man"
M. Douglas, J. MacGowran, Ensemble
Scene 4
"One Kind Word"
L. Driscoll
Scene 5
"Old Sayin's"
S. Booth, M. Douglas
"What Is the Stars?"
M. Douglas, J. MacGowran
"Old Sayin's" (reprise)
S. Booth, M. Douglas
Scene 6
"You Poor Thing"
J. Stapleton, N. Andrews, S. Thompson, B. Garrick
Scene 7
"Dublin Night" (Ballet)
T. Rall, G. de Lappe, Ensemble
(*Ballet Music by* Trude Rittman and Marc Blitzstein.)
Scene 8
"My True Heart"
M. Amundsen, E. Hammond
Scene 9
"On a Day Like This" (Finale Act 1)
S. Booth, M. Douglas, Ensemble
Jig
H. Parker, E. Kelton
Slip Jig
G. Tetley
Shillelagh Dance
C. Hood, E. Martinez, C. Bennett, S. Hunter
Jig
S. Booth, M. Douglas, Ensemble

ACT 2
Scene 1
"Bird Upon the Tree"
S. Booth, M. Amundsen
Scene 2
The Party
(a) "Music in the House"
M. Douglas, Ensemble
(b) "It's Not Irish" (Gramophone)
A. Rubin
(c) "It's Not Irish" (Quartet)
A. Rubin, R. Froehlich, R. Rue, M. Douglas
(d) "The Liffey Waltz"
Ensemble
"Hymn"
R. Hoyem
"Johnny" (Ballet)
T. Rall, G. de Lappe
(*Ballet Music by* Marc Blitzstein.)
Scene 3
"You Poor Thing" (reprise)
J. Stapleton, N. Andrews, S. Thompson, B. Garrick
Scene 5
"For Love"
M. Amundsen
"One Kind Word" (reprise)
L. Driscoll
Scene 6
"Where?"
S. Booth
Scene 7
Finale Act 2
S. Booth, M. Amundsen, M. Douglas, J. MacGowran

1959.05 LUTE SONG

A Revival of the Love Story With Music in Two Acts, 16 Scenes[9]. Book by Sidney Howard and Will Irwin from the famous Chinese play "Pi-Pa-Ki." Music by Raymond Scott. Lyrics by Bernard Hanighen. Directed by John Paul. Choreography by Yeichi Nimura. Musical director, Sylvan Levin. (Orchestrations by Raymond Scott.) Scenery, Costumes and lighting by Robert Edmond Jones. Art director, Watson Barratt. Costume supervisor, Ruth Morley. Produced by the New York City Center Light Opera Company (Jean Dalrymple, Director). Opened 12 March 1959 at the New York City Center and closed 22 March 1959 after 14 performances.

CAST (in order of their appearance): *The Manager, The Honorable Tschang*: CLARENCE DERWENT. *First Propertyman*: Andre Gregory. *Second Propertyman*: Epy Baca. *Tsai-Yong*, the Husband: SHAI-K-OPHIR. *Tsai*, the father: TONIO SELWART. *Madame Tsai*, the Mother: ESTELLE WINWOOD. *Tchao-ou-Niang*, the Wife: DOLLY HAAS. *Prince Nieou*, the Imperial Preceptor: PHILIP BOURNEUF. *Princess Nieou-Chi*, his daughter: LEUEEN MacGRATH. *Si-Tchun*, a Lady in Waiting: Rain Winslow. *Waiting Women*: Maxine Taylor, Margaret Sheehan. *Hand Maiden*: Shizu Moriya. *Chi-Mao-Chiu Players*: Isabel Farrell, Trudi Gasparinetti, Sigrid Geiger, Barbara Monte. *Youen-Kong*, the Steward: JOSEPH DAUBENAS. *Marriage Broker*: Diane De Brett. *A Sweeper of Heaven and Earth*: ASIA. *Imperial Chamberlain*: DONALD SYMINGTON. *Food Commissioner*: Gene Galvin. *First Clerk*: Anthony Edwards. *Second Clerk*: Epy Baca. *First Applicant*: John Darren. *Second Applicant*: Donald Hotton. *Street Beggar*: Mark Fleischman. *Crippled Beggar*: Michael De Marco. *Blind Beggar*: Alan Kirk. *Imperial Guards*: Anthony Edwards, Carl Clark. *Imperial Attendants*: Bob Daley, Michael Fesco, Arnott Mader, Sheldon Ossosky. *The Genie*: DONALD SYMINGTON. *The White Tiger*: ASIA. *The Ape*: Dean Crane. *Phoenix Birds*: Asia, Dean Crane. *Li-Wang*: Ted Van Griethuysen. *Priest of Amida Buddha*: Tom Emlyn Williams. *A Bonze*: Gene Galvin. *Two Lesser Bonzes*: Andre Gregory, Epy Baca. *A Rich Man*: Wesley Owen. *The Lion*: Dean Crane, Dick Colacino. *Ribbon Spinner*: Asia. *Children*: Olivia Johnson, Gloria Kaye, Coco Ramirez, Tina Ramirez. *Palace Guards*: Walter Adams, Peter Deign, Paul Eden, John Pero, Vic Vallaro. *A Secretary*: Epy Baca.

Travellers on the North Road, Beggars, Guards, Attendants, Gods and Othgers: Isabel Farrell, Trudi Gasparinetti, Sigrid Geiger, Olivia Johnson, Gloria Kaye, Barbara Monte, Shizu Moriya, Coco Ramirez, Tina Ramirez, Margaret Sheehan, Maxine Taylor, Walter Adams, Carl Clark, Dick Colacino, Bob Daley, Peter Deign, Michael de Marco, John Darren, Paul Eden, Anthony Edwards, Michael Fesco, Mark Fleischman, Andre Gregory, Donald Hotton, Alan Kirk, Arnott Mader, Sheldon Ossosky, Wesley Owen, John Pero, Vic Vallaro, Ted Van Griethuysen.

1959.06 FIRST IMPRESSIONS

A Musical Comedy in Two Acts, 15 Scenes. Book by Abe Burrows. Based on the novel "Pride and Prejudice" by Jane Austen and the play of the same name by Helen Jerome. Music and lyrics by Robert Goldman, Glenn Paxton and George Weiss. Directed by Abe Burrows. Choreography by Jonathan Lucas. Production (Settings) designed by Peter Larkin. Costumes

[9]Originally produced in New York 6 February 1946 at the Plymouth Theatre for 142 performances. For Synopsis of Scenes and Musical Numbers, see original 1946 production. For this production, the intermission between Acts 1 and 2 has been eliminated; Act 1, Scene 6 and Act 2, Scene 1 have been combined as one scene.

by Alvin Colt. Lighting by Charles Elson. Musical direction by Frederick Dvonch. Orchestrations by Don Walker. Dance arrangements by John Morris. Vocal arrangements and direction by Buster Davis. Produced by George Gilbert and Edward Spector Productions, Inc. (with the assistance of) The Jule Styne Organization. Opened 19 March 1959 at the Alvin Theatre and closed 30 May 1959 after 84 performances.

CAST (in order of appearance): *Mr. Bennet*: Laurie Main. *Mary Bennet*: Lois Bewley. *Mrs. Bennet*: HERMIONE GINGOLD. *Lydia Bennet*: Lynn Ross. *Kitty Bennet*: Lauri Peters. *Jane Bennet*: PHYLLIS NEWMAN. *Maid*: Beverley Jane Welch. *Elizabeth Bennet*: POLLY BERGEN. *Lady Lucas*: Sibyl Bowan. *Charlotte Lucas*: ELLEN HANLEY. *Caroline Bingley*: Marti Stevens. *Charles Bingley*: DONALD MADDEN. *Fitzwilliam Darcy*: FARLEY GRANGER. *Coachmen*: Garrett Lewis, John Starkweather. *Captain Wickham*: JAMES MITCHELL. *Lieutenant Denny*: Bill Carter. *Lieutenant Rockingham*: Stuart Hodes. *Sir William Lucas*: Richard Bengal. *Butler*: Norman Fredericks. *Mr. Stubbs*: Casper Roos. *Williams*: Jay Stern. *Collins*: CHRISTOPHER HEWETT. *Butler at Rosings*: John Starkweather. *Lady Catherine de Bourgh*: MARY FINNEY. *Lady Anne*: Martha Mathes.

Dancers: Arlene Avril, Janise Gardner, Sally Gura, Harriet Leigh, Martha Mathes, Dorothy Jeanne Mattis, Wendy Nickerson, Alvin Beam, Jim Corbett, Stuart Fleming, Richard Gain, Stuart Hodes, Garrett Lewis, John Starkweather. *Singers*: Adrienne Angel, Suzie Baker, Marian Haraldson, Jeannine Masterson, Louise Pearl, Beverley Jane Welch, Stuart Damon, Norman Fredericks, Warren Hays, Casper Roos, Tony Rossi, Jay Stern.

Act 1, Scene 1: Longbourn. Home of the Bennets in Hertfordshire, England, 1813. *Scene 2*: A Road in Meryton. *Scene 3*: The Assembly at Meryton. *Scene 4*: Longbourn. *Scene 5*: Netherfield Hall. *Scene 6*: Longbourn. *Scene 7*: The Garden at Netherfield Hall. *Scene 8*: The Lawn at Netherfield Hall. *Scene 9*: Longbourn.

Act 2, Scene 1: A Church in Kent. *Scene 2*: Rosings. Home of Lady Catherine de Bourgh in Kent. *Scene 3*: A Street in Meryton. *Scene 4*: Longbourn. *Scene 5*: Longbourn. *Scene 6*: Netherfield Hall.

ACT 1[10]
Scene 1
"Five Daughters"
H. Gingold
"I'm Me"
P. Bergen, L. Bewley, L. Ross, L. Peters, P. Newman
Scene 2
"Have You Heard the News?"
H. Gingold, Townspeople
Scene 3
The Assembly Dance
Townspeople, Officers
"A Perfect Evening"
F. Granger, P. Bergen
Scene 4
"As Long as There's a Mother"
H. Gingold, M. Benentt, L. Ross, L. Peters, P. Newman
Scene 5
"Love Will Find Out the Way"
P. Bergen
"Gentlemen Don't Fall Wildly in Love"
F. Granger
Scene 6
"Fragrant Flower"
C. Hewett, P. Bergen
Scene 7
"I Feel Sorry for the Girl"
P. Newman, D. Madden, Ensemble
Dance
L. Bewley, B. Carter, L. Ross, J. Mitchell, L. Peters, S. Hodes
Scene 8
"I Suddenly Find It Agreeable"
P. Bergen, F. Granger
"This Really Isn't Me"
P. Bergen
Scene 9
Finaletto
H. Gingold, L. Bewley, L. Ross, L. Peters, P. Newman

[10]Added during run to the beginning of Act 1, Scene 5:
"Jane"
D. Madden, F. Granger

ACT 2
Scene 1
"Wasn't It a Simply Lovely Wedding?"
P. Bergen, H. Gingold, E. Hanley, C. Hewett, Ensemble
Scene 2
"A House in Town"
H. Gingold
"The Heart Has Won the Game"
F. Granger
"I'm Me" (reprise)
P. Bergen
Scene 3
Dance
J. Mitchell, L. Ross, Officers
Scene 5
"Let's Fetch the Carriage"
P. Bergen, H. Gingold
Scene 6
"The Heart Has Won the Game" (reprise)
F. Granger, P. Bergen

1959.07 MARIA GOLOVIN

A Revival of the Musical Drama (Opera) in Three Acts, 7 Scenes[11]. Libretto and music by Gian Carlo Menotti. Staged by Kirk Browning. Conducted by Herbert Grossman. Chorus master, Gino Smart. Scenery by Rouben Ter-Arutunian. Lighting by Lee Watson. Costumes by Ruth Morley. Produced by the New York City Opera Company. Opened 30 March 1959 at the New York City Center and closed 23 April 1959 after 2 performances in repertory.

CAST (in order of appearance): *Donato*: RICHARD CROSS. *Agata*: REGINA SARFATY. *The Mother*: PATRICIA NEWAY. *Dr. Zuckertanz*: NORMAN KELLEY. *Maria Golovin*: ILONA KOMBRINK. *Trottolo*: Craig Sechler. *The Prisoner*: CHESTER LUDGIN.

1959.08 STREET SCENE

A Revival of the American Opera (Dramatic Musical) in Two Acts, 3 Scenes[12]. Book by Elmer Rice from his play of the same name. Music by Kurt Weill. Lyrics by Langston Hughes. Staged by Herbert Machiz. Conducted by Samuel Krachmalnick. Scenery and costumes by Paul Sylbert. Children's number supervised by Robert Joffrey. Chorus master, Gino Smart. (Orchestrations by Kurt Weill.) Produced by the New York City Opera Company. Opened 2 April 1959 at the New York City Center and closed 29 April 1959 after 7 performances in repertory.

CAST (in order of appearance): *Abraham Kaplan*: Howard Fried. *Greta Fiorentino*: Dolores Mari, Jacquelynne Moody (alt.). *Carl Olsen*: Arnold Voketaitis. *Emma Jones*: RUTH KOBART. *Olga Olsen*: Beatrice Krebs. *Shirley Kaplan*: Florence Anglin. *Mrs. Davis*: Marie Louise. *Henry Davis*: Andrew Frierson. *Willie Maurrant*: Michael Mann. *Anna Maurrant*: WILMA SPENCE, Elisabeth Carron (alt.). *Sam Kaplan*: DAVID POLERI, Frank Poretta (alt.). *Daniel Buchanan*: Keith Kaldenberg. *Frank Maurrant*: WILLIAM CHAPMAN. *George Jones*: Arthur Newman. *Steve Sankey*: Arthur Storch, David Frank (alt.). *Lippo Fiorentino*: JACK DE LON. *Jennie Hildebrand*: Nancy Dussault. *Second Graduate*: Fiddle Viracola. *Third Graduate*: Jennie Andrea. *Mrs. Hildebrand*: Elizabeth Mannion. *Charlie Hildebrand*: Richard Clemence. *Mary Hildebrand*: Lynn Taussig. *Grace Davis*: Sharon Williams. *Rose Maurrant*: HELENA SCOTT, Joy Clements (alt.). *Harry Easter*: Scott Merrill. *Mae Jones*: Sondra Lee. *Dick McGann*: Richard Tone. *Vincent Jones*: Albert Lewis. *Dr. John Wilson*: John Macurdy. *Officer Harry Murphy*: Dan Merriman. *City Marshall James Henry*: George Del Monte. *Fred Cullen*: William Zachariasen, William Saxon (alt.). *First Nursemaid*: Mary LeSawyer. *Second Nursemaid*: Greta Wolff.

Policemen, Milkman, Old Clothes Man, Music Pupil, Interne, Ambulance Driver, Married Couple, Passersby, Neighbors, Children, etc.: New York City Opera Chorus.

[11]Originally produced in New York 5 November 1958 at the Martin Beck Theatre for 5 performances. For Synopsis of Scenes, see original 1958 production. Performed as an opera; no individual musical numbers listed in program.

[12]Originally produced in New York 9 January 1947 at the Adelphi Theatre for 148 performances. For Synopsis of Scenes and Musical Numbers, see original 1947 production.

1959.09

THE DEVIL AND DANIEL WEBSTER

A Revival of the Musical Folk Play (Opera) in One Act[13]. Book and lyrics by Stephen Vincent Benét. Adapted from his own short story of the Faust legend. Music by Douglas Moore. Staged by John Houseman. Conductor, Max Goberman. Scenery and costumes by Rouben Ter-Arutunian. Choreography by Robert Joffrey. Produced by the New York City Opera. Opened 5 April 1959 at the New York City Center amd closed 26 (matinee) April 1959 after 3 performances in repertory. (Preceded by the opera "The Scarf," Music by Lee Hoiby, Libretto by Harry Duncan.)

CAST (in order of appearance): *Jabez Stone*: Joshua Hecht. *Mary Stone*: ADELAIDE BISHOP. *Daniel Webster*: WALTER CASSEL. *A Fiddler*: Keith Kaldenberg. *Mr. Scratch*: NORMAN KELLEY. *Justice Hathorne*: Emile Renan. *Clerk of the Court*: Arthur Newman.

Jury of the Dead: *Walter Butler*: Chester Ludgin. *Blackbeard Teach*: George Del Monte. *King Philip*: Arnold Voketaitis. *Simon Girty*: Grant Williams. *Others*: Jack De Lon, Howard Fried, Andrew Frierson, Paul Huddleston, John Macurdy, Dan Merriman, William Nahr, Harry Theard.

1959.10

REGINA

A Revival of the Musical Drama (Opera) in Three Acts, Prologue and 4 Scenes[14]. Written and composed by Marc Blitzstein. Based on the play "The Little Foxes" by Lillian Hellman. Staged by Herman Shumlin. Conducted by Samuel Krachmalnick. Scenery by Howard Bay. Costumes designed by Aline Bernstein. Choreography by Robert Joffrey. (Orchestrations by Marc Blitzstein.) Produced by the New York City Opera Company. Opened 19 April 1959 at the New York City Center and closed 1 May 1959 after 2 performances in repertory.

CAST (in order of appearance): *Addie*, Cook: CAROL BRICE. *Cal*, Butler: ANDREW FRIERSON. *Alexandra Giddens*, Regina's Daughter: MARGOT MOSER. *Birdie Hubbard*, Oscar's Wife: ELISABETH CARRON. *Oscar Hubbard*, Regina's Brother: EMILE RENAN. *Leo Hubbard*, Oscar's Son: LOREN DRISCOLL. *Regina Giddens*: BRENDA LEWIS. *William Marshall*: ERNEST McCHESNEY. *Benjamin Hubbard*, Regina's Brother: GEORGE IRVING. *Horace Giddens*, Regina's Husband: JOSHUA HECHT. *Manders*: Edson Hoel. *Servants, Townspeople, Field Workers*: New York City Opera Chorus.

1959.11

DESTRY RIDES AGAIN

A Musical in Two Acts, 12 Scenes. Book by Leonard Gershe. Based on the story (novel of the same name) by Max Brand. Music and lyrics by Harold Rome. (Settings) Designed by Oliver Smith. Costumes by Alvin Colt. Lighting by Jean Rosenthal. Musical direction and vocal arrangements by Lehman Engel. Orchestrations by Philip J. Lang. Dance music arranged by Genevieve Pitot. Entire production directed and choreographed by Michael Kidd. Produced by David Merrick in association with Max Brown. Opened 23 April 1959 at the Imperial Theatre and closed 18 June 1960 after 473 performances.

CAST (in order of appearance): *Prologue*: Don Crabtree, David London, Lanier Davis, Nolan Van Way. *Bartender*: Ray Mason. *Frenchy*: DOLORES GRAY. *Wash*: JACK PRINCE. *Sheriff Keogh*: Oran Osburn. *Kent's Gang (3)*: *Gyp Watson*: MARC BREAUX. *Bugs Watson*: SWEN SWENSON. *Rockwell*: GEORGE REEDER. *Mayor Slade*: DON McHENRY. *Claggett*: Don Crabtree. *Kent*: SCOTT BRADY. *Chloe*: LIBI STAIGER. *Rose Lovejoy*: Elizabeth Watts. *Jack Tyndall*: Nolan Van Way. *Destry*: ANDY GRIFFITH. *Stage Driver*: Chad Block. *Ming Li*: Reiko Sato. *Mrs. Claggett*: May Muth. *Bailey*: Ray Mason. *Clara*: ROSETTA LE NOIRE. *Dimples*: Sharon Shore.

Rose Lovejoy Girls: Lynne Broadbent, Joan Broderick, Shelah Hackett, Reiko Sato, Sharon Shore, Carol Stevens. *Frenchy's Girls*: Shelley Chaplan, Lillian D'Honau, Maureen Hopkins, Betty Jenkins, Jillana, Andrina Miller, Shirley Nelson, Adriane Rogers, Carol Warner. *Cowboys*: Jack Beaber, Chad Block, Mel Davidson, Al Lanti, Ken Malone, Frank Pietri, John Ray, Larry Roquemore, Merritt Thompson. *Townspeople*: Maria Graziano, Betty Kent, Sheila Mathews, May Muth, Don Crabtree, Lanier Davis, Ralph Farnworth, David London, Ray Mason, Oran Osburn, Nolan Van Way.

Act 1, Scene 1: The Last Chance Saloon in the western town of Bottleneck, just before the turn of the century. *Scene 2*: The Last Chance Saloon. *Scene 3*: A Street. *Scene 4*: A Corral. *Scene 5*: French's House. *Scene 6*: Paradise Alley. *Scene 7*: A Road in Bottleneck. *Scene 8*: The Last Chance Saloon.

Act 2, Scene 1: Outside the Jailhouse. *Scene 2*: Frenchy's House. *Scene 3*: The Sheriff's Office. *Scene 4*: The Last Chance Saloon.

ACT 1

Scene 1

"Bottleneck"
Patrons of the Last Chance Saloon
"Ladies"
D. Gray, Girls
"Hoop-de-Dingle"
J. Prince, Patrons of the Saloon

Scene 2

"Tomorrow Morning"
A. Griffith

Scene 3

"Ballad of the Gun"
A. Griffith, J. Prince

Scene 4

"The Social"
Townspeople of Bottleneck, S. Swenson, G. Reeder

Scene 5

"I Know Your Kind"
D. Gray
"I Hate Him"
D. Gray

Scene 6

"(Rose Lovejoy of) Paradise Alley"
Cowboys, Rose Lovejoy Girls
"Anyone Would Love You"
A. Griifth, D. Gray

Scene 7

"Once Knew a Fella"
A. Griffith, J. Prince, Friends

Scene 8

"Every Once in a While"
M. Breaux, S. Swenson, G. Reeder, Cowboys, Saloon Girls
"Fair Warning"
D. Gray

ACT 2

Scene 1

"Are You Ready, Gyp Watson?"
(D. Gray,) Friends of Gyp Watson (Ensemble)
"Not Guilty"
The Jury (Male Ensemble)
"Only Time Will Tell"
A. Griffith
"Respectability"[15]
E. Watts, Girls

Scene 2

"That Ring on the Finger"
D. Gray, Girls
"Once Knew a Fella" (reprise)
A. Griffith, D. Gray
"I Say Hello"
D. Gray

Scene 4

(Finale: "Ballad of the Gun" reprise)
(Chorus)

1959.12

THE NERVOUS SET

A Musical in Two Acts, 10 Scenes. Book by Jay Landesman and Theodore J. Flicker. Based on the novel of the same name by Jay Landesman. Music by Tommy Wolf. Lyrics by Fran Landesman. Directed by Theodore J. Flicker. Settings and lighting by Paul Morrison. Costumes by Theoni Vachlioti Aldredge. Music arrangements and direction by Tommy Wolf. Produced by Robert Lantz. Opened 12 May 1959 at the Henry Miller's Theatre and closed 30 May 1959 after 23 performances.

13Originally produced in New York 18 May 1939 at the Martin Beck Theatre for 6 performances. For Synopsis of Scene, see original 1939 production; no individual musical numbers listed.

14Originally produced in New York 31 October 1949 at the 46th Street Theatre for 56 performances. For Synopsis of Scenes and Musical Numbers, see original 1949 production. For this revival, an intermission was added between Act 1, Scenes 1 and 2. The Jazz Band was totally eliminated.

15Dropped for national tour.

CAST (in order of appearance): *Bunny Carwell*: LARRY HAGMAN. *Brad*: RICHARD HAYES, Don Heller (alt.). *Danny*: THOMAS ALDREDGE. *Jan*: TANI SEITZ. *Yogi*: DEL CLOSE. *A Customer*: Barry Primus. *Landlady*: Florence Gassner. *Joan*: Arlene Corwin. *Sari Shaw*: Janice Meshkoff. *Danny's Girl*: Elvira Pallas. *Max the Millionaire*: GERALD HIKEN. *Henry Calhoun*: David Sallade. *Katherine Sloan-Wittiker*: Florence Gassner. *Irving*: Don Heller. *Tony*: Lee Lindsey. *Rejected Boy*: Zale Kessler.

Act 1, Scene 1: Sunday Afternoon, late summer. Washington Square Park, New York City. Now. *Scene 2*: The following spring, Brad and Jan's apartment on Perry Street. *Scene 3*: That weekend. Jan's parents' home, Fairfield County, Connecticut. *Scene 4*: The same evening. The bottom of an unfilled pool. *Scene 5*: Later. Inside the house again. *Scene 6*: The next weekend. Bummy Carwell's apartment on Avenue A.

Act 2, Scene 1: A few days later. Brad and Jan's apartment. *Scene 2*: Later the same day. The Melancholy Pigeon. *Scene 3*: That evening. Katherine Sloan Wittiker's apartment on Sutton Place. *Scene 4*: Later at Brad and Jan's apartment.

ACT 1

"Man, We're Beat"
(The Company)
"New York"
(R. Hayes, T. Aldredge, T. Seitz)
"What's to Lose"
(T. Seitz, R. Hayes)
"Stars Have Blown My Way"
(T. Seitz, R. Hayes)
"Fun Life"
(R. Hayes)
"How Do You Like Your Love?"
(D. Close)
"Party Song"
(The Company)
"If I Could Put You in a Song"
"Night People"
(R. Hayes, T. Seitz)
"I've Got a Lot to Learn About Life"
(T. Seitz)
"Rejection"
(T. Aldredge, Company)
"The Ballad of the Sad Young Men"
(T. Seitz)

ACT 2

"A Country Gentleman"
(R. Hayes, T. Seitz)
"Max the Millionaire"
(G. Hiken, R. Hayes, D. Close, T. Aldredge)
"Laugh, I Thought I'd Die"
(R. Hayes)
"Travel the Road of Love"
(L. Hagman, Company)
("Fun Life" reprise)
(The Company)

1959.13

GYPSY

A Musical in Two Acts, 17 Scenes. Book by Arthur Laurents. Suggested by the memoirs (of the same name) by Gypsy Rose Lee. Music by Jule Styne. Lyrics by Stephen Sondheim. Settings and lighting by Jo Mielziner. Costumes designed by Raoul Pène du Bois. Entire production directed and choreographed by Jerome Robbins. Musical direction by Milton Rosenstock. Orchestrations by Sid Ramin with Robert Ginzler. Dance music arranged by John Kander. Additional dance music by Betty Walberg. Produced by David Merrick and Leland Hayward. Opened 21 May 1959 at the Broadway Theatre, vacationed from 11 July 1960 and resumed 13 August 1960 at the Imperial Theatre, and closed 25 March 1961 after 702 performances.

CAST (in order of appearance): *Uncle Jocko*: Mort Marshall. *George*: Willy Sumner. *Arnold* and His Guitar: John Borden. *Balloon Girl*: Jody Lane. *Baby Louise*: Karen Moore. *Baby June*: JACQUELINE MAYRO. *Rose*: ETHEL MERMAN. *Pop*: Erv Harmon. *Newsboys*: Bobby Brownell, Gene Castle, Steve Curry, Billy Harris. *Weber*: Joe Silver. *Herbie*: JACK KLUGMAN. *Louise*: SANDRA CHURCH. *June*: Lane Bradbury. *Tulsa*: PAUL WALLACE. *Yonkers*: David Winters. *Angie*: Ian Tucker. *L.A.*: Michael Parks. *Kringelein*: Loney Lewis. *Mr. Goldstone*: Mort Marshall. *Farm Boys*: Marvin Arnold, Ricky Coll, Don Emmons, Michael Parks, Ian Tucker, Paul Wallace, David Winters. *Miss Cratchitt*: Peg Murray. *Hollywood Blondes (6)*: *Agnes*: Marilyn Cooper. *Marjorie May*: Patsy Bruder. *Dolores*: Marilyn D'Honau. *Thelma*: Marle Letowt. *Edna*: Joan Petlak. *Gail*: Imelda de Martin. *Pastey*: Richard Porter. *Tessie Tura*: MARIA KARNILOVA. *Mazeppa*: FAITH DANE. *Cigar*: Loney Lewis. *Electra*: CHOTZI FOLEY. *Showgirls*: Kathryn Albertson, Gloria Kristy, Denise McLaglen, Barbara London, Theda Nelson, Carroll Jo Towers, Marie Wallace. *Maid*: Marsha Rivers. *Phil*: Joe Silver. *Bougeron-Cochon*: George Zima. *Cow* Willy Sumner, George Zima.

Act 1, Scene 1: The Stage of a Vaudeville Theatre in Seattle, early 1920s. *Scene 2*: The Kitchen of a frame house, shortly afterward. *Scene 3*: A car enroute from Seattle to Los Angeles. *Scene 4*: Backstage of a Vaudeville Theatre in Los Angeles. *Scene 5*: The Stage of the Vaudeville Theatre in Los Angeles, then Akron, Ohio. *Scene 6*: Two plaster-cracked hotel rooms in Akron, Ohio. *Scene 7*: A Chinese Restaurant in New York City. *Scene 8*: The Stage of Grantziger's Palace Theatre, New York City. *Scene 9*: Grantziger's Office. *Scene 10*: A theatre alley outside the stage door of a vaudeville theatre in Buffalo. *Scene 11*: A railroad platform in Omaha, Nebraska.

Act 2, Scene 1: In the Texas desert. Late afternoon. *Scene 2*: Backstage of a Burlesque Theatre in Wichita, Kansas. *Scene 3*: A backstage corridor. *Scene 4*: The dressing room and corridor. Wichita, then Detroit, Philadelphia, New York City. *Scene 5*: A dressing room backstage at Minsky's Burlesque, New York City. *Scene 6*: An empty stage.

ACT 1

Scene 1
"May We Entertain You"
J. Mayro, K. Moore
Scene 2
"Some People"
E. Merman
Scene 3
Traveling
Scene 4
"Small World"
E. Merman, J. Klugman
Scene 5
Baby June and her Newsboys
(J. Mayro, B. Brownell, G. Castle, S. Curry, B. Harris)
Scene 6
"Mr. Goldstone, I Love You"
E. Merman, (Boys)
"Little Lamb"
S. Church
Scene 7
"You'll Never Get Away from Me"
E. Merman, J. Klugman
Scene 8
Dainty June and her Farmboys
(L. Bradbury, S. Church, M. Arnold,
R. Coll, D. Emmons, M. Parks, I. Tucker, P. Wallace, D. Winters)
Scene 9
"If Momma Was Married"
S. Church, L. Bradbury
Scene 10
"All I Need Is the Girl"
P. Wallace, S. Church
Scene 11
"Everything's Coming Up Roses"
E. Merman

ACT 2

Scene 1
"Madame Rose's Toreadorables"
S. Church, Toreadorables
"Together, Wherever We Go"
E. Merman, S. Church, J. Klugman
Scene 2
"You Gotta Have a Gimmick"
M. Karnilova, F. Dane, C. Foley
Scene 4
"Small World" (reprise)
E. Merman
"Let Me Entertain You"
S. Church, Company
Scene 6
"Rose's Turn"
E. Merman

1959–1960 SEASON

Chita Rivera in BYE BYE BIRDIE (Photo: Friedman-Abeles)
Billy Rose Theatre Collection, New York Public Library for the Performing Arts

1959–1960 SEASON

1959.14 **BILLY BARNES REVUE**

A Musical Revue in Two Acts, 28 Scenes[1]. Music and lyrics by Billy Barnes. Sketches and dialogue by Bob Rodgers. (Settings) Designed by Glenn Holse. Musical director, Billy Barnes. Lighting by Peggy Clark. Costumes supervised by Berman Costume Company. Associate musical director, Armin Hoffman. New York costume supervsion by Peggy Morrison. At the Pianos, Billy Barnes and Armin Hoffman. Produced by George Eckstein in association with Bob Reese. Opened 4 August 1959 at the John Golden Theatre, moved 28 September 1959 to the Lyceum Theatre and closed 17 October 1959 after 87 performances. Transferred Off-Broadway 20 October 1959 to the Carnegie Hall Playhouse and closed 29 November 1959 after 48 additional performances. Total performances : 199.

CAST: JOYCE JAMESON, BERT CONVY, PATTI REGAN, KEN BERRY, ANN GUILBERT, BOB RODGERS, JACKIE JOSEPH, LEN WEINRIB.

ACT 1

Scene 1

"Do a Revue!"
The Company

Scene 2

"Where Are Your Children?"
K. Berry, B. Convy, J. Joseph, A. Guilbert, P. Regan, L. Weinrib

Scene 3

"Las Vegas"
Herman: B. Rodgers. *Girl with Hat*: A. Guilbert. *Tanya*: J. Jameson. *Her Fellas*: B. Convy, K. Berry.

Scene 4

Medic
Surgeon: L. Weinrib. *Staff*: A. Guilbert, P. Regan.

Scene 5

"Foolin' Ourselves"
B. Convy, K. Berry

Scene 6

Safari a la Marilyn
Papa: L. Weinrib. *Arthur*: B. Rodgers. *Marilyn*: J. Jameson.

Scene 7

The Pembrooke Story
Arthur: K. Berry. *Edythe*: A. Guilbert. *Miss O'Brien*: J. Joseph. *John*: B. Convy. *Peter*: L. Weinrib.

Scene 8

"Whatever" (Whatever Happened? No. 1)
P. Regan

Scene 9

"City of the Angels"
Lilly: J. Jameson. *Lolly*: A. Guilbert. *Dolly*: J. Joseph.

Scene 10

"Listen to the Beat!"
Host: L. Weinrib. *Jack*: K. Berry. *Mary Lou*: A. Guilbert. *Dean*: B. Convy. *Sarah*: J. Jameson. *The Prophet*: L. Weinrib. *Beatniks*: B. Rodgers, P. Regan, J. Joseph.

Scene 11

Home in Mississippi (Parody of "Cat on a Hot Tin Roof")
Maggie: P. Regan. *Big Daddy*: L. Weinrib. *Big Mama*: A. Guilbert. *Brick*: B. Rodgers. *No-neck Monsters*: Themselves.

Scene 12

"Tyler My Boy"
B. Convy

Scene 13

"Whatever Happened?" (No. 2)
P. Regan

Scene 14

The Thirties
Narrator: B. Rodgers. *Peddler*: P. Regan. *Fred*: K. Berry. *Ginger*: J. Jameson. *Forgotten Woman*: A. Guilbert. *Forgotten Man*: L. Weinrib. *Shirley*: J. Jameson. *Daddy*: B. Convy. *Step-Mommy*: P. Regan. *Gold Digger*: J. Joseph. *J. N.*: L. Weinrib. *Sam*: K. Berry. *Ruby*: A. Guilbert. *Dick*: B. Convy. *Jeanette*: J. Jameson. *Nelson*: B. Rodgers.

ACT 2

Scene 1

A Dissertation on Transportation, or, It All Started With the Wheel
Principal: B. Rodgers. *P. T. A. President*: J. Jameson. *Teacher*: P. Regan. *Sweet Little Girl*: J. Joseph. *Sour Little Girl*: A. Guilbert. *Teacher's Pet*: K. Berry. *Bully*: L. Weinrib. *Bert Convy*: B. Convy.

Scene 2

"The Fights"
Introduced by A. Guilbert. *Shirley*: J. Jameson. *Harry*: B. Rodgers.

Scene 3

The Vamp and Friends
Vamp: A. Guilbert. *Champ*: K. Berry. *Tramp*: P. Regan. *Camp*: L Weinrib.

Scene 4

"Blocks"
Husband: B. Rodgers. *Wife*: J. Joseph.

Scene 5

Hellahahana
Natives: B. Convy, K. Berry, J. Jameson, L. Weinrib, J. Joseph. *Turista*: A. Guilbert.

Scene 6

"Whatever Happened to" (No. 3)
P. Regan

Scene 7

World at Large
Moderator: B. Convy.

Scene 8

World at Large No. 1
Rosabelle Haley: J. Jameson. *Warden*: L. Weinrib. *Matron*: A. Guilbert.

Scene 9

Station Break
Fire Prevention Queen: P. Regan.

Scene 10

World at Large No.2
Mr. Lernstein: B. Rodgers. *Choral Group*: Choral Group (The Company).

Scene 11

World at Large Preview
Oed: K. Berry. *Jo*: P. Regan.

Scene 12

"(Have I Stayed) Too Long at the Fair"
J. Jameson

Scene 13

"One of Those Days"
Poor Soul: L. Weinrib. *Ads*: B. Convy, J. Joseph, K. Berry.

Scene 14

Finale
The Company

1959.15 **AN EVENING WITH YVES MONTAND**

A Solo Performance in Two Acts. Staged and lighted by Yves Montand. Produced by Norman Granz in association with Jacques Canetti. Opened 22 September 1959 at the Henry Miller's Theatre, moved 12 October 1959 to the Longacre Theatre and closed 31 October 1959 after 42 performances.

CAST: YVES MONTAND. *Piano*: Bob Castella. *Accordionist*: Nick Perito. *Guitar*: Jim Hall. *Clarinet*: Jimmy Guiffre. *Bass*: Al Hall. *Drums*: Charles Persip. *Trombone*: Billy Byers.

ACT 1

"Les Amis" (The Friends)
(*Music by* Bob Castella. *Lyrics by* Francis Lemarque.)

[1]Originally produced Off-Broadway 9 June 1959 at the York Playhouse for 64 performances.

"La Fete A Loulou" (The Birthday of Loulou)
(*Music by* Bob Castella. *Lyrics by* Rene Rouzaud.)
"Une Demoiselle Sur Une Balancoire" (A Young Lady in a Swing)
(*Music by* Mireille. *Lyrics by* Jean Nohain.)
"Ma Mome, Ma P'tite Mome"
(*Music by* Marguerite Monnot. *Lyrics by* Henri Contet.)
"Sir Godfrey"
(*Music by* Georges Liferman. *Lyrics by* Jacques Mareuil.)
"Le Carosse" (The Golden Chariot)
(*Music by* Mireille. *Lyrics by* Henri Contet.)
"Luna-Park"
(*Music by* Loulou Gaste. *Lyrics by* Jean Guigo.)
"Les Feuilles Mortes" (Autumn Leaves)
(*Music by* Joseph Cosma. *Lyrics by* Jacques Prevert.)
"Les Grands Boulevards"
(*Music by* Norbert Glanzberg. *Lyrics by* Jacques Plante.)
"Flamenco De Paris"
(*Music and Lyrics by* Leo Ferré.)
"Un Garcon Dansait" (A Boy Was Dancing)
(*Music by* Georges Liferman. *Lyrics by* Jacques Mareuil.)

ACT 2

"Les Petits Riens" (The Little Daily Nothings)
(*Music and Lyrics by* Francis Lemarque.)
"Simple Comme Bonjour" (Simple as Bonjour)
(*Music by* Henri Crolla. *Lyrics by* Jacques Prevert.)
"Mais Qu'est-ce que J'ai?" (What's Wrong With Me?)
(*Music by* Henri Betti. *Lyrics by* Edith Piaf.)
"La Marie-Vision" (Marie's Mink Coat)
(*Music by* Marc Henyral. *Lyrics by* Roger Varanay.)
"Planter Cafe"
(*Music by* Emil Stern. *Lyrics by* Eddy Marnay.)
"Le Chef D'Orchestre Est Amoureux" (The Conductor Is in Love)
(*Music by* Georges Liferman. *Lyrics by* Jacques Mareuil.)
"A Paris"
(*Music and Lyrics by* Francis Lemarque.)
"Il Fait Des . . . " (Le Fanatique de Jazz)
(*Music by* Edouard Chekle. *Lyrics by* Edith Piaf.)
"Mon Menage a Moi"
(*Music by* Norbert Glanzberg. *Lyrics by* Jean Constantin.)

1959.16

DIE FLEDERMAUS

A Revival of the Operetta in Three Acts[2]. (Original Libretto by Carl Haffner and Richard Genée. Lyrics by Richard Genée. Based on the comedy "Le Réveillon" by Henri Meilhac and Ludovic Halévy.) English libretto by Ruth and Thomas Martin. Music by Johann Strauss. Staged by Michael Pollock. Conducted by Julius Rudel. Produced by the New York City Opera. Opened 26 September 1959 at the New York City Center and closed 24 October 1959 after 3 performances in repertory.

CAST: *Rosalinda*: BEVERLY BOWER. *Eisenstein*: ERNEST McCHESNEY. *Adele*: JACQUELYNNE MOODY. *Sally*: Jennie Andrea. *Alfred*: Thomas Hayward. *Prince Orlofsky*: JACK HARROLD. *Falke*: CHESTER LUDGIN. *Frank*: PAUL UKENA. *Frosch*: Philip Bruns. *Blind*: Grant Williams. *Solo Dancers*: Diane Consoer, Jonathan Watts. *Ensemble*: New York City Opera Chorus.

1959.17

STREET SCENE

A Revival of the American Opera (Dramatic Musical) in Two Acts, 3 Scenes[3]. Book by Elmer Rice from his play of the same name. Music by Kurt Weill. Lyrics by Langston Hughes. Staged by Herbert Machiz. Conducted by Samuel Krachmalnick. Scenery and Costumes by Paul Sylbert. Children's Number supervised by Robert Joffrey. Chorus Master, Gino Smart. (Orchestrations by Kurt Weill.) Produced by the New York City Opera Company. Opened 27 September 1959 at the New York City Center and closed 15 October 1959 after 2 performances in repertory Reopened 13 February 1960 at the New York City Center and closed 19 February 1960 after 3 additional performances. Total this season: 5 performances.

CAST (in order of appearance): *Abraham Kaplan*: Grant Williams. *Greta Fiorentino*: Dolores Mari. *Carl Olsen*: Arnold Voketaitis. *Emma Jones*: RUTH KOBART. *Olga Olsen*: Beatrice Krebs. *Shirley Kaplan*: Florence Anglin. *Mrs. Davis*: Marie Louise. *Henry Davis*: Andrew Frierson. *Willie Maurrant*: Michael Mann. *Anna Maurrant*: ELISABETH CARRON. *Sam Kaplan*: FRANK PORETTA. *Daniel Buchanan*: Keith Kaldenberg. *Frank Maurrant*: WILLIAM CHAPMAN. *George Jones*: Chester Ludgin. *Steve Sankey*: Arthur Storch. *Lippo Fiorentino*: JACK HARROLD. *Jennie Hildebrand*: Nancy Dussault. *Second Graduate*: Sylvia De Van. *Third Graduate*: Jennie Andrea. *Mrs. Hildebrand*: Sophia Steffan. *Charlie Hildebrand*: Richard Clemence. *Mary Hildebrand*: Lynn Taussig. *Grace Davis*: Sharon Williams. *Rose Maurrant*: HELENA SCOTT, Joy Clements (alt.). *Harry Easter*: Seth Riggs. *Mae Jones*: Sondra Lee. *Dick McGann*: Richard Tone. *Vincent Jones*: Albert Lewis. *Dr. John Wilson*: John Macurdy. *Officer Harry Murphy*: Dan Merriman. *City Marshall James Henry*: George Del Monte. *Fred Cullen*: William Zakariasen. *First Nursemaid*: Mary LeSawyer. *Second Nursemaid*: Rita Metzger.

Policemen, Milkman, Old Clothes Man, Music Pupil, Interne, Ambulance Driver, Married Couple, Passersby, Neighbors, Children, etc.: New York City Opera Chorus.

1959.18

THE MIKADO, or The Town of Titipu

A Revival of the Comic Opera in Two Acts[4]. Libretto by William S. Gilbert. Music by Arthur Sullivan. Staged by Dorothy Raedler. Scenic and lighting design by Donald Oenslager. Costume design by Patton Campbell. Conducted by Robert Irving. Produced by the New York City Opera. Opened 1 October 1959 at the New York City Center and closed 1 November 1959 after 4 performances in repertory.

CAST: *The Mikado of Japan*: GEORGE GAYNES. *Nanki-Poo*, his son, disguised as a wandering minstrel in love with Yum-Yum: FRANK PORETTA. *Ko-Ko*, Lord High Executioner of Titipu: NORMAN KELLEY. *Pooh-Bah*, Lord High Everything Else: HERBERT BEATTIE. *Pish-Tush*, a Noble Lord: Robert Kerns. *Yum-Yum, Pitti-Sing, Peep-Bo*, three sisters, wards of Ko-Ko: BARBARA MEISTER, NANCY DUSSAULT, SOPHIA STEFFAN. *Katisha*: CLARAMAE TURNER. *Chorus of School Girls, Nobles, Guards and Coolies*: New York City Opera Chorus.

1959.19

HAPPY TOWN

A Musical Comedy in Two Acts, 23 Scenes. Book adapted (from an original by Harry M. Haldane) by Max Hampton. Music by Gordon Duffy. Lyrics by Harry M. Haldane. Additional Music and lyrics by Paul Nassau. Directed by Allan A. Buckhantz. Choreography by Lee Scott. Settings By Curt Nations. Costumes by J. Michael Travis. Lighting by Paul Morrison. Musical direction and vocal arrangements by Samuel Krachmalnick. Orchestrations by Nicholas Carras. Associate director, Ernest Sarracino. Produced by b & m Productions. Opened 7 October 1959 at the 54th Street Theatre and closed 10 October 1959 after 5 performances.

CAST (in order of appearance): *Lint Richards*: George Blackwell. *Bub Richards*: Bruce MacKay. *Sib Richards*: George Ives. *Glenn Richards*: Michael Kermoyan. *Janice Dawson*: CINDY ROBBINS. *Craig Richards*: BIFF McGUIRE. *Clint Yoder*: TOM WILLIAMS. *Bobbie Jo Hartman*: Alice Clift. *Molly Bixby*: LEE VENORA. *Judge Ed Bixby*: DICK ELLIOTT. *Jim Jo Jamieson*: Frederic Tozere. *A Reporter*: Rico Froehlich. *Pert Hawkins*: RALPH DUNN. *Claney*: Charles May. *Doc Spooner*: WILL WRIGHT. *Mrs. Hawkins*: Liz Pritchett. *Reverend Hornblow*: EDWIN STEFFE. *Mult*: Roy Wilson. *Luke Granger*: Chester Watson. (*Susan Grey*: Leigh Evans.)

Townswomen of Back-A-Heap: Diana Baron, Lillian Bozinoff, Alice Clift, Colleen Corkrey, Dori Davis, Isabelle Farrell, Laurie Franks, Rita Golden, Connie Greco, Marian Haraldson, Marilyn Harris, Judy Keirn, Maxine Kent, Patricia Mount, Robbi Palmer. *Townsmen of Back-A-Heap*: John Buwen, Bob Daley, Rico Froehlich, James Gannon, George Jack, Danny Joel, Charles May, Jim McAnany, Nixon Miller, Howard Parker, Tom Pocoroba, Stewart Rose, Roy Wilson.

---

[2]First English Language Production in New York 16 March 1885 at the Casino Theatre for 42 performances. First New York production of this adaptation 20 December 1950 at the Metropolitan Opera House. For Synopsis of Scenes and Musical Numbers, see May 1954 revival.

[3]Originally produced in New York 9 January 1947 at the Adelphi Theatre for 148 performances. For Synopsis of Scenes and Musical Numbers, see original 1947 production.

[4]First presented in New York 20 July, 10-29 August 1885 at the Union Square and People's Theatres for 22 performances. First authorized production presented 19 August 1885 at the Fifth Avenue Theatre by Richard D'Oyly Carte for 250 performances. For Synopsis of Scenes and Musical Numbers, see 19 August 1885 D'Oyly Carte production.

Act 1, Scene 1: A Private Office in the T.B.A. Exchange. *Scene 2*: Back-A-Heap, Texas. The Main Street. A few hours later. *Scene 3*: Bixby's Super Market. A little later. *Scene 4*: The Main Street. Immediately following. *Scene 5*: Bixby's Super Market. Immediately following. *Scene 6*: The T.B.A. Office. A little later. *Scene 7*: The Main Street. That evening. *Scene 8*: Back-A-Heap Town Hall. Immediately following. *Scene 9*: The Main Street. Immediately following. *Scene 10*: Fairgrounds. Next morning. *Scene 11*: The T.B.A. Office. *Scene 12*: The Prairie.

Act 2, Scene 1: The Main Street. Late the next day. *Scene 2*: E. Street. Immediately following. *Scene 3*: The T.B.A. Office. At about the same time. *Scene 4*: Fairgrounds. Two weeks later. *Scene 5*: A Street. Immediately following. *Scene 6*: The Main Street. *Scene 7*: T.B.A. Office. *Scene 8*: Main Street, Later. *Scene 9*: Bixby's Super Market. *Scene 10*: A Street, Immediately following. *Scene 11*: Town Hall, later.

ACT 1

Scene 1

"It Isn't Easy"
C. Robbins, M. Kermoyan, B. MacKay, G. Blackwell, G. Ives

Scene 2

"Celebration!"
Townspeople

"Something Special"
B. McGuire

Scene 4

"The Legend of Black-Eyed Susan Grey" (Dance)
L. Evans, Townspeople

"Opportunity!"
B. McGuire, E. Steffe, L. Pritchett, Townspeople

"As Busy As Anyone Can Be"
T. Williams, Girls

"Heaven Protect Me!"
C. Robbins, Girls

Scene 7

"I Feel Like a Brother to You"
B. McGuire, L. Venora

Scene 8

"Hoedown!"
Townspeople

Scene 9

"I Am What I Am!"
B. McGuire, L. Venora

"The Beat of a Heart"
L. Venora

"Mean"
C. Robbins

Scene 11

"It Isn't Easy" (reprise)
M. Kermoyan, B. MacKay, G. Blackwell, G. Ives

Scene 12

"When the Time Is Right"
E. Steffe

ACT 2

Scene 1

"Pick-Me-Up!"
Townspeople

Scene 2

"I'm Stuck With Love"
L. Venora

Scene 3

"It Isn't Easy" (reprise)
M. Kermoyan, B. MacKay, G. Blackwell, G. Ives

Scene 4

"Nothing in Common"
C. Robbins, L. Venora

"Talkin' 'Bout You"
C. Robbins, T. Williams, Townspeople

"Something Special" (reprise)
B. McGuire, L. Venora

Scene 8

"Y' Can't Win"
C. Robbins

Scene 11

"Opportunity" (reprise)
Entire Company

1959.20 AT THE DROP OF A HAT

An After Dinner Farrago (Intimate Revue) in Two Acts. Music by Donald Swann. Words by Michael Flanders. Produced by Alexander H. Cohen in association with Joseph I. Levine. Lighting by Ralph Alswang. Frontcloth by Al Hirschfeld. Opened 8 October 1959 at the John Golden Theatre and closed 14 May 1960 after 216 performances.

CAST: MICHAEL FLANDERS, DONALD SWANN.

ACT 1

"Song of Reproduction"

"The Hog Beneath the Skin" (The Warthog)

"A Transport of Delight"

"The Youth of the Heart"
Lyrics by Sydney Carter.)

"Greensleeves"

"The Wompom"

"Sea Fever"

"A Gnu"

"Judgement of Paris"

Songs for Our Time: ("Philological Waltz," "Satellite Moon," "A Happy Song")

ACT 2

"A Song of the Weather"

"The Reluctant Cannibal"

"In the Bath"

"Design for Living"

"Tried by the Centre Court"

"Misalliance"

"Kokoraki" (A Greek Song)

"Madeira, M' Dear?"

"The Hippopotamus"

1959.21 THE MERRY WIDOW

A Revival of the Operetta in Three Acts[5]. Music by Franz Lehár. Original German libretto (Die Lustige Witwe) by Victor Léon and Leo Stein after "L'Attaché d'Ambassade." English libretto by Adrian Ross. Staged by Michael Pollock. Conducted by Julius Rudel. Produced by the New York City Opera. Opened 10 October 1959 at the New York City Center and closed 24 October 1958 after 4 performances in repertory.

CAST: *Sonia*: BEVERLY BOWER. *Prince Danillo*: JOHN REARDON. *Baron Popoff*: JACK HARROLD. *Natalie*: Helena Scott. *De Jolidon*: Frank Poretta. *Marquis de Cascada*: Arnold Voketaitis. *St. Brioche*: Chester Ludgin. *Admiral Khadja*: Dan Merriman. *Mme. Khadja*: Dorothy White. *General Novikovich*: Grant Williams. *Mme. Novikovich*: Lynda Jordan. *Nish*: Roy Stuart. *Lo-Lo*: Lynn Starling. *Solo Dancers*: Dianne Consoer, Jonathan Watts. *Ensemble*: New York City Opera Chorus.

1959.22 TAKE ME ALONG

A Musical in Two Acts, 13 Scenes. Book by Joseph Stein and Robert Russell. Based on the play "Ah, Wilderness!" by Eugene O'Neill. Music and lyrics by Bob Merrill. Dances and musical numbers Staged by Onna White. Production (Settings) sesigned by Oliver Smith. Costumes by Miles White. Lighting by Jean Rosenthal. Musical direction and vocal arrangements by Lehman Engel. Ballet and incidental music by Laurence Rosenthal.

[5]Originally produced in New York 21 October 1907 at the New Amsterdam Theatre for 416 performances. For Synopsis of Scenes and Musical Numbers, see original 1907 production.

Orchestrations by Philip J. Lang. Directed by Peter Glenville. Produced by David Merrick. Opened 22 October 1959 at the Sam S. Shubert Theatre and closed 17 December 1960 after 448 performances.

CAST (in order of appearance): *Nat Miller*: WALTER PIDGEON. *Mildred Miller*: Zeme North. *Art Miller*: James Cresson. *Tommy Miller*: Luke Halpin. *Essie Miller*: UNA MERKEL. *Lily*: EILEEN HERLIE. *Richard Miller*: ROBERT MORSE. *Muriel Macomber*: Susan Luckey. *Dave Macomber*: Fred Miller. *Sid*: JACKIE GLEASON. *Wint*: Peter Conlow. *Lady Entertainers*: Valerie Harper, Diana Hunter, Rae McLean. *Bartender*: Jack Collins. *Belle*: Arlene Golonka. *The Drunk*: Gene Varrone. *Bar Patrons*: Elna Laun, Paula Lloyd, Janice Painchaud, Jack Konzal, Pat Tolson, Lee Howard. *Salesman*: Bill McDonald. *Beardsley Dwarf*: Charles Bolender. *Salome*: Rae McLean.

Townswomen: Nicole Barth, Renee Byrns, Lyn Connorty, Barbara Doherty, Katia Geleznova, Valerie Harper, Diana Hunter, Elna Laun, Paula Lloyd, Nancy Lynch, Rae McLean, Janice Painchaud. *Townsmen*: Alvin Beam, Frank Borgman, John Carter, Lee Howard, Jack Konzal, Bill McDonald, Henry Michel, Jack Murray, John Nola, Bill Richards, Harry Lee Rogers, Walter Strauss, Jimmy Tarbutton, Gene Varrone, Marc West, Pat Tolson, Rusty Parker, Chad Block, Bill Starr.

Act 1, Scene 1: The Miller Home in Centerville, Connecticut, 1910. Early the morning of July 4th. *Scene 2*: The Macomber Home. The same morning. *Scene 3*: The Car Barn. Later that morning. *Scene 4*: The Miller Home. A little later. *Scene 5*: A Street. *Scene 6*: The Picnic Grounds. That afternoon. *Scene 7*: The Miller Home. That evening.

Act 2, Scene 1: Bar Room of the Pleasant Beach House. The same night. *Scene 2*: The Miller Home. Later that night. *Scene 3*: Richard's Bedroom. Afternoon of the following day. *Scene 4*: The Beach. That evening. *Scene 5*: The Miller Home. A little later. *Scene 6*: The Car Barn. Later that evening.

ACT 1

Scene 1

"The Parade" (Marvelous Fire Machine)
W. Pidgeon, Townspeople

"Oh, Please"
W. Pidgeon, U. Merkel, E. Herlie, Family

Scene 2

"I Would Die"
S. Luckey, R. Morse

Scene 3

"Sid, Ol' Kid"
J. Gleason, Townspeople

Scene 4

"Staying Young"
W. Pidgeon

"I Get Embarassed"
J. Gleason, E. Herlie

"We're Home"
E. Herlie

Scene 5

"Take Me Along"
J. Gleason, W. Pidgeon

Scene 6

"For Sweet Charity" (Volunteer Firemen Picnic)
J. Gleason, W. Pidgeon, V. Harper, D. Hunter, R. McLean, Townsmen

Scene 7

"Pleasant Beach House" (Wint's Song)
P. Conlow

"That's How It Starts"
R. Morse

ACT 2

Scene 1

"The Beardsley Ballet"
R. Morse, S. Luckey, C. Bolender, R. McLean, Ensemble

Scene 2

"Oh, Please" (reprise)
W. Pidgeon, U. Merkel

"Promise Me a Rose" (A Slight Detail)
E. Herlie, J. Gleason

"Staying Young" (reprise)
W. Pidgeon

Scene 3

"Little Green Snake"
J. Gleason

Scene 4

"Nine O'Clock"
R. Morse

Scene 5

"But Yours"
J. Gleason, E. Herlie

Scene 6

"Take Me Along" (reprise)
E. Herlie, J. Gleason, Townspeople

1959.23 THE GIRLS AGAINST THE BOYS

A Musical Revue in Two Acts, 20 Scenes. Sketches and lyrics by Arnold B. Horwitt. Music by Richard Lewine. Additional music by Albert Hague. Sketches directed by Aaron Ruben. Dances and musical numbers staged by Boris Runanin. Scenery and lighting by Ralph Alswang. Costumes by Sal Anthony. Dance music arranged by John Morris. Musical director, Irving Actman. Orchestrations by Sid Ramin and Robert Ginzler. Produced by Albert Selden. Opened 2 November 1959 at the Alvin Theatre and closed 14 November 1959 after 16 performances.

CAST: BERT LAHR, NANCY WALKER, SHELLEY BERMAN, DICK VAN DYKE, Joy Nichols, Imelda De Martin, Richard France, June L. Walker, Maureen Bailey, Buzz Halliday, Mace Barrett.

Ensemble: Caroljane Abney, Sandra Devlin, Ray Pointer, Noel Schwartz, Martin Charnin, Bob Roman, Cy Young, Jo Ann Tenney, Roger LePage, Mal Throne, Mona Pivar, Al Fiorella, Margaret Gathright, Mitchell Nutick, Beatrice Salten, Jim Sisco, Ellen Graff.

ACT 1

Scene 1

"The Girls Against the Boys"
D. Van Dyke, M. Barrett, B. Halliday, Ensemble

Scene 2

"Rich Butterfly"
Husband: S. Berman. *Wife*: N. Walker.

Scene 3

Can We Save Our Marriage?
Counselor: D. Van Dyke. *Stella*: J. L. Walker. *Harry*: B. Lahr.

Scene 4

"I Gotta Have You"
I. DeMartin, R. France, C. Abney, S. Devlin, R. Pointer, N. Schwartz

Scene 5

Home Late (based on an idea by Robert Mott)
Husband: D. Van Dyke. *Wife*: B. Halliday.

Scene 6

I Remember
B. Lahr
Butler: M. Barrett.

Scene 7

Assignation
Jock: D. Van Dyke. *Cynthia*: J. Nichols. *Essie*: N. Walker. *Waiter*: M. Charnin. *Counterman*: R. Pointer. *Man at Center Table*: B. Roman. *Max*: N. Schwartz. *Other Patrons*: C. Young, J. A. Tenny, R. LePage, M. Throne, M. Pivar, A. Fiorella.

Scene 8

Comic Monologue (Phone Call With Jewish Father)
(*by* Shelley Berman)S. Berman

Scene 9

"Where Did We Go? Out"
M. Barrett, M. Bailey, R. France, I. DeMartin
(by permission of Robert Paul Smith)

Scene 10

"Too Young to Live"
B. Lahr, N. Walker

Scene 11

"Overspend"
S. Berman, J. Nichols, Ensemble

ACT 2

Scene 1

"Girls and Boys"

Observer: M. Barrett. *Mother*: J. Nichols. *Groom*: D. Van Dyke. *Bride*: I. DeMartin. *Best Man*: R. France. *Father*: B. Roman. *Maid of Honor*: M. Bailey. *Bridesmaids*: M. Pivar, M. Gathright, S. Devlin, B. Halliday. *Guests*: Ensemble.

Scene 2

Nightflight

(*by* Arnold Horwitt and Aaron Ruben)

Passenger: B. Lahr. *Girl*: J. Nichols. *Man*: M. Throne. *Hostess*: J. L. Walker. *Mother*: B. Halliday. *Four People*: M. Barrett, C. Young, B. Roman, N. Popova.

Scene 3

"Light Travelin' Man"

(*Music by* Albert Hague.)S. Berman, R. France

Girls: S. Devlin, C. Abney, M. Gathright.

Scene 4

He and She

Introduction: S. Berman. *He*: D. Van Dyke. *Goat*: N. Schwartz. *Skunks*: C. Abney, R. LePage. *Rabbits*: M. Nutick, B. Salten. *Ducks*: R. Pointer, M. Pivar. *Wolf*: A. Fiorella. *Lamb*: J. A. Tenney. *She*: N. Walker. *Snake*: S. Devlin. *It*: J. Sisco.

Scene 5

"Old-Fashioned Girl"

Doorman: M. Throne. *Monroe Fuller*: B. Lahr. *Tawny*: J. L. Walker. *Usher*: B. Salten. *Treasurer*: S. Devlin. *Male Dancer*: R. LePage. *Show Girls*: B. Halliday, M. Gathright, C. Abney, J. A. Tenney, E. Graff, M. Pivar.

Scene 6

Comic Monologue: (Phone Call to Girl Friend After a Date)

(*by* Shelley Berman)

S. Berman

Scene 7

Hostility

(*by* Arnold Horwitt and Aaron Ruben)

Husband: B. Lahr. *Wife*: N. Walker.

Scene 8

"Nobody Else But You"

(*Music by* Albert Hague.)B. Lahr, N. Walker

Scene 9

Finale

Entire Company

1959.24 THE SOUND OF MUSIC

A Musical Play in Two Acts, 19 Scenes. Book by Howard Lindsay and Russel Crouse. Suggested by the book "The Trapp Family Singers" by Maria Augusta Trapp. Music by Richard Rodgers. Lyrics by Oscar Hammerstein II. Entire production directed by Vincent J. Donahue. Musical numbers staged by Joe Layton. Scenic production by Oliver Smith. Costumes by Lucinda Ballard; Mary Martin's clothes[6] by Mainbocher. Lighting by Jean Rosenthal. Musical director, Frederick Dvonch. Choral arrangements by Trude Rittman. Orchestrations by Robert Russell Bennett. Produced by Leland Hayward, Richard Halliday, Richard Rodgers and Oscar Hammerstein II. Opened 16 November 1959 at the Lunt-Fontanne Theatre, vacationed 2-16 July 1961, moved 6 November 1962 to the Mark Hellinger Theatre, and closed 15 June 1963 after 1443 performances.

CAST (in order of appearance): *Maria Rainer*, a Postulant at Nonnberg Abbey: MARY MARTIN. *Sister Berthe*, Mistress of Novices: Elizabeth Howell. *Sister Margaretta*, Mistress of Postulants: Muriel O'Malley. *The Mother Abbess*: PATRICIA NEWAY. *Sister Sophia*: Karen Shepard. *Captain Georg von Trapp*: THEODORE BIKEL. *Franz*: John Randolph. *Frau Schmidt*, the Housekeeper: Nan McFarland. *Children of Captain von Trapp (7)*: *Liesl*: Lauri Peters. *Friedrich*: William Snowden. *Louisa*: Kathy Dunn. *Kurt*: Joseph Stewart. *Brigitta*: Marilyn Rogers. *Marta*: Mary Susan Locke. *Gretl*: Evanna Lien. *Rolf Gruber*: Brian Davies. *Elsa Schraeder*: MARION MARLOWE. *Ursula*: Luce Ennis. *Max Detweiler*: KURT KASZNAR. *Herr Zeller*: Stefan Gierasch. *Baron Elberfeld*: Kirby Smith. *A Postulant*: Sue Yaeger. *Admiral Von Schreiber*: Michael Gorrin.

Neighbors of Captain von Trapp, Nuns, Novices, Postulants, Contestants in the Festival Concert: Joanne Birks, Patricia Brooks, June Card, Dorothy Dallas, Ceil Delli, Luce Ennis, Cleo Fry, Barbara George, Joey Heatherton, Lucas Hoving, Patricia Kelly, Maria Kova, Shirley Mendonca, Kathy Miller, Lorna Nash, Keith Prentice, Nancy Reeves, Bernice Saunders, Connie Sharman, Gloria Stevens, Tatiana Troyanos, Mimi Vondra.

Act 1, Scene 1: Nonnberg Abbey in Austria early in 1938. *Scene 2*: Mountainside near the Abbey. *Scene 3*: The office of the Mother Abbess, the next morning. *Scene 4*: A corridor in the Abbey. *Scene 5*: The living room of the Trapp Villa, that afternoon. *Scene 6*: Outside the Trapp Villa, that evening. *Scene 7*: Maria's bedroom, late that evening. (*Scene 7a*: A Hallway in the Trapp Villa.) *Scene 8*: The terrace of the Trapp Villa, one week later. *Scene 9*: A hallway in the Trapp Villa, one week later. *Scene 10*: The living room, the same evening. *Scene 11*: A corridor in the Abbey. *Scene 12*: The office of the Mother Abbess, three days later.

Act 2, Scene 1: The terrace, the same day. *Scene 2*: A corridor in the Abbey, two weeks later. *Scene 3*: The office of the Mother Abbess, immediately following. *Scene 4*: A cloister overlooking the chapel. *Scene 5*: The living room, one month later. *Scene 6*: The concert hall, three days later. *Scene 7*: The garden of Nonnberg Abbey, that night.

ACT 1

Scene 1

Preludium

Nuns

Scene 2

"The Sound of Music"

M. Martin

Scene 3

"Maria"

P. Neway, M. O'Malley, E. Howell, K. Shepard

"My Favorite Things"

M. Martin, P. Neway

Scene 5

"Do-Re-Mi"

M. Martin, Children

Scene 6

"You Are Sixteen" (Sixteen Going on Seventeen)

L. Peters, B. Davies

Scene 7

"The Lonely Goatherd"

M. Martin, Children

Scene 8

"How Can Love Survive?"

M. Marlowe, K. Kasznar, T. Bikel

"The Sound of Music" (reprise)

M. Martin, T. Bikel, Children

Scene 10

("Laendler" Dance)

(M. Martin, T. Bikel)

"So Long, Farewell"

Children

Scene 12

"Climb Every Mountain"

P. Neway

ACT 2

Scene 1

"No Way to Stop It"

T. Bikel, K. Kasznar, M. Marlowe

"(An) Ordinary Couple"

M. Martin, T. Bikel

Scene 4

Processional

Ensemble

("Maria" reprise)

(Ensemble)

Scene 5

"You Are Sixteen" (reprise)

M. Martin, L. Peters

"Do-Re-Mi" (reprise)

M. Martin, T. Bikel, Children

[6]Miss Martin's postulant costume and last two costumes designed by Lucinda Ballard.

Scene 6
"Edelweiss"
T. Bikel, M. Martin, Children
"So Long, Farewell" (reprise)
M. Martin, T. Bikel, Children
Scene 7
"Climb Every Mountain" (reprise)
Company

1959.25 FIORELLO!

A Musical in Two Acts, a Prologue and 19 Scenes. Book by Jerome Weidman and George Abbott. Music by Jerry Bock. Lyrics by Sheldon Harnick. Choeography by Peter Gennaro. Scenery, costumes and lighting by William and Jean Eckart. Musical direction, Hal Hastings. Orchestrations by Irwin Kostal. Dance music arranged by Jack Elliott. Production directed by George Abbott. Produced by Robert E. Griffith and Harold S. Prince. Opened 23 November 1959 at the Broadhurst Theatre, moved 9 May 1960 to the Broadway Theatre and closed 28 October 1961 after 795 performances.

CAST (in order of appearance): *Announcer*: Del Hortsmann. *Fiorello*: TOM BOSLEY. *Neil*: Bob Holiday. *Morris*: NATHANIEL FREY. *Mrs. Pomerantz*: Helen Verbit. *Mr. Lopez*: H. F. Green. *Mr. Zappatella*: David Collyer. *Dora*: PAT STANLEY. *Marie*: PATRICIA WILSON. *Ben*: HOWARD DA SILVA. *Ed Peterson*: Del Horstmann. *Second Player*: Stanley Simmonds. *Third Player*: Michael Quinn. *Fourth Player*: Ron Husmann. *Fifth Player*: David London. *Sixth Player*: Julian Patrick. *Seedy Man*: Joseph Toner. *First Heckler*: Bob Bernard. *Second Heckler*: Michael Scrittorale. *Third Heckler*: Jim Maher. *Fourth Heckler*: Joseph Toner. *Nina*: Pat Turner. *Floyd*: MARK DAWSON. *Sophie*: Lynn Ross. *Thea*: ELLEN HANLEY. *Secretary*: Mara Landi. *Commissioner*: Frederic Downs. *Politician*: H. F. Green. *Frankie Scarpini*: Michael Scrittorale. *Mitzi*: EILEEN RODGERS. *Florence*: Deedy Irwin. *Reporter*: Julian Patrick. *First Man*: Scott Hunter. *Second Man*: Michael Scrittorale. *Tough Man*: David London. *Derby*: Bob Bernard. *Frantic*: Stanley Simmonds. *Judge Carter*: Joseph Toner.

Singers: David Collyer, Barbara Gilbert, Del Horstmann, Deedy Irwin, Mara Landi, David London, Julian Patrick, Ginny Perlowin, Patsy Peterson, Silver Saundors, Ron Husmann. *Dancers*: Charlene Carter, Bob Bernard, Elaine Cancilla, Ellen Harris, Patricia Harty, Scott Hunter, Bob La Crosse, Lynda Lynch, James Maher, Gregg Owen, Lowell Purvis, Dellas Rennie, Lynn Ross, Dan Siretta, Michael Scrittorale, Pat Turner.

Prologue: WNYC Radio Station Studios, New York City. 1914.

Act 1, Scene 1: Law Offices of Fiorello H. LaGuardia in Greenwich Village. *Scene 2*: Main Room of the Ben Marino Association. *Scene 3*: A Street outside strike headquarters. *Scene 4*: Fiorello's Office immediately following. *Scene 5*: A Street Corner. *Scene 6*: The same, after Fiorello's election. *Scene 7*: The Roof of a Greenwich Village Tenement House. *Scene 8*: Fiorello's office in the Congressional Office Building in Washington. *Scene 9*: A Street. *Scene 10*: The Main Room of the Ben Marino Association. *Scene 11*: A Pathé News Screening; a ship's gangplank.

Act 2, Scene 1: The LaGuardia Home. Ten years later. *Scene 2*: The Terrace of Floyd and Dora McDuff's Penthouse Home. *Scene 3*: Fiorello's Law Office. *Scene 4*: Madison Avenue and 105th Street. *Scene 5*: Fiorello's Law Office. *Scene 6*: Radio Announcement *Scene 7*: The Main Room of the Ben Marino Association. *Scene 8*: Fiorello's Office.

ACT 1
Scene 1
"On the Side of the Angels"
B. Holiday, N. Frey, P. Wilson
Scene 2
"Politics and Poker"
H. DaSilva, Politicians
Scene 3
"Unfair"
T. Bosley, P. Stanley, Girls
Scene 4
"Marie's Law"
P. Wilson, N. Frey
Scene 5
"The Name's LaGuardia"
T. Bosley, Company
Scene 6
"The Bum Won"
H. DaSilva, Politicians
Scene 7
"I Love a Cop"
P. Stanley
Scene 9
"I Love a Cop" (reprise)
P. Stanley, M. Dawson
Scene 10
"Till Tomorrow"
E. Hanley, Company
Scene 11
"Home Again"
Company

ACT 2
Scene 1
"When Did I Fall in Love"
E. Hanley
Scene 2
"Gentleman Jimmy"
E. Rodgers, Dancing Girls
Scene 6
"Gentleman Jimmy" (reprise)
Company
Scene 7
"Little Tin Box"
H. DaSilva, Politicians
"The Very Next Man"
P. Wilson
("Politics and Poker" reprise)
(H. DaSilva, Politicians)
Scene 8
"The Very Next Man" (reprise)
P. Wilson
Finale ("The Name's LaGuardia" reprise)
Politicians

1959.26 ONCE UPON A MATTRESS

A Musical (Comedy) in Two Acts, a Prologue and 17 Scenes[7]. Book by Jay Thompson, Marshall Barer and Dean Fuller. (Based on the story "The Princess and the Pea" by Hans Christian Andersen.) Music by Mary Rodgers. Lyrics by Marshall Barer. Directed by George Abbott. Dances and musical numbers staged by Joe Layton. Scenery and costumes by William and Jean Eckart. Lighting by Tharon Musser. Musical direction, Hal Hastings. Orchestrations by Hershy Kay, Arthur Beck and Carroll Huxley. Dance music arranged by Roger Adams. Orchestra conducted by Clay Warnick. Produced by T. Edward Hambleton, Norris Houghton, William and Jean Eckart. Opened 25 November 1959 at the Alvin Theatre, moved 24 February 1960 to the Winter Garden, moved 25 April 1960 to the Cort Theatre, moved 9 May 1960 to the St. James Theatre and closed 2 July 1960 after 244 performances. Total: 460 performances.

---

[7]Originally produced Off-Broadway 11 May 1959-15 November 1959 at the Phoenix Theatre for 216 performances. Those actors who originated their roles Off-Broadway but did not transfer to Broadway are listed below: *Prince*: Jim Maher. *Queen*: Gloria Stevens. *Lady Rowena*: Dorothy Aull. *Lady Merrill*: Patsi King. *Lady Lucille*: Luce Ennis. *Sir Studley*: Jerry Newby. *The King*: JACK GILFORD. *Jester*: MATT MATTOX. *Lady Beatrice*: Gloria Stevens. *Sir Luce*: Tom Mixon. *Lady Mabelle*: Chris Karner. *Nightingale of Samarkand*: Ginny Perlowin. *Lord Howard*: Howard Parker. *Sir Steven*: Jim Stevenson. Several minor Lords and Ladies from the Ensemble roles also changed character names.

CAST (in order of appearance): *Minstrel*: HARRY SNOW. *Prince*: Gene Kelton. *Princess*: Chris Karner. *Queen*: Dorothy Frank. *Wizard*: Robert Weil. *Princess Number Twelve*: Mary Stanton. *Lady Rowena*: Patti Karr. *Lady Merrill*: Cheryl Kilgren. *Prince Dauntless*: JOE BOVA. *The Queen*: JANE WHITE. *Lady Lucille*: Dorothy Aull. *Lady Larken*: ANNE JONES. *Sir Studley*: Tom Mixon. *The King*: WILL LEE. *Jester*: JERRY NEWBY. *Sir Harry*: DAN RESIN. *Princess Winnifred*: CAROL BURNETT. *Sir Harold*: David Neuman. *Lady Beatrice*: Dorothy Frank. *Sir Luce*: Stuart Hodes. *Lady Mabelle*: Marjorie Pragon. *Nightingale of Samarkand*: Gina Viglione. *Lady Dorothy*: Dorothy D'Honau. *Sir Nicholas*: Peter Holmes. *Sir Joseph*: Joseph Carow. *Lord Howard*: Gene Kelton. *Lady Jerane*: Jerane Michel. *Lord Casper*: Casper Roos. *Sir Steven*: Jack Schwartz. *Sir Paul*: Paul Richards.

The action takes place in a small kingdom in medieval times.

Act 1, Scene 1: Throne Room. *Scene 2*: The Yellow Gallery. *Scene 3*: Courtyard. *Scene 4*: A Corridor. *Scene 5*: Winnifred's Dressing Chamber. *Scene 6*: The Grey Gallery. *Scene 7*: On the Greensward. *Scene 8*: The Yellow Gallery. *Scene 9*: Great Hall.

Act 2, Scene 1: Castle. *Scene 2*: Winnifred's Dressing Chamber. *Scene 3*: A Corrdior. *Scene 4*: Wizard's Chamber. *Scene 5*: The Grey Gallery. *Scene 6*: The Bed Chamber. *Scene 7*: A Corridor. *Scene 8*: Breakfast Hall.

ACT 1

Prologue

"Many Moons Ago"
H. Snow, Court

Scene 1

"An Opening for a Princess"
J. Bova, A. Jones, Knights and Ladies

"In a Little While"
A. Jones, D. Resin

Scene 2

"In a Little While" (reprise)
A. Jones, D. Resin

Scene 3

"Shy"
C. Burnett, T. Mixon, Knights and Ladies

"The Minstrel, the Jester and I"
W. Lee, H. Snow, J. Newby

Scene 4

"Sensitivity"
J. White, R. Weil

Scene 5

"(The) Swamps of Home"
C. Burnett, J. Bova, Ladies

Scene 7

"Normandy"
H. Snow, J. Newby, W. Lee, A. Jones

Scene 9

"Spanish Panic"
H. Snow, J. Michel, D. Frank, J. White, C. Burnett, J. Bova, Knights and Ladies

"Song of Love"
J. Bova, C. Burnett, Knights and Ladies

ACT 2

Scene 1

"Quiet"
J. Newby, (J. White), Knights and Ladies

Scene 2

"Happily Ever After"
C. Burnett

Scene 3

"Man to Man Talk"
W. Lee, J. Bova

Scene 5

"Very Soft Shoes"
J. Newby, Knights and Ladies

Scene 6

"Yesterday I Loved You"
D. Resin, A. Jones

Scene 7

"Lullaby"
G. Viglione

Scene 9

Finale
Entire Court

1959.27

SARATOGA

A Musical Comedy in Two Acts, 17 Scenes. (Book) Dramatized and directed by Morton DaCosta. Based on the novel "Saratoga Trunk" by Edna Ferber. Music by Harold Arlen. Lyrics (and additional music) by Johnny Mercer. Settings and costumes by Cecil Beaton. Choreography by Ralph Beaumont. Lighting by Jean Rosenthal. Musical direction by Jerry Arlen. Vocal arrangements by Herbert Greene. Orchestrations by Philip J. Lang. Music for dances by Genevieve Pitot. Produced by Robert Fryer. Opened 7 December 1959 at the Winter Garden and closed 13 February 1960 after 80 performances.

CAST (in order of appearance): *Cupide*: TUN TUN. *Clio Dulaine*: CAROL LAWRENCE. *Kakou*: CAROL BRICE. *Belle Piquery*: ODETTE MYRTIL. *The Drapery Man*: Mark Zeller. *The Carpenter*: Albert Popwell. *Shorty*: Augie Rios. *Maudey*: Brenda Long. *The Charwoman*: Virginia Capers. *Mrs. LeClerc*: Martha King. *M. Augustin Haussy*: Richard Graham. *Clint Maroon*: HOWARD KEEL. *M. Begué*: Truman Gaige. *Grandmother Dulaine*: Natalie Core. *Madame Dulaine*: Beatrice Bushkin. *Charlotte Thérèse*: Jeannine Masterson. *Léon*, a Waiter: Mark Zeller. *Editor*: Truman Gaige. *Haberdashery Clerk*: Frank Green. *Fabric Salesman*: Barney Johnston. *M. LaFosse*: Lanier Davis. *Mrs. Sophie Bellop*: EDITH KING. *Mrs. Porcelain*: Natalie Core. *Mr. Gould*: Truman Gaige. *Bart Van Steed*: WARDE DONOVAN. *Mr. Bean*: James Millhollin. *Daisy Porcelain*: Gerrianne Raphael. *Clarissa Van Steed*: Isabella Hoopes. *Miss Diggs*: Janyce Wagner.

Children: Brenda Long, Linda Wright, Augie Rios, Wayne Robertson. *Townspeople, Guests, etc.*: Betsy Bridge, Beatrice Bushkin, Virginia Capers, Martha King, Ina Kurland, Jeannine Masterson, Carol Taylor, Gerrianne Raphael, Lois Van Pelt, Janyce Wagner, Beverley Jane Welch, Socrates Birsky, John Blanchard, Joseph Crawford, Lanier Davis, Paul Dixon, Vito Durante, José Falcion, Julius Fields, John Ford, Jerry Fries, Gene Gavin, Frank Green, Nathaniel Horne, Barney Johnston, Louis Kosman, Jack Matthew, Oran Osburn, John Pero, Harold Pierson, Albert Popwell, Charles Queenan, Mark Zeller, Merritt Thompson.

Act 1, Scene 1: The Rampart Street House, New Orleans, 1880. *Scene 2*: Exterior of the Rampart Street House. *Scene 3*: The Waterfront Market. *Scene 4*: The Museum. *Scene 5*: Begué's Restaurant. *Scene 6*: The Garden of the Rampart Street House. *Scene 7*: The Casino. *Scene 8*: The United States Hotel, Saratoga. *Scene 9*: Clint and Clio's Rooms in the United States Hotel.

Act 2, Scene 1: The Springs, Saratoga. *Scene 2*: Corridor of the United States Hotel. *Scene 3*: Clint's and Clio's Rooms. *Scene 4*: The Verandah. *Scene 5*: The Corridor. *Scene 6*: On a Flatcar and at the Railroad Station, Binghamton, New York. *Scene 7*: The Corridor. *Scene 8*: The Ballroom of the United States Hotel.

ACT 1

Scene 1

"I'll Be Respectable"
C. Lawrence

"One Step—Two Step"
C. Lawrence, A. Rios, B. Long, Ensemble

"Gettin' a Man"
O. Myrtil, C. Brice
(*Music by* Johnny Mercer.)

Scene 3

"Petticoat High"
V. Capers, C. Lawrence, O. Myrtil, Tun Tun, Ensemble

Scene 5

"Why Fight This?"
C. Lawrence, H. Keel
(*Music by* Johnny Mercer.)

"(A) Game of Poker"
H. Keel, C. Lawrence

Scene 6

"Love Held Lightly"
O. Myrtil

"(A) Game of Poker" (reprise)
C. Lawrence, H. Keel, O. Myrtil

Scene 7

"The Gamblers" (dance)
C. Lawrence, Gamblers, Croupiers

"Saratoga"
H. Keel, C. Lawrence

Scene 8
"Saratoga" (reprise)
Ensemble
"The Gossip Song"
E. King, Ensemble
Scene 9
"Countin' Our Chickens"
C. Lawrence, H. Keel
"You or No One"
H. Keel

ACT 2
Scene 1
"The Cure"
Ensemble
"The Men Who Run the Country"
The Robber Barons
(*Music by* Johnny Mercer.)
Scene 3
"The Man in My Life"
C. Lawrence, H. Keel
Scene 4
"The Polka" (dance)
C. Lawrence, W. Donovan, Ensemble
"Love Held Lightly" (reprise)
C. Lawrence
Scene 5
"Goose Never Be a Peacock"
C. Brice
Scene 6
"Dog Eat Dog"
H. Keel, His Men
"The Railroad Fight" (dance)
H. Keel, Tun Tun, the Men
Scene 8
"Petticoat High" (reprise)
C. Lawrence, Ensemble

1960.01 BEG, BORROW OR STEAL

A Musical Comedy in Two Acts, 21 Scenes. Book and lyrics by Bud Freeman, from an (unpublished) story ("Steal—A Disc Jockey's Handbook") by Marvin Seiger and Bud Freeman. Music by Leon Pober. Staged by Billy Matthews. Dances and musical mumbers by Peter Hamilton. Directed by David Doyle. Scenery, costumes and lighting by Carter Morningstar. Musical direction by Hal Hidey. Orchestrations by Peter Matz and Hal Hidey. Produced by Eddie Bracken, with Carroll and Harris Masterson. Opened 10 February 1960 at the Martin Beck Theatre and closed 13 February 1960 after 5 performances.

CAST (in order of appearance): *Mrs. Plonsky*: Jean Bruno. *Junior*: BIFF McGUIRE. *Ollie*: Estelle Parsons. *Phil*: Betty Rhodes. *Judy*: Karen Sargent. *Clara*: BETTY GARRETT. *Pistol*: EDDIE BRACKEN. *Rafe*: LARRY PARKS. *Jason*: Roy Stuart. *Ethel*: Bernice Massi. *Lovers*: Mary Sullivan, Del Hanley. *Modern Dance Leader*: Sally Lee. *Dance Class*: Carmen Morales, Garold Gardner Ellen Halpin, Willard Nagel. *Rug Hooker*: Michael Davis. *Pottery Girl*: Colleen Corkrey. *Bar Girl*: Esther Horrocks. *Knitters*: Fran Leone, Keith Willis. *Painter*: Tom Hester. *Chess Players*: Michael Stuart, Arthur Whitfield. *Flamenco Dancers*: Adriana Keathley, Harold DaSilva. *Guitarist*: Fred Kimbrough. *Kibitzer*: Mara Wirt. *Poet*: John Tormey. *Poetry Lovers*: Shelia Dee, Georgia Kennedy, Virginia Barnes. *Sculptor*: Chuck Arnett. *Model*: Beti Seay. *Mobile Artist*: Lucinda Stevens. *Frieda*: Claiborne Carey. *Patriot*: Jack Drummond. *Sam Lee Howard*: Richard Armbruster. *Muscle*: Bill Linton. *Koppisch*: Richard Woods. *Blanding*: David Doyle.

Act 1, Scene 1: The Street. A run-down section of a monster American city in the 1950s. *Scene 2*: The Store. *Scene 3*: The Street. *Scene 4*: The Pit. *Scene 5*: The Park. *Scene 6*: The Street. *Scene 7*: The Pit. *Scene 8*: Rafe's Attic. *Scene 9*: The Store. *Scene 10*: The Street. *Scene 11*: The Pad. *Scene 12*: The Pit.

Act 2, Scene 1: The Office. Six months later. *Scene 2*: The Street. *Scene 3*: Chez Pit. *Scene 4*: The Office. *Scene 5*: The Street. *Scene 6*: The Pad. *Scene 7*: Chez Pit. *Scene 8*: The Street. *Scene 9*: The Store.

ACT 1
"Some Little People"
Ensemble
"Rootless"
B. McGuire
"What Are We Gonna Do Tonight?"
E. Parsons, B. Rhodes, K. Sargent
"Poetry and All That Jazz"
C. Cary, Ensemble
"Don't Stand Too Close to the Picture"
L. Parks, B. Garrett, Ensemble
"Beg, Borrow or Steal," Recitative
L. Parks
"Beg, Borrow or Steal"
L. Parks
"No One Knows Me"
B. Garrett
"Zen Is When"
E. Bracken, B. McGuire, B. Massi, R. Stuart
Ballet
Ensemble
Soloist: C. Corkrey. *The Lovers*: C. Morales, A. Whitfield.
"Clara"
B. McGuire
"You've Got Something to Say"
L. Parks, B. Garrett
"You've Got Something to Say" (reprise)
L. Parks, B. Garrett, E. Bracken, B. McGuire, Company

ACT 2
"Presenting Clara Spencer"
B. Garrett, assisted by K. Willis, M. Stuart,
C. Arnett, H. DaSilva, W. Nagel, G. Gardner, A. Whitfield
"I Can't Stop Talking"
B. Garrett, B. McGuire
"It's All in Your Mind"
L. Parks, B. Garrett
"In Time"
B. McGuire
"Think"
B. Garrett
"Little People"
E. Bracken, Company
Danced by K. Willis, S. Lee, M. Stuart.
"Rafesville, U.S.A."
B. Massi, R. Stuart
"Beg, Borrow or Steal"
L. Parks, Ensemble
"Let's Be Strangers Again"
B. Garrett, B. McGuire
"Little People" (reprise)
Entire Company

1960.02 THE CRADLE WILL ROCK

A Revival of the Play in Music in One Act[8], 10 Scenes. Play, music and lyrics by Marc Blitzstein. Staged by Howard DaSilva. Scenic design by David Hays. Costume design by Ruth Morley. Choreographed by Billy Parsons. Conducted by Lehman Engel. Produced by the New York City Opera. Opened 11 February 1960 at the New York City Center and closed 21 February 1960 after 4 performances in repertory.

CAST: *Moll*: TAMMY GRIMES. *Gent*: Seth Riggs. *Dick*: Arnold Voketaitis. *Cop*: Dan Merriman. *Reverend Salvation*: Kenneth Smith. *Editor Daily*: Jack Harrold. *Yasha*: Michael Wager. *Dauber*: Chandler Cowles. *President Prexy*: John Macurdy.

[8]First presented in New York 16 June 1937 at the Venice Theatre for 19 performances, subsequently at the Mercury and Windsor Theatres for 112 performances. For Synopsis of Scenes and Musical Numbers, see original 1937 production.

Professor Trixie: Philip Bruns. *Professor Mamie*: Maurice Stern. *Professor Scoot*: Howard Fried. *Doctor Specialist*: Joshua Hecht. *Harry Druggist*: WILLIAM GRIFFIS. *Clerk*: Lehman Engel. *Mr. Mister*: CRAIG TIMBERLAKE. *Mrs. Mister*: RUTH KOBART. *Junior Mister*: Keith Kaldenberg. *Sister Mister*: Nancy Dussault. *Steve*: Frank Poretta. *Sadie Polock*: Sophie Ginn. *Gus Polock*: Robert Kerns. *Bugs*: George Del Monte. *Larry Foreman*: DAVID ATKINSON. *Ella Hammer*: JANE JOHNSTON. *Reporters*: Seth Riggs, William Zachariiesen. *Ensemble*: New York City Opera Chorus.

1960.03 THE CONSUL

A Revival of the Opera (Musical Drama) in Three Acts, 6 Scenes[9]. Libretto and music by Gian-Carlo Menotti. Conductor, Werner Torkanowsky. Settings and costumes by Horace Armistead. Lighting by Jean Rosenthal. Magic sequences created and staged by Fred Keating. Staged by Gian-Carlo Menotti. Produced by the New York City Opera Company. Opened 14 February 1960 at the New York City Center and closed 21 February 1960 after 2 performances in repertory.

CAST: (in order of appearance): *John Sorel*: CHESTER LUDGIN. *Magda Sorel*: PATRICIA NEWAY. *The Mother*: EVELYN SACHS. *Secret Police Agent*: JOSHUA HECHT. *First Plainclothesman*: William Zachariasen. *Second Plainclothesman*: Sam Kirkham. *The Secretary*: REGINA SARFATY. *Mr. Kofner*: ARNOLD VOKETAITIS. *The Foreign Woman*: MARIA MARLO. *Anna Gomez*: Maria Di Gerlando. *Vera Boronel*: Ruth Kobart. *Nika Magadoff* (The Magician): JACK HARROLD. *Assan*: Dan Merriman. *Voice on the Record*: Mabel Mercer.

1960.04 A THURBER CARNIVAL

A Revue in Two Acts, 15 Scenes. Play (sketches, lyrics) by James Thurber. Conceived and directed by Burgess Meredith. Music composed and performed by Don Elliott. Scenery by Marvin Reiss. Associate director, James Starbuck. Men's costumes by Ramsé Stevens. Women's clothes from Jenkins Gowns. Lighting by Paul Morrison. Produced by Michael Davis, Helen Bonfils and Haila Stoddard. Opened 26 February 1960 at the ANTA Theatre, closing 25 June 1960 after 127 performances; re-opened a return engagement 5 September 1960 at the ANTA Theatre and closed 26 November 1960 after 96 perfornances. Total: 223 performances.

CAST: TOM EWELL, PEGGY CASS, PAUL FORD, ALICE GHOSTLEY, JOHN McGIVER, WYNNE MILLER, PETER TURGEON, Charles Braswell, Margo Lundgreen, Don Elliott Quartet (Don Elliott, Jack Six, Jim Raney, Ronnie Bedford).

ACT 1

Scene 1

"Word Dance (Part 1)"
(*Staged by* James Starbuck.)P. Cass, P. Turgeon, P. Ford, W. Miller, J. McGiver, M. Lungreen, A. Ghostley, C. Braswell, (Don Elliott Quartet)

Scene 2

The Night the Bed Fell
T. Ewell

Scene 3

Fables (Part 1):
(*Staged by* James Starbuck.)

A. The Wolf at the Door
Narrator: A. Ghostley. *Daughter*: W. Miller. *Mother*: P. Cass. *Father*: P. Ford. *Wolf*: C. Braswell.

B. The Unicorn in the Garden
Narrator: P. Turgeon. *Man*: P. Ford. *She*: A. Ghostley. *Psychiatrist*: J. McGiver. *Policeman*: C. Braswell.

C. The Little Girl and the Wolf
Narrator: P. Cass. *Wolf*: P. Ford. *Little Girl*: W. Miller.

Scene 4

If Grant Had Been Drinking at Appomattox
Narrator: P. Turgeon. *Shultz*: C. Braswell. *Grant*: T. Ewell. *Lee*: P. Ford. *Lee's Staff Man*: J. McGiver. *Officer*: P. Turgeon.

Scene 5

Casuals of the Keys
Visitor: J. McGiver. *Darrel Darke*: P. Ford.

Scene 6

The Macbeth Murder Mystery
He: T. Ewell. *She*: P. Cass.

Scene 7

"Gentlemen Shoppers"
Narrator: P. Turgeon. *Salesgirl*: A. Ghostley. *Westwater*: J. McGiver. *Bargirl*: W. Miller. *Anderson*: T. Ewell. *Bailey*: P. Ford.

Scene 8

The Last Flower
T. Ewell

ACT 2

Scene 1

(The) Pet Department
Announcer: P. Turgeon. *The Pet Counsellor*: T. Ewell. *Miss Whittaker*: A. Ghostley. *A Girl*: W. Miller.

Scene 2

Mr. Preble Gets Rid of His Wife
Preble: P. Ford. *Miss Daley*: W. Miller. *Mrs. Preble*: P. Cass.

Scene 3

File and Forget
James Thurber: T. Ewell. *Miss Bagley*: M. Lungreen. *Miss Alma Winege*: P. Cass. *Miss Wynne*: W. Miller. *Jeannette Gaines*: A. Ghostley. *Clint Jordan*: P. Ford. *H. F. Cluffman*: J. McGiver.

Scene 4

Take Her Up Tenderly
John: P. Ford. *Nellie*: A. Ghostley. *Lou*: P. Cass.

Scene 5

Fables (Part 2)
(*Staged by* James Starbuck.)

A. The Owl Who Was God
Narrator: A. Ghotsley. *Owl*: J. McGiver.*Moles*: P. Tugeon, C. Braswell. *Secretary Bird*: P. Ford. *Red Fox*: M. Lungreen.

B. The Clothes Moth and the Luna Moth
Narrator: T. Ewell. *Luna Moth*: W. Miller. *Clothes Moth*: C. Braswell.

Scene 6

The Secret Life of Walter Mitty
Narrator: P. Turgeon. *Walter Mitty*: T. Ewell. *Mrs. Mitty*: P. Cass. *First Voice*: C. Braswell. *Lieut. Berg*: P. Turgeon. *Nurse*: W. Miller. *Dr. Renshaw*: J. McGiver. *Dr. Benbow*: C. Braswell. *Dr. Remington*: P. Turgeon. *Mr. Pritchard-Mitford*: P. Ford. *The Leader*: P. Ford.

Scene 7

"Word Dance (Part 2)"
(*Staged by* James Starbuck.)
T. Ewell, J. McGiver, W. Miller, P. Cass, A. Ghostley, M. Lundgreen, P. Ford, P. Turgeon, C. Braswell, Don Elliott Quartet

1960.05 GREENWILLOW

A Musical Comedy in Two Acts, 15 Scenes. Book by Lesser Samuels and Frank Loesser. Based on the novel of the same name by B. J. Chute. Music and lyrics by Frank Loesser. Directed by George Roy Hill. Choreography by Joe Layton. Settings by Peter Larkin. Costumes by Alvin Colt. Lighting by Feder. Orchestrations by Don Walker. Musical direction by Abba Bogin. Produced by Robert A. Willey in association with Frank Productions, Inc. Opened 8 March 1960 at the Alvin Theatre and closed 28 May 1960 after 95 performances.

CAST (in order of appearance): *Jabez Briggs*: John Megna. *Clara Clegg*: Dortha Duckworth. *Mrs. Hasty*: Maggie Task. *Mr. Preebs*: Jordon Howard. *Mrs. Lunny*: Marie Foster. *Reverend Lapp*: WILLIAM CHAPMAN. *Gramma Briggs*: PERT KELTON. *Maidy*: Elaine Swann. *Emma*: Saralou Cooper. *Gideon Briggs*: ANTHONY PERKINS. *Dorrie Whitbred*: ELLEN McCOWN. *Amos Briggs*: Bruce MacKay. *Micah Briggs*: Ian Tucker. *Martha Briggs*: Lynn Brinker. *Sheby Briggs*: Brenda Harris. *Thomas Clegg*: Lee Cass. *Reverend Birdsong*: CECIL KELLAWAY. *Young Churchgoer*: Thomas Norden. *Will*: David Gold. *Nell*: Margery Gray. *Andrew*: Grover Dale.

Singers: Kenny Adams, Betsy Bridge, Marie Foster, Rico Froehlich, Russell Goodwin, Jordon Howard, Marion Mercer, Carl Nicholas, Virginia Oswald, Bob

[9]Originally produced in New York 15 March 1950 at the Ethel Barrymore Theatre for 269 performances. For Synopsis of Scenes and Musical Numbers, see original 1950 production.

Roman, Shelia Swenson, Maggie Task, Karen Thorsell. *Dancers*: Jere Admire, Don Atkinson, Estelle Aza, Joan Coddington, Ethelyne Dunfee, Richard Englund, David Gold, Margery Gray, Mickey Gunnerson, Patsi King, Jack Leigh, Nancy Van Rhein, Jimmy White.

The action takes place during four seasons in and about the (New England) village of Greenwillow.

Act 1, Scene 1: The Square. *Scene 2*: Briggs Farm. *Scene 3*: The Mill. *Scene 4*: The Willow. *Scene 5*: The Square. *Scene 6*: Cleggs Farm. *Scene 7*: The Mill. *Scene 8*: Briggs Farm. *Scene 9*: The Church. *Scene 10*: The Square.

Act 2, Scene 1: The Square. *Scene 2*: Briggs Farm. *Scene 3*: Cleggs House. *Scene 4*: The Square. *Scene 5*: Briggs Farm.

ACT 1

"A Day Borrowed from Heaven"
The Villagers

"A Day Borrowed from Heaven" (reprise)
A. Perkins

"Dorrie's Wish"
E. McCown

"The Music of Home"
B. MacKay, A. Perkins, the Villagers

"Gideon Briggs, I Love You"
A. Perkins, E. McCown

"The Autumn Courting" (dance)
All the Villagers

"The Call to Wander"
B. MacKay

"Summertime Love"
A. Perkins, the Villagers

"Walking Away Whistling"
E. McCown

"The Sermon"
W. Chapman, C. Kellaway

"Could've Been a Ring"
L. Cass, P. Kelton

"Gideon Briggs, I Love You" (reprise)
E. McCown

"Halloweve" (dance)
The Young Villagers

"Never Will I Marry"
A. Perkins

"Greenwillow Christmas" (Carol)
L. Brinker, Villagers

ACT 2

"The Music of Home" (reprise)
The Villagers

"Faraway Boy"
E. McCown

"Clang Dang the Bell"
A. Perkins, P. Kelton, L. Brinker, I. Tucker, B. Harris, J. Megna

"What a Blessing"
C. Kellaway

"He Died Good"
The Villagers

"The Spring Courting" (dance)
G. Dale, E. McCown, the Young Villagers

"Summertime Love" (reprise)
A. Perkins

"What a Blessing" (reprise)
C. Kellaway

"The Call"
A. Perkins

The Music of Home" (reprise)
All of Greenwillow

1960.06 BYE BYE BIRDIE

A Musical (Comedy) in Two Acts, 18 Scenes. Book by Michael Stewart. Music by Charles Strouse. Lyrics by Lee Adams. Scenery by Robert Randolph. Costumes by Miles White. Lighting by Peggy Clark. Musical director, Elliott Lawrence. Orchestrations by Robert Ginzler. Dance arrangements by John Morris. Additional scoring by Elliott Lawrence. Directed and choreographed by Gower Champion. Associate choreographer, Gene Bayliss. Film sequences by Robert J. McCarty in association with Robert Gaffney. Produced by Edward Padula in association with L. Slade Brown. Opened 14 April 1960 at the Martin Beck Theatre, moved 24 October 1960 to the 54th Street Theatre, moved 16 January 1961 to the Sam S. Shubert Theatre, and closed 7 October 1961 after 607 performances.

CAST (in order of appearance): *Albert Peterson*: DICK VAN DYKE. *Rose Grant*: CHITA RIVERA. *Teenagers (17)*: *Helen*: Karin Wolfe. *Nancy*: Marissa Mason. *Alice*: Sharon Lerit. *Margie Ann*: Louise Quick. *Penelope Ann*: Lada Edmund. *Deborah Sue*: Jessica Albright. *Suzie*: Lynn Bowin. *Linda*: Judy Keirn. *Carol*: Penny Ann Green. *Martha Louise*: Vicki Belmonte. *Harold*: Michael Vita. *Karl*: Jerry Dodge. *Harvey*: Dean Stolber. *Henry*: Ed Kresley. *Arthur*: Bob Spencer. *Freddie*: Tracy Everitt. *Peyton*: Gary Howe. *Ursula Merkle*: BARBARA DOHERTY. *Kim MacAfee*: SUSAN WATSON. *Mrs. MacAfee*: MARIJANE MARICLE. *Mr. MacAfee*: PAUL LYNDE. *Teen Trio*: Louise Quick, Jessica Albright, Vicki Belmonte. *Sad Girl*: Sharon Lerit. *Another Sad Girl*: Karin Wolfe. *Mae Peterson*: KAY MEDFORD. *Reporters*: Lee Howard, Jim Sisco, Don Farnworth, John Coyle. *Conrad Birdie*: DICK GAUTIER. *Guitar Man*: Kenny Burrell. *Conductor*: Kasimir Kokich. *Cheerleaders*: Judy Keirn, Lynn Bowin. *Mayor*: Allen Knowles. *Mayor's Wife*: Amelia Haas. *Hugo Peabody*: MICHAEL J. POLLARD. *Randolph MacAfee*: JOHNNY BORDEN. *Mrs. Merkle*: Pat McEnnis. *Old Woman*: Dori Davis. *Neighbors*: Amelia Haas, Jeannine Masterson, Ed Becker, Oran Osburn, George Blackwell, Lee Howard. *Mr. Henkel*: Charles Nelson Reilly. *Gloria Rasputin*: NORMA RICHARDSON. *Ed Sullivan's Voice*: Will Jordan. *TV Stage Manager*: Tony Mordente. *Charles F. Maude*: George Blackwell. *Shriners*: Allen Knowles, John Coyle, Dick Crowley, Don Farnworth, Bud Fleming, Kasimir Kokich, Jim Sisco.

Act 1, Scene 1: Office of Almaelou Music, New York. *Scene 2*: Sweet Apple, Ohio. *Scene 3*: MacAfee Home, Sweet Apple. *Scene 4*: Pennsylvania Station, New York. *Scene 5*: Railroad Station, Sweet Apple. *Scene 6*: Courthouse Steps, Sweet Apple. *Scene 7*: MacAfee Home, Sweet Apple. *Scene 8*: Stage, Central Movie Theatre, Sweet Apple. *Scene 9*: Backstage Office, Central Movie Theatre, Sweet Apple. *Scene 10*: Stage, Central Movie Theatre, Sweet Apple.

Act 2, Scene 1: MacAfee Home, Sweet Apple. *Scene 2*: Street Outside MacAfee Home. *Scene 3*: MacAfee's Back Door. *Scene 4*: Maude's Roadside Retreat. *Scene 5*: Private Dining Room, Maude's Roadside Retreat. *Scene 6*: Back Door, Maude's Roadside Retreat. *Scene 7*: The Ice House. *Scene 8*: Railroad Station, Sweet Apple.

ACT 1

Scene 1

"An English Teacher"
C. Rivera, D. Van Dyke

Scene 2

"The Telephone Hour"
Sweet Apple Kids (Teenagers)

Scene 3

"How Lovely to Be a Woman"
S. Watson

Scene 4

"We Love You, Conrad!"
L. Quick, J. Albright, V. Belmonte

"Put on a Happy Face"
D. Van Dyke, S. Lerit, K. Wolfe

"Normal American Boy"
C. Rivera, D. Van Dyke, Chorus

Scene 5

"One Boy"
S. Watson, J. Albright, S. Lerit

"One Boy" (reprise)
C. Rivera

Scene 6

"Honestly Sincere"
D. Gautier, Townspeople

Scene 7

"Hymn for a Sunday Evening"
P. Lynde, M. Maricle, S. Watson, J. Borden, Neighbors

Scene 9

"How to Kill a Man" (ballet)
C. Rivera, D. Van Dyke, Company

Scene 10

"One Last Kiss"
D. Gautier, Company

ACT 2

Scene 1

"What Did I Ever See in Him?"

C. Rivera, S. Watson

Scene 2

"A Lot of Livin' to Do"

D. Gautier, S. Watson, Teenagers

Scene 3

"Kids"

P. Lynde, M. Maricle

Scene 4

"Baby, Talk to Me"

D. Van Dyke, Quartet

Scene 5

"Shriners' Ballet"

C. Rivera, Shriners

Scene 6

"Kids" (reprise)

P. Lynde, M. Maricle, J. Borden, Townspeople

Scene 7

"Spanish Rose"

C. Rivera

Scene 8

"Rosie"

D. Van Dyke, C. Rivera

1960.07 FROM A TO Z

A Musical Revue in Two Acts, 27 Scenes. (Sketches by Woody Allen, Herbert Farjeon, Don Parks, Nina Warner Hook. Music and lyrics by Jay Thompson, Dickson Hughes, Everett Sloane, Jack Holmes, Mary Rodgers, Marshall Barer, Paul Klein, Fred Ebb, Norman Martin, Don Parks, William Dyer, Lee Goldsmith, Charles Zwar, Alan Melville.) Directed by Christopher Hewett. Choreography by Ray Harrison. Sets, lighting and costumes by Fred Voelpel. Miss Gingold's gowns by Scaasi. Musical direction and vocal arrangements by Milton Greene. Orchestrations by Jay Brower and Jonathan Tunick. Dance arrangements by Jack Holmes. Produced by Carroll and Harris Masterson. Opened 20 April 1960 at the Plymouth Theatre and closed 7 May 1960 after 21 performances.

CAST: HERMIONE GINGOLD, ELLIOTT REID, ALVIN EPSTEIN, LOUISE HOFF, NORA KOVACH, KELLY BROWN, PAULA STEWART, Stuart Damon, Bob Dishy, Isabelle Farrell, Beryl Towbin, Michael Fesco, Larry Hovis, Virginia Vestoff, Doug Spingler.

ACT 1

Scene 1 (A)

"Best Gold"

H. Gingold, N. Kovach,
K. Brown, M. Fesco, D. Spingler, B. Towbin, V. Vestoff, S. Damon, P. Stewart
(*Music and Lyrics by* Jerry Herman.)

Scene 2 (B)

Bardolatry

L. Hoff, E. Reid

Scene 3 (C)

"Pill Parade"

(*Music and Lyrics by* Jay Thompson.)

Narrator: A. Epstein. *Average Man*: K. Brown. *Vitamins*: M. Fesco, D. Spingler. *Benzabang*: B. Towbin. *Pilltown*: V. Vestoff. *Sexaphine*: N. Kovach. *One More Pill*: I. Farrell.

Scene 4 (D)

"Togetherness"

(*Music and Lyrics by* Dickson Hughes and Everett Sloane.)

Grandmother: H. Gingold. *Father*: E. Reid. *Mother*: L. Hoff. *Daughter*: P. Stewart. *Son*: S. Damon.

Scene 5 (E)

Pschological Warfare

(*by* Woody Allen)

Sergeant: A. Epstein. *Privates*: L. Hovis, D. Spingler. *Enemy*: B. Dishy. *Medics*: S. Damon, M. Fesco.

Scene 6 (F)

"Balloons"

N. Kovach, K. Brown, M. Fesco, D. Spingler, B. Towbin, V. Vestoff
(*Music and Lyrics by* Jack Holmes.)

Scene 7 (G)

Music Talk

H. Gingold

Scene 8 (H)

"Hire a Guy"

(*Music by* Mary Rodgers. *Lyrics by* Marshall Barer.)

The Star: L. Hoff. *The Director*: E. Reid. *The Writer*: S. Damon. *Patsy*: B. Dishy.

Scene 9 (I)

"Interlude"

(*Music by* Jack Holmes.)

Ladies: B. Towbin, V. Vestoff, I. Farrell. *Gentlemen*: K. Brown, M. Fesco, D. Spingler. *A Stranger*: N. Kovach. *A Man*: S. Damon.

Scene 10 (J)

Hit Parade

(*by* Woody Allen)

Girl: H. Gingold. *Boy*: A. Epstein.

Scene 11 (K)

Coventional Behavior

E. Reid

Scene 12 (L)

"I Said to Love"

L. Hoff
(*Music by* Paul Klein. *Lyrics by* Fred Ebb.)

Scene 13 (M)

Winter in Palm Springs

(*by* Herbert Farjeon)

Colonel Spicer: A. Epstein. *Mrs. Twiceover*: H. Gingold. *Alice*: B. Towbin.

Scene 14 (N)

"Charlie"

P. Stewart
(*Music by* Norman Martin. *Lyrics by* Fred Ebb.)

Scene 15 (O)

"The Sound of Schmaltz" (Parody of "the Sound of Music")

(*Words by* Don Parks. *Music by* William Dyer.)

Head Nanny: L. Hoff. *Nannies*: N. Kovach, B. Towbin, V. Vestoff, I. Farrell. *Alicia Cadwallader-Smith*: H. Gingold. *Baron von Klaptrap*: E. Reid. *Children*: K. Brown, A. Epstein, M. Fesco, D. Spingler, S. Damon, B. Dishy, P. Stewart.

Scene 1: The Offices of "International Nannies, Ltd." (with an interlude in Central Park). *Scene 2*: The von Klaptrap Nursery. *Scene 3*: Baron von Klaptrap's Apartment. *Scene 4*: The von Klaptrap Living Room.

ACT 2

Scene 1 (P)

"Grand Jury Jump"

N. Kovach, P. Stewart, B. Towbin, V. Vestoff, I. Farrell,
K. Brown, S. Damon, M. Fesco, D. Spingler, L. Hovis
(*Music by* Paul Klein. *Lyrics by* Fred Ebb.)

Scene 2 (Q)

"South American Way"

A. Epstein, B. Dishy
(*Music by* Norman Martin. *Lyrics by* Noman Martin and Fred Ebb.)

Scene 3 (R)

Snapshots

(*by* Herbert Farjeon)

She: H. Gingold. *He*: E. Reid.

Scene 4 (S)

"Time Step"

K. Brown
(*Music by* Paul Klein. *Lyrics by* Fred Ebb.)

Scene 5 (T)

Bobo

E. Reid

Scene 6 (U)

"Queen of Song"

H. Gingold
(*Music and Lyrics by* Eric Maschwitz and Jack Strachey.)

Scene 7 (V)

Surprise Party

(*by* Woody Allen)

Fred: B. Dishy. *Harry*: K. Brown. *Myrna*: L. Hoff. *Linda*: B. Towbin. *Ruthie*: N. Kovach. *Rita*: I. Farrell. *Virginia*: V. Vestoff. *Blonde*: P. Stewart.

Scene 8 (W)

"Countermelody"

P. Stewart, S. Damon

(*Music by* Mary Rodgers and Jay Thompson. *Lyrics by* Marshall Barer.)

Scene 9 (X)

Park Meeting

(*by* Nina Warner Hook)

Governess: H. Gingold. *Woman*: L. Hoff.

Scene 10 (Y)

"Red Shoes"

(*Music by* Jack Holmes.)

Introduced by B. Dishy. *Danced by* I. Farrell, M. Fesco, L. Hovis, D. Spingler, B. Towbin, V. Vestoff.

Scene 11 (Z)

"Four for the Road"

H. Gingold

(*Music by* Paul Klein. *Lyrics by* Lee Goldsmith and Fred Ebb.)

Scene 12 (&)

"What Next?"

The Company

(*Music by* Charles Zwar. *Lyrics by* Alan Melville.)

1960.08 WEST SIDE STORY

A Return Engagement of the Musical in Two Acts, 15 Scenes[10]. Book by Arthur Laurents. Based on a conception of Jerome Robbins. Music by Leonard Bernstein. Lyrics by Stephen Sondheim. Entire production directed and choreographed by Jerome Robbins. Scenic production by Oliver Smith. Costumes by Irene Sharaff. Lighting by Jean Rosenthal. Co-choreographer, Peter Gennaro. Assistant dance director, Howard Jeffrey. Musical direction, Joseph Lewis. Orchestrations by Leonard Bernstein, with Sid Ramin, Irwin Kostal. Produced by Robert E. Griffith and Harold S. Prince by arrangement with Roger L. Stevens. Opened 27 April 1960 at the Winter Garden and closed 10 December 1960 after 249 performances. Total performances, including original run: 981.

CAST: *THE JETS*: *Riff*, the Leader: THOMAS HASSON. *Tony*, his friend: LARRY KERT. *Action*: George Liker. *A-Rab*: Alan Johnson. *Baby John*: Barry Burns. *Big Deal*: Martin Charnin. *Diesel*: Donald Corby. *Snowboy*: Eddie Gaspar. *Mouth Piece*: Eddie Miller. *Tiger*: Richard Corrigan. *Gee-Tar*: Glenn Gibson. *Their Girls*: *Graziella*: Sandy Leeds. *Velma*: Audrey Hays. *Clarice*: Lee Lewis. *Pauline*: Judy Aldene. *Anybodys*: Pat Birch. *Minnie*: Barbara Monte.

THE SHARKS: *Bernardo*, the Leader: GEORGE MARCY. *Maria*, his Sister: CAROL LAWRENCE. *Anita*, his Girl: ALLYN ANN McLERIE. *Chino*, his Friend: Miguel De Vega. *Pepe*: Ben Vargas. *Indio*: Robert Avian. *Luis*: Sterling Clark. *Estella*: Danii Prior. *Burro*: Vince Baggetta. *Nibbles*: Ed Dutton. *Toro*: Kent Thomas. *Moose*: Marc Scott. *Their Girls*: *Rosalia*: Gloria Lambert. *Teresita*: Hope Clarke. *Francisca*: Anna Marie Moylan. *Marguerita*: Poligena Rogers. *Consuelo*: Genii Prior.

THE ADULTS: *Doc*: ALBERT M. OTTENHEIMER. *Schrank*: Ted Gunther. *Krupke*: Roger Franklin. *Gladhand*: Ross Hertz.

1960.09 FINIAN'S RAINBOW

A Revival of the Musical in Two Acts, 10 Scenes[11]. Book by E. Y. Harburg and Fred Saidy. Lyrics by E. Y. Harburg. Music by Burton Lane. Directed and choreographed by Herbert Ross. Scenery and lighting by Howard Bay. Costumes by Stanley Simmons. Orchestrations by Robert Russell Bennett and Don Walker. Musical director, Max Meth. Produced by the New York City Center Light Opera Company (Jean Dalrymple, Director.) Opened 27 April 1960 at the New York City Center, closing 8 May 1960 after 15 performances; re-opened 23 May 1960 at the 46th Street Theatre under the auspices of Robert Fryer and Lawrence Carr with John F. Herman and Theatrical Interests Plan, Inc. and closed 1 June 1960 after 12 additional performances. Total: 27 performances.

CAST[12] (in order of appearance): *Buzz Collins*: Eddie Bruce. *Sheriff*: Tom McElhany, (Tom McElhany). *First Sharecropper*: John McCurry. *Second Sharecropper*: Knute Sullivan. *Susan Mahoney*: ANITA ALVAREZ. *Henry*: Michael Darden. *Finian McLonergan*: BOBBY HOWES. *Sharon McLonergan*: JEANNIE CARSON. *Sam*: Arthur Garrison. *Woody Mahoney*: BIFF McGUIRE. Og, a Leprechaun: HOWARD MORRIS. *Senator Billboard Rawkins*: SORRELL BOOKE. *First Geologist*: Barney Johnston. *Second Geologist*: Robert Guillaume. *Howard*: Jim McGillan. *Diane*: Patty Austin. *Mr. Robust*: Edgar Daniels. *Mr. Shears*: Joe Ross. *First Passion Pilgrim Gospeller*: Jerry Laws. *Second Passion Pilgrim Gospeller*: Bill Glover. *Third Passion Pilgrim Gospeller*: Tiger Haynes. *First Deputy*: Don Gray. *Second Deputy*: Larry Mitchell.

Singers: Issa Arnal, Nan Courtney, Marnell Higley, Mary Louise, Lispet Nelson, Stephanie Reynolds, Alice Elizabeth Webb, Beverly Jane Welch, John Boni, Hugh Dilworth, Bill Glover, Don Gray, Robert Guillaume, Tiger Haynes, Barney Johnston, Jerry Laws, John McCurry, Larry Mitchell, Knute Sullivan. *Dancers*: Marilynn Allwyn, Ellen Halpin, Sally Lee, Diane McDaniel, Carmen Morales, Mavis Ray, Sandra Roveta, Jacqueline Walcott, Myrna White, Julius C. Fields, Jerry Fries, Gene Gavin, Loren Hightower, Nat Horne, Ronald Lee, Paul Olsen, Wakefield Poole, Jaime Juan Rogers, Ron Schwinn.

1960.10 CHRISTINE

A Musical in Two Acts, 18 Scenes. Book by Pearl S. Buck and Charles K. Peck, Jr. Based on the book "My Indian Family" by Hilda Wernher. Music by Sammy Fain. Lyrics by Paul Francis Webster. (Direction uncredited[13].) Choreography and musical numbers by Hanya Holm. Consultant on Indian customs, Bhaskar. Settings and lighting by Jo Mielziner. Costumes by Alvin Colt. Vocal and dance arrangements by Trude Rittman. Orchestrations by Philip J. Lang. Associate producer, Ben Frye. Produced by Oscar S. Lerman and Martin B. Cohen in association with Walter Cohen. Opened 28 April 1960 at the 46th Street Theatre and closed 7 May 1960 after 12 performances.

CAST (in order of appearance): *Beggar*: Joseph Crawford. *Servants to Dr. Singh*: Arthur Tookoyan, Tony Gardell, John Anania. *Auntie*: NANCY ANDREWS. *Uncle*: PHIL LEEDS. *Rainath*: BHASKAR. *Jaya*: Leslye Hunter. *Rajendra*: Augie Rios. *Krishna*: Steve Curry. *Mohan Roy*: Jonathan Morris. *Servant to Mohan Roy*: Nicholas Bianchi. *Station Master*: Louis Polacek. *Sita Roy*: JANET PAVEK. *Lady Christine FitzSimons*: MAUREEN O'HARA. *Dr. Rashil Singh*: MORLEY MEREDITH. *Dr. MacGowan*: Daniel Keyes. *The Matchmaker*: Barbara Webb. *The Prospective Brides (5)*: *Tara*: Mai-Lan. *Lakshmi*: Jinja. *Amora*: Laurie Archer. *Twins*: Anjali Devi, Sasha. *Children of the Town*: Donna Lyn, Jan Rhodes, Louis Hernandez. *Priest*: John Anania.

Townspeople, Hindus, Muslims, Vendors, Beggars: *Dancers*: Laurie Archer, Sandra Bowman, Anjali Devi, Jinja, Mai-Lan, Jonalee Sanford, Sasha, Vito Durante, Dino Laudicino, Joseph Nelson, Alan Peterson, Joe Rocco, Gil Schwartz. *Singers*: Bea Barrett, Diana Corto, Marceline Dacker, Josephine Lang, Jen Nelson, Barbara Webb, John Anania, Nicholas Bianchi, Joseph Crawford, Tony Gardell, Louis Polacek, Arthur Tookoyan.

The story is laid in the little town of Akbarabad, India, at the present time.

Act 1, Scene 1: The Railroad Station in Akbarabad. *Scene 2*: The Study in Dr. Rashil Singh's home. *Scene 3*: Outside the Clinic. *Scene 4*: The Living Room, six days later. *Scene 5*: The Veranda, two months later. *Scene 6*: The Living Room. *Scene 7*: The Veranda. *Scene 8*: The Drawing Room. *Scene 9*: The Clinic. *Scene 10*: The City Square.

Act 2, Scene 1: The Veranda at Rashil's house. *Scene 2*: An open plain. *Scene 3*: A Shrine. *Scene 4*: The Living Room. *Scene 5*: The Veranda. *Scene 6*: The Drawing Room. *Scene 7*: The Veranda. *Scene 8*: Mohan Roy's Home.

ACT 1

"Welcome Song"

N. Andrews, P. Leeds, Bhaskar, Children, Chorus

"My Indian Family"

M. O'Hara

[10]Originally produced in New York 26 September 1957 at the Winter Garden for 732 performances. For Synopsis of Scenes and Musical Numbers, see original 1957 production.

[11]Originally produced in New York 10 January 1947 at the 46th Street Theatre for 725 performances. For Synopsis of Scenes and Musical Numbers, see original 1947 production. Michael Kidd's original choreography credited in "Dance of the Golden Crock."

[12]Cast changes for the transfer were as follows: *Sheriff*: Judson Morgan. *Susan Mahoney*: CARMEN GUTIERREZ. *Mr. Shears*: Cris Alexander. Withdrawn from the ensemble were *Singers*: Marnell Higley, John Boni, Hugh Dilworth, Don Gray. *Dancers*: Marilynn Allwyn, Ellen Halpin, Mavis Ray, Gene Gavin, Jaime Juan Rogers. Added to singing ensemble was Don Grilley.

[13]Direction credited to Edward Chodorov prior to New York opening.

"A Doctor's Soliloquy"
M. Meredith
"UNICEF Song"
Children
"My Little Lost Girl"
M. O'Hara, M. Meredith
"I'm Just a Little Sparrow"
L. Hunter, N. Andrews, Bhaskar, Servants, Children
"We're Just a Pair of Sparrows"
M. O'Hara, L. Hunter
Cobra Ritual Dance
Bhaskar, Dancers
"How to Pick a Man a Wife"
N. Andrews, P. Leeds
"The Lovely Girls of Akbarabad"
B. Weeb, Chorus
"Room in My Heart"
M. O'Hara
"The Divali Festival"
Bhaskar, Dancers, Singers
"I Never Meant to Fall in Love"
M. Meredith, M. O'Hara

ACT 2

"Freedom Can Be a Most Uncomfortable Thing"
N. Andrews, Friends
"Ireland Was Never Like This"
M. O'Hara, Dancers
"He Loves Her"
J. Pavek
"Christine"
M. Meredith
"Room in My Heart" (reprise)
M. O'Hara
"Freedom Can Be a Most Uncomfortable Thing" (reprise)
N. Andrews, P. Leeds
a. Kathak (Plate Dance)
Bhaskar, Girls
b. Kathakali
Dancing Boys
c. Bharatha Natyan
Bhaskar, Dancing Girls and Boys
"The Woman I Was Before"
M. O'Hara
"A Doctor's Soliloquy" (reprise)
M. O'Hara, M. Meredith
"I Never Meant to Fall in Love" (reprise)
M. O'Hara, M. Meredith

1960.11 THE KING AND I

A Revival of the Musical Play in Two Acts, 17 Scenes[14]. Book and lyrics by Oscar Hammerstein II. Music by Richard Rodgers. Based on the novel "Anna and the King of Siam" by Margaret Landon. Settings by Jo Mielziner. Costumes by Irene Sharaff, supervised by Stanley Simmons. Lighting by Klaus Holm. Choreography by Jerome Robbins, reproduced by Yuriko. Orchestrations by Robert Russell Bennett. Musical director, Pembroke Davenport. Directed by John Fearnley. Produced by the New York City Center Light Opera Company (Jean Dalrymple, Director). Opened 11 May 1960 at the New York City Center and closed 29 May 1960 after 15 performances.

CAST (in order of appearance): *Captain Orton*: Sam Kirkham. *Louis Leonowens*: Richard Mills. *Anna Leonowens*: BARBARA COOK. *The Interpreter*: Murray Gitlin. *The Kralahome*: Ted Beniades. *The King*: FARLEY GRANGER. *Phra Alack*: Mark Satow. *Lun Tha*: SETH RIGGS. *Tuptim*: JOY CLEMENTS. *Lady Thiang*: ANITA DARIAN. *Prince Chulalongkorn*: Miki Lamont. *Princess Ying Yaowalak*: Susan Lynn Kikuchi. *Sir Edward Ramsay*: Claude Horton.

The Small House of Uncle Thomas: *Narrator*: JOY CLEMENTS. *Uncle Thomas*: Bettina Dearborn. *Little Eva*: Wonci Lui. *Topsy*: Julie Oser. *Eliza*: YURIKO. *King Simon*: GEMZE DE LAPPE. *Angel*: MARION JIM. *Drummer*: Murray Gitlin.

Princes and Princesses: Alfred De Arco, Delfino De Arco, Evelyn Eng, Vivian Hernandez, Lauretta Lee, Roger Mahabirishingh, Richard Mills, Paul Petrillo, Ado Sato, Claudia Satow. *The Royal Dancers*: Diane Adler, Fumi Akimoto, Ted August, Ethel Bell, Paula Chin, Barbara Creed, Bettina Dearborn, Barrie Duffus, Victor Duntiere, Jan Goldin, Marion Jim, Wonci Lui, Julie Oser, Wintress Perkins, Joysanne Sidimus, Nancy Stevens, Roland Vasquez. *Singers (Wives, Priests, Amazons, Slaves)*: Jyll Alexander, Jennie Andrea, Irving Barnes, Ellen Berse, Jim Connor, Marvin Goodis, Ann Marisse, Claire Richard, Beatrice Ruth.

[14]Originally produced in New York 29 March 1951 at the St. James Theatre for 1246 performances. For Synopsis of Scenes and Musical Numbers, see original 1951 production.

1960–1961 SEASON

Richard Burton in CAMELOT (Photo: Friedman-Abeles)
Billy Rose Theatre Collection, New York Public Library for the Performing Arts

1960–1961 SEASON

1960.12 VINTAGE '60

A Musical Revue in Two Acts, 31 Scenes. Written by Jack Wilson, Alan Jeffreys, Maxwell Grant. Choreography and staging by Jonathan Lucas. Comedy direction by Michael Ross. Set design by Fred Voelpel. Costumes by Raymond Aghayan. Original men's costumes by Ret Turner. Costumes for New York production supervised by Fred Voelpel. Musical arrangements by Allyn Ferguson. Musical direction by Gershon Kingsley. Entire production supervised by Michael Ross. Produced by David Merrick, with Zev Bufman, George Skaff, Max Perkins. Opened 12 September 1960 at the Brooks Atkinson Theatre and closed 17 September 1960 after 8 performances.

CAST: BARBARA HELLER, FAY DeWITT, DICK PATTERSON, MICKEY DEEMS, EMMALINE HENRY, BERT CONVY, Sylvia Lewis, Marc Wilder, Garrett Lewis, Bob Trevis, Bonnie Scott, Michele Lee, Larry Billman, Vilma Auld, Harvey Church, Sue Sellors, Robert Lone.

ACT 1

Scene 1

"The Time Is Now"

The Company

(*Music by* Mark Bucci. *Lyrics by* David Rogers.)

Scene 2

Well Dressed Man

(*by* Mickey Deems)

Announcer: D. Patterson. *Well Dressed Man*: M. Deems.

Scene 3

"More"

(*Music and Lyrics by* Jack Wilson and Alan Jeffreys.)

Girl: B. Heller. *Dancers*: M. Wilder, G. Lewis, L. Billman.

Scene 4

"All American"

(*Music by* Mark Bucci. *Lyrics by* David Rogers.)

First Scientist: G. Lewis. *Second Scientist*: M. Deems. *Third Scientist*: D. Patterson. *Officer*: B. Lone.

Scene 5

Conversation Piece

(*by* Mickey Deems)

Wife: F. DeWitt. *Husband*: M. Deems.

Scene 6

"Isms"

B. Heller

(*Music by* David Baker. *Lyrics by* Sheldon Harnick.)

Scene 7

"Five Piece Band"

(*Music and Lyrics by* Jack Wilson, Alan Jeffreys, Maxwell Grant.)

Singer: M. Lee. *Band*: M. Wilder, G. Lewis, L. Billman, H. Church, B. Lone.

Scene 8

Two Piece Band

(*by* Barbara Heller and Fay DeWitt)

Band: B. Heller, F. DeWitt.

Scene 9

Here I Am

(*by* Jack Wilson and Alan Jeffreys)

Man: M. Deems. *Secretary*: L. Billman.

Scene 10

Moral Climate

(*by* Maxwell Grant and Alan Jeffreys)

First Couple: B. Heller, L. Billman. *Second Couple*: F. DeWitt, D. Patterson.

Scene 11

Cat

(*by* Jack Wilson and Alan Jeffreys)

Cat: G. Lewis. *First Girl*: B. Scott. *Second Girl*: S. Lewis. *Third Girl*: S. Sellors.

Scene 12

Dueling

(*by* Maxwell Grant, Alan Jeffreys and Phil Green)

D. Patterson

Scene 13

"Down in the Streets"

F. DeWitt

(*Music and Lyrics by* Tommy Garlock and Alan Jeffreys.)

Chorus: M. Wilder, G. Lewis, H. Church, L. Billman, B. Lone.

Scene 14

Raven

(*by* Jack Wilson and Alan Jeffreys)

Man: D. Patterson. *Raven*: S. Lewis.

Scene 15

Our Town

(*by* William Lanteau)

Narrator: M. Deems. *Lucy Platz*: B. Heller. *Lorretta Crawford*: E. Henry. *Villain*: B. Trevis. *Dancer*: L. Billman. *Pilot*: D. Patterson. *Nurse*: V. Auld.

Scene 16

"Convention"

(*Sketch, Music and Lyrics by* Jack Wilson, Alan Jeffreys, Maxwell Grant.)

Announcer: B. Trevis. *M.C.*: M. Deems. *Barbara Bitton*: B. Heller. *Representative from New York*: L. Billman. *First Stripper*: E. Henry. *Second Stripper*: S. Lewis. *Richard Nixon*: D. Patterson. *Representative from Arkansas*: M. Wilder. *Representative from California*: G. Lewis. *Pat Nixon*: F. DeWitt. *G.O.P. Chorus and Dancers*: B. Scott, M. Lee, V. Auld, S. Sellors, H. Church, B. Lone.

ACT 2

Scene 1

"Do It in Two"

B. Scott

(*Music and Lyrics by* Jack Wilson and Alan Jeffreys.)

Lead Dancers: M. Wilder, S. Lewis. *Dancers*: G. Lewis, M. Lee, L. Billman, V. Auld, S. Sellors, H. Church, B. Lone.

Scene 2

"Dublin Town"

F. DeWitt

(*Music by* Paul Klein. *Lyrics by* Fred Ebb and Lee Goldsmith.)

Scene 3

Strained Relations

(*by* Alan Jeffreys and Maxwell Grant)

Announcer: E. Henry. *The Group*: L. Billman, M. Deems, F. DeWitt, B. Heller, M. Wilder, E. Henry, D. Patterson, B. Scott, G. Lewis, S. Lewis.

Scene 4

Treat 'Em Rough

(*by* Ronald Axe, William Link, Richard Levinson)

Friend: M. Deems. *Boy*: D. Patterson. *Girl*: F. DeWitt.

Scene 5

Angry Young Girl

(*by* Jack Wilson)B. Heller

(*Background Music by* Armin Hoffman.)

Scene 6

"No Words" (dance)

(*by* Jack Wilson, Alan Jeffreys, Maxwell Grant)

Lead Dancer: M. Wilder. *Dancers*: S. Lewis, V. Auld, S. Sellors, L. Billman, G. Lewis, H. Church, B. Lone.

Scene 7

"Forget Me"

(*Music by* David Baker. *Lyrics by* Sheldon Harnick.)

Girl: B. Heller. *Boy*: G. Lewis.

Scene 8

Mother and Son

(*by* Maxwell Grant and Alan Jeffreys)

Mother: E. Henry. *Son*: M. Deems.

Scene 9

The Man

(*by* Jack Wilson, Alan Jeffreys and Maxwell Grant)

Dino: B. Convy. *Shirley*: B. Scott. *Peter*: L. Billman. *Franky*: D. Patterson.

Scene 10

"Tranquilizers"

(*Music and Lyrics by* Bud McCreery.)

F. DeWitt

Scene 11

Vanityades

(*by* David Rogers)

Husband: M. Deems. *Wife*: B. Heller.

Scene 12
The Lobster and the Crab
(*by* Mickey Deems) M. Deems
Scene 13
"Afraid of Love"
(*Sketch by* Michael Ross. *Music and Lyrics by* Alice Clark and David Morton.)
Woman: B. Heller. *Waiters*: M. Wilder, L. Billman.
Scene 14
The Kinney System Parking Lot Plot
The Company
(*by* Jack Wilson, Alan Jeffreys, Maxwell Grant)
Scene 15
Finale
The Company

1960.13 IRMA LA DOUCE

A Musical Comedy in Two Acts, 20 Scenes. Original (French) book and lyrics by Alexandre Breffort. Music by Marguerite Monnot. English book and lyrics by Julian More. Directed by Peter Brook. Choreography by Onna White. Settings and costumes by Rolf Gerard. Lighting by Joe Davis. Orchestrations by Andre Popp. Additional orchestrations by Robert Ginzler. Dance music by John Kander. Vocal arrangements by Bert Waller and Stanley Lebowsky. Musical director, Stanley Lebowsky. Produced by David Merrick in association with Donald Albery and H. M. Tennent, Ltd. and by arrangement with Henry Hall. Opened 29 September 1960 at the Plymouth Theatre, moved 30 October 1961 to the Alvin Theatre, and closed 31 December 1961 after 527 performances.

CAST (in order of appearance): *Bob-Le-Hotu*, Proprietor of the Bar-des-Inquiets: CLIVE REVILL. *Irma-La-Douce*, a Poule: ELIZABETH SEAL. *A Client*: Eddie Gasper. *Jojo-Les-Yeux-Sales*, a Mec: ZACK MATALON. *Roberto-Les-Diams*, a Mec: Aric Lavie. *Persil-Le-Noir*, a Mec: Osborne Smith. *Frangipane*: Stuart Damon. *Polyte-Le-Mou*, a Mec: Fred Gwynne. *Police Inspector*: George S. Irving. *Nestor-Le-Fripe*, a Law Student: KEITH MICHELL. *M. Bougne*, a Ballroom Owner: George Del Monte. *Counsel for the Prosecution*: Rico Froehlich. *Counsel for the Defense*: Rudy Tronto. *An Usher*: Elliott Gould. *An Honest Man*: Joe Rocco. *Court Gendarme*: Byron Mitchell. *First Warder*: Elliott Gould. *Second Warder*: George Del Monte. *Third Warder*: Rico Froehlich. *A Priest*: Elliott Gould. *A Tax Inspector*: Rudy Tronto.
Gendarmes, Prisoners, Irma's Admirers: George Del Monte, Michael Fesco, Rico Froehlich, Eddie Gasper, Elliott Gould, Byron Mitchell, Rudy Tronto.

Act 1, Scene 1: Outside the Bar-des-Inquiets, Pigalle, Paris, France. *Scene 2*: Inside the Bar. *Scene 3*: Irma's Room. *Scene 4*: The Bridge Caulaincourt. *Scene 5*: Hotel Rapid—Bedroom. *Scene 6*: The Bar. *Scene 7*: Hotel Rapid. *Scene 8*: Nestor and Irma's Room. *Scene 9*: Narrow Street. *Scene 10*: The Banks of the Seine. *Scene 11*: The Bar.

Act 2, Scene 1: A Low Court. *Scene 2*: Prison Ship. *Scene 3*: The Street outside Irma's House. *Scene 4*: Devil's Island. *Scene 5*: The Raft. *Scene 6*: A Paris Street. *Scene 7*: The Police Station. *Scene 8*: The Street. *Scene 9*: Irma's Room.

ACT 1
Scene 1
"Valse Milieu"
C. Revill
Scene 2
"Sons of France"
Z. Matalon, A. Lavie, O. Smith, F. Gwynne, G. S. Irving
"The Bridge of Caulaincourt"
E. Seal, K. Michell
Scene 3
"Our Language of Love"
E. Seal, K. Michell
Scene 4
"She's Got the Lot"
G. S. Irving, Irma's Admirers
Scene 5
"Our Language of Love" (reprise)
E. Seal
Scene 6
"Dis-Donc"
E. Seal
"Le Grisbi is le Root of le Evil in Man"
C. Revill, K. Michell, Z. Matalon, A. Lavie, O. Smith
Scene 8
"Wreck of a Mec"
K. Michell
Scene 9
"That's a Crime"
C. Revill, K. Michell, Z. Matalon, A. Lavie, O. Smith

ACT 2
Scene 1
"The Bridge of Caulaincourt" (reprise)
E. Seal, K. Michell
Scene 2
"From a Prison Cell"
K. Michell, Z. Matalon, A. Lavie, O. Smith
Scene 3
"Irma-la-Douce"
E. Seal
Scene 4
"There Is Only One Paris for That"
K. Michell, Z. Matalon, A. Lavie, O. Smith, Prisoners
Scene 5
"The Freedom of the Seas"
K. Michell, Z. Matalon, A. Lavie, O. Smith
Storm Ballet (Arctic Ballet)
E. Seal, Company
Scene 6
"There Is Only One Paris for That" (reprise)
K. Michell, Z. Matalon, A. Lavie, O. Smith
"Our Language of Love" (reprise)
E. Seal
Scene 7
"But"
K. Michell, G. S. Irving, R. Tronto, G. Del Monte, F. Gwynne
Scene 9
"Christmas Child" (Finale)
Company

1960.14 THE MIKADO, or The Town of Titipu

A Revival of the Comic Opera in Two Acts[1]. Libretto by William S. Gilbert. Music by Arthur Sullivan. Staged by Dorothy Raedler. Scenic and lighting design by Donald Oenslager. Costume design by Patton Campbell. Conducted by Robert Irving. Produced by the New York City Opera. Opened 30 September 1960 at the New York City Center and closed 29 October 1960 after 4 performances in repertory.

CAST: *The Mikado of Japan*: JAMES PEASE. *Nanki-Poo*, his son, disguised as a wandering minstrel in love with Yum-Yum: FRANK PORETTA. *Ko-Ko*, Lord High Executioner of Titipu: NORMAN KELLEY. *Pooh-Bah*, Lord High Everything Else: HERBERT BEATTIE. *Pish-Tush*, a Noble Lord: William Metcalf. *Yum-Yum, Pitti-Sing, Peep-Bo*, three sisters, wards of Ko-Ko: BARBARA MEISTER, NANCY DUSSAULT, SOPHIA STEFFAN. *Katisha*: RUTH KOBART. *Chorus of School Girls, Nobles, Guards and Coolies*: New York City Opera Chorus.

1960.15 THE PIRATES OF PENZANCE, or The Slave of Duty

A Revival of the Comic Opera in Two Acts[2]. Libretto by William S. Gilbert. Music by Arthur Sullivan. Staged by Dorothy Raedler. Costume design by Patton Campbell. Conducted by Robert Irving. Produced by the New York

[1]First presented in New York 20 July, 10-29 August 1885 at the Union Square and People's Theatres for 22 performances. First authorized production presented 19 August 1885 at the Fifth Avenue Theatre by Richard D'Oyly Carte for 250 performances. For Synopsis of Scenes and Musical Numbers, see 19 August 1885 D'Oyly Carte production.
[2]First presented in New York 31 December 1879 at the Fifth Avenue Theatre for a total of 91 performances in two engagements. For Synopsis of Scenes and Musical Numbers, see original 1879 production.

City Opera. Opened 6 October 1960 at the New York City Center and closed 4 November 1960 after 4 performances in repertory.

CAST: *Major General Stanley*: WILLIAM CHAPMAN. *The Pirate King*: ARNOLD VOKETAITIS. *Samuel*, his Lieutenant: William Metcalf. *Frederic*, the Pirate Apprentice: FRANK PORETTA. *Sergeant of Police*: HERBERT BEATTIE. *Mabel, Edith Kate, Isabel*, General Stanley's Daughters: BARBARA MEISTER, JOY CLEMENS, SOPHIA STEFFAN, Ritz Metzger. *Ruth*, Pirate Maid-of-all-work: RUTH KOBART. *Chorus of Pirates, Police and General Stanley's Daughters*: New York City Opera Chorus.

1960.16 AN EVENING WITH MIKE NICHOLS AND ELAINE MAY

A Comedy Revue in Two Acts. (Conceived and written by Mike Nichols and Elaine May.) Directed by Arthur Penn. Designed by Marvin Reiss. Music composed by William Goldenberg. Costumes by Hazel Roy. Associate producer, Peter S. Katz. Produced by Alexander H. Cohen (A Nine O'Clock Theatre Production). Opened 8 October 1960 at the John Golden Theatre and closed 1 July 1961 after 306 performances.

CAST: MIKE NICHOLS, ELAINE MAY.

The program will be announced by the performers. Sketches performed by Nichols and May were drawn from the following:

Adultery
Telephone
Mother and Son
Disc Jockey
The Dawn of Love, or The Sun Also Rises in an Automobile
P.T.A.Chairman
Boss and Secretary (Cocktail Piano)
Spy Sketch (Mysterioso)
Dentist (Second Piano Concerto)
"Everybody's Doin' It"
(Music and Lyrics by Irving Berlin.)
Bach to Bach
Tango
Psychiatrist (Sonata for Piano and Celeste)
Father and Daughter (Chopin)
Pirandello sketch
Interview of Screen Star as Gertrude Stein

1960.17 LAUGHS AND OTHER EVENTS

A One Man Musical Revue in Two Acts. Staged by Tony Charmoli. (Settings) Designed and lighted by John Robert Lloyd. Produced by Martin Tahse. Opened 10 October 1960 at the Ethel Barrymore Theatre and closed 15 October 1960 after 8 performances.

CAST: STANLEY HOLLOWAY.
Musicians: Richmond Gale and Arthur Siegel (Pianos), Jerry Silverman (Banjo), Allan Atlas (Concertina).

ACT 1
"A Cup O' Tea"
"I Knew a Private"
Gunner Joe
(*Monologue by* George Edgar.)
"You Gotta Get Aut"
"My Word, You Do Look Queer"
(*Music and Lyrics by* R. P. Weston and Bert Lee.)
"Poppies"
The 'Ole in the Ark
(*Monologue by* Stanley Holloway.)
"Je Sais Que Vous Etes Jolie"
"The Christening"
"The Little Shirt My Mother Made for Me"
(*Music and Lyrics by* H. Wincott.)
"And Yet I Don't Know" (Buying a Wedding Present)
(*Music and Lyrics by* R. P. Weston.)
"Signalman Dan"
The Lion and Albert
(*Monologue by* Marriott Edgar.)
Old Tavern Songs:
"Champagne Charlie"
"So We Will Sing"
"(Shelling) Green Peas"
"Going to the Derby"

ACT 2
"Sentry Song"
On Strike
(*Monologue by* Charles Pond.)
"I Love Mary"
Three Ha' Pence a Foot
(*Monologue by* Marriott Edgar.)
"(Oh,) I Must Go Home Tonight"
(*Music and Lyrics by* William Hargreaves.)
"Old Sam" (Sam, pick oop tha' Musket)
(*Monologue by* Stanley Holloway. *Music by* Wolseley Charles.)
"Brahn Boots"
(*Music and Lyrics by* R. P. Weston and Bert Lee.)
"The Gay Young Farmer"
Return of Albert
(*Monologue by* Marriott Edgar.)
"Two Lovely Black Eyes"
(*Music and Lyrics by* Charles Coburn.)
"Wotcher" (Knock'd 'Em in the Old Kent Road)
(*Music and Lyrics by* Charles Ingle.)
"A Little Bit of Cucumber"
(*Music and Lyrics by* T. W. Connor.)
"I'm 'Enery the VIII, (I Am)"
(*Music and Lyrics by* Fred Murray and R. P. Weston.)
"Any Old Iron"
(*Music and Lyrics by* Charles Collins, E. A. Sheppard, Fred Tarry.)
"It'll All Be the Same (A Hundred Years from Now)"
(*Music and Lyrics by* Arthur Anderson and Melville Gideon.)

1960.18 THE WALL

A Drama (with music) in Two Acts by Millard Lampell. Based on the novel of the same name by John Hersey. Songs adapted from the Yiddish by Robert DeCormier and Millard Lampell. Directed by Morton DaCosta. Settings and lighting by Howard Bay. Costumes by Noel Taylor. Produced by Kermit Bloomgarden and Billy Rose. Opened 11 October 1960 at the Billy Rose Theater and closed 4 March 1961 after 162 performances.

CAST (in order of appearance): *Pavel Menkes*: Vincent Gardenia. *Fishel Shpunt*: Joseph Buloff. *Dolek Berson*: GEORGE C. SCOTT. *German Private*: James Nielsen. *Katz*: James Ray. *Reb Mazur*: Muni Seroff. *Halinka Apt*: Claudette Nevins. *Clerk*: Joseph Bernard. *Rachel Apt*: Yvonne Mitchell. *Symka Berson*: Marian Seldes. *Mordecai Apt*: Michael Ebert. *Pan Apt*: David Opatoshu. *David Apt*: Paul Mace. *Stefan Mazur*: Robert Drivas. *Rutka Mazur*: Leila Martin. *Pan Kogan*: Truman Gaige. *Pani Kogan*: Marketa Kimbrell. *Regina Kogan*: Lorraine Abate. *German Sergeant*: Robert Burr. *Man and Wife*: James Stevenson, Alberta Nelson. *Woman in Babushka*: Rita Karin. *Rappaport*: Leon B. Stevens. *Beggar Man*: Don Doherty. *Beggar Children*: Rochelle Horowitz, Richard Carafa. *German Oficer*: Norbert Horowitz. *Woman in Selection*: Honey MacKenzie. *Slonim*: Sol Frieder.
Men and Women of the Ghetto: Joe Alfasa, Alice Beardsley, Al Verb, Kenneth Reid.

The action covers the period from the spring of 1940 to the spring of 1943 on a street in Warsaw.

MUSICAL NUMBERS
"Oy, a nacht a sheyne" (Oh, What a Lovely Night)
"Sheyn bin ich, sheyn" (Pretty am I, So Pretty)
"Tsipele" (Little Tsipele)
(*Music by* I. Glatstein. *Yiddish Lyrics by* M. Broderson.)
"Van der ershter vet lachn" (Who will be the first to laugh)
(*Music and Yiddish Lyrics by* M. Gebirtig.)
"Shtil, di nacht iz oysgeshternt" (Silent, the starry night)
(*Words by* Hirsch Glick.)

"Yisrolik" (My name is Yisrolik)
(*Music by* M. Weksler. *Yiddish Lyrics by* L. Rosenthal.)
"Farvos iz der himl geven nechtn loyter?" (Why was the sky so bright yesterday?)
(*Words by* L. Opeskin.)
"Oyf dem zamd fun negev" (On the sands of the Negev)
(*Music*: Anonymous. *Yiddish Lyrics by* M. L. Gisser, based on Israeli Hebrew text by R. Klatchkin.)
"A mame's nign" (A mother's melody)
(*Words by* R. Lifshitz.)
"Findjan" (arabic term for the steaming kettle)
(*Music*: Anonymous. *Yiddish Lyrics by* R. Karpinovitch, based on an Israeli Hebrew text by H. Feiner.)
"Oy, dortn, dortn ibern vaserl" (Oh, there across the water)
"Frunze verde" (Green leaves)
(*Music from* a Roumanian doina. *Lyrics by* I. Horowitz.)
"Noch a glezele tey" (Another little cup of tea)
(*Music and Lyrics by* M. Gebirtig.)
"Idish" (Yiddish)
(*Music from* a popular tango. *Yiddish Lyrics by* I. Kotliar.)
"Motele"
(*Music and Lyrics by* M. Gebirtig.)

1960.19 TENDERLOIN

A Musical Comedy in Two Acts, 23 Scenes and an Epilogue. Book by George Abbott and Jerome Weidman. Based on the novel of the same name by Samuel Hopkins Adams. Music by Jerry Bock. Lyrics by Sheldon Harnick. Directed by George Abbott. Dances and musical numbers staged by Joe Layton. Sets and costumes by Cecil Beaton. (Lighting uncredited.) Musical direction by Hal Hastings. Orchestrations by Irwin Kostal. Dance music arranged by Jack Elliott. Produced by Robert E. Griffith and Harold S. Prince. Opened 17 October 1960 at the 46th Street Theatre and closed 23 April 1961 after 216 performances.

CAST (in order of appearance): *Tommy*: RON HUSMANN. *Nita*: EILEEN RODGERS. *Lieut. Schmidt* (The Pantata): RALPH DUNN. *Reverend Brock*: MAURICE EVANS. *Gertie*: LEE BECKER (Theodore). *Margie*: Margery Gray. *Dorothy*: Dorothy Frank. *Girl*: Patsy Peterson. *Young Man*: Dargan Motgomery. *Jessica*: IRENE KANE. *Laura*: WYNNE MILLER. *Ellington*: Gordon Cook. *Joe*: REX EVERHART. *Purdy*: RAYMOND BRAMLEY. *Martin*: Lanier Davis. *Deacon*: ROY FANT. *Frye*: EDDIE PHILLIPS. *Rooney*: Jordan Howard. *Nellie*: Marguerite Shaw. *Becker*: Michael Roberts. *Callahan*: Jack McCann. *Prostitutes*: Erin Martin, Margery Gray. *Drunk*: Bob Fitch. *Maggie*: Pat Turner. *Liz*: Christine Norden. *Mrs. Barker*: Elaine Rogers. *Chairman*: Joe Hill.

Dancers: Jere Admire, David Evans, Bob Fitch, Dorothy Frank, Margery Gray, Mickey Gunnersen, Sandy Leeds, Jack Leigh, Erin Martin, Marjorie Pragon, Wakefield Poole, Ronald B. Stratton, Jayne Turner, Pat Turner. *Singers*: Charles Aschmann, Carvel Carter, Nancy Emes, John Ford, Stokeley Gray, Maria Graziano, Joe Hill, Jordan Howard, Gail Johnston, Jack McCann, Dargan Montgomery, Patsy Peterson, Claire Richard, Michael Roberts, Elaine Rogers.

Act 1, Scene 1: Limbo; Reverend Brock's Church. New York City, 1890s. *Scene 2*: A Street outside the Church. *Scene 3*: Parish House. *Scene 4*: A Street in front of the Nineteenth Precinct. *Scene 5*: The Nineteenth Precinct Police Station. *Scene 6*: Precinct street. *Scene 7*: The Living Room of Laura Crosbie's Fifth Avenue House. *Scene 8*: A Street in front of Clark's. *Scene 9*: Clark's, a popular Tenderloin haunt. *Scene 10*: Street in front of Clark's. *Scene 11*: A Beach. *Scene 12*: A Street in front of Clark's. *Scene 13*: Clark's, 11:00PM.

Act 2, Scene 1: Central Park. *Scene 2*: A Street. *Scene 3*: Clark's. *Scene 4*: The Trial. *Scene 5*: Clark's. *Scene 6*: The Parish House at night. *Scene 7*: Precinct street. *Scene 8*: The Courtroom. *Scene 9*: A Street. *Scene 10*: Parish House. *Epilogue*: Detroit.

ACT 1
Scene 1
"Bless This Land"
The Choir
"Little Old New York"
E. Rodgers, L. Becker, Company
Scene 3
"Dr. Brock"
M. Evans
"Artificial Flowers"
R. Husmann
"What's In It for You?"
M. Evans, R. Husmann
Scene 6
"Reform"
L. Becker, N. Emes, C. Carter
Scene 7
"Tommy, Tommy"
W. Miller
Scene 9
"Artificial Flowers" (Reprise)
M. Gray
"The Picture of Happiness"
R. Husmann
Dance
L. Becker, E. Phillips, Company
Scene 11
"Dear Friend"
M. Evans, W. Miller, I. Kane, J. Turner
"The Army of the Just"
M. Evans, L. Davis, J. Leigh, C. Aschmann, S. Gray
Scene 13
"How the Money Changes Hands"
M. Evans, E. Rodgers, C. Norden, E. Phillips, L. Becker, Company

ACT 2
Scene 1
"Good Clean Fun"
M. Evans, Company
"My Miss Mary"
R. Husmann, W. Miller, Singers
Scene 3
"My Gentle Young Johnny"
E. Rodgers
Scene 4
"The Trial"
Company
Scene 5
"The Tenderloin Celebration"
E. Phillips, L. Becker, Company
Scene 9
"Reform" (reprise)
L. Becker, M. Gray, C. Norden, Company
Scene 10
"Tommy, Tommy" (reprise)
W. Miller
Epilogue
"Little Old New York" (Detroit reprise)
Company

1960.20 THE UNSINKABLE MOLLY BROWN

A Musical Comedy in Two Acts, 20 Scenes. Book by Richard Morris. Music and lyrics by Meredith Willson. Directed by Dore Schary. Musical numbers staged by Peter Gennaro. Costumes by Miles White. Sets by Oliver Smith. Lighting by Peggy Clark. Orchestrations by Don Walker. Vocal arrangements and musical direction by Herbert Greene. Ballet music arranged by Sol Berkowitz. Associate producer, Walter Reilly. Produced by the Theatre Guild and Dore Schary. Opened 3 November 1960 at the Winter Garden and closed 10 February 1962 after 532 performances.

CAST (in order of appearance): *Molly Tobin*: TAMMY GRIMES. *Michael Tobin*: Sterling Clark. *Aloysius Tobin*: Bill Starr. *Patrick Tobin*: Bob Daley. *Father Flynn*: Norman Fredericks. *Shamus Tobin*: CAMERON PRUD'HOMME. *Brawling Miners*: Alex Stevens, Joe Pronto. *Charlie*: Woody Hurst. *Chistmas Morgan*: Joseph Sirola. *Burt*: Tom Larson. *Banjo*: Billy Faier. *Prostitutes*: Rae McLean, Anna Maria Moylan, Lynn Gay Lorino. *Johnny 'Leadville' Brown*: HARVE PRESNELL, (James Hurst, alt.). *Gitter*: Joe Pronto. *A Boy*: Paul Floyd. *Sheriff*: Terry Violino. *Mrs. McGlone*: EDITH MEISER. *Monsignor Ryan*: Jack Harrold. *Roberts*: Christopher Hewett. *Professor Gardella*: Dale Malone. *Germaine*: June Card. *Princess DeLong*: Mony Dalmes. *Prince DeLong*: Mitchell Gregg. *Countess Ethanotous*: Wanda Saxon. *Jenab-ashros*: Marvin Goodis. *Grand Duchess Marie Nicholaiovna*: Patricia Kelly. *Count Feranti*: Michael Davis. *Duchess of Burlingame*: Barbara Newman. *Duke of Burlingame*: Ted Adkins. *Baron of Auld*: Bob Daley. *Malcolm Broderick*: Barney Johnston. *Mrs. Wadlington*:

Lynne Osborne. *Mr. Wadlington*: Norman Fredericks. *Young Waiter*: Michael Davis. *Maitre D'*: Dale Malone. *Page*: Bobby Brownell. *Male Passenger*: Marvin Goodis. *Mother*: Nada Rowand. *Wounded Sailor*: Bill Starr.

Singers: June Card, Ceil Delli, Pat Finch, Marian Heraldson, Patricia Kelly, Lynne Osborne, Nada Rowland, Wanda Saxon, Michael Davis, Norman Fredericks, Marvin Goodis, Woody Hurst, Barney Johnson, Tom Larson, Dale Malone, Louis Polacek. *Dancers*: Barbara Gine, Diana Hunter, Lynn Gay Lorino, Susan May, Anna Marie Moylan, Rae McLean, Barbara Newman, Nanette Rosen, Ted Adkins, Sterling Clark, Bob Daley, Vito Durante, Don Emmons, Joe Pronto, Mark Ross, Bill Starr, Alex Stevens, Terry Violino.

Act 1, Scene 1: Exterior of the Tobin Shack, Hannibal, Missouri. The turn of the century. *Scene 2*: The road by the Tobin shack. Sun-up the next morning. *Scene 3*: The Saddle Rock Saloon. Leadville, Colorado. Weeks later. *Scene 4*: The street in front of the Saddle Rock. Sunday night, three weeks later. *Scene 5*: Johnny's log cabin. A month later. *Scene 6*: The same, three weeks later. *Scene 7*: Pennsylvania Avenue, Denver, Colorado. Six months later. *Scene 8*: The Terrace of Mrs. McGlone's Denver Mansion. Later that evening. *Scene 9*: Pennsylvania Avenue. Immediately following. *Scene 10*: The Red Parlor of the Browns' Denver Mansion. The evening of their house-warming.

Act 2, Scene 1: The Browns' Paris Salon. A spring afternoon, years later. *Scene 2*: Upper hallway of the Brwons' Denver Mansion. An evening months later. *Scene 3*: The Red Parlor, 8 P.M. that evening. *Scene 4*: The Red Parlor. Next morning. *Scene 5*: The street in front of the Saddle Rock. Months later. *Scene 6*: Monte Carlo. A club off the Casino. Early spring, 1912. *Scene 7*: Outside the club. A moment later. *Scene 8*: The mid-Atlantic. Shortly after 2:30 A.M. April 15, 1912. *Scene 9*: Upper hallway, Brown home. Two weeks later. *Scene 10*: The Rockies.

ACT 1

Scene 1

"I Ain't Down Yet"
T. Grimes, S. Clark, B. Starr, B. Daley

Scene 3

"Belly Up to the Bar, Boys"
T. Grimes, J. Sirola, Miners

Scene 4

"I've A'ready Started In"
H. Presnell, J. Sirola, W. Hurst, T. Larson, J. Pronto

Scene 5

"I'll Never Say No"
H. Presnell

"My Own Brass Bed"
T. Grimes

Scene 7

"The Denver Police"
M. Ross, T. Violino, D. Emmons

Scene 8

"Beautiful People of Denver"
T. Grimes

"Are You Sure?"
T. Grimes, Guests

Scene 10

"I Ain't Down Yet" (reprise)
T. Grimes, H. Presnell

ACT 2

Scene 1

"Happy Birthday, Mrs. J. J. Brown"
M. Dalmes, M. Gregg, International Set

"Bon Jour" (The Language Song)
T. Grimes, M. Gregg, International Set

"If I Knew"
H. Presnell

Scene 2

"Chick-a-Pen"
T. Grimes, H. Presnell

Scene 5

"Keep-a-Hoppin'"
H. Presnell, His Leadville Friends

"Leadville Johnny Brown" (Soliloquy)
H. Presnell

Scene 6

"Up Where the People Are" (dance)
Monte Carlo Guests

"Dolce Far Niente"/("I May Never Fall in Love With You")
M. Gregg, T. Grimes

Scene 10

"I Ain't Down Yet" (reprise)
H. Presnell, T. Grimes, Leadville Friends

1960.21 CAMELOT

A Musical in Two Acts, 20 Scenes. Book and lyrics by Alan Jay Lerner. Based on the novel "The Once and Future King" by T. H. White. Music by Frederick Loewe. Staged by Moss Hart. Choreography and musical numbers by Hanya Holm. Scenic production by Oliver Smith. Costumes designed by Adrian and Tony Duquette. Lighting by Feder. Musical director, Franz Allers. Orchestrations by Robert Russell Bennett and Philip J. Lang. Dance and choral arrangements, Trude Rittman. Produced by Alan Jay Lerner, Frederick Loewe and Moss Hart. Opened 3 December 1960 at the Majestic Theatre and closed 5 January 1963 after 873 performances.

CAST (in order of appearance): *Sir Dinadan*: JOHN CULLUM. *Sir Lionel*: Bruce Yarnell. *Merlyn*: David Hurst. *Arthur*: RICHARD BURTON. *Guenevere*: JULIE ANDREWS. *Nimue*: Marjorie Smith. *A Page*: Leland Mayforth. *Lancelot*: ROBERT GOULET. *Dap*: Michael Clarke-Laurence. *Pelinore*: ROBERT COOTE. *Clarius*: Richard Kuch. *Lady Anne*: Christina Gillespie. *A Lady*: Leesa Troy. *Sir Sagramore*: James Gannon. *A Page*: Peter De Vise. *Herald*: John Starkweather. *Lady Catherine*: Virginia Allen. *Mordred*: RODDY McDOWALL. *Sir Ozanna*: Michael Kermoyan. *Sir Gwilliam*: Jack Dabdoub. *Morgan Le Fey*: M'EL DOWD. *Tom*: Robin Stewart.

Singers: Joan August, Mary Sue Berry, Marnell Bruce, Judy Hastings, Benita James, Marjorie Smith, Shelia Swenson, Leesa Troy, Dorothy White, Frank Bouley, Jack Dabdoub, James Gannon, Murray Goldkind, Warren Hays, Paul Huddleston, Michael Kermoyan, Donald Maloof, Larry Mitchell, Paul Richards, John Taliaferro. *Dancers*: Virginia Allen, Judi Allinson, Laurie Archer, Carlene Carroll, Joan Coddington, Katia Geleznova, Adriana Keathley, Dawn Mitchell, Claudia Schroeder, Beti Seay, Jerry Bowers, Peter Deign, Randy Doney, Richard Englund, Richard Gain, Gene GeBauer, James Kirby, Richard Kuch, Joe Nelson, John Starkweather, Jimmy Tarbutton.

Act 1, Scene 1: A hilltop near Camelot—a long time ago. *Scene 2*: Near Camelot—immediately following. *Scene 3*: Arthur's Study—Five years later. *Scene 4*: A Roadside near Camelot—A few months later. *Scene 5*: A Park near the Castle—Immediately following. *Scene 6*: A Terrace of the Castle—A few weeks later. *Scene 7*: The Tents outside the Jousting Field—A few days later. *Scene 8*: The Grandstand of the Field. *Scene 9*: The Tents Outside the Jousting Field—Immediately following. *Scene 10*: The Terrace—Two years later. *Scene 11*: The Corridor leading to the Great Hall—Immediately following. *Scene 12*: The Great Hall—Immediately following.

Act 2, Scene 1: The Castle Garden—A few years later. *Scene 2*: The Terrace—A few weeks later. *Scene 3*: Near the Forest of Morgan Le Fey—A few days later. *Scene 4*: The Forest of Morgan Le Fey—Immediately following. *Scene 5*: Corridor—That night. *Scene 6*: The Queen's Bedchamber—Immediately following. *Scene 7*: Camelot—Several days later. *Scene 8*: A Battlefield near Joyous Gard—A few weeks later.

ACT 1[3]

Scene 1

"I Wonder What the King is Doing Tonight?"
R. Burton

"The Simple Joys of Maidenhood"
J. Andrews

"Camelot"
R. Burton, J. Andrews

Scene 2

"Follow Me"
M. Smith

Scene 4

"C'est Moi"
R. Goulet

Scene 5

"The Lusty Month of May"
J. Andrews, Ensemble

"Then You May Take Me to the Fair"[4]
J. Andrews, J. Cullum, J. Gannon, B. Yarnell

---

[3]After opening, the following changes were made to Act 1:
"Camelot" (reprise)(Added to Scene 3)
R. Burton, J. Andrews
Scene 9 revised as The Terrace—Immediately following.
Scene 10 dropped.

[4]Dropped after opening.

Scene 6
"How to Handle a Woman"
R. Burton
Scene 8
"The Jousts"
R. Burton, J. Andrews, Ensemble
Scene 9
"Before I Gaze at You Again"
J. Andrews

ACT 2
Scene 1
"If Ever I Would Leave You"
R. Goulet
"The Seven Deadly Virtues"
R. McDowall
Scene 2
"What Do the Simple Folk Do?"
J. Andrews, R. Burton
Scene 4
"The Persuasion"
R. McDowall, M. Dowd
Scene 5
"Fie on Goodness!"
Knights
Scene 6
"I Loved You Once in Silence"
J. Andrews
Scene 7
"Guenevere"
Ensemble
Scene 8
"Camelot" (reprise)
R. Burton

1960.22 WILDCAT

A Musical Comedy in Two Acts, 19 Scenes. Book by N. Richard Nash. Music by Cy Coleman. Lyrics by Carolyn Leigh. Settings by Peter Larkin. Costumes by Alvin Colt. Lighting by Charles Elson. Musical direction, dance and vocal arrangements by John Morris. (Musical) arrangements and orchestrations by Robert Ginzler and Sid Ramin. Directed and choreographed by Michael Kidd. Produced by Michael Kidd and N. Richard Nash. Opened 16 December 1960 at the Alvin Theatre and closed 3 June 1961 after 171 performances.

CAST (in order of appearance): *Jane Jackson*: PAULA STEWART. *Wildcat Jackson* (Wildy): LUCILLE BALL. *Sheriff Sam Gore*: HOWARD FISCHER. *Barney*: Ken Ayers. *Luke*: Anthony Saverino. *Countess Emily O'Brien*: EDITH KING. *Joe Dynamite*: KEITH ANDES. *Hank*: CLIFFORD DAVID. *Miguel*: H. F. Green. *Sookie*: DON TOMKINS. *Matt*: CHARLES BRASWELL. *Corky*: Bill Linton. *Oney*: SWEN SWENSON. *Sandy*: Ray Mason. *Tattoo*: Bill Walker. *Cisco*: Al Lanti. *Postman*: Bill Richards. *Inez*: Marsha Wagner. *Blonde*: Wendy Nickerson.

Singers: Ken Ayers, Lee Green, Jan Leighton, Urylee Leonardos, Virginia Oswald, Anthony Saverino, Jeanne Steel, Gene Varrone. *Dancers*: Robert Bakanic, Barbara Beck, Mel Davidson, Penny Ann Green, Valarie Harper, Lucia Lambert, Ronald Lee, Jacqueline Maria, Wendy Nickerson, Frank Pietri, Bill Richards, Adriane Rogers, John Sharpe, Gerald Teijelo, Marsha Wagner.

Act 1, Scene 1: A Street in Centavo City, a border town, in 1912. *Scene 2*: A Pairie. Sunset, a few days later. *Scene 3*: The Street. The following morning. *Scene 4*: The Plaza in the Mexican part of town. Sunset, the same day. *Scene 5*: The Countess' Sitting Room. The following morning. *Scene 6*: Sookie's House. An hour later. *Scene 7*: Prairie. The same evening. *Scene 8*: The Street. An hour later. *Scene 9*: Plaza. Late afternoon, the following day. *Scene 10*: The Jail. A half hour later. *Scene 11*: Sookie's Hill. Early evening, the same day.

Act 2, Scene 1: The Countess' Sitting Room. Two days later. *Scene 2*: On the way tot he Fiesta. The following afternoon. *Scene 3*: The Plaza. Immediately following. *Scene 4*: The Street. A few days later. *Scene 5*: Sookie's House. Derrick Day, the following day. *Scene 6*: Sookie's Hill. Immediately following. *Scene 7*: Outside Miguel's Cantina. Evening, two days later. *Scene 8*: Sookie's Hill. The following day.

ACT 1
Scene 1
"I Hear"
People of Centavo City
Scene 2
"Hey Look Me Over"
L. Ball, P. Stewart
Scene 3
"Wildcat"
L. Ball, Townspeople
Scene 4
"You've Come Home"
K. Andes
Scene 6
"What Takes My Fancy"
L. Ball, D. Tomkins
Scene 7
"You're a Liar"
L. Ball, K. Andes
Scene 8
"One Day We Dance"
C. David, P. Stewart
Scene 9
"Give a Little Whistle and I'll Be There"
L. Ball, K. Andes, Crew, Townspeople
Scene 11
"Tall Hope"
B. Walker, S. Swenson, R. Mason, C. Braswell, Crew

ACT 2
Scene 1
"Tippy Tippy Toes"
L. Ball, E. King
Scene 3
"El Sombrero"
L. Ball, A. Lanti, S. Swenson, Crew, Townspeople
Scene 6
"Corduroy Road"
K. Andes, Crew, Townspeople
Scene 7
"You've Come Home" (reprise)
K. Andes
Scene 8
Finale
Entire Company

1960.23 DO RE MI

A Musical in Two Acts, 16 Scenes. Book by Garson Kanin. (Based on his novel of the same name.) Music by Jule Styne. Lyrics by Betty Comden and Adolph Green. Scenery by Boris Aronson. Costumes by Irene Sharaff. Musical direction by Lehman Engel. Choreography by Marc Breaux and Deedee Wood. Lighting by Al Alloy. Associate director, William Hammerstein. Orchestrations, Luther Henderson. Vocal arrangements and Vocal direction, Buster Davis. Dance arrangements by David Baker. Directed by Garson Kanin. Associate producer, Jones Harris. Produced by David Merrick. Opened 26 December 1960 at the St. James Theatre, closing 24 July-19 August 1961 for a 1 month vacation, moved 25 December 1961 to the 54th Street Theatre, and closed 13 January 1962 after 400 performances.

CAST (in order of appearance): *The Casa Girls*: Marilyn Allwyn, Diane Ball, Sandra Devlin, Regina Groves, Nancy Van Rhein, Carol Stevens, Dean Taliaferro. *The Dance Team*: Patti Karr, Ray Kirchner. *Kay Cram*: NANCY WALKER. *Hubert Cram* (Hubie): PHIL SILVERS. *Waiter*: Frank Derbas. *John Henry Wheeler*: JOHN REARDON. *The Swingers*: Betty Kent, Donna Sanders, Suzanne Shaw. *Headwaiter*: Marc Jordan. *Fatso O'Rear*: GEORGE MATHEWS. *Skin Demopoulos*: GEORGE GIVOT. *Brains Berman*: DAVID BURNS. *Thelma Berman*: Marilyn Child. *Interviewer*: David Gold. *Photographer*: Stuart Hodes. *Wheeler's Secretaries*: Carol Stevens, Dean Taliaferro. *James Russell Lowell IV*: Chad Block. *Sumo Student*: Ray Kirchner. *Tilda Mullen*:

NANCY DUSSAULT. *Wolfie*: Al Nesor. *Marsha*: Carolyn Ragaini. *Lou*: Steve Roland. *Gretchen*: Betty Kent. *Recording Engineer*: Albert Linville. *Maitre D'*: Bob McClure. *Animal Girls*: Marilyn Allwyn, Diane Ball, Sandra Devlin, Regina Groves, Patti Karr, Nancy Van Rhein, Carol Stevens, Dean Taliaferro. *Moe Shtarker*: Al Lewis. *Commentators*: Bob McClure, Allan Stevenson. *Senator Rogers*: Albert Linville. *Senator Redfield*: Edward Grace. *Chief Counsel*: Steve Roland. *Fatso's Lawyer*: Marc Jordan. *Brain's Lawyer*: Pat Tolson.

The Public: Marilyn Allwyn, Doria Avila, Diane Ball, Frank Derbas, Sandra Devlin, David Gold, Edward Grace, Regina Groves, Stuart Hodes, Curtis Hood, Daniel Jasinski, Marc Jordan, Patti Karr, Betty Kent, Ray Kirchner, Barbara Lang, Josephine Lang, Bob McClure, Ken Malone, Jim Marley, James Moore, Dawn Nickerson, Ed Pfeiffer, Carolyn Ragaini, Steve Roland, Donna Sanders, Suzanne Shaw, Carol Stevens, Liza Stuart, Dean Taliaferro, Pat Tolson, Nancy Van Rhein, Richard Young.

Act 1, Scene 1: The Casacabana. New York City, now. *Scene 2*: Hubie and Kay's Bedroom. *Scene 3*: Fatso's Ice Cream Parlor. *Scene 4*: Brains' Chicken Farm. A Box at Hialeah. A Street. *Scene 5*: John Henry Wheeler's Office. *Scene 6*: The Zen Pancake Parlor. *Scene 7*: The Music Enterprise Associates, Inc. *Scene 8*: The Zen Pancake Parlor. *Scene 9*: All Over Town. *Scene 10*: A Recording Studio. *Scene 11*: The Imperial Room.

Act 2, Scene 1: Hubie and Kay's Bedroom. *Scene 2*: John Henry Wheeler's Office. *Scene 3*: The Music Enterprise Associates, Inc. *Scene 4*: The City. *Scene 5*: A Hearing Room in the Senate Office Building, Washington, D.C.

ACT 1
Scene 1
"Waiting, Waiting"
N. Walker
"All You Need Is a Quarter"
B. Kent, D. Sanders, S. Shaw
Scene 2
"Take a Job"
P. Silvers, N. Walker
Scene 3
The Juke Box Hop (dance)[5]
Fatso's Customers
Scene 4
"It's Legitimate"
P. Silvers, G. Mathews, D. Burns, G. Givot, The Loaders
Scene 5
"I Know About Love"
J. Reardon
Scene 7
The Auditions
C. Ragaini, S. Roland, B. Kent
Scene 8
"Cry Like the Wind"
N. Dussault
"Ambition"
P. Silvers, N. Dussault
Scene 9
Success
Tilda Mullen Fans, N. Dussault, P. Silvers, G. Mathews, D. Burns, G. Givot
Scene 10
"Fireworks"
N. Dussault, J. Reardon
Scene 11
"What's New at the Zoo"
N. Dussault, the Animal Girls
"Asking for You"
J. Reardon
"The Late, Late Show"
P. Silvers

ACT 2
Scene 1
"Adventure"
P. Silvers, N. Walker
Scene 2
"Make Someone Happy"
J. Reardon, N. Dussault
Scene 3
"Don't Be Afraid of a Teardrop"[6]
P. Silvers, G. Mathews, D. Burns, G. Givot
Scene 4
The Juke Box Trouble (dance)
A. Lewis, Cohorts, Company
Scene 5
"V.I.P."
The Public, P. Silvers
"All of My Life"
P. Silvers
Finale
P. Silvers, N. Walker, Company

1961.01

SHOW GIRL

A Small (Musical) Revue in Two Acts, 16 Scenes. Sketches, music and lyrics by Charles Gaynor. Additional sketches by Ernest Chambers. Settings by Oliver Smith. Costumes by Miles White. Lighting by Peggy Clark. Musical direction and orchestrations, Robert Hunter. Additional orchestrations, Clare Grundman. Sketches staged by Charles Gaynor. Musical numbers staged by Richard D'Arcy. Entire production supervised by Oliver Smith. Miss Channing's gowns by Orry-Kelly. Produced by Oliver Smith, James A. Doolittle and Charles Lowe. Opened 12 January 1961 at the Eugene O'Neill Theatre and closed 8 April 1961 after 100 performances.

CAST: CAROL CHANNING, JULES MUNSHIN, LES QUAT' JEUDIS (Raoul Curet, George Denis, André Fuma, Roger Lagier).

ACT 1
Scene 1
Opening—"The Girl in the Show"
C. Channing
Scene 2
Report from Las Vegas
C. Channing
Scene 3
Theatre Piece
Lynn: C. Channing. *Alfred*: J. Munshin.
Scene 4
"Calypso Pete"
C. Channing
Scene 5
Report from Paris: ("Mamba-Java")
Les Quat' Jeudis
(*Music and Lyrics by* Noel Guyves.)
Scene 6
Keeping Up with the Noahs
(*by* Ernest Chambers)
Naomi: C. Channing. *Elijah*: J. Munshin.
Scene 7
"The Girl Who Lived in Montparnasse"
J. Munshin, Les Quat' Jeudis
Scene 8
Carol's Musical Theatre:
C. Channing
a. The Opening Choruses:
"Join Us in a Little Cup of Tea" (from LEND AN EAR)
"This is a Darned Fine Funeral"
b. The Love Songs
"In Our Teeny Little Weeny Nest for Two" (from LEND AN EAR)
"Love Is a Sickness"
c. The Dance Numbers
"The Yahoo Step" (from LEND AN EAR)
"Switchblade Bess"

[5]Added after opening: The Juke Box Twist.

[6]Dropped after opening.

ACT 2
Scene 1
"The Story of Marie"
C. Channing, Les Quat' Jeudis
Scene 2
S. Eureka Presents
(*by* Ernest Chambers. *Music by* Charles Gaynor.)
J. Munshin
Scene 3
"My Kind of Love"
C. Channing, J. Munshin
Scene 4
The Inside Story (Cecilia Sisson sketch)
Scene 5
The Foreign Star (Marlene Dietrich sketch)
Scene 6
Les Quat' Jeudis
Scene 7
The Palace Theatre:
("You Haven't Lived Until You've Played the Palace"/
"Somewhere There's a Little Bluebird")
C. Channing
Scene 8
Finale
C. Channing, Company

1961.02 THE CONQUERING HERO

A Musical Comedy in Two Acts, 16 Scenes. Book by Larry Gelbart. Based on the screenplay "Hail, the Conquering Hero" by Preston Sturges. Music by Moose Charlap. Lyrics by Norman Gimbel. Settings by Jean Rosenthal and William Pitkin. Costumes designed by Patton Campbell. Lighting by Jean Rosenthal. (Musical) arrangements and orchestrations by Robert Ginzler and Sid Ramin. Dance music arranged by Fred Werner. Musical direction and choral arrangements by Sherman Frank. (Direction and choreography uncredited, by Bob Fosse prior to opening.) Produced by Robert Whitehead and Roger L. Stevens by special arrangement with Emka Ltd. Opened 16 January 1961 at the ANTA Theatre and closed 21 January 1961 after 8 performances.

CAST (in order of appearance): *Doorman*: Lee Barry. *Pfc. Doyle*: Walter Farrell. *Pfc. O'Dell*: Bob Dixon. *Cpl. Ganz*: Bill McDonald. *Pfc. Pasco*: Bernie Meyer. *Sgt. Murdock*: LIONEL STANDER. *Nightclub Performer*: Marilyn Stark. *Master of Ceremonies*: Bob Kaliban. *Waiter*: Erik Kristen. *Nightclub Manager*: William LeMassena. *Woodrow Truesmith*: TOM POSTON. *MP*: Burt Bier. *Bartender*: Samye Van. *A General*: T. J. Halligan. *Conductor*: Don Morgan. *Mayor Noble*: FRED STEWART. *Judge Callan*: William LeMassena. *Forrest Noble*: John McMartin. *Whiteman*: Bob Kaliban. *Mrs. Noble*: Edith Gresham. *Rev. Cox*: Geoffrey Bryan. *Sue Anne Barnes*: JANE MASON. *Ronnie*: Richard Buckley. *Mrs. Truesmith*: Elizabeth Kerr. *Libby Callan*: KAY BROWN. *Gene*: Kenny Kealy. *Doc Johnson*: T. J. Halligan. *The Enemy Captain*: John Aristides. *Effie*: Brina Dexter.

Dancers: Margery Beddow, Pat Ferrier, Reby Howells, Shellie Farrell, Marlene Dell, Betty Hyatt Linton, Kathe Howard, William Guske, John Aristides, Dale Moreda, Erik Kristen, Dick Korthaze, Michel Stuart, James Senn. *Singers*: Georgia Creighton, Brina Dexter, Marianne Gale, Charlotte Frazier, Marilyn Stark, Shirley Chester, Burt Bier, Lee Barry, Ed Mastin, Don Morgan, Tony Craig, Charles Rule.

Act 1, Scene 1: The 'Chez Victory' Club. *Scene 2*: The Train. *Scene 3*: The Station at Hillsdale. *Scene 4*: The Truesmith Porch. *Scene 5*: The Church. *Scene 6*: The Truesmith House. *Scene 7*: The River Bank. *Scene 8*: Woodrow's Room. *Scene 9*: The Campaign.

Act 2, Scene 1: The Election. *Scene 2*: The Town Hall. *Scene 3*: The House. *Scene 4*: The Railroad Station. *Scene 5*: The Mayor's Office. *Scene 6*: The Town Hall. *Scene 7*: The Station.

ACT 1
Scene 1
"Girls! Girls!"
L. Barry, Marines
"Five Shots of Whiskey"
L. Stander, B. Dixon, W. Farrell, B. McDonald, B. Meyer
Scene 3
"Hail, the Conquering Hero!"
T. Poston, Company
"Must Be Given to You"
Company
Scene 4
"Wonderful, Marvelous You"
T. Poston, K. Brown, K. Kealey
Scene 5
"Truth"
Entire Company
"Won't You Marry Me?"
K. Brown
Scene 7
The River Bank
J. Mason, T. Poston
Scene 8
"Only Rainbows"
T. Poston, B. Dixon, W. Farrell, B. McDonald
Scene 9
The Campaign
T. Poston, Ensemble

ACT 2
Scene 2
"One Mother Each"
L. Stander, B. Dixon, W. Farrell, B. McDonald, B. Meyer
"Must Be Given to You" (reprise)
Entire Company
Scene 3
"I'm Beautiful"
K. Brown, Marines
Scene 4
"Rough Times"
K. Brown, K. Kealey
Scene 5
"Yours, All Yours"
T. Poston, J. Mason, Ensemble
Scene 7
"Won't You Marry Me?" (reprise)
T. Poston
"Hail, the Conquering Hero"/"Only Rainbows" (reprise)
Entire Company

1961.03 THE MIKADO, or The Town of Titipu

A Revival of the Comic Opera in Two Acts[7]. Libretto by William S. Gilbert. Music by Arthur Sullivan. Staged by Dorothy Raedler. Scenery and lighting by Donald Oenslager. Costumes by Patton Campbell. Conductors, Robert Irving, Felix Popper. Chorus master, William Jonson. Produced by the New York City Center Gilbert and Sullivan Company (Julius Rudel, General Director). Opened 17 January 1961 at the New York City Center and closed 5 February 1961 after 8 performances in repertory.

CAST: *The Mikado of Japan*: GEORGE GAYNES, ARNOLD VOKETAITIS. *Nanki-Poo*: FRANK PORETTA, CARL OLSEN. *Ko-Ko*: NORMAN KELLEY, RAYMOND ALLEN. *Pooh-Bah*: HERBERT BEATTIE, SPIRO MALAS. *Pish-Tush*: WILLIAM METCALF. *Three Sisters, Wards of Ko-Ko*: *Yum-Yum*: BARBARA MEISTER. *Pitti-Sing*: JANET PAVEK. *Peep-Bo*: SOPHIA STEFFAN. *Katisha*: RUTH KOBART, EVELYN SACHS.

[7]First presented in New York 20 July, 10-29 August 1885 at the Union Square and People's Theatres for 22 performances. First authorized production presented 19 August 1885 at the Fifth Avenue Theatre by Richard D'Oyly Carte for 250 performances. For Synopsis of Scenes and Musical Numbers, see 19 August 1885 D'Oyly Carte production.

Chorus of School Girls, Nobles, Guards and Coolies: Paula Coonen, Donna Curtis, Harris Davis, Marceline Decker, David Dodds, Glenn Dowlen, Beverly Evans, Margaret Goz, Norman Grogan, Helen Guile, Edson Hoel, Alan Keene, Carmen Lindsay, Dean Linton, George McWhorter, Kellis Miller, John Minto, Hanna Owen, Charlotte Povia, Betty Jane Schwering, John Smith, Stephanie Reynolds, Mara Yaven, Don Yule, Mariano Parra.

1961.04 THE PIRATES OF PENZANCE, or The Slave of Duty

A Revival of the Comic Opera in Two Acts[8]. Libretto by William S. Gilbert. Music by Arthur Sullivan. Staged by Dorothy Raedler. Scenery by H. A. Condell. Costumes by Patton Campbell. Conductors, Julius Rudel, Kurt Safir. Chorus master, William Jonson. Produced by the New York City Center Gilbert and Sullivan Company (Julius Rudel, General director). Opened 19 January 1961 at the New York City Center and closed 29 January 1961 after 6 performances in repertory.

CAST: *Major-General Stanley*: COLEY WORTH. *The Pirate King*: WILLIAM CHAPMAN. *Samuel*: MAURICE STERN. *Frederic*: FRANK PORETTA, WILLIAM DIARD. *Sergeant of Police*: HERBERT BEATTIE, SPIRO MALAS. *General Stanley's Daughters (4)*: *Mabel*: JACQUELYNNE MOODY. *Edith*: JOY CLEMENTS. *Kate*: SOPHIA STEFFAN. *Isabel*: Stephanie Reynolds. *Ruth*: BEATRICE KREBS. *Chorus of Pirates, Police and General Stanley's Wards*: same as THE MIKADO above.

1961.05 THE GONDOLIERS, or The King of Barataria

A Revival of the Comic Opera in Two Acts[9]. Libretto by William S. Gilbert. Music by Arthur Sullivan. Staged by Dorothy Raedler. Scenery and costumes by Ed Wittstein. Conductor, Julius Rudel. Chorus master, William Jonson. Produced by the New York City Center Gilbert and Sullivan Company (Julius Rudel, General director). Opened 25 January 1961 at the New York City Center and closed 2 February 1961 after 4 performances in repertory.

CAST: *The Duke of Plaza-Toro*: NORMAN KELLEY. *Luiz*: WILLIAM DIARD. *Don Alhambra Del Bolero*: GEORGE GAYNES. *Marco Palmieri*: JOHN ALEXANDER, FRANK PORETTA. *Giuseppe Palmieri*: RICHARD FREDERICKS. *Antonio*: William Metcalf. *Francesco*: Maurice Stern. *Giorgio*: Norman Grogan. *The Duchess of Plaza-Toro*: EVELYN SACHS. *Casilda*: BARBARA MEISTER. *Gianetta*: JANET PAVEK, JOY CLEMENTS. *Tessa*: CECILIA WARD. *Fiametta*: Doris Yarick. *Vittoria*: Sophia Steffan. *Giulia*: Beverly Evans. *Inez*: Gladys Kriese. *Solo Cachucha Dancers*: Adele Valle, Mariano Parra. *Chorus of Gondoliers, Contadine, Men-at-Arms, Heralds and Pages*: same as THE MIKADO above.

1961.06 H.M.S. PINAFORE, or The Lass That Loved a Sailor

A Revival of the Comic Opera in Two Acts[10]. Libretto by William S. Gilbert. Music by Arthur Sullivan. Staged by Allen Fletcher. Scenery and costumes by Patton Campbell. Conductors, Robert Irving, Felix Popper. Chorus master, William Jonson. Produced by the New York City Center Gilbert and Sullivan Company (Julius Rudel, General director). Opened 1 February 1961 at the New York City Center and closed 4 February 1961 after 4 performances in repertory.

CAST: *The Rt. Hon. Sir Joseph Porter, K.C.B.*, First Lord of the Admiralty: COLEY WORTH. *Captain Corcoran*, Commander of the *H.M.S. Pinafore*: WILLIAM CHAPMAN. *Ralph Rackstraw*, Able Seaman: FRANK PORETTA, CARL OLSEN. *Dick Deadeye*, Able Seaman: PAUL UKENA, HERBERT BEATTIE. *Bill Bobstay*, Boatswain: Richard Fredericks. *Bob Becket*: John Macurdy. *Josephine*, the Captain's Daughter: DORIS YARICK, JOY CLEMENTS. *Hebe*, Sir Joseph's First Cousin: Cecilia Ward. *Little Buttercup*, Mrs. Cripps, a Portsmouth bum-boat woman: BEATRICE KREBS, GLADYS KRIESE. *First Lord's Sisters, His Cousins, His Aunts, Sailors, Marines, etc.*: same as THE MIKADO above.

1961.07 13 DAUGHTERS

A Musical in Two Acts, a Prologue and 14 Scenes. Book, music and lyrics by Eaton Magoon, Jr. Additional book material by Leon Tokatyan. Choreography by Rod Alexander. Staged by Billy Matthews. Scenery designed and lighted by George Jenkins. Costumes by Alvin Colt. Musical direction and vocal arrangements by Pembroke Davenport. Orchestrations by Joe Glover. Additional orchestrations by Robert Russell Bennett. Assistant to the choreographer and Hawaiian consultant, Nona Beamer. Dance arrangements by Bob Atwood. Produced by Jack H. Silverman. Opened 2 March 1961 at the 54th Street Theatre and closed 25 March 1961 after 28 performances.

CAST (in order of appearance): *Kahuna*: Paul Michael. *Young Kahuna and Chanter*: Keola Beamer. *Boys*: Miki Lamont, Augie Rios, Delphino De Arco, Ado Sato, Steve Curry. *Kinau*: SYLVIA SYMS. *Chun*: DON AMECHE. *Emmaloa*: MONICA BOYAR. *Mana*, Prince of Hawaii: ED KENNEY. *Malia*: DIANA CORTO. *Kamakia*: Honey Sanders. *William*: JOHN BATTLES. *Jacques*: RICHARD TONE. *Isabel*: GINA VIGLIONE. *Susie*: Constance Di Giovanni. *Sally*: Vivian Hernandez. *Willoughby*: STANLEY GROVER. *Jane*: Diana Baffa. *Maude*: Karen Lynn Reed. *Desdemona*: Shirley De Burgh. *Cora*: Jo Anne Leeds. *Mary*: Nikki Sowinski. *May*: Connie Burnett. *Millie Lee*: Gloria Gabriel. *Minnie Lou*: Jeanne Armin. *Cecilia*: ISABELLE FARRELL. *Governors*: Paul Michael, Jack Murray, Jack Mathers, Irving Barnes. *Prime Minister*: George Hirose. *Keoki*, King of Hawaii: GEORGE LIPTON. *David Scott*, Attorney General: Konrad Matthaei. *Guards*: Bill Jason, Jose Ahumada. *Governor's Wives*: Kelli Scott, Doris Galiber, Lynn Barret, Veronica McCormick. *Sir Cyril*: Peter Pagan. *Assistant Consul*: Nathaniel White.

Singers: Irving Barnes, Lynn Barret, Doris Galiber, Jack Mathers, Paul Michael, Jack Murray, Veronica McCormick, Kelli Scott. *Dancers*: Jeanne Armin, Diana Baffa, Carlos Bas, Keola Beamer, Connie Burnett, Shirley De Burgh, Humberto D'Elia, Antony De Vecchi, Gloria Gabriel, Blair Hammond, Jo Anne Leeds, Roger LePage, Carlos Macri, Michael Maurer, Jerome Michael, Mitchel Nutick, Candy Recla, Nikki Sowinski, Mary Zahn. *Children*: Steve Curry, Delfino De Arco, Constance Di Giovanni, Vivian Hernandez, Miki Lamont, Karen Lynn Reed, Augie Ross, Ado Sato. *Servants*: Jose Ahumada, Kalani Cockett, Bill Jason.

The action takes place in Hawaii in the late nineteenth century.

Prologue: The Valley.

Act 1, Scene 1: Chun's House. 26 years later. *Scene 2*: King's Pavilion. *Scene 3*: By a Stream. *Scene 4*: Mission School. *Scene 5*: By a Stream. *Scene 6*: The Valley. *Scene 7*: Emmaloa's Bedroom. *Scene 8*: The Gold Pavillion of the Waikiki Hotel.

Act 2, Scene 1: Chun's House. *Scene 2*: Chun's Shop. *Scene 3*: Chun's House. *Scene 4*: A Beach near Honolulu Harbor. *Scene 5*: King's Pavilion. *Scene 6*: The Valley.

ACT 1

Prologue

"Kuli Kuli"
S. Syms, Company

"House on the Hill"
D. Ameche

Scene 1

"13 Daughters"
D. Ameche, the Daughters

"Paper of Gold" (dance)
R. Tone, the Daughters

Scene 3

"Let-A-Go Your Heart"
E. Kenney, D. Corto

Scene 4

"Alphabet Song" (*Music by* Nona Beamer.)
The Children

Scene 5

"Throw a Petal"
D. Corto

"When You Hear the Wind"
E. Kenney

Scene 6

"Ka Wahine Akamai"(Smart Woman)
S. Syms, H. Sanders, M. Boyar, Daughters, Suitors

[8]First presented in New York 31 December 1879 at the Fifth Avenue Theatre for a total of 91 performances in two engagements. For Synopsis of Scenes and Musical Numbers, see original 1879 production.

[9]Originally presented in New York 7 January 1890 at Park Theatre for 103 performances. For Synopsis of Scenes and Musical Numbers, see original 1890 production.

[10]Originally presented in New York 15 January 1879 at the Standard Theatre for 175 performances. For Synopsis of Scenes and Musical Numbers, see original 1879 production.

Scene 7

"You Set My Heart To Music"
M. Boyar, D. Ameche, G. Viglione

Scene 8

"13 Daughters" (reprise)
D. Ameche, Daughters, Suitors

"The Cotillion"
Company

ACT 2

Scene 1

"Old Maids"
Daughters

Scene 2

"Oriental Plan"[11]
D. Ameche
(*Music and Lyrics by* Sherman Edwards and Sid Wayne.)

Scene 3

"Hoomalimali" (Baiting the Hook)
S. Syms

"My Pleasure"
S. Grover, G. Viglione

"Puka Puka Pants"
I. Farrell, R. Tone

Scene 4

"My Hawaii"
E. Kenney

Scene 6

Hiiaka Ritual Dance
Dancers

"Hiiaka"
M. Boyar

"House on the Hill" (reprise)
D. Ameche

"My Hawaii" (reprise)
Company

1961.08 THE HAPPIEST GIRL IN THE WORLD

A Musical Comedy in Two Acts, 14 Scenes. Book by Fred Saidy and Henry Myers. Story by E. Y. Harburg (with a bow to Aristophanes "Lysistrata" and Bulfinch). Music by Jacques Offenbach. Lyrics by E. Y. Harburg. Settings and lighting by William and Jean Eckart. Costumes by Robert Fletcher. Choreography by Dania Krupska. Musical direction and vocal arrangements by Robert DeCormier. Orchestrations by Robert Russell Bennett and Hershy Kay. Dance arrangements by Gerald Alters. Musical research by Jay Gorney. Directed by Cyril Ritchard. Electronic tonalities by Louis and Bebe Barron. Produced by Lee Guber. Opened 3 April 1961 at the Martin Beck Theatre and closed 24 June 1961 after 97 performances.

CAST (in order of appearance): *First Courier*: Alton Ruff. *Second Courier*: Ronald B. Stratton. *First Minister*: TED THURSTON. *Second Minister*: DON CRABTREE. *Third Minister*: RICHARD WINTER. *Chief of State*: CYRIL RITCHARD. *A Herald*: Don Atkinson. *General Kinesias*: BRUCE YARNELL. *Phoebe*: Rita Metzger. *Lysistrata*: DRAN SEITZ. *Captain Crito*: JOHN NAPIER. *Jupiter*: MICHAEL KERMOYAN. *Juno*: LU LEONARD. *Bacchus*: TED THURSTON. *Mercury*: Don Atkinson. *Apollo*: JOHN NAPIER. *Neptune*: RICHARD WINTER. *Aphrodite*: JOY CLAUSSEN. *Pluto*: CYRIL RITCHARD. *Diana*: JANICE RULE. *Amaryllis*: JOY CLAUSSEN. *Myrrhina*: LU LEONARD. *A Heckler*: CYRIL RITCHARD. *Daphne*: Norma Donaldson. *Hector*: David Canary. *Ataraxohymonides*: John Wheeler. *Ulysses*: RICHARD WINTER. *Sergeant*: DON CRABTREE. *A Gay Blade*: CYRIL RITCHARD. *A Wine Smuggler*: CYRIL RITCHARD. *Sentinel*: Nancy Windsor. *The Pied Piper of Hamelin*: CYRIL RITCHARD. *Theodora*: Lainie Kazan. *Spartan Woman*: Maura K. Wedge. *A Playwright*: CYRIL RITCHARD. *Rhodope*: Janice Painchaud. *An Ambassador*: CYRIL RITCHARD.

Singers: Ellen Berse, Joy Claussen, Norma Donaldson, Lainie Kazan, Leonora Lanzillotti, Rita Metzger, Elaine Spaulding, Maura K. Wedge, Nancy Windsor, David Canary, Jeff Killian, Paul Merrill, Theodore Morill, Arthur Tookoyan, Mark Tully, John Wheeler, Richard Winter. *Dancers*: Bonnie Brandon, Candace Caldwell, Natasha Grishin, Judith Haskell, Lisa James, Gloria Kaye, Susan May, Carmen Morales, Janice Painchaud, Bill Atkinson, Don Atkinson, Grant Delaney, Victor Duntiere, Louis Kosman, Alton Ruff, Kenneth Scott, Ron Sequoio, Ronald B. Stratton.

Act 1, Scene 1: Office of the Chief of State of Athens. 400 B.C. *Scene 2*: The Rotunda. *Scene 3*: The Agora. *Scene 4*: Patio of the General's Home. *Scene 5*: Atop Mount Olympus. *Scene 6*: Garden of the General's Home. *Scene 7*: The Agora. *Scene 8*: The Patio. *Scene 9*: Lysistrata's Boudoir.

Act 2, Scene 1: The Public Baths. *Scene 2*: Outside the Citadel. *Scene 3*: The Patio. *Scene 4*: Steps leading to the Temple of Diana. *Scene 5*: The Agora.

ACT 1

"The Olympics" (ballet)
(Dance Ensemble)

"Cheers for the Hero"
Ensemble

"The Glory That Is Greece"
C. Ritchard, B. Yarnell, Ensemble

"The Happiest Girl in the World"
D. Seitz, B. Yarnell

"The Greek Marine"
C. Ritchard, T. Thurston, D. Crabtree, R. Winter, Soldiers

"Shall We Say Farewell"
D. Seitz

"Never Be-Devil the Devil"
C. Ritchard

"Whatever That May Be"
J. Rule, the Gods

"Eureka"
M. Kermoyan, the Gods

Diana's Arrival in Athens (dance)
J. Rule

"The Oath"
D. Seitz, Women

"Diana's Transformation"
C. Ritchard, J. Rule, Two Suitors

"Vive la Virtue!"
C. Ritchard, J. Rule

"Adrift on a Star"
D. Seitz, B. Yarnell

"The Happiest Girl in the World" (reprise)
D. Seitz, B. Yarnell

Finale (Act 1)
D. Seitz, B. Yarnell, Ensemble

ACT 2

"That'll Be the Day"
Men

"How Soon, Oh Moon?"
D. Seitz, N. Windsor, Women

"Love-Sick Serenade"
C. Ritchard, L. Leonard

"Five Minutes of Spring"
B. Yarnell, D. Seitz, J. Rule

"The Greek Marine" (reprise)
Soldiers

"Five Minutes of Spring" (reprise)
Soldiers

"Never Trust a Virgin"
C. Ritchard, Women

"Entrance of the Courtesans"
Women

"The Pied Piper's Can-Can"
C. Ritchard, Dancers

"Vive la Virtue!" (reprise)
C. Ritchard, J. Rule

Finale (Act 2)
Entire Company

---

[11]Replaced during run by:
"Nothing Man Cannot Do"
D. Ameche

1961.09

SHOW BOAT

A Revival of the Musical Play in Two Acts, 15 Scenes[12]. Music by Jerome Kern. Book and Lyrics by Oscar Hammerstein II. Based on the novel of the same name by Edna Ferber. Staged by Dania Krupska. Choreography by Arthur Partington. Scenery and lighting by Howard Bay. Costumes by Stanley Simmons. Musical director and conductor, Julius Rudel. Assistant conductor and choral director, William Jonson. (Orchestrations by Robert Russell Bennett.) Produced by the New York City Center Light Opera Company (Jean Dalrymple, Director). Opened 12 April 1961 at the New York City Center and closed 23 April 1961 after 14 performances.

CAST (in order of their appearance): *Pete*: William Coppola. *Windy McLain*: Scott Moore. *Queenie*: CAROL BRICE. *Captain Andy*: JOE E. BROWN. *Parthy Ann Hawkes*: ISABELLA HOOPES. *Ellie*: JANE KEAN. *Frank*: RICHARD FRANCE. *Julie*: ANITA DARIAN. *Steve*: HERBERT FIELDS. *Gaylord Ravenal*: ROBERT ROUNSEVILLE. *Sheriff Ike Vallon*: John Martin. *Magnolia*: JO SULLIVAN. *Joe*: ANDREW FRIERSON. *Rubberface*: J. Patrick Carter. *Backwoodsman*: Norman A. Grogan. *Jeb*: Feodore Tedick. *Miss Parkington*: Carmen Lindsay. *Barker*: Henry Lawrence. *Old Sport*: Jack Rains. *Ethel*: Alyce Webb. *Landlady*: Claire Waring. *Al*: John Smith. *Mazie*: Sherry McCutcheon. *Jim*: Henry Lawrence. *Jake*: William Coppola. *Pianist*: John Cooke. *Charley*: Ned Wright. *Man With Guitar*: J. Patrick Carter. *Mother Superior*: Miriam Lawrence. *Kim*, as a child: Bridget Knapp. *Dottie*: Helen Guile. *Dolly*: Mara Wirt. *Headwaiter*: Feodore Tedick. *Old Lady on Levee*: Sarah Floyd. *Kim*, in her Twenties: Jo Sullivan.

Singers: Beverly Evans, Helen Guile, Miriam Lawrence, Carmen Lindsay, Hanna Owen, Betty Jane Schwering, Mara Wirt, Maggie Worth. John Bessinger, Lawrence Bogue, William Coppola, J. Patrick Carter, Norman A. Grogan, Henry Lawrence, Kellis Miller, Jack Rains, John J. Smith, Feodore Tedick. *Dancers*: Mimi Alexander, Margery Beddow, Geralyn Donald, Ellen Halpin, Linda Howe, Bettye Jenkins, Sherry McCutcheon, Barbara Monte. Todd Butler, Garold Gardner, Eric Kristen, Ronnie Snook. *Jubilee Singers*: Issa Arnal, Ruby Green Aspinall, Kay Barnes, Claretta Freeman, H. Scott Gibson, Joli Gonsalves, Robert Henson, Wanza King, Mary Louise, Rosalie Maxwell, Caryl Paige, Charles Scott, Alyce E. Webb, Arthur Williams, Ned Wright. *Jubilee Dancers*: Leu Comacho, Julius Fields, LaVinnia Hamilton, Nathaniel Horne, Bernard Johnson, Jan Aubrey Mickens, Joan Peters, Harold Pierson, Ronald Platts, Ella Thompson, Glory Van Scott, Myrna White.

1961.10

CARNIVAL

A Musical Comedy in Two Acts, 24 Scenes. Book by Michael Stewart. (Based on the novela "The Love of Seven Dolls" by Paul Gallico and its film adaptation "Lili" by Helen Deutsch.) Music and lyrics by Bob Merrill. Directed and choreographed by Gower Champion. Settings and lighting by Will Steven Armstrong. Costumes by Freddy Wittop. Musical direction and vocal arrangements by Saul Schechtman. Orchestrations by Philip J. Lang. Dance arrangements by Peter Howard. Associate choreographer, Gene Bayliss. Puppets created and supervised by Tom Tichenor. Designer and supervisor of magic and illusion, Roy Benson. Produced by David Merrick. Opened 13 April 1961 at the Imperial Theatre, moved 21 December 1962 to the Winter Garden, and closed 5 January 1963 after 719 performances.

CAST (in order of appearance): *Jacquot*: PIERRE OLAF. *Mr. Schlegel*: HENRY LASCOE. *Grobert*: Will Lee. *Roustabouts*: George Marcy, Tony Gomez, John Nola, Buff Shurr. *Cyclist*: Bob Murray. *Miguelito*: George Marcy. *Dog Trainer*: Paul Sydell. *Wardrobe Mistress*: Carvel Carter. *Harem Girls*: Nicole Barth, Iva March, Beti Seay. *Bear Girl*: Jennifer Billingsley. *Princess Olga*: Luba Lisa. *Band*: C. B. Bernard, Peter Lombard. *Stilt-Walker*: Dean Crane. *Jugglers*: Martin Brothers. *Clowns*: Bob Dixon, Harry Lee Rogers. *Strongman*: Pat Tolson. *Gladys Zuwicki*: Mary Ann Niles. *Gloria Zuwicki*: Christine Bartel. *Gypsy*: Anita Gillette. *Marco the Magnificent*: JAMES MITCHELL. *The Incomparable Rosalie*: KAYE BALLARD. *Greta Schlegel*: June Meshonek. *Lili*: ANNA MARIA ALBERGHETTI. *Paul Berthalet*: JERRY ORBACH. *Blue Birds*: Nicole Barth, Jennifer Billingsley, Iva March, Beti Seay. *Aerialist*: Dean Crane. *Dr. Glass*: Igors Gavon.

Act 1, Scene 1: The Carnival Area on the outskirts of a town in Southern Europe. *Scene 2*: The Puppet Booth. *Scene 3*: Inside Schlegel's Office. *Scene 4*: The Carnival Area. *Scene 5*: The Carnival Area. *Scene 6*: Interior of Main Tent. *Scene 7*: Carnival Area at Night.

Act 2, Scene 1: The Midway. *Scene 2*: Trailer Camp. *Scene 3*: Outside Main Tent.

ACT 1

Scene 1

"Direct from Vienna"
K. Ballard, J. Meshonek, Carnival People

"A Very Nice Man"
A. M. Alberghetti

Scene 2

"Fairyland"
Puppets

"I've Got to Find a Reason"
J. Orbach

"Mira" (Can You Imagine That?)
A. M. Alberghetti

"Sword, Rose and Cape"
J. Mitchell, G. Marcy, T. Gomez, J. Nola, B. Shurr

Scene 3

"Humming"
K. Ballard, J. Meshonek

Scene 4

"Yes, My Heart"
A. M. Alberghetti

Scene 5

"Everybody Likes You"
J. Orbach

Scene 6

"Magic, Magic"
J. Mitchell, K. Ballard, A. M. Alberghetti

"Tanz Mit Mir" (Dance With Me)
N. Barth, J. Billingsley, I. March, B. Seay

"Carnival Ballet"
A. M. Alberghetti, Carnival People, Townspeople

Scene 7

"Mira" (reprise)
A. M. Alberghetti

Theme from 'Carnival'("Love Makes the World Go Round")
A. M. Alberghetti, Puppets

ACT 2

Scene 1

"Yum Ticky" (Ticky Tum Tum)
A. M. Alberghetti, Puppets

"The Rich"
A. M. Alberghetti, Puppets

Theme from 'Carnival' (reprise)
A. M. Alberghetti, Puppets

"Beautiful Candy"
A. M. Alberghetti, Puppets, Vendors

"Her Face"
J. Orbach

"Grand Imperial Cirque de Paris"
P. Olaf, Carnival People

Scene 2

"I Hate Him"/"Her Face" (reprise)
A. M. Alberghetti/J. Orbach

Scene 3

"Grand Imperial Cirque de Paris" (reprise)
Carnival People

"Always, Always You"
J. Mitchell, K. Ballard

"She's My Love"
J. Orbach

1961.11

YOUNG ABE LINCOLN

A Musical in Two Acts, 7 Scenes[13]. Book by Richard N. Bernstein and John Allen. Music by Victor Ziskin. Lyrics by Joan Javits. Special dialogue and lyrics by Arnold Sundgaard. Musical director, Victor Ziskin. Musical numbers Staged by Rhoda Levine. Sets, costumes and lighting by Fred Voelpel.

---

[12]First presented December 27, 1927 at the Ziegfeld Theatre for 572 performances. This revised version first presented 5 January 1946 at the Ziegfeld Theatre for 418 performances. For Synopsis of Scenes and Musical Numbers, see 1946 revival. Act 2, Scene 8 reset on the Levee at Natches.

[13]First produced in New York Off-Broadway 3-8 April 1961 at the York Theatre for 18 performances. This show played 3 matinees daily in its first engagement at the York, 12 matinees weekly at the Eugene O'Neill, and a split schedule of tour dates and regular matinees in its return to the York.

Directed by Jay Harnick. Produced by Arthur Shimkin. Opened 25 April 1961 at the Eugene O'Neill Theatre and closed 7 May 1961 after 27 performances. Re-opened Off-Broadway 10 May 1961 at the York Playhouse and closed 24 June 1961 after 48 additional performances, and 34 performances touring in New York City area schools. Total at the York and O'Neill Theatres: 93 performances.

CAST: *Abe Lincoln*: DARRELL SANDEEN. *William Berry*: Lou Cutell. *Minnie*: Joan Kibrig, (Travis Hudson). *Ann Rutledge*: Judy Foster. *John McNeil*: Ray Hyson. *Bowling Green*: Tom Noel. *Ninian Edwards*: Dan Resin. *Josh*: Ken Kercheval, (Jack Kauflin). *Jack Armstrong*: Robert Darnell. *Seth*: Ralston Hill. *Hannah*: Barbara Cornett. (Actors who originated roles but did not come to Broadway are listed in parentheses; the roles of Hannah and Seth were added for the Broadway run.)

Act 1, Scene 1: The Town Square of New Salem, Illinois in 1833. *Scene 2*: A Drill Field.

Act 2, Scene 1: A Grove in New Salem, Illinois. *Scene 2*: Ann's Room. *Scene 3*: A Clearing in the Woods. *Scene 4*: The Election Site. *Scene 5*: The Election Site.

ACT 1
Scene 1
"The Same Old Me"
Company
"Cheer Up!"
J. Kibrig, L. Cutell
"You Can Dance"
J. Foster, D. Sandeen
"Someone You Know"
D. Sandeen, J. Foster
"I Want to be a Little Frog in a Little Pond"
D. Sandeen, J. Kibrig, L. Cutell, T. Noel, D. Resin, J. Foster
"Clarey Grove Song"
R. Darnell, R. Hyson, K. Kercheval
"Don't P-P-Point Them Guns at Me"
R. Darnell, R. Hyson, K. Kercheval
Scene 2
"The Captain Lincoln March" (Drill Song)
L. Cutell, K. Kercheval, R. Hyson, R. Hill, T. Noel, D. Sandeen
"Run, Indian, Run" (Run Injuns)
R. Darnell, R. Hyson, K. Kercheval, L. Cutell, R. Hill, D. Sandeen

ACT 2
Scene 1
"Welcome Home March"
Company
"Vote for Lincoln"
D. Resin, T. Noel, R. Darnell, R. Hyson, K. Kercheval, L. Cutell, R. Hill
"I Want to Be a Little Frog in a Little Pond" (reprise)
D. Sandeen, Men
Scene 3
"Cheer Up" (reprise)
J. Kibrig, L. Cutell
Scene 4
"Frontier Politics"
D. Resin, R. Darnell, R. Hyson, K. Kercheval, R. Hill, T. Noel, L. Cutell
Scene 5
Finale ("The Same Old Me" reprise)
Company

1961.12 SOUTH PACIFIC

A Revival of the Musical Play in Two Acts, 23 Scenes[14]. Music by Richard Rodgers. Lyrics by Oscar Hammerstein II. Book by Oscar Hammerstein II and Joshua Logan. Adapted from James A. Michener's novel "Tales of the South Pacific." Directed by John Fearnley. Scenery by Jo Mielziner, adapted by Paul Morrison. Original costumes by Motley. Costumes by Stanley Simmons. Musical director, Julius Rudel. (Orchestrations by Robert Russell Bennett.) Produced by the New York City Center Light Opera Company (Jean Dalrymple, Director). Opened 26 April 1961 at the New York City Center and closed 14 May 1961 after 23 performances.

CAST (in order of appearance): *Ngana*: Vivian Hernandez. *Jerome*: Delfino De Arco. *Henry*: Viraj Amonsin. *Ensign Nellie Forbush*: ALLYN ANN McLERIE. *Emile DeBecque*: WILLIAM CHAPMAN. *Bloody Mary*: ROSETTA LeNOIRE. *Bloody Mary's Assistant*: Musa Williams. *Abner*: Jim McMillan. *Stewpot*: JEFF HARRIS. *Luther Billis*: DORT CLARK. *Professor*: Art Ostrin. *Lt. Joseph Cable, U.S.M.C.*: STANLEY GROVER. *Capt. George Brackett, U.S.N.*: EDMUND BAYLIES. *Cmdr. William Harbison, U.S.N.*: WESLEY ADDY. *Yeoman Herbert Quale*: Kenny Adams. *Sgt. Kenneth Johnson*: Daniel P. Hannafin. *Cpl. Richard West*: Don Becker. *Seabee Morton Wise*: Jim Conner. *Sgt. Juan Cortez*: Saran Wallach. *Seaman Tom O'Brien*: Robert Lenn. *Radio Operator Bob McCaffery*: John Aman. *Cpl. Hamilton Steeves*: Thomas Edwards. *Staff Sgt. Guilio Fascinato*: Richard Nieves. *Seaman James Hayes*: Ralph Vucci. *Lt. Genevieve Marshall*: Barbara Saxby. *Ensign Dinah Murphy*: Maggie Worth. *Ensign Janet MacGregor*: Betty Jane Schwering. *Ensign Cora MacRae*: Penny Fuller. *Ensign Bessie Noonan*: Francesca Bell. *Ensign Pamela Whitmore*: Miriam Lawrence. *Ensign Sue Yaeger*: Sybil Scotford. *Ensign Lisa Minelli*: Karen Styne. *Liat*: COCO RAMIREZ. *Lt. Buzz Adams*: Don Corby. *Shore Patrol Officer*: Casper Roos. *Islanders*: Mark Richard Satow, Ado Sato, Eigel Silju.

1961.13 PORGY AND BESS

A Revival of the Folk Opera in Two Acts, 9 Scenes[15]. Book by DuBose Heyward adapted from the play "Porgy" by DuBose and Dorothy Heyward. Music by George Gershwin. Lyrics by DuBose Heyward and Ira Gershwin. Directed by William Ball. Choral director and associate conductor, William Jonson. Settings by Stephen O. Saxe. Costumes by Stanley Simmons. Musical director, Julius Rudel. Lighting by Paul Morrison. Produced by the New York City Center Light Opera Company (Jean Dalrymple, Director). Opened 17 May 1961 at the New York City Center and closed 28 May 1961 after 16 performances.

CAST (in order of appearance): *Clara*: BILLIE LYNN DANIEL. *Mingo*: Jerry Laws. *Sportin' Life*: RAWN SPEARMAN. *Jake*: IRVING BARNES, LEONARD PARKER (alt.). *Serena*: BARBARA WEBB. *Robbins*: Ned Wright. *Jim*: Scott Gibson. *Peter*, the Honey Man: Joseph Crawford. *Lily*, the Strawberry Woman: Edna Ricks. *Maria*: CAROL BRICE. *Porgy*: WILLIAM WARFIELD, IRVING BARNES (alt.). *Crown*: JAMES RANDOLPH. *Bess*: LEESA FOSTER, MARTHA FLOWERS (alt.). *Policemen*: Harry Bessinger, Howard Poyro. *Detective*: William Coppola. *Police Sergeant*: Norman Grogan. *Undertaker*: Wanza King. *Annie*: Alyce Webb. *Frazier*: Eugene Brice. *Nelson*: Arthur Williams. *Strawberry Woman*: Doreese Duquan. *Crabman*: Clyde Turner. *Coroner*: Eugene Wood.

Residents of Catfish Row: Ruby Green Aspinall, Kay Barnes, Phyllis Bash, Catherine Eason, Claretta Freeman, Victoria Harrison, Lillian Hayman, Joan Montgomery, Janet Moodyors, Caryl Paige, Joyce Phipps, Eloise C. Uggams, Catherine Van Buren, Glory Van Scott, Catherine Wallace, William H. Eaton, Jr., Cortez Franklin, Joli Gonsalves, Robert Guillaume, Elijah Hodges, Cullen Maiden, Tony L. Martinez, Garrett Morris, Garwood Perkins, Harold Pierson, John Richardson, Mal Scott, James Wamen, Laurence Watson. *Children*: Joey Lewis, Donna Mills, Cederic Rose, Lisa Scott, Alan Weeks, Jerry Wimberly.

1961.14 DONNYBROOK!

A Musical Comedy in Two Acts, 22 Scenes. Book by Robert E. McEnroe. Based on the film "The Quiet Man," (screenplay by Frank S. Nugent based on the short story of same name published in collection "Green Rushes") by Maurice Walsh. Music and lyrics by Johnny Burke. Directed and choreographed by Jack Cole. (Settings and costumes) Designed by Rouben Ter-Arutunian. Lighting by Klaus Holm. Musical direction and vocal arrangements by Clay Warnick. (Musical) arrangements and orchestrations by Robert Ginzler. Ballet music arranged and orchestrated by Laurence Rosenthal. Produced by Fred Hebert and David Kapp. Opened 18 May 1961 at the 46th Street Theatre and closed 15 July 1961 after 68 performances.

CAST (in order of appearance): *Willie O'Bantie*: Bruce MacKay. *Matthew Gilbane*: James Gannon. *Gavin Collins*: Alfred DeSio. *Old Man Toomey*: CLARENCE NORDSTROM. *Tim O'Connell*: Darrell J. Askey. *Will Danaher*: PHILIP BOSCO. *Ellen Roe Danaher*: JOAN FAGAN. *Esme Gillie*: Marissa Mason. *Sadie McInty*: SIBYL BOWAN. *Birdy Monyhan*: GRACE CARNEY. *Mikeen Flynn*: EDDIE FOY (JR.) *John Enright*: ART LUND. *Father Finucane*: Charles Welch. *An Irish Boy*: Eddie Ericksen.

---

[14]First produced in New York 7 April 1949 at the Majestic Theatre for 1925 performances. For Synopsis of Scenes and Musical Numbers, see original 1949 production.

[15]First produced in New York 10 October 1935 at the Alvin Theatre for 124 performances. For Synopsis of Scenes and Musical Numbers, see original 1935 production.

Jamie, a Bartender: George Harwell. *Kathy Carey*: SUSAN JOHNSON. *Principal Dancer*: Norman Maen.

Singing Ensemble: Georgia Creighton, Charlote Frazer, Nancy Foster, Dee Harless, Georgia Kennedy, Maudeen Sullivan, Darrell J. Askey, Eddie Ericksen, John Ford, George Harwell, Charles Rule, Bob Murdock. *Dancing Ensemble*: Gloria Ann Bowen, Judy Dunford, Mickey Gunnersen, Marissa Mason, Carol Sherman, Suanne Shirley, Pamela Wood, John Aristides, Robert Evans, Larry Fuller, William Guske, David Lober, George Martin, Keith Stewart.

Act 1, Scene 1: Overture. *Scene 2*: Kitchen of Will Danaher's house. *Scene 3*: The Countryside *Scene 4*: Outside "White O'Morn" Cottage. *Scene 5*: Carey's Pub. *Scene 6*: The Countryside. *Scene 7*: The Interior of Enright's Cottage. *Scene 8*: The Church. *Scene 9*: Kathy's Sitting Room; the Irish Countryside. *Scene 10*: Kitchen of Will Danaher's house. *Scene11*: Danaher's Backyard. *Scene 12*: The Danaher Parlor.

Act 2, Scene 1: The Low Road. *Scene 2*: The Interior of "White O'Morn" Cottage. *Scene 3*: The High Road. *Scene 4*: The Interior of "White O'Morn" Cottage. *Scene 5*: Carey's Pub. *Scene 6*: The (Gravestone in the Ruins of the) Church Yard. *Scene 7*: The Interior of "White O'Morn" Cottage. *Scene 8*: Railway Station. *Scene 9*: (A Rock Wall in) Danaher's Field. *Scene 10*: The Interior of "White O'Morn" Cottage.

ACT 1

Scene 1

"Overture"
E. Ericksen, S. Bowan, G. Carney, C. C. Welch, J. Fagan, Dancing Ensemble

Scenes 2 and 3

"Sez I"
J. Fagan, C. Nordstrom, B. Mackay, J. Gannon, A. Desio, D. J. Askey

Scene 5

"The Day the Snow Is Meltin'"
E. Ericksen

"Sad Was the Day"
S. Johnson, Ensemble

"Donnybrook"
Ensemble

Scene 6

"The Day the Snow Is Meltin'" (reprise)
E. Ericksen, A. DeSio, D. J. Askey, A. Lund

Scene 7

"Ellen Roe"
A. Lund

Scene 8

"Sunday Morning"
Ensemble

"The Loveable Irish"
A. Lund, C. C. Welch

Scene 9

"I Wouldn't Bet One Penny"
S. Johnson, E. Foy

Scene 10

"He Makes Me Feel I'm Lovely"
J. Fagan

Scene 11

"The Courting"
Ensemble

"I Have My Own Way"
A. Lund, J. Fagan

Scene 12

"A Toast to the Bride"
C. Nordstrom, Ensemble

ACT 2

Scene 1

"Wisha Wurra"
E. Foy, C. Nordstrom, B. MacKay, J. Gannon, A. DeSio

Scene 3

("Wisha Wurra" reprise)
E. Foy, C. Nordstrom, B. MacKay, J. Gannon, A. DeSio

"He Makes Me Feel I'm Lovely" (reprise)
J. Fagan

Scene 4

"A Quiet Life"
A. Lund

Scene 5

"Mr. Flynn"
S. Johnson, S. Bowan, G. Carney

"Hornpipe Dance"[16]

"Dee-lightful is the Word"
E. Foy, S. Johnson

Scene 6

"For My Own"
J. Fagan, A. Lund

Scene 10

(Finale "Sez I" reprise)
P. Bosco, A. Lund, Ensemble

1961.15

PAL JOEY

A Revival of the Musical Play in Two Acts, 12 Scenes[17]. Book by John O'Hara based on his collected short stories of the same name. Music by Richard Rodgers. Lyrics by Lorenz Hart. Settings and lighting by Howard Bay. Costumes by Frank Thompson. Musical director, Jay Blackton. (Orchestrations by Don Walker, Hans Spialek.) Choreography by Ralph Beaumont. Directed by Gus Schirmer. Produced by the New York City Center Light Opera Company (Jean Dalrymple, Director). Opened 31 May 1961 at the New York City Center and closed 25 June 1961 after 31 performances.

CAST (in order of appearance): *Mike*: JACK WALDRON. *Joey Evans*: BOB FOSSE. *Kid*: Marjorie Graner. *Gladys*: SHEILA BOND. *Iris*: Lillian D'Honau. *Mickey*: Aura Vainio. *Diane*: Dorothy Dushock. *Dottie*: Billie Mahoney. *Sandra*: Pat Turner. *Adele*: Barbara Monte. *Francine*: Ellen Halpin. *Linda English*: CHRISTINE MATHEWS. *Vera Simpson*: CAROL BRUCE. *Valerie*: Betty Hyatt Linton. *Ernest*: Emory Bass. *Vera's Escort*: Philip Salem. *Victor*: Joe Milan. *Scholtz*: Gene Gavin. *Louis*, (The Tenor): John Lankston. *Melba Snyder*: EILEEN HECKART. *Ludlow Lowell*: HARVEY STONE. *O'Brien*: Charles Reynolds. *Mr. Hoople*: Alexander Clark.

Dancers: Lillian D'Honau, Marilyn D'Honau, Dorothy Dushock, Tina Faye, Ellen Fluhr, Marjorie Graner, Ellen Halpin, Carol Ann Kroon, Sara Letton, Betty Hyatt Linton, Billie Mahoney, Barbara Monte, Mona Pivar, Eleanor Rogers, Marla Stevens, Pat Turner, Aura Vainio, Judith West, Gene Gavin, Tod Jackson, Richard E. Korthaze, Vernon Lusby, Mitchell Nutick, Frank Paige, Alan Peterson, Tom Roba, Philip Salem, Bud Spencer, Vernon Wendorf.

[16]Dropped during run.

[17]Originally produced in New York 25 December 1940 at the Ethel Barrymore Theatre for 374 performances. For Synopsis of Scenes and Musical Numbers, see original 1940 production. For this production, "What Is a Man" replaced "Love Is My Friend" in Act 1, Scene 4; "Joey's Tango" (danced by B. Fosse) added to Act 2, Scene 4 between "Take Him" and the reprise of "Bewitched."

1961–1962 SEASON

Barbara Cook in THE GAY LIFE (Photo: Friedman-Abeles)
Billy Rose Theatre Collection, New York Public Library for the Performing Arts

1961–1962 SEASON

1961.16 THE BILLY BARNES PEOPLE

A Musical Revue in Two Acts, 26 Scenes. Music and lyrics by Billy Barnes. Sketches and direction by Bob Rodgers. Production (settings) designed by Spencer Davies. Costumes by Grady Hunt. Musical arrangements and supervision, Ray Henderson. Cartoons, William Box. Produced by John Pool. Opened 13 June 1961 at the Royale Theatre and closed 17 June 1961 after 7 performances.

CAST: JOYCE JAMESON, DICK PATTERSON, PATTI REGAN, DAVE KETCHUM, KEN BERRY, JACKIE JOSEPH, JACK GRINNAGE, JO ANNE WORLEY.

ACT 1

Scene 1

"If It Wasn't for People"
Entire Cast

Scene 2

"There's Nothing Wrong With Our Values"
J. Jameson, D. Ketchum, P. Regan, D. Patterson

Scene 3

Vegas Revisited
Barker: J. Grinnage. *Statue*: J. Joseph. *Chorus Girl*: P. Regan. *Herman Hepplewhite*: D. Ketchum. *Fellas*: J. Grinnage, D. Patterson. *Opera Diva*: J. A. Worley.

Scene 4

"Don't Bother"
J. Joseph, K. Berry

Scene 5

I Wrote a Book
Authoress: J. Jameson. *Fans*: J. A. Worley, D. Patterson.

Scene 6

"If It Makes You Happy" (The Syndicate Song)
The Boss: D. Ketchum. *His Girl*: J. Joseph. *The Boys*: J. Grinnage, K. Berry.

Scene 7

"Damn-ALot" (Parody of "Camelot"in the style of Brendan Behan)
Introduced by J. Grinnage. *Guenevere*: P. Regan. *Morgan O'Fey*: J. Jameson. *King Arthur*: D. Ketchum. *Lancelot*: D. Patterson.

Scene 8

"What Do Have To Hold On To?"
J. A. Worley

Scene 9

"I Like You"
Romantic Couple: J. Joseph, K. Berry. *Neurotic Couple*: J. A. Worley, J. Grinnage. *Sophisticated Couple*: J. Jameson, D. Patterson.

Scene 10

"Before and After"
D. Ketchum, D. Patterson

Scene 11

"Let's Get Drunk"
K. Berry

Scene 12

"It's Not Easy"
Ethel: P. Regan. *Janet*: J. Jameson. *Adele*: J. A. Worley.

Scene 13

The Speech Teacher
Teacher: D. Patterson. *Client*: J. Grinnage.

Scene 14

"The Matinee"
Entire Cast

ACT 2

Scene 1

"If It Wasn't For People" (reprise)
J. Grinnage
The Couch: J. Joseph, D. Patterson. *The Balcony*: J. A. Worley, D. Ketchum. *Bus Stop*: P. Regan, K. Berry.

Scene 2

Liberated Woman
Sally O'Toole: J. Jameson. *Johnny*, her boy friend: J. Grinnage. *Narrator*: D. Patterson.

Scene 3

"What Do We Have to Hold On To?" (reprise)
J. A. Worley

Scene 4

"The End?"
D. Patterson, K. Berry, D. Ketchum

Scene 5

Alice
Alice: J. Joseph. *Felicia Fashion*: P. Regan. *Marty Market*: D. Patterson. *Housewife*: J. A. Worley. *Mrs. Karr*: J. Jameson. *Mr. Karr*: K. Berry. *Mr. Big Business, Sr.*: D. Ketchum. *Mr. Big Business, Jr.*: J. Grinnage.

Scene 6

Grauman's Chinese
D. Patterson, P. Regan, K. Berry

Scene 7

"Second Best"
J. Jameson

Scene 8

"What Do We Have to Hold On To?" (reprise)
J. A. Worley

Scene 9

"Dolls"
D. Ketchum, D. Patterson, P. Regan

Scene 10

"Where Is the Clown?"
J. Jameson, K. Berry

Scene 11

"Marital Infidelity"
Entire Cast

Scene 12

"I Like You" (reprise)
Entire Cast

1961.17 FROM THE SECOND CITY

A Comedy Revue in Two Acts, 24 Scenes[1]. Scenes and dialogues created by the Company. Director, Paul Sills. Music by William Mathieu. Settings and lighting designed by Frederick Fox. Produced by Max Liebman, Bernard Sahlins, Howard Alk, Paul Sills. Opened 26 September 1961 at the Royale Theatre and closed 9 December 1961 after 87 performances.

CAST: HOWARD ALK, ALAN ARKIN, SEVERN DARDEN, ANDREW DUNCAN, BARBARA HARRIS, MINA KOLB, PAUL SAND, EUGENE TROOBNICK. *At the piano*: Garry Sherman.

ACT 1

Scene 1

Max and Mortiz
S. Darden, H. Alk, B. Harris

Scene 2

Great Books
E. Troobnick, B. Harris, A. Duncan, M. Kolb, S. Darden

[1]Unlike all previous and subsequent Second City productions in Chicago, Off-Broadway and elsewhere, this edition was fully scripted and featured little of the improvisation for which the Second City was known. Following the Broadway run, the Second City re-opened Off-Broadway at the Square East in a series of revues in their traditional format: SEA-COAST OF BOHEMIA, ALARUMS AND EXCURSIONS, TO THE WATER TOWER, WHEN THE OWL SCREAMS, OPEN SEASON AT SECOND CITY, and THE WRECKING BALL.

Scene 3
Hollywood Ten
A. Arkin, M. Kolb, S. Darden
Scene 4
Phono Pal
P. Sand, E. Troobnick
Scene 5
The Hoboken Story (Parody of West Side Story)
P. Sand, B. Harris, A. Duncan, A. Arkin, H. Alk, S. Darden
Scene 6
The Silent Film
S. Darden, E. Troobnick, P. Sand
Scene 7
The Bergman Film
S. Darden, P. Sand, B. Harris
Scene 8
Interview: West Germany
E. Troobnick, A. Arkin
Scene 9
Interview: Louisiana
A. Duncan, S. Darden
Scene 10
A Short Message
M. Kolb, E. Troobnick
Scene 11
Football Comes to the U. of C.
A. Duncan, H. Alk, E. Troobnick, S. Darden
Scene 12
Museum Piece
B. Harris, A. Arkin
Scene 13
"Second City Symphony"

ACT 2
Scene 1
"Tempo"
The Company
Scene 2
Laos
P. Sand, A. Duncan
Scene 3
"I Got Blues"
B. Harris, S. Darden, H. Alk
Scene 4
"Minstrel Show"
E. Troobnick, A. Duncan, P. Sand, H. Alk
Scene 5
A Piece of String
S. Darden, P. Sand
Scene 6
No George Don't
A. Arkin, M. Kolb
Scene 7
News Broadcast—1965
E. Troobnick
Scene 8
First Affair
B. Harris, S. Darden
Scene 9
Mountain Climbing
H. Alk, A. Arkin, P. Sand, A. Duncan, E. Troobnick
Scene 10
Caesar's Wife
M. Kolb, B. Harris, H. Alk
Scene 11
Noah
The Company

1961.18

SAIL AWAY

A Musical Comedy in Two Acts, 18 Scenes. Book, music, lyrics and direction by Nöel Coward. (Settings) designed by Oliver Smith. Costumes by Helene Pons and Oliver Smith. Lighting by Peggy Clark. Musical numbers and dances staged by Joe Layton. Orchestrations by Irwin Kostal. Musical direction and dance arrangements by Peter Matz. Vocal arrangements, Fred Werner. Associate choreographer, Buddy Schwab. Produced by Bonard Productions (Helen G. Bonfils, Haila Stoddard, Donald R. Seawell) in association with Charles Russell. Opened 3 October 1961 at the Broadhurst Theatre and closed 24 February 1962 after 167 performances.

CAST (in order of appearance): *Joe*, the ship's purser: CHARLES BRASWELL. *Shuttleworth*, a steward: Keith Prentice. *Rawlings*, a passenger who drinks: James Pritchett. *Sir Gerald Nutfield*: C. Stafford Dickens. *Lady Nutfield*: Margaret Mower. *Barnaby Slade*: GROVER DALE. *Elmer Candijack*: Henry Lawrence. *Maimie Candijack*, his wife: BETTY JANE WATSON. *Glen Candijack*, their son: Alan Helms. *Shirley Candijack*, their daughter: Patti Mariano. *Mr. Sweeney*: Jon Richards. *Mrs. Sweeney*: PAULA BAUERSMITH. *Elinor Spencer-Bollard*: ALICE PEARCE. *Nancy Foyle*, her neice: PATRICIA HARTY. *Alvin Lush*: PAUL O'KEEFE. *Mrs. Lush*, his mother: EVELYN RUSSELL. *John Van Mier*: JAMES HURST. *Mrs. Van Mier*, his mother: MARGALO GILLMORE. *Mimi Paragon*: ELAINE STRITCH. *Ali*, an Arab guide: CHARLES BRASWELL. *Man from American Express*: Richard Woods.

Passengers, Stewards, Arabs, Italians, Children: Jere Admire, Bobby Allen, Don Atkinson, Gary Crabbe, David Evans, Pat Ferrier, Dorothy Frank, Ann Fraser, James Frasher, Gene Gavin, Paul Gross, S. Curtis Hood, Wish Mary Hunt, Cheryl Kilgren, Bridget Knapp, Nancy Lynch, Patti Mariano, Mary Ellen O'Keefe, Alan Peterson, Dennis Scott, Alice Shanahan, Dan Siretta, Gloria Stevens, Christopher Votos.

Act 1, Scene 1: The Main Hall of the Cunard Steam-Ship, *Coronia* .*Scene 2*: John Van Mier's Cabin. *Scene 3*: The Sun Deck, New York Harbor. *Scene 4*: Elinor Spencer-Bollard's Cabin. *Scene 5*: The Sun-Deck, at sea several days later. *Scene 6*: Mimi Paragon's Cabin. *Scene 7*: The Sun Deck. Moonlight. *Scene 8*: The Promenade Deck. Later that night. *Scene 9*: The Sun Deck. Gibraltar.

Act 2, Scene 1: Tangier. *Scene 2*: Italian Interlude. *Scene 3*: The Ship's Nursery. *Scene 4*: The Sun Deck. The Bay of Naples. *Scene 5*: The Boat Deck. Villefranche. *Scene 6*: The Parthenon. *Scene 7*: The Sun Deck. *Scene 8*: The Promenade Deck. *Scene 9*: The Main Hall.

ACT 1
Scene 1
"Come To Me"
E. Stritch, Stewards
Scene 2
"Sail Away"[2]
J. Hurst
Scene 3
"Come To Me" (reprise)
E. Stritch
"Sail Away" (reprise)
J. Hurst, Company
Scene 4
"Where Shall I Find Him?"
P. Harty
Scene 5
"Beatnik Love Affair"
G. Dale, P. Harty, Passengers
"Later Than Spring"
J. Hurst
"The Passenger's Always Right"
C. Braswell, Stewards
Scene 6
"Useful Phrases"
E. Stritch
Scene 7
"Where Shall I Find Her?" (reprise)
G. Dale
Scene 8
"Go Slow, Johnny"
J. Hurst

[2]Previously used in ACE OF CLUBS, London, 1950.

Scene 9
"You're a Long, Long Way from America"
E. Stritch, Company

ACT 2

Scene 1
"The Customer's Always Right"
C. Braswell, Arabs
"Something Very Strange"
E. Stritch

Scene 2
Italian Interlude
The Company

Scene 3
"The Little Ones' ABC"
E. Stritch, P. O'Keffe, Children

Scene 4
"Don't Turn Away from Love"
J. Hurst

Scene 6
"When You Want Me"
G. Dale, P. Harty

Scene 7
"Later Than Spring" (reprise)
E. Stritch

Scene 8
"Why Do the Wrong People Travel?"
E. Stritch

Scene 9
"When You Want Me" (reprise)
The Company
Finale

THE MIKADO, or The Town of Titipu

1961.19

A Revival of the Comic Opera in Two Acts[3]. Libretto by William S. Gilbert. Music by Arthur Sullivan. Staged by Dorothy Raedler. Scenic design by Donald Oenslager. Costume design by Patton Campbell. Conducted by Emerson Buckley. Produced by the New York City Opera. Opened 8 October 1961 at the New York City Center and closed 4 November 1961 after 3 performances in repertory.

CAST: *The Mikado of Japan*: GEORGE GAYNES. *Nanki-Poo*, his son, disguised as a wandering minstrel in love with Yum-Yum: FRANK PORETTA. *Ko-Ko*, Lord High Executioner of Titipu: NORMAN KELLEY. *Pooh-Bah*, Lord High Everything Else: HERBERT BEATTIE. *Pish-Tush*, a Noble Lord: William Metcalf. *Yum-Yum, Pitti-Sing, Peep-Bo*, three sisters, wards of Ko-Ko: JOY CLEMENTS, JANET BROADHURST, SOPHIA STEFFAN. *Katisha*: GLADYS KRIESE. *Chorus of School Girls, Nobles, Guards and Coolies*: New York City Opera Chorus.

MILK AND HONEY

1961.20

A Musical in Two Acts, 12 Scenes. Book by Don Appell. Music and lyrics by Jerry Herman. Production staged by Albert Marre. Choreography, Donald Saddler. Settings and lighting by Howard Bay. Costumes by Miles White. Orchestrations by Hershy Kay and Eddie Sauter. Choral arrangements, Robert de Cormier. Musical director, Max Goberman. Dance arrangements, Genevieve Pitot. Produced by Gerard Oestreicher. Opened 10 October 1961 at the Martin Beck Theatre and closed 26 January 1963 after 543 performances.

[3]First presented in New York 20 July, 10-29 August 1885 at the Union Square and People's Theatres for 22 performances. First authorized production presented 19 August 1885 at the Fifth Avenue Theatre by Richard D'Oyly Carte for 250 performances. For Synopsis of Scenes and Musical Numbers, see 19 August 1885 D'Oyly Carte production.

CAST (in order of appearance): *Porter*: Burt Bier. *Shepherd Boy*: Johnny Borden. *Policeman*: Ronald Holgate. *Ruth*: MIMI BENZELL. *Phil*: ROBERT WEEDE. *Clara Weiss*: MOLLY PICON. *The Guide*: Ellen Berse. *Mrs. Weinstein*: Addi Negri. *Mrs. Strauss*: Dorothy Richardson. *Mrs. Breslin*: Rose Lischner. *Mrs. Segal*: Diane [Diana] Goldberg. *Mrs. Kessler*: Ceil Delli. *Mrs. Perlman*: Thelma Pelish. *Barbara*, Phil's Daughter: LANNA SAUNDERS. *David*, Barbara's Husband: TOMMY RALL. *Adi*: JUKI ARKIN. *Zipporah*; Ellen Madison. *The Cantors*: Lou Polacek, David London. *Maid of Honor*: Matt Turney. *Wedding Couples*: Jose Gutierrez, Linda Howe, Michael Nestor, Jane Zachary. *Cafe Arab*: Renato Cibelli. *Man of the Moshav*: Art Tookoyan. *Mr. Horowitz*: Reuben Singer.

Soldiers, Hassidim, Arabs, Tourists, etc.: Marceline Decker, Urylee Leonardos, Terry Marone, Sandra Stahl, Marilyn Stark, Patti Winston, Myrna Aaron, Nina Feinberg, Penny Ann Green, Judith Haskell, Linda Howe, Susan May, Matt Turney, Jane Zachary, Burt Bier, Gerald Cardoni, Renato Cibelli, Murray Goldkind, David London, Ed Mastin, Lou Poalcek, Robert Rue, Art Tookoyan, Anthony De Vecchi, Louis Gasparinetti, Jose Gutierrez, Stuart Hodes, Alex Kotimski, Carlos Macri, John Mandia, Michael Nestor, Dom Salinaro, Walter Stratton, Eddie Roll, Ronald Holgate.

Act 1, Scene 1: A Street in Jerusalem. (Present time.) *Scene 2*: Another Street. That night. *Scene 3*: A Moshav in the Desert. A few days later. *Scene 4*: David's House. A week later. *Scene 5*: The Barn. *Scene 6*: A Hill overlooking the Valley. *Scene 7*: The Wedding.

Act 2, Scene 1: Another Part of the Moshav. Next morning. *Scene 2*: The Cafe Hotok, Tel Aviv, the same day. *Scene 3*: A Street in Jerusalem, that night. *Scene 4*: Outside Adi's House. A day later. *Scene 5*: The Airport, Tel Aviv.

ACT 1

Scene 1
"Shepherd's Song"
J. Borden, R. Weede
"Shalom"
R. Weede, M. Benzell

Scene 2
"Independence Day Hora"
Company

Scene 3
"Milk and Honey"
T. Rall, J. Arkin, Company

Scene 4
"There's No Reason in the World"
R. Weede
"Chin Up, Ladies"
M. Picon, Widows

Scene 5
"That Was Yesterday"
M. Benzell, R. Weede, T. Rall, K. Arkin, Company

Scene 6
"Let's Not Waste a Moment"
R. Weede

Scene 7
"The Wedding"
M. Benzell, R. Weede, Company

ACT 2

Scene 1
"Like a Young Man"
R. Weede
"I Will Follow You"
T. Rall

Scene 2
"Hymn to Hymie"
M. Picon

Scene 3
"There's No Reason in the World" (reprise)
M. Benzell

Scene 4
"Milk and Honey" (reprise)
J. Arkin, Company
"As Simple As That"
M. Benzell, R. Weede

Scene 5
"Shalom" (reprise)
M. Benzell, R. Weede, Company

1961.21

LET IT RIDE!

A Musical Comedy in Two Acts, 18 Scenes. Book by Abram S. Ginnes. Based on the play "Three Men on a Horse" by John Cecil Holm and George Abbott. Music and lyrics by Jay Livingston and Ray Evans. Additional material by Ronny Graham. Directed by Stanley Prager. Dances and musical numbers Staged by Onna White. Settings and lighting by William and Jean Eckart. Costumes by Guy Kent. Musical director, Jay Blackton. Vocal director, Jerry Packer. Orchestrations, Raymond Jaimes. Dance music arranged by Billy Goldenberg. Produced by Joel Spector. Opened 12 October 1961 at the Eugene O'Neill Theatre and closed 9 December 1961 after 68 performances.

CAST (in order of appearance): *Erwin*: GEORGE GOBEL. *Audrey*: PAULA STEWART. *Carver*: STANLEY GROVER. *Harry*: HAROLD GARY. *Charlie*: ALBERT LINVILLE. *Frankie*: LARRY ALPERT. *Mabel*: BARBARA NICHOLS. *Patsy*: SAM LEVENE. *Birthday Girls*: Pat Turner, Sandra Devlin, Ann Johnson, Sandy Walsh, Rae McLean, Carol Glade, Sally Lee, Sally Kirk, Barbara Marcon. *Nice Nose Brophy*: DORT CLARK. *Mother*: Maggie Worth. *Chief Schermerhorn*: TED THURSTON. *Repulski*: STANLEY SIMMONDS. *First Cop*: John Ford. *Announcer's Voice*: TED THURSTON.

Dancers: Ted Adkins, Robert Bakanic, Rhett Dennis, Sandra Devlin, Bob Evans, Dick Gingrich, Ann Johnson, Sally Kirk, Sally Lee, Jack Leigh, Vernon Lusby, Rae McLean, Barbara Marcon, Pat Turner, Sandra Walsh, Marty Allen, Marc West. *Singers*: Helen Baisley, Francine Bond, Austin Colyer, Clifford Fearl, John Ford, Carol Glade, Robert Lenn, Virginia Perlowin, Michael Roberts, Maggie Worth.

Act 1, Scene 1: Bus. *Scene 2*: Main Office of Modern Greeting Card Company. *Scene 3*: Street outside Hotel Lavillere. *Scene 4*: Bar, Hotel Lavillere. *Scene 5*: Corridor, Modern Greeting Card Company. *Scene 6*: Patsy's Party. *Scene 7*: Audrey's Porch. *Scene 8*: Mabel's Room.

Act 2, Scene 1: Opening. *Scene 2*: Bar. *Scene 3*: Audrey's Porch. *Scene 4*: Mabel's Room. *Scene 5*: Rogues Gallery. *Scene 6*: Lineup. *Scene 7*: Outside Police Station. *Scene 8*: Erwin's Island. *Scene 9*: Bar. *Scene 10*: Finale.

ACT 1

"Run Run Runn"
Singers, Dancers

"The Nicest Thing"
P. Stewart

"Hey, Jimmy, Joe, John, Jim, Jack"
G. Gobel

"Broads Ain't People"
G. Gobel, H. Gary, L. Alpert, A. Linville

"Let It Ride"
S. Levene, Singers, Dancers

"I'll Learn Ya"
G. Gobel, S. Levene

"Love Let Me Know"
P. Stewart, S. Grover

"Happy Birthday"
Birthday Girls

"Everything Beautiful"
G. Gobel, Birthday Girls

"Who's Doing What to Erwin"
P. Stewart, T. Thurston, S. Grover, M. Worth

"I Wouldn't Have Had To"
B. Nichols

ACT 2

"There's Something About a Horse"
Singers, Dancers

"He Needs You"
G. Gobel, L. Alpert, A. Linville

"Just an Honest Mistake"
T. Thurston, S. Simmonds, Cops

"His Own Little Island"
G. Gobel

"If Flutterby Wins"
G. Gobel, S. Leve, L. Alpert, A. Linville, H. Gary, Hoods

Finale
(Entire Company)

1961.22

HOW TO SUCCEED IN BUSINESS WITHOUT REALLY TRYING

A Musical (Comedy) in Two Acts, 24 Scenes. Book by Abe Burrows, Jack Weinstock and Willie Gilbert. Based on the novel of the same name by Shepherd Mead. Music and lyrics by Frank Loesser. Scenery and lighting by Robert Randolph. Costumes by Robert Fletcher. Choreography by Hugh Lambert. Musical staging by Bob Fosse. Musical direction, Elliot Lawrence. Orchestrations by Robert Ginzler. Directed by Abe Burrows. Produced by Cy Feuer and Ernest H. Martin in association with Frank Productions, Inc. Opened 14 October 1961 at the 46th Street Theatre and closed 6 March 1965 after 1417 performances.

CAST (in order of appearance): *Finch*: ROBERT MORSE. *Gatch*: RAY MASON. *Jenkins*: Bob Kaliban. *Tackaberry*: David Collyer. *Peterson*: Casper Roos. *J. B. Biggley*: RUDY VALLEE. *Rosemary*: BONNIE SCOTT. *Bratt*: PAUL REED. *Smitty*: CLAUDETTE SUTHERLAND. *Frump*: CHARLES NELSON REILLY. *Miss Jones*: RUTH KOBART. *Mr. Twimble*: SAMMY SMITH. *Hedy*: VIRGINIA MARTIN. *Scrubwomen*: Mara Landi, Silver Saundors. *Miss Krumholtz*: Mara Landi. *Toynbee*: RAY MASON. *Ovington*: Lanier Davis. *Policeman*: Bob Murdock. *Womper*: SAMMY SMITH.

Singers: David Collyer, Lanier Davis, Bob Kaliban, Bob Murdock, Casper Roos, Charlotte Frazier, Mara Land, Fairfax Mason, Silver Saundors, Maudeen Sullivan. *Dancers*: Nick Andrews, Tracy Everitt, Stuart Fleming, Richard Korthaze, Dale Moreda, Darrell Notara, Merritt Thompson, Carol Jane Abney, Madilyn Clark, Elaine Cancilla, Suzanne France, Donna McKechnie, Ellie Somers, Rosemarie Yellen.

Act 1, Scene 1: Exterior of the World Wide Wicket Company, Park Avenue, New York City. (Present time.) *Scene 2*: Corridor of the World Wide Wicket Company. *Scene 3*: Outer Office of the World Wide Wicket Company. *Scene 4*: The Mail Room. *Scene 5*: J. B. Biggley's Desk. *Scene 6*: Corridor of the World Wide Wicket Company. *Scene 7*: The Elevator Landing. *Scene 8*: The Outer Office. *Scene 9*: Finch's First Office. *Scene 10*: Plans and Systems Office. *Scene 11*: Corridor. *Scene 12*: The Roof. *Scene 13*: Elevator Landing. *Scene 14*: J. B. Biggley's Office.

Act 2, Scene 1: The Outer Office. *Scene 2*: Finch's New Advertising Office. *Scene 3*: J. B. Biggley's Office. *Scene 4*: Men's Washroom. *Scene 5*: Boardroom. *Scene 6*: Television Show. *Scene 7*: Wrecked Outer Office. *Scene 8*: Elevator Landing. *Scene 9*: J. B. Biggley's Office. *Scene 10*: The Outer Office.

ACT 1

Scene 1

"How To (Succeed)"
R. Morse

Scene 2

"Happy To Keep His Dinner Warm"
B. Scott

Scene 3

"Coffee Break"
C. N. Reilly, C. Sutherland, Office Staff

Scene 4

"The Company Way"
R. Morse, S. Smith

"The Company Way" (reprise)
C. N. Reilly, S. Smith, Office Staff

Scene 6

"A Secretary Is Not a Toy"
P, Reed, C. Nelson Reilly, Office Staff

Scene 7

"Been a Long Day"
R. Morse, B. Scott, C. Sutherland

"Been a Long Day" (reprise)
R. Vallee, V. Martin, C. N. Reilly

Scene 8

"Grand Old Ivy"
R. Morse, R. Vallee

Scenes 11 and 12

"Paris Original"
B. Scott, C. Sutherland, R. Kobart, Secretaries

Scene 14

"Rosemary"
R. Morse, B. Scott

Finaletto
R. Morse, B. Scott, C. N. Reilly

ACT 2

Scene 1

"Cinderella Darling"
B. Scott, C. Sutherland, Secretaries

Scene 2

"Happy To Keep His Dinner Warm" (reprise)
B. Scott

Scene 3

"Love From a Heart of Gold"
R. Vallee, V. Martin

Scene 4

"I Believe in You"
R. Morse, C. N. Reilly, P. Reed, Executives

Scene 6

"The Yo Ho Ho" (Pirate Dance)
The Jolly Wickets and Wickettes

Scene 7

"I Believe in You" (reprise)
B. Scott

Scene 9

"Brotherhood of Man"
R. Morse, R. Vallee, C. N. Reilly, P. Reed, S. Smith, R. Kobart, Office Staff

Scene 10

Finale
Company

1961.23

H.M.S. PINAFORE, or The Lass That Loved a Sailor

A Revival of the Comic Opera in Two Acts[4]. Libretto by William S. Gilbert. Music by Arthur Sullivan. Staged by Allen Fletcher. (Costumes and settings) designed by Patton Campbell. Conducted by Felix Popper. Produced by the New York City Opera. Opened 15 October 1961 at the New York City Center and closed 11 November 1961 after 4 performances in repertory.

CAST: *The Rt. Hon. Sir Joseph Porter, K.C.B.*, First Lord of the Admiralty: NORMAN KELLEY. *Captain Corcoran*, Commanding *H.M.S. Pinafore*: WILLIAM CHAPMAN. *Ralph Rackstraw*, Able Seaman: FRANK PORETTA. *Dick Deadeye*, Able Seaman: PAUL UKENA. *Bill Bobstay*, Bo'sun's Mate: Richard Fredericks. *Bob Beckett*, Carpenter's Mate: John Macurdy. *Josephine*, the Captain's Daughter: DORIS YARICK. *Hebe*, Sir Joseph's First Cousin: Sophia Steffan. *Little Buttercup*, a Portsmouth Bumboat Woman: GLADYS KRIESE. *First Lord's Sisters, his Cousins, his Aunts, Sailors, Marines*: New York City Opera Chorus.

1961.24

KWAMINA

A Musical in Two Acts, 15 Scenes. Book by Robert Alan Arthur. Music and lyrics by Richard Adler. Dances and musical numbers Staged by Agnes de Mille. Settings and lighting designed by Will Steven Armstrong. Costumes designed by Motley. Musical and choral direction, Colin Romoff. Dance arrangements, John Morris. Orchestrations by Sid Ramin, Irwin Kostal. Technical consultant, Albert Opoku. Directed by Robert Lewis. Produced by Alfred de Liagre, Jr. Opened 23 October 1961 at the 54th Street Theatre and closed 18 November 1961 after 32 performances.

CAST (in order of appearance): *Obitsebi*: BROCK PETERS. *Blair*: NORMAN BARRS. *Ako*: Robert Guillaume. *Eve*: SALLY ANN HOWES. *Naii*: ETHEL AYLER. *Akufo*: Joseph Attles. *Kwamina (Peter)*: TERRY CARTER. *Kojo*: Ainsley Sigmond. *Children*: Vaughn Fubler, Renaye Fubler. *Nana Mwalla*: REX INGRAM. *Alla*: Rosalie Maxwell. *Mammy Trader*: Lillian Hayman. *Policemen*: Ronald Platts, Edward Thomas. *Drummers*: Montego Joe, Robert Crowder.

Singers: Issa Arnal, Doresse DuQuan, Victoria Harrison, Lillian Hayman, Lee Hooper, Mary Louise, Rosalie Maxwell, Helen Phillips, Joseph Crawford, Scott Gibson, Wanza King, James Lowe, John Miles, Clark Morgan, Mal Scott, Rawn Spearman, George Tipton, Gordon Watkins, Arthur Wright. *Dancers*: Hope Clark, Doris deMendez, Altovise Gore, Minnie Marshall, Joan Peters, Lucinda Ransom, Joan Seabrook, Barbara Teer, Glory Van Scott, Myrna White, Camille Yarborough, Pepsi Bethel, Zebedee Collins, Julius Fields, Frank Glass, Louis Johnson, Charles Moore, Ronald Platts, Mike Quashie, Charles Queenan, Philip Stamps, Edward Thomas.

The action takes place in a village in West Africa at the present time.

ACT 1

Scene 2

"The Cocoa Bean Song"
R. Guillaume, S. Gibson, G. Watkins, Company

Scene 3

"Welcome Home"
S. Hibson, M. Scott, L. Hooper, M. Quashie, Company
Spear Dancers: C. Moore, C. Queenan. *Fonga*: J. Seabrook, B. Teer, G. Van Scott, M. White.

"The Sun Is Beginning to Crow"
Company

Scene 4

"Did You Hear That?"
S. A. Howes, T. Carter

"You're As English As"
S. A. Howes

Scene 5

"Seven Sheep, Four Red Shirts and a Bottle of Gin"
J. Attles, S. Gibson, C. Queenan, G. Tipton, Company

Scene 6

"Nothing More to Look Forward To"
R. Guillaume, E. Ayler

"What's Wrong WIth Me?"
S. A. Howes

Scene 7

"Something Big"
T. Carter, Company

"Ordinary People"
S. A. Howes, T. Carter

Scene 8

Mammy Traders (dance)
Girl With Parasol: G. Van Scott. *Admirers*: C. Moore, Z. Collins, Dance Company.

Scene 9

"A Man Can Have No Choice"
B. Peters

Scene 10

"What Happened to Me Tonight?"
S. A. Howes

ACT 2

Scene 1

Naii's Nuptial Dance
E. Ayler, H. Clarke, Company

"One Wife"
L. Hayman, R. Maxwell, I. Arnal, V. Harrison, L. Hooper, M. Louise, H. Phillips, Dancers

"Nothing More To Look Forward To" (reprise)
E. Ayler

Scene 2

"Something Big" (reprise)
Company

"Another Time, Another Place"
S. A. Howes

Scene 5

Fetish (dance)
B. Peters
Priests: Z. Collins, F. Glass, C. Moore, M. Quashie, C. Queenan, P. Stamps.

[4]Originally presented in New York 15 January 1879 at the Standard Theatre for 175 performances. For Synopsis of Scenes and Musical Numbers, see original 1879 production.

1961.25

AN EVENING WITH YVES MONTAND

A One Man Show in Two Acts. Staged and lighted by Yves Montand. Conductor, Bob Castella. Produced by Salle Productions, Inc. Presented by Norman Granz in association with Jacques Canetti and Alexander H. Cohen. Opened 24 October 1961 at the John Golden Theatre and closed 16 December 1961 after 55 performances.

CAST: YVES MONTAND.

Accordion: Bob Creash. *Clarinet*: Edmund Hall. *Trombone*: Morty Trautman. *Drums*: Charles Persip. *Bass*: Al Hall. *Guitar*: Jim Hall.

ACT 1

"Je suis venu á pieds"
(*Music and Lyrics by* Francis Lemarque.)
"Battling Joe"
(*Music by* Louis Gaste. *Lyrics by* Jean Guigo.)
"La tête á l'ombre"
(*Music and Lyrics by* Paul Misraki.)
"Une demoiselle sur une balancoire" (A Young Lady in a Swing)
(*Music by* Mireille. *Lyrics by* Jean Nohain.)
"Just in Time" (From BELLS ARE RINGING)
(*Music by* Jule Styne. *Lyrics by* Betty Comden and Adolph Green.)
"Gilet Raye" (The Night Porter)
(*Music by* Louiguy. *Lyrics by* Henri Contet.)
"Sous le ciel de Paris"
(*Music by* Hubert Giraud. *Lyrics by* Jean Drejac.)
"Le carosse" (The Golden Chariot)
(*Music by* Mireille. *Lyrics by* Henri Contet.)
"Les grands boulevards"
(*Music by* Norman Glanzberg. *Lyrics by* Jacques Plante.)
"Flamenco of Paris"
(*Music and Lyrics by* Leo Ferre.)
"Un garçon dansait"
(*Music by* Georges Liferman. *Lyrics by* Jacques Mareuil.)

ACT 2

"Mais qu'est-ce que j'ai?" (What's Wrong With Me?)
(*Music by* Henri Betti. *Lyrics by* Edith Piaf.)
"I've Grown Accustomed to Her Face" (from MY FAIR LADY)
(*Music by* Frederick Loewe. *Lyrics by* Alan Jay Lerner.)
"Dis-moi jo" (Tell Me Jo)
(*Music by* Henri Crolla. *Lyrics by* Jean Cosmos.)
"La Marie vision" (Marie's Mink Coat)
(*Music by* Marc Heyrai. *Lyrics by* Roger Varnay.)
"Planter cafe"
(*Music by* Emil Stern. *Lyrics by* Eddy Marnay.)
"Le chef d'orchestre est amoureux" (The Conductor Is in Love)
(*Music by* Georges Liferman. *Lyrics by* Jacques Mareuil.)
"C'est á l'aube" (Dawn)
(*Music by* Philippe Gerard. *Lyrics by* Flavien Monod.)
"Barbara"
(*Poem by* Jacques Prévert.)
"Á Paris"
(*Music and Lyrics by* Francis Lemarque.)
"Il fait des . . . le fanatique du jazz"
(*Music by* Edouard Chekle. *Lyrics by* Edith Piaf.)
"Mon manege á moi"
(*Music by* Norbert Glanzberg. *Lyrics by* Jean Constantin.)

1961.26

KEAN

A Musical Comedy in Two Acts, a Prologue and 12 Scenes. Book by Peter Stone from the comedy of the same name by Jean-Paul Sartre, based on a play by Alexandre Dumas. Music and lyrics by Robert Wright and George Forrest. Production (settings and costumes) designed by Ed Wittstein. Lighting by John Harvey. Musical direction and vocal arrangements, Pembroke Davenport. Ballet and incidental music, Elie Siegmeister. Staged and choreographed by Jack Cole. Produced by Robert Lantz. Opened 2 November 1961 at the Broadway Theatre and closed 20 January 1962 after 92 performances.

CAST (in order of appearance): *Christie*: Alfred DeSio. *Barnaby*: Christopher Hewett. *Edmund Kean*: ALFRED DRAKE. *Stage Manager*: Alfred Toigo. *Ben*: ROBERT PENN. *Francis*: Arthur Rubin. *Solomon*: TRUMAN SMITH. *Lord Neville*: RODERICK COOK. *Countess Elena De Koeberg*: JOAN WELDON. *Lady Amy Goswell*: PATRICIA CUTTS. *Count De Koeberg*: PATRICK WADDINGTON. *Lord Delmore*: John Lankston. *Major-Domo*: Martin Ambrose. *Prince of Wales*: OLIVER GRAY. *Anna Danby*: LEE VENORA. *Prop Boy*: Eddie Ericksen. *Secretary*: Joseph McGrath. *Maxwell*: Larry Shadur. *Henchman*: Martin Ambrose. *Pott*: George Harwell. *St. Albands*: Rene Jarmon. *Sparrow*: Margaret Gathright. *Bolt*: Gloria Warner. *Tim*: Randy Doney. *David*: John Jordan. *Pip*: Paul Jordan. *Patrick*: Charles Dunn. *Guards*: Larry Shadur, John Wheeler.

Dancers: John Aristides, Barbara Beck, Johanna Carothers, Lois Castle, Charles Corbett, Kenneth Creel, Randy Doney, Judy Dunford, Larry Fuller, Mickey Gunnersen, Pamela Hayford, Jim Hutchison, Lisa James, Rene Jarmon, Richard Lyle, George Martin, Roger Puckett, Suanne Shirley. *Singers*: Martin Ambrose, Charise Amidon, Charles Dunn, Eddie Ericksen, Nancy Foster, Margaret Gathright, Maggie Goz, George Harwell, John Lankston, Joseph McGrath, Lispet Nelson, Mary Nettum, Larry Shadur, Susan Terry, Alfred Toigo, Gloria Warner, John Wheeler.

The action takes place in London in the early nineteenth century.

Prologue: Drury Lane Theatre. The Stage.

Act 1, Scene 1: The Danish Embassy. A Ballroom. *Scene 2*: The Street. Drury Lane. *Scene 3*: Drury Lane Theatre. Kean's Dressing Room. *Scene 4*: The Danish Embassy. A private room. And Carlton House. A private room. *Scene 5*: A Street in front of a Thames-side tavern. *Scene 6*: The Green Frog," a tavern.

Act 2, Scene 1: Drury Lane Theatre. Kean's dressing room. *Scene 2*: Drury Lane Theatre. The stage boxes. *Scene 3*: The Street. Drury Lane. *Scene 4*: Kean's House. A drawing room. *Scene 5*: The Street. Drury Lane. *Scene 6*: Drury Lane Theatre. The Stage.

ACT 1

Prologue
"Penny Plain, Twopence Colored"
A. DeSio
"Man and Shadow"
A. Drake

Scene 1
"Mayfair Affair"
J. Weldon, P. Cutts, Dancing and Singing Ensemble
"Sweet Danger"
J. Weldon, A. Drake

Scene 2
"Queue at Drury Lane"
C. Hewett, R. Penn, A. Rubin, Ensemble
"King of London"
C. Hewett, R. Penn, A. Rubin, Ensemble

Scene 3
"To Look Upon My Love"
A. Drake, T. Smith
"Let's Improvise"
A. Drake, L. Venora
"Elena"
A. Drake, A. Rubin, Ensemble

Scene 4
"Social Whirl"
J. Weldon, P. Cutts, O. Gray, P. Waddington

Scene 5
"The Fog and the Grog"
C. Hewett, R. Penn, A. Rubin, A. Drake, Ensemble

Scene 6
Finale (Act 1)
A. Drake, Ensemble

ACT 2

Scene 1
"Civilized People"
A. Drake, L. Venora, J. Weldon
"Service for Service"
J. Weldon, A. Drake
"Willow, Willow, Willow"
L. Venora

Scene 3
"Fracas at Old Drury"
C. Hewett, R. Penn, A. Rubin, A. DeSio, Ensemble

"Chime In!"
A. DeSio, C. Hewett, R. Penn, A. Rubin, Ensemble
Scene 4
"Swept Away"
J. Weldon, A. Drake
"Domesticity"
L. Venora, A. Drake
Scene 5
"Clown of London"
Ensemble
Scene 6
"Apology?"
A. Drake

1961.27 THE GAY LIFE

A Musical Comedy in Two Acts, 15 Scenes. Book by Fay and Michael Kanin. Suggested by the play "Anatol" by Arthur Schnitzler. Music by Arthur Schwartz. Lyrics by Howard Dietz. Directed by Gerald Freedman. Dances and musical numbers staged by Herbert Ross. Scenic production by Oliver Smith. Costumes by Lucinda Ballard. Lighting by Jean Rosenthal. Orchestrations by Don Walker. Vocal arrangements and musical direction, Herbert Greene. Dance arrangements, Robert Starer. Magical illusions created and designed by Jack Adams. Produced by Kermit Bloomgarden. Opened 18 November 1961 at the Sam S. Shubert Theatre and closed 24 February 1962 after 113 performances.

CAST (in order of appearance): *Max*: JULES MUNSHIN. *Usher*: Sterling Clark. *Anatol*: WALTER CHIARI. *Franz*: LEONARD ELLIOTT. *Helene*: JEANNE BAL. *Liesl Brandel*: BARBARA COOK. *Herr Brandel*: LORING SMITH. *Frau Brandel*: LU LEONARD. *Mimi*: YVONNE CONSTANT. *Proprietor*: Michael Quinn. *The Great Gaston*: Jack Adams. *Otto*: Rico Froehlich. *Waiters*: Ted Lambrinos, Russell Goodwin. *Anna*: Joanne Spiller. *Grandmother*: Aura Vainio. *Photographer*: Gerald Teijelo. *Doorman*: Rico Froehlich. *Headwaiter*: Carl Nicholas. *Waiters*: Hal Norman, Ted Lambrinos. *Magda*: ELIZABETH ALLEN.

Singers: Ken Ayers, Russell Goodwin, Tony LaRusso, Ted Lambrinos, Carl Nicholas, Hal Norman, Michael Quinn, Loyce Baker, Joan Bishop, June Card, Luce Ennis, Jeanne Grant, Carole O'Hara, Nancy Radcliffe, Joanne Spiller. *Dancers*: Kip Andrews, Karoly Barta, Sterling Clark, Thatcher Clarke, Ray Kirchner Louis Kosman, Michel Stuart, Gerald Teijelo, Patrick King, Bonnie Brandon, Carolyn Clark, Marion Fels, Carol Flemming, Leslie Franzos, Bettye Jenkins, Doris Ortiz, Eleonore Treiber, Aura Vainio, Jenny Workman.

Act 1, Scene 1: Vienna, 1904. A church. *Scene 2*: Anatol's Apartment. *Scene 3*: Carlsbad. A pavilion. *Scene 4*: Terrace of the Brandel suite in Carlsbad. *Scene 5*: The casino in Carlsbad. A gala. *Scene 6*: A street in Vienna. Christmas Eve. *Scene 7*: A private room at Scaher's Restaurant. *Scene 8*: The Brandel living room.

Act 2, Scene 1: Sacher's Restaurant. Anatol's bachelor party. *Scene 2*: Anatol's Apartment. *Scene 3*: The Brandel living room. *Scene 4*: A street. Liesl's bedroom. *Scene 5*: Outside the Paprikás Cafe. *Scene 6*: The Paprikás Cafe. *Scene 7*: Anatol's Apartment.

ACT 1
Scene 1
"What a Charming Couple"[5]
Ensemble
Scene 2
"Why Go Anywhere at All?"[6]
J. Bal
Scene 3
"Bring Your Darling Daughter"
J. Munshin, Ensemble
"Now I'm Ready for a Frau"
W. Chiari, J. Munshin
Scene 4
"Magic Moment"
B. Cook
"Who Can? You Can?"
W. Chiari, B. Cook
Scene 5
"Oh Mein, Liebchen"
Ensemble
Liebchen Waltz
J. Workman, L. Franzos, T. Clarke, A. Vainio, L. Kosman, S. Clarke, Ensemble
"The Label on the Bottle"
B. Cook
Danced by L. Kosman, R. Kirchner, M. Stuart.
Scene 6
"This Kind of a Girl"
W. Chiari, B. Cook
Scene 7
"The Bloom Is Off the Rose"
J. Munshin, Male Ensemble
Scene 8
"Who Can? You Can" (reprise)
Ensemble
"Now I'm Ready for a Frau" (reprise)
W. Chiari
"Magic Moment" (reprise)
B. Cook

ACT 2[7]
Scene 1
"I'm Glad I'm Single"
Male Ensemble
Nursemaid: L. Franzos. *Anatol, the Boy*: S. Clark. *Strong Man*: L. Kosman. *Celestina*: M. Fels. *Magda*: J. Workman. *Anatol, the Man*: R. Kirchner. *Third Swan from the Left*: E. Treiber. *Helene*: A. Vainio. *Mimi*: B. Brandon.
"I'm Glad I'm Single" (reprise)
Male Ensemble
"Now I'm Ready for a Frau" (reprise)
W. Chiari, J. Munshin
Scene 2
"Something You Never Had Before"
B. Cook
Scene 3
"You Will Never Be Lonely"
L. Leonard, L. Smith, Ensemble
Scene 4
"You're Not the Type"
W. Chiari, B. Cook
Scene 6
"Come A-Wandering With Me"
E. Allen, Male Dancers
Scene 7
"I Never Had a Chance"
W. Chiari
"I Wouldn't Marry You"
B. Cook
"For the First Time"
W. Chiari

1961.28 SUBWAYS ARE FOR SLEEPING

A Musical Comedy in Two Acts, 18 Scenes. Book and lyrics by Betty Comden and Adolph Green. Suggested by the novel of the same name by Edmund G. Love. Music by Jule Styne. Directed and choreographed by Michael Kidd. Settings and lighting by Will Steven Armstrong. Costumes by Freddy Wittop. Musical direction, Milton Rosenstock. Orchestrations, Philip J. Lang. Associate choreographer, Marc Breaux. Dance music arrangements by Peter Howard. Produced by David Merrick. Opened 27 December 1961 at the St. James Theatre and closed 23 June 1962 after 205 performances.

---

[5]Dropped during the run.
[6]Dropped during the run.

[7]Added during run to Act 2, beginning Scene 7:
"Magic Moment" (reprise)
B. Cook

CAST (in order of appearance): *Sleepers*: Gene Varrone, CY YOUNG, Robert Gorman, JOHN SHARPE. *Myra Blake*: GRAYSON HALL. *Angela McKay*: CAROL LAWRENCE. *Tom Bailey*: SYDNEY CHAPLIN. *Station Guard*: Robert Howard. *J. Edward Sykes*: Joe Hill. *Bill*: Anthony Saverino. *Harry Shelby*: Eugene R. Wood. *Gus Holt*: CY YOUNG. *Charlie Smith*: ORSON BEAN. *Jack*: Gene Varrone. *A Drunk*: Jim Weiss. *Max Hillman*: Gene Varrone. *Martha Vail*: PHYLLIS NEWMAN. *Mr. Pitman*: GORDON CONNELL. *Delivery Boy*: Michael Bennett. *Lancelot Zuckerman*: Horase. *Freddie*: Robert Gorman. *Mac*, a Caretaker: JOHN SHARPE. *Social Worker*: Joe Hill. *Photographer*: JOHN SHARPE. *Models*: Sari Clymas, Diane Ball. *Teenagers*: JOHN SHARPE, Michael Bennett. *Zack Flint*: Lawrence Pool. *Lieut. Pilsudski*: Robert Howard. *Mary Tompkins*: Dean Taliaferro. *Joe*, the Museum Guard: Anthony Saverino. *Relief Doorman*: Robert Howard. *Mr. Barney*: Joe Hill.

Singers: Helen Baisley, Vicki Belmonte, Robert Gorman, Stokely Gray, Joe Hill, Robert Howard, Jeannine Michael, Bruce Payton, Anthony Saverino, Joan Sheller, Ruth Shepard. *Dancers*: Diane Ball, Carlos Bas, Michael Bennett, Pepe de Chazza, Sari Clymas, Joel Craig, Robert Evans, Ted Forlow, Valerie Harper, Reby Howells, Gene Kelton, Victoria Mansfield, Wendy Nickerson, Larry Roquemore, Sandra Roveta, Ron Stratton, Dean Taliaferro, Jim Weiss.

Act 1, Scene 1: A Street in New York at the present time. *Scene 2*: Executive Office of Madame Magazine. *Scene 3*: Grand Central Station. *Scene 4*: A Subway Platform. *Scene 5*: A Corridor in the Brunswick Arms. *Scene 6*: Martha's Room. *Scene 7*: A Street. *Scene 8*: The Egyptian Wing of the Metropolitan Museum. *Scene 9*: A Telephone Booth. *Scene 10*: A Street near Madison Square Park. *Scene 11*: Times Square. *Scene 12*: Rockefeller Plaza.

Act 2, Scene 1: The Subway. *Scene 2*: A Street. *Scene 3*: Martha's Room. *Scene 4*: The French Wing of the Metropolitan Museum. *Scene 5*: A Street. *Scene 6*: A Parking Lot.

ACT 1

Scene 1

"Subways Are For Sleeping"
G. Varrone, C. Young, B. Gorman, J. Sharpe

Scene 2

"Girls Like Me"
C. Lawrence

Scene 3

"Station Rush"
People Who Are Going Places (Ensemble)

"I'm Just Taking My Time"
S. Chaplin

Scene 4

"Subways Directions"
S. Chaplin, C. Lawrence, Subway Riders

"Ride Through the Night"
S. Chaplin, C. Lawrence, Subway Riders

Scene 6

"I Was a Shoo-In"
P. Newman

Scene 7

"Who Knows What Might Have Been"
C. Lawrence, S. Chaplin

Scene 8

"Swing Your Projects"
S. Chaplin

Scene 9

"Strange Duet"
P. Newman, O. Bean

Scene 10

"I Said It and I'm Glad"[8]
C. Lawrence

Scene 11

"Be a Santa"
S. Chaplin, C. Lawrence, Santas, Shoppers

ACT 2

Scene 1

"Subway Incident"
C. Lawrence, Teenagers

Scene 2

"How Can You Describe a Face?"[9]
S. Chaplin

Scene 3

"I Just Can't Wait"
O. Bean

Scene 4

"Comes Once in a Lifetime"
C. Lawrence, S. Chaplin

Scene 6

"What Is This Feeling in the Air?"
S. Chaplin, C. Lawrence, O. Bean, Entire Company

1962.01 A FAMILY AFFAIR

A Musical Comedy in Two Acts. Book and lyrics by James Goldman and William Goldman. Music by John Kander. Directed by Harold Prince. Choreography by John Butler. Musical numbers staged by Bob Herget. Settings and lighting by David Hays. Costumes by Robert Fletcher. Musical and vocal direction, Stanley Lebowsky. Orchestrations by Robert Ginzler. Dance music arranged by Gerald Alters. Produced by Andrew Siff. Opened 27 January 1962 at the Billy Rose Theatre and closed 25 March 1962 after 65 performances.

CAST (in order of appearance): *Sally Nathan*: RITA GARDNER. *Gerry Siegal*: LARRY KERT. *Alfie Nathan*: SHELLEY BERMAN. *Morris Siegal*: MORRIS CARNOVSKY. *Tilly Siegal*: EILEEN HECKART. *Mrs. Forsythe*: PAULA TRUEMAN. *Mother Lederer*: LULU BATES. *Babs Sanditz*: Beryl Towbin. *Selma Siegal*: Barbara Ann Walters. *Cindy*: Joan Lowe. *Jenny Stone*: CATHRYN DAMON. *Irma*: Kelli Scott. *Wilma*: Linda Lavin. *Betty Jane*: Carolsue Shaer. *Marie Rose*: Judi West. *Crying Daughter*: Linda Lavin. *Mother*: Alice Nunn. *Christopher Sanditz*: Randy Garfield. *Mr. Weaver*: JACK DeLON. *Wolfgang Demott*: Sam Greene. *Kenwood Sanditz*: Bill McDonald. *Morton Lederer*: Ferdinand Hilt. *Bernice Lederer*: Lynne Charnay. *Milton Lederer*: Bill Linton. *Helen Lederer*: Yettanda Enelow. *Simon Lederer*: Don Crabtree. *Emil Lederer*: Ed Becker. *Big Sadie Lederer*: Jean Bruno. *Little Sadie Lederer*: Maggie Task. *Sports Announcer*: Sam Greene. *Miss Lumpe*: BIBI OSTERWALD. *Harry Latz*: Gino Conforti. *Fifi of Paris*: Linda Lavin. *Brash Girl*: Charlene Carter. *Quiet Girl*: Linda Lavin. *Stop and Shop Answering Service*: Alice Nunn.

Singers: Ed Becker, Theodora Brandon, Jean Bruno, Yettanda Enelow, Sam, Greene, Linda Lavin, Gary Leatherman, Ripple Lewis, Alice Nunn, Kelli Scott, Maggie Task, Barbara Ann Walters. *Dancers*: Tom Abbott, Robert Bishop, Charlene Carter, Jeremy Ives, Bob LaCrosse, Carolsue Shaer, Judi West.

The action takes place in Chicago and its suburbs at the present time.

ACT 1

"Anything For You"
L. Kert, R. Gardner

"Beautiful"
S. Berman

"Beautiful" (reprise)
E. Heckart

"My Son, the Lawyer"
E. Heckart, L. Bates, B. Towbin, Ladies

"Every Girl Wants to Get Married"
R. Gardner, B. Towbin

"Right Girls"
(*Staged by* John Butler.)
S. Berman, J. DeLon, Gentlemen of the Gym

"Kalua Bay"
(*Staged by* John Butler.)
E. Heckart, M. Carnovsky

"There's a Room in My House"
L. Kert, R. Gardner

"Siegal Marching Song" (Football Game)
B. Towbin, R. Garfield, B. McDonald

"Nathan Marching Song" (Football Game)
S. Berman, Ensemble

"Harmony"
B. Osterwald, J. DeLon, G. Conforti, L. Lavin

[8]Dropped during run.

[9]Dropped during run.

ACT 2

"Now, Morris"
M. Carnovsky

"Wonderful Party"
L. Kert, B. McDonald

"Revenge"
(*Staged by* John Butler.)
S. Berman, (A. Nunn), Voices

"Summer Is Over"
E. Heckart

"Harmony" (reprise)
S. Berman, E. Heckart, B. Osterwald, Ensemble

"I'm Worse Than Anybody"
E. Heckart, M. Carnovsky, S. Berman

"What I Say Goes"
L. Kert

"The Wedding"
Entire Company

1962.02 (LEONARD SILLMAN'S) NEW FACES OF 1962

A Musical Revue in Two Acts, 34 Scenes[10]. Sketches by Ronny Graham, Paul Lynde, Jean Shepherd, Richard Maury, Joey Carter, R. G. Brown. Music and lyrics by June Carroll, Arthur Siegel, David Rogers, Mark Bucci, Jack Holmes, Ronny Graham. Choreography, James Moore. Sketches co-staged by Richard Maury. Settings and lighting by Marvin Reiss. Costumes by Thomas Becher. Orchestrations by Jay Bower, Ted Royal, Mark Bucci, Sy Oliver, David Terry. Dance arrangements by Jack Holmes. Musical director, Abba Bogin. Conceived and directed by Leonard Sillman. Produced by Carroll and Harris Masterson. Opened 1 February 1962 at the Alvin Theatre and closed 24 February 1962 after 28 performances.

CAST: Tom Arthur, Charles Barlow, R. G. Brown, Joey Carter, Jim Corbettt, Juan Carlos Copes, Michael Fesco, Travis Hudson, Helen Kardon, Patti Karr, Sylvia Lord, Erin Martin, Marian Mercer, James Moore, Maria Nieves, Sylvia, Joan Thornton, Mickey Wayland.

ACT 1

Scene 1

"Opening"
Entire Company
(*Music and Lyrics by* Ronny Graham.)
Dialogue: J. Carter. *Introduction*: J. Corbett. *Gowns from the Collection of* Luis Estevéz. *Choreography by* James Moore.

Scene 2

Quickies

Scene 3

The Reds Visit Mount Vernon
(*by* Paul Lynde)
Introduced by P. Karr. *Father*: R. G. Brown. *Mother*: M. Mercer. *George*: J. Carter.

Scene 4

"Moral Rearmament"
T. Hudson, J. Moore, T. Arthur
(*Music and Lyrics by* Jack Holmes.)

Scene 5

"Pi in the Sky"
(*by* Jean Shepherd. *Music by* Mark Bucci.)
Pilot: M. Fesco. *Stewardesses*: M. Nieves, M. Wayland.
Passengers: P. Karr, J. Moore, E. Martin, C. Barlow, J. Thornton, R. C. Brown, M. Mercer, M. Fesco, H. Kardon, J. Corbett.

Scene 6

"In the Morning"
S. Lord
(*Music and Lyrics by* Ronny Graham.)

Scene 7

"Happiness"
(*Music by* Marie Gordon. *Lyrics by* David Rogers.)
Man: R. G. Brown. *Happiness Girls*: J. Thornton, H. Kardon, Sylvia, M. Mercer, T. Hudson, M. Wayland.

Scene 8

"Impressions and Folk Songs"
J. Carter
(*Written by* Joey Carter.)

Scene 9

"Togetherness"[11]
(*Music and Lyrics by* Mavor Moore.)
Cardinal: R. G. Brown. *Bishop*: C. Barlow. *Patriarch*: M. Fesco. *Moderator*: J. Moore.

Scene 10

"Moment of Truth"
P. Karr
(*Music and Lyrics by* Jack Holmes. Suggested by Ronny Graham.)

Scene 11

"I Want You To Be the First To Know"
M. Wayland, .C. Barlow, M. Fesco
(*Music by* Arthur Siegel. *Lyrics by* June Carroll.)
First Couple: J. Moore, E. Martin. *Second Couple*: J. C. Copes, M. Nieves. *Third Couple*: J. Corbett, P. Karr. *Young Man*: T. Arthur.

Scene 12

Lemon Coke[12]
(*by* R. G. Brown)
Boy: R. G. Brown. *Girl*: M. Mercer.

Scene 13

"ABCs"
(*Music by* Mark Bucci. *Lyrics by* David Rogers.)
Girl: H. Kardon. *Children*: E. Martin, M. Nieves, J. Corbett, J. C. Copes, J. Moore.

Scene 14

"It Depends on How You Look at Things"
(*Music by* Arthur Siegel. *Lyrics by* June Carroll.)
Husband: R. G. Brown. *Wife*: T. Hudson. *Things*: H. Kardon, J. Thornton, M. Wayland, E. Martin, P. Karr, M. Nieves, Sylvia.

Scene 15

It Takes a Heap
(*by* Tony Geiss and Paul Lynde)
Introduced by P. Karr. *Foreman*: J. Carter. And M. Fesco, H. Kardon, J. Corbett, M. Wayland, M. Nieves, E. Martin.

Scene 16

"Freedomland"
M. Mercer
(*Music and Lyrics by* Jack Holmes.)

Scene 17

"Over the River and Into the Woods"
S. Lord
(*Music and Lyrics by* Jack Holmes. Gown from the collection of Luis Estevéz.)

Scene 18

Nose Cone
(*by* R. G. Brown)
Reporter: M. Fesco. *Mr. and Mrs. Thurman*: R. G. Brown, M. Mercer.

Scene 19

"Johnny Mishuga"
(*Sketch by* David Rogers. *Music by* Mark Bucci. *Lyrics by* David Rogers and Mark Bucci.)
Introduced by T. Arthur. *Momma*: T. Hudson. *Hymie*: J. Carter. *Waiter*: J. Corbett. *Gringo*: C. Barlow. *Johnny*: R. G. Brown. *Yasmin*: M. Mercer. *Deputy*: J. Moore. *Customers*: E. Martin, P. Karr, Sylvia, M. Nieves, H. Kardon, M. Fesco.

ACT 2

Scene 1

Entr'acte
(*Choreography by* James Moore.)
Introduced by J. Thornton, Sylvia

[10]The Sixth in the series of revues conceived by Leonard Sillman as a showcase for new talent. The first was produced in 1934.

[11]Dropped during run.

[12]Dropped during run.

Dancers: J. Corbett, J. C. Copes, M. Fesco, P. Karr, E. Martin, J. Moore, M. Nieves. *Choreography of Argentinian Section by* Juan Carlos Copes. *Danced by* M. Nieves.

Scene 2

Quickies

Scene 3

The Scarsdale Sentence

(*by* David Rogers)

Introduced by P. Karr. *Bettina*: M. Mercer. *Warren*: R. G. Brown.

Scene 4

Madison Avenue Executive

(*by* Ronny Graham)

Executive: J. Moore.

Scene 5

"Collective Beauty"

(*Music by* William Roy. *Lyrics by* Michael McWhinney.)

Lady: T. Hudson. *Revlonites*: H. Kardon, M. Wayland, C. Barlow, J. Corbett, M. Nieves, P. Karr. *Customers*: E. Martin, Sylvia, J. Thornton.

Scene 6

Happy Person

(*by* Herbert Hartig)

Girl: M. Mercer. *Boy*: R. G. Brown.

Scene 7

Untouchables

(*by* Joey Carter)

E. Martin, C. Barlow

Scene 8

"The Other One"

(*Music by* Arthur Siegel. *Lyrics by* June Carroll.)

Woman: M. Mercer. *Man*: J. Corbett. *Dancers*: P. Karr, Sylvia, J. Thornton, M. Wayland, T. Arthur, C. Barlow, M. Fesco, J. C. Copes. (Gowns by Baba Originals.)

Scene 9

Our Models

J. Thornton, Sylvia

Scene 10

"The Untalented Relative"

(*Music by* Arthur Siegel. *Lyrics by* Joey Carter and Richard Maury.)

Introduced by P. Karr. *Folk Singer*: J. Carter. *Folk*: P. Karr, J. C. Copes, M. Mercer, M. Wayland, J. Moore, M. Fesco, C. Barlow, H. Kardon, E. Martin, J. Corbett.

Scene 11

It's All in a Day's Work

(*by* Joey Carter)

Girl: J. Thornton.

Scene 12

"Love Is Good for You"

S. Lord

(*Music by* Arthur Siegel. *Lyrics by* June Carroll.)

Scene 13

Where Are Our Parents

(*by* Ronny Graham, Arnie Sultan and Marvin Worth)

Father: J. Carter. *Mother*: M. Mercer. *Roger*: R. G. Brown. *Mary*: M. Wayland. *Cop*: J. Corbett.

Scene 14

"Wall Street Reel"

Entire Company

(*Music by* Arthur Siegel. *Lyrics by* Jim Fuerst. *Introduction written by* Richard Maury.) *Introduced by* P. Karr.

Scene 15

Finale

(Entire Company)

1962.03

NO STRINGS

A Musical in Two Acts. Book by Samuel Taylor. Music and lyrics by Richard Rodgers. Directed and choreograhphed by Joe Layton. Settings and lighting by David Hays. Costumes by Fred Voelpel and Donald Brooks. Musical direction and dance arrangements, Peter Matz. Orchestrations by Ralph Burns. Associate choregrapher, Buddy Schwab. Production supervisor, Jerome Whyte. Assistant conductor, Milton Greene. Produced by Richard Rodgers in association with Samuel Taylor. Opened 15 March 1962 at the 54th Street Theatre, moved 1 October 1962 to the Broadhurst Theatre and closed 3 August 1963 after 580 performances.

CAST (in order of appearance): *Barbara Woodruff*: DIAHANN CARROLL. *David Jordan*: RICHARD KILEY. *Jeanette Valmy*: NOELLE ADAM. *Luc Delbert*: ALVIN EPSTEIN. *Mollie Plummer*: POLLY ROWLES. *Mike Robinson*: DON CHASTAIN. *Louis dePourtal*: MITCHELL GREGG. *Comfort O'Connell*: BERNICE MASSI. *Gabrielle Bertin*: Ann Hodges. *Marcello Agnolotti*: Paul Cambeilh.

Dancers: Alan Johnson, Susanne Cansino, Julie Drake, Jean Eliot, Ginny Gan, Ellen Graff, Kay Hudson, Ann Hodges, Diana Hrubetz, Sandy Leeds, Anna Marie Moylan, Patti Pappathatos, Janet Paxton, Dellas Rennie, Bea Salten, Carol Sherman, Mary Zahn, Gene Gebauer, Scott Hunter, Larry Merritt, Michael Maurer, David Neuman, Wakefield Poole, Calvin von Reinhold. *Instrumental Characters*: *Flute*: Walter Wegner. *Clarinet*: Aaron Sachs. *Oboe*: Ernest Mauro. *Trumpet*: James Sedler. *Trombone*: James Dahl. *Drums*: Ronnie Bedford. *Bassoon*: Walter Dane.

The action of the play takes place in Paris, Monte Carlo, Honfleur, Deauville and St. Tropez.

ACT 1

"The Sweetest Sounds"

D. Carroll, R. Kiley

"How Sad"

R. Kiley

"Loads of Love"

D. Carroll

"The Man Who Has Everything"

M. Gregg

"Be My Host"

R. Kiley, B. Massi, D. Chastain, A. Epstein, A. Hodges, Dancers

"La La La"

N. Adam, A. Epstein

"You Don't Tell Me"

D. Carroll

"Love Makes the World Go"

P. Rowles, B. Massi, Dancers

"Nobody Told Me"

R. Kiley, D. Carroll

ACT 2

"Look No Further"

R. Kiley, D. Carroll

"Maine"

R. Kiley, D. Carroll

"An Orthodox Fool"

D. Carroll

"Eager Beaver"

B. Massi, D. Chastain, Dancers

"No Strings"

R. Kiley, D. Carroll

"Maine" (reprise)

D. Carroll, R. Kiley

"The Sweetest Sounds" (reprise)

R. Kiley, D. Carroll

1962.04

ALL AMERICAN

A Musical Comedy in Two Acts, 22 Scenes. Book by Mel Brooks. Based on the novel ("Professor Fodorski") by Robert Lewis Taylor. Music by Charles Strouse. Lyrics by Lee Adams. Entire production directed by Joshua Logan. Scenery and lighting by Jo Mielziner. Costumes by Patton Campbell. Choreography by Danny Daniels. Dance arrangements and musical direction, John Morris. Orchestrations by Robert Ginzler. Musical continuity by Trude Rittman. Produced by Edward Padula in association with L. Slade Brown. Opened 19 March 1962 at the Winter Garden and closed 26 May 1962 after 80 performances.

CAST (in order of appearance): *Airline Stewardess*: Lori Rogers. *Flight Attendant*: Robert Lone. *Head Immigration Officer*: Barney Martin. *Immigration Officer*: Michael Gentry. *Fleisser*: Mort Marshall. *Shindler*: David Thomas. *Feinschveiger*: Bernie West. *Katrinka*: Betty Oakes. *Immigrants*: Will B. Able, Jed Allan, Don Atkinson, Vicki Belmonte, Bonnie Brody, Bill Burns, Trudy Carole, John Drew, Anthony Falco, Mary Jane Ferguson, Catherine Gale, Joseph Gentry, Linda Rae Hager, Warren Hays, Jerry

Howard, Bill Landrum, George Lindsey, Selma Malinou, Joe McWherter, Norman Riggins, Bill Starr, Sharon Vaughn. *Professor Fodorski*: RAY BOLGER. *Taxis*: Michael Gentry, Barney Martin, Fred Randall, Norman Riggins, Will B. Able. *Policeman*: Jed Allan. *Gorilla*: Bob Bakanic. *Bride*: Bonnie Brody. *Mannikin*: Mary Jane Ferguson. *Peddler*: Will B. Able. *Chewing Gum Girl*: Bonnie Brody. *Drunk*: Mort Marshall. *Con Ed Worker*: Joseph Gentry. *Cowboys*: Bill Burns, Robert Lone. *Park Avenue Couple*: Betty Oakes, David Thomas. *Sightseeing Tour Guide*: Bernie West. *Second Sightseeing Tour Guide*: George Lindsey. *Elizabeth Hawkes-Bullock*: EILEEN HERLIE. *Susan*: ANITA GILLETTE. *Edwin Bricker*: RON HUSMANN. *Dr. Snopes*: Bernie West. *Coach Hylkington Stockworth* (Hulk): Mort Marshall. *Assistant Coach*: Barney Martin. *Moose*: George Lindsey. *Football Players*: Jed Allan, Bill Burns, John Drew, Joseph Gentry, Michael Gentry, Jerry Howard, Bill Landrum, Joseph McWherter, Fred Randall, Bill Starr. *President Piedmont*: Will B. Able. *Professor Dawson*: David Thomas. *Professor White*: Warren Hays. *First Boy*: Robert Lone. *First Girl*: Trudy Carole. *Second Girl*: Karen Sargent. *Second Boy*: Ed Kresley. *House Mother*: Betty Oakes. *Baton Twirler*: Karen Sargent. *Red Stern*: Barney Martin. *Henderson*: FRITZ WEAVER. *Whistler's Mother*: Betty Oakes. *Craven*: Jed Allan. *Phillips*: Anthony Falco. *Wyler*: Bill Burns. *Homecoming Queen*: Sharon Vaughn. *Secretary*: Betty Oakes. *Farquar*: Bill Starr. *Fountainhead*: Bob Bakanic.

Singers: Vicki Belmonte, Bonnie Brody, Catherine Gale, Selma Malinou, Lori Rogers, Sharon Vaughn, Jed Allan, Bill Burns, John Drew, Anthony Falco, Warren Hays, Norman Riggins. *Dancers*: Trudy Carole, Cathy Conklin, Mary Jane Ferguson, Linda Rae Hager, Charlene Mehl, Karen Sargent, Don Atkinson, Bob Bakanic, Ed Kresley, Bill Landrum, Robert Lone, Kip Watson. *Swing Boy*: Frank Virgulto.

Act 1, Scene 1: Idlewild Airport, (New York). Today. *Scene 2*: New York and Panorama of America. *Scene 3*: Dean's Office, S.B.I.T. (Southern Baptist Institute of Technology) *Scene 4*: Football Field. *Scene 5*: Classroom, S.B.I.T. *Scene 6*: On the Campus. *Scene 7*: Classroom, S.B.I.T. *Scene 8*: Front Porch of Elizabeth's House. *Scene 9*: Front Porch of Girls' Dormitory. *Scene 10*: Susan's Room in Girls' Dormitory. *Scene 11*: On the Window of Susan's Room. *Scene 12*: Locker Room. *Scene 13*: Football Field and Stadium.

Act 2, Scene 1: Office of Exploiters Unlimited. *Scene 2*: Exterior and Interior of Union Building, S.B.I.T. *Scene 3*: Fodorski's Seduction. *Scene 4*: On the Campus. *Scene 5*: Office of Fodorski Foundation. *Scene 6*: Bricker's Room in Boys' Dormitory. *Scene 7*: On the Campus. *Scene 8*: The Cotton Bowl. *Scene 9*: Classroom, S.B.I.T.

ACT 1[13]

Scene 1

"Melt Us"
R. Bolger, Immigrants

Scene 2

"What a Country!"
R. Bolger, Company

Scene 3

"Our Children"
R. Bolger, E. Herlie

"Animal Attraction"
A. Gillette, R. Husmann

"Our Children" (reprise)
R. Bolger, E. Herlie

Scene 5

"We Speak the Same Language"
R. Bolger, R. Husmann

Scene 6

"I Can Teach Them!"
R. Bolger, E. Herlie, R. Husmann, D. Thomas

Scene 7

"It's Fun to Think"
R. Bolger, Professors, Students

Scene 8

"Once Upon a Time"
R. Bolger, E. Herlie

Scene 10

"Nightlife"
A. Gillette, Girls

Scene 11

"I've Just Seen Her"
R. Husmann

"Once Upon a Time"[14] (reprise)
A. Gillette

Scene 12

"Physical Fitness"
The Football Team

"The Fight Song"
R. Bolger, the Football Team

Scene 13

"What A Country!" (reprise)
R. Bolger, Company

ACT 2

Scene 2

"I Couldn't Have Done It Alone"
R. Husmann, A. Gillette

"If I Were You"
R. Bolger, E. Herlie

Scene 3

"Have a Dream"
R. Bolger, F. Weaver, Company

Scene 4

"I've Just Seen Him" (reprise)
A. Gillette

Scene 5

"I'm Fascinating"
R. Bolger

"Once Upon a Time" (reprise)
E. Herlie

Scene 6

"The Real Me"
E. Herlie

Scene 7

"It's Up to Me"
R. Bolger

Scene 8

"The Fight Song" (reprise)
R. Bolger, Company

Scene 9

"It's Fun to Think" (reprise)
Company

1962.05

I CAN GET IT FOR YOU WHOLESALE

A Musical Play in Two Acts, a Prologue and 17 Scenes. Book by Jerome Weidman based on his novel of the same name. Music and lyrics by Harold Rome. Musical staging by Herbert Ross. Settings and lighting by Will Steven Armstrong. Costumes by Theoni V. Aldredge. Musical direction and vocal arrangements by Lehman Engel. Orchestrations by Sid Ramin. Dance and incidental music arranged by Peter Howard. Directed by Arthur Laurents. Produced by David Merrick. Opened 22 March 1962 at the Sam S. Shubert Theatre and closed 8 December 1962 after 300 performances.

CAST (in order of appearance): *Miss Marmelstein*: BARBRA STREISAND. *Maurice Pulvermacher*: JACK KRUSCHEN. *Meyer Bushkin*: KEN LeROY. *Harry Bogen*: ELLIOTT GOULD. *Tootsie Maltz*: James Hickman. *Ruthie Rivkin*: MARILYN COOPER. *Mrs. Bogen*: LILLIAN ROTH. *Martha Mills*: SHEREE NORTH. *Mario*: William Reilly. *Mitzi*: Barbara Monte. *Eddie*: Edward Verso. *Blanche Bushkin*: BAMBI LINN. *Teddy Asch*: HAROLD LANG. *Buggo*: Kelly Brown. *Miss Springer*: Pat Turner. *Velma*: Francine Bond. *Lenny*: William Sumner. *Norman*: Stanley Simmonds. *Manette*: Luba Lisa. *Gail*: Wilma Curley. *Rosaline*: Marion Fels. *Noodle*: Jack Murray. *Sam*: Don Grilley. *Moxie*: Ed Collins. *Sheldon Bushkin*: Steve Curry. *Edith*: Margaret Gathright.

Prologue: Seventh Avenue, New York City, 1937.

---

[13]During run, the following song was added:
"Back to School Again" (Act 1, beginning Scene 5)
Students

[14]Dropped during run.

[15]Apex Modes changed early in the run to Acme Modes.

Act 1, Scene 1: Office of Maurice Pulvermacher, Inc. *Scene 2*: Seventh Avenue. *Scene 3*: A Bronx Stoop. *Scene 4*: Mrs. Bogen's Kitchen in the Bronx. *Scene 5*: Club Rio Rhumba. *Scene 6*: Mrs. Bogen's Kitchen. *Scene 7*: A Bronx Stoop. *Scene 8*: Apex[15] Modes, Inc. *Scene 9*: Apex Modes Showroom.

Act 2, Scene 1: Harry Bogen's Penthouse. *Scene 2*: Apex Modes Inc. *Scene 3*: Apex Modes Inc. *Scene 4*: The Club Rio Rhumba. *Scene 5*: Apex Modes Showroom. *Scene 6*: Mrs. Bogen's Kitchen. *Scene 7*: Office of Maurice Pulvermacher, Inc. *Scene 8*: Seventh Avenue.

ACT 1
Scene 1
"(He's Not a) Well Man"
B. Streisand, J. Kruschen
Scene 2
"The Way Things Are"
E. Gould
Scene 3
"When Gemini Meets Capricorn"
M. Cooper, E. Gould
Scene 4
"Momma, Momma"
E. Gould, L. Roth
Scene 5
"The Sound of Money"
E. Gould, S. North, B. Monte, W. Reilly, E. Verso
Scene 6
"(The) Family Way"
L. Roth, E. Gould, M. Cooper, H. Lang, B. Linn, K. LeRoy
"Too Soon"
L. Roth
Scene 7
"Who Knows?"
M. Cooper
Scene 8
"Have I Told You Lately?"
B. Linn, K. LeRoy
Scene 9
"Ballad of the Garment Trade"
B. Streisand, M. Cooper, B. Linn, E. Gould, H. Lang, K. LeRoy, Company

ACT 2
Scene 1
"A Gift Today"
S. Curry, E. Gould, L. Roth, B. Linn, K. LeRoy, M. Cooper
Dance
B. Linn, K. LeRoy, S. Curry
Scene 2
"Miss Marmelstein"
B. Streisand
"The Sound of Money" (reprise)
E. Gould
Scene 3
"A Funny Thing Happened" (On My Way to Love)
M. Cooper, E. Gould
Scene 4
"What's In It for Me?"
H. Lang, S. North
Scene 5
"What Are They Doing to Us Now?"
B. Streisand, K. Brown, J. Hickman, L. Lisa, W. Curley, P. Turenr, Creditors
Scene 6
"Eat a Little Something"
L. Roth, E. Gould
Scene 7
Epilogue
The Company

1962.06

THE CONSUL

A Revival of the Opera (Musical Drama) in Three Acts, 6 Scenes[16]. Libretto and music by Gian-Carlo Menotti. Conductor, Werner Torkanowsky. Settings and costumes by Horace Armistead. Staged by Roger Englander Produced by the New York City Opera. Opened 28 March 1962 at the New York City Center and closed 8 April 1962 after 4 performances in repertory.

CAST: (in order of appearance): *John Sorel*: RICHARD FREDERICKS. *Magda Sorel*: PATRICIA NEWAY. *The Mother*: EVELYN SACHS. *Secret Police Agent*: WILLIAM CHAPMAN. *First Plainclothesman*: Glenn Dowlen. *Second Plainclothesman*: Norman Grogan. *The Secretary*: MARIJA KOVA. *Mr. Kofner*: GEORGE GAYNES. *The Foreign Woman*: MARIA MARLO. *Anna Gomez*: Mary LeSawyer. *Vera Boronel*: Teresa Racz *Nika Magadoff* (The Magician): NORMAN KELLEY. *Assan*: Fredric Milstein. *Voice on the Record*: Mabel Mercer.

1962.07

PORGY AND BESS

A Revival of the Folk Opera in Two Acts, 3 Scenes[17]. Book by DuBose Heyward adapted from the play "Porgy" by DuBose and Dorothy Heyward. Music by George Gershwin. Lyrics by DuBose Heyward and Ira Gershwin. Directed by William Ball. Scenic design by Stephen O. Saxe. Costume design by Stanley Simmons. Conducted by Julius Rudel. Produced by the New York City Opera. Opened 31 March 1962 at the New York City Center and closed 7 April 1962 after 6 performances in repertory.

CAST (in order of appearance): *Clara*: GWENDOLYN WALTERS. *Mingo*: Harold Pierson. *Sportin' Life*: RAWN SPEARMAN. *Jake*: IRVING BARNES. *Serena*: BARBARA WEBB. *Robbins*: Ned Wright. *Jim*: Scott Gibson. *Peter*, the Honey Man: Jerry Crawford. *Lily*, the Strawberry Woman: Edna Ricks. *Maria*: CAROL BRICE. *Porgy*: LAWRENCE WINTERS. *Crown*: JAMES RANDOLPH. *Bess*: LEESA FOSTER. *Policemen*: Glenn Dowlen, James Fels. Walter Riemer. *Undertaker*: Wanza King. *Annie*: Alyce Webb. *Frazier*: Eugene Brice. *Strawberry Girl*: Doreese Duquan. *Detective*: Richard Fredericks. *Nelson*: Arthur Williams. *Crab Man*: Clyde Turner. *Coroner*: Richard Krause. *Police Sergeant*: Norman Grogan. *Residents of Catfish Row*: New York City Opera Chorus.

1962.08

IOLANTHE, or The Peer and the Peri

A Revival of the Comic Opera in Two Acts[18]. Libretto by William S. Gilbert. Music by Arthur Sullivan. Staged by Dorothy Raedler. Scenery and costumes by Gordon Micunis. Choreography, Helen Andreau. Conductor, Julius Rudel. Chorus master, William Jonson. Produced by the New York City Center Gilbert and Sullivan Company. Opened 11 April 1962 at the New York City Center and closed 22 April 1962 after 3 performances in repertory.

CAST: *The Lord Chancellor*: NORMAN KELLY. *Lord Mountararat*: ROBERT TREHY. *Lord Tolloller*: RICHARD KRAUSE. *Private Willis* of the Grenadier Guards: GEORGE GAYNES, SPIRO MALAS. *Strephon*, an Arcadian Shepherd: RICHARD FREDRICKS. *Queen of the Fairies*: CLARAMAE TURNER. *Iolanthe*, a Fairy, Strephon's Mother: MARLENA KLEINMAN. *Celia, Leila, Fleta*, Fairies: Shirley Chester, Teresa Racz, Betty Jane Schwering. *The Bee*: Helene Andreu. *The Dragonfly*: Beverly Evans. *The Butterfly*: Helen Guile. *Phyllis*, an Arcadian Shepherdess and Ward in Chancery: DORIS YARICK.

Chorus of Dukes, Marquises, Earls, Viscounts, Barons and Fairies: Helene Andreu, Jon Berberian, Joyce Castle, Micahel Cavallaro, Jerry Crawdord, Harris Davis, Glenn Dowlen, Beverly Evans, James Fels, Norman Grogan, Helen Guile, Betsy Hepburn,

---

[16]Originally produced in New York 15 March 1950 at the Ethel Barrymore Theatre for 269 performances. For Synopsis of Scenes and Musical Numbers, see original 1950 production.

[17]First produced in New York 10 October 1935 at the Alvin Theatre for 124 performances. Originally produced in Three Acts, 9 Scenes. This production dispensed with the scene breaks and second intermission. For Synopsis of Scenes and Musical Numbers, see original 1935 production.

[18]First presented in New York 25 November 1882 at the Standard Theatre for 105 performances. For Synopsis of Scenes and Musical Numbers, see original 1882 production.

Edson Hoel, Leonore Lanzillotti, George McWhorter, Joyce Miko, Kellis Miller, Donald Morgan, Hanna Owen, Mariano Parra, Lorraine Phillips, Charlotte Povia, Lourette Raymon, Betty jane Schwering, John Smith, Maggie Worth.

1962.09 H.M.S. PINAFORE, or The Lass That Loved a Sailor

A Revival of the Comic Opera in Two Acts[19]. Libretto by William S. Gilbert. Music by Arthur Sullivan. Staged by Allen Fletcher. Scenery and costumes by Patton Campbell. Conductor, Felix Popper. Chorus master, William Jonson. Produced by the New York City Center Gilbert and Sullivan Company. Opened 12 April 1962 at the New York City Center and closed 21 April 1962 after 4 performances in repertory.

CAST: *The Rt. Hon. Sir Joseph Porter, K.C.B.*, First Lord of the Admiralty: RAYMOND ALLEN. *Captain Corcoran*, Commander of the *H.M.S. Pinafore*: WILLIAM CHAPMAN. *Ralph Rackstraw*, Able Seaman: CARL OLSEN. *Dick Deadeye*, Able Seaman: ROBERT TREHY. *Bill Bobstay*, Boatswain: David Smith. *Bob Becket*: Spiro Malas. *Josephine*, the Captain's Daughter: DORIS YARICK. *Hebe*, Sir Joseph's First Cousin: Marlena Kleinman. *Little Buttercup*, Mrs. Cripps, a Portsmouth bum-boat woman: GLADYS KRIESE. *First Lord's Sisters, His Cousins, His Aunts, Sailors, Marines, etc.*: same as IOLANTHE above.

1962.10 THE MIKADO, or The Town of Titipu

A Revival of the Comic Opera in Two Acts[20]. Libretto by William S. Gilbert. Music by Arthur Sullivan. Staged by Dorothy Raedler. Scenery and lighting by Donald Oenslager. Costumes by Patton Campbell. Conductors, Dean Ryan, Charles Wilson. Chorus master, William Jonson. Produced by the New York City Center Gilbert and Sullivan Company. Opened 14 April 1962 at the New York City Center and closed 21 April 1962 after 5 performances in repertory.

CAST: *The Mikado of Japan*: GEORGE GAYNES, WILLIAM CHAPMAN. *Nanki-Poo*: WILLIAM DIARD. *Ko-Ko*: KEITH KALDENBERG. *Pooh-Bah*: SPIRO MALAS. *Pish-Tush*: DAVID SMITH. *Three Sisters, Wards of Ko-Ko*: *Yum-Yum*: JOY CLEMENTS. *Pitti-Sing*: BEVERLY EVANS. *Peep-Bo*: SHIRLEY CHESTER. *Katisha*: GLADYS KRIESE. *Chorus of School Girls, Nobles, Guards and Coolies*: same as IOLANTHE above.

1962.11 THE GONDOLIERS, or The King of Barataria

A Revival of the Comic Opera in Two Acts[21]. Libretto by William S. Gilbert. Music by Arthur Sullivan. Staged by Dorothy Raedler. Scenery and costumes by Ed Wittstein. Conductors, Julius Rudel, Felix Popper. Chorus master, William Jonson. Produced by the New York City Center Gilbert and Sullivan Company. Opened 18 April 1962 at the New York City Center and closed 22 April 1962 after 3 performances in repertory.

CAST: *The Duke of Plaza-Toro*: NORMAN KELLEY. *Luiz*: WILLIAM DIARD. *Don Alhambra Del Bolero*: GEORGE GAYNES. *Marco Palmieri*: JON CRAIN. *Giuseppe Palmieri*: WILLIAM METCALF. *Antonio*: David Smith. *Francesco*: Richard Krause. *Giorgio*: Norman Grogan. *The Duchess of Plaza-Toro*: CLARAMAE TURNER. *Casilda*: EILEEN SCHAULER. *Gianetta*: JOY CLEMENTS. *Tessa*: MARLENA KLEINMAN. *Fiametta*: Shirley Chester *Vittoria*: Teresa Racz. *Giulia*: Beverly Evans. *Inez*: Gladys Kriese. *Solo Cachucha Dancers*: Helene Andreu, Mariano Parra. *Chorus of Gondoliers, Contadine, Men-at-Arms, Heralds and Pages*: same as IOLANTHE above.

[19]Originally presented in New York 15 January 1879 at the Standard Theatre for 175 performances. For Synopsis of Scenes and Musical Numbers, see original 1879 production.
[20]First presented in New York 20 July, 10-29 August 1885 at the Union Square and People's Theatres for 22 performances. First authorized production presented 19 August 1885 at the Fifth Avenue Theatre by Richard D'Oyly Carte for 250 performances. For Synopsis of Scenes and Musical Numbers, see 19 August 1885 D'Oyly Carte production.
[21]Originally presented in New York 7 January 1890 at Park Theatre for 103 performances. For Synopsis of Scenes and Musical Numbers, see original 1890 production.

1962.12 A FUNNY THING HAPPENED ON THE WAY TO THE FORUM

A Musical Comedy in Two Acts. Book by Burt Shevelove and Larry Gelbart. Based on the plays ("The Haunted House," "Mostellaria", etc.) of Plautus. Music and lyrics by Stephen Sondheim. Directed by George Abbott. Choreography and musical staging by Jack Cole. Settings and costumes by Tony Walton. Lighting by Jean Rosenthal. Musical direction, Harold Hastings. Orchestrations by Irwin Kostal and Sid Ramin. Dance music arranged by Hal Schaefer. Additional dance music by Betty Walberg. Produced by Harold Prince. Opened 8 May 1962 at the Alvin Theatre, moved 9 March 1964 to the Mark Hellinger Theatre, moved 12 May 1964 to the Majestic Theatre, and closed 29 August 1964 after 964 performances.

CAST (in order of appearance): *Prologus*: ZERO MOSTEL. *The Proteans*: Eddie Phillips, George Reeder, David Evans. *Senex*, a citizen of Rome: DAVID BURNS. *Domina*, his wife: RUTH KOBART. *Hero*, his son: BRIAN DAVIES. *Hysterium*, slave to Senex and Domina: JACK GILFORD. *Lycus*, a dealer in courtesans: JOHN CARRADINE. *Pseudolus*, slave to Hero: ZERO MOSTEL. *Tintinabula*, a courtesan: Roberta Keith. *Panacea*, a courtesan: Lucienne Bridou. *The Geminae*, courtesans: Lisa James, Judy Alexander. *Vibrata*, a courtesan: Myrna White. *Gymnasia*, a courtesan: Gloria Kristy. *Philia*, a virgin: PRESHY MARKER. *Erronius*, a citizen of Rome: RAYMOND WALBURN. *Miles Gloriosus*, a warrior: RONALD HOLGATE.

The time is two hundred years before the Christian era, a day in spring. The place is a street in Rome in front of houses of Erronius, Senex and Lycus.

ACT 1
"Comedy, Tonight"
Z. Mostel, the Proteans, Company
"Love, I Hear"
B. Davies
"Free"
Z. Mostel, B. Davies
"The House of Marcus Lycus"
J. Carradine, Z. Mostel, Courtesans
"Lovely"
B. Davies, P. Marker
"Pretty Little Picture"
Z. Mostel, B. Davies, P. Marker
"Everybody Ought To Have a Maid"
D. Burns, Z. Mostel, J. Gilford, J. Carradine
"I'm Calm"
J. Gilford
"Impossible"
D. Burns, B. Davies
"Bring Me My Bride"
R. Holgate, Z. Mostel, Courtesans, Proteans

ACT 2
"That Dirty Old Man"
R. Kobart
"That'll Show Him"
P. Marker
"Lovely" (reprise)
Z. Mostel, J. Gilford
Funeral Sequence and Dance (Dirge)
Z. Mostel, R. Holgate, Courtesans, Proteans
"Comedy Tonight" (reprise)
The Company

1962.13 CAN-CAN

A Revival of the Musical Comedy in Two Acts, 17 Scenes[22]. Book by Abe Burrows. Music and lyrics by Cole Porter. Directed by Gus Schirmer. Lighting and scenic adaptation of Jo Mielziner's original designs by Helen Pond. Costumes by Stanley Simmons. Choreography by Ellen Ray. Musical

[22]Originally produced in New York 7 May 1953 at the Sam S. Shubert Theatre for 892 performances. For Synopsis of Scenes and Musical Numbers, see original 1953 production. "Every Man Is a Stupid Man" was dropped for this production.

direction by James Leon. (Orchestrations by Philip J. Lang. Dance music arranged by Genevieve Pitot.) Produced by the New York City Center Light Opera Company (Jean Dalrymple, Director). Opened 16 May 1962 at the New York City Center and closed 27 May 1962 after 16 performances.

CAST (in order of appearance): *Bailiff*: Phil Roth. *Registrar*: Peter Saul. *Policemen*: George Del Monte, Darrell Sandeen. *Judge Paul Barriere*: Warner Schreiner. *Court President, Henri Marceaux*: Charles Reynolds. *Judge Aristede Forestier*: GEORGE GAYNES. *Claudine*: MARA LYNN. *Gabrielle*: Maggie Worth. *Marie*: Lillian D'Honau. *Celestine*: Marilyn D'Honau. *Hilaire Jussac*: FERDINAND HILT. *Boris Adzinidzinadze*: GABRIEL DELL. *Hercule*: IGGIE WOLFINGTON. *Theophile*: BOB DISHY. *Etienne*: JACK FLETCHER. *Waiter*: Michael Cavallaro. *La Mome Pistache*: GENEVIEVE. *Second Waiter*: Darrell Sandeen. *Cafe Waiter*: Phil Roth. *Nun*: Nora Bristow. *Model*: Betty Hyatt Linton. *Mimi*: Dorothy D'Honau. *Customers*: Nora Bristow, Darell Sandeen. *Doctor*: Charles Reynolds. *Second*: Darrell Sandeen. *Rainbow*: Victor Duntiere. *Prosecutor*: Jack Davison. (*Principal Dancer*: PETER GLADKE.)

Dancers: Joseph Ahumada, Marilyn Charles, Sterling Clark, Victor Duntiere, Gloria Danyl, Dorothy D'Honau, Lillian D'Honau, Marilyn D'Honau, Don Emmons, Natasha Grishin, Janan Hart, Douglas Hinshaw, Robert Holloway, Betty Hyatt Linton, Sally Lou Lee, David Lober, Jami Landi, Mary Jane Moncrieff, Louise Quick, Peter Saul, Fabian Stuart, Alice Shanahan.

1962.14 BRAVO, GIOVANNI

A Musical Comedy in Two Acts, 22 Scenes. Book by A. J. Russell. Based on the novel ("The Crime of Giovanni Venturi") by Howard Shaw. Music by Milton Schafer. Lyrics by Ronny Graham. Scenery and lighting by Robert Randolph. Costumes by Ed Wittstein. Choreography by Carol Haney. Assistant choreograher, Buzz Miller. Musical direction, Continuity and vocal arrangements by Anton Coppola. (Musical) arrangements and orchestrations by Robert Ginzler. Dance music arranged and orchestrated by Luther Henderson. Directed by Stanley Prager. Produced by Philip Rose. Opened 19 May 1962 at the Broadhurst Theatre, closing for vacation 14 July 1962; re-opened 7 September 1962, and closed 15 September 1962 after 76 performances.

CAST (in order of appearance): *Giovanni Venturi*: CESARE SIEPI. *Signor Bellardi*: GEORGE S. IRVING. *Uriti Waiters*: RICO FROEHLICH, Joe McGrath, Ed Dumont, Barney Johnston. *Amedeo*: DAVID OPATOSHU. *Furniture Dealer*: Harry Davis. *Nino*: Al Sambogna. *Gino*: Thatcher Clarke. *Dino*: Buzz Miller. *Miranda*: MICHELE LEE. *Moscolito*: ARNOLD SOBOLOFF. *Carlo*: AL LANTI. *Signora Pandolfi*: MARIA KARNILOVA. *Musicians*: GENE VARRONE, Nino Banome, RICO FROEHLICH. *Night Club Manager*: BUZZ MILLER. *Professor Panfredoni*: HARRY DAVIS. *Troubador*: GENE VARRONE. *Celestina*: LU LEONARD. *Head Chef*: BUZZ MILLER. *Pizza Maker*: GENE VARRONE. *Salad Chef*: Gene Gavin. *Bakers*: Nino Banome, Larry Fuller. *Soup Cook*: Thatcher Clarke. *Helpers*: Alan Peterson, Alvin Beam, Al Sambogna. *Signora Elli*: Penny Gaston. *La Contessa*: Lainie Kazan. *Signor Brancusi*: John Taliaferro. *Professor Musa*: RICO FROEHLICH. *Brigadiere*: GENE VARRONE. *Policeman*: Barney Johnston.

Singing Ensemble: Jyll Alexander, Norma Donaldson, Penny Gaston, Marcia Gilford, Maria Graziano, Lainie Kazan, Betty Kent, Rita Metzger, Ed Dumont, Tom Head, Barney Johnston, Ronald Knight, Joe McGrath, Richard Park, John Taliaferro. *Dancing Ensemble*: Ann Barry, Ellen Halpin, Shellie Farrell, Michele Franchi, Herad Gruh, Baayork Lee, Barbara Richman, Nikki Sowinski, Nino Banome, Alvin Beam, Thatcher Clarke, Larry Fuller, Gene Gavin, Alan Peterson, Al Sambogna, Claude Thompson.

Act 1, Scene 1: A Piazza in Trastavere, Rome, Italy. Dawn of a spring day, at the present time. *Scene 2*: Giovanni's Restaurant. Three weeks later. *Scene 3*: The Piazza. The following afternoon. *Scene 4*: A Fountain in Rome. The following afternoon. *Scene 5*: The Tunnel. A few nights later. *Scene 6*: A Nightclub in Rome. The following morning. *Scene 7*: The Tunnel. The following night. *Scene 8*: The Etruscan Room in the Villa Guilia Museum. A few days later. *Scene 9*: The Tunnel. A few days later. *Scene 10*: Giovanni's Room. Immediately following. *Scene 11*: The Piazza. Late the following Saturday night.

Act 2, Scene 1: The Tunnel. Noon the following Monday. *Scene 2*: A Street in Rome. A month later. *Scene 3*: The Uriti Kitchen. Immediately following. *Scene 4*: The Street. Immediately following. *Scene 5*: Giovanni's Kitchen. A few days later. *Scene 6*: The Etruscan Restaurant. Six months later. *Scene 7*: Giovanni's Room. A few nightds later. *Scene 8*: The Tunnel. Lunchtime, the following day. *Scene 9*: The Etruscan Restauarnt. Immediately following. *Scene 10*: The Tunnel. Immediately following. *Scene 11*: The Piazza. Immediately following.

ACT 1

Scene 1

"Rome"
C. Siepi

"Uriti"
G. S. Irving, Full Ensemble

Scene 2

"Breachy's Law"
C. Siepi, D. Opatoshu

Scene 3

"I'm All I've Got"
M. Lee

Scene 4

"The Argument"
C. Siepi, G. S. Irving

Scene 6

"Signora Pandolfi"
D. Opatoshu, M. Karnilova, B. Miller, Musicians

"The Kangaroo"
M. Karnilova, B. Miller, Waiters, Musicians, Kitchen Help

Scene 8

"If I Were the Man"
C. Siepi

"Steady, Steady"
M. Lee

Scene 9

"We Won't Discuss It"
C. Siepi, D. Opatoshu

Scene 11

"Ah! Camminare"
G. Varrone, C. Siepi, Entire Company

ACT 2

Scene 1

"Breachy's Law" (reprise)
C. Siepi, D. Opatoshu, M. Karnilova, M. Lee

Scene 3

"Uriti Kitchen"
G. S. Irving, A. Soboloff, A. Lanti, B. Miller,
G. Varrone, G. Gavin, N. Banome, L. Fuller, T. Clarke, Helpers

Scene 4

"Virtue Arrivederci"
G. S. Irving

Scene 6

"Bravo, Giovanni"
C. Siepi, G. S. Irving, Singing Ensemble

"One Little World Apart"
M. Lee

Scene 8

"Connubiality"[23]
M. Karnilova, D. Opatoshu

Scene 10

"Miranda"
C. Siepi

1962.15 BRIGADOON

A Revival of the Musical Play in Two Acts, a Prologue and 11 Scenes[24]. Book and lyrics by Alan Jay Lerner. Music by Frederick Loewe. Dance and musical numbers by Agnes de Mille, assisted by James Jamieson. Directed by John Fearnley. Settings by Oliver Smith. Art director, Watson Barratt. Costumes designed by Stanley Simmons. Musical director, Julius Rudel. Conductor, Don Smith. Produced by the New York City Center Light

[23]During run, replaced by:
"Jump In"
M. Karnilova, D. Opatoshu

[24]Originally produced in New York 13 March 1947 at the Ziegfeld Theatre for 581 performances. For Synopsis of Scenes and Musical Numbers, see original 1947 production.

Opera Company (Jean Dalrymple, Director). Opened 30 May 1962 at the New York City Center and closed 10 June 1962 after 16 performances[25].

CAST (in order of appearance): *Tommy Albright*: PETER PALMER. *Jeff Douglas*: FARLEY GRANGER. *Sandy Dean*: Kenny Adams. *Meg Brockie*: ANN FRASER. *Archie Beaton*: Moultrie Patten. *Harry Beaton*: EDWARD VILLELLA. *Andrew MacLaren*: Alexander Clark. *Fiona MacLaren*: SALLY ANN HOWES. *Jean MacLaren*: Jenny Workman. *Angus MacGuffie*: Walter Blocher. *Charlie Dalrymple*: HARRY SNOW. *Maggie Anderson*: Gemze de Lappe. *Sword Dancers*: Richard Rutherford, James Clouser, James McArdle, David Shields, Frank Andre. *Mr. Lundie*: John C. Becher. *Bagpiper*: Maurice Eisenstadt. *Frank*: Felice Orlandi. *Jane Ashton*: Susan Fellows.

Townsfolk of Brigadoon: *Singers*: Faith Daltry, Beverly G. Evans, Susan Fellows, Helen Guile, Marilyn Mason, Hanna Owen, Betty Jane Schwering, Kelli Scott, Lynn Wendell, Kenny Adams, John Aman, Ken Ayers, Donald E. Becker, Jerry Crawford, Harris W. Davis, Marvin Goodis, Robert Lenn, George T. McWhorter, John Sarkis. *Dancers*: Barbara Beck, Lynn Broadbent, Mickey Gunnerson, Michele D. Hardy, Rosalie Kurowska, Lucia Lambert, Loi Leabo, Anna-Marie, Jane Meserve, Esther Villavicencio, Frank André, Robert Bishop, James Clouser, Ben Gillespie, Art Hutchinson, Vernon Lusby, Jim McArdle, Charles B. McCraw, Richard Rutherford, David Shields.

[25]Vocal arrangements by Frederick Loewe. Orchestrations by Ted Royal. Lighting uncredited.

1962–1963 SEASON

Nancy Andrews (center) in LITTLE ME (Photo: Friedman-Abeles, 1962)
Museum of the City of New York, Gift of Annette Trubowitsch, 88.86.49.4

1962–1963 SEASON

1962.16 FIORELLO!

A Revival of the Musical in Two Acts, a Prologue and 19 Scenes[1]. Book by Jerome Weidman and George Abbott. Music by Jerry Bock. Lyrics by Sheldon Harnick. Scenery and lighting by William and Jean Eckart. Costume supervision by Joseph Codori. Musical direction, Jay Blackton. (Orchestrations by Irwin Kostal. Dance music arranged by Jack Elliott.) Entire production staged and directed by Dania Krupska. Choreography by Kevin Carlisle. Produced by the New York City Center Light Opera Company (Jean Dalrymple, Director). Opened 13 June 1962 at the New York City Center and closed 24 June 1962 after 16 performances.

CAST (in order of appearance): *Announcer*: Del Hortsmann. *Fiorello*: SORRELL BOOKE. *Neil*: Richard France. *Morris*: PAUL LIPSON. *Mrs. Pomerantz*: Helen Verbit. *Mr. Lopez*: Tony Gardell. *Mr. Crawford*: Joseph Crawford. *Dora*: DODY GOODMAN. *Marie*: BARBARA WILLIAMS. *Ben Marino*: ART LUND. *Dealer (Ed Peterson)*: Del Horstmann. *Seedy Man*: Terry Violino. *Third Player*: Michael Quinn. *Fifth Player*: Ned Wright. *Second Player*: Feodore Tedick. *Fourth Player*: Walter P. Brown. *Kibitzer*: Will Roy. *First Heckler*: Mike Scrittorale. *Second Heckler*: Bobby Barry. *Third Heckler*: Louis Kosman. *Fourth Heckler*: Ed Pfeiffer. *Fifth Heckler*: Paul Eden. *Nina*: Jeanna Belkin. *Sophie*: Jami Landi. *Floyd*: DORT CLARK. *Thea*: LOLA FISHER. *Washington Secretary*: Mary Louise. *Senator*: Feodore Tedick. *Drunk*: Louis Kosman. *Butler*: Norman Grogan. *Judge*: Bobby Barry. *Politicians*: Jack Rains, Ned Wright. *Commissioner*: John Martin. *Mitzi*: SHEILA SMITH. *Frank Scarpini*: Mike Scrittorale. *Reporter*: Robert Kya-Hill. *Florence*: Maggie Worth. *Tough Man*: Jack Rains. *Frantic*: Louis Kosman.

Singers: Rosalind Cash, Doreese Du Quan, Joanne Hill, Mary Louise Jones, Bobbi Lange, Estelle Moss, Maura Wedge, Betty Weston, Maggie Worth, Bobby Barry, Walter P. Brown, Joseph Crawford, Tony Gardell, H. Scott Gibson, Norman Grogan, (Edward) Del Horstmann, Robert Kya-Hill, Michael Quinn, Jack K. Rains, Will Roy, Feodore Tedick, Ned Wright. *Dancers*: Chele Abel, Nancy Baron, Margery J. Beddow, Jeanna Belkin, Louise Ferrand, Lois Grandi, Carole Kroon, Jami Landi, Lynn G. Lorino, Carol Sue Shafer, Jere Admire, Jean L. Blanchard, Sterling Clark, Paul Eden, Bob Holloway, Bernard Johnson, Louis Kosman, Ed A. Pfeiffer, Paul R. Roman, Miek Scrittorale, Terry Violino.

1962.17 EDDIE FISHER AT THE WINTER GARDEN

A Variety Show in Two Acts, 4 Scenes. Special material by Gordon Jenkins. Directed by John Fearnley. Settings by Oliver Smith. Lighting by Peggy Clark. Orchestrations by Jerry Fielding. Conducted by Pembroke Davenport. Miss Prowse's numbers staged and choreographed by Tony Charmoli. Miss Prowse's costumes by Ray Aghayan. Associate producer, Bernie Rich. A Ramrod Production. Produced by Monte Proser and Milton Blackstone. Opened 2 October 1962 at the Winter Garden and closed 3 November 1962 after 48 performances.

CAST: EDDIE FISHER, JULIET PROWSE, DICK GREGORY, Nicholas Couacevich, Brad Craig, Norman Edwards, Lance Avant, John Frayer, Burnell Deitch.

ACT 1[2]

Scene 1

"The Broadway Zoo"
(Chorus)
(*Music and Lyrics by* Gordon Jenkins. *Projection Designed by* Glenn Holse.)

Scene 2

Dick Gregory (Comedian)

Scene 3

Miss Juliet Prowse (Song and Dance):
"Bewitched" (from PAL JOEY)
(*Music by* Richard Rodgers. *Lyrics by* Lorenz Hart.)
"Smoke Gets in Your Eyes" (from ROBERTA)
(*Music by* Jerome Kern. *Lyrics by* Otto Harbach.)
Great Heroines of Literature in a Broadway Musical Style:
Joan of Arc, Cleopatra, Camille
(*Music and Lyrics by* Jimmy Van Heusen and Sammy Cahn.)
The Boys: N. Couacevich, L. Avant, B. Craig, J. Frayer, N. Edwards, B. Deitch.

ACT 2

Eddie Fisher (Orchestra conducted by Eddy Samuels.):
"Don't Let It Get You Down" (from HOLD ONTO YOUR HATS)
(*Music by* Burton Lane. *Lyrics by* E. Y. Harburg.)
"Back in Your Own Back Yard" (from the film SAY IT WITH SONGS)
(*Music and Lyrics by* Al Jolson, Billy Rose and Dave Dreyer.)
WEST SIDE STORY Medley: "Tonight", "Maria", "Something's Coming"
(*Music by* Leonard Bernstein. *Lyrics by* Stephen Sondheim.)
"You Made Me Love You" (from THE PASSING SHOW OF 1913, THE HONEYMOON EXPRESS)
(*Music by* James V. Monaco. *Lyrics by* Joseph McCarthy.)
"Never on Sunday" (from the film NEVER ON SUNDAY)
(*Music by* Manos Hadjidakis. *English Lyrics by* Billy Towne.)
"This Nearly Was Mine" (from SOUTH PACIFIC)
(*Music by* Richard Rodgers. *Lyrics by* Oscar Hammerstein II.)
"Mack the Knife" (from THE THREEPENNY OPERA)
(*Music by* Kurt Weill. *Lyrics by* Bertolt Brecht and Marc Blitzstein.)
"Hava Naguila" (*Music and Lyrics adapted by* Sid Danoff.)
"Moon River" (from film BREAK FAST AT TIFFANY'S)
(*Music by* Henry Mancini. *Lyrics by* Johnny Mercer.)

AL JOLSON Medley:
"Swanee" (from SINBAD)
(*Music by* George Gershwin. *Lyrics by* Irving Caesar.)
"About a Quarter to Nine" (from film GO INTO YOUR DANCE)
(*Music by* Harry Warren. *Lyrics by* Al Dubin.)
"Liza" (All the Clouds'll Roll Away) (from SHOW GIRL)
(*Music by* George Gershwin. *Lyrics by* Ira Gershwin and Gus Kahn.)
"I'm Sitting on Top of the World" (from film THE SINGING FOOL)
(*Music by* Ray Henderson. *Lyrics by* Sam M. Lewis and Joe Young.)
"Toot Toot Tootsie, Goodbye" (from BOMBO)
(*Music and Lyrics by* Ted Fio Rito, Robert A. King, Gus Kahn, Ernie Erdman.)
"April Showers" (from BOMBO)
(*Music by* Louis Silvers. *Lyrics by* Buddy G. DeSylva.)
"Waiting for the Robert E. Lee"
(*Music by* Lewis F. Muir. *Lyrics by* L. Wolfe Gilbert.)
"Rock-A-Bye Your Baby With a Dixie Melody" (from SINBAD)
(*Music by* Jean Schwartz. *Lyrics by* Sam M. Lewis and Joe Young)
"Sonny Boy" (from film THE SINGING FOOL)
(*Music by* Ray Henderson. *Lyrics by* Buddy G. DeSylva and Lew Brown.)
"Makin' Whoopee" (from WHOOPEE)
(*Music by* Walter Donaldson. *Lyrics by* Gus Kahn.)

Medley: "Anytime" (*Music and Lyrics by* Herbert Happy Lawson), "I Need You Now" (*Music and Lyrics by* Jimmy Crane and Al Jacobs), "Wish You Were Here" (from WISH YOU WERE HERE, *Music and Lyrics by* Harold Rome.), "Heart" (from DAMN YANKEES, *Music and Lyrics by* Richard Adler and Jerry Ross.), "Oh Mein Papa" (from the Swiss/English musical OH MY PAPA!, *Music by* Paul Burkhard. *English Lyrics by* Geoffrey Parsons and John Turner.)

"What Kind of Fool Am I?" (from STOP THE WORLD—I WANT TO GET OFF)
(*Music and Lyrics by* Leslie Bricusse and Anthony Newley.)
"Mein Shtetele Belz" (That Wonderful Girl of Mine)
(*Music and Lyrics by* Bregman, Vocco, Chester Conn and J. J. Kamen.)
"The Sweetest Sounds" (from NO STRINGS)
(*Music and Lyrics by* Richard Rodgers.)

---

[1]Originally produced in New York 23 November 1959 at the Broadhurst Theatre for 795 performances. For Synopsis and Scenes and Musical Numbers, see original 1959 production. For this production, the following revisions were made:

Act 1, Scene 11 (Gangplank for Returning Soldiers from Overseas: "Home Again") became Act 2, Scene 1. Added to this production (Act 2, Scene 6) was the previously cut song:

"Where Do I Go From Here?"
B. Williams (Marie)

[2]No song list appeared in the program. The following was prepared from reviews and recordings.

1962.18 STOP THE WORLD – I WANT TO GET OFF

A New-Style Musical in Two Acts. Book, Music and lyrics by Leslie Bricusse and Anthony Newley. Setting and lighting by Sean Kenny. Musical supervision, Ian Fraser. Musical director, Milton Rosenstock. Orchestrations by Ian Fraser with David Lindup. Burt Rhodes, Gordon Langford. John Broome's choreography restaged by Virginia Mason. Directed by Anthony Newley. Produced by David Merrick in association with Bernard Delfont. Opened 3 October 1962 at the Sam S. Shubert Theatre, moved 9 September 1963 to the Ambassador Theatre, and closed 1 February 1964 after 556 performances.

CAST: *Littlechap*: ANTHONY NEWLEY. *Evie, Anya, Ilse, Ginnie*: ANNA QUAYLE. *Jane*: Jennifer Baker. *Susan*: Susan Baker. *Chorus (and All Other Roles)*: Rawley Bates, Bonnie Brody, Diana Corto, Jo Anne Leeds, Karen Lynn Reed, Sylvia Tysick, Stephanie Winters, Mark Hunter, Paul Rufo.

ACT 1

"The A.B.C. Song"
(Chorus)
"I Want To Be Rich"
(A. Newley, Chorus)
"Typically English"
(A. Quayle)
"A Special Announcement"
(Chorus)
"Lumbered"
(A. Newley)
"Welcome to Sludgepool"
(Chorus)
"Gonna Build a Mountain"
(A. Newley, Chorus)
"Glorious Russian"
(A. Quayle)
"Meilinki Meilchick"
(A. Newley, A. Quayle)
"Family Fugue"
(A. Newley, A. Quayle, J. Baker, S. Baker)
"Typische Deutsche"
(A. Quayle, Chorus)
"Nag! Nag! Nag!"
(A. Newley, A. Quayle, J. Baker, S. Baker, Chorus)

ACT 2

"All American"
(A. Quayle)
"Once in a Lifetime"
(A. Newley)
"Mumbo Jumbo"
(A. Newley)
"Welcome to Sunvale"
(Chorus)
"Someone Nice Like You"
(A. Newley, A. Quayle)
"What Kind of Fool Am I?"
(A. Newley)

1962.19 THE MIKADO, or The Town of Titipu

A Revival of the Comic Opera in Two Acts[3]. Libretto by William S. Gilbert. Music by Arthur Sullivan. Staged by Dorothy Raedler. Scenic design by Donald Oenslager. Costume design by Patton Campbell. Conducted by William Jonson. Produced by the New York City Opera. Opened 13 October 1962 (matinee) at the New York City Center and closed 4 November 1961 after 2 performances in repertory.

[3]First presented in New York 20 July, 10-29 August 1885 at the Union Square and People's Theatres for 22 performances. First authorized production presented 19 August 1885 at the Fifth Avenue Theatre by Richard D'Oyly Carte for 250 performances. For Synopsis of Scenes and Musical Numbers, see 19 August 1885 D'Oyly Carte production.

CAST: *The Mikado of Japan*: PAUL UKENA. *Nanki-Poo*, his son, disguised as a wandering minstrel in love with Yum-Yum: WILLIAM DIARD. *Ko-Ko*, Lord High Executioner of Titipu: NORMAN KELLEY. *Pooh-Bah*, Lord High Everything Else: SPIRO MALAS. *Pish-Tush*, a Noble Lord: David Smith. *Yum-Yum, Pitti-Sing, Peep-Bo*, three sisters, wards of Ko-Ko: JOY CLEMENTS, BEVERLY EVANS, MARIJA KOVA. *Katisha*: EVELYN SACHS. *Chorus of School Girls, Nobles, Guards and Coolies*: New York City Opera Chorus.

1962.20 MR. PRESIDENT

A Musical Comedy in Two Acts, 22 Scenes. Book by Howard Lindsay and Russel Crouse. Music and lyrics by Irving Berlin. Directed by Joshua Logan. Choreography by Peter Gennaro. Settings and lighting by Jo Mielziner. Costumes by Theoni V. Aldredge. Musical direction, Jay Blackton. Dance arrangements, Jack Elliott. Orchestrations, Philip J. Lang. Produced by Leland Hayward. Opened 20 October 1962 at the St. James Theatre and closed 8 June 1963 after 265 performances.

CAST (in order of appearance): *Manager*: DAVID BROOKS. *President Stephen Decatur Henderson*: ROBERT RYAN. *Nell Henderson*: NANETTE FABRAY. *Walter O'Connor*, a Secretary: Jack Rains. *David Caldwell*: Warren J. Brown. *Leslie Henderson*: ANITA GILLETTE. *Larry Henderson*: JERRY STRICKLER. *Youssein Davair*: JACK WASHBURN. *Tippy Taylor*, a Secretary: Charlotte Fairchild. *Pat Gregory*, of the Secret Service: JACK HASKELL. *Charley Wayne*, of the Secret Service: STANLEY GROVER. *Princess Kyra*: WISA D'ORSO. *Russian Soldier*: Jack Mette. *Colonel Wilson*: Van Stevens. *Mrs. Lotta Pendleton*: Marian Haraldson. *George Perkins*: Beau Tilden. *Mr. Thomas*: Carl Nicholas. *Deborah Chakronin*: Baayork Lee. *Arthur Blanchard*: Jack McMinn. *Radio Operator*: John Aman. *Ali Hassoud*: Anthony Falco. *Abou*: Carlos Bas. *Commentators*: Louis Kosman, Jack McMinn. *A Workman*: Dan Siretta. *Miss Barnes*: Lipset Nelson. *The Deacon*: Carl Nicholas. *Sergeant Stone*, of the Secret Service: Beau Tilden. *Chester Kincaid*: John Cecil Holm. *Betty Chandler*: Carol Lee Jensen. *Spieler*: Jack Rains. *Governor Harmon Bardahl*: DAVID BROOKS.

Singing Ensemble: Kellie Brytt, Marian Haraldson, Carol Lee Jensen, Mary Louise, Donna Monroe, Lispet Nelson, Ruth Shepard, Maggie Worth, John Aman, Anthony Falco, Jack McMinn, Jack Mette, Carl Nicholas, Jack Rains, Van Stevens. *Dancing Ensemble*: Lynn Bernay, Connie Burnett, Baayork Lee, Lynn Gay Lorino, Anna Marie Moylan, Barbara Newman, Lynn Ross, Mari Shelton, Arline Woods, Don Atkinson, Bob Bakanic, Carlos Bas, Sterling Clark, Laverne French, Louis Kosman, Bob LaCrosse, Lowell Purvis, Dan Siretta. *Tahitians*: Louis Kosman, Carlos Bas, Lynn Gay Lorino. *Butterflies*: Anna Marie Moylan, Barbara Newman, Mari Shelton. *Kabuki Spider*: Lowell Purvis. *Japanese Beatniks*: Lynn Ross, Bob Bakanic. *Kabuki Lion*: Anthony Falco. *South Sea Warrior*: Laverne French. *Elephant*: Carlos Bas, Louis Kosman. *Lord Krishna*: Connie Burnett. *East Indian Marching Team*: Lynn Bernay, Anna Marie Moylan, Barbara Newman, Mari Shelton, Arline Woods, Don Atkinson, Sterling Clark, Dan Siretta. *Leader*: Baayork Lee.

Act 1, Scene 1: Oval Room at the White House. *Scene 2*: Private Sitting Room in the White House. *Scene 3*: A Lawn Party in Chevy Chase. *Scene 4*: The President's Bedroom. *Scene 5*: The President's Office. *Scene 6*: The Trip. *Scene 7*: The President's Plane. *Scene 8*: A Street in the Middle East. *Scene 9*: Youssein's Apartment. *Scene 10*: The President's Plane. *Scene 11*: Airfield. *Scene 12*: Television Studios. *Scene 13*: The Private Sitting Room in the White House. *Scene 14*: An Office in the White House. *Scene 15*: The President's Office.

Act 2, Scene 1: A Street in Mansfield. *Scene 2*: The Living Room of the Henderson Home. *Scene 3*: An Anteroom in the White House. *Scene 4*: The Judging Pavilion of the Tioga County Fair. *Scene 5*: The Midway of the Fair. *Scene 6*: Another Part of the Fair. *Scene 7*: The Living Room of the Henderson Home.

ACT 1

Scene 1
"Let's Go Back to the Waltz"
N. Fabray, Ensemble
Scene 2
"In Our Hide-Away"
N. Fabray, R. Ryan
"The First Lady"
N. Fabray
Scene 3
"Meat and Potatoes"
J. Haskell, S. Grover
"I've Got To Be Around"
J. Haskell
"The Secret Service"
A. Gillette
Scene 4
"It Gets Lonely in the White House"
R. Ryan

Scene 5
"Is He the Only Man in the World"
N. Fabray, A. Gillette
Scene 6
"They Love Me"
N. Fabray
Scene 7
"Pigtails and Freckles"
J. Haskell, A. Gillette
Scene 9
"Don't Be Afraid of Romance"
J. Washburn
Scene 13
"Laught It Up"
N. Fabray, R. Ryan, A. Gillette, J. Strickler
Scene 14
"Empty Pockets Filled With Love"
J. Haskell, A. Gillette
Scene 15
"In Our Hide-Away" (reprise)
N. Fabray, R. Ryan

ACT 2
Scene 1
"Glad To Be Home"
N. Fabray, Ensemble
Scene 2
"Laught It Up" (reprise)
N. Fabray, R. Ryan
"You Need a Hobby"
N. Fabray, R. Ryan
Scene 3
"Don't Be Afraid of Romance" (reprise)
J. Washburn
"The Washington Twist"
A. Gillette, Dancers
Scene 4
"Pigtails and Freckles" (reprise)
J. Haskell
Scene 5
"The Only Dance I Know"
W. D'Orso
Scene 6
"Meat and Potatoes" (reprise)
J. Haskell
"Is He the Only Man in the World" (reprise)
A. Gillette
"I'm Gonna Get Him"
N. Fabray, A. Gillette
Scene 7
"This Is a Great Country"
R. Ryan
Finale
Entire Company

1962.21 THE MERRY WIDOW

A Revival of the Operetta in Three Acts[4]. Music by Franz Lehár. Original German book ("Die Lustige Witwe") and lyrics by Victor Léon and Leo Stein after "L'Attaché d'Ambassade" by Henri Meilhac. English libretto by Adrian Ross. Staged by Michael Pollock. Scenic design by George Jenkins. Choreographed by Thomas Andrew. Conducted by Carl Bamberger. Produced by the New York City Opera. Opened 21 October 1962 at the New York City Center and closed 11 November 1962 after 3 performances in repertory.

CAST: *Sonia*: ARLENE SAUNDERS. *Prince Danilo*: JOHN REARDON. *Baron Popoff*: JACK HARROLD. *Natalie*: Nancy Foster. *De Jolidon*: JON CRAIN. *Marquis de Cascada*: David Smith. *St. Brioche*: Richard Krause. *Admiral Khadja*: Thomas Paul. *Mme. Khadja*: Lynda Jordan. *General Novikovich*: Spiro Malas. *Mme. Novikovich*: Charlotte Povia. *Nish*: Roy Stuart. *Head Waiter*: George John Smith. *Lo-Lo*: Helen Guile. *Solo Dancers*: Irene Apinée, Jury Gotshalks. *Ensemble*: New York City Opera Chorus.

1962.22 BAMBOCHE!

A Dance Revue in Three Acts, 13 Scenes. Production created and directed by Katherine Dunham. Settings and costumes by John Pratt. Orchestra under the direction of Leslie Harnley. Produced by Stephen Papich in association with Dorothy Gray and Ludwig Gerber. Opened 22 October 1962 at the 54th Street Theatre and closed 28 October 1962 after 8 performances.

CAST: KATHERINE DUNHAM, BESSIE GRIFFIN.

Katherine Dunham Dancers: VANOYE AIKENS, LUCILLE ELLIS, URAL WILSON, RICARDO AVALOS, Hope Clarke, Joan Seabrook, Odile Reifsteck, Lois Rollins, Maria Costoso, Candy Alexander, Carlton Johnson, Clifford Fears, Glenn Standifer, Wesley Gale, Monique LaSalle, David Henderson, Zach Thompson, Pearl Reynolds. *Singers*: ROBERT GUILLAUME, DOROTHY SPEIGHTS, Rosalie Maxwell, Clark Morgan, Gordon Watkins. *Drummers*: Camara Ladji, Julio Mendez, La Rosa Estrada. *Pianist*: Charles Barnett. *Bass Saxophone*: Jerome Richardson.

The Royal Troupe of Morocco: Che Dad Salem, Messaoud Ben Othman, Abderkader Ben Ahmed, El Kaaoui Allal, Marir Boujema, Driss Beid Mohammed, Hayat Khaddouj, Anouar Rabha, Heto Said Ben Brahim, Abderaham Ali Abderahaman, El Serife Buker, Ahmed Abselam, El Serife Takrchtba, Fatima Lahoucine, Tibikcht Fatima Brahim.

ACT 1
Scene 1
Marrakech!
(Music adapted from original themes by Leslie Harnley.)

The dances of Morocco are as varied as its tribal groups. In the courtyard of the Caliph in Marrakech, dancers gather from the Blue people of Goulimine in the South; from the Gnauwa, the tall dark men of Marrakech; from the Berbers of Khenifra, famous for their beautiful women. The musicians play the violins and the Gaitero, a reed instrument as old as the Sahara. The Koraish are proud of their descendency from tribes older than the Prophet Himself and proud of the many generations of artistry and the special favors they have received from the royal families for generations.

Guitera: E. K. Allal. *Acrobat*: A. B. Ahmed. *Dancing Girls*: H. Clarke, L. Rollins. *Wives of the Sultan*: O. Reifsteck, M. Costoso, C. Alexander, L. Ellis. *Berber Girls of the Khenifra* (in the Dance of the Tasadbat): H. Khaddouj, A. Rabha.

The blue Arab women of Goulimine, near the border of Mauritania, are called "blue" because of the Indigo in the garments which rubs off on the faces of the men and the women. The dance is the mysterious Guedra, believed by some to have been evolved from the Oriental people of the Pacific area.

Guedra Dancers: B. B. Mohammed, E. S. Takrchtba, F. Lahouchine, T. F. Brahim. *Gamni Dancers*: M. B. Othman, M. Boujema.

The chief drummers and dancers of the Gnauwa tribes perform the vigorous Gamni, a men's dance in preparation for war.

The Tjballa Dancer: A. A. Abderahaman.

A young boy from the Tjballa Tribes, dressed and veiled as a woman. He is accompanied by a violin player from their native village of Zahyouka, where the Tjballa has for many generations been popular among the young men.

The Desert Scene (Danse du Ventre)
K. Dunham, V. Aikens, Singers, Dancers, Musicians
Guedra (The Mystic Dance by the blue women of Goulimine)
B. B. Mohammed, E. S. Takrchtba, F. Lahoumine, T. F. Brahim

Scene 2
Brazilian Suite
Choros
H. Clarke, O. Reifsteck, C. Fears, C. Johnson
Variations of a Brazilian Quadrille from the nineteenth century.
Batucada
K. Dunham, V. Aikens, Company

[4]Originally produced in New York 21 October 1907 at the New Amsterdam Theatre for 416 performances. For Synopsis of Scenes and Musical Numbers, see original 1907 production.

A group of fisherwomen from bahia flirt with a woman from their own district.

Los Indios

M. Costoso, J. Seabrook, C. Johnson

High in the Andes, two Indian girls break their journey and meet a flute player.

Scene 3

Haitian Suite

"Yanvalou"

D. Speights, R. Guillaume, Gentlemen of the Company
La Place: U. Wilson.

For many years, Katherine Dunham has studied and participated in the deep mysteries of the Vaudun Cult. More recently, the pleasure-loving side of the Haitian people has attracted her. The Yanvalou is the fluid, hypnotic dance of veneration to Damballa, the Serpent God of the Dahomey.

"Bamboche!"

K. Dunham, V. Aikens, Company
(*Music and Lyrics by* Katherine Dunham.)

Bamboche is Haitian Creole for a "get-together to have a good time."

ACT 2

"The Diamond Thief"

(*Music by* Richard Markowitz. *Lyrics by* Le Clerc.)

Zulu Warrior: V. Aikens. *The Overseer*: A. Cooke. *Leader*: R. Guillaume. *The Diamond Thief*: R. Avalos. *Matriarch*: B. Graham. *Witch Doctor*: U. Wilson. *Lady in the Gold Dress*: K. Dunham. *Waiter*: D. Henderson. *Drummer*: C. Ladji. And Villagers, Patrons of the club, and the miners.

Place: Somewhere in the South of Africa. *Scene 1*: The Diamond Mine. *Scene 2*: Street of the Money Lender. *Scene 3*: The Happy Village. *Scene 4*: "De Highlife Bar" *Scene 5*: The Diamond Mine.

Africa is still full of mysteries and witchdoctors and villages within city squalor which revert to their ancient tribal exhibitions. In our locale, the only place to spend money is where the West filters in—in the native bars and cafes. The mines must be full of dreamers. Although the author has obviously not acquired information firsthand, there must be water girls passing at the end of the day, perhaps even one who would flirt with the overseer to ease the situation of the Diamond Thief. There must be an old, disillusioned Matriarch who has taken to Palm Wine and a Zulu Man still fine and handsome, who helps keep the spirit of Old Africa alive. Undoubtedly, to have money on hand from the sale of the diamond to the money lender would turn the Highlife Bar into a real "Gone" spot. There would be flirtatious girls and even a lady who worked her way up to a gold dress. It would be hard for the diamond thief to decide whether it all happened or not but the villagers are happy because in any event it was a great find.

ACT 3

Scene 1

Interior of The Mission House

Piano Player: C. Barnett. *Preacher*: U. Wilson. *A Worshipper*: R. Guillaume. *The Visiting Evangelist*: B. Griffin. And Congregation Members.

Scene 2

Barrelhouse: Florida Swamp Shimmy, Saturday Afternoon: Jacksonville.

K. Dunham, V. Aikens, Ensemble

Scene 3

Flaming Youth: Charleston, Black Bottom, Mooch, Fishtale, Snakehips

A Memory from the Twenties

Kansas City Woman: B. Griffin. *A Woman from Kansas City*: L. Ellis. *Snakehips*: C. Fears. *Drunken Woman*: L. Rollins.

Scene 4

Nostalgia: Songs from the Turn of the Century

D. Speights, R. Guillaume, R. Maxwell, C. Morgan, G. Watkins

Scene 5

Cakewalk

K. Dunham, V. Aikens, L. Ellis, U. Wilson

From the beginning of the century this dance mania of the athletic and exhibitionistic variation spread to Europe (and) completely conquered any existing dance style.

1962.23 BEYOND THE FRINGE

A (Comedy) Revue in Two Acts. Written by Alan Bennett, Peter Cook, Joanthan Miller and Dudley Moore[5]. Staged by Alexander H. Cohen. Original London production directed by Eleanor Fazan. Setting by John Wyckham. Lighting by Ralph Alswang. Production associates, Andre Goulston, Gabriel Katzka. Originally conceived and produced for the Edinburgh Festival by Jonathan Bassett. A Nine O'Clock Theatre Production. Produced by Alexander H. Cohen by arrangement with William Donaldson and Donald Albery. Opened 27 October 1962 at the John Golden Theatre and closed 30 May 1964 after 673 performances. On 8 January 1964 title changed to BEYOND THE FRINGE '64[6]; see entry immediately below.

CAST: ALAN BENNETT, PETER COOK, JONATHAN MILLER, DUDLEY MOORE.

ACT 1

Steppes in the Right Direction[7]

A. Bennett, P. Cook, J. Miller, D. Moore

Royal Box

(*by* Alan Bennett)
P. Cook, D. Moore

"Man Bites God"

J. Miller, D. Moore

Fruits of Experience (Let's Face It)

(*by* Alan Bennett)
A. Bennett

Bollard

(*by* Peter Cook)
A. Bennett, P. Cook, J. Miller, D. Moore

A Piece of My Mind (The Heat Death of the Universe)

(*by* Jonathan Miller)
J. Miller

"Deutscher Chansons" (Chanson; Die Flabbergast)

(*by* Dudley Moore)
J. Miller, D. Moore

The Sadder and Wiser Beaver

(*by* Peter Cook)
A. Bennett, P. Cook

Groves of Academe (Words . . . and Things)

(*by* Alan Bennett and Peter Cook)
A. Bennett, J. Miller

The Prime Minister Speaks (T.V.P.M.)

(*by* Peter Cook)[8]
P. Cook

"And the Same to You" (piano solo)

(*by* Dudley Moore)
D. Moore

Aftermyth of War

A. Bennett, P. Cook, J. Miller, D. Moore

ACT 2

Civil War

A. Bennett, P. Cook, J. Miller, D. Moore

Real Class

A. Bennett, P. Cook, J. Miller, D. Moore

"Little Miss Britten"

(*by* Dudley Moore)
J. Miller, D. Moore

The Suspense Is Killing Me

(*by* Alan Bennett, Jonathan Miller)
A. Bennett, P. Cook, J. Miller, D. Moore

Purn Shooting

(*by* Jonathan Miller)
J. Miller

---

[5]Unless otherwise indicated below, all material written by all four performers.
[6]Return engagement opened 15 December 1964 at the Ethel Barrymore Theatre for 30 performances; see separate entry in 1964-1965 season.
[7]Dropped during run.
[8]Replaced during the run by:

The Great Train Robbery
(*by* Peter Cook)
A. Bennett, P. Cook

Studio 5 (Interviews)
(*by* Peter Cook, Jonathan Miller)
A. Bennett, P. Cook, J. Miller
Sitting on the Bench
(*by* Peter Cook)
P. Cook
Men Only (Bread Alone)
A. Bennett, P. Cook, J. Miller, D. Moore
Take a Pew
(*by* Alan Bennett)
A. Bennett
"So That's the Way You Like It"
A. Bennett, P. Cook, J. Miller, D. Moore
The End of the World
(*by* Peter Cook)
A. Bennett, P. Cook, J. Miller, D. Moore

1962.23 BEYOND THE FRINGE '64

This revised edition opened 8 January 1964 as part of the show's continuous run. Jonathan Miller was succeeded by Paxton Whitehead.

ACT 1
Home Thoughts from Abroad
A. Bennett, P. Cook, P. Whitehead D. Moore
Royal Box
(*by* Peter Cook)
P. Cook, D. Moore, A. Bennett
"Man Bites God"
P. Whitehead, D. Moore
The English Way of Death
(*by* Alan Bennett)
A. Bennett
Bollard
(*by* Peter Cook)
A. Bennett, P. Cook, P. Whitehead D. Moore
A Piece of My Mind (The Heat Death of the Universe)
(*by* Jonathan Miller)
P. Whitehead
Song ("Little Miss Britten"/"Old Meg She Was a Gypsy"
by Dudley Moore)
D. Moore
The Philosophers
The Great Train Robbery
(*by* Peter Cook)
A. Bennett, P. Cook
Colonel Bogey
The Aftermyth of War
A. Bennett, P. Cook, P. Whitehead D. Moore

ACT 2
Civil War
A. Bennett, P. Cook, P. Whitehead D. Moore
Real Class
A. Bennett, P. Cook, P. Whitehead D. Moore
"Weill Song" (Ballad of Gangster Joe)
(*by* Dudley Moore and Peter Cook)
D. Moore, P. Whitehead
One Leg Too Few
(*by* Peter Cook)
P. Cook, D. Moore
Portraits from Memory
(*by* Jonathan Miller)P. Whitehead
The Death of (Lord) Nelson
(*by* Jonathan Miller)
P. Whitehead
The Scientist (Studio Five Interviews)
P. Cook, A. Bennett
The Doctor
The Duke/Lord Cobbold (Studio Five Interviews)
(*by* Peter Cook, A. Bennett, Jonathan Miller)
P. Cook, A. Bennett, P. Whitehead
The Miner (Sitting on the Bench revised)
(*by* Peter Cook)
P. Cook
The Restaurant
The Sermon (Take a Pew revised)
(*by* Alan Bennett)
So That's the Way You Like It
The End of the World
(*by* Peter Cook)
A. Bennett, P. Cook, P. Whitehead D. Moore

1962.24 NOWHERE TO GO BUT UP

A Musical Comedy in Two Acts, 19 Scenes. Book and lyrics by James Lipton. Music by Sol Berkowitz. Directed by Sidney Lumet. Settings by Peter Larkin. Costumes by Robert Fletcher. Choreography by Ronald [Ron] Field. Lighting by Tharon Musser. (Musical) Arrangements and orchestrations by Robert Ginzler. Vocal arrangements and musical direction by Herbert Greene. Produced by Kermit Bloomgarden and Herbert Greene with Steven H. Scheuer. Opened 10 November 1962 at the Winter Garden and closed 17 November 1962 after 9 performances.

CAST (in order of appearance):*Izzy Einstein*: TOM BOSLEY. *Moe Smith*: MARTIN BALSAM. *Anthony Baiello*: BRUCE GORDON. *Wilma Risque*: DOROTHY LOUDON. *Tommy Dee*: BERT CONVY. *Jean Morgan*: MARY ANN MOBLEY. *Hymie*: PHIL LEEDS. *Beggar*: Bob Avian. *Lady with Laundry*: Sally Ann Carlson. *Hop Wong*: PHIL LEEDS. *Hop Family*: Sally Lee, Jodi Kim Long, Bill Star, Eleanore Treiber. *Policeman*: Rico Froehlich. *Reporters*: H. F. Green, Val Avery, Art Wallace. *Woman with Poodle*: Eleonore Treiber. *Lupo*: FRANK CAMPANELLA. *The Gang*: Marty Allen, Bob Avian, Tod Jackson, Larry Merritt, Frank Pietri, Bill Starr, Gerald Teijelo, James Weiss, Blair Hammond, Michael Maurer. *Stage Manager*: Joel Craig. *La Vie Girls*: Nicole Barth, Sally Ann Carlson, Diane Coupé, Dorothy D'Honau, Lillian D'Honau, Maureen Hopkins, Jami Landi, Sally Lee, Sandra Roveta, Dean Taliaferro, Barbara Marcon, Eleanore Treiber. *Sally*: Sally Lee. *Policeman*: Val Avery. *Guard*: Don Rehg.

Act 1, Scene 1: A Cartoon. *Scene 2*: A Street. *Scene 3*: Hop Wong Laundry. *Scene 4*: A Speakeasy. *Scene 5*: A Street. *Scene 6*: Baiello's Office. *Scene 7*: Backstage Corridor, Club La Vie Est Gaie. *Scene 8*: La Vie Est Gaie. *Scene 9*: Exterior, La Vie Est gaie. *Scene 10*: Baiello's Office. *Scene 11*: Backstage Corridor. *Scene 12*: La Vie Est Gaie.

Act 2, Scene 1: La Vie Est Gaie. *Scene 2*: The La Vie Girls' Dressing Room. *Scene 3*: The Backstage Corridor. *Scene 4*: Exterior, La Vie Est Gaie. *Scene 5*: Baiello's Office. *Scene 6*: The Backstage Corridor, then the City. *Scene 7*: The Distillery.

ACT 1
Scene 2
"Ain't You Ashamed"
T. Bosley, M. Balsam
Scene 3
"The 'We Makin' Cash with Sour Mash, No Rickie-Tickie No Licq-ie' Rag"
P. Leeds
"The 'We Makin' Cash with Sour Mash, No Rickie-Tickie No Licq-ie' Rag" (reprise)
P. Leeds, S. Lee, J. K. Long, B. Starr, E. Treiber, T. Bosley, M. Balsam
Scene 4
"Live a Little"
D. Loudon, T. Bosley, M. Balsam, Company
Scene 6
"Yes, Mr. Baiello"
B. Gordon, The Gang
Dance
The Gang
Scene 7
"When a Fella Needs a Friend"
T. Bosley, M. Balsam, B. Convy, M. A. Mobley
Dance
T. Bosley, M. Balsam, B. Convy, M. A. Mobley
Scene 8
"The Odds and Ends of Love"
D. Loudon
"Nowhere To Go But Up"
D. Loudon, The La Vie Girls

Scene 10
"Take Me Back"
B. Gordon, M. A. Mobley
"Yes, Mr. Baiello" (reprise)
B. Gordon, The Gang
Scene 11
"I Love You for That"
D. Loudon, M. Balsam
Scene 12
"Nowhere To Go But Up" (reprise)
The La Vie Girls

ACT 2
Scene 1
"Baby, Baby"
M. Balsam, D. Loudon
Scene 2
"Natural Allies"
T. Bosley, The La Vie Girls
Scene 4
"Out of Sight, Out of Mind"
B. Convy
Scene 5
"Follow the Leader" Septet
B. Gordon, T. Bosley, M. Balsam, D. Loudon, M. A. Mobley, B. Convy, P. Leeds
Scene 6
"Dear Mom"
T. Bosley, M. Balsam
Responses
B. Gordon, F. Campanella, The Gang
Scene 7
"Nowhere to Go But Up" (reprise/Finale)
T. Bosley, M. Balsam, Company

1962.25 THE MIKADO, or The Town of Titipu

A Revival of the Comic Opera in Two Acts[9]. Libretto by William S. Gilbert. Music by Arthur Sullivan. Costumes designed by Charles Ricketts. Basic unit set for the full repertory designed by Peter Goffin. Director of productions, Herbert Newby. Dances arranged by John Reed. Musical director, Isidore Godfrey. Produced by the D'Oyly Carte Opera Company under the management of Sol Hurok. Opened 13 November 1962 at the New York City Center and closed 9 December 1962 after 10 performances in repertory.

CAST: *The Mikado of Japan*: DONALD ADAMS. *Nanki-Poo*, his son, disguised as a wandering minstrel in love with Yum-Yum: THOMAS ROUND. *Ko-Ko*, Lord High Executioner of Titipu: JOHN REED. *Pooh-Bah*, Lord High Everything Else: KENNETH SANDFORD. *Pish-Tush, Go-To*, Noble Lords: Jeffrey Skitch, George Cook. *Yum-Yum, Pitti-Sing, Peep-Bo*, three sisters, wards of Ko-Ko: JENNIFER TOYE, JOANNE MOORE, PEGGY ANN JONES. *Katisha*: GILLIAN KNIGHT. *Chorus of School Girls, Nobles, Guards and Coolies*: (uncredited).

1962.26 THE GONDOLIERS, or The King of Barataria

A Revival of the Comic Opera in Two Acts[10]. Libretto by William S. Gilbert. Music by Arthur Sullivan. Costumes designed by Charles Ricketts. Basic unit set for the full repertory designed by Peter Goffin. Director of productions, Herbert Newby. Dances arranged by John Reed. Musical director, Isidore Godfrey. Produced by the D'Oyly Carte Opera Company under the management of Sol Hurok. Opened 15 November 1962 at the New York City Center and closed 9 December 1962 after 5 performances in repertory.

CAST: *The Duke of Plaza-Toro*, a Grandee of Spain: JOHN REED. *Luiz*, his attendant: PHILIP POTTER. *Don Alhambra Del Bolero*, The Grand Inquisitor: KENNETH SANDFORD. *Marco Palmieri, Giuseppe Palmieri, Antonio, Francesco, Giorgio*, Venetian Gondoliers: THOMAS ROUND, ALAN STYLER, John Cartier, Joseph Riordan, Anthony Raffell. *Annibale*: John Cartier. *The Duchess of Plaza Del Toro*: GILLIAN KNIGHT. *Casilda*, Her Daughter: JENNIFER TOYE. *Gianetta, Tessa, Fiametta, Vittoria, Giulia*, Contadine: JEAN HINDMARSH, PEGGY ANN JONES, Mary Sansom, Joanne Moore, Anne Sessions. *Inez*, The King's Foster-Mother: Jeanette Roach. *Chorus of Gondoliers, Contadine, Men-at-Arms, Heralds and Pages*: (uncredited).

1962.27 LITTLE ME

A Musical Comedy in Two Acts, 35 Scenes. Book by Neil Simon. Based on the novel of the same name by Patrick Dennis. Music by Cy Coleman. Lyrics by Carolyn Leigh. Musical numbers and dances staged by Bob Fosse. Directed by Cy Feuer and Bob Fosse. Scenery and lighting by Robert Randolph. Costumes by Robert Fletcher. Orchestrations by Ralph Burns. Dance music arranged by Fred Werner. Vocal arrangements by Clay Warnick. Musical direction, Charles Sanford. Produced by Cy Feuer and Ernest H. Martin. Opened 17 November 1962 at the Lunt-Fontanne Theatre and closed 29 June 1963 after 257 performances.

CAST (in order of appearance): *Butler*: John Anania. *Patrick Dennis*: PETER TURGEON. *Miss Poitrine*, today: NANCY ANDREWS. *Momma*: ADNIA RICE. *Belle*: VIRGINIA MARTIN. *George Musgrove* as a boy: John Sharpe. *Brucey*: James Senn. *Ramona*: Else Olufsen. *Noble Eggleston*: SID CAESAR. *Mrs. Eggleston*: NANCY CUSHMAN. *Miss Kepplewhite*: Gretchen Cryer. *Pinchley, Junior*: MICKEY DEEMS. *Nurse*: Margery Beddow. *Mr. Pinchley*: SID CAESAR. *Kleeg*: Burt Bier. *Newsboy*: Michael Smuin. *Bernie Buchsbaum*: JOEY FAYE. *Bennie Buchsbaum*: MORT MARSHALL. *Defense Lawyer*: MICKEY DEEMS. *Val Du Val*: SID CAESAR. *George Musgrove*: SWEN SWENSON. *Fred Poitrine*: SID CAESAR. *Preacher*: Ken Ayers. *German Officer*: MICKEY DEEMS. *General*: Michael Quinn. *Courier*: Eddie Gasper. *Red Cross Nurse*: Sandra Stahl. *Steward*: David Gold. *Otto Schnitzler*: SID CAESAR. *Secretary*: Marcia Gilford. *Production Assistant*: MICKEY DEEMS. *Victor*: Marc Jordan. *Prince Cherney*: SID CAESAR. *Yulnick*: MICKEY DEEMS. *Baby*: VIRGINIA MARTIN. *Noble, Junior*: SID CAESAR.

Singers: Gretchen Cryer, Marcia Gilford, Else Olufsen, Sandra Stahl, Lory Stark, John Anania, Ken Ayers, Burt Bier, Harris Hawkins, Marc Jordan, Michael Quinn. *Dancers*: Barbara Beck, Margery Beddow, Reby Howells, Odette Phillips, Dounia Rathbone, Barbara Sharma, Renata Vaselle, Eddie Gasper, Gene Gavin, David Gold, James Kirby, John Sharpe, Michael Smuin, James Senn, Michel Stuart.

Act 1, Scene 1: Belle's estate in Southampton, Long Island. The present. *Scene 2*: The past. A tumbledown shack in Drifters' Row, Venezuela, Illinois. *Scene 3*: The Eggleston's elegant living room. *Scene 4*: Exterior of the Eggleston home. *Scene 5*: Belle's estate. (The present.) *Scene 6*: Interior of a small-town bank. (The past.) *Scene 7*: A golf course. (The present.) *Scene 8*: A hotel room in Peoria. (The past.) *Scene 9*: A prison. *Scene 10*: A courtroom in Chicago. *Scene 11*: (A Chicago stage.) *Scene 12*; The present. *Scene 13*: The Skylight Roof. Chicago. (The past.) *Scene 14*: The present. *Scene 15*: A small, gaily decorated apartment. (Chicago. The past.) *Scene 16*: (At the front and in Chicago.) *Scene 17*: A base hospital, somewhere in France.

Act 2, Scene 1: Belle's Estate. The present. *Scene 2*: On board the S.S. *Gigantic*, on the North Atlantic. (The past.) *Scene 3*: Belle's Estate. (The present.) *Scene 4*: Hollywood. (The past.) *Scene 5*: Belle in Hollywood. *Scene 6*: The office of the Buchsbaum Brothers. Hollywood. *Scene 7*: A biblical movie set. *Scene 8*: Belle's Estate. (The present.) *Scene 9*: The Casino in Monte Carlo. (The past.) *Scene 10*: (The present.) *Scene 11*: The royal bedchamber of Prince Cherny of Rosenzweig. (The past.) *Scene 12*: The Rumpus Room in Belle's Estate. The present. *Scene 13*: The Dakotas. (The past.) *Scene 14*: The Rumpus Room in Belle's Estate. (The present.) *Scene 15*: The exterior of the house, Belle's Estate. (The past.) *Scene 16*: Belle's Estate. (The present.) *Scene 17*: Belle's Estate. The present.

ACT 1[11]
Scene 1
"The Truth"
N. Andrews, P. Turgeon, Servants
Scene 2
"The Other Side of the Tracks"
V. Martin
"Birthday Party" (The Rich Kids' Rag)
Boys, Girls

[9]First presented in New York 20 July, 10-29 August 1885 at the Union Square and People's Theatres for 22 performances. First authorized production presented 19 August 1885 at the Fifth Avenue Theatre by Richard D'Oyly Carte for 250 performances. For Synopsis of Scenes and Musical Numbers, see 19 August 1885 D'Oyly Carte production.

[10]Originally presented in New York 7 January 1890 at Park Theatre for 103 performances. For Synopsis of Scenes and Musical Numbers, see original 1890 production.

[11]Description of scenes does not appear in programs; list prepared from published script.

Scene 3
"I Love You"
S. Caesar, V. Martin
Scene 4
"The Other Side of the Tracks" (reprise)
V. Martin
Scene 6
"Deep Down Inside"
S. Caesar, V. Martin, M. Deems, Poor People
Scene 9
"Be a Performer!"
M. Marshall, J. Faye
Scene 11
"(Oh! Dem Doggone) Dimples"
V. Martin, Police Escort (Chorus)
Scene 13
"Boom-Boom"
S. Caesar, Girls
"I've Got Your Number"
S. Swenson, V. Martin
Scene 15
"Real Live Girl"
S. Caesar
Scene 17
"Real Live Girl" (reprise)
The Doughboys (Men's Chorus)
"Boom-Boom" (reprise)
V. Martin, Howitzers
ACT 2
Scene 5
"Poor Little Hollywood Star"
V. Martin
Scene 6
("To Be a Performer" reprise)
(M. Marshall, J. Faye)
Scene 8
"Little Me"
N. Andrews, V. Martin
Scene 11
"The Prince's Farewell" (Goodbye)
S. Caesar, M. Deems, Loyal Subjects (Chorus)
Scene 14
"Here's To Us"
N. Andrews, Guests
Scene 17
Finale
S. Caesar, V. Martin

THE PIRATES OF PENZANCE, or The Slave of Duty

1962.28

A Revival of the Comic Opera in Two Acts[12]. Libretto by William S. Gilbert. Music by Arthur Sullivan. Costumes designed by Charles Ricketts. Basic unit set for the full repertory designed by Peter Goffin. Director of productions, Herbert Newby. Dances arranged by John Reed. Musical director, Isidore Godfrey. Produced by the D'Oyly Carte Opera Company under the management of Sol Hurok. Opened 20 November 1962 at the New York City Center and closed 9 December 1962 after 6 performances in repertory.

CAST: *Major General Stanley*: JOHN REED. *The Pirate King*: DONALD ADAMS. *Samuel*, his Lieutenant: Alan Styler. *Frederic*, the Pirate Apprentice: PHILIP POTTER. *Sergeant of Police*: GEORGE COOK. *Mabel, Edith, Kate, Isabel*, General Stanley's Daughters: JEAN HINDMARSH, MARY SANSOM, PEGGY ANN JONES, Pauline Wales. *Ruth*, Pirate Maid-of-all-work: GILLIAN KNIGHT. *Chorus of Pirates, Police and General Stanley's Daughters.*

[12]First presented in New York 31 December 1879 at the Fifth Avenue Theatre for a total of 91 performances in two engagements. For Synopsis of Scenes and Musical Numbers, see original 1879 production.

TRIAL BY JURY

1962.29

A Revival of the Comic Opera in One Act[13]. Libretto by William S. Gilbert. Music by Arthur Sullivan. Costumes designed by George Sheringham. Basic unit set for the full repertory designed by Peter Goffin. Director of productions, Herbert Newby. Dances arranged by John Reed. Musical director, Isidore Godfrey. Produced by the D'Oyly Carte Opera Company under the management of Sol Hurok. Opened 22 November 1962 at the New York City Center and closed 9 December 1962 after 7 performances in repertory.

CAST: *The Learned Judge*: JEFFREY SKITCH. *Counsel for the Plaintiff* ALAN STYLER. *The Defendant*: PHILIP POTTER. *Foreman of the Jury*: Peter Sugden *Usher*: GEORGE COOK. *Associate*: ALAN BARRETT. *The Plaintiff*: MARY SANSOM. *First Bridesmaid*: Dawn Bradshaw. *Chorus of Jurymen, Bridesmaids and Public*: (uncredited).

H.M.S. PINAFORE, or The Lass That Loved a Sailor

1962.30

A Revival of the Comic Opera in Two Acts[14]. Libretto by William S. Gilbert. Music by Arthur Sullivan. Costumes designed by Peter Goffin. Basic unit set for the full repertory designed by Peter Goffin. Director of productions, Herbert Newby. Dances arranged by John Reed. Musical director, Isidore Godfrey. Produced by the D'Oyly Carte Opera Company under the management of Sol Hurok. Opened 22 November 1962 at the New York City Center and closed 9 December 1962 after 7 performances in repertory.

CAST: *The Rt. Hon. Sir Joseph Porter, K.C.B.*, First Lord of the Admiralty: JOHN REED. *Captain Corcoran*, Commanding the *H.M.S. Pinafore*: JEFFREY SKITCH. *Ralph Rackstraw*, Able Seaman: THOMAS ROUND. *Dick Deadeye*, Able Seaman: DONALD ADAMS. *Bill Bobstay*, Bo'sun's Mate: George Cook. *Bob Beckett*, Carpenter's Mate: Anthony Raffell. *Josephine*, the Captain's Daughter: JEAN HINDMARSH. *Hebe*, Sir Joseph's First Cousin: Joanne Moore. *Little Buttercup*, a Portsmouth Bumboat Woman: GILLIAN KNIGHT. *First Lord's Sisters, his Cousins, his Aunts, Sailors, Marines*: (uncredited).

IOLANTHE, or The Peer and the Peri

1962.31

A Revival of the Comic Opera in Two Acts[15]. Libretto by William S. Gilbert. Music by Arthur Sullivan. (Costumes uncredited.) Basic unit set for the full repertory designed by Peter Goffin. Director of productions, Herbert Newby. Dances arranged by John Reed. Musical director, Isidore Godfrey. Produced by the D'Oyly Carte Opera Company under the management of Sol Hurok. Opened 27 November 1962 at the New York City Center and closed 9 December 1962 after 4 performances in repertory.

CAST: *The Lord Chancellor*: JOHN REED. *Earl of Mountararat*: DONALD ADAMS. *Earl Tolloller*: PHILIP POTTER. *Private Willis* of the Grenadier Guards: KENNETH SANDFORD. *Strephon*, an Arcadian Shepherd: JEFFREY SKITCH. *Queen of the Fairies*: GILLIAN KNIGHT. *Iolanthe*, a Fairy, Strephon's Mother: JOANNE MOORE. *Celia, Leila, Fleta*, Fairies: Jennifer Toye, Pauline Wales, Jacqueline Mitchell. *Phyllis*, an Arcadian Shepherdess and Ward in Chancery: MARY SANSOM. *Chorus of Dukes, Marquises, Earls, Viscounts, Barons and Fairies*: (uncredited).

[13]First presented in New York 15 November 1875 at the Eagle Theatre for 8 performances. For Synopsis of Scenes and Musical Numbers, see original 1875 production.
[14]Originally presented in New York 15 January 1879 at the Standard Theatre for 175 performances For Synopsis of Scenes and Musical Numbers, see original 1879 production.
[15]First presented in New York 25 November 1882 at the Standard Theatre for 105 performances. For Synopsis of Scenes and Musical Numbers, see original 1882 production.

1963.01 OLIVER!

A Musical in Two Acts, 12 Scenes. Book, music and lyrics by Lionel Bart. Freely adapted from the novel "Oliver Twist" by Charles Dickens. Directed by Peter Coe. (Scenery) Designed by Sean Kenny. Costumes by M. Berman Ltd. Lighting by John Wyckham. Orchestrations by Eric Rogers. Musical director, Don Pippin. Technical supervisor, Ian Albery. Produced by David Merrick and Donald Albery. Opened 6 January 1963 at the Imperial Theatre, moved 14 September 1964 to the Sam S. Shubert Theatre, and closed 14 November 1964 after 774 performances[16].

CAST: *Oliver Twist*: BRUCE PROCHNIK. *At the Workhouse*: *Mr. Bumble*, the Beadle: WILLOUGHBY GODDARD. *Mrs. Corney*, the Matron: HOPE JACKMAN. *Old Sally*, a pauper: Ruth Maynard. *At the Undertaker's*: *Mr. Sowerberry*, the Undertaker: BARRY HUMPHRIES. *Mrs. Sowerberry*, his wife: HELENA CARROLL. *Charlotte*, their daughter: Cherry Davis. *Noah Claypole*, their apprentice: Terry Lomax. *At the Thieves' Kitchen*: *Fagin*: CLIVE REVILL. *The Artful Dodger*: DAVID JONES. *Nancy*: GEORGIA BROWN. *Bet*: Alice Playten. *Bill Sykes*: DANNY SEWELL. *At the Brownlow's*: *Mr. Brownlow*: GEOFFREY LUMB. *Dr. Grimwig*: JOHN CALL. *Mrs. Bedwin*: Dortha Duckworth.

Workhouse Boys and Fagin's Gang: Johnny Borden, Eugene Endon, Bryant Fraser, Randy Gaynes, Bobby Gold, Sal Lombardo, Christopher Month, Patrick O'Shaughnessy, Alan Paul, Barry Pearl, George Priolo, Robbie Reed, Christopher Votos. *Londoners*: Jed Allan, Barbara Bossert, Jack Davison, James Glenn, Lesley Hunt, John M. Kimbro, Michael Lamont, Allan Lokos, Dodie Marshall, Richard Miller, Moose Peting, Ruth Ramsey, Nita Reiter, Ray Tudor, Maura K. Wedge.

The action takes place about 1850, in the North of England and London.

Act 1, Scene 1: The Workhouse. *Scene 2*: The Workhouse Parlor. *Scene 3*: The Undertaker's. *Scene 4*: Paddington Green. *Scene 5*: The Thieves' Kitchen. *Scene 6*: Streets of London.

Act 2, Scene 1: The "Three Cripples." *Scene 2*: The Brownlow's. *Scene 3*: The Thieves' Kitchen. *Scene 4*: The Workhouse. *Scene 5*: The Brownlow's. *Scene 6*: London Bridge.

ACT 1

"Food, Glorious Food"
The Boys

"Oliver!"
W. Goddard, H. Jackman, B. Prochnik, Boys

"I Shall Scream"
H. Jackman, W. Goddard

"Boy For Sale"
W. Goddard

"That's Your Funeral"
B. Humphries, W. Goddard, H. Carroll

"Where Is Love?"
B. Prochnik

"Consider Yourself"
D. Jones, B. Prochnik, Crowd

"You've Got To Pick a Pocket or Two"
C. Revill, B. Prochnik, Boys

"It's a Fine Life"
G. Brown, A. Playten

"I'd Do Anything"
D. Jones, G. Brown, B. Prochnik, A. Playten, C. Revill

"Be Back Soon"
C. Revill, D. Jones, B. Prochnik, Boys

ACT 2

"Oom-Pah-Pah"
G. Brown, Company

"My Name"
D. Sewell

"As Long as He Needs Me"
G. Brown

"Where Is Love?" (reprise)
D. Duckworth

"Who Will Buy?"
B. Prochnik, Chorus

"It's a Fine Life" (reprise)
D. Sewell, G. Brown, C. Revill, Boys

"Reviewing the Situation"
C. Revill

"Oliver!" (reprise)
W. Goddard, H. Jackman

"As Long As He Needs Me" (reprise)
G. Brown

"Reviewing the Situation" (reprise)
C. Revill

Finale: "Food, Glorious Food"/"Consider Yourself"/"I'd Do Anything"
Full Company

[16]Reopened a return engagement 2 August 1965 at the Martin Beck Theatre for 64 performances; see separate entry in 1964-65 season.

1963.02 MAURICE CHEVALIER

A One Man Show in Two Acts. (Sketches by Maurice Chevalier.) Decor and lighting by Raoul Pene Du Bois. Mr. Chevalier's clothes by Larsen in Paris. Produced by Alexander H. Cohen. Opened 28 January 1963 at the Ziegfeld Theatre and closed 23 February 1963 after 28 performances.

CAST: MAURICE CHEVALIER. *At the piano*: Fred Stamper.

MUSICAL NUMBERS AND SKETCHES[17]

"Thank Heaven for Little Girls" (from the film GIGI)
(*Music by* Frederick Loewe. *Lyrics by* Alan Jay Lerner.)

"Quai de Bercy"
(*Music and Lyrics by* Maurice Chevalier and Louis Poterat Alstone.)

"Le twist Canotier"
(*Music and Lyrics by* Noel Roux and Georges Garvarentz.)

"I Still See Elisa" (from PAINT YOUR WAGON)
(*Music by* Frederick Loewe. *Lyrics by* Alan Jay Lerner.)

"Place Pigalle"
(*Music and Lyrics by* Maurice Chevalier and Louis Poterat Alstone.)

George Gershwin Medley

Spectators
(*by* Maurice Chevalier)

"You Must Have Been a Beautiful Baby" (from film HARD TO GET)
(*Music by* Harry Warren. *Lyrics by* Johnny Mercer.)

"Some of These Days"
(*Music and Lyrics by* Shelton Brooks.)

"Contre l'amour y'a rien à faire"
(*Music and Lyrics by* Michel Rivgauche and Ma. Eva Wallis.)

"How to Handle a Woman" (from CAMELOT)
(*Music by* Frederick Loewe. *Lyrics by* Alan Jay Lerner.)

"Les chapeaux"
(*Music and Lyrics by* Jacques Mareuil and Fred Freed.)

"You Made Me Love You"
(*Music by* James V. Monaco. *Lyrics by* Joseph McCarthy.)

From Rag to Twist
(*by* Maurice Chevalier)

"Yankee Doodle Parisien"
(*Music and Lyrics by* George M. Cohan.)

"There's a Rainbow Round My Shoulder" (from the film THE SINGING FOOL)
(*Music and Lyrics by* Billy Rose, Dave Dreyer and Al Jolson.)

"Ah donnez m'en de la chanson"
(*Music and Lyrics by* Rene Rouzaud and Marguerite Monnot.)

"Louise" (from the film INNOCENTS OF PARIS)
(*Music by* Richard A. Whiting. *Lyrics by* Leo Robin.)

"I'm Glad I'm Not Young Anymore" (from the film GIGI)
(*Music by* Frederick Loewe. *Lyrics by* Alan Jay Lerner.)

"À Las Vegas"
(*Music and Lyrics by* Albert Willemetz and Louiguy)

Accents Melodiques
(*by* Maurice Chevalier)

CAN-CAN Medley
(*Music and Lyrics by* Cole Porter.)

[17]Program Note: These are the songs associated with Chevalier, most of which he will sing in the order that fits the mood and the music with one intermission.

"Mimi" (from the film LOVE ME TONIGHT)
(*Music by* Richard Rodgers. *Lyrics by* Lorenz Hart.)
"Valentine"
(*Music and Lyrics by* Albert Willemetz and Henri Christiné)
Stations of Life
(*by* Maurice Chevalier)
"La tête de roi"
(*Music and Lyrics by* Jean-Pierre Moulin.)

1963.03 THE HOLLOW CROWN

A Royal Revue in Two Acts, 32 Scenes. An entertainment by and about the Kings and Queens of England. Devised and staged by John Barton. Musical director, Brian Priestman. Produced by Bonard Productions (Helen G. Bonfils, Haila Stoddard, Donald R. Seawell) by arrangement with the Governors of the Royal Shakespeare Theatre, Stratford-on-Avon. Opened 29 January 1963 at Henry Miller's Theatre and closed 9 March 1963 after 46 performances.

CAST: MAX ADRIAN, DOROTHY TUTIN, JOHN BARTON, PAUL HARDWICK. *Musicians:* Richard Golding (bass), Stephen Manton (tenor), John Lawrenson (baritone), James Walker (piano and harpsichord).

ACT 1

KINGS ACCORDING TO LEGEND AND THE CHRONICLERS

Scene 1
Prologue: The Hollow Crown
(*by* William Shakespeare)M. Adrian

Scene 2
The Death of Kings (from Stow and the Anglo-Saxon Chronicles)
J. Barton
William I (1066-1087), William II (1087-1100), Henry I (1100-1135), Stephen (1135-1154).

Scene 3
An Anonymous Ballad Concerning Henry II and Queen Elinor (1154-1189)
M. Adrian

Scene 4
Sixteenth and Seventeenth Century Chroniclers (Holinshed, Hall, Baker and Churchill) on Henry II (1154-1189), Richard I (1189-1199), John (1199-1216), Henry III (1216-1272), Edward I (1272-1307), Edward II (1307-1327)
P. Hardwick

Scene 5
Ballade by Richard I made during his captivity in the Castle of Durrenstein
J. Lawrenson

Scene 6
From Froissart's Chronicles (Lord Berners):
Richard II (1377-1399) surrenders at Flint Castle to Henry IV (1399-1413) at that time Duke of Lancaster
J. Barton

Scene 7
'A Partial, Prejudiced and Ignorant Historian' (Jane Austen, aged fifteen) on:
Henry IV (1399-1413), Henry V (1413-1422), Henry VI (1422-1461), Edward IV (1461-1483), Edward V (1483), Richard III (1483-1485), Henry VII (1485-1509), Henry VIII (1509-1547), Edward VI (1547-1553), Mary I (1553-1558), Elizabeth I (1558-1603), James (1603-1625), Charles I (1625-1649).
D. Tutin

Scene 8
Henry V—"Agincourt Song"
S. Manton, J. Lawrenson, R. Golding

THE MONARCHS SPEAK FOR THEMSELVES

Scene 9
Diplomacy: Henry VII sends a secret memorandum to his Ambassadors concerning a proposed marriage between himself and the Queen of Naples, and they reply to it.
M. Adrian, J. Barton

Scene 10
The Queene's Command—
(*Music by* Orlando Gibbons)
J. Walker (harpsichord)

Scene 11
A Speech: Mary I denounces the rebellion of Sir Thomas Wyatt, raised in protest against her proposed marriage to Philip of Spain.
D. Tutin

Scene 12
Henry VIII—"The King's Hunt"
S. Manton, J. Lawrenson, R. Golding

Scene 13
Letters:
Henry VIII proposes to Anne Boleyn, a lady in waiting at his court.
P. Hardwick
Anne Boleyn writes to Henry from the Tower before her execution.
D. Tutin

Scene 14
Poems:
Henry VI: 'Kingdoms are but cares'
J. Barton
Henry VIII: 'As the Holly groweth green'
P. Hardwick
Elizabeth I complains of being importuned with love
D. Tutin
Charles II: 'I pass all my hours in a shady old grove'
M. Adrian

Scene 15
Charles II—"Here's a health unto His Majesty"
S. Manton, J. Lawrenson, R. Golding

ACT 2

THE STUARTS

Scene 1
A Reel by James I
(J. Walker)

Scene 2
James I (1603-1625) blows a 'Counterblast to Tobacco'
M. Adrian

Scene 3
Charles I (1625-1649) confronts John Bradshaw, President of the Court, at his trial for high treason and is condemned to death.
P. Hardwick, J. Barton

Scene 4
Ayre by Charles I
S. Manton

Scene 5
Charles II marries Catharine of Braganza—from a speech to Parliament and a letter to the Lord Chancellor.
M. Adrian, J. Barton

Scene 6
Charles II is anatomised by the Marquis of Halifax, one of his ministers.
J. Barton

Scene 7
"The Vicar of Bray" upholds the Protestant Succession: Charles II (1649-1685), James II (1685-1688), William and Mary (1689-1702), Anne (1702-1714), George I (1714-1727).
R. Golding, J. Lawrenson, S. Manton

THE ILLUSTRIOUS HOUSE OF WINDSOR

Scene 8
Queen Caroline: The death of George II's wife
(*by* Lord Hervey)
P. Hardwick

Scene 9

George II (1727-1760) is buried in Westminster Abbey
(*by* Horace Walpole)
M. Adrian

Scene 10

George III (1760-1820) discusses the Arts with the novelist and diarist Fanny Burney.
D. Tutin

Scene 11

Eulogy on George III and the House of Hanover (Dedicated to Her Majesty Queen Charlotte)

Scene 12

The Regency (1811-1820): The Madness of George III (Marianne Thornton to E. M. Forster)
D. Tutin

Scene 13

William IV (1830-1837) makes a good start. (The Greville Memoirs)
P. Hardwick

THE VICTORIAN AGE

Scene 14

"Ballad to an Absent Friend"
R. Golding or J. Lawrenson
(*Music by* Albert, Prince Consort,with words by his brother, Ernest)

Scene 15

Victoria (1837-1901) describes her Coronation at the age of nineteen (from her private journal).
D. Tutin

Scene 16

Variations on "God Save the King"
(*Music by* Beethoven)
J. Walker (piano)

Scene 17

Epilogue: from the 'Morte D'Arthur'
(*by* Sir Thomas Malory)
M. Adrian, P. Hardwick, J. Barton

1963.04

BRIGADOON

A Revival of the Musical Play in Two Acts, a Prologue and 11 Scenes[18]. Book and lyrics by Alan Jay Lerner. Music by Frederick Loewe. Dance and musical numbers by Agnes de Mille, assisted by James Jamieson. Directed by John Fearnley. Settings by Oliver Smith. Costumes by Stanley Simmons. Lighting by Peggy Clark. Conductor, Julius Rudel. Assistant conductor, Rene Wiegert (Vocal arrangements by Frederick Loewe. Orchestrations by Ted Royal.) Produced by the New York City Center Light Opera Company (Jean Dalrymple, Director). Opened 30 January 1963 at the New York City Center and closed 10 February 1963 after 15 performances.

CAST (in order of appearance): *Tommy Albright*: PETER PALMER. *Jeff Douglas*: RUSSELL NYPE. *Sandy Dean*: William Kennedy. *Meg Brockie*: ANN FRASER. *Archie Beaton*: John Carver. *Harry Beaton*: EDWARD VILLELLA. *Andrew MacLaren*: Frank Milan. *Fiona MacLaren*: SALLY ANN HOWES. *Jean MacLaren*: Virginia Bosler. *Angus MacGuffie*: Daniel Hannafin. *Charlie Dalrymple*: HARRY DAVID SNOW. *Maggie Anderson*: Jenny Workman. *Sword Dancers*: Frank Andre, Ben Gillespie, Loren Hightower, Art Hutchinson, Vernon Lusby, Charles McGraw, Paul Olson. *Mr. Lundie*: John C. Becher. *Bagpiper*: Maurice Eisenstadt. *Frank*: Felice Orlandi. *Jane Ashton*: Kelly Stevens.

Townsfolk of Brigadoon: *Singers*: Penny Gaston, Helen Guile, Betsy Hepburn, Marilyne Mason, Hanna Owen, Julie Sargent, Betty Jane Schwering, Jamie Thomas, Lynn Wendall, Robert Carle, Jerry Crawford, Harry W. Davis, James Fels, Marvin Goodis, William Kennedy, Robert Lenn, Herbert Surface, Ralph Vucci. *Dancers*: Virginia Allen, Lucia Lambert, Loi Leabo, Diana Lee Nielson, Mavis Ray, Dorothy Scott, Evelyn Taylor, Mona Jo Tritsch, Esther Villavicencio, Toodie Wittmer, Frank Andre, Robert Charles Bishop, Dennis Cole, Ben Gillespie, José Gutierrez, Loren Hightower, Art Hutchinson, Vernon Lusby, Charles McCraw, Paul Olson.

[18]Originally produced in New York 13 March 1947 at the Ziegfeld Theatre for 581 performances. For Synopsis of Scenes and Musical Numbers, see original 1947 production.

1963.05

WONDERFUL TOWN

A Revival of the Musical Comedy in Two Acts, 13 Scenes[19]. Book by Joseph Fields and Jerome Chodorov. Based on the play "My Sister Eileen" by Joseph Fields and Jerome Chodorov and the stories by Ruth McKinney. Music by Leonard Bernstein. Lyrics by Betty Comden and Adolph Green. Directed by Gus Schirmer. Musical numbers and dances staged by Ralph Beaumont. Sets by Raoul Pene du Bois. Costumes by Ruth Morley. Lighting by Peggy Clark. Musical conductor, Lehman Engel. Associate conductor, James Leon. (Orchestrations by Don Walker.) Produced by the New York City Center Light Opera Company (Jean Dalrymple, Director). Opened 13 February 1963 at the New York City Center and closed 24 February 1963 after 15 performances.

CAST (in order of appearance): *Guide*: Warren Galjour. *Appopoulos*: PHIL LEEDS. *Lonigan*: Walter Kelvin. *Helen*: PAT TURNER. *Wreck*: STEWART ROSE. *Violet*: Betty Hyatt Linton. *Valenti*: Ted Beniades. *Eileen*: JACQUELYN McKEEVER. *Ruth*: KAYE BALLARD. *A Strange Man*: Eric Barnes. *Drunks*: Steve Elmore, Eric Barnes. *Robert Baker*: ROBERT KAYE. *Associate Editors*: Reid Shelton, Warren Galjour. *Mrs. Wade*: Paula Trueman. *Frank Lippencott*: JIM KIRKWOOD. *Chef*: Taylor Reed. *Waiter*: Vito Durante. *Delivery Boy*: Will Mackenzie. *Chick Clark*: Gabriel Dell. *Shore Patrolman*: Stephen Elmore. *First Cadet*: Dom Salinaro. *Second Cadet*: Jose Ahumada. *Policemen*: Warren Galjour, Reid Shelton. *Ruth's Escort*: Reid Shelton.

Greenwich Villagers: *Singers*: Darrell Jay Askey, Eric Barnes, James E. Carville, Norma Donaldson, Steve Elmore, Lynne Ephron, Maria Graziano, Ginger L. McFadden, Will Mackenzie, Larry Mitchell, Judy Rawlings, Taylor Reed, Will Roy, Patricia Sigris, Elise Warner. *Dancers*: Jose Ahumada, Guy Allen, Gerard Brentte, Vito Durante, Mercedes Ellington, Shellie Farrell, Barbara Heath, Sally Kirk, Svetlana McLee, Eleanor Rogers, Nanette Rosen, Dom Salinaro, Marc Scott, Mark Taylor, Pat Trott, Aura Vainio, Doug Weese, James E. M. Weiss.

1963.06

OKLAHOMA!

A Revival of the Musical Comedy in Two Acts, 6 Scenes[20]. Book and lyrics by Oscar Hammerstein II. Music by Richard Rodgers. Based on the play "Green Grow the Lilacs" by Lynn Riggs. Directed by John Fearnley. (Originally directed by Rouben Mamoulian.) Dances by Agnes de Mille, assisted by Mavis Ray. Conducted by Julius Rudel. Assistant conductor, Rudolph Bennett. Settings by Lemuel Ayers. Costumes by Stanley Simmons. Lighting by Peggy Clark. Produced by the New York City Center Light Opera Company (Jean Dalrymple, Director). Opened 27 February 1963 at the New York City Center and closed 10 March 1963 after 15 performances; re-opened a return engagement 15-26 May 1963 at the New York City Center for 15 additional performances. Total: 30 performances.

CAST (in order of appearance): *Aunt Eller*: BETTY GARDE. *Curly*: PETER PALMER. *Laurey*: LOUISE O'BRIEN. *Will Parker*: RICHARD FRANCE. *Jud Fry*: DANIEL P. HANNAFIN. *Ado Annie Carnes*: FAY DE WITT. *Ali Hakim*: BARRY NEWMAN *Gertie Cummings*: Marilyne Mason. *Curly* (in ballet): GROVER DALE. *Laurey* (in ballet): EVELYN TAYLOR. *Jud* (in ballet): GEORGE CHURCH. *The Child* (in ballet): Judy Thelen. *The Girl Who Falls Down*: Mavis Ray. *Andrew Carnes*: WILLIAM TIERNEY. *Cord Elam*: KERMIT KEGLEY.

Dancers: Virginia Bosler, Lucia Lambert, Loi Leabo, Beatrice Lismore, Marlene Messavage, Susana Aschieri, Judy Thelen, Mona Jo Tritsch, Esther Villavicencio, Toodie Wittmer, Frank Andre, Paul Berne, Dennis Cole, Ben Gillespie, Loren Hightower, Vernon Lusby, Charles McGraw, Paul Olson. *Singers*: Faith Daltry, Penny Gaston, Helen Guile, Marilyne Mason, Hanna Owen, Julie Sargent, Sharon J. Vaughn, Christine Watson, Lynn Wendell, Robert Carle, Jerry Crawford, Harris W. Davis, James Fels, Marvin Goodis, William Kennedy, Robert Lenn, Herbert Surface, Ralph Vucci.

1963.07

JACK BENNY

A Variety Revue in Two Acts, 10 Scenes. Design and lighting by Sam Leve. Musical director, Mahlon Merrick. Producer (for Jack Benny), Irving Fein. Presented by Theatre Guild Productions, Inc. (Don Herbert). Opened 27 February 1963 at the Ziegfeld Theatre and closed 6 April 1963 after 52 performances.

[19]Originally produced in New York 25 February 1953 at the Winter Garden for 559 performances. For Synopsis of Scenes and Musical Numbers, see original 1953 production.

[20]Originally produced in New York 31 March 1943 at the St. James Theatre for 2212 performances. For Synopsis of Scenes and Musical Numbers, see original 1943 production.

CAST: JACK BENNY, JANE MORGAN, Toni Marcus, Clara Ward and the Ward Singers[21], the Half Brothers (Roberto and Al Halfss).

ACT 1

Scene 1

The Half Brothers (Juggling Act)

Scene 2

A Few Minutes With Jack Benny (Comedy)

Scene 3

A Few Songs with Jane Morgan ("Fascination," etc.)

Scene 4

Jane Morgan and Jack Benny

Scene 5

Clara Ward and the Ward Singers

ACT 2

Scene 1

Jack Benny Again

Scene 2

Jane Morgan Again

Scene 3

Buck Benny and the Waukegan Hillbillies with Toni Marcus

Scene 4

Jack Benny and Toni Marcus (Violinist)("Getting to Know You")

Scene 5

Jack Benny

1963.08 TOVARICH

A Musical Comedy in Two Acts, a Prologue and 14 Scenes. Book by David Shaw. Based on the play of the same name by Jacques Deval and its English adaptation by Robert E. Sherwood. Music by Lee Pockriss. Lyrics by Anne Croswell. Directed by Peter Glenville. Dances and musical numbers staged by Herbert Ross. Production designed by Rolf Gerard. Costumes by Motley. Lighting by John Harvey. Vocal arrangements and musical direction by Stanley Lebowsky. Orchestrations by Philip J. Lang. Dance music by Lee Pockriss. Additional dance music, Dorothea Freitag. Associate producer, Monty Shaff. Produced by Abel Farbman and Sylvia Harris in association with Joseph P. Harris. Opened 18 March 1963 at the Broadway Theatre, moved 10 June 1963 to the Majestic Theatre, moved 7 October 1963 to the Winter Garden, and closed 9 November 1963 after 264 performances.

CAST (in order of appearance): *Gorotchenko*: ALEXANDER SCOURBY. *Vassily*: Paul Michael. *Mikail*: JEAN PIERRE AUMONT. *Admiral Boris Soukhomine*: Michael Kermoyan. *Count Ivan Shamforoff*: Gene Varrone. *Baroness Roumel*: Katia Geleznova. *Marina*: Rita Metzger. *M. Chauffourier-Dubieff*: Don McHenry. *Tatiana*: VIVIEN LEIGH. *Natalia Mayovskaya*: LOUISE TROY. *Helen Davis*: MARGERY GRAY. *George Davis*: BYRON MITCHELL. *Charles Davis*: GEORGE S. IRVING. *Grace Davis*: LOUISE KIRTLAND. *Louise*: Maggie Task. *Ballet Master*: Tom Abbott. *Nadia*: Barbara Monte. *Mme. Van Hemert*: Pat [Patricia] Kelly. *Mme. Van Steuben*: Eleonore Treiber. *The Footman at the Davis Home*: Harald Horn. *Night Club Singer*: Dale Malone. *Kukla Katusha*: Bette Jenkins. *Ivan*: William Reilly. *Sergei*: Larry Roquemore. *Kukla's Friends*: Lorenzo Bianco, Antony De Vecchi, William Glassman. *A Footman at the Grand Ball*: Elliott Savage. *Baron General Rasumov*: Harald Horn. *Baroness Rasumov*: Michele Franchi. *Prince Dobrynin*: Antony De Vecchi. *Princess Dobrynin*: Marion Fels. *General Boruvsky*: Dale Malone. *Madame Boruvsky*: Eleonore Treiber. *Count Yuriev Neglinsky*: Tom Abbott. *Lady Soukhomine*: Joan Trona. *Maria Soukhomine*: Bettye Jenkins. *Count Rostoff*: Will Parkins. *Madame Muratova*: Carol Flemming. *Essaul of Cossacks Volinin*: Lorenzo Bianco. *Katrina Volinin*: Barbara Monte. *Elena Volinin*: Charlene Mehl. *Princess Mondrovska*: Pat Kelly. *Igor Mondovsky of the Imperial Corps of Cadets*: William Glassman. *Prince Ossipovsky*: Larry Roquemore. *Colonel Yarov*: William Reilly.

Singing Ensemble: Alice Evans, Pat Kelly, Rita Metzger, Maggie Task, Joan Trona, Del Horstmann, Barney Johnston, Jeff Killion, Dale Malone, Elliott Savage. *Dancing Ensemble*: Marion Fels, Carol Flemming, Michele Franchi, Katia Geleznova, Bette Jenkins, Charlene Mehl, Barbara Monte, Barbara Richman, Eleonore Treiber, Tom Abbott, Lorenzo Bianco, Antony De Vecchi, Harald Horn, William Glassman, Will Parkins, William Reilly, Larry Roquemore.

Prologue: Russia.

Act 1, Scene 1: Tsar Nicholas II's Room at the Palace of Tsarskoe Selo.*Scene 2*: A Garret in Paris, the late 1920s. *Scene 3*: A Corridor in the House of Mr. and Mrs. Davis, Paris. *Scene 4*: The Drawing Room of the Davis House. *Scene 5*: The Rehearsal Room in the Basement of the Kasbek Cafe, Paris. *Scene 6*: The Wintergarden in the Davis House. *Scene 7*: The Drawing Room.

Act 2, Scene 1: A Street Outside the Kasbek Cafe. *Scene 2*: The Club Room of the Kasbek Cafe. *Scene 3*: A Street Outside the Kasbek Cafe. *Scene 4*: The Drawing Room of the Davis House. *Scene 5*: A Street in Paris. *Scene 6*: The Kitchen of the Davis House. *Scene 7*: A Ballroom.

ACT 1

"Nitchevo"
J. P. Aumont, M. Kermoyan, G. Varrone,
R. Metzger, Singing and Dancing Ensembles

"I Go To Bed"
J. P. Aumont

"You'll Make an Elegant Butler (And I'll Make an Elegant Maid)"
V. Leigh
(*Music and Lyrics by* Joan Javits and Phillip Springer.)

"Stuck With Each Other"
M. Gray, B. Mitchell

"Say You'll Stay"
L. Kirtland, G. S. Irving

"You Love Me"
V. Leigh, J. P. Aumont

"Introduction Tango"
V. Leigh, M. Gray, J. P. Aumont, B. Mitchell

"That Face"
L. Troy

"Wilkes-Barre, P.A."
V. Leigh, B. Mitchell

"No! No! No!"
M. Gray, J. P. Aumont

"A Small Cartel"
L. Kirtland, G. S. Irving, Singing Ensemble

ACT 2

"It Used To Be"
M. Kermoyan, G. Varrone, L. Troy, P. Michael

"Kukla Katusha"
Dancing Ensemble

"Make a Friend"
V. Leigh, M. Gray, L. Troy, J. P. Aumont,
B. Mitchell, M. Kermoyan, G. Varrone, L. Roquemore, W. Reilly

"The Only One"
V. Leigh

"Uh-Oh!"
M. Gray, B. Mitchell

"Managed"
J. P. Aumont

"I Know the Feeling"
V. Leigh

"All for You"
V. Leigh, J. P. Aumont

"Grand Polonaise"
M. Gray, L. Kirtlnad, B. Mitchell, G. S. Irving, Dancing Ensemble

1963.09 MOTHER COURAGE AND HER CHILDREN

A Chronicle of the Thirty Years War (A Play with Songs) in Two Acts, a Prologue and 12 Scenes. Original (German) Play by Bertolt Brecht, adapted (into English) by Eric Bentley. Music by Paul Dessau. Directed by Jerome Robbins. Settings by Ming Cho Lee. Costumes designed by Motley. Lighting by Tharon Musser. Musical direction by Samuel Matlovsky. Produced by Cheryl Crawford and Jerome Robbins. Opened 28 March 1963 at the Martin Beck Theatre and closed 11 May 1963 after 52 performances.

CAST (in order of appearance): *Prologue*: *Mother Courage*: ANNE BANCROFT. *Kattrin*: ZOHRA LAMPERT. *Eilif*: Conrad Bromberg. *Swiss Cheese*: James Catusi. *Scene 1*: *Recruiting Officer*: John Randolph. *Protestant Sergeant*: Louis Guss. *Scene 2*: *Cook*: MIKE KELLIN. *Swedish Commander*: Eugene Roche. *Chaplain*: GENE

[21]Withdrew from production during the run.

WILDER. *Scene 3*: *Ordnance Officer*: Benjamin Hammer. *Yvette Pottier*: BARBARA HARRIS. *One Eye*: John Harkins. *Catholic Sergeant*: Bruce Glover. *Old Colonel*: Donald Hotton. *Scene 4*: *Regimental Clerk*: Harry Eno. *Older Soldier*: Benjamin Hammer. *Young Soldier*: Bruce Glover. *Scene 5*: *First Soldier*: Donald Hotton. *Second Soldier*: Eugene Roche. *Peasant*: John Randolph. *Peasant Woman*: Jane Hoffman. *Act 2, Scene 1*: *Old Woman*: Jane Hoffman. *Young Man*: Richard Morse. *First Soldier*: John Randolph. *Second Soldier*: Eugene Roche. *Scene 3*: *Girl Singer*: BARBARA HARRIS. *Scene 4*: *Lieutenant*: John Harkins. *First Soldier*: Bruce Glover. *Second Soldier*: Donald Hotton. *Third Soldier*: Dick Bradford. *Peasant Woman*: Jane Hoffman. *Peasant*: Louis Guss. *Young Peasant*: Harry Eno.

Act 1, Scene 1: Sweden, 1624. A Highway. *Scene 2*: Poland, 1626. An Officer's Tent. *Scene 3*: Poland, 1626. A Camp. *Scene 4*: Poland, 1629. An Officer's Tent. *Scene 5*: Saxony, 1631. A War-Ravaged Village. *Scene 6*: Bavaraia, 1632. Inside a Tent. *Scene 7*: The same.

Act 2, Scene 1: Alsace, 1632. A Camp. *Scene 2*: Fichtelgebirge, 1634. A Village. *Scene 3*: Fichtelgebirge, 1635. A Highway. *Scene 4*: Saxony, 1636. A Farm. *Scene 5*: Saxony, 1636. The Same Farm.

ACT 1

Scene 1

"Song of Mother Courage"
A. Bancroft

Scene 2

"Song of the Wise Woman and the Soldier"
C. Bromberg

Scene 3

"The Fraternization Song"
B. Harris

"The Song of the Hours"
G. Wilder

Scene 4

"Song of the Great Capitulation"
A. Bancroft

Scene 6

("Emperor Song"/Ballad of the Soldier)
(D. Hotton)

Scene 7

"Song of Mother Courage" (reprise)
A. Bancroft

ACT 2

Scene 1

("Song of Mother Courage" reprise)
(A. Bancroft)

Scene 2

"The Song of the Great Souls of the Earth"
M. Kellin

Scene 3

(Farm Song)
B. Harris

Scene 5

"Lullaby, Baby"
A. Bancroft

"Song of Mother Courage" (reprise)
A. Bancroft

1963.10 DANNY KAYE

A Variety Revue in Two Acts, 4 Scenes. Lighting by David Bines. Choral arrangements and musical direction by Johnny Mann. Girls' fashions by Mr. Mort. (Producer uncredited.) Opened 10 April 1963 at the Ziegfeld Theatre and closed 11 May 1963 after 39 performances.

CAST: DANNY KAYE, SENOR WENCES, THE DUNHILLS (Art Stanley, John Buwen, Jerry Kurland), THE MARQUIS FAMILY, THE JOHNNY MANN SINGERS (Gloria Gilbert, Pat Morling, Karen Wessler, Kelly Wood, Bill DeBell, John Guarnieri, David McDaniel, Tom Traynor, Dick Wessler, Ted Wills). At the piano, Sammy Prager. *At the drums*: Sidney Kaye.

ACT 1

Scene 1

The Dunhills (Dance Trio)

Scene 2

The Marquis Family (Monkey Act; Trainer, Gene Detroy)

Scene 3

Senor Wences (Ventriloquist)

ACT 2[22]

Danny Kaye (with the Johnny Mann Singers):

"Glory Hallelujah Twist"

"Minnie the Moocher"
(*Music and Lyrics by* Cab Calloway, Clarence Gaskill, Irving Mills.)

"I Took My Love to See 'Who's Afraid of Virginia Woolf?'" (Madrigal)

"Tschaikowsky" (from LADY IN THE DARK)
(*Music by* Kurt Weill. *Lyrics by* Ira Gershwin.)

"Dry Bones"

Yoga sketch

Maurice Chevalier impression

"Begin the Beguine" (from JUBILEE)
(*Music and Lyrics by* Cole Porter.)

Harry Lauder impression

Japanese Television Western

"Zoom"

Ludvig von Schtickfritz (Psychiatrist from Dusseldorf)

1963.11 MAN IN THE MOON

A Puppet Musical Entertainment in Two Acts, by Bil and Cora Baird's Marionette Theatre. Book by Arthur Burns. Based on a story by Bil Baird. Music by Jerry Bock. Lyrics by Sheldon Harnick. Directed by Gerald Freedman. (Musical) Arrangements by Alvy West. Produced by Arthur Cantor and Joseph P. Harris. Opened 11 April 1963 at the Biltmore Theatre and closed 21 April 1963 after 7 performances.

CAST: *Act 1*: *Prologue*: Frank Sullivan. *Jerry*: Franz Fazakas. *Flicker Martin*: Bil Baird. *Sleeves*: Michael King. *Skin*: Bob Brown. *Happy*: Faz Korabel. *Nose Nolan*: Frank Sullivan. *Fluffy*: Franz Fazakas. *Mondo*: Bil Baird. *Chandra*: Cora Baird. *The Man in the Moon*: Frank Sullivan. *Buz*: Waxey Gibbons. *The Giant*: Emil Maurer. *Assosrted Moonbirds, Hi-Behinds, Gollywhoppers*: Carl Harms, George Baird, Bob Brown, Mike King.

ACT 1

MAN IN THE MOON

"Look Where I Am"

"Itch to Be Rich"

"Worlds Apart"

"You Treacherous Men"

"Ain't You Never Been Afraid?"

ACT 2

A pageant of puppetry which will include various characters from Asia, Africa, Europe, and both Americas, to be accompanied by classical, folk, and popular music and during which the puppeteers will disclose some of the secrets of the world of marionettes.

1963.12 SOPHIE

A Musical in Two Acts, 20 Scenes. Book by Phillip Bruneau. Based on the life of Sophie Tucker. Music and Lyrics by Steve Allen. Directed by Jack Sydow. Dances and musical numbers staged by Donald Saddler. Settings and lighting by Robert Randolph. Costumes by Fred Voelpel. Musical direction and vocal arrangements by Liza Redfield. (Musical) Arrangements and orchestrations by Sid Ramin and Arthur Beck. Dance music arrangements by Genevieve Pitot. Produced by Len Bedsow and Hal Grossman in association with Michael Pollock and Max Fialkov. Opened 15 April 1963 at the Winter Garden and closed 20 April 1963 after 8 performances.

---

[22]Inasmuch as Danny Kaye's material was not listed in the program, the above list is not in performance order and was prepared from reviews.

CAST (in order of appearance): *Sophie Tucker*: LIBI STAIGER. *Moe*: Douglas Clarke. *Mama*: BERTA GERSTEN. *William Morris*: PHIL LEEDS. *Theona*: Diana Hunter. *Mrs. Quive*: Urylee Leonardos. *Schmidt*: Don Crabtree. *Policemen*: Nat Horne, Ralph McWilliams. *Chris Brown*: TED THURSTON. *Stage Manager*: John Drew. *Girl*: Bella Shalom. *Mother*: Janet Gaylord. *Acrobat*: Tim Harum. *Sylvain Krouse*: PATSI KING. *Stagehand*: Jordan Bowers. *Juggler*: Stuart Hodes. *Mollie*: ROSETTA LeNOIRE. *Marcus Loew*: DAVID THOMAS. *Mickey Muldoon*: EDDIE ROLL. *Harry Emerson*: DAVID THOMAS. *Frank Westphal*: ART LUND. *Queenie*: Maralyn Thoma. *Julian Mitchell*: TED THURSTON. *Sandy*: Richard Hermany. *Nora Bayes*: Betty Colby. *Stella*: Diana Hunter. *Mr. Kilby*: DAVID THOMAS. *Reporters*: Don Crabtree, John Drew, Richard Hermany. *Theatre Manager*: TED THURSTON. *Ted*: Michael Nestor. *Metropole Manager*: DAVID THOMAS.

Ensemble: Jordan Bowers, Carol Carlin, Douglas Clarke, Betty Colby, John Drew, Louise Ferrand, Janet Gaylord, Ellen Graff, Tim Harum, Florence Hayle, Richard Hermany, Stuart Hodes, Nat Horne, Diana Hunter, Urylee Leonardos, Ralph McWilliams, Michael Nestor, Kelli Scott, Beti Seay, Bella Shalom, Maralyn Thoma, Elizabeth Wullen.

The action of the play covers the early years of Sophie Tucker's preofessional life.

Act 1, Scene 1: Sophie Tucker Tonight. *Scene 2*: The Family Restaurant in Hartford. *Scene 3*: Sophie in New York. *Scene 4*: Backstage 125th Street Theatre. *Scene 5*: Theatre Alley. *Scene 6*: Third Avenue "El." *Scene 7*: A Street. *Scene 8*: Gaiety Burlesque Theatre. *Scene 9*: Sophie Trouping. *Scene 10*: Backstage Ziegfeld Follies.

Act 2, Scene 1: Roof of a Theatrical Hotel. *Scene 2*: Frank's Dressing Room. *Scene 3*: Sophie's Dressing Room. *Scene 4*: Freeport Variety Club. *Scene 5*: Hartford Railroad Station. *Scene 6*: Dressing Rooms and On Stage. *Scene 7*: Freeport Variety Club. *Scene 8*: Dockside. *Scene 9*: Dressing Room in London. *Scene 10*: Cafe Metropole, London.

ACT 1
"Red Hot Mama"
L. Staiger
"Sunshine Face"
L. Staiger
"Mr. Henry Jones"
L. Staiger
"Sophie in New York"
L. Staiger, Company
"Patsy"
R. LeNoire
"I'll Show Them All"
L. Staiger
"I'll Show Them All" (reprise)
L. Staiger
"Hold Onto Your Hats"
P. Leeds, R. LeNoire
"Fast Cars and Fightin' Women"
A. Lund
"Queen of the Burlesque Wheel"
P. King, Ensemble
"When You Carry Your Own Suitcase"
L. Staiger, E. Roll, Ensemble
"When You Carry Your Own Suitcase" (reprise)
A. Lund
"When I'm in Love"
L. Staiger, R. LeNoire
"Sailors of the Sea"
Ensemble
"I Want the Kind of a Fella"
L. Staiger
"I'll Show Them All" (reprise)
L. Staiger

ACT 2
"Who Are We Kidding"
E. Roll, P. King
"Don't Look Back"
Entire Company
"I'd Know It"
A. Lund
"You've Got to Be a Lady"
R. LeNoire
"Ragtime"
Ensemble
"Waltz"
L. Staiger, A. Lund, Ensemble
"When I'm in Love" (reprise)
A. Lund
"I Love You Today"
L. Staiger, A. Lund
"With You"
L. Staiger
"Red Hot Mama" (reprise)
L. Staiger
"I've Got 'Em Standin' in Line"
L. Staiger
"They've Got a Lot to Learn"
A. Lund
"Red Hot Mama" (reprise)
L. Staiger

1963.13

HOT SPOT

A Musical Comedy in Two Acts, 24 Scenes. Book by Jack Weinstock and Willie Gilbert. Music by Mary Rodgers. Lyrics by Martin Charnin. Scenery and costumes by Rouben Ter-Arutunian. Lighting by John Harvey. Musical director, Milton Rosenstock. Dance music and vocal arrangements by Trude Rittman and John Morris. (Musical) Arrangements and orchestrations by Luther Henderson and Ralph Burns. Produced by Robert Fryer and Lawrence Carr with John Herman. Opened 19 April 1963 at the Majestic Theatre and closed 25 May 1963 after 43 performances[23].

CAST (in order of appearance): *Anderson*: James Cresson. *Henderson*: Charles Braswell. *Sally Hopwinder*: JUDY HOLLIDAY. *George Higgins*: Conrad Bain. *The Peace Corps (3)*: *Sue Ann*: MARY LOUISE WILSON. *Howard Mason*: Bob McClure. *Vernon Breen*: James Moore. *Harley*, the pilot: George Furth. *Duke*, the co-pilot: James Cresson. *The D'humians (4)*: *Nadir of D'hum*: ARNY FREEMAN. *Shim*: JOSEPH BOVA. *Ministers of State*: Jack Dabdoub, Howard Kahl. *Deva*: Jack Eddleman. *Iram and Rami*: Carmen DeLavallade, Buzz Miller. *Gabriel Snapper*: JOSEPH CAMPANELLA. *Sumner Tubb, Sr.*: HOWARD FREEMAN. *Mrs. Sumner Tubb*: Virginia Craig. *Sumner Tubb, Jr.*: George Furth. *Allison Kent*: Sheila Smith. *Grobanykov*: Gerald Teijelo. *Pulski*: Buzz Miller.

Singers and Dancers: Sandra Devlin, Jill Bartholomew, Virginia Craig, Audre Johnston, Virginia Oswald, John Herbert, Diane Ede, Gloria Mills, Diane Coupe, Dean Taliaferro, Gildo DiNunzio, Marty Allen, Rhett Dennis, David Bean, Jim McArdle, Doria Avila, Bill Richards, Alvin Beam, Jamie Landi, Lee Hopper, Mary Sue Berry, Marnell Bruce, John Cunningham, Frank Bouley.

Act 1, Scene 1: The 6:45 Report. *Scene 2*: Peace Corps Headquarters. *Scene 3*: national Airport. *Scene 4*: In the air over D'hum. *Scene 5*: The D'hum Airstrip. *Scene 6*: The American Consulate in D'hum. *Scene 7*: The Market Place. *Scene 8*: The Clinic. *Scene 9*: The D'hum Airstrip. *Scene 10*: The Palace. *Scene 11*: The 6:45 Report. *Scene 12*: A Beauty Salon in Washington. *Scene 13*: All of D'hum.

Act 2, Scene 1: Exterior of Yakacabana. *Scene 2*: Interior of Yakacabana. *Scene 3*: Moscow. *Scene 4*: A Street in D'hum. *Scene 5*: The back room of the Clinic. *Scene 6*: Snapper's Apartment at the Consulate. *Scene 7*: Outside the Yakacabana. *Scene 8*: The Yakacabana. *Scene 9*: The 6:45 Report. *Scene 10*: The Consulate Yard. *Scene 11*: Peace Corps Headquarters.

ACT 1
"Don't Laugh"
J. Holliday
(*Music by* Mary Rodgers and Stephen Sondheim. *Lyrics by* Martin Charnin and Stephen Sondheim.)
"Don't Laugh" (reprise)
J. Holliday, Peace Corps
"Welcome"
D'humians
Welcome Dance
C. DeLavallade, J. Moore, B. Miller
"This Little Yankee"
J. Campanella

---

[23]Direction and choreography uncredited at time of the opening; Morton DaCosta and Onna White withdrew as director and choreographer prior to opening.

"Smiles"
J. Holliday, J. Eddleman, J. Cunningham, H. Kahl, B. McClure, J. Herbert, D. Bean, A. Beam, B. Miller
"A Little Trouble"
J. Holliday, J. Bova, A. Freeman, D'humians
"You'd Like Nebraska"
J. Moore, C. DeLavallade
"Hey, Love"
J. Holliday
"I Had Two Dregs"
J. Holliday, J. Bova, H. Freeman, D'humians
"Rich, Rich, Rich"
J. Bova, M. L. Wilson, Peace Corps, D'humians

ACT 2
"That's Good—That's Bad"
J. Holliday
Iram and the Royal D'humian Dancers
C. DeLavallade, (Dancers)
"I Think the World of You"
M. L. Wilson, J. Bova
"Gabie"
J. Holliday
"A Matter of Time"
J. Campanella, J. Holliday
"Gabie" (reprise)
J. Campanella
"Big Meeting Tonight"
B. Miller, G. Teijelo, Ensemble
Russian Dance at the Yakacabana
J. Holliday, B. Miller, G. Teijelo
"A Far, Far Better Way"
J. Holliday
"Don't Laugh" (reprise)
J. Holliday, J. Campanella, Ensemble

1963.14 SHE LOVES ME

A Musical Comedy in Two Acts. Book by Joe Masteroff. Based on the play "Parfumerie" by Miklos Laszlo[24]. Music by Jerry Bock. Lyrics by Sheldon Harnick. Musical numbers Staged by Carol Haney. Directed by Harold Prince. Settings and lighting by William and Jean Eckart. Costumes by Patricia Zipprodt. Musical direction by Harold Hastings. Orchestrations by Don Walker. Incidental music arranged by Jack Elliott. Produced by Harold Prince in association with Lawrence Kasha and Philip C. McKenna. Opened 23 April 1963 at the Eugene O'Neill Theatre and closed 11 January 1964 after 301 performances.

CAST (in order of appearance): *Arpad*: RALPH WILLIAMS. *Mr. Sipos*: NATHANIEL FREY. *Miss Ritter*: BARBARA BAXLEY. *Mr. Kodaly*: JACK CASSIDY. *Georg Nowack*: DANIEL MASSEY. *Mr. Maraczek*: LUDWIG DONATH. *Window Shoppers*: Jety Herlick, Judy West. *First Customer*: Marion Delano. *Second Customer*: Peg Murray. *Third Customer*: Trude Adams. *Amalia Balash*: BARBARA COOK. *Fourth Customer*: Judy West. *Fifth Customer*: Jety Herlick. *Sixth Customer*: Vicki Mansfield. *Mr. Keller*: Gino Conforti. *Waiter*: Wood Romoff. *Busboy*: Al De Sio. *Violinist*: Gino Conforti. *Viktor*: Pepe De Chazza. *Stefanie*: Vicki Mansfield. *Magda*: Judy West. *Ferencz*: Bob Bishop. *Couple*: Peg Murray, Joe Ross. *Nurse*: Jety Herlick. *Carolers*: Jo Wilder, Joe Ross, Gino Conforti. *Paul*: Les Martin.

The action takes place in a city in Europe in the 1930s (inside and outside Maraczek's Parfumerie, the Cafe Imperiale, a hospital room and Miss Balash's apartment).

ACT 1
"Good Morning, Good Day"
R. Williams, N. Frey, B. Baxley, J. Cassidy, D. Massey
"Sounds While Selling"
D. Massey, N. Frey, J. Cassidy, M. Delano, P. Murray, T. Adams
"Thank You, Madam"
N. Frey, D. Massey, J. Cassidy, B. Baxley, M. Delano, P. Murray
"Days Gone By"
L. Donath
"No More Candy"
B. Cook
"Three Letters"
B. Cook, D. Massey
"Tonight at Eight"
D. Massey
"I Don't Know His Name"
B. Cook, B. Baxley
"Perspective"
N. Frey
"Goodbye Georg"
D. Massey, B. Baxley, N. Frey, J. Cassidy, R. Williams, Customers
"Will He Like Me?"
B. Cook
"Ilona"
J. Cassidy
"I Resolve"
B. Baxley
"A Romantic Atmosphere"
W. Romoff, A. DeSio, G. Conforti, P. Murray, J. Ross, V. Mansfield, P. DeChazza, J. West, B. Bishop
"Tango Tragique"
D. Massey
"Dear Friend"
B. Cook

ACT 2
"Try Me"
R. Williams
"Days Gone By" (reprise)
L. Donath
"Where's My Shoe?"
B. Cook, D. Massey
"(Vanilla) Ice Cream"
B. Cook
"She Loves Me"
D. Massey
"A Trip to the Library"
B. Baxley
"Grand Knowing You"
J. Cassidy
"Twelve Days to Christmas"
J. West, G. Conforti, J. Ross, Company
"Ice Cream" (reprise){Finale}
B. Cook, D. Massey

1963.15 STREET SCENE

A Revival of the American Opera (Dramatic Musical) in Two Acts, 3 Scenes[25]. Book by Elmer Rice from his play of the same name. Music by Kurt Weill. Lyrics by Langston Hughes. Staged by Herbert Machiz. Conducted by Skitch Henderson. Scenery and costumes by Paul Sylbert. Choreographed by Sondra Lee and Richard Tone. Chorus master, William Jonson. (Orchestrations by Kurt Weill.) Produced by the New York City Opera. Opened 26 April 1963 at the New York City Center and closed 10 May 1963 after 3 performances in repertory.

CAST (in order of appearance): *Abraham Kaplan*: Howard Fried. *Greta Fiorentino*: Dolores Mari. *Carl Olsen*: Arnold Voketaitis. *Emma Jones*: RUTH KOBART. *Olga Olsen*: Muriel Greenspon. *Shirley Kaplan*: Florence Anglin. *Henry Davis*: Andrew Frierson. *Willie Maurrant*: Robert Buckley. *Anna Maurrant*: ELISABETH CARRON. *Sam Kaplan*: William DuPree. *Daniel Buchanan*: L. D. Clements. *Frank Maurrant*: ROBERT TREHY. *George Jones*: Richard Wentworth. *Steve Sankey*: Richard Armbruster. *Lippo Fiorentino*: JACK HARROLD. *Jennie Hildebrand*: Barbara Maier. *Second Graduate*: Anthea DeForest. *Third Graduate*: Marilyn Mason. *Mrs. Hildebrand*: Anita Lynch. *Charlie Hildebrand*: Charles Cash. *Mary Hildebrand*: Neva Small. *Grace Davis*: Andrea Frierson. *Rose Maurrant*: JOY CLEMENTS. *Harry Easter*: John Reardon. *Mae Jones*: Sondra Lee. *Dick McGann*: Richard Tone. *Vincent Jones*: Albert

[24]Elsewhere known as"The Honest Finder" by Aladar Laszlo.

[25]Originally produced in New York 9 January 1947 at the Adelphi Theatre for 148 performances. For Synopsis of Scenes and Musical Numbers, see original 1947 production.

Lewis. *Dr. John Wilson*: Glenn Dowlen. *Officer Harry Murphy*: David Smith. *City Marshall James Henry*: Arthur Graham. *Fred Cullen*: Don Yule. *First Nursemaid*: Helen Guile. *Second Nursemaid*: Lou Ann Wyckoff. *Policemen, Milkman, Old Clothes Man, Music Pupil, Interne, Ambulance Driver, Married Couple, Passersby, Neighbors, Children, etc.*: New York City Opera Chorus.

1963.16 THE BEAST IN ME

A Musical Revue in Two Acts, 11 Scenes. Book and lyrics by James Costigan. Based on the book "Fables for Our Time" by James Thurber. Music by Don Elliott. Conceived by Haila Stoddard. Directed by John Lehne. Musical staging by John Butler. Settings and lighting by Jean Rosenthal. Costumes by Leo Van Witsen. Orchestrations by Bill Byers. Dance arrangements by Judd Woldin. Musical director, Don Elliott. Conductor, Lehman Engel. Produced by Bonard Productions (Helen G. Bonfils, Haila Stoddard, Donald R. Seawell). Opened 16 May 1963 at the Plymouth Theatre and closed 18 May 1963 after 4 performances.

CAST: KAYE BALLARD, ALLYN ANN McLERIE, RICHARD HAYES, BERT CONVY, NANCY HAYWOOD, JAMES COSTIGAN, DON ELLIOTT and His Orchestra.

ACT 1

Scene 1

There's a Beast in Everybody
Entire Company

Scene 2

The Sea and the Shore
Gibbous Female: K. Ballard. *Gibbous Male*: R. Hayes.

Scene 3

The Lover and His Lass
Mrs. Hippo: K. Ballard. *Hippo*: R. Hayes. *Mrs. Parrot*: .A. A. McLerie. *Parrot*: B. Convy. *Girl*: N. Haywood.

Scene 4

The Lady of the Legs
Tourist: R. Hayes. *Frog*: A. A. McLerie. *Restauranteur*: J. Costigan.

Scene 5

Tea for One
Bride: K. Ballard. *Groom*: R. Hayes.

Scene 6

The Wolf Who Went Places
Professor: R. Hayes. *Wolf*: B. Convy. *Wolfess*: A. A. McLerie.

Scene 7

The Unicorn in the Garden
Man: J. Costigan. *Wife*: K. Ballard. *Dr. Clisbie*: R. Hayes. *Policeman*: B. Convy. *Nymphs*: A. A. McLerie, N. Haywood.

ACT 2

Scene 1

The Foolhardy Mouse and the Cautious Cat
Pouncetta: A. A. McLerie. *Mervyn*: J. Costigan. *Ring Leader*: R. Hayes. *The Gang*: K. Ballard, N. Haywood, B. Convy.

Scene 2

A Moment With Mandy
Mandy: K. Ballard. *Daddy*: B. Convy.

Scene 3

The Moth and the Star
Old Moth: J. Costigan. *Mother Moth*: A. A. McLerie. *Father Moth*: R. Hayes.

Scene 4

The Stork Who Married a Dumb Wife
Cigarette Girl: A. A. McLerie. *Spouse*: K. Ballard. *Stork*: R. Hayes. *The Girl*: N. Haywood. *Mysterious Stranger*: B. Convy. *Waiter*: J. Costigan.

Scene 5

The Shore and the Sea
Evangelist: K. Ballard. *Scholarly Lemming*: J. Costigan. *Congregation*: A. A. McLerie, N. Haywood, R. Hayes, B. Convy.

ACT 1

"Percussion"
"So Beautiful"
"You're Delicious"
"J'Ai"
"I Owe Ohio"
"Go, Go, Go!"
"Breakfast"
"Eat Your Nice Lily, Unicorn"
"Bacchanale"

ACT 2

"Calypso Kitty"
"Glorious Cheese"
"Why?"
"What Do You Say"
"When I'm Alone"
"Hallelujah"

1963.17 PAL JOEY

A Revival of the Musical Play in Two Acts, 12 Scenes[26]. Book by John O'Hara based on his collected short stories of the same name. Music by Richard Rodgers. Lyrics by Lorenz Hart. Settings by Howard Bay. Costumes by Frank Thompson. Lighting by Peggy Clark. Musical director and conductor, Pembroke Davenport. (Orchestrations by Don Walker, Hans Spialek.) Choreography by George and Ethel Martin. Directed by Gus Schirmer. Produced by the New York City Center Light Opera Company (Jean Dalrymple, Director). Opened 29 May 1963 at the New York City Center and closed 9 June 1963 after 15 performances.

CAST (in order of appearance): *Mike*: ART BARNETT. *Joey Evans*: BOB FOSSE. *Kid*: Pat Turner. *Gladys*: ELAINE DUNN. *Iris*: Dorothy D'Honau. *Mickey*: Carol Kroon. *Diane*: Dorothy Dushock. *Dottie*: Shellie Farrell. *Sandra*: Mercedes Ellington. *Adele*: Jan LaPrade. *Francine*: Marilyn D'Honau. *Linda English*: RITA GARDNER. *Vera Simpson*: VIVECA LINDFORS. *Valerie*: Betty Hyatt Linton. *Ernest*: Emory Bass. *Vera's Escort*: John Coyle. *Victor*: Charles Basile. *Scholtz*: George Zima. *Louis*, the Tenor: John Lankston. *Melba Snyder*: KAY MEDFORD. *Ludlow Lowell*: JACK DURANT. *Lester*: Lester Wilson. *O'Brien*: George Church. *Mr. Hoople*: John D. Seymour.

Dancers: Nancy Baron, Carol Carlin, Sheila Cass, Dorothy D'Honau, Marilyn D'Honau, Dorothy Dushock, Mercedes Ellington, Shellie Farrell, Judith Haskell, Carole Kroon, Jan LaPrade, Sigyn Lund, Carmen Morales, Barbara Richman, Patricia Sigris, Babs Warden. Alan Castner, Gerard Brentte, John Coyle, Larry Davids, Hamp Dickens, Jim Hovis, Danny Jasinski, David M. Lober, Paul Reid Roman, Bentley Roton, Roy Smith, George Zima.

[26]Originally produced in New York 25 December 1940 at the Ethel Barrymore Theatre for 374 performances. For Synopsis of Scenes and Musical Numbers, see original 1940 production. "What Is a Man" succeeded "Love Is My Friend" in Act 1, Scene 4; "Pal Joey" ("What Do I Care for a Dame?" sung by B. Fosse as Joey) added to Scene 6 after "Bewitched." "Joey's Class Act" (danced by B. Fosse and L. Wilson) added to Act 2, Scene 4 between "Take Him" and the reprise of "Bewitched."

1963–1964 SEASON

Robert Horton and Inge Swenson in 110 IN THE SHADE (Photo: Friedman-Abeles)
Billy Rose Theatre Collection, New York Public Library for the Performing Arts

1963–1964 SEASON

1963.18 THE KING AND I

A Revival of the Musical Play in Two Acts, 17 Scenes[1]. Book and lyrics by Oscar Hammerstein II. Music by Richard Rodgers. Based on the novel "Anna and the King of Siam" by Margaret Landon. Settings by Jo Mielziner. Costumes by Irene Sharaff, supervised by Stanley Simmons. Lighting by Peggy Clark. Choreography by Jerome Robbins, reproduced by Yuriko. Orchestrations by Robert Russell Bennett. Musical director and conductor, Pembroke Davenport. Directed by John Fearnley. Produced by the New York City Center Light Opera Company (Jean Dalrymple, Director). Opened 12 June 1963 at the New York City Center and closed 23 June 1963 after 15 performances.

CAST (in order of appearance): *Captain Orton*: Sam Kirkham. *Louis Leonowens*: Tommy Leap. *Anna Leonowens*: EILEEN BRENNAN. *The Interpreter*: Paul Flores. *The Kralahome*: Ken LeRoy. *The King*: MANOLO FABREGAS. *Phra Alack*: John Garces. *Lun Tha*: L. D. CLEMENTS. *Tuptim*: JOY CLEMENTS. *Lady Thiang*: ANITA DARIAN. *Prince Chulalongkorn*: Ramon Caballero. *Princess Ying Yaowalak*: Lisa Jo Abe. *Sir Edward Ramsay*: John D. Seymour.

The Small House of Uncle Thomas: *Narrator*: JOY CLEMENTS. *Uncle Thomas*: Bettina Dearborn. *Little Eva*: Susan L. Kikuchi. *Topsy*: Paula Chin. *Eliza*: YURIKO. *King Simon*: Linda Hodes. *Angel*: Marion Jim. *Drummer*: Jim E. McMillan. *Buddha*: Lisa Jo Abe.

Princes and Princesses: David Aguilar, Paul Chin, Delfino DeArco, Capri Hermany, Roma Hermany, Vivian Hernandez, Lawrence Kikuchi, Susan I. Kikuchio, Peter Martinez, Ado Sato, Ramon Torres. *The Royal Dancers*: Susan Ascheri, Hadassah Badoch, Mavis Ray Booth, Noemi Chiesa, Miriam Cole, Barbara Creed, Victor Duntiere, Carol Fried, Phyllis A. Gutelius, Edith Jerell, Marion Jim, Loi Leabo, Paul E. Olson, Clive Thompson. *Singers (Wives, Priests, Amazons, Slaves)*: Faith Daltry Compo, Harris W. Davis, James Fels, Helene Guile, Janet Hayes, Bill Kennedy, Joy Lynne Sica, Sharon Vaughn, Lynn Wendell.

1963.19 SPOON RIVER ANTHOLOGY

A Theatrical Adaptation (Musical Revue) of the Collected Poems of Edgar Lee Masters of the same title in Two Acts. Conceived and directed by Charles Aidman. Original songs, music by Naomi Caryl Hirshhorn, lyrics by Charles Aidman. Lighting by Jules Fisher. (Setting and costumes uncredited.) Originally produced by the Theatre Group, University Extension, UCLA. Production supervised by Robert Weiner. Produced by Joseph Cates. Opened 29 September 1963 at the Booth Theatre, moved 19 November 1963 to the Belasco Theatre and closed 4 January 1964 after 111 performances.

CAST: BETTY GARRETT, ROBERT ELSTON, JOYCE VAN PATTEN, CHARLES AIDMAN. *Singers*: Naomi Caryl Hirshhorn, Hal Lynch.

ACT 1

"He's Gone Away"
N. C. Hirshhorn
The Hill
C. Aidman
Tom Beatty
C. Aidman
"Illinois"
N. C. Hirshhorn, H. Lynch
Mrs. Williams
J. V. Patten
Dora Williams
B. Garrett
Archibald Higbie
R. Elston
Walter Simmons
C. Aidman
Deacon Taylor
R. Elston
Emily Sparks
B. Garrett
Benjamin Pantier
C. Aidman
Mrs. Banjamin Pantier
J. V. Patten
Emily Sparks
B. Garrett
Reuben Pantier
R. Elston
Emily Sparks
B. Garrett
Margaret Fuller Slack
J. V. Patten
"Soldier, Oh Soldier"
H. Lynch
Knowlt Hoheimer
C. Aidman
Lydia Puckett
B. Garrett
Fiddler Jones
R. Elston
Ollie McGee
B. Garrett
Fletcher McGee
C. Aidman
Hamilton Greene, Elsa Wertman
R. Elston, J. V. Patten
Rosie Roberts
B. Garrett
Russian Sonia
J. V. Patten
Lucius Atherton
R. Elston
"Times Are Gettin' Hard, Boys"
N. C. Hirshhorn
Eugene Carman
C. Aidman
"The Water Is Wide"
N. C. Hirshhorn, H. Lynch
William and Emily
R. Elston, J. V. Patton
"The Water Is Wide" (reprise)
N. C. Hirshhorn, H. Lynch
Yee Bow
B. Garrett
Enoch Dunlap
C. Aidman
Mrs. Kessler
J. V. Patten
Nancy Knapp
B. Garrett
George Gray
C. Aidman
Harry Wilmans
R. Elston
Nellie Clark
J. V. Patten
"Paper of Pins"
N. C. Hirshhorn, H. Lynch
Roscoe Purkapile
C. Aidman
Mrs. Purkapile
B. Garrett
A. D. Blood
R. Elston
Shack Dye
C. Aidman
"Freedom"
H. Lynch

[1]Originally produced in New York 29 March 1951 at the St. James Theatre for 1246 performances. For Synopsis of Scenes and Musical Numbers, see original 1951 production.

Hannah Armstrong
B. Garrett
Faith Matheny
J. V. Patten

ACT 2
"Three Nights Drunk"
N. C. Hirshhorn, H. Lynch
Judge Selah Lively
C. Aidman
Zilpha Marsh
B. Garrett
Searcy Foote
R. Elston
Mrs. Charles Bliss
J. V. Patten
"Far Away from Home"
H. Lynch
Pauline Barrett
B. Garrett
The Village Atheist
R. Elston
Mabel Osborne
J. V. Patten
Franklin Jones
C. Aidman
"In the Night"
N. C. Hirshhorn
Dippold the Optician
C. Aidman, Company
"In the Night" (reprise)
N. C. Hirshhorn
Elijah Browning
R. Elston
"Mornin's Come"
N. C. Hirshhorn, H. Lynch
Alexander Throckmorton
C. Aidman
Amanda Barker
B. Garrett
Willard Fluke
R. Elston
Lois Spears
J. V. Patten
"God Bless the Moon"
N. C. Hirshhorn
"Sow Took the Measles"
H. Lynch
Abel Melveney
R. Elston
Hod Putt
C. Aidman
Ida Frickey
B. Garrett
Silas Dement
C. Aidman
Aner Clute, Daily Fraser
J. V. Patten, B. Garrett
'Indignation' Jones
R. Elston
Minerva Jones
J. V. Patten
Doctor Meyers
C. Aidman
Mrs. Meyers
B. Garrett
"Who Knows Where I'm Goin'?"
H. Lynch
Reverend and Mrs. Sibley
R. Elston, J. V. Patten
"My Rooster"
N. C. Hirshhorn
Willie Metcalf
C. Aidman
"I Am, I Am"
N. C. Hirshhorn
"A Horse Named Bill"
H. Lynch
Batterton Dobyns
R. Elston
Flossie Cabanis
B. Garrett
Hortense Robbins
J. V. Patten
Frank Drummer
R. Elston
Barney Hainsfeather
C. Aidman
"Spoon River"
N. C. Hirshhorn, H. Lynch
Lucinda Matlock
B. Garrett
Petit, the Poet
R. Elston
Anne Rutledge
J. V. Patten
"Spoon River"
N. C. Hirshhorn, H. Lynch
Last Poem (Epilogue)
C. Aidman

THE STUDENT GYPSY, or The Prince of Liederkranz

1963.20

A Musical Comedy in Two Acts, 14 Scenes. Book, music, lyrics and direction by Rick Besoyan. Musical numbers staged by Ray Harrison. Sets and costumes by Raoul Pene Du Bois. Lighting by Paul Morrison. Musical direction by Shepard Coleman. Orchestrations and (musical) arrangements by Arnold Goland. Produced by Sandy Farber. Opened 30 September 1963 at the 54th Street Theatre and closed 12 October 1963 after 16 performances.

CAST (in order of appearance): *'Papa' Johann Sebastian Glockenspiel*, Proprietor of the Round Robin Tavern: ALLEN SWIFT. *Ginger Glockenspiel*, Papa Johann's adopted daughter: MITZIE WELCH. *Edelweiss Glockenspiel*, another adopted daughter: JOLEEN FODOR. *Merry May Glockenspiel*, another adopted daighter: EILEEN BRENNAN. *Rudolph von Schlump*, a Grenadier: DON STEWART. *Muffin T. Ragamuffin D D., Ret.*, a Vagabond: DOM DE LUISE. *Gryphon Allescu*, the Gypsy Prince: BILL FLETCHER. *Zampa Allescu*, the Gypsy Queen: SHANNON BOLIN. *Colonel Helmet Blunderbuss*, another Grenadier: DICK HOH. *Pfc. Wolfgang Humperdinck*, another Grenadier: EDWARD MILLER. *Osgood the Good*, King of Liederkranz: Donald Babcock. *Elsie Umlaut*, his Ward: Linda Segal.

The Glockenspiel Girls: *Brunhilde*: Rosemary McNamara. *Puppchen*: Mary Jay. *Dresden*: Jean Palmerton. *Ermintrout*: Maria Garziano. *Shoenheit*: Jacque Dean. *Rosalinde*: Ann Collins. *Zucker*: Jean Middlebrooks. *Schmetterling*: Katherine Sutter. *Pampelmuse*: Jamie Simmons. *Privates in the Royal Grenadiers*: *Offenbach*: Ralph Vucci. *Romberg*: Doug Robinson. *Korngold*: Robert Edsel. *Straus II*: Marc Destin. *Von Weber*: Richard Marshall. *Mozart*: William Wheless. *Lehar*: Nino Galanti. *Von Flotow*: Tony Marlowe. *Sullivan*: Arnold Whyler.

The action takes place late in the nineteenth century in the Kingdom of Singspielia.

Act 1, Scene 1: The Border of Singspielia. A summer afternoon. *Scene 2*: In front of the Round Robin Tavern. *Scene 3*: A Forest Path. *Scene 4*: In front of Muffin's Wagon. *Scene 5*: In front of the Tavern. *Scene 6*: Inside the Tavern. *Scene 7*: Muffin's Wagon. *Scene 8*: In front of the Tavern.

Act 2, Scene 1: The Grenadier's Campsite. That evening. *Scene 2*: The Wine Cellar. *Scene 3*: The Path. *Scene 4*: Muffin's Wagon. *Scene 5*: In front of the Tavern. *Scene 6*: The Border of Singspielia.

ACT 1

"Welcome Home Anthem"
Glockenspiel Girls

"Singspielia"
Glockenspiel Girls

"Romance"
E. Brennan, Glockenspiel Girls

"Somewhere"
D. Stewart

"It's a Wonderful Day to Do Nothing"
D. DeLuise

"The Gypsy Life"
S. Bolin, D. DeLuise, E. Brennan

"The Grenadiers' Marching Song"
D. Hoh, Grenadiers

"Welcome Home Anthem" (reprise)
Glockenspiel Girls

"Greetings"
Grenadiers

"Kiss Me"
Glockenspiel Girls, Grenadiers

"Ting-A-Ling Dearie"
M. Welch, D. Hoh

"Merry May"
D. DeLuise, E. Brennan

"Seventh Heaven Waltz"
E. Brenna, D. Stewart

"A Gypsy Dance"
S. Bolin, D. DeLuise, B. Fletcher

"Walk-On"
S. Bolin

"You're a Man" (Finale Act 1)
Tutti (Entire Company)

ACT 2

"A Whistle Works"
E. Miller

"Gypsy of Love"
D. Stewart

"Our Love Has Flown Away"
E. Brennan

"A Woman Is a Woman Is a Woman"
D. Hoh, D. Stewart, D. DeLuise

"Romance" (reprise)
Glockenspiel Girls

"Very Much in Love"
M. Welch, Glockenspiel Girls

"My Love Is Yours"
D. Stewart, E. Brennan

"There's Life in the Old Folks Yet"
A. Swift, S. Bolin, D. Babcock

"The Drinking Song"
E. Brennan, D. DeLuise, M. Welch, D. Hoh

Finale Act 2
Tutti (Entire Company)

1963.21 HERE'S LOVE

A Musical in Two Acts, 23 Scenes. Book, music and lyrics by Meredith Willson. Based on "Miracle on 34th Street," story by Valentine Davies, screenplay by George Seaton. Directed by Stuart Ostrow. Settings by William and Jean Eckart. Costumes by Alvin Colt. Lighting by Tharon Musser. Musical direction, vocal arrangements and additional scoring by Elliot Lawrence. Orchestrations by Don Walker. Dance music arranged by Peter Howard. Dance and musical numbers staged by Michael Kidd. Produced by Stuart Ostrow. Opened 3 October 1963 at the Sam S. Shubert Theatre and closed 25 July 1964 after 338 performances.

CAST (in order of appearance): *Mr. Kris Kringle*: LAURENCE NAISMITH. *Fred Gaily*: CRAIG STEVENS. *Susan Walker*: VALERIE LEE. *Marvin Shellhammer*: FRED GWYNNE. *Doris Walker*: JANIS PAIGE. *Clerks*: Michael Bennett, Gene Kelton, Bill Stanton, Patrick Cummings, Diane Ball, Sandra Roveta, Patti Pappathatos, Elaine Cancilla. *R. H. Macy*: PAUL REED. *Harry Finfer*: Sal Lombardo. *Mrs. Finfer*: Mara Landi. *Hendrika*: Kathy Cody. *Hendrika's New Mother*: Suzanne France. *Miss Crookshank*: Reby Howells. *Mr. Psawyer*: DAVID DOYLE. *Governor*: Darrell Sandeen. *Mayor*: Hal Norman. *Mr. Gimbel*: William Griffis. *Policeman*: Bob McClure. *Clara*: Mary Louise. *Judge Martin Group*: CLIFF HALL. *District Attorney Thomas Mara*: Larry Douglas. *Tammany O'Halloran*: Arthur Rubin. *Nurse*: Leesa Troy. *Marines*: John Sharpe, Bob McClure, Darrell Sandeen. *Girl Scout Leader*: Mara Landi. *Bailiff*: Del Horstmann. *Mailman*: Hal Norman. *Thomas Mara, Jr.*: Ronnie Kroll. *Murphy*: William Griffis.

Children: Debbie Breen, Kathy Cody, Sal Lombardo, Ronnie Kroll, Terrin Miles. *Dancers*: Diane Ball, Michael Bennett, Duane Bodin, Elaine Cancilla, Patrick Cummings, Suzanne France, Reby Howells, Gene Kelton, Baayork Lee, David Lober, Bill Louther, Patti Pappathatos, Sandra Roveta, John Sharpe, Bill Stanton, Carolsue Shaer. *Singers*: Ceil Delli, Penny Gaston, Del Horstmann, Mara Landi, Mary Louise, Bob McClure, Hal Norman, Darrell Sandeen, Leesa Troy.

Act 1, Scene 1: West 73rd Street, New York City. Thursday morning, Thanksgiving Day. *Scene 2*: Assembly Parade Area. Immediately following. *Scene 3*: Along Central park West. Immediately following. *Scene 4*: 34th Street Roof. Immediately following. *Scene 5*: Doris Walker's Apartment. That evening. *Scene 6*: Briefing Room at Macy's. 3 P.M., the next afternoon. *Scene 7*: Macy's Toy Department, Elevators, Escalator, and into Herald Square. Immediately following. *Scene 8*: Playground in Central Park. Later that afternoon. *Scene 9*: Doris Walker's Office. In the meantime. *Scene10*: Fred Gaily's Apartment. After work that day. *Scene 11*: On the way to Doris' Apartment. Immediately following. *Scene 12*: Store Psychologist's Office at Macy's. The following Monday morning. *Scene 13*: Macy's Toy Department. That evening. *Scene 14*: The Party. *Scene 15*: Macy's Toy Department.

Act 2, Scene 1: Judge Martin Group's Chambers. Several Weeks later, December 19th, morning. *Scene 2*: In Isolation. Later that day. *Scene 3*: Fred's Apartment. That evening. *Scene 4*: A Corridor in the New York Supreme Court. 10 A.M. the next day. *Scene 5*: The Courtroom. Immediately following. *Scene 6*: The Courthouse Corridor. 3 P.M. the following Tuesday afternoon, December 24th. *Scene 7*: The Courtroom. Immediately following. *Scene 8*: Macy's Living Room Display. Christmas Eve, immediately following.

ACT 1

Scene 3

"The Big Clown Balloons"
Paradesters

Scene 5

"Arm in Arm"
J. Paige, V. Lee

"You Don't Know"
J. Paige

Scene 6

"The Plastic Alligator"
F. Gwynne, Clerks

Scene 7

"The Bugle"
L. Naismith, K. Cody

"Here's Love"
L. Naismith, C. Stevens, V. Lee, Ensemble

Scene 8

"My Wish"
C. Stevens, V. Lee

Scene 9

"Pine Cones and Holly Berries"
L. Naismith, J. Paige, F. Gwynne

Scene 10

"Look Little Girl"
C. Stevens

Scene 11

"Look Little Girl" (reprise)
J. Paige

Scene 13

"Expect Things To Happen"
L. Naismith

Scene 14
"Love Come Take Me Again" (Waltz)
Ballet Corps

ACT 2[2]
Scene 2
"Pine Cones and Holly Berries" (reprise)
L. Naismith, V. Lee
Scene 3
"She Hadda Go Back"
C. Stevens, Marines
Scene 5
"That Man Over There"
P. Reed
"My State"
J. Paige, P. Reed, F. Gwynne, A. Rubin, C. Hall
Scene 6
"Nothin' in Common"
J. Paige
Scene 7
"That Man Over There" (reprise)
Court Personnel, Spectators

1963.22 GENTLEMEN, BE SEATED!

A Musical Entertainment in Two Acts, 22 Scenes. Book by Jerome Moross and Edward Eager. Music by Jerome Moross. Lyrics by Edward Eager. Directed by Robert Turoff. Scenic design by William Pitkin. Costume design by Henry Heymann. Lighting by Jules Fisher. Choreographed by Paul Draper, assisted by Bob Bernard. Conducted by Emerson Buckley. Produced by the New York City Opera. Opened 10 October 1963 at the New York City Center and closed 10 November 1963 after 3 performances in repertory.

CAST (in order of appearance): *Interlocutor, (Mr. Brady)*: DICK SHAWN. *Mr. Tambo*: Avon Long. *Mr. Bones*: Charles Atkins. *The Comedienne, (Dowager, Belle Boyd, Dorothea Dix)*: ALICE GHOSTLEY. *The Contralto, (Harriet Tubman, Amanda)*: Carol Brice. *Johnny Reb*: William McDonald. *Billy Yank*: Richard Fredricks. *Southern Girl*: June Card. *Northern Girl*: Mary Burgess. *Mr. Banjo*: Bernard Addison. *The Character Actor, (The Senator, The General, The Pinkerton Man. Mr. Brady's Assistant)*: RICHARD KRAUSE. *Mr. Taps*: PAUL DRAPER. *Ermyntrude*: Charlotte Povia. *Farmer McLean*: David Smith. *Miss Florida Cotton*: Michele Hardy. *Two Soldiers*: Kellis Miller, Don Henderson. *Drill Team*: Bob Bernard, John Tormey, Rec Russell, Bob Ellis. *Horse*: Bob Bernard, Bob Ellis. *Two Other Soldiers*: Kellis Miller, Don Yule. *Two Girls*: Joyce Miko, Beverly Evans. *Four Nurses*: Joyce Miko, Candida Pilla, Beverly Evans, Charlotte Povia. *Minstrels, Waltzers, Soldiers, Nurses, Spectators, Slaves, etc.*: New York City Opera Chorus.

ACT 1[3]
Scene 1
"Grand March"
A. Long, C. Atkins, Chorus, W. McDonald, R. Fredericks, J. Card, M. Burgess
Scene 2
"In the Sunny Old South"
D. Shawn, A. Long, C. Atkins, Chorus
Scene 3
"The Freedom Train"
C. Brice
Scene 4
"Waltzing in the Shadow"
D. Shawn, W. McDonald, R. Fredericks, Chorus
Scene 5
"Fare You Well"
J. Card, W. McDonald, M. Burgess, R. Fredericks
Scene 6
"Why Ain't We Got a Dome?"
A. Long, C. Atkins, D. Shawn
"Tap Dance Drill"
P. Draper, Men's Dance Ensemble
Scene 7
"O, the Picnic in Manassas"
A. Ghostley, R. Krause, C. Povia
Scene 8
"Mocking Bird"
J. Card
Scene 9
"Shiloh"
W. McDonald, Men's Chorus
Scene 10
"The Ballad of Belle Boyd" (Belle Boyd's Back in Town)
Ladies' Chorus
"I Spy"
A. Ghostley
"It's the Witching Hour by the Old Water Tower"
Men's Chorus, A. Ghostley
"I'm a Pinkerton Man"
R. Krause
"Belle Boyd, Where Have You Been?"
Ladies' Chorus
Scene 11
"'Mancipation"
A. Long, C. Atkins, C. Brice
"Pardon, Ma'am"?
"Look Who I Am, Surpise! Surprise!"?
Scene 12
"This Isn't a Gentleman's War Anymore"
D. Shawn
Scene 13
"The Contraband Ball"
A. Ghostley, J. Card, C. Atkins, A. Long, R. Fredericks, Chorus
"O, Miss Walkaround, Come Walking Out With Me"
D. Shawn, A. Ghostley, R. Fredericks, A. Long, C. Atkins, J. Card, Entire Company

ACT 2
Scene 1
"Gentlemen, Be Seated"
D. Shawn
Scene 2
"It's Quiet on the Potomac Tonight"
A. Long, C. Atkins
Scene 3
"The Ballad of Stonewall Jackson"
W. McDonald, Men's Chorus
Scene 4
"I'm Mathew P. Brady, the Camera Man"
D. Shawn,. R. Krause
"Miss Dorothea Dix"
A. Ghostley, Nurses, D. Shawn
Scene 5
"I Can't Remember"
M. Burgess
Scene 6
"From Atlanta to the Sea"
R. Fredericks, C. Brice, Chorus
Scene 7
"What Has Become of Beauty?"
D. Shawn
Scene 8
"Have You Seen Him, Did He Pass This Way?"
C. Brice

---

[2]Added to Act 2, Scene 7 after "That Man Over There" for tour:
"Love Come Take Me Again" (vocal)
Lisa Kirk (Doris)

[3]Scenes and Musical Numbers not in program. List prepared from production manuscript, score and recording.

Scene 9

"This Was the War, What Did It Do for Me and You?"
Entire Company

1963.23

THE MIKADO,

or The Town of Titipu

A Revival of the Comic Opera in Two Acts[4]. Libretto by William S. Gilbert. Music by Arthur Sullivan. Staged by Dorothy Raedler. Scenic design by Donald Oenslager. Costume design by Patton Campbell. Lighting by Jules Fisher. Conducted by William Jonson. Produced by the New York City Opera. Opened 12 October 1963 at the New York City Center and closed 9 November 1963 after 3 performances in repertory.

CAST: *The Mikado of Japan*: PAUL UKENA. *Nanki-Poo*, his son, disguised as a wandering minstrel in love with Yum-Yum: WILLIAM DIARD. *Ko-Ko*, Lord High Executioner of Titipu: NORMAN KELLEY. *Pooh-Bah*, Lord High Everything Else: SPIRO MALAS. *Pish-Tush*, a Noble Lord: David Smith. *Yum-Yum, Pitti-Sing, Peep-Bo*, three sisters, wards of Ko-Ko: CAROL BERGEY, MARY BURGESS, MARLENA KLEINMAN. *Katisha*: MURIEL GREENSPON. *Chorus of School Girls, Nobles, Guards and Coolies*: New York City Opera Chorus.

1963.24

THE MERRY WIDOW

A Revival of the Operetta in Three Acts[5]. Music by Franz Lehár. Original German book (Die Lustige Witwe) and lyrics by Victor Léon and Leo Stein after "L'Attaché d'Ambassade." English libretto by Adrian Ross. Staged by Michael Pollock. Scenic design by George Jenkins. Lighting by Jules Fisher. Choreographed by Thomas Andrew. Conducted by Carl Bamberger. Produced by the New York City Opera. Opened 13 October 1963 (matinee) at the New York City Center and closed 10 November 1963 after 4 performances in repertory.[6]

CAST: *Sonia*: ARLENE SAUNDERS. *Prince Danilo*: JOHN REARDON. *Baron Popoff*: JACK HARROLD. *Natalie*: Gillian Grey. *De Jolidon*: FRANK PORETTA. *Marquis de Cascada*: David Smith. *St. Brioche*: Richard Krause. *Admiral Khadja*: Thomas Paul. *Mme. Khadja*: Charlotte Povia. *General Novikovich*: R. G. Webb. *Mme. Novikovich*: Lynda Jordan. *Nish*: Coley Worth. *Head waiter*: Harris Davis. *Clo-Clo*: Helen Guile. *Solo Dancers*: Rochelle Zide, Ron Sequoio. *Ensemble*: New York Citry Opera.

1963.25

JENNIE

A Musical in Two Acts, 14 Scenes. Book by Arnold Schulman. Suggested by "Laurette"[7] by Marguerite Courtney by arrangement with Alan J. Pakula. Music by Arthur Schwartz. Lyrics by Howard Dietz. Directed by Vincent J. Donahue. Choreography by Matt Mattox. Settings by George Jenkins. Costumes by Irene Sharaff. Lighting by Jean Rosenthal. Musical director, John Lesko. Orchestrations by Philip J. Lang and Robert Russell Bennett. Dance music, vocal arrangements and incidental music by Trude Rittman. Produced by Cheryl Crawford and Richard Halliday. Opened 17 October 1963 at the Majestic Theatre and closed 28 December 1963 after 82 performances.

CAST (in order of appearance): THE MOUNTIE GETS HIS MAN, or, CHANG LU, KING OF THE WHITE SLAVES: *The Evil Chang Lu*: Kirby Smith. *Randolph of the Royal Mounted*: GEORGE WALLACE. *Misguided Coolies (2)*: *Lu Wong*: Gerald Teijelo. *Dong Foo*: Robert Murray. *Our Melissa*: MARY MARTIN. *The Bear*: Jeremiah Morris. *Wicked Owner of a House of Ill Repute*: Elaine Swann. *A Tragic Virgin Sold into White Slavery*: Linda Donovan. *A Sinful Woman of Ill Repute*: Sharon Vaughn. *A Croupier*: Steve Elmore. *A Woodsman*: Rico Froehlich. *A Pioneer Woman*: Julie Sargant.

Jennie Malone: MARY MARTIN. *James O'Connor*: GEORGE WALLACE. *Bessie Mae Sue*: Elaine Swann. *Stella*: Linda Donovan. *Sydney Harris*: JEREMIAH MORRIS. *Frank Granada*: Rico Froehlich. *Casey O'Harrison*: Steve Elmore. *Gregory Hyman*: Kirby Smith. *Sheriff Pugsley*: Jay Velie. *Abe O'Shaughnessy*: JACK DE LON. *Kevin O'Conner*: Brian Chapin. *Lois Houser*: IMELDA DeMARTIN. *O'Conner's Wardrobe Mistress*: Bernice Saunders. *Deputies*: Martin Ambrose, Oran Osburn. *Linda O'Conner*: CONNIE SCOTT. *Nellie Malone*: ETHEL SHUTTA. *Delivery Man*: Stephen Elmore. *Charlie the Juiceman*: Stan Watt. *Flower Girl*: Debbie Scott. *Rita Bradley*: Diane Coupe. *Christopher Lawrence Cromwell*: ROBIN BAILEY. *Shine Boy*: Robert Murray. *Teddy*: Sean Peters. *Gentleman*: Jay Velie. *Stage Manger*: Stan Watt. *Piano Player*: Woody Kessler. *The Pony*: Misty. *Fire Chief*: Jay Velie.

THE SULTAN'S FIFTIETH BRIDE: *Sultan*: Kirby Smith. *Harem Girls*: Diane Coupe, Sally Ackerman, Linda Donovan. *Guardians*: Gerald Teijelo, Robert Murray, Al Sambogna. *Eunuchs*: Blair Hammond, Martin Ambrose. *Indian Fakir*: Jeremiah Morris. *Shalamar*: MARY MARTIN. *Omar*: GEORGE WALLACE.

Dancing Ensemble: Sally Ackerman, Diane Coupe, Mollie Sterns, Blair Hammond, Robert Murray, Al Sambogna, Gerald Teijelo. *Singing Ensemble*: Lispet Nelson, Julie Sargant, Bernice Saunders, Sharon Vaughn, Martin Ambrose, Steve Elmore, Rico Froehlich, Oran Osburn.

Act 1, Scene 1: The Stage of a Theatre in a small town in South Dakota. Early Spring 1906. Melodrama: 'The Mountie Gets His Man." *Scene 2*: Backstage immediately after. *Scene 3*: The town square, a few minutes later. *Scene 4*: Living room of Nellie Malone's Brownstone. New York City, two months later. *Scene 5*: Stage door alley, New York City. The next morning. *Scene 6*: Exterior Nellie Malone's Brownstone, a few hours later. *Scene 7*: Christopher Lawrence Cromwell's New York Town House. Eight weeks later. *Scene 8*: The living room of Nellie Malone's Brownstone. The following Sunday afternoon.

Act 2, Scene 1: Seattle, Washington. Several weeks later. *Scene 2*: O'Conner's Crystal Palace, backstage. Three weeks later. *Scene 3*: Several hours later. *Scene 4*: On stage. Imemdiately after. *Scene 5*: Several hours later. Melodrama: 'The Sultan's Fiftieth Bride." *Scene 6*: Seattle Railroad Station.

ACT 1

Scene 2

"Waitin' For the Evening Train"
M. Martin, G. Wallace

Scene 3

"When You're Far Away From New York Town"
J. De Lon, Company

"I Still Look at You That Way"
M. Martin

Scene 4

"When You're Far Away from New York Town" (reprise)
B. Chapin, Sewing Girls

"For Better or Worse"
E. Shutta

Scene 5

"Born Again"
M. Martin, J. De Lon, Company

"Over Here"
R. Bailey, M. Martin

Scene 6

"Before I Kiss the World Goodbye"
M. Martin

Scene 7

"Sauce Diable" (dance)
Dance Company

"Where You Are"
R. Bailey, M. Martin

"The Jig"
R. Bailey, M. Martin, Company

Scene 8

"See Seattle"
G. Wallace

ACT 2

Scene 1

"High Is Better Than Low"
G. Wallace, M. Martin, Company

[4]First presented in New York 20 July, 10-29 August 1885 at the Union Square and People's Theatres for 22 performances. First authorized production presented 19 August 1885 at the Fifth Avenue Theatre by Richard D'Oyly Carte for 250 performances. For Synopsis of Scenes and Musical Numbers, see 19 August 1885 D'Oyly Carte production.

[5]Originally produced in New York 21 October 1907 at the New Amsterdam Theatre for 416 performances. For Synopsis of Scenes and Musical Numbers, see original 1907 production.

[6]Costumes uncredited; one reviewer noted the costumes were acquired from a production from Casa Manana Musicals, Inc. Texas.

[7]Biography of Laurette Taylor.

"The Night May Be Dark"
M. Martin, E. Shutta
Scene 2
Dance Rehearsal
Harem Girls
"I Believe in Takin' a Chance"
G. Wallace, J. De Lon
Scene 4
"Welcome"
Harem Girls
"Lonely Nights"
M. Martin
Scene 6
"Before I Kiss the World Goodbye" (reprise)
M. Martin

1963.26 110 IN THE SHADE

A Musical Play in Two Acts, 11 Scenes. Book by N. Richard Nash. Based on his play "The Rainmaker." Music by Harvey Schmidt. Lyrics by Tom Jones. Directed by Joseph Anthony. Musical numbers staged by Agnes de Mille. Settings by Oliver Smith. Costumes by Motley. Lighting by John Harvey. Musical director, Don Pippin. Orchestrations by Hershy Kay. Dance music by Billy Goldenberg. Vocal arranger, Robert De Cormier. Produced by David Merrick. Opened 24 October 1963 at the Broadhurst Theatre and closed 8 August 1964 after 330 performances.

CAST (in order of appearance): *Toby*: GEORGE CHURCH. *File*: STEPHEN DOUGLASS. *H.C. Curry*: WILL GEER. *Noah Curry*: STEVE ROLAND. *Jimmy Curry*: SCOOTER TEAGUE. *Lizzie Curry*: INGA SWENSON. *Snookie*: LESLEY WARREN. *Mrs. Jensen*: Diane Deering. *Phil Mackey*: Seth Riggs. *Tommy*: Christopher Votos. *Belinda*: Renee Dudley. *Gershy Toops*: Don Crabtree. *Gil Demby*: Jerry Dodge. *Olive Barrow*: Leslie Franzos. *Wally Skacks, III*: Loren Hightower. *Maurine Toops*: Evelyn Toops. *Bo Dollivon*: Vernon Lusby. *Mr. Curtis*: Robert Shepard. *Bill Starbuck*: ROBERT HORTON. *Wally Skacks*: Carl Nicholas.

Townspeople: Lynne Broadbent, Leslie Franzos, Lucia Lambert, Paula Lloyd, Evelyn Taylor, Esther Villavicencio, Florence Willson, Don Atkinson, Frank Derbas, Jerry Dodge, Ben Gillespie, Loren Hightower, Vernon Lusby, Arthur Whitfield, Barbara Bossert, Gretchen Cryer, Dori Davis, Diane Deering, Corlyn Kemp, Urylee Leonardos, Donna Sanders, Clifford Fearl, David London, Carl Nicholas, Stan Page.

The play takes place in a western state from dawn to midnight of a summer day in a time of drought.

Act 1, Scene 1: The Depot. *Scene 2*: File's Office. Main Street. *Scene 3*: A Picnic Area, near the Bandstand. *Scene 4*: The Rainwagon. *Scene 5*: Another Picnic Area. *Scene 6*: The Edge of the Woods.

Act 2, Scene 1: The Pavilion. *Scene 2*: The Rainwagon. *Scene 3*: A Picnic Area. *Scene 4*: The Rainwagon. *Scene 5*: Near the Bandstand.

ACT 1
"(Gonna Be) Another Hot Day"
S. Douglass, Townspeople
"Lizzie's Coming Home"
W. Geer, S. Roland, S. Teague
"Love, Don't Turn Away"
I. Swenson
"Poker Polka"
S. Douglass, W. Geer, S. Roland
"Hungry Men"
Townspeople
"The Rain Song"
R. Horton, Townspeople
"You're Not Foolin' Me"
I. Swenson, R. Horton
"Raunchy"
I. Swenson, W. Geer
"A Man and a Woman"
I. Swenson, S. Douglass
"Old Maid"
I. Swenson
ACT 2
"Everything Beautiful Happens at Night"
G. Church, S. Teague, L. Warren, Townspeople
"Melisande"
R. Horton
"Simple Little Things"
I. Swenson
"Little Red Hat"
L. Warren, S. Teague
"Is It Really Me?"
I. Swenson, R. Horton
"Wonderful Music"
S. Douglass, R. Horton, I. Swenson
Finale ("The Rain Song")
Full Company

1963.27 TAMBOURINES TO GLORY

A Gospel Singing Play in Two Acts, 10 Scenes. Play (book and lyrics) by Langston Hughes. Based on his novel of the same name Music by Jobe Huntley. Directed by Nikos Psacharopoulos. Settings and costumes by John Conklin. Lighting by Peter Hunt. Choral director, Clara Ward. Dance assistant, Judd Jones. Musical consultant, Abba Bogin. Produced by S. & H. Venture (Joel Schenker and Hexter Productions, Inc.) in association with Sydney S. Baron. Opened 2 November 1963 at the Little Theatre and closed 23 November 1963 after 24 performances.

CAST (in order of appearance): *C. J. Moore*: ROBERT GUILLAUME. *Marshalls*: Rudy Challenger, Garwood Perkins. *Essie Belle Johnson*: ROSETTA LE NOIRE. *Youth*: Clyde Williams. *Mattie Morningside*: Rosalie King. *Laura Wright Reed*: HILDA SIMMS. *Policeman*: Rudy Challenger. *Big-Eyed Buddy Lomax*: LOUIS [Lou] GOSSETT. *Birdie Lee*: CLARA WARD. *Gloria Dawn*: ANNA ENGLISH. *The Gloriettas*: Helen Ferguson, Tina Sattin. *Bartender*: Garwood Perkins. *Brother Bud*: BROTHER JOHN SELLERS. *Brother Clyde*: Clyde Williams. *Marietta Johnson*: MICKI GRANT. *Deacons*: Clark Morgan, Garwood Perkins, BROTHER JOHN SELLERS, Laurence Watson. *Deaconess Lucy Mae Hobbs*: Lynn Hamilton. *Chicken-Crow-For-Day*: JOSEPH ATTLES. *Ministers of Music*: Clyde Williams, Alton Williams. *Windus*: Rudy Challenger. *Prison Warden*: Garwood Perkins.

Tambourine Temple Choir, Passersby, Cabarte Patrons, Neighborhood Folk: Rudy Challenger, Voyla Crowley, Dorothy Drake, Helen Ferguson, Claretta Freemon, Carl Hall, Alma Hubbard, Judd Jones, Rosalie King, Julie Merrell, Theresa Merritt, Clark Morgan, Garwood Perkins, Tina Sattin, Adele Schofield, Laurence Watson.

The action of the play takes place in Harlem, New York City, some time in the past.

Act 1, Scene 1: A Sidewalk in Harlem. Early spring. *Scene 2*: A street corner. A week later. *Scene 3*: A Night Club. Immediately following. *Scene 4*: A Store Front Church. Autumn. *Scene 5*: Laura's Living Room. A few months later. *Scene 6*: Tambourine Temple.

Act 2, Scene 1: The Living Room, again. Summer night. *Scene 2*: The Robing Room of Tambourine Temple. Late Summer. *Scene 3*: A Jail. The next day. *Scene 4*: Tambourine Temple. A few days later.

MUSICAL NUMBERS
"Nobody Knows the Trouble I've Seen"
"O, What Blessings to Receive"
"Travelling Show"
"The New York Blues"
"Scat With Me"
"Moon Outside My Window"
"As I Go"
"Just To Be a Flower in the Garden of the Lord"
"I've Come Back to the Fold"
"I'm Goin to Testify"
"Away from Temptation"
"Devil, Devil, Take Yourself Away"
"Yes, Ma'am"
"Fix Me"
"Just Trust in Him"
"God's Got a Way"
"Let the Church Say Amen"
"God's Love Can Save"
"If You've Got a Tambourine Shake It for the Glory of God" (Tambourines to Glory)

1963.28 THE GOLDEN AGE

An Entertainment (Revue) in the Words and Music of the Elizabethan Age, in Two Acts. Devised by Richard Johnson. Directed by Douglas Campbell. Music devised and directed by Sydney Beck. Men's evening wear by After Six. Gowns by Domingo A. Rodriguez. Produced by Santa Fe Productions, Inc. Presented by Arthur Cantor and E. E. Fogelson. Opened 18 November 1963 at the Lyceum Theatre and closed 23 November 1963 after 7 performances.

CAST: DOUGLAS CAMPBELL, NANCY WICKWIRE, DOUGLAS RAIN, LESTER RAWLINS. *Singers*: Betty Wilson (soprano), James Stover (tenor), Gordon Myers (baritone). *Consort of Instruments*: Blanche Winogrom (virginals, cittern), James Tyler (lute, tenor viol and recorders), Leonid Bolotine (pandora and violin), Robert Kuehn (bass viol).

ACT 1

SPRING AND SUMMER

Elizabeth Regina
(Sir John Davies)
D. Rain, D. Campbell, L. Rawlins

"Blow, Shepherds, Blow!"
(Thomas Morley)
B. Wilson, J. Stover, G. Myers

See Where She Sits
(Edmund Spenser)
The Company

"The Shepherd's Delight"
(Anonymous)
Consort, B. Wilson, J. Stover, G. Myers

The Fair Milkmaid
(Sir Thomas Overbury)
L. Rawlins

I Would I Had Some Flowers
(Shakespeare)
N. Wickwire

The Countryman's Letter
(Nicholas Breton)D. Campbell

Ah, What Is Love?
(Robert Greene)
N. Wickwire

"It Was a Lover and His Lass"
(Morley)
B. Wilson, J. Stover, Virginals

Shakespeare: 'As You Like It'

Phillidah Flouts Me
(Anonymous)
D. Rain

The Shepherd To His Love
(Christopher Marlowe)
D. Campbell

The Shepherdess Replies
(Sir Walter Raleigh)
N. Wickwire

"I Care Not for These Ladies"
(Thomas Campion)
G. Myers, Lute, Bass Viol

The Country Life
(Thomas Dekker)
L. Rawlins

Shepherd and Courtier
(Shakespeare: 'As You Like It')
D. Campbell, D. Rain

"Lord Souche's Masque"
(Anonymous)
Consort

Royal Progress
(Edited from various sourecs)
The Company

"Michells Galliard"
(Anonymous)The Consort

"Now Is the Month of Maying"
(Morley)
B. Wilson, J. Stover, G. Myers, Consort

An English Housewife
(Gervase Markham)
D. Rain

Oh, These Men
(Shakespeare: 'Othello'
N. Wickwire

"Sigh No More Ladies"
(Shakespeare: 'Much Ado About Nothing')
(Music: Sixteenth Century Manuscript)
B. Wilson, J. Stover, Bass Viol

Doctors—Good and Bad
(Nicholas Breton)
L. Rawlins

What Is't You Lack?
(Anonymous Masque)
B. Wilson, J. Stover, G. Myers, Virginals

Neurosis
(Reginald Scot)
D. Rain

To Bed With Mirth
(Andrew Boorde)
N. Wickwire

"Lullaby"
(Thomas Dekker, *Music by* Sydney Beck)
B. Wilson, Pandora

"The Hunt Is Up"
(Anonymous, *Music by* Sydney Beck)
B. Wilson, J. Stover, G. Myers

Hunting
(Gervase Markham)
D. Campbell

"The King's Hunt"
(John Bull)
Virginals

Football
(Philip Stubbes)
D. Rain

The Road to London
(Thomas Deloney)
The Company

"To Portsmouth"
(Melville Collection)
B. Wilson, J. Stover, G. Myers

A Good Sherris-Sack
(Shakespeare)
D. Campbell

The Nut Brown Ale
D. Rain, L. Rawlins

Troll the Bowl
(Thomas Dekker)
L. Rawlins

A Drinking Song
The Company

ACT 2

FALL AND WINTER

Barafostus Dreame
(Anonymous, *Music by* Sydney Beck)
The Consort

It Is Now the Seventh Hour
(Nicholas Breton)
N. Wickwire

"The Cries of London"
(Anonymous, Sixteenth Century Manuscript)
B. Wilson, J. Stover, G. Myers, Consort

Where Be These Boys
(Thomas Dekker: 'A Shoemaker's Holiday')
The Company

London
(Thomas Dekker)
D. Rain

London: A Foreigner's View
(Edited from various sources)
D. Campbell, N. Wickwire, D. Rain

The Theatre
(Thoams Platter) The Company
"Irish Jig"
(Anonymous) Virginals
Sermon
(Edited from various sources) D. Rain
How to Behave at the Theatre
(Thomas Dekker) D. Campbell
"Oxenford's March"
(Anonymous) The Consort
Prologue: The Armada
(Shakespeare) L. Rawlins
The Queen Speaks
(Queen Elizabeth) N. Wickwire
"Joyne Hands"
(Thomas Morley) The Consort
Happy and Glorious
(Sir John Hayward) L. Rawlins
The Queen in Her Good Court
(Paul Hentzner) D. Campbell, D. Rain, L. Rawlins
The Golden Speech
(Queen Elizabeth) N. Wickwire
"The Queen's Galliard"
(John Dowland) Lute, Pandora
To Ride Comely
D. Campbell
A Courtier To All Men's Thinking
(Charles Ascham) D. Rain
Why Do You Stand Bare Headed?
D. Campbell, D. Rain
"Winter Song"
(*Music by* Sydney Beck) J. Stover, Virginals
Shakespeare: 'As You Like It'
Storm At Sea
(John Jane) L. Rawlins
The Peril of Waters
(The Bible, Psalm 107) The Company
"In Darkness Let Me Dwell"
(John Dowland) G. Myers, Virginals, Bass Viol
Tichborne's Elegy
(Chidlock Tichborne) D. Campbell
The Queen Repents
(Queen Elizabeth) N. Wickwire
That Time of Year
(Shakespeare) D. Rain
His Pilgrimage
(Sir Walter Raleigh) L. Rawlins
"A Carol for New Year's Day"
B. Wilson, J. Stover, G. Myers, Consort
(William Byrd, *Music by* Sydney Beck)
Epilogue
(Richard Breton) D. Campbell

1963.29 THE GIRL WHO CAME TO SUPPER

A Musical Comedy in Two Acts, 16 Scenes. Book by Harry Kurnitz. Based on the play "The Sleeping Prince" by Terence Rattigan. Music and lyrics by Nöel Coward. Entire production staged by Joe Layton. Scenery by Oliver Smith. Costumes by Irene Sharaff. Lighting by Peggy Clark. Musical direction and vocal arrangements by Jay Blackton. Orchestrations by Robert Russell Bennett. Dance music arranged by Genevieve Pitot. Produced by Herman Levin. Opened 8 December 1963 at the Broadway Theatre and closed 14 March 1964 after 112 performances.

CAST (in order of appearance): *Jessie Maynard*: Marian Haraldson. *Mary Morgan*: FLORENCE HENDERSON. *Tony Morelli*: Jack Eddleman. *Mr. Grimes*: Peter Pagan. *Violetta Vines*: Maggie Worth. *Peter Northbrook*: RODERICK COOK. *Colonel Hofmann*: Chris Gampel. *Grand Duke Charles, Prince Regent of Carpathia*: JOSE FERRER. *First Girl*: Donna Monroe. *Second Girl*: Ruth Shepard. *Major-Domo*: Carey Nairnes. *King Nicholas III of Carpathia*: SEAN SCULLY. *Simka*: Murray Adler. *Queen Mother*: IRENE BROWNE. *Ada Cockle*: TESSIE O'SHEA. *Baroness Brunheim*: Lucie Lancaster. *Lady Sunningdale*: Ilona Murai.

Dancers: Nancy Lynch, Julie Drake, Sheila Forbes, Jami Landi, Sandy Leeds, Carmen Morales, Ilona Murai, Mari Shelton, Gloria Smith, Mary Zahn, Ivan Allen, Robert [Bob] Fitch, Jose Gutierrez, Peter Holmes, Scott Ray, Paul Reid Roman, Dan Siretta, Mike Toles. *Singers*: Jermey Brown, Kellie Brytt, Carol Glade, Marian Haraldson, Elaine Labour, Donna Monroe, Ruth Shepard, Maggie Worth, Jack Eddleman, John Felton, Dell Hanley, Barney Johnston, Art Matthews, Bruce Peyton, Jack Rains, Mitchell Taylor.

The play takes place in London, just prior to and during the Coronation of His Majesty George V.

Act 1, Scene 1: Backstage at the Majestic Theatre. *Scene 2*: A Dressing Room Backstage. *Scene 3*: Backstage. *Scene 4*: The Regent's Apartment, Carpathian Embassy, Belgrave Square. *Scene 5*: St. Martin's Lane. *Scene 6*: Trafalgar Square. *Scene 7*: St. Martin's Lane. *Scene 8*: The Regent's Apartment. The next morning. *Scene 9*: The Great Hall of the Embassy.

Act 2, Scene 1: Westminster Abbey. *Scene 2*: The Regent's Apartment. *Scene 3*: A Drawing Room, Carpathian Embassy. *Scene 4*: The Foreign Office Ball. *Scene 5*: St. Martin's Lane. *Scene 6*: The Regent's Apartment, after the Ball. *Scene 7*: The Regent's Apartment. The next morning.

ACT 1
Scene 1
"Swing Song"
M. Haraldson, J. Eddleman, Ensemble
"Yasni Kozkolai" (Carpathian National Anthem)
Ensemble
"My Family Tree"
J. Ferrer, R. Cook, Regent's Aides
Scene 2
"I've Been Invited to a Party"
F. Henderson
Scene 3
Waltz
Ensemble
"I've Been Invited to a Party" (reprise)
F. Henderson
Scene 4
"When Foreign Princes Come to Visit Us"
C. Nairnes, Footmen
"Sir or Ma'am"
R. Cook
"Soliloquies"
J. Ferrer, F. Henderson
"Lonely"
J. Ferrer
Scene 6
"London Is a Little Bit of All Right"
"What Ho, Mrs. Brisket"
"Don't Take Our Charlie for the Army"
"Saturday Night at the Rose and Crown"
T. O'Shea, S. Scully, Ensemble
Scene 7
"London Is a Little Bit of All Right" (reprise)
T. O'Shea
Scene 8
"Here and Now"
F. Henderson
"I've Been Invited to a Party" (reprise)
F. Henderson
Scene 9
"Soliloquies" (reprise)
J. Ferrer, F. Henderson
ACT 2
Scene 1
"Coronation Chorale"
F. Henderson, J. Ferrer, Principals, Ensemble
Scene 2
"How Do You Do, Middle Age?"
J. Ferrer
Scene 3
"Here and Now" (reprise)
F. Henderson

Scene 4
"The Stingaree"
J. Ferrer, I. Murai, Ensemble
"Curt, Clear and Concise"
J. Ferrer, R. Cook
"Tango"
J. Ferrer, F. Henderson, Dancing Ensemble
Scene 5
"The Cocoanut Girl":
"Welcome to Pootzie Van Doyle"/"Paddy MacNeil and His Automobile"/"Swing Song"/"Six Lillies of the Valley"/"The Walla Walla Boola"
F. Henderson
Scene 6
"This Time It's True Love"
F. Henderson
Scene 7
"This Time It's True Love" (reprise)
J. Ferrer
"I'll Remember Her"
J. Ferrer

1963.30 DOUBLE DUBLIN

An Entertainment (Revue) in Two Acts. Supervised by Gus Schirmer. Musical direction by Baldwin Bergersen. Setting and lighting by Helen Pond and Herbert Senn. Musical numbers edited by David Nillo. Music arranged and played by Baldwin Bergersen. Produced by Josephine Forrestal Productions, Inc. Opened 26 December 1963 at the Little Theatre and closed 28 December 1963 after 4 performances.

CAST: JOHN MOLLOY, NOEL SHERIDAN, DEIRDRE O'CALLAGHAN, PATRICIA BROGAN.

ACT 1
Audience Reflections
J. Molloy, N. Sheridan
Window Dressing
J. Molloy
100, 000 Welcomes
N. Sheridan
Darts
J. Molloy
Rural Character
J. Molloy
"Gaelic Air"
D. O'Callaghan
The Importance of Behan
N. Sheridan
Amateur Theatricals
J. Molloy, N. Sheridan, P. Brogan, D. O'Callaghan
Joyce's Dublin
J. Molloy, N. Sheridan, P. Brogan, D. O'Callaghan
"Dublin Saunter"
D. O'Callaghan
"Irish Jig"
P. Brogan

ACT 2
Irish Station Break
Four Portraits
J. Molloy
Bonnet Trimmed With the Blue
D. O'Callaghan, N. Sheridan
Folk Singer
J. Molloy, N. Sheridan
Keeping Up With the Jones
N. Sheridan
The Fish Gutter
J. Molloy
"I Was Strolling"
D. O'Callaghan
Portrait in Oils
N. Sheridan
"The Green Bushes"
D. O'Callaghan
Matchmaker
J. Molloy, N. Sheridan
Finale
The Company

1964.01 HELLO, DOLLY!

A Musical Comedy in Two Acts, 15 Scenes. Book by Michael Stewart. Based on the play "The Matchmaker" by Thornton Wilder. Music and lyrics by Jerry Herman. Directed and choreographed by Gower Champion. Settings by Oliver Smith. Costumes by Freddy Wittop. Lighting by Jean Rosenthal. Musical direction and vocal arrangements by Shepard Coleman. Orchestrations by Philip J. Lang. Dance and incidental music arranged by Peter Howard. Assistant to the director, Lucia Victor. A David Merrick-Champion Five Inc. Production. Produced by David Merrick. Opened 16 January 1964 at the St. James Theatre and closed 27 December 1970 after 2844 performances[8].

CAST (in the order of appearance): *Mrs. Dolly Gallagher Levi*: CAROL CHANNING. *Ernestina*: Mary Jo Catlett. *Ambrose Kemper*: Igors Gavon. *Horse*: Jan LaPrade, Bonnie Mathis. *Horace Vandergelder*: DAVID BURNS. *Ermengarde*: Alice Playten. *Cornelius Hackl*: CHARLES NELSON REILLY. *Barnaby Tucker*: JERRY DODGE. *Irene Molloy*: EILEEN BRENNAN. *Minnie Fay*: SONDRA LEE. *Mrs. Rose*: Amelia Haas. *Rudolph*: David Hartman. *Judge*: Gordon Connell. *Court Clerk*: Ken Ayers.

Townspeople, Waiters, Etc.: Nicole Barth, Monica Carter, Carvel Carter, Amelia Haas, Jan LaPrade, Joan Buttons Leonard, Marilyne Mason, Bonnie Mathis, Else Olufsen, Yolanda Poropat, Bonnie Schon, Barbara Sharma, Mary Ann Snow, Jamie Thomas, Pat Trott, Ken Ayers, Alvin Beam, Joel Craig, Dick Crowley, Gene Gebauer, Joe Helms, Richard Hermany, Neil Jones, Charles Karel, Paul Kastl, Jim Maher, Joe McWherter, John Mineo, Randy Phillips, Lowell Purvis, Michael Quinn, Will Roy, Paul Solen, Ronnie Young.

The action takes place in Yonkers and New York City in the 1890s.

Act 1, Scene 1: Along Fourth Avenue, New York City. *Scene 2*: Grand Central Station. *Scene 3*: A Street in Yonkers. *Scene 4*: Vandergelder's Hay and Feed Store, Yonkers. *Scene 5*: The Yonkers Depot. *Scene 6*: Outside Mrs, Malloy's Hat Shop. Water Street, New York City. *Scene 7*: Inside the Hat Shop. *Scene 8*: A Quiet Street. *Scene 9*: Fourteenth Street.

Act 2, Scene 1: In front of the Hoffman House Hotel on Fifth Avenue. *Scene 2*: Outside the Harmonia Gardens Restaurant on the Battery. *Scene 3*: Inside the Harmonia Gardens Restaurant. *Scene 4*: Tableaux Vivantes. *Scene 5*: A Courtroom on Centre Street. *Scene 6*: The Hay and Feed Store, Yonkers.

ACT 1[9]
Scene 2
"I Put My Hand In"
C. Channing, Company
Scene 4
"It Takes a Woman"
D. Burns, Instant Glee Club
"Put on Your Sunday Clothes"
C. N. Reilly, J. Dodge, C. Channing, I. Gavon, A. Playten
Scene 5
"Put on Your Sunday Clothes" (reprise)
The People of Yonkers
Scene 7
"Ribbons Down My Back"
E. Brennan

---

[8]Pearl Bailey and Cab Calloway headed an all-black cast which performed two years of the show's continuous run (889 performances) 12 November 1967-20 December 1969; see separate entry in 1967-1968 season.
[9]When Ethel Merman assumed the role of Dolly Levi in March 1970, added were:
"World, Take Me Back"
E. Merman
(added to Act 1, Scene 4 between "It Takes a Woman" and "Sunday Clothes")
"Love, Look in My Window" (Act 1, Scene 8)
E. Merman

"Motherhood"
C. Channing, D. Burns, E. Brennan, S. Lee, C. N. Reilly, J. Dodge
"Dancing"
C. Channing, C. N. Reilly, J. Dodge, S. Lee, E. Brennan, Dancers
Scene 9
"Before the Parade Passes By"
C. Channing, D. Burns, Company

ACT 2
Scene 1
"Elegance"
E. Brennan, C. N. Reilly, S. Lee, J. Dodge
Scene 3
"The Waiter's Gallop"
D. Hartman, Waiters
"Hello, Dolly!"
C. Channing, D. Hartman, Waiters, Cooks
Scene 4
"Come and Be My Butterfly"[10]
I. Gavon, Muses, Nymphs, Flowers, Butterflies
Scene 5
"It Only Takes a Moment"
C. N. Reilly, E. Brennan, Prisoners, Policemen
"So Long Dearie"
C. Channing, D. Burns
Scene 6
"Hello, Dolly!" (reprise)
C. Channing, D. Burns
Finale
Company

1964.02 JOSEPHINE BAKER AND HER COMPANY

A Musical Revue in Two Acts, 12 Scenes. Production consultant and staging by Felix G. Gerstman. Miss Baker's costumes by Christian Dior, Pierre Balmain, House of Lanvin, and Balenciaga. Scenery by Joseph Hansen. Musical director, Gershon Kingsley. Lighting by Michael Price. Produced by Sherman S. Krellberg. Opened 4 February 1964 at the Brooks Atkinson Theatre and closed 16 February 1964 after 16 performances; reopened 31 March 1964 at the Henry Miller's Theatre and closed 19 April 1964 after 24 additional performances. Total: 40 performances.

CAST: JOSEPHINE BAKER, GEOFFREY HOLDER, AVIV DANCERS (Frances Alenikoff, Larry Bianco, Mary Ann Bruning, Carol Flemming, Jerry Scott), Eliezer Adoram (Singer, Accordionist, Music director for the Aviv Dancers), LARL BECHAM TRIO (Primitive and Modern Dance Group).

ACT 1
Scene 1
"Avec" (from the French revue PARIS MES AMOURS)
(*Music and Lyrics by* Henri Betti, Bruno Coquatrix and Andre Hornez.)
"Quand tu m'embrasse"
(*Music and Lyrics by* Charles Aznavour and Eddie Barclay.)
"Make Believe" (from SHOWBOAT)
(*Music by* Jerome Kern. Lyrics by Oscar Hammerstein II.)
"Quando, Quando"
(*Music by* Tony Renis. *Italian Lyrics by* A. Testa.)
J. Baker
Scene 2
Geoffrey Holder
Scene 3
"Don't Touch My Tomatoes" (from the French revue PARIS MES AMOURS)
(*Music and Lyrics by* Henry Lemarchand and Jo Bouillon.)
J. Baker
Scene 4
Larl Becham Trio
Scene 5
"La Seine"
(*Music and Lyrics by* Guy Lafarge and Flavien Monod. *English Lyrics by* Geoffrey Parsons.)
"Hello, Young Lovers" (from THE KING AND I)
(*Music by* Richard Rodgers. *Lyrics by* Oscar Hammerstein II.)
"Mon bateau blanc"
(*Music and Lyrics by* Gilbert Becaud and Maurice Vidalin.)
"Felicida" (Esto es Felicidad)
J. Baker
(*Music and Lyrcis by* Oscar de la Rosa, Bobby Collazo, Carlos Menendez.)
Scene 6
Israeli Festival (Variations and Debka)
Polynka (A Russian Peasant Dance)
The Aviv Dancers
Scene 7
"(En) Avril à Paris"
(*Music and Lyrics by* Charles Trenet.)/
"April in Paris" (from WALK A LITTLE FASTER)
(*Music by* Vernon Duke. *Lyrics by* E. Y. Harburg. *French Lyrics by* Duck.)
"Addios, Addios"
"Bill" (from SHOWBOAT)
(*Music by* Jerome Kern. *Lyrics by* P. G. Wodehouse.)
"Je pars"
(*Music and Lyrics by* Morton and Selma Craft.)
J. Baker

ACT 2
Scene 1
"Melodie perdue"
(*Music and Lyrics by* Hubert Giraud and Jean Broussolle.)
"(You Are My) Lucky Star" (from film BROADWAY MELODY OF 1936)
(*Music by* Nacio Herb Brown. *Lyrics by* Arthur Freed.)
"Enamorada"
(*Music and Lyrics by* Augusto Alguerro and Leon Arias Rafael.)
"J'ai deux amours"
(*Music and Lyrics by* Georges Koger, Henri Varna, and Vincent Scotto.)
J. Baker
Scene 2
The Aviv Dancers
Scene 3
"Hava Naguila"
(*Arranged by* Harry Belafonte and Lorin.)
J. Baker
Scene 4
Geoffrey Holder
Scene 5
"Fan, Fan"
"La Novia"
(*Music and Lyrics by* J. Prieto.)
"Et pourtant"
(*Music by* Georges Garvarentz. *Lyrics by* Charles Aznavour.)
"Dans mon village"
(*Music and Lyrics by* Henry Lemarchand and Francis Lopez.)
"J'attendrai"
(*Music and Lyrics by* Rastelli, Dino Olivieri and Louis Poterat.)
J. Baker

1964.03 RUGANTINO

A Roman Musical Spectacle (Musical Comedy) in Two Acts, 24 Scenes, in Italian[11]. Book, lyrics and direction by (Pietro) Garinei and (Sandro) Giovannini. Book in collaboration with Festa Campanile and Massimo

[10]Dropped early in the run and replaced by:
"The Polka Contest"
I. Gavon, A. Playten, E. Brennan, C. N. Reilly, S. Lee, J. Dodge, Ensemble

[11]Presented with English subtitles projected on a screen. Title consultant was Herman G. Weinberg with title coordination by Jack Harrold and projection by Bob Swanson, Telesync.

Franciosa. Music by Armando Trovaioli. English version [supertitles] by Alfred Drake. Lyric translation by Edward Eager. Scenery and costumes by Giulio Coltellacci. Musical numbers staged by Dania Krupska. Musical director, Anton Coppola. Scenic supervision, Eldon Elder. Lighting by Vannio Vanni. Technical direction by Ralph Alswang. Production associate, Andre Goulston. Produced by Alexander H. Cohen and Jack Hylton. Opened 6 February 1964 at the Mark Hellinger Theatre and closed 29 February 1964 after 28 performances.

CAST (in order of appearance): *Rugantino*: NINO MANFREDI. *Mariotto*: Goffredo Spinedi. *Rubastracci*: Giuseppe Pennese. *Strappalenzola*: Fernando Martino. *Brother Tappetto*: Lino Benedetti. *Bellachioma*: Toni Ventura. *The Brigadier*: Willy Colombini. *Chief Bandit*: Armando Silverini. *Rosetta*: ORNELLA VANONI. *Gnecco*, Rosetta's husband: RENZO PALMER. *Mastro Titta*: ALDO FABRIZI. *Bojetto*, Mastro Titta's son: CARLO DELLE PIANE. *Donna Marta Paritelli*: FRANCA TAMANTINI. *Don Nicoló Paritelli*: Toni Ucci. *Eusebia*: BICE VALORI. *The Barber*: Giorgio Zaffaroni. *Thorwaldsen*, the sculptor: Cesare Gelli. *Don Fulgenzio*: Giorgio Fabretti. *The Troubador* (Calascione): LANDO FIORINI. *The Lover*: Marcello Serrallonga. *The Goat Keeper*: Luciano Bonanni. *Old Lady of the Cats*: Simona Sorlisi. *Cardinal Severini*: Gino Mucci. *Gentleman*: Angelo Pericet. *Gendarmes*: Renato Ghigi, Angelo Michelotti.

Dancers and Singers: Goffredo Spinedi, Toni Ventura, Willy Colombini, Giorgio Zaffaroni, Marcello Serrallonga, Angelo Infanti, Luciano Bernardi, Fernando Martino, Franco Di Toro, Gabriele Villa, Giuseppe Pennese, Lino Benedetti, Josephine Spinedi, Gianna Zorini, Lettie Zaffaroni, Gina Sampieri, Lida Vianello, Renata Zamengo, Brigitte Kirfel, Gabriella Panenti, Carla Russo, Barbara Schaub, Yvonne De Vintar, Maurizia Camilli. *Chorus of Nora Orlandi*: Armando Silverini, Ercole Vulpiani, Margherita Brancucci, Raffaella Caratelli.

The action takes place in Rome in the year 1830 during the reign of Pope Pius VIII.

Act 1, Scene 1: The Square before Mastro Titta's Tavern. *Scene 2*: Rosetta's Bedroom. *Scene 3*: A Room in the Paritelli Palace. *Scene 4*: The Square. *Scene 5*: Rosetta's Bedroom. *Scene 6*: The Square. *Scene 7*: Outside the Paritelli Palace. *Scene 8*: The Docks. *Scene 9*: The Dining Hall of Paritelli Palace. *Scene 10*: The Street-Barber's. *Scene 11*: The Studio of the Sculptor, Thorwaldsen. *Scene 12*: The Parish Church. *Scene 13*: The Square. *Scene 14*: San Michele Prison. *Scene 15*: The Square on Lantern Night. *Scene 16*: Rosetta's Bedroom.

Act 2, Scene 1: A Corner of Campo Vaccino. *Scene 2*: The Square before the Church of San Pasquale. *Scene 3*: A Corner of the Forum frequented by the hungry stray cats of Rome. *Scene 4*: The Square. *Scene 5*: The Churchyard. *Scene 6*: Mastro Titta's Cellar. *Scene 7*: San Michele Prison. *Scene 8*: A Square in Rome at dawn.

ACT 1

"The Game of Morra" (La Morra)
The Men
"Rugantino in the Stocks" (La Berlina)
Rugantino's 'Friends'
"A House Is Not the Same Without a Woman" (E Bello Avè 'na Donna Dentro Casa)
A. Fabrizi
"Nothing to Do" (Ballata Di Rugantino)
N. Manfredi, the Romans
"Just Look!" (Anvedi Sì Che Paciocca)
O. Vanoni, L. Fiorini, Boys
"The Saltarello"
B. Valori, A. Fabrizi, Ensemble
"Tirrallallera" (Tirollallero)
L. Fiorini
"The Headsman and I"
B. Valori
"Nothing To Do" (reprise)
N. Manfredi
"Ciumachella" (Ciumachella De Trastevere)
L. Fiorini
"Lantern Night"
Ensemble
"Roma" (Roma Nun Fa La Stupida Stasera)
N. Manfredi, O. Vanoni, B. Valori, A. Fabrizi, Ensemble

ACT 2

"Ciumachella" (reprise)
Ensemble
"I'm Happy" (Tira a Campà)
N. Manfredi
"Just Stay Alive" (Sempre Boia È)
A. Fabrizi, Ensemble
"San Pasquale"
B. Valori, Spinsters
"Passatella" (The Drinking Game)
L. Fiorini, G. Spinedi, N. Manfredi, Boys
"It's Quick and Easy" ('Na Botta E Via)
O. Vanoni, Boys
"Dance of the Candle Killers"
Ensemble
"Boy and Man" (È L'Omo Mio)
O. Vanoni
Finale
B. Valori, O. Vanoni, A. Fabrizi, N. Manfredi

1964.04

FOXY

A Musical Comedy in Two Acts, 14 Scenes. Book by Ian McLellan Hunter and Ring Lardner, Jr. Suggested by Ben Jonson's play "Volpone." Music by Robert Emmett Dolan. Lyrics by Johnny Mercer. Directed by Robert Lewis. Choreography and musical numbers staged by Jack Cole. Scenery and lighting by Robert Randolph. Costumes by Robert Fletcher. Musical direction and vocal arrangements by Don Pippin. Orchestrations by Eddie Sauter and Hal Schaefer. Dance music arranged by Hal Schaefer. Produced by David Merrick. Opened 16 February 1964 at the Ziegfeld Theatre and closed 18 April 1964 after 72 performances.

CAST (in order of appearance): *Doc*: LARRY BLYDEN. *Foxy*: BERT LAHR. *Bedrock*: ROBERT H. HARRIS. *Buzzard*: EDWARD GREENHALGH. *Shortcut*: GERALD HIKEN. *Drunk*: Tony Kraber. *Mountie*: John Hallow. *Brandy*: CATHRYN DAMON. *Oliver*: Will Parkins. *Celia*: JULIENNE MARIE. *First Prospector*: Newt Sullivan. *Second Prospector*: Eddie James. *Third Prospector*: Herb Fields. *Stirling*: David Rounds. *First Eskimo*: John Waller. *Second Eskimo*: John Aristides. *Lord Rottingham*: ANTHONY KEMBLE COOPER. *Clergyman*: John Taliaferro. *Ben*: JOHN DAVIDSON. *Laurette*: Mary Ann Corrigan. *Marie*: Constance Meng. *Bellboy*: John Taliferro.

Prospectors: John Aristides, Carlos Bas, Charles Cagle, George Del Monte, Lang Des Jardins, Herbert Fields, Tim Harum, Lee Howard, Eddie James, John Keatts, Robert LaCrosse, Will Parkins, Newt Sullivan, John Taliaferro, John Waller. *Saloon Girls*: Helen Baisley, Mary Ann Corrigan, Virginia Craig, Judith Dunford, Alice Glenn, Marlena Lustik, Ethel Martin, Constance Meng, Nancy Myers, Shelly Rann, Sueanne Shirley, June Eve Story, Susan Terry.

Act 1, Scene 1: Trading Post, Alaska. *Scene 2*: Brandy's Saloon. *Scene 3*: Buzzard's Cabin. *Scene 4*: Buzzard's Cabin. *Scene 5*: Steamboat Landing. *Scene 6*: Buzzard's Cabin. *Scene 7*: Brandy's Saloon.

Act 2, Scene 1: Outside Hotel. *Scene 2*: Hotel Room. *Scene 3*: Outside Hotel. *Scene 4*: Buzzard's Cabin. *Scene 5*: Front Street—Saloon. *Scene 6*: Brandy's Office. *Scene 7*: Brandy's Saloon.

ACT 1

Prologue
L. Blyden
"Many Ways to Skin a Cat"
B. Lahr, L. Blyden
"Rollin' in Gold"
C. Damon, Ensemble
"My Weight in Gold"
J. Marie
"Money Isn't Everything"
B. Lahr, L. Blyden, R. H. Harris, G. Hiken, E. Greenhalgh, Ensemble
"Larceny and Love"
C. Damon, L. Blyden
"Ebeneezer McAfee III"
Ensemble
"Talk to Me, Baby"
J. Marie, J. Davidson
"This Is My Night to Howl"
G. Hiken, J. Davidson, Ensemble
"Bon Vivant"
B. Lahr, Ensemble
Finale Act 1
Ensemble

ACT 2

Entr'acte
Ensemble
"It's Easy When You Know How"
L. Blyden

"Run, Run, Run Cinderella"
J. Marie
"Talk To Me, Baby" (reprise)
J. Davidson
"I'm Way Ahead of the Game"
C. Damon, L. Blyden
"A Case of Rape"
J. Marie, J. Davidson, Ensemble
"In Loving Memory"
B. Lahr, L. Blyden, R. H. Harris, G. Hiken, E. Greenhalgh, Ensemble
Finale
B. Lahr, L. Blyden, Ensemble

1964.05 WHAT MAKES SAMMY RUN?

A Musical Comedy in Two Acts, 16 Scenes. Book by Budd and Stuart Schulberg. Based on the novel of the same name by Budd Schulberg. Music and lyrics by Ervin Drake. Directed by Abe Burrows. Musical staging by Matt Mattox. Settings and lighting by Herbert Senn and Helen Pond. Costumes by Noel Taylor. Vocal arrangements and musical direction by Lehman Engel. Orchestrations by Don Walker. Dance arrangements by Arnold Goland. Orchestrations by Don Walker. Production supervised by Robert Weiner. A Cates Brothers Production in association with Beresford Productions Ltd. Produced by Joseph Cates. Opened 27 February 1964 at the 54th Street Theatre and closed 12 June 1965 after 540 performances.

CAST (in order of appearance): *Al Manheim*: ROBERT ALDA. *Sammy Glick*: STEVE LAWRENCE. *O'Brien*: RALPH STANTLEY. *Osborn*: John Dorrin. *Bartender*: Ralph Vucci. *Julian Blumberg*: George Coe. *Rita Rio*: GRACIELA DANIELE. *Tracy Clark*: RICHARD FRANCE. *Lucky Dugan*: Edward McNally. *Shiek Orsini*: BARRY NEWMAN. *Technical Advisor*: Bob Maxwell. *Sidney Fineman*: ARNY FREEMAN. *Kit Sargent*: SALLY ANN HOWES. *H. L. Harrington*: WALTER KLAVUN. *Laurette Harrington*: BERNICE MASSI. *Seymour Glick*: MACE BARRETT.

Singing Ensemble: Lillian Bozinoff, Natalie Costa, Judith Hastings, Jamie Simmons, Darrell J. Askey, John Dorrin, Richard Terry, Ralph Vucci. *Dancing Ensemble*: Diaan Ainslee, Nancy Carnegie, Barbara Gine, Lavina Hamilton, Bella Shalom, Maralyn Thoma, Jean Blanchard, Marco Gomez, Buck Heller, Nat Horne, Jack Kresy. *Swing Couple*: Lynn Gremmler, Doug Spingler.

The action takes place in New York and Hollywood a generation ago.

Act 1, Scene 1: The City Room of the *New York Record*. *Scene 2*: Joe's Bar. *Scene 3*: The *New York Record*. *Scene 4*: World-Wide Pictures Sound Stage. *Scene 5*: The Studio Street. *Scene 6*: The Sound Stage. *Scene 7*: The Patio of Fineman's Mansion. *Scene 8*: Kit's House.

Act 2, Scene 1: The Court of Grauman's Chinese Theatre. *Scene 2*: Joe's Bar. *Scene 3*: Kit's Terrace. *Scene 4*: The World-Wide Penthouse in New York. *Scene 5*: Kit's Terrace. *Scene 6*: Sammy's Office. *Scene 7*: Sammy's Mansion. *Scene 8*: Sammy's Mansion.

ACT 1
Scene 1
"A New Pair of Shoes"
S. Lawrence, R. Alda, Ensemble
Scene 2
"You Help Me"
S. Lawrence, R. Alda
Scene 4
"A Tender Spot"
S. A. Howes
Scene 5
"Lites-Camera-Platitude"
S. Lawrence, S. A. Howes, R. Alda
Scene 6
"My Hometown"
S. Lawrence
"Monsoon" (Ballet)
G. Daniele, R. France, Ensemble
Scene 7
"I See Something"
B. Massi, S. Lawrence
Scene 8
"Maybe Some Other Time"
S. A. Howes, R. Alda
"You Can Trust Me"
S. Lawrence
"A Room Without Windows"
S. A. Howes, S. Lawrence
"Kiss Me No Kisses"
S. A. Howes, S. Lawrence

ACT 2
Scene 1
"I Feel Humble"
S. Lawrence, B. Newman, Ensemble
Scene 3
"Something to Live For"
S. A. Howes
Scene 4
"Paint a Rainbow"
G. Daniele, R. France, Ensemble
"You're No Good"
B. Massi, S. Lawrence
Scene 5
"Something To Live For" (reprise)
R. Alda
Scene 6
"My Hometown" (reprise)[12]
S. Lawrence
"The Friendliest Thing"
B. Massi
Scene 7
"Wedding of the Year"
Ensemble
Scene 8
"Some Days Everything Goes Wrong"
S. Lawrence

1964.06 LA VIE PARISIENNE

A Revival of the Opéra-Bouffe in Four Acts, in French[13]. Libretto by Henri Meilhac and Ludovic Halévy. Music by Jacques Offenbach. Decor and costumes by Jean-Denis Malcles. Directed by Jean-Louis Barrault. Dances arranged by Roger Stefani. Orchestra conducted by Andre Girard. The Theatre De France Company produced by Sol Hurok, by arrangement with the Government of the French Republic. Opened 10 March 1964 at the New York City Center and closed 15 March 1964 after 8 performances.

CAST: *Bobinet*: Jean-Pierre Granval. *Gardefeu*: Jean Desailly. *The Baron*: Pierre Bertin. *The Brazilian*: JEAN-LOUIS BARRAULT. *Frick, Prosper, Alfred*: JEAN PAREDES. *Gontran, Urbain*: Dominique Santarelli. *Joseph*: Robert Lombardi. *Alphonse*: Regis Outin. *The Man Who Waits*: Michel Bertay. *Metella*: SUZY DELAIR. *The Baroness*: Sarah Sanders. *Gabrielle*: Simone Valère. *Pauline*: Denise Benoît. *The Sweeper*: Marie-Helene Daste.

Chorus and French Can-Can: Judith Alexandre, Dominique Arden, Paulette Attie, Christine Bottai, Claudie Bourlon, Josette Grisy, Sabine Lods, Jane Martel, Nicole Levat, Celine Salles, Andre Batisse, Georges Coste, Henri Gilabert, Jean-Guy Henneveux, Bernard Laik, Gilbert Lefevre, Luis Masson, Gerard Quenez, Stanislas Staskewitsch, Jean Winkler.

1964.07 THE YEOMEN OF THE GUARD, or The Merryman and His Maid

A Revival of the Comic Opera in Two Acts[14]. Libretto by William S. Gilbert. Music by Arthur Sullivan. Staged by Allen Fletcher. Scenery by Stephen O. Saxe. Costumes by Alvin Colt. Conducted by Julius Rudel. Produced by the New York City Center Gilbert and Sullivan Company. Opened 18 March 1964 at the New York City Center and closed 29 March 1964 after 3 performances in repertory.

[12]Dropped from programs during run.
[13]First produced in New York 29 March 1869 at the Theatre Francais. For Synopsis of Scenes and Musical Numbers, see original 1869 production.
[14]First presented in New York 17 October 1888 at the Casino Theatre for 100 performances. For Synopsis of Scenes and Musical Numbers, see original 1888 production.

CAST: *Sir Richard Cholmondeley*, Lieutenant. of the Tower: PAUL UKENA. *Colonel Fairfax* under sentence of death: ROBERT ROUNSEVILLE. *Sergeant Meryll* of the Yeomen of the Guard: GEORGE GAYNES. *Leonard Meryll*, his Son: RICHARD KRAUSE. *Jack Point*, a Strolling Jester: NORMAN KELLEY. *Wilfred Shadbolt*, Head Jailor and Assistant Tormentor: HERBERT BEATTIE. *The Headsman*: Thomas Andrew. *First Yeoman*: Herbert Pordum. *Second Yeoman*: Sean Barker. *First Citizen*: Harris Davis. *Second Citizen*: Glenn Dowlen. *Elsie Maynard*, a Strolling Player: MARY JENNINGS. *Phoebe Meryll*, Sergeant Meryll's Daughter: MARY BURGESS. *Dame Carruthers*, Housekeeper to the Tower: EVELYN SACHS. *Kate*, her Niece: VIRGINIA BITAR.

Chorus of Yeomen of the Guard, Gentlemen, Citizens, etc.: Barbara Beaman, Paul Corder, Harris Davis, Marceline Decker, Anthea de Forest, Glen Dowlen, Roebrt Edwards, Beverly Evans, Frederic Griesinger, Helen Guile, Don Henderson, Lila Herbert, David Hicks, Lynda Jordan, Robert Lee Kelly, Kellis Miller, Hanna Owen, Richard G. Park, Charlotte Povia, Lourette Raymon, Anthony Safina, Alexander Savchuck, John Smith, Dale Westerman, Lou Ann Wyckoff, Marie Young.

1964.08 H.M.S. PINAFORE, or The Lass That Loved a Sailor

A Revival of the Comic Opera in Two Acts[15]. Libretto by William S. Gilbert. Music by Arthur Sullivan. Staged by Allen Fletcher. Scenery and costumes by Patton Campbell. Conductors, Felix Popper and Charles Wilson. Produced by the New York City Center Gilbert and Sullivan Company. Opened 20 March 1964 at the New York City Center and closed 2 April 1964 after 5 performances in repertory.

CAST: *The Rt. Hon. Sir Joseph Porter, K.C.B.*, First Lord of the Admiralty: RAYMOND ALLEN. *Captain Corcoran*, Commander of the *H.M.S. Pinafore*: WILLIAM CHAPMAN. *Ralph Rackstraw*, Able Seaman: ROBERT ROUNSEVILLE. *Dick Deadeye*, Able Seaman: PAUL UKENA. *Bill Bobstay*, Boatswain: Sean Barker. *Bob Becket*: Lee Cass. *Josephine*, the Captain's Daughter: CAROL BERGEY. *Hebe*, Sir Joseph's First Cousin: Marlena Kleinman. *Little Buttercup*, Mrs. Cripps, a Portsmouth bum-boat woman: EVELYN SACHS. *First Lord's Sisters, His Cousins, His Aunts, Sailors, Marines, etc.*: same as THE YEOMEN OF THE GUARD above.

1964.09 THE MIKADO, or The Town of Titipu

A Revival of the Comic Opera in Two Acts[16]. Libretto by William S. Gilbert. Music by Arthur Sullivan. Staged by Dorothy Raedler. Scenery by Donald Oenslager. Costumes by Patton Campbell. Conductor, Dean Ryan. Produced by the New York City Center Gilbert and Sullivan Company. Opened 22 March 1964 at the New York City Center and closed 5 April 1964 after 6 performances in repertory.

CAST: *The Mikado of Japan*: GEORGE GAYNES. *Nanki-Poo*: WILLIAM DIARD. *Ko-Ko*: NORMAN KELLEY. *Pooh-Bah*: HERBERT BEATTIE. *Pish-Tush*: DAVID SMITH. *Three Sisters, Wards of Ko-Ko*: *Yum-Yum*: CAROL BERGEY. *Pitti-Sing*: MARY BURGESS. *Peep-Bo*: MARLENA KLEINMAN. *Katisha*: EVELYN SACHS. *Chorus of School Girls, Nobles, Guards and Coolies*: same as THE YEOMEN OF THE GUARD above.

1964.10 PATIENCE, or Bunthorne's Bride

A Revival of the Comic Opera in Two Acts[17]. Libretto by William S. Gilbert. Music by Arthur Sullivan. Scenery and costumes designed by Motley. Staged by Dorothy Raedler. Solo dance choreography by Thomas Andrew. Conductor, Julius Rudel. Produced by the New York City Center Gilbert and Sullivan Company. Opened 25 March 1964 at the New York City Center and closed 5 April 1964 after 4 performances in repertory.

CAST: *Colonel Calverley*: WILLIAM CHAPMAN. *Major Murgatroyd*: James Wilson. *Lieut. the Duke of Dunstable*: RICHARD KRAUSE. *Reginald Bunthorne*, a Fleshly Poet: EMILE RENAN. *Archibald Grosvenor*, an Idyllic Poet: DAVID SMITH. *Mr. Bunsthorne's Solicitor*: Thomas Andrew. *The Lady Angela, The Lady Saphir, The Lady Ella, The Lady Jane*, Rapturous Maidens: MARLENA KLEINMAN, HELEN GUILE, Virginia Bitar, CLARAMAE TURNER. *Patience*, a Dairy Maid: LEE VENORA. *Chorus of Rapturous Maidens and Officers of the Dragoon Guards*: same as THE YEOMEN OF THE GUARD above.

[15]Originally presented in New York 15 January 1879 at the Standard Theatre for 175 performances. For Synopsis of Scenes and Musical Numbers, see original 1879 production.

[16]First presented in New York 20 July, 10-29 August 1885 at the Union Square and People's Theatres for 22 performances. First authorized production presented 19 August 1885 at the Fifth Avenue Theatre by Richard D'Oyly Carte for 250 performances. For Synopsis of Scenes and Musical Numbers, see 19 August 1885 D'Oyly Carte production.

[17]First presented in New York 22 September 1881 at the Standard Theatre for 177 performances. For Synopsis of Scenes and Musical Numbers, see original 1881 production.

1964.11 FUNNY GIRL

A Musical in Two Acts, 22 Scenes. Book and story[18] by Isobel Lennart. Music by Jule Styne. Lyrics by Bob Merrill. Directed by Garson Kanin. Musical numbers staged by Carol Haney. Scenery and lighting by Robert Randolph. Costumes by Irene Sharaff. Musical director, Milton Rosenstock. Orchestrations by Ralph Burns. Vocal arrangements by Buster Davis. Dance orchestrations by Luther Henderson. Associate producer, Al Goldin. Associate director, Lawrence Kasha. Produced by Ray Stark in association with Seven Arts Productions. Opened 26 March 1964 at the Winter Garden, moved 14 March 1966 to the Majestic Theatre, moved 28 November 1966 to the Broadway Theatre, and closed 1 July 1967 after 1348 performances.

CAST (in order of appearance): *Fanny Brice*: BARBRA STREISAND. *John*: Robert Howard. *Emma*: Royce Wallace. *Mrs. Brice*: KAY MEDFORD. *Mrs. Strakosh*: JEAN STAPLETON. *Mrs. Meeker*: Lydia S. Fredericks. *Mrs. O'Malley*: Joyce O'Neil. *Tom Keeney*: JOSEPH MACAULAY. *Eddie Ryan*: DANNY MEEHAN. *Heckie*: Victor R. Helou. *Workmen*: Robert Howard, Robert Henson. *Snub Taylor*: Buzz Miller. *Trombone Smitty*: Blair Hammond. *Five Finger Finney*: Alan (E.) Weeks. *Trumpet Soloist*: Dick Perry. *Bubbles*: Shellie Farrell. *Polly*: Joan Lowe. *Maude*: Ellen Halpin. *Nick Arnstein*: SYDNEY CHAPLIN. *Showgirls*: Sharon Vaughn, Diana Lee Nielsen. *Stage Director*: Marc Jordan. *Florenz Ziegfeld, Jr.*: ROGER DeKOVEN. *Mimsey*: Sharon Vaughn. *Ziegfeld Tenor*: John Lankston. *Ziegfeld Lead Dancer*: George Reeder. *Adolph*: John Lankston. *Mrs. Nadler*: Rose Randolf. *Paul*: Larry Fuller. *Cathy*: Joan Cory. *Vera*: Lainie Kazan. *Jenny*: Diane Coupe. *Ben*: Buzz Miller. *Mr. Renaldi*: Marc Jordan. *Mike Halsey*: Robert Howard.

Showgirls: Prudence Adams, Joan Cory, Diane Coupe, Lainie Kazan, Diana Lee Nielsen, Sharon Vaughn, Rosmarie Yellen. *Singers*: Lydia S. Fredricks, Mary Louise, Jeanne McLaren, Joyce O'Neil, Rose Randolf, Stephanie Reynolds, Victor R. Helou, Robert Henson, Robert Howard, Marc Jordan, John Lankston, Albert Zimmerman. *Dancers*: Edie Cowan, Christine Dalsey, Shellie Farrell, Ellen Halpin, Rosemary Jelinic, Karen Kristin, Joan Lowe, Jose Ahumada, Bud Fleming, Larry Fuller, Blair Hammond, John Nola, Alan Peterson, Alan E. Weeks.

The action takes place in various theatres, onstage and backstage, on New York's Lower East Side, in Baltimore, and on Long Island shortly before and after World War I.

Act 1, Scene 1: Backstage, Fanny's Dressing Room, about 1910. *Scene 2*: Kenney's Music Hall, backstage. *Scene 3*: In front of Kenney's Music Hall. *Scene 4*: A backyard in Fanny's neighborhood, 6 A.M. *Scene 5*: Kenney's Music Hall—on stage. *Scene 6*: Keeney's Music Hall, backstage and the Chorus Dressing Room, immediately following. *Scene 7*: Mrs. Brice's Kitchen. Months later. *Scene 8*: The New York Theatre—backstage. *Scene 9*: On the Stage of the New York Theatre, the grand finale of the Ziegfeld Follies. *Scene 10*: In front of the Follies curtain, immediately following. *Scene 11*: Outside the house at 24 Henry Street. *Scene 12*: The interior of Mrs. Brice's saloon. *Scene 13*: A private dining room in Baltimore. *Scene 14*: The Baltimore Railroad Terminal.

Act 2, Scene 1: The Arnstein Long Island Mansion, unfurnished and at night. *Scene 2*: Mrs. Brice's saloon. *Scene 3*: The New Amsterdam Theatre—backstage, around 1920. *Scene 4*: The New Amsterdam Theatre—on stage. *Scene 5*: Fanny's dressing room—immediately following. *Scene 6*: The study of the Arnstein house. *Scene 7*: The New Amsterdam Theatre—a bare stage rehearsal. *Scene 8*: The New Amsterdam Theatre—backstage, Fanny's dressing room.

ACT 1[19]

Scenes 1 and 2

"If A Girl Isn't Pretty"
J. Stapleton, K. Medford, D. Meehan, Chorus

Scene 3

"I'm the Greatest Star"
B. Streisand

Scene 5

"Cornet Man"
B. Streisand, B. Miller, Chorus

Scene 7

"Who Taught Her Everything"

[18]The life of Fanny Brice.

[19]Added to programs for National Tour, Act 1, Scene 7 (beginning):
Rehearsal (Downtown Rag)
Ziegfeld Company

K. Medford, D. Meehan
Scene 9
"His Love Makes Me Beautiful"
J. Lankston, Ziegfeld Girls, B. Streisand
Scene 10
"I Want To Be Seen With You Tonight"
S. Chaplin, B. Streisand
Scene 11
"Henry Street"
Chorus
"People"
B. Streisand
Scene 13
"You Are Woman"
S. Chaplin, B. Streisand
Scene 14
"Don't Rain on My Parade"
B. Streisand

ACT 2
Scene 1
"Sadie, Sadie"
B. Streisand, Friends
Scene 2
"Find Yourself a Man"
J. Stapleton, K. Medford, D. Meehan
Scenes 3 and 4
"Rat-Tat-Tat-Tat"
Ziegfeld Company, B. Streisand
Scene 5
"Who Are You Now?"
B. Streisand
Scene 7
"The Music That Makes Me Dance"
B. Streisand
Scene 8
"Don't Rain on My Parade" (reprise)
B. Streisand

THE GONDOLIERS, or The King of Barataria

1964.12

A Revival of the Comic Opera in Two Acts[20]. Libretto by William S. Gilbert. Music by Arthur Sullivan. Staged by Dorothy Raedler. Scenery and costumes by Ed Wittstein. Conductor, Felix Popper. Cachucha dance choreography by Thomas Andrew. Produced by the New York City Center Gilbert and Sullivan Company. Opened 27 March 1964 (matinee) at the New York City Center and closed 27 March 1964 (evening) after 2 performances in repertory.

CAST: *The Duke of Plaza-Toro*: NORMAN KELLEY. *Luiz*: THEODORE MORILL. *Don Alhambra Del Bolero*: GEORGE GAYNES. *Marco Palmieri*: CHARLES HINDSLEY. *Giuseppe Palmieri*: SEAN BARKER. *Antonio*: David Smith. *Francesco*: Herbert Pordum. *Giorgio*: John Smith. *The Duchess of Plaza-Toro*: CLARAMAE TURNER. *Casilda*: DONNA PRECHT. *Gianetta*: MARY JENNINGS. *Tessa*: MARLENA KLEINMAN. *Fiametta*: Virginia Bitar *Vittoria*: Mary Burgess. *Giulia*: Beverly Evans. *Inez*: Charlotte Povia. *Solo Cachucha Dancers*: Rochelle Zide, Thomas Andrew. *Chorus of Gondoliers, Contadine, Men-at-Arms, Heralds and Pages*: same as THE YEOMEN OF THE GUARD above.

THE PIRATES OF PENZANCE, or The Slave of Duty

1964.13

A Revival of the Comic Opera in Two Acts[21]. Libretto by William S. Gilbert. Music by Arthur Sullivan. Staged by Dorothy Raedler. Scenery by H. A. Condell. Conductor, Herbert Grossman. Produced by the New York City Center Gilbert and Sullivan Company. Opened 28 March 1964 at the New York City Center and closed 31 March 1964 after 4 performances in repertory.

CAST: *Major General Stanley*: EMILE RENAN. *The Pirate King*: WILLIAM CHAPMAN *Samuel*, his Lieutenant: William Ledbetter. *Frederic*, the Pirate Apprentice: CHARLES HINDSLEY. *Sergeant of Police*: HERBERT BEATTIE. *Mabel, Edith Kate, Isabel*, General Stanley's Daughters: ANNE ELGAR, VIRGINIA BITAR, MARY BURGESS, Helen Guile. *Ruth*, Pirate Maid-of-all-work: MURIEL GREENSPON. *Chorus of Pirates, Police and General Stanley's Daughters*: Same as THE YEOMEN OF THE GUARD above.

IOLANTHE, or The Peer and the Peri

1964.14

A Revival of the Comic Opera in Two Acts[22]. Libretto by William S. Gilbert. Music by Arthur Sullivan. Staged by Dorothy Raedler. Scenery and costumes by Gordon Micunis. Choreography, Thomas Andrew. Conductor, William Jonson. Produced by the New York City Center Gilbert and Sullivan Company. Opened 3 April 1964 at the New York City Center and closed 4 April 1964 after 3 performances in repertory.

CAST: *The Lord Chancellor*: NORMAN KELLY. *Lord Mountararat*: DAVID SMITH. *Lord Tolloller*: RICHARD KRAUSE. *Private Willis* of the Grenadier Guards: GEORGE GAYNES. *Strephon*, an Arcadian Shepherd: WILLIAM LEDBETTER. *Queen of the Fairies*: CLARAMAE TURNER. *Iolanthe*, a Fairy, Strephon's Mother: MARLENA KLEINMAN. *Celia, Leila, Fleta*, Fairies: Virginia Bitar, Mary Burgess, Beverly Evans. *The Bee*: Rochelle Zide. *The Dragonfly*: Hanna Owen. *The Butterfly*: Helen Guile. *Phyllis*, an Arcadian Shepherdess and Ward in Chancery: CAROL BERGEY. *Chorus of Dukes, Marquises, Earls, Viscounts, Barons and Fairies*: Same as THE YEOMEN OF THE GUARD above.

ANYONE CAN WHISTLE

1964.15

A Musical (Fable) in Two Acts, 12 Scenes. Book by Arthur Laurents. Music and Lyrics by Stephen Sondheim. Scenery by William and Jean Eckart. Costumes by Theoni V. Aldredge. Lighting by Jules Fisher. Dances and musical numbers staged by Herbert Ross. Entire Production directed by Arthur Laurents. Orchestrations by Don Walker. Vocal arrangements and musical direction by Herbert Greene. Dance arrangements by Betty Walberg. Associate producer, Arlene Sellers. Produced by Kermit Bloomgarden and Diana Krasny. Opened 4 April 1964 at the Majestic Theatre and closed 11 April 1964 after 9 performances.

CAST (in order of appearance): *Sandwich Man*: Jeff Killion. *Baby Joan*: Jeanne Tanzy. *Mrs. Schroeder*: Peg Murray. *Treasurer Cooley*: Arnold Soboloff. *Chief Magruder*: James Frawley. *Comptroller Schub*: GABRIEL DELL. *Cora Hoover Hooper*: ANGELA LANSBURY. *The Boys*: Sterling Clark, Harvey Evans, Larry Roquemore, Tucker Smith. *Fay Apple*: LEE REMICK. *J. Bowden Hapgood*: HARRY GUARDINO. *Dr. Detmold*: Don Doherty. *George*: Larry Roquemore. *June*: Janet Hayes. *John*: Harvey Evans. *Martin*: Lester Wilson. *Old Lady*: Eleonore Treiber. *Telegraph Boy*: Alan Johnson. *Osgood*: Georgia Creighton.

Cookies, Townspeople, Tourists: Susan Borree, Georgia Creighton, Janet Hayes, Bettye Jenkins, Patricia Kelly, Barbara Lang, Paula Lloyd, Barbara Monte, Odette Phillips, Hanne-Marie Reiner, Eleonore Treiber, Sterling Clark, Eugene Edwards, Harvey Evans, Dick Ensslen, Loren Hightower, Alan Johnson, Jeff Killion, Jack Murray, William Reilly, Larry Roquemore, Tucker Smith, Don Stewart, Lester Wilson.

The action takes place in a not too distant town. The time is now.

Act 1, Scene 1: The Town. *Scene 2*: The Miracle. *Scene 3*: The Interrogation. *Scene 4*: The Celebration. *Scene 5*: The Romance. *Scene 6*: The Parade. *Scene 7*: The Release.

Act 2, Scene 1: The Conspiracy. *Scene 2*: The Confrontation. *Scene 3*: The Cookie Chase. *Scene 4*: The Farewell. *Scene 5*: The End.

ACT 1
Scene 1
"I'm Like the Bluebird"
Company
"Me and My Town"
A. Lansbury, Boys
Scene 2
"Miracle Song"
A. Lansbury, A. Soboloff, Company

---

[20] Originally presented in New York 7 January 1890 at Park Theatre for 103 performances. For Synopsis of Scenes and Musical Numbers, see original 1890 production.

[21] First presented in New York 31 December 1879 at the Fifth Avenue Theatre for a total of 91 performances in two engagements. For Synopsis of Scenes and Musical Numbers, see original 1879 production.

[22] First presented in New York 25 November 1882 at the Standard Theatre for 105 performances. For Synopsis of Scenes and Musical Numbers, see original 1882 production.

Scene 3
"Simple"
H. Guardino, Company
Scene 4
"A-1 March"
Company
Scene 5
"Come Play Wiz Me"
L. Remick, H. Guardino, Boys
"Anyone Can Whistle"
L. Remick
Scene 6
"A Parade in Town"
A. Lansbury
Scene 7
"Everybody Says Don't"
H. Guardino
Ballet
L. Remick, H. Guradino, Cookies
Variation 1: L. Hightower, O. Phillips, E. Treiber. *Variation 2*: B. Monte. *Variation 3*: A. Johnson, P. Lloyd. *Variation 4*: T. Smith. *Variaton 5*: L. Wilson, H. Reiner. *Variation 6*: W. Reilly, S. Clark, E. Ttreiber, L. Roquemore, H. Evans, B. Jenkins.

ACT 2
Scene 1
"I've Got You to Lean On"
A. Lansbury, G. Dell, A. Soboloff, J. Frawley, Boys
Scene 2
"See What It Gets You"
L. Remick
Scene 3
"The Cookie Chase" (Waltzes)
A. Lansbury, L. Remick, G. Dell, Company
Dancing Deputies: L. Roquemore, T. Smith, H. Evans. *Old Lady*: E. Treiber. *Waltz 1*: O. Phillips. *Waltz 2*: B. Monte. *Waltz 3*: B. Jenkins, A. Johnson. *Waltz 4*: G. Dell, P. Lloyd, H. Reiner, S. Borree, P. Kelly. *Waltz 5*: S. Clark. *Waltz 6*: B. Jenkins. *Pas De Deux*: H. Reiner, W. Reilly. *Gallop*: L. Hightower. *Finale*: Company.
Scene 4
"With So Little to Be Sure Of"
L. Remick, H. Guardino
Scene 5
Finale
Company

1964.16 HIGH SPIRITS

An Improbable Musical Comedy in Two Acts, 12 Scenes. Book, music and lyrics by Hugh Martin and Timothy Gray. based on the play "Blithe Spirit" by Nöel Coward. Directed by Nöel Coward[23]. Settings and costumes by Robert Fletcher. Miss Grimes' costume by Valentina. Lighting by Jules Fisher. Musical direction, Fred Werner. Vocal direction and arrangements by Hugh Martin and Timothy Gray. Orchestrations by Harry Zimmerman. Dance music by Billy Goldenberg. Dances and musical numbers staged by Danny Daniels. Produced by Lester Osterman, Robert Fletcher and Richard Horner. Opened 7 April 1964 at the Alvin Theatre and closed 27 February 1965 after 375 performances.

CAST (in order of appearance): *Charles Condomine*: EDWARD WOODWARD. *Edith*: Carol Arthur. *Ruth Condomine*: LOUISE TROY. *Mrs. Bradman*: Margaret Hall. *Dr. Bradman*: Lawrence Keith. *Madame Arcati*: BEATRICE LILLIE. *Elvira*: TAMMY GRIMES. *Bob*: Robert Lenn. *Beth*: Beth Howland. *Rupert*: Gene Castle.

Singing and Dancing Ensemble: Adrienne Angel, Syndee Balaber, Gene Castle, Jerry Craig, Jackie Cronin, Altovise Gore, Judith Haskell, Beth Howland, Jack Kauflin, Bill Kennedy, Al Lanti, Miriam Lawrence, Renee Lee, Robert Lenn, Alex MacKay, Jacqueline Maria, Stan Mazin, Joe McGrath, Don Percassi, Kathy Preston, Sybil Scotford, Tom Thornton, Ronnie Walken, Anne Wallace.

Act 1, Scene 1: The Condomines' living room. *Scene 2*: A road on the Heath; immediately following. *Scene 3*: The Condomines' living room, after dinner. *Scene 4*: The Condomines' terrace, the next morning. *Scene 5*: The Inner Circle, early that evening. *Scene 6*: The Condomines' living room, immediately following. *Scene 7*: The Roof Garden of the Grovechester Hotel, immediately following.

Act 2, Scene 1: The Condomines' living room, immediately following. *Scene 2*: Madame Arcati's Bedroom, the following morning. *Scene 3*: The Condomines' living room, that afternoon. *Scene 4*: The Inner Circle, that evening. *Scene 5*: The Condomines' living room, several hours later.

ACT 1
"Was She Pettier Than I?"
L. Troy
"The Bicycle Song"
B. Lillie, Ensemble
"You'd Better Love Me"
T. Grimes
"Where Is the Man I Married?"
E. Woodward, L. Troy
"The Sandwich Man"
R. Lenn, B. Howland
"Go Into Your Trance"
B. Lillie, Ensemble
"Where Is the Man I Married?" (reprise)
L. Troy
"Forever and a Day"
E. Woodward, T. Grimes
"Something Tells Me"
T. Grimes, Ensemble
"I Know Your Heart"
E. Woodward, T. Grimes
"Faster Than Sound"
T. Grimes, Ensemble

ACT 2
"If I Gave You"
E. Woodward, L. Troy
"Talking to You"
B. Lillie
"Home Sweet Heaven"
T. Grimes
"Something Is Coming to Tea" (Madame Arcati's Tea Party)
B. Lillie, Ensemble
"The Exorcism"
B. Lillie, Ensemble
"What in the World Did You Want?"
E. Woodward, T. Grimes, L. Troy
"Faster Than Sound" (reprise)
Entire Company

1964.17 WEST SIDE STORY

A Revival of the Musical in Two Acts, 15 Scenes[24]. Book by Arthur Laurents. Based on a conception of Jerome Robbins. Music by Leonard Bernstein. Lyrics by Stephen Sondheim. Original production directed and choreographed by Jerome Robbins. This production staged by Gerald Freedman. Choreography re-mounted by Tom Abbott. Original scenic production by Oliver Smith. This production designed by Peter Wolf. Costumes by Irene Sharaff, supervised by Stanley Simmons. Lighting by Jean Rosenthal. Original co-choreographer, Peter Gennaro. Musical direction, Charles Jaffe. (Orchestrations by Leonard Bernstein, with Sid Ramin, Irwin Kostal.) Produced by the New York City Center Light Opera Company (Jean Dalrymple, Director). Opened 8 April 1964 at the New York City Center and closed 3 May 1964 after 31 performances.

CAST: *THE JETS*: *Riff*, the Leader: JAMES MOORE. *Tony*, his friend: DON McKAY. *Action*: JOE BENNETT. *A-Rab*: Mark Jude Sheil. *Baby John*: Steve Curry. *Snowboy*: Barry Burns. *Big Deal*: Larry Moss. *Diesel*: Hamp Dickens. *Gee-Tar*: Danny Lockin. *Mouth Piece*: Joseph Corby. *Tiger*: John McCook. *Their Girls*: *Graziella*: Wilma Curley. *Velma*: Tobie Lynn. *Minnie*: Barbara Rogers. *Clarice*: Gloria Kaye. *Pauline*: Eileen Casey. *Anybodys*: Erin Martin.

[23]Additional direction by Gower Champion uncredited.

[24]Originally produced in New York 26 September 1957 at the Winter Garden for 732 performances and a return engagement of 249 performances. For Synopsis of Scenes and Musical Numbers, see original 1957 production.

THE SHARKS: *Bernardo*, the Leader: JAY NORMAN. *Maria*, his Sister: JULIA MIGENES. *Chino*, his Friend: B. J. DiSimone. *Pepe*: Noel Schwartz. *Indio*: Tim Ramirez. *Luis*: Jo Jo Smith. *Anxious*: Kent Thomas. *Nibbles*: Carlos Gorbea. *Juano*: Richard Balin. *Toro*: Carmine Terra. *Moose*: Eliot Feld. *Their Girls*: *Anita*, his Girl: LUBA LISA. *Rosalia*: Marilyn Cooper. *Consuelo*: Carmen Morales. *Teresita*: Ella Thompson. *Francisca*: Diana Corto. *Estella*: Lolli Hinton. *Marguerita*: Tina Faye.

THE ADULTS: *Doc*: HARRY DAVIS. *Schrank*: Ted Gunther. *Krupke*: Frank Downing. *Gladhand*: Brooks Morton.

1964.18 CAFE CROWN

A Musical Comedy in Two Acts, 12 Scenes. Book by Hy Kraft. Based on his play of the same name. Music by Albert Hague. Lyrics by Marty Brill. Scenery and lighting by Sam Leve. Costumes by Ruth Morley. Directed by Jerome Eskow. Choreography by Ronald [Ron] Field. Dance music by Albert Hague. Orchestrations by Hershy Kay. Vocal arrangements and musical direction by Gershon Kingsley. Additional orchestrations by Bill Stegmeier, Jack Andrews, Jay Brower. Produced by Philip Rose and Swanlee. Opened 17 April 1964 at the Martin Beck Theatre and closed 18 April 1964 after 3 performances.

CAST (in order of appearance): *Dr. Irving Gilbert*: ALAN ALDA. *Mr. Morris*: Ted Thurston. *Nathan the Waiter*: Norman Shelly. *Mme. Cole*: BRENDA LEWIS. *Bloom the Fiddler*: Joe Ross. *First Woman*: Shirley Leinwand. *Second Woman*: Fay Reed. *Mr. Edelman*: Keith Kaldenberg. *Mrs. Edelman*: Ann Marisse. *Beck*: Roy Stuart. *Rubin*: Robert Penn. *Kaplan*: Val Avery. *Mrs. Perlman*: Francine Beers. *Mr. Toplitz*: MARTIN WOLFSON. *Mendel Polan*: Wood Romoff. *Ida Polan*: Renee Orin. *Hymie the Busboy*: SAM LEVENE. *Norma Roberts*: MONTE AMUNDSEN. *David Cole*: TOMMY RALL. *Lipsky*: Michael Vale. *Petty Officer*: Val Avery. *Ship's Captain*: John Anania. *Sarah*: Betty Aberlin. *Samuel Cole*: THEODORE BIKEL. *Burton*: Edwin Bruce.

Singers: Marilyn Murphy, Bonnie Brody, Betty Aberlin, Fay Reed, Ann Marisse, Shirley Leinwand, Stephanie Winters, John Wheeler, Ken Richards. *Dancers*: Geri Spinner, Betty Rosebrock, Bonnie Walker, Cheryl Kilgren, Patsi King, Luigi Gasparanetti, Ean Benjamin, Robert Avian, Keith Stewart, Terry Violino.

The action takes place in and arouynd the Cafe Crown at the corner of Second Avenue and 12th Street in New York City in the early 1930s.

Act 1, Scene 1: The Street. *Scene 2*: Cafe Crown. *Scene 3*: The Stage of Lipsky's Theatre—Act 1. *Scene 4*: Mme. Cole's dressing room. *Scene 5*: Cafe Crown. *Scene 6*: The Street. *Scene 7*: The Stage of Lipsky's Theatre—Act 2.

Act 2, Scene 1: The Street. *Scene 2*: Cafe Crown. *Scene 3*: The Stage of Lipsky's Theatre. *Scene 4*: Cafe Crown. *Scene 5*: The Street.

ACT 1

Scene 1

"You're a Stranger in This Neighborhood"
A. Alda, Company

Scene 2

"What's the Matter With Buffalo?"
S. Levene, A. Alda, Ensemble

"All Those Years"
T. Rall, M. Amundsen

Scene 3

"Au Revoir Poland-Hello New York!"
B. Lewis, Lipsky Theatre Ensemble

Scene 4

"Make the Most of Spring"
B. Lewis

Scene 5

"So Long As It Isn't Shakespeare"
S. Levene, T. Bikel

"A Lifetime Love"
T. Bikel, B. Lewis

Scene 6

"I'm Gonna Move"
T. Rall

Scene 7

"A Mother's Heart"
B. Lewis, B. Aberlin, Lipsky Theatre Ensemble

"On This Wedding Day"
B. Lewis, Wedding Guests

ACT 2

Scene 1

"What's Gonna Be Tomorrow"
Company

Scene 2

"A Man Must Have Something to Live For"
T. Bikel, Ensemble

"That's the Life For Me"
S. Levene, T. Bikel, B. Lewis, Company

"A Lifetime Love" (reprise)
T. Rall, M. Amundsen

Scene 3

"King Lear Ballet"
T. Bikel, T. Rall, Ensemble

Scene 4

"Magical Things In Life"
S. Levene, T. Bikel, Ensemble

"That's the Life For Me" (reprise)
S. Levene, T. Bikel, B. Lewis, A. Alda, Ensemble

Scene 5

"A Man Must Have Something To Live For" (reprise)
Company

1964.19 PORGY AND BESS

A Revival of the Folk Opera in Two Acts, 9 Scenes[25]. Book by DuBose Heyward adapted from the play "Porgy" by DuBose and Dorothy Heyward. Music by George Gershwin. Lyrics by DuBose Heyward and Ira Gershwin. Directed by John Fearnley. Settings by Stephen O. Saxe. Costumes by Stanley Simmons. Lighting by Nananne Porcher. Musical director, Julius Rudel. Choral director and associate conductor, William Jonson. Produced by the New York City Center Light Opera Company (Jean Dalrymple, Director). Opened 6 May 1964 at the New York City Center and closed 17 May 1964 after 15 performances.

CAST (in order of appearance): *Clara*: MARIE YOUNG. *Mingo*: Tony Middleton. *Sportin' Life*: ROBERT GUILLAUME. *Jake*: IRVING BARNES. *Serena*: GWENDOLYN WALTERS. *Robbins*: Eugene Edwards. *Jim*: Garwood Perkins. *Peter*, the Honey Man: Garrett Morris. *Lily*: Frances Haywood. *Maria*: CAROL BRICE. *Porgy*: WILLIAM WARFIELD or IRVING BARNES. *Crown*: WILLIAM DILLARD. *Bess*: VERONICA TYLER or BARBARA SMITH CONRAD. *Policemen*: David Hicks, John Smith. *Detective*: Walter Riemer. *Undertaker*: Wanza King. *Annie*: Alyce Webb. *Frazier*: Al Fann. *Strawberry Woman*: Kay Barnes. *Crab Man*: Clyde Turner. *Scipio*: William Harris. *Pearl*: Lillian Hayman.

Residents of Catfish Row: Ruby Green Aspinall, Kaye Barnes, Phyllis Bash, Elijah Bennett, Joseph Bryant, Paul Corder, Marceline Decker, Beverly Evans, Don Forrest, Beno Foster, Claretta Freemon, Carol Joy George, Carrie Glover, Helen Guile, William G. Harris, Afrika Hayes, Lillian Hayman, Frances W. Haywood, Annette B. Jackson, Martin Jewell, Marva Josie, Wanza King, Thomas Laidman, Dorothy Lane, Garrett Morris, Caryl Paige, Garwood Perkins, Lucinda Ransom, John Richardson, Edna Ricks, Anthony Safina, Clyde Turner, Eloise C. Uggams, James Wamen, Laurence Watson, Alyce Webb, Pauline Weekes, James Wilson, James Wilson, William Wright, Lou Ann Wyckoff. *Children*: Deborah Hall, Benjamin Hines, Norman Hines, Antonell Jones.

1964.20 MY FAIR LADY

A Revival of the Musical (Comedy) in Two Acts, 18 Scenes[26]. Book and lyrics by Alan Jay Lerner. Based on the play "Pygmalion" by George Bernard Shaw, produced on the screen by Gabriel Pascal. Music by Frederick Loewe. Originally staged by Moss Hart. This production directed by Samuel Liff. Choreography and musical numbers staged by Hanya Holm. Production (settings) designed by Oliver Smith. Costumes by Cecil Beaton, supervised by Stanley Simmons. Musical arrangements (Orchestrations) by Robert Russell Bennett and Philip J. Lang. Lighting by Feder. Dance music

---

[25]First produced in New York 10 October 1935 at the Alvin Theatre for 124 performances. For Synopsis of Scenes and Musical Numbers, see original 1935 production. This production was performed in Two Acts, with the interval after "Oh, I Can't Sit Down" (Act 2, Scene 1 in the original). Note the following program changes for this production:
("Ha da da" and) "Leavin' for de Promis' Land" moved to the opening of Act 2, Scene 1 before "It Ain't Necessarily So." "Buzzard Song" reinstated to Act 1, after "I Got Plenty of Nuttin'." "Occupational Humoresque" (Ensemble) added to Act 2, Scene 5 before "Where's My Bess?"

[26]Originally produced in New York 15 March 1956 at the Mark Hellinger Theatre for 2717 peformances. For Synopsis of Scenes and Musical Numbers, see original 1956 production.

arranged by Trude Rittman. Musical director, Anton Coppola. Produced by the New York City Center Light Opera Company (Jean Dalrymple, Director). Opened 20 May 1964 at the New York City Center and closed 28 June 1964 after 47 performances.

CAST (in order of appearance): *Buskers*: Jerry Trent, Myron Curtis, Kiki Minor. *Mrs. Eynsford-Hill*: Claire Waring. *Eliza Doolittle*: MARNI NIXON. *Freddy Eynsford-Hill*: RUSSELL NYPE. *Colonel Pickering*: BYRON WEBSTER. *A Bystander*: Raymond Allen. *Henry Higgins*: MYLES EASON. *Selsey Man*: Charles Penman. *Hoxton Man*: Henry Lawrence. *Another Bystander*: Robert [Bob] Fitch. *First Cockney*: William Krach. *Second Cockney*: Stokely Gray. *Third Cockney*: Richard H. Goodlake. *Fourth Cockney*: Barney Johnston. *Bartender*: Jack Eddleman. *Harry*: Charles Penman. *Jamie*: Raymond Allen. *Alfred P. Doolittle*: REGINALD GARDINER. *Mrs. Pearce*: DOROTHY SANDS. *Mrs. Hopkins*: Olive Reeves-Smith. *Butler*: Stokely Gray. *Servants*: Jeremy Broun, Margaret Broderson, Joyce Dahl, Ruth Shepard, Art Martinson, Stokely Gray. *Mrs. Higgins*: MARGERY MAUDE. *Chauffeur*: Harry Woolever. *Footmen*: William Krach, Richard Park. *Lord Boxington*: Charles Penman. *Lady Boxington*: Olive Reeves-Smith. *Constable*: Harry Woolever. *Flower Girl*: Kiki Minor. *Zoltan Karpathy*: SANDOR SZABO. *Flunkey*: Richard Park. *Queen of Transylvania*: Terry Marone. *Ambassador*: Raymond Allen. *Bartender*: Barney Johnston. *Mrs. Higgins' Maid*: Margaret Cuddy.

Singing Ensemble: Jeremy Broun, Margaret Broderson, Diane Chase, Joyce Dahl, Elaine Labour, Terry Marone, Donna Monroe, Ruth Shepard, Jack Eddleman, Richard H. Goodlake, Stokely Gray, Barney Johnston, William Krach, Henry Lawrence, Art Martinson, Richard Park. *Dancing Ensemble*: Judi Allison, Emily Byrne, Margaret Cuddy, Katia Geleznova, Audrey Hays, Adriana Keathley, Kiki Minor, Molly Molloy, Mari Shelton, Esther Villavicencio, Dick Colacino, Myron Curtis, Robert [Bob] Fitch, Ronn Forella, Dennis Lynch, Joe Nelson, Jerry Trent, R. Michael Steele, Mark West, Harry Woolever.

1964.21 FADE OUT—FADE IN

A Musical Comedy in Two Acts, 19 Scenes. Book and lyrics by Betty Comden and Adolph Green. Music by Jule Styne. Directed by George Abbott. Dances and musical numbers staged by Ernest Flatt. Settings and lighting by William and Jean Eckart. Costumes by Donald Brooks. Musical direction and orchestrations by Ralph Burns and Ray Ellis. Vocal arrangements by Buster Davis. Dance music arranged by Richard De Benedictis. Produced by Lester Osterman and Jule Styne. Opened 26 May 1964 at the Mark Hellinger Theatre and closed 14 November 1964 after 199 performances; re-opened 15 February 1965 at the Mark Hellinger Theatre and closed 17 April 1965 after 72 additional performances. Total: 271 performances.

CAST[27] (in order of appearance): *Byron Prong*: JACK CASSIDY. *Teenagers*: Jodi Perselle, Judy Newman. *Woman*: Diana Ede. *Man*: Darrell J. Askey. *Autograph Kids*: Roger Allan Raby, Charlene Mehl. *Helga Sixtrees*: Judy Cassmore. *Pops*: Frank Tweddell. *Rosco*: Bob Neukum. *Billy Vespers*: Glenn Kezer, (Paul Michael). *Lyman*: John Dorrin. *Hope Springfield*: CAROL BURNETT. *Rex*: Darrell J. Askey. *Chauffeur*: William Louther. *First Girl*: Wendy Taylor. *First Cowboy Extra*: Steve Elmore. *Second Cowboy Extra*: Fred Cline. *Gangster Extra*: Gene Varrone. *Ralph Governor*: MITCHELL JASON. *Rudolf Governor*: DICK PATTERSON. *Nephews (4)*: *George Governor*: Howard Kahl. *Frank Governor*: John Dorrin. *Harold Governor*: Gene Varrone. *Arnold Governor*: Steve Elmore. *Waiters*: Fred Cline, Richard Frisch, Roger Allan Raby. *Publicity Men*: Sean Allan, Darrell J. Askey. *Convicts*: Gene Kelton; William Louther, Ed Pfeiffer, James Von Weiss . *Myra May Melrose*: Virginia Payne. *Seamstress*: Diane Arnold. *Miss Mallory*: Jo Tract. *Custer Corkley*: Dan Resin. *Approval*: Smaxie. *Photographer*: Sean Allan. *Max Welch*: Richard Frisch. *Lou Williams*: TIGER HAYNES. *Dora Dailey*: Aileen Poe. *Lionel Z. Governor*: LOU JACOBI. *Dr. Anton Taurig*: Reuben Singer. *Gloria Currie*: TINA LOUISE. *Madame Barrymore*: Penny Egelston.

Singing Ensemble: Sean Allan, Jackie Alloway, Darrell J. Askey, Fred Cline, John Dorrin, Trish Dwelley, Steve Elmore, Richard Frisch, Howard Kahl, Carolyn Kemp, Betty Kent, Glenn Kezer, Mari Nettum, Bob Neukum, Roger Allan Raby, Jo Tract, Gene Varrone. *Dancing Ensemble*: Virginia Allen, Diane Arnold, Judy Cassmore, Diana Ede, Ernie Horvath, Gene Kelton, William Louther, Charlene Mehl, Judy Newman, Jodi Perselle, Ed Pfeiffer, Carolsue Shaer, Patricia Sigris, Roy Smith, Bill Stanton, Wendy Taylor, James Von Weiss. *Lead Dancer*: Don Crichton.

The action takes place in New York and Hollywood in the mid-1930s.

Act 1, Scene 1: In front of Grauman's Chinese Theatre. *Scene 2*: Gate—F.F.F. Studio. *Scene 3*: On the Lot. *Scene 4*: Executive Dining Room. *Scene 5*: Wardrobe Department. *Scene 6*: On the Set. *Scene 7*: Dora Dailey. *Scene 8*: Dr. Taurig's Office—Vienna. *Scene 9*: On the Set. *Scene 10*: Executive Dining Room. *Scene 11*: The Bungalow.

Act 2, Scene 1: Gate—F.F.F. Studio. *Scene 2*: Dora Dailey. *Scene 3*: Wardrobe Department. *Scene 4*: A Street. *Scene 5*: L. Z.'s Office. *Scene 6*: On the Set. *Scene 7*: In front of Grauman's Chinese Theatre. *Scene 8*: In front of Grauman's Chinese Theatre.

ACT 1[28]

Scene 1[29]
"The Thirties"[30]
J. Cassidy

Scene 2
"It's Good To Be Back Home"
C. Burnett, Ensemble

Scene 4
"Fear"
D. Patterson, M. Jason, Nephews
"Fear" (reprise)
J. Cassidy, Nephews

Scene 5
"Call Me Savage"
C. Burnett, D. Patterson
"The Usher From the Mezzanine"
C. Burnett

Scene 9
"I'm With You"
C. Burnett, J. Cassidy, D. Crichton, Violin Girls, Bow Boys
"The Usher From the Mezzanine"[31] (reprise)
C. Burnett, Ensemble

Scene 10
"My Fortune Is My Face"
J. Cassidy

Scene 11
"Lila Tremaine"
C. Burnett

ACT 2

Scene 1[32]
"Go Home Train"[33]
C. Burnett

Scene 3
"Close Harmony"
L. Jacobi, J. Cassidy, T. Louise, Nephews

Scene 4
"You Musn't Be Discouraged"
C. Burnett, T. Haynes

Scene 5
"The Dangerous Age"
L. Jacobi
"L.Z. in Quest of His Youth" (Ballet)
L. Jacobi, T. Louise, D. Crichton, Ensemble

Scene 6
"The Fiddler and the Fighter"
J. Cassidy, Ensemble
"Fade Out—Fade In"
C. Burnett, J. Cassidy

---

[27]Cast changes for return engagement: *Byron Prong*: DICK SHAWN. *Helga Sixtrees*: Alice Glenn. *Billy Vespers*: Paul Michael. *Rex*: Barney Johnston. *Chauffeur*: John Richardson. *First Girl*: Trish Dwelley. *First Cowboy Extra*: David Cryer. *George Governor*: Paul Eichel. *Arnold Governor*: David Cryer. *Waiters*: Stephen Elmore. *Publicity Men*: Dean Doss, Barney Johnston. *Convicts*: John Richardson, Bill Starr, Jerry Gotham. *Gloria Currie*: JUDY CASSMORE.

[28]For return engagement, added to Act 1, Scene 6:
"My Heart Is Like a Violin"
D. Shawn (Byron Prong)
For return engagement, added to Act 1, Scene 11(now Scene 10) after "Lila Tremaine":
"A Girl To Remember"
C. Burnett

[29]Dropped for the return engagement.

[30]Dropped for the return engagement.

[31]For return engagement, replaced by:
"Notice Me"
D. Patterson

[32]Dropped for the return engagement.

[33]Dropped for the return engagement.

1964–1965 SEASON

Liza Minelli in FLORA, THE RED MENACE (Photo: Friedman-Abeles, 1965)
Museum of the City of New York, The Mary Bryant Collection, 92.52.5.4

1964–1965 SEASON

1964.22 FOLIES BERGÈRE

A Musical Revue in Two Acts, 20 Scenes, in French. Conceived and directed by Michel Gyarmathy. Music by Henri Betti. Additional music by Philippe Gerard. Sets and costumes by Michel Gyarmathy. Choreography by George Reich. Musical director, Joe Basile. Associate producers, Nicholas A. Strater, Alvin Bojar. Produced by Stephen W. Sharmat in association with J. Robert Purdom. An Arthur Lesser Production of Paul Derval's original revue. Opened 2 June 1964 at the Broadway Theatre and closed 14 November 1964 after 191 performances.

CAST: PATACHOU, GEORGES ULMER, LILIANE MONTEVECCHI, LES HOGANAS (Gert Karlsson, Bende Hoganas, Egon Hoganas), THE TROTTER BROTHERS, PAUL SYDELL & SUZY, NICOLE CROISILLE, VASSILI SULIC, MARION CONRAD, EDMÉE REDOUIN, FRANCOISE GRÈS, The Company of Les Folies Bergère.

Dancers: Marisa Barbaria, Sarah Lee Berber, Anik David, Dorothy D'Honau, Claude Duvernoy, Diane Fox, Francoise Grès, Nancy Herselin, Marcella Hude, Yvonne Neisyter, Gordana Pechitch, Pamela Wellman, Diana West, Gerry Atkins, Flavio Bennati, Francis Ciampi, Ralf Harmer, Don Wallwork. *Les Demoiselles des Folies*: Dominique Chevallier, Nicole Gille, Margo Hamilton, Andrée Hechner, Margareta Lindblum, Mary Luger, Mikki Maher, Anna Page, Irene Peterson, Judy Tickner, Isabel Wardrop, Elizabeth West. *Mannequins*: Marion Barker, Monique Carraz, Charlotte DiSica, Francesca Fontaine, Lyn Hobart, Dale Humphries, Dany Latour, Simone Massix, André Penny, Veronica Pierce, Nancy Walker, Sara Brocket.

ACT 1[1]

Scene 1
- Bonjour de Paris
- "Foll' de Broadway"
  - N. Croisille, Dancers, Les Demoiselles des Folies, Mannequins
- "Ta Ra Ra"
  - M. Conrad
- "Bonjour Folies"
  - L. Montevecchi

Scene 2
- "Can-Can"
  - G. Atkins, Dancers

Scene 3
- Georges Ulmer (songs and impressions including "Pigalle," {*Music and Lyrics by* Georges Ulmer, Konyn, Newman}, and parody of a Flamenco song)

Scene 4
- Souper Fin
  - M. Carraz, D. Chevallier, A. Hechner, J. Moussy, D. Wallwork

Scene 5
- Chopin
  - F. Castel, Les Demoiselles des Folies

Scene 6
- Paul Sydell & Suzy (acrobatic dog act)

Scene 7
- Varieté de Danses:
- Charleston
  - N. Croissille, Dancers
- "C'est toi l'plus beau" (Tango)
  - L. Montevecchi, V. Sulic
- Paris Panam
  - Les Demoiselles des Folies
- Paris Swing: "Ca c'est Panam"
  - L. Montevecchi
  - (*Music and Lyrics by* J. Ledru.)
- Les mains
  - F. Grès, Dancers

Scene 8
- Georges Ulmer (songs and impressions)

Scene 9
- Cleopatra (dance)
  - L. Montevecchi, V. Sulic, Dancers, Les Demoiselles des Folies, Mannequins

Scene 10
- Les Hoganas (Slackwire trio)

Scene 11
- "A toute à l'heure"
  - The Company

ACT 2

Scene 1
- Texas de France
  - F. Grès, Dancers

Scene 2
- Georges Ulmer (songs):
- "Darling Be Careful" (La Trapeziste)
  - (*Music and Lyrics by* Georges Ulmer.)

Scene 3
- "Mariage"
  - F. Castel, Singers
- "Hymne à l'amour"
  - Dancers, Les Demoiselles des Folies, Mannequins

Scene 4
- The Trotter Brothers (Puppetry)

Scene 5
- "Gondole à Venise"
  - D. Latour

Scene 6
- Georges Ulmer (songs)

Scene 7
- "Neige"
  - M. Conrad, V. Sulic, Dancers

Scene 8
- Patachou:
- "Paris boheme"
  - (*Music and Lyrics by* P. Gerard.)
- "Mon manege à moi"
  - (*Music and Lyrics by* Constantin Glanzburg.)
- "Pigalle"
  - (*Music and Lyrics by* Georges Ulmer, Konyn, Newman.)
- "What Now My Love?" (Eh Maintenant?)
  - (*Music and Lyrics by* Gilbert Becaud.)
- "I Wish You Love" (Que Reste-til de Nos Amours)
  - (*Music and Lyrics by* Charles Trenet. *English Lyrics by* Albert Beach.)
- "My Man" (Mon Homme)
  - (*English Lyrics by* Channing Pollock. *Music by* Maurice Yvain. *French Lyrics by* Albert Willemetz and Jacques Charles.)

Scene 9
- Finale: "La Musique"
  - Entire Company
  - (*Music and Lyrics by* Drejac and Gerard.)

1964.23 THE KING AND I

A Revival of the Musical Play in Two Acts, 17 Scenes[2]. Book and lyrics by Oscar Hammerstein II. Music by Richard Rodgers. Based on the novel "Anna and the King of Siam" by Margaret Landon. Settings by Paul C. McGuire. Costumes by Irene Sharaff. (Lighting uncredited.) Original choreography by Jerome Robbins, reproduced by Yuriko. Orchestrations by Robert Russell Bennett. Musical director, Franz Allers. Directed by Edward Greenberg. Produced by the Music Theatre of Lincoln Center (Richard

[1]Added during the run:
Cyprés
M. Hardy, M. Conrad, F. Bennati, Les Demoiselles des Folies

[2]Originally produced in New York 29 March 1951 at the St. James Theatre for 1246 performances. For Synopsis of Scenes and Musical Numbers, see original 1951 production.

Rodgers, President and Producing Director). Opened 6 July 1964 at the New York State Theatre and closed 8 August 1964 after 40 performances.

CAST (in order of appearance): *Captain Orton*: Fred Miller. *Louis Leonowens*: James Harvey. *Anna Leonowens*: RISË STEVENS. *The Interpreter*: Rudy Vejar. *The Kralahome*: MICHAEL KERMOYAN. *The King*: DARREN McGAVIN. *Phra Alack*: Stuart Mann. *Tuptim*: LEE VENORA. *Lady Thiang*: PATRICIA NEWAY. *Prince Chulalongkorn*: Barry Rubins. *Princess Ying Yaowalak*: Gina Kaye. *Lun Tha*: FRANK PORETTA. *Sir Edward Ramsay*: ERIC BROTHERSON.

The Small House of Uncle Thomas: *Narrator*: LEE VENORA. *Uncle Thomas*: Bettina Dearborne. *Little Eva*: Susan Kikuchi. *Topsy*: Paula Chin. *Eliza*: Takako. *King Simon*: Linda Hodes. *Angel*: Connie Sanchez. *Drummer*: Jim McMillan.

Princes and Princesses: Kathleen Din, Gina Kaye, Lorrie Kochiyama, Debbie Kogan, May Yee Mark, Annette Misa, Robert Ader, David Aguilar, Delfino DeArco, Lawrence Kikuchi, Eddie Kochiyama, Frank Orlando, Vito Orlando. *The Royal Dancers*: Takako Asakawa, Hadassah Badock, Joan Bates, Lisa Berg, Noemi Chiesa, Paula Chin, Miriam Cole, Bettina Dearborne, Carol Drisin, Carol Fried, Phyllis Gutelius, Linda Hodes, Susan Kikuchi, Jeanne Nichtern, Connie Sanchez, Katherine Wilson. *Wives*: Anita Alpert, Theodora Brandon, Dixie Carter, Sharon Dierking, Mona Elson, Carole O'Hara, Hanna Owen, Jean Palmerton. *Amazons*: Leisha Caryle, Beverly Morrison, Joanna Owens, Jeanne Rodriguez. *Priests, Slaves*: Walter Adams, Henry Baker, Lazar Dano, Victor Duntiere, William Duvall, Julius Fields, Fred Hamilton, Stuart Mann, Jim McMillan, Ken Richards, Anthony Saverino.

1964.24 THE MERRY WIDOW

A Revival of the Operetta in Three Acts, 4 Scenes[3]. Music by Franz Lehár. Original German book (Die Lustige Witwe) and lyrics by Victor Léon and Leo Stein (after "L'Attaché d'Ambassade.") New book by by Milton Lazarus, based on a version by Edwin Lester and the London version by Christopher Hassall. New lyrics by Forman Brown. Directed by Edward Greenberg. Choreography by Zachary Solov. Settings by Rouben Ter-Arutunian. Costumes by Rene Hubert. (Lighting uncredited, by Michael Paul Price for subsequent tour.) Musical director, Franz Allers. Produced by the Music Theatre of Lincoln Center (Richard Rodgers, President and Producing Director). Opened 17 August 1964 at the New York State Theatre and closed 19 September 1964 after 40 performances.

CAST (in order of appearance): *Major Domo*: George Quick. *Nish*: SIG ARNO. *Baron Popoff*: MISCHA AUER. *Natalie, Baroness Popoff*: JOAN WELDON. *Chevalier St. Brioche*: ROBERT GOSS. *Marquis Cascada*: Rudy Vejar. *General Novikovich*: JOSEPH LEON. *Counselor Khadja*: WOOD ROMOFF. *Mme. Sylvanie Khadja*: Luce Ennis. *Mme. Novikovich*: Marian Haraldson. *Captain Pierre Jolidon*: FRANK PORETTA. *Sonia*, the Widow: PATRICE MUNSEL. *Prince Danilo*: BOB WRIGHT. *Girls from Maxim's (6)*: *Lolo*: Carol Flemming. *Clo Clo*: Jean Lee Schoch. *Dodo*: Annette Bachich. *Margot*: Kathy Wilson. *Joujou*: Skiles Ricketts. *Froufrou*: Birgitta Kiviniemi. *Michel*: William Duvall. *Zozo*: Dixie Carter. *Principal Dancers*: Birgitta Kiviniemi, Dmitry Cheremeteff. *Guests, Lackeys, Maids and Musicians*.

Singing Ladies: Theodora Brandon, Dixie Carter, Kenna Christi, Sharon Dierking, Elaine Johnson, Beverly Morrison, Hanna Owen, Jean Palmerton, Dixie Stewart, Peggy Wathen. *Singing Men*: Bruce Carrithers, Ken Corday, Gene Davis, William Duvall, Harrison Fisher, Norman Grogan, Vincent Henry, Stuart Mann, Philip Rash, Ken Richards, Carl Sloat, Stafford Wing. *Dancing Girls*: Annette Bachich, Bonnie Gene Card, Carol Flemming, Debra Lyman, Skiles Ricketts, Jean Lee Schoch, Kathy Wilson. *Dancing Men*: Ian Bruce, Richard Cousins, Jeremy Wilson, Ian Bruce, Richard Cousins, Jeremy Knight-Ives, Richard Maxon, Malcolm McCormick, Bob Remick, George Tregre.

Act 1, Scene 1: A Corridor at the Marsovian Embassy in Paris, 1905. *Scene 2*: The Reception Hall.

Act 2: The Garden Party at Sonia's Villa just outside Paris, a week later.

Act 3: At Maxim's, later that night.

ACT 1

"When in France"
R. Goss, R. Vejar, J. Weldon,
M. Haraldson, L. Ennis, M. Auer, Guests

"A Respectable Wife"
J. Weldon, F. Poretta

"Who Knows the Way to My Heart?"
P. Munsel, R. Goss, R. Vejar, Bachelors

"Maxim's"
B. Wright, Girls from Maxim's

"Riding on a Carousel"
P. Munsel, R. Wright

Finale (Act 1)
P. Munsel, R. Wright, Ensemble

ACT 2

Marsovian Dance
Dancing Ensemble

"Vilia"
P. Munsel

"Women"
M. Auer, S. Arno, J. Leon, W. Romoff, R. Goss, R. Vejar

Czardas and Waltz
P. Munsel, B. Wright, Dancing Ensemble

"Romance"
F. Poretta, J. Weldon

Finale (Act 2)
P. Munsel, B. Wright, F. Poretta, J. Weldon, Ensemble

ACT 3

"Girls at Maxim's"
Maxim Girls, Waiters, P. Munsel

"I Love You So" (The Merry Widow Waltz)
B. Wright, P. Munsel

Finale (Act 3)
Entire Company

[3]Originally produced in New York 21 October 1907 at the New Amsterdam Theatre for 416 performances.

1964.25 WIENER BLUT

A Revival of the Operette in Three Acts, in German[4]. Original Viennese libretto [Vienna Life] by Victor Léon and Leo Stein. Music by Johann Strauss. New adaptation by Tony Niessner. Music arranged by Hans Hagen. Staged by Tony Niessner. Choreography by Fred Meister. Musical director, Oswald Unterhauser. Production designed by Ferry Windberger. Costumes by Hill Rheis-Gromes. Production supervised and lighting by Thomas Skelton. Produced by Harald A. Hoeller. Presented by the Greek Theatre Association—James A. Doolittle and Felix S. Gerstman. Opened 11 September 1964 at the Lunt-Fontanne Theatre and closed 3 October 1964 after 27 performances.

CAST (in order of appearance): *Mistress of Ceremonies*: GITA RENA. *Policeman*: ANDREIJ HALASZ. *Count Balduin Zedlau*, Ambassador from Reuss-Schleiz-Greiz: ERWIN VON GROSS. *Countess Zedlau*, his wife: MARIA KOWA. *Franziska Cagliari*, dancer at the Karntnertor Theatre: CLEMENTINE MAYER. *Pepi Pleininger*, a model: DAGMAR KOLLER. *Josef*, Count Zedlau's valet: HELMUT WALLNER. *Prince Ypsheim-Gindelbach*, Prime Minsiter of Reuss-Schleiz-Greiz: WILHELM POPP. *Kagler*, Cagliari's father: HUGO LINDINGER. *Anna*, Cagliari's maid: Friedericke Mann. *A Coachman*: WERNER KARMAN. *Count Bitowski*: EMMERICH GODIN. *Countess Bitowski*: ELSE PETRY. *French Ambassador*: Eric Herg. *Italian Ambassador*: Martino Stamos. *English Ambassador*: Wolfgang Hackenberg. *Prussian Ambassador*: Gerhard Kurz. *Russian Ambassador*: WERNER KARMAN. *Lisi*, laundrymaid: Friederike Mann. *Lori*, laundrymaid: Silvia Holzmayer. *A Grenadier*: Erich Herg. *A Watchman* (Deutschmeister): Wolfgang Hackenberg. *A Boy Waiter*: Eveline Kollhammer. *Proprietor of Heitzing Casino*: WERNER KARMAN.

Singing Ensemble: Maria Holoubeck, Silvia Holzmayer, Elfriede Knapp, Angelika Lignu, Friederike Mann, Katherine Stellaki, Wolfgang Hackenberg, Erich Herg, Werner Karman, Gerhard Kurz, Martino Stamos, Achilles Talos. *Dancing Soloists*: IWA SLATEWA, FLORA LOJEKOVA, ANDREJ HALASZ, KURT SCHENKER. *Dancing Ensemble*: Hulda Kuchs, Katja Doreen, Eveline Kohlhammer, Edda Green, Katja Pogacnik, Nora Zechner, Ingrid Nedbal.

The action takes place during the Congress of Vienna in 1815.

Act 1: A Street in Vienna on a summer morning. Cagliari's Villa, the same morning.

Act 2: The Palace of Count Bitowski.

Act 3: The garden of the Casino at Hietzing.

ACT 1

Introduction
G. Rena, Ensemble

"Ich such' jetzt da, ich such' jetzt dort"
H. Wallner

[4]Originally produced in New York in English 23 January 1901 at the Broadway Theatre for 35 performances. This is the German language Broadway premiere.

(I Am Looking Here Now, I Am Looking There Now)
"Pepi! Er?" (Pepi, He?)
C. Mayer, H. Wallner
"Na also schreib' und tu' nicht schmieren"
E. Von Gross, H. Wallner
(Go on, Write and Do Not Scribble)
Polka
D. Koller, Mannequins
"Wunsch' guten Morgen, Herr von Pepi"
D. Koller, H. Wallner
(Good Morning, Mr. van Pepi)
Finale Act 1
C. Mayer, H. Wallner, H. Lindinger, W. Popp, E. Von Gross

ACT 2
"Polonaise"
G. Rena, Ensemble
Pas de Deux
F. Lojekova, A. Halasz
"Wiener Blut" (Vienna Life)
M. Kowa, E. Von Gross
"Wiener Frauen singen gern"
C. Mayer, E. Von Gross
(Viennese Women Love to Sing)
"So nimm, mein susser Schatz"
E. Von Gross, D. Koller, H. Wallner
(Take It, My Sweet Darling)
Mazurka
Solo Dancers
"Bohmische Polka" (Bohemian Polka)
D. Koller, H. Lindinger
Czardas
Solo Dancers
"Lagunenwalzer" (Lagoon Waltz)
M. Stamos, Ensemble
Finale Act 2
Ensemble
"An der schonen blauen Donau"[5]
I. Slatewa, K. Schenker, Dancing Ensemble
(The Blue Danube Waltz)

ACT 3
"Geht's und verkauft's mei G'wand"
F. Mann, S. Holzmayer
(Go On and Sell My Suit)
"A'Walzer von Strauss"
H. Lindinger, W. Hackenberg, Singing Ensemble
(A Waltz by Strauss)
Polka
Soloists, Dancing Ensemble
"Accelerationenwalzer"[6] (Acceleration Waltz)
Ensemble
Finale Act 3
G. Rena, Ensemble

1964.26 THE COMMITTEE

A (Comedy) Revue in Two Acts, 20 Scenes. Written and created by the Company. Material subject to change nightly. Incidental music composed by Ellsworth Milburn. Directed by Alan Myerson. Setting and lighting by Ralph Alswang. Produced by Arthur Cantor in association with Committee Productions. Opened 16 September 1964 at the Henry Miller's Theatre and closed 7 November 1964 after 61 performances.

CAST: SCOTT BEACH, HAMILTON CAMP, GARRY GOODROW, LARRY HANKIN, KATHRYN ISH, ELLSWORTH MILBURN, IRENE RIORDAN, DICK STAHL.

ACT 1[7]
Scene 1
The Party
Host: H. Camp. *Hostess*: K. Ish. *Scotty Pritikin*: S. Beach. *Roger*: L. Hankin. *Billie*: I. Riordan. *Jerry*: D. Stahl. *L. R. Truehart*: E. Milburn. *George Phillips*: G. Goodrow.
Scene 2
Introduction
D. Stahl
Scene 3
Sex on the Campus
Sy: L. Hankin. *Sharon*: K. Ish. *Room-mate*: H. Camp.
Scene 4
The Spies
I. Riordan, D. Stahl, H. Camp, L. Hankin, K. Ish, G. Goodrow
Scene 5
Failure 101 (Oral Exam)
Dr. Benway: S. Beach. *Lyman Engel*: G. Goodrow.
Scene 6
Pregnant
D. Stahl, K. Ish
Scene 7
Mechanical Man
The Mechanical Man: H. Camp. *The Bum*: L. Hankin.
Scene 8
Stick To the Point (Interview)
Ron Wunder: S. Beach. *Elizabeth Mainstream Rockwell*: I. Riordan.
Scene 9
Bar Scene
Pianist: E. Milburn. *Waiter*: D. Stahl. *Larry Number 1*: G. Goodrow. *Larry Number 2*: L. Hankin.
Scene 10
Folk Song ("I'm Gonna Ride a Hundred, Hundred, Hundred Miles")
(*Music and Lyrics by* Irene Riordan and Ellsworth Milburn.)
Entire Company

ACT 2
Scene 1
Blue Valley (California) PTA
Moderator: I. Riordan. *Dr. Ernest*: S. Beach. *Dr. Luce*: H. Camp.
Scene 2
Shoe Store
Customer: G. Goodrow. *Salesman*: H. Camp.
Scene 3
Summer Vacation
Pat: K. Ish. *Nikki*: I. Riordan.
Scene 4
Piano Roll (The Virtuoso)
D. Stahl
Scene 5
Electric Chair (Prison Scene)
Warden: H. Camp. *Chaplain*: G. Goodrow. *Prisoner*: L. Hankin. *Governor*: S. Beach.
Scene 6
Public Opinion
I. Riordan, D. Stahl
Scene 7
Liebowitz
H. Camp, K. Ish, S. Beach
Scene 8
Psychiatrist (The Hour)
Patient: D. Stahl. *Doctor*: G. Goodrow.

---

[5]Added to "Wiener Blut" for this production.
[6]Added to "Wiener Blut" for this production.

[7]The above program running order was for the opening night performance. Also performed during run:
Pavlov
Dr. Pavlov: G. Goodrow. *Visitor*: S. Beach.

Scene 9

Superman

Superman: L. Hankin. *Babs' Husband*: S. Beach.

Scene 10

The Orchestra

Conductor: E. Milburn. *Violin*: I. Riordan. *Cello*: S. Beach. *Horn*: H. Camp. *Bassoon*: G. Goodrow. *Oboe*: K. Ish. *Triangle and Cymbals*: D. Stahl. *Tympany and Wood Block*: L. Hankin.

1964.27 FIDDLER ON THE ROOF

A Musical in Two Acts, a Prologue and 18 Scenes. Book by Joseph Stein. Based on stories by Sholom Aleichem's stories ("Tevye's Daughters") by special permission of Arnold Perl. Music by Jerry Bock. Lyrics by Sheldon Harnick. Entire production directed and choreographed by Jerome Robbins. Settings by Boris Aronson. Costumes by Patricia Zipprodt. Lighting by Jean Rosenthal. Orchestrations by Don Walker. Musical direction and vocal arrangements by Milton Greene. Dance music arranged by Betty Walberg. Produced by Harold Prince. Opened 22 September 1964 at the Imperial Theatre, moved 27 February 1967 to the Majestic Theatre, moved 14 December 1970 to the Broadway Theatre, and closed 2 July 1972 after 3242 performances.

CAST (in order of appearance): *Tevye*, the Dairyman: ZERO MOSTEL. *Golde*, his wife: MARIA KARNILOVA. *Their Three Daughters*: *Tzeitel*: JOANNA MERLIN. *Hodel*: JULIA MIGENES. *Chava*: Tanya Everett. *Shprintze*: Marilyn Rogers. *Beilke*: Linda Ross. *Yente*, the Matchmaker: BEATRICE ARTHUR. *Motel*, the Tailor: AUSTIN PENDLETON. *Perchik*, the Student: BERT CONVY. *Lazar Wolf*, the Butcher: Michael Granger. *Mordcha*, the Innkeeper: Zvee Scooler. *Rabbi*: Gluck Sandor. *Mendel*, his son: Leonard Frey. *Avram*, the Bookseller: Paul Lipson. *Nachum*, the Beggar: Maurice Edwards. *Grandma Tzeitel*: Sue Babel. *Fruma-Sarah*: Carol Sawyer. *Constable*: Joseph Sullivan. *Fyedka*: Joe Ponazecki. *Shandel*: Helen Verbit. *The Fiddler*: Gino Conforti.

Villagers: Tom Abbott, John C. Attle, Sue Babel, Sammy Bayes, Robert Berdeen, Lorenzo Bianco, Duane Bodin, Robert Currie, Sarah Felcher, Tony Gardell, Louis Genevrino, Ross Gifford, Dan Jasin, Sandra Kazan, Thom Koutsoukos, Sharon Lerit, Sylvia Mann, Peff Modelski, Irene Paris, Charles Rule, Carol Sawyer, Roberta Senn, Mitch Thomas, Helen Verbit.

The action takes place in Anatevka, a village in Russia in 1905 on the eve of the revolutionary period.

Prologue: The exterior of Tevye's house.

Act 1, Scene 1: The kitchen of Tevye's house. *Scene 2*: The exterior of Tevye's house. *Scene 3* The interior of Tevye's house. *Scene 4*: The Inn, the following evening. *Scene 5*: The street outside the Inn. *Scene 6*: The exterior of Tevye's house. *Scene 7*: Tevye's Bedroom. *Scene 8*: The village street and the interior of Motel's tailor shop. *Scene 9*: Part of Tevye's Yard. Night. *Scene 10*: The entire yard of Tevye's house.

Act 2, Scene 1: The exterior of Tevye's house. *Scene 2*: The village street. *Scene 3*: The exterior of the railroad station. *Scene 4*: The village street, some months later. *Scene 5*: Motel's tailor shop. *Scene 6*: A road. Late afternoon. *Scene 7*: Tevye's barn. *Scene 8*: Outside Tevye's house.

ACT 1

Prologue

"Tradition"

Z. Mostel, Villagers

Scene 1

"Matchmaker, Matchmaker"

J. Merlin, J. Migenes, T. Everett

Scene 2

"If I Were a Rich Man"

Z. Mostel

Scene 3

"Sabbath Prayer"

Z. Mostel, M. Karnilova, Villagers

Scene 4

"To Life"

Z. Mostel, M. Granger, Men

Scene 6

("Tradition" reprise)

(Z. Mostel)

"Miracle of Miracles"

A. Pendleton

Scene 7

"The Tailor Motel Kamzoil"

Z. Mostel, M. Karnilova, S. Babel, C. Sawyer, Villagers

Scene 9

"Sunrise, Sunset"

Z. Mostel, M. Karnilova, Villagers

Scene 10

"Wedding Dance"

Villagers

ACT 2

Scene 1

"Now I Have Everything"

B. Convy, J. Migenes

("Tradition" reprise)

(Z. Mostel)

"Do You Love Me?"

Z. Mostel, M. Karnilova

Scene 2

"I Just Heard"

B. Arthur, Villagers

Scene 3

"Far From the Home I Love"

J. Migenes

Scene 6

("Chavaleh")

(Z. Mostel)

Scene 7

"Anatevka"

Z. Mostel, M. Karnilova, B. Arthur, M. Granger, L. Frey, P. Lipson

Scene 8

Epilogue

Entire Company

1964.28 OH WHAT A LOVELY WAR

A Musical Entertainment (Revue) in Two Acts. Written by Theatre Workshop, Charles Chilton and members of the (original British) cast after a treatment by Ted Allan. Directed by Joan Littlewood. Military advisor, Raymond Fletcher. Setting and lighting by John Bury. Costumes by Una Collins. Choreography by Bob Stevenson. Musical direction by Shepard Coleman. Musical arrangements by Alfred Ralston. Design supervision by Klaus Holm. A Theatre Workshop Group Production. Produced by David Merrick and Gerry Raffles. Opened 30 September 1964 at the Broadhurst Theatre and closed 16 January 1965 after 125 performances.

THE PIERROTS (CAST): *Master of Ceremonies, General Lanrezac, Drill Sergeant*: VICTOR SPINETTI. *France, Belgium*: MURRAY MELVIN. *England, Sir John French, The Padre*: BRIAN MURPHY. *Russia, English Signaller*: Frank Coda. *French Captain, Assassin*: Richard Curnock. *Gendarme*: Peter Dalton. *Russia, Luxembourg Signaller*: Larry Dann. *Moltke, Belgium*: Colin Kemball. *Sir Henry Wilson, German Officer*: Ian Paterson. *Kaiser, Sir Douglas Haig*: George Sewell. *Swimmer, Irish Standard Bearer*: Bob Stevenson.

BARBARA WINDSOR, Fanny Carby, Jack Eddleman, Myvanwy Jenn, Linda Loftis, Reid Shelton, Valerie Walsh.

ACT 1

"Row, Row, Row" (from ZIEGFELD FOLLIES OF 1912)

Ensemble

(*Music by* James V. Monaco. *Lyrics by* William Jerome.)

"We Don't Want to Lose You (Your King and Country Want You)"

The Ladies

(*Music and Lyrics by* Paul Rubens.)

"Belgium Put the Kibosh on the Kaiser"

V. Walsh

(*Music and Lyrics by* Ellerton.)

Medley:

"Are We Downhearted, (No)"

(*Music and Lyrics by* W. David, L. Wright.)

"It's a Long Way to Tipperary"

(*Music and Lyrics by* Jack Judge and Harry H. Williams.)

"Hold Your Hand Out Naughty Boy"
The Men
(*Music and Lyrics by* Murphy and David.)
"I'll Make a Man of You" (from THE PASSING SHOW OF 1914, London)
B. Windsor
(*Music and Lyrics by* Arthur Wimperis and Herman Finck.)
"Pack Up Your Troubles (in Your Old Kit Bag)"
The Men
(*Music by* George Powell. *Lyrics by* George Asaf.)
"Hitchykoo"
F. Carby
(*Music by* Lewis F. Muir and Maurice Abrahams. *Lyrics by* L. Wolfe Gilbert.)
"Heilige Nacht" (Silent Night)
C. Kemball
"Christmas Day in the Cookhouse"
B. Murphy
"Goodbye . . . ee"
V. Spinetti
(*Music by* Bert Lee. *Lyrics by* R. P. Weston.)

ACT 2
"Oh What a Lovely War" (Oh It's a Lovely War)
Ensemble
(*Music and Lyrics by* J. P. Long, M. Scott, revised by B. Kelsey.)
"Gassed Last Night"
The Men
"Roses of Picardy"
L. Loftis, I. Paterson
(*Music by* Haydn Wood. *Lyrics by* Frederick E. Weatherley.)
"Hush Here Comes a Whizzbang"
The Men
(Soldiers' parody of 'Hush, Here Comes the Dream Man')
(*Music and Lyrics by* R. P. Weston, Barnes and Scott.)
"There's a Long Long Trail"
I. Paterson
(*Music by* Zo Elliott. *Lyrics by* Stoddard King.)
"I Don't Want to Be a Soldier"
The Men
(Soldiers' parody of "I'll Make a Man of You" above)
"Kaiser Bill"
The Men
"They Were Only Playing Leapfrog"
(*Music arr. by* Alfred Ralston.)The Men
"Old Soldiers Never Die"
M. Melvin
"If You Want the Old Batallion"
The Men
"Far Far from Wipers"
(*Music and Lyrics by* Bingham and Greene.)C. Kemball
"If the Sergeant Steals Your Rum"
The Men
"I Wore a Tunic (When You Wore a Tulip)"
I. Paterson
(Soldiers' parody of 'When You Wore a Tulip and I Wore a Big Red Rose')
(*Music by* Percy Wenrich. *Lyrics by* Jack Mahoney.)
"Forward Joe Soap's Army"
The Men
"Fred Karno's Army"
The Men
"When This Lousy War Is Over"
C. Kemball
(Parody of "When This Cruel War Is Over" {Weeping, Sad and Lonely})
(*Music by* Henry Tucker. *Lyrics by* Charles Carroll Sawyer.)
"Wash Me in the Water"
The Men
"I Want To Go Home"
(*Music arr. by* Alfred Ralston.)
The Men
"The Bells of Hell"
(*Music arr. by* Alfred Ralston.)
The Men
"Keep the Home Fires Burning"
M. Jenn
(*Music by* Ivor Novello. *Lyrics by* Lena Guilbert Ford.)
"Sister Susie's Sewing Shirts (for Soldiers)"
B. Windsor
(*Music by* Herman Darewski. *Lyrics by* R. P. Weston.)
Finale:
"Chanson de Craonne"
(*Music and Lyrics by* Vaillant and Couturier.)
"I Don't Want to be A Soldier" (reprise)
"And When They Asked Us"
(*Music by* Jerome Kern.)
Ensemble
(Parody to melody of "They Didn't Believe Me" from THE GIRL FROM UTAH)

1964.29 CAMBRIDGE CIRCUS

A Revue in Two Acts, 25 Scenes. Written by the company. Music by Bill Oddie, Hugh MacDonald, David Palmer. Directed by Humphrey Barclay. (Setting) designed by Stephen Mullin. Costumes by Judy Birdwood. Lighting by Robert Darling. Musical arrangements by David Palmer. Produced by Sol Hurok and David Black in association with Jay Julien and Andre Goulston. Opened 6 October 1964 at the Plymouth Theatre and closed 24 October 1964 after 23 performances[8].

CAST: TIM-BROOKE TAYLOR, GRAHAM CHAPMAN, JOHN CLEESE, DAVID HATCH, JO KENDALL, JONATHAN LYNN, BILL ODDIE.

ACT 1
Scene 1
Bring Out the Beast
(*by* Cardinal Richelieu)
Cast
Scene 2
Cloak and Dagger
(*by* John Cleese and David Hatch)
J. Cleese, D. Hatch, J. Lynn
Scene 3
"London Bus"
J. Lynn, T. Brooke-Taylor, D. Hatch, B. Oddie
(*Music by* Bill Oddie. *Lyrics by* Tim Brooke-Taylor.)
Scene 4
Stage Coach
(*by* Graham Chapman and David Lipscomb)
G. Chapman
Scene 5
Final Episode
(*by* John Cleese and Graham Chapman)
Cast
Scene 6
"Traffic Island"
B. Oddie, J. Kendall, J. Cleese, G. Chapman
(*Music and Lyrics by* Bill Oddie.)
Scene 7
"Patients, For the Use of"
T. Brooke-Taylor, B. Oddie, J. Kendall, J. Lynn
(*Music and Lyrics by* Bill Oddie, Tim Brooke-Taylor, and Chris Stuart-Clark.)
Scene 8
"Scatty"
J. Kendall
(*Music and Lyrics by* Bill Oddie and Hugh MacDonald.)

---
[8]Transferred Off-Broadway 28 October 1964 to Square East, closing 13 January 1965 after 90 performances; re-opened as NEW CAMBRIDGE CIRCUS 14 January 1965 at the Square East and closed 21 March 1965 after 78 performances.

Scene 9
How Black Was My Valley
J. Lynn
(*by* David Lewis, John Cassels, Jonathan Lynn.)
Scene 10
"Boring Straight Song"
B. Oddie
(*Music and Lyrics by* Bill Oddie.)
Scene 11
"BBCBC"
D. Hatch, J. Cleese
(*Music by* Bill Oddie. *Lyrics by* John Cleese et. al.)
Scene 12
"Sing, Sing"
B. Oddie, T. Brooke-Taylor, J. Kendall, J. Cleese, G. Chapman
(*Music and Lyrics by* Bill Oddie.)
Scene 13
Humour Without Tears
(*by* Terry Jones)
D. Hatch, T. Brooke-Taylor, B. Oddie, J. Lynn, J. Kendall

ACT 2
Scene 1
"I Wanna Hold Your Handel"
B. Oddie, T. Brooke-Taylor, D. Hatch, J. Lynn
(*Music and Lyrics by* John Cameron.)
(Beatles parody à la Handel)
Scene 2
Prophet
(*by* Graham Chapman)G. Chapman
Scene 3
"West End Saga"
(*by* Cardinal Richelieu)Cast
Scene 4
"Music-Hall 1600"
J. Lynn, T. Brooke-Taylor
(*Music by* Bill Oddie. *Lyrics by* Tim Brooke-Taylor, Chris Stuart-Clark.)
Scene 5
"Those Were the Days"
B. Oddie
(*Music and Lyrics by* Bill Oddie.)
Scene 6
"Pride and Joy"
D. Hatch, J. Kendall
(*Music and Lyrics by* Bill Oddie.)
Scene 7
To Bury Caesar
(*by* Tony Hendra)G. Chapman, D. Hatch
Scene 8
"On Her Majesty's Service" (O.H.M.S.)
B. Oddie, T. Brooke-Taylor, D. Hatch, J. Kendall
(*Music and Lyrics by* Bill Oddie.)
Scene 9
Banana
(*by* Anthony Buffery and Richard Eyre)
J. Lynn, G. Chapman
Scene 10
"Bigger Than Both of Us"
J. Kendall, J. Cleese
(*Music by* Bill Oddie. *Lyrics by* John Cleese.)
Scene 11
Judge Not
(*by* John Cleese)
J. Cleese, B. Oddie, D. Hatch, J. Lynn, T. Brooke-Taylor, G. Chapman
Scene 12
Foot Note
(*by* Cardinal Richelieu)
Cast

1964.30 THE MERRY WIDOW

A Revival of the Operetta in Three Acts[9]. Music by Franz Lehár. Original Viennese libretto ('Die Lustige Witwe') by Victor Léon and Leo Stein after "L'Attaché d'Ambassade" by Henri Meilhac. English libretto by Adrian Ross. Staged by Michael Pollock. Choreographed by Thomas Andrew. Scenic design by George Jenkins. Lighting by Jules Fisher. Conducted by Carl Bamberger. Produced by the New York City Opera. Opened 10 October 1964 at the New York City Center and closed 1 November 1964 after 3 performances in repertory.

CAST: *Sonia*: NADJA WITKOWSKA. *Prince Danilo*: JOHN REARDON. *Baron Popoff*: JACK HARROLD. *Natalie*: Patricia Welting. *De Jolidon*: MICHELE MOLESE. *Marquis de Cascada*: David Smith. *St. Brioche*: Richard Krause. *Admiral Khadja*: William Ledbetter. *Mme. Khadja*: Charlotte Povia. *General Novikovich*: Spiro Malas. *Mme. Novikovich*: Beverly Evans. *Nish*: Coley Worth. *Clo-Clo*: Helen Guile. *Solo Dancers*: Rochelle Zide, Michael Maule. *Ensemble*: New York City Opera Chorus.

1964.31 DIE FLEDERMAUS

A Revival of the Operetta in Three Acts[10]. Original Libretto by Carl Haffner and Richard Genée. Lyrics by Richard Genée. Based on the comedy "Le Réveillon" by Henri Meilhac and Ludovic Halévy. English libretto by Ruth and Thomas Martin. Music by Johann Strauss. Staged by Julius Rudel. Scenic design by William Pitkin. Costume design by Henry Heymann. Choreography by Thomas Andrew. Conducted by Julius Rudel. Opened 11 October 1964 at the New York City Center and closed 7 November 1964 after 4 performances in repertory.

CAST: *Eisenstein*: JOHN REARDON. *Rosalinda*: BEVERLY SILLS. *Adele*: ANNE ELGAR. *Alfred*: Jon Crain. *Falke*: RICHARD FREDERICKS. *Frank*: LEE CASS. *Blind*: Kellis Miller. *Prince Orlofsky*: DAVID SMITH. *Sally*: Beverly Evans. *Frosch*: Coley Worth. *Ivan*: Glenn Dowlen. *Solo Dancers*: Rochelle Zide, Michael Maule. *Ensemble*: New York City Opera Chorus.

1964.32 GOLDEN BOY

A Musical in Two Acts, 20 Scenes. Book by Clifford Odets and William Gibson. Based on Clifford Odets' play of the same name. Music by Charles Strouse. Lyrics by Lee Adams. Directed by Arthur Penn. Sets, costumes and projections designed by Tony Walton. Choreography by Donald McKayle. Assistant choreographer, Jaime Rogers. Lighting by Tharon Musser. Projections devised by Richard Pilbrow. Musical direction and additional musical scoring by Elliott Lawrence. Orchestrations by Ralph Burns. Musical coordinator for Mr. Davis, George Rhodes. Associate producer, George Platt. An Epic Production. Produced by Hillard Elkins. Opened 20 October 1964 at the Majestic Theatre and closed 5 March 1966 after 569 performances.

CAST (in order of appearance): *Tom Moody*: KENNETH TOBEY. *Roxy Gottlieb*: Ted Beniades. *Tokio*: Charles Welch. *Joe Wellington*: SAMMY DAVIS. *Lorna Moon*: PAULA WAYNE. *Mr. Wellington*: Roy Glenn. *Anna*: Jeannette DuBois. *Ronnie*: Johnny Brown. *Frank*: Lou Gossett. *Terry*: Terrin Miles. *Hoodlum*: Buck Heller. *Eddie Satin*: BILLY DANIELS. *Benny*: Benny Payne. *Al*: Albert Popwell. *Lola*: Lola Falana. *Lopez*: Jaime Rogers. *Mabel*: Mabel Robinson. *Les*: Lester Wilson. *Drake*: Don Crabtree. *Fight Announcer*: Maxwell Glanville. *Reporter*: Bob Daley. *Driscoll*: Ralph Vucci.

Ensemble: Marguerite Delaine, Lola Falana, Baayork Lee, Theresa Merritt, Robin Miller, Sally Neal, Louise Quick, Mabel Robinson, Amy Rouselle, Bob Daley, Maxwell Glanville, Buck Heller, Benny Payne, Harold Pierson, Albert Popwell, Kenneth Scott, Stephen Taylor, Ralph Vucci, Lamont Washington, Lester Wilson.

(The action takes place in New York City 1960-1964.)

Act 1, Scene 1: A Boxers' Gymnasium. *Scene 2*: The Wellington kitchen in Harlem. *Scene 3*: Rooftop of the tenement. *Scene 4*: Tom Moody's Office. *Scene 5*: A Schoolyard playground. *Scene 6*: A Harlem street. *Scene 7*: The Wellington kitchen. *Scene 8*: A Railroad depot. *Scene 9*: The road tour. *Scene 10*: Joe's dressing-room in Madison Square Garden.

---

[9]Originally produced in New York 21 October 1907 at the New Amsterdam Theatre for 416 performances. For Synopsis of Scenes and Musical Numbers, see original 1907 production.
[10]First English language production in New York 16 March 1885 at the Casino Theatre for 42 performances. First New York production of this adaptation 20 December 1950 at the Metropolitan Opera House. For Synopsis of Scenes and Musical Numbers, see May 1954 revival.

Act 2, Scene 1: A bar. *Scene 2*: A party at Eddie's penthouse apartment. *Scene 3*: Along the river. *Scene 4*: Dawn in the park. *Scene 5*: Tom's office. *Scene 6*: 127th Street at night. *Scene 7*: The dressing room. *Scene 8*: The boxing ring. *Scene 9*: The dressing room. *Scene 10*: A Harlem street at night.

ACT 1[11]

Scene 1

"Workout"
Boxers

Scene 3

"Night Song"
S. Davis

Scene 4

"Everything's Great"
K. Tobey, P. Wayne

Scene 5

"Gimme Some"
S. Davis, T. Miles

"Stick Around"
S. Davis

Scene 6

"Don't Forget 127th Street"
S. Davis, J. Brown, Company

Scene 8

"Lorna's Here"
P. Wayne

Scene 9

The Road Tour
S. Davis, P. Wayne, K. Tobey, T. Beniades, B. Daniels, C. Welch, Company

"This Is the Life"
B. Daniels, S. Davis, L. Falana, Company

ACT 2

Scene 1

"Golden Boy"
P. Wayne

Scene 2

"While the City Sleeps"
B. Daniels

"While the City Sleeps" (dance)
M. Robinson, J. Rogers, L. Wilson

"Colorful"
S. Davis

Scene 3

"I Want To Be With You"
S. Davis, P. Wayne

Scene 4

"Can't You See It?"
S. Davis

Scene 6

"No More"
S. Davis, Company

Scene 8

The Fight
S. Davis, J. Rogers

[11]For subsequent American road tour prior to London, the script and song order were revised, including the following changes:

"Colorful" (moved to Act 1 Scene 1 after "The Workout")

"Stick Around" and The Road Tour were dropped.

"Yes, I Can!" (added to close Act 1)
S. Davis

"No More" (moved to opening of Act 2)

"Golden Boy" (moved to Act 2, Scene 6, now Lorna's Bedroom)

"You're No Brother of Mine" (added to Act 2, Scene 2, now Scene 3)
S. Davis, Al Kirk (Frank)

"The Riot" (added to Act 2, Scene 8, now Harlem Street)
The Company

"Can't You See It?" dropped.

"What Became of Me" (added to Act 2, Scene 11, now Madison Square Garden)
S. Davis

1964.33 BEN FRANKLIN IN PARIS

A Musical in Two Acts, a Prologue and 14 Scenes. Play and lyrics by Sidney Michaels. Music by Mark Sandrich, Jr. Direction and choreography by Michael Kidd. Costumes by Motley. Production designed by Oliver Smith. Lighting by Jack Brown. Musical direction and vocal arrangements by Don Pippin. Orchestrations by Philip J. Lang. Dance and incidental music by Roger Adams. Produced by George W. George and Frank Granat. Opened 27 October 1964 at the Lunt-Fontanne Theatre and closed 1 May 1965 after 215 performances.

CAST (in order of appearance): *Captain Wickes*: SAM GREENE. *Benjamin Franklin*: ROBERT PRESTON. *Temple Franklin*: FRANKLIN KISER. *Benjamin Franklin Bache*: JERRY SCHAEFER. *Footman*: Anthony Falco. *Louis XVI*: OLIVER CLARK. *Vergennes*: Art Bartow. *Turgot*: Clifford Fearl. *Madame La Comtesse Diane de Vobrillac*: ULLA SALLERT. *British Grenadier*: Roger LaPage. *David Lord Stormont*: BYRON WEBSTER. *French Soldier*: Ron Schwinn. *Pierre Caron de Beaumarchais*: BOB KALIBAN. *Jacques Fincque*: John Taliaferro. *Little Boy*: Stuart Getz. *Pedro Count de Aranda*: JACK FLETCHER. *Bookseller*: Herb Mazzini. *Janine Nicolet*: SUSAN WATSON. *Abbe de Morellet*: Herb Mazzini. *Spanish Aide-de-Camp*: Kip Andrews. *Spanish Soldier*: Art Matthews. *Spanish Ambassador's Daughter*: Suzanne France. *Yvonne*: Lauren Jones.

Singers and Dancers: Barbara Bossert, Mona Crawford, Hilda Harris, Anita Maye, Caroline Parks, Art Bartow, Anthony Falco, Clifford Fearl, John Keatts, Art Matthews, Herb Mazzini, John Taliaferro, Diane Ball, Marilyn Charles, Jean Eliot, Suzanne France, Ellen Graff, Lauren Jones, Sandy Roveta, Kip Andrews, Roger LePage, George Ramos, Eddie Roll, Rec Russel, Ron Schwinn, Lou Zeldis.

The action takes place in France during 1776-1777.

Prologue: At sea aboard the S. S. *Reprisal*.

Act 1, Scene 1: The Docks. *Scene 2*: Versailles. *Scene 3*: Ben's House. *Scene 4*: The Park. *Scene 5*: Sky over Paris. *Scene 6*: The Pont Neuf. *Scene 7*: Paristown. *Scene 8*: ben's House. *Scene 9*: The Vineyards.

Act 2, Scene 1: The Spanish Embassy. *Scene 2*: Versailles. *Scene 3*: Diane's House. *Scene 4*: Ben's House. *Scene 5*: Versailles.

Prologue

"We Sail the Seas"
American Sailors

ACT 1

Scene 1

"I Invented Myself"
R. Preston, Company

Scene 2

"Too Charming"
R. Preston, U. Sallert

Scene 3

"Whatever Became of Old Temple"
F. Kiser

"Half the Battle"
R. Preston, J. Schaefer, J.F. Kiser, B. Kaliban

Scene 4

"A Balloon Is Ascending"[12]
Company

Scene 5

"To Be Alone With You"
R. Preston, U. Sallert, Company

Scene 6

"You're in Paris"
S. Watson, F. Kiser

Scene 8

"How Laughable It Is"
U. Sallert

[12]Dropped during the run.

Scene 9
"Hic Haec Hoc"
Monks
"God Bless the Human Elbow"
R. Preston, J. Fletcher, B. Kaliban, Monks

ACT 2
Scene 1
"When I Dance With the Person I Love"
S. Watson
Scene 3
"Diane Is"
R. Preston
"Look For Small Pleasures"
R. Preston, U. Sallert
Scene 4
"I Love the Ladies"
R. Preston, S. Greene, B. Kaliban, F. Kiser, Sailors
Scene 5
"To Be Alone With You" (reprise)
R. Preston

COMEDY IN MUSIC

1964.34 Opus 2

A New Edition of the Solo Performance in Two Acts[13]. Designed and lighted by Ralph Alswang. A Nine O'Clock Theatre Production. Produced by Alexander H. Cohen. Opened 9 November 1964 at the John Golden Theatre and closed 24 April 1965 after 192 performances.

CAST: VICTOR BORGE, LEONID HAMBRO.

The order of the program will be announced by Mr. Borge.

ACT 1
Steinway
Mike
Mr. Borge
Latecomers
Curtain

ACT 2
Steinway
Mike
Mr. Borge
Mr. Hambro
Steinway Senior
Steinway Junior
Entire Cast
Mr. Borge Entirely Alone
Curtain

1964.35 SOMETHING MORE!

A Musical Comedy in Two Acts, 17 Scenes. Book by Nate Monaster. Based on the novel "Portofino P.T.A." by Gerald Green. Music by Sammy Fain. Lyrics by Marilyn and Alan Bergman. Directed by Jule Styne[14]. Scenery and lighting by Robert Randolph. Costumes by Alvin Colt. Musical direction by Oscar Kosarin. Orchestrations by Ralph Burns. Vocal arrangements by Buster Davis. Dance arrangements and orchestrations by Robert Prince. Dances and musical numbers staged by Bob Herget. Produced by Lester Osterman. Opened 10 November 1964 at the Eugene O'Neill Theatre and closed 21 November 1964 after 15 performances.

CAST (in order of appearance): *Bill Deems*: ARTHUR HILL. *Carol Deems*: BARBARA COOK. *Suzy Deems*: Neva Small. *Freddy Deems*: Kenny Kealy. *Adam Deems*: Eric White. *Julie*: Katey O'Brady. *Dick*: Hal Linden. *Gladys*: Marilyn Murphy. *Joe Santini*: Rico Froehlich. *Tony Santini*: VICTOR R. HELOU. *Policeman*: RICO FROEHLICH. *Mrs. Ferenzi*: PEG MURRAY. *Monte Checkovitch*: RONNY GRAHAM. *Luigi*: VICTOR R. HELOU. *Lepescu*: MICHAEL KERMOYAN. *Marchesa Valentina Crespi*: JOAN COPELAND. *Tony*: Christopher Man. *Maria*: Katey O'Brady. *The King*: Taylor Reed. *The King's Companion*: Connie Sanchez. *Mr. Veloz*: JO JO SMITH. *Mrs. Veloz*: PAULA KELLY. *Commandatorre Vermelli*: James Lavery. *Clubwoman*: Laurie Franks.

Dancers: Joan Bell, Shari Greene, Lynn Kollenberg, Connie Sanchez, Mimi Wallace, Bob Bishop, Steve Jacobs, Richard Lyle, Barry Preston, Bill Starr. *Singers*: Natalie di Silvio, Laurie Franks, Bobbi Lange, Marilyn Muphy, James Lavery, Taylor Reed, Ed Varrato.

Act 1, Scene 1: The Deems' living room, Mineola, New York. *Scene 2*: Same, a few days later. *Scene 3*: Mineola, New York, to Portofino, Italy. *Scene 4*: The Villa, Portofino. *Scene 5*: Portofino Square. *Scene 6*: The road to the Monastery. *Scene 7*: The old Monastery. *Scene 8*: The Villa.

Act 2, Scene 1: 'Bill Remembers'—Later that night. *Scene 2*: In front of the Marchesa's studio. *Scene 3*: The Marchesa's studio. *Scene 4*: In front of the Marchesa's studio. *Scene 5*: The Villa. *Scene 6*: The road to the beach. *Scene 7*: The beach. Dawn. *Scene 8*: The road to the Villa. *Scene 9*: The Villa.

ACT 1
"Something More"
A. Hill
"Who Fills the Bill"
B. Cook, N. Small, K. Nealy, E. White, H. Linden, CommitteeMemebers
"The Straw That Broke the Camel's Back"
A. Hill
"Better All the Time"
B. Cook
"Don't Make a Move"
J. Lavery, V. R. Helou
"Don't Make a Move" (reprise)
J. Lavery, V. R. Helou (Portofini Branch)
"No Questions"
B. Cook
"Church of My Choice"
R. Graham
"Jaded, Degraded Am I!"
R. Graham
"I've Got Nothin' to Do"
B. Cook, P. Murray, N. Small, K. Nealy, E. White
"I've Got Nothin' to Do" (reprise)
P. Murray
"Party Talk"
Guests
"In No Time At All"
J. Copeland
"The Master of the Greatest Art of All"
M. Kermoyan
"Grazie Par Niente"
R. Graham, B. Cook, J. J. Smith, P. Kelly, Guests
"I Feel Like New Year's Eve"
B. Cook
"One Long Last Look"
B. Cook

ACT 2
"Ode to a Key"
A. Hill
"Bravo, Bravo, Novelisto"
A. Hill, R. Froehlich
"Life Is Too Short"
R. Graham, P. Murray
"Il Lago de Innamoratti"
J. J. Smith, P. Kelly, Ensemble
(*Beach Dance composed and arranged by* Robert Prince.)
"Mineola"
B. Cook
"Come Sta"
P. Murray, N. Small, K. Kealy, E. White, K. O'Brady, C. Mann
Finale
A. Hill, B. Cook

[13]An earlier version of "Comedy In Music" was first produced in New York 2 October 1953 at the John Golden Theatre for 849 performances.
[14]Additional direction by Joe Layton unbilled.

1964.36

IOLANTHE, or The Peer and the Peri

A Revival of the Comic Opera in Two Acts[15]. Libretto by William S. Gilbert. Music by Arthur Sullivan. (Costumes uncredited.) Settings designed by Peter Goffin. Director of productions, Herbert Newby. Musical director, Isidore Godfrey. Associate conductor, James Walker. Produced by the D'Oyly Carte Opera Trust, Ltd. under the management of Sol Hurok. Opened 17 November 1964 at the New York City Center and closed 17 December 1964 after 7 performances in repertory.

CAST: *The Lord Chancellor*: JOHN REED. *Earl of Mountararat*: DONALD ADAMS. *Earl Tolloller*: DAVID PALMER. *Private Willis* of the Grenadier Guards: KENNETH SANDFORD. *Strephon*, an Arcadian Shepherd: JEFFREY SKITCH. *Queen of the Fairies*: GILLIAN KNIGHT. *Iolanthe*, a Fairy, Strephon's Mother: GILLIAN HUMPHREYS. *Celia, Leila, Fleta*, Fairies: Margaret Eales, Pauline Wales, Jennifer Marks. *Phyllis*, an Arcadian Shepherdess and Ward in Chancery: VALERIE MASTERSON.

Chorus of Dukes, Marquises, Earls, Viscounts, Barons and Fairies: Glyn Adams, Keith Bonnington, Liam Cummings, Jon Ellison, Eric Greenall, John Hugill, Thomas Lawlor, James Lewington, Gordon Mackenzie, John Maguire, James Marsland, Alfred Oldridge, Derek Peatfield, Vivien Carman, Dawn Davies, Margaret Eales, Gloria Farndell, Abby Hadfield, Susan Maisey, Jennifer Marks, Marian Martin, Joy Mornay, Elizabeth Mynett, Sylvia Vale, Anna Vincent.

1964.37

TRIAL BY JURY

A Revival of the Comic Opera in One Act[16]. Libretto by William S. Gilbert. Music by Arthur Sullivan. Costumes designed by George Sheringham. Setting designed by Peter Goffin. Director of productions, Herbert Newby. Musical directors, Isidore Godfrey, James Walker. Produced by the D'Oyly Carte Trust, Ltd. under the management of Sol Hurok. Opened 19 November 1964 at the New York City Center and closed 19 December 1964 after 10 performances in repertory.

CAST: *The Learned Judge*: JEFFREY SKITCH. *Counsel for the Plaintiff* ALAN STYLER. *The Defendant*: PHILIP POTTER. *Foreman of the Jury*: Anthony Raffell. *Usher*: GEORGE COOK. *Associate*: KEITH BONNINGTON. *The Plaintiff*: JENNIFER TOYE. *First Bridesmaid*: Joy Mornay. *Chorus of Jurymen, Bridesmaids and Public*: same as IOLANTHE above.

1964.38

H.M.S. PINAFORE, or The Lass That Loved a Sailor

A Revival of the Comic Opera in Two Acts[17]. Libretto by William S. Gilbert. Music by Arthur Sullivan. Settings and costumes designed by Peter Goffin. Back cloth, Joseph and Phil Harker. Director of productions, Herbert Newby. Musical directors, Isidore Godfrey, James Walker. Produced by the D'Oyly Carte Opera Trust, Ltd. under the management of Sol Hurok. Opened 19 November 1964 at the New York City Center and closed 19 December 1964 after 10 performances in repertory.

CAST: *The Rt. Hon. Sir Joseph Porter, K.C.B.*, First Lord of the Admiralty: JOHN REED. *Captain Corcoran*, Commanding the *H.M.S. Pinafore*: JEFFREY SKITCH. *Ralph Rackstraw*, Able Seaman: DAVID PALMER. *Dick Deadeye*, Able Seaman: DONALD ADAMS. *Bill Bobstay*, Bo'sun's Mate: George Cook. *Bob Beckett*, Carpenter's Mate: Anthony Raffell. *Josephine*, the Captain's Daughter: ANN HOOD. *Hebe*, Sir Joseph's First Cousin: Pauline Wales. *Little Buttercup*, a Portsmouth Bumboat Woman: GILLIAN KNIGHT. *First Lord's Sisters, his Cousins, his Aunts, Sailors, Marines*: same as IOLANTHE above.

[15]First presented in New York 25 November 1882 at the Standard Theatre for 105 performances. For Synopsis of Scenes and Musical Numbers, see original 1882 production.

[16]First presented in New York 15 November 1875 at the Eagle Theatre for 8 performances. For Synopsis of Scenes and Musical Numbers, see original 1875 production.

[17]Originally presented in New York 15 January 1879 at the Standard Theatre for 175 performances. For Synopsis of Scenes and Musical Numbers, see original 1879 production.

1964.39

ZIZI

A Musical Extravaganza in Two Acts, 8 Scenes, in French. Scenes. Entire production conceived and staged by Roland Petit. Costumes by Yves Saint-Laurent. Musical director and conductor, Michel Mention. Associate conductor, Don Plumby. Produced by Columbia Theatrical Enterprises, Inc. and Claude Giraud Productions under the auspices of the Association Française d'Action Artistique. Opened 21 November 1964 at the Broadway Theatre and closed 2 January 1965 after 49 performances.

CAST: ZIZI JEANMAIRE, FÉLIX BLASZKA.

Roland Petit Corps de Ballet: Théresè Thoreux, Jacqueline de Min, Panchita de Peri, Nicole Dieu, Vladanka Langhofer, Marie Lys Blanc, Jacques Dombrowski, Ben de Rochemont, Daini Kudo, Hans Kroonder, Robert Richemont, Lucien Mars, Peter Smink. *Off-Stage Male Quartet*: The Revelers. *Percussionist*: Gus Wallez. *Accordionist*: Jean Cardon.

ACT 1

Scene 1

Prologue
(*Music by* Ward Swingle.)
Dancers

Scene 2

"La cervelle"
Z. Jeamaire
(*Music by* Jean Ferrat. *Lyrics by* Bernard Dimey.)

I do pretty well without racking my brains, I have all I need. What makes a woman stupid is to have too much brains. Brains, brains, they're no use to me!

"Les bras d'Antoine"
Z. Jeanmaire, F. Blaszka
(*Music and Lyrics by* Guy Béart.)

These are wonderful and exciting things that I feel when I am in the arms of my beloved Antoine.

Scene 3

Pastiches (Ballet Sketches)
Dancers

Scaramouche
(*Music by* Darius Milhaud.)

Tarantelle
(*Music by* Gioacchino Rossini.)

Espana
(*Music by* Emmanuel Chabrier.)
Introductory Duets by J. Dombrowski (dancer), G. Wallez (percussionist).

Scene 4

La chambre
Z. Jeanmaire, F. Blaszka, Company
(*Ballet by* Georges Simenon. *Music by* Georges Auric.)

A police inspector reconstructs a crime, only to find that history repeats itself. A rectangular light, orange colored, in a piece of the night, it is a window, a window is a room, a room is a man's burrow where one is born, one loves, one hates, one dies . . . And sometimes one kills. In a room, once upon a time . . .

Scene 5

"Bacorope"
(*Music by* Michel Mention.)
N. Dieu, L. Mars, Dancers

Scene 6

La chaloupée
Z. Jeanmaire, B. de Rochemont or J. Dombrowski, Company
(*Story by* Marcel Aymé. *Music by* Maurice Thiriet.)

This dance story about a wedding party was written especially for Zizi Jeanmaire and Roland Petit. The theme of the music is adapted from "Valse Chaloupée" by Jacques Offenbach, who in turn took an old French seafarers' dance form as the basis for his lively and rollicking score.

Scene 7

"Quail On Toast With Pink Champagne"
(*Music by* Michel Mention.)
Z. Jeanmaire, Company. Introduction by Félix Blaska.

In this dance sketch (from the ballet "A La Carte" devised by Roland Petit), Roland Petit and Yves Saint-Laurent depict a gourmet delicacy of

the French cuisine: Les Cailles sur Canape, topped off with a glass of bubbling pink champagne, as portrayed by Zizi Jeanmaire.

ACT 2

Zizi sings:

"Les yeux brilliants" (Sparkling Eyes)
Z. Jeanmaire
(*Music by* Francis Lai. *Lyrics by* Bernard Dimey.)

With my sparkling eyes, my smile and the way I talk, you know where I come from.

"Les tatouages" (The Tattoos)
Z. Jeanmaire, F. Blaszka
(*Music by* Michel Legrand. *Lyrics by* Jean Drejac.)

A play on words. T'as tout is also pronounced "tattoo," and means "you have everything."

"Charleston"
Z. Jeanmaire, A. Brigoni, P. Smink, H. Kroonder

"Drole de musique"
Z. Jeanmaire
(*Music and Lyrics by* Christian Guitreau.)

The sound of the accordion reminds me of the little dance halls and bistros where I've left something of myself.

"Frankie et Johnny"
Z. Jeanmaire, J. Dombrowski, F. Blaszka, Company
(*Lyrics by* Boris Vian, from an American folk song)

A French version of the American hit which makes no pretense whatsoever of portraying our authentic Western life.

"Mon truc en plumes"
Z. Jeanmaire, Entire Company
(*Music by* Jean Constantin. *Lyrics by* Bernard Dimey.)

Although the literal translation of this production number is "My Skill With Feathers," the word "truc" as used in French slang is, with its double entendre, untranslatable.

"Mon bonhomme" (My Guy)
Z. Jeanmaire
(*Music and Lyrics by* Jean Ferrat.)

If I call him just my man, or even my master, that wouldn't give you the correct impression of how really sweet he is. Mon Bonhomme, Mon Bonhomme.

"Je te tuerai d'amour" (I Shall Kill You With Love)
Z. Jeanmaire, Rock 'n' Roll Quartet
(*Music by* Johnny Halliday. *Lyrics by* Raymond Queneau.)

This is France's eloquent answer to our rock 'n' roll. Johnny Halliday, who wrote this music, is not only the continental Elvis Presley, but also writes most of his popular material himself.

"Eh l'amour" (Ah, love!)
Z. Jeanmaire, Entire Company
(*Music and Lyrics by* Jean Ferrat.)

This Gallic hymn to l'amour invokes love in all its facets: young innocence, youthful passion, the cheap and transitory varieties as well as loftier emotions. The song is climaxed by a promise of 'seventh heaven'—or even more!

1964.40

BAJOUR

A Musical Comedy in Two Acts, 22 Scenes. Book by Ernest Kinoy. Based on the short stories ("The Gypsy Women," "The King of the Gypsies") by Joseph Mitchell published in *The New Yorker*[18]. Music and lyrics by Walter Marks. Directed by Lawrence Kasha. Musical numbers staged by Peter Gennaro. Scenery by Oliver Smith. Costumes by Freddy Wittop. Lighting by Peggy Clark. Vocal arrangements and musical direction by Lehman Engel. Orchestrations by Mort Lindsey. Dance music arranged by Richard DeBenedictis. Assistant choreographer, Wally Seibert. Produced by Edward Padula, Carroll and Harris Masterson, Norman Twain. Opened 23 November 1964 at the Sam S. Shubert Theatre, moved 10 May 1965 to the Lunt-Fontanne Theatre and closed 12 June 1965 after 232 performances.

CAST (in order of appearance): *Renting Agent*: Dick Ensslen. *Cockeye Johnny Dembo*: HERSCHEL BERNARDI. *Vanno*: Sal Lombardo. *Loopa*: ANTONIA REY. *First Patrolman*: Harry Danner. *Plainclothesman*: Harry Goz. *Second Patrolman*: Paul Sorvino. *Third Patrolman*: Robert Kristen. *Lou MacNiall*: ROBERT BURR. *Emily Kirsten*: NANCY DUSSAULT. *Mrs. Helene Kirsten*: MAE QUESTEL. *Rosa*: Asya. *Mitya*: Vito Durante. *Frankie*: Terry Violino. *Steve*: GUS TRIKONIS. *The King of Newark*: HERBERT EDELMAN. *Anyanka*: CHITA RIVERA. *Marfa*: Jeanne Tanzy. *Olga*: Carmen Morales. *Chairlady*: LUCIE LANCASTER. *Waiter*: Harry Danner. *J. Arnold Foster*: Ralph Farnworth.

Dancers: Asya, Eileen Barbaris, Michael Bennett, Connie Burnett, John Cashman, Betsy Dickerson, Vito Durante, Gene Foote, Bick Goss, Fernando Grahal, Kazimir Kokich, Marc Maskin, Stan Mazin, Carmen Morales, Carolyn Morris, Leland Palmer, Don Rehg, Geri Seignious, Terry Violino, Billi Vitali. *Singers*: Anita Alpert, Harry Danner, Mariana Doro, Dick Ensslen, Peter Falzone, Ralph Farnworth, Harry Goz, Liza Howell, Robert Kirsten, Urylee Leonardos, Evy Love, Madeline Miller, Eugene Morgan, Jeanne Repp, Jessica Quinn, Paul Sorvino.

(The action takes place at the present time in New York City.)

Act 1, Scene 1: The Empty Store. *Scene 2*: The City. *Scene 3*: The Pickpocket and Confidence Squad. *Scene 4*: Emily's Bedroom. *Scene 5*: The Backyard. *Scene 6*: In front of the Store. *Scene 7*: The Store (now the Ofisa). *Scene 8*: In front of the Store. *Scene 9*: The Ofisa. *Scene 10*: An Urban Renewal Site. *Scene 11*: The Ofisa.

Act 2, Scene 1: The Backyard. *Scene 2*: Momma's Kitchen. *Scene 3*: The Backyard. *Scene 4*: The Pickpocket and Confidence Squad. *Scene 5*: The Guggenheim Museum. *Scene 6*: Central Park. *Scene 7*: Momma's Kitchen. *Scene 8*: The Ofisa. *Scene 9*: An Urban Renewal Site. *Scene 10*: The Empty Store. *Scene 11*: The New Jersey Flats.

ACT 1

Scene 1
"Move Over, New York"
H. Bernardi, Ensemble

Scene 3
"Where Is the Tribe For Me?"
N. Dussault

Scene 5
"The Haggle"
C. Rivera, G. Trikonis, Ensemble
"Love-Line"
C. Rivera

Scene 7
"Words, Words, Words"
N. Dussault, H. Bernardi

Scene 9
"Mean"
C. Rivera

Scene 10
"Must It Be Love?"
N. Dussault

Scene 11
"Bajour"
C. Rivera, N. Dussault, H. Bernardi, Ensemble

ACT 2

Scene 1
"Soon"
C. Rivera, G. Trikonis

Scene 3
"I Can"
C. Rivera, N. Dussault

Scene 4
"Living Simply"
R. Burr, N. Dussault, Patrolmen

Scene 6
"Honest Man"
H. Bernardi, H. Edelman

Scene 7
"Guarantees"
M. Questel
"Love Is a Chance"
N. Dussault

Scene 8
"The Sew-Up"
C. Rivera, M. Questel, Ensemble Women

[18]Later published in book form under the collective title "Up in the Old Hotel."

Scene 11

Finale: "Move Over, America"

Ensemble

THE PIRATES OF PENZANCE, or The Slave of Duty

1964.41

A Revival of the Comic Opera in Two Acts[19]. Libretto by William S. Gilbert. Music by Arthur Sullivan. Settings designed by Peter Goffin. (Costumes uncredited) Director of productions, Herbert Newby. Musical directors, Isidore Godfrey, James Walker. Produced by the D'Oyly Carte Opera Trust, Ltd. under the management of Sol Hurok. Opened 24 November 1964 at the New York City Center and closed 20 December 1964 after 8 performances in repertory.

CAST: *Major General Stanley*: JOHN REED. *The Pirate King*: DONALD ADAMS. *Samuel*, his Lieutenant: Anthony Raffell. *Frederic*, the Pirate Apprentice: PHILIP POTTER. *Sergeant of Police*: GEORGE COOK. *Mabel, Edith Kate, Isabel*, General Stanley's Daughters: VALERIE MASTERSON, GILLIAN HUMPHREYS, PEGGY ANN JONES, Pauline Wales. *Ruth*, Pirate Maid-of-all-work: GILLIAN KNIGHT. *Chorus of Pirates, Police and General Stanley's Daughters*: same as IOLANTHE above.

THE MIKADO, or The Town of Titipu

1964.42

A Revival of the Comic Opera in Two Acts[20]. Libretto by William S. Gilbert. Music by Arthur Sullivan. Production directed by Anthony Besch. Costumes designed by Disley Jones and Charles Ricketts. Settings designed by Disley Jones. Director of productions, Herbert Newby. Musical director, Isidore Godfrey, James Walker. Produced by the D'Oyly Carte Opera Trust, Ltd. under the management of Sol Hurok. Opened 26 November 1964 at the New York City Center and closed 16 December 1964 after 10 performances in repertory.

CAST: *The Mikado of Japan*: DONALD ADAMS. *Nanki-Poo*, his son, disguised as a wandering minstrel in love with Yum-Yum: PHILIP POTTER. *Ko-Ko*, Lord High Executioner of Titipu: JOHN REED. *Pooh-Bah*, Lord High Everything Else: KENNETH SANDFORD. *Pish-Tush, Go-To*, Noble Lords: Alan Styler, George Cook. *Yum-Yum, Pitti-Sing, Peep-Bo*, three sisters, wards of Ko-Ko: JENNIFER TOYE, PEGGY ANN JONES, GILLIAN HUMPHREYS. *Katisha*: GILLIAN KNIGHT. *Chorus of School Girls, Nobles, Guards and Coolies*: same as IOLANTHE above.

RUDDIGORE, or The Witch's Curse

1964.43

A Revival of the Comic Opera in Two Acts[21]. Libretto by William S. Gilbert. Music by Arthur Sullivan. Costumes and settings by Peter Goffin. Director of productions, Herbert Newby. Musical directors, Isidore Godfrey, James Walker. Produced by the D'Oyly Carte Opera Trust, Ltd. under the management of Sol Hurok. Opened 3 December 1964 at the New York City Center and closed 18 December 1964 after 5 performances in repertory.

CAST: *Sir Ruthven Murgatroyd*: JOHN REED. *Richard Dauntless*: DAVID PALMER. *Sir Despard Murgatroyd*: KENNETH SANDFORD. *Old Adam Goodheart*: George Cook. *Sir Roderic Murgatroyd*: DONALD ADAMS. *Rose Maybud*: ANN HOOD. *Mad Margaret*: PEGGY ANN JONES. *Dame Hannah*: GILLIAN KNIGHT. *Zorah*: Jennifer Toye. *Ruth*: Jennifer Marks. *Chorus of Officers, Ancestors, Professional Bridesmaids, etc.*: same as IOLANTHE above.

[19]First presented in New York 31 December 1879 at the Fifth Avenue Theatre for a total of 91 performances in two engagements. For Synopsis of Scenes and Musical Numbers, see original 1879 production.

[20]First presented in New York 20 July, 10-29 August 1885 at the Union Square and People's Theatres for 22 performances. First authorized production presented 19 August 1885 at the Fifth Avenue Theatre by Richard D'Oyly Carte for 250 performances. For Synopsis of Scenes and Musical Numbers, see 19 August 1885 D'Oyly Carte production.

[21]First presented in New York 21 February 1887 at the Standard Theatre for 53 performances. For Synopsis of Scenes and Musical Numbers, see original 1887 production.

I HAD A BALL

1964.44

A Musical Comedy in Two Acts. Book by Jerome Chodorov. Music and lyrics by Jack Lawrence and Stan Freeman. Directed by Lloyd Richards. Settings and lighting by Will Steven Armstrong. Costumes by Ann Roth. Musical direction and vocal arrangements by Pembokre Davenport. Dances and musical numbers staged by Onna White. Orchestrations by Philip J. Lang. Dance music arranged by Luther Henderson. Produced by Joseph Kipness. Opened 15 December 1964 at the Martin Beck Theatre and closed 12 June 1965 after 199 performances.

CAST (in order of appearance): *Garside*: BUDDY HACKETT. *Stan the Shpieler*: RICHARD KILEY. *Jeannie*: KAREN MORROW. *The Alley Gang (4)*: *Gimlet*: Al Nesor. *Joe the Muzzler*: Jack Wakefield. *Ma Maloney*: ROSETTA LeNOIRE. *George Osaka*: Conrad Yama. *Morocco*: Morocco. *Lifeguard*: Marty Allen. *Jimmy*: Nathaniel Jones. *Officer Millhauser*: Ted Thurston. *Brooks*: STEVE ROLAND. *Addie*: LUBA LISA. *Children*: Sheldon Golomb, Gina Kaye.

Singers: Miriamne Burton, Jacqueline Carol, Jacque Dean, Marilyn Feder, Shirley Leinwand, Lispet Nelson, Eugene Edwards, Herbert Fields, Murray Goldkind, Marvin Goodis, Herb Surface, John Wheeler. *Dancers*: Mary Ehara, Sandra Lein, Nancy Lynch, Patti Mariano, Alice Shanahan, June Eve Story, Patti Ann Watson, Marty Allen, Doria Avila, Bob Bernard, Ray Gilbert, Edward J. Heim, Gary Hubler, Scott Hunter, John Sharpe.

Act 1: In and around Coney Island on the Fourth of July. The time is the present.

Act 2: Sixty days later.

ACT 1

"Coney Island, U.S.A."
J. Wakefield, R. LeNoire, C. Yama, A. Nesor, Children, Ensemble

"The Other Half of Me"
R. Kiley

"Red-Blooded American Boy"
S. Roland, A. Nesor, J. Wakefield, R. LeNoire, C. Yama

"I Got Everything I Want"
K. Morrow

"Freud"
B. Hackett

"Think Beautiful"
R. LeNoire, K. Morrow, J. Wakefield, C. Yama, A. Nesor, Ensemble

"Addie's at It Again"
L. Lisa, J. Wakefield, C. Yama, A. Nesor

"Faith"
R. Kiley, A. Nesor, J. Wakefield, R. LeNoire, C. Yama, Children, Ensemble

"Can It Be Possible?"
R. Kiley, K. Morrow, S. Roland, L. Lisa, B. Hackett

ACT 2

"The Neighborhood Song"
A. Nesor, J. Wakefield, R. LeNoire, C. Yama, Ensemble

"The Affluent Society"
R. Kiley, S. Roland

"Boys, Boys, Boys"
L. Lisa, Lifeguards

"Fickle Finger of Fate"
R. Kiley

"I Had a Ball"
K. Morrow, A. Nesor, J. Wakefield, R. LeNoire, C. Yama, Morocco, Ensemble

"Almost"[22]
K. Morrow

"You Deserve Me"
B. Hackett, S. Roland, L. Lisa

"You Deserve Me" (reprise)
B. Hackett

"Tunnel of Love Chase"
B. Hackett, R. Kiley, K. Morrow, T. Thurston, Ensemble

[22]Dropped during the run.

1964.45 BEYOND THE FRINGE '65

A Return Engagement of the Revue in Two Acts[23]. Written by Alan Bennett, Peter Cook, Jonathan Miller, Dudley Moore. Staged by Alexander H. Cohen. Original London production staged by Eleanor Fazan. Setting by John Wyckham. Lighting by Ralph Alswang. Production associates, Andre Goulston, Gabriel Katzka. A Nine O'Clock Theatre Production. Produced by Alexander H. Cohen by arrangement with William Donaldson and Donald Albery. Opened 15 December 1964 at the Ethel Barrymore Theatre and closed 9 January 1965 after 30 performances.

CAST: ROBERT CESSNA, DONALD CULLEN, JOEL FABIANI, JAMES VALENTINE.

ACT 1[24]

Home Thoughts from Abroad
Royal Box
The Following Paid Political Broadcast[25]
Bollard
Blue Trousers[26]
Weill Song
The Philosophers
The Great Train Robbery
Colonel Bogey
The Aftermyth of War

ACT 2

Civil War
Real Class
Die Flabbergast[27]
Portraits from Memory
One Leg Too Few
The Death of (Lord) Nelson
The Scientist
The Doctor
The Duke (Studio Five Interviews)
The Miner (Sitting on the Bench revised)
The Restaurant
The Sermon (Take a Pew revised)
So That's the Way You Like It
The End of the World

1964.46 BRIGADOON

A Revival of the Musical Play in Two Acts, a Prologue and 11 Scenes[28]. Book and lyrics by Alan Jay Lerner. Music by Frederick Loewe. Dance and musical Numbers by Agnes de Mille, assisted by James Jamieson. Directed by John Fearnley. Settings by Oliver Smith. Lighting by Peggy Clark. Costumes by Stanley Simmons. Conductor, William Jonson. (Vocal arrangements by Frederick Loewe. Orchestrations by Ted Royal.) Produced by New York City Center Light Opera Company (Jean Dalrymple, Director). Opened 23 December 1964 at the New York City Center and closed 3 January 1965 after 17 performances.

CAST (in order of appearance): *Tommy Albright*: PETER PALMER. *Jeff Douglas*: SCOTT McKAY. *Sandy Dean*: William [Will] Mackenzie. *Meg Brockie*: LOUISE O'BRIEN. *Archie Beaton*: Earl MacDonald. *Harry Beaton*: EDWARD VILLELLA. *Andrew MacLaren*: Alexander Clark. *Jean MacLaren*: Imelda De Martin. *Fiona MacLaren*: LINDA BENNETT. *Angus MacGuffie*: Daniel Hannafin. *Charlie Dalrymple*: HARRY DAVID SNOW. *Maggie Anderson*: Gemze de Lappe. *Sword Dancers*: Ben Gillespie, Paul Olson, Wayne Boyd, Dennis Cole, Charles McCraw, Ron Tassone. *Mr. Lundie*: CLARENCE NORDSTROM. *Bagpiper*: Maurice Eisenstadt. *Frank*: Si Vario. *Jane Ashton*: Sharon Ritchie.

Townsfolk of Brigadoon: *Singers*: Diana Chase, Maria Hero, Linda Johnson, Virginia Kerr, Bobbi Lange, Leonore Lanzillotti, Joyce Olson, Jeanne Shea, Abbie Todd, Sallie Valante, Lynn Wendell, Brown Bradley, Peter Clark, William J. Coppola, Rex Downey, Glenn Kezer, Henry Lawrence, Jim Lynn, Bob Neukum, Stan Page, Stephen Rydell. *Dancers*: Virginia Allen, Lynne Broadbent, Joanna Crosson, Diana Ede, Lucia Lambert, Loi Leabo, Gracia Littauer, Mavis Ray, Judy Thelen, Mona Tritsch, Esther Villavicencio, Toodie Wittner, Paul Berné, Wayne Boyd, Allan Byrns, Dennis Cole, Joseph Fioretti, Ben Gillespie, Charles McCraw, Paul Olson, Victor Pierantozzi, Ron Tassone, Michael Toles.

1965.01 KELLY

A Musical in Two Acts, a Prologue and 13 Scenes. Book and lyrics by Eddie Lawrence. Music by Moose Charlap. Directed and choreographed by Herbert Ross. Scenic production by Oliver Smith. Costumes by Freddy Wittop. Lighting by Tharon Musser. Orchestrations by Hershy Kay. Dance music by Betty Walberg. Associate producer, Robert L. Livingston. Produced by David Susskind and Daniel Melnick in asssociation with Joseph E. Levine. Opened and closed 6 February 1965 at the Broadhurst Theatre after 1 performance.

CAST (in order of appearance): *Hop Kelly*: DON FRANCKS. *Dan Kelly*: WILFRID BRAMBELL. *Jack Mulligan*: MICKEY SHAUGHNESSY. *Augie Masters*: LEON JANNEY. *Stickpin Sidney Crane*: JESSE WHITE. *James*: Steve Elmore. *Carruthers*: Brandon Maggart. *Fay Cherry*: EILEEN RODGERS. *Charlie*: Josip Elic. *Sparkenbroke*, the butler: Bill Richards. *Mayor Tully*: Hamilton Camp. *Englishman*: Thomas Rezarf. *Angela Crane*: ANITA GILLETTE. *Tough Kid*: Barbara Monte. *Three Tough Guys*: Louis Kosman, Anthony De Vecchi, Michael Nestor. *Sailor*: James Moore. *The Redhead*: Lynn Fields. *The Rube*: Sterling Clark. *Young Girl*: Hanne-Marie Reiner. *First Young Man*: Larry Roquemore. *Second Young Man*: Paul Charles. *The Drunk*: Ronald B. Stratton. *Three Ladies*: Leslie Franzos, Eleanore Treiber, Kathleen Doherty. *Lollypop Girl*: Bette Jenkins. *Beggar*: Bill Richards. *Bums*: James Moore, Larry Roquemore, Bill Richards. *Police Chief*: J. Vernon Oaks. *Policeman*: Robert L. Hultman. *Chief Dignitary*: Stanley Simmonds.

Dancing Ensemble: Kathleen Doherty, Lynn Fields, Leslie Franzos, Bette Jenkins, Barbara Monte, Hanne-Marie Reiner, Eleanore Treiber, Sterling Clark, Paul Charles, Antony De Vecchi, Michael Nestor, Bill Richards, Larry Roquemore, Ronald B. Stratton. *Singing Ensemble*: Georgia Creighton, Ceil Delli, Carol Joplin, Lorene Latine, Donna Monroe, Maggie Task, Walter P. Brown, Steve Elmore, Howard Hartman, Robert L. Hultman, J. Vernon Oaks, William Wendt.

Prologue: Under the Bridge.

Act 1, Scene 1: Along the Bowery. *Scene 2*: The Backroom at Augie Masters' Cabaret on the Bowery. *Scene 3*: The Kelly Shack under the Brooklyn Bridge. *Scene 4*: Sid Crane's Mansion. The Oval Room. *Scene 5*: Red Hook, Brooklyn.

Act 2, Scene 1: The Kelly Shack. *Scene 2*: Augie Masters' Cabaret. *Scene 3*: "Me and the Elements." *Scene 4*: At the foot of the Brooklyn Bridge. *Scene 5*: Below the Bridge. *Scene 6*: Atop the Brooklyn Bridge. *Scene 7*: Along the Bowery. *Scene 8*: Augie Masters' Cabaret.

PROLOGUE

"Ode to the Bridge"
D. Francks

ACT 1

Scene 1

"Six Blocks From the Bridge"
J. White, M. Shaughnessy, L. Janney, Company

Scene 2

"That Old Time Crowd"
E. Rodgers, Boys

"Simple Ain't Easy"
D. Francks, E. Rodgers

Scene 3

"I'm Gonna Walk Right Up to Her"
D. Franks, M. Shaughnessy

Scene 4

"A Moment Ago"
A. Gillette, D. Francks

Scene 5

"This Is a Tough Neighborhood"
Entire Company

[23]Originally produced in New York 27 October 1962 at the John Golden Theatre for 673 performances. See original production for authors of individual sketches.

[24]For individual authors of sketches, see original 1962 production.

[25]Not in previous editions of BEYOND THE FRINGE.

[26]Not in previous editions of BEYOND THE FRINGE.

[27]Not in previous editions of BEYOND THE FRINGE.

[28]Originally produced in New York 13 March 1947 at the Ziegfeld Theatre for 581 performances. For Synopsis of Scenes and Musical Numbers, see original 1947 production.

"(I'll) Never Go There Anymore"
A. Gillette, D. Francks

ACT 2
Scene 1
"Life Can Be Beautiful"
E. Rodgers, W. Brambell, Bums
"Everyone Here Loves Kelly"
E. Rodgers
"Ballad to a Brute"
A. Gillette, D. Francks
Scene 2
"Heavyweight Champ of the World"
M. Shaughnessy, Company
Scene 3
"Me and the Elements"
D. Francks, W. Brambell
Scene 4
"Everyone Here Loves Kelly" (reprise)
E. Rodgers, Company
Scene 7
"Never Go There Anymore" (reprise)
A. Gillette
Scene 8
"Everyone Here Loves Kelly" (reprise)
Entire Company

1965.02 BAKER STREET

A Musical Adventure of Sherlock Holmes in Two Acts, a Prologue and 16 Scenes. Book by Jerome Coopersmith. Adapted from the stories ('The Adventure of the Empty House,' 'A Scandal in Bohemia' and 'The Final Problem') by Sir Arthur Conan Doyle. Music and lyrics by Marian Grudeff and Raymond Jessel. Production designed by Oliver Smith. Costumes by Motley. Lighting by Jean Rosenthal. Directed by Harold Prince. Choreography by Lee Becker Theodore. Musical direction by Harold Hastings. Orchestrations by Don Walker. Dance arrangements by John Morris. Production associate, Hildy Parks. Diamond Jubilee Parade by Bil Baird's Marionettes. Produced by Alexander H. Cohen in association with Gabriel Katzka. Opened 16 February 1965 at the Broadway Theatre, moved 3 November 1965 to the Martin Beck Theatre and closed 14 November 1965 after 313 performances.

CAST (in order of appearance): *Captain Gregg*: PATRICK HORGAN. *Dr. Watson*: PETER SALLIS. *Mrs. Hudson*: Paddy Edwards. *Sherlock Holmes*: FRITZ WEAVER. *Inspector Lestrade*: Daniel Keyes. *Irene Adler*: INGA SWENSON. *Daisy*: Virginia Vestoff. *Baxter*: Martin Wolfson. *Wiggins*: TEDDY GREEN. *Duckbellows*: Bert Michaels. *Nipper*: Sal Pernice. *Perkins*: George Lee. *Macipper*: Mark Jude Sheil. *Murillo*: Jay Norman. *The Three Killers*: Avind Harum, Christopher Walken, Tommy Tune. *Tavern Singer*: Gwenn Lewis. *Professor Moriarty*: MARTIN GABEL.

Dancers: Sara Lee Barber, Barbara Blair, Lois Castle, John Grigas, Gwenn Lewis, Diana Saunders. *Singers*: Martin Ambrose, Frank Bouley, Jack Dabdoub, Gay Edmond, Judie Elkins, Maria Graziano, Horace Guittard, Peter Johl, Mara Landi, Hal Norman, Vera Walton.

The action takes place in and around London in 1897, the year in which England celebrated the Diamond Jubilee of the reign of Queen Victoria.

Prologue: Baker Street, London.

Act 1, Scene 1: The Baker Street flat. *Scene 2*: The stage of the Theatre Royal. *Scene 3*: Backstage at the Theatre Royal. *Scene 4*: An alley in Baker Street. *Scene 5*: Irene's flat. *Scene 6*: The Baker Street flat. *Scene 7*: The London underworld. *Scene 8*: Moriarty's ship.

Act 2, Scene 1: A street in London. *Scene 2*: Moriarty's ship. *Scene 3*: Interior of a carriage. *Scene 4*: The cliffs of Dover. *Scene 5*: A part of London. *Scene 6*: The Baker Street flat. *Scene 7*: A hall in London. *Scene 8*: Baker Street.

ACT 1
Scene 1
"It's So Simple"
F. Weaver, P. Sallis, P. Horgan, D. Keyes
Scene 2
"I'm in London Again"
I. Swenson
Scene 4
"Leave It to Us, Guv"
T. Green, the Irregulars (Male Dancers)
Scene 5
"Letters"
I. Swenson
Scene 6
"Cold Clear World"
F. Weaver
"Finding Words for Spring"
I. Swenson
"What a Night This Is Going to Be"
F. Weaver, I. Swenson, P. Sallis, V. Vestoff
Scene 7
"London Underworld" (Ballet)
Company
Scene 8
"I Shall Miss You"
M. Gabel

ACT 2
Scene 1
"Roof Space"
T. Green, the Irregulars (Male Dancers)
Scene 2
"A Married Man"
P. Sallis
"I'd Do It Again"
I. Swenson
Scene 3
"Pursuit"
F. Weaver
Scene 7
"Jewelry"
M. Wolfson, Criminals (Ensemble)

1965.03 PORGY AND BESS

A Revival of the Folk Opera in Two Acts, 3 Scenes[29]. Book by DuBose Heyward adapted from the play "Porgy" by DuBose and Dorothy Heyward. Music by George Gershwin. Lyrics by DuBose Heyward and Ira Gershwin. Directed by Ella Gerber. Scenic design by Roger Sullivan. Costume design by Stanley Simmons. Conducted by Dean Ryan. Produced by the New York City Opera. Opened 5 March 1965 at the New York City Center and closed 14 March 1965 after 6 performances in repertory.

CAST (in order of appearance): *Clara*: CLAUDIA LINDSAY. *Mingo*: Jerry Laws. *Sportin' Life*: AVON LONG. *Jake*: EDWARD PIERSON. *Serena*: SERENA BASH. *Robbins*: Gordon Watkins. *Jim*: Garwood Perkins. *Peter*, the Honey Man: Carrington Lewis. *Lily*, the Strawberry Woman: Helen Dowdy. *Maria*: CAROL BRICE. *Porgy*: ANDREW FRIERSON. *Crown*: JAMES RANDOLPH. *Bess*: JOYCE BRYANT. *Policeman*: Bill Grier. *Undertaker*: Joseph James. *Annie*: Alyce Webb. *Frazier*: Eugene Brice. *Detective*: Jack Bittner. *Crab Man*: Joseph Attles. *Coroner*: Kellis Miller. *Scipio*: Oscar Sylvan. *Dancer*: Glory Van Scott. *Residents of Catfish Row*: New York City Opera Chorus.

1965.04 DIE DREIGROSCHENOPER

A Revival of the Musical [The Threepenny Opera] in Three Acts, 10 Scenes, in German[30]. Music by Kurt Weill. Original German libretto by Bertolt Brecht (and Elisabeth Hauptmann). (Adapted from "The Beggar's

[29]First produced in New York 10 October 1935 at the Alvin Theatre for 124 performances. For Synopsis of Scenes and Musical Numbers, see original 1935 production. Originally produced in Three Acts, 9 Scenes. This production dispensed with the scene breaks and second intermission.
[30]Previously produced in New York in English only: 13 April 1933 at the Empire Theatre for 12 performances as The 3-Penny Opera. 10 March 1954 at the Theatre de Lys (Off-Broadway) for 96 performances; reopened 30 September 1955 at the Theatre de Lys for an additional 2611 performances.

Opera" by John Gay.) Directed by Adolph Rott. Scenic design by Wolfgang Roth. Costume design by Ruth Morley. Conducted by Julius Rudel. Produced by the New York City Opera. Opened 11 March 1965 at the New York City Center and closed 27 March 1965 after 6 performances in repertory.

CAST: *Ansager (Narrator)*: GEORGE S. IRVING. *Jonathan Jeremiah Peachum*: STEFAN SCHNABEL. *Mrs. Peachum*: LILIA SKALA. *Polly Peachum*: ANITA HOEFER. *Macheath*: KURT KASZNAR. *Brown*: Ralph Herbert. *Lucy*: MARION BRASH. *Filch*: Mathew Anden. *Die Platte (the Gang)(6)*: *Hakenfingerjakob*: Sol Frieder. *Münzmatthias*: John Garson. *Trauerweidenwalter*: Paul Andor. *Ede*: Michael Haeusserman. *Sägerobert*: Claus Jurgens. *Jimmy*: Curt Lowens. *Die Spelunken-Jenny*: MARTHA SCHLAMME. *Huren* (Ladies of Ill-Repute): Constance Conrad, Carla Huston, Erna Rossman, Ruth Sobotka, Ludmilla Tchor. *Smith*: David Smith. *Pastor Kimball*: Henry Cordy. *Ensemble*: New York City Opera Chorus.

The action takes place in Soho, London, just before the coronation of Queen Victoria.

Act 1, Scene 1: A Fair in Soho. *Scene 2*: The Shop of Jonathan Jeremiah Peachum, outfitter of beggars. *Scene 3*: The Stable. *Scene 4*: Peachum's Shop.

Act 2, Scene 1: The Stable. *Scene 2*: A Bordello in Turnbridge. *Scene 3*: A Cell in the Old Bailey Prison.

Act 3, Scene 1: The Street Outside Peachum's Shop. *Scene 2*: The Death Cell in the Old Bailey Prison. *Scene 3*: The Gallows.

ACT 1

Scene 1

"Die Moritat von Mackie Messer" (The Ballad of Mack the Knife)
G. S. Irving

Scene 2

"Der Morgenchoral des Peachum" (Mr. Peachum's Morning Hymn)
S. Schnabel

"Der Anstatt-Dass-Song" (Instead-of Song)
L. Skala, S. Schnabel

Scene 3

"Das Hochzeitslied für ärmere Leute" (Wedding Song for Poor People)
Ensemble

"Die Seeräuber-Jenny" (Pirate Jenny)
A. Hoefer

"Der Kanonen-Song" (Cannon Song)
K. Kasznar

"Siehst du den Mond über Soho" (Liebeslied/Love Song)
A. Hoefer, K. Kasznar

Scene 4

"Der Song vom Nein und Ja" (Barbara-Song)

(Einst glaubte ich, als ich noch unschuldig war)
A. Hoefer

"Erstes Dreigroschen-Finale" (Über die Unsicherheit menschlicher Verhältnisse)

(The Uncertainty of Human Conditions)
A. Hoefer, S. Schnabel, L. Skala

ACT 2

Scene 1

"Der Ballade von der sexuellen Hörigkeit" (The Ballad of Sexual Dependency)
L. Skala

Scene 2

"Die Zuhälterballade" (The Procurer's Ballad)
K. Kasznar, M. Schlamme

Scene 3

"Die Ballade vom Angenehmen Leben" (The Ballad of Pleasant Living)
K. Kasznar

"Das Eifersuchtsduett" (The Jealousy Duet)
M. Brash, A. Hoefer

"Zweies Dreigroschen-Finale" (Denn Wovon Lebt Der Mensch?)

(What Keeps a Man Alive?)
K. Kasznar, M. Schlamme, Ensemble

ACT 3

Scene 1

"Die Ballade von der sexuellen Hörigkeit" (reprise)
L. Skala

"Das Lied von der Unzulänglichkeit menschlichen Strebens"

(The Song About Inadequacy)
S. Schnabel

"Salomon-Song" (Song of Solomon)
M. Schlamme

Scene 3

"Ballade, in der Macheath jedermann Abbitte leistet"

(Ballad in which Macheath Asks Everyone for Forgiveness)
K. Kasznar

"Drittes Dreigroschen-Finale" (Auftauchen des Reitenden Boten)

(Act 3 Finale-The Riding Messenger)
A. Hoefer, L. Skala, M. Schlamme, K. Kasznar, R. Herbert, S. Schnabel, Ensemble

"Die Schluss-Strophen der Moritat" (Moritat reprise)
G. S. Irving

1965.05

THIS WAS BURLESQUE

A Musical Satire (Revue) in Two Acts, 24 Scenes[31]. Entire Production supervised and directed by Ann Corio, based on her recollections. (Music, lyrics and special material mostly by Sonny Lester and Bill Grundy.) Musical conductor, Nick Francis. Choreography by Paul Morokoff. Costumes by Rex Huntington. Miss Corio's gowns by Jacks of Hollywood, Martier-Raymond, and Rex Huntington. Produced by Michael P. Iannucci. Opened 16 March 1965 at the Hudson Theatre and closed 6 June 1965 after 124 performances. Total, including previous Off-Broadway run: 1633 performances.

CAST: ANN CORIO, STEVE MILLS, Harry Conley, Dick Bernie, Paul West, Mac Dennison, Dexter Maitland, Kitty Lynne, Marilyn Marshall, Tina Kaye.

The Burley Cuties: Nicole Jaffee, Linda Donovan, Maria Bradley, Barbara Rhodes, Sharon Taylor, Jerry Beth Shotwell, Mary Alagia, Geraldine Barron, Betsy Haug, Rita O'Connor.

ACT 1

Scene 1

Prologue
S. Mills, D. Maitland, M. Dennison, R. O'Connor, B. Haug

Scene 2

"Hello, Everybody"
The Burley Cuties

Scene 3

Flirtation
S. Mills, P. West, A. Corio

Scene 4

"Bill Bailey"
M. Dennison, the Burley Cuties
(*Music and Lyrics by* Hughie Cannon.)

Scene 5

Hee Haw
D. Bernie, D. Maitland, L. Donovan, S. Taylor

Scene 6

Ecdysiast
M. Bradley

Scene 7

Hotel de France
H. Conley, P. West, N. Jaffee

Scene 8

Dance L'Orient (Seduction of the Virgin Princess)
The Burley Cuties
(*Music and Lyrics by* Sonny Lester and Bill Grundy.)

Scene 9

"St. James Infirmary"
M. Dennison, D. Maitland, A. Corio

Scene 10

Exotic
K. Lynne

Scene 11

Schoolroom
D. Bernie, D. Maitland, B. Rhodes, N. Jaffee, M. Bradley

---

[31]First produced in New York Off-Broadway 6 March 1962 at the Casino East Theatre for 1509 performances.

Scene 12
"Les Poules"
The Burley Cuties, 'La Madame' S. Taylor
Scene 13
Mills and West (comedy)
Scene 14
Marilyn Marshall (tassel routine)
Scene 15
Finale—Candy Butcher

ACT 2
Scene 1
"Powder My Back"
L. Donovan, the Burley Cuties
Scene 2
Sutton Place
H. Conley, A. Corio, T. Kay
Scene 3
Tina Kay
Scene 4
White Cargo
S. Mills, P. West, A. Corio, M. Dennison
Scene 5
"Evolution of Dance"
The Burley Cuties
Scene 6
Hall of Fame
A. Corio, L. Donovan
Scene 7
Crazy House
Entire Cast
Scene 8
Ann Corio (Specialty):
["Would You Like to Lay Your Head Upon My Pillow?"]
["A Pretty Girl Is Like a Melody"]
(*Music and Lyrics by* Irving Berlin.)
Scene 9
Finale
(Entire Company)

1965.06 DO I HEAR A WALTZ?

A Musical in Two Acts, 11 Scenes. Book by Arthur Laurents. Based on his play "The Time of the Cuckoo." Music by Richard Rodgers. Lyrics by Stephen Sondheim. Directed by John Dexter. Choreography by Herbert Ross. Scenery and costumes by Beni Montresor. Lighting by Jules Fisher. Orchestrations by Ralph Burns. Musical director, Frederick Dvonch. Dance music arranged by Richard DeBenedictis. Choreographic associate, Wakefield Poole. Production supervisor, Jerome Whyte. Produced by Richard Rodgers. Opened 18 March 1965 at the 46th Street Theatre and closed 25 September 1965 after 220 performances.

CAST (in order of appearance): *Leona Samish*: ELIZABETH ALLEN. *Mauro*: Christopher Votos. *Signora Fioria*: CAROL BRUCE. *Eddie Yaeger*: STUART DAMON. *Jennifer Yaeger*: JULIENNE MARIE. *Mrs. McIlhenny*: MADELEINE SHERWOOD. *Mr. McIlhenny*: JACK MANNING. *Giovanna*: FLEURY D'ANTONAKIS. *Vito*: James Dybas. *Renato Di Rossi*: SERGIO FRANCHI. *Man on Bridge*: Michael Lamont. *Mrs. Victoria Haslam*: Helon Blount.

Singers: Darrell Askey, Syndee Balaber, Bill Berrian, Helon Blount, Rudy Challenger, Pat Kelly, Liz Lamkin, Michael Lamont, James Luisi, Jack Murray, Carl Nicholas, Candida Pilla, Casper Roos, Bernice Saunders, Liza Stuart. *Dancers*: Jere Admire, Bob Bishop, Wayne De Rammelaere, Steve Jacobs, Sandy Leeds, Joe Nelson, Janice Peta, Walter Stratton, Nancy Van Rijn, Mary Zahn.

Act 1, Scene 1: Venice. *Scene 2*: Garden of Pensione Fioria. Evening. *Scene 3*: Di Rossi's Shop. The next day. *Scene 4*: Piazza San Marco. The same evening. *Scene 5*: Interior of Pensione Fioria. The following day. *Scene 6*: Garden of Pensione Fioria. Immediately afterwards.

Act 2, Scene 1: Facade of Pensione Fioria. The same night. *Scene 2*: Outside the Garden of Pensione Flioria. The enxt evening. *Scene 3*: The Piazza. The following morning. *Scene 4*: Garden of Pensione Fioria. That night. *Scene 5*: Same. The next morning.

ACT 1
Scene 1
"Someone Woke Up"
E. Allen
Scene 2
"This Week Americans"
C. Bruce
"What Do We Do? We Fly!"
E. Allen, M. Sherwood, J. Manning, S. Damon, J. Marie
Scene 3
"Someone Like You"
S. Franchi
"Bargaining"
S. Franchi
Scene 4
"Here We Are Again"
E. Allen, J. Dybas, S. Jacobs, S. Leeds, J. Nelson, N Van Rijn, M. Zahn
Scene 5
"Thinking"
S. Franchi, E. Allen
Scene 6
"No Understand"
C. Bruce, S. Damon, F. D'Antonakis
"Take the Moment"
S. Franchi

ACT 2
Scene 1
"Moon in My Window"
J. Marie, C. Bruce, E. Allen
Scene 2
"We're Gonna Be All Right"
S. Damon, J. Marie
"Do I Hear a Waltz?"
E. Allen, Company
Scene 3
"Stay"
S. Franchi
Scene 4
"Perfectly Lovely Couple"
E. Allen, S. Franchi,
J. Manning, M. Sherwood, J. Marie, S. Damon, F. D'Antonakis, C. Bruce
Scene 5
"Thank You So Much"
S. Franchi, E. Allen

1965.07 THE SAINT OF BLEECKER STREET

A Revival of the Opera (Musical Drama) in Three Acts, 5 Scenes[32]. Music and libretto by Gian-Carlo Menotti. Staged by Gian-Carlo Menotti. Production designed by Robert Randolph. Conducted by Vincent La Selva. Produced by the New York City Opera. Opened 18 March 1965 at the New York City Center and closed 28 March 1965 after 2 performances in repertory.

CAST (in order of appearance): *Assunta*: Muriel Greenspon. *Carmela*: Mary Jennings. *Maria Corona*: Anita Darian. *Her Son*: Clyde Ventura. *Don Marco*: Thomas Paul. *Annina*: JOAN SENA. *Michele*: ENRICO DI GIUSEPPE. *Desideria*: BEVERLY WOLFF. *Salvatore*: David Smith. *Concettina*: Wendy Morris. *A Young Man*: Anthony Safina. *A Young Woman*: Charlotte Povia. *Woman*: Anthea De Forest. *Bartender*: Don Henderson. *First Guest*: Richard Krause. *Second Guest*: William Ledbetter.

Neighbors, Friends, Policemen, etc.: New York City Opera Chorus.

[32]Originally produced in New York 27 December 1954 at the Broadway Theatre for 92 performances. For Synopsis of Scenes, see original 1954 production.

1965.08 MAURICE CHEVALIER AT 77

A One Man Show in Two Acts. Lighting by Jean Rosenthal. At the piano, Fred Stamer. Produced by Alexander H. Cohen. Opened 1 April 1965 at the Alvin Theatre and closed 1 May 1965 after 35 performances.

CAST: MAURICE CHEVALIER.

PROGRAM

"Thank Heaven for Little Girls" (from film GIGI)
(*Music by* Frederick Loewe. *Lyrics by* Alan Jay Lerner.)
Stations of Life (*by* Mauruce Chevalier)
"Place Pigalle"
(*Music and Lyrics by* Maurice Chevalier and Alstone.)
Cole Porter Medley
"Valentine"
(*Music and Lyrics by* Albert Willemetz and Henri Christiné.)
"Some People" (from GYPSY)
(*Music by* Jule Styne. *Lyrics by* Stephen Sondheim.)
"Un p'tit air"
(*Music and Lyrics by* Albert Willemetz and Mireille.)
"I Remember It Well" (from film GIGI)
(*Music by* Frederick Loewe. *Lyrics by* Alan Jay Lerner.)
"Un clochard m'a dit"
(*Music and Lyrics by* Noel Roux and Georges Garvarentz.)
"You Brought a New Kind of Love to Me" (from film THE BIG POND)
(*Music and Lyrics by* Sammy Fain, Irving Kahal and Pierre Norman.)
"When You're Smiling (the Whole World Smiles With You)"
(*Music and Lyrics by* Mark Fisher, Joe Goodwin and Larry Shay.)
"Hello, Dolly" (from HELLO, DOLLY!)
(*Music and Lyrics by* Jerry Herman.)
"You Must Have Been a Beautiful Baby" (from film HARD TO GET)
(*Music by* Harry Warren. *Lyrics by* Johnny Merrcer.)
"La leçon de piano"
(*Music and Lyrics by* Maurice Vandair and Henri Betti.)
"Paris tu rajeunis"
(*Music and Lyrics by* Noel Roux and André Popp.)
"Louise" (from film INNOCENTS OF PARIS)
(*Music by* Richard A. Whiting. *Lyrics by* Leo Robin.)
"A Las Vegas"
(*Music and Lyrics by* Albert Willemetz and Louiguy.)
"Hello, Beautiful"
(*Music and Lyrics by* Walter Donaldson.)
"Mimi La Blonde"
(*Music and Lyrics by* Jean Drejac and Heino Gaze.)
Accents melodiques
(*by* Maurice Chevalier)
"I'm Glad I'm Not Young Anymore" (from film GIGI)
(*Music by* Frederick Loewe. *Lyrics by* Alan Jay Lerner.)
"Au revoir"
(*Music and Lyrics by* Jean Drejac and Fred Freed.)
"Mimi" (from film LOVE ME TONIGHT)
(*Music by* Richard Rodgers. *Lyrics by* Lorenz Hart.)
"Ah donnez m'en de la chanson"
(*Music and Lyrics by* Rene Rouzaud and Marguerite Monnot.)
George Gershwin Medley
Spectateurs spectaculaires
(*by* Maurice Chevalier)
"La tendresse"
(*Music and Lyrics by* Noel Roux and Hubert Giraud.)
"Paris je t'aime"
(*Music and Lyrics by* Battaille-Henri and Victor Schertzinger.)
"La miss"
(*Music and Lyrics by* Henri Salvador.)

1965.09 H.M.S. PINAFORE, or The Lass That Loved a Sailor

A Revival of the Comic Opera in Two Acts[33]. Libretto by William S. Gilbert. Music by Arthur Sullivan. Directed by John Bishop. Scenery and costumes by Patton Campbell. Conductor, Felix Popper. Produced by the New York City Center Gilbert and Sullivan Company. Opened 14 April 1965 at the New York City Center and closed 22 April 1965 after 5 performances in repertory.

CAST: *The Rt. Hon. Sir Joseph Porter, K.C.B.*, First Lord of the Admiralty: NORMAN KELLEY. *Captain Corcoran*, Commander of the *H.M.S. Pinafore*: WILLIAM CHAPMAN, RICHARD FREDERICKS. *Ralph Rackstraw*, Able Seaman: JOHN STAMFORD, WILLIAM GREENE. *Dick Deadeye*, Able Seaman: PAUL UKENA. *Bill Bobstay*, Boatswain: William Ledbetter. *Bob Becket*: Lee Cass. *Josephine*, the Captain's Daughter: ANNE ELGAR, CAROL BAYARD. *Hebe*, Sir Joseph's First Cousin: Marlena Kleinman. *Little Buttercup*, Mrs. Cripps, a Portsmouth bum-boat woman: MURIEL GREENSPON.

First Lord's Sisters, His Cousins, His Aunts, Sailors, Marines, etc.: Joan August, Barbara Beaman, Paul Corder, Harris Davis, Marceline Decker, Anthea de Forest, Glenn Dowlen, Joyce Gerber, Margaret Goodman, Helen Guile, Don Henderson, Lila Herbert, David Hicks, Robert Lee Kelly, Jodell Kenting, Hanna Owen, Richard G. Park, Charlotte Povia, Frank Redfield, Anthony Safina, Alexander Savchuck, John Smith, Marie Young, Don Yule. *Solo Dancer*: Rochelle Zide.

1965.10 PATIENCE, or Bunthorne's Bride

A Revival of the Comic Opera in Two Acts[34]. Libretto by William S. Gilbert. Music by Arthur Sullivan. Scenery and costumes designed by Motley. Staged by Dorothy Raedler. Choreography by Thomas Andrew. Conductor, Julius Rudel. Produced by the New York City Center Gilbert and Sullivan Company. Opened 15 April 1965 at the New York City Center and closed 23 April 1965 after 3 peformances in repertory.

CAST: *Colonel Calverley*: WILLIAM CHAPMAN. *Major Murgatroyd*: James Wilson. *Lieut. the Duke of Dunstable*: RICHARD KRAUSE. *Reginald Bunthorne*, a Fleshly Poet: EMILE RENAN. *Archibald Grosvenor*, an Idyllic Poet: DAVID SMITH. *Mr. Bunsthorne's Solicitor*: Thomas Andrew. *The Lady Angela, The Lady Saphir, The Lady Ella, The Lady Jane*, Rapturous Maidens: MARLENA KLEINMAN, HELEN GUILE, Virginia Bitar, CLARAMAE TURNER. *Patience*, a Dairy Maid: PATRICIA WELTING, ANNE ELGAR. *Chorus of Rapturous Maidens and Officers of the Dragoon Guards*: same as H.M.S. PINAFORE above.

1965.11 THE MIKADO, or The Town of Titipu

A Revival of the Comic Opera in Two Acts[35]. Libretto by William S. Gilbert. Music by Arthur Sullivan. Staged by Dorothy Raedler. Scenery by Donald Oenslager. Costumes by Patton Campbell. Conductor, Charles Wilson. Produced by the New York City Center Gilbert and Sullivan Company. Opened 16 April 1965 at the New York City Center and closed 25 April 1965 after 6 performances in repertory.

CAST: *The Mikado of Japan*: GEORGE GAYNES, PAUL UKENA. *Nanki-Poo*: WILLIAM DIARD, RICHARD KRAUSE. *Ko-Ko*: NORMAN KELLEY, JAMES WILSON, HERBERT BEATTIE. *Pooh-Bah*: HERBERT BEATTIE, LEE CASS, NORMAN KELLEY. *Pish-Tush*: DAVID SMITH. *Three Sisters, Wards of Ko-Ko*: *Yum-Yum*: MARY JENNINGS, VIRGINIA BITAR, PATRICIA WELTING. *Pitti-Sing*: MARY BURGESS. *Peep-Bo*: MARLENA KLEINMAN, HELEN GUILE. *Katisha*: CLARAMAE TURNER, ELAINE BONAZZI, MURIEL GREENSPON. *Chorus of School Girls, Nobles, Guards and Coolies*: same as H.M.S. PINAFORE above.

---

[33]Originally presented in New York 15 January 1879 at the Standard Theatre for 175 performances. For Synopsis of Scenes and Musical Numbers, see original 1879 production.
[34]First presented in New York 22 September 1881 at the Standard Theatre for 177 performances. For Synopsis of Scenes and Musical Numbers, see original 1881 production.
[35]First presented in New York 20 July, 10-29 August 1885 at the Union Square and People's Theatres for 22 performances. First authorized production presented 19 August 1885 at the Fifth Avenue Theatre by Richard D'Oyly Carte for 250 performances. For Synopsis of Scenes and Musical Numbers, see 19 August 1885 D'Oyly Carte production.

1965.12 THE PIRATES OF PENZANCE, or The Slave of Duty

A Revival of the Comic Opera in Two Acts[36]. Libretto by William S. Gilbert. Music by Arthur Sullivan. Staged by Dorothy Raedler. Scenery by H. A. Condell. Conductor, Dean Ryan. Produced by the New York City Center Gilbert and Sullivan Company. Opened 20 April 1965 at the New York City Center and closed 24 April 1965 after 4 performances in repertory.

CAST: *Major General Stanley*: EMILE RENAN. *The Pirate King*: PAUL UKENA, WILLIAM CHAPMAN. *Samuel*, his Lieutenant: William Ledbetter. *Frederic*, the Pirate Apprentice: WILLIAM DIARD, WILLIAM GREENE. *Sergeant of Police*: HERBERT BEATTIE, LEE CASS. *Mabel, Edith Kate, Isabel*, General Stanley's Daughters: ANNE ELGAR, VIRGINIA BITAR, MARY BURGESS, Helen Guile. *Ruth*, Pirate Maid-of-all-work: MURIEL GREENSPON. *Chorus of Pirates, Police and General Stanley's Daughters*: Same as H.M.S. PINAFORE above.

1965.13 THE YEOMEN OF THE GUARD, or The Merryman and His Maid

A Revival of the Comic Opera in Two Acts[37]. Libretto by William S. Gilbert. Music by Arthur Sullivan. Staged by Allen Fletcher. Stage director, Ruth M. Hider. Scenery by Stephen O. Saxe. Costumes by Alvin Colt. Conducted by Julius Rudel. Produced by the New York City Center Gilbert and Sullivan Company. Opened 21 April 1965 at the New York City Center and closed 25 April 1965 after 2 performances in repertory.

CAST: *Sir Richard Cholmondeley*, Lieutenant of the Tower: PAUL UKENA. *Colonel Fairfax* under sentence of death): JOHN STAMFORD. *Sergeant Meryll* of the Yeomen of the Guard: GEORGE GAYNES. *Leonard Meryl*, his Son: RICHARD KRAUSE. *Jack Point*, a Strolling Jester: NORMAN KELLEY. *Wilfred Shadbolt*, Head Jailor and Assistant Tormentor: HERBERT BEATTIE. *The Headsman*: Thomas Andrew. *First Yeoman*: William Greene. *Second Yeoman*: William Ledbetter. *First Citizen*: Harris Davis. *Second Citizen*: Glenn Dowlen. *Elsie Maynard*, a Strolling Player: MARY JENNINGS. *Phoebe Meryll*, Sergeant Meryll's Daughter: MARY BURGESS. *Dame Carruthers*, Housekeeper to the Tower: ELAINE BONAZZI. *Kate*, her Niece: VIRGINIA BITAR. *Chorus of Yeomen of the Guard, Gentlemen, Citizens, etc.*: same as H.M.S. PINAFORE above.

1965.14 HALF A SIXPENCE

A Musical Comedy in Two Acts, 18 Scenes. Book by Beverley Cross. Based on the novel "Kipps" by H. G. Wells. Music and Lyrics by David Heneker. Directed by Gene Saks. Dances and musical numbers staged by Onna White. Scenery and costumes by Loudon Sainthill. Lighting by Jules Fisher. Musical direction by Stanley Lebowsky. Costume supervision by Jane Greenwood. Original ballet music by Robert Prince. Assistant choregrapher, Tom Panko. Vocal arrangements by Buster Davis. Orchestrations by Jim Tyler. Dance arrangements and orchestrations by Robert Prince. Associate producer, Jane C. Nusbaum. Produced by Allen-Hodgdon (Lewis Allen, Dana Hodgdon), Stevens Productions and Harold Fielding. Opened 25 April 1965 at the Broadhurst Theatre and closed 16 July 1966 after 512 performances.

CAST (in order of appearance): *Arthur Kipps*: TOMMY STEELE. *Sid Pornick*: WILL MACKENZIE. *Buggins*: NORMAN ALLEN. *Pearce*: GROVER DALE. *Carshot*: William Larsen. *Flo*: Michele Hardy. *Emma*: Reby Howells. *Kate*: Louise Quick. *Victoria*: Sally Lee. *Mr. Shalford*: Mercer McLeod. *Mrs. Walsingham*: Ann Shoemaker. *Mrs. Botting*: Trescott Ripley. *Ann Pornick*: POLLY JAMES. *Young Walsingham*: JOHN CLEESE. *Helen Walsingham*: CARRIE NYE. *Chitterlow*: JAMES GROUT. *Laura*: Eleonore Treiber. *Girl Student*: Rosanna Huffman. *Boy Student*: Sterling Clark. *Photographer*: Sean Allan. *Photographer's Assistant*: Robert Gorman. *First Reporter*: Reid Klein. *Second Reporter*: Fred Cline. *Gwendolin*: Ann Rachel.

Dancers: Diane Blair, Lynn Fields, Sally Ransone, Sterling Clark, Robert Karl, Alan Peterson, Bill Stanton, Ron Schwinn. *Singers*: Sean Allan, Fred Cline, Robert Gorman, Glenn Kezer, Reid Klein, John Knapp, Max Norman, Carol Richards, Ann Rachel, Constance Moffit, Rosanna Huffman.

Act 1, Scene 1: The Emporium. Folkestone, England, 1900. *Scene 2*: The Promenade. *Scene 3*: The Emporium. *Scene 4*: The 'Hope and Anchor' Bar. *Scene 5*: The street. *Scene 6*: The classroom. *Scene 7*: The Emporium. *Scene 8*: The Promenade. *Scene 9*: The old lighthouse. *Scene 10*: The Military Canal Regatta.

Act 2, Scene 1: Mrs. Botting's solarium. *Scene 2*: Kitchen. *Scene 3*: Photographer's Studio. *Scene 4*: Parlor of rented house. *Scene 5*: The Pier. *Scene 6*: The building site. *Scene 7*: The Promenade. *Scene 8*: The bookshop.

ACT 1

Scene 2

"All in the Cause of Economy"
T. Steele, W. Mackenzie, N. Allen, G. Dale

"Half a Sixpence"
T. Steele, P. James

Scene 4

"Money To Burn"
T. Steele, E. Treiber, Men

Scene 8

"A Proper Gentlemen"
T. Steele, W. Mackenzie, N. Allen, G. Dale, Shopgirls

"She's Too Far Above Me"
T. Steele

Scene 9

"If the Rain's Got to Fall"
T. Steele, G. Dale, W. Mackenzie, N. Allen, Shopgirls, Singers, Dancers

Scene 10

"The Old Military Canal"
Singers

("If the Rain's Got to Fall" reprise)
(Singers)

ACT 2

Scene 1

"A Proper Gentleman" (reprise)
T. Steele, A. Shoemaker, C. Nye, T. Ripley, J. Cleese, Party Guests

Scene 2

"Long Ago"
T. Steele, P. James

Scene 3

"Flash Bang Wallop"
T. Steele, P. James,
J. Grout, M. McLeod, G. Dale, W. Mackenzie, N. Allen, Shopgirls, Singers

Scene 4

"I Know What I Am"
P. James

Scene 6

"The Party's on the House"
T. Steele, G. Dale, W. Mackenzie, N. Allen, Shopgirls, Singers, Dancers

"Half a Sixpence" (reprise)
T. Steele, P. James

Scene 7

"All in the Cause of Economy" (reprise)
M. Hardy, G. Dale, W. Mackenzie, N. Allen

Scene 8

Finale
Entire Company

1965.15 GUYS AND DOLLS

A Revival of the Musical Fable (Comedy) in Two Acts, 17 Scenes[38]. Book by Jo Swerling and Abe Burrows. Based on a story and characters by Damon Runyon. Music and lyrics by Frank Loesser. Choreography by Ralph Beaumont. Adaptation of Jo Mielziner's original (scenic) designs by Peter Wolf. Costumes by Frank Thompson. Lighting by Peggy Clark. (Orchestral arrangements by George Bassman and Ted Royal.) Conductor, Irving Actman. Directed by Gus Schirmer. Produced by the New York City Center

[36]First presented in New York 31 December 1879 at the Fifth Avenue Theatre for a total of 91 performances in two engagements. For Synopsis of Scenes and Musical Numbers, see original 1879 production.

[37]First presented in New York 17 October 1888 at the Casino Theatre for 100 performances. For Synopsis of Scenes and Musical Numbers, see original 1888 production.

[38]First presented in New York 24 November 1950 at the 46th Street Theatre for 1200 performances. For Synopsis of Scenes and Musical Numbers, see original 1950 production. "Havana" now retitled "San Juan."

Light Opera Company (Jean Dalrymple, General director). Opened 28 April 1965 at the New York City Center and closed 9 May 1965 after 15 performances.

CAST (in order of appearance): *Nicely-Nicely Johnson*: JACK DE LON. *Benny Southstreet*: JOEY FAYE. *Rusty Charlie*: Ed Becker. *Sarah Brown*: ANITA GILLETTE. *Arvide Abernathy*: CLARENCE NORDSTROM. *Mission Band*: Jeanne Schlegel, CLARENCE NORDSTROM, Maria Hero, CLAIRE WARING, Arthur Santry, Joy Franz. *Harry the Horse*: TOM PEDI. *Lieut. Brannigan*: FRANK CAMPANELLA. *Nathan Detroit*: ALAN KING. *Angie the Ox*: Vern Shinnal. *Miss Adelaide*: SHEILA MacRAE. *Sky Masterson*: JERRY ORBACH. *Joey Biltmore*: Ed Becker. *Mimi*: Ginna Carr. *General Matilda B. Cartwright*: CLAIRE WARING. *Big Jule*: JAKE LaMOTTA. *Drunk*: Stuart Mann. *Waiter*: Philip Lucas.

Dancers: Rita Agnese, Suzanne Channel, Dorothy D'Honau, Tina Faye, Shelley Frankel, Leslie Franzos, Ginny Gan, Altouise Gore, Shari Greene, Maureen Hopkins, Joan Kruger, Violetta Landek, Maria Strattin, Frank Coppola, Luigi Gasparinetti, Fernando Grahal, Mark J. Holliday, Daniel Joel, Carlos Macri, Mitchell Nutick, Paul Owsley, Charles Reeder, Marc Scott, Ronald Stratton. *Singers*: Joy Franz, Maria Hero, Jeanne Schlegel, Ken Ayres, Edward Becker, Walter P. Brown, Victor P. Helou, Henry Lawrence, Philip Lucas, Jim Lynn, Stuart Mann, John Peck, Michael Quinn, Darrell Sandeen, Arthur Santry.

1965.16 KEN MURRAY'S HOLLYWOOD

A Revue (Commentary and Film) in Two Acts, 6 Scenes. (Conceived by Ken Murray.) Designed and lighted by Ralph Alswang. Music arranged and played by Armin Hoffman. A Nine O'Clock Theatre Production. Produced by Alexander H. Cohen in association with Arthur Whitelaw. Opened 10 May 1965 and closed 22 May 1965 after 16 performances.

CAST: KEN MURRAY.

ACT 1

Scene 1

Prelude by Armin Hoffman

Scene 2

Hollywood's Number One Movie Fan Ken Murray

Scene 3

Hollywood Family Album:

A period of retrospection for one generation and a glimpse into an unfamiliar world for the younger set.

Scene 4

San Simeon

The fabulous castle and estate of the late William Randolph Hearst: first showing of films taken some thirty years ago, giving an intimate portrait of this showplace, its owner, and the glamorous people invited there.

ACT 2

Scene 1

Backstage with Bill and Coo
K. Murray

A visit on the set of Ken Murray's Academy Award-winning feature length motion picture, made with three hundred parakeets. 'Bill and Coo' will be re-released soon in your favorite motion picture theatre.

Scene 2

Hollywood Thirty Years Later

Dedicated to all those who cherish the movies as the living historical record of our changing styles, manners and customs.

1965.17 FLORA, THE RED MENACE

A Musical Comedy in Two Acts, 14 Scenes. Book by George Abbott and Robert Russell. Based on the novel "Love Is Just Around the Corner" by Lester Atwell. Music by John Kander. Lyrics by Fred Ebb. Dance and musical numbers staged by Lee Theodore. Settings by William and Jean Eckart. Costumes by Donald Brooks. Lighting by Tharon Musser. Musical direction by Harold Hastings. Orchestrations by Don Walker. Dance arrangements by David Baker. Production supervisor, Ruth Mitchell. Production directed by George Abbott. Produced by Harold Prince. Opened 11 May 1965 at the Alvin Theatre and closed 24 July 1965 after 87 performances.

CAST (in order of appearance): *F.D.R.'s Voice*: Art Carney. *Apple Seller*: J. Vernon Oaks. *Pencil Seller*: Clark Morgan. *Policeman*: Daniel P. Hannafin. *Broker*: Henry LeClair. *Fourth Man*: John Taliaferro. *Woman*: Anne C. Russell. *Fifth Man*: Anthony Falco. *Sixth Man*: Les Freed. *Seventh Man*: Robert [Bob] Fitch. *School Principal*: Abbie Todd. *Flora (Meszaros)*: LIZA MINNELLI. *Harry Toukarian*: BOB DISHY. *Lilly*: Anne C. Russell. *Artists*: Les Freed, John Taliaferro, J. Vernon Oaks, Diane McAfee, Anthony Falco, Marie Santell. *Comrade Galka*: Louis Guss. *Comrade Ada*: MARY LOUISE WILSON. *Comrade Jackson*: Clark Morgan. *Comrade Charlotte*: CATHRYN DAMON. *Elsa*: Stephanie Hill. *The Lady*: DORTHA DUCKWORTH. *Mr. Weiss*: Joe E. Marks. *Bronco Smallwood*: JAMES CRESSON. *Joe*: Danny Carroll. *Katie*: Marie Santell. *Mr. Rearson*: Gordon Dilworth. *Mr. Stanley*: Robert Kaye. *Lulu*: Jamie Donnelly. *Maggie*: Elaine Cancilla.

Dancers: Elaine Cancilla, Ciya Challis, Barbara Doherty, Judith Doren, Ellen Graff, Mary Ann Niles, Phyllis Wallach, Harry Bell, Robert [Bob] Fitch, Marcello Gamboa, Charles Kalan, James McArdle, Neil J. Schwartz. *Singers*: Jamie Donnelly, Barbara Christopher, Diane McAfee, Abbie Todd, Anthony Falco, Les Freed, Daniel P. Hannafin, Henry LeClair, J. Vernon Oaks, John Taliaferro.

Act 1, Scene 1: A street in New York and the High School of Commercial Art. New York City, 1933. *Scene 2*: The advertising office at Garrett and Mellick's Department Store. *Scene 3*: The Park. *Scene 4*: Flora's Studio. *Scene 5*: The Party Meeting. *Scene 6*: Flora's Studio. *Scene 7*: Mr. Stanley's Office at Garrett and Mellick's Department Store. *Scene 8*: Flora's Studio. *Scene 9*: Union Square and the street in front of Harry's house.

Act 2, Scene 1: Harry's apartment. *Scene 2*: The Park. *Scene 3*: Flora's Studio. *Scene 4*: Mr. Stanley's office at Garrett and Mellick's Department Store. *Scene 5*: Flora's Studio.

ACT 1

Scene 1

Prologue
Ensemble

"Unafraid"
L. Minnelli, Students, Ensemble

Scene 2

"All I Need Is One Good Break"
L. Minnelli, B. Dishy, Artists

Scene 3

"Not Every Day of the Week"
L. Minnelli, B. Dishy

Scene 4

"All I Need Is One Good Break" (reprise)
L. Minnelli, S. Hill, D. Duckworth

"Sign Here"
B. Dishy

Scene 5

"The Flame"
M. L. Wilson, B. Dishy, Comrades

Scene 6

"Palomino Pal"
D. Duckworth, J. Cresson

Scene 7

"A Quiet Thing"
L. Minnelli

Scene 8

"Hello Waves"
B. Dishy, L. Minnelli

Scene 9

"Dear Love"
L. Minnelli, Ensemble

ACT 2

Scene 1

"Express Yourself"
C. Damon, B. Dishy

Scene 2

"Knock, Knock"
M. L. Wilson, J. Cresson

Scene 3

Comrade Charlotte's Ballet—"The Tree of Life"
C. Damon, M. L. Wilson, B. Dishy, Ensemble
Trunk: N. J. Schwartz. *Vine*: R. Fitch. *Spirit of Revolution*: M. A. Niles.

Scene 4

"Sing Happy"
L. Minnelli

Scene 5
"You Are You"
J. E. Marks, S. Hill, L. Minnelli, R. Kaye, J. Donnelly, M. Santell, D. Carroll
Finale
Entire Company

1965.18 KISS ME, KATE

A Revival of the Musical Comedy in Two Acts, 17 Scenes[39]. Book by Sam (Samuel) and Bella Spewack. (Based on William Shakespeare's "The Taming of the Shrew.") Music and lyrics by Cole Porter. Directed by John Fearnley and Billy Matthews. Dances and musical numbers staged by Hanya Holm. Scenery by Robert O'Hearn. Costumes by Stanley Simmons after originals by Lemuel Ayers. Lighting by Peggy Clark. Musical director, Pembroke Davenport. (Orchestrations by Robert Russell Bennett.) Dance music arranged by Genevieve Pitot. Produced by the New York City Center Light Opera Company (Jean Dalrymple, Director). Opened 12 May 1965 at the New York City Center and closed 30 May 1965 after 23 performances.

CAST (in order of appearance): *Fred Graham*: BOB [Robert] WRIGHT. *Harry Trevor*: ALEXANDER CLARK. *Lois Lane*: NANCY AMES. *Ralph* (Stage Manager): William H. Batchelder. *Lilli Vanessi*: PATRICIA MORISON. *Paul*: TIGER HAYNES. *Hattie*: ALYCE ELIZABETH WEBB. *Stage Doorman*: Eugene R. Wood. *Bill Calhoun*: KELLY BROWN. *Cab Driver*: Bill [William] Kennedy. *First Man*: JESSE WHITE. *Second Man*: VICTOR HELOU. *Harrison Howell*: Royal Beal. *Specialty Dancers*: Charles Cook, Ernest Brown. *Doctor*: Don Henderson. *Nurses*: Patricia Finch, Lynn Wendell. *Messengers*: Anthony Santiago, Michael Whaley, Loren Hightower. *Banker*: Richard Lyle. *Truck Driver*: Ben Gillespie.

"Taming of the Shrew" Players: *Bianca* (Lois Lane): NANCY AMES. *Baptista* (Harry Trevor): ALEXANDER CLARK. *Gremio* (First Suitor): William Wendt. *Hortensio* (Second Suitor): Stephen John Rydell. *Lucentio* (Bill Calhoun): KELLY BROWN. *Katharine* (Lilli Vanessi): PATRICIA MORISON. *Servants (3)*: *Nathaniel*: Ben Gillespie. *Gregory*: Richard Lyle. *Philip*: Anthony Santiago. *Petruchio* (Fred Graham): BOB [Robert] WRIGHT. *Haberdasher*: Loren Hightower. *Innkeeper*: Philip Rash. *Waiter*: Brown Bradley.

Dancers: Myrna Aaron, Joanna Crosson, Kiki Minor, Rande Rayburn, Joy Serio, Lucia Lambert, Esther Villavicencio, Ben Gillespie, Loren Hightower, Richard Lyle, Paul Plson, Don Redlich, Anthony Santiago, Michael Whaley. *Singers*: Patricia Finch, Margaret Goz, Madeline Kahn, Jeanne Shea, Mauren Smith, Elise Warner, Lynn Wendell, Maggie Worth, Brown Bradley, Jack L. Fletcher, Don Henderson, Bill Kennedy, Philip Rash, Stephen John Rydell, William Wendt.

1965.19 THE ROAR OF THE GREASEPAINT – THE SMELL OF THE CROWD

A Musical Entertainment in Two Acts. Book, music and lyrics by Leslie Bricusse and Anthony Newley. Directed by Anthony Newley. Musical numbers staged by Gillian Lynne. (Production) Designed and lighted by Sean Kenny. Costumes by Freddy Wittop. Musical director, Herbert Grossman. Orchestrations, Philip J. Lang. Vocal and dance music arrangements by Peter Howard. Assistant choreographer, Buff Shurr. Associate producer, Samuel Liff. Produced by David Merrick. Opened 16 May 1965 at the Sam S. Shubert Theatre and closed 4 December 1965 after 232 performances.

CAST (in order of appearance): *Cocky*: ANTHONY NEWLEY. *Sir*: CYRIL RITCHARD. *The Kid*: SALLY SMITH. *The Girl*: JOYCE JILLSON. *The Negro*: GILBERT PRICE. *The Bully*: Murray Tannenbaum.

The Urchins: Rawley Bates, Lori Browne, Lori Cesar, Jill Choder, Gloria Chu, Kay Cole, Marlene Dell, Boni Enten, Mitzi Feinn, Pamela Gruen, Linda Rae Hager, Cyndi Howard, Laura Michaels, Debbie Palmer, Heather Taylor.

The action takes place on a rocky place.

ACT 1
"The Beautiful Land"
The Urchins
"A Wonderful Day Like Today"
C. Ritchard, A. Newley, The Urchins
"It Isn't Enough"
A. Newley, The Urchins
"Things to Remember"
C. Ritchard, S. Smith, The Urchins
"Put It in the Book"
S. Smith, The Urchins
"This Dream"
A. Newley
"Where Would You Be Without Me?"
C. Ritchard, A. Newley, S. Smith
"Look At That Face"
C. Ritchard, S. Smith, The Urchins
"My First Love Song"
A. Newley, J. Jillson
"The Joker"
A. Newley
"Who Can I Turn To (When Nobody Needs Me)?"
A. Newley

ACT 2
"A Funny Funeral"
"That's What It Is To Be Young"
The Urchins
"What a Man!"
A. Newley, C. Ritchard, S. Smith, The Urchins
"Feeling Good"
G. Price, The Urchins
"Nothing Can Stop Me Now!"
A. Newley, The Urchins
"Things to Remember" (reprise)
C. Ritchard
"My Way"
A. Newley, C. Ritchard
"Who Can I Turn To? (reprise)
C. Ritchard
"The Beautiful Land" (reprise)
The Urchins
"Sweet Beginning"
A. Newley, C. Ritchard

[39]First produced in New York 30 December 1948 at the New Century Theatre for 1077 performances. For Synopsis of Scenes and Musical Numbers, see original 1948 production. For this production, former Scene 8 (The Church) was divided into 2 Scenes. "Pavane" for Dancing Ensemble added to Act 2, Scene 8 before "I Am Ashamed That Women Are So Simple."

1965–1966 SEASON

Barbara Harris in ON A CLEAR DAY YOU CAN SEE FOREVER (Photo: Friedman-Abeles)
Billy Rose Theatre Collection, New York Public Library for the Performing Arts

1965–1966 SEASON

1965.20 SOUTH PACIFIC

A Revival of the Musical Play in Two Acts, 23 Scenes[1]. Music by Richard Rodgers. Lyrics by Oscar Hammerstein II. Book by Oscar Hammerstein II and Joshua Logan. Adapted from James A. Michener's novel "Tales of the South Pacific." Directed by James Hammerstein. Dances by Albert Popwell. Scenery by Jo Mielziner. Costumes by Stanley Simmons. Lighting by Peggy Clark. Musical director, Anton Coppola. Orchestrations by Robert Russell Bennett. Produced by the New York City Center Light Opera Company (Jean Dalrymple, Director). Opened 2 June 1965 at the New York City Center and closed 13 June 1965 after 15 performances.

CAST (in order of appearance): *Ngana*: Dana Shimizu. *Jerome*: Keenan Shimizu. *Henry*: Sab Shimono. *Ensign Nellie Forbush*: BETSY PALMER. *Emile DeBecque*: RAY MIDDLETON. *Bloody Mary*: HONEY SAUNDERS. *Bloody Mary's Assistant*: Maureen Tionco. *Abner*: Victor Duntiere. *Stewpot*: TOM PEDI. *Luther Billis*: ALAN NORTH. *Professor*: Mickey [Michael] Karm. *Lt. Joseph Cable, U.S.M.C.*: RICHARD ARMBRUSTER. *Capt. George Brackett, U.S.N.*: MURVYN VYE. *Cmdr. William Harbison, U.S.N.*: SAM KIRKHAM. *Yeoman Herbert Quayle*: Walter P. Brown. *Marine Sgt. Kenneth Johnson*: William Wendt. *Seaman Richard West*: Ken Ayers. *Seabee Morton Wise*: Scott Blanchard. *Seaman Tom O'Brien*: Mel Gordan. *Radio Operator Bob McCaffrey*: Gregg Nickerson. *Staff Sgt. Thomas Hassinger*: Philip Lucas. *Lt. Genevieve Marshall*: Carol Joplin. *Ensign Dinah Murphy*: Terri Baker. *Ensign Janet MacGregor*: Nancy McGeorge. *Ensign Cora MacRae*: Renee Gorsey. *Ensign Bessie Noonan*: Patricia O'Riordan. *Ensign Connie Walewska*: Marlene Kay. *Ensign Pamela Whitmore*: Dorothy Hanning. *Ensign Sue Yaeger*: Jody Lane. *Ensign Teya Ryan*: Mary E. Small. *Ensign Lisa Minelli*: Maria Hero. *Marine Cpl. Hamilton Steeves*: Michael Quinn. *Seaman John Clark*: Don Yule. *Liat*: ELEANOR CALBES. *Lt. Buzz Adams*: Stan Page. *Shore Patrol Officer*: Joe Bellomo.

1965.21 THE MUSIC MAN

A Revival of the Musical Comedy in Two Acts, 16 Scenes[2]. Book, music and lyrics by Meredith Willson. Story by Meredith Willson and Franklin Lacey. Production directed by Gus Schirmer. Choreography by Vernon Lusby based on the original by Onna White. Settings and lighting by Howard Bay. Costumes by Raoul Pene du Bois. Orchestrations by Don Walker. Dance arrangements by Laurence Rosenthal. Musical direction by Liza Redfield. Vocal arrangements by Herbert Greene. Produced by the New York City Center Light Opera Company (Jean Dalrymple, Director). Opened 16 June 1965 at the New York City Center and closed 27 June 1965 after 15 performances.

CAST (in order of appearance): *Travelling Salesmen*: Russell Goodwin, John Herbert, Jack Davison, Ronald B. Stratton, Howard Kahl, Joseph Carow, Ronn Forella. *Charlie Cowell*: ALAN DEXTER. *Conductor*: Van Stevens. *Harold Hill*: BERT PARKS. *Mayor Shinn*: MILO BOULTON. THE BUFFALO BILLS (4): *Ewart Dunlop*: Al Shea. *Oliver Hix*: Wayne Ward. *Jacey Squires*: Vern Reed. *Olin Britt*: Dale Jones. *Marcellus Washburn*: ART WALLACE. *Tommy Djilas*: WILLIAM GLASSMAN. *Marian Paroo*: GAYLEA BYRNE. *Mrs. Paroo*: SIBYL BOWAN. *Amaryllis*: Garda Hermany. *Winthrop Paroo*: DENNIS SCOTT. *Eulalie Mackecknie Shinn*: DORO MERANDE. *Zaneeta Shinn*: SANDY DUNCAN. *Gracie Shinn*: Roma Hermany. *Alma Hix*: Adnia Rice. *Maud Dunlop*: Jeanne Schlegel. *Ethel Toffelmier*: Amelia Varney. *Mrs. Squires*: Paula Trueman. *Constable Locke*: Van Stevens.

River City Townspeople and Kids: Robin Adair, Rita Agnese, Barbara Beck, Carol B. Bostick, Bonnie Gene Card, Joanne Crosson, Suzanne Crumpler, Joan Lindsay, Sandra Ray, Alice Mary Riley, Joy Serio, Betty Chretien, Peggy Cooper, Laurie Franks, Jodell Ann Kenting, Ora McBride, Addi Negri, Jeannette Seibert, Peggy Wathen, Lynn Wendell, Joseph Carow, Ronn Forella, Carlos Macri, David Moffat, Eric Paynter, Michael Scotlin, Ronald B. Stratton, George Tregre, Gary Wales, Arthur Whitfield, Austin Colyer, Jack Davison, Russell Goodwin, John Herbert, Howard Kahl, Ben Laney, Ripple Lewis, Dan Resin, Van Stevens.

[1]First produced in New York 7 April 1949 at the Majestic Theatre for 1925 performances. For Synopsis of Scenes and Musical Numbers, see original 1949 production.

[2]Originally produced in New York 19 December 1957 at the Majestic Theatre for 1375 performances. For Synopsis of Scenes and Musical Numbers, see original 1957 production.

1965.22 KISMET

A Revival of the Musical Arabian Night (Musical Play) in Two Acts, 14 Scenes, a Prologue and an Epilogue[3]. Book by Charles Lederer and Luther Davis. Based on the play of the same name by Edward Knoblock. Music based on themes by Alexander Borodin. Musical adaptation and lyrics by Robert Wright and George Forrest. Production (settings) designed by Lemuel Ayers. Costumes by Frank Thompson. Lighting by Peter Hunt. Orchestral and choral arrangements by Arthur Kay. Musical direction by Franz Allers. Choreography and musical staging by Jack Cole. Production directed by Edward Greenberg. Produced by the Music Theatre of Lincoln Center (Richard Rodgers, Producing Director). Opened 22 June 1965 at the New York State Theatre and closed 31 July 1965 after 39 performances.

CAST (in order of appearance): *Imam of The Mosque*: Rudy Vejar. *Muezzins*: Grant Spradling, Paul Veglia, Vincent Henry, Martin Jewell. *Mullah*: Julius Fields. *First Beggar*: Earle MacVeigh. *Second Beggar*: Robert Lamont. *Third Beggar*: Andre St. Jean. *Dervishes*: Buddy Bryan, Eddie James. *Omar*: DON BEDDOE. *A Public Poet*, later called *Hajj*: ALFRED DRAKE. *Marsinah*, His Daughter: LEE VENORA. *A Merchant*: Neil McNelis. *Hassan-Ben*: Frank Coleman. *Jawan*: TRUMAN GAIGE. *The Bangle Man*: Rudy Vejar. *Street Dancer*: Sally Neal. *Akbar*: Buddy Bryan. *Assiz*: Eddie James. *Chief Policeman*: Alfred Toigo. *Second Policeman*: Allen Peck. *The Wazir of Police*: HENRY CALVIN. *Wazir's Guards*: Nick Littlefield, Jerry Meyers. *Lalume*: ANNE JEFFREYS. *Attendants*: Henry Baker, James Wamen. *Princesses of Ababu*: Reiko Sato, Diana Banks, Nancy Roth. *The Caliph*: RICHARD BANKE. *Slave Girls*: Michele Evans, Carol Hallock, Eleanore Kingsley, Ingeborg Kjeldsen. *Servant*: Paul Veglia. *Princess Zubbediya of Damascus*: Sally Neal. *Ayah to Zubbediya*: Anita Alpert. *Princess Samaris of Bangalore*: BEATRICE KRAFT. *Prosecutor*: Earle MacVeigh. *Widow Yussef*: Anita Alpert.

Singers: Bonnie Glasgow, Bobbi Lange, Joyce McDonald, Lucille Perret, Susan Sanders, Wanda Saxon, Bonnie Ellen Spark, Henry Baker, Frank Coleman, Vincent Henry, Martin Jewell, Richard Khan, Nick Littlefield, Neil McNelis, Bob Neukum, Allen Peck, Grant Spradling, Paul Veglia. *Dancers*: Joanne DiVito, Marti Hespen, Shai Holsaert, Indra-nila, Bette Scott, Susan Sigrist, Jenny Workman, Julius Fields, Andre St. Jean.

1965.23 OLIVER!

A Return Engagement of the Musical in Two Acts, 12 Scenes[4]. Book, music and lyrics by Lionel Bart. Based on the novel "Oliver Twist" by Charles Dickens. Directed by Peter Coe. (Scenery) Designed by Sean Kenny. Costumes by M. Berman Ltd. Lighting by John Wyckham. Orchestrations by Eric Rogers. Musical director, Robert McNamee. Technical supervisor, Ian Albery. Produced by David Merrick and Donald Albery. Opened 2 August 1965 at the Martin Beck Theatre and closed 25 September 1965 after 64 performances. Total, including original run: 838 performances.

CAST: *Oliver Twist*: VICTOR STILES. *Mr. Bumble*, the Beadle: ALAN CROFOOT. *Mrs. Corney*, the Matron: DAWNA SHOVE. *Old Sally*, a pauper: SHERILL PRICE. *Mr. Sowerberry*, the Undertaker: JOHN MIRANDA. *Mrs. Sowerberry*, his wife: SHERILL PRICE. *Charlotte*, their daughter: Lynda Sturner. *Noah Claypole*, their apprentice: Billy Brandon. *Fagin*: ROBIN RAMSAY. *The Artful Dodger*: JOEY BAIO. *Nancy*: MAURA K. WEDGE. *Bet*: Donnie Smiley. *Bill Sykes*: DANNY SEWELL. *Mr. Brownlow*: BRAM NOSSEN. *Dr. Grimwig*: FRED MILLER. *Mrs. Bedwin*: Dodi Protero.

Workhouse Boys and Fagin's Gang: Tommy Battreall, Ronnie K. Douglas, Paul Dwyer, Anthony Endon, Eugene Endon, Harry Gold, Lee Koenig, Bart Larsen, Chritopher Month, Jackie Perkuhn, Sonny Rocco, Ricky Rosenthal, Brett Smiley. *Londoners*: Walter Blocher, Ted Bloecher, Reese Burns, Dominic Chianese, Sally Cooke, Marise Counsell, Georgia Dell, Walter Hook, Lesley Hunt, Michael McCormick, Richard Miller, Moose Peting, Terry Robinson, Virginia Sandifur, Gretchen Van Aken, Richard Wulf.

1965.24 CAROUSEL

A Revival of the Musical Play in Two Acts, 9 Scenes[5]. Based on Ferenc Molnar's play "Liliom" as adapted by Benjamin F. Glazer. Music by Richard Rodgers. Book and lyrics by Oscar Hammerstein II. Directed by Edward

[3]Originally produced in New York 3 December 1953 at the Ziegfeld Theatre for 583 performances. For Synopsis of Scenes and Musical Numbers, see original 1953 production.

[4]Originally produced in New York 6 January 1963 at the Imperial Theatre for 774 performances. For Synopsis of Scenes and Musical Numbers, see original 1963 production.

[5]First produced in New York 19 April 1945 at the Majestic Theatre for 890 performances. For Synopsis of Scenes and Musical Numbers, see original 1945 production.

Greenberg. Choreography by Agnes de Mille, restaged by Gemze deLappe. Settings by Paul C. McGuire. Costumes by Stanley Simmons. Lighting by Peter Hunt. Musical director, Franz Allers. Orchestrations by Don Walker. Produced by the Music Theatre of Lincoln Center (Richard Rodgers, Producing Director). Opened 10 August 1965 at the New York State Theater and closed 18 September 1965 after 47 performances.

CAST (in order of appearance): *Carrie Pipperidge*: SUSAN WATSON. *Julie Jordan*: EILEEN CHRISTY. *Mrs. Mullin*: BENAY VENUTA. *Billy Bigelow*: JOHN RAITT. *Policeman*: Thomas Barry. *Mr. Bascombe*: Ralston Hill. *Nettie Fowler*: KATHERINE HILGENBERG. *Enoch Snow*: REID SHELTON. *Jigger Craigin*: JERRY ORBACH. *Hannah*: Jenny Workman. *Boatswain*: Birl Jonns. *Arminy*: Dixie Carter. *Captain*: John Dorrin. *Heavenly Friend* (Brother Joshua): Gwyllum Evans. *Starkeeper*: EDWARD EVERETT HORTON. *Louise*: Linda Howe. *Carnival Boy*: Birl Jonns. *Enoch Snow, Jr.*: Alan Johnson. *Principal*: John Dorrin.

Singers: Lynn Carroll, Ronn Carroll, Dixie Carter, Cathy Corkill, Gene Davis, Audrey Dearden, John Dorrin, Dorothy Emmerson, Cleo Fry, Ben Laney, Terry Marone, Laried Montgomery, Bob Neukum, Lucille Perret, Joseph Pichette, Philip Rash, Sean Walsh, Peggy Wathen. *Dancers*: Bonnie Gene Card, Dennis Cole, Richard Cousins, Victor Duntiere, Lois Etelman, Frank Hoopman, Anita Jones, Linda Keeler, Lucia Lambert, Arnott Mader, Richard Oliver, Carol Perea, J. Hunter Ross, Terry Ryland, Eva Marie Sage, Melissa Stoneburn, Kathy Wilson, Toodie Wittmer.

1965.25 DIE FLEDERMAUS

A Revival of the Operetta in Three Acts[6]. Original Viennese libretto by Carl Haffner and Richard Genée. Lyrics by Richard Genée. (Based on the comedy "Le Réveillon" by Henri Meilhac and Ludovic Halévy.) English libretto by Ruth and Thomas Martin. Music by Johann Strauss. Scenic design by William Pitkin. Costume design by Henry Heymann. Conducted by Julius Rudel. Produced by the New York City Opera. Opened 25 September 1965 at the New York City Center and closed 7 November 1965 after 4 performances in repertory.

CAST: *Eisenstein*: JOHN STAMFORD. *Rosalinda*: BEVERLY SILLS. *Frank*: RICHARD WENTWORTH. *Prince Orlofsky*: DAVID SMITH. *Alfred*: Jon Crain. *Falke*: WILLIAM LEDBETTER. *Blind*: Kellis Miller. *Adele*: ANNE ELGAR. *Frosch*: Coley Worth. *Sally*: Beverly Evans. *Ivan*: Don Yule. *Solo Dancers*: Nora Kovach, Istvan Rabovsky, Joan Peterson, Betty Ann Terrell. *Ensemble*: New York City Opera Chorus.

1965.26 THE SAINT OF BLEECKER STREET

A Revival of the Opera (Musical Drama) in Three Acts, 5 Scenes[7]. Music and libretto by Gian-Carlo Menotti. Staged by Francis Rizzo. Production designed by Robert Randolph. Produced by the New York City Opera. Opened 29 September 1965 at the New York City Center and closed 9 October 1965 after 2 performances in repertory.

CAST (in order of appearance): *Assunta*: Muriel Greenspon. *Carmela*: Mary Jennings. *Maria Corona*: Anita Darian. *Her Son*: Clyde Ventura. *Don Marco*: Malcolm Smith. *Annina*: JULIA MIGENES. *Michele*: HARRY THEYARD. *Desideria*: BEVERLY WOLFF. *Salvatore*: William Beck. *Concettina*: Wendy Morris. *A Young Man*: Anthony Safina. *A Young Woman*: Jodell Kenting. *Bartender*: Don Henderson. *First Guest*: Richard Krause. *Second Guest*: Wiliiam Ledbetter. *Neighbors, Friends, Policemen, etc.*: New York City Opera Chorus.

1965.27 THE MERRY WIDOW

A Revival of the Operetta in Three Acts[8]. Music by Franz Lehár. Original Viennese libretto ('Die lustige witwe') by Victor Léon and Leo Stein. (Based on the comedy "L'Attaché d'Ambassade" by Henri Meilhac.) English libretto by Adrian Ross. Staged by Jack Harrold. Scenic design by George Jenkins. Lighting by Jules Fisher. Choreographed by Thomas Andrew. Conducted by Charles Wilson. Produced by the New York City Opera. Opened 2 October 1965 at the New York City Center and closed 14 November 1965 after 4 performances in repertory.

CAST: *Sonia*: EILEEN SCHAULER. *Prince Danilo*: DAVID SMITH. *Nish*: Coley Worth. *Baron Popoff*: JACK HARROLD. *Natalie*: Anne Elgar. *De Jolidon*: JOHN CRAIG. *Marquis de Cascada*: William Beck. *St. Brioche*: Richard Krause. *Admiral Khadja*: William Ledbetter. *Mme. Khadja*: Beverly Evans. *General Novikovich*: Jack Bittner. *Mme. Novikovich*: Charlotte Povia. *Clo-Clo*: Helen Guile. *Solo Dancers*: Nora Kovach, Istvan Rabovsky. *Ensemble*: New York City Opera Chorus.

[6]First English language production in New York 16 March 1885 at the Casino Theatre for 42 performances. First New York production of this adaptation 20 December 1950 at the Metropolitan Opera House. For Synopsis of Scenes and Musical Numbers, see May 1954 revival.

[7]Originally produced in New York 27 December 1954 at the Broadway Theatre for 92 performances. For Synopsis of Scenes, see original 1954 production.

[8]Originally produced in New York 21 October 1907 at the New Amsterdam Theatre for 416 performances. For Synopsis of Scenes and Musical Numbers, see original 1907 production.

1965.28 PICKWICK

A Musical ('Designed for the Introduction of Diverting Characters and Incidents Attempting No Ingenuity of Plot'[9]) in Two Acts, 12 Scenes. Book by Wolf Mankowitz. Based on the novel "The Pickwick Papers" by Charles Dickens. Music by Cyril Ornadel. Lyrics by Leslie Bricusse. Directed by Peter Coe. Settings by Sean Kenny. Costumes by Roger Furse and Peter Rice. Lighting by Jules Fisher. Choreography by Gillian Lynne. Musical direction and vocal arrangements by Ian Fraser. Orchestrations by Eric Rogers. Produced by David Merrick in association with Bernard Delfont. Opened 4 October 1965 at the 46th Street Theatre and closed 20 November 1965 after 56 performances.

CAST (in order of appearance): *Hot Toddy Seller*: Jim Connor. *Cold Drinks Seller*: Edmond Varrato. *Bird Seller*: Roger LePage. *Hot Potato Man*: Gerrit de Beer. *Turnkey*: Allan Lokos. *Roker*: Peter Costanza. *Pickwick*: HARRY SECOMBE. *Augustus Snodgrass*: JULIAN ORCHARD. *Tracy Tupman*: John Call. *Nathaniel Winkle*: OSCAR QUITAK. *Sam Weller*: ROY CASTLE. *Mr. Wardle*: MICHAEL LOGAN. *Rachel*: HELENA CARROLL. *Isabella*: Nancy Haywood. *Emily*: Sybil Scotford. *Fat Boy*: Joe Richards. *Mrs. Bardell*: CHARLOTTE RAE. *Bardell, Jr.*: Brian Chapin. *Mary*: Nancy Barrett. *Mr. Jingle*: ANTON RODGERS. *Major Domo*: Jim Connor. *Dr. Slammer*: Peter Costanza. *First Officer*: Richard Neilson. *Second Officer*: Haydon Smith. *Landlord*: Edmond Varrato. *Mrs. Leo Hunter*: Elizabeth Parrish. *Mr. Leo Hunter*: Gerrit de Beer. *Dodson*: MICHAEL DARBYSHIRE. *Fogg*: Tony Sympson. *Wicks*: Haydon Smith. *Jackson*: Keith Perry. *Usher*: Taylor Reed. *Bailiff*: Stanley Simmonds. *Sergeant Buzfuz*: PETER BULL. *Judge*: Richard Neilson. *Sergeant Snubbins*: Allan Lokos. *Jury Foreman*: Roger LePage.

Passersby, Ostlers, Debtors, Maids, Drinkers and Pot Boys: Jill Alexander, Michael Amber, Bill Black, William Coppola, Ann Davies, Selma Marcus, Ann Tell, Bill Nuss, Edmond Varrato, Larry Whiteley, Gerrit de Beer, Clyde Laurents, Keith Perry, Taylor Reed, Bruce Becker, Susan Cartt, Jo Freilich, Mary Keller, Don Lawrence, Ginia Mason, Lani Michaels, Ross Miles, Nancy Stevens, Don Strong, Haydon Smith, Roger LePage. *Children*: Michael Easton, Richard Easton, Tracy Evans, Leslie Ann Mapes, Bonnie Turner.

The action takes place in and around London and Rochester in 1827.

Act 1, Scene 1: The Pickwickians. *Scene 2*: Introduces Mr. Pickwick to a new and not uninteresting scene in the great drama of life. *Scene 3*: The first day's adventures. *Scene 4*: Strongly illustrative of the position, that the course of true love is not a railway. *Scene 5*: Descriptive of a very important proceeding on the part of Mr. Pickwick; no less an epoch in his life, then in his history. *Scene 6*: Too full of adventure to be briefly described.

Act 2, Scene 1: Some account of Eatanswill; the state of parties therein; and of the election of a member to serve in Parliament for that ancient, loyal and patriotic borough. *Scene 2*: How the Pickwickians, when Mr. Pickwick stepped out of the frying pan, walked gently and comfortably into the fire. *Scene 3*: Showing how Dodson and Fogg were men of Business; and how an affecting interview took place between Mr. Weller and his employer. *Scene 4*: Is wholly devoted to a full and faithful report of the memorable trial of Bardell against Pickwick. *Scene 5*: What befell Mr. Pickwick when he got into the Fleet; what prisoners he saw there; and how he passed the night. *Scene 6*: In which the Pickwick Club is finally dissolved and everything concluded to the satisfaction of everybody.

ACT 1

"I Like the Company of Men"
H. Secombe, J. Orchard, J. Call, O. Quitak

"That's What I'd Like for Christmas"
H. Secombe, Company

"The Pickwickians"
H. Secombe, J. Orchard, J. Call, O. Quitak

"A Bit of a Character"
A. Rodgers, J. Orchard, O. Quitak, J. Call

"There's Something About You"
A. Rodgers, H. Carroll, Company

[9]Charles Dickens' preface to "Pickwick Papers."

"A Gentleman's Gentleman"
R. Castle, N. Barrett
"You Never Met a Feller Like Me"
H. Secombe, R. Castle
"I'll Never Be Lonely Again"
H. Secombe, C. Rae

ACT 2
"Fizkin and Pickwick"
The Company
"Very"
A. Rodgers, H. Secombe, M. Logan
"If I Ruled the World"
H. Secombe, Company
"I'll Never be Lonely Again" (reprise)
The Pickwickians
"Talk"
R. Castle, Company
"That's the Law"
H. Secombe, M. Darbyshire, T. Sympson, Company
"Damages"
H. Secombe, C. Rae
Finale
H. Secombe, Company

1965.29 DRAT! THE CAT!

A Musical Spoof in Two Acts, 16 Scenes. Book and lyrics by Ira Levin. Music by Milton Schafer. Directed and choreographed by Joe Layton. Scenery and lighting by David Hays. Costumes by Fred Voelpel. Musical direction and vocal arrangements by Herbert Grossman. Orchestrations by Hershy Kay and Clare Grundman. Dance music by Genevieve Pitot. Produced by Jerry Adler and Norman Rosemont. Opened 10 October 1965 at the Martin Beck Theatre and closed 16 October 1965 after 8 performances.

CAST (in order of appearance): *The Mayor*: Alfred Spindelman. *Pincer*, Superintendent of Police: CHARLES DURNING. *Mallet*, Chief of Detectives : GENE VARRONE. *Roger "Bulldog" Purefoy*, Former Chief of Detectives: David Gold. *Kate Purefoy*, his wife: LU LEONARD. *Emma*, a Patrolwoman: Sandy Ellen. *Bob Purefoy*, the Purefoy's Son, a Patrolman: ELLIOTT GOULD. *The Van Guilder's Butler*: Harry Naughton. *Matilda Van Guilder*, a Socialite: JANE CONNELL. *Lucius Van Guilder*, Her Husband, a Millionaire: JACK FLETCHER. *Alice Van Guilder*, their Daughter: LESLEY ANN WARREN. *The Maid*: Jacque Dean. *The Minister*: Al Lanti. *The Mayor's Wife*: Marian Haraldson. *Julietta Onderdonck*, a Dowager from Boston: Mariana Doro. *The Judge*: David Gold. *The Prosecutor*: Leo Bloom.

Patrolmen: Leo Bloom, Ralph Farnworth, Ian Garry, David Gold, Barney Johnston, Al Lanti, William Lutz, George Marcy, Larry Moss, Harry Naughton, Ronald Paré, James Powers, Dan Siretta, Bill Starr. *Ensemble*: Jeri Barto, Nancy Lynch, Carmen Morales, Mary Zahn, Lillian Bozinoff, Beth Howland, Meg Walter, Margery Gray.

The action takes place in New York City and environs. The time is spring in the latter part of the nineteenth century.

Act 1, Scene 1: Various places in New York City. *Scene 2*: A Bedroom in the Purefoy's Flat. *Scene 3*: Lucius Van Guilder's Study and Counting Room. *Scene 4*: Alice Van Guilder's Boudoir and a Secret Chamber. *Scene 5*: The Purefoy's Kitchen. *Scene 6*: Pier Fourteen. *Scene 7*: Van Guilder's Study and the Garden. *Scene 8*: The Van Guilders' Cellar.

Act 2, Scene 1: Police Headquarters. *Scene 2*: The Cellar. *Scene 3*: Van Guilder's Study. *Scene 4*: The Woods North of the City. *Scene 5*: Various Places in the City. *Scene 6*: The Woods and the City. *Scene 7*: Van Guilder's Study. *Scene 8*: A Courtroom.

ACT 1
Scene 1
"Drat! The Cat!
Citizens, Patrolmen, A. Spindelman, C. Durning, G. Varrone
Scene 2
"My Son, Uphold the Law"
D. Gold, Patrolmen
Scene 3
"Holmes and Watson"
L. A. Warren, E. Gould
"She Touched Me"
E. Gould
Scene 4
"Wild and Reckless"
L. A. Warrne
Scene 5
"She's Roses"
E. Gould, L. Leonard
Scene 6
"Ignoble Theft of the Idol's Eyes" (ballet)
L. A. Warren, Patrolmen, Attendants of the Idol
Property Men: J. Barto, W. Lutz, L. Moss. *Warriors*: I. Garry, G. Marcy, H. Naughton, R. Paré. *Geishas*: N. Lynch, C. Morales, M. Zahn. *Lion*: B. Starr. *High Priest*: D. Gold. *Cantor*: G. Varrone.
Scene 7
"Dancing With Alice"
E. Gould, L. A. Warren, J. Fletcher, J. Connell, Guests
"Drat! The Cat!" (reprise)
J. Fletcher, J. Connell, Guests
Scene 8
"Purefoy's Lament"
E. Gould

ACT 2
Scene 1
"A Pox Upon the Traitor's Brow"
C. Durning, G. Varrone, S. Ellen, Patrolmen
Scene 2
"Deep in Your Heart"
E. Gould
Scene 3
"Let's Go"
L. A. Warren, E. Gould
"It's Your Fault"
J. Fletcher, J. Connell
Scene 4
"Wild and Reckless" (reprise)
E. Gould
Scene 5
"The Upside-Down Thief" (ballet)
E. Gould, Citizens, Patrolmen, L. Leonard
Tenors: R. Farnworth, G. Varrone. *Concert-Goers*: L. Bozinoff, D. Gold, M. Haraldson, J. Powers, M. Walter. *Soprano*: M. Doro. *Mayor's Companion*: M. Gray. *Patrolmen*: I. Garry, A. Lanti, R. Paré, D. Siretta, B. Starr.
Scene 6
"Today Is a Day for a Band to Play"
C. Durning, G. Varrone, S. Ellen, Patrolmen, Citizens
"She Touched Me" (reprise)
E. Gould, L. A. Warren
Scene 7
"I Like Him"
L. A. Warren
Scene 8
"Justice Triumphant"
Entire Company
"Today Is a Day for a Band to Play" (reprise)
Entire Company

1965.30 THE WORLD OF CHARLES AZNAVOUR

Songs of Love and Other Sorrows (A One-Man Show) in Two Acts. All music by Charles Aznavour. Scenery and lighting by Ralph Alswang. Musical director, Henry Byrs. Produced by Norman Twain and Sid Bernstein in association with Henri Goldgram. Opened 14 October 1965 at the Ambassador Theatre and closed 6 November 1965 after 28 performances.

CAST: CHARLES AZNAVOUR.

ACT 1
"Le temps" (There Is a Time)
(*Lyrics by* Davis.)

"Avec"
"For Me Formidable"
(*Lyrics by* Jacques Plante and Gene Lees.)
"Je Te Rechaufferais"
"Who (Will Take My Place?)" (Qui?)
(*Lyrics by* Herbert Kretzmer.)
"J'ai perdu la tête"
(*Lyrics by* Charles Aznavour.)
"Never Again" (A tout jamais)
(*Lyrics by* Falcone.)
"Parceque"
"Isabelle"
(*Lyrics by* Charles Aznavour.)
"The Boss Is Dead"
"Reste" (Stay)
(*Lyrics by* Bachelor.)
"Two Guitars"
"Que c'est triste Venice"(Venice Blue)
(*Lyrics by* F. Dorin.)
"You've Let Yourself Go"(Tu te laisses aller)
(*Lyrics by* Marcel Stellman.)

ACT 2
"I Dig You That Way" (Je T'Aime Comme Ca)
(*Lyrics by* Davis and Falcone.)
"C'est fini"
"The Time Is Now"
"Quant tu viens chez moi"
"L'amour c'est comme un jour"
"I'm Wrong"
"Et pourtant"
(*Lyrics by* Georges Garvarentz.)
"Les comediens"
(*Lyrics by* Jacques Plante.)
"Love At Last You Have Found Me" (J'en deduis que je t'aime)
(*Lyrics by* Worth.)
"Paris Is at Her Best in May" (J'aime Paris au mois de Mai)
(*Lyrics by* Gene Lees and Roche.)
"La Boheme"
"You've Got to Learn" (Il faut savoir)
(*Lyrics by* Marcel Stellman.)
"La Mamma" (For Mama)
(*Lyrics by* Robert Gall.)

1965.31 ON A CLEAR DAY YOU CAN SEE FOREVER

A Musical in Two Acts, 11 Scenes. Book and lyrics by Alan Jay Lerner. Music by Burton Lane. Directed by Robert Lewis. Dances and musical numbers staged by Herbert Ross. Scenery designed by Oliver Smith. Costumes by Freddy Wittop. Lighting by Feder. Orchestrations by Robert Russell Bennett. Music continuity and vocal (arrangements) by Trude Rittman. Dance music by Betty Walberg. Musical direction by Theodore Saidenberg. Miss Harris' modern clothes by Donald Brooks. Production supervisor, Stone Widney. Produced by Alan Jay Lerner in association with Rogo Productions. Opened 17 October 1965 at the Mark Hellinger Theatre and closed 11 June 1966 after 280 performances.

CAST (in order of appearance): *Dr. Mark Bruckner*: JOHN CULLUM. *Mrs. Hatch*: Rae Allen. *Student*: Gerald Teijelo. *Daisy Gamble*: BARBARA HARRIS. *Muriel Bunson*: Barbara Monte. *James Preston*: William Reilly. *Samuel Welles*: Gordon Dilworth. *Mrs. Welles*: Blanche Collins. *Sir Hubert Insdale*: Byron Webster. *Dolly Wainwhistle*: Hanne Marie Reiner. *Blackamoor*: Bernard Johnson. *Bob Brody*: Dan Resin. *Jimmy Dern*: Ken Richards. *Millard Cross*: Gerald M. Teijolo, Jr. *Warren Smith*: WILLIAM DANIELS. *Prudence Cumming*: Barbara Remington. *Edward Moncrief*: CLIFFORD DAVID. *Flora*: Carol Flemming. *Dr. Paul Bruckner*: Gerry Matthews. *Dr. Conrad Bruckner*: Michael Lewis. *Evans Bolagard*: Hamilton Camp. *Themistocles Kriakos*: TITOS VANDIS. *T.A.A. Official*: David Thomas. *Melinda*: BARBARA HARRIS.

Singing Ensemble: Rudy Challenger, Paul Eichel, Eddie Erickson, Stokely Gray, Bennett Hill, Art Matthews, Dan Resin, Ken Richards, Rita Golden, Joy Holly, Zona Kennedy, Pat Lysinger, Caroline Parks, Nancy Reeves, Jeannette Seibert, Dixie Stewart. *Dancing Ensemble*: Sterling Clarke, Luigi Gasparinetti, Bernard Johnson, Louis Kosman, Kazimir Kokich, Marco Pogacar, Ronald B. Stratton, Gerald Teijolo, William Reilly, Rita Agnese, Carol Flemming, Marion Fels, Leslie Franzos, Bettye Jenkins, Charlene Mehl, Barbara Monte, Hanne Marie Reiner, Barbara Remington.

The action takes place in New York City at the present time.

Act 1, Scene 1: A Lecture Room at the Bruckner Clinic. Afternoon, late spring. *Scene 2*: The Solarium of the Bruckner Clinic, several days later. *Scene 3*: Dr. Mark Bruckner's Office, immediately following. *Scene 4*: The Rooftop of Daisy's Apartment. Later that night. *Scene 5*: Dr. Mark Bruckner's Office. The following afternoon. *Scene 6*: Dr. Mark Bruckner's Office. Early evening, a week later.

Act 2, Scene 1: The Solarium of the Bruckner Clinic. A week later. *Scene 2*: Dr. Mark Bruckner's Office. Immediately following. *Scene 3*: The Rooftop of Daisy's Apartment. Late that night. *Scene 4*: Dr. Mark Bruckner's Office. Afternoon, one week later. *Scene 5*: The Municipal Airport. Later that day.

ACT 1[10]
Scene 3
"Hurry! It's Lovely Up Here"
B. Harris
"Ring Out the Bells"[11]
Servants (Ensemble)
"I'll Not Marry"[12]
B. Harris
"On a Clear Day You Can See Forever"
J. Cullum
Scene 4
"On the S.S. *Bernard Cohn*"
B. Harris, B. Monte, W. Reilly, G. M. Teijolo, Jr.
Scene 5
"At the Hellrakers'"[13] (dance)
Dance Ensemble
"Don't Tamper With My Sister"
C. David, Ensemble
"She Wasn't You"
C. David
Scene 6
"Melinda"
J. Cullum

ACT 2
Scene 1
"When I'm Being Born Again"[14]
T. Vandis

---

[10]Added for the 1966 tour was the following:
"Marriage a la Mode"
Solicitor (Fred Bennett), Sir Hubert (Don Wofford), Mr. Welles (Sean Walsh), Mrs. Welles (Elaine Johnson), Ensemble
Added for 1967 tour were the following: "Marriage a La Mode" dropped.
"First Regression"
Melinda (Linda Lavin), Edward (Lester James)
"Solicitor's Song"
Solicitor (George Comtois),Sir Hubert (William J. Coppola), Hubert Insdale (Joseph Pichette), Samuel Welles (Leon Benedict)
"The Spasm"
Muriel (Jodi Perselle), Company
Added for 1968 tour: "First Regression" and "The Spasm" dropped.
"The Gout"
Daisy (Tammy Grimes), Muriel (Sandra Nitz), Chorus
"Trelawney No. 1"
Chorus

[11]Dropped for subsequent 1966 tour.

[12]Replaced immediately after opening with:
"Tosy and Cosh"
B. Harris
Also, the three opening scenes were condensed into one.

[13]Dropped for subsequent 1966 tour.

[14]Retitled for subsequent tours:
"When I Come Around Again"
James Preston (Walter Willison), Students

Scene 2
"What Did I Have That I Don't Have"
B. Harris
Scene 3
"Wait 'Til We're Sixty-Five"
W. Daniels, Rooftoppers (Ensemble)
Scene 4
"Come Back to Me"
J. Cullum
Scene 5
"Come Back to Me" (reprise)
Ensemble
"On a Clear Day You Can See Forever" (reprise)
J. Cullum, (Ensemble)

1965.32 THE ZULU AND THE ZAYDA

A Comedy With Music in Two Acts, 18 Scenes. Play by Howard Da Silva and Feliz Leon. Music and lyrics by Harold Rome. Based on the (short) story "The Zulu and the Zeide" by Dan Jacobson. Directed by Dore Schary. Settings and lighting by William and Jean Eckart. Costumes by Frank Thompson. Musical supervision and orchestrations by Meyer Kupferman. Conductor, Michael Spivakowsky. Language coach, Barbara Masekela. Produced by Theodore Mann and Dore Schary. Opened 10 November 1965 at the Cort Theatre and closed 16 April 1966 after 179 performances.

CAST (in order of appearance): *Johannes*: OSSIE DAVIS. *Koofer*: James Higgins. *Harry Grossman*: Joe Silver. *Helen Grossman*: Sarah Cunningham. *Arthur Grossman*: Philip Vandervort. *David Grossman*: John Pleshette. *Eric*: John Randolph Jones. *Zayda*: MENASHA SKULNICK. *Tommy Layton*: Norman Barrs. *Paulus*: LOUIS [Lou] GOSSETT. *Woman with Baby Carriage*: Sandra Kent. *Policeman*: David Mogck. *Peter*: Peter DeAnda. *John*: Yaphet Kotto. *Joan*: Christine Spencer. *William*: Ed Hall. *Mr. Lamene*: Charles Moore. *Mrs. Lamene*: Ella Thompson. *Groenwald*: Robert Hewitt. *Dyckboom*: Max Jacobs. *Mourner*: Sholom Ludvinsky. *Nurse*: Sandra Kent.

The action takes place in Johannesburg, Republic of South Africa, at the present time.

Act 1, Scene 1: Botanical Gardens. *Scene 2*: Grossman Terrace. *Scene 3*: L&G Hardware Store. *Scene 4*: Grossman Dining Room. *Scene 5*: Grossman Garden. *Scene 6*: Botanical Gardens. *Scene 7*: Grossman Terrace. *Scene 8*: Grossman Dining Room. *Scene 9*: Grossman Garden. *Scene 10*: A Hill. *Scene 11*: Green Meadows.

Act 2, Scene 1: A Jail. *Scene 2*: The Cemetary. *Scene 3*: Grossman Terrace. *Scene 4*: Grossman Dining Room. *Scene 5*: Hospital Corridor. *Scene 6*: Alley. *Scene 7*: Hospital Garden.

ACT 1
Scene 1
"Tkambuza"
O. Davis
Scene 5
"Crocodile Wife"
O. Davis
Scene 8
"It's Good To Be Alive" (Lebe Is Gut)
M. Skulnick, L. Gossett
Scene 9
"The Water Wears Down the Stone"
O. Davis
Scene 10
"Rivers of Tears"
M. Skulnick
Scene 11
"Like the Breeze Blows"
P. DeAnda, C. Spencer, Ensemble
"Oisgetzaichnet" (Out of This World)
M. Skulnick, Ensemble
ACT 2
Scene 1
"Some Things"
Ensemble
Scene 2
"Zulu Love Song"
L. Gossett
Scene 4
"L'Chayim!" (May Your Heart Stay Young)
M. Skulnick
Scene 5
"How Cold, Cold, Cold, an Empty Room"
O. Davis
Scene 6
Eagle Soliloquy
L. Gossett
Scene 7
"It's Good To Be Alive" (reprise)(Finale)
L. Gossett, M. Skulnick

1965.33 SKYSCRAPER

A Musical Comedy in Two Acts, 25 Scenes. Book by Peter Stone. Based on the play "Dream Girl" by Elmer Rice. Music by James Van Heusen. Lyrics by Sammy Cahn. Directed by Cy Feuer. Dances and musical numbers staged by Michael Kidd. Scenery and lighting by Robert Randolph. Costumes by Theoni V. Aldredge. Musical director, John Lesko. Dance music arranged by Marvin Laird. Associate conductor, Fred Manzella. Produced by Cy Feuer and Ernest H. Martin. Opened 13 November 1965 at the Lunt-Fontanne Theatre and closed 11 June 1966 after 248 performances.

CAST (in order of appearance): *Georgina (Allerton)*: JULIE HARRIS. *Mrs. Allerton*: NANCY CUSHMAN. *Mr. Allerton*: DONALD BURR. *Charlotte*: LESLEY STEWART. *Mayor*: Burt Bier. *Doctor*: Richard Korthaze. *Herbert Bushman*: DICK O'NEILL. *Stanley*: REX EVERHART. *Timothy Bushman*: PETER L. MARSHALL. *Roger Summerhill*: CHARLES NELSON REILLY. *Woman Customer*: Georgia Creighton. *Auctioneer*: Burt Bier. *Harry the Waiter*: John Anania. *Cab Driver*: Ken Ayers. *Jazz Musician*: Walter P. Brown. *Photographer*: Christian Gray.
In film sequence: *Paola*: Pola Chapelle. *Francesco*: Paul Sorvino.
Singers: John Anania, Ken Ayers, Burt Bier, Walter P. Brown, Christian Gray, Randy Phillips, Casper Roos, Eleanor Bergquist, Georgia Creighton, Ceil Delli, Maryann Kerrick. *Dancers*: Ray Chabeau, Gene Gavin, Curtis Hood, Gene Kelton, Ray Kirchner, Richard Korthaze, Darrell Notara, Bill Starr, Kent Thomas, Barbara Beck, Trudy Carson, Marilyn Charles, Suzanne France, Ellen Graff, Lauren Jones, Renata Powers.

The action took place yesterday in New York City in and around a large skyscraper and a very small brownstone.

Act 1, Scene 1: Georgina's Bedroom. *Scene 2*: The Construction Site. *Scene 3*: The Bushman Building; Construction Shack. *Scene 4*: The Construction Site. *Scene 5*: Skyscraper—Ground Level. *Scene 6*: The Construction Site. *Scene 7*: The Construction Shack. *Scene 8*: The Construction Site. *Scene 9*: The Litter Bug (Antique Shop). *Scene 10*: The Construction Site. *Scene 11*: The Litter Bug. *Scene 12*: The Construction Site. *Scene 13*: Two Phones. *Scene 14*: Knickerbocker Auction Galleries. *Scene 15*: Two Phones. *Scene 16*: Georgina's Bedroom at night.

Act 2, Scene 1: The Gaiety Delicatessen. *Scene 2*: Limbo. *Scene 3*: The Film Festival. *Scene 4*: The Construction Site. *Scene 5*: Atop the unfinished skyscraper. *Scene 6*: The Construction Site. *Scene 7*: The Litter Bug. *Scene 8*: The Skyscraper—A Dream. *Scene 9*: The Allerton Bedroom.

ACT 1
Scene 1
"Occasional Flight of Fancy"
J. Harris, Officials
Scene 3
"Run For Your Life"
P. L. Marshall, D. O'Neill
Scene 4
"Local 403" (Socially Conscious Iron Workers)
R. Everhart, Construction Workers, Girls
Scene 7
"Opposites"
J. Harris, P. L. Marshall
"Run For Your Life" (reprise)
P. L. Marshall

Scene 10
"Just the Crust"
C. N. Reilly, R. Everhart
Scene 11
"Everybody Has the Right to Be Wrong"
J. Harris, P. L. Marshall
"Everybody Has the Right to Be Wrong" (reprise)
J. Harris
"Wrong!"
J. Harris, N. Cushman, L. Stewart, Customers
Scene 14
"The Auction" (Ballet)
Customers
Scene 16
"Occasional Flight of Fancy" (reprise)
J. Harris

ACT 2
Scene 1
"The Gaiety"
Customers
Scene 5
"More Than One Way"
P. L. Marshall
Scene 6
"Haute Couture"
R. Everhart, Models, Workers
Scene 7
"Don't Worry"
C. N. Reilly, D. O'Neill
"Don't Worry" (reprise)
J. Harris, C. N. Reilly
"I'll Only Miss Her When I Think of Her"
P. L.Marshall
Scene 8
"Spare That Building"
J. Harris, P. L. Marshall, C. N. Reilly, Company

1965.34 MAN OF LA MANCHA

A Musical Play in One Act. Book by Dale Wasserman. [Based on his teleplay "I, Don Quixote."] Suggested by the life and work ("Don Quixote") of Miguel de Cervantes y Saavedra. Music by Mitch Leigh. Lyrics by Joe Darion. Book and musical staging by Albert Marre. Choreography by Jack Cole. Settings and lighting by Howard Bay. Costumes by Howard Bay and Patton Campbell. Musical direction and dance arrangements by Neil Warner. Musical arrangements by Music Makers Inc. An ANTA-Goodspeed Production. Produced by Albert W. Selden and Hal James. Opened 22 November 1965 at the ANTA Washington Square Theatre, moved 19 March 1968 to the Martin Beck Theatre, moved 2 March 1971 to the Eden Theatre (Off-Broadway), moved 25 May 1971 to the Mark Hellinger Theatre and closed 26 June 1971 after 2328 performances.

CAST (in order of appearance): *Don Quixote (Cervantes)*: RICHARD KILEY. *Sancho*: IRVING JACOBSON. *Captain of the Inquisition*: Renato Cibelli. *Aldonza*: JOAN DIENER. *The Innkeeper*: RAY MIDDLETON. *Dr. Carrasco*: JON CYPHER. *The Padre*: ROBERT ROUNSEVILLE. *Antonia*: Mimi Turque. *The Housekeeper*: Eleanore Knapp. *The Barber*: Gino Conforti. *Pedro*, Head Muleteer: Shev Rodgers. *Anselmo*, a Muleteer: Harry Theyard. *Jose*, a Muleteer: Eddie Roll. *Juan*, a Muleteer: John Aristides. *Paco*, a Muleteer: Anthony De Vecchi. *Tenorio*, a Muleteer: Fernando Grahal. *Maria*, the Innkeeper's Wife: Marceline Decker. *Fermina*, a Servant Girl: Gerrianne Raphael. *The Guitarist*: David Serva.

Guards, Men of the Inquisition: Ray Dash, Jonathan Fox, John Fields, Samye Van, David Matson.

The action takes place in a dungeon in Seville at the end of the sixteenth century and in the imagination of Miguel de Cervantes.

MUSICAL NUMBERS
"Man of La Mancha" (I, Don Quixote)
R. Kiley, I. Jacobson, Horses
"It's All the Same"
J. Diener, Muleteers
"Dulcinea"
R. Kiley, Muleteers
"I'm Only Thinking of Him"
R. Rounseville, M. Turque, E. Knapp, J. Cypher
"I Really Like Him"
I. Jacobson
"What Does He Want of Me?"
J. Diener
"Little Bird, (Little Bird)"
S. Rodgers, Muleteers
"Barber's Song"
G. Conforti
"Golden Helmet of Mambrino"
R. Kiley, I. Jacobson, G. Conforti, Muleteers
"To Each His Dulcinea (To Every Man His Dream)"
R. Rounseville
"The Quest" (The Impossible Dream)
R. Kiley
"The Combat"
R. Kiley, J. Diener, I. Jacobson, Muleteers
"The Dubbing" (Knight of the Woeful Countenance)
R. Middleton, J. Diener, I. Jacobson
"The Abduction"
J. Diener, Muleteers
Moorish Dance
Ensemble
"Aldonza"
J. Diener
"The Knight of the Mirrors" (dance)
R. Kiley, J. Cypher, Ensemble
"A Little Gossip"
I. Jacobson
"Dulcinea" (reprise)
J. Diener
"Man of LaMancha" (reprise)
R. Kiley, J. Diener, I. Jacobson
"The Psalm"
R. Rounseville
"The Quest" (reprise)
Company

1965.35 ANYA

A Musical in Two Acts, a Prelude and 12 Scenes. Book by George Abbott and Guy Bolton. Based on the play "Anastasia" by Marcelle Maurette and Guy Bolton. Music and lyrics by Robert Wright and George Forrest. Based on themes by Sergei Rachmaninoff. Directed by George Abbott. Choreography and musical numbers by Hanya Holm. Scenery by Robert Randolph. Costumes by Patricia Zipprodt. Lighting by Richard Casler. Musical direction by Harold Hastings. Orchestrations by Don Walker. Produced by Fred R. Fehlhaber. Opened 29 November 1965 at the Ziegfeld Theatre and closed 11 December 1965 after 16 performances.

CAST (in order of appearance): *Anya*: CONSTANCE TOWERS. *Nurse*: Patricia Hoffman. *Bounine*: MICHAEL KERMOYAN. *Josef*: BORIS APLON. *Count Drivinitz*: Lawrence Brooks. *Count Dorn*: Adair McGowan. *Sergei*: Jack Dabdoub. *Yegor*: Walter Hook. *Katrina*: IRRA PETINA. *Petrovin*: EDWIN STEFFE. *Balalika Player*: Konstantin Pio-Ulsky. *Genia, the Countess Hohenstadt*: KAREN SHEPARD. *Chernov*: GEORGE S. IRVING. *Olga*: Laurie Franks. *Masha*: Rita Metzger. *Sleigh Driver*: Lawrence Boyll. *Anouchka*: Elizabeth Howell. *Tinka*: Barbara Alexander. *Mother*: Maggie Task. *Father*: Michael Quinn. *Dowager Empress*: LILLIAN GISH. *Prince Paul*: JOHN MICHAEL KING. *Countess Drivinitz*: Elizabeth Howell. *First Policeman*: Lawrence Boyll. *Second Policeman*: Bernard Frank. *Police Sergeant*: Howard Kahl. *Baroness Livenbaum*: MARGARET MULLEN.

Dancers: Barbara Alexander, Ciya Challis, Patricia Drylie, Juliette Durand, Kip Andrews, Steven Boockvor, Randy Doney, Joseph Nelson. *Singers*: Laurie Franks, Patricia Hoffman, Rita Metzger, Mia Powers, Lourette Raymon, Diane Tartleton, Maggie Task, Darrel Askey, Lawrence Boyll, Les Freed, Horace Guittard, Walter Hook, Howard Kahl, Adair McGowan, Richard Nieves, J. Vernon Oaks, Robert Sharp, John Taliaferro, Bernard Frank.

Act 1, Scene 1: The Sanitorium. Berlin, 1925. *Scene 2*: The Cafe Czarina. *Scene 3*: The Chateau. *Scene 4*: The Library. *Scene 5*: The Courtyard. *Scene 6*: The Library. *Scene 7*: The Chateau.

Act 2, Scene 1: The Chateau. *Scene 2*: The Empress' Drawing Room in Copenhagen. *Scene 3*: The Courtyard. *Scene 4*: The Library. *Scene 5*: The Chateau.

ACT 1

Choral Prelude (from Piano Concerto No. 1, Op. 1; Etudes Tableaux, Op. 33, No. 2)
Chorus

Scene 1

"A Song from Somewhere" (from Trio Elegiaque, Op. 9; Symphony No. 2, Op. 27; Melodie, Op. 3, No. 5)
C. Towers

Scene 2

"Vodka, Vodka!" (from Polka Italienne)
I. Petina, B. Aplon, Emigres

"So Proud" (from Symphony No. 1, Op. 13; Piano Concerto No. 3, Op. 30)
M. Kermoyan, G. S. Irving, E. Steffe, B. Aplon

"Homeward" (from Prelude, Op. 23, No. 5)
I. Petina, Emigres

Scene 3

"Snowflakes and Sweethearts" (The Snowbird Song) (from Polka on a Theme de W. R.; Valse, Suite for 2 Pianos, Op. 17, No. 2; "Thou, My Beloved Harvest Field," Op. 4, No. 5)
B. Alexander, C. Towers, M. Quinn, M. Task, Peasants

"On That Day" (from String Quartet in G Minor; "A Dream," Op. 38, No. 5)
G. S. Irving, E. Steffe, B. Aplon, I. Petina

Scene 4

"Anya" (reprise)
M. Kermoyan

"Six Palaces" (from Etudes Tableaux, Op. 33, No. 7; Barcarolle, Suite for 2 Pianos, Op. 5, No. 1; Polichinelle, Op. 3, No. 4; Mazurka, Op.10, No. 7)
C. Towers, M. Kermoyan, G. S. Irving, E. Steffe
Livadia, on the Black Sea: *Young Prince Paul*: R. Doney. *Young Anya*: B. Alexander.
The Palace of Peterhof
The Winter Palace: *Dowager Empress*: L. Gish.

Scene 5

"Hand in Hand" (from Romance, Suite for 2 Pianos, Op. 17, No. 3)
C. Towers, J. M. King

"This Is My Kind of Love" (from Piano Concerto No. 2, Op. 18)
C. Towers, M. Kermoyan

Scene 7

"On That Day" (reprise)
J. M. King, Investors

ACT 2

Scene 1

"That Prelude!" (from prelude in C Sharp Minor, Op. 3, No. 2)
M. Kermoyan, I. Petina, E. Steffe, B. Aplon, G. S. Irving, J. Dabdoub, W. Hook, R. Metzger, L. Franks, Policemen

Scene 2

"A Quiet Land" (from Symphony No. 2, Op. 27)
C. Towers

Scene 3

"Here Tonight, Tomorrow Where?" (from Danse Hongroise, Op. 5, No. 2; "So Many Hours," Op. 4, No. 6)
G. S. Irving, E. Steffe, B. Aplon

"Leben Sie Wohl" (from Prelude, Op. 23, No. 5; Polichinelle, Op. 3, No. 4)
I. Petina, Policemen

"If This Is Goodbye" (from Piano Concerto, No. 2, Op. 18)
C. Towers, M. Kermoyan

Scene 4

"Little Hands" (from Vocalise, Op. 34, No. 14)
L. Gish, C. Towers

Scene 5

"All Hail the Empress" (from Symphony No. 1, Op. 13)
Emigres

1965.36

THE YEARLING

A Musical in Two Acts, 16 Scenes. Book by Herbert Martin and Lore Noto. Based on the novel of the same name by Marjorie Kinnan Rawlings. Music by Michael Leonard. Lyrics by Herbert Martin. Directed by Lloyd Richards. Sets and costumes by Ed Wittstein. Lighting by Jules Fisher. Music direction and vocal arrangements by Julian Stein. Orchestrations by Larry Wilcox. Dance music by David Baker. Choreography by Ralph Beaumont. Associate producer, Michael Balistreri. Produced by Lore Noto. Opened 10 December 1965 at the Alvin Theatre and closed 11 December 1965 after 3 performances.

CAST (in order of appearance): *Jody Baxter*: STEVE SANDERS. *Ezra (Penny) Baxter*: DAVID WAYNE. *Ora Baxter*: DOLORES WILSON. *Fodder-Wing*: PETER FALZONE. *Ma Forrester*: Fay Sappington. *Buck Forrester*: Allan Louw. *Arch Forrester*: Rod Barry. *Pack Forrester*: Roy Barry. *Gabby Forrester*: Bob LaCrosse. *Millwheel Forrester*: Tom Fleetwood. *Lem Forrester*: Robert Goss. *Mrs. Hutto*: CARMEN MATHEWS. *Oliver Hutto*: David Hartman. *Eulalie*: Janet Campano. *Twink*: Carmen Alvarez. *Dock Wilson*: Gordon B. Clarke. *Preacher*: Frank Bouley. *Captain*: David Sabin.

Townspeople: Loyce Baker, Lynette Bennett, Lois Grandi, Bobbi Lange, Ruth Lawrence, Barbara Miller, Bella Shalom, Myrna Strom, Mimi Wallace, Trudy Wallace, Vito Durante, Anthony Endon, Harrison Fisher, Scott Hunter, Martin Ross, Herbert Sanders, Ted Sprague.

Act 1, Scene 1: The Baxter Clearing. *Scene 2*: The Forrester Clearing. *Scene 3*: The Woods. *Scene 4*: The Hutto House. *Scene 5*: The Town of Volusia. *Scene 6*: The Glen. *Scene 7*: The Woods. *Scene 8*: The Forrester Clearing. *Scene 9*: The Baxter Cabin.

Act 2, Scene 1: The Baxter Cabin. The week before Christmas. *Scene 2*: Volusia. *Scene 3*: Wharf. *Scene 4*: The Baxter Cabin. *Scene 5*: The Baxter Cabin. *Scene 6*: The Runaway. *Scene 7*: The Baxter Clearing.

ACT 1

Scene 1

"Let Him Kick Up His Heels"
D. Wayne, D. Wilson

Scene 2

"Boy Talk"
S. Sanders, P. Falzone

"Bear Hunt"
D. Wayne, S. Sanders, Forresters

"Some Day I'm Gonna Fly"
S. Sanders, P. Falzone, Forresters

Scene 3

"Lonely Clearing"
D. Wayne

Scene 4

"Everything in the World I Love"
S. Sanders, C. Mathews

Scene 5

"I'm All Smiles"
C. Alvarez

Scene 9

"The Kind of Man a Woman Needs"
D. Wilson

"What a Happy Day"
D. Wilson, S. Sanders, G. B. Clarke, A. Louw, T. Fleetwood

"What a Happy Day" (reprise)
S. Sanders, A. Louw, G. B. Clarke, T. Fleetwood

ACT 2

Scene 1

"Ain't He a Joy?"
D. Wayne, S. Sanders

"Why Did I Choose You?"
D. Wayne, D. Wilson

"One Promise"
D. Wilson

Scene 2

"One Promise" (reprise)
D. Wilson, Townspeople

"Bear Hunt" (reprise)
Entire Company

Scene 3

"Eveything in the World I Love" (reprise)

D. Wayne, S. Sanders, C. Mathews, D. Hartman, C. Alvarez, Townspeople

Scene 4

"What a Happy Day" (reprise)

S. Sanders

Scene 5

"Nothing More"

D. Wayne, S. Sanders

Scene 7

"Everything Beautiful"

D. Wilson

1965.37 LA GROSSE VALISE

A Musical in Two Acts. Book by Robert Dhery. (Based on the French revue "La Grosse Valise.") Music and orchestrations by Gerard Calvi. Lyrics by Harold Rome. Directed by Robert Dhery. Choreography by Colette Brosset. Associate choreographer, Tom Panko. Musical director, Lehman Engel. Scenery and costumes by Jacques Dupont. Scenery and costumes supervised by Frederick Fox. Lighting by John Gleason. Assistant conductor, Karen Gustafson. Associate producer, Arthur Cantor. Produced by Joseph Kipness and Arthur Lesser. Opened 14 December 1965 at the 54th Street Theatre and closed 18 December 1965 after 7 performances.

CAST (in order of appearance): *Traveler to Bordeaux*: Jacques Ebner. *Antoine*, Customs inspector: MICHEL MODO. *Spanish Tourists*: Marcello Gamboa, Diane Coupe. *Pepito*, a customs inspector: GUY GROSSO. *Jean-Loup Roussel*: assistant chief of customs: RONALD FRASER. *La Fouillette*, an airport police offcier: Tony Doonan. *La Nana*: FRANCE ARNELL. *Photographers*: Max Vialle, Bernard Gauthron. *Nicolas*: Brigitte Valadin. *Svatsou*, the clown (M. Cheri): VICTOR SPINETTI. *Vlaminsky*: Guy Bertil. *Raoul*: Barry L. Martin. *Chief of Customs*: John Maxim. *The Little Porter*: Bert Michaels. *DeWalleyne*: Sybil Bartrop. *Baby's Maid*: Maureen Byrnes. *Chef d'Etat*, a diplomatic official: Max Vialle. *Old Lady*: Rita Charisse. *Andre*: Jean-Michel Mole. *Baby*: Joyce Jillson. *Mireille*: Mireille Chazal. *Pedralini*, head scout: John Maxim. *First Scout*: George Tregre. *Bald Man*: Bernard Gauthron. *Berthozeau*: Tony Doonan.

Ensemble: Diane Baffa, Maureen Byrnes, Diane Coupe, Ronn Forella, Marcello Gamboa, Pat Gosling, Carolyn Kirsch, Alex Mackay, Bert Michaels, Donna Sanders, George Tregre, Mary Zahn.

The action takes place in Customs, Orly Airport, Paris, France, at the present time.

ACT 1

"La Grosse Valise"

R. Fraser, V. Spinetti, B. Valadin, Company

"A Big One"

R. Fraser, M. Modo, G. Grosso, V. Spinetti, B. Valadin, Company

"C'est Defendu"

R. Fraser, F. Arnell, G. Groso, M. Modo

"Hamburg Waltz"

All Principals, Dancing Girls and Boys

"Happy Song"

R. Fraser, G. Grosso, M. Modo, J. Maxim

"For You"

J. Jillson

"Sandwich for Two"

V. Spinetti, B. Valadin

'"La Java"

F. Arnell, J. Maxim, J. Jillson, Dancing Girls and Boys

"Xanadu"

F. Arnell, V. Spinetti, R. Fraser

ACT 2

"Slippy Sloppy Shoes"

V. Spinetti, R. Fraser, Dancing Girls and Boys

"Spanish Dance"

R. Fraser, M. Chazal

"For You" (reprise)

R. Fraser, J. Jillson

"Delilah Done Me Wrong"

V. Spinetti, F. Arnell, and the Slaves

"Hawaii"

F. Arnell, J. Jillson, Dancing Girls

1965.38 OKLAHOMA!

A Revival of the Musical Play in Two Acts, 6 Scenes[15]. Book and lyrics by Oscar Hammerstein II. Music by Richard Rodgers. Based on the play "Green Grow the Lilacs" by Lynn Riggs. Entire production directed by John Fearnley. (Originally directed by Rouben Mamoulian.) Original dances by Agnes de Mille, restaged by Gemze de Lappe. Music director, Pembroke Davenport. Assistant conductor, Abba Bogin. Settings by Lemuel Ayers. Costumes by Stanley Simmons. Lighting by Peggy Clark. Produced by the New York City Center Light Opera Company (Jean Dalrymple, Director). Opened 15 December 1965 at the New York City Center and closed 2 January 1966 after 24 performances.

CAST (in order of appearance): *Aunt Eller*: RUTH KOBART. *Curly*: JOHN DAVIDSON. *Laurey*: SUSAN WATSON. *Will Parker*: RICHARD FRANCE. *Jud Fry*: DANIEL P. HANNAFIN. *Ado Annie Carnes*: KAREN MORROW. *Ali Hakim*: JULES MUNSHIN. *Gertie Cummings*: Loi Leabo. *Curly* in ballet: DEAN CRANE. *Laurey* in ballet: SUSAN WATSON. *Jud* in ballet: James Albright. *The Child* in ballet: Jane Levin. *The Girl Who Falls Down*: Loi Leabo. *Andrew Carnes*: SAMMY SMITH. *Cord Elam*: Herbert Surface.

Dancers: *Girls*: Cathy Conklin, Joanne Crosson, Carolyn Dyer, Carol Estey, Sharon Herr, Loi Leabo, Jane Levin, Marie Patrice, Betty Ann Rapine, Rande Rayburn, Julie Theobald, Toodie Wittmer. *Boys*: Don Angelo, Gerry Dalton, Jeremy Ives, Brynnar Mehl, Philip Rice, Bud Spencer, Fabian Suart. *Singers*: *Girls*: Vicki Belmonte, Maria Bradley, Judie Elkins, Jeanne Frey, Marie Hero, Joyce Olson, Susan Sidney, Maggie Worth. *Boys*: Kenny Adams, Brown Bradley, Roger Alan Brown, Joseph Corby, Peter Clark, Lang Des Jardins, Konstantin Moskalenko, Stephen John Rydell, Herbert Surface, Victor Helou.

1965.39 THE PERSECUTION AND ASSASSINATION OF MARAT AS PERFORMED BY THE INMATES OF THE ASYLUM OF CHARENTON UNDER THE DIRECTION OF THE MARQUIS DE SADE (MARAT/SADE)

A Drama with Music in Two Acts, 33 Scenes[16]. (Original German) Play by Peter Weiss. English version by Geoffrey Skelton. Verse adaptation by Adrian Mitchell. Music by Richard Peaslee. Directed by Peter Brook. Settings and properties by Sally Jacobs. Costumes by Gunilla Palmstierna-Weiss. Choreograhy by Malcolm Goddard. Original Lighting by David Read. Lighting and design supervision by Lloyd Burlingame. Assistant to the director, Ian Richardson. Production supervisor, Samuel Liff. (A Royal Shakespeare Company Production.) Produced by the David Merrick Arts Foundation by arrangement with the Governors of the Royal Shakespeare Theatre. Opened 27 December 1965 at the Martin Beck Theatre and closed 30 April 1966 after 145 performances.

CAST (in order of appearance): *M. Coulmier*: CLIFFORD ROSE. *Mme. Coulmier*: Brenda Kempner. *Mlle. Coulmier*: Ruth Baker. *Herald*: MICHAEL WILLIAMS. *Cucururu*: Freddie Jones. *Kokol*: Hugh Sullivan. *Polpoch*: Jonathan Burn. *Rossignol*: Jeanette Landis. *Jacques Roux*: Robert Lloyd. *Charlotte Corday*: GLENDA JACKSON. *Jean-Paul Marat*: IAN RICHARDSON. *Simonne Evrard*: SUSAN WILLIAMSON. *Marquis de Sade*: PATRICK MAGEE. *Duperret*: JOHN STEINER. *Abbot*: Mark Jones. *A Mad Animal*: Morgan Sheppard. *Schoolmaster*: James Mellor. *The Military Representative*: Ian Hogg. *Mother*: Mark Jones. *Father*: Henry Woolf. *A Newly-Rich Lady*: John Hussey. *Voltaire*: John Harwood. *Lavoisier*: Leon Lissek. *Nuns*: Heather Canning, Jennifer Tudor. *Guards*: Timothy Hardy, Stanford Trowell.

Patients: Mary Allen, Michael Farnsworth, Maroussia Frank, Tamara Fuerst, Guy Gordon, Sheila Grant, Michael Percival, Lyn Pinkney, Carol Raymont. *Musicians*: Patrick Gowers (Music director/harmonium/tuba), Richard Callinan (percussion), Michael Gould (trumpet), Nicholas Moes (guitar/harmonium), Rainer Schuelein (flute/piccolo/alto flute).

The action takes place in the Charenton Asylum in France sometime between 1803 and 1814.

Act 1, Scene 1: Assembly. *Scene 2*: Prologue. *Scene 3*: Preparation. *Scene 4*: Presentation. *Scene 5*: Homage to Marat. *Scene 6*: Stifled Unrest. *Scene 7*: Corday Is Introduced. *Scene 8*: I Am the Revolution. *Scene 9*: Corday's First Visit. *Scene 10*: Song

---

[15]Originally produced in New York 31 March 1943 at the St. James Theatre for 2212 performances. For Synopsis of Scenes and Musical Numbers, see original 1943 production.

[16]Scenes and Song Titles do not appear in the program, but have been prepared from the production typescript, published text, musical score and recordings.

and Mime of Corday's Arrival in Paris. *Scene 11*: Death's Triumph. *Scene 12*: Conversation Concerning Life and Death. *Scene 13*: Marat's Liturgy. *Scene 14*: A Regrettable Intervention. *Scene 15*: Continuation of the Conversation Between Marat and Sade. *Scene 16*: The People's Reaction. *Scene 17*: First Conversation between Corday and Duperret. *Scene 18*: Sade Turns His Back on All the Nations. *Scene 19*: First Rabble-Rousing of Jacques Roux. *Scene 20*: Monsieur de Sade Is Whipped. *Scene 21*: Poor Old Marat. *Scene 22*: Second Conversation Between Corday and Duperret. *Scene 23*: These Lies They Tell. *Scene 24*: Song and Mime of the Glorification of the Beneficiary. *Scene 25*: Corday's Second Visit. *Scene 26*: The Faces of Marat.

Act 2, Scene 1: The National Assembly. *Scene 2*: Poor Marat in Your Bathtub Seat. *Scene 3*: Preparations for the Third Visit. *Scene 4*: Corday's Third and Last Visit. *Scene 5*: Interruptus. *Scene 6*: The Murder. *Scene 7*: Epilogue.

ACT 1

Scene 5

"Homage to Marat"
H. Sullivam, J. Burn, F. Jones, J. Landis, Chorus

Scene 7

"The Corday Waltz"
G. Jackson

Scene 10

"Song and Mime of Corday's Arrival in Paris"
H. Sullivam, J. Burn, F. Jones, J. Landis

"The Tumbrel Song"
H. Sullivam, J. Burn, F. Jones, J. Landis

Scene 16

"The People's Reaction"
H. Sullivam, J. Burn, F. Jones, J. Landis, Chorus

Scene 18

"Those Fat Monkeys"
H. Sullivam, J. Burn, F. Jones, J. Landis

Scene 21

"Poor Old Marat"
H. Sullivam, J. Burn, F. Jones, J. Landis

Scene 22

"One Day It Will Come to Pass"
G. Jackson, J. Steiner

Scene 24

"Song and Mime of the Glorification of the Beneficiary"
P. Magee, I. Richardson, H. Sullivam, J. Burn, F. Jones, J. Landis,

ACT 2

Scene 2

"Poor Marat in Your Bathtub Seat"
H. Sullivam, J. Burn, F. Jones, J. Landis

"Poor Old Marat" (reprise)
H. Sullivam, J. Burn, F. Jones, J. Landis

Scene 4

"Copulation Round"
Chorus

Scene 5

"Fifteen Glorious Years"
H. Sullivam, J. Burn, F. Jones, J. Landis, Company

Scene 7

Finale (Epilogue)
Entire Company

1966.01 SWEET CHARITY

A Musical in Two Acts, a Prologue and 18 Scenes. Book by Neil Simon. Based on the film "Le Notte di Cabiria" [Nights of Cabiria] by Federico Fellini, Tullio Pinelli, Ennio Flaiano. Music by Cy Coleman. Lyrics by Dorothy Fields. Conceived, staged and choreographed by Bob Fosse. Scenery and lighting by Robert Randolph. Costumes by Irene Sharaff. Musical direction and dance music arranged by Fred Werner. Orchestrations by Ralph Burns. Production manager, Robert Linden. Associate producer, John Bowab. Assistant conductor, Oscar Kosarin. Produced by Robert Fryer, Lawrence Carr, Joseph P. and Sylvia Harris. Opened 29 January 1966 at the Palace Theatre and closed 15 July 1967 after 608 performances.

CAST (in order of appearance): *Charity*: GWEN VERDON. *Dark Glasses*: Michael Davis. *Bystander*: John Stratton. *Married Couple*: Bud Vest, Elaine Cancilla. *Woman with hat*: Ruth Buzzi. *Football Player*: John Sharpe. *Ice Cream Vendor*: Gene Foote. *Ballplayers*: Harold Pierson, Eddie Gasper. *Career Carl*: Barbara Sharma. *Young Spanish Man*: Lee Roy Reams. *First Cop*: John Wheeler. *Second Cop*: David Gold. *Helene*: THELMA OLIVER. *Carmen*: Carmen Morales. *Nickie*: HELEN GALLAGHER. *Herman*: John Wheeler. *Doorman*: I. W. Klein. *Ursula*: Sharon Ritchie. *Vittorio Vidal*: JAMES LUISI. *Waiter*: John Stratton. *Manfred*: Bud Vest. *Receptionist*: Ruth Buzzi. *Old Maid*: Elaine Cancilla. *Oscar*: JOHN McMARTIN. *Daddy Johann Sebastian Brubeck*: Arnold Soboloff. *Brother Harold*: Harold Pierson. *Brother Eddie*: Eddie Gasper. *Policeman*: Harold Pierson. *Rosie*: Barbara Sharma. *Barney*: David Gold. *Mike*: Michael Davis. *Good Fairy*: Ruth Buzzi.

Singers and Dancers of Times Square: I. W. Klein, Mary Louise, Alice Evans, Betsy Dickerson, Kathryn Doby, Suzanne Charny, Elaine Cancilla, Carmen Morales, Christine Stewart, Charlene Ryan, David Gold, Gene Foote, Harold Pierson, Bud Vest, Darrell Notara, John Sharpe, Eddie Gasper, Michael Davis, Patrick Heim.

The action takes place in and around New York City at the present time.

Act 1, Scene 1: The Park. *Scene 2*: The Hostess Room (of the Fan-Dango Ballroom). *Scene 3*: Fan-Dango Ballroom. *Scene 4*: A New York Street (outside the Pompeii Club). *Scene 5*: (The Interior of the) Pompeii Club. *Scene 6*: Vittorio Vidal's Apartment. *Scene 7*: The Hostess Room. *Scene 8*: YMHA—92nd Street "Y."

Act 2, Scene 1: YMHA—92nd Street "Y." *Scene 2*: The Rhythm of Life Church. *Scene 3*: (On a New York Street) Going Cross-town. *Scene 4*: Charity's Apartment. *Scene 5*: Coney Island. *Scene 6*: The Fan-Dango Ballroom. *Scene 7*: Times Square. *Scene 8*: Barney's Chile Hacienda. *Scene 9*: The Fan-Dango Ballroom. *Scene 10*: The Park.

ACT 1

Prologue

"Charity's Wish" (Charity's Theme)(dance)
G. Verdon

Scene 1

"You Should See Yourself"[17]
G. Verdon

"The Rescue"
The Passers-by

Scene 3

"Big Spender"
H. Gallgher, T. Oliver, the Fan-Dango Girls

"Charity's Soliloquy"
G. Verdon

Scene 5

"Rich Man's Frug"
B. Sharma, E. Gasper, J. Sharpe, Patrons

Scene 6

"If My Friends Could See Me Now"
G. Verdon

"Too Many Tomorrows"
J. Luisi

Scene 7

"There's Gotta Be Something Better Than This"
G. Verdon, H. Gallagher, T. Oliver

Scene 8

"I'm the Bravest Individual"
G. Verdon, J. McMartin

ACT 2

Scene 2

"Rhythm of Life"
A. Soboloff, H. Pierson, E. Gasper, Worshippers

Scene 4

"Baby Dream Your Dream"
H. Gallagher, T. Oliver

Scene 5

"Sweet Charity"
J. McMartin

Scene 6

"Where Am I Going?"[18]
G. Verdon

[17]Dropped shortly after opening.
[18]Dropped shortly after opening.

Scene 9
"I'm a Brass Band"
G. Verdon
Scene 10
"I Love to Cry at Weddings"
J. Wheeler, M. Davis, H. Gallagher, T. Oliver, Girls, Patrons

1966.02 STREET SCENE

A Revival of the American Opera (Musical) in Two Acts, 3 Scenes[19]. Book by Elmer Rice from his play of the same name. Music by Kurt Weill. Lyrics by Langston Hughes. Staged by Herbert Machiz. Choreographed by Richard Tone. Conducted by Charles Wilson. Scenery and costumes by Paul Sylbert. (Orchestrations by Kurt Weill.) Produced by the New York City Opera. Opened 24 February 1966 at the New York State Theatre and closed 19 March 1966 after 6 performances in repertory.

CAST (in order of appearance): *Abraham Kaplan*: Nico Castel. *Greta Fiorentino*: Dolores Mari. *Carl Olsen*: George S. Irving. *Emma Jones*: RUTH KOBART. *Olga Olsen*: Muriel Greenspon. *Shirley Kaplan*: Florence Anglin. *Henry Davis*: Edward Pierson. *Willie Maurrant*: Bruce Papa. *Anna Maurrant*: EILEEN SCHAULER. *Sam Kaplan*: William DuPree. *Daniel Buchanan*: L. D. Clements. *Frank Maurrant*: WILLIAM CHAPMAN. *George Jones*: Jack Bittner. *Steve Sankey*: Richard Armbruster. *Lippo Fiorentino*: JACK DeLON. *Jennie Hildebrand*: Betsy Hepburn. *Second Graduate*: Janet Morris. *Third Graduate*: Lila Herbert. *Mrs. Hildebrand*: Beverly Evans. *Charlie Hildebrand*: Tom Brooke. *Mary Hildebrand*: Jeanne Tanzy. *Grace Davis*: Donna Babbs. *Rose Maurrant*: ANNE ELGAR. *Harry Easter*: Seth Riggs. *Mae Jones*: Sondra Lee. *Dick McGann*: Alan Peterson. *Vincent Jones*: Barney Martin. *Dr. John Wilson*: Don Carlo. *Officer Harry Murphy*: David Smith. *City Marshall James Henry*: Don Yule. *Fred Cullen*: Paul Corder. *First Nursemaid*: Charlotte Povia. *Second Nursemaid*: Marie Wyckoff.

Policemen, Milkman, Old Clothes Man, Music Pupil, Interne, Ambulance Driver, Married Couple, Passersby, Neighbors, Children, etc.: New York City Opera Chorus.

1966.03 WAIT A MINIM!

A Musical Entertainment (Revue fom South Africa) in Two Acts, 24 Scenes. Devised and directed by Leon Gluckman. Musical arrangements[20] and direction by Andrew Tracey. Decor and lighting by Frank Rembach and Leon Gluckman. Decor executed by Frank Rembach. Costumes by Heather Macdonald-Rouse. Choreography by Frank Staff and Kendrew Lascelles. Lighting and design supervision by Klaus Holm. Costume supervision by Patton Campbell. Production supervisior, Lanier Davis. Produced by Frank Productions, Inc. (Allen B. Whitehead, President). Opened 7 March 1966 at the John Golden Theatre and closed 15 April 1967 after 457 performances.

CAST: ANDREW TRACEY, PAUL TRACEY, KENDREW LASCELLES, MICHEL MARTEL, NIGEL PEGRAM, APRIL OLRICH, DANA VALERY, SARAH ATKINSON.

ACT 1[21]
Scene 1
This Is the Land:
"Ndinosara Nani?" (Karanga Folk Song, Southern Rhodesia)
A. Tracey, N. Pegram, M. Martel, D. Valery, P. Tracey
"Hoe Ry Die Boere" (Afrikaans Folk Song)
N. Pegram, P. Tracey, A. Tracey
"This Is Worth Fighting For"[22]
S. Atkinson
"Subuhi Sana" (Swahili)
A. Tracey
"Jikel' Emaweni"[23] (Xhosa Fighting Song, Tanskei)
(arr. by Makeba)
D. Valery
Scene 2
Dingere Dingale:
"Ajade Papa" (Tamil Lullaby)
M. Martel
Dingere Dingale" (Tamil Song)
The Company
"Tuba Man"
K. Lascelles
Scene 3
Over the Hills:
"I Know Where I'm Going" (Irish Folk Song)
P. Tracey, S. Atkinson, A. Tracey
"Over the Hills"
A. Olrich, A. Tracey
"I Gave My Love a Cherry" (English Folk Song)
P. Tracey, D. Valery, M. Martel, N. Pegram, A. Tracey
Scene 4
"Black-White Calypso"
N. Pegram
(*Music and Lyrics by* Jeremy Taylor.)
Scene 5
Die Meistertrinker
"Deutches Weinlied"
The Company
"Gretl's Cow"
A. Olrich
"Eine kleine bombardonmusik" (Mozart)
N. Pegram, A. Tracey, P. Tracey, K. Lascelles
"Watschplattlanz"
The Company
Scene 6
"Buttermilk Hill"[24] (Irish-American)
D. Valery
Scene 7
"Aria"
P. Tracey
Scene 8
"Out of Focus"
The Company
Snap Happy
A. Olrich, K. Lascelles
"Hoshoryu" (Japanese Folk Song)
M. Martel, S. Atkinson
The Gentle Art
K. Lascelles, M. Martel, P. Tracey
Scene 9
"Dirty Old Town"
A. Tracey, P. Tracey, D. Valery, N. Pegram
(*Music and Lyrics by* Ewan MacColl.)
Scene 10
"Last Summer"
A. Tracey, P. Tracey, N. Pegram, K. Lascelles
Scene 11
Vive La Difference:

---

[19]Originally produced in New York 9 January 1947 at the Adelphi Theatre for 148 performances. For Synopsis of Scenes and Musical Numbers, see original 1947 production.

[20]All musical arrangements for WAIT A MINIM! are played by:
Andrew Tracey: Guitar, guitar-lute, bamboo pipe, Portuguese guitar, mandolin, treble and soprano recorder, Rhodesian mbira, Chopi timbila, Lozi drums, tuba, bagpipes, Indian tabla drums, clarient, Trinidadian steel drum, sousaphone, Indian gong.
Paul Tracey: Guitar, H. M. Bull Fiddle, flute, Chopi timbila, Lozi drums, piccolo, melodica, squeezebox, bagpipes, kalimba, tuba, sousaphone, Indian gong.
Nigel Pegram: Guitar, H.M. Bull Fiddle, double respiratory linguaphone, Lozi drums, bagpipes, Japanese koto zither, trombone, Chopi timbila, penny whistle, Indian tanpura drone. *Kendrew Lascelles*: Trumpet. Other percussion instruments by the Company.

[21]The following song was added during the course of the run and subsequent tour:
"Home Sweet Home" (Act 1, Scene 1)

[22]Dropped during run and tour.

[23]Dropped during tour.

[24]Replaced after opening with:
"Johnny Soldier" (Irish-American)
D. Valery

"Lalirette"
P. Tracey, A. Tracey, M. Martel, N. Pegram
"Le Roi A Fait Battre Tambour" (Medieval ballade)
M. Martel, N. Pegram, P. Tracey, A. Tracey
Tour de France
K. Lascelles, A. Olrich, A. Tracey, P. Tracey, M. Martel
Scene 12
"A Piece of Ground"
N. Pegram
(*Music and Lyrics by* Jeremy Taylor.)
Scene 13
"Ayama"
A. Tracey, P. Tracey, M. Martel
Scene 14
North of the 'Popo:
Professor Piercing
P. Tracey
The Chairwoman
N. Pegram
"Mgeniso waMgodo waShambini" (Chopi Timbila)
A. Tracey, P. Tracey, N. Pegram
"Kupura Kupika" (Pounding Song, Nyasaland)
S. Atkinson, D. Valery, A. Olrich
"The Izicatulo Gumboot Dance"
The Company

ACT 2
Scene 1
Tunes of Glory
"The Wee Cooper o' Fife" (Doric Diddling)
P. Tracey, A. Tracey, N. Pegram
"Red Red Rose" (Robert Burns)
P. Tracey
Scene 2
"Hammer Song" (If I Had a Hammer)
A. Tracey, N. Pegram, M. Martel, P. Tracey
(*Music and Lyrics by* Pete Seeger and Lee Hays.)
Scene 3
"London Talking Blues"
N. Pegram
(*Music and Lyrics by* Jeremy Taylor.)
Scene 4
The Love Life of a Gondolier"
K. Lascelles, M. Martel, A. Olrich
Scene 5
"Foyo" (Haitian Patois Lullaby)
P. Tracey, A. Tracey, N. Pegram
Scene 6
"Cool"
D. Valery, P. Tracey, N. Pegram, A. Tracey
(*Music and Lyrics by* Andrew and Paul Tracey.)
Scene 7
On Guard
K. Lascelles, A. Olrich
Scene 8
Sir Oswald Sodde:
Opening Knight
The Company
"Sir Oswald Sodde"
A. Tracey, S. Atkinson, N. Pegram, P. Tracey, M. Martel
(*Music and Lyrics by* Jeffrey Smith.)
Scene 9
"Table Bay"
D. Valery
(Cape Malay, *arranged and adapted by* Stanley Glasser and Adolf Wood.)
Scene 10
This Is South Africa:
"Chuzi Mama Gwabi Gwabi" (Marabi Dance Song)
D. Valery, M. Martel
"Celeste Aida"*
M. Martel
"Cingoma Chakabaruka" (Tumbuka/Henga party song, Nyasaland)
The Company
"Skalo-Zwi"
(*Music by* Stanley Glasser. *Lyrics by* Gwigwi Mrwebe. Pedi Pipe Dance specially arranged by Andrew Tracey.)
D. Valery, Company
"Samandoza-we!" (Ndau, Southern Rhodesia)
The Company
"Amasalela" (Baca Fighting Song, Transkei)
The Company

1966.04 THE CONSUL

A Revival of the Opera (Musical Drama) in Three Acts, 6 Scenes[25]. Libretto and music by Gian-Carlo Menotti. Staged by Gian-Carlo Menotti. Conductor, Vincent La Selva. Settings and costumes by Horace Armistead. Produced by the New York City Opera. Opened 17 March 1966 at the New York State Theatre and closed 23 March 1966 after 3 performances in repertory.

CAST: (in order of appearance): *John Sorel*: SHERRILL MILNES. *Magda Sorel*: PATRICIA NEWAY. *The Mother*: EVELYN SACHS. *Secret Police Agent*: HERBERT BEATTIE. *First Plainclothesman*: Philip Erickson. *Second Plainclothesman*: Richard Park. *The Secretary*: BEVERLY EVANS. *Mr. Kofner*: DAVID SMITH. *The Foreign Woman*: ELISABETH CARRON. *Anna Gomez*: Ludmilla Azova. *Vera Boronel*: Elisabeth Farmer. *Nika Magadoff*, The Magician: GENE BULLARD. *Assan*: Jack Bittner. *Voice on the Record*: Mabel Mercer.

1966.05 POUSSE-CAFÉ

A Musical in Two Acts, a Prologue and 17 Scenes. Book by Jerome Weidman[26]. Music by Duke Ellington. Lyrics by Marshall Barer and Fred Tobias. Entire production directed by José Quintero. Scenery by Will Steven Armstrong. Costumes by Patricia Zipprodt, Albert Wolsky. Lighting by J. C. Fuqua. Musical direction, Sherman Frank. Production consultant, Charles Conaway. Orchestrations by Larry Wilcox. Choreography, Valerie Bettis. Musical numbers and dances staged by Marvin Gordon. Associate producer, Monty Shaff. Produced by Guy de La Passardiere. Opened 18 March 1966 at the 46th Street Theatre and closed 19 March 1966 after 3 performances.

CAST (in order of appearance): *Ellis*: Ellis Larkins. *Havana*: TRAVIS HUDSON. *Duchess*: Madge Cameron. *Monty*: Al Nesor. *Harry*: Tommy Karaty. *Sourball*: Robert Rovin. *Bill*: Ben Bryant. *Arthur Owen, Jr.*: Jeff Siggins. *John Harmon*: GARY KRAWFORD. *Professor George Ritter*: THEODORE BIKEL. *Solange*: LILO. *Sailor*: Dom Angelo. *Policeman*: Hal Norman. *Paul*: Don Crabtree. *Maurice*: Charles Durning. *Artie*: Coley Worth. *Tourist Lady*: Fran Stevens. *Louise*: Marlena Lustik. *Dean Stewart*: Charles Durning. *Danny*: RICHARD TONE.

Ensemble: Dom Angelo, Kay Cole, Joel Conrad, Mervin Crook, Elaine Giftos, Altovise Gore, Peter Hamparian, Jo Ann Lehmann, Marlena Lustik, Iva March, Simon McQueen, Rita O'Connor, Martin Ross, Barbara Saatan, Scotty Salmon.

The action takes place in New Orleans during the early 1920s.

Act 1, Scene 1: Schoolroom. *Scene 2*: Cafe and Bar. *Scene 3*: Solange's Dressing Room. *Scene 4*: Cafe and Bar. *Scene 5*: Dormitory. *Scene 6*: Solange's Dressing Room. *Scene 7*: Same, the next morning. *Scene 8*: Professor's Quarters. *Scene 9*: Professor's Quarters and Solange's Dressing Room. *Scene 10*: Cafe and Bar.

Act 2, Scene 1: Cafe and Bar. *Scene 2*: Solange's Dressing Room. *Scene 3*: Cafe and Bar. *Scene 4*: Professor's Quarters. *Scene 5*: Cafe and Bar. *Scene 6*: Solange's Dressing Room. *Scene 7*: Schoolroom.

ACT 1
"The Spider and the Fly"
T. Hudson, Dance Ensemble
"Rules and Regulations"
T. Bikel, G. Krawford, R. Rovin, B. Bryant, J. Siggins, T. Karaty
"Follow Me Up the Stairs"
Lilo

[25]Originally produced in New York 15 March 1950 at the Ethel Barrymore Theatre for 269 performances. For Synopsis of Scenes and Musical Numbers, see original 1950 production.
[26]Source credit dropped prior to New York opening. Based on the novel "Professor Unrath" by Heinrich Mann. The film "The Blue Angel" by Karl Zuckmayer was adapted from the same source.

"Goodby Charlie"
T. Hudson, Ensemble
"C'est Comme Ça"
Lilo
"Thank You, Ma'am"
T. Bikel, Lilo
"The Eleventh Commandment"
R. Rovin, J. Siggins, B. Bryant, T. Karaty
"Someone to Care For"
T. Bikel
"The Wedding"
Ensemble

ACT 2
"Let's" (Rehearsal Scene)
R. Tone, M. Lustik, Dancers
"The Good Old Days"
T. Hudson, D. Crabtree, A. Nesor, C. Worth, C. Durning
"Easy To Take"
R. Tone, Lilo
"C'est Comme Ça" (reprise)
T. Bikel
"C'est Comme Ça" (reprise)
Lilo
"Let's" (reprise)
Lilo, Dancers
"Old World Charm"
T. Bikel
"The Spider and the Fly" (reprise)
T. Hudson

1966.06 IT'S A BIRD . . . IT'S A PLANE . . . IT'S SUPERMAN

A Musical Comedy in Two Acts, 18 Scenes. Book by David Newman and Robert Benton. Based on the comic strip "Superman.[27]" Music by Charles Strouse. Lyrics by Lee Adams. Directed by Harold Prince. Dances and musical numbers staged by Ernest Flatt. Scenery and lighting by Robert Randolph. Costumes by Florence Klotz. Musical direction, Harold Hastings, Orchestrations by Eddie Sauter. Dance arrangements by Betty Walberg. Filmed sequences by MPO Pictures, Inc. Produced by Harold Prince in association with Ruth Mitchell. Opened 29 March 1966 at the Alvin Theatre and closed 17 July 1966 after 129 performances.

CAST (in order of appearance): *Superman/Clark Kent*: BOB HOLIDAY. *Max Mencken*: JACK CASSIDY. *Lois Lane*: PATRICIA MARAND. *Perry White*: Eric Mason. *Sydney*: LINDA LAVIN. *Dr. Abner Sedgewick*: MICHAEL O'SULLIVAN. *Jim Morgan*: DON CHASTAIN. *Father Ling*: Jerry Fujikawa. *Dong Ling*: Bill Starr. *Tai Ling*: Murphy James. *Fan Po Ling*: Juleste Salve. *Ming Foo Ling*: Michael Gentry. *Joe Ling*: Joseph Gentry. *Suspects (5)*: *One*: Les Freed. *Two*: Dick Miller. *Three*: Dal Richards. *Four*: John Grigas. *Five*: John Smolko.

Citizens of Metropolis: *Byron*, the Bank Guard: Eugene Edwards. *Harvey*, the Tour Guide: Bob Scherkenbach. *Bonnie*, the Moll: April Nevins. *Sue-Ellen*, the Teenager: Tina Faye. *Marnie*, the Model: Judy Newman. *Gordon*, the Student: Bick Goss. *Annette*, the Secretary: Michelle Barry. *Wanda*, the Waitress: Gay Edmond. *Rosalie*, the High School Girl: Marilyne Mason. *Leslie*, the Shopper: Jayme Mylroie. *Cathy*, the Child: Lori Browne. *Barbie*, the Receptioinst: Mara Landi. *Al*, the Bank Robber: George Bunt. *Milton*, the Hood: Dallas Edmunds. *Kevin*, the College Boy: Roy Smith. *William*, the Exchange Student: Haruki Fujimoto.

The action takes place in and around the city of Metropolis, U.S.A. at the present time.

Act 1, Scene 1: Outside the Chase-Metropolis Bank. *Scene 2*: The Office of *The Daily Planet*. *Scene 3*: A Telephone Booth. *Scene 4*: The Nuclear Ractor at M.I.T. *Scene 5*: The Offices of *The Daily Planet*. *Scene 6*: Dr. Sedgewick's Study. *Scene 7*: The Screening Room. *Scene 8*: Dr. Sedgewick's Home. *Scene 9*: The Offices of *The Daily Planet*. *Scene 10*: Atop City Hall Tower. *Scene11*: The M.I.T. Dedication Grounds.

Act 2, Scene 1: The Front Page, one week later. *Scene 2*: Clark Kent's Apartment. *Scene 3*: A Street in Metropolis. *Scene 4*: Dr. Sedgewick's Laboratory. *Scene 5*: Meanwhile. *Scene 6*: An Abandoned Power Station outside Metropolis. *Scene 7*: The Power Station, next morning.

[27]The Superman comic strip first appeared in 1938 from author-illustrators Jerry Siegel and Joe Shuster, published by Detective Comics.

ACT 1
Scene 1
"Doing Good"
B. Holiday
"We Need Him"
J. Cassidy, P. Marand, B. Holiday, Company
Scene 2
"It's Superman"
P. Marand
Scene 4
"We Don't Matter At All"
D. Chastain, P. Marand
"Revenge"
M. O'Sullivan
Scene 5
"The Woman For the Man"
J. Cassidy
"You've Got Possibilities"
L. Lavin
Scene 7
"What I've Always Wanted"
P. Marand
"Revenge" (reprise)
M. O'Sullivan
Scene 8
"Everything's Easy When You Know How"
The Flying Lings
Scene 11
"It's Super Nice"
The Company

ACT 2
Scene 1
"So Long, Big Guy"
J. Cassidy
Scene 2
"The Strongest Man in the World"
B. Holiday
Scene 3
"Ooh, Do You Love You!"
L. Lavin
Scene 4
"You've Got What I Need"
J. Cassidy, M. O'Sullivan
Scene 5
"It's Superman" (reprise)
The Company
Scene 7
"I'm Not Finished Yet"
P. Marand
"Pow! Bam! Zonk!"
B. Holiday, the Flying Lings

1966.07 HOW TO SUCCEED IN BUSINESS WITHOUT REALLY TRYING

A Revival of the Musical (Comedy) in Two Acts, 24 Scenes[28]. Book by Abe Burrows, Jack Weinstock and Willie Gilbert. Based on the novel of the same name by Shepherd Mead. Music and lyrics by Frank Loesser. Scenery by Robert Randolph. Costumes by Stanley Simmons. Lighting by Peggy Clark. Production directed by Gus Schirmer. Original choreography for "The Yo Ho Ho" by Hugh Lambert. Original musical staging by Bob Fosse. Musical direction, Anton Coppola. (Orchestrations by Robert Ginzler.) Original production directed by Abe Burrows. Produced by the New York City Center

[28]Originally opened in New York 14 October 1961 at the 46th Street Theatre for 1417 performances. For Synopsis of Scenes and Musical Numbers, see original 1961 production.

Light Opera Company (Jean Dalrymple, Director). Opened 20 April 1966 at the New York City Center and closed 8 May 1966 after 23 performances.

CAST (in order of appearance): *Finch*: LEN GOCHMAN. *Gatch*: Lang des Jardins. *Jenkins*: Austin Colyer. *Peterson*: Reese Burns. *Tackaberry*: Henry Lawrence. *J. B. Biggley*: BILLY DE WOLFE. *Rosemary*: SHEILA SULLIVAN. *Bratt*: ART BARNETT. *Smitty*: PAT McENNIS. *Frump*: LEE GOODMAN. *Miss Jones*: JUSTINE JOHNSTON. *Mr. Twimble*: LOU CUTELL. *Hedy*: BETTY LINTON. *Scrubwomen*: Natasha Grishin, Renee Gorsey. *Miss Krumholtz*: Del Green. *Ovington*: Richard Davis. *Policeman*: Paul Adams. *Womper*: LOU CUTELL.

Singers: Paul Adams, Reese Burns, Austin Colyer, Lang des Jardins, Walter E. Hook, Mickey Karm, Henry Lawrence, Richard Marr, Marie Bradley, Jane Coleman, Jacque Dean, Renee Gorsey, Del Green, Maria Hero, Judy McMurdo. *Dancers*: Doria Avila, Richard Denny, Garold Gardner, Jerry Kent, Stan Mazin, Leo J. Muller, Terry Nicholson, Roger Allan Raby, Nephele Buecher, Patricia Cope, Mickey Gunnersen, Natasha Grishin, Rosie Holotik, Beth Howland, Joan Lindsay, Sharron Miller.

1966.08 THE MOST HAPPY FELLA

A Revival of the Musical in Three Acts, 11 Scenes[29]. Book, music and lyrics by Frank Loesser. Based on the play "They Knew What They Wanted" by Sidney Howard. Stage direction and choreography by Ralph Beaumont. Settings by Jo Mielziner. Costumes by Frank Thompson. Lighting by Peggy Clark (Orchestrations by Don Walker.) Musical direction, Abba Bogin. Produced by the New York City Center Light Opera Company (Jean Dalrymple, Director). Opened 11 May 1966 at the New York City Center and closed 22 May 1966 after 15 performances.

CAST (in order of appearance): *The Cashier*: Lee Cass. *Cleo*: KAREN MORROW. *Rosabella*: BARBARA MEISTER. *Waitresses*: Joanna Crosson, Rita O'Connor, Joy Serio, Susan Sigrist. *The Postman*: Lee Cass. *Tony*: NORMAN ATKINS. *Marie*: FRAN STEVENS. *Max*: Joe McGrath. *Herman*: JACK DE LON. *Clem*: James Hobson. *Jake*: Robert E. Maxwell, Jr. *Al*: John A. Boni. *Joe*: ART LUND. *Giuseppe*: Montes de Oca. *Pasquale*: Will Roy. *Ciccio*: Ed Becker. *The Doctor*: Carl Nicholas. *The Priest*: Dick Ensslen. *Tessie*: Karen Grant. *Gussie*: Jody La Rocco. *Sissy*: Marci Phillips. *Neighbor Ladies*: Joyce Olson, Rosemary McNamara, Rita Metzger. *Brakeman*: Dale Westerman. *Bus Driver*: Doug Hunt.

All the Neighbors, and All the Neighbors' Neighbors: Lillian Bozinoff, Susan Cogan, Jeanne Frey, Marlene Kay, Evelyn Kingsley, Rosemary McNamara, Rita Metzger, Barbara Miller, LaVergne Monette, Joyce Olson, Patti Winston, Gene Albano, John A. Boni, Marvin Goodis, James Hobson, Doug Hunt, Philip Lucas, Stuart Mann, Robert E. Maxwell, Jr., Joe McGrath, George T. McWhorter, Dale Westerman, Wilson Robey, Diane Arnold, Linda Bonem, Connie Burnett, Kay Cole, Joanna Crosson, Judith Dunford, Ina Kurland, Rita O'Connor, Joy Serio, Susan Sigrist, Myrna Strom, Dom Angelo, Frank Coppola, Vito Durante, Jerry Fries, Bob LaCrosse, Teak Lewis, Carlos Macri, Donald Mark, Victor Pieran, Dom Salinar, Marc Scott.

1966.09 A TIME FOR SINGING

A Musical in Two Acts. Book and lyrics by Gerald Freedman and John Morris. Based on the novel "How Green Was My Valley" by Richard Llewellyn. Music by John Morris. Directed by Gerald Freedman. Choreography by Donald McKayle. Production (settings) designed by Ming Cho Lee. Costumes by Theoni V. Aldredge. Lighting by Jean Rosenthal. Musical direction, Jay Blackton. Orchestrations by Don Walker. Production associate, Hildy Parks. Production supervisor, Jerry Adler. Produced by Alexander H. Cohen in association with Joe Wishy. Opened 21 May 1966 at the Broadway Theatre and closed 25 June 1966 after 41 performances.

CAST (in order of appearance): *David Griffith*: IVOR EMMANUEL. *Paymaster*: Jay Gregory. *Dai Bando*: John Call. *Cyfartha Lewis*: George Mathews. *Gwillym Morgan (Dada)*: LAURENCE NAISMITH. *Davey Morgan*: Gene Rupert. *Ivor Morgan*: Brian Aver. *Ianto Morgan*: George Hearn. *Owen Morgan*: Harry Theyard. *Evan Morgan*: Philip Proctor. *Huw Morgan*: Frank Griso. *Beth Morgan*: TESSIE O'SHEA. *Angharad Morgan*: SHANI WALLIS. *Bronwen Jenkins*: Elizabeth Hubbard. *Mr. Evans*: John Malcolm. *Iestyn Evans*: David O'Brien. *School Teacher*: David Thomas.

Singers: Robert Carle, Ed Ericksen, Jay Gregory, Marian Haraldson, Zona Kennedy, Reid Klein, Henry LeClair, Constance Moffit, Jack Murray, Mari Nettum, Joyce O'Neil, Michael Quinn, Maggie Task, Ann Tell, David Thomas, Maggie Worth. *Dancers*: Bruce Becker, Steven Boockvor, Sandra Brewer, Roger Briant, Sterling Clark, Carolyn Dyer, Mary Ehara, Rodney Griffin, Patty Mount, Mimi Wallace. *Children*: Paul Dwyer, Peter Falzone, Dewey Golkin, Laura Michaels, Janice Notaro.

The action takes place in the memory of David Griffith, flowing freely in time in the Valley, the Town and the Morgan Home in South Wales in 1900.

ACT 1

"Come You Men"
Male Singing Chorus

"How Green Was My Valley"
I. Emmanuel, Chorus

"Old Long John"
Male Singing Chorus

"Here Come Your Men"
Male Singing Chorus

"What a Good Day Is Saturday"
T. O'Shea, L. Naismith, S. Wallis, Brothers, Company

"Peace Come to Every Heart"
Company

"Someone Must Try"
I. Emmanuel

"Oh, How I Adore Your Name"
S. Wallis

"That's What Young Ladies Do"
I. Emmanuel

"When He Looks at Me"
S. Wallis

"Far From Home"
T. O'Shea, S. Wallis, L. Naismith, Brothers

"I Wonder If"
Brothers

"What a Party"
L. Naismith, I. Emmanuel, G. Mathews, J. Call, Brothers

"Let Me Love You"
S. Wallis

"Why Would Anyone Want to Get Married?"
F. Griso, Brothers, T. O'Shea, L. Naismith

"A Time for Singing"
T. O'Shea, Company

ACT 2

"When the Baby Comes"
Company

"I'm Always Wrong"
S. Wallis

"There Is Beautiful You Are"
I. Emmanuel

"Three Ships"
T. O'Shea, E. Hubbard, B. Avery, Company

"Tell Her"
F. Griso, L. Naismith

"There Is Beautiful You Are" (reprise)
I. Emmanuel

"Let Me Love You" (reprise)
S. Wallis, I. Emmanuel

"And the Mountains Sing Back"
I. Emmanuel

"Gone in Sorrow"
Company

"How Green Was My Valley" (reprise)
Company

1966.10 MAME

A Musical in Two Acts, 16 Scenes. Book by Jerome Lawrence and Robert E. Lee. Based on the novel "Auntie Mame" by Patrick Dennis and the play of the same name by Lawrence and Lee. Music and lyrics by Jerry Herman. Directed by Gene Saks. Dances and musical numbers staged by Onna White. Settings by William and Jean Eckart. Costumes by Robert Mackintosh. Lighting by Tharon Musser. Musical direction and vocal arrangements by Don Pippin. Orchestrations by Philip J. Lang. Dance music arranged by Roger Adams. Associate producer, John Bowab. Produced by Robert Fryer, Lawrence Carr, Sylvia and Joseph P. Harris. Opened 24 May 1966 at the Winter Garden, moved 7 October 1969 to the Broadway Theatre, and closed 3 January 1970 after 1508 performances.

[29]Originally produced in New York 3 May 1956 at the Imperial Theatre for 678 performances. For Synopsis of Scenes and Musical Numbers, see original 1956 production.

CAST (in order of appearance): *Patrick Dennis*, age 10: FRANKIE MICHAELS. *Agnes Gooch*: JANE CONNELL. *Vera Charles*: BEATRICE ARTHUR. *Mame Dennis*: ANGELA LANSBURY. *Ralph Devine*: Ronald Young. *Bishop*: Jack Davison. *M. Lindsay Woolsey*: George Coe. *Ito*: Sab Shimono. *Doorman*: Art Matthews. *Elevator Boy*: Stan Page. *Messenger*: Bill Stanton. *Dwight Babcock*: WILLARD WATERMAN. *Art Model*: Jo Tract. *Dance Teacher*: Johanna Douglas. *Leading Man*: Jack Davison. *Stage Manager*: Art Matthews. *Madame Branislowski*: Charlotte Jones. *Gregor*: John Taliaferro. *Beauregard Jackson Pickett Burnside*: CHARLES BRASWELL. *Uncle Jeff*: Clifford Fearl. *Cousin Fan*: Ruth Ramsey. *Sally Cato*: MARGARET HALL. *Mother Burnside*: Charlotte Jones. *Patrick Dennis*, age 19-29: JERRY LANNING. *Junior Babcock*: Tommy Karaty. *Mrs. Upson*: Johanna Douglas. *Mr. Upson*: John C. Becher. *Gloria Upson*: Diana Walker. *Pegeen Ryan*: Diane Coupe. *Peter Dennis*: Michael Maitland.

Mame's Friends: Diana Baffa, Jack Blackton, David Chaney, Pat Cummings, Jack Davison, Hilda Harris, Tommy Karaty, Nicole Karol, Gene Kelton, Nancy Lynch, Art Matthews, Ross Miles, Stan Page, Ruth Ramsey, Betty Rosebrock, Scott Salmon, Bella Shalom, Bill Stanton, John Taliaferro, Jo Tract, Jodi Williams, Kathy Wilson.

Act 1, Scene 1: Somewhere in New York, 1928. *Scene 2*: Mame's Apartment. *Scene 3*: Hallway of Mame's Apartment. *Scene 4*: Mame's Bedroom. *Scene 5*: Mame's Living Room (and all around New York). *Scene 6*: Mame's Apartment. *Scene 7*: Shubert Theatre, New Haven. *Scene 8*: Salon Pour Messieurs. *Scene 9*: Mame's Apartment. *Scene 10*: Peckerwood.

Act 2, Scene 1: Prep School and College (and Singapore). *Scene 2*: Mame's Apartment. *Scene 3*: Mame's Apartment, six months later. *Scene 4*: Upson Farm. *Scene 5*: Mame's Apartment. *Scene 6*: Mame's Apartment, 1946.

ACT 1

Scene 1
"St. Bridget"
F. Michaels, J. Connell

Scene 2
"It's Today"
A. Lansbury, All

Scene 5
"Open a New Window"
A. Lansbury, All

Scene 7
"The Man in the Moon"
B. Arthur, A. Lansbury, All
"My Best Girl"
F. Michaels, A. Lansbury

Scene 9
"We Need a Little Christmas"
A. Lansbury, F. Michaels, J. Connell, S. Shimono, C. Braswell

Scene 10
"The Fox Hunt"
C. Fearl, F. Michaels, R. Ramsey, C. Jones, Cousins
"Mame"
C. Braswell, All

ACT 2

Scene 1
"Mame" (reprise)(The Letter)
F. Michaels, J. Lanning
"My Best Girl" (reprise)
J. Lanning

Scene 2
"Bosom Buddies"
A. Lansbury, B. Arthur

Scene 3
"Gooch's Song"
J. Connell

Scene 4
"That's How Young I Feel"
A. Lansbury, All
"If He Walked into My Life"
A. Lansbury

Scene 5
"It's Today" (reprise)
A. Lansbury, All
"My Best Girl" (reprise)
J. Lanning

Scene 6
"Open a New Window" (reprise)/(Finale)
A. Lansbury, Company

1966.11 WHERE'S CHARLEY?

A Musical Comedy in Two Acts, 9 Scenes[30]. Book by George Abbott. Based on the play "Charley's Aunt" by Brandon Thomas. Music and lyrics by Frank Loesser. Production directed by Christopher Hewett. Choreography by John Sharpe. (Sets uncredited.) Costumes by Frank Thompson. Lighting and additional settings designed by Peggy Clark. Ballet music adapted by Marvin Laird (Orchestrations by Ted Royal, Hans Spialek, Philip J. Lang.) Musical direction by Pembroke Davenport. Produced by the New York City Center Light Opera Company (Jean Dalrymple, Artistic director). Opened 25 May 1966 at the New York City Center and closed 5 June 1966 after 15 performances.

CAST (in order of appearance): *Brassett*: Tom Bate *Professor Fortesque*: Donald Barton. *Jack Chesney*: DAVID SMITH. *Charley Wykeham*: DARRYL HICKMAN. *Kitty Verdun*: KAREN SHEPARD. *Amy Spettigue*: SUSAN WATSON. *Wilkinson*: Emory Bass. *Sir Francis Chesney*: FERDINAND HILT. *Mr. Spettingue*: MORT MARSHALL. *Donna Lucia D'Alvadorez*: ELEANOR STEBER. *Photographer*: Stan Mazin. *Patricia*: Maria Hero. *Reggie*: Austin Colyer. *Photographer's Assistants*: Violetta Landek, Zebra Nevins.

Band Members: Rodd Barry, Dennis Cole, Gordon Cook, Jack Fletcher, Mario Maroze, Doug Spingler. *Dancers*: Rodd Barry, Dennis Cole, Myron Curtis, Richard Denny, Jerry Kent, Don Lawrence, Mario Maroze, Richard Maxon, Stan Mazin, Doug Spingler, Clive Thompson, Cathy Conklin, Mickey Gunnerson, Beth Howland, Violetta Landek, Sara Letton, Sharron Miller, Zebra Nevins, Rande Rayburn, Alice Mary Riley, Skiles Ricketts, Toodie Wittmer. *Singers*: Paul Adams, Austin Colyer, Gordon Cook, Stephen Everett, Jack Fletcher, William James, Konstantion Moskalenko, Hal Norman, Fred Osin, David Wilder, Laverne Burden, Jane Coleman, Renee Gorsey, Maria Hero, Nina Hirschfeld, Miriam Lawrence, Joyce McDonald, Betsy Norden, Mary Ann Rydzeski, Susan Stockwell, Elise Warner.

1966.12 ANNIE GET YOUR GUN

A Revival of the Musical in Two Acts, 8 Scenes[31]. Music and lyrics by Irving Berlin. Book by Herbert and Dorothy Fields. (Book revisions by Dorothy Fields.) Directed by Jack Sydow. Scenery by Paul C. McGuire. Costumes by Frank Thompson. Lighting by Peter Hunt. Dances and production numbers staged by Danny Daniels. Musical director, Franz Alllers. Orchestrations by Robert Russell Bennett. Dance arrangements by Richard De Benedictis. Produced by The Music Theatre of Lincoln Center (Richard Rodgers, President and Producing Director). Opened 31 May 1966 at the New York City Center and closed 9 July 1966 after 47 performances; re-opened 21 September 1966 at the Broadway Theatre and closed 26 November 1966 after 77 additional performances. Total: 124 performances.

CAST (in order of appearance): *Little Boy*: Jeffrey Scott. *Little Girl*: Deanna Melody. *Charlie Davenport*: JERRY ORBACH. *Dolly Tate*: BENAY VENUTA. *Iron Tail*: Brynar Mehl. *Yellow Foot*: Gary Jendell. *Mac* (Property Man): John Dorrin. *Foster Wilson*: Ronn Carroll. *Frank Butler*: BRUCE YARNELL. *Annie Oakley*: ETHEL MERMAN. *Little Jake*, Her Brother: David Manning. *Her Sisters (3)*: *Nellie*: Donna Conforti. *Jessie*: Jeanne Tanzy. *Minnie*: Holly Sherwood. *Col. William F. Cody (Buffalo Bill)*: RUFUS SMITH. *Mrs. Little Horse*: Mary Falconer. *Mrs. Black Tooth*: Jaclynn Villamil. *Mrs. Yellow Foot*: Kuniko Narai. *Indian Boy*: Jeffrey Scott. *Conductor*: Jim Lynn. *Porter*: Beno Foster. *Waiter*: David Forssen. *Major Gordon Lillie*, Pawnee Bill: JACK DABDOUB. *Chief Sitting Bull*: HARRY BELAVER. *The Wild Horse*, Ceremonial Dancer: JAIME ROGERS. *Pawnee's Messenger*: Walt Hunter. *Major Domo*: Ben Laney. *Mr. Schuyler Adams*: Ronn Carroll. *Mrs. Schuyler Adams*: Patricia Hall. *Dr. (Percy) Ferguson*: Marc Rowan. *Mrs. (Percy) Ferguson*: Bobbi Baird. *Mr. T. L. C. Keefer*: Walt Hunter. *Mr. Ernest Henderson*: Grant Spradling. *Mrs. Ernest Henderson*: Lynn Carroll. *Mrs. Sylvia Potter-Porter*: Mary Falconer. *Mr. Clay*: John Dorrin.

Singers: Bobbi Baird, Vicki Belmonte, Chrysten Caroll, Lynn Carroll, Audrey Dearden, Lynn Dovel, Mary Falconer, Patricia Hall, Florence Mercer, Susan Terry, Kenny Adams, Ronn Carroll, John Dorrin, David Forssen, Beno Foster, Walt Hunter, Ben Laney, Jim Lynn, Marc Rowan, Grant Spradling. *Dancers*: Diane Banks, Joanne

---

[30]Originally produced in New York 11 October 1948 at the St. James Theatre for 792 performances. For Synopsis of Scenes and Musical Numbers, see original 1948 production.

[31]First produced in New York 16 May 1946 at the Imperial Theatre for 1147 performances. For this revival, "Why Do You Love I Hope" and "I'd Share It All with You" were dropped. For return engagement detail, see entry in the following season.

DiVito, Rozann Ford, Barbara Hancock, Ruth Lawrence, Kuniko Narai, Eva Marie Sage, Evelyn Taylor, Jaclynn Villamil, Anne Wallace, Bjarne Buchtrup, Tony Catanzaro, Frank Derbas, Ronn Forella, Marcelo Gamboa, Jeremy Ives, Gary Jendell, Daniel Joel, Brynar Mehl, Gene Myers.

Act 1, Scene 1: The Wilson House, a summer hotel on the outskirts of Cincinnati, Ohio. July. *Scene 2*: A Pullman Parlor in an Overland Steam train. Six weeks later. *Scene 3*: The Fair Grounds at Minneapolis, Minnesota. A few days later. *Scene 4*: The Arena of the Big Tent. Later that night.

Act 2, Scene 1: The deck of a cattle boat. Eight months later. *Scene 2*: The ballroom of the Hotel Brevoort, (New York City). The next night. *Scene 3*: Aboard a ferry, en route to Governor's Island. Next morning. *Scene 4*: Governor's Island, near the Fort. Immediately following.

ACT 1

Scene 1

"Colonel Buffalo Bill"
J. Orbach, B. Venuta, Ensemble

"I'm a Bad, Bad Man"
B. Yarnell, Girls

"Doin' What Comes Naturally'
E. Merman, Children, R. Carroll

"The Girl That I Marry"
B. Yarnell

"You Can't Get a Man With a Gun"
E. Merman

"There's No Business Like Show Business"
E. Merman, B. Yarnell, R. Smith, J. Orbach

Scene 2

"They Say It's Wonderful"
E. Merman, B. Yarnell

"Moonshine Lullaby"
E. Merman, Trio, Children

Scene 3

"Wild West Pitch Dance"
J. Rogers, Dancers

"There's No Business Like Show Business" (reprise)
E. Merman

"My Defenses Are Down"
B. Yarnell, Boys

Scene 4

"Wild Horse Ceremonial Dance"
J. Rogers, Braves

"I'm an Indian Too"
E. Merman

"Adoption Dance"
E. Merman, J. Rogers, Braves

"You Can't Get a Man With a Gun" (reprise)
E. Merman

ACT 2

Scene 1

"(I Got) Lost in His Arms"
E. Merman, Singers

Scene 2

"There's No Business Like Show Business" (reprise)
B. Yarnell, B. Venuta, J. Dabdoub, R. Carroll, P. Hall

"I Got the Sun in the Morning"
E. Merman, Company

"Old Fashioned Wedding"[32]
E. Merman, B. Yarnell

"The Girl That I Marry" (reprise)
B. Yarnell

Scene 4

"Anything You Can Do"
E. Merman, B. Yarnell

"There's No Business Like Show Business" (reprise)
Ensemble

Finale: "They Say It's Wonderful" (reprise)
Entire Company

[32]Newly written for this production.

1966–1967 SEASON

Leslie Uggams in HALLELUJAH, BABY!
Billy Rose Theatre Collection, New York Public Library for the Performing Arts

1966–1967 SEASON

1966.13 GUYS AND DOLLS

A Revival of the Musical Fable (Comedy) in Two Acts, 17 Scenes[1]. Book by Jo Swerling and Abe Burrows. Based on a story and characters by Damon Runyon. Music and lyrics by Frank Loesser. Production directed by Gus Schirmer. Choreography by Ralph Beaumont. Adaptation of Jo Mielziner's original designs by Peter Wolf. Costumes by Frank Thompson. (Orchestral arrangements by George Bassman and Ted Royal.) Musical director, Irving Actman. Associate conductor, Abba Bogin. Produced by the New York City Center Light Opera Company (Jean Dalrymple, Director). Opened 8 June 1966 at the New York City Center and closed 26 June 1966 after 23 performances.

CAST (in order of appearance): *Nicely-Nicely Johnson*: DALE MALONE. *Benny Southstreet*: JOE ROSS. *Rusty Charlie*: Ed Becker. *Sarah Brown*: BARBARA MEISTER. *Arvide Abernathy*: CLARENCE NORDSTROM. *Mission Band*: Jeanne Schlegel, Clarence Nordstrom, Carl Nicholas, Susan Cogan, Jeanne Frey. *Harry the Horse*: TOM PEDI. *Lieut. Brannigan*: FRANK CAMPANELLA. *Nathan Detroit*: JAN MURRAY. *Angie the Ox*: Roger Brown. *Miss Adelaide*: VIVIAN BLAINE. *Sky Masterson*: HUGH O'BRIAN. *Mimi*: Rita O'Connor. *General Matilda B. Cartwright*: CLAIRE WARING. *Big Jule*: B. S. PULLY. *Drunk*: Eddie Phillips. *Waiter*: Marvin Goodis.

Dancers: Diane Arnold, Nephele Buecher, Marilyn D'Honau, Judy Dunford, Mercedes Ellington, Shelly Frankel, Altovise Gore, Rose Holotik, Joan Lindsay, Rita O'Connor, Melissa Stoneburn, Maria Strattin, Gerard Brentte, Frank Coppola, Vito Durante, Philip Filiato, Mark Holliday, Robert La Crosse, Teak Lewis, Carlos Macri, Mitchell Nutick, Paul Owsley, Dom Salinaro, Marc Scott. *Singers*: Susan Cogan, Edward Becker, Roger Brown, Joe Bellomo, Reese Burns, Richard Ensslen, Paul Flores, Marvin Goodis, Joseph Gustern, Mark Howard, Doug Hunt, Robert Maxwell, Sean Walsh.

1966.14 SHOWBOAT

A Revival of the Musical Play in Two Acts, 14 Scenes[2]. Music by Jerome Kern. Book and lyrics by Oscar Hammerstein II. Based on the novel of the same name by Edna Ferber. Directed by Lawrence Kasha. Choreography by Ronald [Ron] Field. Scenic production by Oliver Smith. Costumes by Stanley Simmons. Lighting by Jean Rosenthal. Musical director, Franz Allers. Associate conductor, William [Bill] Brohn. Dance arrangements by Richard De Benedictis. New orchestrations by Robert Russell Bennett. Produced by the Music Theater of Lincoln Center (Richard Rodgers, Producing Director). Opened 19 July 1966 at the New York State Theatre and closed 10 September 1966 after 64 performances.

CAST (in order of their appearance): *Rubberface*: Bob La Crosse. *Captain Andy*: DAVID WAYNE. *Windy (McLain)*: David Thomas. *Joe*: WILLIAM WARFIELD. *Queenie*: ROSETTA LeNOIRE. *Ellie*: ALLYN ANN McLERIE. *Frank*: EDDIE PHILLIPS. *Parthy Ann Hawkes*: MARGARET HAMILTON. *Pete*: Bob Monroe. *Julie*: CONSTANCE TOWERS. *Steve*: WILLIAM TRAYLOR. *Gaylord Ravenal*: STEPHEN DOUGLASS. *(Sheriff Ike) Vallon*: Barton Stone. *Magnolia*: BARBARA COOK. *Backwoodsman*: Neil McNelis. *Jeb*: Jess Green. *First Barker*: George McWhorter. *Strong Woman*: D. Spingler. *Second Barker*: Garrett Morris. *Congress of Beauties*: Emilina Escariz, Rita O'Connor, Nancy Van Rijn, Carol Hanzel. *Third Barker*: Neil McNelis. *Fatima*: Sally Neil. *Landlady*: Helen Noyes. *Ethel*: Joyce McDonald. *Sister*: Frances Haywood. *Mother Superior*: Mary Manchester. *Kim*: Maureen McNabb. *Man With Guitar*: Paul Adams. *Doorman at Trocadero*: Edward Taylor. *Drunk*: John Roberson. *Lottie*: Martha Danielle. *Dolly*: Trudy Wallace. *Sally*: Frances Buffalino. *Maisie*: Judith Keller. *A Girl*: Barbara Lindner. *A Man*: Dale Westerman. *Old Lady on Levee*: Helen Noyes.

Female Dancers: Emilina Escariz, Lois Etelman, Carol Hanzel, Vivian Houston, Eileen Lawlor, Sally Neal, Rita O'Connor, Carol Perea, Nancy Van Rijn. *Male Dancers*: Bryant Baker, Allan Byrns, Peter DeNicola, Ronald Dennis, Bob Hall, Bob LaCrosse, Donald Mark, Robert St. John, Doug Spingler. *Female Singers*: Phyllis Bash, Frances Buffalino, Jane Coleman, Martha Danielle, Dolores Godwin, Frances Haywood, Ernestine Jackson, Judith Keller, Mary Manchester, Barbara Lindner, Joyce McDonald, Estella Munson, Geraldine Overstreet, Lorice Stevens, Trudy Wallace. *Male Singers*: Paul Adams, Donald Coleman, Ray Duval, Scott Gibson, Jess Green, Vincent Henry, Richard Kahn, James Kelley, James Kennon-Wilson, George McWhorter, Laried Montgomery, Garrett Morris, Garwood Perkisn, John Roberson, Alan Sanderson, Richard Sparks, Edward Taylor, Clyde Walker, Dale Westerman, Joe Williams, Lee Winston. *Children*: Paul Dwyer, Michael Grady, Lisa Huggins, Jeanne Ladomirak, William Sims.

Act 1, Scene 1: The Levee on the Natchez on the Mississippi, in the 1880s. *Scene 2*: Kitchen pantry of the *Cotton Blossom*. Five minutes later. *Scene 3*: Auditorium and Stage of the *Cotton Blossom*. One hour later. *Scene 4*: Box office, on foredeck. Three weeks later. *Scene 5*: Auditorium and stage during the Third Act of "The Parson's Bride," that night. *Scene 6*: Stage door. *Scene 7*: The top deck. Later that night. *Scene 8*: The Levee at Greenville. Next morning.

Act 2, Scene 1: The Midway Plaisance, Chicago World's Fair, 1893. *Scene 2*: A room on Ontario Street, 1904. *Scene 3*: Trocadero Music Hall. A few days later. *Scene 4*: St. Agatha's Convent. About the same time. *Scene 5*: Trocadero Music Hall. Just before midnight, New Year's Eve, 1905. *Scene 6*: The *Cotton Blossom* at the Greenville levee, 1927.

ACT 1[3]

"Cotton Blossom"
Entire Ensemble
"Show Boat Ballyhoo"
D. Wayne, Showboat Troupe and Ensemble
"Only Make Believe"
S. Douglass, B. Cook
"Ol' Man River"
W. Warfield, Stevedores
"Can't Help Lovin' Dat Man"
C. Towers, R. LeNoire, B. Cook, W. Warfield, Quartette
"Queenie's Ballyhoo"
R. Le Noire, D. Wayne, Ensemble
"Life Upon the Wicked Stage"
A. A. McLerie, Ensemble
"You Are Love"
B. Cook, S. Douglass
Cakewalk and Finale
Entire Company

ACT 2

"At the Fair"
Sightseers, Barkers, Ushers
"Why Do I Love You?"
B. Cook, S. Douglass, Ensemble
"Bill"
C. Towers
(*Lyrics by* P. G. Wodehouse.)
"Can't Help Lovin' Dat Man" (reprise)
B. Cook
Service and Scene Music-St. Agnes Convent
"Only Make Believe" (reprise)
S. Douglass
"Goodbye, My Lady Love"—Cakewalk
E. Phillips, A. A. McLerie
"After the Ball"
B. Cook
"You Are Love" (reprise)
S. Douglass
"Ol' Man River" (reprise)
W. Warfield, Company
A. A. McLerie, E. Phillips
Finale (Act 2)
Entire Company

[1]First presented in New York 24 November 1950 at the 46th Street Theatre for 1200 performances. For Synopsis of Scenes and Musical Numbers, see original 1950 production. Act 1, Scene 8, now set in San Juan, Puerto Rico, and the accompanying dance now named "San Juan."

[2]First presented December 27, 1927 at the Ziegfeld Theatre for 572 performances.

[3]Added to program for subsequent tour:
"I Might Fall Back on You" (Act 1 before "Queenie's Ballyhoo")

1966.15 A HAND IS ON THE GATE

A Evening (Revue) of Poetry and Folk Music by American Negroes in Two Acts[4]. Arranged and directed by Roscoe Lee Browne. Music arranged by Bill Lee and Stuart Scharf. Lighting consultant, Jules Fisher. Associate producer, Stephen Aaron. Produced by Ivor David Balding for The Establishment Theatre Company, Inc. (Ivor David Balding, Peter Cook, Joseph E. Levine, with Rita Fredericks). Opened 21 September 1966 at the Longacre Theatre and closed 8 October 1966 after 20 performances.

CAST: LEON BIBB, ROSCOE LEE BROWNE, GLORIA FOSTER, MOSES GUNN, ELLEN HOLLY, JAMES EARL JONES, JOSEPHINE PREMICE, CICELY TYSON. *Musicians*: Stuart Scharf (guitar), Bill Lee (bass), Floyd Williams (percussionist), Sheldon Powell (flutist).

ACT 1

On Liberty and Slavery
(*by* George Moses Horton)
J. E. Jones

The Negro Speaks of Rivers
(*by* Langston Hughes)
E. Holly

Frederick Douglass
(*by* Robert Hayden)
M. Gunn

We Wear the Mask
(*by* Paul Laurence Dunbar)
C. Tyson

Southern Mansion
(*by* Arna Bontemps)
L. Bibb

from The Dark Symphony: Lento Grave
(*by* Melvin Tolson)
J. Premice

from O Black and Unknown Bards
(*by* James Weldon Johnson)
J. E. Jones, G. Foster, R. L. Browne

"'Buked and Scorned" (Traditional)
L. Bibb

From the Dark Tower
(*by* Countee Cullen)
J. E. Jones

An Old Woman Remembers
(*by* Sterling Brown)
G. Foster

My City
(*by* James Weldon Johnson)
M. Gunn

Sonnet to a Negro in Harlem
(*by* Helene Johnson)
J. Premice

Precocious Curiosity
(*by* Gwendolyn Brooks)
C. Tyson

Mother to Son
(*by* Langston Hughes)
E. Holly

Sence You Went Away
(*by* James Weldon Johnson)
G. Foster

Miss Meleree
(*by* John Holloway)
L. Bibb

When Malindy Sings
(*by* Paul Laurence Dunbar)
C. Tyson

"A Negro Love Song"
(*by* Paul Laurence Dunbar)
R. L. Browne

"Jane Jane" (A Children's Playgame)(Traditional)
Ensemble

[4]First presented in New York Off-Broadway 15 August 1966 at the New York Shakespeare Festival in Central Park for 1 performance.

Ol' Lem
(*by* Sterling Brown)
J. E. Jones, M. Gunn

Runagate Runagate
(*by* Robert Hayden)
G. Foster, J. E. Jones, M. Gunn

Letter from the South
(*by* Robert Hayden)
R. L. Browne

"'Buked and Scorned " (reprise)
L. Bibb

On Neglect
(*by* Roscoe Lee Browne)
E. Holly

After Winter
(*by* Sterling Brown)
M. Gunn

"All Hid" (A Children's Playgame) (Traditional)
Ensemble

"Little Boy, Little Boy" (Traditional)
J. Premice, L. Bibb

For a Lady I Know
(*by* Countee Cullen)
C. Tyson

No Images
(*by* Waring Cuney)
J. E. Jones

Why Try
(*by* Ted Joans)
R. E. Browne

Robert Whitmore
(*by* Frank Marshall Davis)
E. Holly

Epigram
(*by* Armand Lanusse)
J. Premice

Conception
(*by* Waring Cuney)
C. Tyson

Preface to a 20-Volume Suicide Note
(*by* LeRoi Jones)
L. Bibb

"Careless Love"
(*by* W. C. Handy)
J. Premice

Appoggiatura
(*by* Donald Hayes)
M. Gunn

Witch Doctor
(*by* Robert Hayden)
R. L. Browne

You Are a Part of Me
(*by* Frank Yerby)
G. Foster

At Early Morn
(*by* Binga Dismond)
J. E. Jones

"Dink's Song" (Traditional)
J. Premice

ACT 2

Notes for a Movie Script
(*by* M. Carl Holman)
J. E. Jones

"The Ballad of Rudolph Reed"
(*by* Gwendolyn Brooks)
C. Tyson

Four Questions Addressed to His Excellency, The Prime Minister
(*by* James Vaughn)
R. L. Browne

La Vie C'est La Vie
(*by* Jessie Fauset)
E. Holly

Journey to a Parallel
(*by* Bruce Wright)
M. Gunn
The Elevator Man Adheres to His Form
(*by* Margaret Danner)
J. Premice
Ontogeny Recapitulates
(*by* Roscoe Lee Browne)
J. E. Jones
To a Young Poet
(*by* Myron O'Higgins)
G. Foster
Counterpoint
(*by* Owen Dodson)
L. Bibb
. . . Meanwhile a Mississippi Mother Burns Bacon and the Last Quatrain of the Ballad of Emmett Till
(*by* Gwendolyn Brooks)
E. Holly, R. L. Browne
Bound No'th Blues
(*by* Langston Hughes)
G. Foster
Ma Rainey
(*by* Sterling Brown)
J. Premice
Get Up, Blues
(*by* James Emanuel)
C. Tyson
The Rebel
(*by* Mari Evans)
C. Tyson
"Harlem Sweeties"
(*by* Langston Hughes)
L. Bibb, M. Gunn, J. E. Jones, R. L. Browne
from A Street in Bronzeville: Kitchenette
(*by* Gwendolyn Brooks)
J. Premice
Rag Doll and Summer Birds
(*by* Owen Dodson)
E. Holly
Between the World and Me
(*by* Richard Wright)
J. E. Jones
My Angel
(by Jonathan Brooks)
L. Bibb
Look at That Gal
(*by* Julian Bond)
R. L. Browne
"Glory, Glory"
(Traditional)
Ensemble
The Progress
(*by* Gwendolyn Brooks)
M. Gunn
The End of Man Is His Beauty
(*by* LeRoi Jones)
E. Holly
A Moment Please
(*by* Samuel Allen)
J. E. Jones, R. L. Browne
The Distant Drum
(*by* Calvin Hernton)
R. L. Browne
We Have Been Believers
(*by* Margaret Walker)
G. Foster
"Oh Shenandoah"
(Traditional)
L. Bibb
When in Rome
(*by* Mari Evans)
C. Tyson
My Lord, What a Morning
(*by* Waring Cuney)
G. Foster
American Gothic: To Snatch
(*by* Samuel Allen)
J. E. Jones
The Preacher Ruminates
(*by* Gwendolyn Brooks)
J. Premice
Personal
(*by* Gwendolyn Brooks)
R. L. Browne
Alien
(*by* Donald Hayes)
M. Gunn
The Crazy Woman
(*by* Gwendolyn Brooks)
C. Tyson
"If the Birds (Song)"
(*by* Roscoe Lee Browne)
R. L. Browne
"Rocks and Gravel" (Collected by Allan Lomax, arr. by Leon Bibb)
L. Bibb

1966.16 ANNIE GET YOUR GUN

A Return Engagement of the Revival of the Musical in Two Acts, 8 Scenes[5]. Music and lyrics by Irving Berlin. Book by Herbert and Dorothy Fields. (Book revisions by Dorothy Fields.) Directed by Jack Sydow. Scenery by Paul C. McGuire. Costumes by Frank Thompson. Lighting by Peter Hunt. Dances and production numbers staged by Danny Daniels. Musical director, Jonathan Anderson. Orchestrations by Robert Russell Bennett. Dance arrangements by Richard DeBenedictis. Produced by the Music Theatre of Lincoln Center (Richard Rodgers, President and Producing Director). Opened 21 September 1966 at the Broadway Theatre and closed 26 November 1966 after 77 additional performances. Total including first engagement: 124 performances.

CAST (in order of appearance): *Little Boy*: Jeffrey Scott. *Little Girl*: Deanna Melody. *Charlie Davenport*: JIM LYNN. *Dolly Tate*: BENAY VENUTA. *Iron Tail*: Brynar Mehl. *Yellow Foot*: Gary Jendell. *Mac*, Property Man: John Dorrin. *Foster Wilson*: Ronn Carroll. *Frank Butler*: BRUCE YARNELL. *Annie Oakley*: ETHEL MERMAN. *Little Jake*, Her Brother: David Manning. *Her Sisters (3)*: *Nellie*: Donna Conforti. *Jessie*: Jeanne Tanzy. *Minnie*: Holly Sherwood. *Col. William F. Cody (Buffalo Bill)*: RUFUS SMITH. *Mrs. Little Horse*: Mary Falconer. *Mrs. Black Tooth*: Eva Marie Sage. *Mrs. Yellow Foot*: Kuniko Narai. *Indian Boy*: Jeffrey Scott. *Conductor*: Ben Laney. *Porter*: Beno Foster. *Waiter*: David Forssen. *Major Gordon Lillie* (Pawnee Bill): JACK DABDOUB. *Chief Sitting Bull*: HARRY BELAVER. *The Wild Horse* (Ceremonial Dancer): TONY CATANZARO. *Pawnee's Messenger*: Walt Hunter. *Major Domo*: Ben Laney. *Mr. Schuyler Adams*: Ronn Carroll. *Mrs. Schuyler Adams*: Patricia Hall. *Dr. (Percy) Ferguson*: Marc Rowan. *Mrs. (Percy) Ferguson*: Bobbi Baird. *Mr. T. L. C. Keefer*: Walt Hunter. *Mr. Ernest Henderson*: Grant Spradling. *Mrs. Ernest Henderson*: Lynn Carroll. *Mrs. Sylvia Potter-Porter*: Mary Falconer. *Mr. Clay*: John Dorrin. *The Shy Girl*: Diana Banks.

Singers: Bobbi Baird, Chrysten Caroll, Lynn Carroll, Audrey Dearden, Lynn Dovel, Mary Falconer, Patricia Hall, Florence Mercer, Susan Terry, Kenny Adams, Ronn Carroll, John Dorrin, David Forssen, Beno Foster, Walt Hunter, Ben Laney, Jim Lynn, Marc Rowan, Grant Spradling. *Dancers*: Diane Banks, Joanne DiVito, Carolyn Dyer, Rozann Ford, Barbara Hancock, Ruth Lawrence, Kuniko Narai, Eva Marie Sage, Evelyn Taylor, Bjarne Buchtrup, Tony Catanzaro, Frank Derbas, Ronn Forella, Marcelo Gamboa, Jeremy Ives, Gary Jendell, Daniel Joel, Brynar Mehl, Gene Myers.

1966.17 THE CONSUL

A Revival of the Opera (Musical Drama) in Three Acts, 6 Scenes[6]. Libretto and music by Gian-Carlo Menotti. Conductor, Charles Wilson. Settings by Horace Armistead. Staged by Gian-Carlo Menotti. Produced by the New

[5]First produced in New York 16 May 1946 at the Imperial Theatre for 1147 performances. This revival previously presented 31 May 1966 at the New York State Theatre for 47 performances. For Synopsis of Scenes and Musical Numbers, see 1966 revival from previous season.
[6]Originally produced in New York 15 March 1950 at the Ethel Barrymore Theatre for 269 performances. For Synopsis of Scenes and Musical Numbers, see original 1950 production.

York City Opera. Opened 6 October 1966 at the New York State Theatre and closed 30 October 1966 after 2 performances in repertory.

CAST: (in order of appearance): *John Sorel*: DAVID CLATWORTHY *Magda Sorel*: PATRICIA NEWAY. *The Mother*: EVELYN SACHS. *Secret Police Agent*: JOSEPH FAIR. *First Plainclothesman*: Philip Erickson. *Second Plainclothesman*: Richard Park. *The Secretary*: BEVERLY EVANS. *Mr. Kofner*: DAVID SMITH. *The Foreign Woman*: JULIA MIGENES. *Anna Gomez*: LaVergne Monette. *Vera Boronel*: Charlotte Povia. *Nika Magadoff* (The Magician): GENE BULLARD. *Assan*: Jack Bittner. *Voice on the Record*: Mabel Mercer.

1966.18 THE APPLE TREE

A Musical in Three Acts. (3 One Act Musicals.) Book by Jerry Bock and Sheldon Harnick. Based on stories by Mark Twain, Frank R. Stockton and Jules Feiffer. Additional book material by Jerome Coopersmith. Music by Jerry Bock. Lyrics by Sheldon Harnick. Entire production directed by Mike Nichols. Additional musical staging by Herbert Ross. Choreography by Lee Theodore. Production (Settings) and costume design by Tony Walton. Lighting by Jean Rosenthal. Orchestrations by Eddie Sauter. Musical direction and vocal arrangements by Elliot Lawrence. Animation film sequence by Richard Williams. Produced by Stuart Ostrow. Opened 18 October 1966 at the Sam S. Shubert Theatre and closed 25 November 1967 after 463 performances.

ACT 1: "The Diary of Adam and Eve"

Based on the short story "The Diary of Adam and Eve" by Mark Twain. The action takes place on Saturday, 1 June in Eden.

CAST: *Adam*: ALAN ALDA. *Eve*: BARBARA HARRIS. *Snake*: LARRY BLYDEN.

MUSICAL NUMBERS

"Here in Eden"
B. Harris

"Feelings"
B. Harris

"Eve"
A. Alda

"Friends"
B. Harris

"The Apple Tree" (Forbidden Fruit)
L. Blyden

"Beautiful, Beautiful World"
A. Alda

"It's a Fish"
A. Alda

"Go to Sleep, Whatever You Are"
B. Harris

"What Makes Me Love Him"
B. Harris

ACT 2: "The Lady or the Tiger?"

Based on the short story "The Lady or the Tiger?" by Frank R. Stockton. The action takes place a long time ago in a semi-barbaric kingdom.

CAST: *Balladeer*: LARRY BLYDEN. *King Arik*: Marc Jordan. *Princess Barbara*: BARBARA HARRIS. *Prisoner*: Jay Norman. *Prisoner's Bride*: Jaclynn Villamil. *Nadjira*: Carmen Alvarez. *Captain Sanjar*: ALAN ALDA. *Guard*: Robert Klein. *King Arik's Court*: Jackie Cronin, Barbara Lang, Mary Louise, Michael Davis, Neil F. Jones.

MUSICAL NUMBERS

"I'll Tell You a Truth"
L. Blyden

"Make Way"
King's Court, M. Jordan

"Forbidden Love" (In Gaul)
B. Harris, A. Alda

"The Apple Tree" (reprise)
L. Blyden

"I've Got What You Want"
B. Harris

"Tiger, Tiger"
B. Harris

"Make Way" (reprise)
King's Court

"Which Door?"
A. Alda, B. Harris, M. Jordan, King's Court

"I'll Tell You a Truth" (reprise)
L. Blyden

ACT 3: "Passionella"

Based on the novella "Passionella" by Jules Feiffer. The action takes place now and here.

CAST: *Narrator*: LARRY BLYDEN. *Ella and Passionella*: BARBARA HARRIS. *Mr. Fallible*: Robert Klein. *Producer*: Marc Jordan. *Flip, the Prince, Charming*: ALAN ALDA. *Subways Riders, El Morocco Patrons, Fans, Flip's Following Movie Set Crew, etc.*: Carmen Alvarez, Jackie Cronin, Michael Davis, Neil F. Jones, Marc Jordan, Robert Klein, Barbara Lang, Mary Louise, Jay Norman, Jaclynn Villamil.

MUSICAL NUMBERS[7]

"Oh, To Be a Movie Star"
B. Harris

"Gorgeous"
B. Harris

"(Who, Who, Who, Who) Who Is She?"
The Company

"Wealth"
B. Harris

"You Are Not Real"
A. Alda, Company

"George L."
B. Harris, A. Alda

1966.19 THE THREEPENNY OPERA

The Stockholm Marionette Theatre of Fantasy Production of the Musical Play in Two Acts[8]. Text and lyrics by Bert Brecht. Music by Kurt Weill. English adaptation by Marc Blitzstein. Directed by Michael Meschke. Puppets, masques and settings by Franciszka Themerson. Lighting design by Jules Fisher. Choreography by Holger Rosenquist. Produced by Jay K. Hoffman. Opened 27 October 1966 at the Billy Rose Theatre and closed 6 November 1966 after 13 performances.

CAST (in order of *character*, puppet player, spoken voice, singing voice): *A Street Singer, Filch*: Arne Hogsander, Hakan Serner, Gerald Price. *Mr. J. J. Peachum*: Ulf Hakan Jansson, Ingvar Kjellson, Martin Wolfson. *Mrs. Peachum*: Zanza Lidums, Ulla Sjoblom, Charlotte Rae. *Polly Peachum*: Ellika Linden, Helena Brodin, Jo Sullivan. *Macheath (Mack the Knife)*: Per Nielsen, Goran Graffman, Scott Merrill. *Jenny*: Ellika Linden, Ulla Sjoblom, Lotte Lenya. *Tiger Brown*, Commissioner of Police: Arne Hogsander, Jan Blomberg, George Tyne. *Lucy Brown*: Lydia de Lind van Wijngaarden, Meta Velander, Beatrice Arthur. *Mack's Gang (Matt, Jake, Boba, Walt)*: Jan Blomberg/Heinz Spira/Folke Tragardh/Michael Meschke. *Reverend Kimball, Constable Smith, Whores, Beggars, A Crowd, A Horse*: The Company. (*Additional Voices on Recording*: John Astin, Joseph Beruh, Bernard Bogin, Paul Dooley, William Duell.)

MUSICAL NUMBERS (from recording[9])

Prologue
G. Price

"The Ballad of Mack the Knife"
G. Price

"Morning Anthem"
M. Wolfson

"Instead-Of Song"
M. Wolfson, C. Rae

"Army Song"
S. Merrill, G. Tyne, P. Astin, J. Beruh, B. Bogin, P. Dooley

---

[7]Added shortly after opening:
"I Know" (Act 3 before "Wealth")
B. Harris, Company

[8]The performance was accompanied by the MGM recording of the 1954 Theatre de Lys production for musical numbers. This version previously staged in New York with live actors Off-Broadway 10 March 1954 at the Theatre de Lys for 96 performances; returned 30 September 1955 to the Theater de Lys for an additional 2611 performances.

[9]Reviewers remarked that some musical numbers were truncated, edited or dropped.

"Wedding Song"
J. Astin, J. Beruh, B. Bogin, P. Dooley
"Love Song"
S. Merrill, J. Sullivan
"Ballad of Dependency"
C. Rae
First Threepenny Finale: "The World Is Mean"
J. Sullivan, M. Wolfson, C. Rae
Melodrama and "Polly's Song"
S. Merrill, J. Sullivan
"Pirate Jenny"
L. Lenya
"Tango-Ballad"
L. Lenya, S. Merrill
"Ballad of the Easy Life"
S. Merrill
"Barbara Song"
B. Arthur
"Jealousy Duet"
J. Sullivan, B. Arthur
Second Threepenny Finale: "How to Survive"
S. Merrill, C. Rae, Ensemble
"Useless Song"
M. Wolfson
"Solomon Song"
L. Lenya
"Call from the Grave"
S. Merrill
"Death Message"
S. Merrill
Third Threepenny Finale: "The Mounted Messenger"
W. Duell, Ensemble

1966.20 GILBERT BECAUD ON BROADWAY

A One-Man Show in Two Acts. All music composed by Gilbert Becaud. Scenery and lighting by Ralph Alswang. Musical director, Raymond Bernard. Production coordinator, Jean Silly. Produced by Norman Twain. Opened 31 October 1966 at the Longacre Theatre and closed 20 November 1966 after 19 performances.

CAST: GILBERT BECAUD.

ACT 1
"Je t'attends"
"Viens dans la lumière"
"Les jours meilleurs"
"C'était mon copain"
"Age tendre et têtes de bois"
"Le bateau blanc"
"Rosy and John"
"Forever"
"Quand il est mort le poete"
"T'es venu de loin"
"Le pianiste de varsovie"
"La corrida"

ACT 2
"Alors raconte"
"Mon arbre"
"Mademoiselle Lise"
"Sand and Sea"
"L'oiseau de toutes les couleurs"
"The Other Tree"
"L'orange"
"Nathalie"
"Le jour ou la pluie viendra"
"Et maintenant"
"La ballade des baladins"

1966.21 LET'S SING YIDDISH

A Musical Show in Two Acts, in Yiddish. Based on Yiddish folklore, humor and art songs by Itzik Manger, Mordecai Gebirtig, Moris Rosenfeld, M. Nudelman, and Wolf Younin. Directed by Mina Bern. Assistant director and choreographer, Felix Fibich. Music arranged and conducted by Renee Solomon. Literary supervision by Wolf Younin. Production supervisor, Bernard Sauer. "Once Upon a Shtetl" envisioned by Sylvia Younin and Naomi Hoffman. Produced by Ben Bonus. Opened 9 November 1966 at the Brooks Atkinson Theatre and closed 29 January 1967 after 107 performances.

CAST (in order of appearance): *Girl*: SUSAN WALTERS. *Shadchen*: MAX BOZYK. *Neighbor*: ROSE BOZYK. *Minstrel*: MINA BERN. *Organ Grinder*: SMULIK GOLDSTEIN. *Drummer*: BERNARD SAUER. *Yosi-Ber*: BEN BONUS. *Dancers*: Donna Shadden, James May, Martha Pollak, Tamara Woshak, Tony Masullo, Dan Taylor. *Shaindele*: SUSAN WALTERS. *Mother*: ROSE BOZYK. *Boarders (3)*: *Baile*: MINA BERN. *Berl*: MAX BOZYK. *Actor*: BEN BONUS.

Act 1: A European shtetl (little town) before the two World Wars.

Act 2: In America.

ACT 1: "Once Upon a Shtetl"
Shadchen Dance and Wedding Dance
Dance Ensemble
Let's Sing Yiddish (Hassidic Melodies)
B. Bonus, Entire Ensemble
("Amul in a Shtetl;" "Oifn Gonickle;" "Hoifzinger;" "Yussel Baer;" "Odesser Motiven;" "Shaindeleh;" "Nigun.")

ACT 2
"Castle Garden" (Leben Zul Colombus)
S. Walters, B. Sauer, M. Bern, S. Goldstein
"Life in the Shop" (Machinen)
B. Bonus, F. Dancers, M. Bern, S. Walters, B. Sauer, S. Goldstein, H. Rosen
"On the Subway" (Klain Yingeleh)
M. Bozyk, R. Bozyk
"Encounter in the Park"
M. Bozyk, R. Bozyk
"Wishful Thinking" (Shnyderisher Gezong)
M. Bern, B. Bonus
"American in Israel"
M. Bern, B. Sauer, Entire Ensemble
"Let's Sing Yiddish" (Lo'Mir Zingen Yiddish)
B. Bonus, Entire Ensemble
(Ami Gilad, accordianist)

1966.22 THE PIRATES OF PENZANCE, or The Slave of Duty

A Revival of the Comic Opera in Two Acts[10]. Libretto by William S. Gilbert. Music by Arthur Sullivan. Settings designed by Peter Goffin. Director of productions, Herbert Newby. Musical director, Isidore Godfrey. Associate conductor and chorus master, James Walker. Produced by the D'Oyly Carte Opera Trust, Ltd. under the personal supervision of Bridget D'Oyly Carte and under the management of Sol Hurok. Opened 15 November 1966 at the New York City Center and closed 11 December 1966 after 7 performances in repertory.[11]

CAST: *Major General Stanley*: JOHN REED. *The Pirate King*: DONALD ADAMS. *Samuel*, his Lieutenant: Anthony Raffell. *Frederic*, the Pirate Apprentice: PHILIP POTTER. *Sergeant of Police*: GEORGE COOK. *Mabel, Edith Kate, Isabel*, General Stanley's Daughters: VALERIE MASTERSON, PEGGY ANN JONES, PAULINE WALES, Jennifer Marks. *Ruth*, Pirate Maid-of-all-work: CHRISTENE PALMER.

Chorus of Pirates, Police and General Stanley's Daughters: Glyn Adams, John Banks, George Cook, Neville Grave, John Hugill, Thomas Lawlor, Peter Lodwick, Gordon Mackenzie, Ralph Mason, Alfred Oldridge, Clifford Parkes, Anthony Raffell, David Rayson, John Webley, Howard Williamson, Adrienne de Winters, Katherine Dyson,

[10]First presented in New York 31 December 1879 at the Fifth Avenue Theatre for a total of 91 performances in two engagements. For Synopsis of Scenes and Musical Numbers, see original 1879 production.
[11]Costumes uncredited.

Mercia Glossop, Abby Hadfield, Beti Lloyd-Jones, Susan Maisey, Jennifer Marks, Marian Martin, Norma Millar, Alison Parker, Abigail Ryan, Vera Ryan, Anne Sessions, Anna Vincent, Pauline Wales.

THE MIKADO, or The Town of Titipu

1966.23

A Revival of the Comic Opera in Two Acts[12]. Libretto by William S. Gilbert. Music by Arthur Sullivan. Production directed by Anthony Besch. Costumes designed by Charles Ricketts; Nanki-Poo Act 1 Costume designed by Disley Jones. Settings designed by Peter Goffin. Director of productions, Herbert Newby. Musical director, Isidore Godfrey. Associate conductor and chorus master, James Walker. Produced by the D'Oyly Carte Opera Trust, Ltd. under the personal supervision of Bridget D'Oyly Carte and under the management of Sol Hurok. Opened 17 November 1966 at the New York City Center and closed 7 December 1966 after 9 performances in repertory.

CAST: *The Mikado of Japan*: DONALD ADAMS. *Nanki-Poo*, his son, disguised as a wandering minstrel in love with Yum-Yum: PHILIP POTTER. *Ko-Ko*, Lord High Executioner of Titipu: JOHN REED. *Pooh-Bah*, Lord High Everything Else: KENNETH SANDFORD. *Pish-Tush, Go-To*, Noble Lords: Thomas Lawlor, George Cook. *Yum-Yum, Pitti-Sing, Peep-Bo*, three sisters, wards of Ko-Ko: VALERIE MASTERSON, PEGGY ANN JONES, PAULINE WALES. *Katisha*: CHRISTENE PALMER. *Chorus of School Girls, Nobles, Guards and Coolies*: same as THE PIRATES OF PENZANCE above.

CABARET

1966.24

A Musical in Two Acts, 19 Scenes. Book by Joe Masteroff. Based on the play ("I Am a Camera") by John Van Druten and stories ("The Berlin Stories") by Christopher Isherwood. Music by John Kander. Lyrics by Fred Ebb. Directed by Harold Prince. Dances and cabaret numbers by Ronald [Ron] Field. Scenery by Boris Aronson. Costumes by Patricia Zipprodt. Lighting by Boris Aronson. Musical direction by Harold Hastings. Orchestrations by Don Walker. Dance arrangements by David Baker. Produced by Harold Prince in association with Ruth Mitchell. Opened 20 November 1966 at the Broadhurst Theatre, moved 7 March 1967 to the Imperial Theatre, moved 7 October 1968 to the Broadway Theatre, and closed 6 September 1969 after 1166 performances.

CAST (in order of appearance): *Master of Ceremonies*: JOEL GREY. *Clifford Bradshaw*: BERT CONVY. *Ernst Ludwig*: EDWARD WINTER. *Custom Official*: Howard Kahl. *Fraulein Schneider*: LOTTE LENYA. *Herr Schultz*: JACK GILFORD. *Fraulein Kost*: PEG MURRAY. *Telephone Girl*: Tresha Kelly. *Kit Kat Club Kittens*: Maryann Burns, Janice Mink, Nancy Powers, Viola Smith. *Maitre D'*: Frank Bouley. *Max*: John Herbert. *Bartender*: Ray Baron. *Sally Bowles*: JILL HAWORTH. *Two Ladies*: Mary Ehara, Rita O'Connor. *German Sailors*: Bruce Becker, Steven Boockvor, Roger Briant, Edward Nolfi. *Frau Wendel*: Mara Landi. *Herr Wendel*: Eugene Morgan. *Frau Kruger*: Miriam Lehmann-Haupt. *Herr Erdmann*: Sol Frieder. *Kit Kat Girls (6)*: *Maria*: Pat Gosling. *Lulu*: Lynn Winn. *Rosie*: Bonnie Walker. *Fritzie*: Marianne Selbert. *Texas*: Kathie Dalton. *Frenchie*: Barbara Alston. *Bobby*: Jere Admire. *Victor*: Bert Michaels. *Greta*: Jayme Mylroie. *Felix*: Robert Sharp.

The action takes place in Berlin, Germany in 1929-1930 before the start of the Third Reich.

Act 1, Scene 1: The Kit Kat Klub. *Scene 2*: Aboard a European railway train. *Scene 3*: Fraulein Schneider's flat. *Scene 4*: The Kit Kat Klub. New Year's Eve, 1930. *Scene 5*: Cliff's room. *Scene 6*: The Kit Kat Klub. *Scene 7*: Fraulein Schneider's living room. *Scene 8*: The Kit Kat Klub. *Scene 9*: Cliff's room. *Scene 10*: The Kit Kat Klub. *Scene 11*: Fraulein Schneider's living room and Kraulein Kost's room. *Scene 12*: Herr Schultz's fruit shop.

Act 2, Scene 1: The Kit Kat Klub. *Scene 2*: Herr Schultz's shop. *Scene 3*: The Kit Kat Klub. *Scene 4*: Cliff's room. *Scene 5*: The Kit Kat Klub. *Scene 6*: Cliff's room. *Scene 7*: A Railroad compartment, then The Kit Kat Klub.

ACT 1
Scene 1
"Wilkommen"
J. Grey, Company
Scene 3
"So What?"
L. Lenya
Scene 4
"Don't Tell Mama"
J. Haworth, Girls
"Telephone Song"
Company
Scene 5
"Perfectly Marvelous"
B. Convy, J. Haworth
Scene 6
"Two Ladies"
J. Grey, M. Ehara, R. O'Connor
Scene 7
"It Couldn't Please Me More"
L. Lenya, J. Gilford
Scene 8
"Tomorrow Belongs to Me"
J. Grey, Waiters
Scene 9
"Why Should I Wake Up?"
B. Convy, J. Haworth
Scene 10
"The Money Song" (Money)
J. Grey, Cabaret Girls
Scene 11
"Married"
L. Lenya, J. Gilford
Scene 12
"Meeskite"
J. Gilford
"Tomorrow Belongs to Me" (reprise)
P. Murray, E. Winter, Guests

ACT 2
Scene 1
"If You Could See Her"
J. Grey, Girls
Scene 2
"Married" (reprise)
L. Lenya, J. Gilford
Scene 3
"If You Could See Her" (reprise)
J. Grey, J. Admire
Scene 4
"What Would You Do?"
L. Lenya
Scene 5
"Cabaret"
J. Haworth
Scene 7
Finale
B. Convy, J. Haworth, L. Lenya, J. Gilford, J. Grey, Company

RUDDIGORE, or The Witch's Curse

1966.25

A Revival of the Comic Opera in Two Acts[13]. Libretto by William S. Gilbert. Music by Arthur Sullivan. Costumes and settings by Peter Goffin. Musical director, Isidore Godfrey. Associate conductor and chorus master, James Walker. Produced by the D'Oyly Carte Opera Trust, Ltd. under the personal supervision of Bridget D'Oyly Carte and under the management of Sol

[12]First presented in New York 20 July, 10-29 August 1885 at the Union Square and People's Theatres for 22 performances. First authorized production presented 19 August 1885 at the Fifth Avenue Theatre by Richard D'Oyly Carte for 250 performances. For Synopsis of Scenes and Musical Numbers, see 19 August 1885 D'Oyly Carte production.

[13]First presented in New York 21 February 1887 at the Standard Theatre for 53 performances. For Synopsis of Scenes and Musical Numbers, see original 1887 production.

Hurok. Opened 22 November 1966 at the New York City Center and closed 9 December 1966 after 4 performances.

CAST: *Sir Ruthven Murgatroyd*: JOHN REED. *Richard Dauntless*: DAVID PALMER. *Sir Despard Murgatroyd*: KENNETH SANDFORD. *Old Adam Goodheart*: George Cook. *Sir Roderic Murgatroyd*: DONALD ADAMS. *Rose Maybud*: ANN HOOD. *Mad Margaret*: PEGGY ANN JONES. *Dame Hannah*: CHRISTENE PALMER. *Zorah*: Jennifer Marks. *Ruth*: Pauline Wales. *Chorus of Officers, Ancestors, Professional Bridesmaids, etc.*: same as THE PIRATES OF PENZANCE above.

H.M.S. PINAFORE, or The Lass That Loved a Sailor

1966.26

A Revival of the Comic Opera in Two Acts[14]. Libretto by William S. Gilbert. Music by Arthur Sullivan. Settings designed by Peter Goffin. Little Buttercup costume designed by Anne and Janet Grahame-Johnstone. Director of productions, Herbert Newby. Musical director, Isidore Godfrey. Associate conductor and chorus master, James Walker. Produced by the D'Oyly Carte Opera Trust, Ltd. under the personal supervision of Bridget D'Oyly Carte and under the management of Sol Hurok. Opened 23 November 1966 at the New York City Center and closed 10 December 1966 after 8 performances in repertory.

CAST: *The Rt. Hon. Sir Joseph Porter, K.C.B.*, First Lord of the Admiralty: JOHN REED. *Captain Corcoran*, Commanding the *H.M.S. Pinafore*: THOMAS LAWLOR. *Ralph Rackstraw*, Able Seaman: DAVID PALMER. *Dick Deadeye*, Able Seaman: DONALD ADAMS. *Bill Bobstay*, Bo'sun's Mate: George Cook. *Bob Beckett*, Carpenter's Mate: Anthony Raffell. *Josephine*, the Captain's Daughter: ANN HOOD. *Hebe*, Sir Joseph's First Cousin: Pauline Wales. *Little Buttercup*, a Portsmouth Bumboat Woman: CHRISTENE PALMER. *First Lord's Sisters, his Cousins, his Aunts, Sailors, Marines*: same as THE PIRATES OF PENZANCE above.

WALKING HAPPY

1966.27

A Musical in Two Acts, 17 Scenes. Book by Roger O. Hirson and Ketti Frings. Based on the play "Hobson's Choice" by Harold Brighouse. Music by James Van Heusen. Lyrics by Sammy Cahn. Scenery and lighting by Robert Randolph. Costumes by Robert Fletcher. Musical direction and vocal arrangements by Herbert Grossman. Orchestrations by Larry Wilcox. Dance music arranged by Ed Scott. Dances and musical numbers staged by Danny Daniels. Directed by Cy Feuer. Produced by Cy Feuer and Ernest H. Martin by arrangement with Lester Linsk. Opened 26 November 1966 at the Lunt-Fontanne Theatre and closed 16 April 1967 after 161 performances.

CAST (in order of appearance): *Henry Horatio Hobson*: GEORGE ROSE. *George Beenstock*: Ed Bakey. *Minns*: Thomas Boyd. *Denton*: Casper Roos. *Tudsbury*: Carl Nicholas. *Heeler*: Michael Quinn. *Maggie Hobson*: LOUISE TROY. *Alice Hobson*: Sharon Dierking. *Vickie Hobson*: Gretchen Van Aken. *Albert Beenstock*: James B. Spann. *Freddie Beenstock*: Michael Berkson. *Mrs. Hepworth*: Emma Trekman. *Footman*: Steven Jacobs. *Tubby Wadlow*: Gordon Dilworth. *Will Mossop*: NORMAN WISDOM. *Ada Figgins*: Jane Laughlin. *Mrs. Figgins*: Lucille Benson. *The Figgins Brothers*: Ian Garry, Al Lanti. *Customer*: Eleanor Bergquist. *Handbill Boy*: Richard Sederholm. *Thief*: Burt Bier. *Policeman*: Chad Block. *Beggar*: Richard Korthaze.

Townsmen: Burt Bier, Chad Block, Thomas Boyd, Ian Garry, Gene Gavin, Steven Jacobs, Richard Korthaze, Al Lanti, Carl Nicholas, Don Percassi, Michael Quinn, Casper Roos, Richard Sederholm, Dan Siretta. *Townswomen*: Eleanor Bergquist, Diane L. Blair, Sandra Brewer, Ellen Graff, Marian Haraldson, Jane Laughlin, Marie Patrice O'Neill, Nada Rowland, Anne Wallace.

The action takes place in Salford, an industrial town in Lancashire, England, in 1880.

Act 1, Scene 1: The Moonrakers Pub. Night. *Scene 2*: Hobson's Bootery. *Scene 3*: The Cellar of the Bootery. *Scene 4*: The Moonrakers Pub. *Scene 5*: The Park. *Scene 6*: A Street in the poor section of Salford. *Scene 7*: An Alley lit by gaslight. Evening of the same day. *Scene 8*: The Bootery.

Act 2, Scene 1: Mrs. Hepworth's Sitting Room. *Scene 2*: A Cellar. *Scene 3*: Flat Iron Market. *Scene 4*: Will and Maggie's Cellar. *Scene 5*: Outside Moonrakers Pub. Three weeks later. *Scene 6*: Outside Beenstock's Corn Warehouse. *Scene 7*: Hobson's Bootery. *Scene 8*: Inside Beenstock's Corn Warehouse. *Scene 9*: The Mossop Bootery.

ACT 1
Scene 1
"Think of Something Else"
G. Rose, E. Bakey, Townsmen
Scene 2
"Where Was I?"
L. Troy
Scene 3
"How D'ya Talk to a Girl?"
N. Wisdom, G. Dilworth
Scene 4
"Clog and Grog" (dance)
Townsmen
Scene 5
"If I Be Your Best Chance"
N. Wisdom
Scene 6
"A Joyful Thing" (dance)
N. Wisdom, L. Benson, J. Laughlin, Townspeople
Scene 7
"What Makes It Happen?"
N. Wisdom
Scene 8
"Use Your Noggin"
L. Troy, G. Van Aken, S. Dierking

ACT 2
Scene 1
"You're Right, You're Right"[15]
L. Troy
"I'll Make a Man of the Man"
L. Troy
Scenes 2 and 3
"Walking Happy"
N. Wisdom, L. Troy, Townspeople
Scene 4
"I Don't Think I'm in Love"
N. Wisdom, L. Troy
Scenes 5 and 6
"Such a Sociable Sort"
G. Rose, Friends
Scene 7
"It Might As Well Be Her"
N. Wsdom, G. Dilworth
Scene 8
"People Who Are Nice"[16]
G. Rose
Scene 9
"You're Right, You're Right" (reprise)
N. Wisdom, L. Troy, G. Rose
"I Don't Think I'm in Love" (reprise)
N. Wisdom

PATIENCE, or Bunthorne's Bride

1966.28

A Revival of the Comic Opera in Two Acts[17]. Libretto by William S. Gilbert. Music by Arthur Sullivan. Directed and designed by Peter Goffin. Director of productions, Herbert Newby. Musical director, Isidore Godfrey. Associate conductor and chorus master, James Walker. Produced by the D'Oyly Carte

[14]Originally presented in New York 15 January 1879 at the Standard Theatre for 175 performances. For Synopsis of Scenes and Musical Numbers, see original 1879 production.

[15]Dropped during the run.

[16]Dropped during the run.

[17]First presented in New York 22 September 1881 at the Standard Theatre for 177 performances. For Synopsis of Scenes and Musical Numbers, see original 1881 production.

Opera Trust, Ltd. under the personal supervision of Bridget D'Oyly Carte and under the management of Sol Hurok. Opened 29 November 1966 at the New York City Center and closed 11 December 1966 after 4 performances.

CAST: *Colonel Calverley*: DONALD ADAMS. *Major Murgatroyd*: Alfred Oldridge. *Lieut. the Duke of Dunstable*: PHILIP POTTER. *Reginald Bunthorne*, a Fleshly Poet: JOHN REED. *Archibald Grosvenor*, an Idyllic Poet: KENNETH SANDFORD. *Mr. Bunsthorne's Solicitor*: James Marsland. *The Lady Angela, The Lady Saphir, The Lady Ella, The Lady Jane*, Rapturous Maidens: PEGGY ANN JONES, PAULINE WALES, Jennifer Marks, CHRISTENE PALMER. *Patience*, a Dairy Maid: ANN HOOD. *Chorus of Rapturous Maifdens and Officers of the Dragoon Guards*: same as THE PIRATES OF PENZANCE above.

1966.29 I DO! I DO!

A Musical in Two Acts. Book and lyrics by Tom Jones. Based on the play "The Fourposter" by Jan de Hartog. Music by Harvey Schmidt. Directed by Gower Champion. Scenic production by Oliver Smith. Costumes by Freddy Wittop. Lighting by Jean Rosenthal. Musical direction, John Lesko. Orchestrations by Philip J. Lang. Assistant to the director (Production supervisor), Lucia Victor. A David Merrick and Champion-Six Inc. Production. Produced by David Merrick. Opened 5 December 1966 at the 46th Street Theatre and closed 15 June 1968 after 561 performances.

CAST: *She (Agnes)*: MARY MARTIN. *He (Michael)*: ROBERT PRESTON.
At the two pianos: Woody Kessler, Albert Mello.

The action takes place in a bedroom, and covers fifty years of a marriage, beginning just before the turn of the century.

ACT 1

Prologue:
"All the Dearly Beloved"
"Together Forever"
"I Do! I Do!"
M. Martin, R. Preston
"Good Night"
M. Martin, R. Preston
"I Love My Wife"
R. Preston
"Something Has Happened"
M. Martin
"My Cup Runneth Over"
M. Martin, R. Preston
"Love Isn't Everything"
M. Martin, R. Preston
"Nobody's Perfect"
M. Martin, R. Preston
"A Well Known Fact"
R. Preston
"Flaming Agnes"
M. Martin
"The Honeymoon Is Over"
M. Martin, R. Preston

ACT 2

"Where Are the Snows?"
M. Martin, R. Preston
"When the Kids Get Married"
M. Martin, R. Preston
Another Wedding:
"The Father of the Bride"
R. Preston
"What Is a Woman?"
M. Martin
"Someone Needs Me"
M. Martin
"Roll Up the Ribbons"
M. Martin, R. Preston
"This House"
M. Martin, R. Preston

1966.30 A JOYFUL NOISE

A Musical in Two Acts, 12 Scenes. Book by Edward Padula. Based on the novel "The Insolent Breed" by Borden Deal. Music and lyrics by Oscar Brand and Paul Nassau. Directed by Edward Padula. Settings and lighting by Peter Wexler. Costumes by Peter Joseph. Musical direction by Rene Weigert. Orchestrations and vocal arrangements by William Stegmeyer. Dance music by Lee Holdridge. Dances and musical numbers staged by Michael Bennett. Assistant choreographers, Leland Palmer, Jo Jo Smith. Production supervisor, Jeb Schary. Produced by Edward Padula and Slade Brown in association with Sid Bernstein. Opened 15 December 1966 at the Mark Hellinger Thaetre and closed 24 December 1966 after 12 performances.

CAST (in order of appearance): *Shade Motley*: JOHN RAITT. *Brother Locke*: CLIFFORD DAVID. *Walter Wishenant*: GEORGE MATHEWS. *Jenny Lee*: SUSAN WATSON. *Sam Fredrickson*: ART WALLACE. *Miss Jimmie*: LELAND PALMER. *Saw Mill Boys and THE MOTLEY CREW (5)*: *DeWitt*: Eric Weissberg. *Freddy*: Martin Ambrose. *Jaybird*: Charles Morley. *Oscar*: Oatis Stephens. *Tommy*: Tommy Tune. *Bliss Stanley*: SWEN SWENSON. *Stage Manager*: Jack Fletcher. *Director*: Ken Ayers. *Mary Texas*: KAREN MORROW. *Boys*: Paul Charles, Scott Pearson, Alan Peterson, Barry Preston. *Announcer*: Jack Metté. *Bailey*: Jo Jo Smith. *John Tom*: Shawn Campbell.

Townspeople and City People: *Singers*: Veronica McCormick, Jessica Quinn, Diane Tarleton, Linda Theil, Jamie Thomas, Ken Ayers, Jack Fletcher, Stuart Mann, Eric Mason, Jack Metté, Darrell Sandeen. *Dancers*: Christine Bocchino, Susan Donovan, Baayork Lee, April Nevins, Diane Phillips, Joy Serio, Melissa Stoneburn, Carol Lynn Vazquez, Bonnie Ano, Paul Charles, Winston DeWitt Hemsley, Scott Pearson, Alan Peterson, Barry Preston, Steven Ross, Jo Jo Smith, Tommy Tune.

The action takes place yesterday and today in Macedonia and Nashville, Tennessee.

Act 1, Scene 1: A Clearing in the Hills. *Scene 2*: The Town Square. *Scene 3*: A Clearing. *Scene 4*: The Saw Mill. *Scene 5*: The Field. *Scene 6*: The Top of the Valley.

Act 2, Scene 1: Backstage, Nashville. *Scene 2*: A Clearing in Macedonia. *Scene 3*: The Grand Ole Opry. *Scene 4*: The Recording Studio. *Scene 5*: The State Fair. *Scene 6*: The Town Square.

ACT 1

"Long Time Travelin'"
J. Raitt
"A Joyful Noise"
J. Raitt, Townspeople
"I'm Ready"
S. Watson, L. Palmer, Girls
"Spring Time of the Year"
J. Raitt
"I Like to Look My Best"
J. Raitt, A. Wallace, The Saw Mill Boys
"No Talent"
S. Swenson
"Not Me"
S. Watson, L. Palmer
"Until Today"
J. Raitt, S. Watson
"Swinging a Dance"
J. Raitt, Company
"To the Top"
S. Swenson, J. Raitt

ACT 2

"I Love Nashville"
K. Morrow, Boys
"Whither Thou Goest"
C. David
"We Won't Forget to Write"
L. Palmer, A. Wallace, The Saw Mill Boys
Grand Ole Opry:
"Ballad Maker"
J. Raitt, K. Morrow, The Motley Crew, Ensemble
"Barefoot Gal"
K. Morrow
"Clog Dance"
Dance Ensemble
"Fool's Gold"
J. Raitt, K. Morrow, The Motley Crew, Ensemble

"The Big Guitar"
S. Swenson
"Love Was"
S. Watson
"I Say Yes"
J. Raitt, The Motley Crew, Ensemble
"Lord, You Sure Knew How to Make a New Day"
J. Raitt
"A Joyful Noise" (reprise)
J. Raitt, Townspeople

1966.31 CAROUSEL

A Revival of the Musical Play in Two Acts, 9 Scenes[18]. Based on Ferenc Molnar's play "Liliom" as adapted by Benjamin F. Glazer. Music by Richard Rodgers. Book and lyrics by Oscar Hammerstein II. Original production directed by Rouben Mamoulian. Directed by Gus Schirmer. Choreography by Agnes de Mille, restaged by Gemze deLappe. Settings by Paul C. McGuire. Costumes by Stanley Simmons. Lighting by Feder. Musical director, Jonathan Anderson. (Orchestrations by Don Walker.) Produced by the New York City Center Light Opera Company (Jean Dalrymple, Director). Opened 15 December 1966 at the New York City Center and closed 1 January 1967 after 22 performances.

CAST (in order of appearance): *Carrie Pipperidge*: NANCY DUSSAULT. *Julie Jordan*: CONSTANCE TOWERS. *Mrs. Mullin*: Louise Larabee. *Billy Bigelow*: BRUCE YARNELL. *First Policeman*: Paul Adams. *David Bascombe*: Alexander Clark. *Nettie Fowler*: PATRICIA NEWAY. *Enoch Snow*: JACK DE LON. *Jigger Craigin*: MICHAEL KERMOYAN. *Hannah*: Jenny Workman. *Boatswain*: Darrell Notara. *Second Policeman*: Gene Albano. *Captain*: William R. Miller. *Heavenly Friend* (Joshua): Jay Velie. *Starkeeper*: PARKER FENNELLY. *Louise*: Sandy Duncan. *Carnival Boy*: Darrell Notara. *Enoch Snow, Jr.*: Dennis Cole. *Principal*: Philip Ewart.

Townspeople (Singers): Phyllis Bash, Jane Coleman, Mona Elson, Maria Hero, Joyce McDonald, Estella Munson, Marie O'Kelley, Joyce Olson, Eleanor Shaw, Maggie Task, Paul Adams, Gene Albano, Darrell Askey, Bob Barbieri, Austin Colyer, Gordon Cook, Philip Ewart, Marvin Goodis, William Miller, Laried Montgomery, Joe R. Rhyne, Joseph Williams, Jerry Wyatt. *Dancers*: Karen Brock, Linda Caputi, Alice Condodina, Joanna Crosson, Lois Eteleman, Carol Flemming, Joanne Geahry, Mickey Gunnersen, Lucia Lambert, Gilda Mullett, Toddie Wittmer, Roy Barry, Joseph Carow, D. R. Haworth, Curtis Hood, Paul Olson, Vernon Wendorf.

1966.32 AT THE DROP OF ANOTHER HAT

More of their own words and music[19]. (A Musical Revue in Two Acts.) Music by Donald Swann. Lyrics by Michael Flanders. Designed by Ralph Alswang. Associate producer, Sidney Lanier. Production supervisor, Jerry Adler. Production associate, Hildy Parks. A Nine O'Clock Theatre Production. Produced by Alexander H. Cohen. Opened 27 December 1966 at the Booth Theatre and closed 9 April 1967 after 105 performances.

CAST: MICHAEL FLANDERS, DONALD SWANN.

ACT 1
"The Gasman Cometh"
"From Our Bestiary"
"'P** P* B**** B** D*****"
"Bilbo's Song"
(*Lyrics by* J. R. R. Tolkien)
"Slow Train"
"Thermodynamic Duo"
"Sloth"
"More Songs for Our Time"
"In the Desert"
"Los Olividados"
"Motor Perpetuo"
"A Song of Patriotic Prejudice"

ACT 2
"All Gall"
"Horoscope"
"Armadillo Idyll"
"Twenty Tons of T.N.T."
"Ill Wind"
(*Music by* Wolfgang Amadeus Mozart.)
"Food For Thought"
"Prehistoric Complaint"
"Twice Shy"

1967.01 THE PERSECUTION AND ASSASSINATION OF MARAT AS PERFORMED BY THE INMATES OF THE ASYLUM OF CHARENTON UNDER THE DIRECTION OF THE MARQUIS DE SADE

A Revival of the Drama in Two Acts with Music[20]. Play by Peter Weiss. English version by Geoffrey Skelton. Verse adaptation by Adrian Mitchell. Music by Richard Peaslee. Entire production directed by Donald Driver. Scenery by Edward Burbridge. Costumes by Lewis Brown. Lighting by Martin Aronstein. Musical director, Rod Derefinko. Produced by Zev Bufman (The National Players Company Production). Opened 3 January 1967 at the Majestic Theatre and closed 18 February 1967 after 55 performances.

CAST (in order of appearance): *M. Coulmier*: Stephen Elliott. *Mme. Coulmier*: Barbara Cason. *Mlle. Coulmier*: Cynthia Towne. *Marquis de Sade*: WILLIAM ROERICK. *Herald*: Douglas Watson. *Jean-Paul Marat*: DENNIS PATRICK. *Simonne Evrard*: SHELLIE FELDMAN. *Charlotte Corday*: VERNA BLOOM. *Duperret*: Jered Barclay. *Jacques Roux*: Robert Fields. *Cucurucu*: Leonard Drum. *Polpoch*: Igors Gavon. *Kokol*: Gerard Russak. *Rossignol*: Christine Norden. *Mad Animal*: Abe Vigoda. *Schoolmaster*: James Cahill. *Mother*: Fay Chaiken. *Father*: Peter Blaxill. *Voltaire*: John Tormey. *Lavoisier*: Allan Louw. *Patients*: Fayne Blackburn, Imogene Bliss, Beatrice Brooks, Madlyn Cates, Lousie Clay, Zola Long, Helen F. Ross, Carol Teitel, Geri Wolcott. *Nuns*: John Toland, Edmond Varrato. *Guards*: Sam Kirkham, Robert Keegan, Richard Kinter. *Musicians*: Bernie Moore (guitar), Roberta Russell (flute-piccolo), Patrick Harrison (percussion), Frank Emerson (trumpet).

1967.02 SHERRY!

A Musical Comedy in Two Acts, 12 Scenes. Book and lyrics by James Lipton. Based on the play "The Man Who Came to Dinner" by George S. Kaufman and Moss Hart. Music by Laurence Rosenthal. Scenery and lighting by Robert Randolph. Costumes by Robert Mackintosh. Musical direction and vocal arrangements by Jay Blackton. Orchestrations by Philip J. Lang. Dance arrangements by John Morris. Staging and direction supervised by Joe Layton. Associate producer, Marvin A. Krauss. Produced by Lee Guber, Frank Ford and Shelly Gross. Opened 28 March 1967 at the Alvin Theatre and closed 27 May 1967 after 72 performances.

CAST (in order of appearance): *Daisy Stanley*: MARY LOANE. *Miss Preen*: Janet Fox. *John*: Merritt Smith. *Sarah*: Barbara Webb. *Maggie Cutler*: ELIZABETH ALLEN. *Ernest W. Stanley*: DONALD BURR. *Dr. Bradley*: CLIFF HALL. *Sheridan Whiteside*: CLIVE REVILL. *Harriet Stanley*: PAULA TRUEMAN. *Bert Jefferson*: JON CYPHER. *Lorraine Sheldon*: DOLORES GRAY. *Cosette*: June Lynn Compton. *Beverly Carlton*: BYRON WEBSTER. *Westcott*: Haydon Smith. *Billy*: Del Hinkley. *Banjo*: EDDIE LAWRENCE. *Ginger*: Leslie Franzos.

---

[18]First produced in New York 19 April 1945 at the Majestic Theatre for 890 performances. For Synopsis of Scenes and Musical Numbers, see original 1945 production.

[19]A sequel to the authors' previous British revue success, AT THE DROP OF A HAT, which opened 8 October 1959 at the John Golden Theatre for 215 performances.

[20]Originally produced in New York 27 December 1965 at the Martin Beck Theatre for 145 performances. For Synopsis of Scenes and Musical Numbers, see original 1965 production.

Ensemble (Mesalians): Diane Arnold, Edie Cowan, Carol Estey, Leslie Franzos, Altovise Gore, Carol Hanzel, Carol Perea, Peter De Nicola, Frank De Sal, Luigi Gasparinetti, Roger Allan Raby, Haydon Smith, Doug Spingler, Ted Sprague, Lucille Blackton, June Lynn Compton, Rita Metzger, Jeannette Seibert, Trudy Wallace, Herb Fields, Del Hinkley, Joe Kirkland, Duane Morris, Clyde Williams, Denise Nickerson, Glenn Dufford, Robert Fitch.

The action takes place between December 10th and Christmas Day, 1938, in Mesalia, Ohio.

Act 1, Scene 1: The Stanley Living Room. *Scene 2*: Township of Mesalia. *Scene 3*: Exterior of Stanley Residence. *Scene 4*: The Stanley Residence. *Scene 5*: A Jewelry Shop. *Scene 6*: The Stanley Living Room. *Scene 7*: Mansion House Hotel in Mesalia. *Scene 8*: The Stanley Living Room.

Act 2, Scene 1: Billy's Tavern. *Scene 2*: The Stanley Solarium. *Scene 3*: The Stanley Library. *Scene 4*: The Stanley Living Room.

ACT 1

Scene 1

"Turn on Your Radio"
B. Webb, E. Allen, M. Loane, Ensemble

"Why Does the Whole Damn World Adore Me?"
C. Revill

Scene 2

"Meet Mesalia"
E. Allen, J. Cypher, Ensemble

Scene 3

"Maybe It's Time for Me"
E. Allen

Scene 4

"How Can You Kiss Those Good Times Goodbye?"
C. Revill, E. Allen

Scene 5

"With This Ring"
E. Allen, J. Cypher, C. Revill, C. Hall

Scene 6

"Sherry"
D. Gray, C. Revill

"Alas, Lorraine"
B. Webster

"Au Revoir"
B. Webster

Scene 7

"Proposal Duet"
D. Gray, B. Webster

"Listen Cosette"
D. Gray, J. L. Compton

Scene 8

"Christmas Eve Broadcast"
C. Revill, D. Gray, Ensemble

ACT 2

Scene 1

"Putty in Your Hands"
D. Gray, Ensemble

Scene 2

"Harriet's Pavan"
P. Trueman

"Imagine That"
E. Allen, C. Revill

Scene 3

"Marry the Girl Myself"
C. Revill, E. Lawrence

"The Fred Astaire Affair"
C. Revill, E. Lawrence, L. Franzos, Ensemble

"How Can You Kiss Those Good Times Goodbye?" (reprise)
E. Allen

Scene 4

"Putty in Your Hands" (reprise)
D. Gray, C. Revill, E. Lawrence

"Harriet Sedley"
C. Revill, E. Lawrence, D. Burr

1967.03 HELLO, SOLLY!

An American Yiddish Musical Revue in Two Acts, 6 Scenes[21]. (Costumes, settings, lighting, direction uncredited.) Produced by Hal Zeiger. Opened 4 April 1967 at Henry Miller's Theatre and closed 28 May 1967 after 68 performances.

CAST: MICKEY KATZ, LARRY BEST, MICHAEL (GETZEL) ROSENBERG, STAN PORTER, LITTLE TANYA.

ACT 1[22]

Scene 1

Songs, Stories, Instrumentals:
M. Katz

"Darktown Strutter's Ball"
(*Music and Lyrics by* Shelton Brooks.)

"Sunrise, Sunset" (from FIDDLER ON THE ROOF)
(*Music by* Jerry Bock. *Lyrics by* Sheldon Harnick.)

Yiddish Folk Song (Traditional)

Stories, Sing-along, Bepop:

"Die Greene Koseene"
(*Music and Lyrics by* Abe Schwartz and Hyman Prizant.)

"The Wedding Dance"
(*Music by* Mickey Katz.)

Scene 2

Little Tanya
[Old-country ballad; cantorial tune; "People" from FUNNY GIRL. (*Music by* Jule Styne. *Lyrics by* Bob Merrill.)]

Scene 3

Jokes and Stories
L. Best

ACT 2

Scene 1

Songs of Childhood and Israel:
S. Porter, V. Lloyd

Childhood Medley:

"Seise Kinder Yohren"
(*Music and Lyrics by* David Meyerowitz.)

"Zing, Faigele, Zing"
(*Music and Lyrics by* Max Kletter.)

Chassidic Nigun :

"A Zemmer"
(*Music and Lyrics by* Samuel Bugatch.)

"Sheyibone Beis Hamikdosh"
(*Music and Lyrics by* Yisroll Shorr.)

Scene 2

Michael Rosenberg (Comic sketches)

Scene 3

Finale

1967.04 FINIAN'S RAINBOW

A Revival of the Musical in Two Acts, 10 Scenes[23]. Book by E. Y. Harburg and Fred Saidy. Lyrics by E. Y. Harburg. Music by Burton Lane. Directed by Gus Schirmer. Choreographed by Betty Hyatt Linton. Scenery by Howard Bay. Costumes by Frank Thompson. Lighting by Peggy Clark. (Orchestrations by Robert Russell Bennett and Don Walker.) Musical director, Jonathan Anderson. Produced by the New York City Center Light Opera Company (Jean Dalrymple, Director.) Opened 5 April 1967 at the New York City Center and closed 23 April 1967 after 23 performances.

---

[21]Previously produced in New York 10-11 September 1966 at Carnegie Hall for 3 performances, with the same cast, Little Tanya excepted. Dina Claire appeared on the program.

[22]Neither songs nor sketches were listed in the program. The above list was prepared from reviews, press representative materials and recordings.

[23]Originally produced in New York 10 January 1947 at the 46th Street Theatre for 725 performances. For Synopsis of Scenes and Musical Numbers, see original 1947 production.

CAST (in order of appearance): *Sunny* (Harmonica Player): Elliot Levine. *Buzz Collins*: Ronn Carroll. *Sheriff*: Howard Fischer. *First Sharecropper*: John Dorrin *Second Sharecropper*: Laried Montgomery. *Susan Mahoney*: SANDY DUNCAN. *Henry*: Kevin Featherstone. *Maude*: CAROL BRICE. *Finian McLonergan*: FRANK McHUGH. *Sharon McLonergan*: NANCY DUSSAULT. *Woody Mahoney*: STANLEY GROVER. *Og* (A Leprechaun): LEN GOCHMAN. *Senator Billboard Rawkins*: HOWARD I. SMITH. *First Geologist*: Ronald B. Stratton. *Second Geologist*: Clark Salonis. *Howard*: Jim McMillan. *Diane*: Ellen Hansen. *Mr. Robust*: Austin Colyer. *Mr. Shears*: Paul Adams. *First Passion Pilgrim Gospeller*: Jerry Laws. *Second Passion Pilgrim Gospeller*: Tiger Haynes. *Third Passion Pilgrim Gospeller*: John McCurry. *First Deputy*: Paul Eichel. *Second Deputy*: Joey Carow. *John the Preacher*: Garwood Perkins.

Singers: Barbara Christopher, Jane Coleman, Mary Falconer, Ellen Harris, Ernestine Jackson, Mina Jo King, Joyce McDonald, Dixie Stewart, Alyce Webb. Paul Adams, Austin Colyer, John Dorrin, Paul Eichel, Doug Hunt, Elliot Levine, Laried Montgomery, Garrett Morris, Garwood Perkins, Clark Salonis, Grant Spradling. *Dancers*: Mary Barnett, Josetta Cherry, Joanna Crosson, Joanne De Vito, Ruth Lawrence, Sally Lou Lee, Joy Serio, Toodie Wittmer, Mary Zahn. Guy Allen, Bjarne Buchtrup, Joey Carow, Dennis Edenfield, Jerry Fries, Garold Gardner, Ted Goodridge, Mark Holliday, Bob La Crosse, Ronald B. Stratton, Mark Scott. *Children*: Ellen Hansen, Lisa Huggins, Tom Brooke, Kevin Featherstone, William Sims.

1967.05 ILLYA, DARLING

A Musical in Two Acts, 18 Scenes. Book and direction by Jules Dassin. Based on the film "Never on Sunday" (by Jules Dassin.) Music by Manos Hadjidakis. Lyrics by Joe Darion. Scenery by Oliver Smith. Costumes by Theoni V. Aldredge. Lighting by Jean Rosenthal. Musical direction by Karen Gustafson. Dance and musical numbers staged by Onna White. Orchestrations by Ralph Burns. Dance music arranged by Roger Adams. Assistant choreographer, Tom Panko. Produced by Kermit Bloomgarden in association with United Artists. Opened 11 April 1967 at the Mark Hellinger Theatre and closed 13 January 1968 after 320 performances.

CAST (in order of appearance): *Yorgo*: TITOS VANDIS. *Costa*: Thomas Raskin. *Workman*: Dom Angelo. *Tonio*: NIKOS KOURKOULOS. *Captain*: RUDY BOND. *Illya*: MELINA MERCOURI. *Homer Thrace*: ORSON BEAN. *Waiter*: HAROLD GARY. *Garbage*: WILLIAM DUELL. *Despo*: DESPO. *Musician*: Joseph Alfasa. *Little Man*: Gerrit de Beer. *Forward Sailor*: Joseph Corby. *Timid Sailor*: Robert La Tourneaux. *Vassily*: JOE E. MARKS. *Voula*: Lou Rodgers. *Kiki*: Sandy Ellen. *Cassandra*: Gloria Lambert. *Playgoer*: Nick Athas. *Drama Critic*: Fred Burrell. *Wife*: Del Green. *No Face*: HAL LINDEN. *Bodyguards*: Gerrit de Beer, Harry Kalkanis. *The Other Girl*: Ann Barry. *Bouzouki Soloist*: Harry Lemonopoulos.

Ensemble: Ann Barry, Sandy Ellen, Del Green, Eileen Joy Haber, Suzanne Horn, Robert La Tourneaux, Urylee Leonardos, Lou Rodgers, Arthur Shaffer, Maria Strattin, Martin Allen, Dom Angelo, Lonnie Davis, Marcelo Gamboa, Louis Genevrino, Nat Horne, Harry Kalkanis, Robert Karl, Juleste Salve, Bill Starr, Mitch Thomas, Terry Violino, Nick Athas, Edward Becker, Alvin Cohen, Joseph Corby, Gerrit de Beer, Johnny LaMotta, Stephen Lardas, Thomas Raskin, Loukas Skipitaris.

The action takes place in the Port of Piraeus, Greece at the present time.

Act 1, Scene 1: A Shipyard in Piraeus. *Scene 2*: A Bouzouki Place. *Scene 3*: Illya's Bedroom. *Scene 4*: Outside Illya's House. *Scene 5*: Seaside. *Scene 6*: Shipyard. *Scene 7*: Illya's Apartment. *Scene 8*: The Acropolis. *Scene 9*: The Bouzouki Place. *Scene 10*: Illya's Bedroom.

Act 2, Scene 1: Illya's Apartment. *Scene 2*: Outside Illya's House. *Scene 3*: Illya's Bedroom. *Scene 4*: A Street in Piraeus. *Scene 5*: Illya's Apartment. *Scene 6*: Street of the Girls. *Scene 7*: The Bouzouki Place. *Scene 8*: The Port.

ACT 1[24]

"Po, Po, Po"
O. Bean, N. Kourkoulos

Dance
Ensemble

"Zebekiko"
T. Vandis

"Piraeus, My Love"
M. Mercouri, Men

"Golden Land"
O. Bean, Ensemble

"Zebikiko" (reprise)
T. Vandis

"Love, Love, Love"[25]
M. Mercouri

"I Think She Needs Me"
O. Bean

"I'll Never Lay Down Anymore"
Despo

"After Love"[26]
N. Kourkoulos

"Birthday Song"
N. Kourkoulos, R. Bond, Men

"Medea Tango"
M. Mercouri, Men

"Illya, Darling"
M. Mercouri, T. Vandis, Ensemble

ACT 2

"Dear Mr. Schubert"
M. Mercouri

"The Lesson"
M. Mercouri, O. Bean

"Never on Sunday"
M. Mercouri, Ensemble

"Piraeus, My Love" (reprise)
M. Mercouri

"Medea Tango" (reprise)
N. Kourkoulos

"Heaven Help the Sailors on a Night Like This"
Ensemble

Dance
M. Mercouri, O. Bean, T. Vandis, N. Kourkoulos, R. Bond, J. E. Marks, H. Gary, Ensemble

"Ya Chara"
Company

1967.06 HALLELUJAH, BABY!

A Musical in Two Acts, a Prologue and 6 Scenes. Book by Arthur Laurents. Music by Jule Styne. Lyrics by Betty Comden and Adolph Green. Directed by Burt Shevelove. Dances and musical numbers staged by Kevin Carlisle. Settings designed by William and Jean Eckart. Costumes by Irene Sharaff. Lighting by Tharon Musser. Musical direction and vocal arrangements by Buster Davis. Orchestrations by Peter Matz. Dance orchestrations by Luther Henderson. Assistant choreographers, William Guske, Marie Lake. Associate producer, Joe Linhart. Produced by Albert W. Selden and Hal James, Jane C. Nusbaum and Harry Rigby. Opened 26 April 1967 at the Martin Beck Theatre and closed 13 January 1968 after 293 performances.

CAST (in order of appearance): *Georgina*: LESLIE UGGAMS. *Momma*: LILLIAN HAYMAN. *Clem*: ROBERT HOOKS. *Provers*: Clifford Allen, Garrett Morris, Kenneth Scott, Alan Weeks. *Harvey*: ALLEN CASE. *Captain Yankee*: Justin McDonough. *Calhoun*: Lou Angel. *Mary*: BARBARA SHARMA. *Mister Charles*: Frank Hamilton. *Mrs. Charles*: Marilyn Cooper. *Tip and Tap*: Winston DeWitt Hemsley, Alan Weeks. *Cuties*: Hope Clarke, Sandra Lein, Saundra McPherson. *Prince*: Bud Vest. *Princess*: Carol Flemming. *Sugar Daddy*: Darrell Notara. *Bouncer*: Chad Block. *Mistress*: Marilyn Cooper. *Master*: Darrell Notara. *Director*: Alan Peterson. *Ethel*: Marilyn Cooper. *Official*: Chad Block. *Brenda*: Ann Rachel. *Timmy*: Frank Hamilton. *G.I.s*: Winston DeWitt Hemsley, Kenneth Scott, Alan Weeks, Clifford Allen. *Bus Driver*: Lou Angel. *Dorothy*: Marilyn Cooper. *Maid*: Hope Clarke.

Ensemble: Clifford Allen, Barbara Andrews, Lou Angel, Chad Block, Hope Clarke, Norma Donaldson, Carol Flemming, Nat Gales, Maria Hero, Lee Hooper, Alan Johnson, Sandra Lein, Justin McDonough, Saundra McPherson, Garrett Morris, Darrell Notara, Paul Reid Roman, Suzanne Rogers, Kenneth Scott, Ella Thompson, Bud Vest.

The action takes place in this country from the turn of the century until now.

Act 1, Scene 1: 1900s. The kitchen. *Scene 2*: 1920s. A cabaret. *Scene 3*: 1930s. The bread line.

Act 2, Scene 1: 1940s. An Army camp, outside a night club. *Scene 2*: 1950s. A night club. *Scene 3*: 1960s. An apartment.

ACT 1[27]

[24]After opening, Act 1 revised and shortened.
[25]Dropped after opening

[26]Dropped after opening
[27]Added during the run:
"You Ain't Gonna Shake Them Feathers No More"
(added to Act 1, Scene 2, after "Feet Do Yo' Stuff")
R. Hooks

Introduction
Prologue
L. Uggams
Scene 1
"Back in the Kitchen"
L. Hayman
"My Own Morning"
L. Uggams
"The Slice"
R. Hooks, C. Allen, G. Morris, K. Scott, A. Weeks
"Farewell, Farewell"
L. Angel, J. McDonough, L. Uggams, A. Case
Scene 2
"Feet Do Yo' Stuff"
L. Uggams, Chorines, W. D. Hemsley, A. Weeks
"Watch My Dust"[28]
R. Hooks
"Smile, Smile"
R. Hooks, L. Uggams, L. Hayman
Scene 3
"Witches' Brew" (Double, Double)
L. Uggams, B. Sharma, M. Cooper, Company
Breadline Dance
Bums (Ensemble)
"Another Day"
A. Case, R. Hooks, B. Sharma, L. Uggams
"I Wanted to Change Him"[29]
L. Uggams
"Being Good Isn't Good Enough"
L. Uggams

ACT 2
Scene 1
Dance Drill (Clem's Drill)
W. D. Hemsley, A. Weeks, K. Scott, C. Allen
"Talking to Yourself"
L. Uggams, R. Hooks, A. Case
Limbo Dance
Night Club Patrons (Ensemble)
Scene 2
"Hallelujah, Baby!"
L. Uggams, W. D. Hemsley, A. Weeks
"Not Mine"
A. Case
"I Don't Know Where She Got It"
L. Hayman
"Now's the Time"
L. Uggams
Scene 3
"Now's the Time" (Reprise)
Entire Company

"Hey!" (added to Act 1, Scene 2, after "You Ain't Gonna Shake. .")
L. Uggams
Added for subsequent National Tour:
"When the Weather's Better"
Adam Wade (Clem), Kim Weston (Georgina)
(added to Act 1, Scene 1, after "The Slice;" also reprised in Act 1, Scene 3 before "Another Day." for Julius La Rosa (Harvey), Bobbi Baird (Mary).)
"You're Welcome" (added to Act 1, Scene 2, after "Watch My Dust")
K. Weston
"Under the Ropes" (added to Act 2, Scene 2 before "Hallelujah, Baby!")
Dancers
"Freedom March" (added to Act 2, Scene 3, before "Now's the Time" reprise)
Dancers
Dropped for National Tour:
Breadline Dance, "I Wanted to Change Him," Limbo Dance, "Hey!," "You Ain't Gonna Shake Them Feathers No More."

[28]Dropped during the New York run.
[29]Dropped during the New York run.

1967.07 THE SOUND OF MUSIC

A Revival of the Musical Play in Two Acts, 19 Scenes[30]. Book by Howard Lindsay and Russel Crouse. Suggested by the book "The Trapp Family Singers" by Maria Augusta Trapp. Music by Richard Rodgers. Lyrics by Oscar Hammerstein II. Directed by John Fearnley. Musical numbers staged by Reid Klein. Scenery by Oliver Smith. Costumes by Stanley Simmons. Lighting by Peggy Clark. Musical director, Frederick Dvonch. Choral arrangements by Trude Rittman. Orchestrations by Robert Russell Bennett. Produced by the New York City Center Light Opera Company (Jean Dalrymple, Director). Opened 26 April 1967 at the New York City Center and closed 14 May 1967 after 23 performances.

CAST (in order of appearance): *Maria Rainer*, a Postulant at Nonnberg Abbey: CONSTANCE TOWERS. *Sister Berthe*, Mistress of Novices: Jessica Quinn. *Sister Margaretta*, Mistress of Postulants: Nadine Lewis. *The Mother Abbess*: ELEANOR STEBER. *Sister Sophia*: Bernice Saunders. *Captain Georg von Trapp*: BOB WRIGHT. *Franz*, the Butler: Jim Oyster. *Frau Schmidt*, the Housekeeper: Helen Noyes. *Children of Captain Von Trapp* (7): SHERWOOD SISTERS, HAMILTON BROTHERS: *Liesl*: SANDY DUNCAN. *Friedrich*: Gary Hamilton. *Louisa*: Holly Sherwood. *Kurt*: Eric Hamilton. *Brigitta*: Dawn Sherwood. *Marta*: Maindy Sherwood. *Gretl*: Robin Sherwood. *Rolf Gruber*: REID KLEIN. *Elsa Schraeder*: M'EL DOWD. *Ursula*: Alison Sherwood. *Max Detweiler*: CHRISTOPHER HEWETT. *Herr Zeller*: Larry Swanson. *Baron Elberfeld*: Grant Gordon. A *Postulant*: Kyle Sherwood. *Admiral von Schreiber*: Jay Velie.

Neighbors of Captain Von Trapp, Nuns, Novices, Postulants, Contestants in the Festival Concert, and Storm Troopers: Mona Elson, Susan Feldon, Barbara Gregory, Joy Ellyn Holly, Oksana Iwaszczenko, Patti Kogin, Estella Munson, Marilyn Murphy, Joyce Olson, Candida Pilla, Mary Ann Rydzeski, Ellen Shade, Ann Tell, Beverly Jane Welch, Maggie Worth, Bill Galarno, Garold Gardner.

1967.08 SING, ISRAEL, SING

A Musical Offering (Revue) of Yiddish and Israeli Folklore, Humor and Art Songs in Two Acts. Based on texts and music by Asaf Halevi, Moishe Broderson, Z. Berdi Tswever, M. M. Warshavsky, Itzik Manger, L. Neidus, M. Noy (Neu), Shlomo Weisfisch, Joel Chayes, E. Kishon, H. Kon, Ami Gilad. Special material by M. Nudelman. Directed by Mina Bern. Assistant director and choreographer, Felix Fibich. Music arranged and conducted by Ami Gilad. Assistant conductor, Renee Solomon. Libretto by Wolf Younin. Costumes by Judith. Kibbutz envisioned by Sylvia Younin. Production supervisor, Bernard Sauer. Produced by Ben Bonus. Opend 11 May 1967 at the Brooks Atkinson Theatre and closed 21 May 1967 after 14 performances. Re-opened in an English language adaptation 7 June 1967 at the Brooks Atkinson Theatre and closed 11 June 1967 after 8 performances. Total: 22 performances.

CAST (in order of appearance): *Guards*: ITAMAR, BEN BONUS. *Kibbutz Girls*: MINA BERN, SUSAN WALTERS. *Kibbutz Men*: DANIEL FRANKLIN, BERNARD SAUER. *Oldtimers*: MAX BOZYK, ROSE ROZYK. *Kibbutzniks*: Dance Ensemble. *Dora*: ROSE BOZYK. *David*: DANIEL FRANKLIN.

Dance Ensemble: HADASSAH BODOCH, Melita Ross, Donna Shadden, Marsha Wolfson, Edward Effron, Tony Masullo, Ralph Nelson.

Act 1: In the Kibbutz.

[30]Originally produced in New York 16 November 1959 at the Lunt-Fontanne Theatre for 1443 performances. For Synopsis of Scenes and Musical Numbers, see original 1959 production. Dropped for this production: "An Ordinary Couple."
Added for this production:
"My Favorite Things" (reprise)(added to Act 2, Scene 1 opening)
"Something Good" (added to Act 2, before "Processional")
C. Towers
(*Music and Lyrics by* Richard Rodgers, from the film adaptation.)

Act 2: Kumzits (A Joyful Get-Together) in the Kibbutz.

ACT 1

"The Dream"
Itamar, H. Badoch
Mazal, The Bride: S. Walters. *Companions of the Bride*: Dance Ensemble.

"Only I and You"
S. Walters, D. Franklin

Encounter No. 1
S. Goldstein, M. Bern

Bus Station
B. Sauer, M. Bern

Dance of the Rain
Dance Ensemble

"Song of the Rain"
B. Bonus

Encounter No. 2
S. Goldstein, R. Rozyk

The Law Is the Law
(*by* M. Nudelman)
Policewoman: R. Bozyk. *Kibbutznik*: M. Bozyk.

"Meeting"
Entire Ensemble

"Sing Israel Sing"
B. Bonus

ACT 2

Accordionist
A. Gilad

"We the Sheppards"
Itamar, Dance Ensemble

Boy's Dance (Debka)
Itamar, Dance Ensemble, D. Franklin, B. Sauer

"The Bride Sings"
S. Walters

Economics
(*by* M. Nudelman)
M. Bozyk, S. Goldstein

Reminiscing
B. Bonus

Dances of Many Lands
Dance Ensemble

Two American Business Women
(*by* M. Nudelman)
M. Bern, R. Bozyk
Bride's Side: H. Badoch, Itamar, Dance Ensemble, T. Masullo, M. Ross, D. Shadden, M. Wolfson, E. Effron, R. Nelson. *Groom's Side*: *Musicians*: R. Bozyk, M. Bern, S. Walters, S. Goldstein. *Fathers-in-law*: M. Bozyk, M. Bern. *Bride and Groom*: S. Walters, D. Franklin. *Mothers-in-law*: M. Bern, R. Bozyk.

"Wedding Dance"
Entire Ensemble

"Guard of Israel"
B. Bonus

1967.09 WONDERFUL TOWN

A Revival of the Musical Comedy in Two Acts, 13 Scenes[31]. Book by Joseph Fields and Jerome Chodorov. Based on the play "My Sister Eileen" by Joseph Fields and Jerome Chodorov and the stories of the same name by Ruth McKinney. Music by Leonard Bernstein. Lyrics by Betty Comden and Adolph Green. Directed by Gus Schirmer. Musical numbers and dances staged by Ralph Beaumont. Scenery by Raoul Pene du Bois. Costumes by Frank Thompson. Lighting by Peggy Clark. Musical director, Irving Actman. (Orchestrations by Don Walker.) Produced by the New York City Center Light Opera Company (Jean Dalrymple, Director). Opened 17 May 1967 at the New York City Center and closed 4 June 1967 after 23 performances.

CAST (in order of appearance): *Guide*: Austin Colyer. *Appopoulos*: TED THURSTON. *Lonigan*: Ronn Carroll. *Helen*: BETSY VON FURSTENBERG. *Wreck*: JACK KNIGHT. *Violet*: Betty Hyatt Linton. *Speedy Valenti*: George Marcy. *Eileen*: LINDA BENNETT. *Ruth*: ELAINE STRITCH. *A Strange Man*: Richard Miller. *Drunks*: Ben Laney, Henry Lawrence. *Robert Baker*: NOLAN VAN WAY. *Associate Editors*: Paul Adams, Michael Harrison. *Mrs. Wade*: Claire Waring. *Frank Lippencott*: JACK FLETCHER. *Chef*: Marvin Goodis. *Waiter*: Henry LeClair. *Delivery Boy*: Ronny Hedrick. *Chick Clark*: RICHARD FRANCE. *Shore Patrolman*: Edward Taylor. *First Cadet*: Tim Ramirez. *Second Cadet*: Vito Durante. *Ruth's Escort*: Stokely Gray.

Greenwich Villagers: *Singers*: Maria Bradley, Jacqueline Dean, Mona Elson, Joan Nelson, Barbara Miller, Susan Stockwell, Peggy Walthen, Alyce Elizabeth Webb, Maggie Worth. Paul Adams, Austin Colyer, Marvin Goodis, Stokely Gray, Michael Harrison, Ben Laney, Henry Lawrence, Henry LeClair, Richard Miller, Edward Taylor. *Dancers*: Bonnie Ano, Patty Cope, Judith Danford, Shelley Frankel, Judith Haskell, Ellie Knowles, Ina Kurland, Kuniko Narai, Mary Ann Niles. Guy Allen, Rodd Barry, George Bunt, Vito Durante, Raphael Gilbert, Ronnie Headrick, Dan Joel, Tim Ramirez, Tony Stevens.

[31]Originally produced in New York 25 February 1953 at the Winter Garden for 559 performances. For Synopsis of Scenes and Musical Numbers, see original 1953 production.

1967–1968 SEASON

Neva Small and Robin Wilson in HENRY, SWEET HENRY (Photo: Friedman-Abeles)
Billy Rose Theatre Collection, New York Public Library for the Performing Arts

1967–1968 SEASON

1967.10

SOUTH PACIFIC

A Revival of the Musical Play in Two Acts, 23 Scenes[1]. Music by Richard Rodgers. Lyrics by Oscar Hammerstein II. Book by Oscar Hammerstein II and Joshua Logan. Adapted from James A. Michener's novel "Tales of the South Pacific." Directed by Joe Layton. Scenery and costumes by Fred Voelpel. Lighting by Jules Fisher. Musical director, Jonathan Anderson. Orchestrations by Robert Russell Bennett. Produced by the Music Theater of Lincoln Center (Richard Rodgers, Producing director). Opened 12 June 1967 at the New York State Theatre and closed 9 September 1967 after 104 performances.

CAST (in order of appearance): *Ngana*: Dana Shimizu. *Jerome*: Keenan Shimizu. *Henry*: Robert Ito. *Ensign Nellie Forbush*: FLORENCE HENDERSON. *Emile DeBecque*: GIORGIO TOZZI. *Bloody Mary*: IRENE BYATT. *Abner*: Judd Jones. *Stewpot*: Brad Sullivan. *Luther Billis*: DAVID DOYLE. *Professor*: Mickey [Michael] Karm. *Lt. Joseph Cable, U.S.M.C.*: JUSTIN McDONOUGH. *Capt. George Brackett, U.S.N.*: LYLE TALBOT. *Cmdr. William Harbison, U.S.N.*: Bob Monroe. *Yeoman Herbert Quale*: Ted Story. *Sgt. Kenneth Johnson*: William Lutz. *Seaman Richard West*: Mark East. *Seabee Morton Wise*: Gordon Cook. *Seaman Tom O'Brien*: James O'Sullivan. *Radio Operator Bob McCaffrey*: Roger Brown. *Marine Cpl. Hamilton Steves*: Dick Ensslen. *Seabee Thomas Hassinger*: Philip Lucas. *Seabee James Jerome*: Joseph della Sorte. *Pvt. Sven Larsen*: Don Dolan. *Pvt. Jack Walters*: Bob Barbieri. *Pvt. Dick Sederholm*: Jess. Richards. *Seabee Roger Pitt*: Marvin Camillo. *Seabee John Nathan*: David Jarratt. *Seabee Keith Moore*: Dale Westerman. *Lt. Genevieve Marshall*: Jane Coleman. *Ensign Lisa Manelli*: Lisa Damon. *Ensign Connie Walewska*: Martha Danielle. *Ensign Janet MacGregor*: Susan Campbell. *Ensign Bessie Noonan*: JOYCE MARET. *Ensign Rita Adams*: Ann Nathan. *Ensign Sue Yaeger*: Joyce McDonald. *Ensign Cora MacRae*: Lynn Dovel. *Ensign Dinah Murphy*: Bobbi Baird. *Liat*: JOYCE MARET. *Lt. Buzz Adams*: Jack Knight.

1967.11

JUDY GARLAND AT HOME AT THE PALACE

A Variety Revue in Two Acts[2]. Staged by Richard Barstow. Costumes by Bill Smith, Travilla. Lighting by Ralph Alswang. Musical director, Bobby Cole. A Group V Ltd. Production. Produced by Sid Luft. Opened 31 July 1967 at the Palace Theatre and closed 26 August 1967 after 24 performances; reopened a return engagement 25-27 December 1967 at the Felt Forum, Madison Square Garden for 3 additional peformances. Total: 27 performances.

CAST: JUDY GARLAND, John Bubbles, Jackie Vernon, Francis Brunn, Lorna Luft, Joey Luft.

ACT 1

Scene 1

Francis Brunn

Scene 2

John Bubbles (song and dance)

Scene 3

Jackie Vernon (comedy)

ACT 2[3]

Judy Garland:

"I Feel a Song Coming On" (from film EVERY NIGHT AT EIGHT)
(*Music by* Jimmy McHugh. *Lyrics by* Dorothy Fields and George Oppenheimer.)

"Almost Like Being in Love" (from BRIGADOON)
(*Music by* Frederick Loewe. *Lyrics by* Alan Jay Lerner.)

"This Can't Be Love" (from THE BOYS FROM SYRACUSE)
(*Music by* Richard Rodgers. *Lyrics by* Lorenz Hart.)

Medley (of her film hits):

"You Made Me Love You" (from film THE BROADWAY MELODY OF 1938)
(*Music by* James V. Monaco. *Lyrics by* Joseph McCarthy.)

"For Me and My Gal" (from film FOR ME AND MY GAL)
(*Music by* George W. Meyer. *Lyrics by* Edgar Leslie and Ray Goetz.)

"The Trolley Song" (from film MEET ME IN ST. LOUIS)
(*Music and Lyrics by* Hugh Martin and Ralph Blane.)

"What Now My Love"
(*Music by* Gilbert Becaud. *Lyrics by* Carl Sigman.)

(Medley with family):

"Bob White"
J. Garland, L. Luft
(*Music and Lyrics by* Johnny Mercer and Bernard Hanighen.)

"Jamboree Jones"
J. Garland, L. Luft
(*Music and Lyrics by* Johnny Mercer.)

"Together" (from GYPSY)
J. Garland, L. Luft, J. Luft
(*Music by* Jule Styne. *Lyrics by* Stephen Sondheim.)

"Ol' Man River" (from SHOWBOAT)
(*Music by* Jerome Kern. *Lyrics by* Oscar Hammerstein II.)

"That's Entertainment" (from film THE BANDWAGON)
(*Music by* Arthur Schwartz. *Lyrics by* Howard Dietz.)

"I Loved Him, But He Didn't Love Me" (from WAKE UP AND DREAM, London)
(*Music and Lyrics by* Cole Porter.)

"Rock-a-Bye Your Baby With a Dixie Melody" (from SINBAD)
(*Music by* Jean Schwartz. *Lyrics by* Sam M. Lewis and Joe Young)

"Me and My Shadow"
(*Music by* Al Jolson and Dave Dreyer. *Lyrics by* Billy Rose.)

"Over the Rainbow" (from film THE WIZARD OF OZ)
(*Music by* Harold Arlen. *Lyrics by* E. Y. Harburg.)

[1]First produced in New York 7 April 1949 at the Majestic Theatre for 1925 performances. For Synopsis of Scenes and Musical Numbers, see original 1949 production.

[2]Miss Garland appeared before at the Palace Theatre 16 October 1951 for 266 performances, and returned again 26 September 1956 to the Palace, and later to the Metropolitan Opera House (1959) and Carnegie Hall (1961). Details of these performances are beyond the scope of this book.

[3]Not in performance order.

1967.12

BUDDY HACKETT AND EDDIE FISHER

A Two-Man Revue in Two Acts. Musical director, Colin Romoff. (Produced by Hackett Productions and Fisher Productions.) Opened 28 August 1967 at the Palace Theatre and closed 7 October 1967 after 42 performances.

CAST: BUDDY HACKETT (Comedy monologues), EDDIE FISHER. (Songs). (Opening Act alternates nightly.)

Eddie Fisher's repertoire[4]:

"Let Me Entertain You" (from GYPSY)
(*Music by* Jule Styne. *Lyrics by* Stephen Sondheim.)

"The Impossible Dream" (from MAN OF LA MANCHA)
(*Music by* Mitch Leigh. *Lyrics by* Joe Darion.)

"If She Walked Into My Life" (from MAME)
(*Music and Lyrics by* Jerry Herman.)

"Mame" (from MAME)
(*Music and Lyrics by* Jerry Herman.)

"People Like You"
(*Music and Lyrics by* Larry Kusik and Eddie Snyder.)

"Do-Re-Mi" (from THE SOUND OF MUSIC)
(*Music by* Richard Rodgers. *Lyrics by* Oscar Hammerstein II.)

Finale (Duet with Buddy Hackett)

[4]Not in performance order.

1967.13 MARLENE DIETRICH

A One-Woman Show in One Act. Musical arrangements and orchestra conducted by Burt Bacharach. Lighting by Joe Davis. Production supervisor, Jerry Adler. A Nine O'Clock Theatre Production. Produced by Alexander H. Cohen. Opened 9 October 1967 at the Lunt-Fontanne Theatre and closed 18 November 1967 after 48 performances.

CAST: MARLENE DIETRICH.

REPERTOIRE[5]

"I Can't Give You Anything But Love, Baby" (from BLACKBIRDS OF 1928)
(*Music by* Jimmy McHugh. *Lyrics by* Dorothy Fields.)

"You're the Cream in My Coffee" (from HOLD EVERYTHING)
(*Music by* Ray Henderson. *Lyrics by* Buddy G. DeSylva and Lew Brown.)

"My Blue Heaven" (from ZIEGFELD FOLLIES OF 1927)
(*Music by* Walter Donaldson. *Lyrics by* George Whiting.)

"(See What) The Boys in the Back Room (Will Have)" (from film DESTRY RIDES AGAIN)
(*Music by* Frederick Holländer. *Lyrics by* Frank Loesser.)

"The Laziest Gal in Town" (from film STAGE FRIGHT)
(*Music and Lyrics by* Cole Porter.)

"When the World Was Young" (*Original French Lyrics by* Angela Vannier.)
(*Music by* M. Philippe-Gerard. *Lyrics by* Johnny Mercer.)

"Jonny" (from film SONG OF SONGS)
(*Music by* Frederick Holländer. *Lyrics by* Edward Heyman.)

"Go Away from My Window"
(*arr. by* J. J. Niles.)

"I Wish You Love"
(*Music by* Charles Trenet. *Lyrics by* Albert Beach.)

"The War's Over, Seems We Won, Hooray"

"Boomerang Baby"

"(Naughty) Lola" (from film THE BLUE ANGEL)
(*Music and Lyrics by* Frederick Holländer.)

"Don't Ask Me Why"

"Everyone's Gone to the Moon"
(*Music and Lyrics by* Kenneth King.)

"Marie, Marie"
(*Music by* Gilbert Becaud. *Lyrics by* Pierre Delanoe and Kolpe.)

"Lili Marlene"
(*Music by* Norbert Schultze. *Lyrics by* Hans Leip and Tommie Connor.)

"Where Have All the Flowers Gone?"
(*Music and Lyrics by* Pete Seeger.)

"Honeysuckle Rose" (from HOT CHOCOLATES)
(*Music by* Fats Waller. *Lyrics by* Andy Razaf.)

"Falling in Love Again" (from film THE BLUE ANGEL)
(*Music and Lyrics by* Frederick Holländer.)

"La Vie en Rose"
(*Music by* Louiguy. *Lyrics by* Edith Piaf.)

"Shir Hatan"
(*Music and Lyrics by* Z. Sahar.)

1967.14 HENRY, SWEET HENRY

A Musical in Two Acts, 20 Scenes. Book by Nunnally Johnson. Based on the novel "The World of Henry Orient" by Nora Johnson. Music and lyrics by Bob Merrill. Entire Production directed by George Roy Hill. Choreography by Michael Bennett. Scenery and lighting by Robert Randolph. Costumes by Alvin Colt. Musical direction and vocal arrangements by Shepard Coleman. Orchestrations by Eddie Sauter. Dance music by William Goldenberg and Marvin Hamlisch. Associate producer, Joseph H. Shoctor. Produced by Edward Spector Productions and Norman Twain. Opened 23 October 1967 at the Palace Theatre and closed 31 December 1967 after 80 performances.

CAST (in order of appearance): *Kafritz*: ALICE PLAYTEN. *Valerie Boyd*: ROBIN WILSON. *Miss Cooney*: Barbara Beck. *Marian Gilbert*: NEVA SMALL. *Henry Orient*: DON AMECHE. *Stella*: LOUISE LASSER. *Mrs. Gilbert*: Trudy Wallace. *Usherette*: Julie Sargant. *Mrs. Boyd*: CAROL BRUCE. *Russ*: John Mineo. *Captain Kenneth*: George NeJame. *Hal*: Robert Iscove. *Policeman*: Gerard Brentte. *Mr. Boyd*: MILO BOULTON. *Policeman*: Charles Rule. *Big Val*: K. C. TOWNSHEND.

Norton School Students: Chris Bocchino, Lori Cesar, Terry Forman, Joyce James, Baayork Lee, Gina Page, Ilene Schatz, Joy Stark, Rebecca Urich, Pia Zadora. *Knickerbocker Greys*: Paul Charles, Robert Iscove, Joe Mazzello, Kim Milford, John Mineo, George NeJame, Craig Wineline. *Adult Ensemble*: Robert Avian, Barbara Beck, Gerard Brentte, Gene Castle, Robert Fitch, Marvin Goodis, Neil Jones, Mary Ann Kerrick, Priscilla Lopez, Lee Lund, Laried Montgomery, Charles Rule, Julie Sargant, Mary Ann Snow, Trudy Wallace.

The action takes place in present day New York City.

Act 1, Scene 1: A Street in New York City. *Scene 2*: Locker Room. *Scene 3*: Central Park Zoo. *Scene 4*: Two Bedrooms. *Scene 5*: Concert Hall. *Scene 6*: Val's Bedroom. *Scene 7*: Telephone Booths. *Scene 8*: Luncheonette. *Scene 9*: Street Telephone Booth. *Scene 10*: Orient's Apartment—Exterior and Interior.

Act 2, Scene 1: Boyd's Living Room. *Scene 2*: Washington Square. *Scene 3*: Orient's Apartment. *Scene 4*: Boyd's Living Room. *Scene 5*: Exterior School and Locker Room. *Scene 6*: Cocktail Bar. *Scene 7*: Exterior Orient's Apartment. *Scene 8*: Boyd's Living Room. *Scene 9*: Orient's Bedroom. *Scene 10*: Val's Bedroom; Knickerbocker Grey Happening.

ACT 1

Scene 1
"Academic Fugue"
Company

Scene 2
"In Some Little World"
R. Wilson

Scene 3
"Pillar to Post"
D. Ameche, L. Lasser

Scene 4
"Here I Am"
R. Wilson

Scene 6
"Whereas"[6]
R. Wilson, N. Small

Scene 8
"I Wonder How It Is to Dance With a Boy"
N. Small, Girls

Scene 9
"Nobody Steps on Kafritz"
A. Playten

Scene 10
"Henry, Sweet Henry"
R. Wilson, N. Small
"Woman in Love"
R. Wilson, N. Small
"The People Watchers"
Company

ACT 2

Scene 2
"Weary Near to Dyin'"
R. Wilson, Hippies

Scene 5
"Poor Little Person"
A. Playten, Girls, Knickerbocker Greys
"I'm Blue Too"
R. Wilson, N. Small

Scene 6
"To Be Artistic"
D. Ameche, C. Bruce

[5]Not in performance order.

[6]Dropped after opening.

Scene 9
"Forever"
D. Ameche
Scene 10
"Do You Ever Go to Boston"
R. Wilson
Finale: "Here I Am" (reprise)
R. Wilson

1967.15 HELLO, DOLLY!

(All All-Black Cast takes over the) Musical Comedy in Two Acts, 15 Scenes[7]. Book by Michael Stewart. Based on the play "The Matchmaker" by Thornton Wilder. Music and lyrics by Jerry Herman. Directed and choreographed by Gower Champion. Re-staged by Lucia Victor. Settings by Oliver Smith. Costumes by Freddy Wittop. Lighting by Jean Rosenthal. Musical direction, Saul Schechtman. Orchestrations by Philip J. Lang. Dance and incidental music arranged by Peter Howard. Assistant to the director, Lucia Victor. A David Merrick-Champion Five Inc. Production. Produced by David Merrick. Opened 12 November 1967 (as part of the show's continuous run) at the St. James Theatre and closed 20 December 1969 after 889 performances[8].

CAST (in the order of appearance): *Mrs. Dolly Gallagher Levi*: PEARL BAILEY. *Ernestina*: Mary Mable King. *Ambrose Kemper*: Roger Lawson. *Horse*: Diane Conway, Barbara Harper. *Horace Vandergelder*: CAB CALLOWAY. *Ermengarde*: Sherri 'Peaches' Brewer. *Cornelius Hackl*: JACK CROWDER. *Barnaby Tucker*: WINSTON DeWITT HEMSLEY. *Irene Molloy*: EMILY YANCY. *Minnie Fay*: CHRIS CALLOWAY. *Mrs. Rose*: Marie Bryant. *Rudolph*: Morgan Freeman. *Judge*: Walter P. Brown. *Court Clerk*: James Kennon-Wilson.

Townspeople, Waiters, Etc.: Marki Bey, Edloe R. Brown, Dianne Conway, Merle Derby, Dolores Easty, Demarest Gray, Lavinia Hamilton, Barbara Harper, Pattie Harris, Lolli Hinton, Ernestine Jackson, Laverne Ligon, Joni Palmer, Saundra Sharp, Freda Turner, Guy Allen, Bryant Baker, Fred Benjamin, Walter P. Brown, Donald Coleman, Peter Colly, Dowlin Davis, Clifton Davis, Sargent Faulkner, Larry Ferrell, Julius Fields, Ray Gilbert, Olon Godare, Reginald Jackson, Don Jay, Bob Johnson, James Kennon-Wilson, Peter Norman, E. B. Smith, Joe Williams.

1967.16 HOW NOW, DOW JONES

A Musical Comedy in Two Acts, 18 Scenes. Book by Max Shulman. Based on an original idea by Carolyn Leigh. Music by Elmer Bernstein. Lyrics by Carolyn Leigh. Production directed by George Abbott. Scenic production by Oliver Smith. Costumes by Robert Mackintosh. Lighting by Martin Aronstein. Musical direction, dance and vocal arrangements by Peter Howard. Orchestrations by Philip J. Lang. Dances and musical numbers staged by Gillian Lynne. Associate producer, Samuel Liff. Produced by David Merrick by arrangement with Edwin H. Morris and Company. Opened 7 December 1967 at the Lunt-Fontanne Theatre and closed 15 June 1968 after 220 performances.

CAST (in order of appearance): *Cynthia*: BRENDA VACCARO. *Herbert*: JAMES CONGDON. *Broker*: Joe McGrath. *Kate*: MARLYN MASON. *Wingate*: HIRAM SHERMAN. *Nichols*: Bob Gorman. *Judy Evans*: Patti Davis. *Wally*: Alexander Orfaly. *Charley*: ANTHONY [Tony] ROBERTS. *Sue Ellen*: JENNIFER DARLING. *Bradbury*: REX EVERHART. *Waiter*: Tommy Tune. *Senator McFetridge*: BARNARD HUGHES. *Dow*: Stanley Simmonds. *Jones*: Martin Ambrose. *Tycoons*: Frank DeSal, Bob Gorman, John Joy, Alexander Orfaly. *Lion*: Ron Schwinn. *Customers' Men*: Bob Gorman, Frank DeSal, John Joy, Doug Spungler. *Dr. Gilman*: SAMMY SMITH. *Widows: (4)*: *Mrs. Ragosa*: Francesca Smith. *Mrs. Klein*: Fran Stevens. *Mrs. Harris*: Sally DeMay. *Mrs. Callahan*: Lucie Lancaster. *Mrs. Millhauser*: CHARLOTTE JONES. A.K.: ARTHUR HUGHES.

Dancers: Oscar Anthony, Linnea Chandler, Joel Conrad, Patricia Cope, Frank DeSal, Lois Etelman, Cyndi Howard, Yanco Inone, Eileen Lawlor, Debra Lyman, Diana Quijano, Sally Ransone, George Ramos, Ron Schwinn, Doug Spingler, Ron L. Steinbeck, Pat Trott. *Singers*: Martin Ambrose, Leigh Curran, Patti Davis, Bill Gibbens, Bob Gorman, Maria Hero, John Joy, Joe McGrath, Jack Murray, Alexander Orfaly, Anna Pagan, Dixie Stewart, Mara Worth.

The action takes place in present day New York City.

Act 1, Scene 1: Financial District. *Scene 2*: Child's Restaurant. *Scene 3*: Wingate's Private Office. *Scene 4*: Kate's Apartment. *Scene 5*: Wall Street—Early A.M. *Scene 6*: Wingate & Co., Brokers. *Scene 7*: Mrs. Millhauser's Living Room. *Scene 8*: Kate's Apartment. *Scene 9*: Wingate's Private Office. *Scene 10*: Wall Street. *Scene 11*: Dow Jones Office.

Act 2, Scene 1: New York City. *Scene 2*: Wingate's Private Office. *Scene 3*: Mrs. Millhauser's Living Room. *Scene 4*: Cynthia's Apartment. *Scene 5*: Financial District. *Scene 6*: Kate's Apartment. *Scene 7*: Wingate & Co., Brokers.

ACT 1
Scene 1
"A-B-C"
B. Vaccaro, Tourists, Wall Streeters
Scene 2
"They Don't Make 'Em Like That Anymore"
M. Mason, B. Vaccaro
"Live a Little"
A. Roberts, M. Mason, New Yorkers
Crazy Night Ballet
"The Pleasure's About to Be Mine"
A. Roberts, M. Mason
Scene 3
"A Little Investigation"
H. Sherman, B. Hughes, S. Simmonds, M. Ambrose, Tycoons
Scene 4
"Walk Away"
M. Mason
Scene 6
"Goodbye, Failure, Goodbye"
A. Roberts, Customers' Men, Brokers
Scene 7
"Step to the Rear"
A. Roberts, C. Jones, Widows, Ensemble
Scene 8
"Shakespeare Lied"
M. Mason, B. Vaccaro, S. Smith
Scene 11
"Big Trouble"
M. Mason

ACT 2
Scene 1
"Credo"
S. Smith, F. Stevens, Widows, New Yorkers
"One of Those Moments"
M. Mason
Scene 2
"Big Trouble" (reprise)
H. Sherman, Tycoons
Scene 4
"He's Here!"
B. Vaccaro
Scene 5
"Panic"
Entire Cast
Scene 6
"Touch and Go"
A. Roberts, M. Mason
Scene 7
"That's Good Enough For Me"
Entire Cast

[7]Originally produced 16 January 1964 at the St. James Theatre. For Synopsis of Scenes and Musical Numbers, see original 1964 production.
[8]Production resumed with white principals 26 December 1969.

1967.17 BRIGADOON

A Revival of the Musical Play in Two Acts, a Prologue and 11 Scenes[9]. Book and lyrics by Alan Jay Lerner. Music by Frederick Loewe. Original dances and musical numbers staged by Agnes de Mille, restaged by Gemze de Lappe and Dennis Cole. Directed by Gus Schirmer. Settings by Oliver Smith. Lighting by Peggy Clark. Costumes by Stanley Simmons. Musical director, Jonathan Anderson. (Vocal arrangements by Frederick Loewe. Orchestrations by Ted Royal.) Produced by the New York City Center Light Opera Company (Jean Dalrymple, Director). Opened 13 December 1967 at the New York City Center and closed 31 December 1967 after 23 performances.

CAST (in order of appearance): *Tommy Albright*: BILL HAYES. *Jeff Douglas*: RUSSELL NYPE. *Sandy Dean*: Henry Lawrence. *Meg Brockie*: KAREN MORROW. *Archie Beaton*: Earl McDonald. *Harry Beaton*: EDWARD VILLELLA. *Andrew MacLaren*: Alexander Clark. *Jean MacLaren*: Sarah Jane Smith. *Fiona MacLaren*: MARGOT MOSER. *Angus MacGuffie*: Gordon Cook. *Charlie Dalrymple*: EVAN THOMAS. *Maggie Anderson*: Leslie Franzos. *Sword Dancers*: Dennis Cole, Wilfred Schuman. *Mr. Lundi*: William LeMassena. *Bagpiper*: Maurice Eisenstadt. *Frank*: Paul Adams. *Jane Ashton*: Jeanne Murray Vanderbilt.

Townsfolk of Brigadoon: *Singers*: Chris Callen, Phyllis Bash, Jane Coleman, Peggy Cooper, Mona Elson, Marta Heflin, Oksana Iweszczenko, Mina Jo King, Barbara Miller, Roberta Vatske, Paul Adams, Donald Brassington, Edward Becker, Peter Clark, Gordon Cook, Henry Lawrence, Ken Richards, Robert Monteil, Don Wonder. *Dancers*: Anita Arnell, Joanna Crosson, Chele Graham, Jane Jaffe, Nicole Karol, Karen Kristin, Lucia Lambert, Toodie Wittmer, Marget Wyeth, Paul Berne, Scott Hunter, J. David Kirby, William Koch, Dick Korthaze, Wilfred Schuman, Bud Spencer, Ron Tassone, Duane Taylor.

1967.18 HOW TO BE A JEWISH MOTHER

A Comedy with Music in Two Acts. Conceived by Seymour Vall. Based on the book of the same name by Dan Greenburg. Music by Michael Leonard. Lyrics by Herbert Marshall. Directed by Avery Schreiber. Scenery by Robert Randolph. Costumes by Michael Travis. Lighting by John J. Moore. Musical staging by Doug Rogers. Musical direction and arrangements by Julian Stein. Associate producers, Rick Mandell, Margaret Aldrich. Produced by Jon-Lee and Seymour Vall. Opened 28 December 1967 at the Hudson theatre and closed 13 January 1968 after 21 performances.

CAST: MOLLY PICON, GODFREY CAMBRIDGE.

ACT 1

"Once the Man You Laughed At"

"Laugh a Little"

ACT 2

"Since the Time We Met"

"The Wedding Song"

"Child You Are"

1968.01 THE HAPPY TIME

A Musical in Two Acts, 15 Scenes. Book by N. Richard Nash. Based on the novel by Robert L. Fontaine and the play of the same name by Samuel Taylor. Music by John Kander. Lyrics by Fred Ebb. Directed, filmed and choreographed by Gower Champion. Settings by Peter Wexler. Costumes by Freddy Wittop. Lighting by Jean Rosenthal. Film sequences created by Christopher Chapman. Film technical direction by Barry O. Gordon. Orchestrations by Don Walker. Musical direction and vocal arrangements by Oscar Kosarin. Associate choreographer, Kevin Carlisle. Dance and incidental music arrangements by Marvin Laird. Associate producer, Samuel Liff. Produced by David Merrick. Opened 18 January 1968 at the Broadway Theatre and closed 28 September 1968 after 286 performances.

CAST (in order of appearance): *Jacques Bonnard*: ROBERT GOULET. *Suzanne Bonnard*: Jeanne Arnold. *Philippe Bonnard*: GEORGE S. IRVING. *Bibi Bonnard*: MIKE [Michael] RUPERT. *Louis Bonnard*: CHARLES DURNING. *Annabelle Bonnard*: Kim Freund. *Gillie Bonnard*: Julane Stites. *Nanette Bonnard*: Connie Simmons. *Felice Bonnard*: JUNE SQUIBB. *Grandpere Bonnard*: DAVID WAYNE. *The Six Angels*: *Lizette*: Jacki Garland. *Dorine*: Mary Gail Laverenz. *Sylvie*: Tammie Fillhart. *Monique*: Mary Ann O'Reilly. *Bella*: Vicki Powers. *Grace*: Susan Sigrist. *Laurie Mannon*: JULIE GREGG. *Foufie*: Jeffrey Golkin. *Ganache*: Dallas Johann. *Swing Dancer*: Sammy Williams.

Dancers: Ron Abshire, Jovanni Anthony, Quinn Baird, Andy Bew, Blake Brown, Leonard Crofoot, Ron Crofoot, Wayne Dugger, Joe Giamalva, Dallas Johann, Gene Law, Steve Reinhart, Jon Simonson, Michael Stearns. *Singers*: Marc Anthony, Alan Blight, George Connolly, Tom De Mastri, Paul Dwyer, Scott Gandert, Eric Hamilton, Gary Hamilton, Jeffrey Hamilton, Kevin Hamilton, Mark Lonergan, Brian Shyer, Brandy Wayne, Teddy Williams, Marc Winters.

The action takes place in the past in Jacques Bonnard's studio; and earlier still, in his home in a small town in Canada.

Act 1, Scene 1: Jacques' Studio. *Scene 2*: The Bonnard Home. *Scene 3*: The theatre. *Scene 4*: Bibi's bedroom. *Scene 5*: The Classroom. *Scene 6*: The Schoolyard. *Scene 7*: The Bonnard garden.

Act 2, Scene 1: Jacques' studio. *Scene 2*: A street in St. Pierre. *Scene 3*: The gymnasium. *Scene 4*: After the party. *Scene 5*: The Schoolyard. *Scene 6*: Grandpere's room. *Scene 7*: Jacques' studio. *Scene 8*: The School, Bibi's graduation.

ACT 1

Scene 1

"The Happy Time"
R. Goulet, Family

Scene 2

"He's Back"
The Family

Scene 3

"Catch My Garter"
The Six Angels

"Tomorrow Morning"
R. Goulet, D. Wayne, M. Rupert, The Six Angels

Scene 4

"Please Stay"
M. Rupert, R. Goulet

"I Don't Remember You"
R. Goulet

Scene 5

"St. Pierre"
The Glee Club

"I Don't Remember You" (reprise)
J. Gregg, R. Goulet

Scene 6

"Without Me"
M. Rupert, Schoolmates

Scene 7

"The Happy Time" (reprise)
R. Goulet

ACT 2

Scene 1

"(Walking) Among My Yesterdays"
R. Goulet

Scene 2

("Please Stay" reprise)
(J. Gregg)

Scene 3

"The Life of the Party"
D. Wayne, The Six Angels, Schoolboys

Scene 4

"Seeing Things"
R. Goulet, J. Gregg

Scene 5

Ballet
M. Rupert, J. Stites, K. Freund, C. Simmons, Schoolboys

[9]Originally produced in New York 13 March 1947 at the Ziegfeld Theatre for 581 performances. For Synopsis of Scenes and Musical Numbers, see original 1947 production.

Scene 6
"A Certain Girl"
D. Wayne, R. Goulet, M. Rupert
Scene 7
"Being Alive"[10]
R. Goulet
Scene 8
("St. Pierre" reprise)
(Schoolboys)
"The Happy Time" (reprise)
R. Goulet, Entire Company

1968.02 DARLING OF THE DAY

A Musical Comedy in Two Acts, 14 Scenes. Based on the novel "Buried Alive" by Arnold Bennett. Music by Jule Styne. Lyrics by E. Y. Harburg. Directed by Noel Willman. Choreography by Lee Theodore. Scenery by Oliver Smith. Costumes by Raoul Pene du Bois. Lighting by Peggy Clark. Musical direction and vocal arrangements by Buster Davis. Dance music by Trude Rittman. Orchestrations by Ralph Burns. Produced by The Theatre Guild and Joel Schenker. Opened 27 January 1968 at the George Abbott Theatre and closed 24 February 1968 after 33 performances[11].

CAST (in order of appearances): *Oxford*: PETER WOODTHORPE. *Priam Farll*: VINCENT PRICE. *Henry Leek*: Charles Welch. *Old Gentleman*: Carl Nicholas. *Lady Vale*: BRENDA FORBES. *Cabby*: Ross Miles. *Doctor*: Leo Leyden. *Alice Challice*: PATRICIA ROUTLEDGE. *Daphne*: Joy Nichols. *Alf*: TEDDY GREEN. *Bert*: Marc Jordan. *Rosalind*: Beth Howland. *Sydney*: Reid Klein. *Attendant*: Larry Brucker. *Frame Maker*: Paul Eichel. *Duncan*: Mitchell Jason. *Equerry*: John Aman. *The King*: Charles Gerald. *Constable*: John Aman. *Mrs. Leek*: Camila Ashland. *Curates*: Herb Wilson, Fred Siretta. *Pennington*: Micahel Lewis. *Judge*: Leo Leyden.

Singers: Marian Haraldson, Kay Oslin, Jeannette Seibert, Maggie Task, Maggie Worth, John Aman, Larry Brucker, Paul Eichel, Reid Klein, Carl Nicholas, Albert Zimmerman. *Dancers*: Bonnie Ano, Reby Howells, Beth Howland, Georgianne Thon, Phyllis Wallach, Denise Winston, Christopher Chadman, George Lee, Jim May, Ross Miles, Fred Siretta, Herb Wilson.

The action takes place in London and Putney in 1905.

Act 1, Scene 1: Oxford's Art Gallery—London. *Scene 2*: Farll's London House. *Scene 3*: The Pub in Putney. *Scene 4*: Farll's London House. *Scene 5*: London Street. *Scene 6*: Paradise Villa, Putney. *Scene 7*: Oxford's Salon. *Scene 8*: The Thames River Bank. *Scene 9*: Paradise Villa.

Act 2, Scene 1: Oxford's Salon. *Scene 2*: Paradise Villa Garden. *Scene 3*: Putney High Street. *Scene 4*: The Pub. *Scene 5*: The Courtroom.

ACT 1
Scene 1
"Mad For Art"
Art Lovers (Ensemble)
"He's a Genius"
P. Woodthorpe, V. Price, C. Welch
Scene 2
"To Get Out of This World Alive"
V. Price
Scene 3
"It's Enough To Make a Lady Fall in Love"
P. Routledge, T. Green, M. Jordan, Putney Friends (Ensemble)
Scene 5
"A Gentleman's Gentleman"
P. Routledge, T. Green, M. Jordan, V. Price, M. Jason, Bystanders (Ensemble)
Scene 6
"Double Soliloquy"
V. Price, P. Routledge
"Let's See What Happens"
P. Routledge, V. Price
Scene 7
"Panache"
P. Woodthorpe, B. Forbes
Scene 8
"I've Got a Rainbow Working for Me"
V. Price, Putney Friends (Ensemble)
Scene 9
"Money, Money, Money"
T. Green, M. Jordan, R. Klein
"That Something Extra Special"
P. Routledge
"Money, Money, Money" (reprise)
T. Green, M. Jordan, R. Klein

ACT 2
Scene 2
"What Makes a Marriage Merry"
P. Routledge, V. Price, T. Green, M. Jordan, J. Nichols, B. Howland
"He's a Genius" (reprise)
P. Woodthorpe, Assistants
Scene 4
"Not on Your Nellie"
P. Routledge, T. Green, M. Jordan, Putney Friends (Ensemble)
"Sunset Tree"
V. Price, P. Routledge
Scene 5
"Butler in the Abbey"
V. Price, Courtroom (Ensemble)
"Not on Your Nellie" (reprise)
Entire Company

1968.03 GOLDEN RAINBOW

A Musical (Comedy) in Two Acts, 13 Scenes. Book by Ernest Kinoy. Based on a play ("A Hole in the Head") by Arnold Schulman. Music and lyrics by Walter Marks. Directed by Arthur Storch. Choreography by Tom Panko. Scenery and lighting by Robert Randolph. Costumes by Alvin Colt. Musical direction and vocal arrangements by Elliot Lawrence. Orchestrations by Pat Williams and Jack Andrews. Dance music arranged by Marvin Hamlisch and Luther Henderson. Associate choreographer, Martin Allen. Additional scoring by Elliot Lawrence. A Diplomat Production. Produced by Joseph P. Harris and Ira Bernstein. Opened 4 February 1968 at the Sam S. Shubert Theatre and closed 12 January 1969 after 385 performances.

CAST (in order of appearance): *Mr. Novotny*: Alan Kass. *Ally*: SCOTT JACOBY. *Mr. Hausknecht*: Howard Mann. *Eloise*: Linda Jorgens. *Laundryman*: Charles Karel. *Henry*: Will Hussung. *Mr. Diamond*: Sid Raymond. *Larry Davis*: STEVE LAWRENCE. *Mrs. Magruder*: Fay Sappington. *Lou Garrity*: JOSEPH SIROLA. *Jerome Stone*: Gene Foote. *Rosemary Garrity*: Marilyn Cooper. *Gordon*: John Anania. *Mr. Korngold*: Sam Kressen. *First Reporter*: Charles Karel. *Second Reporter*: Lanier Davis. *Lead Dancer*: Diana Saunders. *Judy Harris*: EYDIE GORME. *Georgia*: Carol Conte. *Stripper*: Thelma Sherr. *Sam*: Frank Pietri. *Umbawa*: Larry Merritt. *Persian Girl*: Linda Jorgens. *Cat Girl*: Carole Bishop. *Nebuchadnezzar*: John Anania. *Virgin*: Diana Saunders. *Hero*: Antony DeVecchi. *Stage Manager*: Charles Karel. *Victor*: Lanier Davis. *Gambler*: Michael Vita.

Dancers: Carole Bishop, Carol Conte, Susan Donovan, Antony DeVecchi, Tina Faye, Alice Glenn, Linda Jorgens, Maralyn Miles, Jean Preece, Wayne Boyd, Gene Foote, Blair Hammond, Larry Merritt, Frank Pietri, Tom Rolla, Michael Shawn, Michael Vita. *Showgirls*: Betty Jo Alvies, Bernadette Brookes, Rae Samuels, Thelma Sherr.

The action takes place in Las Vegas—Today.

Act 1, Scene 1: The Strip—Las Vegas. *Scene 2*: Golden Rainbow Lobby. *Scene 3*: The Airport. *Scene 4*: Golden Rainbow Lobby. *Scene 5*: The Algeria Patio Restaurant. *Scene 6*: Golden Rainbow Pantry. *Scene 7*: Golden Rainbow Lobby.

Act 2, Scene 1: Babylon Nightclub. *Scene 2*: Backstage. *Scene 3*: The Desert. *Scene 4*: Golden Rainbow Lobby. *Scene 5*: Babylon Casino. *Scene 6*: The Golden Rainbow.

---

[10]Dropped after opening.
[11]Book uncredited; bookwriter Nunnally Johnson withdrew his name from credits during tryout.

ACT 1
Scene 1
"Golden Rainbow"[12]
Las Vegans (Ensemble)
Scene 2
"We Got Us"
S. Lawrence, S. Jacoby
Scene 3
"He Needs Me Now"
E. Gorme
Scene 4
"Kid"
S. Lawrence
Scene 5
"For Once in Your Life"
E. Gorme, S. Lawrence, Boys
Scene 6
"Taking Care of You"
E. Gorme, S. Jacoby, Friends (Ensemble)
Scene 7
"I've Got To Be Me"
S. Lawrence
ACT 2
Scene 1
"The Fall of Babylon"
Babylonians (Ensemble)
Scene 2
"Taste"
J. Sirola, Friends (Ensemble)
Scene 3
"Desert Moon"
S. Lawrence, E. Gorme
"All in Fun"
S. Lawrence, E. Gorme
Scene 4
"It's You Again"
E. Gorme
Scene 5
"I've Got To Be Me" (reprise)
S. Lawrence
Scene 6
"How Could I Be So Wrong"
E. Gorme
"We Got Us" (reprise)
S. Lawrence, E. Gorme, S. Jacoby
Finale
Entire Company

1968.04 THE GRAND MUSIC HALL OF ISRAEL

A Musical Revue (from Israel) in Two Acts, 13 Scenes, in Hebrew. Staged and choreographed by Jonathan Karmon. Musical direction and arrangements by Itzchak Graziani. Assistant director, Gavri Levi. Costumes designed by Hovav Kruvi; costumes executed by Bertha Kwartz. Lighting by Jules Fisher. Assistant conductor, Ami Gilad. Produced by Lee Guber and Shelly Gross by arrangement with Bruno Coquatrix. Opened 6 February 1968 at the Palace Theatre and closed 31 March 1968 after 64 performances.

CAST: HELENA HENDEL, GEULA GILL and THE HIGH WILLOWS (David Tal, Ygal Hared, Hedva Amrani), ILAN and ILANIT, THE CARMELIM (Ruty, David, Shima, Michal, Hannan), NISHRI, BOAZ and NECHEMIA, ALICE (Abou Samra) and HANNAN (Goldblatt), THE KARMON HISTADRUTH BALLET.

ACT 1[13]
Scene 1
"Israeli Rhapsody"
Karmon Histadruth Ballet
Scene 2
Songs of Youth:
Ilan and Ilanit
"Lavriada"
(*Music and Lyrics by* M. Lavry- Itzchak Graziani.)
"Bekol Makom"
(*Music and Lyrics by* Gilad Ben Shachar.)
"Nagnu Bekol"
(*Music and Lyrics by* Fred-Nil-Drora Chafkin.)
"Shav Ani Eleich"
(*Music and Lyrics by* Gilad Ben Shachar.)
Scene 3
"Dance of the Fisherman"
Karmon Histadruth Ballet
Scene 4
Oriental Rhythms
Boaz and Nechema
Scene 5
The New Sound of Isarel's Hit Parade:
The Carmelim
"Keren Yar"
(*Music and Lyrics by* Naomi Shemer.)
"Shilgia"
(*Music and Lyrics by* Naomi Shemer and Guy Béart.)
"Machar"
(*Music and Lyrics* by Naomi Shemer and Itzchak Graziani.)
Scene 6
"Hassidic"
(*Music by* Gill Aldena.)
Karmon Histadruth Ballet

ACT 2
Scene 1
Desert Rhythms (On the Seaside of the Mediterranean)
Karmon Histadruth Ballet
Scene 2
The Story of Her People in Song
H. Hendel
Scene 3
A day like everyday in a Kibbutz on the Border
Yona, Karmon Histadruth Ballet
Scene 4
Music in a Novel Manner:
"Sabre Dance"
(*Music by* Aram Katchaturian.)
Nishri (xylophone virtuoso)
Scene 5
The New Spirit of a people in their singing style
The High Willows, G. Gill
Scene 6
"The Feasts of the Kibbutz"
Karmon Histadruth Ballet
Scene 7
Shalom from the Grand Music Hall of Israel
Entire Company

[12]Replaced shortly after opening:
"24 Hours a Day"
Las Vegans (Ensemble)

[13]The songs and dances performed were not specifically identified in the program. Above list was prepared from reviews, press releases and cast recording. The latter was made prior to the Broadway run with a somewhat different cast, and the show continued to tour with revised cast, songs and dances subsequent to New York.

1968.05

HERE'S WHERE I BELONG

A Musical in Two Acts, 17 Scenes. Book by Alex Gordon[14]. Based on the novel "East of Eden" by John Steinbeck. Music by Robert Waldman. Lyrics by Alfred Uhry. Entire production directed by Michael Kahn. Dances and musical staging by Tony Mordente. Scenery by Ming Cho Lee. Costumes by Ruth Morley. Lighting by Jules Fisher. Musical direction and vocal arrangements by Theodore Saidenberg. Dance music by Arnold Goland. Orchestrations by Glenn Osser, Norman Leyden and Jonathan Tunick. Produced by Mitch Miller in association with United Artists. Opened and closed 3 March 1968 after 1 performance.

CAST (in order of appearance): *Adam Trask*: PAUL ROGERS. *Caleb Trask (Cal)*: WALTER McGINN. *Aron Trask*: KEN KERCHEVAL. *Lee*: JAMES COCO. *Will Hamilton*: Casper Roos. *Mrs. Bacon*: Bette Henritze. *Mrs. Tripp*: Dena Dietrich. *Mrs. Heink*: Patricia Kelly. *Abra Bacon*: HEATHER MacRAE. *School Children*: Lee Wilson, Tod Miller. *Miss Ida*: Barbara Webb. *Rabbit Holman*: Scott Jarvis. *Faith*: Graciela Daniele. *Eva*: Aniko Morgan. *Della*: Dorothy Lister. *Kate*: NANCY WICKWIRE. *Joe*: Joseph Nelson. *Juana*: Joetta Cherry. *Newspaper Man*: Taylor Reed. *British Purchasing Agent*: Darrell J. Askey.

Townspeople, Field Workers, Denizens of Castroville Street: Darrell J. Askey, Joetta Cherry, Graciela Daniele, Elisa DeMarko, Larry Devon, John Dickerson, Bud Fleming, John William Gardner, Gene Gavin, John Johann, Ray Kirchner, Jane Laughlin, Dorothy Lister, Andy Love, Richard Marr, David McCorkle, Joyce McDonald, Tod Miller, Aniko Morgan, Joan Nelson, Joseph Nelson, Donald Norris, Taylor Reed, Clifford Scott, Joy Serio, Michele Simmons, David Thomas, Barbara Webb, Lee Wilson.

Prologue: The Trask house in Salinas, California, 1915.

Act 1, Scene 1: Castroville, two years later. *Scene 2*: The Trask house, later that day. *Scene 3*: Kate's place, immediately following. *Scene 4*: The streets of Salinas, immediately following. *Scene 5*: The ice house, several weeks later. *Scene 6*: The lettuce fields, six weeks later. *Scene 7*: Near the depot, the same day. *Scene 8*: The train depot, immediately following. *Scene 9*: The Trask house, three days later. *Scene 10*: The willow tree, early the next morning.

Act 2, Scene 1: Salinas, downtown. Two months later. *Scene 2*: The Salinas bank, two weeks later. *Scene 3*: Kate's place, the same day. *Scene 4*: The willow tree, the next day. *Scene 5*: The Trask house, Thanksgiving dinner. *Scene 6*: Outside Kate's, immedately following. *Scene 7*: The Trask house, a few hours later.

ACT 1
Prologue
"We Are What We Are"
P. Rogers, W. McGinn, J. Coco, K. Kercheval
"Cal Gets By"
W. McGinn
Scene 1
"Raising Cain"
W. McGinn, Ensemble
Scene 2
"Soft Is the Sparrow"
K. Kercheval
Scene 4
"Where Have I Been"
P. Rogers, J. Coco, Townspeople (Ensemble)
Scene 5
"No Time"
W. McGinn, K. Kercheval
"Progress"
Male Ensemble
"Good Boy"
Scene 6
Ballet
W. McGinn, J. Cherry, H. MacRae, Dancing Ensemble
Scene 7
"Act Like a Lady"
H. MacRae
Scene 8
"The Send-Off"
Townspeople
Scene 9
"Top of the Train"
P. Rogers, W. McGinn
Scene 10
"Waking Up Sun"
H. MacRae, W. McGinn

ACT 2
Scene 1
"Pulverize the Kaiser"
B. Henritze, D. Dietrich, P. Kelly, Townspeople
"Where Have I Been" (reprise)
P. Rogers
Scene 3
"You're Mama's"
N. Wickwire
Scene 4
"Here's Where I Belong"
W. McGinn, H. MacRae
Scene 5
"We're a Home"
P. Rogers, J. Coco, K. Kercheval, H. MacRae, W. McGinn

1968.06

THE EDUCATION OF H*Y*M*A*N K*A*P*L*A*N

A Musical in Two Acts, 13 Scenes. Book by Benjamin Bernard Zavin. Based on the collected stories (of the same name) by Leo Rosten. Music and lyrics by Paul Nassau and Oscar Brand. Production directed by George Abbott. Settings by William and Jean Eckart. Costumes by Winn Morton. Lighting by Martin Aronstein. Musical direction and vocal arrangements by Julian Stein. Orchestrations by Larry Wilcox. Dance music arranged by Lee Holdridge. Dances and musical numbers staged by Jaime Rogers. Associate producer, David W. Sampliner. Produced by Andre Goulston/Jack Farren and Stephen Mellow. Opened 4 April 1968 at the Alvin Theatre and closed 27 April 1968 after 28 performances.

CAST (in order of appearance): *Jimmy*: Stephen Bolster. *Pushcart Vendor*: Dick Ensslen. *Old Clothes Man*: Cyril Murkin. *Kathy McKenna*: Donna McKechnie. *Sam Pinsky*: NATHANIEL FREY. *Reuben Plonsky*: David Gold. *Giovanni Pastora*: Dick Latessa. *Mrs. Moskowitz*: Honey Sanders. *Sarah Moskowitz*: Susan Camber. *Mr. Parkhill*: GARY KRAWFORD. *Fanny Gidwitz*: Maggie Task. *Rose Mitnick*: BARBARA MINKUS. *Hyman Kaplan*: TOM BOSLEY. *Eileen Higby*: Dorothy Emmerson. *Marie Vitale*: Beryl Towbin. *Mrs. Mitnick*: Mimi Sloan. *Officer Callahan*: Wally Engelhardt. *Yissel Fishbein*: HAL LINDEN. *Guard*: David Ellin. *Judge Mahon*: Rufus Smith.

Dancers: Pamlea Barlow, Mickie Bier, Susan Camber, Joanne DiVito, Andrea Duda, Lee Lund, Kuniko Narai, Eileen Woliner, Takeshi Hamagaki, Yanco Inone, Pat Matera, Barry Preston, George Ramos, Steven Ross. *Singers*: Alice Cannon, Martha Danielle, Trudy Wallace, Edward Becker, David Ellin, Jack Fletcher.

The action takes place in New York City, the Lower East Side, from 1919-1920.

Act 1, Scene 1: A Street on the Lower East Side. *Scene 2*: Mr. Parkhill's Classroom. *Scene 3*: Teachers' Room. *Scene 4*: Mr. Parkhill's Classroom. *Scene 5*: Rose Mitnick's Apartment. *Scene 6*: A Street. *Scene 7*: Mr. Parkhill's Classroom. *Scene 8*: A Street.

Act 2, Scene 1: Kaplan's Flat. *Scene 2*: Mr. Parkhill's Classroom. *Scene 3*: Ellis Island Deportation Room. *Scene 4*: Judge Mahon's Chambers. *Scene 5*: Hyman Kaplan's Shop. *Scene 6*: Street in front of the School. *Scene 7*: A U.S. Courtroom.

ACT 1
Scene 1
"Strange New World"
G. Krawford
Scene 2
"OOOO-EEEE"
T. Bosley, B. Minkus, G. Krawford, Students
Scene 3
"A Dedicated Teacher" ("Teachers on Parade")
D. Emmerson, B. Towbin, G. Krawford
Scene 4
"Lieben Dich"
T. Bosley

[14]Book credited to Terrence McNally during tryout and previews. There is no such person as "Alex Gordon."

"Loving You"
B. Minkus
Scene 5
"The Day I Met Your Father"
M. Sloan
Scene 6
"Anything Is Possible"
T. Bosley, Students, Dancers, Singers
Scene 8
"Spring in the City"
D. McKechnie, D. Latessa, D. Gold, N. Frey, H. Sanders, M. Task, Dancers, Singers

ACT 2
Scene 1
"Old Fashioned Husband"
H. Linden
Scene 2
"Julius Caesar" ("Shakespeare")
T. Bosley
Scene 3
"I Never Felt Better in My Life"
T. Bosley, Dancers, Singers
Scene 5
"When Will I Learn"
B. Minkus
Scene 6
"All American"
N. Frey, Students

1968.07 GEORGE M!

A Musical in Two Acts, a Prologue, Epilogue and 16 Scenes. Book by Michael Stewart, John and Fran Pascal. (Suggested by the life of George M. Cohan.) Music and lyrics by George M. Cohan. Lyric and musical revisions by Mary Cohan. Entire production directed and choreographed by Joe Layton. Musical supervision by Laurence Rosenthal. Scenery by Tom John. Costumes by Freddy Wittop. Lighting by Martin Aronstein. Musical direction and vocal arrangements by Jay Blackton. Orchestrations by Philip J. Lang. Production supervisor, Jose Vega. Produced by David Black, Konrad Matthaei and Lorin E. Price. Opened 10 April 1968 at the Palace Theatre and closed 26 April 1969 after 435 performances.

CAST (in alphabetical order): *Dog Trainer, Second Pianist, Fay Templeton's maid Rose*: Loni Ackerman. *Living Statue, Secretary in Cohan & Harris office*: Jonelle Allen. *Fay Templeton, Draper's Assistant, Wardrobe Lady*: JACQUELINE ALLOWAY. *Living Statue, Pushcart Girl*: Karin Baker. *First Little Girl, Mrs. Red Deer, Sharpshooter's Assistant, Little Girl with Fay Templeton*: Susan Batson. *Acrobat, Boy in Pushcart*: Billy Brandon. *Dr. Webb, E. F. Albee, Living Statue, Ben, Mayor*: Roger Braun. *Louis Behman, Bell Ringer, Vendor, Fay Templeton's Manager (Freddie)*: DANNY CARROLL. *Willie in 'Popularity,' Sharpshooter, Walt* (Stage Manager of 'I'd Rather Be Right'): GENE CASTLE. *Jerry Cohan*: JERRY DODGE. *Ethel Levey*: JAMIE DONNELLY. *Stagehand, Dog Trainer, Louie, Congressman Burkhardt, Actor in Strike Scene*: James Dybas. *Sam Harris, Violinist, Bell Ringer*: Harvey Evans. *George M. Cohan*: JOEL GREY. *Nellie Cohan*: BETTY ANN GROVE. *Second Little, Girl, Acrobat*: Patti Mariano. *Ventriloquist, Ma Templeton*: Angela Martin. *Archie, Draper, Dockhand, Judge Anspacher, First Policeman in "Nellie Kelly," Man on Street*: John Mineo. *Agnes Nolan*: JILL O'HARA. *Josie Cohan*: BERNADETTE PETERS. *First Pianist, Acrobat, Bell Ringer, Piano Player in Cohan & Harris Office*: Scott Salmon. *Living Statue, Pushcart Girl*: Kathie Savage. *Madame Grimaldi, Mrs. Baker, Flamethrower's Assistant*: JANIE SELL. *Buck and Winger, Designer's Assistant, Sailor, Frankie*: Alan Weeks. *Saxophonist, Flamehrower, Bell Ringer, Ship's Captain, Alderman Hailey, Accordionist in 'Harrigan,' Director of 'I'd Rather Be Right'*: Ronald Young.

Prologue. Act 1, Scene 1: Providence, Rhode Island, 1878. *Scene 2*: Onstage, Columbia Theatre, Cedar Rapids. *Scene 3*: Street in Cedar Rapids. *Scene 4*: Madame Grimaldi's Boarding House. *Scene 5*: En route to New York. *Scene 6*: Adams Street Theatre, various other theatres, New York, 1901-1903. *Scene 7*: General Area, New York, then in front of Savoy Theatre. *Scene 8*: Stage of Liberty Theatre, New York.

Act 2, Scene 1: Office of Cohan & Harris; Fay Templeton's Apartment. *Scene 2*: Onstage, New Amsterdam Theatre. *Scene 3*: Rector's Restaurant, January 1, 1907. *Scene 4*: Street Outside Rector's, next morning. *Scene 5*: The Years till 1919. *Scene 6*: The years till 1937. *Scene 7*: Midtown New York, February 1937. *Scene 8*: Stage of the Alvin Theatre. *Epilogue*.

ACT 1
Scene 2
"Musical Moon" (from THE LITTLE MILLIONAIRE)
J. Dodge, B. A. Grove
"Oh, You Wonderful Boy" (revised, from THE LITTLE MILLIONAIRE)
B. Peters
"All Aboard for Broadway" (from GEORGE WASHINGTON, JR.)
J. Grey, J. Dodge, B. A. Grove, B. Peters
Scene 3
"Musical Comedy Man"[15] (revised, from THE HONEYMOONERS)
J. Grey, J. Dodge, B. A. Grove, B. Peters, Full Company
Scene 5
"All Aboard for Broadway" (reprise)
J. Grey, J. Dodge, B. A. Grove, B. Peters, Full Company
Scene 6
"I Was Born in Virginia" (from GEORGE WASHINGTON, JR.)
J. Donnelly
"Twentieth Century Love" (from THE MERRY MALONES)
J. Grey, J. Dodge, B. A. Grove, B. Peters, J. Donnelly
Scene 7
"My Town"
J. Grey
Scene 8
"Billie" (from BILLIE)
J. O'Hara
"Push Me Along in My Pushcart" (from THE GOVERNOR'S SON, 1906 revival)
J. Donnelly, Pushcart Girls
"Ring to the Name of Rose" (from THE RISE OF ROSIE O'REILLY)
B. Peters, Bell Ringers
"Popularity"
G. Castle, Full Company
"Give My Regards to Broadway" (from LITTLE JOHNNY JONES)
J. Grey, Full Company

ACT 2
Scene 1
"Forty Five Minutes from Broadway"
(from FORTY FIVE MINUTES FROM BROADWAY)
J. Grey, L. Ackerman
"So Long Mary" (from FORTY FIVE MINUTES FROM BROADWAY)
J. Grey, H. Evans, L. Ackerman, D. Carroll, A. Martin
"Down by the Erie (Canal)" (from HELLO, BROADWAY!)
J. Allen, Politicians, S. Batson, Full Company
Scene 2
"Mary" (as "Mary's a Grand Old Name" from FORTY FIVE MINUTES FROM BROADWAY)
J. Alloway
Scene 3
"All Our Friends" (revised, "They're All My Boys" from LITTLE NELLIE KELLY)
H. Evans, Full Company
Scene 5
"Yankee Doodle Dandy"(as "Yankee Doodle Boy" from LITTLE JOHNNY JONES)
"Harrigan" (from FIFTY MILES FROM BOSTON)
"Nellie Kelly, I Love You" (from LITTLE NELLIE KELLY)
"Over There"
"You're a Grand Old Flag" (from GEORGE WASHINGTON, JR.)
J. Grey, Full Company

[15]Replaced for subsequent national tour by:
"The Four of Us" (revised "The Two of Us," from BILLIE)

Scene 6

"The City" (Montage of "The Man Who Owns Broadway" from THE MAN WHO OWNS BROADWAY)

Full Company

Scene 8

"I'd Rather Be Right" (from I'D RATHER BE RIGHT)

J. Grey, Company

(*Music by* Richard Rodgers. *Lyrics by* Lorenz Hart.)

"Give My Regards to Broadway" (reprise)

J. Grey

Epilogue[16]

"Dancing Our Worries Away" (revised, from LITTLE NELLIE KELLY)

"The Great Easter Sunday Parade"

"Hannah's a Hummer" (from THE WISE GUY)

"Barnum and Bailey Rag" (from HELLO, BROADWAY!)

"The Belle of the Barber's Ball" (from COHAN AND HARRIS MINSTRELS)

"The American Ragtime" (from THE AMERICAN IDEA)

"All in the Wearing" (from LITTLE NELLIE KELLY)

"I Want to Hear a Yankee Doodle Tune" (from MOTHER GOOSE)

Full Company

(Recording at end of epilogue by George M. Cohan.)

Four Cohans (Edie Cowan, Darryl Hickman, Linda Larson, Ted Pritchard)

1968.08 I'M SOLOMON

A Musical Fable in Two Acts. Book by Anne Croswell and Dan Almagor. Based on the (Israeli) drama "King Solomon and the Cobbler" by Sammy Gronemann. American adaptation in collaboration with Zvi Kolitz. Music by Ernest Gold. Lyrics by Anne Croswell. Entire production directed and supervised by Michael Benthall. Settings by Rouben Ter-Arutunian. Costumes by Jane Greenwood. Lighting by Martin Aronstein. Musical direction and vocal arrangements by Gershon Kingsley. Orchestrations by Hershy Kay. Special material by David Finkle and Bill Weeden. Dance arrangements by Dorothea Freitag. Dances and musical numbers staged by Donald McKayle. Associate producers, Philip Turk and Kalman Ginzburg. Produced by Zvi Kolitz, Solomon Sagall, and Abe Margolies. Opened 23 April 1968 at the Mark Hellinger Theatre and closed 27 April 1968 after 7 performances.

CAST (in order of appearance): *Meir*, the Drummer: Meir Alon. *Ali*, the Flute Player: Al DeSio. *Isaac*, a Tavern Keeper: John Dorrin. *Tavern Dancer*: Sally Neal. *Yoni*, a Cobbler: DICK SHAWN. *Na'Ama*, his wife: KAREN MORROW. *Yoel*, Temple Building Supervisor: Kenneth Scott. *Mago*, Architect of the Temple: John LaMotta. *Lemech*, a Dyer: Eddie Ericksen. *Aviva*, a Harlot: Alice Evans. *Bruria*, a Harlot: Lynn Archer. *An Officer of the Royal Guard*: Gordon Cook. *Ben Hesed*, Commander of the Royal Guard: PAUL REED. *Princess Nofrit*, Solomon's Favorite Wife: Barbara Webb. *F'htar*, her Slave: Mary Barnett. *Solomon*: DICK SHAWN. *Bathsheba*, Solomon's Mother: CARMEN MATHEWS. *An Ambassador*: Nat Horne. *Ranor*, Ambassador of the Queen of Sheba: Fred Pinkard. *Aide to Ranor*: Garrett Morris. *Rachel*, one of Solomon's wives: Caryl Tenney. *Makedah*, a Member of the Queen of Sheba's Party: SALOME JENS.

Solomon's Concubines: Jeri Barto, Connie Burnett, Miriam Ehrenberg, Carol Flemming, Mary Jane Houdina, Nina Janik, Carol Manning, Sally Neal, Martha Pollak, Renee Rose, Joan Tannen, Nina Trasoff, Myrna White. *Other Wives*: Lynn Archer, Chris Callan, Jacque Dean, Alice Evans, Carol Flemming, Marsha Hastings, Mary Jane Houdina, Sherry Lambert, Carol Manning, Sally Neal, Joan Tannen. *People of Jerusalem, Guards, Slaves, etc.*: Clifford Allen, Meir Alon, Jari Barto, Connie Burnett, Chris Callan, Al Cohen, Gordon Clark, Nikolas Dante, Jacque Dean, Esteban DeLeon, Al DeSio, John Dorrin, Miriam Ehrenberg, Eddie Ericksen, Carol Flemming, Stokely Gray, Rodney Griffin, Jerry Grimes, Marsha Hastings, Nat Horne, Mary Jane Houdina, Jason Howard, Nina Janik, Sherry Lambert, John LaMotta, Carol Manning, Garrett Morris, Sally Neal, Keith Perry, Martha Pollak, Ken Richards, Renee Rose, Jeffrey Shawn, Clay Taliaferro, Joan Tannen, Caryl Tenney, Nina Trasoff, Kyle Weaver, Bruce Wells, Myrna White.

The action takes place from the morning of one day to noon of the next, in and around Jerusalem, about 100 B.C.

ACT 1

"David and Bathsheba"

D. Shawn, People of Jesusalem

"Hail the Son of David!"

D. Shawn, Courtiers, Solomon's Wives

"Preposterous"

D. Shawn

"Have You Heard?"

People of Jerusalem

"The Citation"

P. Reed

"In Love With a Fool"

K. Morrow

"Someone Like Me"

D. Shawn

"In Someone Else's Sandals"

D. Shawn, C. Mathews, Slaves, Concubines

"The Three Riddles"

(*Lyrics by* Erich Segal.)

F. Pinkard, P. Reed, D. Shawn, People of Jerusalem

ACT 2

"Once in 2.7 Years"

Solomon's Wives

"Have You Ever Been Alone With a King Before?"

D. Shawn, K. Morrow

(*Music by* Bill Weeden. *Lyrics by* David Finkle.)

"Lord I Am But a Little Child"

D. Shawn

"I Am What I Am"

D. Shawn

"Something in His Eyes"

K. Morrow

"That Guilty Feeling"

D. Shawn

(*Music by* Bill Weeden. *Lyrics by* David Finkle.)

"Time to Let Go"

C. Mathews

"With Your Hand in My Heart"

D. Shawn, K. Morrow, C. Mathews, People of Jerusalem

"Lord I Am But a Little Child" (reprise)

Entire Company

1968.09 THE PIRATES OF PENZANCE, or The Slave of Duty

A Revival of the Comic Opera in Two Acts[17]. Libretto by William S. Gilbert. Music by Arthur Sullivan. Directed by Allen Fletcher. Scenery by Lloyd Evans. Costumes by Patton Campbell. Lighting by Hans Sondheimer. Conductor, Felix Popper. Produced by the New York City Center Gilbert and Sullivan Company (Felix Popper, General director). Opened 25 April 1968 at the New York City Center and closed 19 May 1968 after 7 performances in repertory.

CAST: *Major General Stanley*: DOUGLAS WATSON, EMILE RENAN. *The Pirate King*: WILLIAM CHAPMAN. *Samuel*, his Lieutenant: William Ledbetter. *Frederic*, the Pirate Apprentice: FRANK PORETTA, JOHN HARGER STEWART. *Sergeant of Police*: JACK BITTNER. *Mabel, Edith Kate, Isabel*, General Stanley's Daughters: PATRICIA WISE or MARGOT MOSER, ELLEN SHADE, JANET WINBURN, Diana Kehrig. *Ruth*, Pirate Maid-of-all-work: MURIEL GREENSPON.

Chorus of Pirates, Police and General Stanley's Daughters: Arlene Adler, Ronald Bentley, Don Carlo, Anthony Darius, Harris Davis, Joseph Galiano, Nino Garcia, Pearle Goldsmith, Marilyn Armstrong, Harriet Greene, Don Henderson, Lila Herbert, Douglas Hunnikin, Suzy Hunter, Diana Kehrig, Karl Patrick Krause, Donna Owen, Hanna Owen, Raymond Papay, Richard Park, Leo Postrel, Joaquin Romaguera, Stefanya Weicker, Maria West, Marie Young.

[16]Epilogue (excepting the Cohan recording) dropped from programs during the New York run.

[17]First presented in New York 31 December 1879 at the Fifth Avenue Theatre for a total of 91 performances in two engagements. For Synopsis of Scenes and Musical Numbers, see original 1879 production.

H.M.S. PINAFORE,

1968.10 or The Lass That Loved a Sailor

A Revival of the Comic Opera in Two Acts[18]. Libretto by William S. Gilbert. Music by Arthur Sullivan. Directed by Allen Fletcher. Scenery and costumes by Patton Campbell. Lighting by Hans Sondheimer. Conductor, Thomas P. Martin. Produced by the New York City Center Gilbert and Sullivan Company (Felix Popper, General director). Opened 27 April 1968 at the New York City Center and closed 19 May 1968 after 8 performances in repertory.

CAST: *The Rt. Hon. Sir Joseph Porter, K.C.B.*, First Lord of the Admiralty: RAYMOND ALLEN, ROBERT TREHY. *Captain Corcoran*, Commander of the *H.M.S. Pinafore*: RICHARD FREDERICKS. *Ralph Rackstraw*, Able Seaman: ENRICO DiGIUSEPPE, EVAN THOMAS. *Dick Deadeye*, Able Seaman: PAUL UKENA, DON YULE. *Bill Bobstay*, Boatswain: Robert Hale. *Bob Becket*: Will Roy. *Josephine*, the Captain's Daughter: JOY CLEMENTS, BARBARA BLANCHARD. *Cousin Hebe*, Sir Joseph's First Cousin: Janet Winburn. *Little Buttercup*, Mrs. Cripps, a Portsmouth bum-boat woman: JOAN KAPLAN. *First Lord's Sisters, His Cousins, His Aunts, Sailors, Marines, etc.*: same as THE PIRATES OF PENZANCE above.

1968.11

HAIR

The American Tribal Love-Rock Musical in Two Acts[19]. Book and lyrics by Gerome Ragni and James Rado. Music by Galt MacDermott. Directed by Tom O'Horgan. Dance director, Julie Arenal. Musical director, Galt MacDermott. Costumes by Nancy Potts. Scenery by Robin Wagner. Lighting by Jules Fisher. Sound by Robert Kiernan. Executive producer, Bertrand Castelli. Produced by Michael Butler. The Natoma Production. Opened 29 April 1968 at the Biltmore Theatre and closed 1 July 1972 after 1750 performances.

CAST (in order of appearance): *Claude*: JAMES RADO. *Ron*: RONALD DYSON. *Berger*: GEROME RAGNI. *Woof*: STEVE CURRY. *Hud*: LAMONT WASHINGTON. *Sheila*: LYNN KELLOGG. *Jeanie*: SALLY EATON. *Dionne*: MELBA MOORE. *Crissy*: SHELLEY PLIMPTON. *Mother*: SALLY EATON, JONATHAN KRAMER, PAUL JABARA. *Father*: Robert I. Rubinsky, Suzanne Norstrand, LAMONT WASHINGTON. *Principal*: Robert I. Rubinsky, Suzanne Norstrand, LAMONT WASHINGTON. *Tourist Couple*: JONATHAN KRAMER, Robert I. Rubinsky. *Waitress*: Diane Keaton. *Young Recruit*: JONATHAN KRAMER. *General Grant*: PAUL JABARA. *Abraham Lincoln*: Lorri Davis. *Sergeant*: Donnie Burks. *Parents*: Diane Keaton, Robert I. Rubinsky. *The Tribe*: Donnie Burks, Lorri Davis, Leata Galloway, Steve Gamet, Walter Harris, Diane Keaton, Hiram Keller, Marjorie LiPari, Emmaretta Marks, Natalie Mosco, Suzannah Norstrand, Robert I. Rubinsky.

The action takes place in New York City, mostly the East Village, at the present time.

ACT 1[20]

"Aquarius"
R. Dyson, Company
"Donna"
G. Ragni, Company
"Hashish"
Company
"Sodomy"
S. Curry, Company
"Colored Spade"
L. Washington, Company
"Manchester (England)"
J. Rado, Company
"Ain't Got No"
S. Curry, L. Washington, M. Moore, Company
"I Believe in Love"
L. Kellogg
"Air"
S. Eaton, S. Plimpton, M. Moore, Company
"Initials"
Company
"I Got Life"
J. Rado, Company
"Going Down"
G. Ragni, Company
"Hair"
J. Rado, G. Ragni, Company
"My Conviction"
J. Kramer
"Easy To Be Hard"
L. Kellogg
"Hung"[21]
G. Ragni, Company
"Don't Put It Down"
G. Ragni, S. Curry
"Frank Mills"
S. Plimpton
"Hare Krishna" ("Be-In")
Company
"Where Do I Go?"
J. Rado, Company

ACT 2

"Electric Blues"
S. Norstrand, L. Galloway, S. Gamet, P. Jabara
"Black Boys"
D. Keaton, S. Norstrand, N. Mosco
"White Boys"
M. Moore, L. Davis, E. Marks
"Walking in Space"
Company
"Abie Baby"
L. Washington, R. Dyson, D. Burks, L. Davis
"Prisoners in Niggertown" ("3-5-0-0")
R. Dyson, W. Harris, Company
"What a Piece of Work is Man"
R. Dyson, W. Harris
"Good Morning Starshine"
L. Kellogg, M. Moore, Company
"The Bed"
Company
"The Flesh Failures"
("Let the Sunshine In")
J. Rado, L. Kellogg, M. Moore, Company

---

[18]Originally presented in New York 15 January 1879 at the Standard Theatre for 175 performances. For Synopsis of Scenes and Musical Numbers, see original 1879 production.

[19]First produced in New York Off-Broadway 29 October-10 December 1967 at the Anspacher Theatre for 49 performances; re-opened at the Cheetah 22 December 1967-28 January 1968 for 45 performances. Original Off-Broadway Credits (where different from Broadway): Directed by Gerald Freedman. Scenery by Ming Cho Lee. Costumes by Theoni V. Aldredge. Lighting by Martin Aronstein. Musical director, John Morris. Associate producer, Bernard Gersten. Manager, David Black. Produced by the New York Shakespeare Festival (Joseph Papp, Producer). Dropped from Off-Broadway production prior to Broadway:
"Red, Blue and White" (Act 1)
"Exanaplanetooch" (Act 2)
"(The) Climax" (Act 2)

[20]Added after Broadway opening:
"Dead End" (Act 1)
M. Moore, L. Galloway, E. Marks, S. Norstrand, Joe Morton
Added for various touring productions:
"Kama Sutra" (Act 1)
Company
"Hello There" (Act 1)
Berger
"Oh Great God of Power" (Act 2)
Berger, Company

[21]Dropped after Broadway opening.

1968.12

THE MIKADO, or The Town of Titipu

A Revival of the Comic Opera in Two Acts[22]. Libretto by William S. Gilbert. Music by Arthur Sullivan. Directed by Jack and Virginia Frymire. Scenery by Donald Oenslager. Costumes by Patton Campbell. Conductor, Byron Dean Ryan. Produced by the New York City Center Gilbert and Sullivan Company (Felix Popper, General director). Opened 1 May 1968 at the New York City Center and closed 14 May 1968 after 8 performances in repertory.

CAST: *The Mikado of Japan*: PAUL UKENA. *Nanki-Poo*: FRANK PORETTA. *Ko-Ko*: JOHN LANKSTON. *Pooh-Bah*: RICHARD WENTWORTH. *Pish-Tush*: WILLIAM LEDBETTER. *Three Sisters, Wards of Ko-Ko*: *Yum-Yum*: CAROL BERGEY. *Pitti-Sing*: MARY BURGESS. *Peep-Bo*: JANET WINBURN. *Katisha*: MURIEL GREENSPON. *Solo Dancer*: Miyoko Watanabe. *Chorus of School Girls, Nobles, Guards and Coolies*: same as THE PIRATES OF PENZANCE above.

1968.13

(LEONARD SILLMAN'S) NEW FACES OF 1968

A Musical Revue in Two Acts, 32 Scenes[23]. Entire production conceived and staged by Leonard Sillman. Sketches by Ronny Graham, Peter DeVries, William F. Brown, Kenny Solms, Gail Parent, Jack Sharkey, David Axelrod, Robert Klein, Norman Kline. Continuity and additional dialogue by William F. Brown. Music and lyrics by Ronny Graham, June Carroll, Arthur Siegel, Clark Gesner, Sam Pottle, David Axelrod, Jerry Powell, David Shire, Richard Maltby, Jr., Murray Grand, Paul Nassau, Hal Hackady, Alonzo Levister, Kenny Solms, Gail Parent, Gene P. Bissell, Carl Friberg, Fred Hellerman, Frank Minkoff, Michael McWhinney, Sydney Shaw, Michael Cohen, Tony Geiss. Choreographed and directed by Frank Wagner. Settings and costumes by Winn Morton. Light design by Paul Sullivan. Production coordinator, Jacqueline Adams. Orchestrations by Lanny Meyers. Musical direction, Ted Simons. An All-Corduroy Production. Produced by Jack Rollins. Opened 2 May 1968 at the Booth Theatre and closed 15 June 1968 after 52 performances.

CAST: Michael K. Allen, Suzanne Astor, Rod Barry, Gloria Bleezarde, Trudy Carson, Marilyn Child, Dottie [Dorothy] Frank, Elaine Giftos, Madeline Kahn, Robert Klein, Joe Kyle, Robert Lone, Brandon Maggart, George Ormiston, Rod Perry, Nancie Phillips, Leonard Sillman.

ACT 1

Scene 1

"Illustrated Overture"

Scene 2

Definitions
(*by* Random House)
Girl: G. Bleezarde. *Boy*: R. Barry.

Scene 3

Welcome
The Producer: L. Sillman.

Scene 4

"Opening"
Entire Company
(*Music and Lyrics by* Ronny Graham.)

Scene 5

Audition
(*by* Robert Klein)
The Auditioner: R. Klein.

Scene 6

"By the Sea"
B. Maggart
(*Music and Lyrics by* Clark Gesner.)

Scene 7

"Where Is the Waltz?"
M. K. Allen
(*Music and Orchestration by* Alonzo Levister. *Lyrics by* Paul Nassau.)
Danced by D. Frank, E. Giftos, T. Carson.

Scene 8

"A New Waltz"
M. Child
(*Music by* Fred Hellerman. *Lyrics by* Frank Minkoff.)
Danced by R. Lone, J. Kyle.

Scene 9

Happy Landings
(*by* Jack Sharkey)
Airline Stewardess: M. Kahn.

Scene 10

"The Girl in the Mirror"
R. Parry
(*Music by* Fred Hellerman. *Lyrics by* Fran Minkoff.)

Isolation
J. Kyle, G. Bleezarde

Scene 11

The American Hamburger League[24]
(*by* Norman Kline)
Introduction: R. Barry. *Beth*: M. Kahn. *Helene*: M. Child. *Rex*: B. Maggart. *Dexter*: G. Ormiston. *Wayne*: R. Klein.

Isolation
T. Carson, R. Barry

Scene 12

Love Songs:

"Something Big"
G. Ormiston, E. Giftos
(*Music by* Sam Pottle. *Lyrics by* David Axelrod.)

"Love in a Tempo"
R. Klein
(*Music and Lyrics by* Ronny Graham.)

"Hungry"
S. Astor, (R. Barry)
(*Music and Lyrics by* Murray Grand.)

Scene 13

"Luncheon Ballad"
S. Astor, M. Child, M. Kahn, N. Phillips
(*Music by* Jerry Powell. *Lyrics by* Michael McWhinney.)

Scene 14

The Underachiever
(*by* Peter De Vries)
Introduction: G. Bleezarde. *Freshman*: R. Klein. *Freshman's Wife*: M. Kahn.

Scene 15

"You're the One I'm For"
B. Maggart
(*Music and Lyrics by* Clark Gesner.)

Scene 16

"Where Is Me?"
M. Child
(*Music by* Arthur Siegel. *Lyrics by* June Carroll.)

Isolation— "Right About Here"
M. K. Allen
(*Music and Lyrics by* Arthur Siegel.)

Scene 17

Gospel According to Jack
(*by* William F. Brown)
S. Astor, R. Barry, T. Carson,
M. Child, D. Frank, M. Kahn, R. Klein, R. Lone, B. Maggart, R. Perry

Scene 18

Mama Doll
(*by* Charles Tobias and Nat Simon; *Conception by* George Ormiston and Nancie Phillips.)
Doll: N. Phillips. *Little Boy*: G. Ormiston.

---

[22]First presented in New York 20 July, 10-29 August 1885 at the Union Square and People's Theatres for 22 performances. First authorized production presented 19 August 1885 at the Fifth Avenue Theatre by Richard D'Oyly Carte for 250 performances. For Synopsis of Scenes and Musical Numbers, see 19 August 1885 D'Oyly Carte production.

[23]The Seventh in the series of revues conceived by Leonard Sillman as a showcase for new talent. The first was produced in 1934.

[24]Dropped after opening.

Scene 19
"Toyland"
(*Dialogue, Music and Lyrics by* Gene P. Bissell.)
Production Singer: M. Kahn. *Compere*: R. Klein.

ACT 2
Introduction
L. Sillman, G. Bleezarde
Scene 1
"Hullabaloo At Thebes"
(*Music and Lyrics by* Ronny Graham.)
Introduction: L. Sillman. *Oedipus*: R. Klein. *Jocasta*: S. Astor.
Antigone: T. Carson. *Ismene*: E. Giftos.
Scene 2
"#X9RL-220"
G. Bleezarde
(*Music by* Jerry Powell. *Lyrics by* Michael McWhinney.)
Scene 3
"You Are"
B. Maggart
(*Music and Lyrics by* Clark Gesner.)
Scene 4
"Evil"
M. K. Allen
(*Music and Lyrics by* Sydney Shaw.)
Scene 5
The Refund
(by Peter De Vries)
Introduction and Clarification: G. Ormiston.
Fred Abernathy: R. Klein. *Ben Abernathy*: B. Maggart.
Sarah Cobleigh: D. Frank.
Scene 6
"Prisms"
M. Child
(Music by Carl Friberg. Lyrics by Hal Hackady.)
Scene 7
"Tango"
The Company
(Music by Sam Pottle. Lyrics by David Axelrod.)
Introduction: L. Sillman.
Isolation—Cymbals and Tambourines
G. Bleezarde, R. Lone
(*Music and Lyrics by* Arthur Siegel.)
Scene 8
"Philosophy"
R. Perry
(*Music by* Carl Friberg. *Lyrics by* Hal Hackady.)
Danced by D. Frank, J. Kyle, E. Giftos.
Scene 9
The Pile-Up
B. Maggart
Scene 10
"Das Chicago Song"
M. Kahn
(*Music by* Michael Cohen. *Lyrics by* Tony Geiss.)
Scene 11
"Missed America"
(*Dialogue, Music and Lyrics by* Kenny Solms and Gail Parent.
Additional Dialogue by Ronny Graham.)
M. C.: G. Ormiston. *Miss Alabama*: N. Phillips. *Miss Minnesota*:
D. Frank. *Miss Connecticut*: S. Astor.
Scene 12
"Die Zusammenfügung"
(*Music by* Sam Pottle. *Lyrics by* David Axelrod.)
Introduction: G. Bleezarde. *Scheiss*: B. Maggart. *Pfeiffer*: R. Klein.
Heidi: M. Kahn. *The Connection*: G. Ormiston.
Scene 13
Opening Reprise
Introduction: L. Sillman.

Scene 13
"The Girl of the Minute"
Entire Company
(*Music by* David Shire. *Lyrics by* Richard Maltby, Jr.)

THE YEOMEN OF THE GUARD, or The Merryman and His Maid

1968.14

A Revival of the Comic Opera in Two Acts[25]. Libretto by William S. Gilbert. Music by Arthur Sullivan. Staged by Allen Fletcher. Scenery by Stephen O. Saxe. Costumes by Alvin Colt. Lighting by Hans Sondheimer. Conducted by Felix Popper. Produced by the New York City Center Gilbert and Sullivan Company (Felix Popper, General director). Opened 8 May 1968 at the New York City Center and closed 12 May 1968 after 3 performances in repertory.

CAST: *Sir Richard Cholmondeley*, Lieutenant of the Tower: ROBERT HALE. *Colonel Fairfax* under sentence of death: FRANK PORETTA. *Sergeant Meryll* of the Yeomen of the Guard: PAUL UKENA. *Leonard Meryll*, his Son: JOHN LANKSTON. *Jack Point*, a Strolling Jester: ROBERT TREHY. *Wilfred Shadbolt*, Head Jailor and Assistant Tormentor: JACK BITTNER. *First Yeoman*: Evan Thomas. *Second Yeoman*: David Hicks. *First Citizen*: Harris Davis. *Second Citizen*: Don Henderson. *Elsie Maynard*, a Strolling Player: MARGOT MOSER. *Phoebe Meryll*, Sergeant Meryll's Daughter: MARY BURGESS. *Dame Carruthers*, Housekeeper to the Tower: ELLEN ALEXANDER. *Kate*, her Niece: FREDREIKA WISEHART. *Chorus of Yeomen of the Guard, Gentlemen, Citizens, etc.*: same as THE PIRATES OF PENZANCE above.

PATIENCE, or Bunthorne's Bride

1968.15

A Revival of the Comic Opera in Two Acts[26]. Libretto by William S. Gilbert. Music by Arthur Sullivan. Directed by Leon Major. Scenery and costumes designed by Motley. Lighting by Hans Sondheimer. Conductor, Felix Popper. Produced by the New York City Center Gilbert and Sullivan Company (Felix Popper, General director). Opened 15 May 1968 at the New York City Center and closed 17 May 1968 after 3 performances in repertory.

CAST: *Colonel Calverley*: WILLIAM CHAPMAN. *Major Murgatroyd*: Nico Castel. *Lieut. the Duke of Dunstable*: JOHN LANKSTON. *Reginald Bunthorne*, a Fleshly Poet: EMILE RENAN. *Archibald Grosvenor*, an Idyllic Poet: WILLIAM METCALF. *Mr. Bunsthorne's Solicitor*: John Henry Thomas . *The Lady Angela, The Lady Saphir, The Lady Ella, The Lady Jane*, Rapturous Maidens: MARY BURGESS, HELEN GUILE, Fredreika Wisehart, CLARAMAE TURNER. *Patience*, a Dairy Maid: JOY CLEMENTS. *Chorus of Rapturous Maidens and Officers of the Dragoon Guards*: same as THE PIRATES OF PENZANCE above.

THE KING AND I

1968.16

A Revival of the Musical Play in Two Acts, 17 Scenes[27]. Book and lyrics by Oscar Hammerstein II. Music by Richard Rodgers. Based on the novel "Anna and the King of Siam" by Margaret Landon. Directed by John Fearnley. Settings by Paul C. McGuire. Costumes by Irene Sharaff, supervised by Frank Thompson. Lighting by Feder. Original choreography by Jerome Robbins, reproduced by Yuriko. (Orchestrations by Robert Russell Bennett.) Musical director, Jonathan Anderson. Produced by the New York City Center Light Opera Company (Jean Dalrymple, Director). Opened 23 May 1968 at the New York City Center and closed 9 June 1968 after 22 performances.

CAST (in order of appearance): *Captain Orton*: Sam Kirkham. *Louis Leonowens*: Eric Hamilton. *Anna Leonowens*: CONSTANCE TOWERS. *The Interpreter*: Paul Flores.

---

[25]First presented in New York 17 October 1888 at the Casino Theatre for 100 performances. For Synopsis of Scenes and Musical Numbers, see original 1888 production.
[26]First presented in New York 22 September 1881 at the Standard Theatre for 177 performances. For Synopsis of Scenes and Musical Numbers, see original 1881 production.
[27]Originally produced in New York 29 March 1951 at the St. James Theatre for 1246 performances. For Synopsis of Scenes and Musical Numbers, see original 1951 production.

The Kralahome: Ted Beniades. *The King*: MICHAEL KERMOYAN. *Phra Alack*: Robert Lenn. *Lun Tha*: STANLEY GROVER. *Tuptim*: ELEANOR CALBES. *Lady Thiang*: ANITA DARIAN. *Prince Chulalongkorn*: Michael Thom. *Princess Ying Yaowalak*: Dana Shimizu. *Sir Edward Ramsay*: Christopher Hewett.

The Small House of Uncle Thomas: *Narrator*: Eleanor Calbes. *Uncle Thomas*: Diane Adler. *Little Eva*: Wonci Lui. *Topsy*: Paula Chin. *Eliza*: YURIKO. *King Simon*: Carol Fried. *Angel*: Jaclynn Villamil. *Drummer*: Lazar Dano. *Buddha*: Lawrence Kikuchi.

Princes and Princesses: Caryn Chow, Sonja Furiya, Dana Shimizu, Rachel Ticotin, Nancy Ticotin, Russell Chow, Lewis Gerardo, Lewis Gerardo, Lawrence Kikuchi, Jaime Roque, Jason Rosen, Keenan Shimizu, Marcus Ticotin. *Royal Dancers*: Diane Adler, Paula Chin, Carol Fried, Linda Gumiela, Joann Ogawa, Margot Parsons, Kathleen Pierini, Susan Platt, Juanita Londono, Wonci Lui, Stephanie Satie, Britt Swanson, Margot Travers, Jaclynn Villamil, Rebecca West, Lazar Dano, Gary Dutton, Vito Durante, Rodger Gerhardstein, Tim Ramirez. *Singers* (Wives, Priests, Amazons and Slaves): Joan diDonato, Lee Hooper, Charlotte Marcheret, Betsy Norden, Barbara Reisman, Rebecca West, Maggie Worth, Larry Devon, Beno Foster, Richard Kie Wye Khan.

1968–1969 SEASON

Angela Lansbury and Kurt Petersen in DEAR WORLD (Photo: Friedman-Abeles)
Billy Rose Theatre Collection, New York Public Library for the Performing Arts

1968.17 MY FAIR LADY

A Revival of the Musical (Comedy) in Two Acts, 18 Scenes[1]. Book and lyrics by Alan Jay Lerner. Based on the play "Pygmalion" by George Bernard Shaw, produced on the screen by Gabriel Pascal. Music by Frederick Loewe. Originally staged by Moss Hart. This production directed by Samuel Liff. Choreography and musical numbers staged by Hanya Holm, restaged by Harry Woolever. Production (settings) designed by Oliver Smith. Costumes by Cecil Beaton, supervised by Stanley Simmons. Musical arrangements (orchestrations) by Robert Russell Bennett and Philip J. Lang. Lighting by Feder. Dance music arranged by Trude Rittman. Musical director, Anton Coppola. Produced by the New York City Center Light Opera Company (Jean Dalrymple, Director). Opened 13 June 1968 at the New York City Center and closed 30 June 1968 after 22 performances.

CAST (in order of appearance): *Buskers*: George Bunt, John Johann, Kiki Minor. *Mrs. Eynsford-Hill*: Claire Waring. *Eliza Doolittle*: INGA SWENSON. *Freddy Eynsford-Hill*: EVAN THOMAS. *Colonel Pickering*: BYRON WEBSTER. *A Bystander*: James Beard. *Henry Higgins*: FRITZ WEAVER. *Selsey Man*: Charles Goff. *Hoxton Man*: Jack Fletcher. *First Cockney*: Laried Montgomery. *Second Cockney*: Stokely Gray. *Third Cockney*: Jack Fletcher. *Fourth Cockney*: William James. *Bartender*: Larry Devon. *Harry*: Charles Goff. *Jamie*: James Beard. *Alfred P. Doolittle*: GEORGE ROSE. *Mrs. Pearce*: Leta Bonynge. *Mrs. Hopkins*: Blanche Collins. *Butler*: William James. *Servants*: Jeanne Shea, Hanna Owen, Maggie Worth, Joyce Olson, William James, Stokely Gray. *Mrs. Higgins*: Margery Maude. *Chauffeur*: Todd Butler. *Footmen*: Darrell Sandeen, Peter Costanza. *Lord Boxington*: James Beard. *Lady Boxington*: Blanche Collins. *Constable*: Richard Maxon. *Flower Girl*: Kiki Minor. *Zoltan Karpathy*: ERIK RHODES. *Flunkey*: Darrell Sandeen. *Queen of Transylvania*: Maggie Worth. *Ambassador*: Charles Goff. *Bartender*: Darrell Sandeen. *Mrs. Higgins' Maid*: Jeanne Shea.

Singing Ensemble: Marcia Brushingham, Spring Fairbank, Maryann Kerrick, Joyce Olson, Hanna Owen, Jeanne Shea, Barbara Sorenson, Maggie Worth, Jim Connor, Peter Costanza, Larry Devon, Jack Fletcher, Stokely Gray, William James, Laried Montgomery, Darrell Sandeen. *Dancing Ensemble*: Lisa Ackerman, Judith Austin, Cindi Bulak, Joyce Maret, Mari McKinn, Kiki Minor, Skiles Ricketts, Britt Swanson, Margot Travers, Oscar Anthony, George Bunt, Todd Butler, Richard Dodd, Joe Helm, John Johann, Donald Mark, Richard Maxon, Duane Taylor, Jimmy White.

1968.18 WEST SIDE STORY

A Revival of the Musical in Two Acts, 15 Scenes[2]. Book by Arthur Laurents. Based on a conception of Jerome Robbins. Music by Leonard Bernstein. Lyrics by Stephen Sondheim. Original direction and choreography by Jerome Robbins, reproduced for this production by Lee Theodore. Scenery by Oliver Smith. Costumes by Winn Morton. Lighting by Peter Hunt. Musical director, Maurice Peress. Orchestrations by Leonard Bernstein, with Sid Ramin, Irwin Kostal. A Lincoln Center Festival '68 Production. Produced by The Music Theater of Lincoln Center (Richard Rodgers, President and Producing director). Opened 24 June 1968 at the New State Theatre and closed 7 September 1968 after 89 performances.

CAST: *THE JETS*: *Riff*, the Leader: AVIND HARUM. *Tony*, his friend: KURT PETERSON. *Action*: Ian Tucker. *A-Rab*: Robert LuPone. *Baby John*: Stephen Reinhardt. *Snowboy*: George Ramos. *Big Deal*: Roger Briant. *Diesel*: Victor Mohica. *Gee-Tar*: Chuck Beard. *Mouth Piece*: Joseph Pichette. *Tiger*: Kenneth Carr. *Their Girls*: *Graziella*: Garet De Troia. *Velma*: Nancy Dalton. *Minnie*: Rachel Lampert. *Clarice*: Sherry Lynn Diamant. *Pauline*: Carol Hanzel. *Pucky*: Jeanne Frey. *Anybodys*: Lee Lund.

THE SHARKS: *Bernardo*, the Leader: ALAN CASTNER. *Maria*, his Sister: VICTORIA MALLORY. *Anita*, his Girl: BARBARA LUNA. *Chino*, his Friend: Bobby Capo, Jr. *Pepe*: Edgar Coronado. *Indio*: Peter De Nicola. *Luis*: Pat Matera. *Anxious*: Steven Gelfer. *Nibbles*: Ramon Caballero. *Juano*: Pernett Robinson. *Toro*: Byron Wheeler. *Moose*: George Comtois. *Their Girls*: *Rosalia*: Kay Oslin. *Consuelo*: Lee Hooper. *Teresita*: Connie Burnett. *Francisca*: Eileen Barbaris. *Estella*: Judith Lerner. *Marguerita*: Carol Lynn Vasquez. *Felicia*: Diane McAfee.

THE ADULTS: *Doc*: MARTIN WOLFSON. *Schrank*: Joseph Mascolo. *Krupke*: Josip Elic. *Gladhand*: Bill McCutcheon.

[1]Originally produced in New York 15 March 1956 at the Mark Hellinger Theatre for 2717 peformances. For Synopsis of Scenes and Musical Numbers, see original 1956 production.

[2]Originally produced in New York 26 September 1957 at the Winter Garden for 732 performances. For Synopsis of Scenes and Musical Numbers, see original 1957 production.

1968.19 NOËL COWARD'S SWEET POTATO

A Musical Revue in Two Acts. Words and Music by Noël Coward. From a conception by Roderick Cook. Material assembled and adapted by Roderick Cook and Lee Theodore. Directed and choreographed by Lee Theodore. Settings by Helen Pond and Herbert Senn. Costumes by David Toser. Lighting by Peter Hunt. Musical supervision and arrangements by Fred Werner. Musical direction and vocal arrangements by Charles Schneider. Co-choreographer, Robert Tucker. Production supervisor, Robert Linden. Assistant choreographer, Vito Durante. Produced by Robert L. Steele in association with The Erani Corporation. Opened 29 September 1968 at the Ethel Barrymore Theatre and closed 12 October 1968 after 17 performances; re-opened 1 November 1968 at the Booth Theatre and closed 23 November 1968 after 27 additional performances. Total: 44 performances.

CAST: GEORGE GRIZZARD, DORTHY LOUDON[3], CAROLE SHELLEY, ARTHUR MITCHELL, TOM KNEEBONE, BONNIE SCHON, Ian Tucker, Robert LuPone, Stephen Reinhardt.

ACT 1

A Beginning (dance)
The Company

"Useful Phrases" (from SAIL AWAY)
G. Grizzard, D. Loudon, A. Mitchell, B. Schon

"Dance, Little Lady" (from THIS YEAR OF GRACE)
B. Schon, Boys
(*Musical Arrangement by* Roland Hanna.)

"Mad Dogs and Englishmen" (from WORDS AND MUSIC, London; SET TO MUSIC)
G. Grizzard, D. Loudon, C. Shelley, T. Kneebone

"World Weary" (from THIS YEAR OF GRACE)
A. Mitchell, B. Schon, Boys

"A Bar on the Piccola Marina"
G. Grizzard

Literature
D. Loudon, T. Kneebone

"Why Does Love Get in the Way?" (from ACE OF CLUBS, London)
C. Shelley

"Men About Town" (from TONIGHT AT 8:30)
G. Grizzard, D. Loudon, T. Kneebone

"Matelot" (from SIGH NO MORE, London)
A. Mitchell, C. Shelley, B. Schon

Eve
T. Kneebone

"Consecutive Fifths"
G. Grizzard
(*Music by* Fred Werner and Roderick Cook.)

"Mad About the Boy" (from WORDS AND MUSIC, London; SET TO MUSIC)
D. Loudon, C. Shelley, B. Schon, Boys

"I Wonder What Happened to Him?" (from SIGH NO MORE, London)
G. Grizzard, T. Kneebone

Karate
B. Schon

"A Room With a View" (from THIS YEAR OF GRACE)
D. Loudon

Waltzes (dance)
G. Grizzard, Boys

"I Like America" (from ACE OF CLUBS, London)
The Company

ACT 2

"Let's Do It"
The Company
(*Music by* Cole Porter.)

[3]Succeeded by MARY LOUISE WILSON for return engagement.

"Three White Feathers" (from WORDS AND MUSIC, London; SET TO MUSIC)
D. Loudon, T. Kneebone
"Don't Put Your Daughter on the Stage, Mrs. Worthington"
G. Grizzard, Boys
"Headless Dance"
A. Mitchell, R. Carter
(*Music from* "Never Again.")
"Alice (Is At It Again)"
T. Kneebone
Social Grace
A. Mitchell, B. Schon, I. Tucker, D. Loudon, T. Kneebone
"Sweet Potato" (dance)
C. Shelley, Boys
Party Chat/Amanda, Elyot and Friends
C. Shelley, G. Grizzard, Company
"If Love Were All" (from BITTER SWEET)
D. Loudon
Sex Talk
T. Kneebone
"Sunset in Samolo"
C. Shelley
(*Music by* Fred Werner and Roderick Cook.)
"Teach Me to Dance Like Grandma" (from THIS YEAR OF GRACE)
D. Loudon, A. Mitchell
(The) Boy Actor
G. Grizzard
"World Weary" (reprise)
The Company
An Ending
The Company

1968.20 MARLENE DIETRICH

A Return Engagement of the One Woman Show in One Act[4]. (Musical) Arrangements by Burt Bacharch. Conductor, Stan Freeman. Production supervisor, Jerry Adler. Lighting by Joe Davis. A Nine O'Clock Theater Production. Produced by Alexander H. Cohen. Opened 3 October 1968 at the Mark Hellinger Theatre and closed 30 November 1968 after 64 performances.

CAST: MARLENE DIETRICH.

REPERTOIRE[5]
"Look Me Over Closely"
"You're the Cream in My Coffee" (from HOLD EVERYTHING)
(*Music by* Ray Henderson. *Lyrics by* Buddy G. DeSylva and Lew Brown.)
"Boomerang Baby"
"My Blue Heaven"
(*Music by* Walter Donaldson. *Lyrics by* George Whiting.)
"(Naughty) Lola" (from film THE BLUE ANGEL)
(*Music and Lyrics by* Frederick Holländer.)
"Where Have All the Flowers Gone?"
(*Music and Lyrics by* Pete Seeger.)
"The Laziest Gal in Town" (from film STAGE FRIGHT)
(*Music and Lyrics by* Cole Porter.)
"Shir Hatan Biem"
(*Music and Lyrics by* Z. Sahar.)
"When the World Was Young"
(*Original French Lyrics by* Angela Vannier.)
(*Music by* M. Philippe-Gerard. *Lyrics by* Johnny Mercer.)
"La Vie en Rose"
(*Music by* Louiguy. *Lyrics by* Edith Piaf.)
"Jonny" (from film SONG OF SONGS)
(*Music by* Frederick Holländer. *Lyrics by* Edward Heyman.)
"Go 'Way from My Window"
(*arr. by* J. J. Niles.)
"Lili Marlene"
(*Music by* Norbert Schultze. *Lyrics by* Hans Leip and Tommie Connor.)
"Das Lied Ist Aus" (Frag' nicht warum ich gehe)
(*Music and Lyrics by* Walter Reisch, A. Robinson, Robert Stoltz.)
"I Wish You Love"
(*Music by* Charles Trenet. *Lyrics by* Albert Beach.)
"Marie, Marie"
(*Music by* Gilbert Becaud. *Lyrics by* Pierre Delanoe and Kolpe.)
"Honeysuckle Rose" (from HOT CHOCOLATES)
(*Music by* Fats Waller. *Lyrics by* Andy Razaf.)
"White Grass"
"Everyone's Gone to the Moon"
(*Music and Lyrics by* Kenneth King.)
"Falling in Love Again" (from film THE BLUE ANGEL)
(*Music and Lyrics by* Frederick Holländer.)

[4]Previously presented in New York 9 October October 1967 at the Lunt-Fontanne Theatre for 48 performances.
[5]Not in performance order.

1968.21 GILBERT BECAUD SINGS LOVE

A One Man Show in Two Acts[6]. All music composed by Gilbert Becaud. Lyrics by Pierre Delanoe, Louis Amade, Maurice Vidalin, Charles Aznavour, Jean Broussolle, Mack David, Carl Sigman, Gilbert Becaud. Scenery and lighting by Ralph Alswang. Musical director, Raymond Bernard. Produced by Norman Twain and Marcel Akselrod by arrangement with Felix Marouani. Opened 6 October 1968 at the Cort Theatre and closed 26 October 1968 after 24 performances.

CAST: GILBERT BECAUD.

ACT 1
"Le jour ou la pluie viendra"
"Les jours meilleurs"
"C'etait mon copain"
"Le bateau blanc"
"Rosy and John"
"L'étoile"
"La grande roue"
"Je t'attends"
"Je partirai"
"T'es venu de loin"
"Le pianiste de Varsovie"
"Cornelius"

ACT 2
"L'oiseau de toutes les couleurs"
"The Other Three"
"Les cerisiers sont blancs"
"La grosse noce"
"La riviere"
"Les cloches"
"Je reviens te chercher"
"Nathalie"
"Et maintenant"
"L'important c'est la Rosa"

1968.22 THE MEGILLA OF ITZIK MANGER

A Yiddish-English Musical in Two Acts, a Prologue and 26 Scenes, in Yiddish. Entire production adapted and staged by Shmuel Bunim. (Based on the poems of Itzik Manger and the Book of Esther.) Music by Dov Seltzer. (Yiddish lyrics by Itzik Manger.) English commentaries by Joe

[6]Gilbert Becaud previously presented in New York 31 October 1966 at the Longacre Theatre for 19 performances.

Darion. Lighting by Eldon Elder. Original Israeli production designed by Shlomo Vitkin. Musical conductor, Max Meth. Assistant director, Amnon Kabatchnik. Produced by Zvi Kolitz, Solomon Sagall and Alice Peerce. Opened 9 October 1968 at the John Golden Theatre and closed 15 December 1968 after 78 performances. Re-opened a return engagement 19 April 1969 at the Longacre Theatre and closed 27 April 1969 after 12 additional performances. Total: 90 performances.

CAST: *Interlocutor, Fastrigosso, Fanfosso, and other assorted characters*: MIKE BURSTEIN. *Ahasueras, Mordechai, Etc. Etc.*: PESACH BURSTEIN. *Vashti, Zeresh, Innkeeper and Various Mothers*: LILLIAN LUX. *Haman, Tailor, Fanfosso's Daughter and different Jews*: ZISHA GOLD. *Esther, Tailor's Apprentice, First Girl, Second Girl and other girls*: SUSAN WALTERS[7]. *Second Interlocutor, Vayzatha and characters of assorted sexes*: ARIEL FURMAN. *Market People, Palace attendants, street crowds, wedding guests, etc. etc.*: The Company.

(The action takes place in Biblical times.)

Act 1, Scene 1: Why Mordechai, the sage, hung around the King's Palace. *Scene 2*: Queen Vashti's boudoir. *Scene 3*: Scandal in the Palace. *Scene 4*: Vashti walks her last, long mile. *Scene 5*: Esther wants to be taken to the King. *Scene 6*: Esther's wedding. *Scene 7*: Mordechai returns home drunk from the wedding. *Scene 8*: Outside the Palace, a lover cries for his lost love. *Scene 9*: Inside the Palace, Queen Esther can't sleep. *Scene 10*: Outside the Palace, Fastrigossa does sleep. He dreams of Esther. *Scene 11*: Jews in trouble come to Mordechai for help. *Scene 12*: Politics in the bedroom. *Scene 13*: Fastrigossa sends a love song to Esther.

Act 1, Scene 1: Fastrigossa attacks the King in the Marketplace and Haman telephones the news to his son, the editor. *Scene 2*: The tailors wet their whistles. *Scene 3*: The King is glad to be alive. *Scene 4*: Mordechai visits Esther in the Palace. *Scene 5*: Now Haman can't sleep. *Scene 6*: Haman, the charmer, comes to charm Esther. *Scene 7*: In the tailor shop, a party suit is being made for Haman. *Scene 8*: Fastrigossa's mother cries for her son and blames Esther and Mordechai for his death. *Scene 9*: Haman waits for his party suit. *Scene 10*: The day of the big masquerade. *Scene 11*: Caught in the act. *Scene 12*: Haman goes to the gallows. *Scene 13*: Finale.

ACT 1

Prologue

"The Tailor's Megilla"
Full Company

Scene 1

"Theme of the Megilla" (Der Nigun Fun Der Megille)
(Full Company)

Scene 3

"Oom Pa Pa Pa" (Drinking Song) (Dem Melech's Sudeh)
(Full Company)

Scene 4

"Vashti's Farewell" (Vashti's Kloglid)
(L. Lux)

Scene 5

"Song of the Walnut Tree" (Der Alter Nussenboim)
(Full Company)

"Theme of the Megilla" (reprise)

Scene 8

"Fastrigossa's Lament" (Di Elegiye Fun Fastrigosso)
(M. Burstein)

Scene 9

"Fastrigossa's Lament" (reprise)

"Song of the Golden Peacock" (Das Lid Fun Der Goldener Paveh)
(Full Company)

Scene 13

"Fly Little Bird" (Flits Fegelech)
(M. Burstein, Company)

ACT 2

Scene 1

"Gevald Aria" (Gevald)
(Full Company)

Scene 2

"The Tailor's Drinking Song" (Come In to the Tavern)
(Kum Arain in Shenk)
(Full Company)

Scene 3

"S'a Mechaye" (The King's Song)
(It's a Groove)
(P. Burstein)

Scene 4

"Song of the Walnut Tree" (reprise)

Scene 7

"The Tailors' Song" (From Stopchet to Kolomay) (Dos Shneider Lid)
(Full Company)

Various reprises

"Revolutionary Song" (Mir Velen Nisht Fasten)
(Full Company)

Scene 8

"A Mother's Tears" (Fastrigossa's Mame)
(L. Lux)

Scene 10

"'Cause Uncle Mordecai Is So Smart" (Der Fetter Mord'che Heist)
(M. Burstein, L. Lux)

Scene 12

"Chiribim"
(Full Company)

Scene 13

"Lechaim" for All (A Toast to the Players)
(Full Company)

1968.23 HER FIRST ROMAN

A Musical in Two Acts, a Prologue and 11 Scenes. Book, music and lyrics by Ervin Drake. Based on the play "Caesar and Cleopatra" by George Bernard Shaw. Dances and musical scenes staged by Dania Krupska. Entire production under the supervision by Derek Goldby. Sets and costumes by Michael Anania. Lighting by Martin Aronstein. Orchestrations and vocal arrangements by Don Walker. Musical direction, dance and incidental music by Peter Howard. Production supervised by Robert Weiner and George Thorn. Produced by Joseph Cates and Henry Fownes in association with Warner Brothers-7 Arts. Opened 20 October 1968 at the Lunt-Fontanne Theatre and closed 2 November 1968 after 17 performances.

CAST (in order of appearance): *Ftatateeta*: CLAUDIA McNEIL. *Rufio*: BRUCE MacKAY. *Roman Centurion*: Jack Dabdoub. *Caesar*: RICHARD KILEY. *Cleopatra*: LESLIE UGGAMS. *Iras*: BARBARA SHARMA. *Charmian*: Diana Corto. *Achillas*: Larry Douglas. *Pothinus*: Earl Montgomery. *Ptolemy*: Phillip Graves. *Britannus*: Brooks Morton. *Roman Sentry*: George Blackwell. *Apollodorous*: Cal Bellini. *Palace Official*: Marc Jordan.

Roman Soldiers: John Baylis, Paul Berné, George Blackwell, Gerry Buckhardt, Robert Carle, Gordon Cook, Bill Gibbens, Scott Hunter, Sean Nolan, Doug Spingler, Don StomsVik, Ronald Stratton. *Egyptians*: Pamela Barlow, Diana Corto, Priscilla Lopez, Sally Neal, Trina Parks, Suzanne Rogers, Renee Rose, Geri Seignious, Henry Baker, Marc Jordan, George Nestor, Alexander Orfaly, Kenneth Scott.

The action takes place in Egypt from October 48 through March 47 B.C.

ACT 1

Prologue

"What Are We Doing in Egypt?"
B. MacKay, J. Dabdoub, Roman Soldiers

Scene 1

"Hail to the Sphinx"
R. Kiley

"Save Me From Caesar"
L. Uggams, R. Kiley

Scene 2

"Many Young Men from Now"
L. Uggams

Scene 4

"Ptolemy"
L. Uggams, Egyptian Women

Scene 5

"Old Gentleman"
R. Kiley

[7]Succeeded by Evelyn Kingsley for return engagement.

Scene 6
"Her First Roman"
B. MacKay, B. Morton, Roman Soldiers
Scene 7
"Magic Carpet"
L. Uggams, C. Bellini, Egyptians
Scene 8
"Rome"
R. Kiley
"The Things We Think We Are"
R. Kiley, L. Uggams, B. Morton, B. MacKay

ACT 2
Scene 1
"I Cannot Make Him Jealous"
L. Uggams
Scene 2
"The Dangerous Age"
B. MacKay, B. Morton
"In Vino Veritas"
R. Kiley, B. MacKay, B. Morton, C. Bellini
"Caesar Is Wrong"
R. Kiley
"Just For Today"
L. Uggams

1968.24 MAGGIE FLYNN

A Musical in Two Acts, a Prologue and 17 Scenes. Book, music and lyrics by Hugo Peretti, Luigi Creatore and George David Weiss. Book in collaboration with Morton Da Costa. Based on an idea by John Flaxman. Entire production directed by Morton Da Costa. Choreography by Brian MacDonald. Setings by William and Jean Eckart. Costumes by W. Robert LaVine. Lighting by Tharon Musser. Musical direction and vocal arrangements by John Lesko. Orchestrations by Philip J. Lang. Dance music arrranged by Trude Rittman. Produced by John Bowab in association with Harris Associates, Inc.and Levin-Townshend Enterprises, Inc. Opened 23 October 1968 at the ANTA Theatre and closed 5 January 1969 after 82 performances.

CAST (in order of appearance):*Mulligan Sergeant*: David Vosburg. *Sprague Sergeant*: Larry Pool. *Garibaldi Sergeant*: James Senn. *Donnelly*: Austin Colyer. *O'Malley*: George Tregre. *First Soldier*: Roger Bigelow. *Carter*: Charles Rule. *O'Brien*: Stanley Simmonds. *Clancy*: Mario Maroze. *Timmy*: WILLIAM JAMES. *Walter*: Douglas Grant. *Maggie Flynn*: SHIRLEY JONES. *William*: Clarence Espinosa. *Andrew*: Giancarlo Esposito. *Erasmus*: Vincent Esposito. *Violet*: Sharon Brown. *Hyacinth*: Jewel Hoston. *Iris*: Irene Cara. *Pansy*: Stephanie Mills. *Chrysanthemum*: Cheri Welles. *Mary O'Cleary*: JENNIFER DARLING. *Bob Jefferson*: Bill Barrian. *Will Jefferson*: Mitch Taylor. *Fireman*: Charles Rule. *Officer O'Reilly*: Nick Malekos. *Effram*: PETER NORMAN. *Molly*: Hazel Steck. *Mick*: John Stanzel .*Bellini*: Robert Mandan. *Atlas*: Robert Roman. *Phineas*: JACK CASSIDY. *Young Girl*: Kathleen Robey. *Goliath*: Roy Barry. *Lena*, The Gorilla: James Senn. *Acrobats*: George Bunt, Don Bonnell. *Colonel John Farraday*: ROBERT KAYE. *Mrs. Vanderhoff*: SIBYL BOWAN. *Mrs. Opdyke*: Jeannette Seibert. *Second Lady*: June Eve Story. *Mrs. Savage*: Sandie Fields. *Mrs. Van Stock*: Hazel Steck. *Deaf Lady*: Betty Hyatt Linton. *Captain Piedmont*: Charles Rule. *Lieutenant*: Larry Pool. *General Parkinton*: Robert Mandan. *Soldier Ed Waters*: Dallas Johann. *Tessie*: Hazel Steck. *Ladies of the Evening*: Reby Howells, Sandie Fields.

The action takes place in various streets of New York City in 1863.

Prologue: Streets of New York City, 1863.

Act 1, Scene 1: Dormitory and Facade of Meagan Orphan Home. *Scene 2*: Barlow's Saloon. *Scene 3*: Christopher Street. *Scene 4*: Dressing Tent. *Scene 5*: Parlor and Facade of Orphanage. *Scene 6*: The Kitchen of Orphanage and Street. *Scene 7*: Kitchen of Orphanage. *Scene 8*: Solarium of Vanderhoff Mansion. *Scene 9*: Union Army Headquarters and the Kitchen.

Act 2, Scene 1: Barlow's Saloon and a Street. *Scene 2*: Veranda of the Vanderhoff Mansion. *Scene 3*: The Basement of the Orphanage. *Scene 4*: The Parlour. *Scene 5*: A Jail. *Scene 6*: The Jail Office. *Scene 7*: Various New York Streets. *Scene 8*: The Kitchen and Front of the Orphanage.

ACT 1
Prologue
"(They're) Never Gonna Make Me Fight"
W. James, Men
Scene 1
"It's a Nice Cold Morning"
S. Jones, Children
Scene 2
"I Wouldn't Have You Any Other Way"
S. Jones, Saloon Boys
Scene 3
"Learn How to Laugh"
J. Cassidy, Townspeople
Scene 4
"Maggie Flynn"
J. Cassidy
Scene 5
"The Thank You Song"
S. Jones, J. Darling, Children
"Look Around Your Little World"
R. Kaye, J. Cassidy
Scene 6
"Maggie Flynn" (reprise)
J. Cassidy, S. Jones, Children, Saloon Boys
Scene 7
"I Won't Let It Happen Again"
S. Jones
Scene 8
"How About a Ball?"
J. Cassidy, S. Jones, S. Bowan, Ladies
Scene 9
"Pitter Patter"
J. Cassidy
"I Won't Let It Happen Again" (reprise)
S. Jones

ACT 2
Scene 1
"Never Gonna Make Me Fight" (reprise)
A. Colyer, S. Simmonds, W. James, Men
Scene 2
"Why Can't I Walk Away?"
J. Cassidy
Scene 3
"The Game of War"
Children
Scene 5
"Mr. Clown"
J. Cassidy, S. Jones, Children, Bums, Ladies of the Evening
"Pitter Patter" (reprise)
S. Jones
Scene 7
The Riot
Full Company
Scene 8
"Don't You Think It's Very Nice?"
S. Jones, J. Cassidy, Children
(Finale:) "Mr. Clown," "Maggie Flynn" (reprises)
S. Jones, J. Cassidy

1968.25 H.M.S. PINAFORE, or The Lass That Loved a Sailor

A Revival of the Comic Opera in Two Acts[8]. Libretto by William S. Gilbert. Music by Arthur Sullivan. Settings and costumes designed by Peter Goffin. Back cloth, Joseph and Phil Harker. Director of productions, Herbert

[8]Originally presented in New York 15 January 1879 at the Standard Theatre for 175 performances. For Synopsis of Scenes and Musical Numbers, see original 1879 production.

Newby. Musical director, James Walker. Chorus master and assistant conductor, William Cowley. Produced by the D'Oyly Carte Opera Trust, Ltd. under the personal supervision of Bridget D'Oyly Carte and under the management of Sol Hurok. Opened 29 October 1968 at the New York City Center and closed 14 November 1968 after 4 performances in repertory.

CAST: *The Rt. Hon. Sir Joseph Porter, K.C.B.*, First Lord of the Admiralty: JOHN REED. *Captain Corcoran*, Commanding *H.M.S. Pinafore*: THOMAS LAWLOR. *Ralph Rackstraw*, Able Seaman: RALPH MASON. *Dick Deadeye*, Able Seaman: DONALD ADAMS. *Bill Bobstay*, Bo'sun's Mate: George Cook. *Bob Becket*, Carpenter's Mate: Clifford Parkes. *Josephine*, the Captain's Daughter: VALERIE MASTERSON, SUSAN JACKSON. *Hebe*, Sir Joseph's First Cousin: Pauline Wales. *Little Buttercup*, Mrs. Cripps, a Portsmouth Bumboat Woman: CHRISTENE PALMER.

First Lord's Sisters, his Cousins, his Aunts, Sailors, Marines: Glyn Adams, John Ayldon, Derek Booth, Jeffrey Cresswell, George Cook, Jon Ellison, Arthur Jackson, Gordon Mackenzie, Clifford Parkes, Brian Peach, David Rayson, Brian Sharpe, Michael Tuckey, John Webley, Howard Williamson, David Young, Brenda Atherton, Susan Minshull-Browne, Christine Bull, Anne Eggleston, Julia Goss, Frances Gregory, Glenys Groves, Anne Guthrie, Abby Hadfield, Beti Lloyd-Jones, Elizabeth Lowry, Marian Martin, Beverly Mino, Elizabeth Mynett, Alison Parkor, Anne Sessions.

PATIENCE, or Bunthorne's Bride

1968.26

A Revival of the Comic Opera in Two Acts[9]. Libretto by William S. Gilbert. Music by Arthur Sullivan. Settings and costumes designed by Peter Goffin. Director of productions, Herbert Newby. Musical director, James Walker. Chorus master and assistant conductor, William Cowley. Produced by the D'Oyly Carte Opera Trust, Ltd. under the personal supervision of Bridget D'Oyly Carte and under the management of Sol Hurok. Opened 31 October 1968 at the New York City Center and closed 13 November 1968 after 4 performances.

CAST: *Colonel Calverley*: DONALD ADAMS. *Major Murgatroyd*: Howard Williamson. *Lieut. the Duke of Dunstable*: RALPH MASON. *Reginald Bunthorne*, a Fleshly Poet: JOHN REED. *Archibald Grosvenor*, an Idyllic Poet: KENNETH SANDFORD. *Mr. Bunsthorne's Solicitor*: James Marsland. *The Lady Angela, The Lady Saphir, The Lady Ella, The Lady Jane*, Rapturous Maidens: PEGGY ANN JONES, PAULINE WALES, Anne Sessions, CHRISTENE PALMER. *Patience*, a Dairy Maid: SUSAN JACKSON. *Chorus of Rapturous Maidens and Officers of the Dragoon Guards*: same as H.M.S. PINAFORE above.

THE MIKADO, or The Town of Titipu

1968.27

A Revival of the Comic Opera in Two Acts[10]. Libretto by William S. Gilbert. Music by Arthur Sullivan. Production directed by Anthony Besch. Costumes designed by Charles Ricketts. Nanki-Poo, Act 1 Costume designed By Disley Jones. Scenery by Peter Goffin. Director of productions, Herbert Newby. Musical director, James Walker. Chorus master and assistant conductor, William Cowley. Produced by the D'Oyly Carte Opera Trust, Ltd. under the personal supervision of Bridget D'Oyly Carte and under the management of Sol Hurok. Opened 1 November 1968 at the New York City Center and closed 16 November 1968 after 8 performances in repertory.

CAST: *The Mikado of Japan*: DONALD ADAMS. *Nanki-Poo*, his son, disguised as a wandering minstrel in love with Yum-Yum: PHILIP POTTER. *Ko-Ko*, Lord High Executioner of Titipu: JOHN REED. *Pooh-Bah*, Lord High Everything Else: KENNETH SANDFORD. *Pish-Tush, Go-To*, Noble Lords: Thomas Lawlor, George Cook. *Yum-Yum, Pitti-Sing, Peep-Bo*, three sisters, wards of Ko-Ko: VALERIE MASTERSON, PEGGY ANN JONES, PAULINE WALES. *Katisha*: CHRISTENE PALMER, BETTI LLOYD-JONES. *Chorus of School Girls, Nobles, Guards and Coolies*: same as H.M.S. PINAFORE above.

THE PIRATES OF PENZANCE, or The Slave of Duty

1968.28

A Revival of the Comic Opera in Two Acts[11]. Libretto by William S. Gilbert. Music by Arthur Sullivan. Settings designed by Peter Goffin. Director of productions, Herbert Newby. Musical director, James Walker. Chorus master and assistant conductor, William Cowley. Produced by the D'Oyly Carte Opera Trust, Ltd. under the personal supervision of Bridget D'Oyly Carte and under the management of Sol Hurok. Opened 6 November 1968 at the New York City Center and closed 17 November 1968 after 4 performances in repertory.[12]

CAST: *Major General Stanley*: JOHN REED, HOWARD WILLIAMSON. *The Pirate King*: DONALD ADAMS. *Samuel*, his Lieutenant: John Webley. *Frederic*, the Pirate Apprentice: PHILIP POTTER. *Sergeant of Police*: GEORGE COOK. *Mabel, Edith Kate, Isabel*, General Stanley's Daughters: VALERIE MASTERSON, PEGGY ANN JONES, PAULINE WALES, Julia Goss. *Ruth*, Pirate Maid-of-all-work: CHRISTENE PALMER. *Chorus of Pirates, Police and General Stanley's Daughters*: same as H.M.S. PINAFORE above.

IOLANTHE, or The Peer and the Peri

1968.29

A Revival of the Comic Opera in Two Acts[13]. Libretto by William S. Gilbert. Music by Arthur Sullivan. Director of productions, Herbert Newby. Settings designed by Peter Goffin. Musical director, James Walker. Chorus master and assistant conductor, William Cowley. Produced by the D'Oyly Carte Opera Trust, Ltd. under the personal supervision of Bridget D'Oyly Carte and under the management of Sol Hurok. Opened 8 November 1968 at the New York City Center and closed 15 November 1968 after 4 performances in repertory[14].

CAST: *The Lord Chancellor*: JOHN REED. *Earl of Mountararat*: DONALD ADAMS. *Earl Tolloller*: RALPH MASON. *Private Willis* of the Grenadier Guards: KENNETH SANDFORD. *Strephon*, an Arcadian Shepherd: THOMAS LAWLOR. *Queen of the Fairies*: CHRISTENE PALMER. *Iolanthe*, a Fairy, Strephon's Mother: PEGGY ANN JONES. *Celia, Leila, Fleta*, Fairies: Anne Sessions, Pauline Wales, Alison Parker. *Phyllis*, an Arcadian Shepherdess and Ward in Chancery: SUSAN JACKSON. *Chorus of Dukes, Marquises, Earls, Viscounts, Barons and Fairies*: same as H.M.S. PINAFORE above.

ZORBA

1968.30

A Musical in Two Acts, 17 Scenes. Book by Joseph Stein. Adapted from the novel "Zorba the Greek" by Nikos Kazantzakis. Music by John Kander. Lyrics by Fred Ebb. Directed by Harold Prince. Choreographed by Ron Field. Scenic production by Boris Aronson. Costumes by Patricia Zipprodt. Lighting by Richard Pilbrow. Musical direction by Harold Hastings. Orchestrations by Don Walker. Dance music arranged by Dorothea Freitag. Production consultant, Vassili Lambrinos. Associate choreographer, Tom Rolla. Produced by Harold Prince in association with Ruth Mitchell. Opened 17 November 1968 at the Imperial Theatre and closed 9 August 1969 after 305 performances.

CAST: *Constable*: David Wilder. *Nikos*: JOHN CUNNINGHAM. *Alexis*: Alex Petrides. *Hortense*: MARIA KARNILOVA. *Manolako*: James Luisi. *Panayotis*: Nat Horne. *Widow*: CARMEN ALVAREZ. *Mimiko*: Al De Sio. *Konstandi*: Joseph Alfasa. *Sofia*: Marsha Tamaroff. *Kyriakos*: Jerry Sappir. *Leader*: LORRAINE SERABIAN. *Kanakis*: Ali Hafid. *Konstantinos*: Angelo Saridis. *Marina*: Alicia Helen Markarian. *Fivos*: Gerrit De Beer. *Efterpi*: Lee Hooper. *Zorba*: HERSCHEL

---

[9]First presented in New York 22 September 1881 at the Standard Theatre for 177 performances. For Synopsis of Scenes and Musical Numbers, see original 1881 production.

[10]First presented in New York 20 July, 10-29 August 1885 at the Union Square and People's Theatres for 22 performances. First authorized production presented 19 August 1885 at the Fifth Avenue Theatre by Richard D'Oyly Carte for 250 performances. For Synopsis of Scenes and Musical Numbers, see 19 August 1885 D'Oyly Carte production.

[11]First presented in New York 31 December 1879 at the Fifth Avenue Theatre for a total of 91 performances in two engagements. For Synopsis of Scenes and Musical Numbers, see original 1879 production.

[12]Costumes uncredited.

[13]First presented in New York 25 November 1882 at the Standard Theatre for 105 performances. For Synopsis of Scenes and Musical Numbers, see original 1882 production.

[14]Costumes uncredited.

BERNARDI. *Loukas*: Loukas Skiptaris. *Meropi*: Juliette Durand. *Aristos*: Charles Kalan. *Georgi*: John La Motta.

Antonis: Anthony Marciona. *Tasso*: Susan Marciona. *Thanos*: Lewis Gundunas. *Pavli*: Richard Dmitri. *Father Zacharia*: Gerard Russak. *Aliki*: Miriam Welch. *Mavrodani*: Paul Michael. *Chyristo*: Louis Garcia. *Zacharias*: Edward Nolfi. *Belly Dancer*: Jemela Omar. *Old Man*: Robert Bernard. *Katapolis*: Richard Nieves. *Despo*: Nina Dova. *Irini*: Connie Burnett. *Athena*: Peggy Cooper. *Grigoris*: Wayne Boyd. *Vasilis*: Martin Meyers.

Instrumental Interlude Soloists: Jerry Sappir, Ali Hafid, Angelo Saridis.

The action takes place in a Bouzouki Circle at the present time, and Piraeus, Greece and the island of Crete, in 1924.

Act 1, Scene 1: A Bouzouki Circle. *Scene 2*: A Waterfront Café in Piraeus. *Scene 3*: The Exterior of a Village Café, adjacent shops and Village Church in Crete. *Scene 4*: The Garden of Hortense's Inn. *Scene 5*: Hortense's Bedroom. *Scene 6*: The Entrance to the Mine. *Scene 7*: Exterior of Hortense's Inn, the next morning. *Scene 8*: Interior of a Café in Khania. *Scene 9*: Interior and Exterior of the Widow's Home, dusk of the next day.

Act 2, Scene 1: The Village Square. *Scene 2*: Exterior of the Cottage in Hortense's garden. *Scene 3*: A Road. *Scene 4*: The Village Square. *Scene 5*: The Entrance to the Mine. *Scene 6*: Hortense's Bedroom. *Scene 7*: The Road leading out of the Village. *Scene 8*: A Bouzouki Circle.

ACT 1
Scene 1
"Life Is"
L. Serrabian, the Company
Scene 2
"The First Time"
H. Bernardi
Scene 3
"The Top of the Hill"
L. Serrabian, Chorus
Scene 4
"No Boom Boom"
M. Karnilova, H. Bernardi, J. Cunningham, The Admirals
"Vive La Difference"
The Admirals, Dancers
Scene 6
"The Butterfly"
J. Cunningham, L. Serrabian, C. Alvarez, Chorus
Scene 7
"Goodbye, Canavaro"
M. Karnilova, H. Bernardi
Scene 8
Belly Dance
J. Omar
"Grandpapa"
H. Bernardi, L. Serrabian, Chorus
"Only Love"
M. Karnilova
"The Bend of the Road"
L. Serrabian, Chorus
"Only Love" (reprise)
L. Serrabian

ACT 2
Scene 1
Bells[15]
Dancers
Scene 2
"Y'assou"[16]
J. Cunningham, H. Bernardi, M. Karnilova, L. Serrabian, Chorus
Scene 3
"Why Can't I Speak?"[17]
C. Alvarez, L. Hooper
Scene 5
Mine Celebration
H. Bernardi, Company
Scene 6
"The Crow"
L. Serrabian, Women
"Happy Birthday"
M. Karnilova
Scene 7
"I Am Free"
H. Bernardi
Scene 8
"Life Is" (reprise)
L. Serrabian, the Company

[15]Dropped for subsequent national tour.
[16]Replaced for subsequent national tour by:
"Bouboulina"
John Raitt (Zorba), Barbara Baxley (Hortense), Chita Rivera (Leader), Chorus
[17]Replaced for subsequent national tour by:
"That's a Beginning"
Marsha Tamaroff (Widow), Gary Krawford (Nikos), C. Rivera

1968.31 PROMISES, PROMISES

A Musical in Two Acts, 14 Scenes. Book by Neil Simon. Based on the film "The Apartment" by Billy Wilder and I.A.L. Diamond. Music by Burt Bacharach. Lyrics by Hal David. Directed by Robert Moore. Musical numbers staged by Michael Bennett. Settings by Robin Wagner. Costumes by Donald Brooks. Lighting by Martin Aronstein. Musical direction and dance arrangements by Harold Wheeler. Orchestrations by Jonathan Tunick. Associate producer, Samuel Liff. Assistant choreographer, Bob Avian. Sound created by Admins, Ltd. Produced by David Merrick. Opened 1 December 1968 at the Sam S. Shubert Theatre and closed 1 January 1972 after 1281 performances.

CAST (in order of appearance): *Chuck Baxter*: JERRY ORBACH. *J. D. Sheldrake*: EDWARD WINTER. *Fran Kubelik*: JILL O'HARA. *Bartender Eddie*: Ken Howard. *Mr. Dobitch*: Paul Reed. *Sylvia Gilhooley*: Adrienne Angel. *Mr. Kirkeby*: Norman Shelly. *Mr. Eichelberger*: Vince O'Brien. *Vivien Della Hoya*: Donna McKechnie. *Dr. Dreyfuss*: A. LARRY HAINES. *Jesse Vanderhof*: Dick O'Neill. *Dentist's Nurse*: Rita O'Connor. *Company Nurse*: Carole Bishop. *Company Doctor*: Gerry O'Hara. *Peggy Olson*: Millie Slavin. *Lum Ding Hostess*: Baayork Lee. *Waiter*: Scott Pearson. *Madison Square Garden Attendant*: Michael Vita. *Dining Room Hostess*: Betsy Haug. *Miss Polansky*: Margo Sappington. *Miss Wong*: Baayork Lee. *Bartender Eugene*: Michael Vita. *Marge MacDougall*: Marian Mercer. *Clancy's Lounge Patrons*: Carole Bishop, Rita O'Connor, Julane Stites, Rod Barry, Gene Cooper, Bob Fitch, Neil F. Jones, Scott Pearson, Michael Shawn. *Clancy's Employees*: Graciela Daniele, Betsy Haug, Margo Sappington. *Helen Sheldrake*: Kay Oslin. *Karl Kubelik*: Ken Howard. *New Young Executive*: Rod Barry. *Interns and Dates*: Barbara Alston, Graciela Daniele, Gerry O'Hara, Michael Shawn.

Orchestra Voices: Kelly Britt, Margot Hanson, Bettye McCormick, Ilona Simon.

The action takes place in New York at the present time.

Act 1, Scene 1: The Offices of Consolidated Life; Second Avenue Bar. *Scene 2*: Chuck's Apartment House. *Scene 3*: Medical Office. *Scene 4*: Mr. Sheldrake's Office. *Scene 5*: Lobby. *Scene 6*: Lum Ding's Restauarnt and Madison Square Garden. *Scene 7*: Lobby, Executive Dining Room; Executive Sun Deck. *Scene 8*: At the Elevator. *Scene 9*: Nineteenth Floor Christmas Party.

Act 2, Scene 1: Clancy's Lounge. *Scene 2*: Chuck's Apartment. *Scene 3*: The Offices of Consolidated Life. *Scene 4*: Lum Ding's Restaurant and Street. *Scene 5*: Chuck's Apartment.

ACT 1
Scene 1
"Half As Big As Life"
J. Orbach
("Grapes of Roth" dance)
(Dancers)
Scene 2
"Upstairs"
J. Orbach
Scene 3
"You'll Think of Someone"
J. O'Hara, J. Orbach
Scene 4
"Our Little Secret"
J. Orbach, E. Winter
Scene 5
"She Likes Basketball"
J. Orbach

Scene 6

"Knowing When to Leave"

J. O'Hara

Scene 7

"Where Can You Take a Girl?"

P. Reed, N. Shelly, V. O'Brien, D. O'Neill

"Wanting Things"

E. Winter

Scene 9

"Turkey Lurkey Time"

D. McKechnie, M. Sappington, B. Lee

ACT 2

Scene 1

"A Fact Can Be a Beautiful Thing"

J. Orbach, M. Mercer, Bar Patrons

Scene 2

"Whoever You Are"

J. O'Hara

"A Young Pretty Girl Like You"

J. Orbach, A. L. Haines

"I'll Never Fall in Love Again"

J. O'Hara, J. Orbach

Scene 4

"Promises, Promises"

J. Orbach

1968.32 CARNIVAL

A Revival of the Musical (Comedy) in Two Acts, 24 Scenes[18]. Book by Michael Stewart. Based on the story ("The Seven Souls of Clement O'Reilly" by Paul Gallico and its film adaptation "Lili") by Helen Deutsch. Music and lyrics by Bob Merrill. Directed by Gus Schirmer. Re-staging of Gower Champion's original choreography by John Nola. Production (settings) and lighting by Feder. Costumes by Harry Curtis, based on originals by Freddy Wittop. Musical and vocal arrangements by Saul Schechtman. Musical director, Peter Howard. Orchestrations by Philip J. Lang. Dance arrangements by Peter Howard. Designer and supervisor of magic and illusion, Jack Adams. Produced by the New York City Center Light Opera Company (Jean Dalrymple, Director). Opened 12 December 1968 at the New York City Center and closed 5 January 1969 after 30 performances.

CAST (in order of appearance): *Jacquot*: PIERRE OLAF. *Mr. Schlegel*: Carmine Caridi. *Grobert*: George Nestor. *Roustabouts*: Chuck Beard, Marcelo Gamboa, Fred Randall, Steven Ross, Paul Solen. *Dog Trainer*: Leonard Brook. *Wardrobe Mistress*: Maria Hero. *Harem Girls*: Nina Janik, Dottie Lester, Maralyn Miles, Linda Rankin. *Bear Girl*: Maureen Hopkins. *Princess Olga*: Dorothy D'Honau. *Band*: Art Ostrin, Nate Barnett. *Stilt-Walker*: Dean Crane. *Jugglers*: Martin Brothers. *Clowns*: Dean Crane, John Drew. *Strongman*: David Berk. *Gladys Zuwicki*: Mary Ann Niles. *Gloria Zuwicki*: Christine Bartel. *Gypsy*: Roberta Vatske. *Marco the Magnificent*: RICHARD FRANCE. *The Incomparable Rosalie*: KAREN MORROW. *Greta Schlegel*: Jennifer Rose. *Lili*: VICTORIA MALLORY. *Paul (Berthalet)*: LEON BIBB. *Blue Birds*: Nina Janik, Dottie Lester, Maralyn Miles, Linda Rankin. *Aerialist*: Dean Crane. *Dr. Glass*: Robert L. Hultman. *Puppets performed by* Richard Barclay.

1969.01 THE FIG LEAVES ARE FALLING

A Musical in Two Acts, a Prologue and 20 Scenes. Book and lyrics by Allan Sherman. Music by Albert Hague. Production directed by George Abbott. Dances and musical numbers staged by Eddie Gasper. Settings by William and Jean Eckart. Costumes by Robert Mackintosh. Lighting by Tharon Musser. Musical direction by Abba Bogin. Orchestrations by Manny Albam. Dance music arranged and orchestra conducted by Jack Lee. Produced by Joseph P. Harris, Lawrence Carr and John Bowab in association with Harris Associates, Inc., and Levin-Townshend Enterprises, Inc. Opened 2 January 1969 at the Broadhurst Theatre and closed 4 January 1969 after 4 performances.

CAST (in order of appearance): *Harry Stone*: BARRY NELSON. *Lillian Stone*: DOROTHY LOUDON. *Pookie Chapman*: JENNY O'HARA. *Mr. Mittleman*: Jay Barney. *Hodgekins*: Joe McGrath. *Reverend Walters*: Darrell Sandeen. *Gelb*: Frank DeSal. *Mildred*: Jean Even. *Grace*: Mara Landi. *Mimsy*: Marilyne Mason. *Charley Montgomery*: KENNETH KIMMINS. *Marty*: Patrick Spohn. *Mother-in-Law*: Helon Blount. *Billy*: David Cassidy. *Cecelia*: Louise Quick. *LeRoy*: Alan Weeks. *Queen Victoria*: Frank DeSal. *Mary Queen of Scots*: Anna Pagan. *Elizabeth Marsden*: Pat Trott. *Mao-Tse*: John Joy. *Marlene*: Jean Even. *Cynthia*: Jocelyn McKay.

Dancers: Jean Even, Mary Jane Houdina, Renata Powers, Sally Ransone, Charlene Ryan, Pat Trott, Frank DeSal, John Medeiros, Michael Misita, Lathan Sanford, Tony Stevens, Patrick Spohn, Pi Douglas. *Singers*: Sherry Lambert, Mara Landi, Rosemary McNamara, Anna Pagan, Jocelyn McKay, Edmund Gaynes, John Joy, Joe McGrath, Darrell Sandeen, Alan Weeks.

(The action trakes place in New York City and Larchmont at the present time.)

Prologue: Larchmont, New York.

Act 1, Scene 1: The Stone's Living Room in Larchmont. *Scene 2*: Limbo. *Scene 3*: Harry's Office. *Scene 4*: The Park. *Scene 5*: Harry's Office. *Scene 6*: The Stone's Living Room; Off to Europe. *Scene 7*: The Stone's Living Room. *Scene 8*: Limbo. *Scene 9*: The Love-in in the Park. *Scene 10*: Limbo. *Scene 11*: The Stone's Bedroom: Nightmare.

Act 2, Scene 1: The Fig Leaves Are Falling. *Scene 2*: Limbo. *Scene 3*: The Stone's Living Room. *Scene 4*: The Theatre. *Scene 5*: Limbo. *Scene 6*: Charley's Apartment. *Scene 7*: Pookie's Pad. *Scene 8*: Limbo. *Scene 9*: The Colorful Living Room: The Ending (?).

ACT 1

Prologue

"All Is Well in Larchmont"

Choir

Scene 1

"Not Tonight"

D. Loudon

Scene 2

"Like Yours"

J. O'Hara, Wallstreeters

Scene 3

"The Fig Leaves Are Falling"

J. O'Hara, B. Nelson

Scene 4

"Give Me a Cause"

The Protestors

Scene 5

"Today I Saw a Rose"

B. Nelson

Scene 6

"We"

D. Loudon

Scene 7

"For Our Sake"

D. Cassidy, L. Quick

Scene 9

"Light One Candle"

A. Weeks, F. DeSal, A. Pagan, Hippies, Yippies, Et Al

Scene 10

"Oh, Boy"

Choir

ACT 2

Scene 1

"The Fig Leaves Are Falling"

The Boys Club

Scene 3

"For the Rest of My Life"

D. Loudon

Scene 4

"I Like It"

B. Nelson, J. O'Hara

Scene 5

"All of My Laughter"

D. Loudon

[18]First produced in New York 13 April 1961 at the Imperial Theatre for 719 performances. For Synopsis of Scenes and Musical Numbers, see original 1961 production.

Scene 7

"Did I Ever Really Live?"
B. Nelson

"Old Fashioned Song"
K. Kimmins, Ensemble

"Lillian, Lillian, Lillian"
D. Loudon, L. Quick, D. Cassidy

1969.02 CELEBRATION

A Musical in Two Acts. Words (book and lyrics) by Tom Jones. Music by Harvey Schmidt. Directed by Tom Jones. Musical numbers staged and choreographed by Vernon Lusby. Settings, lighting and costumes designed by Ed Wittstein. Musical direction by Rod Derefinko. Orchestrations by Jim Tyler. Production coordination by Robert Alan Gold. A Portfolio Production. Produced by Cheryl Crawford and Richard Chandler. Opened 22 January 1969 at the Ambassador Theatre and closed 26 April 1969 after 110 performances.

CAST (in order of appearance): *Potemkin*: KEITH CHARLES. *Orphan*: MICHAEL GLENN-SMITH. *Angel*: SUSAN WATSON. *Rich*: TED THURSTON.

Revelers: Glenn Bastian, Cindi Bulak, Stephan de Ghelder, Leah Horen, Patricia Lens, Norman Mathews, Frank Newell, Pamela Peadon, Felix Rice, Sally Riggs, Gary Wales, Hal Watters.

The action takes place on a platform on New Year's Eve.

ACT 1

"Celebration"
K. Charles, the Revelers

"Orphan in the Storm"
M. Glenn-Smith, the Revelers

"Survive"
K. Charles, the Revelers

"Somebody"
S. Watson, the Hittites

"Bored"
T. Thurston

"My Garden"
M. Glenn-Smith, the Revelers

"Where Did It Go"
T. Thurston, the Sycophants

"Love Song"
S. Watson, K. Charles, T. Thurston, M. Glenn-Smith, the Revelers

"To the Garden"
Everyone

ACT 2

"I'm Glad To See You've Got What You Want"
S. Watson, M. Glenn-Smith

"It's You Who Makes Me Young"
T. Thurston, the Revelers

"Not My Problem"
K. Charles, the Machines

"Fifty Million Years Ago"
M. Glenn-Smith

"The Beautician Ballet"
T. Thurston, the Revelers

"Saturnalia"
K. Charles, the Revelers

"Under the Tree"
S. Watson, the Animals

"Winter and Summer"
Everyone

"Celebration" Finale
Everyone

1969.03 RED, WHITE AND MADDOX

A Thing With Music (Musical Comedy) in Two Acts. Book, music and lyrics by Don Tucker and Jay Broad. (Inspired by the political career of Governor Lester Maddox of Georgia.) Staged by Don Tucker and Jay Broad. Sets and costumes by David Chapman. Design supervision and lighting by Richard Casler. Visual materials by Bill Diehl, Jr. Associate producers, William Domnitz, Arthur Miller. A Theatre Atlanta Production. Produced by Edward Padula. Opened 26 January 1969 at the Cort Theatre and closed 1 March 1969 after 41 performances.

CAST (in alphabetical order): *Alberta*: Georgia Allen. *Student Leader*: Fran Brill. *Cynical Campaigner*: Lois Broad. *Senator*: Ronald Bush. *Air Force General*: Fred Chappell. *Governor of Indiana*: Mitchell Edmonds. *Standard Bearer*: Karl Emery. *The Interlocutor*: Clarence Felder. *General of the Armies*: Gary Gage. *Radio Commentator*: William Gammon. *Lester Maddox*: JAY GARNER. *Student Delegate*: Elaine Harris. *Buttercup Boy*: Ted Harris. *Bombardier*: Christopher Lloyd. *Rock Singer*: Bettye Malone. *Boy from the New Left*: Ted Martin. *The Redneck*: Sandy McCallum. *Virginia Maddox*: Muriel Moore. *Girl from the New Left*: Arlene Nadel. *Political Commentator*: Steve Renfroe. *Little Mary Sue*: Judy Schoen. *Protestor*: Susan Shaloub. *C.I.A. Chief*: William Troutman. *Rock Singer*: James Weston.

Act 1: One hundred years later.

Act 2: One hundred years too late.

ACT 1

"What America Means To Me"
(Entire Company)

"Givers and Getters"
(Company)

"Jubilee Joe"
(Company)

"Ballad of a Redneck"
(Men)

"First Campaign Song"
(Salvation Army Band/Company)

"Hoe Down"
(Entire Company)

"Phooey"
(J. Garner)

"Second Campaign Song"
(Salvation Army Band/Company)

"God Is an American"
(Entire Company)

ACT 2

"Hip-Hooray for Washington"
(J. Garner)

"City Life"
(Company)

"Song of the Malcontents"
(Company)

"The General's Song"
(Company)

"Little Mary Sue"
(Company)

"Billy Joe Ju"
(Company)

"The Impeachment Waltz"
(Company)

"Red, White and Maddox Kazoo March"
(Entire Company)

1969.04 CANTERBURY TALES

A Musical in Two Acts, 10 Scenes[19]. Book by Martin Starkie and Nevill Coghill. Based on Nevill Coghill's translation of Geoffrey Chaucer's

[19]For subsequent National Tour, The Nun's Priest's Tale was reinstated from the London production after The Miller's Tale:

CAST: *Miller*: PATRICK HINES. *Nicholas*: WALTER McGINN. *Alison*: LOUISA FLANINGAM. *The Carpenter*: RAY WALSTON. *Absalom*: Terry Eno. *Gervase*: PATRICK HINES. *Robin*: David Steele. *The Two Parishioners*: Marybeth Lahr, Leslie Bromley.

"Chanticleer"
Company (as above)

"Canterbury Tales." Music by Richard Hill and John Hawkins. Lyrics by Nevill Coghill. Directed by Martin Starkie (after the original London production[20]). Musical numbers and dances staged by Sammy Bayes. Musical direction, vocal and dance arrangements by Oscar Kosarin. Orchestrations by Richard Hill and John Hawkins. Scenery by Derek Cousins. Costumes by Loudon Sainthill. Lighting by Jules Fisher. Scenery supervised by Richard Seger. Assistant choreographer, Bert Michaels. Produced by Management Three Productions Ltd. (Jerry Weintraub, Martin Kummer) and Frank Productions Inc. (Allen B. Whitehead) by arrangement with Classic Presentations Ltd. Opened 3 February 1969 at the Eugene O'Neill Theatre and closed 18 May 1969 after 122 performances.

CAST (in order of appearance): *The Pilgrims*: *Chaucer*: MARTYN GREEN. *Host*: EDWIN STEFFE. *Miller*: ROY COOPER. *Wife of Bath*: HERMIONE BADDELEY. *Cook*: DAVID THOMAS. *Merchant*: LEON SHAW. *Knight*: REID SHELTON. *Steward*: GEORGE ROSE. *Prioress*: ANN GARDNER. *Nun*: EVELYN PAGE. *Priest*: GARNETT SMITH. *Clerk of Oxford*: BRUCE HYDE. *Squire*: ED EVANKO. *Friar*: DICK [Richard] ENSSLEN. *Pardoner*: GARNETT SMITH. *Summoner*: BERT MICHAELS. *The Sweetheart*: SANDY DUNCAN.

THE MILLER'S TALE: *Nicholas*: ED EVANKO. *Alison*: SANDY DUNCAN. *Carpenter*: GEORGE ROSE. *Absalom*: BRUCE HYDE. *Gervase*: ROY COOPER. *Robin*: Terry Eno. *Parishioners*: Mary Jo Catlett, Suzan Sidney.

THE STEWARD'S TALE: *Miller*: ROY COOPER. *Miller's Wife*: EVELYN PAGE. *Molly*: SANDY DUNCAN. *Alan*: ED EVANKO. *John*: BRUCE HYDE.

THE MERCHANT'S TALE: *January*: GEORGE ROSE. *Justinus*: MARTYN GREEN. *Placebo*: GARNETT SMITH. *May*: SANDY DUNCAN. *Damian*: ED EVANKO. *Pluto*: ROY COOPER. *Prosperpina*: ANN GARDNER. *Duenna*: EVELYN PAGE. *Page*: Tod Miller. *Bridesmaids*: Patricia Michaels, Marianne Selbert, Karen Kristin, Joyce Maret. *Attendants*: Terry Eno, Tod Miller, Gene Myers, Ron Schwinn, Jack Fletcher.

THE WIFE OF BATH'S TALE: *King*: REID SHELTON. *Queen*: ANN GARDNER. *Old Woman*: HERMIONE BADDELEY. *Young Knight*: BRUCE HYDE. *Executioner*: Roger Franklin. *Courtiers*: Terry Eno, Ron Schwinn, Tod Miller, Gene Myers. *Court Ladies*: Karen Kristin, Marianne Selbert, Joyce Maret, Patricia Michaels. *Housewife*: Mary Jo Catlett. *Sweetheart*: SANDY DUNCAN.

Other Pilgrims, Workmen: Terry Eno, Jack Fletcher, Tod Miller, Gene Myers, Ron Schwinn, David Thomas. *Village Girls*: Mary Jo Catlett, Betsy Dickerson, Karen Kristin, Joyce Maret, Patricia Michaels, Marianne Selbert, Suzan Sidney.

The action passes between the Tabard Inn, London and Canterbury Cathedral in the spring during the latter part of the fourteenth century.

Act 1, Scene 1: The Tabard Inn, Southwark, London, on a fine Spring day in 1387. *Scene 2*: On the Road. *Scene 3*: The Miller's Tale. *Scene 4*: On the Road. *Scene 5*: The Steward's Tale. *Scene 6*: The Road.

Act 2, Scene 1: Another Ale House en route to Canterbury. *Scene 2* :The Merchant's Tale. *Scene 3*: The Wife of Bath's Tale. *Scene 4*: Canterbury.

ACT 1

Scene 1

"Song of Welcome"
E. Steffe, Company

"Good Night Hymn"
Company

"Canterbury Day"
Company

Scene 2

"Pilgrim Riding Music"
Company

Scene 3

"I Have a Noble Cock"
E. Evanko

"Darling, Let Me Teach You How to Kiss"
B. Hyde

"There's the Moon"
E. Evanko, S. Duncan

Scene 4

"It Depends on What You're At"
H. Baddeley, E. Page, Company

"Love Will Conquer All"
A. Gardner, S. Sidney, Company

Scene 5

"Beer Is Best"
R. Cooper, E. Page, E. Evanko, B. Hyde, S. Duncan

Scene 6

"Canterbury Day" (reprise)
Company

ACT 2

Scene 1

"Come On and Marry Me Honey"
H. Baddeley, Company

Mug Dance
Company

"Where Are the Girls of Yesterday"
E. Steffe, Company

Scene 2

"Hymen, Hymen"
Company

"If She Has Never Loved Before"
G. Rose

"I'll Give My Love a Ring"
E. Evanko, S. Duncan

"Pear Tree Quintet"
E. Evanko, G. Rose, R. Cooper, A. Gardner, S. Duncan

Scene 3

"I Am All A-Blaze"
E. Evanko

"Love Pas de Deux"
M. Selbert, R. Schwinn

"What Do Women Want?"
B. Hyde, Court Ladies

Scene 4

"April Song"
Company

"Love Will Conquer All" (reprise)
A. Gardner, S. Sidney, Company

1969.05

DEAR WORLD

A Musical in Two Acts, 7 Scenes. Book by Jerome Lawrence and Robert E. Lee. Based on the play "The Madwoman of Chaillot" by Jean Giraudoux as adapted by Maurice Valency. Music and lyrics by Jerry Herman. Directed and choreographed by Joe Layton. Scenic production by Oliver Smith. Costumes by Freddy Wittop. Lighting by Jean Rosenthal. Musical direction and vocal arrangements by Don Pippin. Orchestrations by Philip J. Lang. Dance and incidental (music) arrangements by Dorothea Freitag. Associate producer, Hildy Parks. Production supervisor, Jerry Adler. Produced by Alexander H. Cohen. Opened 6 February 1969 at the Mark Hellinger Theatre and closed 31 May 1969 after 132 performances.

CAST (in order of appearance): *The Chairman of the Board*: William Larsen. *Board Members*: Clifford Fearl, Charles Karel, Zale Kessler, Charles Welch. *Prospector*: Joe Masiell. *Julian*: KURT PETERSON. *Nina*: PAMELA HALL. *The Waiter*: Gene Varrone. *The Busboy*: Ty McConnell. *The Doorman*: Michael Davis. *The Juggler*: Ted Agress. *The Peddler*: John Taliaferro. *The Deaf-Mute*: MIGUEL GODREAU. *Countess Aurelia*, The Madwoman of Chaillot: ANGELA LANSBURY. *The Sewerman*: MILO O'SHEA. *Gabrielle*, The Madwoman of Montmartre: JANE CONNELL. *Constance*, The Madwoman of the Flea Market: CARMEN MATHEWS.

People of Paris: Nicole Barth, Bruce Becker, Toney Brealond, Jane Coleman, Jack Davison, Jacque Dean, Richard Dodd, John Grigas, Marian Haraldson, Tony Juliano, Gene Kelton, Carolyn Kirsch, Urylee Leonardos, Larry Merritt, Ruth Ramsey, Orrin Reiley, Patsy Sabline, Connie Simmons, Margot Travers, Mary Zahn.

The action takes place in Paris during an early spring.

Act 1, Scene 1: The luxurious batteau of the Chairman of the Board, afloat on the Seine. *Scene 2*: The Cafe Francais and a slice of surrounding Chaillot. *Scene 3*: The sewers underneath Paris.

Act 2, Scene 1: The Countess' Apartment underneath the Cafe Francais. *Scene 2*: A street in Chaillot in the rain. *Scene 3*: The Flea Market (Marché Aux Pouces) at midnight. *Scene 4*: The Countess' Apartment; the Park at Colombes.

ACT 1

Scene 1

"The Spring of Next Year"
W. Larsen, J. Masiell, C. Fearl, C. Karel, Z. Kessler, C. Welch

[20]Original London production was directed by Vlado Habunek, and co-directed by Martin Starkie.

Scene 2
"Each Tomorrow Morning"
A. Lansbury, All
"I Don't Want to Know"
A. Lansbury
"I've Never Said I Love You"
P. Hall
Scene 3
"Garbage"
M. O'Shea, A Lansbury, J. Connell, C. Mathews, All
"I Don't Want to Know" Ballet
Entire Company
"Dear World"
A. Lansbury, All

ACT 2
Scene 1
"Kiss Her Now"
A. Lansbury
The Tea Party:
"Memory"
C. Mathews
"Pearls"
A. Lansbury, J. Connell
"Dickie"
J. Connell
"Voices"
C. Mathews
"Thoughts"
A. Lansbury
"And I Was Beautiful"
A. Lansbury
Scene 2
"Each Tomorrow Morning" (reprise)
K. Peterson
Scene 3
"One Person"
A. Lansbury, All
Scene 4
Finale
Entire Company

1969.06

1776

A Musical in One Act, 7 Scenes. Book by Peter Stone. Based on a conception of Sherman Edwards (about the making of the Declaration of Independence). Music and lyrics by Sherman Edwards. Scenery and lighting by Jo Mielziner. Costumes by Patricia Zipprodt. Musical direction by Peter Howard. Orchestrations by Eddie Sauter. Directed by Peter Hunt. Musical numbers staged by Onna White. Dance music arrangements by Peter Howard. Vocal arrangements by Elise Bretton. Produced by Stuart Ostrow. Opened 16 March 1969 at the 46th Street Theatre, moved to 26 April 1971 the Majestic Theatre, and closed 13 February 1972 after 1217 performances.

CAST: *Members of the Continental Congress*: *John Hancock*, President: David Ford. *Dr. Josiah Bartlett*, New Hampshire: Paul-David Richards. *John Adams*, Massachusetts: WILLIAM DANIELS. *Stephen Hopkins*, Rhode Island: ROY POOLE. *Roger Sherman*, Connecticut: David Vosburgh. *Lewis Morris*, New York: Ronald Kross. *Robert Livingston*, New York: Henry LeClair. *Reverend Jonathan Witherspoon*, New Jersey: Edmund Lyndeck. *Benjamin Franklin*, Pennsylvania: HOWARD DaSILVA. *John Dickinson*, Pennsylvania: PAUL HECHT. *James Wilson*, Pennsylvania: Emory Bass. *Caesar Rodney*, Delaware: Robert Gaus. *Colonel Thomas McKean*, Delaware: Bruce MacKay. *George Read*, Delaware: Duane Bodin. *Samuel Chase*, Maryland: Philip Polito. *Richard Henry Lee*, Virginia: Ronald Holgate. *Thomas Jefferson*, Virginia: Ken Howard. *Joseph Hewes*, North Carolina: Charles Rule. *Edward Rutledge*, South Carolina: CLIFFORD DAVID. *Dr. Lyman Hall*, Georgia: Jonathan Moore.

Charles Thomson, Congressional Secretary: Ralston Hill. *Andrew McNair*, Congressional Custodian: William Duell. *A Leather Apron*: B. J. Slater. *Courier*: Scott Jarvis. *Abigail Adams*: Virginia Vestoff. *Martha Jefferson*: Betty Buckley.

The action takes place in a single setting representing the Chamber and an Anteroom of the Continental Congress, a Mall, High Street, and Thomas Jefferson's Room, in Philadelphia, and certain reaches of John Adams' mind, in May, June and July, 1776

Scene 1: The Chamber of the Continental Congress. *Scene 2*: The Mall. *Scene 3*: The Chamber. *Scene 4*: Jefferson's Room above High Street. *Scene 5*: The Chamber. *Scene 6*: The Congressional Anteroom. *Scene 7*: The Chamber.

MUSICAL NUMBERS
Scene 1
"Sit Down, John"
W. Daniels, Congress
"Piddle, Twiddle and Resolve"
W. Daniels
"Till Then"
W. Daniels, V. Vestoff
Scene 2
"The Lees of Old Virginia"
R. Holgate, H. DaSilva, W. Daniels
Scene 3
"But, Mr. Adams"
W. Daniels, H. DaSilva, K. Howard, D. Vosburgh, H. LeClair
Scene 4
"Yours, Yours, Yours"
W. Daniels, V. Vestoff
"He Plays the Violin"
B. Buckley, H. DaSilva, W. Daniels
Scene 5
"Cool, Cool, Considerate Men"
P. Hecht, the Conservatives
"Momma, Look Sharp"
S. Jarvis, W. Duell, B. J. Slater
Scene 6
"The Egg"
H. DaSilva, W. Daniels, K. Howard
Scene 7
"Molasses to Rum"
C. David
"Yours, Yours, Yours" (reprise)
V. Vestoff
"Is Anybody There?"
W. Daniels
(Finale)
(The Congress)

1969.07

COME SUMMER

A Musical in Two Acts. Book and lyrics by Will Holt. Based on the novel "Rainbow on the Road" by Esther Forbes. Music by David Baker. Entire production directed and staged by Agnes de Mille. Scenic production by Oliver Smith. Costumes designed by Stanley Simmons. Lighting designed by Thomas Skelton. Musical direction by Milton Rosenstock. Dance music by David Baker and John Berkman. Orchestrations by Carlyle Hall. Vocal arangements and musical continuity by Trude Rittman. Directoral assistant, James Mitchell. Choreographic assistant, Vernon Lusby. Produced by Albert W. Selden and Hal James. Opened 18 March 1969 at the Lunt-Fontanne Theatre and closed 22 March 1969 after 7 performances.

CAST (in order of appearance): *Phineas Sharp*: RAY BOLGER. *Nathaniel Burnap*: WILLIAM COTTRELL. *Jude Scribner*: DAVID CRYER. *Dorinda Pratt*: MARGARET HAMILTON. *Labe Pratt*: JOHN GERSTAD. *Submit Pratt* (Mitty): CATHRYN DAMON. *Mrs. Meserve*: Dorothy Sands. *Emma Faucett*: BARBARA SHARMA. *Francis Faucett*: WILLIAM LE MASSENA. *Dancing Lovers*: Evelyn Taylor, David Evans. *Head Logger*: William Glassman.

The Populace: Marcia Brushingham, Ellen Everett, Sunny Hannum, Lucia Lambert, Mary Ann Rydzeski, Lana Sloniger, Sarah Jane Smith, Britt Swanson, Jeanette Williamson, Toodie Wittmer, Jenny Workman, James Albright, Paul Berné, Bjarne Buchtrup, Dennis Cole, Leonard John Crofoot, Harry Endicott, David Evans, William Glassman, Walter Hook, Doug Hunt, Del Horstmann, John Johann.

The action takes place in the towns and surrounding countryside along the Connectcut River in New England during the peddlers' season, early spring to late fall in the year 1840, just before the factories took over.

ACT 1

"Good Time Charlie"
R. Bolger, Peddlers
"Think Spring"
R. Bolger, D. Cryer, Populace
"Wild Birds Calling"
D. Cryer, C. Damon
"Goodbye, My Bachelor"
R. Bolger
"Fine, Thank You, Fine"
B. Sharma
"Road to Hampton"
D. Cryer
"Come Summer"
R. Bolger, D. Cryer, B. Sharma, C. Damon, E. Taylor, D. Evans
"Let Me Be"
C. Damon, D. Cyrer
"Feather in My Shoe"
R. Bolger
"The Logger's Song"
R. Bolger, D. Cryer, Loggers, Populace

ACT 2

"Jude's Holler"
D. Cryer, Populace
"Faucett Falls Fancy"
R. Bolger, Populace
"Rockin'"
B. Sharma, D. Cryer
"Skin and Bones"
R. Bolger
"Moonglade"
R. Bolger, D. Cryer, C. Damon, B. Sharma, M. Hamilton, J. Gerstad, W. LeMassena, Populace
"Women"
C. Damon
"No"
R. Bolger, Populace
"So Much World"
D. Cryer

1969.08 BILLY

A Musical in One Act. Book by Stephen Glassman. Suggested by Herman Melville's novel "Billy Budd." Music and lyrics by Ron Dante and Gene Allan. Sets by Ming Cho Lee. Costumes by Theoni V. Aldredge. Lighting by Martin Aronstein. Directed by Arthur A. Seidelman. Musical sequences staged by Grover Dale. Vocal arrangements and orchestrations by Ronald Frangipane. Dance music arranged by Coleridge Perkinson. Special arrangements and incidental music by Wally Harper. Sound by Admins. Ltd. A Vanark Enterprises Ltd. Production. Produced by Bruce W. Stark in assoication with Joseph H. Shoctor. Opened and closed 22 March 1969 at the Billy Rose Theatre after 1 performance.

CAST: Officers: *Captain Edward Vere*: LAURENCE NAISMITH. *Lieutenant William Radcliffe*: WILLIAM COUNTRYMAN. *Lieutenant Roger Mordant*: Michael Tartel. *John Claggart*, Master-at-Arms: JOHN DEVLIN. *Corporal John Bernard*: Simm Landres. *Marine Corporals*: Laried Montgomery, Danny Villa.
Seamen: *Billy Budd*: ROBERT SALVIO. *Dansker*: JOHN BEAL. *Whiskers*: DOLPH SWEET. *Campbell*: GEORGE MARCY. *Boscombe*: ALAN WEEKS. *Boyer*: IGORS GAVON. *Gilbert*: Al Cohen. *Donald Taff*: Peter De Maio. *Rawley*: Danny Carroll. *John Thorp*: Joseph Dellasorte. *Stafford*: Bill Schustik. *Fallon*: Pascual Vaquer. *Smithy*: Howard Girven. *Stoker*: Laried Montgomery. *Rush*: Steven Boockvor. *Potter*: Christopher Chadman. *Roper*: Michael Peters. *Marsten*: Tim Ramirez. *Harker*: Ron Tassone. *Seeger*: Frank DeSal. *Grimer*: DeWayne Oliver. And *Molly*: BARBARA MONTE.

The action takes place aboard a Man-of-War in 1796.

MUSICAL NUMBERS

"Prelude"
"Molly"
R. Salvio
"Chanty"
B. Schustik, P. Vaquer, H. Girven, L. Montgomery
"Watch Out for Claggart"/"Work"
A. Weeks, J. Devlin, The Crew
"Shaking Hands With the Wind"
R. Salvio
"Whiskers' Dance"
D. Sweet, The Crew
"It Ain't Us Who Make the Wars"
G. Marcy, The Crew
"The Bridge to Nowhere"
L. Naismith
"It Ain't Us Who Make the Wars" (reprise)
The Crew
"There in the Dark"/"Afraid"
J. Devlin, R. Salvio
"In the Arms of a Stranger"
J. Beal
"The Fiddlers' Green"
R. Salvio, J. Dellasorte, I. Gavon, P. DeMaio, The Crew
"Molly" (reprise)
B. Monte
"Requiem"
R. Salvio

1969.09 BUT NEVER JAM TODAY

An Afro-American Adaptation of Lewis Carroll's "Alice's Adventures in Wonderland" and "Through the Looking Glass" in Two Acts[21]. Conceived and directed by Vinnette Carroll. Music by Gershon Kingsley. Additional music and lyrics by Robert Lorimer. Choreography by Talley Beatty. Associate choreographer, Herman Howell. Settings by Donald Padgett. Costumes by K. T. Fries. Lighting by Marshall Williams. Gospel arrangements, Alex Bradford. Drums, Danny Barrajanos. Produced by the City Center of Music and Drama (Norman Singer, General administration) as part of BLACK EXPO '69. Opened and closed 23 April 1969 at the New York City Center after 1 performance.

CAST (in order of appearance): *Alice*: MARIE THOMAS. *White Rabbit*: TOMMY PINNOCK. *Caterpillar*: MARVIN CAMILLO. *Black Queen*: JOSEPH PERRY. *Cheshire Cat*: LOLA HOLMAN. *First Cook*: Verna Gillis. *Second Cook*: Winston Savage. *Duchess*: CYNTHIA TOWNS. *Mad Hatter*: SHERMAN HEMSLEY. *March Hare*: Thelma Drayton. *Dormouse*: Wai Ching Ho. *White Queen*: CYNTHIA TOWNS. *Two of Spades*: LOLA HOLMAN. *Five of Spades*: ALEX ALEXANDER. *Seven of Spades*: SHERMAN HEMSLEY. *Queen of Hearts*: ALEX ALEXANDER. *King of Hearts*: STERLING ROBERTS. *Knave of Hearts*: Burt Rodriguez. *Gryphon*: LOLA HOLMAN. *Humpty Dumpty*: MARVIN CAMILLO. *Mock Turtle*: ALEX ALEXANDER. *Herald*: Danny Barrajanos.
Members of Jury: Dance Corps. *Citizens of Wonderland*: Angel Caballero, Johnny Harris, Ernest Holly. *Dancers*: Charles Augins, Glen Brooks, Annette Brown, Delores Brown, Matt Cameron, Hope Clarke, Jacquelynne Curry, Trina Frazier, Joan Peters, Gail Reece, Danny Sloan, Andy Torres.

Scene 1: Alice by the River. *Scene 2*: Dance of the Alices. *Scene 3*: Advice from a Caterpillar. *Scene 4*: Black Queen. *Scene 5*: The Duchess' Nursery. *Scene 6*: A Mad Tea Party. *Scene 7*: Alice and the White Queen. *Scene 8*: The Croquet Game. *Scene 9*: Humpty Dumpty. *Scene 10*: The Mock Turtle Story. *Scene 11*: Alice's Evidence. *Scene 12*: Queen Alice.

1969.10 TRUMPETS OF THE LORD

(A Program of Spoken Word, Poetry, Sermons, Spirituals and Gospel Music in One Act[22].) Adapted by Vinnette Carroll from "God's Trombones" by

[21]No song list available. A revised version was later presented on Broadway 31 July 1979 at the Longacre Theatre for 7 performances.
[22]First produced in New York Off-Broadway 29 December 1963 at the Astor Place Theatre for 160 performances.

James Weldon Johnson. Directed by Theodore Mann. Musical adaptations, arrangements and direction by Howard A. Roberts. Scenery by Marsha L. Eck. Costumes by Domingo A. Rodriguez. Lighting by Jules Fisher. Produced by Circle-in-the-Square (Theodore Mann, Artistic director; Paul Libin, Managing director; Gillian Walker, Associate director). Opened 29 April 1969 at the Brooks Atkinson Theatre and closed 3 May 1969 after 7 performances.

CAST: *Sister Henrietta Pinkston*: THERESA MERRITT. *Reverend Bradford Parham*: LEX MONSON. *Reverend Ridgely Washington*: BERNARD WARD. *Reverend Marion Alexander*: CICELY TYSON.

Female Voices: Berniece Hall, Ella Eure, Camille Yarbrough. *Male Voices*: Earl Baker, Bill Glover, Milton Grayson, William Stewart. *Musicians*: Robert Henson (piano), Percy Brice (drums).

MUSICAL NUMBERS

"So Glad I'm Here"
Company
"Call to Prayer"
Company
"Listen Lord—A Prayer"
B. Parham
"Amen Response"
Company
"In His Care"
B. Glover, B. Hall, Company
"The Creation"
B. Parham
"God Lead Us Along"
H. Pinkston
Noah Medley:
"Noah Built the Ark"
M. Alexander
"Run Sinner Run"
C. Yarbrough, Company
"Didn't It Rain"
B. Hall, Company
"The Judgement Day"
R. Washington
"In That Great Gettin' Up Morning"
R. Washington, Company
Funeral Suite:
"Soon One Morning"
B. Hall, Company
"There's a Man"
H. Pinkston, E. Baker, Company
"Go Down Death"
B. Parham
"He'll Understand"
H. Pinkston
"Were You There"
M. Alexander
"Calvary"
Male Voices
"Crucifixion"
Female Voices
Freedom Suite:
"Reap What You Sow"
M. Alexander, Company
"I Shall Not Be Moved"
Company
"We Are Soldiers"
Company
"Woke Up This Morning"
Company
"Let My People Go"
R. Washington
"We Shall Overcome"
H. Pinkston, Company
"Jacob's Ladder"
Company
"God Be With You"
Postlude

1969.11 FIESTA IN MADRID

A Zarzuela in Two Acts, 4 Scenes, in Spanish. Adapted by Tito Capobianco from "La Verbena de La Paloma" ('The Festival of the Dove' with Music) by Tomás Bretón. (Original Spanish libretto by Ricardo de la Vega.) Conceived and directed by Tito Capobianco. Conductor, Odon Alonso. Associate director, Elena Denda. Choreography by Teresa. Settings and costumes by Jose Varona. Associate set designer, David Mitchell. Choral director, Martinez Palomo. Lyric arrangement by G. Roepke and J. Varona. Lighting by Hans Sondheimer. Produced by the City Center of Music and Drama, Inc. (Norman Singer, General administrator). Opened 28 May 1969 at the New York City Center and closed 15 June 1969 after 23 performances.

CAST (in order of appearance): *Photographer*: Chavo Ximenez. *Don Hilarión*: NICO CASTEL. *Don Sebastian*: Alfonso Manosalvas. *Don Pepe*: Nino Garcia. *Seña Rita*: CLARAMAE TURNER. *Julián*: FRANCO IGLESIAS. *Susana*: ISABEL PENAGOS. *Teresa*: TERESA. *Casta*: KAY CREED. *Tia Antonia*: Antonia Rey. *First Maid*: MURIEL GREENSPON. *Three Grenadiers*: Roberto Lorca, Luis Olivares, Monolo Rivera. *Policeman*: Dan Kingman. *First Little Sailor*: MURIEL GREENSPON. *Juggler*: Harry De Dio.

Singing Ensemble: Arlene Adler, Marilyn Armstrong, Renee Herman, Suzy Hunter, Diana Kehrig, Donna Owen, Hanna Owen, Frances Pavlides, Sandra Jean Schaeffer, Henrietta Valor, Maria West, Marie Young, Ron Bentley, George Bohachevsky, Don Carlo, Tony Darius, Harris Davis, Joseph Galiano, Nino Garcia, Don Henderson, Douglas Hunnikin, Karl Krause, Raymond Papay, Dick Park. *Dancers*: Martha Calzado, Deardra Correa, Andrea Del Conte, Liliana Morales, Juana Ortega, Dini Roman.

The action takes place in Madrid in the nineteenth century.

Act 1, Scene 1: A Square in Madrid. *Scene 2*: The Cafe Cantante.

Act 2, Scene 1: The Verbena (Festival). *Scene 2*: A Park.

ACT 1

Scene 1

"Fiesta in Madrid"
Chorus, Dancers
"Times Have Changed" (Los tiempos han cambiado)
N. Castel, A. Manosalvas, N. Garcia
"I Also Have a Heart" (Tambien yo, tego mi corazoncito)
F. Iglesias, C. Turner
"The Tarantula"
I. Penagos, Friends
"Blondes and Brunettes, I Like Them All" (Las rubias y las moreans!)
N. Castel
"On a Girl's Hard Life" (Pobre chica, la que tiene que servir)
The Maids
(*Music by* Federico Chueca and Joaquin Valverde. *Lyrics by* J. Perez.)
"Patio Espanol"
(*Music by* Ruperto Chapi.)
Dancers

Scene 2

"Flamenco Song" (Canto flamenco)
K. Creed, A. Rey, I. Penagos, Chorus, Dancers
"The Grenadiers" (Los granaderos)
R. Lorca, L. Olivares, M. Rivera
"O, What a Lovely Evening" (Qué, hermosa noche me espera!)
N. Castel, K. Creed, I. Penagos, A. Rey
"Forget That Girl, Once and For All" (Olvida esa muchacha para siempre)
C. Turner, F. Iglesias
"Where Are You Going Wearing That Shawl from Manila?"
(Donde vas con mantòn de Manila)
I. Penagos, F. Iglesias
"The Fight" (La pelea)
I. Penagos, K. Creed, A. Rey, F. Iglesias,
C. Turner, N. Castel, D. Kingman, Chorus, Dancers

ACT 2

Scene 1

"The Streets of Madrid" (Las calles de Madrid)
Chorus
(*Music by* Federico Chueca and Joaquin Valverde. *Lyrics by* J. Perez.)

"Who Cares for Love?" (Que te importa que no venga)
I. Penagos
(*Music by* José Serrano. *Lyrics by* V. Sevilla and Carreño.)

"The Barquilleros" (Los barquilleros)
Chorus, Dancers
(*Music by* Federico Chueca and Joaquin Valverde. *Lyrics by* J. Perez.)

"Danza Espanola"
(*Music by* Gimenez.)
Dancers

"Three Little Sailors" (Los marineritos)
Soloists, Chorus
(*Music by* Federico Chueca and Joaquin Valverde. *Lyrics by* J. Perez.)

"Mazurka"
Chorus, Dancers

"The Best Women in the World" (Las mejores majeres del mundo)
C. Turner
(*Music by* J. Ileo. *Lyrics by* Perrin & Palacios.)

"The Milord's Waltz" (Caballero de gracià)
N. Castel
(*Music by* Federico Chueca and Joaquin Valverde. *Lyrics by* J. Perez.)

"The Second Fight" (La pelea)
C. Turner, N. Castel, F. Iglesias,
K. Creed, I. Penagos, A. Rey, D. Kingman, Chorus, Dancers

Scene 2

"You Are the Only One for Me" (Tu eres ese)
I. Penagos, F, Iglesias
(*Music by* Ruperto Chapi. *Lyrics by* Fernández Shaw and José Lopez Silva.)

"Fiesta in Madrid" (reprise)
Soloists, Chorus, Dancers

1969–1970 SEASON

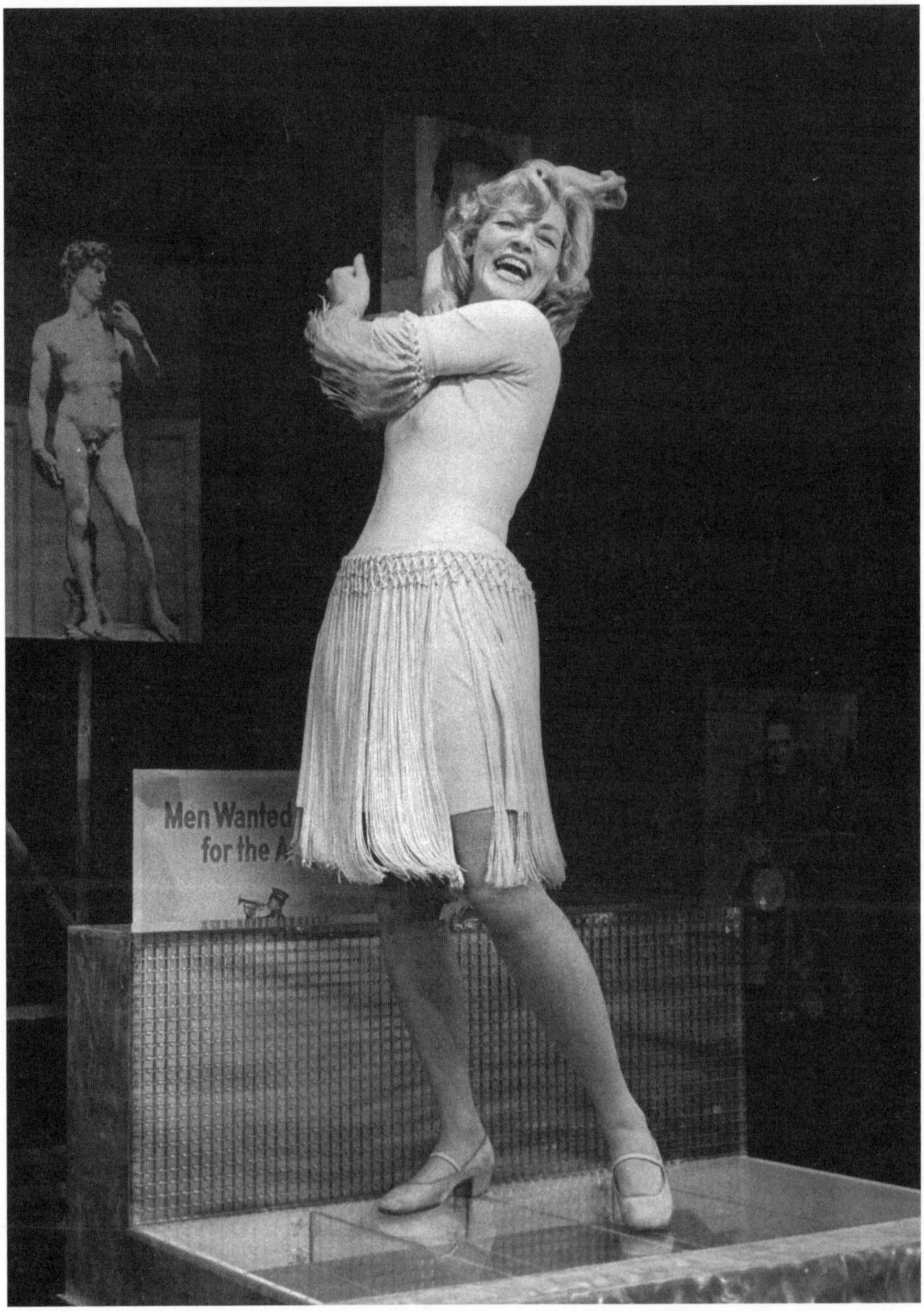

Lauren Bacall in APPLAUSE (Photo: Friedman-Abeles)
Billy Rose Theatre Collection, New York Public Library for the Performing Arts

1969–1970 SEASON

1969.12 OKLAHOMA!

A Revival of the Musical Play in Two Acts, 6 Scenes[1]. Book and lyrics by Oscar Hammerstein II. Music by Richard Rodgers. Based on the play "Green Grow the Lilacs" by Lynn Riggs. Entire production directed by John Fearnley. Original direction by Rouben Mamoulian Choreography by Gemze de Lappe. Original choreography by Agnes de Mille. Music director, Jay Blackton. Scenery and lighting by Paul C. McGuire. Costumes by Miles White. Produced by the Music Theater of Lincoln Center (Richard Rodgers, President and Producing Director). Opened 23 June 1969 at the New York State Theatre and closed 6 September 1969 after 88 performances.

CAST (in order of appearance): *Aunt Eller*: MARGARET HAMILTON. *Curly*: BRUCE YARNELL. *Laurey*: LEE BEERY. *Ike Skidmore*: Sam Kirkham. *Slim*: Del Horstmann. *Joe*: Kurt Olson. *Will Parker*: LEE ROY REAMS. *Jud Fry*: SPIRO MALAS. *Ado Annie Carnes*: APRIL SHAWHAN. *Ali Hakim*: TED BENIADES. *Gertie Cummings*: June Helmers. *Curly* (in ballet): Brynar Mehl. *Laurey* (in ballet): Sandra Balesti. *Jud* (in ballet): James Albright. *The Child* (in ballet): Lee Wilson. *The Girl Who Falls Down*: Sandra Balesti. *Donna*: Donna Monroe. *Judith*: Judith McCauley. *Dixie*: Dixie Stewart. *Joyce*: Joyce Tomanec. *Andrew Carnes*: WILLIAM GRIFFIS. *Cord Elam*: John Gerstad.

Dancers: *Girls*: Graciela Daniele, Katherine Gallagher, Mary Lynn McRae, Gilda Mullett, Sally Ransone, Audrey Ross, Lana Sloniger, Eileen Taylor, Lee Wilson, Toodie Wittmer, Jenny Workman, Mary Zahn. *Boys*: Paul Berné, Andy G. Bew, Henry Boyer, Bjarne Buchtrup, Michael Ebbin, William Glassman, Michael Lane, Ralph Nelson. *Singers*: *Girls*: Bobbi Lange, Judith McCauley, Donna Monroe, Eleanor Rogers, Dixie Stewart, Maggie Task, Joyce Tomanec, Maggie Worth. *Boys*: John Almberg, John D. Anthony, Lester Clark, John Dorrin, Mark East, Del Horstmann, Robert Lenn, Joe McGrath, Kurt Olson, Alex Orfaly, Ken Richards, Tom Trelfa.

1969.13 THE NEW MUSIC HALL OF ISRAEL

A New Edition of the Musical Revue in Two Acts, 16 Scenes, in Hebrew[2]. Staged and choreographed by Jonathan Karmon. Costumes by Lydia Pinkus Ganay, executed by Bertha Kwartz. Additional dialogue by Al Fogel. Assistant director, Gavri Levi. Musical direction by Rafi Paz. Produced by Leon H. Gildin. Opened 2 October 1969 at the Lunt-Fontanne Theatre and closed 29 November 1969 after 77 performances.

CAST: GEULA GILL (singer), GERMAINE ONIKOWSKI (Mistress of ceremonies), LEAH DORLY TRIO (Leah Dorly, Ygal Kerza, Ygal Hared), YOEL DAN (singer), ALMONZNINO (shadow artist), ELISHEVA and MICHAEL (rock 'n roll), BOAS (oriental tambour, david flute), PNINA PERY, YONI and DANI (dance soloists).

THE KARMON DANCERS: *Girls*: Adina, Edna, Eva, Geula Haiuta, Iona Miriam, Nava, Ogira, Ora, Riki, Rina, Rinale, Shara, Tami, Tamar. *Boys*: Alex, Aron, Avi, Clod, Ehud, Iosi, Itamar, Moshe, Nathan, Naftali, Oshiri, Tuvia, Zev, Avulun, Zwi, Israel.

ACT 1

Scene 1
  Popular Songs of Israel
Scene 2
  Springtime in Israel
    The Karmon Dancers
Scene 3
  Elisheva and Michael
Scene 4
  Dance of the Fisherman
    The Karmon Dancers
Scene 5
  Pnina Pery and Her Exylaphone[3]
Scene 6
  The Legend of Timna
    The Karmon Dancers
Scene 7
  A New and Humorous Shadow World
    Almoznino
Scene 8
  Leah Dorly Trio (A girl, two boys and two guitars)
Scene 9
  A Hassidik Marriage
    The Karmon Dancers

ACT 2

Scene 1
  Magic of the Negev
    The Karmon Dancers
Scene 2
  The Popular Music of Israel
    Y. Dan
Scene 3
  Rhythms and Dances of the Desert
    Boaz
Scene 4
  Lest We Forget
    The Karmon Dancers
Scene 5
  Songs
    G. Gill
Scene 6
  Mosaic
    The Karmon Dancers
Scene 7
  Israel Joy of Life
    Entire Troupe

1969.14 JIMMY

A Musical Play of the Life and Times of Jimmy Walker in Two Acts, 18 Scenes. Book by Melville Shavelson. Based on the novel "Beau James" by Gene Fowler and the screenplay by Jack Rose and Melville Shavelson. Music and lyrics by Bill and Patti Jacob. Directed by Joseph Anthony. Scenic production by Oliver Smith. Costumes by W. Robert LaVine. Lighting by Peggy Clark. Projections by Charles E. Hoefler, James Hamilton. Musical direction and vocal arrangements by Milton Rosenstock. Musical arrangements by Jack Andrews. Dance arrangements by John Berkman. Musical numbers staged by Peter Gennaro. Assistant choreographer, Bill Guske. Associate producer, Harry Mayer. Produced by Jack L. Warner in association with Don Saxon. Opened 23 October 1969 at the Winter Garden and closed 3 January 1970 after 84 performances.

CAST (in order of appearance): *Jimmy Walker*: FRANK GORSHIN. *Bonnie*: Cindi Bulak. *Jim Hines*: JACK COLLINS. *Al Smith*: WILLIAM GRIFFIS. *Allie Walker*: JULIE WILSON. *Francis Xavier Aloysius O'Toole*: Ed Becker. *Lawrence Horatio Fink*: Stanley Simmonds. *Antonio Viscelli*: Paul Forrest. *Stanislaus Kazimir Wojciezkowski*: Henry Lawrence. *Mrs. Al Smith*: Peggy Hewett. *Miss Manhattan*: Sally Neal. *Miss Bronx*: Andrea Duda. *Miss Brooklyn*: Carol Conte. *Miss Richmond*: Nancy Dalton. *Miss Queens*: Cindi Bulak. *Stage Manager*: Gary Gendell. *Betty Compton*: ANITA GILLETTE. *Texas Guinan*: DOROTHY CLAIRE. *Edward Duryea Dowling*: LARRY DOUGLAS. *Warrington Brock*: Clifford Fearl. *Charley Hand*: EVAN THOMPSON. *Moe*: Del Horstmann. *Izzy*: Carl Nicholas. *Policeman*: Herb Fields. *Photographers*: Andy G. Bew, Tony Stevens. *Secretary*: Barbara Andres. *Reporter*: Frank Newell. *Tailor*: Carl Nicholas. *Politicians*: Del Hortsmann, Ben Laney, Joseph McGrath. *Girl in fur coat*: Carol Conte. *Policeman*: Ben Laney. *Passerby*: Sandi McCreadie. *Mrs. Compton*: SIBYL BOWAN. *Band Vocalist*: Joseph McGrath. *Process Server*: John D. Anthony. *Recorded Impersonations*: Dwight Weist.

[1]Originally produced in New York 31 March 1943 at the St. James Theatre for 2212 performances. For Synopsis of Scenes and Musical Numbers, see original 1943 production.

[2]A previous edition first produced in New York 6 February 1968 under the title GRAND MUSIC HALL OF ISRAEL at the Palace Theatre for 64 performances.

[3]Dropped during New York run.

Dancing Ensemble: Cindi Bulak, Carol Conte, Nancy Dalton, Andrea Duda, Saundra McPherson, Sally Neal, Eileen Shannon, Monica Tiller, Pat Trott, Andy G. Bew, Stephen Boockvor, Christopher Chadman, David Evans, Gary Gendell, Scott Hunter, Frank Newell, Harold Pierson, Tony Stevens. *Singing Ensemble*: Barbara Andres, Gini Eastwood, Barbara Gregory, Peggy Hewett, Mary Louise, Sandi McCreadie, Claire Thiess, Roberta Vatske, John D. Anthony, Ed Becker, Austin Colyer, Herb Fields, Paul Forrest, Del Horstmann, Ben Laney, Henry Lawrence, Joseph McGrath, Carl Nicholas.

The action takes place in New York City between 1925 and 1931.

Act 1, Scene 1: *S.S. Conte Grande*—1931. *Scene 2*: Jimmy's Apartment—1925. *Scene 3*: Tammany Hall—1925. *Scene 4*: Texas Guinan's—1925. *Scene 5*: Betty's Apartment—1925. *Scene 6*: The 1925 Victory Celebration. *Scene 7*: Allie's Bedroom—1925. *Scene 8*: City Hall—1926.

Act 2, Scene 1: Riverside Drive—1929. *Scene 2*: Betty's New Apartmnet—1929. *Scene 3*: Polling Booth—1929. *Scene 4*: Central Park Casino—1929. *Scene 5*: The Street—1930. *Scene 6*: Betty's Dressing Room—1931. *Scene 7*: Washington Square—1931. *Scene 8*: City Hall—1931. *Scene 9*: Yankee Stadium—1931. *Scene 10*: *S. S. Conte Grande*—1931.

ACT 1[4]

Scene 1

"Will You Think of Me Tomorrow?"
F. Gorshin

Scene 2

"The Little Woman"
W. Griffis, J. Collins, F. Gorshin, J. Wilson

Scene 3

"The Darlin' of New York"
J. Collins, W. Griffis, E. Thompson,
J. Wilson, F. Gorshin, Five Lovely Ladies, Campaign Workers

Scene 4

"Oh, Gee!"
A. Gillette

"The Walker Walk"
D. Claire, A. Gillette, F. Gorshin, Guinan Girls, Patrons

Scene 5

"That Old Familiar Ring"
A. Gillette, F. Gorshin

Scene 6

"The Walker Walk" (reprise)
J. Collins, Politicians, Party Workers

Scene 7

"I Only Wanna Laugh"
J. Wilson

Scene 8

"They Never Proved a Thing"
F. Gorshin, J. Collins, P. Forrest,
S. Simmonds, E. Becker, H. Lawrence, C. Fearl, C. Nicholas,
Politicians

"What's Out There for Me?"[5]
F. Gorshin

ACT 2

Scene 1

"Riverside Drive"
F. Gorshin, Strollers

Scene 2

"The Squabble Song"
F. Gorshin, A. Gillette

Scene 4

Medley
J. McGrath

"One in a Million"
F. Gorshin, A. Gillette

Scene 5

"It's a Nice Place to Visit"
P. Forrest, S. Simmonds, E. Becker, H. Lawrence, C. Fearl, C. Conte,
Company

Scene 6

"The Charmin' Son-of-a-Bitch"
J. Wilson

"Jimmy"
A. Gillette

"Five Lovely Ladies" (reprise)
F. Gorshin

Scene 7

"Our Jimmy"
J. Collins, F. Gorshin, J. Wilson, E. Thompson,
W. Griffis, D. Claire, Five Lovely Ladies, Policemen, Spectators

Scene 9

"Life Is a One-Way Street"
F. Gorshin

Scene 10

Finale
F. Gorshin, A. Gillette

[4]Added during the run:
"Five Lovely Ladies" (Act 1, Scene 3)
F. Gorshin

[5]Dropped during the run.

1969.15 BUCK WHITE

A Musical in Two Acts. Book, music and lyrics by Oscar Brown, Jr. Adapted from the play "Big Time Buck White" by Joseph Dolan Tuotti. Staged by Ocar Brown, Jr. and Jean Pace. Musical arrangements by Mike Terry and Merl Saunders. Orchestrations by Mike Terry. Musical direction by Mel Saunders. Scenery by Edward Burbridge. Lighting by Martin Aronstein. Costumes by Jean Pace. Produced by Zev Bufman in association with High John Productions [Oscar Brown, Jr., Jean Pace, Sivuca]. Opened 2 December 1969 at the George Abbott Theatre and closed 6 December 1969 after 7 performances.

CAST: *Hunter*: HERSCHELL BURTON. *Honey Man*: DAVID MOODY. *Weasel*: TED ROSS. *Rubber Band*: CHARLES WELDON. *Jive*: RON RICH. *Buck White*: MUHAMMAD ALI [CASSIUS CLAY]. *Whitey*: EUGENE SMITH. *Black Man*: Don Sutherland.

The action takes place in the meeting hall of the Beautiful Allelujah Days organization.

ACT 1

"Honey Man Song"
D. Moody

"Money, Money, Money"
T. Ross, D. Moody

"Nobody Does My Thing"
H. Burton

"Step Across That Line"
C. Weldon

"H.N.I.C."
R. Rich

"Beautiful Allelujah Days"
R. Rich, T. Ross, H. Burton, C. Weldon, D. Moody

"Tap the Plate"
R. Rich, C. Weldon, D. Moody

"Big Time Buck White Chant"
The Company

ACT 2

"Big Time Buck White Chant" (reprise)
M. Ali, Company

"Better Far"
M. Ali

"We Came in Chains"
M. Ali, Company

"Black Balloons"
M. Ali, Company

"Look at Them"
E. Smith

"Mighty Whitey"
M. Ali, Company
"Get Down"
M. Ali, Company

1969.16 LA STRADA

A Musical in Two Acts, 14 Scenes. Book by Charles K. Peck, Jr. Based on the film of the same name by Federico Fellini, (Tullio Pinelli, Ennio Flaiano). Music and lyrics by Lionel Bart. Additional music and lyrics by Martin Charnin and Elliot Lawrence[6]. Directed by Alan Schneider. Dances and musical numbers staged by Joyce Trisler[7]. Sets by Ming Cho Lee. Costumes by Nancy Potts. Lighting by Martin Aronstein. Musical direction, Harold Hastings. Orchestrations by Eddie Sauter. Dance music arrangements by Peter Howard. Produced by Charles K. Peck, Jr. and Canyon Productions. Opened and closed 14 December 1969 at the Lunt-Fontanne Theatre after 1 performance.

CAST (in order of appearance): *The Old Man*: JOHN COE. *Gelsomina*: BERNADETTE PETERS. *Mother*: ANNE HEGIRA. *Elsa*: Lisa Belleran. *Eva*: Mary Ann Robbins. *Sophia*: Susan Goeppinger. *Zampano*: STEPHEN PEARLMAN. *Castra*: LUCILLE PATTON. *Acrobats*: Paul Charles, Harry Endicott. *Mario*, the Fool: LARRY KERT. *Mama Lambrini*: PEGGY COOPER. *Alberti*: John Coe. *Sister Claudia*: Susan Goeppinger.

Company: Loretta Abbott, Glen Brooks, Henry Brunjes, Connie Burnett, Robert Carle, Paul Charles, Barbara Christopher, Peggy Cooper, Betsy Dickerson, Harry Endicott, Anna Maria Fanizzi, Jack Fletcher, Nino Galanti, Susan Goeppinger, Rodney Griffin, Mickey Gunnersen, Kenneth Kreel, Don Lopez, Joyce Maret, Stan Page, Odette Panaccione, Mary Ann Robbins, Steven Ross, Larry Small, Eileen Taylor.

The action takes place in and around the cities and villages of Southern Italy in the early 1950s.

Act 1, Scene 1: A Desolate Beach near Gelsomina's House. *Scene 2*: Along the Road (La Strada). *Scene 3*: The Outskirts of a Village. *Scene 4*: A Farm House Yard. *Scene 5*: The Farm Stable. *Scene 6*: Along the Road. *Scene 7*: The Alberti Circus Grounds. *Scene 8*: A Performance of the Alberti Circus.

Act 2, Scene 1: The Circus Grounds. *Scene 2*: A Village Square. *Scene 3*: A Convent. *Scene 4*: Along the Road. *Scene 5*: A Camp Site in the Mountains. *Scene 6*: The End of the Road.

ACT 1
Scene 1
"Seagull, Starfish, Pebble"
B. Peters
(*Music by* Elliot Lawrence. *Lyrics by* Martin Charnin.)
Scene 2
"The Great Zampano"
B. Peters, S. Pearlman
"What's Going on Inside?"
S. Pearlman
(*Music by* Elliot Lawrence. *Lyrics by* Martin Charnin.)
Scene 3
"Belonging"
B. Peters
Scene 4
Wedding Dance
(*Dance Music by* Elliott Lawrence.)
Entire Company
Scene 5
"I Don't Like You"
B. Peters
(*Music by* Elliot Lawrence. *Lyrics by* Martin Charnin.)
Scene 6
Encounters
(*Dance Music by* Elliot Lawrence.)
B. Peters, Entire Company
"There's a Circus in Town"
L. Kert

Scene 7
"You're Musical"
L. Kert, B. Peters
(*Music by* Elliot Lawrence.
Lyrics by Martin Charnin.)
Scene 8
"Only More!"
B. Peters
(*Music by* Elliot Lawrence.
Lyrics by Martin Charnin.)

ACT 2
Scene 1
"What a Man"
B. Peters, P. Cooper
(*Music by* Elliot Lawrence.
Lyrics by Martin Charnin.)
"Everything Needs Something"
B. Peters
(*Music by* Elliot Lawrence.
Lyrics by Martin Charnin.)
Scene 2
"Sooner or Later"
L. Kert
(*Music by* Elliot Lawrence.
Lyrics by Martin Charnin.)
"Sooner or Later" (reprise)
B. Peters
Scene 3
Belonging" (reprise)
B. Peters
Scene 6
The End of the Road
Entire Company
(*Music by* Elliot Lawrence.
Lyrics by Martin Charnin.)

1969.17 COCO

A Musical in Two Acts, 9 Scenes. Book and lyrics by Alan Jay Lerner. (Suggested by the life and career of Coco Chanel.) Music by André Previn. Directed by Michael Benthall. Musical numbers and fashion sequences staged by Michael Bennett. Sets and costumes by Cecil Beaton. Lighting by Thomas Skelton. Orchestrations by Hershy Kay. Dance Music continuity by Harold Wheeler. Musical direction by Robert Emmett Dolan. Associate choreographer, Bob Avian. Associate producer, Fred Hebert. Production supervisor, Stone Widney. Film sequences by Milton Olshin, Fred Lemoine. Produced by Frederick Brisson for Brisson Productions, Inc., and by Montfort Productions. Opened 18 December 1969 at the Mark Hellinger Theatre and closed 3 October 1970 after 333 performances.

CAST (in order of appearance): *Coco*: KATHARINE HEPBURN. *Louis Greff*: GEORGE ROSE. *Pignol*: JEANNE ARNOLD. *Helene*: Maggie Task. *Sebastian Baye*: RENÉ AUBERJONOIS. *Armand*: Al DeSio. *Albert*: Jack Beaber. *Docaton*: Eve March. *Georges*: DAVID HOLLIDAY. *Loublaye*: Gene Varrone. *Varne*: Shirley Potter. *Marie*: Margot Travers. *Jeanine*: Rita O'Connor. *Claire*: Graciela Daniele. *Juliette*: Lynn Winn. *Madelaine*: Carolyn Kirsch. *Lucille*: Diane Phillips. *Colette*: Rosemarie Heyer. *Simone*: Charlene Ryan. *Solange*: Suzanne Rogers. *Noelle*: GALE DIXON. *Dr. Petitjean*: Richard Woods. *Claude*: David Thomas. *The Buyers (4)*: *Dwight Berkwit*: Will B. Able. *Eugene Bernstone*: Robert Fitch. *Ronny Ginsborn*: Chad Block. *Phil Rosenberry*: Dan Siretta. *Lapidus*: Gene Varrone. *Nadine*: Leslie Daniel. *Grand Duke Alexandrovitch*: Bob Avian. *Voice (of Grand Duke Alexandrovitch)*: Jack Dabdoub. *Charles*, Duke of Glenallen: Michael Allinson. *Julian Lesage*: Paul Dumont. *Papa*: Jon Cypher.

Models, Seamstresses, Customers, and Fitters: Vicki Allen, Karin Baker, Kathy Bartosh, Kathie Dalton, Alice Glenn, Maureen Hopkins, Linda Jorgens, Tresha Kelly, Nancy Killmer, Jan Metternich, Marilyn Miles, Joann Ogawa, Jean Peerce, Ann Reinking, Skiles Ricketts, Marianne Seibert, Pamela Serpe, Bonnie Walker, Oscar Antony, Roy Barry, William James, Richard Marr, Don Percassi, Gerald Teijelo.

The action takes place in the Maison Chanel, Rue Cambon, Paris—either in the Salon, in the apartment above . . . or in the memory. It begins in the late Fall of 1953 and ends in the late Spring of 1954.

[6]Per insert in opening night program.
[7]Per insert in opening night program.

Act 1, Scene 1: The Salon. *Scene 2*: The Apartment. *Scene 3*: The Salon. *Scene 4*: The Dressing Room. *Scene 5*: The Apartment. *Scene 6*: The Salon.

Act 2, Scene 1: The Salon. *Scene 2*: The Apartment. *Scene 3*: The Salon.

ACT 1
Scene 1
"But That's the Way You Are"[8]
J. Dabdoub
"The World Belongs to the Young"
K. Hepburn, G. Rose, R. Auberjonois, J. Arnold, Company
"Let's Go Home"
D. Holliday
Scene 2
"Mademoiselle Cliche de Paris"
K. Hepburn
"On the Corner of the Rue Cambon"
K. Hepburn
"The Money Rings Out Like Freedom"
K. Hepburn, Ensemble
Scene 3
"A Brand New Dress"
G. Dixon
Scene 4
"A Woman Is How She Loves"
D. Holliday
Scene 5
"Gabrielle"
J. Cypher
"Coco"
K. Hepburn
Scene 6
"The Preparation"
K. Hepburn, Company

ACT 2
Scene 1
"Fiasco"
R. Auberjonois
"When Your Lover Says Goodbye"
G. Rose
Scene 2
"Ohrbach's, Bloomingdale's, Best & Saks"
W. B. Abel, R. Fitch, C. Block, D. Siretta
"Ohrbach's, Bloomingdale's, Best & Saks" (reprise)
K. Hepburn, Ensemble
Scene 3
"Always Mademoiselle"
K. Hepburn

1970.01 CHARLES AZNAVOUR

A One-Man Show in Two Acts[9]. All music and lyrics by Charles Aznavour, except where noted. Musical director and pianist, Henri Byers. Production supervisor, Leon Sanossian. Produced by Norman Twain in association with Albert I. Fill. Opened 4 February 1970 at the Music Box Theatre and closed 22 February 1970 after 23 performances.

CAST: CHARLES AZNAVOUR.

ACT 1
"Le Tamos"
(*Lyrics by* J. Davis.)
"I Will Give to You"
(*English Lyrics by* B. Morrison.)
"Happy Anniversary"
(*English Lyrics by* Herbert Kretzmer.)
"We'll Drift Away"
(*French Lyrics by* Georges Gavarentz. *English Lyrics by* Buddy Kaye.)
"Le Toreador"
"Sunday's Not My Day"
(*French Lyrics by* T. Veran. *English Lyrics by* B. Morrison.)
"Apaga La Luz"
(*English Lyrics by* R. Deleon.)
"Isabelle"
"I Will Warm Your Heart"
(*English Lyrics by* Gene Lees.)
"To My Daughter"
(*English Lyrics by* B. Morrison.)
"Et Pourtant"
(*French Lyrics by* Georges Gavarentz.)
"The Wine of Youth"
(*English Lyrics by* B. Morrison.)
"Yesterday When I Was Young"
(*English Lyrics by* Herbert Kretzmer.)
"Emmenez-Moi"
"It Will Be My Day"
(*English Lyrics by* B. Morrison.)

ACT 2
"All Those Pretty Girls"
(*English Lyrics by* Buddy Kaye.)
"De T'Avoir Aimer"
"My Hand Needs Your Hand"
(*French Lyrics by* Pierre Roche. *English Lyrics by* Buddy Kaye.)
"You've Let Yourself Go"
(*English Lyrics by* Marcel Stellman.)
"Desormais"
(*French Lyrics by* Georges Gavarentz.)
"Who"
(*English Lyrics by* Herbert Kretzmer.)
"Reste"
"Venice Dressed in Blue"
(*Music by* F. Dorin. *English Lyrics by* Buddy Kaye.)
"La Boheme"
(*Music by* Jacques Plante.)
"August Days in Paree"
(*French Lyrics by* Georges Gavarentz. *English Lyrics by* D. Newburg.)
"Les Comediens"
(*Music by* Jacques Plante.)
"And I in My Chair"
(*English Lyrics by* D. Newburg.)
"You've Got to Learn"
(*English Lyrics by* Marcel Stellman.)
"Les Bons Moments"

1970.02 GANTRY

A Musical in Two Acts, 14 Scenes. Book by Peter Bellwood. Adapted from the novel of the same name by Sinclair Lewis. Music by Stanley Lebowsky. Lyrics by Fred Tobias. Directed and staged by Onna White. Scenery by Robin Wagner. Costumes by Ann Roth. Lighting by Jules Fisher. Orchestrations by Jim Tyler. Musical direction by Arthur Rubinstein. Dance arrangements by Dorothea Freitag. Vocal arrangements by Stanley Lebowsky. Assistant choreographer, Patrick Cummings. Production supervised by Robert Weiner. Associate producer, Fred Menowitz. Produced by Joseph Cates and Jerry Schlossberg. Opened and closed 14 February 1970 at the George Abbott Theatre after 1 performance.

CAST (in order of speaking): *Bill Morgan*: Tom Batten. *Sister Doretha*: Dorothea Freitag. *Adelberta Shoup*: Gloria Hodes. *Sharon Falconer*: RITA MORENO. *Elmer Gantry*: ROBERT SHAW. *Jim Lefferts*: Wayne Tippit. *George F. Babbitt*: Ted Thurston. *Reverend Garrison*: Kenneth Bridges. *Trosper*: Bob Gorman. *Gunch*: David Sabin. *Prout*: Zale Kessler. *Reverend Toomis*: David Hooks. *Architect*: Robert Donahue. *Photographer*: James N. Maher. *Deaf Man*: J. Michael Bloom. *Deaf Man's Wife*: Beth Fowler.

[8]Dropped late in the run when Danielle Darrieux assumed the role of Coco.
[9]Charles Aznavour was previously presented on Broadway 14 October 1965 at the Ambassador Theatre for 28 performances.

Townspeople, Revival Troupe, Students, Workmen.: Chuck Beard, J. Michael Bloom, Kenneth Bridges, Patrick Cummings, Robert Donahue, Sandy Ellen, Carol Estey, Beth Fowler, Gloria Hodes, Keith Kaldenberg, Clyde Laurents, Robert Lenn, James N. Maher, Kathleen Robey, Dixie Stewart, Diane Tarleton, Maralyn Thoma, Terry Violino, Mimi Wallace.

Act 1, Scene 1: Revival Tent—Shelton, Illinois. *Scene 2*: Train. *Scene 3*: Revival Tent—Fargo, North Dakota. *Scene 4*: Revival Tent—Page City, Kansas. *Scene 5*: Sister Sharon's Dressing Room. *Scene 6*: Revival Tent—McAllaster, Kansas. *Scene 7*: Sister Sharon's Hotel Suite in Chicago.

Act 2, Scene 1: Revival Tent—Chicago, Illinois. *Scene 2*: Revival Tent Grounds. *Scene 3*: A Warehouse in Georgia. *Scene 4*: Revival Tent. *Scene 5*: The Office of the Church Board. *Scene 6*: The Tabernacle Office. *Scene 7*: Outside the "Waters of Jordan" Tabernacle.

ACT 1
"Wave a Hand"
T. Batten, the Troupe
Gantry Gets the Call:
R. Shaw, the Troupe, Townspeople
"He Was There"
"Play Ball With the Lord"
"Katie Jonas"
R. Moreno
"Thanks, Sweet Jesus!"
R. Shaw, Townspeople
"Someone I've Already Found"
R. Shaw
"He's Never Too Busy"
R. Moreno, R. Shaw, T. batten, G. Hodes, the Troupe
"We're Sharin' Sharon"
R. Shaw

ACT 2
"We Can All Give Love"
R. Moreno, G. Hodes, Townspeople
"Foresight"
T. Thurston, D. Sabin, B. Gorman, Z. Kessler
"These Four Walls"
R. Moreno
"Show Him the Way"
R. Shaw, Townspeople
"The Promise of What I Could Be"
R. Shaw
"Gantry's Reaction"
R. Shaw
"We're Sharin' Sharon" (reprise)
R. Shaw

1970.03 GEORGY

A Musical in Two Acts, 16 Scenes. Book by Tom Mankiewicz. Based on a novel ("Georgy Girl") by Margaret Forster and the screenplay of the same name by Margaret Forster and Peter Nichols. Music by George Fischoff. Lyrics by Carole Bayer. Directed by Peter Hunt. Choreography by Howard Jeffrey. Settings and lighting by Jo Mielziner. Costumes by Patricia Zipprodt. Music direction and vocal arrangementss by Elliot Lawrence. Orchestrations by Eddie Sauter. Dance music arranged by Marvin Laird. Produced by Fred Coe in association with Joseph P. Harris and Ira Bernstein. Opened 26 February 1970 at the Winter Garden and closed 28 February 1970 after 4 performances.

CAST (in order of appearance): *Georgy*: DILYS WATLING. *James Leamington*: STEPHEN ELLIOTT. *Ted*: LOUIS BEACHNER. *Meredith*: MELISSA HART. *Peg*: HELENA CARROLL. *Jos*: JOHN CASTLE. *Peter*: Richard Quarry. *Health Officer*: CYNTHIA LATHAM.

Party Guests, etc.: Kathryn Doby, Sherry Durham, Patricia Garland, Margot Head, Mary Jane Houdina, Jane Karel, Barbara Monte-Britton, Michon Peacock, Mary Zahn, Rick Atwell, Pi Douglass, Arthur Faria, Charlie Goeddertz, Neil Jones, Sal Pernice, Richard Quarry, Allan Sobek, Tony Stevens. *Children*: Kelly Boa, Mona Daleo, Jackie Paris, Donna Sands, Jill Streisant, Dewey Golkin, Anthony Marciona, Roger Morgan, Johnny Welch. *Singers*: Susan Goeppinger, Del Horstmann, Don Jay, Geoff Leon, Regina Lynn.

(The action takes place in present day London.)

Act 1, Scene 1: A Playground. *Scene 2*: Georgy and Meredith's Flat. *Scene 3*: A Street. *Scene 4*: The Flat. *Scene 5*: James Leamington's House. *Scene 6*: The Flat. *Scene 7*: London Streets. *Scene 8*: James Leamington's House. *Scene 9*: The Flat. *Scene 10*: A Street. *Scene 11*: Apollo Cinema, Piccadilly Circus.

Act 2, Scene 1: The Flat. *Scene 2*: A Street. *Scene 3*: James Leamington's House. *Scene 4*: The Flat. *Scene 5*: A Playground.

ACT 1
Scene 1
"Howjadoo"
D. Watling, Children
Scene 2
"Make It Happen Now"
D. Watling
Scene 3
"Ol' Pease Puddin'"
J. Castle, D. Watling
Scene 4
"Just For the Ride"
M. Hart, Men
"So What?"
D. Watling
Scene 5
"Georgy"
S. Elliott
Scene 6
"A Baby, (Mrs. Jones)"/"Howjadoo" (reprise)
D. Watling, J. Castle, M. Hart
Scene 9
"That's How It Is"
D. Watling, S. Elliott
Scene 11
"There's a Comin' Together"
J. Castle, D. Watling, Chorus

ACT 2
Scene 1
"Something Special"
D. Watling, J. Castle
"Half of Me'"
D. Watling
Scene 2
"Gettin' Back to Me"
M. Hart
Scene 3
"Sweet Memory"
L. Beachner, S. Elliott, Chorus
"Georgy" (reprise)
S. Elliott
Scene 4
"Life's a Holiday"
J. Castle, D. Watling
"Make It Happen Now" (reprise)
D. Watling
Scene 5
Finale: "There's a Comin' Together" (reprise)
Company

1970.04 OPERATION SIDEWINDER

A Play with Songs in Two Acts, 12 Scenes. Play by Sam Shepard. Music (songs) composed and performed by The Holy Modal Rounders (Steve Weber, John Wesley Annas, Richard Tyler, Peter Stampfel, Mike McCarty). Directed by Michael A. Schultz. Sets by Douglas W. Schmidt. Costumes by Willa Kim. Lighting by John Gleason. Musical directors, Marvin Sylvor, Jeff Cutler. Produced by The Repertory Theater of Lincoln Center (Jules Irving, Director; Robert Symonds, Associate director) by special arrangement with Alvin Ferleger Associates. Opened 12 March 1970 at the Vivian Beaumont Theatre and closed 25 April 1970 after 52 performances.

CAST (in order of appearance): *Dukie*: Robert Phalen. *Honey*: BARBARA EDA-YOUNG. *Mechanic*: Michael Miller. *Young Man*: ANDY ROBINSON. *Forest Ranger*: Robert Riggs. *Billy*: ROBERTS BLOSSOM. *Colonel Warner*: JOSEPH MASCOLO. *Captain*: Robert Phalen. *Cadet*: GUS FLEMING. *Mickey Free*: DON PLUMLEY. *First Cohort to Mickey Free*: Ralph Drischell. *Second Cohort to Mickey Free*: Arthur Sellers. *Carhop*: Catherine Burns. *Blood*: Garrett Morris. *Blade*: Paul Benjamin. *Dude*: Charles Pegues. *General Browser*: Paul Sparer. *Doctor Vector*: Ray Fry. *Spider Lady*: Michael Levin. *Edith*: Joan Pringle. *Captain Bovine*: Philip Bosco.

Indians: José Barrera, Paul Benjamin, Gregory Borst, Gus Fleming, Robert Keesler, Michael Levin, Clark Luis, Richard Mason, Muriel Miguel, Louis Mofsie, Santos Morales, Garrett Morris, Jean-Daniel Noland. *Desert Tactical Troop*: Robert Riggs, Robert Phalen, Michael Miller.

Act 1, Scene 1: In the desert. *Scene 2*: A garage. *Scene 3*: In the desert. *Scene 4*: The office of Air Force Colonel Warner. *Scene 5*: In the desert. *Scene 6*: A drive-in restaurant. *Scene 7*: The Air Force Laboratory at Fort George. *Scene 8*: In the desert.

Act 2, Scene 1: In the desert. *Scene 2*: The Kiva of the Spider Lady. *Scene 3*: The office of C.I.A. Captain Bovine. *Scene 4*: On a mesa in the desert.

ACT 1[10]

Scene 1

"Do It Girl"
(*Lyrics by* Peter Stampfel and Antonia.)

Scene 2

"Float Me Down Your Pipeline"
(*Lyrics by* Antonia.)

Scene 3

"Generalonely"
(*Lyrics by* Steve Weber.)

Scene 4

"Catch Me"
(*Lyrics by* Sam Shepard.)

Scene 5

"Euphoria"
(*Lyrics by* Robin Remaily.)

Scene 6

"Synergy"
(*Lyrics by* Peter Stampfel and Antonia.)

Scene 7

"Don't Leave Me Dangling in the Dust" (Dusty Fustchuns)
(*Lyrics by* Robin Remaily.)

Scene 8

"Alien Song"
(*Lyrics by* Sam Shepard.)

ACT 2

Scene 1

"Bad Karma"
(*Lyrics by* Peter Stampfel and Antonia.)

Scene 2

"I Disremember Quite Well"
(*Lyrics by* Antonia.)

Scene 3

"C.I.A. Men"
(*Lyrics by* Peter Stampfel, Tuli Tupferburg and Antonia.)

Scene 4

Hopi Chants

1970.05

PURLIE

A Musical (Comedy) in Two Acts, 6 Scenes, a Prologue and an Epilogue. Book by Ossie Davis, Philip Rose and Peter Udell. Based on the play "Purlie Victorious" by Ossie Davis. Music by Gary Geld. Lyrics by Peter Udell. Production directed by Philip Rose. Choreography by Louis Johnson. Scenery by Ben Edwards. Lighting by Thomas Skelton. Costumes by Ann Roth. Orchestrations and choral arrangements by Garry Sherman and Luther Henderson. Musical supervisor, Garry Sherman. Musical conductor, Joyce Brown. Dance music arranged by Luther Henderson. Produced by Philip Rose. Opened 15 March 1970 at the Broadway Theatre, moved 15 December 1970 to the Winter Garden, moved 15 March 1971 to the ANTA Theatre and closed 7 November 1971 after 689 performances.

CAST (in order of appearance): *Purlie*: CLEAVON LITTLE. *Church Soloist*: LINDA HOPKINS. *Lutiebelle*: MELBA MOORE. *Missy*: NOVELLA NELSON. *Gitlow*: SHERMAN HEMSLEY. *Charlie*: C. DAVID COLSON. *Idella*: HELEN MARTIN. *Ol' Cap'n*: JOHN HEFFERNAN.

Dancers: Loretta Abbott, Hope Clark, Judy Gibson, Lavinia Hamilton, Arlene Rowlant, Ella Thompson, Myrna White, Morris Donaldson, George Faison, Al Perryman, Harold Pierson, William Taylor, Larry Vickers. *Singers*: Carolyn Bird, Barbara Christopher, Denise Elliott, Synthia Jackson, Mildred Lane, Alyce Webb, Mildred Pratcher, Peter Colly, Milt Grayson, Tony Middleton, Ray Pollard.

The action takes place in South Georgia not too long ago.

Prologue: Big Bethel, a country church.

Act 1, Scene 1: A shack on the plantation, some time before that of the prologue. *Scene 2*: Outside Ol' Cap'n Commissary. *Scene 3*: Outside Ol' Cap'n Commissary. *Scene 4*: The shack.

Act 2, Scene 1: On the plantation, 4 A.M. *Scene 2*: The shack, just before dawn.

Epilogue: The time and place as in the Prologue.

ACT 1

Prologue

"Walk Him Up the Stairs"
Entire Company

Scene 1

"New Fangled Preacher Man"
C. Little

"Skinnin' a Cat"
S. Hemsley, The Field Hands

"Purlie"
M. Moore

"The Harder They Fall"
C. Little, M. Moore

Scene 2

Charlie's Songs: "The Barrels of War"/"The Unborn Love"
C. D. Colson

"Big Fish, Little Fish"
J. Heffernan, C. D. Colson

Scene 3

"I Got Love"
M. Moore

"Great White Father"
The Cotton Pickers (Ensemble)

"Skinnin' a Cat" (reprise)
S. Hemsley, C. D. Colson

Scene 4

"Down Home"
C. Little, N. Nelson

ACT 2

Scene 1

"First Thing Monday Mornin'"
The Cotton Pickers (Ensemble)

Scene 2

"He Can Do It"
N. Nelson, M. Moore

"The Harder They Fall"[11] (reprise)
S. Hemlsey, M. Moore, N. Nelson

"The World Is Comin' to a Start"
C. D. Colson, Company

Epilogue

"Walk Him Up the Stairs" (reprise)
Entire Company

[10]Also performed: "Hathor" (*Lyrics by* Peter Stampfel.)

[11]Replaced for West Coast tour by:
"Easy Goin' Man"
Barry Smith (Gitlow)

1970.06 BLOOD RED ROSES

A Play With Songs in Two Acts, 9 Scenes. Book and lyrics by John Lewin. Music by Michael Valenti. Directed by Alan Schneider. Musical numbers staged by Larry Fuller. Scenery by Ed Wittstein. Costumes by Deidre Cartier. Lighting by Tharon Musser. Musical direction by Milton Setzer. Orchestrations by Julian Stein and Abba Bogin. Assistant director, Joan Thorne. Produced by Seymour Vall, Louis S. Goldman in association with Rick Mandell and Bjorn I. Swanstrom. Opened and closed 22 March 1970 at the John Golden Theatre after 1 performance.

CAST (in order of appearance): *Grenadier Guards*: William Tost, Bill Gibbens. *Fitzroy Somerset, Lord Raglan, Commander-in-Chief*: Sydney Walker. *Prince Albert*: Ronald Drake. *Queen Victoria*: JEANIE CARSON. *Private William Cockcroft*: JESS RICHARDS. *Private John Smalls*: PHILIP BRUNS. *Alice Crabbe*, a bawd: JEANIE CARSON. *Mr. W. H. Russell*, Correspondent for the London Times: Jay Gregory. *A Russian Soldier*: Charles Abbott. *Cornet Edwin May*, Fourth Light Dragoons: Lowell Harris. *Florence Nightingale*: JEANIE CARSON.

The action takes place in England and the Crimean Peninsula during the Crimean War of 1854-55.

Act 1, Scene 1: Buckingham Palace and Environs. *Scene 2*: A Nighthouse in London. *Scene 3*: The Hills of the Crimea. *Scene 4*: Another Part of the Terrain. *Scene 5*: Stinks—Detail. *Scene 6*: Windsor Castle.

Act 2, Scene 1: The Crimean Plateau. *Scene 2*: The Hospital at Scutari. *Scene 3*: England Again.

ACT 1
Scene 1
"The Cream of English Youth"
Entire British Army
"A Garden in the Sun"
J. Carson, R. Drake, S. Walker
"Song of How Mucked Up Things Are"
P. Bruns, J. Richards
"The Cream of English Youth" (continued)
P. Bruns, J. Richards
Scene 2
"Song of Greater Britain"
J. Carson
Scene 3
"Black Dog Rum"
S. Walker, The Fusiliers
Scene 4
"In the Country Where I Come From"
J. Richards
Scene 5
"The English Rose"
P. Bruns, J. Richards
Scene 6
"Soldiers Prayer"
The Fusiliers

ACT 2
Scene 1
"Blood Red Roses"
J. Richards
"The Fourth Light Dragoons"
L. Harris
"The English Rose" (continued)
P. Bruns
Scene 3
"Song of the Fair Dissenter Lass"
J. Carson
Finale
Entire Company

1970.07 MINNIE'S BOYS

A Musical in Two Acts, 12 Scenes. Book by Arthur Marx and Robert Fisher. (Suggested by the early lives of the Marx Brothers.) Music by Larry Grossman. Lyrics by Hal Hackady. Directed by Stanley Prager. Musical numbers staged by Marc Breaux. Production consultant, Groucho Marx. Settings by Peter Wexler. Costumes by Donald Brooks. Lighting by Jules Fisher. Musical direction and vocal arrangements by John Berkman. Orchestrations by Ralph Burns. Dance arrangements and incidental music by Marvin Hamlisch and Peter Howard. Associate producer, Peter N. Grad. Produced by Arthur Whitelaw, Max J. Brown and Byron Goldman. Opened 26 March 1970 at the Imperial Theatre and closed 30 May 1970 after 80 performances.

CAST (in order of appearance): *Julie Marx* (Groucho): LEWIS J. STADLEN. *Leonard Marx* (Chico): IRWIN PEARL. *Adolph Marx* (Harpo): DANIEL FORTUS. *Herbie Marx* (Zeppo): ALVIN KUPPERMAN. *Milton Marx* (Gummo): GARY RAUCHER. *Mrs. Flanagan*: Jean Bruno. *Mrs. Krupnik*: Jacqueline Britt. *Minnie Marx*: SHELLEY WINTERS. *Sam Marx* (Frenchie): ARNY FREEMAN. *Hochmeister*: MERWIN GOLDSMITH. *Al Shean*: MORT MARSHALL. *Cop*: Doug Spingler. *Sidebark*: Ronn Hansen. *Acrobats*: Evelyn Taylor, David Vaughan, George Bunt. *Cindy*: Marjory Edson. *Maxie*: RICHARD B. SHULL. *Telegraph Boy*: Stephen Reinhardt. *Robwell*: Casper Roos. *Harpist*: Jean Bruno. *Theatre Manager*: Gene Ross. *E. F. Albee*: ROLAND WINTERS. *Mrs. McNish*: JULIE KURNITZ. *Murdoch*: Jacqueline Britt. *Sandow, the Great*: Richard B. Shull. *Miss Taj Mahal*: Lynne Gannaway. *Miss White House*: Marjory Edson. *Miss Eiffel Tower*: Vicki Frederick.

Ensemble: Jacqueline Britt, Jean Bruno, Bjarne Buchtrup, George Bunt, Dennis Cole, Deede Darnell, Joan B. Duffin, Marjory Edson, Vicki Frederick, Marcela Gamboa, Lynne Gannaway, Ronn Hansen, Elaine Manzel, Stephen Reinhardt, Casper Roos, Gene Ross, Carole Schweid, William W. Sean, Doug Spingler, Evelyn Taylor, David Vaughan, Toodie Wittmer, Mary Zahn.

Act 1, Scene 1: The Street. *Scene 2*: The Marx Apartment. *Scene 3*: Backstage Nagadoches. *Scene 4*: Nagadoches Hotel. *Scene 5*: School Act. *Scene 6*: Onstage. *Scene 7*: Backstage Chicago.

Act 2, Scene 1: Mrs. McNish's Boarding House. *Scene 2*: Outside Palace Theatre. *Scene 3*: Albee's Office. *Scene 4*: Minnie's Long Island Home. *Scene 5*: Walnut Street Theatre.

ACT 1
Scene 1
"Five Growing Boys"
S. Winters, Neighbors
Scene 2
"Rich Is"
M. Marshall, S. Winters, A. Freeman,
L. J. Stadlen, D. Fortus, I. Pearl, A. Kupperman, G. Raucher
"More Precious Far"
L. J. Stadlen, A. Kupperman, D. Fortus, S. Winters
Scene 3
"Four Nightingales"
L. J. Stadlen, D. Fortus, A. Kupperman
"Underneath It All"
R. B. Shull, Girls
Scene 4
"Mama, a Rainbow"
D. Fortus, S. Winters
"You Don't Have To Do It for Me"
S. Winters, L. J. Stadlen, D. Fortus, I. Pearl, A. Kupperman
Scene 6
"If You Wind Me Up"
S. Winters, L. J. Stadlen, D. Fortus, I. Pearl, A. Kupperman
Scene 7
"Where Was I When They Passed Out the Luck?"
L. J. Stadlen, D. Fortus, I. Pearl, A. Kupperman

ACT 2
Scene 1
"The Smell of Christmas"
L. J. Stadlen, D. Fortus, I. Pearl, A. Kupperman
"You Remind Me of You"
L. J. Stadlen, J. Kurnitz
Scene 2
"Minnie's Boys"
S. Winters, Company
Scene 4
"Be Happy"
S. Winters, D. Fortus, I. Pearl, A. Kupperman, G. Raucher

Scene 5
"The Act"
L. J. Stadlen, D. Fortus, I. Pearl, A. Kupperman, S. Winters
Finale
The Company

1970.08 LOOK TO THE LILIES

A Musical in Two Acts, 16 Scenes. Book by Leonard Spigelgass. Based on the novel "Lilies of the Field" by William E. Barrett. Music by Jule Styne. Lyrics by Sammy Cahn. Directed by Joshua Logan. Scenery and lighting by Jo Mielziner. Costumes by Carrie F. Robbins. Musical direction, Milton Rosenstock. Vocal arrangements and direction, Buster Davis. Orchestrations by Larry Wilcox. Dance arrangements by John Morris. Audio design (sound) by Robert I. Liftin. Production associate, Joseph Beruh. Produced by Edgar Lansbury, Max J. Brown, Richard Lewine, and Ralph Nelson. Opened 29 March 1970 at the Lunt-Fontanne Theatre and closed 19 April 1970 after 25 performances[12].

CAST (in order of appearance): *Homer Smith*: AL FREEMAN, JR. *Sister Gertrude*: Maggie Task. *Sister Elizabeth*: Virginia Craig. *Sister Agnes*: Linda Andrews. *Mother Maria*: SHIRLEY BOOTH. *Sister Albertine*: TAINA ELG. *Lady Guitarist*: Anita Sheer. *Juanita*: PATTI KARR. *Rosita*: CARMEN ALVAREZ. *Juan Archuleta*: TITOS VANDIS. *Bartender*: Marc Allen, III. *First Policeman*: Joe Benjamin. *Secomnd Policeman*: Richard Graham. *Courtroom Guards*: Paul Eichel, Michael Davis. *Judge*: Joe Benjamin. *District Attorney*: Don Prieur. *Defense Attorney*: Ben Laney. *Monsignor O'Hara*: Richard Graham. *Poker Players*: Michael Davis, Paul Eichel, Don Prieur. *Townspeople*: *Singers*: Marian Haraldson, Sherri Huff, Suzanne Horn, Maggie Worth, Marc Allen, III, Michael Davis, Paul Eichel, Tony Falco, Ben Laney, Don Prieur. *Dancers*: Carol Conte, Maria DiDia, Tina Faye, Ravah Malmuth, Glenn Brooks, Harry Endicott, Gary Gendell, Steven Ross. *Children*: Lisa Bellaran, Lori Bellaran, Ray Bellaran.

Act 1, Scene 1: The Farm. *Scene 2*: Farmhouse Kitchen. *Scene 3*: Juan's Cafe. *Scene 4*: Farmhouse Kitchen. *Scene 5*: The Farm—The next morning. *Scene 6*: Juan's Cafe.

Act 2, Scene 1: Farmhouse Kitchen. *Scene 2*: Courtroom. *Scene 3*: A Bus Stop. *Scene 4*: The Farm. *Scene 5*: Near Casamagordo. *Scene 6*: Juan's Cafe. *Scene 7*: The Farm. *Scene 8*: A Bus Stop. *Scene 9*: Chapel Exterior. *Scene 10*: Chapel Interior.

ACT 1
Scene 1
"Gott Is Gut"
S. Booth, T. Elg, V. Craig, M., Task, L. Andrews
"First Class Number One Bum"
A. Freeman, Jr.
Scene 2
"Himmlisher Vater"
S. Booth, T. Elg, V. Craig, M., Task, L. Andrews
"Follow the Lamb"
A. Freeman, Jr., S. Booth, T. Elg, V. Craig, M., Task, L. Andrews
Scene 3
"Meet My Seester"
P. Karr. C. Alvarez
Scene 4
"Don't Talk About God"
A. Freeman, Jr.
"When I Was Young"
S. Booth
Scene 5
"On That Day of Days"
P. Karr, C. Alvarez, Children, Townspeople
"You're a Rock"
A. Freeman, Jr.
"I Am What I Am"
S. Booth
"I'd Sure Like to Give It a Shot"
A. Freeman, Jr.
Scene 6
"I'd Sure Like to Give It a Shot" (Dance)
A. Freeman, Jr., P. Karr, C. Alvarez, Customers

ACT 2
Scene 1
"I Admire You Very Much, Mr. Schmidt"
T. Elg
Scene 3
"Look to the Lilies"
S. Booth, T. Elg, V. Craig, M., Task, L. Andrews
Scene 4
"Some Kind of Man"
A. Freeman, Jr.
Scene 5
"Homer's Pitch"
A. Freeman, Jr., Townspeople
Scene 7
"Casamagordo, New Mexico"
T. Elg, V. Craig, M., Task, L. Andrews
"One Little Brick at a Time"
A. Freeman, Jr., Townspeople
Scene 8
"I, Yes Me, That's Who"
S. Booth
Scene 9
"Prayer"
Townspeople
Scene 10
"I, Yes Me, That's Who" (reprise)
A. Freeman, Jr.

[12]Choreography uncredited at opening; credited to Joyce Trisler in previews.

1970.09 APPLAUSE

A Musical in Two Acts, 16 Scenes. Book by Betty Comden and Adolph Green. Based on the film "All About Eve" (by Joseph Mankiewicz) and the original story ("The Wisdom of Eve") by Mary Orr. Music by Charles Strouse. Lyrics by Lee Adams. Directed and choreographed by Ron Field. Scenery by Robert Randolph. Costumes by Ray Aghayan. Lighting by Tharon Musser. Musical direction and vocal arrangements by Don Pippin. Orchestrations by Philip J. Lang. Dance and incidental music arranged by Mel Marvin. Production associate, Phyllis Dukore. Choreographic assistant, Tom Rolla. Produced by Joseph Kipness and Lawrence Kasha in association with Nederlander Productions and George M. Steinbrenner III. Opened 30 March 1970 at the Palace Theatre and closed 27 May 1972 after 898 performances.

CAST (in order of appearance): *Tony Announcer*: John Anania. *Tony Host*: Alan King. *Margo Channing*: LAUREN BACALL. *Eve Harrington*: PENNY FULLER. *Howard Benedict*: ROBERT MANDAN. *Bert*: Tom Urich. *Buzz Richards*: BRANDON MAGGART. *Bill Sampson*: LEN CARIOU. *Duane Fox*: LEE ROY REAMS. *Karen Richards*: ANN WILLIAMS. *Bartender*: Jerry Wyatt. *Peter*: John Anania. *Bob*: Howard Kahl. *Piano Player*: Orrin Reiley. *Stan Harding*: Ray Becker. *Danny*: Bill Allsbrook. *Bonnie*: BONNIE FRANKLIN. *Carol*: Carol Petri. *Joey*: Michael Misita. *Musicians*: Gene Kelton, Nat Horne, David Anderson. *TV Director*: Orrin Reiley. *Autograph Seeker*: Carol Petri.

Singers: Laurie Franks, Ernestine Jackson, Sheilah Rae, Jeannette Seibert, Henrietta Valor, Howard Kahl, Orrin Reiley, Jerry Wyatt. *Dancers*: Renee Baughman, Joan Bell, Debi Carpenter, Patti D'Beck, Marilyn D'Honau, Marybeth Kurdock, Carol Petri, Bill Allsbrook, David Anderson, John Cashman, Jon Daenen, Nikolas Dante, Gene Foote, Gene Kelton, Nat Horne, Michael Misita, Ed Nolfi, Sammy Williams.

The action takes place at the present time in and around New York City.

Act 1, Scene 1: The Tony Awards. *Scene 2*: Margo's Dressing Room. *Scene 3*: The Village Bar. *Scene 4*: Margo's Living Room. *Scene 5*: Margo's Dressing Room. *Scene 6*: Joe Allen's (Restaurant). *Scene 7*: Margo's Bedroom. *Scene 8*: Margo's Living Room. *Scene 9*: Backstage.

Act 2, Scene 1: Buzz and Karen's Connecticut Home. *Scene 2*: Margo's Dressing Room. *Scene 3*: Joe Allen's. *Scene 4*: Margo's Living Room. *Scene 5*: Backstage. *Scene 6*: Margo's Dressing Room. *Scene 7*: Backstage.

ACT 1
Scene 2
"Backstage Babble"
First Nighters (Ensemble)
"Think How It's Gonna Be"
L. Cariou
"But Alive"
L. Bacall, Boys
Scene 3
"But Alive" (continued)
L. Bacall, Boys
Scene 4
"The Best Night of My Life"
P. Fuller
"Who's That Girl?"
L. Bacall
Scene 6
"Applause"
B. Franklin, the Gypsies (Ensemble)
Scene 7
"Hurry Back"
L. Bacall
Scene 8
"Fasten Your Seat Belts"
B. Maggart, A. Williams, R. Mandan, L. R. Reams, L. Cariou, Guests
Scene 9
"Welcome to the Theater"
L. Bacall

ACT 2
Scene 1
"Inner Thoughts"
A. Williams, B. Maggart, L. Bacall
"Good Friends"
L. Bacall, A. Williams, B. Maggart
Scene 2
"The Best Night of My Life" (reprise)
P. Fuller
Scene 3
"She's No Longer a Gypsy"
B. Franklin, L. R. Reams, the Gypies (Ensemble)
Scene 4
"One of a Kind"
L. Cariou, L. Bacall
Scene 5
"One Hallow'een"
P. Fuller
Scene 6
"Something Greater"
L. Bacall
Scene 7
Finale
L. Bacall, Company

1970.10 CRY FOR US ALL

A Musical in One Act, 10 Scenes. Book by William Alfred and Albert Marre. Based on the play "Hogan's Goat" by William Alfred. Music by Mitch Leigh. Lyrics by William Alfred and Phyllis Robinson. Book and musical staging by Albert Marre. Choreography by Todd Bolender. Settings and lighting by Howard Bay. Costumes by Robert Fletcher. Musical direction by Herbert Grossman. Music supervision, Sam Pottle. Orchestrations by Carlyle Hall. Production coordinator, Dwight Fyre. Assistant choreographer, John Mandia. Produced by Mitch Leigh in association with C. Gerald Goldsmith. Opened 8 April 1970 at the Broadhurst Theatre and closed 15 April 1970 after 9 performances.

CAST: *Street-rats* (3): *Miggsy*: Scott Jacoby. *Flylegs*: Darel Glaser. *Cabbage*: Todd Jones. *Matt Stanton*, Leader of Brooklyn's Sixth Ward, and owner of the Court Cafe: STEVE ARLEN. *Kathleen Stanton*, his wife: JOAN DIENER. *Edward Quinn*, Mayor of Brooklyn: ROBERT WEEDE. *Peter Boyle*, a hanger-on of Quinn's: TOMMY RALL. *Bessie Legg*, a back-room girl: HELEN GALLAGHER. *Maria Haggerty*, the Stanton's Housekeeper: DOLORES WILSON. *John "Black Jack" Haggerty*, her husband and Assistant Ward Leader: PAUL UKENA. *James "Palsy" Murphy*, Boss of Brooklyn: EDWIN STEFFE. *Father Stanislaus Coyne*, Pastor of St. Mary Star of the Sea: WILLIAM GRIFFIS. *State Senator Thomas Walsh*: Jay Stuart. *Mortyeen O'Brien*, the Fire Commissioner: Charles Rule. *Peter Mulligan*, Chief Clerk of the Police Department: John Ferrante. *Father Maloney*, Priest of the Printers' Church: Elliott Savage. *The Cruelty Man*: Taylor Reed. *Mrs. Teresa Tuohy*: Fran Stevens. *Fiona Quigley*, factory girl: Elaine Cancilla. *Jack O'Banion*, a reporter for The Brooklyn Eagle: Jack Trussel. *Mrs. Mortyeen O'Brien*: Dora Rinehart. *Aloysius "Wishy" Doyle*, Bartender of the Court Cafe: Bill Dance. *Mutton Egan*, thirteen years old: Ronnie Douglas.

The action takes place in Brooklyn during a five-day period around 1 May 1890. The principal locale is the Court Cafe on the corner of Court Street and Fifth Place, Brooklyn: the street outside, the bar and the backroom of the cafe, and the Haggerty parlor which adjoins it. The action also moves to the street outside Ag Hogan's flat, to the Printers' Church in Brooklyn, and to the Boardwalk in Seagate.

Scene 1: Tuesday Evening. *Scene 2*: Wednesday Morning. *Scene 3*: Wednesday Evening. *Scene 4*: Thursday Evening. *Scene 5*: Friday Evening. *Scene 6*: Later Friday Evening. *Scene 7*: Saturday Afternoon. *Scene 8*: Saturday Night. *Scene 9*: Sunday Afternoon. *Scene 10*: Sunday Evening.

MUSICAL NUMBERS
Scene 1
"See No Evil"
S. Jacoby, D. Glaser, T. Jones
"The End of My Race"
S. Arlen
"How Are Ya Since?"
J. Diener, S. Arlen, The Constituents (Ensemble)
Scene 2
"The Mayor's Chair"
R. Weede
"The Cruelty Man"
S. Jacoby, D. Glaser, T. Jones
Scene 3
"The Verandah Waltz"
J. Diener, S. Arlen
Scene 4
"Home Free All"
S. Arlen, S. Jacoby, D. Glaser, T. Jones, The Constituents
"The Broken Heart of the Wages of Sin"
S. Jacoby, D. Glaser, T. Jones
"The Confessional"
S. Arlen, E. Savage
"Who To Love If Not a Stranger?"
J. Diener
Scene 5
"Cry For Us All"
T. Rall, The Mourners (Ensemble)
Scene 6
"Swing Your Bag'
H. Gallagher
"Call in to Her"
J. Diener, S. Arlen
"That Slavery Is Love"
J. Diener
Scene 7
"I Lost It"
S. Jacoby, D. Glaser, T. Jones
Scene 8
"Aggie, Oh Aggie"
R. Weede
Scene 9
"The Leg of the Duck"
T. Rall

"This Cornucopian Land"
S. Arlen, The Constituents
"How Are Ya Since?" (reprise)
J. Diener, R. Weede
"The Broken Heart or the Wages of Sin" (reprise)
S. Jacoby, D. Glaser, T. Jones
Scene 10
"Cry For Us All" (reprise)
The Constituents

1970.11 THE BOY FRIEND

A Revival of the Musical Comedy of the 1920's in Three Acts[13]. Book, music and lyrics by Sandy Wilson. Directed by Gus Schirmer. Dances and musical numbers staged by Buddy Schwab. Settings and costumes by Andrew and Margaret Brownfoot. Costume supervision, Stanley Simmons. Lighting by Tharon Musser. Musical director, Jerry Goldberg. Orchestrations by Ted Royal and Charles L. Cooke. Associate producer, Robert Saxon. Produced by John Yorke, Don Saxon and Michael Hellerman. Opened 14 April 1970 at the Ambassador Theatre and closed 18 July 1970 after 119 performances.

CAST (in order of appearance): *Hortense*: Barbara Andres. *Nancy*: Lesley Secombe. *Maisie*: SANDY DUNCAN. *Fay*: Mary Zahn. *Dulcie*: SIMON MCQUEEN. *Polly*: JUDY CARNE. *Marcel*: Marcelo Gamboa. *Alphonse*: Ken Mitchell. *Pierre*: Arthur Faria. *Madame Dubonnet*: JEANNE BEAUVAIS. *Bobby Van Husen*: HARVEY EVANS. *Percival Browne*: LEON SHAW. *Tony*: RONALD YOUNG. *Phillipe*: Tony Stevens. *Monica*: Carol Culver. *Lord Brockhurst*: DAVID VAUGHAN. *Lady Brockhurst*: Marie Paxton. *Gendarme*: Jeff Richards. *Waiter*: Tony Stevens. *Pepe*: Marcelo Gamboa. *Lolita*: Mary Zahn.

1970.12 PARK

A Musical in Two Acts. Book and lyrics by Paul Cherry. Music by Lance Mulcahy. Directed by John Stix. Scenery and costumes by Peter Harvey. Lighting by Martin Aronstein. Arrangements and musical direction, Oscar Kosarin. Musical staging by Lee Theodore. Produced by Edward Padula, a division of Eddie Bracken Ventures, Inc. Opened 22 April 1970 at the John Golden Theatre and closed 25 April 1970 after 5 performances.

CAST (in order of appearance): *Young Man*: DON SCARDINO. *Young Woman*: JOAN HACKETT. *Man*: DAVID BROOKS. *Woman*: JULIE WILSON.

The action takes place at the present time in Spring in a park.

ACT 1
"All the Little Things in the World Are Waiting"
D. Scardino
"Hello Is the Way Things Begin"
J. Hackett
"Bein' a Kid"
D. Scardino, J. Hackett
"Elizabeth"
D. Brooks
"He Talks To Me"
J. Wilson, D. Brooks
"Tomorrow Will Be the Same"
Quartet
"One Man"
J. Wilson
"Park"
D. Scardino

ACT 2
"I Want It Just to Happen"
J. Hackett
"I Can See"
J. Wilson
"Compromise"
D. Scardino
"Jamie"
D. Scardino, D. Brooks
"Tomorrow Will Be the Same" (reprise)
Ensemble
"I'd Marry You Again"
J. Wilson, D. Brooks
"Bein' a Kid" (reprise)
Quartet
"Park" (reprise)
Quartet

1970.13 COMPANY

A Musical in Two Acts, 11 Scenes. Book by George Furth. Music and lyrics by Stephen Sondheim. Directed by Harold Prince. Musical numbers staged by Michael Bennett. Sets and projections by Boris Aronson. Costumes by D. D. Ryan. Lighting by Robert Ornbo. Musical direction by Harold Hastings. Orchestrations by Jonathan Tunick. Dance music arrangements by Wally Harper. Production supervisor, Ruth Mitchell. Associate choreographer, Bob Avian. Produced by Harold Prince in association with Ruth Mitchell. Opened 26 April 1970 at the Alvin Theatre and closed 1 January 1972 after 690 performances.

CAST: *Robert*: DEAN JONES. *Sarah*: BARBARA BARRIE. *Harry*: CHARLES KIMBROUGH. *Susan*: MERLE LOUISE. *Peter*: JOHN CUNNINGHAM. *Jenny*: TERI RALSTON. *David*: GEORGE COE. *Amy*: BETH HOWLAND. *Paul*: STEVE ELMORE. *Joanne*: ELAINE STRITCH. *Larry*: CHARLES BRASWELL. *Marta*: PAMELA MYERS. *Kathy*: DONNA McKECHNIE. *April*: SUSAN BROWNING.
Vocal Minority: Cathy Corkill, Carol Gelfand, Marilyn Saunders, Dona D. Vaughan.

The action takes place in New York City at the present time.

Act 1, Scene 1: Robert's apartment. *Scene 2*: Sarah and Harry's living room. *Scene 3*: Peter and Susan's terrace. *Scene 4*: Jenny and David's den/playroom. *Scene 5*: A park bench. *Scene 6*: Amy's kitchen.

Act 2, Scene 1: Robert's apartment, as in Act 1, Scene 1.*Scene 2*: Robert's apartment, later. *Scene 3*: Peter and Susan's terrace. *Scene 4*: A private night-club. *Scene 5*: Robert's apartment.

ACT 1
Scene 1
"Company"
D. Jones, Company
Scene 2
"The Little Things You Do Together"
E. Stritch, Company
"Sorry-Grateful"
C. Kimbrough, G. Coe, C. Braswell
Scene 4
"You Could Drive a Person Crazy"
D. McKechnie, S. Browning, P. Myers
"Have I Got a Girl for You"
C. Braswell, J. Cunningham, S. Elmore, G. Coe, C. Kimbrough
"Someone Is Waiting"
D. Jones
Scene 5
"Another Hundred People"
P. Myers
Scene 6
"Getting Married Today"
B. Howland, S. Elmore, T. Ralston

ACT 2
Scene 1
"Side By Side By Side"
D. Jones, Company
"What Would We Do Without You"
D. Jones, Company

[13]Originally produced in New York 30 September 1954 at the Royale Theatre for 483 performances. For Synopsis of Scenes and Musical Numbers, see original 1954 production.

Scene 2

"Poor Baby"

B. Barrie, T. Ralston, M. Louise, B. Howland, E. Stritch

"Tick Tock" (dance)

D. McKechnie

(*Dance Music Arranged by* David Shire.)

"Barcelona"

D. Jones, S. Browning

Scene 4

"The Ladies Who Lunch"

E. Stritch

"Being Alive"

D. Jones

1970–1971 SEASON

Mary McCarty (foreground) in FOLLIES
Martha Swope/TimePix

1970–1971 SEASON

1970.14 BOB AND RAY-- THE TWO AND ONLY

An Entertainment (Comedy revue) in Two Acts. Created and written by Bob Elliott and Ray Goulding. Directed by Joseph Hardy. Scenery by William Ritman. Lighting by Thomas Skelton. Associate producer, Ben Gerard. Produced by Joseph I. and Johanna Levine in association with Hy Saporta. Opened 24 September 1970 at the John Golden Theatre and closed 13 February 1971 after 162 performances.

CAST: BOB ELLIOTT, RAY GOULDING.

A revue of comedy sketches and interviews employing some of the following Bob-and-Ray characterizations:

CAST—IF USED: Hector Lassie, Captain Larson*, Wally Ballou, Dr. Derek Dexter, Ward Smith, Edgar G. Fanshaw, Martin LeSoeur, Good Professor Groggins***, Gabe Preston, McBeebee Twins, Charles (poet)**, Mayor Ralph Moody Thayer, Mary McGoon, John W. Norbis, Harlow P. Whitcomb, Larry Lovebreath, Maitland W. Montmorency, Leonard Bonfiglio, Barry Campbell, Clinton Snidely, Biff Burns, David Chetley, Fielding Backstayge*****, T. WIlton Messy****, Fahnstock P. Bodry, Neil A. Sturbush, T. Wilton Messy, Jr., Stuffy Hodgson, O. Leo Lahey, Thomas E. Röte, Word Carr, Wolfman*****, Gregg Marlowe, Dean Archer Armstead, Mr. Trace, Clyde L. "Hap" Whartney, Mister Science, Arthur Schermerhorn, Komodo Dragon Expert.

*** Missing Quit
*** Transplant Donor (Accidental)
**** Committed
***** Confined
****** In Pound

1970.15 THE ROTHSCHILDS

A Musical in Two Acts, a Prologue and 18 Scenes. Book by Sherman Yellen. Based on the book of the same name by Frederic Morton. Music by Jerry Bock. Lyrics by Sheldon Harnick. Directed and choreographed by Michael Kidd. Settings and costumes by John Bury. Lighting by Richard Pilbrow. Orchestrations by Don Walker. Musical direction and vocal arrangements by Milton Greene. Dance music arranged by Clay Fullum. Production supervision by Michael Thoma. Produced by Lester Osterman (Productions, Richard Horner) and Hillard Elkins (Productions International Corp., Emanuel Azenberg, Robert Malina, George Platt). Opened 19 October 1970 at the Lunt-Fontanne Theatre and closed 2 January 1972 after 505 performances.

CAST (in order of appearance): *Prince William of Hesse*: KEENE CURTIS. *Guard*: Roger Hamilton. *Mayer Rothschild*: HAL LINDEN. *First Urchin*: Michael Maitland. *Second Urchin*: Kim Michels. *Third Urchin*: Robby Benson. *Gutele (Mama) Rothschild*: LEILA MARTIN. *First Vendor*: Thomas Trelfa. *Second Vendor*: Kenneth Bridges. *Third Vendor*: Jon Peck. *General*: Paul Tracey. *Budurus*: LEO LEYDEN. *First Banker*: Elliott Savage. *Second Banker*: Carl Nicholas. *Young Amshel Rothschild*: Lee Franklin. *Young Solomon Rothschild*: Robby Benson. *Young Nathan Rothschild*: Michael Maitland. *Young Jacob Rothschild*: Mitchell Spera. *Blum*: Howard Honig. *Mrs. Kaufman*: Nina Dova. *Mrs. Segal*: Peggy Cooper. *Peasant*: Christopher Chadman. *Amshel Rothschild*: TIMOTHY JEROME. *Solomon Rothschild*: DAVID GARFIELD. *Jacob Rothschild*: CHRIS SARANDON. *Nathan Rothschild*: PAUL HECHT. *Kalman Rothschild*: ALLAN GRUET. *Joseph Fouche*: KEENE CURTIS. *Herries*: KEENE CURTIS. *Sceptic*: Paul Tracey. *Banker*: Roger Hamilton. *Hannah Cohen*: JILL CLAYBURGH. *Prince Metternich*: KEENE CURTIS.

Members of the Hessian Court, People of the Frankfort Ghetto, Members of the Austrian Court, Grenadiers, Couriers, Crowned Heads of Europe, Banker-Brokers: Rick Atwell, Steve Boockvor, Kenneth Bridges, Henry Brunjes, Christopher Chadman, Peggy Cooper, Patrick Cummings, Nina Dova, Vicki Frederick, Penny Guerard, Roger Hamilton, Ann Hodges, Howard Honig, Del Lewis, John Mineo, Carl Nicholas, Jon Peck, Ted Pejovich, Denise Pence, Jean Richards, Elliott Savage, Wilfred Schuman, Lani Sundsten, Paul Tracey, Thomas Trelfa.

The action takes place throughout Europe between 1772 and 1818.

Prologue: Hesse, 1772.

Act 1, Scene 1: The Gate of the Frankfort Ghetto, 1772. *Scene 2*: The Rothschild Shop, Frankfort Ghetto, 1772. *Scene 3*: The Frankfort Fair, 1773. *Scene 4*: The Study of Prince William of Hesse, 1773. *Scene 5*: The Rothschild Shop, 1788. *Scene 6*: The Rothschild Shop, 1788. *Scene 7*: The Rothschild Shop, 1804. *Scene 8*: Prince William's Study, 1804. *Scene 9*: The Rothschild Shop, 1804.

Act 2, Scene 1: The London Royal Stock Exchange, 1805. *Scene 2*: The London Royal Stock Exchange, 1806. *Scene 3*: The Garden of Hannah Cohen, London, 1806-1811. *Scene 4*: The Rothschild Home, 1812. *Scene 5*: The Ballroom at Aix-La-Chappelle, 1818. *Scene 6*: The Rothschild Home, 1818. *Scene 7*: Various European Capitals, 1818. *Scene 8*: The Rothschild Home, 1818. *Scene 9*: Finale.

ACT 1
Prologue
"Pleasure and Privilege"
K. Curtis, Ensemble
Scene 2
"One Room"
H. Linden, L. Martin
Scene 3
"He Tossed a Coin"
H. Linden, T. Trelfa, K. Bridges, J. Peck, Ensemble
Scene 5
"Sons"
H. Linden, L. Martin, L. Franklin, R. Benson, M. Maitland, M. Spera
Scene 7
"Everything"
P. Hecht, L. Martin, D. Garfield, A. Gruet, T. Jerome, C. Sarandon
Scene 8
"Rothschild and Sons"
H. Linden, P. Hecht, D. Garfield, A. Gruet, T. Jerome, C. Sarandon
Scene 9
"Allons"
K. Curtis, Male Ensemble
"Rothschild and Sons" (reprise)
H. Linden, P. Hecht, D. Garfield, A. Gruet, T. Jerome, C. Sarandon
"Sons" (reprise)
L. Martin, H. Linden

ACT 2
Scene 1
Hymn: "Give England Strength"
K. Curtis, Male Ensemble
"This Amazing London Town"
P. Hecht
Scene 2
"They Say"
P. Tracey, Male Ensemble
"I'm in Love! I'm in Love!"
P. Hecht
Scene 3
"I'm in Love! I'm in Love!" (reprise)
J. Clayburgh
Scene 4
"In My Own Lifetime"
H. Linden
Scene 5
"Have You Ever Seen a Prettier Little Congress?"
K. Curtis
"Stability"
K. Curtis, Ensemble
Scene 7
"Bonds"
P. Hecht, D. Garfield, A. Gruet, T. Jerome, C. Sarandon, K. Curtis, Ensemble
Scene 9
(The Will—Finale)
(H. Linden)

1970.16 (PAUL SILLS') STORY THEATRE

An Entertainment in Two Acts, 10 Scenes. Adapted and directed by Paul Sills. Setting and projections by Michael Devine. Costumes by Stephanie Kline. Lighting by H. R. Poindexter. (Songs by Bob Dylan, Country Joe McDonald, George Harrison, Hamid Hamilton Camp.) Music performed by The True Brethren (Raphael Grinage, Lauren Karapetian, Loren Pickford, Lewis Ross). Special consultant, Viola Spolin. Produced by Zev Bufman. Presented with the help and cooperation of City Center of Music and Drama, Inc. (Norman Singer, Executive director), The Shubert

Organization, and Theatre Development Fund, as originally presented at the Mark Taper Forum by Center Theatre Group of Los Angeles (Gordon Davidson, Artistic director). Opened 26 October 1970 at the Ambassador Theatre and closed 3 July 1971 after 245 performances[1].

CAST (in alphabetical order): PETER BONERZ, HAMID HAMILTON CAMP, MELINDA DILLON, MARY FRANN, VALERIE HARPER, RICHARD LIBERTINI, PAUL SAND, RICHARD SCHAAL.

ACT 1[2]

Scene 1

"A Lot Can Happen in a Day"
H. H. Camp
(*Music and Lyrics by* Hamid Hamilton Camp.)

The Little Peasant
Little Peasant: H. H. Camp. *Peasant's Wife*: M. Dillon. *Cowherd*: P. Sand. *Judge*: P. Bonerz. *Farmer's Wife*: V. Harper. *Parson*: R. Libertini. *Farmer*: R. Schaal. *Rich Peasants*: M. Dillon, M. Frann, P. Sand, V. Harper.

Scene 2

The Bremen Town Musicians
Ass: R. Schaal. *Hound*: P. Sand. *Cat*: P. Bonerz. *Cock*: R. Libertini. *Robbers*: V. Harper, H. H. Camp.

Scene 3

Is He Fat
Man #1: H. H. Camp. *Man #2*: R. Schaal. *Sexton*: R. Libertini. *Parson*: P. Bonerz.

Scene 4

The Robber Bridegroom
Miller: R. Schaal. *Daughter*: M. Dillon. *Robber Bridegroom*: P. Sand. *Old Woman*: V. Harper. *Maiden*: M. Frann. *Robbers*: P. Bonerz, R. Schaal, R. Libertini.

"I'll Be Your Baby Tonight"
H. H. Camp
(*Music and Lyrics by* Bob Dylan.)

Scene 5

Henny Penny
Henny Penny: V. Harper. *Cocky Locky*: R. Schaal. *Ducky Daddles*: H. H. Camp. *Goosey Poosey*: M. Dillon. *Turkey Lurkey*: P. Sand. *Foxy Woxy*: R. Libertini.

"Fixin' To Die Rag"
L. Ross
(*Music and Lyrics by* Joe McDonald.)

ACT 2

"About Time"
H.H. Camp
(*Music and Lyrics by* Hamid Hamilton Camp.)

Scene 1

The Master Thief
Old Man, Parson: R. Schaal. *Wife*: M. Dillon. *Master Thief*: P. Bonerz. *Count*: R. Libertini. *Soldiers*: H. H. Camp, R. Schaal, P. Sand. *Countess*: V. Harper. *Clerk*: P. Sand.

"Dear Landlord"
H. H. Camp
(*Music and Lyrics by* Bob Dylan.)

Scene 2

Venus and the Cat
Man: R. Schaal. *Cat*: M. Frann. *Venus*: V. Harper.

Scene3

The Fisherman and His Wife
Narrator: H. H. Camp. *Fisherman*: R. Libertini. *Flounder*: P. Bonerz. *Wife*: M. Dillon.

Scene 4

Two Crows
Crow #1: P. Bonerz. *Crow #2*: H. H. Camp.

Scene 5

The Golden Goose
Mother, Eldest Daughter: V. Harper. *Simpleton*: P. Sand. *Eldest Son, Peasant*: R. Schaal. *Little Gray Man, King*: H. H. Camp. *Second Son, Parson*: R. Libertini. *Second Daughter*: M. Frann. *Sexton*: P. Bonerz. *Princess*: M. Dillon.

"Here Comes the Sun"
L. Ross
(*Music and Lyrics by* George Harrison.)

---

[1]Joined by *METAMORPHOSES* in repertory 22 April 1971.
[2]The order of scenes was substantially revised during the run.

1970.17 LIGHT, LIVELY AND YIDDISH

A Musical in Two Acts, 15 Scenes, in Yiddish. Adaptation by Ben Bonus. Music by Eli Rubinstein. Text and lyrics by Abram Shulman, Wolf and Sylvia Younin. Additional texts by M. Gershenson, Ch. N. Bialik, Ch. Cheffer, Mina Bern. Sets by Josef Ijaky. Costumes by Sylvia Friedlander. Musical conductor, Renee Solomon. Musical staging and choreography by Felix Fibich. Directed by Mina Bern. Produced by Sol Dickstein. Opened 27 October 1970 at the Belasco Theatre and closed 10 January 1971 after 87 performances.

CAST (in order of appearance): *English Narrator*: DAVID ELLIN. *Zelde* with Her Koshik (Basket): MINA BERN. *Rag Seller*: LEON LIEBGOLD. *Dumpling Woman*: REIZL BOZYK. *Bagel Woman*: LILI LILIANA. *Sosye the Peacemaker*: MIRIAM KRESSYN. *Nokhem the Broker*: SEYMOUR REXITE. *Kvas Seller*: David Carey. *Gitele*, the Young Girl: Diane Cypkin. *Hershele of Ostropolie*: DEN BONUS. *Kalmen*, the Rich Man: LEON LIEBGOLD. *Innkeeper*: REIZL BOZYK.

Dancers: Marcia Brooks, Helen Butleroff, Jack Dyville, Harry Endicott, Robyn Kessler, Tony Masullo, Maggie Masullo, Eileen McCabe, Joseph Tripolino.

Act 1: The shtetl.

Act 2: New York City and Tel Aviv, Israel.

ACT 1

"A Yarid" (A Fair)
"Yiddish" (Yiddish)
"Shver Tsu Zain A Tidene" (It's Hard To Be a Jewish Woman)
"Dus Hut Mir Kainer Nit Gezugt" (Nobody Told Me This)
"Tsen Azeyger" (Ten O'Clock)
"Tfile Tsu Got" (Prayer to God)
"Vu Iz Yoysher?" (Where Is Justice?)
"A Freilekhs" (A Joyful Song)

ACT 2

"Light, Lively and Yiddish"—(arrangement of Yiddish Folk Music)
"Khavertes" (Girl Friends)
"Tsu Mayn Dor" (The Song of My Generation)
"Israel" (Israel)
"A Shukh Putser" (Shoe Shine Boy)
"A Briv" (A Letter)
"S'vet Kumen Der Tog" (The Day Will Come)

1970.18 THE PRESIDENT'S DAUGHTER

A Yiddish-American Musical Comedy in Two Acts and a Prologue. Book by H. Kalmanov. Music by Murray Rumshinsky. Lyrics and direction by Jacob Jacobs. Dances staged by Henrietta Jacobson. Musical director, Murray Rumshinsky. Production design by Barry Arnold. Produced by Jacob Jacobs. Opened 3 November 1970 at the Billy Rose Theatre and closed 2 January 1971 after 72 performances.

CAST (in order of appearance): *Frances*: Michele Burke. *Esther*: Charlotte Gingold. *Yanek*: JACK RECHTZEIT. *Minke*: DIANA GOLDBERG. *Freidel*: CHAYELE ROSENTHAL. *Nathan*: JACOB JACOBS. *Sam Golden*: GEORGE GUIDALL. *Reb Yosel*: Jaime Lewin [Herman Levine]. *Bertha*: Thelma Mintz. *Miriam*: Rachela Relis.

The action takes place at the present time in Sam Golden's Flatbush (Brooklyn) home within a period of several weeks.

PROLOGUE

"Women's Liberation"
D. Goldberg, T. Mintz, C. Cooper, R. Relis

ACT 1

"The President's Daughter"
C. Rosenthal

"I Have What You Want!"
D. Goldberg, J. Jacobs

"A Lesson in Yiddish"
J. Rechtzeit

"Everything Is Possible in Life"
C. Rosenthal, G. Guidall
"Welcome, Mr. Golden!"
C. Rosenthal, J. Jacobs, D. Goldberg, C. Cooper, J. Lewin, M. Burke

ACT 2
"Stiochket"
J. Rechtzeit
"Without a Mother"
C. Rosenthal
"Love at Golden Years"
R. Relis, J. Lewin
"If Only I Could Be a Kid Again"
C. Rosenthal
"An Old Man Shouldn't Be Born"
J. Jacobs
"We Two"
D. Goldberg, J. Rechtzeit
"What More Do I Need?"
G. Guidall
"What Would You Do?"
C. Rosenthal, J. Jacobs

1970.19 TWO BY TWO

A Musical in Two Acts. Book by Peter Stone. Based on the play "The Flowering Peach" by Clifford Odets. Music by Richard Rodgers. Lyrics by Martin Charnin. Production conceived and directed by Joe Layton. Scenery by David Hays. Costumes by Fred Voelpel. Lighting by John Gleason. Musical direction by Jay Blackton. Orchestrations by Eddie Sauter. Dance and vocal arrangements by Trude Rittman. Production supervisor, Jerome Whyte. Projections designed by Cris Alexander. Produced by Richard Rodgers. Opened 10 November 1970 at the Imperial Theatre and closed 11 September 1971 after 351 performances.

CAST (in order of appearance): *Noah*: DANNY KAYE. *Esther*: JOAN COPELAND. *Japheth*: WALTER WILLISON. *Shem*: HARRY GOZ. *Leah*: MARILYN COOPER. *Ham*: MICHAEL KARM. *Rachel*: TRICIA O'NEILL. *Goldie*: MADELINE KAHN.

The action takes place before, during, and after the Flood (in biblical times).

Act 1: In and around Noah's home.

Act 2: Forty days and forty nights later. On the ark, and atop Mt. Ararat.

ACT 1
"Why Me?"
D. Kaye
"Put Him Away"
H. Goz, M. Karm, M. Cooper
The Gitka's Song
The Gitka (instrumental)
"Something Somewhere"
W. Willison, the Family
"You Have Got to Have a Rudder on the Ark" D. Kaye, H. Goz, M. Karm, W. Willison
"Something Doesn't Happen"
T. O'Neil, J. Copeland
"An Old Man"
J. Copeland
"Ninety Again!"
D. Kaye
"Two By Two"
D. Kaye, the Family
"I Do Not Know a Day I Did Not Love You"
W. Willison
"Something Somewhere" (reprise)
D. Kaye

ACT 2
"When It Dries"
D. Kaye, the Family
"Two By Two" (reprise)
D. Kaye, J. Copeland
"You"
D. Kaye
"The Golden Ram"
M. Kahn
"Poppa Knows Best"
D. Kaye, W. Willison
"I Do Not Know a Day I Did Not Love You" (reprise)
T. O'Neil, W. Willison
"As Far As I'm Concerned"
H. Goz, M. Cooper
"Hey, Girlie"
D. Kaye
"The Covenant"
D. Kaye

1970.20 THE ME NOBODY KNOWS

A Musical in Two Acts[3]. (Book[4] adapted by Robert H. Livingston and Herb Schapiro.) Based on the book of the same name, edited by Stephen M. Joseph. Music by Gary William Friedman. Lyrics by Will Holt[5]. Original idea and additional lyrics by Herb Schapiro. Directed by Robert H. Livingston. Musical numbers staged by Patricia Birch. Scenery and lighting by Clarke Dunham. Costumes by Patricia Quinn Stuart. Media design and photography by Stan Goldberg and Mopsy. (Musical) Arrangements and orchestrations, Gary William Friedman. Musical director, Edward Strauss. Produced by Jeff Britton in association with Sagittarius Productions, Inc. Opened 18 December 1970 at the Helen Hayes Theatre, closing 28 August 1971; reopened 15 September 1971 at the Longacre Theatre and closed 28 November 1971 after 370 performances. Total, including Off-Broadway: 578 performances.

CAST (in order of appearance): *Rhoda*: Melanie Henderson. *Lillian*: Laura Michaels. *Carlos*: Jose Fernandez. *Millie Mae*: Irene Cara. *Benjamin*: Douglas Grant. *Catherine*: Beverly Ann Bremers. *Melba*: Gerri Dean. *Lloyd*: Northern J. Calloway. *Donald*: Paul Mace. *Clorox*: Carl Thoma. *William*: Kevin Lindsay. *Nell*: Hattie Winston.

The action takes place at the present time in New York's ghetto.

ACT 1
"Dream Babies" (*Lyrics by* Herb Shapiro.)
G. Dean
"Light Sings" (*Lyrics by* Herb Shapiro.)
K. Lindsay, Company
"This World" (*Lyrics by* Herb Shapiro.)
Company
"Numbers"
Company
"What Happens to Life"
L. Michaels, N. J. Calloway
"Take Hold the Crutch"
H. Winston, Company
"Flying Milk and Runaway Plates"
D. Grant, Company
"I Love What the Girls Have"
P. Mace
"How I Feel"
B. A. Bremers, J. Fernandez
"If I Had a Million Dollars"
Company

ACT 2
"Fugue for Four Girls"
I. Cara, L. Michaels, B. A. Bremers, H. Winston
"Rejoice"
C. Thoma

[3]First produced in New York Off-Broadway 18 May 1970 at the Orpheum Theatre for 208 performances.
[4]The spoken text in this production was written by children between the ages of 7—18 attending New York City public schools in Bedford-Stuyvesant, Harlem, Jamaica, Manhattan and the Youth House in the Bronx.
[5]The lyrics (Fugue for Four Girls; Rejoice; The Horse; War Babies) are children's poems, presented exactly as they wrote them. All other lyrics, except where noted, are by Will Holt.

"Sounds"
H. Winston, B. A. Bremers
"The Tree"
J. Fernandez
"Robert, Alvin, Wendell and Jo Jo"
M. Henderson, L. Michaels, I. Cara, K. Lindsay
"Jail-Life Walk"
P. Mace, N. J. Calloway, C. Thoma
"Something Beautiful"
M. Henderson
"Black"
D. Grant, C. Thoma, I. Cara, N. J. Calloway, G. Dean, H. Winston, M. Henderson, K. Lindsay
"The Horse" (The White Horse)
N. J. Calloway
"Let Me Come In"
Company
"War Babies"
N. J. Calloway

1970.21 LOVELY LADIES, KIND GENTLEMEN

A Musical Comedy in Two Acts, 15 Scenes. Book by John Patrick. Based on the novel "The Teahouse of the August Moon" by Vern J. Sneider and the play of the same name by John Patrick. Music and lyrics by Stan Freeman and Franklin Underwood. Directed by Lawrence Kasha. Dances and musical numbers staged by Marc Breaux. Scenic production by Oliver Smith. Costumes by Freddy Wittop. Lighting by Thomas Skelton. Musical direction and choral arrangements by Theodore Saidenberg. Orchestrations by Philip J. Lang. Dance arrangements by Albert Mello. Associate choreographer, Gary Menteer. Associate producer, Angus Equities, Inc. Produced by Herman Levin. Opened 28 December 1970 at the Majestic Theatre and closed 9 January 1971 after 16 performances.

CAST (in order of appearance): *Sakini*: KENNETH NELSON. *Missionary*: David Steele. *Colonel Wainwright Purdy III*: DAVID BURNS. *Sergeant Gregovich*: LOU WILLS. *Captain Fisby*: RON HUSMANN. *Old Lady*: Sachi Shimizu. *Daughter*: Tisa Chang. *Children*: June Angela, Gene Profanato, Dana Shimizu. *Lady Astor*: Herself. *Ancient Man*: Sab Shimono. *Mr. Seiko*: Alvin Lum. *Miss Higa Jiga*: Lori Chinn. *Mr. Oshira*: David Thomas. *Mr. Hokaida*: Big Lee. *Lotus Blossom*: ELEANOR CALBES. *Mr. Keora*: Sab Shimono. *Captain McLean*: REMAK RAMSAY. *Logan*: David Steele. *Miller*: James Weston. *O'Malley*: Stephen Bolster. *Cabot*: Stuart Craig Wood. *Stock*: James B. Spann. *Lipshitz*: Kirk Norman. *Swenson*: James Hobson. *Cardone*: Dennis Roth. *Mancini*: Richard Nieves. *Colombo*: Charlie J. Rodriguez.

Okinawans and Americans: Barbara Coggin, Catherine Dando., Joan Nelson, Sumiko, Tisa Chang, Lori Chinn, Christi Curtis, Marjory Edson, Rosalie King, Sylvia Nolan, Jo Ann Ogawa, Sachi Shimizu, Susan Sigrist, Stephen Bolster, James Hobson, Alvin Lum, Richard Nieves, Kirk Norman, Charlie J. Rodriguez, Dennis Roth, Sab Shimono, James B. Spann, David Steele, James Weston, Stuart Craig Wood, Henry Boyer, Paul Charles, Charlie Goeddertz, J. J. Jepson, Tim Ramirez, Steven Ross, Joe Milan, Ken Urmston.

The action takes place on the island of Okinawa during a few months in 1946.

Act 1, Scene 1: Okinawa. *Scene 2*: Purdy's Office. *Scene 3*: Outside Purdy's Office. *Scene 4*: Village Square in Tobiki. Fisby's Office. *Scene 5*: Outskirts of Tobiki. *Scene 6*: Purdy and Fisby's Office. *Scene 7*: Village Square in Tobiki; Fisby's Office; On the way to Big Koza. *Scene 8*: The Grove. *Scene 9*: Outskirts of Tobiki.

Act 2, Scene 1: The Teahouse. *Scene 2*: Village Street. *Scene 3*: Fisby's Office. *Scene 4*: Village Street. *Scene 5*: Village Shacks. *Scene 6*: The Teahouse.

ACT 1
Scene 1
"With a Snap of My Finger"
K. Nelson, Okinawans, G.I.s
Scene 2
"Right Hand Man"
D. Burns, K. Nelson, R. Husmann, G.I.s
Scene 4
"Find Your Own Cricket"
K. Nelson, D. Thomas, L. Chinn, Villagers
"One Side of World"
K. Nelson
Scene 5
"Geisha"
E. Calbes
"You Say—They Say"
K. Nelson, Villagers
"This Time"
R. Husmann
Scene 7
"Simple Words"
E. Calbes
"Garden Guaracha"
R. Ramsay
("Find Your Own Cricket" reprise)
(K. Nelson, Villagers)
Scene 8
("Simple Words" reprise)
(R. Husman, E. Calbes)
"If It's Good Enough for Lady Astor"
R. Husmann, R. Ramsay, K. Nelson, Villagers
Scene 9
("Batata")(K. Nelson, R. Husman, R. Ramsay, D. Thomas, Villagers)

ACT 2
Scene 1
"Chaya"
K. Nelson, Villagers
"Call Me Back"
R. Husmann, R. Ramsay, K. Nelson
Scene 2
"Lovely Lades, Kind Gentlemen"
K. Nelson
Scene 3
"You've Broken a Fine Woman's Heart"
D. Burns
("Right Hand Man" reprise)
(K. Nelson)
Scene 5
"One More for the Last One"
K. Nelson, L. Wills, G.I.s, Villagers
Scene 6
("With a Snap of My Finger" reprise)
(K. Nelson)

1971.01 SOON

A Rock Opera in Two Acts, a Prologue and 10 Scenes. (Book) Adaption by Martin Duberman. Based on an original story by Joseph Martinez Kookoolis, Scott Fagan. Music by Joseph M. Kookoolis and Scott Fagan. Lyrics by Scott Fagan. Scenery by Kert Lundell. Lighting by Jules Fisher. Costumes by David Chapman. Orchestrations by Howard Wyeth, Jon Huston. Musical direction by Louis St. Louis. Vocal arrangements by Louis St. Louis and Jacqueline Penn. Choreography by Fred Benjamin. Additional staging by Gerald Freedman. Audio design by Jack Shearing. Produced by Bruce W. Stark and Sagittarius Productions, Inc. Opened 12 January 1971 at the Ritz Theatre and closed 13 January 1971 after 3 performances.

CAST (in order of appearance): *Kelly*: BARRY BOSTWICK. *Annie*: MARTA HEFLIN. *Wilson Wilson*: DENNIS BELLINE. *Michael*: RICHARD GERE. *Neil*: JOSEPH CAMPBELL BUTLER. *Henry*: PETER ALLEN. *Groupies (5)*: *Hope*: Marion Ramsey. *Faith*: Leata Galloway. *Charity*: Vickie Sue Robinson. *Rita*: Pamela Pentony. *Sharon*: Nell Carter. *Henry's Friends (3)*: *Jimmy*: Singer Williams. *Bobby*: Michael Jason. *Phil*: John C. Nelson. *Record Company Executives (4)*: *Mr. Par* (Corporation Head): Del Hinkley. *Elsworth Median* (Technical Advisor): Angus Cairns. *Gran Statisto* (Comptroller): Larry Spinelli. *Al Ti Telson* (Electronic Expert): Paul Eichel. *Songwriter*: Tony Middleton. *Psychedelic Necktie*: Pendleton Brown.

Act 1, Scene 1: On the Road. The Country. *Scene 2*: Coming to the City. *Scene 3*: The City. *Scene 4*: Henry's Office. *Scene 5*: The Club. *Scene 6*: Around the City. *Scene 7*: The Offices of the Music Industry.

Act 2, Scene 1: A Series of Recording Sessions. *Scene 2*: City Downs. *Scene 3*: On the Tour.

ACT 1
Prologue
"Let the World Begin Again"
Scene 1
"In Your Hands"
"I See the Light"/"Gentle Sighs"
Scene 2
"Roll Out the Morning"
Scene 3
"Everybody's Running"
Scene 4
"Henry Is Where It's At"
Scene 5
"Music, Music"
"Glad to Know Ya"
"Rita Cheeta"
Scene 6
"Henry's Dream Theme"
"To Touch the Sky"
Scene 7
The Chase:
"Everybody's Running"
"Marketing, Marketing"
"Sweet Henry Loves You"
"One More Time"
"Straight"
"Wait"

ACT 2
Scene 1
"Faces, Names, Places"
"Annie's Thing"
"Doing the High"
"Soon"
Scene 2
"Country Store Living"
"What's Gonna Happen to Me"
"On the Charts"
"Molecules"
"So Much That I Know"
"Child of Sympathy"
"Frustration"
Scene 3
"Doing the High" (reprise)
"It Won't Be Long"

1971.02 ARI

A Musical in Two Acts, 18 Scenes. Book and lyrics by Leon Uris. Based on his novel "Exodus." Music by Walt Smith. Production directed by Lucia Victor. Choreography by Talley Beatty. Scenery by Robert Randolph. Costumes by Sara Brook. Lighting by Nananne Porcher. Vocal arrangements and musical direction, Stanley Lebowsky. Orchestrations by Philip J. Lang. Dance and incidental music by Peter Howard. Additional music by William Fisher. Associate producers, Ronald Reckseit, Lisa Lipsky. Produced by Ken Gaston and Leonard J. Goldberg in association with Henry Stern. Opened 15 January 1971 at the Mark Hellinger Theatre and closed 30 January 1971 after 19 performances.

CAST (in order of appearance): *Joab*: JOSEPH DELLA SORTE. *Zev*: MARK ZELLER. *David*: MARTIN ROSS. *Mandria*, the Greek: C. K. ALEXANDER. *General Sutherland*: JACK GWILLIM. *Major Caldwell*: JAMIE ROSS. *Ari Ben Canaan*: DAVID CRYER. *Mark Parker*: NORWOOD SMITH. *Kitty Fremont*: CONSTANCE TOWERS. *Dov*: JOHN SAVAGE. *Karen*: JACQUELINE MAYRO. *Benjy*: Roger Morgan. *Armeteau*: Alexander Orfaly. *Friend of Armeteau*: Ed Becker. *Captain Henley*: Casper Roos.

Refugee Children: Tracey Eman, Kelley Boa, Mona Daleo, Toni Lund, Lynn Reynolds, Timmy Ousey, Todd Jones, Johnny Welch, Tony Dean. *Refugees and British Soldiers*: *Dancers*: Bryant Baker, Bjarne Buchtrup, Ron Crofoot, Richard Dodd, Pi Douglass, Richard Maxon, Ronn Steinman, Carol Estey, Reggie Israel, Karen L. Jablons, Joanna Mendl, Gayle Pines, Deborah Strauss. *Singers*: Ed Becker, Ted Bloecher, Bennett Hill, Henry Lawrence, Art Mathews, Casper Roos, D. Brian Wallach, Bonnie Marcus, Patricia Noal, Susan Schevers, Suzanne Horn.

The action takes place on the island of Cyprus in 1947.

Act 1, Scene 1: Beach near Famagusta, Cyprus, at night. *Scene 2*: Mandria's House, immediately after. *Scene 3*: A Waterfront Cafe, the next night. *Scene 4*: Detention Camp, Children's Compound, the following afternoon. *Scene 5*: A Waterfront Cafe, Quayside, Larnaca, a few days later. *Scene 6*: Detention Camp, Children's Compound, the following week. *Scene 7*: A Military Camp, a week later. *Scene 8*: Detention Camp, a few days later. *Scene 9*: The Dispensary. *Scene 10*: Mandrias' House, a few days later. British H.G. the same day. Mandria's House, the following afternoon.

Act 2, Scene 1: A Hidden Cove, the next morning. *Scene 2*: General Sutherland's Quarters, noon. *Scene 3*: Detention Camp, 2:00 P.M. *Scene 4*: Military Camp, 5:00 P.M. *Scene 5*: Dockside, Kyrenia, 6:00 P.M. *Scene 6*: Parker's Hotel's Room, immediately thereafter. *Scene 7*: Aboard the *Exodus*, Kyrenia Harbor, 80th hour of the hunger strike through 120 hour. *Scene 8*: Dockside, Kyrenia, immediately thereafter.

ACT 1
"Children's Lament"
Children
Scene 1
"Yerushaliam"
D. Cryer
"The Saga of Haganah"
M. Ross, M. Zeller, J. Della Sorte, C. K. Alexander
Scene 2
"The Saga of Haganah" (reprise)
C. K. Alexander
Scene3
"Give Me One Good Reason"
C. Towers
Scene 4
"Dov's Nightmare"
J. Savage, Victims of the Holocaust
"Karen's Lullaby"
J. Mayro
Scene 5
"Aphrodite"
C. K. Alexander, A. Orfaly
Scene 6
"My Galilee"
D. Cryer, Palestinians
Scene 7
"The Lord Helps Those Who Help Themselves"
M. Ross, Palestinians
Scene 8
"Alphabet Song"
C. Towers, Children
Tactics
Scene 9
"Give Me One Good Reason" (reprise)
C. Towers
Scene 10
"My Brother's Keeper"
D. Cryer

ACT 2
Scene 1
"The Exodus"
M. Ross, Ensemble
Scene 2
"He'll Never Be Mine"
C. Towers
Scene 3
"One Flag"
J. Mayro, Children
Scene 4
"The Lord Helps Those Who Help Themselves" (reprise)
C. K. Alexander

Scene 7
"I See What I Choose to See"
J. Mayro, J. Savage
"Hora-Galilee" (dance)
J. Mayro, J. Savage, Children, Palestinians
"Ari's Promise"
D. Cryer
Scene 8
Finale: "Ari's Promise" (reprise)
The Company
"The Exodus" (reprise)

1971.03 NO, NO, NANETTE

The New 1925 Musical (A Revival of the Musical Comedy) in Three Acts[6]. Book by Otto Harbach and Frank Mandel. (Book) Adapted and directed by Burt Shevelove. (Based on the comedy "My Lady Friends" by Frank Mandel and Emil Nyitray, based on the story "Oh, James"/"His Lady Friends" by May Edington). Music by Vincent Youmans. Lyrics by Irving Caesar and Otto Harbach. Dances and musical numbers staged by Donald Saddler. (Settings and costumes) Designed by Raoul Pene du Bois. Lighting by Jules Fisher. Musical direction and vocal arrangements by Buster Davis. Orchestrations by Ralph Burns. Dance music arranged and incidental music composed by Luther Henderson. Colston and Clements at the Twin Pianos. Sound by Jack Shearing. Assistant choreographer, Mary Ann Niles. Entire production supervised by Busby Berkeley. Produced by Pyxidium Ltd. (Cyma Rubin)[7]. Opened 19 January 1971 at the 46th Street Theatre and closed 4 February 1973 after 861 performances.

CAST (in order of appearance): *Pauline*: PATSY KELLY. *Lucille Early*: HELEN GALLAGHER. *Sue Smith*: RUBY KEELER. *Jimmy Smith*: JACK GILFORD. *Billy Early*: BOBBY VAN. *Tom Trainor*: Roger Rathburn. *Nanette*: SUSAN WATSON. *Flora Latham*: K. C. Townshend. *Betty Brown*: Loni Zoe Ackerman. *Winnie Winslow*: Pat Lysinger. THE BUSBY BERKELEY GIRLS.

Nanette's Friends: Bob Becker, John Beecher, Joretta Bohannon, Roger Braun, Marcia Brushingham, Kenneth Carr, Jennie Chandler, Kathy Conry, Christine Cox, Kevin Daly, Ed Dixon, Ellen Elias, Mercedes Ellington, Jon Engstrom, Marian Haraldson, Gregg Harlan, Jamie Haskins, Gwen Hillier, Sayra Hummel, Scott Hunter, Dottie Lester, Cheryl Locke, Joanne Lotsko, Mary Ann Niles, Kate O'Brady, Sue Ohman, Jill Owens, Ken Ploss, John Roach, Linda Rose, Ron Schwinn, Sonja Stuart, Monica Tiller, Pat Trott, Phyllis Wallach.

The action takes place on a weekend in early summer of 1925.

Act 1: The home of James Smith, New York City.

Act 2: The garden of Chickadee Cottage, Atlantic City.

Act 3: The living room at Chickadee Cottage, Atlantic City.

ACT 1
"Too Many Rings Around Rosie"
H. Gallagher, Boys, Girls
"I've Confessed to the Breeze"
S. Watson, R. Rathburn
"Call of the Sea"
B. Van, Girls
"I Want to Be Happy"
J. Gilford, S. Watson, R. Keeler, Boys, Girls
"No, No, Nanette"
S. Watson, R. Rathburn
Finaletto Act 1
S. Watson, Boys, Girls

ACT 2
"Peach on the Beach"
S. Watson, Boys, Girls
"Tea for Two"
S. Watson, R. Rathburn, Boys, Girls
"You Can Dance With Any Girl at All"
H. Gallagher, B. Van
Finaletto Act 2
Entire Company

ACT 3
"Telephone Girlie"
B. Van, L. Z. Ackerman, K. C. Townshend, P. Lysinger
"Where-Has-My Hubby-Gone-Blues"
H. Gallagher, Boys
"Waiting for You"
S. Watson, R. Rathburn
"Take a Little One-Step" (from *LOLLIPOP*)
R. Keeler, B. Van, H. Gallagher, P. Kelly, Boys, Girls
(*Lyrics by* Zelda Sears.)
Finale
Entire Company

[6]Originally produced in New York 16 September 1925 at the Globe Theatre for 321 performances.

[7]This revival originally conceived by Harry Rigby.

1971.04 OH! CALCUTTA!

A Musical Entertainment (Revue) in Two Acts, 13 Scenes[8]. Devised by Kenneth Tynan. Entire production conceived and directed by Jacques Levy. Contributors: Samuel Beckett, Jules Feiffer, Dan Greenburg, John Lennon, Jacques Levy, Leonard Melfi, David Newman and Robert Benton, Sam Shepard, Clovis Trouille, Kenneth Tynan, Sherman Yellen. Music and lyrics by The Open Window (Robert Dennis, Peter Schickele, Stanley Walden). Choreography by Margo Sappington. Scenery by James Tilton. Lighting by David F. Segal. Costumes by Fred Voelpel. Projected media designs by Gardner Compton and Emile Ardolino. Still photography by Michael Childers. Musical director, Norman Bergen. Production supervisor, Michael Thoma. An E.P.I.C. Production. Opened 25 February 1971 at the Belasco Theatre and closed 12 August 1972 after 606 performances. Total for Broadway and Off-Broadway runs: 1310 performances.

CAST: Mel Auston, Raina Barrett, Ray Edelstein, Samantha Harper, Patricia Hawkins, William Knight, Mitchell McGuire, Pamela Pilkenton, Gary Rethmeier, Nancy Tribush.

ACT 1
Prologue
Scene 1
Taking Off the Robe ("Oh! Calcutta!")
The Company
Scene 2
Dick & Jane
R. Barrett, G. Rethmeier
Scene 3
"Suite for Five Letters"
M. McGuire, S. Harper, P. Hawkins, W. Knight, P. Pilkenton
Scene 4
"(Will Answer All) Sincere Replies" (Song and Sketch)
C. Howard, S. Harper, G. Retheimer, J. Shearer
Scene 5
"Paintings of Clovis Trouille"
The Open Window
Scene 6
"Jack & Jill" (Song and Sketch)
P. Hawkins, M. McGuire
Scene 7
Delicious Indignities, (or The Deflowering of Helen Axminster)
S. Harper, W. Knight
(*Scene*: An Elegantly Appointed Study in Knightsbridge, 1896.)
Scene 8
Was It Good For You Too? ("Green Pants," "I Like the Look")
R. Barrett, C. Howard, W. Knight, P. Pilkenton, G. Retheimer, J. Shearer
(*Scene*: A Doctor's Office.)

ACT 2[9]
Scene 1
"Much Too Soon"
The Company, The Open Window
(*Music and Lyrics by* The Open Window and Jacques Levy.)

[8]Originally produced in New York Off-Broadway 17 June 1969 at the Eden Theatre for 704 performances.

[9]Added during run to open Act 2:
Who: Whom ("Exchanges of Information")
R. Barrett, C. Howard, D. Rosenbaum

Scene 2
"One on One" (Clarence and Mildred)
M. Auston, P. Pilkenton
Scene 3
Rock Garden
W. Knight, M. McGuire
(*Scene*: Saturday afternoon, just after lunch before the ball game.)
Scene 4
Four in Hand
M. Auston, M. McGuire, G. Retheimer, J. Shearer
Scene 5
"Coming Together, Going Together"
The Company
(Medley: "I Don't Have a Song to Sing," "I'm an Actor," "Ballerina," "I Want It," "Freeze Music," "I Want It" reprise)

1971.05 FOLLIES

A Musical in One Act. Book by James Goldman. Music and lyrics by Stephen Sondheim. Directed by Harold Prince and Michael Bennett. Choreography by Michael Bennett. Scenic Production designed by Boris Aronson. Costumes by Florence Klotz. Lighting by Tharon Musser. Musical direction by Harold Hastings. Orchestrations by Jonathan Tunick. Dance music arrangements by John Berkman. Production supervisor, Ruth Mitchell. Associate choreographer, Bob Avian. Produced by Harold Prince in association with Ruth Mitchell. Opened 4 April 1971 at the Winter Garden and closed 1 July 1972 after 522 performances.

CAST (in order of appearance): *Major-Domo*: Dick Latessa. *Sally Durant Plummer*: DOROTHY COLLINS. *Young Sally*: Marti Rolph. *Christine Crane*: ETHEL BARRYMORE COLT. *Willy Wheeler*: Fred Kelly. *Stella Deems*: MARY McCARTHY. *Max Deems*: John J. Martin. *Heidi Schiller*: Justine Johnston. *Chauffeur*: John Grigas. *Meredith Lane*: SHEILA SMITH. *Chet Richards*: Peter Walker. *Roscoe*: MICHAEL BARTLETT. *Deedee West*: Helon Blount. *Sandra Donovan*: Sonja Levkova. *Hattie Walker*: ETHEL SHUTTA. *Young Hattie*: Mary Jane Houdina. *Emily Whitman*: Marcie Stringer. *Theodore Whitman*: Charles Welch. *Vincent*: Victor Griffin. *Vanessa*: Jayne Turner. *Young Vincent*: Michael Misita. *Young Vanessa*: Graciela Daniele. *Solange LaFitte*: FIFI D'ORSAY. *Carlotta Campion*: YVONNE DE CARLO. *Phyllis Rogers Stone*: ALEXIS SMITH. *Benjamin Stone*: JOHN McMARTIN. *Young Phyllis*: Virginia Sandifur. *Young Ben*: Kurt Peterson. *Buddy Plummer*: GENE NELSON. *Young Buddy*: Harvey Evans. *Dimitri Weisman*: Arnold Moss. *Kevin*: Ralph Nelson. *Young Heidi*: Victoria Mallory.

Party Musicians: Taft Jordan, Aaron Bell, Charles Spies, Robert Curtis. *Showgirls*: Suzanne Briggs, Trudy Carson, Kathie Dalton, Ursula Maschmeyer, Linda Perkins, Margot Travers. *Singers and Dancers*: Graciela Daniele, Mary Jane Houdina, Rita O'Connor, Julie Pars, Suzanne Rogers, Roy Barry, Steve Boockvor, Michael Misita, Joseph Nelson, Ralph Nelson, Ken Urmston, Donald Weismuller.

The action takes place at the present time on the stage of the Weisman Theatre in New York.

MUSICAL NUMBERS
"Beautiful Girls"
M. Bartlett, Company
"Don't Look at Me"
D. Collins, J. McMartin
"Waiting for the Girls Upstairs"
G. Nelson, J. McMartin, A. Smith, D. Collins, H. Evans, K. Peterson, V. Sandifur, M. Rolph
"Rain on the Roof"
M. Stringer, C. Welch
"Ah, Paris!"
F. D'Orsay
"Broadway Baby"
E. Shutta
"The Road You Didn't Take"
J. McMartin
"Bolero d'Amour" (dance)
V. Griffin, J. Turner
"In Buddy's Eyes"
D. Collins
"Who's That Woman?"
M. McCarty, Company
"I'm Still Here"
Y. DeCarlo
"Too Many Mornings"
J. McMartin, D. Collins
"The Right Girl"
G. Nelson
"One More Kiss"
J. Johnston, V. Mallory
"Could I Leave You?"
A. Smith
Loveland:
1—The Folly of Love
"Loveland"
Ensemble
The Spirit of First Love: K. Dalton. *The Spirit of Young Love*: M. Travers. *The Spirit of True Love*: S. Briggs. *The Spirit of Pure Love*: T. Carson. *The Spirit of Romantic Love*: L. Perkins. *The Spirit of Eternal Love*: U. Maschmeyer.
2—The Folly of Youth
Scene: A Bower in Loveland.
"You're Gonna Love Tomorrow"
K. Peterson, V. Sandifur
"Love Will See Us Through"
H. Evans, M. Rolph
3—Buddy's Folly
Scene: A Thoroughfare in Loveland.
"The God-Why-Don't You-Love-Me Blues"
G. Nelson
(With the assistance of S. Rogers, R. O'Connor.)
4—Sally's Folly
Scene: A Boudoir in Loveland.
"Losing My Mind"
D. Collins
5—Phyllis's Folly
Scene: A Honky-Tonk in Loveland.
"The Story of Lucy and Jessie"
A. Smith, Dance Ensemble
6—Ben's Folly
Scene: A Supper Club in Loveland.
"Live, Laugh, Love"
J. McMartin, Dancing Ensemble

1971.06 JOHNNY JOHNSON

A Revival of the Legend (Play) with Music in Two Acts, 14 Scenes[10]. Play (book and lyrics) by Paul Green. Music by Kurt Weill. Directed by José Quintero. Choreography by Bertram Ross. Scenery designed by Peter Harvey. Costumes designed by Robert Fletcher. Lighting designed by Roger Morgan. Musical direction by Joseph Klein. Orchestrations by Kurt Weill. Produced by Timothy Gray and Robert Fletcher in association with Midge La Guardia. Opened and closed 11 April 1971 at the Edison Theatre after 1 performance.

CAST (in order of appearance): *Johnny Johnson*: RALPH WILLIAMS. *Minny Belle Tompkins*: ALICE CANNON. *Villagers*: Entire Company. *His Honor The Mayor*: PAUL MICHAEL. *Miz Smith*: June Helmers. *Grandpa Joe*: JAMES BILLINGS. *Photographer*: BOB LYDIARD. *Messenger*: Christopher Klein. *Anguish Howington*: GORDON MINARD. *Aggie (Tompkins)*: CHARLOTTE JONES. *Recruiting Sergeant*: ALEXANDER ORFALY. *Captain Valentine*: NORMAN CHASE. *Dr. McBray*: WAYNE SHERWOOD. *Private Jessell*: Clay Johns. *Goddess of Liberty*: Nadine Lewis. *Wounded French Soldiers*: James Billings, Clay Johns, Paul Michael, Gordon Minard, Alexander Orfaly, Norman Riggins, Wayne Sherwood. *English Sergeant*: NORMAN RIGGINS. *Corporal George*: ALEXANDER ORFALY. *Private Fairfax*: Paul Michael. *Private Goldberger*: JAMES BILLINGS. *Private Harwood*: GORDON MINARD. *Private Svenson*: Clay Johns. *Private (Patrick) O'Day*: Wayne Sherwood. *Johann Lang*, German Sniper: BOB LYDIARD. *French Nurse*: JUNE HELMERS. *Orderly*: Clay Johns. *Doctor*: Norman Riggins. *Sister from the Organization for the Delight of Soldiers Disabled in the Lien of Duty*: Charlotte Jones. *Chief (of the Allied High Command)*: JAMES BILLINGS. *Belgian Major-General*: ALEXANDER ORFALY. *British Commander*: Clay Johns. *French Major-General*: NORMAN RIGGINS. *American Commander*: PAUL MICHAEL. *Scottish Colonel*: Wayne Sherwood. *Captain*: Alexander Orfaly. *Lieutenant*: Clay Johns. *American Priest*: Norman Riggins. *German*

---

[10]Originally produced in New York 19 November 1936 at the 44th Street Theatre for 68 performances. For Musical Numbers, see original 1936 production. The script was revised from Three Acts, 13 Scenes, to Two Acts, 14 Scenes, with the first two acts combined into one.
Added for this production:
"The Sergeant's Chant" (Act 1, after "Farewell, Goodbye")
A. Orfaly
Dropped from this production:
"How Sweetly Friendship Binds"

Priest: Wayne Sherwood. *Military Policeman*: Clay Johns. *Dr. Mahodan*: JAMES BILLINGS. *Miss Newro*: Charlotte Jones. *Dr. Frewd*: ALEXANDER ORFALY. *Brother Thomas*: Paul Michael. *Brother George*: CLAY JOHNS. *Brother Theodore*: NORMAN RIGGINS. *Anguish Howington, Jr.*: Christopher Klein.

Act 1, Scene 1: A village somewhere in America, 1917. *Scene 2*: Minnie Belle's home, a few days later. *Scene 3*: A Recruiting Office, next day. *Scene 4*: The New York Harbor, sometime later. *Scene 5*: A road somewhere in France, several weeks later. *Scene 6*: A trench in the front, some days later. *Scene 7*: A shell-battered churchyard near the front line, before dawn the next day.

Act 2, Scene 1: An army hospital in France, a few days later. *Scene 2*: A French chateau behind the front lines, the next night. *Scene 3*: The edge of a great battlefield, later the same night. *Scene 4*: On the battlefield, a few minutes later. *Scene 5*: A psychiatrist's office in America, some weeks later. *Scene 6*: An insane asylum or house of balm, some years later. *Scene 7*: A street corner in an American city, much later.

1971.07 70, GIRLS, 70

A Musical in Two Acts, a Prologue and 18 Scenes. Book by Fred Ebb and Norman L. Martin. Based on the play "A Breath of Spring" by Peter Coke. Adapted by Joe Masteroff. Music by John Kander. Lyrics by Fred Ebb. Directed by Paul Aaron. Dances and musical numbers staged by Onna White. Sets and lighting by Robert Randolph. Costumes by Jane Greenwood. Musical direction and vocal arrangements by Oscar Kosarin. Orchestrations by Don Walker. Dance music by Dorothea Freitag. Associate choreographer, Martin Allen. Entire production supervised by Stanley Prager. Produced by Arthur Whitelaw in association with Seth Harrison. Opened 15 April 1971 at the Broadhurst Theatre and closed 15 May 1971 after 35 performances.

CAST (in alphabetical order): Thomas Anderson, Tommy Breslin, HANS CONRIED, Robert G. Dare, Sally DeMay, JOEY FAYE, DOROTHEA FREITAG, Ruth Gillette, Lloyd Harris, LILLIAN HAYMAN, HENRIETTA JACOBSON, GIL LAMB, LUCIE LANCASTER, Marjorie Leach, Abby Lewis, Steve Mills, MILDRED NATWICK, Naomi Price, LILLIAN ROTH, GOLDYE SHAW, Beau Tilden, Bobbi Tremain, Jay Velie, COLEY WORTH.

The action takes place at the present time in New York City.

Act 1, Scene 1: The Cornucopia Tea Room. *Scene 2*: The Broadhurst Theatre. *Scene 3*: Ida's Room. *Scene 4*: The Broadhurst Theatre. *Scene 5*: Sadie's Fur Salon. *Scene 6*: The Broadhurst Theatre. *Scene 7*: Lobby of the Sussex Arms. *Scene 8*: The Broadhurst Theatre. *Scene 9*: Bloomingdale's. *Scene 10*: Lobby of the Sussex Arms.

Act 2, Scene 1: The Broadhurst Theatre. *Scene 2*: Arctic Cold Storage Co. *Scene 3*: The Broadhurst Theatre. *Scene 4*: Lobby of the Sussex Arms. *Scene 5*: The Broadhurst Theatre. *Scene 6*: The Coliseum. *Scene 7*: The Broadhurst Theatre. *Scene 8*: A Chapel.

ACT 1
Prologue
"Old Folks"
Company
Scene 1
"Home"
M. Natwick, L. Roth, L. Lancaster, G. Lamb, H. Conried, L. Hayman, G. Shaw
Scene 2
"Broadway, My Street"
L. Hayman, G. Shaw, T. Anderson, J. Faye, L. Harris, H. Jacobson, B. Tilden, B. Tremain, J. Velie, C. Worth
Scene 4
"The Caper"
H. Conried
Scene 6
"Coffee in a Cardboard Cup"
L. Hayman, G. Shaw
Scene7
"You and I, Love"
S. Mills, A. Lewis, T. Anderson, R. Gillette, L. Harris, B. Tremain, J. Velie, C. Worth
"Do We?"
L. Lancaster, G. Lamb
"Hit It, Lorraine"
M. Natwick, H. Conried, L. Roth, L. Lancaster, D. Freitag
Scene 9
"See the Light"
L. Roth, J. Faye, C. Worth, T. Anderson, J. Velie

ACT 2
Entr'acte
R. Gillette, J. Faye, L. Harris, J. Velie
Scene1
"Boom Ditty Boom"
M. Natwick, H. Conried, L. Roth, G. Lamb, L. Hayman, L. Lancaster, G. Shaw
Scene 2
"Believe"
L. Hayman, M. Natwick, H. Conried, L. Roth, G. Lamb, L. Lancaster, G. Shaw
Scene 3
"Go Visit"
T. Breslin, H. Jacobson
Scene 4
"70, Girls, 70"
The Company
Scene 5
"The Elephant Song"
M. Natwick, L. Hayman, G. Shaw
Scene 8
"Yes"
M. Natwick, Company

1971.08 (OVID'S) METAMORPHOSES

An Entertainment in Two Acts, 10 Scenes. Adapted and translated with lyrics by Arnold Weinstein from Ovid's 'Metamorphoses.' Music composed and performed by The True Brethren. Directed by Paul Sills. Settings by James Trittipo. Costumes by Noel Taylor. Lighting by H. R. Poindexter. Produced by Zev Bufman. Opened 22 April 1971 at the Ambassador Theatre and closed 3 July 1971 after 35 performances[11].

CAST (in alphabetical order): Lewis Arquette, Regina Baff, Charles Bartlett, Hamid Hamilton Camp, Melinda Dillon, MacIntyre Dixon, Mary Frann, Valerie Harper, Paula Kelly, Richard Libertini, Paul Sand, Richard Schaal, Avery Schreiber, Penny White.

ACT 1
Scene 1
IO was the daughter of a priest, beloved (suddenly) of Jove, who changed her into a cow to protect her from the jealousy of his wife, Juno. Juno was not deceived, however, and tormented Io with a gadfly who drove her from continent to continent until she recovered her human form.
Scene 2
VULCAN AND VENUS AND MARS: Vulcan god of fire, artist in iron and other forged metals, was thrown from Olympus by his mother, Juno, because he was lame and ugly. In revenge Vulcan made a golden throne with magic chains and trapped Juno in it. He also trapped Venus, goddess of love (one of his several wives) and his brother Mars, god of war, in a golden net as they were making love.
Scene 3
PELEUS AND THETIS: Pelus was king of Iolchos. Thetis, a sea nymph, was a comfort to many of the gods, but when it was foretold that her son would be greater than his father, the gods decided to marry her to a mortal, and thus she was given to Peleus as his wife. She changed herself into many forms to avoid him, but he overcame her resistance in a grotto by the sea.
Scene 4
PROCRIS AND CEPHALUS: The hunter Cephalus, though loving his wife Procris, spends 60 days with Aurora. Upon his return he finds Procris in mourning and disguises himself as a merchant to test her fidelity by offering her gifts. Procris is enraged and flees to join Diana, but is eventually reunited with Cephalus, presenting him the spear of Diana. On his next hunting trip, Procris follows him and Cephalus thinking she is an animal in the bush, fires the spear. Procris dies in his arms.
Scene 5
CALLISTO was a nymph a hunting companion of Diana, goddess of chastity and the hunt. Jove fell in love with Callisto, changed himself into Diana, and raped her. When Diana found that Callisto was pregnant she banned her from the tribe. An angry Juno changes her into a bear. When Callisto's son, Orion, was at the point of killing her with his bow, Jove changed them into the constellation of the Archer and the Bear.

ACT 2
Scene 1
PICUS AND CANENS: Picus was a king and a forest god associated with Mars. He was faithful to his wife, the beautiful nymph Canens, and resisted the sorceress Circe, who consequently turned him into a predatory bird, sacred to the Romans.

[11]Performed in rotating repertory with *PAUL SILLS' STORY THEATRE*.

Scene 2

PYGMALION (was) revolted by the women he saw around him, (and) created a statue of the ideal woman. He fell in love with it and with this love brought it to life as Galatea.

Scene 3

EUROPA, a professor's daughter, was picking flowers with her playmates when Jove fell in love with her. He turned himself into a bull and carried her off to Crete where she became a mother and a goddess. It may be that Europa's mother was Africa.

Scene 4

PHAETHON discovered that his real father was Apollo, god of the sun, of poetry and of the bow. To prove his parentage, he demanded the privilege of driving for one day the horses who drew the chariot of the sun.

Scene 5

BAUCIS AND PHILEMON were mortals.

1971.09 FRANK MERRIWELL, or Honor Challenged

A Musical in Two Acts, 12 Scenes. Book by Skip Redwine, Larry Frank and Heywood Gould. (Based on the novel "Frank Merriwell's School Days" by Burt L. Standish [Gilbert Patten].) Music and lyrics by Skip Redwine and Larry Frank. Directed and choreographed by Neal Kenyon. Scenery designed by Tom John. Costumes designed by Frank Thompson. Lighting designed by John Gleason. Orchestrations by Arnold Goland. Musical direction and vocal arrangements by Jack Lee. Conducted by and dance arrangements by Jack Holmes. Associate producer, Aaron Ziegelman. Assistant choreographer, Bonnie Ano. Production coordinator, Don Eckstein. Produced by Sandy Farber and Stanley Barnett in association with Nate Friedman. Opened and closed 24 April 1971 at the Longacre Theatre after 1 performance.

CAST (in order of appearance): *Clyde*: J. J. Jepson. *Ned*: Larry Ross. *Hugh*: WALTER BOBBIE. *Belinda Belle Snodd*: NEVA SMALL. *Snella Jean*: Lori Cesar. *Una Marie*: Ellie Smith. *Professor Burrage*: Thomas Ruisinger. *Mrs. Snodd*: LIZ SHERIDAN. *Esther Carmichael*: Jennifer Williams. *Bart Hodge*: Peter Shawn. *Tad Jones*: Gary Keith Steven. *Frank Merriwell*: LARRY ELLIS. *Inza Burrage*: LINDA DONOVAN. *Manuel*: BILL HINNANT.

Act 1, Scene 1: Fardale Train Station: The Blow of a Coward. *Scene 2*: Picnic Grounds: Death at the Picnic. *Scene 3*: Fardale Caves: Explosion in Tunnel G. *Scene 4*: Mrs. Snodd's Boarding House: War! *Scene 5*: Professor's Laboratory: The Spanish Spy. *Scene 6*: Mrs. Snodd's Boarding House: By Fair Means or Foul. *Scene 7*: Picnic Grounds: Terror at the Junction.

Act 2, Scene 1: Picnic Grounds: A Hatred Grows. *Scene 2*: On the Campus: Waterloo. *Scene 3*: Picnic Grounds: Into the Enemy's Hands. *Scene 4*: Burrage Front Porch: Frank Is Missing. *Scene 5*: Fardale Caves: Death By Dynamite.

ACT 1

Scene 1

"There's No School Like Our School"
Students, Local Girls

"Howdy, Mr. Sunshine"
L. Ellis, G. K. Steven

Scene 2

"Prim and Proper"
Students, Local Girls

"Inza"
L. Ellis

Scene 4

"Look for the Happiness Ahead"
L. Ellis, All

Scene 6

"I'd Be Crazy to Be Crazy Over You"
N. Small, P. Shawn

Scene 7

"Now It's Fall"
Students

"The Fallin'-Out-of-Love Rag"
N. Small, Students, Local Girls, L. Ellis

ACT 2

Scene 1

"Frank, Frank, Frank"
All

Scene 2

"In Real Life"
L. Ellis

"The Broadway of My Heart"
T. Ruisinger, L. Sheridan

Scene 3

"Winter's Here"
Students

"The Pure in Heart"
L. Ellis, All

"I Must Be Crazy" (reprise)
N. Small

"Don't Turn His Picture to the Wall"
G. K. Steven, Students, Local Girls

Scene 5

"Manuel Your Friend"
B. Hinnant

"The Pure in Heart" (reprise)
L. Ellis

"Look For the Happiness Ahead" (reprise)
All

1971.10 EARL OF RUSTON

A Country Rocker (Musical) in One Act. Book and lyrics by C. C. Courtney and Ragan Courtney. Music by Peter Link. (Music) Played by Goatleg (Leon Medica, Bootsie Normand, Chip McDonald, Bobby Thomas). Directed by C. C. Courtney. Production designed by Neil Peter Jampolis. Production manager, Martin Herzer. Produced by David Black. Opened 5 May 1971 at the Billy Rose Theatre and closed 8 May 1971 after 5 performances.

CAST: *Earl*: C. C. COURTNEY and RAGAN COURTNEY. *Leda Pearl Crump*: JEAN WALDO BECK. *Herself*: LEECY R. WOODS MOORE. *Sheriff/Bass Guitar*: Leon Medica. *Mr. Turner/Lead Guitar*: Bootsie Normand. *Reverend Reynolds/Rhythm Guitar*: Chip McDonald. *The Doctor/Drums*: Bobby Thomas. *Ernestine*: Lynda Lawley. *Mary Lee Woods*: Bonnie Guidry. *Pianist*: John Bergeron.

The action takes place in Ruston, Louisiana.

MUSICAL NUMBERS

"Just Your Old Friend"
"Earl Is Crazy"
"Guitar Song"
"Easy to Be Lonely"
"Standing"
"Der Blues"—Traditional
"Probably"
(*Music by* C. C. Courtney and Ragan Courtney.)
"Mama, Earl Done Ate the Toothpaste Again"
(*Music by* C. C. Courtney.)
"Silvers Theme"
"Mama, Mama, Mama"
"I've Been Sent Back to the First Grade"
(*Music by* C. C. Courtney.)
"The Revival"
"My Name Is Leda Pearl"
(*Music by* C. C. Courtney.)
"Insane Poontang"
(*Music by* C. C. Courtney and Ragan Courtney.)
"You Still Love Me"
(*Music by* C. C. Courtney.)
"Earl Was Ahead"

1971–1972 SEASON

Cyril Ritchard and Robert Morse in SUGAR
Martha Swope/TimePix

1971–1972 SEASON

1971.11 YOU'RE A GOOD MAN, CHARLIE BROWN

A Musical Entertainment in Two Acts[1]. Book by John Gordon[2]. Based on the comic strip "Peanuts" by Charles M. Schulz. Music and lyrics by Clark Gesner. Directed by Joseph Hardy. Sets and costumes by Alan Kimmel. Lighting by Jules Fisher. Musical staging by Patricia Birch. Musical supervision, arrangements and additional material by Joseph Raposo. Associate producer, Warren Lockhart. Musical director, Jack Holmes. Produced by Arthur Whitelaw and Gene Persson. Opened 1 June 1971 at the John Golden Theatre and closed 27 June 1971 after 31 performances. Total, including Broadway and Off-Broadway runs: 1628 performances.

CAST (in order of speaking): *Linus*: Stephen Fenning. *Charlie Brown*: Dean Stolber. *Patty*: Lee Wilson. *Schroeder*: Carter Cole. *Snoopy*: Grant Cowan. *Lucy*: Liz O'Neal.

Scene: An average day in the life of Charlie Brown.

ACT 1

"You're a Good Man, Charlie Brown"
Entire Company
"Schroeder"
L. O'Neal, C. Cole
"Snoopy"
G. Cowan, D. Stolber
"My Blanket and Me"
S. Fenning
"Kite"
D. Stolber
"Dr. Lucy" (The Doctor Is In)
L. O'Neal, D. Stolber
"Book Report"
D. Stolber, L. O'Neal, S. Fenning, C. Cole

ACT 2

"The Red Baron"
G. Cowan
"T.E.A.M." (The Baseball Game)
Entire Company
"Glee Club Rehearsal"
Entire Company
"Little Known Facts"
L. O'Neal, S. Fenning, D. Stolber
"Suppertime"
G. Cowan
"Happiness"
Entire Company

1971.12 JESUS CHRIST SUPERSTAR

A Musical in Two Acts, 11 Scenes. Music by Andrew Lloyd Webber. Lyrics by Tim Rice. Conceived for the stage and directed by Tom O'Horgan. Scenic design by Robin Wagner. Costumes designed by Randy Barcelo. Lighting designed by Jules Fisher. Sound designed by Abe Jacob. Musical direction by Marc Pressel. Orchestrations by Andrew Lloyd Webber. Production supervisor, Charles Gray. Assistant conductor, Seymour Miroff. Musical supervisor, Mel Rodnon. Associate producers, (Tyler) Gatchell and (Peter) Neufeld. Produced by Robert Stigwood in association with MCA Inc. by arrangement with David Land. Opened 12 October 1971 at the Mark Hellinger Theatre and closed 1 July 1973 after 711 performances.

CAST (in order of appearance): *Judas Iscariot*: BEN VEREEN. *Jesus of Nazareth*: JEFF FENHOLT. *Mary Magdalene*: YVONNE ELLIMAN. *First Priest*: Alan Braustein. *Second Priest*: Michael Meadows. *Caiaphas*: BOB BINGHAM. *Annas*: PHIL JETHRO. *Third Priest*: Steven Bell. *Simon Zealotes, Merchant, Leper*: DENNIS BUCKLEY. *Pontius Pilate*: BARRY DENNEN. *Peter, Merchant, Leper*: MICHAEL JASON. *Maid By the Fire, Leper*: Linda Rios. *Soldier, Judas' Tormentor*: Tom Stovall. *Old Man, Apostle, Merchant, Leper*: Peter Schlosser. *Soldier, Judas' Tormentor*: Paul Sylvan. *King Herod, Merchant, Leper*: PAUL AINSLEY. *Cured Leper, Temple Lady*: Robin Grean. *Cured Leper, Apostle, Merchant, Tormentor (Judas' Death)*: James Sbano. *Cured Leper, Temple Lady*: Laura Michaels. *Cured Leper, Apostle, Merchant, Tormentor (Judas' Death)*: Clifford Lipson. *Cured Leper, Temple Lady, Reporter*: Bonnie Schon. *Cured Leper, Apostle, Reporter*: Pi Douglass. *Cured Leper, Apostle Woman, Temple Lady*: Celia Brin. *Cured Leper, Apostle, Tormentor (Judas' Death)*: Dennis Cooley. *Reporter, Apostle, Temple Lady, Leper*: Anita Morris. *Reporter, Leper*: Ted Neeley. *Reporter, Apostle Woman, Temple Lady, Leper*: Kay Cole. *Reporter, Leper*: Kurt Yaghjian. *Reporter, Leper*: Margaret Warncke. *Reporter, Apostle, Leper*: Willie Windsor. *Reporter, Apostle Woman, Temple Lady, Leper*: Ferne Bork. *Reporter, Apostle, Leper*: Samuel E. Wright. *Apostle Woman, Temple Lady, Leper*: Denise Delapenha. *Apostle, Merchant, Leper, Tormentor*: Robalee Barnes. *Apostle, Leper, Reporter, Tormentor (Judas' Death)*: Doug Lucas. *Soul Girl, Leper*: Charlotte Crossley. *Soul Girl, Leper*: Cecelia Norfleet. *Soul Girl, Leper*: Janet Powell. *Judas' Tormentor, Soldier*: Edward Barton. *Judas' Tormentor, Soldier*: Tony Gardner. *And various Palm Sunday Attendants, Alabaster Monsters, the Mob, and Members of the Crowd.*

RANDALL'S ISLAND: Elliott Randall (Electric, Acoustic), Paul Fleisher (Soprano Sax, Tenor Sax, Baritone Sax, Flute, Clarinet), Pot Namanworth (Piano, Organ), Allen Herman (Drums, Percussion), Gary King (Bass Guitar), Jim Miller (Rhythm Guitar).

The action depicts the last seven days in the life of Jesus of Nazareth.

Act 1, Scene 1: Opening. *Scene 2*: Bethany, Friday Night. *Scene 3*: Jerusalem, Sunday. *Scene 4*: Pontius Pilate's house, Monday. *Scene 5*: Tuesday.

Act 1, Scene 1: Thursday night. *Scene 2*: The Garden. *Scene 3*: Pilate's Palace, Friday. *Scene 4*: House of Herod. *Scene 5*: Pilate's Palace. *Scene 6*: Golgotha.

ACT 1

Scene 1
"Heaven on their Minds"
B. Vereen

Scene 2
"What's the Buzz"
J. Fenholt, Y. Elliman, Apostles, Women
"Strange Thing Mystifying"
B. Vereen, J. Fenholt, Apostles, Women
"Everything's All Right"
Y. Elliman, B. Vereen, J. Fenholt, Apostles, Women

Scene 3
"This Jesus Must Die"
B. Bingham, P. Jethro, Priests, Company
"Hosanna"
B. Bingham, J. Fenholt, Company
"Simon Zealotes"
D. Buckley, Company
"Poor Jerusalem"
J. Fenholt

Scene 4
"Pilate's Dream"
B. Dennen
"The Temple"
J. Fenholt, Company
"I Don't Know How to Love Him"
Y. Elliman, J. Fenholt

Scene 5
"Damned For All Time"
B. Vereen, P. Jethro, B. Bingham, Priests

ACT 2

Scene 1
"The Last Supper"
J. Fenholt, B. Vereen, Apostles

Scene 2
"Gethsemane"
J. Fenholt
"The Arrest"
M. Jason, J. Fenholt, Apostles, Reporters, B. Bingham, P. Jethro
"Peter's Denial"
L. Rios, M. Jason, T. Stovall, P. Schlosser, Y. Elliman

[1]Originally produced in New York Off-Broadway 7 March 1967 at the Theater 80 St. Marks for 1,597 performances.
[2]John Gordon is a pseudonym for Clark Gesner and the collective company of the Original Off-Broadway Cast who devised the show.

Scene 3
"Pilate and Christ"
B. Dennen, T. Stovall, J. Fenholt, Company
Scene 4
"King Herod's Song"
P. Ainsley
"Could We Start Again, Please"
Y. Elliman, M. Jason
"Judas' Death"
B. Vereen, P. Jethro, B. Bingham
Scene 5
"Trial Before Pilate"
B. Dennen, B. Bingham, J. Fenholt, the Mob
"Superstar"
B. Vereen, Company
Scene 6
"The Crucifixion"
J. Fenholt, Company
"John 19:41"
Orchestra

1971.13 AIN'T SUPPOSED TO DIE A NATURAL DEATH

Tunes from Blackness (A Musical) in Two Acts. Book, words and music by Melvin Van Peebles. Directed by Gilbert Moses. Scenery by Kert Lundell. Costumes by Bernard Johnson. Lighting by Martin Aronstein. Musical direction and supervision by Harold Wheeler. Sound by Jack Shearing. Associate producer, Howard Friedman. Produced by Eugene V. Wolsk, Charles Blackwell, Emanuel Azenberg and Robert Malina. Opened 20 October 1971 at the Ethel Barrymore Theatre, moved 17 November 1971 to the Ambassador Theatre and closed 30 July 1972 after 325 performances.

CAST (in order of appearance): Gloria Edwards, Dick Williams, Ralph Wilcox, Joe Fields, Marilyn B. Coleman, Arthur French, Carl Gordon, Madge Wells, Lauren Jones, Clebert Ford, Sati Jamal, Jimmy Hayeson, Toney Brealond, Beatrice Winde, Albert Hall, Garrett Morris, Bill Duke, Minnie Gentry.

The action takes place here and now.

ACT 1
"Just Don't Make No Sense"
A. French
"(The) Coolest Place in Town"
G. Edwards
"You Can Get Up Before Noon Without Being a Square"
R. Wilcox
"Mirror Mirror on the Wall"
J. Fields
"Come Raising Your Leg on Me"
M. B. Coleman
"You Gotta Be Holdin' Out Five Dollars on Me"
C. Gordon, M. Wells
"Sera Sera Jim"
L. Jones
"Catch That on the Corner"
C. Ford
"The Dozens"
J. Hayeson
"Funky Girl on Motherless Broadway"
T. Brealond

ACT 2
"Tenth and Greenwich"
B. Winde
"Heh Heh (Chuckle) Good Mornin' Sunshine"
A. French
"You Ain't No Astronaut"
J. Hayeson
"Three Boxes of Longs Please"
A. Hall
"Lily Done the Zampoughi Every Time I Pulled Her Coattail"
G. Morris, B. Alston
"I Got the Blood"
B. Duke
"Salamaggi's Birthday"
D. Williams
"Come on Feet Do Your Thing"
S. Jamal
"Put a Curse on You"
M. Gentry
(Finale: "Just Don't Make No Sense" reprise)
(Entire Company)

1971.14 TO LIVE ANOTHER SUMMER— TO PASS ANOTHER WINTER

A Musical Entertainment (Revue from Israel[3]) in Two Acts. Written by Hayim Hefer. Music by Dov Seltzer. Additional music by David Krivoshei, Alexander Argov, Naomi Shemer. Additional lyrics by Naomi Shemer. Lyrics translated mostly by David Paulsen. Directed and choreographed by Jonathan Karmon. Production (settings, lighting) designed by Neil Peter Jampolis. Costumes by Lydia Pincus Gany. Music arranged and conducted by David Krivoshei. Musical supervisor, Gary McFarland. Sound designed by Anthony Alloy. Production supervisor, Martin Herzer. Produced by Leonard Soloway. Opened 21 October 1971 at the Helen Hayes Theatre, moved 10 January 1972 to the Lunt-Fontanne Theatre and closed 19 March 1972 after 173 performances.

CAST: RIVKA RAZ, ARIC LAVIE, YONA ATARI, ILI GORLIZKI, HANAN GOLDBLATT.

Singers: Abigail Atarri, Lisa Butbul, David Devon, Rafi Ginat, Sarah Golan, Ronit Goldblatt, Moses Goldstein, Lenore Grant, Mordechai Hamer, Yochai Azani, Judith Rosenberg, Tslila Steren, Hillik Zadok. *Dancers*: Zvulun Cohen, Claude Dolgicer, Katya Dror, David Glazer, Nava Harari, Yuval Harat, Hama Kiviti, Ruth Lerman, Joseph Maimon, Riki Oren, Adam Pasternak, Hadassa Shachar, Ofira Tishler, Tuvia Tishler, Efraim Zamir, Miriam Zamir.

ACT 1
"Son of Man"
R. Raz, A. Lavie, Company
(*Translated by* David Axelrod.)
"The Sacrifice"
A. Lavie, Y. Hazani, Company
"What Are the Basic Things?"
I. Gorlizki, Company
(*Translated by* Lillian Burstein.)
"The Grove of Eucalyptus"
R. Raz, Company
(*Music and Lyrics by* Naomi Shemer. *Translated by* George Sherman.)
"The Tradition That Was Destroyed: Hasidic Medley"
H. Goldblatt, I. Gorlizki, R. Raz, Y. Atari, Company
(*Music by* Sarah and Ehud Zweig, David Weinkranz, Rabbi Carlibach.)
"The Boy With the Fiddle"
A. Lavie
(*Music by* Alexander Argov.)
"Can You Hear My Voice?"
Y. Atari, Company
(*Music by* Samuel Kraus. *Lyrics by* Rachel. *Translated by* George Sherman.)
"Mediteranee"
Company
"When My Man Returns"
R. Raz
(*Music by* George Moustaki.)
"Better Days"
Y. Atari, Company
"Ha'am Haze"
Company

ACT 2
"To Live Another Summer, To Pass Another Winter"
Y. Atari, A. Lavie, H. Goldblatt, R. Raz, Company

[3]The entire company of "To Live Another Summer, To Pass Another Winter" comes from Israel.

"Hora Hora"
Company
(*Music by* Alexander Argov.)
"Noah's Ark"[4]
I. Gorlizki
(*Music by* Naomi Shemer.)
"Don't Destroy the World"
A. Lavie
(*Lyrics in collaboration with* Hayim Guri.)
"Give Shalom and Sabbath to Jeruslaem"
Company
"Sorry We Won"
I. Gorlizki, Y. Atari, H. Goldblatt
(*Music by* David Krivoshei.)
"I'm Alive"
R. Raz, Company
(*Music by* David Krivoshei.)
"Give Me a Star"
R. Raz, A. Lavie, Company
(*Music by* David Krivoshei.)
Finale
Company

1971.15 ON THE TOWN

A Revival of the Musical Comedy in Two Acts, 17 Scenes[5]. Book and lyrics[6] by Betty Comden and Adolph Green. Book based on an idea by Jerome Robbins. Music by Leonard Bernstein. Directed and choreographed by Ron Field. Scenery designed by James Trittipo. Costumes designed by Ray Aghayan, Bob Mackie. Lighting designed by Tharon Musser. Musical direction by Milton Rosenstock. Orchestrations by Leonard Bernstein, Hershy Kay. Assistant choreographer, Michael Shawn. Musical co-ordinator, Dorothea Freitag. Associate producers, Rick Mandell, Allen Litke. The Ron Field Production. Produced by Jerry Schlossberg and Vista Productions. Opened 31 October 1971 at the Imperial Theatre and closed 1 January 1972 after 65 performances.

CAST (in order of appearance): *Workman*: David Wilder. *Chip*: JESS RICHARDS. *Ozzie*: REMAK RAMSAY. *Gabey*: RON HUSMANN. *Flossie*: Carol Petri. *Flossie's Friend*: Marybeth Kurdock. *Bill Poster*: Don Croll. *Little Old Lady*: Zoya Leporska. *Announcer*: Orrin Reiley. *Ivy Smith*: DONNA McKECHNIE. *Hildy*: BERNADETTE PETERS. *S. Uperman*: David Wilder. *Figment*: Orrin Reiley. *Claire*: PHYLLIS NEWMAN. *Maude P. Dilly*: Fran Stevens. *Pitkin*: Tom Avera. *Lucy Schmeeler*: Marilyn Cooper. *Gina Henie*: Gina Paglia. *Master of Ceremonies at Diamond Eddie's*: Dennis Roth. *Diana Dream*: Sandra Dorsey. *Master of Ceremonies at Congacabana*: Don Croll. *Senorita Dolores*: Laura Kenyon. *Bimmy*: Larry Merritt. *Coney Island Zoot Suit Dancers*: John Mineo, Tony Stevens.

Singers: Martha Danielle, Sandra Dorsey, Bobbi Franklin, Laura Kenyon, Gail Nelson, Marie Santell, Don Croll, Richard Marr, Orrin Reiley, Dennis Roth, Luke Stover, David Wilder, Craig Yates. *Dancers*: Carole Bishop, Eileen Casey, Jill Cook, Nancy Dalton, Marybeth Kurdock, Nancy Lynch, Gina Paglia, Pamela Peadon, Carol Petri, Andy G. Bew, Paul Charles, Larry Merritt, John Mineo, Jeff Phillips, Ken Scalice, Doug Spingler, Tony Stevens, Chester Walker.

The action takes place in New York City in June, 1944.

Act 1, Scene 1: Brooklyn Navy Yard. *Scene 2*: Subway Train. *Scene 3*: New York Street. *Scene 4*: Miss Turnstiles. *Scene 5*: Taxi Cab. *Scene 6*: Museum of Natural History. *Scene 7*: New York Street. *Scene 8*: Carnegie Hall. *Scene 9*: Claire's Apartment. *Scene 10*: Hildy's Apartment. *Scene 11*: Times Square.

Act 2, Scene 1: Night Clubs, (a) Diamond Eddie's Manhattan Roof, (b) Congacabana, (c) Slam-Bang. *Scene 2*: Subway Train. *Scene 3*: Imaginary Coney Island. *Scene 4*: Coney Island Express. *Scene 5*: Coney Island. *Scene 6*: Brooklyn Navy Yard.

ACT 1
"I Feel Like I'm Not Out of Bed"
Workmen
"New York, New York"
J. Richards, R. Ramsay, R. Husman
"Miss Turnstiles Ballet"
Contestants, D. McKechnie, Manhatanites
"Come Up to My Place"
B. Peters, J. Richards
"I Get Carried Away"
P. Newman, R. Ramsay
"Lonely Town"
R. Husmann, New Yorkers
"Do, Re, Do"
D. McKechnie, F. Stevens, Teachers, Students
"I Can Cook Too"
B. Peters, J. Richards
"Lucky to Be Me"
R. Husmann, New Yorkers
"Times Square Ballet"
Entire Company

ACT 2
So Long Baby Ice Revue
G. Paglia, Skaters
Nightclub Song ("I'm Blue")
S. Dorsey
Nightclub Song (Spanish)
L. Kenyon
"You Got Me"
P. Newman, R. Ramsay, B. Peters, J. Richards
"I Understand"
T. Avera, M. Cooper
"Playground of the Rich Ballet"
R. Husmann, D. McKechnie, High Society Dancers
"Some Other Time"
P. Newman, B. Peters, J. Richards, R. Ramsay
"Coney Island Hep Cats" (dance)
C. Petri, M. Kurdock, J. Mineo, T. Stevens
"New York, New York" (reprise)
Entire Company

1971.16 THE GRASS HARP

A Musical in One Act, 6 Scenes. Book and lyrics by Kenward Elmslie. Based on the novel and play of the same name by Truman Capote. Music by Claibe Richardson. Directed by Ellis Rabb. (Scenery) Design and lighting by James Tilton. Costumes by Nancy Potts. Musical director, Theodore Saidenberg. Musical arrangements by J. (Billy) Ver Planck. Choreography by Rhoda Levine. Additional orchestrations by Jonathan Tunick, Robert Russell Bennett. Dance and incidental music by John Berkman. Associate producer, Michael Kasdan. Technical advisor, Frank Hauser. A Production of the University of Michigan Professional Theatre Program. Produced by Theatre 1972 (Richard Barr, Charles Woodward, Michael Harvey.) Opened 2 November 1971 at the Martin Beck Theatre and closed 6 November 1971 after 7 performances.

CAST (in order of appearance): *Dolly Talbo*: BARBARA COOK. *Collin Talbo*: RUSS THACKER. *Catherine Creek*: CAROL BRICE. *Verena Talbo*: RUTH FORD. *Maude Riordan*: Christine Stabile. *Dr. Morris Ritz*: MAX SHOWALTER. *Judge Cool*: JOHN BARAGREY. *Babylove*: KAREN MORROW. *Heavenly Pride and Joys*: Kelly Boa, Trudy Bordoff, Colin Dufy, Eva Grant, David Craig Moskin. *Sheriff Amos Legrand*: Harvey Vernon.

The action takes place at the Talbo House, in Joy City and in River Woods, in the past.

Scene 1: The Talbo Backyard. *Scene 2*: The Talbo House. *Scene 3*: The Tree-house in River Woods. *Scene 4*: The Jail. *Scene 5*: Joy City. *Scene 6*: The Tree-house.

MUSICAL NUMBERS
Scene 1
"Dropsy Cure Weather"
B. Cook, C. Brice, R. Thacker
"This One Day"
R. Thacker

---

[4]Dropped during run and national tour and replaced with:
"I Never Wanted to Be a Hero"
H. Goldblatt, Company
(*Music by* David Krivoshei. .)
[5]Originally produced in New York 28 December 1944 at the Adelphi Theatre for 462 performances.
[6]Additional lyrics by Leonard Bernstein.

"This One Day" dance
R. Thacker, C. Stabile

Scene 2

"Think Big Rich"
M. Showalter

"If There's Love Enough"
C. Brice

"Yellow Drum"
B. Cook, C. Brice, R. Thacker

Scene 3

"Marry With Me"
C. Brice

"I'll Always Be in Love"
B. Cook

"Floozies"
R. Thacker

The Babylove Miracle Show:

"Call Me Babylove"
K. Morrow

"Walk into Heaven"
K. Morrow

"Hang a Little Moolah on the Washline"
K. Morrow, the Pride'n Joys

"Talkin' in Tongues"
K. Morrow

"Whooshin' Through My Flesh"
K. Morrow, C. Brice, B. Cook, R. Thacker, Company

"Walk into Heaven" (reprise)
K. Morrow

"Something For Nothing"
M. Showalter

Scene 4

"Indian Blues"
C. Brice, Company

"Take a Little Sip"
R. Thacker, B. Cook, C. Brice, C. Stabile, Company

Scene 5

"Yellow Drum" (reprise)
Company

"What Do I Do Now?"
R. Ford

Scene 6

"Pick Yourself a Flower"
K. Morrow, Company

"The Flower Fortune Dance"
Company

"Reach Out"
B. Cook, Company

1971.17 ONLY FOOLS ARE SAD

A Musical from Israel (Ish Hassid Haya[7]) in Two Acts, in Hebrew and English. Book by Dan Almagor, based on old Hassidic stories and parables. Translated by Shimon Wincelberg and Valerie Arnon. Music derived from Hassidic songs, arranged by Yohanan Zarai and Gil Aldema. Lyrics translated by Robert Friend. Directed by Yossi Yzraely. Musical instructor and advisor, Hanna Hakohen. Scenery by Dani Kanavan. Scenery supervised by Herbert Senn. Costumes supervised by Helen Pond. Lighting by Yehiel Orgal. Lighting supervised by Robert Brand. Consultant on English speech, Nora Dunfee. Produced by Yaacov Agmon under the patronage of the Prime Minister of Israel, Mrs. Golda Meir. Opened 22 November 1971 at the Edison Theatre and closed 26 March 1972 after 144 performances.

CAST: Galia Ishay, Danny Litanny, Don Maseng, Shlomo Nitzan, Michal Noy, Aviva Schwarz.

[7]In literal English, Once There Was a Hassid.

ACT 1[8]

"Once There Was a Melody . . . "
Entire Company

Isaac, the Baker (The Treasure)
Narrators: D. Litanny, M. Noy. *Issac*: G. Ishay.

"A Merry Melody"
Entire Company

Berl, the Tailor (Opening a New Account)
Berl, the tailor: D. Maseng. *Rabbi Levy Itzhak*: S. Nitzan.

The Promise That Was Kept
Narrator: D. Litanny.

Don't Suck the Bones[9]
Narrator: S. Nitzan.

Eat, Lord, and Enjoy
Narrator: M. Noy.

"Tell Me What the Rain Is Saying"[10]
A. Schwarz (soloist)

Don't Sell It Cheap[11]
Narrator: S. Nitzan.

The Woman who sold her place in Paradise[12]
Narrator: M. Noy. *The woman*: G. Ishay.

"A Drinking Song"
D. Maseng (soloist)

The Ten Ruble Note
Narrator: S. Nitzan.

"Kol Rinah Vishu'ah"
Entire Company

Gedaliah, the tar-maker
Narrator: A. Schwarz. *Rabbi Israel Ba'al Shem Tov*: S. Nitzan. *Gedaliah, the tar-maker*: D. Litanny.

ACT 2

The Goat
Narrators: D. Maseng, M. Noy. *The son*: G. Ishay.

"Forest, Forest"[13]
M. Noy (soloist)

Smoking on the Sabbath
Narrator: S. Nitzan.

"Bim-Bam-Bom"
Entire Company

Waiting for the Messiah
Narrator: M. Noy. *Rabbi Moshe Teitelbaum*: D. Maseng.

The Passing of the Ba'al Shem Tov
Narrator: D. Litanny.

Haim, the goose-herder
G. Ishay

Getzl, the shoemaker (Aleph . . . beth)
D. Litanny

The Rabbi who promised to wait
Narrator: S. Nitzan.

A Letter to the Rabbi
D. Maseng (soloist)

[8]Added during the run:

The Rich and the Poor (Act 1)
S. Nitzan

"Veha'er Eineinu" (Carlebach) (Act 1)
Entire Company

The Hassid's Dilemma (Act 1)
Narrator: S. Nitzan.

The Beggar and the Rabbi (Act 1)
Narrator: S. Nitzan.

"Hoshia et Amecha" (Act 2)
Entire Company

[9]Dropped during the run.
[10]Dropped during the run.
[11]Dropped during the run.
[12]Dropped during the run.
[13]Dropped during the run.

"Angel, Angel . . . "
G. Ishay
"Only Fools Are Sad"
A. Schwarz (soloist)
"Avreymele Melamed"
D. Litanny, S. Nitzan, D. Maseng (soloists)
"A Sabbath Song"
S. Nitzan (soloist)
"And God Said unto Jacob"
D. Litanny (soloist)

1971.18 TWO GENTLEMEN OF VERONA

A Musical in Two Acts[14]. Book by John Guare and Mel Shapiro. Based on the play of the same name by William Shakespeare. Music by Galt MacDermott. Lyrics by John Guare. Directed by Mel Shapiro. Setting by Ming Cho Lee. Costumes by Theoni V. Aldredge. Lighting by Lawrence Metzler. Choreography by Jean Erdman. Musical supervision by Harold Wheeler. Additional musical staging by Dennis Nahat. Sound by Jack Shearing. Associate producer, Bernard Gersten. Produced by the New York Shakespeare Festival (Joseph Papp, Producer). Opened 1 December 1971 at the St. James Theatre and closed 20 May 1973 after 614 performances. Total including Broadway and Off-Broadway runs: 628 performances.

CAST (in order of appearance): *Thurio*: Frank O'Brien. *Speed*: Jose Perez. *Valentine*: CLIFTON DAVIS. *Proteus*: RAUL JULIA. *Julia*: DIANA DAVILA. *Lucetta*: Alix Elias. *Launce*: JOHN BOTTOMS. *Antonio*: Frederic Warriner. *Crab*: Phineas. *Duke of Milan*: NORMAN MATLOCK. *Silvia*: JONELLE ALLEN. *Tavern Host*: Frederic Warriner. *Eglamour*: ALVIN LUM.

Quartet: Black Passion: Sheila Gibbs, Signa Joy, Kenneth Lowry, Sakinah Mahammud. *Citizens of Verona and Milan*: Loretta Abbott, Christopher Alden, Roger Briant, Douglas Brickhouse, Stockard Channing, Paul DeJohn, Nancy Denning, Richard DeRusso, Arthur Erickson, Georgyn Geetlein, Sheila Gibbs, Jeff Goldblum, Edward Henkel, Albert Insinnia, Jane Jaffe, Signa Joy, Kenneth Lowry, Sakinah Mahammud, Otis Sallid, Madeline Swift.

The action takes place in Verona, Milan and the Forest.

ACT 1[15]
"Summer, Summer"
Ensemble
"I Love My Father"
Ensemble
"That's a Very Interesting Question"
R. Julia, C. Davis
"I'd Like to be a Rose"
R. Julia, C. Davis
"Thou, Julia, Thou Has Metamorphosed Me"
R. Julia
"Symphony"
R. Julia, Ensemble
"I Am Not Interested in Love"
D. Davila
"Love, Is That You?"
F. O'Brien, G. Geetlein
"Thou, Proteus, Thou Has Metamorphosed Me"
D. Davila
"What Does a Lover Pack?"
D. Davila, R. Julia, Ensemble
"Pearls"
J. Bottoms
"I Love My Father" (reprise)
R. Julia
"Two Gentlemen of Verona"
D. Davila, A. Elias
"Follow the Rainbow"
C. Davis, J. Perez, R. Julia, J. Bottoms, D. Davila, A. Elias
"Where's North?"
C. Davis, J. Perez, V. Matlock, J. Allen, F. O'Brien, Ensemble
"Bring All the Boys Back Home"
N. Matlock, F. O'Brien, Ensemble
"Love's Revenge"
C. Davis
"To Whom It May Concern Me"
J. Allen, C. Davis
"Night Letter"
J. Allen, C. Davis
"Love's Revenge" (reprise)
C. Davis, R. Julia, J. Perez, J. Bottoms
"Calla Lily Lady"
R. Julia

ACT 2
"Land of Betrayal"
A. Elias
"Thurio's Samba"
F. O'Brien, N. Matlock, Ensemble
"Hot Lover"
J. Bottoms, J. Perez
"What a Nice Idea"
D. Davila
"Who Is Silvia"
R. Julia, F. Warriner, Ensemble
"Love Me"
J. Allen, Ensemble
"Eglamour"
A. Lum, J. Allen
"Kidnapped"
D. Davila, N. Matlock, R. Julia, F. O'Brien, Ensemble
"Mansion"
C. Davis
"Eglamour" (reprise)
J. Allen, A. Lum
"What's a Nice Girl Like Her"
R. Julia
"Dragon Fight"
Dragon, A. Lum, R. Julia, C. Davis
"Don't Have the Baby"
D. Davila, A. Elias,, J. Perez, C. Davis
"Love Is That You" (reprise)
F. O'Brien, A. Elias
"Milkmaid"
J. Bottoms, S. Gibbs
Finale: "I Love My Father," "Love Has Driven Me Sane"
Full Company

[14]First produced Off-Broadway as *THE TWO GENTLEMEN OF VERONA* 27 July 1971 at the Delacorte Theatre for 14 performances, plus 23 performances on the New York Shakespeare Festival Mobile Tour throughout New York City.
[15]No song list appears in the program. Song list prepared from the production manuscript and recording.

1971.19 WILD AND WONDERFUL

A "Big City" Fable (Musical) in Two Acts. Book by Phil Phillips. Based on an original work by Bob Brotherton and Bob Miller. Music and lyrics by Bob Goodman. Settings by Stephen Hendrickson. Directed by Burry Fredrik. Dances and musical numbers staged by Ronn Forella. Costumes by Frank Thompson. Lighting by Neil Peter Jampolis. Musical direction, vocal arrangements and dance music composed and arranged by Thom Janusz. Orchestrations by Luther Henderson. Associate producer, John C. O'Regan. Produced by Rick Hobard in association with Raymonde Weil. Opened and closed 7 December 1971 at the Lyceum Theatre after 1 performance.

CAST (in order of appearance): *Jenny*: LAURA McDUFFIE. *Charlie*: WALTER WILLISON. *Lionel Masters*: ROBERT BURR. *Brother John*: LARRY SMALL. *Father Desmond*: TED THURSTON.

(Ensemble): *Yveline*: Yveline Baudez. *Pam*: Pam [Pamela] Blair . *Mary Ann*: Mary Ann Brauning. *Carol*: Carol Conte. *Bob*: Bob Daley. *Anna Maria*: Anna Maria Fanizzi. *Marcelo*: Marcelo Gamboa *Adam*: Adam Grammis. *Patti*: Patti Haine. *Ann*: Ann Reinking. *Jimmy*: Jimmy Roddy. *Steven*: Steven Vincent. *Eddie*: Eddie Wright, Jr.

The action takes place in The Big City.

ACT 1
"Wild and Wonderful" Dance
Company
"My First Moment"
L. McDuffie
"I Spy"
W. Willison
"Desmond's Dilemma"
T. Thurston, L. Small
"Moment Is Now"
W. Willison, Ensemble
"Something Wonderful Can Happen"
L. McDuffie
"Chances"
L. McDuffie, R. Burr, .A Reinking, M. A. Bruning, C. Conte, A. M. Fanizzi
"Jenny"
W. Willison
"Fallen Angels"
L. Small, Dropouts
Dance
P. Blair, J. Roddy, Dropots

ACT 2
"Petty Crime"
L. McDuffie, Judge, Company
"Come a Little Closer"
L. McDuffie, W. Willison
"Is This My Town"
L. McDuffie
"You Can Reach the Sun"
L. Small, Dropouts
"A Different Kind of World"
T. Thurston
"Wait For Me"
W/ Willison
"Wild and Wonderful" (reprise)
Company

1971.20 INNER CITY

A Street Cantata in Two Acts, 10 Scenes. Based on the book "The Inner City Mother Goose" by Eve Merriam. Music by Helen Miller. Lyrics by Eve Merriam. Conceived and directed by Tom O'Horgan. Scenery by Robin Wagner. Costumes by Joseph G. Aulisi. Lighting by John Dodd in association with Jane Reisman. Orchestrations and (musical) arrangements by Gordon (Lowry) Harrell. Musical direction by Clay Fullum. Vocal arrangements by Helen Miller. Sound by Gary Harris. Associate producers, Harvey Milk, John M. Nagel. Production co-ordinator, Charlotte Dicker. Produced by Joseph Kipness, Lawrence Kasha, Tom O'Horgan in association with RCA Records. Opened 19 December 1971 at the Ethel Barrymore Theatre and closed 11 March 1972 after 97 performances.

CAST: Joy Garrett, Carl Hall, Delores Hall, Fluffer Hirsch, LINDA HOPKINS, Paulette Ellen Jones, Larry Marshall, Allan Nicholls, Florence Tarlow.

The action takes place at the present time in New York City.

Act 1, Scene 1: Nub of the Nation. *Scene 2*: Urban Mary. *Scene 3*: Deep in the Night. *Scene 4*: Take-a-Tour, Congressman. *Scene 5*: The Spirit of Education

Act 2, Scene 1: Wisdom. *Scene 2*: Starlight. *Scene 3*: Crooked Man. *Scene 4*: Kindness. *Scene 5*: If.

ACT 1
Scene 1
"Fee Fi Fo Fum"
L. Hopkins
"Now I Lay Me"
C. Hall, D. Hall, A. Nicholls
"Locks"/"I Had a Little Teevee"
F. Hirsch
"Hushabye Baby"/"My Mother Said"
P. E. Jones
"Diddle Diddle Dumpling"/"Rub A Dub Dub"
L. Marshall
"You'll Find Mice"
L. Hopkins
"Ding Dong Bell"
C. Hall, Cast
"The Brave Old City of New York"
J. Garrett
"Urban Renewal"
L. Hopkins
"The Nub of the Nation"
Cast
Scene 2
"Mary, Mary"
Cast
"City Life"
F. Tarlow
"One Misty Moisty Morning"
L. Marshall
"Jack Be Nimble"
C. Hall, F. Hirsch, L. Marshall
"If Wishes Were Horses"
D. Hall
Scene 3
"One Man"/"Deep in the Night"
L. Hopkins
Scene 4
"Statistics"/"12 Rooftops Leaping"/"Take-A-Tour, Congressman"
Cast
"Simple Simon"
L. Marshall, A. Nicholls, Cast
"Poverty Program"
Cast
"One, Two"
C. Hall, Cast
"Tom, Tom"
A. Nicholls
"Hickety, Pickety"
Cast
"Half Alive"
D. Hall
Scene 5
"This Is the Way We Go to School"
Cast
"The Spirit of Education"
F. Tarlow
"Little Jack Horner"
Cast
"Subway Dream"
L. Marshall
"Christmas Is Coming"
F. Hirsch
"I'm Sorry Says the Machine"
L. Marshall, Cast
"Jeremiah Obadiah"
L. Marshall
"Riddle Song"
Cast
"Shadow of the Sun"
Cast

ACT 2
Scene 1
"Boys and Girls Come Out to Play"
Cast
"Summer Nights"
J. Garrett, D. Hall, P. E. Jones
"Lucy Locket"
F. Hirsch
"Winter Nights"
L. Hopkins, F. Tarlow

"Wisdom"
L. Marshall
"The Hooker" (You Make It Your Way)
J. Garrett
Scene 2
"Wino Will"/"Man in the Doorway"
P. E. Jones
"Starlight, Starbright"
D. Hall
"The Cow Jumped Over the Moon"
L. Marshall
"The Dealer" (You Push It You Way)
A. Nicholls
Scene 3
"Taffy"
C. Hall, F. Hirsch, Cast
"Numbers"
L. Marshall, Cast
"The Pickpocket"
C. Hall
"Law and Order"
D. Hall
Scene 4
"Kindness"
A. Nicholls, Cast
"As I Went Over"
A. Nicholls
"There Was a Little Man"
Cast
"Who Killed Nobody"
Cast
Scene 5
"It's My Belief"
L. Hopkins
"Street Sermon"
C. Hall
"The Great If"
C. Hall
"On This Rock"
Cast
"The Great If" (reprise)
Cast

1971.21 ANNE OF GREEN GABLES

A Musical in Two Acts, 23 Scenes. (Book) Adapted by Donald Harron. Based on the novel of the same name by Lucy M. Montgomery. Music by Norman Campbell. Lyrics by Donald Harron and Norman Campbell. Additional lyrics by Mavor Moore and Elaine Campbell. Directed and choreographed by Alan Lund. Production (scenery) designed by Murray Laufer. Costumes by Marie Day. Lighting by Ronald Montgomery. Musical director and orchestrations by John Fenwick. Associate music director, Fen Watkin. Associate lighting designer, Gary Craswell. A Canadian National Musical Theatre Production. Produced by the New York City Center of Music and Drama (Norman Singer, Executive director) in association with the Charlottetown Festival (Prince Edward Island, Canada). Opened 21 December 1971 at the New York City Center and closed 2 January 1972 after 16 performances.

CAST (in order of appearance): *Mrs. Rachel Lynde*: Maud Whitmore. *Mrs. MacPherson*: Cleone Duncan. *Mrs. Barry*: Nancy Kerr. *Mrs. Sloane*: Flora MacKenzie. *Mrs. Pye*: Kathryn Watt. *The Minister*: Lloyd Malenfant. *Reverend Smythe Hawkinson*: Jack Northmore. *Earl*, the mailman: Bill Hosie. *Cecil*, the farmer: George Merner. *Marilla Cuthbert*: ELIZABETH MAWSON. *Matthew Cuthbert*, her brother: PETER MEWS. *Anne Shirley*: GRACIE FINLEY. *Mrs. Spencer*: Flora MacKenzie. *Mrs. Blewett*: Roma Hearn. *Diana Barry*: Glenda Landry.

Young Ladies at Avonlea School: *Prissy Andrews*: Sharlene McLean. *Josie Pye*: Barbara Barsky. *Ruby Gillis*: Patti Toms. *Tillie Boulter*: Lynn Marsh. *Gertie Pye*: Deborah Miller. *Boys at Avonlea School*: *Gilbert Blythe*: JEFF HYSLOP. *Charlie Sloane*: George Juriga. *Moody MacPherson*: Dan Costain. *Gerry Buote*: Andre Denis. *Tommy Sloane*: John Powell. *Malcolm Andrews*: Calvin MacRae.

Mr. Phillips, the schoolmaster: Jack Northmore. *Lucilla*, clerk in Blair's store: Cleone Duncan. *Miss Stacy*, the schoolmistress: Roma Hearn. *Stationmaster*: Bill Hosie.

The action takes place at the turn of the century in Avonlea, a tiny village in Prince Edward Island, Canada's smallest province.

Act 1, Scene 1: The Church Parlor, Avonlea. *Scene 2*: Bright River Railroad Station. *Scene 3*: The House at Green Gables. *Scene 4*: On the way to Mrs. Blewett's. *Scene 5*: Mrs. Blewett's House. *Scene 6*: On the way back to Green Gables. *Scene 7*: Green Gables. *Scene 8*: Green Gables. *Scene 9*: On the way to the Schoolhouse. *Scene 10*: The Schoolhouse. *Scene 11*: All over town. *Scene 12*: On the way to Green Gables. *Scene 13*: On the way to the Picnic; the Picnic.

Act 2, Scene 1: Outside the Schoolhouse. *Scene 2*: Schoolyard. *Scene 3*: Green Gables. *Scene 4*: Green Gables. *Scene 5*: The Nature Hunt. *Scene 6*: The Store at Carmody. *Scene 7*: The Schoolhouse. *Scene 8*: On the way home from School. *Scene 9*: Kitchen, Green Gables. *Scene 10*: Green Gables.

ACT 1
(Overture: "Anne of Green Gables")
(Chorus)
Scene 1
"Great Workers for the Cause"
M. Whitmore, Ladies
"Where Is Matthew Going?"
Townspeople
Scene 2
"Gee, I'm Glad I'm No One Else But Me"
G. Finley
Scene 3
"We Clearly Requested (A Boy)" (Trio)
E. Mawson, G. Finley, P. Mews
Scene 5
"The Facts"
G. Finley, F. MacKenzie, R. Hearn, E. Mawson
Scene 6
"Where'd Marilla Come From?" (reprise)
B. Hosie, G. Merner, Ladies
Scene 7
"Humble Pie"
P. Mews, G. Finley
"Oh, Mrs. Lynde!" (Apology)
G. Finley
Scene 9
"Back to School/ (School) Ballet"
Pupils
Scene 10
"Avonlea We Love Thee"
J. Northmore, Pupils
"Wondrin'"
J. Hyslop
Scene 11
"Did You Hear?"
B. Barsky, K. Watt, C. Duncan, N. Kerr, B. Hosie, G. Merner, M. Whitmore
Scene 13
"Ice Cream"
G. Landry, Company
"The Picnic"
Company
ACT 2
Scene 1
"Where Did the Summer Go To?"
The Pupils
"Kindred Spirits"
G. Finley, G. Landry
Scene 2
"Open the Window!"
R. Hearn, Pupils
Scene 3
"The Words"
P. Mews

Scene 5
"Open the Window!" (reprise)
R. Hearn, Pupils
"Nature Hunt Ballet"
Pupils
"I'll Show Him"
G. Finley, J. Hyslop
Scene 6
"General Store"
C. Duncan, P. Mews, Townspeople
Scene 7
"Pageant Song"
Pupils
"If It Hadn't Been for Me"
Company
Scene 8
"Where Did the Summer Go To?" (reprise)
G. Finley, J. Hyslop, Pupils
Scene 9
"Anne of Green Gables"
P. Mews
Scene 10
"The Words" (reprise)
E. Mawson
"Wondrin'" (reprise)
G. Finley, J. Hyslop
(Finale: "Ice Cream" reprise)
(Company)

1972.01 THE SIGN IN SIDNEY BRUSTEIN'S WINDOW

A Play With Music in Three Acts, 8 Scenes. (Original) Play by Lorraine Hansberry. Adapted by Robert Nemiroff and Charlotte Zaltzberg. Music by Gary William Friedman. Lyrics by Ray Errol Fox. Directed by Alan Schneider. Musical staging by Rhoda Levine. Scenery by William Ritman. Costumes by Theoni V. Aldredge. Lighting by Richard Nelson. Musical director, Mack Schlefer. Music orchestrated and arranged by Gary William Friedman. Associate producer, Robert Nemiroff. Produced by Robert Renfield. Opened 26 January 1972 at the Longacre Theatre and closed 29 January 1972 after 5 performances.

CAST (in order of appearance): *Singers*: Pendleton Brown, Richard Cox, John Lansing, Arnetia Walker. *Sidney Brustein*: HAL LINDEN. *Alton Scales*: John Danelle. *Iris Parodus Brustein*: ZOHRA LAMPERT. *Wally O'Hara*: MASON ADAMS. *Max*: Dolph Sweet. *Mavis Parodus Bryson*: FRANCES STERNHAGEN. *David Ragin*: WILLIAM ATHERTON. *Gloria Parodus*: Kelly Wood.
Singers: Pendleton Brown, Richard Cox, John Lansing, Arnetia Walker.

The action takes place in the Brustein's apartment and adjoining courtyard in Greenwich Village, New York City, in the early 1960s.

Act 1, Scene 1: Early evening, the late spring. *Scene 2*: Dusk. The following week.

Act 2, Scene 1: Just before daybreak. The following day. *Scene 2*: Evening. Late summer. *Scene 3*: Later that evening. *Scene 4*: Election Night. Early fall.

Act 3, Scene 1: Several hours later. *Scene 2*: Early the next morning.

MUSICAL NUMBERS
"Can a Flower Think?"
"In Another Life"
"Mountain Girl"
"To the People"
"While There's Still Time"
"Things As They Are"
"Sweet Evenin'"

1972.02 THE SELLING OF THE PRESIDENT

A Musical in Two Acts. Book by Jack O'Brien and Stuart Hample. Based on the book of the same name by Joe McGinniss. Music by Bob James. Lyrics by Jack O'Brien. Scenery by Tom John. Costumes by Nancy Potts. Lighting by Thomas Skelton. Musical staging by Ethel Martin. Musical direction by Harold Hastings. Orchestrations by Jonathan Tunick. Multi-media designed by William Claxton, Mort Kasman, Gary Youngman, Jim Sant'Andrea. Produced by John Flaxman in association with Harold Hastings and Franklin Roberts. Opened 22 March 1972 at the Sam S. Shubert Theatre and closed 25 Marrch 1972 after 5 performances[16]).

CAST: *Senator George W. Mason*: PAT HINGLE. *Grace Mason*: BARBARA BARRIE. *Senator Hiram Robinson*: Richard Goode. *Sydney Wales*: ROBERT FITZSIMMONS. *Irene Jantzen*: KAREN MORROW. *Ted Bacon*: ROBERT DARNELL. *Ward Nichols*: JOHN GLOVER. *Johnny Olson*: JOHNNY OLSON. *Arthur Hayes*: John Bentley.
Television's Top Singers and Dancers: *Minister*: Tim Noble. *Captain Terror*: Steve Schochet. *Timmy*: Sheilah Rae. *Creepy*: Philip M. Thomas. *Davey*: Tim Noble. *Ghoulie*: Pi Douglass. *Van Denisovich*: Rick Atwell. *Casey Steele*: Jamie Carr. *Franklin Douglass Pierce*: Pi Douglass. *Bonnie Sue Taylor*: Suellen Estey. *Gloria Miller*: Delores Hall. *Linda Allington*: Pamela Myers. *Ralph Reeder*: Tim Noble. *Burgundy Moore*: Trina Parks. *Molly Kilgallen*: Sheilah Rae. *Inga Brand*: Deborah St. Darr. *Barney Zawicki*: Steve Schochet. *Dr. Lloyd Blenheim*: Bill Reinecke. *Mrs. Pearline Gibbons*: Lurlu Lindsay. *Mr. Warren Stevenson*: Peter Grounds. *Randall Phillips*: Philip M. Thomas. *Fleetwing Horn*: Vilma Vaccaro. *Julie Milano*: Pam Zarit. And George Andrew Robinson, Michael Serrecchia.

The action takes place in 1976 in a television studio.

ACT 1
"Something Holy"
D. Hall, Company
"If You Like People"
S. Estey, T. Noble
"Sunset"
P. Douglass, T. Noble, A. Robinson, S. Schochet
"Little Moon"
V. Carr, V. Vaccaro
"Come-on-a-Good-Life"
P. Douglass, T. Parks, P. Thomas, D. Hall
"I've Got to Trust You"
P. Myers
"If You Like People" (reprise)
Company
"Mason Cares"
S. Estey, S. Rae, D. St. Darr, P. Zarit
"On the Winning Side"
P. Myers
"Captain Terror"
S. Rae, S. Schochet, P. Douglass, P. Thomas
"He's a Man"
T. Parks, P. Zarit, D. Hall
ACT 2
"Stars of Glory"
T. Noble
"Terminix"
S. Schochet, D. St. Darr, S. Estey, P. Myers
"Take My Hand"
J. Carr, D. Hall, S. Schochet, V. Vaccaro
"A Passacaglia"
Company
"We're Gonna Live It Together"
Company
"America"
Company

1972.03 A FUNNY THING HAPPENED ON THE WAY TO THE FORUM

A Revival of the Musical Comedy in Two Acts[17]. Book by Burt Shevelove and Larry Gelbart. Based on the plays ("The Haunted House," "Mostellaria",

[16]Direction uncredited at opening; credited to Robert H. Livingston prior to opening.
[17]Originally produced in New York 8 May 1962 at the Alvin Theatre for 964 performances. For Synopsis of Scenes and Musical Numbers, see original 1962 production. Added for this production:

etc.) of Plautus. Music and lyrics by Stephen Sondheim. Directed by Burt Shevelove. A Larry Blyden Production. Choreography by Ralph Beaumont. Settings by James Trittipo. Costumes by Noel Taylor. Lighting by H. R. Poindexter. Musical and vocal direction by Milton Rosenstock. Orchestrations by Irwin Kostal and Sid Ramin. Dance music arranged by Hal Schaefer, Richard De Benedictis. Produced by David Black in association with Seymour Vall and Henry Honeckman. Opened 30 March 1972 at the Lunt-Fontanne Theatre and closed 12 August 1972 after 156 performances.

CAST (in order of appearance): *Prologus*: PHIL SILVERS. *Senex*, a Roman citizen: LEW PARKER. *Domina*, his wife: LIZABETH PRITCHETT. *Hero*, his son, in love with Philia: JOHN HANSEN. *Hysterium*, slave to Senex and Domina: LARRY BLYDEN. *Pseudolus*, slave to Hero: PHIL SILVERS. *Lycus*, a buyer and seller of courtesans: CARL BALLANTINE. *Erronius*, an old man: REGINALD OWEN. *Miles Gloriosus*, a warrior: CARL LINDSTROM. *Tintinabula*, a courtesan: Lauren Lucas. *Panacea*, a courtesan: Gloria Mills. *The Geminae*, courtesans: Trish Mahoney, Sonja Haney. *Vibrata*, a courtesan: Keita Keita. *Gymnasia*, a courtesan: Charlene Ryan. *Philia*, a virgin: PAMELA HALL. *The Proteans*: Joe Ross, Bill Starr, Chad Block.

1972.04 SUGAR

A Musical Comedy in Two Acts, 15 Scenes. Book by Peter Stone. Based on the film "Some Like It Hot" by Billy Wilder and I.A.L. Diamond, based on a story by Robert Thoeren. Music by Jule Styne. Lyrics by Bob Merrill. Directed and choreographed by Gower Champion. Settings by Robin Wagner. Costumes by Alvin Colt. Lighting by Martin Aronstein. Musical direction and vocal arrangements by Elliot Lawrence. Orchestrations by Philip J. Lang. Dance music arrangements by John Berkman. Associate choreographer, Bert Michaels. Produced by David Merrick. Opened 9 April 1972 at the Majestic Theatre and closed 23 June 1973 after 505 performances.

CAST (in order of appearance): *Sweet Sue*: SHEILA SMITH. *(Her) Society Syncopaters*: *Piano*: Harriett Conrad. *Drums*: Linda Gandell. *Bass*: Nicole Barth. *Trumpets*: Leslie Latham, Marylou Sirinek. *Trombones*: Terry Cullen, Kathleen Witmer. *Saxophones*: Pam Blair, Eileen Casey, Debra Lyman, Sally Neal, Mary Zahn.

Bienstock: ALAN KASS. *Joe*: TONY ROBERTS. *Jerry*: ROBERT MORSE. *Spats Palazzo*: STEVE CONDOS. *Dude*: Gerard Brentte. *Spat's Gang*: Andy Bew, Roger Bigelow, Gene Cooper, Arthur Faria, Gene GeBauer, John Mineo, Don Percassi. *Knuckles Norton*: Dick Bonelle. *First Poker Player*: Igors Gavon. *Knuckles' Gang*: Ken Ayers, Richard Maxon, Dale Muchmore, Alexander Orfaly. *Sugar Kane*: ELAINE JOYCE. *Cabdriver*: Ken Ayers. *Olga*: Eileen Casey. *Sunbathers*: Nicole Barth, Pam Blair, Eileen Casey, Robin Hoctor, Debra Lyman, Peggy Lyman, Sally Neal, Pamela Sousa. *Train Conductor*: George Blackwell. *Bellboy*: Andy Bew. *Osgood Fielding, Jr.*: CYRIL RITCHARD. *"Chicago" Singers*: Ken Ayers, George Blackwell, Dick Bonelle, Igors Gavon, Hal Norman.

The action takes place in Chicago, Miami and in between in 1931.

Act 1, Scene 1: Chicago Theatre. *Scene 2*: Backstage Chicago Theatre. *Scene 3*: Chicago Street. *Scene 4*: Clark Street Garage. *Scene 5*: Dearborn Street Railroad Station. *Scene 6*: The Dixie Flyer. *Scene 7*: The Seminole-Ritz Hotel Veranda. *Scene 8*: Josephine and Daphne's Hotel Room.

Act 2, Scene 1: The Beach. *Scene 2*: The Hotel Veranda. *Scene 3*: The New Caledonia Yacht. *Scene 4*: Josephine and Daphne's Hotel Room. *Scene 5*: The Hotel Night Club. *Scene 6*: The Hotel Service Corridor. *Scene 7*: The New Caledonia Yacht.

ACT 1[18]

"Windy City Marmalade"
S. Smith, Society Syncopaters

"Penniless Bums"
R. Morse, T. Roberts, Unemployed Musicians

"Tear the Town Apart" (dance)
S. Condos, Spats' Gang

"The Beauty That Drives Men Mad"
R. Morse, T. Roberts

"We Could Be Close"
R. Morse, E. Joyce

"Sun on My Face"
R. Morse, T. Roberts, E. Joyce, S. Smith, A. Kass, Ensemble

"November Song"
C. Ritchard, Millionaires

"(Doin' It For) Sugar"
R. Morse, T. Roberts

ACT 2

"Hey, Why Not!"
E. Joyce, Ensemble

"Beautiful Through and Through"
C. Ritchard, R. Morse

"What Do You Give to a Man Who's Had Everything?"
T. Roberts, E. Joyce

"Magic Nights"
R. Morse

"It's Always Love"
T. Roberts

"When You Meet a Man in Chicago"
R. Morse, T. Roberts, E. Joyce, S. Smith, All-Girl Band and Chorus Line

1972.05 THAT'S ENTERTAINMENT

A Musical (Revue) in Two Acts. Music by Arthur Schwartz. Lyrics by Howard Dietz. Orchestrations, arrangements and musical direction by Luther Henderson. Choreography by Larry Fuller. Production directed by Paul Aaron. Scenery and lighting designed by David F. Segal. Costumes by Jane Greenwood. Sound designed by Anthony Alloy. Produced by Gordon Crowe in association with J. Robert Breton. Opened 14 April 1972 at the Edison Theatre and closed 16 April 1972 after 4 performances.

CAST (in alphabetical order): *Greg*: David Chaney. *Richard*: Jered Holmes. *Carol*: Judith Knaiz. *Adele*: Michon Peacock. *Lena*: Vivian Reed. *Jack*: Scott Salmon. *Lucille*: Bonnie Schon. *Donald*: Michael Vita. *Sam*: Alan Weeks.

ACT 1

Overture
The Company

Medley:
"We Won't Take It Back" (from *INSIDE U.S.A.*)
"Hammacher Schlemmer, I Love You" (from *THE LITTLE SHOW*)
"Come, Oh, Come" (from *INSIDE U.S.A.*)
M. Peacock, B. Schon, S. Slamon, D. Chaney

"I'm Glad I'm Single" (from *THE GAY LIFE*)J. Holmes

"You're Not the Type" (from *THE GAY LIFE*)/"Miserable with You" (*from THE BANDWAGON*)
J. Knaiz, J. Holmes

"Something to Remember You By" (from *THREE'S A CROWD*)
J. Knaiz

"Hottentot Potentate" (from *AT HOME ABROAD*)
V. Reed, A. Weeks

"Day After Day" (from *FLYING COLORS*)/"Fly by Night" (from *BETWEEN THE DEVIL*)
Company

"Everything"
J. Holmes

"Farewell" (Act 1, after "Comedy Tonight")
L. Pritchett

"Echo Song" (Act 2, after "That Dirty Old Man")
J. Hansen, P. Hall

Dropped for this production:
"Pretty Little Picture," "That'll Show Him"

Note change:
"The House of Marcus Lycus" (revised as solo)
C. Ballantine

[18]For subsequent national tour, the following songs were added:

"See You Around" (Act 1, after "The Beauty That Drives Men Mad")
L. Palmer (Sugar)

"Nice Ways" (Act 1, after "We Could Be Close")
Leland Palmer

"Don't Be Afraid" (Act 2, replacing "What Do You Give. .")
Larry Kert (Joe), L. Palmer

"I'm Engaged" (Act 2, after "Magic Nights")
R. Morse

"People in My Life" (Act 2, after "I'm Engaged")
L. Kert

Dropped for tour:
"Sun on My Face," "What Do You Give to a Man Who's Had Everything?," "It's Always Love."

"Blue Grass" (from *INSIDE U.S.A.*)
A. Weeks
"Fatal Fascination" (from *FLYING COLORS*)/"White Heat" (from *THE BANDWAGON*)
B. Schon
"Right at the Start of It" (from *THREE'S A CROWD*)
A. Weeks
"Confession" (from *THE BANDWAGON*)
J. Knaiz, M. Vita
"Smoking Reefers" (from *FLYING COLORS*)
V. Reed
"How High Can a Little Bird Fly?"(from *THE GIBSON FAMILY*, radio; *FOLLOW THE SUN*, London)
S. Salmon
"Keep Off the Grass"
D. Chaney
"I See Your Face Before Me" (from *BETWEEN THE DEVIL*)
M. Vita, M. Peacock
"Experience" (from *BETWEEN THE DEVIL*)
D. Chaney
"Two Faced Woman" (from *FLYING COLORS*)
A. Weeks
"Foolish Face" (from *THE SECOND LITTLE SHOW*)
S. Salmon
"By Myself" (from *BETWEEN THE DEVIL*)
V. Reed
"That's Entertainment" (from *THE BANDWAGON* film)
M. Vita

ACT 2
Dance Medley:
"You and the Night and the Music" (from *REVENGE WITH MUSIC*)/
"Louisiana Hayride" (from *FLYING COLORS*)
"Dancing in the Dark" (from *THE BANDWAGON*)
The Company
"Triplets" (from *BETWEEN THE DEVIL*)
B. Schon, D. Chaney, J. Holmes
"High and Low" (from *THE BANDWAGON*)
S. Salmon
"How Low Can a Little Worm Go?"
J. Knaiz
"Absent Minded"
J. Holmes
"High Is Better Than Low" (from *JENNIE*)
J. Knaiz, S. Salmon
"If There Is Someone Lovelier Than You" (from *REVENGE WITH MUSIC*)D. Chaney
"I've Made a Habit of You" (from *THE LITTLE SHOW*)
B. Schon
"I Guess I'll Have to Change My Plan" (from *THE LITTLE SHOW*)
A. Weeks
"New Sun in the Sky" (from *THE BANDWAGON*)
V. Reed
"Farewell My Lovely" (from *AT HOME ABROAD*)
M. Peacock
"Alone Together" (from *FLYING COLORS*)
M. Vita
"(A) Shine on Your Shoes" (from *FLYING COLORS*)
The Company

1972.06 LOST IN THE STARS

A Revival of the Musical Play in Two Acts, 18 Scenes[19]. Words (book and lyrics) by Maxwell Anderson. Music by Kurt Weill. Based on the novel "Cry, the Beloved Country" by Alan Paton. Directed by Gene Frankel. Scenery by Oliver Smith. Costumes by Patricia Quinn Stewart. Lighting by Paul Sullivan. Musical direction by Karen Gustafson. Choreography and musical staging by Louis Johnson. Musical arrangements and orchestrations by Kurt Weill. Projections by Alec Nesbitt. Produced by The John F. Kennedy Center for the Performing Arts (Roger L. Stevens, Diana Shumlin, producers). Opened 18 April 1972 at the Imperial Theatre and closed 21 May 1972 after 39 performances.

CAST (in order of appearance): *Answerer*: Lee Hooper. *Dancer*: Harold Pierson. *Leader*: ROD PERRY. *Drummer*: Babafumi Akunyun. *Stephen Kumalo*: BROCK PETERS. *Grace Kumalo*: ROSETTA LeNOIRE. *Stationmaster*: Adam Petroski. *The Young Man*: Sid Marshall. *The Woman*: Ruby Greene Aspinall. *Arthur Jarvis*: Don Fenwick. *James Jarvis*: JACK GWILLIM. *Edward Jarvis*: David Jay. *Mrs. Jarvis*: Karen Ford. *John Kumalo*: LEONARD JACKSON. *Paulus*: Leonard Hayward. *William*: Harold Pierson. *Alex*: Giancarlo Esposito. *Foreman*: Mark Dempsey. *Mrs. M'Kize*: Alyce Elizabeth Webb. *Hlabeni*: Garrett Saunders. *Eland*: Peter Bailey-Britton. *Linda*: Marki Bey. *Johannes Pafuri*: Autris Paige. *Matthew Kumalo*: DAMON EVANS. *Absalom Kumalo*: GILBERT PRICE. *Rose*: Judy Gibson. *Irina*: MARGARET COWIE. *First Policeman*: Mark Dempsey. *Second Policeman*: Roy Hausen. *Servant*: Richard Triggs. *The Guard*: Roy Hausen. *Burton*: Alexander Reed. *The Judge*: STAATS COTSWORTH. *McRae*: Leonard Hayward.

Singers: Lana Caradimas, Suzanne Cogan, Karen Ford, Aleesa Foster, Ruby Greene Aspinall, Amelia Haas, Edna Husband, Urylee Leonardos, Rona Leslie Pervil, Therman Bailey, Donald Coleman, Raymond Frith, Leonard Hayward, Autris Paige, Mandingo Shaka, Richard Triggs. *Dancers*: Michael Harrison, Wayne Stevenson Hayes, Oba-Ya, Michael Oiwake.

Time: The Present. *Opening*: Ndotsheni—a Small Village in South Africa. *Act 1, Scene 1*: Stephen Kumalo's Home. *Scene 2*: The Railroad Station. *Scene 3*: Johannesburg. John Kumalo's Tobacco Shop. *Scene 4*: The Search: (1) The Factory Office, (2) Mrs. M'Kize's House, (3) Hlabeni's House, (4) Parole Office. *Scene 5*: Stephen's Shantytown Lodging. *Scene 6*: A Dive in Shantytown. *Scene 7*: A Street in Shantytown. *Scene 8*: Irina's Hut in Shantytown. *Scene 9*: Arthur Jarvis' Home. *Scene 10*: A Street in Shantytown. *Scene 11*: Prison. *Scene 12*: A Street in Shantytown.

Act 2, Scene 1: Johannesburg. Stephen's Shantytown Lodging. *Scene 2*: Arthur Jarvis' Doorway. *Scene 3*: The Courtroom. *Scene 4*: Prison Cell. *Scene 5*: Stephen's Chapel. *Scene 6*: Stephen Kumalo's Home.

ACT 1
Opening
"The Hills of Ixtapo"
R. Perry, L. Hooper, Singers
Scene 1
"Thousands of Miles"
B. Peters
Scene 2
"Train to Johannesburg"
R. Perry, Singers
Scene 4
"The Search"
B. Peters, R. Perry, Singers
Scene 5
"The Little Grey House"
B. Peters, Singers
Scene 7
"Stay Well"
G. Price
Scene 8
"Trouble Man"
M. Cowie
Scene 9
"Murder in Parkwold"
Singers
Scene 10
"Fear"
Singers
Scene 12
"Lost in the Stars"
B. Peters, Singers

ACT 2
Opening
"The Wild Justice"
R. Perry, Singers
Scene 1
"O Tixo, Tixo, Help Me"
B. Peters

[19]Originally produced in New York 30 October 1949 at the Music Box Theatre for 281 performances.

Scene 4
"Cry, the Beloved Country"
R. Perry, Singers
Scene 5
"Big Mole"
G. Esposito
Scene 6
"Thousands of Miles" (reprise)
Singers

1972.07 DIFFERENT TIMES

A Musical in Two Acts in a Prologue, 15 Scenes and Epilogue. Book, music, lyrics and direction by Michael Brown. Dances and musical numbers staged by Tod Jackson. Scenery and costumes by David Guthrie. Lighting by Martin Aronstein. Orchestrations by Norman Paris, Arthur Harris, Ted Simons. Musical direction, dance and vocal arrangements by Rene Wiegert. Audio (sound) by Jack Shearing. Produced by Bowman Productions Inc. (Arthur C. Twitchell, Jr., President) with William L. Witt and William J. Gumperz. Opened 1 May 1972 at the ANTA Theatre and closed 20 May 1972 after 24 performances.

CAST (in order of appearance): *Stephen Adams Levy*: SAM STONEBURNER. *Margaret Adams*: BARBARA WILLIAMS. *Gregory Adams*: JAMIE ROSS. *Mrs. Daniel Webster Hepplewhite*: MARY JO CATLETT. *Mrs. Hepplewhite's Mother*: PATTI KARR. *Nelle Harper*: Joyce Nolen. *Larry Lawrence Levy*: JOE MASIELL. *Angela Adams*: Candace Cook. *Doughboys*: Terry Nicholson, Ronnie DeMarco, David K. Thorne. *Officer*: Ronald Young. *Marianne*: Dorothy Frank. *Columbia*: Karin Baker. *The Kaiser*: MARY JO CATLETT. *Elsie*: MARY BRACKEN PHILLIPS. *Bobby*: Ronald Young. *Marilyn*: Dorothy Frank. *The Hazelnuts*: Candace Cook, Dorothy Frank, Karin Baker, Joyce Nolen. *Hazel Hughes*: MARY JO CATLETT. *Lady Ffenger*: MARY JO CATLETT. *Hattie, Pauline, and Mae Verne*: Dorothy Frank, Candace Cook, Karin Baker. *The Keynoters*: Terry Nicholson, Mary Bracken Phillips, David K. Thorne, Ronald Young. *Kimberley Langley*: PATTI KARR. *Abigail*: MARY BRACKEN PHILLIPS. *Mrs. Callahan*: MARY JO CATLETT. *Josie*: MARY JO CATLETT. *Frank*: RONALD YOUNG. *Joe*: Terry Nicholson. *Don*: David K. Thorne. *Mel*: Ronnie DeMarco. *Stan*: JOE MASIELL. *Linda*: Dorothy Frank. *Frank Gonzales*: RONALD YOUNG.

The action takes place between 1905 and 1970.

Prologue: 1970.

Act 1, Scene 1: The Fair in Portland, Oregon, 1905. *Scene 2*: A hotel room in Portland, 1905. *Scene 3*: A street in Boston, 1915. *Scene 4*: A hotel room in Boston, 1917. *Scene 5*: A theatre stage, 1917. *Scene 6*: A speakeasy in Boston, 1924-1929. *Scene 7*: The Gregory Adams house in Boston, 1929. *Scene 8*: The Bijou Ballroom in Bayonne, 1933.

Act 2, Scene 1: Ffenger, Hall, London, 1942. *Scene 2*: A street in London, 1942. *Scene 3*: The Gregory Adams house in Boston, 1942. *Scene 4*: The Stephen Adams house in Mt. Kisco and Stephen's office in Manhattan, 1963. *Scene 5*: Abigail's room in Manhattan, 1965. *Scene 6*: An art gallery, 1968. *Scene 7*: Central Park, 1970.

Epilogue: 1970.

ACT 1
"Different Times"
S. Stoneburner
"Seeing the Sights"
People of 1905
"The Spirit Is Moving"
B. Williams, People of 1905
"Here's Momma"
B. Williams
"Everything in the World Has a Place"
J. Ross, B. Williams
"I Wish I Didn't Love Him"
B. Williams
"Forward into Tomorrow"
M. J. Catlett, Suffragettes
"You're Perfect"
C. Cooke
"Marianne"
R. Young, Doughboys, D. Frank, K. Baker, M. J. Catlett
"Daddy, Daddy"
C. Cooke, D. Frank, K. Baker, J. Nolen
"I Feel Grand"
M. J. Catlett, C. Cooke, D. Frank, K. Baker, J. Nolen
"Sock Life in the Eye"
J. Masiell
"I'm Not Through"
J. Masiell, Marathon Dancers

ACT 2
"I Miss Him"
D. Frank, C. Cooke, K. Baker
"One More Time"
P. Karr, T. Nicholson, M. B. Phillips, D. K. Thorne, R. Young
"Here's Momma" (reprise)
S. Stoneburner
"I Dreamed About Roses"
S. Stoneburner, P. Karr, U.S.O. Guests
"I Wish I Didn't Love Her" (reprise)
J. Ross
"The Words I Never Said"
S. Stoneburner, P. Karr
"The Life of a Woman"
P. Karr
"Here's Momma" (reprise)
P. Karr, Momma's Poppas
"He Smiles"
M. B. Phillips, M. J. Catlett
"Genuine Plastic"
S. Stoneburner, Gallery Guests
"Thanks a Lot"
R. Young, M. B. Phillips, Guests
"When They Start Again"
M. B. Phillips, R. Young
"Different Times" (reprise)
S. Stoneburner
"The Spirit Is Moving" (reprise)
Company

1972.08 TOMMY

Les Grands Ballets Canadiens in a ballet adaptation of the rock opera in One Act.[20] Music and Lyrics by Peter Townshend, John Entwistle and Keith Moon. Choreography by Fernand Nault. Sets by David Jenkins. Costumes by François Barbeau. Lighting by Nicholas Cernovitch. Film sequences by Luc-Michel Hannaux, Denys Morisset, PauL Vezina, Office du Film du Québec. Produced by Les Grand Ballets Canadiens (Ludmilla Chiriaeff, Founder and Director; Fernand Nault, Associate Artistic Director; Uriel G. Luft, General manager). Opened 3 May 1972 at the New York City Center and closed 28 May 1972 after 31 performances.

CAST: *Tommy*: MANNIE ROWE or ALEXANDER BELIN or VINCENT WARREN. *Mother*: REVA PINCUSOFF or LESLIE-MAY DOWNS or BARBARA WITHEY. *Father*: LASZLO TAMASIK or WILLIAM JOSEF. *Acid Queen*: Janet Snyder or Manon Larin or Sonia Taverner or Hae Shik Kim. *Pin Ball Wizard*: James Bates or Mannie Rowe or Maurice Lemay or Andris Toppe. *The Hawker*: Renald Rabu or Richard Beaty or Wiliam Josef. *Uncle Ernie*: JOHN STANZEL. *Cousin Kevin*: Andris Toppe or Maurice Lemay or Guillermo Gonzales. *The Lover*: David Drummond or James Boyd or Lorne Toumine. *Sally Simpson*: Carole Landry or Eileen Heath or Lorna Cameron.

With Richard Bouchard, Francine Boucher, Robert Dicello, Louise Dore, Gerry Gilbert, Eileen Heath, Barbara Jacobs, Melinda Lawrence, Helen McKergow, Conrad Peterson, Reva Pincusoff, Cathy Sharp, Richard Sugarman, Susan Taylor, Michael Thomas, Laeleen Winchiu, Barbara Withey.

Lead Vocalist on recording: ROGER DALTREY. *The Hawker*: Sonny Boy Williamson.

MUSICAL NUMBERS
"It's a boy"
"You didn't hear it"
"Amazing journey"
"Sparks"

[20]Preceded by two ballets, Ceremony and Hip and Straight. The ballet was performed to the pre-recorded score of *TOMMY* as released on Decca Records.

"Eyesight to the blind"
(*Music and Lyrics by* Sonny Boy Williamson.)
"Christmas"
"Cousin Kevin"
(*Music and Lyrics by* John Entwistle.)
"The acid queen"
"Underture"
"Do you think it's alright"
"Fiddle about"
(*Music and Lyrics by* John Entwistle.)
"Pinball wizard"
"There's a doctor I've found"
"Go to the mirror boy"
"Tommy can you hear me"
"Smash the mirror"
"Sensation"
"Miracle cure"
"Sally Simpson"
"I'm free"
"Welcome"
"Tommy's holiday camp"
(*Music and Lyrics by* Keith Moon.)
"We're not gonna take it"

1972.09 HARD JOB BEING GOD

A Rock Musical in One Act, 14 Scenes. Music and lyrics by Tom Martel. Directed by Bob Yde. Musical staging by Lee Theodore. Production designed by Ray Wilke. Costumes by Mary Whitehead. Lighting by Patrika Brown. Audio (sound) by Bill Sandreuter. Musical director, Roy Bittan. Produced by Bob Yde in association with Andy Wiswell. Opened 15 May 1972 at the Edison Theatre and closed 20 May 1972 after 7 performances.

CAST (in alphabetical order): *Sarah, Jacob's Wife, Slave, Pharaoh's Soldier, Moabite, Judean, Susanna*: Gini Eastwood. *Jacob's Son, Moses, Moabite, David*: Stu Freeman. *God*: Tom Martel. *Slave, Pharaoh's Soldier, Ruth, Judean, Shepherd*: Anne Sarofeen. *Abraham, Jacob, Pharaoh, Moabite, Judean, Amos*: John Twomey.

Scene 1: Anytime, anywhere. *Scene 2*: Canaan, c. 1935 B.C. *Scene 3*: Canaan, c. 1700 B.C. *Scene 4*: Slave Camp in Egypt, c. 1240 B.C. *Scene 5*: Court of Rameses II, Pharaoh of Egypt, same day, c. 1240 B.C. *Scene 6*: The foot of Mt. Sinai, three months later. *Scene 7*: The Land of Moab, 1110 B.C. *Scene 8*: Jerusalem, 1005 B.C. *Scene 9*: Israel, c. 812 B.C. *Scene 10*: Israel, c. 780 B.C. *Scene 11*: On the banks of the Jordan River, 760 B.C. *Scene 12*: A pasture in Judah, 750 B.C. *Scene 13*: Feast Day, Royal Shrine of Bethel in Israel, 749 B.C. *Scene 14*: Anytime, anywhere.

MUSICAL NUMBERS

Scene 1
"Hard Job Being God"
T. Martel, Company
Scene 2
"Wherever You Go"
G. Eastwood, J. Twomey
Scene 3
"Famine"
J. Twomey, G. Eastwood, S. Freeman
Scene 4
"Buy a Slave"
Egyptian Slave Merchants
"Prayer"
Hebrew Slaves
Scene 5
"Moses' Song"
S. Freeman, J. Twomey
"The Ten Plagues"
J. Twomey, Soldiers, S. Freeman
"Passover"
Soldiers, J. Twomey, S. Freeman, Slaves
Scene 6
"The Eleven Commandments"
S. Freeman, Freed Slaves
Scene 7
"Tribes"
Hebrew Woman, the Tribes
"Ruth"
S. Freeman, J. Twomey, A. Sarofeen
Scene 8
"Festival"
Judeans
"Hail, David"
Judeans, S. Freeman
"A Very Lonely King"
S. Freeman
Scene 9
"Battle"
Scene 10
"You're on Your Own"
Hebrews, T. Martel
Scene 11
"A Psalm of Peace"
G. Eastwood, Hebrews
Scene 12
"I'm Countin' on You"
T. Martel, J. Twomey
Scene 13
"Shalom L'chaim!"
Hebrews
"Amos Gonna Give You Hell"
A. Sarofeen
Scene 14
"What Do I Have to Do?"
T. Martel Company

1972.10 DON'T PLAY US CHEAP

A Comedy Musical in Two Acts. Book, words, music and direction by Melvin Van Peebles. Scenery by Kert Lundell. Costumes by Bernard Johnson. Lighting by Martin Aronstein. Musical supervision by Harold Wheeler. Produced by Melvin Van Peebles. Opened 16 May 1972 at the Ethel Barrymore Theatre and closed 1 October 1972 after 164 performances.

CAST: *Mr. Percy*: Thomas Anderson. *Mrs. Washington*: Joshie Jo Armstead. *Harold Johnson, Rat*: Nate Barnett. *Mr. Johnson, Cockroach*: Frank Carey. *Mr. Bowser*: Robert Dunn. *Earnestine*: Rhetta Hughes. *Trinity*: Joe Keyes, Jr. *Mrs. Bowser*: Mabel King. *David*: Avon Long. *Mr. Washington*: George 'Ooppee' McCurn. *Miss Maybell*: Esther Rolle. *Mrs. Johnson*: Jay Vanleer.

The action takes place here (in Miss Maybell's apartment in Harlem) "a coupla days before tomorrow."

ACT 1
"Some Days It Seems That It Just Don't Even Pay to Get Out of Bed"
N. Barnett, F. Carey
"Break That Party"
A. Long, J. Keyes, Jr.
"8 Day Week"
T. Anderson, Company
"Saturday Night'
Company
"I'm a Bad Character"
J. Keyes, Jr., Company
"You Cut Up the Clothes in the Closet of My Dreams"
J. J. Armstead
"It Makes No Difference"
E. Rolle, Company
"Quittin' Time"
G. McCurn, Company

ACT 2

"Ain't Love Grand"
R. Hughes, Company

"The Book of Life"
R. Dunn, Company

Quartet:

"Ain't Love Grand" (reprise)
R. Hughes

"Know Your Business"
E. Rolle

"Big Future"
F. Carey, J. Vanleer

"Break That Party" (reprise)
A. Long, J. Keyes, Jr.

"Feast on Me"
M. King, Company

"The Phoney Game"
A. Long, Company

"(If You See a Devil) Smash Him"
Company

1972.11 HEATHEN!

A Musical in Two Acts, 21 Scenes. Book by Sir Robert Helpmann and Eaton Magoon, Jr. Music and lyrics by Eaton Magoon, Jr. Directed by Lucia Victor. Choreography by Sammy Bayes. Setting by Jack Brown. Costumes by Bruce Harrow. Lighting by Paul Sullivan. Orchestrations by Larry Fallon. Musical director, Clay Fullum. Associate choreographer, Dan Siretta. Musical supervision, vocal and dance and incidental music by Mel Marvin. Produced by Leonard J. Goldberg and Ken Gaston in association with R. Paul Woodville. Opened and closed 21 May 1972 at the Billy Rose Theatre after 1 performance.

CAST (in order of appearance): *Reverend Jonathan Beacon, Jonathan*: RUSS THACKER. *Kalialani, Kalia*: YOLANDE BAVAN. *Mano'Ula, Mano*: EDWARD RAMBEAU. *The Muggers*: Dennis Dennehy, Justis Skae, Sal Pernice. *Reverend Hiram Burnham*: Dan Merriman. *Hepsibah Burnham*: Ann Hodges. *Church Elders*: Christopher Barrett, Mary Walling, Michael Serrecchia. *Kaha Kai, The Chanter*: Dennis Dennehy. *Alika*: MOKIHANA. *Tourists*: Ann Hodges, Dan Merriman. *Hawaiian Boy*: Charles Goeddertz. *Policeman*: Christopher Barrett. *Pueo*: Honey Sanders. *Momona-Nui*: Tina Santiago. *Boys in Jail*: Charles Goeddertz, Michael Serrecchia, Quitman Fludd.

The Girls and Boys of Past and Present: Nancy Dafgek, Jaclyn Villamil, Mary Walling, Karen Kristin, Dennis Dennehy, Randy DiGrazio, Quitman Fludd, Charles Goeddertz, Sal Pernice, Michael Serrecchia, Justis Skae.

The action takes place in Hawaii in 1819 (the past) and 1972 (the present).

Act 1, Scene 1: A beach by a sea wall, Waikiki, 1972. *Scene 2*: A Church in Boston, 1819. *Scene 3*: Aboard a ship at sea, 1819. *Scene 4*: Mano'ula's Canoe at Sea, 1819. *Scene 5*: The Kona shore, 1819. *Scene 6*: The beach, Waikiki, 1972. *Scene 7*: A grove naer Jonathan's hut, 1819. *Scene 8*: A Jail in Honolulu, 1972. *Scene 9*: On the edge of the village, 1819. *Scene 10*: The Heiau, A Council Meeting, 1819. *Scene 11*: Mano'ula's Compound, 1819. *Scene 12*: Past and Present Blend.

Act 2, Scene 1: A Jail in Honolulu, 1972. *Scene 2*: The Church Grounds, Dedication Ceremony, 1819. *Scene 3*: Waikiki Beach Bar, 11972. *Scene 4*: Mano'ula's Compound, 1819. *Scene 5*: Riding the Breakers, 1819. *Scene 6*: A Corner of the Compound, 1819. *Scene 7*: Kalialani's hut, 1819. *Scene 8*: The village under the eruption of Mauna Loa, 1819. *Scene 9*: Past and Present Blend.

ACT 1

Scene 1

"Paradise"
R. Thacker, Beach People

Scene 2

"The Word of the Lord"
D. Merriman, A. Hodges, C. Barrett, M. Walling, M. Serrecchia

Scene 3

"My Sweet Tomorrow"
R. Thacker

Scene 4

"A Man Among Men"
E. Rambeau, Rowers

Scene 5

"Aloha"
Company

"Kalialani"
Y. Bavan

Scene 7

"No Way in Hell"
R. Thacker, Y. Bavan, E. Rambeau

Scene 9

"Battle Cry"
Y. Bavan

Scene 10

"This Is Someone I Could Love"
E. Rambeau

Scene 11

"House of Grass"
E. Rambeau

Scene 12

"Kava Ceremony"
Company

ACT 2

Scene 1

"For You Brother"
R. Thacker, C. Goeddertz, M. Serrecchia, Q. Fludd

Scene 2

"Spear Games"
Company

"Christianity"
Company

Scene 3

"This Is Someone I Could Love" (reprise)
Y. Bavan

Scene 4

"Heathen"
R. Thacker

Scene 5

"Heathen" (reprise)
R. Thacker, E. Rambeau

Scene 6

"More Better Go Easy"
Mokihana

Scene 9

"Eighth Day"
Company

1972–1973 SEASON

Glynis Johns in A LITTLE NIGHT MUSIC
Martha Swope/TimePix

1972–1973 SEASON

1972.12 GREASE

A New 50's Rock 'N Roll Musical (Comedy) in Two Acts, 12 Scenes[1]. Book, music and lyrics by Jim Jacobs and Warren Casey. Directed by Tom Moore. Musical numbers and dances staged by Patricia Birch. Musical supervision and orchestrations by Michael Leonard. Musical direction, vocal and dance arrangements by Louis St. Louis. Scenery by Douglas W. Schmidt. Costumes by Carrie F. Robbins. Lighting by Karl Eigsti. Sound by Jack Shearing. Produced by Kenneth Waissman and Maxine Fox in association with Anthony D'Amato. Opened 7 June 1972 at the Broadhurst Theatre, moved 21 November 1972 to the Royale Theatre, moved 11 February 1980 to the Majestic Theatre and closed 13 April 1980 after 3388 performances (including Off-Broadway run).

CAST[2] (in order of appearance): *Miss Lynch*: Dorothy Leon. *Patty Simcox*: Ilene Kristen. *Eugene Florczyk*: Tom Harris. *Jan*: Garn Stephens. *Marty*: Meg Bennett. *Betty Rizzo*: ADRIENNE BARBEAU. *Doody*: James Canning. *Roger*: Walter Bobbie. *Kenickie*: Timothy Meyers. *Sonny LaTierri*: Jim Borrelli. *Frenchy*: Marya Small. *Sandy Dumbrowski*: CAROLE DEMAS. *Danny Zuko*: BARRY BOSTWICK. *Vince Fontaine*: Gardner Hayes. *Johnny Casino*: Alan Paul. *Cha-Cha Di Gregorio*: Kathi Moss. *Teen Angel*: Alan Paul.

The action takes place in the late 1950s.

Act 1, Scene 1: (Rydell High Class of '59) Reunion. *Scene 2*: Cafeteria and School Steps. *Scene 3*: Pajama Party. *Scene 4*: Street Corner. *Scene 5*: Schoolyard. *Scene 6*: Park.

Act 2, Scene 1: Kids' Homes. *Scene 2*: School Gym. *Scene 3*: Front of Burger Palace. *Scene 4*: Drive-In Movie. *Scene 5*: Jan's Party. *Scene 6*: Burger Palace.

ACT 1
Scene 1
"Alma Mater"
D. Leon, I. Kristen, T. Harris
"Alma Mater" Parody
Pink Ladies, Burger Palace Boys
Scene 2
"Summer Nights"
C. Demas, B. Bostwick, Pink Ladies, Burger Palace Boys
"Those Magic Changes"
J. Canning, Burger Palace Boys, Pink Ladies
Scene 3
"Freddy, My Love"
M. Bennett, G. Stephens, M. Small, A. Barbeau
Scene 4
"Greased Lightnin'"
T. Meyers, Burger Palace Boys
Scene 6
"Mooning"
W. Bobbie, G. Stephens
"Look at Me, I'm Sandra Dee"
A. Barbeau
"We Go Together"
Pink Ladies, Burger Palace Boys
ACT 2
Scene 1
"Shakin' at the High School Hop"
Entire Company
"It's Raining on Prom Night"
C. Demas
Radio Voice: K. Moss.
Scene 2
"Shakin' at the High School Hop" (reprise)
Entire Company
"Born to Hand-Jive"
A. Paul, Company
Scene 3
"Beauty School Dropout"
A. Paul, M. Small, Choir
Scene 4
"Alone at a Drive-In Movie"
B. Bostwick, Burger Palace Boys
Scene 5
"Rock 'N' Roll Party Queen"
J. Canning, W. Bobbie
"There Are Worse Things I Could Do"
A. Barbeau
"Look at Me, I'm Sandra Dee" (reprise)
C. Demas
Scene 6
"All Choked Up"
C. Demas, B. Bostwick, Company
Finale: "We Go Together" (reprise)
Entire Company

[1]First produced in New York Off-Broadway 14 February 1972 at the Eden Theatre for 128 performances.
[2]Original artists who created their roles Off-Broadway but did not transfer to Broadway: *Marty*: Katie Hanley. *Vince Fontaine*: Don Billett. Note: Pink Ladies include Rizzo, Frenchy, Marty, Jan. Burger Palace Boys include Kenickie, Doody, Roger, Sonny.

1972.13 DON'T BOTHER ME, I CAN'T COPE

A Musical Entertainment (Revue) in Two Acts[3]. Conceived and directed by Vinnette Carroll. (Music and Lyrics) Written by Micki Grant. Choreographer, George Faison. Scenery by Richard A. Miller, supervised by Neil Peter Jampolis. Costumes by Edna Watson, supervised by Sara Brook. Lighting by B. J. Sammler, supervised by Ken Billington. Musical direction and arrangements by Danny Holgate. Production supervisor, Sam Ellis. An Urban Arts Corps Production. Associate producer, Gordon, Gray, Jr. Produced by Edward Padula and Arch Lustberg, in association with Ford's Theater Society (Washington, D.C.). Opened 13 June 1972 at the Edison Theatre and closed 26 October 1974 after 1065 performances (including Playhouse run).

CAST (in alphabetcial order): ALEX BRADFORD, HOPE CLARKE, MICKI GRANT, BOBBY HILL, ARNOLD WILKERSON.
Singers: Alberta Bradford, Charles Campbell, Marie Thomas. *Dancers*: Thommie Bush, Gerald G. Francis, Ben Harney, Leona Johnson.

ACT 1[4]
"I Gotta Keep Movin'"
Alex Bradford, Alberta Bradford, C. Campbell, B. Hill
Danced by B. Harney.

[3]Originally produced 19 April 1972 at the Playhouse Theatre for 63 performances.
[4]Added during the run:
"Lock Up the Doors" (Act 1)
"Children's Rhymes" (Act 1)
Company
"Ghetto Life" (Act 1)
Company
"My Love's So Good" (Act 1)
"Love Mississippi" (Act 2)
"Storefront Church" (Act 2)
Added for National Tours:
Billie Holliday Song (Act 1)
Sheila Ellis
"Prayer" (Act 2)
S. Ellis, Every Hayes, Pat Estwick, Esther Williams, Alton Lathrop
"Sermon" (Act 2)
E. Hayes, Company
"Universe in Mourning" (Act 2)
Vivian Reed

"Harlem Streets"
Dancers
"Lookin' Over from Your Side"
B. Hill
"Don't Bother Me, I Can't Cope"
Entire Company
"When I Feel Like Moving"
H. Clarke, Dancers
"Help"
H. Clarke, Dancers
"Fighting for Pharaoh"
Alex Bradford, B. Hill, Alberta Bradford, C. Campbell
"Good Vibrations"
A. Bradford, Company
"Love Power"
B. Hill, H. Clarke, Company
"You Think I Got Rhythm"
Dancers
"They Keep Coming"
Entire Company
"My Name Is Man"
A. Wilkerson

ACT 2
"Questions"
M. Grant
"It Takes a Whole Lot of Human Feeling"
M. Grant
"You Think I Got Rhythm?" (reprise)
A. Wilkerson, M. Grant
"Time Brings About a Change"
M. Grant, Alex Bradford, Alberta Bradford, C. Campbell, M. Thomas, A. Wilkerson
"So Little Time"
M. Grant
"Thank Heaven for You"
B. Hill, M. Grant
"Show Me That Special Gene"
L. Johnson, M. Thomas, M. Grant
"So Long Sammy"
B. Hill
Danced by H. Clarke, Dancers
"All I Need"
Alberta Bradford, Company
"I Gotta Keep Movin'" (reprise)
M. Grant, Alex Bradford, Company

1972.14 MAN OF LA MANCHA

A Revival of the Musical Play in One Act[5]. Book by Dale Wasserman. Suggested by the life and work ("Don Quixote") of Miguel de Cervantes y Saavedra. Music by Mitch Leigh. Lyrics by Joe Darion. Book and musical staging by Albert Marre. Choroegraphy by Jack Cole. Settings and lighting by Howard Bay. Costumes by Howard Bay and Patton Campbell. Dance arrangements by Neil Warner. Musical arrangements by Music Makers Inc. Musical direction by Joseph Klein. Produced by Albert W. Selden and Hal James by arrangement with Lincoln Center. Opened 22 June 1972 at the Vivian Beaumont Theatre and closed 21 October 1972 after 140 performances.

CAST (in order of appearance): *Don Quixote (Cervantes)*: RICHARD KILEY, DAVID ATKINSON (matinees). *Sancho*: IRVING JACBSON, EDMOND VARRATO (opening and matinees). *Captain of the Inquisition*: Renato Cibelli. *Aldonza*: JOAN DIENER, GERRIANNE RAPHAEL (matinees). *The Innkeeper*: JACK DABDOUB. *Dr. Carrasco*: LEE BERGERE. *The Padre*: ROBERT ROUNSEVILLE. *Antonia*: Diane Barton. *The Housekeeper*: Eleanore Knapp. *The Barber*: Ted Forlow. *Pedro*, Head Muleteer: Shev Rodgers. *Anselmo*, a Muleteer: Ted Forlow. *Jose*, a Muleteer: Hector (Jaime) Mercado. *Juan*, a Muleteer: John Aristides. *Paco*, a Muleteer: Bill Stanton. *Tenorio*, a Muleteer: Fernando Grahal. *Maria*, the Innkeeper's Wife: Rita Metzger. *The Dancing Horses*: Fernando Grahal, Hector (Jaime) Mercado. *The Horses at the Well*: Jeff Killion, Shev Rodgers. *Fermina*, a slavey and Moorish Dancer: Laura Kenyon. *Guitarist*: Stephen Sahlein.

Guards, Men of the Inquisition: Jeff Killion, David Wasson, Robert Cromwell, William Tatum.

1972.15 (LEONARD BERNSTEIN'S) MASS

A Theatre Piece for Singers, Players and Dancers in One Act, 17 Scenes. Music by Leonard Bernstein. Texts from the liturgy of the Roman Mass. English texts by Stephen Schwartz and Leonard Bernstein. Directed by Gordon Davidson. Choreography by Alvin Ailey. Settings by Oliver Smith. Costumes by Frank Thompson. Lighting by Gilbert V. Hemsley, Jr. Staged by Gordon Davidson and Alvin Ailey. Musical director, Maurice Peress. Production coordinator, Diana Shumlin. Sound by Richard Guy. Associate conductor, Thomas Pierson. Associate producer, Schuyler G. Chapin. Produced by the John F. Kennedy Center for the Performing Arts (Roger L. Stevens and Martin Feinstein, Producers) and Sol Hurok. Opened 28 June 1972 at the Metropolitan Opera House and closed 22 July 1972 after 22 performances.

CAST: *Celebrant*: ALAN TITUS or DAVID CRYER.

Singing Ensemble: John D. Anthony, Cheryl Barnes, Jacqueline Britt, Jane Coleman, David Cryer, Magaret Cowie, Ed Dixon, Leigh Dodson, Eugene Edwards, Thom Ellis, Lowell Harris, Lee Hooper, Gary Lipps, Linda Lloyd, Linda Marks, Larry Marshall, Gina Penn, John Bennett Perry, Mary Bracken Phillips, Neva Small, David Spangler, Alan Titus. *The Alvin Ailey American Dance Theatre*: *Acolytes*: Judith Jamison, Dudley Williams, Clive Thompson, Linda Kent, Kenneth Pearl, Sylvia Waters, Estelle E. Spurlock. *Dancing Ensemble*: Kelvin Rotardier, Sara Yarborough, Mari Kajiwara, John Parks, Hector Mercado, Leland Schwantes, Clover Mathis, Lynne Dell Walker.

The Norman Scribner Choir: *Sopranos*: Juanita Brown, Carol Gericke, Diane Higginbotham, Vicki Johnstone, Janet Kenney, Katherine Ray, Cynthia Richards, Diana Rothman, Sandra Willets. *Altos*: Barbara Boller, Catherine Bounds, Alicia Kopfstein-Penk, Patricia George, Suzanne Grant, Raina Mann, Anne Miller, Janet Sooy, Joy Wood. *Tenors*: Barry Butts, David Coon, Robert Dorsey, Michael Hume, William Jones, Robert Kimball, John Madden, Robert Stevenson, Robert Whitney. *Basses*: Earl Baker, Glenn Cunningham, Albert deRuiter, Richard Frisch, Arphelius Paul Gatling, Charles Greenwell, Walter Richardson, Ronald Roxbury, Michael Tronzo. *The Berkshire Boys' Choir*: David Abell, Ben Borsch, Timothy Brown, Chris Cole, Sammy Coleman, Peter Coulianos, Thomas Ettinghausen, Liam Fennelly, Tim Ferrell, Jonathan Gram, Bruce Haynes, Richard Michael, Michael Miller, Chris Negus, Edward Rosen, Robert Rough, Miles Smith, Richard Swan, David Voorhees.

Antiphon: Betty Allen, Karen Altman, Dominic Cossa, Raymond deVoll. *Responsory*: Adrienne Albert, Maeretha Stewart, June Magruder, Charles Magruder, John Manno, William Elliot. *Second Introit*: Leonard Arner (oboe).

Scene 1: Devotions Before Mass: 1. Antiphon: Kyrie Eleison. 2. Hymn: A Simple Song. 3. Psalm: A New Song. 4: Responsory: Alleluia. *Scene 2*: First Introit: Rondo. 1. Prefatory Prayers (Kyrie, Asperges, Introibo, etc.). 2. Thrice-triple Canon: Dominus Vobiscum. *Scene 3*: Second Introit. 1. In Nomine Patris. 2. Prayer for the Congregation (Chorale: Almighty Father). *Scene 4*: Confession. 1. Confiteor. 2. Strophe: I Don't Know. 3. Strophe: Easy. *Scene 5*: Meditation #1. *Scene 6*: Gloria. 1. Gloria Tibi. 2. Gloria in Excelsis. 3. Strophe: Half of the People. 4. Strophe: Thank You. *Scene 7*: Meditation #2. *Scene 8*: Epistle: The Word of the Lord. *Scene 9*: Gospel-Sermon: God Said. *Scene 10*: Credo. 1. Credo in Unum Deum ... 2. Strophe: Non Credo. 3. Strophe: Hurry. 4. Strophe: World Without End. Strophe: I Believe in God. *Scene 11*: Meditation #3: De Profundis, part 1. *Scene 12*: Offertory: De Profundis, part 2. *Scene 13*: The Lord's Prayer: 1. Our Father. 2. Strophe: I Go On. *Scene 14*: Sanctus. *Scene 15*: Agnus Dei. *Scene 16*: Fraction: Things Get Broken. *Scene 17*: Pax: Communion.

MUSICAL NUMBERS
Scene 1
"A Simple Song"
A. Titus or D. Cryer
Scene 4
"I Don't Know"
G. Lipps, N. Small, E. Dixon
"Easy"
E. Edwards, L. Lloyd, D. Spangler
Scene 6
"Gloria Tibi"
A. Titus or D. Cryer

[5]First produced in New York 22 November 1965 at the ANTA Washington Square Theatre for 2328 performances. For Synopsis of Scenes and Musical Numbers, see original 1965 production.

"Thank You"
L. Hooper
Scene 8
"The Word of the Lord"
A. Titus or D. Cryer
Scene 9
"God Said"
L. Marshall
Scene 10
"Non Credo"
J. B. Perry or D. Cryer
"Hurry"
G. Penn
"World Without End"
M. B. Phillips
"I Believe in God"
T. Ellis
Scene 13
"Our Father"
A. Titus or D. Cryer
"I Go On"
A. Titus or D. Cryer
Scene 16
"Things Get Broken"
A. Titus or D. Cryer
Scene 17
"Secret Songs"
M. Cowie, G. Lipps, J. D. Anthony, L. Dodson, E. Dixon

1972.16 JACQUES BREL IS ALIVE AND WELL AND LIVING IN PARIS

A Musical Revue in Two Acts[6]. Music by Jacques Brel. Production conception, English lyrics and additional material by Eric Blau. Based on Jacques Brel's lyrics and commentary. Directed by Moni Yakim. Musical direction by Mort Shuman. Music arranged and conducted by Wolfgang Knittel. (Scenery by Les Lawrence.) Produced by Bill Levine. Opened 15 September 1972 at the Royale Theatre and closed 28 October 1972 after 51 performances. (Total including Broadway and Off-Broadway runs 1897 performances.)

CAST: ELLY STONE, JOE MASIELL, GEORGE BALL, HENRIETTA VALOR, Janet McCall (alt.), Joseph Neal (alt.).

ACT 1
"Marathon"
Company
"Alone"
G. Ball
"Madeleine"
Company
"I Loved"
E. Stone
"Mathilde"
J. Masiell
"Bachelor's Dance"
G. Ball
"Timid Frieda"
H. Valor
"My Death"
E. Stone
"Girls & Dogs"
J. Masiell, G. Ball
"Jackie"
J. Masiell
"The Statue"
G. Ball
"Desperate Ones"
Company
"Sons Of"
E. Stone
"Amsterdam"
J. Masiell

ACT 2
"The Bulls"
G. Ball
"Old Folks"
E. Stone
"Marieka"
E. Stone
"Brussels"
H. Valor
"Fannette"
G. Ball
"Funeral Tango"
J. Masiell
"Middle Class"
J. Masiell, G. Ball
"You're Not Alone"
E. Stone
"Next"
J. Masiell
"Carousel"
E. Stone
"If We Only Have Love"
Company

[6]Originally produced in New York Off-Broadway 22 January 1968 at the Village Gate for 1847 performances.

1972.17 FROM ISRAEL WITH LOVE

(A Musical Revue from Israel in Two Acts.) Director, Avi David. Musical director, Rafi Ben-Moshe. Choreography by Yakov Kalusky. Produced by Pageant Productions P.T.Y. Ltd. (Executive producers, Jerome M. Lapin, Regina A. Lapin. Executive director, David A. Toben. Producer, Colonel Saul Biber. Director International Operations, Herman E. Schner.) Opened 2 October 1972 at the Palace Theatre and closed 8 October 1972 after 10 performances.

CAST: Micha Adir, Dani Amihud, Chaya Arad, Itzik Barak, Shara Badishy, Eti Brechner, David Dardashi, Irith Esched, Tami Gall, Israel Klugman, Elis Menahemi, Malli Noy, Yacov Noy, Nathan Okev, Gadi Oron, Varda Sagy, Reuven Shenar, Yonnith Shoham, Nurit Zeevi, *Musicians*: David Rosenthal, Izhack Lichtenfeld, Juda Asher Shkolnik, Oded Pintus, Shymel Aroukh, Ilan Gilboa.

ACT 1[7]
"Israel Israel"
(*Music and Lyrics by* Shlomo Carlebach.)
"From the South Good Will Come" (Midarom Tipatach Hatova)
(*Music and Lyrics by* Avraham Zigman.)
"Call for Freedom"
"Three Legs"
"We Take Whatever Comes"
Ballet
"Jerusalem of Gold" (Yerushalaim Shel Zahavi)
(*Music and Lyrics by* Naomi Shemer.)
"Natasha"
(*Music and Lyrics by* Dan Almagor and Y. Kalusky.)

ACT 2
"A Beach Song"
"Night, Night, A Lullaby"

[7]Note: Neither Songs nor Dances were credited to individual performers in the program. Composer and lyricist credits taken from recording.

"From Across the River (Me'ever Lanahar)
(*Music and Lyrics by* S. Tschernichovsky and E. Rubinstein.)
"Coffee Song"
"The Parachutist"
"My Dear Son"
Potpourri, Israeli Style:
"Hava Nagila;" "Again the Night Falls;" Dance: Debka.
"I Am Dying"
"A Song of Peace" (Shir La Shalom)
(*Music and Lyrics by* Yaakov Rotblit, Yair Rosenbloom.)

1972.18

DUDE

The Highway Life (A Musical) in Two Acts. Book and lyrics by Gerome Ragni. Music by Galt MacDermott. Directed and staged by Tom O'Horgan. Production (set) designed by Eugene Lee, Roger Morgan, Franne Lee. Costumes designed by Randy Barcelo. Musical arrangements and orchestrations by Horace Ott. Musical direction by Thomas Pierson. Produced by Adela and Peter Holzer. Opened 9 October 1972 at the Broadway Theatre and closed 21 October 1972 after 16 performances.

CAST: *The Theater Stars*: *#33*: ALLAN NICHOLLS. *Dude*: RALPH CARTER. *Mother Earth*: SALOME BEY. *Bread*: DELORES HALL.

The Shubert Angels: Karen Maria Faatz, Katie Field, Helen Jennings, David Kruger, Cary Mark, Mark Perman, Aida Random, Lynn Reynolds.

The Theatre Wings: *Hero*: Alan Braunstein. *Halo*: Sandra Loys Toder. *Echo*: Dawn Johnson. *Solo*: Michael Jason. *Reba*: RAE ALLEN. *Harold*: WILLIAM REDFIELD. *Suzie Moon*: NELL CARTER. *Zero*: James Patrick Farrell III. *Nero*: Leata Galloway. *Sissy*: David Lasley. *Electric Bill*: Jim Turner. *Shadow*: Dale Soules. *Shade*: Barbara Monte-Britton. *Esso*: Bobby Alessi. *Extra*: Billy Alessi. *Meadow*: Michael Meadows. *World War Too*: Georgianna Holmes. *Noname*: Carol Estey. *Texaco*: Dennis Simpson. *Dude*: NAT MORRIS.

ACT 1
Overture
A. Nicholls, Company
"Theatre/Theatre"
A. Nicholls, The Theater Wings, The Shubert Angels
"A-Stage"
A. Nicholls
"The Mountains"
S. Bey
"Pears and Peaches"
The Shubert Angels
"Eat It"
The Pioneers
"Wah Wah"
N. Carter
"Suzie Moon"
N. Carter
"Y.O.U."
N. Morris
"I Love My Boo Boo"
A. Nicholls, N. Carter, D. Hall, S. Bey
"Hum Drum Life"
S. L. Toder, A. Braunstein, D. Hall, S. Bey
"Who's It?"
N. Morris, The Shubert Angels, The Theatre Wings
"Talk to Me About Love"
N. Morris, J. P. Farrell
"Goodbyes"
R. Allen
"I'm Small"
A. Braunstein
"You Can Do Nothing About It"
L. Galloway
"The Handsomest Man"
D. Lasley
"Electric Prophet"
J. Turner
"No One"
S. Bey

ACT 2
"Who Will Be the Children"
The Shubert Angels
"Go Holy Ghost"
The Shubert Angels
"A Song to Sing"
N. Morris, D. Hall, L. Galloway, D. Lasley, The Theatre Wings, The Shubert Angels
"A Dawn"
A. Braunstein, S. L. Toder, The Theatre Wings
"The Days of This Life"
Bobby Alessi, Billy Alessi, N. Morris, J. P. Farrell
"I Never Knew"
S. Bey
"Air Male"
The Theatre Wings
"Undo"
D. Hall
"The Earth"
W. Redfield, R. Allen
"My Darling I Love You March"
The Theatre Wings, The Shubert Angels
"So Long Dude"
The Theatre Wings
"Dude All Dude"
The Theatre Wings, The Shubert Angels
"Peace Peace"
The Shubert Angels
"Jesus Hi"
The Shubert Angels
"Baby Breath"
S. Bey, D. Hall, A. Nicholls, The Theatre Wings, The Shubert Angels
"Sweet Dreams"
A. Nicholls, Company

1972.19

HURRY, HARRY

A Musical Comedy in Two Acts, 19 Scenes. Book by Jeremiah Morris, Lee Kalcheim, Susan Perkis. Music by Bill Weeden. Lyrics by David Finkle. Directed by Jeremiah Morris. Choreography by Gerald Teijelo. Scenery designed by Fred Voelpel. Lighting designed by Martin Aronstein. Costumes designed by Sara Brook. Orchestrations and musical supervision, Lee Norris. Musical direction, Arthur Azener. Associate producer, Ed Lewis. Produced by Peter N. Grad. Opened 12 October 1972 at the Ritz Theatre and closed 13 October 1972 after 2 performances.

CAST (in order of appearance): *Harrison Fairchild IV*: SAMUEL D. RATCLIFFE. *Harrison Fairchild III*: PHIL LEEDS. *Patience Fairchild*: LIZ SHERIDAN. *Muffy Weathersford*: MARY BRACKEN PHILLIPS. *Nick*: Louis Criscuolo. *Marco*: Jack Landron. *Stavos*: Robert Darnell. *Helena*: Randee Heller. *Mama*: LIZ SHERIDAN. *Town Drunk*: PHIL LEEDS. *Melina*: Donna Liggitt Forbes. *Exodus*: Robert Darnell. *Genesis*: Jack Landron. *Deutronomy*: Louis Criscuolo. *Dr. Krauss*: PHIL LEEDS. *Writers*: Louis Criscuolo, Robert Darnell, Randee Heller, Jack Landron, Liz Sheridan. *Starlet*: Donna Liggitt Forbes. *Native #1*: Robert Darnell. *Native #2*: Donna Liggitt Forbes. *Native #3*: Liz Sheridan. *Native #4*: Randee Heller. *Native #5*: Jack Landron. *Witch Doctor*: Louis Criscuolo. *Chief*: PHIL LEEDS. *Star*: LIZ SHERIDAN. *Chorus Boys*: Louis Criscuolo, Robert Darnell, Jack Landron, Phil Leeds. *Not-So-Grand Lamas*: Louis Criscuolo, Donna Liggitt Forbes, Randee Heller, Jack Landron, Phil Leeds, Liz Sheridan. *Grand Lama*: Robert Darnell. *Winston*: Robert Darnell. *Gypsy*: Randee Heller. *Uncle Larry*: PHIL LEEDS. *Congregation*: Louis Criscuolo, Robert Darnell, Donna Liggitt Forbes, Randee Heller, Jack Landron, Phil Leeds, Liz Sheridan.

Act 1, Scene 1: The Wedding Day. *Scene 2*: Taverna in Greece. *Scene 3*: Airport. *Scene 4*: Psychiatrist's Office. *Scene 5*: Hollywood. *Scene 6*: Street in Hollywood. *Scene 7*: Psychiatrist's Office. *Scene 8*: Africa. *Scene 9*: Alone in the World.

Act 2, Scene 1: Psychiatrist's Office. *Scene 2*: Shubert Theatre. *Scene 3*: Psychiatrist's Office. *Scene 4*: Lamasery. *Scene 5*: Psychiatrist's Office. *Scene 6*: A Street. *Scene 7*: Gyspy's Store. *Scene 8*: Church. *Scene 9*: Alone in the World. *Scene 10*: Beach.

ACT 1
Scene 1
"I'm Gonna"
S. D. Ratcliffe
Scene 2
"When a Man Cries"
L. Criscuolo, L. Sheridan, R. Heller, J. Landron, R. Darnell, P. Leeds, D. L. Forbes
Scene 3
"A Trip Through My Mind"
M. B. Phillips, Dead Sea Scrolls
Scene 5
"Life"
S. D. Ratcliffe, the Writers
Scene 6
"Love Can"
M. B. Phillips
Scene 8
"Africa Speaks"
Natives, L. Criscuolo
Scene 9
"Somewhere in the Past"
S. D. Ratcliffe
ACT 2
Scene 2
"Hurry, Harry"
L. Sheridan, Chorus Boys
Scene 3
"Goodbye"
M. B. Phillips
Scene 5
"You Won't Be Happy"
S. D. Ratcliffe, P. Leeds
Scene 8
"He Is My Bag"
S. D. Ratcliffe, Congregation
Scene 9
"Somewhere in the Past" (reprise)
S. D. Ratcliffe, M. B. Phillips
Scene 10
Finale

1972.20 PACIFIC PARADISE

A Maori Musical Revue from New Zealand in Two Acts, 4 Scenes. Directed by Jack Regas. Maori Cultural Director, Arapata Whaanga. Choral director, Kelly Harris. Opening narration compiled and edited by Kit Regas. Lighting by Four Star Stage Lighting. Sound by Masque Sound. Produced by Irving Sudrow. Opened 16 October 1972 at the Palace Theatre and closed 21 October 1972 after 5 performances.

CAST: THE NEW ZEALAND MAORI COMPANY: Faule Bryant, Huri Callaghan, Matekino Callaghan, Sera Chase, Tiramate Dennis, Karen Donaghy, Cecilia Eparaima, Richard Eparaima, Kuini Farthing, Joshua Gardiner, Dawn Hepari, Lena Hiha, Christine Hikuroa, Eva Hona, Te Kani Horsefall, Bernadette Huata, Paraire Huata, Hemi Huata, Ngamoni Huata, Rongo Kahu, Sonny Keepa, Rachel Kewene, Tangiwai Kingi, Karu Kukutai, Josephine Loader, Putiputi Mackey, Gabrielle Mareikura, Rose Maxwell, Terry Maxwell, Kipa Morehu, Gordon Moses, Helen Moses, Philip Munro, Betty Nathan, James Nathan, Brenda Nepe, Dianne Nukutarwhiti, Iti Paenga, Tomaurangi Paki, Thomas Ratima, Kuini Reedy, Percy Reedy, Rimupae Rennie, Derna Richardson, Keren Ricka, Barbara Ringiao, Norga Ringaio, James Robert, Pauline Ruru, Abie Scott, Roberta Smiler, Josephine Smiler, Hineawe Smith, Nagatai Stockman, Raana Tangira, Wiremu Tangira, Irirangi Tahuriorangi, Reverend Anaru Takurua, Putiputi Tonihi, Rongo Tuhura, Atareta Waerea, Royal Walker, Tom Ward, Vicky Ward, Leona Watene, Muriel Wehi, Ngapo Wehi, Tiu Yaes, ARAPATA WHAANGA.

Act 1, Scene 1: Maori Welcome Ceremony. *Scene 2*: Legend of the Great Maori Migration. *Scene 3*: Village Life in the New Land.

Act 2: Maori Festival.

ACT 1
Scene 1
Wero (Warrior's Challenge)
Karanga
Elder women of the tribes call upon the spirit of their ancestors to give them strength to welcome you.
Utaina (Chant of Assembly)
Te Urunga Tu (Traditional Welcome Dance)
"Karanga Tia" (Action song expressing their joy that you are here)
Scene 2
Poroporoaki (Entrance of the Tohunga, the High Preist)
Tohunga: A. Whaanga.
Whakaara (Calling of the people together for discussion)
Whaikorero
In the beginning, in the legendary land of Hawaiiki, the rulers have decreeed that no man may own his own property. All people are welcome to stay but all properties must be shared. Tales of a new land far to the south have created great debate among the Maori tribal chiefs. Some are opposed but many are in favor of seeking a new home far across the seas. In the end, the Tohunga makes the decision. The people agree.
"E Oho Te Whaanau" (Song of Decision. We will go together.)
Tohi Waka (Blessing of the canoes.)
"Uia Mai Koia" (Canoe song. The long hazardous voyage begins.)
Ma Tangi
Our minds are ever thoughtful of the ones we left behind.
Poi Waka
Using their poi balls as paddles, the women demonstrate their fervor in assisting the men. Time passes. The ocean is great. Supplies fade. Disheartened and near starvation, the Maories through suppplication, prayer and faith in their gods, finally sight the distant land of the long low clouds.
Kura Ti Waka
In their final vigorous efforts to reach the shore, the men dedicate themselves and their women to the perpetuation of their race.
"Ti Tiro Mai" (Song of Thanksgiving)
Scene 3
"Taku Patu" (Introductory song)
"Karu" (Song of the fisherman)
He Manuhiri
A visiting tribe approaches the village. They are challenged and in turn counter-challenge. A visiting maiden attracts the eye of a young warrior of the village. He is rebuked by her would-be suitor. A battle follows.
"Po Karekare Ana" (Love song)
With the blessing of the Tohunga, the young couple are joined in marriage.
Tu Mara Mara (A chant uniting the tribes)
Paki Kini (Dance of jubilation)
ACT 2
Poi dances
a. Short single poi. b. Short double poi. c. Long single poi. d. Long double poi. e. Combinations.
"Tangi Hia" (Action song of joy at being here.)
Pana Pana/Rua Moko (Dance to the earthquake gods.)
Tititoria (Women's stick games)
"Koroki" (Song of courtship)
Peru-Peru (A Tai Aha {Spear} Haka)
Ti Rakau (Exercise for timing and agility)
Three and Four Poi Competitions
E Te Hokowhitu and
Pa Aki Kini (Two evolutionary treatments of familiar music)
"E Pare Ra" (A song of departure)
Po Ata Ro
Without metals, using only woods, stone (including the famous New Zealand jade or greenstone), the Maori (pronounced MOW-RY) developed one of the most outstanding cultural nations of the South Pacific. From birth, the male and female child were cherished and taught the arts of oratory, song, dexterity of movement and feats of strength and endurance. Facial grimaces, protruding tongue, eyes rolling, the Maori both intimidates his enemy and intrigues his friends.

Traditional music was based on the quarter tone scale. Today, possessing a natural flair for the rich harmonies, he revels in the Western usage of the half tone scale.

The poi, made of swamp reed (raupo), rolled into a ball and fastened with varying lengths of flax fiber aided the women in attracting the men by demonstration of their grace and dexterity. It also strengthened them for battle in the event their men were overcome in war.

The haka (Men's dances) are of many variations and for many purposes. A display of agreessive manliness in war. A dance to placate the gods, to recall tribal victories, to dispel fear of the unknown. A chance to display manly energy and prowess.

The tiki is highly prized as a personal adornment worn like a pendant around the neck. fashioned from greenstone, as is implied by its foetal form, it is symbolic of the power of creativeness, the sacred attribute of Deity.

1972.21 MOTHER EARTH

A Musical (Revue) in Two Acts, 18 Scenes. Sketches and lyrics by Ron Thronson. Music by Toni Shearer. Directed by Ray Golden. Musical staging by Lynne Morris. Consultant, Kermit Bloomgarden. Scenery by Alan Kimmel. Costumes by Mary McKinley. Lighting by Paul Sullivan. Musical direction and supervision by Larry White. Orchestrations by Alf Clausen. Visuals by Kenneth Shearer. Dance arrangements by Sande Campbell. Associate producers, Howard Butcher IV, Graeme Howard. Entire production supervised by Roger Ailes. Produced by Roger Ailes. Opened 19 October 1972 at the Belasco Theatre and closed 28 October 1972 after 12 performances.

CAST (in alphabetical order): Gail Boggs, Frank T. Coombs, Kimberly Farr, Kelly Garrett, Will Jacobs, Carol Kristy, Laura Michaels, John Bennett Perry, Rick Podell, Charlie J. Rodriguez.

ACT 1

Scene 1

Out of Space

"Mother Earth"
K. Garrett, Company

Scene 2

The Client

"The Time of Our Life"
L. Michaels, C. J. Rodriguez

"Corn on the Macabre"
C. Kristy, R. Podell, G. Boggs
(*Music and Lyrics by* Ron Thronson, Roger Ailes, Ray Golden.)

Scene 3

The Mask Parade

"Too Many Old Ideas"
K. Garrett

Scene 4

The Cheerleader
(*by* Jerry Patch, William Black and Ray Golden)

Uneasy Rider

Landscape With Figures

"Room to Be Free"
R. Podell

Scene 5

Model Wife

"Rent a Robot"
W. Jacobs

Scene 6

A Hike in the Woods
(*by* Jerry Patch and William Black)

Flash Gordon

"Plow It All Under"
C. Kristy, Company

Scene 7

Ewe Turn
(*by* Ray Golden)

The Offal Truth (Ain't It Offal)
(*by* Jack Marlowe and Ray Golden)

The Killathon
(*by* Ron Thronson, Roger Ailes and Ray Golden)

"Taking the Easy Way Out"
J. B. Perry, F. T. Coombs, C. J. Rodriguez

Scene 8

Joggers

"Ozymandias"
J. B. Perry

"Talons of Time"
K. Garrett

"Corn on the Macabre" (reprise)
L. Michaels, K. Farr, F. T. Coombs

Scene 9

The Nursery

"Save the World for Children"
G. Boggs

"Sail On Sweet Universe"
K. Garrett, Company

ACT 2

Scene 1

"Mater Terra"
Company

"Xanadu"
C. Kristy, Company

Scene 2

Breath-Out

"Ecology Waltz"
(*Lyrics by* Ray Golden.)
K. Farr, R. Podell

Scene 3

Chic Diners

"Corn on the Macabre" (reprise)
C. Kristy, C. J. Rodriguez, G. Boggs

Scene 4

Women Shoppers
(*by* Ron Thronson and Ray Golden)

The Swan

"Good Morning World"
J. B. Perry

Scene 5

The Last Redwoods

The Animals
(*by* Ray Golden)

"Tiger! Tiger!"
K. Garrett

Scene 6

Concrete Proposal

"Happy Mother's Day, Mother Earth"
C. J. Rodriguez

Scene 7

Radioactive Terminate

"Pills"
K. Garrett, G. Boggs, C. Kristy, Company
(*Music and Lyrics by* Ray Golden.)

Scene 8

The Billboards
(*by* Jack Marlowe and Ray Golden)

"Corn on the Macabre" (reprise)
K. Garrett, R. Podell, F. T. Coombs

Scene 9

Total Recall
(*by* Ray Golden)

Finale

1972.22 PIPPIN

A Musical Comedy in One Act, 8 Scenes. Book by Roger O. Hirson. Music and lyrics by Stephen Schwartz. Directed and choreographed by Bob Fosse. Scenery by Tony Walton. Costumes by Patricia Zipprodt. Lighting by Jules Fisher. Musical direction by Stanley Lebowsky. Orchestrations by Ralph

Burns. Dance arrangements by John Berkman. Sound by Abe Jacob. Produced by Stuart Ostrow. Opened 23 October 1972 at the Imperial Theatre, moved 15 March 1977 to the Minskoff Theatre, and closed 12 June 1977 after 1944 performances.

CAST (in order of appearance): *Leading Player*: BEN VEREEN. *Pippin*: JOHN RUBINSTEIN. *Charles*: ERIC BERRY. *Lewis*: Christopher Chadman. *Fastrada*: LELAND PALMER. *Musician*: John Mineo. *The Head*: Roger Hamilton. *Berthe*: IRENE RYAN. *Beggar*: Richard Korthaze. *Peasant*: Paul Solen. *Noble*: Gene Foote. *Field Marshall*: Roger Hamilton. *Catherine*: JILL CLAYBURGH. *Theo*: Shane Nickerson.

(*The Players*: Candy Brown, Kathryn Doby, Jennifer Nairn-Smith, Ann Reinking, Pamela Sousa.)

The action takes place in 780 A.D. and thereabouts, in the Holy Roman Empire and thereabouts.

Scene 1: The Opening. *Scene 2*: Home. *Scene 3*: War. *Scene 4*: The Flesh. *Scene 5*: Revolution. *Scene 6*: Encouragement. *Scene 7*: The Hearth. *Scene 8*: The Finale.

MUSICAL NUMBERS

Scene 1

"Magic to Do"
B. Vereen, Players

"Corner of the Sky"
J. Rubinstein

Scene 2

"Welcome Home"
E. Berry, J. Rubinstein

Scene 3

"War Is a Science"
E. Berry, J. Rubinstein

"Glory"
B. Vereen

Scene 4

"Simple Joys"
B. Vereen

"No Time at All"
I. Ryan, The Boys

"With You"
J. Rubinstein, The Girls

Scene 5

"Spread a Little Sunshine"
L. Palmer

"Morning Glow"
J. Rubinstein

Scene 6

"On the Right Track"
B. Vereen, J. Rubinstein

Scene 7

"Kind of Woman"
J. Clayburgh, The Girls

"Extraordinary"
J. Rubinstein

"Love Song"
J. Rubinstein, J. Clayburgh

Scene 8

Finale
The Players

1972.23 LYSISTRATA

A Musical in One Act. Play by Aristophanes. Adapted (from the Greek) by Michael Cacoyannis. Music by Peter Link. Sets by Robin Wagner. Costumes by Willa Kim. Lighting by Jules Fisher. Sound by Abe Jacob. Associate producer, Ira Resnick. Musical director, [Henry] 'Bootsie' Normand. Produced by David Black and David Seltzer. Opened 13 November 1972 at the Brooks Atkinson Theatre and closed 18 November 1972 after 8 performances.

CAST (in order of appearance): *Lysistrata*: MELINA MERCOURI. *Kalonike*: EVELYN RUSSELL. *Myrrhine*: Priscilla Lopez. *Lampito*: Madeleine Le Roux. *Corinthian Woman*: Lynda Sue Marks. *Theban Woman*: Andrea Levine. *Policewoman*: Marylou Perhacs. *Omicron*: JOHN BENTLEY. *Phi-Chi*: GORDON CONNELL. *Omega*: Joseph Palmieri. *Upsilon*: David Thomas. *Epsilon*: JACK FLETCHER. *Gamma*: JANE CONNELL. *Alphabeta*: Avril Gentles. *Deltazeta*: MARY JO CATLETT. *Theta*: Patti Karr. *Iota*: Gayla Osbourne. *Commissioner*: PHILIP BRUNS. *Woman A*: Cynthia Bullens. *Woman B*: Joanne Nail. *Woman C*: Joy Franz. *Kinesias*: RICHARD DMITRI. *Spartan Herald*: Stephen Macht. *Spartan Delegate*: Charles E. Siegel.

MUSICAL NUMBERS

"A Woman's Hands"
M. Mercouri

"On, On, On"
M. Mercouri, Women

"Many the Beasts"
Men

"Are We Strong?"
M. Mercouri, Women

"And We Are In"
M. Mercouri, Women

"Lysistrata"
M. Mercouri, Women

"I Miss My Man"
P. Lopez

"To Touch the Sky"
M. Mercouri, Women

"A Woman's Hands" (reprise)
M. Mercouri

"Eels Are a Girl's Best Friend"
Women

"Let Me Tell You a Little Story"
Men, Women

"Kalimera"
M. Mercouri, Company

1972.24 AMBASSADOR

A Musical in Two Acts, 19 Scenes. Book by Don Ettlinger and Anna Marie Barlow. Based on the novel "The Ambassadors" by Henry James. Music by Don Gohman. Lyrics by Hal Hackady. Directed by Stone Widney. Musical staging and choreography by Joyce Trisler. Sets and costumes by Peter Rice. American production supervised by Robert Guerra. Costumes supervised by Sara Brook. Lighting by Martin Aronstein. Musical arrangements and vocal arrangements by Herbert Grossman. Orchestrations by Philip J. Lang. Dance arrangements by Trude Rittman. Associate producer, Dan Rodden. Produced by Gene Dingenary, Miranda d'Ancona and Nancy Levering. Opened 19 November 1972 at the Lunt-Fontanne Theatre and closed 25 November 1972 after 9 performances.

CAST (in order of appearance): *Flower Girl*: Patricia Arnell. *Lewis Lambert Strether*: HOWARD KEEL. *Waymarsh*: DAVID SABIN. *Marie de Vionnet*: DANIELLE DARRIEUX. *Gloriani*: CARMEN MATHEWS. *Waiter*: Dwight Arno. *Bilham*: Michael Goodwin. *Chad*: Michael Shannon. *Jeanne de Vionnet*: ANDREA MARCOVICCI. *Dancing Master*: Larry Giroux. *Artist*: Larry Giroux. *Guide*: Jack Trussel. *Waiter*: Robert L. Hultman. *Innkeeper's Wife*: Marsha Tamaroff. *Bellboy*: Nikolas Dante. *Lady in Park*: Dixie Stewart. *Amelia Newsome*: M'el Dowd. *Germaine*: Patricia Arnell. *Cabaret Dancers*: Alex Hoff, Phillip Filiato, Suzanne Sponsler, Larry Giroux. *Headwaiter*: Robert L. Hultman. *Hotel Manager*: Jack Trussel.

People of Paris: Janis Ansley, Patricia Arnell, Dwight Arno, Marcia Brooks, Nikolas Dante, Richard Dodd, Vito Durante, Phillip Filiato, Lynn Fitzpatrick, Larry Giroux, Charlie Goeddertz, Gerald Haston, Alexis Hoff, Robert L. Hultman, Douglas E. Hunnikin, Genette Lane, Betsy Ann Leadbetter, Nancy Lynch, Linda-Lee MacArthur, Adam Petroski, Dean Russell, Salicia Saree, Ellie Smith, Suzanne Sponsler, Dixie Stewart, Marsha Tamaroff, Jack Trussel, Chester Walker.

The action takes place in Paris in 1906.

Act 1, Scene 1: The Tuileries. *Scene 2*: Chad's Apartment. *Scene 3*: Gloriani's Garden. *Scene 4*: Terrace of Lambert's Apartment. *Scene 5*: A Park. *Scene 6*: Notre Dame Cathedral. *Scene 7*: The Left Bank. *Scene 8*: Terrace of Lambert's Apartment. *Scene 9*: An Inn at St. Cloud.

Act 2, Scene 1: The Tuileries. *Scene 2*: Terrace (of) Lambert's Apartment. *Scene 3*: A Secluded Part of the Bois de Boulogne. *Scene 4*: Chad's Apartment. *Scene 5*: Marie's Garden. *Scene 6*: Le Petit Moulin Cabaret. *Scene 7*: Marie's Garden. *Scene 8*: A Bridge. *Scene 9*: The Hotel Lobby. *Scene 10*: A Bridge.

ACT 1
Scene 1
"Lilas"
P. Arnell
"Lambert's Quandary"
H. Keel
"I Know the Man"
D. Darrieux
Scene 3
"The Right Time, the Right Place"
Gloriani's Guests (Ensemble)
"She Passed My Way"
D. Darrieux, Guests
"Valse"
Gloriani's Guests (Ensemble)
Scene 4
"Something More"
H. Keel
Scene 5
"Love Finds the Lonely"
A. Marcovicci
Scene 6
"Kyrie Eleison"
Choir
Scene 7
"Surprise"
D. Darrieux, H. Keel, People of the Left Bank (Ensemble)
Scene 8
"Happy Man"
H. Keel

ACT 2
Scene 1
"Lilas, What Happened to Paris"
H. Keel, P. Arnell
Scene 2
"Young With Him"
D. Darrieux
"Too Much to Forgive"
H. Keel
Scene 3
"Why Do Women Have to Call It Love?"
C. Mathews, D. Sabin
Scene 5
"Mama"
A. Marcovicci
"That's What I Need Tonight"
D. Darrieux, H. Keel
Scene 6
"Maxixe-Habanera"
Cabaret Dancers, People of Paris
"That's What I Need Tonight" (reprise)
H. Keel, D. Darrieux, People of Paris
"Gossip"
Ladies of Paris
Scene 7
"Not Tomorrow"
D. Darrieux
Scene 8
"All of My Life"
H. Keel
Scene 9
"Thank You, No"
H. Keel

1972.25 VIA GALACTICA

A Musical in Two Acts, 7 Scenes. Book by Christopher Gore and Judith Ross. Music by Galt MacDermott. Lyrics by Christopher Gore. Entire production conceived and directed by Peter Hall. Production (setting) and costumes designed by John Bury. Lighting by Lloyd Burlingame. Musical director, Thomas Pierson. Vocal arrangements by Joyce Brown. Orchestrations by Bhen Lazaroni, Horace Ott, Danny Hurd. Sound by Jack Shearing. Ensemble movement by George Faison. Produced by George W. George and Barnard S. Strauss in association with Nat Shapiro. Opened 28 November 1972 at the Uris Theatre and closed 2 December 1972 after 7 performances.

CAST: *The Storyteller*: Irene Cara. *Gabriel Finn*: RAUL JULIA. *Hels (Mikelli)*: DAMON EVANS. *April Whitney*: EDLOE. *Omacha*: VIRGINIA VESTOFF. *Dr. Isaacs*: KEENE CURTIS. *Provo*: Bill Starr.

On Earth: *Spokesman*: James Dybas. *Old Man*: Chuck Cissel. *Blue People*: Mark Baker, Jacqueline Britt, Melanie Chartoff, Richard DeRusso, Sylvia DiGiorgio, Livia Genise, Marion Killinger, Toni Lund, Bob Spencer, Bonnie Walker.

On Ithaca: *Diane*: Livia Genise. *Nicklas*: Peter Nissen. *The Roustabout*: Alex Ander. *The Cook*: Mark Baker. *The Mute's Friend*: Robert Blankshine. *The Gypsy*: Jacqueline Britt. *The Boy*: Ralph Carter. *The Geologist*: Melanie Chartoff. *The Student*: Chuck Cissel. *The Mute*: Lili Cockerille. *The Lady*: Lorrie Davis. *The Mechanic*: Richard DeRusso. *The Teacher*: Sylvia DiGiorgio. *The Entertainer*: James Dybas. *The Writer*: Livia Genise. *The Politician*: Marion Killinger. *The Child*: Toni Lund. *The Cripple*: Veronica Redd. *The Tailor*: James Rivers. *The Carpenter*: Richard Ryder. *The Doctor*: Stan Shaw. *The Gambler*: Leon Spelman. *The Janitor*: Bob Spencer. *The Nurse*: Bonnie Walker. *The Grandmother*: J. H. Washington.

(The action takes place a thousand years from now on Earth, on a remote asteroid called Ithaca, and in outer space.)

ACT 1
"Via Galactica"
I. Cara
"We Are One"
The Blue People
"Helen of Troy"
R. Julia
"Oysters"
D. Evans, Edloe
"The Other Side of the Sky"
D. Evans
"Children of the Sun"
V. Vestoff
"Different"
Edloe, Company
"Take Your Hat Off"
V. Vestoff, Company
"Ilmar's Tomb"
V. Vestoff
"Shall We Friend?"
R. Julia
"The Lady Isn't Looking"
V. Vestoff
"Hush"
R. Julia
"Cross on Over"
K. Curtis, V. Vestoff, Company
"The Gospel of Gabriel Finn"
R. Julia

ACT 2
"Terre Haute High"
Edloe
"Life Wins"
V. Vestoff
"The Worm Germ"
B. Starr
"Isaac's Equation"
K. Curtis
"Dance the Dark Away"
I. Cara, Company
"Four Hundred Girls Ago"
R. Julia
"All My Good Mornings"
V. Vestoff
"Isaac's Equation" (reprise)
K. Curtis

"Children of the Sun" (reprise)
V. Vestoff, R. Julia
"New Jerusalem"
Company

Holiday in the Kibbutz
Karmon Israeli Dancers
Finale
Entire Company

1972.26 PURLIE

A Return Engagement of the Musical Comedy in Two Acts, a Prologue, 6 Scenes and an Epilogue[8]. Book by Ossie Davis, Philip Rose and Peter Udell. Based on the play "Purlie Victorious" by Ossie Davis. Music by Gary Geld. Lyrics by Peter Udell. Production directed by Philip Rose. Choreography by Louis Johnson. Scenery by Ben Edwards. Lighting by Thomas Skelton. Costumes by Ann Roth. Orchestrations and choral arrangements by Garry Sherman and Luther Henderson. Musical supervisor, Garry Sherman. Musical conductor, Charles Austin. Dance music arranged by Luther Henderson. Produced by Philip Rose. Opened 27 December 1972 at the Billy Rose Theatre and closed 7 January 1973 after 14 performances.

CAST (in order of appearance): *Purlie*: ROBERT GUILLAUME. *Church Soloist*: SHIRLEY MONROE. *Lutiebelle*: PATTI JO. *Missy*: LAURA COOPER. *Gitlow*: SHERMAN HEMSLEY. *Field Hands*: Every Hayes, Lonnie McNeil, Ted Ross. *Charlie*: DOUGLAS NORWICK. *Idella*: HELEN MARTIN. *Ol' Cap'n*: ART WALLACE.

Dancers: Darlene Blackburn, Deborah Bridges, Raphael Gilbert, Linda Griffin, Every Hayes, Reggie Jackson, Alton Lathrop, Robert Martin, Karen E. McDonald, Lonnie McNeil, Debbie Palmer, Andre Peck, Zelda Pulliam. *Singers*: Demarest Grey, Barbara Joy, Ursuline Kairson, Shirley Monroe, Alfred Rage, Beverly G. Robnett, Ted Ross, Frances Salisbury, Vanessa Shaw, David Weatherspoon, Joe Williams, Jr.

1973.01 GRAND MUSIC HALL OF ISRAEL

A Return Engagement of the Israeli Revue in Two Acts[9]. Conceived, directed and choreographed by Jonathan Karmon. Assistant director, Gavri Levi. Musical director, Rafi Paz. Costumes by Lydia Pinkus Ganay. Produced by Madison Square Garden Productions and Hy Einhorn. Opened 4 January 1973 at the Felt Forum and closed 14 January 1973 after 15 performances.

CAST: SHOSHANA DAMARI, RON ELIRAN, MYRON COHEN (Special Guest Host), ARIELA, THE MARGANIOT (Zlila, Leah), THE TAL U'MATAR (Shlomo on drums, flute, voice; Yehezkel, sitar).

THE KARMON ISRAELI DANCERS AND SINGERS: *Girls*: Tami Tomer, Ofira Ofir, Dassy Shahar, Rima Meir, Ora Mor, Brurira Aviv, Varda Amir, Tirza Barir, Ruth Ramati. *Boys*: Tuvia Ofir, Itamar Gur, Arie Baror, Ephraim Zamir, Zvi Granit, Zvika Zohar, Shimon Ashkenzi, Jonathan Nahorai, Avi Zah.

ACT 1
Israeli Rhapsody (A Mosaic of Israeli Folk Dances)
Israeli Songs
The Marganiot
The Fishermen of Kineret
Karmon Israeli Dancers
Rhythm and Sound of the Desert
The Tal U'Matar
A Night on the Gilboa Mountains
Karmon Israeli Singers
Ron Eliran (songs)
A Panorama of Hassidic Life
Karmon Israeli Dancers and Singers

ACT 2
The Mediterranean Flavor
Karmon Israeli Dancers
Ariela (xylophone specialty)
Fire in the Mountains
Karmon Israeli Dancers
Shoshana Damari (songs)

1973.02 TRICKS

A Musical Comedy in Two Acts, a Prologue and Epilogue. Book and direction by Jon Jory. Based on a play by Moliere ("Les Fourberies de Scapin," or"Monsieur Scapin."). Music by Jerry Blatt. Lyrics by Lonnie Burstein. Choreography by Donald Saddler. Scenery by Oliver Smith. Costumes by Miles White. Lighting by Martin Aronstein. Orchestrations by Bert de Coteau. Dance and incidental music arranged by Peter Howard. Conductor, David Frank. Sound by Jack Shearing. Associate producer, Samuel Liff. Produced by Herman Levin. Opened 8 January 1973 at the Alvin Theatre and closed 13 January 1973 after 8 performances.

CAST (in order of appearance): *Property Mistress*: Adale O'Brien. *Octave*, son of Argante, in love with Hyacinthe: Walter Bobbie. *Sylvestre*, Octave's servant: Christopher Murney. *Scapin*, Leandre's servant: RENE AUBERJONOIS. *Hyacinthe*, daughter of Geronte, in love with Octave: Carolyn Mignini. *Argante*, father of Octave: Mitchell Jason. *Geronte*, father of Leandre: Tom Toner. *Leandre*, son of Geronte, in love with Zerbinetta: Randy Herron. *Zerbinetta*, a Gypsy Queen, in love with Leandre: June Helmers. *Pantanella*: Suzanne Walker. *Isabella*: Jo Anne Ogawa. *Carmella*: Lani Sundsten. *Gondolier*: John Handy.

The Commedia: *Arlecchino/Lead Singer*: Joe Morton. *Charlotta*: Charlotte Crossley. *Ernestina*: Ernestine Jackson. *Shezwae*: Shezwae Powell.

The action takes place in and around Venice.

ACT 1
Prologue: "Love or Money"
The Commedia
"Who Was I?"
W. Bobbie, The Commedia
"Trouble's a Ruler"
R. Auberjonois, C. Murney, W. Bobbie
"Enter Hyacinthe"
W. Bobbie, The Commedia
"Believe Me"
W. Bobbie, C. Mignini, The Commedia
"Tricks"
R. Auberjonois, C. Murney
"A Man of Spirit"
The Commedia
"Where Is Respect?"
M. Jason, T. Toner
"Somebody's Doin' Somebody All the Time"
R. Auberjonois, The Commedia
"A Sporting Man"
R. Auberjonois, The Commedia

ACT 2
"Scapin"
J. Morton
"Anything Is Possible"
R. Auberjonois, C. Murney
"How Sweetly Simple"
C. Mignini, J. Helmers
"Gypsy Girl"
J. Helmers, The Commedia
Epilogue: "Life Can Be Funny"
The Company

1973.03 SHELTER

A Musical in Two Acts. Book and lyrics by Gretchen Cryer. Music by Nancy Ford. Directed by Austin Pendleton. Musical staging by Sammy Bayes. Settings, costumes, projections designed by Tony Walton. Lighting and projections devised by Richard Pilbrow. Orchestrations and electronic arrangements by Thomas Pierson. Music direction and vocal arrangements by Kirk Nurock. Associate producer, Julie Hughes. Produced by Richard Fields and Peter Flood. Opened 6 February 1973 at the John Golden Theatre and closed 4 March 1973 after 31 performances.

---

[8]Originally produced in New York 15 March 1970 at the Broadway Theatre for 689 performances. For Synopsis of Scenes and Musical Numbers, see original 1970 production.

[9]First produced in New York 6 February 1968 at the Palace Theatre for 64 performances, and as *NEW MUSIC HALL OF ISRAEL* 2 October 1969 at the Lunt-Fontanne Theatre for 77 performances.

CAST: *Maud*: MARCIA RODD. *Michael*: TERRY KISER. *Wednesday November*: SUSAN BROWNING. *Gloria*: JOANNA MERLIN. *Television Crew*: Charles Collins, Britt Swanson. *Arthur* (not seen): TONY WELLS. *Voice of the Director* (not seen): Philip Kraus.

The action takes place at the present time in a television studio set.

ACT 1
- Overture
  - T. Wells
- "Changing"
  - M. Rodd, T. Wells
- "Welcome to a New World"
  - T. Kiser, T. Wells
- "It's Hard to Care"
  - T. Kiser, T. Wells, M. Rodd
- "Woke Up Today"
  - M. Rodd, T. Wells
- "Mary Margaret's House in the Country"
  - M. Rodd, T. Wells
- "Woman on the Run"
  - T. Wells
- "Don't Tell Me It's Forever"
  - M. Rodd, T. Kiser, T. Wells

ACT 2
- "Sunshine"
  - T. Wells
- "I Bring Him Seashells"
  - S. Browning
- "She's My Girl"
  - T. Kiser, M. Rodd, T. Wells
- "Welcome to a New World" (reprise)
  - M. Rodd, T. Kiser, T. Wells, S. Browning
- "He's a Fool"
  - S. Browning, M. Rodd
- "Going Home with My Children"
  - M. Rodd, T. Wells
- "Sleep, My Baby, Sleep"
  - T. Wells

1973.04 A LITTLE NIGHT MUSIC

A Musical in Two Acts, a Prologue and 15 Scenes. Book by Harold Wheeler. Suggested by a film ("Smiles of a Summer Night") by Ingmar Bergman. Music and lyrics by Stephen Sondheim. Directed by Harold Prince. Choreography by Patricia Birch. Scenic production designed by Boris Aronson. Costumes designed by Florence Klotz. Lighting designed by Tharon Musser. Musical director, Harold Hastings. Orchestrations by Jonathan Tunick. Production supervisor, Ruth Mitchell. Sound by Jack Mann. Produced by Harold Prince in association with Ruth Mitchell. Opened 25 February 1973 at the Sam S. Shubert Theatre, moved 18 September 1973 to the Majestic Theatre, and closed 3 August 1974 after 601 performances.

CAST (in order of appearance): *Mr. Lindquist*: Benjamin Rayson. *Mrs. Nordstrom*: Teri Ralston. *Mrs. Anderssen*: Barbara Lang. *Mr. Erlanson*: Gene Varrone. *Mrs. Segstrom*: Beth Fowler. *Frederika Armfeldt*: Judy Kahan. *Madame Armfeldt*: HERMIONE GINGOLD. *Frid*, her butler: GEORGE LEE ANDREWS. *Henrik Egerman*: MARK LAMBERT. *Anne Egerman*: VICTORIA MALLORY. *Fredrik Egerman*: LEN CARIOU. *Petra*: D. JAMIN-BARTLETT. *Desiree Armfeldt*: GLYNIS JOHNS. *Malla*, her maid: Despo. *Bertrand*, a page: Will Sharpe Marshall. *Count Carl-Magnus Malcolm*: LAURENCE GUITTARD. *Countess Charlotte Malcolm*: PATRICIA ELLIOTT. *Osa*: Sherry Mathis.

The action takes place in Sweden at the turn of the century.

Act 1, Scene 1: The Egerman Rooms. *Scene 2*: Stage of Local Theatre. *Scene 3*: The Egerman Rooms. *Scene 4*: Desiree's Digs. *Scene 5*: Breakfast Room in (the) Malcolm Country House. *Scene 6*: Egerman Rooms. *Scene 7*: Armfeldt Terrace.

Act 2, Scene 1: The Armfeldt Lawn. *Scene 2*: The Other Part of the Garden. *Scene 3*: Armfeldt Terrace. *Scene 4*: The Dining Room. *Scene 5*: Armfeldt Garden; Another Part of the Garden. *Scene 6*: Desiree's Bedroom. *Scene 7*: The Trees. *Scene 8*: Armfeldt House and Garden.

ACT 1
- Overture
  - B. Rayson, T. Ralston, B. Lang, G. Varrone, B. Fowler
- Prologue
- "Night Waltz"
  - Company

Scene 1
- "Now"
  - L. Cariou
- "Later"
  - M. Lambert
- "Soon"
  - V. Mallory, M. Lambert, L. Cariou
- "The Glamorous Life"
  - J. Kahan, G. Johns, Despo, H. Gingold, T. Ralston, B. Fowler, B. Lang, B. Rayson, G. Varrone

Scene 2
- "Remember?"
  - B. Rayson, T. Ralston, B. Lang, G. Varrone, B. Fowler

Scene 3
- "Remember?" (continued)
  - B. Rayson, T. Ralston, B. Lang, G. Varrone, B. Fowler

Scene 4
- "You Must Meet My Wife"
  - G. Johns, L. Cariou
- "Liaisons"
  - H. Gingold
- "In Praise of Women"
  - L. Guittard

Scene 5
- "In Praise of Women" (continued)
  - L. Guittard

Scene 6
- "Every Day a Little Death"
  - P. Elliott, V. Mallory

Scene 7
- "A Weekend in the Country"
  - Company

ACT 2
- Entr'acte, Scenes 1 and 2
- "The Sun Won't Set"
  - B. Lang, B. Fowler, T. Ralston, B. Rayson, G. Varrone

Scene 3
- "It Would Have Been Wonderful"
  - L. Cariou, L. Guittard

Scene 4
- "Perpetual Anticipation"
  - T. Ralston, B. Fowler, B. Lang

Scene 6
- "Send in the Clowns"
  - G. Johns

Scene 7
- "The Miller's Son"
  - D. Jamin-Bartlett

Scene 8
- Finale
  - Company

1973.05 IRENE

A Revival of the Musical Comedy in Two Acts, 10 Scenes[10]. (New) Book by Hugh Wheeler and Joseph Stein from an adaptation by Harry Rigby. Based

[10]Originally produced in New York 18 November 1919 at the Vanderbilt Theatre for 675 performances.

on the original play by James Montgomery. Music by Harry Tierney. Lyrics by Joseph McCarthy. Additional music and lyrics by Charles Gaynor and Otis Clements. Directed by Gower Champion. Musical numbers staged by Peter Gennaro. Production (settings) and costumes designed by Raoul Pene du Bois. Debbie Reynolds' costumes designed by Irene Sharaff. Lighting designed by David F. Segal. Music and vocal direction by Jack Lee. Orchestrations by Ralph Burns. Dance arrangements and incidental music by Wally Harper. Sound designed by Anthony Alloy. Music consultant and co-ordinator, Joseph A. McCarthy. Associate producer, Steven Beckler. Assistant choreographers, Mary Ann Niles and Tony Stevens. Produced by Harry Rigby, Albert W. Selden and Jerome Minskoff. Opened 13 March 1973 at the Minskoff Theatre and closed 7 September 1974 after 605 performances.

CAST (in order of appearance): *Mrs. O'Dare*: PATSY KELLY. *Jane Burke*: Janie Sell. *Helen McFudd*: Carmen Alvarez. *Jimmy O'Flaherty*: Bruce Lea. *Irene O'Dare*: DEBBIE REYNOLDS. *Emmeline Marshall*: RUTH WARRICK. *Clarkson*: Bob Freschi. *Donald Marshall*: MONTE MARKHAM. *Ozzie Babson*: Ted Pugh. *Madame Lucy*: GEORGE S. IRVING. *Arabella Thornsworthy*: Kate O'Brady.

Debutantes: Arlene Columbo, Meg Bussert, Carrie Fisher, Dorothy Wyn Gehgan, Marybeth Kurdock, Frances Ruth Lea, Jeanne Lehman, Kate O'Brady, Julie Pars, Pamela Peadon, Pat Trott, Sandra Voris, Jeanette Williamson, Penny Worth. *Ninth Avenue Fellas*: Paul Charles, Dennis Edenfield, David Evans, Bob Freschi, John Hamilton, Bruce Lea, Joe Lorden, Bryan Nicholas, Robert Rayow, Dennis Roth, Kenn Scalice, Ron Schwinn, David Steele, Albert Stephenson.

(The action takes place in New York City and on Long Island in 1919.)

Act 1, Scene 1: The Piano Store. *Scene 2*: The Music Room of the Marshall Estate. *Scene 3*: Ninth Avenue. *Scene 4*: Madame Lucy's Salon. *Scene 5*: The Front of the Piano Store. *Scene 6*: The Palais Royale.

Act 2, Scene 1: The Palais Royale. *Scene 2*: The Piano Store. *Scene 3*: Outside the Marquee Tent. *Scene 4*: The Italian Garden.

ACT 1

Scene 1

"The World Must be Bigger Than an Avenue"
D. Reynolds
(*Music by* Wally Harper. *Lyrics by* Jack Lloyd.)

Scene 2

"The Family Tree"[11]
R. Warrick, Debutantes

"Alice Blue Gown"[12]
D. Reynolds

"They Go Wild, Simply Wild, Over Me"
G. S. Irving, Debutantes
(*Music by* Fred Fisher. *Lyrics by* Joseph McCarthy.)

Scene 3

"An Irish Girl"
D. Reynolds, Company
(*Music and Lyrics by* Charles Gaynor and Otis Clements.)

Scene 4

"Stepping on Butterflies"
G. S. Irving, D. Reynolds, C. Alvarez, J. Sell
(*Music by* Wally Harper.)

Scene 5

"Mother Angel Darling"
D. Reynolds, P. Kelly
(*Music and Lyrics by* Charles Gaynor.)

Scene 6

"The Riviera Rage"
D. Reynolds, Company
(*Music by* Wally Harper.)

ACT 2

Scene 1

"The Last Part of Every Party"[13]
Company

"We're Getting Away With It"[14]
G. S. Irving, C. Alvarez, J. Sell, T. Pugh

Scene 2

"Irene"[15]
D. Reynolds, Company

Scene 3

"The Great Lover Tango"
M. Markham, C. Alvarez, J. Sell
(*Music and Lyrics by* Charles Gaynor and Otis Clements.)

"You Made Me Love You" (from *THE HONEYMOON EXPRESS*)
D. Reynolds, M. Markham
(*Music by* James Monaco. *Lyrics by* Joseph McCarthy.)

"You Made Me Love You" (reprise)
G. S. Irving, P. Kelly

Scene 4

Finale
Company

1973.06 SEESAW

A Musical in Two Acts, 18 Scenes. Book by Michael Bennett. Based on the play "Two for the Seesaw" by William Gibson. Music by Cy Coleman. Lyrics by Dorothy Fields. Directed and choreographed by Michael Bennett. Co-choreographer, Grover Dale. Associate choreographers, Bob Avian, Tommy Tune. Scenery by Robin Wagner. Costumes by Ann Roth. Lighting by Jules Fisher. Musical direction and vocal arrangements by Don Pippin. Orchestrations by Larry Fallon. Dance arrangements supervised by Cy Coleman. Dance arrangemenbts by Elman Anderson, Cy Coleman, Marvin Hamlisch and David Spangler. Media art and photography by Sheppard Kerman. Sound by Dick Maitland, Bob Ring, Lou Gonzales. Produced by Joseph Kipness and Lawrence Kasha, James Nederlander, George M. Steinbrenner III, Lorin E. Price. Opened 18 March 1973 at the Uris Theatre, moved 1 August 1973 to the Mark Hellinger Theatre and closed 8 December 1973 after 296 performances.

CAST (in order of appearance): *Jerry Ryan*: KEN HOWARD. *Gittel Mosca*: MICHELE LEE. *David*: TOMMY TUNE. *Sophie*: CECELIA NORFLEET. *Julio Gonzales*: GIANCARLO ESPOSITO. *Sparkle*: LaMONTÉ PETERSON. *Nurse*: Judy [Judith] McCauley. *Ethel*: Cathy Brewer-Moore.

Citizens of New York City: John Almberg, Steve Anthony, Cathy Brewer-Moore, Eileen Casey, Wayne Cilento, Patti D'Beck, Terry Deck, Judy Gibson, Felix Greco, Mitzi Hamilton, Loida Iglesias, Bobby Johnson, Baayork Lee, Amanda McBroom, Judy McCauley, Anita Morris, Gerry O'Hara, Michon Peacock, Frank Pietri, Yolanda Raven, Michael Reed, Orrin Reiley, Don Swanson, William Swiggard, Tom Urich, Dona D. Vaughn, Clyde Walker, Thomas J. Walsh, Chris Wilzak.

The action takes place in New York City at the present time.

Act 1, Scene 1: Prologue. *Scene 2*: Times Square Area. *Scene 3*: Dance Studio on West 54th Street. *Scene 4*: Japanese Restaurant on 46th Street and Lincoln Center. *Scene 5*: Eas 116th Street. *Scene 6*: Gittel's Apartment in the East Village. *Scene 7*: Jerry's Apartment. *Scene 8*: Gittel's Apartment, then the street. *Scene 9*: The Banana Club. *Scene 10*: Gittel's Apartment.

Act 2, Scene 1: St. Vincent's Hospital. *Scene 2*: Dance Studio. *Scene 3*: Jerry's Apartment. *Scene 4*: Backstage at the Theatre. *Scene 5*: Central Park, later that night. *Scene 6*: Gittel's Apartment; phone booth at Kennedy Airport. *Scene 7*: Gittel's Apartment, 2:00A.M. *Scene 8*: Gittel's Apartment; Jerry's Apartment, a few days later.

ACT 1

Scene 1

"Seesaw"
Full Company

Scene 2

"My City"
K. Howard, Neighborhood Girls

Scene 3

"Nobody Does It Like Me"
M. Lee

[11]From the original production of "Irene" in 1919.
[12]From the original production of "Irene" in 1919.
[13]From the original production of "Irene" in 1919.
[14]From the original production of "Irene" in 1919.
[15]From the original production of "Irene" in 1919.

Scene 4
"In Tune"
M. Lee, K. Howard
Scene 5
"Spanglish"
G. Esposito, M. Lee, K. Howard, C. Norfleet, Full Company
Scene 6
"Welcome to Holiday Inn"
M. Lee
Scene 7
"You're a Lovable Lunatic"
K. Howard
Scene 8
"He's Good for Me"
M. Lee
Scene 9
"Ride Out the Storm"[16]
L. Peterson, C. Norfleet, Full Company

ACT 2
Scene 1
"We've Got It"
K. Howard
"Poor Everybody Else"
M. Lee
Scene 2
"Chapter 54, Number 1909"
T. Tune, K. Howard, M. Lee, Dance Company
Scene 4
"The Concert"
M. Lee, Dance Company
"It's Not Where You Start"
T. Tune, Full Company
Scene 8
"I'm Way Ahead"/"Seesaw" (reprise)
M. Lee

1973.07

CYRANO

A Musical in Two Acts, 5 Scenes. Book and lyrics by Anthony Burgess. Based on his adaptation of Edmond Rostand's play "Cyrano de Bergerac." Music by Michael J. Lewis. Directed by Michael Kidd. Costumes by Desmond Heeley. Settings by John Jensen. Lighting by Gilbert V. Hemsley, Jr. Musical direction by Thomas Pierson. Orchestrations by Philip J. Lang. Sound by Abe Jacob. Incidental music Arranged by Clay Fullum. Dueling scenes staged by Patrick Crean, Erik Fredricksen. Produced by Richard Gregson and APJAC International. Opened 13 May 1973 at the Palace Theatre and closed 23 June 1973 after 49 performances.

CAST (in order of appearance): *Candle Lighters*: Paul Berget, Anthony Inneo. *Doorman*: Bob Heath. *Foodseller*: Tovah Feldshuh. *Marquis in Yellow*: Danny Villa. *Musketeer*: Michael Nolan. *Cavalryman*: Donavan Sylvest. *Pickpocket*: Geoff Garland. *Citizen*: James Richardson. *Citizen's Brother*: Tim Nissen. *The Marquis in Red*: Alexander Orfaly. *The Marquis in Beige*: Joel Craig. *Ragueneau*, a baker and poet: ARNOLD SOBOLOFF. *Christian de Neuvillette*: MARK LAMOS. *Madame Aubry*: Betty Leighton. *Ladies of the French Academy (4)*: *Madame de Guemene*: Janet McCall. *Barthenoide*: Patricia Roos. *Felixerie*: Mimi Wallace. *Urimedonte*: Mary Straten. *Le Bret*, Captain of the Gascons: JAMES BLENDICK. *Roxana*: LEIGH BEERY. *Roxana's Duenna*: Anita Dangler. *Count de Guiche*, Guardian of Roxana: LOUIS TURENNE. *Viscount de Valvert*: J. Kenneth Campbell. *Actors*: Anthony Inneo, Richard Schneider. *Actresses*: Vicki Frederick, Jill Rose. *Jodelet*, a farceur: Michael Goodwin. *Montfleury*, a romantic tragedian: PATRICK HINES. *Cyrano de Bergerac*: CHRISTOPHER PLUMMER. *Lise*, Ragueneau's wife: Betty Leighton. *Boys after Pies*: Tim Nissen, Paul Berget. *Bakery Staff*: J. Kenneth Campbell, Geoff Garland, Janet McCall, Michael Nolan, James Richardson, Patricia Roos, Mary Straten. *Gascon Cadets and Soldiers*: J. Kenneth Campbell, Joel Craig, Michael Goodwin, Bob Heath, Anthony Inneo, Gale McNeeley, Michael Nolan, James Richardson, Richard Schneider, Donovan Sylvest, Danny Villa. *Theophraste Renaudot*: George Spelvin. *Cyrano's Pages*: Paul Berget, Tim Nissen. *Capucine Monk*: Geoff Garland. *Sister Marguerite*: Betty Leighton. *Sister Marthe*: Anita Dangler. *Sister Claire*: Patricia Roos. *Nuns*: Tovah Feldshuh, Vicki Frederick, Janet McCall, Jill Rose, Mary Straten, Mimi Wallace.

The action takes place in Paris and environs in 1640, and in 1654.

Act 1, Scene 1: A theatre, Paris, 1640. *Scene 2*: Ragueneau's bakery, Paris.

Act 2, Scene 1: The balcony of Roxana's house, Paris. *Scene 2*: A battle camp near Arras. *Scene 3*: A convent, Paris, 14 years later.

ACT 1
Scene 1
"Cyrano's Nose" (Nose Song)
C. Plummer
"La France, La France"
Company
"Tell Her"
J. Blendick, C. Plummer
"From Now Till Forever"
C. Plummer, Company
Scene 2
"Bergerac"
C. Plummer, L. Beery
"Pocapdedious"
Cadets
"No, Thank You"
C. Plummer
"From Now Till Forever" (reprise)
C. Plummer, M. Lamos

ACT 2
Scene 1
"Roxana"
M. Lamos, Company
"It's She and It's Me"
M. Lamos
"You Have Made Me Love"
L. Beery
"Thither, Thother, Thide of the"
C. Plummer
"Pocapedious" (reprise)
Cadets
Scene 2
"Paris Cuisine"
C. Plummer, J. Blendick, Cadets
"Love Is Not Love"
L. Beery
Scene 3
"Autumn Carol"
L. Beery, Nuns
"I Never Loved You"
C. Plummer

1973.08

NASH AT NINE

A Wordsical (Musical Revue) in One Act structured from the works of Ogden Nash. Verses and Lyrics by Ogden Nash. Music by Milton Rosenstock. Conceived and directed by Martin Charnin. Orchestrations and musical supervision by John Morris. Musical direction, Karen Gustafson. Sets by David Chapman. Costumes by Theoni V. Aldredge. Lighting by Martin Aronstein. Produced by Les Schecter and Barbara Schwei in association with SRO Enterprises and Arnold Levy. Opened 17 May 1973 at the Helen Hayes Theatre and closed 2 June 1973 after 21 performances.

CAST: E. G. MARSHALL, VIRGINIA VESTOFF, Steve Elmore, Bill Gerber, Richie Schechtman.

MUSICAL NUMBERS[17]

Seaside Serenade; Farenheit Gesundheit; The Sniffle; Coefficients of Expansion (A Guide to the Infant Season); To a Small Boy Standing on

[16]Replaced for the subsequent National Tour by:
"The Party's on Me"
Lucie Arnaz (Gittel), Company

[17]The following are not so much song titles as they are a comprehensive list of the Ogden Nash verses as adapted and presented.

My Shoes While I Am Wearing Them; The Madcap Zoologist; The Panther, The Armadillo; The Canary; The Shrew; Experiment Degustatory; The Pig; A Bulletin Has Just Come In; The Fly; The Octopus; The Eel; The Kipper; The Clam; The Guppy; Barmaids Are Diviner Than Mermaids; But I Could Not Love Thee, Ann, So Much, Loved I Not Honoré More; The Armchair Golfer, or, Whimpers of a Shortchanged Viewer; Song of the Open Road; From an Antique Land; Any Millenniums Today, Lady?; Give-Away, Give-Away, Banker Man; I Will Arise and Go Now; Always Marry an April Girl; The Anniversary; Love Under the Republicans (or Democrats); A Word to Husbands; I'm Sure She Said Six-Thirty; To My Valentine; Reflections on Ice-Breaking; I Do, I Will, I Have; The Private Dining Room; One Third of a Calendar; Tin Wedding Whistle; What's in a Name? Here's What's in a Name, or, I Wonder What Became of John and Mary?;No Trouble at All, It's as Easy as Falling Off a Portable Bar; Grandpa Is Ashamed; A Brief Guide to New York; Requiem; The Pizza; All Quiet Along the Potomac, Except the Letter G; Shrinking Song; Suppose I Darken Your Door; You and Me and P. B. Shelley; Come, Come, Kerouac! My Generation is Beater than Yours; The Clean Platter; Coffee With the Meal; The Middle; The Return; Peekaboo, I Almost See You; Modest Meditations on the Here, The Heretofore, and the Hereafter; Birthday on the Beach; A Lady Thinks She Is Thirty; Crossing the Border; For a Good Dog.

1973–1974 SEASON

Ralph Carter in RAISIN
Martha Swope/TimePix

1973–1974 SEASON

1973.09 THE DESERT SONG

A Revival of the Musical in Two Acts, Eight Scenes[1]. Book and lyrics by Otto Harbach and Oscar Hammerstein II. Music by Sigmund Romberg. Directed by Henry Butler. Choreography by David Nillo. Costumes supervised by Sara Brook. Scenery and lighting by Clarke Dunham. Musical direction by Al Cavaliere. Dance arrangements by Dorothea Freitag. A Lehman Engel Production. Produced by Moe Septee in association with Jack L. Wolgin and Victor H. Potamkin. Opened 5 September 1973 at the Uris Theatre and closed 16 September 1973 after 15 performances.

CAST (in order of appearance): *Mindar*: Nicholas Scarpinati. *Sid El Kar*: JOHN RIBECCHI. *Hadji*: Dick Ensslen. *Palace Guard*: Frederick G. Sampson III. *Hassi*: MANDINGO SHAKA. *Neri*: Ruby Greene Aspinall. *Red Shadow/Pierre Birabeau*: DAVID CRYER. *Benjamin Kidd*: JERRY DODGE. *Captain Paul Fontaine*: STANLEY GROVER. *Lieutenant Davergne*: Kent Cottam. *Sergeant Boussac*: William Leyerle. *Azuri*: GLORIA ROSSI. *Azuri Dancing Girls*: Kita Bouroff, Lana Caradimas, Urylee Leonardos, Jane Lucas, Sandra Mannis, Dundi Wright. *Edith*: Osceola Davis. *Susan*: BRITT SWANSON. *General Birabeau*: SHEPPERD STRUDWICK. *Margot Bonvalet*: CHRIS CALLAN, Carol Jeanne Tenney (matinees). *Clementina*: GLORIA ZAGLOOL. *Ali Ben Ali*: MICHAEL KERMOYAN.

Ensemble: Ruby Greene Aspinall, Marsha Bagwell, Rita Oney Best, Kita Bouroff, Lana Caradimas, Jacqueline Clark, Osceola Davis, Karen Ford, Bonnie Hinson, Urylee Leonardos, Rona Leslie, Jane Lucas, Sandra Mannis, Berdeen E. Pigorsh, Brenda Schaffer, Dundi Wright, Donald Coleman, Bill Collins, Austin Colyer, Kent Cottam, Ronald De Felice, Dennis Dohman, Dick Ensslen, William Leyerle, Frederick G. Sampson III, Nicholas Scarpinati, Peter Schroeder, Arthur Shaffer, Anthony Tamburello, David Vogel, David Weatherspoon.

1973.10 RAISIN

A Musical in Two Acts, a Prologue and 14 Scenes. Book by Robert Nemiroff and Charlotte Zaltzberg. Based on Lorraine Hansberry's play "A Raisin in the Sun." Music by Judd Woldin. Lyrics by Robert Brittan. Directed and choreographed by Donald McKayle. Scenery by Robert U. Taylor. Costumes by Bernard Johnson. Lighting by William Mintzer. Musical director and conductor, Howard A. Roberts. Orchestrations by Al Cohn, Robert Freedman. Vocal arrangements by Joyce Brown, Howard A. Roberts. Dance arrangements by Judd Woldin. Incidental arrangements by Dorothea Freitag. Associate producers, Sydney Lewis, Jack Friel. First presented by Arena Stage in Washington, D.C. Produced by Robert Nemiroff. Opened 18 October 1973 at the 46th Street Theatre, moved 14 January 1975 to the Lunt-Fontanne Theatre and closed 8 December 1975 after 847 performances.

CAST (in order of appearance): *People of the Southside*: Chuck Thorpes, Eugene Little, Karen Burke, Zelda Pulliam, Elaine Beener, Renee Rose, Paul Carrington, Marenda Perry, Gloria Turner, Don Jay, Glenn Brooks, Marilyn Hamilton.

Pusher: Al Perryman. *Victim*: Loretta Abbott. *Ruth Younger*: ERNESTINE JACKSON. *Travis Younger*: RALPH CARTER. *Mrs. Johnson*: HELEN MARTIN. *Walter Lee Younger*: JOE MORTON. *Beneatha Younger*: DEBORAH ALLEN. *Lena Younger (Mama)*: VIRGINIA CAPERS. *Bar Girl*: Elaine Beener. *Bobo Jones*: Ted Ross. *Willie Harris*: Walter P. Brown. *Joseph Asagai*: ROBERT JACKSON. *African Drummer*: Chief Bey. *Pastor*: Herb Downer. *Pastor's Wife*: Marenda Perry. *Karl Lindner*: Richard Sanders.

The action takes place in Chicago in the 1950s.

Prologue: Night, The Block, Southside Chicago. *Act 1, Scene 1*: The Younger family living room/kitchenette. Early morning. *Scene 2*: The Southside and the Loop. Morning rush-hour. *Scene 3*: The apartment. Late afternoon. *Scene 4*: A Southside bar. That night. *Scene 5*: The apartment. Next morning. *Scene 6*: That night, the apartment.

Act 2, Scene 1: A Southside Church. Sunday morning. *Scene 2*: The bar. *Scene 3*: The Block and the apartment. That night. *Scene 4*: The apartment. Moving Day, some weeks later. *Scene 5*: The Block. Immediately following. *Scene 6*: The apartment, shortly later. *Scene 7*: The front stoop. Immediately following. *Scene 8*: The apartment. Immediately following.

ACT 1
Prologue (jazz ballet)
Company
Scene 1
"Man Say"
J. Morton
"Whose Little Angry Man"
E. Jackson
Scene 2
"Runnin' to Meet the Man"
J. Mortn, Company
Scene 3
"A Whole Lotta Sunlight"
V. Capers
Scene 4
"Booze"
E. Beener, T. Ross, J. Morton, W. P. Brown, Company
Scene 5
"Alaiyo"
R. Jackson, D. Allen
Scene 6
("Same Old Color Scheme")(recorded)
(E. Beener)
"African Dance"
D. Allen, J. Morton, Company
"Sweet Time"
E. Jackson, J. Morton
"You Done Right"
J. Morton

ACT 2
Scene 1
"He Come Down This Morning"
H. Downer, M. Perry, V. Capers, H. Martin, E. Jackson, R. Carter, Company
Scene 3
"It's a Deal"
J. Morton
Scene 4
"Sweet Time" (reprise)
E. Jackson, J. Morton
Scene 5
"Sidewalk Tree"
R. Carter
Scene 6
"Not Anymore"
J. Morton, E. Jackson, D. Allen
Scene 7
"Alaiyo" (reprise)
R. Jackson
Scene 8
"It's a Deal"[2] (reprise)
J. Morton
"Measure the Valleys"
V. Capers
"He Come Down This Morning" (reprise)

1973.11 MOLLY

A Musical in Two Acts, 14 Scenes. Book by Louis Garfinkle and Leonard Adelson. Based on characters from (the radio series) "The Goldbergs" by Gertrude Berg. Music by Jerry Livingston. Lyrics by Leonard Adelson and Mack David. Directed by Alan Arkin. Dances by Grover Dale. Musical

[1]Originally produced in New York 30 November 1926 at the Casino Theatre for 471 performances. For Synopsis of Scenes and Song List, see original 1926 production. New lyrics by Edward Smith written for "Has Anyone Seen My Bennie?," It," and "One Good Boy Gone Wrong."

[2]For International Tour, replaced by:
"Walter Lee Younger and Son"
Nate Barnett (Walter Lee)

direction and vocal arrangements by Jerry Goldberg. Orchestrations by Eddie Sauter. Dance arrangements by Arnold Gross. Scenery by Marsha L. Eck. Costumes by Carrie F. Robbins. Lighting by Jules Fisher. Sound by Gary Harris. Associate producers, Larry Fallon, Richard Vonella. Musical consultant, Ronald Snyder. Produced by Don Saxon/Don Kaufman/George Daley, in association with Complex IV. Opened 1 November 1973 at the Alvin Theatre and closed 29 December 1973 after 68 performances.

CAST (in order of appearance): *Angelina Frazini*: Suzanne Walker. *Mrs. Sullivan*: CAMILA ASHLAND. *Mr. Sullivan*: Eddie Phillips. *Mrs. Frazini*: Justine Johnson. *Molly (Goldberg)*: KAY BALLARD. *Mrs. Kramer*: Molly Stark. *Belle Seidenschneer*: RUTH MANNING. *Mrs. Bloom*: Hazel Weber Steck. *Mrs. Dutton*: Toni Darnay. *Rosalie (Goldberg)*: LISA ROCHELLE. *Jake (Goldberg)*: LEE WALLACE. *Uncle David*: ELI MINTZ. *Sammy (Goldberg)*: DANIEL FORTUS. *Stella Hazelcorn*: CONNIE DAY. *Michael Stone*: SWEN SWENSON. *Cousin Simon*: MITCHELL JASON. *Max*: Martin Garner.

Ensemble: *Skeeter*: Don Bonnell. *Ralph*: Rodney Griffin. *Reggie*: Bob Heath. *Harold*: Don Percassi. *Vinnie*: Sal Pernice. *Sheala*: Linda Rose. *George*: Leland Schwantes. *Walter*: Gerald Teijelo. *Ellen*: Mimi Wallace. *Sarah*: Miriam Welch.

The action takes place in the Bronx in the spring of 1933.

Act 1, Scene 1: (Opening.) *Scene 2*: The Goldberg Apartment. *Scene 3*: The Front Sidewalk. *Scene 4*: The Rooftop. *Scene 5*: The Sidewalk. *Scene 6*: Belle's Apartment. *Scene 7*: A Street. *Scene 8*: The Goldberg Apartment. *Scene 9*: The Goldberg Apartment. The following day.

Act 2, Scene 1: The Mandarin Palace. *Scene 2*: Outside the Mandarin Palace. *Scene 3*: The Goldberg Apartment. *Scene 4*: The Goldberg Kitchen. *Scene 5*: The Goldberg Apartment.

ACT 1

Scene 1

"There's a New Deal on the Way"
S. Walker, Company
(*Lyrics by* Mack David.)

"If Everyone Got What They Wanted"
K. Ballard, Company
(*Lyrics by* Mack David.)

Scene 2

"A Piece of the Rainbow"
K. Ballard
(*Lyrics by* Mack David.)

Scene 3

"Cahoots"
S. Swenson, K. Ballard
(*Lyrics by* Mack David.)

Scene 4

"Sullivan's Got a Job"
Company
(*Lyrics by* Leonard Adelson.)

"In Your Eyes"
D. Fortus
(*Lyrics by* Mack David.)

Scene 5

"Cahoots" (reprise)
R. Manning, K. Ballard

Scene 8

"High Class Ladies and Elegant Gentlemen"
S. Swenson, C. Day, K. Ballard, L. Wallace, D. Fortus, L. Rochelle
(*Lyrics by* Mack David.)

"So I'll Tell Him"
K. Ballard
(*Lyrics by* Mack David.)

Scene 9

"Appointments"
E. Mintz
(*Lyrics by* Leonard Adelson.)

"There's Gold on the Trees"
L. Wallace, K. Ballard, Company
(*Lyrics by* Mack David.)

ACT 2

Scene 1

"The Mandarin Palace on the Grand Concourse"
Company
(*Lyrics by* Mack David.)

"I Want to Share It All With You"
S. Swenson, C. Day, Company
(*Lyrics by* Mack David.)

Scene 2

"In Your Eyes" (reprise)
D. Fortus

Scene 3

"I Was There"
K. Ballard, L. Wallace
(*Lyrics by* Mack David.)

"Oak Leaf Memorial Park"
K. Ballard
(*Lyrics by* Leonard Adelson.)

"If Everyone Got What They Wanted" (reprise)
E. Mintz, L. Rochelle

"I See a Man"
K. Ballard
(*Music and Lyrics by* Norman L. Martin.)

Scene 5

"The Tremont Avenue Cruisewear Fashion Show"
Company
(*Lyrics by* Leonard Adelson.)

"I've Got a Molly"
L. Wallace
(*Lyrics by* Leonard Adelson.)

"Go in the Best of Health"
K. Ballard
(*Lyrics by* Leonard Adelson.)

1973.12

GIGI

A Musical in Two Acts, 15 Scenes. Book and lyrics by Alan Jay Lerner. Based on the novel of the same name by Colette (and the film of the same name by the musical's authors.) Music by Frederick Loewe. Directed by Joseph Hardy. Dances and musical numbers staged by Onna White. Scenic production by Oliver Smith. Costumes by Oliver Messel. Lighting by Thomas Skelton. Orchestrations by Irwin Kostal. Dance arrangements by Trude Rittman. Musical associate, Harper MacKay. Associate dance director, Martin Allen. Musical direction by Ross Reimueller. Assisant music director, Bruce Ferden. Production coordinator, Herb Adams. A Los Angeles-San Francisco Civic Light Opera Production. Produced by Saint-Subber and Edwin Lester. Opened 13 November 1973 at the Uris Theatre and closed 10 February 1974 after 103 performances.

CAST (in order of speaking appearance): *Honore Lachailles*: ALFRED DRAKE. *Gaston Lachailles*: DANIEL MASSEY. *Liane d'Exelmans*: Sandahl Bergman. *Inez Alvarez* (Mamita): MARIA KARNILOVA. *Gigi*: KARIN WOLFE. *Aunt Alicia*: AGNES MOOREHEAD. *Charles*, her butler: Gordon De Vol. *A French Head Waiter, Receptionist, Telephone Installer, Maitre d'Hotel*: Joe Ross. *Waiters*: Leonard John Crofoot, Thomas Stanton. *Liane's Dance Partner*: Thomas Anthony. *Artist*: Patrick Spohn. *A Count*: Joel Pressman. *Sandomir*: Randy Di Grazio. *Dancing Teacher*: Gregory Drotar. *Manuel*: Truman Gaige. *Maitre Du Fresne*: GEORGE GAYNES. *Maitre Duclos*: Howard Chitjian. *Law Clerks*: Leonard John Crofoot, Thomas Stanton. *Little Girls*: Patricia Daly, Jill Turnbull.

Ensemble: Thomas Anthony, Alvin Beam, Russ Beasley, Robyn Blair, Leonard John Crofoot, Gordon De Vol, Randy Di Grazio, John Dorrin, Gregory Drotar, Janis Eckhart, Margit Haut, Andy Keyser, Beverly Kopels, Diane Lauridsen, Merilee Magnuson, Kelley Maxwell, Vickie Patik, Joel Pressman, Patrick Spohn, Thomas Stanton, Cherie Suzanne, Marie Tillmanns, Sallie True.

The action takes place in Paris mostly at the turn of the century.

Act 1, Scene 1: The Pre-Catelan Restauarnt in the Bois, Paris. A September afternoon, 1900. *Scene 2*: Mamita's Apartment. Immediately following. *Scene 3*: Aunt Alicia's Apartment. Immediately following. *Scene 4*: The Restaurant of the Eiffel Tower. Evening. *Scene 5a*: Alicia's Apartment. Midday, the following day. *Scene 5b*: Apartment of Honore Lachailles. Simultaneously. *Scene 5c*: Alicia's Apartment. As before. *Scene 5d*: Honore's Dressing Room. As before. *Scene 6*: Mamita's Apartment. Two weeks later. *Scene 7a*: The Lobby of the Grand Hotel, Trouville. The following afternoon. *Scene 7b*: The Beach at Trouville.

Act 2, Scene 1: Mamita's Apartment. Early afternoon. Three weeks later. *Scene 2*: The Street outside Mamita's apartment. Immediately following. *Scene 3*: The Office of Maitre DuFresne. A day or two later. *Scene 4*: Mamita's Apartment. The following day. *Scene 5*: A Street Café. An hour later.*Scene 6*: Mamita's Apartment. Later that day. *Scene 7*: Maxim's. That night. *Scene 8*: Mamita's Apartment. Immediately following.

ACT 1
Scene 1
"Thank Heaven for Little Girls"
A. Drake
"It's a Bore"
A. Drake, D. Massey
Scene 3
"The Earth and Other Minor Things"[3]
K. Wolfe
Scene 4
"Paris Is Paris Again"[4]
A. Drake, Ensemble
"She's Not Thinking of Me"
D. Massey
Scene 5
"It's a Bore" (reprise)
A. Drake, D. Massey, T. Gaige, A. Moorehead
Scene 6
"The Night They Invented Champagne"
K. Wolfe, D. Massey, M. Karnilova
Scene 7a
"I Remember It Well"
A. Drake, M. Karnilova
Scene 7b
"I Never Want to Go Home Again"[5]
K. Wolfe, Ensemble
ACT 2
Scene 2
"Gigi"
D. Massey
Scene 3
"The Contract"[6]
A. Moorehead, M. Karnilova, H. Chitjian, G. Gaynes
Scene 5
"I'm Glad I'm Not Young Anymore"
A. Drake
Scene 6
"In This Wide, Wide World"[7]
K. Wolfe
Scene 8
"Thank Heaven for Little Girls" (reprise)
A. Drake

1973.13 GOOD EVENING

A Comedy (Revue) With Music in Two Acts. (Sketches, music and lyrics) Written by Peter Cook and Dudley Moore. Directed by Jerry Adler. (Set, costumes, lighting) Designed by Robert Randolph. Film sequences directed by Joe McGrath. Produced by Alexander H. Cohen and Bernard Delfont in association with Donald Langdon for Hemdale, Ltd. Opened 14 November 1973 at the Plymouth Theatre and closed 30 November 1974 after 438 performances.

CAST: PETER COOK, DUDLEY MOORE.

ACT 1
Hello
On Location
"Madrigal"
Six of the Best
"Die Flabbergast" (German Lied)
Down the Mine
"One Leg Too Few"
"Chanson"
Soap Opera[8]
ACT 2
Gospel Truth
Mini-Drama[9]
"The Kwai Sonata"
(Variations on theme from "Bridge Over the River Kwai" in the style of Bach, Mozart, Chopin, etc.)
The Frog and Peach
An Appeal
"Tea for Two"[10]

1973.14 BETTE MIDLER

A Musical Revue in Two Acts. Special material by Bill Hennessey, Bruce Vilanch. Musical director, Barry Manilow. Lighting by John Tedesco. Choreography by Andre De Shields and Michael Bennett. Set by Richard Mason. Sound by Claire Brothers. Costumes by Bob DeMora. Produced by Aaron Russo in association with Ron Delsener. Opened 3 December 1973 at the Palace Theatre and closed 23 December 1973 after 19 performances.

CAST: BETTE MIDLER. *The Harlettes*: (Charlotte Crossley, Robin Grean, Sharon Redd), 'Nick Brown's Hawaii '73' (*Vocals*: Jimmy Kaina; *Toere*: Marvin Stein; *Dancers*: Betty Kawamura, Cindy Curtin, Helen Estol). *Musicians*: Luther Rix, Frank Vento, Will Lee, Don Grolnick.

MUSICAL NUMBERS[11]
"Friends"
(*Music and Lyrics by* Mark Klingman and Buzzy Linhart.)
"Delta Dawn"
(*Music and Lyrics by* Alex Harvey and Larry Collins.)
"Bad Sex"
(*Music and Lyrics by* Bill Hennessey and Bruce Vilanch.)
"Uptown"
(*Music and Lyrics by* Thomas McKinney.)
"Da Doo Run Run"
(*Music and Lyrics by* Jeff Barry, Ellie Greenwich, Phil Spector.)
"In the Mood"
(*Music by* Joe Garland. *Lyrics by* Andy Razaf.)
"Drinkin' Again"
(*Music and Lyrics by* Doris Tauber and Johnny Mercer.)
"Am I Blue?" (from *ON WITH THE SHOW*, film)
(*Music by* Harry Akst. *Lyrics by* Grant Clarke.)
"Do You Want to Dance?"
(Music and Lyrics by Bobby Freeman.)
"Optimistic Voices" (from *THE WIZARD OF OZ*, film)
(*Music by* Harold Arlen and Herbert Stothart. *Lyrics by* E. Y. Harburg.)
"Lullabye of Broadway" (from *GOLDDIGGERS OF 1935*, film)
(*Music by* Harry Warren. *Lyrics by* Al Dubin.)
"Boogie Woogie Bugle Boy"
(*Music and Lyrics by* Don Raye and Hughie Price.)
"Superstar"
(*Music and Lyrics by* Leon Russell and Bonnie Bramlett.)
"Hello in There"
(*Music and Lyrics by* John Prine.)
"(Your Love Keeps Lifting Me) Higher and Higher"
(*Music and Lyrics by* Gary Lee Jackson, Raymond Miner, Carl W. Smith.)

[3]Newly written for this stage presentation of "Gigi" and not from the original film.
[4]Newly written for this stage presentation of "Gigi" and not from the original film.
[5]Newly written for this stage presentation of "Gigi" and not from the original film.
[6]Newly written for this stage presentation of "Gigi" and not from the original film.
[7]Newly written for this stage presentation of "Gigi" and not from the original film.

[8]Replaced during run by "Tea for Two."
[9]Dropped for subsequent road tour.
[10]Dropped during run and replaced by "Resting."
[11]Not in performance order. Barry Manilow opened the second act with a set of his own songs.

1973.15 THE PAJAMA GAME

A Revival of the Musical Comedy in Two Acts[12]. Book by George Abbott and Richard Bisssell. Based on the novel "7 1/2 Cents" by Richard Bissell. Music and lyrics by Richard Adler and Jerry Ross. Production (scenery, costumes) designed by David Guthrie. Lighting by John Gleason. Musical numbers stagedby Zoya Leporska. Original choreography by Bob Fosse. Musical director, Joyce Brown. Orchestrations by Don Walker. Production directed by George Abbott. Produced by Richard Adler and Bert Wood in association with Nelson Peltz. Opened 9 December 1973 at the Lunt-Fontanne Theatre and closed 3 February 1974 after 65 performances.

CAST (in order of appearance): *Hines*: CAB CALLOWAY. *Prez*: Marc Jordan. *Joe*: Gerrit de Beer. *Hasler*: Willard Waterman. *Gladys*: SHARON MILLER. *Sid Sorokin*: HAL LINDEN. *Mabel*: Mary Jo Catlett. *First Helper*: David Brummel. *Second Helper*: John Engstrom. *Charlie*: Tiger Haynes. *Babe Williams*: BARBARA McNAIR. *Mae*: Margret Coleman. *Brenda*: Chris Calloway. *Poopsie*: Wyetta Turner. *Salesman*: Hal Norman. *Pop*: Baron Wilson.

Dancers: Dru Alexandrine, Eileen Casey, Vicki Frederick, Mickey Gunnersen, Sally Neal, Jo Ann Ogawa, P. J. Benjamin, Hank Brunjes, Jon Engstrom, Ben Harney, Randal Harris, David Kresser, Jr., Cameron Mason, Chester Walker. *Singers*: Chalyce Brown, Susan Dyas, Rebecca Hoodwin, Patricia Moline, Marie Santell, Cynthia White, Gerrit deBeer, David Brummel, Doug Carfrae, Stan Page, Ward Smith, Teddy Williams.

1973.16 THE BEGGAR'S OPERA

A Revival of the Ballad Opera in Three Acts[13]. Book, music and lyrics by John Gay. Directed by Gene Lesser. Musical direction and arrangements by Roland Gagnon. Dance arranged by Elizabeth Keen. Settings by Robert Yodice. Costumes by Carrie F. Robbins. Lighting by Martin Aronstein. Produced by The City Center Acting Company (John Houseman, Artistic Director.) Opened 22 December 1973 at the Billy Rose Theatre and closed 31 December 1973 after 6 performances in repertory.

CAST (in order of appearance): *Filch*: Norman Snow. *Beggar*: Benjamin Hendrickson. *Peachum*: DAVID OGDEN STIERS. *Mrs. Peachum*: MARY LOU ROSATO. *Polly Peachum*: CYNTHIA HERMAN. *Macheath*: KEVIN KLINE. *Matt of the Mint*: Richard Ooms. *Jemmy Twitcher*: Peter Dvorsky. *Harry Paddington*: Joel Colodner. *Wat Dreary*: David Schramm. *Crook Finger'd Jack*: Jared Sakren. *Nimming Ned*: Gerald Shaw. *Mrs. Trapes*: Nita Angeletti. *Dolly Trull*: Leah Chandler. *Jenny Diver*: MARY-JOAN NEGRO. *Suky Tawdry*: Gisela Caldwell. *Betty Coaxer*: Mary Lou Rosato. *Lockit*: SAM TSOUTSOUVAS. *Lucy Lockit*: PATTI LuPONE

1973.17 AN EVENING WITH JOSEPHINE BAKER

A Musical Revue in Two Acts[14]. Stage director, Patrick Horrigan. Lighting consultant, Don Stern. Sound consultant, Robert F. Maybaum. Produced by Jack Jordan and Howard Sanders. Opened 31 December 1973 at the Palace Theatre and closed 6 January 1974 after 7 performances.

CAST: JOSEPHINE BAKER, Roberta Lorco and Company (Paco Juanas, Guitarist; Domingo Alverado, Singer), Michael Powell Ensemble (Michael Powell, Joey Coleman, Leeroy Cooks, Vinson Cunningham, Bernadette Doctor, Dorthea Doctor, Norman Hawkins, Ricardo Portlette, Charlene Ricks, Barbara Rolle, Calvin Van Meter, Esther Westbrook, Peggy Williams, Shirley Williams), Baby Laurence (tap percussionist), G. Keith Alexander (M.C.).

ACT 1

"People" (from *FUNNY GIRL*.)
(*Music by* Jule Styne. *Lyrics by* Bob Merrill.)
"Sourire (a la Vie)"
"(It's) Impossible"
(*Music and Lyrics by* Armando Manzanero and Sid Wayne.)
"Avec"
(*Music and Lyrics by* Henri Betti, Bruno Coquatrix and Andre Hornez.)
"Love Story" (from the film *LOVE STORY*)
(*Music by* Francis Lai. *Lyrics by* Carl Sigman.)
"Hello Young Lovers" (from *THE KING AND I*)
(*Music by* Richard Rodgers. *Lyrics by* Oscar Hammerstein II.)
Medley

ACT 2

"Lend Your Ear"
"Si Me Faltas Tu"
(*Music and Lyrics by* Armando Manzanero.)
My Fair Lady Medley
(*Music by* Frederick Loewe. *Lyrics by* Alan Jay Lerner.)
"Demain"
(*Music and Lyrics by* Donaggio, Pallavicini, Annoux and Vallade.)
"La Vie en Rose"
Music and Lyrics by Edith Piaf and Louiguy.)
"Yesterday"
(*Music and Lyrics by* John Lennon and Paul McCartney.)
"J'ai Deux Amours"
(*Music and Lyrics by* Vincent Scotto, Georges Koger and Henri Varna.)
"My Sweet Lord"
(*Music and Lyrics by* George Harrison.)

1974.01 LIZA

A Musical Revue in Two Acts. (Continuity) Written by Fred Ebb. Directed by Bob Fosse. Choreographed by Bob Fosse and Ron Lewis. Original musical material by Fred Ebb and John Kander. Musical coordinator, Marvin Hamlisch. Musical conductor, Jack French. Lighting designed by Jules Fisher. Audio design. Phil Ramone. Sound by Stan Miller. Production coordinator, Bill Liberman. Produced by the Shubert Organization in association with Ron Delsener. Opened 6 January 1974 at the Winter Garden Theatre and closed 26 January 1974 after 24 performances.

CAST: LIZA MINNELLI.
Dancers: Pam Barlow, Spencer Henderson, Jimmy Roddy, Sharon Wylie.

MUSICAL NUMBERS[15]

"If You Could Read My Mind"
(*Music and Lyrics by* Gordon Lightfoot.)
"Come Back to Me" (from *ON A CLEAR DAY YOU CAN SEE FOREVER*)
(*Music by* Burton Lane. *Lyrics by* Alan Jay Lerner.)
"Shine on Harvest Moon" (from *ZIEGFELD FOLLIES OF 1908*)
(*Music and Lyrics by* Nora Bayes and Jack Norworth.)
"Exactly Like Me"
(*Music by* John Kander. *Lyrics by* Fred Ebb.)
"The Circle"
(Music by Edith Piaf. English Lyrics by Fred Ebb.)
"More Than You Know" (from *GREAT DAY*)
(*Music by* Vincent Youmans. *Lyrics by* Billy Rose and Edward Eliscu.)
"I'm One of the Smart Ones"
(*Music by* John Kander. *Lyrics by* Fred Ebb.)
"Natural Man"
(*Music and Lyrics by* Bobby Hebb and Sandy Baron.)
"I Can See Clearly Now"
(*Music and Lyrics by* Johnny Nash.)
"And I in My Chair"
(*Music and Lyrics by* Jeff Davis, Charles Aznavour and Fred Ebb.)

---

[12]Originally produced in New York 13 May 1954 at the St. James Theatre for 1063 performances. For this production, the Act 2 "Jealousy Ballet" was dropped. "7 1/2 Cents" was staged by Jerome Robbins. Replacing the "Hey There" Act 2 reprise was a new song:
"Watch Your Heart"
B. McNair
(*Music and Lyrics by* Richard Adler.)

[13]First produced in New York 3 December 1750 at the Theatre in Nassau Street for 2 performances. For Synopsis of Scenes and Musical Numbers, see original 1750 production.

[14]Josephine Baker And Her International Revue with Bricktop and the George Faison Universal Dance Experience previously produced 5-8 June 1973 at Carnegie Hall for 4 performances.

[15]Not in performance order. Program provided no song list; list prepared from recording.

"There Is a Time"
(*Music and Lyrics by* Jeff Davis, Charles Azanvour and Gene Lees.)
"A Quiet Thing" (from *FLORA, THE RED MENACE*)
(*Music by* John Kander. *Lyrics by* Fred Ebb.)
"Anywhere You Are"
(*Music by* John Kander. *Lyrics by* Fred Ebb.)
"I Believe You"
(*Music by* John Kander. *Lyrics by* Fred Ebb.)
"Cabaret" (from *CABARET*)
(*Music by* John Kander. *Lyrics by* Fred Ebb.)
"Ring Them Bells" (from television special *LIZA WITH A 'Z'*)
(*Music by* John Kander. *Lyrics by* Fred Ebb.)
"I Gotcha"
(*Music and Lyrics by* Joe Tex.)
"Bye Bye Blackbird"
(*Music by* Ray Henderson. *Lyrics by* Mort Dixon.)

1974.02 LORELEI, or Gentlemen Still Prefer Blondes

A Musical Comedy in Two Acts, 10 Scenes, a Prologue and an Epilogue. New book by Kenny Solms and Gail Parent. Based on the musical comedy "Gentlemen Prefer Blondes"[16] with book by Anita Loos and Joseph Fields. Music by Jule Styne. Lyrics by Leo Robin. New music by Jule Styne. New lyrics by Betty Comden and Adolph Green. Directed by Robert Moore. Choreography by Ernest Flatt. Scenery by John Conklin. Costumes by Alvin Colt. Miss Channing's costumes by Ray Aghayan and Bob Mackie. Lighting by John Gleason. Musical direction by Milton Rosenstock. Orchestrations by Philip J. Lang, Don Walker. Vocal arrangements by Hugh Martin and Buster Davis. Dance music arrangements by Jay Thompson. A Music Fair Enterprises Inc. Production. Produced by Lee Guber and Shelly Gross. Opened 27 January 1974 at the Palace Theatre and closed 3 November 1974 after 320 performances.

CAST (in order of appearance): *Lorelei Lee*: CAROL CHANNING. *Henry Spofford*: LEE ROY REAMS. *Mrs. Ella Spofford*: DODY GOODMAN. *Lord Francis Beekman*: JACK FLETCHER. *Lady Phyllis Beekman*: Jean Bruno. *Josephus Gage*: BRANDON MAGGART. *Dorothy Shaw*: TAMARA LONG. *Gus Esmond*: PETER PALMER. *Bartender*: Ray Cox. *Frank*: Steve Short. *George*: Bob Daley. *Pierre*: Ray Cox. *Charles*: Robert Riker. *Robert Lemanteur*: Robert Fitch. *Louis Lemanteur*: Ian Tucker. *Lobster* (Un Delicieux Pince Rouge!): Brenda Holmes. *Caviar* (Un Bon Oeuf!): Linda McClure. *Pheasant* (Un Oiseau Dans Le Matin!): Aniko Farrell. *Salade* (A Votre Sante!): Marie Halton. *Dessert* (Vive La Glace Chaude!): CAROL CHANNING. *Maitre d'*: Willard Beckham. *Simone Duval*: Sherrill Harper. *Master of Ceremonies*: Robert Riker. *Announcer*: Ray Cox. *Engineer*: Bob Daley. *Mr. Esmond*: David Neuman. *Bridesmaids*: Aniko Farrell, Marie Halton, Sherrill Harper, Linda McClure.

Passengers, Tourists, Olympic Team, Wedding Guests: Aniko Farrell, Joela Flood, Marie Halton, Marian Haraldson, Sherrill Harper, Brenda Holmes, Linda Lee McArthur, Linda McClure, Susan Ohman, Gina Ramsel, Roxanna White, Willard Beckham, Ray Cox, Bob Daley, Bob Fitch, Gregg Harlan, Wayne Mattson, Jonathan Miele, Jeff Richards, Robert Riker, Rick Schneider, Steve Short, Don Swanson, Ian Tucker.

The action takes place aboard the *Ile de France*, in Paris and in New York.
Prologue: Dockside, New York, 1944. *Act 1, Scene 1*: The Pier of the *Ile de France*. *Scene 2*: The Deck of the *Ile de France*. *Scene 3*: Lorelei's Suite on the *Ile de France*. *Scene 4*: The Eiffel Tower. *Scene 5*: Lorelei's Suite, The Ritz Hotel, Paris.
Act 2, Scene 1: Pre-Catalin Nightclub. *Scene 2*: A Paris Street. *Scene 3*: Lorelei's Suite, The Ritz Hotel, Paris. *Scene 4*: On the Way Home. *Scene 5*: The Central Park Casino, New York. *Epilogue*: The present.

ACT 1
Prologue
"Looking Back"
C. Channing
(*Lyrics by* Betty Comden and Adolph Green.)
Scene 1
"Bye Bye Baby"
P. Palmer, C. Channing, Passengers, Tourists
Scene 2
"(It's) High Time"
T. Long, D. Goodman, Passengers
"(I'm Just a Little Girl from) Little Rock"
C. Channing
Scene 3
"I Love What I'm Doing"
T. Long
"It's Delightful Down in Chile"
C. Channing, J. Fletcher, Stewards
Scene 4
"I Won't Let You Get Away"
L. R. Reams, T. Long
(*Lyrics by* Betty Comden and Adolph Green.)
Scene 5
"Keeping Cool With Coolidge"
L. R. Reams, T. Long, D. Goodman, Guests
"Men"
C. Channing
(*Lyrics by* Betty Comden and Adolph Green. *Dance Supervised by* Robert Tucker.)

ACT 2
Scene 1
"Coquette"
T. Long, C. Channing, Showgirls
"Mamie Is Mimi"
C. Channing, B. Fitch, I. Tucker
Scene 2
"Diamonds Are a Girl's Best Friend"
C. Channing
"Homesick (Blues)"
C. Channing, P. Palmer
Scene 3
"Miss Lorelei Lee"
L. R. Reams, T. Long, D. Goodman, B. Maggart, B. Fitch, I. Tucker, Wedding Guests
(*Lyrics by* Betty Comden and Adolph Green.)
Scene 4
"Button Up With Esmond"
C. Channing, Bridesmaids
Scene 5
"Diamonds Area Girl's Best Friend" (reprise)
C. Channing
Epilogue
Finale—"Lorelei"
C. Channing, Company
(*Lyrics by* Betty Comden and Adolph Green.)

1974.03 RAINBOW JONES

A Musical in Two Acts, 11 Scenes. Book, music and lyrics by Jill Williams. Directed by Gene Persson. Musical direction and vocal arrangements by Danny Holgate. Musical staging by Sammy Bayes. Set design by Richard Ferrer. Costume design by James Berton Harris. Lighting by Spencer Mosse. Orchestrations by Preston Sandiford. Produced by Rubykate Inc. (Gene Persson) in association with Phil Gillin and Gene Bambic. Opened and closed 13 February 1974 at the Music Box Theatre after 1 performance.

CAST (in order of appearance): *Rainbow Jones*: RUBY PERSSON. *Leona*: PEGGY HAGEN LAMPREY. *Bones*: ANDY ROHRER. *C. A. Fox*: GIL ROBBINS. *Cardigan*: STEPHANIE SILVER. *Joey Miller*: PETER KASTNER. *Aunt Felicity*: KAY ST. GERMAIN. *Uncle Ithaca*: DANIEL KEYES.

The action takes place at the present time in New York City and on Uncle Ithaca's farm.

Act 1, Scene 1: Noon, Central Park. *Scene 2*: Later, Aunt Felicity's Apartment. *Scene 3*: A few hours later, Joey Miller's Office. *Scene 4*: Minutes later, Central Park. *Scene 5*: That evening, Aunt Felicity's Apartment. *Scene 6*: The next day at noon, Central Park.

---
[16]Originally produced in New York 8 December 1949 at the Ziegfeld Theatre for 740 performances.

Act 2, Scene 1: A few minutes later, Central Park. *Scene 2*: A week later, Uncle Ithaca's Farm. *Scene 3*: A moment later, Central Park. *Scene 4*: A week later, the Parlour Car of the Ohio Express/Felicity's Apartment. *Scene 5*: A few hours later, Central Park.

ACT 1

Prologue

"A Little Bit of Me in You"
P. H. Lamprey, A. Rohrer, G. Robbins, S. Silver

Scene 1

"Free and Easy"
R. Persson

Scene 2

"Do Unto Others"
R. Persson, P. H. Lamprey, A. Rohrer, G. Robbins, S. Silver

Scene 3

"I'd Like to Know You Better"
P. Kastner

Scene 4

"Bad Breath"
P. H. Lamprey, A. Rohrer, G. Robbins, S. Silver

"I'd Like to Know You Better" (reprise)
P. Kastner, R. Persson, P. H. Lamprey, A. Rohrer, G. Robbins, S. Silver

Scene 5

"Alone, At Last, Alone"
K. St. Germain

Scene 6

"Free and Easy" (reprise)
R. Persson

"Her Name Is Leona"
R. Persson, P. H. Lamprey, A. Rohrer, G. Robbins, S. Silver

"We All Need Love"
P. H. Lamprey, A. Rohrer, G. Robbins, S. Silver

ACT 2

Scene 1

"We All Need Love" (reprise)
P. H. Lamprey, A. Rohrer, G. Robbins, S. Silver

"The Only Man for the Job"
A. Rohrer

Scene 2

"It's So Nice"
K. St. Germain, D. Keyes

Scene 3

"Wait a Little While"
P. H. Lamprey

Scene 4

"It's So Nice" (reprise)
R. Persson, K. St. Germain, D. Keyes, P. Kastner

"One Big Happy Family"P. Kastner, P. H. Lamprey, A. Rohrer, G. Robbins, S. Silver

Scene 5

"Who Needs the Love of a Woman"
P. Kastner, R. Persson

"We All Need Love"/"A Little Bit of Me in You" (reprise)
P. Kastner, R. Persson, P. H. Lamprey, A. Rohrer, G. Robbins, S. Silver

1974.04

SEXTET

A Musical in One Act. Book by Harvey Perr and Lee Goldsmith. Music by Lawrence Hurwitt. Lyrics by Lee Goldsmith. Direction and choreography by Jered Barclay. Scenery by Peter Harvey. Costumes by Zoe Brown. Lighting by Marc B. Weiss. Orchestrations and musical direction by David Frank. Sound by Gary Harris. Assistant choreographher, Mary Jane Houdina. Produced by Balemar Productions and Lawrence E. Sokol. Opened 3 March 1974 at the Bijou Theatre and closed 10 March 1974 after 9 performances.

CAST (in order of appearance): *David*: Robert Spencer. *Paul*: John Newton. *Fay*: Mary Small. *Kenneth*: Harvey Evans. *Ann*: Dixie Carter. *Leonard*: Jerry Lanning.

The action takes place at the present time in a New York City apartment.

MUSICAL NUMBERS

"Nervous"
Company

"What the Hell Am I Doing Here?"
J. Newton

"Keep on Dancing"
R. Spencer, H. Evans, M. Small, J. Newton

"Spunk"
M. Small, R. Spencer, H. Evans

"Visiting Rights"
D. Carter

"Going-Staying"
Company

"I Wonder"
D. Carter, M. Small

"Women and Men"
J. Lanning, R. Spencer, H. Evans

"I Love You All the Time"
J. Lanning

"Keep On Dancing" (reprise)
Company

"Hi"
H. Evans

"It'd Be Nice"
M. Small

"Roseland"
Company

"How Does It Start?"
R. Spencer

"Someone to Love"
Company

1974.05

OVER HERE!

A Musical in Two Acts. Book by Will Holt. Music and lyrics by Richard M. Sherman and Robert B. Sherman. Directed by Tom Moore. Musical numbers and dances staged by Patricia Birch. Musical coordination, vocal arrangements, Special dance music by Louis St. Louis. Orchestrations by Michael Gibson and Jim Tyler. Musical director, Joseph Klein. Scenery by Douglas W. Schmidt. Costumes by Carrie F. Robbins. Lighting by John Gleason. Media design by Stan J. Goldberg, Jeanne H. Livingston. Sound design by Jack Shearing. Associate producer, Lou Kramer. Produced by Kenneth Waissman and Maxine Fox. Opened 6 March 1974 at the Sam S. Shubert Theatre and closed 4 January 1975 after 341 performances.

CAST (in order of appearance): *Make-out*: Jim Weston. *Norwin Spokesman*: DOUGLASS WATSON. *Father*: MacIntyre Dixon. *Mother*: Bette Henritze. *Rankin*: William Griffis. *Donna*: Marilu Henner. *Wilma*: Phyllis Somerville. *Maggie*: Ann Reinking. *Mitzi*: JANIE SELL. *Misfit*: John Travolta. *Utah*: Treat Willaims. *Lucky*: John Mineo. *Sarge*: William Newman. *Sam*: Samuel E. Wright. *June*: APRIL SHAWHAN. *Bill*: John Driver. *Pauline de Paul*: MAXENE ANDREWS. *Paulette de Paul*: PATTY ANDREWS.

The action takes place in the 1940s.

ACT 1

"The Beat Begins" (Overture)
The Big Band, Company

"Since You're Not Around"
J. Weston, Company

"Over Here"[17]
P. Andrews, M. Andrews

"Buy a Victory Bond"
Company

"My Dream for Tomorrow"
A. Shawhan, Company

[17]Messrs. Sherman and St. Louis wish to acknowledge the creative contribution of Walter Weschler on these numbers.

"Charlie's Place"
M. Andrews, A. Reinking, J. Mineo, The Big Band, Company
"Hey Yvette"/"The Grass Grows Green"
D. Watson, W. Griffis, M. Dixon
"My Dream for Tomorrow" (reprise)
A. Shawhan, J. Driver
"The Good-Time Girl"
P. Andrews, Company
"Wait for Me Marlena"
J. Sell, Company
"We Got It"[18]
P. Andrews, M. Andrews, J. Sell, Company

ACT 2
"The Beat Continues" (Entre'Act)
The Big Band, Company
"Wartime Wedding"
P. Andrews, M. Andrews, Company
"Don't Shoot the Hooey to Me, Louie"
S. E. Wright
"Where Did the Good Times Go?"
P. Andrews
"Dream Drummin'"/"Soft Music"
J. Travolta, The Big Band, Company
"The Big Beat"[19]
P. Andrews, M. Andrews, J. Sell
"No Goodbyes"
P. Andrews, M. Andrews, Company

1974.06

CANDIDE

A Revival of the Musical in One Act, 33 Scenes[20]. (New) Book adapted from Voltaire's satire (of the same name) by Hugh Wheeler. (Original book by Lillian Hellman.) Music by Leonard Bernstein. Lyrics by Richard Wilbur. Additional lyrics by Stephen Sondheim and John Latouche. Directed by Harold Prince. Choreography by Patricia Birch. Production (settings, costumes) designed by Eugene and Franne Lee. Lighting by Tharon Musser. Musical direction by John Mauceri. Orchestrations by Hershy Kay. Production supervisor, Ruth Mitchell. Produced by The Chelsea Theatre Center of Brooklyn (Robert Kalfin, Artistic director; Michael David, Executive director; Burl Hash, Productions director) in conjunction with Harold Prince and Ruth Mitchell. Opened 10 March 1974 at the Broadway Theatre and closed 4 January 1976 after 740 performances. (Total including Off-Broadway run 788 performances.)

CAST (in order of appearance): *Dr. Voltaire, Dr Pangloss, Governor, Host, Sage*: LEWIS J. STADLEN. *Chinese Coolie, Soldier, Priest, Spanish Don, Sailor, Lion, Guest*: Jim Corti. *Candide*: MARK BAKER. *Huntsman, First Recruiting Officer, Agent, Spanish Don, Cartagenian Sailor, Eunuch*: David Horwitz. *Paquette*: DEBORAH ST. DARR. *Baroness, Harpsichordist, Penitente, Steel Drummer, Houri*: Mary-Pat Green. *Baron, Grand Inquisitor, Slave Driver, Captain, Guest*: Joe Palmieri. *Cunegonde*: MAUREEN BRENNAN. *Maximilian*: SAM FREED. *Servant, Agent of The Inquisition, Spanish Don, Cartagenian Sailor*: Robert Hendersen. *Second Recruiting Officer, Aristocrat, Cartagenian*: Peter Vogt. *Penitente, Whore, Houri*: Gail Boggs. *Penitente, Cartagenian, Houri*: Lynne Gannaway. *Aristocrat, Cartagenian, Second Sheep*: Carolann Page. *Bulgarian Soldier, Aristocrat, Vendor, Sailor, Pygmy, Cow*: Carlos Gorbea. *Bulgarian Soldier, Penitente, Cartagenian Sailor, Cow*: Kelly Walters. *Westphalian Soldier, Agent, Governor's Aide, Pirate, Guest*: Chip Garnett. *Rich Jew, Judge, Man in Black, Cartagenian, Pirate, German, Botanist, Guest*: Jeff Keller. *Aristocrat, Cartagenian, Houri*: Becky McSpadden. *Aristocrat, Whore, Houri, Cunegonde* (alternate): Kathryn Ritter. *Lady with Knitting, Cartagenian, First Sheep*: Renee Semes. *Old Lady*: JUNE GABLE. *Swing Girl*: Rhoda Butler.

(The action takes place in Westphalia and throughout the world in the eighteenth century. Scenes overlap and are played simultaneously.)

Scene 1: Voltaire's Bedroom. *Scene 2*: A Forest Glade. *Scene 3*: The Baroness' Boudoir. *Scene 4*: The Baronial Garden. *Scene 5*: Maximilian's Bedroom. *Scene 6*: The Castle Schoolroom. *Scene 7*: The Baronial Orchard. *Scene 8*: The Baronial Banquet Hall. *Scene 9*: A Desolate Heath in Westphalia. *Scene 10*: The Baronial Chapel. *Scene 11*: A Meadow by Moonlight. *Scene 12*: The Battlefield. *Scene 13*: A Village Square. *Scene 14*: A Bedchamber in the Jew's Palace. *Scene 15*: (The Earthquake;) A Destroyed Fishing Village. *Scene 16*: The Central Square in Lisbon. *Scene 17*: A Room in a Lisbon Palace. *Scene 18*: A Room in the Inn outside Cadiz. *Scene 19*: The Central Plaza at Cadiz. *Scene 20*: The Grand Plaza at Cartagena, Colombia. *Scene 21*: The Slave Market at Cartagena. *Scene 22*: A Ship at Sea. *Scene 23*: The Cathedral of the Jesuits at Montevideo. *Scene 24*: Eldorado. *Scene 25*: The Rocky Shore. *Scene 26*: A Clearing in the Jungle. *Scene 27*: The Grand Plaza, Cartagena, Colombia. *Scene 28*: The Dock at Cartagena. *Scene 29*: A Desert Island. *Scene 30*: A Hall in a Palace in Constantinople. *Scene 31*: A Street Outside the Palace. *Scene 32*: The Cave of the Wisest Man in the World. *Scene 33*: Candide's Farm.

MUSICAL NUMBERS
Scenes 2, 3, 4, 5
"Life Is Happiness Indeed"
M. Baker, M. Brennan, S. Freed, D. St. Darr
Scene 6
("Parade" instrumental)
"The Best of All Possible Worlds"
L. J. Stadlen, M. Baker, M. Brennan, S. Freed, D. St. Darr
Scene 7
"Oh Happy We"
M. Baker, M. Brennan
Scene 9
"It Must Be So"
M. Baker
Scene 10
"O Misere"
C. Page, L. Gannaway, G. Boggs, R. Hendersen
Scene 12
"Oh Happy We" (reprise)
M. Baker, M. Brennan
Scene 14
"Glitter and Be Gay"
M. Brennan
Scene 16
"Auto da Fé" (What a Day)
Company
"This World"
M. Baker
Scene 17
"You Were Dead, You Know"
M. Baker, M. Brennan
Scene 19
"I Am Easily Assimilated"
J. Gable, J. Corti, R. Hendersen, D. Horwitz
"I Am Easily Assimilated" (reprise)
J. Gable, M. Baker, M. Brennan
Scene 21
"My Love"
L. J. Stadlen
Scene 22
("Barcarolle" instrumental)
Scene 23
"Alleluia"
Company
Scene 24
("Eldorado" instrumental)
Scenes 24, 25, 26
"Sheep's Song"
C. Page, R. Semes, J. Corti, D. St. Darr, M. Baker

[18]Messrs. Sherman and St. Louis wish to acknowledge the creative contribution of Walter Weschler on these numbers.
[19]Messrs. Sherman and St. Louis wish to acknowledge the creative contribution of Walter Weschler on these numbers.
[20]This revival first produced Off-Broadway 11 December 1973 at the Chelsea Theater Center, Brooklyn Academy of Music for 48 performances; original production first produced in New York 1 December 1956 at the Martin Beck Theatre for 73 performances.

Scene 28
"Bon Voyage" (Schottische)
L. J. Stadlen, Company
Scene 29
"The Best of All Possible Worlds" (reprise)
J. Gable, M. Baker, D. St. Darr, R. Semes, C. Page
Scene 30
("Constantinople" instrumental)
"You Were Dead, You Know" (reprise)
M. Baker, M. Brennan
Scene 32
("Barcarolle" reprise instrumental)
Scene 33
"Make Our Garden Grow"
Company

THE MIKADO, or The Town of Titipu

1974.07

A Revival of the Comic Opera in Two Acts[21]. Libretto by William S. Gilbert. Music by Arthur Sullivan. Directed and choreographed by Jack Eddleman. Scenic design by Donald Oenslager. Costume design by Patton Campbell. Lighting by Hans Sondheimer. Conducted by Judith Somogi. Chorus master, Chris Nance. Produced by the New York City Opera. Opened 17 March 1974 at the New York State Theatre and closed 20 April 1974 after 5 performances in repertory.

CAST: *The Mikado of Japan*: EDWARD PIERSON. *Nanki-Poo*, his son, disguised as a wandering minstrel in love with Yum-Yum: GARY GLAZE. *Ko-Ko*, Lord High Executioner of Titipu: JAMES BILLINGS. *Pooh-Bah*, Lord High Everything Else: ARA BERBERIAN. *Pish-Tush*, a Noble Lord: Thomas Jamerson. *Yum-Yum, Pitti-Sing, Peep-Bo*, three sisters, wards of Ko-Ko: GLENYS FOWLES, JEANNE PILAND, PULI TORO. *Katisha*: BETTY ALLEN. *Chorus of School Girls, Nobles, Guards and Coolies*: New York City Opera Chorus.

THE CONSUL

1974.08

A Revival of the Opera (Musical Drama) in Three Acts, 6 Scenes[22]. Libretto and music by Gian-Carlo Menotti. Conductor, Christopher Keene. Settings by Horace Armistead. Staged by Gian-Carlo Menotti. Produced by the New York City Opera. Opened 27 March 1974 at the New York State Theatre and closed 28 April 1974 after 4 performances in repertory.

CAST: (in order of appearance): *John Sorel*: JOHN DARRENKAMP *Magda Sorel*: OLIVIA STAPP. *The Mother*: MURIEL COSTA-GREENSPON. *Secret Police Agent*: EDWARD PIERSON. *First Plainclothesman*: Jack Sims. *Second Plainclothesman*: Ray Van Orden. *The Secretary*: SANDRA WALKER. *Mr. Kofner*: DON YULE. *The Foreign Woman*: JUDITH DE ROSA. *Anna Gomez*: Barbara Hocher. *Nika Magadoff* (The Magician): NICO CASTEL. *Vera Boronel*: Virginia Brobyn. *Assan*: William Ledbetter. *Voice on the Record*: Mabel Mercer.

MUSIC! MUSIC!

1974.09

A Cavalcade (Revue) of American Music with footnotes by Alan Jay Lerner in Two Acts, Ninteen Scenes. Entire production staged and directed by Martin Charnin. Choreographed by Tony Stevens. Scenery by David Chapman. Costumes by Theoni V. Aldrdge. Lighting by Martin Aronstein. Vocal arrangements and musical direction by John Lesko. Orchestrations by Elliot Lawrence with Al Cohn, William Elton. Dance arrangements by Wally Harper. Associate producers, Howard Effron, Helen Haskell and Myles Spector. Producers for the City Center: Robert P. Brannigan, Chuck Eisler. Produced by The New York City Center of Music and Drama (Norman Singer, Executive director) and Alvin Bojar. Opened 11 April 1974 at the New York City Center and closed 12 May 1974 after 37 performances.

CAST: GENE NELSON, LARRY KERT, KAREN MORROW, DONNA McKECHNIE, ROBERT GUILLAUME, WILL MacKENZIE, GAIL NELSON, TED PRITCHARD, ARNOLD SOBOLOFF, RUSS THACKER.

Singing and Dancing Ensemble: Renée Baughman, Trish Garland, Denise Mauthé, Michon Peacock, Tom Offt, Michael Radigan, Yoalnda R. Raven, Fred Soiffer, Thomas J. Walsh.

Act 1: 1895-1941. *Scene 1*: Storyville. *Scene 2*: The Great White Way. *Scene 3*: World War I. *Scene 4*: The Princess Theatre. *Scene 5*: Those #%*$20's. *Scene 6*: Tin Pan Alley. *Scene 7*: Prohibition. *Scene 8*: The Boom. *Scene 9*: The Bust. *Scene 10*: Catfish Row. *Scene 11*: New York to Los Angeles.

Act 2: 1941-1974. *Scene 1*: World War II. *Scene 2*: The Great White Way Revisited. *Scene 3*: Rock and Roll. *Scene 4*: New Haven and Broadway. *Scene 5*: The New Frontier. *Scene 6*: The Great Society? *Scene 7*: Yesterday's Children. *Scene 8*: To Be Continued . . .

ACT 1
Scene 1
"Basin Street Blues"
(*Music and Lyrics by* Spencer Williams.)
"When the Saints Go Marching In" (traditional)
Scene 2
"The Merry Widow Waltz" (from *THE MERRY WIDOW*)
(*Music by* Franz Lehár.)
"Yankee Doodle Dandy" (from *LITTLE JOHNNY JONES*)
(*Music and Lyrics by* George M. Cohan.)
Scene 3
"Over There"
(*Music and Lyrics by* George M. Cohan.)
"I Didn't Raise My Boy to Be a Soldier"
(*Music and Lyrics by* Alfred Bryan and Al Piantadosi.)
"How Ya Gonna Keep 'Em Down on the Farm?"
(*Music by* Walter Donaldson. *Lyrics by* Sam Lewis, Joe Young.)
"Hinky Dinky Parlay Voo"
(*Music and Lyrics by* Al Dubin, Irving Mills, Jimmy McHugh and Julian Dash.)
Scene 4
"Look for the Silver Lining" (from *SALLY*)
(*Music by* Jerome Kern. *Lyrics by* Buddy G. DeSylva.)
"Bill" (from *SHOWBOAT*)
(*Music by* Jerome Kern. *Lyrics by* P. G. Wodehouse.)
Scene 5
"Yes Sir, That's My Baby"
(*Music by* Walter Donaldson. *Lyrics by* Gus Kahn.)
Scene 6
Gershwin Medley:
"Fascinating Rhthm"
"Somebody Loves Me"
"The Babbitt and the Bromide"
"Funny Face"
"(I'll Build a) Stairway to Paradise"
"The Man I Love"
"Oh, Lady Be Good"
"Someone to Watch Over Me"
Scene 7
"Manhattan" (from *THE GARRICK GAIETIES OF 1925*)
(*Music by* Richard Rodgers. *Lyrics by* Lorenz Hart.)
Scene 8
"The Girl Friend" (from *THE GIRL FRIEND*)
(*Music by* Richard Rodgers. *Lyrics by* Lorenz Hart.)
"Stouthearted Men" (from *THE NEW MOON*)
(*Music by* Sigmund Romberg. *Lyrics by* Oscar Hammerstein II.)
"Lucky Lindy"
(*Music and Lyrics by* Abel Bauer and L. Wolfe Gilbert.)

[21]First presented in New York 20 July, 10-29 August 1885 at the Union Square and People's Theatres for 22 performances. First authorized production presented 19 August 1885 at the Fifth Avenue Theatre by Richard D'Oyly Carte for 250 performances. For Synopsis of Scenes and Musical Numbers, see 19 August 1885 D'Oyly Carte production.

[22]Originally produced in New York 15 March 1950 at the Ethel Barrymore Theatre for 269 performances. For Synopsis of Scenes and Musical Numbers, see original 1950 production.

Scene 9

"Brother, Can You Spare a Dime?" (from *AMERICANA, 1932*)
(*Music by* Jay Gorney. *Lyrics by* E. Y. Harburg.)

"I'll See You Again" (from *BITTER SWEET*)
(*Music and Lyrics by* Noël Coward.)

"Great Day" (from *GREAT DAY*)
(*Music by* Vincent Youmans. *Lyrics by* Billy Rose and Edward Eliscu.)

"Stormy Weather"
(*Music by* Harold Arlen. *Lyrics by* Ted Koehler.)

Scene 10

"Bess You Is My Woman Now" (from *PORGY AND BESS*)
(*Music by* George Gershwin. *Lyrics by* Ira Gershwin and DuBose Heyward.)

"I Loves You Porgy" (from *PORGY AND BESS*)
(*Music by* George Gershwin. *Lyrics by* Ira Gershwin and DuBose Heyward.)

Scene 11

"Hooray for Hollywood" (from film *HOLLYWOOD HOTEL*)
(*Music by* Richard A. Whiting. *Lyrics by* Johnny Mercer.)

"Lullaby of Broadway" (from film *GOLDDIGGERS OF 1935*)
(*Music by* Harry Warren. *Lyrics by* Al Dubin.)

ACT 2

Scene 1

"In the Mood"
(*Music by* Joe Garland. *Lyrics by* Andy Razaf.)

"There Are Such Things"
(*Music and Lyrics by* George W. Meyer, Abel Baer and Stanley Adams.)

"The White Cliffs of Dover"
(*Music and Lyrics by* Walter Kent and Nat Burton.)

Scene 2

OKLAHOMA! Medley
(*Music by* Richard Rodgers. *Lyrics by* Oscar Hammerstein II.)

"Call Me Mister" (from *CALL ME MISTER*)
(*Music and Lyrics by* Harold Rome.)

"The Composers' Song" (A Recitation by Alan Jay Lerner.)

Scene 3

Rock and Roll Recitation

Scene 4

"Whiffenpoof Song" (Parody)

MY FAIR LADY Medley
(*Music by* Frederick Loewe. *Lyrics by* Alan Jay Lerner.)

Scene 5

WEST SIDE STORY Medley
(*Music by* Leonard Bernstein. *Lyrics by* Stephen Sondheim.)

Dance Segment from *THE MUSIC MAN, CAMELOT, BYE BYE BIRDIE* and *GYPSY.*

Scene 6

HELLO, DOLLY! Medley
(*Music and Lyrics by* Jerry Herman.)

FIDDLER ON THE ROOF Medley
(*Music by* Jerry Bock. *Lyrics by* Sheldon Harnick.)

Scene 7

"Abraham, Martin and John"
(*Music and Lyrics by* Dick Holler.)

"Mamam" (from *MATA HARI*)
(*Music by* Edward Thomas. *Lyrics by* Martin Charnin.)

Scene 8

"I Believe in Music"
(*Music and Lyrics by* Mac Davis.)

1974.10 WORDS AND MUSIC

A Musical Revue of the Lyrics of Sammy Cahn in One Act. (Music by James Van Heusen, Saul Chaplin, Jule Styne, Gene De Paul, Nicholas Brodszky, Alex Stordahl, Paul Weston, Jimmy Lunceford.) Directed by Jerry Adler. Musical director, Richard Leonard. (Setting, costumes) Designed by Robert Randolph. Lighting by Marc B. Weiss. Produced by Alexander H. Cohen in association with Harvey Granat. Opened 16 April 1974 at the John Golden Theatre and closed 3 August 1974 after 127 performances.

CAST: SAMMY CAHN, KELLY GARRETT, SHIRLEY LEMMON, JON PECK.

MUSICAL NUMBERS

"Call Me Irresponsible" (from *PAPA'S DELICATE CONDITION*, film)
"Shake Your Head from Side to Side"
"Rhythm Is Our Business"
"Please Be Kind"
"I've Heard That Song Before" (from *YOUTH ON PARADE*, film)
"Five Minutes More" (from *SWEETHEART OF SIGMA CHI*, film)
"I'll Walk Alone" (from *FOLLOW THE BOYS*, film)
"It's Been a Long, Long Time"
"It's Magic" (from *ROMANCE ON THE HIGH SEAS*, film)
"Guess I'll Hang My Tears Out to Dry" (from *GLAD TO SEE YOU*)
"The Christmas Waltz"
"Teach Me Tonight"
"Three Coins in the Fountain" (from film of the same name)
"Be My Love" (from *THE TOAST OF NEW ORLEANS*, film)
"I'll Never Stop Loving You" (from *LOVE ME OR LEAVE ME*, film)
"Thoroughly Modern Millie" (from film of the same name)
"You'll Never Know"
"All the Way" (from *THE JOKER IS WILD*, film)
"The Tender Trap" (from film of the same name)
"Everybody Has the Right to Be Wrong" (from *SKYSCRAPER*)
"I'll Only Miss Him When I think of Him" (from *SKYSCRAPER*)
"Walking Happy" (from show of the same name)
"Papa, Won't You Dance With Me" (from *HIGH BUTTON SHOES*)
"Day By Day"
"Let It Snow! Let It Snow! Let It Snow!"
"A Touch of Class" (from film of the same name)
"You're My Girl" (from *HIGH BUTTON SHOES*)
"Saturday Night (Is the Loneliest Night of the Week)"
"I Should Care" (from *THRILL OF A ROMANCE*, film)
"Put 'Em in a Box, (Tie 'Em with a Ribbon, and Throw 'Em in the Deep Blue Sea)" (from *ROMANCE ON THE HIGH SEAS*, film)
"The Second Time Around" (from *HIGH TIME*, film)
"Pocketful of Miracles" (from film of the same name)
"I Fall in Love Too Easily" (from *ANCHORS AWEIGH*, film)
"I Wonder Why"
"Until the Real Thing Comes Along"
"Love and Marriage" (from *OUR TOWN*, TV musical)
"The Things We Did Last Summer"
"Time After Time" (from *IT HAPPENED IN BROOKLYN*, film)
"Come Fly With Me" (from film of the same name)
"High Hopes" (from *A HOLE IN THE HEAD*, film)
"My Kind of Town (Chicago Is)" (from *ROBIN AND THE SEVEN HOODS*, film)

1974.11 SAMMY

A Musical Revue in Two Acts. Musical conductor (for Mr. Davis), George Rhodes. Stage director, Darrell Giddens. Musical coordinator, Mel Rodnon. Produced by Nederlander in association with Sy Marsh. Opened 23 April 1974 at the Uris Theatre and closed 4 May 1974 after 14 performances.

CAST: SAMMY DAVIS, JR., FREDA PAYNE, THE NICHOLAS BROTHERS (Harold, Fayard).

MUSICAL NUMBERS[23]

Scene 1

"I've Gotta Be Me" (from *GOLDEN RAINBOW*)
(*Music and Lyrics by* Walter Marks.)

---

[23] No song list appeared in the program. List was prepared from press reviews, and is neither complete nor in performance order.

"Another Spring"
"The Impossible Dream" (from *MAN OF LAMANCHA*)
(*Music by* Mitch Leigh. *Lyrics by* Joe Darion.)
"Goldfinger" (from film of the same name)
(*Music by* John Barry. *Lyrics by* Leslie Bricusse and Anthony Newley.)
"What Kind of Fool Am I?" (from *STOP THE WORLD-I WANT TO GET OFF*)
(*Music and Lyrics by* Leslie Bricusse and Anthony Newley.)
"Who Can I Turn To?" (from *THE ROAR OF THE GREASPAINT-THE SMELL OF THE CROWD*)
(*Music and Lyrics by* Leslie Bricusse and Anthony Newley.)
"The Candy Man" (from *WILLY WONKA AND THE CHOCOLATE FACTORY*, film)
(*Music and Lyrics by* Leslie Bricusse and Anthony Newley.)
"Gonna Build a Montain" (from *STOP THE WORLD-I WANT TO GET OFF*)
"Once in a Lifetime" (from *STOP THE WORLD-I WANT TO GET OFF*)
S. Davis
(*Music and Lyrics by* Leslie Bricusse and Anthony Newley.)
Scene 2
Medley of Songs from their films *DOWN ARGENTINA WAY, TIN PAN ALLEY, ZIEGFELD FOLLIES*
The Nicholas Brothers
"Ol' Man River" (from *SHOWBOAT*)
(*Music by* Jerome Kern. *Lyrics by* Oscar Hammerstein II.)
The Nicholas Brothers
Scene 3
"The Man I Love"
(*Music by* George Gershwin. *Lyrics by* Ira Gershwin.)
"What a Little Moonlight Can Do" (from *ROADHOUSE NIGHTS*, film)
(*Music and Lyrics by* Harry Woods.)
"Cool Blues"
"Band of Gold" (*Music and Lyrics by* Ronald Dunbar, Edythe Wayne.)
"Carousel" (from *JACQUES BREL IS ALIVE AND LIVING IN PARIS*)
(*Music and Lyrics by* Jacques Brel.)
F. Payne
Scene 4
"I'll Never Smile Again"
(*Music and Lyrics by* Ruth Lowe.)
"Witchcraft"
(*Music by* Cy Coleman. *Lyrics by* Carolyn Leigh.)
"Come Fly With Me" (from film of the same name)
(*Music by* James Van Heusen. *Lyrics by* Sammy Cahn.)
"(I Did It) My Way"
(*Music by* Caliude Revaux and Claude François. *English Lyrics by* Paul Anka.)
"Mr. Bojangles"
(*Music and Lyrics by* Jerry Jeff Walker.)
"For Once In My Life"
(*Music by* Orlando Murden. *Lyrics by* Ronald Millar.)
"The Lady Is a Tramp" (from *BABES IN ARMS*)
(*Music by* Richard Rodgers. *Lyrics by* Lorenz Hart.)
"Come on, Baby"
"Ya Got Trouble" (from *THE MUSIC MAN*)
(*Music and Lyrics by* Meredith Willson.)
"Birth of the Blues" (from *GEORGE WHITE'S SCANDALS OF 1926*)
(*Music by* Ray Henderson. *Lyrics by* Buddy G. DeSylva, Lew Brown.)S. Davis

1974.12 RIDE THE WINDS

A Musical in Two Acts. Book, music and lyrics by John Driver. Directed by Lee D. Sankowich. Choreography by Jay Norman. Orchestrations, vocal arrangements and musical direction by Robert Brandzel. Technical advisor, Sensei Yoshiteru Otani. Sets and costumes by Samuel C. Ball. Lighting by Jeff Davis. Produced by Berta Walker and Bill Tchakirides. Opened 16 May 1974 at the Bijou Theatre and closed 18 May 1974 after 3 performances.

CAST (in order of appearance): *Musashi*: IRVING (ALLEN) LEE. *Yamada*: SAB SHIMONO. *Sensei (Honored Teacher) Takuan*: ERNESTO GONZALEZ. *Joshu*: NATE BARNETT. *Inari*: CHIP ZIEN. *Banzo*: TOM MATSUSAKA. *Ya Ta*: Fanny Cerito Assoluta. *Lan*: ELAINE PETRICOFF. *Toki*: MARION JIM. *Oda*: ALEXANDER ORFALY. *Tellers*: Laura May Lewis, John Gorrin. *Priests, Students, Soldiers*: Kenneth Frett, John Gorrin, Richard Loreto, Ken Mitchell.

Act 1: A feudal country in the Far East. The action takes place around a monastery along a mountain road.

Act 2: Four years later.

ACT 1
"Run, Musashi, Run"
The Company
"The Emperor Me"
I. Lee
"The Gentle Buffoon"
N. Barnett, T. Matsusaka
"Those Who Speak"
I. Lee, N. Barnett, T. Matsusaka
"Flower Song"
E. Gonzalez, E. Petricoff, N. Barnett, Ensemble
"You're Loving Me"
I. Lee
"Breathing the Air"
M. Jim
"Remember That Day"
E. Gonzalez, S. Shimono
"Tengu"
Ensemble

ACT 2
"Ride the Winds"
The Company
"Are You a Man"
E. Petricoff
"Ride the Winds" (reprise)
The Company
"Every Days"
E. Petricoff, M. Jim, Inari Priests
"Loving You"
E. Petricoff, I. Lee
"Pleasures"
A. Orfaly
"Someday I'll Walk"
I. Lee
"That Touch"
E. Petricoff
Finale
The Company

1974.13 THE MAGIC SHOW

A Magic Show with Songs in One Act[24]. Book by Bob Randall. Music and lyrics by Stephen Schwartz. Magic by Doug Henning. Direction and dances by Grover Dale. Setting by David Chapman. Costumes by Randy Barcelo. Lighting by Richard Nelson. Musical director, Stephen Reinhardt. Dance arrangements by David Spangler. Audio design by Phil Ramone. Associate producer, Nan Pearlman. Produced by Edgar Lansbury, Joseph Beruh, Ivan Reitman. Opened 28 May 1974 at the Cort Theatre and closed 31 December 1978 after 1859 performances.

CAST (in order of appearance): *Manny*: ROBERT LuPONE. *Feldman*: DAVID OGDEN STIERS. *Donna*: ANNIE McGREEVEY. *Dina*: CHERYL BARNES. *Cal*: DALE SOULES. *Doug*: DOUG HENNING. *Mike*: Ronald Stafford. *Steve*: Lloyd Sannes. *Charmin*: ANITA MORRIS. *Goldfarb*: Sam Schacht.

The action takes place in the Passaic Top Hat, a nite club in New Jersey.

[24]For subsequent tour, an intermission was added after "Doug's Act" in some cities.

MUSICAL NUMBERS

"Up to His Old Tricks"
Entire Company

"Solid Silver Platform Shoes"
C. Barnes, A. McGreevey

"Lion Tamer"
D. Soules

"Style"
D. O. Stiers, Company

"Charmin's Lament"
A. Morris

"Two's Company"
C. Barnes, A. McGreevey

"The Goldfarb Variations"
C. Barnes, D. O. Stiers, A. McGreevey, R. LuPone, A. Morris

"Doug's Act"
D. Henning

"A Bit of Villainy"
D. O. Stiers, C. Barnes, A. McGreevey

"West End Avenue"
D. Soules

"Sweet, Sweet, Sweet"
A. Morris, R. LuPone, R. Stafford, L. Sannes

"Before Your Very Eyes"
C. Barnes, A. McGreevey, D. O. Stiers

1974–1975 SEASON

Angela Lansbury in GYPSY
Martha Swope/TimePix

1974–1975 SEASON

1974.14 THE MERRY WIDOW

A Revival of the Operetta ('La Viuda Alegre') in Three Acts, in Spanish[1]. Original Viennese libretto by Victor Léon and Leo Stein. (Based on the play "L'Attaché d'ambassade" by Henri Meilhac.) Spanish translation by Miguel Padilla. Music by Franz Lehár. Directed by Miguel de Grandy. Scenery by Sormani di Milano. Costumes by Stivanello. Lighting by Lawrence Metzler. Musical director and conductor, Alfredo Munar. Chorus master, Juan Viccini. Choreographer, Armando Suez. Special consultant, Raymond R. Norat. Produced by VICMAN Productions (Victor del Corral, Manolo Alonso). Opened 4 June 1974 at the New York City Center and closed 9 June 1974 after 7 performances.

CAST (in order of appearance): *Viscount Zancada*: Hernando Chaviano. *Baron Mirko Zeta*: Miguel de Grandy. *Kromow*: Rosendo Gali Menendez. *Raul de Saint Brioche*: Carlos de Leon. *Olga Kromow*: Nydia del Rivero. *Bogdanovitch*: Ruddi Fanetti. *Pritzky*: Jesus Zubizaretta. *Valencienne*: PULI TORO. *Camilo De Rosillon*: RAFAEL LE BRON. *Prascovia*: Lolina Gutierrez. *Niegus*: Manolo Alvan. *Ana De Glavari*: GEORGINA GRANADOS. *Count Danilo*: TOMAS ALVAREZ. *Silviana Bogdanovitch*: Lisette Palacio. *Waiters*: Pablo Alamo, Eddie Gonzales, Mario Santisteban, Pedro Trujillo.

Chorus: German Acosta, Frank Acosta, Jose Calazan, Nina Cruz, Frank Cruz, Isis Figueroa, Lourdes Galaya, Luis Gotay, Orika Gutierrez, Ernesto Gutierrez, Hector Lomba, Maria Mainegra, Rafael Morales, Amparo Navarro, Josefa Navarro, Soledad Navarro, Luis Pena, Juan Sabache, Flora Santana, Antonio Tarazona, Amparo Viccini, Elda Zubizarreta, Mercedes Zubizarreta. *Dancers*: Kate Antrobus, Joan Baker, Marissa Benetsky, Sandy Italiano, Barbara Klein, Henry Boyer, Marcos Dinnerstein, Daryl Gray, Gerald Moreno, Stephen Rockford.

The action takes place in Paris in the 1900s.

1974.15 THE MIKADO, or The Town of Titipu

A Revival of the Comic Opera in Two Acts[2]. Libretto by William S. Gilbert. Music by Arthur Sullivan. Directed and choreographed by Jack Eddleman. Scenic design by Donald Oenslager. Costume design by Patton Campbell. Lighting by Hans Sondheimer. Conducted by Judith Somogi. Chorus master, George Branson Gray. Produced by the New York City Opera. Opened 1 September 1974 at the New York State Theatre and closed 9 November 1974 after 6 performances in repertory; returned to the repertory 9 March 1975 at the New York State Theatre for 3 additional performances. (Total 9 performances this season.)

CAST: *The Mikado of Japan*: EDWARD PIERSON. *Nanki-Poo*, his son, disguised as a wandering minstrel in love with Yum-Yum: GARY GLAZE. *Ko-Ko*, Lord High Executioner of Titipu: JAMES BILLINGS. *Pooh-Bah*, Lord High Everything Else: ARA BERBERIAN. *Pish-Tush*, a Noble Lord: Robert Termine. *Yum-Yum, Pitti-Sing, Peep-Bo*, three sisters, wards of Ko-Ko: GLENYS FOWLES, JEANNE PILAND, PULI TORO. *Katisha*: BETTY ALLEN.

Chorus of School Girls, Nobles, Guards and Coolies: New York City Opera Chorus.

1974.16 DIE FLEDERMAUS

A Revival of the Operetta in Three Acts[3]. Original Viennese libretto by Carl Haffner and Richard Genée. Lyrics by Richard Genée. (Based on the comedy "Le Réveillon" by Henri Meilhac and Ludovic Halévy.) English libretto by Ruth and Thomas Martin. Music by Johann Strauss. Directed by Gerald Freedman. Choreographed by Joyce Trisler. Scenic design by Lloyd Evans. Costume design by Theoni V. Aldredge. Lighting by Hans Sondheimer. Conducted by Mario Bernardi. Opened 18 September 1974 at the New York State Theatre and closed 7 November 1974 after 9 performances in repertory; returned to the repertory 18 March 1975 and closed 16 April 1975 after 4 additional performances. (Total 13 performances this season.)

CAST (in order of appearance): *Alfred*, an itinerant tenor: Gary Glaze. *Adele*, von Eisenstein's chambermaid: RUTH WELTING. *Rosalinda von Eisenstein*: JOHANNA MEIER. *Gabriel von Eisenstein*: ALAN TITUS. *Dr. Blind*, a lawyer: Howard Fried. *Dr. Falke*, a close friend of Eisenstein: DOMINIC COSSA. *Frank*, the prison warden: SPIRO MALAS. *Sally*, Adele's sister: Diana Kehrig. *Ivan*, servant to Orlofsky: Jack Sims. *Prince Orlofsky*, a wealthy, bored Russian: DAVID RAE SMITH. *Frosch*, the jailer: Coley Worth. *Solo Dancers*: Esperanza Galan, Juliu Horvath.

Ensemble: New York City Opera Chorus.

1974.17 GYPSY

A Revival of the Musical Fable in Two Acts[4]. Book by Arthur Laurents. Suggested by the memoirs (of the same name) by Gypsy Rose Lee. Music by Jule Styne. Lyrics by Stephen Sondheim. Scenery and lighting by Robert Randolph. Costumes by Raoul Pene du Bois. Directed by Arthur Laurents. Original New York production Directed and choreographed by Jerome Robbins. Choreography reproduced by Robert Tucker. Musical direction by Milton Rosenstock. Orchestrations by Sid Ramin with Robert Ginzler. Dance music arranged by John Kander. Miss Lansbury's costumes by Robert Mackintosh. Sound design by Jack Mann. Produced by Barry M. Brown, Edgar Lansbury, Fritz Holt and Joseph Beruh. Opened 23 September 1974 at the Winter Garden Theatre and closed 4 January 1975 after 120 performances.

CAST (in order of appearance): *Uncle Jocko*: John C. Becher. *George*: Don Potter. *Clarence* (and His Classic Clarinet): Craig Brown. *Balloon Girl*: Donna Elio. *Baby Louise*: Lisa Peluso. *Baby June*: BONNIE LANGFORD. *Rose*: ANGELA LANSBURY. *Chowsie*: Peewee. *Pop*: Ed Riley. *Newsboys*: Craig Brown, Anthony Marciona, Sean Rule, Mark Santoro. *Weber*: Charles Rule. *Herbie*: REX ROBBINS. *Louise*: ZAN CHARISSE. *June*: MAUREEN MOORE. *Tulsa*: JOHN SHERIDAN. *Yonkers*: Steven Gelfer. L.A.: David Lawson. *Little Rock*: Jay Smith. *San Diego*: Dennis Karr. *Boston*: Serhij Bohdan. *Kringelein*: John C. Becher. *Mr. Goldstone*: Don Potter. *Gigolo*: Edith Ann. *Waitress*: Patricia Richardson. *Miss Cratchitt*: Gloria Rossi. *Hollywood Blondes (5)*: Pat Cody, Jinny Kordek, Jan Neuberger, Marilyn Olson, Patricia Richardson. *Agnes*: Denny Dillon. *Pastey*: Richard J. Sabellico. *Tessie Tura*: MARY LOUISE WILSON. *Mazeppa*: GLORIA ROSSI. *Cigar*: John C. Becher. *Electra*: Sally Cooke. *Maid*: Bonnie Walker. *Phil*: Ed Riley. *Bougeron-Cochon*: Serhij Bohdan.

1974.18 MACK AND MABEL

A Musical Love Story in One Act[5], 14 Scenes. Book by Michael Stewart. Based on an idea by Leonard Spiegelgass. Music and lyrics by Jerry Herman. Directed and choreographed by Gower Champion. Scenic design by Robin Wagner. Costume design by Patricia Zipprodt. Lighting design by Tharon Musser. Musical direction and vocal arrangements by Don Pippin. Orchestrations by Philip J. Lang. Incidental and dance music by John Morris. Associate choreographer, Buddy Schwab. Production supervisor, Lucia Victor. Associate producer, Jack Schlissel. Film coordinator, Andy Stein. Early comedy film from the Killiam Collection. Produced by David Merrick in association with Edwin H. Morris. Opened 6 October 1974 at the Majestic Theatre and closed 30 November 1974 after 65 performances.

CAST (in order of appearance): *Eddie*, the watchman: Stanley Simmonds. *Mack Sennett*: ROBERT PRESTON. *Lottie Ames*: LISA KIRK. *Ella*: Nancy Evers. *Freddie*: Roger Bigelow. *Charlie Muldoon*: Christopher Murney. *Wally*: Robert Fitch. *Frank Wyman*: Jerry Dodge. *Mabel Normand*: BERNADETTE PETERS. *Mr. Kleiman*: Tom Batten. *Mr. Fox*: Bert Michaels. *Iris*, the wardrobe mistress: Marie Santell. *William Desmond Taylor*: JAMES MITCHELL. *Phyllis Foster*: Cheryl Armstrong. *Serge*: Frank Root.

---

[1]Neither Synopsis of Scenes nor Musical Numbers given in program. For Synopsis of Scenes and Musical Numbers in English, see original 1907 production.

[2]First presented in New York 20 July, 10-29 August 1885 at the Union Square and People's Theatres for 22 performances. First authorized production presented 19 August 1885 at the Fifth Avenue Theatre by Richard D'Oyly Carte for 250 performances. For Synopsis of Scenes and Musical Numbers, see 19 August 1885 D'Oyly Carte production.

[3]First English language production presented in New York 16 March 1885 at the Casino Theatre for 42 performances. First New York production of this adaptation 20 December 1950 at the Metropolitan Opera House. For Synopsis of Scenes and Musical Numbers, see May 1954 revival.

[4]Originally produced in New York 21 May 1959 at the Broadway Theatre for 702 performances. For Synopsis of Scenes and Musical Numbers, see original 1959 production. The opening number "May We Entertain You" retitled as "Let Me Entertain You." "Mr Goldstone, I Love You" listed as "Mr. Goldstone." "Dainty June and Her Farmboys" was retitled "The Barnyard" for the national tour. "Together, Wherever We Go" listed as "Together." The Act 2 reprise of "Let Me Entertain You" retitled as "The Strip" performed by Zan Charisse (without Company).

[5]After opening, an intermission was added between Scenes 8 and 9.

The Grips: John Almberg, Roger Bigelow, George Blackwell, Frank Bouley, Gerand Brentte, Lonnie Burr, Chet D'Elia, Igors Gavon, Jonathan Miele, Don Percassi, Frank Root. *Mack Sennett Bathing Beauties*: Cheryl Armstrong, Claudia Asbury, Sandahl Bergman, Chrystal Chambers, Nancy Dafgek, Prudence Darby, Elaine Handel, Paula Lynn, Patricia Michaels, Carol Perea, L. J. Rose, Rita Rudner, Marianne Selbert, Jo Speros, Pat Trott, Geordie Withee.

Scene 1: The Sennett Studios, 1938. *Scene 2*: The Brooklyn Studio, 1911. *Scene 3*: Mack's Office, Brooklyn. *Scene 4*: En route to California. *Scene 5*: Los Angeles, 1912. *Scene 6*: On the Set. *Scene 7*: The Orchid Room of the Hollywood Hotel, 1919. *Scene 8*: On the Set. *Scene 9*: Mack's New Office, 1923. *Scene 10*: Studio Early Next Morning. *Scene 11*: A pier, New York. *Scene 12*: "Vitagraph Varieties of 1929" and the Terrace of William Desmond Taylor's Home. *Scene 13*: Mack's Office—then Mabel's Home. *Scene 14*: The Sennett Studios, 1938.

MUSICAL NUMBERS

Scene 1
"Movies Were Movies"
R. Preston

Scene 2
"Look What Happened to Mabel"
B. Peters, R. Fitch, C. Murney, J. Dodge, Grips

Scene 3
"Big Time"
L. Kirk, the Family

Scene 4
"I Won't Send Roses"
R. Preston
"I Won't Send Roses" (reprise)
B. Peters

Scene 5
"I Wanna Make the World Laugh"
R. Preston, Company

Scene 6
"I Wanna Make the World Laugh" (reprise)
R. Preston, Company

Scene 7
"Wherever He Ain't"
B. Peters, Waiters

Scene 8
"Hundreds of Girls"
R. Preston, Bathing Beauties

Scene 10
"When Mabel Comes into the Room"
Company
"My Heart Leaps Up"
R. Preston

Scene 11
"Time Heals Everything"
B. Peters

Scene 12
"Tap Your Troubles Away"
L. Kirk, Girls

Scene 13
"I Promise You a Happy Ending"
R. Preston

CHARLES AZNAVOUR ON BROADWAY

1974.19

A One-Man Show in Two Acts. Musical director, Aldo Frank. Music coordinator, Mel Rodnon. Lighting, Marc B. Weiss. Production manager, Levon Sayan. (All music by Charles Aznavour except as noted.) A Music Fair-Enterprises Inc. Production. Produced by Lee Guber, Shelly Gross and Joseph Harris. Opened 15 October 1974 at the Minskoff Theatre and closed 27 October 1974 after 16 performances.

CAST: CHARLES AZNAVOUR.

ACT 1
"Le Temps"
(*Music by* J. Davis. *English Lyrics by* Herbert Kretzmer.)
"Happy Anniversary"
(English Lyrics by Herbert Kretzmer.)
"I Live for You"
(*English Lyrics by* Herbert Kretzmer.)
"Un par un"
"Our Love, My Love"
(*Lyrics by* Erich Segal.)
"The Ham"
(*Music by* Georges Garvarentz. *English Lyrics by* B. Morrisson.)
"La Mamma"
(*Lyrics by* Robert Gall.)
"To Die of Love"
English Lyrics by Howard Liebling.)
"No I Could Never Forget"
(*Music by* Georges Garvarentz. *English Lyrics by* Al Kasha and Joel Hirschhorn.)
"I Have Lived"
(*English Lyrics by* Al Kasha and Joel Hirschhorn.)
"La Boheme"
(*Lyrics by* Jacques Plante.)
"What Makes a Man"
(English Lyrics by R. Craig.)
"Emmenez-moi"

ACT 2
"La Baraka"
(*English Lyrics by* Herbert Kretzmer.)
"Reste"
"We Can Never Know"
(*English Lyrics by* Al Kasha and Joel Hirschhorn.)
"You've Let Yourself Go"
(*English Lyrics by* Marcel Stellman.)
"Trousse chemise"
(*Lyrics by* J. Mareuil.)
"The 'I Love You' Song"
(*French Lyrics by* G. Bontempelli. *English Lyrics by* Herbert Kretzmer.)
"She"
(*English Lyrics by* Herbert Kretzmer.)
"Que c'est triste Venise"
(*Lyrics by* F. Dorin.)
"And I in My Chair"
(English Lyrics by D. Newburg.)
"Yesterday When I Was Young"
(*English Lyrics by* Herbert Kretzmer.)
"Isabelle"
"The Old Fashioned Way"
(*Music by* Georges Garvarentz. *English Lyrics by* Al Kasha and Joel Hirschhorn.)
"Les comediens"
(*Lyrics by* Jacques Plante.)
"You've Got to Learn"
(*English Lyrics by* Marcel Stellman.)

ANDY WILLIAMS with MICHEL LEGRAND

1974.20

A Musical Revue in Two Acts. Musical director, Jack Fierman. Set by Neil Peter Jampolis. Lighting by Jane Reisman. Associate conductor, Armand Migniani. Soloist, Eileen Duffy. Stage director, Jerry Grollnek. Sound consultant, Pat Baroo. Produced by Nederlander. Opened 16 October 1974 at the Uris Theatre and closed 27 October 1974 after 15 performances.

CAST: ANDY WILLIAMS, MICHEL LEGRAND.

ACT 1
Michel Legrand conducts his own songs, including a medley from "The Umbrellas of Cherbourg."
Soloist: E Duffy.

ACT 2
Andy Williams, with orchestra conducted by Jack Fierman
Finale: Andy Williams and Michel Legrand

1974.21

TONY BENNETT AND LENA HORNE SING

A Musical Revue in Two Acts. Music directors, Torrie Zito (for Tony Bennett), Robert M. Freedman (for Lena Horne). Production coordinator, Sherman Sneed. Wardrobe for Miss Horne, Georgio Sant'Angelo. Produced by Lee Guber, Shelly Gross and Joseph Harris. Opened 30 October 1974 at the Minskoff Theatre and closed 24 November 1974 after 37 performances.

CAST: TONY BENNETT, LENA HORNE.

ACT 1

Miss Horne will sing the songs of Arlen, Bloom, Denver, Freedman, Kristofferson, Porter Razaf, Raposo, Wonder.

ACT 2

Mr. Bennett will sing the songs of Arlen/Koehler, Bacharach, Cahn/Barrie, Cross/Cory, Ebb, Ellington, Gerhswin, Harrison, McCartney, McHugh, Miller, Newley/Bricusse, Rodgers/Hart, Styne. And a Special Tribute to the great American composer Harold Arlen.

1974.22

ANTHONY NEWLEY & HENRY MANCINI

A Musical Revue in Two Acts. Set designed by Neil Peter Jampolis. Theatre lighting by Jane Reisman. Lighting and sound by Jerry Grollnek, Pat Barso. Conductor for Mr. Newley, Ian Fraser. Produced by Nederlander. Opened 31 October 1974 at the Uris Theatre and closed 10 November 1974 after 15 performances.

CAST: ANTHONY NEWLEY, HENRY MANCINI.

ACT 1: Henry Mancini and His Orchestra

Overture from *TOMMY*
(*Music by* Pete Townshend.)

Medley: "Baby Elephant Walk," "Mr. Lucky"
(*Music by* Henry Mancini.)

Love Theme from *ROMEO AND JULIET* film
(*Music by* Nino Rota.)

Overture from *THAT'S ENTERTAINMENT* film:
"The Trolley Song," "Over the Rainbow," "Hi-Lili Hi-Lo," "It's a Most Unusual Day," "Singin' in the Rain," "San Francisco," "Love," That's Entertainment."

(Theme from) *THE PINK PANTHER* film
(*Music by* Henry Mancini.)

Medley: "Love's Theme" (White); "T.S.O.P." (Gamble/Huff)

The Big Band Montage:
"I'm Getting Sentimental Over You," "Blue Flame," "Let's Dance," "Ciribiribin," "Moonlight Serenade," "Artistry in Rhythm," "Nightmare," "Leapfrog," "Take the A Train."

Theme from *PETER GUNN* (Television)
(*Music by* Henry Mancini.)

Ballads by Mancini:
"Dear Heart," "The Sweetheart Tree," "Days of Wine and Roses," Moon River."

ACT 2: Anthony Newley

It's a Musical World Medley:
"It's a Musical World" (from *THE GOOD OLD BAD DAYS*)

"The Good Old Bad Old Days" (from *THE GOOD OLD BAD DAYS*)

"Gonna Build a Mountain" (from *STOP THE WORLD-I WANT TO GET OFF*)

"On a Wonderful Day Like Today" (from *THE ROAR OF THE GREASEPAINT*)

"Goldfinger" (from *GOLDFINGER* film)

"The Good Things in Life" (from *THE GOOD OLD BAD DAYS*)

"The Candy Man" (from *WILLY WONKA AND THE CHOCOLATE FACTORY* film)

"Once in a Lifetime" (from *STOP THE WORLD-I WNAT TO GET OFF*)
(All of the above *Music and Lyrics by* Leslie Bricusse and Anthony Newley.)

"Talk to the Animals" (from *DR. DOOLITTLE* film)
(*Music and Lyrics by* Leslie Bricusse.)

"Love Has the Longest Memory of All" (from *QUILP* film)
(*Music and Lyrics by* Anthony Newley.)

"Middle Age Rock & Roll Star"
(*Music and Lyrics by* Anthony Newley.)

"No Such Thing as Love"
(*Music and Lyrics by* Ian Fraser and Anthony Newley.)
"Who Can I Turn To?" (from *THE ROAR OF THE GREASEPAINT*)

"Feeling Good" (from *THE ROAR OF THE GREASEPAINT*)

A Broadway Medley:
"Everything's Coming Up Roses" (from *GYPSY*)
"Tonight" (from *WEST SIDE STORY*)
"Get Me to the Church on Time" (from *MY FAIR LADY*)
"My Favorite Things" (from *THE SOUND OF MUSIC*)
"If I Were a Rich Man" (from *FIDDLER ON THE ROOF*)
"People" (from *FUNNY GIRL*)
"I'll Never Fall in Love Again" (from *PROMISES, PROMISES*)
"Hello, Dolly!" (from *HELLO, DOLLY!*)
"What Kind of Fool Am I?" (from *STOP THE WORLD-I WANT TO GET OFF*)

1974.23

MOURNING PICTURES

A Drama with Music in Two Acts. Play by Honor Moore. Music by Susan Ain. Directed by Kay Carney. Music supervisor, Larry Abel. Setting by John Jacobsen. Costumes by Whitney Blausen. Lighting by Spencer Mosse. A Lenox Arts Center/Music-Theatre Performing Group Production (Lyn Austin, Mary Silverman, Producers). Produced by Samuel H. Schwartz. Opened and closed 10 November 1974 at the Lyceum Theatre after 1 performance.

CAST (in order of appearance): *Margaret*: KATHRYN WALKER. *Maggie*: LEORA DANA. *Philip*: DONALD SYMINGTON. *Abigail*: Leslie Ackerman. *David*: Daniel Landon. *Doctors Rumbach, Cassidy, Berryman, Potter*: PHILIP CARLSON. *Singer*: DOROTHEA JOYCE.

The action takes place between March and September in Connecticut, New York and Washington, D.C.

Act 1: March-May.

Act 2: June-September.

ACT 1

"What Will She Leave Me?"
D. Joyce

"It's Such a Beautiful Day"
D. Joyce

"What Are You Saying About Me Now?"
D. Joyce

"Sweet Clear Sun"
D. Joyce

ACT 2

"The Garden"
D. Joyce

"Wait Until the Sun"
D. Joyce

"I Want to Go Home"
D. Joyce

"Paul Arrives"
D. Joyce

"There Is a Birthday"
D. Joyce

1974.24

SGT. PEPPER'S LONELY HEARTS CLUB BAND ON THE ROAD

A Rock Spectacle (Musical Revue) in Two Acts. (Based on the film of the same name by The Beatles.) Music and lyrics by John Lennon and Paul McCartney. Production conceived and adapted (for the Stage) by Robin Wagner and Tom O'Horgan. Entire production directed and staged by Tom O'Horgan. Scenic design by Robin Wagner. Costume design by Randy Barcelo. Lighting design by Jules Fisher. Sound design by Abe Jacob. (Music) Arranged and conducted by Gordon Lowry Harrell. Production supervisor, Richard Scanga. Executive producer, Peter Brown. Associate

producers, (R. Tyler) Gatchell & (Peter) Neufeld. Presented at this theatre by Steven Singer, Steve Metz and Howard Dando. Produced by Robert Stigwood in association with Brian Avnet and Scarab Productions, Inc. Opened 17 November 1974 at the Beacon Theatre and closed 5 January 1975 after 66 performances.

CAST (in order of appearance): *Maxwell's Silver Hammermen (3)*: *Jack*: ALLAN NICHOLLS. *Sledge*: WILLIAM PARRY. *Claw*: B. G. GIBSON. *Billy Shears*: TED NEELEY. *Lucy*: ALAINA REED. *Flattop*: Walter Rivera. *Sun Queen, Lovely Rita, Polythene Pam*: David Patrick Kelly. *Strawberry Fields*: KAY COLE. *Sgt. Pepper*: David Patrick Kelly.

Hammeroids: Blake Anderson, Edward Q. Bhartonn, Arlana Blue, Ron Capozzoli, Michael Meadow, Stoney Reece, Jason Roberts.

ACT 1

"Sgt. Pepper's Lonely Hearts Club Band"
A. Nicholls, W. Parry, B. G. Gibson
"With a Little Help from My Friends"
T. Neeley, A. Nicholls, W. Parry, B. G. Gibson
"Nowhere Man"
A. Nicholls, W. Parry, B. G. Gibson
"With a Little Help from My Friends" (reprise)
T. Neeley, A. Nicholls, W. Parry, B. G. Gibson
"Lucy in the Sky With Diamonds"
A. Reed, T. Neeley, A. Nicholls, W. Parry, B. G. Gibson
"I Want You"
T. Neeley, A. Reed, A. Nicholls, W. Parry, B. G. Gibson
"Come Together"
A. Reed, W. Rivera, Friends
"Nowhere Man" II
A. Nicholls, W. Parry, B. G. Gibson
"Sun Queen'
All
"Lovely Rita"
D. P. Kelly, T. Neeley, A. Nicholls, W. Parry, B. G. Gibson, A. Reed
"Polythene Pam"
D. P. Kelly, T. Neeley, A. Nicholls, W. Parry, B. G. Gibson, A. Reed
"She Came in Through the Bathroom Window"
A. Nicholls, W. Parry, B. G. Gibson
"You Never Give Me Your Money'
T. Neeley, D. P. Kelly, A. Nicholls, W. Parry, B. G. Gibson, A. Reed
"Lovely Rita" (reprise)
T. Neeley, D. P. Kelly, A. Nicholls, W. Parry, B. G. Gibson, A. Reed
"Her Majesty"
T. Neeley
"A Day in the Life"
T. Neeley
"She's Leaving Home"
A. Nicholls, W. Parry, B. G. Gibson
"Strawberry Fields Forever"
K. Cole, T. Neeley
"Getting Better"
T. Neeley, K. Cole, A. Nicholls, W. Parry, B. G. Gibson

ACT 2

"Because"
T. Neeley, K. Cole
"When I'm 64"
T. Neeley, K. Cole
"Because" (reprise)
T. Neeley, K. Cole
"Good Morning, Good Morning"
A. Nicholls, W. Parry, B. G. Gibson
"Being for the Benefit of Mr. Kite"
A. Nicholls, W. Parry, B. G. Gibson, A. Reed
"Oh Darling"
K. Cole
"Fixing a Hole"T. Neeley
"Oh Darling" (reprise)
K. Cole
"Being for the Benefit of Mr. Kite" II
A. Nicholls, W. Parry, B. G. Gibson
"Mean Mr. Mustard"
A. Reed
"Maxwell's Silver Hammer"
A. Nicholls, W. Parry, B. G. Gibson
"Being for the Benefit of Mr. Kite" III
A. Nicholls, W. Parry, B. G. Gibson
"Carry That Weight"
A. Nicholls, W. Parry, B. G. Gibson
"Golden Slumbers"
T. Neeley
"Carry That Weight" (reprise)
A. Nicholls, W. Parry, B. G. Gibson
"The Long and Winding Road"
T. Neeley
"Get Back"
D. P. Kelly, T. Neeley, A. Reed, A. Nicholls, W. Parry, B. G. Gibson
"Sgt. Pepper" (reprise)
All
"The End"
All

1974.25 WHERE'S CHARLEY?

A Revival of the Musical (Comedy) in Two Acts, 5 Scenes[6]. Book by George Abbott. Based on the play "Charley's Aunt" by Brandon Thomas. Music and lyrics by Frank Loesser. Directed by Theodore Mann. Scenery by Marjorie Kellogg. Costumes by Arthur Boccia. Lighting by Thomas Skelton. Choreography by Margo Sappington. Musical direction and new arrangements by Tom Pierson. Dialect coach, Marjorie Phillips. Produced by Circle in the Square, Inc. (Theodore Mann, Artistic director; Paul Libin, Managing director). Opened 19 December 1974 at the Circle-in-the Square Theatre and closed 23 February 1975 after 78 performances.

CAST (in order of appearance): *Brassett*: LOUIS BEACHNER. *Jack Chesney*: JERRY LANNING. *Charley Wykeham*: RAUL JULIA. *Kitty Verdun*: CAROL JO LUGENBEAL. *Amy Spettigue*: MARCIA McCLAIN. *Sir Francis Chesney*: PETER WALKER. *Mr. Spettingue*: TOM ALDREDGE. *Donna Lucia D'Alvadorez*: TAINA ELG. *Reggie*: Dennis Cooley.

Students and Young Ladies: Pamela Burrell, Jacqueline Clark, Dennis Cooley, Karen Jablons, Jack Neubeck, Craig Sandquist, Leland Schwantes, Miriam Welch.

The action takes place during the summer at Oxford University, 1892.

Act 1, Scene 1: A Room at Oxford University. *Scene 2*: The Garden.

Act 2, Scene 1: The Garden. *Scene 2*: Where the Ladies Go. *Scene 3*: The Ballroom.

ACT 1

Scene 1

"Where's Charley?"
L. Beachner, Students, Young Ladies
"The Years Before Us"
Students
"Better Get Out of Here"
M. McClain, C. J. Lugenbeal, R. Julia, J. Lanning
"The New Ashmolean Marching Society and Students' Conservatory Band"
P. Walker, T. Aldredge, L. Beachner, Students, Young Ladies

Scene 2

"My Darling, My Darling"
C. J. Lugenbeal, J. Lanning
"Make a Miracle"
R. Julia, M. McClain
"Serenade With Asides"
T. Aldredge
"Lovelier Than Ever"
T. Elg, P. Walker, Students, Young Ladies
"The Woman in His Room"
M. McClain

[6]Originally produced in New York 11 October 1948 at the St. James Theatre for 792 performances.

"Pernambuco"
R. Julia, the Company

ACT 2

Scene 1

"Where's Charley?" (reprise)
M. McClain

"Once in Love With Amy"
R. Julia

Scene 2

"The Gossips"
Young Ladies

Scene 3

"At the Red Rose Cotillion"
Ensemble

Finale
Ensemble

1974.26 GOOD NEWS

A Revival of the Musical Comedy in Two Acts[7]. Original book by Laurence Schwab, Buddy G. DeSylva and Frank Mandel. Music and lyrics by (Buddy) G. DeSylva, (Lew) Brown and (Ray) Henderson. (Book) Adapted by Garry Marshall. Directed by Michael Kidd. Associate choreographer, Gary Menteer. Settings by Donald Oenslager. Costumes by Donald Brooks. Lighting by Tharon Musser. Orchestrations by Philip J. Lang. Musical direction by Liza Redfield. Sound by Tony Alloy. Musical supervision and vocal arrangements by Hugh Martin and Timothy Gray. Dance music and incidental music composed and arranged by Luther Henderson. Associate producers, Robert Anglund, Stan Hurwitz, Frank Montalvo. Production coordinator, Linda Mann Reed. Produced by Harry Rigby and Terry Allen Kramer. Opened 23 December 1974 at the St. James Theater and closed 4 January 1975 after 16 performances.

CAST (in order of appearance): *Bill Johnson*: GENE NELSON. *Tom Marlowe*: SCOTT STEVENSEN. *Beef Saunders*: Joseph Burke. *Bobby Randall*: WAYNE BRYAN. *Pooch Kearney*: STUBBY KAYE. *Flo*: Rebecca Urich. *Millie*: Paula Cinko. *Pat*: JANA ROBBINS. *Babe O'Day*: BARBARA LAIL. *Windy*: Terry Eno. *Slats*: James [Jimmy] Brennan. *Sylvester*: TOMMY BRESLIN. *Professor Kenyon*: ALICE FAYE. *Connie Lane*: MARTI ROLPH. *Muffin*: Margaret. *Colton Player*: Ernie Pysher. *Happy Days Quartet*: Tim Cassidy, Randall Robbins, Scott Stevensen, David Thome. *Acrobats*: Lisa Guignard, Mary Ann Lipson, Ernie Pysher, Jeff Spielman. *Baton Twirlers*: Tim Cassidy, Lynda Goodfriend, Lisa Guignard. *Tap Dancers*: Terry Eno, Jimmy Brennan.

Coeds: Paula Cinko, Robin Gerson, Lynda Goodfriend, Lisa Guignard, Anne Kaye, Mary Ann Lipson, Sally O'Donnell, Rebecca Urich, Marcia Lynn Watkins. *Boys*: Michael Austin, James Brennan, Tim Cassidy, Ernie Pysher, Randall Robbins, Jeff Spielman, David Thome.

The action takes place in the mid-1930s on and around the campus of Tait College.

ACT 1

Overture
Company

"He's a Ladies' Man" (from *FOLLOW THRU*)
J. Robbins, P. Cinko, R. Urich, Students

"The Best Things in Life Are Free"
A. Faye, Students

"Just Imagine"
M. Rolph, J. Robbins, P. Cinko, R. Urich

"Happy Days"
S. Stevensen, J. Robbins, P. Cinko, R. Urich, T. Breslin, Boys

"Button Up Your Overcoat" (from *FOLLOW THRU*)
W. Bryan, B. Lail

"Lucky in Love"
M. Rolph, S. Stevensen, Students

"You're the Cream in My Coffee" (from *HOLD EVERYTHING*)
A. Faye, G. Nelson

"Varsity Drag"
B. Lail, Students

"Together"[8]
A. Faye

"Tait Song"
G. Nelson, S. Kaye, Students

"Lucky in Love" (reprise)
Company

ACT 2

"Today's the Day"
Girls

"Girl of the Pi Beta Phi"
J. Robbins, Girls

"Good News"
A. Faye, M. Rolph, Students

"Keep Your Sunny Side Up" (from *SUNNY SIDE UP* film)
S. Kaye, Boys

"The Best Things in Life Are Free" (reprise)
M. Rolph, S. Stevensen

"Life Is Just a Bowl of Cherries" (from *GEORGE WHITE'S SCANDALS OF 1931*)
A. Faye, M. Rolph, B. Lail

"The Professor and the Students"
A. Faye, S. Kaye, Students

Finale
Company

1975.01 THE WIZ

A Musical in Two Acts, 16 Scenes and a Prologue. Book by William F. Brown. Based on the novel "The Wizard of Oz" by L. Frank Baum. Music and lyrics by Charlie Smalls. Direction and costume design by Geoffrey Holder. Choreography and musical numbers staged by George Faison. Settings designed by Tom H. John. Lighting design by Tharon Musser. Orchestrations by Harold Wheeler. Musical direction and vocal arrangements by Charles H. Coleman. Dance arrangements by Timothy Graphenreed. Produced by Ken Harper. Opened 5 January 1975 at the Majestic Theatre, moved 25 May 1977 to the Broadway Theatre, and closed 28 January 1979 after 1672 performances.

CAST (in order of appearance): *Aunt Em*: Tasha Thomas. *Toto*: Nancy. *Dorothy*: STEPHANIE MILLS. *Uncle Henry*: Ralph Wilcox. *Tornado*: Evelyn Thomas. *Munchkins*: Phylicia Ayers-Allen, Pi Douglass, Joni Palmer, Andy Torres, Carl Weaver. *Addaperle*: CLARICE TAYLOR. *Yellow Brick Road*: Ronald Dunham, Eugene Little, John Parks, Kenneth Scott. *Scarecrow*: HINTON BATTLE. *Crows*: Wendy Edmead, Frances Morgan, Ralph Wilcox. *Tinman*: TIGER HAYNES. *Lion*: TED ROSS. *Kalidahs*: Phillip Bond, Pi Douglass, Rodney Green, Evelyn Thomas, Andy Torres. *Poppies*: Lettie Battle, Leslie Butler, Eleanor McCoy, Frances Morgan, Joni Palmer. *Field Mice*: Phylicia Ayers-Allen, Pi Douglass, Carl Weaver, Ralph Wilcox. *Gatekeeper*: Danny Beard. *Emerald City Citizens*: Lettie Battle, Leslie Butler, Wendy Edmead, Eleanor McCoy, Frances Morgan, Joni Palmer, Evelyn Thomas, Phillip Bond, Ronald Dunham, Rodney Green, Eugene Little, John Parks, Kenneth Scott, Andy Torres. *The Wiz*: ANDRE De SHIELDS. *Evillene*: MABEL KING. *Lord High Underling*: Ralph Wilcox. *Soldier Messenger*: Carl Weaver. *Winged Monkey*: Andy Torres. *Glinda*: DEE DEE BRIDGEWATER.

Pit Singers: Frank Floyd, Sam Harkness, Jozella Reed, Tasha Thomas.

Prologue: Kansas.

Act 1, Scene 1: Munchkin Land. *Scene 2*: Oz Countryside. *Scene 3*: Woods. *Scene 4*: Jungle. *Scene 5*: Kalidah Country. *Scene 6*: Poppy Field. *Scene 7*: Emerald City. *Scene 8*: Throne Room.

Act 2, Scene 1: West Witch Castle. *Scene 2*: Forest. *Scene 3*: Courtyard. *Scene 4*: Emerald City Gate. *Scene 5*: Throne Room. *Scene 6*: Fairgrounds. *Scene 7*: Outskirts. *Scene 8*: Quadling Country.

ACT 1

Prologue

"The Feeling We Once Had"
T. Thomas

"Tornado Ballet"
Company

[7]Originally produced in New York 6 September 1927 at the 46th Street Theatre for 551 performances.

[8]A DeSylva, Brown and Henderson interpolation written as a popular song, neither for the stage or film.

Scene 1
"He's the Wizard"
. Taylor, Munchkins
Scene 2
"Soon as I Get Home"
S. Mills
"I Was Born on the Day Before Yesterday"
H. Battle, Crows
"Ease on Down the Road"
S. Mills, H. Battle, R. Dunham, E. Little, J. Parks, K. Scott
Scene 3
"Slide Some Oil to Me"
T. Haynes, S. Mills, H. Battle
Scene 4
"Mean Ole Lion"
T. Ross
Scene 5
"Kalidah Battle"
S. Mills, H. Battle, T. Haynes, T. Ross, Kalidahs, R. Dunham, E. Little, J. Parks, K. Scott
Scene 6
"Be a Lion"
S. Mills, T. Ross
"Lion's Dream"
T. Ross, Poppies
Scene 7
"Emerald City Ballet" (Psst)
S. Mills, H. Battle, T. Haynes, T. Ross, Company
(*Music by* Timothy Graphenreed and George Faison.)
Scene 8
"So You Wanted to Meet the Wizard"
A. De Shields
"To Be Able to Feel" (What Would I Do If I Could Feel)
T. Haynes

ACT 2
Scene 1
"No Bad News"
M. King
Scene 2
"Funky Monkeys"
Monkeys
Scene 3
"Everybody Rejoice"
S. Mills, H. Battle, T. Haynes, T. Ross, Winkies
(*Music and Lyrics by* Luther Vandross.)
Scene 5
"Who Do You Think You Are?"
S. Mills, H. Battle, T. Haynes, T. Ross
"Believe in Youself"
A. De Shields
Scene 6
"Y'All Got It!"
A. De Shields
Scene 8
"A Rested Body Is a Rested Mind"
D. D. Bridgewater
"Believe in Yourself" (reprise)
D. D. Bridgewater
"Home"
S. Mills

1975.02 BLACK PICTURE SHOW

A Play (with songs) in One Act by Bill Gunn. Music and lyrics by Sam Waymon. Scenery by Peter Harvey. Costumes by Judy Dearing. Lighting by Roger Morgan. Directed by Bill Gunn. Music conducted by Sam Waymon. Associate producer, Bernard Gersten. Produced by the New York Shakespeare Festival at Lincoln Center (Joseph Papp, Producer). Opened 6 January 1975 at the Vivian Beaumont Theater and closed 9 February 1975 after 40 performances.

CAST: *Vocalist*: Sam Waymon. *J.D.*, Alexander's son: Albert Hall. *Alexander*, a Black artist: DICK ANTHONY WILLIAMS. *Norman*, Alexander's companion: Graham Brown. *Hospital Attendants*: William Leet, Marvin Beck. *Rita*, Alexander's second wife: Carol Cole. *Philippe*, a movie producer: Paul-David Richards. *Jan*, Philippe's wife: Linda Miller.

The action takes place at the present time in a hospital psychiatric unit in the Bronx, New York.

MUSICAL NUMBERS
"I'm So Glad"
"Mose Art" (Second Movement)
"Bird of Paradise"
Variation on "Chopin in E Minor"
"Memory"
"Black Picture Show"
(*Lyrics by* Bill Gunn.)
"Mose Art"
(First Movement)
"Bitch in Heat"
"Digits"
"Science Fiction"
"I Feel So Good"
(*Lyrics by* Bill Gunn.)
"Vintage '51"
"Afghanistan"
"Terminate"

1975.03 SHENANDOAH

A Musical in Two Acts, 18 Scenes and a Prologue. Book by James Lee Barrett and Peter Udell. Based on the film of the same name by James Lee Barrett. Music by Gary Geld. Lyrics by Peter Udell. Directed by Philip Rose. Choreography by Robert Tucker. Scenery by C. Murawski. Lighting by Thomas Skelton. Costumes by Pearl Somner and Winn Morton. Orchestrations by Don Walker. Musical direction by Lynn Crigler. Dance arrangements by Russell Warner. Originally presented by the Goodspeed Opera House (Michael Price, Executive producer). Produced by Philip Rose, Gloria and Louis K. Sher. Opened 7 January 1975 at the Alvin Theatre, moved 29 March 1977 to the Mark Hellinger Theatre, and closed 7 August 1977 after 1050 performances.

CAST (in order of appearance): *Charlie Anderson*: JOHN CULLUM. *Jacob*: TED AGRESS. *James*: JOEL HIGGINS. *Nathan*: Jordan Suffin. *John*: David Russell. *Jenny*: PENELOPE MILFORD. *Henry*: Robert Rosen. *Robert*, the boy: Joseph Shapiro. *Anne*: DONNA THEODORE. *Gabriel*: Chip Ford. *Reverend Byrd*: Charles Welch. *Sam*: GORDON HALLIDAY. *Sergeant Johnson*: Edward Penn. *Lieutenant*: Marshall Thomas. *Tinkham*: Charles Welch. *Carol*: Casper Roos. *Corporal*: Gary Harger. *Marauder*: Gene Masoner. *Engineer*: Ed Preble. *Confederate Sniper*: Craig Lucas.

Ensemble: Ted Carrere, Stephen Dubov, Gary Harger, Brian James, Robert Johanson, Sherry Lambert, Craig Lucas, Gene Masoner, Paul Myrvold, Dan Ormond, Casper Roos, J. Kevin Scannell, Jack Starkey, E. Allan Stevens, Marshall Thomas, Matt Gavin.

The action takes place during the Civil War in the Shenandoah Valley of Virginia.

Prologue: (Outside the Anderson House.)

Act 1, Scene 1: Inside the Anderson House on Sunday morning. *Scene 2*: A Country road. *Scene 3*: Inside the Church. *Scene 4*: A Country road. Moments later. *Scene 5*: The Anderson Farmyard. *Scene 6*: The Anderson Porch. *Scene 7*: Martha's Grave. *Scene 8*: Inside the Anderson Parlor. Evening. *Scene 9*: Anne's Bedroom. Minutes before the wedding. *Scene 10*: Sam and Jenny's Wedding in the farmyard. *Scene 11*: Inside the Anderson Parlor. Moments later. *Scene 12*: Anne's Bedroom.

Act 2, Scene 1: The Anderson Farmyard. Weeks later. *Scene 2*: A wooded area near a railroad track. Night. *Scene 3*: A clearing in the woods. Later that evening. *Scene 4*: Anne's Bedroom. *Scene 5*: Martha's Grave. *Scene 6*: Inside the Church.

ACT 1
Prologue
"Raise the Flag of Dixie"
Confederate and Union Soldiers

Scene 1
"I've Heard It All Before"
J. Cullum
Scene 3
"Pass the Cross to Me"
The Congregation
Scene 4
"Why Am I Me"
J. Shapiro, C. Ford
Scene 5
"Next to Lovin' (I Like Fightin')"
T. Agress, J. Higgins, J. Suffin, D. Russell, R. Rosen
Scene 6
"Over the Hill"
P. Milford
"The Pickers Are Comin'"
J. Cullum
"Next to Lovin'" (reprise)
T. Agress, J. Higgins, J. Suffin, D. Russell, R. Rosen, P. Milford
Scene 7
"Meditation"
J. Cullum
Scene 9
"We Make a Beautiful Pair"
D. Theodore, P. Milford
Scene 10
"Violets and Silverbells"
P. Milford, G. Halliday, Anderson Family
Scene 11
"It's a Boy"
J. Cullum

ACT 2
Scene 1
"Freedom"
D. Theodore, C. Ford
"Violets and Silverbells" (reprise)
J. Higgins, D. Theodore
Scene 2
"Papa's Gonna Make It Alright"
J. Cullum
Scene 3
"The Only Home I Know"
G. Harger, Soldiers
Scene 4
"Papa's Gonna Make It Alright" (reprise)
P. Milford
Scene 5
"Meditation" (reprise)
J. Cullum
Scene 6
"Pass the Cross to Me" (reprise)
The Congregation

1975.04

MAN ON THE MOON

A Musical in One Act, 4 Scenes. Book, music and lyrics by John Phillips. Directed by Paul Morrissey. Sets by John J. Moore. Costumes by Marsia Trinder. Lighting by Jules Fisher. Musical director, Karen Gustafson. Musical arrangements by Michael Gibson and Jim Tyler. Sound by Gary Harris. Costume design supervised by Michael Yeargan. Produced by Andy Warhol in association with Richard Turley. Opened 29 January 1975 at the Little Theatre and closed 1 February 1975 after 5 performances.

CAST: *Dr. Bomb*: HARLAN FOSS. *Ernie Hardy*: ERIC LANG. *Leroy* (Little Red Box): MARK LAWHEAD. *President, King Can*: DENNIS DOHERTY. *Angel*: GENEVIEVE WAITE. *Venus*: MONIQUE VAN VOOREN.

Celestial Choir: *Mercury, Miss America*: Brenda Bergman. *Mars*: John Patrick Sundine. *Neptune*: Jennifer Elder. *Pluto*: E. Lynn Nickerson. *Saturn*: Jeanette Chastonay.

Scene 1: Earth. *Scene 2*: Canis Minor. *Scene 3*: The Moon. *Scene 4*: Earth.

MUSICAL NUMBERS
Scene 1
Prologue
H. Foss
"Boys from the South"
E. Lang
"Midnight Deadline Blastoff"
E. Lang
"Mission Control"
H. Foss, E. Lang, M. Lwhead, D. Doherty, B. Bergman
"Speed of Light"
E. Lang, M. Lawhead
Scene 2
"Though I'm a Little Angel"
G. Waite
"Girls"
D. Doherty, M. Van Vooren, G. Waite
"Canis Minor Bolero Waltz"
D. Doherty, M. Van Vooren, G. Waite
"Starburst"
G. Waite
"Penthouse of Your Mind"
D. Doherty
"Champagne and Kisses"
M. Van Vooren
"Star Stepping Stranger/Convent"
E. Lang, G. Waite
"My Name Is Can"
D. Doherty
"American Man on the Moon"
M. Van Vooren
Scene 3
"Welcome to the Moon"
Company
"Sunny, Sunny Moon"
M. Van Vooren, H. Foss
"Love Is Coming Back"
E. Lang, G. Waite
"Truth Cannot Be Treason"
M. Lawhead
"Place in Space"
E. Lang, G. Waite
Scene 4
"Family of Man"
H. Foss
"Yesterday I Left the Earth"
Company
"Stepping to the Stars"
Company

1975.05

THE NIGHT THAT MADE AMERICA FAMOUS

A Musical Revue in Two Acts, a Prologue and Epilogue. Music and lyrics by Harry Chapin. Directed by Gene Frankel. Choreography by Doug Rogers. Scenery designed by Kert Lundell. Costumes designed by Randy Barcelo. Lighting designed by Imero Fiorentino. Lighting supervised by Fred Allison. Multi-media development consultants, Imero Fiorentino Associates. Multi-media executed by Jim Sant'Andrea. Multi-media under the direction of Joshua White. Musical direction by Stephen Chapin. Dance arrangements by John Morris. Audio design by Michael Solomon. Assistant choreographer, Mercedes Ellington. Musical coordinator, Joseph Stecko. Associate producer, Nan Pearlman. Produced by Edgar Lansbury and Joseph Beruh in association with the Shubert Organization. Opened 26 February 1975 at the Ethel Barrymore Theatre and closed 6 April 1975 after 47 performances.

CAST: HARRY CHAPIN, KELLY GARRETT, DELORES HALL, GILBERT PRICE, BILL STARR, Alexandra Borrie, Mercedes Ellington, Sid Marshall, Ernie Pysher, Lynne Thigpen, Tom Chapin, Stephen Chapin.

The action takes place during the last fifteen years.

Act 1: 1960s.

Act 2: 1970s.

ACT 1

Prologue
Company

"Six String Orchestra"
H. Chapin, Company

"Give Me a Road"
Entire Company

"Sunday Morning Sunshine"
H. Chapin, Company

"It's My Day"
K. Garrett

"Give Me a Cause"
Company

"Welfare Rag"
D. Hall, B. Starr, G. Price, Company

"Better Place to Be"
H. Chapin, Company

"Give Me a Wall"
Company

"Peace Teachers"
K. Garrett

"Pigeon Run"
G. Price

"Changing of the Guard"
G. Price

"When I Look Up"
D. Hall

"Sniper"
H. Chapin, Company

ACT 2

"Great Divide"
H. Chapin

"Taxi"
H. Chapin, K. Garrett

"Cockeyed John"
Entire Company

"Mr. Tanner"
H. Chapin, G. Price

"Maxie"
K. Garrett

"Fugue:

"Love Can't"
B. Starr

"When Maudey Wants a Man"
D. Hall

"I'm a Wonderfully Wicked Woman"
K. Garrett

"Battleground Bummer"
G. Price

"Stoopid"
B. Starr

"Cat's in the Cradle"
H. Chapin, Company

"Cockeyed John, Give Me My Dream"
Company

"Too Much World"
K. Garrett, D. Hall, B. Starr, G. Price, H. Chapin, Company

"As I Grow Older"
K. Garrett

"Beginning of the End"
Company

Epilogue: "The Night That Made America Famous"
H. Chapin, Company

1975.06 GOODTIME CHARLEY

A Musical in Two Acts, 17 Scenes. Book by Sidney Michaels. Music by Larry Grossman. Lyrics by Hal Hackady. Entire production directed by Peter H. Hunt. Dances and musical numbers Staged by Onna White. Scenery by Rouben Ter-Arutunian. Costumes by Willa Kim. Lighting by (Abe) Feder. Orchestrations by Jonathan Tunick. Incidental music by Arthur B. Rubinstein. Dance music by Daniel Troob. Produced by Max Brown and Byron Goldman in association with Robert Victor and Stone Widney. Opened 3 March 1975 at the Palace Theatre and closed 31 May 1975 after 104 performances.

CAST (in order of appearance): *Henry V*: Brad Tyrrell. *Charles VI*: Hal Norman. *Isabella of Bavaria*: Grace Keagy. *Queen Kate*: Rhoda Butler. *Philip of Burgundy*: Charles Rule. *Yolande*: Peggy Cooper. *Marie*: Nancy Killmer. *Pope*: Ed Becker. *Charley*: JOEL GREY. *Archbishop Regnault de Chartres*: JAY GARNER. *General George de La Tremouille*: LOUIS ZORICH. *Servants*: George Ramos, Ross Miles, Pat Swayze, Cam Lorendo. *Agnes Sorel*: SUSAN BROWNING. *Jesters*: Andy Hostettler, Gordon J. Weiss. *Joan of Arc*: ANN REINKING. *Minguet*: RICHARD B. SHULL. *First English Captain*: Charles Rule. *Second English Captain*: Hal Norman. *Third English Captain*: Kenneth Bridges. *Herald*: Hal Norman. *Citizen Trio, Soldier Trio, Peasant Trio Hostile Trio*: Kenneth Bridges, Brad Tyrrell, Ed Becker. *Louis*: Dan Joel. *Chef*: Charles Rule. *First Soldier*: Kenneth Bridges. *Second Soldier*: Brad Tyrrell. *Third Soldier*: Hal Norman. *Guard*: Charles Rule. *Estelle*: Kathe Dezina.

Singers: Rhoda Butler, Peggy Cooper, Kathe Dezina, Nancy Killmer, Jane Ann Sargia, Ed Becker, Kenneth Bridges, Hal Norman, Charles Rule, Brad Tyrrell. *Dancers*: Andy Hostettler, Cam Lorendo, Dan Joel, Glen McClaskey, Ross Miles, Tod Miller, Sal Pernice, George Ramos, Pat Swayze, Gordon Weiss, Jerry Yoder.

The action takes place in France between 1429 and 1461.

Act 1, Scene 1: Prologue; Charley's Nightmare, 6 March, 1429. *Scene 2*: Charley's Bedroom at Chinon, that morning. *Scene 3*: Great Hall, immediately after. *Scene 4*: Charley's Study, that evening. *Scene 5*: Before a Tapestry, immediately after. *Scene 6*: Councul Chamber, three weeks later, April. *Scene 7*: A nearby grove at twilight. *Scene 8*: Castles of the Loire, subsequent weeks. *Scene 9*: Reims Cathedral, late May, 1429.

Act 2, Scene 1: A Formal Garden, late summer. *Scene 2*: Chinon Courtyard, the following spring. *Scene 3*: A Bank of the Vienne River, immediately after sunset. *Scene 4*: Confession Booth, a week later. *Scene 5*: Cell in Rouen, 30 May, 1431. *Scene 6*: Cell and War Tent, that same day, simultaneously. *Scene 7*: Great Hall, three weeks later. *Scene 8*: Epilogue; 32 years later, 28 February 1461.

ACT 1

Scene 1

"History"
B. Tyrrell, H. Norman, G. Keagy, R. Butler, C. Rule, P. Cooper, N. Killmer, E. Becker, Ensemble

Scene 2

"Goodtime Charley"
J. Grey, Ensemble

Scene 3

"Visions and Voices"
A. Reinking

Scene 4

"Bits and Pieces"
J. Grey, A. Reinking

"To Make the Boy a Man"
A. Reinking

Scene 5

"Why Can't We All Be Nice"
J. Grey, S. Browning

Scene 6

"Born Lover"
J. Grey

Scene 7

"I Am Going to Love (The Man You're Going to Be)"
A. Reinking

Scene 8

"Castles of the Loire"
A. Reinking, Soldiers
(*Music by* Arthur B. Rubinstein.)

Scene 9

"Coronation"
J. Grey, A. Reinking, Ensemble

ACT 2

Scene 1

"You Still Have a Long Way to Go"
A. Reinking, J. Grey

Scene 2

"Merci, Bon Dieu"
R. B. Shull, S. Browning

Scene 4

"Confessional"
L. Zorich, J. Garner

Scene 5

"One Little Year"
A. Reinking

Scene 8

"I Leave the World"
J. Grey

1975.07 THE LIEUTENANT

A Rock Opera in Two Acts. Book, music and lyrics by Gene Curty, Nitra Scharfman and Chuck Strand. Directed by William Martin. Choreography by Dennis Dennehy. Scenery and costumes designed by Frank J. Boros. Lighting designed by Ian Calderon. Musical direction by Chuck Strand. Music arranged by Chuck Strand and Gus Montero. Sound designed by Bill Merrill. Originally produced at the Queens Playhouse by Joseph S. Kutzreba. Produced by Joseph S. Kutzreba and Spofford J. Beadle. Opened 9 March 1975 at the Lyceum Theatre and closed 16 March 1975 after 9 performances.

CAST (in order of appearance): *Lieutenant*: EDDIE MEKKA. *Judge*: GENE CURTY. *Recruiting Sergeant*: Joel Powers. *First General*: CHET D'ELIA. *Second General*: EUGENE MOOSE. *Third General*: DANNY TAYLOR. *OCS Sergeant*: GENE CURTY. *Chaplain*: Don McGrath. *Captain*: WALT HUNTER. *Sergeant "C" Company*: Jim Litten. *"C" Company*: Steven Boockvor, Clark James, Jim-Patrick McMahon, Joseph Pugliese, Burt Rodriguez, Tom Tofel. *G.I.*: TOM TOFEL. *Senator*: Joel Powers. *First Congressman*: Don McGrath. *Clergyman*: Jim Litten. *Second Congressman*: Burt Rodriguez. *First Reporter*: Jim Litten. *Second Reporter*: Tom Tofel. *Third Reporter*: Jo Speros. *Prosecutor*: Burt Rodriguez. *Defense Attorney*: Gordon Grody. *New Recruit*: Alan K. Siegel. *Dance Captain*: Jim-Patrick McMahon.

The action alternates between Vietnam and the United States over a three-year period. Act Two takes place two years later.

ACT 1

"The Indictment"
E. Mekka, G. Curty

"Join the Army"
E. Mekka, J. Powers, Recruits

"Look for the Men With Potential"
C. D'Elia, E. Moose, D. Taylor

"Kill"
G. Curty

"I Don't Want to Go Over to Vietnam"
E. Mekka, "C" Company

"Eulogy"
D. McGrath

"At 0700 Tomorrow"
W. Hunter, "C" Company

"Massacre"
W. Hunter, E. Mekka, "C" Company, Vietnamese

"Something's Gone Wrong"
W. Hunter, E. Mekka

"Twenty-Eight"
C. D'Elia, E. Moose, D. Taylor, W. Hunter, E. Mekka

"Let's Believe in the Captain"
C. D'Elia, E. Moose, D. Taylor

"Final Report"
C. D'Elia

"I Will Make Things Happen"
T. Tofel

ACT 2

"He Wants to Put the Army in Jail"
J. Powers, D. McGrath, J. Litten, B. Rodriguez

"There's No Other Solution"
C. D'Elia, E. Moose, D. Taylor

"I'm Going Home"
E. Mekka, "C" Company

"We've Chosen You, Lieutenant"
C. D'Elia, E. Moose, D. Taylor

"The Star of This War"
J. Litten, T. Tofel, J. Speros, E. Mekka

"On Trial for My Life"
E. Mekka

"The Conscience of a Nation"
B. Rodriguez

"Damned No Matter How He Turned"
G. Grody

"On Trial for My Life" (reprise)
E. Mekka

"The Verdict"
G. Curty, Jurors

Finale
A. K. Siegel, J. Powers, The Company

1975.08 THE ROCKY HORROR SHOW

A Rock Musical in One Act, 11 Scenes, a Prologue and Epilogue. Book, music and lyrics by Richard O'Brien. Directed by Jim Sharman. Production (scenery) designed by Brian Thomson. Costumes by Sue Blane. Lighting by Chipmonck. Set supervisor, Peter Harvey. Costume supervisor, Pearl Somner. Sound design, Abe Jacob. Musical director, D'Vaughn Pershing. Assistant director, Nina Faso. (Music) Arrangements by Richard Hartley. Special effects by Robert E. McCarthy. Associate producer, John Beug. A Michael White Production. Produced by Lou Adler. Opened 10 March 1975 at the Belasco Theatre and closed 6 April 1975 after 45 performances.

CAST (in order of appearance): *The Belasco Popcorn Girl* (Trixie): Jamie Donnelly. *Janet*: ABIGALE HANESS. *Brad*: BILL MILLER. *Narrator*: Graham Jarvis. *Riff-Raff*: Ritz O'Brien. *Columbia*: BONI ENTEN. *Magenta*: Jamie Donnelly. *Frank*: TIM CURRY. *Rocky*: KIM MILFORD. *Eddie, Dr. Scott*: MEAT LOAF.

MUSICAL NUMBERS

"Science Fiction"
J. Donnelly

"Wedding Song"
B. Miller, A. Haness

"Over at the Frankenstein Place"
B. Miller, A. Haness

"Sweet Transvestite"
T. Curry

"Time Warp"
J. Donnelly, B. Enten, R. O'Brien, G. Jarvis

"The Sword of Damocles"
K. Milford

"Charles Atlas Song" (I Can Make You a Man)
T. Curry

"What Ever Happened to Saturday Night" (Hot Patootie, Bless My Soul)
M. Loaf

"Charles Atlas Song" (reprise)
T. Curry

"Eddie's Teddy"
M. Loaf, B. Enten, Company

"Once in Awhile"
B. Miller

"Planet Shmanet Janet"
T. Curry

"It Was Great When It All Began" (Floorshow/Rose Tint My World)
Company

"Super Heroes"
Company
"Science Fiction" (reprise)
J. Donnelly
"Sweet Transvestite" (reprise)
Company
"Time Warp" (reprise)
Company

1975.09 DOCTOR JAZZ

A Musical in Two Acts, 20 Scenes. Book, music and lyrics (mostly) by Buster Davis. Direction and choreography by Donald MacKayle. Scenery and costumes by Raoul Pene du Bois. Lighting by (Abe) Feder. Sound by Abe Jacob. Principal orchestrator, Luther Henderson. Associate orchestrators, Dick Hyman, Sy Oliver. Dance music arranger and Incidental music composer, Luther Henderson. Musical director and vocal arrangements by Buster Davis. Associate music director, Joyce Brown. Scenic coordiator, Mason Arvold. Costume coordinator, David Toser. Entire production supervised by John Berry. A Pyxidium Ltd. Production. Produced by Cyma Rubin. Opened 19 March 1975 at the Winter Garden and closed 22 March 1975 after 5 performances.

CAST (in order of appearance): *Steve Anderson*: BOBBY VAN. *Spasm Band*: Quitman D. Fludd III, Bruce Heath, HECTOR JAIME MERCADO, Jeff Veazey. *Jonathan Jackson, Jr.*: JACK LANDRON. *Henry*: Paul Eichel. *Harriet Lee*: PEGGY POPE. *Georgia Sheridan*: LILLIAN HAYMAN. *Edna Mae Sheridan*: LOLA FALANA. *Georgia's Girls*: Bonita Jackson, Michele Simmons, Annie Joe Edwards. *Harriet's Girls*: Gail Benedict, Sarah Coleman, Maggy Gorrill, Kitty Jones, Diana Mirras, Sally Neal, Yolanda R. Raven, Catherine Rice. *Lead Dancer*: HECTOR JAIME MERCADO. *The Group*: Bruce Heath, Bonita Jackson, Sally Neal, Yolanda R. Raven, Michele Simmons. *Rudy*: Paul Eichel. *Pete*: Eron Tabor. *Harry*: Paul Eichel.

Dancers: Gail Benedict, Quitman Fludd III, Maggy Gorrill, Bob Heath, Bruce Heath, David Hodo, Bonita Jackson, Michael Lichtefeld, Hector Jaime Mercado, Diana Mirras, Sally Neal, Yolanda R. Raven, Catherine Rice, Michele Simmons, Dan Strayhorn, Jeff Veazey. *Singers*: James Braet, Annie Joe Edwards, Paul Eichel, Marian Haraldson, Evelyn McCauley, Eron Tabor. *Showgirls*: Sarah Coleman, Kitty Jones. *Onstage Musicians*: George Davis, Jr., Dennis Drury, John Gill, Vince Giordano, Haywood Henry, Danny Moore, San Pilafian, Candy Ross, Bob Stewart, Allan Vache, Warren Vache, Jr., Earl Williams, Francis Williams.

Act 1, Scene 1: A Brothel Quarter in New Orleans, 1917. *Scene 2*: The Street. *Scene 3*: Georgia's Salon. *Scene 4*: Harriet's Boudoir. *Scene 5*: The Street. *Scene 6*: Georgia's Garden. *Scene 7*: The Palace of Pleasure. *Scene 8*: Shanghai Theatre. *Scene 9*: Harriet's Office. *Scene 10*: Shanghai Theatre Stage. *Scene 11*: Backstage. *Scene 12*: Harriet's Office.

Act 2, Scene 1: The Dressing Room—The Lenox Club. *Scene 2*: The Lenox Club. *Scene 3*: The Dressing Room. *Scene 4*: In front of a New York Theatre. *Scene 5*: Dressing Room—a New York Theatre. *Scene 6*: On Stage. *Scene 7*: Dressing Room. *Scene 8*: On Stage.

ACT 1
Scene 1
"Dr. Jazz"
B. Van, Musicians, Spasm Band
(*Music and Lyrics by* King Oliver and Howard Melrose.)
"We've Got Connections"
B. Van, L. Hayman, P. Pope
Scene 3
"Georgia Shows 'Em How"
L. Hayman, Her Girls
Scene 5
"Cleopatra Had a Jazz Band"
B. Van, Ballyhoo Band
(*Music by* J. L. Morgan. *Lyrics by* Jack Coogan.)
Juba Dance
L. Falana, Spasm Band
Scene 7
"Charleston Rag"
Jonathan's Band, Harriet's Girls
(*Music by* Eubie Blake.)
"I've Got Elgin Watch Movements in My Hips"
L. Falana
"Blues My Naughty Sweetie Gave to Me"
Ballyhoo Band
Scene 8
"Good-Time Flat Blues"
L. Hayman
(*Music and Lyrics by* Armand J. Piron.)
Scene 10
"Evolution Papa"
L. Falana, H. J. Mercado, Troupe
Scene 11
Rehearsal Tap
The Group
"Blues My Naughty Sweetie Gave to Me" (reprise)
B. Van
(*Music and Lyrics by* Charles McCarron, Carey Morgan and Arthur Swanstrom.)
"I Love It"
L. Falana
(*Music by* Harry Von Tilzer. *Lyrics by* E. Ray Goetz.)
Scene 12
"Anywhere the Wind Blows"
B. Van

ACT 2
Scene 2
"Those—'Shiek-of-Araby'—Blues"
Singers, Dancers
"Look Out for Lil"
L. Falana, Dancers
Scene 4
"Swanee Strut"
B. Van
Scene 6
"All I Want Is My Black Baby Back"
L. Falana
Scene 7
"Everybody Leaves You"
B. Van
Scene 8
"Free and Easy"
L. Falana, Company
"I Love It" (reprise)
B. Van, L. Falana

1975.10 A LETTER FOR QUEEN VICTORIA

An Opera in Four Acts. Written and directed by Robert Wilson. Music by Alan Lloyd in collaboration with Michael Galasso. Choreography by Andrew DeGroat. Scenery and costume supervision by Peter Harvey. Lighting supervision by Beverly Emmons, assisted by Carol Mullins. Musical direction by Michael Galasso. Sound supervisor, R. O. Willis. Verbal tape constructors by Christopher Knowles. Introductory letter by Stefan Brecht. The Sundance Kid speech by Christopher Knowles. Act 3 dialogue by Cynthia Lubar. First speech of Chinaman by James Neu. Slides by Francis Brooks. Produced by The Byrd Foundation, Inc. Opened 22 March 1975 at the ANTA Theatre and closed 5 April 1975 after 18 performances.

CAST: *Singers*: SHERYL SUTTON, CYNTHIA LUBAR, George Ashley, Stefan Brecht, Kathryn Cation, Alma Hamilton, Christopher Knowles, James Neu, Robert Wilson. *Dancers*: Andrew deGroat, Julia Busto. *Musicians*: Michael Galasso (First Violin), Susan Krongold (Second Violin), Kevin Byrnes (Violin), Laura Epstein (Cello), Kathryn Cation (Flute).

Introduction: *Queen Victoria*: A. Hamilton. *1*: K. Cation. 2: S. Brecht. 3: C. Knowles. 4: R. Wilson.

Act 1: *1*: S. Sutton. 2: C. Lubar. *1A*: G. Ashley. *2A*: S. Brecht. *Pilot*: S. Brecht. *Pilot*: J. Neu. *Billy*: K. Cation. *Warden*: S. Snyder. *Chris*: C. Knowles.

Act 2: *1*: G. Ashley. *2*: C. Lubar. *3*: K. Cation. *4*: S. Brecht. *C.W. Soldier*: S. Sutton. *Warden*: S. Snyder. *Chris*: C. Knowles.

Entractes by Robert Wilson and Christopher Knowles.

Act 3: *1A*: S. Brecht. *2A*: S. Snyder. *1B*: G. Ashley. *2B*: J. Busto. *1C*: C. Knowles. *2C*: S. Sutton. *1D*: J. Neu. *2D*: K. Cation. *1E*: A. deGroat. *2E*: C. Lubar.

Act 4: *1*: J. Neu. *2*: S. Snyder. *2A*: S. Brecht. *3, 1*: S. Sutton. *4, 2*: C. Lubar. *Billy*: K. Cation. *Chris*: C. Knowles. *George*: G. Ashley. *Pilot*: J. Neu. *Pilot*: S. Brecht.

1975.11 THE CONSUL

A Revival of the Opera (Musical Drama) in Three Acts, 6 Scenes[9]. Libretto and Music by Gian-Carlo Menotti. Conductor, Christopher Keene. Settings by Horace Armistead. Staged by Francis Rizzo Produced by the New York City Opera. Opened 22 March 1975 at the New York State Theatre and closed 6 April 1975 after 2 performances in repertory.

CAST: (in order of appearance): *John Sorel*: JOHN DARRENKAMP *Magda Sorel*: OLIVIA STAPP. *The Mother*: MURIEL COSTA-GREENSPON. *Secret Police Agent*: EDWARD PIERSON. *First Plainclothesman*: Jack Sims. *Second Plainclothesman*: Tom Barrett. *The Secretary*: SANDRA WALKER. *Mr. Kofner*: DON YULE. *The Foreign Woman*: JUDITH DE ROSA. *Anna Gomez*: Barbara Hocher. *Nika Magadoff* (The Magician): JOHN LANKSTON. *Vera Boronel*: Sophia Steffan. *Assan*: William Ledbetter. *Voice on the Record*: Mabel Mercer.

1975.12 BETTE MIDLER'S CLAMS ON THE HALF SHELL

A Musical Revue in Two Acts, Special material by Bruce Vilanch, Bill Hennessy, Jerry Blatt. Additional lyrics by Jerry Blatt, Bette Midler. Directed and choreographed by Joe Layton. Settings and costumes designed by Tony Walton. Lighting design by Beverly Emmons. Sound by Stan Miller. Musical director, Don York. Associate choreographer, Andre De Shields. Orchestrations, Jimmie Haskell. Production coordinator, Fritz Holt. Produced by Aaron Russo in association with Ron Delsener. Opened 14 April 1975 at the Minskoff Theatre and closed 22 June 1975 after 80 performances.

CAST: BETTE MIDLER, LIONEL HAMPTON. *The HARLETTES*: Charlotte Crossley, Robin Grean, Sharon Redd.
THE MICHAEL POWELL ENSEMBLE: Michael Powell, Charlene Ricks, Doretha Doctor, Jeannie Paige, Clifford Jamerson, Peggy Williams, Ricardo Portlette, Joey Coleman, Vinson Cunningham, Shirley Underwood, Lee Roy Cooks, Norman P. Hawkins.

MUSICAL NUMBERS[10]

OKLAHOMA! Overture
(*Music by* Richard Rodgers.)
"Nobody Knows the Trouble I've Seen"
"(The) Moon of Manakoora" (from *THE HURRICANE* film)
(*Music by* Alfred Newman. *Lyrics by* Frank Loesser.)
"Ol' Man River" (from *SHOWBOAT*)
(*Music by* Jerome Kern. *Lyrics by* Oscar Hammerstein II.)
Medley of Bette's Hits
"The Bitch Is Back"
(*Music and Lyrics by* Elton John and Bernie Taupin.)
"Delta Dawn"
(*Music and Lyrics by* Alex Harvey and Larry Collins.)
The Toilet Medley (1950s Rock 'n Roll Medley)
"Sentimental Journey"
(*Music and Lyrics by* Bud Green, Les Brown and Ben Homer.)
"Ain't No Love'
(*Music and Lyrics by* John Gary Williams.)
Saloon Sequence:
"Back in the Bars Again"
(*Music and Lyrics by* Susan Taylor.)
"Drinking Again"
(*Music and Lyrics by* Johnny Mercer and Doris Tauber.)
"Fiesta in Rio"
(*Music and Lyrics by* Bette Midler and Jerry Blatt.)
"Strangers in the Night"
(*Music and Lyrics by* Charles Singleton, Eddie Snyder and Bert Kaempfert.)
"Do You Wanna Dance?"
(*Music and Lyrics by* Bobby Freeman.)
"Colette"
"If Love Were All" (from *BITTER SWEET*)
(*Music and Lyrics by* Noel Coward.)
"Friends'
(*Music and Lyrics by* Mark Klingman and Buzzy Linhart.)
"I'm Wishing" (from *SNOW WHITE AND THE SEVEN DWARFS* film)
(*Music by* Larry Churchill. *Lyrics by* Larry Morey.)
"A Dream Is a Wish Your Heart Makes"
(*Music and Lyrics by* Mack David, Al Hoffman and Jerry Livingston.)
"Lullaby of Broadway" (from *GOLDDIGGERS OF 1935* film)
(*Music by* Harry Warren. *Lyrics by* Al Dubin.)
"In the Mood"
(*Music by* Joe Garland. *Lyrics by* Andy Razaf. *Additional Lyrics by* Bette Midler and Barry Manilow.)
"Flying Home"
(*Music by* Lionel Hampton, Benny Goodman and Sid Ramin.)
Lionel Hampton Specialty
"We'll Be Together Again"
(*Music and Lyrics by* Carl Fischer and Frankie Laine.)
"Shiver Me Timbers"
(*Music and Lyrics by* Tom Waits.)
"I Don't Want the Night to End"
(*Music and Lyrics by* Phoebe Snow.)
Those Wonderful Sophie Tucker Jokes
"Hello in There"
(*Music and Lyrics by* John Prine.)
""Higher and Higher"
(*Music and Lyrics by* Gary Lee Jackson, Carl W., Smith and Raynard Miner.)
"Boogie Woogie Bugle Boy"
(*Music and Lyrics by* Don Raye and Hughie Prince.)
"Chapel of Love"
(*Music and Lyrics by* Jeff Barry, Ellie Greenwich and Phil Spector.)

1975.13 RODGERS & HART

A Musical Revue in Two Acts. Music by Richard Rodgers. Lyrics by Lorenz Hart. Concept by Richard Lewine and John Fearnley. Directed by Burt Shevelove. Choreography by Donald Saddler. Music direction and vocal arrangements by Buster Davis. Principal orchestrator and dance music arranger, Luther Henderson. Additional orchestrations by Jim Tyler, Bill Brohn, Robert Russell Bennett. Setting by David Jenkins. Costumes by Stanley Simmons. Lighting by Ken Billington. Assistant Choreographer,

[9]Originally produced in New York 15 March 1950 at the Ethel Barrymore Theatre for 269 performances. For Synopsis of Scenes and Musical Numbers, see original 1950 production.

[10]Added during the run:
"How High the Moon" (from *TWO FOR THE SHOW*)
(*Music by* Morgan Lewis. *Lyrics by* Nancy Hamilton.)
"Deep Purple"
(*Music by* Peter DeRose. *Lyrics by* Mitchell Parish.)
"I've Never Been to Flushing"
"You'll Never Be Lonely"
(*Music and Lyrics by* Tom Pacheco.)
"Bad Sex"
(*Music and Lyrics by* Bill Hennessey and Bruce Vilanch.)

Arthur Faria. Produced by Lester Osterman Productions (Lester Osterman-Richard Horner) in association with Worldvision Enterprises Inc. Opened 13 May 1975 at the Helen Hayes Theatre and closed 16 August 1975 after 108 performances.

CAST (in alphabetical order): Barbara Andres, James [Jimmy] Brennan, Wayne Bryan, David-James Carroll, Jamie Donnelly, Tovah Feldshuh, Mary Sue Finnerty, Laurence Guittard, Stephen Lehew, Jim Litten, Virginia Sandifur, Rebecca York.

During the performance the following songs, in part or in toto, will be performed:

"At the Roxy Music Hall"
(from I MARRIED AN ANGEL)
"Babes in Arms"
(from BABES IN ARMS)
"Bewitched, Bothered and Bewildered"
(from PAL JOEY)
"Blue Moon"
"Blue Room"
(from THE GIRL FRIEND)
"Bye and Bye"
(from DEAREST ENEMY)
"Careless Rhapsody"
(from BY JUPITER)
"Cause We Got Cake"
(from TOO MANY GIRLS)
"Come With Me"
(from THE BOYS FROM SYRACUSE)
"Dear Old Syracuse"
(from THE BOYS FROM SYRACUSE)
"Did You Ever Get Stung?"
(from I MARRIED AN ANGEL)
"Do I Hear You Saying (I Love You)?"
(from PRESENT ARMS)
"Down By the River"
(from MISSISSIPPI film)
"Easy to Remember"
(from MISSISSIPPI film)
"Ev'rybody Loves You (When You're Asleep)"
(from I'D RATHER BE RIGHT)
"Everything I've Got"
(from BY JUPITER)
"Falling in Love With Love"
(from THE BOYS FROM SYRACUSE)
"Flower Garden of My Heart, The"
(from PAL JOEY)
"From Another World"
(from HIGHER AND HIGHER)
"Gateway of the Temple of Minerva, (In) The"
(from BY JUPITER)
"Girl Friend, The"
(from THE GIRL FRIEND)
"Give It Back to the Indians"
(from TOO MANY GIRLS)
"Glad to be Unhappy"
(from ON YOUR TOES)
"Great Big Town" (Chicago)
(from PAL JOEY)
"Happy Hunting Horn"
(from PAL JOEY)
"Have You Met Miss Jones?"
(from I'D RATHER BE RIGHT)
"He and She"
(from THE BOYS FROM SYRACUSE)
"He Was Too Good To Me"
(from THE BOYS FROM SYRACUSE)
"Heart Is Quicker Than the Eye, The"
(from ON YOUR TOES)
"Here in My Arms"
(from DEAREST ENEMY)
"How About It?"
(from AMERICA'S SWEETHEART)
"How Was I To Know?"
(from SHE'S MY BABY)
"I Could Write a Book"
(from PAL JOEY)
"I Didn't Know What Time It Was"
(from TOO MANY GIRLS)
"I Married an Angel"
(from I MARRIED AN ANGEL)
"I Wish I Were in Love Again"
(from BABES IN ARMS)
"I'll Tell the Man in the Street"
(from I MARRIED AN ANGEL)
"Imagine"
(from BABES IN ARMS)
"Isn't It Romantic?"
(from LOVE ME TONIGHT film)
"It Never Entered My Mind"
(from HIGHER AND HIGHER)
"It's Got To Be Love"
(from ON YOUR TOES)
"I've Got Five Dollars"
(from AMERICA'S SWEETHEART)
"Johnny One Note"
(from BABES IN ARMS)
"Jupiter Forbid"
(from BY JUPITER)
"Lady Is a Tramp, The"
(from BABES IN ARMS)
"Love Me Tonight"
(from LOVE ME TONIGHT film)
"Love Never Went to College"
(from TOO MANY GIRLS)
"Lovely Day for a Murder, A"
(from HIGHER AND HIGHER)
"Lover"
(from LOVE ME TONIGHT film)
"Manhattan"
(from GARRICK GAIEITIES, THE 1925)
"Me for You!"
(from HEADS UP!)
"Mimi"
(from LOVE ME TONIGHT film)
"Mountain Greenery"
(from GARRICK GAIETIES, THE 1926)
"My Funny Valentine"
(from BABES IN ARMS)
"My Heart Stood Still"
(from A CONNECTICUT YANKEE)
"My Prince"
(from TOO MANY GIRLS)
"No Place But Home"
(from EVERGREEN)
"Nobody's Heart"
(from BY JUPITER)
"Nothing But You"
(from HIGHER AND HIGHER)
"Oh, Diogenes"
(from THE BOYS FROM SYRACUSE)
"On a Desert Isle With Thee"
(from A CONNECTICUT YANKEE)
"On Your Toes"
(from ON YOUR TOES)
"Quiet Night"
(from ON YOUR TOES)
"Sentimental Me"
(from GARRICK GAIETIES, THE 1925)

"She Could Shake the Maracas"
(ftrom TOO MANY GIRLS)
"Ship Without a Sail, A"
(from HEADS UP!)
"Shortest Day of the Year, The
(from THE BOYS FROM SYRACUSE)
"Sing for Your Supper"
(from THE BOYS FROM SYRACUSE)
"Slaughter on Tenth Avenue"
(from ON YOUR TOES)
"Soon"
(from MISSISSIPPI film)
"Spring Is Here"
(from I MARRIED AN ANGEL)
"Take Him"
(from PAL JOEY)
"Ten Cents a Dance"
(from SIMPLE SIMON)
"There's a Small Hotel"
(from ON YOUR TOES)
"This Can't Be Love"
(from THE BOYS FROM SYRACUSE)
"This Funny World"
(from BETSY)
"This Is My Night to Howl"
(from A CONNECTICUT YANKEE)
"Thou Swell"
(from A CONNECTICUT YANKEE)
"Three B's, The (Bach, Beethoven and Brahams)
(from ON YOUR TOES)
"To Keep My Love Alive"
(from A CONNECTICUT YANKEE revival)
"Two-Day For Keith"
(from ON YOUR TOES)
"Wait Till You See Her"
(from BY JUPITER)
"Where or When"
(from BABES IN ARMS)
"Where's That Rainbow?"
(from PEGGY-ANN)
"Why Can't I?"
(from SPRING IS HERE)
"With a Song in My Heart"
(from SPRING IS HERE)
"You Always Love the Same Girl"
(from A CONNECTICUT YANKEE)
"You Are Too Beautiful"
(from HALLELUJAH, I'M A BUM film)
"You Musn't Kick It Around"
(from PAL JOEY)
"You're Nearer"
(from TOO MANY GIRLS film)
"Zip"
(from PAL JOEY)

1975–1976 SEASON

Donna McKechnie in A CHORUS LINE
Martha Swope/TimePix

1975–1976 SEASON

1975.14 CHICAGO

A Musical Vaudeville in Two Acts, 22 Scenes. Book by Fred Ebb and Bob Fosse. Based on the play of the same name by Maurine Dallas Watkins. Music by John Kander. Lyrics by Fred Ebb. Directed and choreographed by Bob Fosse. Settings by Tony Walton. Costumes by Patricia Zipprodt. Lighting by Jules Fisher. Musical director, Stanley Lebowsky. Orchestrations by Ralph Burns. Dance music arranged by Peter Howard. Sound design by Abe Jacob. Assistant choreographer, Tony Stevens. Produced by Robert Fryer and James Cresson in association with Martin Richards. Opened 3 June 1975 at the 46th Street Theatre and closed 27 August 1977 after 947 performances.

CAST (in order of appearance): *Velma Kelly*: CHITA RIVERA. *Roxie Hart*: GWEN VERDON. *Fred Casely*: Christopher Chadman. *Sergeant Fogarty*: Richard Korthaze. *Amos Hart*: BARNEY MARTIN. *Liz*: Cheryl Clark. *Annie*: Michon Peacock. *June*: Candy Brown. *Hunyak*: Graciela Daniele. *Mona*: Pamela Sousa. *Martin Harrison*: Michael Vita. *Matron*: MARY McCARTY. *Billy Flynn*: JERRY ORBACH. *Mary Sunshine*: M. O'HAUGHEY. *Go-to-Hell Kitty*: Charlene Ryan. *Harry*: Paul Solen. *Aaron*: Gene Foote. *The Judge*: Ron Schwinn. *Court Clerk*: Gary Gendell.

The Band: Sy Berger, Harry Divito, Hank Freedman, Karen Gustafson, John Monaco, Anthony Pagano, Waymon Reed, James Sedlar, Charles Spies, William Stanley, Art Wagner, Frank Wess, Tony Posk.

The action takes place in the late 1920's in Chicago, Illinois.

Act 1, Scene 1: Opening; the Hart Bedroom. *Scene 2*: The bedroom. Three hours later. *Scene 3*: Limbo. *Scene 4*: Limbo. *Scene 5*: The Jail. *Scene 6*: The Visitors' Area. *Scene 7*: Limbo. *Scene 8*: Billy's Office. *Scene 9*: Limbo. *Scene 10*: In the Jail. *Scene 11*: Limbo and Roxie's Cell. *Scene 12*: Limbo and a bedroom, somewhere in Chicago. *Scene 13*: The Jail.

Act 2, Scene 1: The Jail. *Scene 2*: Limbo. *Scene 3*: The Jail. *Scene 4*: An anteroom in the courthouse. *Scene 5*: The anteroom of the courthouse, March 9th. *Scene 6*: The Courtroom. *Scene 7*: A room in the jail. *Scene 8*: The Courtroom. *Scene 9*: The Courtroom.

ACT 1
Scene 1
"All That Jazz"
C. Rivera, Company
Scene 2
"Funny Honey"
G. Verdon
Scene 3
"Cell Block Tango"
C. Rivera, the Girls
Scene 4
"When You're Good to Mama"
M. McCarty
Scene 6
Tap Dance
G. Verdon, B. Martin, Boys
Scene 7
"All I Care About (Is Love)"
J. Orbach, Girls
Scene 8
"A Little Bit of Good"
M. O'Haughey
"We Both Reached for the Gun"
J. Orbach, G. Verdon, M. O'Haughey, Company
Scene 9
"Roxie"
G. Verdon, Boys
Scene 11
"I Can't Do It Alone"
C. Rivera
"Chicago After Midnight"
The Band
Scene 13
"My Own Best Friend"
G. Verdon, C. Rivera

ACT 2
Scene 1
"I Know a Girl"
C. Rivera
"Me and My Baby"
G. Verdon, C. Chadman, G. Foote
Scene 2
"Mister Cellophane"
B. Martin
Scene 3
"When Velma Takes the Stand"
C. Rivera, Boys
Scene 5
"Razzle Dazzle"
J. Orbach, Company
Scene 7
"Class"
C. Rivera, M. McCarty
Scene 9
"Nowadays"
G. Verdon
"Nowadays" (reprise)/"R.S.V.P."/"Keep It Hot"
G. Verdon, C. Rivera

1975.15 A CHORUS LINE

A Musical in One Act[1]. Conceived, choreographed and directed by Michael Bennett. Book by James Kirkwood and Nicholas Dante. Music by Marvin Hamlisch. Lyrics by Edward Kleban. Co-choreographer, Bob Avian. Musical direction and vocal arrangements by Don Pippin. Settings by Robin Wagner. Costumes by Theoni V. Aldredge. Lighting by Tharon Musser. Sound by Abe Jacob. Music coordinator, Robert Thomas. Orchestrations by Billy Byers, Hershy Kay, Jonathan Tunick. Assistant to choreographers and dance captain, Baayork Lee. A New York Shakespeare Festival Production. Associate producer, Bernard Gersten. Produced by Joseph Papp in association with Plum Productions (Michael Bennett). Opened 25 July 1975[2] at the Sam S. Shubert Theatre and closed 28 April 1990 after 6137 performances. (Total including Off-Broadway run, 6238 performances.)

CAST (in alphabetical order): *Roy*: Scott Allen. *Kristine*: Renee Baughman. *Sheila*: Carole (Kelly) Bishop. *Val*: Pamela Blair. *Mike*: Wayne Cilento. *Butch*: Chuck Cissel. *Larry*: Clive Clerk. *Maggie*: Kay Cole. *Richie*: Ronald Dennis. *Tricia*: Donna Drake. *Tom*: Brandt Edwards. *Judy*: Patricia Garland. *Lois*: Carolyn Kirsch. *Don*: Ron Kuhlman. *Bebe*: Nancy Lane. *Connie*: Baayork Lee. *Diana*: Priscilla Lopez. *Zach*: Robert LuPone. *Mark*: Cameron Mason. *Cassie*: Donna McKechnie. *Al*: Don Percassi. *Frank*: Michael Serrecchia. *Greg*: Michel Stuart. *Bobby*: Thomas J. [Thommie] Walsh. *Paul*: Sammy Williams. *Vicki*: Crissy Wilzak.

The action takes place at an audition here and now.

MUSICAL NUMBERS
"I Hope I Get It"
Company
"I Can Do That"
W. Cilento
"And . . . "
T. J. Walsh, R. Dennis, P. Blair, P. Garland
"At the Ballet"
C. Bishop, N. Lane, K. Cole
"Sing!"
R. Baughman, D. Percassi
"Hello Twelve, Hello Thirteen, Hello Love"
Company
"Nothing"
P. Lopez
"Dance: Ten; Looks: Three"
P. Blair
"The Music and the Mirror"
D. McKechnie

[1]Originally produced Off-Broadway 15 April 1975 at the Newman Theatre for 101 performances.
[2]In response to the demand for a Broadway opening night, the critics were re-invited on 19 October 1975.

"One"
Company
"The Tap Combination"
Company
"What I Did for Love"
P. Lopez, Company
"One" (reprise)
Company

The company of *A CHORUS LINE* has collectively appeared in eighty-eight different shows in which they have given a total of 37,095 performances. Collectively they have had 612 years of dance training with 748 teachers—counting duplications. They spend approximately $894 a month on dance lessons. While appearing in the shows mentioned they have sustained 30 back, 26 knee and 36 ankle injuries. The characters portrayed in *A CHORUS LINE* are, for the most part, based upon the lives and experiences of Broadway dancers. This show is dedicated to anyone who has ever danced in a chorus or marched in step . . . anywhere.

1975.16

DIE FLEDERMAUS

A Revival of the Operetta in Three Acts[3]. Original Viennese libretto by Carl Haffner and Richard Genée. Lyrics by Richard Genée. (Based on the comedy "Le Réveillon" by Henri Meilhac and Ludovic Halévy.) English libretto by Ruth and Thomas Martin. Music by Johann Strauss. Production devised and directed by Gerald Freedman. Stage director, Richard Getke. Choreography by Thomas Andrew. Scenery designed by Lloyd Evans. Costume design by Theoni V. Aldredge. Lighting by Hans Sondheimer. Conducted by Alexis Hauser. Chorus prepared by Judith Somogi. Produced by the New York City Opera. Opened 29 August 1975 at the New York State Theatre and closed 1 November 1975 after 5 performances in repertory; returned 29 February 1976 to the New York State Theatre for 5 additional performances. Total: 10 performances this season.

CAST (in order of appearance): *Alfred*, an itinerant tenor: Gary Glaze. *Adele*, von Eisenstein's chambermaid: ARLENE RANDAZZO. *Rosalinda von Eisenstein*: JOHANNA MEIER. *Gabriel von Eisenstein*: ALAN TITUS. *Dr. Blind*, a lawyer: Joaquin Romaguera. *Dr. Falke*, a close friend of Eisenstein: DAVID HOLLOWAY. *Frank*, the prison warden: SPIRO MALAS. *Sally*, Adele's sister: Puli Toro. *Ivan*, servant to Orlofsky: Jack Sims. *Prince Orlofsky*, a wealthy, bored Russian: DAVID RAE SMITH. *Frosch*, the jailer: Coley Worth. *Solo Dancers*: Sandra Balestracci, Esperanza Galan, Juliu Horvath.

Ensemble: New York City Opera Chorus.

1975.17

H.M.S. PINAFORE, or The Lass That Loved a Sailor

A Revival of the Comic Opera in Two Acts[4]. Libretto by William S. Gilbert. Music by Arthur Sullivan. Directed by Jack Eddleman. Choreographed by Thomas Andrew. Scenery and costumes by Patton Campbell. Lighting by Hans Sondheimer. Conductor, David Effron. Produced by the New York City Opera. Opened 27 September 1975 at the New York State Theatre and closed 9 November 1975 after 5 performances in repertory; returned 22 February 1976 to the New York State Theatre and closed 3 April 1976 after 4 additional performances in repertory. Total: 9 performances this season.

CAST: *The Rt. Hon. Sir Joseph Porter, K.C.B.*, First Lord of the Admiralty: JAMES BILLINGS. *Captain Corcoran*, Commander of the *H.M.S. Pinafore*: CHARLES ROE. *Ralph Rackstraw*, Able Seaman: GARY GLAZE. *Dick Deadeye*, Able Seaman: PAUL UKENA. *Bill Bobstay*, Boatswain: William Ledbetter. *Bob Becket*: Irwin Densen. *Josephine*, the Captain's Daughter: DIANA SOVIERO. *Hebe*, Sir Joseph's First Cousin: Puli Toro. *Little Buttercup*, Mrs. Cripps, a Portsmouth bum-boat woman: MURIEL COSTA-GREENSPON.

First Lord's Sisters, His Cousins, His Aunts, Sailors, Marines, etc.: New York City Opera Chorus.

[3]First English language production in New York 16 March 1885 at the Casino Theatre for 42 performances. First New York production of this adaptation 20 December 1950 at the Metropolitan Opera House. For Synopsis of Scenes and Musical Numbers, see May 1954 revival.

[4]Originally presented in New York 15 January 1879 at the Standard Theatre for 175 performances. For Synopsis of Scenes and Musical Numbers, see original 1879 production.

1975.18

THE ROBBER BRIDEGROOM

A Country-Folk Musical in One Act. Book and lyrics by Alfred Uhry. Based on the novella of the same name by Eudora Welty. Music composed and arranged by Robert Waldman. Directed by Gerald Freedman. Choreography by Donald Saddler. Settings designed by Douglas W. Schmidt. Costumes designed by Jeanne Button. Lighting designed by David F. Segal. Music performed by The Wretched Refuse (Bob Jones, Alan Kaufman, David Markowitz, Richard Shulberg, Steve Tannenbaum). Produced by The Acting Company (John Houseman, Artistic director; Margot Harley, Producing director; Porter Van Zandt, Executive director). Opened 7 October 1975 at the Harkness Theatre and closed 18 October 1975 after 15 performances.

CAST (in order of appearance): *Jamie Lockhart*, a robber: KEVIN KLINE. *Mike Fink*, a flatboatman: Norman Snow. *Clemment Musgrove*, a rich planter: David Schramm. *Goat*, a simpleton: Robert Bacigalupi. *Little Harp*, a robber: J. W. Harper. *Big Harp*, the head of a robber: Anderson Matthews. *Neighbors* (6): *Kyle Nunnery*: Brooks Baldwin. *Tom Playmale*: Richard Ooms. *Billy Brenner*: Nicholas Surovy. *John Oglesby*: Roy K. Stevens. *Ernie Summers*: Peter Dvorsky. *Herman McLaughlin*: Michael Tolaydo. *Salome*, Musgrove's second wife: MARY LOU ROSATO. *Rosamund*, Musgrove's daughter: PATTI LuPONE. *Goat's Mother*: Glynis Bell. *Airie*, Goat's sister: Sandra Halperin. *Raven*: Elaine Hausman. *Queenie Sue Stevens*: Cynthia Dickason. *The Fiddler*: Alan Kaufman.

The action takes place in legendary Mississippi.

MUSICAL NUMBERS
"With Style"
K. Kline, Company
"The Real Mike Fink"
K. Kline, D. Schramm, N. Snow
"The Pricklepear Bloom"
M. L. Rosato
"Nothin' Up"
P. LuPone
"Deeper in the Woods"
The Company
"Riches"
D. Schramm, K. Kline, M. L. Rosato, P. LuPone
"Love Stolen"
K. Kline
"Poor Tied Up Darlin'"
J. W. Harper, R. Bacigalupi
"Goodbye Salome"
The Company
"Sleepy Man"
P. LuPone

1975.19

TREEMONISHA

An Opera in Two Acts, 3 Scenes, (Libretto and Music) by Scott Joplin. Production conceived and directed by Frank Corsaro. Choeography by Louis Johnson. Orchestration and music supervision by Gunther Schuller. Conductors, Gunther Schuller, Jose Contreras. Sets and costumes by Franco Colavecchia. Lighting by Nananne Porcher. Artistic consultant, Vera Brodsky Lawrence. Assistant director, David Drisin. A Houston Grand Opera Association Production. Produced by Adela Holzer, James Nederlander and Victor Lurie by arrangement with the Dramatic Publishing Company. Opened 21 October 1975 at the Uris Theatre, moved 3 November 1975 to the Palace Theatre and closed 14 December 1975 after 64 performances.

CAST (in order of appearance): *Zodzetrick*: Ben Harney. *Ned*: WILLARD WHITE. *Monisha*, Ned's wife: BETTY ALLEN, Lorna Myers (matinees). *Treemonisha*, Ned's adopted daughter: CARMEN BALTHROP, Kathleen Battle (matinees). *Remus*: CURTIS RAYAM. *Andy*: Kenenth Hicks. *Lucy*: Cora Johnson. *Parson Alltalk*: EDWARD PIERSON. *Simon*: Raymond Bazemore. *Cephus*: Dwight Ransome. *Luddud*: Dorceal Duckens.

THE LOUIS JOHNSON DANCE THEATRE: *Dancers*: Clyde-Jacques Barrett, Thea Barnes, Dwight Baxter, Renee Brailsford, Karen Burke, Veda Jackson, Reggie Jackson, Julia Lema, Anita Littleman, Rick Odums, Dwayne Phelps, Ivson Polk, Mabel Robinson, Martial Roumain, Katherine Singleton, James Thurston, Bobby Walker, Pamela Wilson. *Chorus*: Earl L. Baker, Kenneth Bates, Barbara Christopher, Steven Cole, Ella Eure, Gregory Gardner, Melvin Jordan, Patricia McDermott, Janette Moody, Marion Moore, Vera Moore, Lorna Myers, Glover Parham, Patricia Pates, William Penn, Dwight Ransom, Cornel Richie, Patricia Rogers, Christine Spencer, Walter Turnbull, Gloria Turner, Peter Whitehead, Arthur Williams, Barbara Young.

The action takes place on a plantation in Arkansas, northeast of the town of Texarcana and three or four miles from the Red River.

Act 1, Scene 1: Morning. *Scene 2*: Afternoon of the same day.

Act 2: That evening.

ACT 1
Scene 1
- Overture
  - B. Harney, Dancers
- "The Bag of Luck"
  - C. Balthrop, B. Allen, C. Rayam, W. White, B. Harney
- "The Corn-Huskers"
  - C. Balthrop, Chorus
- "We're Goin' Around"
  - C. Balthrop, B. Allen, C. Johnson, C. Rayam, W. White, Chorus, Dancers
- "The Wreath"
  - C. Balthrop, B. Allen, C. Johnson
- "The Sacred Tree"
  - B. Allen
- "Surprise"
  - C. Balthrop
- "Treemonisha's Bringing Up"
  - C. Balthrop, B. Allen
- "Good Advice"
  - E. Pierson, Chorus
- "Confusion"
  - B. Allen, C. Johnson, C. Rayam, W. White

Scene 2
- "Superstition"
  - R. Bazemore, D. Ransom
- "Treemonisha in Peril"
  - B. Harney, R. Bazemore, D. Duckens, D. Ransom
- "The Frolic of the Bears"
  - Dancers
- "The Wasp Nest"
  - R. Bazemore, D. Ransom
- "The Rescue"
  - C. Balthrop, C. Rayam
- "We Will Rest Awhile"
  - (Male) Quartet
- "Going Home"
  - C. Balthrop, C. Rayam, the Foreman
- "Aunt Dinah Has Blowed De Horn"
  - Chorus, Dancers

ACT 2
- "I Want to See My Child"
  - B. Allen, W. White
- "Treemonisha's Return"
  - C. Balthrop, B. Allen, C. Rayam, W. White, K. Hicks
- "Wrong Is Never Right"
  - C. Rayam, Chorus
- "Abuse"
  - C. Balthrop, K. Hicks
- "When Villains Ramble Far and Near"
  - W. White
- "Conjuror's Forgiven"
  - C. Balthrop, K. Hicks
- "We Will Trust You as Our Leader"
  - C. Balthrop, B. Allen, C. Johnson, W. White, C. Rayam, K. Hicks, Chorus
- "A Real Slow Drag"
  - Entire Company
- "Aunt Dinah Has Blowed De Horn" (reprise)
  - Entire Company

1975.20 ME AND BESSIE

A Musical Evening (Revue) in Two Acts. Conceived and written by Will Holt and Linda Hopkins. Entire production directed by Robert Greenwald. Special dance sequences by Lester Wilson. Musical direction by Howlett Smith. Setting by Donald Harris. Costumes by Pete Menefee. Lighting by Tharon Musser. A Center Theatre Group/Mark Taper Forum Production. Produced by Lee Apostoleris. Opened 22 October 1975 at the Ambassador Theatre, moved under the auspices of Norman Kean 3 December 1975 to the Edison Theatre and closed 5 December 1976 after 453 performances. (Note: From 24 September-5 December 1976 performances were in repertory with "Oh, Calcutta!")

CAST (in order of appearance): *Bessie Smith*: LINDA HOPKINS. *Man*: Lester Wilson. *Woman*: Gerri Dean.

ACT 1
- "I Feel Good"
- "God Shall Wipe All Tears Away"
- "Moan You Mourners"
- "New Orleans Hop Scop Blues"
- "Romance in the Dark"
  - (*Music and Lyrics by* Lil Green.)
- "Preach Them Blues"
  - (*Music and Lyrics by* Bessie Smith.)
- "A Good Man Is Hard to Find"
  - (*Music and Lyrics by* Eddie Green.)
- "T'Ain't Nobody's Bizness If I Do"
  - (*Music and Lyrics by* Porter Grainger, Clarence Williams, Graham Prince.)
- "Gimme a Pigfoot"
  - (*Music and Lyrics by* Wesley Wilson.)
- "Put It Right Here"
  - (*Music and Lyrics by* Porter Grainger.)
- "You've Been a Good Ole Wagon"
  - (*Music and Lyrics by* J. Henry.)
- "Trombone Cholly"
- "Jazzbo Brown"
- "After You've Gone"
  - (*Music by* Turner Layton. *Lyrics by* Henry Creamer.)

ACT 2
- "There'll Be a Hot Time in the Old Town Tonight"
  - (*Music and Lyrics by* Joseph Hayden and Theodore M. Metz.)
- "Empty Bed Blues"
  - (*Music and Lyrics by* J. C. Johnson.)
- "Kitchen Man"
  - (*Music by* Alex Belledna. *Lyrics by* Andy Razaf.)
- "Mama Don't 'Low"
- "Do Your Duty"
  - (*Music and Lyrics by* Wesley Wilson.)
- "Fare Thee Well"
- "Nobody Knows You When You're Down and Out"
  - (*Music and Lyrics by* Jimmy Cox.)
- "Trouble"
  - (*Music and Lyrics by* D. Akers.)
- "The Man's All Right"

1975.21 HELLO, DOLLY!

A Revival of the Musical Comedy in Two Acts, 15 Scenes[5]. Book by Michael Stewart. Based on the play "The Matchmaker" by Thornton Wilder. Music and lyrics by Jerry Herman. Directed by Lucia Victor. Dances recreated by Jack Craig from original choreography by Gower Champion. Settings by Oliver Smith. Costumes supervised by Robert Pusilo. Lighting by John Gleason. Musical direction by Al Cavaliere. (Vocal arrangements, orchestrations, dance and incidental music uncredited.) Produced by Robert Cherin in association with Theatre Now Inc. Opened 6 November 1975 at the Minskoff Theatre and closed 21 December 1975 after 42 performances.

CAST (in the order of appearance): *Mrs. Dolly Gallagher Levi*: PEARL BAILEY. *Ernestina*: Bessye Ruth Scott. *Ambrose Kemper*: Howard Porter. *Horse*: Kathy Jennings, Karen Hubbard. *Horace Vandergelder*: BILLY DANIELS. *Ermengarde*: Karen Hubbard. *Cornelius Hackl*: TERRENCE EMANUEL. *Barnaby Tucker*: GRENOLDO FRA-

[5]Originally produced in New York 16 January 1964 at the St. James Theatre for 2844 performances. For Synopsis of Scenes and Musical Numbers, see original 1964 production. "Come and Be My Butterfly" was not performed in this revival.

ZIER. *Irene Molloy*: MARY LOUISE. *Minnie Fay*: CHIP FIELDS. *Mrs. Rose*: Birdie M. Hale. *Rudolph*: Jonathan Wynne. *Judge*: Ted Goodridge. *Court Clerk*: Ray Gilbert.

Townspeople, Waiters, Etc.: Sally Benoit, Terry Gene, Pat Gideon, Ann Givin, Birdie M. Hale, Karen Hubbard, Gwen Humble, Eulaulá Jennings, Francie Mendenhall, Bessye Ruth Scott, Sachi Shimizu, Guy Allen, Don Coleman, Richard Dodd, Ray Gilbert, Charles Goeddertz, Ted Goodridge, Clark James, James Kennon-Wilson, Richard Maxon, Charles Neal, Howard Porter, Jimmy Rivers, Ken Rogers, David Staller, Teddy Williams, Jonathan Wynne.

1975.22 A MUSICAL JUBILEE

A Musical Entertainment (Revue) in Two Acts, 10 Scenes. Written by Max Wilk. Devised by Marilyn Clark and Charles Burr. Entire production directed by Morton DaCosta. Musical supervision by Lehman Engel. Musical director, John Lesko. Dance arrangements and musical continuity by Trude Rittman. Orchestrations by Philip J. Lang, Hershy Kay, Elman Anderson. Scenery designed by Herbert Senn. Costumes designed by Donald Brooks. Lighting designed by Thomas Skelton. Choreography by Robert Tucker. Associate producer, Merle D. King. Produced by The Theatre Guild and Jonathan Conrow. Opened 13 November 1975 at the St. James Theatre and closed 1 January 1976 after 92 performances.

CAST: PATRICE MUNSEL, TAMMY GRIMES, CYRIL RITCHARD, JOHN RAITT, DICK SHAWN, LARRY KERT, LILLIAN GISH, Steven Boockvor, Eric Brotherson, Marcia Brushingham, Igors Gavon, Nana, David King, Jeanne Lehman, Bettye Malone, Estella Munson, Julie Pars, Dennis Perren, Leland Schwantes, Craig Yates.

Act 1, Scene 1: Opening. *Scene 2*: American Frontier. *Scene 3*: American Military. *Scene 4*: Old Vienna. *Scene 5*: Britain. *Scene 6*: Early Broadway.

Act 2, Scene 1: The Smart Set. *Scene 2*: Vaudeville. *Scene 3*: Jazz. *Scene 4*: Later Broadway.

ACT 1

Scene 1

"Happy Days"
Entire Company
(*Music by* Johann Strauss II. *Lyrics by* Howard Dietz.)

Scene2

"Whoa-Haw"
L. Kert

"Lorena"
J. Raitt
(*Music by* J. P. Webster. *Lyrics by* Reverend H. D. L. Webster.)

"Sweet Betsy from Pike"
T. Grimes

"Skip to My Lou"
P. Munsel, L. Kert

"Whoa-Haw" (reprise)
Entire Company

Scene 3

"Hold on Abraham"
Ensemble
(*Music and Lyrics by* William L. Bradbury.)

"Bonnie Blue Flag"
L. Kert, S. Boockvor, I. Gavon, D. King, D. Perren, L. Schwantes, C. Yates
(*Music by* Valentine Vousden. *Lyrics by* Harry Macarthy.)

"(It's a Long Way to) Tipperary"
T. Grimes, Male Ensemble
(*Music and Lyrics by* Jack Judge and Harry H. Williams.)

"I Didn't Raise My Boy to be a Soldier"
L. Gish
(*Music by* Al Piantadosi. *Lyrics by* Alfred Bryan.)

"Mademoiselle from Armentieres"
C. Ritchard, D. Shawn
(*Music and Lyrics by* Howard Ross.)

"Over There"
P. Munsel, Male Ensemble
(*Music and Lyrics by* George M. Cohan.)

"Battle Hymn of the Republic"
J. Raitt, Entire Company
(*Lyrics by* Julia Ward Howe.)

Scene 4

"Wien, Wien, You're Calling Me"
(*Music and Lyrics by* Rudolf Sieczynski and King.)

"I'm in Love With Vienna"
(*from THE GREAT WALTZ* film.)
(*Music by* Johann Strauss. *Lyrics by* Oscar Hammerstein II.)
P. Munsel, J. Raitt, Ensemble

"Der Shimmy"
T. Grimes
(*Music by* Emmerich Kálmán. *Lyrics by* King.)

"I've Got Something"
(*Music by* Franz Lehár. *Lyrics by* Harry B. Smith and Robert B. Smith.)
C. Ritchard, M. Brushingham, Nana, J. Lehman, B. Malone, J. Pars, E. Munson

"Oh, the Women"
L. Kert
(*Music by* Franz Lehár.)

"Gypsy Love"
(from *GYPSY LOVE*)
P. Munsel, Ensemble
(*Music by* Franz Lehár. *Lyrics by* Harry B. Smith and Robert B. Smith.)

Scene 5

"And Her Mother Came Too"
(from *A TO Z*, London)
C. Ritchard
(*Music by* Ivor Novello. *Lyrics by* Dion Titheradge.)

Scene 6

"Song of the Vagabonds"
(from *THE VAGABOND KING*)
J. Raitt, Male Ensemble
(*Music by* Rudolf Friml. *Lyrics by* Brian Hooker.)

"Totem Tom Tom"
(from *ROSE MARIE*)
T. Grimes, Female Ensemble
(*Music by* Rudolf Friml. *Lyrics by* Oscar Hammerstein II and Otto Harbach.)

"Serenade"
(from *THE STUDENT PRINCE*)
L. Kert
(*Music by* Sigmund Romberg. *Lyrics by* Dorothy Donnelly.)

Violetta
C. Ritchard, T. Grimes, L. Kert, E. Brotherson

"Moonstruck"
(from *OUR MISS GIBBS*)
L. Gish, Male Ensemble
(*Music by* Lionel Monckton. *Lyrics by* James T. Tanner.)

"You Are Love"
(from *SHOWBOAT*)
P. Munsel, J. Raitt
(*Music by* Jerome Kern. *Lyrics by* Oscar Hammerstein II.)

"I've Told Every Little Star"
(from *MUSIC IN THE AIR*)
D. Shawn, Female Ensemble
(*Music by* Jerome Kern. *Lyrics by* Oscar Hammerstein II.)

"Why Was I Born?"
(from *SWEET ADELINE*)
P. Munsel
(*Music by* Jerome Kern. *Lyrics by* Oscar Hammerstein II.)

"The Best Things in Life Are Free"
(from *GOODNEWS*)
L. Kert, Entire Ensemble
(*Music by* Ray Henderson. *Lyrics by* Buddy G. DeSylva and Lew Brown.)

"They Didn't Believe Me"
(from *THE GIRL FROM UTAH*)
T. Grimes
(*Music by* Jerome Kern. *Lyrics by* Herbert Reynolds [Michael E. Rourke].)

"The Song Is You"
(from *MUSIC IN THE AIR*)
J. Raitt
(*Music by* Jerome Kern. *Lyrics by* Oscar Hammerstein II.)

"Something Seems Tingle Ingleing"
(from *HIGH JINKS*)
(*Music by* Rudolf Friml. *Lyrics by* Otto Harbach.)
C. Ritchard, Female Ensemble

"(I Want to Hear a) Yankee Doodle Tune"
(from *MOTHER GOOSE*, 1903)
D. Shawn, Entire Company
(*Music and Lyrics by* George M. Cohan.)

ACT 2

Scene 1

"We're Blasé"
(from *BOW BELLS*, London)

P. Munsel, J. Raitt, T. Grimes, C. Ritchard
(*Music by* Ord Hamilton. *Lyrics by* Bruce Sievier.)
"Poor Little Rich Girl"
(from *CHARLOT'S REVUE*)
T. Grimes
(*Music and Lyrics by* Noël Coward.)
"You Go to My Head"
J. Raitt
(*Music by* J. Fred Coots. *Lyrics by* Haven Gillespie.)
"Find Me a Primitive Man"
(from *FIFTY MILLION FRENCHMEN*)
P. Munsel, T. Grimes
(*Music and Lyrics by* Cole Porter.)
"I Guess I'll Have to Change My Plan"
(from *THE LITTLE SHOW*)
D. Shawn
(*Music by* Arthur Schwartz. *Lyrics by* Howard Dietz.)
"Sophisticated Lady"
L. Kert
(*Music by* Duke Ellington. *Lyrics by* Mitchell Parish and Irving Mills.)
"Love Me or Leave Me"
(from *WHOOPEE*)
P. Munsel
(*Music by* Walter Donaldson. *Lyrics by* Gus Kahn.)
"Gilbert the Filbert"
(from *THE GIRL FROM UTAH, PASSING SHOW OF 1914*)
C. Ritchard
(*Music by* Herman Finck. *Lyrics by* Arthur Wimperis.)
"We're Blasé" (reprise)
P. Munsel, J. Raitt, C. Ritchard, T. Grimes, D. Shawn, L. Kert

Scene 2
"At the Moving Picture Ball"
Ensemble
(*Music by* Joseph H. Santly. *Lyrics by* Howard Johnson.)
The Green Eye of the Little Yellow God
C. Ritchard, D. Shawn, E. Brotherson
(*by* Reginald Purdell, based on the poem by Milton Hayes)
"I Wanna Be Loved by You"
(from *GOOD BOY*)
P. Munsel, T. Grimes, L. Gish
(*Music by* Harry Ruby. *Lyrics by* Bert Kalmar.)
"Miss Annabelle Lee"
D. Shawn
(*Music by* Lew Pollack. *Lyrics by* Sidney Clare, Harry Richman.)

Scene 3
"How Jazz Was Born"
L. Kert, Ensemble
(*Music by* Fats Waller. *Lyrics by* Andy Razaf and Henry Creamer.)
"Ain't Misbehavin'"
(from *HOT CHOCOLATES*)
L. Kert
(*Music by* Fats Waller and Harry Brooks. *Lyrics by* Andy Razaf.)
"I'm Just Wild About Harry"
(from *SHUFFLE ALONG*)
T. Grimes
(*Music and Lyrics by* Eubie Blake and Noble Sissle.)
"Me and My Shadow"
D. Shawn
(*Music by* Al Jolson and Dave Dreyer. *Lyrics by* Billy Rose.)
"Sometimes I'm Happy"
(from *HIT THE DECK*)
P. Munsel
(*Music by* Vincent Youmans. *Lyrics by* Irving Caesar.)
"Great Day"
(from *GREAT DAY*)
J. Raitt
(*Music by* Vincent Youmans. *Lyrics by* Billy Rose and Edward Eliscu.)
"How Jazz Was Born" (reprise)
P. Munsel, J. Raitt, T. Grimes, D. Shawn, L. Kert, Ensemble

Scene 4
"Lullaby of Broadway"
(from *GOLDDIGGERS OF 1935* film)
Ensemble
(*Music by* Harry Warren. *Lyrics by* Al Dubin.)
"(This Is My) Lucky Day"
(from *GEORGE WHITE'S SCANDALS OF 1926*)
D. Shawn
(*Music by* Ray Henderson. *Lyrics by* B. G. DeSylva and Lew Brown.)
"If You Knew Susie"
(from *BIG BOY*)
C. Ritchard
(*Music by* Joseph Meyer. *Lyrics by* B. G. DeSylva.)
"'S Wonderful"
(from *FUNNY FACE*)
L. Gish
(*Music by* George Gershwin. *Lyrics by* Ira Gershwin.)
"Fascinating Rhythm"
(from *LADY, BE GOOD!*)
L. Kert
(*Music by* George Gershwin. *Lyrics by* Ira Gershwin.)
"Liza" (All the Clouds'll Roll Away)
(from *SHOW GIRL*)
T. Grimes
(*Music by* George Gershwin. *Lyrics by* Gus Kahn and Ira Gershwin.)
"Where or When "
(from *BABES IN ARMS*)
P. Munsel
(*Music by* Richard Rodgers. *Lyrics by* Lorenz Hart.)
"Hallelujah"
(from *HIT THE DECK*)
J. Raitt, Entire Company
(*Music by* Vincent Youmans. *Lyrics by* Leo Robin and Clifford Grey.)

1975.23 BOCCACCIO

A Musical in Two Acts, 8 Scenes. Dramatization (book) and lyrics by Kenneth Cavander. Based on stories[6] from "The Decameron" by Giovanni Boccaccio. Music by Richard Peaslee. Directed by Warren Enters. Musical staging by Julie Arenal. Setting by Robert U. Taylor. Costumes by Linda Fisher. Lighting by Patrika Brown. Musical director, Ken Bichel. Orchestrations and arrangements by Walt Levinsky, Richard Peaslee. Produced by Rita Fredericks, Theatre Now, Inc. and Norman Kean. Opened 24 November 1975 at the Edison Theatre and closed 30 November 1975 after 8 performances.

CAST: *Beltramo (Count of Rossiglione), Egano*: MICHAEL ZASLOW. *Giletta (Beltramo's Wife), Abbess*: VIRGINIA VESTOFF. *Masetto (Beltramo's Younger Brother), Ferondo*: ARMAND ASSANTE. *Beatrice (Beltramo's Widowed Sister), Sister Teresa, Ferondo's Wife*: CAROLINE McWILLIAMS. *Isabella (Masetto's Mistress), Sister Angelica*: D'JAMIN BARTLETT. *Alibech (Masetto's Friend), Sister Makaria*: JILL CHODER. *Rustico (A Cousin), Leonetto, Brother Perdurabo*: MUNSON HICKS. *Anichino (Steward to the Family), Nuto, Abbot*: RICHARD BAUER.

The action takes place at a villa outside Florence in the year 1348.

Act 1, Scene 1: Introduction. The Stories: *Scene 2*: Masetto. *Scene 3*: Anichino. *Scene 4*: Pretend You're Living. *Scene 5*: Devil in Hell.

Act 2, Scene 1: The She Doctor. *Scene 2*: Madonna Isabella. *Scene 3*: Ferondo.

ACT 1
Scene 1
Introduction
The Company
Scene 2
"Masetto's Song"
A. Assante, R. Bauer
"Nuns Song"
V. Vestoff, C. McWilliams, D. Bartlett, J. Choder
"God Is Good"
A. Assante, C. McWilliams, D. Bartlett, J. Choder
"Now My Season's Here"
The Company
Scene 3
"Only in My Song"
R. Bauer
"Egano D'Galluzzi"
R. Bauer, M. Zaslow

[6]The stories in "Boccaccio" are taken from The Decameron: Masetto: Day III, Story 1; Anichino: Day VII, Story 7; Devil in Hell: Day II, Story 10; Madonna Isabella: Day VII, Story 6; The Doctor's Daughter: Day III, Story 9; Ferondo: Day III, Story 8.

"The Men Who Have Loved Me"
C. McWilliams
"In the Garden"
R. Bauer, M. Zaslow
"Lucky Anichino"
The Company
Scene 4
"Pretend You're Living"
D. Bartlett
Scene 5
"Devil in Hell"
J. Choder, M. Hicks, Company

ACT 2
Scene 1
"She Doctor"
V. Vestoff, M. Zaslow
"Lover Like a Blind Man"
V. Vestoff
"If You Had Seen"
V. Vestoff
"Love Was Just a Game"
M. Zaslow
Scene 2
"Madonna Isabella"
D. Bartlett, Company
Scene 3
"My Holy Prayer"
R. Bauer, Monks
"Hold Me Gently"
C. McWilliams

1975.24 VERY GOOD EDDIE

A Revival of the Musical (Comedy) in Two Acts, 3 Scenes[7]. Book by Guy Bolton. Based on a farce ("Over Night") by Philip Bartholomae. Music by Jerome Kern. Lyrics by Schuyler Greene. Production directed by Bill Gile. Dances and musical numbers staged by Dan Siretta. Musical direction and (vocal) arrangements by Russell Warner. Scenery and lighting by Fred Voelpel. Costumes by David Toser. Special consultant, Alfred Simon. A Goodspeed Opera House Producton (Michael Price, Producer). Produced by David Merrick, Max Brown and Byron Goldman. Opened 21 December 1975 at the Booth Theatre and closed 5 September 1976 after 307 performances.

CAST (in order of appearance): *Steward*: JAMES HARDER. *Mr. Dick Rivers*: DAVID CHRISTMAS. *Mme. Matroppo*: TRAVIS HUDSON. *Miss Elsie Lilly*: CYNTHIA WELLS. *M. de Rougemont*: JOEL CRAIG. *Mrs. Georgina Kettle*: SPRING FAIRBANK. *Mr. Eddie Kettle*: CHARLES REPOLE. *Mr. Percy Darling*: NICHOLAS WYMAN. *Mrs. Elsie Darling*: VIRGINIA SEIDEL. *Al Cleveland*: JAMES HARDER. *Miss Lily Pond*: Wendy Young. *Miss Chrystal Poole*: Karen Crossley. *Miss Carrie Closewell*: Gillian Scalici. *Miss Always Innit*: Robin Herbert. *Mr. Tayleurs Dumme*: Russ Beasley. *Mr. Dayr Thurst*: Jon Engstrom. *Mr. Dustin Stacks*: Larry McMillan. *Mr. Rollo Munn*: Hal Shane.

The action takes place in 1913.

Act 1: A Hudson River Dayliner.

Act 2, Scene 1: Lobby of the Honeymoon Inn in the Catskills. That evening. *Scene 2*: The next morning.

ACT 1
"We're on Our Way"
Ensemble
"Some Sort of Somebody"
C. Wells, D. Christmas
(*Lyrics by* Elsie Janis.)
"(When You Wear a) Thirteen Collar"
C. Repole
"Bungalow in Quogue"
(from *THE RIVIERA GIRL*)
V. Seidel, N. Wyman
(*Lyrics by* P. G. Wodehouse.)
"Isn't It Great To Be Married"
V. Seidel, S. Fairbank, C. Repole, N. Wyman
"Good Night Boat"
(from *THE NIGHT BOAT*)
Ensemble
(*Lyrics by* Anne Caldwell and Frank Craven.)
"Left All Alone Again Blues"
(from *THE NIGHT BOAT*)
V. Seidel
(*Lyrics by* Anne Caldwell.)
"Hot Dog!"
(from *THE BUNCH AND JUDY*)
Ensemble
(*Lyrics by* Anne Caldwell.)
"If You're a Friend of Mine"
(from *LADY MARY*, London)
V. Seidel, C. Repole
(*Lyrics by* Graham John.)
"Wedding Bells Are Calling Me"
Ensemble
(*Lyrics by* Harry B. Smith.)

ACT 2
"Honeymoon Inn"
(from *HAVE A HEART*)
C. Wells, Ensemble
(*Lyrics by* P. G. Wodehouse.)
"I've Got to Dance"
(dropped from *VERY GOOD EDDIE*)
J. Craig, Ensemble
"Moon Love"
(from *THE BEAUTY PRIZE*)
T. Hudson, Ensemble
(*Lyrics by* Anne Caldwell.)
"Old Boy Neutral"
C. Wells, D. Christmas
"Babes in the Wood"
V. Seidel, C. Repole
"Katy-did"
(from *OH, I SAY!*)
T. Hudson
(*Lyrics by* Harry B. Smith.)
"Nodding Roses"
C. Wells, D. Christmas
(*Lyrics by* Schuyler Greene and Herbert Reynolds.)
Finale
Ensemble
(*Lyrics by* John E. Hazzard and Herbert Reynolds.)

1976.01 HOME SWEET HOMER

A Musical Romantic Comedy in One Act. Book by Roland Kibbee and Albert Marre. (Suggested by Homer's "Odyssey.") Music by Mitch Leigh. Lyrics by Charles Burr and Forman Brown. Book and musical staging by Albert Marre. Scenery and lighting by Howard Bay. Costumes by Howard Bay and Ray Diffen. Musical direction by Ross Reimueller. Orchestrations by Buryl Red. Produced by The John F. Kennedy Center for the Performing Arts (Kennedy Center Productions Inc.) Opened and closed 4 January 1976 at the Palace Theatre after 1 performance.

CAST: *Odysseus*: YUL BRYNNER. *Penelope*, his wife: JOAN DIENER. *Telemachus*, his son: RUSS THACKER. *Penelope's Suitors (8)*: *Antinous*: MARTIN VIDNOVIC. *Pilokrates*: Ian Sullivan. *Ktesippos*: Bill Mackey. *Eurymachus*: Daniel Brown. *Leokritos*: Brain Destazio. *Pimteus*: John Aristedes. *Melios*: Bill Nabel. *Polybos*: Les Freed. *King Alkinoos*: SHEV RODGERS. *Nausikaa*, his daughter: DIANA DAVILA. *Nausikaa's Handmaidens (3)*: *Therapina*: Suzanne Sponsler. *Melantho*: Cecile Santos. *Hippodameia*: Christine Uchida. *Kerux*: Darel Glaser. *Dekati Evdomi, the Seventeenth*: P. J. Mann.

MUSICAL NUMBERS
"The Sorceress"
J. Diener, The Suitors
"The Departure"
Y. Brynner, P. J. Mann
"Home Sweet Homer"
Y. Brynner
"The Ball"
D. Davila, Handmaidens

[7] Originally produced in New York 23 December 1915 at the Princess Theatre for 341 performances.

"How Could I Dare to Dream?"
Y. Brynner, R. Thacker
"I Never Imagined Goodbye"
J. Diener
"Love Is the Prize"
Y. Brynner
"Penelope's Hand"
M. Vidnovic
"He Will Come Home Again"
R. Thacker
"Did He Really Think"
J. Diener
"I Was Wrong"
Y. Brynner
"The Rose"
J. Diener
"Tomorrow"
M. Vidnovic, The Suitors
"The Contest"
Y. Brynner, R. Thacker, M. Vidnovic, The Suitors

1976.02 PACIFIC OVERTURES

A Musical in Two Acts, 18 Scenes. Book by John Weidman. Music and lyrics by Stephen Sondheim. Additional (book) material by Hugh Wheeler. Directed by Harold Prince. Choreographed by Patricia Birch. Scenic production designed by Boris Aronson. Costumes designed by Florence Klotz. Lighting designed by Tharon Musser. Orchestrations by Jonathan Tunick. Musical direction by Paul Gemignani. Dance music by Daniel Troob. Kabuki consultant, Haruki Fujimoto. Masks and dolls by E. J. Taylor. Sound by Jack Mann. Martial arts sequence by Soon-Teck Oh. Produced by Harold Prince in association with Ruth Mitchell. Opened 11 January 1976 at the Winter Garden Theatre and closed 27 June 1976 after 193 performances.

CAST (in order of appearance): *Reciter*: MAKO. *Abe, First Councilor*: YUKI SHIMODA. *Manjiro*: SAB SHIMONO. *Second Councilor*: JAMES DYBAS. *Shogun's Mother*: Alvin Ing. *Third Councilor*: Freddy Mao. *Kayama*: ISAO SATO. *Tamate (Kayama's Wife), Samurai, Storyteller, Swordsman*: Soon-Teck Oh. *Samurai*: Ernest Aruba, Mark Hsu Syers. *Servant*: HARUKI FUJIMOTO. *Observers*: Alvin Ing, Ricardo Tobia. *Fisherman*: Jae Woo Lee. *Merchant*: Alvin Ing. *Son*: Timm Fujii. *Grandmother*: Conrad Yama. *Thief*: Mark Hsu Syers. *Adams*: Ernest Abuba. *Williams*: Larry Hama. *Commodore Matthew Galbraith Perry*: HARUKI FUJIMOTO. *Shogun's Wife*: Freda Foh Shen. *Physician*: Ernest Harada. *Priests*: Timm Fujii, Gedde Watanabe. *Soothsayer*: Mark Hsu Syers. *Sumo Wrestlers*: Conrad Yama, Jae Woo Lee. *Shogun's Companion*: Patrick Kinser-Lau. *Shogun*: MAKO. *Madam*: Ernest Harada. *Girls*: Timm Fujii, Patrick Kinser-Lau, Gedde Watanabe, Leslie Watanabe. *Old Man*: JAMES DYBAS. *Boy*: Gedde Watanabe. *Warrior*: Mark Hsu Syers. *Imperial Priest*: Tom Matsusaka. *Nobles*: Ernest Abuba, Timm Fujii. *British Admiral*: Ernest Harada. *Dutch Admiral*: Patrick Kinser-Lau. *Russian Admiral*: Mark Hsu Syers. *French Admiral*: JAMES DYBAS. *Lords of the South*: Larry Hama, Jae Woo Lee. *Jonathan Goble*: MAKO. *Japanese Merchant*: Conrad Yama. *Samurai's Daughter*: Freddy Mao. *British Sailors*: Timm Fujii, Patrick Kinser-Lau, Mark Hsu Syers. *Musicians*: Fusako Yoshida, Genji Ito.

Proscenium Servants, Sailors, Townspeople: Susan Kikuchi, Diane Lam, Kim Miyori, Freda Foh Shen, Kenneth S. Eiland, Timm Fujii, Joey Ginza, Patrick Kinser-Lau, Tony Marinyo, Kevin Maung, Dingo Secretario, Mark Hsu Syers, Ricardo Tobia, Gedde Watanabe, Leslie Watannabe. *Musicians*: Fusako Yoshida (Shamisen), Genji Ito (Percussion).

The action takes place in Japan in July of 1853, and from then on.

Act 1, Scene 1: Japan in July 1853; Shogun's Court. *Scene 2*: A small Japanese house in Uraga. *Scene 3*: The Japanese shore. *Scene 4*: The deck of the *U.S.S. Powhatan*. *Scene 5*: The Shogun's chamber. *Scene 6*: The Shogun's chamber; en route to Uraga; the house at Uraga. *Scene 7*: The village of Kanagawa. *Scene 8*: Exchange of gifts. *Scene 9*: Kanagawa. *Scene 10*: The Treaty House at Kanagawa. *Scene 11*: Lion Dance.

Act 2, Scene 1: The Imperial Court at Kyoto. *Scene 2*: The Admirals' Visit. *Scene 3*: The Imperial Court. *Scene 4*: The homes of Kayama and Manjiro. *Scene 5*: Ten years later. *Scene 6*: A private garden. *Scene 7*: Japan 1863-1975.

ACT 1
Scene 1
"The Advantages of Floating in the Middle of the Sea"
Mako, Company
Scene 2
"There Is No Other Way"
S. Oh, Observers
Scene 3
"Four Black Dragons"
J. W. Lee, M. H. Syers, Mako, Townspeople
Scene 5
"Chrysanthemum Tea"
Mako, A. Ing, F. F. Shen M. H. Syers, T. Fujii, G. Watanabe, P. Kinser-Lau, E. Harada, C. Yama, J. W. Lee
Scene 6
"Poems"
I. Sato, S. Shimono
Scene 7
"Welcome to Kanagawa"
E. Harada, Girls
Scene 10
"Someone in a Tree"
J. Dybas, Mako, G. Watanabe, M. H. Syers
Scene 11
"Lion Dance"
H. Fujimoto

ACT 2
Scene 2
"Please Hello"
Y. Shimoda, Mako, A. Ing, E. Harada, P. Kinser-Lau, M. H. Syers, J. Dybas
Scene 4
"A Bowler Hat"
I. Sato, S. Shimono
Scene 6
"Pretty Lady"
T. Fujii, P. Kinser-Lau, M. H. Syers
Scene 7
"Next"
Mako, Company

1976.03 ROCKABYE HAMLET

A Musical in Two Acts, a Prologue and 9 Scenes[8]. Book, music and lyrics by Cliff Jones. (Based on the play "Hamlet" by William Shakespeare.) Directed and choreographed by Gower Champion. Co-choreographer, Tony Stevens. Scenery designed by Kert Lundell. Costumes designed by Joseph G. Aulisi. Lighting designed by Jules Fisher. Sound design by Abe Jacob. Swordplay by Larry Carpenter. Musical direction and vocal arrangements by Gordon Lowry Harrell. Dance music arranged by Doug Katsaros. Special effects by Robert Joyce. Produced by Lester Osterman Productions (Lester Osterman, Richard Horner) and Joseph Kipness in association with Martin Richards and Victor D'Arc and Marilyn Strauss, by arrangement with Champlain Productions, Ltd. Opened 17 February 1976 at the Minskoff Theatre and closed 21 February 1976 after 7 performances.

CAST (in order of appearance): *Horatio*: RORY DODD. *Hamlet*: LARRY MARSHALL. *Claudius*: ALAN WEEKS. *Gertrude*: LAETA GALLOWAY. *Priest*: MEAT LOAF. *Polonius*: RANDAL WILSON. *Ophelia*: BEVERLY D'ANGELO. *Laertes*: KIM MILFORD. *Rosencrantz*: CHRISTOPHER CHADMAN. *Guildenstern*: WINSTON DeWITT HEMSLEY. *Player*: IRVING (ALLEN) LEE. *Playeress/ Honeybelle Huckster*: Judy Gibson.

Acolytes, Swordsmen, Nobles, Courtesans: Tommy Aguilar, Steve Anthony, Terry Calloway, Prudence Darby, George Giraldo, Larry Hyman, Kurt Johnson, Clinton Keen, Paula Lynn, Joann Ogawa, Sandi Orcutt, Merel Poloway, Joseph Pugliese, Yolanda Raven, Michelle Stubbs, Dennis Williams. *Singers*: James Braet, Judy DeAngelis, B. G. Gibson, Judy Gibson, Pat Gorman, Suzanne Lukather, Bruce Paine, William Parry. *Roadies*: Chet D'Elia, David Fredericks, David Lawson, Jeff Spielman.

The entire action takes place at a rock concert.

Act 1, Scene 1: Chapel. *Scene 2*: Throne Room. *Scene 3*: Queen's Bedchamber. *Scene 4*: The Disco. *Scene 5*: The Great Hall.

Act 2, Scene 1: The Chapel. *Scene 2*: Limbo. *Scene 3*: The Graveyard. *Scene 4*: The Great Hall.

[8]"Rockabye Hamlet" was originally commissioned by the Canadian Broadcasting Company's Radio Variety Department and performed as "Kronberg: 1582."

ACT 1
Prologue
"Why Did He Have to Die?"
R. Dodd, Chorus
Scene 1
"The Wedding"
L. Marshall, A. Weeks, L. Galloway, M. Loaf, Chorus
"That It Should Come to This"
L. Marshall
Scene 2
"Set It Right"
A. Weeks, L. Marshall, L. Galloway, Chorus
"Hello-Hello"
B. D'Angelo, L. Marshall
"Don't Unmask Your Beauty to the Moon"
L. Marshall, K. Milford
"If Not to You"
B. D'Angelo, Chorus
"Have I Got a Girl for You"
C. Chadman, W. D. Hemsley, L. Marshall, Chorus
"Tis Pity, Tis True"
R. Wilson, A. Weeks, L. Galloway
Scene 3
"Shall We Dance"
L. Marshall, L. Galloway
"All My Life"
L. Galloway
Scene 4
"Something's Rotten in Denmark"
L. Marshall, I. Lee, J. Gibson, Chorus
"Denmark Is Still"
L. Marshall, B. D'Angelo, Chorus
"Twist Her Mind"
R. Dodd, L. Marshall, B. D'Angelo, Chorus
"Gentle Lover"
B. D'Angelo
"Where Is the Reason"
L. Marshall
Scene 5
"The Wart Song"
Players, Chorus
"He Got It in the Ear"
J. Gibson
"It Is Done"
L. Marshall, R. Dodd

ACT 2
Scene 1
"Midnight—Hot Blood"
L. Marshall
"Midnight Mass"
L. Marshall, L. Galloway, A. Weeks, M. Loaf, Choir
"Hey . . . !"
C. Chadman, W. D. Hemsley, A. Weeks
"Sing Alone"
L. Marshall
Scene 2
"Your Daddy's Gone Away"
R. Dodd
"Rockabye Hamlet"
B. D'Angelo
"All by Yourself"
K. Milford
"Rosencrantz & Guildenstern Boogie"
A. Weeks, Chorus Girls
"Laertes Coercion"
A. Weeks, K. Milford, L. Galloway, Chorus Girls
"The Last Blues"
L. Galloway
Scene 3
"Didn't She Do It for Love"
M. Loaf, A. Weeks, L. Marshall, K. Milford, Chorus
"If My Morning Begins"
L. Marshall
Scene 4
"Swordfight"
A. Weeks, L. Marshall, K. Milford, L. Galloway, R. Dodd, Chorus

1976.04 BUBBLING BROWN SUGAR

A Musical Revue in Two Acts, 9 Scenes[9] . Book by Loften Mitchell. Based on a concept by Rosetta LeNoire. Additional music by Danny Holgate, Emme Kemp, Lillian Lopez. Directed by Robert M. Cooper. Choreography and musical staging by Billy Wilson. Musical direction by Danny Holgate. Sets by Clarke Dunham. Costumes by Bernard Johnson. Lighting by Barry Arnold. Projections by Lucie D. Grosvenor, Clarke Dunham. Choral arrangements by Chapman Roberts. Sound design by Joel S. Fichman. A Media House Production. Produced by J. Lloyd Grant, Richard Bell, Robert M. Cooper, Ashton Springer in association with Moe Septee, Inc. Opened 2 March 1976 at the ANTA Theatre and closed 31 December 1977 after 766 performances.

CAST (in order of appearance): *Skip*: Lonnie McNeil. *Bill*: VERNON WASHINGTON. *Ray*: Newton Winters. *Carolyn*: CAROLYN BYRD. *Norma*: Karen Grannum. *Gene*: Alton Lathrop. *Helen*: Dyann Robinson. *Laura*: Charlise Harris. *Marsha*: VIVIAN REED. *Tony*: Anthony Whitehouse. *Irene Paige*: JOSEPHINE PREMICE. *John Sage*: AVON LONG. *Checkers*: JOSEPH ATTLES. *Jim*: CHIP GARNETT. *Ella*: ETHEL BEATTY. *Time Man*: VERNON WASHINGTON. *Waiter*: Anthony Whitehouse. *Judy*: BARBARA RUBENSTEIN. *Charlie*: BARRY PRESTON. *Gospel Lady's Son*: Alton Lathrop. *Gospel Lady*: CAROLYN BYRD. *Young Irene*: VIVIAN REED. *Young Sage*: Newton Winters. *Young Checkers*: Lonnie McNeil. *Female Nightclub Singer*: CAROLYN BYRD. *The Solitunes*: Alton Lathrop, Lonnie McNeil, Newton Winters. *Male Nightclub Singer*: CHIP GARNETT. *Dusty*: JOSEPH ATTLES. *Rusty*: AVON LONG. *Bumpy*: VERNON WASHINGTON. *Count*: BARRY PRESTON. *Dutch*: Anthony Whitehouse. *Dutch's Girl*: BARBARA RUBENSTEIN. *Emcee*: VERNON WASHINGTON.
Chorus: Murphy Cross, Nedra Dixon, Emme Kemp, Stanley Ramsey.

Act 1, Scene 1: Harlem Today. The rest of the action takes place in old Harlem between 1920 and 1940. *Scene 2*: Downtown Speakeasy. *Scene 3*: 125th Street and Seventh Avenue. *Scene 4*: 135th Street and Lenox Avenue. *Scene 5*: Harlem Night Spots. *Scene 6*: At the Savoy.

Act 2, Scene 1: Lenox Avenue—A few minutes later. *Scene 2*: Another street in Harlem. *Scene 3*: Small's Paradise.

ACT 1
Scene 1
"Harlem '70"[10]
Company
(*Music by* Danny Holgate. *Lyrics by* Loften Mitchell.)
"Bubbling Brown Sugar"[11]
Company
(*Music by* Danny Holgate. *Lyrics by* Lillian Lopez and Emme Kemp.)
"(That's) What Harlem Is to Me" (from CONNIE'S HOT CHOCOLATES OF 1935)
(*Music and Lyrics by* Andy Razaf, Russell Wooding, Paul Denniker.)
J. Premice
Bill Robinson Specialty
V. Washington
"Harlem Sweet Harlem"[12]
Company
(*Music by* Danny Holgate. *Lyrics by* Loften Mitchell.)
"Nobody" (interpolated into ZIEGFELD FOLLIES OF 1910)
A. Long
(*Music and Lyrics by* Axel Rogers and Bert Williams.)
"Goin' Back in Time"[13]
V. Washington
(*Music by* Danny Holgate.)

[9]First produced in New York in an earlier version Off-Off Broadway 14 February 1975 at the AMAS Repertory Theatre for 12 performances.
[10]Original music written for this production.
[11]Original music written for this production.
[12]Original music written for this production.
[13]Original music written for this production.

Scene 2

"Some of These Days"

B. Rubenstein

(*Music and Lyrics by* Shelton Brooks.)

"Moving Uptown"[14]

V. Washington

(*Music by* Danny Holgate. *Lyrics by* Loften Mitchell and Emme Kemp.)

Scene 3

"Strolling"[15]

A. Lathrop, C. Harris, L. McNeil, K. Grannum, N. Winters, D. Robinson

(*Music by* Danny Holgate.)

Scene 4

"I'm Gonna Tell God All My Troubles" (traditional)

A. Lathrop

Medley: "His Eye Is on the Sparrow"/"Swing Low, Sweet Chariot" (traditional)

C. Byrd, Company

"Sweet Georgia Brown"

V. Reed, L. McNeil, N. Winters

(*Music and Lyrics by* Maceo Pinkard, Ben Bernie and Kenneth Casey.)

"Honeysuckle Rose" (from LOAD OF COAL)

J. Premice, A. Long

(*Music by* Fats Waller. *Lyrics by* Andy Razaf.)

Scene 5

"Stormy Monday Blues"

C. Byrd

(*Music and Lyrics by* Earl Hines, Billy Eckstine and Bob Crowder.)

"Rosetta"

A. Lathrop, L. McNeil, N. Winters

(*Music and Lyrics by* Earl Hines and Henri Woode.)

"Sophisticated Lady"

C. Garnett, D. Robinson, V. Washington

(*Music by* Duke Ellington. *Lyrics by* Irving Mills and Mitchell Parish.)

"In Honeysuckle Time (When Emaline Said She'd Be Mine)" (from SHUFFLE ALONG)

A. Long, J. Attles

(*Music by* Eubie Blake. *Lyrics by* Noble Sissle.)

"Solitude"

V. Reed, A. Lathrop, L. McNeil, N. Winters

(*Music by* Duke Ellington. *Lyrics by* Eddie DeLange and Irving Mills.)

Scene 6

"C'mon Up to Jive Time"[16]

V. Washington

(*Music by* Danny Holgate.)

Medley: "Stompin' at the Savoy"

(*Music by* Benny Goodman, Edgar Sampson and Chick Webb. *Lyrics by* Andy Razaf.)

"Take the "A" Train"

(*Music and Lyrics by* Duke Ellington and Billy Strayhorn.)

Company

ACT 2

Scene 1

"Harlem—Time"[17]

V. Washington

(*Music by* Danny Holgate.)

"Love Will Find a Way" (from SHUFFLE ALONG)

C. Garnett, E. Beatty

(*Music by* Eubie Blake. *Lyrics by* Noble Sissle.)

"Dutch's Song"[18]

A. Whitehouse

(*Music and Lyrics by* Emme Kemp.)

"Brown Gal"

A. Long

(*Music and Lyrics by* Avon Long and Lil Armstrong.)

"Pray for the Lights to Go Out"

J. Attles

(*Music and Lyrics by* Renton Tunnan and Will Skidmore.)

Scene 2

"I Got It Bad" (from JUMP FOR JOY)

E. Beatty

(*Music by* Duke Ellington. *Lyrics by* Paul Francis Webster.)

"Harlem Makes Me Feel!"[19]

B. Preston

(*Music and Lyrics by* Emme Kemp.)

Scene 3

"Jim, Jam, Jumpin' Jive"

V. Washington, L. McNeil, N. Winters

(*Music and Lyrics by* Cab Calloway.)

"There'll Be Some Changes Made"

J. Premice

(*Music and Lyrics by* W. Benton Overstreet and Billy Higgins.)

"God Bless the Child"

V. Reed

(*Music and Lyrics by* Arthur Herzog, Jr. and Billie Holliday.)

"It Don't Mean a Thing (If It Ain't Got That Swing)"

C. Garnett, A. Whitehouse, K. Premice, Company

(*Music by* Duke Ellington. *Lyrics by* Irving Mills.)

1976.05

MY FAIR LADY

A Revival of the Musical (Comedy) in Two Acts, 18 Scenes[20]. Book and lyrics by Alan Jay Lerner. Based on the play "Pygmalion" by George Bernard Shaw, produced on the screen by Gabriel Pascal. Music by Frederick Loewe. Directed by Jerry Adler based on the original by Moss Hart. Choreography and musical numbers staged by Crandall Diehl, based on the original by Hanya Holm. Production (settings) designed by Oliver Smith. Costumes designed by Cecil Beaton. Special costume assistant, W. Robert Lavine. Musical arrangements (orchestrations) by Robert Russell Bennett and Philip J. Lang. Lighting designed by John Gleason. Dance music arranged by Trude Rittman. Musical director, Theodore Saidenberg. Produced by Herman Levin. Opened 25 March 1976 at the St. James Theatre and closed 20 February 1977 after 384 performances.

CAST (in order of appearance): *Buskers*: Debra Lyman, Stan Picus, Ernie Pysher. *Mrs. Eynsford-Hill*: Eleanor Phelps. *Freddy Eynsford-Hill*: JERRY LANNING *Eliza Doolittle*: CHRISTINE ANDREAS. *Colonel Pickering*: ROBERT COOTE. *Henry Higgins*: IAN RICHARDSON. *First Cockney*: Kevin Marcum. *Second Cockney*: Jack Starkey. *Third Cockney*: William James. *Fourth Cockney*: Stan Page. *Bartender*: Kevin Lane Dearinger. *Harry*: John Clarkson. *Jamie*: Richard Neilson. *Alfred P. Doolittle*: GEORGE ROSE. *Mrs. Pearce*: Sylvia O'Brien. *Mrs. Hopkins*: Margaretta Warwick. *Butler*: Clifford Fearl. *Servants*: Sonja Anderson, Lynn Fitzpatrick, Karen Gibson, Vickie Patik, Kevin Lane Dearinger. *Mrs. Higgins*: BRENDA FORBES. *Chauffeur*: Jack Karcher. *Footmen*: Kevin Lane Dearinger Stan Page. *Lord Boxington*: John Clarkson. *Lady Boxington*: Margaretta Warwick. *Constable*: Timothy Smith. *Flower Girl*: Dru Alexandrine. *Flunkey*: William James. *Zoltan Karpathy*: JOHN CLARKSON. *Queen of Transylvania*: Karen Gibson. *Ambassador*: Richard Neilson. *Bartender*: Clifford Fearl. *Mrs. Higgins' Maid*: Sonja Stuart.

Singing Ensemble: Sonja Anderson, Alyson Bristol, Lynn Fitzpatrick, Karen Gibson, Cynthia Meryl, Vickie Patik, Kevin Lane Dearinger, Clifford Fearl, William James, Kevin Marcum, Stan Page, Jack Starkey. *Dancing Ensemble*: Dru Alexandrine, Sally Benoit, Marie Berry, Debra Lyman, Mari McMinn, Gina Ramsel, Catherine Rice, Sonja Stuart, Bonnie Walker, Richard Ammon, Jeremy Blanton, David Evans, Jack Karcher, Richard Maxon, Stan Picus, Ernie Pysher, Rick Schneider, Timothy Smith.

1976.06

MONTY PYTHON LIVE!

A Comedy Revue in Two Acts[21]. Conceived and written by Graham Chapman, John Cleese, Terry Gilliam, Eric Idle, Terry Jones, Michael Palin. American scenic supervision by Karl Eigsti. Sound by Abe Jacob. Lighting design by John Gleason. Wardrobe coordinator, Ann Goodson. Produced by Artists Consultants, Inc. (Allen Tinkley, Lou Robin, Tom

[14]Original music written for this production.
[15]Original music written for this production.
[16]Original music written for this production.
[17]Original music written for this production.
[18]Original music written for this production. Dropped for national tour. "Ain't Misbehavin" added for tour.

[19]Original music written for this production.
[20]Originally produced in New York 15 March 1956 at the Mark Hellinger Theatre for 2717 peformances. For Synopsis of Scenes and Musical Numbers, see original 1956 production.
[21]Comedy sketches, with no other performance details given.

Robin). Opened 15 April 1976 at the New York City Center and closed 2 May 1976 after 22 performances.

CAST: GRAHAM CHAPMAN, JOHN CLEESE, TERRY GILLIAM, ERIC IDLE, TERRY JONES, MICHAEL PALIN, Carol Cleveland, Neil Innes.

1976.07 SHIRLEY MacLAINE

A Musical Revue in One Act. Written by Fred Ebb. Music arranged or composed by Cy Coleman. Additional material by Bob Wells. Directed and staged by Tony Charmoli. Musical director, Donn Trenner. Special choreography by Alan Johnson. Lighting design by Richard Winkler. Lighting consultant, Graham Large. Sound consultant, Steve Wooley. Produced by HMT Associates. Opened 19 April 1976 at the Palace Theatre and closed 1 May 1976 after 20 performances; returned 9 July 1976 to the Palace Theatre and closed 24 July 1976 after 20 additional performances. Total: 40 performances.

CAST: SHIRLEY MacLAINE.

Gypsies: Candy Brown[22], Jo Ann Lehmann, Gary Flannery, Adam Grammis, Larry Vickers.

MUSICAL NUMBERS[23]

"If My Friends Could See Me Now" (from *SWEET CHARITY*)
S. MacLaine, A. Grammis, G. Flannery
(*Lyrics by* Dorothy Fields.)

"(My) Personal Property"[24]
(from film SWEET CHARITY)
S. MacLaine
(*Lyrics by* Dorothy Fields.)

"Remember Me?"
(from MR. DODDS TAKES THE AIR film)
S. MacLaine
(*Music by* Harry Warren. *Lyrics by* Al Dubin.)

"Hey, Big Spender"
(from SWEET CHARITY)
C. Brown, J. A. Lehmann, S. MacLaine
(*Lyrics by* Dorothy Fields.)

"I'm a Person Too"
S. MacLaine
(*Lyrics by* Bob Wells.)

"Irma la Douce"[25]
(from IRMA LA DOUCE film)
S. MacLaine
(*Music by* Andre Previn.)

"(The) Gypsy in My Soul"
(from JOHN PAUL JONES, Mask & Wig Show)
S. MacLaine, The Gypsies
(*Music and Lyrics by* Clay Boland and Moe Jaffee.)

"It's Not Where You Start"
(from SEESAW)
S. MacLaine, The Gypsies
(*Lyrics by* Dorothy Fields.)

"Every Little Movement Has a Meaning All Its Own"
(from MADAME SHERRY)
S. MacLaine, The Gypsies
(*Music by* Karl Hoschna. *Lyrics by* Otto Harbach.)

"The Hustle" (The Donkey Serenade)
(from THE FIREFLY film)
S. MacLaine, The Gypsies
(*Music by* Rudolf Friml and Herbert Stothart. *Lyrics by* Robert Wright and George Forrest.)

"(She's a) Star"
S. MacLaine
(*Music and Lyrics by* Serge Lama, A. Dona and Fred Ebb.)

"I'm a Brass Band"
(from SWEET CHARITY)
S. MacLaine, The Gypsies
(*Lyrics by* Dorothy Fields.)

[22]For return engagement Barbara Alston replaced Candy Brown.
[23]Added (after "Remember Me?") for the return engagement:
"Steam Heat" (from *THE PAJAMA GAME*)S. MacLaine, G. Flannery, L. Vickers
(*Music and Lyrics by* Richard Adler and Jerry Ross. *Choreography by* Bob Fosse, recreated by Zoya Leporska.)
[24]Dropped for return engagement.
[25]Dropped for return engagement.

1976.08 REX

A Musical in Two Acts, 23 Scenes. Book by Sherman Yellen. Music by Richard Rodgers. Lyrics by Sheldon Harnick. Directed by Edwin Sherin. Choreography by Dania Krupska. Orchestrations by Irwin Kostal. Musical director, Jay Blackton. Dance arrangements by David Baker. Scenery and costumes by John Conklin. Lighting by Jennifer Tipton. Produced by Richard Adler in association with Roger Berlind and Edward R. Downe, Jr. Opened 25 April 1976 at the Lunt-Fontanne Theatre and closed 5 June 1976 after 48 performances.

CAST (in order of appearance): *Norfolk*: Charles Rule. *Cardinal Wolsey*: WILLIAM GRIFFIS. *Will Somers*: TOM ALDREDGE. *Henry VIII, King of England*: NICOL WILLIAMSON. *Mark Smeaton*: ED EVANKO. *Princess Mary*: GLENN CLOSE. *Queen Catherine of England*: BARBARA ANDRES. *Lady Jane Seymour*: APRIL SHAWHAN. *Francis, King of France*: STEPHEN D. NEWMAN. *English Herald*: Danny Ruvolo. *French Herald*: Jeff Phillips. *Queen Claude of France*: MARTHA DANIELLE. *Anne Boleyn; Princess Elizabeth*: PENNY FULLER. *Dauphin*: KEITH KOPPMEIER. *Comus*: MERWIN GOLDSMITH. *First Guard*: Ken Henley. *Lady Margaret*: MARTHA DANIELLE. *Lady in Waiting*: Melanie Vaughan. *Young Princess Elizabeth*: Sparky Shapiro. *Nurse*: Lillian Shelby. *Second Guard*: Dennis Daniels. *Thomas Cromwell*: Gerald R. Teijelo. *Catherine Howard*: Valerie Mahaffey. *Prince Edward*: MICHAEL JOHN. *Queen Katherine Parr of England*: MARTHA DANIELLE.

Ladies and Gentlemen of the Courts: Dennis Daniels, Harry Fawcett, Paul Forrest, Pat Gideon, Ken Henley, Dawn Herbert, Robin Hoff, Don Johanson, Jim Litten, Craig Lucas, Carol Jo Lugenbeal, Valerie Mahaffey, G. Eugene Moose, Jeff Phillips, Charles Rule, Danny Ruvolo, Lillian Shelby, Jo Speros, Gerald R. Teijelo, Jr., Candace Tovar, John Ulrickson, Melanie Vaughan. *Sword and Morris Dancers*: Dennis Daniels, Ken Henley, Don Johnson, Jim Litten, Jeff Phillips, Danny Ruvolo.

The action takes place during the reign of Henry VIII of England until his death.

Act 1, Scene 1: Greenwich Palace. *Scene 2*: Henry's Tent. *Scene 3*: Field of Cloth of Gold. *Scene 4*: French Pavilion. *Scene 5*: Comus' Chambers. *Scene 6*: Hever Castle. *Scene 7*: Hampton Court Palace. *Scene 8*: Chapel. *Scene 9*: The Throne Room. *Scene 10*: Hampton Court Corridor. *Scene 11*: Queen Anne's Bedroom .*Scene 12*: Comus' Lab. *Scene 13*: The Palace. *Scene 14*: The Tower of London. *Scene 15*: The Coronation. *Scene 16*: The City of London.

Act 1, Scene 1: Hampton Court Palace. Ten years later. *Scene 2*: The Great Wall at Hampton Court Palace. *Scene 3*: The Throne Room. *Scene 4*: Hampton Court Corridor. *Scene 5*: Comus' Laboratory. *Scene 6*: Henry's Bedroom. *Scene 7*: The Throne Room.

ACT 1

Scene 1

"Te Deum"
Company

Scene 2

"No Song More Pleasing"
E. Evanko

Scene 3

"Where Is My Son?"

ACT 1

Scene 1

"Te Deum"
Company

Scene 2

"No Song More Pleasing"
E. Evanko

Scene 3

"Where Is My Son?"
N. Williamson

"The Field of Cloth of Gold"
Company

Scene 4

Basse Dance
Company

Scene 6

"The Chase"
M. Goldsmith, T. Aldredge, E. Evanko, Gentlemen of the Court

Scene 7
"Away From You"
N. Williamson
Scene 8
"As Once I Loved You"
B. Andres
Scene 11
"Elizabeth"
E. Evanko, M. Danielle, M. Vaughan
Scene 12
"What Now?"[26]
N. Williamson
Scene 13
"No Song More Pleasing" (reprise)
A. Shawhan, N. Williamson
"Away from You" (reprise)
P. Fuller
Scene 16
"Te Deum" (reprise)
Company

ACT 2
Scene 1
"Christmas at Hampton Court"
P. Fuller, M. John, G . Close
Scene 2
"The Wee Golden Warrior"
T. Aldredge, M. John, P. Fuller, G. Close
Sword Dance and Morris Dance
Sword and Morris dancers
"The Masque"
Ladies and Gentlemen of the Court
Scene 3
"From Afar"
N. Williamson
Scene 4
"In Time"
P. Fuller, T. Aldredge
Scene 7
"In Time" (reprise)
P. Fuller, M. John
"Te Deum" (reprise)
Company

1976.09 SO LONG, 174th STREET

A Musical in One Act. Scenes. Book by Joseph Stein. Based on his play "Enter Laughing" from the novel by Carl Reiner. Music and lyrics by Stan Daniels. Directed by Burt Shevelove. Choreography by Alan Johnson. Scenery by James Riley. Costumes by Stanley Simmons. Lighting by Richard Nelson. Musical direction by John Lesko. Orchestrations by Luther Henderson. Dance music arrangements by Wally Harper. Production supervisor, Stone Widney. Produced by Frederick Brisson in asssociation with the Harkness Organization and Wyatt Dickerson. Opened 27 April 1976 at the Harkness Theatre and closed 9 May 1976 after 16 performances.

CAST (in order of appearance): *David (Kolowitz)*: ROBERT MORSE. *Stage Manager*: Joe Howard. *Girl*: Freda Soiffer. *Barrymore*: GENE VARRONE. *Pope*: ROBERT BARRY. *King*: Richard Marr. *Roosevelt*: David Berk. *Eleanor Roosevelt*: Nancy Killmer. *Mr. Foreman*: MITCHELL JASON. *Wanda*: LONI ACKERMAN. *Marvin*: LAWRENCE JOHN MOSS. *Miss B*: SYDNEY BLAKE. *Harry Hamburger*: ROBERT BARRY. *Waiter*: GENE VARRONE. *Pike*: GENE VARRONE. *Don Baxter*: Chuck Beard. *Don Darwin*: Michael Blue Aiken. *Angela*: BARBARA LANG. *Marlowe*: GEORGE S. IRVING. *Ziegfeld*: GENE VARRONE. *Papa*: LEE GOODMAN. *Soda Jerk*: James Brennan. *Butler*: GEORGE S. IRVING. *Judge*: GEORGE S. IRVING. *Peabody*: Richard Marr. *Man*: James Brennan.

[26]Replaced after opening with:
"Why?"
N. Williamson

Ensemble: Jill Cook, Nancy Killmer, Meribeth Kisner, Denise Mauthe, Rita Rudner, Freda Soiffer, Michael Blue Aiken, Chuck Beard, David Berk, Joe Howard, Richard Marr, William Swiggard.

The action takes place at the present time and the late 1930's in New York City.

MUSICAL NUMBERS
"David Kolowitz, the Actor"
R. Morse, Ensemble
"It's Like"
R. Morse, L. Ackerman
"Undressing Girls With My Eyes"
R. Morse, L. J. Moss, Girls
"Bolero on Rye"
R. Morse, S. Blake, G. Varrone
"Whoever You Are"
R. Morse
"Say the Words"
B. Lang
"My Son the Druggist"
L. Goodman
"You Touched Her"
R. Morse, L. J. Moss, Men
"Men"
L. Ackerman, J. Brennan, Girls
"Boy Oh Boy"
R. Morse, Company
"The Butler's Song"
G. S. Irving
"Being With You"
L. Ackerman, R. Morse
"If You Want to Break Your Father's Heart"
R. Morse, L. Goodman, G. S.Irving, Jury
"So Long, 174th Street"
R. Morse, Family, Friends, Neighbors
"David Kolowitz, the Actor" (reprise)
Company
Finale
Company

1976.10 THREEPENNY OPERA

A Revival of the Musical in Three Acts[27]. Libretto by Bertolt Brecht. Music by Kurt Weill. New translation by Ralph Manheim and John Willett. Directed by Richard Foreman. Scenic design by Douglas W. Schmidt. Costumes by Theoni V. Aldredge. Lighting by Pat Collins. Sound by Roger Jay (Joseph Dungan). Music direction by Stanley Silverman. Associate producer, Bernard Gersten. A New York Shakespeare Festival Production. Produced by Joseph Papp. Opened 1 May 1976 at the Vivian Beaumont Theatre and closed 23 January 1977 after 306 performances[28]

CAST (in order of appearance): *The Ballad Singer*: Roy Brocksmith. *Mack The Knife* (Macheath): RAUL JULIA. *Jenny Towler*: ELLEN GREENE. *Jonathan Peachum*: C. K. ALEXANDER. *Samuel*, Peachum's Assistant: Tony Azito. *Charles Filch*: Ed Zang. *Mrs. Peachum*: ELIZABETH WILSON. *Matt*: Ralph Driscoll. *Polly Peachum*: CAROLINE KAVA. *Jake*: William Duell. *Bob*: K. C. Wilson. *Ned*: Rik Colitti. *Jimmy*: Robert Schlee. *Walt*: Max Gulack. *Tiger Brown*: DAVID SABIN. *Smith*: Glenn Kezer. *Lucy Brown*: BLAIR BROWN. *A Constable*: John Ridge. *Messenger*: Jack Eric Williams.

Beggars and Policemen: Pendleton Brown, M. Patrick Hughes, George McGrath, Rick Petrucelli, John Ridge, Craig Rupp, Armin Shimerman, Jack Eric Williams, Ray Xifo. *Whores*: Penelope Bodry, Nancy Campbell, Gretel Cummings, Brenda Currin, Mimi Turque.

The action takes place in London at the time of Queen Victoria's Coronation, rearranged in Brecht's imagination.

ACT 1
Prologue
"Ballad of Mack the Knife"
R. Brocksmith, T. Azito, R. Schlee, J. E. Williams

[27]First produced in New York in English 13 April 1933 at the Empire Theatre for 12 performances; revived Off-Broadway in a translation by Marc Blitzstein at the Theatre de Lys 10 March 1954 for 96 performances, 20 September 1955 at the Theatre de Lys for 2,611 performances.
[28]Reopened a return engagement Off Broadway 6-24 July 1977 at the Delacorte Theatre for 20 performances.

Scene 1
"Peachum's Morning Hymn"
C. K. Alexander
"'No They Can't' Song"
C. K. Alexander, E. Wilson
Scene 2
"Wedding Song for the Less Well-Off"
Gang, Beggars
"The Cannon Song"
R. Julia, D. Sabin, Gang
"Liebeslied"
C. Kava, R. Julia
Scene 3
"Barbara Song"
C. Kava
First Threepenny Finale: "Concerning the Insecurity of the Human State"
C. Kava, C. K. Alexander, E. Wilson

ACT 2
Scene 1
"Polly's Lied"
C. Kava, R. Julia
"Ballad of Sexual Obsession"
E. Wilson
Scene 2
"Pirate Jenny"
E. Greene
"Ballad of Immoral Earnings"
E. Greene, R. Julia
Scene 3
"Ballad of Gracious Living"
R. Julia
"Jealousy Duet"
B. Brown, C. Kava
Second Threepenny Finale: "What Keeps Mankind Alive?"
R. Julia, E. Greene, Chorus

ACT 3
Scene 1
"Song of the Insufficiency of Human Endeavor"
C. K. Alexander
"Solomon Song"
E. Greene
Scene 3
"Call from the Grave"
R. Julia
"Ballad in Which Macheath Begs All Men for Forgiveness"
R. Julia
Third Threepenny Finale
D. Sabin, G. Kezer, R. Brocksmith, J. E. Williams, E. Wilson, C. K. Alexander, R. Julia, C. Kava, B. Brown, E. Greene, Chorus
"Ballad of Mack the Knife" (reprise)
R. Brocksmith

1976.11 1600 PENNSYLVANIA AVENUE

A Musical About the Problems of Housekeeping in Two Acts. Book and lyrics by Alan Jay Lerner. Music by Leonard Bernstein. Entire production co-directed, staged and choreographed by Gilbert Moses and George Faison. Scenery designed by Kert Lundell. Costumes coordinated by Whitney Blausen, Dona Granata. Lighting by Tharon Musser. Musical direction, Roland Gagnon. Orchestrations by Sid Ramin and Hershy Kay. Sound design by John McClure. Produced by Roger L. Stevens and Robert Whitehead by arrangement with Saint Subber. Opened 4 May 1976 at the Mark Hellinger Theatre and closed 8 May 1976 after 7 performances.

CAST: *The President*: KEN HOWARD. *The President's Wife*: PATRICIA ROUTLEDGE. *Lud*: GILBERT PRICE. *Seena*: EMILY YANCY. *Little Lud*: Guy Costley. *Stage Manager*: David E. Thomas.

The Thirteen Delegates: *NewYork*: Howard Ross. *Pennsylvania*: Reid Shelton. *New Hampshire*: Ralph Farnworth. *Rhode Island*: J. T. Cromwell. *Connecticut*: Lee Winston. *New Jersey*: Walter Charles. *Virginia*: Edwin Steffe. *North Carolina*: John Witham. *South Carolina*: Richard Muenz. *Delaware*: Alexander Orfaly. *Maryland*: Raymond Cox. *Georgia*: Randolph Riscol.

The Staff: *Henry*: Raymond Bazemore. *Rachel*: Urylee Leonardos. *Coley*: Carl Hall. *Joby*: Janette Moody. *Broom*: Howard Ross. *Jim*: Cornel J. Richie. *Sally*: Louise Heath.

The British: *Ordway*: Walter Charles. *Pimms*: John Witham. *Barker*: Lee Winston. *Glieg*: Raymond Cox. *Maitland*: Alexander Orfaly. *Ross*: Edwin Steffe. *Pratt*: Richard Chappell. *Scott*: J. T. Cromwell. *Budgen*: Richard Muenz. *Cockburn*: Reid Shelton. *Reverend Bushrod*: Bruce A. Hubbard. *Auctioneer*: Lee Winston. *James Hoban*: Edwin Steffe. *Royal Visitor*: Raldolph Riscol. *Secretary of the Senate*: Howard Ross. *Mr. Henry*: Lee Winston. *Senator Roscoe Conkling*: Reid Shelton. *Babcock*: Lee Winston. *Secretary of the Senate*: Howard Ross.

Singers: Raymond Bazemore, Elaine Bunse, Nancy Callman, Richard Chappell, Walter Charles, Raymond Cox, J. T. Cromwell, Beth Fowler, Carl Hall, Louise Heath, Bruce A. Hubbard, Kris Karlowski, Urylee Leonardos, Joyce MacDonald, Janette Moody, Richard Muenz, Sharon Powers, Cornel J. Richie, Randolph Riscol, Martha Thigpen, Lee Winston. *Dancers*: Jo-Ann Baldo, Clyde-Jacques Barrett, Joella Breedlove, Allyne DeChalus, Linda Griffin, Bob Heath, Michael Lichtefeld, Diana Mirras, Hector Jaime Mercado, Cleveland Pennington, Al Perryman, Renee Rose, Juliet Seignious, Thomas J. Stanton, Clayton Strange, Mimi B. Wallace. *Swings*: Leah Randolph, Martial Roumain.

The action takes place at The White House in Washington, D.C.

ACT 1
"Rehearse!"
K. Howard, P. Routledge, G. Price, E. Yancy, Entire Company
"If I Was a Dove"
G. Costley
"On Ten Square Miles by the Potomac River"
K. Howard, Delegates
"Welcome Home Miz Adams"
R. Bazemore, U. Leonardos, Staff
"Take Care of This House"
K. Howard, P. Routeldge, G. Costley, Staff
"The President Jefferson Sunday Luncheon Party March"
K. Howard, G. Costley, Guests
"Seena"
G. Price
"Sonatina (The British)"
R. Shelton, Officers, Citizens
1. Allegro con brio
2. Temp di Menuetto (including an authentic harmonization of "To Anacreon in Heav'n" (1740) later known as "The Star Spangled Banner")
3. Rondo
"Lud's Wedding"/"I Love My Wife"
G. Price, E. Yancy, Staff
"Auctions"
L. Winston, Buyers
"The Little White Lie"
K. Howard, P. Routledge
"We Must Have a Ball"
K. Howard
"The Ball"
Entire Company

ACT 2
"Forty Acres and a Mule"
The Staff
"Bright and Black"
E. Yancy, Staff
"Duet for One" ("The First Lady of the Land")
P. Routledge [as Julia Grant, Lucy Hayes], Company
"The Robber-Baron Minstrel Parade"
The Minstrels
"Pity the Poor"
The Minstrels
"The Red White and Blues"
The Minstrels
"I Love This Land"
K. Howard
"Rehearse!" (reprise)
Entire Company

THE MIKADO,
1976.01 or The Town of Titipu

A Revival of the Comic Opera in Two Acts[29]. Libretto by William S. Gilbert. Music by Arthur Sullivan. Production director, Michael Heyland. Costumes designed by Charles Ricketts. Nanki-Poo, Act 1 Costume designed by Disley Jones. Scenery by Disley Jones. Musical director, Royston Nash. Chorus master and assistant conductor, Glyn Hale. Produced by James M. Nederlander by arrangement with the D'Oyly Carte Opera Trust, Ltd. and Dame Bridget D'Oyly Carte. Opened 5 May 1976 at the Uris Theatre and closed 23 May 1976 after 10 performances in repertory.

CAST: *The Mikado of Japan*: JOHN AYLDON. *Nanki-Poo*, his son, disguised as a wandering minstrel in love with Yum-Yum: GEOFFREY SHOVELTON. *Ko-Ko*, Lord High Executioner of Titipu: JOHN REED. *Pooh-Bah*, Lord High Everything Else: KENNETH SANDFORD. *Pish-Tush, Go-To*, Noble Lords: Michael Rayner, Jon Ellison. *Yum-Yum, Pitti-Sing, Peep-Bo*, three sisters, wards of Ko-Ko: JULIA GOSS, JANE METCALFE, PATRICIA LEONARD. *Katisha*: LYNDSIE HOLLAND.

Chorus of School Girls, Nobles, Guards and Coolies: Michael Buchan, Paul Burrows, Barry Clark, Malcolm Coy, Gareth Jones, Guy Matthews, William Palmerley, Edwin Rolles, Thomas Scholey, Alan Spencer, William Strachan, Paul Waite, Michael Westbury. Caroline Baker, Patricia Ann Bennett, Gillian Burrows, Lorraine Dulcie-Daniels, Anne Egglestone, Josephine Hinchley, Beti Lloyd-Jones, Elsie McDougall, Roberta Morrell, Helen Moulder, Suzanne O'Keefe, Andrea Phillips, Glynis Prendergast, Patricia Rea, Vivien Tierney.

THE PIRATES OF PENZANCE,
1976.13 or The Slave of Duty

A Revival of the Comic Opera in Two Acts[30]. Libretto by William S. Gilbert. Music by Arthur Sullivan. Setting designed by Peter Goffin. Production director, Michael Heyland. Musical director, Royston Nash. Chorus master and assistant conductor, Glyn Hale. Produced by James M. Nederlander by arrangement with the D'Oyly Carte Opera Trust, Ltd. and Dame Bridget D'Oyly Carte. Opened 6 May 1976 at the Uris Theatre and closed 12 May 1976 after 8 performances in repertory[31].

CAST: *Major General Stanley*: JAMES CONROY-WARD. *The Pirate King*: JOHN AYLDON. *Samuel*, his Lieutenant: Jon Ellison. *Frederic*, the Pirate Apprentice: MESTON REID. *Sergeant of Police*: MICHAEL RAYNER. *Mabel, Edith, Kate, Isabel*, General Stanley's Daughters: JULIA GOSS, JANE METCALFE, CAROLINE BAKER, Patricia Ann Bennett. *Ruth*, Pirate Maid-of-all-work: LYNDSIE HOLLAND. *Chorus of Pirates, Police and General Stanley's Daughters*: same as *THE MIKADO* above.

H.M.S. PINAFORE,
1976.14 or The Lass That Loved a Sailor

A Revival of the Comic Opera in Two Acts[32]. Libretto by William S. Gilbert. Music by Arthur Sullivan. Back cloth designed and painted by Joseph and Phil Harker. Production director, Michael Heyland. Musical director, Royston Nash. Chorus master and assistant conductor, Glyn Hale. Produced by James M. Nederlander by arranagement with the D'Oyly Carte Opera Trust, Ltd. and Dame Bridget D'Oyly Carte. Opened 16 May 1976 at the Uris Theatre and closed 19 May 1976 after 4 performances in repertory.

CAST: *The Rt. Hon. Sir Joseph Porter, K.C.B.*, First Lord of the Admiralty: JOHN REED. *Captain Corcoran*, Commanding the *H.M.S. Pinafore*: MICHAEL RAYNER. *Ralph Rackstraw*, Able Seaman: MESTON REID. *Dick Deadeye*, Able Seaman: JOHN AYLDON. *Bill Bobstay*, Bo'sun: Jon Ellison. *Bob Becket*, Bo'sun's Mate, Carpenter's Mate: Michael Buchan. *Josephine*, the Captain's Daughter: BARBARA LILLEY. *Hebe*, Sir Joseph's First Cousin: Patricia Leonard. *Little Buttercup*, Mrs. Cripps, a Portsmouth Bumboat Woman: LYNDSIE HOLLAND. *First Lord's Sisters, his Cousins, his Aunts, Sailors, Marines*: same as *THE MIKADO* above.

1976.15 SOMETHING'S AFOOT

A Murder Mystery Musical in Two Acts. Book, Music and Lyrics by James McDonald, David Vos and Robert Gerlach. Additional music by Ed Linderman. Directed and choreographed by Tony Tanner. Scenery by Richard Seger. Costumes by Walter Watson, Clifford Capone. Lighting by Richard Winkler. Musical director, Buster Davis. Orchestrations by Peter M. Larson. Sound by Robert Weeden. Produced by Emanuel Azenberg, Dasha Epstein and John Mason Kirby. Originally produced by the Goodpseed Opera House (Michael Price, Producer). Opened 27 May 1976 at the Lyceum Theatre and closed 18 July 1976 after 61 performances.

CAST (in order of appearance): *Lettie*: NEVA SMALL. *Flint*: MARC JORDAN. *Clive*: SEL VITELLA. *Hope Langdon*: BARBARA HEUMAN. *Dr. Grayburn*: JACK SCHMIDT. *Nigel Rancour*: GARY BEACH. *Lady Grace Manley-Prowe*: LIZ SHERIDAN. *Colonel Gillweather*: GARY GAGE. *Miss Tweed*: TESSIE O'SHEA. *Geoffrey*: WILLARD BECKHAM.

The action takes place during the late spring of 1935 at Rancour's Retreat, a country estate in the English lake district.

Act 1: The Entrance Hall of Rancour's Retreat.

Act 2: The same, immediately following.

ACT 1[33]

"A Marvelous Weekend"
(Entire Company [exc. W. Beckham])
"Something's Afoot"
(Entire Company [exc. W. Beckham])
"Carry On"
(T. O'Shea, L. Sheridan, N. Small, B. Heuman)
"I Don't Know Why I Trust You (But I Do)"
(B. Heuman, W. Beckham)
"The Man With the Ginger Mustache"
(L. Sheridan)
"Suspicious"
(Entire Company)

ACT 2

"The Legal Heir"
(G. Beach)
"You Fell Out of the Sky"
(B. Heuman)
"Dinghy"
(M. Jordan, N. Small)
"I Owe It All"
(T. O'Shea, B. Heuman, W. Beckham)
"New Day"
(W. Beckham, B. Heuman, Choir)

---

[29]First presented in New York 20 July, 10-29 August 1885 at the Union Square and People's Theatres for 22 performances. First authorized production presented 19 August 1885 at the Fifth Avenue Theatre by Richard D'Oyly Carte for 250 performances. For Synopsis of Scenes and Musical Numbers, see 19 August 1885 D'Oyly Carte production.

[30]First presented in New York 31 December 1879 at the Fifth Avenue Theatre for a total of 91 performances in two engagements. For Synopsis of Scenes and Musical Numbers, see original 1879 production.

[31]Costumes uncredited.

[32]Originally presented in New York 15 January 1879 at the Standard Theatre for 175 performances. For Synopsis of Scenes and Musical Numbers, see original 1879 production.

[33]Inasmuch as this is a murder mystery, the program omits the singers' names, which have been restored above based on the production manuscript.

1976–1977 SEASON

Dorothy Loudon, Robert Fitch, and Barbara Erwin in ANNIE
Martha Swope/TimePix

1976–1977 SEASON

1976.16 AN EVENING WITH DIANA ROSS

A Musical Revue in Two Acts. Special material by Billy Goldenberg and Bill Dyer. Additional material by Bruce Vilanch. Directed by Joe Layton. Musical director, Gil Askey. Lighting designed by John Gleason. Sound consultant, Trevor Jordan. A Danny O'Donovan/Sagittarius Entertainment Presentation. Produced by Danny O'Donovan. Opened 14 June 1976 at the Palace Theatre and closed 3 July 1976 after 18 performances.

CAST: DIANA ROSS, The Jones Girls (Shirley Yuvonne Jones, Brenda Elaine Jones, Valorie Denise Jones). *Mimes*: Hayward Coleman, Don McLeod, Stewart Fischer.

ACT 1

"Here I Am"
(*Music by* Burt Bacharach. *Lyrics by* Hal David.)

"I Wouldn't Change a Thing"
(*Music by* Burt Bacharach. *Lyrics by* Hal David.)

"The Lady Is a Tramp" (from *BABES IN ARMS*)
(*Music by* Richard Rodgers. *Lyrics by* Lorenz Hart.)

"Touch Me in the Morning"
(*Music and Lyrics by* Ron Miller and Michael Masser.)

"One Love in My Lifetime"
(*Music and Lyrics by* Larry Brown, Theresa McFaddin, Leonard Perry.)

"Smile" (Theme from film *MODERN TIMES*)
(*Music by* Charles Chaplin. *Lyrics by* John Turner and Geoffrey Parsons.)

"Love Hangover"
(*Music and Lyrics by* Pam Sawyer and Marilyn McLeod.)

"Girls"
(*Music and Lyrics by* John Phillips.)

Medley from "THE POINT" (*Music and Lyrics by* Harry Nilsson.):

"Everybody's Got 'Em"/"Me and My Arrow"/"Lifeline"

"Lady Sings the Blues" (used in film of the same name)
(*Music and Lyrics by* Billie Holiday and Herbie Nichols.)

"'Tain't Nobody's Bizness"
(*Music and Lyrics by* Porter Grainger, Clarence Williams and Graham Prince.)

"(Aux Iles) Hawaii"
(*Music and Lyrics by* Pascal Bastia and Jean Bastia.)

"Stormy Weather" (from *COTTON CLUB PARADE*, 22nd edition, 1933)
(*Music by* Harold Arlen. *Lyrics by* Ted Koehler.)

"(I Need a Little) Sugar in My Bowl"
(*Music and Lyrics by* C. Williams, D. Small, T. Brymn.)

"My Man" (from *ZIEGFELD FOLLIES OF 1921*)
(*Music by* Maurice Yvain. *Lyrics by* Channing Pollock.)

ACT 2

Motown History

Supremes

Medley from *A CHORUS LINE*:
"Play Me the Music" {"The Music and the Mirror"}, "What I Did for Love," "T & A" {"Dance: Ten, Looks: Three}
(*Music by* Marvin Hamlisch. *Lyrics by* Edward Kleban.)

Theme from "Mahagony" ("Do You Know Where You're Going To?")
(*Music and Lyrics by* Michael Masser and Gerry Goffin.)

"Ain't No Mountain High Enough"
(*Music and Lyrics by* Nick Ashford and Valerie Simpson.)

"Reach Out and Touch"
(*Music and Lyrics by* Nick Ashford and Valerie Simpson.)

1976.17 GODSPELL

A Musical in Two Acts[1]. Conceived and directed by John-Michael Tebelak. Based on The Gospel According to St. Matthew. Music and new lyrics by Stephen Schwartz. Lighting by Spencer Mosse. Costumes by Susan Tsu. Production supervision by Nina Faso. Musical director, Stephen Reinhardt. Sound by Robert Minor. Conductor, Paul Shaffer. Associate producer, Charles Haid. Produced by Edgar Lansbury, Stuart Duncan, Joseph Beruh and The Shubert Organization. Opened 22 June 1976 at the Broadhurst Theatre, moved 15 September 1976 to the Plymouth Theatre, moved 12 January 1977 to the Ambassador Theatre and closed 4 September 1977 after 527 performances. (Total including Off-Broadway run, 2645 performances.)

CAST (in alphabetical order): Lamar Alford, Laurie Faso, Lois Faraker, Robin Lamont, Elizabeth Lathram, Bobby Lee, Tom Rolfing, Don Scardino, Marley Sims, Valerie Williams.

ACT 1

"Tower of Babble"
Company

"Prepare Ye the Way of the Lord"
T. Rolfing, Company

"Save the People"
D. Scardino, Company

"Day By Day"
R. Lamont, Company

"Learn Your Lessons Well"
M. Sims

"Bless the Lord"
V. Williams, Company

"All For the Best"
D. Scardino, T. Rolfing

"All Good Gifts"
L. Alford, Company

"Light of the World"
L. Faso, Company

ACT 2

"Learn Your Lessons Well" (reprise)
L. Alford, Company

"Turn Back, O Man"
L. Foraker, Company

"Alas for You"
D. Scardino

"By My Side"
E. Lathram, Company
(*Music by* Peggy Gordon. *Lyrics by* Jay Hamburger.)

"We Beseech Thee"
B. Lee, Company

"On the Willows"
Band

Finale
Company

1976.18 THE MERRY WIDOW

The Australian Ballet in a ballet adaptation of the operetta in Three Acts, 4 Scenes. Music by Franz Lehàr. Original book by Victor Leon and Leo Stein. English version by Christopher Hassall[2]. Scenario and staging by Robert Helpmann. Choreography by Ronald Hynd. Design (scenery, costumes) by Desmond Heeley. Musical adaptation by John Lanchbery. Lighting supervised by John Gleason. Musical director, John Lanchbery. Conductors, Alan Barker, Alan Abbott. Produced by (Sol) Hurok Concerts Inc. in association with the Australian Ballet Foundation. Opened 22 June 1976 at the New York State Theatre and closed 3 July 1976 after 15 performances.

CAST (Principals, Soloists): *Baron Mirko Zeta*, Pontevedrian Ambassador to France: Robert Olup or Colin Peasley. *Valencienne*, his wife: MARIA LANG or Ai-Gul Gainina or Lucette Aldous. *Count Danilo Danilowitsch*, First Secretary of the Pontevedrian Embassy: JOHN MEEHAN or JONATHAN KELLY. *Camille de Rosillon*, French attaché at the Embassy: WALTER BOURKE or KELVIN COE. *Njegus*, Private Secretary to the Ambassador: RAY POWELL or ALAN ALDER. *Kromow*, Under-Secretary at the Embassy: Dale Baker or Rex McNeill. *Pritschitsch*, Under-Secretary at the Embassy: Mark Brinkley or Paul de Masson. *Hanna Glawari*, a wealthy

[1]Originally produced Off-Broadway 17 May 1971 at the Cherry Lane Theatre for 2118 performances.

[2]Christopher Hassall's new English libretto was first produced by the Sadler's Wells Opera in London in 1958 and has not otherwise been performed in New York. *THE MERRY WIDOW* was first produced in New York 21 October 1907 at the New Amsterdam Theatre for 416 performances.

Pontevedrian widow: MARGOT FONTEYN or MARILYN ROWE. *Pontevedrian Dancer*: Paul Saliba or Danilo Radojevic. *Maitre d' at Chez Maxime*: Paul Saliba.

Guests at the Embassy, Pontevedrians, Can Can Ladies, etc. (Artists): Glenda Allen, Stephen Baynes, Paul Cini, Amanda Clerke, Allan Cross, Michael Curry, Sheree da Costa, Irena Fogerty, Carol Green, Deborah Lerine, Angus Lugsdin, William Pepper, Terese Power, Danilo Radojevic, Martin Raistrick, Lucinda Sharp, Olga Tamara, Meryl Tankard, Nina Thomson, Dennis Trinder, Abril Ward.

The action takes place in Paris in 1905.

Act 1, Scene 1: An ante-room in the Pontevedrian Embassy. *Scene 2*: The ballroom in the Pontevedrian Embassy.

Act 2: The garden of Hanna's villa.

Act 3: Chez Maxime.

1976.19 PAL JOEY

A Revival of the Musical (Play) in Two Acts, 12 Scenes[3]. Book by John O'Hara (based on his collected short stories of the same name). Music by Richard Rodgers. Lyrics by Lorenz Hart. Scenery by John J. Moore. Costumes by Arthur Boccia. Lighting by Ron Wallace. Musical director, Scott Oakley. Choreography by Margo Sappington. Directed by Theodore Mann. Produced by the Circle in the Square Theatre (Theodore Mann, Artistic director; Paul Libin, Managing director). Opened 27 June 1976 at the Circle in the Square Theatre and closed 29 August 1976 after 73 performances[4].

CAST (in order of appearance): *Mike*: HAROLD GARY. *Joey Evans*: CHRISTOPHER CHADMAN. *Kid*: Terri Treas. *Gladys*: JANIE SELL. *Gail*: Gail Benedict. *Murphy*: Murphy Cross. *Rosamund*: Rosamund Lynn. *Marilu*: Marilu Henner. *Debbie*: Deborah Geffner. *Linda English*: BONI ENTEN. *Vera Simpson*: JOAN COPELAND. *Gent*: David Hodo. *Ernest*: Austin Colyer. *Waldo*, the Waiter: Denny Martin Flinn. *Victor*: Michael Leeds. *Delivery Boy*: Kenn Scalice. *Louis*, the Tenor: Adam Petroski. *Melba (Snyder)*: DIXIE CARTER. *Ludlow Lowell*: JOE SIROLA. *O'Brien*: Ralph Farnworth.

Boys and Girls: Gail Benedict, Murphy Cross, Deborah Geffner, Marilu Henner, Rosamund Lynn, Terri Treas, Denny Martin Flinn, David Hodo, Michael Leeds, Kenn Scalice.

1976.20 LET MY PEOPLE COME

A Sexual Musical (Revue) in Two Acts[5]. Music and lyrics by Earl Wilson, Jr. Directed by Phil Oesterman. Choreography by Charles Augins. Set and lighting by Duane F. Mazey. Set and costumes supervised by Douglas W. Schmidt. Lighting supervised by John Gleason. Musical direction and vocal arrangements by Norman Bergen. Conductor, Glen Roven. Produced by Phil Oesterman. Opened 22 July 1976 at the Morosco Theatre and closed 2 October 1976 after 106 performances. (Total including Off-Broadway run, 1273 performances.)

CAST (in alphabetical order): Brandy Alexander, Joanne Baron, Dwight Baxter, Pat Cleveland, Lorraine Davidson, Joelle Erasme, Yvette Freeman, Paul Gillespie, Gloria Goldman, Tulane Howard II, Bob Jockers, Empress Kilpatrick, Dianne Legro, Allan Lozito, Bryan Miller, Rod R. Neves, Rozaa, Don Scotti, Sterling Saint-Jacques, Bryan Spencer, Dean Tait, Lori Wagner, Charles Whiteside.

ACT 1

Opening ("Screw")
The Company

"Mirror"
B. Spencer, G. Goldman, P. Gillespie, E. Kilpatrick, R. Neves, L. Wagner, T. Howard, J. Erasme, D. Tait, P. Cleveland, S. St. Jacques

"Whatever Turns You On"
The Company

"Give It to Me"
L. Davidson, L. Wagner

"Giving Life"
E. Kilpatrick, B. Miller, P. Gillespie, R. Neves, L. Wagner, J. Erasme, D. Tait, P. Cleveland, S. St. Jacques

"The Ad"
C. Whiteside

"Fellatio 101"
A. Lozito, Students

"I'm Gay"
B. Jockers, B. Miller, R. Neves, P. Gillespie

"Linda, Georgina, Marilyn & Me"
J. Baron

"Dirty Words"
The Company

"I Believe My Body"
The Company

ACT 2

"The Showbusiness Nobody Knows"
The Company

"Take Me Home With You"
B. Miller

"Choir Practice"
A. Lozito, Company

"And She Loved Me"
Rozaa, E. Kilpatrick, L. Wagner, J. Erasme

"Poontang"
The Company

"Come in My Mouth"
E. Kilpatrick

"The Cunnilingus Champion of Co. C"
B. Miller, P. Cleveland, J. Baron, C. Whiteside

"Doesn't Anybody Love Anymore"
Roza

"Let My People Come"
The Company

1976.21 GUYS AND DOLLS

A Revival of the Musical Fable of Broadway (Comedy) in Two Acts, 18 Scenes[6]. Book by Jo Swerling and Abe Burrows. Based on a story and characters by Damon Runyon. Music and lyrics by Frank Loesser. Directed and choreographed by Billy Wilson. Scenery by Tom H. John. Costumes by Bernard Johnson. Lighting by Thomas Skelton. (Musical) Arrangements and orchestrations by Danny Holgate, Horace Ott. Musical director, choral arranger, Howard Roberts. Sound design by Sander Hacker. Associate producers, Ashton Springer, Carmen F. Zollo. Entire production under the supervision of Abe Burrows. Produced by Moe Septee in association with Victor Potamkin, and in association with Frank Enterprises and Beresford Productions, Ltd. Opened 21 July 1976 at the Broadway Theatre and closed 13 February 1977 after 239 performances.

CAST (in order of appearance): *Nicely-Nicely Johnson*: KEN PAGE. *Benny Southstreet*: CHRISTOPHE PIERRE. *Rusty Charlie*: Sterling McQueen. *Sister Sarah Brown*: ERNESTINE JACKSON. *Harry the Horse*: John Russell. *Lieut. Brannigan*: CLARK MORGAN. *Nathan Detroit*: ROBERT GUILLAUME. *Angie the Ox*: Jymie Charles. *Miss Adelaide*: NORMA DONALDSON. *Sky Masterson*: JAMES RANDOLPH. *Arvide Abernathy*: EMETT 'BABE' WALLACE. *Agatha*: Irene Datcher. *Calvin*: Bardell Conner. *Martha*: Marion Moore. *Joey Biltmore*: Derrick Bell. *Master of Ceremonies*: Andy Torres. *Waiter*: Derrick Bell. *Mimi*: Prudence Darby. *General (Matilda B.) Cartwright*: EDYE BYRDE. *Big Jule*: Walter White. *Drunk*: Andy Torres.

The Guys: Derrick Bell, Toney Brealond, Jymie Charles, Bardell Conner, Nathan Jennings, Jr., Bill Mackey, Sterling McQueen, Andy Torres, Eddie Wright, Jr. *The Dolls*: Prudence Darby, Jacquelyn DuBois, Anna Maria Fowlkes, Helen Gelzer, Julia Lema, Jacqueline Smith-Lee.

---

[3]Originally produced in New York 25 December 1940 at the Ethel Barrymore Theatre for 374 performances. For Synopsis of Scenes and Musical Numbers, see original 1940 production. "What Is a Man" permanently replaced "Love Is My Friend" in Act 1, Scene 4; "Pal Joey" (What Do I Care for a Dame? sung by C. Chadman as Joey) added to Act 1, Scene 6 after "Bewitched."

[4]Orchestrations uncredited.

[5]Originally produced Off-Broadway 8 January 1974 at the Village Gate for 1167 performances. After the opening, the composer/lyricist and choreographer withdrew their names from the credits, and the running order of songs was substantially rearranged.

[6]First presented in New York 24 November 1950 at the 46th Street Theatre for 1200 performances. For Synopsis of Scenes and Musical Numbers, see original 1950 production. Act 1, Scene 8, now set in San Juan, Puerto Rico, and the accompanying dance now named "El Cafe Felicidad."

1976.22

H.M.S. PINAFORE, or The Lass That Loved a Sailor

A Revival of the Comic Opera in Two Acts[7]. Libretto by William S. Gilbert. Music by Arthur Sullivan. Directed by Jack Eddleman. Choreographed by Thomas Andrew. Scenery and costumes by Patton Campbell. Lighting by Hans Sondheimer. Conductor, John Miner. Produced by the New York City Opera. Opened 3 September 1976 at the New York State Theatre and closed 26 September 1976 after 4 performances in repertory.

CAST: *The Rt. Hon. Sir Joseph Porter, K.C.B.*, First Lord of the Admiralty: JAMES BILLINGS. *Captain Corcoran*, Commander of the *H.M.S. Pinafore*: RICHARD FREDERICKS. *Ralph Rackstraw*, Able Seaman: GARY GLAZE. *Dick Deadeye*, Able Seaman: IRWIN DENSEN. *Bill Bobstay*, Boatswain: WILLIAM LEDBETTER. *Bob Becket*: Philip Steele. *Josephine*, the Captain's Daughter: GLENYS FOWLES. *Hebe*, Sir Joseph's First Cousin: PULI TORO. *Little Buttercup* (Mrs. Cripps), a Portsmouth bum-boat woman: MURIEL COSTA-GREENSPON.

First Lord's Sisters, His Cousins, His Aunts, Sailors, Marines, etc.: New York City Opera Chorus.

1976.23

DIE FLEDERMAUS

A Revival of the Operetta in Three Acts[8]. Original Viennese libretto by Carl Haffner and Richard Genée. Lyrics by Richard Genée. (Based on the comedy "Le Réveillon" by Henri Meilhac and Ludovic Halévy.) English libretto by Ruth and Thomas Martin. Music by Johann Strauss. Production devised and directed by Gerald Freedman. Stage director, Richard Getke. Choreography by Thomas Andrew. Scenery designed by Lloyd Evans Costumes design by Theoni V. Aldredge. Lighting by Hans Sondheimer. Conducted by Imre Pallo. Chorus prepared by Judith Somogi. Produced by the New York City Opera. Opened 11 September 1976 at the New York State Theatre and closed 7 November 1976 after 4 performances in repertory; returned 26 February 1977 to the New York State Theatre and closed 30 April 1977 after 6 performances in repertory. Total, 10 performances this season.

CAST (in order of appearance): *Alfred*, an itinerant tenor: Gary Glaze. *Adele*, von Eisenstein's chambermaid: GIANNA ROLANDI. *Rosalinda von Eisenstein*: JOHANNA MEIER. *Gabriel von Eisenstein*: CHARLES ROE. *Dr. Blind*, a lawyer: Jerold Siena. *Dr. Falke*, a close friend of Eisenstein: THOMAS JAMERSON. *Frank*, the prison warden: SPIRO MALAS. *Sally*, Adele's sister: Diana Kehrig. *Ivan*, servant to Orlofsky: Jack Sims. *Prince Orlofsky*, a wealthy, bored Russian: DAVID RAE SMITH *Frosch*, the jailer: James Billings. *Solo Dancers*: Sandra Balestracci, Esperanza Galan, Juliu Horvath. *Ensemble*: New York City Opera Chorus.

1976.24

THE DEBBIE REYNOLDS SHOW

A Musical Revue in Two Acts. Staged and choreographed by Ron Lewis. Musical conductor, Tom Nygaard. Sets by Billy Morris. Lighting by Jerry Grollnek. Costumes and gowns by Bob Mackie. Sound by Trevor Jordan. Producer, Robert Fallon. Produced by Raymax Productions. Opened 16 September 1976 at the Minskoff Theatre and closed 26 September 1976 after 13 performances.

CAST: DEBBIE REYNOLDS, Bruce Lea, Albert Stevenson, Ray Chabeau, Joel Blum, Louis McKay, Gene Myers, George Eiferman, Penny Worth, Dani McCormack, Steven Lardas.

ACT 1

"Gee, But It's Great to Be Here" (from *HAPPY HUNTING*)
D. Reynolds, Cast
(*Music by* Harold Karr. *Lyrics by* Matt Dubey.)

Medley:

"Reach Out and Touch Somebody's Hand"
(*Music and Lyrics by* Nick Ashford and Valerie Simpson.)

"He's Got the Whole World in His Hands" (traditional)

"Touch a Hand"

"Higher and Higher"
D. Reynolds, Cast
(*Music and Lyrics by* Gary Lee Jackson, Carl W. Smith, Raynard Miner.)

Singers' Medley
S. Lardas, P. Worth, D. McCormick

Film Sequence and Medley
D. Reynolds

"I Ain't Down Yet" (from *THE UNSINKABLE MOLLY BROWN*)
D. Reynolds
(*Music and Lyrics by* Meredith Willson.)

Debbie's Salute to Show Business
Entire Company
("When the Midnight Choo-Choo Leaves for Alabam'"/"Sweet Georgia Brown"/"Me and My Shadow")

ACT 2

IRENE Medley:

"Irene"
(*Music by* Harry Tierney. *Lyrics by* Joseph McCarthy.)

"I'm Always Chasing Rainbows"
(*Music by* Harry Carroll. *Lyrics by* Joseph McCarthy.)

"Alice Blue Gown"
(*Music by* Harry Tierney. *Lyrics by* Joseph McCarthy.)

"You Made Me Love You"
(*Music by* James Monaco. *Lyrics by* Joseph McCarthy.)

Premier Night Impressions
D. Reynolds

Bicentennial Salute to America
Entire Company

1976.25

GOING UP!

A Revival of the Uplifting Musical Comedy in Two Acts, 4 Scenes[9]. Book and lyrics by Otto Harbach. Based on the comedy "The Aviator" by James Montgomery. Music by Louis A. Hirsch. Directed by Bill Gile. Choreography and production numbers by Dan Siretta. Musical direction and vocal arrangements by Lynn Crigler. Costumes by David Toser. Scenic design and lighting supervision by Edward Haynes. Lighting by Peter M. Ehrhardt. Special consultant, Alfred Simon. Musical arranger, Russell Warner. A Goodspeed Opera House Production (Michael Price, Producer). Associate producer, James L. D. Roser. Produced by Ashton Springer, William Callahan, (Norman) Stephens-(Max) Weitzenhoffer Productions in association with Stephen R. Friedman and Irwin Meyer. Opened 19 September 1976 at the John Golden Theatre and closed 30 October 1976 after 49 performances.

CAST (in order of appearance): *Miss Zonne*: PAT LYSINGER. *Alex*: Calvin McRae. *Gus*: Larry Hyman. *John Gordon*: Stephen Bray. *Grace Douglas*: KIMBERLY FARR. *F. H. Douglas*: LEE H. DOYLE. *Jules Gaillard*: MICHAEL TARTEL. *Hopkinson Brown*: WALTER BOBBIE. *Madeline Manners*: MAUREEN BRENNAN. *James Brooks*: NOEL CRAIG. *Robert Street*: BRAD BLAISDELL. *Sam Robinson*: RONN ROBINSON. *Dwayne*: James Bontempo. *Faye*: Deborah Crowe. *Howell*: Michael Gallagher. *Ennis*: Teri Gill. *Mollie*: Barbara McKinley.

Act 1, Scene 1: The Gordon Inn Lobby, Lenox, Massachusetts, 1919 . . . afternoon. *Scene 2*: The Smoking Room . . . later that evening.

Act 2, Scene 1: The Terrace . . . the same evening. *Scene 2*: An Airfield near the Gordon Inn . . . six o'clock the next afternoon.

ACT 1

Scene 1

"Paging Mr. Street"
P. Lysinger, S. Bray, Bellboys, Ensemble

"I Want a Determined Boy"
M. Brennan, W. Bobbie, Four Aviators

"If You Look in Her Eyes"
K. Farr, B. Blaisdell, M. Brennan

"Going Up"
B. Blaisdell, Company

Scene 2

"Hello Frisco"[10]
P. Lysinger, Four Aviators

---

[7]Originally presented in New York 15 January 1879 at the Standard Theatre for 175 performances. For Synopsis of Scenes and Musical Numbers, see original 1879 production.

[8]First English language production in New York 16 March 1885 at the Casino Theatre for 42 performances. First New York production of this adaptation 20 December 1950 at the Metropolitan Opera House. For Synopsis of Scenes and Musical Numbers, see May 1954 revival.

[9]Originally produced in New York 25 December 1917 at the Liberty Theatre for 351 performances.

[10]Originally in *ZIEGFELD FOLLIES OF 1915* (*Lyrics by* Gene Buck).

"Down, Up, Left, Right"
B. Blaisdell, W. Bobbie, N. Craig, R. Robinson
"Kiss Me"
K. Farr, M. Tartel
"(Everybody Ought To Do) The Tickle Toe"
K. Farr, Ensemble

ACT 2
Scene 1
"(There's a) Brand New Hero"
Ensemble
"I'll Think of You"[11]
K. Farr, B. Blaisdell
"I'll Think of You" (reprise)
K. Farr, B. Blaisdell
Scene 2
"Do It for Me"
M. Brennan, W. Bobbie
"My Sumurun Girl"[12]
P. Lysinger, R. Robinson
"Going Up"/"Down, Up, Left, Right"/"The Tickle Toe" (reprises)
Company

1976.26 LA BELLE HÉLÈNE

A Revival of the Opéra-bouffe in Three Acts[13]. Original French libretto by Henri Meilhac and Ludovic Halévy. Music by Jacques Offenbach. English libretto by Geoffrey Dunn, revised by Julius Rudel. Production devised and directed by Jack Eddleman. Scenic designer, Lloyd Evans. Costume design by Patton Campbell. Lighting design by Hans Sondheimer. Choreography by Thomas Andrew. Conducted by Julius Rudel. Produced by the New York City Opera. Opened 21 September 1976 at the New York State Theatre and closed 29 October 1976 after 5 performances in repertory; returned 27 February 1977 to the New York State Theatre and closed 20 April 1977 after 4 performances in repertory. Total: 9 performances this season.

CAST (in order of appearance): *Calchas*, Grand Augur of Jupiter: RICHARD McKEE. *Philocomos*, his servant: Joaquin Romaguera. *First Young Lady*: Joan Campbell. *Second Young Lady*: Myrna Reynolds. *Euthycles*, a blacksmith: Don Yule. *Helen*, Queen of Sparta: KARAN ARMSTRONG. *Daphne*, Helen's attendant: Puli Toro. *Orestes*, Son of Agamemnon: DAVID GRIFFITH. *Daughters of Joy (4)*: *Jocanthis*: Vicki Grof. *Anthea*: Valeria Orlando. *Phantis*: Madeleine Mines. *Chloe*: Joyce Tomanec. *Paris*, son of King Priam: HENRY PRICE. *Ajax I*, King of Salamis: JEROLD SIENA. *Ajax II*, King of the Lochrians: MELVIN LOWERY. *Achilles*, King of Phthiotis: JOHN LANKSTON. *Menelaus*, King of Sparta: JAMES BILLINGS. *Agamemnon*, King of the Kings: DAVID HOLLOWAY. *Living statues*: Sandra Balestracci, Mikhail Korogodsky.

Princes and Princesses, Courtiers, Mourners of Adonis, Helen's Attendants, Guards, People, Slaves, etc.: New York City Opera Chorus.

Act 1: The Oracle . . . Sparta, the Temple of Jupiter.

Act 2: The Siege of Paris . . . Queen Helen's Boudoir.

Act 3: The Caravel of Venus . . . The Beach at Nauplia.

ACT 1
Immortal Jupiter. (Introduction and Chorus)
Chorus
It's Considered as a Moral Duty . . .
K. Armstrong, Girls
We've Had a Night Out . . . (Couplets)
D. Griffith, R. McKee, Chorus
Dear Calchas . . . (Melodrama)
R. McKee
On Mount Ida . . . (The Judgement of Paris)
H. Price (Paris)
The five kings of Greece now enter. (March and Entry of the Kings)
Chorus
Our form is perfectly splendid . . . (Couplets)
J. Siena, D. Griffith, R. McKee, M. Lowery, J. Lankston, J. Billings, D. Holloway
Our Queen is divinely glorious. (March reprise)
Chorus
Crown him! Crown him! (Finale Act 1)
Principals, Chorus

ACT 2
Tonight you must wear . . . (Opening Chorus)
K. Armstrong, P. Toro, Girls
We all begin by truly trying. (Invocation to Venus)
K. Armstrong
Now the four Kings introduce . . . (The Goose March)
All
Let us garland ourselves with roses . . . (Couplets)
D. Griffith
It is Heaven that has sent . . . (Duo/Duet of the Dream)
K. Armstrong, H. Price (Paris)
A husband who . . . (Couplets/Finale Act 2)
K. Armstrong, J. Billings, D. Holloway, H. Price, All

ACT 3
What fun! (Opening Chorus)
Chorus
My dear, you're simply being spiteful! (Couplets)
K. Armstrong
When all of Greece has been ravaged . . . (Patriotic Trio)
D. Holloway, R. McKee, J. Billings
Near a fair Ionian island . . . (Chorus)
Chorus
Are you a Spartan madrigal society . . . (Tyrolienne)
H. Price (Paris), Chorus
Do you see?. . (Finale Act 3)
K. Armstrong, J. Billings, D. Griffith, R. McKee, H. Price (Paris), All

1976.27 OH, CALCUTTA!

A Revival of the Musical Entertainment (Revue) in Two Acts, 11 Scenes[14]. Devised by Kenneth Tynan. Entire production conceived and directed by Jacques Levy. Contributors: Jules Feiffer, Dan Greenburg, Lenore Kandel, John Lennon, Jacques Levy, Leonard Melfi, David Newman and Robert Benton, Sam Shepard, Clovis Trouille, Kenneth Tynan, Sherman Yellen. Music and lyrics by (The Open Window) Robert Dennis, Peter Schickele, Stanley Walden. Additional music and lyrics by Stanley Walden and Jacques Levy. Choreography by Margo Sappington. Scenery by James Tilton. Lighting by Harry Silverglat. Costumes by Kenneth M. Yount, supervised by James Tilton. Projection media design by Gardner Compton. Musical director, Stanley Walden. Produced by Hillard Elkins, Norman Kean and Robert S. Fishko. Opened 24 September 1976 at the Edison Theatre and closed 6 August 1989 after 5959 performances[15].

CAST (in alphabetical order): Haru Aki, Jean Andalman, Bill Bass, Dorothy Chansky, Cress Darwin, John Hammil, William Knight, Cy Moore, Coline Morse, Pamela Pilkenton.

ACT 1
Scene 1
Taking Off the Robe ("Oh! Calcutta!")
The Company
Scene 2
"Will Answer All Sincere Replies" (Song and Sketch)
Sue Ellen: D. Chansky. *Dale*: J. Hammil. *Monte*: W. Knight. *Cherie*: J. Andalman.

[11]Originally in *THE RAINBOW GIRL* (*Lyrics by* Rennold Wolf.)
[12]Originally in *THE WHIRL OF SOCIETY* (*Lyrics by* Al Jolson.)
[13]Originally produced in New York in French 26 March 1868 at the French Theatre for 5 weeks; in English 13 April 1868 as *PARIS AND HELEN, OR THE GREEK ELOPEMENT* at the New York Theatre. Musical numbers did not appear in the program, above list prepared from published libretto.

[14]Originally produced in New York Off-Broadway 17 June 1969 at the Eden Theatre for 710 performances; transferred to Broadway 25 February 1971 at the Belasco Theatre for an additional 606 performances.
[15]From 24 September-7 December 1976 performances alternated with *ME AND BESSIE*.

Scene 3

Rock Garden

Man: W. Knight. *Boy*: C. Darwin.
(*Scene*: Saturday afternoon, just after lunch before the ball game.)

Scene 4

Delicious Indignities, (or The Deflowering of Helen Axminster)

Helen: D. Chansky. *Alfred*: W. Knight.
(*Scene*: An Elegantly Appointed Study in Knightsbridge, 1896.)

Scene 5

"Paintings of Clovis Trouille"

Clovis Trouille, now in his 80's, is one of France's most distinguished living painters. He has been painting in the mainstream of surrealism for the past half century.

"Much Too Soon"

C. Darwin
(*Music and Lyrics by* The Open Window and Jacques Levy.)

"Dance for George"

Danced by P. Pilkenton
(Dedicated to the memory of the late George Welbes.)

Scene 6

"Suite for Five Letters"

J. Hammil, W. Knight, D. Chansky, J. Andalman, P. Pilkenton

Scene 7

One on One

H. Aki, B. Bass

"Clarence"

J. Andalman

ACT 2[16]

Scene 1

"Jack & Jill" (Song and Sketch)

P. Pilkenton, J. Hammil

Scene 2

"Spread Your Love Around"

J. Andalman

"Love Lust Poem"

P. Pilkenton, H. Aki

Scene 3

Was It Good For You Too? ("Green Pants," "I Like the Look")

(*Perlmutter*: C. Darwin. *Interviewer*: H. Aki. *Dr. Bronson*: J. Andalman. *Dr. Jaspers*: W. Knight. *Nurse*: P. Pilkenton. *Attendant*: B. Bass. *Woman*: D. Chansky. *Gypsies*: J. Hammil, H. Aki. *Gypsy Dog*: G. Grover Lightstone. *Scene*: A Doctor's Office.)

Scene 4

"Coming Together, Going Together"

The Company

1976.28 PORGY AND BESS

A Revival of the Folk Opera in Three Acts, 9 Scenes[17]. Book by DuBose Heyward adapted from the play "Porgy" by DuBose and Dorothy Heyward. Music by George Gershwin. Lyrics by DuBose Heyward and Ira Gershwin. Production directed by Jack O'Brien. Sets by Robert Randolph. Additional scenic elements for Kittiwah Island designed by John Rothgeb. Costumes by Nancy Potts. Lighting by Gilbert V. Hemsley, Jr. Musical director and choral director, John DeMain. Choreographer and assistant director, Mabel Robinson. Assistant director, Helaine Head. Production coordinator, M. Jane Weaver. Assistant conductor, Ross Reimueller. Associate conductor, Clay Fullum. Produced by Sherwin M. Goldman and the Houston Grand Opera. Opened 25 September 1976 at the Uris Theatre, moved 7 December 1976 to the Mark Hellinger Theatre and closed 9 January 1977 after 122 performances.

CAST (in order of appearance): *Jasbo Brown*: Ross Reimueller. *Clara*: BETTY D. LANE. *Mingo*: Bernard Thacker. *Jake*: Curtis Dickson. *Sportin' Life*: LARRY MARSHALL. *Robbins*: Glover Parham. *Serena*: WILMA SHAKESNIDER or DELORES IVORY-DAVIS. *Jim*: Hartwell Mace. *Peter*: Mervin Wallace. *Lily*: Myra Merritt. *Maria*: CAROL BRICE. *Scipio*: Alex Carrington. *Porgy*: DONNIE RAY ALBERT, ABRAHAM LIND-OQUENDO or ROBERT MOSLEY. *Crown*: ANDREW SMITH or GEORGE ROBERT MERRITT. *Bess*: CLAMMA DALE, ESTHER HINDS or IRENE OLIVER. *Detective*: Hansford Rowe. *Policeman*: William Gammon. *Undertaker*: Cornel Richie. *Annie*: Shirley Baines. *Frazier*: Raymond Bazemore. *Strawberry Woman*: Phyllis Bash. *Crab Man*: Steven Alex-Cole. *Coroner*: John B. Ross.

Ensemble (Residents of Catfish Row): John D. Anthony, Shirley Baines, Earl Baker, Phyllis Bash, Kenneth Bates, Raymond Bazemore, Barbara Buck, Steven Alex-Cole, Ella Eure, Wilhelmenia Fernandez, Elizabeth Graham, Earl Grandison, Kenneth Hamilton, Betty Harris, Loretta Holkmann, Alma Johnson, Cora Johnson, Roberta Long, Hartwell Mace, Patricia McDermott, Myra Merritt, Naomi Moody, Glover Parham, William Penn, Dwight Ransom, Cornel Richie, Rodrick Ross, Alexander B. Smalls, Bernard Thacker, Mervin Wallace, Barbara Ann Webb, Wardell Woodard, Denice Woods, Barbara L. Young.

1976.29 SIAMSA

A Folk Entertainment in Two Acts by the National Folk Theatre of Ireland[18]. Devised and directed by Pat Ahern. Design consultant, Lona Moran. Choreography by Patricia Hanafin. Wardrobe supervisor, Phyllis O'Donoghue. Technical director, Bernard Brannigan. Produced by (Robert P.) Brannigan-(Charles) Eisler Performing Arts International, Inc. Opened 27 September 1976 at the Palace Theatre and closed 2 October 1976 after 8 performances.

CAST: *The Merrymaker*: Sean O'Mahony. *The Gardener*: Liam Heaslip. *The Shoemaker*: Sean Ahern. *Solo Dancers*: Patricia Hanafin, Jimmy Smith, Jerry Nolan, John McCarthy. *Solo Singers*: Mary Deady, Sean Ahern, Liam Heaslip, Sean O'Mahony. *Folk Dancers*: Philomena Daly, Susan Rohan, Catherine Hurley, Michael O'Shea, Aidan O'Carroll. *Children*: Mary Lyons, Marie O'Donoghue, Sandra O'Reilly, Catherine Spangler, Sean Heaslip, Oliver Hurley, John Fitzgerald. *Musicians*: Pat Kennington, Gerard Buckley, Nicholas McAuliffe, Timmy O'Shea, Pierce Heaslip, Audrey O'Carroll.

ACT 1

"Samhra"—Summertime

Dawn is breaking on a summer's morning over a simple Irish homestead. The people are going about their various chores. The barefoot children are off through the fields to gather wild flowers, or maybe to pick up a tune from the local merrymaker .... They might rob an orchard, that is if the gardener and his helper aren't looking, but there's always the chance of a little help from the daughter of the house ... The farmer has his calves to feed, but for his wife the hens come first ... There's a wandering shoemaker, with a song of a bird's nest in the thatch. The neighbors enjoy the beat of his hammer but soon it's milking time and the cows come home.

Darkness falls, the time for a love song and traditional bonfire revelry. In pagan times fire ceremonies were performed at "Bealtaine" on the eve of May Day. The cattle were driven between two fires to be purified by the smoke and preserved from disease. Each person brought a stick for the fire and the menfolk leaped through the flames. The final scene recalls those ancient forms of fire worship.

ACT 2

Scene 1

"Cois Teallaigh"—by the Fireside

The neighbors quietly gather for an evening's merriment by the open hearth. There are love songs and country dances. There is the traditional blessing of the butter churn and the making of the butter. In those days it was regarded as a token of bad luck if each visitor to the house did not take part in the butter-making. Everybody had to take a turn at the dash of the churn.

---

[16]The running order was frequently altered during the run. Added during run to Act 2:

"Playin'"

J. Hammil

Four in Hand (Sketch restored from Off-Broadway production)

[17]First produced in New York 10 October 1935 at the Alvin Theatre for 124 performances. For Synopsis of Scenes and Musical Numbers, see original 1935 production.This production was performed in Two Acts, with the interval after "What You Want Wid Bess?" (Act 2, Scene 2 in the original). "Buzzard Song" reinstated to Act 1, after "I Got Plenty of Nuttin'."

[18]*SIAMSA* (pronounced Shee-am-sa) is a folk entertainment which recaptures the spirit of the age in Ireland when Irish was the spoken language, the age from which Ireland inherited her great treasures of folk music and song. It aims to show something of the simple way of life of the people who gave her that heritage.

Scene 2

"Casadh an Sugain"—The Twisting of the Rope

A journeyman poet makes himself welcome at the half-door. The young girl plying the spinning wheel attracts his attention and he falls in lvoe with her. All goes well until her father and grandmother disapprove. They devise a plan to get him out. They put him twisting a new rope of hay so that he "twists" himself out of the house—never to return. Incidentally, the floors of the old houses were ususally made of caked mud. So, very often, the half-door was taken down to provide a platform for the stepdancers.

Scene 3

"Siamsa an Fomhair"—A Harvest Merrymaking

Set in the days of the singing scythe, the flying flail and the threshing floor, this scene portrays the older methods of cutting and threshing the corn. The "flail" was the instrument used to beat the corn from the sheaves. The straw was kept for the day of the thatching or the day of the "scollops." A scollop is a piece of stick about the length of a man's arm and pointed at both ends. It is used to secure the fresh straw on a thatched roof.

A day's thatching has left our thatcher tired and weary by evening time. The soft crooning of a young women's song as she tends him on the rooftop puts him to sleep. What happens next is something of a nightmare and he is very much relieved in the end to find it was all a dream. *SIAMSA* concludes with a Harvest Dance Festival.

1976.30 THE ROBBER BRIDEGROOM

A Revival of the (Country-Folk) Musical in One Act[19]. Book and lyrics by Alfred Uhry. Based on the novella of the same name by Eudora Welty. Music composed and arranged by Robert Waldman. Directed by Gerald Freedman. Choreography by Donald Saddler. Settings designed by Douglas W. Schmidt. Costumes designed by Jeanne Button. Lighting designed by David F. Segal. Associate producer, Porter Van Zandt. Produced by John Houseman, Margot Harley, Michael B. Kapon by arrangement with The Acting Company. Originally staged by the Musical Theatre Lab at St. Clement's. Opened 9 October 1976 at the Biltmore Theatre and closed 13 February 1977 after 145 performances.

CAST (in order of appearance): *Jamie Lockhart*, a gentleman robber: BARRY BOSTWICK. *Clement Musgrove*, a rich planter: STEPHEN VINOVICH. *Rosamund*, his daughter: RHONDA COULLET. *Salome*, his second wife: BARBARA LANG. *Little Harp*, a robber: LAWRENCE JOHN MOSS. *Big Harp*, the head of a robber: Ernie Sabella. *Goat*, a simpleton: Trip Plymale. *Goat's Mother*: Susan Berger. *Airie*: Jana Schneider. *A Raven*: Carolyn McCurry.

The Residents of Rodney: *Kyle Nunnery*: George DeLoy. *Harmon Harper*: Gary Epp. *Norman Ogelsby*: B. J. Hardin. *Queenie Brenner*: Mary Murray. *Rose Otto*: Melinda Tanner. *Gerry K. Summers*: Dennis Warning. *K. K. Pone*: Tom Westerman.

The action takes place in and around Rodney, Mississippi.

MUSICAL NUMBERS[20]

"Once Upon the Natchez Trace"
The Company

"Suddenly the Day Looks Sunny"
B. Bostwick

"Two Heads"
E. Sabella, L. J. Moss

"Steal With Style"
B. Bostwick

"Rosamund's Dream"
R. Coullet

"The Pricklepear Bloom"
B. Lang

"Nothin' Up"
R. Coullet

"Deeper in the Woods"
The Company

"Riches"
S. Vinovich, B. Bostwick, B. Lang, R. Coullet

"Little Piece of Sugar Cane"
B. Bostwick, Company

"Love Stolen"
B. Bostwick

"Poor Tied Up Darlin'"
L. J. Moss, T. Plymale

"Mean as a Snake"
C. McCurry

"Goodbye Salome"
The Company

"Sleepy Man"
R. Coullet

"Where Oh Where (Is My Baby Darlin'?)"
B. Bostwick, S. Vinovich, R. Coullet

"Pass Her Along"
The Company

Finale
B. Bostwick, Company

1976.31 THE SAINT OF BLEECKER STREET

A Revival of the Opera (Musical Drama) in Three Acts, 5 Scenes[21]. Music and libretto by Gian-Carlo Menotti. Conducted by Cal Stewart Kellogg. Directed by Francis Rizzo. Sets designed by Beeb Salzer. Costumes designed by Carol Luiken. Choreography by Thomas Andrew. Lighting by Hans Sondheimer. Chorus prepared by Conoley Ballard. Produced by the New York City Opera. Opened 5 November 1976 at the New York Stae Theatre and closed 10 November 1976 after 3 performances in repertory.

CAST (in order of appearance): *Assunta*: Jane Shaulis. *A Young Man*: Howard Hensel. *Maria Corona*: Judith De Rosa. *Her Son*: Ron Boucher. *Carmela*: Diana Soviero. *A Young Woman*: Diana Kehrig. *Don Marco*: Irwin Densen. *Annina*: CATHERINE MALFITANO. *Michele*: ENRICO diGIUSEPPE. *Concettina*: Danielle Brisebois. *Desideria*: JEANNE PILAND. *First Guest*: Jerold Siena. *Second Guest*: Alan Baker. *Salvatore*: William Ledbetter. *Bartender*: Don Henderson. *A Nun*: Charlott Thyssen. *A Young Priest*: Ronald Kelley. *Neighbors*: Kenn Dovel, James Sergi. *Neighbors, Friends, Policemen, etc.*: New York City Opera Chorus.

1976.32 BING CROSBY ON BROADWAY

A Musical Entertainment (Revue) in Two Acts. Staged and directed by Robert Sidney. (Settings and costumes uncredited.) Lighting by Martin Aronstein. Produced by William Loeb. Presented by Robert Paterson. Opened 7 December 1976 at the Uris Theatre and closed 19 December 1976 after 12 performances.

CAST: BING CROSBY, ROSEMARY CLOONEY, JOE BUSHKIN, JOE BUSHKIN QUARTET, Kathryn Crosby, Harry Crosby III, Mary-Frances Crosby, Nathaniel Crosby, Ted Rogers, Billy Byers Orchestra.

MUSICAL NUMBERS[22]

"Where the Blue of the Night (Meets the Gold of the Day)"
(*Music and Lyrics by* Roy Turk, Bing Crosby and Fred E. Ahlert.)

"The Pleasure of Your Company" (from *THE GOOD COMPANIONS*, London)
(*Music by* Andre Previn. *Lyrics by* Johnny Mercer.)

"Mary Lou"
(*Music and Lyrics by* George Waggner, J. Russell Robinson and Abe Lyman.)

"Where the Morning Glories Grow"
(*Music by* Richard A. Whiting. *Lyrics by* Raymond B. Egan and Gus Kahn.)

"At My Time of Life" (from *GREAT EXPECTATIONS*, London)
(*Music by* Cyril Ornadel. *Lyrics by* Hal Shaper.)

"On a Slow Boat to China"
B. Crosby, R. Clooney
(*Music and Lyrics by* Frank Loesser.)

[19]Originally produced by the Acting Company in New York 7 October 1975 at the Harkness Theatre for 15 performances.

[20]For subsequent national tour, an intermission was added after "Love Stolen."

[21]Originally produced in New York 27 December 1954 at the Broadway Theatre for 92 performances. For Synopsis of Scenes, see original 1954 production.

[22]Not in performance order.

"By Myself" (from *BETWEEN THE DEVIL*)
R. Clooney
(*Music by* Arthur Schwartz. *Lyrics by* Howard Dietz.)
"Tenderly"
R. Clooney
(*Music and Lyrics by* Jack Lawrence and Walter Gross.)
"Fifty Ways to Leave Your Lover"
(*Music and Lyrics by* Paul Simon.)
"Send in the Clowns" (from *A LITTLE NIGHT MUSIC*)
(*Music and Lyrics by* Stephen Sondheim.)
"Gone Fishing"
(*Music and Lyrics by* Nick and Charles Kenny.)
"Now You Has Jazz" (from *HIGH SOCIETY*, film)
(*Music and Lyrics by* Cole Porter.)
"The Man That Got Away" (from *A STAR IS BORN*, film)
(*Music by* Harold Arlen. *Lyrics by* Ira Gershwin.)
"Hallelujah!" (from *HIT THE DECK*)
(*Music by* Vincent Youmans. *Lyrics by* Leo Robin and Clifford Grey.)
"Sing (Sing a Song)"
(*Music and Lyrics by* Joe Raposo.)
"You've Got a Friend
(*Music and Lyrics by* Carole King.)
"My Cup Runneth Over" (from *I DO! I DO!*)
(*Music by* Harvey Schmidt. *Lyrics by* Tom Jones.)
"Play a Simple Melody" (from *WATCH YOUR STEP*)
(*Music and Lyrics by* Irving Berlin.)
Family Medley of Songs
(arranged by Ken and Mitzie Welch.)
"The Way We Were" (from *THE WAY WE WERE*, film)
(*Music by* Marvin Hamlisch. *Lyrics by* Marilyn and Alan Bergman.)
"Love Me With All Your Heart"
(*Music and Lyrics by* Mario and Carlos Rigual, Carlos Martinoli and M. Vaughn.)
"Just One of Those Things" (from *JUBILEE*)
R. Clooney
(Music and Lyrics by Cole Porter.)
"A Song for You"
(*Music and Lyrics by* Leon Russell.)
Crosby Medley
"That's What Life Is All About"
(*Music and Lyrics by* Les Reed, Bing Crosby, Peter Dacre, Ken Barnes.)

1976.33

MUSIC IS

A Musical in Two Acts, 14 Scenes and a Prologue. Book by George Abbott. Based on William Shakespeare's comedy "Twelfth Night." Music by Richard Adler. Lyrics by Will Holt. Directed by George Abbott. Musical numbers and dances staged by Patricia Birch. Musical director, Paul Gemignani. Orchestrations by Hershy Kay. Dance and vocal arrangements by William Cox. Scenery designed by Eldon Elder. Costumes by Lewis D. Rampino. Lighting by H. R. Poindexter. Assistant director, Judith Abbott. Additional (musical) arrangements by Jim Tyler. Originally premiered at the Seattle Repertory Theatre. Produced by Richard Adler, Roger Berlind, Edward R. Downe, Jr. Opened 20 December 1976 at the St. James Theatre and closed 26 December 1976 after 8 performances.

CAST (in order of appearance): *William Shakespeare*: DANIEL BEN-ZALI. *Valentine*: WILLIAM McCLARY. *Duke Orsino*: DAVID HOLLIDAY. *Curio*: DAVID BRUMMEL. *Viola*: CATHERINE COX. *Captain*: PAUL MICHAEL. *Clown*: William Shakespeare. *Maria*: LAURA WATERBURY. *Sir Toby Belch*: DAVID SABIN. *Malvolio*: CHRISTOPHER HEWETT. *Olivia*: SHERRY MATHIS. *Antonio*: MARC JORDAN. *Sebastian*: JOEL HIGGINS. *Sir Andrew Aguecheek*: JOE PONAZECKI. *First Officer*: DAVID BRUMMEL. *Second Officer*: Doug Carfrae. *Cupids*: Helena Andreyko, Ann Crowley. *Court Musicians*: Donald Hettinger (reeds), Steve Uscher (guitar).

Members of the Court: Helena Andreyko, Doug Carfrae, Jim Corti, Ann Crowley, Dennis Daniels, Dawn Herbert, Dana Kyle, Wayne Mattson, Jason McAuliffe, Carolann Page, Susan Elizabeth Scott, Denny Shearer, Melanie Vaughan, Mimi B. Wallace.

Act 1, Scene 1: Orsino's Garden. *Scene 2*: The Seacoast. *Scene 3*: Orsino's Garden. *Scene 4*: The Seacoast. *Scene 5*: Olivia's Garden. *Scene 6*: Olivia's Orchard. *Scene 7*: Orsino's Palace.

Act 2, Scene 1: Street with a Tailor Shop. *Scene 2*: A Haystack near Olivia's House. *Scene 3*: Olivia's Orchard. *Scene 4*: A Room in Olivia's House. *Scene 5*: Corridor—Malvolio's Bedroom. *Scene 6*: Olivia's Bedroom. *Scene 7*: Front of Olivia's House.

ACT 1
Prologue
"Music Is"
D. Ben-Zali, Company
Scene 1
"When First I Saw My Lady's Face"
D. Holliday
Scene 2
"Lady's Choice"
C. Cox, P. Michael
Scene 3
"The Time Is Ripe for Loving"
Company
"Should I Speak of Loving You"
C. Cox
Dance for Six
H. Andreyko, A. Crowley, M. B. Wallace, D. Shearer, D. Daniels, J. Corti
Scene 4
"Hate to Say Goodbye to You"
M. Jordan, J. Higgins
Scene 5
"Big Bottom Betty"
D. Ben-Zali
"Twenty One Chateaux"
C. Cox, S. Mathis, Company
"Sudden Lilac"
S. Mathis
Scene 6
"Sing Hi"
D. Sabin, J. Ponazecki, D. Ben-Zali, L. Waterbury
Scene 7
Dance: "Blindman's Buff"
C. Cox, D. Holliday, Company

ACT 2
Scene 1
"The Tennis Song"
D. Holliday, W. McClary, Company
Scene 2
"I Am It"
C. Hewett
Scene 3
"No Matter Where"
S. Mathis, C. Cox
"The Duel"
D. Sabin, C. Cox, J. Ponazecki, D. Ben-Zali
Scene 4
"Please Be Human"
S. Mathis, J. Higgins
Scene 7
"What You Will"
D. Ben-Zali, Entire Company

1976.34

BARRY MANILOW ON BROADWAY

A Musical Revue in Two Acts. Special material by Bruce Sussman. Orchestrations by Gerald Alters. Choreography by Barry Manilow and Lady Flash. Lighting designer, Michael Newton-Brown, supervised by Spencer Mosse. Sound engineer, John Venable. Mr. Manilow's clothes by Patrick Elliott. Lady Flash's clothes by Arthur Boccia. Staging consultant, Jack Hofsiss. Production coordinator, Rick Gross. Produced by Lee Guber, Shelly Gross and Miles Lourie. Opened 21 December 1976 at the Uris Theatre and closed 2 January 1977 after 12 performances.

CAST: BARRY MANILOW, Lady Flash (Debra Byrd, Reparata, Monica Buruss); The City Rhythm Band (Lee Gurst, Alan Axelrod, Keith Loving, Steven Donaghey, Harold 'Ricardo' Alexander).

MUSICAL NUMBERS[23]

[23]Not in performance order.

"Riders to the Stars"
(*Music and Lyrics by* Barry Manilow and Adrienne Anderson.)
"Why Don't We Live Together"
(*Music and Lyrics by* Peter Thom and Phil Galston.)
"Looks Like We Made It"
(*Music and Lyrics by* Richard Kerr and Will Jennings.)
"New York City Rhythm"
(*Music and Lyrics by* Barry Manilow and Marty Panzer.)
A Very Strange Medley:
"Kentucky Fried Chicken"
(*Music and Lyrics by* Al Gorgioni and Rob Nolan.)
"State Farm Insurance"
(*Music and Lyrics by* Barry Manilow and Jerry Gavin.)
"Stridex"
(*Music and Lyrics by* Barry Manilow.)
"Band-Aids"
(*Music and Lyrics by* Barry Manilow.)
"Bowlene"
(*Music and Lyrics by* Barry Manilow and Lois Wise.)
"Dr. Pepper"
(*Music and Lyrics by* Randy Newman and Jake Holmes.)
"Pepsi"
(*Music and Lyrics by* Ellen Starr and Joe McNeil.)
"McDonalds"
(*Music and Lyrics by* Kevin Gavin and Sid Woloshin.)
Jump Shout Boogie Medley:
"Jump Shout Boogie"
(*Music and Lyrics by* Barry Manilow and Bruce Sussman.)
"Avenue C"
(*Music and Lyrics by* B. Clayton, Jon Hendricks and Dave Lambert.)
"Jumpin' at the Woodside"
(*Music and Lyrics by* Jon Hendricks and Count Basie.)
"Cloudburst"
(*Music and Lyrics by* Leroy Kirkland, Jimmy Harris and Jon Hendricks.)
"Bandstand Boogie" (*Music and Lyrics by* C. Albertine, Bob Horn, Les Elgart, Larry Elgart, Barry Manilow, Bruce Sussman.)
"This One's for You"
(*Music and Lyrics by* Barry Manilow and Marty Panzer.)
"Beautiful Music"
(*Music and Lyrics by* Barry Manilow and Marty Panzer.)
"Daybreak"
(*Music and Lyrics by* Barry Manilow and Adrienne Anderson.)
"Lay Me Down"
(*Music and Lyrics by* Larry Weiss.)
"Weekend in New England"
(*Music and Lyrics by* Randy Edelman.)
"Studio Musician"
(*Music and Lyrics by* Rupert Holmes.)
"Could It Be Magic"
(*Music and Lyrics by* Barry Manilow, Adrienne Anderson and F. Chopin.)
"Mandy"
(*Music and Lyrics by* Scott English and Richard Kerr.)
"It's a Miracle"
(*Music and Lyrics by* Barry Manilow and Marty Panzer.)
"It's Just Another New Year's Eve"
(*Music and Lyrics by* Barry Manilow and Marty Panzer.)
"I Write the Songs"
(*Music and Lyrics by* Bruce Johnson.)

1976.35 YOUR ARMS TOO SHORT TO BOX WITH GOD

A Gospel Music in One Act. Conceived from the Book of Matthew by Vinnette Carroll. Music and lyrics by (Professor) Alex Bradford. Additional music and lyrics by Micki Grant. Directed by Vinnette Carroll. Choreography by Talley Beatty. Sets and costumes by William Schroder. Set supervisor, Michael J. Hotopp. Lighting by Gilbert V. Hemsley, Jr. Orchestrations and dance music by H. B. Barnum. Choral arrangements and direction by Chapman Roberts. Developed by the Urban Arts Corp for the Festival of Two Worlds, Spoleto, Italy, Summer 1975. A Ford's Theatre Production. Produced by Frankie Hewitt and The Shubert Organization in association with Theater Now, Inc. Opened 22 December 1976 at the Lyceum Theatre and closed 1 January 1978 after 429 performances.

CAST: SALOME BEY, CLINTON DERRICKS-CARROLL, DAVID ST. CHARLES, SHEILA ELLIS, DELORES HALL, WILLIAM HARDY, JR., HECTOR JAIME MERCADO, MABEL ROBINSON, WILLIAM THOMAS, JR., Deborah Lynn Bridges, Sharon Brooks, Thomas Jefferson Fouse, Jr., Michael Gray, Cardell Hall, Bobby Hill, Lidell Jackson, Edna Krider, Leon Washington, Marilyn Winbush.

ACT 1
"Beatitudes"
Company
"We're Gomnna Have a Good Time"
C. Derricks-Carroll, Company
"There's a Stranger in Town"
C. Derricks-Carroll, B. Hill, Company
"Do You Know Jesus?"/"He's a Wonder"
T. J. Fouse, Jr., Company
"Just a Little Bit of Jesus Goes a Long Way"
D. Hall, Company
"We Are the Priests and Elders"
W. Hardy, Jr., C. Derricks-Carroll, B. Hill, M. Gray
"Something Is Wrong in Jerusalem"
S. Bey, M. Robinson, Company
"It Was Alone"
W. Thomas, Jr., D. St. Charles
"I Ain't Had My Fill"
C. Derricks-Carroll, D. St. Charles
"Be Careful Whom You Kiss"
S. Bey, Company
"I Know I Have to Leave Here"
W. Hardy, Jr., Company
"It's Too Late"
Company
Judas Dance
H. J. Mercado
"Your Arms Too Short to Box With God"
D. Hall, Company
"Give Us Barrabas"
Company
"See How They Done My Lord"
S. bBey, Company
"Come On Down"
S. Ellis, C. Derricks-Carroll, M. Gray
"That's What the Bible Say"
M. Gray, Company
"Were You There When They Crucified My Lord?"
S. Bey
"Can't No Grave Hold My Body Down"
B. Hill, Company
"Beatitudes:" (reprise)
B. Hill, Company
"Didn't I Tell You"
W. Hardy, Jr., Company
"When the Power Comes"
W. Hardy, Jr., Company
"As Long As I Live"
S. Bey
"Everybody Has His Own Way"
C. Derricks-Carroll, M. Gray, T. J. Fouse, Jr.
"I Love You So Much Jesus"
D. Hall
"I Left My Sins Behind Me"
D. Hall, Company
"On That Day"
C. Derricks-Carroll, T. J. Fouse, Jr., B. Hill, M. Gray
"The Band"
W. Hardy, Jr., Company

1976.36 FIDDLER ON THE ROOF

A Revival of the Musical in Two Acts, a Prologue and 18 Scenes[24]. Book by Joseph Stein. Based on stories by Sholom Aleichem's stories (Tevye's

[24]Originally produced in New York 22 September 1964 at the Imperial Theatre for 3242 performances. For Synopsis of Scenes and Musical Numbers, see original 1964 production.

Daughters) by special permission of Arnold Perl. Music by Jerry Bock. Lyrics by Sheldon Harnick. Entire production directed and choreographed by Jerome Robbins. Direction reproduced by Ruth Mitchell. Choreography reproduced by Tom Abbott. Settings by Boris Aronson. Costumes by Patricia Zipprodt. Lighting by Ken Billington. Orchestrations by Don Walker. Musical direction by Milton Rosenstock. Vocal arrangements by Milton Greene. Dance music arranged by Betty Walberg. Originally produced by Harold Prince. Produced by The Shubert Orgzanization and Nederlander Producing Company of America, and the John F. Kennedy Center for the Performing Arts, in association with Theatre Now, Inc. Opened 28 December 1976 at the Winter Garden and closed 21 May 1977 after 167 performances.

CAST (in order of appearance): *Tevye*, the Dairyman: ZERO MOSTEL. *Golde*, his wife: THELMA LEE. *Their Five Daughters*: *Tzeitel*: ELIZABETH HALE. *Hodel*: CHRISTOPHER CALLAN. *Chava*: Nancy Tompkins. *Shprintze*: Davia Sacks. *Beilke*: Tiffany Bogart. *Yente*, the Matchmaker: RUTH JAROSLOW. *Motel*, the Tailor: IRWIN PEARL. *Perchik*, the Student: JEFF KELLER. *Mordcha*, the Innkeeper: Leon Spelman. *Lazar Wolf*, the Butcher: Paul Lipson. *Rabbi*: Charles Mayer. *Mendel*, his son: Paul A. Corman. *Avram*, the Bookseller: Merrill Plaskow II. *Nachum*, the Beggar: David Masters. *Grandma Tzeitel*: Duane Bodin. *Fruma Sarah*: Joyce Martin. *Constable*: Alexander Orfaly. *Fyedka*: Rick Friesen. *Shandel*, Motel's Mother: Jeanne Grant. *Bottle Dancers*: Tog Richards, Myron Curtis, Matthew Inge, Wallace Munro. *The Fiddler*: Sammy Bayes.

Villagers: *Shloime* the Bagel Man: Matthew Inge. *Yitzuk* the Streetsweeper: Don Tull. *Chaim* the Fishmonger: Glen McClaskey. *Duvidel* the Seltzer Man: Wallace Munro. *Surcha*: Lynn Archer. *Label*: Tog Richards. *Schmeril*: David Horwitz. *Yakov* the Knife-seller: Patrick Quinn. *Hershel*: Myron Curtis. *Fredel*: Hope Katcher. *Bluma*: Debra Timmons. *Mirala*: Maureen Sadusk. *Sima*: Lynn Archer. *Rivka*: Joyce Martin. *Yussel*: Duane Bodin. *Vladimer*: Robert L. Hultman. *Sasha*: Wallace Munro. *Bascha*: Shelley Wolf.

1977.01 IPI-TOMBI

A Musical (Revue) of South Africa in Two Acts, 8 Scenes. Conceived, devised and produced by Bertha Egnos. Original music by Bertha Egnos. Lyrics by Gail Lakier. Choreography by Sheila Wartski. Additional choreography by Neil McKay and members of the cast. Scenery by Elizabeth MacLeish. Lighting by Timothy Heale and John Wain. American costume supervision by David Toser. Sound by Sander Hacker. American scenic supervision by Robert D. Mitchell. American lighting supervision by Jeremy Johnson. Produced by A. Deshe (Pashanel) and Topol by arrangement with Ray Cooney Productions, Ltd. and Academy Theatre and Brooke Theatre, Johannesburg. Opened 12 January 1977 at the Harkness Theatre and closed 13 February 1977 after 39 performances.

CAST: Count Wellington Judge, Daniel Pule, Jabu Mbalo, Matthew Bodibe, Gideon Bendile, Elliot Ngubane, Andrew Kau, Sam Hlatshwayo, Philip Gama, David Mthethwa, Shadrack Moyo, Martha Molefe, Dorcas Faku, Lydia Monamodi, Busi Dlamini, Zelda Funami, Thembi Mtshali, Linda Tshabalala, Betty-Boo Hlela, Dudu Nzimande, Coreen Pike, Nellie Khumalo, Junior Tshabalala (Chief Drumemr), Simon Nkosi (Drummer), Ali Lerefolo (Drummer).

Act 1, Scene 1: Village of Tsomo. *Scene 2*: The Baptism. *Scene 3*: Song of Hope. *Scene 4*: The City of Gold.

Act 2, Scene 1: Sunday on the Mines. *Scene 2*: The Township Wedding. *Scene 3*: Workday on the Mine. *Scene 4*: The Warriors.

ACT 1

Overture: "Ipi-Tombi" (Where Are the Girls?)

Scene 1

Daybreak sees the start of a day in the village. The women busy about their duties, grinding corn, preparing food and drink for the return of their menfolk from the hunt.

"Sesiyahamba" (We Are Going About Our Labors)

"Hamba Bhekile" (Let the Drinks Be Served)

"Uthando Luphelile" (Love Is Lost, Love Is Gone)

"Madiwa-Madiwa" (Calling for Rain)

"Qhobosha" (The Unfaithful One Will Die)

"Mokhibo" (The Sotho Girls Dance)

"Ntaba Zenyuka" (The Mountains Are High)

"Orgy, the Temptress"

"Moriva"

"Shamanile"

"Shangaan"

Scene 2

The witch-doctor is the most feared and the most powerful person in the village. Mission stations have labored to bring their faith to the people and break the influence of the witch-doctors. The scene interprets the conflict.

Scene 3

"Nadia" (Song of Hope)

Scene 4

"Emdudeni" (Street Sweepers)

"Oo-Le-Le" (Men always sing about girls. His love is as High as the Snow-capped Mountain.)

"A Xhosa Proposition"

A Xhosa girl laments visiting the town and being robbed. She is accosted by a man. The ensuing conversation is carried out in the "click" language which is the feature of the Xhosa tongue.

"The Refuse Collectors"

It is a peculiarity of Johannesburg that each gang of refuse collectors are always the same tribe. The refuse collection is done "at the double."

"Arieni" (Let's Dance)

"Gum Boot dance"

"Ipi-Tombi" (Where Are the Girls?)

ACT 2

Scene 1

"Bayakhala" (Zulu)(The Child)

Help us, Lord, help us feed the child.

Scene 2

"Mama Tembu's Wedding"

"Baby Baby"

"Phata Phata" (Touch Touch)

Zulu Domestics bring wedding gifts.

"Wishing"

"Zimbaba"

"Baby Baby" (reprise)

Scene 3

"Shosholoza" (A work song)

"Going Home" A song of disillusion.

Scene 4

Prelude to battle. The throb of the drums, the undulating of the women spur on the warriors. The dance movements depict their mode of attack—the boasting of their prowess, the dodging and feinting with their imaginary enemies . . .

1977.02 A PARTY WITH BETTY COMDEN & ADOLPH GREEN

A Revival of the Intimate Revue in Two Acts, 12 Scenes[25]. Sketches and lyrics by Betty Comden and Adolph Green. (Music by Leonard Bernstein, Cy Coleman, Jule Styne, Roger Edens, André Previn, Saul Chaplin.) At the piano, Paul Trueblood. Miss Comden's gowns by Donald Brooks. Executed by John Fitzpatrick. Produced by Arthur Cantor and Leonard Friedman. Opened 10 February 1977 at the Morosco Theatre, moved 21 March 1977 to the Little Theatre and closed 30 April 1977 after 92 performances.

CAST: BETTY COMDEN, ADOLPH GREEN.

ACT 1

Scene 1

Opening ("I Said Good Morning" from *IT'S ALWAYS FAIR WEATHER*, film)

(*Music by* Andre Previn.)

Scene 2

The Revuers—Night Club Act

(*Sketches, Music and Lyrics by* The Revuers {Betty Comden, Adolph Green, Judy Holliday, Alvin Hammer, John Frank}.)

1. The Reader's Digest
2. The Screen Writers ("Beautiful Girl")

[25]First produced in New York Off-Broadway 10 November 1958 at the Cherry Lane Theatre, transferring 23 December 1958 to the John Golden Theatre for a total of 82 performances.

3. The Banshee Sisters
4. "The Baroness Bazooka"

Scene 3
ON THE TOWN Medley
(*Music by* Leonard Bernstein.)
1. "New York, New York"
2. "Lonely Town"
3. "Lucky to Be Me"
4. "Some Other Time"
5. "Carried Away"

Scene 4
WONDERFUL TOWN
(*Music by* Leonard Bernstein.)
1. "A Hundred Easy Ways to Lose a Man"
2. "Ohio"
3. "Wrong Note Rag"

ACT 2

Scene 1
SUBWAYS ARE FOR SLEEPING
(*Music by* Jule Styne.)
"Capital Gains"

Scene 2
TWO ON THE AISLE
(*Music by* Jule Styne.)
1. "If (You Hadn't But You Did)"
2. "Catch Our Act at the Met"

Scene 3
GOOD NEWS (Film)
(*Music by* Roger Edens.)
1. "The French Lesson"

Scene 4
STRAWS IN THE WIND
(*Music by* Cy Coleman.)
1. "The Lost Word"

Scene 5
PETER PAN
(*Music by* Jule Styne.)
1. "Captain Hook's Waltz"
2. "Never Never Land"
3. "Mysterious Lady"

Scene 6
STRAWS IN THE WIND
(*Music by* Cy Coleman.)
1. "Simplified Language"

Scene 7
BONANZA BOUND
(*Music by* Saul Chaplin.)
1. "Inspiration"

Scene 8
BELLS ARE RINGING
(*Music by* Jule Styne.)
1. "Just in Time"
2. "Make Someone Happy" (from *DO RE MI*)
(*Music by* Jule Styne.)
3. "The Party's Over"

1977.03 THE PIRATES OF PENZANCE, or The Slave of Duty

A Revival of the Comic Opera in Two Acts[26]. Libretto by William S. Gilbert. Music by Arthur Sullivan. Production directed by Jack Eddleman. Scenic design by Lloyd Evans. Costume design by Patton Campbell. Lighting design by Hans Sondheimer. Conductor, Judith Somogi. Chorus master, George Branson Gary. Produced by the New York City Opera. Opened 26 March 1977 at the New York State Theatre and closed 17 April 1977 after 4 performances in repertory.

CAST: *Major General Stanley*: JAMES BILLINGS. *The Pirate King*: RICHARD McKEE. *Samuel*, his Lieutenant: William Ledbetter. *Frederic*, the Pirate Apprentice: HENRY PRICE. *Sergeant of Police*: IRWIN DENSEN. *Mabel, Edith, Kate, Isabel*, General Stanley's Daughters: GIANNA ROLANDI, DIANA KEHRIG, SANDRA WALKER, MADELEINE MINES. *Ruth*, Pirate Maid-of-all-work: MURIEL COSTA-GREENSPON. *Solo Dancer*: Mikhail Korogodsky.

Chorus of Pirates, Police and General Stanley's Daughters: New York City Opera Chorus.

1977.04 I LOVE MY WIFE

A Musical in Two Acts, 5 Scenes. Book and lyrics by Michael Stewart. Music composed and arranged by Cy Coleman. Based on a play ("Viens chez-moi, j'habite chez une copine") by Luis Rego. Directed by Gene Saks. Scenery by David Mitchell. Lighting by Gilbert V. Hemsley, Jr. Costumes by Ron Talsky. Musical direction by John Miller. Sound by Lou Gonzalez. Musical numbers staged by Onna White. Associate producer, Frank Montalvo. Produced by Terry Allen Kramer and Harry Rigby by arrangement with Joseph Kipness. Opened 17 April 1977 at the Ethel Barrymore Theatre and closed 20 May 1979 after 857 performances.

CAST (in order of appearance): *Cleo*: ILENE GRAFF. *Monica*: JOANNA GLEASON. *Wally*: JAMES NAUGHTON. *Stanley*: Michael Mark. *Quentin*: Joe Saulter. *Harvey*: John Miller. *Norman*: Ken Bichel. *Alvin*: LENNY BAKER.

The action takes place in Trenton, New Jersey, at the present time.

Act 1, Scene 1: Harvey's Diner. *Scene 2*: A Mover's Life. *Scene 3*: Alvin and Cleo's Apartment.

Act 2, Scene 1: Christmas Eve. *Scene 2*: Wally and Monica's Apartment.

ACT 1

Scene 1
"We're Still Friends"
Full Company
"Monica"
L. Baker, J. Gleason, M. Mark, J. Saulter, J. Miller, K. Bichel
"By Threes"
J. Naughton, L. Baker, J. Miller

Scene 2
"A Mover's Life"
L. Baker, M. Mark, J. Saulter, J. Miller, K. Bichel

Scene 3
"Love Revolution"
I. Graff
"Someone Wonderful I Missed"
J. Gleason, I. Graff
"Sexually Free"
L. Baker, I. Graff, J. Naughton

ACT 2

Scene 1
"Hey There, Good Times"
M. Mark, J. Saulter, J. Miller, K. Bichel

Scene 2
"Lovers on Christmas Eve"
J. Gleason, J. Naughton, K. Bichel
"Scream"
M. Mark, J. Saulter, J. Miller, K. Bichel
"Everybody Today Is Turning On"
L. Baker, J. Naughton
"Married Couple Seeks Married Couple"
L. Baker, I. Graff, J. Naughton, J. Gleason
"I Love My Wife"
L. Baker, J. Naughton

1977.05 SIDE BY SIDE BY SONDHEIM

A Musical Entertainment (Revue) in Two Acts. Music and lyrics by Stephen Sondheim. (Additional) Music by Leonard Bernstein, Mary Rodgers,

[26]First presented in New York 31 December 1879 at the Fifth Avenue Theatre for a total of 91 performances in two engagements. For Synopsis of Scenes and Musical Numbers, see original 1879 production.

Richard Rodgers and Jule Styne. Directed by Ned Sherrin. Musical director, Ray Cook. Musical staging by Bob Howe. Continuity by Ned Sherrin. Scenery by Peter Docherty. Costumes by Florence Klotz. Lighting by Ken Billington. Scenery supervision by Jay Moore. Musical supervision by Paul Gemignani. Sound by Jack Mann. Produced by Harold Prince in association with Ruth Mitchell, by arrangement with The Incomes Company, Ltd. Presented in London by H. M. Tennent LTD and Cameron Mackintosh in association with the Mermaid Theatre. Opened 18 April 1977 at the Music Box, moved 22 February 1978 to the Morosco Theatre and closed 19 March 1978 after 390 performances.

CAST: MILLICENT MARTIN, JULIE N. McKENZIE, DAVID KERNAN, NED SHERRIN. *Pianists*: Daniel Troob, Albin Konopka.

ACT 1[27]

"Comedy Tonight" (from *A FUNNY THING HAPPENED ON THE WAY TO THE FORUM*)

"Love Is in the Air" (dropped from *A FUNNY THING HAPPENED ON THE WAY TO THE FORUM*)

"If Momma Was Married" (from GYPSY)
(*Music by* Jule Styne.)

"You Must Meet My Wife" (from *A LITTLE NIGHT MUSIC*)

"The Little Things You Do Together" (from *COMPANY*)

"Getting Married Today" (from *COMPANY*)

"I Remember"[28] (from *EVENING PRIMROSE*, Television)

"Can That Boy Foxtrot" (dropped from *FOLLIES*)

"Company" (from *COMPANY*)

"Another Hundred People"[29] (from *COMPANY*)

"Barcelona" (from *COMPANY*)

"Marry Me a Little" (dropped from *COMPANY*)

"I Never Do Anything Twice" (from *THE SEVEN PERCENT SOLUTION* film)

"Bring on the Girls" (from *FOLLIES*)

"Ah, Paree!" (from *FOLLIES*)

"Buddy's Blues" (from *FOLLIES*)

"Broadway Baby" (from *FOLLIES*)

"You Could Drive a Person Crazy" (from *COMPANY*)

ACT 2

"Everybody Says Don't" (from *ANYONE CAN WHISTLE*)

"Anyone Can Whistle"[30] (from *ANYONE CAN WHISTLE*)

"Send in the Clowns" (from *A LITTLE NIGHT MUSIC*)

"We're Gonna Be All Right"
(from *DO I HEAR A WALTZ?*)
(*Music by* Richard Rodgers.)

"A Boy Like That"/"I Have a Love"[31] (from *WEST SIDE STORY*)
(*Music by* Leonard Bernstein.)

"The Boy From . . . " (from *THE MAD SHOW*)
(*Music by* Mary Rodgers.)

"Pretty Lady" (from *PACIFIC OVERTURES*)

"You Gotta Have A Gimmick" (from *GYPSY*)
(*Music by* Jule Styne.)

"Losing My Mind" (from *FOLLIES*)

"Could I Leave You?"[32] (from *FOLLIES*)

"I'm Still Here" (from *FOLLIES*)

"Conversation Piece"
(*arranged by* Caryl Brahms and Stuart Pedlar)

"Side By Side By Side" (from *COMPANY*)

[27]The running order was revised repeatedly during the run. Added during the run:

"Waiting For the Girls Upstairs" (from *FOLLIES*)(Act 2)

"Being Alive" (from *COMPANY*)(Act 1)

"The Ladies Who Lunch" (from *COMPANY*)(Act 1)

"The Miller's Son" (from *A LITTLE NIGHT MUSIC*)(Act 2)

"Something's Coming" (from *WEST SIDE STORY*)
(*Music by* Leonard Bernstein.)(Act 2)

"The Two of You"
(written for The Kuklapolitan Players)(Act 1)

"Little Lamb" (from *GYPSY*)
(*Music by* Jule Styne.)(Act 1)

"I Feel Pretty" (from *WEST SIDE STORY*)
(*Music by* Leonard Bernstein.)(Act 2)

Added for subsequent national tour:

"Don't Laugh" (from *HOT SPOT*)
(*Music by* Mary Rodgers.)

[28]Dropped during the run.

[29]Dropped during the run.

[30]Dropped during the run.

[31]Dropped during the run.

[32]Dropped during the run.

1977.06

ANNIE

A Musical in Two Acts, 13 Scenes. Book by Thomas Meehan. Based on the "Little Orphan Annie" comic strip (by Harold Gray). Music by Charles Strouse. Lyrics by Martin Charnin. Musical numbers choreographed by Peter Gennaro. Directed by Martin Charnin. Settings by David Mitchell. Costumes by Theoni V. Aldredge. Lighting by Judy Rasmuson. Musical direction and dance music arranged by Peter Howard. Orchestrations by Philip J. Lang. Produced by Mike Nichols, Irwin Meyer, Stephen R. Friedman, Lewis Allen, Alvin Nederlander Associates, Inc., Icarus Productions in association with Peter Krane. Opened 21 April 1977 at the Alvin Theatre, moved 16 September 1981 to the ANTA Theatre, moved 29 October 1981 to the Eugene O'Neill Theatre, moved 10 December 1981 to the Uris Theatre and closed 2 January 1983 after 2377 performances.

CAST (in order of appearance): *Molly*: Danielle Brisebois. *Pepper*: Robyn Finn. *Duffy*: Donna Graham. *July*: Janine Ruane. *Tessie*: Diana Barrows. *Kate*: Shelley Bruce. *Annie*: ANDREA McARDLE. *Miss Hannigan*: DOROTHY LOUDON. *Bundles McCloskey*: James Hosbein. *Dog Catchers*: Steven Boockvor, Donald Craig. *Sandy*: Himself. *Lieutenant Ward*: Richard Ensslen. *Harry*: RAYMOND THORNE. *Sophie, the Kettle*: LAURIE BEECHMAN. *Grace Farrell*: SANDY FAISON. *Drake*: Edwin Bordo. *Mrs. Pugh*: Edie Cowan. *Cecille*: LAURIE BEECHMAN. *Annette*: Penny Worth. *Oliver Warbucks*: REID SHELTON. *A Star to Be*: LAURIE BEECHMAN. *Rooster Hannigan*: ROBERT FITCH. *Lily*: BARBARA ERWIN. *Bert Healy*: Donald Craig. *Fred McCracken*: Bob Freschi. *Jimmy Johnson*: Steven Boockvor. *Sound Effects Man*: James Hosbein. *Bonnie Boylan*: LAURIE BEECHMAN. *Connie Boylan*: Edie Cowan. *Ronnie Boylan*: Penny Worth. *NBC Page*: Mari McMinn. *Kaltenborn's Voice*: Donald Craig. *FDR*: RAYMOND THORNE. *Ickes*: James Hosbein. *Howe*: Bob Freschi. *Morgenthau*: Richard Ensslen. *Hull*: Donald Craig. *Perkins*: LAURIE BEECHMAN. *Honor Guard*: Steven Boockvor. *Justice Brandeis*: Richard Ensslen.

Hooverville-ites, Policemen, Servants, New Yorkers: Laurie Beechman, Steven Boockvor, Edwin Bordo, Edie Cowan, Donald Craig, Richard Ensslen, Barbara Erwin, Bob Freschi, James Hosbein, Mari McMinn, Penny Worth.

The action takes place 11-25 December 1933 in New York City.

Act 1: 11-19 December 1933. *Scene 1*: The New York Municpal Orphanage (Girls' Annex). *Scene 2*: St. Mark's Place. *Scene 3*: A Hooverville under the 59th Street Bridge. *Scene 4*: The Orphanage. *Scene 5*: The Warbucks Mansion at Fifth Avenue and 82nd Street. *Scene 6*: New York City. *Scene 7*: The Orphanage. *Scene 8*: Warbucks' Study.

Act 2: 21-25 December 1933. *Scene 1*: The NBC Radio Studio at 30 Rockefeller Center and the Orphanage. *Scene 2*: The Orphanage. *Scene 3*: Washington: The White House. *Scene 4*: The Great Hall at the Warbucks Mansion. *Scene 5*: The East Ballroom of the Warbucks Mansion.

ACT 1

Scene 1

"Maybe"A. McArdle

"It's the Hard-Knock Life"
A. McArdle, Orphans

"It's the Hard-Knock Life"
(reprise)Orphans

Scene 2

"Tomorrow"
A. McArdle

Scene 3

"We'd Like to Thank You (Herbert Hoover)"
The Hoover-ites

Scene 4

"Little Girls"
D. Loudon

Scene 5

"I Think I'm Gonna Like It Here"

S. Faison, A. McArdle, E. Bordo, L. Bechman, P. Worth, E. Cowan, Other Servants

Scene 6

"N.Y.C."

R. Shelton, S. Faison, A. McArdle, L. Beechman, New Yorkers

Scene 7

"Easy Street"

D. Loudon, B. Fitch, B. Erwin

Scene 8

"You Won't Be an Orphan For Long"

S. Faison, E. Bordo, E. Cowan, L. Beechman, P. Worth, Servants, R. Shelton

ACT 2

Scene 1

"You're Never Fully Dressed Without a Smile"

D. Craig, L. Beechman, E. Cowan, P. Worth, "The Hour of Smiles" Family

Scene 2

"You're Never Fully Dressed Without a Smile" (reprise)

Orphans

"Easy Street" (reprise)

D. Loudon, B. Fitch, B. Erwin

Scene 3

"Tomorrow" (reprise)

A. McArdle, R. Thorne, R. Shelton, The Cabinet

Scene 4

"Something Was Missing"

R. Shelton

"I Don't Need Anything But You"

R. Shelton, A. McArdle

Scene 5

"Annie"

S. Faison, E. Bordo, The Staff

"Maybe" (reprise)

A. McArdle

"A New Deal for Christmas"

A. McArdle, R. Shelton, S. Faison, R. Thorne, The Staff

1977.07 THE KING AND I

A Revival of the Musical Play in Two Acts, 17 Scenes[33]. Book and lyrics by Oscar Hammerstein II. Music by Richard Rodgers. Based on the novel "Anna and the King of Siam" by Margaret Landon. Original choreography by Jerome Robbins. Entire production directed by Yuriko. Settings by Peter Wolf. Costumes by Stanley Simmons, based on the original costumes by Irene Sharaff. Lighting by Thomas Skelton. (Orchestrations by Robert Russell Bennett.) Musical supervisor, Milton Rosenstock. Musical director, John Lesko. Sound by T. Richard Fitzgerald. Associate producer, Fred Walker. Produced by Lee Guber and Shelly Gross. Opened 2 May 1977 at the Uris Theatre and closed 30 December 1978 after 719 performances.

CAST (in order of appearance): *Captain Orton*: Larry Swansen. *Louis Leonowens*: Alan Amick. *Anna Leonowens*: CONSTANCE TOWERS. *The Interpreter*: Jae Woo Lee. *The Kralahome*: MICHAEL KERMOYAN. *The King*: YUL BRYNNER. *Tuptim*: JUNE ANGELA. *Lady Thiang*: HYE-YOUNG CHOI. *Prince Chulalongkorn*: Gene Profanato. *Princess Ying Yaowalak*: Julie Woo. *Lun Tha*: MARTIN VIDNOVIC. *Sir Edward Ramsay*: JOHN MICHAEL KING.

The Small House of Uncle Thomas (ballet): *Narrator*: JUNE ANGELA. *Uncle Thomas*: Jessicca Chao. *Topsy*: Lei-Lynne Doo. *Little Eva*: Diane Lam. *Eliza*: Susan Kikuchi. *King Simon*: Rebecca West. *Angel*: Patricia Weber. *Royal Dancers*: Dale Hairmoto, Barrett Hong, Faye Fujisaka Mar, Ric Ornellas, Libby Rhodes, Cecile Santos, Hope Sogawa, Chandra Tanna, Patricia K. Thomas, Henry Yu. *Propmen*: Kaipo Daniels, Jae Woo Lee, Thomas J. Rees, Robert Vega.

The Royal Dancers and Wives: Su Applegate, Jessica Chao, Lei-Lynn Doo, Dale Harimoto, Pamela Kait, Susan Kikuchi, Faye Fujisaki Mar, Sumiko Murashima, Libby Rhodes, Cecile Santos, Hope Sogawa, Mary Ann Teng, Patricia K. Thomas. *Princesses and Princes*: Ivan Ho, Clark Huang, Annie Lam, Connie Lam, Jennifer Lam, Paul Siu, Tim Waldrip, Kevan Weber, Kym Weber, Julie Woo, Mary Woo. *Nurses and Amazons*: Sidney Smith, Marianne Tatum, Patricia K. Thomas, Rebecca West. *Priests and Slaves*: Kaipo Daniels, Barrett Hong, Jae Woo Lee, Ric Ornellas, Simeon Den, Chandra Tanna, Robert Vega.

[33]Originally produced in New York 29 March 1951 at the St. James Theatre for 1246 performances. For Synopsis of Scenes and Musical Numbers, see original 1951 production.

1977.08 HAPPY END

A Musical in Three Acts, 4 Scenes and a Prologue[34]. Original German play by Elisabeth Hauptmann. Music by Kurt Weill. (Original German) Lyrics by Bertolt Brecht. Book and lyrics adapted by Michael Feingold. Directed and staged by Robert Kalfin and Patricia Birch. Scenic design by Robert U. Taylor. Costumes by Carrie F. Robbins. Lighting by Jennifer Tipton. Musical direction by Roland Gagnon. Associate producer, Wilder Luke Burnap. Chelsea Theatre Center Production newly conceived by Robert Kalfin. Produced by Michael Harvey and the Chelsea Theater Center (Robert Kalfin, Artistic director; Michael David, Executive director). Opened 7 May 1977 at the Martin Beck Theatre and closed 10 July 1977 after 75 performances. Total including Off-Broadway, 131 performances.

CAST (in order of appearance): *The Gang*: *Bill Cracker*: CHRISTOPHER LLOYD. *Sam "Mammy" Wurlitzer*: BENJAMIN RAYSON. *Dr. Nakamura* ("The Governor"): Tony Azito. *Jimmy Dexter* ("The Reverend"): John A. Coe. *Bob Marker* ("The Professor"): Robert Weil. *Johnny Flint* ("Baby Face"): Raymond Barry. *A Lady in Gray* ("The Fly"): GRAYSON HALL. *Miriam*, the Barmaid: Donna Emmanuel.

The Army: *Lieutenant Lillian Holiday* ("Hallelujah Lil"): MERYL STREEP. *Major Stone*: Liz Sheridan. *Captain Hannibal Jackson*: Joe Grifasi. *Sister Mary*: Prudence Wright Holmes. *Sister Jane*: Alexandra Borrie. *Brother Ben Owens*: Christopher Cara.

The Fold: Kristin Joliff, Frank Kopyc, Tom Mardirosian, Martha Miller, Victor Pappas. *A Cop*: David Pursley.

The action takes place in Chicago in December of 1915.

Act 1: Bill's Beer Hall. 22 December.

Act 2: The Salvation Army Mission, Canal Street. 23 December.

Act 3, Scene 1: The Beer Hall. 24 December. *Scene 2*: The Mission Hall. Later that night.

Prologue

Prologue

Entire Company

ACT 1

"The Bilbao Song"

C. Lloyd, The Gang

"Lieutenants of the Lord"

M. Streep, The Army

"March Ahead"

The Army

"The Sailors' Tango"

M. Streep

ACT 2

"Brother, Give Yourself a Shove"

The Army, The Fold

"Song of the Big Shot"

T. Azito

"Don't Be Afraid"

A. Borrie, The Army, The Fold

"In Our Childhood's Bright Endeavor"

J. Grifasi

"The Liquor Dealer's Dream"

J. Grifasi, T. Azito, A. Borrie, The Army , The Fold

ACT 3

Scene 1

"The Mandalay Song"

B. Rayson, The Gang

"Surabaya Johnny"

M. Streep

"Song of the Big Shot" (reprise)

C. Lloyd

"Ballad of the Lily of Hell"

G. Hall

[34]First produced in New York Off-Broadway 8 March 1977 at the Chelsea Theatre Center of Brooklyn for 56 performances.

Scene 2

"The Happy End"-Finale

Entire Company

TOLLER CRANSTON'S THE ICE SHOW

1977.09

An Ice Skating Revue in Two Acts, 5 Scenes. Original music (and lyrics) by Al Kasha and Joel Hirschhorn[35]. Produced and directed by Myrl A. Schreibman. Set design by Anthony Sabatino, William H. Harris. Costume design by Miles White. Lighting design by D. Scott Linder. Sound Design by Jack Shirk. Choreography and staging by Brian Foley. Additional choreography by Ellen Burka. Music supervision by Bill Courtney. Skating consultant, Bill Turner. Produced by Dennis Bass and Robin Cranston. Opened 19 May 1977 at the Palace Theatre and closed 10 July 1977 after 60 performances.

CAST: TOLLER CRANSTON, JIM MILLNS and COLLEEN O'CONNOR, GORDON McKELLEN, JR., KEN SHELLEY, Wendy Burge, Candy Jones and Don Fraser, Kathy Malmberg, Barbara Berezowski and David Porter, Elizabeth Freeman, Jack Courtney and Emily Benenson, Janet and Mark Hominuke.

ACT 1

Overture & Introduction
Full Company
(*Music and Lyrics by* Al Kasha and Joel Hirschhorn.)

Scene 1: Trilogy

"Thus Spake Zarathustra"
D. Fraser, C. Jones

"Candide"
E. Freeman

"Somewhere"
D. Porter, B. Berezowski

"Captain from Castille"
D. Fraser, C. Jones, E. Freeman, D. Porter, B. Berezowski

"Son of a Gun"
K. Shelley, C. O'Connor

"Let's Hear It for Me"
W. Burge

"Free Again"
K. Malmberg

"On the Waterfront"
J. Courtney, E. Benenson

"Nicholas and Alexandra"
T. Cranston

Scene 2: Dance Medley

"Rock Around the Clock"
C. Jones, D. Fraser

"Charleston"
J. Courtney, E. Benenson

"Tango"
J. Courtney, E. Benenson

"Nola"
C. Jones, D. Fraser

"Sugar Blues"
B. Berezowski, D. Porter

"Fascination, "Varsity Drag," "Darktown Strutters Ball"
All the Couples

"My Wife the Dancer"
G. McKellen, Jr.

Scene 3: Russian Ode

"The Young and the Restless"
J. Millns, C. O'Connor

"Innocence"
J. Hominuke, M. Hominuke

"Love Duet"
T. Cranston, E. Benenson

"The Warlords"
G. McKellen, Jr., J. Courtney

"Loneliness of War"
T. Cranston

"Vision"
D. Porter, B. Berezowski

"Dream of Love"
T. Cranston, E. Benenson

"Emptiness and Longing"
T. Cranston

ACT 2

Scene 1: Toller's Ball

"Le Prophète"
Full Company

"Graduation Ball I"
T. Cranston

"Corsaire I"
D. Fraser, C. Jones

"Graduation Ball II"
T. Cranston

"Corsaire II"
J. Millns, C. O'Connor

"Graduation Ball III"
T. Cranston

"Le Prophète" (reprise)
Full Company

"Gaité Parisienen"
E. Freeman

"Raymonda"
W. Burge

"Pas de Deux"
J. Hominuke, M. Hominuke

"Black Orpheus"
K. Malmberg

"MacArthur Park"
G. McKellen, Jr.

"Tick-Tock"
D. Fraser, C. Jones

Scene 2: Latino

"Rodrigo"
J. Courtney, E. Benenson

"Habanera"
J. Millns, C. O'Connor

"La Carioca"
D. Porter, B. Berezowski

"Scheherezade"
K. Shelley

"A Fifth of Beethoven"
J. Millns, C. O'Connor

"I Pagliacci"
T. Cranston

Finale
Full Company

[35]Much of the musical score was comprised of popular standards from the worlds of popular and classical music; Messrs. Kasha and Hirshhorn's contributions were not individually identified.

1977–1978 SEASON

Judy Kaye and Madeline Kahn in ON THE TWENTIETH CENTURY
Martha Swope/TimePix

1977–1978 SEASON

1977.10 BEATLEMANIA

A Musical Entertainment in Two Acts, 9 Scenes. Songs (music and lyrics) written by John Lennon, Paul McCartney, George Harrison. Editorial content by Robert Rabinowitz, Bob Gill, Lynda Obst. Visuals director, Charles E. Hoeffler. Multi-media images by Robert Rabinowitz, Bob Gill, Shep Kerman, Kathleen Rabinowitz. Original concept by Steven Leber, David Krebs, Jules Fisher. All songs except where indicated licensed by ATV Music Group. Scenery by Robert D. Mitchell. Lighting by Jules Fisher. Sound design by Abe Jacob. Musical supervision by Sandy Yaguda. Special consultant, Murray the K. Production supervised by Jules Fisher. Produced by David Krebs and Steven Leber. Opened 1 June 1977 at the Winter Garden, moved 1 March 1979 to the Lunt-Fontanne Theatre, and closed 17 October 1979 after 1006 performances.

CAST: JOE PECORINO (rhythm guitar), MITCH WEISSMAN (bass guitar), LESLIE FRADKIN (lead guitar), JUSTIN McNEIL (drums).

Act 1, Scene 1: Camelot: Pre-Beatles. *Scene 2*: The Coming. *Scene 3*: Making It. *Scene 4*: Listening. *Scene 5*: Tripping.

Act 2, Scene 1: Dropping Out. *Scene 2*: Flower Power. *Scene 3*: Bottoming Out. *Scene 4*: Moving On.

ACT 1

Scene 1

"Let's Twist Again"
(*Music and Lyrics by* Kal Mann and Dave Appell.)

"Roll Over Beethoven"
(*Music and Lyrics by* Chuck Berry.)

"Bye Bye Love"
(*Music and Lyrics by* Felice Bryant and Boudleaux Bryant.)

"Hound Dog"
(*Music and Lyrics by* Jerry Lieber and Mike Stoller.)

The early 1960's begin with an all-time optimism in America. Youthful and elegant, John F. Kennedy charms the public and press while his First Family welcomes the public into the White House. His assassination on 22 November 1963 shocks the country in a horrifying introduction to what's to become the most turbulent of decades.

Scene 2

"I Want to Hold Your Hand"
(*Music and Lyrics by* John Lennon and Paul McCartney.)

"She Loves You"
(*Music and Lyrics by* John Lennon and Paul McCartney.)

Television viewers watch open-mouthed as a group of four Liverpudlians explode on national television. Shortly after their debut in February 1964, the light-hearted mop-topped jesters begin to win recognition and attention never before given to rock and roll artists.

Scene 3

"Help!"

"If I Fell"

"Can't Buy Me Love"

"Day Tripper"

The "Fab Four" establish themselves as style-getters, innovators, movie stars, recording artists and fashion-makers with a contagious sense of humor, newness and excitement.

Scene 4

"Yesterday"

"Eleanor Rigby'

"We Can Work It Out"

"Nowhere Man"

As the group begins to mature musically, a sense of introspection is felt through their music. Critics begin to give them more serious consideration, while an increasing number and diversity of fans await the changing sounds of each newly released recording.

Scene 5

"A Day in the Life"

"Strawberry Fields Forever"

"Penny Lane"

"Magical Mystery Tour"

"Lucy in the Sky With Diamonds"

Becoming an accepted entity by the "establishment," the group takes on a whole new direction with musical experimentation and sensual, psychedelic perceptions. Their music is becoming a directional for the increasing "counter-culture" and anti-establishment youth movement.

ACT 2

Scene 1

"Lady Madonna"

"The Fool on the Hill"

"Got to Get You into My Life"

"Michelle"

"Get Back"

Their growing musical styles have connected with other cultures and life-styles through a multi-dimensional sound which defies categorization. The country's youth follows suit in more personal, individualized self-exploration and unconventional answers to an unresponsive and static society.

Scene 2

"Come Together"

"With a Little Help from My Friends"

"All You Need Is Love"

Holding its own, the youth movement becomes an established force and reality, influencing all phases of society, as the "hippies" and "street-people" of Haight-Ashbury and New York's Lower East Side reach far beyond their coastal boundaries into the homes of middle-America.

Scene 3

"Revolution"

"Helter Skelter"

"Hey Jude"

The assassinations of Martin Luther King, Jr. and Robert Kennedy traumatize the country. The War in Vietnam rages on, and the confusion, anger and violent confrontations in the streets of the U.S. splinter any hopeful ideals left from the early years of the decade. The group moves towards separation.

Scene 4

"I Am the Walrus"

"The Long and Winding Road"

"Let It Be"

The decade climaxes as the group itself splits apart. Their songs, now individual statements, are reflective of their own personal choices and life-styles, while the wealth of collective material remains, painting a spectrum of images ranging from the innocent to innovators, from the celebrities to the outlaws; always growing, creating and moving beyond their audiences.

1977.11 DIE FLEDERMAUS

A Revival of the Operetta in Three Acts[1]. Original Viennese libretto by Carl Haffner and Richard Genée. Lyrics by Richard Genée. (Based on the comedy "Le Réveillon" by Henri Meilhac and Ludovic Halévy.) English libretto by Ruth and Thomas Martin. Music by Johann Strauss. Production devised and directed by Gerald Freedman. Stage director, Richard Getke. Choreography by Thomas Andrew. Scenery designed by Lloyd Evans Costumes design by Theoni V. Aldredge. Lighting by Hans Sondheimer. Conducted by Julius Rudel. Chorus master, Lloyd Walser. Produced by the

[1]First English language production in New York 16 March 1885 at the Casino Theatre for 42 performances. First New York production of this adaptation 20 December 1950 at the Metropolitan Opera House. For Synopsis of Scenes and Musical Numbers, see May 1954 revival.

New York City Opera. Opened 2 September 1977 at the New York State Theatre and closed 1 November 1977 after 7 performances in repertory; returned 8 March 1978 to the New York State Theatre and closed 11 April 1978 after 3 performances in repertory. Total this season: 10 performances.

CAST (in order of appearance): *Alfred*, an itinerant tenor: Henry Price. *Adele*, von Eisenstein's chambermaid: BEVERLY SILLS. *Rosalinda von Eisenstein*: JOHANNA MEIER. *Gabriel von Eisenstein*: CHARLES ROE. *Dr. Blind*, a lawyer: Melvin Lowery. *Dr. Falke*, a close friend of Eisenstein: DAVID HOLLOWAY. *Frank*, the prison warden: RICHARD McKEE. *Sally*, Adele's sister: Puli Toro. *Ivan*, servant to Orlofsky: Jack Sims. *Prince Orlofsky*, a wealthy, bored Russian: DAVID RAE SMITH. *Frosch*, the jailer: Coley Worth. *Solo Dancers*: Sandra Balestracci, Esperanza Galan, Juliu Horvath. *Ensemble*: New York City Opera Chorus.

1977.12 MAN OF LA MANCHA

A Revival of the Musical Play in One Act[2]. Book by Dale Wasserman. Suggested by the life and work ("Don Quixote") of Miguel de Cervantes y Saavedra. Music by Mitch Leigh. Lyrics by Joe Darion. Production (direction) and musical staging by Albert Marre. Setting and lighting by Howard Bay. Costumes by Howard Bay and Patton Campbell. Music arrangements by Music Makers Inc. Musical direction by Robert Brandzel. Produced by Eugene V. Wolsk. Opened 15 September 1977 at the Palace Theatre and closed 31 December 1977 after 124 performances.

CAST (in order of appearance): *Don Quixote (Cervantes)*: RICHARD KILEY. *Sancho*: TONY MARTINEZ. *The Horse*: Ben Vargas. *The Mule*: Hector Mercado. *The Innkeeper*: BOB WRIGHT. *Maria*, the Innkeeper's Wife: Marceline Decker. *Pedro*, Head Muleteer: Chev Rodgers. *Anselmo*, a Muleteer: Ted Forlow. *Juan*, a Muleteer: Mark Holliday. *Tenorio*, a Muleteer: Ben Vargas. *Paco*, a Muleteer: Anthony DeVecchi. *Jose*, a Muleteer: Hector Mercado. *Aldonza*: EMILY YANCY. *Fermina*, a slavey: Joan Susswein. *Guitarist*: Robin Polseno. *Jorge*, a Muleteer: Edmond Varrato. *Fernando*, a Muleteer: David Wasson. *Antonia*: HARRIETT CONRAD. *The Housekeeper*: MARGRET COLEMAN. *The Padre*: TAYLOR REED. *Dr. Carrasco*: IAN SULLIVAN. *The Barber*: Ted Forlow. *Moorish Dancer*: Joan Susswein. *The Captain of the Inquisition*: Renato Cibelli. *Guards*: Michael St. Paul, David Wasson.

1977.13 ESTRADA

The 1977 Music and Dance Festival (A Russian Language Variety Revue) from the Soviet Union in Two Acts. Artistic director, Nikolai Laktionov. Administrative director, Nadezhda Kazantzeva. Choreographer, Tamara Golovanova. Production supervisor, M. William Lettich. Production manager, Savely Onishchenko. Produced by United Euram. Opened 20 September 1977 at the Majestic Theatre and closed 24 September 1977 after 7 performances.

CAST: NANI BREGVADZE (Singer), GRIGORI DAVIDENKO and VLADIMIR KONONOVICH (Ukranian Comic Dance Team), NATALIA and OLEG KIRIUSHKIN (Mimes), LARISA KUDEYAROVA (Acrobat), YEFIM LEVINSON and GALINA KORZINA (Puppet Masters), ORERA (Georgian Vocal Instrumental Group){Nani Bregvadze, Zurab Yashvili, Vakhtang Kikabidze, Teimuraz Megvinet-Ukhutsesi, Alexander Mandjgaladze, Teimuraz Davitaya, Geno Nadirashvili}, PESNYARY (Pop-Rock Group), VLADIMIR SEROV (Cyclist/Aerialist), SOUVENIR ENSEMBLE (Dance Ensemble); ALLA, VYACHESLAV and VYACHESLAV RASSHIVKIN, JR. (Acrobats).

ACT 1

"Moscow Nights"
(*Music and Lyrics by* V. Soloviev-Sedoy.)
Entire Cast

"Korobeiniki" (Russian Dance)
Souvenir Ensemble

Four Contemporary Byelorussian Folk Songs
Pesnyary Ensemble

"Dva Kuma" (Comic Dance)
V. Kononovich, G. Davidenko

Northern Festive Dance
Souvenir Ensemble

"A Friendship That Never Came to Be"
Souvenir Ensemble

Puppet Sketches
Y. Levinson, G. Korzina

"Barynya" (Russian Dance)
Souvenir Ensemble

ACT 2

Sabre Dance
Souvenir Ensemble

"Give My Regards to Broadway"
Orera Ensemble
(*Music and Lyrics by* George M. Cohan.)

Bicycle on the High Wire
V. Serov

"Serdtse"
Orera Ensemble
(*Music and Lyrics by* I. Dunaevsky.)

"Svetlyachok" (Georgian Folk Song)
Orera Ensemble

"Tbiliso"
N. Bregvadze
(*Music by* Revaz Lagidze. *Lyrics by* Peter Gruzinsky.)

"Dorogoy Dlinoyu" (Old Song)
N. Bregvadze

Acrobatic Sketch with a Hoop
L. Kudeyarova

Gypsy Fantasy
Souvenir Ensemble

Acrobatic Sketch
Alla, 2 Vyacheslav Rasshivkins

Specialty
N. Kiriushkin, O. Kiriushkin

"Potekha" (Comic Dance)
Souvenir Ensemble

Finale
Entire Cast

1977.14 COMEDY WITH MUSIC

A Revival of the Musical Entertainment in Two Acts[3]. Conceived and devised by Victor Borge. Production designed by Neil Peter Jampolis. Miss Mulvey's gown by Donald Brooks. Associate producers, Dean Lenz, Allison McLeod. Produced by The Edgewood Organization (Lewis Friedman, John W. Ballard, Executive directors). Opened 3 October 1977 at the Imperial Theatre and closed 16 November 1977 after 64 performances.

CAST: VICTOR BORGE, MARYLYN MULVEY.

ACT 1

Victor Borge

ACT 2

The Concert
Marylyn Mulvey
Victor Borge
The Audience

1977.15 HAIR

A Revival of the American Tribal Love-Rock Musical in Two Acts[4]. Book and lyrics by Gerome Ragni and James Rado. Music by Galt MacDermott.

---

[2]First produced in New York 22 November 1965 at the ANTA Washington Square Theatre for 2328 performances. For Synopsis of Scenes and Musical Numbers, see original 1965 production.

[3]Originally produced in New York as *COMEDY IN MUSIC* 2 October 1953 at the John Golden Theatre for 849 performances.

[4]First produced in New York Off-Broadway 17 October 1967 at the Anspacher Theatre for 50 performances, at the Cheetah 22 December 1967 for 45 performances; transferred to Broadway 29 April 1968 to the

Directed by Tom O'Horgan. Choreography, Julie Arenal. Musical director, Denzil A. Miller, Jr. Costume design by Nancy Potts. Scenic design by Robin Wagner. Lighting design by Jules Fisher. Sound design by Abe Jacob. Vocal direction by Patrick Flynn. Associate producer, George Milman. Produced by Michael Butler in association with K. H. Nezhad. Opened 5 October 1977 at the Biltmore Theatre and closed 6 November 1977 after 43 performances.

CAST (in order of appearance): *Claude*: RANDALL EASTERBROOK. *Berger*: MICHAEL HOIT. *Woof*: SCOTT THORNTON. *Hud*: CLEAVANT DERRICKS. *Sheila*: ELLEN FOLEY. *Jeanie*: IRIS ROSENKRANTZ. *Dionne*: ALAINA REED. *Crissy*: KRISTEN VIGARD. *Shopping Cart Lady*: Michael Leslie. *Mothers*: ANNIE GOLDEN, LOUIS MATTIOLI, PERRY ARTHUR. *Fathers*: James Rich, Eva Charney, Martha Wingate. *Principals*: Carl Woerner, Michael Leslie, Linda Myers. *Tourist Couple*: Perry Arthur, Carl Woerner. *General Grant*: CARL WOERNER. *Abraham Lincoln*: Linda Myers. *Sergeant*: Byron Utley. *Parents*: Lori Wagner, James Rich.

The Tribe: Perry Arthur, Emily Bindinger, Paul Binotto, Eva Charney, Loretta Devine, Doug Katsaros, Michael Leslie, Louis Mattioli, Linda Myers, Raymond Patterson, James Rich, James Sbano, Deborah Van Valkenburgh, Lori Wagner, Doug Wall, Martha Wingate, Carl Woerner, Charlaine Woodard.

1977.16 THE ACT

A Musical in Two Acts, 16 Scenes. Book by George Furth. Music by John Kander. Lyrcis by Fred Ebb. Directed by Martin Scorsese. Choreography by Ron Lewis. Scenery designed by Tony Walton. Lighting designed by Tharon Musser. Costumes designed by Halston. Sound designed by Abe Jacob. Musical direction by Stanley Lebowsky. Orchestrations by Ralph Burns. Dance music arrangements by Ronald Melrose. Vocal and choral arrangements by Earl Brown. Produced by The Shubert Organization, Cy Feuer and Ernest H. Martin. Opened 29 October 1977 at the Majestic Theatre and closed 1 July 1978 after 233 performances.

CAST (in order of appearance): *Lenny Kanter*: Christopher Barrett. *Michelle Craig*: LIZA MINNELLI. *Nat Schreiber*: Arnold Soboloff. *Dan Connors*: BARRY NELSON. *Arthur*: Roger Minami. *Charley Price*: Mark Goddard. *Molly Connors*: Gayle Crofoot.
The Boys: Wayne Cilento, Michael Leeds, Roger Minami, Albert Stephenson. *The Girls*: Carol Estey, Laurie Dawn Skinner. *Dance Alternates*: Claudia Asbury, Brad Witsger.

The action takes place at the Hotel Las Vegas at the present time and concerns Michelle Craig's nightclub act and her memories.

ACT 1
Scene 1
"Shine It On"
(L. Minnelli, Chorus)
Scene 2
"It's the Strangest Thing"
(L. Minnelli)
Scene 4
"Bobo's"
(L. Minnelli, Dancers)
Scene 5
"Turning" (Shaker Hymn)
Scene 6
"Little Do They Know"
(Boys, Girls)
Scene 7
"Arthur in the Afternoon"
(L. Minnelli, R. Minami)
Scene 9
"Hollywood, California"[5]
(L. Minnelli, Dancers)
Scene 11
"The Money Tree"
(L. Minnelli)
ACT 2
Scene 1
"City Lights"
(L. Minnelli, Chorus)
Scene 2
"There When I Need Him"
(L. Minnelli)
Scene 4
"Hot Enough for You?"
(L. Minnelli, Dancers)
"Little Do They Know" (reprise)
(Boys, Girls)
Scene 5
Finale[6]
"My Own Space"
(L. Minnelli)

1977.17 THE PIRATES OF PENZANCE, or The Slave of Duty

A Revival of the Comic Opera in Two Acts[7]. Libretto by William S. Gilbert. Music by Arthur Sullivan. Production directed by Jack Eddleman. Scenic design by Lloyd Evans. Costume design by Patton Campbell. Lighting design by Hans Sondheimer. Conductor, Judith Somogi. Chorus master, Lloyd Walser. Produced by the New York City Opera. Opened 29 October 1977 at the New York State Theatre and closed 6 November 1977 after 2 performances in repertory.

CAST: *Major General Stanley*: JAMES BILLINGS. *The Pirate King*: RICHARD McKEE. *Samuel*, his Lieutenant: James Sergi. *Frederic*, the Pirate Apprentice: HOWARD HENSEL. *Sergeant of Police*: IRWIN DENSEN. *Mabel, Edith, Kate, Isabel*, General Stanley's Daughters: GIANNA ROLANDI, DIANA KEHRIG, SANDRA WALKER, LUXEMBURG. *Ruth*, Pirate Maid-of-all-work: MURIEL COSTA-GREENSPON. *Solo Dancer*: Rafael Romero. *Chorus of Pirates, Police and General Stanley's Daughters*: New York City Opera Chorus.

1977.18 JESUS CHRIST SUPERSTAR

A Revival of the Musical in Two Acts[8]. Music by Andrew Lloyd Webber. Lyrics by Tim Rice. Directed by William Daniel Grey. Choreography and movement by Kelly Carrol. Musical direction by Peter Phillips.Wardobe supervisor, Joan Lucas. Produced by Hal Zeiger. Opened 23 November 1977 at the Longacre Theatre and closed 12 February 1978 after 96 performances[9].

CAST (in order of appearance): *Judas Iscariot*: PATRICK JUDE. *Jesus of Nazareth*: WILLIAM DANIEL GREY. *Mary Magdalene*: BARBARA NILES. *First Priest, Apostle*: Doug Lucas. *Second Priest, Apostle*: Richard Tolin. *Caiaphas*: CHRISTOPHER CABLE. *Annas*: STEVE SCHOCHET. *Simon Zealotes*: BOBBY LONDON. *Peter*: RANDY MARTIN. *Pontius Pilate*: RANDY WILSON. *Soldier, Tormentor*: D. Bradley Jones. *Soldier, Tormentor*: George Bernhard. *Soul Girls*: Freida Ann Williams, Pauletta Pearson, Claudette Washington. *Maid by the Fire*: Celeste Hogan. *Apostles*: David Cahn, Ken Samuels, Lennie Del Duca. *King Herod*: MARK SYERS.

Biltmore Theatre for 1750 performances. For Synopsis of Scenes and Musical Numbers, see original 1968 production. For this production; the following changes were made:
"Dead End" (added to Act 1 after "Ain't Got No")
"Hung" (dropped)
"Prisoners in Niggertown" retitled "Three-Five-Zero-Zero."
[5]Dropped during run.

[6]Replaced after opening with:
"Walking Papers"
(L. Minnelli)
[7]First presented in New York 31 December 1879 at the Fifth Avenue Theatre for a total of 91 performances in two engagements. For Synopsis of Scenes and Musical Numbers, see original 1879 production.
[8]First produced in New York 12 October 1971 at the Mark Hellinger Theatre for 711 performances. For Synopsis of Scenes and Musical Numbers, see original 1971 production.
[9]This revival was staged concert style; orchestrations, costumes, sets, lighting and sound were uncredited.

1978.01 ELVIS: THE LEGEND LIVES!

A Musical Entertainment in Two Acts, 5 Scenes. Production concept by John Finocchio, Larry Marshak, David Zaan. (Based on the life and music of Elvis Presley.) Directed by Jim Sotos and Henry Scarpelli. Musical director, Peter Dino. Special consultant, Paul Lichter. Title music by Doc Pomus and Bruce Foster. Lighting by Barry Arnold. Sound by Joe Golden. Visual concepts and design by Productions Two. Produced by DL Theatrical Productions Inc. (John Finocchio, Larry Marshak, David Zaan). Opened 31 January 1978 at the Palace Theatre and closed 30 April 1978 after 101 performances.

CAST: RICK SAUCEDO, THE JORDANAIRES (Gordon Stoker, Neal Matthews, Hoyt Hawkins), WILL JORDON, D. J. FONTANA. *Kharisma*: Bernice Frazier, Judith O'Dell, April Epps.

Act 1, Scene 1: The Music That Led to the King of Rock 'n Roll. *Scene 2*: Sun Recording Session. *Scene 3*: The Louisiana Hayride. *Scene 4*: The Ed Sullivan Show.

Act 2: International Hotel, Las Vegas.

ACT 1[10]

Scene 1

"Mood Indigo"

"Anytime"

"When the Saints Go Marching In"

"In the Mood"

"Johnny Be Good"

"C. C. Rider"

Scene 2

"Blue Moon of Kentucky"

"When My Blue Moon Turns to Gold Again"

Scene 3

"Heartbreak Hotel"

"How Great Thou Art"

Scene 4

"Reddy Teddy"/"Tutti Fruiti" medley

"Don't Be Cruel"

"One Night With You"

"Lawdy Miss Clawdy"

"A Fool Such As I"

"Hound Dog"

ACT 2

"Theme from 2001"

"Burning Love"

"Are You Lonesome Tonight?"

"I Just Can't Help Believing"

"You Lost That Lovin' Feeling"

"Polk Salad Annie"

"The Wonder of You"

"My Way"

"Moody Blue"

"Little Darlin'"

"In the Ghetto"

"Whole Lot of Shakin'"/"Hound Dog" (reprise)

"Sweet Caroline"

"Suspicious Minds"

"The Legend Lives On"

"American Trilogy"

[10]This composite score was made up of many rock 'n' roll and pop standards for which no credits were given.

1978.02 ON THE TWENTIETH CENTURY

A Musical Comedy in Two Acts, 15 Scenes. Book and lyrics by Betty Comden and Adolph Green. Based on the play ("Twentieth Century") by Ben Hecht, Charles MacArthur and Bruce Milholland. Music by Cy Coleman. Directed by Harold Prince. Musical numbers staged by Larry Fuller. Scenery designed by Robin Wagner. Costumes designed by Florence Klotz. Lighting designed by Ken Billington. Musical director, Paul Gemigani. Orchestrations by Hershy Kay. Furs by Ben Kahn. Associate producers, Sam Crothers, Andre Pastoria. Produced by The Producers Circle 2, Inc. (Robert Fryer, Mary Lea Johnson, James Cresson, Martin Richards) in association with Joseph Harris and Ira Bernstein. Opened 19 February 1978 at the St. James Theatre and closed 18 March 1979 after 460 performances.

CAST (in order of appearance): *Porters*: Keith Davis, Quitman Fludd III, Ray Stephens, Joseph Wise. *Conductor Flanagan*: TOM BATTEN. *Train Secretary Rogers*: STANLEY SIMMONDS. *Letitia Primrose*: IMOGENE COCA. *Owen O'Malley*: GEORGE COE. *Oliver Webb*: DEAN DITTMAN. *Redcap*: Mel Johnson, Jr. *Congressman Lockwood*: RUFUS SMITH. *Anita*: Carol (Jo) Lugenbeal. *Oscar Jaffee*: JOHN CULLUM. *Max Jacobs*: GEORGE LEE ANDREWS. *Imelda*: Willi Burke. *Maxwell Finch*: David Horwitz. *Mildred Plotka/Lily Garland*: MADELINE KAHN. *Otto Von Bismark*: Sal Mistretta. *Bruce Granit*: KEVIN KLINE. *Agnes*: JUDY KAYE. *Hospital Attendants*: Sal Mistretta, Carol Lurie. *Dr. Johnson*: WILLI BURKE.

Singers: Susan Cella, Maris Clement, Peggy Cooper, Karen Gibson, Carol Lugenbeal, Carol Lurie, Melanie Vaughan, Linda Poser, Ray Gill, Ken Hilliard, David Horwitz, Craig Lucas, Sal Mistretta, Hal Norman, Charles Rule, David Vogel, Gerald Teijelo.

The action takes place in the early 1930s, mainly on the 20th Century Limited (train) from Chicago to New York.

Act 1, Scene 1: Chicago, La Salle Station platform. *Scene 2*: The Observation Car and Drawing Room "A." *Scene 3*: Flashback to the bare stage of a theatre. *Scene 4*: Drawing Room "A." *Scene 5*: The Observation Car and Corridor. *Scene 6*: Drawing Room "B." *Scene 7*: The Observation Car. *Scene 8*: Triple Scene of the Observation Car, Drawing Room "A," Drawing Room "B." *Scene 9*; Drawing Rooms "A" and "B." *Scene 10*: Drawing Room "A."

Act 2, Scene 1: "Drawing Room "A." *Scene 2*: "Drawing Room "B." *Scene 3*: The Observation Car. *Scene 4*: Drawing Room "B" in the middle of the night. *Scene 5*: The Observation Car.

ACT 1[11]

Scene 1

"On the Twentieth Century"
Porters, I. Coca, T. Batten, S. Simmonds, Passengers

Scene 2

"I Rise Again"
J. Cullum, G. Coe, D. Dittman

Scene 3

"Indian Maiden's Lament"
W. Burke, M. Kahn

"Veronique"
M. Kahn, Male Singers

Scene 4

"I Have Written a Play"
T. Batten

Scene 5

"Together"
Porters, Passengers, J. Cullum

Scene 6

"Never"
M. Kahn, G. Coe, D. Dittman

"Our Private World"
M. Kahn, J. Cullum

Scene 7

"Repent"
I. Coca

[11]After opening, added as an additional scene set on stage during a play:
"Stranded Again"
C. Rule (as Bishop), Singers

Scene 8
"Mine"
J. Cullum, K. Kline
Scene 9
"I've Got It All"
M. Kahn, J. Cullum
Scene 10
"On the Twentieth Century" (reprise)
Company
ACT 2
Entr'acte ("Life Is Like a Train")
Porters
Scene 1
"Five Zeros"
G. Coe, D. Dittman, I. Coca, J. Cullum
Scene 2
"Sextet"
G. Coe, D. Dittman, J. Cullum, I. Coca, M. Kahn, K. Kline
Scene 3
"She's a Nut"
Company
"Max Jacobs"
G. L. Andrews
Scene 4
"Babbette"
M. Kahn
Scene 5
"The Legacy"
J. Cullum
"Lily, Oscar"
M. Kahn, J. Cullum

1978.03 TIMBUKTU!

A Musical Fable in Two Acts, 12 Scenes. Book by Luther Davis, based on the musical "Kismet"[12] by Charles Lederer and Luther Davis, from the play of the same name by Edward Knoblock. Music and lyrics by Robert Wright and George Forrest from the themes of Alexander Borodin and African Folk Music. Directed, choreographed and costumed by Geoffrey Holder. Scenery by Tony Straiges. Lighting by Ian Calderon. Sound by Abe Jacob. Musical direction and incidental music by Charles H. Coleman. Additional orchestrations by Bill Brohn. Associate producer, Alan Eichler. Produced by Luther Davis, in association with Sarnoff International Enterprises, William D. Cunningham, John F. Kennedy Center for the Performing Arts. Opened 1 March 1978 at the Mark Hellinger Theatre and closed 10 September 1978 after 243 performances.

CAST (in order of appearance): *The Chakaba*, Stiltwalker: Obba Babatunde. *Beggars*: Harold Pierson, Shezwae Powell, Lewis Tucker. *Hadji*: IRA HAWKINS. *Marsinah*, his daughter: MELBA MOORE. *Witchdoctor*: Harold Pierson. *Child*: Deborah Waller. *M'Ballah of the River*: Daniel Barton. *Najua*, Servant to Sahleem-La-Lume: Eleanor McCoy. *The Wazir*: GEORGE BELL. *Chief Policeman*: BRUCE A. HUBBARD. *Sahleem-La-Lume*: EARTHA KITT. *The Three Princesses of Baguezane*: Deborah K. Brown, Sharon Cuff, Patricia Lumpkin. *Munshi*, Bodyservant to the Mansa: MIGUEL GODREAU. *The Mansa of Mali*: GILBERT PRICE. *Orange Merchant*: Obba Babatunde. *Birds of Paradise*: Miguel Godreau, Eleanor McCoy. *Antelopes*: Obba Babatunde, Luther Fontaine. *Woman in the Garden*: Shezwae Powell. *Zubbediya*: Vanessa Shaw.

Citizens of Timbuktu: Obba Babtunde, Gregg Baker, Daniel Barton, Joella Breedlove, Deborah K. Brown, Tony Carroll, Sharon Cuff, Cheryl Cummings, Luther Fontaine, Michael F. Harrison, Dyane Harvey, Marzetta Jones, Jimmy Justice, Eugene Little, Patricia Lumpkin, Joe Lynn, Tony Ndogo, Harold Pierson, Ray Pollard, Shezwae Powell, Ronald Richardson, Vanessa Shaw, Louis Tucker, Deborah Waller, Renee Warren.

[12]First produced in New York 3 December 1953 at the Ziegfeld Theatre for 583 performances.

The action takes place in Timbuktu, in the ancient empire of Mali, West Africa, in the year 1361 (of Islam 752).

Act 1: From Dawn to Dusk. *Scene 1*: The City Square of Timbuktu—Dawn. *Scene 2*: The Gates of the City. *Scene 3*: The City Square at Market Time. *Scene 4*: A Garden of a House near the Palace. *Scene 5*: A Courtyard of the Palace. *Scene 6*: An Attiring Pavilion in the Palace.

Act 2: From Dusk to Dawn. *Scene 1*: Enroute to the Garden. *Scene 2*: The Garden. *Scene 3*: A Corridor in the Palace. *Scene 4*: The Wazir's Harem. *Scene 5*: Another Part of the Palace. *Scene 6*: Palace Court.

ACT 1
Scene 1
"Rhymes Have I"
I. Hawkins, M. Moore, Beggars
"Fate"
I. Hawkins
Scene 2
"In the Beginning, Woman"[13]
E. Kitt
Scene 3
"Baubles, Bangles and Beads"
M. Moore, Merchants
Scene 4
Dance: Birds in Paradise Garden[14]
"Stranger in Paradise"
G. Price, M. Moore
Scene 5
"Gesticulate"
I. Hawkins, Council
Scene 6
"Night of My Nights"
G. Price, Courtiers
ACT 2
Scene 1
Dance: Nuptual Celebration[15]
People of Mali
Scene 2
"My Magic Lamp"[16]/"Stranger in Paradise"
M. Moore
Scene 4
"Rahadlakum"
E. Kitt, Ladies of the Harem
Scene 5
"And This Is My Beloved"
I. Hawkins, M. Moore, G. Price, G. Bell
Scene 6
"Golden Land, Golden Life"[17]
B. A. Hubbard, Nobles of the Court
"Zubbediya" and Dances
V. Shaw, Ensemble
"Night of My Nights" (reprise)
G. Price, M. Moore, I. Hawkins, Nobles of the Court
"Sands of Time"
I. Hawkins, E. Kitt

[13]Newly written for this production, and not from the original musical score of "Kismet."
[14]Newly written for this production, and not from the original musical score of "Kismet."
[15]Newly written for this production, and not from the original musical score of "Kismet."
[16]Newly written for this production, and not from the original musical score of "Kismet."
[17]Newly written for this production, and not from the original musical score of "Kismet."

1978.04

HELLO, DOLLY!

A Revival of the Musical Comedy in Two Acts, 13 Scenes[18]. Book by Michael Stewart. Based on the play "The Matchmaker" by Thornton Wilder. Music and lyrics by Jerry Herman. Directed by Lucia Victor. Choreographed by Jack Craig. Original production directed and choreographed by Gower Champion. Settings by Oliver Smith. Costumes by Freddy Wittop. Lighting by Martin Aronstein. Musical direction by John DeMain. Conducted by Jack Everly. (Orchestrations uncredited.) Dance and incidental music arranged by Peter Howard. Production supervision by Jerry Herman. Associate producer, Robert A. Buckley. Produced by James M. Nederlander and the Houston Grand Opera Opened 5 March 1978 at the Lunt-Fontanne Theatre and closed 9 July 1978 after 147 performances.

CAST (in the order of appearance): *Mrs. Dolly Gallagher Levi*: CAROL CHANNING. *Ernestina*: P. J. Nelson. *Ambrose Kemper*: Michael C. Booker. *Horse*: Carole Banninger, Debra Pigliavento. *Horace Vandergelder*: EDDIE BRACKEN. *Ermengarde*: K. T. Baumann. *Cornelius Hackl*: LEE ROY REAMS. *Barnaby Tucker*: ROBERT LYDIARD. *Minnie Fay*: ALEXANDRA KOREY. *Irene Molloy*: FLORENCE LACEY. *Mrs. Rose*: Marilyn Hudgins. *Rudolph*: John Anania. *Judge*: Bill Bateman. *Court Clerk*: Randolph Riscol.

Townspeople, Waiters, Etc.: Diane Abrams, Carole Banninger, JoEla Flood, Marilyn Hudgins, Deborah Moldow, Janyce Nyman, Jacqueline Payne, Debra Pigliavento, Theresa Rakov, Barbara Ann Thompson, Richard Ammon, Bill Bateman, Kyle Cittadin, Ron Crofott, Don Edward Detrick, Richard Dodd, Rob Draper, David Evans, Tom Garrett, Charlie Goeddertz, James Homan, Alex MacKay, Richard Maxon, Randy Morgan, Randolph Riscol, Mark Waldrop. *Swing Dancers*: Coby Grossbart, Bubba Rambo.

1978.05

DANCIN'

A Musical Entertainment (Revue) in Three Acts, Thirteen Scenes. (Conceived,) directed and choreographed by Bob Fosse. Scenery designed by Peter Larkin. Cotumes designed by Willa Kim. Lighting designed by Jules Fisher. Music and lyrics by Johann Sebastian Bach, Ralph Burns, George M. Cohan, Neil Diamond, Bob Haggart, Ray Bauduc, Gil Rodin and Bob Crosby, Jerry Lieber and Mike Stoller, Johnny Mercer and Harry Warren, Louis Prima, John Philip Sousa, Carole Bayer Sager and Melissa Manchester, Barry Mann and Cynthia Weil, Felix Powell and George Asaf, Sigmund Romberg and Oscar Hammerstein II, Cat Stevens, Edgard Varèse, Jerry Jeff Walker. Music arranged and conducted by Gordon Lowry Harrell. Orchestrations by Ralph Burns. Sound by Abe Jacob. Associate producer, Patti Grubman. Produced by Jules Fisher, The Shubert Organization, and Columbia Pictures. Opened 27 March 1978 at the Broadhurst Theatre, moved 4 December 1980 to the Ambassador Theatre, and closed 27 June 1982 after 1774 performances.

CAST (in alphabetical order):Gail Benedict, Sandahl Bergman, Karen G. Burke, Rene Ceballos, Christopher Chadman, Wayne Cilento, Jill Cook, Gregory B. Drotar, Vicki Frederick, Linda Haberman, Richard Korthaze, Edward Love, John Mineo, Ann Reinking, Blane Savage, Charles Ward. *Alternates*: Christine Colby, William Whitener, Valerie Miller.

ACT 1

Scene 1

Opening:

Prologue: "Hot August Night"

(*Music and Lyrics by* Neil Diamond.)

"Crunchy Granola Suite"

W. Cilento, J. Mineo

Danced by the Company

(*Music and Lyrics by* Neil Diamond.)

Scene 2

Recollections of an Old Dancer:

"Mr. Bojangles"

W. Cilento

Mr. Bojangles: C. Chadman. *Mr. Bojangles' Spirit*: G. B. Drotar.

(*Music and Lyrics by* Jerry Jeff Walker.)

Scene 3

The Dream Barre:

"Chaconne" (A transcription from Bach's Sonata for Violin Solo No. 4)

A Boy: C. Ward. *A Girl*: A. Reinking. *Ballet Master*: R. Korthaze.

Scene 4

Percussion:

Part 1

R. Ceballos, V. Frederick, L. Haberman

Part 2

C. Chadman, W. Cilento, J. Mineo

Part 3

S. Bergman, G. Benedict, K. G. Burke, J. Cook, G. B. Drotar, E. Love, A. Reinking, B. Savage

Part 4: "Ionisation"

C. Ward

(*Music by* Edgard Varèse.)

ACT 2

Scene 1

Dancin' Man:

"I Wanna Be a Dancin' Man" (from the film *THE BELLE OF NEW YORK*)

The Company

(*Music by* Harry Warren. *Lyrics by* Johnny Mercer.)

Scene 2

Three in One:

"Big Noise from Winnetka"

K. G. Burke, W. Cilento, J. Cook

(*Music and Lyrics by* Bob Haggart, Ray Bauduc, Gil Rodin and Bob Crosby.)

Scene 3

"If It Feels Good, Let It Ride"

Pas de Deux: V. Frederick, C. Ward; R. Ceballos, G. B. Drotar; S. Bergman, B. Savage.

(*Music and Lyrics by* Carole Bayer Sager and Melissa Manchester.)

"Easy"

C. Chadman, W. Cilento, E. Love, J. Mineo

(*Music and Lyrics by* Carole Bayer Sager and Melissa Manchester.)

Danced by A. Reinking

Scene 4

A Manic Depressive's Lament:

"I've Got Them Feelin' Too Good Today Blues"

E. Love

(*Music and Lyrics by* Jerry Leiber and Mike Stoller.)

Scene 5

Fourteen Feet:

"Was Dog a Doughnut"

S. Bergman, C. Chadman, W. Cilento, G. B. Drotar, V. Frederick, A. Reinking, B. Savage

(*Music and Lyrics by* Cat Stevens.)

ACT 3

Scene 1

Benny's Number:

"Sing, Sing, Sing"

(*Music by* Louis Prima.)

Part 1: The Company.

Part 2: *Trombone Solo*: V. Frederick, B. Savage, C. Ward. *Trumpet Solo*: A. Reinking. *Clarinet Solo*: The Company. *Piano Solo*: W. Cilento, J. Mineo.

Scene 2

The Female Star Spot:

"Here You Come Again"

S. Bergman, K. G. Burke, R. Ceballos, V. Frederick

(*Music and Lyrics by* Barry Mann and Cynthia Weil.)

Scene 3

America:

"(I'm a) Yankee Doodle Dandy" (from *LITTLE JOHNNY JONES*)The Company

(*Music and Lyrics by* George M. Cohan.)

"Gary Owen"

G. Benedict, L. Haberman, G. B. Drotar

"Stout Hearted Men" (from *THE NEW MOON*)

S. Bergman, V. Frederick, A. Reinking

(*Music by* Sigmund Romberg. *Lyrics by* Oscar Hammerstein II.)

[18]Originally produced in New York 16 January 1964 at the St. James Theatre for 2844 performances. For Synopsis of Scenes and Musical Numbers, see original 1964 production. "Come and Be My Butterfly" was not performed in this revival. Act 1, Scene 3, and Act 2, Scene 4, were eliminated from this production.

"Under the Double Eagle"
W. Cilento, J. Mineo, B. Savage
"Dixie"
K. G. Burke, E. Love
"When Johnny Comes Marching Home"
A. Reinking
"Rally Round the Flag"
R. Ceballos
"Pack Up Your Troubles in Your Old Kit Bag"
V. Frederick, G. Benedict, J. Mineo
(*Music by* Felix Powell. *Lyrics by* George Asaf.)
"The Stars and Stripes Forever"
C. Ward
(*Music by* John Philip Sousa.)
"Yankee Doodle Disco"
The Company
(*Choreographed by* Christopher Chadman.)

Scene 4
Improvisation:
"Dancin'"
The Company
(*Music by* Ralph Burns.)

1978.06 A HISTORY OF THE AMERICAN FILM

A Play with Music in Two Acts, 35 Scenes. Play (and lyrics) by Chris Durang. Music by Mel Marvin. Entire production directed by David Chambers. Musical staging by Graciela Daniele. Set designed by Tony Straiges. Costumes designed by Marjorie Slaiman. Lighting designed by William Mintzer. Sound design by Lou Shapiro. Musical direction by Clay Fullum. Orchestrations by Robert M. Freedman. Associate producers, Marc Howard, Sheila-Barbara-Dinah Productions. Produced by Judith [Judy] Gordon and Richard S. Bright. Opened 30 March 1978 at the ANTA Theatre and closed 16 April 1978 after 21 performances.

CAST (in alphabetical order): *Contract Player #8, whose roles are Blessed Virgin Mother, Speakeasy Patron, Nurse, Voice of Anna Karenina, Ma Joad, Cucumber Girl, Voice of Sonja Henie*: Maureen Anderman. *Jimmy*: Gary Bayer. *Contract Player #1, whose roles are Michael, Salad Chef*: Walter Bobbie. *Contract Player #5, whose roles are Ticket Man, Newsboy, Young Speakeasy Patron, Young Reporter, Grandma Joad, Mickey*: Jeff Brooks. *Contract Player #7, whose roles are Cop, Bartender, Judge, Edward Mortimer, Von Leffing, Navy Officer, Victor Henreid, Theatre Manager, Voices of Vronsky, John, Academy Award Announcer, F81 Narrator, God*: Bryan Clark. *Contract Player #4, whose roles are Jesus, Ferruchi, Ernie the Reporter, Abdhul, Pa Joad, Make-up Man, Harkness, Uncle Sam, Marine Officer, Robot*: David Cromwell. *Contract Player #10 whose roles are Minstrel, Clarinet Man, "Big" Hit Man, David, Fife*: David Garrison. *Contract Player #3, whose roles are Piano Man, Viola, Indian, Ito, Sailor, Stuart*: Ben Halley, Jr. *Bette*: Swoosie Kurtz. *Contract Player #6, whose roles are Orphanage Lady, Ma O'Reilly, Allison Martimer, Prison Warden, Lettuce Girl, Gold Star Mother, WAC*: Kate McGregor-Stewart. *Eve*: Joan Pape. *Loretta*: April Shawhan. *Hank*: Brent Spiner. *Contract Player #9, whose roles are God, Little Hit Man, Eric, Santa, Snare, Voice of Robot*: Eric Weitz. *Contract Player #2, whose roles are Silent Mother, Bartender's Girl, Clara Mortimer, Carrot Girl*: Mary Catherine Wright. *Pianist* (On-Stage): Robert Fisher.

Theaction takes place in a large movie palace with an upstage balcony.

ACT 1
Scene 1
"The Silent Years" (instrumental)
"Minstrel Song"
D. Garrison
Scene 3
"Shanty Town Romance"
G. Bayer, A. Shawhan
Scene 7
"They Can't Prohibit Love"
S. Kurtz
Scene 12
"We're in a Salad"
B. Spiner, Salad Girls, D. Garrison, E. Weitz, W. Bobbie
Salad Girls: Bean: A. Shawhan. *Tomato*: S. Kurtz. *Celery*: J. Pape. *Cucumber*: M. Anderman. *Lettuce*: K. McGregor-Stewart. *Carrot*: M. C. Wright.
Scene 14
"Euphemism"
A. Shawhan
Scene 18
"Ostende Nobis Tosca"
S. Kurtz, B. Spiner, D. Garrison, E. Weitz
"The Red, the White and the Blue"
J. Pape, Company

ACT 2
Scene 3
"Pretty Pin-Up"
J. Pape, A. Shawhan, S. Kurtz, M. C. Wright
Scene 12
"Apple Blossom Victory"
S. Kurtz, J. Pape, K. McGregor-Stewart
Scene 14
"Isn't It Fun to Be in the Movies"
D. Morrison, E. Weitz
Scene 17
"Search for Wisdom"
G. Boyer, A. Shawhan, Company

1978.07 THE MERRY WIDOW

A Revival of the Operetta in Three Acts, 4 Scenes[19]. Original Viennese libretto ('Die lustige witwe') and lyrics by Victor Léon and Leo Stein (after "L'Attaché d'Ambassade" by Henri Meilhac.) Music by Franz Lehár. New English translation and dialogue by Ursula Eggers and Joseph de Rugeris. New lyrics by Sheldon Harnick. This San Diego Opera production directed by Tito Capobianco. Stage director and choreographer, Gigi Denda. Production (settings, costumes) design by Carl Toms. Lighting design by Ken Billington. Conductor, Julius Rudel. Produced by the New York City Opera. Opened 2 April 1978 at the New York State Theatre and closed 27 April 1978 after 8 performances in repertory.

CAST: *Baron Mirko Zeta*: DAVID RAE SMITH. *Valencienne*: Glenys Fowles. *Count Danilo*: ALAN TITUS. *Anna Glawari*: BEVERLY SILLS. *Camille de Rosillon*: BRUCE REED. *Vicomte Cascada*: HARLAN FOSS. *Raoul St. Brioche*: HOWARD HENSEL. *Bogdanovitch*: JOHN LANKSTON. *Sylviane*: Jane Shaulis. *Kromov*: William Ledbetter. *Olga*: Sandra Walker. *Pritchitch*: Jonathan Green. *Praskovia*: Puli Toro. *Njegus*: JAMES BILLINGS. *(Grisettes:) Lolo*: Candace Itow. *Dodo*: Jane Shaulis. *Jou-Jou*: Sandra Walker. *Frou-Frou*: Toni-Ann Gardella. *Clo-Clo*: Puli Toro. *Margot*: Emilietta Ettlin. *Ensemble*: New York City Opera Chorus.

Act 1: At the Petrovenian Embassy in Paris, 1905.

Act 2: At the home of Hannah Glawari.

Act 3: At Maxim's.

ACT 1
"Thank you for your invitation, sir"
H. Foss, D. R. Smith, Ensemble
"Do listen, please"
G. Fowles, B. Reed
"Gentlemen, how kind" (Anna's entrance)
B. Sills, H. Foss, H. Hensel, Men
"Oh Fatherland" (Maxim's)
A. Titus
"Ladies choice!" (Act 1 Finale)
Company

ACT 2
"If you'll indulge us" (Dances and Vilia)
B. Sills, Ensemble
"Heia! See the horseman come"
B. Sills, A. Titus
"Ev'ry woman . . . "
A. Titus, Men

---

[19]Originally produced in New York 21 October 1907 at the New Amsterdam Theatre for 416 performances.

"I'm often at Maxim's"
A. Titus
"Just as a rosebud blossoms"
G. Fowles, B. Reed
"Ha! Ha! Ha!" (Act 2 Finale)
Company

ACT 3
"Here we are: Grisettes and Playgirls" (Grisette Song)
G. Fowles, Grisettes
"I'm a loyal native son" (Très parisien)
J. Billings, Ensemble
"Strings are sighing" (Waltz)
A. Titus, B. Sills
"Oh the study of feminine ways" (Act 3 Finale)
Company

1978.08 THE SAINT OF BLEECKER STREET

A Revival of the Opera (Musical Drama) in Three Acts, 5 Scenes[20]. Music and libretto by Gian-Carlo Menotti. Conducted by Cal Stewart Kellogg. Directed by Francis Rizzo. Sets designed by Beeb Salzer. Costumes designed by Carol Luiken. Choreography by Thomas Andrew. Lighting by Hans Sondheimer. Chorus master, Lloyd Walser. Produced by the New York City Opera. Opened 13 April 1978 at the New York State Theatre and closed 23 April 1978 after 3 performances in repertory.

CAST (in order of appearance): *Assunta*: Jane Shaulis. *A Young Man*: Alan Kays. *Maria Corona*: Judith De Rosa. *Her Son*: Bobby Scalese. *Carmela*: Diana Soviero. *A Young Woman*: Martha Thigpen. *Don Marco*: Irwin Densen. *Annina*: CATHERINE MALFITANO. *Michele*: ENRICO diGIUSEPPE. *Concettina*: Lila Herbert. *Desideria*: SANDRA WALKER. *First Guest*: Alan Kays. *Second Guest*: Alan Baker. *Salvatore*: William Ledbetter. *Bartender*: Kenn Dovel. *A Nun*: Charlott Thyssen. *A Young Priest*: Ron Boucher. *Neighbors*: Don Henderson, Harris Davis. *Neighbors, Friends, Policemen, etc.*: New York City Opera Chorus.

1978.09 AIN'T MISBEHAVIN'

A Musical Revue in Two Acts, 22 Scenes[21], based on the music of Thomas "Fats" Waller. Conceived and directed by Richard Maltby, Jr. Based on an idea by Murray Horwitz and Richard Maltby, Jr. Musical numbers staged by Arthur Faria. Music supervision by Luther Henderson. Associate director, Murray Horwitz. Orchestrations and arrangements by Luther Henderson. Vocal arrangements by William Elliott, Jeffrey Gutcheon. Sets by John Lee Beatty. Costumes by Randy Barcelo. Lighting by Pat Collins. Sound by Otts Munderloh. Originally produced (Off-Broadway) by the Manhattan Theatre Club. Produced by Emanuel Azenberg, Dasha Epstein, The Shubert Organization, Jane Gaynor and Ron Dante. Opened 9 May 1978 at the Longacre Theatre, moved 29 January 1979 to the Plymouth Theatre, moved 26 January 1981 to the Belasco Theatre and closed 21 February 1982 after 1604 performances. Total, including Off-Broadway, 1632 performances.

CAST: NELL CARTER, ANDRE DeSHIELDS, ARMELIA McQUEEN, KEN PAGE, CHARLAINE WOODARD. *Pianist*: LUTHER HENDERSON.

ACT 1[22]
Scene 1
"Ain't Misbehavin'" (1929)(from *HOT CHOCOLATES*)
Company
(*Music by* Thomas Waller and Harry Brooks. *Lyrics by* Andy Razaf.)
Scene 2
"Lookin' Good But Feelin' Bad" (1929)
Company
(*Lyrics by* Lester A. Santly. *Vocal Arrangement by* Jeffrey Gutcheon.)
Scene 3
"'T Aint Nobody's Biz-ness If I Do" (1922)
A. DeShields, Company
(*Music and Lyrics by* Porter Grainger and Everett Robbins. *Additional Lyrics by* Richard Maltby, Jr. and Murray Horwitz.)
Scene 4
"Honeysuckle Rose" (1929)(from *LOAD OF COAL*)
K. Page, N. Carter
(*Lyrics by* Andy Razaf.)
Scene 5
"Squeeze Me" (1925)
A. McQueen
(*Lyrics by* Clarence Williams.)
Scene 6
"Handful of Keys" (1933)
Company
(*Lyrics by* Richard Maltby, Jr. and Murray Horwitz based on an idea by Marty Grosz. *Vocal Arrangement by* WIlliam Elliott.)
Scene 7
"I've Got a Feeling I'm Falling" (1929)(from *APPLAUSE* film)
N. Carter, Company
(*Music by* Thomas Waller and Harry Link. *Lyrics by* Billy Rose.)
Scene 8
"How Ya Baby" (1938)
A. DeShields, C. Woodard, Company
(*Lyrics by* J. C. Johnson.)
Scene 9
"The Jitterbug Waltz" (1942)
Company
(*Lyrics by* Richard Maltby, Jr. *Vocal Arrangement by* William Elliott.)
Scene 10
"The Ladies Who Sing with the Band" (1943)(from *EARLY TO BED*)
A. De Shields, K. Page
(*Lyrics by* George Marion, Jr.)
"Yacht Club Swing" (1938)
C. Woodard
(*Music by* Thomas Waller and Herman Autry. *Lyrics by* J. C. Johnson.)
"When the Nylons Bloom Again" (1943)(from *EARLY TO BED*)
A. McQueen, C. Woodard, N. Carter
(*Lyrics by* George Marion, Jr.)
"Cash for Your Trash" (1942)
N. Carter
(*Lyrics by* Ed Kirkeby.)
"Off-Time" (1929)
Company
(*Music by* Thomas Waller and Harry Brooks. *Lyrics by* Andy Razaf. *Vocal Arrangement by* Jeffrey McGutcheon.)
Scene 11
"The Joint Is Jumpin'" (1938)
Company
(*Lyrics by* Andy Razaf and J. C. Johnson.)

ACT 2
Scene 1
"Spreadin' Rhythm Around" (1935)(from *KING OF BURLESQUE* film)
Company
(*Music by* Jimmy McHugh. *Lyrics by* Ted Koehler. *Additional Lyrics by* Richard Maltby, Jr.)
Scene 2
"Lounging at the Waldorf" (1936)
A. McQueen, C. Woodard, K. Page, N. Carter
(*Lyrics by* Richard Maltby, Jr. *Vocal Arrangement by* William Elliott.)
Scene 3
"The Viper's Drag" (1934)
A. DeShields, Company
(Traditional-"The Reefer Song")
Scene 4
"Mean to Me" (1929)N. Carter
(*Music and Lyrics by* Roy Turk and Fred E. Ahlert.)

---

[20]Originally produced in New York 27 December 1954 at the Broadway Theatre for 92 performances. For Synopsis of Scenes, see original 1954 production.
[21]First produced in New York Off-Broadway 8 February-5 March 1978 at the Manhattan Theatre Club for 28 performances.
[22]All music by Thomas "Fats" Waller alone, except where indicated. Songs not written by "Fats" Waller were recorded by him.

Scene 5
"Your Feet's Too Big" (1936)
K. Page
(*Music and Lyrics by* Ada Benson and Fred Fisher.)
Scene 6
"That Ain't Right" (1943)
A. DeShields, A. McQueen, Company
(*Music and Lyrics by* Nat King Cole. *Additional Lyrics by* Richard Maltby, Jr. and Murray Horwitz.)
Scene 7
"Keepin' Out of Mischief Now"(1932)
C. Woodard
(*Lyrics by* Andy Razaf.)
Scene 8
"Find Out What They Like (and How They Like It)" (1929)
A. McQueen, N. Carter
(*Lyrics by* Andy Razaf.)
Scene 9
"Fat and Greasy" (1936)
A. DeShields, K. Page
(*Music and Lyrics by* Porter Grainger and Charlie Johnson.)
Scene 10
"Black and Blue" (1929)(from *HOT CHOCOLATES*)
Company
(*Music by* Thomas Waller and Harry Brooks. *Lyrics by* Andy Razaf. *Vocal Arrangements by* William Elliott.)
Scene 11
Finale: songs by others which Fats Waller made hits
Company
"I'm Gonna Sit Right Down and Write Myself a Letter" (1933)
K. Page
(*Music by* Fred E. Ahlert. *Lyrics by* Joe Young.)
"Two Sleepy People" (1938)(from *THANKS FOR THE MEMORY* film)
A. McQueen, K. Page
(*Music by* Hoagy Carmichael. *Lyrics by* Frank Loesser.)
"I've Got My Fingers Crossed" (1935)(from *KING OF BURLESQUE* film)
A. McQueen, C. Woodard, K. Page
(*Music by* Jimmy McHugh. *Lyrics by* Ted Koehler.)
"I Can't Give You Anything But Love" (1928)(from *BLACKBIRDS OF 1928*)
A. DeShields, C. Woodard
(*Music by* Jimmy McHugh. *Lyrics by* Dorothy Fields.)
"It's a Sin to Tell a Lie" (1933)
N. Carter, Company
(*Music and Lyrics by* Billy Mayhew.)
"Honeysuckle Rose" (reprise)Company

1978.10 ANGEL

A Musical in Two Acts, 4 Scenes. Book by Ketti Frings and Peter Udell. Based on the play "Look Homeward Angel" by Ketti Frings, adapted from the novel of the same name by Thomas Wolfe. Music by Gary Geld. Lyrics by Peter Udell. Directed by Philip Rose. Choreography by Robert Tucker. Scenery by Ming Cho Lee. Lighting John Gleason. Costumes by Pearl Somner. Orchestrations by Don Walker. Musical direction and dance arrangements by William Cox. Associate producers, Karen Wald, Norman Main. Originally produced at Northstage, Glen Cove, New York, by Norman Main, Executive producer. Produced by Philip Rose and Ellen Madison. Opened 10 May 1978 at the Minskoff Theater and closed 13 May 1978 after 5 performances.

CAST (in order of appearance): *Helen Gant*: Donna Davis. *Ben Gant*: JOEL HIGGINS. *Mrs. Fatty Pert*: PATTI ALLISON. *Mrs. Snowden*: Grace Carney. *Eugene Gant*: DON SCARDINO. *Eliza Gant*: FRANCES STERNHAGEN. *Will Pentland*: Elek Hartman. *Florry Mangle*: Rebecca Seay. *Mrs. Clatt*: Justine Johnston. *Jake Clatt*: Gene Masoner. *Mr. Farrell*: Billy Beckham. *Miss Brown*: Jayne Barnett. *Laura James*: LESLIE ANN RAY. *W. O. Grant*: FRED GWYNNE. *Dr. Maguire*: Daniel Keyes. *Joe Tarkington*: Rex David Hays. *Reed McKinney*: Carl Nicholas. *Tim Laughran*: Norman Stotz. *Madame Victoria*: PATRICIA ENGLUND.

The action takes place in Altamount, North Carolina, during the autumn of 1916.

Act 1: The Dixieland Boarding Home.

Act 2, Scene 1: Gant's marble yard and shop; one week later. *Scene 2*: Dixieland Boarding House; that evening. *Scene 3*: Dixieland; two weeks later, just before dawn.

ACT 1
Angel Theme
"All the Comforts of Home"
Boarders
"Like the Eagles Fly"
J. Higgins
"Make a Little Sunshine"
F. Sternhagen, D. Scardino, J. Higgins
"Fingers and Toes"
F. Gwynne, N. Stotz, C. Nicholas, R. D. Hays
"Fatty"
J. Higgins
"Astoria Gloria"
P. Allison, Boarders
"Railbird"
D. Scardino
"If I Ever Loved Him"
L. A. Ray
"A Dime Ain't Worth a Nickel"
J. Higgins, P. Allison
"I Got a Dream to Sleep On"
D. Scardino
"Drifting"
F. Sternhagen
ACT 2
Scene 1
"I Can't Believe It's You"
F. Gwynne, P. Englund
"Feelin' Loved"
D. Scardino, L. A. Ray
Scene 2
A Medley
J. Higgins, P. Allison, F. Sternhagen, L. A. Ray
Scene 3
"Tomorrow I'm Gonna Be Old"
F. Gwynne
"Feelin' Loved" (reprise)
D. Scardino, L. A. Ray
"How Do You Say Goodbye"
L. A. Ray
"Gant's Waltz"
F. Gwynne, F. Sternhagen
"Like the Eagles Fly" (reprise)
D. Scardino

1978.11 RUNAWAYS

A Musical Theatre Piece in Two Acts[23]. Written, composed and directed by Liz Swados. Settings by Douglas W. Schmidt, Woods Mackintosh. Costumes by Hilary Rosenfeld. Sound by Bill Dreisbach. Lighting by Jennifer Tipton. Production supervisor, Jay David Cohen. Associate producer, Bernard Gersten. A New York Shakespeare Festival Production. Produced by Joseph Papp. Opened 13 May 1978 at the Plymouth Theatre and closed 31 December 1978 after 199 performances. Total, including Off-Broadway run: 261 peformances.

CAST (in order of appearance): *Hubbell*: Bruce Hlibok. *Interpreter for Hubbell*: Lorie Robinson. *A.J.*: Carlo Imperato. *Jackie*: Rachael Kelly. *Luis*: Ray Contreras. *Nikki Kay Kane*: Nan-Lynn Nelson. *Lidia*: Jossie deGuzman. *Manny*: Randy Ruiz. *Eddie*: Jon Matthews. *Sundar*: Bernie Allison. *Roby*: Venustra K. Robinson. *Lazar*: David Schechter. *Eric*: Evan H. Miranda. *Iggy*: Jonathan Feig. *Jane*: Kate Schellenbach. *Ez*: Leonard D. Brown. *Mex-Mongo*: Mark Anthony Butler. *Melinda*: Trini Alvarado. *Deidre*: Karen Evans. *Mocha*: Sheila Gibbs.

Chorus: Paula Anderson, Kenya Brome, Jerome Dekie, Karin Dekie, Lisa Dekie, John Gallogly, Timmy Michaels, Toby Parker. *Musicians*: *Piano and Toy Drum*: Judith Flesiher. *String Bass*: J. Schimmel. *Congas, Timbales, Bongos, Bells Siren and Others*:

[23]First produced in New York Off-Broadway 9 March 1978 at the Public Theatre Cabaret/Martinson Hall for 62 performances.

Lepoldo F. Fleming. *Trap Set, Triangle, Glass and Ratchet*: David Sawyer. *Saxophones and Flutes*: Patience Higgins. *Guitar*: Elizabeth Swados.

The text for "Runaways" is written by Elizabeth Swados except for the following contributions improvised and formed by the actors: "Hubbell—You Don't Understand"—Bruce Hlibok; Spanish Argument from "Footsteps"—Jossie De Guzman, Randy Ruiz; "Hubbell—Out on the Street"—Bruce Hlibok; "Lazar's Heroes"—David Schechter; "In the Sleeping Line"—"A.J.'s Dream"—Carlo Imperato; "Roby's Dream"—Venustra K. Robinson; "Jackie's Dream"—Diane Lane; "Lazar's Dream"—David Schechter; "Eddie's Dream"—Vincent Stewart; "Nightmares in Spanish"—Jossie De Guzman, Randy Ruiz, Ray Contreras. The director gratefully acknowledges the ideas and help of all the actors in the choreography. All instrumental arrangements are improvised by the team of musicians. English-Spanish translations by Jossie deGuzman.

The action takes place at the present time on a playground.

ACT 1

"You Don't Understand"
B. Hlibok, L. Robinson

"I Had to Go"
C. Imperato, J. Schimmel

"Parent/Kid Dance"
Company

"Appendectomy"
R. Kelly

"Where Do People Go"
Company

"Footstep"
N. Nelson, J. Schimmel, J. deGuzman, R. Ruiz

"Once Upon a Time"
J. deGuzman, Company

"Current Events"
J. Matthews

"Every Now and Then"
C. Imperato, B. Allison, Company

"Out on the Street"
B. Hlibok, L. Robinson

"Minnesota Strip"
V. K. Robinson

"Song of a Child Prostitute"
R. Kelly, J. deGuzman, R. Ruiz, R. Contreras

"Christmas Puppies"
N. Nelson

"Lazar's Heroes"
D. Schechter

"Find Me a Hero"
D. Schechter, Company

"Scrynatchkielooaw"
N. Nelson

"The Undiscovered Son"
E. H. Miranda, J. Fleisher, J. Schimmel

"I Went Back Home"
J. Feig, K. Schellenbach

"This Is What I Do When I'm Angry"
C. Imperato, N. Nelson

"The Basketball Song"
L. Brown, Company
DanceR. Contreras, M. A. Butler

"Spoons"
R. Ruiz

"Lullaby for Luis"
J. deGuzman, R. Contreras, P. Higgins, Company

"We Are Not Strangers"
E. H. Miranda, Company

ACT 2

"In the Sleeping Line"
Company

"Lullaby from Baby to Baby"
T. Alvarado, B. Hlibok

"Tra Gog Vo In Dein Whole"(I Will Not Tell a Soul)
D. Schechter, B. Hlibok

"Revenge Song"
Company

"Enterprise"
K. Evans, N. Nelson, M. A. Butler, Company

"Sometimes"
V. K. Robinson, D. Schechter

"Clothes"
J. Feig

"Mr. Graffiti"
M. A. Butler

"The Untrue Pigeon"
N. Nelson

"Senoras de la Noche"
J. deGuzman, R. Ruiz, N. Nelson

"We Have to Die?"
K. Evans

"Where Are Those People Who Did 'Hair'?"
D. Schechter, K. Evans, Company

"Appendectomy II"
R. Kelly, T. Alvarado

"Let Me Be a Kid"
Company

"To the Dead of Family Wars"
K. Evans

"Problem After Problem"
B. Hlibok, L. Robinson

"Lonesome of the Road"
R. Contreras, B. Allison, Company

1978.12 WORKING

A Musical in Two Acts. Based on the book of the same name by Studs Terkel. Adapted and directed by Stephen Schwartz. Music and lyrics by Craig Carnelia, Micki Grant, Mary Rodgers and Susan Birkenhead, Stephen Schwartz, James Taylor. Dances and musical staging by Onna White. Settings by David Mitchell. Costumes by Marjorie Slaiman. Lighting by Ken Billington. Musical direction and vocal arrangements by Stephen Reinhardt. Orchestrations by Kirk Nurock. Dance and incidental music by Michele Brourman. Associate director, Nina Faso. Sound by Jack Mann. Assistant conductor, Kenneth Bichel. Produced by Stephen R. Friedman and Irwin Meyer in association with Joseph Harris. Opened 14 May 1978 at the 46th Street Theatre and closed 4 June 1976 after 25 performances.

CAST (in order of appearance): *Act 1*: *Mike LeFevre*, steelworker: Brad Sullivan. *Al Calinda*, parking lot attendant: David Langston Smyrl. *Nora Watson*, editor: Patti LuPone. *John Fortune*, advertising copy chief: Steven Boockvor. *Diane Wilson*, secretary: Lynne Thigpen. *Herb Rosen*, corporate executive: Rex Everhart. *Anthony Palazzo*, stonemason: Arny Freeman. *John Rushton*, newsboy: Matthew McGrath. *Rose Hoffman*, teacher: Bobo Lewis. *Babe Secoli*, supermarket checker: Lenora Nemetz. *Brett Meyer*, boxboy: David Patrick Kelly. *Emilio Hernandez*, migrant worker: Joe Mantegna. *Conrad Swibel*, gas meter reader: Matt Landers. *Kate Rushton*, housewife: Susan Bigelow. *Barbara Herrick*, agency vice-president: Robin Lamont. *Terry Mason*, stewardess: Lenora Nemetz. *Jill Torrance*, model: Terri Treas. *Roberta Victor*, call girl: Patti LuPone. *Grace Clements*, millworker: Bobo Lewis. *Bud Jonas*, football coach: Bob Gunton. *Marco Camerone*, hockey player: Steven Boockvor. *Joe Zutty*, retired shipping clerk: Arny Freeman. *Tom Patrick*, fireman: Matt Landers.

Act 2: *Benny Blue*, bar pianist: David Patrick Kelly. *Delores Dante*, waitress: Lenora Nemetz. *Heather Lamb*, telephone operator: Lynne Thigpen. *Fran Swenson*, hotel switchboard operator: Bobo Lewis. *Sharon Atkins*, receptionist: Robin Lamont. *Frank Decker*, interstate trucker: Bob Gunton. *Dave McCormick*, interstate trucker: Joe Mantegna. *Booker Page*, seaman: Rex Everhart. *Lucille Page*, his wife: Bobo Lewis. *Will Robinson*, bus driver: David Langston Smyrl. *Jo Anne Robinson*, his wife: Lynne Thigpen. *Tim Devlin*, salesman: Matt Landers. *Carla Devlin*, his wife: Terri Treas. *Ralph Werner*, tie salesman: Matt Landers. *Cathleen Moran*, hospital aide: Robin Lamont. Charlie Blossom, copy boy: David Patrick Kelly. *Maggie Holmes*, cleaning woman: Lynne Thigpen. *Mike LeFevre*, steelworker: Brad Sullivan.

The action takes place at the present time in numerous places of employment. The characters in "Working" are non-fictional characters. Their names have been changed, but their words have not. Even in the case of song lyrics, the writers have tried to remain as faithful as possible to the character's original words. It is our feeling that the value of this piece stems chiefly from the fact that it is true, and we have made every effort to keep from sliding into the realm of "playwriting."

ACT 1

"All the Livelong Day"
Company
("I Hear America Singing" *Lyrics by* Walt Whitman; *Music and Additional Lyrics by* Stephen Schwartz.)

"Lovin Al"
D. L. Smyrl, Ensemble
(*Music and Lyrics by* Micki Grant.)
"The Mason"
D. P. Kelly
(*Music and Lyrics by* Craig Carnelia.)
"Neat to Be a Newsboy"
M. McGrath, Newsboys
(*Music and Lyrics by* Stephen Schwartz.)
"Nobody Tells Me How"
B. Lewis
(*Music by* Mary Rodgers. *Lyrics by* Susan Birkenhead.)
"Treasure Island Trio"
Danced by T. Treas, L. Nemetz, L. Thigpen
(*Music by* Michele Brourman.)
"Un Mejor Dia Vendra"
J. Mantegna, M. Landers, Migrants
(*Music by* James Taylor. *Spanish Lyrics by* Graciela Daniele and Matt Landers.)
"Just a Housewife"
S. Bigelow, K. Rushton, Housewives
(*Music and Lyrics by* Craig Carnelia.)
"Millwork"
R. Lamont, D. P. Kelly, M. Landers
(*Music by* Michele Brourman and Stephen Schwartz.)*Danced by* T. Treas
"Nightskate"
Danced by S. Boockvor
(*Music by* Michele Brourman and Stephen Schwartz.)
"Joe"
A. Freeman
(*Music and Lyrics by* Craig Carnelia.)
"If I Could've Been"
Company
(*Music and Lyrics by* Micki Grant.)

ACT 2
"It's an Art"
L. Nemetz, Customers
(*Music and Lyrics by* Stephen Schwartz.)
"Brother Trucker"
J. Mantegna, B. Gunton, D. P. Kelly, M. Landers
(*Music and Lyrics by* James Taylor.)
"Husbands and Wives"
Danced by R. Everhart, B. Lewis; D. L. Smyrl, L. Thigpen; M. Landers, T. Treas, couples
(*Music by* Michele Brourman.)
"Fathers and Sons"
B. Gunton
(*Music and Lyrics by* Stephen Schwartz.)
"Cleanin' Women"
L. Thigpen
(*Music and Lyrics by* Micki Grant.)
"Something to Point To"
Company
(*Music and Lyrics by* Craig Carnelia.)

1978–1979 SEASON

Angela Lansbury and Len Cariou in SWEENEY TODD
Martha Swope/TimePix

1978–1979 SEASON

THE BEST LITTLE WHOREHOUSE IN TEXAS

1978.13

A Musical Comedy in Two Acts, a Prologue and 17 Scenes[1]. Book by Larry L. King and Peter Masterson. (Based on a short story by Larry L. King) Music and lyrics by Carol Hall. Directed by Peter Masterson and Tommy Tune. Musical numbers staged by Tommy Tune. Sets by Marjorie Kellogg. Costumes by Ann Roth. Lighting by Dennis Parichy. Musical supervision, direction and vocal arrangements by Robert Billig. Associate choreographer, Thommie Walsh. Produced by Universal Pictures (Stevie Phillips, Producer). Opened 19 June 1978 at the 46th Street Theatre and closed 27 March 1982 after 1584 performances. (Total, including Off-Broadway runs, 1669 performances.)

CAST (in order of appearance): *RIO GRANDE BAND*: Craig Chambers (Band Leader). *Girls*: Lisa Brown, Carol Chambers, Donna King, Susan Mansur, Louise Quick-Bowen, Debra Zalkind. *Cowboys*: Jay Bursky, Bradley Clayton King, Michael Scott, Paul Ukena, Jr. *Farmer*: CLINT ALLMON. *Shy Kid*: Gerry Burkhardt. *Miss Wulla Jean*: Edna Milton. *Travelling Salesman*: JAY GARNER. *Slick Dude*: K. C. Kelly. *Choir*: Jay Bursky, Becky Gelke, Edwina Lewis, Jan Merchant, James Rich, Marta Sanders. *Amber*: PAMELA BLAIR. *Shy*: JOAN ELLIS. *Jewel*: DELORES HALL. *Mona Stangley*: CARLIN GLYNN. *The Girls at Miss Mona's*: *Linda Lou*: Donna King. *Dawn*: Lisa Brown. *Ginger*: Louise Quick-Bowen. *Beatrice*: Jan Merchant. *Taddy Jo*: Carol Chambers. *Ruby Rae*: Becky Gelke. *Eloise*: Marta Sanders. *Durla*: Debra Zalkind.

Leroy Sliney: Bradley Clayton King. *The Dogettes*: Gerry Burkhardt, Jay Bursky, Michael Scott, Paul Ukena, Jr. *Melvin P. Thorpe*: CLINT ALLMON. *Soundman*: K. C. Kelly. *Stage Manager*: Tom Cashin. *Melvin Thorpe Singers*: Becky Gelke, Bradley Clayton King, Susan Mansur, Jan Merchant, James Rich, Marta Sanders. *Sheriff Ed Earl Dodd*: HENDERSON FORSYTHE. *Cameraman*: Tom Cashin. *Scruggs*: JAY GARNER. *Mayor Rufus Poindexter*: J. FRANK LUCAS. *Edsel Mackey*: Don Crabtree. *Doatsey Mae*: SUSAN MANSUR. *Townspeople*: Carol Chambers, Bradley Clayton King, Edna Milton, James Rich, Marta Sanders. *TV Announcer*: Larry L. King. *Angelette Imogene Charlene*: Lisa Brown. *Angelettes*: Louise Quick-Bowen, Becky Gelke, Donna King, Debra Zalkind, Jan Merchant. *TV Colorman*: JAY GARNER. *Senator Wingwoah*: J. FRANK LUCAS. *Aggie #21*: Paul Ukena, Jr. *Aggie #71*: Michael Scott. *Aggie #11*: Jay Bursky. *Ukrainian Placekicker—Aggie #1*: K. C. Kelly. *Aggie #17*: James Rich. *Aggie #7*: Gerry Burkhardt. *Aggie #12—Specialty Dancer*: Tom Cashin. *Aggie #77*: Bradley Clayton King. *Photographers*: Michael Scott, Paul Ukena, Jr. James Rich, Jay Bursky. *Reporter #1*: Susan Mansur. *Reporter #2*: Paul Ukena, Jr., *Governor' Aide*: Jay Bursky. *Governor*: JAY GARNER. *Reporter #3*: Michael Scott. *Alternate Dancers*: Monica Tiller, Jerry Yoder, Gena Ramsel.

The action takes place in the state of Texas.

Act 1, Scene 1: The Chicken Ranch, 1930s. *Scene 2*: The Chicken Ranch, early 1970s. *Scene 3*: Same. *Scene 4*: Melvin P. Thorpe's TV Show. *Scene 5*: Back at the Chicken Ranch. *Scene 6*: Same. *Scene 7*: Courthouse Steps, Gilbert, Texas. *Scene 8*: Texas Twinkle Cafe. *Scene 9*: The Texas Aggie Angelettes at the Football Game. *Scene 10*: After the Game and on the way to the Chicken Ranch. *Scene 11*: The Chicken Ranch. *Scene 12*: The Chicken Ranch, later that night.

Act 2, Scene 1: Same as Act 1, Scene 12; at the State Capitol (Austin). *Scene 2*: The Chicken Ranch. *Scene 3*: Sheriff's Office. *Scene 4*: The Chicken Ranch. *Scene 5*: Same.

ACT 1

Prologue
C. Chambers, The Rio Grande Band

Scene 1
"20 Fans"
C. Glynn, the Girls, the Cowboys, C. Allmon, G. Burkhardt, E. Milton, J. Garner, K. C. Kelly, Choir

Scene 2
"A Lil Ole Bitty Pissant Country Place"
C. Glynn, the Girls

Scene 3
"Girl You're a Woman"
C. Glynn, J. Ellis, D. Hall, the Girls

Scene 4
"Watch Dog Theme"
C. Allmon, the Dogettes
"Texas Has a Whorehouse in It"
C. Allmon, the Thorpe Singers, the Dogettes

Scene 6
"Twenty-Four Hours of Lovin'"
D. Hall, the Girls

Scene 7
"Watchdog Theme" (reprise)
The Dogettes
"Texas Has a Whorehouse in It" (reprise)
C. Allmon, the Dogettes, J. F. Lucas, J. Garner, D. Crabtree, S. mansur, Townspeople

Scene 8
"Doatsey Mae"
S. Mansur

Scene 9
"Angelette March"
L. Brown, the Angelettes

Scene 10
"The Aggie Song"
The Aggies

Scene 11
"Bus from Amarillo"
C. Glynn

ACT 2[2]

Scene 1
"The Sidestep"
J. Garner, J. Bursky, J. F. Lucas, C. Allmon, the Dogettes, Melvin Thorpe Singers

Scene 2
"No Lies"
C. Glynn, D. Hall, the Girls

Scene 3
"Good Ole Girl"
H. Forsythe, the Aggies

Scene 4
"Hard Candy Christmas"
P. Blair, D. King, L. Quick-Bowen, L. Brown, B. Gelke, J. Merchant
"Hard Candy Christmas" (reprise)
The Girls

Scene 5
Finale
The Company

IOLANTHE, or The Peer and the Peri

1978.14

A Revival of the Comic Opera in Two Acts[3]. Libretto by William S. Gilbert. Music by Arthur Sullivan. Costumes and scenery designed by Bruno Santini. Lighting by Joe Davis, assisted by Howard Eaton. Choreography by Virginia Mason. Producer, Michael Heyland. Director of productions, Leonard Osborn. Musical director, Royston Nash. Chorus master and associate conductor, David Mackie. Executive producer, Lillian Libman. Technical consultant, Rouben Ter-Arutunian. Produced by James and Joseph Nederlander in association with the City Center of Music and Drama, Inc. and in association with the D'Oyly Carte Opera Trust, Ltd. and Dame Bridget D'Oyly Carte by arrangement with Barclays Bank International. Opened 17 July 1978 at the New York State Theater and closed 20 July 1978 after 2 performances in repertory.

[1]First produced in New York Off-Broadway 17 April 1978 at the Entermedia Theatre for 85 performances.

2Added for the National Tour to Act 2, Scene 1 after "The Sidestep":
"Lonely at the Top"
Larry Hovis (Melvin P. Thrope), Jeffry George (Co-Dog)

[3]First presented in New York 25 November 1882 at the Standard Theatre for 105 performances. For Synopsis of Scenes and Musical Numbers, see original 1882 production.

CAST: *The Lord Chancellor*: JOHN REED. *Earl of Mountararat*: JOHN AYLDON. *Earl Tolloller*: GEOFFREY SHOVELTON. *Private Willis* of the Grenadier Guards: KENNETH SANDFORD. *Strephon*, an Arcadian Shepherd: GARETH JONES. *Queen of the Fairies*: PATRICIA LEONARD. *Celia, Leila, Fleta*, Fairies: Suzanne O'Keeffe, Lorraine Dulcie Daniels, Patricia Ann Bennett. *Phyllis*, an Arcadian Shepherdess and Ward in Chancery: BARBARA LILLEY.

Chorus of Dukes, Marquises, Earls, Viscounts, Barons and Fairies: Richard Brabrooke, Michael Buchan, Barry Clark, Malcolm Coy, Jon Ellison, Michael Farran-Lee, Gareth Jones, Guy Matthews, Richard Mitchell, Edwin Rolles, Thomas Scholey, Bryan Secombe, Alan Spencer, William Strachan, Kevin West, Patrick Wilkes. Susan Cochrane, Linda D'Arcy, Elizabeth Denham, Madeleine Hudson, Beti Lloyd-Jones, Roberta Morrell, Andrea Phillips, Patricia Rea, Suzanne Sloane.

1978.15 THE MIKADO, or The Town of Titipu

A Revival of the Comic Opera in Two Acts[4]. Libretto by William S. Gilbert. Music by Arthur Sullivan. Costumes designed by Disley Jones. Sets designed by Charles Ricketts; Nanki-Poo, Act 1, designed by Disley Jones. Lighting supervision by Martin Aronstein. Production director, Leonard Osborn. Musical director, Royston Nash. Chorus master and associate conductor, David Mackie. Executive producer, Lillian Libman. Technical consultant, Rouben Ter-Arutunian. Produced by James and Joseph Nederlander in association with the City Center of Music and Drama, Inc. and in association with the D'Oyly Carte Opera Trust, Ltd. and Dame Bridget D'Oyly Carte by arrangement with Barclays Bank International. Opened 18 July 1978 at the New York State Theater and closed 19 July 1978 after 3 performances in repertory.

CAST: *The Mikado of Japan*: JOHN AYLDON. *Nanki-Poo*, his son, disguised as a wandering minstrel in love with Yum-Yum: GEOFFREY SHOVELTON. *Ko-Ko*, Lord High Executioner of Titipu: JOHN REED. *Pooh-Bah*, Lord High Everything Else: KENNETH SANDFORD. *Pish-Tush, Go-To*, Noble Lords: Michael Rayner, Jon Ellison. *Yum-Yum, Pitti-Sing, Peep-Bo*, three sisters, wards of Ko-Ko: JULIA GOSS, JANE METCALFE, ROBERTA MORRELL. *Katisha*, an elderly lady in love with Nanki-Poo: PATRICIA LEONARD. *Chorus of School Girls, Nobles, Guards and Coolies*: same as IOLANTHE above.

1978.16 H.M.S. PINAFORE, or The Lass That Loved a Sailor

A Revival of the Comic Opera in Two Acts[5]. Libretto by William S. Gilbert. Music by Arthur Sullivan. Back cloth designed and painted by Joseph and Phil Harker. Director of productions, Leonard Osborn. Musical director, Royston Nash. Chorus master and associate conductor, David Mackie. Executive producer, Lillian Libman. Technical consultant, Rouben Ter-Arutunian. Produced by James and Joseph Nederlander in association with the City Center of Music and Drama, Inc. and in association with the D'Oyly Carte Opera Trust, Ltd. and Dame Bridget D'Oyly Carte by arrangement with Barclays Bank International. Opened 21 July 1978 at the New York State Theater and closed 22 July 1978 after 3 performances in repertory[6].

CAST: *The Rt. Hon. Sir Joseph Porter, K.C.B.*, First Lord of the Admiralty: JOHN REED. *Captain Corcoran*, Commanding the *H.M.S. Pinafore*: MICHAEL RAYNER. *Ralph Rackstraw*, Able Seaman: MESTON REID. *Dick Deadeye*, Able Seaman: JOHN AYLDON. *Bill Bobstay*, Boatswain: Jon Ellison. *Bob Becket*, Boatswain's Mate: Michael Buchan. *Josephine*, the Captain's Daughter: BARBARA LILLEY. *Hebe*, Sir Joseph's First Cousin: Roberta Morrell. *Little Buttercup*, Mrs. Cripps, a Portsmouth Bumboat Woman: PATRICIA LEONARD. *First Lord's Sisters, his Cousins, his Aunts, Sailors, Marines*: same as IOLANTHE above.

1978.17 THE PIRATES OF PENZANCE, or The Slave of Duty

A Revival of the Comic Opera in Two Acts[7]. Libretto by William S. Gilbert. Music by Arthur Sullivan. Scenery by Peter Goffin. Director of productions, Leonard Osborn. Musical director, Royston Nash. Chorus master and associate conductor, David Mackie. Executive producer, Lillian Libman. Technical consultant, Rouben Ter-Arutunian. Produced by James and Joseph Nederlander in association with the City Center of Music and Drama, Inc. and in association with the D'Oyly Carte Opera Trust, Ltd. and Dame Bridget D'Oyly Carte by arrangement with Barclays Bank International. Opened 24 July 1978 at the New York State Theater and closed 25 July 1978 after 2 performances in repertory.

CAST: *Major General Stanley*: JAMES CONROY-WARD. *The Pirate King*: JOHN AYLDON. *Samuel*, his Lieutenant: Jon Ellison. *Frederic*, the Pirate Apprentice: MESTON REID. *Sergeant of Police*: MICHAEL RAYNER. *Mabel, Edith, Kate, Isabel*, General Stanley's Daughters: JULIA GOSS, LORRAINE DULCIE DANIELS, ROBERTA MORRELL, Patricia Ann Bennett. *Ruth*, Pirate Maid-of-all-work: PATRICIA LEONARD. *Chorus of Pirates, Police and General Stanley's Daughters*: same as IOLANTHE above.

1978.18 STOP THE WORLD-I WANT TO GET OFF

A Revival of the Musical in Two Acts[8]. Book, music and lyrics by Leslie Bricusse and Anthony Newley. Sets and costumes by Santo Loquasto. Lighting by Pat Collins. Music supervised and arranged by Ian Fraser. Musical director, George Rhodes. Orchestrations by Billy Byers, Joseph Lipman. Choreography and musical staging by Billy Wilson. Entire production directed by Mel Shapiro. A Hillard Elkins Production. Associate producers, Barbara Platoff, William Ross. Produced by James and Joseph Nederlander in association with City Center of Music and Drama Inc. Opened 3 August 1978 at the New York State Theatre and closed 27 August 1978 after 29 performances.

CAST (in order of appearance): *Littlechap*: SAMMY DAVIS, JR. *Baton Twirler, Death*: Dennis Daniels. *Schoolgirl*: Donna Lowe. *Evie*: MARIAN MERCER. *First Girl in Crow's Nest*: Debora Masterson. *Second Girl in Crow's Nest*: Joyce Nolen. *Susan*: Wendy Edmead. *Guitar Player*: Patrick Kinser-Lau. *Jane*: Shelly Burch. *Anya*: MARIAN MERCER. *The Boy*: Charles Willis, Jr. *Ilse*: MARIAN MERCER. *Lorene*: MARIAN MERCER. *M.C., Snobbs Country Club*: Dennis Daniels. *M.C., Black Organization*: Edwetta Little. *M.C., Spanish Group*: Patrick Kinser-Lau. *M. C., Hadassah*: Joyce Nolen. *Speaker of the House*: Edwetta Little. *Newscaster*: Donna Lowe. *Solo Singer in Sunvale*: Joyce Nolen.

Ensemble: Marcus B. F. Brown, Dennis Daniels, Karen Giombetti, Linda Griffin, Patrick Kinser-Lau, Edwetta Little, Donna Lowe, Debora Masterson, Billy Newton-Davis, Joyce Nolen, Robert Yori-Tanna.

ACT 1

"I Want To Be Rich"
S. Davis

"Typically English"
M. Mercer

"Lumbered"
S. Davis

"Welcome to Sludgeville"
Chorus

"Gonna Build a Mountain"
S. Davis

"Glorious Russian"
M. Mercer

"Meilinki Meilchick"
S. Davis, M. Mercer

[4]First presented in New York 20 July, 10-29 August 1885 at the Union Square and People's Theatres for 22 performances. First authorized production presented 19 August 1885 at the Fifth Avenue Theatre by Richard D'Oyly Carte for 250 performances. For Synopsis of Scenes and Musical Numbers, see 19 August 1885 D'Oyly Carte production.
[5]Originally presented in New York 15 January 1879 at the Standard Theatre for 175 performances. For Synopsis of Scenes and Musical Numbers, see original 1879 production. No program found for this revival.
[6]Costumes uncredited.

[7]First presented in New York 31 December 1879 at the Fifth Avenue Theatre for a total of 91 performances in two engagements. For Synopsis of Scenes and Musical Numbers, see original 1879 production.
[8]Originally produced in New York 3 October 1962 at the Sam S. Shubert Theatre for 556 performances. Dropped from this production: "The A.B.C. Song," "A Special Announcement," "Nag! Nag! Nag!" (replaced by "Life Is a Woman"). "Welcome to Sludgepool" retitled "Welcome to Sludgeville."

"Family Fugue"
S. Davis, M. Mercer, W. Edmead, S. Burch
"Typische Deutsche"
M. Mercer
"Life Is a Woman"
S. Davis

ACT 2
"All American"
M. Mercer
"Once in a Lifetime"
S. Davis
"Mumbo Jumbo"
S. Davis
"Welcome to Sunvale"
Chorus
"Someone Nice Like You"
S. Davis, M. Mercer
"What Kind of Fool Am I?"
S. Davis

1978.19 NAUGHTY MARIETTA

A Revival of the Musical Comedy in Two Acts, 4 Scenes[9]. Music by Victor Herbert. New book and Additional lyrics by Frederick S. Roffman based on the original by Rida Johnson Young. Directed by Gerald Freedman. Musical numbers staged by Graciela Daniele. Costumes designed by Patricia Zipprodt. Sets designed by Oliver Smith. Lighting designed by Ken Billington. Musical director and conductor, John Mauceri. Chorus master, Lloyd Walser. Production conceived by Frederick S. Roffman. Produced by the New York City Opera. Opened 31 August 1978 at the New York State Theatre and closed 10 September 1978 after 14 performances.

CAST: *Marietta d'Altena*: GIANNA ROLANDI. *Captain Richard Warrington* of Kentucky: JACQUE TRUSSEL. *Etienne Grandet*: ALAN TITUS. *Adah Le Clercq*, his Quadroon Mistress: JOANNA SIMON. *Private Silas Slick* of the Rangers: RUSS THACKER. *Acting Governor Grandet*, Etienne's Father: JAMES BILLINGS. *Florenze*, His Secretary: BROOKS MORTON. *Sergeant Harry Blake* of the Rangers: DON YULE. *Rudolfo*: HARLAN FOSS. *Pierre LaFarge*, Envoy from Napoleon: Richard McKee. *Pirates*: Dan Kingman, James Sergi. *Sister Domenique*: Rita Metzger. *Casquette Girls*: Patricia Price, Sally Lambert, Lee Bellaver. *Ranger*: Herbert Hunsberger. *Town Crier*: Edward Vaughan. *Thomas Bailey*: James Sergi. *Flower Girls*: Susan Delery-Whedon, Sally Lambert. *Flower Vendor*: George Bohachevsky. *Bird Vendor*: Louis Perry. *Fruit Vendor*: Robert Brubaker. *Sugar Cane Vendor*: Harris Davis. *Citizens*: Leslie Luxemburg, Lila Herbert, Marie Young. *Vendor*: Robert Brubaker. *Men*: James Brewer, Louis Perry, Herbert Hunsberger, Edward Caughan. *Giovanni*: Jose Bourbon. *Gambler*: Don Carlo. *Pierre*: Kenn Dovel. *Robillard*: Herbert Hunsberger. *Plauche*: James Brewer. *Beaurivage*: Harris Davis. *Major-Domo*: Glenn Rowen. *Spanish Dancer*: Esperanza Galan. *Quadroons*: Sharon Claveau, Rosalie Tisch, Rita Metzger, Marie Young, Madeleine Soyka, Lila Herbert. *French Girls*: Susan Delery-Whedon, Sally Lambert, Jean Rawn, Myrna Reynolds. *Bordenave*: James Sergi. *Durand*: Louis Perry. *La Fourche*: Dan Kingman. *San Domingo Ladies*: Toni-Ann Gardella, Candace Itow, Rebeka Pradera.
Ensemble: New York City Opera Chorus.

The action takes place in Louisiana in 1803.

Act 1, Scene 1: Barataria, the island hideout of privateers, at the mouth of the Mississippi River. *Scene 2*: The Main Square in New Orleans. *Scene 3*: Rudolfo's Theatre. A week or two later.

Act 2: The Jeunesse Dorée Club in New Orleans.

ACT 1
Prologue
G. Rolandi
"It Never, Never Can Be Love"
G. Rolandi, J. Trussel
Opening Chorus
Ensemble
"This Brave New Land" (from *THE PRINCE ANANAIS*)
J. Simon, A. Titus
(Orchestration by Hershy Kay.)
"Tramp, Tramp, Tramp"
J. Trussel, Rangers
"Taisez-Vous"
Ensemble
"All I Crave Is More of Life"
G. Rolandi
"Italian Street Song"
G. Rolandi, Ensemble
Intermezzo
Orchestra
Opening Music
G. Rolandi, H. Foss
"Naughty Marietta"
G. Rolandi
"If I Were Anyone Else But Me"
R. Thacker, G. Rolandi
Dance
Orchestra
Finale
Principals, Ensemble

ACT 2
"New Orleans Jeunesse Dorée"
Male Ensemble
"You Marry a Marionette"
A. Titus, Men
"'Neath the Southern Moon"
J. Simon
"Loves of New Orleans"
Ensemble
"It's Pretty Soft for Silas"
R. Thacker
"Live for Today"
G. Rolandi, J. Simon, J. Trussel, A. Titus, Ensemble
"The Sweet By and By"
J. Billings
"I'm Falling in Love With Someone"
J. Trussel
"Ah, Sweet Mystery of Life"
G. Rolandi, J. Trussel, Company

1978.20 THE MERRY WIDOW

A Revival of the Operetta in Three Acts, 4 Scenes[10]. Music by Franz Lehár. Original German libretto (Die lustige witwe) and lyrics by Victor Léon and Leo Stein (after "L'Attaché d'Ambassade" by Henri Meilhac.) New English translation and dialogue by Ursula Eggers and Joseph de Rugeris. New lyrics by Sheldon Harnick. This San Diego Opera production directed by Tito Capobianco. Stage director, Antoni Jaworski. Choreographer, Jessica Redel. Production (settings, costumes) design by Carl Toms. Lighting design by Ken Billington. Conductor, Imre Pallo. Produced by the New York City Opera. Opened 17 September 1978 at the New York State Theatre and closed 11 November 1978 after 6 performances in repertory.

CAST: *Baron Mirko Zeta*: DAVID RAE SMITH. *Valencienne*: Diana Soviero. *Count Danilo*: HOWARD HENSEL. *Anna Glawari*: JOHANNA MEIER. *Camille de Rosillon*: BRUCE REED. *Vicomte Cascada*: HARLAN FOSS. *Raoul St. Brioche*: ALAN KAYS. *Bogdanovitch*: Herbert Hunsberger. *Sylviane*: Kathleen Murphy. *Kromov*: William Ledbetter. *Olga*: Myrna Reynolds. *Pritchitch*: Louis Perry. *Praskovia*: Susan Delery-Whedon. *Njegus*: JAMES BILLINGS. *Lolo*: Candace Itow. *Dodo*: Kathleen Murphy. *Jou-Jou*: Myrna Reynolds. *Frou-Frou*: Toni-Ann Gardella. *Clo-Clo*: Susan Delery-Whedon. *Margot*: Raven Wilkinson.
Ensemble: New York City Opera Chorus.

---

[9]Originally produced in New York 7 November 1910 at the New York Theatre for 136 performances. This production has been made possible by deeply appreciated gifts from the Fan Fox and Leslie R. Samuels Foundation, Inc., and by the Victor Herbert Foundation.

[10]Originally produced in New York 21 October 1907 at the New Amsterdam Theatre for 416 performances; this adaptation first produced in New York 2 April 1978 at the New York State Theatre for 8 performances. For Synopsis of Scenes and Musical Numbers, see 1978 revival.

1978.21 EUBIE!

A Musical Revue in Two Acts[11]. Music by Eubie Blake. Conceived and directed by Julianne Boyd. Co-choreographer and musical staging by Billy Wilson. Co-choreography and tap choreography by Henry LeTang. Musical supervision and arangements by Danny Holgate. Set design by Karl Eigsti. Costume design by Bernard Johnson. Lighting design by William Mintzer. Sound design by Lou Gonzalez. Choral arrangements by Chapman Roberts. Musical direction by Vicki Carter. Production supervisor, Ron Abbott. Orchestrations by Neal Tate. Associate producer, John N. Hart, Jr. Produced by Ashton Springer in association with Frank C. Pierson and Jay J. Cohen. Opened 20 September 1978 at the Ambassador Theatre and closed 7 October 1979 after 439 performances.

CAST (in alphabetical order): Ethel Beatty, Terry Burrell, Leslie Dockery, Lynnie Godfrey, Gregory Hines, Maurice Hines, Mel Johnson, Jr., Lonnie McNeil, Janet Powell, Marion Ramsey, Alaina Reed, Jeffery V. Thompson.

ACT 1

Prologue: "Goodnight Angeline" (1919); "Charleston Rag" (1899)

"Shuffle Along" (from *SHUFFLE ALONG*)(1921)
The Company
(*Lyrics by* Noble Sissle.)

"In Honeysuckle Time" (from *SHUFFLE ALONG*)(1921)
L. McNeil, J. Powell, Company
(*Lyrics by* Noble Sissle.)

"I'm Just Wild About Harry" (from *SHUFFLE ALONG*)(1921)
M. Hines, J. Powell, L. Godfrey, M. Ramsey, E. Beatty
(*Lyrics by* Noble Sissle.)

"Baltimore Buzz" (from *SHUFFLE ALONG*)(1921)
L. McNeil, J. V. Thompson, M. Johnson, Jr., J. Powell, G. Hines, L. Dockery
(*Mime Staged by* Dana Manno.)

"Daddy (Won't You Please Come Home)" (from *SHUFFLE ALONG*)(1921)
L. Godfrey
(*Lyrics by* Noble Sissle. *Musical Staging by* Julianne Boyd.)

"There's a Million Little Cupids in the Sky" (1924)
M. Hines, L. McNeil, G. Hines, E. Beatty, M. Johnson, Jr., J. V. Thompson, M. Ramsey, J. Powell, L. Dockery, A. Reed
(*Lyrics by* Noble Sissle.)
(dropped from *THE CHOCOLATE DANDIES*)

"I'm a Great Big Baby" (from *TAN MANHATTAN*)(1940)
J. V. Thompson
(*Lyrics by* Andy Razaf.)

"My Handyman Ain't Handy Anymore" (from *BLACKBIRDS OF 1930*)
A. Reed, M. Johnson, Jr.
(*Lyrics by* Andy Razaf.)

"Low Down Blues" (from *SHUFFLE ALONG*)(1921)
G. Hines
(*Lyrics by* Noble Sissle.)

"Gee, I Wish I Had Someone to Rock Me in the Cradle of Love" (1919)
E. Beatty
(*Lyrics by* Noble Sissle. *Duet arrangement by* Vicki Carter.)

"I'm Just Simply Full of Jazz" (from *SHUFFLE ALONG*)(1919)
The Company
(*Lyrics by* Noble Sissle.)

ACT 2

"High Steppin' Days" (1921)
The Company
(*Lyrics by* Johnny Brandon. 1978)

"Dixie Moon" (from *THE CHOCOLATE DANDIES*)(1924)
M. Johnson, Jr., G. Hines, M. Hines, Company
(*Lyrics by* Noble Sissle.)

"Weary" (from *TAN MANHATTAN*)(1940)
T. Burrell, Company
(*Lyrics by* Andy Razaf.)

"Roll Jordan" (from *BLACKBIRDS OF 1930*)
A. Reed, T. Burrell, J. Powell, Company
(*Lyrics by* Andy Razaf.)

"Memories of You" (from *BLACKBIRDS OF 1930*)
E. Beatty
(*Lyrics by* Andy Razaf.)

"If You've Never Been Vamped by a Brownskin, You've Never Been Vamped at All" (from *SHUFFLE ALONG*)(1921)
M. Ramsey, M. Johnson, Jr., L. Godfrey, G. Hines, J. V. Thompson, L. Dockery, J. Powell, M. Hines, L. McNeil
(*Lyrics by* Noble Sissle.)

"You Got to Git the Gittin While the Gittin's Good" (1956)
M. Hines
(*Lyrics by* F. E. Miller.)

"Oriental Blues"[12] (from *SHUFFLE ALONG*)(1921)
J. V. Thompson, E. Beatty, L. Godfrey, J. Powell, M. Ramsey
(*Lyrics by* Noble Sissle.)

"I'm Craving for That Kind of Love" (from *SHUFFLE ALONG*)(1921)
L. Godfrey
(*Lyrics by* Noble Sissle. *Musical Staging by* Julianne Boyd.)

"Hot Feet" (1958)
G. Hines
(*Lyrics by* Noble Sissle.)

"Goodnight Angeline" (from *SHUFFLE ALONG*)(1919)
E. Beatty, M. Johnson, Jr., L. McNeil, J. Powell
(*Lyrics by* Noble Sissle, James Reese Europe)

Finale
The Company

1978.22 KING OF HEARTS

A Musical in Two Acts, 14 Scenes. Book by Joseph Stein. Based on a screenplay by Philippe de Broca, Maurice Bessy and Daniel Boulanger. Music by Peter Link. Lyrics by Jacob Brackman. Directed and choreographed by Ron Field. Settings by Santo Loquasto. Costumes by Patricia Zipprodt. Lighting by Pat Collins. Musical director, Karen Gustafson. Dance arangements by Dorothea Freitag. Orchestrations by Bill Brohn. Sound design by Jack Shearing. Production associate, Nan Pearlman. Associate producers, Lee Minskoff, Charlotte Dicker. Produced by Joseph Kipness and Patty Grubman in association with Jerome Minskoff. Opened 22 October 1978 at the Minskoff Theatre and closed 3 December 1978 after 48 performances.

CAST: *Inmates*: *Demosthenes* (Le Muet): GARY MORGAN. *Madeleine* (La Madame): MILLICENT MARTIN. *Genevieve* (La Courtisane): Mitzi Hamilton. *Simone* (La Ballerine): Marilyn D'Honau. *Dahlia* (La Servante): Isabelle Farrell. *Raoul* (Le Patron du Cirque): BOB GUNTON. *Jeunefille* (La Jeune Fille): PAMELA BLAIR. *Valerie* (La Flutiste): Neva Rae Powers. *Jacques* (Le Fermier): Rex David Hays. *DuBac* (Le Monseigneur): Michael McCarty. *Therese* (La Maman): Maria Guida. *Isolde* (La Chanteuse d'Opéra): Gerianne Raphael. *Claude* (Le Coiffeur): GORDON J. WEISS. *Guy-Louis* (Le Petit Garcon): Timothy Scott. *M. Clichy* (Le Photographe): David E. Thomas. *Philippe* (Le Maitre d'Hotel): Bryan Nicholas. *Marie-Claire* (La Duchesse): Julia Shelley. *Henri* (Le Duc): Will Roy. *Monsieur Cochon* (Le Porc): Wilbur.

American Soldiers: *Private Johnny Perkins*: DON SCARDINO. *Lieutenant McNeill*: Jay Devlin. *Frank*: Robert Brubach. *Steve*: Harry Fawcett. *Joe*: John Scoullar. *Tom*: Jamie Haskins. *Phillip*: Richard Christopher.

German Soldiers: *Hans*: Scott Allen. *Kapitan Kost*: Alexander Orfaly. *Siegfried*: Scott Barnes. *Fritz*: Roger Berdahl. *Karl*: Timothy Wallace. *Willie*: Karl Heist.

The action takes place during one day in September, 1918, toward the end of World War I in the French town of DuTemps, and the trenches that surround it.

Act 1, Scene 1: DuTemps and the American and German Trenches. *Scene 2*: Asylum of Ste. Anne. *Scene 3*: Outside the Asylum Gate. *Scene 4*: The Main Square of DuTemps. *Scene 5*: Madeleine's Establishment. *Scene 6*: Chamber of Love. *Scene 7*: DuTemps. *Scene 8*: American and German Trenches. *Scene 9*: Roof of Cathedral.

Act 2, Scene 1: An Abandoned Circus. *Scene 2*: Outskirts of DuTemps. *Scene 3*: German and American Trenches. *Scene 4*: The Terrace. *Scene 5*: DuTemps and No Man's Land.

ACT 1

Scene 2

"A Stain on the Name"
Inmates

Scene 4

"Deja Vu"
M. Martin

"Promenade" (The Transformation)
Inmates

[11]Originally presented 2 February 1979 at Theatre-Off-Park for 12 performances in substantially different form as a revival of *SHUFFLE ALONG*.

[12]Replaced for National Tour by:
"Baltimo' Joe" (1935)
(*Revised Lyrics by* Cheryl Hardwick, 1978.)

Scene 5
"Turn Around"
M. Martrin, Inmates
Scene 6
"Nothing, Only Love"
P. Blair, D. Scardino, M. Martin
Scene 7
"King of Hearts"
G. Morgan, P. Blair, B. Gunton, M. Martin, Inmates
"Close Upon the Hour"
D. Scardino
Scene 9
"A Brand New Day"
M. McCarty, D. Scardino, Inmates
ACT 2
Scene 1
"Le Grand Cirque de Provence"
B. Gunton, Inmates
"Hey, Look at Me, Mrs. Draba"
D. Scardino
Scene 3
"Going Home Tomorrow"
Soldiers
Scene 4
"Somewhere Is Here"
M. Martin
"Nothing, Only Love" (reprise)
B. Gunton, M. Martin, P. Blair, D. Scardino
Scene 5
"March, March, March"
D. Scardino, Inmates
"The Battle"
Soldiers

1978.23

STREET SCENE

A Revival of the American Opera (Dramatic Musical) in Two Acts, 3 Scenes[13]. Book by Elmer Rice from his play of the same name. Music by Kurt Weill. Lyrics by Langston Hughes. Directed by Jack O'Brien. Conducted by John Mauceri. Scenery designed by Paul Sylbert. Costumes designed by Nancy Potts. Lighting by Gilbert V. Hemsley, Jr. Choreography by Patricia Birch. Chorus master, Lloyd Walser. Chorus prepared by Leann Hillmer. (Orchestrations by Kurt Weill.) Produced by the New York City Opera. Opened 28 October 1978 at the New York State Theatre and closed 12 November 1978 after 4 performances in repertory.

CAST (in order of appearance): *Greta Fiorentino*: Martha Thigpen. *Emma Jones*: DIANE CURRY. *Olga Olsen*: Rosemarie Freni. *Carl Olsen*: Ralph Bassett. *Neighborhood Woman*: Marie Young. *Shirley Kaplan*: Lynn Cohen. *Abraham Kaplan*: Nico Castel. *Salvation Army Girls*: Myrna Reynolds, Kay Schoenfeld. *Henry Davis*: Andrew Smith. *Willie Maurrant*: Robert Sapolsky. *Anna Maurrant*: EILEEN SCHAULER. *Sam Kaplan*: ALAN KAYS. *Daniel Buchanan*: James Clark. *Mrs. Buchanan*: Lila Herbert. *Frank Maurrant*: WILLIAM CHAPMAN. *George Jones*: Robert Paul. *Steve Sankey*: William Ledbetter. *Lippo Fiorentino*: JONATHAN GREEN. *Mrs. Hildebrand*: Sally Lambert. *Jenny Hildebrand*: Kathleen Hegierski. *Graduates*: Denise Adoff, Vanessa Williams. *Charlie Hildebrand*: Timothy Eaton. *Mary Hildebrand*: Dela Bartolini. *Grace Davis*: Kimara Love. *Rose Maurrant*: CATHERINE MALFITANO. *Harry Easter*: ALAN TITUS. *Mae Jones*: Bronwyn Thomas. *Dick McGann*: Daniel Levans. *Vincent Jones*: Bill Herndon. *Dr. John Wilson*: Don Carlo. *Officer Murphy*: Ken Dovel. *Milkman*: Robert Brubaker. *Joan*: Ann Cawlo. *Myrtle*: Alexandra Sabin. *Workman*: Harris Davis. *Eddie*: John Henry Thomas. *Sally*: Brigitte Stocker. *Joe*: Billy Ross. *Strawberry Seller*: Richard Nelson. *Corn Seller*: Susan Delery-Whedon. *James Henry*: Don Yule. *Fred Cullen*: Alan Baker. *Old Clothes Man*: Dan Kingman. *Men*: Frank Tippie, James Brewer, Herbert Hunsberger. *Grocery Boy*: Ken Rubenfeld. *Ambulance Driver*: Edward Vaughan. *Music Student*: Patricia Charbonneau. *Intern*: James Sergi. *Furniture Mover*: Frank Tippie. *Nursemaids*: Marie Young, Rita Metzger. *Middle-Aged Couple*: Dan Kingman, Harriet Greene. *Off Stage Voices*: Vanessa Williams, Timothy Eaton, Lila Herbert.

[13]Originally produced in New York 9 January 1947 at the Adelphi Theatre for 148 performances. For Synopsis of Scenes and Musical Numbers, see original 1947 production.

1978.24

GOREY STORIES

An Entertainment (Revue) with Music in Two Acts[14]. Written and designed by Edward Gorey. Adaptation by Stephen Currens. Music composed and orchestrated by David Aldrich. Directed by Tony Tanner. Scenery supervised by Lynn Pecktal. Costumes supervised by David Murin. Lighting designed by Roger Morgan. Musical director, Martin Silvestri. Furs by Ben Kahn. Produced by Terry Allen Kramer, Harry Rigby, Hale Matthews and John Wulp. Opened and closed 30 October 1978 at the Booth Theatre after 1 performance.

CAST (in order of appearance): *Mona*, a maid: Gemze de Lappe. *Harold*, a butler: Sel Vitella. *Lady Celia*, the hostess: Julie Kurnitz. *Mary Rosemarch*, a spinster: June Squibb. *Ortenzia Caviglia*, a singer: Susan Marchand. *Little Henry*, a child: Tobias Haller. *Jasper Ankle*, an opera freak: Dennis McGovern. *C. F. Earbrass*, an author: Leon Shaw. *Hamish*, a beautiful young man: John Michalski.

Act 1: Lady Celia's Drawing Room.

Act 2: The summer house.

THE STORIES (in order of appearance)

ACT 1
Assembly
Limericks from The Listing Attic
(Company)
The Hapless Child
(S. Vitella, J. Squibb, L. Shaw, G. deLappe, D. McGovern, J. Michalski, J. Kurnitz, S. Marchand)
"The Wuggly Ump"
(Company)
The Curious Sofa
(Company)
The Sinking Spell
(Company)
The Gilded Bat
(Company)
"The Insect God"
(Company)
The Willowdale Handcar
(Company)
The Doubtful Guest
(Company)
"The Blue Aspic" (an opera)
(Company)
(*Lyrics by* Stephen Currens.)
ACT 2
The Unstrung Harp, or Mr. Earbrass Writes a Novel:
(J. Kurnitz, L. Shaw)
The Pious Infant
(Company)
"The Osbick Bird"
(S. Vitella, T. Haller)
The Deranged Cousins
(L. Shaw, D. McGovern, S. Marchand, J. Squibb)
"The Eleventh Episode"
(J. Squibb, S. Marchand)
The Lost Lions
(J. Michalski, L. Shaw, J. Kurnitz)
The Loathsome Couple
(Company)
"The Gashlycrumb Tinies"
(Company)

1978.25

PLATINUM

A Musical with a Flip Side in Two Acts. Book by Will Holt and Bruce Vilanch based on an original idea by Will Holt. Music by Gary William

[14]First produced in New York Off Broadway 8 December 1977 at the WPA Theatre for 12 performances.

Friedman. Lyrics by Will Holt. Directed and choreographed by Joe Layton. Scenery designed by David Hays. Lighting designed by John Gleason. Costumes designed by Bob Mackie. Orchestrations by Fred Thaler, Jimmie Haskell. (Musical) Arrangements by Fred Thaler, Jimmie Haskell, Gary William Friedman. Musical director, Fred Thaler. Sound by Paramount Sound, Steve Wooley. Multi-media designed by Sheppard Kerman. Produced by Gladys Rackmil, Fritz Holt and Barry M. Brown. Opened 12 November 1978 at the Mark Hellinger Theatre and closed 10 December 1978 after 33 performanes.

CAST (in order of appearance): *Shultz*: Tony Shultz. *Lila Halliday*: ALEXIS SMITH. *Snake*: Ronnie B. Baker. *Minky*: Jonathan Freeman. *Boris*: John Hammil. *Damita*: Damita Jo Freeman. *Robin*: Robin Frean. *Avery*: Avery Sommers. *Jeff Leff*: Stanley Kamel. *Crystal Mason*: LISA MORDENTE. *Dan Danger*: RICHARD COX. *Christine*: Christine Faith. *Wenndy*: Wenndy Leigh MacKenzie. *Alan Fairmont*: Jonathan Freeman. *The Sidemen*: Fred Thaler (Conductor/Piano), Gregory Block (Violon), Dick Frank (Guitar), Steve Mack (Bass), Roy Markowitz (Drums).

"Wings of Destiny" Film Sequence Cast: *War Bride*: Lila Halliday (ALEXIS SMITH). *Mack*: Alan Fairmont. (Jonathan Freeman). "Wings of Destiny" conceived and directed by Joe Layton.

Act 1: The newest environmental recording studio in Hollywood.

Act 2,: Six weeks later.

ACT 1

"Back With a Beat"/"Nothing But"
A. Smith

"Sunset"
L. Mordente, A. Sommers, D. J. Freeman, R. Frean

"Ride, Baby, Ride"
R. Cox, D. J. Freeman, R. Frean, A. Sommers

"Destiny"
A. Smith

"Disco Destiny"[15]
L. Mordente, A. Sommers, D. J. Freeman, R. Frean

"I Am the Light"
R. Cox

"Movie Star Mansions"
R. Cox, A. Smith

ACT 2

"Platinum Dreams"
A. Sommers, D. J. Freeman, R. Frean

"Trials and Tribulations"/"I Like You"
L. Mordente, A. Smith

"1945"
R. Cox, A. Smith

"Too Many Mirrors"
A. Smith

"Old Times, Good Times"[16]
A. Smith, Company

1978.26 (JOHN CURRY'S) ICE DANCING

An Ice-Skating Revue in Two Acts, 10 Scenes. Choreographed by (in alphabetical order) Jean-Pierre Bonnefous, Robert Cohan, John Curry, Norman Maen, Kenneth MacMillan, Peter Martins, Douglas Norwick, Donald Saddler, Twyla Tharp. Settings by Tony Straiges. Costumes supervised by Florence Klotz. Lighting by Marilyn Rennagel. Costumes designed by (in alphabetical order) Nadine Baylis., Sara Brook, Norberto Chiesa, Joe Eula, Florence Klotz, Santo Loquasto, D. D. Ryan. Sound design by Jack Mann. Entire production supervised by Ruth Mitchell. Produced by Charlotte Kirk, David Singer and Cubby Downe in association with Peter Wiese. Opened 21 November 1978 at the Felt Forum, closing 3 December 1978; re-opened 19 December 1978 at the Minskoff Theatre[17] and closed 31 December 1978 after 37 performances.

CAST: JOHN CURRY, JOJO STARBUCK, Ron Alexander, Yvonne Brink, Lorna Brown, Jack Courtney, Patricia Dodd, Cathy Foulkes, Brian Grant, Muki Held, Deborah Page, Paul Toomey.

ACT 1

Scene 1

"Palais de Glace" (World Premiere)
(*Music by* Giacomo Myerbeer. *Costumes Designed by* Florence Klotz. *Choreography by* Donald Saddler.)

Paris 1912: Skating in the afternoon was de rigeur, for where else would you find royalty, Ladies of Paris in all their glamour, famous artists of the day, and rich Americans all cavorting?

Major domo: R. Alexander. *Lovers*: C. Foulkes, J. Courtney. *Famous poet*: P. Toomey. *Famous dancer*: P. Dodd. *American*: L. Brown. *Young Count*: B. Grant. *A darling of Paris, well protected*: M. Held. *Another darling of Paris, very well protected*: J. Starbuck. *Prince*: J. Curry.

Scene 2

"Scoop"
P. Toomey, D. Page, Y. Brink
(Stage premiere: March 1976)(Ice Premiere)
(*Music composed and played by* Donald Ashwander. *Costumes designed by* Sara Brook. *Choreography by* Douglas Norwick. "Scoop" by special permission from The Paper Bag Players.)

Scene 3

"After All" (in Three Movements)
J. Curry
(*Music by* Tomasso Albinoni. *Costume designed by* Santo Loquasto. *Choreography by* Twyla Tharp.)

This work was commissioned by John Curry and the U.S. Olympic Committee especially for Mr. Curry's appearance in "Superskates III" at Madison Square Garden, November 1976.

Scene 4

"Moon Dances" (World Premiere)
M. Held, L. Brown, P. Dodd, R. Alexander, B. Grant, P. Toomey
(*Music by* Camille St-Saens. Choreography by John Curry.)

This work made possible by a generous grant from Chanel, Inc.

Scene 5

"Tango-Tango" (World Premiere)
J. Curry, J. Starbuck
("Tango" by Igor Stravinsky. "Jalousie" by Niels Gade. *Choreography by* Peter Martins. *Costumes designed by* D. D. Ryan.)

This work supported by a generous grant from the Doll Foundation.

ACT 2

Scene 1

"Icemoves" (World Premiere)
J. Curry, C. Foulkes, M. Held, P. Dodd, Y. Brink, L. Brown, D. Page, R. Alexander, J. Courtney
(*Music by* Hector Berlioz. *Costumes designed by* Joe Eula. *Choreography by* Jean-Pierre Bonnefous.)

Scene 2

"Night and Day" pas de deux from MYTH
Night: J. Starbuck. *Day*: J. Courtney.
(Mask of Separation composed by Burt Alcantara. *Costumes designed by* Norberto Chiesa. *Choreography by* Robert Cohan. *Costumes executed by* Suzanne Joelson.)

Scene 3

"Feux Follets"
J. Curry
(*Music by* Franz Liszt. *Costume designed* by Harry Lines. *Choreography by* Kenneth MacMillan.)

Scene 4

"Anything Goes" (World Premiere)
J. Starbuck, J. Courtney, L. Brown, D. Page, D. Barker
(*Music by* Leonard Bernstein. *Choreography by* John Curry.)

Scene 5

"Afternoon of a Faun"
J. Curry, C. Foulkes
(*Music by* Claude Debussy. *Costumes designed by* Nadine Baylis. *Choreography by* Norman Maen.)

1978.27 BALLROOM

A Musical in One Act, 13 Scenes.. Book by Jerome Kass. (Based on his teleplay "Queen of the Stardust Ballroom.") Music by Billy Goldenberg.

[15]Orchestrated by Harold Wheeler.
[16]Orchestrated by Harold Wheeler.
[17]For the Broadway transfer the running order was revised; Angela Adney joined the cast, and Muki Held departed the cast.

Lyrics by Marilyn and Alan Bergman. Directed and choreographed by Michael Bennett. Co-choreographer, Bob Avian. Scenic design by Robin Wagner. Costume design by Theoni V. Aldredge. Lighting design by Tharon Musser. Orchestrations by Jonathan Tunick. Sound by Otts Munderloh. Musical direction by Don Jennings. Co-producers, Bob Avian, Bernard Gersten, Susan MacNair. Produced by Michael Bennett. Opened 14 December 1978 at the Majestic Theatre and closed 24 March 1979 after 116 performances.

CAST: *The Family*: *Bea Asher*: DOROTHY LOUDON. *Helen*, her sister-in-law: Sally-Jane Heit. *Jack*, her brother-in-law: John Hallow. *Diane*, her daughter: Dorothy Danner. *David*, her son: Pater Alzado.

At the Stardust Ballroom: *Alfred Rossi*: VINCENT GARDENIA. *Marlene*: Lynn Roberts. *Nathan Bricker*: Bernie Knee. *Angie*: Patricia Drylie. *Johnny "Lightfeet"*: Howard Parker. *Martha*: Barbara Erwin. *Petey*: Gene Kelton. *Shirley*: Liz Sheridan. *Paul*: Michael Vita. *"Scooter"*: Danny Carroll. *Eleanor*: Jayne Turner. *Pauline Krim*: Janet Stewart White. *Faye*: Roberta Haze. *Harry "the Noodle"*: Victor Griffin. *Marie*: Adriana Keathley. *Emily*: Mary Ann Niles. *Mario*: Terry Violino. *Anitra*: Svetlana McLee Grody. *Carl*: David Evans. *Margaret*: Mavis Ray. *Thomas*: Peter Gladke. *Bill*: Rudy Tronto. *And* Marilyn Cooper, Dick Corrigan, Bud Fleming, Carol Flemming, Mickey Gunnersen, Alferd Karl, Dorothy D. Lister, John J. Martin, Joe Milan, Frank Pietri.

Customer's at Bea's Store: *Natalie*: Marilyn Cooper. *Estelle*: Roberta Haze. *Kathy*: Carol Flemming.

The action takes place in the Bronx at the present time.

Scene 1: Bea's Junk Shop. *Scene 2*: Outside the Stardust Ballroom. *Scene 3*: Stardust Ballroom. *Scene 4*: Bea's Living Room. *Scene 5*: Stardust Ballroom. *Scene 6*: Bea's Living Room. *Scene 7*: Bea's Junk Store. *Scene 8*: Stardust Ballroom. *Scene 9*: Bea's Living Room. *Scene 10*: Stardust Ballroom. *Scene 11*: Outside the Ballroom. *Scene 12*: Bea's Living Room. *Scene 13*: Stardust Ballroom.

MUSICAL NUMBERS

Scene 2

"A Terrific Band and a Real Nice Crowd"
D. Loudon

Scene 3

"A Song for Dancing"
L. Roberts, B. Knee
Danced by the Ballroom Regulars.

"One By One"
L. Roberts, B. Knee
Danced by P. Drylie, H. Parker, the Ballroom Regulars.

"The Dance Montage"
Danced by the Ballroom Regulars

"Dreams"
L. Roberts

"Somebody Did Alright for Herself"
D. Loudon

Scene 5

"The Tango Contest"
Danced by M. A. Niles and T. Violino, D. Loudon and V. Gardenia, B. Erwin and G. Kelton, S. M. Grody and D. Evans, L. Sheridan and M. Vita, M. Ray and P. Gladke, A. Keathley and V. Griffin

"Goodnight Is Not Goodbye"
L. Roberts, B. Knee
Danced by the Ballroom Regulars.

Scene 8

"I've Been Waiting All My Life"
B. Knee
Danced by the Ballroom Regulars.

"I Love to Dance"
D. Loudon, V. Gardenia

Scene 10

"More of the Same"
L. Roberts, B. Knee
Danced by the Ballroom Regulars.

Scene 12

"Fifty Percent"
D. Loudon

Scene 13

"The Stardust Waltz"
Danced by the Ballroom Regulars

"I Wish You a Waltz"
D. Loudon

1978.28

A BROADWAY MUSICAL

A Musical about a Broadway Musical, in Two Acts, a Prologue and 9 Scenes[18]. Book by William F. Brown. Music by Charles Strouse. Lyrics by Lee Adams. Production supervised by Gower Champion. (Direction, choreography uncredited). Sets by Peter Wexler. Costumes by Randy Barcelo. Lighting by John DeSantis. Musical conductor, Kevin Farrell. Orchestrations by Robert M. Freedman. Musical supervision and vocal arrangements by Don Pippin. Dance arrangements by Donald Johnston. Co-choreographer, George Bunt. Sound by Abe Jacob. Production co-ordinator, Barbara-Mae Phillips. Associate producer, Maria DiDia. Produced by Norman Kean and Garth H. Drabinsky. Opened and closed 21 December 1978 at the Lunt-Fontanne Theatre after 1 performance.

CAST (in order of appearance): *Policeman*: Nate Barnett. *James Lincoln*: IRVING ALLEN LEE. *Eddie Bell*: WARREN BERLINGER. *Lonnie Paul*: LARRY RILEY. *Melinda Bernard*: Jackee Harry. *Stan Howard*: ALAN WEEKS. *Maggie Simpson*: PATTI KARR. *Stephanie Bell*: GWYDA DONHOWE. *Kumi-Kumi*: Christina Kumi-Kimball. *Smoke & Fire Back-Up Singers*: Maris Clement, Loretta Devine, Jackee Harry. *Richie Taylor's Lawyers*: Sydney Anderson, Michael Gallagher. *Rehearsal Pianist*: Gwen Arment. *Richie Taylor*: LARRY MARSHALL. *Nathaniel*: Nate Barnett. *Richie's Secretary*: Jo Ann Ogawa. *Shirley Wolfe*: ANNE FRANCINE. *Theater Party Associates*: Sydney Anderson, Maris Clement, Loretta Devine. *Male Dancers*: Albert Stephenson, Robert Melvin, Martin Rabbett. *Sylvester Lee*: TIGER HAYNES. *Louie*: Reggie Jackson. *Jake*: Martin Rabbett. *Big Jake*: Albert Stephenson. *Junior*: Robert Melvin.

Ensemble: Sydney Anderson, Gwen Arment, Nate Barnett, Maris Clement, Prudence Darby, Don Edward Detrick, Loretta Devine, Sharon Ferrol, Michael Gallagher, Scott Geralds, Maggy Gorrill, Jackee Harry, Leon Jackson, Reggie Jackson, Carleton Jones, Christina Kumi-Kimball, Michael Kubala, Robert Melvin, Jo Ann Ogawa, Karen Paskow, Martin Rabbett, Albert Stephenson, Marilynn Winbush, Brad Witsger.

Prologue: One year ago, Times Square. *Act 1, Scene 1*; The same day. Eddie Bell's office. *Scene 2*: Six months later. Eddie and Stephanie Bell's apartment. *Scene 3*: Later. Stan Howard's apartment. *Scene 4*: One week later. A midtown Italian restaurant. *Scene 5*: A few minutes later. On a stage in a theatre on West 44th Street.

Act 2, Scene 1: Early one morning a week later. The Federal Theatre, Washington, D.C. *Scene 2*: Technical run-through and opening night in Washington. *Scene 3*: Later on opening night. The Federal Theatre. *Scene 4*: Later. The bar at the Washington Hotel.

ACT 1

Prologue

"Broadway, Broadway"
New Kids in Town, N. Barnett, I. A. Lee

Scene 1

"A Broadway Musical"
W. Berlinger, I. A. Lee, L. Riley, J. Harry, A. Weeks, P. Karr, Ensemble

Scene 3

"Smoke and Fire"
A. Weeks, I. A. Lee, C. Kumi-Kimball, Ensemble

Scene 4

"Lawyers"
W. Berlinger, G. DonHowe, S. Anderson, M. Gallagher

Scene 5

"Yenta Power"
A. Francine, Theatre Party Associates

"Let Me Sing My Song"
L. Marshall

"A Broadway Musical" (reprise)
W. Berlinger, G. DonHowe, I. A. Lee, A. Francine, P. Karr, L. Riley, A. Weeks, Ensemble

ACT 2

Scene 1

"The 1934 Hot Chocolate Jazz Babies Revue"
T. Haynes, I. A. Lee, Ensemble

Scene 2

"Let Me Sing My Song" (reprise)
L. Marshall, Friends

Scene 3

"It's Time for a Cheer-Up Song"
A. Weeks, P. Karr, L. Riley, I. A. Lee

[18]Originally produced in New York Off-Off Broadway 10 October 1978 at the Theatre of Riverside Church for 26 performances.

"You Gotta Have Dancing"
P. Karr, I. A. Lee, Ensemble
Scene 4
"What You Go Through"
G. DonHowe, W. Berlinger
"Don't Tell Me"
W. Berlinger
"Together"
I. A. Lee, W. Berlinger, Staff

1979.01 MONTEITH & RAND

A Comedy Revue in Two Acts[19]. (Devised by John Monteith and Suzanne Rand.) Assisted by bill-boy russell. Lighting by Gilbert V. Hemsley, Jr. Costumes by Donald Brooks. Produced by James Lipton Productions. Opened 2 January 1979 at the Booth Theatre and closed 10 March 1979 after 79 performances. Total, including Off-Broadway run, 110 performances.

CAST: JOHN MONTEITH, SUZANNE RAND.

1979.02 THE GRAND TOUR

A Musical in Two Acts, a Prologue and 13 Scenes. Book by Michael Stewart and Mark Bramble. Based on the play "Jacobowsky and the Colonel" by Franz Werfel and the American play based on the same, by S. N. Behrman. Music and lyrics by Jerry Herman. Directed by Gerald Freedman. Choreography by Donald Saddler. Sets by Ming Cho Lee. Costumes by Theoni V. Aldredge. Lighting by Martin Aronstein. Musical direction by Wally Harper. Orchestrations by Philip J. Lang. Dance music arranged by Peter Howard. Vocal arrangements by Don Pippin. Assistant choreographer, Mercedes Ellington. Sound by Jack Mann. Produced by James M. Nederlander, Diana Shumlin, Jack Schlissel in association with Carole J. Shorenstein and Stewart F. Lane.Opened 11 January 1979 at the Palace Theatre and closed 4 March 1979 after 61 performances.

CAST (in order of appearance): *S. L. Jacobowsky*: JOEL GREY. *Mme. Bouffier*: Grace Keagy. *Cziesno*: Jack Karcher. *Jeannot*: Mark Waldrop. *Colonel Tadeusz Boleslav Stjerbinsky*: RON HOLGATE. *Szabuniewicz*: Stephen Vinovich. *Chauffeur*: Stan Page. *Captain Meuller*: George Reinholt. *Mme. Vauclain*: Chevi Colton. *Marianne*: FLORENCE LACEY. *Conductor*: Gene Varrone. *Mme. Marville*, an Elegant Lady: Travis Hudson. *A Peasant Woman with Chickens*: Grace Keagy. *Jacques*, the Ejected Passenger: Bob Morrisey. *Hugo*, the Hungarian Hercules: Kenneth Kantor. *Mme. Manzoni*: Chevi Colton. *Stiltwalker*: Papa Clairon. *Bargeman*: Kenneth Kantor. *Man with flower in his lapel*: Jay Stuart. *Papa Clairon*: Jay Pierce. *Claudine*: Jo Speros. *Bride's Mother*: Grace Keagy. *Bride's Father*: Gene Varrone. *Bride's Aunt*: Chevi Colton. *Groom*: Mark Waldrop. *Bride*: Michelle Marshall. *Commissaire of Police*: Bob Morrisey. *Peddler*: Stan Page. *Mother Madeleine*: Travis Hudson.

Refugees, Soldiers, Guests, Sisters, etc.: Bjarne Buchtrup, Carol Dorian, Kenneth Kantor, Jack Karcher, Debra Lyman, Michelle Marshall, Bob Morrisey, Stan Page, Tian Paul, Jay Pierce, Linda Poser, Theresa Rakov, Paul Solen, Jo Speros, Mark Waldrop, Jeff Veazey, Bonnie Young. *Swing Dancers*: Bronna Lipton, Jeff Richards.

The action takes place 13-18 June 1940 between Paris and the Atlantic Coast of France.

Act 1, Scene 1: Square outside the Hotel de La Rose. *Scene 2*: Saint-Cyrille. *Scene 3*: A local train heading West. *Scene 4*: Wagons of the Carnival Manzoni. *Scene 5*: Open spot in the countryside near Rennes. *Scene 6*: Dressing area of the Carnival Manzoni. *Scene 7*: Midway of the Carnival Manzoni.

Act 2, Scene 1: A tree-lined canal in the West of France. *Scene 2*: Cafe of Papa Clairon at St. Nazaire. *Scene 3*: A country road near St. Nazaire. *Scene 4*: 23 Rue Mace. *Scene 5*: Empty street in St. Nazaire. *Scene 6*: The Old Wharf at St. Nazaire.

ACT 1
Prologue
"I'll Be Here Tomorrow"
J. Grey
Scene 1
"For Poland"
R. Holgate, G. Keagy, Parisians
Scene 2
"I Belong Here"
F. Lacey
"Marianne"
R. Holgate
Scene 3
"We're Almost There"
F. Lacey, S. Vinovich, J. Grey, R. Holgate, T. Hudson, G. Varrone, Passengers
Scene 4
"Marianne" (reprise)
J. Grey
Scene 5
"More and More"/"Less and Less"
F. Lacey, R. Holgate
Scene 6
"One Extraordinary Thing"
J. Grey, F. Lacey, R. Holgate, S. Vinovich, the Carnival Manzoni
Scene 7
"One Extraordinary Thing" (reprise)
J. Grey
ACT 2
Scene 1
"Mrs. S. L. Jacobowsky"
J. Grey
Scene 2
"Wedding Conversation"
J. Grey, G. Varrone
"Mazeltov"
G. Varrone, Wedding Guests
Scene 3
"I Think, I Think"
R. Holgate
Scene 4
"For Poland" (reprise)
F. Lacey, T. Hudson, Sisters of Charity
Scene 5
"You I Like"
R. Holgate, J. Grey
Scene 6
"I Belong Here" (reprise)
F. Lacey
"I'll Be Here Tomorrow" (reprise)
J. Grey

1979.03 SARAVÁ

A Musical in Two Acts, 17 Scenes. Book and lyrics by N. Richard Nash. Based on the novel "Dona Flor and Her Two Husbands" by Jorge Amado. Music by Mitch Leigh. Directed and choreographed by Rick Atwell. Sets and costumes by Santo Loquasto. Lighting by David F. Segal. Musical direction and vocal arrangements by David Friedman. Orchestrations by Daniel Troob. Dance arrangements by Dom Salvador. Sound by Robert Kerzman. A Mitch Leigh Production. Produced by Eugene V. Wolsk. Opened in preview 11 January 1979 at the Mark Hellinger Theatre, moved 1 March 1979 to the Broadway Theatre and closed 17 June 1979 after 177 performances[20].

CAST (in order of appearance): *Vadinho*: P. J. BENJAMIN. *Flor*: TOVAH FELDSHUH. *Arigof*: RODERICK SPENCER SIBERT. *Costas*: Doncharles Manning. *Manuel*: Wilfredo Suarez. *Dealer*: Jack Neubeck. *Dionisia*: CAROL JEAN LEWIS. *Policemen*: Lloyd Sannes, Gaetan Young. *Dona Paiva*: BETTY WALKER. *Rosalia*: RANDY GRAFF. *Antonio*: ALAN ABRAMS. *Priest*: Ken Waller. *Teo*: MICHAEL INGRAM. *Senhor Baldez*: Jack Neubeck. *Pinho*: David Kottke.

The People of Bahia: Steve J. Ace, Frank Cruz, Donna Cyrus, Marlene Danielle, Adrienne Frimet, Brenda Garratt, Trudie Green, Jane Judge, David Kottke, Daniel Lorenzo, Doncharles Manning, Jack Neubeck, Thelma Ann Nevitt, Ivson Polk, Wynonna Smith, Michelle Stubbs, Wilfredo Suarez, Ken Waller, Freida Ann Williams, John Leslie Wolfe, Gaetan Young.

The action takes place in Bahia, Brazil, from Carnival to Carnival.

Act 1, Scene 1: A Street. *Scene 2*: Barrabas Casino. *Scene 3*: Kitchen in Flor's House. *Scene 4*: A Cemetery. *Scene 5*: Teo's Pharmacy. *Scene 6*: Bedroom in Flor's House. *Scene 7*: Dionisia's Candomble. *Scene 8*: Teo's Pharmacy. *Scene 9*: Kitchen in Flor's House. *Scene 10*: A Church.

---

[19]Originally produced in New York Off-Broadway 27 July 1978 at Theatre East for 31 performances.

[20]Management never designated an opening night; the New York Times reviewed the show 12 February 1979, Variety 14 February 1979, other press followed by 23 February 1979.

Act 2, Scene 1: A Hotel Terrace. *Scene 2*: Flor's House. *Scene 3*: Barrabas Casino. *Scene 4*: Bedroom in Flor's House. *Scene 5*: Dionisia's. *Scene 6*: A Street. *Scene 7*: Finale.

ACT 1
Scene 1
"Saravá"
P. J. Benjamin, T. Feldshuh, Others
Scene 2
"Makulelé"
W. Suarez, D. Manning, P. J. Benjamin, R. S. Sibert
"Vadinho is Gone"
T. Feldshuh
Scene 4
"Hosanna"
T. Feldshuh, Others
Scene 5
"Nothing's Missing"
M. Ingram, T. Feldshuh
Scene 6
"Nothing's Missing" (reprise)
T. Feldshuh
Scene 7
"I'm Looking for a Man"
C. J. Lewis, Others
Scene 8
"A Simple Man"
M. Ingram
Scene 10
"Viva a Vida"
All

ACT 2
Scene 1
"Muito Bom"
T. Feldshuh, M. Ingram, Others
Scene 2
"Nothing's Missing" (reprise)
T. Feldshuh, M. Ingram
Scene 3
"Play the Queen"
T. Feldshuh, P. J. Benjamin, R. S. Sibert, Others
Scene 4
"Which Way Do I Go?"
T. Feldshuh
"Remember"
P. J. Benjamin
"A Simple Man" (reprise)
M. Ingram
Scene 5
"You Do"
C. J. Lewis, Others
Scene 6
"A Single Life"
P. J. Benjamin
"Vadinho Is Gone" (reprise)
T. Feldshuh
Scene 7
"Saravá" (reprise)
All

1979.04 THEY'RE PLAYING OUR SONG

A Musical Comedy in Two Acts, 13 Scenes. Book by Neil Simon. Music by Marvin Hamlisch. Lyrics by Carole Bayer Sager. Directed by Robert Moore. Musical numbers staged by Patricia Birch. Scenery and projections by Douglas W. Schmidt. Costumes by Ann Roth. Lighting by Tharon Musser. Music direction by Larry Blank. Orchestrations by Ralph Burns, Richard Hazard, Gene Page. Sound by Tom Morse. Produced by Emanuel Azenberg. Opened 11 February 1979 at the Imperial Theatre and closed 6 September 1981 after 1082 performances.

CAST (in order of appearance): *Vernon Gersch*: ROBERT KLEIN. *Sonia Walsk*: LUCIE ARNAZ.

The Voices of Vernon Gersch: Wayne Mattson, Andy Roth, Greg Zadikov. *The Voices of Sonia Walsk*: Helen Castillo, Celia Celnik Matthau, Debbie Shapiro. *The Voice of Phil the Engineer*: Philip Cusack. "I Still Believe in Love" reprise sung by Johnny Mathis.

(The action takes place in New York and California at the present time.)

Act 1, Scene 1: Vernon's Apartment—Central Park West, New York City. *Scene 2*: Vernon's Studio—Five days later. *Scene 3*: Le Club. *Scene 4*: Sonia's Apartment—An hour and a half later. *Scene 5*: On the street. *Scene 6*: On the road. *Scene 7*: A beach house in Quogue, Long Island.

Act 2, Scene 1: Vernon's Apartment—A few days later. *Scene 2*: Vernon's Bedroom—Three weeks later. *Scene 3*: Vernon's Bedroom—The middle of the night. *Scene 4*: A Recording Studio—11:00 AM the next morning. *Scene 5*: A Hospital Room—Los Angeles, a few months later. *Scene 6*: Sonia's Apartment—A few months later.

ACT 1
Scene 1
"Fallin'"
R. Klein
Scene 2
"Workin' It Out"
R. Klein, L. Arnaz, Voices
"If He Really Knew Me"
L. Arnaz, R. Klein
Scene 3
"They're Playing Our Song"
R. Klein, L. Arnaz
Scene 4
"If He Really Knew Me" (reprise)
R. Klein, L. Arnaz
"Right"
L. Arnaz, R. Klein, Voices
Scene 7
"Just for Tonight"
L. Arnaz

ACT 2
Scene 1
"When You're in My Arms"
R. Klein, L. Arnaz, Voices
Scene 4
"I Still Believe in Love"
L. Arnaz
Scene 5
"Fill in the Words"
R. Klein, Vocies

1979.05 WHOOPEE!

A Revival of the Musical Comedy in Two Acts, 12 Scenes[21]. Book by William Anthony McGuire. Based on the play "The Nervous Wreck" by Owen Davis (based on a short story "The Wreck" by E. J. Rath.) Music by Walter Donaldson. Lyrics by Gus Kahn. Entire Production directed by Frank Corsaro. Choreography and musical staging by Dan Siretta. Musical direction by Lynn Crigler. Scenery by John Lee Beatty. Costumes by David Toser. Lighting by Peter M. Erhardt. Sound design by Warren E. Jenkins. Production supervisor, Ron Abbott. Production consultant, G. William Oakley. Music research consultant, Alfred Simon. Assistant choreographer, Larry McMillan. Orchestrations and dance arrangements by Russell Warner. Associate producers, Martin Markinson, Joseph Harris, Donald Tick. Produced by Ashton Springer, Frank C. Pierson, Michael Price. Opened 14 February 1979 at the ANTA Theatre and closed 12 August 1979 after 204 performances.

CAST (in order of appearance): *Sheriff Bob*: J. KEVIN SCANNELL. *Mary Custer*: CAROL SWARBRICK. *Judson Morgan*: BOB ALLEN. *Sally Morgan*: BETH AUSTIN. *Henry Williams*: CHARLES REPOLE. *Wanenis*: FRANC LUZ. *Black Eagle*: LEONARD DRUM. *Chester Underwood*: GARRETT M. BROWN. *Harriet*

[21]Originally produced in New York 4 December 1928 at the New Amsterdam Theatre for 379 performances.

Underwood: CATHERINE COX. *Jerome Underwood*: PETER BOYDEN. *Mort*: VIC POLIZOS. *Andy McNab*: BILL ROWLEY. *Jim*: Al Micacchion. *Slim*: Steven Gelfer. *Jack*: Rick Pessagno. *Pete*: Paul M. Elkin. *Red Buffalo*: Brent Saunders. *Matape*: Candy Darling. *Leslie*: Susan Stroman. *Becky*: Robin Black. *Tilly*: Diane Epstein. *Olive*: Teri Corcoran. *Ensemble Alternates*: Jo-Ann Cifala, Jonathan Aronson.

Act 1, Scene 1: Mission rest, Arizona. *Scene 2*: En route to Black Top Canyon. *Scene 3*: Black Top Canyon. *Scene 4*: En route to the Bar "M" Ranch. *Scene 5*: The Bar "M" Ranch. *Scene 6*: Near the Reservation. *Scene 7*: Outside the Bar "M" Ranch.

Act 2, Scene 1: Outside the Reservation. *Scene 2*: Back at the Reservation. *Scene 3*: In the Wilderness. *Scene 4*: Outside the Bar "M" Ranch. *Scene 5*: In the Desert.

ACT 1[22]

Scene 1

"Let's All Make Whoopee Tonight"
Ensemble

"Makin' Whoopee"
C. Repole, Bridesmaids

"I'm Bringing a Red, Red Rose"
F. Luz

Scene 2

"Go Get 'Im"
J. K. Scannell, Ensemble

Scene 3

"Until You Get Somebody Else"
C. Repole, B. Austin

Scene 4

"Go Get 'Im" (reprise)
J. K. Scannell, Ensemble

Scene 5

"Love Me or Leave Me"
C. Swarbrick, C. Repole

Scene 6

"I'm Bringing a Red, Red Rose" (reprise)
F. Luz, B. Austin

Scene 7

"My Baby Just Cares for Me"
C. Repole, Ensemble

"Go Get 'Im" (finaletto)
J. K. SCannell, Ensemble

ACT 2

Scene 2

"Out of the Dawn"
F. Luz, B. Austin

"The Tapahoe Tap"
Indian Ensemble

Scene 3

"Reaching for Someone"
J. K. Scannell

"You"
C. Cox

Scene 4

"Yes, Sir, That's My Baby"
C. Repole, Ensemble

Scene 5

"Makin' Whoopee" (reprise)
C. Repole, Company

[22]For the subsequent National Tour, the show was renamed *MAKIN' WHOOPEE!*. Numerous alterations were made and the following musical numbers were added:

"Come West, Little Girl, Come West"
Mamie Van Doren (Mary Custer), Cowboys
(replacing "I'm Bring a Red, Red Rose" in Act 1, Scene 1)

"My Heart Is Just a Gypsy"
Imogene Coca (Harriet), Gypsies
(added to Act 1, Scene 3 after "Until You Get Somebody Else")

"Harriet's Ecdysiastical Delight" (dance specialty)(Act 2, Scene 3)
I. Coca

1979.06 SWEENEY TODD- THE DEMON BARBER OF FLEET STREET

A Musical Thriller in Two Acts. Book by Hugh Wheeler. Based on a version of "Sweeney Todd" by Christopher Bond (after the original melodrama by George Dibdin-Pitt). Music and lyrics by Stephen Sondheim. Directed by Harold Prince. Dance and movement by Larry Fuller. Production designed by Eugene Lee. Costumes designed by Franne Lee. Lighting designed by Ken Billington. Orchestrations by Jonathan Tunick. Musical director, Paul Gemignani. Sound by Jack Mann. Assistant to Mr. Prince, Ruth Mitchell. Associate producer, Marc Howard. Produced by Richard Barr, Charles Woodward, Robert Fryer, Mary Lea Johnson, Martin Richards in association with Dean and Judy Manos. Opened 1 March 1979 at the Uris Theatre and closed 29 June 1980 after 557 performances.

CAST (in order of appearance): *Anthony Hope*: VICTOR GARBER. *Sweeney Todd*: LEN CARIOU. *Beggar Woman*: MERLE LOUISE. *Mrs. Lovett*: ANGELA LANSBURY. *Judge Turpin*: EDMUND LYNDECK. *The Beadle*: JACK ERIC WILLIAMS. *Johanna*: SARAH RICE. *Tobias Ragg*: KEN JENNINGS. *Pirelli*: JOAQUIN ROMAGUERA. *Jonas Fogg*: Robert Ousley.

The Company: Duane Bodin, Walter Charles, Carole Doscher, Nancy Eaton, Mary-Pat Green, Cris Groenendahl, Skip Harris, Marthe Ihde, Betsy Joslyn, Nancy Killmer, Frank Kopyc, Spain Logue, Craig Lucas, Pamela McLernon, Duane Morris, Robert Ousley, Richard Warren Pugh, Maggie Task. *Swings*: Heather B. Withers, Robert Hendersen.

The action takes place in London's Fleet Street and environs during the nineteenth century.

ACT 1

"The Ballad of Sweeney Todd"
Company

"No Place Like London"
V. Garber, L. Cariou, M. Louise

"The Barber and His Wife"
L. Cariou

"The Worst Pies in London"
A. Lansbury

"Poor Thing"
A. Lansbury

"My Friend"
L. Cariou, A. Lansbury

"Green Finch and Linnet Bird"
S. Rice

"Ah, Miss"
V. Garber, M. Louise

"Johanna"
V. Garber

"Pirelli's Miracle Elixir"
K. Jennings, L. Cariou, A. Lansbury, Company

"The Contest"
J. Romaguera

"Wait"
A. Lansbury

"Kiss Me"
S. Rice, V. Garber

"Ladies in Their Sensitivities"
J. E. Williams

"Quartet"
S. Rice, V. Garber, J. E. Williams, E. Lyndeck

"Pretty Women"
L. Cariou, E. Lyndeck

"Epiphany"
L. Cariou

"A Little Priest"
L. Cariou, A. Lansbury

ACT 2

"God, That's Good!"
K. Jennings, A. Lansbury, L. Cariou, M. Louise, Customers

"Johanna" (reprise)
V. Garber, L. Cariou, S. Rice, M. Louise

"By the Sea"
A. Lansbury

"Not While I'm Around"
K. Jennings, A. Lansbury
"Parlor Songs"
J. E. Williams, A. Lansbury
"City on Fire!"
Lunatics, S. Rice, V. Garber
Final Sequence
V. Garber, M. Louise, L. Cariou, E. Lyndeck, A. Lansbury, S. Rice, K. Jennings
"The Ballad of Sweeney Todd" (reprise)
Company

1979.07 SPOKESONG, or The Common Wheel

A Play with Songs in Two Acts. Play and lyrics by Stewart Parker. Music by Jimmy Kennedy. Directed by Kenneth Frankel. Set by Marjorie Kellogg. Costumes by Bill Walker. Lighting by John McLain. Musical director and pianist, Tom Fay. Cycle coach, John Jenack. Produced by the Circle-in-the-Square (Theodore Mann, Artistic director; Paul Libin, Managing director) and Long Wharf Theatre (Arvin Brown, Artistic director; M. Edgar Rosenblum, Executive director). Opened 15 March 1979 at the Circle-in-the-Square and closed 20 May 1979 after 77 performances.

CAST (in order of appearance): *The Trick Cyclist*: JOSEPH MAHER. *Frank*: JOHN LITHGOW. *Daisy*: VIRGINIA VESTOFF. *Francis*, Frank grandfather: JOSEF SOMMER. *Kitty*, Francis' wife: MARIA TUCCI. *Julian*, Frank's brother: JOHN HORTON.

The action takes place in the 1970s and the 80 years preceding, in a bicycle shop in Belfast, Northern Ireland.

ACT 1[23]
"Daisy Bell"
J. Maher, Company
(*Music and Lyrics by* Harry Dacre.)
"Daisy Bell" (reprise)
J. Lithgow
"The Parlour Song" (Song of the Spokes)
J. Sommer
"Cocktail Song" (Energy)
J. Maher
"Cowboy Song" (Old Bob)
J. Maher
"Daisy Bell" (reprise)
J. Maher, Company

ACT 2
"Music Hall Song" (Salome Danced)
J. Maher, J. Lithgow
"The Parlour Song" (reprise)
J. Maher
"Army Song"
J. Maher
"Spinning Song"
J. Lithgow
(*Lyrics by* Madelyne Bridges.)
"Army Song" (parody)
J. Maher
"The Anthem (of the Common Wheel)"
M. Tucci, J. Sommer
"Daisy Bell" (reprise)
J. Maher, J. Horton

1979.08 ZOOT SUIT

An American Play (Drama with Music) in Two Acts, 2 Prologues and 20 Scenes. Written and directed by Luis Valdez. Choreographic sequences by Patricia Birch. Musical sequences and production by Daniel Valdez. Setting by Thomas A. Walsh from a concept by Roberto Morales, Thomas A. Walsh. Costumes by Peter J. Hall. Lighting by Dawn Chiang. Sound design by Abe Jacob. Production associate, Kenneth S. Brecher. Assistant director, Jack Bender. Original (Music) arrangements by Dan Kuramoto, Daniel Valdez. Additional orchestrations by Dan Kuramoto. A Mark Taper Forum Production. Produced by The Shubert Organization, Center Theatre Group of Los Angeles and Gordon Davidson in association with Lou Adler. Opened 25 March 1979 at the Winter Garden and closed 29 April 1979 after 41 performances.

CAST (in order of appearance): *El Pachuco*: EDWARD JAMES OLMOS. *Henry Reyna*: DANIEL VALDEZ.
His Family: *Enrique Reyna*: Abel Franco. *Dolores Reyna*: Lupe Ontiveros. *Lupe Reyna*: Roberta Delgado Esparza. *Rudy Reyna*: Tony Plana.
His Friends: *George Shearer*: CHARLES AIDMAN. *Alice Bloomfield*: Karen Hensel.
His Gang: *Della Barrios*: Rose Portillo. *Smiley Torres*: Geno Silva. *Joey Castro*: Mike Gomez. *Tommy Roberts*: Paul Mace. *Elena Torres*: Laura Leyva. *Bertha Villareal*: Angela Moya. *Cholo*: Luis Manuel.
Los Angelinos: *Swabbie*: Dennis Stewart. *Manchuka*: Kim Miyori. *Zooter*: Lewis Whitlock. *Little Blue*: Darlene Bryan.
The Downey Gang: *Rafas*: Miguel Delgado. *Ragman*: Lee Mathis. *Hobo*: Richard Jay-Alexander. *Guera*: Gela Jacobson. *Blondie*: Helena Andreyko. *Hoba*: Michele Mais.
The Law: *Lieutenant Edwards*: Vincent Duke Milana. *Sergeant Smith*: Raymond Barry.
The Press: *Press*: Arthur Hammer. *Cub Reporter*: Dennis Stewart. *Newsboy*: Lee Mathis.
The Court: *Judge Charles*: Vincent Duke Milana. *Bailiff*: Raymond Barry.
The Prison: *Guard*: Vincent Duke Milana.
The Military: *Sailors*: Dennis Stewart, Lee Mathis, Raymond Barry. *Marine*: Richard Jay-Alexander.

The action takes place in the Los Angeles area between the fall of 1942 and the fall of 1944, inspired by the infamous Sleepy Lagoon Murder Trial and subsequent Pachuco riots.

Act 1, Scene 1: Zoot Suit (A Barrio Dance). *Scene 2*: The Mass Arrests. *Scene 3*: Pachuco Yo. *Scene 4*: The Interrogation. *Scene 5*: The Press. *Scene 6*: The People's Lawyer. *Scene 7*: The Saturday Night Dance. *Scene 8*: El Dia de la Raza. *Scene 9*: Opening of the Trial. *Scene 10*: Sleepy Lagoon. *Scene 11*: The Conclusion of the Trial.

Act 2, Scene 1: San Quentin. *Scene 2*: The Letters. *Scene 3*: The Incorrigible Pachuco. *Scene 4*: Major George. *Scene 5*: Solitary. *Scene 6*: Zoot Suit Riots. *Scene 7*: Alice. *Scene 8*: The Winning of the War. *Scene 9*: Return to the Barrio.

ACT 1
Scene 1
"(Put on a) Zoot Suit" (Zoot Suit Theme)
E. J. Olmos, Dancing Couples
(*Music and Lyrics by* Daniel Valdez.)
Scene 4
"Los Chucos Suaves"
E. J. Olmos, Dancers
(*Music and Lyrics by* Lalo Guerrero.)
Scene 7
"Vamos a Bailar"
E. J. Olmos, Dancing Couples
(*Music and Lyrics by* Lalo Guerrero.)

ACT 2
Scene 6
"Chicas Patas Boogie"
Dancing Couples
(*Original Lyrics by* Lalo Guerrero.)

1979.09 CARMELINA

A Musical in Two Acts, 12 Scenes. Book by Alan Jay Lerner and Joseph Stein. Based on the film "Buona Sera, Mrs. Campbell" (by Melvin Frank, Sheldon Keller, Dennis Norden.) Music by Burton Lane. Lyrics by Alan Jay Lerner. Directed by Jose Ferrer. Choreographed by Peter Gennaro. Sets designed by Oliver Smith. Costumes designed by Donald Brooks. Lighting by (Abe) Feder. Sound designed by John McClure. Orchestrations by Hershy Kay. Musical direction by Don Jennings. Vocal arrangements by Maurice Levine. Dance music arrangements by David Krane. A Whitehead-Stevens Production. Produced by Roger L. Stevens, J. W. Fisher, Joan Cullman and Jujamcyn Productions. Opened 8 April 1979 at the St. James Theatre and closed 21 April 1979 after 17 performances.

CAST (in order of appearance): *Bellini*: Marc Jordan. *Mayor Nunzio Manzoni*: Gonzalo Madurga. *Vittorio Bruno*: CESARE SIEPI. *Rosa*: GRACE KEAGY. *Salvatore*: Ian Towers. *Signora Carmelina Campbell*: GEORGIA BROWN. *Signora Bernardi*: Judy Sabo. *Roberto Bonafaccio*: Joseph d'Angerio. *Father Tommaso*: Frank Bouley. *Gia Campbell*: JOSSIE deGUZMAN. *Walter Braddock*: GORDON RAMSEY. *Steve Karzinski*: HOWARD ROSS. *Carlton Smith*: JOHN MICHAEL KING. *Flo Braddock*:

[23]No song list appears in the program. Song titles prepared from the published play text.

VIRGINIA MARTIN. *Mildred Karzinski*: Kita Bouroff. *Katherine Smith*: Caryl Tenney. *Father Federico*: David E. Thomas.

Ensemble: Frank Bouley, Kita Bouroff, Kathryn Carter, Karen DiBianco, Spence Ford, Ramon Galindo, Liza Gennaro, Laura Klein, Michael Lane, Morgan Richardson, Judy Sabo, Charles Spoerri, Caryl Tenney, David E. Thomas, Ian Michael Towers, Kevin Wilson, Lee Winston. *Swing Dancers*: Debra Mathews, Michael Rivera.

The action takes place in 1961 somewhere in Italy.

Act 1, Scene 1: The Piazza of San Forino. *Scene 2*: A short time later in Carmelina's house. *Scene 3*: The wee hours of the following morning. The Piazza. *Scene 4*: Late morning, the following day. *Scene 5*: A short time later. Carmelina's house. *Scene 6*: later. The Piazza. *Scene 7*: Carmelina's house, late that night.

Act 2, Scene 1: Early the following morning. The Piazza. *Scene 2*: Immediately following. Carmelina's house. *Scene 3*: A Church. *Scene 4*: Immediately following. Carmelina's house. *Scene 5*: Immediately following. The Piazza.

ACT 1

Scene 1

"It's Time for a Love Song"
C. Siepi

"Why Him?"
G. Brown, C. Siepi

"I Must Have Her"
C. Siepi

Scene 2

"Someone in April"
G. Brown

"Signora Campbell"
G. Keagy, G. Brown, F. Bouley, G. Madurga, Townspeople

Scene 3

"Love Before Breakfast"
G. Brown, C. Siepi

Scene 4

"Yankee Doodles Are Coming to Town"
Townspeople

Scene 6

"One More Walk Around the Garden"
G. Ramsey, H. Ross, J. M. King

"All That He'd Want Me to Be"
J. deGuzman, Friends

Scene 7

"It's Time for a Love Song" (reprise)
C. Siepi

ACT 2

Scene 1

"Carmelina"
C. Siepi

"The Image of Me"
G. Ramsey, H. Ross, J. M. King

Scene 4

"I'm a Woman"
G. Brown

Scene 5

"The Image of You"
V. Martin, G. Ramsey

"It's Time for a Love Song" (reprise)
G. Brown

1979.10 THE UTTER GLORY OF MORRISSEY HALL

A Musical in Two Acts. Book by Clark Gesner and Nagle Jackson. Music and lyrics by Clark Gesner. Directed by Nagle Jackson. Musical numbers and dances staged by Buddy Schwab. Sets and lighting by Howard Bay. Costumes by David Graden. Musical director, John Lesko. Orchestrations by Jay Blackton, Russell Warner. Dance music arrangements by Allen Cohen. Sound by Charles Bellin. Associate producer, Sandy Stern. Produced by Arthur Whitelaw, Albert W. Selden, H. Ridgely Bullock in association with Marc Howard. Opened and closed 13 May 1979 at the Mark Hellinger Theatre after 1 performance.

CAST: *Administration*: *Julia Faysle*, Headmistress of Morrissey Hall: CELESTE HOLM. *Elizabeth Wilkins*, Secretary: MARILYN CASKEY. *Staff*: *Foresta Studley*: PATRICIA FALKENHAIN. *Teresa Winkle*: Laurie Franks. *Mrs. Delmonde*: TAINA ELG. *Miss Newton*: Karen Gibson. *Mr. Weyburn*, Groundskeeper: John Wardwell.

Sixth Form Students: *Carswell*: Mary Saunders. *Vickers*: Gina Franz. *Boody*: Adrienne Alexander. *Dale*: Jill P. Rose. *Dickerson*: Kate Kelly. *Haverfield*: Polly Pen. *Fifth Form Students*: *Alice*: Cynthia Parva. *Helen*: Becky McSpadden. *Frances*: Dawn Jeffory. *Angela*: Bonnie Hellman. *Marjorie*: Anne Kaye. *Mary*: Lauren Shub.

Visitors: *Richard Tidewell*: Willard Beckham. *Charles Hill*: John Gallogly. *Mr. Osgood*: Robert Lanchester.

The action takes place at the present time in the Morrissey Hall School for Girls in England.

ACT 1

Overture: "At the Fair" from "Country Suite" by Desmond Gorss (1885-1958) arranged and conducted for the Morrissey Hall Concert Orchestra by Evelyn Potts, Director of Music.

"Promenade"
Company

"Proud, Erstwhile, Upright, Fair"
C. Holm, P. Falkenhain, M. Caskey

"Elizabeth's Song"
M. Caskey

"Way Back When"
C. Holm, P. Falkenhain

"Lost"
The Sixth Form

"Morning"
T. Elg, Dancing Class

"The Letter"
B. McSpadden, J. Gallogly, Company

"Oh Sun"
A. Kaye (St. George), B. Hellman (Dragon), B. McSpadden, D. Jeffory, L. Shub (Dryads), T. Elg

"Give Me That Key"
C. Holm, B. McSpadden, M. Caskey

"Duet"
M. Caskey, W. Beckham, Company

ACT 2

"Interlude and Gallop"
Orchestra, Students

"You Will Know When the Time Has Arrived"
L. Franks, M. Saunders, Fifth and Sixth Forms

"You Would Say"
B. McSpadden, J. Gallogly, Fifth Form

"See the Blue"
C. Holm, Flowers (Girls)

"Dance of Resignation"
T. Elg

"Reflection"
C. Holm

"The War" ("Les Preludes" by Franz Liszt.)
Company

"Oh, Sun" (reprise), The Ending
Company

1979.11 UP IN ONE

A Musical Revue in One Act. Conceived by Peter Allen and Craig Zadan. Songs and additional musical material written by Peter Allen with Adrienne Anderson, Jeff Barry, Marvin Hamlisch, Marsha Malamet, Dean Pitchford, Carole Bayer Sager. Additional material by Bruce Vilanch. Directed by Craig Zadan. Choreography by Betsy Haug. Scenery by Douglas W. Schmidt. Lighting by Marilyn Rennagel. Costumes by Charles Suppon. Projections by Douglas W. Schmidt, Wendall K. Harrington. Sound by Tom Morse. Production coordinator, Gregory Connell. Production supervisor, Janet Beroza. Musical direction and arrangements by Marc Shaiman. Special arrangements by Marvin Hamlisch. Assistant director, Neil Meron. A Dee Anthony Production. Executive producer, Vince Mauro. Produced by Ron Delsener. Opened 23 May 1979 at the Biltmore Theatre and closed 30 June 1979 after 46 performances.

CAST: PETER ALLEN, LENORA NEMETZ.

MUSICAL NUMBERS[24] (in alphabetical order)

---

[24]Overture arranged by Marvin Hamlisch. Background Vocals: Janis Cercone, Louis Cortelezzi, Corky Hale, Al Scotti.

"Dixie"
(*Music and Lyrics by* Peter Allen.)
"Don't Cry Out Loud"
(*Music and Lyrics by* Peter Allen and Carole Bayer Sager.)
"Don't Wish Too Hard"
(*Music and Lyrics by* Peter Allen and Carole Bayer Sager.)
"Everything Old Is New Again"
(*Music and Lyrics by* Peter Allen and Carole Bayer Sager.)
"Fly Away" (debut)
(*Music and Lyrics by* Peter Allen and Carole Bayer Sager.)
"Harlem on My Mind" (from *AS THOUSANDS CHEER*)
(*Music and Lyrics by* Irving Berlin.)
"I Could Have Been a Sailor"
(*Music and Lyrics by* Peter Allen.)
"I Could Really Show You Around" (debut)
(*Music and Lyrics by* Peter Allen and Dean Pitchford.)
"I'd Rather Leave While I'm Still in Love"
(*Music and Lyrics by* Peter Allen and Carole Bayer Sager.)
"If You Were Wondering"
(*Music and Lyrics by* Peter Allen.)
"I Go to Rio"
(*Music and Lyrics by* Peter Allen and Adrienne Anderson.)
"I Honestly Love You"
(*Music and Lyrics by* Peter Allen and Jeff Barry.)
"Impatient Heart" (debut)
(*Music and Lyrics by* Peter Allen and Marsha Malamet.)
"I Never Never Thought I'd Break" (debut)
(*Music and Lyrics by* Peter Allen and Dean Pitchford.)
"Just a Gigolo"
(*Music and Lyrics by* Leonello Casucci and Irving Caesar.)
"Love Crazy"
(*Music and Lyrics by* Peter Allen and Adrienne Anderson.)
"Make 'Em Pay" (debut)
(*Music and Lyrics by* Peter Allen and Dean Pitchford.)
"More Than I Like You"
(*Music and Lyrics by* Peter Allen and Carole Bayer Sager.)
"Only Wounded" (debut)
(*Music and Lyrics by* Peter Allen and Carole Bayer Sager.)
"Paris at 21"
(*Music and Lyrics by* Peter Allen.)
"Planes"
(*Music and Lyrics by* Peter Allen and Carole Bayer Sager.)
"Puttin' Out Roots Again"
(*Music and Lyrics by* Peter Allen.)
"6:30 Monday Morning"
(*Music and Lyrics by* Peter Allen.)
"Tenterfield Saddler"
(*Music and Lyrics by* Peter Allen.)
"Two Boys"
(*Music and Lyrics by* Marvin Hamlisch, Carole Bayer Sager, Peter Allen.)
"We've Come to an Understanding"
(*Music and Lyrics by* Peter Allen.)
"What Am I Doing Here?" (debut)
(*Music and Lyrics by* Peter Allen and Dean Pitchford.)
"You Oughta Hear Me Sing" (debut)
(*Music and Lyrics by* Peter Allen and Dean Pitchford.)

1979.12 I REMEMBER MAMA

A Musical in Two Acts, 12 Scenes. Book by Thomas Meehan. Based on the play of the same name by John Van Druten and the stories ("Mama's Bank Account") on which it was based by Kathryn Forbes. Music by Richard Rodgers. Lyrics by Martin Charnin. Additional lyrics by Raymond Jessel. Directed by Cy Feuer. Musical numbers staged by Danny Daniels. Scenery by David Mitchell. Costumes by Theoni V. Aldredge. Lighting by Roger Morgan. Sound by Otts Munderloh. Orchestrations by Philip J. Lang. Musical direction and vocal arrangements by Jay Blackton. Co-producer, Roy Somlyo. Production supervisor Jerry Adler. Produced by Alexander H. Cohen and Hildy Parks. Opened 31 May 1979 at the Majestic Theatre and closed 2 September 1979 after 108 performances.

CAST (in order of appearance): *Katrine*: MAUREEN SILLIMAN. *Christine*: CARRIE HORNER. *Dagmar*: TARA KENNEDY. *Johanne*: KRISTEN VIGARD. *Nils*: IAN ZIERING. *Papa*: GEORGE HEARN. *Mama*: LIV ULLMANN. *Mr. McGuire*: RICHARD ENSSLEN. *Aunt Trina*: ELIZABETH HUBBARD. *Aunt Jenny*: DOLORES WILSON. *Aunt Sigrid*: BETTY ANN GROVE. *Mr. Thorkelson*: ARMIN SHIMERMAN. *Uncle Chris*: GEORGE S. IRVING. *Lucie*: Janet McCall. *Nurse*: Sigrid Heath. *Doctor Anderson*: Stan Page. *Dame Sybil Fitzgibbons*: MYVANWY JEAN.
Steiner Street Neighbors: Austin Colyer, John Dorrin, Mickey Gunnersen, Daniel Harnett, Danny Joel, Jan Kasni, Kevin Marcum, Richard Maxon, Marisa Morell, Frank Pietri, Elissa Wolfe.

Act 1, Scene 1: The kitchen and dining room of the Hansen house on Steiner Street in San Francisco, Spring 1910. *Scene 2*: The Hansen parlor, 21 June 1910, evening. *Scene 3*: The Hansen kitchen, mid-November 1910, early afternoon. *Scene 4*: The hospital, later that day. *Scene 5*: The Hansen kitchen, ten days later, early afternoon. *Scene 6*: Teh Hansen kitchen, early December 1910, a Friday evening.

Act 2, Scene 1: The Hansen back porch, Spring, 1911, evening. *Scene 2*: The Hansen kitchen, later that night and the following morning. *Scene 3*: The Lobby of the Fairmount Hotel, a few hours later. *Scene 4*: Uncle Chris' ranch, mid-May 1911, later afternoon. *Scene 5*: The Hansen kitchen, three days later, evening. *Scene 6*: The Hansen parlor, June 1911.

ACT 1
Scene 1
"I Remember Mama"
M. Silliman
"A Little Bit More"[25]
L. Ullman, G. Hearn, Children
"A Writer Writes at Night"
M. Silliman, L. Ullman
Scene 2
"Ev'ry Day (Comes Something Beautiful)"
L. Ullman, Company
"The Hardangerfjord" (dance)
Company
"You Could Not Please Me More"
G. Hearn, L. Ullman
(*Choreographed by* Graciela Daniele.)
Scene 3
"Uncle Chris"[26]
E. Hubbard, D. Wilson, B. A. Grove
Scene 5
"Easy Come, Easy Go"[27]
G. S. Irving, Friends
Scene 6
"It Is Not the End of the World"
The Family

ACT 2
Scene 1
"Mama Always Makes It Better"
The Children
"Lars, Lars"[28]
L. Ullman
Scene 3
"Fair Trade"
M. Jean, L. Ullman, Friends
Scene 4
"It's Going To Be Good To Be Gone"
G. S. Irving
Scene 5
"Time"
L. Ullman
Scene 6
"I Remember Mama" (reprise)[29]
M. Silliman

[25]Lyrics by Raymond Jessel
[26]Lyrics by Raymond Jessel
[27]Lyrics by Raymond Jessel
[28]Lyrics by Raymond Jessel
[29]Lyrics by Raymond Jessel

1979–1980 SEASON

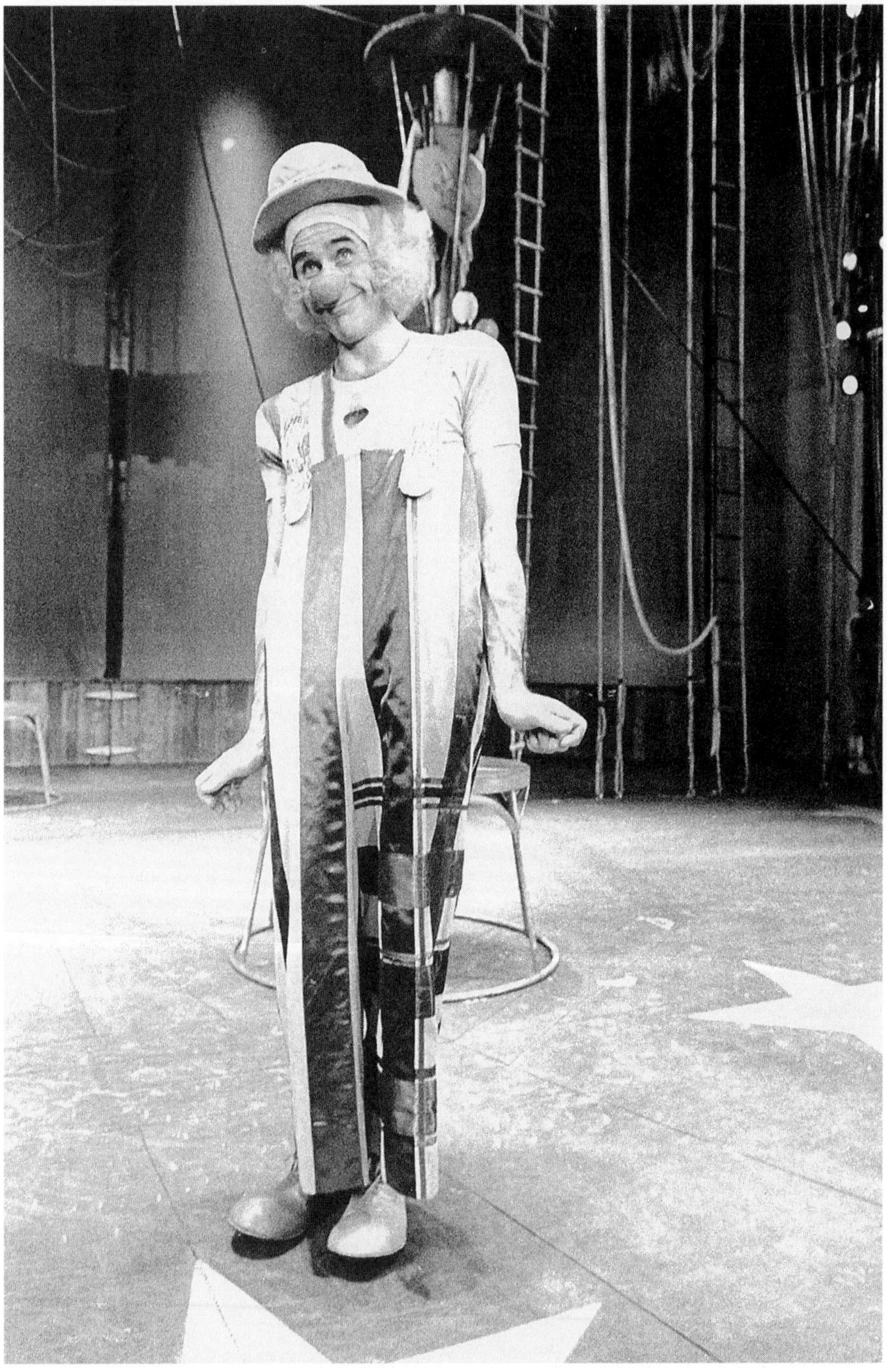

Jim Dale in BARNUM
Martha Swope/TimePix

1979–1980 SEASON

1979.13 A NEW YORK SUMMER

A Musical Revue in One Act, 19 Scenes. Produced and directed by Robert F. Jani. Creative director, Tom Bahler. Production executive, John Jay Moore. Executive musical director, Don Pippin. Art director, John William Keck. Costumes by Frank Spencer; Special costume designs for the Rockettes by Bob Mackie. Lighting by Billy B. Walker. Dialogue and narration by Stan Hart. Choreography and staging by Dru Davis, Violet Holmes, Louis Johnson, Linda Lemac, Howard Parker. Production coordinators, Charles Gillette, Anthony Salerno. Orchestrations by Elman Anderson, Billy Byers, Jack Eskew, Mitch Farber, Allen Faust, Michael Gibson, Quincy Jones, Jay Kennedy, Phil Lang, John Mandel, Peter Matz, Glen Osser, Larry Wilcox, Ray Wright. Produced by the Radio City Music Hall Entertainment Center. Opened 1 June 1979 at the Radio City Music Hall and closed 26 September 1979 after 203 performances.

CAST: KAREN ANDERS, TIM CASSIDY, ANTHONY FALCO, JOHN HALLOW, JOHN J. MARTIN, CHRISTINA SAFFRAN.

THE ROCKETTES: Pauline Achillas, Carol Beatty, Catherine Beatty, Dottie Belle, Susan Boron, Katie Braff, Deniene Bruck, Barbara Ann Cittadino, Eileen Collins, Susanne Doris, Joyce Dwyer, Jody Erickson, Jacqueline Fancy, Deniene Fenn, Phyllis Frew, Prudence Gray, Carol Harbich, Ginny Hounsell, Cynthia Hughes, Holly Jones, Pam Kelleher, Dee Dee Knapp, Judy Little, Leslie Gryszko-McCarthy, Geraldine McDonough, Barbara Moore, Ann Murphy, Joan Peer, Cindy Peiffer, Sheila Phillips, Lorraine Salerno, Jereme Sheehan, Terry Spano, Pam Stacey, Juen Taylor, Susan Theobald, Carol Toman, Rose Ann Woolsey, Phyllis Wujko.

THE APPLES: Steve (Ace) Williams, Stanley Dalton, Rodney Green, Carl Hardy, Mercie J. Hinton, Jr., Ivson (Scooter) Polk.

THE NEW YORKERS: Steve Baumann, Nancy Byne, Lou Ann Csaszar, Scott Dainton, Marcia-Anne Dobres, Christine Doelger, Cecily Douglas, Jeffrey Dreisbach, Barry Eric, Sharon Ferrol, Neal Gold, Lisa Grant, Bill Hedge, Deidre Kane, Dirk Lombard, Michelle Marshall, Tony Moore, Alan Nicholson, Andy Parker, Lorraine Person, Teresa Puente, Joel Rosina, Tina Sherman, Robin Stone, Chris Wheeler, Curtis Worthy.

PRODUCTION DANCERS: Phillip Bond, John Cashman, Jerry James, Mic Kozyra, Tony Lillo, James Parker, Malcolm Perry, Ken Prescott, Robert Raimondo, David Roman, Randy Skinner, J. Thomas Smith. *THE ICE-SKATERS*: Robert Metcalf, Darlene Gilbert.

MUSICAL NUMBERS

Scene 1

"New York, New York" (from *ON THE TOWN*)
The New Yorkers, Entire Company
(*Music by* Leonard Bernstein. *Lyrics by* Betty Comden and Adolph Green.)

"Another Hundred People" (from *COMPANY*)
(*Music and Lyrics by* Stephen Sondheim.)

Scene 2

A Street Scene in Manhattan
The Cabbie: J. Hallow. *Louise*: K. Anders. *Charlie*: J. J. Martin. *Beth*: C. Saffran. *The Policeman*: A. Falco. *Larry*: T. Cassidy.

Scene 3

A Visit to the United Nations featuring the Cherry Blossom Doncho Curtain

The largest silk stage curtain ever woven in Japan was a gift of the people of Tokyo to the people of New York City under their Sister-City Affiliation. It was presented on 4 May 1964 as a symbol of friendship. A masterpiece of the Nishijin weavers of Kyoto, it was made possible by the generosity of the people of Tokyo and scores of Japanese firms and organizations. The Music Hall is the official custodian of this gift to the City of New York.

Scene 4

Central Park in Summertime: A Fantasy at the Turn of the Century

"Put on Your Sunday Clothes" (from *HELLO, DOLLY!*)
(*Music and Lyrics by* Jerry Herman.)

Scene 5

Central Park in Wintertime: A Fantasy on Ice

"Sleigh Ride"
(*Music by* Leroy Anderson. *Lyrics by* Mitchell Parish.)

Scene 6

The Folk Art of New York

Scene 7

The Streets of Harlem: The Apples

Dance Music from *WEST SIDE STORY* (*Music by* Leonard Bernstein.)

Scene 8

Coney Island: "I Thank Heaven"
(*Music by* Tom Bahler. *Lyrics by* Quincy Jones and Mark Vieha.)

Scene 9

"New York at Night"
(*Music and Lyrics by* Tom Bahler and Mark Vieha.)

Scene 10

Broadway — 1979: New York is Dancing:
"I'm Just Wild About Harry" (from *EUBIE!*)
"Not While I'm Around" (from *SWEENEY TODD*)
"Yes, Sir, That's My Baby" (from *WHOOPEE*)
"The Joint Is Jumpin'" (from *AIN'T MISBEHAVIN'*)
"We Go Together" (from, *GREASE*)
"Sing Sing Sing" (from *DANCIN'*)
"One" (from *A CHORUS LINE*)
"They're Playing Our Song" (from *THEY'RE PLAYING OUR SONG*)

Scene 11

Our Salute to Mr. Broadway: George M. Cohan
L. Grant

"I'm a Yankee Doodle Dandy," "Give My Regards to Broadway," You're a Grand Old Flag."

Scene 12

Disco! (pre-recorded)
"Countdown" (performed by Dan Hartman from "Instant Reply" album.)
"Singin' in the Rain" (performed by Sheila and B. Devotions)
"Over the Rainbow" (performed by Meco)
"Mac Arthur Park" (performed by Donna Summer from "Live and More" album)
"La Bamba" (performed by Antonio Rodriguez)
"Brand New Day" (from *THE WIZ* film)

Scene 13

A Street Scene at Night: "New York Lullaby"
(*Music and Lyrics by* Tom Bahler and Mark Vieha.)
Bag Lady: K. Anders.

Scene 14

Shopping on the Avenue: "Avenue, Fifth Avenue"
(*Music and Lyrics by* Tom Bahler and Mark Vieha.)

Scene 15

On Our Way through Rockefeller Center: "A New York Summer"
(*Music and Lyrics by* Tom Bahler and Mark Vieha.)

Scene 16

Radio City Music Hall Movie Memories

Scene 17

The Music and Glamour of the Nation's Showplace

Scene 18

50 Years of America's Rockettes:

"Top Hat, White Tie and Tails" (from *TOP HAT* film)
(*Music and Lyrics by* Irving Berlin.)

"Applause" (from *APPLAUSE*)
(*Music by* Charles Strouse. *Lyrics by* Lee Adams.)

Scene 19

Where in the World But in America: A Finale Tribute to "Lady America" on the beginning of our second half century as New York's Entertainment Center
(New Lyrics set to the Music of "America" by Leonard Bernstein from *WEST SIDE STORY*)Entire Company

1979.14 BRUCE FORSYTHE ON BROADWAY

A One-Man Show in Two Acts. Musical director, Don Hunt. Production supervisor, Peter Mavoides. Lighting by Richard Nelson. Drummer, Freddie Adamson. Produced by Lee Guber and Shelly Gross. A Music Fair Concerts Presentation. Opened 12 June 1979 at the Winter Garden and closed 16 June 1979 after 5 performances.

CAST: BRUCE FORSYTHE.

ACT 1

"Just in Time" (from *BELLS ARE RINGING*)
(*Music by* Jule Styne. *Lyrics by* Betty Comden and Adolph Green.)
Opening Monologue
"It's Never Too Late"
(*Music and Lyrics by* Carmen Lombardo and John Jacob Loeb.)
Piano Solo: "Claire de Lune by Debussy"
"Star Dust"
(*Music by* Hoagy Carmichael. *Lyrics by* Mitchell Parish.)
"Nola"
(*Music by* Felix Arndt. *Lyrics by* Sammy Skylar.)
"Singin' in the Rain" (from *HOLLYWOOD REVUE OF 1929, SINGIN' THE RAIN* films.)
(*Music by* Nacio Herb Brown. *Lyrics by* Arthur Freed.)
"Give Me That Old Soft Shoe" (from *THREE TO MAKE READY*)
(*Music by* Morgan Lewis. *Lyrics by* Nancy Hamilton.)
The Generation Game Sequence (television):
"The Laughing Policeman"
(*Music and Lyrics by* Billie Grey.)
Dance Competition

ACT 2

"My Shining Hour" (from *THE SKY'S THE LIMIT* film)
(*Music by* Harold Arlen. *Lyrics by* Johnny Mercer.)
Noël Coward Impression
The Most Beautiful Girl in the World (sketch)
La Vie en Rose sketch
Valencia sketch
"It's the Ending of My Day"
Savoir Faire Sketch ("Un Homme et Une Femme")
Impressions: Tom Jones, Frank Sinatra, Sammy Davis, Jr., Anthony Newley

1979.15 GOTTU GO DISCO

An Entertainment in Two Acts, a Prologue and 14 Scenes. Book by John Zodrow. Music and lyrics by Kenny Lehman, John Davis, Ray Chew, Nat Adderley, Jr., Thomas Jones, Wayne Morrison, Steve Boston, Eugene Narmore, Betty Rowland, Jerry Powell. Directed by Larry Forde. Choeographed by Jo Jo Smith, Troy Garza. Scenery design by James Hamilton. Lighting by S. A. Cohen. Artistic direction and costumes by Joe Eula. Musical supervision and direction by Kenny Lehman. Vocal direction by Kenny Lehman, Mitch Kerper. Film sequences by Robert Rabinowitz. Sound design by Lenny Will. Associate artistic director, Ron Ferri. Assistant director, Donnis Honeycutt, Jr. Special effects by Chris Langhart. Produced by Jerry Brandt in association with Roy Rifkind, Julie Rifkind, Bill Spitalsky, WKTU—Radio 92. Opened 25 June 1979 at the Minskoff Theater and closed 30 June 1979 after 8 performances.

CAST (in order of appearance): *Narrator, (Vitus)*: JOE MASIELL. *Cassette*: IRENE CARA. *Billy*: PATRICK JUDE. *Minnie*: Lisa Raggio. *Contact*: Laurie Dawn Skinner. *Antwerp*: PATTI KARR. *Lila*: Jane Holzer. *Cubby*: Charlie Serrano. *Snap-Fish*: RHETTA HUGHES. *Pete*: JUSTIN ROSS. *Marc*: Marc Benecke. *Spinner*: Bob Pettie.

Singing Ensemble: Robin Lynn Beck, Gloria Covington, Gerri Griffin, Jack Magradey, Billy Newton-Davis. *Dancing Ensemble*: Connie Marie Brazelton, Prudence Darby, Ronald Dunham, Miguel Gonz, Christine Jacobson, Peter Kapetan, Patrick Kinser-Lau, Julia Lema, Bronna Lipton, Mark Manley, Jodi Moccia, Jamie Patterson, Dee Ranzweiler, Adrian Rosario, Willie Rosario, Sue Samuels. *Swing*:Tony Constantine.

Act 1, Scene 1: The Disco Rag Store. *Scene 2*: Streets of New York; A Bridge in Central Park. *Scene 3*: Antwerp's Apartment. *Scene 4*: Roof Top of Antwerp's Apartment. *Scene 5*: Vitus' Office. *Scene 6*: Various Parts of the Disco Rag Store. *Scene 7*: Sidewalk Outside the Dream Castle Disco. *Scene 8*: The Dream Castle Disco.

Act 2, Scene 1: Vitus' Office; The City. *Scene 2*: Antwerp's Apartment, Roof Top and a Park. *Scene 3*: Various Parts of the Disco Rag Store. *Scene 4*: The King and Queen's Dressing Room. *Scene 5*: A Bridge in Central Park. *Scene 6*: The Dream Castle Disco.

ACT 1

Prologue
"Puttin' It On"
R. L. Beck, Ensemble
(*Music and Lyrics by* Kenny Lehman and Steve Boston, orchestrated by Kenny Lehman.)

Scene 1
"Disco Shuffle"
P. Jude, I. Cara
(*Music and Lyrics by* Ray Chew with assistance by Nat Adderly, Jr.; orchestrated by Ray Chew with vocal arrangements by Nat Adderly, Jr.)

Scene 4
"All I Need"
I. Cara
(*Music and Lyrics by* Thomas Jones and Wayne Morrison, orchestrated by Kenny Lehman.)

Scene 5
"It Won't Work"
J. Masiell
(*Music, Lyrics and Orchestration by* John Davis.)

Scene 6
"Trust Me"
C. Serrano, L. D. Skinner
(*Music and Lyrics by* Kenny Lehman and Steve Boston, orchestrated by Kenny Lehman.)

Scene 7
"In and Out"
M. Beneche, Entire Company
(*Music and Lyrics by* Kenny Lehman and Steve Boston, orchestrated by Kenny Lehman.)

Scene 8
"Got Tu Go Disco"
B. Newton-Davis, Ensemble
(*Music, Lyrics and Orchestration by* John Davis)
"Pleasure Pusher"
J. Ross
(*Music and Lyrics by* Eugene Narmore, orchestrated by Brad Baker.)
"If That Didn't Do It, It Can't Be Done"
Entire Company
(*Music and Lyrics by* Ray Chew with assistance by Nat Adderly, Jr.; orchestrated by Ray Chew with vocal arrangements by Nat Adderly, Jr.)

ACT 2

"Inter-mish-un"
B. Newton-Davis
(*Music and Lyrics by* Kenny Lehman, Thomas Jones and Wayne Morrison.)

Scene 1
"Hanging Over and Out"
J. Masiell
(*Music and Lyrics by* Kenny Lehman and Steve Boston, orchestrated by Kenny Lehman.)

Scene 3
"Chic to Cheap"
R. Hughes
(*Music and Lyrics by* Jerry Powell, orchestrated by Brad Baker.)
"Bad, Glad, Good and Had"
I. Cara
(*Music, Lyrics and Orchestration by* John Davis

Scene 5
"Cassie"
P. Jude
(*Music and Lyrics by* Ray Chew with assistance by Nat Adderly, Jr.; orchestrated by Ray Chew with vocal arrangements by Nat Adderly, Jr.)

Scene 6
"Takin' the Light"
I. Cara, P. Jude, G. Griffin, Ensemble
(*Music and Lyrics by* Kenny Lehman, Thomas Jones and Wayne Morrison, orchestrated by Kenny Lehman.)
"Gettin' to the Top"
P. Karr
(*Music, Lyrics and Orchestration by* John Davis

1979.16 BROADWAY OPRY '79: A Little Country in the Big City

A Country Music Revue in Two Acts. Creative director, Jonas McCord. Talent coordination, Niles Siegel. Scenery and lighting by Michael J. Hotopp and Paul dePass. Sound by Sound Associates. Associate producers, Spyros Venduras, Joseph D'Alesandro. Produced by Family Affair Enterprises, Inc (David S. Fitzpatrick, Edward J. Lynch, Jr., Executive producers.) Opened 27 July 1979 at the St. James Theatre and closed 2 August 1979 after 6 performances[1].

[1]No musical numbers listed in programs.

CAST: TANYA TUCKER, FLOYD CRAMER, DON GIBSON, MICKEY NEWBURY, WAYLON JENNINGS, THE CRICKETS, THE WAYLORS.

1979.17 EVERY GOOD BOY DESERVES FAVOUR

A Play for Actors and Orchestra in One Act. Play by Tom Stoppard. Music by Andre Previn. From an original concept by Trevor Nunn. Directed by Tom Stoppard. Sets and Costumes by Eldon Elder. Lighting by Thomas Skelton. Orchestra conducted by David Gilbert. Sound by Dennis Roe. Produced by The Kennedy Center (Roger L. Stevens) and the Metropolitan Opera. Opened 30 July 1979 at the Metropolitan Opera House and closed 4 August 1979 after 8 performances.

CAST: *Ivanov*: RENÉ AUBERJONOIS. *Alexander*: ELI WALLACH. *Teacher*: CAROL TEITEL. *Sacha*: BOBBY SCOTT. *Doctor*: REMAK RAMSAY. *Colonel Rozinsky*: CARL LOW.

1979.18 BUT NEVER JAM TODAY

A Musical in Two Acts, 16 Scenes[2]. Book by Vinnette Carroll and Bob Larimer. Adapted from the works of Lewis Carroll. Music by Bert Keyes and Bob Larimer. Lyrics by Bob Larimer. Entire production devised and directed by Vinnette Carroll. Choreography by Talley Beatty. Music direction and incidental music by Donald Johnston. Scenery and costumes by William Schroder. Lighting by Ken Billington. Choral arrangements and vocal preparation by Cleavant Derricks. Production supervisor, Robert L. Borod. Sound design by T. Richard Fitzgerald. Orchestrations by Bert Keyes. Special orchestration by H. B. Barnum, Larry Blank. Dance music by H. B. Barnum. Associate producers, Herb Hugel, Gene Messinger. Produced by Arch Nadler, Anita MacShane and the Urban Arts Theatre. Opened 31 July 1979 at the Longacre Theatre and closed 5 August 1979 after 7 performances.

CAST (in order of appearance): *Alice*: MARILYNN WINBUSH. *Caterpillar*: CLEAVANT DERRICKS. *Persona Non Grata*: LYNNE THIGPEN. *Mushrooms*: Brenda Braxton, Clayton Strange, Sharon K. Brooks, Gary Q. Lewis, Celestine DeSaussure, Jeffrey Anderson-Gunter. *The Black Queen*: LYNNE CLIFTON-ALLEN. *The White Rabbit*: JEFFREY ANDERSON-GUNTER. *The Duchess*: REGINALD VEL JOHNSON. *The Cheshire Cat*: JEFFREY ANDERSON-GUNTER. *Cooks*: Cleavant Derricks, Sheila Ellis, Celestine DeSaussure. *The Mad Hatter*: JAI OSCAR ST. JOHN. *The March Hare*: SHEILA ELLIS. *The Dormouse*: Celestine DeSaussure. *The White Queen*: Charlene Harris. *Humpty-Dumpty*: REGINALD VEL JOHNSON. *Tweedledum*: JAI OSCAR ST. JOHN. *Tweedledee*: CLEAVANT DERRICKS. *The Two of Spades*: JAI OSCAR ST. JOHN. *The Five of Spades*: SHEILA ELLIS. *The Seven of Spades*: CLEAVANT DERRICKS. *The Queen of Hearts*: CHARLENE HARRIS. *The King of Hearts*: REGINALD VEL JOHNSON. *Guards*: Clayton Strange, Garry Q. Lewis. *The Mock Turtle*: JEFFREY ANDERSON-GUNTER.

Act 1, Scene 1: Down the Rabbit Hole. *Scene 2*: Interview with a Caterpillar (Square 1). *Scene 3*: The Black Queen (Square 2). *Scene 4*: The Kitchen of the Duchess (Square 3). *Scene 5*: The Cheshire Cat. *Scene 6*: A Mad Party (Square 4). *Scene 7*: The White Queen (Square 5). *Scene 8*: Humpty Dumpty. *Scene 9*: Tweedledum and Tweedledee (Square 6).

Act 2, Scene 1: The Queen of Hearts' Croquet Ground. *Scene 2*: The Queen's Dungeon. *Scene 3*: The Mock Turtle (Square 7). *Scene 4*: The Queen's Dungeon. *Scene 5*: An Examination (Square 8). *Scene 6*: Alice's Reward. *Scene 7*: The Daydream Ends.

ACT 1

"Curiouser and Curiouser"
M. Winbush

"Twinkle Twinkle Little Star"
C. Derricks, L. Thigpen, Company

"Long Live the Queen"
L. Clifton-Allen, M. Winbush

"A Real Life Lullaby"
R. V. Johnson, C. Derricks, S. Ellis, C. DeSaussure

"The More I See People"
J. Anderson-Gunter

"My Little Room"
M. Winbush

"But Never Jam Today"
C. Harris, M. Winbush

"Riding for a Fall"
L. Thigpen, R. V. Johnson, M. Winbush

"All the Same to Me"
J. Oscar St. John, C. Derricks

"I've Got My Orders"
M. Winbush

ACT 2

"God Could Give Me Anything"
J. O. St. John, S. Ellis, C. Derricks

"But Never Jam Today" (reprise)
Company, L. Thigpen

"I Like to Win"
M. Winbush

"And They All Call the Hatter Mad"
L. Thigpen

"Jumping from Rock to Rock"
J. Anderson-Gunter, M. Winbush, Company

"They"
J. O. St. John, S. Ellis, C. Derricks

"Long Live the Queen" (reprise)
The Company

""I've Got My Orders" (reprise)
M. Winbush, Company

[2]Originally produced Off-Off Broadway 23 August 1978 at the Urban Arts Corp for 12 performances. An earlier version developed by Vinnette Carroll but written by different authors was produced at New York City Center 23 April 1969 for 1 performance as part of the Black Expo Festival.

1979.19 GILDA RADNER—LIVE FROM NEW YORK

An Entertainment (Revue) in Two Acts, 14 Scenes. Written by Anne Beatts, Lorne Michaels, Marilyn Suzanne Miller, Don Novello, Michael O'Donoghue, Gilda Radner, Paul Shaffer, Rosie Shuster, Alan Zweibel. Producer and director, Lorne Michaels. Choreography by Patricia Birch. Musical consultation, Paul Shaffer. Music director, Howard Shore. Production design by Eugene Lee, Akira Yoshimura. Costume design by Franne Lee, Karen Roston. Lighting design by Roger Morgan. Sound design by Abe Jacob. Associate producer, Barbara Burns. Presented by Ron Delsener. Opened 2 August 1979 at the Winter Garden and closed 22 September 1979 after 51 performances.

CAST: GILDA RADNER, BOB CHRISTIANSON, FATHER GUIDO SARDUCCI (Don Novello), PAUL SHAFFER, NILS NICHOLS.

Rouge: Diana Grasselli, Myriam Valle, Maria Vidal. *The Candy Slice Group*: John Caruso, Paul Shaffer, Howard Shore, G. E. Smith.

MUSICAL NUMBERS AND SKETCHES

Scene 1

"Let's Talk Dirty to the Animals"
G. Radner
(*Music and Lyrics by* Michael O'Donoghue.)

Scene 2

The Audition: I Love to Be Unhappy
G. Radner
(*Music and Lyrics by* Gilda Radner and Paul Shaffer.)

Scene 3

Father Guido Sarducci: Slide Show
D. Novello

Scene 4

The Judy Miller Show (Little Brownie Girl sketch)

Scene 5

Don Kirschner

Rhonda Weiss introduction
(*by* Anne Beatts and Rosie Shuster.)

Scene 6

Rhonda Weiss and the Rhondettes: "Goodbye Saccharine"
G. Radner
(*Music and Lyrics by* Hardwick, Marilyn Suzanne Miller and Paul Shaffer.)

Scene 7

Father Guido Sarducci: Five Minute University
D. Novello

Scene 8

"If You Look Close"/"Gimme Mick"
G. Radner, Candy Slice Group
(*Music and Lyrics by* Gilda Radner and Paul Shaffer.)

Scene 9

"Lisa Loopner Piano Recital: "The Way We Were" (from film)

G. Radner

(*Sketch by* Anne Beatts and Rosie Shuster. *Music by* Marvin Hamlisch. *Lyrics by* Marilyn and Alan Bergman.)

Scene 10

Father Guido Sarducci: Pay for Your Sins

D. Novello

Scene 11

Emily Litella: Tiny Kingdom (*by* Rosie Shuster)

G. Radner

Scene 12

Nadia Kominich

G. Radner

Scene 13

Roseanne Roseannadanna (*by* Alan Zweibel)

G. Radner

Scene 14

"Honey" (Touch Me with My Clothes On)

G. Radner

(*Music and Lyrics by* Gilda Radner and Paul Shaffer.)

1979.20 NAUGHTY MARIETTA

A Revival of the Musical Comedy in Two Acts, 4 Scenes[3]. Music by Victor Herbert. New book and additional lyrics by Frederick S. Roffman (based on the original by Rida Johnson Young) adapted by Jack Eddleman. Directed by Jack Eddleman. Musical numbers staged by Graciela Daniele. Costumes designed by Patricia Zipprodt. Sets designed by Oliver Smith. Lighting designed by Ken Billington. Musical director and conductor, John Mauceri. Chorus master, Lloyd Walser. Production conceived by Frederick S. Roffman. Produced by the New York City Opera. Opened 30 August 1979 at the New York State Theatre and closed 2 September 1979 after 6 performances.

CAST: *Marietta d'Altena*: ELIZABETH HYNES. *Captain Richard Warrington* of Kentucky: HOWARD HENSEL. *Etienne Grandet*: ALAN TITUS. *Adah Le Clercq*, his Quadroon Mistress: SUSANNE MARSEE. *Private Silas Slick* of the Rangers: LARA TEETER. *Lizette*: Dana Krueger. *Acting Governor Grandet*, Etienne's Father: JAMES BILLINGS. *Florenze*, His Secretary: DAVID GATELY. *Sergeant Harry Blake* of the Rangers: DON YULE. *Rudolfo*: HARLAN FOSS. *Pirates*: Taras Kalba, Michael Rubino. *Town crier*: Edward Zimmerman. *Flower Girls*: Susan Delery-Whedon, Sally Lambert. *Nanette*: Cindy Lynn Aaronson. *Felice*: Sally Lambert. *Fanchon*: Leslie Luxemburg. *Knife Grinder*: Barry Carl. *Flower Vendor*: George Bohachevsky. *Bird Vendor*: Louis Perry. *Fruit Vendor*: Robert Brubaker. *Sugar Cane Vendor*: Harris Davis. *Indian*: Don Carlo. *Pierrot*: José Bourbon. *Graziella*: Toni-Ann Gardella. *Major-Domo*: Glenn Rowen. *Spanish Dancer*: Esperanza Galan. *San Domingo Ladies*: Toni-Ann Gardella, Candace Itow, Rebeka Pradera. *Quadroon Waiters*: Taras Kalba, Michael Rubino, Rafael Romero, José Bourbon. *Man at auction*: Mervin Crook. *Turk*: Barry Carl *Ensemble*: New York City Opera Chorus.

1979.21 THE MERRY WIDOW

A Revival of the Operetta in Three Acts, 4 Scenes[4]. Original Viennese libretto ('Die lustige witwe') and lyrics by Victor Léon and Leo Stein (after "L'Attaché d'Ambassade" by Henri Meilhac.) Music by Franz Lehár. New English translation and dialogue by Ursula Eggers and Joseph de Rugeris. New lyrics by Sheldon Harnick. This San Diego Opera production directed by Tito Capobianco. Stage director, Antoni Jaworski. Choreographer, Jessica Redel. Production (settings, costumes) design by Carl Toms. Lighting design by Ken Billington. Conductor, Imre Pallo. Produced by the New York City Opera. Opened 5 September 1979 at the New York State Theatre and closed 9 September 1978 after 7 performances.

CAST: *Baron Mirko Zeta*: DAVID RAE SMITH. *Valencienne*: Marianna Christos. *Count Danilo*: ALAN TITUS. *Anna Glawari*: DIANA SOVIERO. *Camille de Rosillon*: BRUCE REED. *Vicomte Cascada*: HARLAN FOSS. *Raoul St. Brioche*: ALAN KAYS. *Bogdanovitch*: Herbert Hunsberger. *Sylviane*: Jane Shaulis. *Kromov*: William Ledbetter. *Olga*: Penny Orloff. *Pritchitch*: Louis Perry. *Praskovia*: Susan Delery-Whedon. *Njegus*: JAMES BILLINGS. *Lolo*: Candace Itow. *Dodo*: Jane Shaulis. *Jou-Jou*: Penny Orloff. *Frou-Frou*: Toni-Ann Gardella. *Clo-Clo*: Susan Delery-Whedon. *Margot*: Raven Wilkinson. *Ensemble*: New York City Opera Chorus.

1979.22 PETER PAN, or The Boy Who Wouldn't Grow Up

A Revival of the Musical in Three Acts, 9 Scenes[5]. Book by James M. Barrie, (adaptation uncredited). Music by Mark [Moose] Charlap. Lyrics by Carolyn Leigh. Additional music by Jule Styne. Additional lyrics by Betty Comden and Adolph Green. Original production conceived, directed and choreographed by Jerome Robbins. Entire production directed and choreographed by Rob Iscove. Production (scenery) by Peter Wolf. Costumes designed by Bill Hargate. Lighting designed by Thomas Skelton. Musical and vocal direction by Jack Lee. Sound designed by T. Richard Fitzgerald. Special laser effects by Laser Media. Flying by Foy. Produced by Zev Bufman and James M. Nederlander in association with Jack Molthen, Spencer Tandy and J. Ronald Horowitz. Opened 6 September 1979 at the Lunt-Fontanne Theatre and closed 4 January 1981 after 578 performances.

CAST (in order of appearance): *Michael*: Jonathan Ward. *Nana*: James Cook. *Liza*: Maggy Gorrill. *Wendy*: MARSHA KRAMER. *John*: Alexander Winter. *Mrs. Darling*: BETH FOWLER. *Mr. Darling*: GEORGE ROSE. *Peter Pan*: SANDY DUNCAN. *Lion*: Jim Wolfe. *Turtle*: Cleve Asbury. *Kangaroo*: Reed Jones. *Ostrich*: Maggy Gorrill. *Slightly*: Chris Farr. *Curly*: Michael Estes. *First Twin*: Rusty Jacobs. *Second Twin*: Joey Abbott. *Tootles*: Carl Tramon. *Captain Hook*: GEORGE ROSE. *Nibs*: Dennis Courtney. *Captain Hook*: GEORGE ROSE. *Noodler*: Guy Stroman. *Smee*: ARNOLD SOBOLOFF. *Crocodile*: Kevin McCready. *Tiger Lily*: MARIA POGEE. *Starkey*: Jon Vandertholen. *Cecco*: Trey Wilson. *Mullins*: Steven Yuhasz. *Jukes*: Gary Daniel. *Wendy*, Grown-up: Neva Rae Powers. *Jane*: MARSHA KRAMER. *Tinker Bell*: Laser Media, Inc.

Pirates: William Carmichael, James Cook, Gary Daniel, Dianna Hughes, Guy Stroman, Jon Vandertholen, Trey Wilson, Steven Yuhasz. *Indians*: Cleve Asbury, Maggy Gorrill, Sharon-Ann Hill, Reed Jones, C. J. McCaffrey, Kevin McCready, David Storey, Jim Wolfe. *Trees*: C. J. McCaffrey, Kevin McCready, David Storey.

Act 1, Scene 1: Nursery of the Darling Home.

Act 2, Scene 1: Neverland. *Scene 2*: Path to Lagoon. *Scene 3*: Neverland Forest. *Scene 4*: Home Underground.

Act 3, Scene 1: *The Jolly Roger*. *Scene 2*: Neverland. *Scene 3*: Nursery of the Darling Home. *Scene 4*: The Nursery many years later.

ACT 1

Scene 1

"Tender Shepherd"

B. Fowler, M. Kramer, A. Winter, J. Ward

(*Music by* Mark Charlap. *Lyrics by* Carolyn Leigh.)

"I've Got to Crow"

S. Duncan

(*Music by* Mark Charlap. *Lyrics by* Carolyn Leigh.)

"Neverland"

S. Duncan

(*Music by* Jule Styne. *Lyrics by* Betty Comden and Adolph Green.)

"I'm Flying"

S. Duncan, M. Kramer, A. Winter, J. Ward

(*Music by* Mark Charlap. *Lyrics by* Carolyn Leigh.)

ACT 2

Scene 1

"Morning in Neverland"

Never Animals, Lost Boys

(*Music by* Jule Styne. *Lyrics by* Betty Comden and Adolph Green.)

"Pirate Song"

Pirates

(*Music by* Mark Charlap. *Lyrics by* Carolyn Leigh.)

"A Princely Scheme"

G. Rose, Pirates

(*Music by* Mark Charlap. *Lyrics by* Carolyn Leigh.)

"Indians!"

M. Pogee, Indians

(*Dance Arrangement by* Dorothea Freitag.)

"Wendy"

S. Duncan, Lost Boys

(*Music by* Jule Styne. *Lyrics by* Betty Comden and Adolph Green.)

---

[3]Originally produced in New York 7 November 1910 at the New York Theatre for 136 performances; this version first produced in New York 31 August 1978 at the New York State Theatre for 14 performances. For Synopsis of Scenes and Musical Numbers, see 1978 revival.

[4]Originally produced in New York 21 October 1907 at the New Amsterdam Theatre for 416 performances; this version first produced in New York 2 April 1978 at the New York State Theatre for 8 performances. For Synopsis of Scenes and Musical Numbers, see 1978 revival.

[5]Originally produced in New York 20 October 1954 at the Winter Garden for 152 performances. For this production, "Neverland Waltz," "The Pow Pow Polka," and "To the Ship" were dropped; "Morning in Neverland" was added.

"Another Princely Scheme"
G. Rose, Pirates
(*Music by* Mark Charlap. *Lyrics by* Carolyn Leigh.)
Scene 2
"I Won't Grow Up"
S. Duncan, Lost Boys
(*Music by* Mark Charlap. *Lyrics by* Carolyn Leigh.)
Scene 3
"Mysterious Lady"
S. Duncan, G. Rose, Never Trees
(*Music by* Jule Styne. *Lyrics by* Betty Comden and Adolph Green.)
Scene 4
"Ugg-a-Wugg"
S. Duncan, M. Pogee, Indians, Lost Boys, Darling Children
(*Music by* Jule Styne. *Lyrics by* Betty Comden and Adolph Green.)
"Distant Melody"
M. Kramer
(*Music by* Jule Styne. *Lyrics by* Betty Comden and Adolph Green.)
ACT 3
Scene 1
"Hook's Waltz"
G. Rose, Pirates
(*Music by* Jule Styne. *Lyrics by* Betty Comden and Adolph Green.)
"The Battle"
S. Duncan, G. Rose
(*Music by* Mark Charlap. *Lyrics by* Carolyn Leigh.)
Scene 2
"I've Got to Crow" (reprise)
S. Duncan, Darling Children, Lost Boys
Scene 3
"Tender Shepherd" (reprise)
B. Fowler, M. Kramer, A. Winter, J. Ward
"I Won't Grow Up" (reprise)
The Darling Family, Lost Boys
Scene 4
"Neverland" (reprise)
S. Duncan

1979.23

EVITA

A Musical in Two Acts. Music by Andrew Lloyd Webber. Lyrics by Tim Rice. Directed by Harold Prince. Sets, costumes and projections designed by Timothy O'Brien, Tazeena Firth. Lighting by David Hersey. Sound by Abe Jacob. Choreography by Larry Fuller. Musical director, Rene Wiegert. Orchestrations by Hershy Kay, Andrew Lloyd Webber. Executive producers, R. Tyler Gatchell and Peter Neufeld. Produced by Robert Stigwood in association with David Land. Opened 25 September 1979 at the Broadway Theatre and closed 25 June 1983 after 1568 performances.

CAST (in order of appearance): *Eva*: PATTI LuPONE, Terri Klausner (matinees). *Che*: MANDY PATINKIN. *Peron*: BOB GUNTON. *Peron's Mistress*: Jan Ohringer. *Magaldi*: Mark Syers.

People of Argentina: Seda Azarian, Dennis Birchall, Peppi Borza, Tom Carder, Robin Cleaver, Andy De Gange, Mark East, Teri Gill, Carlos Gorbea, Pat Gorman, Rex David Hays, Terri Klausner, Michael Lichtefeld, Carol Lugenbeal, Paul Lynn, Morgan MacKay, Peter Marinos, Sal Mistretta, Jack Neubeck, Marcia O'Brien, Nancy Opel, Davia Sacks, James Sbano, David Staller, Michelle Stubbs, Robert Tanna, Clarence Teeters, Susan Terry, Phillip Tracy, David Vosburgh, Mark Waldrop, Sandra Wheeler, Brad Witsger, John Leslie Wolfe, Nancy Wood, John Yost. *Children*: Megan Forste, Bridget Francis, Nicole Francis, Michael Pastryk, Christopher Wooten.

The action takes place in Argentina between 1934 and 1952.

ACT 1
"A Cinema in Buenos Aires; July 26, 1952"
Company
"Requiem for Evita"
Company
"Oh What a Circus"
M. Patinkin, Company
"On This Night of a Thousand Stars"
M. Syers
"Eva Beware of the City"
M. Syers, P. LuPone, Family
"Buenos Aires"P. LuPone, Dancers
"Goodnight and Thank You"
M. Patinkin, P. LuPone, Lovers
"The Art of the Possible"
B. Gunton, P. LuPone, Colonels
"Charity Concert"
Company
"I'd Be Surprisingly Good for You"
P. LuPone, B. Gunton
"Another Suitcase in Another Hall"
J. Ohringer
"Peron's Latest Flame"
M. Patinkin, P. LuPone, Company
"A New Argentina"
P. LuPone, B. Gunton, M. Patinkin, Company
ACT 2
"On the Balcony of the Casa Rosada"
B. Gunton, M. Patinkin, Company
"Don't Cry for Me Argentina"
P. LuPone
"High Flying Adored"
M. Patinkin, P. LuPone
"Rainbow High"
P. LuPone, Dressers
"Rainbow Tour"
M. Patinkin, P. LuPone, B. Gunton, Peronists
"The Actress Hasn't Learned (the Lines You'd Like to Hear)"
P. LuPone, M. Patinkin, Company
"And the Money Kept Rolling In (and Out)"
M. Patinkin, Company
"Santa Evita"
Children, Workers
"Waltz for Eva and Che"
P. LuPone, M. Patinkin
"She is a Diamond"
B. Gunton, Officers
"Dice Are Rolling"
B. Gunton, P. LuPone
"Eva's Final Broadcast"
P. LuPone, M. Patinkin
"Montage"
Company
"Lament"
P. LuPone, M. Patinkin

1979.24

THE 1940's RADIO HOUR

A Musical in One Act. (Book) by Walton Jones. Based on an idea by Walton Jones and Carol Lees, as originally presented by the Ensemble Company and Yale Repertory Theatre in New Haven and further developed and presented by the Arena Stage in Washington, D.C. Directed by Walton Jones. Musical numbers staged by Thommie Walsh. Musical supervision and direction by Stanley Lebowsky. Scenic design by David Gropman. Lighting design by Tharon Musser. Costume design by William Ivey Long. Sound design by Otts Munderloh. Orchestrations by Gary S. Fagin. Vocal arrangements by Paul Schierhorn. Produced by Jujamcyn Productions, Joseph Harris, Ira Bernstein and Roger Berlind. Opened 7 October 1979 at the St. James Theatre and closed 6 January 1980 after 105 performances.

CAST (in order of appearance): *Pops Bailey*: Arny Freeman. *Stanley*: John Sloman. *Clifton A. Feddington*: Josef Sommer. *Zoot Doubleman*: Stanley Lebowsky. *Wally Fergusson*: Jack Hallett. *Lou Cohn*: Merwin Goldsmith. *Johnny Cantone*: Jeff Keller. *Ginger Brooks*: Crissy Wilzak. *Connie Miller*: Kathy Andrini. *B. J. Gibson*: Stephen James. *Neal Tilden*: Joe Grifasi. *Ann Collier*: Mary-Cleere Haran. *Geneva Lee Browne*: Dee Dee Bridgewater. *Biff Baker*: John Doolittle.

The Orchestra: *Zoot Doubleman*: Stanley Lebowsky. *Neeley "Flap" Kovacs*: Mauriuice Mark. *Bonnie Cavanaugh*: Jane Ira Bloom. *Custis Jones*: Billy Butler. *Gus Bracken*: Ray Shenfeld. *Scoops Millikan*: Dennis Elliott. *Moe "Lockjaw" Ambrose*: Josh Edwards. *Biff Baker*: John Doolittle. *Fritz Canigliaro*: Joe Petrizzo. *Charlie "Kid Lips" Snyder*: Dennis Anderson. *Ned "Woof" Bennett*: J. D. Parran. *Totts Schoenfeld*: Mel Rodnon. *Fess "Snookie" Davenport*: Rick Centalonza. *Bob "Bobo" Lewis*: Jon Goldman. *Buzz Cranshaw*: Ron Tooley. *Phil Bentley*: Bruce Samuels. *Pieface Minelli*: Lloyd Michels.

The action takes place in the WOV Broadcast Studios, Algonquin Room on the ground floor of the Hotel Astor in New York City on 21 December 1942 about 8P.M.

MUSICAL NUMBERS[6]

---

[6]Song titles do not appear in the program. Above list prepared from production manuscript.

"Chattanooga Choo-Choo" (from *SUN VALLEY SERENADE* film)
J. Sommer, M. C. Haran, D. D. Bridgewater, J. Grifasi, S. James, K. Andrini, C. Wilzak, J. Hallett
(*Music by* Harry Warren. *Lyrics by* Mack Gordon.)

Pepsi Cola Radio Jingle
J. Grifasi, S. James, K. Andrini, C. Wilzak, J. Sommer

"Daddy"
The Band, K. Andrini
(*Music and Lyrics by* Bobby Troupe.)

"Our Love Is Here to Stay" (from *THE GOLDWYN FOLLIES*, film)
J. Keller
(*Music by* George Gershwin. *Lyrics by* Ira Gershwin.)

"That Old Black Magic" (from *STAR SPANGLED RHYTHM* film)
M. C. Haran
(*Music by* Harold Arlen. *Lyrics by* Johnny Mercer.)

"Ain't She Sweet"
J. Doolittle, S. James, C. Wilzak, D. D. Bridgewater, All
(*Music by* Milton Ager. *Lyrics by* Jack Yellen.)

"How About You" (from *BABES ON BROADWAY* film)
S. James, K. Andrini
(*Music by* Burton Lane. *Lyrics by* Ralph Freed.)

"Blue Moon"
J. Grifasi
(*Music by* Richard Rodgers. *Lyrics by* Lorenz Hart.)

"Chiquita Banana"
All Girls
(*Music and Lyrics by* Len Mackenzie, Garth Montgomery and William Wirges.)

"Rose of the Rio Grande"
D. D. Bridgewater, Men, Band
(*Music by* Harry Warren and Ross Gorman. *Lyrics by* Edgar Leslie.)

"I'll Never Smile Again" (from *LAS VEGAS NIGHT* film)
J. Grifasi, S. James, M. C. Haran, C. Wilzak, K. Andrini, J. Keller
(*Music and Lyrics by* Ruth Lowe.)

"Boogie Woogie Bugle Boy"
S. James, K. Andrini, C. Wilzak
(*Music and Lyrics by* Don Raye and Hughie Prince.)

"Blues in the Night" (from *BLUES IN THE NIGHT*, film)
C. Wilzak, Men
(*Music by* Harold Arlen. *Lyrics by* Johnny Mercer.)

"Jingle Bells"
J. Doolittle, J. Grifasi, Group
(Bill Finigan, Glenn Miller, Eddie Saracas arrangement)

"I Got It Bad and That Ain't Good" (from *JUMP FOR JOY*)
D. D. Bridgewater
(*Music by* Duke Ellington. *Lyrics by* Paul Francis Webster.)

"At Last" (from *ORCHESTRA WIVES* film)
S. James
(*Music by* Harry Warren. *Lyrics by* Mack Gordon.)

"Little Brown Jug"
(Bill Finigan arrangement for Glenn Miller)

"Have Yourself a Merry Little Christmas" (from *MEET ME IN ST. LOUIS*, film)
M. C. Haran
(*Music and Lyrics by* Hugh Martin and Ralph Blane.)

"Strike Up the Band" (from *STRIKE UP THE BAND*)
Full Company
(*Music by* George Gershwin. *Lyrics by* Ira Gershwin.)

"I'll Be Seeing You" (from *RIGHT THIS WAY*)
Full Company
(*Music by* Sammy Fain. *Lyrics by* Irving Kahal.)

The Mutual Manhattan Variety Cavalcade ThemeBand
(*Music by* Stanley Lebowsky.)

1979.25 SUGAR BABIES

A Burlesque Musical (Revue) in Two Acts, 24 Scenes. Conceived by Ralph G. Allen and Harry Rigby. Sketches by Ralph G. Allen based on traditional material. Music by Jimmy McHugh. Lyrics by Dorothy Fields, Al Dubin. Additional music and lyrics by Arthur Malvin. Staged and choreographed by Ernest Flatt. Sketches directed by Rudy Tronto. Entire production supervised by Ernest Flatt. Scenery and costumes designed by Raoul Pene du Bois. Lighting designed by Gilbert V. Hemsley, Jr. Vocal arrangements by Arthur Malvin. Additional vocal arrangements by Hugh Martin, Ralph Blane. Musical director, Glen Roven. Orchestrations by Dick Hyman. Dance music arranged by Arnold Gross. Associate producers, Jack Schlissel, Thomas Walton Associates, Frank Montalvo. Produced by Terry Allen Kramer and Harry Rigby in association with Columbia Pictures. 8 October 1979 at the Mark Hellinger Theatre and closed 28 August 1982 after 1208 performances.

CAST (in order of appearance): *Mickey*: MICKEY ROONEY. *Scot*: Scot Stewart. *Jillian*: ANN JILLIAN. *Tom*: Tom Boyd. *Peter*: Peter Leeds. *Jack*: Jack Fletcher. *Jimmy*: Jimmy Mathews. *Ann*: ANN MILLER. *Sid*: SID STONE. And Bob Williams.
The Sugar Babies: Laura Booth, Christine Busini, Diane Duncan, Chris Elia, Debbie Gornay, Barbara Hanks, Jeri Kansas, Barbara Mandra, Robin Manus, Faye Fujisaki Mar, Linda Ravinsky, Michele Rogers, Rose Scudder, Patti Winston. *The Gaiety Quartet*: Jonathan Aronson, Eddie Pruett, Michael Radigan, Jeff Veazey. Hank Brunjes (alt.)

ACT 1

Scene 1
A Memory of Burlesque: "A Good Old Burlesque Show"
M. Rooney, His Friends
(*Music by* Jimmy McHugh. *Lyrics by* Arthur Malvin.)

Scene 2
Welcome to the Gaiety: "Let Me Be Your Sugar Baby"
(*Music and Lyrics by* Arthur Malvin.)
P. Leeds, J. Fletcher, Sugar Babies

Scene 3
Meet Me 'Round the Corner[7]
J. Mathews, S, Stewart, P. Leeds, M. Rooney, R. Scudder, C. Elia, M. Rogers, A. Jillian
One of the most famous of all burlesque scenes, originally based on the Homestead Quartet, a minstrel show afterpiece.

Scene 4
Travelin': "In Louisiana"
A. Miller, Sugar Babies, Gaiety Quartet
(*Music by* Jimmy McHugh. *Lyrics by* Arthur Malvin.)
"I Feel a Song Comin' On" (from *EVERY NIGHT AT EIGHT* film)
(*Music by* Jimmy McHugh. *Lyrics by* Dorothy Fields and George Oppenheimer.)
"Goin' Back to New Orleans"[8]
(*Music and Lyrics by* Arthur Malvin.)

Scene 5
The Broken Arms Hotel
J. Fletcher, T. Boyd, M. Rooney, J. Mathews, R. Scudder

Scene 6
Feathered Fantasy (Salute to Sally Rand): "Sally"
S. Stewart, B. Hanks, Sugar Babies
(*Music by* Jimmy McHugh. *Lyrics by* Arthur Malvin.)

Scene 7
The Pitchman
S. Stone

Scene 8
Ellis Island Lament: "Immigration Rose"
M. Rooney, Gaiety Quartet
(*Music by* Jimmy McHugh. *Lyrics by* Eugene West and Irwin Dash.)
Nearly all Columbia Wheel Burlesque Shows had quartets to support the principal comedian in his specialty turn. Among the more prominent examples are the Church City Boys in Louis Robey's 'Knickerbockers' and The Four Harmonists in 'The Girls from Happyland.'

Scene 9
Scenes from Domestic Life
A. Jillian, J. Mathews, J. Fletcher, P. Leeds, T. Boyd, S. Stewart, R. Manus, L. Booth, D. Gornay

Scene 10
Torch Song (after Bobby Clark)[9]: "Don't Blame Me" (from *CLOWNS IN THE CLOVER*, Chicago)
A. Miller, E. Pruett
(*Music by* Jimmy McHugh. *Lyrics by* Dorothy Fields.)

Scene 11
Orientale: Christine Busini introduced by Jack (Fletcher)

---

[7]During the run replaced by:
"I Want a Girl (Just Like the Girl That Married Dear Old Dad)" (Act 1, Scene 3)
J. Mathews, S, Stewart, P. Leeds, M. Rooney, R. Scudder, C. Elia, M. Rogers, A. Jillian
(*Music by* Harry von Tilzer. *Lyrics by* William Dillon.)

[8]Lyrics revised for subsequent National Tour as "Goin' Back to Cucamonga."

[9]Later billed as A Very Moving Love Song (Salute to Ed Wynn).

Little Egypt, the sensation of the Columbian Exposition of 1893 and many imitators on the variety stages as did La Sylphe, a "Salome" dancer who caused a big stir in burlesque in 1908.

Scene 12

The Little Red Schoolhouse

A. Miller, R. Scudder, D. Duncan, J. Mathews, M. Rooney

Scene 13

The New Candy-Coated Craze: "The Sugar Baby Bounce"

A. Jillian, C. Elia, L. Ravinsky

(*Music and Lyrics by* Jay Livingston and Ray Evans.)

There were many sister acts in burlesque. The Watson Sisters owned their own company in the 1890's. The O'Connor Sisters were first featured in Dave Marion's Own show on the Columbia Wheel in 1923. Not many of the sister acts were comprised of real sisters.

Scene 14

Special Added Attraction: Madame Rentz and her All Female Minstrels featuring the Countess Francine. *Introduction*: J. Fletcher.

"Down at the Gaiety Burlesque"/"Mr. Banjo Man"

A. Miller, M. Rooney, J. Veazey, Sugar Babies

(*Music and Lyrics by* Arthur Malvin.)

One of the earliest of all Burlesque Shows was the Rentz Troupe owned by M. B. Leavitt. Minstrel finales remained popular until 1925. Black light was used on the Variety stage as early as 1904, and there were no fewer than five black light numbers in The Radium Girls of 1919.

ACT 2

Scene 1

Candy Butcher

S. Stone, Gaiety Quartet

Scene 2

Girls and Garters:

"I'm Keeping Myself Available for You"

(*Music by* Jimmy McHugh. *Lyrics by* Arthur Malvin.)

"Exactly Like You"

A. Jillian, Sugar Babies

(*Music by* Jimmy McHugh. *Lyrics by* Dorothy Fields.)

The first girl to throw garters at a Burlesque audience appears to have been Millie de Leon, "The Girls in Blue." Her act was a hot number on the circuits during the first decade of this century. As a result of her generosity, she spent several nights in jail.

Scene 3

Justice Will Out[10]

T. Boyd, P. Leeds, M. Rooney, A. Miller

Scene 4

In a Greek Garden (Salute to Rosita Royce):

"Warm and Willing"

A. Jillian

(*Music by* Jimmy McHugh. *Lyrics by* Jay Livingston and Ray Evans.)

Scene 5

Presenting Madame Alla Gazaza

P. Leeds, S. Stone, A. Miller, J. Veazey, M. Rooney, J. Mathews, J. Fletcher, E. Pruett, A. Jillian, J. Aronson, C. Elia

Scene 6

Tropical Madness: "Cuban Love Song"

S. Stewart, M. Rogers

(*Music by* Jimmy McHugh and Herbert Stothart. *Lyrics by* Dorothy Fields.)

Scene 7

Cautionary Tales

R. Scudder, J. Mathews, E. Pruett, M. Radigan, J. Kansas, J. Fletcher, P. Leeds, T. Boyd, S. Stone

Scene 8

Jimmy McHugh Medley[11]:

M. Rooney, A. Miller

"Every Day Another Tune"

(*Music and Lyrics by* Arthur Malvin.)

"I Can't Give You Anything But Love, Baby"

(*Lyrics by* Dorothy Fields.)

"I'm Shooting High"

(*Lyrics by* Ted Koehler.)

"When You and I Were Young, Maggie Blues"

(*Lyrics by* Jack Frost.)

"On the Sunny Side of the Street"

(*Lyrics by* Dorothy Fields.)

Scene 9

Presenting Bob Williams (Dog Act)[12]

Scene 10

Old Glory: "You Can't Blame Your Uncle Sammy"

Full Company

(*Music by* Jimmy McHugh. *Lyrics by* Al Dubin and Irwin Dash.)

This finale commemorates a famous act, Madame Hilda Case and the Red Raven Cadets, who were headliners on the Empire Circuit in 1905.

1979.26 THE MOST HAPPY FELLA

A Revival of the Musical in Two Acts, 10 Scenes[13]. Book, music and lyrics by Frank Loesser. Based on the play "They Knew What They Wanted" by Sidney Howard. Stage Directed by Jack O'Brien. Choreography by Graciela Daniele. Scenery by Douglas W. Schmidt. Costumes by Nancy Potts. Lighting by Gilbert V. Hemsley, Jr. Orchestrations by Don Walker. Musical direction, Andrew Meltzer. Conductor, Eric Stern. Produced by Sherwin M. Goldman in association with Michigan Opera Theatre (David DiChiera, General director) and Emhan Inc. Opened 11 October 1979 at the Majestic Theatre and closed 25 November 1979 after 53 performances.

CAST (in order of appearance): *The Cashier*: Bill Hastings. *Cleo*: LOUISA FLANINGAM. *Rosabella*: SHARON DANIELS, Linda Michele (matinees). *Waitresses*: Karen Giombetti, Tina Paul, D'Arcy Phifer, Smith Wordes. *Busboy*: Tim Flavin. *The Postman*: Dan O'Sullivan. *Tony*: GIORGIO TOZZI, Frederick Burchinal (matinees). *Marie*: ADRIENNE LEONETTI. *Max*: Steven Alex-Cole. *Herman*: DENNIS WARNING. *Clem*: Dean Badolato. *Jake*: David Miles. *Al*: Kevin Wilson. *Sheriff*: Stephen Dubov. *Joe*: RICHARD MUENZ. *Giuseppe*: Gene Varrone. *Pasquale*: Darren Nimnicht. *Ciccio*: Franco Spoto. *The Doctor*: Joe McGrath. *The Priest*: Lawrence Asher. *Neighbor Ladies*: Melanie Helton, Dee Etta Rowe, Jane Warsaw, Sally Williams. *Brakeman*: Bill Hastings. *Bus Driver*: Michael Capes.

All the Neighbors, and All the Neighbors' Neighbors: Steven Alex-Cole, Lawrence Asher, Dean Badolato, Michael Capes, Richard Croft, Stephen Dubov, Tim Flavin, Karen Giombetti, Bill Hastings, D. Michael Heath, Melanie Helton, David Miles, Tina Paul, D'Arcy Phifer, Patrice Pickering, Candace Rogers, Dee Etta Rowe, Bonnie Simmons, Jane Warsaw, Richard White, Carla Wilkins, Sally Williams, Kevin Wilson, Smith Wordes.

1979.27 STREET SCENE

A Revival of the American Opera (Dramatic Musical) in Two Acts, 3 Scenes[14]. Book by Elmer Rice from his play of the same name. Music by Kurt Weill. Lyrics by Langston Hughes. Directed by Jack O'Brien. Stage Director, Stephen Willems. Conducted by John Mauceri. Scenery designed by Paul Sylbert. Costumes designed by Nancy Potts. Lighting by Gilbert V. Hemsley, Jr. Choreography by Patricia Birch. Chorus master, Lloyd Walser. (Orchestrations by Kurt Weill.) Produced by the New York City Opera. Opened 13 October 1979 at the New York State Theatre and closed 10 November 1979 after 5 performances in repertory.

---

[10]Revised under the titles The Court of Last Resort and The Court of Last Retort.

[11]Added for National Tour with Carol Channing and Robert Morse:

Early Sophie (A Tribute to the Great Sophie Tucker)

C. Channing

"I'm the Last of the Red Hot Mamas"

(*Music by* Milton Ager. *Lyrics by* Jack Yellen.)

"Papa, Don't Go Out Tonight"

(*Music by* Milton Ager. *Lyrics by* Jack Yellen.)

"Some of These Days"

(*Music and Lyrics by* Shelton Brooks.)

[12]During run replaced by:

Bon Appetit

Chaz Chase, C. Elia

and subsequently by Michael Davis (Juggling Specialty).

[13]Originally produced in New York 3 May 1956 at the Imperial Theatre for 678 performances. For Synopsis of Scenes and Musical Numbers, see original 1956 production. Originally presented in Three Acts, 11 Scenes.

[14]Originally produced in New York 9 January 1947 at the Adelphi Theatre for 148 performances. For Synopsis of Scenes and Musical Numbers, see original 1947 production.

CAST (in order of appearance): *Greta Fiorentino*: Martha Thigpen. *Emma Jones*: DIANE CURRY. *Olga Olsen*: Rosemarie Freni. *Carl Olsen*: Ralph Bassett. *Neighborhood Woman*: Marie Young. *Shirley Kaplan*: Carol Rosenfeld. *Abraham Kaplan*: Leo Postrel. *Salvation Army Girls*: Kay Schoenfeld, Cindy Lynn Aaronson. *Henry Davis*: Arthur Woodley. *Willie Maurrant*: Timothy Eaton. *Anna Maurrant*: EILEEN SCHAULER. *Sam Kaplan*: ALAN KAYS. *Daniel Buchanan*: Norman Large. *Mrs. Buchanan*: Lila Herbert. *Frank Maurrant*: WILLIAM CHAPMAN. *George Jones*: Robert Paul. *Steve Sankey*: William Ledbetter. *Lippo Fiorentino*: JONATHAN GREEN. *Mrs. Hildebrand*: Sally Lambert. *Jenny Hildebrand*: Kathleen Hegierski. *Graduates*: Denise Adoff, Vanessa Williams. *Charlie Hildebrand*: Matthew McGrath. *Mary Hildebrand*: Dela Bartolini. *Grace Davis*: Kimara Lovelace. *Rose Maurrant*: CATHERINE MALFITANO. *Harry Easter*: HARLAN FOSS. *Mae Jones*: Bronwyn Thomas. *Dick McGann*: Reed Jones. *Vincent Jones*: Bill Herndon. *Dr. Wilson*: Don Carlo. *Officer Murphy*: Edward Zimmerman. *Milkman*: Robert Brubaker. *Joan*: Ann Cawlo. *Myrtle*: Alizon Hull. *Workman*: Harris Davis. *Eddie*: John Henry Thomas. *Sally*: Suzy Block. *Joe*: Raymond Whitney. *Strawberry Seller*: Richard Nelson. *Corn Seller*: Susan Delery-Whedon. *James Henry*: Don Yule. *Fred Cullen*: Irwin Densen. *Old Clothes Man*: Merle Schmidt. *Men*: Frank Tippie, Barry Carl, Herbert Hunsberger. *Grocery Boy*: Marc Mattaliano. *Ambulance Driver*: Louis Perry. *Music Student*: Susan Eagan. *Intern*: James Sergi. *Furniture Mover*: Frank Tippie. *Nursemaids*: Marie Young, Rita Metzger. *Policemen*: Richard Nelson, Don Henderson. *Middle-Aged Couple*: Harriet Greene, Merle Schmidt. *Off Stage Voices*: Vanessa Williams, Anne Cawlo, Lila Herbert.

1979.28

SNOW WHITE AND THE SEVEN DWARFS

A Musical in One Act. Written for the stage by Joe Cook from the Walt Disney film. (Screenplay by Ted Sears, Otto Englander, Earl Hurd, Dorothy Ann Blank, Richard Creedon, Dick Rickard, Merrill De Maris, Webb Smith.) Music by Frank Churchill. Lyrics by Larry Morey. New music for the stage production by Jay Blackton. New lyrics for the stage production by Joe Cook. Directed and choreographed by Frank Wagner. Executive musical director, Don Pippin. Conductor, Don Smith. Orchestrations by Philip J. Lang. Scenic design by John William Keck. Costume design by Frank Spencer. Mask design and animal costumes by Joe Stephen. Lighting director, Ken Billington. Choral arrangements by Jay Blackton and Don Pippin. Produced by Radio City Music Hall (Robert F. Jani, Producer; John J. Moore, Production executive). Opened 18 October 1979 at the Radio City Music Hall, closing 18 November 1979 after 33 performances; resumed after tour 11 January 1980 and closed 9 March 1980 after 70 additional performances. Total: 103 performances.

CAST (in order of appearance): *Chamberlain*: DAVID PURSLEY. *King*: THOMAS RUISINGER. *Queen*: ANNE FRANCINE. *Snow White*: MARY JO SALERNO. *Miror/Witch*: Charles Hall. *Luna*: YOLANDE BAVAN. *Greta*: Heidi Coe. *Prince Charming*: RICHARD BOWNE. *Mother*: Lauren Lipson. *Huntsman*: BRUCE SHERMAN. *(The Seven Dwarfs)*: *Doc*: DON POTTER. *Happy*: RICHARD DAY. *Grumpy*: BENNY FREIGH. *Sneezy*: LOUIS CARRY. *Bashful*: JAY EDWARD ALLEN. *Sleepy*: JERRY RILEY. *Dopey*: MICHAEL E. KING.

Singers: Ronald Brown, Kenneth Cantor, Peter Constanza, David Dusing, Clifford Fearl, G. Jan Jones, Patricia Landi, Lauren Lipson, Linda Motashami, Dawn Parrish, Caryl Tenney. *Swings*: Tony Gilbert, Marsha Miller. *Dancers*: Conni Brazelton, Beth Buker, Mary-Pat Carey, John Cashman, Danny Clark, Heidi Coe, Joan Cooper, Joy Coronel, Christopher Daniels, Ron Dunham, Alfred Gonzales, Martha Goodman, Jennifer Hammond, Norb Joerder, Janet Marie Jones, David Lee, Kim Leslie, Malcolm Perry, Michael Ragan, Patricia Register, Roger Rouillier, Jerry Sarnat, Hope Sogawa, Reisa Sperling, Thomas J. Stanton, Cassie Stein, Lynn Williford, Kim Woollen. *Swing*: James Paoletti, Jane Wilson.

The action takes place once upon a time in a faraway land.

MUSICAL NUMBERS[15]

"Welcome to the Kingdom"
Company
(*Music by* Jay Blackton. *Lyrics by* Joe Cook.)

"Queen's Presentation"
Company
(*Music by* Jay Blackton. *Lyrics by* Joe Cook. *Music arranged by* Ronald Melrose.)

"I'm Wishing"
M. J. Salerno, H. Coe, Villagers

"One Song"
R. Bowne

"With a Smile and a Song"
M. J. Salerno, Animals

"Whistle While You Work"
M. J. Salerno, Animals

"Heigh-Ho"
The Seven Dwarfs

"Buddle-Uddle-Um-Dum" (The Washing Song)
The Seven Dwarfs

"Will I Ever See Her Again?"
R. Bowne
(*Music by* Jay Blackton. *Lyrics by* Joe Cook.)

"Dwarf's Yodel Song" (The Silly Song)
M. J. Salerno, The Seven Dwarfs, Animals

"Someday My Prince Will Come"
M. J. Salerno

"Heigh-Ho" (reprise)
The Seven Dwarfs

"Here's the Happy Ending" (Finale)
Company
(*Music by* Jay Blackton. *Lyrics by* Joe Cook.)

[15]For the National Tour an intermission was added after "Will I Ever See Her Again?" For the Tour and return engagement, the ensemble was redivided between the King's Court, Queen's Court and Animals.

1979.29

STRIDER

A Play With Music in Two Acts[16]. Play by Mark Rozovsky. Adapted from a story ("Kholstomer: The Story of a Horse") by Leo Tolstoy. English stage version by Robert Kalfin. Based on a translation by Tamara Bering Sunguroff. Directed and staged by Robert Kalfin and Lynne Gannaway. Music originally composed by Mark Rozovsky, S. Vetkin. Oroginal Russian lyrics by Uri Riashentsev. Adapter, composer of new additional music, vocal and instrumental arrangements, and Musical director, Norman L. Berman. New English lyrics by Steve Brown. Production design (scenery) by Wolfgang Roth. Costume designs by Andrew B. Marlay. Lighting design by Robby Monk. Sound design by Gary Harris. A Chelsea Theatre Center Production. Produced by Arthur Whitelaw and Miriam Bienstock in association with Lita Starr. Opened 14 November 1979 at the Helen Hayes Theatre and closed 18 May 1980 after 214 performances. Total, including Off-Broadway run, 403 performances.

CAST (in order of speaking): *Vaska/Mr. Willingstone*: ROGER DeKOVEN. *PrinceSerpuhofsky*: GORDON GOULD. *General/Announcer*: RONNIE NEWMAN. *Viazapurikha/Mathieu/Marie*: PAMELA BURRELL. *Strider*: GERALD HIKEN. *Actors*: Katherine Mary-Brown, Jeannine Khoutieff, Vicki Van Grack. *Groom*: SKIP LAWING. *Gypsy*: Nina Dova. *Count Bobrinsky/Darling/The Lieutenant*: BENJAMIN HENDRICKSON. *Feofan/Fritz*: IGORS GAVON. *Bet Taker*: Vincent A. Feraudo. *Vendor*: Charles Walker. *Actors*: John Brownlee, Nancy Kawalek, Tad Ingram. *Gypsies*: Karen Trott, Steven Blane. (Note: *The Herd*: Chorus.)

Pre-show songs performed by Nina Dova, with Karen Trott, Steven Blane, Paul Kreshka, Bill Tynes.

ACT 1[17]

"Oh Jesus—It's Time to Take Out the Nags"
R. DeKoven

(Only Mortal)
Chorus

"Song of the Herd"
Chorus

"Conversation of Strider and the Herd"
G. Hiken, Chorus

Duet (Warm and Tender)
P. Burrell, G. Hiken

"Darling's Romance"
B. Hendrickson

(Oh, Cruel and Hard of Heart Is Man)
Chorus

"Serpuhovsky's Song"
G. Gould

(Finale Act I: Along the Blacksmith's Alley)
G. Hiken, I. Gavon, G. Gould, Company

ACT 2

"Oh, Jesus—It's Time to Take Out the Nags" (reprise)
R. DeKoven

"Serpuhovsky's Romance"
G. Gould, Chorus

[16]Originally produced in New York Off-Broadway 31 May 1979 at the Chelsea Theatre Center for 187 performances under the title *STRIDER: THE STORY OF A HORSE*.

[17]No song titles appeared in the program. Above list prepared from published text.

(Oh, Hard Is Life for Man and Horse) reprise
N. Dova
"Live Long Enough"[18]
G. Hiken, Chorus
(Strider's Death)
Entire Company

1979.30 BETTE!: DIVINE MADNESS

A Musical Revue in Two Acts. Special material written by Bette Midler, Jerry Blatt, Bruce Vilanch. Staged by Bette Midler and Jerry Blatt. Choreographed by Maria Blakey. Additional choreography by Toni Basil. Musical direction by Tony Berg, Randy Kerber. Lighting designer, Chipmonck. Sound engineer, Bill Darlington. Produced by Ron Delsener. Opened 5 December 1979 at the Majestic Theatre and closed 6 January 1980 after 40 performances.

CAST: BETTE MIDLER, THE STAGGERING HARLETTES (Franny Eisenberg, Linda Hart, Paulette McWilliams), SHABBA-DOO (Adolfo Quinones).

MUSICAL NUMBERS[19]

"Big Noise from Winnetka"
(*Music and Lyrics by* Gil Rodin, Bob Crosby, Bob Haggart, Ray Bauduc.)
"Paradise"
(*Music and Lyrics by* Harry Nilsson, Gil Garfield, Perry Botkin, Jr.)
"Shiver Me Timbers"
(*Music and Lyrics by* Tom Waits)
"The Rose" (from *THE ROSE* film)
(*Music and Lyrics by* Amanda McBroom.)
"Fire Down Below"
(*Music and Lyrics by* Bob Seeger.)
"Stay With Me"
(*Music and Lyrics by* Jerry Ragovoy and George Weiss.)
"Dolores Delago the Toast of Chicago"
"My Mother's Eyes"
(*Music and Lyrics by* Tom Jans.)
"Chapel of Love"
(*Music and Lyrics by* Jeff Barry, Ellie Greenwich, Phil Spector.)
"Boogie Woogie Bugle Boy"
(*Music and Lyrics by* Don Raye and Hughie Prince.)
"E Street Shuffle"
(*Music and Lyrics by* Bruce Springsteen.)
"Summer" (The First Time)
(*Music and Lyrics by* Bobby Goldsboro.)
"Leader of the Pack"
(*Music and Lyrics by* George Morton, Jeff Barry, Ellie Greenwich.)
Those Wonderful Sophie Tucker Jokes
Hang onto My Rainbow Sleeve
Hobo Pantomime
"I'm Ready to Begin Again"
(*Music and Lyrics by* Jerry Leiber and Mike Stoller.)
"Do You Wanna Dance?"
(*Music and Lyrics by* Bobby Freeman.)
"You Can't Always Get What You Want
(*Music and Lyrics by* Mick Jagger and Keith Richards.)
"I Shall Be Released"
(*Music and Lyrics by* Bob Dylan.)

1979.31 OKLAHOMA!

A Revival of the Musical Play in Two Acts, 6 Scenes[20]. Book and lyrics by Oscar Hammerstein II. Music by Richard Rodgers. Based on the play "Green Grow the Lilacs" by Lynn Riggs. Directed by William Hammerstein. Choreography by Agnes de Mille, restaged by Gemze de Lappe. Music director, Jay Blackton. Assistant conductor, Robert Stanley. Scenery by Michael J. Hotopp, Paul dePass. Costumes by Bill Hargate. Lighting by Thomas Skelton. Tap sequences by Miriam Nelson. Rope sequences by Montie Montana. Produced by Zev Bufman and James M. Nederlander in association with Donald C. Carter. Opened 13 December 1979 at the Palace Theatre and closed 31 August 1980 after 301 performances.

CAST (in order of appearance): *Aunt Eller*: MARY WICKES. *Curly*: LAURENCE GUITTARD. *Laurey*: CHRISTINE ANDREAS. *Ike Skidmore*: Robert Ray. *Slim*: Stephen Crain. *Will Parker*: HARRY GROENER. *Jud Fry*: MARTIN VIDNOVIC. *Ado Annie Carnes*: CHRISTINE EBERSOLE. *Ali Hakim*: BRUCE ADLER. *Gertie Cummings*: Martha Traverse. *Curley* (in ballet): DAVID EVANS. *Laurey* (in ballet): LOUISE HICKEY. *Jud* (in ballet): Anthony Santiago. *The Child* (in ballet): Judy Epstein. *Jud's Postcards*: Patti Ross, Ilene Strickler, Susan Whelan. *Andrew Carnes*: Philip Rash. *Cord Elam*: Nick Jolley.

Singers: Sydney Anderson, Stephen Crain, Lorraine Foreman, Nick Holley, John Kildahl, Jessica Molaskey, Joel T. Myers, Philip Rash, Robert Ray, Martha Traverse, M. Lynne Wieneke. *Dancers*: Eric Aaron, Brian Bullard, Phillip Candler, Judy Epstein, David Evans, Tonda Hannum, Louise Hickey, Kristina Koebel, Leslie Morris, Michael Page, Patti Ross, Kevin Ryan, Anthony Santiago, Ilene Strickler, Robert Sullivan, Susan Whelan. *Swings*: Gina Martin, Jerry Ziaja.

1979.32 COMIN' UPTOWN

A Musical in Two Acts, 13 Scenes. Book by Philip Rose and Peter Udell. Based on "A Christmas Carol" by Charles Dickens. Music by Garry Sherman. Lyrics by Peter Udell. Directed by Philip Rose. Choreographed by Michael Peters. Scenery designed by Robin Wagner. Costumes designed by Ann Emonts. Lighting designed by Gilbert V. Hemsley, Jr. Sound Designed by Jack Shearing. Musical director, Howard Roberts. Orchestrations and vocal arrangements by Garry Sherman. Dance music arrangements by Timothy Graphenreed. Associate choreographer, Frances Lee Morgan. Associate producers, Leslie K. Bullock, Anthony Weymouth, Kimako. Produced by W. Ridgely Bullock, Albert W. Selden in association with Columbia Pictures. Opened 20 December 1979 at the Winter Garden and closed 27 January 1980 after 45 performances.

CAST (in order of appearance): *Salvation Army Trio*: DEBORAH LYNN BRIDGES, DEBORAH BURRELL, JENIFER LEWIS. *Shoppers*: Harlem Residents. *Scrooge*: GREGORY HINES. *Bob Crachit*: John Russell. *Tenant's Representative*: LARRY MARSHALL. *Mary* (Recreation Center Director): Saundra McClain. *Minister*: Robert Jackson. *Marley*: TIGER HAYNES. *Christmas Past*: LARRY MARSHALL. *Trio*: DEBORAH LYNN BRIDGES, DEBORAH BURRELL, JENIFER LEWIS. *Time*: Frances Lee Morgan. *Mary* (Younger): Loretta Devine. *Young Scrooge*: Duane Davis. *His Assistant*: Vernal Polson. *Reverend Byrd*: Ned Wright. *Gospel Singer*: Esther Marrow. *Deacon*: John Russell. *Mrs. Crachit, Deacon's Wife*: Virginia McKinzie. *Christmas Present*: SAUNDRA McCLAIN. *Crachit Daughters*: Shirley Black-Brown, Allison R. Manson. *Martha Crachit*: Carol Lynn Maillard. *Tiny Tim*: Kevin Babb. *Christmas Future*: ROBERT JACKSON.

Harlem Residents: Kevin Babb, Shirley Black-Brown, Roslyn Burrough, Barbara Christopher, Duane Davis, Ronald Dunham, Milton Grayson, Linda James, Kevin Jeff, Carol Lynn Maillard, Allison R. Manson, Esther Marrow, Frances Lee Morgan, Raymond Patterson, Vernal Polson, Gloria Sauve, Eric Sawyer, Kiki Shepard, Faruma Williams, Ned Wright.

Act 1, Scene 1: Harlem—125th Street. *Scene 2*: Scrooge's Office. *Scene 3*: Scrooge's Bedroom. *Scene 4*: A Street in Harlem. *Scene 5*: Harlem Baptist Church. *Scene 6*: Scrooge's Bedroom. *Scene 7*: The Crachit Dining Room. *Scene 8*: Outside the Crachit House.

Act 2, Scene 1: Scrooge's Bedroom. *Scene 2*: A Cemetary. *Scene 3*: Another Cemetary. *Scene 4*: Scrooge's Bedroom. *Scene 5*: The Crachit Dining Room.

ACT 1
Scene 1
"Christmas Is Comin' Uptown"
Christmas Shoppers, D. L. Bridges, D. Burrell, J. Lewis, G. Hines
Scene 2
"Somebody's Gotta Be the Heavy"
G. Hines
Scene 3
"Now I Lay Me Down to Sleep"
G. Hines
"Get Your Act Together"
T. Haynes
"Lifeline"
L. Marshall, D. L. Bridges, D. Burrell, J. Lewis
(*Orchestrated by* Willie Strickland.)
Scene 4
"What Better Time for Love"
G. Hines, L. Devine
Scene 5
"It Won't Be Long"
E. Marrow, Congregation

[18]Added during the run on Broadway.
[19]No list of Musical Numbers appears in the program; above list has been prepared from press materials, recordings and the film of the stage production.
[20]Originally produced in New York 31 March 1943 at the St. James Theatre for 2212 performances. For Synopsis of Scenes and Musical Numbers, see original 1943 production.

Scene 6
"Get Down Brother, Get Down"
S. McClain, D. L. Bridges, D. Burrell, J. Lewis
Scene 7
"Sing a Christmas Song"
J. Russell, V. McKinzie, S. Black-Brown, A. R. Manson, the Carolers
"What Better Time for Love" (reprise)
K. Babb, J. Russell, V. McKinzie, S. Black-Brown, A. R. Manson
Scene 8
"Have I Finally Found My Heart?"
G. Hines
ACT 2
Scene 1
"Nobody Really Do"
R. Jackson, D. L. Bridges, D. Burrell, J. Lewis
"Goin', Gone"
R. Jackson
Scene 2
"Get Down, Brother, Get Down" (reprise)
J. Russell, V. McKinzie, S. Black-Brown, A. R. Manson, Mourners
Scene 3
"One Way Ticket to Hell"
D. L. Bridges, D. Burrell, J. Lewis
"Nobody Really Do" (reprise)
R. Jackson, D. L. Bridges, D. Burrell, J. Lewis
Scene 4
"Born Again"
G. Hines
Scene 5
"Born Again" (reprise)
G. Hines, Company

1979.33 THE BABES IN TOYLAND

An Adaptation of the Musical Comedy in Two Acts, a Prologue and 10 Scenes[21]. Original music by Victor Herbert. (Original book and lyrics by Glenn McDonough.) New book adaptation by Ellis Weiner, based on an original idea by Barry Weissler. New music and lyrics by Shelly Markham and Annette Leisten. Directed by Munson Hicks. Choreographed by Tony Stevens. Scenery and costumes by Michael J. Hotopp and Paul de Pass. Puppets by Sid and Marty Krofft. Lighting by Associated Theatrical Designers. Musical direction, Rock Orchestration by Bob Christiansen. Orchestral arrangements by Kirk Nurock. Dance arrangements by Bob Stecko. Produced by American Entertainment Enterprises (Barry and Fran Weissler). Opened 21 December 1979 at the Felt Forum and closed 1 January 1980 after 16 performances.

CAST (in order of appearance): *Tom*: MARK HOLLERAN. *Sugarbear*: ROGER LAWSON. *Horace*: MICHAEL CALKINS. *'The Puppettes'*: Mona Finstoin, Edward T. Jacobs, Robert Hancock, Lynn Hippen, Steve Mathews, Alan F. Seiffert. *Promoter*: Dan Kruger. *Haystack* (Shaggy Dog): Edward T. Jacobs. *Grandfather*: KEN BONAFONS. *Mary*: DEBBIE McLEOD. *Mother Goose*: S. BARKLEY MURRAY. *Barnaby*: C. A. HUTTON. *Old King Cole*: DAN KRUGER. *Jack Be Nimble*: Alan F. Seiffert. *The Old Woman in the Shoe*: Lynn Hippen. *The Children in the Shoe*: Mona Finston, Steve Matthews. *Drummer Boy*: Alan F. Seiffert. *Humpty Dumpty*: , Ken Bonafons, Alan F. Seiffert. *The Wall*: Robert Hancock. *Little Bo Peep*: SHARI WATSON. *Vendors*: Roger Lawson, Mark Holleran, Michael Calkins. *The Shrouds*: S. Barkley Murray, Alan F. Seiffert. *The Toy Soldiers*: Mona Finsten, Robert Hancock, Lynn Hippen, Dan Kruger, Steve Mathews, S. Barkley Murray, Alan F. Seiffert. *Puppeteers*: Mona Finstoin, Robert Hancock, Lynn Hippen, Steve Mathews, Alan F. Seiffert. *Computer Bob*: ROBERT HANCOCK. (Note: The Babes are Tom, Sugarbear, Horace, Mary and Haystack.)

Act 1, Scene 1: The Interior of Grandfather's Toyshop. *Scene 2*: The Town Square of Toyland. *Scene 3*: The Interior of the Old Toy Shop. *Scene 4*: Dream Toyland. *Scene 5*: The Dark Interior of Barnaby's Hide-Out Workshop and Prison in the Closed Tunnel of Love.

Act 2, Scene 1: Central Exterior of Toyland in front of Tunnel of Love. *Scene 2*: The Interior of Barnaby's House of Horrors. *Scene 3*: The Interior of Barnaby's House of Horrors. *Scene 4*: Barnaby's Robot-operated computer room. *Scene 5*: Transition from Laboratory to a modern Disco Toyland.

ACT 1
Prologue
"Big Baby"
The Babes, The Puppettes
"It's a Sweet Life"
The Babes
Scene 2
"Something Must Be Done"
D. Kruger, K. Bonafons, A. F. Sieffert, R. Hancock, S. B. Murray, L. Hippen, M. Finston, S. Mathews, the Babes
"Don't Cry, Bo Peep"
The Babes
"Bare Facts"
The Babes
Scene 3
"Step Out in Front"
D. McLeod, the Babes
Scene 4
"Dream Toyland"
Ladies of the Grand Ballet, Vendors
ACT 2
Scene 2
"The Two of Us"
M. Holleran, D. McLeod
Scene 4
"The March of the Wooden Soldiers"
Toy Soldiers
Scene 5
FinaleCompany

1980.01 CANTERBURY TALES

A Revival of the Musical in Two Acts, 10 Scenes and a Prologue[22]. Book by Martin Starkie and Nevill Coghill. Based on Nevill Coghill's translation of Geoffrey Chaucer's "Canterbury Tales." Music by Richard Hill and John Hawkins. Lyrics by Nevill Coghill. Directed by Robert Johanson. Choreography by Randy Hugill. Musical direction, vocal arrangements by John Kroner. Setting by Michael Anania. Costumes by Sigrid Insull. Lighting by Gregg Marriner. An Equity Library Theatre Production. Produced by Burry Fredrik and Bruce Schwartz. Opened 12 February 1980 at the Rialto Theatre and closed 24 February 1980 after 16 performances. Total, including Off-Broadway run, 46 performances.

CAST (in order of appearance): *Chaucer* (January): Earl McCarroll. *Knight*: Robert Stoeckle. *Squire* (Nicholas/Damian/Horse): Robert Tetirick. *Yeoman* (John/King Arthur): Andy Ferrell. *Prioress*: Mimi Sherwin. *Nun* (Proserpina); K. K. Preece. *Molly* (Guenevere): Kaylyn Dillehay. *May*: Tricia Witham. *Alison* (Sweetheart): Krista Neumann. *Friar* (Justinus): Andrew Traines. *Merchant* (Gervase): Vance Mizelle. *Clerk* (Robin/Page/Horse): Richard Stillman. *Cook* (Miller's Wife/Duenna): Polly Pen. *Miller*: Win Atkins. *Steward* (Carpenter/Placebo): Ted Houck, Jr. *Wife of Bath* (Old Woman): Maureen Sadusk. *Summoner* (Absalon/Alan): Kelly Walters. *Pardonner* (Executioner): Martin Walsh. *Host* (Pluto): George Maguire.

The action takes place on a four day Pilgrimage to Canterbury Carhedral, England in the late 1300s.

ACT 1
Prologue
E. McCarroll, Company
Scene 1
"Welcome Song"
G. Maguire, Company
"Goodnight Hymn"
Company
"Canterbury Day"
Company

[21]First presented in New York as *BABES IN TOYLAND* 13 October 1903 at the Majestic Theatre for 192 performances.

[22]Originally presented in New York 3 February 1969 at the Eugene O'Neill Theatre for 122 performances; this revival previously presented Off-Broadway by the Equity Library Theatre 29 November 1979 at the Master Theatre for 30 performances. For this production, the Mug Dance, "Hymen, Hymen" and "Love Pas de Deux" were dropped. "Pear Tree Quintet" revised as "Pear Tree Sextet." "What Do Women Want?" renamed "What Do Women Most Desire?" Song order rearranged.

Scene 2
"Horse Ride" (Pilgrim Riding Music)
Company
Scene 3
"I Have a Noble Cock"
R. Tetirick
"There's the Moon"
R. Tetirick, K. Neumann
"Darling, Let Me Teach You How to Kiss"
K. Walters
Scene 4
"It Depends on What You're At"
M. Sadusk, K. K. Preece, Company
Scene 5
"Beer Is Best"
W. Atkins, P. Pen, K. Dillehay, K. Walters, A. Ferrell
Scene 6
"Love Will Conquer All"
M. Sherwin, K. K. Preece, Company
"Canterbury Day" (reprise)
Company

ACT 2
Scene 1
"Come On and Marry Me Honey"
M. Sadusk, Company
"Where Are the Girls of Yesterday"
G. Maguire
Danced by K. Neumann, T. Witham, K. Dillehay.
Scene 2
"April Song"
Company
"If She Has Never Loved Before"
E. McCarroll, T. Witham
"I'll Give My Love a Ring"
R. Tetirick, T. Witham
"Pear Tree Sextet"
E. McCarroll, T. Witham, R. Tetirick, G. Maguire, K. K. Preece, V. Mizelle
Scene 3
"What Do Women Most Desire?"
R. Stoeckle, Ladies
"I Am All Ablaze"
R. Stoeckle
Danced by A. Ferrell, K. Dillehay.
Scene 4
"Love Will Conquer All" (reprise)
M. Sherwin, K. K. Preece, Company

1980.02 WEST SIDE STORY

A Revival of the Musical in Two Acts, 15 Scenes[23]. Book by Arthur Laurents. Based on a conception of Jerome Robbins. Music by Leonard Bernstein. Lyrics by Stephen Sondheim. Entire production directed and choreographed by Jerome Robbins. Book Co-directed by Gerald Freedman. Co-choreographer, Peter Gennaro. Choreography reproduced with the assistance of Tom Abbott, Lee Becker Theodore. Scenery designed by Oliver Smith. Costumes designed by Irene Sharaff. Lighting designed by Jean Rosenthal. Musical director, John DeMain. Orchestrations by Leonard Bernstein, with Sid Ramin, Irwin Kostal. Associate producers, Allan Tessler, Steven Jacobson, Stewart F. Lane. Executive producer, Ruth Mitchell. Produced by Gladys Rackmil, The John F. Kennedy Center and James M. Nederlander in association with Zev Bufman Opened 14 February 1980 at the Minskoff Theatre and closed 30 November 1980 after 341 performances.

CAST (in order of appearance): *THE JETS*: *Riff*, the Leader: JAMES J. MELLON. *Tony*, his friend: KEN MARSHALL. *Action*: Mark Bove. *A-Rab*: Todd Lester. *Baby John*: Brian Kaman. *Snowboy*: Cleve Asbury. *Big Deal*: Reed Jones. *Diesel*: Brent Barrett. *Gee-Tar*: G. Russell Weilandich. *Mouthpiece*: Stephen Bogardus. *Tiger*: Mark Fotopoulos. *Their Girls*: *Graziella*: Georganna Mills. *Velma*: Heather Lea Gerdes. *Minnie*: Frankie Wade. *Clarice*: Charlene Gehm. *Pauline*: Nancy Louise Chismar. *Anybodys*: Missy Whitchurch.

THE SHARKS: *Bernardo*, the Leader: HECTOR JAIME MERCADO. *Maria*, his Sister: JOSSIE DE GUZMAN. *Anita*, his Girl: DEBBIE ALLEN. *Chino*, his Friend: Ray Contreras. *Pepe*: Michael Rivera. *Indio*: Darryl Tribble. *Luis*: Adrian Rosario. *Anxious*: Michael DeLorenzo *Nibbles*: Willie Rosario. *Juano*: Michael Franks. *Toro*: Mark Morales. *Moose*: Gary-Michael Davies. *Their Girls*: *Rosalia*: Yamil Borges. *Consuelo*: Nancy Ticotin. *Francisca*: Harolyn Blackwell. *Teresita*: Stephanie E. Williams. *Estella*: Marlene Danielle. *Marguerita*: Amy Lester.

THE ADULTS: *Doc*: SAMMY SMITH. *Schrank*: Arch Johnson. *Krupke*: John Bentley. *Gladhand*: Jake Turner.

1980.03 DIE FLEDERMAUS

A Revival of the Operetta in Three Acts[24]. Original Viennese libretto by Carl Haffner and Richard Genée. Lyrics by Richard Genée. (Based on the comedy "Le Réveillon" by Henri Meilhac and Ludovic Halévy.) English libretto by Ruth and Thomas Martin. Music by Johann Strauss. Production devised and directed by Gerald Freedman. Choreography by Thomas Andrew, restaged by Jessica Redel. Scenery designed by Lloyd Evans Costumes design by Theoni V. Aldredge. Lighting by Hans Sondheimer. Conducted by Imre Pallo. Chorus master, Lloyd Walser. Produced by the New York City Opera. Opened 23 February 1980 at the New York State Theatre and closed 1 March 1980 after 4 performances in repertory.

CAST (in order of appearance): *Alfred*, an itinerant tenor: Gerald Grahame. *Adele*, von Eisenstein's chambermaid: INGA NIELSEN. *Rosalinda von Eisenstein*: MARALIN NISKA. *Gabriel von Eisenstein*: CHARLES ROE. *Dr. Blind*, a lawyer: Norman Large. *Dr. Falke*, a close friend of Eisenstein: DOMINIC COSSA. *Frank*, the prison warden: RICHARD McKEE. *Sally*, Adele's sister: Puli Toro. *Ivan*, servant to Orlofsky: Gary J. Dietrich. *Prince Orlofsky*, a wealthy, bored Russian: DAVID RAE SMITH. *Frosch*, the jailer: Jack Harrold. *Solo Dancers*: Esperanza Galan, Taras Kalba. *Special Guest*: CYNTHIA GREGORY. (Miss Gregory's solo choreographed by Dennis Nahat.) *Ensemble*: New York City Opera Chorus.

1980.04 SILVERLAKE, or A Winter's Tale

A Play with Music (an Opera) in Two Acts, 11 Scenes[25]. Original German libretto ('Der Silbersee') by Georg Kaiser. Music by Kurt Weill. New book by Hugh Wheeler. New lyrics by Lys Symonette. Selections of Weill's incidental music integrated by Lys Symonette. Directed by Harold Prince. Conducted by Julius Rudel. Choreography by Larry Fuller. Scenery and costumes designed by Manuel Lutgenhorst. Lighting designed by Ken Billington. Musical preparation by Robert De Ceunynck, Scott Bergeson. Chorus master, Lloyd Walser. Sound designed by Jack Mann. Produced by the New York City Opera and Gert von Gontard. Opened 20 March 1980 at the New York State Theatre and closed 4 April 1980 after 6 performances in repertory.

CAST (in order of appearance): *Johann*: Harlan Foss. *Dietrich*: Robert McFarland. *Severin*: WILLIAM NEILL. *Heckler*: Edward Zimmerman. *Klaus*: James Clark. *Hans*: Norman Large. *Hunger*: Gary Chryst. *Salesgirls*: Penny Orloff, Jane Shaulis. *Handke*: David Rae Smith. *Officer Olim*: JOEL GREY. *City Inspector*: William Poplaski. *Lottery Agent*: JACK HARROLD. *Doctor*: Richard L. Porter. *Baron Laur*: JACK HARROLD. *Fennimore*: ELIZABETH HYNES. *Liveried Footman*: Gary J. Dietrich. *Frau von Luber*: ELAINE BONAZZI. *Chefs*: Michael Rubino, Rafael Romero. *Ensemble*: New York City Opera Chorus.

The action takes place in and around the mythical village of Silverlake.

Act 1, Scene 1: A Shantytown near Silverlake. *Scene 2*: The Grocery Store in the City. *Scene 3*: By a Country Bridge. *Scene 4*: The Police Station. *Scene 5*: The Hospital. *Scene 6*: Outside the Castle. *Scene 7*: The Castle Dining Room. *Scene 8*: The Great Hall.

Act 2, Scene 1: The Castle Cellars and Attic. *Scene 2*: Various Locations in the Castle. *Scene 3*: On the Road to Silverlake.

ACT 1
Scene 1
Duet of the Woodcutters
H. Foss, R. McFarland
Scene 2
Duet of the Salesgirls
P. Orloff, J. Shaulis

[23]Originally produced in New York 26 September 1957 at the Winter Garden for 732 performances. For Synopsis of Scenes and Musical Numbers, see original 1957 production.

[24]First English language production in New York 16 March 1885 at the Casino Theatre for 42 performances. First New York production of this adaptation 20 December 1950 at the Metropolitan Opera House. For Synopsis of Scenes and Musical Numbers, see May 1954 revival.

[25]Musical Numbers and Scenes do not appear in the program, but have been prepared from the recording and libretto.

Scene 4
In the Police Station: Unseen Chorus
Chorus
Tango
J. Grey, J. Harrold
Unseen Chorus (reprise)
Chorus
Scene 5
Duet in the Hospital
W. Neill, J. Grey
Scene 7
Fennimore's Song
E. Hynes
The Ballad of Caesar's Death
E. Bonazzi
Severin's Revenge Aria
W. Neill
Severin-Fennimore Duet
W. Neill, J. Grey
Scene 8
Act 1 Finale
Chorus

ACT 2
Scene 1
Severin in Chains
W. Neill
First Laur and von Luber Duet
E. Bonazzi, J. Harrold
Scene 2
Friendship Duet
J. Grey, W. Neill
Second Laur and von Luber Duet
E. Bonazzi, J. Harrold
Scene 3
Act 2 Finale
J. Grey, W. Neill, Chorus

1980.05

REGGAE

A Musical Revelation in Two Acts, 11 Scenes. Concept and production by Michael Butler. Story by Kendrew Lascelles. Book by Melvin Van Peebles, Kendrew Lascelles and Stafford Harrison. Music and lyrics by Ras Karbi, Michael Kamen, Kendrew Lascelles, Stafford Harrison, Max Romeo, Randy Bishop, Jackie Mittoo. Directed by Glenda Dickerson. Additional direction by Gui Andrisano. Choreographer, Mike Malone. Musical director, Mike Malone. Cultural consultant dance, Rex Nettleford. Set design by Ed Burbridge. Costume design by Raoul Pene du Bois. Lighting design by Beverly Emmons. Sound design by Lou Gonzalez. Associate musical director, Michael Tschudin. Executive producer, Woodie King. Produced by Michael Butler and Eric Nazhad with David Cogan. Opened 27 March 1980 at the Biltmore Theatre and closed 13 April 1980 after 21 performances.

CAST (in order of appearance): *Anancy, The Spider*: Alvin McDuffie. *Faith*: SHERYL LEE RALPH. *Esau*: PHILIP MICHAEL THOMAS. *Rockets*: OBBA BABATUNDE. *Mrs. Brown*: Fran Salisbury. *Louise*: Louise Robinson. *Ras Joseph*: CALVIN LOCKHART. *Natty*: RAS KARBI. *Gorson*: Charles Wisnet. *Binghi Maytal*: Sam Harkness.
Ensemble: Loretta Abbott, Breeha Clarke, Ralph Glenmore, Jeffrey Anderson Gunter, Thomas Pinnock, Louise Robinson, Kiki Shepard, Beth Shorter, Paul Cook'Tartt, Bruce Taylor, Ras-jawara Tesfa, Avon Testamark, Constance Thomas, Juanita Grace Tyler, Byron Utley, Lewis Whitlock.

The action takes place in one day in Jamaica.

Act 1, Scene 1: Jamaican Airport. *Scene 2*: A Mountain Village. *Scene 3*: A Deserted Greathouse on the Road to Kingston. *Scene 4*: Mrs. Brown's Yard. *Scene 5*: A Road through a Forest. *Scene 6*: A Kingston Rehearsal Hall.

Act 2, Scene 1: Ras Joseph's Yard. *Scene 2*: A Kingston Market. *Scene 3*: On the Edge of the Ghetto. *Scene 4*: The Ghetto. *Scene 5*: The Benefit Concer.

ACT 1
"Junkanoo"
Masquerade Parade
(*Music by* Michael Kamen.)
Scene 1
"Jamaica Is Waiting"
Ensemble
(*Music and Lyrics by* Ras Karbi, Max Romeo, Michael Kamen.)
Scene 2
"Rise Tafari"
Ensemble
(*Music and Lyrics by* Ras Karbi.)
Scene 3
"Farmer"
P. M. Thomas
(*Music and Lyrics by* Max Romeo.)
"Hey Man"
S. L. Ralph, P. M. Thomas
(*Music and Lyrics by* Ras Karbi and Michael Kamen.)
"Mash Em Up"
O. Babatunde, Rude Boys
(*Music and Lyrics by* Kendrew Lascelles, Ras Karbi, Kackie Mittoo and Michael Kamen.)
Scene 4
"Mrs. Brown"
F. Salisbury, L. Robinson, Ensemble
(*Music and Lyrics by* Stafford Harrison and Max Romeo.)
"Everything That Touches You"
F. Salisbury, Mr. Brown
(*Music and Lyrics by* Michael Kamen.)
Scene 5
"Mash Ethiopia"
O. Babatunde, Rude Boys
(*Music and Lyrics by* Kendrew Lascelles, Stafford Harrison, Ras Karbi, Jackie Mittoo, Michael Kamen.)
"Star of Zion"
R. Karbi
(*Music and Lyrics by* Michael Kamen.)
Scene 6
"Reggae Music Got Soul"
S. Harkness, Ensemble
(*Music and Lyrics by* Jackie Mittoo.)
"Talkin' 'Bout Reggae"
S. Harkness, Ensemble
(*Music and Lyrics by* Kendrew Lascelles, Stafford Harrison, Michael Kamen, Jackie Mittoo.)
"Everything That Touches You" (reprise)
S. L. Ralph

ACT 2
Scene 1
"Rise Up Jah-Jah Children"
The Rastas, C. Lockhart
(*Music and Lyrics by* Ras Karbi.)
"No Sinners in Jah Yard"
C. Lockhart, The Rastas
(*Music and Lyrics by* Max Romeo and Ras Karbi.)
Scene 2
"Banana, Banana, Banana"
Ensemble
(*Music and Lyrics by* Ras Karbi and Michael Kamen.)
"Promised Land"
R. Karbi
(*Music and Lyrics by* Ras Karbi.)
Scene 3
"Rasta Roll Call"
C. Lockhart, The Rastas
(*Music and Lyrics by* Ras Karbi.)
"Ethiopian Pageant"
Orchestra
(*Music by* Michael Kamen.)
"Rastafari"
Ensemble
(*Music and Lyrics by* Michael Kamen.)
"Roots of the Tree"
C. Lockhart, The Rastas
(*Music and Lyrics by* Kendrew Lascelles and Ras Karbi.)
"I and I"
S. L. Ralph, P. M. Thomas
(*Music and Lyrics by* Kandrew Lascelles and Max Romeo.)
Scene 4
"Gotta Take a Chance"
O. Babatunde, the Rude Boys
(*Music and Lyrics by* Max Romeo and Michael Kamen.)

"Star of Zion" (reprise)
R. Karbi, S. L. Ralph
"Chase the Devil"
P. M. Thomas
(*Music and Lyrics by* Max Romeo.)
"Now I See It"
S. L. Ralph
(*Music and Lyrics by* Kendrew Lascelles and Randy Bishop.)
Scene 5
"Now I See It" (Reggae)(reprise)
S. L. Ralph, Ensemble
"Everything That Touches You" (reprise)
S. L. Ralph, P. M. Thomas
"Reggaae Music Got Soul" (reprise)
S. L. Ralph, P. M. Thomas, Ensemble
"Jamaica Is Waiting" (reprise)
S. L. Ralph, P. M. Thomas, Ensemble

1980.06

HAPPY NEW YEAR

A Musical in Two Acts. Book by Burt Shevelove. Based on the play "Holiday" by Philip Barry. Music and lyrics by Cole Porter, edited by Buster Davis. Directed by Burt Shevelove. Choreography by Donald Saddler. Musical direction and vocal arrangements by Buster Davis. Orchestrations by Luther Henderson. Additional orchestrations by Daniel Troob. Dance music arrangements by Charles H. Coleman. Production designed by Michael Eagan. Costumes designed by Pierre Balmain. Costumes supervised by John Falabella. Lighting designed by Ken Billington. Sound designed by Tom Morse. Assistant choreographer, Mercedes Ellington. Associate producer, Dorothy Cherry. Produced by Leonard Soloway, Allan Francis, Hale Matthews in association with Marble Arch Productions. Opened 27 April 1980 at the Morosco Theatre and closed 10 May 1980 after 17 performances.

CAST: *The Narrator*: JOHN McMARTIN. *Edward Seton*: WILLIAM ROERICK. *Edward Seton, Jr.* (Ned): RICHARD BEKINS. *Julia Seton*: KIMBERLY FARR. *Linda Seton*: LESLIE DENNISTON. *Johnny Case*: MICHAEL SCOTT.

The Staff: *Frazer*: Roger Hamilton. *Charles*: Morgan Ensminger. *Anderson*: Morgan Ensminger. *Patrick*: J. Thomas Smith. *George*: Tim Flavin. *Thompson*: Tim Flavin. *Steven*: Richard Christopher. *Victor*: Lara Teeter. *Rose*: Lauren Goler. *Nancy*: Lauren Goler. *Maude*: Mary Sue Finnerty. *Miss Madden*: Mary Sue Finnerty. *Mary*: Mary Sue Finnerty. *Annie*: Bobbie Nord. *Bridget*: Michele Marshall. *Miss Madden*: Mary Sue Finnerty.

Some of the Stork Club Set: *Nancy*: Lauren Goler. *Mary*: Mary Sue Finnerty. *Joan*: Michelle Marshall. *Gloria*: Bobbie Nord. *Thompson*: Tim Flavin. *Dixon*: lara Teeter. *Anderson*: Morgan Ensminger. *Harrison*: Richard Christopher.

The action takes place on the five floors in the Fifth Avenue townhouse of Edward Seton in New York City.

Act 1: December 1933.

Act 2: January 1934.

ACT 1[26]
"At Long Last Love"[27]
K. Farr, L. Denniston, R. Bekins
"Ridin' High"[28]
M. Scott, K. Farr
"Let's Be Buddies"[29]
M. Scott, L. Denniston
"Boy, Oh Boy"[30]
L. Denniston
"Easy to Love"[31]
The Young Men
"You Do Something to Me"[32]
M. Scott
"Red, Hot and Blue"[33]
L. Denniston, M. Scott, J. T. Smith, Stork Club Set
"Once Upon a Time"[34]
R. Bekins, L. Denniston
ACT 2
"Night and Day"[35]
J. McMartin, M. Scott
"Let's Make It a Night"[36]
L. Denniston, T. Flavin, L. Teeter
"Ours"[37]
K. Farr
"After You, Who?"[38]
M. Scott
"I Am Loved"[39]
K. Farr
"When Your Troubles Have Started"[40]
L. Denniston, R. Bekins
("Boy, Oh, Boy" reprise)
L. Denniston
("Once Upon a Time" reprise)
R. Bekins, L. Denniston

1980.07

BARNUM

A Musical in Two Acts. Book by Mark Bramble. Music by Cy Coleman. Lyrics by Michael Stewart. Directed and staged by Joe Layton. Scenery designed by David Mitchell. Costumes designed by Theoni V. Aldrdge. Lighting designed by Craig Miller. Sound design by Otts Munderloh. Orchestrations by Hershy Kay. Vocal arrangements by Cy Coleman, Jeremy Stone. Music director, Peter Howard. Circus training by The Big Apple Circus/The New York School for Circus Arts. Associate producers, Steven A. Greenberg, Michael Scharf. Produced by Judy Gordon, Cy Coleman, Maurice Rosenfield, Lois F. Rosenfield in association with Irvin Feld and Kenneth Feld. Opened 30 April 1980 at the St. James Theatre and closed 16 May 1982 after 854 performances.

CAST: *Phineas Taylor Barnum*: JIM DALE. *Chairy Barnum*: GLENN CLOSE. *Ringmaster*: WILLIAM C. WITTER. *Chester Lyman*: TERRENCE V. MANN. *Joice Heth*: TERRI WHITE. *Amos Scudder*: Kelly Walters. *Lady Plate Balancer*: Catherine Carr. *Lady Juggler*: Barbara Nadel. *Chief Bricklayer*: Edward T. Jacobs. *White-faced Clown*: Andy Teirstein. *Sherwood Stratton*: Dirk Lumbard. *Mrs. Sherwood Stratton*: Sophie Schwab. *Tom Thumb*: LEONARD JOHN CROFOOT. *Susan B. Anthony*: Karen Trott. *Julius Goldschmidt*: WILLIAM C. WITTER. *Jenny Lind*: MARIANNE TATUM. *One-Man Band*: Steven Michael. *Wilton*: Bruce Robertson. *Edgar Templeton*: Kelly Walters. *Humbert Morrissey*: TERRENCE V. MANN. *Lady Aerialist*: Robbi Morgan. *James A. Bailey*: WILLIAM C. WITTER. And Ringmasters, Clowns, Bricklayers, Acrobats, Tumblers, Gymnasts, Jugglers, The Bridgeport Pageant Choir, Bands of Every Size Shape and Description, the Mob in general, and Characters too numerous to mention.

Commencing one-half hour before the show: Bradley Steven-Fields. *With tours through The Exhibition of Wonders by* Catherine Carr. *And Musical Diversions in the theatre by* Andy Teirstein, Bruce Robertson. *Pianists*: Karen Gustafson, Peter Phillips.

The action takes place all over America and the major capitals of the world from 1835 to 1880.

ACT 1
"There Is a Sucker Born Ev'ry Minute"
J. Dale
"Thank God I'm Old"
T. White, Tambourine Players
"The Colors of My Life"
J. Dale, G. Close
"One Brick at a Time"
G. Close, J. Dale, Bricklayers
"Museum Song"
J. Dale

---

[26]Incidental Music: "Just One of Those Things," "It's De-Lovely," "Take Me Back to Manhattan," "Make It Another Old-Fashioned, Please," "They Couldn't Compare to You," "You've Got That Thing," "Every Time We Say Goodbye," "Let's Do It," "Where Have You Been?," Let's Fly Away," "Girls," "What Is This Thing Called Love?"
[27]Originally from *YOU NEVER KNOW*, 1938.
[28]Originally from *RED, HOT AND BLUE*, 1936.
[29]Originally from *PANAMA HATTIE*, 1940.
[30]Lyrics by Burt Shevelove.
[31]Originally from *BORN TO DANCE*, film, 1936.
[32]Originally from *FIFTY MILLION FRENCHMEN*, 1929.
[33]Originally from *RED, HOT AND BLUE*, 1936.
[34]From an unproduced musical of the same title.
[35]Originally from *GAY DIVORCE*, 1932.
[36]Intended for *SILK STOCKINGS*, 1955, unused.
[37]Originally from *RED, HOT AND BLUE*, 1936.
[38]Originally from *YOU NEVER KNOW*, 1938.
[39]Originally from *OUT OF THIS WORLD*, 1950.
[40]Dropped from tryout of *RED, HOT AND BLUE*, 1936.

"I Like Your Style"
J. Dale, G. Close
"Bigger Isn't Better"
L. J. Crofoot
"Love Makes Such Fools of Us All"
M. Tatum
"Out There"
J. Dale

ACT 2
"Come Follow the Band"
The Potomac Marching Band and Washingtonians
"Black and White"
G. Close, Choir, T. White, J. Dale, Citizens of Bridgeport
"The Colors of My Life" (reprise)
J. Dale, G. Close
"The Prince of Humbug"
J. Dale
"Join the Circus"
W. C. Witter, All Circus Performers, J. Dale
("There Is a Sucker Born Ev'ry Minute" reprise)
J. Dale

1980.08 A DAY IN HOLLYWOOD/ A NIGHT IN THE UKRAINE

A Musical Double Feature (Two one-act musicals). Book and lyrics by Dick Vosburgh . Music by Frank Lazarus. Directed and choreographed by Tommy Tune. Co-choreographed by Thommie Walsh. Scenery by Tony Walton. Lighting by Beverly Emmons. Costumes by Michel Stuart. Sound design by Otts Munderloh. Musical direction, vocal and dance arrangements by Wally Harper. Co-Producer, Roy Somlyo. Associate producer, Philip M. Getter. Produced by Alexander H. Cohen and Hildy Parks. Opened 1 May 1980 at the John Golden Theatre, moved 17 June 1980 to the Royale Theatre and closed 27 September 1981 after 588 performances.

ACT 1: A DAY IN HOLLYWOOD
A Musical Revue in One Act.

CAST: PRISCILLA LOPEZ, DAVID GARRISON, STEPHEN JAMES, PEGGY HEWETT, FRANK LAZARUS, KATE DRAPER, Niki Harris, Albert Stephenson.

MUSICAL NUMBERS
"Just Go to the Movies"
(The Company)
(*Music and Lyrics by* Jerry Herman.)
"Famous Feet"
(D. Garrison, P. Lopez)
"I Love a Film Cliché"
(F. Lazarus)
(*Music by* Trevor Lyttleton. *Additional Music by* Frank Lazarus.)
"Nelson"
(P. Hewett)
(*Music and Lyrics by* Jerry Herman.)
"The Best in the World"
(P. Lopez)
(*Music and Lyrics by* Jerry Herman.)
"It All Comes Out of the Piano"
(F. Lazarus)
(*Lyrics by* Dick Vosburgh and Frank Lazarus.)
Richard A. Whiting Medley:
(Company)
"Ain't We Got Fun"
(*Lyrics by* Gus Kahn and Raymond B. Egan.)
"Too Marvelous for Words" (from *READY, WILLING AND ABLE* film)
(*Lyrics by* Johnny Mercer.)
"(The) Japanese Sandman"
(*Lyrics by* Raymond B. Egan.)
"On the Good Ship Lollipop" (from *BRIGHT EYES* film)
(*Lyrics by* Sidney Clare.)
"Double Trouble" (from *THE BIG BROADCAST* OF 1936 film)
(*Music by* Ralph Rainger and Richard A. Whiting. *Lyrics by* Leo Robin.)
"Louise" (from *INNOCENTS OF PARIS* film)
(*Lyrics by* Leo Robin.)
"Sleepy Time Gal" (later used in the film of the same name)
(*Music by* Ange Lorenzo and Richard A. Whiting. *Lyrics by* Joseph R. Alden and Raymond B. Egan.)
"Beyond the Blue Horizon" (from *MONTE CARLO* film)
(*Music by* Richard A. Whiting and W. Frank Harling. *Lyrics by* Leo Robin.)
"Thanks for the Memory"
(S. James, K. Draper)
(*Music by* Ralph Rainger. *Lyrics by* Leo Robin.)
"Another Memory"
(S. James, K. Draper)
"Doin' the Production Code"
(P. Lopez, D. Garrison, F. Lazarus, S. James, P. Hewett, K. Draper)
"A Night in the Ukraine"
(Company)

ACT 2: A NIGHT IN THE UKRAINE
A Musical in One Act loosely based on "The Bear" by Anton Chekhov.

CAST: *Mrs. Pavlenko*, a rich widow: PEGGY HEWETT. *Carlo*, her Italian footman: FRANK LAZARUS. *Gino*, her gardener: PRISCILLA LOPEZ. *Serge B. Samovar*, a Moscow lawyer: DAVID GARRISON. *Nina*, Mrs. Pavlenko's daughter: KATE DRAPER. *Constantine*, a coachman: STEPHEN JAMES. *Masha*, a maid: Niki Harris. *Sascha*, a manservant: Albert Stephenson.

Scene: The Morning room of the Pavlenko residence in the Ukraine before the Revolution.

MUSICAL NUMBERS
"Samovar the Lawyer"
(D. Garrison)
"Just Like That"
(K. Draper, S. James)
"Again"
(K. Draper, S. James)
"A Duel! A Duel!"
(P. Hewett, D. Garrison)
"Natasha"
(D. Garrison)
"A Night in the Ukraine"[41] (reprise)
(Company)

1980.09 A ROCKETTE SPECTACULAR

A Musical Revue in One Act, 15 Scenes. Dialogue script writer, Stan Hart. Produced and directed by Robert F. Jani. Executive musical director, Don Pippin. Scenery designed by John William Keck. Rockettes choreographed/staged by Violet Holmes. Costumes designed by Frank Spencer. Miss Rogers choreographed/staged by Howard Parker. Lighting designed by Ken Billington. Conductor, Elman Anderson. Musical routing by Ronald Melrose. Orchestrations by Philip J. Lang, Michael Gibson, Elman Anderson, Arthur Harris, Danny Holgate. Produced by Radio City Music Hall Productions, Inc. Opened 2 May 1980 at the Radio City Music Hall and closed 22 June 1980 after 96 performances.

CAST: GINGER ROGERS, Gail Nelson, Jack Blackton.
Dancers: David Brownlee, John Cashman, Ron Crofoot, David Fredericks, Michael Lang, Bobby [Robert] Longbottom, Daryl Murphy, Scott Plank, Patrick Roddy, David Roman, Brent Saunders, David Scala, Lyn Schaal.
THE ROCKETTES: Pauline Achillas, Carol Beatty, Catherine Beatty, Dottie Belle, Karen Berman, Nina Berman, Susan Boron, Deniene Bruck, Barbara Ann Cittadino, Eileen Collins, Brie Daniels, Susanne Doris, Joyce Dwyer, Jacqueline Fancy, Prudence Gray, Carol Harbich, Ginny Hounsell, Cynthia Hughes, Holly Jones, Pam Kelleher, Dee Dee Knapp, Judy Little, Leslie Gryszko McCarthy, Barbara Moore, Ann Murphy, Lynn Newton, Pam Stacey Pasqualino, Joan Peer, Cindy Peiffer, Geraldine Presky, Sheila Rodriguez, Maryellen Scilla, Terry Spano, Lynn Sullivan, Sunny Summers, Susan Theobald, Carol Toman, Darlene Wendy, Rose Ann Woolsey, Phyllis Wujiko. *Organist*: Timothy Stella.

MUSICAL NUMBERS[42]
Scene 1
The March
The Rockettes
Scene 2
In Their Dressing Room
The Rockettes
Scene 3
In the Star's Dressing Room
G. Rogers, G. Nelson

[41]Added to program shortly after opening.
[42]Running order was revised during the run.

Scene 4
Rockette Rehearsal
The Rockettes, Their Choreographer
Scene 5
In the Star's Dressing Room
G. Rogers, G. Nelson
Scene 6
"My Big Moment"
G. Rogers, The Dancers
(*Music by* Don Pippin. *Lyrics by* Sammy Cahn.)
Scene 7
"Alike, Alike"
The Rockettes
(*Music by* Don Pippin. *Lyrics by* Sammy Cahn.)
Scene 8
Dance Dance Dance
G. Rogers, J. Blackton, The Dancers
("Come Dance With Me")
(J. Blackton, Dancers)
("I Won't Dance"/"Come Dance With Me" Medley)
G. Rogers, J. Blackton, The Dancers
Scene 9
In the Star's Dressing Room
G. Rogers, G. Nelson
Scene 10
Fifty Years of the Rockettes
The Rockettes
Scene 11
Stage-Struck
G. Nelson
("Star")
(G. Nelson)
Scene 12
Five Minutes 'Til Showtime
The Rockettes
Scene 13
Hoedown
The Rockettes, The Dancers
Scene 14
On Her Own
G. Rogers
(*Vocal Introduction for Miss Rogers*: J. Blackton. *Pianist*: William Roy.)
("My Big Moment" reprise)
("Embraceable You" from *GIRL CRAZY*)
("But Not For Me" from *GIRL CRAZY*)
(*Music by* George Gershwin. *Lyrics by* Ira Gershwin.)
("Forty-Second Street" from *FORTY-SECOND STREET* film and show)
("Shuffle Off to Buffalo" from *FORTY SECOND STREET* film and show)
(*Music by* Harry Warren. *Lyrics by* Al Dubin.)"
("Did You Ever See a Dream Walking?" from *SITTING PRETTY* film)
(*Music by* Harry Revel. *Lyrics by* Mack Gordon.)
("We're in the Money" [The Golddiggers' Song] from *GOLDDIGGERS OF 1933* film including pig-Latin chorus)
(*Music by* Harry Warren. *Lyrics by* Al Dubin.)
("Isn't This a Lovely Day?" from *TOP HAT* film)
(*Music and Lyrics by* Irving Berlin.)
("Let's Call the Whole Thing Off" from *SHALL WE DANCE* film)
("They All Laughed" from *SHALL WE DANCE* film)
("They Can't Take That Away from Me" from *SHALL WE DANCE* film)
(*Music by* George Gershwin. *Lyrics by* Ira Gershwin.)
Scene 15
Finale: "You're at the Music Hall"
Company
(*Music by* Don Pippin. *Lyrics by* Sammy Cahn.)

1980.10 BLACK BROADWAY

A Musical Revue in Two Acts, 33 Scenes[43]. Orchestrations and musical arrangements by Dick Hyman. Musical director, Frank Owens. Production designer, Leo Gambacorta. Associate producer, John P. Fleming. Sound by Paul Blank—Omnisound. Produced by George Wein in association with Honi Coles, Robert Kimball and Bobby Short. Opened 4 May 1980 at Town Hall and closed 24 May 1980 after 24 performances.

CAST (in alphabetical order): JOHN W. BUBBLES, NELL CARTER, (CHARLES) HONI COLES, ADELAIDE HALL, GREGORY HINES, BOBBY SHORT, ELISABETH WELCH, EDITH WILSON; Charles "Cookie" Cook, Leslie "Bubba" Gaines, Mercedes Ellington, Carla Earle, Terri Griffin, WyettaTurner.

ACT 1
Overture
(Medley from "*RUNNIN' WILD*": Ginger Brown," "Old-Fashioned Love," Charleston"
(*Music by* James P. Johnson.)
Scene 1
The Story of Black Broadway
B. Short or H. Coles
(*by* George Wein, Dick Hyman, Honi Coles, Robert Kimball.)
Scene 2
"Liza" (Entrance of Copasetics)
G. Hines or H. Coles, C. Cook, B. Gaines
(*Music by* Maceo Pinkard.)
"Blue Turning Gray Over You"
C. Cook
(*Music by* Thoams "Fats" Waller. *Lyrics by* Andy Razaf.)
"I Can't Believe That You're in Love With Me" (from *GAY PAREE*, 1925)
(*Music by* Jimmy McHugh. *Lyrics by* Clarence Gaskill.)
"Perdido"
(*Music by* Juan Tizol. *Lyrics by* Hans Lengsfelder and Ervin Drake.)
"Who"
B Gaines
"Christopher Columbus"
G. Hines or H. Coles, C. Cook, B. Gaines
(*Music by* Leon Berry. *Lyrics by* Andy Razaf.)
Scene 3
"Under the Bamboo Tree" (1902) (from *SALLY IN OUR ALLEY*)
(*Music and Lyrics by* Bob Cole, J. Rosamund Johnson, James Weldon Johnson.)
"(Oh Say,) Wouldn't It Be a Dream" (1905)
(*Music and Lyrics by* Earl Jones and Joe Jordan.)
"Broadway in Dahomey" (from *IN DAHOMEY*, 1903)
B. Short
(*Music and Lyrics by* Alex Rogers, Bert Williams, George Walker.)
Scene 4
"Black and Blue"[44] (from *HOT CHOCOLATES*, 1929)
(*Music by* Thomas "Fats" Waller, Harry Brooks. *Lyrics by* Andy Razaf.)
"He May Be Your Man But He Comes To See Me Sometimes"[45] (from *THE PLANTATION REVUE*, 1922)
E. Wilson
(*Music and Lyrics by* Lemuel Fowler.)
Scene 5
"The Unbeliever" (1920)
B. Short
(*Music and Lyrics by* Chris Smith, Frederick Bryan, Bert Williams.)
Scene 6
The Mayor of Harlem (Patter by Honi Coles)
"Doin' the New Low Down" (from Lew Leslie's *BLACKBIRDS OF 1928*)
G. Hines or H. Coles, C. Cook, B. Gaines, Girls
(*Music by* Jimmy McHugh. *Lyrics by* Dorothy Fields.)
Scene 7
"Creole Love Call"[46] (1928)
(*Music and Lyrics by* Duke Ellington.)

---

[43]First produced in New York 24 June 1979 by the Newport Jazz Festival at Avery Fisher Hall for 1 concert performance. "Program Subject to Change Owing to Magnitude of Production"—Lew Leslie.
[44]Artist introduced song.
[45]Artist introduced song.
[46]Artist introduced song.

"I Must Have That Man"[47] (from Lew Leslie's *BLACKBIRDS OF 1928*)
(*Music by* Jimmy McHugh. *Lyrics by* Dorothy Fields.)
"Diga, Digga Do"[48] (from Lew Leslie's *BLACKBIRDS OF 1928*)
(*Music by* Jimmy McHugh. *Lyrics by* Dorothy Fields.)
"I Can't Give You Anything But Love"[49] (from Lew Leslie's *BLACKBIRDS OF 1928*)
A. Hall
(*Music by* Jimmy McHugh. *Lyrics by* Dorothy Fields.)

Scene 8
Harlem Medley:
B. Short
"She's Tall, She's Tan, She's Terrific" (from *COTTON CLUB PARADE 1937*, 3rd ed.)
(*Music* by J. Fred Coots. *Lyrics by* Benny Davis.)
"Posin'" (from *GRAND TERRACE REVUE*, 1937)
(*Music by* Saul Chaplin. *Lyrics by* Sammy Cahn.)
"Truckin'" (from *COTTON CLUB PARADE*, 26th ed., 1935)
(*Music by* Rube Bloom. *Lyrics by* Ted Koehler.)
"Breakfast in Harlem"
"Gimme a Pigfoot" (*Music and Lyrics by* Wesley Wilson.)

Scene 9
"Ill Wind" (from *COTTON CLUB PARADE*, 24th ed., 1934)
A. Hall
(*Music by* Harold Arlen. *Lyrics by* Ted Koehler.)

Scene 10
"Between the Devil and the Deep Blue Sea" (from *RHYTHMANIA*, Cotton Club, 1931)
A. Hall, B. Short
(*Music by* Harold Arlen. *Lyrics by* Ted Koehler.)

Scene 11
"As Love As I Live" (from *COTTON CLUB PARADE*, 24th ed., 1934)
B. Short
(*Music by* Harold Arlen. *Lyrics by* Ted Koehler.)

Scene 12
"The Brown-Skin Gal in the Calico Gown" (from *JUMP FOR JOY*, 1941)
B. Short
(*Music by* Duke Ellington. *Lyrics by* Paul Francis Webster.)

Scene 13
"Jump For Joy" (from *JUMP FOR JOY*, 1941)
B. Short, Company
(*Music by* Duke Ellington. *Lyrics by* Paul Francis Webster.)

ACT 2

Scene 1
"Cotton Club Stomp" (from *COTTON CLUB REVUE*, 14th ed., 1929)
Frank Owens and Orchestra
(*Music by* Duke Ellington, Johnny Hodges, Harry Carney.)

Scene 2
"Tan Manhattan" (from *TAN MANHATTAN*, 1940)
G. Hines
Music by Eubie Blake. *Lyrics by* Andy Razaf.)

Scene 3
"Charleston Rag"
G. Hines
(*Music by* Eubie Blake.)

Scene 4
Entrance of Elisabeth Welch to "When Lights Are Low" (1936)
(*Music and Lyrics by* Spencer Williams and Benny Carter.)
"Love for Sale" (from *THE NEW YORKERS*, 1930)
(*Music and Lyrics by* Cole Porter.)
"Solomon"[50] (from *NYMPH ERRANT*, 1933, London)
E. Welch
(*Music and Lyrics by* Cole Porter.)

Scene 5
"Charleston"[51] (from *RUNNIN' WILD*, 1923)
E. Welch
(*Music and Lyrics by* Cecil Mack and James P. Johnson.)

[47]Artist introduced song.
[48]Artist introduced song.
[49]Artist introduced song.
[50]Artist introduced song.
[51]Artist introduced song.

Scene 6
Entrance of Nell Carter to Opening Bars of:
"Ain't Misbehavin'" (from *HOT CHOCOLATES*, 1929)
(*Music by* Thomas "Fats" Waller, Harry Brooks. *Lyrics by* Andy Razaf.)
"I've Got a Feeling I'm Falling" (1929)(from *APPLAUSE*, film)
N. Carter
(*Music by* Thomas "Fats" Waller, Harry Link. *Lyrics by* Billy Rose.)

Scene 7
"Legalize My Name" (from *ST. LOUIS WOMAN*, 1946)
N. Carter
(*Music by* Harold Arlen. *Lyrics by* Johnny Mercer.)

Scene 8
A Tribute to Florence Mills: (Scenes 8 & 9)
"I'm a Little Blackbird Looking for a Bluebird" (from *DIXIE TO BROADWAY*, 1924)
E. Wilson
(*Music by* Grant Clarke, Roy Turk. *Lyrics by* George W. Meyer, Arthur Johnston.)

Scene 9
"Silver Rose" (from Lew Leslie's *BLACKBIRDS OF 1926*, London)
E. Welch
(*Music and Lyrics by* George W. Meyer.)

Scene 10
A Tribute to Ethel Waters: (Scenes 10-16)
"Heat Wave" (from *AS THOUSANDS CHEER*, 1933)
N. Carter
(*Music and Lyrics by* Irving Berlin.)

Scene 11
"You're Lucky to Me" (from Lew Leslie's *BLACKBIRDS OF 1930*)
E. Wilson
(*Music by* Eubie Blake. *Lyrics by* Andy Razaf.)

Scene 12
"Suppertime" (from *AS THOUSANDS CHEER*, 1933)
A. Hall
(*Music and Lyrics by* Irving Berlin.)

Scene 13
"Honey in the Honeycomb" (from *CABIN IN THE SKY*, 1940)
N. Carter
(*Music by* Vernon Duke. *Lyrics by* John Latouche.)

Scene 14
"Stormy Weather" (from *COTTON CLUB PARADE*, 22nd ed., 1933)
E. Welch
(*Music by* Harold Arlen. *Lyrics by* Ted Koehler.)

Scene 15
"Taking a Chance on Love" (from *CABIN IN THE SKY*, 1940)
A. Hall, E. Wilson, E. Welch, N. Carter, G. Hines or H. Coles
(*Music by* Vernon Duke. *Lyrics by* John Latouche and Ted Fetter.)

Scene 16
"Dinah" (from *THE PLANTATION REVUE*, 1925)
G. Hines or B. Short
(*Music by* Harry Akst. *Lyrics by* Sam Lewis, Joe Young.)

Scene 17
"Sweet Georgia Brown" (1925)
G. Hines, Ensemble
(*Music and Lyrics by* Ben Bernie, Maceo Pinkard, Kenneth Casey.)

Scene 18
"It Ain't Necessarily So"[52] (from *PORGY AND BESS*, 1935)
"There's a Boat That's Leavin' Soon for New York"[53] (from *PORGY AND BESS*, 1935)
J. W. Bubbles
(*Music by* George Gershwin. *Lyrics by* Ira Gershwin.)

Scene 19
"Memories of You" (from Lew Leslie's *BLACKBIRDS OF 1930*)
J. W. Bubbles, Entire Company
(*Music by* Eubie Blake. *Lyrics by* Andy Razaf.)

Scene 20
"Jump for Joy" (reprise)
Entire Company

[52]Artist introduced song.
[53]Artist introduced song.

1980.11
MUSICAL CHAIRS

A Musical in Two Acts. Book by Barry Berg, Ken Donnelly, Tom Savage. Based on an original story concept by Larry P. Pontillo. Music and lyrics by Tom Savage. Entire production directed and choreographed by Rudy Tronto. Scenery designed by Ernest Allen Smith. Lighting designed by Peggy Clark. Costumes designed by Michael J. Cesario. Director-assistant choreographer, Susan Stroman. Musical direction, Barry H. Gordon. (Music) arrangements and orchestrations by Ada Janik, Dick Leib. Produced by Lesley Savage and Bert Stratford. Opened 14 May 1980 at the Rialto Theatre and closed 25 May 1980 after 15 performances.

CAST (in order of appearance): *Joe Preston*: RON HOLGATE. *Matty*: Ellen McCabe. *Stage Manager*: Douglas Walker. *Sally's Boyfriend*: Scott Ellis. *Millie*: Enid Blaymore. *Roberta*: GRACE KEAGY. *Brad*: Randall Easterbrook. *Miranda*: Leslie-Ann Wolfe. *Lillian*: PATTI KARR. *Harold*: BRANDON MAGGART. *Gary*: JESS RICHARDS. *Janet*: JOY FRANZ. *Brown Suit*: Edward Earle. *Blue Suit*: Tom Breslin. *Tuxedo*: Rick Emery. *Valerie Brooks*: LEE MEREDITH.

The action takes place at the present time in an Off-Broadway theatre on opening night in a section of the audience.

ACT 1

"Tonight's the Night"
Company
"My Time"
R. Holgate
"Who's Who"
Company
"If I Could Be Beautiful"
L. Wolfe, Boys
"What I Could Have Done Tonight"
B. Maggart, J. Franz
"There You Are"
R. Emery
"Sally"
S. Ellis, Company
"Other People"
J. Franz
"My Time" (reprise)
R. Holgate
"Hit the Ladies"
P. Karr, Ladies

ACT 2

"Musical Chairs"
R. Emery, T. Breslin, E. Earle
"Suddenly Love"
J. Richards
"Better Than Broadway"
E. Blaymore, G. Keagy
"Every Time the Music Starts"
R. Easterbrook, Company
"There You Are" (reprise)
R. Emery, R. Holgate, L. Meredith
"My Time" (reprise)
R. Holgate

1980.12
BLACKSTONE!

A Magnificent Musical Magic Show in Two Acts. Directed and choreographed by Kevin Carlisle. Scenery designed by Peter Wolf. Costumes designed by Winn Morton. Lighting designed by Martin Aronstein. Magic production designer, Jack Hart. Musical supervisor-conductor, Milton Setzer. Orchestrations by Richard Bellis. Magic direction, Charles Reynolds. Production supervisor, Jackie Schrock. Illusion supervisor, Bill Smith. Produced by Columbia Artists Theatricals Corporation and Blackstone Magik Enterprises, Inc. Opened 19 May 1980 at the Majestic Theatre and closed 17 August 1980 after 104 performances.

CAST: HARRY BLACKSTONE, GAY BLACKSTONE, BECKY GARRETT, Elaine Barnes, Lynn Castles, Karen Curlee, Ann McLean, Robbin McDowell, Mary McNamara, Reenie Moore, Richard Ruth, Bill Smith, Nikki Summerford, Jim Thompson, John Traub, Michal Weir.

ACT 1

The Vanishing Birdcage
A Salute to Our Heritage
The Wizard
Cassadaga Propaganda
Mysteries of the Orient
Hare
The Incredible Buzzsaw

ACT 2

The Enchanted Garden
Roses for Your Lady
The Wizard Returns
The Extraordinary Floating Lightbulb
Moorish Fantasies
So You Want to Be a Magician
Circus of Mysteries

1980.13
BILLY BISHOP GOES TO WAR

A Play with Music in Two Acts[54]. Written, composed and directed by John Gray, in collaboration with Eric Peterson. (Suggested by the book "Winged Warfare" by Billy Bishop.) Scenery by David Gropman. Lighting by Jennifer Tipton. Sound design by Robert Kerzman. Associate producers, Stephen Graham and Ventures West Capital, Inc. Co-produced by Vancouver East Cultural Centre (Christopher Wootten, Executive Director). First presented in the United States by Arena Stage, Washington, D.C. Produced by Mike Nichols and Lewis Allen. Opened 29 May 1980 at the Morosco Theatre and closed 7 June 1980 after 12 performances. Transferred Off-Broadway 17 June 1980 to the Theatre de Lys and closed 24 August 1980 after 78 additional performances. Total, including Off-Broadway, 90 performances.

CAST: *Billy Bishop, Upperclassman, Adjutant Perrault, Officer, Sir Hugh Cecil, Lady St. Helier, Cedric, Doctor, General John Higgins, Tommy, Lovely Helene, Albert Ball, Walter Bourne, General Hugh M. Trenchard, Servant, King George V*: ERIC PETERSON. *Narrator, Pianist*: JOHN GRAY.

ACT 1

"(We're) Off to Fight the Hun"
E. Peterson, J. Gray
"Canada at War"
E. Peterson, J. Gray
"The Good Ship Caledonia"
"Buried Alive in the Mind"
"December Nights"
E. Peterson, J. Gray
"The RE-7"
"Nobody Shoots No-One in Canada"
E. Peterson, J. Gray
"Lady St. Helier"
E. Peterson
"My First Solo Flight"
E. Peterson
"In the Sky"
E. Peterson, J. Gray

ACT 2

"As Calm as the Ocean"
"Friends Ain't S'posed to Die"
E. Peterson, J. Gray
"General Sir Hugh M. Trenchard"
"The Empire Soirée"
E. Peterson, J. Gray
"(We're) Off to Fight the Hun" (reprise)
E. Peterson, J. Gray
"In the Sky" (reprise)
E. Peterson, J. Gray

[54]No songs were listed in the program. Above list prepared from production typescript and recording.

1980–1981 SEASON

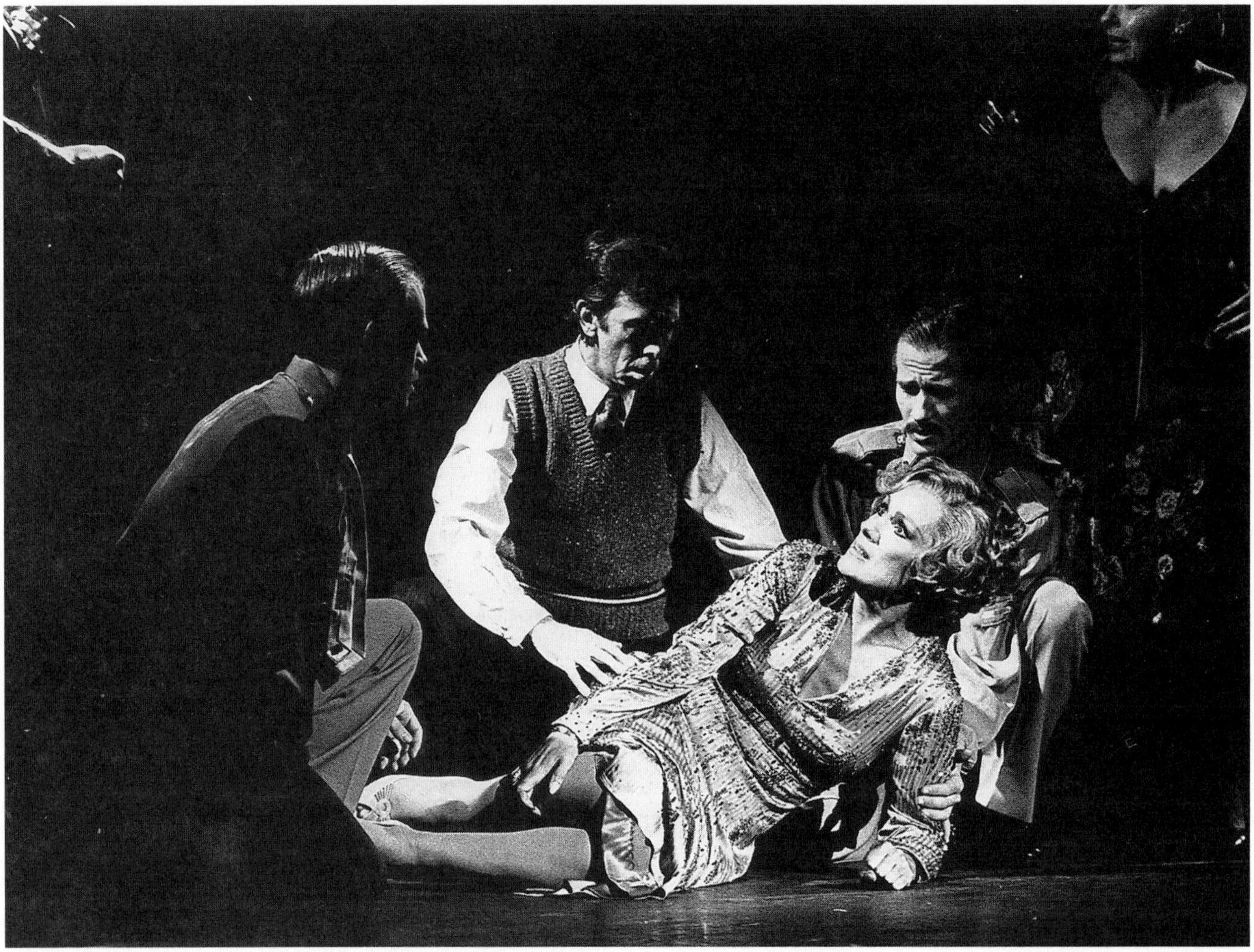

Tammy Grimes (foreground) in 42ND STREET
Martha Swope/TimePix

1980–1981 SEASON

1980.14 YOUR ARMS TOO SHORT TO BOX WITH GOD

A Revival of the Soaring Celebration in Songs and Dance (Gospel Musical) in Two Acts[1]. Conceived from the Book of St. Matthew by Vinnette Carroll. Music and lyrics by Alex Bradford. Additional music and lyrics by Micki Grant. Directed by Vinnette Carroll. Choreography by Talley Beatty. Sets and costumes by William Schroder. Lighting by Richard Winkler. Sound by Abe Jacob. Musical direction by Michael Powell. Orchestrations and dance music by H. B. Barnum. First produced at the Urban Arts Theatre; Producing director, Anita MacShane. Production supervisors, Jerry R. Moore, Richard Martini. Artistic production coordinator, Ralph Farrington. Produced by Tom Mallow in association with James Janek. Opened 2 June 1980 at the Ambassador Theatre, moved 16 September 1980 to the Belasco Theatre, and closed 12 October 1980 after 149 performances.

CAST (in alphabetical order): Adrian Bailey, Julius Richard Brown[2], Cleavant Derricks, Sheila Ellis, Ralph Farrington, Jamil K. Garland, Elijah Gill, William-Keebler Hardy, Jr., Jennifer-Yvette Holliday, Linda James, Garry Q. Lewis, Linda Morton, Jai Oscar St. John, Kiki Shepard, Leslie Hardesty Sisson, Ray Stephens, Quincella Swyningan, Faruma S. Williams, Marilynn Winbush, Linda Young. *Swing Dancers*: Adrian Bailey, Linda James.

ACT 1

"Beatitudes"
Company
(*Music and Lyrics by* Micki Grant.)

"We're Gonna Have a Good Time"
J. R. Brown/C. Derricks, Company
(*Music and Lyrics by* Micki Grant.)

"There's a Stranger in Town"
S. Ellis, Company
(*Music and Lyrics by* Alex Bradford.)

"Do You Know Jesus?"/"He's a Wonder"
J. K. Garland, Company
(*Music and Lyrics by* Alex Bradford.)

"Just a Little Bit of Jesus Goes a Long Way"
J. Holliday
(*Music and Lyrics by* Alex Bradford.)

"We Are the Priests and Elders"
J. R. Brown, C. Derricks, W. Hardy, Jr., J. O. St. John
(*Music and Lyrics by* Micki Grant.)

"Something Is Wrong in Jerusalem"
S. Ellis, Q. Swyningan
(*Music and Lyrics by* Micki Grant.)

"It Was Alone"/"I Know I Have to Leave Here"
J. Holliday, Company
(*Music and Lyrics by* Alex Bradford.)

"Be Careful Whom You Kiss"
S. Ellis, Q. Swyningan
(*Music and Lyrics by* Alex Bradford.)

"Trial"
Company
(*Music and Lyrics by* Micki Grant.)

"It's Too Late"
Company
(*Music and Lyrics by* Micki Grant.)

"Judas Dance" (*Music by* H. B. Barnum.)
R. Farrington

"Your Arms Too Short to Box With God"
J. Holliday, Company
(*Music and Lyrics by* Alex Bradford.)

"Give Us Barabbas"
Company
(*Music and Lyrics by* Alex Bradford.)

"See How They Done My Lord"
S. Ellis, Company
(*Music and Lyrics by* Alex Bradford.)

"Come on Down"
L. E. Young, J. K. Garland, J. O. St. John
(*Music and Lyrics by* Alex Bradford.)

"Can't No Grave Hold My Body Down"
R. Stephens, Company
(*Music and Lyrics by* Alex Bradford.)

"Beatitudes" (reprise)
C. Derricks, Company

ACT 2

"Didn't I Tell You"
J. R. Brown/C. Derricks
(*Music and Lyrics by* Alex Bradford.)

"When the Power Comes"
Company
(*Music and Lyrics by* Alex Bradford.)

"Everybody Has His Own Way"
J. R. Brown/C. Derricks, R. Stephens
(*Music and Lyrics by* Alex Bradford.)

"Down By the Riverside"
C. Derricks, Company

"I Love You So Much Jesus"
J. Y. Holliday
(*Music and Lyrics by* Alex Bradford.)

"The Band"
Company

1980.15 IT'S SO NICE TO BE CIVILIZED

A Musical in Two Acts[3]. Book, music and lyrics by Micki Grant. Directed by Frank Corsaro. Choreography by Mabel Robinson. Musical director, Coleridge-Taylor Perkinson. Scenery and visuals, Charles E. Hoefler. Lighting by Charles E. Hoefler, Ralph Madero. Costume design by Ruth Morley. Orchestrations by Danny Holgate, Neal Tate. Choral arrangements by Tasha Thomas. Dance arrangements by Carl Maultsby. Sound design by Palmer Shannon. Associate producer, Danny Holgate. Produced by Jay Julien, Arnon Milchan, Larry Kalish. Opened 3 June 1980 at the Martin Beck Theatre and closed 8 June 1980 after 8 performances.

CAST (in order of appearance): *Sharkey*: OBBA BABATUNDE. *Mollie*: VIVIAN REED. *Larry*: Larry Stewart. *Sissy*: Vickie D. Chappell. *LuAnne*: Carol Lynn Maillard. *Grandma*: MABEL KING. *Mr. Anderson*: Stephen Pender. *Blade*: Dan Strayhorn. *Rev. Williams*: Eugene Edwards. *Mother*: Deborah Burrell. *Dancing Bag Lady*: Juanita Grace Tyler.

Ensemble: Daria Atanian, Paul Binotto, Sharon K. Brooks, P. L. Brown, Jean Cheek, Vondie Curtis-Hall, Paul Harman, Esther Marrow, Wellington Perkins, Dwayne Phelps, Juanita Grace Tyler. *Dance Alternates*: Allison Rene Manson, Steiv Semien.

The action takes place on Sweetbitter Street over a weekend in late summer.

ACT 1

"Step into My World"
Ensemble

"Keep Your Eye on the Red"
O. Babatunde

"Wake-up, Sun"
O. Babatunde, V. Reed

"Subway Rider"
Ensemble

"God Help Us"
L. Stewart, C. L. Maillard

"Who's Going to Teach the Children?"
M. King

"Out on the Street"
Ensemble

"Welcome, Mr. Anderson"
D. Strayhorn, Gang

"Why Can't Me and You?"
S. Pender

---

[1]Originally produced 22 December 1976 at the Lyceum Theatre for 429 performances.
[2]The roles performed by Julius Richard Brown and Cleavant Derricks are alternated.

[3]First produced in New York Off-Off Broadway 22 February 1979 at AMAS Repertory for 12 performances. Directed by Jeffrey Dunn.

"Why Can't Me and You?" (reprise)
V. D. Chappelle, S. Pender
"Out on the Street" (reprise)
Ensemble
"When I Rise"
E. Edwards
"World Keeps Going Round"
V. Reed, Ensemble

ACT 2
"Antiquity"
Ensemble
"I've Still Got My Bite"
M. King
"Look at Us"
L. Stewart, C. L. Maillard
"Keep Your Eye on the Red"
O. Babatunde
"The American Dream"
S. Pender
"Bright Lights"
V. Reed
"Step into My World" (reprise)
O. Babatunde, V. Reed
"It's So Nice to be Civilized"
S. Pender, V. D. Chappell, The Hawks
"Like a Lady"
V. Reed
"Pass a Little Love Around"
Ensemble

1980.16 THE MUSIC MAN

A Revival of the Musical Comedy in Two Acts, 17 Scenes[4]. Book, music and lyrics by Meredith Willson. Book written in collaboration with Franklin Lacey. Directed and choreographed by Michael Kidd. Sets designed by Peter Wolf. Costumes designed by Stanley Simmons. Lighting designed by Marcia Madeira. Sound designed by Barry Rimler. Orchestrations by Don Walker. Musical and vocal direction by Milton Rosenstock. Produced by James M. Nederlander, Raymond Lussa, Fred Walker. Opened 5 June 1980 at the New York City Center and closed 22 June 1980 after 21 performances.

CAST (in order of appearance): *Travelling Salesmen*: Dennis Holland, Lee Winston, Michael J. Rockne, Randy Morgan, Tom Garrett, Ralph Braun, Andy Hostettler, Larry Cahn. *Charlie Cowell*: JAY STUART. *Conductor*: Peter Wandel. *Harold Hill*: DICK VAN DYKE. *Mayor Shinn*: IGGIE WOLFINGTON. *Ewart Dunlop*: Larry Cahn. *Oliver Hix*: Randy Morgan. *Jacey Squires*: Lee Winston. *Olin Britt*: Ralph Braun. *Marcellus Washburn*: RICHARD WARREN PUGH. *Tommy Djilas*: CALVIN McRAE. *Marian Paroo*: MEG BUSSERT. *Mrs. Paroo*: CAROL ARTHUR. *Amaryllis*: Lara Jill Miller. *Winthrop Paroo*: CHRISTIAN SLATER. *Eulalie MacKecknie Shinn*: JEN JONES. *Zaneeta Shinn*: CHRISTINA SAFFRAN. *Alma Hix*: Marcia Brushingham. *Maud Dunlop*: Mary Gaebler. *Ethel Toffelmier*: P. J. Nelson. *Mrs. Squires*: Mary Roche. *Constable Locke*: Dennis Holland.

River City Townspeople: Victoria Ally, Carol Ann Basch, Dennis Batutis, David Beckett, Mark A. Esposito, Tom Garrett, Liza Gennaro, Dennis Holland, Andy Hostettler, Tony Jaeger, Wendy Kimball, Ara Marx, Darleigh Miller, Gail Pennngton, Rosemary Rado, Michael J. Rockne, Coley Sohn, Peter Wandel.

1980.17 FEARLESS FRANK

A Musical in Two Acts. Book and lyrics by Andrew Davies. (Inspired by "My Life and Loves" by Frank Harris.) Music by Dave Brown. Directed by Robert Gillespie. Musical staging by Michael Vernon. Scenery by Martin Tilley. Costumes supervised by Carrie F. Robbins. Lighting by Ruth Roberts. Orchestrations by Michael Reed. Musical direction and additional arrangements by Michael Rose. Associate producers, Norma Adler, Michael A. Riddell. Originally produced at the King's Head Theatre Club in London. Produced by David Black and Robert Fabian in association with Oscar Lewenstein and Theodore P. Donahue, Jr. Opened 15 June 1980 at the Princess Theatre and closed 25 June 1980 after 12 performances.

CAST: *Frank Harris*: NIALL TOIBIN. *French Waiter, Headmaster, Kendrick, Lord Folkestone, Whistler*: Alex Wipf. *Secretary, Schoolgirl, Jessie, Lilly*: Valerie Mahaffey. *Nellie, Kate, Laura*: Kristen Meadows. *Tobin, Whitehouse, Smith, Chapman, Oscar Wilde*: Steve Burney. *Nursemaid, Actress, Bootblack, Topsy, Newsboy, Enid*: Ann Hodapp. *Cowboy, Carlyle, Mr. Clapton, deMaupassant, Dowson*: OLIVER PIERRE. *Mrs. Mayhew, Mrs. Clapton, Mrs. Clayton*: Evalyn Baron.

And School boys, New Yorkers, Hotel Guests, Cowboys, Cows, Indians, A Crowd, Newsboys, Strollers, Opera Chorus, Harris Detractors, Harris Praisers: The Company.

The action takes place in 1921 in Nice and in the memory of Frank Harris.

ACT 1
"The Man Who Made His Life into a Work of Art"
N. Toibin, Girls
"The Examination Song, or Get Me on That Boat"
A. Wipf, S. Burney, N. Toibin
"Come Help Yourself to America, or Frank in the Melting Pot"
Company
"Halted at the Very Gates of Paradise"—A Song of Frustration
N. Toibin, Girls
"Dandy Night Clerk, or How to Get On in the Hotel Trade"
Company
"Riding the Range"—A Song of the Old West
Company
"Oh Catch Me, Mr. Harris, Cause I'm Falling for You!"
K. Meadows, A. Hodapp, V. Mahaffey, E. Baron, N. Toibin
"The Greatest Man of All"
N. Toibin, Company

ACT 2
"My Poor Wee Lassie"—A Scottish Lament
O. Pierre
"Evening News"—A Song of Success
Company
"Le Maitre de la Conte, or Maupassant Tells All"
O. Pierre
"Oh, Mr. Harris, You're a Naughty Man!"
N. Toibin, E. Baron
"Free Speech, Free Thought, Free Love"
A. Hodapp, N. Toibin, Company
"Mr. Harris, It's All Over Now!"
N. Toibin, Company
"Fearless Frank"
The Company

1980.18 MANHATTAN SHOWBOAT

A Musical Revue in One Act, 10 Scenes. Conceived and produced by Robert F. Jani. Original music and lyrics by Donald Pippin, Sammy Cahn and Nan Mason. Executive musical director, Donald Pippin. Production executive, John J. Moore. Choreographed by Linda Lemac, Howard Parker, Debra Pigliavento, Frank Wagner. Principals Staged by Frank Wagner. Rockettes choreographed by Violet Holmes. Dialogue by Stan Hart. Special material, Nan Mason. Musical routining, Stan Lebowsky. Scenery designed by Robert Guerra. Costumes designed by Frank Spencer, Michael Casey. Lighting designed by David F. Segal. Orchestrations by Elman Anderson, Michael Gibson, Arthur Harris, Philip J. Lang. Produced by Radio City Musical Hall Productions, Inc. Opened 30 June 1980 at the Radio City Music Hall and closed 15 October 1980 after 191 performances.

CAST: *Belle*: KAREN ANDERS. *Edgar*: LOUIS CARRY. *Hiram Boggs*: THOMAS RUISINGER. *Tree*: STEVEN WILLIFORD. *Daisy*: Herself (the baby elephant). *P. T. Barnum*: Tony Moore. *Buffalo Bill*: Buddy Crutchfield. *Annie Oakley*: Luu Ann Csaszar. *Annie*: Laurie Stephenson.

THE ROCKETTES: Pauline Achillas, Carol Beatty, Catherine Beatty, Dottie Belle, Karen Berman, Susan Boron, Deniene Bruck, Barbara Ann Cittadino, Eileen Collins, Brie Daniels, Susan DiGilio, Susanne Doris, Jacqueline Fancy, Alexis Ficks, Mary Ann Fiordalisi, Prudence Gray, Carol Harbich, Ginny Hounsell, Cynthia Hughes, Pam Kelleher, Dee Dee Knapp, Judy Little, Leslie Gryszko McCarthy, Barbara Moore, Ann Murphy, Lynn Newton, Pam Stacey Pasqualino, Joan Peer, Cindy Peiffer, Geraldine Presky, Sheila Rodriguez, Maryellen Scilla, Terry Spano, Lynn Sullivan, Sunny Summers, Susan Theobald, Carol Toman, Darlene Wendy, Rose Ann Woolsey, Phyllis Wujko.

THE NEW YORKERS: Pam Cecil, Joanna Coggins, Lou Ann Csaszar, Buddy Crutchfield, Alvin Davis, Rick Emery, Dale Furry, Bobby Grayson, Phil Hall, Nina

---

[4]Originally produced in New York 19 December 1957 at the Majestic Theatre for 1375 performances. For Synopsis of Scenes and Musical Numbers, see original 1957 production. Original Act 1, Scene 2 was divided in two, yielding an extra scene.

Hennessey, Stephen Hope, Deirdre Kane, Dale Kristien, Andrea Lyman, James Mahady, Tony Moore, Sylvia Nolan, Denise O'Neill, Susan Powers, Cleo Price, Jeffory Robinson, Laurie Stephenson, Bob Teterick, Kay Walbye, Scott Whiteleather, Bob Wrenn.

Dancers: Dennis Angulo, Phillip Bond, Ron Chisholm, Angie Daye, Danute Debney, John Michael Doyle, Glenn Ferrugiari, Doug Fogel, Neisha Folkes, Linda Kay Hamil, Kristie Hannum, Edward Henkel, Ogalyn Jolly, Elisa Lenhart, Kim Leslie, Gail Lohla, Cary Lowenstein, Margaret McGee, Terry McLemore, Ron Meier, Lorena Palacios, James Parker, Debra Pigliavento, Michele Pigliavento, Sam Singhaus, Cassie Stein, Alan Stuart, Karen Toto, Barry Weiss.

Organists: Timothy Stella, David Messineo.

SCENES AND MUSICAL NUMBERS

Scene 1

The Opening

K. Anders, Her Crew

Scene 2

The Circus from our Circus Deck

Scene 3

Nightclubs and Floorshows from our Music Deck

Scene 4

Vaudeville from our Old Troupers Deck

(Bridge Lyrics for Medley by Nan Mason.)

Scene 5

The Sing-A-Long from our Projection Booth Crow's Nest

Scene 6

The Musical Theatre from our Broadway Deck

Scene 7

The Great Revues from our Show Deck

Scene 8

The Rockettes from our Music Hall Deck

Scene 9

Belle's Turn from the Captain's Brig

Scene 10

The Grand Finale: The Ship's Company on Parade

Vocal Solos:

"A Pretty Girl Is Like a Melody" (from *ZIEGFELD FOLLIES OF 1919*)

B. Crutchfield

(*Music and Lyrics by* Irving Berlin.)

"Love Is a Simple Thing" (from *NEW FACES OF 1952*)

C. Price

(*Music by* Arthur Siegel. *Lyrics by* June Carroll.)

"He Takes Me Off His Income Tax" (from *NEW FACES OF 1952*)

C. Price

(*Music by* Arthur Siegel. *Lyrics by* June Carroll.)

Original Songs included:

"Manhattan Showboat"

(*Music by* Donald Pippin. *Lyrics by* Sammy Cahn.)

"There Are No Girls Quite Like Show Girls"

(*Music by* Donald Pippin. *Lyrics by* Sammy Cahn.)

"Right Here"

(*Music by* Donald Pippin. *Lyrics by* Nan Mason.)

1980.19 CAMELOT

A Revival of the Musical in Two Acts, Two Prologues and 14 Scenes[5]. Book and lyrics by Alan Jay Lerner. Based on the novel "The Once and Future King" by T. H. White. Music by Frederick Loewe. Original New York production staged by Moss Hart. Directed by Frank Dunlop. Choreography by Buddy Schwab. Sets and costumes by Desmond Heeley. Lighting design by Thomas Skelton. Musical director, Franz Allers. Orchestra conductor, James Martin. Orchestrations by Robert Russell Bennett and Philip J. Lang. Production supervisor, Jerry Adler. Artistic consultant, Stone Widney. A Dome/Cutler-Herman Production. Produced by Mike Merrick and Don Gregory by arrangement with James M. Nederlander. Opened 8 July 1980 at the New York State Theatre and closed 23 August 1980 after 56 performances.

CAST (in order of appearance): *Arthur*: RICHARD BURTON. *Sir Sagramore*: Andy McAvin. *Merlyn*: JAMES VALENTINE. *Guenevere*: CHRISTINE EBERSOLE. *Sir Dinadan*: WILLIAM PARRY. *Nimue*: Jeanne Caryl. *Lancelot*: RICHARD MUENZ. *Mordred*: ROBERT FOX. *Dap*: Robert Molnar. *Friar*: JAMES VALENTINE. *Lady Anne*: Nora Brennan. *Lady Sybil*: Deborah Magid. *Sir Lionel*: William James. *King Pellinore*: PAXTON WHITEHEAD. *Horrid*: Bob. *Sir Lionel's Squire*: David Gaines. *Sir Sagramore's Squire*: Steve Soborn. *Sir Dinadan's Squire*: Herndon Lackey. *Knights of the Investiture*: Ken Henley, Gary Jaketic, Jack Sharkey, Ronald Bennett Stratton. *Tom*: THOR FIELDS.

Knights, Lords, Ladies of the Court: Nora Brennan, Jeanne Caryl, Melanie Clements, Stephanie Conlow, Van Craig, John Deyle, Debra Dickinson, Richard Dodd, Cecil Fulfer, Davis Gaines, Lisa Ann Grant, Ken Henley, John Herrera, Gary Jaketic, William James, Kelby Kirk, Herndon Lackey, Deborah Magid, Andy McAvin, Laura McCarthy, Robert Molnar, Steve Osborn, Patrice Pickering, Janelle Price, Nancy Rieth, Patrick Rogers, Deborah Roshe, D. Paul Shannon, Jack Starkey, Ronald Bennett Stratton, Sally Ann Swarm, Sally Williams. *Alternates*: Lynn Keeton, Richard Maxon.

Prologue: A Battlefield near Joyous Gard—A long time ago.

Act 1, Scene 1: A Hilltop near Camelot—Eight years earlier. *Scene 2*: Arthur's Study—Five years later. *Scene 3*: A Roadside near Camelot—A few months later. *Scene 4*: A Park near the Castle—Immediately following. *Scene 5*: A Terrace of the Castle—Two months later. *Scene 6*: The Jousting Fields—The next day. *Scene 7*: The Terrace—Early evening of that day. *Scene 8*: The Great Hall—Immediately following.

Prologue: The Castle Garden—A few years later. *Scene 1*: A Cloister on the castle grounds—Immediately following. *Scene 2*: The Terrace—A few weeks later. *Scene 3*: The Forest—The following day. *Scene 4*: The Queen's Bedchamber—Immediately following. *Scene 5*: Camelot—A month later. *Scene 6*: A Battlefield near Joyous Gard—A few weeks later.

ACT 1

Prologue

"Guenevere"

Ensemble

Scene 1

"I Wonder What the King is Doing Tonight?"

R. Burton

"The Simple Joys of Maidenhood"

C. Ebersole

"Camelot"

R. Burton, C. Ebersole

"Follow Me"

J. Caryl

Scene 2

"Camelot" (reprise)

R. Burton, C. Ebersole

Scene 3

"C'est Moi"

R. Muenz

Scene 4

"The Lusty Month of May"

C. Ebersole, Ensemble

Scene 5

"How to Handle a Woman"

R. Burton

Scene 6

"The Jousts"

R. Burton, C. Ebersole, Ensemble

Scene 7

"Before I Gaze at You Again"

C. Ebersole

ACT 2

Scene 1

"If Ever I Would Leave You"

R. Muenz

"The Seven Deadly Virtues"

R. Fox

Scene 2

"What Do the Simple Folk Do?"

C. Ebersole, R. Burton

[5]Originally produced in New York 3 December 1960 at the Majestic Theatre for 873 performances. This revival reduced the number of scenes from 20 to 14. The character of Morgan LeFey has been dropped. Musical Numbers dropped: "Then You May Take Me to the Fair," "The Persuasion." "Guenevere" moved from Act 2, Scene 7 to the beginning of Act 1.

"Fie on Goodness!"
R. Fox, Knights
Scene 4
"I Loved You Once in Silence"
C. Ebersole
Scene 5
"Guenevere" (reprise)
Ensemble
Scene 8
"Camelot" (reprise)
R. Burton

1980.20 FORTY-SECOND STREET

The Song and Dance Fable of Broadway (A Musical) in Two Acts, 16 Scenes. Lead ins and crossovers (Book) by Michael Stewart and Mark Bramble. Based on the novel of the same name by Bradford Ropes (and the Warner Brothers film adapted from it by Rian James and James Seymour.) Music by Harry Warren. Lyrics by Al Dubin. (Other lyrics by Johnny Mercer and Mort Dixon.) Direction and dances by Gower Champion. Scenery design by Robin Wagner. Costumes designed by Theoni V. Aldredge. Lighting designed by Tharon Musser. Musical direction and vocal arrangements by John Lesko. Orchestrations by Philip J. Lang. Dance arrangements by Donald Johnston. Sound by Richard Fitzgerald. Dance assistants, Karin Baker, Randy Skinner. Produced by David Merrick. Opened 25 August 1980 at the Winter Garden, moved 30 March 1981 to the Majestic Theatre, moved 7 April 1987 to the St. James Theatre and closed 8 January 1989 after 3486 performances.

CAST (in order of appearance): *Andy Lee*: DANNY CARROLL. *Oscar*: Robert Colston. *Mac*: Stan Page. *Annie*: KAREN PRUNCZIK. *Maggie Jones*: CAROLE COOK. *Bert Barry*: JOSEPH BOVA. *Billy Lawlor*: LEE ROY REAMS. *Peggy Sawyer*: WANDA RICHERT. *Lorraine*: Ginny King. *Phyllis*: Jeri Kansas. *Julian Marsh*: JERRY ORBACH. *Dorothy Brock*: TAMMY GRIMES. *Abner Dillon*: DON CRABTREE. *Pat Denning*: JAMES CONGDON. *Thugs*: Stan Page, Ron Schwinn. *Doctor*: Stan Page.

Ensemble: Carole Banninger, Steve Belin, Robin Black, Joel Blum, Mary Cadorette, Ronny DeVito, Denise DiRenzo, Mark Dovey, Rob Draper, Brandt Edwards, Jon Engstrom, Sharon Ferrol, Cathy Greco, Dawn Herbert, Christine Jacobsen, Jeri Kansas, Ginny King, Terri Ann Kundrat, Shan Martin, Beth McVey, Maureen Mellon, Sandra Menhart, Bill Nabel, Tony Parise, Don Percassi, Jean Preece, Vicki Regan, Lars Rosager, Linda Sabatelli, Nikki Sahagen, Ron Schwinn, Yveline Semeria, Alison Sherve, Robin Stephens, David Storey, Karen Tamburrelli.

The action takes place during 1933 in New York City and Philadelphia.

Act 1, Scene 1: 42nd Street Theatre, New York City. *Scene 2*: Gypsy Tea Kettle. *Scene 3*: On Stage. *Scene 4*: Dorothy Brock's Dressing Room. *Scene 5*: On Stage. *Scene 6*: Arch Street Theatre, Philadelphia. *Scene 7*: Regency Club and Dorothy Brock's Suite at Hotel Stratford. *Scene 8*; Opening Night, Arch Street Theatre, Philadelphia.

Act 2, Scene 1: Outside Dorothy Brock's Dressing Room, ten minutes later. *Scene 2*: Dressing Rooms at the Arch Street Theatre. *Scene 3*: Stage of the Arch Street Theatre. *Scene 4*: Broad Street Station, Philadelphia. *Scene 5*: 42nd Street Theater, New York City. *Scene 6*: Peggy's Dressing Room. *Scene 7*: Opening Night of "Pretty Lady," 42nd Street Theatre, New York City. *Scene 8*: Backstage.

ACT 1
Scene 1
"Audition" (42nd Street instrumental)
D. Carroll, Ensemble
"Young and Healthy"
L. R. Reams, W. Richert
"Shadow Waltz" (from *GOLDDIGGERS OF 1933* film)
C. Cook, T. Grimes, Girls
"Shadow Waltz" (reprise)
T. Grimes
Scene 2
"Go into Your Dance" (from *GO INTO YOUR DANCE* film, 1935)
C. Cook, W. Richert, K. Prunczik, D. Carroll, G. King, J. Kansas
Scene 3
"You're Getting to Be a Habit With Me"
T. Grimes, L. R. Reams, W. Richert, Ensemble
Scene 5
"Getting Out of Town" (Excerpt from "Gotta Go to Town" from *THE LAUGH PARADE*, film)
J. Congdon, J. Bova, C. Cook, K. Prunczik, T. Grimes, Ensemble
(*Lyrics by* Mort Dixon.)
Scene 6
"Dames" (from *DAMES* film, 1934)
L. R. Reams, Ensemble
Scene 7
"I Know Now" (from *THE SINGING MARINE* film, 1937)
T. Grimes
Scene 8
"I Know Now" (reprise)
L. R. Reams, Girls
"We're in the Money" (from *GOLDDIGGERS OF 1933* film)
K. Prunczik, W. Richert, G. King, J. Kansas, L. R. Reams, Ensemble
Act One Finale
T. Grimes, W. Richert, Full Company
ACT 2
Scene 2
"Sunny Side to Every Situation" (from *HARD TO GET* film, 1938)
K. Prunczik, Ensemble
(*Lyrics by* Johnny Mercer.)
Scene 4
"Lullaby of Broadway" (from *GOLDDIGGERS OF 1935* film)
J. Orbach, Full Company
Scene 6
"About a Quarter to Nine" (from *GO INTO YOUR DANCE* film, 1935)
T. Grimes, W. Richert
Scene 7
"Pretty Lady" Overture
Orchestra
"Shuffle Off to Buffalo"
K. Prunczik, J. Bova, C. Cook, Girls
"Forty-Second Street"
W. Richert, L. R. Reams, Ensemble
Scene 8
"Forty Second Street" (reprise)
J. Orbach

1980.21 THE STUDENT PRINCE

A Revival of the Operetta in Three Acts, a Prologue and 4 Scenes[6]. Music by Sigmund Romberg. Book and lyrics by Dorothy Donnelly. (Based on the play "Old Heidelberg" by Rudolf Bleichmann, adapted from "Alt-Heidelberg" by Wilhelm Meyer-Förster.) Book adaptation by Hugh Wheeler. Conducted by Andrew Meltzer. Directed by Jack Hofsis. Assistant stage Director, Christian Smith. Scenery designed by David Jenkins Costumes designed by Patton Campbell. Lighting designed by Gilbert V. Hemsley, Jr. Choreography by Donald Saddler. Chorus master, Lloyd Walser. Produced by the New York City Opera. Opened 29 August 1980 at the New York State Theatre and closed 7 September 1980 after 13 performances.

CAST (in order of their appearance): *Lackeys*: Edward Zimmerman, Louis Perry, Harris Davis, Mervin Crook. *Dr. Engel*, the Prince's Tutor: DOMINIC COSSA. *Count von Mark*: DAVID RAE SMITH. *Secretaries*: Sven Leaf, Barry Carl. *Prince Karl Franz*: JACQUE TRUSSEL. *Lutz*, valet to the Prince: JAMES BILLINGS. *Gretchen*, Maid at the Inn: MARTHA THIGPEN. *Ruder*: Dan Sullivan. *Nicholas*: Robert LaFosse. *Toni*, a waiter: Jack Harrold. *Hubert*: Harlan Foss. *Detlef*, a student leader: John Lankston. *von Asterberg*, another student leader: Thomas Jamerson. *Lucas*, another student leader: Ralph Bassett. *Freshman*: Louis Perry. *Kathie*, niece of Ruder: LEIGH MUNRO. *Girls*: Madeleine Mines, Jean Rawn, Barbara Wright. *Students*: Dominick Farone, Louis Perry, Merle Schmidt, Spencer Smith. *Grand Duchess Anastasia*: MURIEL COSTA-GREENSPON. *Princess Margaret*, fiancée of Prince Karl Franz: KATHRYN BOULEYN. *Captain Tarnitz*: JOSEPH EVANS. *Countess Leydon*, lady-in-waiting to the Princess: Jane Shaulis. *Huzzars*: Richard Nelson, Herbert Hunsberger, Robert Brubaker, Merle Schmidt. *Friends of the Huzzars*: Madeleine Mines, Jean Rawn, Barbara Wright, Maria Donaldi.

Ensemble: New York City Opera Chorus.

The action takes place in Karlsberg, Germany in the Golden Years.

Prologue: Garden of the Palace at Karlsberg.

---

[6]First produced in New York 2 December 1924 as *THE STUDENT PRINCE IN HEIDELBERG* at the Jolson Theatre for 608 peformances. This production was made possible by a generous and deeply appreciated gift from The Fan Fox and Leslie R. Samuels Foundation, Inc.

Act 1: Garden of the Inn of the Three Golden Apples in Heidelberg.

Act 2: Prince Karl Franz's rooms at the Inn. Four months later.

Act 3, Scene 1: The Royal Palace at Karlsberg. *Scene 2*: Garden of the Inn of the Three Golden Apples. The next day.

PROLOGUE
"By Our Bearing So Sedate"
Lackeys
"Golden Days"
D. R. Smith, J. Trussel
ACT 1
"Garlands Bright With Glowing Flowers"
M. Thigpen, D. Sullivan, Girls
"To the Inn We're Marching" (Students Marching Song)
J. Lankston, R. Bassett, T. Jamerson, Students
"Drink, Drink, Drink" (Drinking Song)
J. Lankston, R. Bassett, T. Jamerson, Students
"Come Boys, Let's All Be Gay, Boys"
L. Munro, J. Lankston, R. Bassett, T. Jamerson, Students
"Drink, Drink, Drink"/"To the Inn We're Marching" (reprise)
J. Lankston, R. Bassett, T. Jamerson, Students
"Heidelberg, Beloved Vision of My Heart"
D. Cossa, J. Trussel, L. Munro, D. Sullivan, M. Thigpen, Girls
"Gaudeamus Igitur"
Students
"Golden Days" (reprise)
D. Cossa
"Deep in My Heart, Dear"
L. Munro, J. Trussel
"Come Sir, Will You Join Our Noble Saxon Corps"
Students
"Overhead the Moon Is Beaming" (Serenade)
J. Trussel, Students
"When the Spring Wakens Everything" (Carnival of Springtime)
Company
ACT 2
"Farmer Jacob Lay Asnoring"
Students
"Student Life"
Company
"Golden Days" (reprise)
J. Trussel, D. Cossa
"Thoughts Will Come to Me"
J. Trussel, D. Cossa
Finale
L. Munro, J. Trussel
ACT 3
Scene 1
Ballet
Orchestra
"Just We Two"
K. Bouleyn, J. Evans, Men
"What Memories, Sweet Rose"
Company
Scene 2
"Let Us Sing a Song"
Students
"If He Knew"
L. Munro, K. Bouleyn
Finale
Company

1980.22 DIE FLEDERMAUS

A Revival of the Operetta in Three Acts[7]. Original libretto by Carl Haffner and Richard Genée. Lyrics by Richard Genée. Based on the comedy "Le Réveillon" by Henri Meilhac and Ludovic Halévy. English libretto by Ruth and Thomas Martin. Production devised and directed by Gerald Freedman. Choreography by Thomas Andrew. Music by Johann Strauss. Scenery designed by Lloyd Evans Costumes design by Theoni V. Aldredge. Lighting by Hans Sondheimer. Conducted by Imre Pallo. Chorus master, Lloyd Walser. Produced by the New York City Opera. Opened 12 September 1980 at the New York State Theatre and closed 20 September 1980 after 4 performances in repertory.

CAST (in order of appearance): *Alfred*, an itinerant tenor: Henry Price. *Adele*, von Eisenstein's chambermaid: INGA NIELSEN. *Rosalinda von Eisenstein*: MARALIN NISKA. *Gabriel von Eisenstein*: ALAN TITUS. *Dr. Blind*, a lawyer: Norman Large. *Dr. Falke*, a close friend of Eisenstein: RICHARD FREDERICKS. *Frank*, the prison warden: HARLAN FOSS. *Sally*, Adele's sister: Puli Toro. *Ivan*, servant to Orlofsky: Gary J. Dietrich. *Prince Orlofsky*, a wealthy, bored Russian: JAMES BILLINGS. *Frosch*, the jailer: Jack Harrold. *Solo Dancers*: Esperanza Galan, Taras Kalba. *Special Guest*: CYNTHIA GREGORY. (Miss Gregory's solo choreographed by Dennis Nahat.)
Ensemble: New York City Opera Chorus.

1980.23 CHARLIE AND ALGERNON

A Very Special Musical in One Act[8]. Book and lyrics by David Rogers. Based on the novel "Flowers for Algernon" by Daniel Keyes. Music by Charles Strouse. Directed by Louis W. Scheeder. Musical director, Conductor, Liza Redfield. Choreography by Virginia Freeman. Orchestrations by Philip J. Lang. Scenery by Kate Edmunds. Costumes by Jess Goldstein. Lighting by Hugh Lester. Sound by William H. Clements. Produced for the Kennedy Center and the Folger Theatre Group by Michael Sheehan and Louis W. Scheeder. Produced by The Kennedy Center, Isobel Robins Konecky, the Fisher Theater Foundation and the Folger Theatre Group. Opened 14 September 1980 at the Helen Hayes Theatre and closed 28 September 1980 after 17 performances.

CAST (in order of appearance): *Charlie*: P. J. BENJAMIN. *Alice Kinnian*: SANDY FAISON. *Dr. Strauss*: EDWARD EARLE. *Dr. Nemur*: ROBERT SEVRA. *Mrs. Donner*: Nancy Franklin. *Lita*: Loida Santos. *Frank*: Patrick Jude. *Charlie's Mother*: Julienne Marie. *Little Charlie*: Matthew Duda. *Charlie's Father*: Michael Vita.

The action takes place at the present time in Brooklyn and Manhattan.

MUSICAL NUMBERS
"Have I the Right"
S. Faison, R. Sevra, E. Earle
"I Got a Friend"
P. J. Benjamin
"I Got a Friend" (reprise)
P. J. Benjamin, S. Faison
"Some Bright Morning"
R. Sevra, P. J. Benjamin, E. Earle, S. Faison
"Jelly Donuts and Chocolate Cake"
N. Franklin, L. Santos, P. Jude
"Hey Look at Me"
P. J. Benjamin, S. Faison
"Reading"
P. J. Benjamin, S. Faison
"No Surprises"
S. Faison
"Midnight Riding"
P. Jude, L. Santos
"Dream Safe With Me"
J. Marie
"Not Another Day Like This"
J. Marie, M. Vita
"Somebody New"
N. Franklin, P. J. Benjamin
"I Can't Tell You"
P. J. Benjamin
"Now"
P. J. Benjamin, S. Faison
"Charlie and Algernon"
P. J. Benjamin

[7]First English language production in New York 16 March 1885 at the Casino Theatre for 42 performances. First New York production of this adaptation 20 December 1950 at the Metropolitan Opera House. For Synopsis of Scenes and Musical Numbers, see May 1954 revival.

[8]Previously produced in London under the title *FLOWERS FOR ALGERNON*.

"The Maze"
P. J. Benjamin
"Whatever Time There Is"
S. Faison, P. J. Benjamin
"Everything Was Perfect"
E. Earle, R. Sevra
"Charlie"
P. J. Benjamin
"I Really Loved You"
P. J. Benjamin
"Whatever Time There Is" (reprise)
S. Faison

INSIDEOUTANDALLAROUND with Shelley Berman

1980.24

A One Man Show in Two Acts. Production supervisor, Kitzi Becker. Production advisor, Richard G. Miller. Produced by Arthur Shafman International, Ltd. Opened 29 September 1980 at the Bijou Theatre and closed 25 October 1980 after 24 performances.

CAST: SHELLEY BERMAN (Comedy monologues).

SILVERLAKE, or A Winter's Tale

1980.25

A Revival of the Play with Music (Opera) in Two Acts, 11 Scenes[9]. Original German libretto (Der Silbersee) by Georg Kaiser. Music by Kurt Weill. New book by Hugh Wheeler. New lyrics by Lys Symonette. Selections of Weill's incidental music integrated by Lys Symonette. Directed by Harold Prince. Conducted by Julius Rudel. Choreography by Larry Fuller. Scenery and costumes designed by Manuel Lutgenhorst. Lighting designed by Ken Billington. Musical preparation by Robert De Ceunynck, Scott Bergeson. Chorus master, Lloyd Walser. Sound designed by Jack Mann. Produced by the New York City Opera and Gert von Gontard. Opened 11 October 1980 at the New York State Theatre and closed 19 October 1980 after 4 performances in repertory.

CAST (in order of appearance): *Johann*: Harlan Foss. *Dietrich*: Robert McFarland. *Severin*: WILLIAM NEILL. *Heckler*: Edward Zimmerman. *Klaus*: James Clark. *Hans*: Norman Large. *Hunger*: Gary Chryst. *Salesgirls*: Penny Orloff, Jane Shaulis. *Handke*: David Rae Smith. *Officer Olim*: JOHN LANKSTON. *City Inspector*: William Poplaski. *Lottery Agent*: JACK HARROLD. *Doctor*: Richard Nelson. *Baron Laur*: JACK HARROLD. *Fennimore*: KATHLEEN HEGIERSKI. *Liveried Footman*: Gary Dietrich. *Frau von Luber*: MURIEL COSTA-GREENSPON. *Chefs*: Michael Rubino, Rafael Romero. *Ensemble*: New York City Opera Chorus.

BRIGADOON

1980.26

A Revival of the Musical Play in Two Acts, 12 Scenes[10]. Book and lyrics by Alan Jay Lerner. Music by Frederick Loewe. Choreography and musical staging by Agnes de Mille, recreated by James Jamieson. Directed by Vivian Matalon. Scenery designed by Michael J. Hotopp and Paul dePass. Costumes designed by Stanley Simmons. Lighting designed by Thomas Skelton. Musical direction and vocal arrangements by Wally Harper. Orchestrations by Mack Schlefer, Bill Brohn. Sound by T. Richard Fitzgerald. A Wolf Trap Production (Craig Hankenson, Executive producer.) Produced by Zev Bufman and The Shubert Organization. Opened 16 October 1980 at the Majestic Theatre and closed 8 February 1981 after 133 performances.

CAST (in order of appearance): *Tommy Albright*: MARTIN VIDNOVIC. *Jeff Douglas*: MARK ZIMMERMAN. *Angus MacGuffie*: Kenneth Kantor. *Archie Beaton*: Casper Roos. *Sandy Dean*: Michael Cone. *Maggie Anderson*: MARINA EGLEVSKY. *Harry Beaton*: JOHN CURRY. *Meg Brockie*: ELAINE HAUSMAN *Andrew MacLaren*: Jack Dabdoub. *Fiona MacLaren*: MEG BUSSERT. *Jean MacLaren*: Mollie Smith. *Charlie Dalrymple*: STEPHEN LEHEW. *Mr. Lundie*: Frank Hamilton. *Jane Ashton*: Betsy Craig.

Townsfolk of Brigadoon: *Singers*: Michael Cone, Betsy Craig, Larry French, Linda Hohenfeld, Michael Hayward-Jones, Joseph Kolinski, Diane Pennington, Cheryl Russell, Linda Wonneberger. *Dancers*: Bill Badolato, Cherie Bower, Amy Danis, Tom Fowler, John Giffin, Mickey Gunnersen, Jennifer Henson, David Hughes, Phil LaDuca, Elena Malfitano, Susie McCarter, Jerry Mitchell, Eric Nesbitt, Holly Reeve, Dale Robbins, Harry Williams. *Swing Dancers/Singers*: Randal Harris, Suzi Winson. *Bagpiper*: Larry Cole.

Act 1, Scene 1: A Hillside in Scotland. *Scene 2*: MacConnachy Square (in the village of Brigadoon). *Scene 3*: A Hillside in Brigadoon. *Scene 4*: The Brockie Shed. *Scene 5*: Outside the MacLaren House.

Act 2, Scene 1: Outside Mr. Lundie's House *Scene 2*: The Glen. *Scene 3*: The Forest. *Scene 4*: Outside the MacLaren House. *Scene 5*: A Hillside in Scotland. *Scene 6*: A Cocktail Bar in New York City. *Scene 7*: A Hillside in Scotland.

ACT 1
Scene 1
"Once in the Highlands"
Ensemble
"Brigadoon"
Ensemble
Scene 2
"Down on MacConnachy Square"
M. Cone, E. Hausman, Townsfolk
"Waitin' for My Dearie"
M. Bussert, Girls
"I'll Go Home With Bonnie Jean"
S. Lehew, Men
Danced by J. Curry, M. Eglevsky Townsfolk.
Scene 3
"The Heather on the Hill"
M. Vidnovic, M. Bussert
"Rain Exorcism"
Townsfolk
Scene 4
"The Love of My Life"
E. Hausman
Scene 5
"Jeannie's Packing Up"
Danced by Girls
"Come to Me, Bend to Me"
S. Lehew
Danced by M. Smith, Girls.
"Almost Like Being in Love"
M. Vidnovic, M. Bussert

ACT 2
Scene 2
"Wedding Dance"
M. Smith, S. Lehew, Townsfolk
"Sword Dance"
J. Mitchell, Sword Dancers, Dancers
Scene 3
"The Chase"
J. Curry, Men of Brigadoon
"There But For You Go I"
M. Vidnovic, M. Bussert
Scene 4
"Steps Stately"
Danced by Townsfolk
"Drunken Reel"
Danced by Townsfolk
"Funeral Dance"
Danced by M. Eglevsky
Scene 5
"From This Day On"
M. Vidnovic, M. Bussert
"Brigadoon" (reprise)
Ensemble

[9]Originally produced in New York 20 March 1980 at the New York State Theatre for 6 performances. For Synopsis of Scenes and Musical Numbers, see March 1980 production.

[10]Originally produced in New York 13 March 1947 at the Ziegfeld Theatre for 581 performances. The original production was in Two Acts, 11 Scenes and a Prologue; for this production the book was revised into Two Acts, 12 Scenes, and scene descriptions, the intermission placement and song order have been slightly altered. "My Mother's Wedding Day" was dropped.

Scene 6
"Come to Me, Bend to Me" (reprise)
M. Bussert
"The Heather on the Hill" (reprise)
M. Bussert
Scene 7
"From This Day On" (reprise)
M. Vidnovic
"Brigadoon" (reprise)
Ensemble

1980.27 TINTYPES

A Musical (Revue) in Two Acts, 13 Scenes[11]. Conceived by Mary Kyte, Mel Marvin and Gary Pearle. Directed by Gary Pearle. Musical staging by Mary Kyte. Settings by Tom Lynch. Costumes by Jess Goldstein. Lighting by Paul Gallo. Sound design by Jack Mann. Musical and vocal arrangements by Mel Marvin. Orchestrations and vocal arrangements by John McKinney. Production coordinator, Brent Peek. An American National Theatre and Academy Production. Originally produced by the Arena Stage, Washington, D.C. Produced by Richmond Crinkley and Royal Pardon Productions, Ivan Bloch, Larry J. Silva, Eve Skina in association with Joan F. Tobin. Opened 23 October 1980 at the John Golden Theatre and closed 11 January 1981 after 93 performances. Total, including Off-Broadway, 230 performances.

CAST (in alphabetical order): Carolyn Mignini, Lynne Thigpen, Trey Wilson, Mary Catherine Wright, Jerry Zaks. *At the Piano*: Mel Marvin.

Act 1, Scene 1: Arrivals. *Scene 2*: Ingenuity and Inventions. *Scene 3*: TR (Teddy Roosevelt). *Scene 4*: Wheels. *Scene 5*: The Factory. *Scene 6*: Anna Held. *Scene 7*: Outside Looking In. *Scene 8*: Fitting In.

Act 2, Scene 1: Panama. *Scene 2*; The Ladies. *Scene 3*: Rich and Poor. *Scene 4*: Vaudeville. *Scene 5*: Finale.

ACT 1
Scene 1
"Ragtime Nightingale"
(*Music and Lyrics by* Joseph F. Lamb.)(1915)
"The Yankee Doodle Boy" (from *LITTLE JOHNNY JONES*, 1904)
(*Music and Lyrics by* George M. Cohan.)
"Ta-Ra-Ra Boom-De-Ay!"
(*Music and Lyrics by* Henry J. Sayers.)(1891)
"I Don't Care"
(*Music by* Harry O. Sutton. *Lyrics by* Jean Lenox.)(1905)
"Come Take a Trip in My Airship"
(*Music and Lyrics by* George Evans and Ren Shields.)(1904)
"Kentucky Babe"
(*Music and Lyrics by* Richard H. Buck and Adam Geibel.)(1896)
"A Hot Time in the Old Town Tonight"
(*Music by* Theodore H. Metz. *Lyrics by* Joe Hayden.)(1896)
"Stars and Stripes Forever"
(*Music by* John Philip Sousa.)(1897)
Scene 2
"Electricity"
(*Music by* Karl Hoschna. *Lyrics by* Harry B. Smith.)(1905)
Scene 3
"El Capitan" (from *EL CAPITAN*, 1896)
(*Music by* John Philip Sousa.)
Scene 4
"Pastime Rag"
(*Music by* Artie Matthews.)(1920)
"Meet Me in St. Louis"
(*Music by* Kerry Mills. *Lyrics by* Andrew B. Sterling.)(1904)
"Solace"
(*Music by* Scott Joplin.)
"Waltz Me Around Again Willie" (from *HIS HONOR, THE MAYOR*, 1906)
(*Music by* Ren Shields. *Lyrics by* Will D. Cobb.)

[11]Originally produced in New York Off-Broadway 17 April 1980 at the Theater at St. Peter's Church for 137 performances.

"Wabash Cannonball" (traditional)
"In My Merry Oldsmobile"
(*Music by* Gus Edwards. *Lyrics by* Vincent P. Bryan.)(1905)
Scene 5
"Wayfaring Stranger" (traditional)
"Sometimes I Feel Like a Motherless Child" (traditional)
"Aye, Lye, Lyu Lye" (traditional)
"I'll Take You Home Again Kathleen"
(*Music and Lyrics by* Thomas P. Westendorf.)(1876)
"America the Beautiful"
(*Music and Lyrics by* Katherine Lee Bates and Samuel Ward.)(1910)
"Wait for the Wagon" (traditional)
"What It Takes to Make Me Love You—You've Got It"
(*Music and Lyrics by* J. W. Johnson and James Reese Europe.)(1914)
Scene 6
"The Maiden With the Dreamy Eyes" (from *THE LITTLE DUCHESS*, 1901)
(*Music by* Bob Cole. *Lyrics by* James Weldon Johnson.)
"If I Were on the Stage (Kiss Me Again)" (from *MADEMOSIELLE MODISTE*, 1905)
(*Music by* Victor Herbert. *Lyrics by* Henry Blossom.)
Scene 7
"Shortnin' Bread"
(traditional; *Music by* Reese 'Pree.)(1905)
"Nobody"
(*Music by* Alex Rogers. *Lyrics by* Bert Williams.)
(interpolated into *ZIEGFELD FOLLIES OF 1910*)
Scene 8
"Elite Syncopations"
(*Music by* Scott Joplin.)(1902)
"I'm Goin' to Live Anyhow, 'Til I Die"
(*Music and Lyrics by* Shepard N. Edmonds.)(1900)

ACT 2
"The Ragtime Dance"
(*Music by* Scott Joplin.)(1902)
Scene 1
"I Want What I Want When I Want It" (from *MADEMOISELLE MODISTE*, 1905)
(*Music by* Victor Herbert. *Lyrics by* Henry Blossom.)
Scene 2
"It's Delightful to Be Married" (from *A PARISIAN MODEL*, 1907)
(*Music by* Vincent Scotto. *Lyrics by* Anna Held.)
"Fifty-Fifty"
(*Music and Lyrics by* Jim Burris and Chris Smith.)(1914)
"American Beauty"
(*Music and Lyrics by* Joseph F. Lamb.)(1913)
Scene 3
"Then I'd Be Satisfied With Life" (from *RUNNING FOR OFFICE*, 1903)
(*Music and Lyrics by* George M. Cohan.)
"Narcissus"
(*Music by* Ethelbert Nevin.)(1891)
"Jonah Man"
(*Music and Lyrics by* Alex Rogers.)(1903)
"When It's All Goin' Out and Nothin' Comin' In" (from *SALLY IN OUR ALLEY*, 1902)
(*Music and Lyrics by* Bert Williams and George Walker.)
"We Shall Not Be Moved" (traditional)
Scene 4
"Hello, Ma Baby"
(*Music by* Joseph E. Howard. *Lyrics by* Ida Emerson.)(1899)
"Teddy Da Roose"
(*Music and Lyrics by* Ed Moran and J. Fred Helf.)(1910)
"A Bird in a Gilded Cage"
(*Music by* Arthur J. Lamb and Harry von Tilzer.)(1900)
"Bill Bailey, Won't You Please Come Home"
(*Music and Lyrics by* Hughie Cannon.)(1902)

"She's Gettin' More Like the White Folks Every Day"
(*Music and Lyrics by* Bert Williams and George Walker.)(1901)
"You're a Grand Old Flag" (frm *GEORGE WASHINGTON, JR.*)(1906)
(*Music and Lyrics by* George M. Cohan.)
"The Yankee Doodle Boy" (reprise)
Scene 5
"Toyland" (from *BABES IN TOYLAND*, 1903)
(*Music by* Victor Herbert. *Lyrics by* Glen MacDonough.)
"Smiles" (from *THE PASSING SHOW OF 1918*)
(*Music by* Lee G. Roberts. *Lyrics by* J. Will Callahan.)

1980.28

QUICK CHANGE

A Revue in Two Acts, 8 Scenes. Written by Bruce Belland, Roy M. Rogosin, Michael McGiveney. Directed by Roy M. Rogosin. Music by Roy M. Rogosin. Lyrics by Bruce Belland. Costumes by Mary Wills. Set by John Shipley, Chris Flower. Sound by Alan Chapman, Eric Neufeld. Production advisor, Richard G. Miller. Produced by Arthur Shafman International Ltd. Opened 30 October 1980 at the Bijou Theatre and closed 2 November 1980 after 5 performances.

CAST: MICHAEL McGIVENEY, assisted by Judith Hudson, Mark Bodine, Chris Flower.

ACT 1
Scene 1
Carnival
Scene 2
The Triumph of Arthur
Scene 3
The Lady Recites
Scene 4
Bill Sikes (from Charles Dickens' "Oliver Twist" celebrating 75 years of family tradition.)
ACT 2
Scene 1
Pitchman and the Cop
Scene 2
Quicker Than the Eye
Scene 3
A Misunderstood Minority
Scene 4
Shoot-Out at Belle's Saloon

1980.29

PERFECTLY FRANK

A Musical Revue in Two Acts, a Prologue and 11 Scenes. Conceived and written by Kenny Solms. Music and lyrics by Frank Loesser. Scenery and costumes designed by John Falabella. Lighting designed by Ken Billington. Musical director, Yolanda Segovia. Directed by Fritz Holt. Choreography by Tony Stevens. Music consultant, Larry Grossman. Orchestrations by Bill Byers. Dance arrangements by Ronald Melrose. Sound designed by Larry Spurgeon. Associate producer, Vivian Serota. Produced by Gladys Rackmill and Fred Levinson in association with Emhan Inc. Opened 30 November 1980 at the Helen Hayes Theatre and closed 13 December 1980 after 17 performances.

CAST (in alphabetical order): Andra Akers, Wayne Cilento, Jill Cook, Don Correia, David Holliday, David Ruprecht, Virginia Sandifur, Debbie Shapiro, Jo Sullivan, Jim Walton.

Act 1, Scene 1: Screen Test. *Scene 2*: USO Show. *Scene 3*: Dressing Room. *Scene 4*: Understudy Rehearsal. *Scene 5*: Manhattan.

Act 2, Scene 1: Rumble Rumble. *Scene 2*: Marriage. *Scene 3*: Rosabella. *Scene 4*: Dressing Room. *Scene 5*: Blues. *Scene 6*: Finale.

ACT 1[12]
Prologue
"Three Cornered Tune" (from *GUYS AND DOLLS*)
Company
"I Hear Music" (from *DANCING ON A DIME* film)
Company
(*Music by* Burton Lane.)
Scene 1
"Kiss the Boys Goodbye" (from *KISS THE BOYS GOODBYE* film)
V. Sandifur
(*Music by* Victor Schertzinger.)
"Snug as a Bug in a Rug" (from *THE GRACIE ALLEN MURDER CASE* film)
V. Sandifur
(*Music by* Matt Malneck.)
"The Moon of Manakoora" (from *THE HURRICANE* film)
V. Sandifur
(*Music by* Alfred Newman.)
"The Boys in the Backroom" (from *DESTRY RIDES AGAIN* film)
V. Sandifur
(*Music by* Frederick Hollander.)
Scene 2
"Murder, He Says" (from *HAPPY GO LUCKY* film)
J. Cook, W. Cilento
(*Music by* Jimmy McHugh)
"Some Like It Hot" (from *SOME LIKE IT HOT* film)
(*Music by* Gene Krupa and Remo Biondi.)
"I Don't Want to Walk Without You" (from *SWEATER GIRL* film)
D. Shapiro
(*Music by* Jule Styne.)
"Roseanna" (from *ROSEANNA McCOY* film)
J. Walton
"I Wish I Didn't Love You So" (from *THE PERILS OF PAULINE* film)
D. Holliday
"Where Are You Now (That I Need You?)" (from *RED, HOT AND BLUE* film)
D. Holliday
"They're Either Too Young or Too Old" (from *THANK YOUR LUCKY STARS*
film)
A. Akers
(*Music by* Arthur Schwartz.)
"What Do You Do in the Infantry?"
A. Akers, Men
"Praise the Lord and Pass the Ammunition"
D. Holliday
"Spring Will Be a Little Late This Year"
J. Sullivan
Scene 3
"I Believe in You" (from *HOW TO SUCCEED IN BUSINESS ....*)
D. Ruprecht, Men
Scene 4
"Make a Miracle" (from *WHERE'S CHARLEY?*)
D. Correia, J. Cook
"My Darling, My Darling" (from *WHERE'S CHARLEY?*)
D. Correia, J. Cook
Scene 5
"My Time of Day" (from *GUYS AND DOLLS*)
D. Holliday
"Two Sleepy People" (from *THANKS FOR THE MEMORY* film)
A. Akers, D. Ruprecht
(*Music by* Hoagy Carmichael.)
"No Two People" (from *HANS CHRISTIAN ANDERSEN* film)
D. Correia, J. Cook
"Baby, It's Cold Outside" (from *NEPTUNE'S DAUGHTER* film)
V. Sandifur, J. Walton
"Luck Be a Lady" (from *GUYS AND DOLLS*)
D. Holliday
"Fugue for Tinhorns" (from *GUYS AND DOLLS*)
D. Shapiro, W. Cilento, D. Holliday
"Take Back Your Mink" (from *GUYS AND DOLLS*)
V. Sandifur

[12]Song list not included in program, but was prepared from management and press materials.

"How'dja Like to Love Me?" (from *COLLEGE SWING* film)
J. Cook
(*Music by* Burton Lane.)
"The Lady's in Love With You" (from *SOME LIKE IT HOT* film)
D. Shapiro
(*Music by* Burton Lane.)
"Guys and Dolls" (from *GUYS AND DOLLS*)
Company
"I've Never Been in Love Before" (from *GUYS AND DOLLS*)
D. Holliday, Company

ACT 2
Entr'acte: Medley from *HANS CHRISTIAN ANDERSEN* film

Scene 1
"Rumble, Rumble, Rumble" (from *THE PERILS OF PAULINE* film)
D. Shapiro, J. Walton, J. Cook

Scene 2
"Standing on the Corner" (from *THE MOST HAPPY FELLA*)
D. Ruprecht, W. Cilento, J. Walton
"Once in Love With Amy" (from *WHERE'S CHARLEY?*)
W. Cilento
"Marry the Man Today" (from *GUYS AND DOLLS*)
V. Sandifur, A. Akers, J. Cook
"Happy To Keep His Dinner Warm" (from *HOW TO SUCCEED IN BUSINESS . . .*)
V. Sandifur
"Never Will I Marry" (from *GREENWILLOW*)
J. Walton
"Adelaide's Lament" (from *GUYS AND DOLLS*)
A. Akers

Scene 3
"Ooh, My Feet!"
"I Like Everybody"
"I Don't Know Nothing About You" (The Letter)
J. Sullivan, D. Holliday
"Somebody Somewhere"
J. Sullivan
"Rosabella"
D. Holliday
"Warm All Over"
J. Sullivan
"Like a Woman Loves a Man"
J. Sullivan
"My Heart Is So Full of You"
D. Holliday
(all of the above from *THE MOST HAPPY FELLA*)

Scene 4
Central Park Duck
J. Sullivan

Scene 5
"Can't Get Out of This Mood" (from *SEVEN DAYS LEAVE* film)
V. Sandifur
(*Music by* Jimmy McHugh.)
"Luck Be a Lady" Dance (from *GUYS AND DOLLS*)
D. Shapiro, D. Correia
"Junk Man"
D. Shapiro
(*Music by* Joseph Meyer.)

Scene 6
"More I Cannot Wish You" (from *GUYS AND DOLLS*)
Company
"If I Were a Bell" (from *GUYS AND DOLLS*)
V. Sandifur, D. Holliday
"Hoop-Dee-Do"
W. Cilento, V. Sandifur, D. Correia, J. Cook
(*Music by* Milton Delugg.)
"Just Another Polka"
Company
(*Music by* Milton Delugg.)
"The New Ashmolean Marching Society and Students Conservatory Band"
(from *WHERE'S CHARLEY?*)
Company
"Bubbles in the Wine"
D. Ruprecht
(*Music by* Lawrence Welk.)
"What Are You Doing New Year's Eve?"
D. Holliday, D. Shapiro
"Sposalizio" (from *THE MOST HAPPY FELLA*)
Company
"Jingle, Jangle, Jingle" (from *THE FOREST RANGERS* film)
W. Cilento, D. Correia
(*Music by* Joseph J. Lilley.)
"Big D" (from *THE MOST HAPPY FELLA*)
J. Cook, W. Cilento, D. Correia, D. Shapiro
"Anywhere I Wander" (from *HANS CHRISTIAN ANDERSEN* film)
J. Sullivan
"Sand in My Shoes" (from *KISS THE BOYS GOODBYE* film)
A. Akers
(*Music by* Victor Schertzinger.)
"Sing a Tropical Song" (from *HAPPY GO LUCKY* film)
D. Ruprecht, A. Akers
(*Music by* Jimmy McHugh.)
"Dolores" (from *LAS VEGAS NIGHTS* film)
D. Holliday, Men
(*Music by* Louis Alter.)
"Sit Down You're Rockin' the Boat" (from *GUYS AND DOLLS*)
Company
"Brotherhood of Man" (from *HOW TO SUCCEED IN BUSINESS . . .*)
Company
"On a Slow Boat to China"
V. Sandifur
"Small Fry" (from *SING YOU SINNERS* film)
J. Cook
(*Music by* Hoagy Carmichael.)
"A Bushel and a Peck" (from *GUYS AND DOLLS*)
A. Akers
"Heart and Soul" (from *A SONG IS BORN* film short)
Company
(*Music by* Hoagy Carmichael.)

1980.30 ONWARD VICTORIA

A Musical in Two Acts, 17 Scenes[13]. Book and lyrics by Charlotte Anker and Irene Rosenberg. Music by Keith Herrmann. Directed by Julianne Boyd. Musical numbers staged by Michael Shawn. Scenic design by William Rittman. Costumes by Theoni V. Aldredge. Lighting by Richard Nelson. Music direction by Larry Blank. Orchestrations by Michael Gibson. Dance arrangements by Donald Johnston. Vocal arrangements by Keith Herrmann, Larry Blank. Sound design by Lewis Mead. Produced by John N. Hart, Jr. in association with Hugh J. Hubbard and Robert M. Browne. Opened and closed 14 December 1980 at the Martin Beck Theatre after 1 performance.

CAST (in order of appearance): *Little Girl*: Lora Jeanne Martens. *Victoria Woodhull*: JILL EIKENBERRY. *Tennie Claflin*: BETH AUSTIN. *Telegraph Boy*: Marty McDonough. *Jim*: Dan Cronin. *Cornelius Vanderbilt*: TED THURSTON. *Mrs. Fleming*: Carrie Wilder. *Mrs. Baxter*: Karen Gibson. *Mrs. Randolph*: Lora Jeanne Martens. *Fleming*: Gordon Stanley. *Randolph*: Marty McDonough. *Baxter*: John Kildahl. *Woman Investor #1*: Carol Lurie. *Johnson*: Scott Fless. *Perkins*: Ian Michael Towers. *William Evarts*: REX HAYS. *Woman Investor #2*: Dru Alexandrine. *Beth Tilton*: MARTHA JEAN STERNER. *Theodore Tilton*: EDMOND GENEST. *Elizabeth Cady Stanton*: LAURA WATERBURY. *Jim's Girlfriend*: Lauren Goler. *Congressman Butler*: Kenneth H. Waller. *Henry Ward Beecher*: MICHAEL ZASLOW. *Susan B. Anthony*: Dorothy Holland. *Grant Speaker*: Kenneth H. Waller. *Eunice Beecher*: Linda Poser. *Charlie Delmonico*: LENNY WOLPE. *Maginnes*: Kenneth H. Waller. *Anthony Comstock*: JIM JANSEN. *Judge*: Kenneth H. Waller. *Fullerton*: LENNY WOLPE.

The action takes place in New York City and Washington, D.C. during 1871.

---

[13]Originally produced in New York Off-Broadway 22 February 1979 by the Joseph Jefferson Theatre Co. at the Greenwich Mews Theatre for 12 performances.

Act 1, Scene 1: New York City, 1871. *Scene 2*: Commodore Cornelius Vanderbilt's Office. *Scene 3*: Victoria's Salon, six months later. *Scene 4*; Plymouth Church, Brooklyn Heights. *Scene 5*; Woodhull and Claflin's Brokerage. *Scene 6*: Washington, D.C., 24 May 1872. *Scene 7*: Victoria's Campaign Tour. *Scene 8*: Beecher's Study—The next day. *Scene 9*: Victoria's Brokerage/Beecher's Study—Three months later. *Scene 10*: Delmonico's Restaurant—Two hours later.

Act 2, Scene 1: Victoria's Brokerage—The next day. *Scene 2*: Beecher's Study—Two months later. *Scene 3*: Steinway Hall. *Scene 4*: Victoria's Brokerage: Two days later. *Scene 5*: Brokerage/Street/Jail. *Scene 6*: Exterior and Interior of Courtroom—*Scene 7Scene 8*

ACT 1

Scene 1

"The Age of Brass"
J. Eikenberry, B. Austin, M. Zaslow, J. Jansen, E. Genest, M. J. Sterner, L. Waterbury, D. Holland, Ensemble

Scene 2

"Magnetic Healing"
J. Eikenberry, B. Claflin, T. Thurston

Scene 3

"Curiosity"
R. Hays, M. J. Sterner, E. Genest, L. Waterbury, T. Thurston, Ensemble

Scene 4

"Beecher's Processional"
M. Zaslow, Ensemble

Scene 5

"I Depend on You"
J. Eikenberry, B. Austin

Scene 7

"Victoria's Banner"[14]
J. Eikenberry, B. Austin, L. Waterbury, D. Holland, Ensemble

"Changes"
J. Eikenberry

Scene 9

"A Taste of Forever"
J. Eikenberry, E. Genest

Scene 10

"Unescorted Women"
L. Wolpe, B. Austin, J. Eikenberry, Ensemble

ACT 2

Scene 1

"Love and Joy"
J. Eikenberry, M. Zaslow

Scene 2

"Everyday I Do a Little Something for the Lord"
J. Jansen

"It's Easy for Her"
M. Zaslow

Scene 3

"You Cannot Drown the Dreamer"
J. Eikenberry, L. Waterbury

Scene 4

"Respectable"
B. Austin

Scene 5

"Read It in the Weekly"
J. Eikenberry, M. Zaslow, E. Genest, B. Austin, J. Jansen, Newsboys, Readers

Scene 6

"A Valentine for Beecher"
Ensemble

"Beecher's Defense"
J. Eikenberry

"Another Life"
J. Eikenberry, M. Zaslow

"You Cannot Drown the Dreamer" (reprise)
J. Eikenberry, B. Austin

[14]Based on Victoria Woodhull's original campaign lyrics.

THE PIRATES OF PENZANCE, or The Slave of Duty

1981.01

A Revival of the Comic Opera in Two Acts[15]. Libretto by William S. Gilbert. Music by Arthur Sullivan. Directed by Wilford Leach. Music adapted and conducted by William Elliott. Choreography by Graciela Daniele. Scenery by Bob Shaw and Wilford Leach, supervised by Paul Eads. Costumes by Patricia McGourty. Lighting by Jennifer Tipton. Sound by Don Ketteler. Production supervisor, Jason Steven Cohen. A New York Shakespeare Festival Production. Produced by Joseph Papp. Opened 8 January 1981 at the Uris Theater, moved 12 August 1981 to the Minskoff Theatre, and closed 28 November 1982 after 772 performances.

CAST (in order of appearance): *The Pirate King*: KEVIN KLINE. *Samuel*, his Lieutenant: Stephen Hanan. *Frederic*, the Pirate Apprentice: REX SMITH. *Ruth*, A Pirate Maid-of-all-work: ESTELLE PARSONS. *Major General Stanley's Daughters (8)*: *Edith*: Alexandra Korey. *Kate*: Marcie Shaw. *Isabel*: Wendy Wolfe. *Mabel*: LINDA RONSTADT. And Robin Boudreau, Maria Guida, Nancy Heikin, Bonnie Simmons. *Major-General Stanley*: GEORGE ROSE. *Sergeant of Police*: TONY AZITO.

Pirates and Police: Dean Badolato, Mark Beudert, Brian Bullard, Scott Burkholder, Walter Caldwell, Tim Flavin, Ray Gill, George Kmeck, Daniel Marcus, G. Eugene Moose, Joseph Neal, Walter Niehenke, Joe Pichette, Ellis Skeeter Williams, Michael Edwin Willson.

ACT 1

"Pour, O Pour the Pirate Sherry"
K. Kline, S. Hanan, R. Smith, Pirates

"When Frederic Was a Little Lad"
E. Parsons

"Oh, Better Far to Live and Die"
K. Kline, Pirates

"Oh, False One, You Have Deceived Me!"
E. Parsons, R. Smith

"Climbing Over Rocky Mountain"
Daughters

"Stop Ladies, Pray!"
R. Smith, Daughters

"Oh, Is There Not One Maiden Breast"
R. Smith, Daughters

"Poor Wandering One"
L. Ronstadt, Daughters

"What Ought We to Do?"
M. Shaw, A. Korey, Daughters

"How Beautifully Blue the Sky"
L. Ronstadt, R. Smith, Daughters

"Stay, We Must Not Lose Our Senses"
R. Smith, Daughters, Pirates

"Hold, Monsters!"
L. Ronstadt, S. Hanan, G. Rose, Daughters, Pirates

"I Am the Very Modern Model of a Modern Major-General"
G. Rose, Ensemble

"Oh, Men of Dark and Dismal Fate"
Ensemble

ACT 2

"Oh, Dry the Glistening Tear"
L. Ronstadt, Daughters

"Then Frederic"
G. Rose, R. Smith

"When the Foreman Bares His Steel"
T. Azito, L. Ronstadt, Police, Daughters

"Now for the Pirates' Lair!"
R. Smith, K. Kline, E. Parsons

"When You Had Left Our Pirate Fold"
E. Parsons, R. Smith, K. Kline

"My Eyes Are Fully Open" (from *RUDDIGORE*)
R. Smith, E. Parsons, K. Kline

[15]First presented in New York 31 December 1879 at the Fifth Avenue Theatre for 91 performances in two engagements. This revival first produced in New York Off-Broadway by the New York Shakespeare Festival 15 July 1980 at the Delacorte Theatre (in Central Park) for 42 performances.

"Away, Away! My Heart's on Fire"
E. Parsons, K. Kline, R. Smith
"All Is Prepared"
L. Ronstadt, R. Smith
"Stay Frederic, Stay!"
L. Ronstadt, R. Smith
"Sorry Her Lot" (from *H.M.S. PINAFORE*)
L. Ronstadt
"No, I Am Brave"
L. Ronstadt, T. Azito, Police
"When a Felon's Not Engaged in His Employment"
T. Azito, Police
"A Rollicking Band of Pirates We"
Pirates, T. Azito, Police
"With Cat-Like Tread Upon Our Prey We Steal"
Pirates, Police, S. Hanan
"Hush, Hush! Not a Word!"
R. Smith, Pirates, Police, G. Rose
"Sighing Softly to the River"
G. Rose, Ensemble
Finale[16]
Ensemble

1981.02 SHAKESPEARE'S CABARET

A Musical Revue in One Act[17]. Concept and music by Lance Mulcahy. (Words by William Shakespeare.) Entire production directed by John Driver. Choreography by Lynne Taylor-Corbett. Scenery and costumes by Frank J. Boros. Lighting by Marc B. Weiss. Orchestrations, vocal arrangements and musical direction by Don Jones. Production advisor, Richard G. Miller. Produced by Arthur Shafman. Opened 21 January 1981 at the Bijou Theatre and closed 8 March 1981 after 54 performances.

CAST (in order of speaking appearance): Patti Perkins, Michael Rupert, Catherine Cox, Larry Riley, Pauletta Pearson, Alan Brasington.

MUSICAL NUMBERS
"If Music and Sweet Poetry Agree" (from *THE PASSIONATE PILGRIM*)
Ensemble
"What Thou See'st When Thou Dost Awake" (*from A MIDSUMMER NIGHT'S DREAM*)
Ensemble
"All That Glitters" (from *THE MERCHANT OF VENICE*)
C. Cox, P. Perkins, P. Pearson
"Why Should This a Desert Be?" (from *AS YOU LIKE IT*)
M. Rupert
"Crabbed Age and Youth" (from *THE PASSIONATE PILGRIM*)
A. Brasington, P. Perkins
"Orpheus and His Lute" (from *HENRY III*)
P. Pearson
"Music With Her Silver Sound" (from *ROMEO AND JULIET*)
C. Cox, M. Rupert, P. Perkins, A. Brasington
"Come Live With Me and Be My Love"
(attributed to Christopher Marlowe, quoted in *TWELFTH NIGHT*)
L. Riley
"Have More Than Thou Showest" (from *KING LEAR*)
M. Rupert, A. Brasington
"Venus and Adonis Suite" (An Erotic Narrative Poem)
Ensemble
Venus sees Adonis bathing naked in the stream. She tries to seduce him. He rejects her. Her premonition of his death. He is killed by the wild boar. Venus mourns his death. She flies off to her home in the skies.
"Tell Me Where Is Fancy Bred?" (from *THE MERCHANT OF VENICE*)
Ensemble
"If Music Be the Food of Love" (from *TWELFTH NIGHT*)
A. Brasington, P. Pearson
"Epitaph for Marina" (from *PERICLES*)
M. Rupert, C. Cox
"The Phoenix and the Turtle"
A. Brasington, P. Perkins, P. Pearson, C. Cox, M. Rupert
"Now" (from *A MIDSUMMER NIGHT'S DREAM*)
L. Riley
"The Willow Song" (from *OTHELLO*)
C. Cox
"Immortal Gods" (from *TIMON OF ATHENS*)
A. Brasington
"Tomorrow Is St. Valentine's Day" (from *HAMLET*)
P. Perkins
"Fathers That Wear Rags" (from *KING LEAR*)
P. Pearson
"The Grave Digger's Song" (from *HAMLET*)
L. Riley
"Now" (reprise)
L. Riley, P. Perkins, P. Pearson, C. Cox, A. Brasington
"Come Unto These Yellow Sands" (from *THE TEMPEST*)
Ensemble
"Shall I Compare Thee to a Summer's Day?" (from *SONNET* 18)
C. Cox, A. Brasington
"Lawn as White as Driven Snow" (from *THE WINTER'S TALE*)
Ensemble
"Rosalynde" (from *AS YOU LIKE IT*)
L.Riley, A. Brasington
"Let the Canakin Clink" (from *OTHELLO*)
Ensemble
"Shakespeare's Epitaph"
Ensemble
"Fear No More the Heat of the Sun" (from *CYMBELINE*)
Ensemble
"Epitaph" (reprise)
Ensemble

1981.03 THE FIVE O'CLOCK GIRL

A Revival of the Musical Comedy in Two Acts, 10 Scenes[18]. Book by Guy Bolton and Fred Thompson. Music and lyrics by Bert Kalmar and Harry Ruby. Entire production directed by Sue Lawless. Musical staging and choreography by Dan Siretta. Scenery by John Lee Beatty. Costumes by Nanzi Adzima. Lighting by Craig Miller. Sound design by Richard Fitzgerald. Music research consultant, Alfred Simon. Orchestrations and dance arrangements by Russell Warner. Assistant choreographer, Larry McMillian. Musical direction by Lynn Crigler. Production consultant, Warren Pincus. A Goodpseed Opera House Production. Produced by Rodger Hess. Opened 28 January 1981 at the Helen Hayes Theatre and closed 8 February 1981 after 14 performances.

CAST (in order of appearance): *Madame Irene*: SHEILA SMITH. *Hudgins*, Mr. Brooks' valet: TED PUGH. *Susan Snow*: PAT STANLEY. *Patricia Brown*: LISBY LARSON. *Gerald Brooks*: ROGER RATHBURN. *Ronnie Webb*: BARRY PRESTON. *Cora Wainwright*: DEE HOTY. *Jasper Cobb*: TIMOTHY WALLACE.

Ensemble: *Jeanie*: Teri Corcoran. *Pete*, the waiter: James Homan. *Rodney*, Madame Irene's escort: Richard Ruth. *Sam*: Rodney Pridgen. *Ethel; Molly* the Maid: Annette Michelle. *Elsie*: Lora Jeanne Martens. *Bunnie*: Jean McLaughlin. *Polly*: Debra Grimm. *Maisie*: Carla Farnsworth-Webb. *Jules*, the Maitre d': Jonathan Aronson. *Detective*: G. Brandon Allen. *Bobby, Policeman*: Gary Kirsch.

The action takes place in New York in the 1920's.

Act 1, Scene 1: A Block Party near Beekman Place. *Scene 2*: On the Telephone. *Scene 3*: Gerry's Apartment. *Scene 4*: The Snowflake Cleaners. *Scene 5*: The Kit Kat Club.

Act 2, Scene 1: Outside the Field and Stream Hotel, Southampton, Long Island. *Scene 2*: The Snowflake Cleaners. *Scene 3*: A Street in New York. *Scene 4*: Roof garden between the Apartments of Gerry and Ronnie. *Scene 5*: The Church.

16The restoration of part of the original New York finale to THE PIRATES OF PENZANCE of 1879 was done by Richard Traubner.
[17]Originally produced 1 February 1980 Off-Broadway at the Colonnades Theatre Lab for 40 performances.

[18]Originally produced in New York as *THE 5 O'CLOCK GIRL* 10 October 1927 at the 44th Street Theatre for 280 performances.

ACT 1
Scene 1
"In the Old Neighborhood"
S. Smith, Ensemble
Scene 2
"Keep Romance Alive" (from *HIPS, HIPS, HOORAY* film)
Telephone Girls
"Thinking of You"
L. Larson, R. Rathburn
Scene 3
"I'm One Little Party"
B. Preston, Female Ensemble
"Up in the Clouds"
L. Larson, R. Rathburn, Ensemble
"My Sunny Tennessee" (from *MIDNIGHT ROUNDERS OF 1921*)
T. Wallace, Ensemble
(*Music and Lyrics by* Bert Kalmar, Harry Ruby, Herman Ruby.)
"Any Little Thing"
P. Stanley, T. Pugh
Scene 5
"Manhattan Walk" (from *GOOD BOY*)
S. Smith, B. Preston, D. Hoty, T. Pugh, Ensemble
(*Music by* Herbert Stothart and Harry Ruby. *Lyrics by* Bert Kalmar.)

ACT 2
Scene 1
"Long Island Low Down" (from *ANIMAL CRACKERS*)
S. Smith, Ensemble
"Who Did? You Did!"
L. Larson, R. Rathburn
"Any Little Thing" (reprise)
P. Stanley
Scene 2
"Nevertheless (I'm in Love With You)" (interpolation)
P. Stanley, T. Pugh
Scene 3
"All Alone Monday" (from *THE RAMBLERS*)
R. Rathburn
Scene 4
"Dancing the Devil Away" (from *LUCKY*)
B. Preston, Ensemble
(*Music by* Harry Ruby. *Lyrics by* Bert Kalmar and Otto Harbach.)
Scene 5
"Up in the Clouds"
L. Larson, R. Rathburn
Finale
Company

1981.04

PIAF

A Drama (with Songs) in Two Acts, 24 Scenes, by Pam Gems. Directed by Howard Davies. Setting by David Jenkins. Costumes by Julie Weiss. Lighting by Beverly Emmons. Produced originally in Great Britain by the Royal Shakespeare Company. Production coordinator, Brent Peek. Sound by Jack Mann. Assistant director, Helaine Head. Musical direction and arrangements, Michael Dansicker. Produced by Elizabeth I. McCann, Nelle Nugent, The Shubert Organization, Ray Larsen in association with Warner Theatre Productions, Inc. Opened 5 February 1981 at the Plymouth Theatre and closed 28 June 1981 after 165 performances.

CAST (in order of appearance): *Emcee/Manager*: David Leary. *Piaf*: JANE LAPOTAIRE. *"Papa" Leplée, owner of Cluny Club*: Peter Friedman. *Toine*: ZOË WANAMAKER. *Emil, maitre d' at Cluny Club*: Nicholas Woodeson. *Legionnaire*: Stephen Davies. *Thugs (3)*: *Jacques*: Lewis Arlt. *Eddie*: Robert Christian. *Little Louis*: Michael Ayr. *Police Inspector*: Kenneth Welsh. *Paul, man with rose*: David Purdham. *German Soldier #1*: Lewis Arlt. *German Soldier #2*: Michael Ayr. *Georges*: Kenneth Welsh. *Butcher*: Robert Christian. *Pierre*, on bicycle; later, *Piaf's Agent*: Stephen Davies. *Marlene*: Jean Smart. *Marcel*: Robert Christian. *American Soldier #1*: David Purdham. *American Soldier #2*: Peter Friedman. *Barman*: Robert Christian. *Madeleine*: Judith Ivey. *Lucien*: Michael Ayr. *Angelo*: Lewis Arlt. *Physiotherapist*: Kenneth Welsh. *Jacko*: Nicholas Woodeson. *Dope Pusher*: Michael Ayr. *Nurse*: Sherry Steiner. *Theo*: David Purdham.

The play is a celebration of the life of Edith Piaf from the late 1920's through 1963.

Act 1, Scene 1: The bare stage of the Cluny Club. *Scene 2*: Outside the Cluny Club. *Scene 3*: Piaf's Room. *Scene 4*: The Cluny Club. *Scene 5*: The Street. *Scene 6*: The Cluny Club. *Scene 7*: A Police Station, and afterwards. *Scene 8*: A classy club. *Scene 9*: Piaf's apartment. *Scene 10*: A Street. *Scene 11*: Piaf's Apartment. *Scene 12*: Josephine's Nightclub. *Scene 13*: Piaf and Marcel.

Act 2, Scene 1: A Stage Dressing Room. *Scene 2*: A Bar. *Scene 3*: Piaf's Apartment. *Scene 4*: A Parisian café. *Scene 5*: A Hospital Waiting Room. *Scene 6*: A Rehearsal Studio. *Scene 7*: Piaf's Apartment. *Scene 8*: A Room at the Ritz. *Scene 9*: An empty stage. *Scene 10*: Piaf's Private Room in a Nursing Home. *Scene 11*: Piaf's Room in the South of France.

ACT 1[19]
Scene 2
"Les Mômes de la Cloche"
J. Lapotaire
(*Music by* Vincent Scotto. *Lyrics by* Decaye.)
Scene 4
"Les Mômes de la Cloche" (reprise)
J. Lapotaire
Scene 6
"La Ville Inconnue"
J. Lapotaire
(*Music by* Charles Dumont. *Lyrics by* Michel Vaucaire.)
Scene 7
"Tu Me Fais Tourner Ma Tête"
J. Lapotaire
Scene 8
"Si Tu Partais"
J. Lapotaire
"L'Accordéoniste" (The Accordionist)
J. Lapotaire
(*Music by* M. Emer. *English Lyrics by* Adrian Mitchell.)
Scene 9
"C'est à Hambourg" (Harbour Girl)
J. Lapotaire
(*Music and Lyrics by* Charles Dumont and Edith Piaf. *English Lyrics by* Pam Gems and Adrian Mitchell.)
Scene 11
"Milord"
J. Lapotaire, Z. Wanamaker
(*Music by* Marguerite Monnot. *Lyrics by* Georges Moustaki.)
"Auprès de Ma Blonde"
J. Lapotaire, Z. Wanamaker
Scene 13
"La Belle Histoire D'Amour"
J. Lapotaire
(*Music and Lyrics by* Edith Piaf and Charles Dumont. *English Lyrics by* Adrian Mitchell.)

ACT 2
Scene 6
"Deep in the Heart of Texas"
S. Davies
(*Music by* Don Swander. *Lyrics by* June Hershey.)
Scene 7
"Le Droit D'Aimer"
J. Lapotaire
Scene 9
"La Goualante du Pauvre Jean" (The Ballad of Poor Old John)
J. Lapotaire
(*Music by* Marguerite Monnot. *Lyrics by* René Rouzoud. *English Lyrics by* Adrian Mitchell.)
Scene 10
"Non, Je Ne Regrette Rien"
J. Lapotaire
(*Music by* Charles Dumont. *Lyrics by* Michel Vaucaire.)

[19]Scene list and song list prepared from production typescript.

Additional Music used:
"Les Trois Cloches" (The Three Bells)
(*Music and Lyrics by* Jean Villard {Gilles}. *English Lyrics by* Bert Reisfeld.)
"Bravo Pour Le Clown"
(*Music and Lyrics by* Henri Contet and Louiguy.)
"Je T'ai Dans le Peau"
"La Vie en Rose"
(*Music and Lyrics by* Edith Piaf and Louiguy. *English Lyrics by* Mack David.)
"Mon Dieu"
(*Music and Lyrics by* Charles Dumont and Michel Vaucaire.)
"Hymne à L'Amour" (If You Love Me)
(*Music by* Marguerite Monnot. *Lyrics by* Edith Piaf. *English Lyrics by* Geoffrey Parsons.)
"Un Sale Petit Brouillard"

1981.05 JACQUES BREL IS ALIVE AND WELL AND LIVING IN PARIS

A Revival of the Musical Entertainment (Revue) in Two Acts[20]. Music by Jacques Brel. Production conception, English lyrics and additional material by Eric Blau. Based on Jacques Brel's lyrics and commentary. Original direction by Moni Yakim. Production supervised by Eric Blau. Produced by Lily Tuner Attractions. Opened 19 February 1981 at Town Hall and closed 8 March 1981 after 21 performances.

CAST: JOE MASIELL, BETTY RHODES, SALLY COOKE, SHAWN ELLIOTT.

1981.06 SOPHISTICATED LADIES

A Musical (Revue) in Two Acts. Music by Duke Ellington. Concept by Donald MacKayle. Directed by Michael Smuin. Musical staging and choreography by Donald MacKayle, Michael Smuin. Co-choreography and tap choreography by Henry LeTang. Musical director, Mercer Ellington. Settings designed by Tony Walton. Costumes designed by Willa Kim. Lighting designed by Jennifer Tipton. Sound designed by Otts Munderloh. Orchestrations by Al Cohn. Musical and dance arrangements by Lloyd Mayers. Vocal arrangements by Malcolm Dodds, Lloyd Mayers. Associate choreographer, Bruce Heath. Assistant choreographer, Mercedes Ellington. Musical consultant and additional arrangements, Paul Chihara. Produced by Roger S. Berlind, Manheim Fox, Sondra Gilman, Burton L. Litwin and Louise Westergaard in association with Belwin Mills Publishing Corporation and Norzar Productions. Opened 1 March 1981 at the Lunt-Fontanne Theatre and closed 2 January 1983 after 767 performances.

CAST: GREGORY HINES, JUDITH JAMISON, PHYLLIS HYMAN, P. J. BENJAMIN, HINTON BATTLE, GREGG BURGE, MERCEDES ELLINGTON, PRISCILLA BASKERVILLE, TERRI KLAUSNER.

Ensemble: Claudia Asbury, Paula Lynn, Wynonna Smith, Adrian Bailey, Michael Lichtefeld, Michael Scott Gregory, T. A. Stephens.

ACT 1[21]

"I've Got To Be a Rug Cutter" (1937)
H. Battle, G. Burge, M. S. Gregory, M. Lichtefeld
(*Music and Lyrics by* Duke Ellington.)
"Music Is a Woman" (Based on "Jubilee Stomp" 1928)
G. Hines, J. Jamison
(*Music by* Duke Ellington. *Lyrics by* John Guare.)
"The Mooche" (1929)
H. Battle, C. Asbury, M. Ellington, P. Lynn, W. Smith
(*Music by* Duke Ellington and Irving Mills.)
"Hit Me With a Hot Note (and Watch Me Bounce)" (1945)
T. Klausner
(*Music by* Duke Ellington. *Lyrics by* Don George.)
"I Love You Madly" (1950)
(*Music and Lyrics by* Duke Ellington.)
"Perdido" (1971)
J. Jamison, G. Burge, H. Battle
(*Music and Lyrics by* Juan Tizol, Ervin Drake, Hans Lengsfelder.)
"Fat and Forty"[22]
P. J. Benjamin
(*Music and Lyrics by* Al Hibbler and Duke Ellington.)
"It Don't Mean a Thing (If It Ain't Got That Swing)" (1929)
P. Hyman, G. Burge, G. Hines, A. Bailey, M. Lichtefeld, M. S. Gregory, T. A. Stephens
(*Music by* Duke Ellington. *Lyrics by* Irving Mills.)
"Bli-Blip" (1941)
P. J. Benjamin, T. Klausner
(*Music by* Duke Ellington. *Lyrics by* Duke Ellington and Irving Mills.)
"Cotton Tail" (1940)
P. J. Benjamin, T. Klausner, Ensemble
(*Music by* Duke Ellington.)
"Take the "A" Train" (1941)
P. Hyman, G. Hines
(*Music by* Billy Strayhorn.)
"Solitude" (1934)
J. Jamison, P. Baskerville
(*Music by* Duke Ellington. *Lyrics by* Eddie DeLange and Irving Mills.)
"Don't Get Around Much Anymore" (1942)
G. Hines
(*Music by* Duke Ellington. *Lyrics by* Bob Russell.)
"I Let a Song Go Out of My Heart" (from *COTTON CLUB PARADE*, 1938)
J. Jamison
(*Music by* Duke Ellington. *Lyrics by* Irving Mills and John Redmond.)
"Caravan" (1937)
G. Burge, M. Ellington, Ensemble
(*Music by* Duke Ellington and Juan Tizot. *Lyrics by* Irving Mills.)
"Something to Live For" (1939)
G. Hines
(*Music and Lyrics by* Duke Ellington and Billy Strayhorn)
"Old Man Blues" (1930)
H. Battle, J. Jamison
(*Music and Lyrics by* Duke Ellington and Irving Mills.)
"Drop Me Off in Harlem" (1933)
H. Battle, P. J. Benjamin, G. Burge, G. Hines, P. Baskerville, Ensemble
(*Music by* Duke Ellington. *Lyrics by* Nick Kenny.)
"Rockin' in Rhythm" (*from EARL CARROLL'S VANITIES OF 1932*)
Company
(*Music by* Duke Ellington, Irving Mills, Harry Carney.)

ACT 2

"Duke's Place" (1957)
G. Hines
(*Music by* Duke Ellington. *Lyrics by* Bill Katz and Robert Thiele.)
"Diminuendo in Blue" (1942)
G. Hines
(*Music by* Duke Ellington.)
"In a Sentimental Mood" (1935)
P. Hyman
(*Music by* Duke Ellington. *Lyrics by* Manny Kurtz and Irving Mills.)
"I'm Beginning to See the Light" (1944)
J. Jamison, G. Hines
(*Music and Lyrics by* Duke Ellington, Don George, Johnnie Hodges, Harry James.)
"Satin Doll" (1958)
P. J. Benjamin
(*Music by* Duke Ellington. *Lyrics by* Billy Strayhorn and Johnny Mercer.)
"Just Squeeze Me" (1946)
T. Klausner
(*Music by* Duke Ellington. *Lyrics by* Lee Gaines.)
"Dancers in Love" (1945)
H. Battle, G. Burge, M. Ellington
(*Music by* Duke Ellington.)

---

[20]Originally produced in New York Off-Broadway 22 January 1968 at the Village Gate for 1847 performances; transferred to Broadway 15 September 1972 at the Royale Theatre for 51 performances. For Synopsis of Musical Numbers, see 1972 production.

[21]Added to Act 1, after "Old Man Blues" for National Tour:
"Prelude to a Kiss" (1938)
Paula Kelly
(*Music by* Duke Ellington. *Lyrics by* Irving Gordon and Irving Mills.)

[22]Replaced during the run and for subsequent tour by:
"Everything But You" (1945)
(*Music by* Duke Ellington, Harry James. *Lyrics by* Don George.)

"Echoes of Harlem" (1936)
H. Battle, G. Burge, Ladies
(*Music by* Duke Ellington.)
"I'm Just a Lucky So-and-So" (1945)
G. Hines, Gentlemen
(*Music by* Duke Ellington. *Lyrics by* Mack David.)
"Hey Baby" (1946)[23]
P. J. Benjamin, M. Ellington
(*Music and Lyrics by* Duke Ellington.)
"Imagine My Frustration" (1966)
T. Klausner, G. Burge
(*Music and Lyrics by* Duke Ellington, Billy Strayhorn, Gerald Wilson.)
"Kinda Dukish" (1955)
G. Hines
(*Music by* Duke Ellington.)
"Ko-Ko" (1939)
G. Hines, A. Bailey, M. S. Gregory, M. Lichtefeld, T. A. Stephens
(*Music by* Duke Ellington.)
"I'm Checking Out Goombye" (1939)
P. Hyman
(*Music and Lyrics by* Duke Ellington and Billy Strayhorn.)
"Do Nothing 'Til You Hear from Me" (1943)
G. Hines
(*Music by* Duke Ellington. *Lyrics by* .Bob Russell)
"I Got It Bad and That Ain't Good" (from *JUMP FOR JOY*, 1941)
P. Hyman
(*Music by* Duke Ellington. *Lyrics by* Paul Francis Webster.)
"Mood Indigo" (1931)
P. Hyman, T. Klausner
(*Music by* Duke Ellington, Irving Mills, Albany "Barney" Bigard.)
"Sophisticated Lady" (1933)
G. Hines, J. Jamison, Company
(*Music by* Duke Ellington. *Lyrics by* Mitchell Parish and Irving Mills.)
"It Don't Mean a Thing" (reprise)
G. Hines, Company

1981.07 BRING BACK BIRDIE

A Musical Comedy in Two Acts, 15 Scenes[24]. Book by Michael Stewart. Music by Charles Strouse. Lyrics by Lee Adams. Production conceived and directed by Joe Layton. Scenery designed by David Mitchell. Costumes designed by Fred Voelpel. Lighting designed by David Hays. Sound designed by Otts Munderloh. Video sequences created by Wakefield Poole, Frank O'Dowd. Musical direction, vocal arrangements by Mark Hummel. Dance music arranged by Daniel Troob. Still photographs by Barbara J. Rossi. orchestral arrangements by Ralph Burns, Stanley Applebaum, Daniel Troob, Philip J. Lang, Jim Tyler, Gary Anderson, Gerald Alters, Scott Kuney, Coleridge-Taylor Perkinson, Charles Strouse. Produced by Lee Guber, Shelly Gross, Slade Brown and Jim Milford. Opened 5 March 1981 at the Martin Beck Theatre and closed 7 March 1981 after 4 performances.

CAST (in order of appearaance): *Storyteller*: Donna Monroe. *Albert*: DONALD O'CONNOR. *Rose*: CHITA RIVERA. *Mtobe*: MAURICE HINES. *Hogan*: Howard Parker. *Albert, Jr.*: Evan Seplow. *Jenny*: Robin Morse. *Gary*: Jeb Brown. *Girl Friends*: Barbara Dare Thomas, Vanessa Bell, Julie Cohen, Christine Langner. *Porter*: Frank DeSal. *Guard*: Howard Parker. *Sunnie*: Betsy Friday. *Tourist*: Bill Bateman. *His Wife*: Zoya Leporska. *Shopping Bag Lady*: Rebecca Renfroe. *Indian Squaw*: Janet Wong. *Indian Brave*: Larry Hyman. *Mae Peterson*, (Delores Zepol): MARIA KARNILOVA. *Mayor C. B. Townshend*, (Conrad Birdie): Marcel Forestieri. *Effie*: Zoya Leporska. *Marshall*: Howard Parker. *"Filth" Group*: Evan Seplow, Jeb Brown, Cleve Asbury, Leon Evans, Mark Frawley. *House Manager*: Peter Oliver Norman. *Chorus Girls*: Betsy Friday, Rebecca Renfroe, Vanessa Bell. *Rose II*: Lynnda Ferguson. *Reverend Sun*: Frank DeSal. *Reporter #1*: Bill Bateman. *Reporter #2*: Donna Monroe. *Reporter #3*: Larry Hyman, Frank DeSal. *Street Cleaner*: Frank DeSal. *Cameraman*: Michael Blevins. *Stage Door Johnnies*: Bill Bateman, Peter Oliver Norman, Cleve Asbury, Frank DeSal. *Birdettes*: Betsy Friday, Rebecca Renfroe, Vanessa Bell. *Walter*: Kevin Petitt.

Act 1, Scene 1: A Darkened Office, (twenty years after 'Bye Bye Birdie'). *Scene 2*: Forest Hills and Environs. *Scene 3*: Peterson Kitchen. *Scene 4*: Port Authority Bus Terminal. *Scene 5*: Bent River Junction, Arizona. *Scene 6*: El Coyote Club. *Scene 7*: Office of Mayor. *Scene 8*: University Stadium.

Act 2, Scene 1: University Staadium. *Scene 2*: Reverend Sun's Compound. *Scene 3*: Office of the Mayor. Main Street, Bent River Junction. *Scene 4*: University Stadium Locker Room. *Scene 5*: Rose's Motel .*Scene 6*: Television Studio. *Scene 7*: The Grammy Show.

ACT 1
Scene 1
"Twenty Happy Years"
C. Rivera, D. O'Connor
Scene 2
"Movin' Out"
R. Morse, J. Brown, Kids
"Half of a Couple"
R. Morse, Girl Friends
Scene 3
"I Like What I Do"
C. Rivera
Scene 4
"Bring Back Birdie"
M. Hines, Company
"Movin' Out" (reprise)
Kids
Scene 5
"Baby You Can Count on Me"
D. O'Connor
Scene 6
"A Man Worth Fightin' For"
C. Rivera, Cowboys
Scene 7
"You Can Never Go Back"
M. Forestieri
Scene 8
"Filth"
E. Seplow, J. Brown, C. Asbury, L. Evans, M. Frawley
"Back in Show Biz Again"
D. O'Connor

ACT 2
Scene 1
"Middle Age Blues"
D. O'Connor
Scene 2
"Inner Peace"
C. Rivera, F. DeSal, Sunnies
Scene 3
"There's a Brand New Beat in Heaven"
M. Hines, The Tucson Tabernacle Choir
"Twenty Happy Years" (reprise)
D. O'Connor
"Well, I'm Not!"
C. Rivera
Scene 4
"When Will Grown-Ups Grow Up?"
Kids
"Middle Age Blues" (reprise)
D. O'Connor
Scene 5
"Young"
D. O'Connor
Scene 7
"I Love 'Em All"
M. Karnilova, Boyfriends
"Bring Back Birdie" (reprise)
M. Forestieri, The Birdettes
"Twenty Happy Years" (reprise)
D. O'Connor, C. Rivera

[23]Dropped for subsequent tour.
[24]Conceived as a sequel by the same authors whose *BYE BYE BIRDIE* opened 14 April 1960 at the Martin Beck Theatre for 607 performances.

1981.08

AMERICA

A Musical Revue in One Act, 11 Scenes. Conceived and produced by Robert F. Jani. Original music and lyrics by Tom Bahler and Mark Vieha. Musical direction and routines by Tom Bahler. Choreography by Violet Holmes, Linda Lemac and Frank Wagner. Principals staged by Frank Wagner. Scenic design by Robert Guerra. Costume design by Michael Casey. Lighting design by Ken Billington. Special material and dialogue by Harvey Jacobs. Orchestrations by Mitch Farber, Robert M. Freedman, Jay Kennedy, Billy May. Synthesizer program and performance by Don Dorsey. Director of the Rockettes, Violet Holmes. Produced by Radio City Music Hall Productions, Inc. Opened 13 March 1981 at the Radio City Music Hall and closed 7 September 1981 after 284 performances.

CAST: *THE AMERICANS*: Wendy Edmead, Jeff Johnson, Reed Jones, Mark Morales, Iris Revson.

THE ROCKETTES: Pauline Achillas, Carol Beatty, Catherine Beatty, Dottie Belle, Susan Boron, Barbara Ann Cittadino, Eileen Collins, Brie Daniels, Susanne Doris, Jacqueline Fancy, Deniene Fenn, Alexis Ficks, Prudence Gray, Jennifer Hammond, Carol Harbich, Terry Spano Higgins, Ginny Hounsell, Cynthia Hughes, Pam Kelleher, Dee Dee Knapp, Judy Little, Kris Mooney, Barbara Moore, Lynn Newton, Pam Stacey Pasqualino, Kerri Pearsall, Joan Peer, Cindy Peiffer, Gerri Presky, Ann Murphy St. John, Lynn Sullivan, Sunny Summers, Susan Theobald, Carol Toman, Patricia Tully, Darlene Wendy, Rose Ann Woolsey, Phyllis Wujko, Joyce Dwyer (Captain).

THE NEW YORKERS: Michael Booker, Andrew Charles, Buddy Crutchfield, Lou Ann Csaszar, Johnny Driscoll, Catherine Fries, Dale Furry, David Holland, Laurie Jaeger, David Michael Johnson, Rena Phillips, Kitty Preston, Cleo Price, Edward Prostak, Lance Roberts, Danny Robins, Lisa Sherman, Marc Villa.

THE DANCERS: Blake Atherton, David Beckett, Ron Chisholm, Rick Conant, Lloyd Culbreath, Renee DuLaney, Byron Easley, Glenn Ferrugiari, Karen Fraction, Michael Graham, Tony Jaegar, David Lee, Kim Leslie, Bronna Lipton, David Roman, Sam Singhaus, Thomas Stanton, Maureen Stevens, Barry Weiss, Kim Woollen.

THE ORGANISTS: Robert Maidhof, George Wesner.

MUSICAL NUMBERS

Scene 1

The Opening

Let music swell the breeze and ring from all the trees sweet freedom's song.

Scene 2

The Story of America

From school house days.

Scene 3

"Fifty Great Places All in One Place"
(*Music and Lyrics by* Tom Bahler and Mark Vieha.)

Scene 4

"The Spirit of America"
(*Music and Lyrics by* Tom Bahler and Mark Vieha.)

Scene 5

A Tour de Force of America

A magical, musical, pictorial entertainement voyage to America's fifty great states.

Scene 6

Hawaii Is the 50th Star

In the flag of the U.S.A.

Scene 7

The Electro-Live-Synthomagnetic Radio City Music Hall Orchestra
Conducted by Kevin Farrell. Assistant Conductor, Paul Bogaev.

Scene 8

Freedom

From Yankee Doodle to Dixie we praise the Lord for our freedom.

Scene 9

A New American Spirit Is Alive

Scene 10

On Parade
(includes "Come Follow the Band" from *BARNUM*)
(*Music by* Cy Coleman. *Lyrics by* Michael Stewart.)

Scene 11

The Finale—America the Beautiful

1981.09

BROADWAY FOLLIES

A Vaudeville Revue in Two Acts, 15 Scenes. Music and lyrics by Walter Marks. Concept and direction by Donald Driver. Choreography by Arthur Faria. Scenery designed by Peter Larkin. Costumes designed by Alvin Colt. Lighting designed by Roger Morgan. Sound designed by Abe Jacob. Musical direction, vocal and dance arrangements by Marvin Laird. Orchestrations by Bill Byers. Talent coordinator, Gilbert Miller. Production supervisor, Robert Strauss. Produced by Edgar Lansbury, Joseph Beruh and James Nederlander. Opened and closed 15 March 1981 at the Nederlander Theatre after 1 performance.

CAST: ROBERT SHIELDS, LORENE YARNELL, TESSIE O'SHEA, Milo & Roger, Scott's Royal Boxers (Katherine and George Scott, Tina Scott), Los Malambos (Guido Lopez, Nicolas Sarrea, Hector Diaz), Michael Davis, Gaylord Maynard & Chief Bearpaw.

Ensemble: Stephen Bourneuf, Kitty Kuhn, Mark Martino, Nancy Meadows, Brad Miskell, Alice Ann Oakes, Aurelio Padron, R. J. Peters, D'Arcy Phifer, Mark Ruhala, Karen Teti, Suzanne Walker.

ACT 1

Scene 1

"Broadway Follies"
Ensemble

Scene 2

Vaudeville
R. Shields, L. Yarnell

Scene 3

Wonderful U
Scott's Royal Boxers, Follies Ensemble

Scene 4

"Piccadilly"
T. O'Shea

Scene 5

The Oasis
Milo & Roger

Scene 6

The Pampas
Los Malambos

Scene 7

The Toyshop
R. Shields, L. Yarnell

Scene 8

"The Paper Bag Rag"
T. O'Shea, Bud's Paper Bag Band

ACT 2

Scene 1

At Home with the Clinkers
R. Shields, L. Yarnell

Scene 2

"The Barnyard"
T. O'Shea, Her Chicks

Scene 3

Specialty
R. Shields

Scene 4

The Saloon
G. Maynard, Belinda, Chief Bearpaw, The Dingbats

Scene 5

Tap My Way to the Stars
L. Yarnell, Ensemble

Scene 6

The Rest of Michael Davis (juggling act)

Scene 7

Grand Parade
Entire Company

1981.10

WOMAN OF THE YEAR

A Musical Comedy in Two Acts, 15 Scenes. Book by Peter Stone. Based on the MGM film of the same name by Ring Lardner, Jr. and Michael Kanin. Music by John Kander. Lyrics by Fred Ebb. Directed by Robert Moore. Musical numbers staged by Tony Charmoli. Settings designed by Tony Walton. Costumes designed by Theoni V. Aldredge. Lighting designed by Marilyn Rennagel. Sound designed by Abe Jacob. Musical direction and vocal arrangements by Donald Pippin. Orchestrations by Michael Gibson. Dance arrangements by Ronald Melrose. Animations by Michael Sporn. Produced by Lawrence Kasha, David S. Landay, James M. Nederlander, Warner Theatre Productions/Claire Nichtern, Carole J. Shorenstein, Stewart F. Lane. Opened 29 March 1981 at the Palace Theatre and closed 13 March 1983 after 770 performances.

CAST (in order of appearance): *Chairperson*: Helon Blount. *Tess Harding*: LAUREN BACALL. *Floor Manager*: Michael O'Gorman. *Chip Salisbury*: Daren Kelly. *Gerald*: RODERICK COOK. *(The Cartoonists {5}): Pinky Peters*: Gerry Vichi. *Phil Witaker*: Tom Avera. *Sam Craig*: HARRY GUARDINO. *Ellis McMaster*: Rex D. Hays. *Abbott Canfield*: Lawrence Raiken. *Murray*: Rex Everhart. *Helga*: Grace Keagy. *Alexi Petrikov*: Eivind Harum. *Cleaning Women*: Helon Blount, Marian Haraldson. *Jan Donovan*: Marilyn Cooper. *Larry Donvan*: Jamie Ross. (*Voice of Katz*: Fred Ebb.)

Chorus: DeWright Baxter, Joan Bell, Helon Blount, Sergio Cal, Donna Drake, Richard Glendon-Larsen, Marian Haraldson, Michael Kubala, Paige Massman, Gene Montoya, Michael O'Gorman, Susan Powers, Daniel Quinn, Robert Warners. *Swings*: Ed Nolfi, Karen Giombetti.

Act 1, Scene 1: Backstage at a Hotel Ballroom. *Scene 2*: A TV Studio and Sam's Studio. *Scene 3*: Tess' Office. *Scene 4*: Sam's Studio. *Scene 5*: The Inkpot. *Scene 6*: Tess' Apartment. *Scene 7*: Around New York .*Scene 8*: Tess' Apartment. *Scene 9*: Tess' Apartment and a Hotel Ballroom.

Act 2, Scene 1: The Street. *Scene 2*: The Inkpot. *Scene 3*: A Ballet Rehearsal Room. *Scene 4*: Sam's Studio. *Scene 5*: Larry's House. *Scene 6*: The TV Studio.

ACT 1[25]
Scene 1
"Woman of the Year"[26]
L. Bacall, Women
Scene 2
"The Poker Game"
H. Guardino, Cartoonists
"See You in the Funny Papers"
H. Guardino
Scene 3
"When You're Right, You're Right"
L. Bacall, R. Cook
Scene 4
"Shut Up, Gerald"
L. Bacall, H. Guardino, R. Cook
"So What Else Is New?"
H. Guardino, F. Ebb
Scene 5
"One of the Boys"
L. Bacall, Cartoonists, R. Everhart, Men
"Table Talk"
L. Bacall, H. Guardino
Scene 6
"The Two of Us"
L. Bacall, H. Guardino
Scene 7
"It Isn't Working"
Cartoonists, D. Kelly, G. Keagy, R. Cook, New Yorkers
Scene 8
"I Told You So"
R. Cook, G. Keagy
Scene 9
"Woman of the Year" (reprise)
L. Bacall
ACT 2[27]
Scene 1
"So What Else Is New?" (reprise)
H. Guardino, F. Ebb
Scene 2
"I Wrote the Book"
L. Bacall, H. Blount, M. Haraldson
Scene 3
"Happy in the Morning"
E. Harum, L. Bacall, Dancers
Scene 4
"Sometimes a Day Goes By"
H. Guardino
Scene 5
"The Grass Is Always Greener"
L. Bacall, M. Cooper
Scene 6
"We're Gonna Work It Out"
L. Bacall, H. Guardino

[25]The subsequent national tour was re-staged in Two Acts, 14 Scenes, and re-choreographed by Joe Layton. Added to Act 1, Scene 8 after "I Told You So:"
"Who Would Have Dreamed"
Raquel Welch (Tess Harding)

[26]New title song written for the national tour.

[27]During the Broadway run, Act 2, Scene 1 was dropped.
For the national tour, the following was added to Act 2, Scene 6 (revised as Scene 5):
"Open the Window, Sam"
L. Bacall

1981.11

AAAH OUI GENTY!

A Marionette Revue in Two Acts. (Conceived by Philippe Genty.) Production supervisor, Christopher Dunlop. Produced by Arthur Shafman. Opened 9 April 1981 at the Bijou Theatre and closed 3 May 1981 after 29 performances.

CAST: *COMPAGNIE PHILIPPE GENTY*: Mary Genty, Philippe Genty, Michel Guillaume, Jean-Louis Heckel.

ACT 1
Signboard
Clown
Signboard
Pierrot
Drifting
ACT 2
Metamorphosis
Signboard
The Offcier
Signboard
Ostrich Ballet

1981.12

COPPERFIELD

A Musical in Two Acts, 19 Scenes. Book, music and lyrics by Al Kasha and Joel Hirschhorn. Based on the novel "David Copperfield" by Charles Dickens. Direction and choreography by Rob Iscove. Set design by Tony Straiges. Costume design by John David Ridge. Lighting design by Ken Billington. Musical direction, vocal arrangements by Larry Blank. Orchestrations by Irwin Kostal. Dance arrangements, incidental music by Donald Johnston. Sound design by John McClure. A Dome Production. Produced by Don Gregory and Mike Merrick. Opened 16 April 1981 at the ANTA Theatre and closed 26 April 1981 after 13 performances.

CAST (in order of appearance): *Dr. Chilip*: Richard Warren Pugh. *Peggotty*: Mary Stout. *Nurse*: Katharine Buffaloe. *Aunt Betsey Trotwood*: CARMEN MATHEWS. *Young David*: EVAN RICHARDS. *Clara Copperfield*: Pamela McLernon. *Mr. Murdstone*: MICHAEL CONNOLLY. *Jane Murdstone*: Maris Clement. *Mr. Micawber*: GEORGE S. IRVING. *Bootmaker*: David Horwitz. *Butcher*: Bruce

Sherman. *Baker*: Richard Warren Pugh. *Mrs. Micawber*: Linda Poser. *Victoria*: Spence Ford. *Vanessa*: Dana Moore. *Constable*: Michael Danek. *Mick Walker*: Gary Munch. *Mealy Potatoes*: Brian Quinn. *Billy Mowcher*: Christian Slater. *Mr. Quinion*: Ralph Braun. *Mr. Dick*: Lenny Wolpe. *Janet*: Darleigh Miller. *Adult David*: BRIAN MATTHEWS. *Mrs. Heep*: Beulah Garrick. *Uriah Heep*: BARRIE INGHAM. *Mr. Wickfield*: Keith Perry. *Agnes Wickfield*: LESLIE DENNISTON. *Dora Spenlow*: MARY MASTRANTONIO. *Julia Mills*: Katharine Buffaloe. *Ticket Taker*: Michael Gorman.

Ensemble: David Ray Bartee, Ralph Braun, Katharine Buffaloe, Maris Clement, Michael Danek, Spence Ford, Michael Gorman, David Horwitz, Pamela McLernon, Darleigh Miller, Dana Moore, Gary Munch, Keith Perry, Linda Poser, Richard Warren Pugh, Brian Quinn, Lynne Savage, Bruce Sherman, Claude Tessier, Missy Whitchurch. *Swing Dancers*: Heather Lee Gerdes, Daniel Dee.

The action takes place in 1812 and 1822 in England.

Act 1, Scene 1: A stormy December night, 1812. The drawing room of the Copperfield cottage in Blunderstone in Suffolk. *Scene 2*: An afternoon in the autumn, 1822. The garden of the Copperfield cottage. *Scene 3*: The following spring. The drawing room of the Copperfield cottage. *Scene 4*: 6:30 in the morning. The Murdstone and Grinby Warehouse. *Scene 5*: Mid-afternoon, the following summer. *Scene 6*: Immediately following. On the road to Dover. *Scene 7*: A few weeks later. *Scene 8*: A week later. On the road near Aunt Betsey's house. *Scene 9*: Immediately following. The parlor of Aunt Betsey's house. (The same), Ten years later. *Scene 10*: A week later. Mr. Wickfield's sitting room in London. *Scene 11*: The following Sunday. Southwark Fair.

Act 2, Scene 1: Several months later. Mr. Wickfield's office. *Scene 2*: Outside the church. *Scene 3*: Several months later. Mr. Wickfield's sitting room. *Scene 4*: Several weeks later. The home of David and Dora Copperfield. *Scene 5*; A street near the Wickfield house. *Scene 6*: The office of Wickfield and Heep. *Scene 7*: The home of David and Dora Copperfield. *Scene 8*: One year later. The London docks.

ACT 1

Scene 1

"I Don't Want a Boy"
C. Mathews, M. Stout, Ensemble

Scene 2

"Mama, Don't Get Married"
E. Richards, P. McLernan, M. Stout

Scene 4

"Copperfield" (TheBottle Song)
E. Richards, R. Braun, B. Quinn, C. Slater, G. Munch, Ensemble

Scene 5

"Something Will Turn Up"
G. S. Irving, E. Richards, Creditors, Ensemble

"Something Will Turn Up" (reprise)
G. S. Irving, E. Richards, Micawber Family

Scene 6

"Anyone"
E. Richards

Scene 9

"Here's a Book"
C. Mathews, L. Wolpe, E. Richards

Scene 10

"'Umble"
B. Ingham, B. Garrick

Scene 11

"The Circle Waltz"
B. Matthews, M. Mastrantonio, L. Denniston, Ensemble

ACT 2

Scene 1

"Up the Ladder"
B. Ingham, G. S. Irving

"I Wish He Knew"
L. Denniston

Scene 2

"The Lights of London"
B. Matthews, M. Mastrantonio

Scene 3

"'Umble" (reprise)
B. Ingham

Scene 4

"I Wish He Knew" (reprise)
L. Denniston

Scene 5

"Something Will Turn Up" (reprise)
G. S. Irving, B. Matthews

Scene 6

"Villainy Is the Matter"
B. Matthews, B. Ingham, G. S. Irving, L. Denniston, C. Mathews, L. Wolpe, B. Garrick, M. Stout, L. Poser

Scene 7

"With the One I Love"
B. Matthews

Scene 8

"Something Will Turn Up" (reprise)
G. S. Irving, Company

1981.13 CAN CAN

A Revival of the Musical (Comedy) in Two Acts, a Prologue and 17 Scenes[28]. Book (revised) by Abe Burrows. Music and lyrics by Cole Porter. Entire production staged and choreographed by Roland Petit. Directed by Abe Burrows. Scenery designed by David Mitchell. Costumes designed by Franca Squarciapino, supervised by Patricia Adshead. Lighting designed by Thomas Skelton. Musical direction, vocal arrangements by Stanley Lebowsky. Orchestrations by Philip J. Lang. Dance arrangements, new dance music by Donald York. Sound by Larry Spurgeon. Produced by James M. Nederlander, Arthur Rubin, Jerome Minskoff, Stewart F. Lane, Carole J. Shorenstein, Charles D. Kelman. Opened 30 April 1981 at the Minskoff Theatre and closed 3 May 1981 after 5 performances.

CAST (in order of appearance): *Policemen*: Tommy Breslin, John Remme, John Dolf, Dennis Batutis, Kevin McCready. *Bailiff*: Joseph Cusanelli. *Judge Paul Barriere*: DAVID BROOKS. *Court President*: Tom Batten. *Judge Aristede Forestier*: RON HUSMANN. *Claudine*: PAMELA SOUSA. *Hilaire Jussac*: SWEN SWENSON. *Boris Adzinidzinadze*: AVERY SCHREIBER. *Waiter*: John Remme. *La Mome Pistache*: ZIZI JEANMAIRE. *Hercule*: MICHAEL DANTUONO. *Theophile*: MITCHELL GREENBERG. *Etienne*: TOMMY BRESLIN. *Photographer*: James Dunne. *Tabac Waiter*: Joseph Cusanelli. *Monarchist*: Tom Batten. *Jail Guard*: John Remme. *Model*: Deborah Carlson. *Adam*: Darrell Barnett. *Eve*: PAMELA SOUSA. *The Snake*: ZIZI JEANMAIRE, Dennis Batutis, James Horvath, Steven LaChance, Kevin McCready. *Mimi*: Donna King. *Apache Leader*: Luigi Bonino. *Patrons*: Nealey Gilbert, Dennis Batutis. *Chief Justice*: Joseph Cusanelli.

Ensemble: Deborah Carlson, Pam Cecil, Edyie Fleming, Nealey Gilbert, Linda Haberman, Nancy Hess, Brenda Holmes, Donna King, Manette LaChance, Meredith McIver, Gail Pennington, Rosemary Rado, Daryl Richardson, Linda Von Germer, Darrell Barnett, Dennis Batutis, John Dolf, James Dunne, James Hovath, Steven LaChance, Kevin McCready, Gregory Schanuel. *Swings*: Kim M. Noor, Bob Renny.

1981.14 THE MOONY SHAPIRO SONGBOOK

A Musical Comedy in Two Acts[29]. Book by Monty Norman and Julian More. Music by Monty Norman. Lyrics by Julian More. Directed by Jonathan Lynn. Musical numbers staged by George Faison. Setting by Saul Radomsky. Costumes by Franne Lee. Lighting by Tharon Musser. Musical direction by Elman Anderson. Dance arrangements by Timothy Graphenreed. Vocal arrangements by Ray Cook. Associate conductor, Irving Joseph. Musical supervisor, Stanley Lebowsky. Sound by Otts Munderloh. Projections by Wendall Harrington. Originally produced on the London stage by Jack Gill for Stoll Productions, Ltd. by arrangement with The Cambridge Theatre Company, Ltd. Produced by Stuart Ostrow in association with T.A.T. Communications Company. Opened and closed 3 May 1981 at the Morosco Theatre after 1 performance.

CAST: JEFF GOLDBLUM plays Himself, Mr. Shapiro, Rocco the Shoeshine Boy, Talking Picture Star, Louis Da Rosa, French Crooner, Street Trumpeter, Fat German, Member of the Big Band Vocal Group, U.S.O. Entertainer, Marvin, Israeli Dancer, Russian Singer, Lee Pyong-Do, Liverpool Pop Group Drummer.

---

[28]Originally produced in New York 7 May 1953 at the Sam S. Shubert Theatre for 892 performances. For Synopsis of Scenes and Musical Numbers, see original 1953 production. "Every Man Is a Stupid Man," "If You Loved Me Truly" dropped for this production.

[29]Produced in London under the title *SONGBOOK*. The show presents the fictitious life and work of a prolific songwriter in revue form.

JUDY KAYE plays Herself, Reverend Mother, Mrs. Shapiro, Mrs. Kleinberg, Salvation Army Girl, Talking Picture Star, Torch Singer, Another Torch Singer, Busby Berkeley Girl, Bella, Fat German, Member of Big Band Vocal Group, Marlene, U.S.O. Entertainer, Rusty, Israeli Dancer, Kim-Sung, Liverpool Pop Singer, Sheila O'Toole.

TIMOTHY JEROME plays Himself, Moony Shapiro, Mr. Woo, Cop, Fat German, U.S.O. Entertainer, Senator "Beanpole" Pickles.

ANNE McGREEVEY plays Herself, Tilly, Mary Cassidy, Mae Feldman, Astrid Kalmar, Talking Picture Star, Dolly Ralston, Busby Berkeley Girl, French Music Hall Singer, Fat German, Member of Big Band Vocal Group, British Comedienne, U.S.O. Entertainer, Bonny Van Heysen, Debbie Stellman, Jude, Israeli Dancer, Russian Singer, KGB Officer, Lin-Chi, Magda Gyor, Liverpool Pop Group Singer.

GARY BEACH plays Himself, Dead End Kid, Rabbi Kotchinsky, Sailor, U.S. Immigration Officer, Talking Picture Star, First Newsboy, Rudy Vallee, Bum, Dancer, Busby Berkeley Tenor, Waiter, Flower Seller, Fat German, Gestapo Officer, Press Photographer, Member of Big Band Vocal Group, Second Newsboy, Prisoner-of-War Guard, U.S.O. Entertainer, Academy Awards Singer, Alvin Burns, Chuck, Israeli Dancer, Schmuel, Russian Singer, Johnny Bakuba, Bob Dylan, Bob Dylan's Spokesman, Benedict Rickenbaker, Leader of the Liverpool Pop Group, British Trades Union Leader, Bonny's Singing Partner.

Back-Up Singers: Philip Hoffman, Audrey Lavine, Brenda Pressley. *March of Time Announcer*: Philip Hoffman.

ACT 1

"Songbook" (from *BALTIMORE BALLYHOO* film, 1948)
Company
"East River Rhapsody" (from revue *FELDMAN FOLLIES OF 1926*)
G. Beach, Company
"Talking Picture Show" (from *EVERMORE* film, 1928)
J. Goldblum, J. Kaye, A. McGreevey, G. Beach
"Meg" (Trunk Song, 1929)
T. Jerome
"Mister Destiny" (from hit recording, 1930)
J. Kaye
"Your Time Is Different to Mine" (from hit recording, 1932)
J. Kaye
"Pretty Face" (from *PRETTY FACES OF 1934* film)
G. Beach, A. McGreevey, J. Kaye
"Je Vous Aime, Milady" (from hit recording, 1935)
J. Goldblum
"Les Halles" (Cabaret Song, 1935)
A. McGreevey
"Olympics'36" (from hit recording, 1936)
Company
"Nazi Party Pooper" (Trunk Song, 1936)
T. Jerome
"I'm Gonna Take Her Home to Momma" (from hit recording, 1938)
A. McGreevey, J. Kaye, J. Goldblum, G. Beach
War Songs 1939-1945:
"Bumpity-Bump"
A. McGreevey
"The Girl in the Window" (Das Mädchen Am Fenster)
J. Kaye
"Victory"
Company
Academy Award-winning Hollywood Evergreens 1945-1948:
"April in Wisconsin" (from *A YANK AT THE VATICAN* film)/
"It's Only a Show" (from *LET'S DO THE SHOW RIGHT HERE* film)/
"Bring Back Tomorrow" (from *BRING BACK TOMORROW* film)
G. Beach
"Songbook" (reprise)(from *BALTIMORE BALLYHOO*, 1948)
Company

ACT 2

"Happy Hickory" (from musical *HAPPY HICKORY*, 1954)
A. McGreevey
HAPPY HICKORY Rejects (Trunk Songs)—
"When a Brother Is a Mother to His Sister"
T. Jerome
"Climbin'"
A. McGreevey
"Don't Play That Lovesong Anymore"
T. Jerome
Vocal Gems from *HAPPY HICKORY*:
"Happy Hickory" (reprise)
Company
"Lovely Sunday Mornin'"
A. McGreevey, G. Beach
"Rusty's Dream Ballet"
J. Kaye, J. Goldblum
"A Storm in My Heart"
G. Beach, A. McGreevey, J. Goldblum, J. Kaye
"The Pokenhatchit Public Protest Committee"
Company
"Happy Hickory" (reprise)
Company
"I Accuse" (from *RED, WHITE AND BLACK*, 1957)
A. McGreevey, J. Kaye
"Messages I" (Trunk Song, 1958)
J. Goldblum
"Messages II" (Version for Bob Dylan, 1963)
G. Beach
"I Found Love" (from hit recording, 1964)
A. McGreevey, J. Kaye, J. Goldblum, G. Beach
"Don't Play that Lovesong Anymore" (Trunk Song)
J. Kaye
"Golden Oldie" (Trunk Song, 1972)
T. Jerome
"Climbin'" (from hit recording, 1972)
A. McGreevey, G. Beach, J. Goldblum, J. Kaye, T. Jerome
"Nostalgia" (Trunk Song, 1977)
J. Goldblum
Finale
Company

1981.15 INACENT BLACK

A Heaven-Sent Comedy (with songs) in Two Acts, 9 Scenes[30]. Play by A. Marcus Hemphill. Original music and lyrics by (Gene) McFadden, (John) Whitehead and (Melba) Moore. Directed by Mikell Pinkney. Scenic design by Felix E. Cochren. Costume design by Marty Pakledinaz. Lighting design by Tim Phillips. Sound design by Joseph Donohue. Musical conductor, Barry Eastmond. Associate director, Ed Cambridge. Produced by Gloria Hope Sher, Marjorie Moon and Jay J. Cohen in association with Zaida Coles Edley and Spirit Will Productions (a subsidiary of Bedford Stuyvesant Restoration Corporation). Opened 6 May 1981 at the Biltmore Theatre and closed 17 May 1981 after 15 performances.

CAST (in order of appearance): *Helwin Rydell*: Gregory Miller. *Mama Essie Rydell*: BARBARA MONTGOMERY. *Mary Rydell*: Reginald Vel Johnson. *Charles Rydell*: Count Stovall. *Percy Rydell*: Bruce Strickland. *Waitress*: Rosanna Carter. *Inacent Black*: MELBA MOORE. *Pretty Pete*: Ronald "Smokey" Stevens. *Carmen Casteel*: Joyce Sylvester. *Sally-Baby Washington*: Lorey Hayes. *Voice of Hamilton Rydell*: Ed Cambridge.

The action takes place in the spring, 1980, in the Rydell Estate Mansion in Old Westbury, Long Island, and in New York City.

Act 1, Scene 1: Friday, 10:15 A.M. Study of the Rydell Mansion in Old Westbury, Long Island, New York. *Scene 2*: Friday, 1:00 P.M. Coffee Shop at New York Port Authority. *Scene 3*: Friday, 4:00 P.M. Rydell Mansion. *Scene 4*: Saturday, 9:00 A.M. Rydell Mansion. *Scene5*: Saturday, Noon. Rydell Mansion.

Act 2, Scene 1: Saturday, 2:30P.M. Near an outside phone booth—New York City. *Scene 2*: Saturday, 3:00 P.M. Central Park—New York City. *Scene 3*: Saturday, 6:00 P.M. Rydell Mansion. *Scene 4*: Sunday, 8:15 P.M. Rydell Mansion.

MUSICAL NUMBERS[31]

"Stand Together"
"He's All That We Need"
"Somebody Told Me"

1981.16 LENA HORNE: THE LADY AND HER MUSIC

A Musical Revue in Two Acts. Production staged by Arthur Faria. Musical direction by Harold Wheeler. Scenery designed by David Gropman.

[30]Originally produced in Brooklyn *as INACENT BLACK AND THE FIVE BROTHERS* by the Billie Holiday Theatre 12 May 1979 for 7 months of performances.
[31]Musical numbers not listed in program; above list prepared from press materials.

Costumes designed by Stanley Simmons. Lighting designed by Thomas Skelton. Musical conductor, Coleridge-Taylor Perkinson. Musical consultants, Luther Henderson, Coleridge Taylor-Perkinson. Miss Horne's Wardobe, Giorgio Sant'Angelo. Assistant conductor, Linda Twine. Produced by James M. Nederlander, Michael Frazier, Fred Walker in association with Sherman Sneed and Jack Lawrence. Opened 12 May 1981 at the Nederlander Theatre and closed 30 June 1982 after 333 performances.

CAST: LENA HORNE.

Lena's Trio: Grady Tate (Drums), Steve Bargonetti (Guitar), Bob Cranshaw (Bass).
The Company: Clare Bathé, Tyra Ferrell, Vondie Curtis-Hall. *Alternates*: Deborah Lynn Bridges, Peter Oliver-Norman.

ACT 1[32]

"From This Moment On" (from *KISS ME KATE* film)
(*Music and Lyrics by* Cole Porter. *Arranged by* Ron Roullier.)

"I Got a Name"
(*Music and Lyrics by* Norman Gimbel, Charles Fox. *Arranged by* Harold Wheeler.)

"I'm Glad There Is You"
(*Music and Lyrics by* Paul Madeira, Jimmy Dorsey. *Arranged by* Lennie Hayton.)

"I Want To Be Happy" (from *NO, NO, NANETTE*)
(*Music by* Vincent Youmans. *Lyrics by* Irving Caesar. *Arranged by* Bob Freedman.)

Cotton Club Revue: (*Arrangements by* Coleridge-Taylor Perkinson.)

"Copper Colored Gal (of Mine)" (from *COTTON CLUB PARADE*, 1936, 27th ed)
(*Music and Lyrics by* Benny Davis and J. Fred Coots.)

"Raisin' the Rent" (from *COTTON CLUB PARADE*, 1933, 22nd ed)
(*Music by* Harold Arlen. *Lyrics by* Ted Koehler.)

"As Long As I Live" (from *COTTON CLUB PARADE*, 1934, 24th ed)
(*Music by* Harold Arlen. *Lyrics by* Ted Koehler.)

"Lady With a Fan" (from *COTTON CLUB PARADE*, 1933, 23rd ed)
(*Music by* Harold Arlen. *Lyrics by* E. Y. Harburg.)

Cotton Club to Hollywood

"Where or When" (from *BABES IN ARMS*)
(*Music by* Richard Rodgers. *Lyrics by* Lorenz Hart. *Arranged by* Harold Wheeler.)

"Can't Help Lovin' Dat Man" (from *SHOWBOAT*)
(*Music by* Jerome Kern. *Lyrics by* Oscar Hammerstein II. *Arranged by* Ron Roullier.)

Hollywood

"Just One of Those Things" (from *JUBILEE*)
(*Music and Lyrics by* Cole Porter. *Arranged by* Ron Roullier.)

"Stormy Weather"
(*Music by* Harold Arlen. *Lyrics by* Ted Koehler. *Arranged by* Bob Freedman.)

"Love" (from *THE ZIEGFELD FOLLIES* film, 1946)
(*Music and Lyrics by* Hugh Martin and Ralph Blane. *Arranged by* Mark Wolfram, Gil Askey, C. T. Perkins.)

Broadway

"Push de Button" (from *JAMAICA*)
(*Music by* Harold Arlen. *Lyrics by* E. Y. Harburg. *Arranged by* Ron Roullier.)

"The Lady Is a Tramp" (from *BABES IN ARMS*)
(*Music by* Richard Rodgers. *Lyrics by* Lorenz Hart. *Arranged by* Mark Wolfram, Gil Askey, C. T. Perkins.)

"Yesterday When I Was Young"
(*Music by* Charles Aznavour. *Lyrics by* Herbert Kretzmer. *Arranged by* Harold Wheeler.)

"Deed I Do"
(*Music by* Walter Hirsch. *Lyrics by* Fred Rose. *Arranged by* Grady Tate and Lena Horne.)

"Life Goes On"
(*Music by* Paul Williams. *Lyrics by* Craig Doerge. *Arranged by* Harold Wheeler.)

ACT 2

"Watch What Happens" (from *THE UMBRELLAS OF CHERBOURG* film)
(*Music by* Michel Legrand. *English Lyrics by* Norman Gimbel. *Arranged by* Gary Anderson.)

"The Surrey With the Fringe on Top" (from *OKLAHOMA!*)
(*Music by* Richard Rodgers. *Lyrics by* Oscar Hammerstein II. *Arranged by* Lennie Hayton.)

"Fly"
(*Music and Lyrics by* Martin Charnin. *Arranged by* Coleridge-Taylor Perkinson.)

"Bewitched" (from *PAL JOEY*)
(*Music by* Richard Rodgers. *Lyrics by* Lorenz Hart. *Arranged by* Harold Wheeler.)

"A Lady Must Live" (from *AMERICA'S SWEETHEART*)
(*Music by* Richard Rodgers. *Lyrics by* Lorenz Hart. *Arranged by* Coleridge-Taylor Perkinson.)

Love This Business

"That's What Miracles Are All About"
(*Music and Lyrics by* Charlie Smalls. *Arranged by* Coleridge-Taylor Perkinson.)

Early Career

"I'm Going to Sit Right Down and Write Myself a Letter"
(*Music by* Fred Ahlert. *Lyrics by* Joe Young. *Arranged by* Coleridge-Taylor Perkinson.)

"Stormy Weather" (reprise)

"If You Believe" (from *THE WIZ*)
(*Music and Lyrics by* Charlie Smalls. *Arranged by* Harold Wheeler and Gary Anderson.)

---

[32]Song list prepared from program and Original Cast live recording. Also performed:

"Better Than Anything"
(*Music and Lyrics by* D. Wheat and William Loughborough.)

1981–1982 SEASON

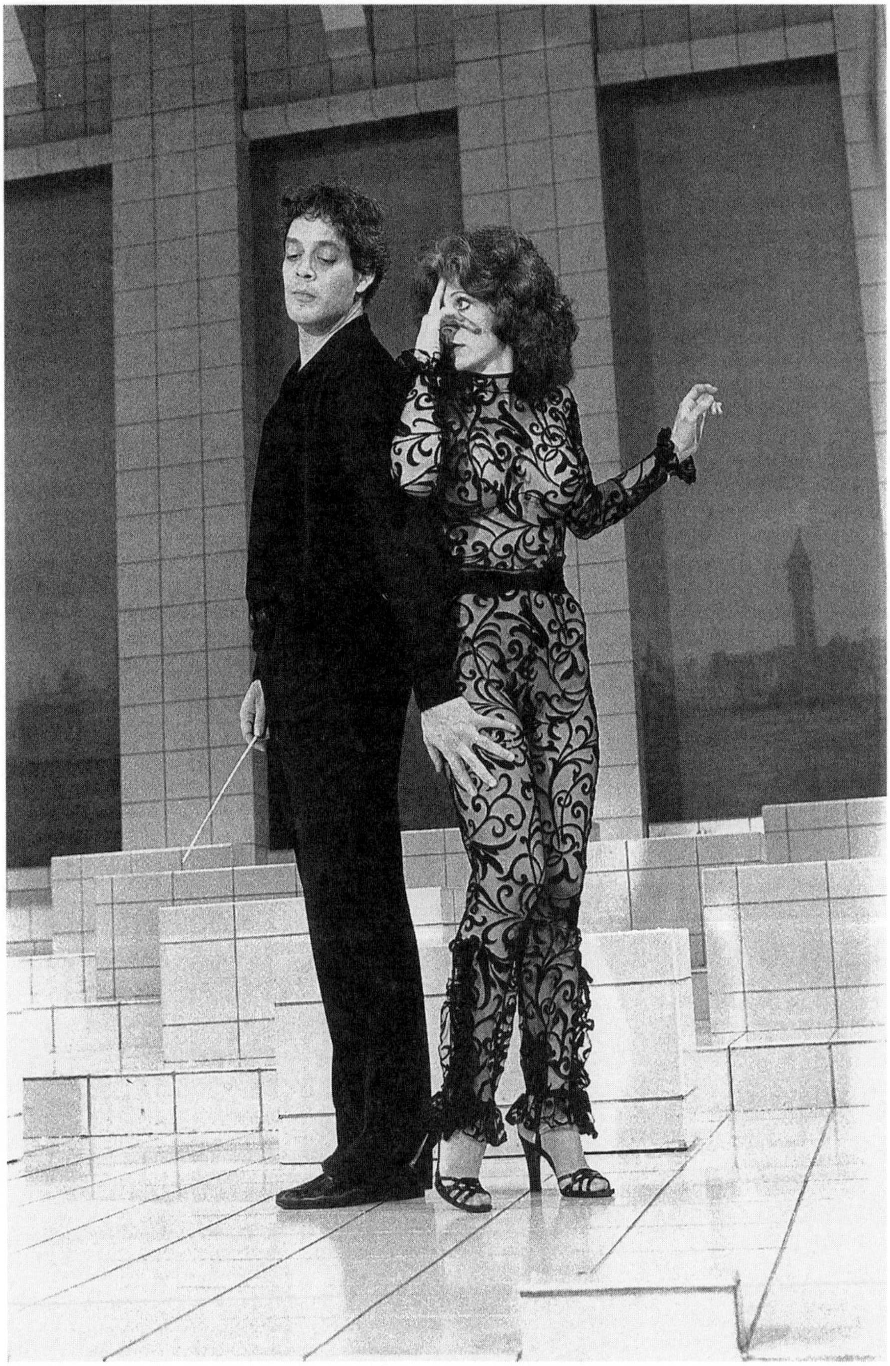

Raul Julia and Anita Morris in NINE
Martha Swope/TimePix

Chorus: Kenneth D. Ard, Marlene Danielle, Robert Hoshour, Renee Dulaney, Timothy Tobin, Teri Gibson, Diane Pennington, Caryn Richmond.

The action takes place in England in 1593. The story of this drama is true and accurate, except for minor adjustments in time for dramatic purpose.

Act 1, Scene 1: Queen Elizabeth's Bed Chamber. 28 May. Late morning. *Scene 2*: Backstage at the Globe Theatre. A few hours later. *Scene 3*: The Mall near St. James Palace. During the Jubilee Festival. *Scene 4*: Sir Walter Raleigh's Observatory. That evening. *Scene 5*: The Privy Council Chamber at St. James Palace. 30 May. Morning.

Act 2, Scene 1: Eleanor Bull's Tavern at Deptford. 30 May. Early evening. *Scene 2*: Deptford Waterfront Docks. 30 May. Later that evening. *Scene 3*: The Courtyard at St. James Palace. A few days later.

ACT 1

Prologue
Chroniclers

"Rocking the Boat"
R. Serra, M. Warncke, S. Hall, Chorus

"Because I'm a Woman"
L. Mordente, L. Del Duca, Jr., J. H. Kurtz

"Live for the Moment"
P. Jude, Company

"Emelia"
L. Del Duca, Jr., P. Jude

"I'm Coming 'Round to Your Point of View"
P. Jude, L. Mordente

"The Ends Justify the Means"
R. Rosen, D. Greenfield

"Higher Than High"
P. Jude, L. Mordente, J. H. Kurtz, L. Del Duca, Jr., Chorus

"Rocking the Boat" (reprise)
Company

ACT 2

Act 2 Prologue
Chroniclers

"Christopher"
L. Mordente, Chorus

"So Do I" (Ode to Virginity)
J. H. Kurtz, Chorus

"Two Lovers"
L. Mordente

"The Funeral Dirge"
J. H. Kurtz, L. Mordente, L. Del Duca, Jr., R. Rosen, S. Hall, M. Warncke

"Live for the Moment" (reprise)
P. Jude, L. Mordente

"Emelia" (reprise)
P. Jude, L. Mordente

"Can't Leave Now"
P. Jude

"Christopher" (reprise)
L. Mordente, L. Del Duca, Jr., Company

"The Madrigal Blues"
P. Jude, Company

1981.25

OH, BROTHER!

A Musical Comedy in One Act. Book[7] and lyrics by Donald Driver. (Suggested by William Shakespeare's "The Comedy of Errors" and the comedies of Plautus.) Music by Michael Valenti. Directed and staged by Donald Driver. Scenery designed by Michael J. Hotopp, Paul DePass. Costumes designed by Ann Emonts. Lighting designed by Richard Nelson. Musical direction, vocal and dance arrangements by Marvin Laird. Sound designed by Richard Fitzgerald. Orchestrations by Jim Tyler. Assistant choreographer, Ahmed Hussein. Produced by Zev Bufman, the John F. Kennedy Center, the Fisher Theater Foundation, Joan Cullman, Sidney Shlenker. Opened 10 November 1981 at the ANTA Theatre and closed 11 November 1981 after 3 performances.

CAST (in order of appearance): *Revolutionary Leader*: LARRY MARSHALL. *Revolutionaries*: Mark Martino, Thomas LoMonaco. *Bugler*: Sal Provenza. *Revolutionary Women*: ALYSON REED, Pamela Khoury, Kathy Mahoney-Bennett, Geraldine Hanning, Suzanne Walker, Karen Teti. *Revolutionaries*: Stephen Bourneuf, Michael-Pierre Dean. *Lew*: RICHARD B. SHULL. *A Camel*: Steve Sterner, Eric Scheps. *Western Mousada*: HARRY GROENER. *Western Habim*: ALAN WEEKS. *Fatatatatatima*: ALYSON REED. *Eastern Habim*: JOE MORTON. *Eastern Mousada*: DAVID-JAMES CARROLL. *Saroyana*: JUDY KAYE. *Musica*: MARY MASTRANTONIO. *Revolutionaries*: Steve Sterner, Eric Scheps. *Balthazar*: BRUCE ADLER. *Ayatollah*: Thomas LoMonaco. *Lillian*: Geraldine Hanning.

The action takes place at the present time on the Persian Gulf.

MUSICAL NUMBERS

"We Love an Old Story"
L. Marshall, Revolutionaries

"I To the World"
H. Groener, A. Weeks, D. Carroll, J. Morton

"How Do You Want Me?"
J. Kaye

"That's Him"
M. Mastrantonio, Revolutionaries

"Everybody Calls Me by My Name"
H. Groener, Revolutionaries

"O.P.E.C. Maiden"
H. Groener, Revolutionaries

"A Man"
D. Carroll

"How Do You Want Me?" (reprise)
J. Kaye

"Tell Sweet Saroyana"
D. Carroll, A. Weeks, Arabs

"What Do I Tell People This Time?"
J. Kaye

"O.P.E.C. Maiden" (reprise)
M. Mastrantonio, Women

"A Loud and Funny Song"
J. Kaye, M. Mastrantonio, A. Reed

"The Chase"
Full Company

"I To the World" (reprise)
H. Groener, A. Weeks, D. Carroll, J. Morton

"Oh, Brother!"
Full Company

1981.26

CAMELOT

A Return Engagement of the Revival of the Musical in Two Acts, 14 Scenes[8]. Book and lyrics by Alan Jay Lerner. Based on the novel "The Once and Future King" by T. H. White. Music by Frederick Loewe. Directed by Frank Dunlop. Choreography by Buddy Schwab. Sets and costumes by Desmond Heeley. Lighting design by Thomas Skelton. Musical director, Franz Allers. Conductor, Terry James. Orchestrations by Robert Russell Bennett and Philip J. Lang. Sound design by John McClure. Musical consultant, Robert Kreis. Artistic consultant, Stone Widney. A Dome/Cutler-Herman Production. Associate producers, Steve Herman, Jon Cutler. Produced by Mike Merrick and Don Gregory. Opened 15 November 1981 at the Winter Garden and closed 2 January 1982 after 57 performances.

CAST (in order of appearance): *Arthur*: RICHARD HARRIS. *Sir Sagramore*: Andy McAvin. *Merlyn*: James Valentine. *Guenevere*: MEG BUSSERT. *Sir Dinadan*: William Parry. *Nimue*: Jeanne Caryl. *Lancelot*: RICHARD MUENZ. *Mordred*: RICHARD BACKUS. *Dap*: Robert Molnar. *Friar*: Vincenzo Prestia. *Lady Anne*: Sally Williams. *Lady Sybil*: Patrice Pickering. *Sir Lionel*: William James. *King Pellinore*: BARRIE INGHAM. *Horrid*: Daisy. *Sir Lionel's Squire*: Steve Osborn. *Sir Sagramore's Squire*: Randy Morgan. *Sir Dinadan's Squire*: Richard Maxon. *Knights of the Investiture*: Bruce Sherman, Jack Sharkey, Ken Henley, Ronald Bennett Stratton. *Tom*: Thor Fields.

Knights, Lords, Ladies of the Court: Elaine Barnes, Marie Berry, Bjarne Buchtrup, Jeanne Caryl, Melanie Clements, John Deyle, Norb Joerder, Kelby Kirk, Debra Dickinson, Kathy Flynn-McGrath, Ken Henley, William James, Dale Kristien, Lorraine Lazarus, Lauren Lipson, Craig Mason, Richard Maxon, Andy McAvin, Robert Molnar, Randy Morgan, Ann Neville, Steve Osborn, Patrice Pickering, Joel Sager, Mariellen Sereduke, D. Paul Shannon, Bruce Sherman, Jack Starkey, Ronald Bennett Stratton, Nicki Wood. *Alternates*: Ellyn Arons, Gary Wales.

---

[7]Program note: Litigation pending W. Shakespeare and Plautus.

[8]Originally produced in New York 3 December 1960 at the Majestic Theatre for 873 performances; this revival previously produced in New York 8 July 1980 at the New York State Theatre for 56 performances. For Synopsis of Scenes and Musical Numbers, see 1980 revival.

1981.27 ## MERRILY WE ROLL ALONG

A Musical Comedy in Two Acts, 17 Scenes. Book by George Furth. Based on the play of the same name by George S. Kaufman and Moss Hart. Music and lyrics by Stephen Sondheim. Production directed by Harold Prince. Choreography by Larry Fuller. Scenery designed by Eugene Lee. Costumes designed by Judith Dolan. Lighting designed by David Hersey. Orchestrations by Jonathan Tunick. Musical director, Paul Gemignani. Sound design by Jack Mann. Dance arrangements by Tom Fay, Arnold Gross. Associate producers, Ruth Mitchell, Howard Haines. Produced by Lord Grade, Martin Starger, Robert Fryer, Harold Prince. Opened 16 November 1981 at the Alvin Theatre and closed 28 November 1981 after 16 performances.

CAST (in order of appearance): *Franklin Shephard*: JIM WALTON. *Mary Flynn*: ANN MORRISON. *Charley Kringas*: LONNY PRICE. *Gussie*: TERRY FINN. *Joe*: JASON ALEXANDER. *Beth*: SALLY KLEIN. *Franklin Shephard (at age 43)*: Geoffrey Horne. *Jerome*: David Cady. *Terry*: Donna Marie Elio. *Ms. Gordon*: Maryrose Wood. *Alex*, Talk Show Host: Marc Moritz. *Gwen Wilson*: Tonya Pinkins. *Ted*: David Loud. *Les*: David Shine. *Mr. Spencer*: Paul Hyams. *Mrs. Spencer*: Mary Johansen. *Meg*: Daisy Prince. *Ru*: Forest D. Ray. *Bartender*: Tom Shea. *Evelyn*: Abby Pogrebin. *Valedictorian*: Giancarlo Esposito. *George*, the Headwaiter: James Bonkovsky. *Girl auditioning*: Marianna Allen. *Nightclub Waitress*: Liz Callaway. *Photographer*: Steven Jacob. *Soundman*: Clark Sayre. *Waiter*: Gary Stevens.

The action moves backwards in time from 1980 to 1955.

Act 1, Scene 1: Lake Forest Academy, Lake Forest, Illinois. 1980. *Scene 2*: Franklin Shepard's house, Bel Air, California. 1979. *Scene 3*: 1979-1976. *Scene 4*: The Polo Lounge of the Beverly Hills Hotel, Beverly Hills, California. 1975. *Scene 5*: A TV Studio, New York City. *Scene 6*: 1973-1969. *Scene 7*: Frank's Apartment. Central Park West, New York City. 1968. *Scene 8*: 1968-1966. *Scene 9*: Outside a courthouse, Centre Street. 1966.

Act 2, Scene 1: Outside a theatre. 1964. *Scene 2*: 1964-1962. *Scene 3*: Joe and Gussie's Apartment, Sutton Place. 1962. *Scene 4*: 1961. *Scene 5*: A small nightclub in Greenwich Village. 1960. *Scene 6*: Frank and Charley's apartment; Joe Josephson's office; Manhattan. 1959-1957. *Scene 7*: A rooftop on West 110th Street. 1957. *Scene 8*: Lake Forest Academy. 1955.

ACT 1

Scene 1
"Merrily We Roll Along"
Company

Scene 2
"Rich and Happy"
J. Walton, Company

Scene 3
"Merrily We Roll Along" (reprise)
Company

Scene 4
"Like It Was"
A. Morrison

Scene 5
"Franklin Shephard, Inc."
L. Price

Scene 6
"Merrily We Roll Along" (reprise)
Company

Scene 7
"Old Friends"
J. Walton, L. Price, A. Morrison

Scene 8
"Merrily We Roll Along" (reprise)
Company

Scene 9
"Not a Day Goes By"
J. Walton
"Now You Know"
A. Morrison, Company

ACT 2

Scene 1
"It's a Hit!"
J. Walton, A. Morrison, L. Price, J. Alexander

Scene 2
"Merrily We Roll Along" (reprise)
Company

Scene 3
"Good Thing Going"
L. Price, J. Walton

Scene 4
"Merrily We Roll Along" (reprise)
Company

Scene 5
"Bobby and Jackie and Jack"
L. Price, S. Klein, J. Walton, D. Loud
"Not a Day Goes By" (reprise)
J. Walton, A. Morrison

Scene 6
"Opening Doors"
J. Walton, L. Price, A. Morrison, J. Alexander, S. Klein

Scene 7
"Our Time"
J. Walton, L. Price, A. Morrison, Company

Scene 8
"The Hills of Tomorrow"
Company

1981.28 ## THE FIRST

A Musical in Two Acts, a Prologue and 17 Scenes. Book by Joel Siegel with Martin Charnin. Music by Bob Brush. Lyrics by Martin Charnin. Entire production staged and directed by Martin Charnin. Musical numbers choreographed by Alan Johnson. Scenery by David Chapman. Costumes by Carrie Robbins. Lighting by Marc B. Weiss. Sound by Louis Shapiro. Consultant, Rachel Robinson. Musical supervision, Orchestrations, dance arrangements by Luther Henderson. Musical conductor, Mark Hummel. Vocal arranger, Joyce Brown. Associate producer, Roger Luby. Produced by Zev Bufman and Neil Bogart, Michael Harvey and Peter A. Bobley. Opened 17 November 1981 at the Martin Beck Theatre and closed 12 December 1981 after 37 performances.

CAST (in order of appearance): *Patsy*, the bartender: Bill Buell. *Leo Durocher*: TREY WILSON. *Clyde Sukeforth*: RAY GILL. *Powers*: Sam Stoneburner. *Thurman*, Brooklyn Eagle Photographer: Thomas Griffith. *Branch Rickey*: DAVID HUDDLESTON. *Cannon*: Jack Hallett. *Holmes*: Stephen Crain. *Sorrentino*, a busboy: Paul Forrest. *People at the Bar* (Bartender, Soldier, and Girl): (D.) Peter Samuel, Bob Morrisey, Kim Criswell. *Jackie Robinson*: DAVID ALAN GRIER. *Third Baseman*: Steven Bland. *Junkyard Jones*: Luther Fontaine. *Catcher*: Michael Edward-Stevens. *Jo-Jo*: Rodney Saulsberry. *Umpire*: Paul Forrest. *Cool Minnie*: CLENT BOWERS. *Softball*: Paul Cook Tartt. *Bucky*: Michael Edward-Stevens. *Equipment Manager*: Steven Bland. *Redcap*: Michael Edward-Stevens. *Rachel Isum*: LONETTE McKEE. *Passengers*: Margaret Lamee, Sam Stoneburner, Rodney Saulsberry, Janet L. Hubert, Thomas Griffith, Kim Criswell, Steven Bland, Bob Morrisey, Stephen Crain, Boncellia Lewis. *Cuban Reporters*: Rodney Saulsberry, Steven Bland. *Swanee Rivers*: Steven Boockvor. *Casey Higgins*: COURT MILLER. *Hatrack Harris*: D. Peter Samuel. *Pee Wee Reese*: Bob Morrisey. *Eddie Stanky*: Stephen Crain. *Dodger Coaches*: Jack Hallett, Bill Buell. *Dodger Rookie*: Thomas Griffith. *Trainer*: Paul Forrest. *Fans*: Boncellia Lewis, Steven Bland, Michael Edward-Stevens, Janet Hubert, Rodney Saulsberry. *Sheriff*: Jack Hallett. *Huey*, a fan: Jack Hallett. *Philadelphia Reporters*: Paul Forrest, Jack Hallett. *Brian Waterhouse*: Bill Buell. *Opal* (on the left): Janet L. Hubert. *Ruby* (on the right): Boncellia Lewis. *Dodger Wives*: Kim Criswell, Margaret Lamee. *Red Barber*: Himself. *Hilda Chester*: Kim Criswell. *Pittsburgh Pirates*: Stephen Crain, Thomas Griffith.

The play dramatizes actual events in the life of Jackie Robinson that occurred between August 1945 and September 1947. Some characters have been created and some chronology and situations have been altered.

Prologue: On the Playing Field.

Act 1, Scene 1: Gallagher's Restaurant, West 52nd Street, New York. *Scene 2*: The Third Base Line; Comiskey Park, Chicago. *Scene 3*: The Locker Room of the Kansas City Monarchs in Chicago. *Scene 4*: Union Station, Chicago. *Scene 5*: Branch Rickey's Office: 215 Montague Street, Brooklyn. *Scene 6*: The Havana Training Camp of the Brooklyn Dodgers. *Scene 7*: Outside a Ballpark; Jacksonville, Florida. *Scene 8*: The Locker Room. *Scene 9*: Branch Rickey's Office. *Scene 10*: The Playing Field.

Act 2, Scene 1: Behind First Base, The Polo Grounds, New York. *Scene 2*: The Dodger Locker Room, Shibe Park, Philadelphia. *Scene 3*: Behind Third Base, Ebbets Field. *Scene 4*: The Front Porch of a Farmhouse, Outside of St. Louis. *Scene 5*: Outside Ebbets Field. *Scene 6*: Inside Ebbets Field. The bottom of the seventh. *Scene 7*: Inside Ebbets Field. The top of the ninth.

ACT 1

Scene 1
"Jack Roosevelt Robinson"
D. Huddleston, T. Wilson, R. Gill

Scene 2
"Dancin' Off Third"
D. A. Grier, L. Fontaine, the Monarchs
Scene 3
"The National Pastime"
C. Bowers, D. A. Grier, L. Fontaine, the Monarchs
Scene 4
"Will We Ever Know Each Other"
D. A. Grier, L. McKee
Scene 5
"The First"
D. A. Grier
Scene 6
"Bloat"
T. Wilson, Reporters, the Dodgers
Scene 7
"The First" (reprise)
D. A. Grier
Scene 8
"It Ain't Gonna Work!"
C. Miller, the Dodgers
"The Brooklyn Dodger Strike"
D. Huddleston, T. Wilson
Scene 9
"Jack Roosevelt Robinson" (reprise)
D. Huddleston
"The First" (reprise)
L. McKee

ACT 2
Scene 1
"You Do-Do-Do-It Good!"
C. Bowers, D. A. Grier, L. Fontaine, the Monarchs, J. Hubert, B. Lewis
Scene 2
"Is This Year Next Year?"
S. Stoneburner, Reporters, D. Huddleston, R. Gill, the Dodgers
Scene 3
"There Are Days And There Are Days"
L. McKee
Scene 4
"It's a Beginning"
D. Huddleston, D. A. Grier
Scene 5
"The Opera Ain't Over"
K. Criswell, the Fans, D. A. Grier, the Dodgers, L. McKee, D. Huddleston

1981.29 DREAMGIRLS

A Musical in Two Acts, 20 Scenes. Book and lyrics by Tom Eyen. Music by Henry Krieger. Directed and choreographed by Michael Bennett. Co-choreographer, Michael Peters. Scenic design by Robin Wagner. Costume design by Theoni V. Aldredge. Lighting design by Tharon Musser. Sound design by Otts Munderloh. Musical supervision and orchestrations, Harold Wheeler. Musical director, Yolanda Segovia. Vocal arrangements, Cleavant Derricks. Produced by Michael Bennett, Bob Avian, Geffen Records, the Shubert Organization. Opened 20 December 1981 at the Imperial Theatre and closed 4 August 1985 after 1522 performances.

CAST (in order of appearance): *The Stepp Sisters*: Deborah Burrell, Vanessa Bell, Tenita Jordan, Brenda Pressley. *Charlene*: Cheryl Alexander. *Joanne*: Linda Lloyd. *Marty*: Vondie Curtis-Hall. *Curtis Taylor, Jr.*: BEN HARNEY. *Deena Jones*: SHERYL LEE RALPH. *The M.C.*: Larry Stewart. *Tiny Joe Dixon*: Joe Lynn. *Lorrell Robinson*: LORETTA DEVINE. *C. C. White*: OBBA BABATUNDE. *Effie Melody White*: JENNIFER HOLLIDAY. *Little Albert and the Tru-Tones*: Wellington Perkins, Charles Bernard, Jamie Patterson, Charles Randolph-Wright, Weyman Thompson. *James Thunder Early*: CLEAVANT DERRICKS. *Edna Burke*: Sheila Ellis. *The James Early Band*: Charles Bernard, Jamie Patterson, Wellington Perkins, Scott Plank, Charles Randolph-Wright, Weyman Thompson. *Wayne*: Tony Franklin. *Dave and the Sweethearts*: Paul Binotto, Candy Darling, Stephanie Eley. *Frank*, a press agent: David Thomé. *Michelle Morris*: Deborah Burrell. *Jerry*, a nightclub owner: Joe Lynn. *The Five Tuxedos*: Charles Bernard, Jamie Patterson, Charles Randolph-Wright, Larry Stewart, Weyman Thompson. *Les Style*: Cheryl Alexander, Tenita Jordan, Linda Lloyd, Brenda Pressley. *Film Executives*: Paul Binotto, Scott Plank, Weyman Thompson. *Mr. Morgan*: Larry Stewart. (N.B. *The Dreamettes, the Dreams* {through Act 1, Scene 11}: J. Holliday, L. Devine, S. L. Ralph. *Deena Jones and The Dreams* thereafter: S. L. Ralph, L. Devine, D. Burrell.)

Announcers, Fans, Reporters, Stagehands, Party Guests, Photographers: Cheryl Alexander, Phylicia Ayers-Allen, Vanessa Bell, Charles Bernard, Paul Binotto, Candy Darling, Ronald Dunham, Stephanie Eley, Sheila Ellis, Tenita Jordan, Linda Lloyd, Joe Lynn, Frank Mastrocola, Jamie Patterson, Wellington Perkins, Scott Plank, Brenda Pressley, David Thomé, Charles Randolph-Wright, Larry Stewart, Weyman Thompson. *Swings*: Brenda Braxton, Milton Craig Nealy.

Act 1: The Early Sixties. *Scene 1*: The Apollo Theatre. *Scene 2*: On the Road. *Scene 3*: A Recording Studio. *Scene 4*: Limbo. *Scene 5*: A Hotel in St. Louis. *Scene 6*: Miami. *Scene 7*: Dressing Room in the Atlantic Hotel. *Scene 8*: Cleveland. *Scene 9*: A TV Studio. *Scene 10*: San Francisco. *Scene 11*: Las Vegas, backstage. *Scene 12*: Las Vegas, on stage.

Act 2: The Early Seventies. *Scene 1*: Las Vegas Hilton. *Scene 2*: Chicago Nightclub. *Scene 3*: Vogue Magazine Photo Call. *Scene 4*: National Democratic Fundraiser. *Scene 5*: A Chicago Recording Studio. *Scene 6*: Los Angeles. *Scene 7*: Chicago. *Scene 8*: New York.

ACT 1
Scene 1
"I'm Looking for Something"
D. Burrell, V. Bell, T. Jordan, B. Pressley
"Goin' Downtown"
W. Perkins, C. Bernard, J. Patterson, C. Randolph-Wright, W. Thompson
"Takin' the Long Way Home"
J. Lynn
"Move (You're Steppin' on My Heart)"
J. Holliday, L. Devine, S. L. Ralph
"Fake Your Way to the Top"
C. Derricks, J. Holliday, L. Devine, S. L. Ralph, The James Early Band
"Cadillac Car"
B. Harney, C. Derricks, O. Babatunde, V. Curtis-Hall, The Company
Scene 2
"Cadillac Car" (reprise)
The Company
Scene 3
"Cadillac Car" (reprise)
The Company
Scene 4
"Cadillac Car" (reprise)
P. Binotto, C. Darling, S. Eley
"Steppin' to the Bad Side"
B. Harney, O. Babatunde, C. Derricks, T. Franklin, J. Holliday, L. Devine, S. L. Ralph, the Company
Scene 5
"Party, Party"
The Company
Scene 6
"I Want You Baby"
C. Derricks, J. Holliday, L. Devine, S. L. Ralph
Scene 7
"Family"
O. Babatunde, B. Harney, C. Derricks, S. L. Ralph, L. Devine
Scene 8
"Dreamgirls"
J. Holliday, L. Devine, S. L. Ralph
"Press Conference"
The Company
"Only the Beginning"
B. Harney, S. L. Ralph, J. Holliday
Scene 9
"Heavy"
J. Holliday, L. Devine, S. L. Ralph
Scene 10
"Heavy" (reprise)
J. Holliday, L. Devine, S. L. Ralph, B. Harney
Scene 11
"It's All Over"
B. Harney, J. Holliday, S. L. Ralph, L. Devine, O. Babatunde, D. Burrell, C. Derricks
"And I Am Telling You I Am Not Going"
J. Holliday

Scene 12
"Love Love You Baby"
L. Devine, S. L. Ralph, D. Burrell

ACT 2
Scene 1
"Dreams" Medley[9]
S. L. Ralph, L. Devine, D. Burrell, Company
Scene 2
"I Am Changing"
J. Holliday
Scene 3
"One More Picture Please"
The Company
"When I First Saw You"
B. Harney, S. L. Ralph
Scene 4
"Got to Be Good Times"
C. Bernard, J. Patterson, C. Randolph-Wright, L. Stewart, W. Thompson
"Ain't No Party"
L. Devine, C. Derricks
"I Meant You No Harm"
C. Derricks
"Quintette"
S. L. Ralph, L. Devine, O. Babatunde, D. Burrell, C. Derricks
"The Rap"
C. Derricks, O. Babatunde, V. Curtis-Hall, D. Thomé, L. Devine, the Company
Scene 5
"I Miss You Old Friend"
J. Holliday, V. Curtis-Hall, O. Babatunde, Les Style
"One Night Only"
J. Holliday
Scene 6
"One Night Only" (reprise)
S. L. Ralph, L. Devine, D. Burrell, Company
Scene 7
"I'm Somebody"
S. L. Ralph, L. Devine, D. Burrell
"Faith in Myself"
J. Holliday
Scene 8
"Hard To Say Goodbye, My Love"
S. L. Ralph, L. Devine, D. Burrell
("Dreamgirls" reprise)
(S. L. Ralph, L. Devine, D. Burrell, J. Holliday)

1982.01 LITTLE ME

A Revival of the Musical Comedy in Two Acts, 19 Scenes[10]. Book (revised) by Neil Simon. Based on the novel of the same name by Patrick Dennis. Music by Cy Coleman. Lyrics by Carolyn Leigh. Directed by Robert Drivas. Choreographed by Peter Gennaro. Sets and costumes by Tony Walton. Lighting by Beverly Emmons. Vocal and dance arrangements by Cy Coleman. Orchestrations by Harold Wheeler. Music director, Donald York. Sound designer, Tom Morse. Produced by Ron Dante, Wayne Rogers, Steven Leber, David Krebs, (J.) McLaughlin, (Marc) Piven, Inc., Warner Theatre Productions, Inc., Emanuel Azenberg. Opened 21 January 1982 at the Eugene O'Neill Theatre and closed 21 February 1982 after 36 performances.

CAST (in order of appearance): *Act 1: Announcer*: Gibby Brand. *Belle* (today): JESSICA JAMES. *Charlie Drake*: Henry Sutton. *Belle*: MARY GORDON MURRAY. *Momma*: Mary Small. *Ramona*: Mary C. Holton. *Cerine*: Gail Pennington. *Bruce*: Brian Quinn. *Noble Eggleston* VICTOR GARBER. *Flo Eggleston*: JAMES COCO. *Greensleeves*: Henry Sutton. *Ms. Kepplewhite*: Maris Clement. *Pinchley Junior*: James Brennan. *Nurse*: Sean Murphy. *Amos Pinchley*: JAMES COCO. *Town Spokesman*: Henry Sutton. *Court Clerk*: Stephen Berger. *Attorney*: Gibby Brand. *Bandleader*: Gibby Brand. *Henchmen*: Bob Freschi, Stephen Berger. *Frankie Polo*: Don Correia. *Val du Val*: VICTOR GARBER. *Fred Poitrine*: VICTOR GARBER. *Boom Boom Girls*: Bebe Neuwirth, Gail Pennington. *Bert*: Mark McGrath. *Sergeant*: Stephen Berger. *Preacher*: Gibby Brand. *German Soldier*: Gibby Brand. *General*: Gibby Brand. *Red Cross Nurse*: Andrea Green.

Act 2: Captain: Bob Freschi. *Steward*: David Cahn. *Sailor I*: Brian Quinn. *Sailor II*: Mark McGrath. *Mr. Worst*: JAMES COCO. *Assistant Director*: Henry Sutton. *Otto Schnitzler*: JAMES COCO. *Pharoah I*: Kevin Winkler. *Croupier*: James Brennan. *Doctor*: Gibby Brand. *Yulnick*: Gibby Brand. *Prince Cherney*: JAMES COCO. *Baby Belle*: MARY GORDON MURRAY. *Noble Junior*: VICTOR GARBER.

Townspeople, Skylight patrons, Nurses, Soldiers, Passengers, International set and Peasants: Stephen Berger, Michael Blevins, David Cahn, Maris Clement, Bob Freschi, Andrea Green, Mary C. Holton, Mark McGrath, Gary Mendelson, Sean Murphy, Bebe Neuwirth, Gail Pennington, Susan Powers, Brian Quinn, Kevin Brooks Winkler. *Swings*: John Hillner, Meredith Murray.

Act 1, Scene 1: The Casa Manana, Hackensack, New Jersey, this evening. Young Belle's home in Twin Jugs, Illinois, years ago. *Scene 2*: Noble Eggleston's home on Quality Hill. Belle's Shack. *Scene 3*: Pinchley's Bank. *Scene 4*: Young Belle's Apartment. *Scene 5*: The Skylight Roof Cafe. *Scene 6*: Young Belle's Apartment. *Scene 7*: Young Belle's Apartment, a few months later. In the trenches in Europe in World War I. *Scene 8*: A base hospital somewhere in France.

Act 2, Scene 1: The Casa Manana, tonight. On board ship, after World War I. *Scene 2*: Older Belle recalls her life back in the United States. *Scene 3*: The Dining Room in the Castle of Phillip Randolph Worst. *Scene 4*: Hollywood set at Paramour Pictures. *Scene 5*: Older Belle recalls her life after Hollwood. *Scene 6*: The Casino at Monte Carlo. *Scene 7*: The Royal Bedchamber of the Prince Cherny of Rosenzweig. *Scene 8*: Older Belle recalls her life after the Prince's funeral. The house on Quality Hill. *Scene 9*: Outside the house on Quality Hill. *Scene 10*: The house on Quality Hill. *Scene 11*: The Casa Manana, tonight.

ACT 1
Scene 1
"Don't Ask a Lady"
J. James
"The Other Side of the Tracks"
M. G. Murray
Scene 2
"The Rich Kids Rag" (The Birthday Party)
Company
"I Love You"
V. Garber, M. G. Murray, Company
"The Other Side of the Tracks" (reprise)
M. G. Murray
Scene 3
"Deep Down Inside"[11]
J. Coco, M. G. Murray, Company
Scene 5
"Boom-Boom"
V. Garber
"I've Got Your Number"
D. Correia
Scene 6
"Real Live Girl"
V. Garber
Scene 8
"Real Live Girl" (reprise)
Doughboys

ACT 2
Scene 1
"I Love You" (reprise)
V. Garber, M. G. Murray
Scene 3
"I Wanna Be Yours"
M. G. Murray, J. Coco
Scene 5
"Little Me"
J. James, M. G. Murray, M. Small

[9]During the run, replaced by a reprise of "Dreamgirls."

[10]Originally produced in New York 17 November 1962 at the Lunt-Fontanne Theatre for 257 performances. "The Truth," "Be a Perfomer!," "Dimples," "Poor Little Hollywood Star" were dropped for this production. "Don't Ask a Lady" and "I Wanna Be Yours" were newly written for this production.

[11]Choreography by Bob Fosse recreated from original production.

Scene 7

"Farewell" (The Prince's Goodbye)

J. Coco, G. Brand, H. Sutton, Company

Scene 8

"Here's To Us"

J. James, Company

Scene 11

(Finale)

J. James, Company

1982.02 THE CURSE OF AN ACHING HEART

A Drama (with Music) in One Act, a Prologue and 5 Scenes. Play (and lyrics) by William Alfred. Music by Claibe Richardson. Directed by Gerald Gutierrez. Sets designed by John Lee Beatty. Costumes designed by Nancy Potts. Lighting designed by Dennis Parichy. Sound designed by David Rapkin. Orchestrations by Bruce Pomohac. Associate producers, David Jiranek, Frederick C. Venturelli. Produced by Margot Harley, John Houseman, Everett King, David Weil, Sidney Shlenker. Opened 25 January 1982 at the Little Theatre and closed 21 February 1982 after 32 performances.

CAST (in order of appearance): *Prologue*: *Frances Walsh*: FAYE DUNAWAY. *Scene 1*: *Frances Anna Duffy*: FAYE DUNAWAY. *Gertrude "Lulu" Fitter*: Audrie Neenan. *Scene 2*: *Frances Anna Duffy*: FAYE DUNAWAY. *John Joseph " Jo Jo" Finn*: Bernie McInerney. *Scene 3*: *Pasquale "Packy" Malardino*: Jon Polito. *Man with newspaper*: Dale Helward. *Herman Crump*: Kurt Knudson. *Martin "Lugs" Walsh*: Terrance O'Quinn. *Fran Duffy*: FAYE DUNAWAY. *Lulu Fitter*: Audrie Neenan. *Minnie Crump*: Francine Beers. *J. Stanislaus McGahey*: Colin Stinton. *Aloysius "Wishy" Burke*: Paul McCrane. *Scene 4*: *Frances Anna Duffy Walsh*: FAYE DUNAWAY. *Gertrude "Lulu" Fitter Malardino*: Audrie Neenan. *Gertrude Graham Finn*: Beverly May. *Scene 5*: *Frances Anna Duffy*: FAYE DUNAWAY. *Martin Thomas Walsh*: Raphael Sbarge. *John Joseph " Jo Jo" Finn*: Bernie McInerney.

Prologue: 1942. *Scene 1*: Friday Night Dreams Come True—1923. *Scene 2*: Clothes Make the Woman—1925. *Scene 3*: The Curse of an Aching Heart—1927. *Scene 4*: All Saints, All Souls—1935. *Scene 5*: Holy Saturday—1942.

MUSICAL NUMBERS[12]

Scene 1

"Love to Your Heart's Desire"

F. Dunaway, A. Neenan

Scene 2

"Make It New"

F. Dunaway

Scene 3

"Spring, Spring, Spring"

J. Polito

"Thorsping"

A. Neenan, F. Dunaway

"I Got Eyes for a Girl on the Car"

J. Polito

"Ain't Love Grand"

A. Neenan, J. Polito

1982.03 JOSEPH AND THE AMAZING TECHNICOLOR DREAMCOAT

A Musical in Two Acts and a Prologue[13]. Music by Andrew Lloyd Webber. Lyrics by Tim Rice. Direction and choreography by Tony Tanner. Scenery by Karl Eigsti. Costumes by Judith Dolan. Lighting by Barry Arnold. Sound by Tom Morse. Musical supervision, arrangements and orchestrations by Martin Silvestri, Jeremy Stone. Musical director, David Friedman. Associate producers, Thomas Pennini, Jean Luskin, Jerome Edson. Produced by Zev Bufman, Susan R. Rose, Melvyn J. Estrin, Sidney Shlenker, Gail Berman by arrangement with The Robert Stigwood Organization Ltd. and David Land. Opened 27 January 1982 at the Royale Theatre and closed 4 September 1983 after 670 performances. Total, including Off-Broadway run: 747 performances.

CAST (in order of appearance): *Narrator*: LAURIE BEECHMAN. *Women's Chorus*: Lorraine Barrett, Karen Bogan, Katharine Buffaloe, Lauren Goler, Randon Lo, Joni Masella, Kathleen Rowe McAllen, Renée Warren. *Jacob*: GORDON STANLEY. *Brothers (11)*: *Reuben*: ROBERT HYMAN. *Simeon*: Kenneth Bryan. *Levi*: STEVE McNAUGHTON. *Napthali*: CHARLIE SERRANO. *Issachar*: Peter Kapetan. *Asher*: David Asher. *Dan*: James Rich. *Zebulon*: Doug Voet. *Gad*: Barry Tarallo. *Benjamin*: PHILIP CARRUBBA. *Judah*: Stephen Hope. *Joseph*: BILL HUTTON. *Ismaelites*: TOM CARDER, DAVID ARDAO. *Potiphar*: DAVID ARDAO. *Mrs. Potiphar*: RANDON LO. *Butler*: Kenneth Bryan. *Baker*: Barry Tarallo. *Pharaoh*: TOM CARDER. *Swings*: Rosalyn Rahn, John Ganzer.

Prologue ("You Are What You Feel")

L. Beechman

ACT 1

"Jacob and Sons"/"Joseph's Coat"

L. Beechman, Brothers, G. Stanley, B. Hutton, Women

"Joseph's Dreams"

L. Beechman, B. Hutton, Brothers

"Poor Poor Joseph"

L. Beechman, Brothers, Women

"One More Angel in Heaven"

S. McNaughton, Brothers

"Potiphar"

L. Beechman, Women, R. Lo, D. Ardao, B. Hutton

"Close Every Door"

B. Hutton, Women

"Stone the Crows"[14]

L. Beechman, T. Carder, B. Hutton, Women, Men

"Pharaoh's Story"

L. Beechman, Women

ACT 2

"Poor, Poor Pharaoh"/"Song of the King"

L. Beechman, T. Carder, Women, Men

"Pharaoh's Dream Explained"

B. Hutton, Women, Men

"Stone the Crows" (reprise)

L. Beechman, T. Carder, B. Hutton, Women, Men

"Those Canaan Days"

R. Hyman, Brothers

"The Brothers Came to Egypt"/"Grovel, Grovel"

L. Beechman, Brothers, B. Hutton, Women

"Who's the Thief?"

B. Hutton, Brothers, Women

"Benjamin Calypso"

C. Serrano, Brothers

"Joseph All the Time"

L. Beechman, B. Hutton, Brothers, Women

"Jacob in Egypt"

B. Hutton, Brothers, Women

"Any Dream Will Do"

B. Hutton, Company

"May I Return to the Beginning"

The Company

1982.04 PUMP BOYS AND DINETTES

A Musical in Two Acts[15]. Conceived and written by the Company (John Foley, Mark Hardwick, Debra Monk, Cass Morgan, John Schimmel, Jim Wann). Scenery by Doug Johnson, Christopher Nowak. Costumes by Patricia McGourty. Lighting by Fred Buchholtz. Sound by Bill Dreisbach.

---

[12]Songs not listed in program. Above list prepared from production typescript.

[13]Originally produced in New York Off-Broadway 18 November 1981 at the Entermedia Theatre for 77 performances. Previously produced Off-Broadway twice at the Brooklyn Academy of Music: 26 December 1976 for 22 performances, and 13 December 1977 for 24 performances.

[14]During the run and for subsequent national tour, replaced by:

"Go, Go Joseph"

L. Beechman, B. Tarallo, K. Bryan, Chorus, B. Hutton, Men

[15]Originally produced Off-Broadway 10 July 1981 at the Westside Arts Theatre for 20 performances, 13 October 1981 at the Colonnades Theatre for 112 performances.

Production coordinator, Sherman Warner. Produced by Dodger Productions (Michael David, Doug Johnson, Rocco Landesman, Des McAnuff, Edward Strong, Sherman Warner), Louis Busch Hager, Marilyn Strauss, Kate Studley, Warner Theatre Productions, Inc. and Max Weitzenhoffer. Opened 4 February 1982 at the Princess Theatre and closed 18 June 1983 after 573 performances.

CAST (in alphabetical order): *Jackson*: John Foley. *L.M.*: Mark Hardwick. *Prudie Cupp*: Debra Monk. *Rhetta Cupp*: Cass Morgan. *Eddie*: John Schimmel. *Jim*: Jim Wann.

ACT 1

"Highway 57"
All
(*Music and Lyrics by* Jim Wann.)

"Taking It Slow"
Pump Boys (Men)
(*Music and Lyrics by* John Foley, Mark Hardwick, John Schimmel, Jim Wann.)

"Serve Yourself"
M. Hardwick
(*Music and Lyrics by* Jim Wann.)

"Menu Song"
Dinettes (Women)
(*Music and Lyrics by* Debra Monk, Cass Morgan.)

"The Best Man"
D. Monk
(*Music and Lyrics by* Jim Wann.)

"Fisherman's Prayer"
Pump Boys
(*Music and Lyrics by* Jim Wann.)

"Caution: Men Cooking"[16]
Pump Boys
(*Music and Lyrics by* Debra Monk, Cass Morgan, Jim Wann, John Foley.)

"Mamaw"
J. Wann
(*Music and Lyrics by* Jim Wann.)

"Be Good or Be Gone"
C. Morgan
(*Music and Lyrics by* Jim Wann.)

"Drinkin' Shoes"
All
(*Music and Lyrics by* Mark Hardwick, Cass Morgan, Debra Monk.)

ACT 2

"Pump Boys"
Pump Boys
(*Music and Lyrics by* Jim Wann.)

"Mona"
J. Foley
(*Music and Lyrics by* Jim Wann.)

"T.N.D.P.W.A.M."
M. Hardwick
(*Music and Lyrics by* Jim Wann.)

"Tips"
Dinettes
(*Music and Lyrics by* Debra Monk, Cass Morgan.)

"Sister"
Dinettes
(*Music and Lyrics by* Cass Morgan.)

"Vacation"
All
(*Music and Lyrics by* Jim Wann.)

"No Holds Barred"
All
(*Music and Lyrics by* Jim Wann, Cass Morgan.)

"Farmer Tan"
M. Hardwick, Dinettes
(*Music and Lyrics by* Jim Wann.)

"Highway 57" (reprise)
All

[16]Replaced after opening with:
"Catfish"
Pump Boys
(*Music and Lyrics by* Jim Wann, Bland Simpson.)

"Closing Time"
All
(*Music and Lyrics by* Jim Wann.)

1982.05 LITTLE JOHNNY JONES

A Revival of the Musical (Comedy) in Two Acts, 8 Scenes[17]. Book, music and lyrics by George M. Cohan. Adapted by Alfred Uhry. Entire production directed by Gerald Gutierrez. Scenery designed by Robert Randolph. Costumes designed by David Toser. Lighting designed by Thomas Skelton. Sound designed by Abe Jacob. Choreography and musical staging by Dan Siretta. Musical direction by Lynn Crigler. Additional orchestrations by Eddie Sauter, Mack Schlefer. Dance arrangements by Russell Warner. Vocal arrangements and additional dance arrangements by Robert Fisher. Musical consultant, Alfred Simon. Production associate, Warren Pincus. Production supervisor, Robert Strauss. Originally produced by the Goodspeed Opera House, East Haddam, Connecticut (Michael P. Price, Executive producer). Presented by James M. Nederlander, Steven Leber, David Krebs, and the John F. Kennedy Center. Opened and closed 21 March 1982 at the Alvin Theatre after 1 performance.

CAST (in order of appearance): *Starter at the Hotel Cecil*: JACK BITTNER. *Anthony Anstey*, a racetrack man: PETER VAN NORDEN. *Florabelle Fly*, Society Editor of the *San Francisco Searcher*: JANE GALLOWAY. *Timothy D. McGee*, another racetrack man: TOM ROLFING. *Goldie Gates*, an American copper heiress: MAUREEN BRENNAN. *Sing-Song*, Sports Editor, *Peking Gazette*: Bruce Chew. *Whitney Wilson*, the great unknown: ERNIE SABELLA. *A Bellboy*: Al Micacchion. *Johnny Jones*, an American jockey: DONNY OSMOND. *Mrs. Kenworth*, Goldie's aunt and guardian: ANNA McNEELY. *Announcer at English Derby*: JACK BITTNER. *Captain Squirvy*: JACK BITTNER. *A Newsboy*: David Fredericks.

American Boys, Porters, Sailors: Richard Dodd, David Fredericks, James Homan, Gary Kirsch, Bobby Longbottom, Al Micacchion, David Monzione, Keith Savage. *American Girls*: Colleen Ashton, Terri Corcoran, Susie Fenner, Linda Gradl, Debra Grimm, Lori Lynott, Annette Michelle, Mayme Paul. *Dance Alternates*: Tammy Silva, Jonathan Aronson, Jamie Torcellini.

The action takes place in England, New York and Saratoga in 1904.

Act 1, Scene 1: Exterior of the Hotel Cecil, London, 1904. *Scene 2*: Interior of the Hotel Cecil, immediately following. *Scene 3*: Hyde Park, immediately following. *Scene 4*: The British Derby, that afternoon.

Act 2, Scene 1: Outside the Pier at Southampton, a week later. *Scene 2*: The Pier itself, immediately following. *Scene 3*: A New York Street, two weeks later. *Scene 4*: Saratoga, the Fourth of July.

ACT 1

Scene 1

"The Cecil in London"
J. Bittner, Ensemble

Scene 2

"Then I'd Be Satisfied With Life"
P. Van Norden

"Yankee Doodle Boy"
D. Osmond, Ensemble

Scene 3

"Oh, You Wonderful Boy" (from *THE LITTLE MILLIONAIRE*, 1911)
M. Brennan, J. Galloway, American Girls

Scene 4

"The Voice in My Heart" (from *LITTLE NELLIE KELLY*, 1922)
A. McNeely, Ensemble

"Finaletto"
Company

ACT 2

Scene 1

"Captain of a Ten Day Boat"
J. Bittner, Ensemble

Scene 2

"Goodbye Flo"
J. Galloway, Sailors

"Life's a Funny Proposition"
D. Osmond

[17]Originally produced in New York 7 November 1904 at the Liberty Theatre for 52 performances.

"Let's You and I Just Say Goodbye" (from *THE RISE OF ROSIE O'REILLY*, 1923)
M. Brennan
"Give My Regards to Broadway"
D. Osmond, Ensemble
Scene 3
"Extra! Extra!"
Newsboys
Scene 4
"American Ragtime" (from *THE AMERICAN IDEA*, 1908)
J. Galloway, T. Rolfing, D. Osmond, Ensemble
Finale
Company

1982.06 ENCORE

Fifty Years of Showstoppers (A Musical Revue) in Two Acts, 11 Scenes. Producer and director, Robert F. Jani. Musical director, Tom Bahler. Scenic designer, Charles Lisanby. Scenic coordinator, Terry Carriker. Production costume designer, Michael Casey. Lighting designer, Ken Billington. Staging and choreography by Adam Grammis, Geoffrey Holder, Frank Wagner, Shozo Nakano, Linda Lemac, Violet Holmes. Conductor, Joseph Klein. Produced by Radio City Music Hall Productions, Inc. Opened 26 March 1982 at the Radio City Music Hall and closed 6 September 1982 after 288 performances.

CAST: WENDY EDMEAD, TOM GARRETT, MICHAEL KUBALA, KUNIKO NARAI, DEBORAH PHELAN, JUSTIN ROSS, LUIS VILLANUEVA, KAREN ZIEMBA.

THE ROCKETTES: Lois Ann Alston, Kathy Beatty, Dottie Belle, Susan Boron, Elizabeth Chanin, Barbara Ann Cittadino, Susan Cleland, Eileen Marie Collins, Brie Daniels, Susanne Doris, Jackie Fancy, Deniene Fenn, Alexis Ficks, Prudence Gray, Jennifer Hammond, Carol Harbich, Cindy Hughes, Stephanie James, Joan Peer Kelleher, Pam Kelleher, Dee Dee Knapp, Judy Little, Sonya Livingston, Leslie Grysko, McCarthy, Mary McNamara, Lynn Newton, Pam Stacey Pasqualino, Kerri Pearsall, Cindy Peiffer, Gerri Presky, Terry Spano, Lynn Sullivan, Susan Theobald, Carol Toman, Pat Tully, Darlene Wendy, Rose Ann Woolsey, Phyllis Wujko.

THE NEW YORKERS: John Aller, David Brownlee, Rick Conant, Dale Furry, Edyie Fleming Geistman, Sonya Hensley, David Michael Johnson, Joe Joyce, Connie Kunkle, Rosemary Loar, Keith Locke, Edward Prostak, Susan Streater, Scott Willis.

Dancers: David Askler, Robert Boling, Leigh Catlett, Cisco X. Drayton, Larry Lynd, Will Mead, Jackie Patterson, David Roman, Stan Shelmire.

ACT 1
Scene 1
"Encore"
Full Company
(*Music by* Stanley Lebowsky. *Lyrics by* Fred Tobias. *Staged and Choreographed by* Adam Grammis assisted by Linda Lemac.)
Scene 2
Our Scrapbook of Memories
G. Hounsell
The Rockette selected to be Radio City Music Hall's Golden Jubilee Ambassador-to-the-World, recalls some of the great moments of the past with the assistance of an animated collage of photos and films.
Scene 3
The Glory of Easter (*Staged and Choreograped by* Linda Lemac.)
Full Company
"The Lord's Prayer"
(*Music by* Albert Hay Malotte.)
"Kamenoi Ostrow"
(*Music by* Anton Rubinstein.)
Originally presented in 1933 during the first year of the Music Hall, the cathedral spectacle quickly became a world-famous tradition, one of hundreds of lavish musical productions presented on The Great Stage through the years.
Scene 4
"Ohka-No-Zu" (Cherry Blossom)
The Rockettes
The Lions: T. Garrett, M. Kubala. (*Staged and Choreographed by* Shozo Nakano, assisted by Violet Holmes.)
The famed Doncho Curtain, a special gift to New York City from its sister city, Tokyo, was presented as an act of friendship in 1964. This magnificent curtain, the largest hand-woven silk, theatrical backdrop ever created, is featured in this international tribute to the Music Hall fiftieth anniversary.
Scene 5
"Rhapsody in Blue"
(*Music by* George Gershwin. *Staged and Choreographed by* Geoffrey Holder, assisted by Linda Lemac.)
Danced by K. Narai, L. Villanueva, The New Yorkers, The Rockettes, The Dancers
Gershwin himself gave his wholehearted approval to the Music Hall's first opulent staging of his "Rhapsody" in a production by Leon Leonidoff. The dance-realization of this Gershwin classic was so well recived that it has been brought back—and reinterpreted—many times, as in this, our Golden Jubilee production.
Scene 6
"Showstoppers"
V. Holmes, The Rockettes
(*Music by* John Kander. *Lyrics by* Fred Ebb. *Staged and Choreographed by* Frank Wagner and Violet Holmes.)
Founded by Russell Markert in 1925, the Rockettes quickly established a new style of American dance that has been widely emulated. Only rarely in their 57-year history has an audience had the opportunity to see how the Rockettes rehearse. Here is a backstage glimpse of the world's most famous precision dance troupe in drill with their real-life, present director.

ACT 2
Scene 1
"Bolero"
(*Music by* Maurice Ravel. *Staged and Choreographed by* Geoffrey Holder, assisted by Linda Lemac.)
Danced by K. Narai, L. Villanueva, The Dancers, The Rockettes
Soon after Arturo Toscanini introduced American audiences to Ravel's "Bolero" in 1929, the peice became a national craze. In February, 1935, barely two months after the Music Hall opened, a production by Leonidoff presented the work for the first time in America in its original dance version. Here, then, is a new interpreation of one of the Hall's most frequently requested favorites.
Scene 2
Fifty Years of American Popular Music
W. Edmead, T. Garrett, M. Kubala, D. Phelan, J. Ross, K. Ziemba, The New Yorkers
(*Staged and Choreographed by* Adam Grammis assisted by Linda Lemac.)
Whether danced, sung or played—or all three—Music Hall audiences have been treated to the best of America's own popular music during each of the past five decades. Here we relive some of the memorable tunes from past shows, songs that came from the great films, recordings and musicals of the day.
Scene 3
Dancing in Diamonds (*Staged and Choreographed by* Violet Holmes.)
"There Are No Girls Like Show Girls"The Rockettes
(*Music by* Donald Pippin. *Lyrics by* Sammy Cahn.)
"Encore"The Rockettes
(*Music by* Stanley Lebowsky. *Lyrics by* Fred Tobias.)
No anniversary tribute to the Music Hall would be complete without honoring the most sparkling act in show business, the Radio City Music Hall Rockettes. The world's most famous line of precision dancers dress their glamorous best to show you why fifty years of dancing at the Music Hall hasn't been nearly long enough.
Scene 4
"That's Entertainment" (from *THE BANDWAGON* film)
The Company
(*Music by* Arthur Schwartz. *Lyrics by* Howard Dietz. *Staged and Choreograped by* Frank Wagner.)
Radio City Music Hall is the greatest motion picture palace in the world having introduced more great stars and films to American audiences than any other theatre. The history of the Hall traces the story of entertainment itself—whole worlds of delight on stage and film that have sustained—and enlivened—the country's spirits for half a century.
Scene 5
A Salute to the Music Hall: "You're at the Music Hall"
Full Company
(*Music by* Donald Pippin. *Lyrics by* Sammy Cahn.)

1982.07 THE GRAND DUCHESS OF GÉROLSTEIN

A Revival of the Opéra-bouffe in Three Acts, 4 Scenes[18]. Original (French) libretto ("La Grande-Duchesse de Gérolstein") by Henri Meilhac and Ludovic Halévy. Music by Jacques Offenbach. English adaptation by Ruth and Thomas Martin. Directed by Jack Hofsis. Conducted by Antonio de Almeida. Choreography by Christopher Chadman. Scenery and costumes designed by John Conklin. Lighting designed by Gilbert V. Helmsley, Jr. Chorus master, Lloyd Walser. Produced by the New York City Opera. Opened 15 April 1982 at the New York State Theatre and closed 24 April 1982 after 5 performances in repretory[19].

CAST (in order of appearance): *Fritz*: HENRY PRICE. *Wanda*: LEIGH MUNRO. *General Boom*: CLAUDE CORBEIL. *Baron Puck*: JAMES BILLINGS. *Nepomuc*: William Ledbetter. *The Grand Duchess*: MURIEL COSTA-GREENSPON. *Prince Paul*: JACK HARROLD. *Notary*: Don Yule. *Baron Grog*: JONATHAN GREEN. *Ensemble*: New York City Opera Chorus.

Act 1: A Military Encampment in a small town of a European Duchy.

Act 2: A Hall in the Palace of the Grand Duchess.

Act 3, Scene 1: The Bridal Suite in the Right Wing. *Scene 2*: A Banquet Hall in the Palace.

1982.08 IS THERE LIFE AFTER HIGH SCHOOL?

A Musical in Two Acts. Book by Jeffrey Kindley. Suggested by the book of the same title by Ralph Keyes. Music and lyrics by Craig Carnelia. Entire production staged by Robert Nigro. Set design by John Lee Beatty. Costumes designed by Carol Oditz. Lighting design by Beverly Emmons. Sound design by Tom Morse. Musical direction and orchestrations by Bruce Coughlin. World premiere at Hartford Stage Company, Hartford, Connecticut. Associate producer, Robert Feiden. Produced by Clive Davis, Francois de Menil, Harris Maslansky, Twentieth-Century Fox Theater Productions, Inc. Opened 7 May 1982 at the Ethel Barrymore Theater and closed 16 May 1982 after 12 performances.

CAST (in alphabetical order): Raymond Baker, Cynthia Carle, Alma Cuervo, Sandy Faison, Harry Groener, Philip Hoffman, David Patrick Kelly, Maureen Silliman, James Widdoes.

ACT 1

"The Kid Inside"
Entire Company

"Things I Learned in High School"
H. Groener

"Second Thoughts"
R. Baker, S. Faison, D. P. Kelly, M. Silliman, J. Widdoes

"Nothing Really Happened"
A. Cuervo, Women

"Beer"
R. Baker, H. Groener, D. P. Kelly

"For Them"
P. Hoffman, Company

"Diary of a Homecoming Queen"
M. Silliman

ACT 2

"Thousands of Trumpets"
J. Widdoes, Company
Drum Major: H. Groener.

"Reunion"
Entire Company

"High School All Over Again"
D. P. Kelly

"Fran and Janie"
S. Faison, M. Silliman

"I'm Glad You Didn't Know Me"
C. Carle, P. Hoffman

1982.09 NINE

A Musical in Two Acts. Book by Arthur Kopit. (Based on an English) Adaptation from the Italian (screenplay for "8 1/2" by Federico Fellini, Tullio Pinelli, Ennio Flaiano) by Mario Fratti. Music and lyrics by Maury Yeston. Directed by Tommy Tune. Scenery by Lawrence Miller. Costumes by William Ivey Long. Lighting by Marcia Madeira. Musical supervision and orchestrations by Jonathan Tunick. Musical director, Wally Harper. Choral composition and musical continuity by Maury Yeston. Artistic associate, Thommie Walsh. Sound by Jack Mann. Initial staged reading, Composer/Librettist Conference, Eugene O'Neill Memorial Theater Center. Associate producer, Mark Beigelman. Presented in association with Shulamith and Michael N. Appell, Jerry Wexler and Michael Kleinman Productions. Produced by Michel Stuart, Harvey J. Klaris, Roger S. Berlind, James M. Nederlander, Francine LeFrak, Kenneth D. Greenblatt. Opened 9 May 1982 at the 46th Street Theatre and closed 4 February 1984 after 732 performances.

CAST: *Guido Contini*: RAUL JULIA. *Guido* at an early age: Cameron Johann. *Luisa*: KAREN AKERS. *Carla*: ANITA MORRIS. *Claudia*: SHELLY BURCH. *Guido's Mother*: TAINA ELG. *Liliane LaFleur*: LILIANE MONTEVECCHI. *Lina Darling*: Laura Kenyon. *Stephanie Necrophorus*: STEPHANIE COTSIRILOS. *Our Lady of the Spa*: KATE DEZINA. *Mama Maddelena*, Chief of Chambermaids: CAMILLE SAVIOLA. *Seraghina*: KATHI MOSS.

The Italians: *Maria*: Jeanie Bowers. *Francesca*: Kim Criswell. *A Venetian Gondolier*: Colleen Dodson. *Giulietta*: Louise Edeiken. *Annabella*: Nancy McCall. *Diana*: Cynthia Meryl. *Renata*: Rita Rehn.

The Germans: *Gretchen von Krupf*: Lulu Downs. *Heidi von Sturm*: Linda Kerns. *Olga von Sturm*: Dee Etta Rowe. *Ilsa von Hesse*: Alaina Warren Zachary.

Young Guido's Schoolmates: Evans Allen, Jadrien Steele, Patrick Wilcox.

(The action takes place in a health spa near Venice and in the mind of Guido Contini.)

ACT 1

"Overture Delle Donne"
Company

"Spa Music"

"Not Since Chaplin"

"Guido's Song"
R. Julia

"Coda di Guido"
Company

"The Germans at the Spa"
C. Saviola, Italians, Germans

"My Husband Makes Movies"
K. Akers

"A Call from the Vatican"
A. Morris

"Only With You"
R. Julia

"Folies Bergere"
L. Montevecchi, S. Cotsirilos, Company

"Nine"
T. Elg, Company

"Ti Voglio Bene"/"Be Italian"
K. Moss, Boys, Company

"The Bells of St. Sebastian"
R. Julia, Boys, Company

ACT 2[20]

"A Man Like You"/"Unusual Way"/"Grand Canal"
S. Burch, R. Julia

"The Grand Canal:"
R. Julia, Company

"Contini Submits"/"The Grand Canal"/"Tarantella"/"Every Girl in Venice"/"Marcia Di Ragazzi"/"Recitativo"/"Amor"/"Recitativo"/"Only You"/Finale

---

[18]First performed in English in New York 17 June 1868 at the New York Theatre for 33 performances.

[19]Note: The Act 2 Finale and the Duchess' Aria which opens Act 3 were recently discovered in France. The current production marks the first time they have been performed since the premiere of the opera in Paris in 1867.

[20]Added for the National Tour, before "The Grand Canal" in Act 2:
"Now's the Moment"
Sergio Franchi (Guido Contini)

"Simple"
A. Morris
"Be On Your Own"
K. Akers
"I Can't Make This Movie"
R. Julia
"Getting Tall"
C. Johann
"Nine"/"Long Ago"/"Nine" (reprise)
R. Julia

1982.10 DO BLACK PATENT LEATHER SHOES REALLY REFLECT UP?

A Musical in Two Acts, 14 Scenes. Book by John R. Powers, based on his novel of the same name. Music and lyrics by James Quinn, Alaric Jans. Directed by Mike Nussbaum. Musical numbers staged by Thommie Walsh. Settings by James Maronek. Costumes by Nancy Potts. Lighting by Marilyn Rennagel. Sound by Richard Fitzgerald. Orchestrations and musical supervision by Jerome Jay Dryer. Musial direction and vocal arrangements by Larry Hochman. Dance arrangements by Peter Larson. Production supervisor, William Gardner. Associate choreographer, Ronna Kaye. Produced by Mavin Productions Inc., Libby Adler Mages, Daniel A. Golman. Opened 27 May 1982 at the Alvin Theatre and closed 30 May 1982 after 5 performances.

CAST (in order of appearance): *Eddie Ryan*: RUSS THACKER. *Secretary*: Amy Miller. *Becky Bakowski*: MAUREEN MOORE. *Sister Melanie*: Amy Miller. *Sister Lee*: Ellen Crawford. *Father O'Reilly*: ROBERT FITCH. *Virginia Lear*: Vicki Lewis. *Felix Lindor*: Don Stitt. *Mike Depki*: Peter Heuchling. *Nancy Ralansky*: Karen Tamburrelli. *Mary Kenny*: Christine Gradl. *Louie Schlang*: Jason Graae. *Sister Helen*: Elizabeth Hansen. *Sister Monica Marie*: Catherine Fries.

Act 1: Elementary School. *Scene 1*: St. Bastion's School: The Present. *Scene 2*: Second Grade at St. Bastion's. *Scene 3*: Confession at St. Bastion's Church. *Scene 4*: The Playground—Fifth Grade. *Scene 5*: Fifth Grade at St. Bastion's. *Scene 6*: Confession at St. Bastion's Church. *Scene 7*: Eighth Grade at St. Bastion's.

Act 2: High School. *Scene 1*: The Freshman Mixer in the Gym of St. Patrick Bremmer High School for Boys. *Scene 2*: The Front Yard of Becky's House—A year later. *Scene 3*: Confession at St. Bastion's Church. *Scene 4*: The Athletic Fields of St. Patrick Bremmer & St. Ann's High Schools—Senior Year. *Scene 5*: The Night of the Senior Prom. *Scene 6*: Becky's Hospital Room. *Scene 7*: The Present.

ACT 1
Scene 1
"Get Ready, Eddie"
The Company
Scene 2
"The Greatest Gift"
E. Hansen, the Kids
Scene 4
"It's the Nuns"
The Kids, the Nuns
"Little Fat Girls"
M. Moore, R. Thacker
Scene 5
"Cookie Cutters"
E. Crawford, M. Moore
Scene 6
"Patron Saints"
R. Fitch, R. Thacker, the Kids, the Nuns
Scene 7
"Private Parts"
R. Fitch, the Boys
"How Far Is Too Far"
The Girls, the Boys
Finale Act 1
The Company

ACT 2
Scene 1
"Doo-waa, Doo-wee"
J. Graae, the Company
"I Must Be in Love"
R. Thacker
Scene 2
"Friends, the Best Of"
M. Moore, R. Thacker
Scene 4
"Mad Bombers and Prom Queens"
D. Stitt, V. Lewis, the Kids
Scene 5
"Late Bloomer and Prom Montage"
R. Thacker, the Kids
Scene 6
"Friends, the Best Of" (reprise)
M. Moore, R. Thacker
Scene 7
"Thank God"
The Company

1982.11 THE BEST LITTLE WHOREHOUSE IN TEXAS

A Return Engagement of the Musical Comedy in Two Acts, a Prologue and 16 Scenes[21]. Book by Larry L. King and Peter Masterson. (Based on a short story by Larry L. King.) Music and lyrics by Carol Hall. Directed by Peter Masterson and Tommy Tune. Musical numbers staged by Tommy Tune. Sets by Marjorie Bradley Kellogg. Costumes by Ann Roth. Lighting by Dennis Parichy. Musical supervision, direction and vocal arrangements by Robert Billig. Associate choreographer, Thommie Walsh. Associate producers, Bonnie Champion, Danny Kreitzberg. Produced by Stevie Phillips in association with Universal Pictures. Opened 31 May 1982 at the Eugene O'Neill Theatre and closed 24 July 1982 after 63 performances.

CAST (in order of appearance): *Band*: Craig Chambers (guitar, narrator), Racine Romaguera (bass), Harvey Shapiro (steel guitar), Pete Blue (piano), Chuck Zeuren (drums), Marty Laster (fiddle). *Girls*: Merilee Magnuson, Mimi Bessette, Roxie Lucas, Ruth Gottschall, Valerie Leigh Bixler. *Cowboys*: Beau Allen, Don Bernhardt, Michael Boyd. *Farmer*: Andy Parker. *Shy Kid*: Eric Aaron. *Miss Wulla Jean*: Louise Quick. *Travelling Salesman*: Patrick Hamilton. *Slick Dude*: Roger Berdahl. *Choir*: Don Bernhardt, Karen Sutherland, Diana Broderick, Merilyn J. Johnson, Clare Fields, George Dvorsky. *Angel*: Susann Fletcher. *Shy*: CHERYL EBARB. *Jewel*: DELORES HALL. *Mona Stangley*: CARLIN GLYNN. *The Girls at Miss Mona's*: *Linda Lou*: Valerie Leigh Bixler. *Dawn*: Mimi Bessette. *Ginger*: Roxie Lucas. *Beatrice*: Clare Fields. *Taddy Jo*: Merilee Magnuson. *Ruby Rae*: Diana Broderick. *Eloise*: Karen Sutherland. *Durla*: Ruth Gottschall.

Leroy Sliney: Roger Berdahl. *The Dogettes*: Don Bernhardt, George Dvorsky, Andy Parker, Joel Anderson. *Melvin P. Thorpe*: CLINTON ALLMON. *Soundman*: Roger Berdahl. *Melvin Thorpe Singers*: Karen Sutherland, Beau Allen, Diana Broderick, Clare Fields, Eric Aaron, Merilee Magnuson. *Sheriff Ed Earl Dodd*: GIL ROGERS *Cameraman*: Eric Aaron. *C. J. Scruggs*: Patrick Hamilton. *Mayor Rufus Poindexter*: J. FRANK LUCAS. *Edsel Mackey*: Robert Moyer. *Doatsey Mae*: BECKY GELKE. *Townspeople*: Beau Allen, Karen Sutherland, Patti D'Beck, Clare Fields, Eric Aaron, Merilee Magnuson. *TV Announcer*: Larry L. King. *Angelette Imogene Charlene*: Mimi Bessette. *Angelettes*: Merilee Magnuson, Ruth Gottschall, Karen Sutherland, Diana Broderick, Valerie Leigh Bixler. *Chip Brewster*: Patrick Hamilton. *Senator Wingwoah*: J. FRANK LUCAS. *Aggie #17*: Michael Boyd. *Aggie #71*: Beau Allen *Aggie #11*: Joel Anderson. *Scandinavian Placekicker—Aggie #1*: Roger Berdahl. *Aggie #21*: Eric Aaron. *Aggie #7*: Don Bernhardt. *Aggie #12*: George Dvorsky. *Aggie #77*: Andy Parker. *Aggie Specialty Dancer*: Tom Cashin. *Photographers*: Beau Allen, Eric Aaron, Michael Boyd, Don Bernhardt. *Reporter #1*: Becky Gelke. *Reporter #2*: Beau Allen. *Governor's Aide*: Joel Anderson. *Governor*: PATRICK HAMILTON. *Reporter #3*: Beau Allen. *Alternate Dancer*: Patti D'Beck.

---

[21]Originally produced in New York Off-Broadway 17 April 1978 at the Entermedia Theatre for 85 performances; transferred to Broadway 19 June 1978 at the 46th Street Theatre for 1584 performances. For Synopsis of Scenes and Musical Numbers, see original 1978 production. For this production, Act 1 ended with Act 1, Scene 10 and "The Aggie Song;" Scene 11 was dropped. "Bus from Amarillo" was moved to Act 2, Scene 4, to follow the reprise of "Hard Candy Christmas."

1982–1983 SEASON

Natalia Makarova and Dina Merrill in ON YOUR TOES
Martha Swope/TimePix

1982–1983 SEASON

1982.12 BLUES IN THE NIGHT

A Musical (Revue) in Two Acts[1]. Conceived and directed by Sheldon Epps. Set design by John Falabella. Costume design by David Murin. Lighting design by Ken Billington. Conductor, Charles Coleman. Musical director, supervisor, vocal arrangements by Chapman Roberts. Co-musical director, arrangements and orchestrator, Sy Johnson. Sound by Bill Merrill, Tay McLaren. Associate producer, Joshua Silver. Produced by Mitchell Maxwell, Alan J. Schuster, Fred H. Krones, M2 Entertainment. Opened 2 June 1982 at the Rialto Theatre and closed 18 July 1982 after 53 performances.

CAST (in order of singing appearance): *Woman #1*: LESLIE UGGAMS. *Woman #2*: DEBBIE SHAPIRO. *Woman #3*: JEAN DuSHON. *Saloon Singer*: Charles Coleman.

The action takes place in a Chicago hotel during 1938.

ACT 1

"Blue Blue"
The Company
(*Music and Lyrics by* Bessie Smith.)

"Four Walls (and One Dirty Window) Blues"
C. Coleman
(*Music and Lyrics by* Willard Robison)

"I've Got a Date With a Dream" (from *MY LUCKY STAR* film)
L. Uggams, D. Shapiro
(*Music by* Harry Revel. *Lyrics by* Mack Gordon.)

"These Foolish Things (Remind Me of You)" (from *NEW FACES*, London)
L. Uggams
(*Music by* Harry Link, Jack Strachey. *Lyrics by* Holt Marvell [Eric Maschwitz].)

"New Orleans Hop Scop Blues"
J. DuShon
(*Music and Lyrics by* George W. Thomas.)

"It Makes My Love Come Down"
L. Uggams, D. Shapiro, J. DuShon
(*Music and Lyrics by* Bessie Smith.)

"Copenhagen"
D. Shapiro
(*Music by* Charlie Davis. *Lyrics by* Walter Melrose.)

"Wild Women Don't Have the Blues"
C. Coleman
(*Music and Lyrics by* Ida Cox.)

"Lover Man"
L. Uggams
(*Music and Lyrics by* Jimmy Davis, Roger "Ram" Ramirez, Jimmy Sherman.)

"Take Me for a Buggy Ride"
J. DuShon
(*Music and Lyrics by* Leola and Wesley Wilson.)

"Willow Weep for Me"
D. Shapiro
(*Music and Lyrics by* Ann Ronnell.)

"Kitchen Man"
J. DuShon
(*Music and Lyrics by* Andy Razaf and Alex Bellenda.)

"Low"
L. Uggams
(*Music and Lyrics by* Vernon Duke, Milton Drake, Ben Oakland.)

"Take It Right Back"
L. Uggams, D. Shapiro, J. DuShon
(*Music and Lyrics by* H. Grey.)

ACT 2

"Wild Women Don't Have the Blues" (reprise)
The Band

"Blues in the Night" (from *BLUES IN THE NIGHT* film)
L. Uggams, D. Shapiro
(*Music by* Harold Arlen. *Lyrics by* Johnny Mercer.)

"Dirty No Gooder Blues"
J. DuShon
(*Music and Lyrics by* Bessie Smith.)

"When a Woman Loves a Man"
C. Coleman
(*Music by* Bernard Hanighen and Gordon Jenkins. *Lyrics by* Johnny Mercer.)

"Am I Blue?" (from *ON WITH THE SHOW* film)
L. Uggams, D. Shapiro, J. DuShon
(*Music by* Harry Akst. *Lyrics by* Grant Clarke.)

"Rough and Ready Man"
L. Uggams
(*Music and Lyrics by* Alberta Hunter.)

"Reckless Blues"
D. Shapiro
(*Music and Lyrics by* Bessie Smith.)

"Wasted Life Blues"
J. DuShon
(*Music and Lyrics by* Bessie Smith.)

"Baby Doll"
C. Coleman
(*Music and Lyrics by* Bessie Smith.)

"Nobody Knows You When You're Down and Out"
L. Uggams, D. Shapiro, J. DuShon
(*Music and Lyrics by* Jimmy Cox.)

"I Gotta Right to Sing the Blues" (from *EARL CARROLL'S VANITIES*, 1932)
L. Uggams, D. Shapiro, J. DuShon
(*Music by* Harold Arlen. *Lyrics by* Ted Koehler.)

"Blue Blue"/"Blues in the Night" (reprise)
L. Uggams, D. Shapiro, J. DuShon

[1]Originally produced Off-Broadway 26 March 1980 at the Production Company for 51 performances.

1982.13 PLAY ME A COUNTRY SONG

A Musical in Two Acts. Book by Jay Broad. Music and lyrics by John R. Briggs, Harry Manfredini. Directed by Jerry Adler. Choreography by Margo Sappington. Scenic design by David Chapman. Costume design by Carol Oditz. Lighting design by Marc B. Weiss. Musical direction, vocal arrangements by Phil Hall. Sound design by Robert Kerzman. Developmental supervision, Milton Moss. Associate producer, Cheryl Raab. Produced by Frederick R. Selch. Opened and closed 27 June 1982 at the Virginia Theatre after 1 performance.

CAST (in order of appearance): *Norm*: Reed Jones. *Ellen*: Mary Gordon Murray. *Tony*: Stephen Crain. *Fred*: Jay Huguely. *Howard*: Ronn Carroll. *Lizzie*: Louisa Flaningam. *Frances*: Karen Mason. *Penny*: Mary Jo Catlett. *Buster*: Kenneth Ames. *Meg*: Candace Tovar. *Jerome*: René Clemente. *Hank*: Rick Thomas.

ACT 1

"Sail Away"
M. G. Murray

"Rodeo Dreams"
R. Jones

"Why Does a Woman Leave Her Man"
J. Huguely

"Eighteen-Wheelin' Baby"
C. Tovar, L. Flaningam, M. J. Catlett, M. G. Murray

"Waitin' Tables"
L. Flaningam, Company

"Playing For Position"
R. Clements, K. Ames

"Just Thought I'd Call"
R. Thomas

"Sing-a-Long"
K. Mason, R. Carroll, Company

"Sail Away"/"If You Don't Mind"
M. G. Murray, S. Crain

"Play Me a Country Song"
Company

ACT 2

"Coffee Beer and Whiskey"
J. Huguely, Company

"Only a Fool"
C. Tovar, R. Thomas

"You Can't Get Ahead"
M. J. Catlett
"You Have to Get It Out to Get Away"
M. G. Murray
"Big City"
K. Ames
"My Sweet Woman"
J. Huguely, Men
"All of My Dreams"
L. Flaningam, Women
"Rodeo Rider"
S. Crain, Company

1982.14 SEVEN BRIDES FOR SEVEN BROTHERS

A Musical in Two Acts, 19 Scenes. Book by Lawrence Kasha and David S. Landay. Music by Gene de Paul. Lyrics by Johnny Mercer. New songs by Al Kasha and Joel Hirschhorn. Based on the MGM film (screenplay by Frances Goodrich, Albert Hackett, Dorothy Kinsley) and the short story "The Sobbin Women" by Stephen Vincent Benet on which it was based. Choreography and musical staging by Jerry Jackson. Directed by Lawrence Kasha. Sets by Robert Randolph. Costumes by Robert Fletcher. Lighting by Thomas Skelton. Sound by Abe Jacob. Musical director, Richard Parrinello. Orchestrations by Irwin Kostal. Dance arrangements by Robert Webb. Associate producers, Martin Gould, Bernard Hodes. Produced by Kaslan Productions (Lawrence Kasha-David S. Landay). Opened 8 July 1982 at the Alvin Theatre and closed 11 July 1982 after 5 performances.

CAST (in order of appearance): (*The Seven Brothers*): *Adam*: DAVID-JAMES CARROLL. *Benjamin*: D. Scot Davidge. *Ephraim*: Jeffrey Reynolds. *Caleb*: Lara Teeter. *Daniel*: Jeff Calhoun. *Frank*: Michael Ragan. *Gideon*: CRAIG PERALTA. *Mr. Bixby*: Fred Curt. *Mrs. Bixby*: Jeanne Bates. *Preacher*: Jack Ritschel. *Mr. Perkins*: Gino Gaudio. *Lumbermen*: James Horvath, Russell Giesenschlag, Don Steffy, Gary Moss, Clark Sterling, Kevin McCready. *Indian*: Conley Schnaterbeck. (*The Seven Brides*): *Milly*: DEBBIE BOONE. *Ruth*: Sha Newman. *Martha*: Laurel van der Linde. *Sarah*: Linda Hoxit. *Liza*: Jan Mussetter. *Alice*: NANCY FOX. *Dorcas*: Manette LaChance. *Jeb*: Russell Giesenschlag. *Zeke*: Kevin McCready. *Carl*: Don Steffy. *Matt*: Gary Moss. *Luke*: James Horvath. *Joel*: Clark Stering. *Dorcas' Sister*: Marylou Hume. *Mrs. Perkins*: Marykatherine Somers. *Townsboy*: David Pavlosky.

Townspeople: Jeanne Bates, Cheryl Randall, Fred Curt, Gino Gaudio, Russell Giesenschlag, James Horvath, Marylou Hume, Kevin McCready, Gary Moss, David Davlovsky, Jack Ritschel, Conley Schnaterbeck, Sam Singhaus, Marykatherine Somers, Don Steffy, Clark Sterling, Stephanie Stromer.

The action takes place in the Pacific Northwest during the 1850's.

Act 1, Scene 1: On the Road. *Scene 2*: The Town Square. *Scene 3*: The Restaurant. *Scene 4*: The Pontipee House. *Scene 5*: The Pontipee House. Later the same evening. *Scene 6*: The Pontipee House. The next morning. *Scene 7*: Church Yard. *Scene 8*: The Road Home. *Scene 9*: The Pontipee House. *Scene 10*: The Barn.

Act 2, Scene 1: The Town. *Scene 2*: Echo Pass. *Scene 3*: The Pontipee Yard. *Scene 4*: The Barn. *Scene 5*: The Pontipee Yard. *Scene 6*: The Trapping Cabin. *Scene 7*: The Pontipee House. *Scene 8*: The Woods. *Scene 9*: Church Yard.

ACT 1
Scene 1
"Bless Your Beautiful Hide"
D. Carroll
Scene 3
"Wonderful Wonderful Day"
D. Boone, Brides, Townspeople
Scene 4
"One Man"
D. Boone
(*Music and Lyrics by* Al Kasha and Joel Hirschhorn.)
Scene 6
"Goin' Courting"
D. Boone, The Brothers
Scene 7
"Social Dance"
D. Boone, D. Carroll, Brides, Brothers, Suitors, Townspeople
Scene 9
"Love Never Goes Away"
D. Carroll, D. Boone, C. Peralta
(*Music and Lyrics by* Al Kasha and Joel Hirschhorn.)
Scene 10
"Sobbin' Women"
D. Carroll, Brothers

ACT 2
Scene 2
"The Townsfolk's Lament"
Suitors, Townspeople
(*Music and Lyrics by* Al Kasha and Joel Hirschhorn.)
Scene 3
"A Woman Ought To Know Her Place"
D. Carroll
(*Music and Lyrics by* Al Kasha and Joel Hirschhorn.)
Scene 4
"We Gotta Make It Through the Winter"
The Brothers
(*Music and Lyrics by* Al Kasha and Joel Hirschhorn.)
"You Gotta Make It Through the Winter" (reprise)
D. Boone, Brides
Scene 5
"Spring Dance"
Brides, Brothers
Scene 6
"A Woman Ought To Know Her Place" (reprise)
D. Carroll, C. Peralta
Scene 7
"Glad That You Were Born"
D. Boone, Brides, Brothers
(*Music and Lyrics by* Al Kasha and Joel Hirschhorn.)
Scene 9
"Wedding Dance"
D. Boone, D. Carroll, Brides, Brothers, Townspeople

1982.15 MANHATTAN RHYTHM

A Dance Revue in Two Acts, 8 Scenes. Conceived and staged by Jon Devlin. Additional choreography by Jay Norman, Mary Delia Quigley, Harry Bell. Musical arrangements by Richard Dimino; additional horn arrangements by Smithcox Organization. Costumes by David Toser. Lighting by David Adams. Sound by Gary Harris. Fantasy creatures, Richard Tautkus. Produced by Barbara Moore. Opened 21 July 1982 at the Savoy Theatre and closed 14 August 1982 after 27 performances.

CAST: JON DEVLIN AND HIS COMPANY: *Female Dancers*: Virginia Clark East, Lyn Gendron, Anne Marie Giambattista, Kim Kuhlman, Diana Laurenson (Dance Captain), Linda Paul, Lisa Rudy, Lauren Salerno. *Male Dancers*: Louis Albert, Richard Loreto, Ralph Rodriguez, Steven Van Dyke (Dance Captain). *Singers*: Armour Gomez, Teri Hiatt, Karen Quackenbush, Bonnie Sue Taylor.

Act 1, Scene 1: Jazz. *Scene 2*: Big Band 40's. *Scene 3*: Broadway. *Scene 4*: Disc Space Fantasy.

Act 2, Scene 1: Rock n' Roll n' Rock Medley. *Scene 2*: Latin. *Scene 3*: Country/Western. *Scene 4*: Top Hits.

ACT 1
Scene 1
Opening
The Company
"Love For Sale"
T. Hiatt
Danced by J. Devlin, L. Rudy, A. M. Giambattista, D. Laurenson, K. Kuhlman, V. C. East, S. Van Dyke, R. Loreto, L. Albert.
"Manhattan Rhythm Blues"
Danced by J. Devlin, L. Gendron.
"All Blues"
Dance Solo: A. M. Giambattista.
Danced by V. C. East, L. Rudy, D. Laurenson, L. Salerno, L. Paul, K. Kuhlman.
"Take Five"
Danced by S. Van Dyke, R. Loreto, L. Albert.
"Walkin' Sally"
Danced by D. Laurenson, L. Paul, A. M. Giambattista.
Scene 2
"One O'Clock Jump"/"In the Mood"
T. Hiatt

Danced by J. Devlin. *Backup Vocals*: B. S. Taylor, A, Gomez, K. Quackenbush.

"Fifty-Seventh Street"

Danced by L. Albert, K. Kuhlman, S. Van Dyke, D. Laurenson, R. Rodriguez, A. M. Giambattista, L. Paul, L. Gendron.

Scene 3

Crossover

V. C. East

Medley

K. Quackenbush, B. S. Taylor, A. Gomez

Danced by A. M. Giambattista, L. Salerno, R. Loreto, R. Rodriguez, S. Van Dyke.

(*Additional Choreography by* Mary Delia Quigley.)

"You Can Dance"

T. Hiatt

Danced by S. V. Dyke, R. Rodriguez.

(*Additional Choreography by* Harry Bell.)

Scene 4

Star Trek Medley/Star Wars Cantina

Danced by L. Gendron, R. Loreto, L. Salerno, L. Albert, D. Laurenson, A. M. Giambattista, L. Rudy, S. Van Dyke, R. Rodriguez.

ACT 2

Scene 1

Rock n' Roll n' Rock Medley

The Company

(*Additional Choreography by* Jay Norman.)

Scene 2

Mambo/Cha-Cha/Mambo

Danced by A. M. Giambattista, D. Laurenson, V. C. East, L. Salerno, J. Devlin, L. Gendron.

Merengue

Danced by A. M. Giambattista, L. Gendron, V. C. East, L. Salerno.

Spanish Cape

Danced by J. Devlin.

Tango

Danced by J. Devlin, D. Laurenson.

Samba

Danced by The Compnay.

Duo: J. Devlin, A. M. Giambattista.

Scene 3

"Hey Good Lookin'"

B. S. Taylor

"Lady"

A. Gomez

"9 to 5"

K. Quackenbush

"Never Ending Love"

The Company

Scene 4

"Guilty"

T. Hiatt, A. Gomez

"Physical"

Danced by B. S. Taylor, S. Van Dyke, R. Rodriguez.

"Out Here on My Own"

T. Hiatt

"Fame"

Danced by D. Laurenson, A. M. Giambattista, L. Gendron, V. C. East.

"Celebration"

The Company

(*Additional Choreography by* Jay Norman.)

1982.16 THE MERRY WIDOW

A Revival of the Operetta in Three Acts, 4 Scenes[2]. Music by Franz Lehár. Original German libretto (Die Lustige Witwe) by Victor Léon and Leo Stein (after "L'Attaché d'Ambassade.") English version by Adrian Ross. Directed by Bill Gile. Choreography by Donald Saddler. Scenery designed by Helen Pond and Herbert Senn. Costumes designed by Suzanne Mess. Lighting designed by Gilbert V. Helmsley, Jr. Conductor, Scott Bergeson. Produced by the New York City Opera. Opened 7 September 1982 at the New York State Theatre and closed 13 November 1982 after 13 performances in repertory.

CAST (in order of appearance): *Baron Popoff*: JACK HARROLD. *Natalie*: Susanne Marsee. *M. de St. Brioche*: WILLIAM EICHORN. *Marquis de Cascada*: Thomas Jamerson. *Sylviane*: Bonnie Kirk. *Olga*: Janis Eckhart. *General Novikovich*: Douglas Perry. *Vicomte Camille de Jolidon*: JOSEPH EVANS. *Counsellor Khadja*: William Ledbetter. *Nisch*: James Billings. *Sonia*: ELIZABETH HYNES. *Prince Danilo*: ALAN TITUS. *Head Waiter*: Robert Brubaker. *Zozo*: Susan Elizabeth Scott. *Lolo*: Rebeka Pradera. *Dodo*: Esperanza Galan. *Jou-Jou*: Candace Itow. *Frou-Frou*: Victoria Rinaldi. *Clo-Clo*: Kate Langan. *Margot*: Tamara Mark. *Chorus of Marsovian and Parisian Society, Dancers, Servants and Waiters*: New York City Opera Chorus.

1982.17 YOUR ARMS TOO SHORT TO BOX WITH GOD

A Revival of the Gospel Musical in Two Acts[3]. Conceived from the Book of St. Matthew by Vinnette Carroll. Music and lyrics by Alex Bradford and Micki Grant. Entire production directed by Vinnette Carroll. Choreography by Talley Beatty, restaged by Ralf Paul Haze. Sets and costumes by William Schroder. Lighting by Richard Winkler. Sound by R. Shepard, Jim Esher. Musical direction, arrangements by Michael Powell. Orchestrations and dance music by H. B. Barnum. Associate producer, Jerry R. Moore. Coproducers, Anita MacShane, The Urban Arts Theatre. Produced by Barry and Fran Weissler. Opened 9 September 1982 at the Alvin Theatre and closed 7 November 1982 after 69 performances.

CAST: PATTI LaBELLE, AL GREEN, Julius Richard Brown, Nora Cole, Jamil K. Garland, Eijah Gill, L. Michael Gray, Ralf Paul Haze, Cynthia Henry, The Bobby Hill, Rufus E. Jackson, Elmore James, Linda James, Tommi Johnson, Janice Nunn Nelson, Dwayne Phelps, Quincella, Kiki Shepard, Leslie Hardesty Sisson, Marilynn Winbush.

ACT 1

"Beatitudes"

Company

(*Music and Lyrics by* Micki Grant.)

"We're Gonna Have a Good Time"

P. LaBelle, Company

(*Music and Lyrics by* Micki Grant.)

"Me and Jesus"

A. Green, Company

(*Music and Lyrics by* Micki Grant.)

"There's a Stranger in Town"

A. Green

(*Music and Lyrics by* Alex Bradford.)

"Running for Jesus"

J. N. Nelson, Company

(*Music and Lyrics by* Inez Andrews.)

"We Are the Priests and Elders"

J. R. Brown, T. B. Hill, L. M. Gray, E. James

(*Music and Lyrics by* Micki Grant.)

"Something Is Wrong in Jerusalem"

N. Cole, Quincella

(*Music and Lyrics by* Micki Grant.)

"It Was Alone"/"I Know I Have to Leave Here"

E. Gill, T. Johnson, Company

(*Music and Lyrics by* Alex Bradford.)

"Be Careful Whom You Kiss"

E. Gill, R. P. Haze, N. Cole, Quincella

(*Music and Lyrics by* Alex Bradford.)

"Trial"

Company

(*Music and Lyrics by* Micki Grant.)

"It's Too Late"

Company

(*Music and Lyrics by* Micki Grant.)

[2]Originally produced in New York 21 October 1907 at the New Amsterdam Theatre for 416 performances. For Synopsis of Scenes and Musical Numbers, see original 1907 production. Interpolated into this production:

"One Love in a Lifetime" (from *GIUDITTA*)

(*Music by* Franz Lehár. *Original Lyrics by* Paul Knepler and Fritz Löhner. *New English Lyrics by* Scott Bergeson.)

[3]Originally produced in New York 22 December 1976 at the Lyceum Theatre for 429 performances.

"Judas' Dance"
R. P. Haze
(*Music and Lyrics by* H. B. Barnum.)
"Your Arms Too Short to Box With God"
P. LaBelle, Company
(*Music and Lyrics by* Alex Bradford.)
"Give Us Barrabas"
Company
(*Music and Lyrics by* Alex Bradford.)
"See How They Done My Lord"
N. Cole, Company
(*Music and Lyrics by* Alex Bradford.)
"Come on Down"
M. M. Gray, J. K. Garland, L. James
(*Music and Lyrics by* Alex Bradford.)
"Veil of the Temple"
P. LaBelle, Company
"Can't No Grave Hold My Body"
L. M. Gray, Quincella, E. Gill, Company
(*Music and Lyrics by* Alex Bradford.)
"Beatitudes" (reprise)
P. LaBelle, A. Green, Company

ACT 2
"Didn't I Tell You"
A. Green, Company
(*Music and Lyrics by* Alex Bradford.)
"Couldn't Keep It to Myself"
A. Green, Company
(*Music and Lyrics by* Alex Bradford.)
"When the Power Comes"
A. Green, Company
(*Music and Lyrics by* Alex Bradford.)
"Everybody Has His Own Way"
A. Green, J. R. Brown, T. B. Hill, T. Johnson
(*Music and Lyrics by* Alex Bradford.)
"Down By the Riverside"
L. M. Gray, A. Green, Company
"I Love You So Much Jesus"
P. LaBelle
(*Music and Lyrics by* Alex Bradford.)
"As Long as I Live"
T. Johnson
(*Music and Lyrics by* Alex Bradford.)
"On That Day"
T. B. Hill, Company
(*Music and Lyrics by* Alex Bradford.)
"The Band"
Company
(*Music and Lyrics by* Alex Bradford.)

1982.18 A DOLL'S LIFE

A Musical in Two Acts, 16 Scenes. Book[4] and lyrics by Betty Comden and Adolph Green. Music by Larry Grossman. Production directed by Harold Prince. Musical director, Paul Gemignani. Orchestrations by Bill Byers. Choreography by Larry Fuller. Scenery designed by Timothy O'Brien, Tazeena Firth. Costumes designed by Florence Klotz. Lighting designed by Ken Billington. Sound by Jack Mann. Produced by James M. Nederlander, Sidney Shlenker, Warner Theatre Productions, Inc., Joseph Harris, Mary Lea Johnson, Martin Richards, Robert Fryer in association with Harold Prince. Opened 23 September 1982 at the Mark Hellinger Theatre and closed 26 September 1982 after 5 performanes.

CAST: *Nora*: BETSY JOSLYN. *Actor, Torvald, Johan*: GEORGE HEARN. *Otto*: PETER GALLAGHER. *Eric*: EDMUND LYNDECK. *Astrid*: Barbara Lang. *Audition Singer, Selma, Jacqueline*: Penny Orloff. *Conductor, Mr. Gustafson, Escamillo, Audition Singer, Loki, Mr. Zetterling*: Norman A. Large. *Stage Hand, Dr. Berg, Audition Singer, Ambassador*: David Vosburgh. *Stage Manager, Hamsun, Petersen, Warden, Nilson*: Michael Vita. *Dowager*: Diane Armistead. *Musician, Mr. Kloster*: Gordon Bovinet. *Camilla Forrester*: Willi Burke. *Assistant Stage Manager, Helga*: Patti Cohenour. *Prison Guards*: John Corsaut, David Cale Johnson. *Helmer's Maid, Waitress*: Carol Lurie. *Musician, Waiter*: Larry Small. *Waiter, Audition Singer, Muller*: Paul Straney. *Maid, The Widow*: Olga Talyn. *Ivar*: Jim Wagg. *Emmy*: Kimberly Stern. *Bob*: David Seaman. *Woman in White*: Lisa Peters. *Woman in Red*: Peri Gill. *Woman in Black*: Patricia Parker. *Man in Black*: David Evans.

The action takes place at a rehearsal of Ibsen's "A DOLL'S HOUSE: in 1982.

Act 1, Scene 1: A Rehearsal of Ibsen's "A Doll's House"—1982. *Scene 2*: The Train. *Scene 3*: The Cafe Europa. *Scene 4*: Street Outside the Cafe Europa. *Scene 5*: Otto's Room. *Scene 6*: Backstage at the Opera. *Scene 7*: An Opera Reading. *Scene 8*: Otto's Room. *Scene 9*: Cannery. *Scene 10*: Prison. *Scene 11*: The Opera House.

Act 2, Scene 1: Eric's Bedroom. *Scene 2*: Billiard Room. *Scene 3*: Billiard Room. The next morning. *Scene 4*: The Grand Cafe. Spring, Fall, Winter. *Scene 5*: The Living Room.

ACT 1
Scene 1
Prologue
B. Joslyn, Company
Scene 2
"A Woman Alone"
B. Joslyn, P. Gallagher, N. A. Large, Company
Scene 3
"Letter to the Children"
B. Joslyn
"New Year's Eve"
E. Lyndeck, G. Hearn, D. Vosburgh, N. A. Large
Scene 5
"Stay with Me, Nora"
P. Gallagher, B. Joslyn
Scene 7
The Opera Audition:
"Arrival"
B. Lang
"Loki and Baldur"
P. Gallagher, (Audition) Singers
"You Interest Me"
G. Hearn
"Departure"
B. Lang, Company
Scene 8
"Letter from Klemnacht"
B. Lang
"Learn to Be Lonely"
B. Joslyn
Scene 9
"Rats and Mice and Fish"
Women
Scene 10
"Jailer, Jailer"/"Letter to the Children" (reprise)
B. Joslyn, Women
Scene 11
Excerpts from 'Loki and Baldur'
Company
"Rare Wines"
E. Lyndeck, G. Hearn

ACT 2
Scene 1
"No More Mornings"
B. Joslyn
Scene 2
"There She Is"
G. Hearn, E. Lyndeck, P. Gallagher
"Power"
B. Joslyn
Scene 3
"Letter to the Children" (reprise)
B. Joslyn
"At Last"
G. Hearn
Scene 4
"The Grand Cafe"
Company

[4]Conceived by its authors as a response to the play "A Doll's House" by Henrik Ibsen.

Scene 5
Finale
Company

1982.19

CATS

A Musical in Two Acts, a Prologue and 20 Scenes. Based on T.S. Eliot's "Old Possum's Book of Practical Cats."[5] Music by Andrew Lloyd Webber. Directed by Trevor Nunn. Associate director, choreography by Gillian Lynne. (Scenic and costume) Design by John Napier. Lighting by David Hersey. Sound design by Martin Levan. Musical director, Rene Wiegert. Production musical director, Stanley Lebowsky. Orchestrations by David Cullen, Andrew Lloyd Webber. Executive producers, R. Tyler Gatchell Jr., Peter Neufeld. Produced by Cameron Mackintosh, The Really Useful Company (Limited), David Geffen, The Shubert Organization. Opened 7 October 1982 at the Winter Garden and closed 10 September 2000 after 7485 performances.

CAST (in amphibolical order): *Alonzo*: Hector Jaime Mercado. *Bustopher Jones, Asparagus, Growltiger*: Stephen Hanan. *Bombalurina*: Donna King. *Carbucketty*: Steven Gelfer. *Cassandra*: René Ceballos. *Coricopat, Mungojerrie*: René Clemente. *Demeter*: Wendy Edmead. *Etcetera, Rumpleteazer*: Christine Langner. *Grizabella*: BETTY BUCKLEY. *Jellylorum, Griddlebone*: Bonnie Simmons. *Jennyanydots*: Anna McNeely. *Mistoffolees*: Timothy Scott. *Munkustrap*: Harry Groener. *Old Deuteronomy*: Ken Page. *Plato, Macavity, Rumpus Cat*: Kenneth Ard. *Pouncival*: Herman W. Sebek. *Rum Tum Tugger*: Terrence Mann. *Sillabub*: Whitney Kershaw. *Skimbleshanks*: Reed Jones. *Tantomile*: Janet L. Hubert. *Tumblebrutus*: Robert Hoshour. *Victoria*: Cynthia Onrubia. *The Cats Chorus*: Walter Charles, Susan Powers, Carol Richards, Joel Robertson.

Act 1: "When cats are maddened by the midnight dance"

Act 2: "Why will the summer day delay—when will time flow away"

ACT 1
Prologue
"Jellicle Songs for Jellicle Cats"
The Company
(*Additional Material written by* Trevor Nunn and Richard Stilgoe.)

Scene 1
"The Naming of Cats"
The Company

Scene 2
"Invitation to the Jellicle Ball"
Victoria: C. Onrubia. *Mistoffolees*: T. Scott.

Scene 3
"The Old Gumbie Cat"
Jennyanydots: A. McNeely. *Cassandra*: R. Ceballos. *Bombalurina*: D. King. *Jellylorum*: B. Simmons.

Scene 4
"Rum Tum Tugger"
T. V. Mann

Scene 5
"Grizabella, the Glamour Cat"
Grizabella: B. Buckley. *Dememter*: W. Edmead. *Bombalurina*: D. King.

Scene 6
"Bustopher Jones"
Bustopher: S. Hanan. *Jennyanydots*: A. McNeely. *Jellylorum*: B. Simmons. *Bombalurina*: D. King.

Scene 7
"Mungojerrie and Rumpleteazer"
Mistoffolees: T. Scott. *Mungojerrie*: R. Clemente. *Rumpleteazer*: C. Langner.

Scene 8
"Old Deuteronomy"
Munkustrap: H. Groener. *The Rum Tum Tugger*: T. V. Mann. *Old Deuteronomy*: K. Page.

Scene 9
"The Aweful Battle of the Pekes and Pollicles" together with "The Marching Song of the Pollicle Dogs"
Munkustrap: H. Groener. *The Rumpus Cat*: K. Ard.

Scene 10
"The Jellicle Ball"
The Company

Scene 11
"Memory"
Grizabella: B. Buckley.
(*Lyrics by* Trevor Nunn, based on poems by T. S. Eliot.)

ACT 2
Scene 1
"The Moments of Happiness"
Old Deuteronomy: K. Page.

Scene 2
"Gus: The Theatre Cat"
Jellylorum: B. Simmons. *Asparagus*: S. Hanan.

Scene 3
"Growltiger's Last Stand"
Growltiiger: S. Hanan. *Griddlebone*: B. Simmons. *The Crew*: H. Groener, R. Jones, T. V. Mann, T. Scott. *Siamese Acrobat*: S. Gelfer.

Scene 4
"Skimbleshanks"
Skimbleshanks: R. Jones.

Scene 5
"Macavity"
Demeter: W. Edmead. *Bombalurina*: D. King. *Alonzo*: H. J. Mercado. *Macavity*: K. Ard. *Munkustrap*: H. Groener.

Scene 6
"Mr. Mistoffolees"
Mistoffolees: T. Scott. *The Rum Tum Tugger*: T. V. Mann.

Scene 7
"Memory" (reprise)
Grizabella: B. Buckley.

Scene 8
"The Journey to the Heavyside Layer"
The Company

Scene 9
"The Ad-Dressing of Cats"
Old Deuteronomy: K. Page.

1982.20

CANDIDE

A Revival of the Musical in Two Act, 23 Scenes[6]. Book[7] adapted from Voltaire's satire (of the same name) by Hugh Wheeler. (Original Book by Lillian Hellman.) Music by Leonard Bernstein. Lyrics by Richard Wilbur. Additional lyrics by Stephen Sondheim and John Latouche. Directed by Harold Prince. Choreography by Patricia Birch. Scenery designed by Clarke Dunham. Costumes designed by Judith Dolan. Lighting designed by Ken Billington. Conducted by John Mauceri. Orchestrations by Leonard Bernstein and Hershy Kay. Chorus master, David Leighton. Set graphics by Donald Beckman. Produced by the New York City Opera. Opened 13 October 1982 at the New York State Theatre and closed 2 November 1982 after 7 performances in repertory.

CAST (in order of appearance): *Voltaire*: JOHN LANKSTON. *Candide*: DAVID EISLER. *Huntsman*: Don Yule. *Paquette*: DEBORAH DARR. *Baroness*: Bonnie Kirk. *Baron*: JACK HARROLD. *Cunegonde*: ERIE MILLS. *Maximilian*: SCOTT REEVE.

[5]A Note on the Text: Most of the poems comprising "Old Possum's Book of Practical Cats" (1939) have been set to music complete and in their originally published form; a few have been subject to a minor revision of tense or pronoun, and eight lines have been added to "The Song of the Jellicles."

However, some of our lyrics, notably "The Marching Song of the Pollicle Dogs" and the story of "Grizabella" were discovered among the unpublished writings of Eliot.

The prologue is based on ideas and incorporates lines from another unpublished poem, entitled "Pollicle Dogs and Jellicle Cats." Growltiger's aria is taken from an Italian translation of "Practical Cats."

"Memory" includes lines from and is suggested by "Rhapsody on a Windy Night," and other poems of the Prufrock period. All other words in the show are taken from the Collected Poems. —Trevor Nunn

[6]Original production first produced in New York 1 December 1956 at the Martin Beck Theatre for 73 performances; revised version first produced Off-Broadway 11 December 1973 at the Chelsea Theater Center, Brooklyn Academy of Music for 48 performances; transferred 5 March 1974 to the Broadway Theatre for 740 performances.

[7]Hugh Wheeler and Harold Prince made further small changes to the 1974 script for this new 'Opera House' version.

Servant of Maximilian: JAMES BILLINGS. *Dr. Pangloss*: JOHN LANKSTON. *Bulgarian Soldiers*: Don Yule, JAMES BILLINGS. *Westphalian Soldiers*: Andy Roth, William Ledbetter. *Don Isaachar*, the Jew: JAMES BILLINGS. *Grand Inquisitor*: JACK HARROLD. *Calliope Player*: Bonnie Kirk. *Heresy Agent*: Ralph Bassett. *Inquisition Agents*: Gary Dietrich, William Poplaski. *Judge*: JAMES BILLINGS. *Old Lady*: MURIEL COSTA-GREENSPON. *Dons*: Robert Estner, Andy Roth, Michael Rubino, Don Yule, William Ledbetter, Ralph Bassett. *Businessman*: JOHN LANKSTON. *Governor*: JOHN LANKSTON. *Governor's Aide*: Andy Roth. *Slave Driver*: JACK HARROLD. *Father Bernard*: JAMES BILLINGS. *Sailors*: Gary Dietrich, William Poplaski, Andy Roth, Jeffrey Smith. *Pirates*: John Henry Thomas, William Ledbetter. *Pink Sheep*: Ivy Austin, Rhoda Butler. *Lion*: James Sergi. *Pasha-Prefect*: JACK HARROLD. *First Gambler*: JAMES BILLINGS. *Second Gambler (Police Chief)*: JOHN LANKSTON. *Sage*: JOHN LANKSTON.

(The action takes place in Westphalia and throughout the world in the eighteenth century. Scenes overlap and are played simultaneously.)

Scene 1: Dr. Voltaire's Traveling Freak Show. *Scene 2*: The Castle and Gardens. *Scene 3*: A Desolate Heath. *Scene 4*: The Baronial Chapel. *Scene 5*: A Meadow by Moonlight and The Battlefield. *Scene 6*: Cunegonde's Room. *Scene 7*: Destroyed Village. *Scene 8*: Central Square in Lisbon. *Scene 9*: A Lisbon Street. *Scene 10*: Cunegonde's Room. *Scene 11*: A Room in the Inn at Cadiz. *Scene 12*: Central Plaza at Cadiz.

Act 2, Scene 1: Plaza Grande, Cartagena. *Scene 2*: A Ship at Sea. *Scene 3*: Montevideo Cathedral. *Scene 4*: A Jungle. *Scene 5*: Eldorado and a Jungle. *Scene 6*: A Jungle and Sheep Meadow. *Scene 7*: Ballroom in Cartagena and The Dock. *Scene 8*: A Desert Island. *Scene 9*: A Hall in the Palace. *Scene 10*: The Cave of the Wisest Man. *Scene 11*: Candide's Farm.

ACT 1

"Life Is Happiness Indeed"
D. Eisler, E. Mills, S. Reeve, D. Darr

("Fanfare" instrumental)

"The Best of All Possible Worlds"
J. Lankston, D. Eisler, E. Mills, S. Reeve, D. St. Darr

"Oh Happy We"
D. Eisler, E. Mills

(Candide Begins His Travels)

"It Must Be So" (Candide's Meditation)
D. Eisler

(Westphalian Fanfare, Chorale, Battle Music)
(Chorus)

"It Must Be So" (instrumental reprise)

"Glitter and Be Gay"
E. Mills

"Dear Boy"
J. Lankston, Men's Chorus

"Auto da Fé" (What a Day)
Company

"Candide's Lament" (This World)
D. Eisler

"You Were Dead, You Know"
D. Eisler, E. Mills

"I Am Easily Assimilated"
M. Costa-Greenspon, Dons

Quartet Finale
D. Eisler, E. Mills, M. Costa-Greenspon, J. Lankston, Chorus

ACT 2

"Ballad of the New World"
D. Eisler, Chorus

"My Love"
J. Lankston, S. Reeve

(Barcarolle)

"Alleluia"
S. Reeve, E. Mills, J. Lankston, Chorus

("Eldorado" instrumental)

"Sheep Song"
I. Austin, R. Butler, J. Sergi, D. Darr, D. Eisler, Chorus

"Governor's Waltz"

"Bon Voyage" (Schottische)
J. Lankston, Company

"Quiet"
M. Costa-Greenspon, D. Darr, D. Eisler

"The Best of All Possible Worlds" (reprise)
M. Costa-Greenspon, D. Eisler, D. Darr

("Constantinople" instrumental)

"What's the Use"
J. Harrold, J. Billings, J. Lankston

"You Were Dead, You Know" (reprise)
D. Eisler, E. Mills

"Make Our Garden Grow"
Company

1982.21 THE GRAND DUCHESS OF GEROLSTEIN

A Revival of the Opéra-bouffe in Two Acts, 4 Scenes[8]. Original (French) libretto (La Grande-Duchesse de Gérolstein) by Henri Meilhac and Ludovic Halévy. Music by Jacques Offenbach. English adaptation by Ruth and Thomas Martin. Directed by Jack Hofsiss. Conducted by Scott Bergeson. Choreography by Christopher Chadman. Scenery and costumes designed by John Conklin. Lighting designed by Gilbert V. Helmsley, Jr. Chorus master, David Leighton. Produced by the New York City Opera. Opened 23 October 1982 (matinee) at the New York State Theatre and closed 3 November 1982 after 3 performances in repertory.

CAST (in order of appearance): *Fritz*: CAROLL FREEMAN. *Wanda*: CLAUDETTE PETERSON. *General Boom*: SPIRO MALAS. *Baron Puck*: JAMES BILLINGS. *Nepomuc*: WILLIAM LEDBETTER. *The Grand Duchess*: SUSANNE MARSEE. *Prince Paul*: RON [Ronald] RAINES. *Baron Grog*: NICO CASTEL. *Ensemble*: New York City Opera Chorus.

1982.22 ROCK 'N' ROLL! THE FIRST 5,000 YEARS

A Rock Musical Revue in Two Acts. Conceived by Bob Gill and Robert Rabinowitz. Musical continuity and supervision by John Simon. Special consultant, Dick Clark. Directed and choreographed by Joe Layton. Scenery by Mark Ravitz. Costumes by Franne Lee. Lighting by Jules Fisher. Sound by Bran Ferren. Orchestrations, dance and vocal arrangements by John Simon. Musical direction by Andrew Dorfman. Media by Gill & Rabinowitz. Co-choreographer, Jerry Grimes. Associate producers, Charles Koppelman, Martin Bandier. Produced by Jules Fisher and Annie Fargue in association with Dick Clark, Inc., Fred Disipio. Opened 24 October 1982 at the St. James Theater and closed 31 October 1982 after 9 performances.

CAST: Rob Barnes, Joyce Leigh Bowden, Ka-Ron Brown, Sandy Dillon, Andrew Dorfman, Rich Hebert, Lon Hoyt, William Gregg Hunter, Bill Jones, Jenifer Lewis, Dave MacDonald, Wendy Leigh MacKenzie, Karen Mankes, Bob Miller, Michael Pace, Raymond Patterson, Marion Ramsey, Jim Riddle, Shaun Solomon, Tom Teeley, Russell Velazquez, Barbara Walsh, Patrick Weathers, Carl E. Weaver, Lillias White.

ACT 1

"Love Is a Many Splendored Thing" (from the film)
Frank Sinatra (recording)
(*Music by* Sammy Fain. *Lyrics by* Paul Francis Webster.)

"Tutti Frutti"
C. Weaver, Compnay
(*Music and Lyrics by* Richard Penniman, D. La Bostrie, Joe Lubin.)

"Rock Around the Clock"
J. Riddle, Company
(*Music and Lyrics by* Max Friedman and Jimmy DeKnight.)

"Blueberry Hill"
W. G. Hunter, Company
(*Music and Lyrics by* Al Lewis, Larry Stock, Vincent Rose.)

"Wake Up Little Susie"
R. Velazquez, T. Teeley, Company
(*Music and Lyrics by* Boudleaux and Felice Bryant.)

"Great Balls of Fire"
T. Teeley, Company
(*Music and Lyrics by* Otis Blackwell and Jack Hammer.)

"Johnny B Goode"
C. E. Weaver, Company
(*Music and Lyrics by* Chuck Berry.)

---

[8]First performed in English in New York 17 June 1868 at the New York Theatre for 33 performances. For Synopsis of Scenes and Musical Numbers, see 1982 revival.

"Heartbreak Hotel"
P. Weathers, Company
(*Music and Lyrics by* Mae Boren Axton, Tommy Durden, Elvis Presley.)

"Hound Dog"
P. Weathers, Company
(*Music and Lyrics by* Jerry Lieber and Mike Stoller.)

"Love Me Tender"
P. Weathers, Company
(*Music and Lyrics by* Vera Matson and Elvis Presley.)

"Why Do Fools Fall in Love"
C. E. Weaver, R. Barnes, S. Solomon, W. G. Hunter, R. Patterson, Company
(*Music and Lyrics by* Frank Lymon and Morris Levy.)

"Sh-Boom" (Life Could Be a Dream)
D. MacDonald, Company
(*Music and Lyrics by* James Edwards, Carl Feaster, James Keyes, Floyd F. McRae.)

"Will You Still Love Me Tomorrow"
M. Ramsey, Company
(*Music and Lyrics by* Gerry Goffin and Carole King.)

"Da Doo Ron Ron"
W. L. MacKenzie, Company
(*Music and Lyrics by* Jeff Barry, Ellie Greenwich, Phil Spector.)

"The Twist"
R. Patterson, Company
(*Music and Lyrics by* Hank Ballard.) *Featured Dancer:* K. Brown.

"Land of a Thousand Dances"
W. G. Hunter, Company.
(*Music and Lyrics by* Chris Kenner and Antoine Domino.) *Featured Dancer:* K. Brown.

"I'll Be There"
R. Barnes, Company
(*Music and Lyrics by* Hal Davis, Berry Gordy, Bob West, Willie Hutch.)

"You Keep Me Hanging On"
J. Lewis, L. White, M. Ramsey, Company
(*Music and Lyrics by* Eddie Holland, Lamont Dozier, Bryant Holland.)

"Proud Mary"
M. Ramsey, Company
(*Music and Lyrics by* John C. Fogerty.)

"A Hard Day's Night" (from film)
J. Riddle, R. Velazquez, T. Teeley, B. Miller, Company
{*Music and Lyrics by* John Lennon and Paul McCartney.}

"I Got You Babe"
K. Mankes, M. Pace, Company
(*Music and Lyrics by* Sonny Bono.)

"Good Vibrations"
R. Hebert, C. E. Weaver, J. Riddle, Company
(*Music and Lyrics by* Brian Wilson and Mike Love.)

"Here Comes the Sun"
T. Teeley, Company
(*Music and Lyrics by* George Harrison.)

"The Sunshine of Your Love"
T. Teeley, R. Velazquez, Company
(*Music and Lyrics by* Jack Bruce, Eric Clapton, Peter Brown.)

"Blowin' in the Wind"
P. Weathers, Company
(*Music and Lyrics by* Bob Dylan.)

"Like a Rolling Stone"
P. Weathers, Company
(*Music and Lyrics by* Bob Dylan.)

"Whiter Shade of Pale"
D. MacDonald, Company
(*Music and Lyrics by* Keith Reid and Gary Brooker.) *Featured Dancer:* K. Brown.

"Mrs. Robinson"
R. Velazquez, T. Teeley, Company
(*Music and Lyrics by* Paul Simon.) *Featured Dancer:* K. Brown.

"White Rabbit"
B. Walsh, K. Mankes, W. L. MacKenzie, Company
(*Music and Lyrics by* Grace Slick.)

"Respect"
L. White, Company
(*Music and Lyrics by* Otis Redding.)

"The Night They Drove Old Dixie Down"
P. Weathers, Company
(*Music and Lyrics by* J. Robbie Robertson.)

"People Got to be Free"
R. Velazquez, Company
(*Music and Lyrics by* Edward Brigate, Felix Cavaliere.)

"Cry Baby"
S. Dillon, Company
(*Music and Lyrics by* Burt Russell and Norman Meade.)

"Forever Young"
B. Walsh, Company
(*Music and Lyrics by* Bob Dylan.)

"Everybody's Talking"
M. Pace, Company
(*Music and Lyrics by* Fred Neil.)

"Joy to the World"
R. Velazquez, Company
(*Music and Lyrics by* Hoyt Axton.)

"Both Sides Now"
W. L. MacKenzie, Company
(*Music and Lyrics by* Joni Mitchell.)

"Higher and Higher"
R. Patterson, Company
(*Music and Lyrics by* Renard Miner, Gary Jackson, Carl Smith.)

ACT 2

"Tubular Bells" (instrumental)
B. Miller, Company
(*Music by* Mike Oldfield.)

"I Feel the Earth Move"
J. L. Bowden, Company
(*Music and Lyrics by* Carole King.)

"Satisfaction"
D. MacDonald, Company
(*Music and Lyrics by* Mick Jagger and Keith Richard.)

"When Will I Be Loved"
J. L. Bowden, Company
(Music and Lyrics by Phil Everly.)

"My Generation"
J. Riddle, Company
(*Music and Lyrics by* Peter Townshend.)

"You've Got a Friend"
M. Pace, Company
(*Music and Lyrics by* Carole King.)

"Nothing from Nothing"
W. G. Hunter, Company
(*Music and Lyrics by* Billy Preston and Bruce Fisher.) *Featured Dancer:* K. Brown.

"Say It Loud I'm Black and Proud"
R. Barnes, Company
(*Music and Lyrics by* James Brown.)

"Summer in the City"
J. Riddle, Company
(*Music and Lyrics by* John Sebastian, Steve Boone, Mark Sebastian.) *Featured Dancer:* K. Brown.

"Whole Lotta Love"
R. Velazquez, J. Riddle, Company
(*Music and Lyrics by* John Baldwin, John Bonham, James Patrick Page.)

"Star Spangled Banner" (instrumental)
T. Teeley
(*Music arranged by* Jimi Hendrix.)

"Boogie Woogie Bugle Boy"
J. L. Bowden, Company
(*Music and Lyrics by* Don Raye and Hughie Prince.)

"I Feel Like I'm Gonna Die Rag"
D. MacDonald, Company
(*Music and Lyrics by* Joe McDonald.)

"American Pie"
R. Hebert, Company
(*Music and Lyrics by* Don McLean.)

"Imagine"
T. Teeley, Company
{*Music and Lyrics by* John Lennon.}

"School's Out"
D. MacDonald, Company
(*Music and Lyrics by* Alice Cooper and Michael Bruce.)

"Rock and Roll All Night"
J. Riddle, Company
(*Music and Lyrics by* Paul Stanley and Gene Simmons.)

"Benny and the Jets"
L. Hoyt, Company
(*Music and Lyrics by* Elton John, Bernie Taupin.)
"Space Oddity"
M. Pace, R. Velazquez, Company
(*Music and Lyrics by* David Bowie.)
"Take a Walk on the Wild Side"
P. Weathers, Company
(*Music and Lyrics by* Lou Reed.)
"Everybody Is a Star"
C. E. Weaver, L. White, R. Patterson, W. G. Hunter, Company
(*Music and Lyrics by* Sylvester Stewart.) *Featured Dancer:* K. Brown.
"Stayin' Alive" (from *SATURDAY NIGHT FEVER* film)
L. Hoyt, M. Pace, R. Hebert, Company
(*Music and Lyrics by* Barry Gibb, Robin Gibb, Maurice Gibb.)
"Love to Love You Baby"
J. Lewis, Company
(*Music and Lyrics by* Peter Bellote, Giorgio Morder, Donna Summer.)
"I Will Survive"
L. White, Company
(*Music and Lyrics by* Dino Fekaris, Frederick J. Perren.)
"On the Run" (instrumental)
A. Dorfman, R. Velazquez
(*Music by* Roger Waters, David Gilmour, Rick Wright. *Lyrics by* Roger Waters.)
"Jocko Homo"
D. MacDonald, Company
(*Music and Lyrics by* Mark Mothersbaugh.)
"Message in a Bottle"
L. Hoyt, Company
(*Music and Lyrics by* Sting Summer.)
"Our Lips Are Sealed"
K. Mankes, Company
(*Music and Lyrics by* Jane Weidlin and Terry Hall.)
"Concrete Shoes"
S. Dillon, S. Solomon, Company
(*Music and Lyrics by* Rod Swenson.)
"Rock and Roll Music"
Company
(*Music and Lyrics by* Chuck Berry.)

1982.23 HERMAN VAN VEEN: ALL OF HIM

A Musical Show (One-Man Musical Revue) in Two Acts. Concept by Herman van Veen, Michel Lafaille. English adaptation and lyrics by Christopher Adler. Translations by Patricia Braun. Directed by Michel Lafaille. Set designed by Gerard Jongerius, Ed DeBoer. Costumes designed by Ellen van der Horst. Lighting designed by Rob Munnik. Sound designed by Hans van der Linden. Musical direction, Eric van der Wurff. English associate producer, Patricia Braun. Produced by Joost Taverne, Michael Frazier, Ron van Eeden in association with Harlekyn U.S.A. Company. Opened 8 December 1982 at the Ambassador Theatre and closed 12 December 1982 after 6 performances.

CAST: HERMAN VAN VEEN.

MUSICAL NUMBERS (in alphabetical order)
{*All Lyrics by* Herman van Veen except where noted.}
"A Girl"
(*Music by* Herman van Veen and Erik van der Wurff.)
"A Loose Woman"
(*Music by* Herman van Veen. *Original {Dutch}Lyrics by* Willem Wilmink. *English Lyrics by* Christopher Adler.)
"Cranes"
(*Music traditional with adaptation by* Herman van Veen. *Original {Dutch} Lyrics by* Willem Wilmink. *English Lyrics by* Christopher Adler.)
"Do You Remember"
(*Music by* Herman van Veen. *Original {Dutch} Lyrics by* Hans Lodeizen. *English Lyrics by* Christopher Adler.)
"Hello"
(*Music by* Herman van Veen and Erik van der Wurff.)
"Heroes"
(*Music by* Chris Pilgrim. *Original {Dutrch} Lyrics by* Rob Chrispijn. *English Lyrics by* Christopher Adler.)
"Hole-in-One"
(*Music by* Erik van der Wurff and Herman van Veen.)
"I Don't Want Any Help"
(*Music by* Erik van der Wurff and Herman van Veen. Original {Dutch} Lyrics by Herman van Veen. *English Lyrics by* Christopher Adler.)
"I Won't Let That Happen to Him"
(*Music by* Georges Delerue.)
"Jacob Is Dead"
(*Music by* Herman van Veen.)
"Kitchen Sink"
(*Music by* Erik van der Wurff and Herman van Veen. *Original {Dutch} Lyrics by* Herman van Veen. *English Lyrics by* Christopher Adler.)
"Ode to Suicide"
(*Music by* Joop Stokkermans. *Original {Dutch} Lyrics by* Guus Vleugel. *English Lyrics by* Christopher Adler.)
"Parade of Clowns"
(*Music by* Erik van der Wurff and Herman van Veen. *Original {Dutch} Lyrics by* Ron Chrisijn. *English Lyrics by* Christopher Adler.)
"Sarabande"
(*Music by* J. B. Senaille, Herman van Veen and Erik van der Wurff.)
"Station"
(*Music by* Erik van der Wurff and Herman van Veen.)
"Tell Me Who I Was"
(*Music by* Phillipe-Gerard. *Original French Lyrics by* Gébé. *Dutch Lyrics by* Willem Wilmink. *English Lyrics adapted from the Dutch by* Christopher Adler.)
"The Back of Life"
(*Music by* Herman van Veen. *Original {Dutch} Lyrics by* Willem Wilmink. *English Lyrics by* Christopher Adler.)
"The Fence"
(*Music by* Erik van der Wurff.)
"The Interveiw"
(*Music by* Erik van der Wurff and Herman van Veen.)
"The Rules of the Asylum"
(*Music by* Herman van Veen. *Original {Dutch} Lyrics by* Rob Chrispijn.)
"Time Passed Her By"
(*Original Music and {Dutch} Lyrics by* Jean Ferrat. *English Lyrics by* Christopher Adler.)
"What a Day"
(*Music by* Erik van der Wurff.)

1982.24 ALICE IN WONDERLAND

A Revival of the Fantasy by Lewis Carroll, adapted for the stage in Two Acts by Eva Le Gallienne and Florida Freibus[9]. Music by Richard Addinsell. Set design by John Lee Beatty. Costume design by Patricia Zipprodt. Lighting design by Jennifer Tipton. Puppets by The Puppet People. Music adapted and supervised by Jonathan Tunick. Movement by Bambi Linn. Illustrated by John Tenniel. Sound by Jack Mann. Musical conductor, Les Scott. Special effects by Chic Silber. Entire production conceived and directed by Eva Le Galliennne. Co-directed by John Strasberg. An Eva LeGallienne Production. Produced by Sabra Jones, Anthony D. Marshall in association with WNET/Thirteen. Opened 23 December 1982 at the Virginia Theatre and closed 9 January 1983 after 21 performances.

CAST (in order of appearance): *Singers*: Nancy Killmer, Marti Morris. *Alice*: KATE BURTON. *Small White Rabbit*: Mary Stuart Masterson. *Mouse*: John Remme. *Lory*: John Miglietta. *Duck*: Nicholas Martin. *Dodo*: James Valentine. *Eaglet*: Rebecca Armen. *White Rabbit*: Curt Dawson. *Caterpillar*: John Heffernan. *Fish Footman*: Geddeth Smith. *Frog Footman*: Claude-Albert Saucier. *Duchess*: Edward Zang. *Cook*: Richard Sterne. *Voice of Cheshire Cat*: Geddeth Smith. *March Hare*: Josh Clark. *Mad Hatter*: MacIntyre Dixon. *Dormouse*: Nicholas Martin. *Two of Spades*: Geoff Garland. *Five of Spades*: Rober Ott Boyle. *Seven of Spades*: Steve Massa. *Three of Clubs*: Skip Harris. *Seven of Clubs*: Cliff Rakerd. *Ace of Hearts*: Geddeth Smith. *Two of Hearts*: Rebecca Armen. *Three of Hearts*: John Remme. *Four of Hearts*: Mary Stuart Masterson. *Five of Hearts*: Claude-Albert Saucier. *Six of Hearts*: Marti Morris. *Seven of Hearts*: John Miglietta. *Eight of Hearts*: Nancy Killmer. *Nine of Hearts*: Richard Sterne. *Ten of Hearts*: John Heffernan. *Knave of Hearts*: John Seidman. *Queen of Hearts*: Brian Reddy. *King of Hearts*: Richard Woods. *Gryphon*: Edward Hibbert. *Mock Turtle*: James Valentine. *Red Queen*: Mary Louise Wilson. *Train Guard*: Nicholas Martin. *Man in*

[9]First presented *as ALICE IN WONDERLAND AND THROUGH THE LOOKING GLASS* in New York 12 December 1932 at the Civic Repertory Theatre for 127 performances. For Synopsis of Scenes and Musical Numbers, see original 1932 production.

White Paper: Geddeth Smith. *Goat*: Claude-Albert Saucier. *Tweedledum*: Robert Ott Boyle. *Tweedledee*: John Remme. *White Queen*: EVA Le GALLIENNE, Joan White, alt. *Sheep*: John Heffernan. *Voice of Humpty Dumpty*: Richard Woods. *White Knight*: Curt Dawson. *Front of Horse*: Josh Clark. *Back of Horse*: Cliff Rakerd. *Old Frog*: Edward Hibbert. *Voice of Leg of Mutton*: Steve Massa.

1983.01

MERLIN

A Musical in Two Acts, 12 Scenes. Book by Richard Levinson, William Link. Songs (Music) and incidental music by Elmer Bernstein. Lyrics by Don Black. Magic illusions, Doug Henning. Directed by Ivan Reitman. Choreography by Christopher Chadman, Billy Wilson. Scenic design by Robin Wagner. Costume design by Theoni V. Aldredge. Lighting design by Tharon Musser. Sound design by Abe Jacob. Orchestrations by Larry Wilcox. Music direction, vocal arrangements by David Spear. Dance arrangements by Mark Hummel. Magic consultant, Charles Reynolds. Production supervisor, Jeff Hamlin. Associate producer, Joe Medjuck. Produced by Ivan Reitman, Columbia Pictures Stage Productions, Inc., Marvin A. Krauss, James M. Nederlander. Opened 13 February 1983 at the Mark Hellinger Theatre and closed 7 August 1983 after 199 performances.

CAST (in order of appearance): *Old Merlin*: George Lee Andrews. *Creatures of the Glade*: Robin Cleaver, Ramon Galindo, Todd Lester, Claudia Shell, Robert Tanna. *Young Merlin*: Christian Slater. *The Wizard*: EDMUND LYNDECK. *Merlin*: DOUG HENNING. *Philomena*: Rebecca Wright. *The Queen*: CHITA RIVERA. *The Queen's Companion*: Gregory Mitchell. *Prince Fergus*: NATHAN LANE. *Merlin's Vision*: Debby Henning. *Ariadne*: Michelle Nicastro. *Acolyte*: Alan Brasington. *Earth*: Peggy Parten. *Air*: Robyn Lee. *Fire*: Spence Ford. *Water*: Debby Henning. *Ladies of the Court*: Pat Gorman, Leslie Hicks, Robyn Lee, Peggy Parten, Iris Revson. *Manservant*: Alan Brasington. *Old Soldier*: George Lee Andrews. *Arthur*: Christian Slater.

Ladies of the Ensemble: Robin Cleaver, Spence Ford, Pat Gorman, Andrea Handler, Debby Henning, Leslie Hicks, Sandy Laufer, Robyn Lee, Peggy Parten, Iris Revson, Claudia Shell. *Men of the Ensemble*: David Asher, Ramon Galindo, Todd Lester, Joe Locarro, Fred C. Mann III, Gregory Mitchell, Andrew Hill Newman, Eric Roach, Robert Tanna, Robert Warners.

The action takes place in the time of sorcery.

Act 1, Scene 1: Merlin's Glade. *Scene 2*: The Palace of the Queen. *Scene 3*: The Glade. *Scene 4*: A Crystal Grove. *Scene 5*: A River. *Scene 6*: The Hall of the Angels.

Act 2, Scene 1: A Far Away Village. *Scene 2*: The Palace. *Scene 3*: A Marsh. *Scene 4*: the Palace Ramparts. *Scene 5*: The Queen's Dungeon. *Scene 6*: On the Way to London.

ACT 1

Scene 1

"It's About Magic"
G. L. Andrews, C. Slater, D. Henning, R. Wright, Ensemble

Scene 2

"I Can Make It Happen"
C. Rivera

Scene 3

"Beyond My Wildest Dreams"
M. Nicastro

"Something More"
D. Henning, M. Nicastro

Scene 4

"The Elements"
D. Henning, E. Lyndeck, Ensemble

Scene 5

"Fergus' Dilemma"
N. Lane, Ladies of the Court

Scene 6

"Nobody Will Remember Him"
C. Rivera, E. Lyndeck

ACT 2

Scene 1

"Put a Little Magic in Your Life"
G. L. Andrews, D. Henning, R. Wright, Ensemble

"He Who Knows the Way"
E. Lyndeck

Scene 2

"I Can Make It Happen" (reprise)
C. Rivera

Scene 3

"He Who Knows the Way" (reprise)
E. Lyndeck

Scene 4

"We Haven't Fought a Battle in Years"
N. Lane, Soldiers

Scene 5

"Satan Rules"
C. Rivera

"Nobody Will Remember Him" (reprise)
C. Rivera

Scene 6

"He Who Knows the Way" (reprise)
D. Henning, E. Lyndeck, C. Slater

1983.02

ON YOUR TOES

A Revival of the Musical Comedy in Two Acts, 12 Scenes[10]. Book by Richard Rodgers, Lorenz Hart and George Abbott. Lyrics by Lorenz Hart. Music by Richard Rodgers. Directed by George Abbott. Original choreography by George Balanchine. Additional ballet choreography by Peter Martins. Musical numbers choreographed by Donald Saddler. Production (scenic and costume) design by Zack Brown. Lighting by John McLain. Musical director, conductor, John Mauceri. Original orchestrations by Hans Spialek. Coordinating producer, Charlene Harrington. Produced by Alfred de Liagre, Jr., Roger L. Stevens, John Mauceri, Donald R. Seawell, André Pastoria. Opened 6 March 1983 at the Virginia Theatre and closed 20 May 1984 after 505 performances.

CAST (in order of appearance): *Phil Dolan II*: Eugene J. Anthony. *Lil Dolan*: Betty Ann Grove. *Phil Dolan III, Junior*: Philip Arthur Ross. *Stage Manager*: Dirk Lumbard. *Lola*: Mary C. Robare. *Phil Dolan III*, Junior (15 years later): LARA TEETER. *Miss Pinkerton*: Michaela K. Hughes. *Sidney Cohn*: Peter Slutsker. *Frankie Frayne*: CHRISTINE ANDREAS. *Joe McCall*: Jerry Mitchell. *Vera Barnova*: NATALIA MAKAROVA. *Anushka*: Tamara Mark. *Peggy Porterfield*: DINA MERRILL. *Sergei Alexandrovitch*: GEORGE S. IRVING. *Konstantine Morrosine*: GEORGE DE LA PEÑA. *Oscar*: Eugene J. Anthony. *Stage Doorman*: David Gold. *A Woman Reporter*: Betty Ann Grove. *Dimitri*: Chris Peterson. *Ivan*: Don Steffy. *Louie*: George Kmeck.

Princess Zenobia Ballet: *Princess Zenobia*: NATALIA MAKAROVA. *Beggar*: GEORGE DE LA PEÑA. *Kringa Khan*: George Kmeck. *Ali Shar*: Eugene J. Anthony. *Ahmud Ben B'Du*: David Gold.

Hank Jay Smith: Michael Vita.

On Your Toes Ballet: *Ballet Leaders*: Alexander Filipov, Starr Danias. *Tap Leaders*: Dirk Lumbard, Dana Moore.

Cop: Michael Vita. *Messenger Boy*: Dean Badolato.

Slaughter on Tenth Avenue Ballet: *Hoofer*: LARA TEETER. *Strip Tease Girl*: NATALIA MAKAROVA. *Big Boss*: Michael Vita.

Cop: Jerry Mitchell.

Ensemble: Melody A. Dye, Michaela K. Hughes, Tamara Mark, Dana Moore, Mary C. Robare, Marcia Lynn Watkins, Leslie Woodies, Sandra Zigars, Dean Badolato, Alexander Filipov, Wade Laboissonniere, Dirk Lumbard, Robert Meadows, Jerry Mitchell, Chris Peterson, Don Steffy, Kirby Tepper, David Gold, Georeg Kmeck.

Act 1, Scene 1: A Vaudeville Stage, about 1920. *Scene 2*: The Vaudeville Dressing Room. *Scene 3*: A Classroom of Knickerbocker University—WPA Extension. *Scene 4*: Vera's Apartment, the next morning. *Scene 5*: The Schoolroom. *Scene 6*: The Bare Stage, Cosmopolitan Opera House, the next morning. *Scene 7*: Cosmopolitan Opera House. "Princesse Zenobia" Ballet.

Act 2, Scene 1: The Bare Stage, Cosmopolitan Opera House. *Scene 2*: The Classroom. *Scene3*: The Bare Stage, Cosmopolitan Opera House. *Scene 4*: The Stage Door, Cosmopolitan Opera House. *Scene 5*: Stage of the Cosmopolitan Opera House. "Slaughter on Tenth Avenue" Ballet.

ACT 1

Scene 1

"Two A Day for Keith"
E. J. Anthony, B. A. Grove, P. A. Ross

Scene 3

"Questions and Answers" (The Three B's)
L. Teeter, Students

"It's Got To Be Love"
C. Andreas, L. Teeter, Students

---

[10]Originally produced in New York 11 April 1936 at the Imperial Theatre for 315 performances. For this revival, "The Heart Is Quicker Than the Eye" was moved from Act 1 to Act 2. "The Seduction" and a reprise of "Quiet Night" were added, and the song and scene order, scene descriptions were slightly revised.

Scene 4
"Too Good for the Average Man"
G. S. Irving, D. Merrill
"The Seduction"
N. Makarova, L. Teeter
Scene 5
"There's a Small Hotel"
C. Andreas, L. Teeter
Scene 7
"La Princesse Zenobia" Ballet
ACT 2
Scene 1
"The Heart Is Quicker Than the Eye"
D. Merrill, L. Teeter
"Glad To Be Unhappy"
C. Andreas
Scene 2
"Quiet Night"
M. Vita, Ensemble
"On Your Toes"
C. Andreas, Ensemble
Scene 4
"Quiet Night" (reprise)
G. S. Irving
Scene 5
"Slaughter on Tenth Avenue" Ballet
(Finale)
(Entire Company)

1983.03 CHARLES AZNAVOUR

A Solo Performance in Two Acts[11]. Music director, Aldo Frank. Sound, Robert Kerzman. Wardrobe by Ted Lapidus. Musical coordinator, Bob Cranshaw. Produced by Ron Delsener and Levon Sayan. Opened 14 March 1983 at the Lunt-Fontanne Theater and closed 26 March 1983 after 14 performances.

CAST: CHARLES AZNAVOUR.
Background vocalists: Diana Green, Ednah Holt, Carol Steele.

MUSICAL NUMBERS
(All music and lyrics by Charles Aznavour except where noted.)
"Le Temps"
(*Music by* Davis.)
"In Your Room"
(*Music and Lyrics by* Charles Aznavour and Buddy Kaye.)
"I Didn't See the Time Go By"
(*Music and Lyrics by* Charles Aznavour and Herbert Kretzmer.)
"Etre"
(*Music by* Georges Garaventz.)
"Happy Anniversary"
(*English Lyrics by* Herbert Kretzmer.)
"In Times To Be"
(*French Lyrics by* Jacques Plante. *English Lyrics by* Herbert Kretzmer.)
"L'amour bon dieu"
"I Act As If"
(*Lyrics by* Jacques Plante. *English Lyrics by* Dee Shipman.)
"To Be a Soldier"
(*Music and Lyrics by* Charles Aznavour and Herbert Kretzmer.)
"Nous n'avons pas d'enfant"
(*Music by* Georges Garaventz.)
"I'll Be There"
(*Music by* Georges Garaventz. *Lyrics by* Charles Aznavour and Herbert Kretzmer.)
"Les comediens"
(*Lyrics by* Jacques Plante.)
"She"
"Take Me Along"
"The Happy Days"
"Mon ami mon Judas"
"And I in My Chair"
(English Lyrics by D. Newberg.)
"Isabelle"
"You've Let Yourself Go"
(*English Lyrics by* Marcel Stellman.)
"Mon emouvant amour"
"Ave Maria"
(*Music by* Georges Garaventz.)
"What Makes a Man"
"La Boheme"
(*Lyrics by* Jacques Plante.)
"The Old Fashioned Way"
(*Music by* Georges Garaventz.)
"Yesterday When I Was Young"
(*English Lyrics by* Herbert Kretzmer.)
"You've Got to Learn"
"La Mama"
(*Music by* Robert Gall.)
"Mourir d'aimer"
"Qui, de t'avoir aimee"
"Que c'est triste Venise"
(*Music by* F. Dorin.)
"Non je n'ai rien oublie"
(*Music by* Georges Garaventz.)
"Ils sont tombes"
"The First Dance"

[11]Charles Aznavour previously appeared on Broadway 14 October 1965 at the Ambassador Theatre for 29 performances, and 4 February 1970 at the Music Box Theatre for 23 performances.

1983.04 PORGY AND BESS

A Revival of the Folk Opera in Two Acts, 9 Scenes[12]. Libretto by DuBose Heyward adapted from the play "Porgy" by DuBose and Dorothy Heyward. Music by George Gershwin. Lyrics by DuBose Heyward and Ira Gershwin. Directed by Jack O'Brien Assistant director, production supervisor, Helaine Head. Scenery designer, Douglas W. Schmidt. Costume designer, Nancy Potts. Lighting designer, Gilbert V. Hemsley, Jr. Musical director C. William Harwood. Choreographer, George Faison. Production coordinator, M. Jane Weaver. Assistant conductor, Edward Strauss. Associate conductor, John Miner. Associate producer, Virginia Hymes. Produced by Radio City Music Hall Productions, Inc. (Bernard Gersten, Executive producer) and Sherwin M. Goldman Productions. Opened 7 April 1983 at the Radio City Music Hall and closed 15 May 1983 after 45 performances.

CAST (in order of appearance): *Jasbo Brown*: Edward Strauss. *Clara*: PRISCILLA BASKERVILLE or LUVENIA GARNER. *Mingo*: Timothy Allen. *Jake*: Alexander Smalls or James Tyeska. *Sportin' Life*: LARRY MARSHALL. *Robbins*: Tyrone Jolivet. *Serena*: SHIRLEY BAINES, REGINA McCONNELL, WILMA SHAKESNIDER or VERONICA TYLER. *Jim*: Donald Walter Kase. *Peter*, (the Honey Man): Mervin Bertel Wallace. *Lily*: Y. Yvonne Matthews. *Maria*: LORETTA HOLKMANN or GWENDOLYN SHEPHERD. *Scipio*: Akili Prince. *Porgy*: ROBERT MOSLEY, JR., MICHAEL V. SMARTT, JONATHAN SPRAGUE or JAMES TYESKA. *Crown*: GREGG BAKER or GEORGE ROBERT MERRITT. *Bess*: PRISCILLA BASKERVILLE, HENRIETTA ELIZABETH DAVIS, NAOMI MOODY or DAISY NEWMAN. *Detective*: Larry Storch. *Policeman*: William Moize. *Undertaker*: Joseph S. Eubanks. *Annie*: Lou Ann Pickett. *Frazier*: Raymond H. Bazemore. *Strawberry Woman*: Denice Woods. *Crab Man*: Thomas J. Young. *Nelson*: Everett McCorvey. *Coroner*: Richert Easley.

Ensemble (Residents of Catfish Row): Loretta Abbott, Timothy Allen, Earl L. Baker, Emerson Battles, Raymond H. Bazemore, Shirley Black-Brown, Roslyn Burrough, Vertrelle Cameron, Seraiah Carol, Duane Clenton Carter, Dabriah Chapman, Louise Coleman, Janice D. Dixon, Cisco Xavier Drayton, Alberta M. Driver, Joseph S. Eubanks, Karen E. Eubanks, Lori Eubanks, Beno Foster, Jerry Godfrey, Earl Grandison, Milton B. Grayson, Jr., Elvira Green, Lawrence Hamilton, Gurcell Henry, Lisa D. Holkmann, Janice T. Hutson, David-Michael Johnson, Leavata Johnson, Tyrone Jolivet, Dorothy L. Jones, Donald Walker Kase, Roberta Alexandra Laws, Eugene Little, Ann Marie Mackey, Barbara Mahajan, Amelia Marshall, Richard Mason, Y. Yvonne Matthews, Everett McCorvey, John McDaniels, William Moize, Byron Onque, H. William Penn, Marenda Perry, Lou Ann Pickett, Herbert Lee Rawlings, Jr., Roumel Reaux, David Robertson, Lattilia Ronrico, Renee L. Rose, Myles

[12]First produced in New York 10 October 1935 at the Alvin Theatre for 124 performances.

Gregory Savage, Sheryl Shell, Kiki Shepard, Chuck Thorpes, Mervin Bertel Wallace, Pamela Warrick-Smith, Cornelius White, Rodney Wing, Denice Woods, Thomas J. Young, and Diallobe Dorsey, Angela Holcomb, Robert Kryser, Jason Little, Noelle Richards, Kevin L. Stroman, Charee Adia Thropes, Tarik Winston.

The action takes place in Charleston, South Carolina, in the early 1930's.

Act 1, Scene 1: Catfish Row, a summer evening. *Scene 2*: Serena's Room, the following night. *Scene 3*: Catfish Row, a month later. *Scene 4*: Kittiwah Island, late afternoon.

Act 2, Scene 1: Catfish Row, before dawn, a week later. *Scene 2*: Serena's Room, the dawn of the following day. *Scene 3*: Catfish Row, the next night. *Scene 4*: Catfish Row, the next afternoon. *Scene 5*: Catfish Row, a week later.

ACT 1

Scene 1

"Brown Blues"
Piano

"Summertime"
P. Baskerville

"A Woman Is A Sometime Thing"
A. Smalls, Men

"Here Come De Honey Man"
M. B. Wallace

"They Pass By Singing"
R. Mosley, Jr.

"Oh Little Stars"
R. Mosley, Jr.

Scene 2

"Gone, Gone, Gone"
Ensemble

"Overflow"
Ensemble

"My Man's Gone Now"
S. Baines,

"Leavin' For the Promise' Lan'"
P. Baskerville, Ensemble

Scene 3

"It Takes a Long Pull to Get There"
A. Smalls, Men

"I Got Plenty o' Nuttin'"
R. Mosley, Jr., Ensemble

"Struttin' Style"
L. Holkmann

"Buzzard Song"
R. Mosley, Jr., Ensemble

"Bess, You Is My Woman Now"
R. Mosley, Jr., P. Baskerville

"Oh, I Can't Sit Down"
Ensemble

Scene 4

"I Ain't Got No Shame"
Ensemble

"It Ain't Necessarily So"
L. Marshall, Ensemble

"What You Want With Bess?"
P. Baskerville, G. Baker

ACT 2

Scene 1

"Oh, Doctor Jesus"
S. Baines, L. Holkmann, M. B. Wallce, Y. Y. Matthews, R. Mosley, Jr.

"I Loves You, Porgy"
R. Mosley, Jr., P. Baskerville

Scene 2

"Oh, He'venly Father"
Ensemble

"Oh, de Lawd Shake de Heavens"
Ensemble

"Oh, Dere's Somebody Knockin' at De Do'"
Ensemble

"A Red Headed Woman"
G. Baker, Ensemble

Scene 3

"Clara, Clara"
Ensemble

Scene 4

"There a Boat Dat's Leavin' Soon for New York"
L. Marshall, P. Baskerville

"Good Mornin', Sistuh!"
Ensemble

Scene 5

"Oh, Bess, Oh Where's My Bess"
R. Mosley, Jr., S. Baines, Y. Y. Matthews

"Oh Lawd, I'm On My Way"
R. Mosley, Jr. . Ensemble

1983.05 SHOWBOAT

A Revival of the Musical (Play) in Two Acts, 15 Scenes[13]. Book and lyrics by Oscar Hammerstein II. Based on the novel of the same name by Edna Ferber. Music by Jerome Kern. Directed by Michael Kahn. Choreography by Dorothy Danner. Scenery designed by Herbert Senn, Helen Pond. Costumes designed by Molly Maginnis. Lighting designed by Thomas Skelton. Musical director, John DeMain. Conductor, Jack Everly. Sound by Richard Fitzgerald. A Houston Grand Opera Production. Executive producers, Robert A. Buckley, Douglas Urbanski. Produced by James M. Nederlander, John F. Kennedy Center (Roger L. Stevens, Chairman), Denver Center (Donald R. Seawell, Chairman). Opened 24 April 1983 at the Uris Theatre and closed 26 June 1983 after 73 performances.

CAST (in order of their appearance): *Windy (McLain)*: Richard Dix. *Steve*: Wayne Turnage. *Pete*: Glenn Martin. *Queenie*: KARLA BURNS. *Parthy Ann Hawkes*: AVRIL GENTLES. *Captain Andy*: DONALD O'CONNOR. *Ellie*: PAIGE O'HARA. *Frank*: PAUL KEITH. *Mahoney*: Randy Hansen. *Julie*: LONETTE McKEE. *Gaylord Ravenal*: RON RAINES. *(Sheriff Ike) Vallon*: Jacob Mark Hopkin. *Magnolia*: SHERYL WOODS. *Joe*: BRUCE HUBBARD. *Backwoodsman*: Lewis White. *Jeb*: James Gedge. *Barkers*: Lewis White, Randy Hansen, James Gedge. *La Belle Fatima*: Lynda Karen. *Old Sport*: Larry Hansen. *Landlady*: Mary Rocco. *Jim*: Jacob Mark Hopkin. *Jake*: Randy Hansen. *Young Man with Guitar*: Larry Hansen. *Charlie*: P. L. Brown. *Mother Superior*: Linda Milani. *Young Kim*: Tracy Paul. *Lottie*: Gloria Parker. *Dolly*: Dale Kristien. *Old Lady on Levee*: Mary Rocco. *Older Kim*: Karen Culliver. *Radio Announcer's Voice*: Hal Douglas.

Chorus: *Women*: Vanessa Ayers, Joanna Beck, Karen Culliver, Olivia Detante, Kim Fairchild, Cheryl Freeman, Lynda Karen, Dale Kristien, Linda Milani, Gloria Parker, Veronica Rhodes, Mary Rocco, Molly Wassermann, Carrie Wilder. *Swings*: Jeane July, Suzanne Ishee. *Men*: P. L. Brown, Michael-Pierre Dean, Merwin Foard, Joe Garcia, James Gedge, Michael Gray, Larry Hansen, Randy Hansen, Jacob Mark Hopkin, Glenn Martin, Randy Morgan, Dennis Perren, Leonard Piggee, Alton Spencer, Robert Vincent, Lewis White, Wardell Woodard. *Swings*: Tom Garrett, Ed Battle.

Act 1, Scene 1: The Levee at Natchez on the Mississippi, in the 1880s. *Scene 2*: Kitchen pantry of the *Cotton Blossom*. . Five minutes later. *Scene 3*: Outside a river front gambling saloon. Simultaneously. *Scene 4*: Auditorium and Stage of the *Cotton Blossom*. . One hour later. *Scene 5*: Box office, on foredeck. Three weeks later. *Scene 6*: Auditorium and stage during the Third Act of "The Parson's Bride," that night. *Scene 7*: The top deck. Later that night. *Scene 8*: The Levee at Greenville. Next morning.

Act 2, Scene 1: The Midway Plaisance, Chicago World's Fair, 1893. *Scene 2*: A room on Ontario Street, 1904. *Scene 3*: Rehearsal room, Trocadero Music Hall. A few days later. *Scene 4*: St. Agatha's Convent. About the same time. *Scene 5*: Trocadero Music Hall, New Year's Eve, ringing in the year 1905. *Scene 6*: The deck of the *Cotton Blossom*, 1927. *Scene 7*: The levee at Greenville, the next night.

ACT 1

"Cotton Blossom"
Stevedores, Townspeople

"Show Boat Parade and Ballyhoo"
D. O'Connor, the Showboat Troupe, Townspeople

"Only Make Believe"
R. Raines, S. Woods

"Ol' Man River"
B. Hubbard, Stevedores

"Can't Help Lovin' Dat Man"
L. McKee, R. Le Noire, S. Woods, B. Hubbard, Ensemble

"Life Upon the Wicked Stage"
P. O'Hara, Ensemble

"I Might Fall Back on You"
P, Keith, P. O'Hara

[13]First presented December 27, 1927 at the Ziegfeld Theatre for 572 performances. This production was made possible in part through a major grant from Citibank•Citicorp and a generous gift from Mrs. Edgar Tobin.

"Queenie's Ballyhoo"
R. Le Noire, D. O'Connor, Ensemble
"You Are Love"
S. Woods, R. Raines
Finale
Entire Ensemble

ACT 2
"At the Fair"
Sightseers, Barkers
"Why Do I Love You?"
S. Woods, R. Raines, D. O'Connor, A. Gentles, Ensemble
"Bill" (*Lyrics by* P. G. Wodehouse.)
L. McKee
"Can't Help Lovin' Dat Man" (reprise)
S. Woods
Service and Scene Music-St. Agnes Convent
"Only Make Believe" (reprise)
R. Raines
"Goodbye, My Lady Love"—Cakewalk
P. Keith, P. O'Hara
(*Music and Lyrics by* Joseph E. Howard.)
Magnolia's Debut at the Trocadero Music Hall:
"After the Ball"
S. Woods, Ensemble
(*Music and Lyrics by* Charles K. Harris.)
"Ol' Man River" (reprise)
B. Hubbard
"You Are Love" (reprise)
R. Raines
"Hey Feller"
K. Burns, Ensemble
Finale (Act 2)
Entire Ensemble

1983.06 MY ONE AND ONLY

A Musical in Two Acts, 15 Scenes. Book by Peter Stone and Timothy S. Mayer[14]. Music by George Gershwin. Lyrics by Ira Gershwin. Staged and choreographed by Thommie Walsh and Tommy Tune. Associate choreographer, Baayork Lee. Associate director, Phillip Oesterman. Scenic design by Adrianne Lobel. Costume design by Rita Ryack. Lighting design by Marcia Madeira. Sound design by Otts Munderloh. Musical concept, dance arrangements by Wally Harper. Orchestrations by Michael Gibson. Musical and vocal direction, Jack Lee. Dance arrangements by Peter Larson. Musical consultant, Michael Feinstein. A King Street Production (Bernard Carragher, Obie Bailey, Bernard Bailey). Associate producer, Jonathan Farkas. Produced by Paramount Theatre Productions, Francine LeFrak, Kenneth-Mark Productions (Kenneth D. Greenblatt, Mark S. Schwartz), in association with Jujamcyn Theatres, Tams-Witmark Music Library, Lewis Allen. Opened 1 May 1983 at the St. James Theatre and closed 5 March 1985 after 767 performances.

CAST (in order of appearance): *The New Rhythm Boys*: David Jackson, Ken Leigh Rogers, Ronald Dennis. *Captain Billy Buck Chandler*: TOMMY TUNE. *Mickey*: DENNY DILLON. *Prince Nicolai Erraclyovitch Tchatchavadze*: BRUCE McGILL. *Fish (6)*: *Flounder*: Nana Visitor. *Sturgeon*: Susan Hartley. *Minnow*: Stephanie Eley. *Prawn*: Jill Cook. *Kipper*: Niki Harris. *Anchovie*: Karen Tamburrelli. *Edith Herbert*: TWIGGY. *Right Reverend J. D. Montgomery*: ROSCOE LEE BROWNE. *Reporter*: Jill Cook. *Mr. Magix*: CHARLES "HONI" COLES. *Ritz Quartet*: Casper Roos, Paul David Richards, Carl Nicholas, Will Blankenship. *Policeman*: Paul David Richards. *Stage Doorman*: Paul David Richards. *Mrs. O'Malley*: Ken Leigh Rogers. *Conductor*: Adrian Bailey. *Dancing Gentlemen*: Adrian Bailey, Bar Dell Conner, Ronald Dennis, David Jackson, Alde Lewis, Jr., Bernard Manners, Ken Leigh Rogers. *Achmed*: BRUCE McGILL. *Swings*: Merilee Magnuson, Melvin Washington.

Act 1, Scene 1: Pennsylvania Station, 1 May 1927. *Scene 2*: Billy's Hangar. *Scene 3*: Mr. Magix' Emporial. *Scene 4*: Club Havana. *Scene 5*: Cinema. *Scene 6*: Central Park. *Scene 7*: The Hangar. *Scene 8*: A Deserted Beach.

Act 2, Scene 1: Aquacade. *Scene 2*: Mr. Magix' Emporial. *Scene 3*: Pennsylvania Station. *Scene 4*: The Hangar. *Scene 5*: Club Oasis. *Scene 6*: The Uptown Chapel. *Scene 7*: Bows and Finale.

[14]Adapted from the musical "Funny Face," book by Fred Thompson and Paul Gerard Smith.

ACT 1
Scene 1
"I Can't Be Bothered Now" (from *A DAMSEL IN DISTRESS* film)
The New Rhythm Boys, T. Tune, Twiggy, B. McGill, D. Dillon, Ensemble
"Blah, Blah, Blah" (from *DELICIOUS* film)
T. Tune
Scene 2
"Boy Wanted" (from *A DANGEROUS MAID*)
Twiggy, J. Cook
"Soon" (from *STRIKE UP THE BAND*)
T. Tune
Scene 3
"High Hat" (from *FUNNY FACE*)/"Sweet and Low-Down" (from *TIP-TOES*)
H. Coles, T. Tune, the New Rhythm Boys, Ensemble
Scene 4
"Blah, Blah, Blah" (reprise)
Twiggy
"Just Another Rhumba"[15] (unused, *THE GOLDWYN FOLLIES* film, 1938)
R. L. Browne, Ensemble
Scene 5
"He Loves and She Loves" (from *FUNNY FACE*)
T. Tune, Twiggy
"He Loves and She Loves" (reprise)
Ritz Quartette
Scene 7
"I Can't Be Bothered Now" (reprise)
The New Rhythm Boys
Scene 8
"'S Wonderful" (from *FUNNY FACE*)
T. Tune, Twiggy
"'S Wonderful" (reprise)
Ritz Quartette
"Strike Up the Band" (from *STRIKE UP THE BAND*)
T. Tune

ACT 2
Scene 1
"In the Swim" (from *FUNNY FACE*)/"What Are We Here For" (from *TREASURE GIRL*)
Fish, B. McGill
"Nice Work If You Can Get It" (from *A DAMSEL IN DISTRESS* film)
Twiggy
Scene 2
"My One and Only" (from *FUNNY FACE*)
H. Coles, T. Tune
(Special Material by Charles "Honi" Coles.)
Scene 4
"Funny Face" (from *FUNNY FACE*)
D. Dillon, B. McGill
Scene 5
"My One and Only" (reprise)
T. Tune
Scene 6
"Kickin' the Clouds Away" (from *TELL ME MORE!*)
R. L. Browne, Ensemble
(*Lyrics by* Buddy DeSylva and Ira Gershwin. *Dance Arrangements by* Peter Howard.)
"How Long Has This Been Going On?" (from *ROSALIE*, dropped from *FUNNY FACE*)
Twiggy, T. Tune
Scene 7
"Strike Up the Band" (reprise)
Company

[15]Dropped after opening.

1983.07 THE FLYING KARAMAZOV BROTHERS

An Entertainment in Two Acts. (Conceived by the Cast.) Setting and costumes by Robert Fletcher. Lighting by Marc B. Weiss. Sound by Robert Kerzman. Associate Producers, Harold Thau, Robert Courson. Produced by Mace Neufeld and Viacom International, Inc. Opened 10 May 1983 at the Ritz Theatre and closed 19 June 1983 after 47 performances.

CAST: *Dmitri*: Paul David Magid. *Alyosha*: Randy Nelson. *Fyodor*: Timothy Daniel Furst. *Smerdyakov*: Sam Williams. *Ivan*: Howard Jay Patterson.

Kamikaze Ground Crew (band): Douglas Wieselman, Mike van Liew, Gina Leishman, Bud Chase, Alex Willows.

The action takes place at the present time on the stage of a prestigious Broadway theatre.

"Ivan's Antique Store" and "The Chumleighland March" (*Music by* Thaddeus Spae.)

All other music by Douglas Wieselman.

1983.08 DANCE A LITTLE CLOSER

A Musical in Two Acts, 9 Scenes. Book and lyrics by Alan Jay Lerner. Based on the play "Idiot's Delight" by Robert E. Sherwood. Music by Charles Strouse. Directed by Alan Jay Lerner. Musical staging and choreography by Billy Wilson. Scenery by David Mitchell. Costumes by Donald Brooks. Lighting by Thomas Skelton. Orchestrations by Jonathan Tunick. Musical direction by Peter Howard. Dance music by Glen Kelly. Sound design by John McClure. Production supervisor, Stone Widney. Associate producer, Paul N. Temple. Produced by Frederick Brisson, Jerome Minskoff, James Nederlander, the John F. Kennedy Center (Roger L. Stevens, Chairman). Opened and closed 11 May 1983 at the Minskoff Theatre after 1 performance.

CAST (in order of appearance): *Roger Butterfield*: Don Chastain. *Harry Aikens*: LEN CARIOU. *The Delights (3)*: *Shirley*: Diane Pennington. *Bebe*: Cheryl Howard. *Elaine*: Alyson Reed. *Johannes Hartog*: David Sabin. *Contessa Carla Pirianno*: Elizabeth Hubbard. *Captain Mueller*: Noel Craig. *Charles Castleton*: Brent Barrett. *Edward Dunlop*: Jeff Keller. *Bellboy*: Philip Mollet. *Waiter*: Brian Sutherland. *Reverend Oliver Boyle*: I. M. Hobson. *Hester Boyle*: Joyce Worsley. *Heinrich Walter (Halloway)*: Joseph Kolinski. *Cynthia Brookfield-Bailey*: LIZ ROBERTSON. *Dr. Josef Winkler*: GEORGE ROSE. *Pas de Deux*: *Harry's Double*: Brian Sutherland. *Cynthia's Double*: Robin Stephens. *Rink Attendant*: James Fatta. *Ice Skater*: Colleen Ashton. *Violinist*: James Fatta. *Harry, Harry, Harry, Harry*: Peter Wandel, Philip Mollet, Brian Sutherland, James Fatta.

Hotel Guests: Colleen Ashton, Candy Cook, Mary Dale, James Fatta, Philip Mollet, Linda Poser, Robin Stephens, Brian Sutherland, Peter Wandel. *Swings*: Joanne Genelle, Mark Lamanna.

The action takes place during "the avoidable future" at the Barclay-Palace Hotel on a hillside in the Austrian Alps.

Act 1, Scene 1: The nightclub of the Barclay-Palace Hotel New Year's Eve, shortly before midnight. *Scene 2*: The main entrance lounge of the hotel 2 A.M. that night. *Scene 3*: The Winkler Suite later that night. *Scene 3A*: Harry's Memory. *Scene 4*: A Bedroom in a mid-Western hotel ten years earlier. *Scene 5*: The skating rink at the Hotel New Year's Day morning. *Scene 6*: The nightclub of the hotel that evening.

Act 2, Scene 1: The main entrance lounge of the hotel the following morning. *Scene 2*: Cynthia's memory. *Scene 3*: The main entrance lounge of the hotel immediately following.

ACT 1

Scene 1

"It Never Would've Worked"
L. Cariou, the Delights

"Happy, Happy New Year"
L. Cariou, the Delights, Guests

Scene 2

"No Man Is Worth It"
L. Robertson

"What Are You Going to Do About It?"
L. Cariou, J. Kolinski

Scene 3

"A Woman Who Thinks I'm Wonderful"
G. Rose

Scene 3A

"Pas de Deux"
(*Danced by*) B. Sutherland, R. Stephens

Scene 4

"There's Never Been Anything Like Us"
L. Cariou

"Another Life"
L. Robertson

Scene 5

"Why Can't the World Go and Leave Us Alone?"
B. Barrett, J. Keller

"He Always Comes Home to Me"
L. Robertson

Scene 6

"I Got a New Girl"
L. Cariou, the Delights

"Dance a Little Closer"
L. Cariou, L. Robertson, Guests

"There's Always One You Can't Forget"
L. Cariou

ACT 2

Scene 1

"Homesick"
The Delights

"Mad"
L. Cariou, the Delights

"I Don't Know"
L. Cariou, I. M. Hobson, E. Hubbard, the Delights, B. Barrett, J. Keller, L. Robertson

"Auf Wiedersehen"
G. Rose

"I Never Want To See You Again"
L. Cariou

Scene 2

"On Top of the World"
L. Robertson, Men

Scene 3

"I Got a New Girl" (reprise)
L. Cariou, L. Robertson

"Dance a Little Closer" (reprise)
L. Cariou, L. Robertson

1983–1984 SEASON

George Hearn in LA CAGE AUX FOLLES
Martha Swope/TimePix

1983–1984 SEASON

1983.09 5.6.7.8 . . . DANCE!

A Musical Revue in Two Acts, 10 Scenes. Written by Bruce Vilanch. Original songs by David Zippel and Wally Harper. Directed and choreographed by Ron Field. Associate director, David Rubinstein. Associate choreographer, Marianne Selbert. Musical director, Thomas Helm. Scenery by Tom H. John. Costumes by Lindsay W. Davis. Lighting by Richard Nelson. Film sequences by Christopher Dixon. Musical supervisor, Wally Harper. Orchestrations by Bill Byers. Dance arrangements by Mark Hummel and Donald York. Production coordinator, Stephen Nisbet. Director of the Rockettes, Violet Holmes. Produced by Radio City Music Hall Productions, Inc. (Bernard Gersten, Executive Producer). Opened 15 June 1983 at the Radio City Music Hall and closed 5 September 1983 after 149 performances.

CAST: SANDY DUNCAN, DON CORREIA, BILL IRWN, ARMELIA McQUEEN, KEN SACHA, MARGE CHAMPION.

THE ROCKETTES: Joyce Dwyer, Carol Harbich, Joan Peer Kelleher, Gerri Presky, Susan Boron, Dee Dee Knapp, Deniene Fenn, Barbara Ann Moore, Judy Little, Phyllis Wujiko, Barbara Ann Cittadino, Leslie McCarthy, Eileen M. Collins, Cindy Peiffer, Pauline A. Tzikas, Cynthia Hughes, Susanne Doris, Carol Toman, Pam Kelleher, Jackie Fancy, Ginny Hounsell, Prudence Gray Demmler, Terry Spano, Dottie Belle, Sonya Livingston, Rose Anne Woolsey, Susan Theobald, Carol Beatty, Catherine Beatty, Brie Daniels, Lynn Newton, Darlene Wendy, Lynn Sullivan, Alexis Ficks, Jennifer Hammond, Kerri Pearsall, Patricia Tully, Susan Cleland, Elizabeth Chanin.

Dancers: Robin Alpert, Christine Colby, Carol Estey, Edyie Fleming, Blanche, Sonya Hensley, Jodi Moccia, Gayle Samuels, Gregory Brock, Ciscoe Bruton II, Daniel Esteras, Douglas Graham, Michael Lafferty, Dan McCoy, Rodney Pridgen, Adrian Rosario.

Singers: Freida A. Williams, Holly Lipton Nash, Lois Sage, Roger Berdahl, Michael Halpern, Wayne Mattson, Wes Skelley, Paul Solen.

ACT 1

Scene 1

5-6-7-8 . . . Dance!:
S. Duncan, the Rockettes, Dancers, Singers

Half-Hour
(*Film Sequence by* Christopher Dixon.)

"Five, Six, Seven, Eight . . . Dance!"
(*Music by* Wally Harper. *Lyrics by* David Zippel.)

"Life Is a Dance"
(*Music by* Gavin Christopher.)

Dance
(*Music by* Paul Jabara.)

Scene 2

5-6-7-8 . . . Band!:
S. Duncan, Dancers

"It's Better with a Band"
(*Music by* Wally Harper. *Lyrics by* David Zippel.)

Scene 3

5-6-7-8 . . . Husband!:

Meet Don
(*Film Sequence by* Christopher Dixon.)

"I've Got Your Number" (from *LITTLE ME*)
D. Correia, Dancers, the Rockettes
(*Music by* Cy Coleman. *Lyrics by* Carolyn Leigh.)

"You Musn't Kick It Around" (from *PAL JOEY*)
D. Correia, Dancers, the Rockettes
(*Music by* Richard Rodgers. *Lyrics by* Lorenz Hart.)

"It Only Happens When I Dance With You" (from *EASTER PARADE* film)
(*Music and Lyrics by* Irving Berlin.)
S. Duncan, D. Correia, the Rockettes, Dancers

Scene 4

5-6-7-8 . . . Protest!
A. McQueen, the Rockettes

"Singers' Protest"
(*Music by* Wally Harper. *Lyrics by* David Zippel.)

"One Step" (from *HOW DO YOU DO, I LOVE YOU* and *STARTING HERE, STARTING NOW*)
(*Music by* David Shire. *Lyrics by* Richard Maltby, Jr.)

Scene 5

5-6-7-8 . . . Victory!:
The Company

"It Had to Be You"
(*Music by* Isham Jones. *Lyrics by* Gus Kahn.)

"Bad Habits"
(*Music and Lyrics by* Billy Field and Tom Price.)

"It's Not What You Weigh"
(*Music by* Wally Harper. *Lyrics by* David Zippel.)

"Sing, Sing, Sing"
(*Music by* Louis Prima.)

"Make Way for Tomorrow" (from *COVER GIRL* film)
(*Music by* Jerome Kern. *Lyrics by* Ira Gershwin and E. Y. Harburg.)

ACT 2

Scene 1

5-6-7-8 . . . Marilyn!:
S. Duncan, D. Correia, the Rockettes, Singers

Don's Fantasy
(*Film Sequence by* Christopher Dixon.)

"Cheek to Cheek" (from *TOP HAT* film)
(*Music by* Irving Berlin.)

"I Go to Rio!"
(*Music and Lyrics by* Peter Allen and Adrienne Anderson.)

"I'm Flying" (from *PETER PAN*)
(*Music by* Mark [Moose] Charlap. *Lyrics by* Carolyn Leigh.)

Scene 2

5-6-7-8 . . . Sandy!:
S. Duncan, Male Dancers

"She Just Loves Las Vegas"
(*Music by* Wally Harper. *Lyrics by* David Zippel.)

"Dance With Me"
(*Music and Lyrics by* R. Parker, Jr. and David Rubinson.)

"Neverland" (from *PETER PAN*)
(*Music by* Jule Styne. *Lyrics by* Betty Comden and Adolph Green.)

Scene 3

5-6-7-8 . . . Audition!:
B. Irwin

"Tea for Two" (from *NO, NO NANETTE*)[instrumental]
(*Music by* Vincent Youmans.)

Scene 4

5-6-7-8 . . . Inspirations!:

Dance Teams Medley:
Company
"I Love to Dance" (from *BALLROOM*)
(*Music by* Billy Goldenberg. *Lyrics by* Marilyn and Alan Bergman.)
"Tres Moutarde"
(*Music by* Cecil Macklin.)
"La Cumparsita"
(*Music by* G. H. Matos Rodriguez.)
"The Continental" (from *THE GAY DIVORCEE* film)
(*Music by* Con Conrad.)
"Our Love Is Here to Stay" (from *THE GOLDWYN FOLLIES* film)
(*Music by* George Gershwin. *Lyrics by* Ira Gershwin.)

"Where Did You Learn to Dance" (from *I LOVE MELVIN* film)
S. Duncan, M. Champion
(*Music by* Josef Myrow. *Lyrics by* Mack Gordon.)

"I Love to Dance" (reprise)
M. Champion, D. Correia, Dancers

Scene 5

5-6-7-8 . . . Finale:
Company

"Broadway Rhythm" (from *BROADWAY MELODY OF 1936* film)
(*Music by* Nacio Herb Brown. *Lyrics by* Arthur Freed.)

"Body Language"
(*Music and Lyrics by* Steve Sperry and Barry Fasman.)

"Five, Six, Seven, Eight . . . Dance!" (reprise)

1983.10

MAME

A Revival of the Musical in Two Acts, 16 Scenes[1]. Book by Jerome Lawrence and Robert E. Lee. Based on the novel "Auntie Mame" by Patrick Dennis and the play of the same name by Lawrence and Lee. Music and lyrics by Jerry Herman. Directed by John Bowab. Choreography by Diana Baffa-Brill, based on the original by Onna White. Production supervisor, Jerry Herman. Scenery by Peter Wolf, based on the originals by William and Jean Eckart. Costumes by Robert Mackintosh. Lighting by Thomas Skelton. Sound by Christine Voellinger. Musical director, Jim Coleman. Vocal arrangements by Donald Pippin. Orchestrations by Philip J. Lang. Executive producer, Michael Lynne. Associate producer, Manny Kladitis. Produced by the Mitch Leigh Company. Opened 24 July 1983 at the Gershwin Theatre and closed 28 August 1983 after 41 performances.

CAST (in order of appearance): *Patrick Dennis*, age 10: Roshi Handwerger. *Agnes Gooch*: JANE CONNELL. *Vera Charles*: ANNE FRANCINE *Mame Dennis*: ANGELA LANSBURY. *Ralph Devine*: Jacob Mark Hopkin. *Bishop*: Merwin Foard. *M. Lindsay Woolsey*: Donald Torres. *Ito*: SAB SHIMONO. *Doorman*: Brian McAnally *Elevator Boy*: Marshall Hagins. *Messenger*: David Miles. *Dwight Babcock*: WILLARD WATERMAN. *Bubbles the Clown*: Ken Henley. *Dance Teacher*: Louise Kirtland. *Bird Dancers*: Suzanne Ishee, Patrick Sean Murphy. *Leading Man*: Kenneth Kantor. *Stage Manager*: Rchard Poole. *Madame Branislowski*: Fran Stevens. *Gregor*: Ken Henley. *Beauregard Jackson Pickett Burnside*: Scot Stewart. *Uncle Jeff*: Kenneth Kantor. *Cousin Fan*: Carol Lurie. *Sally Cato*: Barbara Lang. *Mother Burnside*: Fran Stevens. *Patrick Dennis*, age 19-29: Byron Nease. *Junior Babcock*: Patrick Sean Murphy. *Mrs. Upson*: Louise Kirtland. *Mr. Upson*: John C. Becher. *Gloria Upson*: Michaela K. Hughes. *Pegeen Ryan*: Ellyn Arons. *Peter Dennis*: Daniel Mahon.

Mame's Friends: Ellyn Arons, Alyson Bristol, Merwin Foard, Marshall Hagins, Ken Henley, Jacon Mark Hopkin, Michaela Hughes, Suzanne Ishee, Kenneth Kantor, Harry Kingsley, Melinda Koblick, David Loring, Carol Lurie, Brian McNally, David Miles, Patrick Sean Murphy, Viewma Negromonte, Michele Pigliavento, Cissy Rebich, Richard Poole, Joseph Rich, Mollie Smith.

1983.11

LA CAGE AUX FOLLES

A Musical in Two Acts, 10 Scenes. Book by Harvey Fierstein. Based on the play of the same name by Jean Poiret. Music and lyrics by Jerry Herman. Directed by Arthur Laurents. Choreography by Scott Salmon. Settngs designed by David Mitchell. Costumes designed by Theoni V. Aldredge. Lighting designed by Jules Fisher. Sound designed by Peter Fitzgerald. Musical direction, vocal arrangements by Donald Pippin. Orchestrations by Jim Tyler. Dance music arrangements by Gordon Lowry Harrell. Assistant choreographer, Richard Balestrino. Executive producers, Barry Brown and Fritz Holt. Produced by Allan Carr, with Kenneth D. Greenblatt, Marvin A. Krauss, Stewart F. Lane, James M. Nederlander, Martin Richards, in association with Jonathan Farkas, John J. Pomerantz, Martin Heinfling. Opened 21 August 1983 at the Palace Theatre and closed 14 November 1987 after 1761 performances.

CAST (in order of appearance): *Georges*: GENE BARRY. *Les Cagelles (12)*: *Chantal*: David Cahn. *Monique*: Dennis Callahan. *Dermah*: Frank DiPasquale. *Nicole*: John Dolf. *Hanna*: David Engel. *Mercedes*: David Evans. *Bitelle*: Linda Haberman. *Lo Singh*: Eric Lamp. *Odette*: Dan O'Grady. *Angelique*: Deborah Phelan. *Phaedra*: David Scala. *Clo-Clo*: Sam Singhaus.

Francis: Brian Kelly. *Jacob*: William Thomas, Jr. *Albin*: GEORGE HEARN. *Jean-Michel*: John Weiner. *Anne*: Leslie Stevens. *Jacqueline*: Elizabeth Parrish. *M. Renaud*: Walter Charles. *St. Tropez Townspeople (8)*: *Mme. Renaud*: Sydney Anderson. *Paulette*: Betsy Craig. *Hercule*: Jack Neubeck. *Etienne*: Jay Pierce. *Babette*: Marie Santell. *Colette*: Jennifer Smith. *Tabarro*: Mark Waldrop. *Pepe*: Ken Ward.

Edouard Dindon: Jay Garner. *Marie Dindon*: Merle Louise. *Swing Performers*: Robert Bruback, Drew Geraci, Jan Leigh Herndon, Leslie Simons.

The action takes place in summer in St. Tropez, France, at the present time.

Act 1, Scene 1: Outside, then inside, the club "La Cage aux Folles." Late afternoon. *Scene 2*: The Apartment of Georges and Albin; onstage at "La Cage aux Folles." *Scene 3*: Offstage at "La Cage aux Folles:" the apartment. *Scene 4*: The Promenade and a Cafe in St. Tropez. *Scene 5*: Offstage and Onstage at "La Cage aux Folles." *Scene 6*: Offstage and Onstage at "La Cage aux Folles."

Act 2, Scene 1: The Promenade and the Cafe in St. Tropez. *Scene 2*: The Apartment. *Scene 3*: Chez Jacqueline, an elegant restaurant. *Scene 4*: The Apartment; the club "La Cage aux Folles."

ACT 1
Scene 1
"We Are What We Are"
Les Cagelles
Scene 2
"A Little More Mascara"
G. Hearn, Friends
Scene 3
"With Anne on My Arm"
J. Weiner
"With You on My Arm" (reprise)
G. Barry, G. Hearn
Scene 4
"The Promenade"
Townspeople
"Song on the Sand"
G. Hearn
Scene 5
"La Cage aux Folles"
G. Hearn, Les Cagelles
Scene 6
"I Am What I Am"
G. Hearn

ACT 2
Scene 1
"Song on the Sand" (reprise)
G. Barry, G. Hearn
"Masculinity"
G. Barry, G. Hearn, Townspeople
Scene 2
"Look Over There"
G. Barry
"Cocktail Counterpoint"
G. Barry, J. Garner, M. Louise, W. Thomas
Scene 3
"The Best of Times"
G. Hearn, E. Parrish, Patrons
Scene 4
"Look Over There" (reprise)
J. Weiner
Grand Finale
(Entire Company)

1983.12

THE MERRY WIDOW

A Revival of the Operetta in Three Acts[2]. (Music by Franz Lehár. Original German libretto (Die Lustige Witwe) by Victor Léon and Leo Stein (after "L'Attaché d'Ambassade.") English version by Adrian Ross. Directed by Ronald Bentley. Choreography by Donald Saddler. Scenery designed by Helen Pond and Herbert Senn. Costumes designed by Suzanne Mess. Lighting designed by Gilbert V. Helmsley, Jr. Conductor, Eric Knight. Chorus master, Joseph Colaneri. Produced by the New York City Opera. Opened 2 October 1983 at the New York State Theatre and closed 13 November 1983 after 6 performances in repertory.

CAST (in order of appearance): *Baron Popoff*: JACK HARROLD. *Natalie*: Susanne Marsee. *M. de St. Brioche*: WILLIAM EICHORN. *Marquis de Cascada*: Thomas Jamerson. *Sylviane*: Debra Vanderlinde. *Olga*: Joyce Castle *General Novikovich*: Jonathan Green. *Vicomte Camille de Jolidon*: Alan Kays. *Counsellor Khadja*: William Ledbetter. *Nisch*: Gerald Isaac. *Sonia*: KAREN HUFFSTODT. *Prince Danilo*: CRIS GROENENDAAL. *Head Waiter*: Mervin Crook. *Zozo*: Anny DeGange. *Lolo*: Joan Mirabella. *Dodo*: Esperanza Galan. *Jou-Jou*: Candace Itow. *Frou-Frou*: Victoria Rinaldi. *Clo-Clo*: Raven Wilkinson. *Margot*: Jean Barber. *Chorus of Marsovian and Parisian Society, Dancers, Servants and Waiters*: New York City Opera Chorus.

---

[1]Originally produced in New York 24 May 1966 at the Winter Garden for 1508 performances. For Synopsis of Scenes and Musical Numbers, see original 1966 production.

[2]Originally produced in New York 21 October 1907 at the New Amsterdam Theatre for 416 performances. For Synopsis of Scenes and Musical Numbers, see original 1907 production. Interpolated into this production:
"Girls Were Made to Love and Kiss" (from *PAGANINI*)
(*Music by* Franz Lehar. *Original German Lyrics by* Paul Knepler and Bela Jenbach. *English Lyrics by* A. P. Herbert.)

1983.13

CANDIDE

A Revival of the Musical in Two Act, 23 Scenes[3]. (New) Book adapted from Voltaire's satire (of the same name) by Hugh Wheeler. (Original book by Lillian Hellman.) Music by Leonard Bernstein. Lyrics by Richard Wilbur. Additional lyrics by Stephen Sondheim and John Latouche. Directed by Harold Prince. Stage director, Arthur Masella. Choreography by Patricia Birch. Scenery designed by Clarke Dunham. Costumes designed by Judith Dolan. Lighting designed by Ken Billington. Conducted by Scott Bergeson. Orchestrations by Leonard Bernstein and Hershy Kay. Chorus prepared by Mitchell Krieger. Produced by the New York City Opera. Opened 16 October 1983 (matinee) at the New York State Theatre and closed 30 October 1983 after 5 performances in repertory.

CAST (in order of appearance): *Voltaire*: JOHN LANKSTON. *Candide*: CRIS GROENENDAAL. *Huntsman*: Don Yule. *Paquette*: MARIS CLEMENT. *Baroness*: Bonnie Kirk. *Baron*: JACK HARROLD. *Cunegonde*: CLAUDETTE PETERSON. *Maximilian*: SCOTT REEVE. *Servant of Maximilian*: JAMES BILLINGS. *Dr. Pangloss*: JOHN LANKSTON. *Bulgarian Soldiers*: Don Yule, JAMES BILLINGS. *Westphalian Soldiers*: Andy Ferrell, William Ledbetter. *Don Isaachar*, the Jew: JAMES BILLINGS. *Grand Inquisitor*: JACK HARROLD. *Calliope Player*: Bonnie Kirk. *Heresy Agent*: Ralph Bassett. *Inquisition Agents*: Gary Dietrich, William Selissen. *Judge*: JAMES BILLINGS. *Old Lady*: MURIEL COSTA-GREENSPON. *Dons*: Vasilis Iracledes, Brian Kaman, Michael Rubino, Don Yule, William Ledbetter, Ralph Bassett. *Businessman*: JOHN LANKSTON. *Governor*: JOHN LANKSTON. *Governor's Aide*: Andy Ferrell. *Slave Driver*: JACK HARROLD. *Father Bernard*: JAMES BILLINGS. *Sailors*: Gary Dietrich, William Selissen, Andy Ferrell, Travis Wright. *Pirates*: John Henry Thomas, William Ledbetter. *Pink Sheep*: Ivy Austin, Rhoda Butler. *Lion*: Robert Brubaker. *Pasha-Prefect*: JACK HARROLD. *First Gambler*: JAMES BILLINGS. *Second Gambler (Police Chief)*: JOHN LANKSTON. *Sage*: JOHN LANKSTON.

1983.14

ZORBA

A Revival of the Musical in Two Acts, 15 Scenes[4]. Book (revised) by Joseph Stein. Adapted From the novel "Zorba the Greek" by Nikos Kazantzakis. Music by John Kander. Lyrics by Fred Ebb. Directed by Michael Cacoyannis. Choreographed by Graciela Daniele. Scenic design by David Chapman. Costumes designed by Hal George. Lighting designed by Marc B. Weiss. Sound system designed by T. Richard Fitzgerald. Musical direction by Randolph Mauldin. Orchestrations by Don Walker. Dance arrangements by Tom Fay. Associate producer, Alecia Parker. Produced by Barry and Fran Weissler, Kenneth-John Productions (Kenneth D. Greenblatt, John J. Pomerantz). Opened 16 October 1983 at the Broadway Theatre and closed 2 September 1984 after 362 performances.

CAST (in order of appearance): *The Woman*: DEBBIE SHAPIRO. *Konstandi, Turkish Dancer, Russian Admiral*: Frank DeSal. *Thanassai, French Admiral, Monk*: John Mineo. *Constable*: Raphael LaManna. *Athena, Crow*: Suzanne Costallos. *Niko*: ROBERT WESTENBERG. *Zorba*: ANTHONY QUINN. *Despo, Crow*: Panchali Null. *Marika, Crow*: Angelina Fiordellisi. *Katina*: Susan Terry. *Vassilakas*: Chip Cornelius. *Marinakos, Monk*: Peter Marinos. *Mimiko*: Aurelio Padron. *Katapolis, Monk*: Peter Kevoian. *Yorgo, Italian Admiral*: Richard Warren Pugh. *Sophia, Crow*: Pamela Trevisani. *Mavrodani*: Charles Karel. *Pavli*: Thomas David Scalise. *Manolakas*: Michael Dantuono. *The Widow*: TARO MEYER. *Priest, English Admiral*: Paul Straney. *Madame Hortense*: LILA KEDROVA. *Marsalias, Monk*: Rob Marshall. *Anagnosti*: Tim Flavin. *Maria, Cafe Whore*: Karen Giombetti.

The action takes place in Piraeus, Greece and the island of Crete.

Act 1, Scene 1: A Market Place, Piraeus. *Scene 2*: A Café, Piraeus. *Scene 3*: A Crete Village. *Scene 4*: Hortense's Garden. *Scene 5*: Interior of Hortense's Inn. *Scene 6*: The Mine Site. *Scene 7*: A Village Street. *Scene 8*: A Bar in Piraeus. *Scene 9*: A Village Street.

Act 2, Scene 1: Hortense's Garden. *Scene 2*: The Widow's House. *Scene 3*: The Church Square. *Scene 4*: Entrance to the Mine. *Scene 5*: Hortense's Bedroom. *Scene 6*: The Port, Piraeus.

ACT 1
Scene 1
"Life Is"
D. Shapiro, Company
Scene 2
"The First Time"
A. Quinn
Scene 3
"The Top of the Hill"
D. Shapiro, Chorus
Scene 4
"No Boom Boom"
L. Kedrova, Admirals, A. Quinn, R. Westenberg
Scene 5
"Vive La Difference"
The Admirals,
Scene 6
"Mine Song"
Company
Scene 7
"The Butterfly"
T. Meyer, R. Westenberg, D. Shapiro
"Goodbye, Canavaro"
L. Kedrova, A. Quinn, R. Westenberg
Scene 8
"Grandpapa"
A. Quinn, D. Shapiro, Chorus
(*Additional Choreography by* Theodore Pappas.)
Scene 9
"Only Love"
L. Kedrova
"The Bend of the Road"
D. Shapiro
"Only Love" (reprise)
D. Shapiro

ACT 2
Scene 1
"Y'assou"
Company
"Woman"
A. Quinn
Scene 2
"Why Can't I Speak?"/"That's a Beginning"
T. Meyer, R. Westenberg, D. Shapiro
Scene 3
Easter Dance
Company
Scene 4
Miners' Dance
The Men
Scene 5
"The Crow"
D. Shapiro, Crows, Monks
"Happy Birthday"
L. Kedrova
Scene 6
"I Am Free"
A. Quinn

1983.15

AMEN CORNER

A Musical in Two Acts, 6 Scenes. Book by Philip Rose, Peter Udell. Based on the play "The Amen Corner" by James Baldwin. Music by Garry Sherman. Lyrics by Peter Udell. Directed by Philip Rose. Choreography by Al Perryman. Scenery by Karl Eigsti. Costumes by Felix E. Cochren. Lighting by Shirley Prendergast. Orchestratons by Garry Sherman, Dunn Pearson. Vocal arrangements by Garry Sherman. Dance arrangements by Dunn Pearson, George Butcher. Musical direction by Margaret Harris. Sound by Peter Fitzgerald. Associate producer, Philip Rose. Produced by Prudhomme Productions (Edward Mann, Judith Henry, Joel Goldstein, Gil

[3]Original production first produced in New York 1 December 1956 at the Martin Beck Theatre for 73 performances; revised version first produced Off-Boadway 11 December 1973 at the Chelsea Theater Center, Brooklyn Academy of Music for 48 performances; transferred 5 March 1974 to the Broadway Theatre for 740 performances. For Synopsis of Scenes and Musical Numbers, see 1982 revival.

[4]Originally produced in New York 17 November 1968 at the Imperial Theatre for 305 performances. For this revival, the book was revised from 17 to 15 Scenes; Belly Dance, and Bells, were dropped. Added were "Woman," "That's a Beginning" and Easter Dance.

Gerard). Opened 10 November 1983 at the Nederlander Theatre and closed 4 December 1983 after 29 performances.

CAST (in order of speaking): *Margaret Alexander*, Pastor of the Church: RHETTA HUGHES. *Sister Moore*, elder of the Church: Jean Check. *Odessa*, Margaret's older sister: RUTH BROWN. *David*, Margaret's son: KEITH LORENZO AMOS. *Sister Boxer*, elder of the Church: Helena-Joyce Wright. *Brother Boxer*, elder of the Church: Chuck Cooper. *Luke*, Margaret's husband: ROGER ROBINSON.

Members of the Congregation: Loretta Abbott, Leslie Dockery, Cheryl Freeman, Gene Lewis, Denise Morgan, Lewis Robinson, Renee Rose, Vanessa Shaw, Jeffery V. Thompson. *Dancers*: Loretta Abbott (Captain), Leslie Dockery, Renee Rose. Swings: Venida Evans, Leonard Piggee.

The action takes place in a sanctified storefront church in Harlem and in the adjoining apartment early in the 1960's.

Act 1, Scene 1: Church, Sunday morning. *Scene 2*: Apartment. Later that morning. *Scene 3*: Apartment, late afternoon the following Saturday. *Scene 4*: Church, same afternoon. *Scene 5*: Apartment, same afternoon.

Act 2: Apartment, early Sunday morning.

ACT 1

Scene 1

"Amen Corner"
R. Hughes

Scene 2

"That Woman Can't Play No Piano"
K. L. Amos, Friends

"In the Real World"
C. Cooper

"You Ain't Gonna Pick Up Where You Left Off"
R. Hughes, R. Robinson

Scene 3

"In the Real World" (reprise)
H. Wright

"We Got a Good Thing Goin'"
R. Robinson, K. L. Amos

Scene 4

"In His Own Good Time"
H. Wright, C. Cooper, J. Cheek, R. Brown, Congregation

Scene 5

"Heat Sensation"
R. Robinson

"Everytime We Call It Quits"
R. Robinson

ACT 2

"Somewhere Close By"
R. Brown

"Leanin' on the Lord"
H. Wright, C. Cooper, J. Cheek, R. Brown, Congregation

"I'm Already Gone"
K. L. Amos

"Love Dies Hard"
R. Hughes

"Everytime We Call It Quits" (reprise)
R. Robinson, R. Hughes

"Rise Up and Stand Again"
R. Hughes

1983.16 LA TRAGÉDIE DE CARMEN

An Adaptation of Georges Bizet's opera 'Carmen' in One Act (in French). (Original Libretto by Henri Meilhac and Ludovic Halévy, based on the novel "Carmen" by Prosper Merimée.) Adaptation by Marius Constant, Jean-Claude Carrière, Peter Brook. Directed by Peter Brook. Musical director, Marius Constant. Scenery by Jean-Guy Lecat. Costumes by Chloé Obolensky. Conductors, Randall Behr, Roger Cantrell. Artistic advisor, Bernard Lefort. Associate director, Maurice Benichou. As originally presented in Paris at The Bouffes du Nord by the Théâtre National de L'Opéra de Paris and the Centre International de Créations Théâtrales, Micheline Rozan, Producer. Co-Producer, Roy A. Somlyo. Produced by Alexander H. Cohen and Hildy Parks in association with James Nederlander, Jr. and Arthur Rubin. Opened 17 November 1983 at the Vivian Beaumont Theater and closed 28 April 1984 after 187 performances[5].

CAST: *Carmen*: Cynthia Clarey or Hélèle Delavault or Emily Golden or Eva Saurova or Patricia Schuman. *Don José*: Evan Bortnick or Laurence Dale or Howard Hensel or James Hoback or Peter Puzzo. *Micaëla*: Anne Christine Biel or Véronique Dietschy or Agnès Host or Beverly Morgan. *Escamillo*: Carl Johan Falkman or Jake Gardner or Ronald Madden or John Rath. *Lillas Pastia*: Andreas Katsulas or Alain Maratrat. *Lieutenant Zuniga, Old Woman*: Jean-Paul Denizon or Andreas Katsulas. *Garcia*, Carmen's husband: Tapa Sudana or Andreas Katsulas.

1983.17 MARILYN: AN AMERICAN FABLE

A Musical in Two Acts, 16 Scenes. Libretto (Book) by Patricia Michaels. Music and lyrics by Jeanne Napoli, Doug Frank, Gary Portnoy, Beth Lawrence, Norman Thalheimer. Directed and Choreographed by Kenny Ortega. Scenery design by Tom H. John. Costume design by Joseph G. Aulisi. Lighting design by Marcia Madeira. Sound design by T. Richard Fitzgerald. Musical supervision, direction, vocals and orchestral arrangements by Steven Margoshes. Orchestrations by Bill Brohn. Dance arrangements and additional orchestrations by Donald Johnston. Additional dance arrangements by Ronald Melrose. Consultant producer, Janet Robinson. Music consultants, Fred Bestall, Lance Reynolds. Assistant director, Greg Smith. Assistant choreographer, Veda Jackson. Associate producers, Peter Duke, Paul Faske, France Weiner. Produced by Malcolm Cooke, William May, Dolores Quinton, James Kabler, Joseph DioGuardi, John Ricciardelli, Arnold Bruck, Tom Kaye, Leo Rosenthal, Harper Sibley, June Curtis, Renee Blau in association with Jerome Minskoff. Opened 20 November 1983 at the Minskoff Theatre and closed 3 December 1983 after 16 performances.

CAST (in order of appearance): *Young Norma Jean*: KRISTI COOMBS. *Destiny*: PEGGIE BLUE, MICHAEL KUBALA, T. A. [Ty] STEPHENS. *Norma Jean/Marilyn Monroe*: ALYSON REED. *Jim Dougherty*: GEORGE DVORSKY. *Pat*: Debi Monahan. *Factory Girls*: Melissa Bailey, Deborah Dotson, Jodi Marzorati, Mary Testa, Dooba Wilkins. *Photographer*: JAMES HASKINS. *Servicemen*: Gary-Michael Davies, Mark Ziebell. *Agent*: MITCHELL GREENBERG. *Studio Head*: ALAN NORTH. *Director*: Gary-Michael Davies. *Assistant Director*: Ty Crowley. *Camera Man*: Ed Forsyth. *Hairdresser*: Deborah Dotson. *Designer*: Michael Rivera. *Hedda*: Mary Testa. *Louella*: Melissa Bailey. *Joe DiMaggio*: SCOTT BAKULA. *Sis*: LISE LANG. *Tommy*: WILLY FALK. *Coach/Companion*: Dooba Wilkins. *Arthur Miller*: WILL GERARD. *Strasberg*: Steve Schocket. *Acting Coach*: Ty Crowley.

Ensemble: Melissa Bailey, Eileen Casey, Andrew Charles, Kevin Cort, Ty Crowley, Gary-Michael Davies, Deborah Dotson, Mark Esposito, Ed Forsyth, Marcial Gonzalez, Christine Gradl, Marguerite Lowell, Jodi Marzorati, Debi Monahan, Michael Rivera, Steve Schocket, Mary Testa, Dooba Wilkins, Mark Ziebell. *Swings*: Ivson Polk, Maryellen Scilla.

The action takes place from 1934 to 1962 in Hollywood and New York City.

Act 1, Scene 1: Under the Hollywood Hills, 1934-1942. *Scene 2*: The Parachute Factory, 1945. *Scene 3*: Overseas. *Scene 4*: Studio's Executive Office. *Scene 5*: The Soundstage, 1948-1953. *Scene 6*: Outside the Studio. *Scene 7*: The Soundstage, 1955. *Scene 8*: Marilyn's Dressing Room. *Scene 9*: DiMaggio's Restaurant. *Scene 10*: Premier Night.

Act 2, Scene 1: Marilyn's Bedroom. *Scene 2*: Soundstage. *Scene 3*: New York City, 1956-1960. *Scene 4*: New York Penthouse. *Scene 5*: New York to Hollywood. *Scene 6*: Soundstage.

ACT 1

Scene 1

"A Single Dream"
K. Coombs, P. Blue, M. Kubala, T. A. Stephens
(*Music and Lyrics by* Jeanne Napoli and Doug Frank.)

"Jimmy Jimmy"
P. Blue, M. Kubala, T. A. Stephens, A, Reed, G. Dvorsky, D. Monahan, Ensemble
(*Music and Lyrics by* Jeanne Napoli and Doug Frank.)

"Church Doors"
P. Blue, M. Kubala, T. A. Stephens
(*Music and Lyrics by* Beth Lawrence and Norman Thalheimer.)

Scene 2

"Swing Shift"
Factory Girls
(*Music and Lyrics by* Beth Lawrence and Norman Thalheimer.)

Scene 3

"The Golden Dream"
G. Dvorksy, Servicemen
(*Music and Lyrics by* Beth Lawrence and Norman Thalheimer.)

[5]On 19 March 1984 an English language version titled simply *CARMEN* by Sheldon Harnick was added to the performance schedule in rotating repertory with the original French language version. The production was performed as an opera with no individual musical numbers listed

Scene 4
"When You Run the Show"
A. North, M. Greenberg
(*Music and Lyrics by* Beth Lawrence and Norman Thalheimer.)
Scene 5
"Gossip"
M. Testa, M. Bailey
(*Music and Lyrics by* Komack and Doug Frank.)
"Cold Hard Cash"
A. Reed, Men
(*Music by* Wally Harper. *Lyrics by* David Zippel.)
Scene 6
"I'm a Fan"
W. Falk, L. Lang
(*Music and Lyrics by* Beth Lawrence and Norman Thalheimer.)
Scene 7
"Finally"
S. Bakula, A. Reed
(*Music and Lyrics by* Beth Lawrence and Norman Thalheimer.)
"Church Doors" (reprise)
P. Blue, M. Kubala, T. A. Stephens
Scene 10
"It's a Premiere Night"
The Company
(*Music and Lyrics by* Beth Lawrence and Norman Thalheimer.)
"A Single Dream" (reprise)
A. Reed

ACT 2
Scene 1
"We'll Help You Through the Night"
P. Blue, M. Kubala, T. A. Stephens
(*Music and Lyrics by* Jeanne Napoli, Dawson, Turner.)
Scene 2
"Run Between the Raindrops"
A. Reed
(*Music and Lyrics by* Jeanne Napoli and Gary Portnoy.)
"You Are So Beyond"
W. Falk
(*Music and Lyrics by* Jeanne Napoli and Doug Frank.)
Scene 3
"Cultural Pursuits"
A. Reed, W. Gerard, Ensemble
(*Music and Lyrics by* Doug Frank.)
"Church Doors" (reprise)
P. Blue, M. Kubala, T. A. Stephens
Scene 4
"Don't Hang Up the Telephone"
S. Bakula
(*Music and Lyrics by* Jeanne Napoli and Gary Portnoy.)
Scene 5
"All Roads Lead to Hollywood"
A. Reed, Company
(*Music and Lyrics by* Beth Lawrence and Norman Thalheimer.)
Scene 6
"My Heart's an Open Door"
A. Reed, S. Bakula
(*Music and Lyrics by* Beth Lawrence and Norman Thalheimer.)
"Miss Bubbles"
A. Reed, Men's Ensemble
(*Music and Lyrics by* Jeanne Napoli, Doug Frank and Gary Portnoy.)
"The Best of Me"
A. Reed
(*Music and Lyrics by* Beth Lawrence and Norman Thalheimer.)
"A Single Dream" (reprise)
A. Reed
Finale: "We Are the Ones"
The Company
(*Music and Lyrics by* Beth Lawrence and Norman Thalheimer.)

1983.18

DOONESBURY

A Musical in Two Acts, 13 Scenes. Book and lyrics by Garry Trudeau, based on his comic strip of the same name. Music by Elizabeth Swados. Directed by Jacques Levy. Choreography by Margo Sappington. Scenery designed by Peter Larkin. Costumes designed by Patricia McGourty. Lighting designed by Beverly Emmons. Sound designed by Tom Morse. Orchestrations by Elizabeth Swados. Arrangements and musical direction by Jeff Waxman. Produced by James Walsh in association with Universal Pictures. Opened 21 November 1983 at the Biltmore Theatre and closed 19 February 1984 after 104 performances.

CAST (in order of appearance): *Roland*: Reathel Bean. *Mike Doonesbury*: Ralph Bruneau. *Mark*: Mark Linn-Baker. *B.D.*: Keith Szarabajka. *Boopsie*: Laura Dean. *Zonker*: Albert Macklin. *Duke*: Gary Beach. *Honey*: Lauren Tom. *J.J.*: Kate Burton. *Joanie*: Barbara Andres. *Provost*: Peter Shawn. *Voice of President Reagan*: Reathel Bean.

The action takes place on Graduation weekend in Walden, an off-off-campus house.

Act 1, Scene 1: Walden, Living Room. *Scene 2*: Walden, Back Porch. *Scene 3*: Los Angeles County Courtroom. *Scene 4*: Walden, Living Room. *Scene 5*: Los Angeles County Courtroom. *Scene 6*: Walden, Living Room. *Scene 7*: WBBY, Radio Station. *Scene 8*: Walden Living Room.

Act 2, Scene 1: Walden, Living Room. *Scene 2*: Walden, Front Yard. *Scene 3*: Walden Puddle. *Scene 4*: Walden, Living Room. *Scene 5*: Commencement Exercises.

ACT 1[6]
Scene 1
"Graduation"
R. Bean, R. Bruneau, K. Szarabajka, L. Dean, M. Linn-Baker, A. Macklin
"Just One Night"
R. Bruneau
Scene 2
"I Came to Tan"
A. Macklin, Ensemble
Scene 3
"Guilty"
G. Beach, Ensemble
Scene 4
"I Can Have It All"
L. Dean, Ensemble
Scene 6
"Get Together"
K. Burton, R. Bruneau
Scene 7
"Baby Boom Boogie Boy"
M. Linn-Baker, R. Bean, Ensemble
Scene 8
"Another Memorable Meal"
R. Bruneau, K. Szarabajka, L. Dean, M. Linn-Baker, A. Macklin, K. Burton, B. Andres

ACT 2
Scene 1
"Just a House"
Ensemble
Scene 2
"Complicated Man"
L. Tom, L. Dean
Scene 3
"Real Estate"
G. Beach, A. Macklin
Scene 4
"Mother"
K. Burton, B. Andres
"It's the Right Time to be Rich"
K. Szarabajka, R. Bean

[6]For subsequent national tour, "Just One Night" moved from Act 1, Scene 1, to Act 1, Scene 6, replacing "Get Together." Added to Act 1, Scene 5:
"The Chairman's Song"
The Chairman, Duke, Honey, Ensemble

"Muffy and the Topsiders"
L. Dean, R. Bruneau, M. Linn-Baker, A. Macklin
"Just One Night" (reprise)
R. Bruneau, K. Burton
Scene 5
"Graduation" (reprise)
Ensemble

1983.19 BABY

A Musical in Two Acts, 24 Scenes. Book by Sybille Pearson. Based on a story developed with Susan Yankowitz. Music by David Shire. Lyrics by Richard Maltby, Jr. Directed by Richard Maltby, Jr. Musical staging by Wayne Cilento. Scenery by John Lee Beatty. Costumes by Jennifer von Mayrhauser. Lighting by Pat Collins. Film design by John Pieplow. Film sequences by Lennart Nilsson, Bo G. Erikson, Carl O. Lofman, Swedish Television. Orchestrations by Jonathan Tunick. Music direction, Peter Howard. Sound design by Jack Mann. Sound Textures, Electronic programming by Dan Wyman. Associate producers, Ronald Licht, Robert A. Stewart, J. C. Associates, Elaine Yaker, Karen Howard, Lillian Steinberg. Produced by James B. Freydberg, Ivan Bloch, Kenneth-John Productions (Kenneth D. Greenblatt, John J. Pomerantz), Suzanne J. Schwartz in association with Manuscript Productions. Opened 4 December 1983 at the Ethel Barrymore Theater and closed 1 July 1984 after 241 performances.

CAST (in order of appearance): *Lizzie Fields*: LIZ CALLAWAY. *Danny Hooper*: TODD GRAFF. *Arlene MacNally*: BETH FOWLER. *Alan MacNally*: JAMES CONGDON. *Pam Sakarian*: CATHERINE COX. *Nick Sakarian*: MARTIN VIDNOVIC. *Nurse*: Barbara Gilbert. *Doctor*: John Jellison. *Mr. Weiss*: Philip Hoffman. *Dean Webber*: Dennis Warning. *Mr. Hart*: Dennis Warning. *Intern*: Lon Hoyt. *First Woman*: Judith Thiergaard. *Second Woman*: Lisa Robinson. *Third Woman*: Kirsti Carnahan. *Fourth Woman*: Barbara Gilbert. *Fifth Woman*: Judith Thiergaard. *Sixth Woman*: Kim Criswell.
People in the Town: Kirsti Carnahan, Kim Criswell, Barbara Gilbert, Philip Hoffman, Lon Hoyt, John Jellison, Lisa Robinson, Judith Thiergaard, Dennis Warning. *Swings*: Judith Bliss, Michael Waldron.

The action takes place at the present time from March through November.

Act 1, Scene 1: A College Town. March to early April. *Scene 2*: Danny and Lizzie's Apartment. Early April. *Scene 3*: Alan and Arlene's Bedroom. *Scene 4*: Nick and Pam's Bedroom. *Scene 5*: A Doctor's Witing Room. Mid-April. *Scene 6*: The Track. *Scene 7*: On the Campus. *Scene 8*: A Doctor's Office. Early May. *Scene 9*: A Baseball Field. *Scene 10*: Alan and Arlene's Bedroom. *Scene 11*: A Bus Station. Mid-May. *Scene 12*: Alan and Arlene's House. *Scene 13*: Nick and Pam's Bedroom. *Scene 14*: Graduation. Early June. *Scene 15*: Danny and Lizzie's Apartment. Mid-July.

Act 2, Scene 1: The Town. Late August. *Scene 2*: A Doctor's Office. Early September. *Scene 3*: On the Campus. *Scene 4*: Nick and Pam's Bedroom. *Scene 5*: Alan and Arlene's Porch. *Scene 6*: Danny and Lizzie's Apartment. Mid-September. *Scene 7*: Nick and Pam's Bedroom. Mid-October. *Scene 8*: Alan and Arlene's Porch. *Scene 9*: All Three Bedrooms. Mid-November.

ACT 1[7]
Scene 1
"We Start Today"
T. Graff, L. Callaway, J. Congdon, B. Fowler, M. Vidnovic, C. Cox, People in the Town
Scene 2
"What Could Be Better?"
T. Graff, L. Callaway
Scene 3
"The Plaza Song"
J. Congdon, B. Fowler
Scene 4
"Baby, Baby, Baby"
M. Vidnovic, C. Cox, J. Congdon, B. Fowler, T. Graff, L. Callaway
Scene 5
"I Want It All"
C. Cox, L. Callaway, B. Fowler
Scene 6
"At Night She Comes Home to Me"
M. Vidnovic, T. Graff
Scene 7
"What Could Be Better?" (reprise)
T. Graff, L. Callaway
Scene 9
"Fatherhood Blues"
T. Graff, J. Congdon, M. Vidnovic, P. Hoffman, D. Warning
Scene 13
"Romance"
M. Vidnovic, C. Cox
"I Chose Right"
T. Graff
Scene 14
"We Start Today" (reprise)
Ensemble
Scene 15
"The Story Goes On"
L. Callaway

ACT 2
Scene 1
"The Ladies Singin' Their Song"
L. Callaway, the Women in the Town
Scene 2
"Baby, Baby, Baby" (reprise)
B. Fowler
Scene 4
"Romance" (reprise)
M. Vidnovic, C. Cox
Scene 5
"Easier to Love"
J. Congdon
Scene 6
"Two People in Love"
T. Graff, L. Callaway
Scene 7
"With You"
M. Vidnovic, C. Cox
Scene 8
"And What If We Had Loved Like That"
J. Congdon, B. Fowler
Scene 9
"We Start Today" (reprise)
T. Graff, L. Callaway, M. Vidnoiv, C. Cox, J. Congdon, B. Fowler
"The Story Goes On" (reprise)
Company

1983.20 PEG

A Musical Autobiography in Two Acts. Story and new lyrics by Peggy Lee. New music by Paul Horner. Directed by Robert Drivas. Creative consultant, Cy Coleman. Musical direction, Larry Fallon. Scenery designed by Tom H. John. Costumes designed by Florence Klotz. Lighting designed by Thomas Skelton. Sound consultant, Phil Ramone. Vocal arrangements by Ray Charles. Sound design by Jan Nebozenko. Orchestrations by Artie Butler, Larry Fallon, Dominic Frontiere, Bill Holman, Gordon Jenkins, Philip J. Lang, Johnny Mandel, Billy May, Leon Pendarvis, Don Sebesky, Larry Wilcox, Torrie Zito, (Benny Carter, Randy Newman). (Choral arrangements by Ray Charles.) Produced by Zev Bufman, Marge and Irv Cowan, Georgia Frontiere. Opened 14 December 1983 at the Lunt-Fontanne Theater and closed 17 December 1983 after 5 performances.

CAST: PEGGY LEE.
Quartet: Michael Renzi (Piano), Grady Tate (Drums), Jay Leonhart (Bass), Bucky Pizzarelli (Guitar).

ACT 1
"Fever"
(*Music and Lyrics by* Johnny Davenport and Eddie Cooley.)
"Soul"
(*Music by* Paul Horner. *Lyrics by* Peggy Lee. *Orchestration by* Don Sebesky. *Choral Arrangement by* Ray Charles.)

[7] In the subsequent tour and other regional productions, the song "Patterns' sung by Arlene (B. Fowler) was restored to Act 1.

"Daddy Was a Railroad Man"
(*Music by* Paul Horner. *Lyrics by* Peggy Lee. *Orchestration by* Larry Wilcox. *Choral Arrangement by* Ray Charles.)

"Mama"
(*Music by* Paul Horner. *Lyrics by* Peggy Lee. *Orchestration by* Gordon Jenkins. *Choral Arrangement by* Ray Charles.)

"That Old Piano"
(*Music by* Paul Horner. *Lyrics by* Peggy Lee. *Orchestration by* Billy May.)

"One Beating a Day"
(*Music by* Paul Horner. *Lyrics by* Peggy Lee. *Orchestration by* Leon Pendarvis. *Choral Arrangement by* Ray Charles.)

"That's How I Learned to Sing the Blues"
(*Music by* Paul Horner. *Lyrics by* Peggy Lee. *Orchestration by* Billy May. *Choral Arrangement by* Ray Charles.)

"Goody Goody"
(*Music by* Matt Malneck. *Lyrics by* Johnny Mercer. *Orchestration by* Mike Renzi. *Choral Arrangement by* Ray Charles.)

"Sometimes You're Up"
(*Music by* Paul Horner. *Lyrics by* Peggy Lee. *Orchestration by* Philip J. Lang. *Choral Arrangement by* Ray Charles.)

"He'll Make Me Believe That He's Mine"
(*Music by* Paul Horner. *Lyrics by* Peggy Lee. *Orchestration by* Johnny Mandel.)

"Why Don't You Do Right?"
(*Music and Lyrics by* Joe McCoy. *Orchestration by* Bill Holman. *Choral Arrangement by* Ray Charles.)

ACT 2

"I Love Being Here With You"
(*Music and Lyrics by* Peggy Lee. *Orchestration by* Larry Wilcox.)

"The Other Part of Me"
(*Music by* Paul Horner. *Lyrics by* Peggy Lee. *Orchestration by* Dominic Frontiere. *Choral Arrangement by* Ray Charles.)

"I Don't Know Enough About You"
(*Music and Lyrics by* Peggy Lee and Dave Barbour. *Orchestration by* Tore Zito.)

"Angels on Your Pillow"
(*Music by* Paul Horner. *Lyrics by* Peggy Lee. *Orchestration by* Don Sebesky.)

"It's a Good Day"
(*Music and Lyrics by* Peggy Lee and Dave Barbour *Orchestration by* Larry Fallon. *Choral Arrangement by* Ray Charles.)

"Manana"
(*Music and Lyrics by* Peggy Lee and Dave Barbour. *Orchestration by* Leon Pendarvis. *Choral Arrangement by* Ray Charles.)

"What Did Dey Do to My Goil?"
(*Music by* Paul Horner. *Lyrics by* Peggy Lee. *Orchestration by* Philip J. Lang. *Choral Arrangement by* Ray Charles.)

"Stay Away from Louisville Lou"
(*Music by* Paul Horner. *Lyrics by* Peggy Lee. *Orchestration by* Billy May.)

"No More Rainbows"
(*Music by* Paul Horner. *Lyrics by* Peggy Lee. *Orchestration by* Artie Butler. *Choral Arrangement by* Ray Charles.)

"Flowers and Flowers"
(*Music by* Paul Horner. *Lyrics by* Peggy Lee. *Orchestration by* Tore Zito. *Choral Arrangement by* Ray Charles.)

"Lover" (from *LOVE ME TONIGHT* film)
(*Music by* Richard Rodgers. *Lyrics by* Lorenz Hart. *Orchestration by* Sy Oliver.)

"Big Spender" (from *SWEET CHARITY*)
(*Music by* Cy Coleman. *Lyrics by* Dorothy Fields. *Orchestration by* Bill Holman and Dave Grusin.)

"I'm a Woman"
(*Music and Lyrics by* Jerry Lieber and Mike Stoller. *Orchestration by* Benny Carter.)

"Is That All There Is?"
(*Music and Lyrics by* Jerry Lieber and Mike Stoller. *Orchestration by* Randy Newman.)

"There Is More"
(*Music by* Paul Horner. *Lyrics by* Peggy Lee. *Orchestration by* Don Sebesky. *Choral Arrangement by* Ray Charles.)

Bows and Exit Music
(*Orchestration by* Philip J. Lang.)

1983.21 THE TAP DANCE KID

A Musical in Two Acts, 15 Scenes. Book by Charles Blackwell. Based on the novel "Nobody's Family Is Going to Change" by Louise Fitzhugh. Music by Henry Krieger. Lyrics by Robert Lorick. Directed by Vivian Matalon. Dances and musical staging by Danny Daniels. Musical supervision, orchestra and vocal arrangements by Harold Wheeler. Scenic production by Michael J. Hotopp and Paul DePass. Costumes by William Ivey Long. Lighting by Richard Nelson. Musical And vocal direction by Don Jones. Dance music arrangements by Peter Howard. Sound design by Jack Mann. Assistant choreographer, D. J. Giagni. Scenic photography by Mark Feldstein. Associate producers, Mark Beigelman, Richard Chwatt. Produced by Stanley White, Evelyn Barron, Harvey J. Klaris, Michel Stuart in association with Michel Kleinman Productions. Opened 21 December 1983 at the Broadhurst Theatre, moved 27 March 1984 to the Minskoff Theatre and closed 11 March 1985 after 669 performances.

CAST (in order of appearance): *Willie*: ALFONSO RIBEIRO. *Ginnie*: HATTIE WINSTON. *Dulcie*: BARBARA MONTGOMERY. *Emma*: MARTINE ALLARD. *William*: SAMUEL E. WRIGHT. *Dipsey*: HINTON BATTLE. *Mona*: Karen Paskow. *Carole*: JACKIE LOWE. *Daddy Bates*: ALAN WEEKS. *Winslow*: Michael Blevins. *Joe*: Jackie Patterson. *Offstage Voice*: Lloyd Culbreath.

Little Rio Dancers and New Yorkers: Leah Bass, Kevin Berdini, Michael Blevins, Karen Curlee, Suzzanne Douglas, Rick Emery, Karen E. Fraction, D. J. Giagni, J. J. Jepson, Karen Paskow, Rodney Alan McGuire, Jackie Patterson, Mayme Paul, Jamie M. Pisano, Ken Prescott, Oliver Woodall, James Young. *Swings*: Llloyd Culbreath, Linda Von Germer.

The action takes place at the present time in New York City's Roosevelt Island and Manhattan.

Act 1, Scene 1: Dining Room. *Scene 2*: Dipsey's Loft. *Scene 3*: William's Study. *Scene 4*: Playground. *Scene 5*: Manhattan. *Scene 6*: The Fabulous Westway Hotel Ballroom. *Scene 7*: William's Study. *Scene 8*: Terrace.

Act 2, Scene 1: Dining Room. *Scene 2*: Playground. *Scene 3*: Dipsey's Loft. *Scene 4*: Willie's Bedroom. *Scene 5*: Manhattan. *Scene 6*: Dispey's Loft. *Scene 7*: Street.

ACT 1[8]

Scene 1

"Another Day"[9]
H. Winston, M. Allard, A. Ribeiro

Scene 3

"Four Strikes Against Me"
M. Allard

"Class Act"
H. Winston, H. Battle, A. Weeks

Scene 4

"They Never Hear What I Say"
M. Allard, A. Ribeiro

"Dancing Is Everything"
A. Ribeiro

Scene 5

"Crosstown"
A. Ribeiro, New Yorkers

Scene 6

"Fabulous Feet"
H. Battle, J. Lowe, Dancers

"I Could Get Used to Him"
J. Lowe, Dancers

---

[8]For the subsequent national tour, substantial changes were made to the book and score as follows: Production re-directed by by Jerry Zaks.

New Act 1, Scene 1

"Dipsey's Comin' Over"
Dulé Hill (Willie)

New Act 1, Scene 2: Rehearsal Studio

"High Heels"
H. Battle, Theresa Hayes (Carole), Dancers

"Something Better, Something More"
H. Battle

Act 2, Scene 2 and 3 reversed

New Act 2, Scene 4: Rehearsal Studio

"Dipsey's Vaudeville"
Dancers, H. Battle, T. Hayes

"I Remember How It Was" (moved from Scene 3)

Former Scene 4 now Scene 5

New Act 2, Scene 6 (replacing former Scenes 5 and 6): A Theatre.

[9]Dropped for subsequent tnational tour.

Scene 8
"Man in the Moon"
H. Battle

ACT 2

Scene 1
"Like Him"
M. Allard, H. Winston

Scene 2
"Someday"
M. Allard, A. Ribeiro

Scene 3
"My Luck Is Changing"
H. Battle
"I Remember How It Was"
H. Winston

Scene 4
"Lullabye"
H. Winston
"Tap Tap"
A. Weeks, A. Ribeiro, H. Battle

Scene 5
"Dance If It Makes You Happy"
A. Ribeiro, H. Battle, A. Weeks, J. Lowe, Dancers

Scene 6
"William's Song"
S. E. Wright

Scene 7
"Class Act" (Finale)
The Family

1984.01 THE RINK

A Musical in Two Acts. Book by Terrence McNally. Music by John Kander. Lyrics by Fred Ebb. Directed by A. J. Antoon. Choreography by Graciela Daniele. Scenery designed by Peter Larkin. Costumes designed by Theoni V. Aldredge. Lighting designed by Marc B. Weiss. Sound designed by Otts Munderloh. Musical director, Paul Gemignani. Dance arrangements by Tom Fay. Orchestrations by Michael Gibson. Assistant choreographer, Tina Paul. Associate producer, Tina Chen. Executive producer, Robin Ullman. Produced by Jules Fisher, Roger Berlind, Joan Cullman, Milbro Productions (Jim Milford, Slade Brown), Kenneth-John Productions (Kenneth D. Greenblatt-John Pomerantz) in association with Jonathan Farkas and Jujamcyn Theatres. Opened 9 February 1984 at the Martin Beck Theatre and closed 4 August 1984 after 204 performances.

CAST (in order of appearance):*Angel*: LIZA MINNELLI. *Little Girl*: Kim Hauser. *The Wreckers (6)*: *Lino*: Jason Alexander. *Buddy*: Mel Johnson, Jr. *Guy*: Scott Holmes. *Lucky*: Scott Ellis. *Tony*: Frank Mastrocola. *Ben*: Ronn Carroll. *Anna*: CHITA RIVERA. *Dino*: Scott Holmes. *Dino's Father*: Ronn Carroll. *Lenny*: Jason Alexander. *Hiram*: Mel Johnson, Jr. *Tom*: Frank Mastrocola. *Sugar*: Scott Ellis. *Punk*: Frank Mastrocola. *Punk*: Scott Ellis. *Punk*: Jason Alexander. *Mrs. Silverman*: Ronn Carroll. *Mrs. Jackson*: Mel Johnson, Jr. *Arnie*: Scott Ellis. *Charlie*: Mel Johnson, Jr. *Uncle Fausto*: Jason Alexander. *Suitor*: Scott Ellis. *Suitor*: Mel Johnson, Jr. *Suitor*: Frank Mastrocola. *Father Rocco*: Scott Holmes. *Bobby Perillo*: Scott Ellis. *Sister Philomena*: Ronn Carroll. *Peter Reilly*: Frank Mastrocola. *Junior Miller*: Mel Johnson, Jr. *Debbie Duberman*: Scott Holmes. *Danny*: Scott Ellis.

The action takes place in a roller rink somewhere on the Eastern seaboard during the 1970's.

ACT 1
"Colored Lights"
L. Minnelli
"Chief Cook and Bottle Washer"
C. Rivera
"Don't Ah Ma Me"
C. Rivera, L. Minnelli
"Blue Crystal"
S. Holmes
"Under the Roller Coaster"
L. Minnelli
"Not Enough Magic"
S. Holmes, L. Minnelli, C. Rivera, S. Ellis, M. Johnson, Jr., F. Mastrocola, J. Alexander, R. Carroll
"We Can Make It"
C. Rivera
"After All These Years"
The Wreckers
"Angel's Rink and Social Center"
L. Minnelli, the Wreckers
"What Happened to the Old Days?"
C. Rivera, R. Carroll, M. Johnson, Jr.
"Colored Lights" (reprise)
L. Minnelli

ACT 2[10]
"The Apple Doesn't Fall Very Far"
C. Rivera, L. Minnelli
"Marry Me"
J. Alexander
"We Can Make It" (reprise)
C. Rivera
"Mrs. A"
C. Rivera, L. Minnelli, J. Alexander, Suitors
"The Rink"
The Wreckers
"Wallflower"
C. Rivera, L. Minnelli
"All the Children in a Row"
L. Minnelli, S. Ellis

1984.02 THE HUMAN COMEDY

A Musical in Two Acts, 17 Scenes[11]. Libretto by William Dumaresq. Based on the novel of the same name by William Saroyan. Music by Galt MacDermott. Directed by Wilford Leach. Scenery by Bob Shaw. Costumes by Rita Ryack. Lighting by James F. Ingalls. Sound by Tom Morse. Music director, orchestrator, Galt MacDermott. Conductor, Tania León. Projections, Wendall Harrington. A New York Shakespeare Festival Production. Associate producer, Jason Steven Cohen. Produced by Joseph Papp and the Shubert Organization. Opened 5 April 1984 at the Royale Theatre and closed 15 April 1984 after 13 performances.

CAST (in order of singing): *Trainman*: David Lawrence Johnson. (*The Family, 4*): *Ulysses Macauley*: JOSH BLAKE. *Mrs. Kate Macauley*: BONNIE KOLOC. *Homer Macauley*: STEPHEN GEOFFREYS. *Bess Macauley*: MARY [Elizabeth] MASTRANTONIO. *Helen*: Anne Marie Bobby. *Miss Hicks*: Laurie Franks. *Spangler*: REX SMITH. *Thief*: Christopher Edmonds. *Mr. Grogan*: GORDON CONNELL. *Felix*: Daniel Noel. *Beautiful Music*: Debra Byrd. *Mary Arena*: Caroline Peyton. *Mexican Woman*: Olga Merediz. *Voice Of Matthew Macauley*: Grady Mulligan. *Marcus Macalay*: Don Kehr. *Tobey*: JOSEPH KOLINSKI. *Soldiers*: Kenneth Bryan, Louis Padilla, Michael Willson. *A Neighbor*: Kathleen Rowe McAllen. *Diana Steed*: Laeta Galloway. *Minister*: Walter Hudson. *Townspeople*: Marc Stephen Delgatto, Lisa Kirchner, Vernon Spencer, Dan Tramon.

The action takes place in 1943 in a little town in California.

Act 1, Scene 1: At a Train Crossing. *Scene 2*: At Home. *Scene 3*: At School. *Scene 4*: At the Telegraph Office. *Scene 5*: Message. *Scene 6*: At Home. *Scene 7*: Message. *Scene 8*: At the Telegraph Office. *Scene 9*: At Home.

Act 2, Scene 1: At the Debarkation Center. *Scene 2*: At Home. *Scene 3*: War Front. *Scene 4*: Home Front. *Scene 5*: At War and at Home. *Scene 6*: At the Telegraph Office. *Scene 7*: In the Park. *Scene 8*: Home.

ACT 1
"In a Little Town in California"
Company

Scene 1
"Hi Ya Kid"
D. L. Johnson, J. Blake

Scene 2
"We're a Little Family"
B. Koloc, S. Geoffreys, J. Blake, M. E. Mastrantonio

---

[10]Added to the close of Act 2 after opening:
"Coda"
C. Rivera, L. Minnelli

[11]Originally produced in New York Off-Broadway 20 December 1983 at the Public Theatre/Anspacher for 79 performances.

Scene 3
"The Assyrians"
A. M. Bobby, L. Franks
"Noses"
S. Geoffreys
Scene 4
"You're a Little Young for the Job"
R. Smith, S. Geoffreys
"I Can Carry a Tune"
S. Geoffreys
"Happy Birthday"
S. Geoffreys
"Happy Anniversary"
S. Geoffreys, R. Smith, G. Connell
"I Think the Kid Will Do"
G. Connell, R. Smith
"Beautiful Music"
D. Byrd, Company
"Cocoanut Cream Pie"
G. Connell, S. Geoffreys
"When I Am Lost"
S. Geoffreys, D. Byrd, Company
Scene 5
"I Said, Oh No"
M. E. Mastrantonio, C. Peyton, O. Merediz
Scene 6
"Daddy Will Not Be Walking Through The Door"
B. Koloc
"The Birds in the Sky"
M. E. Mastrantonio
"Remember Always to Give"
B. Koloc
"Long Past Sunset"
D. Kehr
Scene 7
"Don't Tell Me"
C. Peyton, D. Kehr, the Family, Company
Scene 8
"The Fourth Telegram"
R. Smith, G. Connell
"Give Me All the Money"
C. Edmonds, R. Smith
Scene 9
"Everything Is Changed"
S. Geoffreys, B. Koloc
"The World Is Full of Loneliness"
B. Koloc
"Hi Ya Kid" (reprise)
D. L. Johnson, J. Blake, Company
ACT 2
Scene 1
"How I Love Your Thingamajig"
Soldiers
"Everlasting"
J. Kolinski
"An Orphan, I Am"
J. Kolinski
"I'll Tell You About My Family"
D. Kehr
Scene 2
"I Wish I Were a Man"
C. Peyton
Scene 3
"Marcus, My Friend"
J. Kolinski
"My Sister Bess"
D. Kehr
Scene 4
"I've Known a Lot of Guys"
L. Galloway
"Diana"
R. Smith
Scene 5
"Dear Brother"
S. Geoffreys, D. Kehr
"The Birds in the Trees"/"A Lot of Men" (reprise)
L. Galloway, R. Smith
"Parting"
B. Koloc, Wives, Sweethearts, Mothers, Freinds, Soldiers
Scene 6
"Mr. Grogan, Wake Up"
S. Geoffreys
"Hello Doc"
R. Smith
Scene 7
"What Am I Supposed to Do?"
S. Geoffreys, R. Smith
Scene 8
"Long Past Sunset"
B. Koloc, Company
"I'm Home"
J. Kolinski
"Somewhere, Someone"
M. E. Mastrantonio
"I'll Always Love You"
C. Peyton, Company
"Hi Ya Kid" (reprise)
D. L. Johnson, J. Blake, Company
"Fathers and Mothers (And You and Me)"
Company

1984.03 DIE FLEDERMAUS

A Revival of the Operetta in Three Acts, in German[12]. Original libretto by Carl Haffner and Richard Genée. Lyrics by Richard Genée. Based on the comedy "Le Réveillon" by Henri Meilhac and Ludovic Halévy. Music by Johann Strauss. Produced (Staged) by Karl Dönsch. Sets by Pantelis Dessyllas. Costumes by Fred Adlmüller and Alice Maria Schlesinger. Choreography by Gerhard Senft. Chorus master, Franz Gerstacker. Lighting, Mark W. Stanley. Conductors, Franz Bauer-Theussl, Rudolf Bibl. A Vienna Volksoper Production. Produced by Kazuko Hillyer International. Opened 10 April 1984 at the New York State Theatre and closed 20 April 1984 after 5 performances in repertory.

CAST: *Gabriel von Eisenstein*, a man of leisure: PETER MINICH. *Rosalinda*, his wife: BARBARA DANIELS. *Frank*, the prison governor: Karl Dönsch. *Prinz Orlofsky*: DAGMAR KOLLER. *Alfred*, tenor, one of Rosalinda's former suitors: ADOLPH DALLAPOZZA. *Dr. Falke*, a Notary: RUSSELL SMYTHE. *Dr. Blind*, a Solicitor: Rudolf Wasserlof. *Adele*, Rosalinda's maid: ELISABETH KALES. *Ida*, her sister: Guggi Loewinger. *Frosch*, the prison warden: Ossy Kolman.

Ballet: Polka: "Thunder and Lightning (op. 314): Christina Klein, Elisabeth Stelzer, Istvan Bernath and the corps de ballet. Waltz: "Blue Danube" (op. 314): Melitta Ogrisse, Ivan Jakus, and the corps de ballet. *Chorus*: Vienna Volsoper Chorus.

1984.04 THE MERRY WIDOW

A Revival of the Operetta (DIE LUSTIGE WITWE) in Three Acts, 4 Scenes, in German[13]. Music by Franz Lehár. Original German book and lyrics by Victor Léon and Leo Stein (after "L'Attaché d'Ambassade" by Henri Meilhac.) Produced (Staged) by Robert Herzl. Choreography by Gerhard Senft. Settings by Pantelis Dessyllas. Costumes by Barbara Bilabel, Alice Maria Schlesinger. Lighting, Mark W. Stanley. Conductors, Franz Bauer-Theussl, Rudolf Bibl. Chorus master, Franz Gerstacker. A Vienna Volksoper Production. Produced by Kazuko Hillyer International. Opened

[12]First English language production in New York 16 March 1885 at the Casino Theatre.
[13]Originally produced in New York in English 21 October 1907 at the New Amsterdam Theatre for 416 performances.

11 April 1984 at the New York State Theatre and closed 21 April 1984 after 5 performances in repertory.

CAST: *Baron Mirko Zeta*, Pontevedrinian Ambassador in Paris: KARL DÖNSCH. *Valencienne*, his wife: MELANIE HOLIDAY. *Count Danilo Danilowitsch*, Secretary of the Pontevedrinian Embassy: EBERHARD WAECHTER. *Hanna Glawari*, the Widow: IRJANA IROSCH. *Camille de Rosillon*: RICHARD KARCZYKOWSKI. *Vicomte Cascada*: Peter Drahosch. *Raoul de St. Brioche*: HEINZ HELLBERG. *Bogdanowitsch*, Pontevedrinian Consul: WOLFGANG DAUSCHA. *Sylviane*, his wife: Renate Krula. *Kromow*, Councellor: Hans Kraemmer. *Olga*, his wife: Magdalena Emesz. *Pritschitsch*, Military attaché: Wolfgang Jeschek. *Praskowia*, his wife: Sonja Mottl. *Njegus*, Major-domo of the Pontevedrinian Embassy: ERICH KUCHAR.

Ballet: Act 2, "Kolo": Melitta Ogrise, Elisabeth Stelzer, Istvan Bernath, Zdislav Zelinka and the corps de ballet. Act 3, "Zwanzinette": Christina Klein, Zdislav Zelinka, Lili Clemente, Felicitas Prikopa, Istvan Bernath, Istvan Varga. "Nachledil-March": Gabriella Masek, Percy Kofranek, Peter Gavrikov, men of the corps de ballet. "Can Can": Corps de de ballet. *Chorus*: Vienna Volksoper Chorus.

1984.05 CZARDAS PRINCESS

A Revival of the Operetta, DIE CSÁRDÁSFÜRSTIN,{The Gypsy Princess} in Three Acts[14], in German. Original (Viennese) book and lyrics by Leo Stein and Bela Jenbach. Music by Emmerich Kálmán. Produced (staged) by Robert Herzl. Sets by Pantelis Dessyllas. Costumes by Silvia Strahammer. Choreography by Michael Maurer. Lighting Mark W. Stanley. Chorus master, Karl Heinz Dold. Conductors, Franz Bauer-Theussl, Rudolf Bibl. A Vienna Volksoper Production. Produced by Kazuko Hillyer International. Opened 12 April 1984 at the New York State Theatre and closed 20 April 1984 after 4 performances in repertory.

CAST: *Leopold Maria, Prince von und Lippert-Weylersheim*: RUDOLF WASSERLOF. *Anhilte*, his wife: Sonja Mottl. *Edwin Ronald*, his son: FRANZ WAECHTER. *Countess Anastasia*, his niece: ELISABETH KALES. *Baron Eugen von Rohnsdorff*, army captain, his nephew: PETER DRAHOSCH. *Count Boni Kácsiánu*: JACK POPPELL. *Feri von Kerekes*, called 'Feri bácsi': SÁNDOR NÉMETH. *Sylva Varescu*, a cabaret singer: MELENA RUDIFERIA. *Wilhlem von Billing*, ambassador: Wolfgang Dauscha. *Siggi Gross*, manager of the Orpheum in Budapest: Helmut Randers. *Sandor von Kiss*, a Notary, syndic of the Orpheum: Rudolf Katzboeck. *Max*, head-waiter of the Grand Hotel, Vienna: Josef Forstner.

Chorus: Vienna Volksoper Chorus.

ACT 1

"Heia, heia in den Bergen ist mein Heimatland"

"Alle sind wir Sünder"

"Sylva, ich will nur dich-Ja Mädchen gibt es wunderfeine"

"Aus ist's mit der Liebe-Ganz ohne Weiber geht die Chose nicht"

"O jag' dem Glück nicht nach"

"Ich Edwin Ronald-Hochzeitstanz-Ja so ein Teufelsweib"

ACT 2

"Erstrahlen die Lichter"

"Ich warte auf das grosse Wunder-Machen wir's den Schwalben nach"

"Heller Jubel"

"Liebchen, mich reisst es"

"Mädel guck-Das ist die Liebe"

"Tanzen möcht' ich-Tausend kleine Engel singen"

"Verzeih' Papa-Lieben sich zwei Menschenkinder"

ACT 3

"Nimm, Zigeunder, deine Geige-Jaj Mamám, Bruderherz ich kauf mir die Welt"

"Mädel guck-Das ist die Liebe"

"Tausend kleine Engel singen"

1984.06 SHIRLEY MacLAINE ON BROADWAY

A Musical Entertainment (Revue) in One Act. Original music and lyrics by Marvin Hamlisch, Christopher Adler. Additional material by Larry Grossman, Buz Kohan. Staged and choreographed by Alan Johnson. Lighting design by Ken Billington. Costumes by Pete Menefee. Musical director, Jack French. Associate lighting designer, Jeffrey Schissler. Producer, Michael Flowers. Presented by Guber/Gross Productions (Lee Guber, Shelly Gross) and The Nederlander Organization. Opened 19 April 1984 at the Gershwin Theatre and closed 27 May 1984 after 46 performances.

CAST: SHIRLEY MacLAINE. *Company*: Mark Reina, Larry Vickers, Jamilah Lucas, Antonette Yuskis. *Swing*: Gary Flannery.

MUSICAL NUMBERS[15]

"Now"

Harold Arlen Medley (with a little Gershwin):

"If I Only Had a Brain"

"Get Happy"

"I've Got the World on a String"

"S'Wonderful"

Hooker Medley:

"If They Could See Me Now"

"In the Movies"

Monologues from 3 of Shirley's non-musical films:

"Terms of Endearment"

"Some Came Running"

"The Turning Point"

Tribute to the dance styles of Bob Fosse, Michael Kidd and new black choreographers (George Faison, Billy Wilson, Geoffrey Holder)

Anecdotes about mountain climbing in the Himalayas

"Life Is Just a Bowl of Cherries" (from *GEORGE WHITE'S SCANDALS OF 1931*)

(*Music by* Ray Henderson. *Lyrics by* Lew Brown and Buddy DeSylva.)

"Nobody Does It Better" (from *SEESAW*)

(*Music by* Cy Coleman. *Lyrics by* Dorothy Fields.)

"A Cockeyed Optimist" (from *SOUTH PACIFIC*)

(*Music by* Richard Rodgers. *Lyrics by* Oscar Hammerstein II.)

"Imagine"

(Music and Lyrics by John Lennon.)

1984.07 OLIVER!

A Revival of the Musical in Two Acts, 12 Scenes[16]. Book, music and lyrics by Lionel Bart. Based on the novel "Oliver Twist" by Charles Dickens. Directed by Peter Coe. (Production) Designed by Sean Kenny. Lighting design by Andrew Bridge. Sound design by Jack Mann. Orchestrations by Eric Rogers. Musical Director, John Lesko. Associate director, Geoffrey Ferris. Executive producers, R. Tyler Gatchell, Jr., Peter Neufeld. Produced by Cameron Mackintosh, Carole J. Shorenstein, James M. Nederlander by arrangement with The Southbrook Group. Opened 29 April 1984 at the Mark Hellinger Theatre and closed 13 May 1984 after 17 performances.

CAST: *Oliver Twist*: BRADEN DANNER.

At the Workhouse: *Mr. Bumble*, the Beadle: MICHAEL McCARTY. *Mrs. Bumble*, the Matron: ELIZABETH LARNER. *Old Sally*, a Pauper: Susan Willis.

At the Undertaker's: *Mr. Sowerberry*, the Undertaker: RODERICK HORN. *Mrs. Sowerberry*, his wife: FRANCES CUKA. *Charlotte*, their daughter: Andi Henig. *Noah Claypole*, their apprentice: Alan Braunstein.

At the Thieves' Kitchen: *Fagin*: RON MOODY. *The Artful Dodger*: DAVID GARLICK. *Nancy*: PATTI LuPONE. *Bet*: Sarah E. Litzsinger. *Bill Sykes*: GRAEME CAMPBELL. *Bullseye*: Vito, Buffy.

At the Brownlow's: *Mr. Brownlow*: MICHAEL ALLINSON. *Dr. Grimwig*: Louis Beachner. *Mrs. Bedwin*: ELIZABETH LARNER.

Workhouse Boys and Fagin's Gang: Robert David Cavanaugh, Samir Chowdhury, Ruben Cuevas, Roshi Handwerger, Cameron Johann, Mark Manasseri, Michael Manasseri, Kipp Marcus, Shawn Morgal, Brian Noodt, Roy Nygaard, R. D. Robb, Dennis Singletary, Zachary A. Stier. *Londoners*: Diane Armistead, Louis Beachner, Alan Braunstein, Frances Cuka, W. P. Dremak, Gregg Edelman, Tony Gilbert, Eleanor Glockner, Beth Guiffre, Jan Horvath, Michael McCarty, William McClary, Marcia Mitzman, Martin Moran, Barbara Moroz, Cheryl Russell, Clark Sayre, Jane Strauss, Susan Willis.

---

[14]First produced in New York in English as "The Riviera Girl" 24 September 1917 for 78 performances.

[15]Note: No song list included in program. Above list prepared from press files and recordings.

[16]Originally produced in New York 6 January 1963 at the Imperial Theatre for 774 performances. For Synopsis of Scenes and Musical Numbers, see original 1963 production.

1984.08

SUNDAY IN THE PARK WITH GEORGE

A Musical in Two Acts[17]. Book by James Lapine[18]. Music and Lyrics by Stephen Sondheim. Directed by James Lapine. Scenery by Tony Straiges. Costumes by Patricia Zipprodt, Ann Hould-Ward. Set and costume designs adapted from the Georges Seurat painting entitled "Sunday Afternoon on the Island of the Grand Jatte." Lighting by Richard Nelson. Special effects, Bran Ferren. Sound by Tom Morse. Movement by Randolyn Zinn. Musical direction, Paul Gemignani. Orchestrations by Michael Starobin. Produced by The Shubert Organization and Emanuel Azenberg by arrangement with Playwrights Horizons. Opened 2 May 1984 at the Booth Theatre and closed 13 October 1985 after 604 performances.

CAST (in order of appearance): *Act 1*: *George*, an artist: MANDY PATINKIN. *Dot*, his mistress: BERNADETTE PETERS. *An Old Lady*: BARBARA BRYNE. *Her Nurse*: Judith Moore. *Franz*, a servant: Brent Spiner. *A Boy Bathing in the river*: Danielle Ferland. *A Young Man sitting on the bank*: Nancy Opel. *A Man lying on the bank*: Cris Groenendaal. *Jules*, another artist: CHARLES KIMBROUGH. *Yvonne*, his wife: DANA IVEY. *A Boatman*: William Parry. *Celeste #1*: Melanie Vaughan. *Celeste #2*: Mary D'Arcy. *Louise*, the daughter of Jules and Yvonne: Danielle Ferland. *Frieda*, a cook: Nancy Opel. *Louis*, a baker: Cris Groenendaal. *A Soldier*: Robert Westenberg. *A Man with bicycle*: John Jellison. *A Little Girl*: Michele Rigan. *A Woman with baby carriage*: Sue Anne Gershenson. *Mr.*: Kurt Knudson. *Mrs.*: Judith Moore.

Act 2: *George*, an artist: MANDY PATINKIN. *Marie*, his grandmother: BERNADETTE PETERS. *Dennis*, a technician: Brent Spiner. *Bob Greenberg*, the museum director: CHARLES KIMBROUGH. *Naomi Eisen*, a composer: DANA IVEY. *Harriet Pawling*, a patron of the arts: Judith Moore. *Billy Webster*, her friend: Cris Groenendaal. *A Photographer*: Sue Anne Gershenson. *A Museum Assistant*: John Jellison. *Charles Redmond*, a visiting curator: WILLIAM PARRY. *Alex*, an artist: Robert Westenberg. *Betty*, an artist: Nancy Opel. *Lee Randolph*, the museum's publicist: Kurt Knudson. *Blair Daniels*, an art critic: BARBARA BRYNE. *A Waitress*: Melanie Vaughan. *Elaine*: Mary D'Arcy.

Act 1 takes place on a series of Sundays from 1884 to 1886 and alternates between a park on an island in the Seine just outside of Paris, and Georges' studio. Act 2 takes place in 1984 at an American art museum, and on the island in the Seine.

ACT 1
"Sunday in the Park With George"
B. Peters
"No Life"
C. Kimbrough, D. Ivey
"Color and Light"
B. Peters, M. Patinkin
"Gossip"
M. Vaughan, M. D'Arcy, W. Parry, J. Moore, B. Bryne, C. Kimbrough, D. Ivey
"The Day Off"
M. Patinkin, J. Moore, B. Spiner, N. Opel, W. Parry, R. Westenberg, M. Vaughan, M. D'Arcy, D. Ivey, D. Ferland, C. Kimbrough, C. Groenendaal
"Everybody Loves Louis"
B. Peters
"Finishing the Hat"
M. Patinkin
"We Do Not Belong Together"
B. Peters, M. Patinkin
"Beautiful"
B. Bryne, M. Patinkin
"Sunday"
Company

ACT 2
"It's Hot Up Here"
Company
"Chromolume #7"
M. Patinkin, B. Peters
"Putting It Together"
M. Patinkin, Company
"Children and Art"
B. Peters
"Lesson #8"
M. Patinkin
"Move On"
M. Patinkin, B. Peters
"Sunday" (reprise)
Company

1984.09

THE WIZ

A Revival of the Musical in Two Acts, a Prologue and 15 Scenes[19]. Book by William F. Brown. Based on the novel "The Wizard of Oz" by L. Frank Baum. Music and lyrics by Charlie Smalls. Direction and costume design by Geoffrey Holder. Choreography and musical numbers staged by George Faison. Scenery designed by Peter Wolf. Lighting designed by Paul Sullivan. Orchestrations by Harold Wheeler. Musical direction and vocal arrangements by Charles Coleman. Dance arrangements by Timothy Graphenreed. Sound by Gary M. Stocker. Produced by Tom Mallow, James Janek and the Shubert Organization. Opened 24 May 1984 at the Lunt-Fontanne Theater and closed 3 June 1984 after 13 performances.

CAST (in order of appearance): *Aunt Em*: PEGGIE BLUE. *Toto*: Toto. *Dorothy*: STEPHANIE MILLS. *Uncle Henry*: David Weatherspoon. *Tornado*: Daryl Richardson. *Munchkins*: Carol Dennis, Ada Dyer, Lawrence Hamilton, Sam Harkness, David Weatherspoon. *Addaperle*: JUANITA FLEMING. *Yellow Brick Road*: Alfred L. Dove, Germaine Edwards, Dwight Leon, David Robertson. *Scarecrow*: CHARLES VALENTINO. *Sunflowers*: Carol Dennis, Ada Dyer, Sam Harkness, David Weatherspoon. *Crows*: Paula Anita Brown, Marvin Engran, Jasmine Guy. *Tinman*: HOWARD PORTER. *Lion*: GREGG BAKER. *Strangers*: Carol Dennis, Sam Harkness, David Weatherspoon. *Kalidahs*: Marvin Engran, Jasmine Guy, Lawrence Hamilton, Raymond C. Harris, Gigi Hunter, Martial Roumain. *Poppies*: Sharon Brooks, Paula Anita Brown, Carla Earle, Tanya Gibson, Gigi Hunter, Daryl Richardson. *Chief of Field Mice*: Ada Dyer. *Field Mice*: Lawrence Hamilton, David Weatherspoon. *Royal Gatekeeper*: Sam Harkness. *Head of the Society of Emerald City*: Sharon Brooks.

Emerald City Citizens: Paula Anita Brown, Roslyn Burrough, Carol Dennis, Alfred L. Dove, Ada Dyer, Carla Earle, Germaine Edwards, Marvin Engran, Tanya Gibson, Jasmine Guy, Lawrence Hamilton, Sam Harkness, Raymond C. Harris, Gigi Hunter, Dwight Leon, Daryl Richardson, David Robertson, Martial Roumain, David Weatherspoon.

The Wiz: CARL HALL. *Evillene*: ELLA MITCHELL. *Lord High Underling*: Lawrence Hamilton. *Soldier Messenger*: Marvin Engran. *Winged Monkey*: Germaine Edwards. *Glinda*: ANN DUQUESNAY.

[17]Orginally produced in New York Off-Broadway 9 July 1983 at Playwrights Horizons for 25 performances.
[18]Although suggested by the life of Georges Seurat and by his painting "A Sunday Afternoon on the Island of La Grande Jatte," all characters in "Sunday in the Park With George" are products of the authors' imaginations.

[19]Originally produced in New York 5 January 1975 at the Majestic Theatre for 1672 performances. For Synopsis of Scenes and Musical Numbers, see original 1975 production. For this production, the original Act 2, Scene 4 (Emerald City Gate), was dropped.

1984–1985 SEASON

Stubby Kaye in GRIND
Martha Swope/TimePix

1984–1985 SEASON

1984.10 GOTTA GETAWAY!

A Magical Musical Voyage (Revue) in Two Acts, 11 Scenes. Conceived and created by Stephen Nisbet, James Lecesne. Writer, James Lecesne. Directed and choreographed by Larry Fuller. Co-choreographer, Marianne Selbert. Producer-Artistic director, Patricia Morinelli. Associate producer, Stephen Nisbet. Original music by Marc Elliot, Chip Orton, Gene Palumbo, Marc Shaiman, Eric Watson. Musical director, Gene Palumbo. Orchestrations by Michael Gibson, Bill Brohn. Conductor, Robert Billig. Vocal arrangements, Gene Palumbo, Robert Billig. Dance arrangements by Michael Rice. Scenery by Eduardo Sicangco. Costumes by Michael Casey. Lighting by Clarke W. Thornton. Music video by Neil Wagman. Produced by Radio City Music Hall Productions, Inc. Opened 13 June 1984 at the Radio City Music Hall and closed 3 September 1984 after 149 performances.

CAST: LILIANE MONTEVECCHI, TONY AZITO, LORETTA DEVINE, ALYSON REED, RON and JOY HOLIDAY.

THE ROCKETTES: Pauline Achillas, Carol Beatty, Katherine Beatty, Dottie Belle, Susan Boron, Elizabeth Chanin, Barbara Ann Cittadino, Susan Cleland, Eileen Collins, Brie Daniels, Prudence Gray Demmler, Susanne Doris, Jackie Fancy, Deniene Fenn, Alexis Ficks, Carol Harbich, Jennifer Hammond, Ginny Hounsell, Cindy Hughes, Joan Peer Kelleher, Pam Kelleher, DeeDee Knapp, Judy Little, Sonya Livingston, Leslie Gryszko McCarthy, Mary McNamara, Barbara Moore, Lynn Newton, Kerri Pearsall, Gerri Presky, Terry Spano, Pamela Stacy Pasqualino, Lynn Sullivan, Susan Theobald, Carol Toman, Patricia Tully, Rose Ann Woolsey, Darlene Wendy.

Cruisettes: Arminae Azarian, Ellia English, Connie Kunkle, Jacqueline Reilly, Freida Williams.

Stewards: Ciscoe Bruton, John Clonts, Joe DeGunther, Brian Feehan, Darrell Greene, Marc Hunter, David Michael Johnson, Robert Kellett, Lacy Darryl Phillips, Jeff Shade, Paul Solen, Alan Stuart, John M. Wiltberger.

Act 1, Scene 1: Bon Voyage. *Scene 2*: Shipshape. *Scene 3*: 50,000 Leagues under the Sea. *Scene 4*: The Poop Deck. *Scene 5*: Island Hopping.

Act 2, Scene 1: Ohh, La La Paris. *Scene 2*: Up in the Air. *Scene 3*: A Wild Holiday. *Scene 4*: The Forbidden City. *Scene 5*: The Stardeck. *Scene 6*: Land Ho.

ACT 1

Scene 1

"Gotta Getaway"
L. Montevecchi, A. Reed, L. Devine, T. Azito
(*Video Sequence Directed by* Neil Wagman.)

"Gotta Getaway"
A. Reed, L. Devine, T. Azito
(*Music and Lyrics by* Glenn Roven.)

"I'm Throwing a Ball Tonight" (from *PANAMA HATTIE*)
L. Montevecchi, A. Reed, L. Devine, T. Azito, The Rockettes, Cruisettes, Stewards
(*Music and Lyrics by* Cole Porter.)

"Use Your Imagination" (from *OUT OF THIS WORLD*)
L. Montevecchi
(*Music and Lyrics by* Cole Porter.)

Scene 2

"Too Marvelous for Words" (from *READY, WILLING AND ABLE* film)
(*Music by* Richard A. Whiting. *Lyrics by* Johnny Mercer.)

"This Heart of Mine" (from *ZIEGFELD FOLLIES* film)
A. Reed, J. Clonts, R. Kellett, B. Feehan, M. Hunter, Stewards
(*Music by* Harry Warren. *Lyrics by* Arthur Freed.)

Scene 3

"Bubble Bubble"
L. Devine, The Rockettes, Cruisettes
(*Music by* Gene Palumbo. *Lyrics by* Chip Orton.)
Mermen: C. Bruton, D. Greene, J. Shape, L. Philips. *Divers*: T. Azito, D. M. Johnson, A. Stuart. *Sea Nymphs*: R. Woolsey, G. Hounsell, S. Cleland, J. Hammond. *Seaweed*: M. McNamara, J. Little, K. Beatty. *Mermaids*: B. Chanin, S. Livingston, P. Tully, L. Sullivan, T. Spano.

Scene 4

"La Cumparsita"
L. Montevecchi, J. DeGunther
(*Music by* G. H. Matos Rodriguez. *Original Choreography by* George Reich.)

Scene 5

"Here in Minipoora"
T. Azito, L. Devine, A. Reed, The Rockettes, Stewards, Cruisettes
(*Music and Lyrics by* Marc Elliot and Marc Shaiman.)

"Hot VooDoo" (from *BLONDE VENUS* film)
L. Montevecchi, Full Company
(*Music by* Sam Coslow. *Lyrics by* Ralph Rainger.)
Dancing Trees: C. Beatty, P. Stacey, L. Newton.

ACT 2

Scene 1

"Hello Beautiful"
T. Azito, Folies Showgirls
(*Music and Lyrics by* Walter Donaldson.)
Showgirls: B. Daniels, T. Spano, C. Hughes, B. A. Cittadino, K. Pearsall, C. Beatty, P. Tully, L. G. McCarthy, L. Newton, R. Woolsey, S. Cleland, P. G. Demler.

"Le Dernier Pierrot"
L. Montevecchi
(*Music by* Pierre Porte. *Lyrics by* Pascal Sevran.)

"Folies Bergeres" (from NINE)
L. Montevecchi, The Rockettes, Stewards
(*Music and Lyrics by* Maury Yeston.)

"(I'll Build a) Stairway to Paradise" (from *GEORGE WHITE'S SCANDALS OF 1922*)
L. Montevecchi, T. Azito, The Rockettes, Stewards
(*Music by* George Gershwin. *Lyrics by* Buddy DeSylva and Ira Gershwin.)

Scene 2

"Higher and Higher"
The Cruisettes: A. Azarian, E. English, J. Reilly, F. Williams.
(*Music and Lyrics by* Gary Jackson, Carl Smith, Raynard Miner.)

Scene 3

The Holidays (Dancers, Acrobats, Animal Trainers)
R. Holiday, J. Holiday, Cats

Scene 4

"Come to the Supermarket in Old Peking" (from *ALADDIN*, TV Musical)L. Devine
(*Music and Lyrics by* Cole Porter.)

"Peking Ballet"
A. Reed, J. Shade, The Stewards, Rockettes
(*Original Ballet Music by* Eric Watson. *Masks by* Willa Shalit.)

Scene 5

"Once You've Seen a Rainbow"
A. Reed, L. Devine, L. Montevecchi
(*Music and Lyrics by* Gene Palumbo and Chip Orton.)

Scene 6

"Manhattan"
T. Azito, The Stewards
(*Music and Lyrics by* Marc Elliot and Marc Shaiman.)

"Take Good Care of That Lady"
L. Devine, A. Reed, L. Montevecchi, T. Azito, Full Company
(*Music and Lyrics by* Marc Elliot and Marc Shaiman.)

1984.11 CANDIDE

A Revival of the Musical in Two Act, 23 Scenes[1]. (New) Book adapted from Voltaire's satire (of the same name) by Hugh Wheeler. (Original book by Lillian Hellman.) Music by Leonard Bernstein. Lyrics by Richard Wilbur. Additional lyrics by Stephen Sondheim and John Latouche. Directed by Harold Prince. Stage directors, Arthur Masella and Albert Sherman. Choreography by Patricia Birch. Scenery designed by Clarke Dunham. Costumes designed by Judith Dolan. Lighting designed by Ken Billington. Conducted by John Mauceri. Orchestrations by Leonard Bernstein and Hershy Kay. Chorus Master, Joseph Colaneri. Produced by the New York City Opera. Opened 18 July 1984 at the New York State Theatre and closed 22 July 1984 after 7 performances.

CAST (in order of appearance): *Voltaire*: JOHN LANKSTON. *Candide*: DAVID EISLER. *Huntsman*: Don Yule. *Paquette*: DEBORAH DARR. *Baroness*: Carol Sparrow. *Baron*: JACK HARROLD. *Cunegonde*: LEIGH MUNRO. *Maximilian*: SCOTT REEVE. *Servant of Maximilian*: JAMES BILLINGS. *Dr. Pangloss*: JOHN

[1]Original production first produced in New York 1 December 1956 at the Martin Beck Theatre for 73 performances; revised version first produced Off-Boadway 11 December 1973 at the Chelsea Theater Center, Brooklyn Academy of Music for 48 performances; transferred 5 March 1974 to the Broadway Theatre for 740 performances. For Synopsis of Scenes and Musical Numbers, see 1982 revival.

LANKSTON. *Bulgarian Soldiers*: Don Yule, JAMES BILLINGS. *Westphalian Soldiers*: Scott Evans, William Ledbetter. *Don Isaachar*, the Jew: JAMES BILLINGS. *Grand Inquisitor*: JACK HARROLD. *Calliope Player*: Carol Sparrow. *Heresy Agent*: Ralph Bassett. *Inquisition Agents*: Gary Dietrich, Michael Martorano. *Judge*: JAMES BILLINGS. *Old Lady*: MURIEL COSTA-GREENSPON. *Dons*: Vasilis Iracledes, Scott Evans, Richard Smith, Don Yule, William Ledbetter, Ralph Bassett. *Businessman*: JOHN LANKSTON. *Governor*: JOHN LANKSTON. *Governor's Aide*: Scott Evans. *Slave Driver*: JACK HARROLD. *Father Bernard*: JAMES BILLINGS. *Sailors*: Gary Dietrich, Michael Martorano, Scott Evans, Travis Wright. *Pirates*: John Henry Thomas, William Ledbetter. *Pink Sheep*: Ivy Austin, Susan Delery-Whedon. *Lion*: Robert Brubaker. *Pasha-Prefect*: JACK HARROLD. *First Gambler*: JAMES BILLINGS. *Second Gambler (Police Chief)*: JOHN LANKSTON. *Sage*: JOHN LANKSTON.

1984.12 THE MIKADO, or The Town of Titipu

A Revival of the Comic Opera in Two Acts[2]. Libretto by William S. Gilbert. Music by Arthur Sullivan. Directed by Lofti Mansouri. Choreography by Patricia Birch. Scenery and costumes designed by Thierry Bosquet. Lighting designed by John Gleason. Conducted by David Stahl. Chorus master, Jospeh Colaneri. Produced by the New York City Opera. Opened 6 September 1984 at the New York State Theatre and closed 9 September 1984 after 6 performances in repertory.

CAST (in order of appearance): *Pooh-Bah*, Lord High Everything Else: RICHARD McKEE. *Pish-Tush*, a Noble Lord: Dominic Cossa. *Nanki-Poo*, his son, disguised as a wandering minstrel in love with Yum-Yum: BRUCE REED. *Ko-Ko*, Lord High Executioner of Titipu: JAMES BILLINGS. *Yum-Yum, Pitti-Sing, Peep-Bo*, three sisters, wards of Ko-Ko: ELIZABETH HYNES, CYNTHIA ROSE, LOUISA JONASON. *Katisha*: ELAINE BONAZZI. *The Mikado of Japan*: WILLIAM WILDERMANN. *Chorus of School Girls, Nobles, Guards and Coolies*: New York City Opera Chorus.

1984.13 SWEENEY TODD- THE DEMON BARBER OF FLEET STREET

A Revival of the Musical Thriller in Two Acts[3]. Book by Hugh Wheeler. Based on a version of "Sweeney Todd" by Christopher Bond (after the original melodrama by George Dibdin-Pitt). Music and Lyrics by Stephen Sondheim. Directed by Harold Prince. Choreography by Larry Fuller. Scenery designed by Eugene Lee. Costumes designed by Franne Lee. Lighting designed by Ken Billington. (Orchestrations by Jonathan Tunick.) Conductor, Paul Gemignani. Assistant to Mr. Prince, Arthur Masella. Assistant stage directors, Raymond Menard, Albert Sherman. Produced by the New York City Opera. Opened 11 October 1984 at the New York State Theatre and closed 16 November 1984 after 13 performances. in repertory.

CAST (in order of appearance): *Anthony Hope*: CRIS GROENENDAAL. *Sweeney Todd*: TIMOTHY NOLEN. *Beggar Woman*: ADAIR LEWIS. *Mrs. Lovett*: ROSALIND ELIAS. *Judge Turpin*: WILLIAM DANSBY. *The Beadle*: JOHN LANKSTON. *Johanna*: LEIGH MUNRO. *Tobias Ragg*: PAUL BINOTTO. *Pirelli*: JEROLD SIENA. *Jonas Fogg*: William Ledbetter. *Ensemble*: New York City Opera Chorus.

1984.14 THE THREE MUSKETEERS

A Revival of the Musical Adventure in Two Acts, 17 Scenes[4]. (Original) Book by William Anthony McGuire. New version by Mark Bramble. Based on the novel of the same name by Alexandre Dumas. Music by Rudolf Friml. Lyrics by P. G. Wodehouse and Clifford Grey. Directed by Joe Layton. Choreography by Lester Wilson. Fights by Steve Dunnington. Scenery designed by Nancy Winters. Costumes designed by Freddy Wittop. Lighting designed by Ken Billington. Sound designed by Jan Nebozenko. Music adapted, arranged and supervised by Kirk Nurock. Conductor, Gordon Lowry Harrell. Orchestrations by Larry Wilcox. Vocal and fight arrangements by Kirk Nurock. Dance arrangements by Wally Harper, Mark Hummel. Produced by Irvin Feld, Kenneth Feld, Ina Lea Meibach, Jerome Minskoff. Opened 11 November 1984 at the Broadway Theatre and closed 18 November 1984 after 9 performances.

CAST (in order of appearance): *Queen Anne of France*: Darlene Anders. *Lady Constance Bonacieux*: LIZ CALLAWAY. *Cardinal Richelieu*: ED DIXON. *Sergeant Jussac*: Raymond Patterson. *Innkeeper*: J. P. Dougherty. *The Duke of Buckingham*: Joseph Kolinski. *The Compte de la Rochefort*: Michael Dantuono. *Milady de Winter*: MARIANNE TATUM. *D'Artagnan*: MICHAEL PRAED. *Athos*: CHUCK WAGNER. *Aramis*: BRENT SPINER. *Porthos*: RON TAYLOR. *Selenus*: J. P. Dougherty. *Laundress*: Susan Goodman. *de Beauverais*: Steve Dunnington. *Captain Treville*: Peter Samuel. *King Louis XIII*: Roy Brocksmith. *Tavern Wench*: Susan Goodman. *Chambermaid*: Elisa Fiorillo. *Patrick*: Perry Arthur. *Major Domo*: J. P. Dougherty.

Cardinal's Guards: Bill Badolato, Steve Dunnington, Craig Heath Nim, Steve Marder, Mark McGrath, Sal Viviano, Faruma Williams. *Citizens of Poissy, Paris, Calais, The King's Musketeers, and Characters Too Numerous to Mention*: Janet Aldrich, Perry Arthur, Bill Badolato, Tina Belis, Steven Blanchard, Steve Dunnington, Elisa Fiorillo, Terri Garcia, Susan Goodman, Patty Holley, Jeff Johnson, Steve Marder, Mark McGrath, Craig Heath Nim, Susan Postel, Wynonna Smith, Sal Viviano, Faruma Williams, Sandra Zigars. *Swings*: De Dwight Baxter, Kirsti Carnahan, Craig Frawley, Jacqueline Smith-Lee.

The action takes place in 1626 in France and England.

Act 1, Scene 1: France. April, 1626. *Scene 2*: Poissy, A Market Town outside Paris. *Scene 3*: Paris, the Night of All Fool's Eve. *Scene 4*: Garden at the Convent of Carmier. *Scene 5*: Streets of Paris. *Scene 6*: The Laundry at Number 7 Rue de Colombier. *Scene 7*: The Cardinal's Chamber in the Louvre. *Scene 8*: Gardens of the Tuileries. *Scene 9*: Palace Corridor into the Great Hall. *Scene 10*: On the Road to Calais.

Act 2, Scene 1: The Golden Lily Tavern, Calais. *Scene 2*: Streets of Calais and the Ship to England. *Scene 3*: The Duke of Buckingham's Castle in England. *Scene 4*: Milady's Bedroom at the Golden Lily Tavern, Calais. *Scene 5*: The Road to Paris. *Scene 6*: All over Paris. *Scene 7*: The Hotel de Ville.

ACT 1

Scene 1

Prologue
C. Wagner, B. Spiner, R. Taylor, R. Brocksmith, P. Samuel, D. Anders, L. Callaway, R. Patterson, J. P. Dougherty, J. Kolinski, M. Dantuono, M. Tatum, M. Praed

Scene 2

"Gascony Bred"
M. Praed, J. P. Dougherty, All

"All for One"
C. Wagner, B. Spiner, R. Taylor

"Only a Rose"
M. Praed, L. Callaway

"My Sword and I"
M. Praed, All

Scene 3

Carnival of Fools
Full Company

Scene 4

"L'Amour Toujours L'Amour"
J. Kolinski, D. Anders

Scene 5

"Come to Us"
M. Tatum, R. Patterson

Scene 6

"March of the Musketeers"
C. Wagner, B. Spiner, R. Taylor, M. Praed, All

Scene 7

"Bless My Soul"
E. Dixon, M. Tatum, M. Dantuono

Scene 8

"Only a Rose" (reprise)
L. Callaway, M. Praed, All

Scene 10

Act 1 Finale
M. Praed, C. Wagner, B. Spiner, R. Taylor, Full Company

ACT 2

Scene 1

"Vive la France"
R. Brocksmith, Company

"The Actor's Life"
C. Wagner, B. Spiner, R. Taylor, M. Praed

---

[2]First presented in New York 20 July, 10-29 August 1885 at the Union Square and People's Theatres for 22 performances. First authorized production presented 19 August 1885 at the Fifth Avenue Theatre by Richard D'Oyly Carte for 250 performances. For Synopsis of Scenes and Musical Numbers, see 19 August 1885 D'Oyly Carte production.

[3]Originally produced in New York 1 March 1979 at the Uris Theatre for 557 performances. For Synopsis of Scenes and Musical Numbers, see original 1979 production.
Restored for this production:
"Johanna" (Act 1, after "The Contest")
W. Dansby

[4]Originally produced in New York 13 March 1928 at the Lyric Theatre for 318 performances.

"My Belle"
M. Praed, L. Callaway

Scene 2

"The Chase"
Full Company

"My Belle" (reprise)
M. Praed, C. Wagner, B. Spiner, R. Taylor

Scene 3

"Dreams"
J. Kolinski

Scene 4

"L'Amour Toujours L'Amour" (reprise)
M. Tatum

Scene 5

"All for One" (reprise)
C. Wagner, B. Spiner, R. Taylor, M. Praed

Scene 6

"Gossip"
C. Wagner, B. Spiner, R. Taylor, M. Praed, M. Tatum, R. Patterson, E. Dixon, L. Callaway, P. Samuel, R. Brocksmith, D. Anders, Full Company

Scene 7

Finale
Full Company

1984.15 HAARLEM NOCTURNE

A Musical (Revue) in One Act[5]. Conceived by André de Shields. Written and directed by André DeShields, Murray Horwitz. Musical direction, orchestrations, vocal arrangements by Marc Shaiman. Scenic design by David Chapman. Costume design by Jean-Claude Robin. Lighting design by Marc B. Weiss. Sound design by Bill Dreisbach. Associate producer, Alecia Parker. Produced by Barry and Fran Weissler by special arrangement with Black Goat Entertainment. Opened 18 November 1984 at the Latin Quarter and closed 30 December 1984 after 49 performances.

CAST: ANDRÉ DeSHIELDS, DEBRA BYRD, ELLIA ENGLISH, MARC SHAIMAN, FREIDA WILLIAMS.

MUSICAL NUMBERS

"Love in the Morning"
A. DeShields, Ladies
(*Music and Lyrics by* Steven Lemberg.)

"Wishful Thinking"
A. DeShields, Ladies
(*Music and Lyrics by* Kenny Moore, Martri McCall and Zedrick Turnbough.)

"New York Is a Party"
A. DeShields, Ladies
(*Music by* Marc Shaiman. *Lyrics by* Robert I.)

"Jungle Hip Hop"
A. DeShields, Ladies
(*Music and Lyrics by* André DeShields.)

"Sweet Dreams Are Made of This"
The Ladies
(*Music by* Annie Lennox. *Lyrics by* D. A. Stewart.)

"What Becomes of the Broken-Hearted"
A. DeShields, Ladies
(*Music and Lyrics by* W. Witherspoon, P. Riser, J. Dean.)

"Love's Sad Glance"
The Ladies
(*Music by* Marc Shaiman. *Lyrics by* Ula Hedwig.)

"Secret Love"
D. Byrd, The Ladies
(*Music by* Kenny Moore. *Lyrics by* Alex Brown.)

"Say It Again"
F. Williams, Ladies
(*Music and Lyrics by* Dennis Andreopolous.)

"Heads or Tails"
A. DeShields, Ladies
(*Music and Lyrics by* Dennis Andreopolous.)

"Hit the Road Jack"
E. English, A. DeShields, Ladies
(*Music and Lyrics by* Percy Mayfield.)

"Waterfaucet Blues"
E. English
(Traditional blues; *Music and Lyrics adapted by* Micki Grant.)

"Streetcorner Symphony"
A. DeShields, Ladies
("The Way We Were," *Music by* Marvin Hamlisch. Lyrics by Marilyn and Alan Bergman. "Release Yourself" *Lyrics by* Larry Graham.)

"Bad Boy"
A. DeShields, Ladies
(*Music and Lyrics by* Lil Armstrong.)

"Symphony Rap"
A. DeShields, Ladies
(*Music and Lyrics by* André DeShields.)

"Mary Mack"
A. DeShields, F. Williams, Ladies
(traditional children's song)

Pastiche
The Ladies
("Locomotion" by Carole King, Gerry Goffin; "My Boyfriend's Back" by Bob Feldman, Gerald Goldstein, Richard Gottehrer; "Chapel of Love" by Jeff Barry, Ellie Greenwich, Phil Spector; "Soldier Boy" by Florence Green, Luther Dixon; "Come and Get These Memories" by Eddie Holland, Lamont Dozier, Brian Holland; "Da Doo Run Run" by Jeff Barry, Ellie Greenwich, Phil Spector; "Wishing and Hoping" by Burt Bacharach, Hal David; "He's So Fine" by Ronald Mack; "My Sweet Lord" by George Harrison; "Please Mr. Postman" by Brian Holland, Robert Bateman, Freddie Gorman; "Tell Him" by Burt Russell; "Baby Love" by Eddie Holland, Brian Holland, Lamont Dozier; "And Then He Kissed Me" by Jeff Barry, Ellie Greenwich, Phil Spector; "Leader of the Pack" by Jeff Barry, Ellie Greenwich, Phil Spector; "The Shoop Shoop Song" by Rudy Clark; "He's Sure the Boy I Love" by Cynthia Weil, Barry Mann; "My Boyfriend's Back"; I Can Never Go Home Anymore" by George Morton; "He's a Rebel" by Gene Pitney; "The Girl I'm Gonna Marry" by Ellie Greenwich, Tony Powers, Phil Spector; "Not Too Young to Get Married" by Jeff Barry, Ellie Greenwich, Phil Spector, Thomas Elliott; "Memories" by Andrew Lloyd Webber, Trevor Nunn.)

"Lush Life"
A. DeShields
(*Music and Lyrics by* Billy Strayhorn.)

"Haarlem Nocturne"
The Ladies
(*Music by* Earle Hagen. *Lyrics by* Dick Rogers.)

"B.Y.O.B."
A. DeShields, Ladies
(*Music and Lyrics by* André DeShields.)

"Now Is the Time"
A. DeShields, Ladies
(*Music and Lyrics by* André DeShields.)

1984.16 DOUG HENNING AND HIS WORLD OF MAGIC

A Magic Revue in Two Acts. Conceived and directed by Doug Henning. Staged and choreographed by Charlene Painter. Music composed and directed by Peter Matz. Costumes by Jeff Billings; Additional costumes by Bill Hargate. Set by Bill Bohnert. Lighting design by Michael McGiveney. Music designer and coordinator, Jim Steinmeyer. Head illusion engineer and additional illusions, William Kennedy. Illusions design and construction, John Gaughan. Magical consultant, Charles Reynolds. Animal trainer, Rick Glassey. Produced by James M. Nederlander and Arthur Rubin. Opened 11 December 1984 at the Lunt-Fontanne Theatre and closed 27 January 1985 after 60 performances.

CAST: DOUG HENNING, DEBBY HENNING, Victor Heineman, D. J. Mergenthaler, Gina Rose, Kathleen White.

The production includes illusions and magic that Doug Henning has performed in the theatre (The Magic Show, Merlin) and on television during the past ten years, such as 'The Tunnel of Awe' and 'The Miracle Levitation Vanish.' Others include conjuring a 450-pound tiger and a Burmese panther, and sleight-of-hand magic visible to the audience on giant television screens. Mr. Henning saws two women in half, transports himself from inside a sack to the inside of a stuffed animal.

1985.01 THE KING AND I

A Revival of the Musical Play in Two Acts, 17 Scenes[6]. Book and lyrics by Oscar Hammerstein II. Music by Richard Rodgers. Based on the novel

[5]Originally produced Off-Broadway 19 January 1984 at B.Y.O.B. Cabaret Downstairs at La Mama.

[6]Originally produced in New York 29 March 1951 at the St. James Theatre for 1246 performances. For Synopsis of Scenes and Musical Numbers, see original 1951 production. Yul Brynner also appeared in a revival of *THE KING AND I* 2 May 1977 at the Uris Theatre for 719 performances.

"Anna and the King of Siam" by Margaret Landon. Original choreography by Jerome Robbins; choreography reproduced by Rebecca West. Directed by Mitch Leigh. Settings designed by Peter Wolf. Costumes by Stanley Simmons, based on the original costumes designed by Irene Sharaff. Lighting designed by Ruth Roberts. (Orchestrations uncredited.) Production supervisor, Conwell Worthington II. Musical director, Richard Parrinello. Sound designed by Scott Marcellus. Associate producer, Manny Kladitis. Executive producer, Milton Hershon. Produced by the Mitch Leigh Company. Opened 7 January 1985 at the Broadway Theatre and closed 30 June 1985 after 191 performances.

CAST (in order of appearance): *Louis Leonowens*: Jeffrey Bryan Davis. *Captain Orton*: Burt Edwards. *Anna Leonowens*: MARY BETH PEIL. *The Interpreter*: Jae Woo Lee. *The Kralahome*: JONATHAN FARWELL. *The King*: YUL BRYNNER. *Lead Royal Dancer*: Kathy Lee Brynner. *Lun Tha*: Sal Provenza. *Tuptim*: PATRICIA WELCH. *Lady Thiang*: IRMA-ESTEL LaGUERRE. *Prince Chulalongkorn*: Araby Abaya. *Princess Ying Yaowalak*: Yvette Laura Martin. *Fan Dancer*: Patricia Weber. *Sir Edward Ramsay*: Edward Crotty.

The Small House of Uncle Thomas (ballet): *Uncle Thomas*: Hope Sogawa. *Little Eva*: Evelina Deocares. *Topsy*: Deborah Harada. *Eliza*: Kathy Lee Brynner. *King Simon*: Rebecca West. *Angel*: Patricia Weber.

The Royal Dancers and Wives: Marla F. Bingham, Young-Hee Cho, Carolyn DeLany, Evelina Deocares, Deborah Harada, Valerie Lau-Kee, Suzen Murakoshi, Hope Sogawa, Sylvia Yamada. *Princesses and Princes*: Max Barabas, Michael Bulos, Amy Chin, Lisa Chui, Mark Damrongsri, Kate Gwon, Tracie Mon-Ting Lee, Michelle Nigalan, Steven Tom, Luke Trainer, Annie Woo. *Nurses and Amazons*: Alis-Elaine Anderson, Joyce Campana, Mariann Cook, Janet Jordan. *Priests and Slaves*: Cornel Chan, Kaipo Daniels, Gary Bain Domasin, Stanley Earl Harrison, Thomas Heath, Andre Lengyel, Ron Stefan.

1985.02 HARRIGAN 'N HART

A Musical in Two Acts, 16 Scenes. Book by Michael Stewart. Based on material compiled by Nedda Harrigan Logan and "The Merry Partners" by E. J. Kahn, Jr. (New) Music by Max Showalter. (New) Lyrics by Peter Walker. Songs of the Period by Edward Harrigan (Lyrics) and David Braham (Music). Entire production directed by Joe Layton. Choreographed by D. J. Giagni. Scenic design by David Mitchell. Costume design by Ann-Hould Ward. Lighting design by Richard Nelson. Music supervision, orchestrations and arrangements by John McKinney. Musical director, Peter Howard. Sound design by Otts Munderloh. Originally produced by the Goodspeed Opera House (Michael P. Price, Executive director). Produced by Elliott Martin, Arnold Bernhard and The Shubert Organization. Opened 31 January 1985 at the Longacre Theatre and closed 3 February 1985 after 5 performances.

CAST (in order of appearance): *Stetson*: Mark Fotopoulos. *Edward Harrigan*: HARRY GROENER. *Tony Hart*: MARK HAMILL. *Archie White*: Clent Bowers. *Old Colonel*: Cleve Asbury. *The Colonel's Wife*: Barbara Moroz. *Eleanor*: Roxie Lucas. *Andrew LeCouvrier*: Mark Fotopoulos. *Martin Hanley*: Oliver Woodall. *Sam Nichols*: Clent Bowers. *Alfred J. Dugan*: Christopher Wells. *Felix Barker*: Clent Bowers. *Judge*: Mark Fotopoulos. *Annie Braham Harrigan*: Tudi Roche. *Johnny Wild*: Mark Fotopoulos. *Billy Gross*: Cleve Asbury. *Chester Fox*: Kenston Ames. *Lily Fay*: Merilee Magnuson. *Elsie Fay*: Barbara Moroz. *Ada Lewis*: Roxie Lucas. *Mrs. Annie Yeamons*: ARMELIA McQUEEN. *Jennie Yeamons*: Amelia Marshall. *Harry Mack*: Christopher Wells. *Photographer*: Kenston Ames. *Judge Hilton*: Christopher Wells. *Nat Goodwin*: Cleve Asbury. *Captain*: Mark Fotopoulos. *Newsboy*: Kenston Ames. *Newsgirl*: Amelia Marshall. *Belle*: Barbara Moroz. *Gerta Granville*: CHRISTINE EBERSOLE. *Adelaide Harrigan*: Merilee Magnuson. *Uncle Albert*: Clent Bowers. *Newspaperman*: Kenston Ames. *William Gill*: Mark Fotopoulos. *Doctor*: Christopher Wells. *Nurse*: Merilee Magnuson. *Swings*: Michael Gorman, Alison Mann.

The action takes place from 1871 to 1888.

Act 1, Scene 1: Stetson's American Music Hall, Galesburg, Illinois, 1871. *Scene 2*: New York City. *Scene 3*: The Theatre Comique. *Scene 4*: U. S. Courthouse, Worcester, Massachusetts. *Scene 5*: The Theatre Comique. *Scene 6*: The Theatre Comique. *Scene 7*: Outside the New Theatre Comique, Opening Night. *Scene 8*: Old Nieuw Amsterdam. *Scene 9*: A Restaurant, later that evening. *Scene 10*: The New Theatre Comique.

Act 2, Scene 1: New York City and the Park Theatre. *Scene 2*: Harrigan's Tour, 1880 to 1886. *Scene 3*: Backstage, Wallack's Theatre. *Scene 4*: New York City. *Scene 5*: New York Hospital. *Scene 6*: The Park Theatre, 22 March 1888

ACT 1

Scene 1

"Put Me in My Little Bed"
M. Hamill

"Wonderful Me"
H. Groener, M. Hamill

Scene 3

"Mulligan Guard"
H. Groener, M. Hamill
(*Music by* David Braham. *Lyrics by* Edward Harrigan.)

Scene 4

"Put Me in My Little Bed" (reprise)
M. Hamill

Scene 5

"I Love to Follow a Band"
H. Groener, Company
(*Music by* David Braham. *Lyrics by* Edward Harrigan.)

"Such an Education Has My Mary Ann"
H. Groener, M. Hamill, Company
(*Music by* David Braham. *Lyrics by* Edward Harrigan.)

"Maggie Murphy's Home"
T. Roche, H. Groener, C. Bowers, Company
(*Music by* David Braham. *Lyrics by* Edward Harrigan.)

"McNally's Row of Flats"
A. McQueen, Company
(*Music by* David Braham. *Lyrics by* Edward Harrigan.)

"Something New, Something Different"
H. Groener, M. Hamill, Company

Scene 6

"That's My Partner"
H. Groener, M. Hamill

Scene 8

"She's Our Gretel"
H. Groener, M. Hamill, A. McQueen, Company
(*Music by* David Braham. *Lyrics by* Edward Harrigan.)

Scene 9

"What You Need Is a Woman"
C. Ebersole

Scene 10

"Knights of the Mystic Star"
A. McQueen, Company
(*Music by* David Braham. *Lyrics by* Edward Harrigan.)

"Girl of the Mystic Star"
C. Ebersole, Men
(*Music by* David Braham. *Lyrics by* Edward Harrigan.)

"Mulligan Guard" (reprise)
H. Groener, M. Hamill

ACT 2

Scene 1

"Skidmore Fancy Ball"
C. Bowers, C. Wells, M. Fotopoulos, C. Asbury
(*Music by* David Braham. *Lyrics by* Edward Harrigan.)

"Sweetest Love"
R. Lucas, B. Moroz
(*Music by* David Braham. *Lyrics by* Edward Harrigan.)

"The Old Barn Floor"
M. Fotopoulos, A. Marshall, K. Ames, M. Magnuson

"Silly Boy"
C. Ebersole, C. Asbury, C. Wells
(*Music by* David Braham. *Lyrics by* Edward Harrigan.)

"Mulligan Guard" (reprise)
H. Groener, M. Hamill, Company

"We'll Be There"
H. Groener, M. Hamill, Company

Scene 2

"Ada with the Golden Hair"
T. Roche, M. Fotopoulos, C. Asbury
(*Music by* David Braham. *Lyrics by* Edward Harrigan.)

"That Old Featherbed"
C. Wells, M. Magnuson, B. Moroz
(*Music by* David Braham. *Lyrics by* Edward Harrigan.)

"Sam Johnson's Colored Cakewalk"
C. Bowers, A. Marshall
(*Music by* David Braham. *Lyrics by* Edward Harrigan.)

"Dip Me in the Golden Sea"
H. Groener, A. McQueen, Company
(*Music by* David Braham. *Lyrics by* Edward Harrigan.)

"That's My Partner" (reprise)
H. Groener

Scene 3

"I've Come Home to Stay"
M. Hamill
(*Music by* David Braham. *Lyrics by* Edward Harrigan.)

"If I Could Trust Me"
M. Hamill

Scene 4

"Maggie Murphy's Home" (reprise)
O. Woodall, M. Magnuson, A. McQueen, R. Lucas

"I've Come Home to Stay" (reprise)
M. Hamill, Girls

Scene 5

"I Need This One Chance"
C. Ebersole

Scene 6

"I Love to Follow a Band" (reprise)
T. Roche, Company

"Mulligan Guard" (reprise)
H. Groener, M. Hamill, A. McQueen

"Something New, Something Different" (reprise)
H. Groener, M. Hamill, Company

1985.03 LEADER OF THE PACK

A Musical (Revue) in One Act[7]. Music and lyrics by Ellie Greenwich and Friends. Liner notes (Book) by Anne Beatts. Additional material by Jack Heifner. Based on the original play by Melanie Mintz. Directed and choreographed by Michael Peters. Settings designed by Tony Walton. Costumes designed by Robert de Mora. Lighting designed by Pamela Cooper. Musical director and musical adapter, Jimmy Vivino. Vocal arrangements by Marc Shaiman. Dance arrangements by Timothy Graphenreed. Sound designed by Abe Jacob. Produced by The Pack (Elizabeth I. McCann, Nelle Nugent, Francine LeFrak, Clive Davis, John Hart Associates, Inc., Rodger Hess, Richard Kagan). Opened 8 April 1985 at the Ambassador Theater and closed 21 July 1985 after 120 performances.

CAST (in order of appearance): *Darlene Love*: DARLENE LOVE. *Annie Golden*: ANNIE GOLDEN. *Young Ellie Greenwich* (1960's): DINAH MANOFF. *Rosie*, Ellie's Mother: Zora Rasmussen. *Shelley*: Barbara Yeager. *Mickey*: Jasmine Guy. *Jeff Barry*: PATRICK CASSIDY. *Gus Sharkey*: DENNIS BAILEY. *D. J. Voice*: Peter Neptune. *Waitress*: Jasmine Guy. *Lounge Singer*: Pattie Darcy. *Dance Couple*: Shirley Black-Brown, Keith McDaniel. *Gina*: Gina Taylor. *Ellie Greenwich* (1980's): ELLIE GREENWICH.

Girls and Guys: Shirley Black-Brown, Pattie Darcy, Christopher Gregory, Jasmine Guy, Danny Herman, Lon Hoyt, Keith McDaniel, Jodi Moccia, Peter Neptune, Zora Rasmussen, Joey Sheck, Gina Taylor, Barbara Yeager.

The action takes place here and now . . . and in the days of beehives and 45s.

MUSICAL NUMBERS

"Be My Baby"
A. Golden, Girls
(*Music and Lyrics by* Ellie Greenwich, Jeff Barry, Phil Spector.)

"Wait 'Til My Bobby Gets Home"
D. Love, Company
(*Music and Lyrics by* Ellie Greenwich, Jeff Barry, Phil Spector.)

"A . . . . My Name Is Ellie"
D. Manoff
(*Music and Lyrics by* Ellie Greenwich.)

"Jivette Boogie Beat"
D. Manoff, B. Yeager, J. Guy
(*Music and Lyrics by* Ellie Greenwich.)

"Why Do Lovers Break Each Others Hearts"
D. Love, Company
(*Music and Lyrics by* Ellie Greenwich, Tony Powers, Phil Spector.)

"Today I Met the Boy I'm Gonna Marry"
D. Love, Company
(*Music and Lyrics by* Ellie Greenwich, Tony Powers, Phil Spector.)

"I Wanna Love Him So Bad"
D. Manoff, Girls
(*Music and Lyrics by* Ellie Greenwich, Jeff Barry, Phil Spector.)

"Do Wah Diddy"
P. Cassidy, Guys
(*Music and Lyrics by* Ellie Greenwich, Jeff Barry.)

"And Then He Kissed Me"
D. Manoff, Girls
(*Music and Lyrics by* Ellie Greenwich, Jeff Barry, Phil Spector.)

"Hanky Panky"
P. Cassidy, Guys
(*Music and Lyrics by* Ellie Greenwich, Jeff Barry.)

"Not Too Young (to Get Married)"
D. Love, Girls
(*Music and Lyrics by* Ellie Greenwich, Jeff Barry, Phil Spector.)

"Chapel of Love"
Entire Company
(*Music and Lyrics by* Ellie Greenwich, Jeff Barry, Phil Spector.)

"Baby I Love You"
A. Golden, Girls
(*Music and Lyrics by* Ellie Greenwich, Jeff Barry, Phil Spector.)

"Leader of the Pack"
A. Golden, Company
(*Music and Lyrics by* Ellie Greenwich, Jeff Barry, George "Shadow" Morton.)

"Look of Love"
P. Darcy
(*Music and Lyrics by* Ellie Greenwich, Jeff Barry.)

"Christmas—Baby Please Come Home"
D. Love, Girls
(*Music and Lyrics by* Ellie Greenwich, Jeff Barry, Phil Spector.)

"I Can Hear Music"
A. Golden, P. Darcy, K. McDaniel, L. Hoyt
(*Music and Lyrics by* Ellie Greenwich, Jeff Barry, Phil Spector.)

"Rock of Rages"
D. Manoff
(*Music and Lyrics by* Ellie Greenwich, Jeff Kent.)

"Keep It Confidential"
G. Taylor, Company
(*Music and Lyrics by* Ellie Greenwich, Jeff Kent, Ellen Foley.)

"Da Doo Ron Ron"
E. Greenwich, Guys
(*Music and Lyrics by* Ellie Greenwich, Jeff Barry, Phil Spector.)

"What a Guy"
E. Greenwich, Company
(*Music and Lyrics by* Ellie Greenwich, Jeff Barry, Phil Spector.)

"Maybe I Know"
E. Greenwich, Girls
(*Music and Lyrics by* Ellie Greenwich, Jeff Barry.)

"River Deep, Mountain High"
D. Love, Company
(*Music and Lyrics by* Ellie Greenwich, Jeff Barry, Phil Spector.)

"We're Gonna Make It (After All)"
E. Greenwich, D. Love, A. Golden, Company
(*Music and Lyrics by* Ellie Greenwich.)

1985.04 TAKE ME ALONG

A Revival of the Musical in Two Acts, 15 Scenes[8]. Book (revised) by Joseph Stein and Robert Russell. Based on the play "Ah, Wilderness!" by Eugene O'Neill. Music and lyrics by Bob Merrill. Directed by Thomas Gruenewald. Choreography and musical staging by Dan Siretta. Scenery by James Leonard Joy. Costumes by David Toser. Lighting by Craig Miller. Musical direction by Lynn Crigler. Dance arrangements by Allen Cohen. Orchestrations by Philip J. Lang. Additional orchestrations by Lynn Crigler, Allen Cohen. Sound by Jan Nebozenko. A Goodspeed Opera House Production (Michael P. Price, Executive director). Produced by the John F. Kennedy Center. Opened and closed 14 April 1985 at the Martin Beck Theatre after 1 performance.

CAST (in order of appearance): *Nat Miller*, Editor of the Centerville Globe: ROBERT NICHOLS. *Essie Miller*, Nat's wife: BETTY JOHNSON. *Arthur Miller*, Richard's older brother, at Yale: STEPHEN McDONOUGH. *Mildred Miller*, the youngest Miller: ALYSON KIRK. *Lily Miller*, Nat's sister: BETH FOWLER. *Muriel Macomber*, Macomber's daughter and friend to Richard: TARYN GRIMES. *Richard Miller*, Nat's younger son: GARY LANDON WRIGHT. *David Macomber*, dry goods store owner: Richard Korthaze. *Sid Davis*, Essie's brother: KURT KNUDSON. *Belle*, a travelling artiste for hire: NIKKI SAHAGEN. *Wint*, Arthur's friend: Joel Whittaker. *Bartender*: David Vosburgh. *The Salesman*: John Witham.

Trolley Conductors, Firemen, Townsfolk, Bar Patrons, Ladies of the Evening: Kathy Andrini, Blake Atherton, Michael Kelly Boone, Ed Brazo, Richard Dodd, Andy Hostettler, Richard Korthaze, Patrick S. Murphy, Mercedes Perez, Keith Savage, David Vosburgh, Joel Whittaker, Betty Winsett, John Witham.

The action takes place in Centerville, Conncecticut, in 1906.

---

[7]Originally produced Off-Broadway 17 January 1984 at the Bottom Line.

[8]Originally produced in New York 22 October 1959 at the Sam S. Shubert Theatre for 448 performances. Dropped for this production were: "For Sweet Charity," "The Beardsley Ballet" and "Pleasant Beach House" (Wint's Song).

Act 1, Scene 1: The Miller Home. *Scene 2*: The Macomber Yard. *Scene 3*: The Centerville Car Barn. *Scene 4*: The Miller Home. *Scene 5*: The Picnic Grounds. *Scene 6*: The Miller Home. *Scene 7*: The Miller Home.

Act 2, Scene 1: The Pleasant Beach House. *Scene 2*: The Miller Home. *Scene 3*: The Miller Home. *Scene 4*: Richard's Bedroom. *Scene 5*: The Dock. *Scene 6*: The Miller Home. *Scene 7*: The Miller Home. *Scene 8*: The Centerville Car Barn.

ACT 1

Scene 1

"Marvelous Fire Machine" (The Parade)
R. Nichols, Ensemble

"Oh, Please"
B. Johnson, R. Nichols

"Oh, Please" (reprise)
B. Johnson, R. Nichols, B. Fowler, S. McDonough, A. Kirk

Scene 2

"I Would Die"
G. L. Wright, T. Grimes

Scene 3

"Sid, Ole Kid"
K. Knudson, N. Sahagen, Townspeople

Scene 4

"Staying Young"
R. Nichols

"I Get Embarassed"
K. Knudson, B. Fowler

"We're Home"
B. Fowler

"Take Me Along"
K. Knudson, R. Nichols

Scene 5

"Take Me Along" (reprise)
Company

"The Only Pair I've Got"[9]
N. Sahagen, Ensemble

"In the Company of Men"[10]
K. Knudson, R. Nichols, Male Ensemble

Scene 6

"Knights on White Horses"[11]
B. Fowler, B. Johnson

Scene 7

"That's How It Starts"
G. L. Wright

ACT 2

Scene 1

"If Jesus Don't Love Ya"[12]
G. L. Wright, N. Sahagen, Ensemble

Scene 2

"Oh, Please" (reprise)
R. Nichols, B. Johnson

Scene 3

"Promise Me a Rose" (A Slight Detail)
B. Fowler,

"Staying Young" (reprise)
R. Nichols

Scene 4

"Little Green Snake"
K. Knudson

Scene 5

"Nine O'Clock"
G. L. Wright

"Nine O'Clock" (reprise)
G. L. Wright, T. Grimes

Scene 6

"But Yours"
K. Knudson, B. Fowler

Scene 8

Finale
B. Fowler, K. Knudson

[9]Newly written for this production.
[10]Newly written for this production.
[11]Newly written for this production.
[12]Newly written for this production.

1985.05 GRIND

A Musical in Two Acts, a Prologue and 23 Scenes. Book by Fay Kanin. Music by Larry Grossman. Lyrics by Ellen Fitzhugh. Directed by Harold Prince. Choreographed by Lester Wilson. Scenery designed by Clarke Dunham. Costumes designed by Florence Klotz. Lighting designed by Ken Billington. Musical director, Paul Gemignani. Orchestrations by Bill Byers. Additional orchestrations by Jim Tyler, Harold Wheeler. Dance music arrangements by Tom Fay. Sound by Otts Munderloh. Assistant choreographer, Larry Vickers. Executive producers, Ruth Mitchell and Sam Crothers. Produced by Kenneth D. Greenblatt, John J. Pomerantz, Mary Lea Johnson, Martin Richards, James M. Nederlander, Harold Prince, Michael Frazier in association with Susan Madden Samson and Jonathan Farkas. Opened 16 April 1985 at the Mark Hellinger Theatre and closed 22 June 1985 after 79 performances.

CAST (in order of appearance): *Leroy*: BEN VEREEN. *Harry*: LEE WALLACE. *Gus*: STUBBY KAYE. *Solly*: JOEY FAYE. *Vernelle*: Marion Ramsey. *(Earle's Pearls, 4)*: *Ruby*: Hope Clarke. *Fleta*: Valarie Pettiford. *Kitty*: Candy Brown. *Linette*: Wynonna Smith. *Maybelle*: Carol Woods. *Mechanical Man*: Jackie Jay Patterson. *Knockabouts*: Leonard John Crofoot, Ray Roderick, Kelly Walters, Steve Owsley, Malcolm Perry. *Romaine*: Sharon Murray. *Satin*: LEILANI JONES. *Louis*, the Stage Manager: Brian McKay. *Mike*, the Doorman: Oscar Stokes. *Stooge*: Leonard John Crofoot. *Doyle*: TIMOTHY NOLEN. *Grover*: Donald Acree. *Mrs. Faye*: Ruth Brisbane. *Toughs*: Leonard John Crofoot, Ray Roderick, Kelly Walters, Steve Owsley, Malcolm Perry.

The action takes place in and around Harry Earle's Burlesque Theatre in Chicago, Illinois during 1933.

Prologue: Harry Earle's Burlesque Theatre.

Act 1, Scene 1: Backstage. *Scene 2*: Onstage. *Scene 3*: In the Wings. *Scene 4*: Onstage. *Scene 5*: The Alley next to the Theatre. *Scene 6*: Girls' Dressing Room; Backstage. *Scene 7*: The Alley. *Scene 8*: Onstage. *Scene 9*: The Alley. *Scene 10*: Backstage. *Scene 11*: Mrs. Fay's Kitchen. *Scene 12*: On the Street.

Act 2, Scene 1: Backstage. *Scene 2*: Onstage. *Scene 3*: Stage Right Wing. *Scene 4*: Onstage. *Scene 5*: Backstage. *Scene 6*: Backstage. *Scene 7*: The Alley. *Scene 8*: Satin's Room. *Scene 9*: Onstage. *Scene 10*: Backstage. *Scene 11*: Onstage.

ACT 1

Prologue

"This Must Be the Place"
Company

Scene 2

"Cadava"
J. Faye, S. Kaye, S. Murray

Scene 4

"A Sweet Thing Like Me"
L. Jones, Earle's Pearls

Scene 5

"I Get Myself Out"
S. Kaye

Scene 6

"My Daddy Always Taught Me to Share"
B. Vereen

Scene 7

"All Things to One Man"
L. Jones

Scene 8

"The Line"
B. Vereen, Earle's Pearls

Scene 9

"Katie My Love"
T. Nolen

Scene 10

"The Grind"
S. Kaye, Company

"Yes, Ma'am"
T. Nolen

Scene 11

"Why, Mama, Why"
L. Jones, B. Vereen

Scene 12

"This Crazy Place"
B. Vereen, Company

ACT 2

Scene 1

"From the Ankles Down"

B. Vereen, Earle's Pearls

"Who Is He?"

L. Jones

"Never Put It in Writing"

S. Kaye

"I Talk, You Talk"

T. Nolen

Scene 4

"Timing"

S. Murray, J. Faye

Scene 5

"These Eyes of Mine"

C. Woods, Company

Scene 6

"New Man"

B. Vereen

(*Dance Music Arranged by* Gordon Lowry Harrell.)

Scene 8

"Down"

T. Nolen

Scene 9

"A Century of Progress"

B. Vereen, L. Jones, Earle's Pearls

Scene 11

Finale

Company

BIG RIVER: The Adventures of Huckleberry Finn

1985.06

A Musical in Two Acts, 18 Scenes. Book by William Hauptman. Adapted from the novel "The Adventures of Huckleberry Finn" by Mark Twain. Music and lyrics by Roger Miller. Production staged by Des McAnuff. Scenery by Heidi Landesman. Costumes by Patricia McGourty. Lighting by Richard Riddell. Sound by Otts Munderloh. Musical supervision by Daniel Troob. Orchestrations by Steven Margoshes and Danny Troob. Dance and incidental music by John Richard Lewis. Musical direction and vocal arrangements by Linda Twine. Choreography by Janet Watson. Stage movement and fights by B. H. Barry. Originally produced by The American Repertory Theatre, Cambridge, Massachusetts (Robert Brustein, Artistic director); subsequently produced by The LaJolla Playhouse, LaJolla, California (Des McAnuff, Artistic director). Associate producers, Arthur Katz, Emily Landau, Frederic H. Mayerson, TM Productions, Inc. Produced by Rocco Landesman, Heidi Landesman, Rick Steiner, M. Anthony Fisher and Dodger Productions. Opened 25 April 1985 at the Eugene O'Neill Theatre and closed 20 September 1987 after 1005 performances.

CAST (in order of appearance): *In St. Petersburg, and later on the Illinois shore and Jackson's Island*: *Mark Twain*: GORDON CONNELL. *Huckleberry Finn*: DANIEL H. JENKINS. *Widow Douglas*: Susan Browning. *Miss Watson*: Evalyn Baron. *Jim*: RON RICHARDSON. *Tom Sawyer*: John Short. *Ben Rogers*: William Youmans. *Jo Harper*: Andi Henig. *Simon*: Aramis Estevez. *Dick*: Michael Brian. *Pap Finn*: John Goodman. *Judge Thatcher*: Ralph Byers. *Woman in Shanty*: Evalyn Baron.

On the River, south of St. Louis: *Slaves and Overseers on a Flatboat*: Carol Dennis, Elmore James, Jennifer Leigh Warren, Franz Jones, Aramis Estevez, John Goodman, William Youmans, Michael Brian.

On the River, near Cairo, Illinois: *Three Men on a Skiff*: Ralph Byers, Reathel Bean, Elmore James.

On the Riverbank in Kentucky: *The King*: BOB GUNTON. *The Duke*: RENE AUBERJONOIS. *Soldiers and Citizens*: The Company.

In Bricktown, Arkansas: *Hank*: William Youmans. *Andy*: Michael Brian. *Lafe*: Reathel Bean. *Townspeople*: The Company.

In Hillsboro, Arkansas: *A Young Fool*: William Youmans. *Mary Jane Wilkes*: PATTI COHENOUR. *Susan Wilkes*: Peggy Harmon. *Joanna Wilkes*, a hare-lip: Andi Henig. *Bill*, a servant: Franz Jones. *Counselor Robinson*: Reathel Bean. *Alice*, their slave: Carol Dennis. *Alice's daughter*: Jennifer Leigh Warren. *Mourners*: The Company. *Sheriff Bell*: John Goodman. *Harvey Wilkes*: Ralph Byers. *Man in the Crowd*: Michael Brian. *Harmonia Player*: Evalyn Baron. *Mourners and Mob*: The Company.

On a Farm near Hilsboro: *Sally Phelps*: Susan Browning. *Silas Phelps*: Ralph Byers. *Doctor*: Gordon Connell. *Hired Hands*: Reathel Bean, Michael Brian, John Goodman.

The action takes place along the Missippi River Valley, sometime in the 1840's.

Act 1, Scene 1: The Widow Douglas' home in St. Petersburg, Missouri. *Scene 2*: A Cave by the River. *Scene 3*: The Widow Douglas' home. *Scene 4*: A Cabin on the Illinois shore. *Scene 5*: The Cabin; Jackson's Island. *Scene 6*: A Cabin on the Missouri shore; a Raft on the River. *Scene 7*: On the Raft in the moonlight, approaching Cairo, Illinois. *Scene 8*: On the Riverbank in Kentucky; on the Raft downriver.

Act 2, Scene 1: On the Raft in Tennessee. *Scene 2*: In Bricktown, Arkansas. *Scene 3*: On the Raft in a nearby cove. *Scene 4*: In Hillsboro, Arkansas; the Wilkes' Farm near Hillsboro. *Scene 5*: Next day at the Farm. *Scene 6*: The Farm; the Cemetery. *Scene 7*: To the Shore and the Raft. *Scene 8*: A Country Road; the Phelps Farm near Hillsboro. *Scene 9*: The Phelps Farm, that night; the Raft. *Scene 10*: The Phelps Farm.

ACT 1

Scene 1

"Do You Want to Go to Heaven"

The Company

Scene 2

"The Boys"

J. Short, the Gang

"Waiting for the Light to Shine"

D. H. Jenkins

Scene 4

"Guv'ment"

J. Goodman

Scene 5

"Hand for the Hog"

J. Short

"I Huckleberry Me"

D. H. Jenkins

Scene 6

"Muddy Water"

R. Richardson, D. H. Jenkins

Scene 7

"Crossing Over"

Slaves, Overseer

"River in the Rain"

D. H. Jenkins, R. Richardson

Scene 8

"When the Sun Goes Down in the South"

R. Auberjonois, B. Gunton, D. H. Jenkins

ACT 2

Scene 2

"The Royal Nonesuch"

R. Auberjonois, Company

Scene 3

"Worlds Apart"

R. Richardson, D. H. Jenkins

Scene 4

"Arkansas"

W. Youmans

"How Blest We Are"

J. L. Warren, Company

"You Ought To Be Here With Me"

P. Cohenour, P. Harmon, A. Henig

Scene 5

"How Blest We Are" (reprise)

C. Dennis

"Leaving's Not the Only Way to Go"

P. Cohenour, R. Richardson, D. H. Jenkins

Scene 7

"Waiting for the Light to Shine" (reprise)

D. H. Jenkins

Scene 8

"Free at Last"

R. Richardson

Scene 10

"River in the Rain" (reprise)

D. H. Jenkins, R. Richardson

"Muddy Water" (reprise)

The Company

1985–1986 SEASON

Betty Buckley (left) in DROOD
Martha Swope/TimePix

1985–1986 SEASON

1985.07 TANGO ARGENTINO

A Dance Revue in Two Acts. Conceived and directed by Claudio Segovia, Héctor Orezzoli. Choreography by Juan Carlos Copes. Musical directors, José Libertella, Luis Stazo, Osvaldo Berlingieri. Scenery and costumes by Héctor Orezzoli, Claudio Segovia. Originally commissioned by the Festival d'Automne, Paris. Produced by Mel Howard and Donald K. Donald. Opened 25 June 1985 at the New York City Center and closed 30 June 1985 after 7 performances; re-opened 9 October 1985 at the Mark Hellinger Theater and closed 30 March 1986 after 199 performances. Total: 206 performances.

CAST: *Singers*: Raúl Lavié, Jovita Luna, Elba Berón, Alba Solís.
Dancers: Naanim Timoyko (soloist), Juan Carlos Copes, María Nieves, Nélida and Nelson, Gloria and Eduardo, Mayoral and Elsa María, Virulazo and Elvira, The Dinzels (Gloria, Rodolfo), Maria and Carlos Rivarola.
Musicians: *Sexteto Mayor*: José Libertella (bandoneón); Luis Stazo (bandoneón); Mario Abramovich (violin); Eduardo Walczak (violin); Oscar Palermo (piano); Osvaldo Aulicino (bass). And: Osvaldo Berlingieri (piano); Oscar Ruben Gonzalez (bandoneón, flute); Rodolfo Fernandez (violin); Juan Schiaffino (violin); Dino Carlos Quarleri (violoncello); Lisandro Adrover (bandoneón).

ACT 1[1]

"Quejas de Bandoneon"
(*Music by* J. de Dios Filiberto.)

"El Apache Argentino"
(*Music by* M. Aróztegui, A. Mathón.)
Ballet
Two thugs entwine and dance the tango.

"El Esquinazo"
(*Music by* A. Villoldo.)
Ballet
Couples of "outsiders" dance the "milonga."

"Milonga del Tiempo Heroico"
(*Music by* F. Canaro.)
J. C. Copes, M. Nieves

"La Puñalada"
(*Music by* P. Castellanos, E. C. Flores.)
O. Berlingieri, Orchestra

"La Morocha"
(*Music by* E. Saborido, A. Villoldo.)
Gloria, M. Rivarola
Two young girls dance the tango "discreetly."

"El Choclo"
(*Music and Lyrics by* A. Villoldo, E. S. Discépolo.)
E. Berón
"With this tango, the tango was born and, weeping, fled the mud, searching for the sky . . . "

"La Cumparsita"
(*Music by* G. H. Matos Rodriguez.)
M. Rivarola, C. Rivarola
European dance hall

"Mi Noche Triste"
(*Music and Lyrics by* S. Castriotta, P. Contursi.)
R. Lavié
For me there is no consolation and that's why I get drunk, to forget our love.

"Orgullo Criollo"
(*Music by* J. DeCaro, P. Laurenz.)
Virulazo, Elvira
Choreography: Virulazo.

"De Mi Barrio"
(*Music and Lyrics by* R. Goyeneche.)
J. Luna

"Bandoneones"
J. Libertella, L. Stazo, L. Adrover, O. R. González

"Milonguita"
The story of the young girl of the barrio who, seduced by a ruffian, follows the road of her ruin.

"Milonguita"
(*Music by* E. Delfino, S. Linning.)

"Divina"
(Music by J. Mora, J. de la Calle.)

"Melenita de Oro"
(*Music by* E. Delfino, S. Linning.)

"Re-fa-si"
(*Music by* E. Delfino.)
Milonguita: N. Timoyko. *The Ruffian*: J. C. Copes. *The Ruffian's Accomplice*: Nélida. *The Bridegroom*: Nelson. *The Cabaret's Customers*: Eduardo, Mayoral, C. Rivarola. *The Prostitutes*: Gloria, E. Maria, G. Dinzel, M. Rivarola.

"Nostalgias"
(*Music by* J. C. Cobian, E. Cadícamo.)
Sexteto Mayor
Bandoneon, groan your gray tando, perhaps you also suffer from love.

"Cuesta Abajo"
(Music and Lyrics by Gardel, Le Pera.)
R. Lavié
I carry my shame everywhere, shame to have been and pain of being no more.

"El Entrerriano"
(*Music by* R. Mendizabal.)
G. Dinzel, R. Dinzel.
Choreography: R. Dinzel.

"Canaro en Paris"
(*Music by* Scarpino, Caldarella.)
O. Berlingieri, Orchestra

"Taquito Militar"
(*Music by* M. Mores.)
J. C. Copes, M. Nieves, Nélida and Nelson, Gloria and Eduardo

ACT 2

"Milongueando en El 40"
(*Music by* Armando Pontier.)
Gloria and Eduardo
Choreography: Eduardo.

"Uno"
(*Music and Lyrics by* E. S. Discépolo, M. Mores.)
A. Solís

---

[1]The program which appears below is from the Broadway engagement at the Mark Hellinger. The running order and selection of music was subject to change during the run and subsequent national tour. The City Center engagement was produced in association with the 55th Street Dance Theatre Foundation, Inc. The program and cast changes appear below.

Appearing at City Center, and not at the Mark Hellinger:
Singers: Roberto Goyeneche, María Graña. *Added for Broadway*: Alba Solís. *Dancers*: Virulazo and Elvira. *Musicians*: unchanged.
Music dropped after City Center engagement:

"Cancion Desesperada"
(*Music and Lyrics by* E. S. Discépolo.)
M. Graña
I am a desperate song.

"Caseron de Tejas"
(*Music and Lyrics by* S. Piana, C. Castillo.)/

"Sin Palabras"
(*Music and Lyrics by* M. Mores, E. S. Discépolo.)
M. Graña
The piano music will drift in from the dimly lit room, to sing the pure tenderness of the waltz.

"Malena"
(*Music and Lyrics by* L. Demare, C. Castillo.)
R. Goyeneche
Malena grieves like a bandoneón.

"El Motivo"
(*Music and Lyrics by* J. C. Cobián, P. Contursi.)
R. Goyeneche
The nostalgia of those days of pleasure and love has lost its flavor, today it invites tears.

One is so alone with her pain, one is so blind in her sorrow.

"La Ultima Curda"

(*Music and Lyrics by* A. Troilo, C. Castillo.)
A. Solís

Life is an absurd wound.

"La Yumba"

(*Music by* O. Pugliese.)
Mayoral, E. María
Choreography: Mayoral.

"Nunca Tuvo Novio"

(*Music and Lyrics by* E. Cadícamo, A. Bardi.)
R. Lavié, O. Berlingieri, Orchestra

Poor and alone, you are without illusion, without faith.

"Jealousy" [Celos]

(*Music by* J. Gade.)
Nélida and Nelson
Choreography: Nélida and Nelson.

"Desencuentro"

(*Music and Lyrics by* A. Troilo, C. Castillo.)
E. Berón

Your luck is so bad that when you want to put the last bullet in your pistol in your head—it won't fire.

"Tanguera"

(*Music by* M. Mores)
Orchestra

"Verano Porteño"

(*Music by* Astor Piazzolla.)
J. C. Copes, M. Nieves

"Balada Para Mi Muerte"

(*Music and Lyrics by* Astor Piazzolla and H. Ferrer.)
J. Luna

I'll toss the cloak of dawn around my shoulders, my next to last whiskey will age in its glass, my death, in love, will arrive on a tango step, and I will die precisely at six o'clock.

"Adios Nonino"

(*Music by* Astor Piazzolla.)
Sexteto Mayor

"Danzarin"

(*Music by* J. Plaza.)

"Quejas de Bandoneon"

(*Music by* J. de Dios Filiberto.)
Ballet

The dance floor fills with the sound of the orchestra, and under the spotlights, the marionettes embrace.

1985.08 SINGIN' IN THE RAIN

A Musical in Two Acts, 17 Scenes. Adaptation (book) by Betty Comden and Adolph Green. Based on their screenplay for the MGM film of the same name. Music by Nacio Herb Brown. Lyrics by Arthur Freed. Directed and choreographed by Twyla Tharp with some original choreography by Gene Kelly and Stanley Donen. Scenery by Santo Loquasto. Costumes by Ann Roth. Lighting by Jennifer Tipton. Sound by Sound Associates. Film sequences by Gordon Willis. Music supervision and arrangements by Stanley Lebowsky. Music director, Robert Billig. Orchestrations by Larry Wilcox. Associate Producer, Eugene V. Wolsk. Produced by Maurice Rosenfield, Lois F. Rosenfield, and Cindy Pritzker, Inc. Opened 2 July 1985 at the Gershwin Theatre and closed 18 May 1986 after 367 performances.

CAST (in order of appearance): *Dora Bailey*: Melinda Gilb. *Cosmo Brown*: PETER SLUTSKER. *Lina Lamont*: FAYE GRANT. *Don Lockwood*: DON CORREIA. *R. F. Simpson*: HANSFORD ROWE. *Roscoe Dexter*: RICHARD FANCY. *Rod*: Robert Radford. *Kathy Selden*: MARY D'ARCY. *Sid Phillips*: Martin Van Treuren. *Phoebe Dinsmore*: Jacque Dean. *Diction Coach*: Austin Colyer. *Sound Engineer*: John Spalla. *Ticket Taker*: Martin Van Treuren. *A Warner Brother*: Austin Colyer. *Zelda Zanders*: Mary Ann Kellogg.

Ensemble: Ray Benson, John Carrafa, Richard Colton, Austin Colyer, Jacqe Dean, Diane Duncan, Yvonne Dutton, Craig Frawley, Melinda Gilb, Katie Glasner, Barbara Hoon, David-Michael Johnson, Mary Ann Kellogg, Raymond Kurshals, Alison Mann, Barbara Moroz, Kevin O'Day, Robert Radford, Tom Rawe, Gene Sager, John Spalla, Amy Spencer, Cynthia Thole, Martin Van Treuren, Shelley Washington, Laurie Williamson. *Swings*: Cheri Butcher, Brad Moranz, David Askler.

Cast in Film Sequences: *"The Royal Rascal"*: *Philippe*: D. Correia. *Jeanette*: F. Grant. *Enemies of the King*: R. Benson, C. Frawley, G. Sager, M. Van Treuren.

"Talking Picture Demonstration": *Man on Screen*: J. Spalla.

"The Dueling Cavalier" and "The Dancing Cavalier": *Yvonne*: F. Grant. *Lady-in-Waiting*: C. Thole. *Ladies of the Court*: D. Duncan, A. Mann, B. Moroz. *Pierre*: D. Correia. *Manservant*: G. Sager. *Villain*: M. Van Treuren.

The action takes place in Hollywood in the 1920's.

Act 1, Scene 1: The Premiere of "The Royal Rascal." Grauman's Chinese Theatre, September, 1927. *Scene 2*: Altoona, Pennsylvania—a vaudeville theatre, ten years earlier. *Scene 3*: Grauman's Chinese Theatre, onstage and backstage, at the premiere. *Scene 4*: Hollywood Boulevard, later that evening. *Scene 5*: The Coconut Grove party after the premiere. *Scene 6*: The Studios of Monumental Pictures. Silent Stage, 7 October, 1927. *Scene 7*: Shooting "The Duelling Cavalier," a silent film. *Scene 8*: An empty soundstage. *Scene 9*: Diction lessons. *Scene 10*: Shooting "The Duelling Cavalier" as a talking picture. *Scene 11*: Conversion of "The Duelling Cavalier" to a Musical. The Glendale Theatre, sneak preview of "The Dueling Cavalier" as a talkie, January 1928. *Scene 12*: Don's home, later that evening. *Scene 13*: A street near Kathy's house.

Act 2, Scene 1: Filming musical numbers at Warner Brothers Studio. *Scene 2*: Monumental Pictures' recording studio. (a.) The next day. (b.) Later that week. *Scene 3*: Title production number in "The Dancing Cavalier." *Scene 4*: Grauman's Chinese Theatre, the premiere of "The Dancing Cavalier."

ACT 1[2]

Scene 2

"Fit as a Fiddle"[3]

D. Correia, P. Slutsker
(*Music and Lyrics by* Arthur Freed, Al Hoffman, Al Goodhart.)

Scene 4

"Beautiful Girl" (from *GOING HOLLYWOOD* film)

D. Correia, Fans

Scene 5

"I've Got a Feelin' You're Foolin'" (from *BROADWAY MELODY OF 1936* film)

M. D'Arcy, Coconut Grove Coquettes

Scene 6

"Make 'Em Laugh"

P. Slutsker

"Hub Bub"

P. Slutsker, Studio Stage Hands
(*Music by* Stanley Lebowsky.)
Studio Stage Hands: J. Carrafa, R. Colton, R. Kurshals, K. O'Day, R. Radford, T. Rawe.

Scene 8

"You Are My Lucky Star" (from *BROADWAY MELODY OF 1936* film)

D. Correia, M. D'Arcy

Scene 9

"Moses Supposes"[4]

D. Correia, P. Slutsker
(*Music by* Roger Edens. *Lyrics by* Betty Comden and Adolph Green.)

Scene 12

"Good Mornin'"[5] (from *BABES IN ARMS* film)

D. Correia, M. D'Arcy, P. Slutsker

Scene 13

"Singin' in the Rain"[6] (from *HOLLYWOOD REVUE OF 1929* film)

D. Correia

---

[2]All of the songs listed below appeared in the original MGM film, with the exception of "Hub Bub," "Rag Doll," "Temptation," "Takin' Miss Mary to the Ball," "Love Is Where You Find It," and "Blue Prelude" which were added for this production. A substantially revised production (Two Acts, 19 Scenes) was mounted for a national tour under the direction of Lawrence Kasha, choreography by Peter Gennaro, sets by Peter Wolf, costumes by Robert Fletcher, lighting by Thomas Skelton. All of the song additions which appear in the note above were dropped. Added to Act 2, Scene 3 was:

"What's Wrong with Me?" (from *THE KISSING BANDIT* film)

Jennifer Smith (Lina Lamont)
(*Music by* Nacio Herb Brown. *Lyrics by* Edward Heyman.)

[3]As choreographed by Gene Kelly and Stanley Donen in the film.
[4]As choreographed by Gene Kelly and Stanley Donen in the film.
[5]As choreographed by Gene Kelly and Stanley Donen in the film.
[6]As choreographed by Gene Kelly and Stanley Donen in the film.

ACT 2

Scene 1

"(The) Wedding of the Painted Doll" (from *BROADWAY MELODY* film)

D. Duncan, Y. Dutton, K. Glasner, K. O'Day, A. Spencer, C. Thole

"Rag Doll"

R. Colton, B. Hoon, R. Kurshals

"Temptation" (from *GOING HOLLYWOOD* film)

M. Gilb

Dancers: M. A. Kellogg, R. Radford, S. Washington.

"Takin' Miss Mary to the Ball" (from *ON AN ISLAND WITH YOU* film)

(*Lyrics by* Edward Heyman.) R. Benson, A. Mann

Dancing Horse: J. Carrafa, T. Rawe.

"Love Is Where You Find It" (from *THE KISSING BANDIT* film)

(*Lyrics by* Earl Brent.) Ensemble

Scene 2

"Would You?" (from *SAN FRANCISCO* film)

M. D'Arcy

Scene 3

"Broadway Rhythm" (from *BROADWAY MELODY OF 1936* film)

The Company

"Blue Prelude"

The Company

(*Music and Lyrics by* Joe Bishop and Gordon Jenkins.)

Court at Frolic: R. Benson, J. Carraf, R. Colton, K. Glasner, B. Hoon, M. A. Kellogg, R. Kurshals, R. Radford, T. Rawe, A. Spencer, C. Thole, S. Washington. *Pierre*: D. Correia. *Manservant*: G. Sager. *Villain*: M. Van Treuren. *Ladies of the Court*: D. Duncan, A. Mann, B. Moroz. *Apache Dancers*: J. Carrafa, R. Colton, Y. Dutton, K. Glasner, B. Hoon, M. A. Kellogg, R. Kurshals, K. O'Day, T. Rawe, A. Spencer. *Chanteuse*: L. Williamson. *Danseuse*: S. Washington. *Savate Fighters*: R. Benson, R. Kurshals. *Peasants*: A. Colyer, J. Dean, C. Frawley, M. Gilb, D. Johnson, J. Spalla.

Scene 4

"Would You?" (reprise)

M. D'Arcy

"You Are My Lucky Star" (reprise)

D. Correia, M. D'Arcy, Company

"Singin' in the Rain" (reprise)

The Company

1985.09 THE STUDENT PRINCE

A Revival of the Operetta in Three Acts, a Prologue and 4 Scenes[7]. Music by Sigmund Romberg. Book and lyrics by Dorothy Donnelly. (Based on the play "Old Heidelberg" by Rudolf Bleichmann, adapted from "Alt-Heidelberg" by Wilhelm Meyer-Förster.) Book adaptation by Hugh Wheeler. Conducted by Paul Gemignani. Directed by Jack Hofsis. Stage director, Christian Smith. Scenery designed by David Jenkins Costumes designed by Patton Campbell. Lighting designed by Gilbert V. Hemsley, Jr. Choreography by Donald Saddler. Chorus master, Joseph Colaneri. Produced by the New York City Opera. Opened 5 July 1985 at the New York State Theatre and closed 21 July 1985 after 9 performances in repertory.

CAST (in order of their appearance): *Lackeys*: Edward Zimmerman, Louis Perry, George Wyman, Neil Eddinger. *Dr. Engel*, the Prince's Tutor: ADIB FAZAH. *Count von Mark*: DAVID RAE SMITH. *Secretaries*: Glenn Rowen, Jonathan Guss. *Prince Karl Franz*: JERRY HADLEY. *Lutz*, valet to the Prince: JACK HARROLD. *Gretchen*, Maid at the Inn: CAROL SPARROW. *Ruder*: Joseph McKee. *Nicholas*: Douglas Hamilton. *Toni*, a waiter: James Billings. *Hubert*: William Ledbetter. *Detlef*, a student leader: Stephen O'Mara. *von Asterberg*, another student leader: Robert Brubaker. *Lucas*, another student leader: Wilbur Pauley. *Freshman*: Louis Perry. *Kathie*, niece of Ruder: ELIZABETH HYNES. *Girls*: Madeleine Mines, Paula Hostetter, Beth Pensiero. *Grand Duchess Anastasia*: MURIEL COSTA-GREENSPON. *Princess Margaret*, fiancée of Prince Karl Franz: CYNTHIA ROSE. *Captain Tarnitz*: Cris Groenendaal. *Countess Leydon*, lady-in-waiting to the Princess: Jane Shaulis. *Huzzars*: George Wyman, Glenn Rowan, Neil Eddinger, Gregory Moore. *Friends of the Huzzars*: Madeliene Mines, Paula Hostetter, Beth Pensiero, Jill Bosworth. *Ensemble*: New York City Opera Chorus.

[7]First produced in New York as "The Student Prince in Heidelberg" 2 December 1924 at the Jolson Theatre for 608 performances. For Synopsis of Scenes and Musical Numbers, see 1980 revival.

1985.10 THE MIKADO, or The Town of Titipu

A Revival of the Comic Opera in Two Acts[8]. Libretto by William S. Gilbert. Music by Arthur Sullivan. Directed by Lofti Mansouri. Stage director, Christian Smith. Choreography by Patricia Birch. Scenery and costumes designed by Thierry Bosquet. Lighting designed by John Gleason. Conducted by David Stahl. Chorus master, Jospeh Colaneri. Produced by the New York City Opera. Opened 13 July 1985 (matinee) at the New York State Theatre and closed 16 October 1985 after 12 performances in repertory.

CAST (in order of appearance): *Nanki-Poo*, his son, disguised as a wandering minstrel in love with Yum-Yum: DAVID EISLER. *Pish-Tush*, a Noble Lord: David Hamilton. *Pooh-Bah*, Lord High Everything Else: JOSEPH McKEE. *Ko-Ko*, Lord High Executioner of Titipu: JACK HARROLD. *Yum-Yum, Pitti-Sing, Peep-Bo*, three sisters, wards of Ko-Ko: CLAUDETTE PETERSON, DIANNE IAUCO, CAROL SPARROW. *Katisha*: JOYCE CASTLE. *The Mikado of Japan*: WILLIAM WILDERMANN. *Chorus of School Girls, Nobles, Guards and Coolies*: New York City Opera Chorus.

1985.11 THE MERRY WIDOW

A Revival of the Operetta in Three Acts and a Prologue[9]. Music by Franz Lehár. Original German book (Die Lustige Witwe) and lyrics by Victor Léon and Leo Stein after "L'Attaché d'Ambassade" by Henri Meilhac. English version by Adrian Ross. Directed by Ronald Bentley. Conducted by Imre Pallo. Set designers, Helen Pond and Herbert Senn. Costume designer, Suzanne Mess. Lighting designer, Gilbert V. Hemsley, Jr. Chorus master, Joseph Colaneri. Produced by the New York City Opera Company. Opened 30 August 1985 at the New York State Theatre and closed 3 November 1985 after 12 performances in repertory.

CAST (in order of appearance): *Baron Popoff*: JACK HARROLD. *Natalie*: Susanne Marsee. *General Novikovich*: Douglas Perry. *Counsellor Khadja*: William Ledbetter. *Marquis de Cascada*: William Parcher. *Sylviane*: Ruth Golden. *M. de St. Brioche*: JOHN LANKSTON. *Olga*: Jane Bunnell. *Vicomte Camille de Jolidon*: MARK THOMSEN. *Nisch*: James Billings. *Sonia*: LEIGH MUNRO. *Count Danilo*: ALAN TITUS. *Head Waiter*: Mervin Crook. *Zozo*: Ivy Austin. *Lolo*: Joan Mirabella. *Dodo*: Esperanza Galan. *Jou-Jou*: Candace Itow. *Frou-Frou*: Victoria Rinaldi. *Clo-Clo*: Victoria Rinaldi. *Margot*: Jean Barber. *Chorus of Marsovian and Parisian Society, Dancers, Servants and Waiters*: New York City Opera Chorus.

1985.12 SONG & DANCE

A Musical in Two Acts. Music by Andrew Lloyd Webber. Lyrics by Don Black. American adaptation, additional lyrics and direction by Richard Maltby, Jr. Choreography by Peter Martins. Entire production supervised by Richard Maltby, Jr. and Peter Martins. Orchestrations by Andrew Lloyd Wbber and David Cullen. Musical advisor, David Caddick. Musical supervision and direction, John Mauceri. Associate tap choreographer, Gregg Burge. Settings by Robin Wagner. Costumes by Willa Kim. Lighting by Jules Fisher. Sound by Martin Levan. Executive producers, R. Tyler Gatchell, Jr., Peter Neufeld. A Cameron Mackintosh/Shubert Organization Production. Produced by Cameron Mackintosh, Inc., The Shubert Organization, F. W. M. Producing Group by arrangement with The Really Useful Company, (Inc). Opened 18 September 1985 at the Royale Theater and closed 8 November 1986 after 474 performances.

CAST: *Act 1*: *Emma*: BERNADETTE PETERS.

The action takes place at the present time in New York and Los Angeles.

ACT 1: SONG

"Take That Look Off Your Face"

[8]First presented in New York 20 July, 10-29 August 1885 at the Union Square and People's Theatres for 22 performances. First authorized production presented 19 August 1885 at the Fifth Avenue Theatre by Richard D'Oyly Carte for 250 performances. For Synopsis of Scenes and Musical Numbers, see 19 August 1885 D'Oyly Carte production.

[9]Original New York production first presented 21 October 1907 at the New Amsterdam Theatre for 416 performances. For Synopsis of Scenes and Musical Numbers, see original 1907 production.

Interpolated into this production:

"Girls Were Made to Love and Kiss" (from PAGANINI)

(*Music by* Franz Lehar. *Original German Lyrics by* Paul Knepler and Bela Jenbach. *English Lyrics by* A. P. Herbert.)

"Let Me Finish"
"So Much to Do in New York"
"First Letter Home"
"English Girls"
"Capped Teeth and Caesar Salad"
"You Made Me Think You Were in Love"
"So Much to Do in New York" (reprise)
"Second Letter Home"
"Unexpected Song"
"Come Back with the Same Look in Your Eyes"
"Take That Look Off Your Face" (reprise)
"Tell Me on a Sunday"
"I Love New York"
"So Much to Do in New York" (reprise)
"Married Men"
"Third Letter Home"
"Let Me Finish" (reprise)
"What Have I Done?"
Finale (Take That Look Off Your Face)

ACT 2: DANCE

CAST: *Act 2*: *Joe*: CHRISTOPHER D'AMBOISE.
The Women: Charlotte d'Amboise, Denise Faye, Cynthia Onrubia, Mary Ellen Stuart. *The Men*: Gregg Burge, Gen Horiuchi, Gregory Mitchell, Scott Wise.
A city street: *Man from the streets*: Gregg Burge. *A street outside a disco*: *Woman in gold*: Mary Ellen Stuart. *Her Two Escorts*: Scott Wise, Gregory Mitchell. *A bar*: *Woman in blue*: Charlotte d'Amboise. A *Customer*: Gen Horiuchi. *Two Singles*: Cynthia Onrubia, Denise Faye. *Wall Street*: *Woman in Grey Flannel*: Cynthia Onrubia.

The action takes place at the present time in New York.

Scene 1: A New York subway station. *Scene 2*: The city. *Scene 3*: A street outside a disco. *Scene 4*: Billboards. *Scene 5*: A bar. *Scene 6*: A city street. *Scene 7*: Wall Street. *Scene 8*: A park. *Scene 9*: Fifth Avenue. *Scene 10*: A department store fashion show. *Scene 11*: New York.

1985.13 KISMET

A Revival of the Musical Play (Musical Arabian Night) in Two Acts, 15 Scenes[10]. Book by Charles Lederer and Luther Davis. Based on the play of the same name by Edward Knoblock. Music based on themes by Alexander Borodin. Musical adaptation and lyrics by Robert Wright and George Forrest. Directed by Frank Corsaro. Conducted by Scott Bergeson. Set and costume designer, Lawrence Miller. Lighting designer, Mark W. Stanley. Chorus master, Joseph Colaneri. Produced by the New York City Opera. Opened 3 October 1985 at the New York State Theatre and closed 17 November 1985 after 13 performances in repertory.

CAST (in order appearance): *Imam of The Mosque*: James Clark. *Silk Dancers*: Ashley Janeway, Jean Barber, Malcolm Grant, Terry Lacy. *Muezzins*: Louis Perry, Glenn Rowen, Bernard Waters, George Wyman. *Beggars*: Don Yule, Robert Brubaker. *Dervishes*: Vasilis Iracledes, Richard Smith. *Omar*: JAMES BILLINGS. *A Public Poet, later called Hajj*: THEODORE BAERG. *Marsinah*, His Daughter: MICHEL McBRIDE. *Businessman*: William Ledbetter. *Hassan-Ben*: Ralph Bassett. *Jawan*: JOHN LANKSTON. *Bangle Man*: James Clark. *Silk Merchants*: Louis Perry, Bernard Waters. *Brave Merchant*: Harris Davis. *Young Women*: Madeleine Mines, Mary Ann Rydzeski. *Pearl Merchant*: William Ledbetter. *Slave Merchant*: Mervin Crook. *Informer*: William Ledbetter. *Policemen*: Ralph Bassett, Robert Brubaker. *Chief of Police*: Don Yule. *Wazir of Police*: RICHARD McKEE. *Wazir's Guards*: Jeff Davis, Eric Miller, Donald R. Richardson, Elliot Santiago, Frank Sollito. *Slave Girls*: Jean Barber, Stephanie Godino, Ashley Janeway. *Harem Girl*: Deborah Saverance. *Lalume*: JOYCE CASTLE. *Princesses of Ababu*: Shannon Bresnahan, Joan Mirabella, Victoria Rinaldi. *The Caliph*: MARK THOMSEN. *Widow Yussef*: Jane Shaulis. *Ayah to Lalume*: Mary Ann Rydzeski. *Princess Zubbediya of Damascus*: Esperanza Galan. *Ayah to Zubbediya*: Jane Shaulis. *Princess Samaris of Bangalore*: Candace Itow. *Prosecutor*: James Clark. *Spies*: Ralph Bassett, Robert Brubaker, William Ledbetter. *Guest*: Louis Perry. *Ensemble*: New York City Opera Chorus.

[10]Originally produced in New York 3 December 1953 at the Ziegfeld Theatre for 583 performances. For Synopsis of Scenes and Musical numbers, see original 1953 production.

1985.14 LA GATTA CENERENTOLA

Favola in musica (a fable in music) in Three Acts [Cinderella the Cat], in Italian. Book, music and lyrics by Roberto De Simone. Directed by Roberto de Simone. Scenery by Mauro Carosi. Costumes by Odette Nicoletti. Musical director, Renato Piemontese. Produced by the Italian Government with special assistance from the America-Italy Society in celebration of the City of New York's Italian Cultural Month. Opened 19 October 1985 at the Vivian Beaumont Theatre and closed 20 October 1985 after 2 performances.

CAST (from the Ente Teatro Cronaca of Naples): *Jesce sole*: Antonella D'Agostino. *La donna della cabala*: Ofelia De Simone. *La zingara*: Ofelia De Simone. *Il canto dei turchi*: Virgilio Villani. *Bene mio*: Virgilio Villani. *La voce del rosario*: Virgilio Villani. *Asso di bastoni*: Virgilio Villani. *Il ballo di S. Giovanni*: Lello Giulivo, Giuseppe De Vittorio. *La gatta cenerentola*: VALERIA BAIANO. *La matrigna*: RINO MARCELLI. *La pettinatrice* (a door-to-door Neapolitan hair-dresser): Isa Danielli. *La sorella Patrizia*: Giuseppe De Vittorio. *La sarta orfana di madre*: Patrizia Spinosi. *Il monacello* (a magic Neapolitan figure): Giovanni Mauriello. *Cuccurucú*: Giovanni Mauriello. *Il femminella*: Giovanni Mauriello. *Vurria addeventare*: Gianni Lamagna. *La cameriere di Palazzo Reale*: Anna Incoronato, Patrizia Spinosi, Adria Mortari, Anna Spagnuolo, Antonella D'Agostino. *La voce castrata*: Gianfranco Mari. *Il militaire francese*: Gianfranco Mari. *Il militaire spagnuolo*: Lello Giulivo. *La canzone dei militari*: Luciano Catapano, Gianni Lamagna. *L'angoscia, la crisi e la violenza delle lavandaie*: Isa Danielli.

ACT 1[11]
"Jesce Sole"
"E' Nata"
"Villanella di Cenerentola"
"Canzoni dei Sette Mariti"
"Canzone delle Sei Sorelle"
"Duetto (mamma mamma che bella cosa)"
"Rosario"
"Canzone del Monacello"

ACT 2
"Villanella a Ballo (vurria addeventare)"
"Moresca"
"Madrigale"
"Tarantella (oi mamma ca mò vene)"

ACT 3
"Coro dei Soldati"
"1°Coro Delle Lavandaie"
"2°Coro Delle Lavandaie"
"Canzone della Zingara"
"Il Suicidio del Femminella"
"Jesce Sole"
"Scena Delle Ingiurie"
Finale

1985.15 MAYOR

A Musical in Two Acts, 19 Scenes[12]. Book by Warren Leight. Based on the book "Mayor" by Edward I. Koch. Music and lyrics by Charles Strouse. Directed by Jeffrey B. Moss. Choreography by Barbara Siman. Sets and costumes designed by Randy Barcelo. Lighting designed by Richard Winkler. Musical director and arranger, Michael Kosarin. Orchestrations by Christopher Bankey. Sound by Lewis Mead. Assistant choreographer, Laurie Brongo. Associate producer, Sam Crothers. Produced by Martin Richards, Jerry Kravat, Mary Lea Johnson with the New York Music Company. Opened 23 October 1985 at the Latin Quarter and closed 5 January 1986 after 70 performances. Total, including Off-Broadway run: 268 performances.

CAST (in alphabetical order): Douglas Bernstein, Marion J. Caffey, Nancy Giles, Ken Jennings, Ilene Kristen, Kathryn McAteer, John Sloman, Lenny Wolpe (as the Mayor).

The action takes place at the present time in New York City.

[11]No songs listed in program.List prepared from Italian cast recording.
[12]Originally produced in New York Off-Broadway 13 May 1985 at the Top of the Village Gate for 198 performances.

Act 1, Scene 1: Gracie Mansion. *Scene 2*: Midtown Street. *Scene 3*: City Hall. *Scene 4*: Street. *Scene 5*: Outside Third Avenue Tunnel. *Scene 6*: Limbo. *Scene 7*: An Office. *Scene 8*: Street.

Act 2, Scene 1: Central Park. *Scene 2*: Offices at City Hall. *Scene 3*: City Hall. *Scene 4*: On the Subway. *Scene 5*: Gracie Mansion—At a Mirror. *Scene 6*: Posh Grand Ballroom—Helmsley Palace Hotel. *Scene 7*: Street, outside the Helmsley Palace Hotel—Night. *Scene 8*: Gracie Mansion—the Mayor's Bedroom. *Scene 9*: Limbo. *Scene 10*: Mayor's Bedroom. *Scene 11*: Limbo.

ACT 1

Scene 1

"Mayor"

Mayor: L. Wolpe

Scene 2

"You Can Be a New Yorker Too!"

Businessman: J. Sloman. *Out of Towner*: D. Bernstein. *Bicycle Messenger*: M. J. Caffey. And Company.

Scene 3

Board of Estimate

Mayor: L. Wolpe. *Carol Bellamy*: K. McAteer. *Leona Helmsley*: I. Kristen. *Harrison J. Goldin*: D. Bernstein. *Security Guard*: M. J. Caffey.

"You're Not the Mayor"

Carol Bellamy: K. McAteer. *Security Guard*: M. J. Caffey. *Aide*: K. Jennings.

"Mayor" (reprise)

Mayor: L. Wolpe.

Scene 4

Critics

K. Jennings, M. J. Caffey, K. McAteer

"March of the Yuppies"

N. Giles, J. Sloman, D. Bernstein, Company

Scene 5

The Ribbon Cutting

"Hootspa"

Mayor: L. Wolpe. *John V. Lindsay*: J. Sloman. *Abe Beame*: K. Jennings.

Scene 6

Alternate Side

K. McAteer

Scene 7

"Coalition"

M. J. Caffey, I. Kristen, D. Bernstein

Scene 8

("Coalition" reprise)

M. J. Caffey, I. Kristen, D. Bernstein

"What You See Is What You Get"

Sue Simmons: N. Giles. *Mayor*: L. Wolpe. And Company.

ACT 2

Scene 1

In the Park

Company

"Ballad"

I. Kristen, J. Sloman

Scene 2

On the Telephone

Mayor: L. Wolpe. *Carol Bellamy*: K. McAteer.

Scene 3

"I Want to Be the Mayor"

Harrison J. Goldin: D. Bernstein.

Scene 4

Subway: "The Last 'I Love New York' Song"

Company

Scene 5

"Ballad" (reprise)

(*Lyrics by* Warren Leight.)

Mayor: L. Wolpe.

Scene 6

Testimonial Dinner: "Good Times"

Mayor: L. Wolpe. *John Cardinal O'Connor*: D. Bernstein. *Bess Myerson*: N. Giles. *Leona Helmsley*: I. Kristen. *Harry Helmsley*: J. Sloman. *David Rockefeller*: K. Jennings. *Waiter*: M. J. Caffey.

Scene 7

"We Are One" (I'll Never Leave You)

Homeless People: M. J. Caffey, K. McAteer. *Leona Helmsley*: I. Kristen. *Harry Helmsley*: J. Sloman.

Scene 8

"How'm I Doin'?"

Mayor: L. Wolpe. And Company.

Scene 10

"Mayor" (reprise)

Mayor: L. Wolpe.

Scene 11

"My City"

Company

1985.16

PIPINO IL BREVE

A Musical [Pippin the Short] in Three Acts, in Italian, performed with Puppets. Book, music and lyrics by Tony Cucchiara. Directed by Giuseppe DiMartino. Produced by the Italian Government with special assistance from the America-Italy Society in celebration of the City of New York's Italian Cultural Month. Opened 25 October 1985 at the Vivian Beaumont Theatre and closed 26 October 1985 after 2 performances.

CAST: *Pipino il Breve, Berta la piedona, Belisenda, Filippo, Falista, Marante, Belisario di Magonza, Bernardo di Chiaramonte, Morando de Ribera, Aquilone di Baviera, Lamberto, La lamentatricell cantastorie*: Teatro Stabile di Catania of Sicily.

MUSICAL NUMBERS[13]

"Figlia"

"Chilpericu III"

"Di Berta e Pipinu Cuntamu La Storia"

"La Partenza di L'Ambasceria"

"Figlia"

"La Me Ventura"

"U Corredu"

"Duetto d'Amore"

"Chistu Succedi da Mill'anni"

"Matruzza Mia"

"Viva Viva La Regina"

"Picchi' Chiangi Sta Beddra Rigina"

"Berta Filava"

"Viva Carlu Magnu"

1985.17

THE NEWS

A Musical in Two Acts. Story (Book) by Paul Schierhorn, David Rotenberg, R. Vincent Park. Music and lyrics by Paul Schierhorn. Directed by David Rotenberg. Choreography by Wesley Fata. Scenery by Jane Musky. Costumes by Richard Hornung. Lighting by Norman Coates. Sound by Gary Scott Peck/ATI. Conductor, John Rinehimer. (Musical) Arrangements by John Rinehimer, Paul Schierhorn. Supervisor, Orchestrator, John Rinehimer. Originally presented at the Burt Reynolds Jupiter Theatre (Karen Poindexter, Managing director). Associate producers, Patricia Bayer, Annette R. McDonald, Quentin H. McDonald. Produced by Zev Bufman, Kathleen Lindsey, Nicholas Neubauer, R. Vincent Park, Martin and Janice Barandes. Opened 7 November 1985 at the Helen Hayes Theatre and closed 9 November 1985 after 4 performances.

CAST (in order of appearance): *Reporter*: Cheryl Alexander. *Circulation Editor*: Frank Baier. *Executive Editor*: JEFF CONAWAY. *Killer*: ANTHONY CRIVELLO. *City Editor*: Michael Duff. *Feature Editor*: Jonathan S. Gerber. *Talk Show Host*: Anthony Hoylen. *Reporter*: Patrick Jude. *Girl*: LISA MICHAELIS. *Reporter*: Charles Pistone. *Sports Editor*: John Rinehimer. *Style Editor*: Peter Valentine. *Managing Editor*: Billy Ward.

[13]Taken from cast recording.

The action takes place in the City Room of a large metropolitan newspaper, the bedroom of a 15-year old girl, a one room apartment, and a city street.

ACT 1

"I Am the News"
J. Conaway, Company

"They Write the News"
J. Conaway

"Mirror, Mirror"
L. Michaelis

"Front Page Exposé"
J. Conaway, Reporters

"Dad"
L. Michaelis

"Hot Flashes" (I)
Reporters

"She's on File"
J. Conaway

"Super Singo"
J. Conaway, Reporters

"Dear Felicia"
J. Conaway, F. Baier

"Horoscope"
C. Alexander, P. Jude, C. Pistone, Band

"Hot Flashes" (II)
Band, Reporters

"Classifieds"/"Personals"
Band, Reporters, L. Michaelis, A. Crivello

"Wonderman"
L. Michaelis

"Shooting Stars"
A. Crivello

"What's the Angle"
Reporters, J. Conaway

"The Contest"
J. Conaway, Reporters, J. S. Gerber, Band

"Dear Editor"
A. Crivello

"Editorial"
J. Conaway, Reporters, A. Crivello, Band

ACT 2

"Hot Flashes" (Financial)
Band

"Talk to Me"
A. Crivello, L. Michaelis

"Pyramid Lead"
J. Conaway, Reporters

"Beautiful People"
J. Conaway, C. ALexander, A. Crivello, Reporters, Band

"Hot Flashes" (III)
Reporters, Band

"Sports"
Reporters, Band

"Open Letter"
J. Conaway, A. Crivello, Company

"Mirror, Mirror" (reprise)
L. Michaelis

"Ordinary, Extraordinary Day"
A. Crivello, L. Michaelis

"What's the Angle" (reprise)
Reporters, Band

"Violent Crime"
J. Conaway, L. Michaelis, Reporters

"What in the World"
P. Jude, Reporters, Band

"Acts of God" (Births, Death and the Weather)
Company

1985.18

THE MYSTERY OF EDWIN DROOD

A Musical in Two Acts, 12 Scenes[14]. Book, music and lyrics by Rupert Holmes. Suggested by the unfinished novel of the same name by Charles Dickens. Directed by Wilford Leach. Choreography by Graciela Daniele. Scenery by Bob Shaw. Costumes by Lindsay W. Davis. Lighting by Paul Gallo. Sound by Tom Morse. Magic lantern projections by James Cochrane. Orchestrations by Rupert Holmes. Musical direction by Michael Starobin. A New York Shakespeare Festival. Associate producer, Jason Steven Cohen. Opened 2 December 1985 at the Imperial Theatre and closed 16 May 1987 after 608 performances.

CAST[15] (in order of appearance): *Mayor Thomas Sapsea/Mr. William Cartwright, Your Chairman*: GEORGE ROSE. *Stage Manager and Barkeep/Mr. James Throttle*: Peter McRobbie. *John Jasper/Mr. Clive Paget*: HOWARD MCGILLIN. *The Reverend Crisparkle/Mr. Cedric Moncrieffe*: GEORGE N. MARTIN. *Edwin Drood/Miss Alice Nutting*: BETTY BUCKLEY. *Rosa Bud/Miss Deidre Peregrine*: PATTI COHENOUR. *Alice/Miss Isabel Yearsley*: Judy Kuhn. *Beatrice/Miss Florence Gill*: Donna Murphy. *Helena Landless/Miss Janet Conover*: JANA SCHNEIDER. *Neville Landless/Mr. Victor Grinstead*: JOHN HERRERA. *Durdles/Mr. Nick Cricker*: JEROME DEMPSEY. *Deputy/Master Nick Cricker*: STEPHEN GLAVIN. *The Princess Puffer/Miss Angela Prysock*: CLEO LAINE. *Shade of Jasper/Mr. Harry Sayle*: Nicholas Gunn. *Shade of Drood/Mr. Montague Pruitt*: Brad Miskell. *Clients of Princess Puffer (2)*: *Mr. Alan Eliot*: Herndon Lackey. *Mr. Christopher Lyon*: Rob Marshall. *Succubae (4)*: *Miss Gwendolyn Pynn*: Francine Landes. *Miss Sarah Cook*: Karen Giombetti. *Miss Florence Gill*: Donna Murphy. *Miss Isabel Yearsley*: Judy Kuhn. *Satyr/Master Nick Cricker*: STEPHEN GLAVIN. *Servants (3)*: *Mr. Philip Bax*: JOE GRIFASI. *Miss Violet Balfour*: Susan Goodman. *Miss Gwendolen Pynn*: Francine Landes. *Harold/Mr. James Throttle*: Peter McRobbie. *Julian/Mr. Alan Eliot*: Herndon Lackey. *Horace/Mr. Brian Pankhurst*: Charles Goff. *Bazzard/Mr. Philip Bax*: JOE GRIFASI.

Citizens of Cloisterham: Karen Giombetti, Charles Goff, Susan Goodman, Nicholas Gunn, Judy Kuhn, Herndon Lackey, Francine Landes, Rob Marshall, Peter McRobbie, Brad Miskell, Donna Murphy, Joe Pichette.

The action takes place at the Music Hall Royale this evening. Opening comments by Your Chairman, Mr. William Cartwright, immediately followed by the Music Hall Royale's presentation of "The Mystery of Edwin Drood."

Act 1: The Situation. *Scene 1*: The home of John Jasper at Minor Canon Corner in the cathedral city of Cloisterham, (England). A morning in late December. *Scene 2*: The conservatory at the Nun's House, a seminary for young women in Cloisterham High Street. Later that morning. *Scene 3*: Cloisterham High Street, outside the residence of Mayor Thomas Sapsea. The following afternoon. *Scene 4*: The opium den of Princess Puffer in the East End of London. Dawn, the next day. *Scene 5*: Cloisterham High Street. That afternoon. *Scene 6*: The crypts of Cloisterham Cathedral. Late that night. *Scene 7*: The ruins of Cloisterham. Christmas Eve. *Scene 8*: The home of John Jasper. A short time later. *Scene 9*: Minor Canon Corner. Christmas day and night.

Act 2: The Sleuths. *Scene 1*: Cloisterham Station. Six months later. *Scene 2*: Cloisterham High Street. *Scene 3*: The Voting; the Solution.

ACT 1

"There You Are"
G. Rose, Company

Scene 1

"A Man Could Go Quite Mad"
H. McGillin

"Two Kinsmen"
B. Buckley, H. McGillin

Scene 2

"Moonfall"
P. Cohenour

"Moonfall" (reprise)
P. Cohenour, J. Schneider, J. Kuhn, D. Murphy

Scene 4

"The Wages of Sin"
C. Laine

[14]Originally produced Off-Broadway 4 August 1985 at the Delacorte Theatre, Central Park, for 27 performances. Late in the Broadway run the title of the show was altered to DROOD.

[15]The theatrical characters from "The Mystery of Edwin Drood" appear in regular typeface; the Victorian music hall actors' names performing "The Mystery of Edwin Drood" appear in italics.

"Jasper's Vision"
N. Gunn, B. Miskell, Succubae, S. Glavin
Scene 5
"Ceylon"
B. Buckley, P. Cohenour, J. Schneider, J. Herrera, Ensemble
"Both Sides of the Coin"
H. McGillin, G. Rose, Ensemble
Scene 7
"Perfect Strangers"
B. Buckley, P. Cohenour
Scene 8
"No Good Can Come from Bad"
J. Herrera, B. Buckley, P. Cohenour, J. Schneider, G. N. Martin, H. McGillin, J. Grifasi
Scene 9
"The Name of Love"/"Moonfall" (reprise)
P. Cohenour, H. McGillin, Ensemble

ACT 2
Scene 1
"Settling Up the Score"
Dick Datchery, C. Laine, Ensemble
Scene 2
"Off to the Races"
G. Rose, J. Dempsey, S. Glavin, Ensemble
"Don't Quit While You're Ahead"
C. Laine, Company
Scene 3
(The Voting: "Settling Up the Score" reprise)
Company
"The Garden Path to Hell"
C. Laine
("The Solution")
Entire Company

1985.19 JERRY'S GIRLS

A Broadway Entertainment (Musical Revue) in Two Acts[16]. Music and lyrics by Jerry Herman. Staged and directed by Larry Alford. Choreography by Wayne Cilento. Concepts by Larry Alford, Wayne Cilento, Jerry Herman. Scenery designed by Hal Tine. Costumes designed by Florence Klotz. Lighting designed by Tharon Musser. Sound designed by Peter Fitzgerald. Dance arranger, Mark Hummel. Musical supervisor, Donald Pippin. Orchestrations by Christopher Bankey, Joseph Gianono, Jim Tyler. Musical director, Janet Glazener. Produced by Zev Bufman, Kenneth-John Productions (Kenneth D. Greenblatt, John J. Pomerantz). Opened 18 December 1985 at the St. James Theatre and closed 20 April 1986 after 139 performances.

CAST (in order of appearance): (*Ensemble*:) Ellyn Arons, Kirsten Childs, Kim Crosby, Anita Ehrler, Terri Homberg, Robin Kersey, Joni Masella, Deborah Phelan. DOROTHY LOUDON, LESLIE UGGAMS, CHITA RIVERA.
Swing: Jacquey Maltby. *Onstage Pianist*: Sue Anderson.

ACT 1
"It Takes a Woman" (from *HELLO, DOLLY!*)
Ensemble
"It Takes a Woman" (reprise)
Ensemble
"Just Leave Everything to Me" (from *HELLO, DOLLY!* film)
D. Loudon
"Put on Your Sunday Clothes" (from *HELLO, DOLLY!*)
D. Loudon, Ensemble
"It Only Takes a Moment" (from *HELLO, DOLLY!*)
L. Uggams
"Wherever He Ain't" (from *MACK AND MABEL*)
C. Rivera
"We Need a Little Christmas" (from *MAME*)
E. Arons, K. Childs, K. Crosby, A. Ehrler, D. Phelan
"Tap Your Troubles Away" (from *MACK AND MABEL*)
D. Loudon, C. Rivera, L. Uggams, Ensemble
"I Won't Send Roses" (from *MACK AND MABEL*)
L. Uggams
Vaudeville Medley:
"Two-a-Day" (from *PARADE*)
D. Loudon
"Bosom Buddies" (from *MAME*)
C. Rivera, L. Uggams
"The Man in the Moon" (from *MAME*)
D. Loudon
"So Long Dearie" (from *HELLO, DOLLY!*)
C. Rivera
"Take It All Off" (from *JERRY'S GIRLS*)
K. Crosby, T. Homberg, R. Kersey, J. Masella, D. Loudon
"Two-a-Day" (reprise)
D. Loudon, C. Rivera, Ensemble
"Shalom" (from *MILK AND HONEY*)
L. Uggams
"Milk and Honey" (from *MILK AND HONEY*)
L. Uggams, E. Arons, K. Childs, K. Crosby, T. Homberg, R. Kersey, D. Phelan
"Before the Pararde Passes By" (from *HELLO, DOLLY!*)
C. Rivera
"Have a Nice Day" (cut from *LA CAGE AUX FOLLES*)
D. Loudon, E. Arons, K. Childs, K. CRosby, T. Homberg, R. Phelan, J. Masella
"Showtune" (from *PARADE*)
C. Rivera, Ensemble
"If He Walked into My Life" (from *MAME*)
L. Uggams
"Hello, Dolly!" (from *HELLO, DOLLY!*)
D. Loudon, L. Uggams, C. Rivera, Ensemble

ACT 2
Movies Medley:
"Just Go to the Movies"
E. Arons, K. Childs, K. Crosby, T. Homberg, D. Phelan
(from *A DAY IN HOLLYWOOD/A NIGHT IN THE UKRAINE*)
"Movies Were Movies" (from *MACK AND MABEL*)
L. Uggams
"Look What Happened to Mabel" (from *MACK AND MABEL*)
C. Rivera
"Nelson"
D. Loudon
(from *A DAY IN HOLLYWOOD/A NIGHT IN THE UKRAINE*)
"Just Go to the Movies" (reprise)
"I Don't Want to Know" (from *DEAR WORLD*)
C. Rivera
"It's Today" (from *MAME*)
L. Uggams, E. Arons, K. Crosby, A. Ehrler, T. Homberg, R. Kersey, J. Masella, D. Phelan
"Mame" (from *MAME*)
D. Loudon, E. Arons, K. Crosby, A. Ehrler, T. Homberg, R. Kersey, J. Masella, D. Phelan
"Kiss Her Now" (from *DEAR WORLD*)
L. Uggams, K. Childs
"The Tea Party" (from *DEAR WORLD*):
"Dickie"
D. Loudon
"Voices"
L. Uggams
"Thoughts"
C. Rivera
"Time Heals Everything" (from *MACK AND MABEL*)
D. Loudon
"That's How Young I Feel" (from *MAME*)
C. Rivera, A. Ehrler, J. Masella

[16]Originally produced Off-Broadway in an earlier version 17 August 1981 at Ted Hook's Onstage for 101 performances.

"My Type" (from *NIGHTCAP*)
D. Loudon

LA CAGE AUX FOLLES Medley:

"La Cage Aux Folles"
C. Rivera, K. Childs, A. Ehrler, T. Homberg, R. Kersey, J. Masella, D. Phelan

"Song on the Sand"
D. Loudon, K. Childs, T. Homberg, R. Kersey, D. Phelan

"I Am What I Am"
L. Uggams

"The Best of Times"
D. Loudon, C. Rivera, L. Uggams, Ensemble

1985.20 WIND IN THE WILLOWS

A Musical in Two Acts, 15 Scenes. Book by Jane Iredale. Based on the novel of the same name by Kenneth Grahame. Music by William Perry. Lyrics by Roger McGough, William Perry. Staged by Tony Stevens. Choreography by Margery Beddow. Scenery by Sam Kirkpatrick. Costumes by Freddy Wittop. Lighting by Craig Miller. Sound by Jack Mann. Musical supervision by Jonathan Tunick. Orchestrations by William D. Brohn. Dance and incidental music by David Krane. Musical director and vocal arrangements by Robert Rogers. Production supervisor, Stephen Zweigbaum. Asisstant choreographer, James Brennan. Fights by Conal O'Brien. Originally produced by the Folger Theatre, Washington, D.C. Produced by RLM Productions, Inc. (Michael Bright, Richard Ericson, Laura Harris, Renny Serre) and Liniva Productions, Inc. Opened 20 December 1985 at the Nederlander Theatre and closed 22 December 1985 after 4 performances.

CAST (in order of appearance): *Mole*: VICKI LEWIS. *Mother Rabbit*: Nora Mae Lyng. *Father Rabbit*: John Jellison. *Rat*: DAVID (James) CARROLL. *Toad*: NATHAN LANE. *Chief Stoat*: Donna Drake. *Badger*: IRVING BARNES. *Chief Weasel*: P. J. BENJAMIN. *Wayfarer Rat*: Jackie Lowe. *Police Sergeant*: Scott Waara. *Court Clerk*: Kenston Ames. *Judge*: John Jellison. *Prosecutor*: Michael Byers. *Jailer's Daughter*: Nora Mae Lyng. *Jailer*: Michael Byers.

Ensemble: Kenston Ames, Shell M. Benjamin, Michael Byers, Jackie Lowe, Marguerite Lowell, Nora Mae Lyng, Mary C. Robare, Jamie Rocco, Ray Roderick, Scott Waara. *Swings*: Teresa Payne-Rohan, Kevin Winkler.

Act 1, Scene 1: A Meadow in Spring. *Scene 2*: The River. *Scene 3*: The Wild Wood. *Scene 4*: The Lawns of Toad Hall. *Scene 5*: Rat's Dock in Summer. *Scene 6*: The Wild Wood. *Scene 7*: The Car Park at the Red Lion Inn. *Scene 8*: A Meadow in Autumn.

Act 2, Scene 1: The Courtroom. *Scene 2*: Rat's Dock in Autumn. *Scene 3*: Toad Hall. *Scene 4*: A Jail Cell. *Scene 5*: The Woods. *Scene 6*: Rat's Dock. *Scene 7*: The Grand Dining Room at Toad Hall.

ACT 1

Scene 1

"The World Is Waiting for Me"
V. Lewis

Scene 2

"When Springtime Comes to My River"
D. Carroll

"Messing About in Boats"
D. Carroll, V. Lewis

Scene 3

"Evil Weasel"
P. J. Benjamin, D. Drake, Weasels, Stoats

Scene 4

"That's What Friends Are For"
N. Lane, D. Carroll, V. Lewis, the Rabbits

Scene 6

"Follow Your Instinct"
V. Lewis, the Rabbits, Weasels, Stoats

Scene 7

"The Gasoline Can-Can"
N. Lane, the Rabbits

"You'll Love It in Jail"
P. J. Benjamin, D. Drake, N. Lane, the Policemen

Scene 8

"Mediterranean"
J. Lowe

"The Day You Came into My Life"
V. Lewis

ACT 2

Scene 1

"S-S-S-Something Comes over Me"
N. Lane

Scene 2

"I'd Be Attracted"
V. Lewis, D. Carroll

"When Springtime Comes to My River" (reprise)
D. Carroll

"The Day You Came into My Life" (reprise)
V. Lewis

Scene 3

"Moving Up in the World"
P. J. Benjamin, D. Drake, Weasels, Stoats

Scene 4

"Brief Encounter"
N. Lane, N. M. Lyng

Scene 5

"Where Am I Now?"
N. Lane

"The Wind in the Willows"
The Company

Scene 6

"That's What Friends Are For" (reprise)
N. Lane, D. Carroll, I. Barnes, The Rabbits

Scene 7

"Come What May"
The Company

1985.21 THE ROBERT KLEIN SHOW!

An Entertainment (Revue) in Two Acts. Written and conceived by Robert Klein. Musical director, Bob Stein. Produced by Circle-in-the-Square (Theodore Mann, Artistic director; Paul Libin, Producing Director). Opened 20 December 1985 at the Circle-in-the-Square and closed 4 January 1986 after 16 performances.

CAST: ROBERT KLEIN, KENNY RANKIN.

1986.01 JEROME KERN GOES TO HOLLYWOOD

A Musical Revue in Two Acts. Conceived by David Kernan. Written by Dick Vosburgh. Music by Jerome Kern. Lyrics by Oscar Hamerstein II, Dorothy Fields, Ira Gershwin, Otto Harbach, Johnny Mercer, E. Y. Harburg, Jimmy McHugh, P. G. Wodehouse, Buddy DeSylva, Gus Kahn, Bernard Dougall, Herbert Reynolds. Directed by David Kernan. Set design by Colin Pigott. Costume design by Christine Robinson. Lighting design by Ken Billington, Musical director, Peter Howard. Sound design by Tony Meola. Musical consultant, Clive Chaplin. Additional staging, Irving Davies. Produced by Arthur Cantor, Bonnie Nelson Schwartz by arrangement with Peter Wilson and Showpeople. Opened 23 January 1986 at the Ritz Theatre and closed 1 February 1986 after 13 performances.

CAST (in alphaabetical order): ELAINE DELMAR, SCOTT HOLMES, LIZ ROBERTSON, ELISABETH WELCH.

ACT 1[17]

"The Song Is You" (from *MUSIC IN THE AIR*, 1934)
Ensemble
(*Lyrics by* Oscar Hammerstein II.)

[17]Dates that appear below are the year the song first appeared on screen.

"I've Told Every Little Star" (from *MUSIC IN THE AIR*, 1934)
Ensemble
(*Lyrics by* Oscar Hammerstein II.)
"Let's Begin" (from *ROBERTA*, 1935)
E. Delmar
(*Lyrics by* Otto Harbach.)
"I Won't Dance" (from *ROBERTA*, 1935)
L. Robertson
(*Lyrics by* Otto Harbach, Oscar Hammerstein II, Jimmy McHugh, Dorothy Fields.)
"Californ-i-ay" (from *CAN'T HELP SINGING*, 1944)
(*Lyrics by* E. Y. Harburg.)
E. Delmar, S. Holmes, L. Robertson
"I'll Be Hard to Handle" (from *ROBERTA*, 1935)L. Robertson
(*Lyrics by* Bernard Dougall.)
"Smoke Gets in Your Eyes" (from *ROBERTA*, 1935)
E. Welch
(*Lyrics by* Otto Harbach.)
"Yesterdays" (from *ROBERTA*, 1935)
S. Holmes, L. Robertson
(*Lyrics by* Otto Harbach.)
"Bojangles of Harlem" (from *SWING TIME*, 1936)
E. Delmar, S. Holmes, L. Robertson
(*Lyrics by* Dorothy Fields.)
"I'm Old-Fashioned" (from *YOU WERE NEVER LOVELIER*, 1942)
E. Delmar
(*Lyrics by* Johnny Mercer.)
"Make Believe" (from *SHOW BOAT*, 1936)
L. Robertson
(*Lyrics by* Oscar Hammerstein II.)
"Why Do I Love You?" (from *SHOW BOAT*, 1951)
L. Robertson
(*Lyrics by* Oscar Hammerstein II.)
"I Have the Room Above Her" (from *SHOW BOAT*, 1936)
S. Holmes
(*Lyrics by* Oscar Hammerstein II.)
"I Still Suits Me" (from *SHOW BOAT*, 1936)
S. Holmes, E. Welch
(*Lyrics by* Oscar Hammerstein II.)
"Day Dreaming" (1941)
E. Delmar, S. Holmes, L. Robertson
(*Lyrics by* Gus Kahn.)
"I Dream Too Much" (from *I DREAM TOO MUCH*, 1935
(*Lyrics by* Dorothy Fields.)
E. Delmar, S. Holmes, L. Robertson
"Can I Forget You?" (from *HIGH, WIDE AND HANDSOME*, 1937)
(*Lyrics by* Oscar Hammerstein II.)
E. Delmar, S. Holmes, L. Robertson
"Pick Yourself Up" (from *SWING TIME*, 1936)
E. Delmar, L. Robertson
(*Lyrics by* Dorothy Fields.)
"She Didn't Say Yes" (from *THE CAT AND THE FIDDLE*, 1934)
E. Welch
(*Lyrics by* Otto Harbach.)
"The Folks Who Live on the Hill" (from *HIGH, WIDE AND HANDSOME*, 1937)
(*Lyrics by* Oscar Hammerstein II.)
S. Holmes
"Long Ago and Far Away" (from *COVER GIRL*, 1944)
Ensemble
(*Lyrics by* Ira Gershwin.)

ACT 2
"The Show Must Go On" (from *COVER GIRL*, 1944)
Ensemble
(*Lyrics by* Ira Gershwin.)
"Don't Ask Me Not to Sing" (from *ROBERTA*, 1935)
S. Holmes
(*Lyrics by* Otto Harbach.)
"The Way You Look Tonight" (from *SWING TIME*, 1936)
S. Holmes
(*Lyrics by* Dorothy Fields.)
"A Fine Romance" (from *SWING TIME*, 1936)
E. Delmar, S. Holmes
(*Lyrics by* Dorothy Fields.)
"Lovely to Look At" (from *ROBERTA*, 1935)
E. Welch
(*Lyrics by* Dorothy Fields, Jimmy McHugh.)
"Just Let Me Look at You" (from *JOY OF LIVING*, 1938)
L. Robertson
(*Lyrics by* Dorothy Fields.)
"Who?" (from *SUNNY*, 1930)
Ensemble
(*Lyrics by* Otto Harbach and Oscar Hammerstein II.)
"Remind Me" (from *ONE NIGHT IN THE TROPICS*, 1940)
E. Delmar
(*Lyrics by* Dorothy Fields.)
"The Last Time I Saw Paris" (from *LADY BE GOOD*, 1940)
S. Holmes
(*Lyrics by* Oscar Hammerstein II.)
"Ol' Man River" (from *SHOW BOAT*, 1929)
E. Delmar, S. Holmes, L. Robertson
(*Lyrics by* Oscar Hammerstein II.)
"Why Was I Born?" (from *SWEET ADELINE*, 1935)
E. Welch
(*Lyrics by* Oscar Hammerstein II.)
"Bill" (from *SHOW BOAT*, 1936)
L. Robertson
(*Lyrics by* P. G. Wodehouse, Oscar Hammerstein II.)
"Can't Help Lovin' Dat Man" (from *SHOW BOAT*, 1936)
E. Delmar
(*Lyrics by* Oscar Hammerstein II.)
"All the Things You Are" (from *BROADWAY RHYTHM*, 1943)
(*Lyrics by* Oscar Hammerstein II.)
E. Delmar, S. Holmes, L. Robertson
"I've Told Every Little Star" (reprise)
E. Welch
"They Didn't Believe Me" (from *TILL THE CLOUDS ROLL BY*, 1946)
Ensemble
(*Lyrics by* Herbert Reynolds.)
"Till the Clouds Roll By" (from *TILL THE CLOUDS ROLL BY*, 1946)
Ensemble
(*Lyrics by* Guy Bolton and P. G. Wodehouse.)
"Look for the Silver Lining" (from *SALLY*, 1929)
Ensemble
(*Lyrics by* Buddy deSylva.)
"Make Way for Tomorrow" (from *COVER GIRL*, 1944)
Ensemble
(*Lyrics by* E. Y. Harburg, Ira Gershwin.)

1986.02 UPTOWN . . . IT'S HOT!

A Musical (Revue) in Two Acts, 5 Scenes and a Prologue. Conceived, directed and choreographed by Maurice Hines. Narrations written by Jeffery V. Thompson, Marion Ramsey. Scenery designed by Tom McPhillips. Costumes designed by Ellen Lee. Lighting designed by Marc B. Weiss. Musical direction and supervision, Frank Owens. Dance arrangements by Frank Owens and Thom Bridwell. Production supervisor, Beverley Randolph. Assistant choreographer, Mercedes Ellington. Associate producer, Stanley Kay. Produced by Allen Spivak and Larry Magid. Opened 28 January 1986 at the Lunt-Fontanne Theatre and closed 16 February 1986 after 24 performances.

CAST: MAURICE HINES, MARION RAMSEY, JEFFERY V. THOMPSON, LAWRENCE HAMILTON, TOMMI JOHNSON, ALISA GYSE.

Ensemble: Sheila D. Barker, Toni-Maria Chalmers, Leon Evans, Michael Franks, Robert H. Fowler, Lovette George, Ruthanna Graves, Yolanda Graves, Emera Hunt, Leslie Williams-Jenkins, Lisa Ann Malloy, Delphine T. Mantz, Gerry McIntyre, Christopher T. Moore, Elise Neal, Leesa M. Osborn, Marishka Shanice Phillips, R. LaChanze Sapp, Cheryl Ann Scott, Darious Keith Williams.

Act 1, Scene 1: 1930s. *Scene 2*: 1940s.

Act 2, Scene 1: 1950s and 1960s. *Scene 2*: 1970s. *Scene 3*: 1980s.

ACT 1

Prologue

J. V. Thompson, A. Gyse, L. Hamilton, T. Johnson, M. Ramsey, M. Hines, Men Ensemble

Scene 1

"Swing That Music"
M. Ramsey
(*Music and Lyrics by* Louis Armstrong and H. Gerlach.)

"Cotton Club Stomp"
M. Ramsey, Ensemble
(*Music by* Duke Ellington.)

Three Gents:
L. Hamilton, C. T. Moore, R. H. Fowler

"Daybreak Express"
(*Music by* Duke Ellington.)

"Tap Along with Me"
(*Music by* F. Owens.)

"Dinah"
(*Music by* Harry Akst. *Lyrics by* Sam M. Lewis, Joe Young.)

That Shot 'Em!
(*Adaptation by* Marion Ramsey, Jefffery V. Thompson.)
J. V. Thompson, M. Ramsey, T. Johnson, R. H. Fowler

Stormy Weather Medley:
M. Hines, A. Gyse

"When Your Lover Has Gone"
(*Music and Lyrics by* E. A. Swan.)

"Ill Wind"
(from *COTTON CLUB PARADE*, 1934)
(*Music by* Harold Arlen. *Lyrics by* Ted Koehler.)

"Body and Soul"
(from *THREE'S A CROWD*)
(*Music by* Johnny Green. *Lyrics by* Edward Heyman, Robert Sour, Frank Eyton.)

"Stormy Weather"
(*Music by* Harold Arlen. *Lyrics by* Ted Koehler.)

"Diga Diga Doo" (from *BLACKBIRDS OF 1928*)
(*Music by* Jimmy McHugh. *Lyrics by* Dorothy Fields.)
M. Ramsey, G. McIntyre, D. T. Mantz, Ensemble

"Lady Be Good"
M. Hines
(*Music by* George Gershwin.)

Cab Calloway and the Nicholas Brothers:

"Jim Jam Jumpin'"
T. Johnson, L. Evans, D. K. Williams
(*Music by* Cab Calloway.)

Scene 2

Big Band Tribute

Chick Webb Theme Song: "Let's Get Together"
Orchestra
(*Music by* Chick Webb.)

"A-Tisket, A-Tasket"
A. Gyse
(*Music and Lyrics by* Ella Fitzgerald and Van Alexander.)

Jitterbuggin': "Jumpin' at the Woodside"
M. Hines,
M. Ramsey, J. V. Thompson, L. Hamilton, D. T. Mantz, S. Barker, Ensemble
(*Music by* Count Basie.)

ACT 2

Scene 1

Doo Woppers: "Why Do Fools Fall in Love"
A. Gyse, L. Hamilton, T. Johnson
(*Music and Lyrics by* Frank Lymon and Morris Levy.)

The Apollo: Master of Ceremonies
J. V. Thompson

The Gospel Caravan:

"His Eye Is on the Sparrow" (traditional)
L. Hamilton

"Amazing Grace" (traditional)
A. Gyse

"Just a Closer Walk with Thee" (traditional)
T. Johnson

"Old Landmark"
L. Hamilton, A. Gyse, T. Johnson, R. L. Sapp, Ensemble
(*Music and Lyrics by* M. A. Brunner.)

Good Mornin' Judge
(*Adaptation by* Jeffery V. Thompson.)
Judge Pigmeat: J. V. Thompson. *De District Attorney*: M. Ramsey. *The Defendant*: A. Gyse. *Sonny Rayburn*: M. Hines.

Rock & Roll Medley:

"You Send Me"
T. Johnson
(*Music and Lyrics by* L. C. Cooke.)

"Blueberry Hill"
J. V. Thompson
(*Music and Lyrics by* Al Lewis, Larry Stock, Vincent Rose.)

"Tutti Frutti"
G. McIntyre
(*Music and Lyrics by* Richard Penniman, D. LaBostrie, Joe Lubin.)

"Johnny B. Goode"
L. Hamilton, Ensemble Men
(*Music and Lyrics by* Chuck Berry.)

Battle of the Groups:
"Will You Still Love Me Tomorrow?"
T. Chalmers, L. Williams-Jenkins, D. T. Mantz, C. A. Scott
(*Music and Lyrics by* Gerry Goffin and Carole King.)

"Be My Baby"
A. Gyse, S. D. Barker, E. Neal
(*Music and Lyrics by* Phil Spector, Ellie Greenwich, Jeff Barry.

"Don't Mess with Bill"
R. L. Sapp, L. A. Mallory, L. M. Osborn
(*Music and Lyrics by* W. Smokey Robinson.)

"Dancin' in the Streets"
Y. Graves, L. George, E. Hunt
(*Music and Lyrics by* Marvin Gaye, I. Hunter, W. Stevenson.)

"Stop! in the Name of Love"
M. Ramsey, R. Graves, M. S. Phillips
(*Music and Lyrics by* Brian Holland, Lamont Dozier, Eddie Holland.)

"Ain't Too Proud to Beg"
L. Hamilton, D. K. Williams, L. Evans, T. Johnson, G. McIntyre
(*Music and Lyrics by* Eddie Holland, Norman Whitfield.)

"Proud Mary"
M. Ramsey, R. Graves, M. S. Phillips, C. A. Scott
(*Music and Lyrics by* John C. Fogerty.)

Scene 2

Station WHOT
J. V. Thompson

Stevie Wonder Medley
(*Music and Lyrics by* Stevie Wonder and Leon Evans):

"Superstition"
Ensemble Dancers

"Keep on Running"
M. Hines (Devil)

"Higher Ground"
A. Gyse (Victim)

"Do I Do"
L. Hamilton (Angel)

Scene 3

Radio Playoffs
M. Ramsey, L. Hamilton, R. L. Sapp, L. Evans, G. McIntyre, M. Hines

"Express"
M. Ramsey, J. V. Thompson, Ensemble Dancers
(*Music and Lyrics by* B. T. Express.)

Rappers
L. Hamilton, J. V. Thompson

"1999"
Full Company
(*Music and Lyrics by* Prince.)

1986.03

THE AMERICAN DANCE MACHINE

A Theatre Dance Revue in Two Acts, 15 Scenes[18]. Entire production concieved, supervised and directed by Lee Theodore. Musical director and orchestrator, James Raitt. Lighting designer, Curt Osterman. Produced by the American Dancemachine, Inc. in association with 55th Street Dance Theater Foundation, Inc. Opened 4 February 1986 at the New York City Center and closed 16 February 1986 after 16 performances.

CAST: DICK CAVETT (Special Guest Host), HAROLD CROMER, TINKA GUTRICK, KELBY KIRK, AJA MAJOR, Newton Cole, Joe Deer, Dan Fletcher, Kim Freshwater, Camille Ross, David Storey, Dannul Dailey, Jennifer Dempster, Brian Duguay, Diana Losk, Michael Lott, Mark Curtis Smith, Donna Smythe, Lynn Sterling, 'Ali Theodore, Kyle Williams.

ACT 1

Scene 1

"The Whip Dance" (from *DESTRY RIDES AGAIN*, 1959)
M. Lott, N. Cole, M. C. Smith
(*Choreography by* Michael Kidd, reconstructed by Swen Swenson. *Music and Lyrics by* Harold Rome.)

Scene 2

"Popularity" (from *GEORGE M!*, 1968)
D. Fletcher, Ensemble
(*Choreography by* Joe Layton. *Music and Lyrics by* George M. Cohan.)

Scene 3

"June Is Bustin' Out All Over" (from *CAROUSEL*, 1945)
C. Ross, Female Ensemble
(*Choreography by* Agnes deMille, reconstructed by Gemze deLappe. *Music by* Richard Rodgers. *Lyrics by* Oscar Hammerstein II.)

Scene 4

"Shriners' Ballet" (from *BYE BYE BIRDIE*, 1960)
T. Gutrick, Male Ensemble
(*Choreography by* Gower Champion, reconstructed by Edmond Kresley. *Music by* Charles Strouse. *Lyrics by* Lee Adams.)

Scene 5

"Won't You Charleston With Me?" (from *THE BOY FRIEND*, 1970 revival)
A. Major, B. Duguay
(*Choreography by* Buddy Schwab, reconstructed by Eleanor Treiber. *Music and Lyrics by* Sandy Wilson.)

Scene 6

"The Telephone Dance" (from *CABARET*, 1966)
T. Gutrick, D. Dailey, Ensemble
(*Choreography by* Ron Field, reconstructed by Marianne Seibert. *Music by* John Kander. *Lyrics by* Fred Ebb.)

Scene 7

"The Clog Dance" (from *WALKING HAPPY*, 1966)
D. Fletcher, Male Ensemble
(*Choreography and Reconstruction by* Danny Daniels. *Introduction by* Joe Deer. *Music by* James Van Heusen. *Lyrics by* Sammy Cahn. *Dance Arrangement by* Ed Scott.)

Scene 8

"Floyd's Guitar Blues" (from the Katherine Dunham Repertory)
T. Gutrick, J. Deer
(*Choreography by* Katherine Dunham, reconstructed by Glory Van Scott. *Music by* Floyd Smith.)

Scene 9

"Charlie's Place" (from *OVER HERE*, 1974)
A. Major, D. Storey, Ensemble
(*Choreography and Reconstruction by* Patricia Birch. *Music and Lyrics by* Richard Sherman and Robert Sherman.)

Intermission: Historical material performed by Harold Cromer, arranged by Harold Cromer in collaboration with Albert Murray. "Mr. Bojangles" score composed by Jerry Jeff Walker.

ACT 2

Scene 1

"If the Rain's Gotta Fall" (from *HALF A SIXPENCE*, 1965)
K. Kirk, Ensemble
(*Choreography by* Onna White, reconstructed by Eleanor Treiber and Tom Panko. *Music and Lyrics by* David Heneker.)

Scene 2

"Satin Doll" (from *THE ED SULLIVAN SHOW*, TV, 1962)
K. Williams, C. Ross, L. Sterling

"Me and My Gal" (from *THE ED SULLIVAN SHOW*, TV, 1962)
T. Gutrick, A. Theodore
(*Choreography by* Carol Haney, reconstructed by Buzz Miller. *Music by* Duke Ellington, Billy Strayhorn, Johnny Mercer. *Arrangement by* Luther Henderson.)

Scene 3

"Little Old New York" (from *TENDERLOIN*, 1960)
A. Major, K., Freshwater, Ensemble
(*Choreography by* Joe Layton, reconstructed by Joe Layton and Lee Theodore. *Music by* Jerry Bock. *Lyrics by* Sheldon Harnick.)

Scene 4

"Come to Me, Bend to Me" (from *BRIGADOON*, 1947)
K. Kirk

"The Funeral Dance" (from *BRIGADOON*, 1947)
T. Gutrick, Female Ensemble
(*Choreography by* Agnes deMille, recomstructed by Gemze deLappe. *Music by* Frederick Loewe. *Lyrics by* Alan Jay Lerner.)

Scene 5

"You Can Dance with Any Girl at All" (from *NO, NO, NANETTE*, 1971 revival)
A. Major, K. Kirk
(*Choreography by* Donald Saddler, reconstructed by Donald Saddler. *Music by* Vincent Youmans. *Lyrics by* Irving Caesar and Otto Harbach.)

Scene 6

"The Aggie Song" (from *THE BEST LITTLE WHOREHOUSE IN TEXAS*, 1978)
N. Cole, Male Ensemble
(*Choreography by* Tommy Tune, reconstructed by Jerry Yoder. *Music and Lyrics by* Carol Hall.)

1986.04

BRIGADOON

A Revival of the Musical Play in Two Acts, Eleven Scenes[19]. Book and lyrics by Alan Jay Lerner. Music by Frederick Loewe. Original dances by Agnes de Mille, recreated by James Jamieson. Directed by Gerald Freedman. Set and costume designer, Desmond Heeley. Lighting designer, Duane Schuler. Conductor, Paul Gemignani. Chorus master, Joseph Colaneri. Sound consultant, Farrel Becker. Produced by the New York City Opera. Opened 1 March 1986 at the New York State Theatre and closed 30 March 1986 after 40 performances[20].

CAST (in order of appearance): *Tommy Albright*: RICHARD WHITE or JOHN LESLIE WOLFE. *Jeff Douglas*: TONY ROBERTS. *Maggie Anderson*: TINKA GUTRICK. *Archie Beaton*: William Ledbetter. *Angus MacGuffie*: Don Yule. *Meg Brockie*: JOYCE CASTLE or MARCIA MITZMAN. *Stuart Dalrymple*: Robert Brubaker. *Sandy Dean*: Gregory Moore. *Harry Beaton*: LUIS PEREZ. *Andrew MacLaren*: David Rae Smith. *Fiona MacLaren*: SHERYL WOODS or BEVERLY LAMBERT. *Jean MacLaren*: Camille Ross. *Charlie Dalrymple*: CRIS GROENENDAAL or DAVID EISLER. *Fish Monger*: Stephanie Godino. *Mr. Lundie*: James Billings. *Sword Dancers*: Terry Lacy, Joe Deer. *Bagpiper*: Stephen Fox. *Frank*: Ralph Bassett. *Jane Ashton*: Alison Bevan.

Townsfolk of Brigadoon: *Singers*: *New York City Opera Chorus*: Marilyn Armstrong, Lee Belaver, George Bohachevsky, Jill Bosworth, Don Carlo, Mervin Crook, Harris Davis, Neil Eddinger, Harriet Green, Jonathan Guss, Don Henderson, Lila Herbert, Ron Hilley, Paula Hostetter, Rita Metzger, Madeline Mines, Gregory Moore, Beth Pensiero, Louis Perry, J. Randolph Peyton, Bridget Ramos, Frank Ream, Glenn Rowen, Mary Ann Rydzeski, Deborah Saverance, Susan Schafer, Carolyn Sielski, Frank Tippie,

[18]A previous edition was presented Off-Broadway 14 June 1978 at the Century Theatre for 198 performances. Between 1978 and 1986 the company toured widely with an changing repertory.

[19]Originally produced in New York 13 March 1947 at the Ziegfeld Theatre for 581 performances. For Synopsis of Scenes and Musical Numbers, see original 1947 production.

[20]Orchestrations uncredited.

Catherine Williams, George Wyman, Marie Young, Edward Zimmerman. *New York City Opera Dancers*: Jean Barber, Savia Berger, Jose Bourbon, Kathy Bradney, Joe Deer, Esperanza Galan, Stephanie Godino, Malcolm Grant, Vasilis Iracledes, Candace Itow, Ashley Janeway, Terry Lacy, Marc Mahler, Fritz Masten, Joan Mirabella, Louis Navarette, Daniel Pelzig, Deidre Sheehan, Richard Smith, Anina von Molnar.

1986.05

THE FLYING KARAMAZOV BROTHERS

Juggling and Cheap Theatrics (A Vaudeville Revue) in Two Acts. Conceived, written and directed by the Flying Karamazov Brothers. Sets by Seiza de Tarr. Lighting by Eben Sprinsock. Produced by Lincoln Center Theatre (Gregory Mosher, Artistic director; Bernard Gersten, Executive producer). Opened 1 April 1986 at the Vivian Beaumont Theatre and closed 20 April 1986 after 24 performances; re-opened (Off Broadway) 23 April 1986 at the Mitzi Newhouse Theater and closed 4 May 1986 after 16 additional performances. Total: 40 performances.

CAST: *Fyodor*: TIMOTHY DANIEL FURST. *Dmitri*: PAUL DAVID MAGID. *Alyosha*: RANDY NELSON. *Ivan*: HOWARD JAY PATTERSON. *Smerdyakov*: SAM WILLIAMS.

1986.06

BIG DEAL

A Musical in Two Acts, 24 Scenes. (Book) Written by Bob Fosse. Based on the film "Big Deal on Madonna Street," (Screenplay by Susi Cecchi D'Amico, Mario Monicelli, Agenore Incrocci and Furio Scarpelli.) Directed and choreographed by Bob Fosse. Scenery by Peter Larkin. Costumes by Patricia Zipprodt. Lighting by Jules Fisher. Orchestrations by Ralph Burns. Sound by Abe Jacob. Associate choreographer, Christopher Chadman. Music arranged and conducted by Gordon Lowry Harrell. Executive producer, Jules Fisher. Produced by The Shubert Organization, Roger Berlind, Jerome Minskoff in association with Jonathan Farkas. Opened 10 April 1986 at the Broadway Theatre and closed 8 June 1986 after 70 performances.

CAST (in order of appearance): *Lilly*: LORETTA DEVINE. *First Narrator*: Wayne Cilento. *Second Narrator*: Bruce Anthony Davis. *Kokomo*: Gary Chapman. *Otis*: Alde Lewis, Jr. *Charley*: CLEAVANT DERRICKS. *Pearl*: Valarie Pettiford. *Slick*: Larry Marshall. *Sunnyboy*: Mel Johnson, Jr. *Willie*: ALAN WEEKS. *Judge and Bandleader*: Bernard J. Marsh. *Band Singer*: Valarie Pettiford. *Phoebe*: Desiree Coleman. *Dancin' Dan*: Gary Chapman. *First Shadow*: Valarie Pettiford. *Second Shadow*: Barbara Yeager. *Little Willie*: Roumel Reaux. *Announcer*: Candace Tovar.

Dancers: Ciscoe Bruton II, Lloyd Culbreath, Kim Darwin, Cady Huffman, Amelia Marshall, Frank Mastrocola, Stephanie Pope, Roumel Reaux, George Russell, Candace Tovar. *Alternates*: Bryant Baldwin, Diana Laurenson, Vince Cole. *On-Stage Band*: Brian Brake (drums), Leonard Oxley (piano), William Shadel (clarinet), Joe Mosello (trumpet), Earl May (bass), Britt Woodman (trombone).

The action takes place in the 1930's on the South Side of Chicago, Illinois.

Act 1, Scene 1: Prologue. *Scene 2*: Locker Room and Fight Arena. *Scene 3*: The Judge's Chambers. *Scene 4*: Prsion Yard. *Scene 5*: Gem Theatre. *Scene 6*: The Men's Room at the Gem Theatre. *Scene 7*: A Camera Store. *Scene 8*: Cottage Grove Avenue. *Scene 9*: Pool Hall. *Scene 10*: Cottage Grove Avenue. *Scene 11*: Paradise Ballroom. *Scene 12*: Alley Outside Dancehall.

Act 2, Scene 1: Prologue. *Scene 2*: Slick's Apartment. *Scene 3*: Willie's House. *Scene 4*: A Pawnshop. *Scene 5*: Slick's Apartment. *Scene 6*: Charlie's Room. *Scene 7*: Lily's Rented Room. *Scene 8*: Refreshment Stand of Gem Theatre. *Scene 9*: Lily's Rented Room. *Scene 10*: The Robbery. *Scene 11*: The Fantasies. *Scene 12*: A Street.

ACT 1

Scene 1

"Life Is Just a Bowl of Cherries" (from *GEORGE WHITE'S SCANDALS OF 1931*)
(*Music by* Ray Henderson. *Lyrics by* Buddy DeSylva, Lew Brown.)
L. Devine

"For No Good Reason at All"
W. Cilento, B. A. Davis
(*Music and Lyrics by* Abel Baer, Samuel W. Lewis, Joe Young.)

Scene 2

"Charley My Boy"
C. Derricks
(*Music and Lyrics by* Ted Fiorito and Gus Kahn.)

Scene 3

"I've Got a Feelin' You're Foolin'" (from *BROADWAY MELODY OF 1936*, film)
G. Chapman, C. Derricks, B. J. Marsh, W. Cilento, B. A. Davis
(*Music by* Nacio Herb Brown. *Lyrics by* Arthur Freed.)

Scene 4

"Ain't We Got Fun"
The Prisoners
(*Music by* Richard A. Whiting. *Lyrics by* Gus Kahn and Raymond Egan.)

Scene 5

"For No Good Reason at All" (reprise)
W. Cilento, B. A. Davis, The Dancers

Scene 8

"Chicago"
W. Cilento, B. A. Davis
(*Music and Lyrics by* Fred Fisher.)

Scene 9

"Pick Yourself Up" (from *SWING TIME* film)
C. Derricks, A. Weeks, L. Marshall, M. Johnson, Jr., A. Lewis, Jr.
(*Music by* Jerome Kern. *Lyrics by* Dorothy Fields.)

Scene 10

"I'm Just Wild About Harry" (from *SHUFFLE ALONG*)
L. Devine
(*Music by* Eubie Blake. *Lyrics by* Noble Sissle.)

Scene 11

"Beat Me Daddy Eight to the Bar"
B. J. Marsh, Band, Dancers
(*Music and Lyrics by* Don Raye, Hughie Prince, Eleanor Sheehy.)

"The Music Goes 'Round and 'Round"
B. J. Marsh, Band
(*Music by* Edward Farley and Michael Riley. *Lyrics by* Red Hodgson.)

Scene 12

"Life Is Just a Bowl of Cherries" (reprise)
L. Devine

ACT 2

Scene 1

"Now's the Time to Fall in Love"
W. Cilento, B. A. Davis, Dancers
(*Music and Lyrics by* Al Sherman and Al Lewis.)

Scene 2

"Ain't She Sweet"
M. Johnson, Jr., D. Coleman, W. Cilento, B. A. Davis, Dancers
(*Music by* Milton Ager. *Lyrics by* Jack Yellen.)

Scene 3

"Everybody Loves My Baby"
A. Weeks, W. Cilento, B. A. Davis
(*Music and Lyrics by* Jack Palmer and Spencer Williams.)

"Me and My Shadow"
G. Chapman, V. Pettiford, B. Yeager
(*Music by* Al Jolson and Dave Dreyer. *Lyrics by* Billy Rose.)

Scene 5

"Love Is Just Around the Corner" (from *HERE IS MY HEART*, film)
W. Cilento, B. A. Davis
(*Music by* Lewis E. Gensler. *Lyrics by* Leo Robin.)

Scene 7

"Just a Gigolo"
B. J. Marsh, C. Derricks
(*Music by* Leonello Casucci. *Original German Lyrics by* Julius Brammer. *English Lyrics by* Irving Caesar.)

"Who's Your Little Who-Zis?"
B. J. Marsh, V. Pettiford
(*Music by* Hal Goering and Ben Bernie. *Lyrics by* Walter Hirsch.)

Scene 9

"Yes Sir, That's My Baby"
C. Derricks
(*Music by* Walter Donaldson. *Lyrics by* Gus Kahn.)

"Button Up Your Overcoat" (from *FOLLOW THRU*)
L. Devine
(*Music by* Ray Henderson. *Lyrics by* Buddy DeSylva, Lew Brown.)

Scene 11

"Daddy, You've Been a Mother to Me"

A. Weeks, R. Reaux

(*Music and Lyrics by* Fred Fisher.)

"Hold Tight—Hold Tight"

A. Lewis, Jr., Ladies

(*Music and Lyrics by* Leonard Ware, Willie Spottswood, Ed Robinson, Ben Smith, Sidney Bechet.)

"Happy Days Are Here Again" (from *CHASING RAINBOWS*, film)

L. Marshall, D. Coleman, M. Johnson, Jr., Company

(*Music by* Milton Ager. *Lyrics by* Jack Yellen.)

"I'm Sitting on Top of the World"

C. Derricks, Company

(*Music by* Ray Henderson. *Lyrics by* Samuel L. Lewis, Joseph Young.)

Scene 12

"Life Is Just a Bowl of Cherries' (reprise)

L. Devine

1986.07

SWEET CHARITY

A Revival of the Musical in Two Acts, a Prologue and 19 Scenes[21]. Book (revised) by Neil Simon. Based on the film "Le Notte di Cabiria" [Nights of Cabiria], screenplay by Federico Fellini, Tullio Pinelli, Ennio Flaiano. Music by Cy Coleman. Lyrics by Dorothy Fields. Original production conceived, staged and choreographed by Bob Fosse. Scenery and lighting by Robert Randolph. Costumes by Patricia Zipprodt. Musical direction by Fred Werner. Orchestrations by Ralph Burns. Sound by Otts Munderloh. Production manager, Phil Friedman. Assisant to Mr. Fosse, Gwen Verdon. Directed and choreographed by Bob Fosse. Produced by Jerome Minskoff, James M. Nederlander, Arthur Rubin, Joseph Harris. Opened 27 April 1986 at the Minskoff Theatre and closed 15 March 1987 after 368 performances.

CAST (in order of appearance): *Charity*: DEBBIE ALLEN. *Dark Glasses*: David Warren Gibson. *Married Couple*: Quin Baird, Jan Horvath. *First Young Man*: Jeff Shade. *Woman with hat*: CELIA TACKABERRY. *Ice Cream Vendor*: Kelly Patterson. *Young Spanish Man*: Adrian Rosario. *A Cop*: Tanis Michaels. *Helene*: ALLISON WILLIAMS. *Nickie*: BEBE NEUWIRTH. *Herman*: LEE WILKOF. *Panhandler*: CELIA TACKABERRY. *Doorman*: Tom Wierney. *Ursala*: CARRIE NYGREN. *Vittorio Vidal*: MARK JACOBY. *Waiter*: Tom Wierney. *Manfred*: Fred C. Mann III. *Receptionist*: Celia Tackaberry. *Old Maid*: Jan Horvath. *Oscar*: MICHAEL RUPERT. *Daddy Johann Sebastian Brubeck*: IRVING ALLEN LEE. *Brother Harold*: Tanis Michaels. *Brother Ray*: Stanley Wesley Perryman. *Rosie*: Dana Moore. *Mike*: Michael Davis. *Good Fairy*: CELIA TACKABERRY.

Singers and Dancers of Times Square: Quin Baird, Christine Colby, Alice Everett Cox, David Warren Gibson, Kim Morgan Greene, Jan Horvath, Jane Lanier, Fred C. Mann III, Alison Reneé Manson, Tanis Michaels, Dana Moore, Kelly Patterson, Stanley Wesley Perryman, Mimi Quillin, Adrian Rosario, Jeff Shade, Tom Wierney. *Alternates*: Michelle O'Steen, Chet Walker.

---

[21]Originally produced in New York 29 January 1966 at the Palace Theatre for 608 performances. For Synopsis of Scenes and Musical Numbers, see original 1966 production. "You Should See Yourself" retained for this production; "Charity's Soliloquy" (Act 1, Scene 3) dropped. New music written for "I'm the Bravest Individual" (Act 1, Scene 8) and the title song, "Sweet Charity" (Act 2, Scene 5).

1986–1987 SEASON

Teresa Stratas in RAGS
Martha Swope/TimePix

1986–1987 SEASON

1986.08

CANDIDE

A Revival of the Musical in Two Act, 23 Scenes[1]. (New) Book adapted from Voltaire's satire (of the same name) by Hugh Wheeler. (Original book by Lillian Hellman.) Music by Leonard Bernstein. Lyrics by Richard Wilbur. Additional lyrics by Stephen Sondheim and John Latouche. Directed by Harold Prince. Stage director, Arthur Masella. Choreography by Patricia Birch. Scenery designed by Clarke Dunham. Costumes designed by Judith Dolan. Lighting designed by Ken Billington. Conducted by Scott Bergeson. Orchestrations by Leonard Bernstein and Hershy Kay. Additional orchestrations by John Mauceri. Chorus master, Joseph Colaneri. Produced by the New York City Opera. Opened 1 July 1986 at the New York State Theatre and closed 6 July 1986 after 8 performances; re-opened 11 November 1986 and closed 16 November 1986 after an additional 8 performances. Total: 16 performances.

CAST (in order of appearance): *Voltaire*: JOHN LANKSTON. *Candide*: DAVID EISLER. *Huntsman*: Don Yule. *Paquette*: DEBORAH DARR. *Baroness*: Ruth Golden. *Baron*: JACK HARROLD. *Cunegonde*: ERIE MILLS. *Maximilian*: SCOTT REEVE. *Servant of Maximilian*: JAMES BILLINGS. *Dr. Pangloss*: JOHN LANKSTON. *Bulgarian Soldiers*: Don Yule, JAMES BILLINGS. *Westphalian Soldiers*: William Ledbetter, Andy Roth. *Don Isaachar*, the Jew: JAMES BILLINGS. *Grand Inquisitor*: JACK HARROLD. *Calliope Player*: Ruth Golden. *Heresy Agent*: Ralph Bassett. *Inquisition Agents*: Gary Dietrich, Douglas Hamilton. *Judge*: JAMES BILLINGS. *Old Lady*: MURIEL COSTA-GREENSPON. *Dons*: Vasilis Iracledes, Scott Evans, Richard Smith, Don Yule, William Ledbetter, Ralph Bassett. *Businessman*: JOHN LANKSTON. *Governor*: JOHN LANKSTON. *Governor's Aide*: Andy Roth. *Slave Driver*: JACK HARROLD. *Father Bernard*: JAMES BILLINGS. *Sailors*: Gary Dietrich, Douglas Hamilton, Andy Roth, Scott Evans. *Pirates*: John Henry Thomas, William Ledbetter. *Pink Sheep*: Ivy Austin, Rhoda Butler. *Lion*: Robert Brubaker. *Pasha-Prefect*: JACK HARROLD. *First Gambler*: JAMES BILLINGS. *Second Gambler (Police Chief)*: JOHN LANKSTON. *Sage*: JOHN LANKSTON.

1986.09

KISMET

A Revival of the Musical Play (Musical Arabian Night) in Two Acts, 15 Scenes[2]. Book by Charles Lederer and Luther Davis. Based on the play of the same name by Edward Knoblock. Music based on themes by Alexander Borodin. Musical adaptation and lyrics by Robert Wright and George Forrest. Directed by Frank Corsaro. Choreographer, Randolyn Zinn. Conducted by Paul Gemignani. Set and costume designer, Lawrence Miller. Lighting designer, Mark W. Stanley. Chorus master, Joseph Colaneri. Produced by the New York City Opera. Opened 8 July 1986 at the New York State Theatre and closed 13 July 1986 after 8 performances.

CAST (in order appearance): *Imam of The Mosque*: James Clark. *Silk Dancers*: Ashley Janeway, Jean Barber, Terry Lacy, Fritz Masten. *Muezzins*: Louis Perry, Frank Ream, Glenn Rowen, George Wyman. *Beggars*: Don Yule, Robert Brubaker. *Dervishes*: Vasilis Iracledes, Richard Smith. *Omar*: JAMES BILLINGS. *A Public Poet*, later called *Hajj*: TIMOTHY NOLEN. *Marsinah*, His Daughter: DIANA WALKER. *Businessman*: William Ledbetter. *Hassan-Ben*: Ralph Bassett. *Jawan*: JOHN LANKSTON. *Swains*: Terry Lacy, Fritz Masten.. *Bangle Man*: James Clark. *Silk Merchants*: Louis Perry, Frank Ream. *Brave Merchant*: Harris Davis. *Young Women*: Madeleine Mines, Mary Ann Rydzeski. *Pearl Merchant*: William Ledbetter. *Slave Merchant*: Mervin Crook. *Informer*: William Ledbetter. *Policemen*: Ralph Bassett, Robert Brubaker. *Chief of Police*: Don Yule. *Wazir of Police*: JACK HARROLD. *Wazir's Guards*: Jeff Davis, Eric Miller, Donald R. Richardson, Elliot Santiago, Frank Sollito. *Slave Girls*: Jean Barber, Savia Berger, Ashley Janeway. *Harem Girl*: Rebecca Rosales. *Lalume*: SUSANNE MARSEE. *Princesses of Ababu*: Stephanie Godino, Joan Mirabella, Victoria Rinaldi. *The Caliph*: CRIS GROENENDAAL. *Widow Yussef*: Rebecca Russell. *Ayah to Lalume*: Mary Ann Rydzeski. *Princess Zubbediya of Damascus*: Esperanza Galan. *Ayah to Zubbediya*: Rebecca Russell *Princess Samaris of Bangalore*: CANDACE ITOW. *Prosecutor*: James Clark. *Spies*: Ralph Bassett, Robert Brubaker, William Ledbetter. *Guest*: Louis Perry. *Ensemble*: New York City Opera Chorus.

1986.10

DIE FLEDERMAUS

A Revival of the Operetta in Three Acts[3]. Original libretto by Carl Haffner and Richard Genée. Lyrics by Richard Genée. Based on the comedy "Le Réveillon" by Henri Meilhac and Ludovic Halévy.) English version by Ruth and Thomas Martin. Music by Johann Strauss. Devised and directed by Gerald Freedman. Stage director, Christian Smith. Set designer, Lloyd Evans. Costume designer, Thierry Bosquet. Choreographer, Thomas Andrew. Lighting designer, Hans Sondheimer. Conductor, Imre Pallo. Produced by the New York City Opera. Opened 18 July 1986 at the New York State Theatre and closed 8 November 1986 after 9 performances in repertory.

CAST (in order of appearance): *Alfred*, an itinerant tenor: MICHAEL COUSINS. *Adele*, Rosalinda's chambermaid: CLAUDETTE PETERSON. *Rosalinda von Eisenstein*: LEIGH MUNRO. *Gabriel von Eisenstein*: THEODORE BAERG. *Dr. Blind*, a lawyer: Jerold Siena. *Dr. Falke*, a close friend of Eisenstein: WILLIAM PARCHER. *Frank*, the prison warden: Richard McKee. *Sally*, Adele's sister: Alison Bevan. *Ivan*, servant to Orlofsky: Larry Becker. *Prince Orlofsky*, a wealthy bored Russian: JAMES BILLINGS. *Guest Artist*: Patricia McBride. *Solo Dancer*: Esperanza Galan. *Frosch*, the jailer: Jack Harrold. *Ensemble*: New York City Opera Chorus.

1986.11

HONKY TONK NIGHTS, or How Billy Sampson and Company Left Hell's Kitchen for the Promised Land and What They Found There

A Musical Comedy in Two Acts. Book and lyrics by Ralph Allen, David Campbell. Music by Michael Valenti. Direction and choreography by Ernest O. Flatt. Associate choreographer, Toni Kaye. Scenery by Robert Cothran. Costumes by Mardi Phillips. Lighting by Natasha Katz. Sound by Jack Mann. Musical direction, vocal arrangements by George Broderick. Orchestrations by Jim Tyler. Dance arrangements by David Krane. Produced by Edward H. Davis and Allen M. Shore in association with Marty Feinberg and Schellie Archbold. Opened 7 August 1986 at the Biltmore Theatre and closed 9 August 1986 after 4 performances.

CAST (in order of appearance): *Barney Walker*: JOE MORTON. *Billy Sampson*: IRA HAWKINS. *Armistead Sampson*: DANNY STRAYHORN. *Lily Meadows*: TERESA BURRELL. *George Gooseberry*: REGINALD VelJOHNSON. *Ruby Bush*: Yolanda Graves. *Ivy Vine*: Kyme. *Countess Aida*: Susan Beaubian. *Kitty Stark*: Robin Kersey. *Montgomery Boyd*: M. Demby Cain. *Winston Grey*: Keith Rozie. *Sparks Roberts*: Lloyd Culbreath. *Patron*: Charles Bernard Murray.

Sampson Philharmonia: George Broderick, Kaman Adilifu, John Gale, Robert Keller, David Krane, Gregory Maker, James Sedlar, Andrew Stein, Quinten White.

Act 1: Sampson's Music Hall, on a winter evening. New York City's Hell's Kitchen, 1912.

Act 2: The Promised Land Saloon, summer, 1922, Harlem.

ACT 1

"The Honky Tonk Nights Rag, or Professor Walker and His Solo Symphony"
The Sampson Philharmonia

"Honky Tonk Nights"
I. Hawkins and His Company

"Hot and Bothered"
T. Burrell

"Roll With the Punches"
J. Morton, D. Strayhorn, S. Beaubian, Kyme, R. Kersey, Y. Graves

"Lily of the Alley"
D. Strayhorn, K. Rozie, M. D. Cain, L. Culbreath, J. Morton, T. Burrell

"Choosing a Husband's a Delicate Thing"
D. Strayhorn, J. Morton, R. VelJohnson

[1]Original production first produced in New York 1 December 1956 at the Martin Beck Theatre for 73 performances; revised version first produced Off-Boadway 11 December 1973 at the Chelsea Theater Center, Brooklyn Academy of Music for 48 performances; transferred 5 March 1974 to the Broadway Theatre for 740 performances. For Synopsis of Scenes and Musical Numbers, see 1982 revival.

[2]Originally produced in New York 3 December 1953 at the Ziegfeld Theatre for 583 performances. For Synopsis of Scenes and Musical numbers, see original 1953 production.

[3]First English language production in New York 16 March 1885 at the Casino Theatre for 42 performances. First New York production of this adaptation 20 December 1950 at the Metropolitan Opera House. For Synopsis of Scenes and Musical Numbers, see May 1954 revival.

"Little Dark Bird"
T. Burrell
"Withered Irish Rose"
J. Morton, D. Strayhorn, R. VelJohnson, M. D. Cain, T. Burrell
"Tapaholics"
L. Culbreath, Kyme, M. D. Cain
"Eggs"
J. Morton, T. Burrell
"A Ticket to the Promised Land"
The Sampson Company

ACT 2
"The Promised Land"
The Pyromaniacs
"Stomp the Blues Away"
The Sampson Company
"I've Had It"
J. Morton, T. Burrell
"The Sampson Beauties"
Kyme, R. Kersey, Y. Graves
"The Reform Song"
J. Morton, R. VelJohnson, D. Strayhorn
"I Took My Time"
T. Burrell
"The Brothers Vendetto"
J. Morton, R. VelJohnson, D. Strayhorn
"A Man of Many Parts"
J. Morton
Finale
The Sampson Company

1986.12

ME AND MY GIRL

A Musical Comedy in Two Acts, a Prologue and 9 Scenes. Book and lyrics by L. Arthur Rose and Douglas Furber. Music by Noel Gay. Book revised by Stephen Fry; contributions to revisions by Mike Ockrent. Directed by Mike Ockrent. Choreography by Gillian Gregory. Set design by Martin Johns. Costume designs by Ann Curtis. Lighting design by Chris Ellis, Roger Morgan. Musical direction by Stanley Lebowsky. Sound design by Tom Morse. Orchestrations and dance arrangements by Chris Walker. Produced by Richard Armitage, Terry Allen Kramer, James M. Nederlander, Stage Promotions Limited & Co. Opened 10 August 1986 at the Marquis Theatre and closed 31 December 1989 after 1420 performances.

CAST (in order of appearance): *Lady Jacqueline Carstone*: JANE SUMMERHAYS. *The Honorable Gerald Bolingbroke*: NICK ULLETT. *Lord Battersby*: Eric Hutson. *Lady Battersby*: Justine Johnston. *Herbert Parchester*: TIMOTHY JEROME. *Sir Jasper Tring*: Leo Leyden. *Maria*, Duchess of Dene: JANE CONNELL. *Sir John Tremayne*: GEORGE S. IRVING. *Charles Heathersett*, the Butler: THOMAS TONER. *Bill Snibson*: ROBERT LINDSAY. *Sally Smith*: MARYANN PLUNKET. *Pub Pianist*: John Spalla. *Mrs. Worthington-Worthington*: Gloria Hodes. *Lady Diss*: Elizabeth Larner. *Lady Brighton*: Susan Cella. *Bob Barking*: Kenneth H. Waller. *Telegraph Boy*: Bill Brassea. *Mrs. Brown*: Elizabeth Larner. *Constable*: Eric Johnson.

Ensemble: Cleve Asbury, Bill Brassea, Jonathan Brody, Frankie Cassidy, Susan Cella, Sheri Cowart, Bob Freschi, Ann-Marie Gerard, Larry Hensen, Ida Henry, Randy Hills, Gloria Hodes, K. Craig Innes, Eric Johnson, Michael Hayward-Jones, Barry McNabb, Donna Monroe, Barbara Moroz, Cindy Oakes, William Ryall, John Spalla, Cynthia Thole, Mike Turner, Kenneth H. Waller. *Swings*: Corinne Melancon, Tony Parise.

The action takes place in the late 1930's, in and around Hareford Hall, Hampshire, Mayfair and Lambeth.

Prologue: Mayfair.

Act 1, Scene 1: Hareford Hall, Hampshire. *Scene 2*: The Kitchen. *Scene 3*: The Drawing Room. *Scene 4*: The Hareford Arms. *Scene 5*: The Terrace.

Act 2, Scene 1: The Garden at Hareford Hall. The next afternoon. *Scene 2*: The Library. *Scene 3*: Lambeth. *Scene 4*: Hareford Hall.

ACT 1
Scene 1
"A Weekend at Hareford"
Ensemble
"Thinking of No-One But Me"
J. Summerhays, N. Ullett
"The Family Solicitor"
T. Jerome, G. S. Irving, J. Connell, N. Ullett, E. Hutson, J. Johnston
"Me and My Girl"
R. Lindsay, M. Plunkett
Scene 2
"An English Gentleman"
T. Toner, Staff
Scene 3
"You Would If You Could"
J. Summerhays, R. Lindsay
"Hold My Hand" (from *HOLD MY HAND*, London)
R. Lindsay, M. Plunkett, Dancers
Scene 4
"Once You Lose Your Heart"
M. Plunkett
Scene 5
"Preparation Fugue"
The Company
"The Lambeth Walk"
R. Lindsay, M. Plunkett, Company

ACT 2
Scene 1
"The Sun Has Got His Hat On"[4]
N. Ullett, J. Summerhays, Ensemble
"Take It on the Chin"
M. Plunkett
Scene 2
"Once You Lose Your Heart" (reprise)
M. Plunkett
"Song of Hareford"
J. Connell, R. Lindsay, Ensemble
"Love Makes the World Go Round" (from *THESE FOOLISH THINGS*, London)
R. Lindsay, G. S. Irving
Scene 3
"Leaning on a Lamppost" (from *FEATHER YOUR NEST*, film)
R. Lindsay, Ensemble
Scene 4
Finale
The Company

1986.13

RAGS

A Musical in Two Acts, 22 Scenes. Book by Joseph Stein. Music by Charles Strouse. Lyrics by Stephen Schwartz. Directed by Gene Saks. Musical staging by Ron Field. Sets designed by Beni Montresor. Costumes designed by Florence Klotz. Lighting designed by Jules Fisher. Sound designed by Peter Fitzgerald. Musical direction and additional arrangements by Eric Stern. Orchestrations by Michael Starobin. Production supervisor, Robert V. Straus. Associate producer, Madeline Lee Gilford. Produced by Lee Guber, Martin Heinfling, Marvin A. Krauss. Opened 21 August 1986 at the Mark Hellinger Theatre and closed 23 August 1986 after 4 performances.

CAST (in order of appearance): *Homesick Immigrant*: Andy Gale. *Rebecca Hershkowitz*: TERESA STRATAS. *David Hershkowitz*: JOSH BLAKE. *Guards*: John Aller, Peter Samuel. *The Americans*: Michael Cone, Michael Davis. *Bella Cohen*: JUDY KUHN. *Avram Cohen*: DICK LATESSA. *Anna Blumberg*: EVALYN BARON. *Jack Blumberg*: MORDECAI LAWNER. *Ben*: LONNY PRICE. *Recruiters*: Andy Gale, Stan Rubin. *Nathan's Landlady*: Irma Rogers. *Millie*, her neighbor: Bonnie Schon. *Editor of newspaper*: Stan Rubin. *Social Worker*: Joanna Glushak. *Klezmorim*: Teddy Bragin (tuba), Sean Mahony (trombone), Bruce Engel (trumpet), Harold Seletsky (clarinet), Marshall Coid (violin). *Mr. Bronstein*: Stan Rubin. *Sweatshop Workers (3)*: *Rosa*: Audrey Lavine. *Esther*: Joan Finkelstein. *Sam*: Gabriel Barre. *Saul*, a union organizer: TERRENCE MANN. *Cigar Boss*: Peter Samuel. *Rachel Halpern*: MARCIA LEWIS. *An Avid Shopper*: Joanna Glushak. *Mr. Rosen*: John Aller. *Hamlet*: Peter Samuel. *Ophelia*: Joanna Glushak. *Gertrude*: Irma Rogers. *Rosencrantz*: Michael Cone. *Laertes*: Gabriel Barre. *Frankie*: Michael Cone. *Mike*: Michael Davis. *"Big Tim" Sullivan*: REX EVERHART. *Mr. Harris*: LARRY KERT. *Irish Tenor on Recording*: Michael Cone. *Ragman*: Gabriel Barre. *Wealthy New Yorkers*: Bill Hastings, John Aller,

[4]An interpolation, not in the original English 1937 production.

Michael Davis, Joan Finkelstein, Joanna Glushak, Wendy Kimball, Robert Radford, Peter Samuel, Catherine Ulissey. *Man on Stilts*: Gabriel Barre. *Thugs*: Andy Gale, Peter Samuel. *A Passerby*: Stan Rubin. *Morris*. a little boy: Devon Michaels. *His Mother*: Bonnie Schon. *Violinist*: Marshall Coid. *His Mother*: Irma Rogers. *Irish Girl*: Wendy Kimball. *Her Mother*: Audrey Lavine. *Italian Tenor*: Andy Gale. *His Mother*: Joanna Glushak. *Mrs. Sullivan*: Bonnie Schon. *Herschel Cohen*: John Aller. *Swings*: Patti Mariano, Cissy Rebich, Mark Fotopoulos.

The action takes place during 1910 on the Lower East Side of New York City.

Act 1, Scene 1: Ellis Island, April 1910. *Scene 2*: Battery Park, immediately following. *Scene 3*: East Side Streets and Blumberg Tenement Apartment. That afternoon. *Scene 4*: East Broadway and Offices of the Lower East Side. The next few days. *Scene 5*: A Street and Sweatshops. A few days later. *Scene 6*: Outside Bronstein's Sweatshop. Later that day and weeks following. *Scene 7*: A Yiddish Theatre. A few weeks later. *Scene 8*: Suffolk Street and under the Brooklyn Bridge. Later that night. *Scene 9*: McCarthy's Bar. *Scene 10*: The Blumberg Apartment. Evening, 3 July. *Scene 11*: Suffolk Street and Above Fourteenth Street. Immediately following. *Scene 12*: The Street Market. 4 July. *Scene 13*: The Blumberg Apartment. Immediately following.

Act 2, Scene 1: The Rooftop. Evening, 4 July. *Scene 2*: The Rooftop. Later that night. *Scene 3*: The Street Market. The next day. *Scene 4*: A few days later. *Scene 5*: The Lower East Side Democratic Club. A week later. *Scene 6*: The Blumberg Apartment. Some time later. *Scene 7*: Bronstein's Sweatshop. *Scene 8*: Union Square, A Protest Demonstration. Later that day. *Scene 9*: Suffolk Street and Battery park. A few weeks later.

ACT 1

Scene 1

"I Remember"
A. Gale

Scene 2

"Greenhorns"
M. Cone, New Immigrants

Scene 3

"Brand New World"
T. Stratas, J. Blake

Scene 4

"Children of the Wind"
T. Stratas, D. Latessa, J. Blake

Scene 5

"Penny a Tune"
M. Lewis, Klezmorim, Peddlers, Workers

Scene 6

"Easy for You"
T. Mann, T. Stratas, J. Blake

Scene 7

"Hard to Be a Prince"
P. Samuel, Company

Scene 8

"Blame It on the Summer Night"
T. Stratas, Clarinetist

Scene 9

"What's Wrong with That?"
M. Cone, M. Davis, R. Everhart, L. Kert

Scene 10

"For My Mary"
M. Cone, L. Price

Scene 11

"Rags"
J. Kuhn, D. Latessa

Scene 12

"On the Fourth of July"
Picnickers (Company)

Scene 13

"To America"
T. Stratas, L. Kert

ACT 2

Scene 1

"Yankee Boy"
L. Kert, Neighbors

Scene 2

"Uptown"
L. Kert, T. Stratas

"Wanting"
T. Stratas, T. Mann

Scene 3

"Three Sunny Rooms"
M. Lewis, D. Latessa

Scene 4

"The Sound of Love"
L. Price, J. Blake, Shoppers

"For My Mary" (reprise)
J. Kuhn, L. Price

Scene 5

"Democratic Club Dance"
T. Stratas, R. Everhart, L. Kert, B. Schon, Democrats

Scene 7

"Bread and Freedom"
A. Lavine, T. Stratas, J. Finkelstein, G. Barre

Scene 8

"Dancing with the Fools"
T. Stratas, L. Kert, Strikers

Scene 9

Finale
T. Stratas, J. Blake, The Americans, New Immigrants

1986.14

THE NEW MOON

A Revival of the Operetta in Two Acts, 7 Scenes[5]. Book by Oscar Hammerstein II, Frank Mandel and Laurence Schwab. Music by Sigmund Romberg. Lyrics by Oscar Hammerstein II. New adaptation of the book and lyrics by Robert Johanson. Conductor, Jim Coleman. Director and choreographer, Robert Johanson. Set designer, Michael Anania. Costume designer, Andrew Marlay. Lighting designer, Mark W. Stanley. Chorus master, Joseph Colaneri. Produced by the New York City Opera. Opened 26 August 1986 at the New York State Theatre and closed 7 September 1986 after 16 performances.

CAST (in order of appearance): *Julie*, Marianne's maid: JOYCE CAMPANA. *Alexander*, Bondservant to Beaunoir: GERALD ISAAC. *M. Beaunoir*, Marianne's father, owner of *The New Moon*: Jack Harrold. *Captain Duval*, Commander of *The New Moon*, suitor to Marianne: Joseph McKee. *Vicomte Ribaud*, the great French detective: DAVID RAE SMITH. *Fouchette*, informer for Ribaud: Allen Riberdy. *Robert Mission*, Bondservant to Beaunoir, formerly a nobleman: RICHARD WHITE or DAVIS GAINES. *Besac*, Boatswain on*The New Moon*: Richard McKee. *Jacques*, ship's carpenter on *The New Moon*: Michael Brown. *Marianne Beaunoir*, Beaunoir's daughter: LEIGH MUNRO or MARYANNE TALESE. *Proprietor*: Harris Davis. *Spaniard*: Terry Lacy. *Flower Dancer*: Esperanza Galan. *Philippe Dupres*, French exile, Robert's comrade: MICHAEL COUSINS or MARK THOMSEN. *Clotilde Lombaste*, leader of the brides bound for Martinique: MURIEL COSTA-GREENSPON. *Admiral de Jean*, commander of the new French Navy: John Lankston. *Servants, Courtiers, Ladies, Sailors, Pirates, Tavern Wenches, Brides and French Soldiers*: New York City Opera Chorus.

The action takes place in New Orleans, Louisiana, 1792.

Act 1, Scene 1: Ballroom of M. Beaunoir. *Scene 2*: Cafe Creole, shortly thereafter. *Scene 3*: Ballroom of M. Beanoir, later that night.

Act 2, Scene 1: Deck of *The New Moon*, three days later. *Scene 2*: Isle of Pines, one year later. *Scene 3*: Marianne's cabin, immediately thereafter. *Scene 4*: The stockade, the next morning.

ACT 1[6]

Scene 1

Opening
J. Campana, Servants, Courtiers

---

[5]First presented in New York 19 September 1928 at the Imperial Theatre for 509 performances. The original production was performed in Three Acts, 8 Scenes.

[6]No song list was included in the program for this production. The list below was prepared from Robert Johanson's previous production of THE NEW MOON at Papermill Playhouse.

"Marianne"
R. White
"Marianne" (reprise)
L. Munro, M. Brown, Sailors
"The Girl on the Prow"
L. Munro, R. McKee, Sailors
"Gorgeous Alexander"
G. Isaac, J. Campana, Servants
"An Interrupted Love Song"
J. McKee
"Marianne" (reprise)
R. White

Scene 2
"Tavern Song"
Sailors, Wenches
"Softly, as in a Morning Sunrise"
M. Cousins, Men
"Stouthearted Men"
R. White, M. Cousins, Men

Scene 3
"One Kiss"
L. Munro, Ladies
"Wanting You"
L. Munro, R. White
Finale
Ensemble

ACT 2
Scene 1
"Chanty"
R. McKee, Sailors
"Funny Little Sailor Man"
M. Costa-Greenspon, R. McKee, Sailors, Brides
"Lover Come Back to Me"
L. Munro
"Stouthearted Men" (reprise)
R. White, Ensemble

Scene 2
"Lover Come Back to Me" (reprise)
R. White, M. Cousins, L. Munro

Scene 3
"Love Is Quite a Simple Thing"
J. Campana, M. Costa-Greenspon
"One Kiss" (reprise)
L. Munro, R. White

Scene 4
Finale
Ensemble

1986.15 ROWAN ATKINSON AT THE ATKINSON

An Evening of Comedy in Two Acts. Written by Richard Curtis, Rowan Atkinson, Ben Elton. Music by Howard Goodall. Directed by Mike Ockrent. Musical director, Steven Margoshes. (Set) Design by Will Bowen. Lighting design by Mark Henderson. Sound design by Tony Meola. Production supervisor, Mitchell Erickson. Produced by Arthur Cantor in association with Caroline Hirsch, Peter Wilson, Tony Aljoe.Opened 14 October 1986 at the Brooks Atkinson Theatre and closed 18 October 1986 after 6 performances.

CAST: ROWAN ATKINSON, ANGUS DEAYTON.

The "Schoolmaster" monologue was written by Richard Sparks.

1986.16 RAGGEDY ANN

A Musical Adventure in Two Acts. Book by William Gibson. (Based on characters created by Johnny Gruelle in the "Raggedy Ann Stories.") Music and lyrics by Joe Raposo. Directed and choreographed by Patricia Birch. Set design by Gerry Hariton, Vicki Baral. Costume design by Carrie Robbins. Lighting design by Marc B. Weiss. Sound design by Abe Jacob. Flying by Foy. Musical supervision, dance arrangements by Louis St. Louis. Orchestrations by Stan Applebaum. Musical directors, Ross Allen, Roy Rogosin. Conductor, Ross Allen. Originally produced for the stage by Empire State Institute for the Performing Arts (Patricia B. Snyder, Producing director). Produced by Jon Silverman Associates, Ltd., the (John F.) Kennedy Center, the Empire State Institute for the Performing Arts, Donald K. Donald, in association with CBS. Opened 16 October 1986 at the Nederlander Theatre and closed 19 October 1986 after 5 performances.

CAST (in order of appearance): *Doctors*: Dick Decareau, Joe Barrett, Richard Ryder. *Poppa*: BOB MORRISEY. *Marcella*: LISA RIEFFEL. *Raggedy Ann*: IVY AUSTIN. *Raggedy Andy*: SCOTT SCHAFER. *Baby Doll*: CAROLYN MARBLE. *Panda*: MICHELAN SISTI. *General D*: LEO BURMESTER. *Bat*: GAIL BENEDICT. *Wolf*: GORDON [JOSEPH] WEISS. *Camel with the wrinkled knees*: JOEL AROESTE. *Mommy*: ELIZABETH AUSTIN.

Company: Melinda Buckley, Gregory Butler, Anny DeGange, Susann Fletcher, Michaela Hughes, Steve Owsley, Andrea Wright. *Swing*: Helena Andreyko.

The action takes place sometime earlier in this century on the New York riverfront.

ACT 1
"Gingham and Yarn"
Company
"Carry On"
B. Morrisey
"Diagnosis"
D. Decareau, J. Barrett, R. Ryder
"The Light"
Dolls, L. Rieffel
"Make Believe"
I. Austin, L. Burmester
"Blue"
J. Aroeste, I. Austin
"Make Believe" (reprise)
S. Schafer, L. Rieffel, Dolls, Company
"Make Believe" (reprise)
I. Austin, L. Rieffel
"Something in the Air"
Company
"Delighted"
Clouds
"So Beautiful"
I. Austin, L. Rieffel, Clouds
"A Heavenly Chorus"
Yellow Yum Yum
"The Shooting Star"
E. Austin, B. Morrisey, The Rat in the Rolls Royce
"The Wedding"
Company
"Rag Dolly"
I. Austin

ACT 2
"Gingham and Yarn" (reprise)
Company
"You'll Love It"
G. Benedict, S. Schafer, the Batettes
"A Little Music"
L. Rieffel, J. Aroeste, I. Austin, Dolls
"Gone"
Dolls, Company
"Why Not"
E. Austin
"What Did I Lose?"
E. Austin
"Somewhere"
I. Austin
"Welcome to L.A."
Nurses
"Diagnosis" (reprise)
Doctors
"I Come Riding"
L. Burmester

"Gingham and Yarn" (reprise)
Company
"Rag Dolly" (Finale)
Company

1986.17 FLAMENCO PURO

A Dance Revue in Two Acts. Conceived, directed and designed by Claudio Segovia and Hector Orezzoli. Sound by F. Richard Fitzgerald. Associate producer, Marilynn LeVine. Produced by Mel Howard and Donald K. Donald. Opened 19 October 1986 at the Mark Hellinger Theatre and closed 30 November 1986 after 53 performances.

CAST (in alphabetical order): *Dancers*: Manuela Carrasco, José Cortés (El Biencasao), Antonio Montoya (El Farruco), Pilar Montoya (La Faraona), Rosario Montoya (La Farruquita), Eduardo Serrano (El Guito), Angelita Vargas.

Singers: Juan José Amador, Diego Camacho (El Boquerón), Adela Chaqueta, Enrique (El Extremeño), Fernanda de Utrera, Juan Fernández (El Moreno), Antonio Núñez (El Chocolate).

Guitarists: Joaquin Amador, Ramón Amador, Agustin Carbonell (El Bola), José Carmona Carmona (El Habichuela), Juan Carmona Carmona (El Habichuela), José Miguel Carmona Niño.

ACT 1
"Bulerias"
The Entire Company
My sorrow is great/My fatigue is great/I'll take them to the grave with me/
And say nothing to anyone.
Sallow, with rings under her eyes?/Don't ask her what's wrong/
She is truly in love.
I am brown and poor/Even browner is Cinnamon.
"Martinete"
A. Núñez
A primal scream, with artifice is "truth in a clenched fist."
"Toque"
Pepe Habichuela
"Cana"
(*Danced by*) M. Carrasco, P. Montoya, R. Montoya, A. Vargas
Singers: Enrique, D. Cumacho, J. Fernández. *Guitars*: A. Carbonell, Juan C. Carmona, J. Amador.
Cafe Cantate:
"Alegrias"A. Chaqueta
My child has a balcony
Which faces the rising sun
The sun rises, my child rises
And God's grace rises too.
I spread my hair out on a branch
On a branch
And the name of the person who will unravel it
Is Manuel
"Romeras"
(Danced by) J. Cortés
"Garrotin"
(Danced by) A. Vargas
"Romance"
(Danced by) M. Carrasco
"Farruca"
(Danced by) E. Serrano
"Alegrias"
(Danced by) R. Montoya
Singers: D. Camacho, Enrique, J. J. Amador, J. Fernández. *Guitars*: J. Amador, R. Amador, A. Carbonell, J. M. Carmona.
"Fandangos"
F. de Utrera, A. Núñez, Juan Carmona Carmona, José Carmona Carmona

I am not afraid of death/Because death is a natural thing/ I am more afraid of life/Because I don't know where it will lead me/With this head of mine.

If I call you sun I abuse you/If I call you moon I wound you/And when I call you morning star/It seems as if I am killing you/Would you like, perhaps, for me to call you sky?

"Tarantos"
The Entire Company
Don't be afraid Señora
It's just a miner singing
A miner with a sore throat
Because of the dust in his path
I lost my handkerchief
While leaving the mine
And who has found it?
A gypsy that I love
And he doesn't want to give it back.

ACT 2
"Tangos"
(Danced by) A. Chaqueta, R. Montoya, P. Montoya
Singers: Enrique, J. Fernández, J. J. Amador. *Guitars*: A. Carbonell, J. M. Carmona.
Hold your tongue, Hold your tongue
Because I have hidden things about you.
Little secrets that no one knows.
All black eyes/Are to be taken prisoner tomorrorw.
Yours are so black/You must cover your face with a veil.
"Tientos"
(Danced by) A. Vargas
Guitars: José Carmona Carmona, Juan Carmona Carmona. *Singer*: D. Camacho.
Listening to her I trembled/She told me my fortune.
But what she didn't tell me
Is that I have begun to hate my love/for the rest of my life.
What kind of bird is singing on the green olive?
Tell him to stop!
He's hurting my ears.
"Soleares"
F. de Utrera
Guitar: José Carmona Carmona. *Danced by* E. Serrano. *Guitars*: A. Carbonell, Juan Carmona Carmona. *Singers*: Enrique, J. J. Amador. *Danced by* M. Carrasco. *Guitars*: J. Amador, R. Amador. *Singers*: Enrique, J. J. Amador.
Perhaps I was born on a Tuesday
Because this bad luck of mine
Follows me everywhere.
"Seguiriya"
(Danced by) A. Montoya, A. Núñez
Guitars: José Carmona Carmona, R. Amador. *Singer*: J. Fernández.
Ay, Don't knock at this door
For the love of God don't knock
The gypsy inside
Is dead by my fault.
"Bulerias"
Entire Company

1986.18 INTO THE LIGHT

A Musical in Two Acts, a Prologue, 13 Scenes and an Epilogue. Book by Jeff Tambornino. Music by Lee Holdridge. Lyrics by John Forster. Directed by Michael Maurer. Choreography by Mary Jane Houdina. Scenery, projections by Neil Peter Jampolis, Hervig Libowitzky. Costumes by Karen Roston. Lighting by Neil Peter Jampolis. Sound design by Jack Mann. Musical direction by Peter Howard. Orchestrations by Ira Hearshen. Laser design by Marilyn Lowey. Special laser effects by Laser Media. Synthesizer programming by Jeff Waxman. Produced by Joseph Z. Nederlander, Richard Kughn, Jerrold Perenchio. Opened 22 October 1986 at the Neil Simon Theatre and closed 26 October 1986 after 6 performances.

CAST (in order of speaking): *Friend*: ALAN MINTZ. *Mathew Prescott*: DANNY GERARD. *Kate Prescott*: SUSAN BIGELOW. *James Prescott*: DEAN JONES. *Colonel*: Ted Forlow. *Major*: David Young. *Father Frank Girella*: WILLIAM PARRY. *Peter Vonn*: LENNY WOLPE. *Nathan Gelb*: Peter Walker. *Vijay Bannerjee*: Mitchell Greenberg. *Phyllis Terwilliger*: Kathryn McAteer. *Paul Cooper*: Alan Brasington. *Don Cesare*: CASPER ROOS. *Archbishop Parisi*: TOM BATTEN. *Signor Bocciarelli*: Gordon Stanley.

Ensemble: Michael Duran, David Young, Deborah Carlson, Terri Homberg, Valerie DePena. *Swings*: Cheri Butcher, Ron Chisholm.

The action takes place at the present time during late summer in Los Alamos, New Mexico, and in Turin, Italy.

Act 1, Scene 1: James Prescott's office and the Prescott home. *Scene 2*: The lab at Los Alamos. *Scene 3*: The Prescott home. late at night. *Scene 4*: The next morning. *Scene 5*: Turin, Italy. The Council Chambers of Il Centro di Sindonologia. *Scene 6*: The Precott home. *Scene 7*: The airport and lab at Los Alamos.

Act 2, Scene 1: Turin, Italy. *Scene 2*: Turin, Italy. *Scene 3*: The Prescott home. *Scene 4*: The testing room, St. John's Cathedral. *Scene 5*: Albergo Excelsiore. *Scene 6*: The testing room.

ACT 1
Prologue: "Poltergeists"
D. Gerard, S. Bigelow
Scene 1
"Neat/Not Neat"
D. Jones, W. Parry, S. Bigelow
"It Can All Be Explained"
D. Jones, W. Parry
Scene 2
"The Data"
D. Jones, Team
Scene 3
"A Talk About Time"
D. Jones, K. Bigelow
Scene 4
"Trading Solos"
W. Parry, D. Gerard, A. Mintz
Scene 5
"Let There Be Light"
D. Jones, C. Roos, W. Parry, G. Stanley, T. Batten
Scene 6
"Wishes"
D. Gerard
Scene 7
"The Three of Us"
S. Bigelow, D. Jones
"Rainbow Logic"
D. Jones

ACT 2
Scene 1
"Fede Fede"
C. Roos, T. Batten, Team
Scene 2
"To Measure the Darkness"
D. Jones, S. Bigelow
Scene 4
"The Testing"
D. Jones, Team
Scene 5
"The Rose and I"
S. Bigelow
Scene 6
"The Testing" continued
D. Jones, Team
"Measure the Darkness" (reprise)
D. Jones
"Be There"
D. Jones, D. Gerard
Epilogue: "Into the Light"
Company

1986.19 OH, COWARD!

A Revival of the Musical Revue in Two Acts, 18 Scenes[7]. Words and music by Noël Coward. Devised and Directed by Roderick Cook. Settings by Helen Pond, Herbert Senn. Costumes by David Toser. Lighting by F. Mitchell Dana. Musical director, Dennis Buck. Musical arrangements by Rene Wiegert. Executive producer, Richard Seader. Produced by Raymond J. Greenwald. Opened 17 November 1986 at the Helen Hayes Theater and closed 3 January 1987 after 56 performances.

CAST: RODERICK COOK, CATHERINE COX, PATRICK QUINN.

Act 1, Scene 1: Introduction. *Scene 2*: Oh Coward! *Scene 3*: England. *Scene 4*: Family Album. *Scene 5*: Music Hall. *Scene 6*: If Love Were All. *Scene 7*: Travel. *Scene 8*: Finale Act 1.

Act 2, Scene 1: Mad Dogs and Englishmen. *Scene 2*: A Marvelous Party. *Scene 3*: Design for Dancing. *Scene 4*: You Were There. *Scene 5*: Theatre. *Scene 6*: Love. *Scene 7*: Women. *Scene 8*: World Weary. *Scene 9*: Let's Do It. *Scene 10*: Finale.

ACT 1
Scene 1
The Boy Actor
C. Cox, P. Quinn, R. Cook
Scene 2
"Something to Do With Spring" (from *WORDS AND MUSIC*, London)
"Bright Young People" (from *COCHRAN'S 1931 REVUE*, London)
"Poor Little Rich Girl" (from *ON WITH THE DANCE*, London)
"Zigeuner" (from *BITTER SWEET*)
"Let's Say Goodbye" (from *WORDS AND MUSIC*, London)
"This Is a Changing World" (from *PACIFIC 1860*, London)
"We Were Dancing" (from *TONIGHT AT 8:30*)
"Dance Little Lady" (from *THIS YEAR OF GRACE*)
"(A) Room with a View" (from *THIS YEAR OF GRACE*)
"Sail Away" (from *ACE OF CLUBS*, London; *SAIL AWAY!*)
C. Cox, P. Quinn, R. Cook
Scene 3
"London Is a Little Bit of All Right" (from *THE GIRL WHO CAME TO SUPPER*)
P. Quinn
"The End of the News" (from *SIGH NO MORE*)
C. Cox, R. Cook
"The Stately Homes of England" (from *OPERETTE*, London; *SET TO MUSIC*)
P. Quinn, R. Cook
"London Pride"
C. Cox
Scene 4
Auntie Jessie
R. Cook
"Uncle Harry" (from *PACIFIC 1860*, London)
C. Cox, P. Quinn
Scene 5
Introduction
R. Cook
"Chase Me Charlie" (from *ACE OF CLUBS*, London)
C. Cox
"Saturday Night at the Rose and Crown"
(from *THE GIRL WHO CAME TO SUPPER*)
C. Cox, P. Quinn, R. Cook
"Island of Bollamazoo" (from *OPERETTE*, London)
P. Quinn
"What Ho, Mrs. Brisket" (from *THE GIRL WHO CAME TO SUPPER*)
R. Cook
"Has Anybody Seen Our Ship?" (from *TONIGHT AT 8:30*)
C. Cox, P. Quinn, R. Cook
"Men About Town" (from *TONIGHT AT 8:30*)
P. Quinn, R. Cook
Scene 6
"If Love Were All" (from *BITTER SWEET*)
Scene 7
Too Early or Too Late
R. Cook
"Why Do the Wrong People Travel?" (from *SAIL AWAY!*)
C. Cox, P. Quinn

[7]Originally produced Off-Broadway 4 October 1972 at the New Theatre for 295 performances.

"The Passenger's Always Right" (from *SAIL AWAY!*)
C. Cox, P. Quinn, R. Cook
Scene 8
"Mrs. Worthington"
C. Cox, P. Quinn, R. Cook

ACT 2
Scene 1
"Mad Dogs and Englishmen" (from *WORDS AND MUSIC* London; *THIRD LITTLE SHOW*)
C. Cox, P. Quinn, R. Cook
Scene 2
"The Party's Over Now" (from *WORDS AND MUSIC*, London; *SET TO MUSIC*)
R. Cook
Scene 3
"Dance Little Lady" (from *THIS YEAR OF GRACE*)
C. Cox, P. Quinn, R. Cook
Scene 4
"You Were There" (from *TONIGHT AT 8:30*)
P. Quinn
Scene 5
"Three White Feathers" (from *WORDS AND MUSIC*, London)
C. Cox, R. Cook
The Star, P. Quinn
The Critic, R. Cook
The Elderly Actress, C. Cox
Scene 6
Gertie
R. Cook
Loving
P. Quinn
I Am No Good at Love
R. Cook
Sex Talk
P. Quinn
A Question of Lighting
P. Quinn, R. Cook
"Mad About the Boy" (from *WORDS AND MUSIC*, London; *SET TO MUSIC*)
C. Cox
Scene 7
Introduction
R. Cook
"Nina" (from *SIGH NO MORE*, London)
P. Quinn
"Mrs. Wentworth-Brewster" (A Bar on the Piccola Marina)
R. Cook
Scene 8
"World Weary" (from *THIS YEAR OF GRACE*)
C. Cox, P. Quinn, R. Cook
Scene 9
"Let's Do It"
(*Music by* Cole Porter.) C. Cox, P. Quinn, R. Cook
Scene 10
"Where Are the Songs We Sung?" (from *OPERETTE*, London)
P. Quinn
"Someday I'll Find You" (from *PRIVATE LIVES*)
R. Cook
"I'll Follow My Secret Heart" (from *CONVERSATION PIECE*)
C. Cox
"If Love Were All" (reprise)
C. Cox, P. Quinn, R. Cook
"Play, Orchestra, Play" (from *TONIGHT AT 8:30*)
C. Cox, P. Quinn, R. Cook
"I'll See You Again" (from *BITTER SWEET*)
C. Cox, P. Quinn, R. Cook

1986.20

SMILE

A Musical in Two Acts. Book and lyrics by Howard Ashman. Based on the film of the same name with screenplay by Jerry Belson. Music by Marvin Hamlisch. Directed by Howard Ashman. Musical staging by Mary Kyte. Scenic design by Douglas W. Schmidt. Costume design by William Ivey Long. Lighting design by Paul Gallo. Sound design by Otts Munderloh. Musical director, Paul Gemignani. Orchestrations by Sid Ramin, Bill Byers, Dick Hazard, Torrie Zito. Vocal arrangements by Buster Davis. Associate producers, Barbara Livitz, Ronald and Barbara Balser. Produced by Lawrence Gordon, Richard Kagan, Sidney Shlenker. Opened 24 November 1986 at the Lunt-Fontanne Theatre and closed 3 January 1987 after 48 performances.

CAST: *Contestants*: *Robin Gibson*, Antelope Valley: ANNE MARIE BOBBY. *Doria Hudson*, Yuba City: JODI BENSON. *Sandra-Kay Macafee*, Bakersfield: VEANNE COX. *Maria Gonzales*, Salinas: CHERYL-ANN ROSSI. *Shawn Christianson*, La Jolla: TIA RIEBLING. *Valerie Sherman*, Sacramento: LAUREN GOLER. *Heidi Anderson*, Anaheim: Deanna D. Wells. *Patti-Lynn Bird*, El Centro: Mana Allen. *Debralee Davis*, Eureka: Andrea Leigh-Smith. *Kate Gardner*, Fresno: Mia Malm. *Linda Lee*, San Francisco: Valerie Kau-Lee. *Kimberly Lyons*, Palo Alto: Julie Tussey. *Gina Minelli*, San Luis Obispo: Donna Marie Elio. *Dana Simpson*, Sausalito: Renée Veneziale. *Connie-Sue Whipple*, Visalia: Cindy Oakes. *Cookie Wilson*, Carson: Nikki Rene. *Joanne Marshal*, last year's winner: Mia Malm.
Adults: *Brenda DiCarlo Freelander*: MARSHA WATERBURY. *Big Bob Freelander*: JEFF McCARTHY. *Tommy French*, the pageant choreographer: MICHAEL O'GORMAN. *Dale Wilson-Shears*, chairman of the Young American Miss Foundation: RICHARD WOODS. *Ted Farley*, an Emcee: DICK PATTERSON. *Carol*, Brenda's assistant: Ruth Williamson. *Tony*, a volunteer: Jeffrey Wilkins. *Robin's Mom, Judge, Volunteer*: Laura Gardner. *Photographer, Judge, Volunteer*: K. C. Wilson.
Kids: *Little Bob Freelander*: Tommy Daggett. *Freddy*: Andrew Cassese.
Swings: Michael Bologna, Susan Dow, Linda Hess, Woody Howard, Joyce Nolen.

Act 1: Santa Rosa Junior College, (Santa Rosa, California). Three days last summer.

Act 2: Santa Rosa Junior College. Saturday night.

ACT 1
Prologue
The Contestants
"Orientation/Postcard #1"
M. Waterbury, A. M. Bobby, Contestants
"Disneyland"
J. Benson
"Shine"
The Contestants, M. O'Gorman, M. Waterbury
"Postcard #2"
A. M. Bobby
"Nerves"
The Contestants
"Young and American" (Preliminary Night)
The Contestants
"Until Tomorrow Night"
The Contestants, M. Waterbury, J. McCarthy

ACT 2
"Postcard #3/Dressing Room Scene"
A. M. Bobby, J. Benson, D. Patterson, Contestants
"Smile"
D. Patterson, Contestants
"In Our Hands"
The Contestants
"Pretty as a Picture"
D. Patterson, J. McCarthy, A. M. Bobby, Contestants

1986.21

THE WORLD ACCORDING TO ME

A One Man Comedy Revue in Two Acts. Created and written by Jackie Mason. Supervised by Ron Clark. Scenery and lighting by Neil Peter Jampolis. Sound by Bruce D.Cameron. Associate producer, Jyll Rosenfeld. Produced by Nick Vanoff. Opened 22 December 1986 at the Brooks Atkinson Theater and closed 2 January 1988 after 367 performances.

CAST: JACKIE MASON (stand-up comedy, monologues, impressions.

THE MIKADO,

1987.01 or The Town of Titipu

A Revival of the Comic Opera in Two Acts[8]. Libretto by William S. Gilbert. Music by Arthur Sullivan. Directed and choreographed by Brian Macdonald. Set design by Susan Benson and Douglas McLean. Costumes designed by Susan Benson. Lighting designed by J. Michael Whitfield. Musical direction, additional musical arrangements by Berthold Carriere. Orchestra of the New York Opera Repertory Theater. A Stratford Festival of Canada Production. Produced by Ed and David Mirvish and Brian Macdonald. Opened 13 January 1987 at the New York City Center and closed 18 January 1987 after 7 performances; re-opened 2 April 1987 at the Virginia Theatre and closed 3 May 1987 after 38 additional performances. Total: 45 performances.

CAST: *The Mikado of Japan*: AVO KITTASK. *Nanki-Poo*, his son, disguised as a wandering minstrel in love with Yum-Yum: JOHN KEANE. *Ko-Ko*, Lord High Executioner of Titipu: ERIC DONKIN. *Pooh-Bah*, Lord High Everything Else: RICHARD McMILLAN. *Pish-Tush*, a Noble Lord: Paul Massel. *Yum-Yum, Pitti-Sing, Peep-Bo*, three sisters, wards of Ko-Ko: MARIE BARON, KAREN WOOD, KAREN SKIDMORE. *Katisha*, an elderly lady in love with Nanki-Poo: ARLENE MEADOWS. *Tumbler*: David Gonzales.

Chorus of School Girls, Nobles, Guards and Coolies: Stephen Beamish, Timothy Cruickshank, Aggie Cekuta Elliot, Glori Gage, Paul Gatchell, Larry Herbert, Deborah Joy, Devid Keeley, Calla Krause, Richard March, Janet Martin, Dale Mieske, Lyndsay Richardson, Bradley C. Rudy, Joy Thompson-Allen, Marcia Tratt, Jim White.

1987.02 STARDUST

A Musical Revue in Two Acts[9]. Lyrics by Mitchell Parish. Music by Hoagy Carmichael, Benny Goodman, Duke Ellington, Leroy Anderson, others. Based on an idea by Burton L. Litwin and Albert Harris. Conceived and directed by Albert Harris. Musical staging by Patrice Soreiro. Musical supervision and direction, vocal arrangements, orchestrations by James Raitt. Scenery by David Jenkins. Costumes by Mardi Philips. Lighting by Ken Billington. Sound by Gary Harris. Associate producer, Richard Jay Smith. Tap dance created and staged by Henry LeTang. Produced by Burton L. Litwin, Howard Rose, Martin I. Rein, Louise Westergaard in association with Paula Hutter Gilliam[10]. Opened 19 February 1987 at the Biltmore Theatre and closed 17 May 1987 after 118 performances. Total including Off-Broadway run: 177 performances.

CAST (in alphabetical order): MICHELE BAUTIER, MAUREEN BRENNAN, KIM CRISWELL, ANDRE DeSHIELDS, JASON GRAAE, JIM WALTON.

ACT 1

"Carolina Rolling Stone"
J. Graae, Company
(*Music by* Eleanor Young, Harry D. Squires. 1921)

"Riverboat Shuffle"
A. DeShields, Company
(*Music by* Hoagy Carmichael, Dick Voynow, Irving Mills. 1924)

"One Morning in May"[11]
M. Brennan
(*Music by* Hoagy Carmichael. 1933)

"Sweet Lorraine"
J. Walton
(*Music by* Cliff Burwell. 1928)

"Sentimental Gentleman from Georgia"
M. Bautier, M. Brennan, K. Criswell
(*Music by* Frank Perkins. 1932)

"Sophisticated Lady"
M. Bautier
(*Music by* Duke Ellington. *Co-Lyricist*: Irving Mills. 1933)

"Dixie After Dark"
A. DeShields, J. Walton
(*Music by* Ben Oakland, Irving Mills. 1934)

"Stairway to the Stars"
K. Criswell
(*Music by* Matty Malneck, Frank Signorelli. 1935)

"Wealthy, Shmelthy, as Long as You're Healthy"
J. Graae
(*Music by* Sammy Fain. 1935)

The 1930's Unrequited Love Montage:

"Hands Across the Table" (from *CONTINENTAL VARIETIES*)
M. Bautier
(*Music by* Jean Delettre. 1934)

"You're So Indiff'rent"
J. Graae
(*Music by* Sammy Fain. 1935)

"It Happens to the Best of Friends"
K. Criswell
(*Music by* Rube Bloom. 1934)

"I Would If I Could But I Can't"
J. Walton
(*Music by* Bing Crosby, Alan Grey. 1933.

"The Scat Song"
A. DeShields, M. Brennan
(*Music by* Frank Perkins, Cab Calloway. 1932)

"Sidewalks of Cuba" (from *COTTON CLUB PARADE OF 1934*)
K. Criswell, J. Graae
(*Music by* Ben Oakland, Irving Mills. 1934)

"Evenin'"[12]
M. Bautier
(*Music by* Harry White. 1934)

"Deep Purple"
A. DeShields, Company
(*Music by* Peter DeRose. 1934)

ACT 2

"Sophisticated Swing"
K. Criswell, M. Brennan, J. Walton
(*Music by* Will Hudson. 1936)

"Midnight at the Onyx"
A. DeShields, M. Brennan, J. Walton
(*Music by* Will Hudson. 1937)

"Tell Me Why"
(J. Graae)
(*Music by* Michael Edwards, Sigmund Spaeth. 1945)

"Does Your Heart Beat for Me?"
J. Graae
(*Music by* Russ Morgan, Arnold Johnson. 1936)

"Stars Fell on Alabama"
J. Walton, M. Brennan
(*Music by* Frank Perkins. 1934)

"Don't Be That Way"
A. DeShields, M. Bautier
(*Music by* Benny Goodman, Edgar Sampson. 1935)

"Organ Grinder's Swing"
A. DeShields, J. Graae, J. Walton
(*Music by* Will Hudson. *Co-Lyricist*: Irving Mills. 1936)

"Moonlight Serenade"
Company
(*Music by* Glenn Miller. 1939)

"Star Dust"
M. Bautier

---

[8]First presented in New York 20 July, 10-29 August 1885 at the Union Square and People's Theatres for 22 performances. First authorized production presented 19 August 1885 at the Fifth Avenue Theatre by Richard D'Oyly Carte for 250 performances. For Synopsis of Scenes and Musical Numbers, see 19 August 1885 D'Oyly Carte production. Added to the Ensemble for the Broadway run: Elizabeth Adams, David Playfair, Gerald Smuin, , Steve Yorke. Dropped from Ensemble for Broadway run: Calla Krause, Dale Mieske, Bradley C. Rudy. Added for Broadway run: Conductor, Fen Watkin. Additional Tumbler {Acrobat}: Walter Quigley.

[9]Originally produced Off-Broadway 11 November 1986 at Theater Off Park for 59 peformances.

[10]Late in Broadway run William H. Kessler joined as a co-producer.

[11]Dropped late in Broadway run.

[12]Replaced late in run by:
"The Lamp Is Low" M. Bautier
(*Music by* Peter DeRose, Bert Shefter, adapted from Maurice Ravel's 'Pavanne pour une Infante Defunte.' 1939)

(*Music by* Hoagy Carmichael. 1929)

Your Cavalcade of Hits: *Host*: A. DeShields.

"Belle of the Ball"
J. Graae, M. Brennan
(*Music by* Leroy Anderson. 1951)

"The Syncopated Clock"
M. Brennan, J. Graae, K. Criswell, J. Walton
(*Music by* Leroy Anderson. 1946)

"Take Me in Your Arms"
M. Brennan
(*Music by* Fred Markush. 1932)

"Ciao, Ciao, Bambino"
K. Criswell
(*Music by* Domenico Modugno. 1959)

"Sleigh Ride"
M. Brennan, J. Graae, K. Criswell, J. Walton
(*Music by* Leroy Anderson. 1949)

"Volare"
J. Walton, Company
(*Music by* Domenico Modugno. 1958)

"Your Cavalcade of Hits" Theme
Music by James Raitt. *Lyrics by* Jay Jeffries.

"Happy Cigarettes" Theme
Music by James Raitt. *Lyrics by* Peter Jablonski.

"Ruby" (from *RUBY GENTRY*, film)
A. DeShields
(*Music by* Heinz Roemheld. 1953)

"Forgotten Dreams"
Company
(*Music by* Leroy Anderson. 1954)

"Star Dust" (reprise)
Company

1987.03

SOUTH PACIFIC

A Revival of the Musical Play in Two Acts, 23 Scenes[13]. Book by Oscar Hammerstein II and Joshua Logan. Adapted from James A. Michener's novel "Tales of the South Pacific." Music by Richard Rodgers. Lyrics by Oscar Hammerstein II. Direction and musical staging by Gerald Freedman. Scenery and costumes by Desmond Heeley. Lighting by Duane Schuler. Choreography by Janet Watson. Sound by Thomas Maher. Musical director, Paul Gemignani. Orchestrations by Robert Russell Bennett. Produced by the New York City Opera. Opened 28 February 1987 at the New York State Theatre and closed 26 April 1987 after 68 performances.

CAST (in order of appearance): *Ngana*: Lynn Chen or Allegra Forste. *Jerome*: Robin Ria or Peter Yarin. *Henry*: Thomas Ikeda. *Ensign Nellie Forbush*: SUSAN BIGELOW or MARCIA MITZMAN. *Emile DeBecque*: JUSTINO DIAZ or STANLEY WEXLER. *Bloody Mary*: MURIEL COSTA-GREENSPON or CAMILLE SAVIOLA. *Bloody Mary's Assistant*: Raven Wilkinson. *Luther Billis*: TONY ROBERTS. *Lt. Joseph Cable, U.S.M.C.*: RICHARD WHITE or CRIS GROENENDAAL. *Capt. George Brackett, U.S.N.*: JAMES BILLINGS. *Cmdr. William Harbison, U.S.N.*: Daren Kelly or Joseph Culliton. *Lt. Buzz Adams*: Ralph Bassett. *Seaman Tom O'Brien*: Terry Lacy. *Cpl. Hamilton Steeves, U.S.M.C.*: Ron Hilley. *Abner*: Charles Mandracchia. *Sgt. Kenneth Johnson*: Gregory Moore. *Radio Operator Bob McCaffrey*: Jonathan Guss. *Stewpot*: John Welch. *Professor*: Jeff Blumenkrantz. *Private Victor Jerome*: Andrew Cuk. *Pvt. Sven Larsen*: Edward Zimmerman. *Yeoman Herbert Quale*: Frank Ream. *Sgt. Jack Waters*: Louis Perry. *Seabee Richard West*: Robert Brubaker. *Seabee Morton Wise*: William Dyszel. *Staff-Sgt. Thomas Hassinger*: David Frye. *Seabee Joseph Grant*: Don Yule. *Lt. Genevieve Marshall*: Michele McBride. *Ensign Lisa Minelli*: Ivy Austin. *Ensign Connie Walewska*: Deborah Darr. *Ensign Janet MacGregor*: Janet Villas. *Ensign Bessie Noonan*: Paula Hostetter. *Ensign Rita Adams*: Deanna Wells. *Ensign Sue Yaeger*: Tina Johnson. *Ensign Cora MacRae*: Sylvia Rhyne. *Ensign Dinah Murphy*: Kay Schoenfeld. *Liat*: ANN YEN or ADRIENNE TELEMAQUE. *Marcel*: Henry Ravelo.

[13]First produced in New York 7 April 1949 at the Majestic Theatre for 1925 performances. For Synopsis of Scenes and Musical Numbers, see original 1949 production. For this production, the Act 1 Finale was listed under the title"This Is How It Feels"/"I'm Gonna Wah That Man Right Out-a My Hair" (reprise); The Soft Shoe Dance (Act 2, Scene 1) dropped.

1987.04

LES MISÉRABLES

A Musical in Two Acts, a Prologue and 4 Scenes. Original French text by Alain Boublil and Jean-Marc Natel. Additional material by James Fenton. Based on the novel of the same name by Victor Hugo. Music by Claude-Michel Schönberg. (English) Lyrics by Herbert Kretzmer. Directed and adapted by Trevor Nunn and John Caird. Orchestral score by John Cameron. Musical supervision and direction by Robert Billig. Sound by Andrew Bruce/Autograph. (Settings) Designed by John Napier. Lighting by David Hersey. Costumes by Andreane Neofitou. Executive producers, Martin McCallum, Richard-Jay Alexander. Original London production produced by Cameron Mackintosh and the Royal Shakespeare Company. Produced by Cameron Mackintosh in association with the John F. Kennedy Center. Opened 12 March 1987 at the Broadway Theatre, moved 16 October 1990 to the Imperial Theatre, and is still running at this time!

CAST (in order of appearance): *Prologue, 1815*: *Jean Valjean*: COLM WILKINSON. *Javert*: TERRENCE MANN. *Chain Gang*: Kevin Marcum, Paul Harman, Anthony Crivello, John Dewar, Joseph Kolinski, Leo Burmester, David Bryant, Alex Santoriello, Michael Maguire. *Farmer*: Jesse Corti. *Labourer*: Alex Santoriello. *Innkeeper*: John Norman. *Innkeeper's Wife*: Susan Goodman. *The Bishop of Digne*: Norman Large. *Constables*: Marcus Lovett, Steve Shocket.

Montreuil-sur-Mer, 1823: *Fantine*: RANDY GRAFF. *Foreman*: Paul Harman. *Workers*: Jesse Corti, John Dewar. *Women Workers*: Cindy Benson, Marcie Shaw, Jane Bodle, Joanna Glushak. *Factory Girl*: Ann Crumb. *Sailors*: Jospeh Kolinski, Kevin Marcum, John Dewar. *Whores*: Susan Goodman, Joanna Glushak, Jane Bodle, Kelli James, Ann Crumb, Frances Ruffelle, Judy Kuhn, Gretchen Kingsley-Weihe. *Old Woman*: Cindy Benson. *Crone*: Marcie Shaw. *Pimp*: Steve Shocket. *Bamatabois*: Anthony Crivello. *Fauchelevent*: Steve Shocket.

Montfermeil, 1823: *Young Cosette*: Donna Vivino. *Madame Thénardier*: JENNIFER BUTT. *Thénardier*: LEO BURMESTER. *Young Eponine*: Chrissie McDonald. *Drinker*: Jesse Corti. *Young Couple*: Alex Santoriello, Gretchen Kingsley-Wiehe. *Drunk*; John Norman. *Diners*: Norman Large, Joanna Glushak. *Other Drinkers*: Steve Shocket, Anthony Crivello, Kevin Marcum, Ann Crumb, Susan Goodman, Cindy Benson. *Young Man*: Joseph Kolinski. *Young Girls*: Jane Bodle, Kelli James. *Old Couple*: Marcie Shaw, John Dewar. *Travelers*: Paul Harman, Marcus Lovett.

Paris, 1832: *Gavroche*: Braden Danner. *Old Beggar Woman*: Susan Goodman. *Young Prostitute*: Ann Crumb. *Pimp*: John Norman. *Eponine*: FRANCES RUFFELLE. *Thénardier's Gang (4)*: *Montparnasse*: Alex Santoriello. *Babet*: Marcus Lovett. *Brujon*: Kevin Marcum. *Claquesous*: Steve Schocket. *Enjolras*: MICHAEL MAGUIRE. *Marius*: DAVID BRYANT. *Cosette*: JUDY KUHN. *Combeferre*: Paul Harman. *Feuilly*: Joseph Kolinski. *Courfeyrac*: Jesse Corti. *Joly*: John Dewar. *Grantaire*: Anthony Crivello. *Lesgles*: Norman Large. *Jean Prouvaire*: John Norman.

Prologue: Digne, (France). 1815.

Act 1, Scene 1: Montreuil-sur-Mer, 1823. *Scene 2*: Montfermeil, 1823. *Scene 3*: Paris, 1832.

Act 2: Paris, 1832.

ACT 1

Prologue

Prologue
The Company

"Soliloquy"
C. Wilkinson

"At the End of the Day"
Unemployed, Factory Workers

Scene 1

"I Dreamed a Dream"
R. Graff

"Lovely Ladies"
Ladies, Clients

"Who Am I?"
C. Wilkinson

"Come to Me"
R. Graff, C. Wilkinson

"Castle on a Cloud"
D. Vivino

"Master of the House"
L. Burmester, J. Butt, Customers

"Thénardier Waltz (of Treachery)"
L. Burmester, J. Butt, C. Wilkinson

Scene 2

"Look Down"
B. Danner, Beggars

"Stars"
T. Mann
"Red and Black"
M. Maguire, D. Bryant, Students
"Do You Hear the People Sing?"
M. Maguire, Students, Citizens

Scene 3

"In My Life"
J. Kuhn, C. Wilkinson, D. Bryant, F. Ruffelle
"A Heart Full of Love"
J. Kuhn, D. Bryant, F. Ruffelle
"One Day More"
The Company

ACT 2

"On My Own"
F. Ruffelle
"A Little Fall of Rain"
F. Ruffelle, D. Bryant
"Drink with Me to Days Gone By"
A. Crivello, Students, Women
"Bring Him Home"
C. Wilkinson
"Dog Eats Dog"
L. Burmester
"Soliloquy" (Javert's Suicide)
T. Mann
"Turning"
Women
"Empty Chairs at Empty Tables"
D. Bryant
"Wedding Chorale"
Guests
"Beggars at the Feast"
L. Burmester, J. Butt
Finale
The Company

1987.05 STARLIGHT EXPRESS

A Musical in Two Acts. Music by Andrew Lloyd Webber. Lyrics by Richard Stilgoe. Directed by Trevor Nunn. Choreographed by Arlene Phillips. (Sets, costumes) Designed by John Napier. Lighting by David Hersey. Sound by Martin Levan. Musical director, Paul Bogaev. Musical direction and supervision, David Caddick. Orchestrations by David Cullen, Andrew Lloyd Webber. Production advisor, Arthur Cantor. Originally produced on the London stage by The Really Useful Company. Executive producer, Gatchell & Neufeld Ltd. Produced by Martin Starger and Lord Grade in association with MCA Music Entertainment Group, Stage Promotions (Four)/Strada Holdings, Weintraub Entertainment Group, Inc. Opened 15 March 1987 at the Gershwin Theatre and closed 8 January 1989 after 761 performances.

CAST (in order of appearance): *Bobo*: A. C. Ciulla. *Expresso*: Philip Clayton. *Weltschaft*: Michael Berglund. *Turnov*: William (Christopher) Frey. *Hashamoto*: D. Michael Heath. *Prince of Wales*: Sean McDermott. *Greaseball*: ROBERT TORTI. *Greaseball's Gang*: Todd Lester, Sean Grant, Ronald Garza, Angel Vargas, Joey McKneely, Gordon Owens. *Rusty*: GREG MOWRY. *Pearl*: REVA RICE. *Dinah*: JANE KRAKOWSKI. *Ashley*: ANDREA McARDLE. *Buffy*: JAMIE BETH CHANDLER. *Rocky I*: Frank Mastrocola. *Rocky II*: Sean Grant. *Rocky III*: Ronald Garza. *Rocky IV*: Angel Vargas. *Dustin*: MICHAEL SCOTT GREGORY. *Flat-Top*: Todd Lester. *Red Caboose*: BERRY K. BERNAL. *Krupp*: Joey McKneely. *Wrench*: Christina Youngman. *Joule*: Nicole Picard. *Volta*: Mary Ann Lamb. *Purse*: Gordon Owens. *Electra*: KEN ARD. *Poppa*: STEVE FOWLER. *Belle*: Janet Williams Adderley.

Voice of the Boy: Braden Danner. *Voice of the Mother*: Melanie Vaughan. *Starlight Chorus*: Paul Binotto, Lon Hoyt, Melanie Vaughan, Mary Windholtz. *Swing*: Anthony Galde.

(The action takes place in the imagination of the boy.)

ACT 1[14]

"Rolling Stock"
R. Torti, Greaseball's Gang
"Engine of Love"[15]
G. Mowry, R. Rice, J. Krakowski, A. McArdle, J. B. Chandler
"Lotta Locomotion"
J. Krakowski, A. McArdle, J. B. Chandler, G. Mowry
"Freight"
The Company
"AC/DC"
K. Ard, J. McKneely, C. Youngman, N. Picard, M. A. Lamb, G. Owens, Company
"Pumping Iron"
R. Torti, R. Rice, J. Krakowski, A. McArdle, J. B. Chandler, N. Picard, M. A. Lamb, C. Youngman
"Freight" (reprise)
The Company
"Make Up My Heart"
R. Rice
"Race One"
R. Torti and J. Krakowski, M. Berglund and N. Picard, W. Frey and B. K. Bernal, K. Ard and R. Rice
"There's Me"
B. K. Bernal, J. Krakowski
"Poppa's Blues"
S. Fowler, F. Mastrocola, S. Grant, R. Garza, A. Vargas, G. Mowry
"Belle"
J. W. Adderley, S. Fowler, F. Mastrocola, S. Grant, R. Garza, A. Vargas, G. Mowry, M. S. Gregory, T. Lester
"Race Two"
A. C. Ciulla and J. B. Chandler, K. Rose and M. A. Lamb, P. Clayton and A. McArdle, S. Fowler and M. S. Gregory
"Laughing Stock"
The Company
"Starlight Express"
G. Mowry

ACT 2[16]

"Silver Dollar"
The Company
"U.N.C.O.U.P.L.E.D."
J. Krakowski, A. McArdle, J. B. Chandler
"Rolling Stock" (reprise)
J. Krakowski, A. McArdle, J. B. Chandler
"Wide Smile, High Style, That's Me"
B. K. Bernal, K. Ard, J. McKneely, C. Youngman, N. Picard, M. A. Lamb, G. Owens
"First Final"
R. Torti and R. Rice, K. Ard and J. Krakowski, K. Rose and M. A. Lamb, S. Fowler and B. K. Bernal
"Right Place, Right Time"
F. Mastrocola, S. Grant, R. Garza, A. Vargas
"I Am the Starlight"
G. Mowry, S. Fowler

---

[14]The subsequent national tour, subtitled "Tracking Across America" made the following revisions:

"Taunting Rusty" (added after "Engine of Love") Greaseball and Gang

"Belle" was dropped.

"Silver Dollar" was replaced by "The Rap."

The national tour was directed and choreographed by Arlene Phillips, tour lighting by Rick Belzer and Ted Mather, associate scenic designer Raymond Huessy, produced by James M. Nederlander, Columbia Artists Management, Inc., Concert Productions International and Pace Theatrical Group.

[15]Devised from an original lyric by Peter Reeves.

[16]During the Broadway run, the song order in Act 2 was revised as follows: "Chase" was dropped; after "Final Selection," the order was "One Rock & Roll Too Many," "Only You," and "Light at the End of the Tunnel."

"Final Selection"
G. Mowry, M. S. Gregory, J. Krakowski, K. Ard, R. Rice, R. Torti, B. K. Bernal

"Only You"
R. Rice, G. Mowry

"Chase"
The Company

"One Rock & Roll Too Many"
R. Torti, K. Ard, B. K. Bernal

"Light at the End of the Tunnel"
The Company

1987.06 BARBARA COOK: A CONCERT FOR THE THEATRE

A One Woman Show in Two Acts. Music arranged and conducted by Wally Harper. Scenery by John Falabella. Costumes by Joseph G. Aulisi. Lighting by Richard Winkler. Sound by Fred Miller. Keyboard coordinator, John Clifton. Associate producer, Perry B. Granoff. Produced by Jerry Kravat, The Shubert Organization, Emanuel Azenberg. Opened 15 April 1987 at the Ambassador Theater and closed 26 April 1987 after 13 performances.

CAST: BARBARA COOK.
Musicians: Wally Harper (piano), John Beal (bass), Charles Loeb (guitar), John Redsecker (drums), David Carey (percussion), Mack Schlefer (keyboard), John Clifton (keyboard), Lawrence Feldman (reeds).

MUSICAL NUMBERS

"Sing a Song with Me"
(*Music by* Wally Harper. *Lyrics by* Paul Zakrzewski.)

"Let Me Sing a Simple Song"
(from *MASS*)
(*Music by* Leonard Bernstein. *Lyrics by* Stephen Schwartz.)

"Come Rain or Come Shine" (from *ST. LOUIS WOMAN*)
(*Music by* Harold Arlen. *Lyrics by* Johnny Mercer.)

"The Man I Love" (dropped from *LADY BE GOOD* and *STRIKE UP THE BAND*)
(*Music by* George Gershwin. *Lyrics by* Ira Gershwin.)

"A Foggy Day" (from *A DAMSEL IN DISTRESS* film)
(*Music by* George Gershwin. *Lyrics by* Ira Gershwin.)

"Sweet Georgia Brown"
(*Music and Lyrics by* Maceo Pinkard, Ben Bernie, Kenneth Casey.)

"If Love Were All" (from *BITTER SWEET*)
(*Music and Lyrics by* Noël Coward.)

"Them There Eyes"
(*Music and Lyrics by* Maceo Pinkard, Ben Bernie, Kenneth Casey.)

"Widescreen"
(*Music and Lyrics by* Rupert Holmes.)

"Stars"
(*Music and Lyrics by* Laura Nyro.)

"Wait Till You See Him" (from *BY JUPITER*)
(*Music by* Richard Rodgers. *Lyrics by* Lorenz Hart.)

"I Love a Piano" (from *STOP! LOOK! LISTEN!*)
(*Music and Lyrics by* Irving Berlin.)

"I See Your Face Before Me" (from *BETWEEN THE DEVIL*)
(*Music by* Arthur Schwartz. *Lyrics by* Howard Dietz.)

"Change Partners" (from *CAREFREE* film)
(*Music and Lyrics by* Irving Berlin.)

"Mr. Snow" (from *CAROUSEL*)
(*Music by* Richard Rodgers. *Lyrics by* Oscar Hammerstein II.)

"Dear Friend"/"Ice Cream" (from *SHE LOVES ME*)
(*Music by* Jerry Bock. *Lyrics by* Sheldon Harnick.)

"Till There Was You" (from *THE MUSIC MAN*)
(*Music and Lyrics by* Meredith Willson.)

"An Ingenue"
(*Music by* Wally Harper. *Lyrics by* David Zippel.)

"I Can Cook Too" (from *ON THE TOWN*)
(*Music by* Leonard Bernstein. *Lyrics by* Betty Comden and Adolph Green.)

"He Was Too Good To Me" (from *SIMPLE SIMON*)
(*Music by* Richard Rodgers. *Lyrics by* Lorenz Hart.)

"Losing My Mind" (from *FOLLIES*)
(*Music and Lyrics by* Stephen Sondheim.)

"Carolina in the Morning" (from *THE PASSING SHOW OF 1922*)
(*Music by* Walter Donaldson. *Lyrics by* Gus Kahn.)

"Why Did I Choose You?" (from *THE YEARLING*)
(*Music by* Michael Leonard. *Lyrics by* Herbert Martin.)

"In Between Goodbyes"
(*Music by* Wally Harper. *Lyrics by* David Zippel.)

1987–1988 SEASON

Joanna Gleason in INTO THE WOODS
Martha Swope/TimePix

1987–1988 SEASON

1987.07 DREAMGIRLS

A Revival of the Musical in Two Acts, 20 Scenes[1]. Book and lyrics by Tom Eyen. Music by Henry Krieger. Directed and choreographed by Michael Bennett. Co-choreographer, Michael Peters. Scenic design by Robin Wagner. Costume design by Theoni V. Aldredge. Lighting design by Tharon Musser. Sound design by Otts Munderloh. Musical supervision and orchestrations, Harold Wheeler. Musical coordinator, Yolanda Segovia. Musical director, Marc Falcone. Vocal arrangements, Cleavant Derricks. Production supervised by Bob Avian. Produced by Marvin A. Krauss and Irving Siders. Opened 28 June 1987 at the Ambassador Theatre and closed 29 November 1987 after 177 performances.

CAST (in order of appearance): *The Stepp Sisters*: Susan Beaubian, Rhetta Hughes, R. LaChanze Sapp, Lorraine Velez. *Charlene*: Yvette Louise Cason. *Joanne*: Lynda McConnell. *Marty*: Roy L. Jones. *Curtis Taylor, Jr.*: WEYMAN THOMPSON. *Deena Jones*: ALISA GYSE. *The M.C.*: Vernon Spencer. *Tiny Joe Dixon*: Leonard Piggee. *Lorrell Robinson*: ARNETIA WALKER. *C. C. White*: KEVYN MORROW. *Effie Melody White*: LILLIAS WHITE. *Little Albert and the Tru-Tones*: Bobby Daye, Robert Clater, Matthew Dickens, Germaine Edwards, Robert Fowler. *James Thunder Early*: HERBERT L. RAWLINGS, JR. *Edna Burke*: Fuschia Walker. *The James Early Band*: Robert Clater, Bobby Daye, Matthew Dickens, Germaine Edwards, Robert Fowler, David Thomé. *Wayne*: Milton Craig Nealy. *Dave and the Sweethearts*: Stephen Bourneuf, Shirley Tripp, Lorraine Velez. *Frank*, a press agent: Tim Cassidy. *Dwight*, a TV Director: David Thomé. *TV Stage Manager*: Stephen Bourneuf. *Michelle Morris*: Susan Beaubian. *Jerry*, a nightclub owner: Leonard Piggee. *Carl*, a piano player: Robert Fowler. *The Five Tuxedos*: Robert Clater, Bobby Daye, Matthew Dickens, Germaine Edwards, Robert Fowler. *Les Style*: Yvette Louise Cason, Rhetta Hughes, Lynda McConnell, R. LaChanze Sapp. *Film Executives*: Matthew Dickens, Robert Fowler, David Thomé. *Mr. Morgan*: Vernon Spencer. *Security Guard*: Leonard Piggee.

Party Guests, Photographers: Stephen Bourneuf, Yvette Louise Cason, Tim Cassidy, Robert Clater, Bobby Daye, Matthew Dickens, Germaine Edwards, Robert Fowler, Rhetta Hughes, Lynda McConnell, Milton Craig Nealy, Leonard Piggee, R. LaChanze Sapp, Vernon Spencer, David Thomé, Shirley Tripp, Fuschia Walker. *Swings*: Brenda Braxton, Graciela Simpson, Phillip Gilmore, Darryl Eric Tribble. (N.B. *The Dreamettes, the Dreams* {through Act 1, Scene 11}: L. White, A. Walker, A. Gyse. *Deena Jones and The Dreams* thereafter: A, Gyse, A. Walker, S. Beaubian.)

1987.08 THE STUDENT PRINCE

A Revival of the Operetta in Three Acts, a Prologue and 4 Scenes[2]. Music by Sigmund Romberg. Book and lyrics by Dorothy Donnelly. (Based on the play "Old Heidelberg" by Rudolf Bleichmann, adapted from "Alt-Heidelberg" by Wilhelm Meyer-Förster.) Book adaptation by Hugh Wheeler. Conducted by Jim Coleman. Directed by Jack Hofsis. Stage director, Christian Smith. Scenery designed by David Jenkins. Costumes designed by Patton Campbell. Lighting Designed by Gilbert V. Hemsley, Jr. Choreography by Donald Saddler, restaged by Jessica Redel. Chorus Master, Joseph Colaneri. Produced by the New York City Opera. Opened 7 July 1987 at the New York State Theatre and closed 8 November 1987 after 14 performances in repertory.

CAST (in order of their appearance): *Lackeys*: Edward Zimmerman, Louis Perry, George Wyman, Neil Eddinger, Glenn Rowen, Gregory Moore. *Dr. Engel*, the Prince's Tutor: BRIAN STEELE or CHESTER LUDGIN. *Count von Mark*: DAVID RAE SMITH. *Secretaries*: Glenn Rowen, Jonathan Guss. *Prince Karl Franz*: JOHN STEWART or JON GARRISON. *Lutz*, valet to the Prince: JAMES BILLINGS or JACK HARROLD. *Gretchen*, Maid at the Inn: SUSANNE MARSEE. *Ruder*: Joseph McKee. *Nicholas*: Douglas Hamilton. *Toni*, a waiter: Jack Harrold or James Billings. *Hubert*: William Ledbetter. *Detlef*, a student leader: Stanley Cornett. *von Asterberg*, another student leader: Robert Brubaker. *Lucas*, another student leader: Robert Ferrier. *Freshman*: Louis Perry. *Kathie*, niece of Ruder: CLAUDETTE PETERSON or LEIGH MUNRO. *Girls*: Madeleine Mines, Paula Hostetter, Beth Pensiero, Jill Bosworth. *Grand Duchess Anastasia*: MURIEL COSTA-GREENSPON. *Princess Margaret*, fiancée of Prince Karl Franz: LISBETH LLOYD or CYNTHIA ROSE. *Captain Tarnitz*: CRIS GROENENDAAL. *Countess Leydon*, lady-in-waiting to the Princess: Rebecca Russell. *Huzzars*: Edward Zimmerman, Louis Pewrry, George Wyman, Neil Eddinger, Glenn Rowen, Gregory Moore. *Friends of the Huzzars*: Madeleine Mines, Paula Hostetter, Beth Pensiero, Jill Bosworth. *Ensemble*: New York City Opera Chorus.

1987.09 SWEENEY TODD- THE DEMON BARBER OF FLEET STREET

A Revival of the Musical Thriller in Two Acts[3]. Book by Hugh Wheeler. Based on a version of "Sweeney Todd" by Christopher Bond (after the original melodrama by George Dibdin-Pitt). Music and lyrics by Stephen Sondheim. Directed by Harold Prince. Choreography by Larry Fuller, recreated by William Kirk. Production designed by Eugene Lee. Costumes designed by Franne Lee. Lighting designed by Ken Billington. Orchestrations by Jonathan Tunick. Musical director, Paul Gemignani. Stage director, Arthur Masella. Produced by the New York City Opera. Opened 29 July 1987 at the New York State Theater and closed 4 October 1987 after 11 performances in repertory.

CAST (in order of appearance): *Anthony Hope*: CRIS GROENENDAAL. *Sweeney Todd*: STANLEY WEXLER or TIMOTHY NOLEN. *Beggar Woman*: BROOKS ALMY or IVY AUSTIN. *Mrs. Lovett*: MARCIA MITZMAN or JOYCE CASTLE. *Judge Turpin*: JOSEPH McKEE or WILL ROY. *The Beadle*: JOHN LANKSTON. *Johanna*: SUSAN POWELL or LEIGH MUNRO. *Tobias Ragg*: ROBERT JOHANSON. *Pirelli*: JEROLD SIENA. *Jonas Fogg*: William Ledbetter. *The Company*: New York City Opera Chorus.

1987.10 THE DESERT SONG

A Revival of the Operetta {Musical} in Two Acts, 7 Scenes[4]. Book and lyrics by Otto Harbach and Oscar Hammerstein II. New adaptation of book and lyrics by Robert Johanson. Music by Sigmund Romberg. Directed and choreographed by Robert Johanson. Conductor, Jim Coleman. Costume designer, Suzanne Mess. Set design, Michael Anania. Lighting design, Mark W. Stanley. Chorus master, Joseph Colaneri. Produced by the New York City Opera. Opened 25 August 1987 at the New York State Theatre and closed 6 September 1987 after 16 performances.

CAST (in order of appearance): *Sid El Kar*: MICHAEL COUSINS or JOHN STEWART. *Hassi*: KENNETH KANTOR. *Hadji*: William Ledbetter. *Neri*: Joyce Campana. *Red Shadow/Pierre Birabeau*: RICHARD WHITE. *Benjamin Kidd*: PHILIP WILLIAM McKINLEY. *Azuri*: LOUISE HICKEY. *Captain Paul Fontaine*: THEODORE BAERG or CRIS GROENENDAAL. *Sergeant LaVergne*: David Frye. *Susan*: LILLIAN GRAFF. *Edith*: Paula Hostetter. *General Birabeau*: DAVID RAE SMITH. *Margot Bonvalet*: LINDA MICHELE or JANE THORNGREN. *Ali Ben Ali*: RAYMOND BAZEMORE. *Clementina*: JOYCE CAMPANA. *Nogi*: Robert Brubaker. *Ensemble*: New York City Opera Chorus.

The action takes place in Morocco in the 1930's.

Act 1, Scene 1: Retreat of the "Red Shadow" in the Riff Mountains. *Scene 2*: Near the desert, outside General Birabeau's house. *Scene 3*: The garden of General Birabeau's home, the same day.

Act 2, Scene 1: The Great Hall of Ali Ben Ali. The following day. *Scene 2*: The room of the Silken Couch. *Scene 3*: The edge of the desert. *Scene 4*: Back at General Birabeau's, two nights later.

ACT 1[5]

Scene 1

"High on a Hill"
M. Cousins, Riffs

"The Riff Song"
R. White, Riffs

---

[1]Originally produced in New York 20 December 1981 at the Imperial Theatre for 1522 performances. For Synopsis of Scenes and Musical Numbers, see original 1981 production.

[2]First produced in New York as "The Student Prince in Heidelberg" 2 December 1924 at the Jolson Theatre for 608 peformances; this adaptation first produced in New York 29 August 1980 at the New York State Theatre for 13 performances. For Synopsis of Scenes and Musical Numbers, see 1980 revival.

[3]Originally produced in New York 1 March 1979 at the Uris Theatre for 557 performances. For Synopsis of Scenes and Musical Numbers, see original 1979 production.

[4]Originally produced in New York 30 November 1926 at the Casino Theatre for 471 performances.

[5]No song list was included in the program for this production. The list below was prepared from Robert Johanson's previous production of THE DESERT SONG at Papermill Playhouse.

"My Margot"
T. Baerg, Soldiers
Scene 2
"Why Did We Marry Soldiers?"
L. Graff, Women
Scene 3
"French Military Marching Song"
L. Michele, Company
"Romance"
L. Michele, Women
"I Want a Kiss"
L. Michele, T. Baerg
"It"
P. W. McKinley, L. Graff
"The Desert Song"
R. White, L. Michele
Finale, Act 1
Full Company
ACT 2
Scene 1
"Song of the Brass Key"
J. Campana, Harem Girls
"One Good Boy Gone Wrong"
P. W. McKinley, J. Campana
"Eatern Western Love"
R. Bazemore, M. Cousins
"One Alone"
R. White, Men
Scene 2
"The Sabre Song"
L. Michele
"The Desert Song" (reprise)
R. White, L. Michele
Scene 3
"One Alone" (reprise)
R. White, L. Michele, M. Cosuins, T. Baerg, R. Bazemore, Men
Scene 4
"It" (reprise)
P. W. McKinley, L. Graff
"Dance of Triumph"
L. Hickey
Finale, Act 2
Full Company

1987.11 DIE FLEDERMAUS

A Revival of the Operetta in Three Acts[6]. Music by Johann Strauss. Original libretto by Carl Haffner and Richard Genée. Lyrics by Richard Genée. Based on the comedy "Le Réveillon" by Henri Meilhac and Ludovic Halévy. English libretto by Ruth and Thomas Martin. Production devised and directed by Gerald Freedman. Stage director, Christian Smith. Choreography by Thomas Andrew. Scenery designed by Lloyd Evans Costumes design by Thierry Bosquet. Lighting design by Hans Sondheimer. Conducted by Imre Pallo. Chorus master, Joseph Colaneri. Produced by the New York City Opera. Opened 26 September 1987 at the New York State Theatre and closed 31 October 1987 (matinee) after 5 performances in repertory.

CAST (in order of appearance): *Alfred*, an itinerant tenor: Michael Cousins. *Adele*, Rosalinda's chambermaid: CLAUDETTE PETERSON. *Rosalinda von Eisenstein*: LEIGH MUNRO. *Gabriel von Eisenstein*: THEODORE BAERG. *Dr. Blind*, a lawyer: Jonathan Green. *Dr. Falke*, a close friend of Eisenstein: WILLIAM PARCHER. *Frank*, the prison warden: JOSEPH McKEE. *Sally*, Adele's sister: Alison Bevan. *Ivan*, servant to Orlofsky: Larry Becker. *Prince Orlofsky*, a wealthy, bored Russian: JAMES BILLINGS. *Guest Artist*: PATRICIA McBRIDE. *Solo Dancer*: Esperanza Galan. *Frosch*, the jailer: Jack Harrold. *Ensemble*: New York City Opera Chorus.

---

[6]First English Language Production in New York 16 March 1885 at the Casino Theatre for 42 performances. First New York production of this adaptation 20 December 1950 at the Metropolitan Opera House. For Synopsis of Scenes and Musical Numbers, see May 1954 revival.

1987.12 ROZA

A Musical in Two Acts. Book and lyrics by Julian More. Based on the novel "La Vie Devant Soi" by Romain Gary. Music by Gilbert Becaud. Directed by Harold Prince. Musical staging by Patricia Birch. Costumes by Florence Klotz. Scenery by Alexander Okun. Lighting by Ken Billington. Sound by Otts Munderloh. Musical direction, vocal and dance arrangements by Louis St. Louis. Orchestrations by Michael Gibson. Production consultant, Mervyn Nelson. Executive producer, Ruth Mitchell. Associate producer, Allen M. Shore. Produced by The Producers Circle Company (Mary Lea Johnson, Martin Richards, Martin Richards, Sam Crothers) and the Shubert Organization by arrangement with Les Editions Musicales et Artistiques (EMA). Opened 1 October 1987 at the Royale Theatre and closed 11 October 1987 after 12 performances.

CAST (in order of appearance): *Madame Roza*: GEORGIA BROWN. *Max*: Al DeCristo. *Raoul*: Ira Hawkins. *Madame Bouaffa*: Michele Mais. *Jasmine*: Yamil Borges. *Hamil*: Neal Ben-Ari. *Doctor Katz*: Jerry Matz. *Madame Katz*: Marcia Lewis. *Michel*: David Shoichi Chan. *Banania*: Mandla Msomi. *Salima*: Monique Cintron. *Young Momo*: Max Loving. *Lola*: BOB GUNTON. *Young Moise*: Stephen Rosenberg. *Woman*: Thuli Dumakude. *Man*: Richard Frisch. *Moise*: Joey McKneely. *Momo*: Alex Paez. *Yussef Kadir*: Neal Ben-Ari.

The action takes place in a house in Belleville, an immigrant quarter of Paris, inhabited by many different ethnic groups.

Act 1: 1970.

Act 2: 1974.

ACT 1
"Happiness"
G. Brown
"Max's Visit"
A. DeCristo, G. Brown
"Different"
B. Gunton, G. Brown, M. Lewis, M. Mais, Y. Borges
"Is Me"
M. Loving, S. Rosenberg, M. Cintron,
D. S. Chan, M. Msomi, M. Mais, Y. Borges
"Get the Lady Dressed"
G. Brown, B. Gunton, M. Loving,
S. Rosenberg, M. Cintron, D. S. Chan, M. Msomi
"Hamil's Birthday"
Company
"Bravo Bravo"
G. Brown
"Moon Like a Silver Window"
M. Loving, A. Paez, Company
ACT 2
"Merci"
A. Paez, J. McKneely
"House in Algiers"
G. Brown
"Yussef's Visit"
N. Ben-Ari, G. Brown, A. Paez, J. McKneely, B. Gunton
"Life Is Ahead of Me"
A. Paez
"Sweet Seventeen"
M. Mais, Y. Borges, A. Paez, J. McKneely
"Lola's Ceremony"
B. Gunton, Company
"Don't Make Me Laugh"
G. Brown, B. Gunton
"Live a Little"
G. Brown
Finale
Company

1987.13 MORT SAHL ON BROADWAY

A One Man Show in One Act. Lighting by Roger Morgan. Executive producer, Marvin A. Krauss. Produced by James L. Nederlander and Arthur Rubin. Opened 11 October 1987 at the Neil Simon Theatre and closed 1 November 1987 after 25 performances.

CAST: MORT SAHL.

1987.14

LATE NITE COMIC

A Musical in Two Acts, 21 Scenes. Book by Allan Knee. Music and lyrics by Brian Gari. Directed by Philip Rose[7]. Choreographed by Dennis Dennehy. Scenery designed by Clarke Dunham. Costumes designed by Gail Cooper-Hecht. Lighting designed by Ken Billington. Musical direction by Gregory J. Dlugos. Orchestrations by Larry Hochman. Vocal and dance arrangements by James Raitt. Sound designed by Abe Jacob. Produced by Rory Rosegarten. Opened 15 October 1987 at the Ritz Theatre and closed 17 October 1987 after 4 performances.

CAST: *David Ackerman*: ROBERT LuPONE. *Gabrielle*: TERESA TRACY. *Susan, Hooker*: Pamela Blasetti. *Club Owner, Hooker*: Kim Freshwater. *Jenny, Hooker*: Lauren Goler. *Cecil, Club Owner, Voice of God, Krazy Korn Emcee*: Patrick Hamilton. *Hooker*: Judine Hawkins. *Tanya, Delilah*: Aja Major. *Club Owner, Mike, Las Vegas Emcee*: Michael McAssey. *Hooker, Metropolitan Ballerina*: Sharon Moore. *Nat, Bartender, David's Alter Ego, Metropolitan Male Dancer*: Mason Roberts. *Clara, Hooker*: Susan Santoro. *Club Owner, Bartender, Busboy*: Don Stitt.

Ensemble: Pamela Blasetti, Kim Freshwater, Lauren Goler, Judine Hawkins, Aja Major, Sharon Moore, Susan Santoro, Don Stitt. *Swings*: Danielle P. Connell, Barry Finkel.

The action takes place at the present time in New York and Las Vegas.

Act 1, Scene 1: A piano lounge. *Scene 2*: Comedy Clubs. *Scene 3*: Streets of New York. *Scene 4*: David's Apartment. *Scene 5*: Streets of New York. *Scene 6*: David's Apartment. *Scene 7*: Streets of New York. *Scene 8*: David's Apartment. *Scene 9*: Streets of New York. *Scene 10*: Krazy Korn Club. *Scene 11*: David's Apartment.

Act 2, Scene 1: Mr. Ribs' Club. *Scene 2*: A Hooker's Bar. *Scene 3*: Club Dressing Room. *Scene 4*: Bloomingdale's. *Scene 5*: Apartment Stoop. *Scene 6*: Metropolitan Opera House. *Scene 7*: Streets of New York. *Scene 8*: David's Apartment. *Scene 9*: The Comedy Circuit. *Scene 10*: Las Vegas.

ACT 1

Scene 1

"Gabrielle"
R. LuPone

Scene 2

"The Best in the Business"
R. LuPone, Club Owners

Scene 4

"Clara's Dancing School"
T. Tracy, S. Santoro

"This Lady Isn't Right for Me"
R. LuPone, A. Major, L. Goler, P. Blasetti, T. Tracy

Scene 7

"Having Someone"
R. LuPone, Club Owners

Scene 8

"Stand-Up"
R. LuPone

Scene 9

"The Best in the Business" (reprise)
R. LuPone

Scene 10

"Late Nite Comic"
R. LuPone

"Stand-Up" (reprise)
R. LuPone

Scene 11

"It Had to Happen Sometime"
R. LuPone, T. Tracy

"When I Am Movin'"
T. Tracy

"Think Big"
R. LuPone, M. Roberts

ACT 2

Scene 2

"Relax With Me, Baby"
R. LuPone, M. Roberts, Hookers

[7]Succeeded by Tony Stevens, uncredited.

Scene 6

"Dance"
R. LuPone, T. Tracy, Ensemble

Scene 9

"Late Nite Comic" (reprise)
R. LuPone

Scene 10

"It's Such a Different World"
R. LuPone, Vegas Girls, Vegas Guys

"It Had to Happen Sometime" (reprise)
R. LuPone, T. Tracy

"Gabrielle"/"Yvonne"
R. LuPone

1987.15

ANYTHING GOES

A Revival of the Musical Comedy in Two Acts, 13 Scenes[8]. Original book by Guy Bolton and P. G. Wodehouse, Howard Lindsay and Russel Crouse. New book by Timothy Crouse and John Weidman. Music and lyrics by Cole Porter. Settings and costumes by Tony Walton. Lighting by Paul Gallo. Musical director, Edward Strauss. Orchestrations by Michael Gibson. Dance arrangements by Tom Fay. Sound by Tony Meola. Choreographed by Michael Smuin. Directed by Jerry Zaks. Produced by Lincoln Center Theater (Gregory Mosher, Artistic director; Bernard Gersten, Executive producer). Opened 19 October 1987 at the Vivian Beaumont Theatre and closed 3 September 1989 after 804 performances.

CAST (in order of appearance): *Louie*: Eric Y. L. Chan. *Elisha Whitney*: REX EVERHART. *Fred*: Steve Steiner. *Billy Crocker*: HOWARD McGILLIN. *Reno Sweeney*: PATTI LuPONE. *Young Girl*: Michele Pigliavento. *Sailor*: Alec Timerman. *Captain*: David Pursley. *Purser*: Gerry Vichi. *Reporter #1*: Robert Kellett. *Photographer*: Gerry McIntyre. *Reporter #2*: Larry Cahn. *Purity*: Daryl Richardson. *Chastity*: Maryellen Scilla. *Virtue*: Jane Lanier. *Minister*: Richard Korthaze. *Luke*: Stanford Egi. *John*: Toshi Toda. *Hope Harcourt*: KATHLEEN MAHONY-BENNETT. *Mrs. Evangeline Harcourt*: ANNE FRANCINE. *Lord Evelyn Harcourt*: ANTHONY HEALD. *G-Man #1*: Dale Hensley. *G-Man #2*: Leslie Feagan. *Erma*: LINDA HART. *Moonface Martin*: BILL McCUTCHEON. *Woman in Bathchair*: Jane Seaman. *Her Niece*: Alice Ann Oakes. *Countess*: Pat Gorman. *Thuggish Sailors*: Mark Chmiel, Dan Fletcher, Darryl Phillips. *Ship's Crew and Passengers*: Ensemble.

Chanty Quartet: Steve Steiner, Larry Cahn, Dale Hensley, Leslie Feagan. *Dancing Ensemble*: Eric Y. L. Chan, Mark Chmiel, Dan Fletcher, Robert Kellett, Jane Lanier, Gerry McIntyre, Alice Ann Oakes, Lacy Darryl Phillips, Michele Pigliavento, Daryl Richardson, Maryellen Scilla, Alec Timerman, Barbara Yeager. *Swings*: Robert Ashford, Amy O'Brien.

Act 1, Scene 1: A Bar. *Scene 2*: The Ships' Deck. *Scene 3*: The Ship's Deck. *Scene 4*: Mr. Whitney's Cabin. *Scene 5*: The Ship's Deck. *Scene 6*: Lord Evelyn's Stateroom. *Scene 7*: The Ships' Deck. *Scene 8*: The Ships' Deck.

Act 2, Scene 1: The Ships' Nightclub. *Scene 2*: The Brig. *Scene 3*: The Ships' Deck. *Scene 4*: The Brig. *Scene 5*: The Ships' Deck.

ACT 1

("Anything Goes")
(Recording sung by Cole Porter)

Scene 1

"I Get a Kick Out of You"
P. LuPone

"(There's) No Cure Like Travel"
(dropped from original production)
A. Timerman, M. Pigliavento, Ship's Crew

Scene 2

"Bon Voyage"
Company

Scene 3

"You're the Top"
P. LuPone, H. McGillin

"Easy to Love"
(from *BORN TO DANCE*, film) H. McGillin

[8]Originally produced in New York 21 November 1934 at the Alvin Theater for 420 performances.

Scene 4
"I Want to Row with the Crew"
(from *PARANOIA*, Yale) R. Everhart
Scene 5
"Sailor's Chanty" (There'll Always Be a Lady Fair)
Chanty Quartet
"Friendship"
(from *DUBARRY WAS A LADY*) P. LuPone, B. McCutcheon
Scene 7
"It's Delovely"
(from *RED HOT AND BLUE*) H. McGillin, K. Mahony-Bennett
Scene 8
"Anything Goes"
P. LuPone, Company

ACT 2
Scene 1
"Public Enemy #1"
Company
"Blow, Gabriel, Blow"
P. LuPone, Company
"Goodbye, Little Dream, Goodbye"
(from *O MISTRESS MINE*, London)
K. Mahoney-Bennett
Scene 2
"Be Like the Bluebird"
B. McCutcheon
"All Through the Night"
H. McGillin, K. Mahoney-Bennett, Men
Scene 3
"The Gypsy in Me"
A. Heald
Scene 5
"Buddie, Beware"
L. Hart, Sailors
"I Get a Kick Out of You" (reprise)
Company

1987.16 CABARET

A Revival of the Musical in Two Acts[9]. Book (revised) by Joe Masteroff. Based on the play ("I Am a Camera") by John Van Druten and stories ("The Berlin Stories") by Christopher Isherwood. Music by John Kander. Lyrics by Fred Ebb. Directed by Harold Prince. Dances and cabaret numbers staged by Ron Field. Scenic design, David Chapman based on original set design by Boris Aronson. Costume design by Patricia Zipprodt. Lighting design by Marc B. Weiss. Sound design by Otts Munderloh. Musical director, Donald Chan. Musical supervisor, Donald Pippin. Orchestrations by Don Walker. Additional orchestrations by Michael Gibson. Dance arrangements by Ronald Melrose. Associate producer, Alecia Parker, in association with Phil Witt. Produced by Barry and Fran Weissler. Opened 29 October 1987 at the Imperial Theatre, moved 9 February 1988 to the Minskoff Theatre and closed 4 June 1988 after 262 performances.

CAST (in order of appearance): *The Emcee (Master of Ceremonies)*: JOEL GREY. *Clifford Bradshaw*: GREGG EDELMAN. *Ernst Ludwig*: DAVID STALLER. *Customs Official*: David Vosburgh. *Fraulein Schneider*: REGINA RESNIK. *Fraulein Kost*: NORA MAE LYNG. *Herr Schultz*: WERNER KLEMPERER. *Telephone Girl*: Ruth Gottschall. *Sally Bowles*: ALYSON REED. *Girl Orchestra*: Sheila Cooper (tenor sax), Barbara Merjan (drums), Panchali Null (trombone), Eve Potfora (piano). *Two Ladies*: Ruth Gottschall, Sharon Lawrence. *Maitre D'*: David Vosburgh. *Max*: Jon Vandertholen. *Kissing Couple*: Mark Dovey, Sharon Lawrence. *German Sailors*: Jim Wolfe, Mark Dovey, Greg Schanuel. *Frau Wendel*: Mara Landi. *Kit Kat Girls*: Laurie Crochet, Noreen Evans, Caitlin Larsen, Sharon Lawrence, Mary Rotella. *First Waiter*: Stan Chandler. *Bobby*: Michelan Sisti. *Victor*: Lars Rosager.

Ensemble: Stan Chandler, Laurie Crochet, Bill Derifield, Mark Dovey, Noreen Evans, Karen Fraction, Laura Franks, Ruth Gottschall, Caitlin Larsen, Sharon Lawrence, Mary Munger, Pachali Null, Steve Potfora, Lars Rosager, Mary Rotella, Gregory Schanuel, Michelan Sisti, Jon Vandertholen, David Vosburgh, Jim Wolfe. *Swings*: Candy Cook, Aurelio Padron.

[9]Originally produced in New York 20 November 1966 at the Broadhurst Theatre for 1166 performances. For Synopsis of Scenes and Musical Numbers, see original 1966 production. Dropped from this production:
"Meeskite."
Added for this production:
"Don't Go" (replacing "Why Should I Wake Up?")
G. Edelman
"I Don't Care Much" (added Act 2, after "What Would You Do?")
J. Grey

1987.17 DON'T GET GOD STARTED

A Musical in Two Acts. Written by Ron Milner. Story and idea development by Barry Hankerson, Ron Milner. Music and lyrics by Marvin Winans. Directed by Ron Milner. Scenic design by Llewellen Harrison. Costume design by Victoria Shaffer. Lighting design by Shirley Prendergast. Sound by Scott Marcellus. Vocal and musical arranger, Ronald Winans. Musical director, Steven Ford. Additional staging by Conni Marie Brazelton. Artistic consultant, Woodie King, Jr. Associate producers, Reuben Cannon, Bernard Parker. Produced by Barry Hankerson, Quentin Perry and Jeffrey Day Sharp. Opened 29 October 1987 at the Longacre Theatre and closed 10 January 1988 after 86 performances.

CAST: *Female Lead Vocalist*: VANESSA BELL ARMSTRONG. *Wise Old Man, The Reverend*: Ernie Banks. *Claudette, Sister Needlove*: Conni Marie Brazelton. *Wise Old Woman*: Marilyn Coleman. *Jack, Silk*: GIANCARLO ESPOSITO. *Sylvia, Barbara Ann*: CHIP FIELDS. *Male Lead Vocalist*: BE BE WINANS. *Robert, Lawrence, Buzz*: Marvin Wright-Bey.

Choir: Donald Albert, Margaret Bell, Susan Dawn Carson, Victor Trent Cook, Starletta DuPois, Patty Heaton, Keith Laws, Andrea McClurkin, Nadine Middlebrook Norwood, Stefone Pettis, Sylvia Simmons, Monique Williams, Angie Winans, Debbie Winans, Ronald Wyche.

ACT 1
"Cry Loud (Lift Your Voice Like a Trumpet)"
V. B. Armstrong, B. B. Winans
"Slipping Away from You"
V. B. Armstrong, B. B. Winans
"After Looking for Love"
V. B. Armstrong
"Change Your Nature"
B. B. Winans
"What's Wrong with Our Love"
V. B. Armstrong, B. B. Winans
"Don't Turn Your Back"
V. B. Armstrong
"Turn Us Again"
V. B. Armstrong, B. B. Winans

ACT 2
"Abide With Me" (Hymn)
B. B. Winans
"Let the Healing Begin"
V. B. Armstrong, B. B. Winans, Choir
"Renew My Mind"
Choir
"Denied Stone"
V. B. Armstrong, B. B. Winans
"He'll Make It Alright"
Choir
"Can I Build My Home in You"/"Bring Back the Days of Yea and Nay"
V. B. Armstrong, B. B. Winans
"Always"
V. B. Armstrong
"I Made It" (reprise)
V. B. Armstrong, B. B. Winans
"Millions"
"Still in Love with You"
B. B. Winans
"It's Alright Now" (reprise)
Choir

1987.18

INTO THE WOODS

A Musical in Two Acts. Book by James Lapine[10]. Music and lyrics by Stephen Sondheim. Directed by James Lapine. Musical staging by Lar Lubovitch. Settings designed by Tony Straiges. Costumes by Ann Hould-Ward, based on original concepts by Patricia Zipprodt and Ann Hould-Ward. Lighting by Richard Nelson. Magic consultant, Charles Reynolds. Sound by Alan Stieb, James Brousseau. Orchestrations by Jonathan Tunick. Originally produced by the Old Globe Theatre, San Diego, California. Executive producer, Michael David. Associate producers, Gregory Mosher, Paula Fisher, David B. Brode, The Mutual Benefit Companies/Fifth Avenue Productions. Produced by Heidi Landesman, Rocco Landesman, Rick Steiner, M. Anthony Fisher, Frederic H. Mayerson, Jujamcyn Theatres. Opened 5 November 1987 at the Martin Beck Theatre and closed 3 September 1989 after 764 performances.

CAST (in order of appearance): *Narrator*: TOM ALDREDGE. *Cinderella*: Kim Crosby. *Jack*: Ben Wright. *Baker*: CHIP ZIEN. *Baker's Wife*: JOANNA GLEASON. *Cinderella's Stepmother*: Joy Franz. *Florinda*: Kay McClelland. *Lucinda*: Lauren Mitchell. *Jack's Mother*: Barbara Bryne. *Little Red Ridinghood*: Danielle Ferland. *Witch*: BERNADETTE PETERS. *Cinderella's Father*: Edmund Lyndeck. *Cinderella's Mother*: Merle Louise. *Mysterious Man*: TOM ALDREDGE. *Wolf*: ROBERT WESTENBERG. *Rapunzel*: Pamela Winslow. *Rapunzel's Prince*: Chuck Wagner. *Grandmother*: Merle Louise. *Cinderella's Prince*: ROBERT WESTENBERG. *Steward*: Philip Hoffman. *Giant*: Merle Louise. *Snow White*: Jean Kelly. *Sleeping Beauty*: Maureen Davis.

ACT 1

Prologue: "Into the Woods"
Company

"Hello, Little Girl"
R. Westenberg, D. Ferland

"I Guess This Is Goodbye"
B. Wright

"Maybe They're Magic"
J. Gleason

"I Know Things Now"
D. Ferland

"A Very Nice Prince"
K. Crosby, J. Gleason

"Giants in the Sky"
B. Wright

"Agony"
R. Westenberg, C. Wagner

"It Takes Two"
C. Zien, J. Gleason

"Stay With Me"
B. Peters

"On the Steps of the Palace"
K. Crosby

"Ever After"
T. Aldredge, Company

ACT 2

Prologue: "So Happy"
Company

"Agony" (reprise)
R. Westenberg, C. Wagner

"Lament"
B. Peters

"Any Moment"
R. Westenberg, J. Gleason

"Moments in the Woods"
J. Gleason

"Your Fault"
B. Wright, C. Zien, B. Peters, K. Crosby, D. Ferland

"Last Midnight"
B. Peters

"No More"
C. Zien, T. Aldredge

"No One Is Alone"
K. Crosby, D. Ferland, C. Zien, B. Wright

Finale: "Children Will Listen"
B. Peters, Company

1987.19

TEDDY AND ALICE

A Musical in Two Acts, a Prelude and 15 Scenes. Book by Jerome Alden. Music by John Philip Sousa. Adaptations and original music by Richard Kapp. Lyrics by Hal Hackady. Artistic consultant, Alan Jay Lerner. Directed by John Driver. Choreography by Donald Saddler. Additional musical staging by D. J. Giagni. Scenery design by Robin Wagner. Costume design by Theoni V. Aldredge. Lighting design by Tharon Musser. Sound design by Peter Fitzgerald. Orchestrations by Jim Tyler. Vocal arrangements, music supervisor, Donald Pippin. Dance arrangements by Gordon Lowry Harrell. Musical director, Larry Blank. Originally produced at the Tampa Bay Performing Arts Center. Associate producers, Glen Cross, Clarice Swan Fitzgerald, Wilmor Four in association with Jon Cutler. Produced by Hinks Shimberg. Opened 12 November 1987 at the Minskoff Theatre and closed 17 January 1988 after 77 performances.

CAST (in order of appearance): *James Amos*: Tony Floyd. *Belle Hagner*: Karen Ziemba. *J. P. Morgan*: David Green. *Harriman*: John Witham. *Henry Cabot Lodge*: Raymond Thorne. *Elihu Root*: Gordon Stanley. *William Howard Taft*: Michael McCarthy. *Theodore 'Teddy' Roosevelt*: LEN CARIOU. *Edith Roosevelt*: BETH FOWLER. *Ted Roosevelt, Jr.*: Robert D. Cavanaugh. *Kermit Roosevelt*: Seth Granger. *Ethel Roosevelt*: Sarah Reynolds. *Archie Roosevelt*: Richard H. Blake. *Quentin Roosevelt*: John Daman. *Ida Tarbel*: Mary Jay. *Wheeler*: John Remme. *Officer O'Malley*: Christopher Wells. *Alice Roosevelt*: NANCY HUME. *Eleanor Roosevelt*: Nancy Opel. *Nick Longworth*: RON RAINES. *Franklin Roosevelt*: Alex Kramarevsky. *Admiral Murphy*: David Green. *Samuel Gompers*: John Witham. *Elliott Roosevelt*: Ken Hilliard. *Ghost*: Pamela McLernon.

Servants, Reporters, Tea Party Ladies, Marines, Ambassadors: Ellyn Aarons, Ruth Bormann, Kathleen Gray, Ken Hilliard, Alex Kramarevsky, Mark Lazore, Keith Locke, Pamela McLernon, Elizabeth Mozer, Keith Savage, Jeff Shade. *Swings*: Kaylyn Dillehay, Travis Layne Wright.

Act 1, Scene 1: Interior of the White House, Fall 1901, shortly after President McKinley's assassination. *Scene 2*: White House Yard. *Scene 3*: The President's Office. *Scene 4*: Alice's Dressing Room, different day. *Scene 5*: Presidential Bedroom Suite. *Scene 6*: Rose Garden of the White House, later that evening. *Scene 7*: Public Area in the White House, later that evening. *Scene 8*: North Portico of the White House, three weeks later. *Scene 9*: Republican National Convention, Summer 1904.

Act 2, Scene 1; Main Entrance Hall, Summer 1904. *Scene 2*: Area of Birch Trees near the White House, same day. *Scene 3*: Election Day. *Scene 4*: The President's Office. *Scene 5*: Campsite near the White House in the Woods. *Scene 6*: East Room of the White House.

ACT 1

Prelude: "The Thunderer"
Orchestra

Scene 1

"This House"
L. Cariou, Family, Friends, Staff, Reporters

Scene 2

"But Not Right Now"
N. Hume

Scene 3

"She's Got to Go"
M. McCarty, G. Stanley, R. Thorne

Scene 4

"The Fourth of July"
N. Hume, N. Opel

Scene 5

"Charge"
L. Cariou, B. Fowler, R. D. Cavanaugh, S. Granger, S. Reynolds, R. D. Blake, J. Daman

"Battlelines"
B. Fowler

Scene 6

"The Coming-Out Party Dance"
L. Cariou, N. Hume, R. Raines, B. Fowler, Guests

"Leg O' Mutton"
N. Hume, R. Raines, Guests

[10]Inspired by the Fairy Tales of Jacob and Wilhelm Grimm.

"Not Love"
R. Raines, M. McCarty, G. Stanley, R. Thorne
Scene 7
"Her Father's Daughter"
L. Cariou
"Perfect for Each Other"
R. Raines
Scene 8
"He's Got to Go" (reprise)
M. McCarty, G. Stanley, R. Thorne, R. Raines
Scene 9
"Wave the Flag"
L. Cariou, B. Fowler, N. Opel, R. D. Cavanaugh, S. Granger, S. Reynolds, R. H. Blake, J. Daman, J. Witham, D. Green, Hecklers, Supporters

ACT 2
Scene 1
"(The) Fourth of July" (reprise)
L. Cariou
"(The) Fourth of July" (reprise)
N. Hume, N. Opel, B. Fowler, Ladies
Scene 2
"Nothing to Lose"
R. Raines, N. Hume
Scene 3
"Election Eve"
M. McCarty, G. Stanley, R. Thorne, J. Witham, D. Green, Reporters
Scene 4
"Perfect for Each Other" (reprise)
N. Hume
Scene 5
"Can I Let Her Go?"
L. Cariou
Scene 6
"Private Thoughts"
M. McCarty, G. Stanley, R. Thorne, B. Fowler, R. D. Cavanaugh, S. Reynolds, S. Granger, R. H. Blake, J. Daman, Servants, Staff, Reporters
"This House" (reprise)
L. Cariou, B. Fowler, Guests

1987.20 PENN & TELLER

A Magic Revue in Two Acts, 12 Scenes[11]. Directed by Art Wolff. Set by John Lee Beatty. Lighting by Dennis Parichy. Sound by Chuck London Media/Stuart Werner. Director of Covert Activities, Marc Garland. Produced by Richard Frankel, Thomas Viertel, Steven Baruch. Opened 1 December 1987 at the Ritz Theatre and closed 20 March 1988 after 130 performances.

CAST: PENN JILLETTE, TELLER.

ACT 1
Casey at the Bat
A Card Trick
Cups and Balls
Suspension
Domestication of Animals
East Indian Needle Mystery
Quote of the Day

ACT 2
Another Card Trick
MOFO the Psychic Gorilla
How We Met
Shadows
10 in 1

[11]A previous edition of "Penn & Teller" appeared Off-Broadway 18 April 1985 at the Westside Arts/Downstairs Theatre for 666 performances.

1988.01 THE PHANTOM OF THE OPERA

A Musical in Two Acts, a Prologue and 19 Scenes. Book by Richard Stilgoe, Andrew Lloyd Webber. (Based on the novel of the same name [Le Fantôme de l'Opéra] by Gaston Leroux.) Music by Andrew Lloyd Webber. Lyrics by Charles Hart. Additional lyrics by Richard Stilgoe. Directed by Harold Prince. Musical staging and choreography by Gillian Lynne. Production design (sets and costumes) by Maria Björnson. Lighting by Andrew Bridge. Sound by Martin Levan. Musical supervision and direction by David Caddick. Orchestrations by David Cullen, Andrew Lloyd Webber. Produced by Cameron Mackintosh and the Really Useful Company. Opened 26 January 1988 at the Majestic Theater and is still running at the present time!

CAST: *The Phantom of the Opera*: MICHAEL CRAWFORD. *Christine Daaé*: SARAH BRIGHTMAN, PATTI COHENOUR (alt.) *Raoul*, Vicomte de Chagny: STEVE BARTON. *Carlotta Guidicelli*: JUDY KAYE. *Monsieur André*: Cris Groenendaal. *Monsieur Firmin*: Nicholas Wyman. *Madame Giry*: Leila Martin. *Ubaldo Piangi*: David Romano. *Meg Giry*: Elisa Heinsohn. *Monsieur Reyer*: Peter Kevoian. *Auctioneer*: Richard Warren Pugh. *Porter, Marksman*: Jeff Keller. *Monsieur Lefèvre*: Kenneth H. Waller. *Joseph Buquet*: Philip Steele. *Don Attilio* ("Il Muto"), *Passarino*: George Lee Andrews. *Slave Master* ("Hannibal"): Luis Perez. *Flunky, Stagehand*: Barry McNabb. *Policeman*: Charles Rule. *Page* ("Don Juan Triumphant"): Olga Talyn. *Potter, Fireman*: William Scott Brown. *Page ("Don Juan Triumphant")*: Candace Rogers-Adler. *Wardrobe Mistress, Confidante* ("Il Muto"): Mary Leigh Stahl. *Princess* ("Hannibal"): Rebecca Luker. *Madame Firmin*: Beth McVey. *Innkeeper's Wife* ("Don Juan Triumphant"): Jan Horvath.

The Ballet Chorus of the Opéra Populaire: Irene Cho, Nicole Fosse, Lisa Lockwood, Lori MacPherson, Dodie Petit, Catherine Ulissey. *Ballet Swing*: Denny Berry. *Swings*: Frank Mastrone, Alba Quezada.

The action takes place in the Paris Opéra House in 1911, and Paris in 1881.

Prologue: The stage of the Paris Opéra House, 1911.

Act 1: Paris, 1881. *Scene 1*: The dress rehearsal of 'Hannibal.' *Scene 2*: After the gala. *Scene 3*: Christine's dressing room. *Scene 4*: The Labyrinthe underground. *Scene 5*: Beyond the lake. *Scene 6*: Beyond the lake, the next morning. *Scene 7*: Backstage. *Scene 8*: The Managers' office. *Scene 9*: A performance of 'Il Muto.' *Scene 10*: The roof of the Opéra House.

Act 2: Six months later. *Scene 1*: The staircase of the Opéra House, New Year's Eve. *Scene 2*: Backstage. *Scene 3*: The Managers' office. *Scene 4*: A rehearsal for 'Don Juan Triumphant.' *Scene 5*: A graveyard in Peros. *Scene 6*: The Opéra House stage before the Premiere. *Scene 7*: 'Don Juan Triumphant.' *Scene 8*: The Labyrinthe underground. *Scene 9*: Beyond the lake.

ACT 1
Scene 1
"Think Of Me"
J. Kaye, S. Brightman, S. Barton
Scene 2
"Angel of Music"
S. Brightman, E. Heinsohn
Scene 3
"Little Lotte"/"The Mirror" (Angel of Music)
S. Barton, S. Brightman, M. Crawford
Scene 4
"The Phantom of the Opera"
M. Crawford, S. Brightman
Scene 5
"The Music of the Night"
M. Crawford
Scene 6
"I Remember"/"Stranger Than You Dreamt It"
S. Brightman, M. Crawford
Scene 7
"Magical Lasso"
P. Steele, E. Heinsohn, L. Martin, Ballet Girls
Scene 8
"Notes"/"Prima Donna"
N. Wyman, C. Groenendaal, S. Barton, J. Kaye, L. Martin, E. Heinsohn, M. Crawford
Scene 9
"Poor Fool, He Makes Me Laugh"
J. Kaye, Company

Scene 10
"Why Have You Brought Me Here"/"Raoul, I've Been There"
S. Barton, S. Brightman
"All I Ask of You"
S. Barton, S. Brightman
"All I Ask of You" (reprise)
M. Crawford

ACT 2
Scene 1
"Masquerade"/"Why So Silent"
Full Company
Scene 3
"Notes"/"Twisted Every Way"
C. Groenendaal, N. Wyman, J. Kaye, D. Romano, S. Barton, S. Brightman, L. Martin, M. Crawford
Scene 5
"Wishing You Were Somehow Here Again"
S. Brightman
"Wandering Child"/"Bravo Bravo" (Bravo, Monsieur)
M. Crawford, S. Brightman, S. Barton
Scene 7
"The Point of No Return"
M. Crawford, S. Brightman
Scene 8
"Down Once More"/"Track Down This Murderer"
Full Company

1988.02 SARAFINA!

A Musical in Two Acts[12]. (Book) Written by Mbongeni Ngema. Music and lyrics by Mbongeni Ngema. Additional songs by Hugh Masekela. Musical arrangements by Mbongeni Ngema and Hugh Masekela. Conceived and directed by Mbongeni Ngema. Set and costumes by Sarah Roberts. Lighting by Mannie Manim. Conductor, additional choreography by Ndaba Mhlongo. Sound by Tom Sorce. First presented by the Committed Artists and the Market Theatre at the Market Theatre, Johannesburg, (South Africa) June 1987. A Committed Artists Production. Produced by Lincoln Center Theatre (Gregory Mosher, Artistic director; Bernard Gersten, Executive producer) in association with Lucille Lortel, The Shubert Organization. Opened 28 January 1988 at the Cort Theatre and closed 2 July 1989 after 597 performances.

CAST: *Magundane*: Ntomb'khona Dlamini. *Scabha*: Khumbuzile Dlamini. *Colgate*: Pat Mlaba. *Teaspoon*: Lindiwe Dlamini. *Crocodile*: Dumisani Dlamini. *Silence*: Congo Hadebe. *Stimela Sase-Zola*: Nhlanhla Ngema. *S'Ginci*, Police Sergeant: Mhlathi Khuzwayo. *Sarafina*: Leleti Khumalo. *Mistress It's a Pity*: Baby Cele. *Dumadu*: Nonhlanhla Mbambo. *China*: Linda Mchunu. *Lindiwe*: Lindiwe Hlengwa. *Zandile*: Zandile Hlengwa. *Siboniso*: Siboniso Khumalo. *Timba*: Cosmas Sithole. *Priest*: Thandani Mavimbela. *Charnele*: Charnele Dozier Brown. *Mubi*: Mubi Mofokeng. *Nandi*: Nandi Ndlovu. *Thandekile*: Thandekile Nhlanhla. *Police Lieutenant*: Pumi Shelembe. *Kipizane*: Kipizane Skweyiya. *Thandi*: Thandi Zulu.

Musicians: Master Mathibe, Eddie Mathibe (keyboards), Makate Peter Mofolo , Ray Molefe (trumpets), Douglas Mnisi (lead guitar), Bruce Mwansla (drums), S'Manga Nhlebela (bass).

The action takes place at Morris Isaacson High School in Soweto, South Africa in 1976.

ACT 1
"Zibuuylle Emasisweni" (It's Finally Happening)
Company
"Niyayibona Lento Engiyibonayo" (Do You See What I See)
Company
"Sarafina"
M. Khuzwayo, N. Ngema
(*Music and Lyrics by* Hugh Masekela.)
"The Lord's Prayer"
B. Cele, Company
"Yes! Mistress It's a Pity"
B. Cele, Company
(*Music and Lyrics by* Hugh Masekela and Mbongeni Ngema.)

[12]Originally produced Off-Broadway 25 October 1987 at the Mitzi Newhouse Theatre for 81 performances.

"Give Us Power"
T. Zulu, N. Dlamini, B. Cele, Company
"Afunani Amaphoyisa eSoweto" (What Is the Army Doing in Soweto?)
Company
"Nkosi Sikeleli'Afrika"
Company
"Freedom Is Coming Tomorrow"
Company
Entr'acte: "Excuse Me Baby Please, Please If You Don't Mind Baby, Thank You"
Band
(*Music and Lyrics by* Hugh Masekela.)

ACT 2
"Meeting Tonight"
T. Nhlanhla, Company
(*Music and Lyrics by* Hugh Masekela.)
"We Are Guerillas"
T. Nhlanhla, Company
"Uyamemeza Ungoma"
T. Zulu
"We Will Fight for Our Land"
T. Mavimbela, T. Zulu, D. Dlamini, Company
"Mama"
N. Dlamini, T. Nhlanhla, B. Cele, Company
"Sechaba"
Company
(*Music and Lyrics by* Hugh Masekela.)
"Isizwe" (The Nation Is Dying)
T. Nhlanhla
"Goodbye"
B. Cele
(*Music and Lyrics by* Hugh Masekela.)
"Kilimanjaro"
Company
"Africa Burning in the Sun"
Company
(*Music and Lyrics by* Hugh Masekela.)
"Stimela Sasezola"
N. Ngema, Company
"Olayithi" (It's All Right)
Company
"Bring Back Nelson Mandela"
L. Khumalo, Company
(*Music and Lyrics by* Hugh Masekela.)
"Wololo!"
Company

1988.03 RODNEY DANGERFIELD ON BROADWAY

A Comedy Revue in Two Acts. Production designer, Steven A. Cohen. Sound designer, Peter Fitzgerald. Produced by James M. Nederlander. Opened 2 February 1988 at the Mark Hellinger Theatre and closed 7 February 1988 after 6 performances.

CAST: RODNEY DANGERFIELD, Bob Nelson.

1988.04 THE MUSIC MAN

A Revival of the Musical (Comedy) in Two Acts, 17 Scenes[13]. Book, music and lyrics by Meredith Willson. Book written in collaboration with Franklin Lacey. Directed by Arthur Masella. Choreographed by Marcia Milgrom Dodge. Sets designed by David Jenkins. Costumes designed by Andrew Marlay. Lighting designed by Duane Schuler. Orchestrations by Don Walker. Chorus master, Joseph Colaneri. Conductor, Donald Pippin.

[13]Originally produced in New York 19 December 1957 at the Majestic Theatre for 1375 performances. For Synopsis of Scenes and Musical Numbers, see original 1957 production. Original Act 1, Scene 2 has been divided in two, yielding an extra scene.

Produced by the New York City Opera. Opened 26 February 1988 at the New York State Theatre and closed 10 April 1988 after 51 performances.

CAST (in order of appearance): *Travelling Salesmen*: WIlliam Ledbetter, James Clark, Robert Brubaker, Stanley Wexler, Jonathan Green. *Newpaper Readers*: Louis Perry, Neil Eddinger. *Charlie Cowell*: Rex D. Hays. *Conductor*: Ralph Bassett or John Henry Thomas. *Harold Hill*: BOB GUNTON. *Mayor Shinn*: RICHARD McKEE. *Eulalie MacKecknie Shinn*: MURIEL COSTA-GREENSPON. *Zaneeta Shinn*: JILL POWELL. *Gracie Shinn*: Alexandra Steinberg. *Alma Hix*: Bridget Ramos. *Ethel Toffelmier*: Ivy Austin. *Maud Dunlop*: Lee Belaver. *Mrs. Squires*: Rita Metzger. *Jacey Squires*: Jonathan Green. *Marcellus Washburn*: JAMES BILLINGS. *Ewart Dunlop*: James Clark. *Oliver Hix*: Robert Brubaker. *Olin Britt*: Don Yule. *Marian Paroo*: LEIGH MUNRO. *Mrs. Paroo*: BROOKS ALMY. *Amaryllis*: Allegra Victoria Forste *Winthrop Paroo*: JOEL CHAIKEN. *Tommy Djilas*: STEVEN M. SCHULTZ *Constable Locke*: William Ledbetter. *River City Townspeople*: New York City Opera Chorus.

1988.05 THE GOSPEL AT COLONUS

A Musical in Two Acts[14]. Book and lyrics by Lee Breuer. Based on an adaptation of Sophocles' "Oedipus at Colonus" in the version by Robert Fitzgerald and incorporates passages from both Sophocles' "Oedipus Rex" and "Antigone" in the versions by Dudley Fitts and Robert Fitzgerald. Music by Bob Telson. Directed by Lee Breuer. Production and set design by Alex Yerxa. Costume design by Ghretta Hynd. Lighting design by Julie Archer. Sound design by David Hewitt, Ron Lorman. Originally produced by the Brooklyn Academy of Music Next Wave Festival. Executive producers, Michael David, Edward Strong, Sherman Warner. Produced by Dodger Productions, Liza Lorwin, Louis Busch Hager, Playhouse Square Center (Cleveland, Ohio), Fifth Avenue Productions (Karen Walter Goodwin, Elizabeth Williams). Opened 24 March 1988 at the Lunt-Fontanne Theatre and closed 15 May 1988 after 61 performances.

CAST: *Messenger*, a visiting pastor who narrates the role of Oedipus and performs the role of Messenger as a sermon: MORGAN FREEMAN. *Oedipus*, a soloist and gospel quintet who sing portions of the role of Oedipus: CLARENCE FOUNTAIN AND THE FIVE BLIND BOYS OF ALABAMA (Bobby Butler, Jimmy L. Carter, J. T. Clinkscales, Reverend Olice Thomas, Joseph Watson). *Antigone*, an evangelist who performs the role of Antigone and selected choral material: ISABELL MONK. *Theseus*, the assistant pastor of the church who performs the role of Theseus: Reverend Earl F. Miller. *Ismene*: Jevetta Steele and the J. D. Steele Singers (J. D. Steele, Fred Steele, Janice Steele, Jevetta Steele). *Creon*, a deacon of the church who performs the role of Creon: Robert Earl Jones. *Polyneices*, a member of the congregation who performs the role of Polyneices: Kevin Davis. *Choragos*: Martin Jacox, J. J. Farley and the Soul Stirrers (Jackie Banks, Martin Jacox, Ben Odom, Willie Rogers). *The Singer*: Sam Butler, Jr. *The Choir Soloist*: Carolyn Johnson-White. *Guest Choir Director*: J. D. Steele.

Chorus: The Institutional Radio Choir: *Altos*: Betty Cooper, Angie Haddock, Vincent Haddock, Jr., Crystal Johnson, Selene Jones, Shellie Jordan, O'Jean Lilly, Janet Napper, Pamela Poitier, Francine Tompkins, Candace White. *Sopranos*: Regina Berry, Katie Braan, Deborah Britt, Sharon K. Driskill, Mary Fischer, Josie Johnson, Carolyn Johnson-White, Ernestine King, Kecia Lewis-Evans. *Tenors*: Charles Bellamy, Lindwood Chamberlain, George Cooper, Hayward Jerome Gregory, Kevin Jackson, Roscoe Robinson, Billy Steele, Ezekiel Tobby, Carl Williams, Jr., Jeff Young.

ACT 1

The Welcome and Quotations
M. Freeman

The Invocation ("Live Where You Can")
Choir, J. Steele (Soloist)

Recapitulation from Oedipus the King
I. Monk, E. F. Miller

Oedipus and Antigone enter Colonus
I. Monk, M. Freeman

Ode to Colonus ("Fair Colonus")
W. Rogers (Solist)

"Stop! Do Not Go On"
S. Butler, Jr. (Soloist), J. J. Farley and the Soul Stirrers

Bridge
C. Fountain and the Five Blind Boys of Alabama

Choral Dialogue: ("Who is This Man?")
M. Jacox, M. Freeman

Ismene Comes to Colonus: "How Shall I See Through My Tears?"
The J. D. Steele Singers, Jevetta Steele (Soloist)

Narrative of Ismene
I. Monk

Tableau, Polyneices and Eteocles
J. D. Steele, F. Steele

The Rite
I. Monk, M. Freeman, C. Fountain

Tableau, Antigone and Ismene
Janice Steele, Jevetta Steele

Dialogue: Chorus Questions Oedipus
M. Jacox, M. Freeman

The Prayer: ("A Voice Foretold")
C. Fountain and the Five Blind Boys of Alabama, S. Butler, Jr.

Oedipus Is Welcomed in Colonus

Peroration
E. F. Miller

Jubilee ("No Never")
M. Jacox, the Soul Stirrers

Bridge
C. Fountain and the Five Blind Boys of Alabama, Choir, Ensemble

Creon Comes to Colonus and the Seizure of the Daughters
R. E. Jones, M. Freeman, C. Fountain and the Five Blind Boys of Alabama

Oedipis Curses Creon (Suite, "All My Heart's Desire")
C. Fountain and the Five Blind Boys of Alabama, Choir, R. E. Jones, M. Freeman

Choral Ode ("Numberless Are the World's Wonders")
J. D. Steele Singers (J. D. Steele, Janice Steele, Soloists), Choir

ACT 2

Oedipus Laments ("Lift Me Up")
C. Fountain and the Five Blind Boys of Alabama

Polyneices' Testimony and Supplication, Oedipus' Curse
K. Davis, M. Freeman, C. Fountain

"Evil"
S. Butler, Jr.

"You Break My Heart"
J. D. Steele, F. Steele, B. Odom

Poem ("Love Unconquerable")
I. Monk

Preaching with Tuned Response
M. Freeman, C. Fountain

Special Effect ("Ah! Heaven's Height Has Cracked!")

The Teachings
M. Freeman, E. F. Miller

The Descent of Oedipus

"Oh Sunlight of No Light"
S. Butler, Jr.

"Eternal Sleep"
W. Rogers, the Soul Stirrers

Mourning
I. Monk, E. F. Miller, Jevetta Steele, Jancie Steele

Doxology, the Paen ("Lift Him Up")
Choir (C. Johnson-White, Soloist)

The Sermon
M. Freeman

Closing Hymn ("Now Let the Weeping Cease")
W. Rogers, the Soul Stirrers, Choir, Ensemble

Benediction
M. Freeman

1988.06 OBA OBA

A Brazilian Extravaganza (Musical Revue) in Two Acts, 13 Scenes. Conceived by Franco Fontana. Musical direction by Wilson Mauro. Choreographer, Roberto Abrahão. Assistant choreographers, Soraya Bastos, Luis Bocanha. Technical consultant, Mario Ruffa. Sound by Peter Fitzgerald. Lighting consultant, Steve Cochrane. Co-producer, Dino Cuzzoni. Produced by Franco Fontana. Opened 29 March 1988 at the Ambassador Theatre and closed 8 May 1988 after 48 performances.

CAST: ELIANA ESTVÃO, NILZE CARVALHO, TOCO PRETO, JAIME SANTOS, Bebeto, Beiçola, Borracha, Brechó, Chita, Claudia Jacomo, Claudinho

[14]Previously produced in Brooklyn 8 November 1983 at the Brooklyn Academy of Music/Carey Playhouse for 30 performances.

Nascimento, Cobra Mansa, Concheta, Gerson do Pandeiro, José Roberto Ferreira, Ledinha da Mangueira, Lindete Souza, Lucia Helena Máximo, Luis Bernardo, Luis Bocanha, Marcia Souza, Marcos Negão, Marquinho da Dona Geralda, Marta Sargentelli, Miguel do Repinique, Milani Nicolau, Olga Maria, Paulo Xavier, Pedro Pottier, Roberto Silva, Rosemary Silva, Soninha Toda Pura, Soraya Bastos, Tomé de Bebedouro, Vivian Machado Soares, Waldir Cavalcanti, Wilmar Vieira, Wilson Mauro.

Ensemble: Claudio Sargentelli, Cristino Ricardo, Dalto Macedo, Garcia de Aragão, Iole Fernandes, Lucelita Barros, Maria Elza de Jesus, Monica Gonçalves, Nino, Ondina Lopes, Vera Lima.

ACT 1

Scene 1

"Xica da Silva"

R. Silva, W. Vieira, Company

The story opens when Brazil is still a land of slaves ruled by the Portuguese. Through her feminine charms the beautiful Xica da Silva wins the heart of the nobleman João Fernandes. As a result she gains her freedom and earns a place in the Portuguese court. As time goes by, Xica becomes a lady and the nobleman bcomes her slave.

Scenes 2 and 4

Homage to Baião and Chorinho

N. Carvalho, T. Preto

Some classics of these two particular kinds of popular music featuring the most expressive Brazilian instruments, the badolim and the cavaquinho, a small guitar with four chords. Pieces such as "Tico, Tico," "Urubu Malandro" and two famous compositions by Waldir Azevedo, "Brasilierinho" and "Delicado," have made Baião and Chorinho famous throughout the world.

Scene 3

"Samba de Roda"

T. Preto, G. Pandeiro, M. Nicolau, C. Jacomo,
Concheta, L. da Mangueira, L. Souza, M. Sargentelli,
O. Maria, R. Silva, S. T. Pura, V. M. Soares

This is a typical dance born in Bahia's public squares and markets. A festive competition among the women of the town. This coquettish contest displays their superiority in performing this particular type of samba.

Scene 5

Homage to the Northeast

J. Santos, Company

The most evocative music and songs of this marvelous, but desolately poor territory, moves from the resigned lamentations of the Acordeon to the explosive reactions of the people who find in song and dance the strength and joy of life.

Scene 6

"Brazil Capela"

E. Estevao

Scene 7

Homage to the Bossanova and Brazilian Music of the Seventies

E. Estevao, N. Carvalho, W. Mauro, W. Cavalcanti

A medley dedicated to that great musical phenomenon of the Sixties that made artists like Tom Jobim, Baden Powell, Vincius de Moraes and songs like "Manhã de Carnaval," "Samba de uma nota so" and "Garota de Ipanema" world-famous.

E. Estevao, M. Sargentelli, O. Maria, S. T. Pura, S. Bastos

A medley dedicated to the artists who still follow the great tradition of Brazilian music, and brilliantly insert their work into the present international musical language, thus maintaing the worldwide prestige of Brazilian popular music.

Scene 8

Tribute to the 'Brazilian Bombshell' Carmen Miranda

N. Carvalho, E. Estavao, L. Souza, Company

ACT 2

Scene 1

"Macumba"

L. de Mangueira, L. Souza, Bebeto,
G. do Pandeiro, O. Maria, L. Bocanha, J. R. Ferrera, M. Sargentelli, Company

This religious African cult with its dances and its saints (Orixa) including the magical appearance of Iemanjã, Queen of the Seas and Fertility.

Scene 2

Afro-Brazilian Folk Songs and Dances:

Berimbau Medley

L. Bocanha, G. do Pandeiro, Brechó, C. Nascimento,
L. Bernardo, R. Silva, T. de Bebedouro, W. Cavalcanti, W. Mauro, J. Santos

Capoeira of Angola

Bebeto, Bericola, Borracha, Chita, C. Mansa,
L. Bocanha, M. Negão, C. Jacomo, Concheta, L. Souza, M. Souza,
M. Sargentelli, O. Maria, R. Silva, S. T. Pura, S. Bastos, V. M. Soares

A tribute to the first struggles against the white masters wherein the slaves used their hands and feet as their only weapon. (Capoeira, which later became a dance.)

Maculele

Brecho, C. Jacomo, C. Nascimento, J. R. Ferreira, L. Souza,
L. H. Máximo, L. Bernardo, M. Souza, M. Sargentelli, P. Xavier,
R. Silva, S. Bastos, T. de Bebedouro, W. Cavalcanti, W. Vieira

Dances that require agility and skill and are carried out with small batons accompanied by the lively rhythm of tambores and agogo.

Acrobatic Capoeira

Bebeto, Beicola, Borracha, Chita, Cobra Mansa, L. Bocanha, M. Negão

Scene 3

Rhythm Beaters

G. do Pandeiro, Bebeto, Borracha, L. Bocanha,
M. da Dona Geralda, M. do Repinique, M. Nicolau, P. Pottier

Various instruments are at first played separately, in order to stress their peculiarities, and then all together in a sweeping progress of rhythm.

Scene 4

Show of Samba Dancers

O. Maria, R. Silva, S. T. Pura

An exaltation of the beauty and charm of the Brazilian Mulatto women through the sensual progress of their samba.

Scene 5

Grand Carnival

Company

The most popular themes of the various carnivals, featuring a parade of the artists who then allow the audience to participate in the great and collective festivities.

1988.07

MAIL

A Musical in Two Acts and a Prologue. Book and lyrics by Jerry Colker. Music by Michael Rupert. Directed by Andrew Cadiff. Choreography by Grover Dale. Scenery and projections by Gerry Hariton, Vicki Baral. Costume design by William Ivey Long. Lighting by Richard Nelson. Sound design by Tom Morse. Multi-image production by Nelson & Sixta. Musical supervision, Paul Gemignani. Orchestrations by Michael Gibson. Musical direction, vocal and dance arrangements by Tom Fay. Assistant choreographer, Stephen Jay. Originally produced by the Pasadena Playhouse, State Theatre of California, Inc. Associate producer, Kenneth Biller. Produced by Michael Frazier, Susan Dietz, Stephen Wells and the John F. Kennedy Center/ANTA (Donald R. Seawell). Opened 14 April 1988 at the Music Box Theatre and closed 14 May 1988 after 36 performances.

CAST (in order of appearance): *Alex*: MICHAEL RUPERT. *Dana*: MARA GETZ. *Radio Announcer*: Rick Stockwell. *Radio Singer*: Mary Bond Davis. *LIFE Execs*: Alan Muraoka, Robert Loftin, Rick Stockwell. *Franklin*: BRIAN MITCHELL. *Sandi*: ANTONIA ELLIS. *Max*: ROBERT MANDAN. *Kathy Sue Binger*: Michelle Pawk. *Billy Ray Binger*: Rick Stockwell. *Assistants*: Alan Muraoka, Robert Loftin. *Power Ladies*: Louise Hickey, Michele Pawk. *Mama Utility*: Mary Bond Davis. *Con Ed Men*: Alan Muraoka, Rick Stockwell, Robert Loftin. *Democratic Party Delegate*: Michelle Pawk. *Brunhilda*: Mary Bond Davis. *Hunter*: Rick Stockwell. *Gypsy*: Louise Hickey. *Boy Scout*: Robert Loftin. *I.R.S. Auditor*: Alan Muraoka. *Operator*: Mary Bond Davis. *Candi Suwinski*: Michelle Pawk. *Harmony Steinberg*: Louise Hickey. *Craterface Callahan*: Robert Loftin. *Takeuchi Fujimoto*: Alan Muraoka. *Mr. Stansbury*: Rick Stockwell. *Lois T. Wertshafter*: Mary Bond Davis. *Pitchman*: Rick Stockwell.

Pitchpeople: Mary Bond Davis, Robert Loftin, Alan Muraoka, Michele Pawk, Rick Stockwell, Louise Hickey. *Swings*: Stephen Jay, Rachelle Ottley.

Prologue: 6:00 A. M. one winter morning. A Manhattan apartment.

Act 1: 11:15 P. M., four months later. The same apartment.

Act 2: The same.

PROLOGUE

"Monolithic Madness"

M. Rupert

ACT 1

"Gone So Long"
M. B. Davis
"Hit the Ground Running"
M. Getz, M. Rupert
"It's Your Life"
A. Muraoka, R. Loftin, R. Stockwell
"Cookin' with Steam"
B. Mitchell
(*Music by* Brian Mitchell and Michael Rupert. *Lyrics by* Jerry Colker. Recorded track arranged and played by Brian Mitchell.)
"It's Just a Question of Technique"
A. Ellis, M. Rupert
"It's None of My Business"
R. Mandan
"Crazy World"
M. Getz
"Ambivalent Rag"
M. Rupert
"It's Your Life" II
A. Muraoka, R. Loftin, R. Stockwell
"You Better Get Outta Town"
M. Pawk, R. Stockwell, A. Muraoka, R. Loftin
"We're Gonna Turn Off Your Juice"
L. Hickey, M. Pawk, M. B. Davis, A. Muraoka, R. Stockwell, R. Loftin
"The World Set on Fire by a Black and a Jew"
B. Mitchell, M. Rupert
"Where Are You/Where Am I?"
M. Getz
"Family Ties"
R. Mandan
"One Lost Weekend"
A. Ellis, M. Rupert, M. Getz
"Junk Mail"/"Disconnected"
Ensemble
"Helplessness at Midnight"
M. B. Davis
"What Have You Been Doing for the Past Ten Years?"
M. Rupert, Ensemble
"A Blank Piece of Paper"
M. Rupert

ACT 2

"Sweepstakes"
M. Rupert, R. Stockwell, Pitchpeople
"It's Getting Harder to LoveYou"
M. Getz, Pitchwomen
"Publish Your Book"
A. Ellis, M. Rupert, Pitchpeople
"Ambivalent Rag" II
M. Rupert
"Pages of My Diary"
M. Getz, M. Rupert, Pitchwomen
"One Step at a Time"/"Ambivalent Rag" III
M. Rupert, Pitchpeople
"Don't Count on It"
A. Ellis, M. Rupert
"Friends for Life"
B. Mitchell, M. Rupert
"Twenty-Nine Years Ago"
R. Mandan, M. Rupert
"Crazy World" (reprise)
M. Rupert
"Sweepstakes" (reprise)
Pitchpeople
"A Blank Piece of Paper" (reprise)
M. Rupert
"Crazy World" (Finale)
M. Rupert, M. Getz

1988.08

MICHAEL FEINSTEIN IN CONCERT

A One Man Show in Two Acts. Conceived by Michael Feinstein, Christopher Chadman. Special material, Bruce Vilanch. Staged by Christopher Chadman. Musical director, Elliot Finkel. Set designed by Andrew Jackness. Lighting designed by Beverly Emmons. Sound designed by Tom Sorce. Orchestrations by Ian Finkel. Special arrangements by David Spear. Associate producers, Jonthan Scharer, Peter Kapp. Produced by Ron Delsener. Opened 19 April 1988 at the Lyceum Theatre and closed 12 June 1988 after 57 performances.

CAST: MICHAEL FEINSTEIN.
Musicians: Eliot Finkel (pianist, conductor), David Finck (bass), Ian Finkel (percussion), Luther Rix (drums), Don de Marco (guitar), Ralph Olsen (woodwinds).

ACT 1

"Isn't It Romantic?" (from *LOVE ME TONIGHT*, film)
(*Music by* Richard Rodgers. *Lyrics by* Lorenz Hart.)
"Taking a Chance on Love" (from *CABIN IN THE SKY*)
(*Music by* Vernon Duke. *Lyrics by* John Latouche and Ted Fetter.)
"You Keep Coming Back Like a Song"(from *BLUE SKIES*, film)
"Be Careful, It's My Heart" (from *HOLIDAY INN*, film)
"It Only Happens When I Dance with You" (from *EASTER PARADE*, film)
"Alexander's Ragtime Band"
(*Music and Lyrics by* Irving Berlin.)
"Lydia, the Tattooed Lady" (from *MARX BROTHERS AT THE CIRCUS*, film)
(*Music by* Harold Arlen. *Lyrics by* E. Y. Harburg.)
"Our Love Is Here to Stay" (from *THE GOLDWYN FOLLIES*, film)
"Fascinatin' Rhythm" (from *LADY, BE GOOD*)
"I Got Rhythm" (from *GIRL CRAZY*)
(*Music by* George Gershwin. *Lyrics by* Ira Gershwin.)
"Sail Away" (from *SAIL AWAY* and *ACE OF CLUBS*, London)
(*Music and Lyrics by* Noël Coward.)
"Sing a Tropical Song" (from *HAPPY GO LUCKY*, film)
(*Music by* Jimmy McHugh. *Lyrics by* Frank Loesser.)
"Another Song about Paris"
(*Music and Lyrics by* Dave Frischberg.)
"Rhode Island Is Famous for You" (from *INSIDE U.S.A.*)
(*Music by* Arthur Schwartz. *Lyrics by* Howard Dietz.)
"Never Never Land" (from *PETER PAN*)
(*Music by* Jule Styne. *Lyrics by* Betty Comden and Adolph Green.)
"Wasn't It Romantic?"
(*Music by* Hugh Martin. *Lyrics by* Marshall Barer.)

ACT 2

"I Want to Hear a Yankee Doodle Tune"
(*Music and Lyrics by* George M. Cohan.)
"Will You Remember Me" (dropped from *LADY, BE GOOD*)
(*Music by* George Gershwin. *Lyrics by* Ira Gershwin.)
"Loopin' the Loop" (dropped from *CHICAGO*)
(*Music by* John Kander. *Lyrics by* Fred Ebb.)
"I Won't Send Roses"/"Time Heals Everything" (from *MACK AND MABEL*)
(*Music and Lyrics by* Jerry Herman.)
"Can Can" (from *CAN CAN*)
(*Music and Lyrics by* Cole Porter.)
"I Can Dream, Can't I?"/"I'll Be Seeing You" (from *RIGHT THIS WAY*)
(*Music by* Sammy Fain. *Lyrics by* Irving Kahal.)
"Old Friends" (from *MERRILY WE ROLL ALONG*)
(*Music and Lyrics by* Stephen Sondheim.)
"Wanna Sing a Show Tune"
(*Music and Lyrics by* Ray Jessel.)
Harry Warren medley:
(*All Music by* Harry Warren.)
"I Found a Million Dollar Baby" (from *BILLY ROSE'S CRAZY QUILT*)
(*Lyrics by* Billy Rose, Mort Dixon.)
"Would You Like to Take a Walk?"
(from *SWEET AND LOW*, *BILLY ROSE'S CRAZY QUILT*)
(*Lyrics by* Billy Rose, Mort Dixon.)

"You're My Everything" (from *THE LAUGH PARADE*)
(*Lyrics by* Mort Dixon, Joe Young.)
"Jeepers Creepers" (from *GOING PLACES*, film)
(*Lyrics by* Johnny Mercer.)
"You Must Have Been a Beautiful Baby" (from *HARD TO GET*, film)
(*Lyrics by* Johnny Mercer.)
"There Will Never Be Another You" (from *ICELAND*, film)
(*Lyrics by* Mack Gordon.)
"About a Quarter to Nine"
(from *GO INTO YOUR DANCE*, film; *42nd STREET*, musical)
(*Lyrics by* Al Dubin.)
"Lulu's Back in Town" (from *BROADWAY GONDOLIER*, film)
(*Lyrics by* Al Dubin.)
"I Got a Gal in Kalamazoo" (from *ORCHESTRA WIVES*, film)
(*Lyrics by* Mack Gordon.)
"Latin from Manhattan" (from *GO INTO YOUR DANCE*, film)
(*Lyrics by* Al Dubin.)
"Forty-Second Street" (from *FORTY-SECOND STREET*, film and show)
(*Lyrics by* Al Dubin.)
"An Affair to Remember" (from film of the same name)
(*Lyrics by* Harold Adamson and Leo McCarey.)
"The More I See You" (from *BILLY ROSE'S DIAMOND HORSESHOE*, film)
(*Lyrics by* Mack Gordon.)
"You'll Never Know" (from *HELLO, FRISCO HELLO!*, film)
(*Lyrics by* Mack Gordon.)
"September in the Rain" (from *MELODY FOR TWO*, film)
(*Lyrics by* Al Dubin.)
"I Had the Craziest Dream" (from *SPRINGTIME IN THE ROCKIES*, film)
(*Lyrics by* Mack Gordon.)
"No Love, No Nothin'" (from *THE GANG'S ALL HERE*, film)
(*Lyrics by* Leo Robin.)
"I Only Have Eyes for You" (from *DAMES*, film)
(*Lyrics by* Al Dubin.)
"I Wanna Be a Dancin' Man"
(from *THE BELLE OF NEW YORK*, film; *DANCIN'*, show)
(*Lyrics by* Johnny Mercer.)
"The Lady in the Tutti Frutti Hat" (from *THE GANG'S ALL HERE*, film)
(*Lyrics by* Leo Robin.)
"On the Atcheson, Topeka and the Santa Fe" (from *THE HARVEY GIRLS*, film)
(*Lyrics by* Johnny Mercer.)
"Lullaby of Broadway"
(from *GOLDDIGGERS OF 1935*, film; *42nd STREET*, show)
(*Lyrics by* Al Dubin.)

"I Love a Piano" (from *STOP! LOOK! LISTEN!*)
(*Music and Lyrics by* Irving Berlin.)

"Along the Way"
(*Music by* Jule Styne. *Lyrics by* Bob Merrill.)

1988.09

CHESS

A Musical in Two Acts, 2 Prologues and 23 Scenes. Book by Richard Nelson. Based on an idea by Tim Rice. Music by Benny Andersson, Björn Ulvaeus. Lyrics by Tim Rice. Directed by Trevor Nunn. Dance staging by Lynne Taylor-Corbett. Scenic design by Robin Wagner. Costume design by Theoni V. Aldredge. Lighting design by David Hersey. Sound design by Andrew Bruce. Musical director and supervisor, Paul Bogaev. Orchestrations and (musical) arrangements by Anders Eljas. Executive producers, (Tyler) Gatchell & (Peter) Neufeld, Ltd. Produced by The Shubert Organization, 3 Knights Ltd. (Benny Andersson, Tim Rice, Björn Ulvaeus), Robert Fox, Ltd. Opened 28 April 1988 at the Imperial Theatre and closed 25 June 1988 after 68 performances.

CAST (in order of appearance): *Gregor Vassey*: Neal Ben-Ari. *Young Florence*: Gina Gallagher. *Freddie*: PHILIP CASNOFF. *Florence*: JUDY KUHN. *Anatoly*: DAVID CARROLL. {David-James Carroll}. *Molokov*: Harry Goz. *Nickolai*: Kurt Johns. *Walter*: Dennis Parlato. *Arbiter*: Paul Harman. *Svetlana*: Marcia Mitzman. *Joe and Harold*, Embassy Officials: Richard Muenz, Eric Johnson.

Ensemble: John Aller, Neal Ben-Ari, Suzanne Briar, Steve Clemente, Katherine Lynne Condit, Ann Crumb, David Cryer, R. F. Daley, Deborah Geneviere, Kurt Johns, Eric Johnson, Paul Laureano, Rosemary Loar, Judy McLane, Jessica Molaskey, Richard Muenz, Kip Niven, Francis Ruivivar, Alex Santoriello, Wysandria Woolsey. *Swings*: Karen Babcock, Craig Wells.

Prologue: Budapest, Hungary, 1956.

Act 1, Scene 1: A large meeting room in the Bangkok Hilton Hotel. Thailand, the present time. *Scene 2*: Hotel hallway and Anatoly's hotel suite. *Scene 3*: Freddie's suite. *Scene 4*: The Chess trade show. *Scene 5*: The Chess Board Arena, and later, elevators, and Anatoly's office. *Scene 6*: Freddie's suite. *Scene 7*: The streets of Bangkok. *Scene 8*: The Generous Sole Restaurant, and Terrace. *Scene 9*: The Chess Board Arena and later, Florence's hotel room. *Scene 10*: Underground parking square below the Arena. *Scene 11*: A small baggage room at the airport and later, a concourse in the airport.

Prologue: Kennedy Airport, New York, eight weeks later.

Act 2, Scene 1: Budapest, Hungary, eight weeks later. *Scene 2*: A chapel of a large cathedral. *Scene 3*: Freddie's suite. *Scene 4*: A walk along the Danube outside the hotel after dinner. *Scene 5*: Svetlana's hotel room. *Scene 6*: Outside the Chess Arena building. *Scene 7*: The Lobby of the Chess Arena. *Scene 8*: An elegant restaurant. *Scene 9*: Freddie's suite. *Scene 10*: The walk along the Danube. *Scene 11*: Anatoly's dressing room. *Scene 12*: A room at the Budapest Airport and later, a hangar.

PROLOGUE
"The Story of Chess"
N. Ben-Ari

ACT 1[15]
Scene 1
"Press Conference" (What a Scene, What a Joy)
P. Casnoff, J. Kuhn, Reporters
Scene 2
"Where I Want to Be"
D. Carroll
Scene 3
"How Many Women" (Argument)
J. Kuhn, P. Casnoff
Scene 4
"Merchandisers' Song"
D. Parlato, Merchandisers
"U.S vs. U.S.S.R."
H. Goz, American and Soviet Delegates
Scene 5
"Chess Hymn"
P. Harman, Company
Quartet ("A Model of Decorum and Tranquility")
H. Goz, J. Kuhn, P. Harman, D. Carroll
Scene 6
"You Want to Lose Your Only Friend?"
J. Kuhn, P. Casnoff
"Someone Else's Story"
J. Kuhn
Scene 7
"One Night in Bangkok"
P. Casnoff, Company
Scene 8
"Terrace Duet"
J. Kuhn, D. Carroll
Scene 9
"So You Got What You Want"
P. Casnoff, J. Kuhn

---

[15]For the National tour presented under the auspices of Tom Mallow in association with William H. Kessler, Michael M. Weatherly, Robert R. Larsen and Pace Theatrical Group, the book was revised by Robert Coe. A new physical production (Sets, David Mitchell; Costumes, Susan Hilferty; Lighting, Ken Billington; Sound, Gary Stocker) was assembled under the direction of Des McAnuff, with choreography by Peter Anastos, additional choreography by Wayne Cilento. The song order was altered substantially. Added were:
"The Russian and Molokov" (added to Act 1, Scene 3)
John Herrera (Anatoly), David Hurst (Molokov)
"Who'd Ever Think It" (Act 1, Scene 8)
Stephen Bogardus (Freddie), Carolee Carmello (Florence)
"The Reporters" (Act 1, final scene before 'Anthem")
Ensemble
"Someone Else's Story" (reprise replaced '"Anthem" at end of show)
C. Carmello
Subsequent tours and revivals implemented a variety of changes to the text and score too numerous to detail here.

"Nobody's Side"
J. Kuhn

Scene 11

"Anthem"
D. Carroll

PROLOGUE[16]

"Arbiter's Song"
P. Harman, Company

ACT 2

Scene 1

"Hungarian Folk Song"
Company

Scene 2

"Heaven Help My Heart"
J. Kuhn

Scene 3

"No Contest" (Winning)
P. Casnoff, D. Parlato

Scenes 4 and 5

"You and I"
D. Carroll, J. Kuhn, M. Mitzman

Scene 6

"A Whole New Board Game"
P. Casnoff

Scene 7

"Let's Work Together"
D. Parlato, H. Goz

Scene 8

"I Know Him So Well"
J. Kuhn, M. Mitzman

Scene 9

"Pity the Child"
P. Casnoff

Scene 10

"Lullaby" ("Apukad Eros Kezen")
N. Ben-Ari, J. Kuhn

Scene 11

"Endgame"
D. Carroll, P. Casnoff, Company

Scene 12

"You and I" (reprise)
D. Carroll, J. Kuhn

"Anthem" (reprise)
J. Kuhn

1988.10 ROMANCE ROMANCE

Two Musicals each in One Act[17]. Book and lyrics by Barry Harman. Music by Keith Herrmann. Directed by Barry Harman. Choreographed by Pamela Sousa. Scenic design by Steven Rubin. Costume design by Steven Jones. Lighting design by Craig Miller. Sound design by Peter Fitzgerald. Musical director, Kathy Sommer. Vocal and dance arrangements by Keith Herrmann. Orchestrations by Michael Starobin. Additional orchestrations by Daniel Troob, Joseph Gianono. Produced by Dasha Epstein, Harve Brosten, Jay S. Bulmash, in association with George Krynicki and Marvin A. Krauss. Opened 1 May 1988 at the Helen Hayes Theater and closed 15 January 1989 after 297 performances.

ACT 1: The Little Comedy

Based on the short story by Arthur Schnitzler (as translated by George Edward Reynolds).

CAST: *Alfred von Wilmers*: SCOTT BAKULA. *Josefine Weninger*: ALISON FRASER. *"Him"*: Robert Hoshour. *"Her"*: Deborah Graham.

The action takes place in Vienna at the turn of the century.

MUSICAL NUMBERS

"The Little Comedy"
S. Bakula, A. Fraser

"Goodbye, Emil"
A. Fraser

"It's Not Too Late"
S. Bakula, A. Fraser

"Great News"
S. Bakula, A. Fraser

"Oh, What a Performance!"
S. Bakula, A. Fraser

"I'll Always Remember the Song"
S. Bakula, A. Fraser

"Happy, Happy, Happy"
S. Bakula

"Women of Vienna"
S. Bakula

"Yes, It's Love"
A. Fraser

"A Rustic Country Inn"
S. Bakula, A. Fraser

"The Night It Had to End"
A. Fraser

"The Little Comedy" (Finale)
S. Bakula, A. Fraser

ACT 2: Summer Share

Based on the play "Pain de Menage" by Jules Renard (as translated by Max Gulack).

CAST: *Lenny*: Robert Hoshour. *Barb*: Deborah Graham. *Sam*: SCOTT BAKULA. *Monica*: ALISON FRASER.

The action takes place in the Hamptons during August of the current year.

MUSICAL NUMBERS

"Summer Share"
All

"Think of the Odds"
D. Graham, R. Hoshour

"It's Not Too Late" (reprise)
S. Bakula, A. Fraser

"Plans A & B"
A. Fraser, R. Hoshour

"Let's Not Talk About It"
S. Bakula, D. Graham

"So Glad I Married Her"
All

"Small Craft Warnings"
D. Graham, R. Hoshour

"How Did I End Up Here?"
A. Fraser

"Words He Doesn't Say"
S. Bakula

"My Love for You"
R. Hoshour, D. Graham

"Moonlight Passing Through a Window"
S. Bakula

"Now"
A. Fraser

"Romantic Notions"
S. Bakula, D. Graham, R. Hoshour, A. Fraser

"Romance, Romance"
All

[16]Dropped after the opening.
[17]Originally produced Off-Broadway 30 October 1987 at the Actors Outlet Theatre for 37 performances.

THE WORLD ACCORDING TO ME

1988.11

A Return Engagement of the One Man Comedy Revue in Two Acts[18]. Written and created by Jackie Mason. Supervised by Ron Clark. Scenery and lighting by Neil Peter Jampolis. Sound by Bruce Cameron. Associate producer, Jyll Rosenfeld. Produced by Nick Vanoff. Opened 3 May 1988 at the Brooks Atkinson Theatre and closed 31 December 1988 after 203 performances. Total including first engagement: 570 performances.

CAST: JACKIE MASON (stand-up comedy, monologues, impressions).

Act 1: Current events and cultural experiences.

Act 2: The ever-popular Gentiles and Jews.

CARRIE

1988.12

A Musical in Two Acts, a Prologue and 13 Scenes. Book by Lawrence D. Cohen. Based on the novel of the same name by Stephen King. Music by Michael Gore. Lyrics by Dean Pitchford. Directed by Terry Hands. Choreography by Debbie Allen. Set design by Ralph Koltai. Costume design by Alexander Reid. Lighting design by Terry Hands. Sound design by Martin Levan. Assistant director, Louis W. Scheeder. Orchestrations by Anders Eljas, Harold Wheeler, Michael Starobin. Music supervisor, Harold Wheeler. Musical director, Paul Schwartz. A Friedrich Kurz/Royal Shakespeare Company Production. Produced by Friedrich Kurz in association with Whitecap Productions (Lawrence D. Cohen, Michael Gore) and Martin Barandes. Opened 12 May 1988 at the Virginia Theatre and closed 15 May 1988 after 5 performances.

CAST: *Margaret White*: BETTY BUCKLEY. *Carrie White*: LINZI HATELEY. *Chris*: Charlotte d'Amboise. *Tommy*: Paul Gyngell. *Miss Gardner*: Darlene Love. *Billy*: Gene Anthony Ray. *Sue*: Sally Ann Triplett.

Ensemble: *Jamie*: Jamie Beth Chandler. *Cathy*: Catherine Doffey. *Michèle*: Michèle du Verney. *Shelley*: Michelle Hodgson. *Rose*: Rosemarie Jackson. *Kelly*: Kelly Littlefield. *Maddy*: Madeleine Loftin. *Michelle*: Michelle Nelson. *Mary Ann*: Mary Ann Oedy. *Squeeze*: Suzanne Maria Thomas. *Gary*: Gary Co-Burn. *Kevin*: Kevin Coyne. *David*: David Danns. *Matthew*: Matthew Dickens. *Eric*: Eric Gilliom. *Kenny*: Kenny Linden. *Joey*: Joey McKneely. *Mark*: Mark Santoro. *Chris*: Christopher Solari. *Scott*: Scott Wise. *Swing Dancers*: Mary Ann Lamb, Darryl Eric Tribble.

The action takes place at the present time.

Prologue: The Gynasium.

Act 1, Scene 1: The Showers. *Scene 2*: The Locker Room. *Scene 3*: The White Home. *Scene 4*: The Drive-In. *Scene 5*: The White Home. *Scene 6*: The Gymnasium. *Scene 7*: The Night Spot. *Scene 8*: The White Home.

Act 2, Scene 1: The Pig Farm. *Scene 2*: The Gymnasium. *Scene 3*: Carrie's Room. *Scene 4*: The Prom. *Scene 5*: Epilogue.

PROLOGUE
"In"
D. Love, Girls

ACT 1
Scene 1
"Dream On"
Girls, L. Hateley

Scene 2
"Carrie"
L. Hateley

Scene 3
"Open Your Heart"
B. Buckley, L. Hateley
"And Eve Was Weak"
B. Buckley, L. Hateley

Scene 4
"Don't Waste the Moon"
S. A. Triplett, P. Gyngell, C. Solari, G. A. Ray, Girls, Boys

Scene 5
"Evening Prayers"
L. Hateley, B. Buckley

Scene 6
"Unsuspecting Hearts"
D. Love, L. Hateley

Scene 7
"Do Me a Favor"
S. A. Triplett, P. Gyngell, C. Solari, G. A. Ray, Girls, Boys

Scene 8
"I Remember How Those Boys Could Dance"
B. Buckley

ACT 2
Scene 1
"Out for Blood"
C. Solari, G. A. Ray, Boys

Scene 2
"It Hurts To Be Strong"
S. A. Triplett

Scene 3
"I'm Not Alone"
L. Hateley
"When There's No One"
B. Buckley

Scene 4
"Wotta Night!"
Girls, Boys
"Unsuspecting Hearts" (reprise)
D. Love, L. Hateley
"Heaven"
P. Gyngell, S. A. Triplett, D. Love, L. Hateley, B. Buckley, Girls, Boys
"Alma Mater"
Girls, Boys, D. Love
"The Destruction"
L. Hateley

Scene 5
"Carrie" (reprise)
B. Buckley

---

[18]Originally produced in New York 22 December 1986 at the Brooks Atkinson Theatre for 367 performances.

1988–1989 SEASON

Mary Ann Lamb, Barbara Yaeger, and JoAnn Hunter in JEROME ROBBINS' BROADWAY
Martha Swope/TimePix

1988–1989 SEASON

AN EVENING WITH ROBERT KLEIN

1988.13

A Revue in One Act[1]. Conceived and written by Robert Klein. Musical director, Bob Stein. Presented by Circle-in-the-Square Theatre (Theodore Mann, Artistic director; Paul Libin, Producing director). Opened 19 June 1988 at the Circle-in-the-Square Theatre and closed 27 June 1988 after 3 performances.

CAST: ROBERT KLEIN.
Vocalists: Betsy Bircher, Catherine Russell.

THE MERRY WIDOW

1988.14

A Revival of the Operetta in Three Acts[2]. Music by Franz Lehár. Original Viennese libretto 'Die lustige witwe' by Victor Léon and Leo Stein (after "L'Attaché d'Ambassade" by Henri Meilhac.) English version by Adrian Ross. Original production (stage direction) by Ronald Bentley. Choreographer, Sharon Halley. Set designers, Helen Pond and Herbert Senn. Costume designer, Suzanne Mess. Lighting designer, Ken Tabachnick. Conductor, Imre Pallo. Assistant stage director, Cynthia Edwards. Chorus master, Joseph Colaneri. Produced by the New York City Opera. Opened 6 July 1988 at the New York State Theatre and closed 25 August 1988 after 5 performances in repertory.

CAST (in order of appearance): *Baron Popoff*: RICHARD MCKEE. *Natalie*: Ruth Golden. *General Novikovich*: John Lankston. *Counsellor Khadja*: Michael Willson. *Marquis de Cascada*: Robert Ferrier. *Sylviane*: Michele McBride. *M. de St. Brioche*: MICHAEL REES DAVIS. *Olga*: Joyce Campana. *Vicomte Camille de Jolidon*: Paul Austin Kelly. *Nisch*: James Billings. *Sonia*: LEIGH MUNRO. *Count Danilo*: RICHARD WHITE. *Head Waiter*: Jonathan Guss. *Zozo*: Ivy Austin. *Lolo*: Joan Mirabella. *Dodo*: Esperanza Galan. *Jou-Jou*: Candace Itow. *Frou-Frou*: Victoria Rinaldi. *Clo-Clo*: Ashley Janeway. *Margot*: Jean Barber. *Chorus of Marsovian and Parisian Society, Dancers, Servants and Waiters*: New York City Opera Chorus.

CANCIONES DE MI PADRE (Songs for My Father)

1988.15

A Romantic Evening in Old Mexico (Musical Revue) in Two Acts, 7 Scenes. (Conceived by Linda Ronstadt.) Directed and choreographed by Michael Smuin. Setting designed by Tony Walton. Costumes by Arturo Ceballos; Manuel. Lighting designed by Jules Fisher. Conductor, Ruben Fuentes. Sponsor, Tecate Imported Beer. Produced by Ira Koslow for Asher/Frost Management. Opened 12 July 1988 at the Minskoff Theatre and closed 30 July 1988 after 18 performances.

CAST: LINDA RONSTADT, DANIEL VALDEZ (vocals).

MARIACHI VARGAS DE TECALITLAN: Jose Martinez Baravas, Mario A. Santiago Miranda, Juan Manuel Biurquis Isiano, Daniel Martinez Rodriquez, Idlefonso Moya Escobedo, Francisco Javier Gonzalez Bautista (violins), Federico Torres Martinez, Rigoberto Mercado Alvarez (trumpets), Natividad Santiago Gonzalez, Victor Cardenas Garcia, Rafael Palomar Ruelas (guitar), Arturo Mendoza Villaluazo, Rubén Fuentes, Pepe Martinez, Juan Pinzon. Silvestre Vargas, Ruben Fuentes, Jose "Pepe" Martinez (directors), Arturo Mendoza (coordinator).

BALLET FOLKLORICO DE LA FONDA, GILBERTO PUENTE (guitar), SAL LOPEZ, URBANIE LUCERO, Mary Louise Diaz, Elsa Annette Estrada, Luis Valdez, Lalo Garcia (dancers).

The setting is a romantic evening in old Mexico.

Act 1, Scene 1: First Mariachi section. *Scene 2*: Traditional Dances—Jalisco costumes. *Scene 3*: Revolutionary section.

Act 2, Scene 1: Mariachi Vargas. *Scene 2*: Ballad section. *Scene 3*: Traditional dances. *Scene 4*: Town courtyard.

ACT 1

Scene 1

"Fanfarria" Mariachi Vargas

"Los Laureles" (The Laurels)
(*Music and Lyrics by* Consuelo Velásquez, José López.)

"Por Un Amor" (For a Love)
(*Music and Lyrics by* Gilberto Parra.)

"La Cigarra" (The Cicada)
(*Music and Lyrics by* Ray Pérez Y Soto.)

"Tú Sólo Tú" (You Only You)
(*Music and Lyrics by* Felipe Valdez Leal.)
L. Ronstadt, I. Moya
Violin Solos: Jose Martinez, Juan Manuel Biurquix.

"Cancion Mexicana" (Mexican Cancion)
(*Music and Lyrics by* Lalo Guerrero.)

Scene 2

"La Negra"
M. L. Diaz, E. Estrada, U. Lucero, L. Garcia, S. Lopez, L. Valdez

"El Gusto"
M. L. Diaz, E. Estrada, U. Lucero, L. Garcia, S. Lopez, L. Valdez

"El Caballito"
S. Lopez, M. L. Diaz

Scene 3

"El Tren Sone"
Mariachi Vargas

"La Rielera" (The Railroad Woman)

"Corrido de Cananea" (Ballad of Cananea)
(L. Ronstadt)
(Traditional; *Music and Lyrics adapted by* Rubén Fuentes.)

"(El) Adios del Soldado" (The Soldier's Farewell)
L. Ronstadt, D. Valdez
(*Music and Lyrics by* Valdez Leal.)
Chorus: M. Santiago, I. M. Escobedo. *Violin Solos*: J. Martinez, J. M. Biurquix.

"Yo Soy el Corrido" (I Am the Ballad)
L. Ronstadt, D. Valdez

"El Sol Que Tú Eres" (The Sun That You Are)
L. Ronstadt, D. Valdez
(Traditional; *Music and Lyrics adapted by* Daniel Valdez.)

"La Rielera" (reprise)

"Viva México"
Company

ACT 2

Scene 1

"Fiesta En Jalisto"

"Las Bodas de Luiz Alonso"

Scene 2

"Hay Unos Ojos" (There Are Some Eyes)
(L. Ronstadt)
(Traditional; *Music and Lyrics adapted by* Rubén Fuentes.)
Violin Solos: J. Martinez, J. M. Biurquix.

"Rogaciano el Huapanguero" (Rogaciano the singer of huapangos)
L. Ronstadt, D. Martinez, I. Moya
(*Music and Lyrics by* Valeriano Trejo.)

"Dos Arbolitos" (Two Little Trees)
L. Ronstadt, D. Martinez, I. Moya
(*Music and Lyrics by* Chuco Martinez Gil.)
Violin Solos: J. Martinez, J. M. Biurquix.

"La Barca de Guaymas" (The Boat from Guaymas)
L. Ronstadt, I. Moya, R. Palaomar
(Traditional, *Music and Lyrics adapted by* Rubén Fuentes.)
Violin Solos: J. Martinez, J. M. Biurquix.

"Amorcito Corazon" (Sweet Love)
D. Valdez

---

[1]A previous production THE ROBERT KLEIN SHOW opened 20 December 1985 at the Circle-in-the-Square for 16 performances.

[2]Originally produced in New York 21 October 1907 at the New Amsterdam Theatre for 416 performances. For Synopsis of Scenes and Musical Numbers, see original 1907 production. Interpolated into this production:
"Girls Were Made to Love and Kiss" (from PAGANINI)
(*Music by* Franz Lehar. *Original German Lyrics by* Paul Knepler and Bela Jenbach. *English Lyrics by* A. P. Herbert.)

Scene 3
"La Bamba"
Dance Company in Vera Cruz costumes
"Malguena Salerosa"
G. Puente
"(El) Jarabe Tapatio"
Dance Company in China Poblana costumes
"El Cascabel"
Mariachi Vargas
Scene 4
"Y Andale" (Get On With It)
L. Ronstadt, D. Martinez
(*Music and Lyrics by* Minerva Elizondo.)
"(El) Crucifijo de Piedra" (The Crucifix of Stone)
(*Music and Lyrics by* Hermanos Cantorale.)
"La Calandria" (The Lark)
L. Ronstadt, D. Martinez, I. Moya
(*Music and Lyrics by* Nicandro Castillo.)
"La Charreada" (A show of skills of the charro, a gentleman cowboy)
(L. Ronstadt)
(*Music and Lyrics by* Felipe Bermejo.)
"Cancion Mixteca" (Song from Mixteca)
(*Music and Lyrics by* Lopez Alaves.)
"Volver, (Volver)" (Return, Return)(from *CHULAS FRONTERAS* film)
Company
(*Music and Lyrics by* F. Maldonado.)

1988.16 THE NEW MOON

A Revival of the Operetta in Two Acts, 7 Scenes[3]. Book by Oscar Hammerstein II, Frank Mandel and Laurence Schwab. Music by Sigmund Romberg. Lyrics by Oscar Hammerstein II. New adaptation of the book and lyrics by Robert Johanson. Conductor, Jim Coleman. Director and choreographer, Robert Johanson. Set designer, Michael Anania. Costume designer, Andrew Marlay. Lighting designer, Mark W. Stanley. Chorus master, Joseph Colaneri. Assistant stage directors, Albert Sherman and Laura Alley. Assistant choreographer, Sharon Halley. Produced by the New York City Opera. Opened 19 July 1988 at the New York State Theatre and closed 24 July 1988 after 7 performances.

CAST (in order of appearance): *Julie*, Marianne's maid: JOYCE CAMPANA. *Alexander*, Bondservant to Beaunoir: GERALD ISAAC. *M. Beaunoir*, Marianne's father, owner of *The New Moon*: James Billings. *Captain Duval*, Commander of *The New Moon*, suitor to Marianne: Joseph McKee. *Vicomte Ribaud*, the great French detective: DAVID RAE SMITH. *Fouchette*, informer for Ribaud: Allen Riberdy. *Robert Mission*, Bondservant to Beaunoir, formerly a nobleman: RICHARD WHITE or WILLIAM PARCHER. *Besac*, Boatswain on*The New Moon*: Kenneth Kantor. *Jacques*, ship's carpenter on *The New Moon*: David Frye. *Marianne Beaunoir*, Beaunoir's daughter: LEIGH MUNRO or JANE THORNGREN. *Proprietor*: Harris Davis. *Spaniard*: Terry Lacy. *Flower Dancer*: Esperanza Galan. *Philippe Dupres*, French exile, Robert's comrade: MICHAEL COUSINS or MICHAEL REES DAVIS. *Clotilde Lombaste*, leader of the brides bound for Martinique: MURIEL COSTA-GREENSPON. *Admiral de Jean*, commander of the new French Navy: John Lankston. *Servants, Courtiers, Ladies, Sailors, Pirates, Tavern Wenches, Brides and French Soldiers*: New York City Opera Chorus.

1988.17 AIN'T MISBEHAVIN'

A Revival of the Musical Revue in Two Acts, 22 Scenes[4]. Based on the music of Thomas "Fats" Waller. Conceived and directed by Richard Maltby, Jr. Based on an idea by Murray Horwitz and Richard Maltby, Jr. Musical staging and choreography by Arthur Faria. Music supervision by Luther Henderson. Associate director, Murray Horwitz. Orchestrations and arrangements by Luther Henderson. Vocal and musical concepts, Jeffrey Gutcheon. Vocal arrangements by William Elliott, Jeffrey Gutcheon. Sets by John Lee Beatty. Costumes by Randy Barcelo. Lighting by Pat Collins. Sound by Tom Morse. Originally produced (Off-Broadway) by the Manhattan Theatre Club. Produced by The Shubert Organization, Emanuel Azenberg, Dasha Epstein, Roger Berlind. Opened 15 August 1988 at the Ambassador Theatre and closed 15 January 1989 after 176 performances.

CAST: NELL CARTER, ANDRE DE SHIELDS, ARMELIA MCQUEEN, KEN PAGE, CHARLAINE WOODARD. *Conductor and Pianist*: LUTHER HENDERSON.

1988.18 NAUGHTY MARIETTA

A Revival of the Musical Comedy in Two Acts, 3 Scenes[5]. Music by Victor Herbert. Book and lyrics adapted by Theodore Pappas based on the original by Rida Johnson Young. Director and choreographer, Theodore Pappas. Costumes designed by Andrew Marlay. Sets designed by Oliver Smith. Lighting designed by Ken Tabachnick. Conductor, Scott Bergeson. Chorus master, Joseph Colaneri. Produced by the New York City Opera. Opened 30 August 1988 at the New York State Theatre and closed 11 September 1988 after 14 performances.

CAST (in order of appearance): *Watchman*: Jonathan Guss. *Flower Girl*: Rebecca Rosales. *Fanchon*: Christine Meadows. *Nanette*: Paula Hostetter. *Felice*: Madeleine Mines. *Etienne Grandet*, alias Bras Pique: RICHARD WHITE. *Adah (Le Clercq)*: SUSANNE MARSEE. *Manuel*: Ralph Bassett. *Pirate*: John Henry Thomas. *Town crier*: William Ledbetter. *Silas Slick*: JACK KENNY. *Harry Blake*: DON YULE. *Captain Richard Warrington*: MICHAEL REES DAVIS. *Lizette*: Ivy Austin. *American Indian*: David Gramlich. *Lieutenant Governor Grandet*: JOSEPH MCKEE. *Florenze*: JOHN LANKSTON. *Marietta d'Altena*: CHERYL PARRISH. *Rudolfo*: JAMES BILLINGS. *Graziella*: Esperanza Galan. *Men*: Neil Eddinger, Louis Perry.
Ensemble: New York City Opera Chorus.

Act 1: A Town Square in New Orleans, 1780.

Act 2, Scene 1: Rudolfo's Theater, ten days later.*Scene 2*: A Men's Club, later that evening.

ACT 1
Opening Chorus
Ensemble
"Tramp, Tramp, Tramp"
M. R. Davis Rangers
"Taisez-Vous"
Rangers, Casquette Girls
"Naughty Marietta"
C. Parrish
"It Never, Never Can Be Love"
C. Parrish, M. R. Davis
"If I Were Anyone Else But Me"
J. Kenny, I. Austin
"'Neath the Southern Moon"
S. Marsee
"Italian Street Song"
C. Parrish, Ensemble
Finale
Principals, Chorus

ACT 2
"All I Crave Is More of Life"
C. Parrish
"You Marry a Marionette"
R. White
Intermezzo
Orchestra
"At the Ball"
Male Ensemble
"Loves of New Orleans"
Ensemble

[3]First presented in New York 19 September 1928 at the Imperial Theatre for 509 performances. For Synopsis of Scenes and Musical Numbers, see 1986 revival.

[4]Originally produced in New York 9 May 1978 at the Longacre Theatre for 1604 performances, transferring from its Off-Broadway debut 8 February 1978 at the Manhattan Theatre Club for 28 performances. For Synopsis of Scenes and Musical Numbers, see original 1978 production.

[5]Originally produced in New York 7 November 1910 at the New York Theatre for 136 performances.

"Mister Right"
I. Austin
"A Royal Whipping Boy"
J. Kenny
"Live for Today"
C. Parrish, S. Marsee, M. R. Davis, R. White, Ensemble
"I'm Falling in Love With Someone"
M. R. Davis
"Ah, Sweet Mystery of Life"
C. Parrish, M. R. Davis
Finale Ultimo
C. Parrish, M. R. Davis, R. White, Chorus

1988.19 MICHAEL FEINSTEIN IN CONCERT: ISN'T IT ROMANTIC

A One Man Show in Two Acts. Special material, Bruce Vilanch. Production staged and supervised by Christopher Chadman. Musical director, conductor, Joel Silberman. Set designed by Andrew Jackness. Lighting designed by Beverly Emmons. Sound designed by Daryl Bornstein. Orchestrations by Ian Finkel. Additional orchestrations by Joseph Gianono, Larry Hochman, Pete Levin, Johnny Mandel, John Oddo. Special arrangements by Stan Freeman and Joel Silberman. Produced by Ron Delsener, Jonathan Scharer. Opened 5 October 1988 at the Booth Theatre and closed 6 November 1988 after 39 performances[6].

CAST: MICHAEL FEINSTEIN.
Musicians: Joel Silberman (pianist, conductor), David Finck (bass), Ian Finkel (xylophone), Dave Ratajczak (drums), John Basile (guitar), Ralph Olsen (woodwinds).

1988.20 LEGS DIAMOND

A Musical in Two Acts, 21 Scenes. Book by Harvey Fierstein, Charles Suppon. Based on the Warner Brothers film "The Rise and Fall of Legs Diamond" (screenplay by Joseph Landon). Music and lyrics by Peter Allen. Directed by Robert Allan Ackerman. Musical numbers choreographed by Alan Johnson. Scenery designed by David Mitchell. Costumes designed by Willa Kim. Lighting designed by Jules Fisher. Sound designed by Peter Fitzgerald. Black art effects consultant, Ted Shapiro. Musical director, vocal arrangements by Eric Stern. Orchestrations by Michael Starobin. Dance music arrangements by Mark Hummel. Associate producer, Kathleen Raitt. Produced by James M. Nederlander, James L. Nederlander, Arthur Rubin, The Entertainment Group (Howard Perloff, Eddie Bruce, Joey Roberts, Marc Rose, Ken Silver), George M. Steinbrenner III, in association with Jonathan Farkas and Marvin A. Krauss (Executive producer). Opened 26 December 1988 at the Mark Hellinger Theatre and closed 19 February 1989 after 64 performances.

CAST (in order of appearance): *Jack Diamond*: PETER ALLEN. *Convicts*: Adrian Bailey, Quin Baird, Frank Cava, Norman Wendall Kauahi, Bobby Moya, Paul Nunes, Keith Tyrone. *Prison Guards*: Stephen Bourneuf, Rick Manning. *Madge*: Brenda Braxton. *Cigarette Girl*: Deanna Dys. *Bones*: Christian Kauffmann. *Augie*: Raymond Serra. *Kiki Roberts*: Randall Edwards. *Devane*: Pat McNamara. *Hotsy Totsy Announcer*: Mike O'Carroll. *Flo*: JULIE WILSON. *Hotsy Totsy Girls*: Carol Ann Baxter, Colleen Dunn, Deanna Dys, Gwendolyn Miller, Wendy Waring. *Moran*: Jim Fyfe. *Arnold Rothstein* (A.R.): JOE SILVER. *Tropicana Announcer*: James Brandt. *Tuxedo Dancers*: Stephen Bourneuf, Jonathan Cerullo, K. Craig Innes, Kevin Weldon. *Latin Dancers*: Frank Cava, Norman Wendall Kauahi, Bobby Moya, Paul Nunes, Keith Tyrone. *Champagne Girls*: Carol Ann Baxter, Gwendolyn Miller. *Showgirls*: Colleen Dunn, Wendy Waring. *Gangsters*: Quin Baird, Stephen Bourneuf, James Brandt, Jonathan Cerullo, Rick Manning, Bobby Moya, Paul Nunes, Mike O'Carroll. *Taxi Dancers*: Frank Cava, K. Craig Innes, Bobby Moya. *Boys from Bay Ridge*: Adrian Bailey, Rick Manning, Bobby Moya. *Mourner*: Ruth Gottschall. *Burlesque Women*: Gwendolyn Miller, Wendy Waring. *Barber*: Mike O'Carroll. *Chinese Waiter*: Norman Wendall Kauahi. *A.R.'s Gang*: Adrian Bailey, Quin Baird, Jonathan Cerullo, Rick Manning, Bobby Moya. *Jack's Gang*: Stephen Bourneuf, Frank Cava, K. Craig Innes, Norman Wendall Kauahi, Paul Nunes, Keith Tyrone. *Policeman*: Paul Nunes. *Jack Diamond's Secretary*: Shelley Wald. *FBI Men*: James Brandt, Rick Manning.
Swings: Dan O'Grady, Jennifer Rymer, Steven Scionti.

The action takes place in and around New York during the 1920's.

Act 1, Scene 1: Pennsylvania State Prison, 1921. *Scene 2*: Pennsylvania Station, New York City. *Scene 3*: The Hotsy Totsy Club and Grill. *Scene 4*: The Backroom of The Hotsy Totsy Club. *Scene 5*: Hotsy Totsy Club Alley. *Scene 6*: The Stage of The Tropicana. *Scene 7*: Times Square. *Scene 8*: The Backroom of the Hotsy Totsy Club. *Scene 9*: Flo's Office. *Scene 10*: The Hotsy Totsy Club and Grill. *Scene 11*: Taxi Dancers' Dressing Room. *Scene 12*: Around New York. *Scene 13*: The Hotsy Totsy Club and Grill.

Act 2, Scene 1: A Funeral Parlor. *Scene 2*: The Streets of New York. *Scene 3*: The Hotsy Totsy Stage and The Tropicana Stage. *Scene 4*: The Ladies' Powder Room of The Hotsy Totsy Club. *Scene 5*: The Backroom of The Hotsy Totsy Club. *Scene 6*: The Hotsy Totsy Stage. *Scene 7*: The Diamond Building. *Scene 8*: The Hotsy Totsy Club and Grill.

ACT 1
Scene 1
"When I Get My Name in Lights"
P. Allen, Ensemble
Scene 3
"Speakeasy"
Ensemble
"Applause"
J. Wilson, The Hotsy Totsy Girls
"Knockers"
P. Allen, The Hotsy Totsy Girls
Scene 6
"I Was Made for Champagne"
R. Edwards, The Tropicana Dancers
"Tropicana Rhumba"
P. Allen, R. Edwards
Scene 7
"Sure Thing Baby"
P. Allen
Scene 8
"Speakeasy Christmas"
The Hotsy Totsy Girls
"Charge It to A.R."
J. Silver, R. Serra, J. Fyfe, C. Kauffmann, Gangsters
Scene 9
"Only an Older Woman"
P. Allen, J. Wilson
Scene 10
"Taxi Dancers' Tango"
P. Allen, Ensemble
Scene 12
"Only Steal from Thieves"
P. Allen, R. Edwards, Gangsters
Scene 13
"When I Get My Name in Lights" (reprise)
P. Allen, Company

ACT 2
Scene 1
"Cut of the Cards"
P. Allen, Company
Scene 2
"Gangland Chase"
P. Allen, Gansters
Scene 3
"Now You See Me, Now You Don't"
P. Allen, R. Edwards, Ensemble
Scene 4
"The Man Nobody Could Love"
R. Edwards, J. Wilson, B. Braxton

[6]No musical numbers listed in program. Michael Feinstein previously appeared in concert at the Lyceum Theatre 19 April 1988 for 57 performances.

Scene 6
"The Music Went Out of My Life"
J. Wilson
Scene 7
"Say It Isn't So"
P. Allen, Company
Scene 8
"All I Wanted Was the Dream"
P. Allen

1989.01 H.M.S. PINAFORE

A Revival of the Comic Opera in Two Acts[7]. Libretto by William S. Gilbert. Music by Arthur Sullivan. Directed by Christopher Renshaw. Choreographed by Stuart Hopps. Conducted by David White. (Settings and costumes) Designed by Tim Goodchild. Original lighting design by Mick Hughes; lighting design by Colin Scott. The New Sadler's Wells Opera production. Produced by the City Center 55th Street Theatre Foundation, Inc., by arrangement with Sadler's Wells Trust, Ltd. Opened 17 January 1989 at the New York City Center and closed 29 January 1989 after 16 performances.

CAST: *The Rt. Hon. Sir Joseph Porter, K.C.B.*, First Lord of the Admiralty: NICKOLAS GRACE. *Captain Corcoran*, Commander of the *H.M.S. Pinafore*: GORDON SANDISON. *Ralph Rackstraw*, Able Seaman: HUGH HETHERINGTON. *Dick Deadeye*, Able Seaman: THOMAS LAWLOR. *Bill Bobstay*, Boatswain: Steven Page. *Bob Becket*: Jeremy Jacka. *Josephine*, the Captain's Daughter: ROSEMARY ASHE. *Little Buttercup*, a Bumboat woman: LINDA ORMINSTON. *Cousin Hebe*, Sir Joseph's First Cousin: Joan Davies.

First Lord's Sisters, Cousins, Aunts, Sailors, Marines, etc.: Brigitta Angsmyr, Jane Cammack, Joan Carroll, David Dyer, Michael Fitchew, George Freeburn, Ann Gall, Claire Hayes, Jeremy Jacka, Robert Jon, Fiona Lamont, Guy Matthews, Tim Menah, Sally-Anne Middleton, Michael Neill, Anne O'Neill, Ian Platt, Elisabeth Stirling, Susan Stubbs, Colin Trickett.

1989.02 BLACK AND BLUE

A Musical Revue in Two Acts. Entire production conceived and directed by Claudio Segovia and Héctor Orrezoli. Choreographers, Cholly Atkins, Henry LeTang, Frankie Manning, Fayard Nicholas. Musical supervision, arrangements, orchestrations by Sy Johnson. Additional arrangements and orchestrations by Luther Henderson. Scenery, costumes designed, and lighting conceived by Claudio Segovia and Héctor Orezzoli. Lighting by Neil Peter Jampolis, Jane Reisman. Sound designed by Abe Jacob. Assistant choreographer, Dianne Walker. Conductor, Leonard Oxley. Associate producer, Marilynn LeVine. Produced by Mel Howard and Donald K. Donald. Opened 26 January 1989 at the Minskoff Theatre and closed 20 January 1991 after 829 performances.

CAST: *The Singers*: RUTH BROWN, LINDA HOPKINS, CARRIE SMITH.

The Hoofers: Bunny Briggs, Ralph Brown, Lon Chaney, Tina Pratt, Jimmy Slyde, Dianne Walker.

The Dancers: Rashamella Cumbo, Tanya Gibson, Germaine Goodson, Angela Hall, Kyme, Valerie Macklin, Deborah Mitchell, Valerie E. Smith, Frederick J. Boothe, Eugene Fleming, Ted Levy, Bernard Manners, Van Porter, Kevin Ramsey, Ken Roberson, Melvin Washington, Ivery Wheeler.

The Younger Generation: Cyd Glover, Savion Glover, Dormeshia Sumbry.

The Musicians: Martin Aubert, Bill Easley, Stephen Furtaldo, Sir Roland Hanna, Haywood Henry, Virgil Jones, Al McKibbon, Leonard Oxley, Jerome Richardson, Grady Tate, Emery Thompson, Claude Williams, Britt Woodman.

ACT 1
Blues: "I'm a Woman"
L. Hopkins, Ruth Brown, C. Smith
(*Music and Lyrics by* McDaniel.)
Hoofers a Cappella
Ralph Brown, B. Manners, S. Glover, B. Briggs, T. Levy, J. Slyde, L. Chaney
"Royal Garden Blues"
Musicians
(*Music and Lyrics by* Spencer Williams and Clarence Williams.)
"St. Louis Blues"
Ruth Brown
(*Music and Lyrics by* W. C. Handy.)
Featured Musicians: R. Hanna, H. Henry, B. Woodman, E. Thompson, G. Tate, M. Aubert.
"Everybody Loves My Baby"
The Dancers
(*Music and Lyrics by* Jack Palmer and Spencer Williams. *Choreography by* Henry LeTang. *Arrangements and orchestrations by* Luther Henderson.)
"After You've Gone"
L. Hopkins, B. Manners, Male Dancers
(*Music by* Henry Creamer. *Lyrics by* Turner Layton.)
"If I Can't Sell It I'll Keep Sittin' on It"
Ruth Brown
(*Music by* Alexander Hill. *Lyrics by* Andy Razaf.)
"I Want a Big Butter and Egg Man"
C. Smith, E. Fleming, K. Ramsey, T. Levy
(*Music and Lyrics by* Percy Venable and Louis Armstrong.)
Featured Musicians: R. Hanna, E. Thompson.
"Rhythm Is Our Business"
S. Glover, C. Glover, D. Sumbry
(*Music by* Jimmie Lunceford and Saul Chaplin. *Lyrics by* Sammy Cahn. *Choreography by* Henry LeTang.)
"Mystery Song"
T. Gibson, R. Cumbo, Valerie E. Smith
(*Music by* Duke Ellington. *Lyrics by* Irving Mills.)
"Stompin' at the Savoy"
J. Slyde
(*Music by* Benny Goodman, Chick Webb, Edgar Sampson. *Lyrics by* Andy Razaf.)
"I've Got a Right to Sing the Blues" (from *EARL CARROLL'S VANITIES OF 1932*)
(*Music by* Harold Arlen. *Lyrics by* Ted Koehler.)
C. Smith
"Black and Tan Fantasy"
B. Briggs, Dancers
(*Music by* Duke Ellington and Bubber Miley.)
Choreography by Frankie Manning.
"Come Sunday"
L. Hopkins
(*Music and Lyrics by* Duke Ellington.)
"Daybreak Express"
Musicians
(*Music by* Duke Ellington.)
"'Tain't Nobody's Bizness If I Do"
Ruth Brown, L. Hopkins
(*Music and Lyrics by* Porter Grainger, Clarence Williams, Graham Prince.)
Featured Musician: R. Hanna.
"That Rhythm Man" (from *HOT CHOCOLATES*)
Dancers
(*Music by* Fats Waller and Harry Brooks. *Lyrics by* Andy Razaf. *Arrangements and orchestrations by* Luther Henderson.)

ACT 2
"Swinging" to "Wednesday Night Hop"
Dancers
(*Music by* Johnson; Johnakins-Kirk.)
"Cry Like a Baby"
"I'm Getting 'Long Alright"
L. Hopkins
(*Music and Lyrics by* R. Sharp and C. Singleton.)
"Memories of You" (from *BLACKBIRDS OF 1930*)
D. Walker, B. Manners, K. Ramsey
(*Music by* Eubie Blake. *Lyrics by* Andy Razaf.)
Choreography by Cholly Atkins.
"Body and Soul" (from *THREE'S A CROWD*)
Ruth Brown
(*Music by* Johnny Green. *Lyrics by* Edward Heyman, Robert Sour, Frank Eyton.)
"I'm Confessing (That I Love You)"
Kyme, B. Manners, F. Boothe, T. Levy, K. Ramsey
(*Music by* Al. J. Neiberg. *Lyrics by* Don Daugherty and Ellis Reynolds.)
Choreography by Cholly Atkins. *Featured Musicians*: C. Williams, M. Aubert.

[7]Originally presented in New York 15 January 1879 at the Standard Theatre for 175 performances. For Synopsis of Scenes and Musical Numbers, see original 1879 production.

"East St. Louis Toodle-oo"
Ralph Brown, L. Chaney
(*Music by* Duke Ellington, {Bubber Miley}.)

"Am I Blue?" (from *ON WITH THE SHOW* film)
C. Smith
(*Music by* Harry Akst. *Lyrics by* Grant Clarke.)
Featured Musican: C. Williams.

"I Can't Give You Anything But Love" (from *BLACKBIRDS OF 1928*)
A. Hall, E. Fleming, Dancers
(*Music by* Jimmy McHugh. *Lyrics by* Dorothy Fields. *Choreography by* Henry LeTang.)

"In a Sentimental Mood"
B. Briggs
(*Music by* Duke Ellington.)
Featured Musician: J. Richardson.

"Black and Blue" (from *HOT CHOCOLATES*)
Ruth Brown, L. Hopkins, C. Smith, J. Slyde, B. Briggs
(*Music by* Fats Waller and Harry Brooks. *Lyrics by* Andy Razaf.)

Finale
S. Glover, C. Glover, D. Sumbry,
J. Slyde, B. Briggs, Ralph Brown, L. Chaney, D. Walker, Dancers
(*Arrangements and orchestrations by* Luther Henderson.)

1989.03 JEROME ROBBINS' BROADWAY

A Musical Revue in Two Acts, a Prologue and 12 Scenes. Entire production directed and choreographed by Jerome Robbins. Dialogue, music and lyrics by James M. Barrie, Irving Berlin, Leonard Bernstein, Jerry Bock, Sammy Cahn, Moose Charlap, Betty Comden, Larry Gelbart, Morton Gould, Adolph Green, Oscar Hammerstein II, Sheldon Harnick, Arthur Laurents, Carolyn Leigh, Stephen Longstreet, Hugh Martin, Jerome Robbins, Richard Rodgers, Burt Shevelove, Stephen Sondheim, Joseph Stein, Jule Styne. Co-director, Grover Dale. Production scenic designer, Robin Wagner. Scenery by Boris Aronson, Jo Mielziner, Oliver Smith, Robin Wagner, Tony Walton. Supervising costume designer, Joseph G. Aulisi. Costumes by Joseph G. Aulisi, Alvin Colt, Raoul Pene du Bois, Irene Sharaff, Tony Walton, Miles White, Patricia Zipprodt. Musical director, Paul Gemignani. Assistants to the choreographer, Cynthia Onrubia, Victor Castelli, Jerry Mitchell. Sound by Otts Munderloh. Lighting designed by Jennifer Tipton. Orchestrations by Sid Ramin, William D. Brohn. Musical continuity by Scott Frankel. Narrative continuity by Jason Alexander. Produced by The Shubert Organization, Roger Berlind, Suntory International Corporation, Byron Goldman, Emanuel Azenberg, in association with Pace Theatrical Group. Opened 26 February 1989 at the Imperial Theatre and closed 1 September 1990 after 634 performances.

CAST (in alphabetical order): JASON ALEXANDER, Richard Amaro, Dorothy Benham, Jeffrey Lee Broadhurst, Christophe Caballero, Mindy Cartwright, Irene Cho, Jamie Cohen, CHARLOTTE D'AMBOISE, Camille de Ganon, Donna Di Meo, Donna Marie Elio, Mark Esposito, SUSANN FLETCHER, Scott Fowler, Angelo H. Fraboni, Ramon Galindo, Nicholas Garr, Gregorey Garrison, Carolyn Goor, Michael Scott Gregory, Andrew Grose, Alexia Hess, NANCY HESS, Louise Hickey, Eric A. Hoisington, Barbara Hoon, JoAnn M. Hunter, Scott Jovovich, Pamela Khoury, SUSAN KIKUCHI (dance captain), MICHAEL KUBALA, ROBERT LA FOSSE, Mary Ann Lamb, JANE LANIER, David Lowenstein, Michael Lynch, Greta Martin, JOEY McKNEELY, Julio Monge, Troy Myers, Maria Neenan, Jack Noseworthy, Steve Ochoa, Kelly Patterson, LUIS PEREZ, FAITH PRINCE, James Rivera, Tom Robbins, George Russell (dance captain), Greg Schanuel, DEBBIE SHAPIRO, Renée Stork, Mary Ellen Stuart, Linda Talcott, Leslie Trayer, Ellen Troy, Andi Tyler, SCOTT WISE, Elaine Wright, Barbara Yeager, Alice Yearsley.

ACT 1

Overture—Prologue
The Setter: J. Alexander.

("Gotta Dance" from *LOOK MA, I'M DANCIN'*")
M. Lynch, Company
(*Music and Lyrics by* Hugh Martin.)

("Papa, Won't You Dance With Me?" from *HIGH BUTTON SHOES*)
(*Music by* Jule Styne. *Lyrics by* Sammy Cahn.) D. Shapiro, Company

("Shall We Dance?" from *THE KING AND I*)
Company
(*Music by* Richard Rodgers. *Lyrics by* Oscar Hammerstein II.)

Scene 1
"New York, New York"
"Sailors on the Town"
"Ya Got Me"
(from *ON THE TOWN*,1944)
Gaby: R. La Fosse. *Chip*: S. Wise. *Ozzie*: M. Kubala. *Hildy*: D. Shapiro. *Claire*: M. E. Stuart. *Dolores Dolores*: N. Hess. *Emcee*: J. Alexander. *First Workman*: D. Lowenstein. *Sailors, Workmen, Dance Hall Hostesses, Passers-by, etc.*: Company.
Book based on an idea by Jerome Robbins. Music by Leonard Bernstein. Book and lyrics by Betty Comden and Adolph Green. Scenery by Oliver Smith. Costumes by Alvin Colt.

Scene 2
"Charleston" From *BILLION DOLLAR BABY* (1945)
Cop: D. Lowenstein. *Doorman*: M. Lynch. *Three Flappers*: B. Yeager, M. A. Lamb, J. M. Hunter. *Socialites*: J. Lanier, N. Garr. *A Timid Girl*: S. Fletcher. *Good Time Charlie*: T. Meyers. *Collegiates*: E. Wright, A. H. Fraboni. *Younger Generation*: C. Caballero, L. Talcott. *Older Generation*: B. Hoon, S. Fowler. *Two Gangsters*: M. S. Gregory, S. Jovovich. *Two Bootleggers*: A. Grose, J. Monge.
Book and lyrics by Betty Comden and Adolph Green. Music by Morton Gould. Scenery by Oliver Smith. Costumes designed by Irene Sharaff.

Scene 3
"Comedy Tonight" From *A FUNNY THING HAPPENED ON THE WAY TO THE FORUM* (1962)
Pseudolus: J. Alexander. *First Protean*: S. Wise. *Second Protean*: J. McKneely. *Third Protean*: M. Kubala. *The Company*: C. d'Amboise, D. Benham, S. Fletcher, M. S. Gregory, A. Grose, R. La Fosse, M. A. Lamb, D. Lowenstein, M. Lynch, J. Noseworthy, K. Patterson, L. Perez, T. Robbins, G. Schanuel, D. Shapiro.
Book by Burt Shevelove and Larry Gelbart. Music and lyrics by Stephen Sondheim. Scenery and costumes by Tony Walton. Dance music arranged by Betty Walberg. Staged by Jerome Robbins.

Scene 4
"I Still Get Jealous" From *HIGH BUTTON SHOES* (1947)
Ma: F. Prince. *Pa*: J. Alexander.
Book by Stephen Longstreet. Music by Jule Styne. Lyrics by Sammy Cahn. Scenery by Oliver Smith. Costumes by Miles White.

Scene 5
"Suite of Dances" From *WEST SIDE STORY* (1957)
(Prologue; The Dance at the Gym; Cool; America; The Rumble; Somewhere.)
Tony: R. La Fosse. *Maria*: A. Hess. *Riff*: S. Wise. *Bernardo*: N. Garr. *Anita*: C. d'Amboise. *Rosalia*: D. Shapiro. *Graziella*: D. Di Meo. *"Somewhere" Soloist*: D. Benham. *The Jets*: J. McKneely, C. Caballero, S. Fowler, A. H. Fraboni, M. S. Gregory, A. Grose, E. A. Hoisington, T. Meyers, J. Noseworthy, K. Patterson, G. Schanuel. *Their Girls*: L. Hickey, B. Hoon, M. A. Lamb, M. Neenan, M. E. Stuart, L. Talcott, L. Trayer, A. Yearsley. *The Sharks*: J. Cohen, M. Esposito, S. Jovovich, D. Lowenstein, M. Lynch, J. Monge, S. Ochoa, J. Rivera. *Their Girls*: I. Cho, D. M. Elio, N. Hess, J. M. Hunter, R. Stork, A. Tyler, E. Wright, B. Yeager.
Based on a conception of Jerome Robbins. Book by Arthur Laurents. Music by Leonard Bernstein. Lyrics by Stephen Sondheim. Scenery by Oliver Smith. Costumes designed by Irene Sharaff. Co-choreographer, Peter Gennaro. Directed and choreographed by Jerome Robbins.

ACT 2

Scene 1
"The Small House of Uncle Thomas" From *THE KING AND I* (1951)
Narrator: B. Yeager. *Eliza*: S. Kikuchi. *King Simon*: J. McKneely. *Little Eva*: L. Talcott. *Topsy*: J. M. Hunter. *Uncle Thomas*: B. Hoon. *Angel/George*: I. Cho. *Royal Dancers*: C. Caballero, D. Di Meo, M. Esposito, E. A. Hoisington, M. Neenan, S. Ochoa, R. Stork, A. Tyler, E. Wright, A. Yearsley. *Royal Singers*: D. Benham, D. M. Elio, L. Trayer, N. Hess, L. Hickey, M. E. Stuart. *Propmen*: J. Cohen, A. H. Fraboni, S. Fowler, N. Garr, S. Jovovich, J. Rivera.
Book and lyrics by Oscar Hammerstein II. Music by Richard Rodgers. Based upon the novel "Anna and the King of Siam" by Margaret Landon. Scenery by Jo Mielziner. Costumes designed by Irene Sharaff. Dance music arranged by Trude Rittman.

Scene 2
"You Gotta Have a Gimmick" From *GYPSY* (1959)
Cigar: J. Alexander. *Louise*: M. A. Lamb. *Tessie*: F. Prince. *Mazeppa*: D. Shapiro. *Electra*: S. Fletcher.
Book by Arthur Laurents. Music by Jule Styne. Lyrics by Stephen Sondheim. Suggested by the memoirs of Gypsy Rose Lee. Scenery by Jo Mielziner. Costumes by Raoul Pene du Bois.

Scene 3

"I'm Flying" From *PETER PAN* (1954)

(Charlap-Leigh)

Peter Pan: C. d'Amboise. *Wendy*: D. Di Meo. *Michael*: L. Talcott. *John*: S. Ochoa.

Book by James M. Barrie. Music by Moose Charlap and Jule Styne. Lyrics by Carolyn Leigh, Betty Comden and Adolph Green. New scenery by Robin Wagner. New costumes by Joseph Aulisi. Flying by Foy.

Scene 4

"On a Sunday by the Sea" From *HIGH BUTTON SHOES* (1947)

Book by Stephen Longstreet. Music by Jule Styne. Lyrics by Sammy Cahn.

Scene 5

"Mr. Monotony" From *MISS LIBERTY* (1949), *CALL ME MADAM* (1950), dropped.

Singer: D. Shapiro. *First Dancer*: L. Perez. *Second Dancer*: J. Lanier. *Third Dancer*: R. La Fosse.

Music and Lyrics by Irving Berlin. New costumes by Joseph Aulisi. Dance music arranged by Genevieve Pitot.

Scene 6

("Tradition;" "The Dream;" "Sunrise, Sunset;" "Wedding Dance.") From *FIDDLER ON THE ROOF* (1964)

Tevye: J. Alexander. *Golde*: S. Fletcher. *Motel Kamzoil*: M. Lynch. *Tzeitel*: A. Tyler. *Grandma Tzeitel*: B. Hoon. *Fruma-Sarah*: N. Hess. *Lazar Wolf*: T. Robbins. *The Rabbi*: T. Meyers. *The Fiddler*: J. McKneely. *Bottle Dancers*: C. Caballero, M. Esposito, S. Jovovich, G. Schanuel. *Villagers, Wedding Guests*: Company.

Book by Joseph Stein. Music by Jerry Bock. Lyrics by Sheldon Harnick. Based on Sholom Aleichem's stories by special arrangement of Arnold Perl. Scenery by Boris Aronson. Costumes by Patricia Zipprodt. Dance music arranged by Betty Walberg.

Scene 7

"Some Other Time"

"New York, New York" (reprise)

Finale from *ON THE TOWN* (1944)

Gaby: R. La Fosse. *Chip*: S. Wise. *Ozzie*: M. Kubala. *Hildy*: D. Shapiro. *Claire*: M. E. Stuart. *Ivy*: A. Hess. *Three Sailors*: C. Caballero, K. Patterson, M. S. Gregory. And the Full Company.

Setting for "Broadway at Night" designed by Robin Wagner.

1989.04 THE PAJAMA GAME

A Revival of the Musical Comedy in Two Acts, 17 Scenes[8]. Book by George Abbott and Richard Bisssell. Based on the novel "7 1/2 Cents" by Richard Bissell. Music and lyrics by Richard Adler and Jerry Ross. Director and choreographer, Theodore Pappas. Conductor, Peter Howard. Set designer, Michael Anania. Costume designer, by Marjorie McCown. Lighting designer, Ken Tabachnick. Chorus Master, Joseph Colaneri. Produced by the New York City Opera. Opened 3 March 1989 at the New York State Theatre and closed 16 April 1989 after 51 performances.[9]

CAST (in order of appearance): *Hines*: AVERY SALTZMAN. *Prez*: David Green. *Joe*: Jim Borstelmann. *Hasler*: Steve Pudenz. *Gladys*: LENORA NEMETZ. *Mae*: Susan Nicely. *Brenda*: Joyce Campana. *Poopsie*: Lillian Graff. *Sid Sorokin*: RICHARD MUENZ. *Charlie*: Louis Perry. *First Helper*: Scott Robertson. *Second Helper*: David Koch. *Mabel*: Brooks Almy. *Babe Williams*: JUDY KAYE. *Max*: Don Yule. *Pat*: Paula Hostetter. *Pop*: William Ledbetter. *Steam Heat Boys*: Jim Borstelmann, David Koch. *Ensemble*: New York City Opera Chorus.

1989.05 CHU CHEM

The First Chinese-Jewish Musical in Two Acts[10]. Book by Ted Allan. Music by Mitch Leigh. Lyrics by Jim Haines, Jack Wohl. Entire production staged by Albert Marre. Scenery by Robert Mitchell. Costumes by Kenneth M. Yount. Lighting by Jason Sturm. Sound by Gary M. Stocker. Musical, vocal direction by Don Jones. Orchestrations by Michael Gibson. Production supervisor, Dwight Frye. A Jewish Repertory Theatre Production. Produced by The Mitch Leigh Company and William D. Rollnick. Opened 7 April 1989 at the Ritz Theatre and closed 14 May 1989 after 45 performances.

CAST: *The Oriental Company*: *The Prince*: KEVIN GRAY. *The Elder*: Alvin Lum. *Hong Ho*, the Governor: Chev Rodgers. *The Prince's Brother*: Hechter Ubarry. *Dah-ah-Dil, Concubine, Villager*: Zoie Lam. *The Prompter*: Timm Fujii. *Na Mi, Concubine, Villager*: Simone Gee. *Lei-An, Concubine, Villager*: Keelee Seetoo. *Shu-Wo, Propman, Villager*: Kenji Nakao. *Ho-Ke, Propman, Villager*: Jason Ma. *Nu-Wo, Propman, Villager*: Paul Nakauchi. *Chueh-Wu, Propman, Guard*: Nephi Jay Wimmer. *The Westerners*: *Chu Chem*: MARK ZELLER. *Lotte*: EMILY ZACHARIAS. *Jacob*: Irving Burton.

The action takes place some six hundred years ago in China.

ACT 1

"Orient Yourself"
Oriental Company

"What Happened, What?"
M. Zeller, I. Burton

"Welcome"
Villagers

"You'll Have to Change"
E. Zacharias

"Love Is"
K. Gray

"I'll Talk to Her"
M. Zeller, K. Gray, H. Ubarry

"Shame on You"
M. Zeller, K. Gray, Concubines

"It Must be Good for Me"
E. Zacharias

"I'll Talk to Her" (reprise)
M. Zeller, K. Gray

"You'll Have to Change" (reprise)
K. Gray

"The River"
E. Zacharias, K. Gray, Propmen

"We Dwell in Our Hearts"
M. Zeller, E. Zacharias, K. Gray

ACT 2

"Re-Orient Yourself"
Oriental Company

"What Happened, What?" (reprise)
I. Burton

"I Once Believed"
E. Zacharias

"It's Possible"
M. Zeller

"Our Kind of War"
Company

"Boom!"
C. Rodgers

Finale
Company

1989.06 THE WIZARD OF OZ

A Musical Spectacle in Two Acts. Based on the novel of the same name by L. Frank Baum and the MGM film adaptation by Noel Langley, Florence Ryerson, Edgar Allan Woolf. Book by Michel M. Grilikhes. Original music by Harold Arlen. Original lyrics by E. Y. Harburg. Original incidental music by Herbert Stothart. Directed and produced by Michel M. Grilikhes. Dances by Onna White. Costumes by Bill Campbell. Art director, Jeremy Railton. Scenery designed by Stephen Ehlers. Musical supervisor, Tom Worrall. Dimensional sound by John Neal. Associate choreographer, Jim Tyler. Dance arrangements by Jackie Shaw O'Neill. Sponsors, Purina Dog Chow, Downy Fabric Softener. Produced by M.M.G. Arena Productions.

---

[8]Originally produced in New York 13 May 1954 at the St. James Theatre for 1063 performances. For Synopsis of Scenes and Musical Numbers, see original 1954 production. The action was reset to June 1957.

[9]Orchestrations uncredited.

[10]Originally produced in New York Off-Broadway 22 December 1988 at the Jewish Repertory Theatre for 20 performances. An earlier version starring Menasha Skulnick and Molly Picon was presented in Philadelphia in December 1966 but closed before reaching New York.

Opened 22 March 1989 at Radio City Music Hall and closed 9 April 1989 after 37 performances.

CAST: *Dorothy*: GRACE GREIG. *Aunt Em, Glinda*: LINDA JOHNSON. *Uncle Henry*: John Sovec. *Zeke, Cowardly Lion*: GUY ALLEN. *Hunk, Scarecrow*: JOE MCDONOUGH. *Hickory, Tin Woodsman*: JOE GIUFFRE. *Miss Gulch, Wicked Witch of the West*: POLLY SEALE. *Professor Marvel, Wizard, Gate Keeper*: BART WILLIAMS. *Toto*: Toby, Coby, Patrick, Darrin, or Misty.

MUSICAL NUMBERS[11]

"Over the Rainbow"
"Munchkinland"
"Ding Dong! The Witch Is Dead"
"Follow the Yellow Brick Road"
"If I Only Had a Brain"
"If I Only Had a Heart"
"Lions and Tigers and Bears"
"If I Only Had the Nerve"
"Optimistic Voices"
"The Merry Old Land of Oz"
"If I Were King of the Forest"
"Courage"
"There's No Place Like Home"
Finale

1989.07 WELCOME TO THE CLUB

A Musical in Two Acts. Book by A. E. Hotchner. Music by Cy Coleman. Lyrics by Cy Coleman and A. E. Hotchner. Directed by Peter Mark Schifter. Musical numbers staged by Patricia Birch. Scenery designed by David Jenkins. Costumes designed by William Ivey Long. Lighting designed by Tharon Musser. Sound designed by Otts Munderloh. Orchestrations by Doug Katsaros. Vocal arrangements by Cy Coleman, David Pogue. Musical director, David Pogue. Associate producer, Robert R. Larsen. Produced by Cy Coleman, A. E. Hotchner, William H. Kessler, Jr., Michael M. Weatherly in association with Raymond J. Greenwald. Opened 13 April 1989 at the Music Box Theatre and closed 22 April 1989 after 13 performances.

CAST (in order of appearance): *Arlene Meltzer*: MARILYN SOKOL. *Milton Meltzer*: AVERY SCHREIBER. *Gus Bottomly*: Bill Buell. *Aaron Bates*: Scott Wentworth. *Bruce Aiken*: Samuel E. Wright. *Kevin Bursteter*: Scott Waara. *Betty Bursteter*: Jodi Benson. *Carol Bates*: Marcia Mitzman. *Eve Aiken*: Terri White. *Winona Shook*: Sally Mayes.

The action takes place at the present time in a section of a New York City jail exclusively reserved for alimony delinquents.

ACT 1

"A Place Called Alimony Jail"
Husbands, Wives
"Pay the Lawyer"
Husbands
"Mrs. Meltzer Wants the Money Now!"
M. Sokol, Husbands
"That's a Woman"
S. Wentworth, M. Mitzman, Wives
"Piece of Cake"
T. White, S. E. Wright
"Rio"
A. Schreiber, M. Sokol, Wives, B. Buell
"Holidays"
M. Sokol
"The Trouble with You"
S. Wentworth, M. Mitzman, Husbands, Wives
"Mother-in-Law"
Husbands
"At My Side"
S. E. Wright, S. Waara

[11]The cast performed to pre-recorded dialogue and music from the 1939 film, whose songs are listed below.

ACT 2

"Southern Comfort"
S. Mayes, S. Wentworth, Wives, Husbands
"The Two of Us"
S. E. Wright, A. Schreiber
"It's Love! It's Love!"
B. Buell, Husbands
"The Name of Love"
M. Mitzman
"Miami Beach"
M. Sokol, Husbands
"Guilty"
S. Mayes
"Love Behind Bars"
S. Mayes, S. Wentworth, Wives
"At My Side" (reprise)
S. Waara, J. Benson
"It Wouldn't Be You"
Husbands, Wives

1989.08 BARRY MANILOW AT THE GERSHWIN

A Musical Revue in Two Acts. Written by Ken and Mitzie Welch, Roberta Kent, Barry Manilow. Concept by Ernie Chambers, Jack Feldman, Roberta Kent, Barry Manilow, Bruce Sussman. Production created and directed by Joe Gannon. Production (set, costumes) designer, Jeremy Railton. Lighting designer, J. T. McDonald. Music directors, Bud Harner, Ron Pedley. Original production created and produced by Joe Gannon. Presented by Garry C. Kief, James M. Nederlander, James L. Nederlander, Arthur Rubin. Opened 18 April 1989 at the Gershwin Theatre and closed 10 June 1989 after 44 performances[12].

CAST: BARRY MANILOW.

Musicians: Vanessa Brown (percussion, vocals), Debra Byrd (vocals), Billy Kidd (keyboards, vocals), Marc Levine (bass guitar, vocals), Joe Melotti (keyboards, vocals), John Pondel (guitar, vocals), Dana Robbins (woodwinds, vocals), Bud Harner (drums), Ron Pedley (keyboards).

1989.09 STARMITES

A Musical in Two Acts, a Prologue, 9 Scenes and an Epilogue[13]. Book by Stuart Ross and Barry Keating. Music and lyrics by Barry Keating. Directed and staged by Larry Carpenter. Choreography by Michele Asaf. Assistant choreographer, T. C. Charlton. Sets by Lowell Detweiler. Costumes by Susan Hirschfeld. Lighting by Jason Kantrowitz. Sound by John Kilgore. Musical direction, dance arrangements by Henry Aronson. Orchestrations, sound effects by James McElwane. Vocal arrangements, associate musical director, Dianne Adams. Associate producers, Peter Bogyo, John Burt, Severn Sandt. Produced by Hinks Shimberg, Mary Keil, Steven Warnick. Opened 27 April 1989 at the Criterion Center Stage Right and closed 18 June 1989 after 60 performances.

CAST (in order of appearance): *On Earth*: *Eleanor*: LIZ LARSEN. *Mother*: SHARON MCKNIGHT.

Innerspace: *Shak Graa*: Ariel Grabber. *Spacepunk*: BRIAN LANE GREEN. *Trinkulus*: GABRIEL BARRE.

Starmites: *Ack Ack Ackerman*: Bennett Cale. *Herbie Harrison*: Victor Trent Cook. *Dazzle Razzledorf*: Christopher Zelno. *Diva*: SHARON MCKNIGHT. *Bizarbara*: LIZ LARSEN.

Banshees: *Shotzi*: Mary Kate Law. *Canibelle*: Gwen Stewart. *Balbraka*: Freida Williams. *Maligna*: Janet Aldrich. *Droids*: John-Michael Flate, Ric Ryder.

The action takes place now on Earth and in Innerspace.

Prologue: Eleanor's Bedroom, Planet Earth.

[12]Musical numbers not listed in program.
[13]Originally produced Off-Broadway 23 October 1980 at the Ark Theatre for 20 performances; subsequently produced 24 April 1987 by Musical Theatre Works at the CSC Theatre for 16 performances.

Act 1, Scene 1: A Sacrificial Lab in Innerspace. *Scene 2*: Shriekwood Forest. *Scene 3*: Castle Nemesis: The Great Hall. *Scene 4*: The Castle Mortuary. *Scene 5*: Castle Nemesis: The Great Hall.

Act 2, Scene 1: Castle Nemesis: The Great Hall. *Scene 2*: The Chamber of Psychosorcery. *Scene 3*: Castle Nemesis: The Great Hall. *Scene 4*: A Sacrificial Lab in Innerspace.

Epilogue: Eleanor's Bedroom, Planet Earth.

ACT 1
Prologue
"Superhero Girl"
L. Larsen
Scene 1
"Starmites"
Starmites, B. L. Green
"Trink's Narration"
G. Barre, Starmites
"Afraid of the Dark"
B. L. Green, Starmites, L. Larsen, G. Barre
Scene 2
"Little Hero"
L. Larsen
"Attack of the Banshees"
Banshees
Scene 3
"Hard to Be Diva"
S. McKnight, Banshees
Scene 4
"Love Duet"
B. L. Green, L. Larsen
Scene 5
"The Dance of Spousal Arousal"
Banshees, L. Larsen
Finaletto
Company

ACT 2
Scene 1
"Bizarbara's Wedding"
L. Larsen, Banshees
"Milady"
B. L. Green, Starmites
Scene 2
"Beauty Within"
S. McKnight, L. Larsen
Scene 3
"The Cruelty Stomp"
G. Barre, Company
"Reach Right Down"
Starmites, S. McKnight, Banshees
Scene 4
"Immolation"
L. Larsen, A. Grabber, B. L. Green
"Starmites"/"Diva" (reprise)
S. McKnight, Starmites, Banshees
Epilogue
Finale
Company

GHETTO: The Last Performance in the Vilna Ghetto

1989.10

A Drama with Music in Two Acts, 22 Scenes. Play by Joshua Sobol. Translated (from the Hebrew) by David Lan. English lyrics by Jeremy Sams. Directed by Gedalia Besser. Musical direction, orchestrations, arrangements of authentic ghetto songs by William Schimmel. Movement by Nir Ben Gal, Liat Dror. Fight direction, B. H. Barry. Set by Adrian Vaux. Costumes by Edna Sobol. Lighting by Kevin Rigdon. This translation was commissioned by the Royal National Theatre of Great Britain. Produced by Circle in the Square (Theodore Mann, Artistic director; Paul Libin, Producing director). Opened 30 April 1989 at the Circle in the Square and closed 28 May 1989 after 33 performances.

CAST (in order of appearance): *Srulik*, a ventriloquist: AVNER EISENBERG. *Kittel*: STEPHEN MCHATTIE. *Hayyah*: HELEN SCHNEIDER. *The Dummy*: Gordon Joseph Weiss. *Gens*: GEORGE HEARN. *The Hassid*: Jerry Matz. *Weiskopf*: DONAL DONNELLY *Kruk*: JARLATH CONROY. *Haiken*: Marshall Coid. *Reed Player*: David Hopkins. *Guitar Player*: Barry Mitterhoff. *Accordion Player*: William Swindler. *Miriam*: Julie Goell. *Ooma, Dr. Weiner*: Alma Cuervo. *The Rich Man*: Richard M. Davidson. *Dr. Gottlieb*: Jerry Matz. *A Judge*: David Rosenbaum. *Luba*: Andrea Clark Libin. *Yankel*: Jon Rothstein. *Yitzhak Geivish*: Matthew P. Mutrie. *Elia Geivish*: Jonathan Mann. *Dessler*: William Verderber. *Jewish Policeman Averbuch*: Ahvi Spindell. *Jewish Policeman Levas*: Angelo Ragonesi. *A Woman*: Julie Anne Eigenberg. *German Soldiers*: Brain Maffitt, Spike McClure.

The action opens in an apartment in Tel Aviv in 1983, and thereafter takes place in and around the theatre in the Vilna ghetto under the Nazi occupation from September 1941 to its liquidation two years later.

ACT 1[14]
Scene 2
"Unter Daine Vaisse Shteren" (In the sky the stars all glisten . . .)
H. Schneider
"Hot Zich Mir Di Shich Zerissn" (Someone stole my overcoat . . .)
A. Eisenberg, H. Schneider, G. D. Weiss
Scene 9
"Vei Zu Di Teg" (Ah my children, my children . . .)
Actors
"Swanee" (from *SINBAD*)
H. Schneider
(*Music by* George Gershwin. *Lyrics by* Irving Caesar.)
Scene 11
"Shtiler, Shtiler" (Go to sleep my little flower . . .)
Scene 12
"Lullaby" (Hush my child, the winds are blowing . . .)
A. Cuervo

ACT 2
Scene 1
"Yidishe Brigades" (Forget the sun—forget the flowers . . .)
Company
"Isrulik" (I'm Isrulik—the orphan of the ghetto . . .)
J. Mann
Scene 3
"Isrulik" (reprise)
A. Cuervo, Company
Scene 4
"Friling" (I walk through the ghetto alone and forsaken . . .)
H. Schneider
"Je t'aime—c'est fou" (Je suis peut etre mal foutoe . . .)
H. Schneider
(*Music by* Jeremy Sams. *Lyrics by* Joshua Sobol.)
"Mir Lebn Eibik" (We'll live forever—year after year . . .)
Company
Scene 5
"Dremlen Feigl" (Birds are dreaming in the treetops . . .)
H. Schneider
Scene 8
"Mayday Song" (We've dragged through the mud . . .)
H. Schneider
"Zog Nit Keinmol" (Never say the final journey is at hand . . .)

[14] No song list appears in the program. The list below was prepared from the production typescript.

Scene 11
"Pak Zich Ain" (Move along, move along, every Jew knows this song . . .)
G. J. Weiss

1989.11 LEGENDS IN CONCERT

A Musical Revue in Two Acts[15]. Created and directed by John Stuart. Choreography by Inez Mourning. Musical director, Kerry McCoy. Lighting, production consultatnt, Dennis Condon. Costumes by Betty Lurenz. Technical consultant, Ron Popp. Multi-media design, Media Innovations/Joseph Jarred. Lasers, Mark Fisher. Supervisor in charge of production, Steve Yuhasz. Associate producers, Don Saxon, Robert R. Blume, Malcolm Allen. Produced by John Stuart. Opened 4 May 1989 at the Academy Theatre and closed 28 May 1989 after 22 performances.

CAST (in order of appearance): *Jack Benny*: Eddie Carroll. *Al Jolson*: Clive Baldwin. *Buddy Holly*: George Trullinger. *Liberace*: Daryl Wagner. *Marilyn Monroe*: Katie LaBourdette. *Nat King Cole*: Donny Ray Evins. *Judy Garland*: Julie Sheppard. *John Lennon*: Randy Clark. *Another Guest*: Tony Roi.
Singer/Dancers: Renee Chambers, Troy Christian, Vincent D'Elia, Elena Ferrante, Debby Kole, Gary La Rosa, Michael Roberts, Marrielle Monte.

[15]An evening of impersonations. No musical numbers were listed in the program.

1989–1990 SEASON

Danny Strayhorn, David Jackson, and Jane Krakowski in GRAND HOTEL
Martha Swope/TimePix

1989–1990 SEASON

ELVIS: A ROCKIN' REMEMBRANCE

1989.12

A Musical Biography of Elvis Presley in Two Acts, a Prologue and 10 Scenes. (Book) Written by Robert Rabinowitz. Entire production directed and choreographed by Patricia Birch. Scenery designed by Douglas W. Schmidt. Costumes designed by Jeanne Button. Lighting designed by Jules Fisher, Peggy Eisenhauer. Sound designed by Otts Munderloh. Media film designed and directed by Robert Rabinowitz. Film sequences produced by Chrisann Verges. Projection supervision, Bran Ferren. Musical supervisors, Phil Ramone, Robby Merkin. Musical director, Terry Mike Jeffrey. Orchestrations and vocal arrangements by Robby Merkin. Assistant director, John Mineo. Produced by Jules Fisher, Rodger Hess, Magic Promotions Inc., Pace Theatrical Group, Concert Productions International, Marvin A. Krauss, Act III Communications Inc., Joseph Rascoff, Julian and Jean Aberbach, Mark Levy, in association with the estate of Elvis Presley. Presented by Madison Square Garden Enterprises. Opened 6 June 1989 at the Beacon Theatre and closed 30 June 1989 after 31 performances.

CAST: *Young Elvis*: TERRY MIKE JEFFREY. *Heyday Elvis*: JOHNNY SEATON. *Older Elvis*: JULIAN WHITAKER. *Principal Dancers*: Dannul Dailey, Tinka Gutrick.
Company (in alphabetical order): Helena Andreyko, Darren Dollar, James Ellis, Collette Hill, Debbie Jeffrey, Leonard Joseph, Paul Mahos, Pat Moya, David Mullen, Kaye Pryor, Carol Denise Smith, Trish Vevera, Patrick Weathers. *Swing*: Harrison Beal.

Prologue: America Sends Mixed Signals.

Act 1, Scene 1: The Eisenhower Years. The last throes of innocence. *Scene 2*: Elvis finds his fans and his fans find a new rebel hero and an independent lifestyle. *Scene 3*: Graceland. *Scene 4*: Dreams and nightmares.

Act 2, Scene 1: The unreal world of Hollywood clashes with the real world of the Sixties. *Scene 2*: "Here I am strange and afraid in a world I never made." *Scene 3*: Las Vegas I. A New Elvis. *Scene 4*: A Carousel. *Scene 5*: Las Vegas II and after. *Scene 6*: A new beginning.

PROLOGUE

"By and By" (traditional)
D. Jeffrey

"Let the Good Times Roll"
J. Ellis
(*Music and Lyrics by* Leonard Lee.)

"Boogie-Woogie Bugle Boy"
(Andrews Sisters)
(*Music and Lyrics by* Don Raye and Hughie Prince.)

"(Gimme That) Old Time Religion" (traditional)

"Oh, Happy Days"
L. Joseph, Company
(*Music and Lyrics by* Edwin Hawkins.)

ACT 1

Scene 1

"That's All Right Mama"
T. M. Jeffrey, K. Freeman, K. McCann, W. Pryor
(*Music and Lyrics by* Arthur Crudup.)

"Blue Moon of Kentucky"
T. M. Jeffrey, Company
(*Music and Lyrics by* Bill Monroe.)

"I Don't Care if the Sun Don't Shine"
T. M. Jeffrey, Company
(*Music and Lyrics by* Mack David.)

"Mystery Train"
T. M. Jeffrey, Company
(*Music and Lyrics by* Herman Parker, Jr. and Sam C. Phillips.)

"Heartbreak Hotel"
J. Seaton, Company
(*Music and Lyrics by* Mae Boren Axton, Tommy Burden and Elvis Presley.)

"Mama Don't Allow"
P. Mahos
(Traditional; *Additional Lyrics by* Robby Merkin.)

"Can't Nobody Do Me Like Jesus"
L. Joseph, C. Hill, D. Jeffrey, K. Pryor
(Traditional; *Additional Lyrics by* Robby Merkin.)

Scene 2

"All Shook Up"
J. Seaton
(*Music and Lyrics by* Otis Blackwell and Elvis Prelsey.)

"Don't Be Cruel"
J. Seaton
(*Music and Lyrics by* Otis Blackwell and Elvis Prelsey.)

"Shake, Rattle and Roll"
J. Seaton, Company
(*Music and Lyrics by* Charles Calhoun.)

"Treat Me Nice"
J. Seaton, T. Gutrick
(*Music and Lyrics by* Jerry Lieber and Mike Stoller.)

"Hound Dog"
J. Seaton, Company
(*Music and Lyrics by* Jerry Lieber and Mike Stoller.)

"In the Garden" (traditional)
C. Hill, K. Pryor, D. Jeffrey, P. Moya
Saxophone Solo: T. M. Jeffrey.

Scene 3

"Baby Let's Play House"
J. Seaton, Company
(*Music and Lyrics by* Arthur Gunter.)

"Teddy Bear"
J. Seaton, Company
(*Music and Lyrics by* Bernie Lowe and Kal Mann.)

"Hot Dog Buddy"
J. Seaton, Company
(*Music and Lyrics by* Bill Haley.)

"Return to Sender"
J. Seaton, Company
(*Music and Lyrics by* Otis Blackwell and Winfield Scott.)

"Long Tall Sally"
J. Seaton, Company
(*Music and Lyrics by* Robert Blackwell, Enotris Johnson, Richard Penniman.)

"Great Balls of Fire"
J. Seaton, Company
(*Music and Lyrics by* Jack Hammer.)

"The Great Pretender"
J. Seaton, Company
(*Music and Lyrics by* Buck Ram.)

Scene 4

"Love Me Tender"
J. Seaton
(*Music and Lyrics by* Vera Matson and Elvis Presley.)

"I Want You, I Need You, I Love You"
J. Seaton, D. Dailey, D. Mullen, P. Mahos, D. Dollar
(*Music and Lyrics by* Ira Kosloff and Maurice Mysels.)

"It's Now or Never"
J. Seaton, D. Dailey, T. Gutrick
(*Music and Lyrics by* Wally Gold and Aaron Schroeder.)

"A Big Hunk of Love"
J. Seaton, D. Dailey
(*Music and Lyrics by* Aaron Schroeder and Sid Wyche.)

ACT 2

"Amazing Grace"
T. M. Jeffrey (off-stage)
(*Music and Lyrics by* Elvis Presley.)

Scene 1

"Jailhouse Rock"
J. Seaton, Company
(*Music and Lyrics by* Jerry Lieber and Mike Stoller.)

"Wear My Ring Around Your Neck"
J. Seaton, P. Weathers, Company
(*Music and Lyrics by* Bert Carroll, Russell Moody.)

"Surrender"
J. Seaton, P. Weathers, Company
(*Music and Lyrics by* Doc Pomus, Mort Shuman.)

"Mean Woman Blues"
J. Seaton, P. Weathers, Company
(*Music and Lyrics by* Claude DeMetrius.)

"You're the Devil in Disguise"
J. Seaton, P. Weathers, Company
(*Music and Lyrics by* Bernie Baum, Bill Giant, Florence Kaye.)
"G. I. Blues"
J. Seaton, P. Weathers, Company
(*Music and Lyrics by* Roy C. Bennett and Sid Tepper.)
"Rock-a-Hula Baby"
J. Seaton, Company
(*Music and Lyrics by* Fred Wise, Ben Weisman, Dolores Fuller.)
"Bossa Nova Baby"
T. M. Jeffrey, T. Gutrick, D. Dailey
(*Music and Lyrics by* Jerry Lieber and Mike Stoller.)
"Blue Hawaii" (from the films *BLUE HAWAII, WAIKIKI WEDDING*)
(*Music by* Ralph Rainger. *Lyrics by* Leo Robin.) J. Seaton, C. Hill
"Backlash Blues"
J. Seaton, C. Hill
(*Music and Lyrics by* Nina Simone and Langston Hughes.)
Drum Solo: W. Pryor.

Scene 2
"Are You Lonesome Tonight?"
J. Whitaker, T. M. Jeffrey
(*Music and Lyrics by* Lou Handman and Roy Turk.)
Monologue: J. Seaton.

Scene 3
"2001: Thus Spake Zarathustra"
J. Seaton, Company
(*Music by* Richard Strauss.)
"CC Rider"
J. Seaton, Company
(*Music and Lyrics by* Elvis Presley.)
"Burning Love"
J. Seaton, Company
(*Music and Lyrics by* Denis Linde.)
"Can't Help Falling in Love"
J. Seaton, Company
(*Music and Lyrics by* Luigi Creatore, Hugo Peretti, George Weiss.)

Scene 4
"My Way"
J. Whitaker
(*Music and Lyrics by* Paul Anka.)

Scene 5
"Battle Hymn" (traditional)
T. M. Jeffrey, Company (off-stage)
"Suspicious Minds"
J. Whitaker, Company
(*Music and Lyrics by* Mark James.)
"If I Can Dream"
J. Whitaker, Company
(*Music and Lyrics by* W. Earl Brown.)
"Blue Suede Shoes"
J. Whitaker
(*Music and Lyrics by* Carl Lee Perkins.)

Scene 6
"Precious Memories"
D. Jeffrey, C. D. Smith
"Blue Suede Shoes" (reprise)
J. Seaton

1989.13

THE MERRY WIDOW

A Revival of the Operetta in Three Acts, 4 Scenes[1]. Music by Franz Lehár. Original German book and lyrics by Victor Léon and Leo Stein (after "L'Attaché d'Ambassade.") English version by Adrian Ross. This San Diego Opera production directed by Tito Capobianco. Original production (direction) by Ronald Bentley. Stage director, Cynthia Edwards. Choreographer, Sharon Halley. Set designers, Helen Pond and Herbert Senn. Lighting design by Ken Tabachnick. Conductor, Imre Pallo. Chorus master, Joseph Colaneri. Produced by the New York City Opera. Opened 8 July 1989 at the New York State Theatre and closed 1 August 1989 after 4 performances in repertory.

CAST (in order of appearance): *Baron Popoff*: RICHARD MCKEE. *Natalie*: Ruth Golden. *General Novikovich*: JOHN LANKSTON. *Counsellor Khadja*: Michael Willson. *Marquis de Cascada*: ROBERT FERRIER. *Sylviane*: Lisbeth Lloyd. *M. de St. Brioche*: RICHARD BYRNE. *Olga*: Joyce Campana. *Vicomte Camille de Jolidon*: PAUL AUSTIN KELLY. *Nisch*: JAMES BILLINGS. *Count Danilo*: RICHARD MUENZ. *Sonia*: MICHELE MCBRIDE. *Head Waiter*: Jonathan Guss. *Zozo*: Ivy Austin. *Lolo*: Joan Mirabella. *Dodo*: Esperanza Galan. *Jou-Jou*: Candace Itow. *Frou-Frou*: Victoria Rinaldi. *Clo-Clo*: Stephanie Godino. *Margot*: Jean Barber. *Ensemble*: New York City Opera Chorus.

1989.14

CANDIDE

A Revival of the Musical in Two Act, 23 Scenes[2]. (New) Book adapted from Voltaire's satire (of the same name) by Hugh Wheeler. (Original book by Lillian Hellman.) Music by Leonard Bernstein. Lyrics by Richard Wilbur. Additional lyrics by Stephen Sondheim and John Latouche. Directed by Harold Prince. Stage director, Albert Sherman. Choreography by Patricia Birch. Scenery designed by Clarke Dunham. Costumes designed by Judith Dolan. Lighting designed by Ken Billington. Conducted by Scott Bergeson. Orchestrations by Leonard Bernstein and Hershy Kay; additional orchestrations by John Mauceri. Chorus master, Joseph Colaneri. Produced by the New York City Opera. Opened 18 July 1989 at the New York State Theatre and closed 10 September 1989 (matinee) after 14 performances.

CAST (in order of appearance): *Voltaire*: JOHN LANKSTON. *Candide*: MARK BEUDERT. *Huntsman*: Don Yule. *Paquette*: MARIS CLEMENT. *Baroness*: Christine Meadows *Baron*: Richard McKee. *Cunegonde*: CYNDIA SIEDEN. *Maximilian*: JAMES JAVORE. *Servant of Maximilian*: James Billings. *Dr. Pangloss*: JOHN LANKSTON. *Bulgarian Soldiers*: Don Yule, James Billings. *Westphalian Soldiers*: William Ledbetter, Jose Traba. *Don Isaachar*, the Jew: JAMES BILLINGS. *Grand Inquisitor*: RICHARD MCKEE. *Calliope Player*: Christine Meadows. *Heresy Agent*: Ralph Bassett. *Inquisition Agents*: Gary Dietrich, Kirk Griffith. *Judge*: JAMES BILLINGS. *Old Lady*: MURIEL COSTA-GREENSPON. *Dons*: Daniel Albert, William Ward, Joey R. Smith, Don Yule, William Ledbetter, Ralph Bassett. *Businessman*: John Lankston. *Governor*: JOHN LANKSTON. *Governor's Aide*: Daniel Albert. *Slave Driver*: Richard McKee. *Father Bernard*: James Billings. *Sailors*: Gary Dietrich, Kirk Griffith, Jose Traba, Daniel Albert. *Pirates*: John Henry Thomas, William Ledbetter. *Pink Sheep*: Andrea Green, Karen Ziemba. *Lion*: Michael Willson *Pasha-Prefect*: RICHARD MCKEE. *First Gambler*: JAMES BILLINGS. *Second Gambler (Police Chief)*: JOHN LANKSTON. *Sage*: JOHN LANKSTON.

1989.15

THE MIKADO, or The Town of Titipu

A Revival of the Comic Opera in Two Acts[3]. Libretto by William S. Gilbert. Music by Arthur Sullivan. Director, Lofti Mansouri. Stage director, David Pfeiffer. Conductor, Peter Howard. Choreographer, Patricia Birch. Set and costume designer, Thierry Bosquet. Lighting designer, John Gleason. Chorus master, Joseph Colaneri. Produced by the New York City Opera. Opened 29 July 1989 at the New York State Theatre and closed 18 August 1989 after 4 performances in repertory.

CAST (in order of appearance): *Nanki-Poo*, his son, disguised as a wandering minstrel in love with Yum-Yum: PAUL AUSTIN KELLY. *Pish-Tush*, Noble Lord: William Parcher. *Pooh-Bah*, Lord High Everything Else: JOSEPH MCKEE. *Ko-Ko*, Lord High Executioner of Titipu: JAMES BILLINGS. *Yum-Yum*, *Pitti-Sing*, *Peep-Bo*, three sisters, wards of Ko-Ko: LISA SAFFER, CHRISTINE MEADOWS, BARBARA SHIRVIS. *Katisha*: JANE SHAULIS. *The Mikado of Japan*: RICHARD MCKEE. *Chorus of School Girls, Nobles, Guards and Coolies*: New York City Opera Chorus.

---

[1]Originally produced in New York 21 October 1907 at the New Amsterdam Theatre for 416 performances. For Synopsis of Scenes and Musical Numbers, see 1907 production.

[2]Original production first produced in New York 1 December 1956 at the Martin Beck Theatre for 73 performances; revised version first produced Off-Boadway 11 December 1973 at the Chelsea Theater Center, Brooklyn Academy of Music for 48 performances; transferred 5 March 1974 to the Broadway Theatre for 740 performances; this version first produced 13 October 1982 at the New York State Theatre for 7 performances in repertory. For Synopsis of Scenes and Musical Numbers, see 1982 revival.

[3]First presented in New York 20 July, 10-29 August 1885 at the Union Square and People's Theatres for 22 performances. First authorized production presented 19 August 1885 at the Fifth Avenue Theatre by Richard D'Oyly Carte for 250 performances. For Synopsis of Scenes and Musical Numbers, see 19 August 1885 D'Oyly Carte production.

1989.16 MANDY PATINKIN IN CONCERT: DRESS CASUAL

A One Man Musical Revue in One Act[4]. Lighting by Richard Nelson. Produced by Ron Delsener. Opened 1 August 1989 at the Helen Hayes Theatre and closed 16 September 1989 after 49 performances.

CAST: MANDY PATINKIN.
Piano: Paul Ford.

MUSICAL NUMBERS[5]

"Soliloquy" (from *CAROUSEL*)
(*Music by* Richard Rodgers. *Lyrics by* Oscar Hammerstein II.)

Medley from *PAL JOEY*
("Great Big Town" [Chicago]; "You Musn't Kick It Around"; "I Could Write a Book"; "Happy Hunting Horn"; "What Do I Care for a Dame?;" "Do It the Hard Way"; "I'm Talking to My Pal"[6])
(*Music by* Richard Rodgers. *Lyrics by* Lorenz Hart.)

"Buddy's Blues" (from *FOLLIES*)
(*Music and Lyrics by* Stephen Sondheim.)

"When the Red, Red Robin Comes Bob, Bob, Bobbin' Along"
(*Music and Lyrics by* Harry Woods.)

"And the Band Played On"
(*Music by* John F. Palmer. *Lyrics by* Charles B. Ward.)

"Over the Rainbow" (from *THE WIZARD OF OZ* film)
(*Music by* Harold Arlen. *Lyrics by* E. Y. Harburg.)

"Pennies from Heaven" (from *PENNIES FROM HEAVEN* film)
(*Music by* Arthur Johnston. *Lyrics by* Johnny Burke.)

"Top Hat, White Tie and Tails" (from *TOP HAT* film)
(*Music and Lyrics by* Irving Berlin.)

"Puttin' on the Ritz"
(*Music and Lyrics by* Irving Berlin.)

"Alexander's Ragtime Band"
(*Music and Lyrics by* Irving Berlin .)

"Sonny Boy" (from *THE SINGING FOOL* film)
(*Music and Lyrics by* Al Jolson, Buddy DeSylva, Lew Brown, Ray Henderson.)

"No One Is Alone" (from *INTO THE WOODS*)
(*Music and Lyrics by* Stephen Sondheim.)

"No More" (from *INTO THE WOODS)*
(*Music and Lyrics by* Stephen Sondheim.)

"A-Tisket, A-Tasket" (from *COTTON CLUB PARADE* 1938)(5th edition)
(*Music and Lyrics by* Ella Fitzgerald, Al Feldman.)

"Coffee in a Cardboard Cup" (from *70 GIRLS 70*)
(*Music by* John Kander. *Lyrics by* Fred Ebb.)

1989.17 SHENANDOAH

A Revival of the Musical in Two Acts, 18 Scenes and a Prologue[7]. Book by James Lee Barrett, Peter Udell and Philip Rose. Based on the film of the same name by James Lee Barrett. Music by Gary Geld. Lyrics by Peter Udell. Directed by Philip Rose. Choreography by Robert Tucker. Original set design by Kert Lundell, adapted by Reginald Bronskill. Costumes by Guy Geoly. Lighting by Stephen Ross. Musical direction by David Warrack. Produced by Howard Hurst, Sophie Hurst, Peter Ingster. Opened 8 August 1989 at the Virginia Theatre and closed 2 September 1989 after 31 performances.[8]

CAST (in order of appearance): *Charlie Anderson*: JOHN CULLUM. *Jacob*: BURKE LAWRENCE. *James*: CHRISTOPHER MARTIN. *Nathan*: Nigel Hamer. *John*: Stephen McIntyre. *Jenny*: TRACEY MOORE. *Henry*: Robin Blake. *Robert*, the boy: Jason Zimbler. *Anne*: CAMILLA SCOTT. *Gabriel*: Roy McKay. *Reverend Byrd*: Donald Saunders. *Sam*: THOMAS CAVANAGH. *Sergeant Johnson*: Jim Selman. *Lieutenant*: Casper Roos. *Tinkham*: Richard Liss. *Carol*: Jim Bearden. *Corporal*: Stephen Simms. *Marauder*: Sam Mancuso. *Engineer*: Donald Saunders. *Confederate Snipers*: David Connolly, Gerhard Kruschke.

Ensemble: Henry Alessan, Jim Bearden, Mark Bernkoff, David Connolly, Lesley Corne, Mark Ferguson, Brian Gow, Jennifer Griffin, Gerhard Kruschke, Richard Liss, Robert Longo, Sam Mancuso, Casper Roos, Fernando Santos, Jim Selman, Stephen Simms. *Swing*: Paul Malloy.

1989.18 THE DESERT SONG

A Revival of the Musical in Two Acts, 7 Scenes[9]. Book and lyrics by Otto Harbach and Oscar Hammerstein II. Music by Sigmund Romberg. New adaptation of book and lyrics by Robert Johanson. Director and choreographer, Robert Johanson. Conductor, James Allen Gahres. Co-choreographer, Sharon Halley. Set designer, Michael Anania. Costume designer, Suzanne Mess. Lighting designer, Mark W. Stanley. Chorus master, Joseph Colaneri. Produced by the New York City Opera. Opened 29 August 1989 at the New York State Theatre and closed 3 September 1989 after 7 performances.

CAST (in order of appearance): *Sid El Kar*: MICHAEL COUSINS. *Hassi*: ERICK DEVINE. *Hadji*: William Ledbetter. *Neri*: Joyce Campana. *Benjamin Kidd*: PHILIP WILLIAM MCKINLEY. *Azuri*: LOUISE HICKEY. *Captain Paul Fontaine*: LOUIS OTEY. *Sergeant La Vergne*: David Frye. *Susan*: LILLIAN GRAFF. *Edith*: Paula Hostetter. *Margot Bonvalet*: MICHELE MCBRIDE. *General Birabeau*: RON PARADY. *Pierre Birabeau*, Red Shadow: RICHARD WHITE. *Ali Ben Ali*: RAYMOND BAZEMORE. *Clementina*: JOYCE CAMPANA. *French Girls, Spanish Cabaret Girls and Soldiers' Wives, Native Dancers, Servants and Soldiers*: New York City Opera Chorus.

The action takes place in Morocco in the 1930s.

Act 1, Scene 1: Retreat of the Red Shadow in the Riff Mountains. *Scene 2*: Near the desert, outside General Birabeau's house. *Scene 3*: The garden of General Birabeau's home, the same day.

Act 2, Scene 1: The Great Hall of Ali Ben Ali. The following day. *Scene 2*: The room of the Silken Couch. *Scene 3*: The edge of the desert. *Scene 4*: Back at General Birabeau's, two nights later.

ACT 1[10]

Scene 1

"High on a Hill"
M. Cousins, Riffs

"The Riff Song"
R. White, Riffs

"My Margot"
L. Otey, Soldiers

Scene 2

"Why Did We Marry Soldiers?"
L. Graff, Women

Scene 3

"French Military Marching Song"
M. McBride, Company

"Romance"
M. McBride, Women

"I Want a Kiss"
M. McBride, L. Otey

"It"
P. W. McKinley, L. Graff

"The Desert Song"
R. White, M. McBride

Finale, Act 1
Full Company

ACT 2

Scene 1

"Song of the Brass Key"
J. Campana, Harem Girls

"One Good Boy Gone Wrong"
P. W. McKinley, J. Campana

---

[4]Originally produced Off-Broadway 27 February 1989 at the Public Theatre for 6 performances.
[5]Not in performance order.
[6]Dropped from original production of PAL JOEY.
[7]Originally produced in New York 7 January 1975 at the Alvin Theatre for 1050 performances. For Synopsis of Scenes and Musical Numbers, see original 1975 production. Act 1 was set in Spring, Act 2 in Autumn.
[8]Dance arrangements, orchestrations uncredited.

[9]Originally produced in New York 30 November 1926 at the Casino Theatre for 471 performances.
[10]No song list appears in program; this list prepared from the Papermill Playhouse production where this adaptation premiered. Dropped for this production: "I'll Be a Buoyant Girl," "Then You'll Know," "Let Love Go," "One Flower in Your Garden," "Farewell," and "All Hail to the General," "Let's Have a Love Affair;" also Act 2, Scene 2.

"Eastern Western Love"
R. Bazemore, M. Cousins
"One Alone"
R. White, Men
Scene 2
"The Saber Song"
M. McBride
"The Desert Song" (reprise)
R. White, M. McBride
Scene 3
"One Alone" (reprise)
R. White, M. McBride, M. Cousins, L. Otey, R. Bazemore, Men
Scene 4
"It" (reprise)
P. W. McKinley, L. Graff
Dance of Triumph
J. Campana
Finale, Act 2
Full Company

1989.19

SWEENEY TODD-THE DEMON BARBER OF FLEET STREET

A Revival of the Musical Thriller in Two Acts[11]. Book by Hugh Wheeler. Based on a version of "Sweeney Todd" by Christopher Bond (after the original melodrama by George Dibdin-Pitt). Music and lyrics by Stephen Sondheim. Directed by Susan H. Schulman. Choreography by Michael Lichtefeld. Scenic design by James Morgan. Costumes designed by Beba Shamash. Lighting designed by Mary Jo Dondlinger. Musical direction and design, David Krane. Assistant musical director, Jan Rosenberg. Originally directed on Broadway by Harold Prince. Produced Off-Off Broadway by the York Theatre Company (Janet Hayes Walker, Producing Director). Produced by the Circle in the Square Theatre (Theodore Mann, Artistic director; Paul Libin, Producing director.) Opened 14 September 1989 at the Circle in the Square Theatre and closed 25 February 1990 after 189 performances.

CAST (in order of appearance): *Jonas Fogg*: Tony Gilbert. *Policeman*: David E. Mallard. *Bird Seller*: Ted Keegan. *Dora*: Sylvia Rhyne. *Mrs. Mooney*: Mary Philips. *Anthony Hope*: Jim Walton. *Sweeney Todd*: BOB GUNTON. *Beggar Woman*: SuEllen Estey. *Mrs. Lovett*: BETH FOWLER. *Judge Turpin*: David Barron. *The Beadle*: Michael McCarty. *Johanna*: Gretchen Kingsley. *Tobias Ragg*: Eddie Korbich. *Pirelli*: Bill Nabel.

1989.20

DANGEROUS GAMES

A Musical in Two Acts (2 One-Act Musicals)[12]. Book by Jim Lewis and Graciela Daniele. Music by Astor Piazzolla. Lyrics by William Finn. Conceived, choreographed and directed by Graciela Daniele. Co-choreographer, Tina Paul. Scenic design, Tony Straiges. Costume design, Patricia Zipprodt. Lighting design, Peggy Eisenhauer. Sound design, Otts Munderloh. Musical direction and arrangements by James Kowal. Musical consultant and arrangements by Rodolfo Alchourron. Fight direction by B. H. Barry (Tango), Luis Perez (Orfeo). Originally produced by the American Music Theatre Festival, Philadelphia; Spoleto Festival USA, Charleston, and La Jolla Playhouse, San Diego. Produced by Jules Fisher, James M. Nederlander, Arthur Rubin in association with Mary Kantor. Opened 19 October 1989 at the Nederlander Theatre and closed 21 October 1989 after 4 perfomances.

ACT 1: Tango

CAST: *Tango*: *Delia*, the Madam: Dana Moore. *The Men (3)*: *Felipe*: Philip Jerrry. *Ricardo*: Richard Amaro. *Carlos*: Ken Ard. *The Women (4)*: *Renata*: René Ceballos. *Diana*: Diana Laurenson. *Maria*: Malinda Shaffer. *Adriana*: Adrienne Hurd-Sharlein. *The Brothers (2)*: *Juan*: John Mineo. *Gregorio*: Gregory Mitchell, Luis Perez (alt.). *Cristina*, the new whore: Tina Paul, Elizabeth Mozer (alt.).

ACT 2: Orfeo

CAST: *Orfeo*: Gregory Mitchell, Luis Perez (alt.). *Dicha*: René Ceballos. *Aurora*, a child: Danyelle Weaver. *Pluton*: Ken Ard. *Nora/Lascivia*: Tina Paul, Elizabeth Mozer (alt.). *Antares/Altivo*: John Mineo. *Mira/Codicia*: Dana Moore. *Lyrae/LaGula*: Malinda Shaffer. *Cleo/Envidia*: Diana Laurenson. *Alberio/Ira*: Marc Villa. *Ursula/Malicia*: Adrienne Hurd-Sharlein. *Leon/Mentira*: Phillip Jerry. *Arturo/Charon/Perez*: Richard Amaro. *Bombo Player*: Adrian Brito. *Swings*: Frank Cava; Mamie Duncan-Gibbs.

Quintet: Rodolfo Alchourron (guitar), Jorge Alfano (bass, bamboo flute), Miguel Arrabal (bandoneon), Jon Kass (violin), James Kowal (piano, conductor), René Ceballos (offstage vocals).

"Desaparecidos" is the Spanish word for "the ones who have disappeared," and refers specifically to those individuals arrested by the Argentina military dictatorship (who are never heard from again).

Dedicated to the "desaparecidos" of Argentina and numerous other countries around the world. "Orfeo" is an attempt to give new meaning to the age-old myth of Orpheus and Eurydice. In the original myth, Orpheus, whose job it is to raise the sun, falls in love with Eurydice. But Eurydice dies. Orpheus' love for Eurydice is so great that he goes after her to Hell. He plays his magic lute so beautifully that Pluto, King of Hell, permits Orpheus to take Eurydice back to the living. But on one condition: Orpheus must not turn around and look at Eurydice before leaving Hell. He turns around to look at Eurydice too early, and loses Eurydice forever.

In "Orfeo," the story is reset in Argentina, and told through the eyes of a young girl whose parents have "been disappeared." Pursued by the same man who kidnapped her parents, Aurora manages to escape and falls asleep. In her dream version of the myth, the child comes to understand that only by confronting the truth head-on will she ever be able to wake up from this all-too-real nightmare.

1989.21

TAKARAZUKA

A Musical Revue (from Japan) in Two Acts, 11 Scenes. Artistic directors, Shinju Ueda, Hirotoshi Ohara. Composers and arrangers, Takio Terada, Kenji Yoshizaki, Kaoru Irie, Kazuakira Hashimoto, Toshiko Yonekawa. Conductor, Kazuakira Hashimoto. Choreographers, Yoshijiro Hanayagi, Mayumi Nishizaki, Eiken Fujima, Hagi Hanayagi, Kiyomi Hayama, Taku Yamada, Roger Minami. Set design by Hideo Ishihama, Toshiaki Sekiya. Costume design by Harumi Tokoro, Kikue Nakagawa, Ikuei Touda. Lighting design by Naoji Imai, supervised by Ken Billington. Assistant directors, Masazumi Tani, Masaya Ishida. President, Haruhiko Saka. Produced by Kohei Kobayashi. Opened 25 October 1989 at the Radio City Music Hall and closed 29 October 1989 after 6 performances.

CAST: YURI MATSUMOTO, JUNKO TAKARA, AKIRA BAN, MIZUKI OURA, KAE SEGAWA, MITO HIBIKI, YU SHION, AI KODAMA, MIRA ANJU, YUKI AMAMI.

(*Company*:) Yu Asuka, Yo Natsumi, Miya Aoi, Manami Kozue, Yuka Shima, Nachi Mineoka, Kanade Nazuki, Hikaru Senju, Mitsuru Aiko, Aya Maiki, Mayu Omine, Michuru Namine, Naoki Ema, Chitose Kagami, Chie Kinami, Risa Wakao, Ayu Mitsuki, Natsuki Yuma, Fubuki Takane, Rio Hanbusa, Katusra Godai, Nari Asaoka, Ai Otohara, Ginka Itsuki, Yuka Shino, Yuzumi Mari, Mami Natsuki, Hajime Wako, Reo Kazami, Maika Tomo, Ko Minoru, Ayano Ogishiro, Yoko Hana, Shun Tasai, Yura Natsukawa, Mire Aika, Chikoto Yumeno, Mitsuki Mario, Satomi Akino, Tatsuki Koju, Konomi Akane, Yuki Maori, Aki Itsumine, Serika Moemi, Kei Miyabi, Shoko Kirihara, Jun Shibuki, Akari Michi, Rei Natsushiro, Hibiki Takumi, Mai Gojo.

ACT 1: Takarazuka Dance Festival
Scene 1
Prologue/"Takarazuka March" (Ondo Takarazuka Koshinkyoku)
M. Oura, Y. Matsumoto, Company
(*Composer/Arranger*: Takio Terada. *Lyricist*: Ken Kumon. *Choreographer*: Eiken Fujima.)

---

[11]Originally produced in New York 1 March 1979 at the Uris Theatre for 557 performances; this revival first produced Off-Off Broadway 31 March 1989 at the York Theatre for 24 performances. For Synopsis of Scenes and Musical Numbers, see original 1979 production. Omitted from this production: "The Barber and His Wife," "Quartet (Act 1)." Restored for this production:
"Johanna" (Act 1, after "The Contest")
D. Barron
(Not the same song as "Johanna" as sung by J. Walton above.)
Added to this production:
"Wigmaker Sequence" (Act 2, after "By the Sea")
J. Walton, B. Gunton, Quintet
The last two musical numbers have been retitled "The Judge's Return" and Final Scene.

[12]No individual song titles given in the program.

A medley of traditional Japanese dances set to modern music in celebration of Takarazuka.

Scene 2

"Snow, Moon and Flower" (Utsukushiki Nippon)

Y. Shion, M. Hibiki, A. Kodama, R. Natsushiro, Company

(*Composer*: Takio Terada. *Arranger*: Kaoru Irie. *Lyricist*: Shinji Ueda. *Choreographer*: Yoshijiro Hanayagi.)

A selection of delicate dances that celebrate the transient beauty of snow, moon and flowers as the seasons change.

Scene 3

"Icy Moon" (Koreru Tsuki)

M. Oura, M. Hibiki, A. Kodama, A. Ban, Company

(*Composer*: Takio Terada. *Arranger*: Kaoru Irie. *Lyricist*: Shinji Ueda. *Choreographer*: Yoshijiro Hanayagi.)

A Noh dancer performs ritualistically before statues of the Buddha and summons spirits whose dances and costumes are reminiscent of Japan in the eighth century.

Scene 4

"Swirling Snow" (Yuki Shimaki)

A. Mitsuki, Y. Matsumoto, Company

(*Composer*: Takio Terada. *Arranger*: Kaoru Irie. *Lyricist*: Shinji Ueda. *Choreographer*: Yoshijiro Hanayagi.)

A traveller rests against a torii gate to reflect on her life. A vision of a young and beautiful self rises from the snow and dances for a lover who will never return.

Scene 5

"The Cherry Flower" (Sakura/Sakura Gensokyoku)

M. Kozue, Company

(*Composers/Arrangers*: Toshiko Yonekawa, Takio Terada. *Choreographer*: Mayumi Nishizaki.)

Koto players and dancers perform in a tribute to the national flower of Japan.

ACT 2: Takarazuka Forever, a Grand Revue

Scene 1

Prologue (*Choreographer*: Roger Minami.)

"Takarazuka Forever"

A. Kodama, Company

(*Composer/Arranger*: Kenji Yoshizaki. *Lyricist*: Hirotoshi Ohara.)

Dance

M. Oura, Company

"A Pretty Girl Is Like a Melody"

M. Oura, Y. Amani, Company

(*Composer/Lyricist*: Irving Berlin. *Arranger*: Kenji Yoshizaki.)

Scene 2

Flower Fantasy (*Choreographer*: Taku Yamada.)

"I'll String Along with You"

Y. Shion, M. Kozue, Company

(*Composer*: Harry Warren. *Arranger*: Kazuakira Hashimoto. *Lyricist*: Al Dubin.)

"I Only Have Eyes for You"

A. Kodama, A. Ban, K. Segawa, M. Anju, M. Hibiki, Y. Shima, Y. Shino

(*Composer*: Harry Warren. *Arranger*: Kazuakira Hashimoto. *Lyricist*: Al Dubin.)

Scene 3

Arabian Dream (*Choreographer*: Kiyomi Hayama.)

"Too Close for Comfort" (from *MR. WONDERFUL*)

J. Takara, Y. Ammi, Company

(*Composer*: Jerry Bock. *Arranger*: Kenji Yoshizaki. *Lyricists*: Larry Holofcener, George Weiss.)

Dance/Polovtsian (from "*Prince Igor*")

M. Oura, A. Kodama, Company

(*Composer*: Alexander Borodin. *Arranger*: Takio Terada.)

Scene 4

Keep Young and Beautiful (*Choreographer*: Taku Yamada.)

"American Beauty Rose"

Y. Shion, Company

(*Composer*: Read Evans, Hal David, Arthur Altman. *Arranger*: Kenji Yoshizaki.)

"Keep Young and Beautiful"

M. Hibiki, Company

(*Composer*: Harry Warren. *Arranger*: Kazuakira Hashimoto. *Lyricist*: Al Dubin.)

"You Stepped Out of a Dream"

M. Oura, Company

(*Composer*: Nacio Herb Brown. *Arranger*: Kazuakira Hashimoto. *Lyricist*: Gus Kahn.)

"The Lady Is a Tramp"

M. Oura, M. Hibiki, Company

(*Composer*: Richard Rodgers. *Arranger*: Kazuakira Hashimoto. *Lyricist*: Lorenz Hart.)

Scene 5

Piano Fantasy

"Play a Simple Melody"

Y. Shion

(*Composer/Lyricist*: Irving Berlin. *Arranger*: Kazuakira Hashimoto. *Choreographer*: Kiyomi Hayama.)

"Shaking the Blues Away"

M. Oura, Company

(*Composer/Lyricist*: Irving Berlin. *Arranger*: Kazuakira Hashimoto. *Choreographer*: Roger Minami.)

"Rhapsody in Blue"

M. Oura, M. Hibiki, K. Segawa, M. Anju, Company

(*Composer*: George Gershwin. *Arranger*: Kenji Yoshizaki. *Choreographer*: Roger Minami.)

Scene 6

Finale (*Choreographer*: Kiyomi Hayama.)

"The Words Are in My Heart"

N. Mineoka, Company

(*Composer*: Harry Warren. *Arranger*: Kazuakira Hashimoto. *Lyricist*: Al Dubin.)

"In the Cool, Cool, Cool of the Evening"

Y. Shion, M. Hibiki, Company

(*Composer*: Hoagy Carmichael. *Arranger*: Kazuakira Hashimoto. *Lyricist*: Johnny Mercer.)

"Something's Gotta Give"

M. Oura, K. Segawa, M. Anju, N. Yuma, Y. Amami

(*Composer/Lyricist*: Johnny Mercer. *Arranger*: Kazuakira Hashimoto.)

"Takarazuka Forever" (reprise)

M. Oura, M. Hibiki, A. Kodama, Y. Shion, N. Mineoka, Company

SID CAESAR & COMPANY: Does Anybody Know What I'm Talking About?

1989.22

A Musical Revue in Two Acts[13]. Directed by Martin Charnin. Original songs by Martin Charnin. Scenery and lighting by Neil Peter Jampolis. Costumes by Karen Roston. Sound by Bruce Cameron. Musical director, Elliot Finkel. Originally presented by Art D'Lugoff at the Village Gate. Associate producers, J. Scott Broder, Sonny Bloch., Robert Courson. Produced by Ivan Bloch and Harold Thau in association with Larry Spellman. Opened 1 November 1989 at the John Golden Theatre and closed 5 November 1989 after 5 performances.

CAST: SID CAESAR, Lee Delano, Linda Hart, Lubitza [Luba] Gregus, Peter Shawn, Laura Turnbull, Erick Devine, Carolyn Michel.

SCENES AND MUSICAL NUMBERS

Sleep

S. Caesar

A Boy at His First Dance

S. Ceasar

A Man Walking Down the Aisle

S. Ceasar

Zero Hour

S. Caesar

A Man with His Wife Arguing to the First Movement of Beethoven's Fifth Symphony

S. Caesar, L. Turnbull

The Last Angry Bull

S. Caesar, L. Gregus, L. Delano,
L. Hart, P. Shawn, L. Turnbull, E Devine, C. Michel

At the Movies

S. Caesar, L. Hart, L. Delano, P. Shawn

[13]Originally produced Off-Broadway 22 June 1989 at the Vilage Gate for 72 performances.

We Aren't Fooling Anyone
Company
The World Through the Eyes of a Baby
S. Caesar
The Penny Candy Gum Machine
S. Caesar
The Grieg Piano Concerto
S. Caesar
The Professor
S. Caesar, L. Delano
"Make a New Now, Now!"
S. Caesar, Company

1989.23 MEET ME IN ST. LOUIS

A Musical in Two Acts, 14 Scenes. Based on "The Kensington Stories" by Sally Benson and the MGM motion picture "Meet Me in St. Louis." Book by Hugh Wheeler. Music and lyrics by Hugh Martin and Ralph Blane. Directed by Louis Burke. Choreography by Joan Brickhill. Assistant director, Lonnie Chase. Associate choreographer, Herman-Jay Muller. Production (settings, costumes) design by Keith Anderson. Lighting by Ken Billington. Musical supervisor, Milton Rosenstock. Musical director, Bruce Pomohac. Orchestrations by Michael Gibson. Dance arranger, James Raitt. Sound by Alan Stieb, James Brousseau. Vocal arrangers, Hugh Martin, Bruce Pomohac. Ice choreographer, Michael Tokar. Associate producers, Loren Krok, P. K. Sloman, L. Everett Chase. Produced by Brickhill-Burke Productions (Louis Burke, Joan Brickhill), Christopher Seabrooke and EPI Products. Opened 2 November 1989 at the Gershwin Theater and closed 10 June 1990 after 253 performances.

CAST (in order of appearance): *Lon Smith*: Michael O'Steen. *Randy Travis*: Brian Jay. *Katie*: BETTY GARRETT. *Motorman*: Jim Semmelman. *Tootie Smith*: COURTNEY PELDON. *Mrs. Smith*: CHARLOTTE MOORE. *Grandpa Prophater*: MILO O'SHEA. *Esther Smith*: DONNA KANE. *Rose Smith*: Juliet Lambert. *John Truitt*: Jason Workman. *Agnes Smith*: Rachael Graham. *Mr. Alonzo Smith*: GEORGE HEARN. *Warren Sheffield*: Peter Reardon. *Ida Boothby*: Naomi Reddin. *Douglas Moore*: Gregg Whitney. *Eve Finley*: Shauna Hicks. *Dr. Bond*: Gordon Stanley. *Lucille Ballard*: Karen Culliver. *Clinton A. Badger*: Craig A. Meyer.

Ensemble: Kevin Backstrom, Dan Buelow, Victoria Lynn Burton, Karen Culliver, Deanna Dys, H. David Gunderman, Shauna Hicks, K. Craig Innes, Brian Jay, Rachel Jones, Nancy Lemenager, Joanne McHugh, Frank Maio, Carol Lee Meadows, Craig A. Meyer, Christopher Lee Michaels, Ron Morgan, Georga L. Osborne, Rachelle Ottley, Christina Pawl, Naomi Reddin, Carol Schuberg, Jim Semmelman, Ken Shepski, Gordon Stanley, Sean Frank Sullivan, Cynthia Thole, Gregg Whitney, Kyle Whyte, Lee Wilson.

The action takes place in and around the Smith family home, 5135 Kensington Avenue, St. Louis—from summer 1903 to the spring of 1904 and the opening of the Louisiana Purchase Exposition.

Act 1, Scene 1: Street outside the Smith Family Home—Summer 1903. *Scene 2*: Interior of the Smith House. *Scene 3*: Lon's Princeton Party. *Scene 4*: Preparing for Hollywood. *Scene 5*: The Girls' Bedroom and the Smith Home. *Scene 6*: Esther's Dream. *Scene 7*: The Bedroom again—the next morning.

Act 2, Scene 1: The Frozen Pond—before Thanskgiving. *Scene 2*: The Smith Home—preparing for Thanksgiving. *Scene 3*: Tree-Trimming Time. *Scene 4*: Snowy Men—Christmas Eve. *Scene 5*: The Ball and Portico Outside. *Scene 6*: Back Home—later that evening. *Scene 7*: The Louisiana Purchase Exposition—Spring 1904.

ACT 1[14]
Scene 1
"Meet Me in St. Louis"
Ensemble
(*Music by* Kerry Mills. *New Lyrics by* Hugh Martin and Ralph Blane.)
Scene 2
"Meet Me in St. Louis" (reprise)
M. O'Shea, C. Peldon
"The Boy Next Door"
D. Kane
"Be Anything But a Girl"[15]
M. O'Shea, R. Graham, C. Peldon
Scene 3
"Skip to My Lou"
J. Lambert, D. Kane, M. O'Steen, G. Whitney, J. Workman, P. Reardon, Company
(Traditional; *New Lyrics by* Hugh Martin and Ralph Blane.)
"Under the Bamboo Tree" (If You Lak-a Me Like I Lak-a You) (from *SALLY IN OUR ALLEY*)
D. Kane, C. Peldon
(*Music and Lyrics by* Bob Cole and J. Rosamund Johnson.)
"Banjos"[16]
M. O'Steen, Company
Scene 4
"Ghosties and Ghoulies and Things That Go Bump in the Night"[17]
B. Garrett, R. Graham, C. Peldon, Neighborhood Kids
"Halloween Ballet"[18]
Company
Scene 5
"Wasn't It Fun?"[19]
G. Hearn, C. Moore
Scene 6
"The Trolley Song"
D. Kane, Company
ACT 2
Scene 1
"Ice"[20]
J. Lambert, P. Reardon, G. Whitney, Company
Featured Skaters: R. Ottley, R. Morgan.
"Raving Beauty"[21] (from *BEST FOOT FORWARD*, 1963 revival)
P. Reardon, G. Whitney, J. Lambert
Scene 2
"A Touch of the Irish"[22]
B. Garrett, D. Kane, J. Lambert
"You Are For Loving" (from *BEST FOOT FORWARD*, 1963 revival)
J. Workman, D. Kane
Scene 3
"A Day in New York"
G. Hearn, Family
Scene 5
"The Ball"[23]
M. O'Shea, Company
"Diamonds in the Starlight"[24]
J. Workman, D. Kane
Scene 6
"Have Yourself a Merry Little Christmas"
D. Kane
Scene 7
"Paging Mr. Sousa"[25]
G. Hearn, Company

---

[14]For subsequent national tour, the show was substantially revised; Act 1, Scenes 1 and 7 were dropped, and the Ice Skating sequence (Act 2, Scene 1) was reset inside the Smith Family Home. Added for the national tour:
"Whenever I'm With You" (Act 1, Scene 3)
Billy Barnes (Grandpa), Family
"You'll Hear a Bell" (Act 1, Scene 3)
Jo Ann Cunningham (Mrs. Smith)
"Over the Bannister" (Act 1, Scene 5)
Stuart Larson (John Tuitt)
"What's His Name?" (Act 2, Scene 3)
Barbara Sharma (Katie)

[15]Dropped for national tour.
[16]For national tour, moved to Act 2, Scene 4.
[17]Dropped for national tour.
[18]Dropped for national tour.
[19]For national tour, moved to Act 2, Scene 3.
[20]Dropped for national tour.
[21]Dropped for national tour.
[22]Dropped for national tour.
[23]Dropped for national tour.
[24]Dropped for national tour.
[25]Dropped for national tour.

Finale
Company

1989.24 3 PENNY OPERA

A Revival of the Musical in Three Acts, a Prologue and 9 Scenes[26]. Book and lyrics by Bertolt Brecht. (Newly) Translated by Michael Feingold. Music by Kurt Weill. Directed by John Dexter. Musical staging by Peter Gennaro. Music director, Julius Rudel. Scenery and costumes by Jocelyn Herbert. Lighting by Andy Phillips, Brian Nason. Sound by Peter Fitzgerald. Additional orchestrations, musical continuity by Julius Rudel. Associate producers, Margo Lion, Hiroshi Sugawara, Lloyd Philips, Kiki Mayake, Nancy Ellison. Produced by Jerome Hellman in association with Haruki Kadokawa and James M. Nederlander. Opened 5 November 1989 at the Lunt-Fontanne Theatre and closed 31 December 1989 after 65 performances.

CAST (in order of appearance): *A Ballad Singer*: Ethyl Eichelberger. *Jenny Diver*, a whore: SUZZANNE DOUGLAS. *Jonathan Jeremiah Peachum*, head of a gang of beggars: ALVIN EPSTEIN. *Filch*, beggar: Jeff Blumenkrantz. *Mrs. Peachum*: GEORGIA BROWN. *Polly Peachum*, their daughter: MAUREEN MCGOVERN. *Macheath*, head of a gang of crooks: STING. *Macheath's Gang (6)*: *Matt of the Mint*: JOSH MOSTEL. *Crook-Finger Jack*: Mitchell Greenberg. *Sawtooth Bob*: David Schechter. *Ed*: Philip Carroll. *Walter (called "Walt Dreary)*: Tom Robbins. *Jimmy*: Alex Santoriello. *Tiger Brown*, Chief of London Police: LARRY MARSHALL. *Whores (6)*: *Dolly*: Anne Kerry Ford. *Betty*: Jan Horvath. *Vixen*: Teresa de Zarn. *Molly*: Nancy Ringham. *Suky Tawdry*: K. T. Sullivan. *Old Whore*: Fiddle Viracola. *Smith*, a police constable : David Pursley. *Policemen*: MacIntyre Dixon, Michael Piontek. *Lucy*, Brown's daughter: KIM CRISWELL.

Beggars, Bystanders: Philip Carroll, MacIntyre Dixon, Michael Piontek, David Schechter, Steven Major West.

The action takes place in London during the nineteenth century.

Prologue: Street Fair in Soho.

Act 1, Scene 1: Peachum's Shop. Wednesday morning. *Scene 2*: A deserted stable. 5:00 p.m. *Scene 3*: Peachum's Shop. Thursday morning.

Act 2, Scene 1: The stable. Thursday afternoon. *Scene 2*: A whorehouse in Turnbridge. Later that afternoon. *Scene 3*: Old Bailey Jail. Immediately afterward.

Act 3, Scene 1: Peachum's shop. Late that night. *Scene 2*: Lucy's Room in the Old Bailey. *Scene 3*: Macheath's Cell in the Old Bailey. 6:00 a.m. Friday.

ACT 1
Prologue
"Ballad of Mack the Knife (Moritat)"
E. Eichelberger
Scene 1
"Peachum's Morning Hymn"
A. Epstein
"Why-Can't They Song"
A. Epstein, G. Brown
Scene 2
"Wedding Song"
Gang
"Pirate Jenny"
M. McGovern
"Soldiers' Song"
Sting, L. Marshall
"Wedding Song" (reprise)
Gang
"Love Song"
Sting, M. McGovern
Scene 3
"Barbara Song"
M. McGovern
First 3 Penny Finale
M. McGovern, A. Epstein, G. Brown

ACT 2
Scene 1
"Melodrama and Polly's Song"
Sting, M. McGovern
Interlude
"Ballad of the Prisoner of Sex"
G. Brown
Scene 2
"Pimp's Ballad" (Tango)
Sting, S. Douglas
Scene 3
"Ballad of Living in Style"
Sting
"Jealousy Duet"
K. Criswell, M. McGovern
Second 3 Penny Finale
Sting, G. Brown, Chorus

ACT 3
Scene 1
"Ballad of the Prisoner of Sex" (reprise)
G. Brown
"Song of Futility"
A. Epstein
Scene 2
"Lucy's Aria"
K. Criswell
Interlude
"Solomon Song"
S. Douglas
Scene 3
"Call from the Grave"
Sting
"Epitaph"
Sting
"March to the Gallows"
Orchestra
Third 3 Penny Finale
Entire Company

[26]Originally produced as "The 3-Penny Opera" in New York 13 April 1933 at the Empire Theatre for 12 performances. An Off-Broadway revival (in an adaptation by Marc Blitzstein) at the Theatre de Lys 10 March 1954 for 94 performances, and its return engagement 30 September 1955 for 2611 performances established the show's international reputation.

1989.25 PRINCE OF CENTRAL PARK

A Musical in Two Acts. Book by Evan H. Rhodes, based on his novel of the same name. Music by Don Sebesky. Lyrics by Gloria Nissenson. Directed and choreographed by Tony Tanner. Scenery and costumes by Michael Bottari, Ronald Case. Lighting by Norman Coates. Musical direction, vocal arrangements by Joel Silberman. Sound by Daryl Bornstein. Associate choreographer, Stephen Bourneuf. Supervisor, orchestrator, Don Sebesky. Dance arrangements by Henry Aronson. Originally produced at Jan McArt's Cabaret Theatre, Key West, Florida; subsequently produced at the Al Hirschfeld Theatre, Miami Beach, Florida. Associate producer, Belle M. Deitch. Executive producer, Karen Poindexter. Produced by Abe Hirschfeld and Jan McArt. Opened 9 November 1989 at the Belasco Theater and closed 11 November 1989 after 4 performances.

CAST (in order of appearance): *Jay-Jay*: RICHARD H. BLAKE. *School Guard*: Sel Vitella. *Street People*: John Hoshko, Adrian Bailey. *Agnes*: Bonnie Perlman. *Officer Washinski*: Ruth Gottschall. *Bag Lady*: Marilyn Hudgins. *Anna Squagliatoria*: Bonnie Perlman. *May Berg*: Anne-Marie Gerard. *Aerobics Instructor*: Stephen Bourneuf. *Margie Miller*: JO ANNE WORLEY. *Sally*: CHRIS CALLEN. *Officer Simpson*: Adrian Bailey. *Stock Broker*: John Hoshko. *Fist*: Sean Grant. *Bird Brain*: Jason Ma. *Feather*: Alice Yearsley. *Elmo*: ANTHONY GALDE. *Park Ranger Rupp*: Sel Vitella. *Carpenter*: Terry Eno. *Young Richard*: John Hoshko. *Young Margie* Ruth Gottschall. *Ballet Dancer*: Alice Yearsley. *Floor Walker*: Marilyn Hudgins. *Maitre d'*: Terry Eno. *Waiter*: Sel Vitella. *Twitchy*: Anne-Marie Gerard. *Aerobics Students*: Adrian Bailey, Terry Eno, Ruth Gottschall, Anne-Marie Gerard, John Hoshko, Sel Vitella.

Tap Dancers: Adrian Bailey, Stephen Bourneuf, Ruth Gottschall, John Hoshko, Jason Ma, Bonnie Perlman, Alice Yearsley. *Swings*: Terry Iten, Jody Keith Barrie.

The action takes place in and around New York City's Central Park at the present time.

ACT 1

"Here's Where I Belong"
R. H. Blake, Ensemble
"All I've Got Is Me"
R. H. Blake
"New Leaf"
J. A. Worley, Aerobics Club
"Follow the Leader"
A. Galde, Gang, R. H. Blake
Montage: "Here's Where I Belong"
Ensemble
"We Were Dancing"
J. A. Worley, J. Hoshko, R. Gottschall
"One of a Kind"
J. A. Worley, R. H. Blake
"I Fly By Night"
A. Galde, Gang
"Zap"
J. A. Worley, R. H. Blake, Ensemble

ACT 2

"Good Evening"
Ensemble
"All I've Got Is Me" (reprise)
J. A. Worley, R. H. Blake
"They Don't Give You Life at Sixteen"
A. Galde, Ensemble
"Red"
J. A. Worley, Ensemble
"I Fly By Night" (reprise)
A. Galde, Gang, R. H. Blake
"The Prince of Central Park"
R. H. Blake
"One of a Kind" (reprise)
J. A. Worley

1989.26 GRAND HOTEL

A Musical in One Act, 20 Scenes. Book by Luther Davis, based on the novel of the same name by Vicki Baum, by arrangement with Turner Entertainment Co., owner of the MGM film. Music and lyrics by Robert Wright and George Forrest. Additional music and lyrics by Maury Yeston. Directed and choreographed by Tommy Tune. Setting design by Tony Walton. Costume design by Santo Loquasto. Lighting design by Jules Fisher. Sound design by Otts Munderloh. Orchestrations by Peter Matz. Musical and vocal direction by Jack Lee. Music supervision and additional music by Wally Harper. Associate director, Bruce Lumpkin. Production associate, Kathleen Raitt. Associate producers, Sandra Greenblatt, Martin R. Kaufman, Kim Poster. Produced by Martin Richards, Mary Lea Johnson, Sam Crothers, Sander Jacobs, Kenneth D. Greenblatt, Paramount Pictures, Jujamcyn Theatres in association with Patty Grubman and Marvin A. Krauss. Opened 12 November 1989 at the Martin Beck Theatre, moved 3 February 1992 to the Gershwin Theatre, and closed 19 April 1992 after 1018 performances.

CAST (in order of appearance): *Colonel Dr. Otternschlag*: JOHN WYLIE. *The Doorman*: Charles Mandracchia. *The Countess*: Yvonne Marceau. *The Gigolo*: Pierre Dulaine. *Madame Peepee*: Kathi Moss. *Rohna*, the Grand Concierge: REX D. HAYS. *Bellboys (4)*: *Georg Strunk*: Ken Jennings. *Kurt Krönenberg*: Keith Crowningshield. *Hanns Bittner*: Gerrit de Beer. *Willibald*, captain: J. J. Jepson. *Erik*, Front Desk: BOB STILLMAN. *The Telephone Operators (3)*: *Hildegarde Bratts*: Jennifer Lee Andrews. *Siegfriede Holzheim*: Suzanne Henderson. *Wolffe Bratts*: Lynette Perry. *The Chauffeur*: Ben George. *Zinnowitz*, the lawyer: Hal Robinson. *General Director Preysing*, Saxonia Mills: TIMOTHY JEROME. *Flaemmchen*, the Typist: JANE KRAKOWSKI. *Otto Kringelein*, the Bookkeeper: MICHAEL JETER. *Raffaela*, the confidante: KAREN AKERS. *Sandor*, the Impresario: Mitchell Jason. *(Victor) Witt*, Company Manager: Michel Moinot. *Elizaveta Grishinskaya*, the Ballerina: LILIANE MONTEVECCHI. *Felix von Gaigern*, the Baron: DAVID (James) CARROLL. *The Jimmys*: David Jackson, Danny Strayhorn. *The Scullery Workers (4)*: *Ernst Schmidt*: Henry Grossman. *Franz Kohl*: William Ryall. *Werner Holst*: David Elledge. *Gunther Gustaffson*: Walter Willison. *Hotel Courtesan*: Suzanne Henderson. *Trudie*, the maid: Jennifer Lee Andrews.

Swings: Michael DeVries, Niki Harris, Glenn Turner.

The action takes place in the Grand Hotel in Berlin, 1928.

Scene 1: The Grand Hotel Lobby and far below in the Scullery. *Scene 2*: The Moroccan Coffee Bar. *Scene 3*: A corner of The Grand Ballroom. *Scene 4*: The Ladies Powder Room. *Scene 5*: Men's Washroom and The Hotel Bar. *Scene 6*: The Baron's Room. *Scene 7*: The Yellow Pavilion. *Scene 8*: The Hotel Conference Room. *Scene 9*: Backstage at the Opera House. *Scene 10*: The Financial Corner of the Hotel Lobby. *Scene 11*: The Roof of the Grand Hotel .*Scene 12*: Grushinskaya's Suite. *Scene 13*: Raffalela's Room. *Scene 14*: The Hotel Conference Room and just inside the ever-revolving door. *Scene 15*: Raffaela's Room. *Scene 16*: Grishinskaya's Suite. *Scene 17*: The Hotel Bar. *Scene 18*: A Cross Corridor upstairs in the Hotel/ the Doctor's Room/Presying's Room/Flemmchen's adjoining room/Kringelein's Room/The Bedchamber of The Countess and The Gigolo. *Scene 19*: Grushinskaya's Suite/Kringelein's Room/Preysing's Room. *Scene 20*: The Lobby of the Grand Hotel.

MUSICAL NUMBERS

The Presentation of the Company:
"The Grand Parade"
J. Wylie, Company
(*Additional music and lyrics by* Maury Yeston.)

Scene 1
"As It Should Be"
D. Carroll
(*Lyrics revised by* Maury Yeston.)
"Some Have, Some Have Not"
Scullery Workers
(*Lyrics revised by* Maury Yeston.)
"At the Grand Hotel"
M. Jeter
(*Additional music and lyrics by* Maury Yeston.)
"Table with a View"
M. Jeter
(*Lyrics revised by* Maury Yeston.)

Scene 2
"Maybe My Baby Loves Me"
D. Jackson, D. Strayhorn, J. Krakowski

Scene 3
"Fire and Ice"
L. Montevecchi, Ensemble
(*Lyrics revised by* Maury Yeston.)
"Twenty-two Years"
K. Akers
(*Additional music and lyrics by* Maury Yeston.)
"Villa on a Hill"
K. Akers

Scene 4
"I Want to Go to Hollywood"
J. Krakowski
(*Additional music and lyrics by* Maury Yeston.)

Scene 5
"Everybody's Doing It"
H. Robinson
(*Additional music and lyrics by* Maury Yeston.)
"The Crooked Path"
T. Jerome
(*Lyrics revised by* Maury Yeston.)

Scene 6
"As It Should Be" (reprise)
D. Carroll
(*Lyrics revised by* Maury Yeston.)

Scene 7
"Who Couldn't Dance with You?"
J. Krakowski, D. Carroll, M. Jeter

Scene 8
"The Boston Merger"
H. Robinson, T. Jerome, Shareholders
(*Lyrics revised by* Maury Yeston.)

Scene 9
"No Encore"
L. Montevecchi

Scene 11
"Fire and Ice" (reprise)
Company
(*Lyrics revised by* Maury Yeston.)
Scene 12
"Love Can't Happen"
D. Carroll, L. Motevecchi
(*Additional music and lyrics by* Maury Yeston.)
Scene 13
"What She Needs" (What You Need)
K. Akers
(*Lyrics revised by* Maury Yeston.)
Scene 16
"Bonjour Amour"
L. Montevecchi
(*Additional music and lyrics by* Maury Yeston.)
Scene 17
"Happy"
D. Jackson, D. Strayhorn
"We'll Take a Glass Together"
M. Jeter, D. Carroll
(*Lyrics revised by* Maury Yeston.)
Scene 18
"I Waltz Alone"
J. Wylie
(*Lyrics revised by* Maury Yeston.)
"Roses at the Station"
D. Carroll
(*Additional music and lyrics by* Maury Yeston.)
Scene 19
"How Can I Tell Her?"
K. Akers
(*Lyrics revised by* Maury Yeston.)
Scene 20
"As It Should Be" (reprise)
B. Stillman, Company
(*Lyrics revised by* Maury Yeston.)
"Some Have, Some Have Not" (reprise)
Scullery Workers
(*Lyrics revised by* Maury Yeston.)
"The Grand Parade"
Company
(*Additional music and lyrics by* Maury Yeston.)
The Grand Finale:
"The Grand Waltz"
Entire Company

1989.27 GYPSY

A Revival of the Musical Fable in Two Acts[27]. Book by Arthur Laurents. Suggested by the memoirs (of the same name) by Gypsy Rose Lee. Directed by Arthur Laurents. Original production directed and choreographed by Jerome Robbins; choreography reproduced by Bonnie Walker. Music by Jule Styne. Lyrics by Stephen Sondheim. Scenery design by Kenneth Foy. Costume design by Theoni V. Aldredge. Lighting design by Natasha Katz. Sound design by Peter Fitzgerald. Musical director, Eric Stern. Orchestrations by Sid Ramin, Robert Ginzler. Dance music arrangements, John Kander. Produced by Barry and Fran Weissler, Kathy Levin, Barry Brown in association with Tokyo Broadcasting System International, Inc. and Pace Theatrical Group. Opened 16 November 1989 at the St. James Theatre and closed 6 January 1991 after 476 performances; played a return engagement 28 April 1991 at the Minskoff Theater for 105 performances (see separate entry in 1990-1991 season). Total: 581 performances.

CAST (in order of appearance): *Uncle Jocko*: Tony Hoty. *George*: John Remme. *Clarence* (and his classic clarinet): Bobby John Carter. *Balloon Girl*: Jeana Haege. *Baby Louise*: Kristen Mahon. *Baby June*: Christen Tassin. *Rose*: TYNE DALY. *Chowsie*: Peewee. *Pop*: Ronn Carroll. *Newsboys*: Demetri Callas, Bobby John Carter, Danny Cistone, Jason Miner. *Weber*: Mace Barrett. *Herbie*: JONATHAN HADARY. *Louise*: CHRISTA MOORE. *June*: Tracy Venner. *Tulsa*: Robert Lambert. *Yonkers*: Bruce Moore. *L.A.*: Craig Waletzko. *Kansas*: Ned Hannah. *Flagstaff*: Paul Geraci. *St. Paul*: Alec Timerman. *Mr. Goldstone*: John Remme. *Miss Cratchitt*: Barbara Erwin. *Hollywood Blondes (5)*: Barbara Folts, Teri Furr, Nancy Melius, Michele Pigliavento, Robin Robinson. *Agnes*: Lori Ann Mahl. *Pastey*: Jim Bracchitta. *Tessie Tura*: Barbara Erwin. *Mazeppa*: Jana Robbins. *Electra*: Anna McNeely. *Cigar*: Ronn Carroll. *Maid*: Ginger Prince. *Phil*: Mace Barrett. *Bougeron-Cochon*: Jim Bracchitta. *Swings*: Julie Graves, Eric H. Kaufman.

1989.28 VICTOR BORGE ON BROADWAY

A Musical Entertainment in Two Acts[28]. Conceived by Victor Borge. Assistant to Mr. Borge, Jim Colias. Produced by Music Fair Productions, Inc. (Shelly Gross) Opened 5 December 1989 at the Brooks Atkinson Theatre and closed 10 December 1989 after 8 performances.

CAST: VICTOR BORGE.

1989.29 CITY OF ANGELS

A Musical in Two Acts, 37 Scenes. Book by Larry Gelbart. Music by Cy Coleman. Lyrics by David Zippel. Directed by Michael Blakemore. Musical numbers staged by Walter Painter. Scenic design by Robin Wagner. Costume design by Florence Klotz. Lighting design by Paul Gallo. Sound design by Peter Fitzgerald, Bernard Fox. Orchestrations by Bill Byers. Vocal arrangements by Cy Coleman, Varon Gershovsky. Musical direction by Gordon Lowry Harrell. Fight staging by B. H. Barry. Produced by Nick Vanoff, Roger Berlind, Jujamcyn Theatres, Suntory International Corporation, The Shubert Organization. Opened 11 December 1989 at the Virginia Theatre and closed 19 January 1992 after 878 performances.

MOVIE CAST (in order of appearance): *Stone*: JAMES NAUGHTON. *Orderlies*: James Hindman, Tom Galantich. *Oolie*: RANDY GRAFF. *Alaura Kingsley*: DEE HOTY. *Big Six*: Herschel Sparber. *Sonny*: Raymond Xifo. *Jimmy Powers*: Scott Waara. *The Angel City Four*: Peter Davis, Amy Jane London, Gary Kahn, Jackie Presti. *Munoz*: Shawn Elliott. *Officer Pasco*: Tom Galantich. *Bobbi*: KAY MCCLELLAND. *Irwin S. Irving*: RENE AUBERJONOIS. *Peter Kingsley*: Doug Tompos. *Margaret*: Carolee Carmello. *Luther Kingsley*: Keith Perry. *Dr. Mandril*: James Cahill. *Mallory Kingsley*: Rachel York. *Mahoney*: James Hindman. *Yamato*: Alvin Lum. *Commissioner Gaines*: Evan Thompson. *Margie*: Eleanor Glockner. *Bootsie*: Jacquey Maltby.

HOLLYWOOD CAST (in order of appearance): *Stine*: GREGG EDELMAN. *Buddy Fidler*: RENE AUBERJONOIS. *Shoeshine*: Evan Thompson. *Gabby*: KAY MCCLELLAND. *Barber*: James Cahill. *Donna*: RANDY GRAFF. *Anna*: Eleanor Glockner. *Jimmy Powers*: Scott Waara. *The Angel City Four*: Peter Davis, Amy Jane London, Gary Kahn, Jackie Presti. *Carla Haywood*: DEE HOTY. *Del Dacosta*: James Hindman. *Pancho Vargas*: Shawn Elliott. *Werner Kriegler*: Keith Perry. *Gerald Pierce*: Doug Tompos. *Avril Raines*: Rachel York. *Gene*: Tom Galantich. *Cinematographer*: Alvin Lum. *Stand-In*: Carolee Carmello. *Hairdresser*: Eleanor Glockner. *Studio Cops*: Herschel Sparber, Raymond Xifo.

Swings: Chrissy Faith, Marcus Neville.

---

[27]Originally produced in New York 21 May 1959 at the Broadway Theatre for 702 performances. For Synopsis of Scenes and Musical Numbers, see original 1959 production. For this revival, several songs were retitled in the program:

"May We Entertain You" (Act 1, Scene 1) retitled "Let Me Entertain You."

"Mr. Goldstone, I Love You" (Act 1, Scene 6) retitled "Mr. Goldstone."

"Let Me Entertain You" (Act 2, Scene 4) retitled "The Strip."

Dropped: Traveling (Act 1, Scene 3), "Small World" (reprise) (Act 2, Scene 4).

[28]Victor Borge has appeared previously in Broadway in his one-man shows:

Comedy in Music, 2 October 1953, John Golden Theatre, 849 performances.

Comedy in Music, Opus 2, 9 November 1964, John Golden Theatre, 192 performances.

Comedy with Music, 3 October 1977, Imperial Theatre, 64 performances.

The action takes place in Los Angeles during the late 1940's.

Act 1, Scene 1: L.A. County Hospital. *Scene 2*: Stone Office, one week earlier. *Scene 3*: Writer's Cell, Master Pictures Studio. *Scene 4*: Buddy Fidler's Office. *Scene 5*: Stone's Office. *Scene 6*: Stine's Bedroom, The Garden of Allah. *Scene 7*: Stone's Bungalow. *Scene 8*: Buddy's Office. *Scene 9*: Stone's Bungalow. *Scene 10*: A Cocktail Lounge. *Scene 11*: Bobbi's Dressing Room. *Scene 12*: Writer's Cell. *Scene 13*: The Kingsley Mansion. *Scene 14*: The Solarium. *Scene 15*: The Search. *Scene 16*: Stone's Bungalow. *Scene 17*: Donna's Bedroom. *Scene 18*: Stone's Bungalow. *Scene 19*: L.A. County Morgue. *Scene 20*: Buddy's Office. *Scene 21*: The Morgue.

Act 2, Scene 1: A Recording Studio. *Scene 2*: A Bel-Air Bedroom. *Scene 3*: L.A. County Jail. *Scene 4*: Oolie's Bedroom. *Scene 5*: Donna's Bedroom. *Scene 6*: A Bel-Air Garden. *Scene 7*: Buddy's Study. *Scene 8*: The Jail. *Scene 9*: Buddy's Study. *Scene 10*: Alaura's Bedroom. *Scene 11*: Buddy's Office. *Scene 12*: Stine's Apartment, New York. *Scene 13*: The Red Room. *Scene 14*: The Kingsley Solarium. *Scene 15*: Writer's Cell. *Scene 16*: A Soundstage, Master Pictures Studio.

ACT 1

Prelude: Theme from "City of Angels"
Angel City 4

Scene 2
"Double Talk"
J. Naughton, D. Hoty

Scene 4
"Double Talk" (reprise)
R. Auberjonois, G. Edelman

Scene 6
"What You Don't Know About Women"
K. McClelland, R. Graff

Scene 7
"Ya Gotta Look Out for Yourself"
S. Waara, The Angel City 4

Scene 8
"The Buddy System"
R. Auberjonois, R. Graff

Scene 10
"With Every Breath I Take"
K. McClelland

Scene 14
"Tennis Song"
J. Naughton, D. Hoty

Scene 15
"Ev'rybody's Gotta Be Somewhere"
J. Naughton, The Angel City 4

Scene 16
"Lost and Found"
R. York

Scene 21
"All Ya Have to Do Is Wait"
S. Elliott, A. Lum, J. Hindman, T. Galantich
"You're Nothing Without Me"
G. Edelman, J. Naughton

ACT 2

Scene 1
"Stay With Me"
S. Waara, The Angel City 4

Scene 4
"You Can Always Count on Me"
R. Graff

Scene 5
"You Can Always Count on Me" (reprise)
R. Graff

Scene 12
"It Needs Work"
K. McClelland

Scene 13
"With Every Breath I Take" (reprise)
J. Naughton, K. McClelland

Scene 15
"Funny"
G. Edelman

Scene 16
"You're Nothing Without Me" (reprise)
J. Naughton, G. Edelman, K. McClelland

1990.01 JUNON AND AVOS-THE HOPE

A Soviet Rock Musical in Two Acts, a Prologue and Epilogue (in Russian). Book and lyrics by Andrey Voznesensky. Music by Alexis Ribnikov. Directed by Mark Zakharov. Choreography by Vladimir Vassiliev. Sets by Oleg Sheintsiss. Costumes by Valentina Komolova. Sound by Abe Jacob. English narrative written by Susan Silver and Albert Todd. America producer, Lucy Jarvis. Presented by Pierre Cardin, by special arrangement with Lencom Theatre and the Theatre Union of the U.S.S.R. Opened 7 January 1990 at the New York City Center and closed 4 February 1990 after 35 performances.

CAST: *Count Nikolai Rezanov*, Chamberlain of Emperor Alexander I: NIKOLAI KARACHENTSEV. *Conchita*, Maria de la Concepcione de Arguello: YELENA SHANINA. *First Conjurer*: Yury Naumkin. *Second Conjurer*: Gennady Trofimov. *Burning Heretic, Fernando Lopez, the Theatrical Narrator*: ALEXANDER ABDULOV. *Vision of a woman with an infant*: Ludmilla Porgina. *Count Alexey Rumiantsev/The Governor of San Francisco*: Vladimir Shiryayev. *Naval Officers*: Vladimir Belousov, Boris Chunayev, Vladimir Kuznetsov, Rady Ovchinnikov. *Padre Abella*: Villor Kuznetsov. *Interpreter*: Rady Ovchinnikov. *Spanish Ladies*: Irena Alfiorova, Tatiana Derbeneva, Ludmilla Porgina, Alexandra Zakharova, Tatiana Rudina, Ludmilla Artemieva. *Conchita's Messenger*: Yury Zelenin. *The Singing Monk*: Alexander Sado.

The Russian Sailors, Spaniards, the Shareholders of the Russian-American Company, the monks, chimeras and others: Vladislav Victor Rakov, Alexander Sririn, Nikolai Shusharin, Alexander Karnaushkin, Igor Fokin, Andrey Leonov, Sergey Chonishvilli, Oleg Ruduk, Leonid Luvinsky, Leonid Gromov, Denis Karasiov.

The Choir: *Sopranos*: Irena Musayelian, Valentina Prokhorova, Zinaida Morozova, Natlia Mishenko. *Altos*: Irena Kushnarenko, Valeria Zhivova, Lilia Semashko, Yelena Rudnitskaya. *Tenor*: Vladimir Tursky. *Basses*: Alexey Larin, Valdimir Prokhorov, Sergey Stepanchenko.

Rock Group Araks: *Keyboards*; Sergey Rudnitsky. *Bass Guitar*: Seregy Rizhov. *Vocals*: Alexander Sado, Nikolai Parfenyuk, Pavel Smeian. *Guitar/Violin/Cello*: Sergey Berezkin. *Drums*: Anatoly Abromov. *Brass*: Yakov Levda, Victor Denisov.

Storyteller (Narration in English): PHILIP CASNOFF.

The action takes place in Russia and San Francisco from 1806 to 1842.

MUSICAL NUMBERS[29]

"I Will Never See You Again, I Will Never Forget You"
"Avos" (the hope for good luck)
"The White Wild Rose"
"Hallelejuah to Love"

1990.02 THE SOUND OF MUSIC

A Revival of the Musical (Play) in Two Acts, 19 Scenes[30]. Book by Howard Lindsay and Russel Crouse. Suggested by the book "The Trapp Family Singers" by Maria Augusta Trapp. Music by Richard Rodgers. Lyrics by Oscar Hammerstein II. Directed by James Hammerstein. Musical staging by Joel Bishoff. Set and lighting designer, Neil Peter Jampolis. Costume designer, Suzanne Mess. Conductor, Richard Parrinello. Orchestrations by Robert Russell Bennett. Sound by Abe Jacob. Chorus master, Joseph Colaneri. Produced by the New York City Opera in association with James M. Nederlander. Opened 8 March 1990 at the New York State Theatre and closed 22 April 1990 after 54 performances.

CAST (in order of appearance): *Maria Rainer*, a Postulant at Nonnberg Abbey: DEBBY BOONE. *Sister Berthe*, Mistress of Novices: Jill Bosworth *Sister Margaretta*, Mistress of Postulants: Michele McBride. *The Mother Abbess*: CLAUDIA CUMMINGS. *Sister Sophia*: Robin Tabachnik. *Captain Georg von Trapp*:

---

[29]Performed as an opera without individual scenes or musical numbers listed. The plot synopsis however included the following song titles.

[30]Originally produced in New York 16 November 1959 at the Lunt-Fontanne Theatre for 1443 performances. For Synopsis of Scenes and Musical Numbers, see original 1959 production.

LAURENCE GUITTARD. *Franz*, the butler: David Rae Smith. *Frau Schmidt*, the housekeeper: Ellen Tovatt. *Children of Captain von Trapp (7)*: *Liesl*: EMILY LOESSER. *Friedrich*: Richard H. Blake. *Louisa*: Kelly Karbacz. *Kurt*: Ted Huffman. *Brigitta*: Kia Graves. *Marta*: Lauren Gaffney. *Gretl*: Mary Mazzello. *Rolf Gruber*: Marc Heller. *Elsa Schraeder*: MARIANNE TATUM. *Ursula*: Bridget Ramos. *Max Detweiler*: WERNER KLEMPERER. *Herr Zeller*: Louis Perry. *Baron Elberfeld*: William Ledbetter. *Postulant*: Barbara Shirvis. *Admiral von Schreiber*: Glenn Rowen.

Neighbors of Captain von Trapp, Nuns, Novices, Postulants, Contestants in the Festival Concert: New York City Opera Chorus.

1990.03 OBA OBA '90

A New Edition of the Brazilian Extravaganza (Revue) in Two Acts, 13 Scenes[31]. (Conceived and directed by Franco Fontana.) Musical director, Wilson Mauro. Choreographer, Roberto Abrahão. Lighting consultant, Giancarlo Campora. Produced by Franco Fontana. Opened 15 March 1990 at the Marquis Theatre and closed 22 April 1990 after 45 performances.

CAST: SONIA SANTOS, JAIME SANTOS, TOCO PRETO, PAULO RAMOS.
(in alphabetical order): Aderson Cirne, Amilton Lino, Andrea Candida, Bananal, Betho Filho, Branca de Neve, Carlos Leça, Carlos Oliveira, Cesar de Alabama, Claudia Capoeira, Curimã, Delma de Oliviera, Edgar Pretinho, Edilson Nery, Edmilson Nery, Edson Escovão, Eliane Garcia, Elisangela Maia, Evelyn Eduardo, Formiguinha, Gerson Galante, Glaucia Ribeiro, Heron DeAngola, Ivon Rosas, Janete Santos, Jorge Rum, Julio Peluchi, Katia Rio, Maguila Meneses, Malaguti, Mara Boeing, Maranhão, Marcelo Boim, Mario Capoeira, Marquinho da Dona Geralda, Marta Jacintho, Mauro Boim, Meia-Noite, Mirna Montenegro, Monica Acioli, Norberto Queiroz, Pé de Cão, Pelé, Pena Rodrigues, Renny Flores, Robertinho da Cuica, Rui Lima, Val Ventilador, Velly Bahia, Vivian M. Soares, Wilson Mauro.

ACT 1

Scene 1

Liberation from Slavery

The suffering of black slaves in prison. Their consciousness of their condition. The final unification of all blacks until freedom was achieved.

Scenes 2 and 4

Homage to "Chorinho"

Some classics of this particular kind of popular music feature the most expressive Brazilian instrument, the cavaquinho, a small guitar with four chords. Pieces such as "Carinhoso," "Urubu Malandro" and "Tico Tico" have made Chorinho famous throughout the world.

Scene 3

Samba de Roda-Lambada

This is a typical dance born in Bahia's public squares and markets—a festive competition among the women of the town. This coquettish contest displays their superiority in performing this particular type of samba. Lambada is a sexy popular dance from northeast Brazil that is becoming very popular and successful all over the world.

Scene 5

Homage to the Northeast

The most evocative music and songs of this marvelous, but desolately poor, territory move from the resigned lamentations of the Acordeom to the explosive reactions of the people who find in song and dance the strength and joy of life.

Scene 6

Brazil Capela

Scene 7

Homage to the Bossa Nova and the Seventies

The Bossa Nova—a medley dedicated to that great musical phenomenon of the sixties that made artists Tob Jobim, Baden Powell and Vinicius de Moraes and the songs "Wave," Samba de uma nota so" and "Garota de Ipanema" world-famous. The Seventies—a medley dedicated to the music of the seventies that made famous artists Jorge Ben and Sergio Mendess, and the songs "Mais Que Nada," "Taj Mahal" and Pais Tropical."

Scene 8

Tribute to the 'Brazilian Bombshell' Carmen Miranda

ACT 2

Scene 1

Macumba

The religious African cult with its dances and its saints (Orixa) including the magical appearance of Iemanja, Queen of the Seas and Fertility.

Scene 2

Afro-Brazilian Folk Songs and Dances; Berimbau Medley

Capoeira of Angola:

A tribute to the struggles against the white masters wherein the slaves used their hands and feet as their only weapon (Capoeira, which later became a dance).

Maculele:

Dances that require agility and skill and are carried out with small batons accompanied by the lively rhythm of tambores and agogo.

Acrobatic Capoeira

Scene 3

Rhythm Beaters

Various instruments are at first played separately, in order to stress their peculiarities, and then all together in a sweeping progress of rhythm.

Scene 4

Show of Samba Dancers

An exaltation of the beauty and charm of the Brazilian mulatto women through the sensual progress of their samba.

Scene 5

Grand Carnival

The most popular themes of the various carnivals, featuring a parade of the artists who then allow the audience to participate in the great and collective festivals.

[31]First produced in New York 29 March 1988 at the Ambassador Theatre for 46/53? performances.

1990.04 ASPECTS OF LOVE

A Musical in Two Acts, a Prologue and 34 Scenes. Book adaptation by Andrew Lloyd Webber. Based on the novel of the same name by David Garnett. Music by Andrew Lloyd Webber. Lyrics by Don Black and Charles Hart. Directed by Trevor Nunn. Choreography by Gillian Lynne. Production design (costumes, settings) by Maria Björnson. Lighting by Andrew Bridge. Sound by Martin Levan. Production musical director, Paul Bogaev. Orchestrations by David Cullen, Andrew Lloyd Webber. Produced by The Really Useful Company (Bridget Hayward, producer). Opened 8 April 1990 at the Broadhurst Theatre and closed 2 March 1991 after 377 performances.

CAST: *Rose Vibert*, a French actress: ANN CRUMB. *Alex Dillingham*, a young Englishman: MICHAEL BALL. *George Dillingham*, Alex's uncle, an English painter: KEVIN COLSON. *Giulietta Trapani*, an Italian sculptress: KATHLEEN ROWE MCALLEN. *Marcel Richard*, an actor manager: WALTER CHARLES. *Jenny Dillingham*, age 12: Deanna du Clos. *Jenny Dillingham*, age 14: Danielle du Clos. *Elizabeth*, George's housekeeper: Suzanne Briar. *Hugo Le Muenier*, Rose's friend: Don Goodspeed. *Jerome*, George's gardener: Philip Clayton.

At the Cafe: *Actors*: Philip Clayton, John Dewar, Marcus Lovett, Kurt Johns. *Actresses*: Elinore O'Connell, Lisa Vroman, Wysandria Woolsey. *Stage Manager*: Don Goodspeed. *Assistant Stage Manager*: Jane Todd Baird. *Waiter*: Gregory Mitchell. *Man on Date*: Eric Johnson. *His Date*: Suzanne Briar.

At the Fairground: *First Barker*: Eric Johnson. *Second Barker*: Kurt Johns. *Alex's Friends*: Don Goodspeed, Philip Clayton. *Their Girlfriends*: Elinore O'Connell, Lisa Vroman. *Alex's Date*: Jane Todd Baird. *War Veteran*: John Dewar. *His Wife*: Suzanne Briar. *Local Men*: Marcus Lovett, Gregory Mitchell. *Local Woman*: Wysandria Woolsey. *In Venice*: *Gondolier*: Kurt Johns. *Hotel Cashier*: Lisa Vroman. *Nun*: Elinore O'Connell. *Doctor*: John Dewar. *Hotleier*: Eric Johnson. *Pharmacist*: Wysandria Woolsey. *Registrar*: Eric Johnson. *Assistant Registrar*: John Dewar.

In Rose's Dressing Room: *Rose's Friends*: Jane Todd Baird, Suzanne Briar, Philip Clayton, John Dewar, Kurt Johns, Eric Johnson, Marcus Lovett, Gregory Mitchell, Elinore O'Connell, Lisa Vroman, Wysandria Woolsey.

At the Circus: *Clowns*: Gregory Mitchell, Marcus Lovett, Philip Clayton, John Dewar. *Knife Thrower*: Kurt Johns. *His Assistant*: Wysandria Woolsey.

At the Wake: *The Young Peasant*: Gregory Mitchell.

Swings: Wiley Kidd, Brad Oscar, Anne Marie Runolfsson.

The action takes place on the (European) continent between 1947-1964.

Prologue: On the Terrace at Pau, 1964.

Act 1, Scene 1: France, 1947. A Small Theatre in Montpellier. *Scene 2*: A Cafe in Montpellier. *Scene 3*: The Railway Station. *Scene 4*: In a Train Compartment. *Scene 5*: The House at Pau. *Scene 6*: A Sculpture Exhibition in Paris. *Scene 7*: In many rooms in the House at Pau. *Scene 8*: On the Terrace. *Scene 9*: Outside the bedroom. *Scene 10*: Up in the Pyrenees. *Scene 11*: The House at Pau. *Scene 12*: The Railway Station. *Scene 13*: Two Years pass . . . A Fairground in Paris. *Scene 14*: George's Flat in Paris. *Scene 15*:

Giulietta's Studio in Venice. *Scene 16*: A Registry Office. *Scene 17*: A Military Camp in Malaya.

Act 2, Scene 1: Thirteen years later . . . A Grand Theatre in Paris. *Scene 2*: At the Stage Door. *Scene 3*: George's House in Pau. *Scene 4*: A Cafe in Venice/The House at Pau. *Scene 5*: The Garden at Pau. *Scene 6*: The Countryside around the House. *Scene 7*: Two years pass . . . The Garden at Pau. *Scene 8*: On the Terrace., *Scene 9*: Up in the Pyrenees. *Scene 10*: In the Vineyard at Pau. *Scene 11*: A Circus in Paris. *Scene 12*: Outside the Circus. *Scene 13*: Jenny's Bedroom in Paris. *Scene 14*: The Vineyards at Pau. *Scene 15*: A Hayloft. *Scene 16*: On the Terrace.

ACT 1

Prologue

"Love Changes Everything"
M. Ball

Scene 2

"Parlez-vous français?"
A. Crumb, M. Ball, Ensemble

Scene 4

"Seeing Is Believing"
M. Ball, A. Crumb

Scene 6

"A Memory of a Happy Moment"
K. Colson, K. R. McAllen

Scene 10

"Chanson d'enfance"
A. Crumb

Scene 13

"Everybody Loves a Hero"
Barkers, Ensemble

Scene 14

"She'd Be Far Better Off with You"
M. Ball, K. Colson, A. Crumb, S. Briar

Scene 15

"Stop. Wait. Please."
K. R. McAllen, K. Colson, Ensemble

ACT 2

Scene 1

"Leading Lady"
W. Charles, Ensemble

Scene 3

"Other Pleasures"
K. Colson

Scene 4

"There Is More to Love"
K. R. McAllen, A. Crumb

Scene 5

"Mermaid Song"
D. Du Clos, M. Ball

Scene 8

"The First Man You Remember"
K. Colson, D. Du Clos

Scene 11

"The Journey of a Lifetime"
Company

Scene 12

"Falling"
K. Colson, A. Crumb, M. Ball, D. Du Clos

Scene 14

"Hand Me the Wine and the Dice"
K. R. McAllen, Ensemble

Scene 16

"Anything But Lonely"
A. Crumb

1990.05

TRULY BLESSED: A Musical Celebration of Mahalia Jackson

A Musical in Two Acts, 14 Scenes. Written, conceived, original music and lyrics by Queen Esther Marrow. Additional music and lyrics, original (musical) arrangements by Reginald Royal. Directed by Robert Kalfin. Choreography by Larry Vickers. Musical supervision and orchestrations by Joseph Joubert. Scenery and lighting design by Fred Kolo. Costume design by Andrew B. Marlay. Sound design by Peter Fitzgerald. Production supervisor, Mortimer Halpern. Originally produced by Ford's Theatre, Washington, D.C. Produced by Howard Hurst, Philip Rose, Sophie Hurst in association with Frankie Hewitt. Opened 22 April 1990 at the Longacre Theatre and closed 20 May 1990 after 33 performances.

CAST: *Mahalia Jackson*: QUEEN ESTHER MARROW.
Ensemble: Carl Hall, Lynette G. DuPré, Doug Eskew, Gwen Stuart.

Act 1, Scene 1: Opening. *Scene 2*: New Orleans. *Scene 3*: Going to Chicago. *Scene 4*: The Church. *Scene 5*: Touring. *Scene 6*: On the Backsteps. *Scene 7*: Mayor Daley and the Rally. *Scene 8*: Mr. Sigmund Galloway. *Scene 9*: On Top of the World.

Act 2, Scene 1: Carnegie Hall. *Scene 2*: The March on Washington. *Scene 3*: Mahalia in the Berkshires. *Scene 4*: In the Holy Land. *Scene 5*: Epilogue and Celebration.

ACT 1

"I Found the Answer"
(*Music and Lyrics by* Johnny Lange.)

"St. Louis Blues"
(*Music and Lyrics by* W. C. Handy.)

"It's Amazing What God Can Do"
(*Music and Lyrics by* Reginald Royal.)

Medley: "On the Battlefield for My Lord"/"Glory Hallelujah"

"He May Not Come When You Want Him"

"Lord, I'm Determined"
(*Music and Lyrics by* Queen Esther Marrow.)

"Happy Days Are Here Again" (from *CHASING RAINBOWS* film)
(*Music by* Milton Ager. *Lyrics by* Jack Yellen.)

"Precious Lord"
(*Music and Lyrics by* Thomas A. Dorsey.)

"Jesus Remembers When Others Forget"
(*Music by* Joseph Joubert. *Lyrics by* Thomas A. Dorsey.)

"Thank You for the Change in My Life"
(*Music and Lyrics by* Queen Esther Marrow.)

"Come on Children, Let's Sing"

ACT 2

"Even Me"
(*Arranged by* Roberta Martin.)

"Didn't It Rain"

Spiritual Medley:
"Wade in the Water"
"Old Ship of Zion"
"Battle Hymn of the Republic"
(Traditional; *Lyrics by* Julia Ward Howe.)
"I've Been Buked"
"Soon I Will Be Done"

"His Gift to Me"
(*Music and Lyrics by* Reginald Royal.)

"Move on up a Little Higher"
(*Music and Lyrics by* Mahalia Jackson.)

"Rusty Bell"

"Truly Blessed"
(*Music and Lyrics by* Reginald Royal.)

"He's Got the Whole World in His Hands"
(Traditional; *adapted by* Geoff Love.)

1990.06

A CHANGE IN THE HEIR

A Musical Comedy in Two Acts and a Prologue. Book by George H. Gorham and Dan Sticco. Music by Dan Sticco. Lyrics by George H. Gorham. Directed and choreographed by David H. Bell. Sets by Michael Anania. Costumes by David Murin. Lighting by Jeff Davis. Musical director

and dance arrangements by Rob Bowman. Orchestrations by Robby Merkin. World premiere originally produced by New Tuners, Theatre, Chicago. Produced by Stewart F. Lane. Opened 29 April 1990 at the Edison Theater and closed 13 May 1990 after 17 performances.

CAST (in order of appearance): *Aunt Julia*: BROOKS ALMY. *Giles*: Brian Sutherland. *Edwin*: J. K. Simmons. *Nicholas*: David Gunderman. *Countess*: Connie Day. *Lady Enid*: Mary Stout. *Prince Conrad*: JUDY BLAZER. *Princess Agnes*: JEFFREY HERBST. *Martha*: Jan Neuberger. *Lady Elizabeth*: Jennifer Smith.

Prologue: Once upon a time, long, long ago, in a castle far, far away.

Act 1: Twenty years later, Friday and Saturday.

Act 2: Sunday morning.

ACT 1

Prologue
Company

"Here I Am"
J. Blazer

"The Weekend"
B. Almy, C. Day, J. Neuberger, M. Stout, J. K. Simmons, B. Sutherland

"Look at Me"
J. Herbst, J. Blazer

"Take a Look at That"
J. Herbst, J. Smith

"The Quintet"
J. K. Simmons, M. Stout, J. Herbst, C. Day, J. Blazer

"Can't I?"
J. Blazer

"When"
B. Almy, J. Neuberger

"A Fairy Tale"
J. Herbst, J. Blazer

"An Ordinary Family"
Company

ACT 2

"Happily Ever After After All"
J. Herbst

"Can't I?" (reprise)
J. Blazer

"Duet"
J. Herbst, J. Blazer

"Hold That Crown"
B. Almy

"By Myself"
J. Blazer, Company

Finale
Company

1990–1991 SEASON

Keith Carradine in THE WILL ROGERS FOLLIES
Martha Swope/TimePix

1990–1991 SEASON

A LITTLE NIGHT MUSIC

1990.07

A Revival of the Musical in Two Acts, a Prologue and 15 Scenes[1]. Book by Harold Wheeler. Suggested by a film ("Smiles of a Summer Night") by Ingmar Bergman. Music and lyrics by Stephen Sondheim. Directed by Scott Ellis. Choreography by Susan Stroman. Sets designed by Michael Anania. Costumes designed by Lindsay W. Davis. Lighting designed by Dawn Chiang. Conductor, Paul Gemignani. Orchestrations by Jonathan Tunick. Sound by Abe Jacob. Produced by the New York City Opera. Opened 3 August 1990 at the New York State Theatre and closed 7 November 1990 after 11 performances in repertory.

CAST (in order of appearance): *Mrs. Segstrom*: Susanne Marsee. *Mr. Lindquist*: Ron Baker. *Mrs. Nordstrom*: Lisa Saffer. *Mrs. Anderssen*: Barbara Shirvis. *Mr. Erlanson*: Michael Rees Davis. *Frederika Armfeldt*: Danielle Ferland. *Madame Armfeldt*: REGINA RESNICK. *Frid*, her butler: DAVID COMSTOCK. *Henrik Egerman*: KEVIN P. ANDERSON. *Anne Egerman*: BEVERLY LAMBERT. *Fredrik Egerman*: GEORGE LEE ANDREWS. *Petra*: SUSAN TERRY. *Desirée Armfeldt*: SALLY ANN HOWES. *Malla*, her maid: Raven Wilkinson. *Bertrand*, a page: Michael Rees Davis. *Count Carl-Magnus Malcolm*: MICHAEL MAGUIRE. *Countess Charlotte Malcolm*: MAUREEN MOORE. *Osa*: Judith Jarosz. *Serving Gentlemen*: Michael Cornell, Ernest Foederer, Kent A. Heacock, Ronald Kelly, Brian Michels, Brian Quirk, Christopher Sheperd, John Henry Thomas.

STREET SCENE

1990.08

A Revival of the American Opera (Dramatic Musical) in Two Acts, 3 Scenes[2]. Book by Elmer Rice from his play of the same name. Music by Kurt Weill. Lyrics by Langston Hughes. Production directed by Jack O'Brien, restaged by Jay Lesenger. Conducted by Chris Nance. Scenery designed by Paul Sylbert. Costumes designed by Marjorie McCown. Lighting by Gilbert V. Hemsley, Jr. Choreography by Patricia Birch. Chorus Master, Joseph Colaneri. (Orchestrations by Kurt Weill.) Produced by the New York City Opera. Opened 7 September 1990 at the New York State Theatre and closed 29 September 1990 after 6 performances in repertory.

CAST (in order of appearance): *Greta Fiorentino*: Rachel Rosales. *Emma Jones*: JOYCE CASTLE. *Olga Olsen*: Susanne Marsee. *Carl Olsen*: Robert Ferrier. *Neighborhood Woman*: Lisa Jablow. *Shirley Kaplan*: Elinor Basescù. *Abraham Kaplan*: David Rae Smith. *Salvation Army Girls*: Deborah Williams, Kathleen Smith. *Henry Davis*: Eugene Perry. *Willie Maurrant*: Keith Cacciola-Morales. *Anna Maurrant*: MARGARET CUSACK. *Sam Kaplan*: KEVIN P. ANDERSON. *Daniel Buchanan*: Peter Blanchet. *Mrs. Buchanan*: Lila Herbert. *Frank Maurrant*: WILLIAM PARCHER. *George Jones*: William Ledbetter. *Steve Sankey*: Richard Maynard. *Lippo Fiorentino*: JONATHAN GREEN. *Mrs. Hildebrand*: Jennifer Lane. *Jenny Hildebrand*: Robin Tabachnik. *Graduates*: Alexis Martin, Karla Simmons. *Charlie Hildebrand*: Derek Dreyer. *Mary Hildebrand*: Rachel Samberg. *Grace Davis*: Melissa Martin. *Rose Maurrant*: SHERYL WOODS. *Harry Easter*: HARLAN FOSS. *Mae Jones*: Jeanette Palmer. *Dick McGann*: John MacInnis. *Vincent Jones*: David Comstock. *Dr. Wilson*: Don Henderson. *Officer Murphy*: David Frye. *Milkman*: Ian D. Klapper. *Joan*: Allegra Victoria Forste. *Myrtle*: Francesca LaGuardia. *Workman*: Louis Perry. *Eddie*: Gregory Moore. *Sally*: Kelley Faulkner. *Joe*: Michael Cole. *Strawberry Seller*: Marty Singleton. *Corn Seller*: Rita Metzger. *James Henry*: Don Yule. *Fred Cullen*: Jonathan Guss. *Old Clothes Man*: Don Henderson. *Grocery Boy*: Kent A. Heacock. *Ambulance Driver*: Ronald Kelley. *Music Student*: Jane Cummins. *Intern*: John Henry Thomas. *Furniture Movers*: Glenn Rowen, Webster Latimer. *Nursemaids*: Lee Bellaver, Susan Ward. *Policemen*: Michael Putsch, Neil Eddinger. *Middle-Aged Couple*: Harris Davis, Rita Metzger.

[1]Originally produced in New York 25 February 1973 at the Sam S. Shubert Theatre for 601 performances. For Synopsis of Scenes and Musical Numbers, see original 1973 production.
[2]Originally produced in New York 9 January 1947 at the Adelphi Theatre for 148 performances. For Synopsis of Scenes and Musical Numbers, see original 1947 production.

MICHAEL FEINSTEIN IN CONCERT: PIANO AND VOICE

1990.09

A One Man Show in Two Acts[3]. Special material, Bruce Vilanch. Production staged and supervised by Christopher Chadman. Musical director, Ian Finkel. Lighting by David Agress. Sound designed by Daryl Bornstein. Johnny Mercer material arranged by Stan Freeman. Produced by Ron Delsener. Opened 2 October 1990 at the John Golden Theatre and closed 27 October 1990 after 30 performances.

CAST: MICHAEL FEINSTEIN[4].
Musicians: Ian Finkel (xylophone), David Fink (bass), Martin Fischer (drums), Bruce Uchitel (guitar).

ACT 1
"I Hear Bells" (from *LOVE MATCH*)
(*Music by* David Shire. *Lyrics by* Richard Maltby, Jr.)
"Manhattan" (from *GARRICK GAIETIES OF 1925*)
(*Music by* Richard Rodgers. *Lyrics by* Lorenz Hart.)
"Make Believe" (from *SHOWBOAT*)
(*Music by* Jerome Kern. *Lyrics by* Oscar Hammerstein II.)
"I Have Dreamed" (from *THE KING AND I*)
(*Music by* Richard Rodgers. *Lyrics by* Oscar Hammerstein II.)
"Sweet and Low Down" (from *TIP TOES*)
(*Music by* George Gershwin. *Lyrics by* Ira Gershwin.)
"The Man I Love"[5] (alternate lyric as "The Girl I Love")
(*Music by* George Gershwin. *Lyrics by* Ira Gershwin.)
"I'll Build a Stairway to Paradise" (from *GEORGE WHITE'S SCANDALS* 1922)
(*Music by* George Gershwin. *Lyrics by* B. G. DeSylva.)
"Sister Susie's Sewing Shirts for Soldiers"
(*Music by* Hermann Darewski. *Lyrics by* R. P. Weston.)
"Where Do You Start"
(*Music by* Johnny Mandel. *Lyrics by* Marilyn and Alan Bergman.)
"Let Me Love You"
(*Music and Lyrics by* Bart Howard.)
"Wait Till You See Her" (from *BY JUPITER*)
(*Music by* Richard Rodgers. *Lyrics by* Lorenz Hart.)
"The Most Beautiful Girl in the World" (from *JUMBO*)
(*Music by* Richard Rodgers. *Lyrics by* Lorenz Hart.)
"Lover" (from *LOVE ME TONIGHT* film)
(*Music by* Richard Rodgers. *Lyrics by* Lorenz Hart.)
BURTON LANE Medley:
"Babes on Broadway" (from *BABES ON BROADWAY* film)
(*Music by* Burton Lane. *Lyrics by* E. Y. Harburg, Ralph Freed.)
"How About You?" (from *BABES ON BROADWAY* film)
(*Music by* Burton Lane. *Lyrics by* E. Y. Harburg, Ralph Freed.)
"Anything Can Happen in New York" (from *BABES ON BROADWAY* film)
(*Music by* Burton Lane. *Lyrics by* E. Y. Harburg, Ralph Freed.)
"On a Clear Day You Can See Forever" (from show of same name)
(*Music by* Burton Lane. *Lyrics by* Alan Jay Lerner.)
"No One Is Alone" (from *INTO THE WOODS*)
(*Music and Lyrics by* Stephen Sondheim.)

ACT 2
"The Old Music Master" (from *TRUE TO LIFE* film)
(*Music by* Hoagy Carmichael. *Lyrics by* Johnny Mercer.)
Tin Pan Alley/Broadway Medley:
"Are You Havin' Any Fun?" (from *GEORGE WHITE'S SCANDALS* 1939)
(*Music by* Sammy Fain. *Lyrics by* Jack Yellen.)
"On the Sunny Side of the Street" (*LEW LESLIE'S INTERNATIONAL REVUE*)
(*Music by* Jimmy McHugh. *Lyrics by* Dorothy Fields.)

[3]Michael Feinstein appeared on Broadway in his previous one man shows:
MICHAEL FEINSTEIN IN CONCERT, 19 April 1988, Lyceum, 62.
MICHAEL FEINSTEIN IN CONCERT: ISN'T IT ROMANTIC?, 5 October 1988, Booth, 38.
[4]On opening night, composer Burton Lane joined the performance as a special guest star.
[5]Dropped from *LADY, BE GOOD*, *STRIKE UP THE BAND* and *ROSALIE*.

"The Best Things in Life Are Free" (from *GOOD NEWS*)
(*Music by* Ray Henderson. *Lyrics by* Buddy G. DeSylva, Lew Brown.)
"I Can't Give You Anything But Love" (from *BLACKBIRDS OF 1928*)
(*Music by* Jimmy McHugh. *Lyrics by* Dorothy Fields.)
"Love Will Find a Way" (from *SHUFFLE ALONG*)
(*Music by* Eubie Blake. *Lyrics by* Noble Sissle.)

"Whatever Happened to Melody?"
(*Music and Lyrics by* Cynthia Thompson, Ray Jessel and Bryn Celli Ddu.)

"Holiday for Strings"
(*Music by* David Rose. *Lyrics by* Sammy Gallop.)

"Rhode Island Is Famous for You" (from *INSIDE U.S.A.*)
(*Music by* Arthur Schwartz. *Lyrics by* Howard Dietz.)

"Killing Time"
(*Music by* Jule Styne. *Lyrics by* Carolyn Leigh)

"The Music That Makes Me Dance" (from *FUNNY GIRL*)
(*Music by* Jule Styne. *Lyrics by* Bob Merrill.)

Johnny Mercer Medley:
"Too Marvelous for Words" (from *READY, WILLING, AND ABLE* film)
(*Music by* Richard Whiting. *Lyrics by* Johnny Mercer.)
"Lazybones"
(*Music and Lyrics by* Johnny Mercer and Hoagy Carmicahael.)
"Hooray for Hollywood" (from *HOLLYWOOD HOTEL* film)
(*Music by* Richard Whiting. *Lyrics by* Johnny Mercer.)
"I'm Old-Fashioned" (from *YOU WERE NEVER LOVELIER* film)
(*Music by* Jerome Kern. *Lyrics by* Johnny Mercer.)
"The Girl Friend of the Whirling Dervish" (from *GARDEN OF THE MOON* film)
(*Music by* Harry Warren. *Lyrics by* Johnny Mercer.)
"Glow Worm"
(*Music by* Paul Lincke. *Lyrics by* Lilla Cayley Robinson, Johnny Mercer.)
"Satin Doll"
(*Music by* Billy Strayhorn and Duke Ellington. *Lyrics by* Johnny Mercer.)
"Laura" (from *LAURA* film)
(*Music by* David Raksin. *Lyrics by* Johnny Mercer.)
"Dream"
(*Music and Lyrics by* Johnny Mercer.)
"Come Rain or Come Shine" (from *ST. LOUIS WOMAN*)
(*Music by* Harold Arlen. *Lyrics by* Johnny Mercer.)

"Where Would I Be Without You"

"I Love a Piano" (from *STOP! LOOK! LISTEN!*)
(*Music and Lyrics by* Irving Berlin.)

1990.10 BUGS BUNNY ON BROADWAY

A Musical Revue in Two Acts. Created and conducted by George Daugherty. Music by Carl Stalling and Milt Franklyn, based upon the works of von Suppé, Rossini, Wagner, J. Strauss, Donizetti and Liszt. Animation directed by Chuck Jones, Friz Freleng, Robert McKimson, Robert Clampett. Voice characterizations by Mel Blanc and Arthur Q. Bryan. Scenic design by Michael Giaimo. Art direction by Darrel Van Citters. Lighting design by Bob Jared. Executive producer for the Nederlander Corporation, Peter H. Russell. Executive producer, Steven Goldberg. Produced by Warner Brothers, in association with Industrial FX Productions Inc. (Producer, George Daugherty.) Opened 4 October 1990 at the Gershwin Theatre and closed 7 October 1990 after 5 performances.

CAST: BUGS BUNNY, ELMER FUDD, PORKY PIG, DAFFY DUCK, Giovanni Jones, Granny, Baby Daffy Duck.

ACT 1

The Merrie Melodies Theme

The Ride of the Valkyries
(*Music by* Richard Wagner.)

Baton Bunny
(*Guest Conductor*: Bugs Bunny.)
(*Music by* Franz von Suppé. Based upon "Morning, Noon and Night in Vienna." Animation directed by Chuck Jones.)

Excerpt from "What's Up, Doc?"
(*Animation directed by* Robert McKimson. *Musical Direction by* Carl W. Stalling.)

Hungarian Rhapsody No. 2
(*Music by* Franz Liszt.)

High Note
(*Original score by* Milt Franklyn after Johann Strauss. Based upon "The Blue Danube." *Animation directed by* Chuck Jones.)

A Salute to Carl Stalling
(*Music by* Carl W. Stalling. Score from "Jumping Jupiter.")

The Rabbit of Seville
Bugs Bunny, Elmer Fudd
(*Music by* Gioacchino Rossini, arranged by Milt Franklyn. Based upon "The Barber of Seville" Overture. *Animation directed by* Chuck Jones. *Voice characterization by* Mel Blanc and Arthur Q. Bryan.)

ACT 2

Excerpt from "This Is a Life?"
Bugs Bunny, Daffy Duck, Elmer Fudd, Granny
(*Music by* Milt Franklyn. *Animation Direction by* Friz Freleng. *Voice characterization by* Mel Blanc.)

A Corny Concerto
Bugs Bunny, Porky Pig, Baby Daffy Duck
(*Music by* Carl W. Stalling. Based upon "Tales of the Vienna Woods" and "The Blue Danube" by Johann Strauss. *Animation Direction by* Robert Clampett.)

Morning, Noon and Night in Vienna

Rhapsody Rabbit
Bugs Bunny
(*Music by* Franz Liszt. Based on the Second Hungarian Rhapsody. Music originally arranged by Carl W. Stalling. *Animation Direction by* Friz Freleng. *Voice characterization by* Mel Blanc.)

Long-Haired Hare
Bugs Bunny, Giovanni Jones
(*Original Score by* Carl W. Stalling, after Wagner, Donizetti and Rossini. *Animation Directed by* Chuck Jones. *Voice characterization by* Mel Blanc.)

What's Opera, Doc?
Bugs Bunny, Elmer Fudd
(*Music by* Richard Wagner, arranged by Milt Franklyn. Based upon music from "The Flying Dutchman," "Die Walküre," Siegfreid" and "Tannhauser." *Directed by* Chuck Jones. *Voice characterizations by* Mel Blanc and Arthur Q. Bryan.)

1990.11 JACKIE MASON: BRAND NEW

A One Man Comedy Revue in Two Acts[6]. Production design and lighting by Neil Peter Jampolis. Sound design by Bruce Cameron. Opening sequence directed by David Niles. Executive producer, Jyll Rosenfeld. Produced by Old Friends Group (Michael Simoff, Eric P. Aschenberg). Opened 17 October 1990 at the Neil Simon Theatre and closed 30 June 1991 after 216 performances.

CAST: JACKIE MASON (stand-up comedy, monologues, impressions).

1990.12 ONCE ON THIS ISLAND

A Musical in One Act[7]. Book and lyrics by Lynn Ahrens. Based on the novel "My Love, My Love" by Rosa Guy. Music by Stephen Flaherty. Directed and choreographed by Graciela Daniele. Set by Loy Arcenas. Costumes by Judy Dearing. Lighting by Allen Lee Hughes. Sound by Scott Lehrer. Orchestrations by Michael Starobin. Musical director, Steve Marzullo. Associate choreographer, Willie Rosario. Vocal and dance arrangements, musical continuity by Stephen Flaherty. Percussion concepts, Norbert Goldberg. Produced by The Shubert Organization, Capital Cities/ABC Inc., Suntory International Corporation, and James Walsh in association with Playwrights Horizons. Opened 18 October 1990 at the Booth Theatre and closed 1 December 1991 after 469 performances.

CAST (in alphabetical order): *The Storytellers*: *Daniel*: JERRY DIXON. *Erzulie*, Goddess of Love: Andrea Frierson. *Mama Euralie*: Sheila Gibbs. *Ti Moune*: LaCHANZE. *Asaka*, Mother of the Earth: Kecia Lewis-Evans. *Little Ti Moune*: Afi

---

[6]Previously produced Off-Broadway 27 January 1990 at the Public Theatre for 18 performances, and 5 May 1990 for 12 additional performances. Previous editions of Jackie Mason's one man show have been presented 22 December 1986 at the Brooks Atkinson Theatre for 367 performances; 3 May 1988 at the Brooks Atkinson for 203 performances.

[7]Originally produced Off-Broadway 6 May 1990 at Playwrights Horizons for 60 performances.

McClendon. *Armand*: Gerry McIntyre. *Agwe*, God of Water: Milton Craig Nealy. *Andrea*: Nikki Rene. *Papa Ge*: Demon of Death: Eric Riley. *Tonton Julian*: Ellis E. Williams.

The action takes takes place on an island in the French Antilles at night, in a storm.

MUSICAL NUMBERS
"We Dance"
Storytellers
"One Small Girl"
S. Gibbs, E. E. Williams, A. McClendon, Storytellers
"Waiting for Life"
La Chanze, Storytellers
"And the Gods Heard Her Prayer"
K. Lewis-Evans, M. C. Nealy, E. Riley, A. Frierson
"Rain"
M. C. Nealy, Storytellers
"Pray"
La Chanze, E. E. Williams, S. Gibbs, Guard, Storytellers
"Forever Yours"
La Chanze, J. Dixon, E. Riley
"The Sad Tale of the Beauxhommes"
G. McIntyre, Storytellers
"Ti Moune"
S. Gibbs, E. E. Williams, La Chanze
"Mama Will Provide"
K. Lewis-Evans, Storytellers
"Waiting for Life" (reprise)
La Chanze
"Some Say"
Storytellers
"The Human Heart"
A. Frierson, Storytellers
"Pray" (reprise)
Storytellers
"Some Girls"
J. Dixon
"The Ball"
N. Rene, J. Dixon, La Chanze, Storytellers
"Forever Yours" (reprise)
E. Riley, La Chanze, A. Frierson, Storytellers
"A Part of Us"
S. Gibbs, A. McClendon, E. E. Williams, Storytellers
"Why We Tell the Story"
Storytellers

1990.13

THE MIKADO, or The Town of Titipu

A Revival of the Comic Opera in Two Acts[8]. Libretto by William S. Gilbert. Music by Arthur Sullivan. Production (direction), Lofti Mansouri. Conductor, Chris Nance. Stage director, David Pfeiffer. Set and costume designer, Thierry Bosquet. Lighting designer, John Gleason. Choreographer, Patricia Birch. Chorus master, Joseph Colaneri. Produced by the New York City Opera. Opened 20 October 1990 at the New York State Theatre and closed 9 November 1990 after 5 performances in repertory.

CAST (in order of appearance): *Nanki-Poo*: CARROLL FREEMAN. *Pish-Tush*: WILLIAM PARCHER. *Pooh-Bah*: JOSEPH McKEE. *Ko-Ko*: JAMES BILLINGS. *Yum-Yum*: LISA SAFFER. *Pitti-Sing*: BRONWYN THOMAS. *Peep-Bo*: MICHELE MCBRIDE. *Katisha*: JOSEPH GAYER. *The Mikado of Japan*: RICHARD McKEE. *Chorus of School Girls, Nobles, Guards and Coolies*: New York City Opera Chorus.

[8]First presented in New York 20 July, 10-29 August 1885 at the Union Square and People's Theatres for 22 performances. First authorized production presented 19 August 1885 at the Fifth Avenue Theatre by Richard D'Oyly Carte for 250 performances. For Synopsis of Scenes and Musical Numbers, see 19 August 1885 D'Oyly Carte production.

1990.14

OH, KAY!

A Revival of the Musical Comedy in Two Acts, 8 Scenes[9]. Book by Guy Bolton and P. G. Wodehouse, adaptation by James Racheff. Concept, direction and choreography by Dan Siretta. Musical direction, vocal and additional dance arrangements by Tom Fay. Orchestrations by Arnold Goland. Dance arrangements by Donald Johnston. Scenic design by Kenneth Foy. Costume design by Theoni V. Aldredge. Lighting design by Craig Miller. Sound by Jan Nebozenko. Associate producer, Leo K. Cohen. Executive producer, Natalie Lloyd. Inspired by the Goodspeed Opera House (East Haddam, Connecticut) and Birmingham (Michigan) productions. Produced by David Merrick. Opened 1 November 1990 at the Richard Rodgers Theatre and closed 5 January 1991 after 77 performances. (Reopened 2-16 April 1991 at the Lunt-Fontanne Theatre with a revised cast for 16 additional previews, but closed before its scheduled re-opening[10].)

CAST (in order of appearance): *Billy Lyles*: GREGG BURGE. *Dolly Greene*: Kyme. *Duke*: Stanley Wayne Mathis. *Nick*: David Preston Sharpe. *Joe*: Fracaswell Hyman. *Waiter, Jake*: Frantz Hall. *Larry Potter*: Kevin Ramsey. *Shorty*: HELMAR AUGUSTUS COOPER. *Sam*: David Preston Sharpe. *B.J.*: Keith Robert Bennett. *Floyd*: Frederick J. Boothe. *Zeke*: Ken Roberson. *Jimmy Winter*: BRIAN MITCHELL. *Constance DuGrasse*: Tamara Tunie Bouquett. *Chauffeur*: Byron Easley. *Kay Jones*: ANGELA TEEK. *Janson*: Mark Kenneth Smaltz. *Reverend Alphonse DuGrasse*: Alexander Barton. *Duo Pianists*: Donald Johnston, Robert Colston.

Ensemble: Keith Robert Bennett, Jacquelyn Bird, Frederick J. Boothe, Cheryl Burr, Byron Easley, Robert H. Fowler, Karen E. Fraction, Frantz Hall, Garry Q. Lewis, Greta Martin, Sharon Moore, Elise Neal, Ken Roberson, David Preston Sharp, Allyson Tucker, Mona Wyatt.

The action takes place in Harlem in 1926.

Act 1, Scene 1: Onstage at the Paradise Club. *Scene 2*: Backstage at the Paradise Club. *Scene 3*: Jimmy Winter's townhouse, late that night. *Scene 4*: Jimmy Winter's townhouse, the next morning.

Act 2, Scene 1: Jimmy's Terrace, that afternoon. *Scene 2*: Onstage at the Paradise Club. *Scene 3*: Backstage at the Paradise Club. *Scene 4*: Onstage at the Paradise Club.

ACT 1
Scene 1
"Slap That Bass" (from *SHALL WE DANCE* film)
G. Burge, Kyme, Ensemble
Scene 3
"When Our Ship Comes Sailing In"[11]
S. W. Mathis, H. A. Cooper, Male Ensemble
"Dear Little Girl"
B. Mitchell, H. A. Cooper
"Maybe"
B. Mitchell, A. Teek
Scene 4
"You've Got What Gets Me" (from *GIRL CRAZY* film)
G. Burge, Kyme
"Do, Do, Do"
B. Mitchell, A. Teek
"Clap Yo' Hands"
K. Ramsey, Ensemble

[9]Originally produced in New York 8 November 1926 at the Imperial Theater for 256 performances.

[10]For revised version, the creative credits remained the same, except that the set design was uncredited. The new cast appears below with cast changes marked with an *. The roles of Duke, Joe, Waiter, Jake, Sam, Floyd were eliminated.

CAST (in order of appearance): *Billy Lyles*: GREGG BURGE. *Dolly Greene*: Kyme. *Kay Jones*: RAE DAWN CHONG*. *Nick*: David Preston Sharpe. *Zeke*: Ken Roberson. *Larry Potter*: Kevin Ramsey. *Shorty*: HELMAR AUGUSTUS COOPER. *B.J.*: Keith Robert Bennett. *Jimmy Winter*: RON RICHARDSON*. *Constance DuGrasse*: Natalie Oliver*. *Chauffeur*: Byron Easley. *Janson*: Mark Kenneth Smaltz. *Reverend Alphonse DuGrasse*: Alexander Barton. *Duo Pianists*: David Evans*, Robert Colston.

Ensemble: added were Frederick J. Boothe (previously in a featured role), Melissa Haizlip, Sara Beth Lane, Ken Leigh Rogers; dropped was Mona Wyatt.

Added to Act 2, Scene 1, after "Fidgety Feet":
"Ask Me Again" (reprise)
R. Richardson

[11]Dropped from original 1926 production.

ACT 2
Scene 1
"Oh, Kay!"
G. Burge, A. Teek, Ensemble
(*Lyrics by* Ira Gershwin and Howard Dietz.)
"Ask Me Again" (interpolation)
A. Teek
"Fidgety Feet"
S. W. Mathis, Ensemble
"Someone to Watch Over Me"
A. Teek
Scene 2
"Heaven on Earth"
K. Ramsey, S. W. Mathis, G. Burge
(*Lyrics by* Ira Gershwin and Howard Dietz.)
Scene 4
"Show Me the Town"[12]
"Sleepless Nights"
A. Teek, G. Burge, Kyme, K. Ramsey, Ensemble
"Someone to Watch Over Me" (reprise)
B. Mitchell, A. Teek

1990.15 BUDDY: THE BUDDY HOLLY STORY

A Musical in Two Acts. Based on the life and career of Buddy Holly. (Book) Written by Alan Janes, from an idea by Laurie Mansfield. (Music and lyrics by Buddy Holly and various writers.) Directed by Rob Bettinson. (Set) Designed by Andy Walmsley. Costumes by Bill Butler, Carolyn Smith. Lighting by Graham McLusky. Musical director, Paul Jury. Musical consultant, Bruce Welch. Sound by Rick Price. All jingles composed by Paul Jury. Executive producer, Brian Sewell. Associate producer, Contracts International, Ltd. Produced by Paul Elliott, Laurie Mansfield and Greg Smith (for International Artistes), David Mirvish. Opened 4 November 1990 at the Sam S. Shubert Theatre and closed 19 May 1991 after 225 performances.

CAST (in order of appearance): *Act 1*: *Hipockets Duncan*: Fred Sanders. *Jingle Singers*: Jo Lynn Burks, Caren Cole, Liliane Stilwell. *The Hayriders*: Melanie Doane, Kevin Fox, Tom Nash, Steve Steiner, Don Stitt. *Engineer (KDAV)*: Philip Anthony. *Buddy Holly*: PAUL HIPP. *Joe B. Mauldin*: Bobby Prochaska. *Jerry Allison*: Russ Jolly. *Boppers and Autograph Hunters*: Jill Hennessy, Paul McQuillan, Ken Triwush. *Decca Session Musicians*: Kevin Fox, Tom Nash, Ken Triwush, Steve Steiner. *Decca Producer*: David Mucci. *Decca Engineers*: Paul McQuillan, Don Stitt. *Norman Petty*: Kurt Ziskie. *Vi Petty*: Jo Lynn Burks. *Fourth Cricket*: Ken Triwush. *DJ (WCLS)*: David Mucci. *DJ (WWOL)*: Philip Anthony. *DJ (WDAS)*: Demo Cates. *DJ (KPST)*: Don Stitt. *Candy*: Melanie Doane. *Couples in Woods*: Jo Lynn Burks, Caren Cole, Kevin Fox, Jill Hennessy, Liliane Stilwell, Ken Triwush. *Apollo Singers*: Sandra Caldwell, Denese Matthews, Lorraine Scott. *Musicians at Apollo*: Demo Cates, Alvin Crawford, Jerome Smith, Jr., James H., Wiggins, Jr. *Performer at Apollo*: Jerome Smith, Jr. *DJ at Apollo*: Don Stitt. *Man at Apollo*: Demo Cates.

Act 2: *Jingle Singers, WWOL*: Sandra Caldwell, Denese Matthews, Lorraine Scott. *Maria Elena*: Jill Hennessy. *Murray Deutch*: Steve Steiner. *Shirley*: Caren Cole. *Maria Elena's Aunt*: Liliane Stilwell. *English DJ*: Paul McQuillan. *Photographers*: Members of the Company. *Peggy Sue*: Melanie Doane. *DJ (KRWP)*: Kurt Ziskie. *Clearlake MC*: Don Stitt. *The Big Bopper*: David Mucci. *Dion*: Paul McQuillan. *The Belmonts*: Russ Jolly, Tom Nash. *Richie Valens*: Philip Anthony. *Tommy*: Ken Triwush. *Mary Lou Sokoloff*: Caren Cole. *Jack Daw*: Steve Steiner. *The Snowbirds*: Jo Lynn Burks, Caren Cole, Melanie Doane, Jill Hennessy, Liliane Stilwell. *Band and Back-Up Singers at Clearlake*: Members of the Company.

The action covers the life of Buddy Holly with a re-creation of his last concert in Clear Lake, Iowa on 2 February 1959.

ACT 1[13]
"Texas Rose"
(*Music and Lyrics by* Paul Jury.)
"Flower of My Heart"
(*Music and Lyrics by* Paul Jury.)
"Ready Teddy"
(*Music and Lyrics by* John Marascolo and Robert Blackwell.)
"That's All Right"
(*Music and Lyrics by* Arthur Crudup.)
"That'll Be the Day"
(*Music and Lyrics by* Jerry Allison, Buddy Holly, Norman Petty.)
"Blue Days, Black Nights"
(*Music and Lyrics by* Ben Hall.)
"Changing All These Changes"
(*Music and Lyrics by* J. Denny.)
"Peggy Sue"
(*Music and Lyrics by* Jerry Allison, Buddy Holly, Norman Petty.)
"(I'm) Looking for Someone to Love"
(*Music and Lyrics by* Buddy Holly, Norman Petty.)
"Mailman Bring Me No More Blues"
(*Music and Lyrics by* Ruth Roberts, Bill Klatz, Stanley Clayton.)
"Maybe Baby"
(*Music and Lyrics by* Buddy Holly, Norman Petty.)
"Everyday"
(*Music and Lyrics by* Charles Hardin, Norman Petty.)
"Sweet Love"
(*Music and Lyrics by* Paul Jury and Caren Cole.)
"You Send Me"
(*Music and Lyrics by* Sam Cooke.)
"Not Fade Away"
(*Music and Lyrics by* Charles Hardin and Norman Petty.)
"Words of Love"
(*Music and Lyrics by* Buddy Holly.)
"Oh Boy"
(*Music and Lyrics by* Norman Petty, Sonny West, Bill Tilghman.)
ACT 2
"Listen to Me"
(*Music and Lyrics by* Charles Hardin and Norman Petty.)
"Well All Right"
(*Music and Lyrics by* Jerry Allison, Buddy Holly, Norman Petty, Joe Maudlin.)
"It's So Easy to Fall in Love"
(*Music and Lyrics by* Buddy Holly, Norman Petty.)
"Think It Over"
(*Music and Lyrics by* Jerry Allison, Buddy Holly, Norman Petty.)
"True Love Ways"
(*Music and Lyrics by* Buddy Holly, Norman Petty.)
"Why Do Fools Fall in Love"
(*Music and Lyrics by* Frank Lymon, Morris Levy.)
"Chantilly Lace"
(*Music and Lyrics by* J. P. Richardson.)
"Peggy Sue Got Married"
(*Music and Lyrics by* Buddy Holly.)
"Heartbeat"
(*Music and Lyrics by* Bob Montgomery, Norman Petty.)
"La Bamba"
(*Traditional, adapted by* Richie Valens.)
"Raining in My Heart"
(*Music and Lyrics by* Felice and Boudleaux Bryant.)
"It Doesn't Matter Anymore"
(*Music and Lyrics by* Paul Anka.)
"Rave On"
(*Music and Lyrics by* Norman Petty, Bill Tilghman, Sonny West.)
"Johnny B. Goode"
(*Music and Lyrics by* Chuck Berry.)

1990.16 THOSE WERE THE DAYS

An English-Yiddish Musical Revue in Two Acts. Concept and continuity by Zalmen Mlotek, Moishe Rosenfeld. (Music and lyrics by M. Warshavsky, M. Gebirtig, A. Lebedeff, Itsik Manger, W. Younin, J. Rumshinsky, Mani Lieb, Gene Raskin, Mel Tolkin, Ben Bonus, Ben Yomen, Hymie Jacobson, Chana Mlotek, Gioacchino Rossini, R. Abelson, M. Rosenfeld, Jack Yellen, Lew Pollack, Jacob Jacobs, Sholom Secunda, Sammy Cahn, Saul Chaplin, Bella Meisel, Herman Yablokoff, Nellie Cashman, Samuel Steinberg. Scenes by I. L. Peretz, Sholom Aleichem, and others. Additional material by Ernesto Lecuona, Jacques Offenbach, Miriam Makeba, Frank Loesser, Manos

[12]Dropped from original 1926 production, restored here for the first time.
[13]Publishers, not authors or vocalists, listed in the program.

Hadjidakis, Billy Towne, Bruce Adler, Robert Abelson, Mina Bern, Eleanor Reissa.) Directed and choreographed by Eleanor Reissa. Musical director, Zalmen Mlotek. Costumes by Gail Cooper-Hecht. Lighting by Tom Sturge. Sound by Jim Badrak, Alan Gregorie. Produced by Moe Septee in association with Victor H. Potamkin, Zalmen Mlotek, Moishe Rosenfeld. Opened 7 November 1990 at the Edison Theatre and closed 24 February 1991 after 126 performances.

CAST: BRUCE ADLER, MINA BERN, ELEANOR REISSA, ROBERT ABELSON, LORI WILNER, The Golden Land Klezmer Orchestra.

Act 1: The Shtetl.

Act 2: The Music Hall.

ACT 1

Prologue—Nigunim (melodies)
Company
"Lomir Loybn" (Let Us Praise)(folksong)
"Sha Shtil" (The Rabbi's Coming)(folksong)

"Oyfn Pripetshik" (At the Fireplace)
B. Adler
(*Music and Lyrics by* M. Warshavsky.)

On a Moonlit Night (based on a story by I. L. Peretz)
E. Reissa, L. Wilner

"Ver Der Ershter Vet Lahkn" (Who Will Laugh First?)
E. Reissa, L. Wilner
(*Music and Lyrics by* M. Gebirtig.)

"Motele"
R. Abelson, E. Reissa
(*Music and Lyrics by* M. Gebirtig.)

"Hudl Mitn Shtrudl" (Hudl with the Shtrudl)
B. Adler
(*Music and Lyrics by* A. Lebedeff.)

Kasrilevke Restoran (A Restaurant in Kasrilevke)
B. Adler, R. Abelson, M. Bern
(Based on a story by Sholom Aleichem)

"Di Dinst" (The Maid)(folksong)
E. Reissa

Shalakh-Mones (Gifts for Purim)
E. Reissa, L. Wilner
(Based on a story by Sholom Aleichem)

"Yosl Ber"
B. Adler, L. Wilner, E. Reissa
(*Music*, Folk-melody. *Lyrics by* Itsik Manger.)

"Halevay Volt Ikh Singl Geven" (I Wish I Were Single Again)
R. Abelson, M. Bern
(American folksong adapted by W. Younin.)

"Shloymele-Malkele"
L. Wilner, B. Adler
(Music by J. Rumshinsky.)

"Mamenyu Tayere" (Dear Mama)
L. Wilner, M. Bern
(*Music*, Folk-melody. *Lyrics by* Mani Leib, from the repertoire of Menashe Oppenheim.)

"Nokhumke, Mayn Zun" (Nochum, My Son)(folksong)
R. Abelson, B. Adler

"Saposhkelekh" (The Boots)
E. Reissa
(*Folksong*, from the research of Michael Alpert.)

"The Wedding"
Company

"Khosn-Kale mazl-Tov" (Congratulations to the Bride and Groom) (folksong)

"Di Rod" (The Circle)
(*Music and Lyrics by* M. Warshavsky.)

"Der Ayznban" (The Train) (folksong)

"Yoshke Fort Avek" (Yoshke's Going Away) (folksong)

"Mayn Alte Heym"
(from the "Forbidden Songs" of Soviet Jews as recorded by David Eshet)

ACT 2

"Those Were the Days"
E. Reissa, R. Abelson
(*Music and Lyrics by* Gene Raskin.)

Shpil Gitar (Play Guitar)
L. Wilner

"The Palace of the Czar"
B. Adler
(*Music and Lyrics by* Mel Tonkin.)

"Shabes, Shabes, Shabes" (Welcoming the Sabbath)
M. Bern
(*Music by* Ben Yomen. *Lyrics by* Ben Bonus.)

Chelm
Company

"Litvak/Galitsyaner"
B. Adler, E. Reissa
(*Music and Lyrics by* Hymie Jacobson.)

Di Mame (The Mother)
M. Bern

"Yiddish International Radio Hour"
Company
(*Yiddish Lyrics by* Chana Mlotek.)

"Figaro's Aria" (from The Barber of Seville)
R. Abelson
(*Music by* Giaocchino Rossini. *Yiddish Lyrics by* Ron Abelson, Moishe Rosenfeld.)

"My Yiddishe Mame"
E. Reissa
(*Music by* Lew Pollack. *Lyrics by* Jack Yellen.)

"Hootsatsa"
B. Adler
(Based on a song by Fishl Kanapoff.)

"Bei Mir Bistu Schoen" (To Me, You're Beautiful)
E. Reissa, L. Wilner, B. Adler
(*Music by* Sholom Secunda. *Yiddish Lyrics by* Jacob Jacobs. *English Adaptation by* Sammy Cahn, Saul Chaplin.)

"In an Orem Shtibele" (In a Poor Little House)(folksong)
M. Bern

"A Khanzndl Oyf Shabes" (A Cantor for the Sabbath)(folksong)
R. Abelson

"Papirosn" (Cigarettes)
L. Wilner
(*Music and Lyrics by* Bella Meisel, Herman Yablokoff.)

"Yosl, Yosl"
E. Reissa
(*Music by* Samuel Steinberg. *Lyrics by* Nellie Cashman.)

"Rumania, Rumania"
B. Adler
(*Music and Lyrics by* A. Lebedeff, Sholom Secunda.)

"Those Were the Days" (Finale)
Company

1990.17

SHOGUN: THE MUSICAL

A Musical in Two Acts. Book and lyrics by John Driver. Based on the novel "Shogun" by James Clavell. Music by Paul Chihara. Directed and choreographed by Michael Smuin. Scenery designed by Loren Sherman. Costumes designed by Patricia Zipprodt. Lighting designed by Natasha Katz. Sound by Tony Meola. Orchestrations by David Cullen, Steven Margoshes. Musical director, Edward G. Robinson. Fight instructor, Masahiro Kunii. Co-choreographer, Kirk Peterson. Assistant director, J. Steven White. Production supervision, Jeremiah J. Harris. Co-producers, Hiroshi Sugawara, Lloyd Phillips. Produced by James Clavell, Joseph Harris, Haruki Kadokawa. Opened 20 November 1990 at the Marquis Theater and closed 20 January 1991 after 72 performances.

CAST (in order of appearance): *John Blackthornean* English sea captain of the *Erasmus*: PHILIP CASNOFF. *The Crew of the Erasmus* (3): *Roper*: Ron Navarre. *Pieterzoon*: Lee Lobenhofer. *Sonk*: Terry Lehmkuhl. *Father Alvito*, a Portuguese priest: John Herrera. *Lord Buntaro*, Daimyo of Anjiro Province, married to Lady Mariko: Joseph Foronda. *Omi*, a Samurai in love with Kiku: Eric Chan. *A Captured Samurai*: Tito Abeleda. *Gyoko*, Madam of the Tea House, owner of Kiku's contract: Freda Foh Shen. *Kiku*, courtesan of the first class: JoAnn M. Hunter. *First Samurai Guard*: Darren Lee. *Second Samurai Guard*: Marc Oka. *Third Samurai Guard*: Owen Johnston. *Lord Toranaga*, Overlord of Central Province, second most powerful Daimyo in Japan, member of Council of Regents: FRANCIS RUIVIVAR. *Sazuko*, Toranaga's youngest consort: Jenny Woo. *Osagi*, son of Lord Toranaga: Jason Ma. *Lady Mariko* educated by

the Jesuits, married to Lord Buntaro: JUNE ANGELA. *Captain General Ferriera,* Portuguese Captain of the Black Ship: Lee Lobenhofer. *The Courtier of Osaka*: Darren Lee. *Catholic Daimyos*: Cholsu Kim, Marc Oka, Kenji Nakao. *Lord Ishido,* the most powerful Daimyo in Japan: Alan Muraoka. *A Ninja*: Andrew Pacho. *Fujiko,* widow of Osagi, consort to Blackthorne: Leslie Ishii. *Ishido's Head Samurai*: Tito Abeleda. *Osaka Guards*: Kenji Nakao, Andrew Pacho. *Ishido's General,* Challenger to Omi at river crossing: Jason Ma. *Chimmoko,* maid to Lady Mariko: Kiki Moritsugu. *An Acolyte*: Jason Ma. *Slatterns of the Hovel*: Tina Horii, Linda Igarashi, Chi-En Telemaque. *The Red Guards of Osaka Castle*: Marc Oka, Alan Ariano. *Ninja Attackers*: Cheri Nakamura, Andrew Pacho, Darren Lee, Owen Johnston, Tito Abeleda, Jason Ma, Terry Lehmkuhl, Cholsu Kim, Ron Navarre. *Taiko Drummers*: Jason Ma, Marc Oka, Leslie Ishii, Lee Lobenhofer.

Swings and Other Dancers: Ted Hewlett, Herman Sebek, Victoria Lee, Lyd-Lyd Gaston.

The action takes place in Japan between April and July 1600.

ACT 1

"Karma"
Orchestra

"Night of Screams"
P. Casnoff, Sailor, Ensemble

"This Is Samurai"
Samurai

"How Nice to See You"
F. Ruivivar, J. Foronda, J. Herrera, J. Angela

"Impossible Eyes"
J. Angela, P. Casnoff

"He Let Me Live"
J. Angela

"Honto"
P. Casnoff

"Assassination"
J. Herrera, L. Lobenhofer

"Shogun"
Hostages

"Royal Blood"
A. Muraoka, F. Ruivivar

"An Island"
F. Ruivivar

"No Word for Love"
J. Angela

"Mad Rum Below/Escape"
P. Casnoff, Ensemble

"Karma" (reprise)
F. Ruivivar, Ensemble

"Born to Be Together"
J. Angela, P. Casnoff

ACT 2

"Fireflies"
Ensemble, J. Angela, P. Casnoff

"Sail Home"
P. Casnoff

"Rum Below"
P. Casnoff, F. Ruivivar, Ensemble

"Pillowing"
F. Foh Shen, J. M. Hunter, Ladies

"Born to Be Together" (reprise)
J. Angela, P. Casnoff

"No Man"
P. Casnoff

"Cha-No-Yu"
J. Angela, J. Foronda

"Absolution"
J. Herrera, J. Ma, Ensemble, J. Angela

"Poetry Competition"
A. Muraoka, J. Woo, J. Angela

"Death Walk"
Ensemble, P. Casnoff

"One Candle"
J. Angela, P. Casnoff

"Ninja Raid"
Orchestra

"One Candle" (reprise)
J. Angela, P. Casnoff

"Winter Battle"
Orchestra

"Resolutions"
F. Ruivivar, Ensemble

"Trio"
F. Ruivivar, P. Casnoff, J. Angela

Finale
Ensemble

1990.18 FIDDLER ON THE ROOF

A Revival of the Musical in Two Acts, Two Prologues, an Epilogue and 17 Scenes[14]. Book by Joseph Stein. Based on stories by Sholom Aleichem's stories (Tevye's Daughters) by special permission of Arnold Perl. Music by Jerry Bock. Lyrics by Sheldon Harnick. Original production directed and choreographed by Jerome Robbins. Direction reproduced by Ruth Mitchell. Choreography reproduced by Sammy Dallas Bayes. Scenery by Boris Aronson. Costumes based on original designs by Patricia Zipprodt. Lighting by Ken Billington. Sound by Peter Fitzgerald. Orchestrations by Don Walker. Musical direction, vocal arrangements by Milton Greene. Associate producer, Alecia Parker. Produced by Barry and Fran Weissler and Pace Theatrical Group, in association with C. Itoh & Co., Ltd./Tokyo Broadcasting System International, Inc., A. Deshe (Pashanel). Opened 18 November 1990 at the Gershwin Theatre and closed 16 June 1991 after 241 performances.

CAST (in order of appearance): *Tevye,* the Dairyman: TOPOL. *Golde,* his wife: MARCIA LEWIS. *Their Three Daughters*: *Tzeitel*: Sharon Lawrence. *Hodel*: Tia Riebling. *Chava*: Jennifer Prescott. *Shprintze*: Kathy St. George. *Beilke*: Judy Dodd. *Motel,* the Tailor: Jack Kenny. *Perchik,* the Student: Gary Schwartz. *Fyedka*: Ron Bohmer. *Lazar Wolf,* the Butcher: Mark Zeller. *Mordcha,* the Innkeeper: David Masters. *Nachum,* the Beggar: Michael J. Farina. *Yente,* the Matchmaker: RUTH JAROSLOW. *Rabbi*: Jerry Matz. *Avram,* the Bookseller: Jerry Jarrett. *Constable*: Mike O'Carroll. *Mendel,* the Rabbi's son: David Pevsner. *The Fiddler*: Stephen Wright. *Grandma Tzeitel*: Kathy St. George. *Fruma-Sarah*: Jeri Sager. *Shandel,* Motel's Mother: Panchali Null. *Bottle Dancers*: Kenneth M. Daigle, David Enriquez, Craig Gahnz, Keith Keen. *Russian Dancers*: Brian Arsenault, Michael Berresse, Brian Henry.

Villagers: Brian Arsenault, Michael Berresse, Joanne Borts, Stacey Lynn Brass, Gerry Burkhardt, Lisa Cartmell, Kenneth M. Daigle, David Enriquez, Craig Gahnz, Brian Henry, Todd Heughens, Keith Keen, Brad Little, Panchali Null, Marty Ross, Jeri Sager, Beth Thompson, Jeffrey Wilkins, Lou Williford. *Alternate Villagers*: James Horvath, Lori Ada Jaroslow, Laura Patinkin, Gary John La Rosa. *Swings*: Chris Jamison, Newton Cole.

1990.19 AN EVENING WITH HARRY CONNICK JR. AND HIS ORCHESTRA

A One Man Musical Revue in Two Acts. Directed by Joe Layton. Conductor, Marc Shaiman. Musical director, Benjamin Jonah Wolfe. Scenery design by John Falabella. Lighting designer, Marilyn Lowey. Wardrobe by Alexander Julian. Executive producer, Ann Marie Wilkins. Presented by Radio City Music Hall Productions (Ed Micone, Scott Sanders, producers) and James L. Nederlander. Opened 23 November 1990 at the Lunt-Fontanne Theatre and closed 8 December 1990 after 13 performances[15].

CAST: HARRY CONNICK JR.

Musicians: Marc Shaiman (conductor), Benjamin Jonah Wolfe (bass), Shannon Powell (drums), Leroy Jones (trumpet), Jerry Weldon (tenor saxophone), Lucien Barbarin (trombone), Russell Malone (guitar), Craig Klein (trombone), Mark Mullins (trombone), Jeremy Davenport (trumpet), Roger Ingram (trumpet), Dan Miller (trumpet), Ned Goold (tenor saxophone), Brad Leali (alto saxophone), William Campbell (alto saxophone), Dave Schumacher (baritone saxophone).

[14]Originally produced in New York 22 September 1964 at the Imperial Theatre for 3242 performances. For Synopsis of Scenes and Musical Numbers, see original 1964 production. "Chavaleh" appears in the program for this revival.

[15]Musical numbers not listed in program.

1990.20

PETER PAN

A Revival of the Musical in Three Acts, Seven Scenes[16]. Book by James M. Barrie[17]. Music by Mark Charlap. Lyrics by Carolyn Leigh. Additional music by Jule Styne. Additional lyrics by Betty Comden and Adolph Green. Original production conceived, directed and choreographed by Jerome Robbins. Directed by Fran Soeder. Choreographed by Marilyn Magness. Neverland sets by James Leonard Joy; (original scenery by The Edgewood Organization). Costumes designed by Mariann Verheyen. Lighting designed by Natasha Katz. Musical supervision and direction by Kevin Farrell. New orchestrations by Brian W. Tidwell. Additional (music) arrangements by M. Michael Fauss, Kevin Farrell. Sound designed by Peter Fitzgerald. Flying by Foy. A McCoy-Rigby Entertainment Production. Produced by James M. Nederlander, Arthur Rubin, Thomas P. McCoy, Keith Stava, P.P. Investments, Jon B. Platt. Opened 13 December 1990 at the Lunt-Fontanne Theatre and closed 20 January 1991 after 45 performances.

CAST (in order of appearance): *Wendy Darling*: CINDY ROBINSON. *John Darling*: BRITT WEST. *Michael Darling*: CHAD HUTCHISON. *Liza*: Anne McVey. *Nana*: Bill Bateman. *Mrs. Darling*: LAUREN THOMPSON. *Mr. Darling*: STEPHEN HANAN. *Peter Pan*: CATHY RIGBY. *Never Bear*: Adam Ehrenworth. *Curly*: Alon Williams. *First Twin*: Janet Kay Higgins. *Second Twin*: Courtney Wyn. *Slightly*: Christopher Ayres. *Tootles*: Julian Brightman. *Mr. Smee*: DON POTTER. *Cecco*: Calvin Smith. *Gentleman Starkey*: Carl Packard. *Noodler*: Barry Ramsey. *Bill Jukes*: Andy Ferrara. *Captain Hook*: STEPHEN HANAN. *Crocodile*: Barry Ramsey. *Tiger Lily*: HOLLY IRWIN.

Pirates and Indians: Bill Bateman, Andy Ferrara, Anne McVey, Christian Monte, Carl Packard, Barry Ramsey, Joseph Savant, Calvin Smith, Timothy Talman, David Thome, John Wilkerson.

Wendy, Grown-up: LAUREN THOMPSON. *Jane*: CINDY ROBINSON.

Act 1: The Nursery of the Darling Residence.

Act 2, Scene 1: Neverland. *Scene 2*: Cavern (Marooner's Rock). *Scene 3*: The Home Underground.

Act 3, Scene 1: The Pirate Ship *Scene 2*: The Nursery of the Darling Residence. *Scene 3*: The Nursery many years later.

ACT 1

"Tender Shepherd"
L. Thompson, C. Robinson, B. West, C. Hutchison

"I've Got to Crow" (I Gotta Crow)
C. Rigby

"Neverland"
C. Rigby
(*Music by* Jule Styne. *Lyrics by* Betty Comden and Adolph Green.

"I'm Flying"
C. Rigby, C. Robinson, B. West, C. Hutchison

ACT 2

Scene 1

"Pirate March"
S. Hanan, Pirates

"A Princely Scheme" (Hook's Tango)
S. Hanan, Pirates
(*Music by* Trude Rittman. *Lyrics by* Carolyn Leigh.

"Indians!"
H. Irwin, Indians

"Wendy"
C. Rigby, Boys
(*Music by* Jule Styne. *Lyrics by* Betty Comden and Adolph Green.

"Tarantella" (Another Princely Scheme)
S. Hanan, Pirates

Scene 2

"I Won't Grow Up"
C. Rigby, C. Robinson, Lost Boys

Scene 3

"Ugg-aWugg"
C. Rigby, H. Irwin, C. Robinson, Boys, Indians
(*Music by* Jule Styne. *Lyrics by* Betty Comden and Adolph Green.

"Distant Melody"
C. Rigby
(*Music by* Jule Styne. *Lyrics by* Betty Comden and Adolph Green.

ACT 3

Scene 1

"(Captain) Hook's Waltz"
S. Hanan, Pirates
(*Music by* Jule Styne. *Lyrics by* Betty Comden and Adolph Green.

"I've Got to Crow" (reprise)
C. Rigby, Company

Scene 2

"Tender Shepherd" (reprise)
C. Robinson, B. West, C. Hutchison

"I Won't Grow Up" (reprise)
The Darling Family, Lost Boys

Scene 3

"Neverland" (reprise)
C. Rigby

[16]Originally produced in New York 20 October 1954 at the Winter Garden for 152 performances. For this production, "Neverland Waltz," "The Pow Pow Polka," "Dangerous Lady," "To the Ship," "The Battle," "Morning in Neverland" dropped from the program; the 9 Scenes of previous productions consolidated into 7 Scenes.

[17]Book adaptation uncredited.

1991.01

MULE BONE

A Comedy with Songs in Two Acts, 2 Prologues and 3 Scenes. Play by Langston Hughes and Zora Neale Thurston. (Based on her short story "The Bone of Contention.") Prologue and epilogue by George Houston Bass. Music by Taj Mahal. (Lyrics by Langston Hughes.) Directed by Michael Schultz. Sets by Edward Burbridge. Costumes by Lewis Brown. Lighting by Allen Lee Hughes. Sound by Serge Ossorguine. Musical supervisor, Taj Mahal. Fights by Ron Van Clief. Dances staged by Dianne McIntyre. Produced by Lincoln Center Theatre (Gregory Mosher, Director; Bernard Gersten, Executive producer). Opened 14 February 1991 at the Ethel Barrymore Theatre and closed 14 April 1991 after 67 performances.

CAST (in order of appearance): *Zora*: Joy Lee. *Dave Carter*: Eric Ware. *Jim*: KENNY NEAL. *Daisy*: Akosua Busia. *Deacon Hambo*: Sonny Jim Gaines. *Old Man Brazzle*: Clebert Ford. *Lum Boger*: Paul S. Eckstein. *Lige Mosely*: Reggie Montgomery. *Robena*: Pauline Meyer. *Joe Lindsay*: Allie Woods, Jr. *Walter Thomas*: Donald Griffin. *Mayor Joe Clark*: SAMUEL E. WRIGHT. *Sister Blunt*: Ebony Jo-Ann. *Senator*: Pee Wee Love. *Teets*: Joy Lee. *Bootsie*: Vanessa Williams. *Mattie Clark*: Myra Taylor. *Luther*: Bron Wright. *Matilda*: Shareen Powlett. *Willie Lewis*: Robert Earl Jones. *Tony Taylor*: Mansoor Najeeullah. *Sister Taylor*: Marilyn Coleman. *Reverend Simms*: Leonard Jackson. *Jesse, Julius*: T. J. Jones. *Katie Pitts*: Theresa Merritt. *Sister Lewis*: Frances Foster. *Sister Thomas*: Fanni Green. *Sister Hambo*: Edwina Lewis. *Sister Lindsay*: Peggy Pettitt. *Reverend Singletary*: Arthur French.

The action takes place in Eatonville, Florida, on Saturday, 8 November during the 1920's.

Prologue: Just outside of Eatonville.

Act 1: Joe Clark's General Store.

Prologue: A barn. Dave Carter's house. Saturday night.

Act 2, Scene 1: Macedonia Baptist Church. The following Monday. *Scene 2*: A high stretch of railroad tracks a mile out of town. The same day. late afternoon.

ACT 1

"Jubilee" (Opening Theme)

"Graveyard Mule" (Hambone Rhyme)
(*Lyrics by* George Houston Bass.)

"Me and the Mule"

"Song for a Banjo Dance"

"But I Rode Some"

"Hey Hey Blues"

"Shake That Thing"
(*Music by* "Poppa" Charlie Jackson.)

ACT 2

"Crossing" (Lonely Day)

"Bound No'th Blues"

Finale

1991.02

PENN & TELLER: THE REFRIGERATOR TOUR

An Evening of Magic and Mayhem in Two Acts. (Conceived by Penn & Teller. Original music by Gary Stockdale.) Set by John Lee Beatty. Lighting by Dennis Parichy. Sound by T. Richard Fitzgerald, Craig Van Tassell. Director of covert activities, Robert P. Libbon. Director of internal affairs, Mike Wills. Associate producer, Marc Routh. Produced by Richard Frankel, Thomas Viertel and Steven Baruch. Opened 3 April 1991 at the Eugene O'Neill Theatre and closed 29 June 1991 after 103 performances[18].

CAST: PENN JILLETTE, TELLER, Carol Jenkins.

ACT 1

Amana Damocles

A Card Trick

"Liftoff to Love/Ripoff of Love"
(*Written by* Gary Stockdale, Penn Jillette and Teller. *Performed by* Gary Stockdale.)

Two Modern Fakir Tricks

Quotation of the Day

Two Houdini Tricks

ACT 2

Mofo, the Psychic Gorilla

By Buddha, This Duck Is Immortal!

Cuffed to a Creep

"Burnin' Luv"
(*Written by* Gary Stockdale.)

Shadows

King of Animal Traps

1991.03

MISS SAIGON

A Musical in Two Acts, 6 Scenes. Book by Alain Boublil, Claude-Michel Schönberg. Additional material by Richard Maltby, Jr. Music by Claude-Michel Schönberg. Lyrics by Richard Maltby, Jr., Alain Boublil, adapted from original French lyrics by Alain Boublil. Directed by Nicholas Hytner. Musical staging by Bob Avian. Production (settings) designed by John Napier. Costumes by Andreane Neofitou, Suzy Benzinger. Lighting by David Hersey. Sound by Andrew Bruce. Orchestrations by William D. Brohn. Musical supervision, David Caddick, Robert Billig. Conductor, Robert Billig. Associate director, Mitchell Lemsky. Associate producer, Martin McCallum. Executive producers, Mitchell Lemsky, Richard Jay-Alexander. Produced by Cameron Mackintosh. Opened 11 April 1991 at the Broadway Theatre and closed 28 January 2001 after 4125 performances.

CAST (in order of appearance): *Saigon, 1975*: *The Engineer*: JONATHAN PRYCE. *Kim*: LEA SALONGA, KAM CHENG (alt.). *Gigi*: Marina Chapa. *Mimi*: Sala Iwamatsu. *Yvette*: Imelda de los Reyes. *Yvonne*: JoAnn M. Hunter. *Bar Girls*: Raquel C. Brown, Annette Calud, Mirla Criste, Jade Stice, Melanie Mariko Tojio. *Chris*: WILLY FALK. *John*: HINTON BATTLE. *Marines*: Paul Dobie, Michael Gruber, Leonard Joseph, Paul Matsumoto, Sean McDermott, Thomas James O'Leary, Gordon Owens, Christopher Pecaro, Matthew Pedersen, Kris Phillips, W. Ellis Porter, Alton F. White, Bruce Winant. *Barmen*: Zar Acayan, Alan Ariano, Jason Ma. *Vietnamese Customers*: Tony C. Avanti, Eric Chan, Francis J. Cruz, Darren Lee, Ray Santos, Nephi Jay Wimmer. *Thuy*: BARRY BERNAL. *Embassy Workers, Inhabitants of Saigon, Vendors*: Company.

Ho Chi Minh City, April 1978: *Ellen*: LIZ CALLAWAY. *Tam*: Brian R. Baldomero or Philip Lyle Kong. *Guards*: Tony C. Avanti, Francis J. Cruz. *Assistant Commissar*: Eric Chan. *Dragon Acrobats*: Darren Lee, Michael Gruber, Nephi Jay Wimmer. *Soldiers*: Zar Acayan, Alan Ariano, Jason Ma, Paul Matsumoto, Ray Santos, Nephi Jay Wimmer. *Citizens of Ho Chi Minh City, Refugees*: Company.

U.S.A., September 1978: *Conference Delegates*: Company.

Bangkok, October 1978: *Hustlers*: Zar Acayan, Jason Ma, Paul Matsumoto, Ray Santos, Nephi Jay Wimmer. *Owner of the Moulin Rouge*: Francis J. Cruz. *Inhabitants of Bangkok, Bar Girls, Vendors, Tourists*: Company.

Saigon, April 1975: *Schultz*: Thomas James O'Leary. *Antoine*: Alton F. White. *Reeves*: Bruce Winant. *Gibbons*: Paul Dobie. *Troy*: Leonard Joseph. *Nolen*: Gordon Owens. *Huston*: Matthew Pedersen. *Frye*: Sean McDermott. *Marines, Vietnamese Civilians*: Company.

Bangkok, October 1978: *Inhabitants of Bangkok, Customers of the Moulin Rouge*: Company.

Swings: Sylvia Dohi, Henry Menendez, Todd Zamarripa.

Act 1, Scene 1: Saigon, 1975. *Scene 2*: Ho Chi Minh City (formerly Saigon), April 1978.

Act 2, Scene 1: U.S.A., September 1978. *Scene 2*: Bangkok, October 1978. *Scene 3*: Saigon, April 1975.*Scene 4*: Bangkok, October 1978.

ACT 1

Scene 1

"The Heat Is On in Saigon"
J. Pryce, Girls, Marines, Company

"The Movie in My Mind"
M. Chapa, L. Salonga, Girls

"The Transaction"
H. Battle, J. Pryce, W. Falk, Company

"Why God Why?"
W. Falk

"Sun and Moon"
L. Salonga, W. Falk

"The Telephone"
H. Battle, W. Falk, J. Pryce

"The Ceremony"
L. Salonga, W. Falk, Girls

"The Last Night of the World"
L. Salonga, W. Falk

Scene 2

"The Morning of the Dragon"
Company, B. K. Bernal, J. Pryce

"I Still Believe"
L. Salonga, L. Callaway

"Back in Town"
L. Salonga, J. Pryce, B. K. Bernal

"You Will Not Touch Him"
L. Salonga, B. K. Bernal

"If You Want to Die in Bed"
J. Pryce

"I'd Give My Life for You"
L. Salonga, Company

ACT 2

Scene 1

"Bui-Doi"
H. Battle, Company

Scene 2

"What a Waste"
J. Pryce, Company

"Please"
H. Battle, L. Salonga

Scene 3

"The Guilt Inside Your Head" (The Fall of Saigon, April 1975)
B. K. Bernal, L. Salonga, W. Falk, H. Battle, Company

Scene 4

"Sun and Moon" (reprise)
L. Salonga

"Room 317"
L. Callaway, L. Salonga

"Now That I've Seen Her"
L. Callaway

"The Confrontation"
L. Callaway, W. Falk, H. Battle

"The American Dream"
J. Pryce, Company

"Little God of My Heart"
L. Salonga, B. R. Baldomero

[18]Reopened Off-Broadway as PENN & TELLER ROT IN HELL 30 July 1991 at the John Houseman Theatre closing 19 January 1992 after 200 performances.

1991.04 LIZA MINNELLI: STEPPING OUT AT RADIO CITY

A Musical Revue in Two Acts. Special musical material, John Kander and Fred Ebb. Directed by Fred Ebb. Musial director, Bill LaVorgna. Choreography by Susan Stroman; additional choreography by Lisa Mordente. Musical supervision, Marvin Laird, Glen Roven. Vocal arranger, Billy Stritch. Scenic designer, Michael J. Hotopp. Costume designer, Julie Weiss. Lighting designer, David Agress. Sound designer, Hank Catteneo. Musical arrangements by Marvin Laird, Artie Schreck, Mike Abene, Ralph Burns, Torrie Zito, Glen Roven, Russell Kassoff, Billy Stritch, Peter Howard, Pet Shop Boys. Executive producers, Eliot Weisman, Premiere Artists Services, Inc. Produced by Radio City Music Hall Productions (Scott Sanders, Ed Micone). Opened 23 April 1991 at the Radio City Music Hall and closed 12 May 1991 after 15 performances; returned 24 January 1992 to Radio City Music Hall and closed 1 February 1992 after 7 additional performances. Total: 22 performances.

CAST: LIZA MINNELLI.
Ensemble (in alphabetical order): Mamie Duncan-Gibbs, Sherry Dundish, Roxanne Dundish, Ruth Gotschall, Joanne McHugh, Joanna Noble, Jeanette Palmer (swing), Irma Rogers, Jessica Sheridan, Dorothy Stanley, Terri White, Monica Wemitt, Tara Young.

Act 1: Liza in Concert.

Act 2: Liza and Friends.

ACT 1
"The Nearness of You"
(*Music by* Hoagy Carmichael. *Lyrics by* Ned Washington.)
"Teach Me Tonight"
(*Music by* Gene de Paul. *Lyrics by* Sammy Cahn.)
"Who Would Have Dreamed?"
"Cottage for Sale"
(*Music by* Willard Robison. *Lyrics by* Larry Conley.)
"Some People" (from *GYPSY*)
(*Music by* Jule Styne. *Lyrics by* Stephen Sondheim.)
"Sara Lee"
(*Music by* John Kander. *Lyrics by* Fred Ebb.)
"Sorry I Asked"
(*Music by* John Kander. *Lyrics by* Fred Ebb.)
"Similar Features"
"Le Temps"
"Quiet Love"
"What Makes a Man a Man"
"Sailor Boy"
"Live Alone and Like It"
(*Music and Lyrics by* Stephen Sondheim.)
"Seeing Things" (from *THE HAPPY TIME*)
(*Music by* John Kander. *Lyrics by* Fred Ebb.)
Vincent Minnelli Tribute
"Stepping Out" (from *STEPPING OUT*, film)
(*Music by* John Kander. *Lyrics by* Fred Ebb.)
"Losing My Mind" (from *FOLLIES*)
(*Music and Lyrics by* Stephen Sondheim.)
"(But) The World Goes Round" (from *NEW YORK, NEW YORK* film)
(*Music by* John Kander. *Lyrics by* Fred Ebb.)
"All By Myself"
(*Music and Lyrics by* Irving Berlin.)

ACT 2
"Hey Liza It's Me"
(*Music by* John Kander. *Lyrics by* Fred Ebb.)
Men Medley with the Demon Divas:
"Natural Man"
"The Man I Love"
(*Music by* George Gershwin. *Lyrics by* Ira Gershwin.)
"Not for the Life of Me"
"Drum Dance"
"Old Friend"
"My Buddy"
Bob Fosse Tribute
Medley:
"Pack Up Your Troubles (in Your Old Kit Bag)"
(*Music by* Felix Powell. *Lyrics by* George Asaf.)
"It's a Long Way To Tipperary"
(*Music and Lyrics by* Jack Judge and Harry M. Williams.)
"Imagine"
(*Music and Lyrics by* John Lennon.)
Group Stepping Out
"New York, New York" (from *NEW YORK, NEW YORK* film)
(*Music by* John Kander. *Lyrics by* Fred Ebb.)

1991.05 THE SECRET GARDEN

A Musical in Two Acts, a Prologue and 18 Scenes. Book and lyrics by Marsha Norman. Based on the novel of the same name by Frances Hodgson Burnett. Music by Lucy Simon. Directed by Susan H. Schulman. Choreography by Michael Lichtefeld. Scenery by Heidi Landesman. Costumes by Theoni V. Aldredge. Lighting by Tharon Musser. Sound by Otts Munderloh. Orchestrations by William D. Brohn. Musical direction, vocal arrangements by Michael Kosarin. Dance arrangements by Jeanine Levenson. Associate producers, Greg C. Mosher, Rhoda Mayerson, Playhouse Square Center (Lawrence J. Wilker, President), Dorothy and Wendell Cherry, Margo Lion, 126 Second Avenue Corporation (Hal Luftig, Alan D. Perry). Produced by Heidi Landesman, Rick Steiner, Frederic H. Mayerson, Elizabeth Williams, Jujamcyn Theatres/TV Asahi, Dodger Productions (Michael David, Doug Johnson, Rocco Landesman, Des McAnuff, Edward Strong, Sherman Warner). Opened 25 April 1991 at the St. James Theatre and closed 3 January 1993 after 706 performances.

CAST: *Lily*: REBECCA LUKER. *Mary Lennox*: DAISY EAGAN, Kimberly Mahon (alt.)
In Colonial India, 1906: *Fakir*: Peter Marinos. *Ayah*: Patricia Phillips. *Rose*, Mary's mother: Kay Walbye. *Captain Albert Lennox*, Mary's father: Michael DeVries. *Lieutenant Peter Wright*: Drew Taylor. *Lieutenant Ian Shaw*: Paul Jackel. *Major Holmes*: Peter Samuel. *Claire*, his wife: Rebecca Judd. *Alice*, Rose's friend: Nancy Johnston.
At Misselthwaite Manor, North Yorkshire, England, 1906: *Archibald Craven*, Mary's uncle: MANDY PATINKIN. *Dr. Neville Craven*, his brother: ROBERT WESTENBERG. *Mrs. Medlock*, the housekeeper: BARBARA ROSENBLAT. *Martha*, a chambermaid: ALISON FRASER. *Dickon*, her brother: JOHN CAMERON MITCHELL. *Ben*, the gardener: TOM TONER. *Colin*: JOHN BABCOCK. *Jane*: Teresa De Zarn. *William*: Frank DiPasquale. *Betsy*: Betsy Friday. *Timothy*: Alec Timerman. *Mrs. Winthrop*: Nancy Johnston.
Swings: Kevin Ligon, Bill Nolte, Jane Seaman, Jennifer Smith.

The action takes place in 1906.

Opening (Prologue): India; The Library at Misselthwaite Manor; A Train Platform in Yorkshire; The Door to Misselthwaite Manor; Mary's Room; The Gallery.

Act 1, Scene 1: Mary's Sitting Room. *Scene 2*: The Ballroom. *Scene 3*: In the Maze/The Greenhouse; The Edge of the Moor. *Scene 4*: Archibald's Library. *Scene 5*: The Gallery. *Scene 6*: The Hallway. *Scene 7*: Colin's Room. *Scene 8*: On the Grounds/The Door to the Garden.

Act 2, Scene 1: The Tea Party Dream/The Other Side of the Door. *Scene 2*: Archibald's Dressing Room. *Scene 3*: Colin's Room. *Scene 4*: The Greenhouse. *Scene 5*: Colin's Room. *Scene 6*: In the Maze/The Garden. *Scene 7*: The Library. *Scene 8*:Mary's Room/Paris. *Scene 9*: Archibald's Rooms in Paris. *Scene 10*: The Garden.

ACT 1[19]
Opening
"Opening Dream"
R. Luker, P. Marinos, D. Eagan, Company
"There's a Girl"
Company
"House Upon the Hill"
Company

[19]Added to Act 1, beginning of Scene 6 for national tour:
"I Heard Someone Crying" (reprise)
[Mary Lennox], Company

"I Heard Someone Crying"
D. Eagan, M. Patinkin, R. Luker, Company
Scene 1
"A Fine White Horse"
A. Fraser
Scene 2
"A Girl in the Valley"
R. Luker, M. Patinkin, Dancers
Scene 3
"It's a Maze"
T. Toner, D. Eagan, J. C. Mitchell
"Winter's on the Wing"
J. C. Mitchell
"Show Me the Key"
D. Eagan, J. C. Mitchell
Scene 4
"A Bit of Earth"
M. Patinkin
Scene 5
"Storm I"
Company
"Lily's Eyes"
M. Patinkin, R. Westenberg
Scene 6
"Storm II"
D. Eagan, Company
Scene 7
"Round-Shouldered Man"
J. Babcock
Scene 8
"Final Storm"
Company

ACT 2
Scene 1
"The Girl I Meant to Be"
D. Eagan, Company
Scene 2
"Quartet"
M. Patinkin, R. Westenberg, K. Walbye, R. Luker
Scene 3
"Race You to the Top of the Morning"
M. Patinkin
Scene 4
"Wick"
J. C. Mitchell, D. Eagan
Scene 5
"Come to My Garden"
R. Luker, J. Babcock
Scene 6
"Come Spirit, Come Charm"
D. Eagan, A. Fraser, J. C. Mitchell, P. Marinos, P. Phillips, R. Luker, Company
"A Bit of Earth" (reprise)
R. Luker, K. Walbye, M. DeVries
Scene 7
"Disappear"
R. Westenberg
Scene 8
"Hold On"
A. Fraser
"Letter Song"
D. Eagan, A. Fraser
Scene 9
"Where in the World"
M. Patinkin
"How Could I Ever Know?"
R. Luker, M. Patinkin
Scene 10
Finale
Company

1991.06

GYPSY

A Return Engagement of the Revival of the Musical Fable in Two Acts[20]. Book by Arthur Laurents. Suggested by the memoirs (of the same name) by Gypsy Rose Lee. Directed by Arthur Laurents. Original choreography of Jerome Robbins, reproduced by Bonnie Walker. Music by Jule Styne. Lyrics by Stephen Sondheim. Scenery design by Kenneth Foy. Costume design by Theoni V. Aldredge. Lighting design by Natasha Katz. Sound by Peter Fitzgerald. Musical direction by Michael Rafter. Orchestrations by Sid Ramin with Robert Ginzler. Dance music arranged by John Kander. Produced by Barry and Fran Weissler, Kathy Levin, Barry Brown, in association with Tokyo Broadcasting System International and Pace Theatrical Group. Opened 28 April 1991 at the Minskoff Theater and closed 28 July 1991 after 105 performances. Total including first engagement: 581 performances.

CAST (in order of appearance): *Uncle Jocko*: Stan Rubin. *George*: Victor Raider-Wexler. *Clarence* (and His Classic Clarinet): Bobby John Carter. *Balloon Girl*: Jeana Haege. *Baby Louise*: Kristen Mahon. *Baby June*: Susan Cremin. *Rose*: TYNE DALY. *Pop*: Ronn Carroll. *Newsboys*: Bobby John Carter, Thomas Fox, Danny Cistone, Tony Yazbeck. *Weber*: Richard Levine. *Herbie*: JONATHAN HADARY. *Louise*: CRISTA MOORE. *June*: TRACY VENNER. *Tulsa*: ROBERT LAMBERT. *Yonkers*: Bruce Moore. *L.A.*: Craig Waletzko. *Kansas*: Paul Geraci. *Flagstaff*: Kevin Petitto. *St. Paul*: Cory English. *The Cow*: Crista Moore, Barbara Folts, Robin Robinson, Cory English, Kevin Petitto. *Kringelein*: Stan Rubin. *Mr. Goldstone*: Victor Raider-Wexler. *Miss Cratchitt*: Barbara Erwin. *Hollywood Blondes (5)*: Teri Furr, Barbara Folts, Nancy Melius, Michele Pigliavento, Robin Robinson. *Agnes*: Lori Ann Mahl. *Pastey*: Jeff Brooks. *Tessie Tura*: BARBARA ERWIN. *Mazeppa*: JANA ROBBINS. *Electra*: ANNA McNEELY. *Cigar*: Ronn Carroll. *Maid*: Ginger Prince. *Phil*: Richard Levine. *Bougeron-Couchon*: Jeff Brooks. *Swings*: Laurie Crochet, George Smyros.

1991.07

THE WILL ROGERS FOLLIES: A Life in Revue

A Musical in Two Acts, a Prelude and 12 Scenes. Book by Peter Stone. Inspired by the words of Will and Betty Rogers. Music by Cy Coleman. Lyrics by Betty Comden and Adolph Green. Directed and choreographed by Tommy Tune. Settings design by Tony Walton. Costume design by Willa Kim. Lighting design by Jules Fisher. Sound design by Peter Fitzgerald. Projection design by Wendall K. Harrington. Orchestrations by Billy Byers. Musical direction by Eric Stern. Associate director, Phillip Oesterman. Associate choreographer, Jeff Calhoun. Produced by Pierre Cossette, Martin Richards, Sam Crothers, James M. Nederlander, Stewart F. Lane, Max Weitzenhoffer, in association with Japan Satellite Broadcasting. Opened 1 May 1991 at the Palace Theatre and closed 5 September 1993 after 983 performances.

CAST (in order of appearance): *Ziegfeld's Favorite*: CADY HUFFMAN. *Will Rogers*: KEITH CARRADINE. *Unicyclist*: Vince Bruce. *Wiley Post*: PAUL UKENA. JR. *Clem Rogers*: DICK LATESSA. *Will's Sisters*: Roxane Barlow, Maria Calabrese, Colleen Dunn, Dana Moore, Wenda Waring, Leigh Zimmerman. *Betty Blake*: DEE HOTY. *The Wild West Show (Trainers)*: Tom and Bonnie Brackney, with B.A., Cocoa, Gigi, Rusty, Trixie, Zee. *Betty's Sisters*: Roxane Barlow, Maria Calabrese, Colleen Dunn, Dana Moore, Wenda Waring, Leigh Zimmerman. *Will Rogers, Jr.*: Rick Faugno. *Mary Rogers*: Tammy Minoff. *James Rogers*: Lance Robinson. *Freddy Rogers*: Gregory Scott Carter. *Roper*: Vince Bruce.

The Will Rogers Wranglers: John Ganun, Troy Britton Johnson, Jerry Mitchell, Jason Opsahl. *The New Ziegfeld Girls*: Roxane Barlow, Maria Calabrese, Ganine Derleth, Rebecca Downing, Colleen Dunn, Sally Mae Dunn, Toni Georgiana, Eileen Grace, Luba Gregus, Tonia Lynn, Dana Moore, Aimee Turner, Jillana Urbina, Wendy Waring, Christina Youngman, Leigh Zimmerman. *The Voice of Mr. Ziegfeld*: Gregory Peck. *Swings*: Mary Lee DeWitt, Jack Doyle, Angie L. Schworer.

The action takes place in the Palace Theatre at the present time.

Act 1, Scene 1: The Follies. *Scene 2*: The Ranch. *Scene 3*: The Moon. *Scene 4*: The Follies. *Scene 5*: The St. Louis Exposition. *Scene 6*: Vaudeville. *Scene 7*: The Follies.

Act 2, Scene 1: The Follies. *Scene 2*: The Convention. *Scene 3*: The Hollywood Ranch. *Scene 4*: The Bare Stage. *Scene 5*: The Finale.

---

[20] Originally produced in New York 21 May 1959 at the Broadway Theatre for 702 performances; this production originally opened 16 November 1989 at the St. James Theatre for 476 performances. For Synopsis of Scenes and Musical Numbers, see original 1959 production and 1989 revival.

ACT 1
Prelude
"Let's Go Flying"
(Chorus)
Scene 1
"Will-a-Mania"
C. Huffman, Company
"Give a Man Enough Rope"
K. Carradine, The Will Rogers Wranglers
Scene 2
"It's a Boy"
D. Latessa, Will's Sisters
"So Long Pa"
K. Carradine
Scene 3
"My Unknown Someone"
D. Hoty
Scene 5
"We're Heading for a Wedding"
K. Carradine, D. Hoty
Scene 6
"The Big Time"
K. Carradine, D. Hoty, the Children
"My Big Mistake"
D. Hoty
Scene 7
"The Powder Puff Ballet" (My Big Mistake)
The New Ziegfeld Girls
"Marry Me Now"/"I Got You"
K. Carradine, D. Hoty
Wedding Finale
(Company)

ACT 2
Scene 1
"Give a Man Enough Rope" (reprise)
K. Carradine, The Will Rogers Wranglers
"Look Around"
K. Carradine
Scene 2
"Favorite Son"
K. Carradine, Chorus
Scene 3
"No Man Left for Me"
D. Hoty
"Presents for Mrs. Rogers"
K. Carradine, The Will Rogers Wranglers, The New Ziegfeld Girls
Scene 4
"Will-a-mania" (reprise)
K. Carradine, D. Latessa
"Without You" ("I Got You" reprise)
D. Hoty
Scene 5
"Never Met a Man I Didn't Like"
K. Carradine, Company

1991–1992 SEASON

Gregory Hines and Stanley Wayne Mathis in JELLY'S LAST JAM
Martha Swope/TimePix

1991–1992 SEASON

1991.08 A LITTLE NIGHT MUSIC

A Revival of the Musical in Two Acts, a Prologue and 15 Scenes[1]. Book by Harold Wheeler. Suggested by a film ("Smiles of a Summer Night") by Ingmar Bergman. Music and Lyrics by Stephen Sondheim. Directed by Scott Ellis. Choreography by Susan Stroman. Sets designed by Michael Anania. Costumes designed by Lindsay W. Davis. Lighting designed by Dawn Chiang. Conductor, Paul Gemignani. (Orchestrations by Jonathan Tunick.) Sound designed by Abe Jacob. Produced by the New York City Opera. Opened 9 July 1991 at the New York State Theatre and closed 10 August 1991 after 7 performances in repertory.

CAST (in order of appearance): *Mrs. Segstrom*: Susanne Marsee. *Mr. Lindquist*: Ron Baker. *Mrs. Nordstrom*: Lisa Saffer. *Mrs. Anderssen*: Barbara Shirvis. *Mr. Erlanson*: Peter Blanchet. *Frederika Armfeldt*: Danielle Ferland. *Madame Armfeldt*: ELAINE BONAZZI. *Frid*, her butler: David Fuller. *Henrik Egerman*: KEVIN P. ANDERSON. *Anne Egerman*: BEVERLY LAMBERT. *Fredrik Egerman*: GEOERGE LEE ANDREWS. *Petra*: JOANNA GLUSHAK. *Desirée Armfeldt*: SALLY ANN HOWES. *Malla*, her maid: Raven Wilkinson. *Bertrand*, a page: Peter Blanchet. *Count Carl-Magnus Malcolm*: MICHAEL MAGUIRE. *Countess Charlotte Malcolm*: MAUREEN MOORE. *Osa*: Judith Jarosz. *Serving Gentlemen*: Kent A. Heacock, Ronald Kelly, Jeff Kensmoe, Ian D. Klapper, Brian Michaels, Brian Quirk, John Henry Thomas, Mike Timoney.

1991.09 THE MOST HAPPY FELLA

A Revival of the Musical in Three Acts, 10 Scenes[2]. Book, music and lyrics by Frank Loesser. Based on the play "They Knew What They Wanted" by Sidney Howard. Directed by Arthur Allan Seidelman. Conducted by Chris Nance. Choreography by Dan Siretta. Set designer, Michael Anania. Costume designer, Beba Shamash. Lighting designer, Mark W. Stanley. Sound designer, Abe Jacob. Orchestrations by Don Walker. Chorus master, Joseph Colaneri. Produced by the New York City Opera. Opened 4 September 1991 at the New York State Theatre and closed 18 October 1991 after 10 performances in repertory.

CAST (in order of appearance): *The Cashier*: William Ledbetter. *Cleo*: KAREN ZIEMBA or JOANNA GLUSHAK. *Rosabella*: ELIZABETH WALSH or MICHELE MCBRIDE. *Waitresses*: Jean Barber, Joan Mirabella, Deidre Sheehan. *Busboys*: Dean Dufford, Michael Langlois. *The Postman*: William Ledbetter. *Tony*: LOUIS QUILICO or JOHN FIORITO. *Marie*: ELAINE BONAZZI or SUSANNE MARSEE. *Max*: Ron Hilley. *Herman*: LARA TEETER or BRIAN QUINN. *Clem*: Gregory Moore. *Jake*: David Frye. *Al*: Jonathan Guss. *Joe*: BURKE MOSES or JOHN LESLIE WOLFE. *Giuseppe*: Arthur Rubin. *Pasquale*: Richard Byrne. *Ciccio*: John Lankston. *The Doctor*: Peter Blanchet. *The Priest*: Don Yule. *Tessie*: Alice Roberts. *Gussie*: Zachary London. *Artie*: Jonathan Zwi. *Neighbors*: Harris Davis, Michael Langlois, Louis Perry, Phillip Sneed, William Ward, Edward Zimmerman. *Neighbor Ladies*: Lee Bellaver, Esperanza Galan, Stephanie Godino, Rita Metzger. *Station Attendant*: James Russell.

1991.10 BARRY MANILOW'S SHOWSTOPPERS

A Musical Revue in Two Acts. Written by Mitzie Welch, Ken Welch, Barry Manilow. Directed by Kevin Carlisle. Creative consultant, Roberta Kent. Set design by Jim Youmans. Costume design by Phillip Dennis. Lighting by Don Holder. Sound design by Jon Weston. Musical director, Kevin Bassinson. Vocal director, Debra Byrd. Produced by Kevin Carlisle, Ken Welch, Mitzie Welch and Garry Kief. Opened 25 September 1991 at the Paramount Theatre (at Madison Square Garden) and closed 28 September 1991 after 4 performances.

CAST: BARRY MANILOW, Kevin Brackett, Donna Cherry, Craig Meyer, Michelle Nicastro, Debra Byrd.

In addition to Mr. Manilow's repertoire [see below], the following songs may be included in tonight's performance:

MUSICAL NUMBERS[3]

"All I Need Now Is the Girl" (from *GYPSY*)
(*Music by* Jule Styne. *Lyrics by* Stephen Sondheim.)
"But the World Goes 'Round" (from *AND THE WORLD GOES ON*)
(*Music by* John Kander. *Lyrics by* Fred Ebb.)
"Dancing in the Dark" (from *THE BANDWAGON*)
(*Music by* Arthur Schwartz. *Lyrics by* Howard Dietz.)
"Fascinating Rhythm" (from *LADY BE GOOD*)
(*Music by* George Geshwin. *Lyrics by* Ira Gershwin.)
"Fugue for Tinhorns" (from *GUYS AND DOLLS*)
(*Music and Lyrics by* Frank Loesser.)
"Give My Regards to Broadway" (from *LITTLE JOHNNY JONES*)
(*Music and Lyrics by* George M. Cohan.)
"Guys and Dolls" (from *GUYS AND DOLLS*)
(*Music and Lyrics by* Frank Loesser.)
"I'll Be Seeing You" (from *RIGHT THIS WAY*)
(*Music by* Sammy Fain. *Lyrics by* Irving Kahal.)
"Let Freedom Ring" (from *WE THE PEOPLE*, CBS Television Special)
(*Music by* Barry Manilow. *Lyrics by* Bruce Sussman and Jack Feldman.)
"Luck Be a Lady" (from *GUYS AND DOLLS*)
(*Music and Lyrics by* Frank Loesser.)
"Memory" (from *CATS*)
(*Music by* Andrew Lloyd Webber. *Lyrics by* T. S. Eliot.)
"Never Met a Man I Didn't Like" (from *THE WILL ROGERS FOLLIES*)
(*Music by* Cy Coleman. *Lyrics by* Betty Comden and Adolph Green.)
"Old Friends" (from *MERRILY WE ROLL ALONG*)
(*Music and Lyrics by* Stephen Sondheim.)
"Once in Love with Amy" (from *WHERE'S CHARLEY?*)
(*Music and Lyrics by* Frank Loesser.)
"Real Live Girl" (from *LITTLE ME*)
(*Music by* Cy Coleman. *Lyrics by* Carolyn Leigh.)
"The Kid Inside" (from *IS THERE LIFE AFTER HIGH SCHOOL?*)
(*Music and Lyrics by* Craig Carnelia.)
"Where or When" (from *BABES IN ARMS*)
(*Music by* Richard Rodgers. *Lyrics by* Lorenz Hart.)
"Who Needs to Dream" (from *COPACABANA*, CBS Television Film)
(*Music by* Barry Manilow and Artie Butler. *Lyrics by* Bruce Sussman and Jack Feldman.)
"You Can Have the TV" (from *NOTES*)
(*Music and Lyrics by* Craig Carnelia.)

REPERTOIRE[4]

"I Got Rhythm" (from *GIRL CRAZY*)
(*Music by* George Gershwin. *Lyrics by* Ira Gershwin.)
"Rhapsody in Blue"
(*Music by* George Gershwin.)
"Trying to Get the Feeling Again"
(*Music and Lyrics by* David Pomeranz.)
"Tonight" (from *WEST SIDE STORY*)
(*Music by* Leonard Bernstein. *Lyrics by* Stephen Sondheim.)
"Somewhere in the Night"
(*Music by* Richard Kerr. *Lyrics by* Will Jennings.)
"Cabaret" (from *CABARET*)
(*Music by* John Kander. *Lyrics by* Fred Ebb.)
"Daybreak"
(*Music and Lyrics by* Barry Manilow and Adrienne Anderson.)
"76 Trombones" (from *THE MUSIC MAN*)
(*Music and Lyrics by* Meredith Willson.)
"It's a Miracle"
(*Music and Lyrics by* Barry Manilow and Marty Panzer.)
"Even Now"
(*Music by* Barry Manilow. *Lyrics by* Marty Panzer.)
"Mandy" (from *YIP YIP YAPHANK, ZIEGFELD FOLLIES OF 1919*)
(*Music and Lyrics by* Irving Berlin.)
"Read 'Em and Weep"
(*Music and Lyrics by* Jim Steinman.)

---

[1]Originally produced in New York 25 February 1973 at the Sam S. Shubert Theatre for 601 performances. For Synopsis of Scenes and Musical Numbers, see original 1973 production.

[2]Originally produced in New York 3 May 1956 at the Imperial Theatre for 678 performances. For Synopsis of Scenes and Musical Numbers, see original 1956 production. For this production, Act 2, Scenes 1 and 2 have been combined.

[3]Not in performance order.

[4]These songs represent Barry Manilow's current repertoire, as recorded on the album of the same name.

"NYC Rhythm"
(*Music and Lyrics by* Barry Manilow.)
"I Am Your Child"
(*Music and Lyrics by* Barry Manilow.)

1991.11 ANDRÉ HELLER'S WONDERHOUSE

An Entertainment in One Act. Entire production created, designed and directed by André Heller. Assistant director, Ivana De Vert. Rideau de Scène, Erté. Costumes by Susanne Schmoegner. Lighting by Pluesch. Sound by T. Richard Fitzgerald. English language adaptation by Mel Howard. Incidental music arranged and orchestrated by Andrew Powell. Band conductor, J. Leonard Oxley. Executive producer, Norman Rothstein. Originally produced in Europe by Peter Schwenkow and Stefan Seigner in association with Vereinigte Buehnen Wien. Produced by Mel Howard in association with Jean D. Weill. Opened 20 October 1991 at the Broadhurst Theatre and closed 27 October 1991 after 9 performances[5].

CAST: *Igor*: BILLY BARTY. *Olga*: PATTY MALONEY. *The Stagehand*, Gunila Carina Evalena Winniwingquist: GUNILLA WINGQUIST. *Guests*: RAO, CARLO OLDS, MACAO, BARONESS JEANNETTE LIPS VON LIPSTRILL, OMAR PASHA, MARION AND ROBERT KONYOT, EZIO BEDIN, MILO and ROGER, Aroon Kalan (assistant to Milo and Roger).

The action takes place in the old Wonderhouse Theatre at present.

1991.12 BRIGADOON

A Revival of the Musical Play in Two Acts, 11 Scenes[6]. Book and lyrics by Alan Jay Lerner. Music by Frederick Loewe. Original dances by Agnes deMille, recreated by James Jamieson. Directed by Gerald Freedman. Set and costume designer, Desmond Heeley. Lighting designer, Duane Schuler. Conductor, Paul Gemignani. Orchestrations by Ted Royal. Chorus master, Joseph Colaneri. Sound by Abe Jacob. Produced by the New York City Opera. Opened 7 November 1991 at the New York State Theatre and closed 17 November 1991 after 12 performances.

CAST (in order of appearance): *Tommy Albright*: JOHN LESLIE WOLFE or GEORGE DVORSKY. *Jeff Douglas*: TONY ROBERTS. *Maggie Anderson*: JOAN MIRABELLA. *Archie Beaton*: William Ledbetter. *Angus MacGuffie*: Don Yule. *Meg Brockie*: JOYCE CASTLE or LOUISA FLANIGAM. *Stuart Dalrymple*: Richard Byrne. *Sandy Dean*: Gregory Moore. *Harry Beaton*: SCOTT FOWLER. *Andrew MacLaren*: David Rae Smith. *Fiona MacLaren*: MICHELE MCBRIDE or ELIZABETH WALSH. *Jean MacLaren*: Camille de Ganon. *Charlie Dalrymple*: DAVID EISLER or ROBERT TATE. *Fish Monger*: Stephanie Godino. *Mr. Lundie*: Ron Randell. *Sword Dancers*: Joe Deer, William Ward. *Bagpiper*: Stephen Fox. *Frank*: Jonathan Guss. *Jane Ashton*: Leslie Farrell. *Townsfolk of Brigadoon*: New York City Opera Chorus, New York City Opera Dancers.

1991.13 PETER PAN

A Return Engagement of the Revival of the Musical in Three Acts, 7 Scenes[7]. Book by James M. Barrie[8]. Music by Mark [Moose] Charlap. Lyrics by Carolyn Leigh. Additional music by Jule Styne. Additional lyrics by Betty Comden and Adolph Green. Original production conceived, directed and choreographed by Jerome Robbins. Directed by Fran Soeder, restaged by Bill Bateman. Choreographed by Marilyn Magness. Scenery designed by Michael J. Hotopp, Paul dePass, James Leonard Joy. Costumes designed by Mariann Verheyen. Lighting designed by Natasha Katz. Musical director, Brian W. Tidwell. Musical supervisor, Kevin Farrell. Additional (musical) arrangements by M. Michael Fauss, Kevin Farrell. Sound designed by Peter Fitzgerald. Flying by Foy. Produced by Thomas P. McCoy, Keith Stava, P.P. Investments, Jon B. Platt. Opened 27 November 1991 at the Minskoff Theatre and closed 5 January 1992 after 48 performances.

CAST (in order of appearance): *Wendy Darling*: CINDY ROBINSON. *John Darling*: DAVID BURDICK. *Michael Darling*: JOEY CEE. *Liza*: Anne McVey. *Nana*: Bill Bateman. *Mrs. Darling*: LAUREN THOMPSON. *Mr. Darling*: J. K. SIMMONS. *Peter Pan*: CATHY RIGBY. *Curly*: Alon Williams. *First Twin*: Janet Kay Higgins. *Second Twin*: Courtney Wyn. *Slightly*: Christopher Ayres. *Tootles*: Julian Brightman. *Mr. Smee*: DON POTTER. *Cecco*: Calvin Smith. *Gentleman Starkey*: Carl Packard. *Captain Hook*: J. K. SIMMONS. *Crocodile*: Barry Ramsey. *Tiger Lily*: MICHELLE SCHUMACHER. *Pirates and Indians*: Bill Bateman, Andy Ferrara, Anne McVey, Charlie Matcus, Carl Packard, Barry Ramsey, Joseph Savant, Calvin Smith, David Thome, John Wilkerson.
Wendy, Grown-up: LAUREN THOMPSON. *Jane*: CINDY ROBINSON.
Ensemble Swing: Jim Alexander.

1991.14 CATSKILLS ON BROADWAY

An Evening of Comedy in One Act, 4 Scenes. Conceived by Freddie Roman. Entire production supervised by Larry Arrick. Set design by Lawrence Miller. Lighting design by Peggy Eisenhauer. Sound design by Peter Fitzgerald. Musical director, Barry Levitt. Opening musical sequence arranged by Don Pippin. Projection design by Wendall K. Harrington. Creative consultant, Richard Vos. Associate producer, Sandra Greenblatt. Presented by Kenneth D. Greenblatt, Stephen D. Fish, and 44 Productions (Michael G. Miller, Jeff Schwartz). Opened 5 December 1991 at the Lunt-Fontanne Theatre and closed 3 January 1993 after 452 performances.

CAST (in order of appearance): FREDDIE ROMAN, MARILYN MICHAELS, DICK CAPRI, MAL Z. LAWRENCE.

SCENES
Freddie Roman (stand-up comedy)
Marilyn Michaels (impressions, songs)
Dick Capri (stand-up comedy)
Mal Z. Lawrence (stand-up comedy)

1991.15 NICK & NORA

A Musical in Two Acts, 14 Scenes. Book by Arthur Laurents. Based on characters created by Dashiell Hammett and "The Thin Man" motion pictures owned by Turner Entertainment Co. Music by Charles Strouse. Lyrics by Richard Maltby, Jr. Directed by Arthur Laurents. Scenic design by Douglas W. Schmidt. Costume design by Theoni V. Aldredge. Lighting design by Jules Fisher. Choreography by Tina Paul. Orchestrations by Jonathan Tunick. Musical and vocal direction by Jack Lee. Dance and incidental music by Charles Strouse. Dance and incidental music arrangements by Gordon Lowry Harrell. Sound design by Peter Fitzgerald. Animals by William Berloni Theatrical Animals, Inc. Production supervisor, Janet Beroza. Assistant choreographer, Luis Perez. Associate musical director, Patrick Scott Brady. Produced by Terry Allen Kramer, Charlene and James M. Nederlander, Daryl Roth, Elizabeth Ireland McCann, in association with James Pentecost and Charles Suisman. Opened 8 December 1991 at the Marquis Theater and closed 15 December 1991 after 9 performances.

CAST (in order of appearance): *Asta*: Riley. *Nora Charles*: JOANNA GLEASON. *Nick Charles*: BARRY BOSTWICK. *Tracy Gardner*: CHRISTINE BARANSKI. *Yukido*: THOM SESMA. *Mavis*: Kathy Morath. *Delli*: Kristen Wilson. *Max Bernheim*: REMAK RAMSAY. *Victor Moisa*: CHRIS SARANDON. *Spider Malloy*: JEFF BROOKS. *Lorraine Bixby*: FAITH PRINCE. *Edward J. Connors*: KIP NIVEN. *Lieutenant Wolfe*: MICHAEL LOMBARD. *Maria Valdez*: YVETTE LAWRENCE. *Lily Connors*: DEBRA MONK. *Selznick*: Hal Robinson. *Monsignor Flaherty*: John Jellison. *Mariachi*: Tim Connell, Kris Phillips. *Waitress*: Kristen Wilson.
Swings: Mark Hoebee, Cynnthia Thole.

The action takes place in Hollywood, 1937.

Act 1, Scene 1: Nick & Nora's bungalow, The Garden of Allah. *Scene 2*: The Studio. *Scene 3*: Lorraine's (Max's version). *Scene 4*: The Studio. *Scene 5*: Nick & Nora's bungalow. *Scene 6*: Lorraine (Victor's version). *Scene 7*: Beverly Hills. *Scene 8*: Lorraine's.

Act 2, Scene 1: Victor's villa. *Scene 2*: Nick & Nora's bungalow. *Scene 3*: Lorraine's (Maria's version). *Scene 4*: Lorraine's. *Scene 5*: The Big Bamboo. *Scene 6*: Tracy's terrace.

ACT 1
Scene 1
"Is There Anything Better Than Dancing?"
B. Bostwick, J. Gleason, C. Baranski
Scene 2
"Everybody Wants to Do a Musical"
C. Baranski

---

[5]No musical numbers listed in program.
[6]Originally produced in New York 13 March 1947 at the Ziegfeld Theatre for 581 performances. For Synopsis of Scenes and Musical Numbers, see original 1947 production.
[7]Originally produced in New York 20 October 1954 at the Winter Garden for 152 performances; this production previously presented in New York 13 December 1990 at the Lunt-Fontanne Theatre for 45 performances. For Synopsis of Scenes and Musical Numbers, see 1990 revival.
[8]Adaptation uncredited.

Scene 3
"Not Me"
R. Ramsay, F. Prince, K. Niven
Scene 4
"Swell"
B. Bostwick, J. Brooks, J. Gleason, C. Sarandon
Scene 5
"As Long as You're Happy"
B. Bostwick, J. Gleason
"People Get Hurt"
D. Monk
Scene 6
"Men"
F. Prince, C. Sarandon, K. Niven, C. Baranski
Scene 7
"May the Best Man Win"
B. Bostwick, J. Gleason, C. Baranski
"Detectiveland"
Company
Scene 8
"Look Who's Alone Now"
B. Bostwick

ACT 2
Scene 1
"Class"
C. Sarandon
Scene 2
"Let's Go Home"
J. Gleason
Scene 4
"A Busy Night at Lorraine's"
B. Bostwick, J. Gleason, J. Brooks, Suspects
Scene 5
"Boom Chicka Boom"
Y. Lawrence, T. Connell, K. Phillips
Scene 6
"Let's Go Home" (reprise)(Married Life)
B. Bostwick, J. Gleason

1992.01 THE MOST HAPPY FELLA

A Revival of the Musical in Two Acts, 11 Scenes[9]. Book, music and lyrics by Frank Loesser. Based on the play "They Knew What They Wanted" by Sidney Howard. Entire production directed by Gerald Gutierrez. Choreography by Liza Gennaro. Sets by John Lee Beatty. Costumes by Jess Goldstein. Lighting by Craig Miller. Duo piano arrangements by Robert Page under the supervision of Frank Loesser. Musical direction, Tim Stella. Artistic associate, Jo Sullivan. Originally produced by the Goodspeed Opera House Production. Produced by The Goodspeed Opera House, Center Theater Group/Ahmanson Theatre, Lincoln Center Theatre, The Shubert Organization, and Japan Satellite Broadcasting/Stagevision. Opened 13 February 1992 at the Booth Theatre and closed 30 August 1992 after 229 performances.

CAST (in order of appearance): *The Cashier*: Tad Ingram. *Cleo*: LIZ LARSON. *Rosabella*: SOPHIE {Schwab} HAYDEN. *Postman*: TAD INGRAM. *Tony*: SPIRO MALAS. *Herman*: SCOTT WAARA. *Clem*: Bob Freschi. *Jake*: John Soroka. *Al*: Ed Romanoff. *Marie*: CLAUDIA CATANIA. *Max*: Bill Badolato. *Joe*: CHARLES PISTONE. *Pasquale*: Mark Lotito. *Ciccio*: BUDDY CRUTCHFIELD. *Giuseppe*: BILL NABEL. *The Priest*: Bill Badolato. *Doctor*: TAD INGRAM.

The Folks of San Francisco and Napa Valley: John Aller, Anne Allgood, Bill Badolato, Molly Brown, Kyle Craig, Mary Helen Fisher, Bob Freschi, Ramon Galindo, T. Doyle Leverett, Ken Nagy, Gail Pennington, Ed Romanoff, Jane Smulyan, John Soroka, Laura Streets, Thomas Titone, Melanie Vaughan. *Swings*: Robert Ashford, Keri Lee.

1992.02 CRAZY FOR YOU

A Musical Comedy in Two Acts, 17 Scenes. Book by Ken Ludwig. Co-conceived by Ken Ludwig and Mike Ockrent, inspired by material (the musical "Girl Crazy," with original book) by Guy Bolton and John McGowan. Music by George Gershwin. Lyrics by Ira Gershwin, (Gus Kahn, Desmond Carter). Directed by Mike Ockrent. Choreography by Susan Stroman. Scenic design by Robin Wagner. Costume design by William Ivey Long. Lighting design by Paul Gallo. Sound design by Otts Munderloh. Orchestrations by William D. Brohn, (Sid Ramin). Musical director, Paul Gemignani. Musical consultant, Tommy Krasker. Dance and incidental music arranged by Peter Howard. Fights by B. H. Barry. Associate director, Steven Zweigbaum. Associate producers, Richard Godwin, Valerie Gordon. Produced by Roger Horchow and Elizabeth Williams. Opened 19 February 1992 at the Sam S. Shubert Theatre and closed 7 January 1996 after 1622 performances.

CAST (in order of appearance): *Tess*: BETH LEAVEL. *Patsy*: STACEY LOGAN. *Bobby Child*: HARRY GROENER. *Bela Zanger*: BRUCE ADLER. *Sheila*: Judine Hawkins Richard. *Mitzi*: Paula Leggett. *Susie*: Ida Henry. *Louise*: Jean Marie. *Betsy*: Peggy Ayn Maas. *Margie*: Salomé Mazard. *Vera*: Louise Ruck. *Elaine*: Pamela Everett. *Irene Roth*: MICHELE PAWK. *Mother*: JANE CONNELL. *Perkins*: Gerry Burkhardt. *Cactus*: Gerry Burkhardt. *Moose, Mingo, Sam*: THE MANHATTAN RHYTHM KINGS: Brian M. Nalepka, Tripp Hanson, Hal Shane. *Junior*: Casey Nicholaw. *Pete*: Fred Anderson. *Jimmy*: Michael Kubala. *Billy*: Ray Roderick. *Wyatt*: Jeffrey Lee Broadhurst. *Harry*: Joel Goodness. *Polly Baker*: JODI BENSON. *Everett Baker*: RONN CARROLL. *Lank Hawkins*: JOHN HILLNER. *Eugene*: STEPHEN TEMPERLEY. *Patricia*: AMELIA WHITE.

Ensemble: Fred Anderson, Jeffrey Lee Broadhurst, Gerry Burkharrdt, Pamela Everett, Joel Goodness, Tripp Hanson, Ida Henry, Michael Kubala, Paula Leggett, Stacey Logan, Penny Ayn Maas, Jean Marie, Salomé Mazzard, Brian M. Nalepka, Casey Nicholaw, Judine Hawkins Richard, Ray Roderick, Louise Ruck, Hal Shane. *Swings*: Ken Lundie, Chris Peterson, Maryellen Scilla.

Act 1, Scene 1: Backstage at the Zangler Theatre, New York City, in the 1930s. *Scene 2*: 42nd Street, outside the theatre. *Scene 3*: Main Street, Deadrock, Nevada. *Scene 4*: Lank's Saloon. *Scene 5*: In the Desert. *Scene 6*: The Gaiety Theatre. *Scene 7*: Main Street, Deadrock, three days later. *Scene 8*: The Lobby of the Gaiety Theatre, two weeks later. *Scene 9*: The Stage of the Gaiety Theatre. *Scene 10*: The Gaiety Theatre Dressing Rooms, opening night. *Scene 11*: Main Street, Deadrock.

Act 2, Scene 1: Lank's Saloon, later that evening. *Scene 2*: Lank's Saloon, the next morning. *Scene 3*: The Gaiety Theatre, backstage. *Scene 4*: The Auditorium of the Gaiety Theatre. *Scene 5*: New York, six weeks later. *Scene 6*: Main Street, Deadrock, six days later.

ACT 1
Scene 1
"K-ra-azy for You" (from *TREASURE GIRL*)
H. Groener
Scene 2
"I Can't Be Bothered Now" (from *A DAMSEL IN DISTRESS* film)
H. Groener, Girls
Scene 3
"Bidin' My Time" (from *GIRL CRAZY*)
T. Hanson, B. M. Nalepka, H. Shane
"Things Are Looking Up" (from *A DAMSEL IN DISTRESS* film)
H. Groener
Scene 4
"Could You Use Me?" (from *GIRL CRAZY*)
J. Benson, H. Groener
Scene 5
"Shall We Dance?" (from *SHALL WE DANCE* film)
J. Benson, H. Groener
Scene 7
"Someone to Watch Over Me" (from *OH, KAY!*)
J. Benson
Scene 9
"Slap That Bass" (from *SHALL WE DANCE* film)
H. Groener, B. M. Nalepka, B. Leavel, S. Logan, Company
(*Orchestrations by* Sid Ramin.)
"Embraceable You" (from *GIRL CRAZY*)
J. Benson, H. Groener
Scene 10
"Tonight's the Night"[10]
Company
(*Lyrics by* Ira Gershwin and Gus Kahn.)
Scene 11
"I Got Rhythm" (from *GIRL CRAZY*)
J. Benson, H. Groener, Company

[9]Originally produced in New York 3 May 1956 at the Imperial Theatre for 678 performances. For Synopsis of Scenes and Musical Numbers, see original 1956 production.

[10]Previously unused.

ACT 2
Scene 1
"The Real American Folk Song Is a Rag" (from *LADIES FIRST*)
T. Hanson, B. M. Nalepka, H. Shane
"What Causes That?" (from *TREASURE GIRL*)
H. Groener, B. Adler
Scene 2
"Naughty Baby"[11]
M. Pawk, J. Hillner
(*Lyrics by* Ira Gershwin and Desmond Carter.)
Scene 4
"Stiff Upper Lip" (from *A DAMSEL IN DISTRESS* film)
H. Groener, J. Benson, S. Temperley, A. White, Company
"They Can't Take That Away from Me" (from *SHALL WE DANCE* film)
H. Groener
"But Not For Me" (from *GIRL CRAZY*)
J. Benson
Scene 5
"Nice Work If You Can Get It" (from *A DAMSEL IN DISTRESS* film)
H. Groener, Girls
Scene 6
Finale
Company

1992.03 FIVE GUYS NAMED MOE

A Musical (Revue) in Two Acts, based on the music made popular by Louis Jordan. Book by Clarke Peters. Music and lyrics by Louis Jordan, (Leo Hickman, Dallas Bartley, Larry Wynn, Jerry Bresler, Morry Lasco, Dick Adams, Fleecie Moore, Claude Demetriou, Jon Hendricks, Lora Lee, Johnny Burke, Jimmy Van Heusen, Sid Robin, Bill Davis, Don Wolf, Johnny Lange, Hy Heath, Joe Willoughby, Dr. Walt Merrick, Ellis Walsh, Busby Meyers, R. McCoy, C. Singleton, Browley Bri, Sam Theard, Spencer Lee, Joan Whitney, Alex Kramer, Jo Greene, Vaughn Horton, Denver Darling, Milton Gabler, Joseph Meyer, Buddy Bernier, Robert Emmerich, S. Austin.) Directed and choreographed by Charles Augins. (Setting) Designed by Tim Goodchild. Costumes by Noel Howard. Lighting by Andrew Bridge. Sound by Tony Meola/Autograph. Orchestrations by Neil McArthur. Vocal arrangements, musical supervision by Chapman Roberts. Musical direction, musical supervision, Reginald Royal. Executive producer, Richard Jay Alexander. Originally produced at The Theatre Royal, Stratford East (England). Produced by Cameron Mackintosh. Opened 8 April 1992 at the Eugene O'Neill Theatre and closed 2 May 1993 after 445 performances.

CAST (in order of appearance): *Nomax*: JERRY DIXON. *Big Moe*: DOUG ESKEW. *Four-Eyed Moe*: MILTON CRAIG NEALY. *No Moe*: KEVIN RAMSEY. *Eat Moe*: JEFFREY D. SAMS. *Little Moe*: GLENN TURNER.

ACT 1
"Early in the Morning"
(*Music and Lyrics by* Louis Jordan, Leo Hickman, Dallas Bartley.)
"Five Guys Named Moe"
(*Music and Lyrics by* Larry Wynn and Jerry Bresler.)
"Beware Brother Beware"
(*Music and Lyrics by* Morry Lasco, Dick Adams, Fleecie Moore.)
"I Like 'em Fat Like That"
(*Music and Lyrics by* Claude Demetriou and Louis Jordan.)
"Messy Bessy"
(*Music and Lyrics by* Jon Hendricks.)
"Pettin' and Pokin'"
(*Music and Lyrics by* Lora Lee.)
"Life Is So Peculiar" (from *MR. MUSIC* film)
(*Music and Lyrics by* Johnny Burke and James Van Heusen.)
"I Know What I've Got"
(*Music and Lyrics by* Sid Robin and Louis Jordan.)
"Azure Te"
(*Music and Lyrics by* Bill Davis and Don Wolf.)
"Safe, Sane and Single"
(*Music and Lyrics by* Louis Jordan, Johnny Lange, Hy Heath.)
"Push Ka Pi Shi Pie"
(*Music and Lyrics by* Joe Willoughby, Louis Jordan, Dr. Walt Merrick.)

[11]Previously unused.

ACT 2
"Saturday Night Fish Fry"
(*Music and Lyrics by* Ellis Walsh, Louis Jordan.)
"What's the Use of Getting Sober"
(*Music and Lyrics by* Busby Meyers.)
"If I Had Any Sense"
(*Music and Lyrics by* Rose Marie McCoy, Charles. Singleton.)
"Dad Gum Your Hide Boy"
(*Music and Lyrics by* Browley Bri.)
The Cabaret:
"Let the Good Times Roll"
(*Music and Lyrics by* Fleecie Moore, Sam Theard.)
"Reet, Petite and Gone"
(*Music and Lyrics by* Spencer Lee, Louis Jordan.)
"Caldonia"
(*Music and Lyrics by* Fleecie Moore.)
"Ain't Nobody Here But Us Chickens"
(*Music and Lyrics by* Joan Whitney, Alex Kramer.)
"Don't Let the Sun Catch You Crying"
(*Music and Lyrics by* Jo Greene.)
"Choo, Choo, Ch'boogie"
(*Music and Lyrics by* Vaughn Horton, Denver Darling, Milton Gabler.)
"Look Out Sister"
(*Music and Lyrics by* Sid Robin, Louis Jordan.)
Medley:
"Hurry Home"
(*Music and Lyrics by* Joseph Meyer, Buddy Bernier, Robert Emmerich.)
"Is You Is or Is You Ain't Ma' Baby?" (from FOLLOW THE BOYS film)
(*Music and Lyrics by* Billy Austin, Louis Jordan.)
"Five Guys Named Moe" (Finale)

1992.04 GUYS AND DOLLS

A Revival of the Musical Fable of Broadway in Two Acts, 17 Scenes[12]. Book by Jo Swerling and Abe Burrows. Based on a story and characters by Damon Runyon. Music and lyrics by Frank Loesser. Directed by Jerry Zaks. Choreographed by Christopher Chadman. Settings by Tony Walton. Costumes by William Ivey Long. Lighting by Paul Gallo. Orchestrations by George Bassman, Ted Royal, Michael Starobin, (Michael Gibson, Danny Troob). Dance music by Mark Hummel. Sound by Tony Meola. Assistant choreographer, Linda Haberman. Associate producers, Playhouse Square Center (Cleveland), David B. Brode. Executive producer, David Strong Warner, Inc. Produced by Dodger Productions, Roger Berlind, Jujamcyn Theatres/TV Asahi, Kardana Productions, Inc. and the John F. Kennedy Center. Opened 14 April 1992 at the Martin Beck Theatre and closed 8 January 1995 after 1143 performances.

CAST (in order of appearance): *Nicely-Nicely Johnson*: WALTER BOBBIE. *Benny Southstreet*: J. K. SIMMONS. *Rusty Charlie*: Timothy Shew. *Sister Sarah Brown*: JOSIE DE GUZMAN. *Arvide Abernathy*: JOHN CARPENTER. *Agatha*: Eleanor Glockner. *Calvin*: Leslie Feagan. *Martha*: Victoria Clark. *Harry the Horse*: Ernie Sabella. *Lieut. Brannigan*: STEVE RYAN. *Nathan Detroit*: NATHAN LANE. *Angie the Ox*: Michael Goz. *Miss Adelaide*: FAITH PRINCE. *Sky Masterson*: PETER GALLAGHER. *Joey Biltmore*: Michael Goz. *Hot Box Master of Ceremonies*: Stan Page. *Mimi*: Denise Faye. *General Matilda B. Cartwright*: RUTH WILLIAMSON. *Big Jule*: Herschel Sparber. *Drunk*: Robert Michael Baker. *Waiter*: Kenneth Kantor. *Crapshooter Dance Lead*: Scott Wise.

Other Guys: Robert Michael Baker, Gary Chryst, Lloyd Culbreath, R. F. Daley, Randy André Davis, David Elder, Cory English, Mark Esposito, Leslie Feagan, Michael Goz, Kenneth Kantor, Carlos Lopez, John MacInnis, Stan Page, Timothy Shew, Scott Wise. *Other Dolls*: Tina Marie DeLeone, Denise Faye, JoAnn M. Hunter, Nancy Lemenager, Greta Martin, Pascale Faye-Williams. *Swings*: Larry Cahn, Susan Misner, Steven Sofia.

1992.05 METRO

A Musical in Two Acts, 17 Scenes. Original (Polish) book and lyrics by Agata Miklaszewska and Maryna Miklaszewska. English book by Mary Bracken Phillips and Janusz Józefowicz. Music by Janusz Stoklosa. English lyrics by Mary Bracken Phillips. Direction and choreography by Janusz Józefowicz. Scenery by Janusz Sosnowski. Costumes by Juliet Polcsa, Marie

[12]First presented in New York 24 November 1950 at the 46th Street Theatre for 1200 performances. For Synopsis of Scenes and Musical Numbers, see original 1950 production."Travelling Light" omitted for this production.

Anne Chiment. Lighting by Ken Billington. Sound by Jaroslaw Regulski. Laser effects by Mike Deissler. Musical direction, vocal and orchestral arrangements by Janusz Stoklosa. American dance supervisor, Cynthia Onrubia. Executive producer, Donald C. Farber. Originally produced at the Dramatyczny Theatre in Warsaw, Poland. Produced by Wiktor Kubiak. Opened 16 April 1992 at the Minskoff Theatre and closed 26 April 1992 after 13 performances.

CAST: *Anka*: KATARZYNA GRONIEC, Robyn Griggs (alt.) *Jan*: ROBERT JANOWSKI, Rohn Seykell (alt.). *Edyta*: Edyta Górniak. *Max*: Mariusz Czajka. *Philip*: Olek Krupa, Janusz Józefowicz (alt.). *Viola*: Violetta Klimczewska. *Iwona*: Iwona Runowska.

Ensemble: Krzysztof Adamski, Monika Ambroziak, Andrew Appolonow, Jacek Badurek, Alicja Borkowska, Michal Chamera, Pawel Cheda, Magdalena Depczyk, Jaroslaw Derybowski, Wojciech Dmochowski, Malgorzata Duda, Katarzyna Galica, Katarzyna Gawel, Denisa Geislerova, Lidia Groblewska, Piotr Hajduk, Joanna Jagla, Jaroslaw Janikowski, Adam Kamien´, Grzegorz Kowalczyk, Andrzej Kubicki, Katarzyna Lewandowska, Barbara Melzer, Michal Milowicz, Radoslaw Natkan´ski, Polina Oziernych, Marek Palucki, Beata Pawlik, Katarzyna Skarpetowska, Igor Sorine, Ewa Szawlowska, Marc Thomas, Ilona Trybula, Beata Urban´ska, Kamila Zapytowska.

Act 1, Scene 1: A Theatre somewhere in Europe. *Scene 2*: A Metro somewhere in Europe. *Scene 3*: The Theatre. *Scene 4*: The Metro. *Scene 5*: The Theatre. *Scene 6*: The Metro. *Scene 7*: Audition results. *Scene 8*: Tower of Babel.

Act 2, Scene 1: The Metro. *Scene 2*: Philip's Office. *Scene 3*: Abandoned subway station. *Scene 4*: The Metro. *Scene 5*: The Metro. *Scene 6*: The Metro. *Scene 7*: Pieniadze. *Scene 8*: The Metro. *Scene 9*: The Metro.

ACT 1[13]
Scene 2
"Metro"
R. Janowski, Company
Scene 3
"My Fairy Tale"
Basia, A. Borkowska, D. Geislerova
Dancers: I. Runowska, L. Groblewska, V. Klimczewska.
Scene 4
"But Not Me"
R. Janowski, Company
Scene 5
"Windows"
K. Groniec
Scene 7
"Bluezwis"
R. Janowski, W. Dmochowski, Company
"Love Duet I"
K. Groniec, R. Janowski
Scene 8
"Tower of Babel"
Company

ACT 2
Scene 1
"Benjamin Franklin"
R. Janowski, Company
Scene 3
"Uciekali"
R. Janowski, Company
Scene 5
"Waiting"
E. Gorniak, K. Groniec, Dancers
Scene 7
"Pieniadze"
Company
Scene 8
"Love Duet II"
K. Groniec, R. Jankowski
Scene 9
"Dreams Don't Die"
K. Groniec

1992.06 THE HIGH ROLLERS SOCIAL AND PLEASURE CLUB

A Musical Revue in Two Acts. Conceived by Judy Gordon. Directed and choreographed by Alan Weeks. Arrangements, musical direction, orchestrations by Allen Toussaint. Scenery by David Mitchell. Costumes by Theoni V. Aldredge. Lighting by Beverly Emmons. Sound by Peter Fitzgerald. Music advisors, Jerry Wexler, Charles Neville. Associate director, Bruce Heath. Production supervisor, Mary Porter Hall. Associate producers, Nicholas Evans, Donald Tick, Mary Ellen Ashley, Irving Welzer. Produced by Judy Gordon, Dennis Grimaldi, Allen M. Shore, Martin Markinson. Opened 22 April 1992 at the Helen Hayes Theatre and closed 2 May 1992 after 14 performances.

CAST (in order of appearance): *Wonder Boy #1*: Keith Robert Bennett. *Queen*: DEBORAH BURRELL-CLEVELAND. *King*: Lawrence Clayton. *Jester*: Eugene Fleming. *Sorcerer*: Michael McElroy. *Enchantress*: VIVIAN REED. *Princess*: Nikki Rene. *Wonder Boy #2*: Tarik Winston. And ALLEN TOUSSAINT.

The High Roller Band: Allen Tousaint (conductor, piano), Carl Maultsby (associate conductor), Frank Canino (bass), Gary Keller (saxophone), Joel Helleny (trombone), Steve Johns (drums), Darryl Shaw (trumpet), Bob Rose (guitar).

The action takes place in the High Rollers Social and Pleasure Club, New Orleans, with a side trip to the Bayou at the time of Mardi Gras.

ACT 1
"Tu Way Pocky Way"
E. Fleming
(Traditional; arranged by the Wild Magnolias.)
"Open Up"
Band
"Mr. Mardi Gras"
Company
(*Music and Lyrics by* Allen Toussaint.)
Piano Solo
A. Toussaint
"Chicken Shack Boogie"
E. Fleming, Company
(*Music and Lyrics by* Lola Ann Callum and Amos Milburn.)
"Lady Marmalade"
V. Reed, M. McElroy, Company
(*Music and Lyrics by* Kenny Nolan.)
"Don't You Feel My Leg"
D. Burrell-Cleveland, L. Clayton, E. Fleming, M. McElroy
(*Music and Lyrics by* Danny Barker and Blue Lu Barker.)
"You Can Have My Husband" (Don't Mess with My Man)
V. Reed
(*Music and Lyrics by* Dorothy Labostrie.)
"Fun Time"
K. R. Bennett, T. Winston
(*Music and Lyrics by* Allen Toussaint.)
Rock Medley:
Company
"It Will Stand"
(*Music and Lyrics by* Norman Johnson.)
"Mother-in-Law"
(*Music and Lyrics by* Allen Toussaint.)
"Working in a Coal Mine"
(*Music and Lyrics by* Allen Toussaint.)
"Lipstick Traces (on a Cigarette)"
(*Music and Lyrics by* Naomi Neville.)
"Rockin' Pneumonia"
(*Music and Lyrics by* Huey P. Smith.)
"(Sittin' in) Ya Ya"
(*Music and Lyrics by* Lee Dorsey, Clarence Lewis, Morgan Robinson.)
"Feet Don't Fail Me Now" (My Feet Can't Fail Me Now)
K. R. Bennett, T. Winston
(*Music and Lyrics by* Mad Musicians.)
"Ooh Poo Pa Doo"
E. Fleming
(*Music and Lyrics by* Jesse Hill.)
"Dance the Night (Away with You)"
(*Music and Lyrics by* Doc Pomus and Mac Rebennack.)
"Such a Night"
L. Clayton, D. Burrell-Cleveland
(*Music and Lyrics by* Mac Rebennack.)
"All These Things"
V. Reed, M. McElroy
(*Music and Lyrics by* Naomi Neville.)
"Mellow Sax"
N. Rene, G. Keller (saxophone), Company
(*Music and Lyrics by* Roy Montrell.)
"Sea Cruise"
V. Reed, D. Burrell-Cleveland, N. Rene
(*Music and Lyrics by* Huey P. Smith.)

[13]Final running order for opening night as per program insert.

"Jambalaya (on the Bayou)"
E. Fleming, Company
(*Music and Lyrics by* Hank Williams.)

ACT 2

"Tu Way Pocky Way" (reprise)
E. Fleming

"Bourbon Street Parade"
Company
(*Music and Lyrics by* Paul Barbarin.)

"(I Ain't Gonna Give Nobody None o' This) Jelly Roll"
K. R. Bennett, T. Winston
(*Music and Lyrics by* Spencer Williams, Clarence Williams.)

"Heebie Jeebie Dance"
N. Rene, D. Burrell-Cleveland, V. Reed
(*Music by* Boyd Atkins.)

"I Like It Like That"
E. Fleming, Company
(*Music and Lyrics by* Chris Kenner.)

"Fiyou on the Bayou" (Fire on the Bayou)
Company
(*Music and Lyrics by* Arthur Neville, Jr., Leo Nocentelli.)

"Marie Laveau"
V. Reed
(*Music and Lyrics by* Shel Silverstein, Baxter Taylor III.)

"Walk on Gilded Splinters"
Company
(*Music and Lyrics by* Mac Rebennack.)

"Black Widow Spider"
L. Clayton
(*Music and Lyrics by* Mac Rebennack.)

"Tell It Like It Is"
(*Music and Lyrics by* Lee Diamond, George Davis.)

"You're the One"
D. Burrell-Cleveland, L. Clayton
(*Music and Lyrics by* Adolph Smith, Cosmo Matassa.)

"Let the Good Times Roll"
Company
(*Music and Lyrics by* Leonard Lee.)

"Challenge Dance"
E. Fleming, L. Clayton, M. McElroy, K. R. Bennett, T. Winston

"Mos Scoscious"
M. McElroy, N. Rene
(*Music and Lyrics by* Mac Rebennack.)

"We All Need Love"
V. Reed
(*Music and Lyrics by* Allen Toussaint.)

"Tu Way Pocky Way" (reprise)
E. Fleming

"Injuns Here We Come"
K. R. Bennett, Company
(*Music and Lyrics by* The Wild Magnolias and Wilson Turbinton.)

"Golden Crown"
Company
(*Music and Lyrics by* Theodore Dollis.)

"Jockomo"
Company
(*Music and Lyrics by* James Crawford.)

"Hey Mama"
Company

"(When the) Saints Go Marchin' In"
Company

1992.07 MAN OF LA MANCHA

A Revival of the Musical Play in One Act[14]. Book by Dale Wasserman. Suggested by the life and work ("Don Quixote") of Miguel de Cervantes y Saavedra. Music by Mitch Leigh. Lyrics by Joe Darion. Entire production staged by Albert Marre. Sets by Howard Bay. Costumes by Howard Bay and Patton Campbell. Lighting by Gregory Allen Hirsch. Sound by Jon Weston. Musical director, Brian Salesky. Dance arrangements by Neil Warner. Executive producer, Manny Kladitis. Produced by The Mitch Leigh Company. Opened 24 April 1992 at the Marquis Theatre and closed 26 July 1992 after 108 performances[15].

CAST: *Cervantes/Don Quixote*: RAUL JULIA. *Aldonza/Dulcinea*: SHEENA EASTON. *Sancho*: TONY MARTINEZ. *Governor/Pedro*, the Head Muleteer: CHEV RODGERS. *The Padre*: DAVID WASSON. *Dr. Carrasco*: IAN SULLIVAN. *The Innkeeper*: DAVID HOLLIDAY. *Antonia*: VALERIE DE PENA. *The Housekeeper*: MARCELINE DECKER. *The Barber*: Ted Forlow. *Paco*, a Muleteer/*The Mule*: Hechter Ubarry. *Juan*, a Muleteer/*The Horse*: Jean-Paul Richard. *Manuel*, a Muleteer: Luis Perez. *Tenorio*, a Muleteer: Gregory Mitchell. *Jose*, a Muleteer: Bill Santora. *Jorge*, a Muleteer: Chet D'Elia. *Maria*, the Innkeeper's Wife: Tanny McDonald. *Fermina*, a slavey/*Moorish Dancer*: Joan Susswein Barber. *Captain of the Inquisition*: Jon Vandertholen. *Guitarists*: Robin Polseno, David Serva. *Guards*: Chet D'Elia, Darryl Ferrera. *Swing*: Rick Manning.

1992.08 JELLY'S LAST JAM

A Musical in Two Acts, 12 Scenes. Book by George C. Wolfe. (Suggested by the life and music of Jelly Roll Morton.) Music by Jelly Roll Morton; additional music composed by Luther Henderson. Lyrics by Susan Birkenhead. Directed by George C. Wolfe. Choreography by Hope Clarke. Tap choreography by Gregory Hines, Ted L. Levy. Musical adaptation, orchestrations, musical supervision by Luther Henderson. Musical director, Linda Twine. Scenic design by Robin Wagner. Costumes designed by Toni-Leslie James. Lighting design by Jules Fisher. Sound design by Otts Munderloh. Mask and puppet design by Barbara Pollitt. Associate producers, Peggy Hill Rosencranz, Marilyn Hall, Dentsu Inc. Executive producer, David Strong Warner, Inc. Produced by Margo Lion and Pamela Koslow in association with Polygram Diversified Entertainment, 126 Second Avenue Corporation/Hal Luftig, Rodger Hess, Jujamcyn Theatres/TV Asahi, and Herb Alpert. Opened 26 April 1992 at the Virginia Theatre and closed 5 September 1993 after 569 performances.

CAST (in order of appearance): *Chimney Man*: KEITH DAVID. *The Hunnies*: Mamie Duncan-Gibbs, Stephanie Pope, Allison M. Williams. *The Crowd*: Ken Ard, Adrian Bailey, Sherry D. Boone, Brenda B. Braxton, Mary Bond Davis, Ralph Deaton, Melissa Haizlip, Cee-Cee Harshaw, Ted L. Levy, Stanley Wayne Mathis, Victoria Gabrielle Platt, Gil Pritchett III, Michelle M. Robinson. *Jelly Roll Morton*: GREGORY HINES.

The People of His Past: *Young Jelly*: SAVION GLOVER. *The Sisters*: Victoria Gabrielle Platt, Sherry D. Boone. *The Ancestors*: Adrian Bailey, Mary Bond Davis, Ralph Deaton, Ann Duquesnay, Melissa Haizlip. *Miss Mamie*: Mary Bond Davis. *Buddy Bolden*: Ruben Santiago-Hudson. *Too-Tight Nora*: Brenda Braxton. *Three Finger Jake*: Gil Pritchett III. *Gran Mimi*: Ann Duquesnay. *Jack the Bear*: STANLEY WAYNE MATHIS. *Foot-in-Yo-Ass Sam*: Ken Ard. *Anita*: TONYA PINKINS. *The Melrose Brothers*: Don Johanson, Gordon Joseph Weiss. *Swings*: Ken Roberson, Janice Lorraine-Holt.

Jelly's Red Hot Peppers: Brian Grice (drums), Ben Brown (bass), Steve Bargonetti (banjo), Virgil Jones (trumpet), Britt Woodman (trombone), Bill Easley (clarinet).

The action takes place in The Jungle Inn, a lowdown club somewhere 'tween Heaven 'n' Hell on the eve of Jelly Roll Morton's death.

Act 1, Scene 1: The Jam. *Scene 2*: In the Beginning. *Scene 3*: Goin' Uptown. *Scene 4*: The Journey to Chicago. *Scene 5*: Chicago! *Scene 6*: Jelly 'n' Anita. *Scene 7*: The Midnite Inn.

Act 2, Scene 1: The Chimney Man Takes Charge. *Scene 2*: The New York Suite. *Scene 3*: The Last Chance. *Scene 4*: Central Avenue. *Scene 5*: The Last Rites.

ACT 1

Scene 1

"Jelly's Jam" (adapted from "King Porter Stomp")
The Hunnies, The Crowd

"In My Day" (adapted from "Wild Man Blues")
G. Hines, The Hunnies

Scene 2

"The Creole Way"
(*Music by* Luther Henderson.)
A. Bailey, M. B. Davis, R. Deaton, A. Duquesnay, M. Haizlip, S. Glover

"The Whole World's Waitin' to Sing Your Song"
(adapted from "My Little Dixie Home")

"Street Scene"(*Music by* Luther Henderson.)
G. Hines, S. Glover, The Street Crowd

---

[14]First produced in New York 22 November 1965 at the ANTA Washington Square Theatre for 2328 performances. For Synopsis of Scenes and Musical Numbers, see original 1965 production.

[15]Orchestrations uncredited.

Scene 3
"Michigan Water" (traditional)
M. B. Davis, R. Santiago-Hudson
The Banishment:
"Get Away Boy" (*Music by* Luther Henderson.)
"Lonely Boy Blues" (traditional)
A. Duquesnay, S. Glover, G. Hines
Scene 4
"Somethin' More" (adapted from "Pretty Lil")
G. Hines, S. W. Mathis, K. David, The Hunnies, The Crowd
"That's How You Jazz"
G. Hines, S. W. Mathis, The Dance Hall Crowd
Scene 5
"The Chicago Stomp" (adapted from "Burnin' the Iceberg")
G. Hines, The Red Hot Peppers, K. David, The Hunnies, The Chicago Crowd
Scene 6
"Play the Music for Me" (adapted from "Dead Man Blues")
T. Pinkins
"Lovin' Is a Lowdown Blues" (adapted from "Jungle Blues")
The Hunnies
Scene 7
"Dr. Jazz"
G. Hines, The Crowd
(*Music by* King Oliver and Walter Melrose.)

ACT 2
Scene 2
"Good Ole New York" (adapted from "Hyena Stomp")
K. David, The Hunnies, G. Hines, The New York Crowd
"Too Late, Daddy"
G. Hines, The Harlem Crowd
(*Music by* Luther Henderson.)
"That's the Way We Do Things in New Yawk"
(adapted from "Shreveport Stomp") G. Hines, D. Johanson, G. J. Weiss
Jelly's Isolation Dance
G. Hines, S. Glover
Scene 3
"The Last Chance Blues" (adapted from "Blue Blood Stomp")
G. Hines, T. Pinkins
Scene 5
"The Last Rites" (includes "Creole Boy")
G. Hines, K. David, The People of His Past
(*Music by* Luther Henderson, Jelly Roll Morton.)

1992.09

FALSETTOS

A Musical in Two Acts[16]. Book by William Finn and James Lapine. Music and lyrics by William Finn. Directed by James Lapine. Set design by Douglas Stein. Costume design by Ann Hould-Ward. Lighting design by Frances Aronson. Sound design by Peter Fitzgerald. Musical arrangements by Michael Starobin. Musical direction, Scott Frankel. Associate producer, Alecia Parker. Produced by Barry and Fran Weissler, in association with James and Maureen O'Sullivan Cushing and Masakazu Shibaoka Broadway Pacific. Opened 29 April 1992 at the John Golden Theatre and closed 27 June 1993 after 487 performances.

CAST (in order of appearance): *Marvin*: MICHAEL RUPERT. *Whizzer*: STEPHEN BOGARDUS. *Mendel*: CHIP ZIEN. *Jason*: JONATHAN KAPLAN, ANDREW HARRISON LEEDS (alt.). *Trina*: BARBARA WALSH. *Charlotte*: HEATHER MACRAE. *Cordelia*: CAROLEE CARMELLO.

Act 1: 1979.

Act 2: 1981.

ACT 1
"Four Jews in a Room Bitching"
S. Bogardus, M. Rupert, J. Kaplan, C. Zien
"A Tight Knit Family"
M. Rupert, C. Zien
"Love Is Blind"
M. Rupert, J. Kaplan, S. Bogardus, C. Zien, B. Walsh
"Thrill of First Love"
M. Rupert, S. Bogardus
"Marvin at the Psychiatrist" (A Three-Part Mini-Opera)
J. Kaplan, C. Zien, S. Bogardus, M. Rupert
"Everyone Tells Jason to See a Psychiatrist"
J. Kaplan, M. Rupert, B. Walsh, S. Bogardus
"This Had Better Come to a Stop"
M. Rupert, S. Bogardus, J. Kaplan, B. Walsh, C. Zien
"I'm Breaking Down" (from *IN TROUSERS*)
B. Walsh
"Jason's Therapy"
C. Zien, B. Walsh, S. Bogardus, M. Rupert, J. Kaplan
"A Marriage Proposal"
C. Zien, B. Walsh, J. Kaplan
"A Tight Knit Family" (reprise)
M. Rupert, C. Zien
"Trina's Song"
B. Walsh
"March of the Falsettos"
C. Zien, M. Rupert, J. Kaplan, S. Bogardus
"Trina's Song" (reprise)
B. Walsh
"The Chess Game"
M. Rupert, S. Bogardus
"Making a Home"
C. Zien, J. Kaplan, B. Walsh, S. Bogardus
"The Games I Play"
S. Bogardus, C. Zien, B. Walsh, J. Kaplan
"Marvin Goes Crazy"
M. Rupert, C. Zien, J. Kaplan, B. Walsh, S. Bogardus
"I Never Wanted to Love You"
M. Rupert, C. Zien, J. Kaplan, B. Walsh, S. Bogardus
"Father to Son"
M. Rupert, J. Kaplan

ACT 2
"Welcome to Falsettoland"
Company
"The Year of the Child"
Company
"Miracle of Judaism"
Company
"Sitting Watching Jason (Play Baseball)"
Company
"A Day in Falsettoland"
Company
"Everyone Hates His Parents"
C. Zien, J. Kaplan, M. Rupert, B. Walsh
"What More Can I Say"
M. Rupert, S. Bogardus
"Something Bad Is Happening"
H. MacRae, C. Carmello
"Holding to the Ground"
B. Walsh
"Days Like This I Almost Believe in God"
Company
"Cancelling the Bar Mitzvah"
J. Kaplan, C. Zien, B. Walsh
"Unlikely Lovers"
M. Rupert, S. Bogardus, H. MacRae, C. Carmello
"Another Miracle of Judaism"
J. Kaplan
"You Gotta Die Sometime"
S. Bogardus
"Jason's Bar Mitzvah"
Company
"What Would I Do?"
M. Rupert, S. Bogardus

[16] Act 1 previously presented Off-Broadway as MARCH OF THE FALSETTOS 9 April 1981 at Playwrights Horizons and the Westside Arts Theatre for 298 performances, and Act 2 as FALSETTOLAND 28 June 1990 at Playwrights Horizons and the Lucille Lortel Theatre for 238 performances.

1992–1993 SEASON

Chita Rivera in KISS OF THE SPIDER WOMAN
Martha Swope/TimePix

1992–1993 SEASON

1992.10 110 IN THE SHADE

A Revival of the Musical in Two Acts, 11 Scenes[1]. Book by N. Richard Nash. Based on his play "The Rainmaker." Music by Harvey Schmidt. Lyrics by Tom Jones. Original direction by Joseph Anthony. Dances and musical numbers originally staged by Agnes de Mille. Directed by Scott Ellis. Choreographed by Susan Stroman. Set designer, Michael Anania. Costume design, Lindsay W. Davis. Lighting design, Jeff Davis. Sound design, Abe Jacob. Conductor, Paul Gemignani. Orchestrations by Hershy Kay; additional orchestrations by William D. Brohn. (Original dance music by William Goldenberg); additional dance music arrangements by Peter Howard. Chorus master, Joseph Colaneri. Fight coordinator, Steve Hall. Dialect coach, K. C. Ligon. Produced by the New York City Opera. Opened 18 July 1992 at the New York State Theatre and closed 15 November 1992 after 12 performances in repertory

CAST (in order of appearance): *Tommy*: Robert Mann Keyser. *Dance Couple*: Jennifer Paulson Lee, John Scott. *File*: RICHARD MUENZ. *Jimmy Curry*: DAVID AARON BAKER. *Noah Curry*: WALTER CHARLES. *H.C. Curry*: HENDERSON FORSYTHE. *Lizzie Curry*: KAREN ZIÉMBA. *Snookie Updegraff*: CRISTA MOORE. *Bill Starbuck*: BRIAN SUTHERLAND. *Townspeople*: New York City Opera Chorus.

The action takes place in a western state during a 24-hour period, on a summer day in a time of drought.

Act 1, Scene 1: A fence and a windmill. *Scene 2*: The depot. *Scene 3*: A street in Three Point, File's office. *Scene 4*: The park. *Scene 5*: Outside the Curry house. *Scene 6*: An open space.

Act 1, Scene 1: The park. *Scene 2*: Starbuck's truck. *Scene 3*: A picnic area. *Scene 4*: An open space. *Scene 5*: A fence and a windmill.

ACT 1
- "Gonna Be Another Hot Day"
  R. Muenz, Townspeople
- "Lizzie's Coming Home"
  D. A. Baker, W. Charles, H. Forsythe
- "Love, Don't Turn Away"
  K. Ziémba
- "Overhead"[2]
  Townspeople
- "Poker Polka"
  D. A. Baker, W. Charles, H. Forsythe, R. Muenz
- "Why Can't They Leave Me Alone"[3]
  R. Muenz
- "Come on Along"[4]
  Townspeople
- "Rain Song"
  B. Sutherland, Townspeople
- "You're Not Foolin' Me"
  K. Ziémba, B. Sutherland
- "Cinderella"[5]
  Children
- "Raunchy"
  K. Ziémba
- "A Man and a Woman"
  R. Muenz, K. Ziémba
- "Old Maid"
  K. Ziémba

[1]Originally produced in New York 24 October 1963 at the Broadhurst Theatre for 330 performances. Dropped from the original production was "Hungry Men."
[2]Newly written song for this production.
[3]Newly written song for this production.
[4]Newly written song for this production.
[5]Newly written song for this production.

ACT 2
- "Come on Along" (reprise)
  Townspeople
- "Everything Beautiful Happens at Night"
  Townspeople
- "Shooting Star"[6]
  B. Sutherland
- "Melisande"
  B. Sutherland
- "Simple Little Things"
  K. Ziémba
- "Little Red Hat"
  D. A. Baker, C. Moore
- "Is It Really Me?"
  K. Ziémba, B. Sutherland
- "Wonderful Music"
  B. Sutherland, R. Muenz, K. Ziémba
- Finale: "Rain Song"
  Company

1992.11 ANNA KARENINA

A Musical in Two Acts, a Prologue and 19 Scenes. Book and lyrics by Peter Kellogg. Based on the novel of the same name by Leo Tolstoy. Music by Daniel Levine. Directed by Theodore Mann. Musical sequences staged by Patricia Birch. Musical direction and dance music arrangements by Nicholas Archer. Scenic design by James Morgan. Costume design by Carrie Robbins. Lighting design by Mary Jo Dondlinger. Sound design by Fox and Perla. Orchestrations by Peter Matz. Associate choreographer, Jonathan Cerullo. Produced by Circle in the Square Theatre (Theodore Mann, Artistic director; Robert A. Buckley, Managing director; Paul Libin, Consulting producer). Opened 26 August 1992 at the Circle in the Square Theatre and closed 11 October 1992 after 46 performances.

CAST (in order of appearance): *Count Alexis Vronsky*: SCOTT WENTWORTH. *Anna Karenina*: ANN CRUMB. *Constantine Levin*: GREGG EDELMAN. *Train Conductor*: David Pursley. *Prince Stephen Oblonsky*, "Stiva": JERRY LANNING. *Princess Kitty Scherbatsky*: MELISSA ERRICO. *Dunyasha*, Kitty's maid: Naz Edwards. *Korsunsky*, Master of Ceremonies: Gabriel Barre. *Men at the Ball*: Larry Hansen, Ray Wills. *Guard at the Station*: Larry Hansen. *Masha*, woman at the station: Amelia Prentice. *Seryozha Karenin*, Anna's son: ERIC HOUSTON SAARI. *Annushka*, Karenin's maid: Darcy Pulliam. *Nicolai Karenin*, Anna's husband: JOHN CUNNINGHAM. *Fyodor*, a servant: David Pursley. *Basso*: David Pursley. *Princess Elizabeth Tversky*, Betsy: Jo Ann Cunningham. *Woman at Party*: Naz Edwards. *Finance Minister*: Ray Wills. *Man at Party*: Gabriel Barre. *Prince Yashvin*, a Captain: Ray Wills. *Vasily*, Vronsky's servant: Larry Hansen. *Levin's Foreman*: David Pursley. *Peasant*: Gabriel Barre. *Gina*: Amelia Prentice.

Swings: Jonathan Cerullo, Audrey Lavine. *Extras*: Jeremy Black, Billy Hipkins.

The action takes place in the 1870's.

Act 1: Russia.

Act 2: Russia and Italy.

Prologue: St. Petersburg Train Station.

Act 1, Scene 1: Moscow Train Station, next morning. *Scene 2*: Kitty Scherbatsky's house, later the same day. *Scene 3*: A Ball, a few days later. *Scene 4*: A small station between Moscow and St. Petersburg, the next night. *Scene 5*: Anna's House in St. Petersburg. *Scene 6*: Prince Tversky's home, that night. *Scene 7*: Croquet Lawn, several weeks later. *Scene 8*: Kitty's House. *Scene 9*: A small dance in St. Petersburg. *Scene 10*: On the way home. *Scene 11*: Anna's House. *Scene 12*: Vronsky's apartment.

Act 2, Scene 1: Anna's House, three months later. *Scene 2*: Levin's Estate and Italy. *Scene 3*: A Villa in Rome. *Scene 4*: Kitty's House. *Scene 5*: A Hotel in Moscow. *Scene 6*: Karenin's House. *Scene 7*: St. Petersburg Train Station.

ACT 1
Prologue
- "On a Train"
  A. Crumb, S. Wentworth, G. Edelman, Chorus

[6]Newly written song for this production.

Scene 1
"There's More to Life Than Love"
J. Lanning, A. Crumb
Scene 2
"How Awful"
M. Errico
"Would You?"
G. Edelman
"In a Room"
G. Edelman, M. Errico, A. Crumb, S. Wentworth
Scene 3
Waltz and Mazurka
A. Crumb, M. Errico, S. Wentworth, J. Lanning, Chorus
Scene 5
"Nothing Has Changed"
A. Crumb
Scene 6
"Lowlands"
D. Pursley
Scene 7
"Rumors"
Chorus
Scene 8
"How Many Men?"
M. Errico
Scene 9
"We Were Dancing"
S. Wentworth
Scene 10
"I'm Lost"
A. Crumb
Scene 11
"Karenin's List"
J. Cunningham
Scene 12
"Waiting for You"
A. Crumb, S. Wentworth

ACT 2
Scene 1
"This Can't Go On"
A. Crumb, S. Wentworth, J. Cunningham
Scene 2
"Peasants' Idyll"
Chorus
"That Will Serve Her Right"
G. Edelman
Scene 3
"Everything's Fine"
A. Crumb, S. Wentworth
Scene 4
"Would You?" (reprise)
G. Edelman, M. Errico
Scene 5
"Everything's Fine" (reprise)
A. Crumb
Scene 6
"Only at Night"
J. Cunningham
Scene 7
Finale
A. Crumb, Chorus

1992.12 MUSIC OF ANDREW LLOYD WEBBER

A Musical Revue in Two Acts. Directed by Arlene Phillips. Production (scenic) designer, Marc B. Weiss. Costume coordinator, Frank Krenz. Sound designer, Martin Levan. Production musical supervisor, Michael Reed. Musical director, Paul Bogaev. Produced by Broadway in Concert, Inc. (LIVENT), Pace Theatrical Group by arrangement with The Really Useful Company and Superstar Ventures. Opened 22 September 1992 at the Radio City Music Hall and closed 4 October 1992 after 14 performances.

CAST: MICHAEL CRAWFORD, TIM DONOGHUE, WILLY FALK, MARK HARDY, JULIET LAMBERT, JIMMY LOCKETT, DONNA LEE MARSHALL, GARY MAUER, CATHY PORTER, TAMI TAPPAN, TY TAYLOR, ELIZABETH WARD, GAY WILLIS, LAURIE BEECHMAN, LUANN ARONSON, Ensemble.

ACT 1
Jesus Christ Superstar Overture
Orchestra
"Jesus Christ Superstar" (from *JESUS CHRIST SUPERSTAR*)
(*Lyrics by* Tim Rice.) W. Falk, Company
"Potiphar" (from *JOSEPH AND THE AMAZING TECHNICOLOR DREAMCOAT*)
(*Lyrics by* Tim Rice.) D. L. Marshall, W. Falk, M. Hardy, J. Lockett, T. Taylor
"Close Every Door" (from *JOSEPH AND THE AMAZING TECHNICOLOR DREAMCOAT*)
(*Lyrics by* Tim Rice.) T. Donoghue
"A Pharaoh's Story" (from *JOSEPH AND THE AMAZING TECHNICOLOR DREAMCOAT*)
(*Lyrics by* Tim Rice.) L. Beechman
"Starlight Express" (from *STARLIGHT EXPRESS*)
(*Lyrics by* Richard Stilgoe.) G. Mauer, J. Lockett
"Unexpected Song" (from *SONG & DANCE*)
(*Lyrics by* Don Black.) L. Aronson
"Another Suitcase in Another Hall" (from *EVITA*)
(*Lyrics by* Tim Rice.) L. Aronson
"Memory" (from *CATS*)
(*Text and additional lyrics by* Trevor Nunn after T. S. Eliot.) L. Beechman
"Mr. Mistoffelees" (from *CATS*)
(*Text by* T. S. Eliot.) T. Taylor, Company
"Jellicle Ball" (from *CATS*)
(*Orchestration by* David Cullen.) Orchestra
"Amigos Para Siempre" (Friends for Life)
(*Lyrics by* Don Black.) G. Willis, W. Falk
"I Don't Know How to Love Him" (from *JESUS CHRIST SUPERSTAR*)
(*Lyrics by* Tim Rice.) C. Porter
"Everything's Alright" (from *JESUS CHRIST SUPERSTAR*)
(*Lyrics by* Tim Rice.) C. Porter, G. Mauer, T. Taylor
"Gethsemane" (from *JESUS CHRIST SUPERSTAR*)
(*Lyrics by* Tim Rice.) M. Crawford

ACT 2
Evita Suite Orchestra
"Don't Cry for Me Argentina" (from *EVITA*)
(*Lyrics by* Tim Rice.) E. Ward
"And the Money Kept Rolling In" (from *EVITA*)
(*Lyrics by* Tim Rice.) M. Crawford, Company
"Pie Jesu" (from *REQUIEM*)
G. Willis, T. Tappan, Company
The Phantom of the Opera Overture
Orchestra
"Think of Me" (from *THE PHANTOM OF THE OPERA*)
(*Lyrics by* Charles Hart. *Additional Lyrics by* Richard Stilgoe.) J. Lambert
"The Phantom of the Opera" (from *THE PHANTOM OF THE OPERA*)

(*Lyrics by* Charles Hart. *Additional Lyrics by* Richard Stilgoe and Mike Batt.)
M. Crawford, J. Lambert

"All I Ask of You" (from *THE PHANTOM OF THE OPERA*)
(*Lyrics by* Charles Hart. *Additional Lyrics by* Richard Stilgoe.)
M. Crawford, C. Porter

"Wishing You Were Somehow Here Again" (from *THE PHANTOM OF THE OPERA*)
(*Lyrics by* Charles Hart. *Additional Lyrics by* Richard Stilgoe.) J. Lambert

"Masquerade" (from *THE PHANTOM OF THE OPERA*)
(*Lyrics by* Charles Hart. *Additional Lyrics by* Richard Stilgoe.) Company

"The Music of the Night" (from *THE PHANTOM OF THE OPERA*)
(*Lyrics by* Charles Hart. *Additional Lyrics by* Richard Stilgoe.) M. Crawford

1992.13

OBA OBA '93

A New Edition of the Brazilian Musical Revue in Two Acts, 13 Scenes[7]. (Conceived and directed by Franco Fontana) Musical direction, Wilson Mauro. Choreography by Roberto Abraho. Produced by Franco Fontana. Opened 1 October 1992 at the Marquis Theatre and closed 11 November 1992 after 45 performances.[8]

CAST: ELIANA ESTAVO, Ailto Souza, Ana Careca, Ana Paula Dos Reis, Angela Mara, Arlindo Pipiu, Carlos Leca, Carlos Oliveira, Carlos Silva, Casemiro Raposo, Chico Filho, Claudia Lisboa, Claudio Nascimento, Claudio Sampaio, Claudio Santos, Cobrinha Mansa, Christiane Moreira, Edgar Aguiar, Edval Boa Morte, Eliane Garcia Emerson Bernardes, Formiguinha, Gamo, Giovani Ramos, Ilson Helvecio, Iris Da Rocha, Jaime Santos, Jones Santana, Jorge Boa Morte, Jorge Rum, Julio Peluchi, Lu Viana, Luciano Ribeiro, Mac, Marcia Labios de Mel, Marcio Do Repenique, Marquinho Da Geralda, Mauricio De Souza, Mercia Alexandre, Messias Bastos, Monica Acioli, Nelaci Costa, Nilton Maravilha, Patricia Dantas, Patricia Moreira, Paulo W. Takase, R. Malaguti, Ray Do Pandeiro, Ratinho, Rita De Cassia Nobre, Roberto Silva, Rodman Clayson, Rose Perola, Sergio Rocha, Sete Mola, Sonia Regina Maraes, Toco Preto, Valeria Matos, Wellington Gusmao, Wilson Mauro.

Scene 1

Origins of Brazil

Before the Portuguese people came to Brazil, it was a jungle full of beautiful nature—wonderful flora and fauna—and the only human beings living there were the native Indians. These people lived completely free in this natural paradise until Europeans came to Brazil with African slaves. Today, Brazil is touted as the world's cultural melting pot—and the apparently seamless integration of blacks, native Indians and white Europeans to create "the Brazilian" is witness to that. But it was not always so. Until the liberation of slaves, proclaimed by Princess Isabel of Portugal in 1888, the pain of blacks captive in Brazil was unmatched elsewhere in the Americas. Even after gaining their freedom, Afro-Brazilians had to struggle within a society full of discrimination. It was only through the attempted unification of all blacks that they began to rebuild and recovered their culture, brutally interrupted by slavery. This opening act portrays the stages of black culture in Brazil, from the early days of slavery to the redemption.

Scene 2

Homage to "Chorinho"

Chorinho is a Portuguese word that literally means "little cry." One would not guess that meaning, however, by listening to this lively rhythm that flourished in the turn of the nineteenth century in urban areas of Brazil, especially Sao Paulo and Rio de Janeiro. The cavaquinho, a type of ukelele, which is the centerpiece of any typical chorinho band, requires an amazing level of dexterity by the player. The cavaquinho sounds like a high-pitched lament, a little cry indeed, even when it is played in cheerful songs such as "Tico Tico No Fuba" or "Urubu Malandro," both of which were written by Brazil's most important chorinho composer, Zequinha de Abreu.

Scene 3a

Samba de Roda

In the public squares of Sao Salvador, the beautiful and mystic capital of Bahia, one may inadvertently run into an improvised competition of bliss and grace among women. The natives refer to this competition as Samba de Roda, roughly translated as "Samba in a Circle," a popular Bahia tradition whose roots are lost in the past. This competition is one of joy, with the girls taking turns flaunting their natural talents.

Scene 3b

Lambada

Another popular dance comes from Belem at the border of the Eastern Amazon: the now world-famous Lambada. Unlike Samba de Roda which is unqiuely Brazilian, the Lambada shares common ground with Caribbean culture; the rhythm bears a striking resemblance to Santo Domingo's merengue. The dance—voluptuous, sensual and downright carnal—is a lifesize reflection of one of the strongest aspects of Brazilian culture, one that can be found throughout the giant country: the lust for love.

Scene 3c

Samba Reggae

This dance was born just a few months ago in the town of Salvador, Bahia. In this short time, there has been an explosion of popularity of this dance, which is now becoming the rage throughout cities in Brazil. The rhythm which underscores this dance combines the traditional samba with reggae music from the Caribbean. This is the first time that this dance form is being presented in the United States.

Scene 4

Homage to the Northeast

It has been said that despite personal and national tragedies, Brazilians have a natural joie de vivre. From the desolate and poor Northeast—where droughts may last for many years in a row, destroying crops and spreading hunger—comes songs of lament seasoned with ever-lasting hope. Eventually, the mourn of the accordion resolves in an outburst of a people that learned to extract the good from bad situations and dance with candid jubilation.

Scene 5

Brazil Cappela

Ary Barroso's "Aquarela do Brazil"—"Brazilian Colors" in English—has become a classic that has risen to the level of an "alternative" Brazilian national anthem. The poetic lyrics rhapsodize about the exuberant natural splendors of Brazil. So strong is the chant that it demands no more than the superb voice of Eliana Estevao to bring it to life.

Scene 6

Homage to the Bossa Nova and the Seventies

The Bossa Nova is undisputed as the most precious artistic gift Brazil has given to the world. This musical revolution started in the mid-1950s with a handful of young composers in Rio de Janeiro and it spread throughout the world to such an extent that virtually all modern pop music—from jazz to heavy metal—shows some level of Bossa Nova influence, with its new concepts of harmonization, rhythmic division and melody writing. At the center of it all, one man guided the legion of followers that even today continues growing—Antonio Carlos Jobim. The composer of the revolutionary "Desafinado," the delightful "Girl from Ipanema" and dozens of other tunes that worked their way up the jazz and pop charts, Jobim is one of the most appreciated musicians in the world today.

Scene 7

Tribute to Carmen Miranda—the 'Brazilian Bombshell'

The first wave of Brazilian music ever to reach the United States came through the body and soul of Carmen Miranda. Born in Portugal, Carmen became an emblem of Brazil and managed to represent a comprehensive culture which encompassed the much wider and larger Hispanic community of Latin America. Her 'chica-chica-boom,' peculiar arm dance, colorful clothes and fruit basket hat are easily recognized in the U.S. But behind the outrageous facade was an authentic singer whose interpretations still rank among the best ever.

[7]Previous editions presented in New York 29 March 1988 at the Ambassador Theatre for 46 performances; 15 March 1990 at the Marquis Theatre for 45 performances.

[8]Settings and costumes uncredited.

ACT 2

Scene 1

Macumba

Brazil is the largest Catholic country in the world, but it is also true that many Brazilians are devoted to a second religion: the Macumba. Macumba is a type of voodoo, equivalent to Santeria in Cuba and Puerto Rico, and it has its roots in the same boats that brought the African slaves to Brazil and those other Caribbean countriies. The saints of Macumba (Oxossi, Yemanja, Xango, Obatala, and others) represent a blending of Catholic divinities with primitive African gods in an ambiance of magic and mystery that commences as the drums start echoing and a trance takes over the stage. As they say in the Macumba worship places, "Sarava!"

Scene 2

Afro-Brazilian Folk Songs and Dances—Berimbau Medley

Capoeira of Angola:

Capoeira is one of the principal elements of black culture in Brazil, where it arrived with the first boats coming from Angola. Deprived by their masters of carrying any kind of weapons, the slaves kept the tradition of capoeira as a means of conquering, and then defending, their freedom in the new land. To elude their white masters, blacks disguised capoeira in a dance to the rhythm of berimbau, pandeiro, ganga and caxixi. The berimbau is one of the many intriguing musical instruments developed by black culture in Brazil. It consists of a wood arch, bent by a string of metal wire; the resulting tension gives the wire a distinctive sound that can be "tuned" when pressed with a round metal chip by one hand and struck with a wood stick by the other. The sound is transmitted to an open, hollow coconut shell connected to the string through another piece of wire. A small caxixi—a device which produces a shaker-like sound—completes the set. The player hits the single string with the wood stick, tunes it with the metal chip, shakes the caxixi and presses the coconut shell back and forth against his thorax, and the resulting sound creates an atmosphere that can become a musical event in itself, or the background to a capoeira dance.

Maculele:

The dance of the Maculele, like Capoeira, was born in Bahia from the traditions brought by African slaves. Also like Capoeira, the dance is a practical disguise of a type of martial art. The batons used by the dancers can be replaced by swords and other types of mortal weapons, making it a very dangerous dance. Today, there are several Maculele groups, not only in Bahia, but in many other areas of Brazil, including the industrialized Sao Paulo.

Acrobatic Capoeira:

For the capoerista, the practice is more than a dance and more than a martial art—it is a philosophy, a way of life. The acrobatic capoeira here takes the form of a jogo, an exceedingly dangerous contest in which the opponents attempt to best one another combining traditional moves and individual improvisations. Oba Oba's capoeiristas, recruited among the best in the country, perform incredible acrobatic feats that are at once mighty and gracious.

Scene 3

Partido Alto

One of the most genuine expressions of Brazilian urban music in Partido Alto. Literally, the name means "High Party," in reference to the most distinguished members of a school of samba. Those are usually from the Ala de Compositores, a group of composers in charge of preparing the songs that will be sung during Carnival. They get together to improvise verses around some theme of the moment. A similar variation of Partido Alto is the Pagode—roughly meaning 'mockery'—in which sambistas joke around in a type of jam session with plenty of room for improvisation. As one would expect, in both cases the rhythm is the same that marks the Carnival parades—only a bit slower and with a more important role reserved to the acoustic guitar and the cavaquinho. In a typical Partido Alto or Pagode, a chorus is repeated by all members of the group and the improvised verses are sung alternately by each individual. Sometimes the verses express a duel between two members of the group, the winner being the one who has the last word.

Scene 4

Rhythm Beaters

The magic of the samba is rooted in many different percussion instruments: the humorous cuica—a drum that has the unique characteristic of being played from the inside, where a piece of wood attached to the skin is rubbed by the skillful hands of the player; the surdo—a huge drum that produces the bass-beat; the tamborins—high-pitched, small drums that are played with a stick; and finally, the father of it all, the pandeiro. The pandeiro, known to Americans as tambourine, is the central instrument of any samba group. Its round shape and leather skin remind its players of a soccer ball and it is almost inevitable that the two Brazilian passions—soccer and samba—come together in the performance.

Scene 5

Show of Samba Dancers

Joining the rhythm beaters are a group of mulatto women in a joyous display of samba dancing. The mulatto is perhaps the best expression of a possible "Brazilian race." Resulting from a mixture of the white Portuguese with the black Africans, the mulatto has more than just skin color to prove such inheritance. The duality of the African and the European continents is merged into the mulatto, transforming one single body into the conveyor of master and slave, pose and humbleness, sorrow and happiness, sensuality and innocence, and, most of all, beauty and strength.

Scene 6

Grand Carnival

Carnival is undoubtedly the greatest popular party in the whole world. It developed out of a Portuguese tradition of pagan parties which marked the four days preceding the grieving sobriety of Lent. In Brazil, Carnival has become a tapestry into which millions of lives are woven during day-to-day preparations. Carnival takes place 40 days before Lent; it starts on a Friday evening and lasts through the following Ash Wednesday. During these five nights and four days, certain morals take a vacation and perhaps the world becomes a better place in which to live. Although it is celebrated throughout the country, it is in Rio de Janeiro that the Carnival became the symbol that the world has learned to admire. In Oba Oba, the traditional parade of Rio de Janeiro's Schools of Samba is recreated to give a truthful taste of Brazil.

1992.14

REGINA

A Revival of the Musical Drama (Opera) in Three Acts, a Prologue and 4 Scenes[9]. Text and music by Marc Blitzstein. Based on the play "The Little Foxes" by Lillian Hellman. Directed by Rosalind Elias. Conducted by Laurie Ann Hunter. Set design by James Leonard Joy. Costume design by Joseph A. Citarella. Lighting design by Jeff Davis. Chorus master, Joseph Colaneri. (Orchestrations by Marc Blitzstein.) Produced by the New York City Opera. Opened 9 October 1992 at the New York State Theatre and closed 24 October 1992 after 4 performances in repertory.

CAST (in order of appearance): *Addie*, Regina's housekeeper: DENISE WOODS. *Cal*, Regina's houseman: MICHAEL LOFTON. *Alexandra Giddens*, Zan, Regina's daughter: ELIZABETH FUTRAL. *Birdie Hubbard*, Oscar's wife: SHERYL WOODS. *Oscar Hubbard*, Regina's brother: RON BAKER. *Leo Hubbard*, Birdie and Oscar's son: JOHN DANIECKI. *Regina Giddens*: LEIGH MUNRO. *William Marshall*, a businessman from Chicago: PAUL AUSTIN KELLY. *Benjamin Hubbard*, Regina's brother: ANDREW WENTZEL. *Horace Giddens*, Regina's husband: LEROY LEHR. *Townspeople*: New York City Opera Chorus.

1992.15

GYPSY PASSION

A Return Engagement of the Flamenco Musical Revue in Two Acts, 8 Scenes[10]. (Conceived) and directed by Tomas Rodriguez-Pantoja.

[9]Originally produced in New York 31 October 1949 at the 46th Street Theatre for 56 performances. For Synopsis of Scenes and Musical Numbers, see original 1949 production.

[10]Originally produced in New York 22 April 1992 at Town Hall for 15 performances.

Traditional music and lyrics from Spanish Gypsy Life. Artistic and musical director, Manuel Morao. Choreography by Gitanos de Jerez. Scenery by David Sumner. Costumes by Mercedes Muñiz. Lighting by Tom Sturge. Sound by Otts Munderloh. Production supervisor, Carlos Gorbea. Produced by Roy A. Somlyo and Andalucia Productions for the Government of Andalucia, Spain. Opened 17 November 1992 at the Plymouth Theatre and closed 2 January 1993 after 54 performances. Total including prior Town Hall engagement: 69 performances.

CAST: *First Generation*: MANUEL MORAO, Lorenzo Galvez, Manuel Moneo, Juana la del Pipa. *Second Generation*: Antonio el Pipa, Sara Baras, Concha Vargas, Juan Antonio Ogalla, Pepe de la Joaquina, Luis Moneo, Antonio Moreno, Carmen de la Jeroma. *Third Generation*: Manuela Nuñez, Mercedes Ruiz, Patricia Valdés, Estephania Aranda. And Maria Gonzalez.

Act 1, Scene 1: The Patriarch. *Scene 2*: The Forest outside Seville. *Scene 3*: In Seville, the next day. *Scene 4*: Seville, the market place.

Act 2, Scene 1: Romance. *Scene 2*: The Wedding. *Scene 3*: At work. *Scene 4*: Finale.

ACT 1

Scene 1

"Toná"
M. Morao (singer)
The chief of the gypsies, the oldest and wisest of the tribe, tells the story of his people in song.

Scene 2

"Villancico"
Entire Company

"Soleá"
J. la del Pipa (singer), C. Vargas (dancer), M. Morao, L. Moneo, A. Moreno (guitarists)

"Cantiña"
P. de la Juaquina (singer), A. el Pipa (dancer), M. Morao, L. Moneo, A. Moreno (guitarists)

"Tangos"
J. la del Pipa (singer/dancer)

"Tanguillos"
J. la del Pipa (singer/dancer), M., Nuñez, M. Ruiz, P. Valdés, E. Aranda (dancers), M. Morao, L. Moneo, A. Moreno (guitarists)

"Seguirillas"
M. Moneo (singer), S. Baras (dancer), M. Morao, L. Moneo, A. Moreno (guitarists)
Gypsies prepare to spend the night in a gypsy camp, before going to the city market in the morning to trade their handicrafts. The birth of a child heightens the joy and excitement in the camp.

Scene 3

"Zapateado"
Entire Company

"Taranto"
L. Galvez, J. A. Ogalla, C. de la Jeroma (dancers), M. Morao (guitarist)
After conducting their business, the adults go to a tavern where they sing and dance the Flamenco.

Scene 4

"Bulerias"
P. de la Joaquina, J. la del Pipa (singers), M. Nuñez, M. Ruiz, P. Valdés, E. Aranda (dancers), L. Moneo, A. Moreno (guitarists)
After the business is conducted, the children express their emotions in a natural and spontaneous way.

ACT 2

Scene 1

"Alegrias"
P. de la Joaquina (singer), A. el. Pipa, S. Baras, J. A. Ogalla, C. de la Jeroma (dancers), M. Morao, L. Moneo, A. Moreno (guitarists)
Two young adults who have fallen in love express their emotions in song and dance.

Scene 2

"Alboreá"
Entire Company

"El Polo de Tobalo"
P. de la Joaquina (singer), A. el Pipa, S. Baras (dancers), M. Morao, L. Moneo, A. Moreno (guitarists)
The young lovers receive their families' approval to marry. The marriage ceremony takes place with the traditional gypsy rites and the new couple promises to perpetuate the gypsy heritage.

Scene 3

"Martinetes"
L. Galvez, M. Moneo, P. de la Joaquina (singers), A. el Pipa, S. Baras (dancers)
The new husband must work long hours in his father's blacksmith shop to support his bride.

Scene 4

"Bulerias" (reprise/finale)
Entire Company
Always a unique and happy people devoted to tradition, the gypsies embrace their treasured Flamenco in an affirmation of joy and celebration of life.

1992.16 3 FROM BROOKLYN

A Musical Revue in One Act. Conceived and directed by Sal Richards. Original music and lyrics by Sandi Merle and Steve Michaels. Musical director, Steve Michaels. Set design, Charles E. McCarry. Lighting design, Phil Monat. Sound design, Raymond D. Schilke. Produced by Michael Frazier, Larry Spellman, Don Ravella. Opened 19 November 1992 at the Helen Hayes Theatre and closed 27 December 1992 after 45 performances.

CAST: SAL RICHARDS, ROSLYN KIND, (BOBBY) ALTO & (BUDDY) MANTIA, ADRIANNE TOLSCH, RAYMOND SERRA (Cosmo the Cabbie). *THE BQE DANCERS*: Guy Richards, John Michaels, Damon Rusignola.

The action takes place on a street in Brooklyn at the present time.

MUSICAL NUMBERS[11]

"People" (from *FUNNY GIRL*)
R. Kind
(*Music by* Jule Styne. *Lyrics by* Bob Merrill.)

"I've Gotta Be Me" (from *GOLDEN RAINBOW*)
R. Kind
(*Music and Lyrics by* Walter Marks.)

"Take a Trip"
R. Kind

"Meadowlark" (from *THE BAKER'S WIFE*)
R. Kind
(*Music and Lyrics by* Stephen Schwartz.)

"3 from Brooklyn"
(Company)
(*Music by* Steve Michaels. *Lyrics by* Sandi Merle.)

1992.17 MY FAVORITE YEAR

A Musical in Two Acts, 15 Scenes. Book by Joseph Daugherty. Based on the film of the same name; screenplay by Norman Steinberg, Dennis Palumbo, from a story by Dennis Palumbo. Music by Stephen Flaherty. Lyrics by Lynn Ahrens. Directed by Ron Lagomarsino. Musical staging by Thommie Walsh. Sets by Thomas Lynch. Costumes by Patricia Zipprodt. Lighting by Jules Fisher. Sound by Scott Lehrer. Musical director, Ted Sperling. Orchestrations by Michael Starobin. Dance music arrangements by Wally Harper. Fight director, B. H. Barry. Produced by Lincoln Center Theatre (Andre Bishop, Artistic director; Bernard Gersten, Executive producer) in association with AT&T OnStage. Opened 10 December 1992 at the Vivian Beaumont Theatre and closed 10 January 1993 after 37 performances.

CAST (in order of appearance): *Benjy Stone*: EVAN PAPPAS. *King Kaiser*: TOM MARDIROSIAN. *Sy Benson*: JOSH MOSTEL. *K. C. Downing*: LANNYL STEPHENS. *Alice Miller*: ANDREA MARTIN. *Herb Lee*: ETHAN PHILLIPS. *Belle Steinberg Carroca*: LAINIE KAZAN. *Leo Silver*: PAUL STOLARSKY. *Alan Swann*: TIM CURRY. *Rookie Carroca*: THOMAS IKEDA. *Tess*: Katie Finneran. *Uncle Morty*: David Lipman. *Aunt Sadie*: Mary Stout.

[11]Not in performance order.

Ensemble: Leslie Bell, Maria Calabrese, Kevin Chamberlin, Colleen Dunn, Katie Finneran, James Gerth, Michael Gruber, David Lipman, Roxie Lucas, Nora Mae Lyng, Michael McGrath, Alan Muraoka, Jay Poindexter, Russell Ricard, Mary Stout, Thomas Titone, Bruce Winant, Christina Youngman. *Swings*: Robert Ashford, Aimee Turner.

The action takes place in New York City in 1954.

Act 1, Scene 1: The Broadcast Studio. *Scene 2*: The Writers' Office, morning. *Scene 3*: The Writers' Office, later that day. *Scene 4*: Swann's Waldorf Suite. *Scene 5*: Streets of New York. *Scene 6*: The Broadcast Studio. *Scene 7*: The Ladies' Room. *Scene 8*: The Broadcast Studio. *Scene 9*: Belle's Apartment.

Act 2, Scene 1: Central Park. *Scene 2*: The Plaza Hotel. *Scene 3*: Swann's Waldorf Suite. *Scene 4*: The Broadcast Studio. *Scene 5*: Swann's Dressing Room. *Scene 6*: The Broadcast Studio.

ACT 1

Scene 1

"Twenty Million People"
E. Pappas, Company

Scene 2

"Larger Than Life"
E. Pappas

Scene 3

"The Musketeer Sketch"
E. Pappas, J. Mostel, T. Mardirosian, A. Martin, L. Stephens, P. Stolarsky, E. Phillips

Scene 4

"Waldorf Suite"
E. Pappas

"Rookie in the Ring"
L. Kazan

Scene 5

"Manhattan"
T. Curry, E. Pappas, Ensemble
(*Orchestration by* Danny Troob.)

Scene 6

"Naked in Bethesda Fountain"
J. Mostel, A. Martin, P. Stolarsky, E. Phillips, L. Stephens

"The Gospel According to King"
T. Mardirosian, T. Curry, Company

"The Musketeer Sketch Rehearsal"
E. Pappas, T. Curry, Ensemble

Scene 7

"Funny/The Duck Joke"
L. Stephens, A. Martin

Scene 8

"The Musketeer Sketch Rehearsal" (Part 2)
T. Mardirosian, T. Curry, Ensemble

Scene 9

"Welcome to Brooklyn"
D. Lipman, T. Ikeda, L. Kazan, M. Stout, E. Pappas, T. Curry, Neighbbors

"If the World Were Like the Movies"
T. Curry

ACT 2

Scene 1

"Exits"
T. Curry

Scene 3

"Shut Up and Dance"
L. Stephens, E. Pappas

Scene 4

"Professional Showbizness Comedy"
A. Martin, T. Mardirosian, Ensemble

Scene 5

"The Lights Come Up"
T. Curry, E. Pappas

Scene 6

"Maxford House"
Maxford House Girls

"The Musketeer Sketch Finale"
Company

"My Favorite Year"
E. Pappas, Company

1992.18

TOMMY TUNE TONITE!

A Song and Dance Act (Musical Revue) in One Act. Directed by Jeff Calhoun. Choreographic contributions by Charles "Honi" Coles, Tripp Hanson, Allan Johnson, Leslie J. Lockery, Ann Reinking, Hal Shane, Ron Young. Setting design by Tony Walton. Costume design by Willa Kim. Lighting design by Jules Fisher, Peggy Eisenhauer. Sound design by David Dansky. Musical direction, Michael Biagi. (Musical) arrangements and/or orchestrations by Michael Biagi, Randall Biagi, Wally Harper, Bob Holloway, Dick Lieb, Peter Matz, Michael Reeder, Alex Rybeck, Don Sebesky, Harold Wheeler. Overture arranged by Mark Hummel, orchestrated by Don Sebesky. Associate producers, Phillip Oesterman, David Wolfe. Produced by Pierre Cossette, James M. Nederlander, William E. Simon. Opened 27 December 1992 and closed 3 January 1993 after 10 performances.

CAST: TOMMY TUNE, Robert Fowler, Frantz Hall.

MUSICAL NUMBERS

"Tap Your Troubles Away" (from *MACK AND MABEL*)
(*Music and Lyrics by* Jerry Herman.)

"Let's Face the Music and Dance" (from *FOLLOW THE FLEET* film)
(*Music and Lyrics by* Irving Berlin.)

"A Song for Dancing" (from *BALLROOM*)
(*Music by* William Goldenberg. *Lyrics by* Marilyn and Alan Bergman.)

"Dancing in the Dark" (from *THE BANDWAGON*)
(*Music by* Arthur Schwartz. *Lyrics by* Howard Dietz.)

"Everything Old Is New Again"
(*Music by* Peter Allen. *Lyrics by* Carole Bayer Sager.)

"You're the Top" (from *ANYTHING GOES*)
(*Music and Lyrics by* Cole Porter.)

"Puttin' on the Ritz" (from *PUTTIN' ON THE RITZ* film)
(*Music and Lyrics by* Irving Berlin.)

"Someone to Watch Over Me" (verse only) (from *OH, KAY!*)
(*Music by* George Gershwin. *Lyrics by* Ira Gershwin.)

"Star Dust" (verse only)
(*Music by* Hoagy Carmichael. *Lyrics by* Mitchell Parish.)

"Blue Skies" (from *BETSY*
(*Music and Lyrics by* Irving Berlin.)

"The Old Soft Shoe" (from *THREE TO MAKE READY*)
(*Music by* Morgan Lewis. *Lyrics by* Nancy Hamilton.)

"Once in Love With Amy" (from *WHERE'S CHARLEY?*)
(*Music and Lyrics by* Frank Loesser.)

"I'm Building Up to an Awful Let-Down" (from *RISE AND SHINE*, London)
(*Music by* Fred Astaire. *Lyrics by* Johny Mercer.)

"They Can't Take That Away from Me" (from *SHALL WE DANCE* film)
(*Music by* George Gershwin. *Lyrics by* Ira Gershwin.)

"Taking a Chance on Love" (from *CABIN IN THE SKY*)
(*Dance music only by* Vernon Duke.)

"In the Still of the Night" (from *ROSALIE* film)
(*Music and Lyrics by* Cole Porter.)

"You Go to My Head"
(*Music by* J. Fred Coots. *Lyrics by* Haven Gillespie.)

Recollections of the Variety Arts Studios and Broadway

"Broadway Melody" (from *THE BROADWAY MELODY* {1929})
(*Music by* Nacio Herb Brown. *Lyrics by* Arthur Freed.)

"Please Don't Monkey With Broadway"
(from *BROADWAY MELODY OF 1940* film)
(*Music and Lyrics by* Cole Porter.)
"Sam the Old Accordion Man"
(*Music and Lyrics by* Walter Donaldson.)
"When the Midnight Choo-Choo Leaves for Alabam'"
(*Music and Lyrics by* Irving Berlin.)
"Strike Up the Band" (from *STRIKE UP THE BAND*)
(*Dance Music only by* George Gershwin.)
"Shanghai Lil" (from *FOOTLIGHT PARADE* film)
(*Music by* Harry Warren. *Lyrics by* Al Dubin.)
"Top Hat, White Tie and Tails" (from *TOP HAT* film)
(*Music and Lyrics by* Irving Berlin.)
Finale

1993.01

FOOL MOON

A Comedy Performance Revue in Two Acts. Created by Bill Irwin and David Shiner. (Original music and lyrics by the Red Clay Ramblers.) Set design by Douglas Stein. Costume design by Bill Kellard. Lighting design by Nancy Schertler. Sound design by Tom Morse. Flying by Foy. Producing associate, Nancy Harrington. Produced by James B. Freydberg, Kenneth Feld, Jeffrey Ash, Dori Berinstein. Opened 25 February 1993 at the Richard Rodgers Theatre and closed 5 September 1993 after 207 performances.

CAST (in order of appearance): DAVID SHINER, BILL IRWIN.
THE RED CLAY RAMBLERS: Clay Buckner (fiddle, harmonica), Chris Frank (piano, tuba, accordion, ukelele), Jack Herrick (trumpet, bass, banjolin, tin whistle, concertina), Tommy Thompson (banjos), Rob Ladd (drums).

ACT 1
Opening
D. Shiner, B. Irwin, Red Clay Ramblers, 2 Ushers
"Fire and Sugar" (traditional)
Red Clay Ramblers
Encounter
D. Shiner, B. Irwin
"Old Jim Canaan's"
Red Clay Ramblers
(*Music and Lyrics by* Reverend Robert Wilkins.)
Dance Solo
D. Shiner
Dance to the Left
B. Irwin, Stage Manager
Big Night Out
D. Shiner, B. Irwin, an Audience Member

ACT 2
"I Crept into the Crypt (and Cried)"
Red Clay Ramblers
(*Music and Lyrics by* Elizabeth Anderson.)
Improvisation in Public
D. Shiner, an Audience Memeber
Harlequin/Pantalone
B. Irwin, Red Clay Ramblers, D. Shiner
"Hiawatha's Lullaby"
Red Clay Ramblers
(*Music by* Walter Donaldson. *Lyrics by* Joe Young.)
"Tea for Two" (from *NO, NO NANNETTE*)
D. Shiner, B. Irwin
(*Music by* Vincent Youmans. *Lyrics by* Irving Caesar.)
Conductor
B. Irwin, Red Clay Ramblers
Cinema
D. Shiner, 4 Audience Members
"Valley of the Dry Bones" (traditional; a capella)
Red Clay Ramblers, D. Shiner, B. Irwin
Dance/"Fire and Sugar" (reprise)
B. Irwin, D. Shiner, Red Clay Ramblers

1993.02

THE GOODBYE GIRL

A Musical in Two Acts, 21 Scenes. Book by Neil Simon. (Based on his screenplay for the film of the same name.) Music by Marvin Hamlisch. Lyrics by David Zippel. Directed by Michael Kidd. Musical staging by Graciela Daniele. Scenery and costumes by Santo Loquasto. Lighting by Tharon Musser. Sound design by Tom Clark. Musical direction, Jack Everly. Assistant choreographer, Willie Rosario. Orchestrations by Billy Byers, Torrie Zito. Conductor, Jack Everly. Production supervisor, Peter Lawrence. Dance musical arranged by Mark Hummel. Associate producer, Kaede Seville. Produced by Office Two-One Inc., Gladys Nederlander, Stewart F. Lane, James M. Nederlander, Richard Kagan, Emanuel Azenberg. Opened 4 March 1993 at the Marquis Theatre and closed 15 August 1993 after 188 performances.

CAST (in order of appearance): *Lucy*: TAMMY MINOFF. *Paula*: BERNADETTE PETERS. *Billy*: Scott Wise. *Donna*: Susann Fletcher. *Jenna*: Cynthia Onrubia. *Cynthia*: Erin Torpey. *Melanie*: Lisa Molina. *Mrs. Crosby*: CAROL WOODS. *Elliott*: MARTIN SHORT. *Mark*: John Christopher Jones. *Stage Manager*: Darlesia Cearcy. *First Man at Theatre*: Larry Sousa. *Woman at Theatre*: Mary Ann Lamb. *Second Man at Theatre*: Rick Crom. *Cast of 'Richard III'*: Barry Bernal, Darlesia Cearcy, Jamie Beth Chandler, Dennis Daniels, Denise Faye, Nancy Hess, Joe Locarro, Rick Manning, Cynthia Onrubia, Linda Talcott, Scott Wise. *Audience at 'Richard III'*: Rick Crom, Ruth Gottschall, Sean Grant, Mary Ann Lamb, Larry Sousa. *Mark's Mother*: Ruth Gottschall. *TV Stage Manager*: Rick Crom. *Ricky Simpson Announcer*: Rick Crom. *Ricky Simpson*: John Christopher Jones. *Swings*: Ned Hannah, Michele Pigliavento.

Act 1, Scene 1: Paula's apartment. *Scene 2*: A dance studio. *Scene 3*: In front of Paula's building. *Scene 4*: Paula's apartment. *Scene 5*: Paula's apartment. *Scene 6*: An off-off-Broadway theater. *Scene 7*: Central Park. *Scene 8*: Paula's apartment. *Scene 9*: An off-off-Broadway theater.

Act 2, Scene 1: Paula's apartment. *Scene 2*: Paula's apartment. *Scene 3*: The Ricky Simpson Show. *Scene 4*: Paula's apartment. *Scene 5*: Paula's apartment. *Scene 6*: The rooftop of Paula's building. *Scene 7*: Paula's apartment. *Scene 8*: A schoolyard. *Scene 9*: The lake in Central Park. *Scene 10*: A TV Studio. *Scene 11*: Paula's apartment. *Scene 12*: In front of Paula's building.

ACT 1
Scene 1
"This Is as Good as It Gets"
B. Peters, T. Minoff
"No More"
B. Peters
Scene 2
"A Beat Behind"
B. Peters, S. Wise, Ensemble
Scene 3
"This Is as Good as It Gets" (reprise)
T. Minoff, L. Molina, E. Torpey
Scene 4
"My Rules"/("Elliot Garfield Grant")
M. Short, B. Peters
"Good News, Bad News"
M. Short, B. Peters, T. Minoff
Scene 5
"Good News, Bad News" (reprise)
C. Woods
Scene 7
"Footsteps"
B. Peters, T. Minoff
Scene 8
"How Can I Win?"
B. Peters
Scene 9
"Richard Interred"
M. Short, B. Peters, T. Minoff, J. C. Jones, C. Woods, S. Fletcher, Ensemble

ACT 2
Scene 1
"How Can I Win?" (reprise)
B. Peters

Scene 2
"Good News, Bad News" (reprise)
M. Short
Scene 3
"Too Good to Be Bad"
B. Peters, S. Fletcher, C. Onrubia
Scene 4
"2 Good 2 B Bad" (reprise)
C. Woods
Scene 5
"Who Would've Thought?"
B. Peters, M. Short, T. Minoff, L. Molina, E. Torpey
Scene 6
"Paula" (An Improvised Love Song)"
M. Short, B. Peters
Scene 8
"Who Would've Thought?" (reprise)
T. Minoff, L. Molina, E. Torpey
Scene 9
"I Can Play This Part"
M. Short
Scene 10
"Jump for Joy"
B. Peters, Ensemble
Scene 11
"What a Guy"
B. Peters
Scene 12
Finale
B. Peters, M. Short, T. Minoff

1993.03

THE WIZ

A Revival of the Musical in Two Acts, a Prologue and 16 Scenes[12]. Book by William F. Brown. Based on the novel "The Wonderful Wizard of Oz" by L. Frank Baum. Music and lyrics by Charlie Smalls. Directed and choreographed by George Faison. Scenic design by Randel Wright. Costumes by Jonathan Bixby. Lighting by Jonathan McLain. Musical direction and dance arrangements by Timothy Graphenreed. Sound by Abe Jacob. Produced by Atlanta's Theatre of the Stars (Christopher B. Manos, producer) and Robert L. Young and Associates, in association with The National Black Arts Festival. Opened 16 March 1993 at the Beacon Theater and closed 28 March 1993 after 16 performances.

CAST (in order of appearance): *Aunt Em*: TONI SEAWRIGHT. *Toto*: Mischief. *Dorothy*: STEPHANIE MILLS. *Uncle Henry*: Maurice Lautner. *Tornado*: Evelyn Thomas. *Munchkins*: Inaya Jafan Davis, Bobby Daye, Kellie Turner, Virginia Ann Woodruff. *Addaperle*: EBONY JO-ANN. *Yellow Brick Road*: Christopher Davis, James A. Ervin, Cornell Ivey, Neil Whitehead. *Scarecrow*: GARRY Q. LEWIS. *Crows*: Evelyn Ebo, Gina Reneé Ellis, Roland Hayes, Frederick Moore, April Nixon, John Eric Parker, Katherine J. Smith. *Tinman*: EUGENE FLEMING. *Lion*: H. CLENT BOWERS. *Kalidahs*: Evelyn Ebo, Roland Hayes, Frederick Moore, April Nixon, Katherine J. Smith, Evelyn Thomas, Rachel Tecora Tucker. *Poppies*: Evelyn Ebo, Gina Reneé Ellis, April Nixon, Katherine J. Smith, Rachel Tecora Tucker. *Field Mice*: Inaya Jafan Davis, Cornell Ivey, John Eric Parker, Virginia Ann Woodruff. *Gatekeeper*: Bobby Daye. *The Wiz*: ANDRE DE SHIELDS. *Evillene*: ELLA MITCHELL. *Lord High Underling*: Maurice Lautner. *Soldier Messenger*: Roland Hayes. *Winged Monkey*: Cornell Ivey.

Winged Monkeys: Christopher Davis, Evelyn Ebo, James A. Ervin, Roland Hayes, Frederick Moore, April Nixon, John Eric Parker, Katherine J. Smith, Rachel Tecora Tucker, Neil Whitehead. *Emerald City Citizens*: Christopher Davis, Inaya Jafan Davis, Bobby Daye, Evelyn Ebo, Gina Reneé Ellis, James A. Ervin, Roland Hayes, Cornell Ivey, Maurice Lautner, Frederick Moore, April Nixon, John Eric Parker, Katherine J. Smith, Evelyn Thomas, Rachel Tecora Tucker, Kellie Turner, Neil Whitehead, Virginia Ann Woodruff. *Glinda*: TONI SEAWRIGHT. *Swings*: Raymond C. Harris, Maureen Brown.

[12]Originally produced in New York 5 January 1975 at the Majestic Theatre for 1672 performances. For Synopsis of Scenes and Musical Numbers, see original 1975 production. For this production, reprises of "Ease on Down the Road" for Dorothy, Scarecrow, Tinman, Lion (Scene 4 only) and "Yellow Brick Road" were added at the end of Act 1, Scenes 3 and 4.

1993.04

THE SONG OF JACOB ZULU

A Drama with Music in Two Acts by Tug Yourgrau. Original music composed by Ladysmith Black Mambazo. Lyrics by Tug Yourgrau and Ladysmith Black Mambazo. Directed by Eric Simonson. Set design by Kevin Rigdon. Costume design, Erin Quigley. Lighting design, Robert Christen. Sound design, Rob Milburn. Dialect coach, Gillian Lane-Plescia. Fight director, Ned Mochel. Produced by the Steppenwolf Theatre, Randall Arney, Stephen Eich, Albert Poland, Susan Liederman, Bette Cerf Hill, in association with Maurice Rosenfield. Opened 24 March 1993 at the Plymouth Theatre and closed 9 May 1993 after 53 performances.

CAST (in alphabetical order): *Marty Frankel*: Gerry Becker. *Mrs. Zulu, Mrs. Mgobese, Ma Buthelezi*: Pat Bowie. *Judge Neville*: Robert Breuler. *John Dawkins, Dr. Shaw*: David Connelly. *Martin Zulu, Zebulun, Guerrilla*: Leelai Demoz. *Jacob Zulu*: K. TODD FREEMAN. *Mrs. Sabelo, Beauty Dlamini, Guerrilla*: Erika L. Heard. *Mr. Vilakazi, Fumani, Guerrilla*: Danny Johnson. *Policeman, Mbongeni, Michael Dube, Guerrilla, Philip Zulu*: Gary DeWitt Marshall. *Reverend Zulu, Mr. X, Itshe*: ZAKES MOKAE. *Magistrate, Mr. Van Heerden, Mr. Jeppe*: Don Oreskes. *Aunt Miriam, Student, Ruth Dube*: Tania Richard. *Interpreter, Policeman, Student, Jacob's Superior*: Seth Sibanda. *Anthony Dent, Lieutenant Malan*: Alan Wilder. *Michael Jeppe, Lieutenant Kramer*: Nicholas Cross Wodtke. *Policeman, Uncle Mdishwa, Teacher, Percy, Commissar*: Cedric Young.

Chorus Leader: JOSEPH SHABALA. *Chorus*: LADYSMITH BLACK MAMBAZO: Jabulani Dubazana, Abednego Mazibuko, Albert Mazibuko, Geophrey Mdletshe, Russel Mthembu, Inos Phungula, Jockey Shabalala, Ben Shabalala, Joseph Shabalala.

Act 1, Scene 1: Shaka's Rock Shopping Mall, Natal, South Africa. 24 December 1985. *Scene 2*: Interrogation Room at a Jail in Pietermaritzburg. 29 December 1985. *Scene 3*: Visitors room, Eshowe Courthouse Jail. 6 February 1986. *Scene 4*: Eshowe Courtroom. Immediately afterward. *Scene 5*: The Jail Visitors Room. 7 February 1986. *Scene 6*: The Courtroom. Later the same day. *Scene 7*: A kraal, a traditional home, in Zululand; A Hospital in Pietermaritzburg. 8 February 1986. *Scene 8*: The Visitors Room. Later the same day. *Scene 9*: The Courtroom., 9 February 1986. *Scene 10*: The main room of the Zulu home in Imbali. Afternoon, the same day. *Scene 11*: A street near Imbali High School; one week later. A field on the edge of Imbali, two months later. A street in Imbali, later that afternoon. *Scene 12*: The main room of the Zulu home in Imbali. October 1984. *Scene 13*: Interrogation room at a jail in Pietermaritzburg; three days later. A street near Imbali High School; one week later. The Zulu home, one week later. Outside a store in Imbali, late October 1984. *Scene 14*: Outside the house in Imbali, later the same night. The South African border with Swaziland.

Act 2, Scene 1: Ma Buthelezi's home near Piet Retief, near the Swaziland border. Late evening in October 1984. The South African/Swazi border later that night. *Scene 2*: A street in Matola, asuburb of Maputo, Mozambique, two days later; before sunset. *Scene 3*: An Umkhonto we Sizwe training camp in Angola. October 1985; across the border in South Africa, mid-November 1985. *Scene 4*: The Courtroom, 10 February 1986; the same, morning of 11 February 1986. *Scene 5*: Jacob's cell, that evening. *Scene 6*: The courtroom, 12 February 1986; Pretoria Central Prison, 29 April 1986.

ACT 1[13]
Scene 1
"Lalelani!" (Listen!)
Scene 2
You are the one . . .
Scene 3
Cabanga! Imagine, imagine, imagine . . .
Jesus is my Savior . . .
Scene 4
"Ayikanoni!" (The time is not right!)
Blood river, Blood river. .
Scene 5
Oh, Jacob!
Scene 7
Our brother acts so strangely
Scene 8
"Ingane yeZulu!" (Child of Heaven!)
Scene 9
Boycott Bantu Education . . .

[13]List of musical numbers taken from published text (Arcade Publishing Co., New York, 1993).

Scene 11
The mouth is still, but the blood will tell . . .
Scene 12
Oh, Zulu, Zulu! Children of Heaven . . .
Scene 14
"Baba nomana" (Oh, Papa and Mama)

ACT 2
Scene 1
Wo ngaze ngahamba, ngahamba wema (I am wandering and roving all over)
It is dark in my mind, it is dark in my heart . . .
Scene 3
Wo ngaze ngahamba, ngahamba wema (reprise)
Scene 4
"Ingane yeZulu!" (Child of Heaven!)(reprise)
Scene 5
Uyezwa uyezwa uyezka na! (Do you hear, do you hear . . .)
Child of Heaven
Scene 6
Wozani! Wozani sihambe (Come see the wounds of Christ in heaven. .)
"Lalelani!" (Listen!) (reprise)
"Nkosi Sikelel' iAfrika" (God Bless Africa)
(*Music and Lyrics by* Enoch Sontonga; translated by Rev. Philip Notombela, Tug Yourgrau.)

1993.05 AIN'T BROADWAY GRAND

A Musical in Two Acts, 18 Scenes. Book by Thomas Meehan and Lee Adams. (Inspired by the Michael Todd biography "A Valuable Property" by Michael Todd, Jr. and Susan McCarthy Todd.) Music by Mitch Leigh. Lyrics by Lee Adams. Directed by Scott Harris. Choreography by Randy Skinner. Scenery designed by David Mitchell. Costumes designed by Suzy Benzinger. Lighting designed by Ken Billington. Sound by Otts Munderloh. Musical direction, Nicholas Archer. Musical supervision, vocal arrangements by Neil Warner. Orchestrations by Chris Bankey. Dance arrangements by Scot Woolley. A Tra La La Inc. Production. Produced by Arthur Rubin. Opened 18 April 1993 at the Lunt-Fontanne Theatre and closed 9 May 1993 after 25 performances.

CAST (in order of appearance): *Bobby Clark*: GERRY VICHI. *Gypsy Rose Lee*: DEBBIE SHAPIRO GRAVITTE. *Mike Todd*: MIKE BURSTYN. *Harriet Popkin*: Alix Korey. *Lou*, the Stage Manager: Bill Nabel. *Murray Pearl*: Mitchell Greenberg. *Reuben Pelish*: David Lipman. *Joan Blondell*: MAUREEN McNAMARA. *Marvin Fischbein*: Gabriel Barre. *Waldo Klein*: Bill Kux. *Wally Farfle*: Scott Elliott. *Dexter Leslie*: Richard B. Shull. *Jaeger*: Merwin Goldsmith. *Lindy's Waiters*: Bill Corcoran, Jerold Goldstein, Bill Nabel. *Thelma*: Caitlin Carter. *Floyd*: Patrick Wetzel. *Rocco*: Luis Perez. *Frankie*, the Bartender: Scott Fowler. *Herbie*, the Office Boy: Jerold Goldstein.

'Of The People,' Part 1: *The President and His Cabinet*: Timothy Albrecht, Bill Corcoran, Scott Elliott, Scott Fowler, Jerold Goldstein, Joe Istre, Rod McCune, Bill Nabel, Luis Perez, Mimi Cichanowicz Quillin, Patrick Wetzel. *Riverside Drive Streetwalker*: Beverly Britton. *Lili*: Ginger Prince. *Sheryl*: Jennifer Frankel. *Linda*: Mimi Cichanowicz Quillin.

'Of the People,' Part 2: *The President and His Cabinet*: Leslie Bell, Beverly Britton, Caitlin Carter, Colleen Dunn, Jennifer Frankel, Lauren Golar-Kosarin, Elizabeth Mills, Ginger Prince, Mimi Chicanowicz Quillin, Carol Denise Smith. *Ensemble*: Timothy Albrecht, Leslie Bell, Beverly Britton, Caitlin Carter, Bill Corcoran, Colleen Dunn, Scott Elliott, Scott Fowler, Jennifer Frankel, Jerold Goldstein, Lauren Goler-Kosarin, Joe Istre, Rod McCune, Elizabeth Mills, Bill Nabel, Luis Perez, Ginger Prince, Mimi Cichanowicz Quillin, Carol Denise Smith, Patrick Wetzel. *Swings*: Kelli Barclay, James Horvath, Lynn Sullivan.

The action takes place in the summer and early fall, 1948.

Act 1, Scene 1: The stage of the Alvin Theatre. *Scene 2*: Backstage at the Alvin Theatre. *Scene 3*: Backstage at a production meeting. *Scene 4*: Lindy's Restaurant. *Scene 5*: The Bar at "21." *Scene 6*: Todd's office. *Scene 7*: 'Of the People' show curtain. *Scene 8*: The Oval Office. *Scene 9*: The stage of the Colonial Theatre, Boston.

Act 2, Scene 1: The street in front of Lindy's. *Scene 2*: Todd's suite, Ritz-Carlton Hotel, Boston. *Scene 3*: Riverside Drive, near Grant's tomb. *Scene 4*: A costume shop. *Scene 5*: Rehearsal backstage at the Alvin Theatre. *Scene 6*: The Beverly Hills Hotel, Beverly Hills, California. *Scene 7*: Behind the curtain at the Alvin Theatre. *Scene 8*: The Oval Office. *Scene 9*: Backstage at the Alvin Theatre.

ACT 1
Scene 1
"Girls Ahoy!"
G. Vichi, D. S. Gravitte, Ensemble
Scene 2
"Ain't Broadway Grand"
M. Burstyn, A. Korey, M. Greenberg, D. Lipman, Ensemble
"Class"
M. Burstyn, Chorus Girls
Scene 3
"The Theatre, the Theatre"
G. Barre, B. Kux
"Ain't Broadway Grand" (reprise)
M. Burstyn, A. Korey, M. Greenberg, R. B. Shull, G. Barre, B. Kux, S. Elliott, Ensemble
Scene 4
"Lindy's"
M. Goldsmith, Waiters, Company
"It's Time to Go"
D. S. Gravitte, Ensemble
Scene 5
"Waiting in the Wings"
M. McNamara
"You're My Star"
M. Burstyn, Ensemble
Scene 8
"A Big Job"
President, Ensemble
Scene 9
"Ain't Broadway Grand" (reprise)
Company

ACT 2
Scene 1
"Ain't Broadway Grand" (reprise)
M. Goldsmith, Waiters
Scene 2
"They'll Never Take Us Alive"
M. Burstyn, A. Korey, M. Greenberg
Scene 3
"On the Street"
M. Burstyn
"The Man I Married"
M. McNamara, Female Ensemble
Scene 4
"Maybe, Maybe Not"
D. S. Gravitte
Scene 5
"Tall Dames and Low Comedy"
G. Vichi, Ensemble
Scene 6
"He's My Guy"
M. McNamara
Scene 8
"A Big Job" (reprise)
President, Ensemble
Scene 9
"You're My Star" (reprise)
M. Burstyn
"Ain't Broadway Grand" (reprise)
Company

1993.06 (THE WHO'S) TOMMY

A Musical in Two Acts, 22 Scenes[14]. Book by Pete Townshend and Des McAnuff. Music and lyrics by Pete Townshend. Additional music and lyrics by John Entwistle and Keith Moon. Directed by Des McAnuff. Choreographed by Wayne Cilento. Scenery by John Arnone. Costumes by David C. Woolard. Lighting by Chris Parry. Projections by Wendall K. Harrington. Sound by Steve Canyon Kennedy. Musical supervision and direction, Joseph Church. Video by Batwin + Robin Productions, Inc. Orchestrations by Steven Margoshes. Special effects, Gregory Meeh. Flying by Foy. Fight direction by Steve Rankin. Technical supervision by Gene O'Donovan. Executive producers, David, Strong, Warner, Inc., Scott Zeiger/Gary Gunas. Associate producer, John F. Kennedy Center. Executive producers, David, Strong, Warner, Inc. and Scott Zeiger/Gary Gunas. Produced by Pace Theatrical Group and Dodger Productions with Kardana Productions, Inc. Opened 22 April 1993 at the St. James Theatre and closed 17 June 1995 after 900 performances.

CAST (in order of appearance): *Mrs. Walker*: MARCIA MITZMAN. *Captain Walker*: JONATHAN DOKUCHITZ. *Uncle Ernie*: PAUL KANDEL. *Minister*: Bill Buell. *Mr. Simpson*: Bill Buell. *Minister's Wife*: Jody Gelb. *Nurse*: Lisa Leguillou. *Officer #1*: Michael McElroy. *Officer #2*: Timothy Warmen. *Allied Soldier #1*: Donnie Kehr. *Allied Soldier #2*: Michael Arnold. *Lover*: Lee Morgan. *Tommy*, age 4: Carly Jane Steinborn or Crysta Macalush. *Tommy*: MICHAEL CERVERIS. *Judge*: Tom Flynn. *Tommy*, age 10: Buddy Smith. *Cousin Kevin*: Anthony Barrile. *Kevin's Mother*: Maria Calabrese. *Kevin's Father*: Tom Flynn. *Local Lads, later Security Guards*: Michael Arnold, Paul Dobie, Christian Hoff, Donnie Kehr, Michael McElroy, Timothy Warmen. *Local Lasses*: Maria Calabrese, Tracy Nicole Chapman, Pam Klinger, Lisa Leguillou, Alice Ripley, Sherie Scott. *Hawker*: Michael McElroy. *Harmonica Player*: Lee Morgan. *The Gypsy*: Cheryl Freeman. *First Pinball Lad*: Donnie Kehr. *Second Pinball Lad*: Christian Hoff. *Specialist*: Norm Lewis. *Specialist's Assistant*: Alice Ripley. *News Vendor*: Tom Flynn. *Sally Simpson*: Sherie Scott. *Mrs. Simpson*: Pam Klinger. *Mr. Simpson*: Bill Buell. *D.J.*: Tom Flynn.

Ensemble: Michael Arnold, Bill Buell, Maria Calbrese, Tracy Nicole Chapman, Paul Dobie, Tom Flynn, Jody Gelb, Chistian Hoff, Donnie Kehr, Pam Klinger, Lisa Leguillou, Norm Lewis, Michael McElroy, Lee Morgan, Alice Ripley, Sherie Soctt, Timothy Warmen. *Swings*: Victoria Lecta Cave, Romain Frugé, Todd Hunter, Trecy Langran.

Act 1, Scene 1: 22 Heathfield Gardens, London, England/POW Camp, Germany, 1941. *Scene 2*: Hospital/POW Camp, 1945. *Scene 3*: 22 Heathfield Gardens. *Scene 4*: English Courtroom. *Scene 5*: Hospital. *Scene 6*: Church/The home of the relatives, 1950. *Scene 7*: 22 Heathfield Gardens. *Scene 8*: 22 Heathfield Gardens/A youth club. *Scene 9*: Psychiatric clinic. *Scene 10*: 22 Heathfield Gardens. *Scene 11*: The Isle of Dogs. *Scene 12*: Amusement Arcade.

Act 2, Scene 1: The Sunlight Laundry. *Scene 2*: Research Laboratory. *Scene 3*: The Street/22 Heathfield Gardens. *Scene 4*: 22 Heathfield Gardens. *Scene 5*: The Streets of London, 1961-1963. *Scene 6*: Holiday Camp. *Scene 7*: The Simpsons'. *Scenes 8, 9, and 10*: Heathfield Gardens.

ACT 1
Overture: 1941
Company
Scene 1
"Captain Walker"
Officers
Scene 2
"It's a Boy"
Nurses, M. Mitzman
"We've Won"
J. Dokuchitz, Allied Soldiers
Scene 3
"Twenty-One"
M. Mitzman, L. Morgan, J. Dokuchitz
"Amazing Journey"
M. Cerveris
Scene 5
"Sparks" (instrumental)
"Amazing Journey" (reprise)
M. Cerveris
Scene 6
"Christmas"
J. Dokuchitz, M. Mitzman, B. Buell, J. Gelb, Ensemble
"See Me, Feel Me"
M. Cerveris
Scene 7
"Do You Think It's Alright"
J. Dokuchitz, M. Mitzman
"Fiddle About"
P. Kandel, Ensemble
(*Music and Lyrics by* John Entwistle.)
"See Me, Feel Me" (reprise)
M. Cerveris
Scene 8
"Cousin Kevin"
P. Kandel, Ensemble
(*Music and Lyrics by* John Entwistle.)
"Sensation"
M. Cerveris, Ensemble
Scene 9
"Sparks" (reprise, instrumental)
Scene 10
"Eyesight to the Blind"
M. McElroy, L. Morgan, Ensemble
(Additional material *Music and Lyrics by* Sonny Boy Williamson.)
Scene 11
"Acid Queen"
C. Freeman
Scene 12
"Pinball Wizard"
Local Lads, A. Barrile, Ensemble

ACT 2
Underture (Entr'acte): 1960
(Ensemble)
Scene 1
"There's a Doctor"
J. Dokuchitz, M. Mitzman
Scene 2
"Go to the Mirror"
N. Lewis, A. Ripley, J. Dokuchitz, M. Mitzman
"Listening to You"
M. Cerveris, C. J. Steinborn, B. Smith
Scene 3
"Tommy Can You Hear Me"
Local Lads
Scene 4
"I Believe My Own Eyes"
J. Dokuchitz, M. Mitzman
"Smash the Mirror"
M. Mitzman
"I'm Free"
M. Cerveris
Scene 5
"Miracle Cure"
T. Flynn, Local Lads
"Sensation" (reprise)
M. Cerveris, Ensemble
"I'm Free"/"Pinball Wizard" (reprise)
M. Cerveris, Company
Scene 6
"Tommy's Holiday Camp"
P. Kandel
(*Music and Lyrics by* Keith Moon.)

[14]A ballet adaptation of TOMMY performed to the pre-recorded score by The Who was performed 3 May 1972 at the New York City Center by Les Ballets Canadiennes for 31 performances; see entry in that season.

Scene 7
"Sally Simpson"
A. Barrile, Security Guards, S. Scott, B. Buell, P. Klinger
Scene 8, 9, 10
"Welcome"
M. Cerveris, Ensemble
"We're Not Going to Take It"
M. Cerveris, Ensemble
"See Me, Feel Me"/"Listening to You" (reprises)/Finale
M. Cerveris, Company

"Light Romance"
S. Lawrence, W. Evans
"Madman"
W. Evans
"Tell Me It's Not True"
S. Lawrence, Full Company

1993.07 BLOOD BROTHERS

A Musical in Two Acts. Book, music and lyrics by Willy Russell. Directed by Bill Kenwright and Bob Tomson. Set and costume design by Andy Walmsley. Lighting design by Joe Atkins. Sound design by Paul Astbury. Production musical direction, Rod Edwards. Musical direction, Rick Fox. (Musical) arrangemnts, Del Newman. Associate producer, Jon Miller. Technical supervision, Gene O'Donovan. Produced by Bill Kenwright. Opened 25 April 1993 at the Music Box Theatre and closed 30 April 1995 after 839 performances.

CAST (in order of appearance): *Mrs Johnstone*: STEPHANIE LAWRENCE. *Narrator*: WARWICK EVANS. *Mrs. Lyons*: BARBARA WALSH. *Mr. Lyons*: Ivar brogger. *Mickey*: CON O'NEILL. *Eddie*: MARK MICHAEL HUTHINSON. *Sammy*: James Clow. *Linda*: JAN GRAVESON. *Perkins*: Sam Samuelson. *Donna Marie, Miss Jones*: Regina O'Malley. *Policeman, Teacher*: Robin Haynes. *Brenda*: Anne Torsiglieri.
Other Parts: Ivar Brogger, Kerry Butler, James Clow, Robin Haynes, Philip Lehl, Regina O'Malley, Sam Samuelson, John Schiappa, Anne Torsiglieri, Douglas Weston.

The action takes place in Liverpool, England.

ACT 1
"Marilyn Monroe"
S. Lawrence
"My Child"
S. Lawrence, B. Walsh
"Easy Terms"
S. Lawrence
"Shoes Upon the Table"
W. Evans
"Easy Terms" (reprise)
S. Lawrence
"Kids Game"
J. Clow, J. Graveson, C. O'Neill, Ensemble
"Shoes Upon the Table" (reprise)
W. Evans
"Shoes Upon the Table" (reprise)
W. Evans
"Bright New Day" (Prelude)
S. Lawrence
"Long Sunday Afternoon"/"My Friend"
C. O'Neill, M. M. Hutchinson
"Bright New Day"
S. Lawrence, Full Company

ACT 2
"Marilyn Monroe" (reprise)
S. Lawrence
"Shoes Upon the Table" (reprise)
W. Evans
"That Guy"
C. O'Neill, M. M. Hutchinson
"Shoes Upon the Table" (reprise)
W. Evans
"I'm Not Saying a Word"
M. M. Hutchinson
"Take a Letter, Miss Jones"
I. Brogger, R. O'Malley, Ensemble
"Marilyn Monroe" (reprise)
S. Lawrence

1993.08 TANGO PASIÓN

A Dance Musical in Two Acts, and a Prologue. Entire production conceived by Mel Howard. Choreography by Hector Zaraspe. Orchestrations, arrangements, musical direction and original music, José Libertella, Luis Stazo. Sets based on paintings by Ricardo Carpani. Costume and scenic design by John Falabella. Lighting by Richard Pilbrow, Dawn Chiang. Sound design by Jan Nebozenko. Originally presented at the Coconut Grove Playhouse, Miami, Florida (Arnold Mittelman, Producing artistic director). Executive producer, Norman Rothstein. Produced by Mel Howard, Donald K. Donald and Irving Schwartz. Opened 28 April 1993 at the Longacre Theatre and closed 2 May 1993 after 5 performances.

CAST (in order of appearance): *Ricardo*, the artist: Alberto del Solar. *Pedro Montero*: Jorge Torres. *Lila Quintana*: Pilar Alvarez. *Lucas*, the Maitre d': Osvaldo Cliento. *Juan Larossa*: Gustavo Russo. *Señorita Virginia*: Veronica Gardella. *Carmela*, the Waitress: Alejandra Mantinan. *Julio Camargo*: Marcelo Bernadaz. *Dr. Bertolini*: Luis Castro. *Señora Rosalinda Bertolini*: Claudia Mendoza. *Carlos Bronco*: Armando Orzuza. *Señora Dora Bronco*: Daniela Arcuri. *Grisel*, Carlos' Mistress: Graciela Garcia. *Romero Brandán*, the Spoiler: Jorge Romano. *Rosendo Frías*, Pool Player: Fernando Jimenez. *Angela*, Rosendo's Girlfriend: Judit Aberastain. *Rodolfo*, the Club Singer: Daniel Bouchet. *Flora Rosa*, the Club Singer: Yeni Patiño. *Zully*, the Lieutenant's Date: Viviana Laguzzi. *The Lieutenant*: Juan Corvalan. *Ludmilla Orlinskaya*, the European Movie Star: Gunilla Wingquist.
Sexteto Mayor: José Libertella, Luis Stazo (bandoneon), Mario Abramovich, Eduardo Walczak (violin), Oscar Palermo (piano), Osvaldo Aulicino (bass). And Tomás Giannini (bandoneon), Juan Zunini (keyboards, synthesizer), Jorge Orlando (percussion). *Dancing Couples*: Armando & Daniela, Fernando & Judit, Gustavo & Alejandra, Jorge & Pilar, Juan & Viviana, Luis & Claudia, Marcelo & Veronica, Osvaldo & Graciela. *Other dancers*: Jorge Romano, Gunila Wingquist. *Singers*: Daniel Bouchet, Alberto del Solar, Yeni Patiño.

Prologue: The present.

Act 1: The late 1940's.

Act 2: The present.

ACT 1[15]
How could I forget you, my Cafetín of Buenos Aires?
"Mi Buenos Aires Querido" (Gardel)
"Payadora" (Plaza)
Company
"Cafetín de Buneos Aires" (Mores, Discépolo)
A. del Solar (singer)
Sitting at your tables which ask no questions, I wept the bitter tears of my first heartbreak ...
"El Internado" (Canaro)
Armando & Daniela (dancers)
"El Moleston" (Libertella, Stazo)
Romano (dancer)
"Taquito Militar" (Mores)
Romano & Graciela (dancers)
"Nostalgias" (Cadicamo, Cabián)
D. Bouchet (singer)
I lift my glass and make a toast to the cruel misfortunes of love ...
"Chique" (Brignolo)
Luis & Claudia (dancers)
"Uno" (Mores)
Y. Patiño (singer)
One crawls and slithers between thorns simply trying to feel love ...
"La Cumparsita" (Rodríguez)

[15]Opening night song list prepared as per program insert.

"Recitado"
A. del Solar
I wasted my life shuffling empty dreams ...
"Canto"
D. Bouchet
If only you knew how much I still love you ...
"Danza"
Juan & Viviana
"Copete" (Anon.)
Fernando & Judit (dancers)
"Milonga del 900" (Piana)
Gustavo, Fernando, Marcelo, Osvaldo, Armando, Juan (dancers)
"La Tablada" (Canaro)
Osvaldo & Graciela
"Ojos Negros" (Anon.)
Gunilla, Osvaldo, Alberto
"Hotel Victoria" (Latasa)
Yeni, Juan, Osvaldo, Romano, Armando, Gustavo (dancers)
"El Firulete" (Mores)
Armando, Daniela, Gustvao, Alejandra, Luis, Claudia, Juan, Viviana
"Ojos Negros" (reprise)
Luis, Gunilla, Juan (dancers)
"Orgullo Criollo" (Decaro, Laurenz)
Gustavo & Alejandra
"Preludio a Francini" (Abramovich, Stazo)
Luis & Claudia
"El Dia Que Me Quieras" (Gardel, Le Pera)
D. Bouchet, Y. Patiño (singers)
The soft sound of your breathing caresses my daydreams ...
"Milonga de Mis Amores" (Laurenz)
Fernando & Judit (dancers)
"Responso" (Troilo)
Romano & Claudia (dancers)
"Re Fa Si" (Delfino)
Company
"Canaro en Paris" (Scarpino)
Sexteto Mayor, Company

ACT 2
I am because you have dreamed me.
"Rapsodia de Arrabal" (Libertella)
A. del Solar, Jorge & Pilar
"Bailonga" (Mores)
Company
"Melancolico" (Plaza)
Armando, Daniela, Osvaldo, Graciela (dancers)
"A Media Luz" (Donato)
Y. Patiño, D. Bouchet (singers), Luis, Gunilla, Alejandra, Judit, Claudia, Verónica (dancers)
When the lights are low, love casts a magic spell ...
"Seleccion de Milongas" (Castellanos, Villoldo, Laurenz)
Juan, Gustavo, Fernando, Romano (dancers)
"Asi Se Baila El Tango" (Marvil)
A. del Solar (singer)
This is how you tango; the arm, like a serpent, coils, around the waist ...
"Quejas de Bandoneon" (Filiberto)
Jorge & Pilar (dancers)
"Celos" (Gadé)
Sexteto Mayor
"Balada Para Un Loco" (Piazzolla, Ferrer)
Luis, Pilar, Gunilla (dancers), A. del Solar (singer)
Love me just as I am: loco, loco, loco!
"Melancolico Buenos Aires" (Piazzolla)
Marcelo & Verónica (dancers)
"Libert Tango" (Piazzolla)
Graciela, Viviana, Alejandra, Judit, Osvaldo, Juan, Gustavo, Fernando (dancers)
"Verano Porteño" (Piazzolla)
Juan, Jorge (dancers)
"Fuga Y Misterio" (Piazzolla)
Marcelo, Luis, Gustavo, Viviana (dancers)
"Adios Nonino" (Piazzolla)
Sexteto Mayor
Provocacion:
"Paris Otoñal" (Libertella)/
"Balada Para Mi Vida" (Libertella, Ferrer)
Jorge, Pilar, Company (dancers), A. del Solar, Y. Patiño, D. Bouchet (singers)
We will be lovers forever, passionate for eternity, two fires of God ...
"Onda 9" (Piazzolla)
Company

1993.09 KISS OF THE SPIDER WOMAN

A Musical in Two Acts, a Prologue and 19 Scenes. Book by Terrence McNally, based on the novel of the same name by Manuel Puig. Music by John Kander. Lyrics by Fred Ebb. Directed by Harold Prince. Choreography by Vincent Patterson; additional choreography by Rob Marshall. Scenic design and projections, Jerome Sirlin. Costumes designed by Florence Klotz. Lighting design by Howell Binkley. Sound design by Martin Levan. Musical supervision, conductor, Jeffrey Huard. Orchestrations by Michael Gibson. Dance music by David Krane. Produced by Livent (U.S.) Inc. (Garth Drabinsky, Myron I. Gottlieb). Opened 3 May 1993 at the Broadhurst Theatre and closed 1 July 1995 after 906 performances.

CAST (in order of appearance): *Molina*: BRENT CARVER. *Warden*: HERNDON LACKEY. *Valentin*: ANTHONY CRIVELLO. *Esteban*: Philip Hernandez. *Marcos*: Michael McCormick. *Spider Woman, Aurora*: CHITA RIVERA. *Aurora's Men, Prisoners*: Keith McDaniel, Robert Montano, Dan O'Grady, Raymond Rodriguez. *Molina's Mother*: MERLE LOUISE. *Marta*: KIRSTI CARNAHAN. *Escaping Prisoner*: Colton Green. *Religious Fanatic, Prisoner*: John Norman Thomas. *Amnesty International Observer, Prisoner Emilio*: Joshua Finkel. *Prisoner Fuentes*: Gary Schwartz. *Gabriel, Prisoner*: Jerry Christakos. *Window Dresser at Montoya's, Prisoner*: Aurelio Padron.
Swings: Gregory Mitchell, Colton Green.

The action takes place in a prison in Latin America sometime in the recent past.

Prologue: A Prison. *Act 1, Scene 1*: The Prison; Molina's Cell. *Scene 2*: The Prison. *Scene 3*: Molina and Valentin's Cell. *Scene 4*: The Prison. *Scene 5*: The Cell. *Scene 6*: The Prison. *Scene 7*: Warden's Office. *Scene 8*: The Prison; the Cell. *Scene 9*: The Cell. *Scene 10*: The Infirmary. *Scene 11*: The Cell. *Scene 12*: Molina's movie; the Cell.

Act 2, Scene 1: The Cell. *Scene 2*: Limbo; Warden's Office. *Scene 3*: The Cell. *Scene 4*: Kiss of the Spider Woman. *Scene 5*: The Cell. *Scene 6*: The Prison; Warden's Office; Molina's Apartment; A Park; Molina's Mother's Apartment. *Scene 7*: The Interrogation Room; A Theatre.

ACT 1
Prologue
C. Rivera, Prisoners
Scene 1
"Her Name Is Aurora"
B. Carver, C. Rivera, Aurora's Men, Prisoners
Scene 2
"Over the Wall"
Prisoners
Scene 3
"Bluebloods"
B. Carver
"Dressing Them Up"/"I Draw the Line"
B. Carver, A. Crivello
"Dear One"
M. Louise, K. Carnahan, A. Crivello, B. Carver
Scene 4
"Over the Wall" II
Prisoners, B. Carver, A. Crivello
Scene 5
"Where You Are"
C. Rivera, Aurora's Men, Prisoners

Scene 6
"Over the Wall" III-"Marta"
A. Crivello, Prisoners
Scene 7
"Come"
C. Rivera
Scene 8
"I Do Miracles"
C. Rivera, K. Carnahan
Scene 9
"Gabriel's Letter"/"My First Woman"
J. Christakos, A. Crivello
Scene 10
"Morphine Tango"
Orderlies
"You Could Never Shame Me"
M. Louise
"A Visit"
C. Rivera, B. Carver
Scene 11
"She's a Woman"
B. Carver
Scene 12
"Gimme Love"
C. Rivera, B. Carver, Aurora's Men

ACT 2
Scene 1
"Russian Movie"/"Good Times"
C. Rivera, B. Carver, A. Crivello
"The Day After That"
A. Crivello, Families of the Disappeared
Scene 2
"Mama, It's Me"
B. Carver
Scene 3
"Anything for Him"
C. Rivera, B. Carver, A. Crivello
Scene 4
"Kiss of the Spider Woman"
C. Rivera
Scene 6
"Over the Wall" IV-"Lucky Molina"
H. Lackey, Prisoners
Scene 7
"Only in the Movies"
B. Carver, People in His Life (Company)

1993–1994 SEASON

Sally Murphy and Michael Hayden in CAROUSEL
Joan Marcus/Photofest

1993–1994 SEASON

1993.10 **SHE LOVES ME**

A Revival of the Musical (Comedy) in Two Acts[1]. Book by Joe Masteroff. Based on the play "Illatszertár" [Parfumerie] by Miklos Laszlo. Music by Jerry Bock. Lyrics by Sheldon Harnick. Directed by Scott Ellis. Musical staging by Rob Marshall. Settings by Tony Walton. Costume design by David Charles, Jane Greenwood. Lighting design by Peter Kaczorowski. Sound by Tony Meola. Musical direction by David Loud. Orchestrations[2] by Fred Matosich, Jr., Don Walker (original orchestrations). Produced by The Roundabout Theatre Company (Todd Haimes, Artistic director; Gene Feist, Founding director). Opened 10 June 1993 at the Criterion Center Stage Right and closed 1 August 1993 after 61 performances; reopened 7 October 1993 at the Brooks Atkinson Theatre under the commercial auspices of James M. Nederlander, Elliott Martin, with Herbert Wasserman, Freddy Bienstock, Roger L. Stevens and closed 19 June 1994 after an additional 294 performances. Total: 355 performances.

CAST (in order of appearance): *Ladislav Sipos*: LEE WILKOF. *Arpad Laszlo*: BRAD KANE. *Ilona Ritter*: SALLY MAYES. *Steven Kodaly*: HOWARD McGILLIN. *Georg Nowack*: BOYD GAINES. *Mr. Maraczek*: LOUIS ZORICH. *First Customer*: Tina Johnson. *Second Customer*: Kristi Lynes. *Third Customer*: Trisha Gorman. *Fourth Customer*: Cynthia Sophiea. *Fifth Customer*: Laura Waterbury. *Amalia Balash*: JUDY KUHN[3]. *Keller*: Nick Corley. *Headwaiter*: JONATHAN FREEMAN. *Busboy*: Joey McKneely.

Ensemble: Bill Badolato, Peter Boynton, Nick Corley, Trisha Gorman, Tina Johnson, Kristi Lynes, Joey McKneely, Cynthia Sophiea, Laura Waterbury. *Swings*: Mary Illes, Mason Roberts.

1993.11 **CAMELOT**

A Revival of the Musical in Two Acts, 16 Scenes[4]. Book and lyrics by Alan Jay Lerner. Based on the novel "The Once and Future King" by T. H. White. Music by Frederick Loewe. Original New York production staged by Moss Hart. Directed and choreographed by Norbert Joerder. Scenic production supervision and additional design by Neil Peter Jampolis. Costume supervision and additional design by Franne Lee. Sound design by Tom Morse. Musical director, conductor, John Visser. Produced by Music Fair Productions, Inc. (Shelly Gross, Executive producer). Opened 21 June 1993 at the Gershwin Theatre and closed 7 August 1993 after 56 performances[5].

CAST (in order of appearance): *Sir Dinadan*: RICHARD SMITH. *Sir Lionel*: Virl Andrick. *Merlyn*: JAMES VALENTINE. *Arthur*: ROBERT GOULET. *Sir Sagramore*: Cedric C. Cannon. *Lady Anne*: Jean Mahlmann. *Guenevere*: PATRICIA KIES. *Nimue*: Vanessa Shaw. *Lancelot*: STEVE BLANCHARD. *Dap*: Newton R. Gilchrist. *Pellinore*: JAMES VALENTINE. *Mordred*: TUCKER MCCRADY. *Tom of Warwick*: CHRIS VAN STRANDER.

Ensemble: Virl Andrick, Steve Asciolla, Greg Brown, Cedrick C. Cannon, Ben Starr Coates, William Thomas Evans, Newton R. Gilchhrist, Lisa Guignard, Theresa Hudson, Brian Jefferey Hurst, Donald Ives, Ted Keegan, Karen Longwell, Jean Malhlmann, Raymond Sage, Barbara Scanlon, Vanessa Shaw, Richard Smith, Verda Lee Tudor, Kimberly Wells. *Swings*: Tina Belis, Michael J. Novin.

Act 1, Scene 1: A hilltop near Camelot—a long time ago. *Scene 2*: The forest—immediately following. *Scene 3*: Arthur's Study—Five years later. *Scene 4*: A roadside near Camelot—A few months later. *Scene 5*: A park near the Castle. *Scene 6*: Arthur's study—A few weeks later. *Scene 7*: The grandstand of the jousting field. *Scene 8*: Arthur's study. *Scene 9*: The Great Hall.

Act 2, Scene 1: The Castle Garden—A few years later. *Scene 2*: The Terrace—A few weeks later. *Scene 3*: Near the Forest of Morgan Le Fey—A few days later. *Scene 4*: The Forest of Morgan Le Fey—Immediately following. *Scene 5*: Corridor—That night. *Scene 6*: The Queen's Bedchamber—Immediately following. *Scene 7*: Camelot—Several days later. *Scene 8*: A Battlefield near Joyous Gard—A few weeks later.

ACT 1[6]
Scene 1
"I Wonder What the King is Doing Tonight?"
R. Goulet
"The Simple Joys of Maidenhood"
P. Kies
"Camelot"
R. Goulet, P. Kies
"Camelot" (reprise)
R. Goulet, P. Kies
Scene 2
"Follow Me"
M. Smith
Scene 3
"Camelot" (reprise)
R. Goulet, P. Kies
Scene 4
"C'est Moi"
S. Blanchard
Scene 5
"The Lusty Month of May"
P. Kies, Ensemble
Scene 6
"How to Handle a Woman"
R. Goulet
Scene 7
"The Jousts"
R. Goulet, P. Kies, Ensemble
Scene 8
"Before I Gaze at You Again"
P. Kies

ACT 2
Scene 1
"Madrigal"
Court Dancers, Musicians
"If Ever I Would Leave You"
S. Blanchard
"The Seven Deadly Virtues"
T. McCrady
Scene 2
"Fie on Goodness!"
T. McCrady, Knights
Scene 3
"What Do the Simple Folk Do?"
P. Kies, R. Goulet
Scene 5
"I Loved You Once in Silence"
P. Kies
Scene 6
"Guenevere"
Ensemble
Scene 7
"Camelot" (reprise)
R. Goulet

1993.12 **THE STUDENT PRINCE**

A Revival of the Operetta in Three Acts, a Prologue and 4 Scenes[7]. Music by Sigmund Romberg. Book and lyrics by Dorothy Donnelly. Book adaptation

---

[1]Originally produced in New York 23 April 1963 at the Eugene O'Neill Theatre for 301 performances. For Synopsis of Scenes and Musical Numbers, see original 1963 production. A shortened version of "Thank You, Madam" was performed at the close of "Sounds While Selling." "Tango Tragique" was omitted from this production, but performed as an instrumental during the scene. "A Romantic Atmosphere" orchestrated by David Krane. "Days Gone By" (reprise) dropped from Act 2.
[2]David Krane joined Frank Matosich, Jr. in revising Don Walker's orchestrations.
[3]Succeeded by DIANE FRATANTONI for the commercial transfer.
[4]Originally produced in New York 3 December 1960 at the Majestic Theatre for 873 performances.
[5]Orchestrations uncredited.

[6]For this production, "Then You May Take Me to the Fair" and "The Persuasion" were omitted; "The Madrigal" was added.
[7]First produced in New York 2 December 1924 at the Jolson Theatre for 608 performances; this adaptation first produced by the NYC Opera 29 August 1980. For Synopsis of Scenes and Musical Numbers, see 1980 revival.

by Hugh Wheeler. Conducted by Scott Bergeson. Production (original direction) by Jack Hofsis. Stage director, Christian Smith. Scenery designed by David Jenkins. Costumes designed by Patton Campbell. Lighting designed by Gilbert V. Hemsley, Jr. Choreography by Donald Saddler, restaged by Jessica Redel. Chorus master, Joseph Colaneri. Produced by the New York City Opera. Produced by the New York City Opera. Opened 14 August 1993 at the New York State Theatre and closed 28 August 1993 after 15 performances.

CAST (in order of their appearance): *Lackeys*: Steven Raiford, Louis Perry, Edward Zimmerman, Ron Hilley. *Dr. Engel*, the Prince's Tutor: LOUIS OTEY. *Count von Mark*: DAVID RAE SMITH. *Secretaries*: Michael Lockley, Jonathan Guss. *Prince Karl Franz*: MICHAEL REES DAVIS. *Lutz*, valet to the Prince: JAMES BILLINGS. *Gretchen*, Maid at the Inn: SANDRA RUGGLES. *Ruder*: Joseph McKee. *Nicholas*: Gunnar Waldman. *Toni*, a waiter: Jonathan Green. *Hubert*: William Ledbetter. *Detlef*, a student leader: Gordon Gietz. *von Asterberg*, another student leader: Ron Baker. *Lucas*, another student leader: David Langan. *Freshman*: Steven Raiford. *Kathie*, niece of Ruder: MICHELE PATZAKIS. *Girls*: Madeleine Mines, Paula Hostetter, Jill Bosworth, Beth Pensiero. *Grand Duchess Anastasia*: MURIEL COSTA-GREENSPON. *Princess Margaret*, fiancée of Prince Karl Franz: MICHELE MCBRIDE. *Captain Tarnitz*: JEFF MATSEY. *Countess Leydon*, lady-in-waiting to the Princess: Dulcy Reyes. *Huzzars*: James Russell, Michael Lockley, Daniel Shigo, Richard Pearson. *Friends of the Huzzars*: Madeleine Mines, Paula Hostetter, Beth Pensiero, Jill Bosworth. *Ensemble*: New York City Opera Chorus.

1993.13 THE MIKADO, or The Town of Titipu

A Revival of the Comic Opera in Two Acts[8]. Libretto by William S. Gilbert. Music by Arthur Sullivan. Stage director, Christian Smith. Choreography by Patricia Birch, restaged by Helen Andreyko. Conductor, Steven Mosteller. Scenery and costumes by Thierry Bousquet. Lighting by John Gleason. Chorus master, Joseph Colaneri. Produced by the New York City Opera. Opened 12 September 1993 at the New York State Theatre and closed 19 October 1993 after 7 performances in repertory.

CAST: *The Mikado of Japan*: RICHARD MCKEE. *Nanki-Poo*, his son, disguised as a wandering minstrel in love with Yum-Yum: PAUL AUSTIN KELLY. *Ko-Ko*, Lord High Executioner of Titipu: JAMES BILLINGS. *Pooh-Bah*, Lord High Everything Else: JOSEPH MCKEE. *Pish-Tush*, Noble Lord: Jeff Matsey. *Yum-Yum, Pitti-Sing, Peep-Bo*, three sisters, wards of Ko-Ko: ABBIE FURMANSKY, SANDRA GELB, FRANCES PALLOZZI. *Katisha*: CHRISTENE PALMER, BETTI LLOYD-JONES. *Chorus of School Girls, Nobles, Guards and Coolies*: New York City Opera Chorus.

1993.14 CINDERELLA

A Musical in Two Acts, a Prologue and 10 Scenes. Book and lyrics (for television) by Oscar Hammerstein II. Book adapted by Steve Allen, adapted for the stage by Robert Johanson. Music by Richard Rodgers. Directed and choreographed by Robert Johanson. Co-choreographer, Sharon Halley. Set designer, Henry Bardon. Costume designer, Gregg Barnes. Lighting designer, Jeff Davis. Sound designer, Abe Jacob. Conductor, Eric Stern. Orchestrations by Robert Russell Bennett. Chorus master, Joseph Colaneri. Assistant stage director, Paul L. King. Produced by the New York City Opera. Opened 9 November 1993 at the New York State Theatre and closed 21 November 1993 after 14 performances.

CAST (in order of appearance): *Fairy Godmother*: SALLY ANN HOWES. *Royal Herald*: Ron Baker. *Little Girl*: Abigail Mentzer. *Cinderella's Stepmother*: NANCY MARCHAND. *Cinderella's Stepsisters (2)*: *Joy*: ALIX KOREY. *Portia*: JEANETTE PALMER. *Cinderella*: CRISTA MOORE. *Dog*: Andrew Pacho. *Cat*: Debbi Fuhrman. *Queen*: MARIA KARNILOVA. *King*: GEORGE S. IRVING. *Royal Chef*: Jonathan Green. *Royal Steward*: John Lankston. *Prince*: GEORGE DVORSKY. *Youngest Fairy*: Stephanie Godino. *Tiara Fairy*: Shawn Stephens. *Ensemble*: New York City Opera Chorus.

Prologue: A Public Square.

Act 1, Scene 1: The Kitchen. *Scene 2*: Royal Dressing Room. *Scene 3*: Back in the Kitchen. *Scene 4*: A Magical Place.

Act 2, Scene 1: The Palace Ballroom. *Scene 2*: A Garden at the Palace. *Scene 3*: The Palace Ballroom. *Scene 4*: Back in the Kitchen. *Scene 5*: Garden at the Palace. *Scene 6*: The Palace Ballroom.

ACT 1[9]
Prologue
"The Prince Is Giving a Ball"
R. Baker, Townspeople
Scene 1
"In My Own Little Corner"
C. Moore
Scene 2
"The Prince Is Giving a Ball" (reprise)
Townspeople
"Your Majesties"
G. S. Irving, M. Karnilova, J. Lankston, J. Green, Ensemble
"The Loneliness of Evening"[10]
G. Dvorsky
"My Best Love"[11]
G. S. Irving, G. Dvorsky
Scene 3
"Impossible"
C. Moore, S. A. Howes
Scene 4
"The Gavotte"
Ensemble

ACT 2
Scene 1
"Ten Minutes Ago"
C. Moore, G. Dvorsky
Scene 2
"Stepsisters' Lament"
A. Korey, J. Palmer
Scene 3
"Waltz for a Ball"
Ensemble
"If I Weren't King"[12]
G. S. Irving
"Do I Love You Because You're Beautiful?"
C. Moore, G. Dvorsky
Scene 4
("When You're Driving Through the Moonlight")
C. Moore, N. Marchand, A. Korey, J. Palmer
"A Lovely Night"
C. Moore, N. Marchand, A. Korey, J. Palmer
Scene 6
Finale
Company

1993.15 JOSEPH AND THE AMAZING TECHNICOLOR DREAMCOAT

A Revival of the Musical in Two Acts, a Prologue and 21 Scenes[13]. Music by Andrew Lloyd Webber. Lyrics by Tim Rice. Based on the Old Testament story. Directed by Stephen Pimlott. Choreography by Anthony Van Laast. (Scenery and costume) Design by Mark Thompson. Lighting design by Andrew Bridge. Sound design by Martin Levan. Musical direction by Patrick Vaccariello. Musical supervision by Michael Reed. Orchestrations by John Cameron. An Andrew Lloyd Webber Production. Produced by James M. Nederlander and Terry Allen Kramer. Opened 10 November 1993 at the Minskoff Theatre and closed 29 May 1994 after 231 performances.

CAST: *Joseph*: MICHAEL DAMIAN. *Narrator*: KELLI RABKE. *Pharaoh*: ROBERT TORTI. *Jacob/Potiphar/Guru*: CLIFFORD DAVID. *Butler*: Glenn Sneed. *Baker*: Bill Nolte. *Mrs. Potiphar*: JULIE BOND. *Apache Dancers*: Tina Ou, Tim Schultheis.

---

[8]First presented in New York 20 July, 10-29 August 1885 at the Union Square and People's Theatres for 22 performances. First authorized production presented 19 August 1885 at the Fifth Avenue Theatre by Richard D'Oyly Carte for 250 performances. For Synopsis of Scenes and Musical Numbers, see 19 August 1885 D'Oyly Carte production.

[9]Musical numbers not listed in programs.
[10]Dropped from SOUTH PACIFIC before its opening.
[11]Dropped from FLOWER DRUM SONG before its opening.
[12]Newly interpolated.
[13]Originally produced in New York Off-Broadway 18 November 1981 at the Entermedia Theatre for 77 performances; transferred 27 January 1982 to the Royale Theatre for 670 performances. Total: 747 performances. Previously produced Off-Broadway twice at the Brooklyn Academy of Music: 26 December 1976 for 22 performances, and 13 December 1977 for 24 performances.

Brothers and Wives: *Reuben*: MARC KUDISCH. *Reuben's Wife*: Michelle Murlin. *Simeon*: Neal Ben-Ari. *Simeon's Wife*: Mindy Franzese. *Levi*: ROBERT TORTI. *Levi's Wife*: Jocelyn Vodovoz Cook. *Napthali*: DANNY BOLERO. *Napthali's Wife*: Mamie Duncan-Gibbs. *Issachar*: Bill Nolte. *Isaachar's Wife*: Jacquie Porter. *Asher*: Timothy Smith. *Asher's Wife*: Lisa Akey. *Dan*: Joseph Savant. *Dan's Wife*: Sarah Miles. *Zebulun*: Tim Schultheis. *Zebulun's Wife*: Diana Brownstone. *Gad*: Glenn Sneed. *Gad's Wife*: Gina Trano. *Benjamin*: TY TAYLOR. *Benjamin's Wife*: Tina Ou. *Judah*: Gerry McIntyre. *Judah's Wife*: Susan Carr George.

Swings: Ron Kellum, Andrew Makay, Janet Rothermel, Kelli Severson, Gina Trano, Matthew Zarley.

Children's Choirs: The Carolabbe Chorus, La Petite Musicale, Long Island Performing Arts Center Choir, The William F. Halloran Vocal Ensemble.

ACT 1
Prologue ("You Are What You Feel")
K. Rabke
Scene 1
"Any Dream Will Do"
M. Damina, Children
Scene 2
"Jacob and Sons"/"Joseph's Coat"
K. Rabke, Brothers, Wives, Children, C. David, M. Damian
Scene 3
"Joseph's Dreams"
K. Rabke, M. Damian, Brothers, Female Ensemble
Scene 4
"Poor Poor Joseph"
K. Rabke, Brothers, Children
Scene 5
"One More Angel in Heaven"
M. Kudisch, M. Murlin, K. Rabke, Brothers, Wives, C. David, Children
Scene 6
"Potiphar"
K. Rabke, Ensemble, J. Bond, C. David, M. Damian
Scene 7
"Close Every Door"
M. Damian, Children
Scene 8
"Go, Go, Go Joseph"
K. Rabke, G. Sneed, B. Nolte, Ensemble, C. David, Children

ACT 2
Scene 1
"Pharaoh's Story"
K. Rabke, Children
Scene 2
"Poor, Poor Pharaoh"/"Song of the King"
K. Rabke, G. Sneed, C. David, Children, Men
Scene 3
"Pharaoh's Dream Explained"
M. Damian, Ensemble, Children
Scene 4
"Stone the Crows"
K. Rabke, C. David, Children, M. Damian, Female Ensemble
Scene 5
"Those Canaan Days"
P. Harman, C. David, Brothers, Apache Dancers
Scene 6
"The Brothers Came to Egypt"/"Grovel, Grovel"
K. Rabke, Brothers, M. Damian, Female Ensemble, Children
Scene 7
"Who's the Thief?"
M. Damian, Brothers, Female Ensemble, Children
Scene 8
"Benjamin Calypso"
G. McIntyre, Brothers, Female Ensemble, Children
Scene 9
"Joseph All the Time"
K. Rabke, M. Damian, Children, Brothers, Female Ensemble
Scene 10
"Jacob in Egypt"
K. Rabke, M. Damian, Children, Ensemble
Scene 11
"Any Dream Will Do"
M. Damian, K. Rabke, Ensemble, C. David, Children
Scene 12
"Close Every Door" (reprise)
M. Damian, Children
Scene 13
"Joseph Megamix"
The Company

1993.16

A GRAND NIGHT FOR SINGING

A Musical Revue in Two Acts[14]. Conceived and directed by Walter Bobbie. Music by Richard Rodgers. Lyrics by Oscar Hammerstein II. Settings by Tony Walton. Costume design by Martin Pakledinaz. Lighting design by Natasha Katz. Sound by Tony Meola. Orchestrations by Michael Gibson, Jonathan Tunick. Musical direction and arrangements by Fred Wells. Additional staging by Pamela Sousa. Produced by The Roundabout Theatre Company (Todd Haimes, Artistic director; Gene Feist, Founding director). Opened 17 November 1993 at the Criterion Center Stage Right and closed 2 January 1994 after 52 performances.

CAST (in order of appearance): MARTIN VIDNOVIC, JASON GRAAE, VICTORIA CLARK, ALYSON REED, LYNNE WINTERSTELLER

ACT 1
"Carousel Waltz" (from *CAROUSEL*)/
"So Far" (from *ALLEGRO*)/
"It's a Grand Night For Singing" (from *STATE FAIR* film)
Company
"The Surrey with the Fringe on the Top" (from *OKLAHOMA!*)
J. Graae
"Stepsisters' Lament" (from *CINDERELLA*)
L. Wintersteller, V. Clark
"We Kiss in a Shadow" (from *THE KING AND I*)
M. Vidnovic
"Hello, Young Lovers" (from *THE KING AND I*)
Company
"A Wonderful Guy" (from *SOUTH PACIFIC*)
A. Reed
"I Cain't Say No" (from *OKLAHOMA!*)
V. Clark
"Maria" (from *THE SOUND OF MUSIC*)
J. Graae
"Do I Love You Because You're Beautiful?" (from *CINDERELLA*)
L. Wintersteller
"Honey Bun" (from *SOUTH PACIFIC*)
M. Vidnovic, Company
"The Gentleman Is a Dope" (from *ALLEGRO*)
A. Reed
"Don't Marry Me" (from *FLOWER DRUM SONG*)
M. Vidnovic, J. Graae, L. Wintersteller, V. Clark
"I'm Gonna Wash That Man Right Outa My Hair" (from *SOUTH PACIFIC*)
A. Reed, L. Wintersteller, V. Clark
"If I Loved You" (from *CAROUSEL*)
V. Clark
"Shall We Dance?" (from *THE KING AND I*)
L. Wintersteller, J. Graae
"That's the Way It Happens" (from *ME AND JULIET*)
A. Reed, J. Graae
"All at Once You Love Her" (from *PIPE DREAM*)
M. Vidnovic, J. Graae
"Some Enchanted Evening" (from *SOUTH PACIFIC*)
Company

ACT 2
"Oh, What a Beautiful Mornin'" (from *OKLAHOMA!*)
M. Vidnovic
"Wish Them Well" (from *ALLEGRO*)
Company

---

[14]Originally produced Off-Broadway as a nightclub revue 2 March-10 April 1993 at Rainbow and Stars for 60 performances.

"The Man I Used To Be" (from *PIPE DREAM*)
V. Clark, A. Reed, J. Graae
(*Dance arrangements by* Wally Harper.)
"It Might As Well Be Spring" (from *STATE FAIR*)
L. Wintersteller
"Kansas City" (from *OKLAHOMA!*)
Company
"When the Children Are Asleep" (from *CAROUSEL*)
"I Know It Can Happen Again" (from *ALLEGRO*)
"My Little Girl" (excerpt from "Soliloquy," from *CAROUSEL*)
Company
"It's Me" (from *ME AND JULIET*)
A. Reed, J. Graae, M. Vidnovic
(*Dance arrangements by* Wally Harper.)
"Love, Look Away" (from *FLOWER DRUM SONG*)
V. Graae
"When You're Driving Through the Moonlight" (from *CINDERELLA*)
"A Lovely Night" (from Cinderella)
V. Clark, M. Vidnovic, A. Reed, J. Graae
"Something Wonderful" (from *THE KING AND I*)
L. Wintersteller
"This Nearly Was Mine" (from *SOUTH PACIFIC*)
M. Vidnovic
"Impossible" (from *CINDERELLA*)
"I Have Dreamed" (from *THE KING AND I*)
Company

1993.17 CYRANO: THE MUSICAL

A Musical in Two Acts, 3 Scenes. Based on the play "Cyrano de Bergarac" by Edmond Rostand. (Original Dutch) Book and lyrics by Koen van Dijk. Music by Ad van Dijk. English lyrics by Peter Reeves; additional lyrics by Sheldon Harnick. Directed by Eddy Habbema. Scenery designed by Paul Gallis. Costumes designed by Yan Tax. Lighting designed by Reinier Twebeeke. Sound designed by Rogier van Rossum. Associate set design, Duke Durfee. Associate costume design, Marcia K. McDonald. Associate lighting design, Brian Nason. Associate sound design, Steve Canyon Kennedy. Orchestrations by Don Sebesky, Tony Cox. Special effects, Gregory Meeh. Associate director, Eleanor Fazan. Fight director, Malcolm Ranson. Executive producer, Robin DeLevita. Produced by Joop van den Ende in association with Peter Kulok. Opened 21 November 1993 at the Neil Simon Theatre and closed 20 March 1994 after 137 performances.

CAST (in order of appearance): *Man*: Geoffrey Blaisdell. *Le Bret*: PAUL SCHOEFFLER. *Ragueneau*: ED DIXON. *Christian*: PAUL ANTHONY STEWART. *DeGuiche*: TIMOTHY NOLEN. *Roxane*: ANNE RUNOLFSSON. *Valvert*: Adam Pelty. *Chaperone*: Joy Hermalyn. *Montfleury*: Mark Agnes. *Cyrano*: BILL VAN DIJK, Jordan Bennett (alternate). *Captain de Castel Jaloux*: Geoffrey Blaisdell. *Mother Superior*: Elizabeth Acosta. *Novice*: Michele Ragusa.

Opera Audience, Cadets, Precieuses, Chefs, Waitresses, Nuns: Elizabeth Acosta, Mark Agnes, Carina Andersson, Christopher Eaton Baily, James Barbour, Geoffrey Blaisdell, Michelle Dawson, Jeff Gardner, Daniel Guzman, Joy Hermalyn, Bjørn Johnson, Peter Lockyer, Stuart Marland, Kerry O'Malley, Adam Pelty, Tom Polum, Michele Ragusa, Sam Scalamoni, Robin Skye, Tami Tappan, Ann van Cleave, Charles West. *Swings*: Ted Keegan, Rose McGuire, Christian Nova.

Act 1: Paris, 1640.

Act 2, Scene 1: A besieged camp near Arras, a few month later. *Scene 2*: Paris, seven years later.

ACT 1
Prologue
G. Blaisdell, P. Schoeffler, E. Dixon, Ensemble
"Opera, Opera"
Ensemble
"Aria"
M. Agnes, B. Van Dijk, Ensemble
"One Fragment of a Moment"
P. A. Stewart, A. Runolfsson
"Confrontation"
Ensemble
"The Duel"
B. Van Dijk, Ensemble
"Where's All This Anger Coming From"
P. Schoeffler, B. Van Dijk
"Loving Her"
B. Van Dijk, P. A. Stewart
"A Message from Roxane"
J. Hermalyn, B. Van Dijk
"Ragueneau's Patisserie"
E. Dixon, Chefs, Waitresses
"Roxane's Confession"
A. Runolfsson, B. Van Dijk
"What a Reward"
T. Nolen, P. Schoeffler, E. Dixon
"Hate Me"
B. Van Dijk
"Courage Makes a Man"
Cadets, G. Blaisdell
"Cyrano's Story"
B. Van Dijk, P. A. Stewart
"A Letter for Roxane"
B. Van Dijk, P. A. Stewart
"I Have No Words"
P. A. Stewart
"Two Musketeers"
B. Van Dijk, P. A. Stewart
"An Evening Made for Lovers"
Ensemble
"Balcony Scene"
A. Runolfsson, P. A. Stewart, B. Van Dijk
"Poetry"
B. Van Dijk, A. Runolfsson
"Moonsong"
B. Van Dijk
"Stay With Me!"
Ensemble

ACT 2
Scene 1
"Every Day, Every Night"
B. Van Dijk, P. A. Stewart, Cadets
"A White Sash"
T. Nolen, B. Van Dijk, Cadets
"When I Write"
B. Van Dijk
"Two Musketeers" (reprise)
P. A. Stewart, B. Van Dijk
"Rhyming Menu"
A. Runolfsson, E. Dixon, Ensemble
"Even Then"
A. Runolfsson
"Tell Her Now"
P. A. Stewart, B. Van Dijk
"The Evening"
B. Van Dijk, Cadets
"Even Then" (reprise)
A. Runolfsson, B. Van Dijk
"The Battle"
Ensemble
"Everything You Wrote"
A. Runolfsson
Scene 2
"He Loves To Make Us Laugh"
Nuns, E. Acosta
"A Visit from DeGuiche"
T. Nolen, A. Runolfsson, E. Acosta
"Opera, Opera" (reprise)
Ensemble
"An Old Wound"/"The Letter"/"Moonsong"
B. Van Dijk, A. Runolfsson

1993.18 MY FAIR LADY

A Revival of the Musical (Comedy) in Two Acts, 18 Scenes[15]. Book and lyrics by Alan Jay Lerner. Based on the play "Pygmalion" by George Bernard Shaw, produced on the screen by Gabriel Pascal. Music by Frederick Loewe. Directed by Howard Davies. Choreography by Donald Saddler. Scenic design based on original designs by Ralph Koltai. Costume design by Patricia Zipprodt. Lighting design by Natasha Katz. Sound design by Peter Fitzgerald. Musical and vocal direction, Jack Lee. Production supervisor, Craig Jacobs. Associate producer, Alecia Parker. Produced by Barry and Fran Weissler, Jujamcyn Theatres in association with Pace Theatrical Group, Tokyo Broadcasting System International and Martin Rabbett. Opened 9 December 1993 at the Virginia Theatre and closed 1 May 1994 after 165 performances.

CAST (in order of appearance): *Eliza Doolittle*: MELISSA ERRICO. *Freddy Eynsford-Hill*: ROBERT SELLA. *Mrs. Eynsford-Hill*: Lisa Merrill McCord. *Colonel Pickering*: PAXTON WHITEHEAD. *Professor Henry Higgins*: RICHARD CHAMBERLAIN. *The 'Loverly Quartet'*: Jeffrey Wilkins, Bruce Moore, Michael Gerhart, Jamie Mackenzie. *George* the Bartender: Bill Ullman. *Jamie*: Michael J. Farina. *Harry*: James Young. *Mrs. Pearce*: GLYNIS BELL. *Butler*: Jeffrey Wilkins. *Alfred P. Doolittle*: JULIAN HOLLOWAY. *Servants*: Edwardyne Cowan, Michael Gerhart, Marilyn Kay Huelsman, Corinne Melançon, Meg Tolin. *Charles*, the Chauffeur: Michael Gerhart. *Mrs. Higgins*: DOLORES SUTTON. *Lord Boxington*: Jeffrey Wilkins. *Lady Boxington*: Marnee Hollis. *Policeman*: Ron Schwinn. *Flower Girl*: Corinne Melançon. *Footman*: Ben George. *Professor Zoltan Karpathy*: James Young. *Queen of Transylvania*: Patti Karr. *Mrs. Higgins' Maid*: Sue Delano.

Ensemble: Edwardyne Cowan, Laurie Crochet, Alexander de Jong, Sue Delano, Rebecca Downing, Michael J. Farina, Ben George, Michael Gerhart, Marnee Hollis, Marilyn Kay Huelsman, Patti Karr, Tom Kosis, John Vincent Leggio, Jamie MacKenzie, Lisa Merrill McCord, Corinne Melançon, Bruce Moore, Ron Schwinn, Meg Tolin, Bill Ullman, Jeffrey Wilkins, James Young. *Swings*: Newton Cole, Wendy Oliver, John Scott.

The action takes place in London in 1912.

Act 1, Scene 1: Outside Covent Garden. *Scene 2*: The Pub—Tottenham Court Road. *Scene 3*: Higgins' Laboratory. *Scene 4*: Higgins' Laboratory. *Scene 5*: Higgins' Laboratory—The Lessons. *Scene 6*: The Bed. *Scene 7*: Outside Ascot. *Scene 8*: Ascot. *Scene 9*: Wimpole Street. *Scene 10*: Higgins' Laboratory.

Act 2, Scene 1: The Ballroom. *Scene 2*: Higgins' Laboratory. *Scene 3*: Wimpole Street. *Scene 4*: Covent Garden. *Scene 5*: Higgins' Laboratory. *Scene 6*: The Garden of Mrs. Higgins. *Scene 7*: Wimpole Street. *Scene 8*: Higgins' Laboratory.

ACT 1
Scene 1
"Why Can't the English?"
R. Chamberlain
"Wouldn't It Be Loverly"
M. Errico, Quartet
Scene 2
"With a Little Bit of Luck"
J. Holloway, J. Young, M. J. Farina, Company
Scene 3
"I'm an Ordinary Man"
R. Chamberlain
Scene 5
"Just You Wait"
M. Errico
"The Servants' Chorus"
Servants
"The Rain in Spain"
R. Chamberlain, M. Errico, P. Whitehead
Scene 6
"I Could Have Danced All Night"
M. Errico
Scene 8
"Ascot Gavotte"
Company
Scene 9
"On the Street Where You Live"
R. Sella

ACT 2
Scene 1
"The Embassy Waltz"
Company
Scene 2
"You Did It"
R. Chamberlain, P. Whiehead, Servants
"Just You Wait" (reprise)
M. Errico
Scene 3
"On the Street Where You Live" (reprise)
R. Sella
"Show Me"M. Errico
Scene 4
"Wouldn't It Be Loverly" (reprise)
Company
"Get Me to the Church on Time"
J. Holloway, Company
Scene 5
"Hymn to Him"
R. Chamberlain
Scene 6
"Without You"
M. Errico
Scene 7
"I've Grown Accustomed to Her Face"
R. Chamberlain

[15]Originally produced in New York 15 March 1956 at the Mark Hellinger Theatre for 2717 peformances. For this production, Street Entertainers (Act 1, Scene 1) and "With a Little Bit of Luck" (reprise) were dropped. The Ballroom Scene/"Embassy Waltz" was moved from the close of Act 1 to the Opening of Act 2.

1993.19 THE RED SHOES

A Musical in Two Acts, 19 Scenes. Book by Marsha Norman. Based on the film of the same name, screenplay by Emeric Pressburger. Music by Jule Styne. Lyrics by Marsha Norman and Paul Stryker [Bob Merrill]. Directed by Stanley Donen. Choreographed by Lar Lubovitch. Scenery by Heidi Landesman. Costumes by Catherine Zuber. Lighting by Ken Billington. Sound by Tony Meola. Musical direction and vocal arrangements by Don Pippin. Ballet and dance music arrangements by Gordon Harrell. Orchestrations by Sid Ramin, William D. Brohn. Flying by Foy. Associate producer, Jujamcyn/The Broadway Fund. Produced by Martin Starger in association with MCA/Universal and James M. Nederlander. Opened 16 December 1993 at the Gershwin Theatre and closed 19 December 1993 after 5 performances.

CAST (in order of appearance): *Grisha Ljubov*: GEORGE DE LA PEÑA. *Irina Boronskaya*: LESLIE BROWNE. *Ivan Boleslavsky*: Jon Marshall Sharp. *Livy*: Robert Jensen. *Sergei Ratov*: TAD INGRAM. *Dmitri*: Charles Goff. *Boris Lermontov*: STEVE BARTON. *Julian Craster*: HUGH PANARO. *Lady Ottoline Neston*: Pamela Burrell. *Victoria Page*: MARGARET ILLMAN, Amy Wilder (alternate). *Miss Hardiman*: Lydia Gaston. *Miss Lovat*: Laurie Gamache. *Dr. Copelias*: Daniel Wright. *James* ("Les Sylphides"): Scott Fowler. *Marguerite*: Jamie Chandler-Torns. *The Priest*: Robert Jensen. *Jean Louis*: Scott Fowler, Don Bellamy (alternate). *The Angel*: Jeff Lander.

The Company of The Ballet Lermontov: Jennifer Alexander, Anita Intrieri, Don Bellamy, Robert Jensen, Mucuy Bolles, Christina Johnson, Jamie Chandler-Torns, Jeff Lander, Geralyn Del Corso, Christina Marie Norrup, Scott Fowler, Oscar Ruge, Antonia Franceschi, Laurie Gamache, Jonathan Riseling, Lydia Gaston, Joan Tsao, Nina Goldman, James Weatherstone, Daniel Wright. *Swings*: Kellye Gordon, James Hadley, Alexies Sánchez, Catherine Ulissey, Aliceann Wilson.

The action takes place in the world of The Ballet Lermontov in London, Paris and Monte Carlo, in 1921-1922.

Act 1, Scene 1: Covent Garden Opera House—London. *Scene 2*: Lady Neston's Town House—Mayfair, London. *Scene 3*: Covent Garden Rehearsal Hall. *Scene 4*: Julian's Hotel Room—Paris. *Scene 5*: Paris Opera House—Lermontov's Office. *Scene 6*: Paris Opera House—On stage. *Scene 7*: Paris Opera House—Rehearsal hall and on stage. *Scene 8*: Monte Carlo Opera House—Vicky's Dressing Room. *Scene 9*: Lermontov's Villa—Monte Carlo. *Scene 10*: Monte Carlo Opera House—On stage. *Scene 11*: A Promenade—Monte Carlo. *Scene 12*: A Restaurant—Monte Carlo. *Scene 13*: Monte Carlo Opera House—On stage.

Act 2, Scene 1: Monte Carlo Opera House—Rehearsal Hall. *Scene 2*: Monte Carlo Opera House—Lermontov's Office. *Scene 3*: Vicky and Julian's flat—London/Monte Carlo Opera House—Lermontov's Office. *Scene 4*: Monte Carlo Opera House—Backstage. *Scene 5*: Monte Carlo Opera House—Vicky's Dressing Room. *Scene 6*: Monte Carlo Opera House—The Ballet of the Red Shoes.

ACT 1
Scene 1
"Swan Lake"
L. Browne, J. M. Sharp, G. De La Peña, Company

"I Make the Rules"
S. Barton, G De La Peña
Scene 3
"The Audition"
M. Illman
"Corps de Ballet"
G. De La Peña, Company
Scene 4
"When It Happens to You"
H. Panaro
Scene 6
"Top of the Sky"
S. Barton, M. Illman
Scene 7
Ballet Montage (Swan Lake, Coppelia, Sleeping Beauty, Les Sylphides, Swan Lake)
M. Illman, Company
Scene 9
"It's a Fairy Tale"
S. Barton, H. Panaro, G. De La Peña, T. Ingram, C. Goff
Scene 11
"Be Somewhere"
H. Panaro
Scene 12
"The Rag"
G. De La Peña, Company
Scene 13
"Am I To Wish Her Love"
S. Barton, M. Illman

ACT 2
Scene 1
"Do Svedanya"
G. De La Peña, T. Ingram, Company
Scene 2
"Come Home"
S. Barton
Scene 3
"When You Dance for a King"
S. Barton, M. Illman
Scene 6
The Ballet of the Red Shoes
The Girl: M. Illman. *The Shoemaker*: G. De La Peña. *The Young Man*: S. Fowler.

1994.01 DAMN YANKEES

A Revival of the Musical in Two Acts[16]. Book by George Abbott and Douglass Wallop[17]. Based on the novel "The Year the Yankees Lost the Pennant" by Douglass Wallop. Music and lyrics by Richard Adler and Jerry Ross. Directed by Jack O'Brien. Choreographed by Rob Marshall. Scenic design by Douglas W. Schmidt. Costume design by David C. Woolard. Lighting design by David F. Segal. Sound design by Jonathan Deans. Special effects design by Gregory Meeh. Orchestrations by Douglas Besterman. Dance arrangements by Tom Fay; additional dance arrangements by David Krane. Vocal arrangements and musical supervision by James Raitt. Assistant director, Will Roberson. Assistant choreographer, Kathleen Marshall. Originally produced by The Old Globe Theatre, San Diego, California. Associate producers, Thomas Hall, Jennifer Manocherian, Jonathan Pillot, Andrea Pines, TDI, Mark Balsam, Meyer Ackerman, Julian Schlossberg,Workin' Man Films, Inc. Produced by Mitchell Maxwell, PolyGram Diversified Entertainment, Dan Markley, Kevin McCollum, Victoria Maxwell, Fred H. Krones, Andrea Nasher, The (Richard) Frankel•(Thomas) Viertel•(Steven) Baruch Group, Paula Heil Fisher, Julie Ross, in association with Jon B. Platt, Alan J. Schuster and Peter Breger. Opened 3 March 1994 at the Marquis Theatre, closing 1 January 1995 after 342 performances; re-opened 28 February 1995 at the Marquis Theatre and closed 6 August 1995 after 184 additional performances. Total: 526 performances.

CAST (in order of appearance): *Meg Boyd*: LINDA STEPHENS. *Joe Boyd*: DENNIS KELLY. *Sister*: Susan Mansur. *Gloria Thorpe*: VICKI LEWIS. *Applegate*: VICTOR GARBER. *Joe Hardy*: JARROD EMICK. *Rocky*: Scott Wise. *Smokey*: Jeff Blumenkrantz. *Sohovik*: Gregory Jbara. *Mickey*: John Ganun. *Vernon*: Joey Pizzi. *Del*: Scott Robertson. *Ozzie*: Michael Winther. *Bubba*: Cory English. *Henry*: Bruce Anthony Davis. *Bomber*: Michael Berresse. *Van Buren*: DICK LATESSA. *Betty*: Paula Leggett Chase. *Donna*: Nancy Ticotin. *Kitty*: Cynthia Onrubia. *Photographer*: Amy Rider. *Rita*: Amy Rider. *Welch*: Terrence P. Currier. *Lola*: BEBE NEUWIRTH. (Note: The Senators include Rocky, Smokey, Sohovik, Mickey, Vernon, Del, Ozzie, Bubba, Henry, Bomber.)
Swings: Mark Santoro, Robyn Peterman.

(The action takes place the year the Yankees lost the pennant in the 1950s.)

ACT 1
"Six Months Out of Every Year"
L. Stephens, D. Kelly, S. Mansur, V. Lewis, Husbands, Wives
"Goodbye, Old Girl"
D. Kelly, J. Emick
"Blooper Ballet"[18]
The Senators
"Heart"
D. Latessa, The Senators
"Shoeless Joe from Hannibal, Mo."
V. Lewis, The Senators
"Shoeless Joe from Hannibal, Mo." (reprise)
V. Lewis, J. Emick, Ensemble
"A Little Brains—A Little Talent"
B. Neuwirth
"A Man Doesn't Know"
L. Stephens, J. Emick
"Whatever Lola Wants (Lola Gets)"
B. Neuwirth

ACT 2
"Who's Got the Pain?"
B. Neuwirth, The Senators
"The Game"
The Senators
"Near To You"
J. Emick, S. Bolin
"Those Were the Good Old Days"
V. Garber
"Two Lost Souls"
B. Neuwirth, V. Garber
"A Man Doesn't Know" (reprise)
L. Stephens, D. Kelly
Finale: "Heart" (reprise)
Company

1994.02 CAROUSEL

A Revival of the Musical Play in Two Acts, 9 Scenes[19]. Book and lyrics by Oscar Hammerstein II. Based on Ferenc Molnar's play "Liliom" as adapted by Benjamin F. Glazer. Music by Richard Rodgers. Directed by Nicholas Hytner. Choreography by Sir Kenneth MacMillan, staged by Jane Elliott. Sets and costumes by Bob Crowley. Lighting by Paul Pyant. Sound by Steve Canyon Kennedy. Musical director, Eric Stern. Orchestrations by William D. Brohn. Fight direction by David Leong. Dances for the original Theatre Guild production by Agnes de Mille. Originally produced by The Royal National Theatre (Great Britain). Produced by the Lincoln Center Theatre (André Bishop, Artistic director; Bernard Gersten, Executive producer), by arrangement with The Royal National Theatre, Cameron Mackintosh and The Rodgers and Hammerstein Organization. Opened 24 March 1994 at the Vivian Beaumont Theatre and closed 17 January 1995 after 322 performances.

[16]Originally produced in New York 5 May 1955 at the 46th Street Theatre for 1019 performances. Song order, vocals and reprises have been substantially revised from the original; "Who's Got the Pain?" moved from the end of Act 1 to the opening of Act 2.
[17]Uncredited book revisions by George Abbott and Jack O'Brien.
[18]New for this production.
[19]First produced in New York 19 April 1945 at the Majestic Theatre for 890 performances. For Synopsis of Scenes and Musical Numbers, see original 1945 production. For this production, "The Carousel Waltz" became the Prologue. "The Highest Judge of All" was omitted from this production.

CAST (in order of appearance): *Carrie Pipperidge*: AUDRA ANN MC DONALD. *Julie Jordan*: SALLY MURPHY. *Mrs. Mullin*: KATE BUDDEKE. *Billy Bigelow*: MICHAEL HAYDEN. *Policeman*: Taye Diggs. *David Bascombe*: Robert Breuler. *Nettie Fowler*: SHIRLEY VERRETT. *Enoch Snow*: EDDIE KORBICH. *Jigger Craigin*: FISHER STEVENS. *Innkeeper*: Rebecca Eichenberger. *Captain*: Brian d'Arcy James. *Heavenly Friend*: Lauren Ward. *Starkeeper*: JEFF WEISS. *Louise*SANDRA BROWN. *Fairground Boy*: JON MARSHALL SHARP. *Enoch Snow, Jr.*: Duane Boutté. *Margaret Snow*: Lovette George. *Other Snow Children*: Philipp Lee Carabuena, Cece Cortes, Lyn Nagel, Cindy Robinson, Tiffany Sampson, tse-Mach Washington.

Principal: Brian d'Arcy James. *Dr. Selden*: Jeff Weiss. *Robert Allen*: Steven Ochoa. *Hannah Bentley*: Cindy Robinson. *Peter Bentley, Jr.*: Tony Capone. *Abbie Chase*: Natascia A. Diaz. *Charles "Chip" Chase*: Alexies Sânchez. *Jonathan Chase*: Robert Cary. *Virginia Frazer*: Rebecca Eichenberger. *Buddy Hamlin*: Devin Richards. *Cyrus Hamlin*: Taye Diggs. *Arminy Livermore*: Paula Newsome. *Hudson Livermore*: Brian d'Arcy James. *William Osgood*: Rocker Verastique. *Ornn Peesley*: Duane Boutté. *Susan Peters*: Linda Gabler. *Myrtle Robbins*: Lacey Hornkohl. *Ella Sanborn*: Alexia Hess. *Jenny Sanborn*: Lauren Ward. *Martha Sewell*: Keri Lee. *Liza Sinclair*: Endalyn Taylor-Shellman. *Penny Sinclair*: Lovette George. *Henry Sears*: Jeffrey James. *Abner Sperry*: Michael O'Donnell. *Ben Sperry*: Glen Harris. *Sadie Sperry*: Dana Stackpole.

Louise's Friends: Robert Cary, Glen Harris, Steven Ochoa, Michael O'Donnell, Alexie Sanchez, Rocker Verastique. *Swings*: Robert Cary, Lisa Mayer, Donna Rubin, Thomas Titone, Reggie Valdez.

1994.03 JACKIE MASON: POLITICALLY INCORRECT

A One Man Comedy Revue in Two Acts[20]. Written and created by Jackie Mason. Production design and lighting by Neil Peter Jampolis. Sound design by Bruce Cameron. Produced by Jyll Rosenfeld. Opened 5 April 1994 at the John Golden Theatre and closed 4 June 1995 after 347 performances.

CAST: JACKIE MASON (stand-up comedy, monologues, impressions).

1994.04 (DISNEY'S) BEAUTY AND THE BEAST

A Musical in Two Acts. Book by Linda Woolverton (based on her screenplay for the Walt Disney animated film of the same name). Music by Alan Menken. Lyrics by Howard Ashman and Tim Rice. Directed by Robert Jess Roth. Choreography by Matt West. Scenic design by Stan Meyer. Costume design by Ann Hould-Ward. Lighting design by Natasha Katz. Sound design by T. Richard Fitzgerald. Illusions by Jim Steinmeyer, John Gaughan. Prosthetics, John Dods. Musical direction and incidental music arrangements by Michael Kosarin. Orchestrations by Danny Troob. Musical supervision and vocal arrangements by David Friedman. Fight director, Rick Sordelet. Dance arrangements by Glen Kelly. Produced by Walt Disney Productions (Ron Logan, Robert McTyre, Theatrical Production Division). Opened 18 April 1994 at the Palace Theatre and closed 5 September 1999 after 2250 performances; re-opened 12 November 1999 at the Lunt-Fontanne Theatre (see separate entry in 1999-2000 season) and is still running at this time!

CAST (in order of appearance): *Enchantress*: Wendy Oliver. *Young Prince*: Harrison Beal. *Beast*: TERRENCE MANN. *Belle*: SUSAN EGAN. *Lefou*: KENNY RASKIN. *Gaston*: BURKE MOSES. *Three Silly Girls*: Sarah Solie Shannon, Paige Price, Linda Talcott. *Maurice*: TOM BOSLEY. *Cogsworth*: HEATH LAMBERTS. *Lumiere*: GARY BEACH. *Babette*: STACEY LOGAN. *Mrs. Potts*: BETH FOWLER. *Chip*: BRIAN PRESS. *Madame de la Grande Bouche*: ELEANOR GLOCKNER. *Monsieur D'Arque*: Gordon Stanley.

Townspeople, Enchanted Objects: Joan Barber, Roxane Barlow, Harrison Beal, Michael-Demby Cain, Kate Dowe, David Elder, Merwin Foard, Gregorey Garrison, Jack Hayes, Kim Huber, Elmore James, Rob Lorey, Patrick Loy, Barbara Marineau, Joanne McHugh, Anna McNeeley, Bill Nabel, Wendy Oliver, Vince Pesce, Paige Price, Sarah Solie Shannon, Gordon Stanley, Linda Talcott, Wysandra Woolsey. *Voice of Prologue Narrator*: David Ogden Stiers. *Swings*: Alisa Klein, Dan Mojica, Joan Barber, Kate Dowe, Gregorey Garrison, Rob Lorey.

ACT 1[21]

Prologue
Enchantress

"Belle"
S. Egan, B. Moses, K. Raskin, Silly Girls, Townspeople

"No Matter What"
T. Bosley, S. Egan
(*Lyrics by* Tim Rice.)

"No Matter What" (reprise)
T. Bosley

"Me"
B. Moses, S. Egan
(*Lyrics by* Tim Rice.)

"Belle" (reprise)
S. Egan

"Home"
S. Egan
(*Lyrics by* Tim Rice.)

"Home" (reprise)
B. Fowler

"Gaston"
K. Raskin, B. Moses, Silly Girls, Tavern Patrons

"Gaston" (reprise)
B. Moses, K. Raskin

"How Long Must This Go On?"
T. Mann
(*Lyrics by* Tim Rice.)

"Be Our Guest"
G. Beach, B. Fowler, H. Lamberts, E. Glockner, B. Press, S. Logan, Enchanted Objects

"If I Can't Love Her"
T. Mann
(*Lyrics by* Tim Rice.)

ACT 2[22]

Wolf Chase

"Something There"
S. Egan, T. Mann, G. Beach, B. Fowler, H. Lamberts

"Human Again"
G. Beach, E. Glockner, H. Lamberts, B. Fowler, S. Logan, B. Press, Enchanted Objects

"Maison des Lunes"
B. Moses, K. Raskin, G. Stanley
(*Lyrics by* Tim Rice.)

"Beauty and the Beast"
B. Fowler

"If I Can't Love Her" (reprise)
T. Mann

"The Mob Song"
B. Moses, K. Raskin, G. Stanley, Townspeople

"The Battle"
Company

"Transformation"
T. Mann, D. Eagan
(*Lyrics by* Tim Rice.)

"Beauty and the Beast" (reprise)
Company

1994.05 PASSION

A Musical in One Act, 16 Scenes. Book by James Lapine, based on the film "Passione D'Amore" by Ettore Scola, and the novel on which it was based, "Fosca" by I. U. Tarchetti. Music and lyrics by Stephen Sondheim. Directed by James Lapine. Set design by Adrianne Lobel. Costume design by Jane Greenwood. Lighting design by Beverly Emmons. Sound design by Otts Munderloh. Musical direction by Paul Gemignani. Orchestrations by Jonathan Tunick. Associate director, Jane Comfort. Produced by The Shubert Organization, Capital Cities/ABC, Roger Berlind, and Scott Rudin, by arrangement with Lincoln Center Theatre. Opened 9 May 1994 at the Plymouth Theatre and closed 7 January 1995 after 280 performances.

---

[20]Previous editions of Jackie Mason's one man show have been presented as THE WORLD ACCORDING TO ME 22 December 1986 at the Brooks Atkinson Theatre for 367 performances; returned 3 May 1988 at the Brooks Atkinson for 203 performances; JACKIE MASON: BRAND NEW 17 October 1990 at the Neil Simon Theatre for 216 performances.

[21]All lyrics by Howard Ashman except where noted.

[22]In September 1998 the following new song was added for Toni Braxton as Belle, before "The Mob Song":

"A Change in Me"
T. Braxton
(*Lyrics by* Tim Rice.)

CAST (in order of speaking): *Clara*: MARIN MAZZIE. *Giorgio (Bachetti)*: JERE SHEA. *Colonel Ricci*: GREGG EDELMANN. *Doctor Tambourri*: TOM ALDREDGE. *Lieutenant Torasso*: Francis Ruivivar. *Sergeant Lombardi*: Marcus Olson. *Lieutenant Barri*: William Parry. *Major Rizzolli*: Cris Groenendaal. *Private Augenti*: George Dvorsky. *Fosca*: DONNA MURPHY. *Fosca's Mother*: Linda Balgord. *Fosca's Father*: John Leslie Wolfe. *Ludovic*: Matthew Porretta. *Mistress*: Juliet Lambert.

The action takes place in Milan and a remote military outpost, in 1863.

Scene 1: Clara's bedroom in Milan. *Scene 2*: The Officers' Dining Quarters in a remote part of Italy; Outdoors; the Dining Quarters. *Scene 3*: The Castle Garden. *Scene 4*: The Dining Quarters. *Scene 5*: The Courtyard; Fosca's Drawing Room/Clara's Bedroom. *Scene 6*: Fosca's Drawing Room; the Doctor's Office. *Scene 7*: Fosca's Bedroom. *Scene 8*: The Billiard Room; flashback to Fosca's past. *Scene 9*: The Mountainside, a distance from the outpost. *Scene 10*: The Parade Ground; Giorgio's bedroom. *Scene 11*: A Train compartment to Milan; back at the Courtyard. *Scene 12*: A Bench near the Milan Train Station. *Scene 13*: A Christmas party at the Dining Quarters. *Scene 14*: Fosca's Bedroom. *Scene 15*: An Open Field. *Scene 16*: A hospital; Giorgio's past.

MUSICAL NUMBERS[23]

Scene 1
- "Happiness"
  - M. Mazzie, J. Shea

Scene 2
- "First Letter"
  - M. Mazzie, J. Shea, T. Aldredge, G. Edelman
- "Second Letter"
  - M. Mazzie, J. Shea
- "Third Letter"
  - M. Mazzie, J. Shea, Soldiers
- "Fourth Letter"
  - M. Mazzie, J. Shea
- "I Read"
  - D. Murphy
- Transition
  - J. Shea, Men

Scene 3
- "Garden Sequence"
  - J. Shea, D. Murphy

Scene 4
- Transition
  - Soldiers

Scene 5
- "Trio"
  - D. Murphy, J. Shea, M. Mazzie
- Transition
  - Attendants

Scene 6
- Solders' Gossip
  - Soldiers

Scene 7
- "I Wish I Could Forget You"
  - D. Murphy, J. Shea

Scene 8
- "Soldiers' Gossip" (1)
  - Soldiers
- Flashback
  - D. Murphy, G. Edelman, L. Balgord, J. L. Wolfe, M. Porretta, J. Lambert

Scene 9
- "Sunrise Letter"
  - M. Mazzie, J. Shea
- "Is This What You Call Love?"
  - J. Shea

Scene 10
- "Soldiers' Gossip" (2)
  - Soldiers

Scene 11
- Transition
  - C. Groenendaal
- "Forty Days"
  - M. Mazzie
- "Loving You"
  - D. Murphy
- Transition
  - Woman, Man
- "Soldiers' Gossip" (3)
  - Soldiers

Scene 12
- Letter from Clara
  - M. Mazzie

Scene 13
- Christmas Carol (in Italian)
  - F. Ruivivar
- "Farewell Letter"
  - M. Mazzie, J. Shea

Scene 14
- "No One Has Ever Loved Me"
  - J. Shea, D. Murphy

Scene 16
- Finale
  - Company

[23]Neither a Synopsis of Scenes nor list of Musical Numbers appear in the program. Above list was prepared from the published text and cast recording.

1994.06 THE BEST LITTLE WHOREHOUSE GOES PUBLIC

A Musical Comedy in Two Acts, a Prologue and 15 Scenes[24]. Book by Larry L. King and Peter Masterson. Music and lyrics by Carol Hall. Directed by Peter Masterson and Tommy Tune. Choreography by Jeff Calhoun, Tommy Tune. Scenery designed by John Arnone. Costumes designed by Bob Mackie. Lighting designed by Jules Fisher, Peggy Eisenhauer. Sound by Tony Meola. Musical and vocal direction, Karl Jurman. Musical supervision, vocal and dance arrangements by Wally Harper. Orchestrations by Peter Matz. Musical advisor, Robert Billig. Video by Batwin + Robin Productions, Inc. Associate director, Phillip Oesterman. Associate choreographer, Niki Harris. Production supervisor, Gene O'Donovan. Produced by Stevie Phillips and MCA/Universal. Opened 10 May 1994 at the Lunt-Fontanne Theatre and closed 21 May 1994 after 15 performances.

CAST (in order of appearance): *Showroom Headliner*: Troy Britton Johnson. *Showroom Patrons*: Gerry Burkhardt, Laurel Lynn Collins, Sally Mae Dunn, Tom Flagg, Joe Hart, Don Johanson, Mark Manley, Mary Frances McCatty, Casey Nicholaw, Louise Ruck, William Ryall, Shaver Tillitt, Jillana Urbina, Richard Vida, Theara J. Ward. *Street Whores*: Pamela Everett, Ganine Giorgione, Amy Heggins, Lainie Sakakura, Christina Youngman. *Ralph J. Bostick*: Danny Rutigliano. *Comedian*: JIM DAVID. *Las Vegas Legends*: Mary Frances McCatty, Don Johanson, Laurel Lynn Collins, Gerry Burkhardt, Sally Mae Dunn, Theara J. Ward, William Ryall. *I.R.S. Director*: KEVIN COONEY. *Schmidt*, his assistant: DAVID DOTY. *Terri Clark*: GINA TORRES. *Mona Stangley*: DEE HOTY. *A Client of the Whorehouse*: Joe Hart. *Sam Dallas*: SCOTT HOLMES. *B. S. Bullshit*: DAVID DOTY. *Senator A. Harry Hardast*: RONN CARROLL. *Lotta Lovingood*: Pamela Everett. *The President of the United States*: DAVID DOTY. *His Hairdresser*: JIM DAVID.

The Working Girls and the Wall Street Wolves: Gerry Burkhardt, Laurel Lynn Collins, Sally Mae Dunn, Pamela Everett, Tom Flagg, Ganine Giorgione, Joe Hart, Amy N. Heggins, Don Johanson, Troy Britton Johnson, Mark Manley, Mary Frances McCatty, Casey Nicholaw, Louise Ruck, Danny Rutigliano, William Ryall, Lainie Sakakura, Shaver Tillitt, Jillana Urbina, Richard Vida, Theara J. Ward, Christina Youngman. *Swings*: Niki Harris, Vincent D'Elia.

Prologue: The showroom, Las Vegas.

Act 1, Scene 1: Conference Room, I.R.S., Washington, D.C. *Scene 2*: Cactus Motel, somewhere in Texas. *Scene 3*: In the shadows of the Washington Monument. *Scene 4*: In the kitchen of the whorehouse, Nevada. *Scene 5*: The parlor of the whorehouse and Wall Street, New York.

Act 2, Scene 1: On the information highway. *Scene 2*: Air Force One—on the tarmac, LAX. *Scene 3*: I.R.S. Director's Georgetown home. *Scene 4*: Sam Dallas' apartment, Washington, D.C. *Scene 5*: An I.R.S. corridor. *Scene 6*: The hearing. *Scene 7*: Larry King Live. *Scene 8*: Sam Dallas' dressing room, Washington, D.C. *Scene 9*: The Stallion Fields Whorehouse, Nevada. *Scene 10*: The steps of our nation's Capitol.

[24]Conceived by the same authors as a sequel to their Broadway musical "The Best Little Whorehouse in Texas" which opened 19 June 1978 at the 46th Street Theatre for 1584 performances.

ACT 1
Prologue
"Let the Devil Take Us"
Las Vegas Legends, Showroom Patrons, Street Whores, D. Rutigliano
Scene 2
"Nothin' Like a Picture Show"
D. Hoty
"I'm Leavin' Texas"
D. Hoty, Texans
Scene 4
"It's Been a While"
S. Holmes, D. Hoty
Scene 5
"Brand New Start"
S. Holmes, D. Hoty, G. Torres, K. Cooney, D. Doty, Working Girls, Wall Street Wolves

ACT 2
Scene 1
"The Smut Song"
R. Carroll
"Call Me"
D. Hoty, Girls, Couch Potaotoes (Men)
Scene 4
"Change in Me"
S. Holmes
Scene 6
"Here for the Hearing"
Ladies, Senators
Scene 7
"Piece of the Pie"
D. Hoty, S. Holmes, Ladies
Scene 8
"Change in Me" (reprise)
S. Holmes
Scene 10
"If We Open Our Eyes"
Entire Company

1994.07

GREASE

A Revival of the Musical (Comedy) in Two Acts, 13 Scenes[25]. Book, music and lyrics by Jim Jacobs and Warren Casey. Directed and choreographed by Jeff Calhoun. Scenic design by John Arnone. Costume design by Willa Kim. Lighting design by Howell Brinkley. Sound design by Tom Morse. Musical direction, vocal and dance music arrangements by John McDaniel. Orchestrations by Steven Margoshes. Associate choreographer, Jerry Mitchell. Associate producer, Alecia Parker. A Tommy Tune Production. Produced by Barry and Fran Weissler and Jujamcyn Theatres, in association with Pace Theatrical Group and TV Asahi. Opened 11 May 1994 at the Eugene O'Neill Theatre and closed 23 February 1997 after 1150 performances; re-opened 8 April 1997 at the Eugene O'Neill Theatre and closed 25 January 1998 after an additional 353 performances. Total: 1503 performances.

CAST (in order of appearance): *Vince Fontaine*: Brian Bradley. *Miss Lynch*: MARCIA LEWIS. *Patty Simcox*: Michelle Blakeley. *Eugene Florczyk*: Paul Castree. *Jan*: Heather Stokes. *Marty*: Megan Mullally. *Betty Rizzo*: ROSIE O'DONNELL. *Doody*: SAM HARRIS. *Roger*: Hunter Foster. *Kenickie*: Jason Opsahl. *Sonny Latierri*: Carlos Lopez. *Frenchy*: Jessica Stone. *Sandy Dumbrowski*: SUSAN WOOD. *Danny Zuko*: RICKY PAULL GOLDIN. *The Heartbeats*: Katy Grenfell, Janice Lorraine Holt, Lorna Shane. *The Straight A's*: Clay Adkins, Patrick Boyd, Denis Jones. *The Dream Mooners*: Patrick Boyd, Katy Grenfell. *Cha-Cha DeGregorio*: Sandra Purpuro. *Teen Angel*: BILLY PORTER.

Ensemble: Clay Adkins, Melissa Bell, Patrick Boyd, Katy Grenfell, Ned Hannah, Janice Lorraine Holt, Denis Jones, Allison Metcalf, H. Hylan Scott II, Lorna Shane. *Swings*: Patti D'Beck, Brian-Paul Mendoza.

(The action takes place in the late 1950s.)

Act 1, Scene 1: Rydell High. *Scene 2*: Cafeteria. *Scene 3*: School Hallway. *Scene 4*: Marty's Bathroom. *Scene 5*: Street Corner. *Scene 6*: Bleachers. *Scene 7*: School Yard. *Scene 8*: The Lockers.

Act 2, Scene 1: Rydell High Boy's Gym. *Scene 2*: Outside the Burger Palace. *Scene 3*: Twi-Light Drive-In. *Scene 4*: Rizzo's Rec Room. *Scene 5*: Burger Palace.

ACT 1[26]
Scene 1
"Alma Mater"[27]
M. Lewis, Company
"We Go Together"
Pink Ladies, Burger Palace Boys
Scene 2
"Summer Nights"
S. Wood, R. P. Goldin, Pink Ladies, Burger Palace Boys
Scene 3
"Those Magic Changes"
S. Harris, Company
Scene 4
"Freddy, My Love"
M. Mullally, Pink Ladies
Scene 5
"Greased Lightnin'"
J. Opsahl, Burger Palace Boys
"Greased Lightnin'" (reprise)
R. O'Donnell, Burger Palace Boys
Scene 6
"Rydell Fight Song"[28]
S. Wood, M. Blakely, Cheerleading Squad
Scene 7
"Mooning"
H. Foster, H. Stokes
"Look at Me, I'm Sandra Dee"
R. O'Donnell
Scene 8
"Since I Don't Have You"[29]
S. Wood
(*Music and Lyrics by* Joseph Rock, James Beaumont and the Skyliners.)
"We Go Together" (reprise)
Company

ACT 2
Scene 1
"Shakin' at the High School Hop"
The Four Straight A's
"It's Raining on Prom Night"
S. Wood, The Four Straight A's
"Born to Hand-Jive"
P. Castree, M. Lewis, Company
Scene 2
"Beauty School Dropout"
B. Porter, J. Stone, Company
Scene 3
"Alone at a Drive-In Movie"
R. P. Goldin
Scene 4
"Rock 'N' Roll Party Queen"
S. Harris, J. Opsahl
"There Are Worse Things I Could Do"
R. O'Donnell
"Look at Me, I'm Sandra Dee" (reprise)
S. Wood, R. O'Donnell
Scene 5
Finale[30]
Company

---

[25]Originally produced in New York Off-Broadway 14 February 1972 at the Eden Theatre for 128 performances; transferred 7 June 1972 to the Broadhurst Theatre for a total of 3388 performances, including Off-Broadway run.

[26]Pink Ladies include Rizzo, Frenchy, Marty, Jan. Burger Palace Boys include Kenickie, Doody, Roger, Sonny. For this revival, the role of Johnny Casino and the reprise of "Shakin' at the High School Hop" were dropped.
[27]Revised as an "a cappella" version of "We Go Together."
[28]Not in the original production, but added for this production.
[29]Not in the original production, but added for this production.
[30]Includes "All Choked Up."

1994–1995 SEASON

Alan Campbell and Betty Buckley in SUNSET BOULEVARD
Joan Marcus/Photofest

1994–1995 SEASON

SHOWBOAT

1994.08

A Revival of the Musical (Play) in Two Acts, 20 Scenes[1]. Music by Jerome Kern. Book and lyrics by Oscar Hammerstein II. Based on the novel of the same name by Edna Ferber. Directed by Harold Prince. Choreography by Susan Stroman. Production (scenery) design by Eugene Lee. Costumes designed by Florence Klotz. Lighting design by Richard Pilbrow. Orchestrations by Robert Russell Bennett, William D. Brohn. Production musical supervisor, Jeffrey Huard. Dance music arranged by David Krane. Sound design by Martin Levan. Assistant to Mr. Prince, Ruth Mitchell. Produced by LIVENT (U.S.) Inc. (Garth Drabinsky, Chairman and Chief executive officer; Myron I. Gottlieb, President.) Opened 2 October 1994 at the Gershwin Theatre and closed 5 January 1997 after 946 performances.

CAST (in order of their appearance): *Steve*: DOUG LABRECQUE. *Queenie*: GRETHA BOSTON. *Pete*: David Bryant. *Parthy Ann Hawkes*: ELAINE STRITCH. *Windy (McLain)*: Ralph Williams. *Cap'n Andy*: JOHN MCMARTIN. *Ellie*: DOROTHY STANLEY. *Frank*: JOEL BLUM. *Julie*: LONNETTE MCKEE. *Gaylord Ravenal*: MARK JACOBY. *(Sheriff Ike) Vallon*: Jack Dabdoub. *Magnolia*: REBECCA LUKER. *Joe*: MICHEL BELL. *Dealer*: Bob Walton. *Jeb*: David Earl Hart. *Backwoodsman*: Mike O'Carroll. *Young Kim*: Larissa Auble. *Ethel*: Danielle Greaves. *Landlady*: Lorraine Foreman. *Mother Superior*: Sheila Smith. *Jim*: Mike O'Carroll. *Jake*: Bob Walton. *Charlie*: Michael Scott. *Lottie*: Louise-Marie Mennier. *Dottie*: Karen Curlee. *Drunk*: David Bryant. *Radio Announcer*: Michael Scott. *Kim*: Tammy Amerson. *Old Lady on Levee*: Sheila Smith.

Ensemble: Van Abrahams, Timothy Albrecht, Derin Altay, Kevin Bagby, Hal Beasley, Timothy Robert Blevins, David Bryant, Joseph Cassidy, Roosevelt André Credit, Karen Curlee, Jack Dabdoub, Debbie de Coudreaux, Lorraine Foreman, Jose Garcia, Ron Gibbs, Steve Girardi, Danielle Greaves, Jeff Hairston, Lorna Hampson, Linda Hardwick, Pamela Harley, David Earl Hart, Richard L. Hobson, Michel LaFlèche, Karen Lifshey, Kim Lindsay, Jesse Means II, Louise-Marie Mennier, Kiri-Lyn Muir, Panchali Null, Mike O'Carroll, Amy Jo Phillips, Catherine Pollard, Jimmy Rivers, Michael Scott, Jill Slyter, Bob Walton, Laurie Walton, Cheryl Warfield, Jo Ann Hawkins White, Dathan B. Williams, Gay Willis, Lonel Woods, Darlene B. Young. *Swings*: Dannis Daniels, David Dannehl, Tari Kelly, Richie McCall, Kimberley Michaels, Louise St. Cyr. *Children*: Larissa Auble, Kimberly Jean Brown, Joran Corneal, Edwin Hodge. *Band on the Cotton Blossom*: Derin Altay (cymbals), Bob Walton (glockenspiel), Paul Gallo (clarinet), Dan Levine (trombone), Michael Scott (bass drums), Nathan Durham (tuba), Brian Miller (flute).

Act 1, Scene 1: The Levee at Natchez on the Mississippi River in 1887. *Scene 2*: Kitchen pantry of the *Cotton Blossom*. Five minutes later. *Scene 3*: Natchez. Outside a riverfront gambling saloon. *Scene 4*: Auditorium of the *Cotton Blossom*. *Scene 5*: The windows of Magnolia's cabin and Ravenal's room. *Scene 6*: Fort Adams. Box office on the foredeck of the *Cotton Blossom*. *Scene 7*: Auditorium and stage of the *Cotton Blossom*. *Scene 8*: Upper deck of the *Cotton Blossom*. *Scene 9*: The Levee in Natchez.

Act 2, Scene 1: The levee in Natchez. Exterior of the *Cotton Blossom*. (1889). *Scene 2*: Magnolia's room on the *Cotton Blossom*. *Scene 3*: Montage I. Chicago (1889); On the Dock at Natchez (1899); Chicago, outside the Palmer House Hotel (1899). *Scene 4*: Chicago. A room in a boarding house. *Scene 5*: Chicago. St. Agatha's Convent. *Scene 6*: Chicago. Rehearsal at the Trocadero Night Club. *Scene 7*: Entrance to the Palmer House Hotel, New Year's Eve, 1899. *Scene 8*: Trocadero Night Club. *Scene 9*: Montage II (1900-1921). The Levee at Natchez. The streets of Chicago. The revolving door of the Palmer House Hotel. *Scene 10*: The levee at Natchez (1927). *Scene 11*: Later on the levee.

ACT 1

Scene 1
"Cotton Blossom"
Stevedores, Gals, Townspeople
"Cap'n Andy's Ballyhoo"
J. McMartin, E. Stritch, the Showboat Troupe, Stevedores, Gals, Townspeople
"Where's the Mate for Me?"
M. Jacoby
"Make Believe"
M. Jacoby, R. Luker
"Ol' Man River"
M. Bell, Stevedores

Scene 2
"Can't Help Lovin' Dat Man"
L. McKee, G. Boston, M. Bell, R. Luker, Ensemble

Scene 3
"Till Good Luck Comes My Way"
M. Jacoby, D. Bryant, J. Blum, Townsmen

Scene 4
"Mis'ry's Comin' Aroun'"
G. Boston, Stevedores, Gals

Scene 5
"I Have the Room Above Her"
M. Jacoby, R. Luker

Scene 6
"Life Upon the Wicked Stage"
D. Stanley, Townswomen
"Queenie's Ballyhoo"
G. Boston, Stevedores, Gals

Scene 8
"You Are Love"
M. Jacoby, R. Luker

Scene 9
Act 1 Finale: "The Wedding Celebration"
Company

ACT 2

Scene 2
"Why Do I Love You?"
E. Stritch, Company

Scene 3
"Dandies on Parade"
City Folk

Scene 5
"Alma Redemptoris Mater" (Hymn)
Choir
"Ol' Man River" (reprise)
M. Bell

Scene 6
"Bill"
L. McKee
(*Lyrics by* P. G. Wodehouse, revised by Oscar Hammerstein II.)
"Can't Help Lovin' Dat Man" (reprise)
R. Luker

Scene 8
"Goodbye, My Lady Love"
J. Blum, D. Stanley
(*Music and Lyrics by* Joseph E. Howard.)
"After the Ball" (from *A TRIP TO CHINATOWN*)
R. Luker, Ensemble
(*Music and Lyrics by* Charles K. Harris.)

Scene 9
"Ol' Man River" (reprise)
M. Bell

Scene 10
"Dance Away the Night"
R. Luker

Scene 11
"Kim's Charleston"
T. Amerson, E. Stritch, Company
Act 2 Finale
M. Bell, Company

WONDERFUL TOWN

1994.09

A Revival of the Musical Comedy in Two Acts, 13 Scenes[2]. Book by Joseph Fields and Jerome Chodorov. Based on the play "My Sister Eileen" by

[1]First presented in New York 27 December 1927 at the Ziegfeld Theatre for 572 performances.

[2]Originally produced in New York 25 February 1953 at the Winter Garden for 559 performances. For Synopsis of Scenes and Musical Numbers, see original 1953 production. "Conquering New York" Ballet dropped from this production.

Joseph Fields and Jerome Chodorov (and the stories of the same name by Ruth McKinney). Music by Leonard Bernstein. Lyrics by Betty Comden and Adolph Green. Directed by Richard Sabellico. Conductor, Eric Stern. Choreographer, Tina Paul. Set designer, Michael Anania. Costume designer, Gail Baldoni. Lighting designer, Jeff Davis. Sound designer, Abe Jacob. Chorus master, Joseph Colaneri Assistant stage director, Paul L. King. (Orchestrations uncredited.) Produced by the New York City Opera. Opened 8 November 1994 at the New York State Theatre and closed 20 November 1994 after 14 performances.

CAST (in order of their appearance): *Tour Guide*: William Ledbetter. *Appopolous*: LARRY BLOCK. *Lonigan*: Don Yule. *Helen*: MEGHAN STRANGE. *Wreck*: TIMOTHY WARMEN. *Violet*: Amanda Green. *Speedy Valenti*: Carlos Lopez. *Eileen Sherwood*: CRISTA MOORE. *Ruth Sherwood*: KAY MCCLELLAND. *Fletcher*: Gary Jackson. *Drunks*: Mason Roberts, Louis Perry. *Eskimo Pie Man*: Mason Roberts. *Robert Baker*: RICHARD MUENZ. *Associate Editors*: John Lankston, William Ledbetter. *Rexford*: Gary Jackson. *Mr. Mallory*: Louis Perry. *Danny*: Jeffrey Weber. *Party Guest*: Marilyn Armstrong. *Trent*: Daniel Shigo. *Mrs. Wade*: Susan Browning. *Frank Lippencott*: DON STEPHENSON. *Chef*: William Ledbetter. *Waiter*: Daniel Shigo. *Delivery Boy*: Larry Sousa. *Chick Clark*: STEPHEN BERGER. *Shore Patrolman*: Ron Hilley. *First Cadet*: Larry Sousa. *Second Cadet*: Mason Roberts. *Brazilian Ambassador*: John Lankston. *Solo Policeman*: John Lankston. *Policemen*: Ron Hilley, Louis Perry, William Ledbetter, Jeffrey Weber. *Ruth's Escort*: Gary Jackson. *Flower Sellers*: Paula Hostetter, Melissa Maravell. *Customer*: Beth Pensiero. *Children*: Zoe Startz Barton, Simon Behr, Dov Lebowitz-Nowak, Sebastian Perez, Jacqueline Rosenfield, Rachel Rosenfield.

1994.10 SUNSET BOULEVARD

A Musical in Two Acts, 21 Scenes. Book and lyrics by Don Black and Christopher Hampton. Based on the film and screenplay of the same name by Billy Wilder. Music by Andrew Lloyd Webber. Directed by Trevor Nunn. Musical staging by Bob Avian. Production (settings) design by John Napier. Costume design by Anthony Powell. Lighting design by Andrew Bridge. Sound design by Martin Levan. Musical supervision and direction by David Caddick. Musical director, Paul Bogaev. Orchestrations by David Cullen and Andrew Lloyd Webber. Associate production design, Peter David Gould. Production supervision, Peter Lawrence. Produced by The Really Useful Company (Edgar Dobie, President). Opened 17 November 1994 at the Minskoff Theatre and closed 22 March 1997 after 977 performances.

CAST: *Norma Desmond*: GLENN CLOSE. *Joe Gillis*: ALAN CAMPBELL. *Max von Mayerling*: GEORGE HEARN. *Betty Schaefer*: ALICE RIPLEY. *Cecil B. DeMille*: Alan Oppenheimer. *Artie Green*: Vincent Tumeo.

(Ensemble): *First Harem Girl, Beautician*: Sandra Allen. *Young Writer, Salesman, DeMille's Assistant*: Bryan Batt. *Heather, Second Masseuse*: Susan Dawn Carson. *Cliff, Salesman, Young Guard*: Matthew Dickens. *Third Harem Girl (Jean), Beautician, Hedy Lamarr*: Colleen Dunn. *Morino, Salesman, Hog Eye*: Steven Stein-Grainger. *Lisa, Doctor*: Kim Huber. *First Financeman, Film Actor, Salesman*: Rich Hebert. *Katherine, Psychiatrist*: Alicia Irving. *Second Harem Girl, Beautician*: Lada Boder. *Mary, First Masseuse*: Lauren Kennedy. *Sheldrake, Police Chief*: Sal Mistretta. *John, Salesman, Victor Mature*: Mark Morales. *Myron, Manfred*: Rick Podell. *Second Financeman, Salesman, Party Guest*: Tom Alan Robbins. *Jonesy, Sammy, Salesman*: David Eric. *Choreographer, Salesman*: Rick Sparks. *Joanna, Astrologer*: Wendy Walter.

The action takes place in Los Angeles, 1949-1950.

Act 1, Scene 1: Exterior/Dawn, the House on Sunset. *Scene 2*: Exterior/Day, Paramount Studios. *Scene 3*: Exterior/Day, on the road. *Scene 4*: Exterior/Day, the Garage on Sunset. *Scene 5*: Interior/Day and Evening, the house on Sunset. *Scene 6*: Interior/Night, Norma's Guest House. *Scene 7*: Interior/Evening, Schwab's Drugstore. *Scene 8*: Exterior/Night, the Terrace on Sunset. *Scene 9*: Interior/Evening, the House on Sunset. *Scene 10*: Interior/Day, the House on Sunset. *Scene 11*: Interior/Night, the House on Sunset. *Scene 12*: Interior/Night, Artie Green's Apartment. *Scene 13*: Interior/Night, the House on Sunset.

Act 2, Scene 1: Exterior/Day, Norma's Swimming Pool. *Scene 2*: Exterior/Day, Paramount Studio. *Scene 3*: Interior/Night, Betty's office at Paramount. *Scene 4*: Interior/Day, the House on Sunset. *Scene 5*: Interior/Exterior/Night, Betty's office/Paramount backlot. *Scene 6*: Exterior/Night, the House on Sunset. *Scene 7*: Exterior/Interior/Night, the House on Sunset. *Scene 8*: Exterior/Interior/Dawn, the House on Sunset.

ACT 1
Scene 1
Prologue
A. Campbell
Scene 2
"Let's Have Lunch"
A. Campbell, Ensemble
Scene 5
"Surrender"
G. Close
"With One Look"
G. Close
"Salome"
G. Close, A. Campbell
Scene 6
"The Greatest Star of All"
G. Hearn
Scene 7
"Every Movie's a Circus"
A. Campbell, A. Ripley, V. Tumeo, Ensemble
"Girl Meets Boy"
A. Campbell, A. Ripley
Scene 9
"New Ways to Dream"
G. Close
Scene 10
"The Lady's Paying"
R. Podell, G. Close, A. Campbell, Salesmen
Scene 11
"The Perfect Year"
G. Close, A. Campbell
Scene 12
"This Time Next Year"
A. Campbell, A. Ripley, V. Tumeo, Ensemble

ACT 2
Scene 1
"Sunset Boulevard"
A. Campbell
"The Perfect Year" (reprise)
G. Close
Scene 2
"As If We Never Said Goodbye"
G. Close
"Surrender" (reprise)
A. Oppenheimer
Scene 3
"Girl Meets Boy" (reprise)
A. Ripley, A. Campbell
Scene 4
"Eternal Youth Is Worth a Little Suffering"
Norma's Consultants
Scene 5
"Too Much in Love to Care"
A. Ripley, A. Campbell
Scene 6
"New Ways to Dream" (reprise)
G. Hearn
Scene 7
"Sunset Boulevard" (reprise)
A. Campbell, A. Ripley
Scene 8
"The Greatest Star of All" (reprise)
G. Hearn, G. Close
"Surrender" (reprise)
G. Close

1944.11 THE FLYING KARAMAZOV BROTHERS DO THE IMPOSSIBLE!

A Comedy Revue in Two Acts. (Conceived by the Flying Karamazov Brothers.) Musical direction by Doug Wieselman. Produced by An Imagination Company, Ltd., Herb Goldsmith Productions Ltd, and Jujamcyn Theatres. Opened 20 November 1994 at the Helen Hayes Theatre and closed 1 January 1995 after 50 performances.

CAST: *Dmitri Karamazov*: PAUL MAGID. *Ivan Karamazov*: HOWARD JAY PATTERSON. *Rakitin Karamazov*: MICHAEL PRESTON. *Smerdyakov Karamazov*: SAM WILLIAMS. The Kamakaze Ground Crew.

1994.12 A CHRISTMAS CAROL

A Musical in One Act, 14 Scenes. Book by Mike Ockrent and Lynn Ahrens. Based on the novel of the same name by Charles Dickens. Music by Alan Menken. Lyrics by Lynn Ahrens. Directed by Mike Ockrent. Choreographed by Susan Stroman. Setting design by Tony Walton. Costume design by William Ivey Long. Lighting design by Jules Fisher and Peggy Eisenhauer. Sound design by Tony Meola. Projections by Wendall K. Harrington. Flying by Foy. Production supervisor, Gene O'Donovan. Associate director, Steven Zweigbaum. Associate choreographer, Chris Peterson. Musical direction by Paul Gemignani. Orchestrations by Michael Starobin. Dance arrangements and incidental music by Glen Kelly. Executive producer, Dodger Productions. Producer, Tim Hawkins. Presented by Nickleodeon Family Classics and Madison Square Garden. Opened 1 December 1994 at the Paramount Theatre, Madison Square Garden and closed 1 January 1995 after 71 performances[3].

CAST (in order of their appearance): *Punch and Judy Man*: Christopher Sieber. *Punch and Judy Woman*: Donna Lee Marshall. *Organ Grinder*: Robert Ousley. *Grave Digger*: Bill Nolte. *Mr. Smythe*: JOSEPH KOLINSKI. *Jack Smythe*: Andy Jobe. *Grace Smythe*: Lindsay Jobe. *Scrooge*: WALTER CHARLES. *Crachit*: NICK CORLEY. *Charity Men*: Robert Ousley, Martin Van Treuren, Walter Willison. *Old Joe*: Ken McMullen. *Match Girl*: Arlene Pierret. *Street Urchins and Children*: Matthew F. Byrne, Jacy de Filippo, Justin Bartholomew Kamen, Olivia Oguma, Christopher Mark. *Sandwich Board Man*: MICHAEL MANDELL. *Fred*: ROBERT WESTENBERG. *Jonathan*: Jason Fuchs. *Lamplighter*: KEN JENNINGS. *Blind Hag*: Andrea Frierson Toney. *Mrs. Mops*: Darcy Pulliam. *Ghost of Jacob Marley*: JEFF KELLER. *Ghost of Christmas Past*: KEN JENNINGS. *Judge*: Michael H. Ingram. *Scrooge at 8*: David Gallagher. *Fan at 6*: Mary Elizabeth Albano. *Scrooge's Mother*: Andrea Frierson Toney. *Scrooge's Father*: Michael X. Martrin. *Mr. Kent*: Ken McMullen. *Scrooge at 12*: Ramzi Khalaf. *Fan at 10*: Jacy de Filippo, Olivia Oguma. *Fezziwig*: Gerry Vichi. *Scrooge at 18*: Michael Christopher Moore. *Marley*, as a young man: Christopher Sieber. *Mrs. Fezziwig*: Mary Stout. *Emily*: Emily Skinner. *Ghost of Christmas Present*: MICHAEL MANDELL. *Tiny Tim*: Matthew Mezzacappa. *Mrs. Crachit*: Joy Hermalyn. *The Crachit Children*: Mary Elizabeth Albano, Betsy Chang, David Gallagher, Sean Thomas Morrissey. *Sally*, Fred's wife: Natalie Toro. *Undertakers*: Michael X. Martin, Christopher Sieber. *Ghost of Christmas Future*: Theara J. Ward.

Business Men, Ghosts, Gifts and the People of London: Mary Elizabeth Albano, Joan Barber, Renée Bergeron, Christophe Caballero, Betsy Chang, Candy Cook, Madeleine Doherty, Mark Dovey, Donna Dunmire, Andrea Frierson Toney, David Gallagher, Melissa Haizlip, Joy Hermalyn, Michael H. Ingran, Don Johanson, Eric H. Kaufman, John-Charles Kelly, Ramzi Khalaf, David Lowenstein, Seth Malkin, Donna Lee Marshall, Michael X. Martin, Carol Lee Meadows, Michael Christopher Moore, Sean Thomas Morrissey, Ken McMullen, Karen Murphy, Bill Nolte, Robert Ousley, Tom Pardoe, Gail Pennington, Angela Piccinni, Arlene Pierret, Darcy Pulliam, Josef Reiter, Pamela Remler, Sam Reni, Eric Riley, Rommy Sandhu, Christopher Sieber, Emily Skinner, Erin Stoddard, Mary Stout, Tracy Terstriep, Natalie Toro, Martin Van Treuren, Gerry Vichi, Theara J. Ward, Walter Willison. *Angels*: Blessed Sacrament Chorus of Staten Island, Public School 26 Chorus, Righteousness Unlimited, William F. Halloran Vocal Ensemble-School 22. *Swings*: Leslie Bell, Matthew F, Byrne, Jacy de Filippo, Mark S. Hoebee, Michael Hayward-Jones, Justine Bartholomew Kamen, Olivia Oguma, Christopher Mark Petrizzo, P. J. Smith, Matthew J. Vargo, Billy Vitelli, Cynthia Thole, Whitney Webster.

The action takes place in London, 1880.

Scene 1: A Graveyard near St. Paul's Cathedral, Christmas Eve. *Scene 2*: The Royal Exchange. *Scene 3*: The Street. *Scene 4*: Scrooge's House. *Scene 5*: Scrooge's Bed Chamber. *Scene 6*: The Law Courts. *Scene 7*: The Factory. *Scene 8*: Fezziwig's Banking House. *Scene 9*: Montage. *Scene 10*: A Starry Night. *Scene 11*: All Over London. *Scene 12*: The Graveyard. *Scene 13*: Scrooge's Bed Chamber. *Scene 14*: The Street, Christmas Day.

MUSICAL NUMBERS

Scene 1
"The Years Are Passing By"
B. Nolte

Scene 2
"Jolly, Rich and Fat" (A Jolly Good Time)
Charity Men, Smythe Family, Businessmen, Wives, Children
"Nothing to Do With Me"
W. Charles, N. Corley

Scene 3
"Street Song" (Nothing to Do With Me)
People of London, W. Charles, R. Westenberg, J. Fuchs, M. Mandell, K. Jennings, A. F. Toney, A. Jobe

Scene 4
"Link By Link"
J. Keller, W. Charles, Ghosts

Scene 5
"The Lights of Long Ago" (Part 1)
K. Jennings

Scene 6
"God Bless Us, Everyone"
A. F. Toney, M. E. Albano, D. Gallagher

Scene 7
"A Place Called Home"
R. Khalaf, J. de Filippo/O. Oguma, W. Charles

Scene 8
"Mr. Fezziwig's Annual Christmas Ball"
G. Vichi, M. Stout, Guests
"A Place Called Home" (reprise)
E. Skinner, M. C. Moore, W. Charles

Scene 9
"The Lights of Long Ago" (Part 2)
M. C. Moore, C. Sieber, E. Skinner, People from Scrooge's Past

Scene 10
"Abundance and Charity"
M. Mandell, W. Charles, Christmas Presents

Scene 11
"Christmas Together"
M. Mezzacappa, N. Corley, J. Hermalyn, Crachit Children, R. Westenberg, N. Toro, W. Charles, People of London

Scene 12
"Dancing on Your Grave"
Grave Diggers, T. J. Ward, Monks, Businessmen, D. Pulliam, M. X. Martin, C. Sieber, K. McMullen, J. Kolinski, N. Corley
"Yesterday, Today and Tomorrow"
W. Charles, Angels, People of London

Scene 13
"The Years Are Passing By" (reprise)
J. Fuchs

Scene 14
"Nothing to Do With Me" (reprise)
W. Charles
"Christmas Together" (reprise)
People of London
"God Bless Us, Everyone" (Finale)
Company

1994.13 COMEDY TONIGHT

A Comedy Revue in One Act. (Assembled by Alexander H. Cohen.) Special material for Ms. Loudon contributed by Bruce Vilanch. Directed by Alexander H. Cohen. Musical staging by Albert Stephenson. Sets by Ray Klausen. Costumes by Alvin Colt. Lighting by Richard Nelson. Sound by Bruce D. Cameron. Musical director, Peter Howard. Associate producer, Hildy Parks. Produced by Alexander H. Cohen and Max Cooper. Opened 18 December 1994 at the Lunt-Fontanne Theatre and closed 24 December 1994 after 8 performances.

CAST: JOY BEHAR, MICHAEL DAVIS, DOROTHY LOUDON, MORT SAHL.

SCENES
Joy Behar (stand-up comedy)
Michael Davis (juggling and comedy)
Dorothy Loudon (songs and comedy):
"Fifty Percent" (from *BALLROOM*)
(*Music by* William Goldenberg. *Lyrics by* Marilyn and Alan Bergman.)
Mort Sahl (political satire and comedy)

[3]The production played an irregular schedule of multiple daily performances.

1995.01 YOUNG MAN, OLDER WOMAN

A Musical Comedy in Two Acts. Book by Doug and Helen Smith. Songs by Millie Jackson, PJaye Scott, Douglas Knyght-Smith, Reynaldo Rey, Jolyon Skinner. (Directed by Millie Jackson. Produced by Millie Jackson.) Opened 10 January 1995 at the Beacon Theatre and closed 5 February 1995 after 28 performances.[4]

CAST: *Millie*: MILLIE JACKSON. *Reynaldo*: REYNALDO REY. *Doctor Lester*, the Psychiatrist: Douglas Knyght. *Connie Vertible*, Dr. Lester's nurse: Kenneth "Chocolate Thunder" Montague. *Millie's Daughter*: Keisha Jackson. *Background Singers*.

MUSICAL NUMBERS

"Baby I'm Ready Now"
(*Music and Lyrics by* Millie Jackson, PJaye Scott, Douglas Knyght-Smith.)

"Living with a Stranger"
(*Music and Lyrics by* PJaye Scott, Douglas Knyght-Smith.)

"The Weight of Love"
(*Music and Lyrics by* Millie Jackson, Reynaldo Rey.)

"You Gonna Miss Me"
(*Music and Lyrics by* PJaye Scott, Douglas Knyght-Smith.)

"Don't Wanna B N Luv"
(*Music and Lyrics by* PJaye Scott, Douglas Knyght-Smith.)

"When a Woman Makes Up her Mind"
(*Music and Lyrics by* PJaye Scott, Douglas Knyght-Smith.)

"I Wish It Would Rain Down"
(*Music and Lyrics by* Phil Collins.)

"Someday We'll All Be Free"
(*Music and Lyrics by* Donny Hathaway.)

"Taking My Life Back"
(*Music and Lyrics by* Millie Jackson, Jolyon Skinner.)

"People in My Head"
(*Music and Lyrics by* Millie Jackson, PJaye Scott, Douglas Knyght-Smith.)

"Young Man, Older Woman"
(*Music and Lyrics by* Millie Jackson, Jolyon Skinner.)

1995.02 JESUS CHRIST SUPERSTAR

A Revival of the Musical in Two Acts[5]. Music by Andrew Lloyd Webber. Lyrics by Tim Rice. Directed and choreographed by Tony Christopher. Scenery by Bill Stabile. Costumes by David Paulin. Lighting by Rick Belzer. Sound by Jonathan Deans. Musical director, Craig Barna. Special effects, Gregg Stephens. Associate choreographer, Larry Vickers. Executive producer, Forbes Candlish. Produced by Landmark Entertainment Group, Magic Promotions & Theatricals, TAP Productions. Opened 17 January 1995 at the Paramount Theatre, Madison Square Garden and closed 29 January 1995 after 16 performances.

CAST: *Jesus of Nazareth*: TED NEELEY. *Judas Iscariot*: CARL ANDERSON. *Mary Magdalene*: SYREETA WRIGHT. *Caiaphas*: David Bedella. *Annas*: Danny Zolli. *First Priest*: Mark Slama. *Second Priest*: Michael Guarnera. *Third Priest*: Gary Bankston. *Simon (Zealotes)*: Lawrence Clayton. *Pontius Pilate*: DENNIS DEYOUNG. *Tormentors*: Carol Bentley, Shannon Falank, Kristen Young. *Peter*: Mike Eldred. *King Herod*: Douglass Fraser. *Maid by the Fire*: Karen Byers. *Soldier by the Fire*: Mark C. Reis. *Old Man by the Fire*: Pressley Sutherland. *Soul Sisters*: Karen Byers, J. Kathleen Lamb, Hillary Turk. *Apostles, Their Women, The People of Bethany and Jerusalem*: Gary Bankston, Carol Bentley, Kevin Bernard, Karen Byers, Phil Dominguez, Mike Eldred, Shannon Falank, Robert H. Fowler, Michael Guarnera, Vanessa A. Jones, Eileen Kaden, J. Kathleen Lamb, Mark C. Reis, Mark Slama, Pressley Sutherland, Hillary Turk, Kritsen Young. *Swings*: Michelle DeJean, Jill B. Gounder, Hans Kriefall, Cindi Parise, Larry Vickers.

[4]No program available. Details prepared from recordings, press materials.

[5]First produced in New York 12 October 1971 at the Mark Hellinger Theatre for 711 performances. For Synopsis of Scenes and Musical Numbers, see original 1971 production.

1995.03 SMOKEY JOE'S CAFE: The Songs Of Leiber And Stoller

A Musical Revue in Two Acts. Words and music by Jerry Leiber and Mike Stoller. Directed by Jerry Zaks. Musical staging by Jerry McKneely. Original concept by Stephen Helper and Jack Viertel. Co-conceived with additional musical staging by Otis Sallid. Scenery design by Heidi Landesman. Costume design by William Ivey Long. Lighting design by Timothy Hutton. Sound design by Tony Meola. Orchestrations by Steven Margoshes. Arranged and conducted by Louis St. Louis. Production supervisor, Steven Beckler. Associate producers, Marc Routh, Rhoda Mayerson, Thomas Glaser. Produced by Richard Frankel, Thomas Viertel, Steven Baruch, Jujamcyn Theatres/Jack Viertel, Rick Steiner, Frederic H. Mayerson, Center Theatre Group/Ahmanson Theatre/Gordon Davidson. Opened 2 March 1995 at the Virginia Theatre and closed 16 January 2000 after 2036 performances.

CAST (in alphabetical order): KEN ARD, ADRIAN BAILEY, BRENDA BRAXTON, VICTOR TRENT COOK, B. J. CROSBY, PATTIE DARCY JONES, DELEE LIVELY, FREDERICK B. OWENS, MICHAEL PARK.

ACT 1[6]

"Neighborhood"
Company
(*Music and Lyrics by* Jerry Leiber, Mike Stoller, Ralph Dino.)

"Young Blood"
A. Bailey, with F. B. Owens, K. Ard, V. T. Cook
(*Music and Lyrics by* Jerry Leiber, Mike Stoller, Doc Pomus.)

"Falling"
D. Lively

"Ruby Baby"
M. Park, with A. Bailey, F. B. Owens, K. Ard, V. T. Cook

"Dance With Me"
K. Ard, B. J. Crosby, with A. Bailey, F. B. Owens, K. Ard, V. T. Cook
(*Music and Lyrics by* Jerry Leiber, Mike Stoller, Louis Lebish, George Treadwell, Irv Nathan.)

"Neighborhood" (reprise)
B. J. Crosby, B. Braxton, D. Lively, P. D. Jones

"Keep On Rollin'"
V. T. Cook, with A. Bailey, K. Ard, F. B. Owens

"Searchin'"
V. T. Cook, A. Bailey, K. Ard, F. B. Owens

"Kansas City"
B. J. Crosby, P. D. Jones, M. Park

"Trouble"
D. Lively, B. Braxton

"Love Me/Don't"
A. Bailey, P. D. Jones

"Fools Fall in Love"
B. J. Crosby

"Poison Ivy"
K. Ard, with A. Bailey, F. B. Owens, V. T. Cook

"Don Juan"
B. Braxton

"Shoppin' for Clothes"
V. T. Cook, F. B. Owens, with A. Bailey, K. Ard, M. Park
(*Music and Lyrics by* Jerry Leiber, Mike Stoller, Kent Harris.)

"I Keep Forgettin'"
P. D. Jones

"On Broadway"
A. Bailey, F. B. Owens, K. Ard, V. T. Cook
(*Music and Lyrics by* Jerry Leiber, Mike Stoller, Barry Mann, Cynthia Weil.)

"D. W. Washburn"
V. T. Cook, Company

"Saved"
B. J. Crosby, Company

[6]All music and lyrics by Jerry Leiber and Mike Stoller, except where noted below.

ACT 2

"That Is Rock & Roll"
Company
"Yakety Yak"
Company
"Charlie Brown"
Company
"Stay a While"
L. St. Louis, David Keyes (synthesizer)
"Pearl's a Singer"
P. D. Jones
(*Music and Lyrics by* Jerry Leiber, Mike Stoller, Ralph Dino, John Sembello.)
"Teach Me How to Shimmy"
M. Park, D. Lively, with A. Bailey, V. T. Cook
"You're the Boss"
F. B. Owens, B. Braxton
"Smokey Joe's Café"
F. B. Owens, Company
"Loving You"
K. Ard, Company
"Treat Me Nice"
V. T. Cook
"Hound Dog"
B. J. Crosby
"Little Egypt"
F. B. Owens, with A. Bailey, K. Ard, M. Park, V. T. Cook
"I'm a Woman"
B. J. Crosby, B. Braxton, D. Lively, P. D. Jones
"There Goes My Baby"
A. Bailey, with F. B. Owens, K. Ard, M. Park, V. T. Cook
(*Music and Lyrics by* Jerry Leiber, Mike Stoller, Benjamin Nelson, Lover Patterson, George Treadwell.)
"Love Potion #9"
A. Bailey, with F. B. Owens, K. Ard, M. Park, V. T. Cook
"Some Cats Know"
B. Braxton
"Jailhouse Rock"
M. Park, Company
"Fools Fall in Love" (reprise)
B. J. Crosby
"Spanish Harlem"
K. Ard, B. Braxton
(*Music and Lyrics by* Phil Spector, Jerry Leiber.)
"I (Who Have Nothing)"
V. T. Cook
(*Music and Lyrics by* Jerry Leiber, Mike Stoller, Carlo Donida.)
"Neighborhood" (reprise)
P. D. Jones
"Stand By Me"
A. Bailey, Company
(*Music and Lyrics by* Jerry Leiber, Mike Stoller, Ben E. King.)
"That Is Rock & Roll" (Finale)
Company

1995.04 MAMA I WANT TO SING PART 2

A Gospel Musical in Two Acts[7]. Book and lyrics by Vy Higginsen and Ken Wydro. Original music by Wesley Naylor. Music arranged and conducted by Wesley Naylor. Set design by Charles McClannahan. Lighting design by Marshall Williams. Directed by Ken Wydro. Choreography by Cisco Drayton. Produced by Vy Higginsen and Ken Wydro. Opened 7 March 1995 at the Paramount Theatre, Madison Square Garden, and closed 12 March 1995 after 8 performances.

CAST: *Doris Winter*: DESIREE COLEMAN-JACKSON. *Mama Winter*: SHIRLEY CAESAR. *Sister Carrie*: VANESSA BELL ARMSTRONG. *Reverend Julian Simmons*: MARK KIBBLE. *Minister of Music*: Pierre Cook. *Little Doris*: Knoelle Higginson Wydro. *Narrator*: Hazel Smith. And the Mt. Calvary Choir.

The New York Reach Ensemble: *Sopranos*: Anissia Bunton, Marilyn Davis, Kim Summerson, Michelle C. White, Jannis Winstead. *Altos*: Shannon Cooper, Robin Cunningham, Kimberly Marshall, Diane Spann-Miller, Anita Wells. *Tenors*: Daryl Banks, Tyrone Flowers, Willie Heard, Damon Horton, Ronnie McLeod. *The Halos*: Kim Summerson, Diane Spann-Miller, Anita Wells.

ACT 1

Choir Rehearsal
P. Cook, Mt. Calvary Choir
"The Spirit of Your Father"
S. Caesar
"The Lord Is Blessing Me"
M. Kibble, Mt. Calvary Choir
"Faith"
V. B. Armstrong, Mt. Calvary Choir
"Sermon"
M. Kibble
"Because He Lives"
D. Coleman-Jackson, Mt. Calvary Choir
"Something Pretty"
D. Coleman-Jackson, M. Kibble
"Finding a Man Ain't Easy"
V. B. Armstrong, S. Caesar, D. Coleman-Jackson
"We Belong Together"
D. Coleman-Jackson, M. Kibble
"Bless You, My Children"
S. Caesar, Mt. Calvary Choir

ACT 2

"Stay Close to the Music"
D. Coleman-Jackson, The Halos
"Long Distance Love"
Las Vagas Hotel, Julian's Apartment, New York
"New Life on the Planet"
D. Coleman-Jackson
"Mt. Calvary Baptism Day"
Baptism at Mt. Calvary
"Sister Carrie's Song"
V. B. Armstrong, Mt. Calvary Choir
"The Promise of the Future"
M. Kibble
"To Love Is To Serve"
D. Coleman-Jackson, M. Kibble
"Please Understand"
D. Coleman-Jackson
"Something to Remember Me By"
V. B. Armstrong
"Where Is My Mommy, Please"
K. H. Wydro, S. Caesar
"Alone on the Road"
S. Caesar
"Going Home"
S. Caesar
Finale Medley
Company

[7]Originally opened Off-Broadway 25 March 1990-30 March 1991 at the Heckscher Theatre in repertory with "Mama I Want to Sing, Part 1."

1995.05 HOW TO SUCCEED IN BUSINESS WITHOUT REALLY TRYING

A Revival of the Musical (Comedy) in Two Acts[8]. Book by Abe Burrows, Jack Weinstock and Willie Gilbert. Based on the novel of the same name by

[8]Originally opened in New York 14 October 1961 at the 46th Street Theatre for 1417 performances. For Musical Numbers, see original 1961 production. For this production, "Cinderella Darling" was dropped from the opening of Act 2 and replaced by:

"How to Succeed" (reprise)
V. Clark, K. Lynes, Women

Shepherd Mead. Music and lyrics by Frank Loesser. Scenery design by John Arnone. Costume design by Susan Hilferty. Lighting design by Howell Binkley. Directed by Des McAnuff. Choreography by Wayne Cilento. Video design by Batwin + Robin Productions, Inc. Sound design by Steve Canyon Kennedy. Music direction and vocal arrangements by Ted Sperling. Orchestrations by Danny Troob; additional orchestrations by David Siegel, Robert Ginzler. Dance arrangements by Jeanine Tesori. Incidental music arranged by Ted Sperling. Executive producer, Dodger Productions. Associate producer, Whistlin' Dixie. Originally produced by LaJolla Playhouse, LaJolla, California (Michael Greif, artistic director; Terrence Dwyer, managing director). Produced by Dodger Productions (Michael David, Doug Johnson, Des McAnuff, Rocco Landesman, Edward Strong, Sherman Warner), Kardana Productions, Inc. (John N. Hart, Jr., Mort Swinsky), The John F. Kennedy Center (James D. Wolfensohn, chairman; Lawrence J. Wilker, president), the Nederlander Organization (James M. Nederlander). Opened 23 March 1995 at the Richard Rodgers Theatre and closed 14 July 1996 after 548 performances.

CAST (in order of their appearance): *Voice of the Narrator*: Walter Cronkite. *J. Pierrepont Finch*: MATTHEW BRODERICK. *Milt Gatch*: Tom Flynn. *Jenkins*: Jay Aubrey Jones. *Davis*: William Ryall. *Bert Bratt*: JONATHAN FREEMAN. *Tackaberry*: Martin Moran. *J. B. Biggley*: RONN CARROLL. *Rosemary Pilkington*: MEGAN MULLALLY. *Smitty*: VICTORIA CLARK *Bud Frump*: JEFF BLUMENKRANTZ. *Miss Krumholtz*: Kristi Lynes. *Office Boy*: Randl Ask. *Security Guard*: Kevin Bogue. *Henchmen*: Jack Hayes, Jerome Vivona. *Miss Jones*: LILLIAS WHITE. *Twimble*: GERRY VICHI. *Hedy La Rue*: LUBA MASON. *Toynbee*: Tom Flynn. *Scrubwomen*: Rebecca Holt, Carla Renata Williams. *Dance Soloist*: Nancy Lemenager. *Ovington*: Randl Ask. *TV Announcer*: Randl Ask. *Wickets and Wickettes*: Kevin Bogue, Maria Calabrese, Jack Hayes, Nancy Lemenager, Kristi Lynes, Aiko Nakasone, Jerome Vivona, Carla Renata Williams. *Wally Womper*: GERRY VICHI.

Ensemble: Randl Ask, Kevin Bogue, Maria Calabrese, Tom Flynn, Jack Hayes, Rebecca Holt, Jay Aubrey Jones, Nancy Lemenager, Martin Moran, Aiko Nakasone, William Ryall, Jerome Vivona, Carla Renata Williams. *Swings*: Jeffry Denman, Tom Flagg, Pamela Gold.

The action takes place in 1961 at the World Wide Wicket Company in New York City.

1995.06 THE MERRY WIDOW

A Revival of the Operetta in Three Acts, 4 Scenes[9]. Music by Franz Lehár. Original German book and lyrics by Victor Léon and Leo Stein (after "L'Attaché d'Ambassade.") (New) English book adaptation by Robert Johanson. (New) English lyrics by Albert Evans. Production director, Robert Johanson. Choreographer, Sharon Halley. Set design by Michael Anania. Costume design by Gregg Barnes. Lighting design by Mark W. Stanley. Sound design by Abe Jacob. Chorus master, Joseph Colaneri. Conductor, Eric Stern. Produced by the New York City Opera. Opened 26 March 1995 at the New York State Theatre and closed 22 April 1995 after 7 performances in repertory.

CAST: *Baron Mirko Zeta*: GEORGE S. IRVING. *Valencienne*: Elizabeth Futral. *Kromov*: Joseph McKee. *Olga*: Beth McVey. *Bogdanovitch*: JOHN LANKSTON. *Sylviane*: Suzanne Ishee. *Njegus*: ROBERT CREIGHTON. *Camille de Rosillon*: CARLO SCIBELLI. *Vicomte Cascada*: JEFFREY LENTZ. *Raoul de St. Brioche*: JAMES BOBICK. *Hanna (Glawari)*: JANE THORNGREN. *Count Danilo*: MICHAEL HAYES. *Lolo*: Jean Barber. *Dodo*: Stephanie Godino. *Jou-Jou*: Christiane Farr. *Frou-Frou*: Kathy Meyer. *Clo-Clo*: Debbi Fuhrman. *Margot*: Joan Mirabella. *Young Danilo*: John MacInnis. *Young Hanna*: Christane Farr. *Ensemble*: New York City Opera Chorus.

Act 1: The Marsovian Embassy. Paris, early 1900's.

Act 2: The Garden of Mme. Glawari's villa.

Act 3: Chez Maxim.

ACT 1[10]
- "For Marsovia"
  - G. S. Irving, E. Futral, J. Lentz, J. Bobick, C. Scibelli, Marsovians, Parisians
- "A Respectable Wife"
  - E. Futral, C. Scibelli
- "Gentlemen, I Pray" (The Widow's Entrance)
  - J. Thorngren, Men
- "Maxim's"
  - M. Hayes, R. Creighton, Grisettes
- "The Quarrel"
  - J. Thorngren, M. Hayes
- Finale, Act 1
  - J. Thorngren, M. Hayes, Full Company

ACT 2
- "Marsovian Dances"
  - Company
- "Vilia"
  - J. Thorngren, Company
- "Women"
  - M. Hayes, G. S. Irving, R. Creighton, J. Lankston, J. McKee, J. Bobick, J. Lentz, C. Scibelli
- "Marsovian Dances" (reprise)
  - J. Thorngren, M. Hayes, Dancers
- "Romance"
  - E. Futral, C. Scibelliil
- "Summerhouse Quintet"
  - J. Thorngren, M. Hayes, E. Futral, C. Scibelli, G. S. Irving
- Finale, Act 2
  - J. Thorngren, M. Hayes, Company

ACT 3
- "Cakewalk"
  - Full Company
- "Another Frenchman" (Njegus' Song)
  - R. Creighton, Women
- "I'll Remember"[11]
  - E. Futral, C. Scibelli
- "Cancan"
  - J. Thorngren, Grisettes, Company
- "Yours Is My Heart"[12]
  - M. Hayes
- "The Merry Widow Waltz"
  - M. Hayes, J. Thorngren
- Finale, Act 3
  - Company

1995.07 GENTLEMEN PREFER BLONDES

A Revival of the Musical Comedy in Two Acts, 11 Scenes[13]. Book by Joseph Fields and Anita Loos[14], adapted from her novel of the same name. Music by Jule Styne. Lyrics by Leo Robin. Directed by Charles Repole. Choreographed by Michael Lichtefeld. Scenery and costume designed by Eduardo Sicangco. Lighting design by Kirk Bookman. Sound design by T. Richard Fitzgerald. Orchestrations by Douglas Besterman. Musical supervision and vocal arrangements by Michael O'Flaherty. Dance music by Gordon Harrell. Musical director, Andrew Wilder. Associate producer, Sue Frost. Executive producer, Manny Kladitis. Produced by National Actors

[9]Originally produced in New York 21 October 1907 at the New Amsterdam Theatre for 416 performances.

[10]No song list appears in the New York City Opera program. Song list prepared from the previous Papermill Playhouse production where this adaptation premiered.

[11]Interpolation "Meine Lippen, sie kuessen so heiss" from GIUDITTA.

[12]Interpolation "Dein ist mein ganzes Herz" (Yours Is My Heart) from *THE LAND OF SMILES*.

[13]Originally produced in New York 8 December 1949 at the Ziegfeld Theatre for 740 performances.

[14]Book revisions were uncredited. The book was drastically revised, songs reassigned, dropped and moved within the show, which was revised from 12 to 11 scenes. "Homesick Blues" was retitled "Homesick." The "Sunshine" song lyrics were largely dropped and its music formed the basis for the dance sequence "Sunshine Montage." "You Say You Care" was excised from the plot and became incidental music in the final scene for the Park Casino Trio. The following musical numbers were dropped:

"Bye Bye Baby" (reprises), the Practice Scherzo, "In the Champs de Mers" (dance), "House on Rittenhouse Square," "Coquette" and "Button Up with Esmond."

Theatre (Tony Randall, Founder and artistic directior) in association with The Goodspeed Opera House (Michael P. Price, Executive producer). Opened 10 April 1995 at the Lyceum Theatre and closed 30 April 1995 after 24 performances.

CAST (in order of their appearance): *Dorothy Shaw*: KAREN PRUNZIK. *Lorelei Lee*: K. T. SULLIVAN. *Gus Esmond*: ALLEN FITZPATRICK. *Lady Phyllis Beekman*: CAROL SWARBRICK. *Sir Francis Beekman*: DAVID PONTING. *Mrs. Ella Spofford*: SUSAN RUSH. *Henry Spofford*: GEORGE DVORSKY. *Josephus Gage*: JAMIE ROSS. *Steward*: Dick Decareau. *Frank*: Craig Waletzko. *George*: Ken Nagy. *Mime*: Joe Bowerman. *Robert Lemanteur*: Craig Waletzko. *Louie Lemanteur*: John Hoshko. *Tango Couples*: Paula Grider, Joe Bowerman, Lisa Hanna, Ken Nagy, Richard Costa, Lorinda Santos. *Park Casino Trio*: Angela Bond, John Hoshko, Craig Waletzko. *Mr. Esmond, Sr.*: Dick Decareau.

Ensemble: Angela Bond, Joe Bowerman, Richard Costa, Paula Grider, Lisa Hanna, Bryan S. Haynes, John Hoshko, Ken Nagy, Wendy Roberts, Lorinda Santos, Craig Waletzko. *Swings*: Melissa Bell, Marty McDonough.

Time: 1926.

Act 1, Scene 1: Onstage and backstage at Club Purgatory, New York City. *Scene 2*: The French Line Pier in New York, midnight sailing. *Scene 3*: The Sun Deck of the *Ile de France*, three days out. *Scene 4*: Lorelei's Suite on the *Ile de France*, later that day. *Scene 5*: Paris. *Scene 6*: Lorelei's suite at The Ritz in Paris, evening.

Act 2, Scene 1: Onstage at the Club Cocteau in Paris, the next evening. *Scene 2*: Dorothy's dressing room backstage, immediately following. *Scene 3*: Streets of Paris, in front of the Café Rouge. *Scene 4*: Lorelei's Suite, 3 A.M. *Scene 5*: The Central Park Casino, New York, 10 days later.

ACT 1
Scene 1
Opening
K. Prunzik, Men
"It's High Time"
K. T. Sullivan, K. Prunzik
Scene 2
"It's High Time" (reprise)
Company
"Bye, Bye Baby"
A. Fitzpatrick, K. T. Sullivan, Company
Scene 3
"I'm Just A Little Girl from Little Rock"
K. T. Sullivan
"I'm Atingle, I'm Aglow"
J. Ross, K. T. Sullivan, K. Prunzik, S. Rush
"I Love What I'm Doing"
K. Prunzik, Olympic Men
Scene 4
"Just a Kiss Apart"
G. Dvorsky, K. Prunzik
"It's Delightful Down in Chile"
D. Ponting, K. T. Sullivan
Scene 5
"Sunshine Montage"
J. Bowerman, Company
Scene 6
"I'm Atingle, I'm Aglow" (reprise)
J. Ross, Company
Finale Act 1
K. T. Sullivan

ACT 2
Scene 1
"Mamie Is Mimi"
K. Prunzik, Company
Scene 2
"Diamonds Are a Girl's Best Friend"
K. T. Sullivan
Scene 3
"A Ride on a Rainbow" (from *RUGGLES OF RED GAP*, television)
G. Dvorsky, K. Prunzik, Tango Couples
Scene 4
"Gentlemen Prefer Blondes"
K. T. Sullivan, A. Fitzpatrick
"Homesick"
A. Fitzpatrick, K. T. Sullivan, K. Prunzik, G. Dvorsky, S. Rush, J. Ross
Scene 5
"I Love What I'm Doing" (reprise)
Trio
"You Say You Care"
Trio
"Keeping Cool With Coolidge"
Company
Finale
Company

1995–1996 SEASON

Julie Andrews (center) and Members of the Company of VICTOR/VICTORIA
Joan Marcus/Photofest

1995–1996 SEASON

1995.08 BUTTONS ON BROADWAY

Celebrating his 60th Anniversary in Show Business (A One Man Show in Two Acts). Musical director, Bryan Louiselle. Scenic design by Nancy Thun. Lighting design by Ken Billington. Sound design by Lewis Mead. Produced by Don Gregory. Opened 8 June 1995 at the Ambassador Theatre and closed 16 July 1995 after 33 performances.

CAST: RED BUTTONS (comedy, impressions, a few songs[1]).

1995.09 CHRONICLE OF A DEATH FORETOLD

A Musical in One Act. Based on the novel (of the same name) by Gabriel García Márquez. Adapted by Graciela Daniele and Jim Lewis. Music by Bob Telson. Additional material by Michael John LaChiusa. Conceived, directed and choreographed by Graciela Daniele. Sets by Christopher Barreca. Costumes by Toni-Leslie James. Lighting by Jules Fisher, Beverly Emmons. Sound by Tony Meola. Musical director, dance music arrangements by Steve Sandberg. (Music) Arrangements by Bob Telson. Associate choreographer, Willie Rosario. Sponsored by A&T. Production made possible by grants from The Rockefeller Foundation, The Gilman and Gonzalez-Falla Theatre Foundation, Inc. Produced by Linclon Center Theatre (André Bishop, Artistic director; Bernard Gersten, Executive producer), by arangement with INTAR Hispanic American Arts Center. Opened 15 June 1995 at the Plymouth Theatre and closed 16 July 1995 after 37 performances[2].

CAST: *Santiago Nasar*: GEORGE DE LA PEÑA. *Cristo*, his friend: JULIO MONGE. *Placida*, Santiago's mother: YOLANDE BAVAN. *Victoria*, the cook: Myra Lucretia Taylor. *Divina*, her daughter: Monica McSwain. *Angela Vicario*: SAUNDRA SANTIAGO. *Pura Vicario*, her mother: Ivonne Coll. *Pablo Vicario*, Angela's brother: LUIS PEREZ. *Pedro Vicario*, Angela's brother: GREGORY MITCHELL. *Bayardo San Roman*: ALEXANDRE PROIA. *Clotilde*, the bodega keeper: TONYA PINKINS. *Flora*, Santiago's fiancée: Lisa Leguillou. *Faustino*, a butcher: Lazaro Perez. *Xius*, a widower: Norberto Kerner. *Colonel Aponte*: Nelson Roberto Landrieu. *Father Amador*: Jaime Tirelli. *Margot*, a novice: René M. Ceballos. *Maria*: Denise Faye.

Place and time: An isolated Latin American town in the past and present.

1995.10 THE MIKADO, or The Town of Titipu

A Revival of the Comic Opera in Two Acts[3]. Libretto by William S. Gilbert. Music by Arthur Sullivan. Production (direction), Lofti Mansouri. Stage director, Christian Smith. Conductor, Randall Craig Fleischer. Set and costume designer, Thierry Bosquet. Lighting designer, John Gleason. Choreographer, Patricia Birch; choreography re-staged by Helena Andreyko. Chorus master, Joseph Colaneri. Produced by the New York City Opera. Opened 23 September 1995 at the New York State Theatre and closed 4 November 1995 after 4 performances in repertory; returned 3 March 1996 and closed 18 April 1996 after 4 additional performances. Total this season: 8 performances.

CAST (in order of appearance): *Nanki-Poo*: MATTHEW CHELLIS. *Pish-Tush*: JAMES BOBICK. *Pooh-Bah*: JOSEPH MCKEE. *Ko-Ko*: JAMES BILLINGS. *Yum-Yum*: BARBARA SHIRVIS. *Pitti-Sing*: ANGELA HORN. *Peep-Bo*: DIANNA HELDMAN. *Katisha*: JOYCA CASTLE. *The Mikado of Japan*: RICHARD MCKEE. *Chorus of School Girls, Nobles, Guards and Coolies*: New York City Opera Chorus.

[1]Included "Sam, You Made the Pants Too Long"
[2]No individual scenes or musical numbers were listed.
[3]First presented in New York 20 July, 10-29 August 1885 at the Union Square and People's Theatres for 22 performances. First authorized production presented 19 August 1885 at the Fifth Avenue Theatre by Richard D'Oyly Carte for 250 performances. For Synopsis of Scenes and Musical Numbers, see 19 August 1885 D'Oyly Carte production.

1995.11 COMPANY

A Revival of the Musical Comedy in Two Acts, 11 Scenes[4]. Book by George Furth. Music and lyrics by Stephen Sondheim. Directed by Scott Ellis. Choreographed by Rob Marshall. Set by Tony Walton. Costumes by William Ivey Long. Lighting by Peter Kaczorowski. Sound by Tony Meola. Projections by Wendall K. Harrington. Musical direction by David Loud. Orchestrations by Jonathan Tunick. Fights by David Leong. Assistant choreographer, Sarah Miles. Originally produced (and directed) on Broadway by Harold Prince. Original dance arrangements by Wally Harper. Original 'Tick Tock' dance music arrangements by David Shire. Produced by The Roundabout Theatre Company (Todd Haimes, Artistic director; Ellen Richard, Managing director). Opened 5 October 1995 at the Criterion/Stage Right and closed 3 December 1995 after 68 performances.

CAST: *Robert*: BOYD GAINES. *Sarah*: KATE BURTON. *Harry*: ROBERT WESTENBERG. *Susan*: PATRICIA BEN PETERSON. *Peter*: JONATHAN DOKUCHITZ. *Jenny*: DIANA CANOVA. *David*: JOHN HILLNER. *Amy*: VEANNA COX. *Paul*: DANNY BURSTEIN. *Joanne*: DEBRA MONK. *Larry*: TIMOTHY LANDFIELD. *Marta*: LA CHANZE. *Kathy*: CHARLOTTE D'AMBOISE. *April*: JANE KRAKOWSKI.

1995.12 PATTI LUPONE ON BROADWAY

A One Woman Show in Two Acts. Conceived and directed by Scott Wittman. Written by Jeffrey Richman. Musical director, Dick Gallagher. Musical arrangements, John McDaniel. Lighting by John Hastings. Sound by Otts Munderloh. Additional musical arrangements by Steven D. Bowen, Dick Gallagher, Glen Roven, Marc Shaiman, Jonathan Tunick. Produced by Jujamcyn Theatres (James H. Binger, Chairman; Rocco Landesman, Preident; Paul Libin, Producing Director; Jack Viertel, Creative Director). Opened 12 October 1995 at the Ritz Theatre and closed 25 November 1995 after 46 performances.

CAST: PATTI LUPONE.
The Mermen: Byron Motley, Josef Powell, Gene Van Buren, John West.

MUSICAL NUMBERS[5]

"I Get a Kick Out of You" (from *ANYTHING GOES*)
(*Music and Lyrics by* Cole Porter.)
"I'm a Stranger Here Myself" (from *ONE TOUCH OF VENUS*)
(*Music by* Kurt Weill. *Lyrics by* Ogden Nash.)
"It Never Was You" (from *KNICKERBOCKER HOLIDAY*)
(*Music by* Kurt Weill. *Lyrics by* Maxwell Anderson.)
"Everything Happens to Me"
(*Music by* Matt Dennis. *Lyrics by* Tom Adair.)
"Lush Life"
(*Music and Lyrics by* Billy Strayhorn.)
"Ain't Nobody Here But Us Chickens" (interpolated into *FIVE GUYS NAMED MOE*)
(*Music and Lyrics by* Alex Kramer and Joan Whitney.)
"I've Got the Sun in the Morning" (from *ANNIE GET YOUR GUN*)
(*Music and Lyrics by* Irving Berlin.)
"Dirty Hands! Dirty Face!" (from *BOMBO*)
(*Music by* James V. Monaco. *Lyrics by* Al Jolson, Grant Clarke and Edgar Leslie.)
"(And) His Rocking Horse Ran Away" (from *AND THE ANGELS SING* film)
(*Music by* Johnny Burke. *Lyrics by* Jimmy Van Heusen.)
"My Ship" (from *LADY IN THE DARK*)
(*Music by* Kurt Weill. *Lyrics by* Ira Gershwin.)
"Surabaya Johnny" (from *HAPPY END*)
(*Music by* Kurt Weill. *Lyrics by* Bertolt Brecht.)

[4]Originally produced in New York 26 April 1970 at the Alvin Theatre for 690 performances. For Synopsis of Scenes and Musical Numbers, see original 1970 production. The Vocal Minority were dropped for this revival. Added for this production:
"Marry Me a Little" (Act 1 closing)
B. Gaines
[5]Miss LuPone accompanied by The Mermen on "Ain't Nobody Here But Us Chickens," "I Got the Sun in the Morning," "Sleepy Man," "Anything Goes," "Moonshine Lullaby," and "Heaven."

"Calling You" (from film *BAGDAD CAFE*)
(*Music and Lyrics by* Bob Telson.)
"Get Here"
(*Music and Lyrics by* Brenda Russell.)
"Come to the Supermarket in Old Peking" (from TV musical *ALADDIN*)
(*Music and Lyrics by* Cole Porter.)
"Being Alive" (from *COMPANY*)
(*Music and Lyrics by* Stephen Sondheim.)
"Looking for Love on Broadway"
(*Music and Lyrics by* James Taylor.)
"Don't Cry for Me Argentina" (from *EVITA*)
(*Music by* Andrew Lloyd Webber. *Lyrics by* Tim Rice.)
"Sleepy Man" (from *THE ROBBER BRIDEGROOM*)
(*Music by* Robert Waldman. *Lyrics by* Alfred Uhry.)
"Meadowlark" (from *THE BAKER'S WIFE*)
(*Music and Lyrics by* Stephen Schwartz.)
"As Long as He Needs Me" (from *OLIVER!*)
(*Music and Lyrics by* Lionel Bart.)
"Nickel Under Your Foot" (from *THE CRADLE WILL ROCK*)
(*Music and Lyrics by* Marc Blitzstein.)
"I Dreamed a Dream" (from *LES MISERABLES*)
(*Music by* Claude-Michel Schönberg. *Lyrics by* Alain Boublil and Herbert Kretzmer.)
"Anything Goes" (from *ANYTHING GOES*)
(*Music and Lyrics by* Cole Porter.)
"Moonshine Lullaby" (from *ANNIE GET YOUR GUN*)
(*Music and Lyrics by* Irving Berlin.)
"Heaven"
(*Music and Lyrics by* Julie Gold.)
"Lost in the Stars" (from *LOST IN THE STARS*)
(*Music by* Kurt Weill. *Lyrics by* Maxwell Anderson.)
"Bewitched" (from *PAL JOEY*)
(*Music by* Richard Rodgers. *Lyrics by* Lorenz Hart.)

1995.13 HELLO, DOLLY!

A Revival of the Musical Comedy in Two Acts, 13 Scenes[6]. Book by Michael Stewart. Based on the play "The Matchmaker" by Thornton Wilder. Music and lyrics by Jerry Herman. Original production directed and choreographed by Gower Champion. Directed and staged by Lee Roy Reams. Associate choreographer, Bill Bateman. Set design by Oliver Smith. Costume design by Jonathan Bixby. Lighting design by Ken Billington. Sound design by Peter Fitzgerald. Musical director and conductor, Jack Everly. Musical supervision, Tim Stella. Orchestrations by Philip J. Lang. Dance arrangements by Peter Howard. Production supervisor, Jerry Herman. Scenic supervision by Rosaria Sinisi. Produced by Manny Kladitis, Magic Promotion and Theatricals (Lee D. Marshall, Joe Marsh, Glenn Bechdel), Pace Theatrical Group (Allen Becker, Brian Becker, Miles Wilkin, Scott Zeiger). Opened 19 October 1995 at the Lunt-Fontanne Theatre and closed 28 January 1996 after 116 performances.

CAST (in the order of appearance): *Mrs. Dolly Gallagher Levi*: CAROL CHANNING. *Ernestina*: Monica M. Wemitt. *Ambrose Kemper*: James Darrah. *Horse*: Sharon Moore, Michele Tibbitts. *Horace Vandergelder*: JAY GARNER. *Ermengarde*: Christine DeVito. *Cornelius Hackl*: MICAHEL DEVRIES. *Barnaby Tucker*: CORY ENGLISH. *Minnie Fay*: LORI ANN MAHL. *Irene Molloy*: FLORENCE LACEY. *Mrs. Rose*: Elizabeth Green. *Rudolph*: Steve Pudenz. *Stanley*: Julian Brightman. *Judge*: Bill Bateman. *Court Clerk*: Halden Michaels.

Townspeople, Waiters, Etc.: John Bantay, Desta Barbieri, Bill Bateman, Kimberly Bellmann, Bruce Blanchard, Stephen Bourneuf, Julian Brightman, Holly Cruikshank, Simone Gee, Jason Gillman, Milica Govich, Elizabeth Green, Donald Ives, Dan LoBuono, Jim Madden, Halden Michaels, Sharon Moore, Michael Quinn, Robert Randle, Mitch Rosengarten, Mary Setrakian, Clarence M. Sheridan, Randy Slovacek, Roger Preston Smith, Ashley Stover, Michele Tibbitts. *Swings*: Kevin M. Burrows, Jennifer Joan Joy, John Salvatore, Matthew A. Sipress.

[6]Originally produced in New York 16 January 1964 at the St. James Theatre for 2844 performances. For Synopsis of Scenes and Musical Numbers, see original 1964 production. As in previous revivals, "Come and Be My Butterfly" was not performed. Act 1, Scene 3, and Act 2, Scene 4, were eliminated. "The Polka Contest" followed "Hello, Dolly!" in Act 2, Scene 3.

1995.14 SWINGING ON A STAR

A Musical Revue in Two Acts, 7 Scenes. Lyrics by Johnny Burke. Music by Johnny Burke, Erroll Garner, Robert Haggart, Arthur Johnston, James Monaco, Harold Spina, Jimmy Van Heusen. Written and directed by Michael Leeds. Choreographed by Kathleen Marshall. Scenery designed by James Youmans. Costumes designed by Judy Dearing. Lighting designed by Richard Nelson. Orchestrations and vocal arrangements by Barry Levitt. Dance arrangements by Peter Howard. Additional orchestrations by Brian Besterman. Sound designer, T. Richard Fitzgerald. Video and projections by Batwin + Robin Productions, Inc. Assistant musical director and additional arrangements by Ron Drotos. Production coordinator, Todd Little. Musical direction by Barry Levitt. Originally produced by the Goodspeed Opera House, George Street Playhouse. Produced by Richard Seader, Mary Burke Kramer, Paul B. Berkowsky. Opened 22 October 1995 at the Music Box Theatre and closed 14 January 1996 after 97 performances.

CAST (in alphabetical order): TERRY BURRELL, LEWIS CLEALE, KATHY FITZGERALD, EUGENE FLEMING, ALVALETA GUESS, LORI HART, MICHAEL MCGRATH.

Act 1, Scene 1: Speakeasy, Chicago. *Scene 2*: Depression, The Bowery. *Scene 3*: Radio Show, New York City. *Scene 4*: USO Show, the Pacific Islands.

Act 2, Scene 1: Ballroom, Hotel Roosevelt, Akron, Ohio. *Scene 2*: Road to Paramount Studios, Hollywood. *Scene 3*: Supper Club, the Present.

ACT 1

Scene 1

"You're Not the Only Oyster in the Stew"
A. Guess, L. Hart, K. Fitzgerald
(*Music by* Harold Spina.)
"Chicago Style" (from *ROAD TO BALI* film)
E. Fleming, L. Hart, K. Fitzgerald, M. McGrath
(*Music by* Jimmy Van Heusen.)
"Ain't It a Shame About Mame" (from *RHYTHM ON THE RIVER* film)
E. Fleming, T. Burrell
(*Music by* James Monaco.)
"What's New"
L. Hart
(*Music by* Robert Haggart.)
"Doctor Rhythm" (dropped from *DOCTOR RHYTHM* film)
A. Guess, E. Fleming
(*Music by* James Monaco.)
(*Choreographed by* Kathleen Marshall and Eugene Fleming.)
The Waiter: M. McGrath. *Mame*: T. Burrell. *Escort*: L. Cleale. *Cleo*: A. Guess. *Jeannie*: L. Hart. *Flora*: K. Fitzgerald. *Ben*: E. Fleming.

Scene 2

"Pennies from Heaven" (from *PENNIES FROM HEAVEN* film)
L. Cleale
(*Music by* Arthur Johnston.)
"When Stanislaus Got Married" (from *AND THE ANGELS SING* film)
M. McGrath, A. Guess, L. Hart, E. Fleming, T. Burrell
(*Music by* Jimmy Van Heusen.)
"His Rocking Horse Ran Away" (from *AND THE ANGELS SING* film)
K. Fitzgerald
(*Music by* Jimmy Van Heusen.)
"Annie Doesn't Live Here Anymore"
L. Cleale, M. McGrath, E. Fleming
(*Music by* Harold Spina. *Lyrics by* Joe Young, Johnny Burke.)
The Homeless Man: L. Cleale. *The Street People*: A. Guess, L. Hart, E. Fleming, T. Burrell. *The Polish Gentleman*: M. McGrath. *The Housewife*: K. Fitzgerald. *The Suitors*: L. Cleale, M. McGrath, E. Fleming.

Scene 3

"Annie Doesn't Live Here Anymore" (reprise)
M. McGrath, L. Hart, L. Cleale, E. Fleming, A. Guess, T. Burrell
"Scatterbrain" (from *SCATTERBRAIN* film)
M. McGrath
(*Music by* Keene Bean, Frankie Masters.)
"One, Two, Button Your Shoe" (from *PENNIES FROM HEAVEN* film)
L. Hart, M. McGrath
(*Music by* Arthur Johnston.)
"Whoopsie Daisy Day"
L. Cleale, E. Fleming, A. Guess, T. Burrell
(*Music by* Johnny Burke.)

"What Does It Take To Make You Take to Me?"
K. Fitzgerald
(*Music by* Jimmy Van Heusen.)
"Irresistible"
L. Cleale, K. Fitzgerald, E. Fleming, A. Guess, T. Burrell.
(*Music by* Harold Spina.)
"An Apple for the Teacher" (from *THE STAR MAKER* film)
All
(*Music by* Arthur Johnston.)
The Burkettes: E. Fleming, A. Guess, T. Burrell.
The Announcer: L. Cleale. *Buddy*: M. McGrath.
Betty: L. Hart. *Vicky Voyay*: K. Fitzgerald.

Scene 4
"Thank Your Lucky Stars and Stripes" (from *PLAYMATES* film)
M. McGrath, E. Fleming
(*Music by* Jimmy Van Heusen.)
"Personality" (from *ROAD TO UTOPIA* film)
K. Fitzgerald, L. Hart, T. Burrell
(*Music by* Jimmy Van Heusen.)
"There's Always the Blues"
A. Guess
(*Music by* Joe Bushkin.)
"Polka Dots and Moonbeams"
L. Cleale
(*Music by* Jimmy Van Heusen.)
"Swinging on a Star" (from *GOING MY WAY* film)
All
(*Music by* Jimmy Van Heusen.)
"(Thank Your Lucky) Stars and Stripes" (reprise)
All
Don Carter: M. McGrath. *Buzz Albright*: E. Fleming. *Miss South Dakota*: K. Fitzgerald. *Miss North Carolina*: L. Hart. *Miss Rhiengold*: T. Burrell. *Lena George*: A. Guess. *Eddie*: L. Cleale.

ACT 2

Scene 1
"Don't Let That Moon Get Away" (from *SING YOU SINNERS* film)
E. Fleming
(*Music by* James Monaco.)
"All You Want to Do Is Dance"(from *DOUBLE FOR NOTHING* film)
(*Music by* Arthur Johnston.)
"You Danced with Dynamite"
K. Fitzgerald, M. McGrath
(*Music by* Jimmy Van Heusen.)
"Imagination"
T. Burrell, E. Fleming, L. Hart
(*Music by* Jimmy Van Heusen.)
"It Could Happen to You" (from *AND THE ANGELS SING* film)
A. Guess
(*Music by* Jimmy Van Heusen.)
The Manager: L. Cleale. *The Coat Check Girl*: L. Hart.
The Waiter: E. Fleming. *The Vocalist*: T. Burrell. *The Man*: M. McGrath. *The Date*: K. Fitzgerald. *The Woman Alone*: A. Guess.

Scene 2
"Apalachicola" (from *ROAD TO RIO* film)
L. Cleale, M. McGrath, K. Fitzgerald
(*Music by* Jimmy Van Heusen.)
"You Don't Have to Know the Language" (from *ROAD TO RIO* film)
L. Cleale, M. McGrath, K. Fitzgerald, L. Hart, T. Burrell
(*Music by* Jimmy Van Heusen.)
"Going My Way" (from *GOING MY WAY* film)
L. Cleale
(*Music by* Jimmy Van Heusen.)
"Shadows on the Swanee"
A. Guess, L. Cleale, M. McGrath
(*Music by* Harold Spina. *Lyrics by* Joe Young, Johnny Burke.)
"Rhythm on the River" (from *RHYTHM ON THE RIVER* film)
All
(*Music by* James Monaco.)
"Road to Morocco" (from *ROAD TO MOROCCO* film)
L. Cleale, M. McGrath, K. Fitzgerald
(*Music by* Jimmy Van Heusen.)
Assistant Director: E. Fleming. *Bing*: L. Cleale. *Bob*: M. McGrath. *Dorothy*: K. Fitzgerald. *Girls*: L. Hart, T. Burrell. *Southern Woman*: A. Guess.

Scene 3
"But, Beautiful" (from *ROAD TO RIO* film)
T. Burrell
(*Music by* Jimmy Van Heusen.)
"Moonlight Becomes You" (from *ROAD TO MOROCCO* film)
L. Cleale
(*Music by* Jimmy Van Heusen.)
"Sunday, Monday or Always" (from *DIXIE* film)
A. Guess
(*Music by* Jimmy Van Heusen.)
"Misty"
E. Fleming
(*Music by* Erroll Garner.)
"Here's That Rainy Day" (from *CARNIVAL IN FLANDERS*)
K. Fitzgerald
(*Music by* Jimmy Van Heusen.)
"Pennies from Heaven" (reprise)
All
"Swinging on a Star" (reprise)
All
The Lovers: L. Hart and L. Cleale, A. Guess and M. McGrath, T. Burrell and E. Fleming, K. Fitzgerald.

1995.15 VICTOR/VICTORIA

A Musical Comedy in Two Acts, 16 Scenes. Book by Blake Edwards. (Based on the musical film of the same name, screenplay by Blake Edwards, which was based on the German Ufa film "Viktor und Viktoria" conceived by Hans Hoemburg and written by Rheinhold Schuenzer.) Music by Henry Mancini. Lyrics by Leslie Bricusse. Directed by Blake Edwards. Choreographed by Rob Marshall. Additional musical material by Frank Wildhorn. Scenic design by Robin Wagner. Costume design by Willa Kim. Lighting design by Jules Fisher and Peggy Eisenhauer. Sound design by Peter Fitzgerald. Orchestrations by Billy Byers. Dance and incidental music by David Krane. Fight staging by B. H. Barry. Music direction and vocal arrangements by Ian Fraser. Assistant director, Kirsten Sanderson. Assistant choreographers, Cynthia Onrubia and Sarah Miles. Executive producers, Edwards-Adams Theatrical Inc., Metropolitan Theatrical Entertainment Inc. Co-producers, Robin De Levita, Jeff Rowland. Associate producers, Joop Van Den Ende, Tina Vanderheyden, TDI, Ogden Entertainment. Produced by Blake Edwards, Tony Adams, John Scher, Endemol Theater Productions, Inc., Polygram Broadway Ventures, Inc. Opened 25 October 1995 at the Marquis Theatre and closed 27 July 1997 after 738 performances[7].

CAST (in order of appearance): *Carroll Todd* (Toddy): TONY ROBERTS. *Les Boys*: Michael Demby-Cain, Angelo Fraboni, Darren Lee, Michael O'Donnell, Vince Pesce, Arte Phillips, Rocker Verastique. *Richard Di Nardo*: MICHAEL CRIPE. *Henri Labisse*: ADAM HELLER. *Gregor*: Casey Nicholaw. *Madame Roget*: Jennifer Smith. *Victoria Grant* (Victor): JULIE ANDREWS. *Choreographer*: Christopher Innvar. *Miss Selmer*: Cynthia Sophiea. *André Cassell*: RICHARD B. SHULL. *Jazz Singer*: Devin Richards. *Jazz Hot Musicians*: Michael Demby-Cain, Arte Phillips, Rocker Verastique. *Jazz Hot Ensemble*: Roxane Barlow, Caitlin Carter, Pascale Faye, Angelo Fraboni, Amy Heggins, Darren Lee, Aixa M. Rosario Medina, Casey Nicholaw, Michael O'Donnell, Cynthia Onrubia, Vince Pesce. *Norma Cassidy*: RACHEL YORK. *King Marchan*: MICHAEL NOURI. *Squash* (Mr. Bernstein): GREGORY JBARA. *Louis Says Ensemble*: Roxane Barlow, Michael-Demby Cain, Caitlin Carter, Pascale Faye, Angelo Fraboni, Amy Heggins, Darren Lee, Aixa M. Rosario Medina, Michael O'Donnell, Cynthia Onrubia, Vince Pesce, Arte Phillips, Devlin Richards, Jennifer Smith, Cynthia Sophiea, Rocker Verastique. *Chambermaid*: Jennifer Smith. *Apache Dancers*: Angelo Fraboni, Darren Lee, Michael O'Donnell, Vince Pesce, Arte Phillips, Rocker Verastique. *Street Singer*: Tara O'Brien. *Norma's Girls*: Roxane Barlow, Caitlin Carter, Pascale Faye, Amy Heggins, Aixa M. Rosario Medina, Cynthia Onrubia. *Sal Adretti*: Ken Land. *Clam*: Mark Lotito. *Juke*: Casey Nicholaw.

Ensemble: Roxane Barlow, Michael-Demby Cain, Caitlin Carter, Pascale Faye, Angelo Fraboni, Amy Heggins, Darren Lee, Aixa M. Rosario Medina, Tara O'Brien, Michael O'Donnell, Cynthia Onrubia, Vince Pesce, Arte Phillips, Devlin Richards, Jennifer Smith, Rocker Verastique. *Swings*: Mark S. Hoebee, Elizabeth Mozer, Scott Taylor.

---

[7]Subsequent national tour produced by NETworks, in association with the Jeriko Touring Company. Directed by Mark Hoebee, choreographed by Dan Mojica.

Act 1, Scene 1: Small Square/Chez Lui. *Scene 2*: Small Square/Toddy's Flat. *Scene 3*: Backstage at Cassell's. *Scene 4*: Cassell's Nightclub. *Scene 5*: Backstage at Cassell's. *Scene 6*: Left Bank Cafe. *Scene 7*: Paris Hotel Suites.

Act 2, Scene 1: Cassell's Nightclub. *Scene 2*: Victoria's Dressing Room. *Scene 3*: Paris Hotel Suites. *Scene 4*: Chez Lui. *Scene 5*: Small Square. *Scene 6*: Paris Hotel Suites. *Scene 7*: Chicago Speakeasy. *Scene 8*: Paris Hotel Suites. *Scene 9*: Cassell's Nightclub.

ACT 1
Scene 1
"Paris By Night"
T. Roberts, Les Boys
Scene 2
"If I Were a Man"[8]
J. Andrews
"Trust Me"
T. Roberts, J. Andrews
(*Music by* Frank Wildhorn.)
Scene 4
"Le Jazz Hot"
J. Andrews, Ensemble
Scene 6
"The Tango"
J. Andrews, R. York
Scene 7
"Paris Makes Me Horny"[9]
R. York
"Crazy World"[10]
J. Andrews

ACT 2
Scene 1
"Louis Says"[11]
J. Andrews, Ensemble
(*Music by* Frank Wildhorn.)
Scene 3
"King's Dilemma"
M. Nouri
Scene 4
"Apache"
Les Boys
"You & Me"
T. Roberts, J. Andrews
Scene 5
"Paris By Night" (reprise)
T. O'Brien
Scene 6
"Almost a Love Song"
M. Nouri, J. Andrews
Scene 7
"Chicago, Illinois"
R. Yorke, Girls
Scene 8
"Living in the Shadows"
J. Andrews
(*Music by* Frank Wildhorn.)
Scene 9
"Victor/Victoria"
J. Andrews, T. Roberts, Company
"Who Can I Tell?"
Liza Minnelli (Victoria Grant)
(*Music and Lyrics by* Leslie Bricusse.)

[8]Dropped during the run.
[9]Dropped for subsequent national tour.
[10]Replaced in January 1997 by:
"Who Can I Tell?"
Liza Minnelli (Victoria Grant)
(*Music and Lyrics by* Leslie Bricusse.)
[11]"Louis Says" and the entire Act 2, Scene 1 dropped during the run.

1995.16 FOOL MOON

A Revival of the Comedy Performance Revue in Two Acts[12]. Created by Bill Irwin and David Shiner. (Original music and lyrics by the Red Clay Ramblers.) Set design by Douglas Stein. Costume design by Bill Kellard. Lighting design by Nancy Schertler. Sound design by Tom Morse. Flying by Foy. Producing associate, Nancy Harrington. Associate producer, Daniel F. Kearns. Produced by James B. Freydberg, Kenneth Feld, Jeffrey Ash, Dori Berinstein. Opened 29 October 1995 at the Ambassador Theatre and closed 7 January 1996 after 81 performances.

CAST (in order of appearance): DAVID SHINER, BILL IRWIN.
THE RED CLAY RAMBLERS: Clay Buckner (fiddle), Chris Frank (piano, accordion, trombone, ukelele), Jack Herrick (bass, trumpet, mellophone, banjolin, tin whistle), Mark Roberts (banjo, flute, oboe, tin whistle, keyboard), Rob Ladd (drums, ukelele).

ACT 1[13]
Opening
D. Shiner, B. Irwin, Red Clay Ramblers, 2 Ushers
"Fire and Sugar" (traditional)
Red Clay Ramblers
Encounter
D. Shiner, B. Irwin
"Wa-Hoo"[14]
Red Clay Ramblers
Dance Solo
D. Shiner
Dance to the Left
B. Irwin, Stage Manager
Big Night Out
D. Shiner, B. Irwin, an Audience Member

ACT 2
"Pal-Yat-Chee"[15]
Red Clay Ramblers
Improvisation in Public
D. Shiner, an Audience Memeber
Harlequin/Pantalone
B. Irwin, Red Clay Ramblers, D. Shiner
"Hiawatha's Lullaby"
Red Clay Ramblers
(*Music by* Walter Donaldson. *Lyrics by* Joe Young.)
"Tea for Two" (from *NO, NO NANETTE*)
D. Shiner, B. Irwin
(*Music by* Vincent Youmans. *Lyrics by* Irving Caesar.)
Conductor
B. Irwin, Red Clay Ramblers
Cinema
D. Shiner, 4 Audience Members
"Valley of the Dry Bones" (traditional; a capella)
Red Clay Ramblers, D. Shiner, B. Irwin
"Melancholy Moon Song"[16]
Red Clay Ramblers, B. Irwin, D. Shiner
"Fire and Sugar" (reprise)
B. Irwin, D. Shiner, Red Clay Ramblers

1995.17 THE MANY VOICES OF DANNY GANS

A One Man Revue in One Act. Production supervisor, Chip Lightman. Lighting, John Featehrstone, Fred Irish, Norm Schwab. Sound, On Stage Audio. Produced by the Nederlander Organization. Opened 8 November 1995 at the Neil Simon Theatre and closed 12 November 1995 after 6 performances.

[12]Originally produced in New York 25 February 1993 at the Richard Rodgers Theatre for 207 performances.
[13]Scenes and Musical Numbers not identified in programs; list prepared from producers' materials.
[14]Not in previous 1992 production.
[15]Not in previous 1992 production.
[16]Not in previous 1992 production.

CAST: DANNY GANS (impressionist). *The Band*: Pat Caddick (keyboards, vocals), Rapahel Erardy (drums, vocals); Tim Manfredi (keyboards, guitar, vocals).

1995.18 CINDERELLA

A Revival of the Musical in Two Acts, a Prologue and 10 Scenes[17]. Book and lyrics (for television) by Oscar Hammerstein II. Book adapted (for the stage) by Steve Allen, Robert Johanson. Music by Richard Rodgers. Directed and choreographed by Robert Johanson. Co-choreographer, Sharon Halley. Scenery by Henry Bardon. Costumes by Gregg Barnes. Lighting by Jeff Davis. Sound by Abe Jacob. Conductor, Rob Fisher. Orchestrations by Robert Russell Bennett. Chorus master, Joseph Colaneri. Produced by the New York City Opera. Opened 9 November 1995 at the New York State Theatre and closed 19 November 1995 after 12 performances.

CAST (in order of appearance): *Fairy Godmother*: SALLY ANN HOWES. *Royal Herald*: Stephen Howell. *Little Girl*: Elizabeth Dietrich. *Cinderella's Stepmother*: JEAN STAPLETON. *Cinderella's Stepsisters (2)*: *Joy*: ALIX KOREY. *Portia*: JEANETTE PALMER. *Cinderella*: REBECCA BAXTER. *Dog*: Andrew Pacho. *Cat*: Debbi Fuhrman. *Queen*: JANE POWELL. *King*: GEORGE S. IRVING. *Royal Chef*: Joel Sorenson. *Royal Steward*: John Lankston. *Prince*: GEORGE DVORSKY. *Youngest Fairy*: Stephanie Godino. *Tiara Fairy*: Irina Dvorovenko. *Ensemble*: New York City Opera Chorus.

1995.19 A CHRISTMAS CAROL

A Revival of the Musical in One Act, 13 Scenes[18]. Book by Mike Ockrent and Lynn Ahrens. Based on the novel of the same name by Charles Dickens. Music by Alan Menken. Lyrics by Lynn Ahrens. Directed by Mike Ockrent. Choreographed by Susan Stroman. Setting design by Tony Walton. Costume design by William Ivey Long. Lighting design by Jules Fisher and Peggy Eisenhauer. Sound design by Tony Meola. Projections by Wendall K. Harrington. Flying by Foy. Production supervisor, Gene O'Donovan. Associate director, Steven Zweigbaum. Associate choreographer, Chris Peterson. Musical direction by Paul Gemignani. Orchestrations by Michael Starobin and Douglas Besterman. Dance arrangements and incidental music by Glen Kelly. Executive producer, Dodger Productions. Producer, Tim Hawkins. Presented by Madison Square Garden. Opened 30 November 1995 at the Paramount, Madison Square Garden and closed 31 December 1995 after 70 performances[19].

CAST (in order of appearance): *Beadle*: David Lowenstein. *Mr. Smythe*: JAMES JUDY. *Grace Smythe*: Cara Horner, Joanna Howard. *Scrooge*: TERRENCE MANN. *Crachit*: NICK CORLEY. *Charity Men*: Robert Ousley, Wayne W. Pretlow, Walter Willison. *Old Joe*: Ken McMullen. *Street Urchins and Children*: Matthew Ballinger, Zachary Petkanas, Paul Franklin Dano, Christopher Mark Petrizzo, Olivia Oguma, Diana Mary Rice. *Mrs. Crachit*: Robin Baxter. *Tiny Tim*: Zachary London, Chris Marquette. *Poulterer*: Walter Willison. *Sandwichboard Man*: BEN VEREEN. *Fred*: STEVE BLANCHARD. *Jonathon*: Jason Fuchs, Evan J. Newman. *Lamplighter*: KEN JENNINGS. *Blind Hag*: Nicole Arrington. *Mrs. Mops*: Karen Murphy. *Ghost of Jacob Marley*: PAUL KANDEL. *Ghost of Christmas Past*: KEN JENNINGS. *Lights of Christmas Past*: Matthew Baker, Sean Thomas Morrissey, Rommy Sandhu, Tom Pardoe. *Judge*: Michael H. Ingram. *Scrooge at 8 years*: Matthew Ballinger, Zachary Petkanas. *Fan at 6*: Diana Mary Rice, Olivia Oguma. *Scrooge's Mother*: Barbara Marineau. *Scrooge's Father*: Michael X. Martin. *Mr. Hawkins*: Kenneth McMullen. *Scrooge at 12 years*: Paul Franklin Dano, Christopher Mark Petrizzo. *Fan at 10 years*: Eliza Atkins Clark, Nathalie Paulding. *Fezziwig*: Michael Cone. *Scrooge at 18 years*: Tom Stuart. *Young Marley*: Ken Barnett. *Mrs. Fezziwig*: Joy Hermalyn. *Emily*: Emily Skinner. *Ghost of Christmas Present*: BEN VEREEN. *The Crachit Children*: Eliza Atkins Clark, Nathalie Paulding, Anthony Roth Costanzo, Bobby Steggert, Sean Thomas Morrissey. *Sally*, Fred's wife: Stephanie Bast. *Ignorance*: Matthew Ballinger, Zachary Petkanas. *Undertakers*: Michael X. Martin, Ken Barnett. *Ghost of Christmas Future*: Theara J. Ward.

Business Men, Gifts, Ghosts and the People of London: Farah Alvin, Nicole Arrington, Matthew Baker, Ken Barnett, Stephanie Bast, Robin Baxter, Amy B. Blake, Steve Blanchard, Brad Bradley, Michael Cone, Candy Cook, Donna Dunmire, Peter Gregus, Jeffrey Hankinson, Melissa Haizlip, Joy Hermalyn, Michael H. Ingram, James Judy, David Lowenstein, Barbara Marineau, Michael X. Martin, Dana Lynn Mauro, Carol Lee Meadows, Sean Thomas Morrissey, Kenneth McMullen, Karen Murphy, Robert Ousley, Tom Pardoe, Gail Pennington, Angela Piccinni, Wayne W. Pretlow, Josef Reiter, Eric Riley, Pamela Remler, Sam Reni, Rommy Sandhu, Emily Skinner, Erin Stoddard, Tom Stuart, Tracy Terstreip, Theara J. Ward, Walter Willison. *Swings*: Rachel Black, Jillian Bowen, Rob Donohoe, Mathis M. Fender, Nicholas Gould, Jack Ingram, Dana Leigh Jackson, Don Johanson, Nicole Napolitano, Christian Stuck, Cynthia Thole, Matthew J. Vargo, Jeff Williams. *Angels*: P.S. 26 Chorus, Bronx; William Alexander Middle School 51, Brooklyn; Roy H. Mann Concert Choir, Brooklyn; Park Middle School Chorus, Scotch Plains, New Jersey. *The Red Children's Cast*: Matthew Ballinger, Jason Fuchs, Joanna Fuchs, Joanna Howard, Chris Marquette, Nathalie Paulding, Christopher Mark Perizzo, Diana Mary Rice, Bobby Steggert. *The Green Children's Cast*: Eliza Atkins Clark, Anthony Roth Constanzo, Paul Franklin Dano, Cara Horner, Zach London, Evan J. Newman, Olivia Oguma, Zachary Petkanas.

1996.01 RIVERDANCE

A Dance Revue in Two Acts. Music by Bill Whelan. Poetry by Theo Dorgan. Directed by John McColgan. Choreography by Michael Flatley, Jean Butler, Colin Dunne, Tara Little, Moscow Folk Ballet Company, Maria Pages, Tarik Winston. Scenery and painted projections by Robert Ballagh. Costumes by Jen Kelly. Lighting by Rupert Murray. Sound by Michael O'Gorman. Orchestrations by Nick Ingman, Bill Whelan. Projections by Chris Slinsgby. Produced by Moya Doherty. Opened 13 March 1996 at the Radio City Music Hall and closed 17 March 1996 after 8 performances.[20]

CAST: *Narrator*: JOHN KAVANAGH. *Solo Dancers*: JEAN BUTLER, COLIN DUNNE, MARIA PAGES, TARIK WINSTON, DANIEL WOOTEN. *Solo Singer*: IVAN THOMAS. Company of 30.

1996.02 THE MERRY WIDOW

A Revival of the Operetta in Three Acts, 4 Scenes[21]. Music by Franz Lehár. Original German book and lyrics by Victor Léon and Leo Stein (after "L'Attaché d'Ambassade.") (New) English book adaptation by Robert Johanson. (New) English lyrics by Albert Evans. Production director, Robert Johanson. Choreographer, Sharon Halley. Set design by Michael Anania. Costume design by Gregg Barnes. Lighting design by Mark W. Stanley. Sound design by Abe Jacob. Chorus master, Joseph Colaneri. Conductor, Alexander Sander. Produced by the New York City Opera. Opened 23 March 1996 at the New York State Theatre and closed 19 April 1996 after 6 performances in repertory.

CAST (in order of appearance): *Baron Mirko Zeta*, Marsovian Ambassador to Paris: GEORGE S. IRVING. *Valencienne*, his wife: Patricia Johnson. *Kromov*, Masovian General: Joseph McKee. *Olga*, wife of Kromov: Beth McVey. *Bogdanovich*, Marsovian Consul: JOHN LANKSTON. *Sylviane*, wife of Bogdanovich: Suzanne Ishee. *Njegus*, aide to Baron Zeta: ROBERT CREIGHTON. *Camille de Rosillon*, Valencienne's admirer, a Parisian: CARLO SCIBELLI. *Vicomte Cascada*, an eligible Parisian: MATTHEW CHELLIS. *Raoul de St. Brioche*, another eligible Parisian: SHON SIMS. *Hanna*, the widow Glawari: JANE THORNGREN. *Count Danilo*, nephew of the King of Marsovia: MICHAEL HAYES. *Lolo*: Jean Barber. *Dodo*: Stephanie Godino. *Jou-Jou*: Julie Stahl. *Frou-Frou*: Kathy Meyer. *Clo-Clo*: Debbi Fuhrman. *Margot*: Joan Mirabella. *Young Hanna*: Julie Stahl. *Young Danilo*: Marty McDonough. *Chorus of Marsovian and Parisian Society, Dancers, Servants and Waiters*: New York City Opera Chorus.

---

[17]Originally produced in New York 9 November 1993 at the New York State Theatre for 14 performances. For Synopsis of Scenes and Musical Numbers, see original 1993 production.

[18]Originally produced in New York 1 December 1994 at the Paramount, Madison Square Garden for 71 performances. For Synopsis of Scenes and Musical Numbers, see original 1994 production.

[19]The production played an irregular schedule of multiple daily performances. For this revival the following changes were made:
Scene 1 and "The Years Are Passing By" were dropped.
Added to Scene 2 (former Scene 3) before "Street Song":
"You Mean More to Me"
N. Corley, Z. London or C. Marquette
"The Years Are Passing By" (reprise) in former Scene 13 (new Scene 12) was replaced by:
"London Town Carol"
J. Fuchs or E. J. Newman

[20]For Synopsis of Scenes and Musical Numbers, see return engagement 2 October 1996.

[21]Originally produced in New York 21 October 1907 at the New Amsterdam Theatre for 416 performances.

1996.03 LOVE THY NEIGHBOR

A One Man Comedy Revue in Two Acts[22]. Written and created by Jackie Mason. Production design and lighting by Neil Peter Jampolis. Sound design by Charles McIntyre. Executive producer, Jyll Rosenfeld. Produced by Abe Hirschfeld. Opened 24 March 1996 at the Booth Theatre and closed 5 January 1997 after 236 performances.

CAST: JACKIE MASON (stand-up comedy, monologues, impressions).

1996.04 STATE FAIR

A Musical in Two Acts, 18 Scenes. Book by Tom Briggs and Louis Mattioli, based on the screenplay for the film "State Fair" by Oscar Hammerstein II and the novel of the same name by Philip Stong. Music by Richard Rodgers. Lyrics by Oscar Hammerstein II. Co-directed by James Hammerstein and Randy Skinner. Choreography by Randy Skinner. Scenic design by James Leonard Joy. Costume design by Michael Bottari and Ronald Case. Lighting design by Natasha Katz. Sound design by Brian Ronan. Musical direction and vocal arrangements by Kay Cameron. Orchestrations by Bruce Pomohac. Dance arrangements by Scot Woolley. Produced by David Merrick, the Theatre Guild, Philip Langner, Robert Franz, Natalie Lloyd, Jonathan C. Herzog, Meredith Blair, Gordon Smith. Executive producer, Thomas Viertel. Associate producers, Mark N. Sirangello and the PGI Entertainment Company. Pre-Broadway National Tour (also) produced by Sonny Everett, Bonnie Nelson Schwartz, Matt Garfield, Ron Kumin; Associate producers, David Young and Norma Langworthy, by arrangement with Celia Lipton Productions, Inc, in association with the North Carolina School of the Arts Foundation. Opened 27 March 1996 at the Music Box Theatre and closed 30 June 1996 after 118 performances.

CAST (in order of appearance): *Abel Frake*: JOHN DAVIDSON. *Gus*, the Frake's hired man: James Patterson. *Melissa Frake*, Abel's wife: KATHRYN CROSBY. *Wayne Frake*, their son: BEN WRIGHT. *Dave Miller*, the local storekeeper: Charles Goff. *Eleanor*, Wayne's girlfriend: Susan Haefner. *Margy Frake*, Wayne's sister: ANDREA MCARDLE. *Harry*, Margy's boyfriend: Peter Benson. *Uncle Sam*: Michael Lee Scott. *Fair Announcer*: J. Lee Flynn. *Midway Cow*: Kelli Barclay. *Midway Pig*: Jackie Angelescu. *The Houp-La Barker*: Tim Fauvell. *Emily Arden*: DONNA MCKECHNIE. *The Astounding Stralenko*: Steve Steiner. *Vivian*, a cooch dancer: Tina Johnson. *Jeanne*, a cooch dancer: Leslie Bell. *Mrs. Edwin Metcalf* of Pottsville: Jacquiline Rohrbacker. *Pat Gilbert*, a newspaper reporter: SCOTT WISE. *Charlie*, a newspaper photographer: Darrian C. Ford. *Lem*, a farmer: John Wilkerson. *Clay*, a farmer: J. Lee Flynn. *Hank Munson*, a farmer: Newton R. Gilchrist. *The Chief of Police*: Steve Steiner. *Violet*, his daughter: Jackie Angelescu. *The Fairtones*: Ian Knauer, James Patterson, Michael Lee Scott, Scott Willis. *Judge Heppenstahl*: Charles Goff.

Barkers, Vendors, Judges, Fairgoers: Kelli Barclay, Leslie Bell, Linnea Dakin, Suellen Estey, Tim Fauvell, Amy Gage, Susan Haefner, Tina Johnson, Ian Knauer, James Patterson, Michael Lee Scott, Mary C Sheehan, Steve Steiner, Scott Willis. *Roustabouts*: Michael Lee Scott, Scott Willis. *Swings*: Julie Lira, John Scott.

The action takes place over five days in late August of 1946 on the Frake Farm in Brunswick, Iowa and at the State Fair in Des Moines.

Act 1, Scene 1: The Frake Farm, a Tuesday afternoon in late August. *Scene 2*: On the Road to Des Moines. Wednesday morning before dawn. *Scene 3*: The Midway at the Hoop-La Booth. Later that morning. *Scene 4*: The Midway at the Temple of Wonder. Later that morning. *Scene 5*: The Beer Tent. That afternoon. *Scene 6*: Outside the Dairy Pavilion. Later that afternoon. *Scene 7*: The Starlight Dance Meadow. That evening. *Scene 8*: Camper's Hill. Thursday morning. *Scene 9*: Exhibition Hall. That afternoon. *Scene 10*: A Nearby Hillside. Early that night. *Scene 11*: The Starlight Dance Meadow. Later that night.

Act 2, Scene 1: Outside the Livestock Pavilion. Friday afternoon. *Scene 2*: Outside the Dairy Pavilion. Early that night. *Scene 3*: The Starlight Dance Meadow. Immediately following. *Scene 4*: The Hillside. Later that night. *Scene 5*: Camper's Hill. Later that night. *Scene 6*: On the Midway. Immediately following. *Scene 7*: The Frake Farm. Saturday night after supper.

ACT 1
Scene 1
Opening ("Our State Fair")[23]
J. Davidson, K. Crosby, B. Wright
"It Might As Well Be Spring"[24]
A. McArdle
Scene 2
"Driving at Night"
J. Davidson, K. Crosby, B. Wright, A. McArdle
Scene 3
"Our State Fair" (reprise)
Ensemble
Scene 4
"That's For Me"[25]
B. Wright
Scene 5
"More Than Just a Friend"[26] (Sweet Hog of Mine)
J. Davidson, N. R. Gilchrist, J. Sloman, J. L. Flynn
(*Lyrics by* Richard Rodgers.)
Scene 6
"Isn't It Kinda Fun?"[27]
S. Wise, A. McArdle
Scene 7
"You Never Had It So Good"
D. McKechnie, the Fairtones
Scene 8
"It Might As Well Be Spring" (reprise)
A. McArdle
"When I Go Out Walking With My Baby"
J. Davidson, K. Crosby
Scene 10
"So Far" (from *ALLEGRO*)
B. Wright, D. McKechnie
Scene 11
"It's a Grand Night for Singing"[28]
Company

ACT 2
Scene 1
"The Man I Used To Be" (from *PIPE DREAM*)
S. Wise, T. Johnson, L. Bell
"All I Owe Ioway"[29]
J. Davidson, Company
Scene 2
"The Man I Used To Be" (reprise)
S. Wise
"Isn't It Kinda Fun?" (reprise)
A. McArdle
Scene 3
"That's the Way It Happens" (from *ME & JULIET*)
D. McKechnie, the Fairtones
Scene 5
"Boys and Girls Like You and Me"
J. Davidson, K. Crosby
Scene 6
"The Next Time It Happens" (from *PIPE DREAM*)
A. McArdle

---

[22]Previous editions of Jackie Mason's one man show have been presented as THE WORLD ACCORDING TO ME 22 December 1986 at the Brooks Atkinson Theatre for 367 performances; returned 3 May 1988 at the Brooks Atkinson for 203 performances; JACKIE MASON: BRAND NEW 17 October 1990 at the Neil Simon Theatre for 216 performances; JACKIE MASON: POLITICALLY INCORRECT, 5 April 1994 at the John Golden Theatre for 347 performances.

[23]Songs included in the original 1945 film.
[24]Songs included in the original 1945 film.
[25]Songs included in the original 1945 film.
[26]Written for the 1962 film.
[27]Songs included in the original 1945 film.
[28]Songs included in the original 1945 film.
[29]Songs included in the original 1945 film.

1996.05 THE KING AND I

A Revival of the Musical Play in Two Acts[30]. Book and lyrics by Oscar Hammerstein II. Music by Richard Rodgers. Based on the novel "Anna and the King of Siam" by Margaret Landon. Musical staging by Lar Lubovitch. (Original) Choreography by Jerome Robbins, supervised by Susan Kikuchi. Directed by Christopher Renshaw. Scenic design by Brian Thomson. Costume design by Roger Kirk. Lighting design by Nigel Levings. Orchestrations by Robert Russell Bennett. Additional orchestrations by Bruce Coughlin. Musical director, Michael Rafter. Musical supervisor, Eric Stern. Sound by Tony Meola and Lewis Mead. Produced by Dodger Productions, The John F. Kennedy Center, James M. Nederlander, Perseus Productions with John Frost and the Adelaide Festival Centre in association with The Rodgers and Hammerstein Organization. Opened 11 April 1996 at the Neil Simon Theatre and closed 22 February 1998 after 781 performances[31].

CAST (in order of appearance): *Captain Orton*: John Curless. *Louis Leonowens*: Ryan Hopkins. *Anna Leonowens*: DONNA MURPHY. *The Interpreter*: Alan Muraoka. *The Kralahome*: RANDALL DUK KIM. *The King of Siam*: LOU DIAMOND PHILLIPS. *Lun Tha*: JOSE LLANA. *Tuptim*: JOOHEE CHOI. *Lady Thiang*: TAEWON KIM. *Prince Chulalongkorn*: John Chang. *Princess Yaowlak*: Lexine Bondoc. *Sir Edward Ramsay*: Guy Paul.

Royal Wives, Slaves, Courtiers, Guards, Monks, English Guests, Market People: Tito Abeleda, John Bantay, Camille M. Brown, Benjamin Bryant, Meng-Chen Chang, Kam Cheng, Vivien Eng, Lydia Gaston, Margaret Ann Gates, C. Sean Kim, Shawn Ku, Doan Mackenzie, Paolo Montalban, Alan Muraoka, Paul Nakauchi, Tina Ou, Andrew Pacho, Mami Saito, Lainie Sakakura, Carol To, Yolanda Tolentino, Tran T. Thuc Hanh, Yan Ying, Kayoko Yoshioka, Greg Zane. *The Royal Children*: Kelly Jordan Bit, Lexine Bondoc, Kailip Boonrai, Jacqueline Te Lem, Erik Lin-Greenberg, Kenji Miyata, Brandon Marshall Ngai, Amy Y. Tai, Jenna Noelle Ushkowitz, Shelby Rebecca Wong, Jeff G. Yalun.

The Small House of Uncle Thomas (ballet): *Eliza*: Yan Ying. *Simon of Legree*: Tito Abeleda. *Angel George*: Meng-Chen Chang. *Little Eva*: Tran T. Thuc Hanh. *Topsy*: Tina Ou. *Uncle Thomas*: Mami Saito. *Dogs*: John Bantay, Doan Mackenzie, Greg Zane. *Guards*: Andrew Pacho, C. Sean Kim, Shawn Ku. *Propmen*: Benjamin Bryant, Paolo Montalban, Alan Muraoka, Paul Nakauchi. *Archers*: Camille M. Brown, Vivien Eng, Lainie Sakakura, Kayoko Yoshioka. *Singers*: Kam Cheng, Margaret Ann Gates, Carol To, Yolanda Tolentino.

1996.06 A FUNNY THING HAPPENED ON THE WAY TO THE FORUM

A Revival of the Musical Comedy in Two Acts[32]. Book by Burt Shevelove and Larry Gelbart. Based on the plays ("The Haunted House," "Mostellaria", etc.) of Plautus. Music and lyrics by Stephen Sondheim. Directed by Jerry Zaks. Choreographed by Rob Marshall. Set and costume design by Tony Walton. Lighting by Paul Gallo. Sound by Tony Meola. Musical director, Eddie Strauss. Orchestrations by Jonathan Tunick. Dance music arrangements by David Chase. Associate producer, Marc Routh. Produced by Jujamcyn Theatres, Scott Rudin/Paramount Pictures, The Viertel-Baruch-Frankel Group (Tom Viertel-Steven Baruch-Richard Frankel), Roger Berlind, Dodger Productions. Opened 18 April 1996 at the St. James Theatre and closed 4 January 1998 after 715 performances.

CAST (in order of appearance): *Prologus*, an actor: NATHAN LANE. *The Proteans*: Brad Aspel, Cory English, Ray Roderick. *Hero*, son of Senex and Domina: JIM STANEK. *Philia*, a virgin: JESSICA BOEVERS. *Senex*, a citizen of Rome: LEWIS J. STADLEN. *Domina*, his wife: MARY TESTA. *Hysterium*, slave to Senex and Domina: MARK LINN-BAKER. *Lycus*, a buyer and seller of courtesans: ERNIE SABELLA. *Pseudolus*, slave to hero: NATHAN LANE. *Tintinabula*, a courtesan: Pamela Everett. *Panacea*, a courtesan: Leigh Zimmerman. *The Geminae*, courtesans: Susan Misner, Lori Werner. *Vibrata*, a courtesan: Mary Ann Lamb. *Gymnasia*, a courtesan: Stephanie Pope. *Erronius*, an citizen of Rome: WILLIAM DUELL. *Miles Gloriosus*, a warrior: CRIS GROENENDAAL.

1996.07 BRING IN 'DA NOISE, BRING IN 'DA FUNK

A Rap/Tap Discourse on the Staying Power of the Beat (Musical Revue), in Two Acts, 6 Scenes[33]. Choreographer, Savion Glover. Based on an idea by Savion Glover and George C. Wolfe. Book by Reg E. Gaines. Music by Daryl Waters, Zane Mark and Ann Duquesnay. Conceived and directed by George C. Wolfe. Scenic design by Riccardo Hernandez. Costume design by Paul Tazewell. Lighting design by Jules Fisher, Peggy Eisenhauer. Sound design by Dan Moses Schreier. Projection design by Batwin + Robin Productions, Inc. Music supervision and orchestrations by Daryl Waters. Music direction by Zane Mark. Vocal arrangements by Ann Duquesnay. Dramaturg, Shelby Jiggetts. Produced by the Joseph Papp Public Theater/New York Shakespeare Festival (George C. Wolfe, Producer; Rosemarie Tichler, Artistic producer; Laurie Beckelman, Exectutive director; Joey Parner, Executive producer), by special arrangement with The Shubert Organization. Associate producer, Wiley Hausam. Opened 24 April 1996 at the Ambassador Theatre and closed 10 January 1999 after 1123 performances.

CAST (in order of appearance): SAVION GLOVER, BAAKARI WILDER, JIMMY TATE, VINCENT BINGHAM, JEFFREY WRIGHT, ANN DUQUESNAY, JARED CRAWFORD, RAYMOND KING, DULÉ HILL.

Act 1, Scene 1: In 'Da Beginning. *Scene 2*: Som'thin from Nuthin'. *Scene 3*: Urbanization.

Act 2, Scene 1: Where's the Beat? *Scene 2*: Street Corner Symphony. *Scene 3*: Noise/Funk.

ACT 1

Scene 1

"Bring in 'Da Noise, Bring in 'Da Funk"
Company

"The Door to Isle Gorée"
J. Wright

"Slave Ships"
A. Duquesnay, S. Glover

Scene 2

"Som'thin from Nuthin'"/"The Circle Stomp"
B. Wilder, D. Hill, J. Tate, V. Bingham, A. Duquesnay, J. Wright

"The Pan Handlers"
J. Crawford, R. King

Scene 3

"The Lynching Blues"
B. Wilder, A. Duquesnay, Company

"Chicago Bound"
S. Glover, A. Duquesnay, Company

"Shifting Sounds"
J. Wright

"Industrialization"
S. Glover, B. Wilder, J. Tate, V. Bingham, J. Crawford, R. King

"The Chicago Riot Rag"
S. Glover, B. Wilder, J. Tate, V. Bingham, J. Crawford

"I Got the Beat"/"Dark Tower"
A. Duquesnay, J. Wright, Company

"The Whirligig Stomp"
Company

[30] Originally produced in New York 29 March 1951 at the St. James Theatre for 1246 performances. For Synopsis of Scenes and Musical Numbers, see original 1951 production.

[31] Added to this production were two new dance numbers, choreography by Lar Lubovitch, with Richard Rodgers' melodies arranged by Eric Stern:

"Royal Dance Before the King" (Act 1, before "My Lord and Master")
Company

"Procession of the White Elephant" (Act 2, after "Shall We Dance")
Company

"Western People Funny" was dropped from this production.

"The Royal Bangkok Academy" (though not in the program) was performed in a shortened form.

[32] Originally produced in New York 8 May 1962 at the Alvin Theatre for 964 performances. For Synopsis of Scenes and Musical Numbers, see original 1962 production. Dropped for this production: "Pretty Little Picture."

[33] Originally produced Off-Broadway 18 November 1995-28 January 1996 in the Newman Theatre at the Joseph Papp Public Theater/New York Shakespeare Festival for 85 performances.

ACT 2
Scene 1
Where's the Beat?:
The Voice: J. Wright. *The Chanteuse*: A. Duquesnay. *The Kid*: D. Hill. *Grin & Flash*: J. Tate, V. Bingham. *Uncle Huck-A-Buck*: B. Wilder. *Li'l Darlin'*: S. Glover.
"Now That's Tap"
J. Tate, V. Bingham
"The Uncle Huck-A-Buck Song"
B. Wilder, S. Glover, Company
"Kid Go!"
D. Hill, Company
"The Lost Beat Swing"
A. Duquesnay, Company
"Green, Chaney, Buster, Slyde"
S. Glover
Scene 2
"1956—Them Conkheads"
A. Duquesnay, Company
"1967—Hot Fun"
A. Duquesnay, J. Wright, Company
"1977—Blackout"
S. Glover, B. Wilder, J. Tate, V. Bingham
"1987—Gospel/Hip Hop Rant"
J. Wright, S. Glover, A. Duquesnay
Scene 3
"Drummin'"
J. Crawford, R. King
"Taxi"
S. Glover, J. Tate, B. Wilder, V. Bingham
"Conversations"
J. Crawford, R. King, S. Glover, J. Tate, B. Wilder, V. Bingham
"Hittin'"
S. Glover, B. Wilder, J. Tate, V. Bingham, J. Crawford, R. King, J. Wright
"Bring in 'Da Noise, Bring in 'Da Funk" (reprise)
Company

1996.08

BIG

A Musical in Two Acts, 14 Scenes. Book by John Weidman. Based on the Twentieth Century Fox film of the same name with screenplay by Gary Ross and Anne Spielberg. Music by David Shire. Lyrics by Richard Maltby, Jr. Directed by Mike Ockrent. Choreography by Susan Stroman. Scenic design by Robin Wagner. Costume design by William Ivey Long. Lighting design by Paul Gallo. Sound by Steve Canyon Kennedy. Special effects design by Gregory Meeh. Orchestrations by Douglas Besterman. Dance music arranged by David Krane. Additional vocal arrangements by Patrick Scott Brady. Magic consultant, Charles Reynolds. Electronic music designed by Brian Besterman. Musical direction by Paul Gemignani. Associate director, Steven Zweigbaum. Assistant choreographer, Ginger Thatcher. Co-produced by Pachyderm Entertainment, Fuji Television Network, Inc./Kyodo Tokyo, Inc. Associate producer, Daniel F. Kearns. Producing associate, Michelle Leslie. Produced by James B. Freydberg, Kenneth Feld, Laurence Mark and Kenneth D. Greenblatt in association with F.A.O. Schwarz, Fifth Avenue. Opened 28 April 1996 at the Sam S. Shubert Theatre and closed 13 October 1996 after 193 performances.

CAST (in order of appearance): *Cynthia Benson*: Lizzy Mack. *Young Josh*: PATRICK LEVIS. *Tiffany*: Samantha Robyn Lee. *Maggie*: Lori Aine Bennett. *Mrs. Baskin*: BARBARA WALSH. *Mr. Baskin*: John Sloman. *Mr. Kopecki*: Ray Wills. *Billy*: BRETT TABISEL. *Mrs. Kopecki*: Donna Lee Marshall. *Carnival Man*: Clent Bowers. *Derek*: Alex Sanchez. *Zoltar*: Himself. *Josh Baskin*: DANIEL JENKINS. *Panhandler*: Ray Wills. *Arcade Man*: Frank Mastrone. *Derelict*: John Sloman. *Matchless*: Frank Vlastnik. *Paul*: GENE WEYGANDT. *Susan*: CRISTA MOORE. *MacMillan*: JON CYPHER. *Starfighter*: Brandon Espinoza. *F.A.O. Sales Executive*: Joan Barber. *Birnbaum*: Frank Vlastnik. *Lipton*: Frank Mastrone. *Barrett*: Clent Bowers. *Miss Watson*: Jan Neuberger. *Deathstarettes*: Joyce Chittick, CJay Hardy. *Larry Johnson*: John Sloman. *Nick*: Ray Wills. *Tom*: John Sloman. *Diane*: Donna Lee Marshall. *Abigail*: Jill Matson. *Skatephone*: Spencer Liff. *Kid with Walkman*: Enrico Rodriguez. *Skateboard Romeo*: Graham Bowen.

Parents, Shoppers, Executives and Office Staff: Joan Barber, Clent Bowers, Joyce Chittick, CJay Hardy, Donna Lee Marshall, Frank Mastrone, Jill Matson, Jan Neuberger, Alex Sanchez, John Sloman, Frank Vlastnik, Ray Wills. *The Big Kids*: Lori Aine Bennett, Graham Bowen, Brandon Espinoza, Samantha Robyn Lee, Spencer Liff, Lizzy Mack, Enrico Rodriguez. *Swings*: Stacey Todd Holt, Joseph Medeiros, Corinne Melancon, Kari Pickler.

Act 1, Scene 1: The Neighborhood, New Jersey. *Scene 2*: The Baskin Home. *Scene 3*: Port Authority Bus Terminal. *Scene 4*: F.A.O.Schwarz. *Scene 5*: The Offices of MacMillan Toys. *Scene 6*: Josh's Loft. *Scene 7*: A New York Restaurant.

Act 2, Scene 1: The Mall. *Scene 2*: Susan's Office. *Scene 3*: The Offices of MacMillan Toys. *Scene 4*: An Eastside Apartment. *Scene 5*: The Roof Terrace. *Scene 6*: The Neighborhood. *Scene 7*: A Warehouse.

ACT 1
Scene 1
"Can't Wait"
P. Levis, B. Walsh, B. Tabisel, Kids, Parents
"Talk to Her"
B. Tabisel, P. Levis
"The Carnival"
Company
Scene 2
"This Isn't Me"
D. Jenkins
Scene 3
"I Want To Go Home"
D. Jenkins
Scene 4
"The Time of Your Life"
The Kids
"Fun"
J. Cypher, D. Jenkins, Company
Scene 5
"Dr. Deathstar"
J. Chittick, C. Hardy
"Josh's Welcome"
C. Moore, G. Weygandt, Executives
"Here We Go Again"
C. Moore
Scene 6
"Stars, Stars, Stars"
D. Jenkins, C. Moore
Scene 7
"Tavern Foxtrot"
G. Weygandt, Company
"Cross the Line"
D. Jenkins, Kids, Company

ACT 2
Scene 1
"It's Time"
B. Tabisel, Kids
"Stop, Time"
B. Walsh
"Happy Birthday, Josh"
Kids
Scene 2
"Dancing All the Time"
C. Moore
"I Want to Know"
P. Levis
Scene 3
"Coffee, Black"
D. Jenkins, J. Cypher, J. Neuberger, F. Vlastnik, C. Bowers, F. Mastrone, Executives and Staff
Scene 4
"The Real Thing"
R. Wills, J. Sloman, D. L. Marshall, J. Matson
Scene 5
"One Special Man"
C. Moore

Scene 6
"When You're Big"
D. Jenkins
"Skateboard Romance"
Kids
Scene 7
"I Want to Go Home"/"Stars, Stars, Stars" (reprise)
D. Jenkins, C. Moore

1996.09

RENT

A Musical in Two Acts[34]. Book, music and lyrics by Jonathan Larson,[35] (inspired by Giaccomo Puccini's "La Bohème," libretto by Luigi Illica and Giuseppe Giacosa, after Henri Murger's "Scènes de la Vie de Bohème.") Directed by Michael Greif. Choreography by Marlies Yearby. Set design by Paul Clay. Costume design by Angela Wendt. Lighting design by Blake Burba. Sound design by Kurt Fischer. Music supervision and additional arrangements by Tim Weil. Musical arranger, Steve Skinner. Film by Tony Gerber. Produced by Jeffrey Seller, Kevin McCollum, Allan S. Gordon and New York Theatre Workshop. Opened 29 April 1996 at the Nederlander Theatre and is still running at this time!

CAST (in order of appearance): *Roger Davis*: ADAM PASCAL. *Mark Cohen*: ANTHONY RAPP. *Tom Collins*: JESSE L. MARTIN. *Benjamin Coffin III*: TAYE DIGGS. *Joanne Jefferson*: FREDI WALKER. *Angel Schunard*: WILSON JERMAINE HEREDIA. *Mimi Marquez*: DAPHNE RUBIN-VEGA. *Maureen Johnson*: IDINA MENZEL. *Mark's Mom, Alison, others*: Kristen Lee Kelly. *Christmas caroler, Mr. Jefferson, a pastor, and others*: Byron Utley. *Mrs. Jefferson, woman with bags, and others*: Gwen Stewart. *Gordon, the man, Mr. Grey and others*: Timothy Britten Parker. *Man with squeegee, a waiter, and others*: Gilles Chiasson. *Paul, a cop, and others*: Rodney Hicks. *Alexi Darling, Roger's mom, and others*: Aiko Nakasone.

Swings: Yassmin Alers, Darius de Haas, Shelley Dickinson, David Driver, Mark Setlock, Simone.

ACT 1
"Tune Up"/"Voice Mail #1"
A. Rapp, A. Pascal, K. L. Kelly, J. L. Martin, T. Diggs
"Rent"
Company
"You Okay Honey?"
W. J. Heredia, J. L. Martin
"One Song Glory"
A. Pascal
"Light My Candle"
A. Pascal, D. Rubin-Vega
("Voice Mail #2")
(B. Utley, G. Stewart)
"Today 4 U"
W. J. Heredia
"You'll See"
T. Diggs, A. Rapp, J. L. Martin, A. Pascal, W. J. Heredia
"Tango: Maureen"
A. Rapp, F. Walker
"Life Support"
R. Hicks, T. B. Parker, Company
"Out Tonight"
D. Rubin-Vega
"Another Day"
A. Pascal, D. Rubin-Vega, Company
"Will I?"
Company
"On the Street" (X-M Bells #2/Bummer)
Company
"Santa Fe"[36]
J. L. Martin, Company
"We're Okay"
F. Walker
"I'll Cover You"
W. J. Heredia, J. L. Martin
"Christmas Bells"
Company
"Over the Moon"
I. Menzel
"La Vie Bohème"/"I Should Tell You"[37]
Company

ACT 2
"Seasons of Love"
Company
"Happy New Year"/"Voice Mail #3"
D. Rubin-Vega, A. Pascal, A. Rapp, I. Menzel, F. Walker, J. L. Martin, W. J. Heredia, K. L. Kelly, A. Nakasone, T. Diggs
"Take Me or Leave Me"
I. Menzel, F. Walker
"Without You"
A. Pascal, D. Rubin-Vega
"Voice Mail #4"
A. Nakasone
"Contact"
Company
"I'll Cover You" (reprise)
J. L. Martin, Company
"Halloween"
A. Rapp
"Goodbye, Love"
A. Rapp, D. Rubin-Vega, A. Pascal, I. Menzel, F. Walker, J. L. Martin, T. Diggs
"What You Own"
B. Utley, A. Rapp, J. L. Martin, T. Diggs, A. Pascal
"Voice Mail #5"
A. Nakasone, Mimi's Mom, B. Utley, K. L. Kelly
Finale/"Your Eyes"
A. Pascal, Company

[34]Originally produced by the New York Theatre Workshop as a work in progress 29 October-6 November 1995 and then Off-Broadway 13 February-31 March 1996 for 51 performances. Dropped from Off-Broadway production:
"Door"/"Wall"
A. Rapp, A. Pascal

[35]In late 1998, dramaturge Lynn Thomson was granted co-authorship credit by court settlement.

[36]Additional lyrics by Billy Aronson.

[37]Additional lyrics by Billy Aronson.

1996–1997 SEASON

Michael Mulheren, Henry Stram, Ted Sperling, Brian d'Arcy James, David Elder, and Martin Moran in TITANIC
Joan Marcus/Photofest

1996–1997 SEASON

1996.10 FOUR SAINTS IN THREE ACTS

A Revival of the Opera in a Prelude and Four Acts[1]. Words by Gertrude Stein. Music by Virgil Thomson. Scenario by Maurice Grosser. Production conceived, designed and directed by Robert Wilson. Conductor, Dennis Russell Davies. Costumes designed by Francesco Clemente. Lighting designed by Jennifer Tipton, Robert Wilson. Chorus master, Richard Bado. Text edited for projection by Francis Rizzo. Produced by Lincoln Center Festival 96 (John Rockwell, Director). Opened 1 August 1996 at the New York State Theatre and closed 3 August 1996 after 4 performances[2].

CAST (in order of vocal appearance): *St. Stephen*: John McVeigh. *St. Settlement*: Nicole Heaston. *St. Plan*: Eric Owens. *St. Sarah*: Jill Grove. *Commère*: MARIETTA SIMPSON. *Compère*: WILBUR PAULEY. *St. Theresa I*: ASHLEY PUTNAM. *St. Theresa II*: SUZANNA GUZMAN. *St. Ignatius*: SANFORD SYLVAN. *St. Cecilia*: Jonita Lattimore. *St. Celestine*: Beth Clayton. *St. Lawrence*: Chuck Winkler. *St. Chavez*: Gran Wilson. *St. Jan*: Brett Scharf. *St. Genevieve*: Audrey Vallance. *St. Anne*: Barbie Brandon. *St. Answers*: Mark Swindler. *St. Placide, St. Vincent, St. Eustace*: Eric Edlund. *St. Absalom, St. Phillip*: Matthew A. Kreger. *Acrobat*: John M. Phillips.

Houston Grand Opera Chorus: Barbie Brandon, Sandra Tye Campbell, Beth Clayton, Kelley Leigh Cooksey, Eric Edlund, Lisa Fjoslien, Jill Grove, Derek W. Henry, Matthew A. Kreger, Kimberly Lane, Jonita Lattimore, Kathleen M. Manley, John McVeigh, Kevin M. Moody, Eric Owens, Bret Scharf, Marc Shreiner, Susan Stone, Nark Swindler, Denise Thorson, Audrey Vallance, Nathan Wight, Chuck Winkler, James Marley Winslow.

Prelude: A choral introduction to all the Saints.

Act 1: On the steps of Avila Cathedral. "A Pageant, or Sunday School Entertainment."

Act 2: A garden party in the country near Barcelona.

Act 3: A monastery garden on the coast near Barcelona.

Act 4: The Saints in heaven.

1996.11 H.M.S. PINAFORE, or The Lass That Loved a Sailor

A Revival of the Comic Opera in Two Acts[3]. Libretto by William S. Gilbert. Music by Arthur Sullivan. Directed by James Billings. Choreographer, Jessica Redel. Conductor, John McGlinn. Set designer, Michael Anania. Costume designer, Joseph A. Citarella. Lighting designer, Jeff Davis. Chorus master, Joseph Colaneri. Produced by the New York City Opera. Opened 20 September 1996 at the New York State Theatre and closed 9 November 1996 after 9 performances in repertory.

CAST (in order of appearance): *Captain Corcoran*, Commanding the *H.M.S. Pinafore*: VICTOR BENEDETTI. *Bill Bobstay*, Boatswain's Mate: James Bobick. *Bob Becket*, Carpenter's Mate: Don Yule. *Little Buttercup*, (Mrs. Cripps), a Portsmouth Bumboat Woman: DIANA DANIELE. *Dick Deadeye*, Able Seaman: JOSEPH MCKEE. *Ralph Rackstraw*, Able Seaman: GEORGE DYER. *Josephine*, the Captain's Daughter: BARBARA SHIRVIS. *The Rt. Hon. Sir Joseph Porter, K.C.B.*, First Lord of the Admiralty: JAMES BILLINGS. *Cousin Hebe*, Sir Joseph's First Cousin: Angela Horn.

First Lord's Sisters, his Cousins, his Aunts, Sailors, Marines: New York City Opera Chorus: Marilyn Armstrong, Lee Bellaver, George Bohachevsky, Jill Bosworth, Frank Burzio, Mervin Crook, Harris Davis, Neil Eddinger, Bernadette Fiorella, Don Henderson, Bridget R. Hendrix, Ron Hilley, Gregory Hostetler, Paula Hostetter, Katherine Keyes, April Lindevald, Melissa Maravell, Andrea Miller, Madeleine Mines, Roger Ohlsen, Beth Pensiero, Louis Perry, Mary Ann Rydzeski, Daniel Shigo, Boyd Schlaefer, Phillip Sneed, Matthew Surapine, Verda Lee Tudor, Jeffrey Weber, Leslie Wilk, Deborah Williams, Edward Zimmerman. *New York City Opera Dancers*: Joan Barber, Martha Chapman-Verges, Gregorio DeSilva, Erica Fischbach, Esperanza Galan, Gary Giffune, Stephanie Godino, Randall Graham, Tyler Ingram, Susannah Israel, Candace Itow, Violetta Klimczewska, Ruth-Ellen Kroll, Terry Lacy, Fritz Masten, Joan Mirabella, John Radwick, Brandon L. Saxon, Deirdre Sheehan, Philipp Verges, Yurly Vodolaga, William Ward.

1996.12 RIVERDANCE

A Return Engagement of the Dance Revue in Two Acts, 13 Scenes[4]. Music by Bill Whelan. Poetry by Theo Dorgan. Directed by John McColgan. Choreography by Michael Flatley, Jean Butler, Colin Dunne, Tara Little, Moscow Folk Ballet Company, Paula Nic Cionnaith, Maria Pagés, Tarik Winston. Scenery and painted projections by Robert Ballagh. Costumes by Jen Kelly. Lighting by Rupert Murray. Sound by Michael O'Gorman. Orchestrations by Nick Ingman, Bill Whelan. Projection design by Chris Slinsgby. Produced by Abhann Productions Ltd. (Moya Doherty, producer). Opened 2 October 1996 at the Radio City Music Hall and closed 20 October 1996 after 21 performances.

CAST: *Narrator*: JOHN CAVANAGH. *Solo Dancers*: COLIN DUNNE, EILEEN MARTIN, MARIA PAGES. With TARIK WINSTON, EILEEN IVERS, IVAN THOMAS, DANIEL B. WOOTEN, HERBIN VAN CAYSEELE. *Solo Singers*: KATIE MCMAHON, MORGAN CROWLEY.

Irish Dance Troupe: Sarah Berry, Dearbhail Bates, Natalie Biggs, Lorna Bradley, Martin Brennan, Rachel Byrne, Yzanne Cloonan, Andrea Curley, Jo Ellen Forsyth, Fiona Gallagher, Susan Ginnety, Deirdre Goulding, Paula Goulding, Conor Hayes, Miceál Hopkins, Donnacha Howard, Kellie Hughes, Ciara Kennedy, Sinéad Lightley, Eileen Martin, Stephen McAteer, Sorcha McCaul, Kevin McCormack, Jonathan McMorrow, Aoibheann O'Brien, Niamh O'Brien, Cormac Ó Sé, Ursula Quigley, Joan Rafter, Pat Roddy, Sheila Ryan, Anthony Savage, Glenn Simpson, Claire Usher, J. R. Vancheri, Raymond Walls, Leanda Ward. *Moscow Folk Ballet*: Svetlana Kossoroukova, Ilia Stretsov, Tatiana Nedostop, Marina Taranda, Iouri Oustiougov, Serguei Iakoubov, Iouri Shishkine, Olena Krutsenko. *Riverdance Singers*: Derek Byrne, Patrick Connolly, Jennifer Curran, Tony Davoren, Maire Lang, Kay Lynch, Lorraine Nolan, Cathal Synnott (choirmaster). *Drummers*: Abraham Doron, Vinny Ozborne, Andrew Reilly, Derek Tallon.

ACT 1

Scene 1

Introduction

"Reel Around the Sun"

(*Choreographed by* Michael Flatley.)

Cornora; The Chroos Reel; Reel Around the Sun.

Scene 2

"The Heart's Cry"

Scene 3

Women of Ireland:

(*Choreographed by* Jean Butler.)

The Countess Cathleen; Women of Sidhe.

Scene 4

"Caoineadh Chú Chulainn" (Lament)

Scene 5

Thunderstorm

(*Choreographed by* Michael Flatley.)

Scene 6

"Shivna"

(*Choreographed by* Moscow Folk Ballet Company.)

Scene 7

Firedance

(*Choreographed by* Maria Pagés.)

Scene 8

Slip into Spring—The Harvest

Scene 9

Riverdance: "Cloudsong," "Dance of the Riverwoman," Earthrise, Riverdance

(*Choreographed by* Mavis Ascott; *Irish Step Dance Choreography by* Michael Flatley; *Female Solo Choreography by* Jean Butler.)

ACT 2

Scene 1

Introduction

---

[1]First produced in New York 20 February 1934 at the 44th Street Theatre for 32 performances; re-opened 2 April 1934 at the Empire Theatre for an additional 16 performances. Total: 48 performances.

[2]Performed as an opera with no intermission; no individual musical numbers listed.

[3]Originally presented in New York 15 January 1879 at the Standard Theatre for 175 performances. For Synopsis of Scenes and Musical Numbers, see original 1879 production.

[4]First produced in New York 13 March 1996 at the Radio City Music Hall for 8 performances

American Wake (Nova Scotia Set, "Lift the Wings")
(*Choreographed by* Michael Flatley, Paula Nic Cionnath.)
Scene 2
The Harbour of the New World:
"Heal Their Hearts"—Freedom
Trading Tips
(*Choreographed by* Colin Dunne, Tarik Winston.)
Morning in Macedonia (The Russian Dervish)
(*Choreographed by* Moscow Folk Ballet Company.)
Oscail an Doras (Open the Door)
Heartbeat of the World—Andalucia
(*Choreographed by* Maria Pagés, Colin Dunne.)
Scene 3
"Home and the Heartland"
(*Choreographed by* Michael Flatley, Colin Dunne, Jean Butler.)
Scene 4
Riverdance International

1996.13 BRIGADOON

A Revival of the Musical Play in Two Acts, 11 Scenes[5]. Book and lyrics by Alan Jay Lerner. Music by Frederick Loewe. Original dances by Agnes de Mille. Choreography recreation and additional choreography by Gemze de Lappe. Stage director, Christian Smith. Original set and costume designer, Desmond Heeley. Lighting designer, Duane Schuler. Conductor, John McGlinn. Orchestrations by Ted Royal. Dance arrangements by Trude Rittman. Vocal arrangements by Frederick Loewe. Sound design, Abe Jacob. Chorus master, Joseph Colaneri. Produced by the New York City Opera. Opened 13 November 1996 at the New York State Theatre and closed 24 November 1996 after 14 performances.

CAST (in order of appearance): *Tommy Albright*: BRENT BARRETT. *Jeff Douglas*: SEAN DONNELLAN. *Maggie Anderson*: LESLIE BROWNE. *Archie Beaton*: William Ledbetter. *Angus MacGuffie*: James Bobick. *Meg Brockie*: JUDY KAYE. *Stuart Dalrymple*: Joel Sorenson. *Sandy Dean*: Ron Hilley. *Harry Beaton*: ROBERT LAFOSSE *Andrew MacLaren*: Don Yule. *Fiona MacLaren*: REBECCA LUKER. *Jean MacLaren*: Elizabeth Ferrell. *Charlie Dalrymple*: GEORGE DYER. *Mr. Lundie*: George Hall. *Sword Dancers*: Philipp Verges, William Ward. *Bagpiper*: Stephen Frank. *Frank*: Jon Brent Curry. *Jane Ashton*: Stacy Lee Tilton.

Townsfolk of Brigadoon: *New York City Opera Chorus*: same as H.M.S. PINAFORE above. *New York City Opera Dancers*: same as H.M.S. PINAFORE above.

1996.14 CHICAGO

A Revival of the Musical (Vaudeville) in Two Acts[6]. Book by Fred Ebb and Bob Fosse. Based on the play of the same name by Maurine Dallas Watkins. Music by John Kander. Lyrics by Fred Ebb. Original production directed and choreographed by Bob Fosse. Directed by Walter Bobbie. Choreographed by Ann Reinking in the style of Bob Fosse. Scenic design by John Lee Beatty. Costume design by William Ivey Long. Lighting design by Ken Billington. Music director, Rob Fisher. Original orchestrations by Ralph Burns. Dance music arranged by Peter Howard. Sound design by Scott Lehrer. Script adaptation by David Thompson. Associate producer, Alecia Parker. Presesnted in association with Pace Theatrical Group. Produced by Barry and Fran Weissler in association with Kardana Productions Inc. Opened 14 November 1996 at the Richard Rodgers Theatre, moved 12 February 1997 to the Sam S. Shubert Theatre and is still running at this time!

CAST (in order of appearance): *Velma Kelly*: BEBE NEUWIRTH. *Roxie Hart*: ANN REINKING. *Fred Casely*: Michael Berresse. *Sergeant Fogarty*: Michael Kubala. *Amos Hart*: JOEL GREY. *Liz*: Denise Faye. *Annie*: Mamie Duncan-Gibbs. *June*: Mary Ann Lamb. *Hunyak*: Tina Paul. *Mona*: Caitlin Carter. *Matron "Mama" Morton*: MARCIA LEWIS. *Billy Flynn*: JAMES NAUGHTON. *Mary Sunshine*: D. SABELLA. *Go-to-Hell Kitty*: Leigh Zimmerman. *Harry*: Rocker Verastique. *Aaron*: David Warren-Gibson. *The Judge*: Jim Bortselmann. *Martin Harrison*: Bruce Anthony Davis. *Court Clerk*: John Mineo.

1996.15 A CHRISTMAS CAROL

A Revival of the Musical in One Act, 13 Scenes[7]. Book by Mike Ockrent and Lynn Ahrens. Based on the novel of the same name by Charles Dickens. Music by Alan Menken. Lyrics by Lynn Ahrens. Directed by Mike Ockrent. Choreographed by Susan Stroman. Setting design by Tony Walton. Costume design by William Ivey Long. Lighting design by Jules Fisher and Peggy Eisenhauer. Sound design by Tony Meola. Projections by Wendall K. Harrington. Flying by Foy. Associate director, Steven Zweigbaum. Associate choreographer, Chris Peterson. Musical direction by Paul Gemignani. Orchestrations by Michael Starobin and Douglas Besterman. Dance arrangements and incidental music by Glen Kelly. Executive producer, Dodger Productions. Producer, Tim Hawkins. Presented by Madison Square Garden. Opened 26 November 1996 at the (Paramount) Theatre, Madison Square Garden and closed 5 January 1997 after 90 performances.

CAST (in order of appearance): *Beadle*: David Lowenstein. *Mr. Smythe*: JAMES JUDY. *Grace Smythe*: Jennifer Blain, Cara Horner. *Scrooge*: TONY RANDALL. *Crachit*: NICK CORLEY. *Charity Men*: Michael H. Ingram, Keith Byron Kirk, Seth Malkin. *Old Joe*: Don Mayo. *Street Urchins*: Matthew Hoffman, Christopher Mark Petrizzo, Zachary Stefan Petkanas, Gemini Quintos, Diana Mary Rice, Evan Silverberg. *Mrs. Crachit*: Robin Baxter. *Tiny Tim*: Matthew Ballinger, Pierce Cravens. *Poulterer*: Michael H. Ingram. *Sandwichboard Man*: BEN VEREEN. *Jonathon*: Jason Fuchs, Evan J. Newman. *Lamplighter*: KEN JENNINGS. *Blind Hag*: Joan Barber. *Fred*: GREG ZERKLE. *Mrs. Mops*: Corinne Melancon. *Ghost of Jacob Marley*: PAUL KANDEL. *Ghost of Christmas Past*: KEN JENNINGS. *Lights of Christmas Past*: Matthew Baker, Christopher F. Davis, Sean Thomas Morrissey, David Rosales. *Judge*: Michael H. Ingram. *Scrooge at 8 years*: Zachary Stefan Petkanas, Evan Silverberg. *Fan at 6*: Gemini Quintos, Diana Mary Rice. *Scrooge's Mother*: Joan Barber. *Scrooge's Father*: Michael X. Martin. *Mr. Hawkins*: Don Mayo. *Scrooge at 12 years*: Matthew Hoffman, Christopher Mark Petrizzo. *Fan at 10 years*: Eliza Atkins Clark, Elizabeth Lundberg. *Fezziwig*: Ray Friedeck. *Scrooge at 18 years*: Michael Moore. *Young Marley*: Ken Barnett. *Mrs. Fezziwig*: Joy Hermalyn. *Emily*: Emily Skinner. *Fiddler*: Brad Bradley. *Ghost of Christmas Present*: BEN VEREEN. *The Crachit Children*: Eliza Atkins Clark, Matthew Hoffman, Elizabeth Lundberg, Sean Thomas Morrissey, Christopher Mark Petrizzo. *Sally*, Fred's wife: Whitney Webster. *Ignorance*: Zachary Stefan Petkanas, Evan Silverberg. *Undertakers*: Ken Barnett, Michael X. Martin. *Ghost of Christmas Future*: VALENTINA KOZLOWA.

Business Men, Gifts, Ghosts and the People of London: Matthew Baker, Joan Barber, Ken Barnett, Robin Baxter, Leslie Bell, Carol Bentley, Brad Bradley, Betsy Chang, Candy Cook, Rosa Curry, Christopher F. Davis, Ray Friedeck, Peter Gregus, Jeffrey Hankinson, Joy Hermalyn, Michael H. Ingram, James Judy, Louisa Kendrick, Carrie Kenneally, Keith Byron Kirk, David Lowenstein, Jason Ma, Seth Malkin, Donna Lee Marshall, Michael X. Martin, Dana Lynn Mauro, Don Mayo, Elizabeth Mills, Corinne Melancon, Michael Moore, Seth Thomas Morrissey, Adam Pelty, Gail Pennington, Angela Piccinni, Pamela Remler, Samuel Reni, David Rosales, Emily Skinner, Whitney Webster, Greg Zerkle. *Swings*: Rachel Black, Rob Donohoe, Jesse

[5]Originally produced in New York 13 March 1947 at the Ziegfeld Theatre for 581 performances. For Synopsis of Scenes and Musical Numbers, see original 1947 production.

[6]Originally produced in New York 3 June 1975 at the 46th Street Theatre for 947 performances. For Synopsis of Scenes and Musical Numbers, see original 1975 production. This revival was based on the Encore Series concert production 2-4 May 1996 at the New York City Center for 4 performances with much the same cast and creative team. For this production, "Chicago After Midnight" was dropped. "Nowadays" (reprise/"R.S.V.P."/"Keep It Hot" were replaced by:
"Honey Rag"
A. Reinking, B. Neuwirth
Finale
Company

[7]Originally produced in New York 1 December 1994 at the Paramount, Madison Square Garden for 71 performances. For Synopsis of Scenes and Musical Numbers, see original 1994 production. For this year's and the 1995 revival the following changes were made:
Scene 1 and "The Years Are Passing By" were dropped.
Added to Scene 2 (former Scene 3) before "Street Song":
"You Mean More to Me"
N. Corley, M. Ballinger or P. Cravens
"The Years Are Passing By" (reprise) in former Scene 13 (new Scene 12) was replaced by:
"London Town Carol"
J. Fuchs or E. J. Newman
Note: The production played an irregular schedule of multiple daily performances.

Adam Eisenberg, Nicholas Gould, Dana Leigh Jackson, Don Johanson, Robin Lewis, Grace Ann Pisani, Jordan Siwek, Lindsay Sperber, Cynthia Thole, Brandon Urbanowitz, Jeff Williams. *Angels*: Bergen Beach School, P.S. 26 Chorus, Terrill Middle School, P.S. 250 Concert Choral *The Red Children's Cast*: Jennifer Blain, Pierce Cravens, Jason Fuchs, Matthew Hoffman, Elizabeth Lundberg, Grace Ann Pisani, Gemini Quintos, Evan Silverberg, Jordan Siwek. *The Green Children's Cast*: Matthew Ballinger, Eliza Atkins Clark, Nicholas Gould, Cara Horner, Evan Jay Newman, Zachary Stefan Petkanas, Christopher Mark Petrizzo, Diana Mary Rice, Lindsay Sperber, Brandon Urbanowitz.

1996.16 JUAN DARIÉN

A Revival of the Carnival Mass in One Act[8], 14 Scenes, a Prologue and an Epilogue. Conceived by Julie Taymor and Elliot Goldenthal. Music and original lyrics by Elliot Goldenthal. Based on a tale by Horacio Quirogà. Directed by Julie Taymor. Sets and costumes by G. W. Mercier and Julie Taymor. Puppetry and masks by Julie Taymor. Lighting design by Donald Holder. Sound by Tony Meola. Musical direction by Richard Cordova. Produced by Lincoln Center Theatre Co. (André Bishop, Artistic director; Bernard Gersten, Executive producer) in association with Music-Theatre Group (Lyn Austin, Diane Wondisford, Producers). Opened 24 November 1996 at the Vivian Beaumont Theatre and closed 5 January 1997 after 49 performances.

CAST: *Plague Victims*: The Company. *Mother (Dancer)*: ARIEL ASHWELL. *Mother (Vocalist)*: ANDREA FRIERSON TONEY. *Hunter*: Kristofer Batho. *Mr. Bones*: BRUCE TURK. *Shadows*: The Company, led by Stephen Kaplin. *Juan (Puppet)*: Kristofer Batho, Andrea Kane, Barbara Pollitt. *Juan (Boy)*: DANIEL HODD. *Schoolteacher*: BRUCE TURK. *Schoolchildren*: The Company. *Drunken Couple*: Kristofer Batho, Andrea Kane. *Señor Toledo*: Martín Santangelo. *Circus Tigers*: The Company. *Circus Barker, Street Singer*: DAVID TONEY. *Old Woman*: Ariel Ashwell. *Green Dwarf*: Andrea Kane, Sophia Salguero. *Marie Posa*: Sophia Salguero. *Ballad of Return Soloist*: IRMA-ESTEL LAGUERRE.

The action takes place in a South American jungle and a nearby village.

Prologue: Darkness; A Church in the Jungle. *Scene 1*: The Jungle. *Scene 2*: The Plague; A Village in Mourning. *Scene 3*: A Prayer Answered; The Transformation. *Scene 4*: The Nurturing; Juan's Ritual Baptism. *Scene 5*: Night in the Village. *Scene 6*: Journey to School; The Parting. *Scene 7*: School: Discipline, Fact. *Scene 8*: The Mother Dies. *Scene 9*: The Carnival. *Scene 10*: Discovery; Suspicion. *Scene 11*: The Interrogation; Schoolroom 2. *Scene 12*: The Torture and Retransformation of Juan Darién. *Scene 13*: The Jaguars' Congress; Retribution. *Scene 14*: The Mother's Grave and the Return to the Jungle. *Epilogue*: The Jungle.

MUSICAL NUMBERS[9]

Prologue
Agnus Dei
 Chorus
Lacrymosa
 Chorus, A. Ashwell, A. F. Toney
Mr. Bones Fanfare (dance)
 B. Turk
Jaguar Cub Approach
 A. Ashwell, A. F. Toney
Mr. Bones' Two-Step (dance)
 B. Turk
The Hunter's Entrance
Gloria
 Chorus, A. Ashwell, A. F. Toney
Initiation
A Round at Midnight
Sanctus
 A. Ashwell, A. F. Toney
School
 D. Hodd
Recordare
 A. Ashwell, A. F. Toney, D. Hodd, Chorus
Carnaval
 D. Toney
Lullabye
 D. Toney
 (*Lyrics by* Elliot Goldenthal.)
Trance
 D. Hodd
 (*Lyrics by* Horacio Quirogà.)
Dies Irae
 D. Toney, Chorus, D. Hodd, A. Ashwell, A. F. Toney
Lacrymosa II/Retribution
 Chorus, D. Hodd, A. Ashwell, A. F. Toney
"The Ballad of Return"
 I. LaGuerre
 (*Lyrics by* Elliot Goldenthal.)

[8]Originally produced in New York Off-Broadway 4 March 1988 at St. Clement's Theatre for 23 performances; revived 26 December 1989 at St. Clement's Theatre for 48 performances.

[9]Musical Numbers not listed in the program. Above listing prepared from libretto in the theatre program and the recording of the original concert version.

1996.17 GREASE

A Revival of the Musical (Comedy) in Two Acts, 12 Scenes[10]. Book, music and lyrics by Jim Jacobs and Warren Casey. Directed and choreographed by Jeff Calhoun. Scenic design by John Arnone. Costume design by Willa Kim. Lighting design by Howell Brinkley. Sound design by Tom Morse. Musical supervision, vocal and dance music arrangements by John McDaniel. Musical direction, John Samorian. Orchestrations by Steven Margoshes. Associate choreographer, Jerry Mitchell. Associate producer, Alecia Parker. A Tommy Tune Production. Produced by Barry and Fran Weissler and Jujamcyn Theatres, in association with Pace Theatrical Group and TV Asahi. Opened 29 November 1996 at the New York City Center and closed 1 December 1996 after 5 performances.

CAST (in order of appearance): *Vince Fontaine*: PETER SCOLARI. *Miss Lynch*: MIMI HINES. *Sonny*: Stephen Gnojewski. *Kenickie*: Steve Geyer. *Frenchy*: Alisa Klein. *Doody*: Roy Chicas. *Betty Rizzo*: JASMINE GUY. *Marty*: Cathy Trien. *Roger*: David Josefsberg *Jan*: Farah Alvin. *Danny Zuko*: ADRIAN ZMED. *Eugene Florczyk*: Christopher Youngsman. *Patty Simcox*: Stephanie Seeley. *Sandy Dumbrowski*: Christiane Noll. *The Heartbeats*: Denise Boccanfuso, Stefani Rae, Joelle Letta. *The Dream Mooners*: Shannon Bailey, Stefani Rae. *The Straight A's*: Shannon Bailey, Christopher Youngsman, Alan Jenkins, Daniel Paulus. *Cha-Cha DeGregorio*: Lori Lynch. *Teen Angel*: Kevin Anthony.

Ensemble: Shannon Bailey, Denise Boccanfuso, Ashton Byrum, Scot Fedderly, Alan Jenkins, Michelle Kittrell, Joelle Letta, Daniel Paulus, Stefani Rae, Mary Ruvolo. *Swings*: Thomas Scott, Jeanna Schweppe, Timothy Edward Smith. {Note: Pink Ladies include Rizzo, Frenchy, Marty, Jan. Burger Palace Boys include Kenickie, Doody, Roger, Sonny.}

1996.18 ONCE UPON A MATTRESS

A Revival of the Musical Comedy in Two Acts[11]. Book (revised) by Jay Thompson, Marshall Barer and Dean Fuller. (Based on the story "The Princess and the Pea" by Hans Christian Andersen.) Music by Mary Rodgers. Lyrics by Marshall Barer. Directed by Gerald Gutierrez. Choreographed by Liza Gennaro. Scenery by John Lee Beatty. Costumes by Jane Grrenwood. Lighting by Pat Collins. Sound by Tom Morse. Musical direction and vocal arrangements by Eric Stern. Orchestrations by Bruce Coughlan. Dance arrangements by Tom Fay. Executive producer, Dodger Management Group. Produced by Dodger Productions and Joop Van Den

[10]Originally produced in New York Off-Broadway 14 February 1972 at the Eden Theatre for 128 performances; transferred 7 June 1972 to the Broadhurst Theatre for a total of 3388 performances, including Off-Broadway run. This version originally produced 11 May 1994 at the Eugene O'Neill Theatre for 1503 performances; this national touring company played simultaneously with the Broadway company of GREASE! at the Eugene O'Neill for 3 days. For this touring production, Act 2, Scenes 4 and 5 have been combined, eliminating the Burger Palace set.

[11]Originally produced Off-Broadway 11 May 1959 at the Phoenix Theatre for 216 performances; transferred to Broadway 25 November 1959 at the Alvin Theatre for an additional 244 performances. Total: 460 performances. For Musical Numbers, see original 1959 production. For this production, a new song was added to Act 2, after "Quiet":

"Goodnight, Sweet Princess"
 D. A. Baker

Ende. Opened 19 December 1996 at the Broadhurst Theatre and closed 1 June 1997 after 187 performances.

CAST: *King Sextimus*: HEATH LAMBERTS. *Queen Aggravain*: MARY LOU ROSATO. *Prince Dauntless*: DAVID AARON BAKER. *Winnifred*, Princess of Farfelot: SARAH JESSICA PARKER. *Sir Harry*, Knight of the Herald: LEWIS CLEALE. *Lady Larken*, a Lady in Waiting: JANE KRAKOWSKI. *Jester*: DAVID HIBBARD. *Master Merton*, confidante to the Queen: Tom Alan Robbins. *The Nightingale of Samarkand*, a royal pet: Ann Brown. *The Royal Cellist*: Laura Bontrager. *The Royal Ballet*: Arte Phillips, Pascale Faye. *Minstrel*, a travelling player: LAWRENCE CLAYTON. *Player Queen*: David Jennings. *Player Prince*: David Elder. *Player Princess*: Bob Walton. *Other Players*: Arte Phillips, Nick Cokas, Stephen Reed.

Knights, Lords and Ladies attending the Queen: Nick Cokas, David Elder, David Jennings, Sebastian LaCause, Jason Psahl, Arte Phillips, Stephen Reed, Bob Walton, Ann Brown, Maria Calabrese, Thursday Farrar, Pascale Faye, Janet Metz, Tina Ou, Aixa M. Rosario Medina, Jennifer Smith. *Swings*: Pamela Gould, Thomas Titone.

The action takes place in and about the castle in the spring, 1428.

1997.01 MANDY PATINKIN IN CONCERT

A One Man Show in One Act. At the piano, Paul Ford. Produced by Dodger Endemol Theatricals[12]. Opened 1 March 1997 at the Lyceum Theatre and closed 23 March 1997 after 17 performances[13].

CAST: MANDY PATINKIN.

MUSICAL NUMBERS[14]

"Beat Out Dat Rhythm on a Drum" (from *CARMEN JONES*)
(*Music by* Georges Bizet. *Lyrics by* Oscar Hammerstein II.)
"School Days"
(*Music by* Gus Edwards. *Lyrics by* Will D. Cobb.)
"Time in a Bottle"
(*Music and Lyrics by* Jim Croce.)
"Inchworm" (from *HANS CHRISTIAN ANDERSEN* film)
(*Music and Lyrics by* Frank Loesser.)
"The Wrong Note Rag" (from *WONDERFUL TOWN*)
(*Music by* Leonard Bernstein. *Lyrics by* Betty Comden and Adolph Green.)
"A-Tisket, A-Tasket"
(*Music and Lyrics by* Van Alexander and Ella Fitzgerald.)
"You Are Beautiful" (from *FLOWER DRUM SONG*)
(*Music by* Richard Rodgers. *Lyrics by* Oscar Hammerstein II.)
"Not a Day Goes By" (from *MERRILY WE ROLL ALONG*)
(*Music and Lyrics by* Stephen Sondheim.)
"Sam, You Made the Pants Too Long"
(*Music by* Isham Jones. *Lyrics by* Sam M. Lewis, Milton Berle, Fred Whitehouse.)
"Cohen Owes Me $97"
(*Music and Lyrics by* Irving Berlin.)
"Loving You" (from *PASSION*)
(*Music and Lyrics by* Stephen Sondheim.)
"If I Loved You" (from *CAROUSEL*)
(*Music by* Richard Rodgers. *Lyrics by* Oscar Hammerstein II.)
"When I Grow Too Old to Dream" (from *THE NIGHT IS YOUNG* film)
(*Music by* Sigmund Romberg. *Lyrics by* Oscar Hammerstein II.)
"Remember" (*A LITTLE NIGHT MUSIC*)
(*Music and Lyrics by* Stephen Sondheim.)
"Ya Got Trouble" (from *THE MUSIC MAN*)
(*Music and Lyrics by* Meredith Willson.)
"Frankfurter Sandwiches"
(*Music and Lyrics by* Al Dubin, Harry Pease and Ed G. Nelson.)
"Honey Bun" (from *SOUTH PACIFIC*)
(*Music by* Richard Rodgers. *Lyrics by* Oscar Hammerstein II.)
"And the Band Played On"
(*Music by* John Palmer. *Lyrics by* Charles B. Ward.)
"Marie"
(*Music and Lyrics by* Randy Newman.)
"Once Upon a Time" (from *ALL AMERICAN*)
(*Music by* Charles Strouse. *Lyrics by* Lee Adams.)
"Taxi"
(*Music and Lyrics by* Harry Chapin.)
"Soliloquy" (from *CAROUSEL*)
(*Music by* Richard Rodgers. *Lyrics by* Oscar Hammerstein II.)
"Waters of March"
(*Music and Lyrics by* Antonio Carlos Jobim.)
"How Glory Goes" (from *FLOYD COLLINS*)
(*Music and Lyrics by* Adam Guettel.)
"Bring Him Home" (from *LES MISERABLES*)
(*Music by* Alain Boublil, Claude-Michel Schönberg. *Lyrics by* Herbert Kretzmer.)
"Carefully Taught" (from *SOUTH PACIFIC*)
(*Music by* Richard Rodgers. *Lyrics by* Oscar Hammerstein II.)
"Children Will Listen" (from *INTO THE WOODS*)
(*Music and Lyrics by* Stephen Sondheim.)
"Pennies from Heaven" (from *PENNIES FROM HEAVEN* film)
(*Music by* Arthur Johnston. *Lyrics by* Johnny Burke.)
"Oh, What a Circus" (from *EVITA*)
(*Music by* Andrew Lloyd Webber. *Lyrics by* Tim Rice.)
"Experiment" (from *NYMPH ERRANT*)
(*Music and Lyrics by* Cole Porter.)
"Over the Rainbow" (from *THE WIZARD OF OZ* film)
(*Music by* Harold Arlen. *Lyrics by* E. Y. Harburg.)
"White Christmas" (from *HOLIDAY INN* film)
(*Music and Lyrics by* Irving Berlin.)
"God Bless America"
(*Music and Lyrics by* Irving Berlin.)
"As Time Goes By" (from *EVERYBODY'S WELCOME*)
(*Music and Lyrics by* Herman Hupfeld.)
(*Yiddish Lyrics [for 3 songs above] by* Henry Sapoznik.)
"Rockabye Your Baby with a Dixie Melody" (from *SINBAD*)
(*Music by* Jean Schwartz. *Lyrics by* Sam M. Lewis, Joe Young.)

1997.02 THE MIKADO, or The Town of Titipu

A Revival of the Comic Opera in Two Acts[15]. Libretto by William S. Gilbert. Music by Arthur Sullivan. Production (direction), Lotfi Mansouri. Stage direction, Christian Smith. Conductor, Randall Craig Fleischer. Set and costume designer, Thierry Bosquet. Lighting designer, John Gleason. Choreographer, Patricia Birch. Chorus master, Gary Wedow. Produced by the New York City Opera. Opened 8 March 1997 at the New York State Theatre and closed 23 April 1997 after 6 performances in repertory.

CAST (in order of appearance): *Nanki-Poo*: MATTHEW CHELLIS. *Pish-Tush*: SHON SIMS. *Pooh-Bah*: JOSEPH MCKEE. *Ko-Ko*: JAMES BILLINGS. *Yum-Yum*: BARBARA SHIRVIS. *Pitti-Sing*: ANGELA HORN. *Peep-Bo*: DEANE MEEK. *Katisha*: CYNTHIA MUNZER. *The of Japan*: RICHARD MCKEE. *Chorus of School Girls, Nobles, Guards and Coolies*: New York City Opera Chorus.

1997.03 PLAY ON!

A Musical in Two Acts. Book by Cheryl L. West. (Based loosely on "Twelfth Night" by William Shakespeare.) Songs (music) by Duke Ellington. Conceived and directed by Sheldon Epps. Choreographed by Mercedes Ellington. Arrangements, musical supervision, orchestrations by Luther Henderson. Scenic design, James Leonard Joy. Costume design, Marianna Elliott. Lighting design, Jeff Davis. Sound design, Jeff Ladman. Creative

[12]Billed as a benefit engagement for 5 charities: Association to Benefit Children; Crohn's and Colitis Foundation; National Dance Institute; Peace Now; Physicians for Human Rights.
[13]Played an irregular schedule of 5 performances a week.
[14]No songs listed in program. Not in performance order; not all songs performed at all performances.

[15]First presented in New York 20 July, 10-29 August 1885 at the Union Square and People's Theatres for 22 performances. First authorized production presented 19 August 1885 at the Fifth Avenue Theatre by Richard D'Oyly Carte for 250 performances. For Synopsis of Scenes and Musical Numbers, see 19 August 1885 D'Oyly Carte production.

consultant, Louis Johnson. Creative historic consultant, Frankie Manning. Musical director, J. Leonard Oxley. Originally produced at the Old Globe Theatre, San Diego, California. Associate producers, Leon Memoli, David Levy, Nancy Eichorn, Louis F. Raizin, James L. Simon, Fred H. Krones. Produced by Mitchell Maxwell, Eric Nederlander, Thomas Hall, Hal Luftig, Bruce Lucker, Mike Skipper, Victoria Maxwell, in association with Kery Davis, Alan J. Shuster. Opened March 20 1997 at the Brooks Atkinson Theatre and closed 11 May 1997 after 61 performances.

CAST (in order of appearance): *Vy*: CHERYL FREEMAN. *Jester*: ANDRÉ DESHIELDS. *Sweets*: LARRY MARSHALL. *Miss Mary*: YVETTE CASON. CC: Crystal Allen. *Duke*: CARL ANDERSON. *Rev*: LAWRENCE HAMILTON. *Lady Liv*: TONYA PINKINS

Denizens of Harlem: Ronald "Cadet" Bastine, Jacqueline Bird, Wendee Lee Curtis, Byron Easley, Alan H. Green, Frantz G. Hall, Gil P., Lacy Darryl Phillips, Lisa Scialabba, Erika Vaughn, Karen Callaway Williams. *Swings*: Germaine Goodson, Bryan S. Haynes, Stacie Precia, William Wesley.

Time: The Swingin '40's.

Location: The Magical Kingdom of Harlem.

Act 1, Scene 1: Grand Central Station. *Scene 2*: 125th Street. *Scene 3*: The Duke's Apartment. *Scene 4*: The Cotton Club. *Scene 5*: Lady Liv's Dressing Room. *Scene 6*: The Cotton Club. *Scene 7*: *Scene 8*: The Cotton Club. *Scene 9*: *Scene 10*: The Cotton Club.

Act 2, Scene 1: The Cotton Club. *Scene 2*: Lady Liv's Dressing Room. *Scene 3*: The Cotton Club. *Scene 4*: Outside of the Cotton Club. *Scene 5*: The Cotton Club. *Scene 6*: Lady Liv's Apartment. *Scene 7*: Outside of the Cotton Club. *Scene 8*: The Duke's Apartment. *Scene 9*: 125th Street.

ACT 1
Scene 1
"Take the A Train"
C. Freeman, Ensemble
(*Music and Lyrics by* Billy Strayhorn.)
Scene 2
"Drop Me Off in Harlem"
C. Freeman, Denizens of Harlem
(*Music by* Duke Ellington. *Lyrics by* Nick Kenny.)
"I've Got to Be a Rug Cutter"
A. DeShields, C. Freeman, Cotton Club Dancers
(*Music and Lyrics by* Duke Ellington.)
Scene 3
"I Let a Song Go Out of My Heart"
C. Anderson
(*Music and Lyrics by* Duke Ellington, Irving Mills, Henry Nemo, John Redmond.)
Scene 4
"C Jam Blues"
Cotton Club Dancers
(*Music by* Duke Ellignton.)
"Mood Indigo"
T. Pinkins
(*Music and Lyrics by* Duke Ellington, Irving Mills, Albany Bigard.)
Scene 5
"Don't Get Around Much Anymore"
C. Freeman, T. Pinkins
(*Music by* Duke Ellington. *Lyrics by* Bob Russell.)
"Don't You Know I Care"
L. Hamilton
(*Music by* Duke Ellington. *Lyrics by* Mack David.)
Scene 6
"It Don't Mean a Thing If It Ain't Got That Swing"
A. DeShields, Y. Cason, L. Marshall, L. Hamilton
(*Music by* Duke Ellington. *Lyrics by* Irving Mills.)
Scene 7
"I Got It Bad and That Ain't Good" (from JUMP FOR JOY)
C. Anderson, C. Freeman
(*Music by* Duke Ellington. *Lyrics by* Paul Francis Webster.)
"Hit Me With a Hot Note and Watch Me Bounce"
C. Freeman, Duke's Band
(*Music by* Duke Ellington. *Lyrics by* Don George.)
Scene 9
"I'm Just a Lucky So and So"
A. DeShields, Cotton Club Dancers
(*Music by* Duke Ellington. *Lyrics by* Mack David.)
Scene 10
"Everything But You"
T. Pinkins, C. Freeman
(*Music and Lyrics by* Duke Ellington, Don George, Harry James.)
"Solitude"
C. Freeman, C. Anderson, T. Pinkins, L. Hamilton
(*Music and Lyrics by* Duke Ellington, Eddie DeLange, Irving Mills.)

ACT 2
Scene 1
"Black Butterfly"
Lady Liv's Escorts
(*Music and Lyrics by* Duke Ellington, Ben Carruthers, Irving Mills.)
"I Ain't Got Nothin' But the Blues"
T. Pinkins
(*Music by* Duke Ellington. *Lyrics by* Don George.)
Scene 3
"I'm Beginning to See the Light"
L. Hamilton, Cotton Club Dancers
(*Music by* Duke Ellington, Don George, Harry James, Johnny Hodges.)
"I Got It Bad and That Ain't Good" (reprise)
L. Hamilton
Scene 4
"I Didn't Know About You"
C. Freeman
(*Music by* Duke Ellington. *Lyrics by* Bob Russell.)
Scene 5
"Rocks in My Bed"
L. Marshall, A. DeShields
(*Music and Lyrics by* Duke Ellington.)
Scene 6
"Something to Live For"
L. Hamilton, T. Pinkins
(*Music by* Duke Ellington. *Lyrics by* Billy Strayhorn.)
Scene 7
"Love You Madly"
Y. Cason, L. Marshall
(*Music and Lyrics by* Duke Ellington.)
Scene 8
"Prelude to a Kiss"
C. Freeman, C. Anderson
(*Music and Lyrics by* Duke Ellington, Irving Gordon, Irving Mills.)
Scene 9
"In a Mellow Tone"
C. Freeman, C. Anderson, T. Pinkins, L. Hamilton, Denizens of Harlem
(*Music by* Duke Ellington. *Lyrics by* Milt Gabler.)

1997.04

ANNIE

A Revival of the Musical in Two Acts, 13 Scenes[16]. Book by Thomas Meehan. Based on the "Little Orphan Annie" comic strip (by Harold Gray). Music by Charles Strouse. Lyrics by Martin Charnin. Musical numbers choreographed by Peter Gennaro. Directed by Martin Charnin. Settings by Kenneth Foy. Costumes by Theoni V. Aldredge. Lighting by Ken Billington. Sound by T. Richard Fitzgerald. Musical direction and supervision by Keith Levinson. (Original orchestrations by Philip J. Lang.) Associate producers, Tamar Climan and Herb Goldsmith. Produced by Timothy Childs, Rodger Hess and Jujamcyn Theatres, in association with Terri B. Childs and Al

[16]Originally opened 21 April 1977 at the Alvin Theatre for 2377 performances. For Synopsis of Scenes and Musical Numbers, see original 1977 production. For this production, a new song was added to Act 1, Scene 7, before "Easy Street":
"You Make Me Happy"
N. Carter, C. Dunn
After the opening, Act 1, Scene 3 was dropped, including "We'd Like to Thank You, (Herbert Hoover)."

Nocciolino. Opened 26 March 1997 at the Martin Beck Theatre and closed 19 October 1997 after 240 performances.

CAST (in order of appearance): *Annie*: BRITTNY KISSINGER. *Molly*: Christiana Anbri. *Pepper*: Cassidy Ladden. *Duffy*: Mekenzie Rosen-Stone. *July*: Casey Tuma. *Tessie*: Lyndsey Watkins. *Kate*: Melissa O'Malley *Miss Hannigan*: NELL CARTER. *Bundles McCloskey*: Michael E. Gold. *Apple Seller*: Brad Wills. *Dog Catchers*:Tom Treadwell, Sutton Foster. *Sandy*: Cindy Lou. *Sergeant Thayer*: Michael E. Gold. *Lieutenant Ward*: Drew Taylor. *Sophie, the Kettle*: Barbara Tirrell. *Fred*: Tom Treadwell. *Grace Farrell*: COLLEEN DUNN. *Drake*: MichaelJohn McGann. *Mrs. Pugh*: Barbara Tirrell. *Cecille*: Sutton Foster. *Mrs. Greer*: Elizabeth Richmond. *Annette*: Kelley Swaim. *Oliver Warbucks*: CONRAD JOHN SCHUCK. *A Star to Be*: Sutton Foster. *Rooster Hannigan*: JIM RYAN. *Lily*: KAREN BYERS-BLACKWELL. *Bert Healy*: MichaelJohn McGann. *Fred McCracken*: Brad Wills. *Jimmy Johnson*: Tom Treadwell. *Sound Effects Man*: Michael E. Gold. *Bonnie Boylan*: Elizabeth Richmond. *Connie Boylan*: Kelley Swaim. *Ronnie Boylan*: Sutton Foster. *Oxydent "Hour of Smiles" Producer*: Jennifer L. Neuland. *H.V. Kaltenborn's Voice*: Bryan Young. *F.D.R.*: RAYMOND THORNE. *Ickes*: Brad Wills. *Howe*: Tom Treadwell. *Hull*: Drew Taylor. *Perkins*: Barbara Tirrell. *Morganthau*: MichaelJohn McGann. *Honor Guard*: Michael E. Gold. *Justice Brandeis*: Drew Taylor.

Hooverville-ites, Warbucks' Staff, New Yorkers: Sutton Foster, Michael E. Gold, MichaelJohn McGann, Jennifer L. Neuland, Elizabeth Richmond, Kelley Swaim, Drew Taylor, Barbara Tirrell, Tom Treadwell, Brad Wills.

1997.05

DREAM

A Musical Revue in Two Acts, 5 Scenes. Based on the lyrics of Johnny Mercer. Music by Harold Arlen, Rube Bloom, Hoagy Carmichael, Walter Donaldson, Duke Ellington, Ziggy Elman, Bernie Hanighen, Jerome Kern, Matt Malneck, Henry Mancini, Johnny Mercer, David Raksin, Victor Schertzinger, Billy Strayhorn, James Van Heusen, Harry Warren, Richard Whiting. Conceived by Louise Westergaard and Jack Wrangler. Directed and choreographed by Wayne Cilento. Scenic design, David Mitchell. Costume design, Ann Hould-Ward. Lighting design, Ken Billington. Sound design, Peter Fitzgerald. Musical supervision and vocal arrangements, Donald Pippin. Musical direction and vocal arrangements, Bryan Louiselle. Dance music arrangements, Jeanine Tesori. Orchestrations by Dick Lieb. Originally staged and developed at Tennessee Repertory Theatre, Nashville, Tennessee (Mac Pirkle, Artistic director; Brian J. Laczko, Managing director). Associate producers, Nicole Michelle Cuillo, Nancy LaVista, L. Michael Post, Elisa Sterling. Produced by Louise Westergaard, Mark Schwartz Bob Cuillo, Roger Dean, Obie Bailey, Stephen O'Neil, Abraham Salaman. Opened 3 April 1997 at the Royale Theatre and closed 6 July 1997 after 109 performances.

CAST: LESLEY ANN WARREN, JOHN PIZZARELLI, MARGARET WHITING, BROOKS ASHMANSKAS, JONATHAN DOKUCHITZ, CHARLES MCGOWAN, JESSICA MOLASKEY, DARCIE ROBERTS, Todd Bailey, Angelo Fraboni, Amy Heggins, Jennifer Lamberts, Nancy Lemenager, Susan Misner, Kevyn Morrow, Timothy Edward Smith, Ray Kennedy (John Pizzarelli Trio, piano), Martin Pizzarelli (John Pizzarelli Trio, bass). *Understudies/Swings*: Jeffrey Denman, Jody Ripplinger, Bill Szobody, Deborah Yates.

Act 1, Scene 1: Savannah—The Age of Innocence. *Scene 2*: Magnicificent Obsession—The Age of Decadence. *Scene 3*: Rainbow Room.

Act 2, Scene 1: Hollywood Canteen. *Scene 2*: Academy Awards.

ACT 1

Scene 1

"Dream"
D. Roberts, J. Molaskey, N. Lemenager, Company
(*Music by* Johnny Mercer.)

"Lazybones"
A. Heggins, K. Morrow, J. Dokuchitz, Company
(*Music by* Hoagy Carmichael.)

"On Behalf of the Travelling Salesmen"
B. Ashmanskas, T. E. Smith
(*Music by* Walter Donaldson.)

"Pardon My Southern Accent"
L. A. Warren
(*Music by* Matt Malneck.)

"You Must Have Been a Beautiful Baby" (from *HARD TO GET* film)
C. McGowan, D. Roberts
(*Music by* Harry Warren.)

"Have You Got Any Castles, Baby?" (from *VARSITY SHOW* film)
J. Dokuchitz, L. A. Warren, Company
(*Music by* Richard Whiting.)

"Goody, Goody"
L A. Warren, Company
(*Music by* Matt Malneck.)

"Skylark"
J. Molaskey
(*Music by* Hoagy Carmichael.)

"The Dixieland Band"
J. Dokuchitz, Company
(*Music by* Bernie Hanighen.)

Scene 2

"I Had Myself a True Love"
"I Wonder What Became of Me" (from *ST. LOUIS WOMAN*)
L. A. Warren, D. Roberts
(*Music by* Harold Arlen.)

"Jamboree Jones Jive"
John Pizzarelli Trio, Company
(*Music by* Johnny Mercer.)

"Fools Rush In"
John Pizzarelli Trio, Company
(*Music by* Rube Bloom.)

"Come Rain or Come Shine" (from *ST. LOUIS WOMAN*)
B. Ashmanskas
(*Music by* Harold Arlen.)

"Out of This World" (from film of the same name)
D. Roberts
(*Music by* Harold Arlen.)

"I Remember You" (from *THE FLEET'S IN* film)
J. Molaskey
(*Music by* Victor Schertzinger.)

"Blues in the Night" (from film of the same name)
L. A. Warren
(*Music by* Harold Arlen.)

"One for My Baby" (from *THE SKY'S THE LIMIT* film)
M. Whiting
(*Music by* Harold Arlen.)

Scene 3

"You Were Never Lovelier" (from film of the same name)
J. Dokuchitz
(*Music by* Jerome Kern.)

"Satin Doll"
S. Misner, Men
(*Music by* Billy Strayhorn and Duke Ellington.)

"I'm Old Fashioned" (from You Were Never Lovelier film)
D. Roberts, J. Dokuchitz
(*Music by* Jerome Kern.)

"Dearly Beloved" (from You Were Never Lovelier film)
J. Dokuchitz, D. Roberts
(*Music by* Jerome Kern.)

"This Time the Dream's on Me" (from Blues In The Night film)
L. A. Warren, J. Pizzarelli, M. Whiting
(*Music by* Harold Arlen.)

"Something's Gotta Give" (from Daddy Long Legs film)
J. Molaskey
(*Music by* Johnny Mercer.)

"Too Marvelous for Words" (from Ready, Willing and Able film)
C. McGowan, Company
(*Music by* Richard Whiting.)

ACT 2

Scene 1

"I Thought About You"
J. Pizzarelli
(*Music by* James Van Heusen.)

"And the Angels Sing"
Orchestra
(*Music by* Ziggy Elman.)

"The Fleet's In" (from film of the same name)
Men
(*Music by* Victor Schertzinger.)

"G.I. Jive"
L. A. Warren, J. Molaskey, N. Lemenager
(*Music by* Johnny Mercer.)

"I'm Doin' It for Defense" (from Star Spangled Rhythm film)
D. Roberts
(*Music by* Harold Arlen.)

"Tangerine" (from *THE FLEET'S IN* film)
B. Ashmanskas, Company
(*Music by* Victor Schertzinger.)
"Day In—Day Out"
M. Whiting
(*Music by* Rube Bloom.)
"Jeepers Creepers" (from *GOING PLACES* film)
John Pizzarelli Trio, Company
(*Music by* Harry Warren.)
"That Old Black Magic" (from *STAR SPANGLED RHYTHM* film)
L. A. Warren
(*Music by* Harold Arlen.)
"Laura" (from film of the same name)
J. Dokuchitz
(*Music by* David Raksin.)
"You Go Your Way"
Company
(*Music by* Johnny Mercer.)
"My Shining Hour" (from *THE SKY'S THE LIMIT* film)
M. Whiting, Company
(*Music by* Harold Arlen.)

Scene 2

"Hooray for Hollywood" (from *HOLLYWOOD HOTEL* film)
B. Ashmanskas, A. Fraboni, K. Morrow, T. E. Smith
(*Music by* Richard Whiting.)
"Accentuate the Positive" (from *HERE COME THE WAVES* film)
B. Ashmanskas, A. Fraboni, K. Morrow, T. E. Smith, N. Lemenager
(*Music by* Harold Arlen.)
"In the Cool, Cool of the Evening" (from *HERE COMES THE GROOM* film)
M. Whiting, John Pizzarelli Trio, Company
(*Music by* Hoagy Carmichael.)
"Charade" (from film of the same name)
(*Music by* Henry Mancini.)
"The Days of Wine and Roses" (from film of the same name)
J. Dokuchitz, J. Molaskey, Company
(*Music by* Henry Mancini.)
"Moon River" (from *BREAKFAST AT TIFFANY'S* film)
L. A. Warren
(*Music by* Henry Mancini.)
"On the Atchison, Topeka and the Santa Fe" (from *THE HARVEY GIRLS* film)
(*Music by* Harry Warren.) Company

1997.06

TITANIC

A Musical in Two Acts, a Prologue and Twenty-Three Scenes. Story and book by Peter Stone. Music and lyrics by Maury Yeston. Directed by Richard Jones. Choreographed by Lynne Taylor-Corbett. Scenic and costume design, Stewart Laing. Lighting design, Paul Gallo. Sound design, Steve Canyon Kennedy. Orchestrations by Jonathan Tunick. Music supervision and direction, Kevin Stites. Executive producer, Dodger Management Group. Produced by Dodger Endemol Productions, Richard Pechter, The John F. Kennedy Center for the Performing Arts. Opened 23 April 1997 at the Lunt-Fontanne Theatre and closed 28 March 1999 after 804 performances.

CAST: *Officers and Crew of the R.M.S. Titanic*: *Captain E. J. Smith*: JOHN CUNNINGHAM. *First Officer William Murdoch*: David Costabile. *Second Officer Charles Lightoller*: John Bolton. *Third Officer William Pitman*: Matthew Bennett. *Frederick Barrett*, Stoker: Brian d'Arcy James. *Harold Bride*, Radioman: Martin Moran. *Henry Etches*, First Class Steward: Allan Corduner. *Frederick Fleet*, Lookout: David Elder. *Quartermaster Robert Hichens*: Adam Alexi-Malle. *Fourth Officer Joseph Boxhall*: Andy Taylor. *Chief Engineer Joseph Bell*: Ted Sperling. *Wallace Hartley*, Orchestra Leader: Ted Sperling. *Bandsman Bricoux*: Adam Alexi-Malle. *Bandsman Taylor*: Andy Taylor. *Stewardess Robinson*: Michele Ragusa. *Stewardess Hutchinson*: Stephanie Park. *Bellboy*: Mara Stephens.

Passengers aboard R.M.S. Titanic: *First Class*: *J. Bruce Ismay*: DAVID GARRISON. *Thomas Andrews*: MICHAEL CERVERIS. *Isidor Straus*: LARRY KEITH. *Ida Straus*: ALMA CUERVO. *J. J. Astor*: WILLIAM YOUMANS. *Madeline Astor*: Lisa Datz. *Benjamin Guggenheim*: Joseph Kolinski. *Mme. Aubert*: Kimberly Hester. *John B. Thayer*: Michael Mulheren. *Marion Thayer*: Robin Irwin. *George Widener*: Henry Stram. *Eleanor Widener*: Jody Gelb. *Charlotte Cardoza*: Becky Ann Baker. *J. H. Rogers*: Andy Taylor. *The Major*: Matthew Bennett. *Edith Corse Evans*: Mindy Cooper. And David Elder, Erin Hill, Theresa McCarthy, Charles McAteer, Jennifer Piech, Clarke Thorell.

Second Class: *Charles Clarke*: DON STEPHENSON. *Caroline Nevlle*: JUDITH BLAZER. *Edgar Beane*: BILL BUELL. *Alice Beane*: VICTORIA CLARK. And John Bolton, Mindy Cooper, David Costabile, David Elder.

Third Class: *Kate McGovern*: Jennifer Piech. *Kate Murphey*: Theresa McCarthy. *Kate Mullins*: Erin Hill. *Jim Farrell*: Clarke Thorell. And Adam Alexi-Malle, Becky Ann Baker, Matthew Bennett, Mindy Cooper, Alma Cuervo, Liza Datz, Jody Gelb, Kimberly Hester, Robin Irwin, Larry Keith, Joseph Kolinski, Michael Mulheren, Charles McAteer, Ted Sperling, Mara Stephens, Henry Stram, Andy Taylor, William Youmans.

On Shore: *Frank Carlson*: Henry Stram.

Swings: Melissa Bell, Kay Walbye, Jonathan Brody, John Jellison, Drew McVety.

The action takes place between 10-15 April 1912. All characters and events are based on fact.

Prologue: Harland & Wolff, Shipbuilders, Aberdeen, Scotland.

Act 1, Scene 1: Southampton: The Ocean Dock. *Scene 2*: Aboard the *R.M.S. Titanic*. The stern. *Scene 3*: The Dock. *Scene 4*: The Bridge and Boiler Room #6. *Scene 5*: The Saloon ("D") Deck. *Scene 6*: The First Class Dining Saloon. *Scene 7*: The Bridge. *Scene 8*: The Middle ("F") Deck. The Third Class Commissary. *Scene 9*: The Bridge. *Scene 10*: The Radio Room. *Scene 11*: The Boat Deck: First Class Promenade. *Scene 12*: "A" Deck. *Scene 13*: The Bridge: then The Promenade ("B") Deck, The Saloon ("D") Deck, The Middle ("F") Deck; The First Class Smoke Room and The Crow's Nest.

Act 2, Scene 1: First, Second, Third Class Corridors, and The Bridge. *Scene 2*: The First Class Grand Salon. *Scene 3*: ("E") Deck: A Stairwell. *Scene 4*: The Boat Deck. *Scene 5*: The Radio Room. *Scene 6*: At the Lifeboats. *Scene 7*: Portholes. *Scene 8*: The Upper Promenade ("A") Deck. *Scene 9*: The First Class Smoke Room. *Scene 10*: The Aftermath.

The Decks:

Boat Deck: The Bridge, the Radio Room, the Life Boats
Upper Promenade (A) Deck: First Class Promenade, First Class Reading and Writing Room, First Class Smoke Room
Promenade (B) Deck: First Class Promenade
Upper (C) Deck: Second Class Promenade
Saloon (D) Deck: First Class Dining Saloon; Second Class Promenade
Main (E) Deck: Second Class Cabins
Middle (F) Deck: Third Class Dining Saloon; Third Class Promenade
Lower (G) Deck: Third Class (Steerage) Dormitories
Orlop (H) Deck: Boiler Room #6

Act 1

Prologue: "In Every Age"
M. Cerveris
The Launching:
"How Did They Build Titanic?"
B. James
"There She Is"
B. James, M. Moran, D. Elder
"Loading Inventory"
J. Cunningham, Stevedores, Ship's Personnel
"The Largest Moving Object"
D.Garrison, J. Cunningham, M. Cerveris
"I Must Get On That Ship"
M. Bennett, Second and Third Class Passengers
"The First Class Roster"
M. Bennett, V. Clark
"Godspeed Titanic"
The Company
"Barrett's Song"
B. James
"What a Remarkable Age This Is!"
A. Corduner, Staff and First Class Diners
"To Be a Captain"
D. Costabile
"Lady's Maid"
J. Piech, T. McCarthy, E. Hill, Steerage
"The Proposal"
B. James
"The Night Was Alive"
M. Moran
"Hymn"
The Company
"Doing the Latest Rag"
T. Sperling, A. Alexi-Malle, A. Taylor, Company

"I Have Danced"
V. Clark, B. Buell
"No Moon"
D. Elder, Company
"Autumn"
T. Sperling

ACT 2
"Wake up, Wake up!"
A. Corduner, Stewards, Company
"Dressed in Your Pajamas in the Grand Salon"
The Company
"The Staircase"
C. Thorell, J. Piech, T. McCarthy, E. Hill
"The Blame"
D. Garrison, M. Cerveris, J. Cunningham
To the Lifeboats:
"Getting in the Lifeboat"
M. Mulheren, R. Irwin
"I Must Get on That Ship" (reprise)
D. Costabile, J. Bolton, A. Corduner, M. Stephens, Passengers
"Lady's Maid" (reprise)
C. Thorell
"Canons"
Company
"The Proposal" (reprise)
B. James
"The Night Was Alive" (reprise)
M. Moran
"We'll Meet Tomorrow"
D. Stephenson
"Still"
L. Keith, A. Cuervo
"To Be a Captain" (reprise)
A. Corduner
"Mr. Andrews' Vision"
M. Cerveris
"In Every Age" (reprise)
The Company
Finale
The Company

1997.07

STEEL PIER

An American Fable (Musical) in Two Acts, 20 Scenes. Book by David Thompson. Music by John Kander. Lyrics by Fred Ebb. Conceived by Scott Ellis, Susan Stroman and David Thompson. Directed by Scott Ellis. Choreography by Susan Stroman. Setting design, Tony Walton. Costume design, William Ivey Long. Lighting design, Peter Kaczorowski. Sound design, Tony Meola. Dance and incidental music arrangements, Glen Kelly. Projections, Wendall K. Harrington. Orchestrations by Michael Gibson. Musical direction and vocal arrangements by David Loud. Associate producer, Pace Theatrical Group. Produced by Roger Berlind. Opened 24 April 1997 at the Richard Rodgers Theatre and closed 28 June 1997 after 76 performances.

CAST (in order of appearance): *Bill Kelly*: DANIEL MCDONALD. *Rita Racine*: KAREN ZIEMBA. *Shelby Stevens*: DEBRA MONK. *Mick Hamilton*: GREGORY HARRISON. *Mr. Walker*: Ronn Carroll. *Buddy Becker*: Joel Blum. *Bette Becker*: Valerie Wright. *Johnny Adel*: Timothy Warmen. *Dora Foster*: Alison Bevan. *Happy McGuire*: Jim Newman. *Precious McGuire*: Kristen Chenoweth. *Luke Adams*: John C. Havens. *Mick's Picks*: Mary Illes, Rosa Curry, Sarah Solie Shannon. *Corky*: Casey Nicholaw. *Dr. Johnson*: John MacInnes. *Sonny*: Gregory Mitchell. *Preacher*: Adam Pelty. *The Flying Dunlaps*: Leigh-Anne Wencker, Jack Hayes, JoAnn M. Hunter, Robert Fowler, John MacInnis.

Steel Pier Marathon Couples: *Couple #39*: K. Ziemba, D. McDonald. *Couple #32*: D. Monk, J. C. Havens. *Couple #17*: V. Wright, J. Blum. *Couple #4*: K. Chenoweth, J. Newman. *Couple #26*: A. Bevan, T. Warmen. *Couple #46*: J. M. Hunter, G. Mitchell. *Couple #8*: D. L. Mauro, A. Blankenbuehler. *Couple #50*: E. Mills, J. Hayes. *Couple #68*: L. Wencker, R. Fowler. *Couple #71*: I. Gilliams, A. Pelty. *Couple #51*: S. S. Shannon, C. Nicholaw. *Couple #54*: M. Illes, B. Bradley. *Couple #65*: R. Curry, J. MacInnis. *Couple #18*: L. Wencker, J. Hayes. *Couple #41*: I. Gilliams, J. MacInnis. *Couple #11*: R. Curry, R. Fowler. *Couple #30*: E. Mills, A. Pelty. *Couple #25*: K. Chenoweth, G. Mitchell. *Couple #19*: M. Illes, C. Nicholaw. *Couple #14*: L.Wencker, B. Bradley. *Couple #40*: I. Gilliams, R. Fowler. *Couple #55*: S. S. Shannon, B. Bradley. *Couple #34*: R. Curry, J. Hayes. *Couple #62*: M. Illes, T. Warmen. *Swings*: Julio Augustin, Leslie Bell, Angelique Ilo, Scott Taylor.

Place: Steel Pier, Atlantic City, New Jersey. *Time*: August, 1933.

Act 1, Scene 1: The Beach/The Boardwalk. *Scene 2*: The Steel Pier Ballroom. *Scene 3*: Mick Hamilton's Office. *Scene 4*: The Rest Stations. *Scene 5*: The Steel Pier Ballroom. *Scene 6*: Behind the Bandstand. *Scene 7*: The Steel Pier Ballroom. *Scene 8*: Mick Hamilton's Office. *Scene 9*: The Steel Pier Ballroom. *Scene 10*: The Diving Horse Tank. *Scene 11*: The Steel Pier Ballroom/The Trenton Air Show.

Act 2, Scene 1: The Rest Stations. *Scene 2*: A Corridor near the Dance Floor. *Scene 3*: The Steel Pier Ballroom. *Scene 4*: Outside the Steel Pier Ballroom. *Scene 5*: The Rooftop of the Ballroom. *Scene 6*: The Steel Pier Ballroom. *Scene 7*: The Women's Rest Station. *Scene 8*: The Steel Pier Ballroom. *Scene 9*: The Women's Rest Station/Outside the Steel Pier.

ACT 1
Scene 1
"Waiting to Ride"
K. Ziemba
Scene 2
"Everybody Dance"
G. Harrison, M. Illes, R. Curry, S. S. Shannon
"Second Chance"
D. McDonald
Scene 4
"In Here"
D. Monk, J. Blum, J. Newman, V. Wright, J. C. Havens, K. Ziemba, T. Warmen, K. Chenoweth, A. Bevan, D. McDonald
Scene 5
"Montage I"
The Company
Scene 6
"Winning"
G. Harrison, Company
Scene 7
"Dance with Me"/"The Last Girl"
G. Harrison, K. Ziemba, D. McDonald, Company
"Montage II"
The Company
Scene 9
"Everybody's Girl"
D. Monk
Scene 10
"Wet"
K. Ziemba, D. McDonald
Scene 11
"Lovebird"
K. Ziemba
"Everybody Dance" (reprise)
G. Harrison, Company

ACT 2
Scene 1
"Leave the World Behind"
D. McDonlad, K. Ziemba, Company
Scene 3
"Montage III"
The Company
Scene 4
"Somebody Older"
D. Monk
Scene 5
"Running in Place"
K. Ziemba
Scene 6
"Lookin' for Love"
G. Harrison

"Two Little Words"
K. Chenoweth, M. Illes, R. Curry, S. S. Shannon
"First You Dream"
D. McDonald, K. Ziemba
Scene 8
"Steel Pier"
G. Harrison, K. Ziemba, M. Illes, R. Curry, S. S. Shannon
Scene 9
"Steel Pier" (reprise)
The Company

1997.08

THE LIFE

A Musical in Two Acts. Book by David Newman, Ira Gasman and Cy Coleman. Based on an original idea by Ira Gasman. Music by Cy Coleman. Lyrics by Ira Gasman. Directed by Michael Blakemore. Choreographed by Joey McKneely. Scenic design by Robin Wagner. Costumes design by Martin Pakledinaz. Lighting design by Richard Pilbrow. Sound design by Peter Fitzgerald. Music direction by Gordon Lowry Harrell. Orchestrations by Don Sebesky and Harold Wheeler. Dance and vocal arrangements by Cy Coleman and Doug Katsaros. Originally produced in New York City by Westbeth Theater Center (Arnold Engelman, Producing director). Produced by Roger Berlind, Martin Richards, Cy Coleman and Sam Crothers. Opened 26 April 1997 at the Ethel Barrymore Theatre and closed 7 June 1998 after 465 performances.

CAST (in order of appearance): *Jojo*: SAM HARRIS. *Carmen*: Lynn Sterling. *Chichi*: Sharon Wilkins. *Frenchie*: Katy Grenfell. *Tracy*: Judine Richárd. *Bobby*: Mark Bove. *Oddjob*: Michael Gregory Gong. *Silky*: Rudy Roberson. *Slick*: Mark Anthony Taylor. *Memphis*: CHUCK COOPER. *April*: Felicia Finley. *Snickers*: GORDON JOSEPH WEISS. *Lacy*: VERNEL BAGNERIS. *Queen*: PAMELA ISAACS. *Sonja*: LILLIAS WHITE. *Fleetwood*: KEVIN RAMSEY. *Mary*, (Angel): BELLAMY YOUNG. *Doll House Dancer*: Stephanie Michels. *Street Evangelists*: Judine Richárd, Rudy Roberson, Mark Anthony Taylor. *Cop*: Mark Bove. *Shoeshine*: Michael Gregory Gong. *Lou*: RICH HEBERT. *Shatellia*: Mark Anthony Taylor. *Enrique*: Rudy Roberson. *Monte Hustlers*: Mark Bove, Michael Gregory Gong, Mark Anthony Taylor.

Ensemble: Mark Bove, Felicia Finley, Chris Ghelfi, Michael Gregory Gong, Katy Grenfell, Stephanie Michels, Judine Richárd, Rudy Roberson, Lynn Sterling, Mark Anthony Taylor, Sharon Wilkins. *Swing*: Tracy Nicole Chapman.

Place: 42nd Street, (New York City.) *Time*: Then.

ACT 1
"Check It Out!"
The Company
"Use What You Got"
S. Harris, Company
"A Lovely Day to Be Out of Jail"
P. Isaacs, L. White
"A Piece of the Action"
K. Ramsey
"The Oldest Profession"
L. White
"Don't Take Much"
C. Cooper
"Go Home"
P. Isaacs, B. Young
"You Can't Get to Heaven"
P. Isaacs, L. White, Street Evangelists
"My Body"
K. Grenfell, S. Wilkins, J. Richárd, L. Sterling, L. White, P. Isaacs, F. Finley
"Why Don't They Leave Us Alone"
M. G. Gong, M. Bove, R. Roberson, M. A. Taylor, G. J. Weiss, F. Finley, L. Sterling, S. Wilkins, K. Grenfell, P. Isaacs, L. White, J. Richárd
"Easy Money"
B. Young, S. Harris, K. Ramsey
"He's No Good"
P. Isaacs
"I'm Leaving You"
P. Isaacs
"The Hookers' Ball"
V. Bagneris, Company

ACT 2
"Step Right Up"
R. Roberson, M. A. Taylor, M. G. Gong, M. Bove
"Mr. Greed"
S. Harris, M. Bove, M. G. Gong, R. Roberson, M. A. Taylor
"My Way or the Highway"
C. Cooper, P. Isaacs
"People Magazine"
R. Hebert, B. Young
"We Had a Dream"
P. Isaacs
"Use What You Got" (reprise)
B. Young, R. Hebert, S. Harris
"'Someday' Is For Suckers"
L. White, K. Grenfell, F. Finley, M. A. Taylor, L. Sterling, J. Richárd, S. Wilkins
"My Friend"
P. Isaacs, L. White
"We Gotta Go"
K. Ramsey, P. Isaacs
"Check It Out!" (reprise)
Company

1997.09

JEKYLL & HYDE

A Musical in Two Acts, 26 Scenes. Based on the novel "The Strange Case of Dr. Jekyll and Mr. Hyde" by Robert Louis Stevenson. Conceived for the stage by Steve Cuden and Frank Wildhorn. Book and lyrics by Leslie Bricusse. Music by Frank Wildhorn. Scenic design by Robin Phillips and James Noone. Costume design by Ann Curtis. Lighting design by Beverly Emmons. Properties and set dressing by Christina Poddubiuk. Sound design by Karl Richardson and Scott Stauffer. Orchestrations by Kim Scharnberg. Musical director, Jeremy Roberts. Musical conductor, Jason Howland. Vocal arrangements by Jason Howland and Ron Melrose. Musical supervisor, Jeremy Roberts. Special effects design by Gregory Meeh. Fight coordinator, J. Allen Suddeth. Choreography by Joey Pizzi. Directed by Robin Phillips. Previous developmental productions by the Alley Theatre (Houston), 5th Avenue Musical Theatre (Seattle), and Theatre Under the Stars (Houston). Associate producer, Bill Young. Executive producer, Gary Gunas (PACE). Produced by PACE Theatrical Group (Allen Becker, Brian Becker, Miles Wilkin, Scott Zieger) and Fox Theatricals (Michael Leavitt, David Fay, Leon Strauss, Robert Baudendistel, Harvey Harris), in association with Jerry Frankel, Magicworks Entertainment (Joe Marsh, Lee Marshall, Brad Krassner) and the Landmark Entertainment Group (Tony Christopher, Gary Goddard). Opened 28 April 1997 at the Plymouth Theatre and closed 7 January 2001 after 1543 performances[17]

CAST (in order of appearance): *John Utterson*: GEORGE MERRITT. *Sir Danvers Carew*: BARRIE INGHAM. *Dr. Henry Jekyll*: ROBERT CUCCIOLI, ROBERT EVAN (Wednesday, Saturday matinees). *An Old Man*, in the mental hospital: David Chaney. *Mental Patients*: David Koch, Bill E. Dietrich. *Doctor*: Donald Grody. *Attendants*: Frank Mastrone, Charles E. Wallace. *Nurses*: Emily Scott Skinner, Jodi Stevens. *Kate*, a cockle seller: Leah Hocking. *Alice*, a scullery maid: Emily Scott Skinner. *Molly*, a fish gutter: Jodi Stevens. *Bet*, a scullery maid: Jodi Stevens. *Polly*, a scrubber woman: Bonnie Schon. *Mike*, a clerk: John Treacy Egan. *Albert*, a barman: Frank Mastrone. *Davie*, a barrow boy: David Chaney. *Ned*, a sailor: David Koch. *Bill*, a docker: Bill E. Dietrich. *Jack*, a beggar: Charles E. Wallace. *Mr. Simon Stride*: Raymond Jaramillo McLeod. *Rupert*, Bishop of Basingstoke: Michael Ingram. *The Right Honorable Archibald Proops*: Brad Oscar. *Lord Savage*: Martin Van Truren. *Lady Beaconsfield*: Emily Zacharias. *General Lord Glossop*: Geoffrey Blaisdell. *Emma Carew*, Jekyll's fiancée: CHRISTIANE NOLL. *First Gentleman*: Frank Mastrone. *Second Gentleman*: Brad Oscar. *Manservant at Sir Danvers'*: David Chaney. *Under Footman*: Charles E. Wallace. *Grooms*: Bill E. Dietrich, John Treacy Egan. *Housemaids*: Emily Scott Skinner, Jodi Stevens. *Guinevere*, manageress of "The Red Rat": Emily Zacharias. *Lucy*, the main attraction at "The Red Rat": LINDA EDER. *Three Toughs*, of "The Red Rat": Bill E. Dietrich, David Koch, Charles E. Wallace. *Two Whores*: Emily Scott Skinner, Bonnie Schon. *Siegfried*, The Pianist at "The Red Rat": Geoffrey Blaisdell. *The Spider*, proprietor of "The Red Rat": Martin Van Treuren. *Sir Douglas*: Michael Ingram. *Sir Peter*: Brad Oscar. *Lord G*: Donald Grody. *Poole*, Jekyll's manservant: Donald Groody. *Edward Hyde*, Jekyll's "other half": ROBERT CUCCIOLI, ROBERT EVAN (Wednesday, Saturday matinees). *Dog*: B.J. *A Young*

[17]Subsequent national tour directed by David Warren, choreographed by Jerry Mitchell. Direction and scenic design based on Robin Phillips' original Broadway production. Dropped for subsequent tour were: "Good 'n' Evil," "His Work and Nothing More," "No One Knows Who I Am," "Obsession," "Dear Lord and Father of Mankind."

Girl, managed by Gwinny: Jodi Stevens. *A Newsboy*: Bill E. Dietrich. *A Priest*, at the Bishop's funeral: Frank Mastrone. *Mr Bisset*, an apothecary: David Chaney. *Policemen*: Michael Ingram, Geoffrey Blaisdell. *A Maitre d'Hotel*, at a social club: David Chaney. *A Doorman*, at the same: Charles E. Wallace. *Barrow Boys*: Michael Ingram, Brad Oscar, Geoffrey Blaisdell. *Boy Soprano*, at the wedding: LINDA EDER. *Bridesmaids*: Emily Scott Skinner, Jodi Stevens. *Priest at wedding*: David Chaney. *Curate*: Charles E. Wallace. *Choir Boy*: Bill E. Dietrich. *Swings*: Paul Hadobas, Rebecca Spencer.

(The action takes place in nineteenth century London.)

Act 1, Scene 1: A London Street. *Scene 2*: The Violent Ward, St. Jude's Hospital. *Scene 3*: A London Square. *Scene 4*: St. Jude's Hospital. *Scene 5*: The sidewalk, Regent's Park. *Scene 6*: Sir Danvers Carew's Home, Regent's Park. *Scene 7*: Dock Side, London's East End. *Scene 8*: Backstage at The Red Rat. *Scene 9*: The Red Rat. *Scene 10*: Harley Street. *Scene 11*: Dr. Jekyll's Consulting Room. *Scene 12*: Dr. Jekyll's Laboratory. *Scene 13*: The East End. *Scene 14*: Harley Street. *Scene 15*: Dr. Jekyll's Consulting Room, The Carew House. *Scene 16*: Dr. Jekyll's Consulting Room. *Scene 17*: The Embankment, Westminster.

Act 2, Scene 1: A London Street, Outside the Cathedral, A Pharmacy, Harley Street, Supper Club Entrance in the West End, Platform at Victoria Station. *Scene 2*: Dr. Jekyll's Laboratory. *Scene 3*: The Carew House, The River Bank. *Scene 4*: The Bridge, London's East End. *Scene 5*: Dr. Jekyll's Laboratory. *Scene 6*: Lucy's Room, above The Red Rat. *Scene 7*: Dr. Jekyll's Laboratory. *Scene 8*: Westminster. *Scene 9*: St. Anne's Church, Westminster.

ACT 1[18]

Scene 2
"Lost in the Darkness"
R. Cuccioli (Jekyll)
Scene 3
"Façade"
Ensemble
Scene 4
"Jekyll's Plea"
R. Cuccioli (Jekyll), Board of Governors
Scene 5
"Façade" (reprise)
Ensemble
Scene 6
"Emma's Reasons"
R. J. McLeod, C. Noll
"Take Me As I Am"
R. Cuccioli (Jekyll), C. Noll
Scene 7
"Façade" (reprise)
Ensemble
Scene 8
"No One Knows Who I Am"
C. Noll

---

[18]National tour restaged in Two Acts, a Prologue and Sixteen Scenes, with scene and song changes as follows:

Prologue: A London Street. *Act 1, Scene 1*: The Violent Ward, St. Jude's Hospital. *Scene 2*: A London Square. *Scene 3*: St. Jude's Hospital. *Scene 4*: Sir Danvers Carew's Home, Regent's Park. *Scene 5*: The Red Rat. *Scene 6*: Outside Dr. Jekyll's Laboratory. *Scene 7*: The Streets of London. *Scene 8*: Jekyll's Study. *Scene 9*: Shabby Street near The Red Rat.

Act 2, Scene 1: London Montage. *Scene 2*: Dr. Jekyll's Laboratory. *Scene 3*: Outside The Red Rat. *Scene 4*: Dr. Jekyll's Laboratory. *Scene 5*: Lucy's Room, above The Red Rat. *Scene 6*: Dr. Jekyll's Laboratory. *Scene 7*: St. Anne's Church, Westminster.

ACT 1
Scene 1
"Lost in the Darkness"
[Dr. Jekyll]
"I Need to Know"
[Dr. Jekyll]
Scene 2
"Façade"
[Ensemble]
Scene 3
"Board of Governors" (Jekyll's Plea)
[Dr. Jekyll, Board of Governors]
"Pursue the Truth"
[Dr. Jekyll, John Utterson]
Scene 4
"The Engagement Party"
[Sir Danvers, Simon Stride, Emma Carew]
"Take Me As I Am"
[Dr. Jekyll, E. Carew]
"Letting Go"
[Sir Danvers, E. Carew]
Scene 5
"Bring on the Men"
[Lucy, Ensemble]
Scene 6
"This Is the Moment"
[Dr. Jekyll]
"The Transformation"
[Dr. Jekyll]
(*Lyrics by* Steve Cuden, Leslie Bricusse and Frank Wildhorn.)
Scene 7
"Alive!"
[Edward Hyde, Lucy]
(*Lyrics by* Steve Cuden, Leslie Bricusse and Frank Wildhorn.)
Scene 8
"Sympathy, Tenderness"
[Lucy]
"Someone Like You"
[Lucy]
Scene 9
"Alive!" (reprise)[Edward Hyde]

ACT 2
Scene 1
"Murder, Murder!"
[Ensemble]
(*Lyrics by* Steve Cuden, Leslie Bricusse and Frank Wildhorn.)
Scene 2
"Once Upon a Dream"
[Emma Carew]
(*Lyrics by* Steve Cuden, Leslie Bricusse and Frank Wildhorn.)
"Streak of Madness"
[Emma Carew, Dr. Jekyll]
"In His Eyes"
[Lucy, Emma Carew]
Scene 3
"(It's a) Dangerous Game"
[Lucy, Edward Hyde]
"Façade" (reprise)
[Spider, Ensemble]
Scene 4
"The Way Back"
[Dr. Jekyll]
Scene 5
"A New Life"
[Lucy]
"Sympathy, Tenderness"
[Edward Hyde]
Scene 6
"Confrontation"
[Dr. Jekyll and Edward Hyde]
Scene 7
"Facade" (reprise)
[Ensemble]
"Final Transformation"
[Dr. Jekyll)

Scene 9
"Good 'N' Evil"
L. Eder
Scene 11
"This Is the Moment"
R. Cuccioli (Jekyll)
Scene 13
"Alive!"
R. Cuccioli (Hyde)
Scene 15
"His Work, and Nothing More"
R. Cuccioli (Jekyll), G. Merritt, B. Ingram, C. Noll
Scene 16
"Someone Like You"
L. Eder
Scene 17
"Alive!"
R. Cuccioli (Hyde), Ensemble

ACT 2
Scene 1
"Murder, Murder!"
B. E. Dietrich, Ensemble
Scene 2
"Once Upon a Dream"
C. Noll
"Obsession"
R. Cuccioli (Jekyll)
Scene 3
"In His Eyes"
L. Eder, C. Noll
Scene 4
"(It's a) Dangerous Game"
R. Cuccioli (Hyde), L. Eder
Scene 5
"The Way Back"
R. Cuccioli (Jekyll)
Scene 6
"A New Life"
L. Eder
"Sympathy, Tenderness"
R. Cuccioli (Hyde)
Scene 7
"Lost in the Darkness" (reprise)
R. Cuccioli (Jekyll)
"Confrontation"
R. Cuccioli (as Jekyll and Hyde)
Scene 8
"Facade" (reprise)
Ensemble
Scene 9
"Dear Lord and Father of Mankind"
L. Eder (Boy Soprano)

1997.10 CANDIDE

A Revival of the Musical in Two Act[19]. Book adapted from Voltaire's satire (of the same name) by Hugh Wheeler[20]. Music by Leonard Bernstein. Lyrics by Richard Wilbur. Additional lyrics by Stephen Sondheim and John Latouche. Directed by Harold Prince. Choreography by Patricia Birch. Scenery designed by Clarke Dunham. Costumes designed by Judith Dolan. Lighting designed by Ken Billington. Sound designed by Jonathan Deans. Music continuity and additional orchestrations by John Mauceri. Musical supervision and direction by Eric Stern. Orchestrations by Leonard Bernstein and Hershy Kay. Produced by LIVENT (U.S.) Inc. (Garth Drabinsky, Chairman). Opened 29 April 1997 at the Gershwin Theatre and closed 27 July 1997 after 103 performances.

CAST (in order of appearance): *Voltaire*: JIM DALE. *Candide*: JASON DANIELEY. *Paquette*: STACEY LOGAN. *Baroness Von Thunder*: Julie Johnson. *Baron Von Thunder*: MAL Z. LAWRENCE. *Cunegonde*: HAROLYN BLACKWELL, GLENDA BALKAN (alt.). *Maximilian*: BRENT BARRETT. *Hugo*, Maximilian's Servant: ARTE JOHNSON. *Old Lady*: ANDREA MARTIN. *Dr Pangloss*: JIM DALE. *Governor*: JIM DALE. *Radu*, A Bulgarian Soldier: ARTE JOHNSON. *Second Bugarian Soldier*: Paul Harman. *Don Isaachar*, The Rich Jew: ARTE JOHNSON. *Grand Inquisitor*: MAL Z. LAWRENCE. *Heresy Agent*: David Girolmo. *Judge Gomez*: ARTE JOHNSON. *Businessman*: JIM DALE. *Governor*: JIM DALE. *Governor's Aide*: Allen Hidago. *Columbo*, A Slave Driver: MAL Z. LAWRENCE. *Father Bernard*: ARTE JOHNSON. *Sheep One*: Nanne Puritz. *Sheep Two*: D'Vorah Bailey. *Lion*: Seth Malkin. *Pasha-Prefect of Constantinople*: MAL Z. LAWRENCE. *Turhan Bey*, A Constantinople Gambler: ARTE JOHNSON. *Second Gambler* (Police Chief): JIM DALE. *Sage*: JIM DALE. *Ensemble*: D'Vorah Bailey, Mary Kate Boulware, Diana Brownstone, Alvin Crawford, Chrisopher F. Davis, Sherrita Duran, Deanna Dys, David Girolmo, Paul Harman, Joy Hermalyn, Allen Hidalgo, Wendy Hilliard, Elizabeth Jimenez, Julie Johnson, Ken Krugman, Chad Larget, Shannon Lewis, Seth Malkin, Andrew Pacho, Nanne Puritz, Owen Taylor, Eric Van Hoven. *Swings*: Matthew Aibel, Rachel Coloff, Joseph P. McDonnell, Starla Pace.

ACT 1
"Life Is Happiness Indeed"
J. Dale, J. Danieley, H. Blackwell, B. Barrett, S. Logan
(*Lyrics by* Stephen Sondheim.)
"(The) Best of All Possible Worlds"
J. Dale, J. Danieley, H. Blackwell, B. Barrett, S. Logan, Ensemble
"Oh Happy We"
J. Danieley, H. Blackwell
"It Must Be So"
J. Danieley
"Westphalian Chorale"
Ensemble
(*Lyrics by* Leonard Bernstein.)
"Glitter and Be Gay"
H. Blackwell
"Auto-da-fé" (What a Day)
Full Company
(*Lyrics by* John Latouche, Stephen Sondheim.)
"Candide's Lament" (This World)
J. Danieley
(*Lyrics by* Stephen Sondheim.)
"You Were Dead, You Know"
J. Danieley, H. Blackwell
(*Lyrics by* John Latouche.)
"I Am (So) Easily Assimilated"
A. Martin, Dons, Company
(*Lyrics by* Leonard Bernstein.)
Quartet Finale
J. Danieley, H. Blackwell, J. Dale, A. Martin, Ensemble

ACT 2
"Ballad of the New World"
J. Danieley, Ensemble
"My Love"
J. Dale, B. Barrett
(*Lyrics by* John Latouche, Richard Wilbur.)
"Alleluia"
Ensemble
"Sheep Song"
N. Puritz, D. Bailey, S. Malkin, S. Logan
(*Lyrics by* Stephen Sondheim.)
"Bon Voyage" (Schottische)
J. Dale, Company
"Quiet"
A. Martin, J. Danieley, S. Logan
"(The) Best of All Possible Worlds" (reprise)
J. Danieley, S. Logan, A. Martin, N. Puritz, D. Bailey
"What's the Use"
M. Z. Lawrence, A. Johnson, J. Dale, Ensemble

[19]This revival first produced on Broadway 8 March 1974 at the Broadway Theatre for 740 performances; original production 1 December 1956 at the Martin Beck Theatre for 73 performances. For Synopsis of Scenes and Musical Numbers, see 1974 revival.
[20]Original book by Lillian Hellman.

"You Were Dead, You Know" (reprise)
J. Danieley, H. Blackwell
"Make Our Garden Grow"
Full Company

1997.11 THE WIZARD OF OZ

A Musical Spectacle in One Act, 16 Scenes[21]. Based on the novel of the same name by L. Frank Baum and the MGM film adaptation by Noel Langley, Florence Ryerson, Edgar Allan Woolf. Book by John Kane for the Royal Shakespeare Company. Music by Harold Arlen. Lyrics by E. Y. Harburg. Background music by Herbert Stothart. Directed by Robert Johanson. Choreographed by Jamie Rocco. Scenic design by Michael Anania. Costume design by Gregg Barnes. Lighting design by Timothy Hunter. Sound design by David R. Paterson. Musical director, Jeffrey Rizzo. Production originally presented at the Papermill Playhouse, New Jersey. Produced by Madison Square Garden Productions (Tim Hawkins, producer). Opened 15 May 1997 at the Theatre at Madison Square Garden and closed 8 June 1997 after 45 performances[22].

CAST (in order of appearance) In Kansas: *Dorothy*: JESSICA GROVÉ. *Toto*: Plenty. *Aunt Em*: JUDITH MCCAULEY. *Uncle Henry*: Roger Preston Smith. *Hunk*: LARA TEETER. *Hickory*: MICHAEL GRUBER. *Zeke*: KEN PAGE. *Almira Gulch*: ROSEANNE (BARR). *Professor Marvel*: GERRY VICHI.

In Oz: *Glinda*, the Good Witch: JUDITH MCCAULEY. *Mayor of Munchkinland*: Louis Carry. *Barristers*:Wendy Coates, Jonas Moscartolo. *Coroner*: Derrick McGinty *The Wicked Witch of the West*: ROSEANNE (BARR). *The Scarecrow*: LARA TEETER. *The Tinman*: MICHAEL GRUBER. *The Cowardly Lion*: KEN PAGE. *The Wizard of Oz*: GERRY VICHI. *Nikko*, Commander of the Flying Monkeys: Martin Klebba. *Winkie General*: Roger Preston Smith.

Munchkins, Crows, Apple Trees, Poppies, Citizens of Oz, Flying Mionkeys and Winkies: Vivian Y. Bayubay, Maggie Keenan Bolger, Patrick Boyd, Kai Braithwaite, Lindsy Canuel, Casey Colgan, Christine DeVito, Chantele M. Doucette, Peter William Dunn, Danielle Lee Greaves, Gail Cook Howell, Heidi Karol Johnson, Martin Klebba, Benjamin E. Lear, Don Mayo, M. Kathryn Quinlan, Gemini Quintos, D. J. Salisbury, Dana Scarborough, Samantha Sensale, Evan Silverberg, Andrea Szucs, Christopher Trousdale, Wendy Watts. *Swings*: Lenny Daniel, Jamie Waggoner. *Children's Choirs*: Oaks School #3 (Oceanside, New York), Public School 312 (Brooklyn, New York), Public School 95 (Queens, New York), Terrill Middle School (Scotch Plains, New Jersey).

Scene 1: The Gale's Farm in Kansas. *Scene 2*: Professor Marvel's Wagon. *Scene 3*: The Gale's Farm. *Scene 4*: Munchkinland. *Scene 5*: A Cornfield. *Scene 6*: An Apple Orchard. *Scene 7*: A Wild Forest. *Scene 8*: A Field of Poppies. *Scene 9*: Outside the Gates of the Emerald City. *Scene 10*: Inside the Emerald City. *Scene 11*: The Wizard's Chamber. *Scene 12*: The Haunted Forest. *Scene 13*: Inside the Witch's Castle. *Scene 14*: The Wizard's Chamber. *Scene 15*: Inside the Emerald City. *Scene 16*: The Gale's Farm in Kansas.

MUSICAL NUMBERS
Scene 1
"Over the Rainbow"
J. Grové
Scene 3
The Cyclone
Scene 4
"Come Out, Come Out"
J. McCauley, J. Grové, Munchkins
"Ding Dong! The Witch Is Dead"
J. McCauley, L. Carry, W. Coates, J. Moscartolo, D. McGinty, Munchkins
"Follow the Yellow Brick Road"
J. Grové, Munchkins
Scene 5
"If I Only Had a Brain"
L. Teeter, J. Grové, Crows
"We're Off to See the Wizard"
J. Grové, L. Teeter
Scene 6
"If I Only Had a Heart"
M. Gruber, J. Grové, L. Teeter, Apple Trees
"We're Off to See the Wizard" (reprise)
J. Grové, L. Teeter, M. Gruber
Scene 7
"Lions and Tigers and Bears"
J. Grové, L. Teeter, M. Gruber
"If I Only Had the Nerve"/"We're Off to See the Wizard" (reprise)
K. Page, J. Grové, M. Gruber, L. Teeter
Scene 8
"Poppies"/"Optimistic Voices"
J. McCauley, J. Grové, L. Teeter, M. Gruber, K. Page, Roseanne, Poppies
Scene 9
"Optimistic Voices" (reprise)
Female Chorus
Scene 10
"(The) Merry Old Land of Oz"
J. Grové, L. Teeter, M. Gruber, K. Page, Guard, Citizens of Oz
"(If I Were) King of the Forest"
K. Page, J. Grové, M. Gruber, L. Teeter
Scene 12
"March of the Winkies"
Winkies
Scene 13
"Ding Dong! The Witch Is Dead" (reprise)
Winkies, J. Grové, K. Page, L. Teeter, M. Gruber
Scene 15
"Over the Rainbow" (reprise)
J. McCauley
Scene 16
Finale
Company

1997.12 KING DAVID

A Musical Concert in Two Acts, Ten Scenes. Book and lyrics by Tim Rice. Based on the story of the shepherd boy who was chosen to be King of Israel. Music by Alan Menken. Directed by Mike Ockrent. Scenic design by Tony Walton. Costume design by William Ivey Long. Lighting design by David Agress. Sound design by Jonathan Deans. Musical direction, vocal and incidental music arrangements by Michael Kosarin. Orchestrations by Douglas Besterman. Co-producer, Ritza B. Barath. Produced by Walt Disney Theatrical Productions and André Djaoui. Opened 18 May 1997 at the New Amsterdam Theatre and closed 23 May 1997 after 6 performances.

CAST (in order of appearance): *David*: MARCUS LOVETT. *Bathsheba*: ALICE RIPLEY. *Young Solomon*: Daniel James Hodd. *Joab*: STEPHEN BOGARDUS. *Samuel*: PETER SAMUEL. *Saul*: MARTIN VIDNOVIC. *Agag*: Timothy Robert Blevins. *Jesse*: Michael Goz. *Abner*: TIMOTHY SHEW. *Jonathan*: ROGER BART. *Michal*: JUDY KUHN. *Goliath*: BILL NOLTE. *Young Absalom*: Dylan Lovett. *Absalom*: ANTHONY GALDE. *Uriah*: Peter C. Ermides. *Abishag*: Kimberly JaJuan.

Ensemble: Mark Agnes, Joan Barber, Stephanie Bast, Robin Baxter, Kristen Behrendt, Timothy Robert Blevins, Benjamin Brecher, Timothy Breese, Kirsti Carnahan, Nick Cavarra, Philip A. Chaffin, Michael DeVries, Peter C. Ermides, Hunter Foster, Ray Friedeck, Anthony Galde, Michael Goz, Ellen Hoffman, Kimberly JaJuan, James Javore, Keith Byron Kirk, Ann Kittredge, David Lowenstein, Barbara Marineau, Donna Lee Marshall, Michael X. Martin, Karen Murphy, Bill Nolte, Ilysia Pierce, Ron Sharpe, Timothy Shew, Rachel Ulanet, Andrew Varela, Melanie Vaughan, Sally Wilfert, Laurie Williamson.

Act 1, Scene 1: Prologue. *Scene 2*: Samuel. *Scene 3*: Saul. *Scene 4*: Goliath. *Scene 5*: Jonathan. *Scene 6*: Exile.

Act 2, Scene 1: David the King. *Scene 2*: Bathsheba. *Scene 3*: Absalom. *Scene 4*: David's Final Days.

ACT 1
Scene 1
Prologue
M. Lovett, A. Ripley, D. J. Hodd, S. Bogardus, Chorus
Scene 2
"Israel and Saul"
S. Bogardus, P. Samuel, M. Vidnovic, Chorus
"Samuel Confronts Saul"
M. Vidnovic, P. Samuel, T. R. Blevins, Chorus

[21]THE WIZARD OF OZ was previously produced in a different adaptation 22 March 1989 at Radio City Music Hall for 37 performances.
[22]Performed an irregular performance schedule of 12 performances a week.

"Samuel Anoints David"
S. Bogardus, P. Samuel, M. Goz, M. Lovett, Chorus
Scene 3
"The Enemy Within"
M. Vidnovic, Chorus
"There is a View . . . "
S. Bogardus, T. Shew, M. Vidnovic, Chorus
"Psalm 8"
M. Lovett
"Genius from Bethlehem"
M. Vidnovic, M. Lovettt, T. Shew, S. Bogardus, R. Bart, J. Kuhn
Scene 4
"The Valley of Elah"
B. Nolte, T. Shew, S. Bogardus, M. Lovett, M. Vidnovic, Soldiers
"Goliath of Gath"
B. Nolte, M. Lovett, S. Bogardus, Soldiers, Chorus
"Sheer Perfection"
S. Bogardus, M. Vidnovic, M. Lovett, J. Kuhn
Scene 5
"Saul Has Slain His Thousands"
S. Bogardus, Chorus
"You Have It All"
M. Vidnovic, R. Bart, M. Lovett
"Psalm 23"
M. Vidnovic, M. Lovett
"You Have It All"/"Sheer Perfection" (reprises)
R. Bart, S. Bogardus, J. Kuhn, M. Lovett
Scene 6
"Hunted Partridge on the Hill"
S. Bogardus, M. Vidnovic, J. Kuhn, M. Lovett, Men
"The Death of Saul"
M. Vidnovic, R. Bart, P. Samuel, Chorus
"How Are the Mighty Fallen"
M. Lovett, Chorus

ACT 2
Scene 1
"This New Jerusalem"
M. Lovett, A. Galde, R. Bart, S. Bogardus, Chorus
"David and Michal"
M. Lovett, S. Bogardus, J. Kuhn
"The Ark Brought to Jerusalem"
M. Lovett, Chorus
"Never Again"
J. Kuhn, M. Lovett
Scene 2
"How Wonderful the Peace"
A. Galde, S. Bogardus, M. Lovett, Chorus
"Off Limits"
A. Ripley, M. Lovett, S. Bogardus
"Warm Spring Night"
M. Lovett
"When in Love"
A. Ripley
"Uriah's Fate Sealed"
M. Lovett, S. Bogardus, A. Ripley, Chorus
"Atonement"
M. Lovett, M. Vidnovic, P. Samuel, A. Ripley, Chorus
Scene 3
"The Caravan Moves On"
S. Bogardus, A. Galde, M. Lovett, M. Vidnovic, P. Samuel, Men
"Death of Absalom"
S. Bogardus, A. Galde
"Absalom My Absalom"
M. Lovett
Scene 4
"Solomon"
D. J. Hodd, S. Bogardus, M. Lovett, A. Ripley
"David's Final Hours"
J. Kuhn, M. Lovett, S. Bogardus, A. Ripley, B. Nolte, M. Vidnovic, R. Bart, P. Samuel, Chorus
"The Long Long Day"
M. Lovett
"This New Jerusalem"
D. J. Hodd, Company

1997–1998 SEASON

Emily Skinner and Alice Ripley in SIDE SHOW
Joan Marcus/Photofest

1997–1998 SEASON

1997.13 FOREVER TANGO

A Dance Revue in Two Acts. Created and directed by Luis Bravo. Musical direction and arrangements by Lisandro Adrover. Choreography by the dancers. Costume design, Argemira Affonso. Lighting design, Luis Bravo. Sound design, Tom Craft. Associate producer, Joe Watson. Produced by Steven Baruch, Richard Frankel, Thomas Viertel, Marc Routh, Jujamcyn Theatres, Interamerica, Inc. Opened 19 June 1997 at the Walter Kerr Theatre, closing 5 April 1998; moved 15 April 1998 to the Marquis Theatre, and closed 1 August 1998 after 453 performances.

CAST: *Dancers*: Miriam Larici, Diego DiFalco, Luis Castro and Claudia Mendoza, Carlos Gavito and Marcela Durán, Jorge Torres and Karina Piazza, Carlos Vera and Laura Marcarie, Guillermo Merlo and Cecilia Saia, Gabriel Ortega and Sandra Bootz, Pedro Calveyra and Nora Robles, Carolina Zokalski. *Singer*: Carlos Morel.

Musicians: *Bandoneóns*: Lisandro Adrover, Hector Del Curto, Carlos Niesi, Victor Lavallen. *Violins*: Humberto Ridolfi, Rodion Boshoer. *Viola*: Oscar Hasbun. *Cello*: Dino Quarleri. *Bass*: Silvio Acosta. *Piano*: Fernando Marzan. *Keyboard*: Mario Araolaza.

ACT 1

"Preludio del Bandoneón y la Noche"
M. Larici, D. DiFalco
Conception: Luis Bravo.
A metaphorical scene composed and written from the mind of a bandoneón virtuoso. The image presented is of a bandoneón in search of passion. The metaphor represents both. The bandoneón—personified by the male dancer—gives birth to the woman, his dream and his ideal. She is born of his dream, but is lost and becomes the night, where he pursues her.

Overture
Forever Tango Orchestra
(*Music by* Lisandro Adrover.)

"El Suburbio"

This typical scene of the 1880s takes place in a brothel located between the barrio and the city where people of all classes meet. The choreography of the fight, as the two "compadritos" fight for a woman, asserts their power.

"A Los Amigos"
Forever Tango Orchestra
(*Music by* A. Pontier.)

"Derecho Viejo"
K. Piazza, J. Torres
(*Music by* E. Arolas.)
A scene in the famous Hansen House in the early 1900s as the tango began to spread throughout Buneos Aires. People of all classes gathered to dance the prohibited "tango" at one of the city's most reputable dance spots.

"El Dia Que Me Quieras"
C. Morel
(*Music and Lyrics by* C. Gardel and A. Lepera.)
The song is the romantic wish of the singer wishing for his unachievable dream. Carlos Gardel, Argentina's most famous singer, made this one of the tango's most popular songs of the 1930s.

"La Mariposa"
L. Macarie, C. Vera
(*Music by* O. Pugliese.)

"Comme Il Faut"
S. Bootz, G. Ortega
(*Music by* E. Arolas.)
The tango, prohibted in Buenos Aires, was introduced to Parisian high society in the 1930s. Only after it was accepted by Parisian aristocracy was it finally welcomed by Buenos Aires' "good families." The tango eventually broke the barrier that separated Buenos Aires' rich elite from the lower classes near the port. The scene reflects years when the tango won legitimacy in Buenos Aires as it became the craze of Paris salons.

"Berretín"
Forever Tango Orchestra
(*Music by* P. Laurenz.)
A piece to the essential emotion of the tanguero. The love that can not be because it does not exist. The infatuation.

"La Tablada"
C. Mendoza, L. Castro
(*Music by* F. Canaro.)
This dance is in the typical style of the pretentious Argentine middle class. More than a tango, it is a playful exaggeration. By the 1920s, the street tough of the turn of century known as the compadron, had been replaced by the compadrito—a middle class imitation. The narcissistic gestures of the male dancer and his exaggerated "macho" act were part of the role but also underlined by his obsessive insecurity. The woman, in turn, plays the coquette.

"Milongueando En El '40"
C. Saia, G. Merlo
(*Music by* A. Pontier.)

"S.V.P."
M. Durán, C. Gavito
(*Music by* Astor Piazzolla.)
Like the initial dream, this dance is a testimony to the encounter—or disencounter between man and woman. The dancers search for each other with the intensity born of passion. Yet, they walk away from each other at the end of the dance, in this allegory of the duality of passion and lust, search, and desperation and loss that is the tango, leaving us with the sense of incompleteness of the porteño.

"Responso"
Forever Tango Orchestra
(*Music by* A. Troilo.)

"Azabache"
(Entire) Company
(*Music by* E. M. Fracini.)
In the early 1900s, the residents of San Telmo gathered to dance "Candombes." Descendants of African slaves brought to Rio de la Plata by the Conquistadores in the 1700s stayed behind, mixing their rhythms in this precursor of the milonga and the tango.

ACT 2

"Tanguera"
N. Robles, P. Calveyra
(*Music by* M. Mores.)
From the 1950s, she was the woman with an attitude where only the most brazen dared to show their lust for life and their carnality dancing a tango.

"A Evaristo Carriego"
M. Durán, C. Gavito
(*Music by* E. Rovira.)
The eternal fantasy. The impossibility of an older man with a younger woman. They meet again, and finally, he seduces her. This is the ultimate conquest. She has given herself to him, submitted to his will. Yet he is empty, incomplete. Having lost the challenge of her seduction, he remains aloof and distant. Once again—like the tango—he is alone.

"Payadora"
Forever Tango Orchestra
(*Music by* J. Plaza.)

"Quejas De Bandoneón"
L. Marcarie, C. Vera
(*Music by* J. de Dios Filiberto.)
Bandoneón, instrument of tears and pain, solitude and melancholy. Its high wailing laments fill the nights of arrabales in Buenos Aires.

"Gallo Ciego"
K. Piazza, J. Torres
(*Music by* A. Bardi.)

"Balda Para un Loco"
C. Morel
(*Music by* Astor Piazzolla. *Lyrics by* H. Ferrer.)
The eternal "crazy." Always in love; with a flower, with a cloud, with a wisp of air—he is the kite taken by the wind, floating in every direction and searching . . . searching for what? The perfect flower, the music of a garbage can, a street horn or . . . perhaps . . . just to turn the corner and run in "Her." A toast to the "crazy!"

"La Cumparista"
C. Saia, G. Merlo; K. Piazza, J. Torres; M. Durán, C. Gavito
(*Music by* G. M. Rodriguez.)
Three couples in this tribute to the most famous of all tangos.

"Jealousy"
Forever Tango Orchestra
(*Music by* Jacob Gade.)

"Felicia"
C. Mendoza, L. Castro
(*Music by* E. Saborido.)
The is a tribute to the "compadrito" born of Italian culture. Like the wise guys of the New York streets, these characters were also important to the Buenos Aires tango scene. The eternal cat and mouse game between man and woman.
"Adiós Nonino"
Forever Tango Orchestra
(*Music by* Astor Piazzolla.)
Astor Piazzolla wrote this mournful tribute to his father, Nonino, upon his death. It was first played during his funeral.
"Libertango"
C. Saia, G. Merlo
(*Music by* Astor Piazzolla.)
Romance del Bandoneón y la Noche: "Tus Ojos de Cielo"
M. Larici, D. DiFalco
(*Music by* Lisandro Adrover. *Conception*: Luis Bravo.)
And the metaphor continues between the bandoneón and its passion for the night. In the end, she returns to her origins in the emotions of the bandoneón.
"Lo Que Vendrá" (Finale)
(Dance) Company
(*Music by* Astor Piazzolla.)

1997.14 UMABTHA: THE ZULU MACBETH

A Revival of the Zulu Musical in Two Acts[1]. Written and directed by Welcome Msomi. Music by Welcome Msomi with traditional songs. Assistant director and vocal arranger, Thuli Dumakude. Choreographed by Thuli Dumakude, Mduduzi Zwane, Mafika Mgwazi. Original lighting by Mannie Manim; lighting for this production by France Mavana and Denis Hutchinson. Sound by Emmanuel McGarth. A Production of the Johannesburg Civic Theater. Produced by Lincoln Center Festival 97. Opened 21 July 1997 at the New York State Theatre and closed 27 July 1997 after 7 performances.

CAST: *Mabatha* (Macbeth), the King's cousin: THABANI PATRICK TSHANINI. *Ka Madonsela* (Lady Macbeth): DIEKENTSENG MNISI. *Dangane* (Duncan), the King: LAWRENCE MASONDO. *Donebane* (Donaldbain), the Prince: BUYANI SHANGASE. *Makhiwane* (Malcolm), the Prince: MARTIN JWARA. *Mafudu* (Macduff), the King's cousin: Qond'okwakhe Mngwengwe. *Bhangane* (Banquo), the King's Induna/*Isipoki* (Spirit): Qed'umunyu Zungu. *Folose* (Fleance), Bhangane's son/*Isipoki* (Spirit): Shaun Dugen. *Isangoma 1, 2, 3* (Witches): S'bongile Ngqulunga, Promise S'thembile Jali, Mary-Anne Busi Mchunu.

Ka Makhawulana (Lady Macduff), Maludu's wife: Philile Sibiya. *Indodana* (Mafudu's son): Skhumbuzo Nsele. *Sidakwa*: Skhumbuzo Nsele. *The King's Guard*: Skhumbuzo Nsele. *Isipoki (Spirit)*: Skhumbuzo Nsele. *Hoshweni* (Ross)/*Isipoki* (Spirit): Zam'akhule Ngiba. *Linalo* (Lennox)/*Isipoki* (Spirit): Cyprian Nzama. *Anganao* (Angus)/ *Inceku/Isipoki/uMbulali II*: Thakozani Makhoba. *Inceku/Dance Captain*: Mduduzi Zwane. *Imbongi*, the King's praise singer/*Isipoki*: Pa Vusi Chili. *Inyanga/Isipoki*: Thal'ithemba Mthembu. *Isalukozi*, the nurse: Thokozile Gumede. *Msimbithi*, the messenger: Philani Radebe. *KaMadonsela understudy I/Intombi* (Maiden): Bulelwa Maqungo. *KaMadonsela understudy II/Intombi* (Maiden): Gcinile Nkosi. *Mabatha understudy/Inceku* (King's servant): Vumisani Ndlavu. *Mafudu understudy/Inceku* (King's servant): Xolani Ncobeni.

Izintombi (Maidens): Thembelihle Chiliza, Bongiwe Hlophe, Nomthandaze Langa, Lady-Fair Mngadi, Thandekile Msomi, Ntombifuthi Nzama, Winile Sibiya. *Drummers*: William Lembede, Bernard Hlophe, Jacob Makatsanyane, David Msimango, Bong'nkosi Nxumalo. *Igoso*, Captain of the Warriors: Mafika Ngwazi. *Iphini* (understudies): Joseph Mngumi, Prince Gambushe, Zafuka Qwatubane. *Umbulali I* (Murderer)/*Ibutho* (Warrior): Mbongwa Njilo. *Umbali II* (Murderer)/ *Ibutho* (Warrior): Bhekisisa Mthembu. *Amabutho*, Warriors: Bhekumuthi Cele, Magazine Amon Cele, Mazwi Cele, Kufakwakhe Dlamini, France Duna, Zwelibanzi Gansa, Mbokodo Mhlongo, Sipho Mngadi, Bhekuyise Mnyandu, Mkhanyiselwa Mvundla, Xolani Ngubane, Alpheus Ngwazi, Nkosibuka Qumbisa.

MUSICAL NUMBERS[2]
"Bayeza Abangoma"
"Wathukuthela"
"Wangishiya U Mabatha"
"Washumlilo"
"Qon Qo Qo"
"Umngcwabo"
"Udumo Lonke Mbathazeli"
"Kwasa Kusile"
"Shayani Izandla"
"Indlu Kamalandela"
"Bhula Wenyanga"
"Obani Labaya"

1997.15 1776

A Revival of the Musical in Two Acts, 7 Scenes[3]. Book by Peter Stone. Based on a conception of Sherman Edwards (about the making of the Declaration of Independence). Music and lyrics by Sherman Edwards. Directed by Scott Ellis. Musical staging by Kathleen Marshall. Settings designed by Tony Walton. Costumes designed by William Ivey Long. Lighting designed by Brian Nason. Sound designed by Brian Ronan. Orchestrations by Brian Besterman. Dance arrangements by Peter Howard. Musical direction by Paul Gemignani. Dialects by K. C. Ligon. Produced by the Roundabout Theatre Company (Todd Haimes, Artistic director; Ellen Richard, General manager). Opened 14 August 1997 at the Criterion Center Stage Right and closed 16 November 1997 after 109 performances; re-opened 3 December 1997 at the Gershwin Theatre under the commercial auspices of James M. Nederlander, Stewart F. Lane, Rodger Hess, Bill Haber, Robert Halmi, Jr., Dodger Endemol Theatrical Productions and Hallmark Entertainment, and closed 14 June 1998 after 224 additional performances. Total: 333 performances.

CAST: *Members of the Continental Congress*: *John Hancock*, President: Richard Poe. *Dr. Josiah Bartlett*, New Hampshire: Michael X. Martin. *John Adams*, Massachusetts: BRENT SPINER. *Stephen Hopkins*, Rhode Island: TOM ALDREDGE. *Roger Sherman*, Connecticut: John Herrera. *Lewis Morris*, New York: Tom Riis Farrell. *Robert Livingston*, New York: Daniel Marcus. *Reverend Jonathan Witherspoon*, New Jersey: Jerry Lanning. *Benjamin Franklin*, Pennsylvania: PAT HINGLE. *John Dickinson*, Pennsylvania: MICHAEL CUMPSTY. *James Wilson*, Pennsylvania: Michael Winther. *Caesar Rodney*, Delaware: Michael McCormick. *Colonel Thomas McKean*, Delaware: Bill Nolte. *George Read*, Delaware: Kevin Ligon. *Samuel Chase*, Maryland: Ric Stoneback. *Richard Henry Lee*, Virginia: Merwin Foard. *Thomas Jefferson*, Virginia: Paul Michael Valley. *Joseph Hewes*, North Carolina: David Lowenstein. *Edward Rutledge*, South Carolina: GREGG EDELMAN. *Dr. Lyman Hall*, Georgia: Brian Sutherland.

Charles Thomson, Congressional Secretary: Guy Paul. *Andrew McNair*, Congressional Custodian: MacIntyre Dixon. *A Leather Apron*: Joseph Cassidy. *Courier*: Dashiell Eaves. *Abigail Adams*: Linda Emond. *Martha Jefferson*: Lauren Ward. *Painter*: Ben Sheaffer.

1997.16 THE LAST EMPRESS

A Musical in Two Acts, a Prologue, Epilogue and 13 Scenes, in Korean. Book by Mun Yul Yi. Adaptation by Kwang Lim Kim. Music by Hee Gab Kim. Lyrics by In Ja Yang. Directed by Ho Jin Yun. Choreography by Byung Goo Seo. Costume design by Hyun Sook Kim. Scenic design by Dong Woo Park. Lighting design by Hyung O Choi. Sound by Ki Young Kim. Musical direction by Kolleen Park. Orchestrations and additional music by Peter Casey. Executive producer, Young Hwan Kim. Associate producers, Sang Ryul Lee, Su Mun Lee, Young il Yang, Woo Jong Lee. Produced by Arts Communications Seoul Company (A-Com). Opened 15 August 1997 at the New York State Theater and closed 24 August 1997 after 12 performances[4].

CAST: *Queen Min*, Ja-young Min: WONJUNG KIM, TAEWON KIM (alternate). *Taewongun*, King Kojung's Father: JAE HWAN LEE. *King Kojung*: HEE SUNG YU. *Inoue*, Ambassador of Japan: HEE JUNG LEE. *Itoh Hirobumi*, Prime Minister of Japan: MU YEOL CHOI. *Kye Hun Hong*, General Hong: MIN SOO KIM. *Miura*

---

[1]A Production of the Johannesburg Civic Theatre (South Africa). Previously produced in New York Off-Broadway 9 April 1979 at the Entermedia Theatre for 41 performances. The 1979 production was performed in Two Acts, 21 Scenes.

[2]No Scenes or Musical Numbers listed in programs. List of musical numbers prepared from 1979 production and recordings.

[3]Originally produced in New York 16 March 1969 at the 46th Street Theatre for 1217 performances. For Synopsis of Scenes and Musical Numbers, see original 1969 production. For this revival, an intermission was added after Scene 5; the reprise of "Yours, Yours, Yours" in the final scene was renamed "Compliments."

[4]Returned 31 July-23 August 1998 to the New York State Theatre for 29 additional performances; see separate entry in following season.

Goroh, Ambassador of Japan: SUNG KI KIM. *Chillyunggun*, Shaman: HYUN DONG KIM. *Four Japanese Merchants*: Hak Jun Kim, Do Kyung Kim, Ho Jin Kim, Sang Hoe Park. *Park, Kim*, Court Ladies: Young Ju Jeong, He Jung Kim. *Weber*, Russian Envoy: David DeWitt. *Sontag*, Russian Lady: Mary Jo Todaro. *Young Queen*: Anne Chun. *Prince*: Hyun Dong Kim. *Foreign Envoys*: Tom Schmid, Eric Morgan, Claire Beckman, Samantha Camp.

Chorus/Dancers: So Youn An, Geon Ryeong Bae, Eun Jung Cho, Im Su Choi, Se Hwan Choi, Jeong Ju Doh, Soon Chul Hyun, Young Ju Jeong, Woo Jeong Jeoung, Do Hyeong Kim, Hakjun Kim, Hak Muk Kim, Ho Jin Kim, Hyun Dong Kim, Soo Jin Kim, Young Ju Kim, Young Ok Kim, Min Kyeng Kwak, He Jeong Lee, Jae Gu Lee, Ji Eun Lee, Ji Youn Lee, Kyoung Woo Lee, Sung Ho Lee, Hyo Jung Moon, Sang Hoe Park, Seung Jun Seo, Hyo In Shin, Chan Youn.

ACT 1
Prologue
"Japan's Choice"
Scene 1
"The Day We Greet the New Queen"
Scene 2
"Taewongun's Regency"
"King & Courtesans"
"Your Highness Is Beautiful"
"Look on Me"
Scene 3
"Marketplace"
"Four Japanese Merchants"
"Fight at the Marketplace"
"I Am Hong Kye-Hun"
"A Wish for a Prince"
"The Shaman"
"Knock Knock"/"Song of the Soldiers"
Scene 4
"Grow Big and Strong, Dear Prince"
"You Are the King of Chosun"
"Until the World Needs Me Again"
Scene 5
"Kojong's Imperial Conference"
"It's All a Scheme"
"Seven Foreign Envoys"
"Four Japanese"
"Itoh's Ambition"
Scene 6
"Uprising of the Old Line Units"
"Military Mutiny of 1882"
"Back at the Seat of Power"
"I Miss You, My Dear Queen"
"We Shall Return"
"Wu Chang-Ching and Taewongun"
Scene 7
"Taewongun Is Taken to China"
"Inoe Threatens King Kojong"
"Queen Min's Return"
"We Shall Rise Again"
"Meeting of Japan's Chosun Policy"

ACT 2
Scene 1
"Dancing at the Grand Banquet"
"Come Celebrate Our Reforms"
"Elizabeth I of Chosun"
"Negotiations at the Grand Banquet"
"New Morning Is Dawning in Chosun"
"Isn't It Strange, Snowflakes Are Falling"
Scene 2
"You Shall Drink Miura's Wine"
"Tripartite Intervention and the Atami House Conspiracy"
"Isn't It Strange, Snowflakes Are Falling" (reprise)
Scene 3
"Chosun Is Tangun's Land"
"Miura's Audience with the King"
Scene 4
"The French Lesson"
"When the Wine Gets Cold"
"Welcome, Ladies"
"Ritual for Murder"
Scene 5
"Prince and Queen"
"Where Was It That We Met"
"You Are My Destiny"
"Take Away the Darkening Sky"
Scene 6
"Do Not Hurt the Queen"
"The Last of Hyong Kye-Hun"
"Queen Min Chased by the Beasts"
"Find the Queen, Kill the Fox"
"How Will I Live Now"
Epilogue
"Rise, People of Chosun"

1997.17 SIDE SHOW

A Musical in Two Acts, Five Scenes. Book and lyrics by Bill Russell[5]. Music by Henry Krieger. Directed and choreographed by Robert Longbottom. Scenic design by Robin Wagner. Costume design by Gregg Barnes. Lighting design by Brian MacDevitt. Sound design by Tom Clark. Orchestrations by Harold Wheeler. Musical direction, dance and vocal arrangements by David Chase. Associate producer, Ginger Montel. Produced by Emanuel Azenberg, Joseph Nederlander, Herschel McKenna, Janice McKenna and Scott Nederlander. Opened 16 October 1997 at the Richard Rodgers Theatre and closed 3 January 1998 after 90 performances.

CAST (in alphabetical order): *Reptile Man*: Barry Finkel. *Bearded Lady*: Andy Gale. *Roustabout*: Billy Hartung. *Snake Girl*: Emily Hsu. *Fortune Teller*: Alicia Irving. *Fakir*: Devavand N. Janki. *The Boss*: KEN JENNINGS. *Jake*: NORM LEWIS. *Sixth Exhibit*: Judy Malloy. *Sheik*: David Masenheimer. *Terry Connor*: JEFF MCCARTHY. *Roustabout*: David McDonald. *Geek*: Philip Officer. *Buddy Foster*: HUGH PANARO. *Dolly Dimples*: Verna Pierce. *Violet Hilton*: ALICE RIPLEY. *Roustabout*: Jim T. Ruttman. *Daisy Hilton*: EMILY SKINNER. *Harem Girl*: Jenny-Lynn Duckling. *Harem Girl*: Susan Taylor. *Roustabout*: Timothy Warmen. *Harem Girl*: Darlene Wilson.

Reporters, Vaudevillians, the Follies Company, Party Guests, Radio Show Singers, the Movie Crew, Hawkers: Side Show Cast. *Swings*: John Paul Almon, Kelly Cole, John Frenzer, Michelle Millerick, J. Robert Spencer.

Act 1, Scene 1: The Midway. *Scene 2*: Vaudeville.

Act 1, Scene 1: The Follies. *Scene 2*: On the Road. *Scene 3*: The Texas Centennial.

ACT 1
Scene 1
"Come Look at the Freaks"
K. Jennings, Company
"Like Everyone Else"
E. Skinner, A. Ripley
"You Deserve a Better Life"
J. McCarthy
"Crazy, Deaf and Blind"
K. Jennings
"The Devil You Know"
N. Lewis, Attractions
"More Than We Bargained For"
J. McCarthy, H. Panaro

[5]Inspired by the lives of Daisy and Violet Hilton, Siamese twins who earned their living as musical performers in sideshows, carnivals, and vaudeville.

"Feelings You've Got to Hide"
E. Skinner, A. Ripley
"When I'm By Your Side"
E. Skinner, A. Ripley
"Say Goodbye to the Freak Show"
Company
Scene 2
"Overnight Sensation"
J. McCarthy, Reporters
"Leave Me Alone"
E. Skinner, A. Ripley
"We Share Everything"
E. Skinner, A. Ripley, Vaudevillians
"The Interview"
E. Skinner A. Ripley, Reporters
"Who Will Love Me As I Am"
E. Skinner, A. Ripley
ACT 2
Scene 1
"Rare Songbirds on Display"
Company
"New Year's Day"
J. McCarthy, H. Panaro, N. Lewis, E. Skinner, A. Ripley, Company
"Private Conversation"
J. McCarthy
Scene 2
"One Plus One Equals Three"
H. Panaro, E. Skinner, A. Ripley
"You Should Be Loved"
N. Lewis
"They Hardly Know I'm Around"
A. Ripley, H. Panaro, E. Skinner
"Tunnel of Love"
J. McCarthy, H. Panaro, E. Skinner, A. Ripley
Scene 3
"Beautiful Day for a Wedding"
K. Jennings, Hawkers
"She's Gone"
A. Ripley
"Marry Me, Terry"
E. Skinner
"I Will Never Leave You"
E. Skinner, A. Ripley
Finale
Company

1997.18 TRIUMPH OF LOVE

A Musical Comedy in Two Acts. Book by James Magruder. Based on (his own translation of) the French play of the same name by Pierre Marivaux. Music by Jeffrey Stock. Lyrics by Susan Birkenhead. Directed by Michael Mayer. Choreographed by Doug Varone. Set design by Heidi Ettinger. Costume design by Catherine Zuber. Lighting design by Paul Gallo. Sound design by Brian Ronan. Musical supervisor/arrangements, Michael Kosarin. Orchestrations by Bruce Coughlin. Music direction, Patrick Brady. Produced by Margo Lion, Metropolitan Entertainment Group (Jeff Rowland), Jujamcyn Theatres, in association with Pace Theatrical Group, The Baruch-Frankel-Viertel Group[6], Alex Hitz. Associate producers, Charles Kelman, Productions Inc., Marc Routh. Opened 23 October 1997 at the Royale Theatre and closed 4 January 1998 after 84 performances.

CAST (in order of appearance): *Agis*, a student of reason: Christopher Sieber. *Hesione*, his aunt, a philosopher: BETTY BUCKLEY. *Dimas*, the gardener: Kevin Chamberlin. *Harlequin*, the valet: Roger Bart. *Hermocrates*, a philosopher, brother to Hesione: F. MURRAY ABRAHAM. *Princess Léonide*: SUSAN EGAN. *Corine*, her maid servant: NANCY OPEL.

The action takes place in the garden retreat of the philosopher Hermocrates, an eighteenth century Greco-French topiary labyrinth.

ACT 1
"This Day of Days"
B. Buckley, R. Bart, K. Chamberlin, C. Sieber, F. M. Abraham
"Anything"
S. Egan
"The Bond That Can't Be Broken"
S. Egan, C. Sieber
"Mr. Right"
N. Opel, R. Bart
(*Music by* Van Dyke Parks.)
"You May Call Me Phocion"
S. Egan, B. Buckley
"Mr. Right" (reprise)
N. Opel, K. Chamberlin
"Emotions"
F. M. Abraham, S. Egan
"The Sad and Sordid Saga of Cécile"
S. Egan, C. Sieber, N. Opel, R. Bart, K. Chamberlin
"Serenity"
B. Buckley
"Issue in Question"
C. Sieber
"Teach Me Not to Love You"
The Company
ACT 2
"Have a Little Faith"
N. Opel, S. Egan, R. Bart, K. Chamberlin
(*Music by* Michael Kosarin.)
"The Tree"
B. Buckley, F. M. Abraham
"What Have I Done?"
S. Egan
"Henchmen Are Forgotten"
R. Bart, K. Chamberlin, N. Opel
"Love Won't Take No for an Answer"
F. M. Abraham, B. Buckley, C. Sieber
"This Day of Days" (reprise)
S. Egan, C. Sieber, N. Opel, R. Bart, K. Chamberlin

1997.19 THE SCARLET PIMPERNEL

A Musical Adventure in Two Acts. Book and lyrics by Nan Knighton. Based on the novel of the same name by Baroness Orczy[7]. Music by Frank Wildhorn. Directed by Peter Hunt. Choreographed by Adam Pelty. Scenery by Andrew Jackness. Costumes by Jane Greenwood. Lighting by Natasha Katz. Sound by Karl Richardson. Fight director, Rick Sordelet. Orchestrations by Karl Richardson. Musical direction and vocal arrangements by Ron Melrose. Produced by Pierre Cossette, Bill Haber, Hallmark Entertainment, Ted Forstmann, with Kathleen Raitt. Opened 9 November 1997 at the Minskoff Theatre; closed 3-9 October 1998 for revision; resumed 10 October 1998 (see detail below) and closed 30 May 1999 after 640 performances[8].

CAST (in order of appearance): *Madame St. Cyr*: Marine Jahan. *St. Cyr*: Timothy Shew. *Marie*: Elizabeth Ward. *Tussaud*: Philip Hoffman. *Dewhurst*: James Judy. *Chauvelin*: TERRENCE MANN. *Percy (Blakeney)*: DOUGLAS SILLS. *Marguerite (St. Just)*: CHRISTINE ANDREAS. *Lady Digby*: Sandy Rosenberg. *Lady Llewellyn*: Pamela Burrell. *Armand St. Just*: GILLES CHIASSON. *Ozzy*: Ed Dixon. *Farleigh*: Allen Fitzpatrick. *Leggett*: Bill Bowers. *Elton*: Adam Pelty. *Hal Hastings*: William Thomas Evans. *Ben*: Dave Clemmons. *Neville*: R. F. Daley. *Robespierre*: David Cromwell. *Grappin*: Ken Labey. *Coupeau*: Eric Bennyhoff. *Mercier*: Jeff Gardner. *Jessup*: James Dybas. *Prince of Wales*: David Cromwell. *French Mob and Soldiers/ British Guest and Servants*: Stephanie Bast, Nick Cavarra, Sutton Foster, Melissa Hart, Lauri Landry, Alison Lory, Don Mayo, Kevyn Morrow, Katie Nutt, Terry Richmond, Craig Rubano, Charles West. *Fisherman*: David Cromwell. *Swings*: Paul Castree, Sarah Knapp, Catherine LaValle, Ed Sala.

The action takes place from May into July, 1794, in England and France.

---

[6]Steve Baruch, Richard Frankel, ThomasViertel.

[7]Pen name for Mrs. Montague Barstow.

[8]Played a return engagement 10 September 1999 at the Neil Simon Theatre for 132 additional performances; for detail of revised production, see entry in 1999-2000 season.

ACT 1
"Madame Guillotine"
French Chorus
"Believe"
D. Sills, C. Andreas, British Chorus
"Vivez!"
C. Andreas, S. Rosenberg, P. Burrell, D. Sills, et al
"Prayer"
D. Sills
"Into the Fire"
D. Sills, His Men
"Falcon in the Dive"
T. Mann
'When I Look at You"
C. Andreas
"The Scarlet Pimpernel"
D. Sills, C. Andreas, G. Chiasson, S. Rosenberg, P. Burrell, Servants
"Where's the Girl?"
T. Mann
"When I Look at You" (reprise)
D. Sills
"The Creation of Man"
D. Sills, D. Cromwell, Percy's Men
"The Riddle"
T. Mann, C. Andreas, D. Sills, et al

ACT 2
"They Seek Him Here"
D. Sills, D. Cromwell, S. Rosenberg, P. Burrell, et al
"Only Love"
C. Andreas
"She Was There"
D. Sills
"Storybook"
C. Andreas {Leontine}, French Chorus
"Where's the Girl?" (reprise)
T. Mann
"Lullaby"
Chorus Solos {Helene, Chloe}
"You Are My Home"
C. Andreas, G. Chiasson, French Prisoners
"Believe" (reprise)
Company

Reconstructed version previewed from 10 October 1998, opened 4 November 1998 at the Minskoff Theatre. (All credits same as above except the following.) Directed and choreographed by Robert Longbottom. Assistant choreographers, Tom Kosis and Darlene Wilson. Dance arrangements by David Chase. Executive producer, Tim Hawkins. Produced by Radio City Entertainment and Ted Forstmann, by arrangement with Pierre Cossette, Bill Haber, Hallmark Entertainment and Kathleen Raitt.

CAST (in order of appearance): *Marguerite (St. Just)*: RACHEL YORK. *Chauvelin*: REX SMITH. *Percy (Blakeney)*: DOUGLAS SILLS. *Marie*: Elizabeth Ward. *Armand St. Just*: JAMES BOHANEK. *Tussaud*: Philip Hoffman. *Coupeau*: Timothy Eric Hart. *Mercier*: Jeff Gardner. *Ozzy*: Harvey Evans. *Farleigh*: Tom Zemon. *Dewhurst*: James Judy. *Jessup*: James Dybas. *Ben*: Ken Land. *Hastings*: William Thomas Evans. *Neville*: Stephen Hope. *Leggett*: Douglas Storm. *Hal*: Michael Hance. *Robespierre*: David Cromwell. *Lady Digby*: Sandy Rosenberg. *Lady Llewellyn*: Pamela Burrell. *Prince of Wales*: Davd Cromwell. *Jailer*: T. Doyle Leverett.

French Mob and Soldiers/British Guest and Servants: Stephanie Bast, Nick Cavarra, Michael Halling, Marine Jahan, John Lathan, Alison Lory, Mark McGrath, Katie Nutt, Jessica Philips, Terry Richmond, Craig Rubano, Cynthia Sophiea, Charles West. *Swings*: Drew Garaci, Stephen Hope, Sarah Knapp, James Van Treuren.

The action takes place from May into July, 1794, in England and France.

ACT 1[9]
"Storybook"
R. York, French Ensemble
"Madame Guillotine"
R. Smith
"Believe"
D. Sills, R. York, British Chorus
"You Are My Home"
D. Sills, R. York
Wedding Dance
Ensemble
"Prayer"
D. Sills
"Into the Fire"
D. Sills, the League
The Rescue
Ensemble
"Falcon in the Dive"
R. Smith
"When I Look at You"
R. York
"Where's the Girl?"
R. Smith
"You Are My Home" (reprise)
R. York, J. Bohanek
"The Creation of Man"
D. Sills, the League
"The Riddle"
R. Smith, R. York, D. Sills, et al

ACT 2
"The Scarlet Pimpernel"
D. Sills, R. York, Ball Guests
"They Seek Him Here"
D. Sills, S. Rosenberg, P. Burrell, D. Cromwell, et al
The Gavotte
Ensemble
"She Was There"
D. Sills
"Storybook" (reprise)
R. York, French Girls
"Where's the Girl?" (reprise)
R. Smith
"Into the Fire" (reprise)
The League
"I'll Forget You"
R. York
The Duel
D. Sills, R. Smith, R. York
"When I Look at You" (reprise)
D. Sills, R. York
"Into the Fire" (reprise)
Company

[9]Dropped from first production: "Vivez," "Believe," "Only Love," and Lullaby. Added for reconstructed version: Wedding Dance, The Rescue, The Gavotte, The Duel, "I'll Forget You," "She Was There."

1997.20 THE LION KING

A Musical in Two Acts, 20 Scenes. Book by Roger Allers and Irene Mecchi. Based on the Disney film of the same name, screenplay by Irene Mecchi, Jonathan Roberts and Linda Woolverton. Music by Elton John. Lyrics by Tim Rice. Additional music and lyrics by Lebo M, Mark Mancina, Jay Rifkin, Julie Taymor, Hans Zimmer. Directed by Julie Taymor. Choreographed by Garth Fagan. Scenic design by Richard Hudson. Costume design by Julie Taymor. Mask and puppet design by Julie Taymor and Michael Curry. Lighting design by Donald Holder. Sound design by Tony Meola. Musical director, Joseph Church. Orchestrations by Robert Elhai, David Metzger, Bruce Fowler. Associate producer, Donald Franz. Produced by Walt Disney Theatrical Productions. Opened 13 November 1997 at the New Amsterdam Theatre and is still running at this time!

CAST (in order of appearance): *Rafiki*: TSIDII LE LOKA. *Mufasa*: SAMUEL E. WRIGHT. *Sarabi*: Geena Breedlove. *Zazu*: GEOFF HOYLE. *Scar*: JOHN VICKERY. *Young Simba*: SCOTT IRBY-RANNIAR. *Young Nala*: KAJUANA SHUFORD. *Shenzi*: TRACY NICOLE CHAPMAN. *Banzai*: STANLEY WAYNE MATHIS. *Ed*: KEVIN CAHOON. *Timon*: MAX CASELLA. *Pumbaa*: TOM ALAN ROBBINS. *Simba*: JASON RAIZE. *Nala*: HEATHER HEADLEY.

Ensemble Singers: Eugene Barry-Hill, Gina Breedlove, Ntomb'khona Dlamini, Sheila Gibbs, Lindiwe Hlengwa, Christopher Jackson, Vanessa A. Jones, Faca Kulu, Ron Kunene, Philip Dorian McAdoo, Sam McKelton, Lebo M, Nandi Morake. *Ensemble Dancers*: Camille M. Brown, Iresol Cardona, Mark Allan Davis, Lana

Gordon, Timothy Hunter, Michael Joy, Aubrey Lynch II, Karine Plantadit-Bageot, Endalyn Taylor-Shellman, Levensky Smith, Ashi K. Smythe, Christine Yasunaga. *Swings*: Lindiwe Dlamini, Sonya Leslie, Peter Anthony Moore, Nhlanhla Ngema, Rachel Tecora Tucker, Frank Wright II.

Act 1, Scene 1: Pride Rock. *Scene 2*: Scar's Cave. *Scene 3*: Rafiki's Tree. *Scene 4*: The Pridelands. *Scene 5*: Scar's Cave. *Scene 6*: The Pridelands. *Scene 7*: Elephant Graveyard. *Scene 8*: Under the Stars. *Scene 9*: Elephant Graveyard. *Scene 10*: The Gorge. *Scene 11*: Pride Rock. *Scene 12*: Rafiki's Tree. *Scene 13*: The Desert/The Jungle.

Act 2, Scene 1: Scar's Cave. *Scene 2*: The Pridelands. *Scene 3*: The Jungle. *Scene 4*: Under the Stars. *Scene 5*: Rafiki's Tree. *Scene 6*: The Jungle. *Scene 7*: Pride Rock.

ACT 1
Scene 1
"Circle of Life"
T. LeLoka, Ensemble
Scene 4
"The Morning Report"
G. Hoyle, S. Irby-Ranniar, S. E. Wright
Scene 6
"I Just Can't Wait To Be King"
S. Irby-Ranniar, K. Shuford, G. Hoyle, Ensemble
Scene 7
"Chow Down"
T. N. Chapman, S. W. Mathis, K. Cahoon
Scene 8
"They Live in You"
S. E. Wright, Ensemble
Scene 9
"Be Prepared"
J. Vickery, T. N. Chapman, S. W. Mathis, K. Cahoon, Ensemble
Scene 11
"Be Prepared" (reprise)
J. Vickery, Ensemble
Scene 13
"Hakuna Matata"
M. Casella, T. A. Robbins, S. Irby-Ranniar, J. Raise, Ensemble
ACT 2
Entr'acte
"One By One"
Ensemble
Scene 1
"The Madness of King Scar"
J. Vickery, G. Hoyle, S. W. Mathis, T. N. Chapman, K. Cahoon, H. Headley
Scene 2
"Shadowland"
H. Headley, T. LeLoka, Ensemble
Scene 4
"Endless Night"
J. Raize, Enseble
Scene 6
"Can You Feel the Love Tonight"
M. Casella, T. A. Robbins, J. Raize, H. Headley, Ensemble
"He Lives in You" (reprise)
T. LeLoka, J. Raize, Ensemble
Scene 7
"King of Pride Rock"/"Circle of Life" (reprise)
Ensemble

1997.22 A CHRISTMAS CAROL

A Revival of the Musical in One Act, 13 Scenes[10]. Book by Mike Ockrent and Lynn Ahrens. Based on the story of the same name by Charles Dickens. Music by Alan Menken. Lyrics by Lynn Ahrens. Directed by Mike Ockrent. Choreographed by Susan Stroman. Setting design by Tony Walton. Costume design by William Ivey Long. Lighting design by Jules Fisher and Peggy Eisenhauer. Sound design by Tony Meola. Projections by Wendall K. Harrington. Flying by Foy. Associate director, Steven Zweigbaum. Associate choreographer, Chris Peterson. Musical direction by Paul Gemignani. Orchestrations by Michael Starobin and Douglas Besterman. Dance arrangements and incidental music by Glen Kelly. Executive producer, Dodger Productions. Producer, Tim Hawkins. Presented by Madison Square Garden. Opened 18 November 1997 at the (Paramount) Theatre, Madison Square Garden and closed 4 January 1998 after 96 performances.

CAST (in order of appearance): *Beadle*: Del-Bourree Bach. *Mr. Smythe*: CHRIS VASQUEZ. *Grace Smythe*: Tavia Riveé Jefferson, Olivia Oguma *Scrooge*: HAL LINDEN, RODDY MCDOWALL. *Crachit*: TED GROSS. *Charity Men*: Roland Rusinek, Wayne Pretlow, Erik Stein. *Old Joe*: Kenneth McMullen. *Street Urchins*: Paul Franklin Dano, Anthony Blair Hall, Zoe Petkanas, Gemini Quintos, Joseph Louis Santos III, Evan Silverberg. *Mrs. Crachit*: Robin Baxter. *Tiny Tim*: Christopher Cordell, Patrick J. P. Duffey. *Poulterer*: Roland Rusinek. *Sandwichboard Man*: KEN PAGE. *Jonathon*: Adam Barruch, Christopher Marquette. *Lamplighter*: JOEL BLUM. *Blind Hag*: Debra Cardona. *Fred*: PAUL JACKEL. *Mrs. Mops*: Marilyn Pasekoff. *Ghost of Jacob Marley*: PAUL KANDEL. *Ghost of Christmas Past*: JOEL BLUM. *Lights of Christmas Past*: Matthew Baker, Christopher F. Davis, Sean Haythe, Sean Thomas Morrissey. *Judge*: Roland Rusinek. *Scrooge at 8 years*: Anthony Blair Hall, Joseph Louis Santos III. *Fan at 6*: Zoe Petkanas, Gemini Quintos. *Scrooge's Mother*: Debra Cardona. *Scrooge's Father*: Wayne Schroder. *Mr. Hawkins*: Kenneth McMullen. *Scrooge at 12 years*: Paul Franklin Dano, Evan Silverberg. *Fan at 10 years*: Elizabeth Lundberg, Jenell Slack. *Fezziwig*: Ray Friedeck. *Scrooge at 18 years*: Tom Stuart. *Young Marley*: Ken Barnett. *Mrs. Fezziwig*: Joy Hermalyn. *Emily*: Kate Dawson. *Fiddler*: Brad Bradley. *Ghost of Christmas Present*: KEN PAGE. *The Crachit Children*: Paul Franklin Dano, Elizabeth Lundberg, Sean Thomas Morrissey, Jenell Slack, Evan Silverberg. *Sally*, Fred's wife: Whitney Webster. *Ignorance*: Anthony Blair Hall, Joseph Louis Santos III. *Want*: Zoe Patkanas, Gemini Quintos. *Undertakers*: Ken Barnett, Wayne Schroder. *Ghost of Christmas Future*: CHRISTINE DUNHAM.

Business Men, Gifts, Ghosts and the People of London: Del-Bourree Bach, Matthew Baker Ken Barnett, Robin Baxter, Leslie Bell, Carol Bentley, Renée Bergeron, Brad Bradley, Debra Cardona, Candy Cook, Christopher F. Davis, Kate Dawson, Ray Friedrick, Peter Gregus, James Hadley, Sean Smythe, Joy Hermalyn, Paul Jackel, Louisa Kendrick, Carrie Kenneally, Donna Lee Marshall, Kenneth McMullen, Aiza M. Rosaio-Medina, Elizabeth Mills, Sean Thomas Morrissey, Christopher Nilsson, Marilyn Pasekoff, Meredith Patterson, Wayne Pretlow, Gail Pennington, Josef Reiter, Pamela Remler, Samuel Reni, Ronald Rusinek, Vikki Schnurr, Erik Stein, Tom Stuart, Chris Vasquez, Whitney Webster. *Swings*: Rachel Black, Alex Brumel, Dana Chechile, Alexander Dollin, Rob Donohoe, Carissa Farina, Brett Figliozzi, Matt L. Hedge, Yvonne Meyer, Rommy Sandhu, Scott Taylor, Cythia Thole, Jeff Williams. *Angels*: Park Middle School, M. S. 330; South Side Middle School, P.S. 95. *Red Children's Cast*: Adam Barruch, Alex Brumel, Dana Chechile, Christopher Cordell, Paul Franklin Dano, Anthony Blair Hall, Matt L. Hedge, Elizabeth Lundberg, Olivia Oguma, Zoe Petkanas.*Green Children's Cast*: Alexander Dollin, Patrick J. P. Duffey, Carissa Farina, Brett Figliozzi, Tavia Riveé Jefferson, Christopher Marquette, Gemini Quintos, Joseph Louis Santos III, Evan Silverberg, Jenell Slack.

1997.21 STREET CORNER SYMPHONY

A Retro Musical (Revue) in One Act. Conceived and staged by Marion J. Caffey. Scenic design by Neil Peter Jampolis. Costume design by Jonathan Bixby. Lighting design by Jules Fisher and Peggy Eisenhauer. Sound design by Jonathan Deans. Vocal arrangements by Michael McElroy. Musical supervision, orchestrations and dance music arrangements by Daryl Waters. Musical director, Lon Hoyt. Associate producer, Sharleen Cooper Cohen. Produced by Kenneth Waissman and Brian Bantry[11]. Opened 24 November 1997 at the Brooks Atkinson Theatre and closed 1 February 1998 after 80 performances.

---

[10]Originally produced in New York 1 December 1994 at the Paramount, Madison Square Garden for 71 performances. For Synopsis of Scenes and Musical Numbers, see original 1994 production. For this year's and the 1995 and 1996 revivals the following changes were made:
Scene 1 and "The Years Are Passing By" were dropped.
Added to Scene 2 (former Scene 3) before "Street Song":
"You Mean More to Me"
N. Corley, M. Ballinger or P. Cravens
"The Years Are Passing By" (reprise) in former Scene 13 (new Scene 12) was replaced by:
"London Town Carol"
J. Fuchs or E. J. Newman
Note: The production played an irregular schedule of multiple daily performances.

[11]Kenneth Waissman withdrew as co-producer after the opening.

CAST (in order of appearance): *Clarence*: EUGENE FLEMING. *The Narrator/ Cynthia*: CAROL DENNIS. *Jessie-Lee*: JOSE LLANA. *Sukki*: CATHERINE MORIN. *C.J.*: C. E. SMITH. *Debbie*: DEBRA WALTON. *Chip*: VICTOR TRENT COOK. *Susan*: STACY FRANCIS.

Scene: The Neighborhood—The 1960s. The Fantasy Concert—The 1970s.

MUSICAL NUMBERS

"Dancing in the Street"
The Guys
(*Music and Lyrics by* Marvin Gaye, William Stevenson and Ivy Jo Hunter.)

"Dance to the Music"
Company
(*Music and Lyrics by* Sylvester Stewart.)

"The Way You Do the Things You Do"
V. T. Cook, E. Fleming, the Guys
(*Music and Lyrics by* William Robinson and Robert Rogers.)

"I Wanna Know Your Name"
V. T. Cook, Company
(*Music and Lyrics by* Kenneth Gamble and Leon Huff.)

"My Boyfriend's Back"
C. Morin, D. Walton, S. Francis
(*Music and Lyrics by* Robert Feldman, Gerald Goldstein and Richard Gottehrer.)

"It's in His Kiss" (Shoop Shoop Song)
S. Francis, C. Morin, D. Walton
(*Music and Lyrics by* Rudy Clark.)

"Try a Little Tenderness"
E. Fleming
(*Music and Lyrics by* Harry Woods, Jimmy Campbell and Reg Connelly.)

"Respect"
C. Dennis, the Girls
(*Music and Lyrics by* Otis Redding.)

"Baby Workout"
J. Llana, D. Walton, Company
(*Music and Lyrics by* Alonzo Tucker and Jackie Wilson.)

"Dance Chant"
Company
(Based on an idea of and inspired by Andre De Shields.)

"Baby Workout" (reprise)
J. Llana, D. Walton, Company

"Unchained Melody" (from *UNCHAINED MELODY* film)
C. E. Smith
(*Music by* Alex North. *Lyrics by* Hy Zaret.)

"Psychedelic Shack"
Company
(*Music and Lyrics by* Norman J. Whitfield and Barrett Strong.)

"Cloud Nine"
Company
(*Music and Lyrics by* Norman J. Whitfield and Barrett Strong.)

"I Want to Take You Higher"
Company
(*Music and Lyrics by* Sylvester Stewart.)

"Ohio"
J. Lana, Company
(*Music and Lyrics by* Neil Young.)

"Machine Gun"
J. Llana
(*Music and Lyrics by* Jimi Hendrix.)

"American Pie"
C. Dennis
(*Music and Lyrics by* Don McLean.)

"Love's in Need of Love Today"
C. Dennis
(*Music and Lyrics by* Stevie Wonder.)

"Get Ready"
V. T. Cook, Company
(*Music and Lyrics by* William Robinson, Jr.)

"Want Ads"
S. Francis, C. Morin, D. Walton
(*Music and Lyrics by* J. Perry, B. Perkins and G. Johnson.)

"Love Train"
E. Fleming, the Guys
(*Music and Lyrics by* Kenneth Gamble and Leon Huff.)

"Oh Girl"
J. Llana, the Guys
(*Music and Lyrics by* Eugene Record.)

"Betcha By Golly Wow"
V. T. Cook, the Guys
(*Music and Lyrics by* Thomas Bell and Linda Creed.)

"Heaven Must Be Missing an Angel"
The Guys
(*Music and Lyrics by* Frederick J. Perren and Kenneth St. Lewis.)

"The Tracks of My Tears"
S. Francis
(*Music and Lyrics by* Marvin Tarplin, Warre Moore and William Robinson, Jr.)

"Can I?"
V. T. Cook
(*Music and Lyrics by* Herman Griffth and Hal Davis.)

"Midnight Train to Georgia"
C. Dennis, with E. Fleming, J. Llana, C. E. Smith
(*Music and Lyrics by* James D. Weatherly.)

"Mr. and Mrs. Jones"
The Guys
(*Music and Lyrics by* Kenneth Gamble, Leon Huff and Cary Gilbert.)

"Proud Mary"
D. Walton, C. Morin, S. Francis
(*Music and Lyrics by* John Fogerty.)

"Hold On I'm Coming"
C. E. Smith, E. Fleming
(*Music and Lyrics by* Isaac Hayes, Jr. and David Porter.)

"Soul Man"
C. E. Smith, E. Fleming
(*Music and Lyrics by* Isaac Hayes and David Porter.)

"End of the Road"
C. Dennis, Company
(*Music and Lyrics by* Antonio Reid, Daryl Simmons and Kenneth Edmonds.)

"Love Train" (reprise)
Company

1998.01 RAGTIME

A Musical in Two Acts, 18 Scenes, a Prologue and Epilogue. Book by Terrence McNally. Based on the novel of the same name by E. L. Doctorow. Music by Stephen Flaherty. Lyrics by Lynn Ahrens. Directed by Frank Galati. Musical staging by Graciela Daniele. Production design by Eugene Lee. Costume design by Santo Loquasto. Lighting design by Jules Fisher and Peggy Eisenhauer. Sound design by Jonathan Deans. Musical director, David Loud. Orchestrations by William David Brohn. Dance music arranged by David Krane. Vocal arrangements by Stephen Flaherty. Projections designed by Wendall K. Harrington. Magic illusions by Franz Harary. Associate choreographghfer, Willie Rosario. Produced by LIVENT (US) Inc.[12] (Garth Drabinksy, Chairman; Myron I. Gottlieb, President). Opened 18 January 1998 at the Ford Center for the Performing Arts and closed 16 January 2000 after 861 performances.

CAST (in order of appearance): *The Little Boy*: Alex Strange. *Father*: MARK JACOBY. *Mother*: MARIN MAZZIE. *Mother's younger brother*: STEVEN SUTCLIFFE. *Grandfather*: Conrad McLaren. *Coalhouse Walker*: BRIAN STOKES MITCHELL. *Sarah*: AUDRA MCDONALD. *Booker T. Washington*: Tommy Hollis. *Tateh*: PETER FRIEDMAN. *The Little Girl*: Lea Michele. *Harry Houdini*: Jim Corti. *J. P. Morgan*: Mike O'Carroll. *Henry Ford*: Larry Daggett. *Emma Goldman*: JUDY KAYE. *Evelyn Nesbit*: LYNNETTE PERRY. *Stanford White*: Kevin Bogue. *Harry K. Thaw*: Colton Green. *Admiral Peary*: Rod Campbell. *Matthew Henson*: Duane Martin Foster. *Judge*: Mike O'Carroll. *Foreman*: Conrad McLaren. *Reporter*: Jeffrey Kuhn. *Kathleen*: Anne Kanengeiser. *Policeman*: Larry Dagget. *Doctor*: Bruce Winant. *Dirty Old Man*: Bruce Winant. *Policeman*: Colton Green. *Sarah's Friend*: Vanessa Townsell-Crisp. *Trolley Conductor*: Gordon Stanley. *Willie Conklin*: David Mucci. *Fireman*: Jeffrey Kuhn. *Brigit*: Anne. L. Nathan. *Conductor*: Joe Locarro. *Town Hall Bureaucrat*: Larry Dagget. *Second Bureaucrat*: Anne Kanengeiser. *Clerk*: Jeffrey Kuhn. *White Lawyer*: Brce Winant. *Black Lawyer*: Duane Martin Foster. *Reporters*: Rod Campbell, Godon Stanley. *Welfare Official*: Anne Kanengeiser. *Baron's Assistant*: Anne L. Nathan. *Gang Member*: Duane Martin Foster. *Pas de Deux*: Monica L. Richards, Keith LaMelle Thomas. *Charles S. Whitman*: Gordon Stanley. *Little Coalhouse*: (to be announced).

The Ensemble: Shaun Amyot, Darlene Bel Grayson, Kevin Bogue, Sondra M. Bonitto, Jamie Chandler-Torns, Ralph Deaton, Rodrick Dixon, Bernard Dotson, Donna Dunmire, Adam Dyer, Duane Martin Foster, Patty Goble, Colton Green, Elisa

[12]In September 1999 SFX Entertainment Group acquired the assets of LIVENT and became the show's producer.

Heinshohn, Anne Kanengeiser, Jeffrey Kuhn, Joe Langworth, Joe Locarro, Anne L. Nathan, Pachali Null, Mimi Quillen, Monica L. Richards, Orgena Rose, Gordon Stanley, Angela Teek, Keith LaMelle Thomas, Allyson Tucker, Leon Williams, Bruce Winant. *Swings*: Karen Andrew, John D. Baker, Mark Cassius, Dioni Michelle Collins, Mary Sharon Dziedzic, Valerie Hawkins, Kennl Hobson, Todd Thurston.

Act 1, Scene 1: Dock in the New York Harbor/At sea. *Scene 2*: A vaudeville theater, New York City. *Scene 3*: Mother's garden, New Rochelle. *Scene 4*: Ellis Island/Lower East Side. *Scene 5*: The Tempo Club/Harlem/Ford's assembly line. *Scene 6*: Railroad station, New Rochelle. *Scene 7*: Emerald Isle Firehouse. *Scene 8*: Mother's house, New Rochelle. *Scene 9*: A hillside above New Rochelle. *Scene 10*: A union hall in New York City/Lawrence, Massachusetts/A train. *Scene 11*: New Rochelle and New York City.

Act 2, Scene 1: The streets of New Rochelle/Mother's house. *Scene 2*: The Polo Grounds. *Scene 3*: Mother's house. *Scene 4*: Atlantic City/Million Dollar Pier/Boardwalk. *Scene 5*: Harlem/Coalhouse's hideout. *Scene 6*: The beach, Atlantic City. *Scene 7*: The Morgan Library, New York City.

ACT 1

Prologue

"Ragtime"
Company

Scene 1

"Goodbye, My Love"
M. Mazzie

"Journey On"
M. Jacoby, P. Friedman, M. Mazzie

Scene 2

"The Crime of the Century"
L. Perry, S. Sutcliffe, Ensemble

Scene 3

"What Kind of Woman"
M. Mazzie

Scene 4

"A Shtetl Iz Amereke"
P. Friedman, L. Michele, Immigrants

"Success"
P. Friedman, M. O'Carroll, J. Corti, Ensemble

Scene 5

"Gettin' Ready Rag"
B. S. Mitchell, Ensemble

"Henry Ford"
L. Daggett, B. S. Mitchell, Ensemble

Scene 6

"Nothing Like the City"
P. Friedman, M. Mazzie, A. Strange, L. Michele

Scene 8

"Your Daddy's Son"
A. McDonald

"New Music"
M. Jacoby, M. Mazzie, S. Sutcliffe, B. S. Mitchell, A. McDonald, Ensemble

Scene 9

"Wheels of a Dream"
B. S. Mitchell, A. McDonald

Scene 10

"The Night That Goldman Spoke at Union Square"
S. Sutcliffe, J. Kaye, Ensemble

"Lawrence, Massachusetts"
Ensemble

"Gliding"
P. Friedman

Scene 11

"Justice"
B. S. Mitchell, Ensemble

"President"
A. McDonald

"Till We Reach That Day"
V. Townsell-Crisp, B. S. Mitchell, J. Kaye, S. Sutcliffe, M. Mazzie, P. Friedman, Ensemble

ACT 2

Entr'acte

"Harry Houdini, Master Escapist"
A. Strange, J. Corti

Scene 1

"Coalhouse's Soliloquy"
B. S. Mitchell

"Coalhouse Demands"
Company

Scene 2

"What a Game"
M. Jacoby, A. Strange, Ensemble

Scene 3

"Atlantic City"
L. Perry, J. Corti

"New Music" (reprise)
M. Jacoby

Scene 4

"Atlantic City" (Part 2)
Ensemble

"The Crime of the Century"/"Harry Houdini, Master Escapist" (reprise)
L. Perry, J. Corti

"Buffalo Nickel Photoplay, Inc."
Baron Ashkenazy

"Our Children"
M. Mazzie, Baron Ashkenazy

Scene 5

"Sarah Brown Eyes"
B. S. Mitchell, A. McDonald

"He Wanted to Say"
J. Kaye, S. Sutcliffe, B. S. Mitchell, Coalhouse's Men

Scene 6

"Back to Before"
M. Mazzie

Scene 7

"Look What You've Done"
T. Hollis, B. S. Mitchell, Coalhouse's Men

"Make Them Hear You"
B. S. Mitchell

Epilogue

"Ragtime"/"Wheels of a Dream" (reprise)
Company

1998.02

CAPEMAN

A Musical in Two Acts, 9 Scenes. Music, book and lyrics by Paul Simon. Book and lyrics by Derek Walcott. Directed and choreographed by Mark Morris[13]. Sets and costumes by Bob Crowley. Lighting by Natasha Katz. Sound by Peter J. Fitzgerald. Projections by Wendell K. Harrington. Orchestrator, Stanley Silverman. Musical director, Oscar Hernandez. Co-producer, Stephen Eich. Produced by Plenaro Productions (Dan Klores, Brad Grey, Edgar Dobie), James L. Nederlander, in association with Dreamworks Records and King World Productions Inc. Opened 29 January 1998 at the Marquis Theatre and closed 28 March 1998 after 68 performances.

CAST (in order of appearance): *Children's Choir*: Evan Newman, Sebastian Pérez, Khalid Rivera, Amanda Vacharat, Tara Ann Villaneuva. *Salvador Agrón*, (ages 36 to 42): RUBEN BLADES. *Carlos Apache*: Julio Monge. *Angel Soto*: Raymond Rodriguez. *Sal Agrón*, (ages 16 to 20): MARC ANTHONY. *Frenchy Cordero*: Ray Rodríguez-Rosa. *Babu Charlie Cruz*: Lugo. *Tony Hernandez*: Renoly Santiago. *Reverend González*: Philip Hernández. *Bernadette*: Sophia Salguero. *Yolanda*: Natascia A. Díaz. *Cookie*: Élan. *Salvi Agrón* (age 7): Evan Newman. *Aurea Agrón* (age 8): Tara Ann Villaneuva. *Esmeralda Agrón*: EDNITA NAZARIO. *Carmen*: Claudette Sierra. *Santero/Lazarus*: Nestor Sanchez. *Doo-Wop Group*: Milton Cardona, Ray De La Paz, Myrna Lynn Gomila, Roger Mazzeo, Frank Negrón, Yassmin Alers, Kia Joy Goodwin. *Mrs. Young*: Cass Morgan. *Mrs. Krzesinski*: Luba Mason. *Aurea Agrón* (age 30): Michelle Ríos. *Wahzinak*: Sara Ramirez. *First Inmate*: John Lathan. *The Warden*: John Jellison. *Virgil*, a guard: Stephen Lee Anderson. *The Master of Ceremonies*: Ray De La Paz.

Parade Attendants, Vendors, Parade Officials, People at the Asilo, Guests, Celebrants, People on New York Street, Inmates, Guards, Immigrants, Party Guests, Three Kings, Sales Clerks, Boys, Orphans, Border Patrol: Yassmin Alers, Stephen Lee Anderson,

[13]Additional directorial assistance by Jerry Zaks; choreographic assistance by Joey McNeeley.

Milton Cardona, René M. Ceballos, Tony Chiroldes, Ray De La Paz, Élan, José Joaquín García, Kia Joy Goodwin, Elise Hernández, John Jellison, Lugo, Luba Mason, Roger Mazzeo, Claudia Montiel, Marisol Morales, Frank Negrón, Evan Newman, Sebastian Perez, Mark Price, Sara Ramirez, Khalid Rivera, Ray Rodríguez-Rosa, Raymond Rodriguez, Ramón Saldaña, Claudette Sierra, Amanda Vacharat, Tara Ann Villanueva. *Swings*: Lada Boder, Osborn Focht, Jason Martinez.

Act 1, Scene 1: New York City, 1979. *Scene 2*: Puerto Rico, early 1950s. *Scene 3*: New York City, 1959. *Scene 4*: New York City, 1962.

Act 2, Scene 1: New York City, 1963. *Scene 2*: Various prisons in New York state, 1963-76. *Scene 3*: Fishkill Prison, 1976-77. *Scene 4*: The desert, Arizona, 1977. *Scene 5*: New York City, 1979.

ACT 1

Scene 1

"El Coquí"
Children's Choir, R. Blades

"Puerto Rican Day Parade"
Parade Singers, Ensemble

"Born in Puerto Rico"
R. Baldes, M. Anthony, J. Monge, R. Rodriguez, R. Rodríguez-Rosa, Lugo, R. Santiago, P. Hernández, N. Sanchez

Scene 2

"In Mayagüez"
R. Blades, E. Nazario, Nuns, Children

"Carmen"
E. Nazario, C. Sierra

"The Santero"
N. Sanchez, E. Nazario, Celebrants

"Chimes"
E. Nazario

"Christmas in the Mountains"
Three Kings, C. Sierra, E. Nazario, Guests

Scene 3

"Satin Summer Nights"
M. Anthony, S. Salguero, Élan, R. Santiago, Doo-Wop Group

"Bernadette"
M. Anthony, S. Salguero, Doo-Wop Group

"The Vampires"
R. Santiago, M. Anthony, J. Monge, R. Rodriguez, R. Rodríguez-Rosa, Lugo, Doo-Wop Group

"Shopliftin' Clothes"
M. Anthony, R. Santiago, Sales Clerks, J. Monge, Doo-Wop Group

"Dance to a Dream"
J. Monge, N. A. Díaz, S. Salguero, M. Anthony

"Quality"
S. Salguero, N. Díaz, Élan, R. Blades, Doo-Wop Group

"Manhunt"
R. Blades, J. Monge, M. Anthony, R. Santiago, Ensemble

"Can I Forgive Him"
E. Nazario, C. Morgan, L. Mason

"Adios Hermanos"
M. Anthony, R. Blades, M. Ríos, R. Santiago, S. Salguero, N. Díaz, N. Sanchez, Ensemble

Scene 4

"Jesús Es Mi Señor"
Congregants, P. Hernández, E. Nazario, M. Ríos, S. Salguero, N. Díaz, N. Sanchez

ACT 2

Scene 1

"Sunday Afternoon"
E. Nazario

Scene 2

"Time is an Ocean"
M. Anthony, R. Blades, E. Nazario

Scene 3

"Wahzinak's First Letter"
S. Ramirez

"Killer Wants to Go to College"
J. Lathan, J. Jellison, Inmates

"Virgil"
S. L. Anderson, J. Jellison

"My Only Defense"
M. Anthony

"Wahzinak's Letter (Duet)"
R. Blades, S. Ramirez

"Virgil and the Warden"
J. Lathan, R. Blades, J. Jellison

Manhunt (Instrumental)

"Trailways Bus"
N. Sanchez, S. Ramirez, R. Blades, Border Patrolman

Scene 4

"The Mission"
R. Blades, N. Sanchez

"El Malecón"
R. Blades

"Children's Chimes"
E. Newman, T. A. Villaneuva, P. Hernández, Orphans

"You Fucked Up My Life"
R. Rodriguez, Lugo, M. Anthony, R. Santiago, R. Rodríguez-Rosa, R. Blades, Doo-Wop Group

"Lazarus"/"Last Drop of Blood"
N. Sanchez, R. Blades, C. Morgan, Ensemble

"Wahzinak's Last Letter"
S. Ramirez

Scene 5

"El Coquí" (reprise)
Children's Choir, R. Blades

"Tony Hernandez"
R. Blades, R. Santiago

"Carlos and Yolanda"
R. De La Paz, M. Ríos, R. Blades, J. Monge, N. Díaz, Ensemble

"Sal's Last Song"
R. Blades, E. Nazario

"Esmeralda's Dream"
E. Nazario, M. Anthony, Doo-Wop Group

1998.03 THE SOUND OF MUSIC

A Revival of the Musical (Play) in Two Acts[14]. Book by Howard Lindsay and Russel Crouse. Suggested by the book "The Trapp Family Singers" by Maria Augusta Trapp. Music by Richard Rodgers. Lyrics by Oscar Hammerstein II. Directed by Susan Schulman. Choreography by Michael Lichtefeld. Scenery by Heidi Ettinger. Costumes by Catherine Zuber. Lighting by Paul Gallo. Sound design by Tony Meola. Orchestrations by Bruce Coughlin. Dance and incidental music arrangements by Jeanine Tesori. Original orchestrations by Robert Russell Bennett. Original choral and dance arrangements by Trude Rittmann. Musical direction by Michael Rafter. Associate producers, James D. Stern, Pace Theatrical Group. Produced by Hallmark, Steven Baruch, Richard Frankel, Thomas Viertel, Jujamcyn Theaters, in association with the Rodgers and Hammerstein Organzation, Charles Kelman Productions, Simone Genatt Haft, Marc Routh, Jay Binder, Robert Halmi, Jr. Opened 12 March 1998 at the Martin Beck Theatre and closed 20 June 1999 after 533 performances.

CAST (in order of appearance): *Sister Margaretta*, Mistress of Postulants: Jeanne Lehman. *Sister Berthe*, Mistress of Novices: Gina Ferrall *The Mother Abbess*: PATTI COHENOUR. *Sister Sophia*: Ann Brown. *Maria Rainer*, a Postulant at Nonnberg Abbey: REBECCA LUKER. *Captain Georg von Trapp*: MICHAEL SIBERRY. *Franz*, the butler: John Curless. *Frau Schmidt*, the housekeeper: Patricia Conolly. *Children of Captain von Trapp (7)*: *Liesl*: SARA ZELLE. *Friedrich*: Ryan Hopkins. *Louisa*: Natalie Hall. *Kurt*: Matthew Ballinger. *Brigitta*: Tracy Alison Walsh. *Marta*: Andrea Bowen. *Gretl*: Ashley Rose Orr. *Rolf Gruber*: Dashiell Eaves. *Ursula*, a maid: Lynn C. Pinto. *Elsa Schraeder*: JAN MAXWELL. *Max Detweiler*: FRED APPLEGATE. *Herr Zeller*: Timothy Landfield. *Baron Elberfeld*: Gannon McHale. *Baroness Elberfeld*: Martha Hawley. *A New Postulant*: Laura Benanti. *Admiral von Schreiber*: Reno Roop.

Neighbors and Servants of Captain von Trapp, Nuns, Novices, Postulants, Priests, Clerics, Nazis, Contestants in the Festival Concert: Anne Allgood, Joan Barber, Laura

[14]Originally produced in New York 16 November 1959 at the Lunt-Fontanne Theatre for 1443 performances. For Synopsis of Scenes (dropped for this revival), see original 1959 production. Dropped for this production: "An Ordinary Couple." The order of songs has been rearranged to correspond more closely to the film version.

Benanti, Ann Brown, Patricia Connoly, Gina Ferrall, Natalie Hgall, Martha Hawley, Kelly Cae Hogan, Siri Howard, Matt Loney, Patricia Phillips, Lynn C. Pinto, Reno Roop, Kristie Dale Sanders, Ben Sheaffer, Sara Zelle. *Swings*: Tad Ingram, Betsi Morrison, Margaret Shafer.

ACT 1

Preludium
P. Cohenour, J. Lehmann, G. Ferrall, A. Brown, Nuns, Novices, Postulants

"The Sound of Music"
R. Luker

"Maria"
P. Cohenour, J. Lehmann, G. Ferrall, A. Brown

"I Have Confidence"[15]
R. Luker
(*Lyrics by* Richard Rodgers.)

"Do-Re-Mi"
R. Luker, Children

"(You Are) Sixteen Going on Seventeen"
S. Zelle, D. Eaves

"My Favorite Things"
R. Luker, P. Cohenour

"How Can Love Survive?"
J. Maxwell, F. Applegate

"The Sound of Music" (reprise)
M. Siberry, Children, R. Luker

"So Long, Farewell"
Children

"Morning Hymn"
P. Cohenour, Nuns, Novices, Postulants

"Climb Every Mountain"
P. Cohenour

ACT 2

Opening, Act 2
F. Applegate, Children

"No Way to Stop It"
J. Maxwell, F. Applegate, M. Siberry

"Something Good"[16]
R. Luker, M. Siberry

Wedding Processional
P. Cohenour, Nuns, Novices, Postulants

"Sixteen Going on Seventeen" (reprise)
R. Luker, S. Zelle

"The Lonely Goatherd"
R. Luker, M. Siberry, Children

"Edelweiss"
M. Siberry, R. Luker, Children

"So Long, Farewell" (reprise)
R. Luker, M. Siberry, Children

Finale Ultimo
P. Cohenour, Nuns, Novices, Postulants

1998.04

CABARET

A Revival of the Musical in Two Acts[17]. Book (revised) by Joe Masteroff. Based on the play ("I Am a Camera") by John Van Druten and stories ("The Berlin Stories") by Christopher Isherwood. Music by John Kander. Lyrics by Fred Ebb. Directed by Sam Mendes. Co-directed and choreographed by Rob Marshall. Set designed by Robert Brill. Costumes designed by William Ivey Long. Lighting designed by Peggy Eisenhauer and Mike Baldassari. Sound designed by Brian Ronan. Musical director, Patrick Vaccariello. Orchestrations by Michael Gibson. Dance music arranged by David Krane. Original dance music arranged by David Baker. Produced by the Roundabout Theatre Company. Opened 19 March 1998 at the Kit Kat Klub (Henry Miller's Theatre); suspended 21 July 1998 and resumed 20 August 1998; moved 13 November 1998 to Studio 54 and is still running at this time!

CAST (in order of appearance): *Emcee*: ALAN CUMMING. *The Kit Kat Girls (6)*: *Rosie*: Christina Pawl. *Lulu*: Erin Hill. *Frenchie*: Joyce Chittick. *Texas*: Leenya Rideout. *Fritzie*: Michele Pawk. *Helga*: Kristin Olness. *The Kit Kat Boys (4)*: *Bobby*: Michael O'Donnell. *Victor*: Brian Duguay. *Hans*: Bill Szobody. *Herman*: Fred Rose. *Sally Bowles*: NATASHA RICHARDSON. *Clifford Bradshaw*: JOHN BENJAMIN HICKEY. *Ernst Ludwig*: DENIS O'HARE. *Customs Official*: Fred Rose. *Fraulein Schneider*: MARY LOUISE WILSON. *Fraulein Kost*: MICHELLE PAWK. *Rudy*: Bill Szobody. *Herr Schultz*: RON RIFKIN. *Gorilla*: Joyce Chittick. All other parts played by members of the company. *Swings*: Linda Romoff, Vance Avery.

The action takes place in Berlin, Germany, 1929-30.

ACT 1[18]

"Wilkommen"
A. Cumming, The Kit Kat Klub

"So What?"
M. L. Wilson

"Don't Tell Mama"
N. Richardson, the Kit Kat Girls

"Mein Herr"[19] (from film *CABARET*)
N. Richardson, the Kit Kat Girls

"Perfectly Marvelous"
J. B. Hickey, N. Richardson

"Two Ladies"
A. Cumming, E. Hill, M. O'Donnell

"It Couldn't Please Me More"
M. L. Wilson, R. Rifkin

"Tomorrow Belongs to Me"
A. Cumming

"Maybe This Time"[20] (from film *CABARET*)
N. Richardson

"Money" (The Money Song)
A. Cumming, the Kit Kat Girls

"Married"
M. L. Wilson, R. Rifkin

"Tomorrow Belongs to Me" (reprise)
M. Pawk, D. O'Hare, Company

ACT 2

"Kick Line" (dance)
The Kit Kat Club

"Married" (reprise)
R. Rifkin

"If You Could See Her"
A. Cumming, J. Chittick

"What Would You Do?"
M. L. Wilson

"I Don't Care Much" (from film *CABARET*)
A. Cumming

"Cabaret"
N. Richardson

Finale
Company

1998.05

HIGH SOCIETY

A Musical Comedy in Two Acts, 16 Scenes. Book by Arthur Kopit. Based on the the play "The Philadelphia Story" by Philip Barry and the Turner Entertainment Company film "High Society." Music and lyrics by Cole Porter. Additional lyrics by Susan Birkenhead. Directed by Christopher Renshaw[21]. Musical staging by Lar Lubovitch[22]. Scenery by Loy Arcenas. Costumes by Jane Greenwood. Lighting by Howell Binkley. Sound by Tony Meola. Musical direction by Paul Gemignani. Dance music arrangements by Glen Kelly. Ocrhestrations by William David Brohn. Associate producer,

---

[15]Written for the film version.

[16]Written for the film version. Replaced "(An) Ordinary Couple" from the original production.

[17]Originally produced in New York 20 November 1966 at the Broadhurst Theatre for 1166 performances. For Synopsis of Scenes and Musical Numbers, see original 1966 production.

[18]Dropped for this revival: "Meeskite."

[19]Replaced "Telephone Song."

[20]Replaced "Why Should I Wake Up?"

[21]Program credit to the contrary, Des McAnuff assumed the direction during previews.

[22]Program credit to the contrary, Wayne Cilento assumed the choreography duing previews.

Kevin C. Whitman. Produced by Lauren Mitchell and Robert Gallus, Hal Luftig and Richard Samson, Dodger Endemol Theatricals in association with Bill Haber. Originally produced by American Conservatory Theater, San Francisco (Carey Perloff, Artistic director; Heather Kitchen, Managing director). Opened 27 April 1998 at the St. James Theatre and closed 30 August 1998 after 144 performances.

CAST (in order of appearance): *Polly*, Downstairs Maid: Jennifer Smith. *Arthur*, Butler: Glenn Turner. *Chester*, House Man: Barry Finkel. *Sunny*, Scullery Maid: Kisha Howard. *Stanley*, House Boy: Jeff Skowron. *Patsy*, Cook: Betsy Joslyn. *Peg*, Upstairs Maid: Dorothy Stanley. *Edmund*, Major Domo: William Ryall. *Margaret Lord*: LISA BANES. *Dinah Lord*: ANNA KENDRICK. *Tracy Lord*: MELISSA ERRICO. *Uncle Willie*: JOHN MCMARTIN. *C. K. Dexter Haven*: DANIEL MCDONALD. *Mike Connor*: STEPHEN BOGARDUS. *Liz Imbrie*: RANDY GRAFF. *George Kittredge*: MARC KUDISCH. *Seth Lord*: Daniel Gerroll. *Swings*: Vince Pesce, Solie Shannon.

The action takes place on a glorious weekend in June 1938 in Oyster Bay, Long Island.

Act 1, Scene 1: The Lord's Estate. *Scene 2*: Tracy's Room. *Scene 3*: The Veranda. *Scene 4*: The Nursery. *Scene 5*: The Grounds. *Scene 6*: The South Parlor. *Scene 7*: The Pavilion. *Scene 8*: The Pool.

Act 2, Scene 1: Uncle Willie's House, very early Sunday morning. *Scene 2*: Uncle Willie's Ballroom. *Scene 3*: Dexter's House. *Scene 4*: Uncle Willie's Kitchen. *Scene 5*: Uncle Willie's Grounds. *Scene 6*: The Lord's Pool. *Scene 7*: The Lord's Garden. *Scene 8*: The Terrace, the next morning.

ACT 1

Scene 1

"High Society"[23]
The Household Staff

Scene 2

"Ridin' High" (from *RED, HOT AND BLUE*)
M. Errico, Household Staff

Scene 3

"(I'm) Throwing a Ball Tonight"[24] (from *PANAMA HATTIE*)
L. Banes, M. Errico, J. McMartin, A. Kendrick

Scene 4

"Little One"
D. McDonald, A. Kendrick

Scene 5

"Who Wants To Be a Millionaire?"
S. Bogardus, R. Graff

Scene 6

"I Love Paris" (from *CAN CAN*)
A. Kendrick, M. Errico

Scene 7

"She's Got That Thing" (from *FIFTY MILLION FRENCHMEN*)
J. McMartin, D. McDonald, Company

Scene 8

"Once Upon a Time"[25]
M. Errico

"True Love"
D. McDonald, M. Errico

ACT 2

Scene 1

"High Society"[26] (reprise)
Household Staff

Scene 2

"Let's Misbehave"[27] (from *PARIS*)
M. Errico, J. McMartin, Company

"I'm Getting Myself Ready for You" (from *THE NEW YORKERS*)
J. McMartin, R. Graff

Scene 3

"Once Upon a Time"[28] (reprise)
D. McDonald

"Just One of Those Things" (from *JUBILEE*)
D. McDonald

Scene 4

"Well, Did You Evah?"[29]
Household Staff, M. Errico, J. McMartin, R. Graff

Scene 5

"You're Sensational"
S. Bogardus

"Say It with Gin" (from *THE NEW YORKERS*)
J. McMartin

"Ridin' High" (reprise)
L. Banes

Scene 6

"It's All Right with Me" (from *CAN CAN*)
M. Errico

Scene 7

"He's a Right Guy" (from *SOMETHING FOR THE BOYS*)
R. Graff

Scene 8

"(I Love You) Samantha"
D. McDonald

"True Love" (reprise)
M. Errico, D. McDonald

1998.06 THE WIZARD OF OZ

A Revival of the Musical Spectacle in One Act, 16 Scenes[30]. Based on the novel of the same name by L. Frank Baum and the MGM film adaptation by Noel Langley, Florence Ryerson, Edgar Allan Woolf. Book by John Kane (for the Royal Shakespeare Company), adapted by Robert Johanson. Music by Harold Arlen. Lyrics by E. Y. Harburg. Background music by Herbert Stothart. Directed by Robert Johanson. Choreographed by Jamie Rocco; associate choreographer, Donna Drake. Scenic design by Michael Anania. Costume design by Gregg Barnes. Lighting design by Timothy Hunter. Sound design by David R. Paterson, Mark Menard. Flying by Foy. Animals by William Berloni. Special effects by Ian O'Connor. Musical direction and additional orchestration by Jeff Rizzo. Production originally presented at the Papermill Playhouse, New Jersey (Angelo Del Rossi, Producer) Produced by Madison Square Garden Productions (Tim Hawkins, producer); presented by Cold-Eeze. Opened 6 May 1998 at the Theatre at Madison Square Garden and closed 31 May 1998 after 38 performances[31].

CAST (in order of appearance) In Kansas: *Dorothy*: JESSICA GROVÉ. *Toto*: Plenty. *Aunt Em*: JUDITH MCCAULEY. *Uncle Henry*: Bob Dorian. *Hunk*: LARA TEETER. *Hickory*: DIRK LUMBARD. *Zeke*: KEN PAGE. *Almira Gulch*: EARTHA KITT. *Professor Marvel*: MICKEY ROONEY.

In Oz: *Glinda*, the Good Witch: JUDITH MCCAULEY. *Mayor of Munchkinland*: Eugene Pidgeon. *Barristers*: Steve Babiar, Wendy Coates. *Coroner*: P.J. Terranova. *Lollipop Guild*: Martin Klebba, Mark Povinelli, Deborah Wilson. *The Wicked Witch of the West*: EARTHA KITT. *The Scarecrow*: LARA TEETER. *Crows*: Renee Bonadio, Christine DeVito, Martin Klebba. *Crow Voices*: D'Ambrose Boyd, Casey Colgan, Daniel Herron, D. J. Salisbury, Russell Warfield. *The Tinman*: DIRK LUMBARD. *Apple Trees*: Casey Colgan, Daniel Herron, D. J. Salisbury. *Apple Tree Voices*: Gail Cook Howell, Heidi Karol Johnson, Angela Robinson. *The Cowardly Lion*: KEN PAGE. *The Wizard of Oz*: MICKEY ROONEY. *Nikko*, Commander of the Flying Monkeys: Martin Klebba. *Winkie General*: Bob Dorian.

Munchkins, Crows, Apple Trees, Poppies, Citizens of Oz, Flying Monkeys and Winkies: Steve Babiar, Renee Bonadio, D'Ambrose Boyd, Bill Brassca, Wendy Coates, Casey Colgan, Christine DeVito, Kassandara Marie Hazard, Kristopher Michael Hazard, Daniel Herron, Gail Cook Howell, Shauna Markey, Andrea McCormick, Caroline McMahon, Eugene Pidgeon, Mark Povinelli, Angela Robinson, Mary Ruvolo, D. J. Salisbury, Kristi Sperling, Andrea Szücs, Leslie Stump-Vanderpool, P.J. Terranova, Russell Warfield, Wendy Watts, Deborah Wilson. *Swings*: Lenny Daniel, Donna Drake, Ron Gibbs, Jamie Waggoner. *Children's Choirs*.

---

[23]New lyrics by Susan Birkenhead.
[24]New lyrics by Susan Birkenhead.
[25]New lyrics by Susan Birkenhead.
[26]New lyrics by Susan Birkenhead.
[27]Additional lyrics by Susan Birkenhead.
[28]New lyrics by Susan Birkenhead.
[29]New lyrics by Susan Birkenhead.
[30]This adaptation previously produced in New York 15 May 1997 at the Theatre at Madison Square Garden for 45 performances. THE WIZARD OF OZ was previously produced in a different adaptation 22 March 1989 at Radio City Music Hall for 37 performances.
[31]Performed an irregular performance schedule of 12 performances a week.

1998–1999 SEASON

Members of the Company of FOSSE
Joan Marcus/Photofest

1998–1999 SEASON

AN EVENING WITH JERRY HERMAN

1998.07

A Musical Revue in Two Acts. Music and lyrics by Jerry Herman. Directed by Lee Roy Reams. Set design, Kenneth Foy. Lighting design, Ken Billington. Sound design, Peter Fitzgerald. Produced by Manny Kladitis and Jon Wilner, in association with Magicworks Entertainment and PACE Theatrical Group, Inc. Opened 28 July 1998 at the Booth Theatre and closed 23 August 1998 after 28 performances.

CAST: JERRY HERMAN (piano, vocals), LEE ROY REAMS (vocals), FLORENCE LACEY (vocals), Jered Egan (bass).

ACT1

"Shalom" (from *MILK AND HONEY*)
F. Lacey, L. R. Reams

"Put On Your Sunday Clothes" (from *HELLO, DOLLY!*)
L. R. Reams

"It Only Takes a Moment" (from *HELLO, DOLLY!*)
L. R. Reams

"Before the Parade Passes By" (from *HELLO, DOLLY!*)
L. R. Reams

"So, Long Dearie" (from *HELLO, DOLLY!*)
F. Lacey

"Ribbons Down My Back" (from *HELLO, DOLLY!*)
F. Lacey

"Dancing" (from *HELLO, DOLLY!*)
F. Lacey

"Penny in My Pocket" (dropped from *HELLO, DOLLY!*)
L. R. Reams

"Hello, Dolly!" (from *HELLO, DOLLY!*)
F. Lacey, L. R. Reams, J. Herman

"It's Today" (from *MAME*)
L. R. Reams

"Gooch's Song" (from *MAME*)
J. Herman

"We Need a Little Christmas" (from *MAME*)
F. Lacey, J. Herman

"If He Walked into My Life" (from *MAME*)
F. Lacey

"Mame" (from *MAME*)
F. Lacey, L. R. Reams, J. Herman

ACT 2

"I Don't Want to Know" (from *DEAR WORLD*)
F. Lacey

"Movies Were Movies" (from *MACK AND MABEL*)
F. Lacey, L. Reams, J. Herman

"I Won't Send Roses" (from *MACK AND MABEL*)
L. R. Reams

"Hundreds of Girls" (from *MACK AND MABEL*)
J. Herman

"Time Heals Everything" (from *MACK AND MABEL*)
F. Lacey

"Tap Your Troubles Away" (from *MACK AND MABEL*)
L. R. Reams

"Movies Were Movies" (reprise)
F. Lacey, L. R. Reams, J. Herman

"I Belong Here" (from *THE GRAND TOUR*)
F. Lacey

"Mrs. S. L. Jacobowsky" (from *THE GRAND TOUR*)
L. R. Reams

"I'll Be Here Tomorrow" (from *THE GRAND TOUR*)
J. Herman

"La Cage Aux Folles" (from *LA CAGE AUX FOLLES*)
L. R. Reams

"Song on the Sand" (from *LA CAGE AUX FOLLES*)
F. Lacey

"I Am What I Am" (from *LA CAGE AUX FOLLES*)
L. R. Reams

"The Best of Times" (from *LA CAGE AUX FOLLES*)
F. Lacey, L. R. Reams, J. Herman

"The Best Christmas of All"[1] (from *MRS SANTA CLAUS*, Television)
F. Lacey, L. R. Reams

THE LAST EMPRESS

1998.08

A Revised Version of the Musical in Two Acts, a Prologue, Epilogue and 13 Scenes, in Korean[2]. Book by Mun Yol Yi. Adaptation by Kwang Lim Kim. Music by Hee Gab Kim. Lyrics by In Ja Yang. Directed by Ho Jin Yun. Choreography by Byung Goo Seo. Costume design by Hyun Sook Kim. Scenic design by Dong Woo Park. Lighting design by Hyung O Choi. Sound design by Ki Young Kim. Musical direction by Kolleen Park. Orchestrations and additional music by Peter Casey. Executive producer, Young Hwan Kim. Associate producers, Sang Ryul Lee, Su Mun Lee, Young Il Yang, Mun Yol Yi, Hee Hwan Lee, Woo Jong Lee. Produced by Arts Communications Seoul Company (A-Com). Opened 4 August 1998 at the New York State Theater and closed 23 August 1998 after 24 performances.

CAST: *Queen Min*, Ja-young Min: TAEWON YI KIM, WONJUNG KIM(alternate). *Taewongun*, King Kojung's Father (Regent): SUNG HOON LEE. *King Kojung*: HEE SUNG YU. *Inoue*, Ambassador of Japan: HEE JUNG LEE. *Itoh Hirobumi*, Prime Minister of Japan: YOUNG CHAE CHOI. *Kye Hun Hong*, General Hong: MIN SOO KIM. *Miura Goroh*, Ambassador of Japan: SUNG KI KIM. *Yuan Shi Kai*, Ambassador of China: SUNG HO LEE. *Chillyunggun*, Shaman: HYUN DONG KIM. *Park, Kim*, Court Ladies: Young Joo Jeong, Hyo Jung Moon. *German Envoy*: Peter Marinos. *(Lady) Sontag*, Russian Lady: Mary Jo Todaro. *French Envoy*: Paul Taylor. *Lady Underwood*: Marci Reid. *Weber*, Russian Envoy: Al Bundonis. *Prince*: Jung Hoon Woo. (*Child*: Eun Soo Jang. *Royal Tutor*: Kyoung Woo Lee. *Japanese Military Officer*: Hak Muk Kim.)

Chorus/Dancers: So Youn An, Ji Soo Choi, So Young Choi, Jeong Ju Doh, Eun Kyoung Han, Mi Kyung Jung, Do Hoon Kim, Do Hyeong Kim, Tai Hyun Kim, Ho Jin Kim, Sang Jin Kim, Young Ju Kim, Sun Mi Kim, Hak Muk Kim, Bong Soo Kim, So Yeoun Kim, So Young Kim, Sang Yun Kim, Yu Lim Kwak, Ji Eun Lee, Soo Hyoung Lee, Kyoung Woo Lee, Ji Youn Lee, Sang Ho Park, Yong Park, Sang Ryu, Beom Seok Seo, Eun Kyoung Yoon, Chan Yun.

ACT 1

Prologue

"Japan Has Chosen"
S. K. Kim, Japanese Assassins

Scene 1

"The Day We Greet the New Queen"
Sung Hoon Lee, H. S. Yu, T. Y. Kim, The Company

Scene 2

"Regency of the King's Father"
Sung Hoon Lee, Subjects

"Soft is the Spring Breeze"
H. S. Yu, Court Ladies

"Your Highness Is So Beautiful"
Court Ladies

"There Is a Star in My Heart"
T. Y. Kim

"The Examination for State Military Service"
M. S. Kim, Sung Hoon Lee, H. S. Yu, Applicants

"A Wish for a Prince"
T. Y. Kim, H. S. Yu, Sung Hoon Lee, Court Ladies, Subjects

"Shaman Rite (for Child Bearing)"
H. D. Kim, Shamans

Scene 3

"Open Up the Door"
Sung Hoon Lee, Foreigners

"Song of the Soldiers"
Soldiers, People

Battle Against the Foreigners

Scene 4

"Grow Big and Strong, Dear Prince"
Court Ladies

---

[1]Dropped during the run and replaced by:
"You I Like" (from *THE GRAND TOUR*)
J. Herman, L. R. Reams, F. Lacey

[2]First produced in New York 15 August 1997 at the New York State Theater for 12 performances.

"You Are the King of Chosun"
T. Y. Kim, H. S. Yu, Court Ladies
"Until the World Needs Me Again"
Sung Hoon Lee
Scene 5
"Kojong's Imperial Conference"
H. S. Yu, Subjects
"It's All a Scheme"
T. Y. Kim
"Seven Foreign Envoys"
Foreign Envoys
Scene 6
"New Army Unit, Old Army Unit"
Soldiers, Japanese Merchants
Military Mutiny of 1882
"Back at the Seat of Power"
Sung Hoon Lee
"I Miss You, My Dear Queen"
H. S. Yu
"We Shall Return to the Palace"
T. Y. Kim, H. S. Yu, M. S. Kim
Scene 7
"Regent and Chinese"
Sung Hoon Lee, Sung Ho Lee
"Regent Is Taken to China"
Sung Hoon Lee
"Inoue Threatens King Kojong"
H. J. Lee
"Queen Min's Return"
The Company
"We Shall Rise Again"
T. Y. Kim, H. S. Yu, M. S. Kim, The Company
"Meeting on Japan's Chosun Policy"
Y. J. Choi, S. K. Kim, Japanese Cabinet Members

ACT 2
Scene 1
Dance at the Grand Banquet
"Come Celebrate Our Reforms"
T. Y. Kim, H. S. Yu
"Queen Elizabeth of Chosun"
Wives of the Foreign Envoys
"Negotiations at the Grand Banquet"
H. J. Lee, T. Y. Kim, Foreign Envoys
"The Sun Is Rising in Chosun"
The Company
"Isn't It Strange, Snowflakes Are Falling"
E. S. Jang
Scene 2
"You Shall Drink the Wine Offered by Miura"
T. Y. Kim
"Tripartite Intervention and the Atami House Conspiracy"
T. Y. Kim, H. S. Yu, A. Bundonis, P. Marinos, P. Taylor, S. K. Kim, Assassins
"Isn't It Strange, Snowflakes Are Falling" (reprise)
E. S. Jang
Scene 3
"New Era for the Prince"
K. W. Lee, T. Y. Kim, H. S. Yu
"Miura's Audience with the King"
S. K. Kim, T. Y. Kim, H. S. Yu
Scene 4
"The Situation Has Quickly Been Changed"
S. K. Kim
"The Queen Is Studying French Today"
M. J. Todaro
"By the Time This Drink Gets Cold"
S. K. Kim, Assassins
"Welcome"
Wives of the Foreign Envoys, T. Y. Kim
Ritual for 'Fox Hunt'
Scene 5
"The Prince and Queen"
J. H. Woo, T. Y. Kim
"Where Was It That We Met"
T. Y. Kim, M. S. Kim
"You Are My Destiny"
M. S. Kim
"Thunder and Lightning"
J. H. Woo, T. Y. Kim
"Light Up My Darkest Night"
T. Y. Kim
Scene 6
"Do Not Harm the Queen"
Sung Hoon Lee, H. M. Kim
"The Last of General Hong"
M. S. Kim
"The Queen Is Hunted Down"
T. Y. Kim, Y. J. Jeong
"Find the Queen, Kill the Fox"
Assassins, Court Ladies
"How Will I Live From Now On?"
J. H. Woo
"The World After the Death"
H. S. Yu, Sung Hoon Lee
Epilogue
"Rise, People of Chosun"
T. Y. Kim, The Company

1998.09

RIVERDANCE

A Return Engagement of the Dance Revue in Two Acts, 13 Scenes[3]. Music by Bill Whelan. Poetry by Theo Dorgan. Directed by John McColgan. Choreography by Michael Flatley, Jean Butler, Colin Dunne, Tara Little, Moscow Folk Ballet Company, Paula Nic Cionnaith, Maria Pagés, Tarik Winston. Scenery and painted projections by Robert Ballagh. Costumes by Jen Kelly. Lighting by Rupert Murray. Sound by Michael O'Gorman. Orchestrations by Nick Ingman, Bill Whelan. Projection design by Chris Slinsgby. Musical director, Eoghan O'Neill. Produced by Abhann Productions Ltd. (Moya Doherty, producer). Opened 24 September 1998 (matinee) at the Radio City Music Hall and closed 11 October 1998 after 23 performances.

CAST: *Narrator*: JOHN CAVANAGH. *Solo Dancers*: EILEEN MARTIN, PAT RODDY. *Solo Singers*: KATIE MCMAHON.

Irish Dance Troupe: Andrea Curley (Dance Captain), Dearbhail Bates (Assistant Dance Captain), Sarah Berry, Tara Barry, Natalie Biggs, Lorna Bradley, Martin Brennan, Rachel Byrne, Zeph Caissie, Melissa Convery, Jo Ellen Forsyth, Susan Ginnety, Paula Goulding, Sinéad Green, Gary Healy, Donnacha Howard, Sean Kelliher, Nicola Leonard, Matt Martin, Sorcha McCaul, Jonathan McMorrow, Paula McNelis, Joe Moriarty, Niall Mulligan, Aoibheann O'Brien, Niamh O'Brien, Ursula Quigley, Katie Regan, Ann Ryan, Lisa Ryan, Sheila Ryan, Anthony Savage, Anthony Sharkey, Ryan Sheridan, Claire Usher, Leanda Ward. *Firedance/Andalucia*: Nuria Brisa, Marta Jiménez Luis, Aranxta Jurado. *Moscow Folk Ballet*: Serguei Iakoubov, Svetlana Kossoroukova, Olena Krutsenko, Tatiana Nedostop, Iouri Oustiougov, Iouri Shishkine, Ilia Stretsov, Marina Taranda. *Riverdance Singers*: Derek Byrne, Derek Collins, Patrick Connolly, Jennifer Curran, Tony Davoren (Soloist—Oscail an Doras), Johanna Higgins, Maire Lang, Denise O'Kane, Cathal Synnott (choirmaster). *Trading Taps*: Robert Reed, Toby Harris, Donnell A. Russell. *Heal Their Hearts*: Charles Gray. *Slip into Spring/Home and the Heartland*: Eileen Ivers (Fiddle Player). *Drummers*: Abraham Doron, Vinny Ozborne, Darren Smith, David Tilly.

1998.10

SWAN LAKE

A Ballet in Two Acts, a Prologue and 11 Scenes. Music by Peter Ilyich Tchaikovsky. Directed and choreographed by Matthew Bourne. (Scenery and costumes) Designed by Lez Brotherson. Lighting by Rick Fisher. Musical director, David Frame. Orchestrations by David Cullen. Sound by Mark Menard. Conductor, David Frame. Associate conductor, Jack Buckhannan. Executive Management (North America), Martin McCallum and Alan Wasser. Produced by Adventures in Motion Picturess (Katharine Doré, Producing Director) and Cameron Mackintosh. Opened 8 October 1998 at the Neil Simon Theatre and closed 24 January 1999 after 124 performances.

---

[3]First produced in New York 13 March 1996 at the Radio City Music Hall for 8 performances, returned 2 October 1996 to the Radio City Music Hall for 21 performances. For Synopsis of Scenes and Musical Numbers, see October 1996 engagement.

CAST: *The Swan*: ADAM COOPER, WILL KEMP. *The Prince*: SCOTT AMBLER, BEN WRIGHT. *The Queen*: ISABEL MORTIMER, MARGUERITE PORTER. *The Prince's Girlfriend*: EMILY PIERCY. *The Private Secretary*: BARRY ATKINSON. *The Young Prince*: ANDREW WALKINSHAW. *Company*: Detlev Alexander, Jacqueline Anderson, Sarah Barron, Wilson E. Batista, Andrew Corbett, Saranne Curtin, Matthew Dalby, Vicky Evans, Ramon Flowers, Christopher Freeman, Jeffrey Lane Freeze, Nina Goldman, Gino Grenek, Heather Habens, Ben Hartley, Floyd Hendricks, Hans-Werner Klohe, Martin Lofsnes, Michela Meazza, Mark Mitchell, Neil Penlington, Arthur Pita, Colin Ross-Waterson, Tom Searle, Kirsty Tapp, Alan Vincent, Tom Ward, Ewan Wardrop, William Yong.

Prologue: The Prince's Bedroom.

Act 1, Scene 1: The Prince's Bedroom. *Scene 2*: The Palace. *Scene 3*: The Opera House. The Ballet. *Scene 4*: The Prince's Private Quarters. *Scene 5*: The Street. *Scene 6*: A Seedy Club [Club Swank]. *Scene 7*: The Street. *Scene 8*: A City Park.

Act 2, Scene 1: The Palace Gates. *Scene 2*: The Royal Ball. *Scene 3*: The Prince's Bedroom.

ACT 1

Scene 1

Maids, Valet and Footmen: The Company.

Scene 2

Cadets, Dignitaries, Officals, Soldiers, etc.: The Company.

Scene 3

The Queen's Escort: N. Penlington. *The Moth Maiden*: M. Meazza. *The Nobleman*: E. Wardrop. *Butterfly Maidens*: S. Barron, S. Curtin, H. Habens, I. Mortimer. *Evil Forest Troll*: D. Alexander. *His Attendants*: J. Anderson, V. Evans.

Scene 6

Club Owner: A. Vincent. *Barmaid*: J. Anderson. *Fan Dancer*: H. Habens. *Hostesses*: S. Barron, S. Curtin. *Party Girls*: V. Evans, I. Mortimer. *East End Gangsters*: B. Hartley, M. Loftsnes. *Sailors*: D. Alexander, H. Klohe. *Barflies*: A. Corbett, N. Goldman, C. Ross-Waterson. *Pop Idol*: N. Penlington. *Pimp*: A. Pita. *Juvenile Delinquent*: A. Walkinshaw.

Scene 8

Swans: The Company. *Duet*: A. Cooper or S. Ambler, W. Kemp or B. Wright. *Cygnets*: D. Alexander, W. E. Batista, R. Flowers, B. Hartley. *Solo*: W. Kemp or B. Wright. *Big Swans*: A. Corbett, H. Klohe, A. Pita, A. Vincent.

ACT 2

Scene 1

Doorman, Royal Spotters, Autograph Hunters, Paparazzi: The Company.

Scene 2

The German Princess: H. Habens. *The Spanish Princess*: J. Anderson. *The Hungarian Princess*: S. Barron. *Princess of Monaco*: I. Mortimer. *The Italian Princess*: S. Curtin. *The French Princess*: N. Goldman. *The Romanian Princess*: V. Evans. *The Royal Escorts*: The Company.
The Russian Dance: A. Cooper or W. Kemp, S. Barron, V. Evans, H. Habens.
The Spanish Dance: D. Alexander, J. Anderson, the Company.
The Neapolitan Dance: S. Curtin, E. Wardrop, the Company.
Czardas: A. Cooper or W. Kemp, S. Ambler or B. Wright, N. Goldman, E. Piercy, the Company.

Scene 3

Doctor, Nurses, Swans: The Company.

1998.11 MANDY PATINKIN IN CONCERT: MAMALOSHEN

A One-Man Revue of Yiddish Song in One Act[4]. (Conceived by Mandy Patinkin.) Piano, Lawrence Yurman. Violin, Saeka Matsuyama. Musical arrangements by Paul Ford and Eric Stern. Scenic consultant, Eric Renschler. Lighting design, Eric Cornwell. Sound design, Otts Munderloh. Produced by Dodger Endemol Theatricals[5]. Opened 13 October 1998 at the Belasco Theatre and closed 7 November 1998 after 28 performances.[6]

CAST: MANDY PATINKIN.

MUSICAL NUMBERS[7]

"Rozhinkes Mit Mandlen" (Raisins and Almonds)
A mother rocks her child, wishes him everything
(*Music and Lyrics by* Abraham Goldfaden, Henry Lefkowitch, Stanley Lionel.)

"Mayn Mirl" (Maria)(from *WEST SIDE STORY*)
(*Music by* Leonard Bernstein. *English lyrics by* Stephen Sondheim.)

"Yome, Yome . . . " (Traditional)
A mother questions her daughter.

"Belz"
Remembering a little town called Belz
(*Music and Lyrics by* Alexander Olshanetsky and Jacob Jacobs.)

"Tsen Kopikes" (Ten Kopecks)(Traditional)
A guy wants ten pennies to romance his girl.

"Supercalifragilisticexpialidocious" (from *MARY POPPINS*, film)
(*Music and English Lyrics by* Richard M. Sherman and Robert B. Sherman.)

"The Hokey Pokey"
(*Music and Lyrics by* Charles Mack, Taft Baker and Roland LaPrise.)

"Papirosin" (Cigarettes)
A boy sells cigarettes to survive the war.
(*Music and Lyrics by* Herman Yablokoff.)

"Motl Der Opreyter"
A sweatshop worker struggles to support his family.
(*Music and Lyrics by* Chaim Towber and H. Solomonson.)

"Unter Dayne Vayse Shtern" (Under Your White Stars)
A holocaust song.
(*Music and Lyrics by* Abraham Sutzkever and Abraham Brudno.)

"Lid Fun Titanic" (Song of the Titanic)
A ship is lost at sea—hope survives.
(*Music and Lyrics by* Joshua Rayzner.)

"Hey, Tsigelekh" (Hey, Little Goats)
The diaspora.
(*Music and Lyrics by* Mordecai Gebirtig.)

"Take Me Out to the Ball Game"
(*Music by* Albert Von Tilzer. *English Lyrics by* Jack Norworth.)

"God Bless America"
(*Music and English Lyrics by* Irving Berlin.)

"Der Alter Tzigayner" (The Old Gypsy)
The old gypsy fiddler plays an unfogettable tune.
(*Music by* Abraham Ellstein. *Lyrics by* Jacob Jacobs.)

"White Christmas" (from film of the same name)
(*Music and English Lyrics by* Irving Berlin.)

"Oyfn Pripetshik"
Children learn their ABC's at the fireplace.
(*Music and Lyrics by* Mark M. Warshawsky.)

"American Tune"
Our journey to America.
(*Music and American Lyrics by* Paul Simon.)

1998.12 AZNAVOUR ON BROADWAY

A One-Man Show in Two Acts. Musical director, Russell Kassoff. Mr. Aznavour's clothing by Francesco Smalto. Produced by Delsenerslater/SFX Entertainment (Ron Delsener-Slater) by special arrangement with Lévon Sayan. Opened 20 October 1998 at the Marquis Theatre and closed 15 November 1998 after 24 performances.

CAST: CHARLES AZNAVOUR.

MUSICAL NUMBERS[8]

"Je Bois"
"Sa Jeunesse"
"Yesterday, When I Was Young"
(*Music and French lyrics by* Charles Aznavour. *English lyrics by* Herbert Kretzmer.)
"La Mamma"
"What Makes a Man"

[4]Mamaloshen means "mother tongue" in Yiddish.
[5]Dodger Productions: Michael David, Doug Johnson, Des McAnuff, Rocco Landesman, Edward Strong and Sherman Warner. Endemol Theatre Productions: Joop van den Ende and Robin de Levita.
[6]Previously produced Off-Broadway at the Angel Orensantz Centre 21 July 1998- 22 August 1998 for 30 performances. Program note: "Special thanks to Judy Blazer and her glorious voice and to Zalman Mlotek and his wonderful Yiddish Chorale" (performances on tape).

[7]Dropped after Off-Broadway engagement: "A Day in the Park."
[8]Musical numbers not listed in programs.

1998.13 FOOTLOOSE

A Musical in Two Acts, 18 Scenes. Book by Dean Pitchford and Walter Bobbie. Based on the film of the same name, screenplay by Dean Pitchford. Music by Tom Snow. Lyrics by Dean Pitchford. Additional songs by Kenny Loggins and Eric Carmen. Directed by Walter Bobbie. Choreographed by A. C. Ciulla. Scenery designed by John Lee Beatty. Costumes designed by Toni-Leslie James. Lighting designed by Ken Billington. Sound designed by Tony Meola. Orchestrations by Danny Troob. Music supervision and vocal arrangements by Doug Katsaros. Dance music arrangements by Joe Baker. Produced by Madison Square Garden Productions (Tim Hawkins, Producer) and Dodger Endemol Productions[9]. Opened 22 October 1998 at the Richard Rodgers Theatre and closed 2 July 2000 after 737 performances.

CAST (in order of appearance): *Ren McCormack*: JEREMY KUSHNIER. *Ethel McCormack*: CATHERINE COX. *Shaw Moore*: STEPHEN LEE ANDERSON. *Vi Moore*: DEE HOTY. *Ariel Moore*: JENNIFER LAURA THOMPSON. *Lulu Warnicker*: Catherine Campbell. *Wes Warnicker*: Adam LeFevre. *Eleanor Dunbar*: Donna Lee Marshall. *Doreen*: Donna Lee Marshall. *Coach Dunbar*: JOHN HILLNER. *Rusty*: STACY FRANCIS. *Urleen*: Kathy Deitch. *Wendy Jo*: Rosalind Brown. *Chuck Cranston*: BILLY HARTUNG. *Lyle*: Jim Ambler. *Travis*: Bryant Carroll. *Cop*: Nick Sullivan. *Country Fiddler*: Nick Sullivan. *Betty Blast*: Robin Baxter. *Irene*: Robin Baxter. *Willard Hewitt*: TOM PLOTKIN. *Saloon Keeper*: John Deyle *Principal Clerk*: John Deyle. *Cowboy Bob*: Artie Harris. *Jeter*: Artie Harris. *Bickle*: Hunter Foster. *Garvain*: Paul Castree.

Ensemble: Billy Angell, Angela Brydon, Paul Castree, Hunter Foster, Kristen Leigh Gorski, Artie Harris, Sean Haythe, Lori Holmes, Daniel Karaty, Katharine Leonard, Mark Myars, JoAnna Ross, Serena Soffer, Ron Todorowski. *Swings*: Ben Cameron, Sean Haythe, Paige Hinton, Jeanine Meyers, Orfeh.

Scene: Somewhere in the heartland of America in the recent past.

Act 1, Scene 1: City of Chicago; Town of Bomont, Church. *Scene 2*: Church Yard. *Scene 3*: Burger Blast Restaurant. *Scene 4*: High School Hallway. *Scene 5*: Street Corner; Principal's Office; Warnicker Home. *Scene 6*: Moore Home. *Scene 7*: Burger Blast Restaurant. *Scene 8*: Plains of Bomont. *Scene 9*: Moore Home. *Scene 10*: High School Gymnasium.

Act 2, Scene 1: The "Bar-B-Q" Country & Western Bar. *Scene 2*: Moore Home. *Scene 3*: Lot behind the Feed and Fuel. *Scene 4*: The Potawney Bridge. *Scene 5*: Bomont Town Hall. *Scene 6*: Church. *Scene 7*: Church Yard. *Scene 8*: High School Gymnasium.

ACT 1

Scene 1

"Footloose"
J. Kushnier, Company
(*Music by* Kenny Loggins. *Lyrics by* Kenny Loggins, Dean Pitchford.)

"On Any Sunday"[10]
S. L. Anderson, Company

Scene 3

"The Girl Gets Around"
B. Hartung, J. L. Thompson, B. Carroll, J. Ambler
(*Music by* Sammy Hagar.)

Scene 4

"I Can't Stand Still"[11]
J. Kushnier

Scene 5

"Somebody's Eyes"
S. Francis, R. Brown, K. Deitch, Company

Scene 6

"Learning To Be Silent"[12]
D. Hoty, C. Cox

Scene 7

"Holding Out for a Hero"
J. L. Thompson, S. Francis, R. Brown, K. Deitch
(*Music by* Jim Steinman.)

Scene 9

"Somebody's Eyes" (reprise)
S. Francis, R. Brown, K. Deitch

"Heaven Help Me"
S. L. Anderson

Scene 10

"I'm Free"
(*Music by* Kenny Loggins.)
"Heaven Help Me"/"On Any Sunday" (reprise)
J. Kushnier, S. L. Anderson, Company

ACT 2

Scene 1

"Still Rockin'"/"Let's Make Believe We're in Love?"[13]
R. Baxter, Country Kickers

"Let's Hear It for the Boy"
S. Francis, Company

Scene 2

"Can You Find It in Your Heart?"[14]
D. Hoty

Scene 3

"Mama Says"[15]
T. Plotkin, the Boys

Scene 4

"Almost Paradise"
J. Kushnier, J. L. Thompson
(*Music by* Eric Carmen.)

Scene 5

"Dancing Is Not a Crime"[16]
J. Kushnier, the Boys

Scene 6

"I Confess"[17]
S. L. Anderson

"On Any Sunday" (reprise)
Company

Scene 7

"Can You Find It in Your Heart?" (reprise)
S. L. Anderson

Scene 8

"Footloose" (reprise)
Company

1998.14 SANDRA BERNHARD: I'M STILL HERE DAMN IT!

A One-Woman Show in One Act[18]. (Conceived and written by Sandra Bernhard.) Director, Marty Callner. Scenic consultant, Paul Holt. Lighting consultant, Allen Branton. Sound consultant, Nelson-O'Reilly Productions, Inc. Special material, musical director, Mitchell Kaplan. Produced by Contemporary Productions (An SFX Entertainment Company) and Arielle Tepper. Opened 5 November 1998 at the Booth Theatre and closed 3 January 1999 after 51 performances.

CAST: SANDRA BERNHARD.

The Band: Mitchell Kaplan (keyboards), Denise Fraser (drums, percussion), Dan Petty (guitar), Michael Stanzilis (bass guitar), Soumaya Akaaboune (gembe, vocals).

MUSICAL NUMBERS[19]

"Walk Tall"
(*Music and Lyrics by* Mitchell Kaplan and Sandra Bernhard.)

"On the Runway"
(*Music and Lyrics by* Mitchell Kaplan, Sandra Bernhard and Derrick Smit.)

"Nightingale"
(*Music and Lyrics by* Mitchell Kaplan and Sandra Bernhard.)

"God Is Good"
(*Music and Lyrics by* Mitchell Kaplan and Sandra Bernhard.)

"Midnight Train to Georgia"
(*Music and Lyrics by* Jim Weatherly.)

---

[9]Dodger Productions: Michael David, Doug Johnson, Des McAnuff, Rocco Landesman, Edward Strong and Sherman Warner. Endemol Theatre Productions: Joop van den Ende and Robin de Levita.
[10]Newly written for the stage, and not in the original film.
[11]Newly written for the stage, and not in the original film.
[12]Newly written for the stage, and not in the original film.
[13]Newly written for the stage, and not in the original film.
[14]Newly written for the stage, and not in the original film.
[15]Newly written for the stage, and not in the original film.
[16]Newly written for the stage, and not in the original film.
[17]Newly written for the stage, and not in the original film.
[18]Previously produced Off-Broadway 11 November 1997 at the Westbeth Theatre Center.
[19]Musical numbers not listed in programs. List prepared from press materials, reviews, recordings; not in performance order.

1998.15

LITTLE ME

A Revival of the Musical Comedy in Two Acts[20]. Book (revised) by Neil Simon. Based on the novel of the same name by Patrick Dennis. Music by Cy Coleman. Lyrics by Carolyn Leigh. Directed and choreographed by Robert Marshall. Set design by David Gallo. Costume design by Anne Hould-Ward. Lighting design by Kenneth Posner. Sound design by Brian Ronan. Orchestrations by Harold Wheeler. Musical director, David Chase. Dance music arranged by David Krane. Projection design by Jan Hartley. Associate director and choreographer, Cynthia Onrubia. Produced by Roundabout Theatre Company (Todd Haimes, Artistic Director; Ellen Richard, Managing Director). Opened 12 November 1998 at the Roundabout Theatre/Stage Right and closed 7 February 1999 after 101 performances.

CAST (in order of appearance): *Belle*: FAITH PRINCE. *Belle's Boys*: Michael Arnold, Jeffrey Hankinson, Ned Hannah, Denis Jones. *Momma*: RUTH WILLIAMSON. *Ramona*: Andrea Chamberlain. *Bruce*: MICHAEL MCGRATH. *Cerine*: Cynthia Onrubia. *Noble Eggleston* MARTIN SHORT. *Mrs. Eggleston*: RUTH WILLIAMSON. *Greensleeves*: Michael McEachran. *Maid*: Christine Pedi. *Lucky*: MICHAEL PARK. *Miss Kepplewhite*: Christine Pedi. *Pinchley Junior*: Brooks Ashmanskas. *Nurse*: Kimberly Lyon. *Amos Pinchley*: MARTIN SHORT. *Kleeg*: Peter Benson. *Newsboys*: Michael Arnold, Jeffrey Hankinson. *Bernie Buchsbaum*: MICHAEL MCGRATH. *Benny Buchsbaum*: MARTIN SHORT. *Attorney*: Peter Benson. *Chain Gang*: Michael Arnold, Jeffrey Hankinson, Ned Hannah, Denis Jones. *Maitre D'*: Peter Benson. *Boom Boom Girls*: Kimberly Lyon, Joanne McHugh, Cynthia Onrubia. *Val du Val*: MARTIN SHORT. *Colette*: Roxane Barlow. *Kitty*: Cynthia Onrubia. *Suzie*: Joanne McHugh. *Roxane*: Roxane Barlow. *Christine*: Christine Pedi. *Bert*: MICHAEL MCGRATH. *Soldier*: Denis Jones. *Fred Poitrine*: MARTIN SHORT. *Sergeant*: Michael McEachran. *Preacher*: Peter Benson. *German Soldier*: MICHAEL MCGRATH. *General*: Peter Benson. *Army Nurse*: Christine Pedi. *Captain*: Peter Benson. *Steward*: Brooks Ashmanskas. *First Sailor*: Ned Hannah. *Second Sailor*: Jeffrey Hankinson. *Assistant Director*: Brooks Ashmanskas. *Secretary*: Christine Pedi. *Otto Schnitzler*: MARTIN SHORT. *Movie "King"*: Michael McEachran. *Victor*: Peter Benson. *Prince Cherney*: MARTIN SHORT. *Yulnick*: MICHAEL MCGRATH. *Casino Woman*: Christine Pedi. *Doctor*: Brooks Ashmanskas. *Justices*: Denis Jones, Jeffrey Hankinson. *The Drunk*: MARTIN SHORT. *Party Guests, Rich Kids, Drifter's Row Townspeople, Courtroom Dancers, Skylight Roof Patrons, Nurses, Soldiers, Medics, Passengers, Biblical Slaves, Casino Patron Patrons and Mourners*. *Swings*: Joey Pizzi, Josh Prince, Courtney Young.

Scenes: The Present: Southampton, 1962. The Past: Venezuela, Illinois; Chicago; Somewhere in France; On the North Atlantic; Hollywood; Monte Carlo; A Principality in Middle Europe.

ACT 1[21]

"Little Me"
F. Prince, Belle's Boys

"The Other Side of the Tracks"
F. Prince

"Rich Kids Rag" (The Birthday Party)
Rich Kids, M. Short [Noble]

"I Love You"
M. Short [Noble], F. Prince, Company

"The Other Side of the Tracks" (reprise)
F. Prince

"Deep Down Inside"
F. Prince, M. Short [Pinchley], Company

"Be a Perfomer"
M. McGrath, M. Short [Bernie], F. Prince

"Dimples"
F. Prince, Her Chain Gang

"Boom-Boom"
M. Short [Val du Val], Boom Boom Girls

"I've Got Your Number"
M. Park

"Real Live Girl"
M. Short [Fred Poitrine]

"Real Live Girl" (reprise)
M. Short [Fred Poitrine], Soldiers

Finale (Act 1)
F. Prince

ACT 2

"I Love Sinking You"
F. Prince, M. Short [Fred Poitrine], Company

"Poor Little Hollywood Star"
F. Prince

"(The Prince's) Goodbye" (Farewell)
M. Short [Prince Cherney], M. McGrath, Company

"Here's To Us"
F. Prince, Company

[20]Originally produced in New York 17 November 1962 at the Lunt-Fontanne Theatre for 257 performances.

[21]Not used in this production: "The Truth" (original 1962 production), and "I Wanna Be Yours" and "Don't Ask a Lady" (both from the 1982 revival). "I Love Sinking You" is a revised version of "I Love You."

1998.16

ON THE TOWN

A Revival of the Musical Comedy in Two Acts, 17 Scenes[22]. Book and lyrics[23] by Betty Comden and Adolph Green. Book based on an idea by Jerome Robbins. Music by Leonard Bernstein. Directed by George C. Wolfe. Choreographed by Keith Young. Set design by Adrianne Lobel. Costume design by Paul Tazewell. Lighting design by Paul Gallo. Sound design by Jon Weston. Musical direction by Kevin Stites. Orchestrations by Bruce Coughlin. Produced by The Joseph Papp Public Theater/New York Shakespeare Festival (George C. Wolfe, Producer; Rosemarie Tichler, Artistic Producer; Mark Litvin, Managing Director). Opened 22 November 1998 at the Gershwin Theatre and closed 17 January 1999 after 65 performances.

CAST (in order of appearance): *Workman*: Gregory Emanuel Rahming. *Quartet*: Tom Aulino, Christopher F. Davis, Blake Hammond, John Jellison. *Ozzie*: ROBERT MONTANO. *Chip*: JESSE TYLER FERGUSON. *Gabey*: PERRY LAYLON OJEDA. *Flossie*: Linda Mugleston. *Flossie's Friend*: Chandra Wilson. *Subway Bill Poster*: John Jellison. *Little Old Lady*: MARY TESTA. *Mannequins*: Dottie Earle, Jennifer Frankel, Amy Heggins, Judine Richard. *Miss Turnstiles Announcers*: Nora Cole, Gregory Emanuel Rahming. *Ivy Smith*: TAI JIMENEZ. *Policeman*: Christopher F. Davis. *Mr. S. Uperman*: Blake Hammond. *Hildy Esterhazy*: LEA DELARIA. *Waldo Figment*: Tom Aulino. *Claire DeLoone*: SARAH KNOWLTON. *Primitive Man and Woman*: Stephen Campanella, Judine Richàrd. *Pas de Deux Dancers*: Kristine Bendul, Darren Gibson. *Madame Maude P. Dilly*: MARY TESTA. *Women of Carnegie Hall*: Nora Cole, Linda Mugleston, Chandra Wilson. *Pitkin W. Bridgework*: JONATHAN FREEMAN. *Lucy Schmeeler*: ANNIE GOLDEN. *Diamond Eddie's Girls*: Kristine Bendul, Jennifer Frankel, Amy Heggins, Keenah Reid, Judine Richàrd. *Master of Ceremonies*: Blake Hammond. *Diana Dream/Dolores Dolores*: Nora Cole. *Rajah Bimmy*: John Jellison.

Dance Ensemble: Brad Aspel, Tom Aulino, Kristine Bendul, Stephen Campanella, R. J. Durell, Dottie Earle, Jennifer Frankel, Edgard Gallardo, Darren Gibson, Amy Heggins, John Jellison, Darren Lee, Keenah Reid, Judine Richard. *The People of New York*: Tom Aulino, Blake Hammond, John Jellison, Linda Mugleston, Gregory Emanuel Rahming, Chandra Wilson. *Swings*: Kim Craven, Sloan Just, Rommy Sandhu, Scott Spahr.

The action takes place in New York City in June, 1944.

Act 1, Scene 1: The Brooklyn Navy Yard. *Scene 2*: A Subway Train in Motion. *Scene 3*: A New York Street. *Scene 4*: Presentation of Miss Turnstiles. *Scene 5*: A Taxi Cab. *Scene 6*: The Museum of Natural History. *Scene 7*: A Busy New York Street. *Scene 8*: A Corridor and Studio in Carnegie Hall. *Scene 9*: Central Park. *Scene 10*: Claire's and Hildy's Apartments. *Scene 11*: Times Square.

Act 2, Scene 1: Night Clubs, (a) Diamond Eddie's Club, (b) The Congacabana, (c) The Slam Bang Club. *Scene 2*: The Subway Train to Coney Island. *Scene 3*: The Dream Coney Island. *Scene 4*: Subway Platform. *Scene 5*: The Real Coney Island. *Scene 6*: The Brooklyn Navy Yard.

ACT 1

Scene 1

"I Feel Like I'm Not Out of Bed"
G. E. Rahming, Quartet

"New York, New York"
R. Montano, J. T. Ferguson, P. L. Ojeda, Full Company

Scene 3

"Gabey's Coming"
R. Montano, J. T. Ferguson, P. L. Ojeda, Mannequins

Scene 4

"Presentation of Miss Turnstiles" (Ballet)
N. Cole, G. E. Rahming, T. Jimenez, Dance Ensemble

[22]Originally produced in New York 28 December 1944 at the Adelphi Theatre for 462 performances. For Synopsis of Scenes and Musical Numbers, see original 1944 production. This revival originated in an open air production 17-31 August 1997 at the Delacorte Theatre (Off-Broadway) for 14 performances. For this revival, the previously unused "Gabey's Comin'" was added to Act 1, Scene 3.

[23]Additional lyrics by Leonard Bernstein.

Scene 5
"Come Up to My Place"
L. DeLaria, J. T. Ferguson
Scene 6
"(I Get) Carried Away"
S. Knowlton, R. Montano, S. Campanella, J. Richàrd
Scene 7
"Lonely Town"
P. L. Ojeda, Dance Ensemble
Scene 8
"Carnegie Hall Pavane" (Do, Do, Re, Do)
T. Jimenez, M. Testa, Women of Carnegie Hall
Scene 9
"Lucky to Be Me"
P. L. Ojeda, Ensemble
Scene 10
"I Understand"
J. Freeman
"I Can Cook Too"
L. DeLaria
Scene 11
"Times Square Ballet"
Full Company

ACT 2
Scene 1a
"So Long Baby"
Diamond Eddie's Girls
"I Wish I Was Dead" (I'm Blue)
N. Cole [Diana Dream]
Scene 1b
"I Wish I Was Dead" (I'm Blue)
N. Cole [Dolores Dolores]
"You Got Me"
L. DeLaria, S. Knowlton, R. Montano, J. T. Ferguson
Scene 1c
"I Understand"
J. Freeman, A. Golden
Scene 2
Subway Ride
P. L. Ojeda, People of New York
Scene 3
Imaginary Coney Island (Ballet)
P. L. Ojeda, T. Jimenez, Dance Ensemble
Scene 4
"Some Other Time"
S. Knowlton, L. DeLaria, R. Montano, J. T. Ferguson
Scene 5
"The Real Coney Island"
J. Jellison
Scene 6
"I Feel Like I'm Not Out of Bed" (reprise)
G. E. Rahming
"New York, New York" (reprise)
Entire Company

1998.17

FOOL MOON

A Revival of the Comedy Performance Revue in Two Acts[24]. Created by Bill Irwin and David Shiner. (Original music and lyrics by the Red Clay Ramblers.) Set design by Douglas Stein. Costume design by Bill Kellard. Lighting design by Nancy Schertler. Sound design by Tom Morse. Flying by Foy. Producing associate, Nancy Harrington. Associate producer, Sammi Rose Cannold. Produced by James B. Freydberg, Jeffrey Ash, Dori Berinstein, CTM Productions (David Jiranek, David Weil and Cricket Hooper). Opened 22 November 1998 at the Brooks Atkinson Theatre and closed 3 January 1999 after 49 performances.

CAST (in order of appearance): DAVID SHINER, BILL IRWIN.
THE RED CLAY RAMBLERS: Clay Buckner (fiddle, harmonica), Chris Frank (piano, accordion, trombone, ukelele, tuba, guitar), Jack Herrick (bass, trumpet, mandolin, tin whistle, concertina), Mark Roberts (banjo, flute, oboe, tin whistle, keyboard), Rob Ladd (drums, ukelele).

ACT 1[25]
Opening
D. Shiner, B. Irwin, Red Clay Ramblers, 2 Ushers
"Fire and Sugar" (traditional)
Red Clay Ramblers
Encounter
D. Shiner, B. Irwin
"Wa-Hoo"[26]
Red Clay Ramblers
Dance Solo
D. Shiner
Dance to the Left
B. Irwin, Stage Manager
Big Night Out
D. Shiner, B. Irwin, an Audience Member

ACT 2
"Pal-Yat-Chee"[27]
Red Clay Ramblers
(*Music and Lyrics by* Eddie Maxwell and Spike Jones.)
Improvisation in Public
D. Shiner, an Audience Memeber
Harlequin/Pantalone
B. Irwin, Red Clay Ramblers, D. Shiner
"Hiawatha's Lullaby"
Red Clay Ramblers
(*Music by* Walter Donaldson. *Lyrics by* Joe Young.)
"Tea for Two" (from *NO, NO NANETTE*)
D. Shiner, B. Irwin
(*Music by* Vincent Youmans. *Lyrics by* Irving Caesar.)
Conductor
B. Irwin, Red Clay Ramblers
Cinema
D. Shiner, 4 Audience Members
"Valley of the Dry Bones" (traditional; a capella)
Red Clay Ramblers, D. Shiner, B. Irwin
"Melancholy Moon Song"[28]
Red Clay Ramblers, B. Irwin, D. Shiner
"Fire and Sugar" (reprise)
B. Irwin, D. Shiner, Red Clay Ramblers

1998.18

PETER PAN, or The Boy Who Wouldn't Grow Up

A Revival of the Musical in Three Acts, 7 Scenes[29]. Book by James M. Barrie[30]. Music by Moose [Mark] Charlap. Lyrics by Carolyn Leigh. Additional music by Jule Styne. Additional lyrics by Betty Comden and Adolph Green. Original Broadway production conceived, directed and choreographed by Jerome Robbins. Directed by Glenn Casale. Choreographed by Patti Columbo. Scenery designed by John Iacovelli. Costumes designed by Shigeru Yaji. Lighting designed by Martin Aronstein. Sound designed by Francois Bergeron. Musical direction and vocals arrangements by Craig

---

[24]Originally produced in New York 25 February 1993 at the Richard Rodgers Theatre for 207 performances, and 29 October 1995 at the Ambassador Theatre for 81 performances.

[25]Scenes and Musical Numbers not identified in programs; list prepared from producers' materials. Also performed:
"Old Jim Canaan's" (by Reverend Robert Wilkins.)
"Take Five" (by Paul Desmond)
Love Theme from Romeo And Juliet(film)
(*Music by* Nino Rota.)

[26]Not in previous 1993 production.

[27]Not in previous 1993 production.

[28]Not in previous 1993 production.

[29]Originally produced in New York 20 October 1954 at the Winter Garden for 152 performances. This adaptation previously presented in New York 13 December 1990 at the Lunt-Fontanne Theatre for 45 performances, and 27 November 1991 at the Minskoff Theatre for 48 performances. For Synopsis of Scenes and Musical Numbers, see 1990 revival.

[30]Musical libretto uncredited.

Barna. Flying illusions by ZFX, Inc. Produced by (Thomas P.) McCoy-Rigby Entertainment, The Nederlander Organization and La Mirada Theatre for the Performing Arts, in association with Albert Nocciolino, Larry Payton and J. Lynn Singleton. Opened 23 November 1998 at the Minskoff Theatre and closed 3 January 1999 after 48 performances; returned 7 April 1999 to the Gershwin Theatre and closed 29 August 1999 after 168 additional performances. Total: 216 performances.

CAST (in order of appearance): *Mrs. Darling*: BARBARA MCCULLOH. *Wendy Darling*: ELISA SAGARDIA. *John Darling*: CHASE KNIFFEN. *Michael Darling*: DRAKE ENGLISH. *Liza*: Dana Solimando. *Nana*: Buck Mason. *Mr. Darling*: PAUL SCHOEFFLER. *Peter Pan*: CATHY RIGBY. *Curly*: Alon Williams. *First Twin*: Janet Higgins. *Second Twin*: Doreen Chila. *Slightly*: Scott Bridges. *Tootles*: Aileen Quinn. *Mr. Smee*: MICHAEL NOSTRAND. *Cecco*: Tony Spinosa. *Gentleman Starkey*: Sam Zeller. *Noodler*: Randy Davis. *Bill Jukes*: Buck Mason. *Captain Hook*: PAUL SCHOEFFLER. *Crocodile*: Buck Mason. *Tiger Lily*: DANA SOLIMANDO. *Mermaid*: Barbara McCulloh. *Pirates and Indians*: Kim Arnett, Randy Davis, Jeffrey Elsass, Casey Miles Good, Buck Mason, Brian Shepard, Roger Preston Smith, Tony Spinosa, Sam Zeller.

Wendy, Grown-up: BARBARA MCCULLOH. *Jane*: AILEEN QUINN.

General Understudy: Michelle Berti. *Swing*: William Alan Coats.

1998.19 CHRISTMAS FROM THE HEART

A Christmas Entertainment in One Act, 3 Scenes. Book by Kenny Rogers and Kelly Junkermann Rogers. Music and lyrics by Kenny Rogers, Warren Hartman and Steve Glassmeyer. Beacon Theatre Production directed by Larry Pellegrini. Musical staging by Dani Davis and Adam Pelty. Set design by George Xenos. Costumes design by Frank Krenz and Juan DeArmas. Lighting design by Jeff Metter. Sound design by Keith Bugos. Orcestrator/Musical director, Warren Hartman. Executive producers, Robert Halmi, Jr. and Larry Levinson. Produced by Hallmark Entertainment. Opened 24 November 1998 at the Beacon Theatre and closed 3 January 1999 after 47 performances.

CAST: The Grown-Ups: *Hank Longley*: KENNY ROGERS. *Roscoe Baxter*: Martin Epstein. *Katie*: Jillian Arciero. *Agnes*: Charlotte Franklin. *Rosemary's Mom/Nativity Teacher*: Cara D'Emanuele-Sanders. *Patterson*: James Broderick. *Doug*: Doug Dean. *Mary Claire*: Ellie Dvorkin. *Mary's Assistant*: Johnny Tammaro, Jr.

The Kids: *Rosemary*: Taylor Burgos. *Tray*: Shaw Leggett. *Beckie*: Francesca Mari. *Maleek*: Jeremy Maleel Leggett. *Percival*: Evan Broder. *Kurt*: James Kurlinski.

The Toys: *Jack*: Drew DiStefano. *Bruno*: Steve Calzaretta. *Rags*: Mamie Parris. *Riches*: Topher Goodman. *Foxy*: Kathy Connolly. *Cheeseball*: Heather Feeney. *Sarge*: Stephen G. Kennedy. *Giselle*: Jacqueline Maloney. *Ballerina*: Matina Parisi.

Christmas Sprites: Johnny Tammaro, Jr., Steve Calzaretta, Topher Goodman, Derek Staranowski, Marnie Parris, Ellie Dvorkin, Robin Higginbotham, Julie Foldesi. *Ensemble*: Johnny Tammaro, Jr., Ellie Dvorkin, Robin Higginbotham, Derek Staranowski, Julie Foldesi. *Choir*: The Voice of Praise Choir.

Scene 1: Merryville Town Park. *Scene 2*: Merryville Church. *Scene 3*: Hank Longley's Toy Shoppe.

MUSICAL NUMBERS

Scene 1

"Frosty the Snowman"
The Kids

"Winter Wonderland" (from *ZIEGFELD FOLLIES OF 1934*)
K. Rogers, Ensemble

"Let It Snow, Let It Snow, Let It Snow"
K. Rogers
(*Music by* Jule Styne. *Lyrics by* Sammy Cahn.)

"The Christmas Song"
K. Rogers
(*Music and Lyrics by* Mel Tormé and Robert Wells.)

"White Christmas" (from *WHITE CHRISTMAS* film)
K. Rogers
(*Music and Lyrics by* Irving Berlin.)

"(The) Twelve Days of Christmas"
K. Rogers, Special Guests

"It's Not Just Christmas"
K. Rogers
(*Music and Lyrics by* Debi Smith-Cochran, Anathale G. Sandlin, Bill Swindell, Tina Murrah-Swindell.)

Scene 2

"The Chosen One" "Away in the Manger," "O Holy Night," "Silent Night," "The First Noel," "We Three Kings," "Joy to the World"
(Traditional; *music arranged by* Kenny Rogers, Warren Hartman.)

Scene 3

"Merry Christmas"
Ensemble
(*Music and Lyrics by* Kenny Rogers, Warren Hartman and Steve Glassmeyer.)

"I Want To Be a Christmas Present"
The Toys
(*Music and Lyrics by* Kenny Rogers, Warren Hartman and Steve Glassmeyer.)

"Heroes"
K. Rogers
(*Music and Lyrics by* Kenny Rogers, Warren Hartman and Steve Glassmeyer.)

"Money Isn't What Really Matters"
K. Rogers, The Kids
(*Music and Lyrics by* Kenny Rogers, Warren Hartman and Steve Glassmeyer.)

"Love Me Just For Me"
J. Maloney

"If I Only Had Your Heart"
K. Rogers, J. Maloney
(*Music and Lyrics by* Kenny Rogers, Warren Hartman and Steve Glassmeyer.)

"Mr. Perfect"
The Toys
(*Music and Lyrics by* Kenny Rogers, Warren Hartman and Steve Glassmeyer.)

"I Promise You"
K. Rogers
(*Music and Lyrics by* Kenny Rogers, Warren Hartman and Steve Glassmeyer.)

"The Toy Shoppe"
Ensemble
(*Music and Lyrics by* Kenny Rogers, Warren Hartman and Steve Glassmeyer.)

"'Til the Season Comes 'Round Again" (Finale)
K. Rogers
(*Music and Lyrics by* John Barlow Jarvis and Randy Goodrum.)

1998.20 A CHRISTMAS CAROL

A Revival of the Musical in One Act, 13 Scenes[31]. Book by Mike Ockrent and Lynn Ahrens. Based on the story of the same name by Charles Dickens. Music by Alan Menken. Lyrics by Lynn Ahrens. Directed by Mike Ockrent. Choreographed by Susan Stroman. Setting design by Tony Walton. Costume design by William Ivey Long. Lighting design by Jules Fisher and Peggy Eisenhauer. Sound design by Tony Meola. Projections by Wendall K. Harrington. Flying by Foy. Associate director, Steven Zweigbaum. Associate choreographer, Chris Peterson. Musical direction by Paul Gemignani. Orchestrations by Michael Starobin and Douglas Besterman. Dance arrangements and incidental music by Glen Kelly. Executive producer, Dodger Endemol Theatricals. Producer, Tim Hawkins. Presented by American Express/Madison Square Garden. Opened 2 December 1998 at the (Paramount) Theatre, Madison Square Garden and closed 27 December 1998 after 57 performances.

CAST (in order of appearance): *Beadle*: Del-Bourree Bach. *Mr. Smythe*: CHRIS VASQUEZ. *Grace Smythe*: Netousha Harris, Tavia Riveé Jefferson. *Scrooge*: ROGER DALTREY. *Crachit*: TODD GROSS. *Charity Men*: David Aaron Damane, Roland Rusinek, Wayne Schroder. *Old Joe*: Kenneth McMullen. *Street Urchins*: Dana Chechile, Carissa Farina, Dennis Michael Hall, Jesse McCartney, Gabriel Millman, Stephen Scarpulla. *Mrs. Crachit*: Rachel Black. *Tiny Tim*: Anthony Blair Hall, Christian Valiando. *Poulterer*: Roland Rusinek. *Sandwichboard*: ROZ RYAN. *Jonathon*: Adam Barruch, Kennedy Kanagawa. *Lamplighter*: KEN JENNINGS. *Blind Hag*: Debra Cardona. *Fred*: JOHN SLOMAN. *Mrs. Mopps*: Marilyn Pasekoff. *Ghost of Jacob Marley*: PAUL KANDEL. *Ghost of Christmas Past*: KEN JENNINGS. *Lights of Christmas Past*: Matthew Baker, Ronald Cadet Bastine, Keith Fortner, Michael Lomeka. *Judge*: Roland Rusinek. *Scrooge at 8 years*: Dennis Michael Hall, Stephen Scarpulla. *Scrooge's Mother*: Debra Cardona. *Scrooge's Father*: Wayne Schroder. *Mr. Hawkins*: Kenneth McMullen. *Scrooge at 12 years*: Jesse McCartney, Gabriel Millman. *Fan*: Dana Chechile, Carissa Farina. *Fezziwig*: Daniel Marcus. *Scrooge at 18 years*: Joe Cassidy. *Young Marley*: Ken Barnett. *Mrs. Fezziwig*: Joy Hermalyn. *Emily*:

---

[31]Originally produced in New York 1 December 1994 at the Paramount Theatre, Madison Square Garden for 71 performances. For Synopsis of Scenes and Musical Numbers, see original 1994 production. For this year's and the 1995, 1996 and 1997 revivals the following changes were made:

Scene 1 and "The Years Are Passing By" were dropped.

Added to Scene 2 (former Scene 3) before "Street Song":

"You Mean More to Me"
T. Gross, A. B. Hall or C. Valiando

"The Years Are Passing By" (reprise) in former Scene 13 (new Scene 12) was replaced by:

"London Town Carol"
A. Barruch or K. Kanagawa

Note: The production played an irregular schedule of multiple daily performances.

Kristin Huxhold. *Ghost of Christmas Present*: ROZ RYAN. *The Crachit Children*: Dana Chechile, Carissa Farina, Jesse McCartney, Gabriel Millman. *Sally*, Fred's wife: La Tanya Hall. *Ignorance*: Dennis Michael Hall, Stephen Scarpulla. *Want*: Netousha Harris, Tavia Riveé Jefferson. *Undertakers*: Ken Barnett, Wayne Schroder. *Ghost of Christmas Yet-To-Be*: CHRISTINE DUNHAM.

Business Men, Gifts, Ghosts and the People of London: Lori Alexander, Del-Bourree Bach, Matthew Baker, Ken Barnett, Ronlad Cadet Bastine, Hayes Bergman, Rachel Balck, Liam Burke, Joe Cassidy, Debra Cardona, Candy Cook, David Aaron Damane, Juliet Fischer, Keith Fortner, Peter Gregus, La Tanya Hall, Joy Hermalyn, Kristin Huxhold, Carrie Kinneally, Kate Levering, Michael Lomeka, Daniel Marcus, Kenneth McMullen, Marilyn Pasekoff, Gail Pennington, Meredith Patterson, Pamela Remler, Roland Rusinek, Yasuko Tamaki, Vikki Schnurr, Wayne Schroder, John Sloman, Chris Vasquez. *Swings*: Ron Bagden, Jane Brockman, Ann Kittredge, Robin Lewis, Angela Piccinni, Scott Taylor, Cynthia Thole, Jeff Williams. *Angels*: Terrill Middle School Broadway Chorus, P.S./M.S. 330 Glee Club, South Side Middle School Select Chorus, Eastwood International Children's Choir. *Red Children's Cast*: Adam Barruch, Carissa Farina, Anthony Blair Hall, Dennis Michael Hall, Netousha Harris, Gabriel Millman. *Green Children's Cast*: Dana Chechile, Kennedy Kanagawa, Tavia Riveé Jefferson, Jesse McCartney, Stephen Scarpulla, Chritian Valiando. *Swings*: Barry Cavanagh, Bret Fox, Chloé Zeitounian.

1998.21 PARADE

A Musical in Two Acts. Book by Alfred Uhry. Music and lyrics by Jason Robert Brown. Co-conceived and directed by Harold Prince. Choreographed by Patricia Birch. Settings by Riccardo Hernandez. Costumes by Judith Dolan. Lighting by Howell Binkley. Sound by Jonathan Deans. Musical supervision and direction, Eric Stern. Orchestrations by Don Sebesky. Produced by Lincoln Center Theater Company (André Bishop, Artistic director; Bernard Gersten, Executive producer), in association with LIVENT (US) Inc. Opened 17 December 1998 at the Vivian Beaumont Theatre and closed 28 February 1999 after 84 performances.

CAST (in order of appearance): *Young Soldier*: JEFF EDGERTON. *Aide*: Don Stephenson. *Assistant*: Melanie Vaughan. *Old Soldier*: DON CHASTAIN. *Lucille Frank*: CAROLEE CARMELLO. *Leo Frank*: BRENT CARVER. *Hugh Dorsey*: HERNDON LACKEY. *Governor Slaton*: JOHN HICKOK. *Frankie Epps*: KIRK MCDONALD. *Mary Phagan*: CHRISTY CARLSON ROMANO. *Iola Stover*: Brooke Sunny Moriber. *Jim Conley*: RUFUS BONDS, JR. *J. N. Starnes*: Peter Samuel. *Officer Ivey*: Tad Ingram. *Newt Lee*: RAY ARANHA. *Prison Guard*: Randy Redd. *Mrs. Phagan*: JESSICA MOLASKEY. *Lizzie Phagan*: Robin Skye. *Floyd MacDaniel*: J. B. ADAMS. *Britt Craig*: EVAN PAPPAS. *Tom Watson*: JOHN LESLIE WOLFE. *Angela*: Angela Lockett. *Riley*: J. C. Montgomery. *Luther Rosser*: J. B. ADAMS. *Fiddlin' John*: JEFF EDGERTON. *Judge Roan*: DON CHASTAIN. *Nurse*: Adinah Alexander. *Monteen*: Abbi Hutcherson. *Essie*: Emily Klein. *Mr. Peavy*: Don Stephenson.

Ensemble: Adinah Alexander, Duane Boutté, Diana Brownstone, Thursday Farrar, Will Gartshore, Abbi Hutcherson, Tad Ingram, Emily Klein, Angela Lockett, Megan McGinniss, J. C. Montgomery, Brooke Sunny Moriber, Randy Redd, Joel Robertson, Peter Samuel, Don Stephenson, Bill Szobody, Anne Torsiglieri, Melanie Vaughan, Wysandria Woolsey.

(The action takes place in Marietta and Atlanta, Georgia and environs in 1913.)

ACT 1

"The Old Red Hills of Home" (Prologue)
J. Edgerton, D. Chastain, Ensemble

"The Dream of Atlanta" (Anthem)
Ensemble

"How Can I Call This Home?"
B. Carver, Ensemble

"The Picture Show"
K. McDonald, C. C. Romano

"Leo at Work/What Am I Waiting For?"
B. Carver, C. Carmello

"I am trying to remember . . ." (Interrogation)
R. Aranha, J. Molaskey

"Big News!"
E. Pappas

"There Is a Fountain"/"It Don't Make Sense"[32]
K. McDonald, Ensemble

"Watson's Lullaby"
J. L. Wolfe

"Somethin' Ain't Right"
H. Lackey

"Real Big News"
E. Pappas, Reporters, Ensemble

"You Don't Know This Man"
C. Carmello

The Trial (Finale Act 1):

"It Is Time Now"
J. Edgerton, J. L. Wolfe, Ensemble

"Twenty Miles from Marietta"
H. Lackey

Frankie's Testimony
K. McDonald, C. C. Romano, J. L. Wolfe

"The Factory Girls/Come Up to My Office"
B. S. Moriber, E. Klein, A. Hutcherson, B. Carver

Newt Lee's Testimony
R. Aranha, Ensemble

"My Child Will Forgive Me"
J. Molaskey

"That's What He Said"
R. Bonds, Jr.

"It's hard to speak my heart" (Leo's Statement)
B. Carver

Closing Statement and Verdict
Ensemble

ACT 2

"It Goes On and On"
E. Pappas

"A Rumblin' and a Rollin'"
J. C. Montgomery, A. Lockett, R. Aranha, R. Bonds, Jr.

"Do It Alone"
C. Carmello

"Pretty Music"
J. Hickok

"Letter to the Governor"
D. Chastain

"This Is Not Over Yet"
B. Carver, C. Carmello, Factory Girls, R. Aranha

"Feel the Rain Fall" (Blues)
R. Bonds, Ensemble

"Where Will You Stand When the Flood Comes?"
J. L. Wolfe, H. Lackey, Ensemble

"All the Wasted Time"
B. Carver, C. Carmello

Finale
Ensemble

1998.22 THE FLYING KARAMAZOV BROTHERS: Sharps, Flats and Accidentals

A Vaudeville Revue in Two Acts[33]. Written, directed and produced by the Flying Karamazov Brothers. Music by Doug Wieselman. Ballet choreography by Doug Elkins. Dance costumes by Susan Hilferty. Lighting by David Hutson. Produced by Interpresario and Anne Geenen Productions Inc. in association with Alice Tully Hall. Opened 18 December 1998 at Alice Tully Hall and closed 3 January 1999 after 18 performances.

CAST: *Dimitri*: PAUL MAGID. *Ivan*: HOWARD JAY PATTERSON. *Rakitin*: MICHAEL PRESTON. *Fyodor*: TIM FURST.

1999.01 FOSSE

A Celebration in Song and Dance (a Musical Revue) in Three Acts, Five Parts. Choreography by Bob Fosse. Conceived by Richard Maltby, Jr., Chet Walker and Ann Reinking. Artistic advisor, Gwen Verdon. Choreography recreated by Chet Walker. Co-directed and co-choreographed by Ann Reinking. Production directed by Richard Maltby, Jr. Scenery and costume design by Santo Loquasto. Lighting design by Andrew Bridge. Sound design

[32]Incorporating "There Is a Fountain," traditional hymn by William Cowper, melody by Lowell Mason, 1772.

[33]THE FLYING KARAMAZOV BROTHERS have appeared in their own revues three times before on Broadway (as well as off Broadway and on tour): 10 May 1983 at the Ritz Theatre for 47 performances; 1 April 1986 at the Vivian Beaumont Theatre for 40 performances, and in THE FLYING KARAMAZOV BROTHERS DO THE IMPOSSIBLE! 20 November 1994 at the Helen Hayes Theatre for 50 performances.

by Jonathan Deans. Musical director, Patrick S. Brady. Orchestrations by Ralph Burns and Douglas Besterman. Produced by Livent (U.S.) Inc.[34] Opened 14 January 1999 at the Broadhurst Theatre and closed 25 August 2001 after 1100 performances.

CAST: VALARIE PETTIFORD, JANE LANIER, EUGENE FLEMING, DESMOND RICHARDSON, SERGIO TRUJILLO, KIM MORGAN GREENE, MARY ANN LAMB, DANA MOORE, ELIZABETH PARKINSON, SCOTT WISE, Julio Agustin, Brad Anderson, Andy Blankenbuehler, Marc Calamia, Holly Cruikshank, Lisa Gajda, Scott Jovovich, Christopher R. Kirby, Dede LaBarre, Shannon Lewis, Mary MacLeod, Brad Musgrove, Michael Paternostro, Rachelle Rak, Lainie Sakakura, Alex Sanchez. *Swings*: Bill Burns, Susan Lamontagne, Deborah Leamy, Sean Palmer, Josh Rhodes, J. Kathleen Watkins. (*Music specialties*: Perry Cavari (drums), Mike Hall (bass), Jim Pugh (trombone), Glenn Drewes (trumpet), Walt Weiskopf (clarinet), Jon Werking (piano).)

ACT 1

Prologue:

"Life Is Just a Bowl of Cherries"[35] (from *BIG DEAL*, 1986)
V. Pettiford
(*Music by* Ray Henderson. *Lyrics by* Lew Brown, B. G. DeSylva.)

Fosse's World
B. Musgrove, J. Lanier, Entire Company
(*Music by* Gordon Lowry Harrell, including "Calypso" by G. Harrell, and "Snake in the Grass" by Frederick Loewe from *THE LITTLE PRINCE*. film, 1974. *Staged by* Ann Reinking. *Dance elements inspired by* THE LITTLE PRINCE and signature Fosse styles which appeared in *DAMN YANKEES, REDHEAD, NEW GIRL IN TOWN, LITTLE ME, SWEET CHARITY, HOW TO SUCCEED IN BUSINESS WITHOUT REALLY TRYING, CABARET, CHICAGO*)

"Bye Bye Blackbird" (from *LIZA WITH A "Z"*, television, 1972)
V. Pettiford, J. Agustin, A. Blankenbuehler, M. Calamia, H. Cruikshank, L. Gajda, S. Jovovich, D. LaBarre, M. A. Lamb, S. Lewis, M. MacLeod, D. Moore, E. Parkinson, M. Paternostro, R. Rak, D, Richardson, L. Sakakura, S. Trujillo
(*Music by* Ray Henderson. *Lyrics by* Mort Dixon.)

Part 1: [Chicago - Influences]

From the Edge (from *DANCIN'*, 1978)
B. Anderson, C. K. Kirby, A. Sanchez
(*Music by* Gordon Lowry Harrell.)

Percussion 4 (from *DANCIN'*, 1978)
D. Richardson
(*Music by* Gordon Lowry Harrell.)

"Big Spender" (from *SWEET CHARITY*, 1966)
V. Pettiford, J. Lanier, K. M. Greene, D. LaBarre, M. A. Lamb, S. Lewis, M. MacLeod, D. Moore, E. Parkinson, R. Rak
(*Music by* Cy Coleman. *Lyrics by* Dorothy Fields.)

"Crunchy Granola Suite" (from *DANCIN'*)
B. Anderson, E. Fleming
Danced by J. Agustin, M. Calamia, H. Cruikshank, L. Gajda, S. Jovovich, C. R. Kirby, D. LaBarre, M. A. Lamb, S. Lewis, M. MacLeod, E. Parkinson, M. Paternostro, D. Richardson, L. Sakakura, A. Sanchez.
(*Music and Lyrics by* Neil Diamond.)

Part 2: [Hollywood]

Transition: "Hooray for Hollywood"
(*Music by* Richard Whiting. *Lyrics by* Johnny Mercer.)

"From This Moment On" (from *KISS ME, KATE*, film, 1953)
M. A. Lamb or L. Sakakura (mats.), A. Blankenbuehler
(*Music and Lyrics by* Cole Porter. The first 45 seconds of film choreography by Bob Fosse; originally danced by Bob Fosse and Carol Haney.)

Alley Dance (from *MY SISTER EILEEN*, film, 1955)
"Got No Room for Mr. Gloom"
S. Wise or B. Musgrove (mats.), S. Jovovich
(*Music by* Jule Styne. *Lyrics by* Leo Robin.)

Transition: Dance elements inspired by *RED HEAD* (1959)
Company

Walking the Cat (*Music by* Patrick S. Brady. *Staged by* Ann Reinking.)
"I Wanna Be a Dancin' Man"[36] (from *DANCIN'*, 1978)
E. Fleming, V. Pettiford, J. Lanier, S. Wise, and B. Anderson, A. Blankenbuehler, M. Calamia, L. Gajda, K. M. Greene, C. R. Kirby, M. A. Lamb, S. Lewis, M. McLeod, D. Moore, B. Musgrove, E. Parkinson, A. Sanchez, S. Trujillo
(*Music by* Harry Warren. *Lyrics by* Johnny Mercer. *Dedicated to* Fred Astaire.)

ACT 2

Part 3: [New York]

"Shoeless Joe from Hannbal Mo" (from *DAMN YANKEES*, 1955)
J. Agustin, B. Anderson, A. Blankenbuehler, M. Calamia, E. Fleming, C. R. Kirby, A. Sanchez, S. Trujillo, M. Paternostro, S. Wise
Pitcher: A. Sanchez. *Batters*: B. Anderson, S. Wise. *Bunter*: J. Agustin.
(*Music and Lyrics by* Richard Adler and Jerry Ross.)

Transition: Dance elements inspired by *NEW GIRL IN TOWN*(1957)
A. Sanchez

Nightclubs: The Dance Team of Bob Fosse and Mary Ann Niles:

"Dancing in the Dark"
(*Music by* Arthur Schwartz. *Lyrics by* Howard Dietz.)

"I Love a Piano" (from *STOP! LOOK! LISTEN!*, 1916)
(*Music and Lyrics by* Irving Berlin.) S. Lewis, R. Rak
Danced by S. Wise; E. Parkinson and S. Jovovich; L. Sakakura and A. Blankenbuehler; J. Lanier, M. Paternostro and A. Sanchez; J. Agustin, B. Anderson, M. Calamia, H. Cruikshank, D. LaBarre, M. A. Lamb, M. MacLeod, S. Trujillo.
Dance elements inspired by Fosse/Niles or Fosse appearances on such television shows as Your Hit Parade (1950), the Morey Amsterdam Show (1949), the Colgate Comedy Hour (1951), the motion picture *THE AFFAIRS OF DOBIE GILLIS* (1953), Cavalcade of Stars (1951), The Ed Sullivan Show (1956).
Music arranged by Patrick S. Brady. *Staged by* Ann Reinking.

"Steam Heat"
J. Lanier, M. Paternostro, A. Sanchez
(*Music and Lyrics by* Richard Adler and Jerry Ross.)

"I Gotcha" (from the *LIZA WITH A "Z"*, TV, 1972.)
S. Lewis, B. Musgrove, C. R. Kirby
(*Music and Lyrics by* Joseph Arrington, Jr. [Joe Tex].)

"Rich Man's Frug" (from *SWEET CHARITY*, 1966)
L. Gajda; B. Musgrove, and A. Blankenbuehler; J. Agustin, B. Anderson, M. Calamia, H. Cruikshank, S. Jovovich, C. R. Kirby, D. LaBarre, S. Lewis, M. MacLeod, R. Rak, L. Sakakura, S. Trujillo

The Aloof; The Heavyweight; The Big Finish.
(*Music by* Cy Coleman.)

Transition: My Silky Thoughts
(*Music by* Patrick Brady.)

Cool Hand Luke (from The Bob Hope Special, TV, October 1968)
E. Parkinson, D. Richardson and C. R. Kirby
(*Music by* Lalo Schifrin. *Choreographed for* Gwen Verdon, with Lee Roy Reams and Buddy Vest.)

Transition: "Big Noise from Winnetka"[37] (from *DANCIN'*, 1978)
(*Music by* Ray Bauduc, Bob Haggart. *Lyrics by* Bob Crosby, Gil Rodin.)

"Dancing Dan"[38] (Me and My Shadow) (from *BIG DEAL*, 1986)
(*Music by* Dave Dryer and Al Jolson. *Lyrics by* Billy Rose.)
E. Fleming, K. M. Greene, D. Moore

"Nowadays"/"The Hot Honey Rag" (from *CHICAGO*, 1975)
V. Pettiford, J. Lanier
(*Music by* John Kander. *Lyrics by* Fred Ebb.)

ACT 3

Part 4: [Complexities]

"Glory" (from *PIPPIN*, 1972)
E. Fleming
Danced by C. R. Kirby, J. Agustin, B. Anderson, A. Blankenbuehler, M. Calamia, S. Jovovivh, M. A. Lamb, B. Musgrove, E. Parkinson, M. Paternostro, L. Sakakura, A. Sanchez.
(*Music and Lyrics by* Stephen Schwartz.)

"Manson Trio" (from *PIPPIN*, 1972)
E. Fleming, D. LaBarre, M. McLeod
(*Music and Lyrics by* Stephen Schwartz.)

"Mein Herr" (from *CABARET*, film, 1972)
V. Pettiford, and H. Cruikshank, L. Gajda, K. M. Greene, S. Lewis, D. Moore, R. Rak
(*Music by* John Kander. *Lyrics by* Fred Ebb.)

"Take Off with Us" (Three Pas de Deux from *ALL THAT JAZZ*, film, 1979)
M. Calamia and L. Sakakura; M. A. Lamb and E. Parkinson; B. Musgrove and D. Richardson
(*Music by* Stanley R. Lebowsky. *Lyrics by* Fred Tobias.)

"Razzle Dazzle" (from *CHICAGO*, 1975)
S. Wise, K. M. Greene, D. Moore
(*Music by* John Kander. *Lyrics by* Fred Ebb.)

---

[34]In September 1999 SFX Entertainment Group acquired the assets of LIVENT and became the show's producer.

[35]Song first introduced to Broadway by Ethel Merman in *GEORGE WHITE'S SCANDALS* (1931).

[36]Song first introduced on film by Fred Astaire in *THE BELLE OF NEW YORK*, 1951.

[37]First introduced by its authors on film in *LET'S MAKE MUSIC* in 1941.

[38]First introduced as a popular song by Al Jolson and Ted Lewis in 1927.

"Who's Sorry Now?"[39] (from *ALL THAT JAZZ*, film, 1979)
H. Cruikshank, L. Gajda, D. LaBarre, M. A. Lamb, S. Lewis, M. MacLeod, E. Parkinson, R. Rak, L. Sakakura
(*Music by* Harry Ruby. *Lyrics by* Ted Snyder and Bert Kalmar.)
"There'll Be Some Changes Made"[40] (from *ALL THAT JAZZ*, film, 1979)
J. Lanier, K. M. Greene, D. Moore
(*Music by* W. Benton Overtstreet. *Lyrics by* Billy Higgins.)
"Mr. Bojangles"[41] (from *DANCIN'*, 1978)
A. Blankenbuehler
Mr. Bojangles: S. Trujillo. *The Spirit*: D. Richardson.
(*Music and Lyrics by* Jerry Jeff Walker.)
"Life Is Just a Bowl of Cherries" (reprise)
V. Pettiford

Part 5: Finale

Benny Goodman's "Sing Sing Sing"[42] (from *DANCIN'*, 1978)
(*Music and Lyrics by* Louis Prima.)/
"Christopher Columbus"
(*Music and Lyrics by* Andy Razaf and Leon Berry.) Entire Company
Drums: P. Cavari. *Bass*: M. Hall. *Trombone solo*: J. Pugh.
Danced by H. Cruikshank, C. R. Kirby, D. Richardson.
Trumpet solo: G. Drewes.
Danced by E. Parkinson.
Clarinet solo: W. Weiskopf.
Danced by V. Pettiford, J. Lanier, M. MacLeod, D. Moore, K. M. Greene, M. A. Lamb, R. Rak, J. Agustin, B. Anderson, M. Calamia, C. Kirby, A. Sanchez, S. Trujillo, M. Paternostro.
Piano solo: J. Werking.
Danced by S. Wise, E. Fleming.

1999.02 (DEIN PERRY'S) STEEL CITY

A Dance Revue in One Act[43]. Conceived, directed and choreographed by Dein Perry. Music (and lyrics) by Tim Finn. Sets designed by Brian Thomson. Costumes by Michael Wilkinson. Lighting by Trudy Dalgleish. Sound by Darryl Lewis. Produced by Garry Van Egmond for Theaters and Concerts International. Opened 26 January 1999 at Radio City Music Hall and closed 30 January 1999 after 7 performances.

CAST: DEIN PERRY, Paul Davis, Nathan Sheens, Lee McDonald, Grant Turner, Sheldon Perry, Brian Burke, Dan Clemente, Steven Grace, Andrew Harrison, Nigel Long, Sean Mulligan, Shane Preston, Glen Rhule, Dean Street, Aaron Sweetman, Melissa Gibson, Brooke Henderson, Leah Howard, Rebecca Jeffs, Rachel Schmaltz, Ann Tsirigotis.

MUSICAL NUMBERS

"Steel City"
Truss Dance
"Spirit Level"
"Old Car"
"Drop Out"
(*Music and Lyrics by* Tim Finn and M. Azcona.)
"Walking"
"Smoke Duet"
"Rock & Roll Girl"
"Absail"
"Forklifts"
"Where I Live"
(*Music and Lyrics by* Tim Finn and M. Chunn.)
"New Car"
"Road Trip"
(*Music and Lyrics by* Tim Finn and M. Azcona.)
"Glide"

Finale

1999.03 YOU'RE A GOOD MAN, CHARLIE BROWN

A Revival of the Musical Entertainment in Two Acts[44]. Book[45], music and lyrics by Clark Gesner. Based on the comic strip "Peanuts" by Charles M. Schulz. Directed by Michael Mayer. Choreography by Jerry Mitchell. Scenic design by David Gallo. Costume design by Michael Krass. Lighting design by Kenneth Posner. Sound design by Brian Ronan. Musical direction by Kimberly Grigsby. Music supervision, arrangements and additional material by Andrew Lippa. Orchestrations by Michel Gibson. Produced by Michael Leavitt, Fox Theatricals, and Jerry Frankel, Arthur Whitelaw, Gene Persson, in association with Larry Payton. Opened 4 February 1999 at the Ambassador Theatre and closed 13 June 1999 after 150 performances.

CAST (in order of appearance): *Sally*: KRISTIN CHENOWETH. *Schroeder*: STANLEY WAYNE MATHIS. *Linus*: B. D. WONG. *Snoopy*: ROGER BART. *Lucy*: ILANA LEVINE. *Charlie Brown*: ANTHONY RAPP.

Time: An average day in the life of Charlie Brown.

ACT 1

"You're a Good Man, Charlie Brown"[46]
Company
"Schroeder"
I. Levine, S. W. Mathis
"Snoopy"
R. Bart
"My Blanket and Me"
B. D. Wong, Company
"The Kite"
A. Rapp
"The Doctor Is In" (Dr. Lucy)
I. Levine, A. Rapp
"Beethoven Day"
S. W. Mathis
(*Music and Lyrics by* Andrew Lippa.)
"Rabbit Chasing"
K. Chenoweth, R. Bart
"Book Report"
A. Rapp, I. Levine, B. D. Wong, S. W. Mathis

ACT 2

"The Red Baron"
R. Bart
"My New Philosophy"
K. Chenoweth, S. W. Mathis
(*Music and Lyrics by* Andrew Lippa.)
"T.E.A.M." (The Baseball Game)
A. Rapp, Entire Company
"Glee Club Rehearsal"
Entire Company
"Little Known Facts"
I. Levine, B. D. Wong, A. Rapp
"Suppertime"
R. Bart
"Happiness"
Entire Company

1999.04 ANNIE GET YOUR GUN

A Revival of the Musical in Two Acts[47]. Music and lyrics by Irving Berlin. Book by Herbert and Dorothy Fields, revised by Peter Stone. Directed by Graciela Daniele. Choreographed by Graciela Daniele and Jeff Calhoun.

---

[39]First introduced as a popular song in vaudeville by Gus Van and Joe Schenck in 1923.
[40]First introduced as a popular song in vaudeville by Billy Higgins in 1924.
[41]First introduced as a popular song by its author in 1968
[42]First introduced on film in *AFTER THE THIN MAN* in 1936.
[43]Production originated in Australia prior to a 40-city American and Canadian tour. No program found; song list prepared from Australian compact disc (Sony/Columbia), not in performance order.

[44]Originally produced in New York Off-Broadway 7 March 1967 at the Theatre 80 St. Marks for 1,597 performances. Subsequently revived on Broadway 1 June 1971 at the John Golden Theatre for 31 performances.
[45]Original book credited to John Gordon, a pseudonym for Clark Gesner and the collective company of the Original Off-Broadway Cast who devised the show. Book revisions uncredited.
[46]Additional material by Andrew Lippa.
[47]First produced in New York 16 May 1946 at the Imperial Theatre for 1147 performances.

Scenic design by Tony Walton. Costume design by William Ivey Long. Lighting design by Beverly Emmons. Sound by G. Thomas Clark. Musical director and dance music arrangements by Marvin Laird. Orchestrations by Bruce Coughlin. Supervising music director, vocal and incidental music arranger, John McDaniel. Associate producers, Alecia Parker, Judith Ann Abrams. Produced by Barry and Fran Weissler, in association with Kardana, Michael Watt, Irving Welzer and Hal Luftig. Opened 4 March 1999 at the Marquis Theatre and closed 1 September 2001 after 1046 performances.

CAST (in order of appearance): *Buffalo Bill* (Colonel William F. Cody): RON HOLGATE. *Frank Butler*: TOM WOPAT. *Dolly Tate*: VALERIE WRIGHT. *Tommy Keeler*: ANDREW PALERMO. *Winnie Tate*: NICOLE RUTH SNELSON. *Mac*, the Propman: Kevin Bailey. *Charlie Davenport*: PETER MARX. *Foster Wilson*: RONN CARROLL. *Chief Sitting Bull*: GREGORY ZARAGOZA. *Annie Oakley*: BERNADETTE PETERS. *Kids (3)*: *Jessie Oakley*: Cassidy Ladden. *Nellie Oakley*: Mia Walker. *Little Jake*: Trevor McQueen Eaton. *Running Deer*: Kevin Bailey. *Eagle Feather*: Carlos Lopez. *Dining Car Waiter*: Brad Bradley. *Sleeping Car Porter*: Patrick Wetzel. *Pawnee Bill* (Major Gordon Lillie): RONN CARROLL. *Messenger*: Kevin Bailey. *Band Leader*: Marvin Laird. *Mrs. Schuyler Adams*: Julia Fowler. *Silvia Potter-Porter*: Jenny-Lynn Suckling.

Ensemble: Shaun Amyot, Kevin Bailey, Brad Bradley, Randy Donaldson, Madeleine Ehlert, Julia Fowler, Kisha Howard, Adrienne Hurd, Keri Lee, Carlos Lopez, Desiree Parkman, Eric Sciotto, Kelli Bond Severson, Timothy Edward Smith, Jenny-Lynn Suckling, David Villela, Patrick Wetzel. *Swings*: Leasen Beth Almquist, Patti D'Beck, Rick Spaans.

ACT 1[48]

"There's No Business Like Show Business"
T. Wopat, Company

"Doin' What Comes Naturally"
B. Peters, Kids, R. Carroll [Foster Wilson]

"The Girl That I Marry"
T. Wopat, B. Peters

"You Can't Get a Man with a Gun"
B. Peters

"There's No Business Like Show Business" (reprise)
T. Wopat, R. Holgate, P. Marx, B. Peters

"I'll Share It All With You"
A. Palermo, N. R. Snelson, Company

"Moonshine Lullaby"
B. Peters, Kids, Ensemble Trio

"There's No Business Like Show Business" (reprise)
B. Peters

"They Say It's Wonderful"
B. Peters, T. Wopat

"My Defenses Are Down"
T. Wopat, Young Men

The Trick
B. Peters, Company

Finale Act 1: "You Can't Get a Man with a Gun" (reprise)
B. Peters

ACT 2

"The European Tour"
B. Peters, Company

"(I Got) Lost in His Arms"
B. Peters

"Who Do You Love, I Hope"
A. Palermo, N. R. Snelson, Company

"I Got the Sun in the Morning"
B. Peters, Company

"An Old-Fashioned Wedding"
B. Peters, T. Wopat

"The Girl That I Marry" (reprise)
T. Wopat

"Anything You Can Do"
B. Peters, T. Wopat

"They Say It's Wonderful"
B. Peters, T. Wopat, Company

Finale Ultimo
Company

[48]For subsequent national tour, Jeff Calhoun was credited as both director and choreographer. "I'll Share It All with You" and "The European Tour" were both dropped.

1999.05 BAND IN BERLIN

A Musical in One Act. (Book) Written and conceived by Susan Feldman[49]. Production staged and choreographed and co-conceived by Patricia Birch. Directed by Patricia Birch and Susan Feldman. Set design by Douglas W. Schmidt. Costume design by Jonathan Bixby, Gregory Gale. Lighting design by Kirk Bookman. Sound design by David Schnirman. Musical director, Wilbur Pauley. Media design, Richard Law. Filmmakers, Anthony Chase, Eric Rodine. Puppet design by Stephen Kaplin. Assistant director/choreographer, Jonathan Stuart Cerullo. Keyboard arrangements by Robert Wolinsky. Associate producers, Marsha Dubrow, Gilford/Freeley, Kathleen O'Grady, Geoffrey Shearing, Joseph S. Steinberg. Produced by Robert V. Strauss, Jeffrey Ash, Randall L. Wreghitt, Gayle Francis in association with Marcia Roberts, DLT Entertainment/ADF Enterprises, by special arrangement with Art at St. Ann's and American Music Theater Festival (Philadelphia). Opened 7 March 1999 at the Helen Hayes Theatre and closed 21 March 1999 after 17 performances.

CAST: *Roman Cykowski*, on film and voice-over: HUBERT RUBENS.
(HUDSON SHAD): *Ari Leshnikoff*, First Tenor: MARK BLEEKE. *Erich Collin*, Second Tenor: TIMOTHY LEIGH EVANS. *Harry Frommermann*, Lyric Baritone: HUGO MUNDAY. *Roman Cykowski*, Baritone: PETER BECKER. *Robert Biberti*, Bass: WILBUR PAULEY. *Erwin Bootz*, Pianist: ROBERT WOLINSKY.

Time and Place: Memories of Germany 1927-1935.

MUSICAL NUMBERS[50]

Overture

"Schlaf Mein Liebling" (Good Night, Sweetheart)
(*Music by* Ray Noble. *German Lyrics by* Beda [Fritz Löhner].)

Prologue

"Ein Neüer Frühling Wird In Die Heimat Kommen" (A New Spring Will Come to the Homeland)
(*Music and German Lyrics by* Will Meisel, Willy Engelberger and Fritz Rotter.)

The Beginning

"Schöne Isabella Aus Kastilien" (Dearest Isabella from Castille)
(*Music and German Lyrics by* Erwin Bootz and Gerd Karlick. *English lyrics by* Wilbur Pauley.)

"My Little Green Cactus" (Meine kleine Gruner Kaktus)
(*Music and Lyrics by* Dorian and Horda [Bert Reisfeld and Rolf Marbot].)

"Quand Il Pleut"/"Stormy Weather"
(*Music by* Harold Arlen. *English Lyrics by* Ted Koehler.)

The Rise

"Wochenend und Sonnenschein" (Happy Days Are Here Again)
(*Music by* Milton Ager. *English Lyrics by* Jack Yellen. *German Lyrics by* Charles Amberg.)

"Veronika, Der lenz ist Da" (Spring Is Here)
(*Music by* Walter Jurmann. *German Lyrics by* Fritz Rotter. *English Lyrics by* Wilbur Pauley.)

"Die Dorfmusik" (Village Music)
(*Music and Lyrics by* Fryberg, von Donop and Kirsten.)

"Tea for Two" (from *NO, NO, NANETTE*)
(*Music by* Vincent Youmans. *Lyrics by* Irving Caesar.)

World Tour

"Wie Wär's Mal Mit Lissabon?" (What's Happening in Lisbon?"
(*Music and Lyrics by* Werner Bochman and Lehnow.)

It Don't Mean a Thing If It Ain't Got That Swing"
(*Music by* Duke Ellington. *Lyrics by* Irving Mills.)

"Creole Love Call"
(*Music and Lyrics by* Duke Ellington.)

Overture to *THE BARBER OF SEVILLE*
(*Music by* Giaccomo Rossini.)

Performing Under the Third Reich

"Night and Day"/"Nuit et Jour" (from *THE GAY DIVORCE*)
(*Music and Lyrics by* Cole Porter. *French Lyrics by* Emila Renaud.)

"Ein Neuer Frühling Wird In Die Heimat Kommen" (A New Spring Will Come to the Homeland) (reprise)

"Eine Kleine Frühlingsweise" (A Little Spring Melody)
(*Music by* Anton Dvorak. *German Lyrics by* Langsfelder.)

[49]Based on the true story of the Comedian Harmonists, a German vocal sextet whose sudden rise to fame in the 1920s was cut short by the Third Reich.

[50]All music numbers performed by Hudson Shad in German, English and/or French with piano accompaniment.

"Der Onkel Bumba Aus Columba Tanzt Nur Rumba" (When Yuba Plays the Rumba on His Tuba)(from *THE THIRD LITTLE SHOW*)
(*Music and English Lyrics by* Herman Hupfeld. *German Lyrics by* Fritz Rotter and A. Robinson.)

Swansong Tour

"Whistle While You Work" (from *SNOW WHITE AND THE SEVEN DWARFS* film)
(*Music by* Frank Churchill. *Lyrics by* Larry Morey.)

"Die Liebe Kommt Die Liebe Geht" (Love Comes, Love Goes)
(*Music by* Fritz Kreisler. *German Lyrics by* Ernst Marischka. *English Lyrics by* Wilbur Pauley.)

"Baby, (Wo Ist Mein Baby)"
(*Music by* Friedrich Holländer. *Lyrics by* Mehring.)

"Der Alte Cowboy" (The Last Round-Up) (from *ZIEGFELD FOLLIES OF 1934*)
(*Music and English Lyrics by* Billy Hill. *German Lyrics by* Walter.)

Epilogue

"Auf Wiederseh'n, My Dear"
(*Music and English Lyrics by* Al Hoffman, Al Goodheart, Ed Nelson, Milton Ager. *German Lyrics by* Charles Amberg.)

1999.06 ROLLIN' ON THE T.O.B.A.

A Tribute to the Last Days of Black Vaudeville (Musical Revue) in Two Acts, 11 Scenes. Conceived by Ronald "Smokey" Stevens and Jaye Stewart, featuring excerpts from "The Simple Stories" by Langston Hughes. Additional material by Irvin S. Bauer. Set design by Larry W. Brown. Costume design by Michele Reisch. Lighting design by Jon Kusner. Sound design by Shabach Audio. Musical direction and orchestrations by David Alan Bunn. Choreographed by Leslie Dockery. Directed by Ronald "Smokey" Stevens and Leslie Dockery. Associate producers, Martin Shugrue, Carriene Nevin. Produced by John Grimaldi, Ashton Springer, Frenchmen Productions, Inc. Opened 24 March 1999 at the Kit Kat Club (Henry Miller's Theatre) and closed 4 April 1999 after 14 performances[51].

CAST (in order of appearance): *Stevens*: RONALD "SMOKEY" STEVENS. *Stewart*: RUDY ROBERSON. *Bertha Mae Little*: SANDRA REAVES-PHILLIPS.

The action takes place on the T. O. B. A.[52] circuit in 1931.

Act 1, Scene 1: On the Train. *Scene 2*: Monogram Theatre. *Scene 3*: Bertha's Phone Call. *Scene 4*: Dressing Room. *Scene 5*: Royal Theatre. *Scene 6*: Bertha's Letter/On the Train. *Scene 7*: Booker T. Theatre.

Act 2, Scene 1: Regal Theatre. *Scene 2*: Bertha's Show/The Regal Theatre. *Scene 3*: On the Train. *Scene 4*: On the Train.

ACT 1

Overture

"Rollin' on the T.O.B.A."
Entire Company
(*Music and Lyrics by* Ronald "Smokey" Stevens, Sandra Reaves-Phillips, Chapman Roberts, Benny Key and David Alan Bunn.)

Scene 1

Toast to Harlem
R. Roberson, R. S. Stevens

Scene 2

"Bill Robinson Walk"
R. S. Stevens
(*Music by* Bill "Bojangles" Robinson.)

Evolution
(*by* Flournoy Miller and Aubrey Lyles)

"Ugly Chile"
R. Roberson, R. S. Stevens
(*Music by* Clarence Williams. *Lyrics by* Johnny Mercer.)

Scene 3

"Travelin' Blues"
S. Reaves-Phillips
(*Music and Lyrics by* Ronald "Smokey" Stevens and Sandra Reaves-Phillips.)

Scene 4

Lincoln West
(*by* Gwendolyn Brooks)
The Liar (Staggerlee)
(*by* Terrence Cooper) R. Roberson, R. S. Stevens

Scene 5

"(Saturday Night) Fish Fry"
R. Roberson, R. S. Stevens
(*Music and Lyrics by* Ellis Walsh and Louis Jordan.)

Scene 6

"St. Louis Blues"
S. Reaves-Phillips
(*Music and Lyrics by* W. C. Handy.)

Scene 7

"The Poker Game"
R. S. Stevens
(*Sketch by* Bert Williams, set to music "Black and Tan Fantasy" by Duke Ellington.)

"Nobody" (interpolated into *ZIEGFELD FOLLIES OF 1910*)
R. S. Stevens
(*Music and Lyrics by* Bert Williams.)

"Huggin' and Chalkin'"
R. Roberson
(*Music and Lyrics by* Kermit Goell and Clancy Hayes.)

"Sexy Blues"/"You've Taken My Blues and Gone"
S. Reaves-Phillips
(*Music and Lyrics by* Sandra Reaves-Phillips, Chapman Roberts and Ronald "Smokey" Stevens; *Sketch by* Langston Hughes.)

The Car Crash and Broken Dialogue
(*by* Flournoy Miller and Aubrey Lyles)
R. Roberson, R. S. Stevens

Conversationalization
(*by* Flournoy Miller and Aubrey Lyles)
R. Roberson, R. S. Stevens

"Let the Good Times Roll"
Entire Company
(*Music and Lyrics by* Sam Theard and Fleecie Moore.)

ACT 2

Scene 1

"(New Orleans) Hop Scop Blues"
R. S. Stevens
(*Music by* Clarence Williams.)

The Chess Game
R. Roberson, R. S. Stevens
(Sketch set to "Funeral March of the Marionettes," *Music by* Charles Gounod.)

Scene 2

"Take Me as I Am"
S. Reaves-Phillips
(*Music by* Sandra Reaves-Phillips.)

"One Hour Mama"
S. Reaves-Phillips
(*Music and Lyrics by* Porter Grainger.)

"Million Dollar Secret"
S. Reaves-Phillips
(*Music and Lyrics by* Helen Humes and Jules Bihari.)

Freddie and Flo
(*by* Butterbeans and Susie) S. Reaves-Phillips, R. Roberson

"A Good Man is Hard to Find"
S. Reaves-Phillips
(*Music and Lyrics by* Eddie Green.)

"Take Me as I Am" (reprise)
S. Reaves-Phillips

Scene 3

Simple on Integration
(*by* Langston Hughes) R. Roberson, R. S. Stevens

Soul Food
(*by* Langston Hughes) R. Roberson, R. S. Stevens, S. Reaves-Phillips

Scene 4

Banquet in Honor
(*by* Langston Hughes) R. Roberson, R. S. Stevens

I'm Still Here
(*by* Langston Hughes)

[51] First produced by the AMAS Musical Theatre (Rosetta LeNoire, Founder and Artistic Director), and subsequently Off-Broadway 28 January-7 March 1999 at the 47th Street Theatre for 45 performances.

[52] Theatre Owners' Booking Association controlled a circuit of exclusively black theatres.

Trouble in Mind
(*by* Richard Jones) R. Roberson, R. S. Stevens, S. Reaves-Phillips
"Rollin' on the T. O. B. A." (reprise)
Entire Company

1999.07 MARLENE

A Musical Play in Two Acts. Play by Pam Gems. Directed by Sean Matthias. Set designer, John Arnone. Costume designer, David C. Woolard. Lighting designer, Marc Jonathan. Sound designer, Peter J. Fitzgerald. Musical direction, Kevin Amos. Associate producers, Alice Chebba Walsh, Mary Ellen Ashley, Anne L. Bernstein, Kimberly Vaughn, Richard Samson, Jennifer Lee, Herb Goldsmith Productions. Produced by Ric Wanetik and Frederic B. Vogel. Opened 11 April 1999 at the Cort Theatre and closed 2 May 1999 after 25 performances.

CAST (in order of appearance): *Mutti*: Mary Diveny. *Vivian (Hoffman)*: Margaret Whitton. *Marlene Dietrich*: SIÂN PHILLIPS.

Scene: A theatre in Paris. 1969.

ACT 1[53]

"You Do Something to Me" (from *FIFTY MILLION FRENCHMEN*)
(*Music and Lyrics by* Cole Porter.)
"Look Me Over Closely"
(*Music and Lyrics by* Terry Gilkyson.)
"Illusions" (from *ILLUSIONS* film)
(*Music and Lyrics by* Frederick Holländer.)
"Johnny, (wenn Du Geburtstag hast)"(Jonny) (from *SONG OF SONGS* film)
(*Music and Lyrics by* Frederick Holländer.)
"(Ich bin die fesche) Lola" (from *THE BLUE ANGEL* film)
(*Music and Lyrics by* Frederick Holländer.)
"I Wish You Love" (Que Reste-til de Nos Amours)
(*Music and French lyrics by* Charles Trenet . *English lyrics by* Albert Beach.)

ACT 2

"Mein Blondes Baby"
(*Music and Lyrics by* Peter Kreueder and Fritz Rotter.)
"Warum" (Frag' Nicht Warum Ich Gehe)
(*Music by* Robert Stolz. *Lyrics by* Walter Reisch and A. Robinson.)
"The Laziest Girl in Town" (from *STAGE FRIGHT* film)
(*Music and Lyrics by* Cole Porter.)
"The Boys in the Back Room" (See What the Boys in the Back Room Will Have) (from *DESTRY RIDES AGAIN*, film)
(*Music by* Frederick Holländer. *Lyrics by* Frank Loesser.)
"Lili Marlene"
(*Music by* Norbert Schultze. *Original German lyrics by* Hans Leip. *English lyrics by* Tommie Connor.)
"Honeysuckle Rose" (from *LOAD OF COAL* revue)
(*Music by* Fats Waller. *Lyrics by* Andy Razaf.)
"Where Have All the Flowers Gone?"
(*Music and Lyrics by* Pete Seeger.)
"La vie en Rose"
(*Music and French Lyrics by* Edith Piaf and Louiguy.)
"Falling in Love Again" (Ich bin von Kopf bis Fuss auf Liebe eingestellt)
(from *THE BLUE ANGEL*, film)
(*Music by* Frederick Holländer. *Lyrics by* Sammy Lerner.)

1999.08 THE CIVIL WAR

An American Musical Event (a Musical) in Two Acts. Book and lyrics by Frank Wildhorn, Jack Murphy and Gregory Boyd[54]. Music by Frank Wildhorn. Directed by Jerry Zaks. Musical staging by Luis Perez. Scenic design by Douglas W. Schmidt. Costume design by William Ivey Long. Lighting design by Paul Gallo. Sound design by Karl Richardson. Projections by Wendall K. Harrington. Orchestrations by Kim Scharnberg. Musical director, Jeff Lams. Musical supervision, Jason Howland. Vocal director, Dave Clemmons. Battles by David Leong. Originally commissioned and produced by Alley Theatre, Houston, Texas. Executive producer, Gary Gunas, PACE Theatrical Group. Associate producers, I. W. Marks, Michael Skipper and Chris Edgecomb. Produced by Pierre Cossette, PACE Theatrical Group/SFX Entertainment, Bomurwil Productions, Kathleen Raitt, and Jujamcyn Theatres. Opened 22 April 1999 at the St. James Theatre and closed 13 June 1999 after 61 performances.

CAST: Union Army: *Captain Emmet Lochran*: Michael Lanning. *Sergeant Patrick Anderson*: Rod Weber. *Sergeant Byron Richardson*: Royal Reed. *Corporal William McEwen*: Gilles Chiasson. *Private Conrad Bock*: Ron Sharpe. *Private Charles Spencer*: Bart Shatto. *Private Nathaniel Taylor*: John Sawyer.

Of the Confederate Army: *Captain Billy Pierce*: Gene Miller. *Sergeant Virgil Franklin*: Dave Clemmons. *Corporal John Beauregard*: Mike Eldred. *Corporal Henry Stewart*: David M. Lutken. *Private Darius Barksdale*: Anthony Galde. *Private Cyrus Stevens*: Jim Price. *Private Sam Taylor*: Matt Bogart.

Frederick Douglass: Keith Byron Kirk. *Clayton Toler*: Michel Bell. *Bessie Tholer*: Cheryl Freeman. *Benjamin Reynolds*: Lawrence Clayton. *Exter Thomas*: Wayne W. Pretlow. *Harriet Jackson*: Capathia Jenkins. *Liza Hughes*: Cassandra White.

Autolycus Fell: Leo Burmester. *Auctioneer's Assistant*: Dave Clemmons. *Sarah McEwen*: Irene Molloy. *Violet*: Hope Harris. *Mabel*: Beth Leavel. *Mrs. Bixby*: Beth Leavel. *Nurse*: Hope Harris. *Voice of President Lincoln*: David M. Lutken. *Pit Singers*: David Michael Felty, Hope Harris, Monique Midgette, Raun Ruffin. *Swings*: David Michael Felty, Monique Midgette, Chris Roberts, Raun Ruffin.

(The action is set during the American Civil War 1861-1865.)

ACT 1[55]

"A House Divided"
The Citizens
"Freedom's Child"
K. B. Kirk, other Abolitionists
"By the Sword"/"Sons of Dixie"
The Armies
"Tell My Father"
M. Bogart
"The Peculiar Institution"
The Enslaved
"If Prayin' Were Horses"
M. Bell, C. Freeman
"Greenback"
L. Burmester, B. Leavel, H. Harris
"Missing You (My Bill)"
I. Molloy
"Judgement Day"
G. Miller, M. Lanning, M. Bogart, the Armies
"Father, How Long?"
M. Bell
"Someday"
C. Jenkins, C. Freeman, Others
"I'll Never Pass This Way Again"
D. M. Lutken
"How Many Devils?"
The Armies

ACT 2

"Virginia"
G. Miller
"Candle in the Window"
C. Jenkins
"Oh! Be Joyful!"
L. Burmester, R. Reed, R. Sharpe, B. Shatto
"The Hospital"
B. Leavel, H. Harris, Union Soldiers, M. Bell
"If Prayin' Were Horses" (reprise)
M. Bell, C. Freeman
"River Jordan"
L. Clayton, others
"Sarah"
G. Chiasson

---

[53]Some songs performed in excerpt form. All vocals by Siân Phillips.

[54]Authors' note: Many voices inspired the writing of *THE CIVIL WAR*: Sojourner Truth and Abraham Lincoln; Walt Whitman, Sullivan Ballou and Frederick Douglass; Hanna Ropes and R. E. Lee; Henry Kyd Douglas (2nd Virginia) and Henry Pearson (6th New Hampshire), among others.

[55]The subsequent national tour presented by Networks (SFX Entertainment) was directed by Stephen Rayne. Musical staging, by Ken Roberson; Costumes by Christine Hanak; Lighting by Howell Binkley; Sound by Duncan Edwards, other credits unchanged. The order of musical numbers was substantially revised; added were "Brother My Brother," "Old Gray Coat," "I Never Knew His Name," and "The Day the Sun Stood Still."

"The Honor of Your Name"
I. Molloy
"Greenback" (reprise)
L. Burmester, H. Harris
"Northbound Train"
M. Lanning
"Last Waltz for Dixie"
G. Miller, Confederate Soldiers
"The Glory"
M. Lanning, K. B. Kirk, L. Clayton, Full Company

1999.09

IT AIN'T NOTHIN' BUT THE BLUES

A Musical (Revue) in Two Acts. Written by Charles Bevel, Lita Gaithers, Randal Myler, Ron Taylor, Dan Wheetman. Based on an original idea by Ron Taylor. Directed by Randal Myler. Movement, Donald McKayle. Set design, Robin Sanford Roberts. Costume design by Enid Turnbull. Lighting design, Don Darnutzer. Sound design, Jon Weston. Musical direction, Dan Wheetman. Vocal direction, Lita Gaithers. Associate producers, Electric Factory Concerts, Adam and David Friedson, Richard Martini, Marcia Roberts, Murray Schwartz. Associate producer, Ron Taylor. Produced by Eric Krebs, Jonathan Reinis, Lawrence Horowitz, Anita Waxman, Elizabeth Williams, CTM Productions, Anne Squadron, in association with Lincoln Center Theater Company. A production of the Crossroads Theater Company, San Diego Repertory Theatre and Alabama Shakespeare Festival. Opened 24 April 1999 at the Vivian Beaumont Theatre, closing 29 August 1999, moved 9 September 1999 to the Ambassador Theatre and closed 2 January 2000 after 276 performances.[56]

CAST (*The Ensemble*): "MISSISSIPPI" CHARLES BEVEL, GRETHA BOSTON, CARTER CALVERT, ELOISE LAWS, GREGORY PORTER, RON TAYLOR, DAN WHEETMAN.
The Band: Kevin Cooper, Jim Ehinger, Debra Laws, Tony Matthews, Charlie Rhythm, Daryll Whitlow.

ACT 1[57]
"Odun De" (Music traditional[58].)
Company
"Niwah Wechi" (Music traditional[59].)
E. Laws, Company
"Blood Done Signed My Name" (Music traditional.)
R. Taylor, G. Boston
"Raise Them Up Higher" (Music traditional.)
C. Bevel
"Danger Blues" (Music traditional.)
E. Laws
"Black Woman" (Music traditional.)
G. Porter
"I'm Gonna Do What the Spirit Say Do" (Music traditional.)
G. Boston
"I've Been Living with the Blues"
Company
(*Music and Lyrics by* Sonny Terry and Brownie McGhee.)
"Blues Man"
R. Taylor
(*Music and Lyrics by* Z. Z. (Arzelle) Hill.)
"My Home's Across the Blue Ridge Mountains" (Music traditional.)
C. Calvert
""T" for Texas"
D. Wheetman
(*Music and Lyrics by* Jimmie Rogers.)
"Who Broke the Lock?" (Music traditional.)
G. Porter, C. Bevel
"My Man Rocks Me" (Music traditional.)
E. Laws
"St. Louis Blues"
G. Boston
(*Music and Lyrics by* W.C. Handy.)
"Now I'm Gonna Be Bad"
C. Calvert
(*Music and Lyrics by* Dan Wheetman.)
"Walking Blues"
C. Bevel
(*Music and Lyrics by* Ron Taylor.)
"Come On In My Kitchen"
G. Porter
"(*Music and Lyrics by* Robert L. Johnson.)
"Cross Road Blues"
C. Bevel
(*Music and Lyrics by* Robert L. Johnson.)
"I Know I've Been Changed" (Music traditional.)
G. Boston
"Child of the Most High King"
R. Taylor, Men
(Music traditional, arranged by Ron Taylor.)
"Children, Your Line Is Dragging"
G. Porter
(Music traditional, arranged by Fisher Thompson, Sr.)
"Catch on Fire"
Company
(Music traditional, arranged by Lita Gaithers.)

ACT 2
"Let the Good Times Roll"
R. Taylor
(*Music and Lyrics by* Sam Theard and Fleecie Moore.)
"Sweet Home Chicago"
G. Porter, C. Bevel
(*Music and Lyrics by* Robert L. Johnson.)
"Wang Dang Doodle"
G. Boston, C. Calvert, E. Laws
(*Music and Lyrics by* Willie Dixon.)
"Someone Else Is Stepping In"
E. Laws
(*Music and Lyrics by* Denise LaSalle.)
"Please Don't Stop Him"
G. Boston
(*Music and Lyrics by* Herb J. Lance and John Wallace; *additional lyrics and arrangements by* Lita Gaithers.)
"I'm Your Hootchie Coochie Man"
R. Taylor
(*Music and Lyrics by* Willie Dixon, arranged by Ron Taylor.)
"Crawlin' King Snake"
G. Porter
(*Music and Lyrics by* John Lee Hooker.)
"Mind Your Own Business"
D. Wheetman
(*Music and Lyrics by* Hank Williams, Sr.)
"Walking After Midnight"
C. Calvert
(*Music by* Alan Block. *Lyrics by* Don Hecht.)
"I Can't Stop Lovin' You"
C. Bevel
(*Music and Lyrics by* Don Gibson.)
"The Thrill Is Gone"
R. Taylor
(*Music and Lyrics by* Roy Hawkins and Rick Darnell.)
"I Put a Spell on You"
E. Laws
(*Music and Lyrics by* Jay Hawkins.)
"Fever"
C. Calvert
(*Music and Lyrics by* John Davenport and Eddie Cooley.)

---

[56]First produced in New York Off-Broadway 26 March-11 April 1999 at the New Victory Theatre for 15 performances. Returned (Off-Broadway) 28 August 2000 to B.B. King Blues Club for a 6 performances/week run.
[57]Dropped after New Victory Theatre engagement:
"Gabrielle" (Act 1)
D. Wheetman, R. Taylor
(*Music and Lyrics by* Dan Wheetman.)
"Goin' to Lousianne" (Act 1)
R. Taylor
(*Music and Lyrics by* Ron Taylor.)
"How Can I Keep from Singing" (Music traditional.) (Act 1)
C. Calvert
"Go Tell It on the Mountain" (Music traditional.)(Act 1)
E. Laws
[58]Special thanks to Adetunji Joda.
[59]Special thanks to Donald McKayle.

"Candy Man" (Music traditional.)
D. Wheetman
"Goodnight, Irene"
C. Bevel, D. Wheetman
(*Music and Lyrics by* Huddie Ledbetter and John A. Lomax.)
"Strange Fruit"
G. Boston
(*Music and Lyrics by* Lewis Allan.)
"Someday We'll All Be Free"
C. Bevel, G. Porter
(*Music and Lyrics by* Donny Hathaway and Edward Howard, arranged by Charles Bevel.)
"Members Only"
Company
(*Music and Lyrics by* Larry Addison, arranged by Ron Taylor.)
"Let the Good Times Roll" (reprise)
Company

1999.10 THE GERSHWINS' FASCINATING RHYTHM

A Musical (Revue) in One Act. Music by George Gershwin. Lyrics by Ira Gershwin. Conceived for the stage by Mel Marvin and Mark Lamos. Choreographed by David Marques. Directed by Mark Lamos. Source material by Deena Rosenberg. Scneic design, Michael Yeargan. Costume design, Paul Tazewell. Lighting design, Peggy Eisenhauer. Sound design, Abe Jacob. Orchestrations, Larry Hochman. Music direction and supervision, Cynthia Kortman. Musical/vocal arranger, Mel Marvin. Additional arrangements, Paul J. Ascenzo, Joseph Church. First produced at the Hartford Stage Company, and subsequently at the Arizona Theatre Company. Associate producers, Magicworks/SFX Entertainment and Jerry Frankel. Produced by Music Makers Inc. [Mitch Leigh], Columbia Artists, Manny Kladitis. Opened 25 April 1999 at the Longacre Theatre and closed 9 May 1999 after 17 performances.

CAST: MICHAEL BERESSE, DARIUS de HAAS, ADRIANE LENOX, ORFEH, SARA RAMIREZ, PATRICK WILSON, Chris Ghelfi, Tim Hunter, Karen Lifshey, Jill Nicklaus. *Swings*: Brian J. Marcum, Kenya U. Massey.

MUSICAL NUMBERS
"Fascinating Rhythm" (from *LADY, BE GOOD!*)
Company
"I've Got a Crush on You" (from *TREASURE GIRL*; *STRIKE UP THE BAND*)
S. Ramirez, M. Berresse
"Oh, Lady, Be Good!" (from *LADY, BE GOOD!*)
D. de Haas
"High Hat" (from *FUNNY FACE*)
P. Wilson, S. Ramirez
"Clap Yo' Hands" (from *OH, KAY!*)
Orfeh, Company
"(My) Cousin in Milwaukee" (from *PARDON MY ENGLISH*)
"The Lorelei" (from *PARDON MY ENGLISH*)
A. Lenox, Orfeh
"The Man I Love" (dropped from *STRIKE UP THE BAND*, 1927[60])
"Soon" (from *STRIKE UP THE BAND*)
S. Ramirez, P. Wilson
"Love Is Here to Stay" (pas de deux)
J. Nicklaus, M. Berresse
"Little Jazz Bird" (from *LADY, BE GOOD!*)
D. de Haas
"Isn't It a Pity" (from *PARDON MY ENGLISH*)
S. Ramirez, K. Lifshey
"I Love to Rhyme" (from *GOLDWYN FOLLIES*, film)
"Blah, Blah, Blah" (from *DELICIOUS*, film)
"I Got Rhythm" (from *GIRL CRAZY*)
M. Berresse, Company
"Embraceable You" (from *GIRL CRAZY*)
P. Wilson, C. Ghelfi, T. Hunter, K. Lifshey, J. Nicklaus
"Let's Call the Whole Thing Off" (from *SHALL WE DANCE*, film)
D. de Haas, Orfeh
"Nice Work If You Can Get It" (from *A DAMSEL IN DISTRESS*, film)
A. Lenox
"But Not for Me" (from *GIRL CRAZY*)
P. Wilson
"Just Another Rhumba" (from *GOLDWYN FOLLIES*, film, unused)
S. Ramirez, M. Berresse
"Someone to Watch Over Me" (from *OH, KAY!*)
D. de Haas, K. Lifshey, Orfeh, S. Ramirez, P. Wilson
"The Half of It, Dearie, Blues" (from *LADY, BE GOOD!*)
A. Lenox
"Love Is Here to Stay" (from *GOLDWYN FOLLIES*, film)
S. Ramirez
"How Long Has This Been Going On" (from *ROSALIE*)
P. Wilson
"Home Blues" (from *SHOW GIRL*)
S. Ramirez, P. Wilson
(*Lyrics by* Ira Gershwin and Gus Kahn, set to the Homesickness Theme from 'An American in Paris.')
"Who Cares?" (from *OF THEE I SING*)
M. Berresse. Company
"They Can't Take That Away from Me" (from *SHALL WE DANCE*, film)
Company
"Hang on to Me" (from *LADY, BE GOOD!*)
Company

[60]Also intended for but unused in *LADY, BE GOOD!* and ROSALIE.

1999.11 THE WIZARD OF OZ

A Return Engagement of the Musical Spectacle in One Act, 16 Scenes[61]. Based on the novel of the same name by L. Frank Baum and the MGM film adaptation by Noel Langley, Florence Ryerson, Edgar Allan Woolf. Book by John Kane (for the Royal Shakespeare Company), adapted by Robert Johanson. Music by Harold Arlen. Lyrics by E. Y. Harburg. Background music by Herbert Stothart. Directed by Robert Johanson; assistant director, Ron Gibbs. Musical staging by Jamie Rocco; associate choreographer, Donna Drake. Dance and vocal arrangements by Peter Howard. Scenic design by Michael Anania. Costume design by Gregg Barnes. Lighting design by Steve Cochrane. Sound design by David R. Paterson, Mark Menard. Flying by Foy. Animals by William Berloni. Special effects by Ian O'Connor. Musical direction and additional orchestration by Jeff Rizzo. Production originally presented at the Papermill Playhouse, New Jersey (Angelo Del Rossi, Producer). Produced by Madison Square Garden Productions (Tim Hawkins, producer). Opened 6 May 1999 at the Theatre at Madison Square Garden and closed 16 May 1999 after 22 performances[62].

CAST (in order of appearance) In Kansas: *Dorothy*: JESSICA GROVÉ. *Toto*: Plenty. *Aunt Em*: JUDITH MCCAULEY. *Uncle Henry*: Tom Urich. *Hunk*: CASEY COLGAN. *Hickory*: DIRK LUMBARD. *Zeke*: FRANCIS RUIVIVAR. *Almira Gulch*: JOANNE WORLEY. *Professor Marvel*: MICKEY ROONEY.

In Oz: *Glinda*, the Good Witch: JUDITH MCCAULEY. *Lollipop Guild*: Ethan Crough, Martin Klebba, David Steinberg. *Mayor of Munchkinland*: Eugene Pidgeon. *Barristers*: Wendy Coates, Wendy Watts. *Coroner*: Bill Rolon. *The Wicked Witch of the West*: JOANNE WORLEY. *The Scarecrow*: CASEY COLGAN. *Crows*: Shauna Markey, Mary Ruvolo, Martin Klebba. *Crow Voices*: Lenny Daniel, Trent Armand Kendall, Danny Vaccaro. *The Tinman*: DIRK LUMBARD. *Apple Trees*: Lenny Daniel, Bill Rolon, Danny Vaccaro. *Apple Tree Voices*: Karen Babcock, Gail Cook Howell, Christi Moore. *The Cowardly Lion*: FRANCIS RUIVIVAR. *The Wizard of Oz*: MICKEY ROONEY. *Nikko*, Commander of the Flying Monkeys: Martin Klebba. *Winkie General*: Tom Urich.

Munchkins, Poppies, Citizens of Oz, Jitterbugs, Flying Monkeys and Winkies: Karen Babcock, Steve Babiar, Bill Brassea, Alvin Brown, Kelly Burnette, Wendy Coates, Ethan Crough, Lenny Daniel, Gail Cook Howell, Trent Armand Kendall, Martin Klebba, Shauna Markey, Caroline McMahon, Christi Moore, Eugene Pidgeon, Allison Queal, Bill Rolon, Mary Ruvolo, David Steinberg, Danny Vaccaro, Wendy Watts, Deborah Y. Wilson. *Swings*: Ron Gibbs, Kevin Steele, Jamie Waggoner, Emily Westhafer. *Dance Captain*: Ron Gibbs.

[61]This adaptation previously produced in New York 15 May 1997 at the Theatre at Madison Square Garden for 45 performances, and 6 May 1998 at the Theatre at Madison Square Garden for 38 performances. THE WIZARD OF OZ was previously produced on stage in New York in a different adaptation 22 March 1989 at Radio City Music Hall for 37 performances.
[62]Performed an irregular performance schedule of 11 performances a week.

1999–2000 SEASON

Adam Pascal and Heather Headley in AIDA
Joan Marcus/Photofest

1999–2000 SEASON

1999.12 KAT AND THE KINGS

A Musical in Two Acts from South Africa. Book and lyrics by David Kramer. Music and arrangements by Taliep Petersen. Direction by David Kramer. Choreography by Jody J. Abrahams and Loukmaan Adams. Set and costume design by Saul Radomsky. Lighting design by Howard Harrison. Sound design by Orbital Sound/Sebastian Frost. Musical supervision by Gary Hind. Musical direction by Jeff Lams. Produced by Harriet Newman Leve, Judith and David Rosenbauer, in association with Richard Frankel, Marc Routh, Willette Klausner, Kardana-Swinsky Productions, David Kramer, Taliep Petersen, Renaye Kramer, by special arrangement with Paul Elliott, Nick Salmon, Lee Menzies. Opened 19 August 1999 at the Cort Theatre and closed 2 January 2000 after 157 performances.

CAST (in order of appearance): *Kat Diamond*: TERRY HECTOR. *Lucy Dixon*: KIM LOUIS. (*The Kings (4)*: *Young Kat Diamond*: JODY J. ABRAHAMS. *Bingo* LOUKMAAN ADAMS. *Ballie*: JUNAID BOOYSEN. *Magoo*: ALISTAIR IZOBELL.

Act 1: Cape Town, South Africa, 1999. District Six, 1957.

Act 2: Cape Town, South Africa, 1999/1959. Durban, South Africa, 1959.

ACT 1
"Memory"
K. Louis, the Kings
"American Thing"
T. Hector, Company
"My Lucky Day"
J. J. Abrahams, T. Hector
"Mavis"
T. Hector, L. Adams, J. J. Abrahams, J. Booysen, A. Izobell
"Boetie Guitar"
T. Hector, The Kings
"Cavalla Kings"
K. Louis, The Kings
"If Your Shoes Don't Shine"
T. Hector
"Dress to Kill"
K. Louis, The Kings
"Shine"
K. Louis, The Kings
"The Tafelberg Hotel"
K. Louis, The Kings
"Lonely Girl"
L. Adams, A. Izobell, T. Hector, J. J. Abrahams, J. Booysen
"Josephine"
J. Booysen, The Kings
"Wild Time"
Company

ACT 2
"Happy to Be Nineteen"
Company
"Lonely Girl" (reprise)
L. Adams, The Kings
"Oo Wee Bay Bee"
J. J. Abrahams, The Kings
"Only If You Have a Dream"
K. Louis, A. Izobell
"The Last Thing You Need"
J. J. Abrahams, L. Adams, A. Izobell, J. Booysen
"Stupid Boy"
T. Hector
The Claridges Hotel Medley:
"Cavalla Kings" intro
The Kings
"The Singing Sensation"
J. J. Abrahams, K. Louis, The Kings
"The Bell Hop"
L. Adams, The Kings
"Blind Date"
A. Izobell
"Lonely Girl" (reprise)
K. Louis, The Kings
"The Invisible Dog"
L. Adams, The Kings
"Hey Baby"
J. J. Abrahams, The Kings
"Cavalla Kings" (reprise)
K. Louis, The Kings
Skeleton Dance
The Kings
"Lagunya"
L. Adams, J. Booysen, J. J. Abrahams, A. Izobell
"Lucky Day" (reprise)
J. J. Abrahams, T. Hector
Finale:
"The Singing Sensation" (reprise)
J. J. Abrahams, The Kings
"Hey Baby" (reprise)
A. Izobell, The Kings
"We Were Rocking"
T. Hector, Company
"Lagunya" (reprise)
L. Adams, Company
"Wild Time" (reprise)
Company

1999.13 THE SCARLET PIMPERNEL

A Return Engagement of the Musical Adventure in Two Acts[1]. Book and lyrics by Nan Knighton. Based on the novel of the same name by Baroness Orczy[2]. Music by Frank Wildhorn. Directed and choreographed by Robert Longbottom. Scenery by Andrew Jackness. Costumes by Jane Greenwood. Lighting by Natasha Katz. Sound by Karl Richardson. Fight director, Rick Sordelet. Orchestrations by Kim Scharnberg. Musical direction and vocal arrangements by Ron Melrose. Musical supervision, Jason Howland. Assistant choreographers, Tom Kosis and Darlene Wilson. Dance arrangements by David Chase. Executive producer, Tim Hawkins. Produced by Radio City Entertainment and Ted Forstmann. Opened 10 September 1999 at the Neil Simon Theatre and closed 2 January 2000 after 132 performances. Total, including previous engagement: 772 performances.

CAST (in order of appearance): *Marguerite (St. Just)*: CAROLEE CARMELLO. *Chauvelin*: MARC KUDISCH. *Percy (Blakeney)*: RON BOHMER. *Marie*: Elizabeth Ward Land. *Armand St. Just*: KIRK McDONALD. *Tussaud*: David Masenheimer. *Coupeau*: Stephonne Smith. *Mercier*: David St. Louis. *Ozzy*: Harvey Evans. *Elton*: Russell Garrett. *Dewhurst*: Ken Land. *Jessup*: Charles West. *Ben*: James Hindman. *Farleigh*: Matthew Shepard. *Hal*: Danny Gurwin. *Robespierre*: David Cromwell. *Prince of Wales*: Davd Cromwell.

Opera Dancers, Soldiers, Prisoners, British Guests and Servants: Emily Hsu, Alicia Irving, David Masenheimer, Robb McKindles, Katie Nutt, Elizabeth O'Neill, Jessica Phillips, Terry Richmond, Laura Schutter, Charles West. *Swings*: Peter Flynn, Drew Geraci, Cynthia Leigh Heim, Jennifer Smith, James Van Teuren.

(The action takes place from May into July, 1794, in England and France.)

ACT 1[3]

---

[1]Originally produced in New York 9 November 1997 at the Minskoff Theatre; revised version opened 10 October 1998, closing after 640 performances. This third engagement reflected minor changes in the script and score, a smaller cast and orchestra.
[2]Pen name for Mrs. Montague Barstow.
[3]Dropped from first production: "Vivez," "Believe," "Only Love," and Lullaby. Added for reconstructed version: Wedding Dance, The Rescue, The Gavotte, The Duel, "I'll Forget You," "She Was There." Dropped for this return engagement: "Believe," "You Are My Home" (reprise), All Act 2 reprises.

"Storybook"
C. Carmello, French Ensemble
"Madame Guillotine"
M. Kudisch
"You Are My Home"
R. Bohmer, C. Carmello
Wedding Dance
Ensemble
"Prayer"
R. Bohmer
"Into the Fire"
R. Bohmer, the League
The Rescue
Ensemble
"Falcon in the Dive"
M. Kudisch
"When I Look at You"
C. Carmello
"Where's the Girl?"
M. Kudisch
"The Creation of Man"
R. Bohmer, the League
"The Riddle"
M. Kudisch, C. Carmello, R. Bohmer

ACT 2
"The Scarlet Pimpernel"
R. Bohmer, C. Carmello, Ball Guests
"They Seek Him Here"
R. Bohmer
The Gavotte
The Company
"She Was There"
R. Bohmer
"I'll Forget You"
C. Carmello
The Duel
R. Bohmer, M. Kudisch, C. Carmello
"Into the Fire" (reprise)
Company

1999.14 DAME EDNA: THE ROYAL TOUR

An Entertainment in Two Acts. Devised and written (and directed) by Barry Humphries. Music and lyrics by Barry Humphries. Additional material by Ian Davidson. Scenic design by Kenneth Foy. Costume design by Stephen Adnitt. Lighting design by Jason Kantrowitz. Sound design by Peter Fitzgerald. Musical arrangements by Andrew Ross. Artistic associate, Cynthia Onrubia. Associate producers, Skylight Productions, Adam Friedson, David Friedson, Allen Spivak/Larry Magid, Richard Martini. Produced by Leonard Soloway, Chase Mishkin, Steven M. Levy and Jonathan Reinis. Opened 17 October 1999 at the Booth Theatre and closed 2 July 2000 after 297 performances.

CAST: *Dame Edna Everage*: DAME EDNA (Barry Humphries). *The Fingers on the Keyboards*: Andrew Ross. *The Gorgeous Ednaette #1*: Roxane Barlow. *An Equally Gorgeous Ednaette #2*: Tamlyn Brooke Shusterman.

MUSICAL NUMBERS[4]
"It's Edna-Time"
"Look at Me When I'm Talking to You"
"Call Me Old-Fashioned (I'm a Broadway Star)"
"Any Friend of Kenny's Is a Friend of Mine" (Friends of Kenny)
"Come On Possums, Wave Your Gladiola"

[4]Musical numbers not listed in programs.

1999.15 SATURDAY NIGHT FEVER

A Musical in Two Acts, 19 Scenes. Based on the Paramount/RSO Picture, based on a story by Nik Cohn. Screenplay by Norman Wexler. Stage adaptation by Nan Knighton, in collaboration with Arlene Phillips, Paul Nicholas and Robert Stigwood. Songs by the Bee Gees[5]. Directed and choreographed by Arlene Phillips. Scenic designer, Robin Wagner. Costumes designed by Andy Edwards. Broadway Costumes designed by Suzy Benzinger. Lighting by Andrew Bridge. Sound by Mick Potter. Musical director, Martyn Axe. Orchestrations by Nigel Wright. Dance and vocal arrangements by Phil Edwards. Associate producers, Manny Kladitis and David Rocksavage. Produced by Robert Stigwood. Opened 21 October 1999 at the Minskoff Theatre and closed 30 December 2000 after 500 performances.

CAST: *Tony Manero*: JAMES CARPINELLO. *Stephanie Mangano*: PAIGE PRICE. *Annette*: ORFEH. *Bobby C*: PAUL CASTREE. *Joey*: SEAN PALMER. *Double J*: ANDY BLANKENBUEHLER. *Gus*: RICHARD H. BLAKE. *Monty*: BRYAN BATT. *Frank Manero*: Casey Nicholaw. *Flo Manero/Lucille*: Suzanne Costallos. *Frank Junior*: Jerry Tellier. *Fusco/Al*: Frank Mastrone. *Jay Langhart/Becker*: David Coburn. *Chester*: Andre Ward. *Cesar*: Michael Balderrama. *Vinnie*: Chris Ghelfi. *Sal*: Danial Jerod Brown. *Dino*: Brian J. Marcum. *Lou*: Rick Spaans. *Dom*: Miles Alden. *Roberto*: Ottavio. *Antonio*: Drisco Fernandez. *Ike*: David Robertson. *Shirley*: Karine Plantadit-Bageot. *Maria*: Natalie Willes. *Connie*: Jeanine Meyers. *Doreen*: Angelo Pupello. *Linda Manero/patti*: Aliane Baquerot. *Gina*: Rebecca Sherman. *Sophia*: Paula Wise. *Donna*: Shannon Beach. *Rosalie*: Deanna Dys. *Lola*: Jennifer Newman. *Inez*: Danielle Jolie. *Lorelle*: Stacey Martin. *Kenny*: Kristoffer Cusick. *Nick*: Karl duHoffmann. *Rocker*: Roger Lee Israel. *Natalie*: Anne Nicole Biancofiore. *Ann Marie*: Marcia Urani. *Angela*: Gina Philistine.

Swings: Anne Nicole Biancofiore, Kristoffer Cusick, Karl duHoffmann, David Eggers, Roger Lee Israel, Gina Philistine, Amanda Plesa, Marcia Urani.

Time: 1976.or whenever you were 19. *Place*: New York City (Brooklyn and Manhattan.)

Act 1, Scene 1: The Neighborhood. Bay Ridge, Brooklyn. *Scene 2*: The Manero House. *Scene 3*: Outside 2001 Odyssey – Saturday Night. *Scene 4*: Inside 2001 Odyssey – Saturday Night. *Scene 5*: The Neighborhood Paint Store. *Scene 6*: The Manero House. *Scene 7*: Dale Dance Studios. *Scene 8*: The Neighborhood. *Scene 9*: Inside 2001 Odyssey – Saturday Night.

Act 2, Scene 1: The Verrazano Narrows Bridge – Saturday Night. *Scene 2*: Dale Dance Studios. *Scene 3*: The Neighborhood. *Scene 4*: Stephanie's Apartment – Manhattan. *Scene 5*: Bench overlooking Bridge. *Scene 6*: The Neighborhood. *Scene 7*: Inside 2001 Odyssey – Saturday Night. The Dance Competition. *Scene 8*: Exterior 2001 Odyssey – Saturday Night. *Scene 9*: The Verrazano Narrows Bridge – Saturday Night. *Scene 10*: Park Bench near the Bridge.

ACT 1[6]
Scene 1
"Stayin' Alive"
J. Carpinello, the Company
Scene 3
"Boogie Shoes"
J. Carpinello, the Faces
(*Music and Lyrics by* Harry Casey and Richard Finch.)
Scene 4
"Disco Inferno"
B. Batt, the Company
(*Music and Lyrics by* Leroy Green and Ron 'Have Mercy' Kersey.)
"Night Fever"
J. Carpinello, the Company
Scene 7
"Disco Duck"
B. Batt
(*Music and Lyrics by* Rick Dees.)
"More Than a Woman"
J. Carpinello, P. Price

[5]Brothers Gibb: Barry, Robin and Maurice.
[6]Additional music credits:
"A Fifth of Beethoven"
(*Music by* Walter Murphy.)
"Also Spake Zarathustra"
(*Music by* Richard Strauss.)
"Night on Disco Mountain"
(*Music by* David Shire.)

Scene 8
"If I Can't Have You"
Orfeh
Scene 9
"It's My Neighborhood"
The Company
"You Should Be Dancin'"
J. Carpinello, the Company
ACT 2
Scene 1
"Jive Talkin'"
J. Carpinello, Orfeh, the Faces, the Company
Scene 2
"First and Last"
P. Castree
"Tragedy"
P. Castree
Scene 4
"What Kind of Fool"
P. Price
(*Music and Lyrics by* Barry Gibb and Albhy Galuten.)
Scene 7
"Nights on Broadway"
Orfeh, P. Price, the Company
The Dance Competition:
"Open Sesame"
Danced by A. Ward, K. Plantadit-Bageot
(*Music and Lyrics by* Robert Bell, Ronald Bell, George Brown, Charles Smith, Dennis Thomas.)
"More Than a Woman"
Danced by J. Carpinello, P. Price
"Salsation"
Danced by M. Balderrama, N. Willes
(*Music by* David Shire.)
Scene 8
"Immortality"
J. Carpinello
Scene 10
"How Deep Is Your Love"
J. Carpinello, P. Price

1999.16 (DISNEY'S) BEAUTY AND THE BEAST

A Return Engagement of the Musical in Two Acts[7]. Book by Linda Woolverton (based on her screenplay for the Walt Disney animated film of the same name). Music by Alan Menken. Lyrics by Howard Ashman and Tim Rice. Directed by Robert Jess Roth. Choreography by Matt West. Scenic design by Stanley A. Meyer. Costume design by Ann Hould-Ward. Lighting design by Natasha Katz. Sound design by Jonathan Deans. Illusion design by Jim Steinmeyer, John Gaughan. Prosthetics, John Dods. Musical direction and incidental music arrangements by Michael Kosarin. Orchestrations by Danny Troob. Musical supervision and vocal arrangements by David Friedman. Fight director, Rick Sordelet. Dance arrangements by Glen Kelly. Associate producers, Tony McLean and Pam Young. Produced by Walt Disney Theatrical Productions (Peter Schneider, Thomas Schumacher). Opened 12 November 1999 at the Lunt-Fontanne Theatre and is still running at this time!

CAST (in order of appearance): *Enchantress*: Lisa Mayer. *Young Prince*: Michael Lang. *Beast*: STEVE BLANCHARD. *Belle*: ANDREA McARDLE. *Bookseller*: Glenn Rainey. *Lefou*: JAY BRIAN WINNICK. *Gaston*: PATRICK RYAN SULLIVAN. *Three Silly Girls*: Lauren Goler-Kosarin, Linda Talcott Lee, Amanda Watkins. *Maurice*: J. B. ADAMS. *Wolves*: Robert H. Fowler, Jennifer Hampton, Michael Lang, Lisa Mayer. *Cogsworth*: JEFF BROOKS. *Lumiere*: PATRICK PAGE. *Babette*: PAM KLINGER. *Mrs. Potts*: BARBARA MARINEAU. *Chip*: RICKY ASHLEY, MATTHEW DOTZMAN. *Madame de la Grande Bouche*: JUDITH MOORE. *Salt and Pepper*: Robert H. Fowler, Joseph Savant. *Doormat*: Michael Lang. *Cheesegrater*: Kevin M. Burrows. *Monsieur D'Arque*: Glenn Rainey.

Townspeople, Enchanted Objects: Kevin Berdini, Kevin M. Burows, Karl Christian, Kate Dowe, Barbara Folts, Robert H. Fowler, Lauren Goler-Kosarin, Jennifer Hampton, Michael Lang, Robin Lewis, Anna McNeely, William Paul Michals, Lisa Mayer, Bill Nabel, Glenn Rainey, Joseph Savant, Marguerite Shannon, Linda Talcott Lee, Rachel Ulanet, Amanda Watkins. *Voice of Prologue Narrator*: David Ogden Stiers. *Swings*: Karl Christian, Kate Dowe, Barbara Folts, Robin Lewis.

1999.17 ABBY'S SONG

A Musical in Two Acts and a Prologue. Book and lyrics by Mary Pat Kelly. Music by Elliot Willensky. Directed and choreographed by Randy Skinner. Set design, Bill Clarke. Costume design, David C. Woolard. Lighting design, Nancy Schertler. Sound design, Scott Lehrer. Orchestrations, Michael Gibson. Musical direction, vocal and dance arrangements, Stephen Bates. Produced by Spirit Lake Productions, Mickey Kelly, Susan Kelly Panian and Michael Kelly. Opened 14 November 1999 at the New York City Center and closed 28 November 1999 after 16 performances.

CAST (in order of appearance): *The Mentor*: PAUL SORVINO. *Danny* (a young angel): David A. Tay. *Judith*: JUDY MALLOY. *Bertha*: Jacquiline Rohrbacker. *Leah*: Monica L. Patton. *Ethan*: Sebastian Sozzi. *Becky*: Maggie Panian. *Susannah*: Courtney Leigh. *Lilly*: Ally Hilfiger. *John*: JOHN WILKERSON. *Josh*: Daniel Elborne. *Bennie*: Michael-Leon Wooley. *Abby*: JACKIE ANGELESCU. *Ruben*: John Paul Almon.

A story that has grown old lives again when it's retold.

Time: The present. *Place*: Whispering Pines, Montana.

PROLOGUE
"An Ordinary Town"
P. Sorvino
ACT 1
"Woman's Work"
J. Malloy, M. L. Patton, J. Rohrbacker, M. Panian, A. Hilfiger, C. Leigh
"Fly a Rainbow"
J. Angelescu
"Fly a Rainbow" (reprise)
J. Angelescu, D. A. Tay
"More Than Ever"
J. Wilkerson, J. Malloy
"The Wolf Song"
M. Wooley, J. Wilkerson, D. Elborne, S. Sozzi
"I Am Home"
J. P. Almon, M. L. Patton
"Another Girl Who's Just Like Me"
J. Angelescu, M. Panian, A. Hilfiger, C. Leigh, J. Malloy, M. L. Patton
"There's a Price"
J. Rohrbacker, J. Malloy
"You Just Gotta Be You"
D. A. Tay, J. Angelescu
"She Left Without a Word"
J. Malloy
ACT 2
"A Little Girl in the Night"
J. Angelescu, Ensemble
"Beyond"
Men, Boys
"I Did It"
J. Angelescu
"An Angel Has a Message"
D. A. Tay, J. Angelescu
"A Mother's Heart"
J. Malloy, M. L. Patton, J. Rohrbacker
"Pass the Wine"
Men and Boys
"The Revelation"
D. A. Tay, J. Angelescu, Men and Boys

[7]Originally opened 18 April 1994 at the Palace Theatre and closed 5 September 1999 after 2250 performances. For Musical Numbers, see original 1994 production. The added song "A Change in Me" was retained for this engagement.

"How Do You Follow a Star"
J. Angelescu, S. Sozzi
"Who is This Child"
J. Angelescu, J. Wilkerson
"Abby's Song"
Ensemble
"Fly a Rainbow" (reprise)
J. Angelescu, Ensemble
"One Small Voice"
Ensemble

1999.18 TANGO ARGENTINO

A Revival of the Dance Revue in Two Acts[8]. Entire production conceived and directed by Claudio Segovia, Héctor Orezzoli. Choreographic conception, Claudio Segovia. Choreography by the dancers. Musical directors, Osvaldo Berlingieri, Julio Oscar Pane. Scenery, costumes design and lighting conceived by Claudio Segovia and Héctor Orezzoli. Lighting consultatnt, Marcelo Cuervo. Sound design, Gastón Brisky. Executive producers, Daniel Grinbank, Fernando Moya, Isabel Chaput. Produced by DG Producciones, a CIE-R&P Company (Daniel Grinbank, President). Opened 17 November 1999 at the Gershwin Theatre and closed 9 January 2000 after 63 performances.

CAST: *Singers*: Raúl Lavié, María Graña, Jovita Luna, Alba Solís.
Dancers: Nélida and Nelson, Héctor and Elsa María Mayoral, Carlos and Inés Bórquez, Norma and Luis Pereyra, Carlos Copello and Alicia Monti, Roberto Herrera and Lorena Yácono, Guillermina Quiroga, Vanina Bilous, Antonio Cervila Jr., Johana Copes. *Guest Artists*: Juan Carlos Copes, María Nieves, Pablo Verón.
Musicians: Osvaldo Berlingieri (piano); Christian Zárate (piano); Roberto Pansera (bandoneón); Horacio Romo (bandoneón); Rubén Oscar Gonzalez (bandoneón, percussion, flute); Pablo Agri (violin); Pablo Aznarez (violin); Raúl Di Renzo (violin); Gustavo Roberto Mulé (violin); Walter Sebastián Prusac (violin); Leonardo Suarez Paz (violin); Dino Carlos Quarleri (violoncello); Enrique Guerra (contrebass).

ACT 1
"Quejas de Bandoneon"
(*Music by* J. de Dios Filiberto.)
"El Apache Argentino"
(*Music by* M. Aróztegui, A. Mathón.)
A. Cervila Jr., P. Verón, L. Pereyra, J. C. Copes, C. Borquez, C. Copello
"El Porteñíto"
(*Music by* A. Villoldo.)
G. Quiroga, N. Pereyra, A. Monti, J. Copes, I. Borquez
"El Esquinazo"
(*Music by* A. Villoldo.)
P. Verón, G. Quiroga
"La Puñalada"
(*Music by* P. Castellanos, E. C. Flores.)
"El Choclo"
(*Music by* A. Villoldo, E. S. Discépolo.)
Orchestra
"La Cumparsita"
(*Music by* G. H. Matos Rodriguez.) P. Verón, G. Quiroga
"Mi Noche Triste"
(*Music and Lyrics by* S. Castriotta, P. Contursi.)
R. Lavié
"El Entrerriano"
(*Music by* R. Mendizábal.)
N. Pereyra, L. Pereyra
"De Mi Barrio"
(*Music and Lyrics by* R. Goyeneche.)
J. Luna
"Chiqué"
J. C. Copes, J. Copes
"Bandoneones"
R. Pansera, H. Romo, R. González, A. Zárate

[8]First produced in New York 25 June 1985 at the New York City Center for 7 performances; re-opened 9 October 1985 at the Mark Hellinger Theatre and closed 30 March 1986 after 199 performances. Total: 206 performances

Milonguita:
V. Bilous, Nelson, Nélida, A. Cervila Jr., E. Maria, N. Pereyra, I. Bórquez, A. Monti, G. Quiroga, J. Copes, H. Mayoral, L. Pereyra, C. Bórquez, P. Véron, C. Copello
"Milonguita"
(*Music by* E. Delfino, S. Linning.)
"Divina"
(*Music by* J. Mora, J. De la Calle.)
"Melenita de Oro"
(*Music by* E. Delfino, S. Linning.)
"Re-fa-si"
(*Music by* E. Delfino.)
"Nostalgias"
(*Music by* J. C. Cobian, E. Cadícamo.)
Orchestra
"La Yumba"
(*Music by* O. Pugliese.)
I. Bórquez, C. Bórquez
"Cautivo" [song]
M. Graña
"Recuerdo"
(*Music by* O. Pugliese.)
C. Copello, A. Monti
"Canaro en Paris"
(*Music by* A. Scarpino, J. Caldarella.)
Orchestra
"Nocturna"
(*Music by* J. Plaza.)
N. Pereyra, L. Pereyra, I. Bórquez, C. Bórquez, C. Copello, A. Monti, A. Cervila Jr., J. Copes, R. Herrera, L. Yácono

ACT 2
"Milongueando en El 40"[9]
R. Herrera, L. Yácono
"Uno"
(*Music and Lyrics by* E. S. Discépolo, M. Mores.)
"La Ultima Curda" [song][10]
A. Solís
"Milonguero Viejo"
H. Mayoral, E. M. Mayoral
"Celos" (Jealousy)
(*Music by* J. Gade.)
Nélida and Nelson
"Naranjo en Flor"
(*Music and Lyrics by* H. Y. V. Espósito.)
R. Lavié
"Tanguera"
(*Music by* M. Mores)
P. Véron, G. Quiroga
"La Mariposa"
Orchestra
"Patetico"
J. C. Copes, M. Nieves
"Cancion Desesperada" [song]
M. Graña
"Verano Porteño"
(*Music by* Astor Piazzolla.)
V. Bilous, A. Cervila Jr.
"Balada Para Mi Muerte"
(*Music and Lyrics by* Astor Piazzolla and H. Ferrer.)
Orchestra
"Danzarin"
(*Music by* J. Plaza.)
"Quejas de Bandoneon"
(*Music by* J. De Dios Filiberto.)
Dancers

[9]In previous production, the music was credited to Armando Pontier.
[10]In previous production, the music was credited to A. Troilo, C. Castillo.

1999.19 KISS ME, KATE

A Revival of the Musical Comedy in Two Acts, 17 Scenes[11]. Book by Sam and Bella Spewack[12]. (Based on William Shakespeare's "The Taming of the Shrew.") Music and lyrics by Cole Porter. Directed by Michael Blakemore. Choreographed by Kathleen Marshall. Scenery by Robin Wagner. Costumes by Martin Pakledinaz. Lighting by Peter Kaczorowski. Sound design by Tony Meola. Musical director, Paul Gemignani. Orchestrations by Don Sebesky. Produced by Roger Berlind and Roger Horchow. Opened 18 November 1999 at the Martin Beck Theatre and closed 30 December 2001 after 881 performances.

CAST (in order of appearance): *Hattie*: ADRIANE LENOX. *Paul*: STANLEY WAYNE MATHIS. *Ralph* (Stage Manager): Eric Michael Gillett. *Lois Lane*: AMY SPANGLER. *Bill Calhoun*: MICHAEL BERRESSE. *Lilli Vanessi*: MARIN MAZZIE. *Fred Graham*: BRIAN STOKES MITCHELL. *Harry Trevor*: John Horton. *Pops* (Stage Doorman): Robert Ousley. *Cab Driver*: Jerome Vivona. *First Man*: LEE WILKOF. *Second Man*: MICHAEL MULHEREN. *Harrison Howell*: Ron Holgate.

"Taming of the Shrew" Players: *Bianca* (Lois Lane): AMY SPANGLER. *Baptista* (Harry Trevor): MICHAEL BERRESSE. *Gremio* (First Suitor): Kevin Neil McCready. *Hortensio* (Second Suitor): Darren Lee. *Lucentio* (Bill Calhoun): MICHAEL BERRESSE. *Katharine* (Lilli Vanessi): MARIN MAZZIE. *Petruchio* (Fred Graham): BRIAN STOKES MITCHELL. *Nathaniel*: Jerome Vivona. *Gregory*: Vince Pesce. *Philip*: Blake Hammond. *Haberdasher*: Michael X. Martin.

Ensemble: Eric Michael Gillet, Patty Goble, Blake Hammond, JoAnn M. Hunter, Nancy Lemenager, Darren Lee, Michael X. Martin, Kevin Neil McCready, Carol Lee Meadows, Elizabeth Mills, Linda Mugleston, Robert Ousley, Vince Pesce, Cynthia Sophiea, Jerome Vivona.

Act 1, Scene 1: The stage of Ford's Theatre, Baltimore. June. 1948. *Scene 2*: The Backstage Corridor. *Scene 3*: Fred and Lilli's Dressing Rooms. *Scene 4*: Padua. *Scene 5*: Street in Padua (Piazza). *Scene 6*: The Backstage Corridor. *Scene 7*: Fred and Lilli's Dressing Rooms. *Scene 8*: A Country Road in Padua. *Scene 9*: The Church in Padua.

Act 2, Scene 1: Immediately following. The Theatre Alley. *Scene 2*: Before the Curtain. *Scene 3*: Petruchio's House. *Scene 4*: The Backstage Corridor. *Scene 5*: Fred and Lilli's Dressing Rooms. *Scene 6*: The Backstage Corridor. *Scene 7*: Before the Curtain. *Scene 8*: Baptista's House, Padua.

ACT 1

Scene 1
"Another Op'nin', Another Show"
A. Lenox, Company

Scene 2
"Why Can't You Behave?"
A. Spangler, M. Berresse

Scene 3
"Wunderbar"
M. Mazzie, B. S. Mitchell
"So in Love"
M. Mazzie

Scene 4
"We Open in Venice"
B. S. Mitchell, M. Mazzie, A. Spangler, M. Berresse

Scene 5
"Tom, Dick or Harry"
A. Spangler, M. Berresse, K. N. McCready, D. Lee
"I've Come to Wive It Wealthily in Padua"
B. S. Mitchell, Men
"I Hate Men"
M. Mazzie
"Were Thine That Special Face"
B. S. Mitchell

Scene 8
"Cantiamo D'Amore" (I Sing of Love)
Ensemble

Scene 9
"Kiss Me, Kate"
B. S. Mitchell, M. Mazzie, Singing Ensemble

ACT 2

Scene 1
"Too Darn Hot"
S. W. Mathis, Ensemble

Scene 3
"Where Is the Life That Late I Led?"
B. S. Mitchell

Scene 4
"Always True to You (in My Fashion)"
A. Spangler

Scene 5
"From This Moment On"[13]
R. Holgate, M. Mazzie

Scene 6
"Bianca"
M. Berresse, Ensemble
"So in Love" (reprise)
B. S. Mitchell

Scene 7
"Brush Up Your Shakespeare"
L. Wilkof, M. Mulheren

Scene 8
Pavane
A. Spangler, M. Berresse, Ensemble
"I Am Ashamed That Women Are So Simple"
M. Mazzie
"Kiss Me, Kate" (Finale)
Company

1999.20 PUTTING IT TOGETHER

A Musical Review in Two Acts[14]. Music and Lyrics by Stephen Sondheim. Directed by Eric D. Schaeffer. Choreographed by Bob Avian. (Scenery and costumes) Designed by Bob Crowley. Lighting designed by Howard Harrison. Projections designed by Wendall K. Harrington. Miss Burnett's Costumes by Bob Mackie. Sound designed by Andrew Bruce, Mark Menard. Orchestrations by Jonathan Tunick. Musical director, Paul Raiman. Associate director/choreographer, Jodi Moccia. Executive producers, David Caddick and Martin McCallum. Produced by Cameron Mackintosh, in association with the Mark Taper Forum (Gordon Davidson, Artistic Director). Opened 21 November 1999 at the Ethel Barrymore Theatre and closed 20 February 2000 after ?99 performances.

CAST: *The Wife*: CAROL BURNETT. *The Husband*: GEORGE HEARN. *The Younger Man*: JOHN BARROWMAN. *The Younger Woman*: RUTHIE HENSHALL. *The Observer*: BRONSON PINCHOT. *The Wife*, (alternate) at certain performances: KATHIE LEE GIFFORD.

ACT 1
"Invocation and Instructions to the Audience"
(from THE FROGS)
B. Pinchot
"Putting It Together"
(from SUNDAY IN THE PARK WITH GEORGE)
The Company
"Rich and Happy"
(from MERRILY WE ROLL ALONG)
The Company
"Do I Hear a Waltz?"
(from DO I HEAR A WALTZ)
C. Burnett, G. Hearn

---

[11]Originally produced on Broadway 30 December 1948 at the New Century Theatre for 1077 performances.
[12]Uncredited revisions by John Guare.
[13]Originally from the film KISS ME, KATE; dropped from OUT OF THIS WORLD prior to opening.
[14]Original English 1992 production devised by Stephen Sondheim and Julia McKenzie. Previously produced in an earlier version in New York Off-Broadway 2 March-23 May 1993 at the Manhattan Theatre Club for 96 performances. The author and producer have purposely chosen the spelling of the word "review."

"Merrily We Roll Along" #1 (from MERRILY WE ROLL ALONG)
B. Pinchot
"Lovely" (from A FUNNY THING HAPPENED ON THE WAY TO THE FORUM)
The Company
"Hello Little Girl" (from INTO THE WOODS)
G. Hearn, R. Henshall
"My Husband the Pig" (from A LITTLE NIGHT MUSIC, unused)
C. Burnett
"Everyday a Little Death" (from A LITTLE NIGHT MUSIC)
C. Burnett, R. Henshall
"Everybody Ought to Have a Maid" (from A FUNNY THING HAPPENED ON THE WAY TO THE FORUM)
B. Pinchot, C. Burnett
"Have I Got a Girl for You?" (from COMPANY)
J. Barrowman, G. Hearn
"Pretty Women" (from SWEENEY TODD-THE DEMON BARBER OF FLEET STREET)
J. Barrowman, G. Hearn
"Sooner or Later" (from DICK TRACY, film)
R. Henshall
"Bang!" (from A LITTLE NIGHT MUSIC, unused)
J. Barrowman, B. Pinchot, R. Henshall
"Country House" (from FOLLIES, London)
C. Burnett, G. Hearn
"Unworthy of Your Love" (from ASSASSINS)
J. Barrowman, R. Henshall
"Merrily We Roll Along" #2 (from MERRILY WE ROLL ALONG)
B. Pinchot
"Could I Leave You?" (from FOLLIES)
C. Burnett
"Rich and Happy" (reprise)
The Company

ACT 2
"Back in Business" (from DICK TRACY, film)
The Company
"It's Hot Up Here" (from SUNDAY IN THE PARK WITH GEORGE)
The Company
"The Ladies Who Lunch" (from COMPANY)
C. Burnett
"The Road You Didn't Take" (from FOLLIES)
G. Hearn
"Live Alone and Like It" (from DICK TRACY, film)
J. Barrowman
"More" (from DICK TRACY, film)
R. Henshall
"There's Always a Woman" (from ANYONE CAN WHISTLE, unused)
C. Burnett, R. Henshall
"Buddy's Blues" (from FOLLIES)
B. Pinchot
"Good Thing Going" (from MERRILY WE ROLL ALONG)
G. Hearn
"Marry Me a Little" (from COMPANY)
J. Barrowman
"Not Getting Married Today" (from COMPANY)
R. Henshall
"Merrily We Roll Along" #3 (from MERRILY WE ROLL ALONG)
The Company
"Being Alive" (from COMPANY)
The Company
"Like It Was" (from MERRILY WE ROLL ALONG)
C. Burnett
Finale—"Old Friends" (from MERRILY WE ROLL ALONG)
The Company

1999.21 A CHRISTMAS CAROL

A Revival of the Musical in One Act, 13 Scenes[15]. Book by Mike Ockrent and Lynn Ahrens. Based on the story of the same name by Charles Dickens. Music by Alan Menken. Lyrics by Lynn Ahrens. Directed by Mike Ockrent. Choreographed by Susan Stroman. Setting design by Tony Walton. Costume design by William Ivey Long. Lighting design by Jules Fisher and Peggy Eisenhauer. Sound design by Tony Meola. Projections by Wendall K. Harrington. Flying by Foy. Associate directors, Ray Roderick, Steven Zweigbaum. Associate choreographer, Chris Peterson. Musical direction by Paul Gemignani. Orchestrations by Michael Starobin and Douglas Besterman. Dance arrangements and incidental music by Glen Kelly. Executive producer, Dodger Endemol Theatricals. Producer, Tim Hawkins. Presented by American Express/Madison Square Garden. Opened 30 November 1999 at the (Paramount) Theatre, Madison Square Garden and closed 30 December 1999 after 64 performances.

CAST (in order of appearance): *Beadle*: Del-Bourree Bach. *Mr. Smythe*: CHRIS VASQUEZ. *Grace Smythe*: Brittany Alexander Campbell, Marissa Gould. *Scrooge*: TONY ROBERTS. *Bob Crachit*: NICK CORLEY. *Charity Men*: Don Mayo, Roland Rusinek, Wayne Schroder. *Old Joe*: Kenneth McMullen. *Street Urchins*: Andrew Keenan-Bolger, Lexine Bondoc, Johnny Cennicola, Kennedy Kanagawa, Tristin Mays, Jimmy Walsh. *Mrs. Crachit*: Whitney Webster. *Tiny Tim*: Dennis Michael Hall, Patrick Stogner. *Poulterer*: Roland Rusinek. *Sandwichboard Man*: REGINALD VelJOHNSON. *Jonathon*: Matt Bowles, Marshall Pailet. *Lamplighter*: DIDI CONN. *Blind Hag*: Joan Barber. *Fred*: JAMES JUDY. *Mrs. Mopps*: Marilyn Pasekoff. *Ghost of Jacob Marley*: PAUL KANDEL. *Ghost of Christmas Past*: DIDI CONN. *Lights of Christmas Past*: Leo Alvarez, Keith Fortner, Michael Lomeka, David Rosales. *Judge*: Roland Rusinek. *Scrooge at 8 years*: Johnny Cennicola, Jimmy Walsh. *Scrooge's Mother*: Joan Barber. *Scrooge's Father*: Wayne Schroder. *Mr. Hawkins*: Kenneth McMullen. *Scrooge at 12 years*: Andrew Keenan-Bolger, Kennedy Kanagawa. *Fan*: Lexine Bondoc, Tristin Mays. *Fezziwig*: Daniel Marcus. *Scrooge at 18 years*: Joe Cassidy. *Young Marley*: Ken Barnett. *Mrs. Fezziwig*: Debra Cardona. *Emily*: Kristin Huxhold. *Ghost of Christmas Present*: REGINALD VelJOHNSON. *The Crachit Children*: Andrew Keenan-Bolger, Lexine Bondoc, Kenendy Kanagawa, Tristin Mays. *Sally*, Fred's wife: La Tanya Hall. *Ignorance*: Johnny Cennicola, Jimmy Walsh. *Want*: Brittany Alexander Campbell, Marissa Gould. *Undertakers*: Ken Barnett, Wayne Schroder. *Ghost of Christmas Yet-To-Be*: CHRISTINE DUNHAM.

Business Men, Gifts, Ghosts and the People of London: Lori Alexander, Leo Alvarez, Del-Bourree Bach, Joan Barber, Ken Barnett, Hayes Bergman, Liam Burke, Debra Cardona, Joe Cassidy, Candy Cook, Juliet Fischer, Keith Fortner, La Tanya Hall, Kristin Huxhold, James Judy, Carrie Kenneally, Jessica Kostival, Michael Lomeka, Daniel Marcus, Don Mayo, Kenneth McMullen, Marilyn Pasekoff, Meredith Patterson, Gail Pennington, Josef Reiter, David Rosales, Wendy Rosoff, Roland Rusinek, Vikki Schnurr, Wayne Schroder, Erin Stoddard, Chris Vasquez, Whitney Webster. *Swings*: Ron Bagden, Jane Brockman, Jeffrey Hankinson, Ann Kittredge, Adam Pelty, Angela Piccinni, Rommy Sandhu, Cynthia Thole. *Angels*: P.S. 390 and 330 La Petite Musicale, Park Middle School Broadway Chorus, South Side Middle School Chorale, YPC Jubilee Chorus. *Red Children's Cast*: Marissa Gould, Kennedy Kanagawa, Tristin Mays, Marshall Pailet, Patrick Stogner, Jimmy Walsh. *Green Children's Cast*: Andrew Keenan-Bolger, Lexien Bondoc, Matt Bowles, Brittany Alexander Campbell, Johnny Cennicola, Dennis Michael Hall. *Swings*: Patrick Dunn, Bret Fox, Molly Jobe.

1999.22 MARIE CHRISTINE

A Musical in Two Acts and a Prelude. Words and music by Michael John LaChiusa[16]. Directed and choreographed by Graciele Daniele. Sets by

---

[15]Originally produced in New York 1 December 1994 at the Paramount Theatre, Madison Square Garden for 71 performances. For Synopsis of Scenes and Musical Numbers, see original 1994 production. For this year's and the 1995, 1996, 1997 and 1998 revivals the following changes were made: Scene 1 and "The Years Are Passing By" were dropped.
Added to Scene 2 (former Scene 3) before "Street Song":
"You Mean More to Me"
T. Gross, A. B. Hall or C. Valiando
"The Years Are Passing By" (reprise) in former Scene 13 (new Scene 12) was replaced by:
"London Town Carol"
A. Barruch or K. Kanagawa
Note: The production played an irregular schedule of multiple daily performances.

[16]Freely adapted from the legend of Medea.

Christopher Barreca. Costumes by Toni-Leslie James. Lighting by Jules Fisher and Peggy Eisenhauer. Sound by Scott Stauffer. Musical director, David Evans. Orchestrations by Jonathan Tunick. Associate choreographer, Willie Rosario. Fight director, Luis Perez. Produced by Lincoln Center Theater Company (André Bishop, Artistic director; Bernard Gersten, Executive producer). Opened 2 December 1999 at the Vivian Beaumont Theatre and closed 9 January 2000 after 44 performances.

CAST: *Prisoner #1*: Jennifer Leigh Warren. *Prisoner #2*: Andrea Frierson-Toney. *Prisoner #3*: Mary Bond Davis. *Marie Christine L'Adrese*: AUDRA McDONALD, Sherry Boone (alt.). *Marie Christine's Mother*: VIVIAN REED. *Serpent*: Donna Dunmire. *Dante Keyes*: ANTHONY CRIVELLO. *Celeste*, a maid: Lovette George. *Ozelia*, a Maid: Rosena M. Hill. *Jean L'Adrese*: KEITH LEE GRANT. *Paris L'Adrese*: DARIUS deHAAS. *Lisette*, Marie Christine's maid: KIMBERLY JaJUAN. *Joachim*, a valet: André Garner. *Osmond*, a valet: Jim Weaver. *Monsieur St. Vinson*: Jim Weaver. *Monsieur Archambeau*: André Garner. *Beatrice*, Jean's fiancée: Joy Lynn Matthews. *Children*: Powers Pleasant, Zachary Thornton, Joshua Walter. *Magdalena*: MARY TESTA. *Petal*, Magdalena's "daughter": Janet Metz. *Duchess*, Magdalena's "daughter": Kim Huber. *Gates*: SHAWN ELLIOTT. *Bartender*: Peter Samuel. *Bar Patron*: Michael Babin. *Leary*: Michael McCormick. *McMahon*: Mark Lotito. *Esau Parker*: Peter Samuel. *Olivia Parker*: Janet Metz. *Grace Parker*: Kim Huber. *Old Dante*: Michael Babin. *Helena*, Gates' daughter: Donna Dunmire. *Chaka* (drums): David Pleasant.

Ensemble: Franz C. Alderfer, Ana Marie Andricain, Michael Babin, Brent Black, Donna Dunmire, André Garner, Lovette George, Rosena M. Hill, Kim Huber, Mark Lotito, Joy Lynn Matthews, Michael McCormick, Janet Metz, Monique Midgette, Peter Samuel, Jim Weaver.

Prelude: A Prison. *Act 1*: 1894. A park on Lake Pontchartrain outside of New Orleans. Marie Christine's home on Mandolin Street in New Orleans and its interiors, as well as its garconniere and ballroom. A pier.

Act 2: 1899. A saloon in the First Ward, Chicago. An alleyway. A small house and its interior; Interior of a church.

ACT 1

"Before the Morning"
Women
"Mamzell' Marie"
Company
"Ton Grandpere est le soleil"
V. Reed
"Beautiful"
A. McDonald
"The Map of Your Heart"
D. deHaas, K. L. Grant, A. McDonald
"Way Back to Paradise"
A. McDonald, K. JaJuan
"To Find a Lover"
A. McDonald, Company
"The Adventure Never Ends"/"Nothing Beats Chicago"/
"Ocean Is Different"/"Danced with a Girl"
A. Crivello
"Tou Mi Mi"
K. JaJuan
"Miracles and Mysteries"
V. Reed, Prisoners
"I Don't Hear the Ocean"
A. Crivello, A. McDonald
"Bird Inside the House"
Maids and Valets
"All Eyes Look Upon You"
K. L. Grant
"A Month Ago"
Maids
"Danced with a Girl" (reprise)
A. Crivello
"We're Gonna Go to Chicago"
A. Crivello, A. McDonald
"Dansez Calinda"
K. JaJuan
"I Will Give"
A. McDonald, Prisoners
Finale of Act 1
D. deHaas, Company

ACT 2

Opening/"I Will Love You"
Prisoners, A. Crivello, A. McDonald
"Cincinnati"
M. Testa, J. Metz, K. Huber
"You're Looking at the Man"
M. McCormick, M. Lotito, A. Crivello
"The Scorpion"
A. Crivello, A. McDonald
"Lover Bring Me Summer"
J. Metz, K. Huber
"Old Dante'
M. Babin
"Tell Me"
A. McDonald
"Paradise Is Burning Down"
M. Testa
"Prison in a Prison"
A. McDonald, Prisoners, D. Dunmire, A. Crivello
"Better & Best"
M. McCormick, M. Lotito
"Good Looking Woman"
S. Elliott, M. McCormick, M. Lotito
"No Turning Back"
D. deHaas, V. Reed, K. L. Grant, K. JaJuan
"Beautiful" (reprise)
A. McDonald
"A Lovely Wedding"
M. Testa
"I Will Love You" (reprise)
A. McDonald
"Your Name"
A. Crivello
Finale of Act 2
Women

1999.23 MINNELLI ON MINNELLI

A Musical Revue in Two Acts. [Liza sings songs from the movies of Vincente Minnelli.] Directed by Fred Ebb. Choreographed by John DeLuca. Scenery by John Arnone. Costumes by Bob Mackie. Lighting by Howell Binkley. Sound by Peter J. Fitzgerald. Projections by Batwin+Robin. Film sequence prepared by Jack Haley, Jr. Musical arrangements and supervision, Marvin Hamlisch and Billy Stritch. Vocal arranger, Billy Stritch. Dance arrangements, David Krane, Peter Howard. Orchestrations by Michael Abene, William David Brohn, Jorge Calendrelli, Ned Ginsburg, Russell Kassoff, Peter Matz, Don Sebesky, Jonathan Tunick, Torrie Zito. Musical director, Bill LaVorgna. Executive producers, Gary Labriola and Edward J. Micone, Jr. Produced by Radio City Entertainment, LM Concerts, Scott Nederlander and Stewart F. Lane. Opened 8 December 1999 at the Palace Theatre and closed 2 January 2000 after 19 performances.[17]

CAST: LIZA MINNELLI, Jeffrey Broadhurst, Stephen Campanella, Billy Hartung, Sebastian LaCause, Jim Newman; Alex Timmerman [swing].

ACT 1

"If I Had You" (Incidental music THE CLOCK, film)
L. Minnelli
(*Music and Lyrics by* Ted Shapiro, Jimmy Campbell and Reg Connelly.)
"Taking a Chance on Love" (from CABIN IN THE SKY, film[18])
L. Minnelli
(*Music by* Vernon Duke. *Lyrics by* Jonathan Latouche and Ted Fetter.)

[17]Played an irregular holiday performance schedule of approximately 5 performances weekly.
[18]Previously introduced in the stage production of CABIN IN THE SKY in 1940.

"Cabin in the Sky" (from CABIN IN THE SKY, film[19])
L. Minnelli
(*Music by* Vernon Duke. *Lyrics by* Jonathan Latouche.)
"Happiness Is Just a Thing Called Joe" (from CABIN IN THE SKY, film)
L. Minnelli
(*Music by* Harold Arlen. *Lyrics by* E. Y. Harburg.)
"Love" (from ZIEGFELD FOLLIES, film, 1946)
L. Minnelli
(*Music and Lyrics by* Hugh Martin and Ralph Blane.)
"Limehouse Blues" (from ZIEGFELD FOLLIES, film[20], 1946)
L. Minnelli, Men
(*Music by* Philip Braham. *Lyrics by* Douglas Furber.)
"Meet Me in St. Louis" (from MEET ME IN ST. LOUIS, film)
L. Minnelli, Men
(*Music by* Kerry Mills. *Lyrics by* Andrew B. Sterling.)
"Under the Bamboo Tree" (from MEET ME IN ST. LOUIS, film[21])
L. Minnelli, Men
(*Music by* J. Rosamund Johnson. *Lyrics by* Bob Cole.)
"The Boy Next Door" (from MEET ME IN ST. LOUIS, film)
L. Minnelli
(*Music and Lyrics by* Hugh Martin and Ralph Blane.)
"Skip to My Lou" (from MEET ME IN ST. LOUIS, film)
Men
(*Traditional; Music and Lyrics by* Hugh Martin and Ralph Blane.)
"Have Yourself a Merry Little Christmas " (from MEET ME IN ST. LOUIS, film)
L. Minnelli
(*Music and Lyrics by* Hugh Martin and Ralph Blane.)
"That's Entertainment" (from THE BANDWAGON, film)
Men
(*Music by* Arthur Schwartz. *Lyrics by* Howard Dietz.)
"I Guess I'll Have to Change My Plan" (from THE BANDWAGON, film[22])
L. Minnelli, J. Newman
(*Music by* Arthur Schwartz. *Lyrics by* Howard Dietz.)
"By Myself" (from THE BANDWAGON, film[23])
Men
(*Music by* Arthur Schwartz. *Lyrics by* Howard Dietz.)
"That's Entertainment" (reprise)
Men
"Triplets" (from THE BANDWAGON, film[24])
L. Minnelli, B. Hartung, J. Broadhurst
(*Music by* Arthur Schwartz. *Lyrics by* Howard Dietz.)
"Dancing in the Dark" (from THE BANDWAGON, film[25])
J. Newman, S. LaCause, S. Campanella
(*Music by* Arthur Schwartz. *Lyrics by* Howard Dietz.)
"A Shine on Your Shoes" (from THE BANDWAGON, film[26])
L. Minnelli, Men
(*Music by* Arthur Schwartz. *Lyrics by* Howard Dietz.)

ACT 2
Medley:Men
"This Heart of Mine" (from ZIEGFELD FOLLIES, film, 1946)
(*Music by* Harry Warren. *Lyrics by* Arthur Freed.)
"Just in Time" (from BELLS ARE RINGING, film[27])
(*Music by* Jule Styne. *Lyrics by* Betty Comden and Adolph Green.)
"I'll Build a Stairway to Paradise" (from AN AMERICAN IN PARIS, film[28])
(*Music by* George Gershwin. Lyrics by Buddy G. DeSylva and Ira Gershwin.)
"Be a Clown" (from THE PIRATE, film)
(*Music and Lyrics by* Cole Porter.)
"'S Wonderful" (from AN AMERICAN IN PARIS, film[29])
(*Music by* George Gershwin. *Lyrics by* Ira Gershwin.)
"Liza" (All the Clouds'll Roll Away) (from SHOW GIRL)
(*Music by* George Gershwin. *Lyrics by* Gus Kahn and Ira Gershwin.)
Childhood Reminiscences
L. Minnelli
"An American in Paris Ballet" (Film excerpt)
(*Music by* George Gershwin.)
"I Got Rhythm" (from AN AMERICAN IN PARIS, film[30])
L. Minnelli
(*Music by* George Gershwin. *Lyrics by* Ira Gershwin.)
"Baubles, Bangles and Beads" (from KISMET, film[31])
L. Minnelli, Men
(*Music and Lyrics by* Robert Wright and George Forrest, based on themes of Alexander Borodin.)
"The Night They Invented Champagne" (from GIGI, film)
L. Minnelli, Men
(*Music by* Frederick Loewe. *Lyrics by* Alan Jay Lerner.)
"I Remember It Well" (from GIGI, film)
L. Minnelli
(*Music by* Frederick Loewe. *Lyrics by* Alan Jay Lerner. *Additional lyrics by* Fred Ebb.)
"On a Clear Day You Can See Forever" (from ON A CLEAR DAY YOU CAN SEE FOREVER, film[32])
Men
(*Music by* Burton Lane. *Lyrics by* Alan Jay Lerner.)
"Come Back to Me" (from ON A CLEAR DAY YOU CAN SEE FOREVER, film[33]
Men
(*Music by* Burton Lane. *Lyrics by* Alan Jay Lerner.)
"What Did I Have That I Don't Have" (from ON A CLEAR DAY YOU CAN SEE FOREVER, film[34])
L. Minnelli
(*Music by* Burton Lane. *Lyrics by* Alan Jay Lerner.)
Film montage from MADAME BOVARY, THE BAD AND THE BEAUTIFUL, BRIGADOON (The Chase), GIGI (end)
"The Trolley Song" (from MEET ME IN ST. LOUIS, film[35])
L. Minnelli, Men
(*Music and Lyrics by* Hugh Martin and Ralph Blane.)
"If It Wasn't for You (There Wouldn't Be Me)"
L. Minnelli
(*Music by* John Kander. *Lyrics by* Fred Ebb.)

1999.24 SWING!

A Musical (Dance Revue) in Two Acts. Original concept, Paul Kelly. Directed and choreographed by Lynne Taylor-Corbett. Production supervisor, Jerry Zaks. Scenic design by Thomas L. Lynch. Costume design by William Ivey Long. Lighting design by Kenneth Posner. Sound design by

[19]Previously introduced in the stage production of CABIN IN THE SKY in 1940.
[20]Previously introduced to the stage in the London revue A TO Z, then in New York in CHARLOT'S REVUE OF 1924.
[21]Previously introduced to the stage in SALLY IN OUR ALLEY, 1902.
[22]Previously introduced to the stage in THE LITTLE SHOW, 1929.
[23]Previously introduced to the stage in BETWEEN THE DEVIL, 1937.
[24]Previously introduced to the stage in BETWEEN THE DEVIL, 1937.
[25]Previously introduced to the stage in the stage production of THE BANDWAGON, 1931.
[26]Previously introduced to the stage in FLYING COLORS, 1932.
[27]Previously introduced to the stage in BELLS ARE RINGING, 1956.
[28]Previously introduced to the stage in GEORGE WHITE'S SCANDALS OF 1922.
[29]Previously introduced to the stage in FUNNY FACE, 1927.
[30]Previously introduced to the stage in GIRL CRAZY, 1930.
[31]Previously introduced to the stage in KISMET, 1953.
[32]Previously introduced to the stage in ON A CLEAR DAY YOU CAN SEE FOREVER in 1965.
[33]Previously introduced to the stage in ON A CLEAR DAY YOU CAN SEE FOREVER in 1965.
[34]Previously introduced to the stage in ON A CLEAR DAY YOU CAN SEE FOREVER in 1965.
[35]Liza Minnelli accompanied her mother Judy Garland in the film clip of "The Trolley Song."

Peter Fitzgerald. Musical director, Jonathan Smith. Orchestrations by Harold Wheeler. Music supervisor, Michael Rafter. Music direction, Jonathan Smith. Aerial flying by ANTIGRAVITY, Inc. Associate producers, TV/Asahi/Hankyu, MARS Theatrical Productions, Judith Marinoff. Produced by Marc Routh, Richard Frankel, Stephen Baruch, Thomas Viertel, Lorie Cowen Levy/Stanley Shopkorn, Jujamcyn Theaters, in association with BB Promotion, Dede Harris/Jeslo Productions, Libby Adler Mages/Mari Glick, James D. Stern/Douglas L. Meyer and PACE Theatrical Group/SFX. Opened 9 December 1999 at the St. James Theatre and closed 14 January 2001 after 461 performances.

CAST: ANN HAMPTON CALLAWAY, EVERETT BRADLEY, LAURA BENANTI, Laureen Baldovi, Kristine Bendul, Carol Bentley, Caitlin Carter, Geralyn Del Corso, Desirée Duarte, Beverly Durand, Erin East, Scott Fowler, Ryan Francois, Kevin Michael Gaudin, Edgar Godineaux, Aldrin Gonzalez, Janine LaManna, Carlos Sierra-López, Rod McCune, J. C. Montgomery, Arte Phillips, Robert Royston, Jenny Thomas, Keith Lamelle Thomas, Maria Torres, CASEY MacGILL AND THE GOTHAM CITY GATES, MICHAEL GRUBER. *Swings*: Kristine Bendul, Desirée Duarte, Erin East, Kevin Michael Gaudin, Rod McCune.

The Gotham City Gates: Conductor, Piano/Keyboard: Jonathan Smith. *Guitars*: Dan Hovey. *Bass Piano/Keyboard*: Conrad Korsch. *Drums/Percussion*: Scott Neumann. *Woodwinds*: Matt Hong, Lance Bryant. *Associate Conductor, Trumpet*: Douglas Oberhamer. *Trombone*: Steve Armour.

ACT 1[36]

"It Don't Mean a Thing (If It Ain't Got That Swing)"
C. MacGill, The Band
(*Music by* Duke Ellington. *Lyrics by* Irving Mills. *Musical arrangements by* Jonathan Smith and Steve Armour.)

"Airmail Special"
Company
(*Music by* Benny Goodman, James R. Mundy and Charles Christian. *Musical arrangements by* Ian Herman.)

"Jersey Bounce"
(*Music by* B. Plater, T. Bradshaw, E. Johnson, B. Feyhe and Duke Ellington. *Musical arrangements by* Ian Herman.)

"Opus One"
(*Music by* D. George, J. Hodges and H. James. *Musical arrangements by* Ian Herman.)

"Jumpin at the Woodside"
R. Francois, J. Thomas, Company[37]
(*Music by* Count Basie.)

"Bounce Me, Brother (with a Solid Four)" (from BUCK PRIVATES film)
A. H. Callaway, Company
(*Music and Lyrics by* Don Raye and Hughie Prince. *Musical arrangements by* Jonathan Smith.)

"Two and Four"
L. Benanti, C. MacGill, The Band
(*Music and arrangement by* Ann Hampton Callaway.)

"Hit Me with a Hot Note and Watch Me Bounce"
(*Music by* Duke Ellington. *Lyrics by* D. George. *Vocal arrangements by* Michael Rafter.)

"Rhythm"
C. MacGill, M. Gruber, Company
(*Music by* Casey MacGill.)

"Throw That Girl Around"
E. Bradley, Company
(*Music and Lyrics by* Everett Bradley, Ilene Reid and Michael Heitzman. *Dance arrangements by* Everett Bradley and Lynne Taylor-Corbett.)

"Show Me What You Got"
(*Music by* Everett Bradley and Jonathan Smith. *Dance arrangements by* Everett Bradley and Lynne Taylor-Corbett.)
West Coast Couple: B. Durand, A. Gonzalez. *Latin Couple*: C. Sierra-López, M. Torres.

"Bli-Blip" (from JUMP FOR JOY)
A. H. Callaway, E. Bradley
(*Music by* Duke Ellington. *Lyrics by* Sid Kuller. *Vocal arrangements by* Everett Bradley and Ann Hampton Callaway.)

"Billy-A-Dick"
M. Gruber, Company
(*Music by* Hoagy Carmichael. *Lyrics by* Paul Francis Webster. *Additional lyrics by* Sean Martin Hingston.)

"Harlem Nocturne"
C. Carter, C. Korsch
(*Music by* Earle Hagen and Dick Rogers. *Musical arrangements by* Jon C. Cowherd.)

"Kitchen Mechanics' Night Out"
C. MacGill, R. Francois, J. Thomas, Company
(*Music and Lyrics by* Casey MacGill, Jonathan Smith, Lynne Taylor-Corbett and Paul Kelly.)

"Shout and Feel It"
R. Francois, J. Thomas
(*Music by* Count Basie. *Choreographed by* Ryan Francois and Jenny Thomas.)

"Boogie Woogie Bugle Boy (of Company B)" (from BUCK PRIVATES film)
E. Bradley, K. L. Thomas, E. Godineaux, with D. Oberhamer, L. Bryant, M. Hong
(*Music and Lyrics by* Don Raye and Hughie Prince. *Musical arrangements by* Jonathan Smith and Everett Bradley.)

The U.S.O.:

"G.I. Jive"
L. Benanti, G. DelCorso, C. Carter
(*Music and Lyrics by* Johnny Mercer. *Musical arrangements by* Jonathan Smith and Michael Rafter.)

"A String of Pearls"
A. Gonzales, K. L. Thomas, M. Gruber, Company
(*Music by* Jerry Gray. *Lyrics by* Eddie DeLange.)

"I Got a Gal in Kalamazoo"
(*Music by* Harry Warren. *Lyrics by* Mack Gordon.)

"Candy"
(*Music and Lyrics by* Mack David, Joan Whitney and Alex C. Kramer.)

"I'm Gonna Love You Tonight"
L. Benanti, M. Gruber, Company
(*Music by* Casey MacGill. *Lyrics by* Jack Murphy. *Additional lyrics by* Lynne Taylor-Corbett. *Vocal arrangements by* Michael Rafter.)

"I'll Be Seeing You" (from RIGHT THIS WAY)
A. H. Callaway, S. Fowler, C. Bentley
(*Music by* Sammy Fain. *Lyrics by* Irving Kahal. *Vocal arrangements by* Ann Hampton Callaway. *Dance arrangements by* Ian Herman.)

"In the Mood"
Company
(*Music by* Joe Garland. *Lyrics by* Andy Razaf.)

"Don't Sit Under the Apple Tree"
(*Music and Lyrics by* Lew Brown, Sam H. Stept and Charlie Tobias.)

ACT 2

"Swing, Brother, Swing"
A. H. Callaway, L. Benanti, E. Bradley, M. Gruber, C. MacGill, Company[38]
(*Music and Lyrics by* Walter Bishop, Lewis Raymond and Clarence Williams. *Vocal arrangements by* Casey MacGill.)

"Caravan"
The Gotham City Gates
(*Music by* Juan Tizol and Duke Ellington. *Lyrics by* Irving Mills.)

"Dancers in Love"
G. DelCorso, K. L. Thomas
(*Music by* Duke Ellington.)

"Cry Me a River"
L. Benanti, S. Armour
(*Music and Lyrics by* Arthur Hamilton. *Trombone arrangements by* Steve Armour.)

"Blues in the Night"
A. H. Callaway, C. Carter, E. Godineaux
(*Music by* Harold Arlen. *Lyrics by* Johnny Mercer.)

---

[36]All musical arrangements by Jonathan Smith except as noted. Additional musical quotations excerpted from:
"It Had to Be You"
(*Music by* Isham Jones. *Lyrics by* Gus Kahn.)
"The Jumpin' Jive" (Jump, Jive and Wail)
(*Music and Lyrics by* Cab Calloway, Frank Froeba and Jack Palmer.)

[37]Ryan Francois and Jenny Thomas perform their own choreography.

[38]Scott Fowler performs his own choreography.

"Take Me Back to Tulsa"/"Stay a Little Longer"
E. Bradley, M. Gruber, C. MacGill, Company
(*Music by* James Robert Wills and Tommy Duncan.)
"Boogie Woogie Country"
M. Gruber, R. Royston, L. Baldovi, Company[39]
(*Music by* Jack Murphy and Jonathan Smith.)
"All of Me"
E. Bradley, A. H. Callaway
(*Music by* Gerald Marks. *Lyrics by* Seymour Simons. *Vocal arrangements by* Ann Hampton Callaway. *Musical arrangements by* Ann Hampton Callaway and Jon C. Cowherd.)
"I Won't Dance" (from ROBERTA, film)
(*Music by* Jerome Kern. *Lyrics by* Dorothy Fields. *Additional lyrics by* Ann Hampton Callaway. *Vocal arrangements by* Ann Hampton Callaway. *Musical arrangements by* Ann Hampton Callaway and Jon C. Cowherd.)
"Bill's Bounce"
A. Gonzalez, S. Fowler, B. Durand, C. Bentley
(*Music by* Bill Elliott.)
"Stompin' at the Savoy"
A. H. Callaway
(*Music by* Benny Goodman, Edgar M. Sampson, Chick Webb. *Lyrics by* Andy Razaf. *Additional lyrics by* Ann Hampton Callaway. *Vocal arrangements by* Ann Hampton Callaway and Yaron Gershovsky.)
Finale:
"Swing, Brother, Swing" (reprise)
Company
"Sing, Sing, Sing"
(*Music and Lyrics by* Louis Prima, Andy Razaf, L. Berry.)
"It Don't Mean a Thing (If It Ain't Got That Swing)" (reprise)
(*Vocal arrangements by* Yaron Gershovsky. *Musical arrangements by* Ryan Francois and Jonathan Smith.)

1999.25 MUCH ADO ABOUT EVERYTHING

A One-Man Comedy Revue in Two Acts[40]. Written and directed by Jackie Mason. Lighting designer, Stan Crocker. Sound designer, Christopher Cronin. Associate producers, Howard Weiss, Henry Handler, Jam Theatricals (Arny Granat, Jerry Mickelson, Steve Traxler). Executive producers, Jyll Rosenfeld and Fred Krohn. Produced by Raoul Lionel Felder and Jon Stoll. Opened 30 December 1999 at the John Golden Theatre and closed 30 July 2000 after 183 performances.

CAST: JACKIE MASON (stand-up comedy, monologues, impressions).

2000.01 JAMES JOYCE'S THE DEAD

A Musical Play in One Act, Four Scenes[41]. Book by Richard Nelson (adapted from the last chapter of James Joyce's 'The Dubliners"). Music by Shaun Davey. Lyrics[42] conceived and adapted by Richard Nelson and Shaun Davey. Sets by David Jenkins. Costumes by Jane Greenwood. Lighting by Jennifer Tipton. Sound by Scott Lehrer. Orchestrations by Shaun Davey. Musical direction by Charles Prince. Choreographed by Seán Curran. Directed by Richard Nelson. Produced by Gregory Mosher and Arielle Tepper, in association with Playwrights Horizons (Tim Sanford, Artistic Director). Opened 11 January 2000 at the Belasco Theatre and closed 16 April 2000 after 112 performances.

CAST: *The Hostesses* (3): *Aunt Julia Morkan*, a music teacher: SALLY ANN HOWES. *Aunt Kate Morkan*, her sister (also a music teacher): MARNI NIXON. *Mary Jane Morkan*, their niece (also a music teacher): EMILY SKINNER. *The Family* (2): *Gabriel Conroy*, Julia and Kate's nephew: CHRISTOPHER WALKEN. *Gretta Conroy*, Gabriel's wife: BLAIR BROWN. *The Guests* (5): *Mr. Browne*, a friend of the Aunts: BRIAN DAVIES. *Freddy Malins*: STEPHEN SPINELLA. *Mrs. Malins*, Freddy's mother: PADDY CROFT. *Miss Molly Ivors*: ALICE RIPLEY. *Bartell D'Arcy*, an opera singer: JOHN KELLY.

The Help (5): *Lily*, the maid: Brooke Sunny Moriber. *Michael*, a music student of Mary Jane's: Dashiell Eaves. *Rita*, another student of Mary Jane's: Daisy Eagan. *Cellist*, a music student of Julia's: Daniel Barrett. *Violinist*, a music student of Kate's: Louise Owen.

Ghost: *Young Julia Morkan*: DAISY EAGAN.

Setting: The Misses Morkans' annual Christmas-time party. Dublin, near the turn of the century.

Scene 1: The drawing room of the Misses Morkans' flat. *Scene 2*: The drawing room arranged for dinner. *Scene 3*: Aunt Julia's bedroom. *Scene 4*: A room in the Gresham Hotel.

MUSICAL NUMBERS

Scene 1
"Killarney's Lakes"
E. Skinner, M. Nixon, D. Eagan
"Kate Kearney"
D. Eaves, E. Skinner, Company
"Parnell's Plight"
A. Ripley, D. Eaves, C. Walken, B. Brown, Company
"Adieu to Ballyshannon"
C. Walker, B. Brown
"When Lovely Lady"
S. A. Howes, M. Nixon
"Three Jolly Pigeons"
S. Spinella, B. Davies, Company
"Goldenhair"
B. Brown, C. Walken

Scene 2
"Three Graces"
G. Conroy, Company
"Naughty Girls"
S. A. Howes, M. Nixon, E. Skinner, Company
"Wake the Dead"
S. Spinella, Company

Scene 3
"D'Arcy's Aria"
J. Kelly
"Queen of Our Hearts"
B. Davies, S. Spinella, C. Walken, J. Kelly, D. Eaves
"When Lovely Lady" (reprise)
S. A. Howes, D. Eagan

Scene 4
"Michael Furey"
B. Brown
"The Living and the Dead"
C. Walken, Company

2000.02 SQUONK

BigSmörgåsbørdWünderWerk (A Musical Entertainment) in One Act. Created by Steve O'Hearn and Jackie Dempsey in collaboration with the original NY Squonk Ensemble, Casi Pacilio, Kevin Kornicki, Jana Losey and T. Weldon Anderson. Directed by Tom Diamond. Music by Jackie Dempsey with Squonk. Image book, Steve O'Hearn. Lyrics by Jana Losey with Jackie Dempsey. Sets, puppets and costumes by Steve O'Hearn. Lighting by Tim Saternow. Sound, Bernard Fox. Projections by Steve

---

[39]Robert Royston and Laureen Baldovi perform their own choreography.
[40]Previous editions of Jackie Mason's one man show have been presented as THE WORLD ACCORDING TO ME 22 December 1986 at the Brooks Atkinson Theatre for 367 performances; returned 3 May 1988 at the Brooks Atkinson for 203 performances; JACKIE MASON: BRAND NEW 17 October 1990 at the Neil Simon Theatre for 216 performances; JACKIE MASON: POLITICALLY INCORRECT, 5 April 1994 at the John Golden Theatre for 347 performances; LOVE THY NEIGHBOR 24 March 1996 at the Booth Theatre for 236 performances. This edition addressed such topics as the Internet, cell phones, Y2K, Bill Gates, plus 20 minutes of vintage Jackie Mason.
[41]Previously produced in New York Off-Broadway 28 October-28 November 1999 at Playwrights Horizons for 32 performances.
[42]Authors' note: The lyrics to some of these songs have been or adapted from or inspired by a number of eighteenth and nineteenth century Irish poems by Oliver Goldsmith, Lady Sydney Morgan, Michael William Balfe, William Allingham and from an anonymous nineteenth century music hall song. Other lyrics are adapted from Joyce or are original. Lyrics of D'Arcy's Aria were translated into Italian by Ali Davey. Mary Jane's academy piece and additional arrangements by Deborah Abramson. Other party pieces and underscore pieces in Scene 3 derive from works by Thomas Moore.

O'Hearn, with Casi Pacilio and Nick Fox-Geig. Musical direction by Jackie Dempsey. Associate producers, Mastantuono/Palumbo, Eric Falkenstein. Produced by William Repicci, Michael Minichiello, Lauren Doll, Cookie Centracco, Chris Groenewold. Opened 29 February 2000 at the Helen Hayes Theatre and closed 26 March 2000 after 32 performances[43].

CAST (in order of appearance): Jackie Dempsey (keyboard, accordion), Kevin Kornicki (electronic and acoustic percussion, sound textures), Steve O'Hearn (flutes, electronic winds, many-belled trumpet), T. Weldon Anderson (double bass), Jana Losey (vocals).

MUSICAL NUMBERS

Scene 1
tarantella tourner
what stirs

Scene 2
tutti di frutti
gadabout

Scene 3
fête de la tête
eat you up

Scene 4
jardin du jewels
sighs of her eyes

Scene 5
gigue giocoso
dance of the seven vowels

Scene 6
ballata bel canto
whirring of the wheel

Scene 7
tasto solo
tines

Scene 8
voce solomente
spoon

Scene 9
pas de deux
one bite too

Scene 10
basso virtuoso
blade

Scene 11
dansa de la lumiere
in the kitchen of the mountain king

Scene 12
torso con brio
touched

Scene 13
balletto di bocca buffo
dance of the jawbone glee club

Scene 14
diva du jour
whirl din din din

Scene 15
requiem de l'eau
caught

Scene 16
arioso splashetto
drank big drink

Scene 17
duettino pianissimo
in wavelet white

Scene 18
finale toronado
everything stirs

[43]Previously produced Off-Off Broadway 2-28 August 1999 at P.S. 122.

2000.04

DANCING ON DANGEROUS GROUND

An Irish Dance Drama in Two Acts. (Based on the Celtic legend "The Hunt for Dairmuid and Grania.") Original choreography by Jean Butler and Colin Dunne. Music composed by Seamus Egan and performed by Solas. Narrative and lyrics by Johnny Cunningham. Additional Irish Dance choreography by Michael Smith. Directed by Jeremy Sturt. Settings and costumes designed by Tim Hatley. Lighting design by Tom Kenny. Produced by Tricky Feat Ltd., Radio City Entertainment, Electric Factory Concerts, Artiste Management Productions and Creative Management Ltd[44]. Opened 8 March 2000 at Radio City Music Hall and closed 12 March 2000 after 7 performances.

CAST: *Grania*: JEAN BUTLER. *Diarmuid*: COLIN DUNNE. *Finn McCool*: Tony Kemp. *Deirdru*, friend of Grania: Sorcha McCaul. *Oisin*, son of Finn: Glenn Simpson. *Grania's Bodyguards*: Bobby Fox, Ciaran Maguire, Brian Swanton.

Finn McCool's Court, The Fianna/Women of the Court: Mary Ann Bakke, Aisling Barr, Angela Burns, Cara Butler, Marc Daniels, Michael Donegan, Colleen Farrell, Jo Ellen Forsyth, Sinead Gibbons, Roisin Alana Gilfedder, Tara Hegarty, Joel Hanna, Catriona Kelly, Maria Kirby, Leanna Leonard, Ryan McCaffery, Laura Minogue, Ronan Morgan, Mark O'Donnell, Aisling O'Dwyer, Martin Percival, Stephen Scarriff, Martina Stewart, J. R. Vancheri. *The Voice of Finn*: Stanley Townshend.

Solas: Seamus Egan, John Doyle (guitar), Mick McAuley (accordion, tin whistle), Deirdre Scalon (vocals), Ray Fean (percussion). *Soundtrack Musicians*: Noel Eccles (percussion), Dave West (keyboards), Kieran O'Hare (Uilleann pipes), Eoghan O'Neill (bass guitar).

ACT 1

"Finn's Prologue" (Truth is the hardest tale to tell)
From out of Ireland's mythic past comes Finn McCool, the leader of the Fianna. His story unfolds bringing forth Diarmuid and Grania, his fellow players in legend.

At the Court of Finn McCool
We join the court of Finn and meet his household, including Finn's great friend and colleague, Diarmuid, who is revered as the finest of the Fianna. There is an air of joyful anticipation among the court as Grania, Finn's betrothed, is soon to make her appearance.

Grania's Arrival
Grania enters Finn's court for the first time and meets her future husband. Her solo dance for Finn reflects her delight with her betrothed and her respect and admiration for him which is mirrored by his evident affection for her.

The Training
In another part of Finn's fortress home Diarmuid puts the Fianna through its paces in a series of training exercises. With their commander, Finn, in attendance, they display the precision of their skills and Diarmuid shows why he is regarded as being matchless among his peers.

The Gift of the Bodyguards
As a visible token of his love and esteem for Grania, Finn presents her with his warrior son, Oisin, and three other members of his elite military force who are to form her personal retinue of bodyguards.

The Female State of Mind
Led by Grania's friend and confidante, Deirdru, the women of the court take part in a light-hearted dance which expresses their delight at Grania's introduction to the court. Grania acknowledges the compliment by briefly joining their dance under Finn's watchful and admiring gaze.

The Hooley
The off-duty Fianna members join their women-folk for a lively and up-beat dance session on the eve of wedding celebrations that gather momentum with the approach of nightfall.

Diarmuid's Reflection
An encounter with a fiddle player beguiles Diarmuid into a more relaxed and mellow mood, encouraging him into dropping his guard and showing the playful and fun-loving side of his character.

[44]Tricky Feat Ltd. (Ian Allen, Jean Butler, Colin Dunne, Harvey Goldsmith, Producers); Radio City Entertainment (Edward J. Micone, Jr., Executive Vice President and Executive Producer of RCE; Bob Garcia, Vice President Entertainment Finance of RCE); Electric Factory Concerts (Allen Spivak, Larry Magid, Producers).

Meeting in a late-night bar

The arrival of more musicans and party-goers draws Diarmuid into a late-night bar where amidst an ever more boisterous and rowdy session of music and dance he is unexpectedly confronted by another man's bride-to-be.

On Dangerous Ground

Oblivious to their surrounding and companions, Diarmuid's and Grania's smoldering attraction for one another catches fire in a sexy and seductive dance. As their passion threatens to flare over they are drawn back into the company of their fellow revelers, but with their hearts still racing and with eyes only for each other.

ACT 2

At the Wedding of Finn and Grania

Finn's joy as he takes Grania's hand in marriage is tempered by the dread expressed in his later doubts and misgivings;

'Yet though she placed her hand in mine she would not share my glance
And a fear came over me
For her soul seemed to dance with another.'

However, the wedding festivities and dancing continue unabated, but with Diarmuid an increasingly central and provocative figure to whom Grania is constantly drawn.

Grania's Betrayal

With all thoughts of her new husband now obliterated by her wanton passion for Diarmuid, Grania conspires to free herself from her marital vows by enlisting Dierdru aqnd the women of the court to ply Finn and the Fianna with adulterated wine. As Finn and his men sink into comatose sleep, Grania and Diarmuid steal away into the night.

The Lovers in Flight

The lovers have fled deep into the forest and in this secure retreat share some tender moments of a romantic idyll. But both Diarmuid and Grania know that the tranquility of their newfound sanctuary is a temporary lull before the terror of the pursuit that must surely come.

The Fianna Awaken

Arising slowly from long hours of drugged slumber, the Fianna members struggle to shake off their stupor and their stiffness, but succeed in regaining their composure and military bearing before throwing off the ties that bind them.

Finn's Cry for War

Enraged by Grania's betrayal and his womenfolk's part in the flown lovers' act of treachery, Finn calls the Fianna to arms to answer his call for vengeance and, as punishment, compels the women of the court to make ready to join their men in the hunt for the fugitive couple.

The Pursuit and a Death

Driven on the by vengeful Finn, the Fianna remorselessly hunts down the outlawed lovers and at the height of their pursuit Diarmuid and Grania become separated. One by one Diarmuid's every escape route is sealed off until Finn and the pursuers close in on their former comrade with fatal consequences.

Grania's Lament

The Fianna and the women of the court melt away as Grania cradles the body of her one true love. Turning to Finn for consolation she finds only rejection. Utterly alone with her grief she dances herself into a state of inconsolable surrender.

Epilogue

As the dance returns Diarmuid and Grania to their rightful place in legend, Finn concludes our story with words that are full of insight, but also of regret:

'Only the past I hold, for the heart I can't possess
And the heart is every moment our destiny and our time
Till the rivers run backward and the moon no longer turns the tide
So hear me as I tell my truth
All is for love, and all is forever.'

2000.03 PORGY AND BESS

A Revival of the Folk Opera in Two Acts[45]. Book by DuBose Heyward adapted from the play "Porgy" by DuBose and Dorothy Heyward. Music by George Gershwin. Lyrics by DuBose Heyward and Ira Gershwin. Production directed by Tazewell Thompson. Choreography by Julie Arenal. Sets by Douglas W. Schmidt. Costumes by Nancy Potts. Lighting by Robert Wierzel. Fight director, Roddy Kinter. Conductors, John DeMain, Richard Bado. Produced by the New York City Opera (Paul Kellogg, Artistic and General Director). Opened 7 March 2000 at the New York State Theatre and closed 25 March 2000 after 10 performances in repertory.

CAST (in order of appearance): *Jasbo Brown*: Gerald Steichen. *Clara*: ANITA JOHNSON. *Mingo*: Robert Mack. *Jake*: Kenneth Floyd. *Sportin' Life*: DWAYNE CLARK. *Robbins*: Michael Austin. *Serena*: ANGELA SIMPSON or MONIQUE McDONALD. *Jim*: Edward Pleasant. *Peter*: Bert Lindsey. *Lily*: Shirley Russ. *Maria*: SABRINA ELAYNE CARTEN. *Scipio*: Nkosane Jackson. *Porgy*: ALVY POWELL or RICHARD HOBSON. *Crown*: TIMOTHY ROBERT BLEVINS or LESTER LYNCH. *Bess*: MARQUITA LISTER or KISHNA DAVIS. *Detective*: Wynn Harmon. *Policemen*: Michael Hajek, Charles Mandracchia. *Undertaker*: Bryan Jackson. *Annie*: Jeanette Blakeney. *Frazier*: Marvin Lowe. *Strawberry Woman*: Adina Aaron. *Crab Man*: Duane Martin Foster. *Nelson*: E. Mani Cadet. *Coroner*: John Henry Thomas.

(Residents of Catfish Row) Ensemble: Adina Aaron, Jeanette Blakeney, Bert Boone, Elaugh Butler, E. Mani Cadet, Aixa Cruz-Falú, David Aron Damane, Jean Derricotte-Murphy, Devonne Douglas, Mia Douglas, Rochelle Ellis, Duane Martin Foster, Anne Fridal, Chinyelu Ingram, Clinton Ingram, Bryan Jackson, Nicola James, Quanda Johnson, Naomi Elizabeth Jones, Pamela E. Jones, Jason Phillip Knight, Bert Lindsey, Lisa Lockhart, Marvin Lowe, Robert Mack, Edward Pleasant, Dorian Gray Ross, Elizabeth Lyra Ross, Leonard Rowe, Shirley Russ, Martín Solá, Lucy Salome Sträuli, Marcelin Summers, Everett Suttle, Kellie Turner. *Children*: Khalif Diouf, Ayanna Francis, Leilani Irvin, Nkosane Jackson, Kayla Leacock, Grace Price, Afrika Rhames, Khadijha Stewart, Lacey Thomas, Jamal Russ, Verne Watley.

2000.05 RIVERDANCE ON BROADWAY

A Revival of the Dance Revue in Two Acts, 22 Scenes[46]. Music and lyrics by Bill Whelan. Directed by John McColgan. Set design, Robert Ballagh. Lighting design,Rupert Murray. Costume design, Joan Bergin. Sound design, Michael O'Gorman. Orchestrations by Bill Whelan, Nick Ingman, David Downes. Musical director, Cathal Synnott. Original principal Irish dance choreographer, Michael Flatley. Original choreography by Mavis Ascott, Jean Butler, Colin Dunne, Carol Leavy Joyce, Andrei Kisselev, Moscow Folk Ballet Company, Maria Pagés, Tarik Winston. Executive producer, Julian Erskine. Produced by Abhann Productions Ltd. (Moya Doherty, producer). Opened 16 March 2000 at the Gershwin Theatre and closed 26 August 2001 after 605 performances.

CAST: *Solo Dancers*: PAT RODDY, EILEEN MARTIN, MARIA PAGÉS. *Solo Singers*: TSIDII LE LOKA, BRIAN KENNEDY. *Narrator*: LIAM NEESON (voice on tape).

The Riverdance Irish Dance Troupe: Dearbhail Bates, Sarah Berry, Tara Barry, Natalie Biggs, Lorna Bradley, Martin Brennan, Zeph Caissie, Suzanne Cleary, Andrea Curley, Marty Dowds, Lindsay Doyle, Shannon Doyle, Susan Ginnety, Paula Goulding, Conor Hayes, Gary Healy, Matt Martin, Tokiko Masuda, Sinéad McCafferty, Holly McGlinchy, Jonathan McMorrow, Joe Moriarty, Niall Mulligan, Catherine O'Brien, David O'Hanlon, Debbie O'Keeffe, Ursula Quigley, Kathleen Ryan, Anthony Savage, Rosemarie Schade, Ryan Sheridan, Claire Usher, Leanda Ward, Margaret Williams.

The Riverdance Orchestra: Cathal Synnott (Musical director/keyboards), Athena Tergis (Fiddle), Ivan Goff (Uilleann pipes/low whistle), Kenneth Edge (Soprano and alto saxophones), Nikola Parov (Gadulka, Kaval, Gaida and Bouzouki), Eilís Egan (Accordion), Des Moore (Electric and acoustic guitars), Noel Heraty (Percussion), Desi Reynolds (Drums and percussion), Tony Steele (Bass guitar), Robbie Harris (Bodhrán, Darrabukkas, Dunbeg, and Ouda).

The Riverdance Singers: Sara Clancy (soloist), Patrick Connolly, Brian Dunphy, Joanna Higgins, Darren Holden, Michael Londra, Tara O'Beirne, Sherry Steele, Ben Stubbs, Yvonne Woods.

Moscow Folk Ballet Company: Denis Boroditski, Andrei Kisselev, Yulia Koryagina, Olena Krutsenko, Svetlana Malinina, Ilia Streltsov, Vitaly Verterich, Yana Volkova.

The Riverdance Tappers: Walter "Sundance" Freeman, Channing Cook Holmes, Karen Callaway Williams.

The Amanzi Singers: Notombikhona Dlamini, Fana Kekana, Ntombifuthi Pamella Mhlongo, Francina Moliehi Mokubetsi, Keneilwe Margaret Motsage, Isaac Mthethwa, Andile Selby Ndebele, Mbuso Dick Shange.

The Riverdance Drummers: Darren Andrews, Abe Doron, Eamon Ellams, Gary Grant.

ACT 1

Scene 1

Invocation: "Hear My Cry"
B. Kennedy

[45]First produced in New York 10 October 1935 at the Alvin Theatre for 124 performances. For Synopsis of Scenes and Musical Numbers, see original 1935 production. This production was reduced from Three Acts to Two, with its one intermission following the original Act Two, Scene 2.

[46]First produced in New York 13 March 1996 at Radio City Music Hall for 8 performances, returned 2 October 1996 to Radio City Music Hall for 21 performances; returned 24 September 1998 to Radio City Music Hall for an additional 23 performances.

Scene 2
"Reel Around the Sun"
P. Roddy, The Irish Dance Troupe
Scene 3
"The Heart's Cry"
The Riverdance Singers
Scene 4
"The Countess Cathleen"
E. Martin, The Irish Dance Troupe
Scene 5
"Caoineadh Chú Chulainn" (Lament)
I. Goff
Scene 6
"Thunderstorm"
P. Roddy, The Irish Dance Troupe
Scene 7
"Shivna"
Moscow Folk Ballet, The Riverdance Singers
Scene 8
"Firedance"
M. Pagés, The Irish Dance Troupe
Scene 9
"At the Edge of the World"
B. Kennedy
Scene 10
"Slip into Spring-The Harvest"
The Riverdance Orchestra
Scene 11
"Riverdance"
P. Roddy, E. Martin,
The Riverdance Singers and Drummers, The Irish Dance Troupe

ACT 2
Scene 1
"American Wake"
The Company
Scene 2
"Lift the Wings"
B. Kennedy, S. Clancy
Scene 3
Harbour of the New World:
Trading Taps
W. S. Freeman, C. C. Holmes, K. C. Williams
"Amanzi"
Amanzi Singers
"I Will Set You Free"
T. Le Loka, Amanzi Singers
"Let Freedom Ring"
T. Le Loka, Amanzi Singers
Scene 4
"Morning in Macedonia"
The Riverdance Orchestra
Scene 5
"The Russian Dervish"
Moscow Folk Ballet Company
Scene 6
"Heartbeat of the World—Andalucia"
M. Pagés, N. Heraty, P. Roddy
Scene 7
"Rí Rá"
E. Martin, The Irish Dance Troupe,
Moscow Folk Ballet Company, The Riverdance Singers and Drummers
Scene 8
"Homecoming"
A. Tergis, M. Pagés, R. Harris
Scene 9
Anthem: "Endless Journey"
T. Le Loka, B. Kennedy,
Amanzi and Riverdance Singers, The Irish Dance Troupe
Scene 10
"Heartland"
P. Roddy, E. Martin, The Irish Dance Troupe
Scene 11
Finalé
The Company

2000.06

AIDA

A Musical in Two Acts. Book by Linda Woolverton, Robert Falls and David Henry Hwang, suggested by the opera[47]. Music by Elton John. Lyrics by Tim Rice. Directed by Robert Falls. Choreographed by Wayne Cilento. Scenic and costume design by Bob Crowley. Lighting design by Natasha Katz. Sound design by Steve C. Kennedy. Fight direction by Rick Sordelet. Musical arrangements by Guy Babylon, Paul Bogaev. Orchestrations by Steve Margoshes, Guy Babylon and Paul Bogaev. Dance arrangements by Bob Gustafson. Musical direction and vocal arrangements by Paul Bogaev. Associate producer, Marshall B. Purdy. Produced by Hyperion Theatricals[48] (Peter Schneider, Thomas Schumacher, Producers). Opened 23 March 2000 at the Palace Theatre and is still running at this time!

CAST (in order of appearance): *Amneris*: SHERIE RENÉ SCOTT. *Radames*: ADAM PASCAL. *Aida*: HEATHER HEADLEY. *Mereb*: DAMIAN PERKINS. *Zoser*: JOHN HICKOK. *Pharaoh*: DANIEL ORESKES. *Nehebka*: Schele Williams. *Amonasro*: TYREES ALLEN.

Ensemble: Robert M. Armitage, Troy Allan Burgess, Franne Calma, Bob Gaynor, Kisha Howard, Tim Hunter, Youn Kim, Kyra Little, Nekya Unique Massey, Corinne McFadden, Phineas Newborn III, Jody Ripplinger, Raymond Rodriguez, Eric Sciotto, Samuel N. Thiam, Jerald Vincent, Schele Williams, Natalia Zisa. *Swings*: Chris Payne Dupré, Kelli Fournier, Timothy Edward Smith, Endalyn Taylor-Shellman.

(The story is set in ancient Egypt.)

ACT 1
"Every Story Is a Love Story"
S. R. Scott, Company
"Fortune Favors the Brave"
A. Pascal, Soldiers
"The Past is Another Land"
H. Headley
"Another Pyramid"
J. Hickok, Ministers
"How I Know You"
D. Perkins, H. Headley
"My Strongest Suit"
S. R. Scott, Women of the Palace
"Enchantment Passing Through"
A. Pascal, H. Headley
"My Strongest Suit" (reprise)
S. R. Scott, H. Headley
"The Dance of the Robe"
H. Headley, S. Williams, Nubians
"Not Me"
A. Pascal, D. Perkins, H. Headley, S. R. Scott
"Elaborate Lives"
A. Pascal, H. Headley
"The Gods Love Nubia"
H. Headley, J. Hickok, Nubians

ACT 2
"A Step Too Far"
S. R. Scott, A. Pascal, H. Headley

---

[47]The opera AIDA was composed by Giuseppe Verdi to a libretto by Antonio Ghislanzoni and Camille duLocke.
[48]Hyperion is a division of Walt Disney Theatrical Productions.

"Easy as Life"
H. Headley
"Like Father Like Son"
J. Hickok, A. Pascal, Ministers
"Radames' Letter"
A. Pascal
"How I Know You" (reprise)
D. Perkins
"Written in the Stars"
H. Headley, A. Pascal
"I Know the Truth"
S. R. Scott
"Elaborate Lives" (reprise)
H. Headley, A. Pascal
"Every Story Is a Love Story" (reprise)
S. R. Scott

2000.07 CONTACT

A Dance Play in Two Acts, Three Parts, by Susan Stroman and John Weidman[49]. Written by John Weidman. Directed and choreographed by Susan Stroman. Sets by Thomas Lynch. Costumes by William Ivey Long. Lighting by Peter Kaczorowski. Sound by Scott Stauffer. Associate choreographer, Chris Peterson. Produced by Lincoln Center Theater Company (André Bishop, Artistic Director; Bernard Gersten, Executive Producer). Opened 30 March 2000[50] at the Vivian Beaumont Theater and is still running at this time!

CAST (in alphabetical order): JASON ANTOON, John Bolton, Tomé Cousin, Holly Cruikshank, Pascle Faye, BOYD GAINES, Nina Goldman, Peter Gregus, Shannon Hammons, Jack Hayes, SEÁN MARTIN HINGSTON, Stacey Todd Holt, Angelique Ilo, DAVID MacGILLIVRAY, STEPHANIE MICHELS, Mayumi Miguel, Dana Stackpole, SCOTT TAYLOR, Rocker Verastique, Robert Wersinger, DEBORAH YATES, KAREN ZIEMBA. *Swings*: Steve Geary, Joanne Manning.

ACT 1

Part I: SWINGING[51]

A Servant, an Aristocrat, a Girl on a Swing

Scene: A forest glade, 1767.

CAST: *Two Frenchmen*: S. M. Hingston, S. Taylor. *Girl on the Swing*: S. Michels.

MUSIC

"My Heart Stood Still"
Stephane Grappelli
(*Music by* Richard Rodgers.)
Anitra's Dance (from PEER GYNT SUITE No. 1)
Waltz Eugene (from EUGENE ONEGIN, Opus 24)
La Farandole (from L'Arlesienne Suite No. 2)
New York Philharmonic, conducted by Leonard Bernstein

Part II: DID YOU MOVE?

A Wife, a Husband, a Headwaiter

Scene: An Italian restaurant, Queens, 1954.

CAST: *A Wife*: K. Ziemba. *A Husband*: J. Antoon. *A Headwaiter*: D. MacGillivray. *Restaurant Patrons*: T. Cousin, N. Goldman, P. Gregus, D. Stackpole. *Waiters*: S. Taylor, R. Wersinger. *Photographer*: P. Faye. *Cigarette Girl*: S. Hammons. *Uncle Vinnie*: S. M. Hingston. *Headwaiter*: D. MacGillivray. *Busboy*: R. Verastique.

MUSIC

"You're Nobody til Somebody Loves You"
Dean Martin
(*Music and Lyrics by* Russ Morgan, Larry Stock and James Cavanaugh.)
"Powerful Stuff"
The Fabulous Thunderbirds
(*Music and Lyrics by* Wally Wilson, Michael Henderson and Robert S. Field.)
"Put a Lid on It"
Squirrel Nutzippers
(*Music by* Tom Maxwell.)
"Sweet Lorraine"
Stephane Grappelli
(*Music and Lyrics by* Clifford Burwell and Mitchell Parish.)
"Runaround Sue"
Dion
(*Music by* Ernest Maresca, Dion DiMucci.)
"Beyond the Sea"
Royal Crown Revue, conducted by Arte Butler
(*Music by* Charles Trenet and Jack Lawrence.)

ACT 2

Part III: CONTACT

An Advertising Executive, a Bartender, a Girl in a Yellow Dress

Scene: (An apartment and a bar.) New York City, 1999.

CAST: *Michael Wiley*: B. Gaines. *Bartender, Voice Messages*: J. Antoon. *Girl in the Yellow Dress*: D. Yates. *Jack*: J. Hayes. *Johnny*: S. M. Hingston. *Joe*: R. Wersiger. *Clubgoers*: T. Cousin, P. Faye, N. Goldman, P. Gregus, S. Hammons, S. T. Holt, S. Michels, M. Miguel, D. Stackpole, S. Taylor, R. Verastique. *Swings* (for all 3 Parts): S. Geary, A. Ilo, D. MacGillivray, J. Manning.

MUSIC

"See What I Mean?"
Al Cooper and His Savoy Sultans
(*Music by* J. Chapman.)
"Simply Irresistible"
Robert Palmer
(*Music by* Robert Palmer.)
"Do You Wanna Dance?"
Beach Boys
(*Music and Lyrics by* Bobby Freeman.)
"Topsy"
Royal Crown Revue
(*Music by* William Edgar Battle and Eddie Durham.)
"Sing Sing Sing"
Benny Goodman and His Orchestra
(*Music by* Louis Prima, arranged by Benny Goodman.)
"Christopher Columbus"
Benny Goodman and His Orchestra
(*Music and Lyrics by* Andy Razaf.)
"Moondance"
Van Morrison
(*Music by* Van Morrison.)

2000.08 THE WILD PARTY

A Musical in One Act, 5 Scenes. Book by Michael John LaChiusa and George C. Wolfe. Music and lyrics by Michael John LaChiusa. Based on the poem of the same name by Joseph Moncure March. Directed by George C. Wolfe. Choreographed by Joey McKneely. Scenic design, Robin Wagner. Costume design, Toni-Leslie James. Lighting design, Jules Fisher and Peggy Eisenhauer. Sound design, Tony Meola. Musical director, Todd Ellison. Orchestrations by Bruce Coughlin. Associate producer, Wiley Hausam. Produced by the Joseph Papp Public Theatre/New York Shakespeare Festival (George C. Wolfe, Producer), Scott Rudin/Paramount Pictures, Roger Berlind, (Elizabeth) Williams/(Anita) Waxman. Opened 13 April 2000 at the Virginia Theatre and closed 11 June 2000 after 68 performances.

CAST (in order of appearance): *Queenie*: TONI COLLETTE. *Burrs*: MANDY PATINKIN. *Jackie*: Marc Kudisch. *Miss Madelaine True*: Jane Summerhays. *Sally*: Sally Murphy. *Eddie Mackrel*: Norm Lewis. *Mae*: Leah Hocking. *Nadine*: Brooke Sunny Moriber. *Phil D'Armano*: Nathan Lee Graham. *Oscar D'Amano*: Michael McElroy. *Dolores*: EARTHA KITT. *Gold*: Adam Grupper. *Goldberg*: Stuart Zagnit. *Black*: YANCEY ARIAS. *Kate*: TONYA PINKINS.

Time: New York, New York. 1928.

Scene 1: The Vaudeville. *Scene 2*: Promenade of Guests. *Scene 3*: The Party. *Scene 4*: After Midnight Dies. *Scene 5*: Finale.

[49]All the music in CONTACT was pre-recorded.
[50]First produced Off-Broadway 7 October 1999-7 January 2000 at the Mitzi Newhouse Theater for 109 performances.
[51]Inspired by the painting, The Swing, circa 1768, by Jean-Honoré Fragonard.

MUSICAL NUMBERS

Scene 1

"Queenie Was a Blonde"/"Marie Is Tricky"/"Wild Party"
T. Collette, M. Patinkin, Company

Scene 2

"Dry"
M. Patinkin, M. Kudisch, J. Summerhays, S. Murphy, N. Lewis, L. Hocking, N. L. Graham, M. McElroy. E. Kitt

"Welcome to My Party"
T. Collette

"Like Sally"
J. Summerhays

"Breezin' Through Another Day"
M. Kudisch

"Uptown"
N. L. Graham, M. McElroy

"Eddie & Mae"
N. Lewis, L. Hocking

"Gold & Goldberg"
A. Grupper, S. Zagnit

"Moving Uptown"
E. Kitt

Scene 3

"Black Bottom"
T. Collette, Company

"Best Friend"
T. Collette, T. Pinkins

"A Little M-M-M"
N. L. Graham, M. McElroy

"Tabu/Taking Care of the Ladies"
M. McElroy, Y. Arias, Company

"Wouldn't It Be Nice?"
M. Patinkin

"Lowdown-Down"
T. Collette

"Gin"
M. Patinkin, Company

"Wild"
Company

"Need"
J. Summerhays, Company

"Black Is a Moocher"
T. Pinkins

"People Like Us"
T. Collette, Y. Arias

Scene 4

"After Midnight Dies"
S. Murphy

"Godlen Boy"
N. Lewis, N. Graham, M. McElroy

"The Movin' Uptown Blues"
A. Grupper, S. Zagnit

"The Lights of Broadway"
B. S. Moriber

"More"
M. Kudisch

"Love Ain't Nothin'/Welcome to Her Party/ What I Need"
T. Pinkins, M. Patinkin, T. Collette

"How Many Women in the World?"
M. Patinkin

"When It Ends"
E. Kitt

Scene 5

"This is What It Is"
T. Collette

Finale
T. Collette, M. Patinkin, Company

2000.09 JESUS CHRIST SUPERSTAR

A Revival of the Musical in Two Acts[52]. Music by Andrew Lloyd Webber. Lyrics by Tim Rice. Directed by Gale Edwards. Choreography by Anthony Van Laast. Scenic design by Peter J. Davison. Costume design by Roger Kirk. Lighting design by Mark McCullough. Sound design by Richard Ryan. Musical supervisor, Simon Lee. Associate musical supervisor, Kristen Blodgett. Musical director, Patrick Vaccariello. Assistant choreographer, Denny Berry. Orchestrations by Andrew Lloyd Webber. Produced by The Really Useful Superstar Company and Nederlander Producing Company of America Inc. Opened 16 April 2000 at the Ford Center for the Performing Arts and closed 3 September 2000 after 161 performances.

CAST: *Jesus of Nazareth*: GLENN CARTER. *Judas Iscariot*: TONY VINCENT. *Mary Magdalene*: MAYA DAYS. *Pontius Pilate*: KEVIN GRAY. *King Herod*: PAUL KANDEL. *Simon Zealotes*: MICHAEL K. LEE. *Caiaphas*: FREDERICK B. OWENS. *Annas*: RAY WALKER. *Peter*: RODNEY HICKS.

Apostles/Disciples: Christian Borle, Lisa Brescia, D'Monroe, Manoel Feliciano, Somer Lee Graham, J. Todd Howell, Daniel C. Levine, Anthony Manough, Joseph Melendez, Eric Millegan, Michael Seelbach, Alexander Selma, David St. Louis, Shayna Steele, Max Von Essen, Joe Wilson, Jr., Andrew Wright. *Soul Girls/Disciples*: Merle Dandridge, Deidre Goodwin, Lana Gordon. *Priests*: Hank Campbell, Devin Richards, Timothy Warmen. *Swings*: Bernard Dotson, Jessica Phillips, Adam Simmons. *Profiteers, Lepers, Roman Guards, The Mob, Herod's Court and Paparazzi*: Members of the Company.

2000.10 THE GREEN BIRD

A Comedy with Music in Two Acts[53]. (Original Italian) Play by Carlo Gozzi, translated by Albert Bermel and Ted Emery. Original music composed and orchestrated by Elliot Goldenthal. Additional text by Eric Overmeyer. Scenic design by Christine Jones. Costume design by Constance Hoffman. Lighting design by Donald Holder. Sound design, Jon Weston. Mask and puppet design, Julie Taymor. Music director, Richard Martinez. Vocal director, Joe Church. Musical staging by Daniel Ezralow. Directed by Julie Taymor. Produced by Ostar Enterprises Inc. (Robert E. Wankel, Executive Vice President), with Theater for a New Audience (Jeffrey Horowitz, Artistic Director) and Nina Lannan. Opened 18 April 2000 at the Cort Theatre and closed 4 June 2000 after 55 performances.

CAST (in order of appearance): *Brighella*: Reg. E. Cathey. *Pantalone*: Andrew Weems. *Smeraldina*: DIDI CONN. *Truffaldino*: NED EISENBERG. *Barbarina*: Katie MacNichol. *Renzo*: SEBASTIAN ROCHÉ. *The Green Bird*: BRUCE TURK. *Ninetta*: KRISTINE NIELSEN. *Voice of Calmon*: Andrew Weems. *Tartaglia*: DEREK SMITH. *Tartagliona*: EDWARD HIBBERT. *Beautician*: Andrew Weems. *Pompea*: Lee Lewis. *Pierrot*: Andrew Weems. *Voice of Serpentina*: Lee Lewis.

Singing Apples: Sophia Salguero (soloist), Meredith Patterson, Sarah Jane Nelson. *Dancing Waters*: Erico Villanueva (soloist), Ramon Flowers. *Servants/Marching Band/Puppeteers*: Ken Barnett, Ramon Flowers, Sarah Jane Nelson, Meredith Patterson, Sophia Salguero, Erico Villanueva.

The action is set in the imaginary city of Monterotondo, Serpentina's garden, the ogre's mountain lair and other suitably fabulous places.

ACT 1[54]

"Truffaldino's Sausage Shop"

"O Greedy People" (The Apples That Sing)
S. Salguero, S. J. Nelson, M. Patterson
(*Lyrics by* Carlo Gozzi and Albert Bermel.)

---

[52]First produced in New York 12 October 1971 at the Mark Hellinger Theatre for 711 performances. For Synopsis of Scenes and Musical Numbers, see original 1971 production. For this production, the following were added to the list of musical numbers:

"Everything's Alright" (reprise)
(Act 1, after "The Temple")
M. Days, G. Carter

"Blood Money" (added at the close of Act 1, to accompany "Damned for All Time")

[53]An earlier production of this play under the direction of Julie Taymor was presented Off-Broadway 7 March 1996 at the New Victory Theater for 15 performances.

[54]Musical numbers (except for "Oh Foolish Heart") not listed in programs. List prepared from press office materials and Original Cast Recording from DRG Records.

"Tartaglia's Lament"
D. Smith
"The Bickering"
"Calmon, King of Statues"
"Joy to the King"
S. Salguero
(*Lyrics by* Carlo Gozzi and Albert Bermel.)
Ninetta's Hope
"Renzo and Pompea Duet"
S. Roche, L. Lewis
(*Lyrics by* Albert Bermel.)
"Barbarina's Lament"
K. MacNichol
The Waters That Dance
"Serpentina's Garden"
A. Weems
Under Bustle Funk
Green Bird Descent
The Magic Feather
The King's Lament (violin solo)
Accordions and Palace Rhumba

ACT 2
Prologue (Radio Waves)
Acids and Alkalis
Apple Aria (instrumental)
"Oh Foolish Heart" (Finale)
Full Company
(*Lyrics by* David Suehsdorf.)

2000.11 THE MUSIC MAN

A Revival of the Musical Comedy in Two Acts, 18 Scenes[55]. Book, music and lyrics by Meredith Willson. Story by Meredith Willson and Franklin Lacey. Direction and choreography by Susan Stroman. Scenery designed by Thomas Lynch. Costumes designed by William Ivey Long. Lighting designed by Peter Kaczorowski. Sound designed by Jonathan Deans. Musical supervision and direction by David Chase. Orchestrations by Doug Besterman. Dance and incidental music by David Krane. Associate choreographer, Tara Young, Associate director, Ray Roderick. Produced by Dodger Theatricals, John F. Kennedy Center for the Performing Arts, Elizabeth Williams/Anita Waxman, Kardana-Swinsky Productions, Lorie Cowen Levy/Dede Harris. Opened 27 April at the Neil Simon Theatre and closed 30 December 2001 after 685 performances.

CAST (in order of appearance): *Conductor*: Andre Garner. *Charlie Cowell*: RALPH BYERS. *Travelling Salesmen*: Liam Burke, Kevin Bogue, E. Clayton Cornelious, Michael Duran, Blake Hammond, Michael McGurk, Dan Sharkey, John Sloman. *Harold Hill*: CRAIG BIERKO. *Olin Britt*: Michael-Leon Wooley. *Amaryllis*: Jordan Puryear. *Maud Dunlop*: Martha Hawley. *Ewart Dunlop*: Jack Doyle. *Mayor Shinn*: PAUL BENEDICT. *Alma Hix*: Leslie Hendrix. *Ethel Toffelmier*: Tracy Nicole Chapman. *Oliver Hix*: John Sloman. *Jacey Squires*: Blake Hammond. *Marcellus Washburn*: MAX CASELLA. *Tommy Djilas*: CLYDE ALVES. *Marian Paroo*: REBECCA LUKER. *Mrs. Paroo*: KATHERINE McGRATH. *Winthrop Paroo*: MICHAEL PHELAN. *Eulalie Mackecknie Shinn*: RUTH WILLIAMSON. *Zaneeta Shinn*: KATE LEVERING. *Gracie Shinn*: Ann Whitlow Brown. *Mrs. Squires*: Ann Brown. *Constable Locke*: Kevin Bogue.

Residents of River City: Cameron Adams, Kevin Bogue, Sara Brenner, Chase Brock, Liam Burke, E. Clayton Cornelious, Michael Duran, Andre Garner, Ellen Harvey, Mary Illes, Joy Lynn Matthews, Michael McGurk, Robbie Nicholson, Ipsita Paul, Pamela Remler, Dan Sharkey, Lauren Ullrich, Travis Wall. *Swings*: Jennie Ford, Leigh Heim, Jason Snow, Jeff Williams.

Act 1, Scene 1: A Railway Coach, morning, 3 July, 1912. *Scene 2*: Train Depot. River City, Iowa. *Scene 3*: The Center of Town. *Scene 4*: A Street. *Scene 5*: The Paroo's House. *Scene 6*: Madison Gymnasium. 4 July. *Scene 7*: The Center of Town. *Scene 8*: A Street just off the Center of Town. *Scene 9*: Madison Library. *Scene 10*: A Street, the following Saturday, late afternoon. *Scene 11*: The Paroos' Porch, immediately following. *Scene 12*: The Edge of Town, noon, the following Saturday.

Act 2, Scene 1: Madison Gymnasium, the following Tuesday evening. *Scene 2*: The Front of the Hotel, the following Wednesday evening. *Scene 3*: The Paroos' Porch, immediately following. *Scene 4*: Madison Park. *Scene 5*: The Footbridge. *Scene 6*: The Center of Town, immediately following.

ACT 1
Scene 1
"Rock Island"
R. Byers, Travelling Salesmen
Scene 3
"Iowa Stubborn"
Townspeople of River City
"(Ya Got) Trouble"
C. Bierko, Townspeople
Scene 5
"Piano Lesson"
R. Luker, K. McGrath, K. Puryear
"Goodnight, My Someone"
R. Luker
Scene 6
"Seventy Six Trombones"
C. Bierko, Boys, Girls
Scene 7
"Sincere"
M. Wooley, J. Sloman, J. Doyle, B. Hammond
Scene 8
"The Sadder-But-Wiser Girl"
C. Bierko, M. Casella
"Pickalittle (Talkalittle)"
L. Hendrix, T. N. Chapman, R. Williamson, M. Hawley, A. Brown, Ladies of River City
"Goodnight Ladies"
M. Wooley, J. Sloman, J. Doyle, B. Hammond
Scene 9
"Marian the Librarian"
C. Bierko, Boys, Girls
Scene 11
"Gary, Indiana"
C. Bierko, K. McGrath
"My White Knight"
R. Luker
Scene 12
"The Wells Fargo Wagon"
M. Phelan, Townspeople

ACT 2
Scene 1
"It's You"
M. Wooley, J. Sloman, J. Doyle, B. Hammond, C. Bierko, Townspeople
"Pickalittle" (reprise)
R. Williamson, M. Hawley, T. N. Chapman, L. Hendrix, A. Brown, Ladies of River City
Scene 2
"Lida Rose"
M. Wooley, J. Sloman, J. Doyle, B. Hammond
"Will I Ever Tell You?"
R. Luker
Scene 3
"Gary, Indiana" (reprise)
M. Phelan, K. McGrath, R. Luker
Scene 4
"Shipoopi"
M. Casella, C. Bierko, Townspeople
Scene 5
"Till There Was You"
R. Luker

[55]Originally produced in New York 19 December 1957 at the Majestic Theatre for 1375 performances. For Synopsis of Scenes and Musical Numbers, see original 1957 production. Original Act 1, Scene 2 was divided in two, yielding an extra scene.

"Seventy Six Trombones"/"Goodnight, My Someone" (reprise)
C. Bierko, R. Luker
"Till There Was You" (reprise)
C. Bierko

Scene 6
Finale
Company

2000.12 DIRTY BLONDE

A Play (with Songs) in One Act[56]. Play by Claudia Shear, conceived by Claudia Shear and James Lapine. Directed by James Lapine. Musical staging, John Carrafa. Scenic design, Douglas Stein. Costume design, Susan Hilferty. Lighting design, David Lander. Sound design, Dan Moses Schreier. Arrangements, musical direction by Bob Stillman. Produced by The Shubert Organization, Chase Mishkin, Ostar Enterprises, ABC, Inc., in association with the New York Theatre Workshop. Opened 1 May 2000 at the Helen Hayes Theatre and closed 4 March 2001 after 352 performances.

CAST (in order of appearance): *Frank Wallace, Ed Hearn and others*: BOB STILLMAN. *Jo, Mae (West)*: CLAUDIA SHEAR. *Charlie and others*: KEVIN CHAMBERLIN.

MUSICAL NUMBERS[57]

"Dirty Blonde"
(*Music and Lyrics by* Bob Stillman.)

"A Guy What Takes His Time" (from SHE DONE HIM WRONG, film)
(*Music and Lyrics by* Ralph Rainger.)

"Cuddle Up and Cling to Me"
(*Music by* Henry I. Marshall. *Lyrics by* Stanley Murphy.)

"I Found a New Way to Go to Town" (from I'M NO ANGEL, film)
(*Music by* Harvey Brooks. *Lyrics by* Gladys Dubois and Ben Ellison.)

"I'm No Angel" (from I'M NO ANGEL, film)
(*Music by* Harvey Brooks. *Lyrics by* Gladys Dubois and Ben Ellison.)

"I Love It"
(*Music by* Harry Von Tilzer. *Lyrics by* E. Ray Goetz.)

"I Want You, I Need You" (from I'M NO ANGEL, film)
(*Music by* Harvey Brooks. *Lyrics by* Ben Ellison.)

"I Wonder Where My Easy Rider's Gone" (from SHE DONE HIM WRONG, film)
(*Music and Lyrics by* Shelton Brooks.)

"Oh My, How We Posé" (from McALLISTER'S LEGACY)
(*Music by* David Braham. *Lyrics by* Edward Harrigan.)

"Perfect Love"
(*Music and Lyrics by* Garret Frerichs and Oezlem Cetin.)

---

[56]Previously produced Off-Broadway 13 January-13 February 2000 at the New York Theatre Workshop for 33? performances.

[57]Not in performance order. "Dirty Blonde" is the only new song written especially for this production.

2000–2001 SEASON

Carolee Carmello, Lonny Price, and Randy Graff in A CLASS ACT
Joan Marcus/Photofest

2000-2001 SEASON

2000.13

PENN & TELLER

A New Edition of the Comedy Revue in Two Acts. Written by Penn Gillette and Teller. Directed by Ken Krashner Lewis and Nathan Santucci. Opened 6 June 2000 at the Beacon Theatre and closed 11 June 2000 after 8 performances.

CAST: PENN GILLETTE; TELLER.

2000.14

BORSCHT BELT BUFFET ON BROADWAY

A Musical Revue in One Act. Staged by Dan Siretta. Musical director, Zalmen Mlotek. Associate producers, Arnold Graham, Howard Rapp. Produced by NYK Productions, Inc. Opened 24 October 2000 at Town Hall and closed 6 November 2000 after 16 performances.

CAST: BRUCE ADLER, DAVID "Dudu" FISHER, MAL Z. LAWRENCE.

MUSICAL NUMBERS, SPECIALTIES[1]

"Borscht Belt Buffet"
B. Adler, D. Fisher, M. Z. Lawrence
Hebrew language sketch
B. Adler, D. Fisher, M. Z. Lawrence
Bruce Adler Specialty
["It Don't Mean a Thing If It Ain't Got That Swing" (Jewish Be-bop version)
"Style"
"Makin' Whoopee" (from WHOOPEE)(Eddie Cantor impression)
"If I Were the King of the Forest" (Bert Lahr impression)
"You Gotta Start Each Day with a Song" (Jimmy Durante impression)
"Bessie Mae" (Menasha Skulnick impression)
"Singin' in the Rain" (Gene Kelly impression)
"Rockabye Your Baby with a Dixie Melody" (Al Jolson impression)
"The Candy Man" (Sammy Davis impression)
"The Birth of the Blues" (Sammy Davis impression)
"The Palace of the Czar" (from THOSE WERE THE DAYS) (Danny Kaye impression)
Yiddish language sketch
"Oh They Call Me Kullman with a capital K"
Cowboy Medley
"Huz-zah-zah"]
"Romania"
B. Adler, D. Fisher, M. Z. Lawrence
"Dudu" Fisher Specialty
["Shalom" (from MILK AND HONEY, in Hebrew)
"Memory" (from CATS)
"Kol Nidre" (interspersed with musical quotes from LES MISERABLES)
(concluding with "Who Am I?" and "Bring Him Home")
"All I Ask of You" (from THE PHANTOM OF THE OPERA)
"The Phantom of the Opera" (from THE PHANTOM OF THE OPERA)
Broadway Medley (performed in Hebrew)
"Maria" (from WEST SIDE STORY)
"The Music of the Night" (from THE PHANTOM OF THE OPERA)
"Sunrise, Sunset" (from FIDDLER ON THE ROOF)
"Send in the Clowns" (from A LITTLE NIGHT MUSIC)
"Don't Cry for Me, Argentina" (from EVITA)
"Oklahoma" (from OKLAHOMA!)
"All That Jazz" (from CHICAGO)
"Edelweiss" (from THE SOUND OF MUSIC)
"Climb Every Mountain" (from THE SOUND OF MUSIC)
"The Impossible Dream" (from MAN OF LaMANCHA)]
The Audition
B. Adler, D. Fisher, M Z. Lawrence
Mal. Z. Lawrence Specialty
Florida, Lancaster (Penn.), Atlantic City, Catskills sketches
Vocal Medley (including "Killing Me Softly" and "Knock Three Times")
Bruce Springsteen
"Borscht Belt on Broadway" (Finale)
B. Adler, D. Fisher, M. Z. Lawrence

[1]Musical numbers and specialties not listed in programs.

2000.15

THE FULL MONTY

A Musical in Two Acts. Book by Terrence McNally (based on the film of the same name with screenplay by Simon Beaufoy). Music and Lyrics by David Yazbek. Directed by Jack O'Brien. Choreographed by Jerry Mitchell. Scenic design by John Arnone. Costume design by Robert Morgan. Lighting design by Howell Binkley. Sound design by Tom Clark. Orchestrations by Harold Wheeler. Dance arrangements by Zane Mark. Music direction/Vocal and Incidental Music Arrangements by Ted Sperling. Produced by Fox Searchlight Pictures, Lindsey Law, Thomas Hall. Opened 26 October 2000 at the Eugene O'Neill Theatre, still running at time of this writing.

CAST (in order of appearance): *Georgie Bukatinsky*: ANNIE GOLDEN. *Buddy "Keno" Walsh*: Denis Jones. *Reg Willoughby*: TODD WEEKS. *Jerry Lukowski*: PATRICK WILSON. *Dave Bukatinsky*: JOHN ELLISON CONLEE. *Malcolm MacGregor*: JASON DANIELY. *Ethan Girard*: ROMAIN FRUGÉ. *Nathan Lukowski*: Nicholas Cutro or Thomas Michael Fiss. *Susan Hershey*: Laura Marie Duncan. *Joanie Lish*: Jannie Jones. *Estelle Genovese*: Liz McConahay. *Pam Lukowski*: LISA DATZ. *Teddy Slaughter*: Angelo Fraboni. *Molly MacGregor*: Patti Perkins. *Harold Nichols*: MARCUS NEVILLE. *Vicki Nichols*: EMILY SKINNER. *Jeanette Burmeister*: KATHLEEN FREEMAN. *Noah "Horse" T. Simmons*: ANDRÉ DeSHIELDS. *Moving Man*: C. E. Smith. *Police Sergeant*: C. E. Smith. *Social Worker*: Jannie Jones. *Minister*: Jay Douglas. *Tony Giordano*: Jimmy Smagula. *Swings*: Sue-Anne Morrow, Jason Opsahl, Matthew Stocke, Ronald Wyche.

The action is set in Buffalo, New York, at the present time.

ACT 1

"Scrap"
P. Wilson, J. E. Conlee, M. Neville, J. Daniely, R. Frugé, T. Weeks, Men
"It's a Woman's World"
A. Golden, L. M. Duncan, J. Jones, L. McConahay
"Man"
P. Wilson, J. E. Conlee
"Big Ass Rock"
P. Wilson, J. E. Conlee, J. Daniely
"Life with Harold"
M. Neville, E. Skinner
"Big Black Man"
A. DeShields, the Guys
"You Rule My World"
J. E. Conlee, M. Neville
"Michael Jordan's Ball"
The Guys

ACT 2

"Jeanette's Showbiz Number" (Things Could Be Better)
K. Freeman, the Guys
"Breeze Off the River"
P. Wilson
"The Goods"
P. Wilson, J. E. Conlee, M. Neville, J. Daniely, R. Frugé, A. DeShields, the Women
"You Walk with Me"
J. Daniely, R. Frugé
"You Rule My World" (reprise)
A. Golden, E. Skinner
"Let It Go"
P. Wilson, R. Frugé, J. Daniely, J. E. Conlee, A. DeShields, M. Neville, the Company

2000.16 MATTERS OF THE HEART

A One-Woman Concert in Two Acts. Conceived and directed by Scott Wittman. Additional dialogue by John Weidman. Musical direction and arrangements by Dick Gallagher. Lighting by John Hastings. Sound by Mark Fiore. Gowns designed by Oscar de la Renta. Produced by Lincoln Center Theatre (André Bishop, Artistic Director, and Bernard Gersten, Executive Producer). Opened 13 November 2000 at the Vivian Beaumont Theatre and closed 17 December 2000 after 11 performances[2].

CAST: PATTI LuPONE.

ACT 1[3]

"Love Makes the World Go Round" (Theme from CARNIVAL)
(*Music and Lyrics by* Bob Merrill.)
"I'm in Love with a Wonderful Guy" (from SOUTH PACIFIC)
(*Music by* Richard Rodgers. *Lyrics by* Oscar Hammerstein II.)
"God Only Knows"
(*Music and Lyrics by* Brian Wilson.)
"Easy to Be Hard" (from HAIR)
(*Music by* Galt MacDermott. *Lyrics by* James Rado and Gerome Ragni.)
"The Last Time I Saw Richard"
(*Music and Lyrics by* Joni Mitchell.)
"Where Love Resides"
(*Music and Lyrics by* Jimmy Webb.)
"Shattered Illusions"
(*Music and Lyrics by* Adele Anderson and Dillie Keane.)
"Unexpressed"
(*Music and Lyrics by* John Bucchino.)
"Not a Day Goes By" (from MERRILY WE ROLL ALONG)
(*Music and Lyrics by* Stephen Sondheim.)
"Playbill"
(*Music and Lyrics by* John Bucchino.)
"Alone Again (Naturally)"
(*Music and Lyrics by* Gilbert O'Sullivan.)
"Better Off Dead"
(*Music and Lyrics by* Randy Newman.)
"Air That I Breath"
(*Music and Lyrics by* Albert Hammond and Michael Hazelwood.)
"Sand and Water"
(*Music and Lyrics by* Beth Nielson Chapman.)
"Being Alive" (from COMPANY)
(*Music and Lyrics by* Stephen Sondheim.)

ACT 2

"When the World Was Young"
(*Music by* Angele Vannier and Phillipe Bosch. *Lyrics by* Johnny Mercer.)/
"I Never Do Anything Twice" (from THE SEVEN PERCENT SOLUTION, film)
(*Music and Lyrics by* Stephen Sondheim.)
"Back to Before"
(*Music by* Stephen Flaherty. *Lyrics by* Lynn Ahrens.)
"Real Emotional Girl"
(*Music and Lyrics by* Randy Newman.)
"My Father"
(*Music and Lyrics by* Judy Collins.)
"Look Mummy, No Hands"
(*Music and Lyrics by* Dillie Keane.)
"Time After Time"
(*Music and Lyrics by* Cyndi Lauper and Rob Hyman.)
"Another Auld Lang Syne"
(*Music and Lyrics by* Dan Fogelberg.)
"Hello, Young Lovers" (from THE KING AND I)
(*Music by* Richard Rodgers. *Lyrics by* Oscar Hammerstein II.)
"My Best to You"
(*Music and Lyrics by* Gene Willadsen and Isham Jones.)

[2]Played an irregular schedule of Sunday evening and Monday performances concurrent with the run of CONTACT.
[3]Not in performance order.

2000.17 THE ROCKY HORROR SHOW

A Revival of the Rock Musical in Two Acts[4]. Book, music and lyrics by Richard O'Brien. Directed by Christopher Ashley. Choreographed by Jerry Mitchell. Scenic design by David Rockwell. Costume design by David C. Woolard. Lighting design by Paul Gallo. Sound design by Richard Fitzgerald/Domonic Sack. Video design by Batwin + Robin Productions. Musical direction and vocal arrangements by Henry Aronson. New orchestrations by Doug Katsaros. Original orchestrations by Richard Hartley. Produced by Jordan Roth, by arrangement with Christopher Malcolm, Howard Panter and Richard O'Brien for the Rocky Horror Company, Ltd. Opened 15 November 2000 at the Circle-in-the-Square Theatre; closed 23 September 2001; re-opened 30 October 2001 and closed 6 January 2002 after 436 performances.

CAST (in order of appearance): *Usherette*: DAPHNE RUBIN-VEGA. *Usherette*: JOAN JETT. *Janet Weiss*: ALICE RIPLEY. *Brad Majors*: JARROD EMICK. *Narrator*: DICK CAVETT. *Riff Raff*: RAÚL ESPARZA. *Magenta*: DAPHNE RUBIN-VEGA. *Columbia*: JOAN JETT. *Frank 'N' Furter*: TOM HEWITT. *Rocky*: SEBASTIAN LaCAUSE. *Eddie*: LEA DeLARIA. *Dr. Scott*: LEA DeLARIA. *Phantoms*: Kevin Cahoon, Deidre Goodwin, Aiko Nakasone, Mark Price, Jonathan Sharp, James Stovall. *Swings*: John Jeffrey Sharp, Kristen Lee Kelly.

Time: Then and Now. *Place*: Here and There.

ACT 1

"Science Fiction Double Feature"
D. Ruben-Vega, J. Jett [Usherettes], Phantoms
"Damn It, Janet"
J. Emick, A. Ripley, Phantoms
"Over at the Frankenstein Place"
J. Emick, A. Ripley, R. Esparza, Phantoms
"The Time Warp"
R. Esparza, D. Ruben-Vega, J. Jett, D. Cavett, Company
"Sweet Transvestite"
T. Hewitt, J. Emick, R. Esparza, D. Ruben-Vega, J. Jett, Phantoms
"The Sword of Damocles"
S. LaCause, D. Cavett, Company
"I Can Make You a Man" (Charles Atlas Song)
T. Hewitt, Company
"Hot Patootie" (What Ever Happened to Saturday Night)
L. DeLaria [Eddie], Company
"I Can Make You a Man" (reprise)
T. Hewitt, Company

ACT 2

"Touch-A-Touch-A-Touch Me"
A. Ripley, D. Ruben-Vega, J. Jett, Phantoms
"Once in a While"
J. Emick, Phantoms
"Eddie's Teddy"
L. DeLaria [Dr. Scott], D. Cavett, J. Jett, T. Hewitt, Company
"Planet Shmanet – Wise Up Janet Weiss"
T. Hewitt, Company
"Floorshow/Rose Tint My World" (It Was Great When It All Began)
J. Jett, S. LaCause, J. Emick, A. Ripley, T. Hewitt, R. Esparza, Company
"I'm Going Home"
T. Hewitt, Company
"Super Heroes"
J. Emick, A. Ripley, D. Cavett, Phantoms
"Science Fiction Double Feature" [reprise]
D. Ruben-Vega, J. Jett, Phantoms

2000.18 SEUSSICAL

A Musical in Two Acts. Conceived by Eric Idle, Lynn Ahrens and Stephen Flaherty, from the works of Dr. Seuss [Theodore Geisel]. Book by Lynn Ahrens and Stephen Flaherty. Music by Stephen Flaherty. Lyrics by Lynn Ahrens. Directed by Frank Galati, (Rob Marshall). Choreographed by Kathleen Marshall. Scenery by Eugene Lee, (Tony Walton). Costumes by William Ivey Long. Lighting by Natasha Katz. Sound by Jonathan Deans.

[4]Previously produced in New York 10 March 1975 at the Belasco Theatre for 45 performances. The 1975 production was presented in One Act, 11 Scenes, a Prologue and Epilogue.

Orchestrations by Douglas Besterman. Musical director, David Holcenberg. Dance arranger, David Chase. Vocal arranger, Stephen Flaherty. Executive Producers, Gary Gunas and Alecia Parker. Produced by SFX Theatrical Group, Barry and Fran Weissler and Universal Studios, in association with Hal Luftig, Mort Swinsky and Michael Watt. Opened 30 November 2000 at the Richard Rodgers Theatre and closed 20 May 2001 after 197 performances.

CAST: *The Cat in the Hat*: DAVID SHINER. *Horton the Elephant*: KEVIN CHAMBERLIN. *Gertrude McFuzz*: JANINE LaMANNA. *Mayzie LaBird*: MICHELE PAWK. *JoJo*: ANTHONY BLAIR-HALL, Andrew Keenan-Bolger (alt.). *Sour Kangaroo*: Sharon Wilkins. *The Mayor of Whoville*: Stuart Zagnit. *Mrs. Mayor*: Alice Playten. *Cat's Helpers*: Joyce Chittick, Jennifer Cody, Justin Greer, Mary Ann Lamb, Darren Lee, Jerome Vivona. *General Genghis Khan Schmitz*: Erick Devine. *Bird Girls*: Natascia A. Diaz, Sara Gettelfinger, Catrice Joseph. *Wickersham Brothers*: David Engel, Tom Plotkin, Eric Jordan Young. *The Grinch*: William Ryall. *JoJo's Teacher*: Monique L. Midgette. *JoJo's Principal*: Casey Nicholaw. *Vlad Vladikoff*: Darren Lee. *Judge Yertle the Turtle*: Devin Richards. *Marshal of the Court*: Ann Harada.

Citizens of the Jungle of Nool, Whos, Mayor's Aides, Fish, Cadets, Hunters, Circus McGurkus Animals and Performers: Joyce Chittick, Jennifer Cody, Erich Devine, Natascia Diaz, David Engel, Sara Gettelfinger, Justin Greer, Ann Harada, Catrice Joseph, Eddie Korbich, Mary Ann Lamb, Darren Lee, Monique L. Midgette, Casey Nicholaw, Tom Plotkin, Devin Richards, William Ryall, Jerome Vivona, Sharon Wilkins, Eric Jordan Young. *Swings*: Shaun Amyot, Jenny Hill, Michelle Kittrell, David Lowenstein.

ACT 1

"Oh, the Thinks You Can Think!"
D. Shiner, the Company

"Our Story Begins"
D. Shiner

"Horton Hears a Who"
K. Chamberlin, Bird Girls, Citizens of the Jungle of Nool

"Biggest Blame Fool"
S. Wilkins, K. Chamberlin, D. Engel, T. Plotkin, E. J. Young, Bird Girls, J. LaManna, M. Pawk, Citizens of the Jungle of Nool, D. Shiner

"Here on Who"
S. Zagnit, A. Playten, W. Ryall, Whos, K. Chamberlin

"A Day for the Cat in the Hat"
D. Shiner, A. B. Hall, Cat's Helpers

"It's Possible" (In McElligott's Pool)
A. B. Hall, D. Shiner, the Fish

"How to Raise a Child"
S. Zagnit, A. Playten

"The Military"
E. Devine, S. Zagnit, A. Playten, A. B. Hall, Cadets

"Alone in the Universe"
A. B. Hall, K. Chamberlin

"The One Feather Tail of Miss Gertrude McFuzz"
J. LaManna

"Amayzing Mayzie"
M. Pawk, J. LaManna, Bird Girls

"Amayzing Gertrude"
J. LaManna, D. Shiner, Bird Girls

"Monkey Around"
D. Engel, T. Plotkin

"Chasing the Whos"
K. Chamberlin, S. Wilkins, Bad Girls, D. Engel, T. Plotkin, D. Shiner, D. Lee, the Whos

"How Lucky You Are"
D. Shiner

"Notice Me, Horton"
J. LaManna, K. Chamberlin

"How Lucky You Are" (reprise)
M. Pawk, K. Chamberlin, D. Shiner

Act 1 Finale
Full Company

ACT 2

"How Lucky You Are" (reprise)
D. Shiner

"Our Story Resumes"
D. Shiner, K. Chamberlin, S. Zagnit, A. Playten, J. LaManna, Bird Girls

"Egg, Nest and Tree"
S. Wilkins, Bird Girls, D. Engel, T. Plotkin, D. Shiner, Cat's Helpers, Hunters

"The Circus McGurkus"
D. Shiner, K. Chamberlin, Circus McGurkus Animals and Performers

"The Circus on Tour"
K. Chamberlin

"Mayzie in Palm Beach"
M. Pawk, D. Shiner, K. Chamberlin

"Solla Sollew"
K. Chamberlin, Circus McGurkus Animals and Performers, S. Zagnit, A. Playten, A. B. Hall

"The Whos' Christmas Pageant"
W. Ryall, the Whos

"A Message from the Front"
E. Devine, S. Zagnit, A. Playten, Cadets

"Alone in the Universe" (reprise)
A. B. Hall, K. Chamberlin

"Havin' a Hunch"
D. Shiner, A. B. Hall, Cat's Helpers

"All for You"
J. LaManna, Bird Girls

"The People Versus Horton the Elephant"
K. Chamberlin, S. Wilkins, D. Engel, T. Plotkin, A. Harada, D. Richards, Bird Girls, J. LaManna, S. Zagnit, A. Playten, A. B. Hall, Whos, D. Shiner

Finale/"Oh, the Thinks You Can Think!" (reprise)
Full Company

2000.19 A CHRISTMAS CAROL

A Revival of the Musical in One Act, 13 Scenes[5]. Book by Mike Ockrent and Lynn Ahrens. Based on the novel of the same name by Charles Dickens. Music by Alan Menken. Lyrics by Lynn Ahrens. Direction by Mike Ockrent. Choreographed by Susan Stroman. Setting design by Tony Walton. Costume design by William Ivey Long. Lighting design by Jules Fisher and Peggy Eisenhauer. Sound design by Tony Meola. Projections by Wendall K. Harrington. Flying by Foy. Associate director, Ray Roderick. Associate choreographer, Chris Peterson. Musical direction by Paul Gemignani. Orchestrations by Michael Starobin and Douglas Besterman. Dance arrangements and incidental music by Glen Kelly. Executive producer, Howard Kolins. Producer, Marshall Jones. Presented by American Express. Opened 30 November 2000 at the (Paramount) Theatre, Madison Square Garden and closed 31 December 2000 after 63 performances.

CAST (in order of appearance): *Beadle*: Del-Bourree Bach. *Mr. Smythe*: ERIC PINNICK. *Grace Smythe*: Catherine Marie Downey, Amelia Harris. *Scrooge*: FRANK LANGELLA. *Bob Cratchit*: NICK CORLEY. *Charity Men*: Roland Rusinek, Wayne Schroder, Erik Stein. *Old Joe*: Kenneth McMullen. *Street Urchins*: Johnny Cenicola, Patrick Dunn, Nicholas Jonas, Lindsey Pickering, Justin Riordan, Lily Havala Wen. *Mrs. Cratchit*: Whitney Webster. *Tiny Tim*: Patrick Stogner, Jimmy Walsh. *Poulterer*: Roland Rusinek. *Sandwichboard Man*: D'AMBROSE BOYD. *Jonathon*: Gerard Canonico, Scott Owen Cumberbatch. *Lamplighter*: KEN JENNINGS. *Blind Hag*: Joan Barber. *Fred*: JAMES JUDY. *Mrs. Mopps*: Marilyn Pasekoff. *Ghost of Jacob Marley*: PAUL KANDEL. *Ghost of Christmas Past*: KEN JENNINGS. *Lights of Christmas Past*: Leo Alvarez, James Hadley, Deon Ridley, David Rosales. *Judge*: Roland Rusinek. *Scrooge at 8*: Nicholas Jonas, Justin Riordan. *Scrooge's Mother*: Joan Barber. *Scrooge's Father*: Wayne Schroder. *Mr. Hawkins*: Kenneth McMullen. *Scrooge at 12*: Johnny Cenicola, Patrick Dunn. *Fan*: Lindsey Pickering, Lily Havala Wen. *Fezziwig*: Daniel Marcus. *Scrooge at 18*: Joe Cassidy. *Young Marley*: Ken Barnett. *Mrs. Fezziwig*: Kelly Ellenwood. *Emily*: Kate Dawson. *Ghost of Christmas Present*: D'AMBROSE

[5]Originally produced in New York 1 December 1994 at the Paramount Theatre, Madison Square Garden for 71 performances. For Synopsis of Scenes and Musical Numbers, see original 1994 production. For this year's and the 1995, 1996, 1997, 1998, and 1999 revivals the following changes were made:

Scene 1 and "The Years Are Passing By" were dropped.

Added to Scene 2 (former Scene 3) before "Street Song":

"You Mean More to Me"
T. Gross, A. B. Hall or C. Valiando

"The Years Are Passing By" (reprise) in former Scene 13 (new Scene 12) was replaced by:

"London Town Carol"
A. Barruch or K. Kanagawa

Note: The production played an irregular schedule of multiple daily performances.

BOYD. *The Cratchit Children*: Johnny Cenicola, Patrick Dunn, Lindsey Pickering, Lily Havala Wen. *Sally*, Fred's wife: La Tanya Hall. *Ignorance*: Nicholas Jones, Justin Riordan. *Want*: Amelia Harris, Catherine Marie Downey. *Undertakers*: Ken Barnett, Wayne Schroder. *Ghost of Christmas Yet-To-Be*: CHRISTINE DUNHAM.

Business Men, Gifts, Ghosts and the People of London: Leo Alvarez, Del-Bourree Bach, Joan Barber, Ken Barnett, Hayes Bergman, Joe Cassidy, Candy Cook, James Hadley, La Tanya Hall, Amy Heggins, James Judy, Donna Kapral, Carrie Kenneally, Natalie King, Daniel Marcus, Kenneth McMullen, Patrick Mullaney, Shaun R. Parry, Marilyn Pasekoff, Gail Pennington, Erick Pinnick, Deon Ridley, David Rosales, Parisa Ross, Roland Rusinek, Wayne Schroder, Debra Denys Smith, Erik Stein, Yasuko Tamaki, Whitney Webster, Mindy Franzese Wild. *Swings*: Jane Brockman, Rob Donohoe, Donna Dunmire, Jeffrey Hankinson, Ann Kittredge, Cynthia Thole, Matthew J. Vargo, Craig Waletzko. *Angels*: Terrill Middle School Broadway Chorus, YPC Jubilee Chorus, La Petite Musicale, South Side Middle School Chorale. *Red Children's Cast*: Scott Owen Cumberbatch, Catherine Marie Downey, Patrick Dunn, Lindsey Pickering, Justin Riordan. *Green Children's Cast*: Gerard Canonico, Johnny Cenicola, Amelia Harris, Nicholas Jonas, Lily Havala Wen. *Children Swings*: Harley Adams, Allison Fischer, Kenny Gureck.

2000.20

JANE EYRE

A Musical in Two Acts. Book and additional lyrics by John Caird. Based on the novel of the same name by Charlotte Brontë. Music and lyrics by Paul Gordon. Directed by John Caird and Scott Schwartz. Settings by John Napier. Costumes by Andreane Neofitou. Lighting by Jules Fisher and Peggy Eisenhauer. Sound design by Mark Menard and Tom Clark. Dance and movement by Jayne Patterson. Projections design by John Napier, Lisa Podgur Cuscuna, Jules Fisher and Peggy Eisenhauer. Musical director, vocal and incidental music arrangements by Steve Tyler. Orchestrations by Larry Hochman. Produced by Annette Niemtzow, Janet Robinson, Pamela Koslow and Margaret McFeeley Golden, in association with Jennifer Manocherian and Carolyn Kim McCarthy. Opened 10 December 2000 at the Brooks Atkinson Theatre and closed 10 June 2001 after 210 performances.

CAST (in order of appearance): *Jane Eyre*: MARLA SCHAFFEL. *Young Jane*: Lisa Musser. *Young John Reed*: Lee Zarrett. *Mrs. Reed*: Gina Ferrall. *Mr. Brocklehurst*: Don Richard. *Miss Scatcherd*: Marguerite MacIntyre. *Marigold*: MARY STOUT. *Helen Burns*: Jayne Patterson. *Schoolgirls*: Nell Balaban, Andrea Bowen, Elizabeth DeGrazia, Bonnie Gleicher, Rita Glynn, Gina Lamparella. *Mrs. Fairfax*: MARY STOUT. *Robert*: Bruce Dow. *Adele*: Andrea Bowen. *Grace Poole*: Nell Balaban. *Edward Fairfax Rochester*: JAMES BARBOUR. *Bertha*: Marguerite MacIntyre. *Blanche Ingram*: ELIZABETH DeGRAZIA. *Lady Ingram*: Gina Ferrall. *Mary Ingram*: Jayne Patterson. *Young Lord Ingram*: Lee Zarrett. *Mr. Eshton*: Stephen R. Buntrock. *Amy Eshton*: Nell Balaban. *Louisa Eshton*: Gina Lamparella. *Colonel Dent*: Don Richard. *Mrs. Dent*: Marguerite MacIntyre. *Richard Mason*: Bill Nolte. *The Gypsy*: Marje Bubrosa [JAMES BARBOUR]. *Vicar*: Don Richard. *St. John Rivers*: STEPHEN R. BUNTROCK.

Swings: Sandy Binion, Bradley Dean, Erica Schroeder.

The action is set in England in the 1840s at Gateshead Hall, Lowood School, Thornfield Hall and the surrounding Yorkshire Moors.

ACT 1

"The Orphan"
M. Schaffel
"Children of God"
School Girls, D. Richard, G. Ferrall, M. MacIntyre, Ensemble
"Forgiveness"
J. Patterson, L. Musser, M. Schaffel
"The Graveyard"
M. Schaffel, L. Musser, Ensemble
"Sweet Liberty"
M. Schaffel, Ensemble
"Perfectly Nice"
M. Stout, A. Bowen, M. Schaffel
"As Good as You"
J. Barbour
"Secret Soul"
M. Schaffel, J. Barbour
"The Finer Things"
E. DeGrazia
"Oh How You Look in the Light"
J. Barbour, E. DeGrazia, Ensemble
"The Pledge"
M. Schaffel, J. Barbour
"Sirens"
J. Barbour, M. Schaffel, M. MacIntyre

ACT 2

"Things Beyond This Earth"
Ensemble
"Painting Her Portrait"
M. Schaffel
"In the Light of the Virgin Morning"
M. Schaffel, E. DeGrazia
"The Gypsy"
M. Bubrosa
"The Proposal"
M. Schaffel, J. Barbour
"Slip of a Girl"
M. Stout, M. Schaffel, B. Dow, A. Bowen
"The Wedding"
Ensemble
"Wild Boy"
J. Barbour, M. Schaffel, M. MacIntyre, Ensemble
"Sirens" (reprise)
M. Schaffel, J. Barbour
"Farewell Good Angel"
J. Barbour
"My Maker"
M. Schaffel, Ensemble
"Forgiveness" (reprise)
G. Ferrall, M. Schaffel, Ensemble
"The Voice Across the Moors"
S. R. Buntrock, M. Schaffel, J. Barbour
"Poor Sister"
B. Nolte, M. Schaffel
"Brave Enough for Love"
M. Schaffel, J. Barbour, Ensemble

2001.01

A CLASS ACT

A Musical in Two Acts, 17 Scenes[6]. Music and lyrics by Edward Kleban. Book by Linda Kline and Lonny Price. Directed by Lonny Price. Choreographed by Marguerite Derricks. Scenic design by James Noone. Costume design by Carrie Robbins. Lighting design by Kevin Adams. Sound design by Acme Sound Partners. Musical direction, additional arrangements by David Loud. Incidental music by Todd Ellison. Orchestrations by Larry Hochman. Production consultant, Lori Steinberg. Executive producer, East Egg Entertainment. Executive producer, East Egg Entertainment. Associate producers, Robyn Goodman, Tokyo Broadcasting System/Kumiko Yoshii. Marty Bell, Chase Mishkin and Arielle Tepper present the Manhattan Theatre Club Production. Opened 11 March 2001 at the Ambassador Theatre and closed 10 June 2001 after 105 performances.

CAST[7] (in order of appearance): *Lucy et al*: DONNA BULLOCK. *Bobby, (Michael Bennett) et al*: DAVID HIBBARD. *Ed (Kleban)*: LONNY PRICE. *Felicia et al*: SARA RAMIREZ. *Lehman (Engel) et al*: PATRICK QUINN. *Charley, (Marvin Hamlisch) et al*: JEFF BLUMENKRANTZ. *Mona et al.*: NANCY KATHRYN ANDERSON. *Sophie*: RANDY GRAFF.

Act 1, Scene 1: The Shubert Theatre, 1988. *Scene 2*: Hillside Hospital, 1958. *Scene 3*: The Shubert Theatre, 1988. *Scene 4*: The BMI Workshop, 1966. *Scene 5*: Ed's Apartment, 1966. *Scene 6*: Recording Studio/Columbia Records, 1966-1971. *Scene 7*: Outside the Royal Alexandra Theatre, Toronto, 1972.

Act 2, Scene 1: The Shubert Theatre, 1988; Manhattan, 1973. *Scene 2*: Sophie's Laboratory, 1972. *Scene 3*: Central Park, 1973. *Scene 4*: Michael Bennett's Studio, 1973. *Scene 5*: The Public Theatre, 1974-1975. *Scene 6*: Manhattan, 1975-1985. *Scene 7*: Sophie's Laboratory, 1985. *Scene 8*: The BMI Musical Theatre Workshop, 1986. *Scene 9*: St. Vincent's Hospital, 1987. *Scene 10*: The Shubert Theatre, 1988.

---

[6]First produced in New York Off-Broadway 9 November-10 December 2000 at Manhattan Theater Club's City Center Stage II for 38 performances.
[7]At the Manhattan Theatre Club, the following played roles but did not transfer to Broadway: *Felicia*: JULIA MURNEY. *Lehman*: JONATHAN FREEMAN. *Lucy*: CAROLEE CARMELLO. *Charley*: RAY WILLS. Choreography by Scott Wise. Dropped before Broadway were:

"Making Up Ways" (Act 1, Scene 5)
L. Price
"When the Dawn Breaks" (Act 2, Scene 8)
L. Price

ACT 1
Scene 1
"Light on My Feet"
L. Price, Company
(*Additional lyrics by* Brian Stein.)
Scene 2
"The Fountain in the Garden"
Company
"One More Beautiful Song"
L. Price, R. Graff
Scene 4
"Fridays at Four"
Company
"Bobby's Song"
D. Hibbard
"Charm Song"
P. Quinn, Company
"Paris Through the Window"
L. Price, D. Hibbard, J. Blumenkrantz
(*Additional lyrics by* Glenn Slater.)
Scene 5
"Mona"
N. K. Anderson
Scene 6
"Under Separate Cover"
D. Bullock, R. Graff, L. Price
"Don't Do It Again"
S. Ramirez, L. Price
"Gaugin's Shoes"
L. Price, Company
"Don't Do It Again" (reprise)
P. Quinn
Scene 7
"Follow Your Star"
R. Graff, L. Price

ACT 2
Scene 1
"Better"[8]
L. Price, Company
Scene 2
"Scintillating Sophie"
L. Price
"Next Best Thing to Love"
R. Graff
Scene 4
"Broadway Boogie Woogie"
D. Bullock
Scene 5
A CHORUS LINE excerpts ("At the Ballet," "One," "What I Did for Love")
Company
(*Music by* Marvin Hamlisch.)
Scene 6
"Better" (reprise)
L. Price, Company
"I Choose You"
L. Price, D. Bullock
"The Nightmare"
L. Price
Scene 7
"Say Something Funny"
Company
Scene 8
"I Won't Be There"
L. Price
Scene 9
"Self-Portrait"
L. Price
Scene 10
"Self-Portrait" (reprise)
Company

2001.02 FOLLIES

A Revival of the Musical in Two Acts[9]. Book by James Goldman. Music and lyrics by Stephen Sondheim. Directed by Matthew Warchus. Choreography by Kathleen Marshall. Set design by Mark Thompson. Costume design by Theoni V. Aldredge. Lighting design by Hugh Vanstone. Sound design by Jonathan Deans. Original dance music arranged by John Berkman. Additional dance music arranged by David Chase. Associate choreographer, Joey Pizzi. Associate director, Thomas Caruso. Orchestrations by Jonathan Tunick. Musical direction by Eric Stern. Executive producer, Frank P. Scardino. Produced by the Roundabout Theatre (Todd Haimes, Artistic Director; Ellen Richard, Managing Director; Julia C. Levy, Executive Director). Opened 5 April 2001 at the Belasco Theatre and closed 14 July 2001 after 116 performances.

CAST (in order of appearance): *Dimitri Weismann*: LOUIS ZORICH. *Showgirls*: Jessica Leigh Brown, Colleen Dunn, Amy Heggins, Wendy Waring. *Sally Durant Plummer*: JUDITH IVEY. *Sandra Crane*: Nancy Ringham. *Dee Dee West*: Dorothy Stanley. *Stella Deems*: CAROL WOODS. *Sam Deems*: Peter Cormican. *Solange LaFitte*: JANE WHITE. *Roscoe*: Larry Raiken. *Heidi Schiller*: JOAN ROBERTS. *Emily Whitman*: MARGE CHAMPION. *Theodore Whitman*: DONALD SADDLER. *Carlotta Campion*: POLLY BERGEN. *Hattie Walker*: BETTY GARRETT. *Phyllis Rogers Stone*: BLYTHE DANNER. *Benjamin Stone*: GREGORY HARRISON. *Buddy Plummer*: TREAT WILLIAMS. *Young Phyllis*: Erin Dilly. *Young Sally*: Lauren Ward. *Young Dee Dee*: Roxane Barlow. *Young Emily*: Carole Bentley. *Young Carlotta*: Sally Mae. Dunn. *Young Sandra*: Dottie Earle. *Young Solange*: Jacqueline Hendy. *Young Heidi*: Brooke Sunny Moriber. *Young Hattie*" Kelli O'Hara. *Young Stella*: Allyson Tucker. *Young Ben*: Richard Roland. *Young Buddy*: Joey Sorge. *Young Theodore*: Rod McCune. *Kevin*: Stephen Campanella. *"Margie"*: Roxane Barlow. *"Sally"*: Jessica Leigh Brown.

Ladies and Gentlemen of the Ensemble: Roxane Barlow, Carole Bentley, Jessica Leigh Brown, Stephen Campanella, Colleen Dunn, Sally Mae Dunn, Dottie Earle, Aldrin Gonzalez, Amy Heggins, Jacqueline Hendy, Rod McCune, Kelli O'Hara, T. Oliver Reid, Alex Sanchez, Allyson Tucker, Matt Wall, Wendy Waring. *Swings*: Nadine Isenegger, Parisa Ross, Jeffrey Hankinson.

2001.03 BELLS ARE RINGING

A Revival of the Musical Comedy in Two Acts[10]. Book and lyrics by Betty Comden and Adolph Green. Music by Jule Styne. Directed by Tina Landau. Choreography by Jeff Calhoun. Settings by Riccardo Hernandez. Costumes designed by David C. Woolard. Lighting by Donald Holder. Sound design, Acme Sound Partners. Musical Direction and Vocal Arrangements, David Evans. Orchestrations by Don Sebesky. Dance Music Arrangements, Mark Hummel. Associate producers, Alan S. Kopit, Richard Berger. Produced by Mitchell Maxwell, Mark Balsam, Victoria Maxwell, Robert Barandes, Richard Bernstein, Mark Goldberg, James L. Simon, in association with Fred H. Krones and Momentum Productions, Inc. Opened 12 April 2001 at the Plymouth Theatre closed 10 June 2001 after 69 performances.

CAST (in order of appearance): *TV Announcer*: Shane Kirkpatrick. *Telephone Girls*: Caitlin Carter, Joan Hess, Emily Hsu, Alice Rietveld. *Sue*: BETH FOWLER. *Gwynne*: Angela Robinson. *Ella Peterson*: FAITH PRINCE. *Carl*: Julio Agustin. *Inspector Barnes*: ROBERT ARI. *Francis*: JEFFREY BEAN. *Sandor*: DAVID GARRISON. *Jeff Moss*: MARC KUDISCH. *Larry Hastings*: David Brummel. *Louie*: Greg Reuter. *Padie,*

---

[8]Previously interpolated into the Off-Broadway revue THE MADWOMAN OF CENTRAL PARK WEST.

[9]Originally produced in New York 4 April 1971 at the Winter Garden for 522 performances. For Synopsis of Musical Numbers, see original 1971 production. First produced in New York in One Act without intermission, this revival added an intermission after "Too Many Mornings." Bolero d'Amour was revised as Danse d'Amour.

[10]First produced in New York 29 November 1956 at the Sam S. Shubert Theatre for 924 performances. Comden & Green revised the book, the order of songs was revised, and the reprise of "Long Before I Knew You" was reassigned to Jeff (M. Kudisch) and dropped from the program listing. "Better Than a Dream," added during the New York run and for national tour and film version, was retained.

the Street Sweeper: Roy Harcourt. *Ludwig Smiley*: Lawrence Clayton. *Charlie Bessemer*: Josh Rhodes. *Dr. Kitchell*: Martin Moran. *Blake Barton*: Darren Ritchie. *Joey*: Shane Kirkpatrick. *Olga*: Caitlin Carter. *Corvello Mob Men*: David Brummel, Greg Reuter. *Maid*: Linda Romoff. *Paul Arnold*: Lawrence Clayton. *Bridgette*: Joan Hess. *Waiter*: Josh Rhodes. *Man on Street*: Josh Rhodes. *Madame Grimaldi*: Joanne Baum. *Mrs. Mallet*: Joan Hess.

Ensemble: Julio Agustin, Joanne Baum, David Brummel, Caitlin Carter, Lawrence Clayton, Roy Harcourt, Joan Hess, Emily Hsu, Shane Kirkpatrick, Greg Reuter, Josh Rhodes, Alice Rietveld, Darren Ritchie, Angela Robinson, Linda Romoff, *Dancers*: Caitlin Carter, Roy Harcourt, Joan Hess, Emily Hsu, Shane Kirkpatrick, Greg Reuter, Josh Rhodes. *Swings*: James Hadley, Stacey Harris, Marc Oka, Kelly Sullivan.

Time: 1956. *Place*: New York City.

ACT 1

"Bells Are Ringing"
Telephone Girls
"It's a Perfect Relationship"
F. Prince
"Independent"
M. Kudisch, Dancers
"You've Got to Do It"
M. Kudisch
"It's a Simple Little System"
D. Garrison, Ensemble
"It's Better Than a Dream"
F. Prince, M. Kudisch
"Hello, Hello There"
L. Clayton, F. Prince, M. Kudisch, Ensemble
"I Met a Girl"
M. Kudisch, Ensemble
"Is It a Crime?"
F. Prince, R. Ari, J. Bean
"Long Before I Knew You"
F. Prince, M. Kudisch

ACT 2

"Mu-Cha-Cha"
J. Agustin, F. Prince, A. Robinson, Dancers
"Just in Time"
M. Kudisch, F. Prince, Ensemble
(*Original dance arrangements by* John Morris.)
"Drop That Name"
F. Prince, Ensemble
"The Party's Over"
F. Prince
"Salzburg"
B. Fowler, D. Garrison
"The Midas Touch"
M. Moran, Dancers
"I'm Goin' Back"
F. Prince
Finale
The Company

2001.04 BLAST

A Music Revue in Two Acts. Directed by James Mason. Choreography by Jim Moore, George Pinney, John Vanderkolff. Music director, James Prime. Scene and costume design, Mark Thompson. Lighting design, Hugh Vanstone. Orchestrations by James Prime. Sound design, Mark Hood, Bobby Aitken, Tom Morse. Tour direction, Dodger Touring, Big League Theatricals. Associate Producer, Donnie Vandoren. Executive producer, Dodger Management Group. Presented by Cook Group Incorporated and Star of Indiana. Opened 17 April 2001 at the Broadway Theatre and closed 23 September 2001 after 173 performances.

CAST [in alphabetical order]: Trey Allgood III (Visual Ensemble, Voice), Rachel J. Anderson (French Horn, Mellophone, Voice), Nicholas E. Angelis (Snare Drum, Percussion, Voice), Matthew A. Banks (Tuba, Euphonium, Voice), Kimberly Beth Baron (French Horn, Mellophone, Keyboard, Voice), Wesley Bullock (Cornet, Trumpet, Didgerydoo, Voice), Mark Burroughs (Tuba), Jesus Cantu, Jr. (Trumpet, Coronet, Keyboard, Voice, Percussion), Jodina Rosario Carey (Visual Ensemble, Voice), Robert Carmical (Trombone, Baritone, Voice), Alan "Otto" Compton (Percussion, Voice), Dayne Delahoussaye (French Horn, Mellophone, Voice), Karen Duggan (Visual Ensemble, Voice), John Elrod (Trombone, Euphonium, Voice), Brandon J. Epperson (Trombone, Didgerydoo, Bass Trombone, Voice), Kenneth Frisby (Visual Ensemble, Voice), J. Derek Gipson (Trumpet, Piccolo Trumpet, Cornet, Voice), Trevor Lee Gooch (Tuba, Didgerydoo, Percussion, Voice), Casey Marshall Gooding (Trumpet, Piccolo Trumpet, Cornet, Didgerydoo, Voice), Bradley Kerr Green (Trombone, Conductor, Trombonium, Didgerydoo, Voice), Benjamin Taber Griffin (Trombone, Bass Trombone, Euphonium, Trombonium, Didgerydoo, Voice), Benjamin Raymond Handel (Percussion, Voice), Benjamin W. Harloff (Trumpet, Piccolo Trumpet, Flugelhorn, Cornet, Mellophone, Voice), Joe Haworth (Euphonium, Percussion, Voice), Darren M. Hazlett (Percussion, Didgerydoo, Voice), Tim Heasley (Trombone, Percussion, Voice), Freddy Hernandez, Jr. (Trumpet, Mellophone, Didgerydoo, Voice), George Hester (Trumpet, Cornet, Mellophone, Voice), Jeremiah Todd Huber (Visual Ensemble, Percussion, Voice), Martin A. Hughes (Visual Ensemble, Voice), Naoki Ishikawa (Percussion, Voice), Stacy J. Johnson (Visual Ensemble, Voice), Sanford R. Jones (Tuba, Didgerydoo, Voice), Anthony F. Leps (Trumpet, Cornet, Mellophone, Didgerydoo, Percussion, Voice), Ray Linkous (Conductor, Tuba, Didgerydoo, Voice), Jean Marie Mallicoat (Euphonium, Didgerydoo, Percussion, Voice), Jack Mansager (Percussion, Voice), Brian Mayle (Didgerydoo, Percussion, Voice), Dave Millen (Trumpet, Voice), Jim Moore (Visual Ensemble, Voice), Westley Morehead (Trombone, Trombonium, Didgerydoo, Voice), David Nash (Percussion, Voice), Jeffrey A. Queen (Snare Drum, Percussion, Voice), Douglas Raines (Percussion, Didgerydoo, Voice), Chris Rasmussen (Percussion, Voice), Joseph J. Reinhart (Trumpet, Cornet, Voice), Jamie L. Roscoe (Visual Ensemble, Voice), Jennifer Ross (Visual Ensemble, Voice), Christopher Eric Rutt (French Horn, Mellophone, Didgerydoo, Percussion, Voice), Christopher J. Schletter (Trombone, Trombonium, Euphonium, Voice), Andrew Schnieders (Percussion, Voice), Jonathan L. Schwartz (Visual Ensemble, Voice), Greg Seale (Percussion, Voice), Andy Smart (Trumpet, Didgerydoo, Voice), Radiah Y. Stewart (Visual Ensemble, Voice), Bryan Anthony Sutton (Visual Ensemble, Voice), Sean Terrell (Trumpet, Didgerydoo, Voice), Andrew James Toth (Visual Ensemble, Voice), Joni Paige Viertel (French Horn, Mellophone, Didgerydoo, Voice), Kristin Whiting (Visual Ensemble, Voice).

ACT 1

Bolero
(*Music by* Maurice Ravel.)
Color Wheel
(*Music by* J. Lee.)
Split Commentaries
(*Music by* Josh Talbot.)
Everybody Loves the Blues
(*Music by* Maynard Ferguson and Nicholas Lane.)
Loss
(*Music by* Don Ellis.)
"Simple Gifts" (from Old American Songs, Set 1)/Appalachian Spring
(*Music by* Aaron Copland.)
Battery Battle
(*Music by* T. Hannum, J. Lee and P. Rennick.)
Medea
(*Music by* Samuel Barber.)
The Promise of Living (from THE TENDER LAND)
(*Music by* Aaron Copland.)

ACT 2

Color Wheel Too
(*Music by* John Vanderkolff.)
Gee, Officer Krupke (from WEST SIDE STORY)
(*Music by* Leonard Bernstein.)
Lemontech
(*Music by* Jonathan Vanderkolff.)
Tangerinamadidge
(*Music by* James Mason and Jonathan Vanderkolff.)
Land of Make Believe
(*Music by* Chuck Mangione.)
Spiritual of the Earth:
Marimba Spiritual
(*Music by* Minoru Miki.)
Earth Beat
(*Music by* Michael Spiro.)
Malagueña
(*Music by* Ernesto Lecuona.)

2001.05 THE PRODUCERS

A Musical in Two Acts, 18 Scenes. Book by Mel Brooks and Thomas Meehan (based on Mel Brooks' film). Music and lyrics by Mel Brooks. Direction and choreography by Susan Stroman. Scenery designed by Robin Wagner. Costumes designed by William Ivey Long. Lighting designed by

Peter Kaczorowski. Sound designed by Steven C. Kennedy. Orchestrations by Douglas Besterman. Music direction and vocal arrangements, Patrick S. Brady. Musical arrangements and supervision, Glen Kelly. Associate director, Steven Zweigbaum. Associate producers, Frederic H. and Rhoda Mayerson, Lynn Landis. Produced by Rocco Landesman, SFX Theatrical Group, Frankel-Baruch-Viertel-Routh Group[11], Bob and Harvey Weinstein, Rick Steiner, Robert F. X. Sillerman and Mel Brooks, in association with James D. Stern/Douglas Meyer. Opened 19 April 2001 at the St. James Theatre, still running at time of this writing.

CAST (in order of appearance): *The Usherettes*: Bryn Dowling, Jennifer Smith. *Max Bialystock*: NATHAN LANE. *Leo Bloom*: MATTHEW BRODERICK. *Hold-me Touch-me*: Madeleine Doherty. *Mr. Marx*: Ray Wills. *Franz Liebkind*: BRAD OSCAR. *Carmen Ghia*: ROGER BART. *Roger De Bris*: GARY BEACH. *Bryan*: Peter Marinos. *Kevin*: Ray Wills. *Scott*: Jeffry Denman. *Shirley*: Kathy Fitzgerald. *Ulla*: CADY HUFFMAN. *Lick-me Bite-me*: Jennifer Smith. *Kiss-me Feel-me*: Kathy Fitzgerald. *Jack Lepidus*: Peter Marinos. *Donald Dinsmore*: Jeffry Denman. *Jason Green*: Ray Wills. *Lead Tenor*: Eric Gunhus. *Sergeant*: Ray Wills. *O'Rourke*: Abe Sylvia. *O'Riley*: Matt Loehr. *O'Houllihan*: Robert H. Fowler. *Guard*: Jeffry Denman. *Bailiff*: Abe Sylvia. *Judge*: Peter Marinos. *Foreman of the Jury*: Kathy Fitzgerald. *Trustee*: Ray Wills.

Ensemble: Jeffry Denman, Madeleine Doherty, Bryn Dowling, Kathy Fitzgerald, Robert H. Fowler, Ida Gilliams, Eric Gunhus, Kimberly Hester, Naomi Kakuk, Matt Loehr, Peter Marinos, Angie L. Schworer, Jennifer Smith, Abe Sylvia, Tracy Terstriep, Ray Wills. *Swings*: Jim Borstelmann, Adrienne Gibbons, Jamie LaVerdiere, Brad Musgrove, Christina Marie Norrup.

Act 1: New York, 1959. *Scene 1*: Shubert Alley. *Scene 2*: Max's Office, 16 June 1959. *Scene 3*: The Chambers Street Offices of Whitehall and Marx. *Scene 4*: Max's Office. *Scene 5*: The Rooftop of a Greenwich Village Apartment (on Jane Street). *Scene 6*: The Living Room of Renowned Theatrical Director Roger Debris' Elegant Upper East Side Townhouse on a Sunny Tuesday afternoon in June. *Scene 7*: Max's Office. *Scene 8*: Little Old Lady Land.

Act 2, Scene 1: Max's Office, late morning, a few weeks later. *Scene 2*: The Bare Stage of a Broadway Theatre. *Scene 3*: Shubert Alley. *Scene 4*: The stage of The Shubert Theatre. *Scene 5*: Max's Office, later that night. *Scene 6*: The Holding Cell of a New York Courthouse, ten days later. *Scene 7*: A New York Courtroom. *Scene 8*: Sing Sing. *Scene 9*: The Stage of the Shubert Theatre. *Scene 10*: Shubert Alley. *Curtain Call.*

ACT 1

Scene 1

"Opening Night"
Ensemble

"The King of Broadway"
N. Lane, Ensemble

Scene 2

"We Can Do It"
N. Lane, M. Broderick

Scene 3

"I Wanna Be a Producer" ["Unhappy"]
M. Broderick, the Accountants

Scene 4

"We Can Do It" (reprise)
N. Lane, M. Broderick

Scene 5

"In Old Bavaria"
B. Oscar

"Der Guten Tag Hop Clop"
B. Oscar, N. Lane, M. Broderick

Scene 6

"Keep It Gay"
G. Beach, R. Bart, P. Marinos, R. Wills, J. Denman, K. Fitzgerald, N. Lane, M. Broderick

Scene 7

"When You Got It, Flaunt It"
C. Huffman

Scene 8

"Along Came Bialy"
N. Lane, Little Old Ladies

Act One Finale
N. Lane, M. Broderick, B. Oscar, C. Huffman, G. Beach, R. Bart, P. Marinos, R. Wills, J. Denman, K. Fitzgerald

[11]Richard Frankel, Steve Baruch, Tom Viertel, Mark Routh.

ACT 2

Scene 1

"That Face"
M. Broderick, C. Huffman, N. Lane

Scene 2

"Haben Sie Gehoert Das Deutsche Band?" (Have You Ever Heard the German Band?)
R. Wills, B. Oscar

Scene 3

"Opening Night" (reprise)
B. Dowling, J. Smith

"You Never Say 'Good Luck' on Opening Night"
G. Beach, N. Lane, R. Bart, B. Oscar, M. Broderick

Scene 4

"Springtime for Hitler"
E. Gunhus, G. Beach, C. Huffman, Ensemble

Scene 5

"Where Did We Go Right?"
N. Lane, M. Broderick

Scene 6

"Betrayed"
N. Lane

Scene 7

"'Till Him"
M. Broderick, N. Lane

Scene 8

"Prisoners of Love"
The Convicts

Scene 9

"Prisoners of Love" (continued)
G. Beach, C. Huffman, Ensemble

Scene 10

"Prisoners of Love" (reprise); "Leo and Max"
N. Lane, M. Broderick

Curtain Call

"Goodbye!"
The Company

2001.06 THE ADVENTURES OF TOM SAWYER

A Musical in Two Acts, 14 Scenes. Book by Ken Ludwig, based on the novel of the same name by Mark Twain. Music and Lyrics by Don Schlitz. Directed by Scott Ellis. Choreographed by David Marques. Scenic design by Heidi Ettinger. Costume design by Anthony Powell. Lighting design by Kenneth Posner. Sound design by Lew Mead. Musical director, Paul Gemignani. Orchestrations by Michael Starobin. Dance and incidental music by David Krane. Fight director, Rick Sordelet. Produced by James M. Nederlander, James L. Nederlander and Watt/Dobie Productions. Opened 26 April 2001 at the Minskoff Theatre and closed 13 May 2001 after 21 performances.

CAST (in order of appearance): *Tom Sawyer*: JOSHUA PARK. *Ben Rogers*: Tommar Wilson. *George Bellamy*: Joe Gallagher. *Lyle Bellamy*: Blake Hackler. *Joe Harper*: Erik J. McCormack. *Alfred Temple*: Pierce Cravens. *Amy Lawrence*: Ann Whitlow Brown. *Lucy Harper*: Mekenzie Rosen-Stone. *Susie Rogers*: Èlan. *Sabina Temple*: Nikki M. James. *Sally Bellamy*: Stacia Fernandez. *Sereny Harper*: Donna Lee Marshall. *Lucinda Rogers*: Amy Jo Phillips. *Naomi Temple*: Sally Wilfert. *Aunt Polly*: LINDA PURL. *Sid Sawyer*: MARSHALL PAILET. *Doc Robinson*: Stephen Lee Anderson. *Reverend Sprague*: TOMMY HOLLIS. *Lanyard Bellamy*: RICHARD POE. *Gideon Temple*: Ric Stoneback. *Lemuel Dobbins*: JOHN CHRISTOPHER JONES. *Muff Potter*: TOM ALDREDGE. *Huckleberry Finn* JIM POULOS. *Injun Joe*: KEVIN DURANT. *Judge Thatcher*: JOHN DOSSETT. *Becky Thatcher*: KRISTEN BELL. *Widow Douglas*: JANE CONNELL. *Pap*: Stephen Lee Anderson. *Swings*: Patrick Boll, Michael Burton, John Herrera, Kate Reinders, Elise Santora.

The action takes place in St. Petersburg, Missouri, in 1844.

Act 1, Scene 1: A Meadow and the town of St. Petersburg. *Scene 2*: The fence in front of Tom's house. *Scene 3*: The graveyard. *Scene 4*: On the way to church. *Scene 5*: Outside the schoolhouse. *Scene 6*: Inside the schoolhouse. *Scene 7*: The alley behind the jail. *Scene 8*: Inside the courthouse.

Act 2, Scene 1: The school and the town. *Scene 2*: Tom's bedroom. *Scene 3*: Widow Douglas' front porch. *Scene 4*: The picnic grounds, Cardiff Hill. *Scene 5*: McDougal's Cave. *Scene 6*: Inside and outside the church.

ACT 1

Scene 1

"Hey, Tom Sawyer"
J. Park, L. Purl, J. C. Jones, T. Hollis, Townspeople

Scene 2

"Here's My Plan"
J. Park

"Smart Like That"
J. Park, T. Wilson, Boys

Scene 3

"Hands All Clean"
K. Durand

"The Vow"
J. Park, K. Poulos

Scene 4

"Ain't Life Fine"
Townspeople

Scene 5

"It Ain't Just Me"
J. Poulos

Scene 6

"To Hear You Say My Name"
J. Park, K. Bell

Scene 7

"Murrel's Gold"
K. Durand, T. Aldredge, J. Park, J. Poulos

Scene 8

"The Testimony"
J. Park, Townspeople

ACT 2

Scene 1

"Ain't Life Fine" (reprise)
Townspeople

Scene 2

"This Time Tomorrow"
L. Purl

Scene 3

"I Can Read"
J. Poulos, J. Connell

Scene 4

"You Can't Can't Dance"
J. Dossett, L. Purl, Townspeople

"Murrel's Gold" (reprise)
K. Durand

Scene 5

"Angel's Lost"
L. Purl, J. Dossett, Townspeople

"Light"
J. Park

"Angel's Lost" (reprise)
K. Bell

Scene 6

"Light" (reprise)
Townspeople

Finale
J. Park, J. Poulos, K. Bell, Boys, Girls

2001.07 GEORGE GERSHWIN ALONE

A Play with Music in Two Acts. Play by Hershey Felder. Music by George Gershwin. Lyrics by Ira Gershwin. Directed by Joel Zwick. Settings by Yael Pardess. Sound by John Gottlieb. Produced by Richard Willis, Martin Markinson, HTG Productions. Opened 30 April 2001 at the Helen Hayes Theatre and closed 22 July 2001 after 96 performances.

CAST: *George Gershwin*: HERSHEY FELDER.

MUSICAL NUMBERS

"Swanee" (interpolated into SINBAD)
(*Lyrics by* Irving Caesar.)

"Embraceable You" (from GIRL CRAZY)

"Someone to Watch Over Me" (from OH KAY!)

"Bess, You is My Woman Now" (from PORGY AND BESS)
(*Lyrics by* DuBose Heyward and Ira Gershwin.)

"An American in Paris"

"Rhapsody in Blue"

2001.08 42nd STREET

A Revival of the Song and Dance Fable of Broadway (A Musical) in Two Acts, 16 Scenes[12]. Book by Michael Stewart and Mark Bramble. Based on the novel of the same name by Bradford Ropes (and the Warner Brothers film adapted from it by Rian James and James Seymour.) Music by Harry Warren. Lyrics by Al Dubin. (Other lyrics by Johnny Mercer and Mort Dixon.) Original direction and dances by Gower Champion. Staged by Mark Bramble. Musical staging and new choreography by Randy Skinner. Scenery design by Douglas W. Schmidt. Costume design by Roger Kirk. Lighting design by Paul Gallo. Sound design by Peter Fitzgerald. Musical direction by Todd Ellison. Musical adaptation, arrangements and additional orchestrations by Donald Johnston. Orchestrations by Philip J. Lang. Executive producer, Dodger Management Group. Produced by Dodger Theatricals, Joop van den Ende and Stage Holding. Opened 2 May 2001 at the Ford Center for the Performing Arts and is still running at this writing.

CAST (in order of appearance): *Andy Lee*: MICHAEL ARNOLD. *Oscar*: BILLY STRITCH. *Mac*: ALLEN FITZPATRICK. *Annie*: MYLINDA HULL. *Diane*: Tamlyn Brooke Shusterman. *Maggie Jones*: MARY TESTA. *Bert Barry*: JONATHAN FREEMAN. *Billy Lawlor*: DAVID ELDER. *Peggy Sawyer*: KATE LEVERING. *Phyllis*: Catherine Wreford. *Lorraine*: Megan Sikora. *Julian Marsh*: MICHAEL CUMPSTY. *Dorothy Brock*: CHRISTINE EBERSOLE. *Abner Dillon*: MICHAEL McCARTY. *Pat Denning*: RICHARD MUENZ. *Waiters*: Brad Aspel, Mike Warshaw, Shonn Wiley. *Thugs*: Allen Fitzpatrick, Jerry Tellier. *Doctor*: ALLEN FITZPATRICK. (*Standby*: BETH LEAVEL.)

Ensemble: Brad Aspel, Becky Bersteler, Randy Bobish, Chris Clay, Michael Clowers, Maryam Myika Day, Alexander deJong, Amy Dolan, Isabelle Flachsmann, Jennifer Jones, Dontee Kiehn, Renée Klapmeyer, Jessica Kostival, Keirsten Kupiec, Todd Lattimoore, Melissa Rae Mahon, Michael Malone, Jennifer Marquardt, Meredith Patterson, Darin Phelps, Wendy Rosoff, Megan Schenck, Kelly Sheehan, Tamlyn Brooke Shusterman, Megan Sikora, Erin Stoddard, Yasuko Tamaki, Jonathan Taylor, Jerry Tellier, Elisa van Duyne, Erika Vaughn, Mike Warshaw, Merrill West, Shonn Wiley Catherine Wreford. *Swings*: Kelli Barclay, Melissa Giattino, Brian J. Marcum, Luke Walrath.

2001.09 CINDERELLA

A Revival of the Musical in Two Acts, a Prologue and 13 Scenes[13]. Book and lyrics by Oscar Hammerstein II. Music by Richard Rodgers. Adapted for the

---

[12]First produced in New York 25 August 1980 at the Winter Garden for 3486 performances. For Synopsis of Scenes and Musical Numbers, see original 1980 production. For this revival the following changes were made:

"Shadow Waltz" (reprise, dropped from Act 1, Scene 1)

"I Only Have Eyes for You" (from DAMES film)(Added to Act 1, Scene 7, replacing "I Know Now")
C. Ebersole

"Getting Out of Town" (reprise, added to Act 2, Scene 4)
J. Freeman, M. Testa, Full Company

"Montage" (Added to Act 2, Scene 5)
M. Cumpsty, M. Arnold, K. Levering, Ensemble

"With Plenty of Money and You" (from GOLD DIGGERS OF 1937 film) (Added to Act 2, Scene 7, after Overture)
K. Levering, Men

Finale (Act 2, Scene 8)
Full Company

[13]First produced for television in 31 March 1957; this production was adapted from the 2 November 1998 telecast. A previous stage adaptation was presented in New York 9 November 1993 at the New York State Theatre for 14 performances.

stage by Tom Briggs from the teleplay by Robert L. Freedman. Directed by Gabriel Barre. Choreographed by Ken Roberson. Scenic design by James Youmans. Costume design by Pamela Scofield. Lighting design by Tim Hunter. Sound design by Duncan Edwards. Special effects by Gregory Meeh. Puppets designed by Integrity Designworks. Music Director/ Conductor, John Mezzio. Orchestrations by David Siegel. Original orchestrations by Robert Russell Bennett. Musical supervision and arrangements by Andrew Lippa. Executive producer, Ken Gentry. Presented by Radio City Entertainment; National Tour presented by Marshalls. Produced by NETworks. Opened 3 May 2001 at the Theatre at Madison Square Garden and closed 13 May 2001 after 16 performances.

CAST: *The Fairy Godmother*: EARTHA KITT. *Cinderella*: JAMIE-LYNN SIGLER. *Prince Christopher*: PAOLO MONTALBAN. *The Stepmother*: EVERETT QUINTON. *Cinderella's Stepsisters (2)*: *Grace*: NATASHA YVETTE WILLIAMS. *Joy*: ALEXANDRA KOLB. *Lionel*, the Court Herald: Victor Trent Cook. *Queen Constantina*: Leslie Becker. *King Maximilian*: Ken Prymus. *4 White Mice*: Kip Driver, Kevin Duda, Jason Ma, Jason Robinson. *Charles*, a cat: Patrick Wetzel. *A Dove*: André Ward.

Villagers, Merchants, Maidens and Palace Guests: Joanne Borts, Natalie Cortez, Kip Driver, Kevin Duda, Davis Kirby, Amy Nicole Krawcek, Jason Ma, Christy Morton, Kerri Nowe, Monica Patton, Karine Plantadit-Bageot, Christeena Michelle Riggs, Jason Robinson, Jessica Rush, Jonathan Stahl, Kate Strohbehn, Keith L. Thomas, Ron J. Todorowski, André Ward, Patrick Wetzel. *Swings*: Lyn Philistine, Todd L. Underwood.

The action takes place once upon a time in a kingdom far away.

Act 1, Scene 1: The Village Square. *Scene 2*: The Stepmother's Manor House, immediately following. *Scene 3*: The Royal Parlor, immediately following. *Scene 4*: The Manor House, one week later. *Scene 5*: The Pumpkin Patch behind the Manor House. *Scene 6*: Outside the Royal Palace, immediately following.

Act 2, Scene 1: The Royal Ballroom. *Scene 2*: The Royal Gardens, immediately following. *Scene 3*: Outside the Royal Palace, immediately following. *Scene 4*: The Manor House, later that night. *Scene 5*: Throughout the Kingdom, the following day and night. *Scene 6*: The Manor House, the following morning. *Scene 7*: The Wedding Finale.

ACT 1

Prologue
E. Kitt, J. Sigler, Ensemble

Scene 1
"The Sweetest Sounds" (from NO STRINGS)
J. Sigler, P. Montalban
(*Lyrics by* Richard Rodgers.)
"The Prince Is Giving a Ball"
V. T. Cook, E. Quinton, N. Y. Williams, A. Kolb, Villagers

Scene 2
"In My Own Little Corner"
J. Sigler, Animals

Scene 3
"The Sweetest Sounds" (reprise)
J. Sigler, P. Montalban

Scene 4
"In My Own Little Corner" (reprise)
J. Sigler

Scene 5
"Fol-de-Rol" (Godmothers' Song)
E. Kitt
"Impossible"
E. Kitt, J. Sigler
"The Transformation"
E. Kitt, J. Sigler, Animals
"It's Possible!"
J. Sigler, E. Kitt, Horses, Coachman, Footman

ACT 2

Scene 1
"(The) Gavotte"
P. Montalban, Maidens, Other Guests
"The Cinderella Waltz" (Waltz for a Ball)
J. Sigler, P. Montalban, Guests
"Ten Minutes Ago"
P. Montalban, J. Sigler, Company

Scene 2
"Stepsisters' Lament"
N. Y. Williams, A. Kolb
"Do I Love You Because You're Beautiful?"
P. Montalban, J. Sigler

Scene 3
"Ten Minutes Ago" (reprise)
P. Montalban

Scene 4
"When You're Driving Through the Moonlight"
J. Sigler, E. Quinton, N. Y. Williams, A. Kolb, E. Quinton
"A Lovely Night"
J. Sigler, E. Quinton, N. Y. Williams, A. Kolb, Animals
"A Lovely Night" (reprise)
J. Sigler

Scene 5
"The Search"
V. T. Cook, P. Montalban, Maidens

Scene 7
"There's Music in You" (Finale Ultimo)(from MAIN STREET TO BROADWAY film)
E. Kitt, Company

INDEX OF SHOWS

Note: Variant show titles have been indexed for ease of use, so that both PO-CA-HON-TAS and POCAHONTAS, FOLLIES OF 1907 and ZIEGFELD FOLLIES OF 1907, BEAUTY AND THE BEAST and DISNEY'S BEAUTY AND THE BEAST will be found. If a show's title changed during the course of its run, that will be both footnoted and cross-indexed (THE MYSTERY OF EDWIN DROOD, 1985, became DROOD!; PIGGY, 1927, became I TOLD YOU SO).

A la Broadway 1911.26
A la Carte 1927.38
Aaah Oui Genty! 1981.11
Abby's Song 1999.17
About Town (A. Philipp) 1894.10
About Town (Ellis-Herbert-Hubbell) 1906.29
Abyssinia 1906.14
Across the Atlantic 1879.54
Act, The 1977.16
Adam's Temptation, or, Birds of Paradise 1891.10
Adamless Eden!, An 1884.60
Adele 1913.21
Admiral, The 1893.22
Adonis 1884.42, 1886.47, 1888.36, 1893.13, 1899.23
Adonis, or, Ye Statue, Ye Miller, Ye Maiden, and Ye Lordly Villyain 1894.19
Adrienne 1923.16
Adventures of Tom Sawyer, The 2001.06
Afgar 1920.41
Africa 1893.50
Africana (operetta) 1934.37
Africana (revue) 1927.32
L'Afrique 1882.05
Ages Ago 1880.18
Agreeable Surprise, The 1794.01
Ahmed! 1875.06
Aida 2000.06
Ain't Broadway Grand 1993.05
Ain't Misbehavin' 1978.09, 1988.17
Ain't Supposed to Die a Natural Death 1971.13
Ain't it the Truth 1921.41
Air Ship, The 1899.13
Aladdin the Second 1872.34
Aladdin, Jr. 1895.08
Aladdin, or, the Wonderful Lamp 1864.15
Aladdin, or, the Wonderful Scamp 1867.13, 1869.39, 1870.39
Aladdin, the Wonderful Scamp! 1867.26
Aladdin/Sinbad the Sailor 1873.17
Alaskan, The 1907.26
Algeria 1908.24
Algerian, The 1893.40
Alice in Wonderland 1982.24
Alice in Wonderland and Through the Looking Glass 1932.28, 1947.09
Alive and Kicking 1950.02
All Aboard 1913.16
All American 1962.04
All at Sea 1882.28
All for Love 1949.02
All for the Ladies 1912.49
All in Fun 1940.23
All in One 1955.05
All the King's Horses 1934.04
Allah Be Praised! 1944.15
Allegro 1947.17
Allen, Dave, An Evening With 1981.23
Allez-Oop! 1927.35
Alma, Where do You Live? 1910.26
Almost Crazy 1955.11
Alone at Last 1915.27
Along Fifth Avenue 1949.01
Alphonse and Gaston 1902.42
Alsatians, The 1884.60
Always You 1920.01
Amanuensis 1888.15
Ambassador 1972.24
Amber Empress, The 1916.18
Ameer, The 1899.40
Amen Corner 1983.15
America 1893.45, 1913.22, 1981.08
America's Sweetheart 1931.04
American Beauty, An 1896.51
American Dance Machine, The 1986.03
American Idea, The 1908.31
American Maid, The 1913.06
Americana (1926) 1926.21
Americana (1928) 1928.40
Amilie, or, the Love Test 1838.01
Amor di Principe 1911.19
Amorita 1885.63
L'amour que qu'c'est qu'ca? 1886.29
Andalusian, or, the Young Guard, The 1851.02
André Charlot's Revue of 1924 1924.01
André Heller's Wonderhouse 1991.11
Andy Williams With Michel Legrand 1974.20
Angel 1978.10
Angel Face 1919.44
Angel in the Wings 1947.20
Angela 1928.46
Animal Crackers 1928.38
Ankles Aweigh 1955.04
Anna Held's All Star Varieté Jubilee 1913.35
Anna Karenina 1992.11
Anna Russell and Her Little Show 1953.10
Anne of Green Gables 1971.21
Annie 1977.06, 1997.04
Annie Dear 1924.38
Annie Get Your Gun 1946.12, 1958.03, 1966.12, 1966.16, 1999.04
Another Mikado 1885.62
Anthony Newley & Henry Mancini 1974.22
Antiope 1889.33
Anya 1965.35
Anyone Can Whistle 1964.15
Anything Goes 1934.36, 1987.15
Apajune, the Water Sprite 1882.16, 1885.05
Aphrodite 1919.38
Apollo in New York 1854.04
Apollo, or, the Oracle of Delphi 1891.12
Applause 1970.09
Apple Blossoms 1919.27
Apple Tree, The 1966.18
Arabesque 1925.37
Arabian Girl and 40 Thieves, An 1899.21
Arabian Nights, The, or, Aladdin's Wonderful Lamp 1887.32
Araminta's Wedding 1876.37
Arcadia 1886.24, 1888.06
Arcadians, The 1910.05
Archers, The, or, the Mountaineers of Switzerland 1796.01
Ardriell 1889.26
Are You Insured? 1885.29
Are You With It? 1945.18
Ari 1971.02
Arizona 1899.38
Arms and the Girl 1950.04
Around the Clock 1906.40, 1908.02
Around the Map 1915.28
Around the World (Kiralfy) 1875.21
Around the World (M. Klein/Hippodrome) 1911.28
Around the World in Eighty Days 1875.05, 1875.18, 1877.04, 1880.41, 1882.62, 1885.33, 1886.41, 1890.17, 1892.35
Around the World in Eighty Days (Wells-Porter) 1946.13
Arrah-Na-Pogue, or, the Wicklow Wedding 1865.06, 1869.33, 1872.27, 1873.20, 1903.25
Art of Maryland, The 1896.26
Artist's Model, An 1895.43
Artists and Models (1923) 1923.25
Artists and Models (1924) 1924.36
Artists and Models (1927) 1927.58
Artists and Models (1943) 1943.20
Artists and Models (Paris Edition, 1925) 1925.23
Artists and Models (Paris-Riviera Edition of 1930) 1930.20
As Thousands Cheer 1933.22
As You Were 1920.03
As the Girls Go 1948.28
Aspects of Love 1990.04
At Gay Coney Island 1897.07
At Home Abroad 1935.12

At Home With Ethel Waters 1953.12
At the Drop of Another Hat 1966.32
At the Drop of a Hat 1959.20
At the French Ball 1897.22
At the Lower Harbor 1900.06
Atkinson, Rowan: At the Atkinson 1986.15
Atta Boy 1918.38
Aunt Bridget's Baby 1891.14, 1892.06
Aunt Hannah 1900.15
Auto Race, The 1907.54
Awakening of Mr. Pipp, The 1904.14
Azael, the Prodigal 1851.07, 1851.08
Aznavour, Charles, on Broadway 1970.01, 1974.19, 1983.03
Aznavour on Broadway 1998.12
Aznavour, Charles: The World of 1965.30
Azrael; or, the Magic Charm 1873.08
Aztec Romance, An 1912.32
Azurine, or, a Voyage to the Earth 1876.36

Ba-Ta-Clan 1864.11
Baba! 1876.16, 1879.02
Babes and the Baron, The 1905.55
Babes in Arms 1937.05
Babes in Toyland 1903.31, 1905.01, 1929.48, 1930.41, 1979.33
Babes in the Wood, Robin Hood and His Merry, Merry Men, and Harlequin, Who Killed Cock Robin? 1890.50
Babes in the Wood, The 1872.40
Babes in the Wood, or, Who Killed Cock Robin? 1877.43, 1879.33, 1880.70
Babes in the Woods & the Good Little Fairy Birds! or, Who Killed Cock Robin? 1878.20
Babette 1903.37
Babies of the Period, The 1870.29
Babiole 1880.58
Baby 1983.19
Bachelor Belles, The 1910.34
Bad Boy and His Teddy Bears, The 1907.61
Bad Dickey 1869.43
Bagatelle 1875.13
Bagels and Yox 1951.20
Baggage Check, A 1898.10
Bajour 1964.40
Baker, Josephine, An Evening With 1973.17
Baker Street 1965.02
Bal Negre 1946.21
Balieff's Chauve-Souris 1922.06, 1923.28, 1925.03, 1927.51, 1929.05, 1931.38, 1943.11
Balkan Princess, The 1911.06
Balky Princess, The 1911.14
Ballet Ballads 1948.17
Ballet Girl, The 1897.52
Ballet of 1830, The 1912.24
Ballroom 1978.27
Ballyhoo 1930.42
Ballyhoo of 1932 1932.16
Bamboche! 1962.22
Bamboola 1929.25
Band Box Follies, The 1927.40
Band Wagon, The 1931.16
Band in Berlin 1999.05
Bandanna Land 1908.08
Banditti, or, Lamb'd in Corsica 1889.32
Banjo Eyes 1941.13
Bankers and Brokers 1905.31
Bar-Ber Blu 1868.21
Barbara Cook: A Concert for the Theatre 1987.06
Barbara Fidgety 1899.30
Barbe Bleue 1868.18, 1870.45, 1871.28, 1872.33, 1877.38, 1879.55
Barefoot Boy With Cheek 1947.08
Barnum 1980.07
Baron Trenck 1912.10
Baroness Fiddlesticks, The 1904.50
Barrier, The 1950.16
Barry Manilow at the Gershwin 1989.08
Barry Manilow on Broadway 1976.34
Barry Manilow's Showstoppers 1991.10
Barry of Ballymore 1911.04
Basket Maker's Wife, The 1852.06
Basoche, A, or, King of the Students 1893.05
Bathing Girl, The 1895.23
Battle of Port Arthur, The 1907.54
Battle of the Skies, The 1908.26
Battling Butler 1923.36
Bavards, Les 1868.30
Be Yourself 1924.30
Beadle's Pirates for Ten Cents 1880.15
Beast in Me, The 1963.16
Beat the Band 1942.29
Beatlemania 1977.10
Beautiful Galatea, The/Trial by Jury 1882.54
Beautiful Star 1891.34
Beauty Doctor, The 1905.35
Beauty Shop, The 1914.13
Beauty Spot, The 1909.07
Beauty and the Beast 1999.16
Beauty and the Beast, (Disney's) 1994.04
Beauty of Seville, The 1865.07
Becaud, Gilbert, on Broadway 1966.20
Becaud, Gilbert, Sings Love 1968.21
Beg, Borrow or Steal 1960.01
Beggar Student, The 1883.62, 1884.51, 1887.26, 1898.30, 1899.42, 1913.08
Beggar's Holiday 1946.24
Beggar's Opera, The 1750.01, 1854.06, 1855.08, 1859.04, 1928.13, 1957.02, 1973.16
Begum, The 1887.47
Belle Galatea, La 1875.12
Belle Hélène, La 1868.07, 1868.27, 1871.07, 1872.39, 1877.14, 1877.30, 1879.69, 1886.18, 1893.22, 1899.02, 1976.26
Belle L.N., La 1870.17
Belle Paree, La/Bow Sing 1911.12
Belle Sauvage, La 1872.09
Belle of Avenue A, The 1905.39
Belle of Bohemia, The 1900.41
Belle of Bond Street, The 1914.10
Belle of Bridgeport, The 1900.48
Belle of Brittany, The 1909.29
Belle of Broadway, The 1902.10
Belle of London Town, The 1907.05
Belle of Mayfair, The 1906.47
Belle of New York, The 1897.39, 1898.68, 1900.05
Belle of the Barber's Ball, The 1908.22
Belle of the West, The 1905.50
Belle-Poule, La 1877.19
Belles of the Kitchen, The 1871.12, 1872.13, 1873.06, 1873.13, 1875.17, 1876.08, 1881.20
Bellman 1887.28
Bells are Ringing 1956.14, 2001.03
Bells of Corneville!, The 1878.16
Belmont Varieties 1932.19
Ben Franklin in Paris 1964.33
Bennett, Tony and Lena Horne Sing 1974.21
Benny, Jack 1963.07
Beppo 1869.32
Bernard & Collier's Nifties of 1923 1923.33
Bernhard: I'm Still Here Damn It! 1998.14
Best Foot Forward 1941.06
Best Little Whorehouse Goes Public, The 1994.06
Best Little Whorehouse in Texas, The 1978.13, 1982.11
Betsy 1926.51
Betsy, an American Widow 1911.46
Bette Midler 1973.14
Bette Midler's Clams on the Half Shell 1975.12
Bette!: Divine Madness 1979.30
Better 'Ole, The, or, the Romance of Old Bill 1918.31
Better Late than Never! 1859.13
Better Times 1922.30
Betty 1916.20
Betty Lee 1924.47
Betty, be Good 1920.15
Between You and Me and the Post 1867.17
Between the Devil 1937.16
Beyond the Fringe 1962.23
Beyond the Fringe '64 1962.23
Beyond the Fringe '65 1964.45
Bicycle Girl, The 1895.36
Biff! Bing! Bang! 1921.12
Biff-Bang! 1918.17
Big 1996.08
Big Boy 1925.01, 1925.28
Big Deal 1986.06
Big Little Princess, The 1902.29
Big Pony, the Gentlemanly Savage 1887.14
Big River: The Adventures of Huckleberry Finn 1985.06
Big Show, The 1916.15
Big Stick, The 1908.11
Billee Taylor, or, the Reward of Virtue (Pottinger-Stephens) 1881.07, 1882.23, 1882.51, 1882.66, 1885.40, 1898.24
Billie 1928.31
Billion Dollar Baby 1945.20
Billionaire, The 1902.43
Billy 1969.08
Billy Barnes People, The 1961.16
Billy Barnes Revue 1959.14
Billy Bishop Goes to War 1980.13
Billy Rose's Crazy Quilt 1931.13
Billy Taylor, or, the Lass Who Loved a Sailor (Burlesque) 1882.20, 1883.23
Billy the Tailor, or, a Stitch in Time Saves a Patch 1881.17
Bing Crosby on Broadway 1976.32
Bird of Paradise, A (Thompson-Tissington) 1867.08
Bird of Paradise, The (Tully) 1912.03
Bitter Sweet 1929.41, 1934.13
Black Broadway 1980.10
Black Crook 1866.18, 1870.44, 1871.27, 1873.10, 1874.21, 1876.34, 1879.12, 1880.08, 1881.13, 1882.77, 1886.16, 1887.03, 1889.21, 1892.38, 1893.23, 1894.34, 1896.32
Black Domino/Between You and Me and the Post, The 1866.01
Black Hussar, The 1885.28, 1885.67, 1887.18, 1898.37, 1900.29
Black Picture Show 1975.02
Black Rhythm 1936.30
Black Scandals 1928.39
Black Sheep, A, and How it Came Out in the Wash 1896.02
Black Statue, The 1866.32
Black Venus 1881.02, 1883.06
Black and Blue 1989.02
Blackberries of 1932 1932.08
Blackbird, The 1882.50
Blackbirds of 1928 1928.18
Blackbirds of 1930 1930.34
Blackbirds of 1933–34 1933.27

Blackbirds of 1939 1939.14
Blackstone 1980.12
Blast 2001.04
Bless You All 1950.19
Blind Beggars, The 1870.39
Blind Man's Daughter, The 1867.09
Blonde Marie 1937.04
Blonde Sinner, The 1926.20
Blonde in Black, The 1903.16
Blondette, or, the Naughty Prince and Pretty Peasant 1862.09
Blood Brothers 1993.07
Blood Red Roses 1970.06
Bloomer Girl 1944.23, 1947.01
Blossom Time 1921.31, 1923.14, 1923.15, 1924.12, 1926.05, 1931.07, 1938.17, 1943.12
Blue Beard (Farnie) 1877.22, 1884.20, 1892.49
Blue Beard, or, the Mormon, the Maiden and the Little Militaire (Lydia Thompson Troupe) 1871.14, 1872.22
Blue Beard, or, the Punishment of Curiosity (Nixon's Equestrian Troupe) 1860.01
Blue Bird, The 1924.48, 1932.09
Blue Eyes 1921.04
Blue Holiday 1945.07
Blue Jeans 1890.35, 1892.01
Blue Kitten 1922.02
Blue Moon, The 1906.41
Blue Paradise, The 1915.17
Bluebeard, Jr., or, Fatima and the Fairy (Greene-Eustis-Maddern-Braham) 1890.03
Blues in the Night 1982.12
Blues, Ballads and Sin Songs 1954.11
Blushing Bride, The 1922.07
Bob 1883.40
Bob and Ray - the Two and Only 1970.14
Boccaccio 1880.20, 1880.26, 1880.57, 1881.44, 1883.41, 1883.55, 1884.52, 1888.26, 1898.49, 1905.11, 1931.44, 1975.23
Body Beautiful, The 1958.01
Bohea-man's Girl, The 1845.01
Bohemian Girl, The 1844.01, 1852.07, 1853.04, 1854.03, 1855.05, 1858.03, 1859.03, 1864.04, 1864.19, 1867.07, 1868.12, 1869.41, 1872.17, 1874.02, 1877.35, 1878.03, 1882.13, 1882.64, 1884.33, 1885.32, 1889.28, 1896.16, 1898.39, 1898.76, 1900.22, 1911.10, 1933.17
Bohemian Girl, The, or, the Merry Zingara (burlesque) 1870.14
Bombastes Furioso 1924.20
Bombo 1921.34, 1923.12
Bon Garçon, Un 1929.15
Bonnie Scotland 1895.41
Boom-Boom 1929.06
Borge, Victor 1953.13, 1964.34, 1989.28
Borscht Belt Buffet on Broadway 2000.14
Borscht Capades 1951.21
Bottle of Ink, A 1885.04
Bottomland 1927.30
Boulangère a des Écus, La 1877.13, 1877.31, 1879.45
Boulotte! 1875.19
Bow Sing 1911.12
Boy Friend, The 1954.09, 1970.11
Boy Wanted, A 1897.04
Boy With the Boodle, The 1907.38
Boy and the Girl, The 1909.12
Boys & Girls 1891.26
Boys and Betty, The 1908.36
Boys and Girls Together 1940.12
Boys from Syracuse, The 1938.14
Boys of Kilkenny, The 1897.12
Brass Monkey, A 1888.32
Bravo, Giovanni 1962.14
Brazilian, The 1890.19
Breaking into Society 1905.37
Breaking the Spell 1882.59
Brian Boru 1896.41
Bric-à-Brac 1879.52, 1889.34
Bridal Trap, The 1886.34
Bride-Elect, The 1898.25
Brigadoon 1947.07, 1950.10, 1957.03, 1962.15, 1963.04, 1964.46, 1967.17, 1980.26, 1986.04, 1991.12, 1996.13
Brigands, Les 1870.41, 1872.03, 1873.01, 1879.36, 1879.47
Brigands, The 1889.23, 1890.01
Bright Eyes 1910.09
Bright Lights of 1944 1943.16
Bring Back Birdie 1981.07
Bring in 'da Noise, Bring in 'da Funk 1996.07
Bringing Up Father 1925.12
Broadway Brevities of 1920 1920.33
Broadway Follies 1981.09
Broadway Musical, A 1978.28
Broadway Nights 1929.28
Broadway Opry '79: A Little Country in the Big City 1979.16
Broadway Sho-Window 1936.06
Broadway Whirl, The 1921.19
Broadway and Buttermilk 1916.13
Broadway to Paris 1912.43
Broadway to Tokio 1900.07
Broadway, A La 1911.26
Broken Idol, A 1909.17
Bronze Donkey, The 1860.02
Brook, The 1879.32, 1881.01
Brook, The, or, a Jolly Day at the Picnic 1880.11
Brother Max 1885.50
Brother and Sister 1863.09
Brown Buddies 1930.29
Brown's in Town 1899.08
Brownies, The 1894.42
Bruce Forsythe on Broadway 1979.14
Bubbling Brown Sugar 1976.04
Buck White 1969.15
Buddies 1919.31
Buddy Hackett and Eddie Fisher 1967.12
Buddy: The Buddy Holly Story 1990.15
Bugs Bunny on Broadway 1990.10
Bunch and Judy, The 1922.45
Bunch of Keys, A, or, the Hotel 1883.26
Bunk of 1926/1st & 2nd eds 1926.11
Bunty, Bulls and Strings 1912.07
Burgomaster, The 1900.59
Burlesque of La Belle Hélène 1885.39
Burlesque of La Princess de Trébizonde 1886.07
Burlesque of the Merry Widow 1908.01
Buster Brown 1905.05
Busy Izzy 1903.09
Busy Izzy's Boodle 1908.12
But Never Jam Today 1969.09, 1979.18
Buttons on Broadway 1995.08
Buttrio Square 1952.13
Buy-it-Dear, 'Tis Made of Cashmere 1840.03
Buzzin' Around 1920.20
By Jupiter 1942.15
By the Beautiful Sea 1954.02
By the Sad Sea Waves 1899.11
By the Way/1st & 2nd eds 1925.50
Bye Bye Birdie 1960.06
Bye Bye Bonnie 1927.05
Bye, Bye, Barbara 1924.24

C.O.D. 1888.05
Cabalgata 1949.07
Cabaret 1966.24, 1987.16, 1998.04
Cabin in the Sky 1940.17
Cad: The Tomboy 1883.36
Cadet Girl, The 1900.34
Cadi, The 1891.27
Caesar, Sid & Company: Does Anybody Know What I'm Talking About? 1989.22
Cafe Crown 1964.18
Cage aux Folles, La 1983.11
Caliph, The 1896.25
Call Me Madam 1950.15
Call Me Mister 1946.10
Calling All Stars 1934.39
Camargo, La 1880.29
Cambridge Circus 1964.29
Camelot 1960.21, 1980.19, 1981.26, 1993.11
Can-Can 1953.07, 1962.13, 1981.13
Canard à Trois Becs!, Le 1875.30
Canary Cottage 1917.04
Canary, The 1918.34
Canciones di Mi Padre (Songs for My Father) 1988.15
Candide (C. Weidman-G. Pitot-J. Coleman) 1933.12
Candide (L. Bernstein-Latouche-Wilbur) 1956.15, 1974.06, 1982.20, 1983.13, 1984.11, 1986.08, 1989.14, 1997.10
Candy 1892.43
Candy Kid, The 1907.50
Candy Shop, The 1909.09
Canterbury Tales 1969.04, 1980.01
Cape Cod Follies 1929.33
Capeman 1998.02
Capital Prize, A 1885.35
Capitan, El 1896.13, 1897.10, 1898.13
Capt. Jack Sheppard 1886.53
Captain Cook 1897.27
Captain Jinks 1925.29
Captain Karl! 1891.20
Captain Mishler 1884.23
Captain Rufus 1907.29
Captain Thérèse 1892.08
Captain of the Queens's Own 1885.54
Carib Song 1945.13
Caribbean Carnival 1947.19
Carl, the Fiddler 1871.22
Carmelina 1979.09
Carmen Jones 1943.24, 1945.06, 1946.09, 1956.06
Carmen Up too Late, or, the Bold Toreador 1891.35
Carmen, or, Soldiers and Seville-ians 1880.43
Carnival 1961.10, 1968.32
Carnival in Flanders 1953.11
Caroline 1923.03
Carousel 1945.05, 1949.03, 1954.07, 1957.11, 1965.24, 1966.31, 1994.02
Carrie 1988.12
Casino Boy, The 1900.35
Casino Girl, The 1900.20, 1901.08
Castles in Spain 1881.24
Castles in the Air (Kerker) 1890.16
Castles in the Air (Wenrich) 1926.24
Cat and the Fiddle, The (Carter-Sinn) 1907.60
Cat and the Fiddle, The (Kern) 1931.37
Cat's in the Larder, The, or, the Maid With a Parasol 1840.04
Catch a Star 1955.12
Catch of the Season, The 1905.27
Catherine 1898.50, 1899.17, 1903.28
Cats 1982.19
Catskills on Broadway 1991.14
Caviar 1934.15
Celebrated Hard Case, A 1878.01

Celebration 1969.02
Cendrillon 1866.34
Cent Vierges, Les 1872.42, 1874.04, 1877.40
Century Girl 1916.24
Century Midnight Whirl, The 1919.43
Century Revue, The 1920.22
Certain Party, A 1911.17
Chalet, Le 1866.27
Chamberlain Brown's Scrap Book 1932.14
Chamooni III 1859.11
Champagne, Sec 1933.23
Chandeliers, The, or, Venice in New York 1890.09
Change Your Luck 1930.19
Change in the Heir, A 1990.06
Chanson de Fortunio, La 1868.31
Chaperons, The 1902.20
Charity Begins at Home 1880.18
Charity Girl, The 1912.36
Charlatan, The 1898.48
Charles Aznavour on Broadway 1970.01, 1974.19, 1983.03
Charlie and Algernon 1980.23
Charlot Revue of 1926, The 1925.42
Charlot's Revue of 1924 1924.01
Chatter 1885.45
Chauve-Souris 1922.06, 1923.28, 1925.03, 1927.51, 1929.05, 1931.38, 1843.11
Chauve-Souris 1943 1943.11
Check 44, or, Tobogganing 1888.03
Chee-Chee 1928.30
Cheek 1883.43
Cheer Up 1917.16
Cherry Blossoms 1927.14
Chess 1988.09
Chevalier, Maurice, An Evening With 1930.13
Chevaliers Du Pince-Nez, Les 1880.28
Chicago 1975.14, 1996.14
Chieftain, The 1895.26
Chiffon Girl, The 1924.05
Child of Fortune, The 1892.16
Children in the Wood, The 1873.28
Chilpéric 1869.30, 1874.23, 1875.15
Chimes of Normandy, The 1877.36, 1881.05, 1882.08, 1882.36, 1884.32, 1885.38, 1889.29, 1896.20, 1898.74, 1900.09, 1931.41
Chin-Chin, or, a Modern Aladdin 1914.23
China Doll, A 1904.49
China Rose 1925.04
Chinese Honeymoon, A 1902.19, 1904.12
Chinese Love 1921.05
Ching Chow Hi!, or, a cracked piece of China 1870.11, 1876.30
Chip of the Old Block! 1866.35
Chocolate Dandies, The 1924.27
Chocolate Soldier, The 1909.22, 1910.28, 1921.40, 1930.03, 1931.33, 1934.12, 1942.17, 1947.06
Choir Rehearsal, The 1921.05
Chorus Line, A 1975.15
Chow Chow, or, a Tale of Pekin 1872.25
Chris and the Wonderful Lamp 1900.01
Christine 1960.10
Christmas Carol, A 1994.12, 1995.19, 1996.15, 1997.22, 1998.20, 1999.21, 2000.19
Christmas from the Heart 1998.19
Chronicle of a Death Foretold 1995.09
Chu Chem 1989.05
Chu Chin Chow 1917.24, 1919.20
Cigale, La 1878.14, 1891.36, 1892.60
Cinder-le-on! 1867.02
Cinderella 1859.05, 1861.03, 1867.13, 1891.41, 1894.18
Cinderella (Rodgers-Hammerstein) 1993.14, 1995.18, 2001.09
Cinderella at School 1881.11, 1881.27, 1882.34, 1883.31
Cinderella e la Comare, or, the Lover, The Lackey, and the Little Glass Slipper 1866.03
Cinderella on Broadway 1920.19
Cinderella, or, the Little Glass Slipper 1855.02, 1880.55
Cinderella, or, the Lover, the Lackey, and the Little Glass Slipper 1867.22, 1870.36
Cinders 1923.10
Cingalee, The 1904.40
Circus Day 1901.22
Circus Girl, The 1897.20, 1898.29
Circus Princess, The 1927.17
Circus in Town 1887.31
City Chap, The 1925.38
City Directory, The 1890.07, 1890.34, 1893.28
City of Angels 1989.29
Civil War, The 1999.08
Class Act, A 2001.01
Claude Duval, or, Love and Larceny 1882.17
Claudius Nero 1890.40
Clemenceau Case, The 1890.42
Clinging Vine, The 1922.47
Clio 1885.46
Cloches de Corneville, Les 1878.08, 1879.24, 1879.27, 1879.40, 1880.50, 1881.41, 1881.51, 1882.58, 1883.60, 1885.19, 1902.13, 1926.45
Clorinda! The Girl of the Period 1869.27
Clorindy 1898.41
Clover 1889.22
Coco 1969.17
Cocoanuts, The 1925.45, 1927.21
Codfish Aristocracy 1902.26
Coeur et la Main, Le 1883.59
Cohan Revue of 1916, The 1916.02
Cohan Revue of 1918, The 1917.37
Cohan and Harris Minstrels 1908.22, 1909.16
College Widower, The 1904.39
Columbus Reconstructed 1866.16, 1867.18
Columbus el Filibustero!! 1857.08
Comden & Green, A Party With 1958.21, 1977.02
Come Along 1919.08
Come Summer 1969.07
Come of Age 1934.03, 1952.03
Come to Bohemia 1916.07
Comedy Tonight 1994.13
Comedy With Music 1977.14
Comedy in Music 1953.13
Comedy in Music Opus 2 1964.34
Comic Annual, The 1834.01
Comin' Uptown 1979.32
Coming thro' the Rye 1906.04
Committee, The 1964.26
Commodore, The 1886.50
Company 1970.13, 1995.11
Comrades 1893.33
Comte Obligado 1929.13
Con-Curers, The 1897.48
Concert Varieties 1945.10
Connecticut Yankee, A 1927.56, 1943.22
Connick, Jr., Harrn, An Evening With 1990.19
Connie's Hot Chocolates 1929.23
Conquering Hero, The 1961.02
Consul, The 1950.05, 1952.12, 1960.03, 1962.06, 1966.04, 1966.17, 1974.08, 1975.11
Contact 2000.07
Contented Woman, A 1897.01
Continental Varieties 1934.32
Continental Varieties of 1936 1935.19
Conversation Piece 1934.34
Cook, Barbara: A Concert for the Theatre 1987.06
Cook's Tour 1898.38
Coon Hollow 1894.27
Copper and Brass 1957.14
Copperfield 1981.12
Cordelia's Aspirations 1883.63, 1885.22, 1887.16, 1887.45, 1893.10
Corner Grocery, The, or, the Bad Forgetful Boy 1884.26
Corsair, The (Rice-Braham) 1887.43
Corsair, The (Wm. Brough) 1857.07
Corsican Brothers & Co., The, or, What London Laughs At 1884.44
Cosaque, La 1886.09
Count Me In 1942.27
Count of Luxembourg, The 1912.33, 1930.07
Countess Dubarry 1883.08
Countess Maritza 1926.27, 1928.15
Country Girl, A, or, Town and Country Life 1902.30, 1911.22
Country Sport, A 1893.49
Courted into Court 1896.52, 1897.40
Courtin' Time 1951.17
Cousin Lucy 1915.20
Cox and Box, or, the Long Lost Brothers 1879.21, 1934.22, 1936.20, 1939.05, 1944.07, 1951.08
Cradle Will Rock, The 1937.08, 1947.21, 1960.02
Cranks 1956.13
Crazy Patch 1886.01
Crazy With the Heat 1941.03
Crazy for You 1992.02
Crinoline Girl, The 1914.08
Criss Cross 1926.32
Crook, The, or, the Hunchback of Not-er-dam 1873.22
Crosby, Bing: on Broadway 1976.32
Cross My Heart 1928.28
Crowing Hen, The 1886.33
Cry for Us All 1970.10
Crystal Slipper, The, or, Prince Prettiwitz and Little Cinderella 1888.39
Cupid! 1884.61
Curl and the Judge, The 1901.17
Curse of an Aching Heart, The 1982.02
Cyrano 1973.07
Cyrano de Bergerac 1899.28
Cyrano: the Musical 1993.17
Cyranose de Brick-A-Brac 1898.50
Czardas Princess 1984.05

Dick Whittington and His Cat 1891.19
Daffy Dill 1922.26
Dairymaids, The 1907.32
Dalilah 1858.01
Dame Edna: The Royal Tour 1999.14
Damn Yankees 1955.08, 1994.01
Dan's Tribulations 1884.13, 1893.27
Dance Me a Song 1950.03
Dance a Little Closer 1983.08
Dance and Grow Thin 1917.03
Dancin' 1978.05
Dancing Around 1914.22
Dancing Duchess, The 1914.17
Dancing Girl, The 1923.02
Dancing on Dangerous Ground 2000.04
Dangerous Games 1989.20
Dangerous Maid, A 1898.72
Danny Kaye 1963.10
Darkest America 1896.49
Darling of the Day 1968.02
Darling of the Gallery Gods, The 1903.18

Daughter of Madame Angot 1925.51
Daughter of St. Mark, The 1855.06
Daughter of the Regiment, The, or, the 800 Fathers 1870.23
Daughter of the Revolution, A 1895.16
Davis, Sammy 1974.11
Day Before Spring, The 1945.19
Day and a Night in New York, A 1898.47
Day in Hollywood/A Night in the Ukraine, A 1980.08
Dazzler, The 1891.02, 1894.16
Deacon and the Lady, The 1910.29
Deacon's Daughter, The 1887.17, 1887.46
Dead Shot!, The 1875.37
Dear Sir 1924.34
Dear World 1969.05
Dearest Enemy 1925.31
Debbie Reynolds Show, The 1976.24
Débutante, The 1914.30
Deep Harlem 1929.01
Deep River 1926.31
Deep, Deep Sea, The; or, the Sea Serpent! 1834.02
Defender, The 1902.21
Dein Perry's Steel City 1999.02
Delmonico's at Six 1893.42
Deluge, The, or, Paradise Lost 1874.13
Demoiselles de Mme. Angot, Les 1877.18
Depleurisy 1901.17
Deseret, or, the Saint's Difficulties 1880.54
Desert Flower, The 1868.02
Desert Song, The 1926.42, 1946.03, 1973.09, 1987.10, 1989.18
Destry Rides Again 1959.11
Deux Avuegles, Les 1858.02, 1864.01, 1866.29, 1869.09, 1875.27
Devil and Daniel Webster, The 1939.20, 1959.09
Devil's Auction, The, or, the Golden Branch 1867.25, 1883.47
Devil's Deputy, The 1894.29
Dew Drop Inn 1923.13
Diamond Cut Diamond 1858.09
Dick Whittington and His Cat 1872.04
Different Times 1972.07
Dime Novel, The 1883.18
Dirty Blonde 2000.12
Disney's Beauty and the Beast 1999.16
District Leader, The 1906.19
Dixie to Broadway 1924.37
Do Black Patent Leather Shoes Really Reflect Up? 1982.10
Do I Hear a Waltz? 1965.06
Do Re Mi 1960.23
Doctor Jazz 1975.09
Doctor of Alcantara, The 1866.07, 1866.19, 1866.21, 1867.06, 1868.11, 1882.46
Doctor of All-Can-Tear-Her!, The 1866.22
Dodging for a Wife 1866.26
Doing Our Bit 1917.23
Doings of Mrs. Dooley, The 1902.32
Doll Girl, The 1913.20
Doll's Life, A 1982.18
Dollar Princess, The 1909.21
Dolly Varden 1902.03, 1902.31
Dolores 1888.10
Domestic Bliss! 1866.26
Don Caesar 1886.26
Don't Bother Me, I Can't Cope 1972.13
Don't Get God Started 1987.17
Don't Play Us Cheap 1972.10
Donna Juanita 1881.25, 1881.42, 1882.57
Donnybrook! (Burke) 1961.14
Donnybrook! (Ellis) 1886.60
Donovans, The 1875.14
Doonesbury 1983.18
Dora Bella, the Minstrel, the Mission, the Miss, the Mill and the Misery, or the Dyed Hair and the Turned Head! 1869.45
Dorcas 1896.50
Dorothy 1887.44, 1895.20, 1898.57
Double Dublin 1963.30
Doug Henning and His World of Magic 1984.16
Dove of Peace, The 1912.40
Dovetta 1889.19
Down Broadway, or, the Miniature "69th" 1876.19
Down on the Suwanee River 1896.04
Down the Pike 1904.45
Dr. De Luxe 1911.15
Dr. Syntax 1894.24
Dragons de Villars, Les, or, the Hermit's Bell 1869.24, 1877.12, 1878.09, 1882.29
Dramatic Review for 1868, The 1869.04
Drat! The Cat! 1965.29
Dream 1997.05
Dream City 1906.48
Dream Girl, The 1924.23
Dream With Music 1944.18
Dreamgirls 1981.29, 1987.07
Dreams of Three 1919.17
Dreams! or Binks' Photograph Gallery 1882.39
Dreams, or, Fun in a Photograph Gallery 1880.42, 1882.03
Dreigroschenoper, Die 1965.04
Dress Parade, The 1903.18
Dress Rehearsal, The 1889.27
Dressler, Marie: All Star Gambol 1913.07
Drood! 1985.18
Drum Major, The 1889.40
Drum-Major's Daughter, The 1885.07
DuHurry 1901.17
Dubarry was a Lady 1939.30
Dubarry, The 1932.23
Duchess Misbehaves, The 1946.06
Duchess of Dantzic, The 1905.04
Duchess, The 1911.36
Dude 1972.18
Duke of Duluth, The 1905.33
Dumb Girl of Sevilla, The 1890.38
Dunham, Katherine, and Her Company 1950.07, 1955.26 (see also Tropical Revue)
Dwarf's Wedding at the Court of Peter the Great, The 1891.33

Earl Carroll Vanities (1931) 1931.26
Earl Carroll's Sketch Book (1929) 1929.26
Earl Carroll's Sketch Book (1935) 1935.04
Earl Carroll's Vanities (1923) 1923.21
Earl Carroll's Vanities (1924) 1924.31
Earl Carroll's Vanities (1925) 1925.25
Earl Carroll's Vanities (1926) 1925.48, 1926.23
Earl Carroll's Vanities (1927)/International Edition 1927.02
Earl Carroll's Vanities (1928) 1928.23
Earl Carroll's Vanities (1930) 1930.22
Earl Carroll's Vanities (1932) 1932.18
Earl Carroll's Vanities (1940) 1940.02
Earl and the Girl, The 1905.49
Earl of Ruston 1971.10
Early to Bed 1943.07
Earthquake, The 1910.23
East Lynne, or, the Elopement 1870.25
East Wind 1931.39
Easy Dawson 1905.26
Echo, The 1910.20
Ed Wynn Carnival, The 1920.10
Ed Wynn's Grab Bag 1924.35
Eddie Fisher at the Winter Garden 1962.17
Edgewood Folks 1880.37
Edith Piaf and Her Continental Entertainers 1947.18
Edmund Burke 1905.38
Education of H*Y*M*A*N K*A*P*L*A*N, The 1968.06
Edwin and Angelina; or, the Banditti 1796.03
8 Bells 1891.24 1985.40) (see also New 8 Bells, The)
Eileen 1917.07
Eileen Asthore 1906.38
El Capitan 1896.13, 1897.10, 1898.13
Electric Spark, The 1882.80
Elfins and Mermaids 1881.26
Elsie 1923.08
Elsie Janis and Her Gang 1919.40, 1922.03
Elves, or, the Statue Bride, The 1857.02, 1866.06, 1867.14
Elvis: A Rockin' Remembrance 1989.12
Elvis: the Legend Lives! 1978.01
Elysium 1892.24
Emerald Isle, The, or, the Caves of Carrig-Cleena 1902.25
Enchanted Cat, The 1877.05
Enchanted Isle 1927.45
Enchantment 1879.42, 1880.63
Enchantress, The (Balfe) 1846.01, 1852.03, 1852.04, 1854.02, 1854.07, 1862.03, 1863.07
Enchantress, The (Herbert) 1911.38
Encore 1982.06
L'Enfant Prodigue 1893.25
Engaged 1925.21
English Daisy, An 1904.04
Erminie 1886.30, 1888.02, 1889.16, 1889.49, 1893.35, 1897.24, 1898.36, 1899.24, 1903.32, 1921.01
Ernani, or, the Horn of a Dilemma 1868.32
Errand Boy, The 1904.41
Estrada 1977.13
Estrella 1883.67
Eternal Road, The 1937.01
Eubie! 1978.21
Eva 1912.48
Evangeline and the Lone Fisherman 1880.02
Evangeline, or, the Belle of Acadia 1874.11, 1877.21, 1878.02, 1878.19, 1879.01, 1885.58, 1887.01, 1888.13, 1889.13, 1892.04, 1896.35
Evening With Beatrice Lillie, An 1952.11
Evening With Dave Allen, An 1981.23
Evening With Diana Ross, An 1976.16
Evening With Harry Connick, Jr. and His Orchestra, An 1990.19
Evening With Jerry Herman, An 1998.07
Evening With Josephine Baker, An 1973.17
Evening With Maurice Chevalier, An 1930.13
Evening With Mike Nichols and Elaine May, An 1960.16
Evening With Robert Klein, An 1988.13
Evening With Yves Montand, An 1959.15, 1961.25
Every Good Boy Deserves Favour 1979.17
Everybody's Welcome 1931.36
Everything 1918.23
Everywhere I Roam 1938.18
Everywoman (Her Pilgrimate in Quest of Love) 1911.09
Evil Eye, The, or, the Many Merry Mishaps of Nid and the Weird Wonderful Wanderings of Nod 1899.04
Evita 1979.23

Excelsior 1883.48
Excelsior, Jr. 1895.38
Excess Baggage 1927.66
Exhibit II 1899.38
Experience 1914.24, 1918.01
Eyes and Ears in London 1880.19

Face the Music 1932.05, 1933.02
Fad and Folly 1902.40
Fade Out - Fade In 1964.21
Fads and Fancies 1915.05
Fair Co-Ed, The 1909.03
Fair One With the Blonde Wig, The 1870.20, 1872.19, 1876.06
Fair One With the Golden Locks, The 1863.04
Fair in Midgettown, The 1897.35
Fairies' Well, The 1889.38
Fairy Prince O'Donoughue, or, the White Horse of Killarney, 1865.04
Fakir, The 1891.04
Falka 1884.14, 1886.37, 1887.22, 1900.17
Falote, La 1897.11
Falsettos 1992.09
Family Affair, A 1962.01
Family Jars 1867.19, 1871.20
Fanchon 1884.50
Fancy Free 1918.12
Fanny 1954.15
Fantana 1905.03
Fantasma 1889.02
Fantasma, or, Funny Frolics in Fairyland 1884.58
Fascinating Flora 1907.18
Fascinating Widow, The 1911.30
Fashions of 1924 1923.22
Fast and Furious 1931.31
Fatherland 1892.31
Fatinitza 1879.22, 1879.25, 1879.65, 1879.67, 1880.48, 1880.62, 1882.07, 1882.65, 1883.11, 1887.41, 1904.57
Faust 1867.28, 1870.43
Faust Up to Date 1889.54
Faust on Time 1889.42
Faust, or, the Demon, the Doctor and the Devil's Draught 1867.16
Faust, or, the Vicissitudes of a "Girl of the Period" 1870.06
Faustus, or, the Demon of the Drachenfels 1851.01, 1854.01
Fearless Frank 1980.17
Fee-G! 1874.25
Feldprediger, Der 1885.27
Female Drummer, A 1898.78
Femme a Papa, La 1885.57
Fencing Master, The 1892.52, 1898.04
Fiddle-Dee-Dee 1900.38
Fiddler on the Roof 1964.27, 1976.36, 1981.18, 1990.18
Fiddlers Three 1918.26
Field of the Cloth of Gold, The 1869.08
Fiesta in Madrid 1969.11
Fifth Avenue 1877.07
Fifty Miles from Boston 1908.09
Fifty Million Frenchmen 1929.45
Fifty-Fifty, Ltd. 1919.32
Fig Leaves are Falling, The 1969.01
Fille de Madame Angot, La 1873.11, 1874.15, 1874.19, 1875.02, 1875.28, 1876.17, 1876.26, 1877.27, 1879.48, 1881.49, 1883.30, 1883.57, 1884.54, 1887.37, 1890.22, 1893.04, 1926.47
Fille du Tambour-Major, La 1880.44, 1880.49, 1881.54, 1885.20
Fin-Fin, the Pretty Brigand 1885.31
Fine and Dandy 1930.28
Finian's Rainbow 1947.03, 1955.09, 1960.09, 1967.04
Finish of Mr. Fresh, The 1898.70
Finnigan's 400 1899.18
Fiorello! 1959.25, 1962.16
Fioretta 1929.08
Fire Fly, or, the Friend of the Flag 1868.19, 1869.40
Firebrand of Florence, The 1945.04
Firefly, The 1912.46, 1931.45
Fireman's Flame, The 1937.12
First Come-First Served 1853.02
First Impressions 1959.06
First Life Guards at Brighton 1880.01
First, The 1981.28
Fisher, Eddie, at the Winter Garden 1962.17
Fisher Maiden, The 1903.29
Five Guys Named Moe 1992.03
Five O'Clock Girl, The 1927.52, 1981.03
5...6...7...8...Dance! 1983.09
Flag is Born, A 1946.17
Flahooley 1951.15
Flamenco Puro 1986.17
Flams, The 1894.46
Fledermaus 1954.06
Fledermaus, Die 1885.14, 1879.57, 1885.52, 1900.02, 1953.06, 1953.15, 1954.10, 1955.17, 1956.10, 1957.13, 1958.15, 1959.16, 1964.31, 1965.25, 1974.16, 1975.16, 1976.23, 1977.11, 1980.03, 1980.22, 1981.22, 1984.03, 1986.10, 1987.11
Fleur de Thé 1869.05, 1871.24
Fleur-de-Lis 1895.22
Fleurette 1891.21
Flick Flock 1869.38
Flo-Flo (Davis-Whitney) 1904.53
Flo-Flo (Hein-Paulton) 1917.34
Floor Walkers, The 1900.08
Flora Bella 1916.17
Flora, the Red Menace 1965.17
Florida Girl 1925.40
Florodora 1900.51, 1902.05, 1905.13, 1920.09
Flossie 1924.17
Flower Drum Song 1958.19
Flower Girl, The 1905.46
Flower of the Ranch, The 1908.13
Fluffy Ruffles 1908.27
Flying Colors 1932.17
Flying High 1930.11
Flying Karamazov Brothers do the Impossible, The 1994.11
Flying Karamazov Brothers, A: Sharps, Flats and Accidentals 1998.22
Flying Karamazov Brothers, The 1983.07, 1986.05
Fol-De-Rol 1901.28
Folies Bergère 1939.31, 1964.22
Follies (Sondheim) 1971.05, 2001.02
Follies of 1907 (Ziegfeld) 1907.24
Follies of 1908 (Ziegfeld) 1908.19
Follies of 1909 (Ziegfeld) 1909.13
Follies of 1910 (Ziegfeld) 1910.18
Follow Me 1916.25
Follow Thru 1929.03
Follow the Girl (Parenteau-Blossom) 1918.06
Follow the Girls (Charig-Shapiro-Pascal) 1944.14
Fool Moon 1993.01, 1995.16, 1998.17
Fools Rush In 1934.40
Footlights 1927.39
Footloose 1998.13
For Goodness Sake 1922.10
For Your Pleasure 1943.02
Forbidden Melody 1936.27
Foresters, The 1892.14
Forever Tango 1997.13
Forsythe, Bruce: on Broadway 1979.14
Fortune Teller, The 1898.60, 1929.40
Fortunio and His Seven Gifted Servants 1883.37
Fortunio and his Gifted Servants! 1872.16
'49ers, The 1922.42
Forty Thieves, The 1870.21
Forty Thieves, or, Striking Oil in Family Jars!, The 1869.06, 1871.01
Forty-Five Minutes from Broadway 1906.02, 1906.42
Forty-Second Street 1980.20, 2001.08
Fosse 1999.01
4–11–44 1889.15
Four Saints in Three Acts 1934.05, 1952.06, 1996.10
1492, Up to Date or Very Near It 1893.17, 1894.26, 1897.46
45 Minutes from Broadway 1912.11
Foxy 1964.04
Foxy Grandpa 1902.08
Foxy Quiller 1900.50
Fra Diavolo 1866.15, 1884.35, 1885.30, 1892.13, 1898.33, 1900.18, 1901.10
Fra Diavolo, or, the Beauty and the Brigands 1864.13, 1867.23
Fra Diavolo, the Brigand of the Period 1870.18
Fra Diavolo; or, the Inn of Terracina 1864.18, 1867.04, 1868.10
Frank Fay Vaudeville 1939.16
Frank Fay's Fables 1922.08
Frank Merriwell, or, Honor Challenged 1971.09
Frederika 1937.03
Free Lance, The 1906.18
Free for All 1931.28
French Doll, The 1922.09
French Maid, The 1897.37, 1898.51
Friend Fritz 1893.03
Friend and Foe 1882.69
Fritz Among the Gypsies 1883.01
Fritz in England and Ireland 1883.20
Fritz in Ireland 1892.12
Fritz in Ireland, or, the Bell-ringer and the Love of the Shamrock 1884.07
Fritz in Ireland, or, the Bell-ringer of the Rhine and the Love of the Shamrock 1879.63, 1880.39, 1881.52, 1893.38
Fritz in Prosperity 1893.38
Fritz in Tammany Hall 1905.41
Fritz in a Mad House 1893.12, 1894.09
Fritz, Our Cousin German 1870.24, 1871.15, 1873.24, 1887.11
Frivolities of 1920 1920.02
Frolics of a Day 1883.50
From A to Z 1960.07
From Across the Pond 1907.35
From Broadway to Paris 1912.43
From Israel With Love 1972.17
From St. Louis to New Orleans! 1875.37
From Vienna 1939.23
From the Second City 1961.17
Frow-Frow 1870.16, 1876.09
Full Monty, The 2000.15
Fun in a Fog 1873.09
Fun on the Bristol 1880.35, 1881.47, 1892.53
Fun on the Pacific Mail 1894.39
Funabashi 1908.03
Funny Face 1927.59
Funny Girl 1964.11
Funny Mr. Dooley, The 1904.06

Funny Thing Happened on the Way to the Forum, A 1962.12, 1972.03, 1996.06
Funny Valentines 1885.42
Funzapoppin' 1949.06
Furs and Frills 1917.21

Gabriel Grub; or, the Story of the Goblins Who Stole the Sexton! 1873.29
Gaby 1911.18
Gaiety Girl, A 1894.33, 1895.10
Galatea, or, the Black Scupltor 1876.33
Gandolfo! 1884.60
Gang's All Here, The 1931.05
Gans, Danny: The Many Voices of 1995.17
Gantry 1970.02
Garland, Judy, At Home at the Palace 1968.11
Garrett O'Magh 1901.02
Garrick Gaieties, The (1925) 1925.17
Garrick Gaieties, The (1926) 1926.13
Garrick Gaieties, The (1930) 1930.18, 1930.33
Gasparone 1885.11, 1887.20
Gatta Cenerentola, La 1985.14
Gay Divorce 1932.26
Gay Hussars, The 1909.15
Gay Life, The 1961.27
Gay Musician, The 1908.16
Gay New York 1906.10
Gay Paree (1925) 1925.27
Gay Paree (1926) 1926.37
Gay White Way, The 1907.42
Gayest Manhattan 1898.01
Gayest Manhattan, or, Around New York in Ninety Minutes 1897.14
Geezer, The 1896.36
Geisha, The 1896.27, 1897.44, 1898.18, 1913.09, 1931.35
Geneviève de Brabant 1868.26, 1872.31, 1874.17, 1874.18
Gentleman Joe, or, the Hanson Cabby 1896.01
Gentleman Joe, the Hansom Cabby 1896.05
Gentlemen Prefer Blondes 1949.18, 1995.07
Gentlemen, Be Seated! 1963.22
George Gershwin Alone 2001.07
George M! 1968.07
George W. Lederer's Mid-Summer Night Fancies 1903.18
George Washington, Jr. 1906.11, 1907.09
George White's Music Hall Varieties 1932.24
George White's Scandals (1919) 1919.13
George White's Scandals (1920) 1920.17
George White's Scandals (1921) 1921.22
George White's Scandals (1922) 1922.27
George White's Scandals (1923) 1923.18
George White's Scandals (1924) 1924.19
George White's Scandals (1925) 1925.22
George White's Scandals (1926) 1926.16
George White's Scandals (1928) 1928.22
George White's Scandals (1929) 1929.35
George White's Scandals (1931) 1931.30
George White's Scandals (1936) 1935.18
George White's Scandals (1939) 1939.25
Géorgiennes, Les 1871.06
Georgy 1970.03
Gershwins' Fascinating Rhythm, The 1999.10
Get Together 1921.28
Getting Together 1918.10
Getting a Polish 1910.33
Ghetto: The Last Performance in the Vilna Ghetto 1989.10
Giddy Throng, The 1900.56
Gigi 1973.12
Gilbert Becaud Sings Love 1968.21
Gilbert Becaud on Broadway 1966.20
Gilbert and Sullivan Review, A 1905.22
Gilda Radner - Live From New York 1979.19
Gin-Nevieve de Graw 1868.33
Ginger 1923.37
Ginger Snaps 1929.52
Gingerbread Man, The 1905.56
Gingham Girl, The 1922.28
Girl and the Kaiser, The 1910.36
Girl Behind the Counter, The 1907.41
Girl Behind the Gun, The 1918.28
Girl Crazy 1930.31
Girl Friend, The 1926.07
Girl Question, The 1908.23
Girl Wanted 1896.03
Girl Who Came to Supper, The 1963.29
Girl Who Smiles, The 1915.19
Girl and the Gambler, The 1906.34
Girl and the Governor, The 1907.07
Girl and the Wizard, The 1909.24
Girl from Brazil, The 1916.14
Girl from Brighton, The 1912.29
Girl from Broadway, The 1907.04
Girl from Dixie, A 1903.41
Girl from Home, The 1920.13
Girl from Kay's, The 1903.33
Girl from Martin's, The 1899.30
Girl from Montmartre, The 1912.26
Girl from Nantucket, The 1945.17
Girl from Paris, The 1896.48, 1898.05
Girl from Up There, The 1901.01
Girl from Utah, The 1914.18, 1915.18
Girl from Wyoming, The 1938.12
Girl in Pink Tights, The 1954.01
Girl in the Spotlight, The 1920.21
Girl in the Taxi, The 1910.32
Girl in the Train, The 1910.27
Girl o' Mine 1918.02
Girl of My Dreams, The 1911.25
Girl on the Film, The 1913.36
Girlies 1910.17
Girls Against the Boys, The 1959.23
Girls Will be Girls 1904.27
Girls of Gottenburg, The 1908.25
Girls of Holland, The 1907.52
Giroflé-Girofla 1875.04, 1875.11, 1875.26, 1875.29, 1875.38, 1876.20, 1876.21, 1877.11, 1877.33, 1878.18, 1879.23, 1879.49, 1880.56, 1885.23, 1893.07, 1894.14, 1905.08, 1926.40
Girouette, or, the Weathercock 1882.26
Glad Hand 1897.31
Glance at New York in 1848, A 1848.01
Glimpse of the Great White Way, A
Glittering Gloria 1904.08
Glorianna 1918.33
Glorious 7, The 1870.04
Glory 1922.48
Go Easy, Mabel 1922.17
Go to It 1916.22
Go-Go 1923.06
Goddess of Liberty, The 1909.31
Goddess of Truth, The 1896.10
Godspell 1976.17
Going Up 1917.36, 1976.25
Going it Blind 1859.14
Going to the Races 1898.64
Gold Bug, The 1896.30
Golden Age, The 1963.28
Golden Apple, The 1954.03
Golden Boy 1964.32
Golden Butterfly, The (Barnes-Brinkworth) 1870.28, 1872.38
Golden Butterfly, The (DeKoven-Smith) 1908.34
Golden Dawn 1927.63
Golden Horseshoe, The 1898.53
Golden Rainbow 1968.03
Golden Wedding, The 1893.34
Goldilocks 1958.14
Gondoliers, The, or, the King of Barataria 1890.02, 1893.09, 1898.42, 1931.15, 1934.21, 1935.08, 1936.16, 1939.08, 1940.11, 1942.09, 1944.09, 1948.07, 1951.06, 1961.05, 1962.11, 1962.26, 1964.12
Good Boy 1928.25
Good Evening 1973.13
Good Luck, Sam! 1918.36
Good Morning, Dearie 1921.36
Good Morning, Judge 1919.02
Good Mr. Best, The 1897.30
Good News 1927.41, 1974.26
Good Night Paul 1917.18
Good Old Summertime, The 1904.07
Good Thing, A 1896.37
Good Times 1920.26
Good-Bye Bill 1918.14
Goodbye Girl, The 1993.02
Goodtime Charley 1975.06
Gorey Stories 1978.24
Gospel at Colonus, The 1988.05
Gossoon, The 1891.42
Gotta Getaway! 1984.10
Gottu Go Disco 1979.15
Governor's Son, The 1901.07, 1906.21
Governors, The 1898.02
Grab Bag, The 1924.35
Grafter, The 1906.09
Grand Casimir, Le 1883.34, 1885.25, 1885.60
Grand Duchess of Gérolstein, The 1874.22, 1875.23, 1982.07, 1982.21
Grand Duchess, The 1870.40, 1872.20, 1873.21, 1874.01, 1875.22, 1876.27, 1890.11, 1891.17, 1894.48, 1899.10 (see also Grande-Duchesse de Gérolstein, La)
Grand Dutch S, The 1868.05, 1876.05
Grand Hotel 1989.26
Grand Mogol, Le (Audran) 1887.35
Grand Mogul, The (Luders-Pixley) 1907.13
Grand Music Hall of Israel 1968.04, 1973.01
Grand Night for Singing, A 1993.16
Grand Street Follies (1922), The 1922.20
Grand Street Follies (1924), The 1924.14
Grand Street Follies (1925), The 1925.20
Grand Street Follies (1926), The 1926.17
Grand Street Follies (1927), The 1927.23
Grand Street Follies (1928), The 1928.19
Grand Street Follies (1929), The 1929.20
Grand Tour, The 1979.02
Grand Vizier, The 1895.07
Grande-Duchesse de Gérolstein, La 1867.24, 1868.15, 1868.16, 1868.24, 1868.25, 1869.18, 1870.03, 1870.37, 1871.25, 1872.29, 1873.15, 1876.24, 1877.34, 1879.61, 1884.05, 1886.08 (see also Grand Duchess, The; Grand Duchess of Gérolstein, The)
Grass Harp, The 1971.16
Grass Widow, The 1917.32
Grease 1972.12, 1994.07, 1996.17
Great Day 1929.37
Great Decide, The 1906.29
Great Lady 1938.15
Great Scheme, A, Our Dime Museum 1884.17
Great Temptations, The 1926.14
Great Waltz, The 1934.29
Great to be Alive! 1950.06
Greek Slave, A 1899.39
Green Bird, The 2000.10
Green Grow the Lilacs 1931.02

Green Monster, or, the White Knight and the Giant Warrior 1865.05
Green Pastures, The 1930.10, 1935.01, 1951.11
Green-Room Fun 1882.24, 1883.33
Grenfell, Joyce Requests the Pleasure 1955.19
Grenfell, Joyce: Monologues and Songs 1958.10
Greenwich Village Follies (1919), The 1919.18
Greenwich Village Follies (1920), The 1920.28
Greenwich Village Follies (1921), The 1921.27
Greenwich Village Follies (1922), The 1922.32
Greenwich Village Follies (1923), The 1923.31
Greenwich Village Follies (1924), The 1924.32
Greenwich Village Follies (1925), The/1st & 2nd eds 1925.47
Greenwich Village Follies (1928), The 1928.14
Greenwillow 1960.05
Grim Goblin, The 1880.34
Grind 1985.05
Grip, The 1885.66, 1889.18, 1897.43
Grosse Valise, La 1965.37
Gulliver's Travels 1904.20
Gus Edwards' Broadway Sho-Window 1936.06
Guy Mannering, or, the Gipsy's Prophecy 1855.01
Guys and Dolls 1950.17, 1955.06, 1965.15, 1966.13, 1976.21, 1992.04
Gypsy 1959.13, 1974.17, 1989.27, 1991.06
Gypsy Baron, The 1886.04, 1898.14, 1944.26, 1945.15
Gypsy Blonde 1934.17
Gypsy Lady 1946.18
Gypsy Love 1911.37
Gypsy Passion 1992.15
Gypsy, The 1912.42

H.M.S. Pinafore, or, the Lass That Loved a Sailor 1879.05, 1879.06, 1879.07, 1879.08, 1879.13, 1879.14, 1879.16, 1879.17, 1879.28, 1879.29, 1879.30, 1879.58, 1879.59, 1879.66, 1879.70, 1880.12, 1880.53, 1882.12, 1882.22, 1882.40, 1883.21, 1884.30, 1885.16, 1885.37, 1886.17, 1887.25, 1890.18, 1896.19, 1898.09, 1899.07, 1900.26, 1911.21, 1912.22, 1913.12, 1914.11, 1915.13, 1926.08, 1931.12, 1931.23, 1933.11, 1934.10, 1934.26, 1935.10, 1936.10, 1936.21, 1939.06, 1942.02, 1944.06, 1948.06, 1949.14, 1951.04, 1952.18, 1955.22, 1961.06, 1961.23, 1962.09, 1962.30, 1964.08, 1964.38, 1965.09, 1966.26, 1968.10, 1968.25, 1975.17, 1976.14, 1976.22, 1978.16, 1989.01, 1996.11
Haarlem Nocturne 1984.15
Hackettz, Buddy, and Eddie Fisher 1967.12
Hair 1968.11, 1977.15
Hairpin Harmony 1943.18
Half Moon, The 1920.40
Half a King 1896.28, 1897.36
Half a Sixpence 1965.14
Half a Widow 1927.43
Hall of Fame, The 1902.06
Hallelujah, Baby! 1967.06
Ham Tree, The 1905.28, 1906.24
Hamlet (burlesque) 1870.07
Hamlet II (burlesque) 1895.15
Hammerstein's 9 O'Clock Revue 1923.35
Hand is on the Gate, A 1966.15
Hands Up 1915.16
Hanky Panky (Sloane-Goetz) 1912.25
Hanky Panky Land (Coots-Moore) 1921.42
Hans, the Flute Player 1910.24
Hänsel and Gretel 1895.28
Happiest Girl in the World, The 1961.08
Happiest Night of His Life, The 1911.07
Happy 1927.64
Happy Days 1919.22
Happy End 1977.08
Happy Go Lucky 1926.30
Happy Hooligan 1902.09
Happy Hooligan's Trip Around the World 1906.06
Happy Hunting 1956.16
Happy Little Home, A 1895.37
Happy New Year 1980.06
Happy Time, The 1968.01
Happy Town 1959.19
Happy as Larry 1950.01
Happyland, or, the King of Elysia 1905.36
Hard Job Being God 1972.09
Harlem Cavalcade 1942.13
Harlequin Bluebeard, or, the Good Fairy Preciosa and the Bad Demon Rusifusti 1864.23
Harlequin Jack the Giant Killer 1861.01
Harlequin! Demon Statue, the Enchanted Pills and Magic Apple Tree; or, High Diddle Diddle, the Cat's in the Fiddle, the Cow Jumped Over the Moon! 1875.40
Harrigan 'n Hart 1985.02
Harry Delmar's Revels 1927.62
Hassard Short's Ritz Revue 1924.33
Hats Off to Ice 1944.20
Havana 1909.04
Have You Seen Smith? 1898.66
Have a Heart 1917.01
Hayride 1954.08
Hazel Flagg 1953.01
He Came from Milwaukee 1910.25
He Didn't Want to do It 1918.22
He, She, Him and Her 1888.43
Head Over Heels 1918.25
Head Waiters, The 1902.02
Heads Up! 1929.42
Hear! Hear! 1955.13
Heart and Hand 1883.10
Heart of Paddy Whack 1914.29
Heathen 1972.11
Heathen, The (Not the Christian) 1898.50
Heaven on Earth 1948.23
Held, Anna, All Star Variete Jubilee 1913.35
Helen Goes to Troy 1944.16
Helen of Troy, New York 1923.19
Hell/Temptations/Gaby 1911.18
Hello Daddy 1928.50
Hello Lola! 1926.02
Hello Yourself!!!! 1928.41
Hello, Alexander 1919.26
Hello, Broadway! 1914.34
Hello, Dolly! 1964.01, 1967.15, 1975.21, 1978.04, 1995.13
Hello Lester 1920.35
Hello, Paris (J.R. Johnson-Hill) 1911.26
Hello, Paris (Tarbox-Rubens) 1930.37
Hello, Solly! 1967.03
Hellzapoppin' 1938.08
Helter Skelter 1899.17
Hen-Pecks, The 1911.05
Hendrik Hudson, or, the Discovery of Columbus 1890.27, 1894.13
Henning, Doug, and His World of Magic 1984.16
Henry, Sweet Henry 1967.14
Her Family Tree 1920.45
Her First Roman 1968.23
Her Little Highness 1913.27
Her Regiment 1917.28
Her Soldier Boy 1916.26
Here Goes the Bride 1931.42
Here's Howe 1928.17
Here's Love 1963.21
Here's Where I Belong 1968.05
Herman Van Veen: All of Him 1982.23
Herman, Jerry, An Evening With 1998.07
Hero is Born, A 1937.11
Herrmann's Transatlantique Vaudevilles 1889.35
Hey Nonny Nonny! 1932.13
Hiawatha! A long way after Longfellow 1880.10, 1880.67
Hiawatha, or, Ardent Spirits and Laughing Water 1856.04
Hiccory Diccory Dock; or, Harlequin Jack of the Beanstalk! 1869.26
Higgledy-Piggledy 1904.39
High Button Shoes 1947.16
High Jinks 1913.34
High Kickers 1941.09
High Roller, A 1891.18
High Rollers Social and Pleasure Club, The 1992.06
High Society 1998.05
High Spirits 1964.16
High and Lengthy, or, the Steer and the Peri 1883.03
High-Born Lady, A 1898.67
Higher and Higher 1940.06
Highwayman, The 1897.50, 1917.10
Hilarities 1948.21
Hip! Hip! Hooray! (G. Edwards-Smith) 1907.44
Hip-Hip-Hooray (Hubbell-Golden) 1915.24
Hippodrome!, The 1866.20
Hired Girl's Millions, The 1907.28
Hired Girl, A 1898.03
His Excellency 1895.29
His Grace, the Duke! 1876.04
His Honor the Mayor (Edwards-Aarons-Campbell-Skinner) 1906.20, 1907.21
His Honor the Mayor of the Bowery (Samuel Blair Co.) 1905.02
His Honor, the Barber 1911.20
His Little Widows 1917.09
His Majesty 1906.15
His-Mud-Scow Pinafore 1879.09
History of the American Film, A 1978.06
Hit the Deck! 1927.16
Hit the Trail 1954.17
Hitchy-Koo (1917) 1917.12
Hitchy-Koo (1918) 1918.18
Hitchy-Koo (1919) 1919.25
Hitchy-Koo (1920) 1920.39
Hobbies 1879.53, 1881.08
Hodge, Podge & Co. 1900.47
Hogan's Alley 1896.38
Hoity-Toity 1901.17
Hokey-Pokey 1912.07
Hold Everything 1928.36
Hold It! 1948.15
Hold On to Your Hats 1940.10
Hold Your Horses 1933.21
Hole in the Ground, A 1887.29
Holiday on Broadway 1948.13
Holka Polka 1925.36
Hollow Crown, The 1963.03
Hollywood Pinafore, or, the Lad Who Loved a Salary 1945.09
Home Sweet Homer 1976.01
Honey Girl 1920.14
Honeydew 1920.31
Honeymoon Express, The 1913.05
Honeymoon Lane 1926.29
Honeymooners, The 1907.20
Honky Tonk Nights 1986.11
Hook of Holland 1907.63

Hooray for What! 1937.15
Hop O' My Thumb (J. Schonberg) 1870.22
Hop O' My Thumb (S. Rosenfeld-M. Klein) 1913.33
Hop O' My Thumb, or, the Ogre and the Dwarf! (A. Smith-W.T. Peterschen) 1862.02
Horrors 1880.06
Horrors, or, the Marajah of Zogobad 1879.35
Horse Marines 1869.14
Hoss and Hoss 1891.37, 1893.08
Hot Chocolates 1929.23
Hot Mikado, The 1939.17
Hot Old Time, A 1897.33, 1900.24, 1905.14
Hot Rhythm 1930.24
Hot Spot 1963.13
Hot-Cha! (Laid in Mexico) 1932.07
Hotel Mouse, The 1922.12
Hotel Topsy Turvy 1898.63
Hottest Coon in Dixie, The 1901.20
House of Flowers 1954.19
House that Jack Built, The (G.L. Fox) 1864.06
House that Jack Built, The, or, Harlequin and the Fairy Generous (J. Maffit) 1864.02
Houseboat on the Styx, The 1928.49
How Baxter Butted In 1905.51
How Come? 1923.11
How He Won Her 1905.09
How Now, Dow Jones 1967.16
How to Succeed in Business Without Really Trying 1961.22, 1966.07, 1995.05
How to be a Jewish Mother 1967.18
Howdy, Mr. Ice 1948.19
Howdy, Mr. Ice of 1950 1949.05
Hoyden, The 1907.46
Human Comedy, The 1984.02
Hummin' Sam 1933.06
Humming Bird, The 1887.08, 1887.34
Hummings Birds and Onions 1902.29
Humpty Dumpty (G.L. Fox) 1868.06, 1871.18, 1873.02, 1876.03
Humpty Dumpty (J. Maffit) 1880.68, 1881.39, 1888.07
1880.07
HUmpty Dumpty (Collins-McNally) 1904.47
Humpty Dumpty Abroad! (G.L. Fox) 1873.26
Humpty Dumpty Junior, or, the Fairy of the Diamond Mines and the Giant's Festival (Kiralfy) 1870.31
Humpty Dumpty Up to Date (Lilliputians) 1894.30
Humpty Dumpty at Home (G.L. Fox) 1874.09
Humpty Dumpty at School! (G.L. Fox) 1874.03
Humpty Dumpty in Every Clime (G.L. Fox) 1875.32
Humpty Dumpty's Dream (Fox-Fraser) 1878.10
Humpty Dumpty, Volume the Third (Fox-Denier) 1871.11
110 in the Shade 1963.26, 1992.10
Hurdy Gurdy Girl, The 1907.39
Hurly-Burly 1898.50
Hurry, Harry 1972.19
Husband (?), The 1907.31
Hustler, The 1891.40

I Can Get it for You Wholesale 1962.05
I Do! I Do! 1966.29
I Had a Ball 1964.44
I Love My Wife 1977.04
I Married an Angel 1938.05
I Remember Mama 1979.12
I Saltimbanchi 1911.16
I Told You So 1927.04
I'd Rather be Right 1937.13
I'll Say She Is 1924.11
I'm Solomon 1968.08
I, Mary McPain 1902.29
Ice Dancing 1978.26
Ice Show, The (Toller Cranston's) 1977.09
Icetime 1946.14
Icetime of 1948 1947.12
Idea, The 1894.17
Idol's Eye, The 1897.42
If I Were You 1892.57
If the Shoe Fits 1946.22
Ill Treated Il Trovatore!, or, the Mother, the Maiden and the Musicianeer 1880.24, 1864.09
Ill-Fed-Dora 1884.59
Illustrator's Show, The 1936.01
Illya, Darling 1967.05
In Atlantic City 1898.44
In Dahomey 1903.08, 1904.26
In Gay New York 1896.18, 1898.20
In Gay Paree 1899.15, 1899.37
In Gotham 1898.56
In Greater New York 1897.16
In Hayti 1909.18
In Mexico - 1848 (A War-Time Wedding) 1896.42
In New York Town 1905.42
In Newport 1904.56
In Posterland 1902.33
In the Limelight 1911.34
In Town 1897.32
Inacent Black 1981.15
Indiana 1887.04
Indigo 1891.22
Inner City 1971.20
Innocent Eyes 1924.13
Inside U.S.A. 1948.14
Inside the Earth 1909.20
Insideoutandallaround With Shelley Berman 1980.24
International Cup, The 1910.23
International Revue 1930.09
International Soirée 1958.06
Into the Light 1986.18
Into the Woods 1987.18
Investigation 1884.41, 1886.42
Invincibles!, The 1863.01
Invisible Prince, The, or, the Island of Tranquil Delights 1859.07, 1860.03, 1866.08, 1867.15
Iolanthe, or, the Peer and the Peri 1882.78, 1887.21, 1890.48, 1892.40, 1898.52, 1900.04, 1913.13, 1915.14, 1926.10, 1927.57, 1931.20, 1934.11, 1934.24, 1936.11, 1936.19, 1939.04, 1942.07, 1944.10, 1948.03, 1951.07, 1952.19, 1955.24, 1962.08, 1962.31, 1964.14, 1964.36, 1968.29, 1978.14
Iole 1913.37
Ipi-Tombi 1977.01
Irene 1919.36, 1923.09, 1973.05
Irish Aristocracy 1882.81, 1884.19, 1886.23, 1889.51
Irish Artist, The 1894.36, 1896.09
Irish Gentleman, An 1897.47
Irish Heiress, The 1875.34
Irish Minstrel, The 1886.51, 1888.12, 1889.14, 1891.07
Irishman's Love, An 1891.01
Irma la Douce 1960.13
Is There Life After High School? 1982.08
Isham's Octoroons 1899.31
Island of Bachelors!, The 1876.10
Isle O' Dreams, The 1913.03
Isle of Champagne, The 1892.55, 1893.20, 1898.34
Isle of Gold, The 1897.21
Isle of Spice, The 1904.25
It Ain't Nothin' But the Blues 1999.09
It Happened in Nordland 1904.54
It Happens on Ice 1940.16
It's So Nice to be Civilized 1980.15
It's Up to You 1921.08
It's Up to You, John Henry 1905.43
It's a Bird. . .It's a Plane. . .It's Superman 1966.06
Ivanhoe 1869.17
Ivy Leaf, The 1886.10
Ixion, or, the Man at the Wheel 1868.23, 1869.28, 1869.31, 1870.02, 1872.07, 1872.14, 1872.24, 1872.36, 1873.27, 1876.13, 1885.08, 1885.18, 1886.31

J.P. McEvoy's New Americana 1932.20
Jacinta, or, the Maid of Manzanillo 1894.47
Jack Benny 1963.07
Jack and Gill Went Up the Hill 1866.02, 1866.28
Jack and Jill (Barratt-Anderson-Harbach) 1923.07
Jack and Jill (Maffit) 1874.24
Jack and the Beanstalk 1931.46
Jack o' Lantern 1917.22
Jack's Romance 1915.03
Jack-in-the-Box 1886.02
Jackie Mason's World According to Me, The 1986.21, 19988.11
Jackie Mason: Brand New 1990.11
Jackie Mason: Politically Incorrect 1994.03
Jackpot 1944.01
Jack, the Giant Killer 1872.43
Jacques Brel is Alive and Well and Living in Paris 1972.16, 1981.05
Jacquette 1887.24
Jamaica 1957.16
James Joyce's the Dead 2000.01
Jane Eyre 2000.20
Janis, Elsie, and Her Gang 1919.40, 1922.03
Japan by Night 1902.22, 1903.19
Jekyll & Hyde 1997.09
Jelly's Last Jam 1992.08
Jennie 1963.25
Jenny Lind 1860.04, 1863.01, 1866.17
Jerome Kern Goes to Hollywood 1986.01
Jerome Robbins' Broadway 1989.03
Jerry's Girls 1985.19
Jersey Lily, The 1903.27
Jesus Christ Superstar 1971.12, 1977.18, 1995.02, 2000.09
Jewel of Asia, The 1903.06
Jim Jam Jems 1920.35
Jimmie 1920.42
Jimmy 1969.14
Joan of Arc, or, the Merry Maid of Orleans 1892.02
Jocko, or, the Brazilian Ape 1865.10
John Curry's Ice Dancing 1978.26
John Henry 1940.01
John Murray Anderson's Almanac 1953.17
Johnny 2 X 4 1942.11
Johnny Johnson 1936.28, 1971.06
Johnny on the Spot 1899.09
Jolie Parfumeuse, La 1875.07, 1876.31, 1877.16, 1877.29, 1879.34, 1879.46, 1882.55, 1883.61, 1884.45, 1886.22
Jolly Bachelors!, The (Stevens-Darling) 1882.18

Jolly Bachelors, The (Hubbell-McDonough) 1910.01
Jolly Baron, A 1905.32
Jolly Musketeer, The 1898.73
Jolly Surprise, A 1892.19
Jonica 1930.14
Joseph and the Amazing Technicolor Dreamcoat 1982.03, 1993.15
Josephine Baker and Her Company 1964.02
Josephine Sold by Her Sisters 1886.43
Joshua Whitcomb 1876.22, 1878.11, 1880.21, 1881.10, 1882.82, 1886.13
Jotham Valley 1951.05
Jour et la Nuit, Le 1882.30, 1885.17
Joyce Grenfell, Requests the Pleasure 1955.19
Joyce Grenfell: Monologues and Songs 1958.10
Joyce, James, The Dead 2000.01
Joyful Noise, A 1966.30
Juan Darién 1996.16
Jubilee 1935.14
Judy 1927.09
Judy Forgot 1910.30
Judy Garland at Home at the Palace 1967.11
Jumbo 1935.15
Jumping Jupiter 1911.08
June Days 1925.26
June Love 1921.09
Juno 1959.04
Junon and Avos - the Hope 1990.01
Jupiter, or, the King and the Cobbler 1892.20
Just Because 1922.13
Just Fancy! 1927.54
Just a Joke 1906.12
Just a Minute (Archer) 1928.34
Just a Minute (Orlob) 1919.33

Kajanka 1889.50, 1890.25
Karl, the Peddler 1886.56
Kat and the Kings 1999.12
Kate Kip, Buyer 1898.69
Katherine Dunham and Her Company 1950.07, 1955.26 (see also Tropical Revue)
Katinka 1915.29
Katja 1926.33
Katzenjammer Kids, The 1900.53
Kaye, Danny 1963.10
Kean 1961.26
Keep 'Em Laughing 1942.12
Keep Kool 1924.16
Keep Moving 1934.18
Keep Off the Grass 1940.07
Keep Shufflin' 1928.10
Keep it Clean 1929.24
Kelly 1965.01
Ken Murray's Blackouts of 1949 1949.09
Ken Murray's Hollywood 1965.16
Kenilworth 1886.54
Kenilworth, or, Ye Queen, Ye Knight and Ye Maiden 1872.26
Kenilworth, or, Ye Queene, Ye Earle and Ye Maydenne 1867.10, 1869.42
Khedive, The 1891.23
Kid Boots 1923.47
Kid, The 1892.34
Kill Trovatore! 1867.21
Killarney and the Rhine 1898.59
Kilpatrick's Old-Time Minstrels 1930.16
Kim-Ka!, or, the Adventures of an Aeronaut 1875.36
Kindergarden, The (R.G. Morris) 1887.05
Kindergarten, The (R.G. Morris) 1885.06
King Casey 1907.53
King Charming, or, the Blue Bird of Paradise 1855.10
King Cotton, or, the Exiled Prince 1862.08
King David 1997.12
King Dodo 1902.18
King Highball 1902.27
King Kaliko 1892.27
King René's Daughter 1893.44
King and I, The 1951.12, 1956.03, 1960.11, 1963.18, 1964.23, 1968.16, 1977.07, 1985.01, 1996.05
King of Cadonia, The 1910.03
King of Coney Island, The 1857.06
King of Hearts 1978.22
King's Carnival, The 1901.12
King's Fool, The 1890.08
Kismet (Wright-Forest) 1953.16, 1965.22, 1985.13, 1986.09
Kismet, or, Two Tangled Turks (Kerker-Carroll) 1895.21, 1897.02
Kiss Burglar, The 1918.15, 1919.05
Kiss Me! 1927.34
Kiss Me, Kate 1948.32, 1952.02, 1956.05, 1965.18, 1999.19
Kiss Waltz, The 1911.32
Kiss of the Spider Woman 1993.09
Kissing Time 1920.37
Kitty Darlin' 1917.27
Kitty Grey 1909.01
Kitty's Kisses 1926.12
Kitty, The 1888.45
Klein, Robert, An Evening With 1988.13
Knickerbocker Girl, The 1903.17
Knickerbocker Holiday 1938.11
Knickerbockers, The 1893.19
Knight for a Day, A 1907.59
Knights of Song 1938.10
Knotty Affair, A 1891.15
Koh-I-Noor, The 1893.41
Koreans, The 1898.31
Kosher Kitty Kelly 1925.19
Kwamina 1961.24
Kykunkor (The Witch Woman) 1934.16

La-La-Lucille! 1919.12
Lace Petticoat 1927.03
Ladies First 1918.32
Ladies' Paradise, The 1901.18
Lady Billy 1920.43
Lady Butterfly 1923.01
Lady Comes Across, The 1942.01
Lady Do 1927.15
Lady Fingers 1929.07
Lady Luxury 1914.33
Lady Says Yes, A 1945.01
Lady Slavey, The 1896.06, 1898.28
Lady Teazle 1904.55
Lady from Lane's, The 1907.30
Lady in Ermine, The 1922.36
Lady in Red, The 1919.11
Lady in the Dark 1941.04, 1943.03
Lady of the Slipper, The, or, a Modern Cinderella 1912.39
Lady or the Tiger, The 1888.19, 1892.47
Lady, Be Good! 1924.43
Laffing Room Only 1944.30
Lagardère; or, the Hunchback of Paris 1887.27
Lalla Rookh, or, the Fire Worshippers 1859.08
Lalla Rookh, or, the Pearl of India! 1872.10
Lalla Rookh, or, the Prophet Unveiled 1869.34
Lamb of Delft, The 1911.14
Lancers, The 1907.58
Land of Bells, The 1935.02
Land of Joy, The 1917.25
Land of Nod, The 1907.14
Lassie 1920.12
Last Empress, The 1997.16, 1998.08
Last Waltz, The 1921.14
Last of the Hogans, The 1891.45
Last of the Rohans, The 1899.27
Late Nite Comic 1987.14
Later On 1889.09, 1889.41, 1890.29
Lauder, Sir Harry 1928.05, 1930.17
Laugh Parade, The 1931.40
Laugh Time 1943.13
Laugh, Town, Laugh 1942.16
Laughs and Other Events 1960.17
Law! Son-Amble-Ah! 1870.36
Lawn Tennis 1880.47
Leader of the Pack 1985.03
Leather Patch, The 1886.03, 1887.39, 1894.04
Leave it to Jane 1917.17
Leave it to Me 1938.13
Legends in Concert 1989.11
Legs Diamond 1988.20
Lena Horne (and Tony Bennett) Sing 1974.21
Horne, Lena: The Lady and Her Music 1981.16
Lend an Ear 1948.30
Leo and Lotos 1872.37
Leon's La! Bell-L.N. 1868.14
Leon's Own Grand Dutch "S" 1868.05
Leonard Bernstein's Mass 1972.15
Leonard Sillman's New Faces of 1968 1968.13
Leonardo 1895.31
Let 'Em Eat Cake 1933.25
Let Freedom Sing 1942.26
Let George Do It 1912.16
Let My People Come 1976.20
Let it Ride! 1961.21
Let's Face It 1941.08
Let's Go 1918.08
Let's Make an Opera 1950.18
Let's Sing Yiddish 1966.21
Letter for Queen Victoria, A 1975.10
Letty Pepper 1922.14
Lew Leslie's Blackbirds of 1928 1928.18
Lew Leslie's Blackbirds of 1933–1934 1933.27
Lew Leslie's Blackbirds of 1939 1939.14
Lew Leslie's International Revue 1930.09
Li'l Abner 1956.12
Liar, The 1950.11
Liberty Belles, The 1901.21
Liberty Jones 1941.05
Lischen and Fritzchen 1875.15
Lieber Augustin 1913.23
Lieutenant Helene of the Guards 1883.64
Lieutenant, The 1975.07
Life 1876.23
Life Begins at 8:40 1934.19
Life in New York, or, Tom and Jerry on a Visit 1856.02
Life, The 1997.08
Lifting the Cup 1903.18
Lifting the Lid/A Gilbert and Sullivan Review 1905.22
Light, Lively and Yiddish 1970.17
Lilac Domino, The 1914.25
Lili 1885.56
Lillie, Beatrice, An Evening With 1952.11
Lilli Tse 1898.11
lilliputians in Posterland, The 1902.33
Lily of Killarney, or, the Colleen Bawn 1868.01, 1895.13, 1898.06
Linger Longer Letty 1919.37
Lion King, The 1997.20
Lion Tamer, The 1891.47
Lischen et Fritzchen 1868.17, 1870.10, 1875.09
Listen Lester 1918.39
Little Blue Devil, The 1919.34

Little Boy Blue, (Bereny) 1911.44
Little Boy Blue, or, Hush-A-Bye Baby and Patty and Her Pitcher 1867.12
Little Café, The 1913.31
Little Cherub, The 1906.25
Little Christopher 1894.38
Little Christopher Columbus 1894.38
Little Corporal, The 1898.54
Little Detective, The, or, Woman's Cuirosity 1869.44, 1871.21, 1880.17
Little Dew Drop, or, the Fairies' Home in the Palace of Neptune 1867.32
Little Dolly Dimples 1907.19
Little Duchess, The 1901.25
Little Duke, The 1879.15, 1884.34, 1896.12
Little Faust! 1870.26
Little Host, The 1898.77
Little Jack Sheppard 1886.45
Little Jessie James 1923.24
Little Johnny Jones 1904.42, 1907.16, 1982.05
Little Me 1962.27, 1982.01, 1998.15
Little Michus, The 1907.06
Little Millionaire, The 1911.33
Little Miss Bluebeard 1923.26
Little Miss Charity 1920.30
Little Miss Fix-It 1911.13
Little Nell and the Marchioness 1867.20, 1868.04, 1868.22, 1870.34, 1871.13, 1876.35, 1881.18
Little Nellie Kelly 1922.43
Little Nemo 1908.35
Little Night Music, A 1973.04, 1990.07, 1991.08
Little Puck 1888.04, 1888.34, 1890.10
Little Racketeer, A 1932.01
Little Red Riding Hood (Richardson-Rice) 1900.03
Little Red Riding-Hood (Brinkworth-Barnes) 1872.02
Little Show, The 1929.19
Little Simplicity 1918.35
Little Trooper, The 1894.28
Little Tycoon, The 1886.15
Little Whopper, The 1919.28
Little of Everything, A 1904.22
Liza (Minnelli) 1974.01
Liza (Pincard) 1922.44
Liza Minnelli: Stepping Out at Radio City 1991.04
Loan of a Lover, The 1857. 07, 1863.03, 1866.04
Lola from Berlin 1907.37
Lollipop 1924.02
London Follies, The 1911.14
Lonely Romeo, A 1919.14
Lonesome Town 1908.05
Long Legged Letty 1914.21
Look Ma, I'm Dancin'! 1948.08
Look Who's Here 1920.07
Look to the Lilies 1970.08
Looney Park 1903.28
Lorelei, or, Gentlemen Still Prefer Blondes 1974.02
Lorgaire, The 1878.17, 1888.40
Lorraine 1887.12, 1888.24
Lost Boy, The 1905.07
Lost in the Stars 1949.15, 1958.11, 1972.06
Lost, Strayed or Stolen 1896.29
Louie the 14th 1925.08
Louisiana Lady 1947.13
Louisiana Purchase 1940.08
Love Among the Roses!, or, an Ambassador from Below 1870.43
Love Birds 1921.06
Love Call, The 1927.55
Love Cure, The 1909.19
Love Dreams 1921.35
Love Letter, The 1921.33
Love Life 1948.25
Love Mill, The 1918.04
Love Song, The 1925.02
Love Thy Neighbor 1996.03
Love in Ye Days of Charles Ye Second 1884.36
Love is Blind 1859.16
Love o' Mike 1917.02
Love's Labor Lost 1859.15
Love's Lottery 1904.36
Love's Young Dream 1879.50
Lovely Galatea 1889.27
Lovely Ladies, Kind Gentlemen 1970.21
Lovely Lady 1927.68
Lovers and Lunatics 1906.13
Loyalina, or, Brigadier-General Fortunio, and His Seven Gifted Aides-de-Camp 1864.12
Luana 1930.26
Luckee Girl 1928.27
Lucky 1927.12
Lucky Dog, A 1906.35
Lucky Sambo 1925.18
Lucretia Borgia, M.D., La Grande Doctresse 1869.11
Lucretia Borgia, or, the Cup of Cold Poison! 1871.05
Lucrezia Borgia 1873.05
Luna, the Naughty Little Boy who cried for the Moon 1872.08
LuPone, Patti 1995.12, 2000.16
Lurline, or, the Knight and the Naiads 1870.35, 1872.12
Lute Song 1946.05, 1959.05
Lysistrata 1972.23

M'liss, Child of the Sierras 1883.05
M'lle. Nitouche 1885.55, 1885.68
Macbeth 1870.15
Mack and Mabel 1974.18
MacLaine, Shirley 1984.06, 1976.07
Macushla 1912.06, 1920.16
Mad Bargain, A 1893.06
Madam Moselle 1914.14
Madam Piper 1884.21
Madame Angot's Daughter 1880.03
Madame Boniface 1884.43
Madame Favart 1879.43, 1881.46, 1884.02
Madame L'Archiduc 1874.26, 1875.25, 1884.49
Madame Pompadour 1924.39
Madame Sherry 1910.22
Madame Toussante L'Overture's Reception 1896.46
Madame Troubadour 1910.31
Madcap Duchess, The 1913.32
Madcap Princess, A 1904.30
Madcap, The 1928.06
Madeleine, or, the Magic Kiss 1895.06, 1898.40
Madelon 1887.50
Madge Smith, Attorney 1900.55
Magdalena 1948.24
Maggie 1953.02
Maggie Flynn 1968.24
Maggie, the Midget 1888.08
Magic Deer, or, Princess Sweetlips 1852.02
Magic Knight, The 1906.48, 1906.48
Magic Melody, The (Romberg) 1919.35
Magic Melody, The, or, Fortunio's Song (Offenbach) 1900.06
Magic Ring, The 1923.34
Magic Show, The 1974.13
Magic Slipper!, The 1879.38
Magnolia Lady, The 1924.41
Maid Marian 1902.04
Maid and the Magpie, The 1869.47
Maid and the Millionaire, The 1907.23
Maid and the Moonshiner, The 1886.40
Maid and the Mummy, The 1904.24
Maid in America 1915.02
Maid in the Moon, The 1899.26
Maid of Belleville, The 1886.36
Maid of Plymouth, The 1894.03
Maid of the Mountains, The 1918.27
Maids of Athens 1914.09
Mail 1988.07
Maître de Chapelle, Le 1866.23, 1869.19
Major, The 1881.29, 1885.15, 1895.05
Make It Snappy 1922.15
Make Mine Manhattan 1948.04
Make a Wish 1951.13
Mam'selle 'Awkins 1900.16
Mam'selle Napoleon 1903.40
Mam'zelle 1884.62, 1886.48
Mama I Want to Sing Part 2 1995.04
Mama's Baby Boy 1912.20
Mame 1966.10, 1983.10
Mamselle Sallie 1906.44
Mamzelle Champagne 1906.23
Mamzelle Nitouche 1884.46
Man Who Owns Broadway, The 1909.26
Man With Three Wives, The 1913.02
Man from China, The 1904.18
Man from Cook's, The 1912.12
Man from Mars, A 1901.17
Man from Now, The 1906.30
Man in the Moon (Bock-Harnick) 1963.11
Man in the Moon, Jr., The (Englander) 1899.19
Man in the Moon, The (Englander) 1899.19
Man of La Mancha 1965.34, 1972.14, 1977.12, 1992.07
Man on the Moon 1975.04
Mandarin, The 1896.45
Mandy Patinkin in Concert 1997.01
Mandy Patinkin in Concert: Dress Casual 1989.16
Mandy Patinkin in Concert: Mamaloshen 1998.11
Manhattan Beach; or, Love Among the Breakers 1878.21
Manhattan Mary 1927.46
Manhattan Rhythm 1982.15
Manhattan Showboat 1980.18
Manhattan Varieties 1932.19
Manhatters, The 1927.36
Manilow, Barry, at the Gershwin 1989.08
Manilow, Barry, on Broadway 1976.34
Manilow, Barry, Showstoppers 1991.10
Manola!, or, Blonde and Brunette 1882.06
Manteaux Noirs 1882.60
Many Voices of Danny Gans, The 1995.17
Marat/Sade 1965.39, 1967.01
Marcelle 1908.30
Marching By 1932.06
Marguerite 1896.07
Maria Golovin 1958.17, 1959.07
Mariage Aux Lanternes, Le 1864.08, 1869.22
Marie Christine 1999.22
Marie Dressler's All Star Gambol 1913.07
Marilyn: an American Fable 1983.17
Marinka 1945.11
Marionette Players, The 1923.29
Marita 1886.49
Maritana 1848.04, 1855.04, 1864.07, 1864.16, 1867.03, 1868.09, 1884.38, 1898.19, 1900.13

Marjolaine (Hugo Felix) 1922.04
Marjolaine, La (Charles Lecocq) 1877.32, 1879.26, 1879.44, 1883.28
Marjorie 1924.21
Marlene 1999.07
Marlene Dietrich 1967.13, 1968.20
Marlowe 1981.24
Marquis of Michigan, The 1898.58
Marquis, The 1887.33
Marriage Aux Lanterns!, La 1875.12
Marriage Market, The 1913.26
Marriage à la Carte 1911.01
Marriage by Lanterns 1868.20
Marriage of Georgette, The 1855.03
Marrying Mary 1906.27
Marton, la Jolie Bouquetière 1877.08
Marty Malone 1896.24
Mary 1920.38
Mary Jane McKane 1923.45
Mary's Lamb 1908.17
Masaniello 1869.36
Mascot, The 1881.45, 1882.09, 1882.14, 1882.25, 1882.49, 1883.13, 1883.19, 1883.22, 1887.06, 1892.30, 1900.14, 1909.08
Mascotte, La 1881.22, 1881.33, 1881.34, 1881.48, 1882.31, 1882.61, 1883.54, 1884.29, 1884.47, 1885.36, 1885.61, 1887.38, 1926.43
Mascotte, The 1881.21, 1885.09
Mask and Gown 1957.10
Masks and Faces, or, the Miseries of Midgit! 1873.04
Mass 1972.15
Massaniello, Hero and Martyr of Italian Liberty 1859.06
Mathews at Home! 1834.01
Mathias Sandorf 1888.23
Matilda 1906.50
Matinee Girl, The 1926.04
Matinée Idol, A 1910.12
Matrimony 1866.32
Matters of the Heart 2000.16
Maurice Chevalier 1932.04, 1947.05, 1948.12, 1955.14, 1963.02, 1965.08
Mavourneen 1891.28, 1894.20, 1895.30
Max! The Merry Swiss Boy 1873.19
May Day in Town, or, New York in an Uproar 1787.01
May Queen, The 1889.17
May Wine 1935.17
Mayflowers 1925.43
Mayor 1985.15
Mayor of Tokio, The 1905.53
Maytime 1917.15
Mazeppa, or, the Untamed Rocking Horse 1864.05
Mazulm, or, the Night Owl 1864.17
Mazulm, the Night Owl 1888.01
Mazuma Man, The 1907.40
McAllister's Legacy 1885.02
McFadden's Elopement 1894.51
McFadden's Row of Flats 1897.38
McKenna's Flirtation 1889.37, 1891.08
McNooney's Visit 1887.07
McSorley's Inflation 1882.79
Me Nobody Knows, The 1970.20
Me and Bessie 1975.20
Me and Juliet 1953.08
Me and My Girl 1986.12
Me, Him and I 1904.58
Mecca 1920.34
Medal and the Maid, The 1904.03
Medea (burlesque) 1858.04
Medea!, or, the Best of Mothers With a Brute of a Husband 1867.29
The Medium/(The Telephone) 1947.10, 1948.29, 1950.13
Meet Me in St. Louis 1989.23
Meet My Sister 1930.43
Meet the People 1940.21
Megilla of Itzik Manger, The 1968.22
Meller, Raquel 1926.09, 1926.35
Melody 1933.03
Melting of Molly, The 1918.42
Memphis Bound 1945.08
Mephisto and the Four Sensations! 1873.12
Mercenary Mary 1925.16
Merlin 1983.01
Merrily We Roll Along 1981.27
Merry Countess, The (Brandl-Frost) 1895.35
Merry Countess, The (J. Strauss-Anderson) 1912.27
Merry Duchess, The 1883.52
Merry Malones, The 1927.47
Merry Monarch, The 1890.26, 1891.31
Merry Tramps, The 1896.34
Merry War, The 1882.45, 1884.08
Merry Whirl, The 1910.15
Merry Widow and the Devil, The (burlesque) 1908.38
Merry Widow, The 1907.48, 1921.29, 1929.47, 1931.27, 1942.21, 1943.09, 1944.24, 1957.04, 1957.15, 1958.16, 1959.21, 1962.21, 1963.24, 1964.24, 1964.30, 1965.27, 1974.14, 1976.18, 1978.07, 1978.20, 1979.21, 1982.16, 1983.12, 1984.04, 1985.11, 1988.14, 1989.13, 1995.06, 1996.02
Merry World, The (Biddle-Smith) 1895.18
Merry World, The (Rubens-Coots-Grey) 1926.15
Merry, Merry 1925.34
Merry-Go-Round (Souvaine-Gorney) 1927.27
Merry-Go-Round, The (Edwards-West) 1908.15
Messenger Boy, The 1901.19
Messin' Around 1929.18
Metamora, or, the Last of the Pollywogs 1848.02, 1856.04
Metamorphoses 1971.08
Metro 1992.05
Mexican Hayride 1944.02
Mexicana (Hubbell-Smith) 1906.07
Mexicana (Mexican revue) 1939.18
Micaëla 1883.16
Michael Feinstein in Concert 1988.08
Michael Feinstein in Concert: Isn't it Romantic 1988.19
Michael Feinstein in Concert: Piano and Voice 1990.09
Michael Strogoff 1881.30, 1881.31, 1881.32
Michael Todd's Peep Show 1950.12
Michio Itow's Pin Wheel 1922.21
Mickey Finn 1903.13
Mid-Summer Night Fancies 1903.18
Midler, Bette 1973.14
Midler, Bette: Clams on the Half Shell 1975.12
Midler, Bette!: Divine Madness 1979.30
Midnight Assault, or, the Italian Brigands/Love Amongst the 1865.08
Midnight Bell, A 1889.12, 1890.04
Midnight Girl, The 1914.07
Midnight Rounders (1920), The 1920.23
Midnight Rounders of 1921, The 1921.02
Midnight Sons, The 1909.11
Mikado, The, or, the Town of Titipu 1885.43, 1885.47, 1885.48, 1886.12, 1886.25, 1886.55, 1890.14, 1890.20, 1894.23, 1896.17, 1898.21, 1899.16, 1900.27, 1902.22, 1910.14, 1912.23, 1913.11, 1915.09, 1925.13, 1927.44, 1931.10, 1931.25, 1933.08, 1934.07, 1934.27, 1935.05, 1936.04, 1936.13, 1939.03, 1940.13, 1942.04, 1944.04, 1947.22, 1949.10, 1951.01, 1952.14, 1955.18, 1959.18, 1960.14, 1961.03, 1961.19, 1962.10, 1962.19, 1962.25, 1963.23, 1964.09, 1964.42, 1965.11, 1966.23, 1968.12, 1968.27, 1974.07, 1974.15, 1976.12, 1978.15, 1984.12, 1985.10, 1987.01, 1989.15, 1990.13, 1993.13, 1995.10, 1997.02
Military Maid, The 1900.44
Milk White Flag, and its Battle-Scarred Followers on the Field of Mars and in the Courts of venus 1894.37
Milk and Honey 1961.20
Miller's Daughter, The 1893.01
Million Dollars, A 1900.42
Mimic World of 1921, The (J. Schwartz-Murphy-Pollack) 1921.25
Mimic World, The (Furth-Jerome) 1908.21
Mimic and the Maid, The 1907.03
Minnelli, Liza 1974.01
Minnelli, Liza: Stepping Out at Radio City 1991.04
Minnelli on Minnelli 1999.23
Minnie Palmer's Boarding School 1880.25
Minnie's Boys 1970.07
Minstrel of Clare, The 1896.11
Misérables, Les 1987.04
Miss 1917 1917.26
Miss Blythe of Duluth 1892.58
Miss Caprice 1913.23
Miss Daisy 1914.20
Miss Dolly Dollars 1905.29
Miss Esmeralda 1888.41
Miss Helyett 1891.38
Miss Hook of Holland 1907.63
Miss Information 1915.25
Miss Innocence 1908.39, 1909.25
Miss Innocence Abroad 1894.25
Miss Jack 1911.29
Miss Liberty 1949.08
Miss Lotta 1864.14
Miss Manhattan 1897.15
Miss Millions 1919.41
Miss Philadelphia 1897.55
Miss Pocahontas 1907.49
Miss Princess 1912.47
Miss Prinnt 1900.58
Miss Saigon 1991.03
Miss Simplicity 1902.07
Miss Springtime 1916.19
Mlle. Mischief 1908.29
Mlle. Modiste 1905.57, 1907.36, 1913.15, 1929.36
Mlle. Nitouche 1885.55, 1885.68
Mme. Angot 1890.24
Mme. Angot's Child! 1873.18
Mme. Favart 1879.31, 1881.36
Mme. L'Archiduc 1877.17, 1882.53
Mocking Bird, The 1902.37
Modern Eve, A 1915.08
Modest Suzanne 1912.01
Modiste Shop, The 1913.28
Molly 1973.11
Molly Darling 1922.29
Molly May 1910.11
Molly Moonshine 1905.45
Molly O' 1916.08
Monks of Malabar, The 1900.39
Monsieur Beaucaire 1919.42
Monsieur Choufleuri Restera Chez Lui-Le 1874.08
Monsieur Choufleuri at Home! 1876.11
Monsieur Choufleuri! 1873.23
Monsieur Choufleury 1869.12

Monsieur Jacques 1854.05, 1878.22
Monsieur Landry 1869.19
Montand, Yves, An Evening With 1959.15, 1961.25
Monte Carlo 1898.17
Monte Cristo, Jr. (Lutz-Caryll) 1888.11, 1888.38, 1889.30
Monte Cristo, Jr. (Romberg-J. Schwartz) 1919.03
Monteith & Rand 1979.01
Monty Python Live! 1976.06
Moonlight 1924.04
Moonshine 1905.45
Moony Shapiro Songbook, The 1981.14
Mordecai Lyons 1882.74
Morning, Noon and Night 1908.33
Morris Gest's Midnight Whirl 1919.43
Mort Sahl on Broadway 1987.13
Mosquito 1870.19
Most Happy Fella, The 1956.04, 1959.02, 1966.08, 1979.26, 1991.09, 1992.01
Mother 1935.16
Mother Courage and Her Children 1963.09
Mother Earth 1972.21
Mother Goose 1899.22, 1903.39
Mother Goose! and the Fairy Legend of the Golden Egg 1865.02
Motor Girl, The 1909.14
Mountebanks, The 1893.02
Mourning Pictures 1974.23
Mousquetaires au Couvent, Les 1881.50
Mozart 1926.41, 1926.49
Mr. Battling Buttler 1923.36
Mr. Blarney from Ireland 1906.03
Mr. Bluebeard 1903.04
Mr. Coney's Isle 1901.03
Mr. Hamlet of Broadway 1908.44
Mr. Lode of Koal 1909.27
Mr. New York, Esq. 1897.19
Mr. Pickwick 1903.02
Mr. President 1962.20
Mr. Strauss Goes to Boston 1945.12
Mr. Wix of Wickham 1904.34
Mr. Wonderful 1956.02
Mrs. Black is Back 1904.43
Mrs. Delaney of Newport 1903.35
Mrs. Mac, the Mayor 1904.48
Mrs. O'Brien, Esquire 1892.48
Mrs. Partington, or, Home for the Holidays 1862.06
Mrs. Patterson 1954.16
Mrs. Radley Barton's Ball in Greater New York 1897.16
Mrs. Wilson, That's All 1906.43
Mrs. Wilson-Andrews 1906.43
Much Ado About Everything 1999.25
Much Ado About a Merchant of Venice 1869.15
Muddy Day, The 1883.32
Muldoon's Picnic 1882.01, 1883.02
Mule Bone 1991.01
Mulligan Guard Ball, The 1879.04, 1883.46
Mulligan Guard Pic-Nic, The 1878.13, 1880.36, 1883.53
Mulligan Guard's Ball, The 1892.54
Mulligan Guard's Chowder, The 1879.37
Mulligan Guard's Christmas, The 1879.68
Mulligan Guard's Nominee, The 1880.64
Mulligan Guard's Surprise, The 1880.09
Mulligan's Silver Wedding 1881.09
Mum's the Word 1940.20
Murder at the Vanities 1933.20
Murder in the Old Red Barn 1936.03
Murray Anderson's Almanac (1880–1930) 1929.29
Musette; or, the Secret of Guilde Court 1876.32
Music Box Revue (1921–22) 1921.30
Music Box Revue (1922–23) 1922.39
Music Box Revue (1923–24) 1923.32
Music Box Revue (1924–25) 1924.44
Music Hath Charms 1934.43
Music Is 1976.33
Music Man, The 1957.18, 1965.21, 1980.16, 1988.04, 2000.11
Music in May 1929.17
Music in My Heart 1947.14
Music in the Air 1932.22, 1951.22
Music of Andrew Lloyd Webber 1992.12
Music! Music! 1974.09
Musical Chairs 1980.11
Musical Jubilee, A 1975.22
Musketeers, The 1883.12
Musquitoe, La 1840.01
My Antoinette 1901.18
My Aunt Bridget 1886.58, 1890.12, 1890.30, 1894.31
My Best Girl 1912.31
My Boys 1897.49
My Darlin' Aida 1952.15
My Dear Public 1943.14
My Fair Lady 1956.01, 1964.20, 1968.17, 1976.05, 1981.19, 1993.18
My Favorite Year 1992.17
My Girl 1924.40
My Golden Girl 1920.05
My Lady 1901.06
My Lady Molly 1904.01
My Lady Peggy Goes to Town 1903.12
My Lady's Glove 1917.14
My Lady's Maid, or, Lady Madcap 1906.32
My Little Friend 1913.14
My Magnolia 1926.19
My Maryland 1927.42
My One and Only 1983.06
My Princess 1927.50
My Romance 1948.27
My Sweetheart 1882.56, 1884.53, 1887.40
My Tom-Boy Girl 1905.21
Myles Aroon 1889.03, 1889.48, 1891.06, 1896.14
Mystery Moon 1930.21
Mystery of Edwin Drood, The 1985.18

Na-Non (Burlesque of Nanon) 1885.51
Nadjy 1888.20, 1889.04
Naiad Queen, The 1872.06, 1884.27
Naiad Queen, The; or, the Mysteries of the Lurlie Berg! 1841.01
Namiko-San 1927.28
Nancy Brown 1903.07
Nancy Hanks, The 1897.56
Nanon (Genée in German) 1885.01,
Nanon (Genée in English) 1898.15, 1900.23
Nanon, the Hostess of the Golden Lamb (Genée in English) 1885.41, 1892.03
Nash at Nine 1973.08
Natja 1925.06
Natural Gas 1888.17, 1889.06, 1889.39
Nature 1897.29
Naughty Cinderella 1925.41
Naughty Marietta 1910.35, 1929.38, 1931.43, 1978.19, 1979.20, 1988.18
Naughty Naught 1937.02, 1939.10, 1946.19
Naughty Riquette 1926.26
Ne'er too Late to Mend 1859.16
Nearly a Hero 1908.10
Ned Wayburn's Gambols 1929.04
Ned Wayburn's Minstrel Misses 1903.18
Ned Wayburn's Town Topics 1915.22
Needs Must, or, the Ballad Singers 1793.01
Nell Gwynne 1884.57, 1901.11
Nell-Go-In 1900.49
Nellie Bly 1946.04
Neptune's Daughter 1906.46
Nervous Set, The 1959.12
Never Despair 1859.12
Never Homes, The 1911.35
Never Judge by Appearances 1859.09
New 8 Bells, The 1895.40
New Americana 1928.45, 1932.20
New Boys and Girls, The 1892.09
New Chauve-Souris 1931.38
New City Directory, The 1891.43, 1892.36
New Evangeline, The 1880.40
New Faces of 1934 1934.06
New Faces of 1936 1936.12
New Faces of 1943 1942.34
New Faces of 1952 1952.09
New Faces of 1956 1956.08
New Faces of 1962 1962.02
New Faces of 1968 1968.13
New Fritz! Our Cousin German 1878.04, 1878.12
New Girl in Town 1957.07
New Hellzapoppin' 1938.08
New Moon, The 1928.29, 1942.22, 1944.17, 1986.14, 1988.16
New Music Hall of Israel, The 1969.13
New Priorities of 1943 1942.23
"New" Rounders, The 1900.33
New York Summer, A 1979.13
New York as it Is 1848.03
New Yorkers, The (Englander-Hobart) 1901.23
New Yorkers, The (Porter) 1930.40
New Yorkers, The (Schwartz-Myers) 1927.11
Newcomers, The 1923.23
Newley, Anthony, & Henry Mancini 1974.22
Newlyweds and Their Baby, The 1909.05
Newport, or, the Swimmer, the Singer and the Cypher 1879.50
News, The 1985.17
Next President, The 1958.12
Nia-for-li-ca, in the Halls of Montezuma 1878.05
Niagra 1910.23
Nic-Nax of 1926 1926.22
Nichols & May, An Evening With 1960.16
Nick & Nora 1991.15
Nicodemus 1869.02, 1869.14
Nifties of 1923 1923.33
Night Boat, The 1920.04
Night Clerk, The 1895.34
Night That Made America Famous, The 1975.05
Night With the Pierrots, A 1912.09
Night at the Circus, A 1891.44, 1893.26, 1894.43, 1896.40
Night in New York, A 1896.47
Night in Paris, A/1st & 2nd eds 1926.01
Night in Rome, A 1866.14, 1866.24
Night in Spain, A (Messrs. Shubert revue) 1927.19
Night in Spain, A (Valverde) 1917.33
Night in Venice, A (J. Strauss) 1884.18, 1900.30
Night in Venice, A (Messrs. Shubert revue) 1929.22
Night of Love 1941.02
Night of the Fourth, The 1901.04
Nightingale, The 1927.01
Nikita Balieff's New Chauve-Souris 1931.38
Nikki 1931.34

Nimble Nip!, or, Ogre Ugliphiz, Fairy Silvereyes & the Princess with the Strawberry Mask 1875.39
Nina Rosa 1930.27
Nine 1982.09
Nine Fifteen Revue 1930.06
1940! or. .Crummles in Search of Novelty 1840.02
1940's Radio Hour, The 1979.24
90 in the Shade 1915.01
97 or 79 1884.24
Niniche 1885.59
Nisida 1880.66
No Foolin' 1926.18
No More Peace 1938.02
No Other Girl 1924.22
No Strings 1962.03
No for an Answer 1941.01
No, No, Nanette 1925.30, 1971.03
Noble Rouge, A 1929.30
Nobody Home 1915.07
Noces d'Olivette, Les 1881.53
Noces de Jeannette, Les 1861.05, 1866.27, 1872.01
Noël Coward's Sweet Potato 1968.19
Norma on the Half Shell 1867.11
Norman Leslie 1836.01
Normandy Wedding, A 1898.12
Norma; or, Titiens in a Minstrel Band 1876.07
Not Yet, But Soon 1907.12
Nothing But Love 1919.29
Nothing Venture Nothing Have, or, a Courtship in 1640 1859.17
Notoriety 1894.49
Novelty 1856.01
Nowhere to Go But Up 1962.24

O'Brien Girl, The 1921.32
O'Flynn, The 1934.41
O'Neill of Derry 1907.56
O'Nero, or, the Lady of Lions 1890.45
O'Reagans, The 1886.52, 1889.11
Oba Oba 1988.06
Oba Oba '90 1990.03
Oba Oba '93 1992.13
Object of Interest, An 1869.44
Octoroons 1899.31
Odds and Ends of 1917 1917.29
L'Oeil Crevé 1869.03, 1874.07
Of Thee I Sing 1931.48, 1933.13, 1952.07
Of V We Sing 1942.05
Off the Earth 1895.03
Office Boy, The 1903.34
Ogallallas, The 1894.08
Oh Captain! 1958.02
Oh Justine 1917.31
Oh What a Lovely War 1964.28
Oh! Calcutta! 1971.04, 1976.27
Oh! Oh! Delphine! 1912.34
Oh! Oh! Nurse 1925.44
Oh! What a Night 1885.69
Oh, Boy! 1917.06
Oh, Brother! 1981.25
Oh, Coward! 1986.19
Oh, Ernest! 1927.20
Oh, I Say! 1913.29
Oh, Kay! 1926.36, 1928.01, 1990.14
Oh, Lady! Lady! 1918.03
Oh, Look! 1918.07
Oh, My Dear! 1918.37
Oh, Please! 1926.46
Oh, What a Girl! 1919.19
Oily Vet, or, the Wilful Maid and the Sad Sea Dog 1881.12
Oklahoma! 1943.04, 1951.16, 1953.09, 1958.07, 1963.06, 1965.38, 1969.12, 1979.31
Old Bill, M.P. 1926.38
Old Dame Trot and Her Comical Cat 1865.01
Old Dutch 1909.30
Old Homestead, The 1887.02, 1887.42, 1888.25, 1889.43, 1890.36, 1894.52, 1898.45, 1899.32, 1904.32, 1907.43, 1908.32
Old Lady, The/Dreams of Three 1919.17
Old Lavender 1877.24, 1885.49, 1888.14, 1893.46
Old Limerick Town 1902.36
Old Town, The 1910.02
Oliver! 1963.01, 1965.23, 1984.07
Olivette 1880.69, 1881.03, 1881.14, 1881.38, 1881.56, 1882.11, 1882.32, 1882.37, 1882.47, 1882.52, 1882.72, 1883.25, 1884.03, 1884.28, 1896.21, 1899.14
Olympiana, or, a Night With Mitchell 1857.04
On Broadway 1896.39
On Your Toes 1936.05, 1954.12, 1983.02
On a Clear Day You Can See Forever 1965.31
On the Frontier 1888.30
On the Town 1944.33, 1971.15, 1998.16
On the Track! 1871.17
On the Twentieth Century 1978.02
On the Yellowstone 1884.10
Once Over Lightly 1942.33
Once Upon a Mattress 1959.26, 1996.18
Once on This Island 1990.12
Ondina!, or, the Spirit of the Waters 1861.06
One Horse Town, A 1906.28
110 in the Shade 1963.26, 1992.10
One Kiss 1923.44
One Round of Pleasure 1897.25
One Touch of Venus 1943.19
One for the Money 1939.12
One of the Old Stock 1888.31
Only Fools are Sad 1971.17
Only Girl, The 1914.27, 1934.14
Onward Victoria 1980.30
Oolah, The 1889.24
Opera Ball, The 1912.08
Operation Sidewinder 1970.04
Optimists, The 1928.04
Orange Blossoms 1922.33
Orchid, The 1907.15
Orchids Preferred 1937.06
Oriental America, or, In the Isle of San Domingo 1896.46
Origin of the Cakewalk, or, Clorindy 1898.41
Orphée Aux Enfers 1867.05, 1868.13, 1868.28, 1869.10
Orpheus (Burlesque) 1893.01
Orpheus and Eurydice 1883.65
Orpheus in der Unterwelt 1861.02, 1866.33
Orpheus in the Underworld 1956.09
Other Way, The 1899.30
Otoyo 1903.19
Otto, a German 1878.15, 1880.51
Our Belle Hélene 1890.13
Our Bridget's Dreams 1903.30
Our Goblins, or, Fun on the Rhine 1880.32, 1881.16
Our Irish Visitors 1886.46, 1887.23
Our Japanese Embassy 1860.04
Our Jennie 1887.51
Our Miss Gibbs 1910.21
Our Nell 1922.46
Out of This World 1950.20
Over Here! 1974.05
Over the Garden Wall 1885.03, 1886.62
Over the River 1912.02
Over the Top 1917.31
Ovid's Metamorphoses 1971.08
Oxygen 1886.32
Oxygen! or, Gas in Burlesque Metre 1877.23
Oy Is Dus A Leben! 1942.28
Oyster Man, The 1907.55

Pa 1887.09
Pacific Mail, The 1894.39
Pacific Overtures 1976.02
Pacific Paradise 1972.20
Padlocks of 1927 1927.31
Paese Dei Campanelli, Il 1935.02
Page's Revel; or, the Summer Night's Bivouac 1869.02
Paint Your Wagon 1951.24
Painting the Town 1906.39
Pair of Pinks, A 1904.11
Pajama Game, The 1954.05, 1957.08, 1973.15, 1989.04
Pal Joey 1940.22, 1952.01, 1961.15, 1963.17, 1976.19
Panama Hattie 1940.19
Panhandle Pete 1906.31
Panjandrum 1893.16
Pansy 1929.21
Paola, or, the First of the Vendettas 1889.36
Papa's Boy 1905.24
Papa's Darling 1914.26
Papa's Wife 1899.38
Parade (Moross) 1935.03
Parade (J.R. Brown) 1998.21
Paradise Alley 1924.07
Paradise of Mahomet, The 1911.03
Pardon My English 1933.01
Pardon Our French 1950.14
Paris 1928.33
Paris '90 1952.04
Paris and Helen, or, the Grecian Elopement 1868.08
Paris by Night 1904.23
Paris, or, the Apple of Discord 1870.42
Parisian Folly, A 1874.10
Parisian Model, A 1906.45, 1908.04
Parisiana 1928.09
Paris; or, the Judgement 1869.21
Park 1970.12
Park Avenue 1946.20
Parlor Match, A 1890.32, 1892.45, 1896.31
Parlor Match, A, or, Turning a Crank 1884.48
Parlor Match, a, Up to Now 1892.18
Party With Betty Comden & Adolph Green, A 1958.21, 1977.02
Pas Sur la Bouche 1929.16
Passing Show of 1894, The 1894.21
Passing Show of 1912, The/The Ballet of 1830 1912.24
Passing Show of 1913, The 1913.18
Passing Show of 1914, The 1914.16
Passing Show of 1915, The 1915.11
Passing Show of 1916, The 1916.11
Passing Show of 1917, The 1917.08
Passing Show of 1918, The 1918.20
Passing Show of 1919, The 1919.30
Passing Show of 1921, The 1920.47
Passing Show of 1922, The 1922.34
Passing Show of 1923, The 1923.17
Passing Show of 1924, The 1924.29
Passing Show of 1926, The 1926.15
Passion 1994.05
Passionnément! 1929.11
Passions of 1926 1926.15
Pat's New Wardrobe 1888.42, 1889.25
Pat's Wardrobe 1886.61
Patchwork 1875.16

Patience, or, Bunthorne's Bride 1881.37, 1881.43, 1881.57, 1882.38, 1882.42, 1882.48, 1883.15, 1883.24, 1884.31, 1885.34, 1890.47, 1892.37, 1896.22, 1898.65, 1900.21, 1912.18, 1927.25, 1928.20, 1931.17, 1933.14, 1934.33, 1936.23, 1939.11, 1944.11, 1948.10, 1964.10, 1965.10, 1966.28, 1968.15, 1968.26
Patience, or, the Stage-Struck Maidens 1882.04
Patients; or, Bunion-Salve's Bride! 1881.55
Patinkin, Mandy: in Concert 1989.16, 1997.01, 1998.11
Patsy in Politics 1907.34
Patti LuPone on Broadway 1995.12
Paul Clifford 1852.01, 1871.10
Paul Jones 1890.33, 1892.10, 1898.07
Paul Sills' Story Theatre 1970.16
Pearl Maiden, The 1912.05
Pearl and the Pumpkin, The 1905.25
Pearl of Pekin, The 1888.09, 1889.01, 1889.44, 1892.11
Peasant Girl, The 1915.04
Peek-a-Boo 1919.21
Peg 1983.20
Peg o' My Dreams 1924.09
Peggy 1911.45
Peggy Machree 1908.43
Peggy from Paris 1903.24
Peggy-Ann 1926.50
Penelope 1888.33
Penn & Teller 1987.20, 2000.13
Penn & Teller: The Refrigerator Tour 1991.02
Penn's Aunts Among the Pirates, and How They Got There 1881.19
Penny-Ante, or, the Last of the Fairies 1884.25
Pepita, or, the Girl With the Glass Eyes 1886.14
Perfect Fool, The 1921.37
Perfectly Frank 1980.29
Peri, or, the Enchanted Fountain, The 1852.05
Périchole, La 1869.01, 1871.03, 1871.23, 1872.28, 1873.16, 1874.16, 1876.25, 1877.10, 1877.42, 1878.07, 1879.51, 1880.60, 1882.35, 1883.27, 1886.20, 1895.09, 1925.46, 1926.48
Persecution and Assassination of Jean-Paul Marat as Performed by the Inmates of the Asylum of Charenton under the Direction of the Marquis de Sade, The, 1965.39, 1967.01
Pet of the Petticoats, The 1853.03, 1862.07, 1863.02, 1867.19, 1871.20
Pete 1887.48, 1889.07
Peter Gray, or, Ding Dong 1869.27
Peter Pan (Bernstein) 1950.08
Peter Pan (Styne-Comden-Green-Charlap-Leigh) 1954.13, 1979.22, 1990.20, 1991.13, 1998.18
Petit Duc, Le 1879.18, 1879.19, 1879.39, 1880.52
Petit Faust, Le 1870.08, 1870.27, 1870.30, 1872.41, 1874.05, 1875.08, 1875.33, 1877.37, 1879.60
Petite Mariée, La 1877.09, 1877.26, 1879.41, 1885.24
Petite Muette, La 1880.16
Petroliamania, or, Oil on the Brain 1865.03
Phantom of the Opera, The 1988.01
Philémon and Baucis 1893.44
Phoebe of Quality Street 1921.13
Photos 1881.23, 1882.27
Piaf 1981.04
Piaf, Edith, and Her Continental Entertainers 1947.18
Piccoli of Vittorio Podrecca, The 1932.29, 1934.02
Pickwick 1965.28
Pie-Rats of Penn-Yann, The 1881.06
Pied Piper, The 1908.41
Pierrette 1885.12
Pierrot the Prodigal 1916.16, 1925.09
Piff! Paff!! Pouf!!! (Schwartz-Jerome) 1904.15
Piff-Paff!, or, the Magic Armory (Farnie-Connolly) 1877.39
Piggy 1927.04
Pin Wheel 1922.21, 1922.21
Pin-a-4 1886.29
Pink Lady, The 1911.11, 1912.28
Pinocchio 1938.16
Pins and Needles (Labor Stage revue) 1937.14
Pins and Needles 1939 (Labor Stage revue) 1937.14
Pins and Needles! (Albert de Courville revue) 1922.05
Pioneer Days/Neptune's Daughter 1906.46
Pipe Dream 1955.27
Pipino Il Breve 1985.16
Pippin 1972.22
Pippin, or, the King of the Gold Mines 1870.13
Pippins 1890.43
Pique Family!, A Play on the Da-ly, The 1876.02
Pirates of Penzance, The, or, the Slave of Duty 1879.72, 1880.45, 1882.10, 1882.19, 1882.21, 1883.14, 1885.13, 1890.15, 1890.46, 1898.71, 1900.11, 1912.21, 1915.12, 1926.44, 1927.61, 1931.18, 1933.18, 1934.08, 1934.23, 1935.06, 1936.08, 1936.15, 1939.02, 1940.15, 1942.06, 1944.08, 1946.11, 1948.02, 1949.11, 1951.09, 1952.16, 1955.16, 1960.15, 1961.04, 1962.28, 1964.13, 1964.41, 1965.12, 1966.22, 1968.09, 1968.28, 1976.13, 1977.03, 1977.17, 1978.17, 1981.01
Pitter Patter 1920.32
Plain Jane 1924.10
Plain and Fancy 1955.01
Plantation Revue 1922.25
Platinum 1978.25
Play Me a Country Song 1982.13
Play On! 1997.03
Playing the Ponies 1907.62
Playmates 1893.43
Pleasure Bound 1929.09
Pleasure Seekers, The 1913.30
Plighted by Moonlight 1882.43
Plume de ma Tante, La 1958.18
Pluto 1869.07
Pluto, or, the Magic Lyre 1869.46
Po-Ca-Hon-Tas, or, Ye Gentle Savage 1863.10
Po-Ca-Hon-Tas, or, the Gentle Savage 1855.11, 1866.13, 1869.13
Pocahontas, Up to Date 1892.26
Poet and the Puppets, The 1893.11
Police Force, The 1877.03
Policy Kings 1938.19
Policy Players, The 1899.33
Poll and Partner Joe 1872.05, 1872.11
Polly 1929.02
Polly Middles 1892.17
Polly of Hollywood 1927.10
Polly, or, the Pet of the Regiment 1885.26
Polonaise 1945.14
Pom-Pom 1916.04
Pomme d'Api, Le 1880.28
Pont des Soupirs, Le 1871.26
Poor Jonathan 1890.39, 1896.23
Poor Little Ritz Girl 1920.25
Pop 1883.42
Poppy 1923.27
Porgy and Bess 1935.13, 1942.03, 1943.15, 1944.03, 1953.04, 1961.13, 1962.07, 1964.19, 1965.03, 1976.28, 1983.04, 2000.03
Portofino 1958.04
Postillon de Longjumeau, Le 1880.22
Poupée, La 1897.41, 1898.26
Pousse Café (Weber-Fields) 1897.48
Pousse-Café (Ellington-Barer) 1966.05
Pré Aux Clercs, Le 1880.14
Present Arms 1928.16
President's Daughter, The 1970.18
Press Agent, The 1905.52
Pretty Mrs. Smith 1914.21
Prima Donna From the Country, The 1862.06
Prima Donna of a Night 1872.18
Prima Donna, The 1901.09, 1908.40
Prince Achmet! 1880.65
Prince Ananias 1894.45, 1896.43
Prince Conti 1883.29
Prince Kam, or, a Trip to Venus 1894.05
Prince Karl 1886.27
Prince Lavender's Reception 1890.05
Prince Methusalem 1883.44, 1883.45, 1884.63, 1888.22
Prince of Bohemia, The 1910.04
Prince of Central Park 1989.25
Prince of Pilsen, The 1903.10, 1904.16, 1905.16, 1906.16, 1907.17, 1930.01
Prince of Tatters, A 1902.39
Princess April 1924.42
Princess Beggar 1907.01
Princess Bonnie 1895.25
Princess Carpillona, or, the Kings of the Golden Valley 1880.05
Princess Charming 1930.30
Princess Chic, The 1900.12
Princess Flavia 1925.39
Princess Ida, or, Castle Adamant 1884.09, 1886.57, 1925.15, 1934.31, 1936.24, 1955.20
Princess Nicotine 1893.39
Princess Pat, The 1915.23
Princess Toto 1879.71
Princess Virtue 1921.11
Princess de Trébizonde, La 1874.14
Princess of Kensington, A 1903.21
Princess of Madagascar, The 1883.66
Princess of Trébizonde, The 1871.19, 1875.20, 1876.18, 1883.38, 1883.58, 1894.11
Princesse de Trébizonde, La 1880.23
Princesse des Canaries, La 1883.51
Prinz Gemahl, Der 1883.35
Prinz Methusalem 1880.61
Priorities of 1942 1942.10
Prodigal Son, The 1891.05
Producers, The 2001.05
Promises, Promises 1968.31
Promoters, The 1909.06
Protecto 1897.51
Pump Boys and Dinettes 1982.04
Punch, Judy and Company 1903.15
Pupil in Magic, The 1890.31, 1894.01
Puritania, or, the Earl and the Maid of Salem 1892.42
Purlie 1970.05, 1972.26
Purple Road, The 1913.10
Put & Take 1921.26
Putting it Together 1999.20
Puzzles of 1925 1925.05
Pygmalion, or, the Peerless & Beautiful Statue 1869.25
Pyramid, The 1887.19

Quaker Girl, The 1911.39
Queen High 1926.25
Queen o' Hearts 1922.38
Queen of Brilliants, The 1894.41
Queen of Hearts; or, Harlequin, the Knave of Hearts, who stole the Tarts, and the old Woman that lived in a Shoe 1869.35
Queen of a Day, A 1855.07
Queen of the Moulin Rouge, The 1908.42
Queen of the Movies, The 1914.02
Queen's Lace Handkerchief, The 1882.71, 1897.53, 1899.05
Queen's Mate, The 1888.18
Quick Change 1980.28
Quo Vass Iss? 1899.38

Rag Baby, A 1884.16, 1884.37
Ragged Earl, The 1899.03
Ragged Robin 1910.06
Raggedy Ann 1986.16
Rags 1986.13
Ragtime 1998.01
Raiders, The 1905.17
Rain or Shine 1928.08
Rainbow 1928.44
Rainbow Girl, The 1918.11
Rainbow Jones 1974.03
Rainbow Revels 1880.33
Rainbow Rose 1926.06
Rainmaker of Syria, The, or, the Woman King 1893.32
Rainmakers, The 1894.06
Raisin 1973.10
Rambler Rose 1917.19
Ramblers, The 1926.28
Rang Tang 1927.33
Rape of Lucretia, The 1948.31
Raquel Meller 1926.09, 1926.35
Ratcatcher, The, or, the Pied Piper of Hamelin 1885.65
Raymond Hitchcock's Hitchy-Koo 1920 1920.39
Raymond Hitchcock's Pin Wheel 1922.21
Razzle Dazzle 1951.10
Rebel, The 1900.36
Red Canary, The 1914.12
Red Feather 1903.36
Red Hussar, The 1890.23
Red Letter Nights!, or, Catching a Croesus 1884.11
Red Mill, The 1906.33, 1945.16
Red Moon, The 1909.10
Red Pepper 1922.18
Red Petticoat, The 1912.41
Red Robe, The 1928.48
Red Rose, The 1911.23
Red Shoes, The 1993.19
Red Widow, The 1911.41
Red, Hot and Blue 1936.26
Red, White and Maddox 1969.03
Redhead 1959.01
Regatta Girl, The 1900.19
Reggae 1980.05
Regina 1949.16, 1953.05, 1953.14, 1958.13, 1959.10, 1992.14
Rehearsal, The 1893.04
Reign of Error, A 1899.12
Reilly and the 400 1890.49, 1891.25, 1893.15
Reine Indigo, La 1877.41
Remarkable Pipe Dream of Mr. Sherlock Holmes, The 1899.36
Rendezvous, The 1892.49
Rent 1996.09
Reunion in New York 1940.04
Rêve, Le 1898.35
Revels, or, Bon-Ton George, Jr. 1880.59
Revenge With Music 1934.38
Review, or, the Wags of Windsor, The 1853.01
Revue Russe 1922.37
Revue of Revues, The 1911.34
Rex 1976.08
Reynolds, Debbie: The Debbie Reynolds Show 1976.24
Rhapsody 1944.28
Rhapsody in Black 1931.11
Rice's Summer Nights 1898.41
Rich Mr. Hoggenheimer, The 1906.37
Richelieu of the Period! 1871.04
Ride the Winds 1974.12
Riflemen at Vassar, N.G.S.N.Y. 1883.17
Right Girl, The 1921.07
Right This Way 1938.01
Ring and the Keeper, The 1887.40
Ring of Fate, or, Fire, Air, Earth and Water, The 1864.22
Rink, The 1984.01
Rio Rita 1927.08
Rip Van Winkle (Bristow) 1855.09
Rip Van Winkle (Farnie-Planquette) 1882.75
Rip Van Winkle, or, a 20 Year's Snooze (Brinkworth) 1870.32
Ripples 1930.05
Rise of Rosie O'Reilly, The 1923.46
Rising Generation, The 1893.30
Riverdance 1996.01, 1996.12, 1998.09
Riverdance on Broadway 2000.05
Riviera Girl, The 1917.20
Road to Mandalay, The 1916.05
Roar of the Greasepaint - The Smell of the Crowd, The 1965.19
Rob Roy (DeKoven) 1894.40, 1895.24, 1913.25
Rob Roy (Pocock-Davy-Bishop) 1859.01
Robber Baron, The 1901.14
Robber Bridegroom, The 1975.18, 1976.30
Robber of the Rhine, The 1892.25
Robert Grau's American Celebrities 1893.24
Robert Klein: The Show! 1985.21
Robert and Bertrand 1865.07
Roberta 1933.26
Robin Hood (DeKoven) 1891.29, 1892.41, 1892.51, 1893.18, 1893.48, 1895.01, 1896.08, 1898.23, 1900.31, 1902.28, 1912.19, 1929.43, 1932.02, 1944.25
Robin Hood, or, the Maid That was Arch and the Youth That was Archer (Lydia Thompson) 1872.21
Robinson Crusoe (Farnie) 1877.25, 1879.03
Robinson Crusoe (Mexican Juvenile Opera Co.) 1875.24
Robinson Crusoe (Simpson-F.W. Humphrey) 1869.23
Robinson Crusoe and His Man Friday (B.A. Baker) 1869.20
Robinson Crusoe, Esq. and His Man Friday (E.E. Rice) 1880.13
Robinson Crusoe, His Man Friday, Monkey, and the King of Caribee Islands (D. Braham) 1875.31
Robinson Crusoe, Jr. (Romberg-Hanley-Atteridge) 1916.03
Rock 'N' Roll! The First 5,000 Years 1982.22
Rock-a-Bye Baby 1918.16
Rockabye Hamlet 1976.03
Rockette Spectacular, A 1980.09
Rocky Horror Show, The 1975.08, 2000.17
Rodgers & Hart 1975.13
Rodney Dangerfield on Broadway 1988.03
Rogers Brothers in Central Park, The 1900.40
Rogers Brothers in Harvard, The 1902.24
Rogers Brothers in Ireland, The 1905.30
Rogers Brothers in London, The 1903.23
Rogers Brothers in Panama, The 1907.33
Rogers Brothers in Paris, The 1904.31
Rogers Brothers in Wall Street 1899.29
Rogers Brothers in Washington, The 1901.16
Roi Carotte, Le 1872.23
Rollicking Girl, The 1905.20
Rollin' on the T.O.B.A. 1999.06
Roly Poly/Without the Law 1912.44
Roly-Boly Eyes 1919.24
Romance Romance 1988.10
Romance of Athlone, A 1899.01, 1900.10
Roof Scrambler, The 1839.01
Rosalie 1928.03
Rosalinda 1942.31
Rose Girl, The 1921.03
Rose Maid, The 1912.15
Rose de Saint Flour, La 1863.05, 1867.30, 1870.38, 1875.27
Rose of Algeria, The 1909.23
Rose of Auvergne, The 1875.15, 1879.20
Rose of Castile, The 1864.20, 1864.21, 1866.10
Rose of China, The 1919.39
Rose of Panama, The 1912.04
Rose of Persia, The, or, the Story Teller and the Slave 1900.37
Rose of Stamboul, The 1922.11
Rose of the Alhambra, the, or, the Magic Lute 1907.08
Rose-Marie 1924.28, 1927.06
Rosemi-Shell!, or, My Daughter! Oh, My Daughter 1876.01
Ross, Diana, An Evening With 1976.16
Rothschilds, The 1970.15
Roughing It! 1873.03
Round of Pleasure, A 1897.25
'Round New York in 80 Minutes 1899.36
Round the Clock, or, New York by Dark 1872.35, 1873.25, 1874.20
Round the Town 1924.15
Rounders, The 1899.25
Roussotte, La 1886.19
Rowan Atkinson at the Atkinson 1986.15
Royal Chef, The 1904.28
Royal Middy, The 1880.04, 1882.15
Royal Rogue, A 1900.57
Royal Vagabond, The 1919.04
Roza 1987.12
Ruddigore, or, the Witch's Curse 1927.24, 1931.24, 1934.30, 1936.25, 1944.12, 1955.23, 1964.43, 1966.25
Ruddygore, or, the Witch's Curse 1887.10
Rudolph and Adolph 1902.17
Rufus LeMaire's Affairs 1927.13
Rufus Rastus 1906.08
Rugantino 1964.03
Ruggles of Red Gap 1915.32
Rumple 1957.17
Run on the Bank, A 1895.02, 1897.05
Run, Little Chillun' 1933.04, 1943.10
Runaway Colt, A 1895.39
Runaway Girl, A 1898.46, 1900.28
Runaways 1978.11
Runaways, The 1903.14
Runnin' Wild (Johnson-Mack) 1923.39
Running Wild (Vincent-Lee) 1889.05
Running for Office 1903.11
Russell, Anna, and Her Little Show 1953.10
Ruth Selwyn's Nine Fifteen Revue 1930.06

Sadak and Kalasrade!, or, the Waters of Oblivion 1862.01
Sadie Thompson 1944.27
Said Pasha 1889.10
Sail Away 1961.18
Saint of Bleecker Street, The 1954.18, 1965.07, 1965.26, 1976.31, 1978.08
Sally 1920.44, 1923.30, 1948.16
Sally in Our Alley 1902.23
Sally, Irene and Mary 1922.31, 1925.11
Saluta 1934.20
Sambo Girl, The 1905.40
Sammy (Davis) 1974.11
San Toy 1900.43, 1902.12, 1905.18
Sancho Panza 1923.43
Sandra Bernhard: I'm Still Here Damn It! 1998.14
Santa Claus; or, Harlequin Bob Cratchet and Ding Dong Dell! 1877.01
Santa Maria 1896.33
Sapolio 1899.30
Sarafina! 1988.02
Saratoga 1959.27
Saravá 1979.03
Sardanapalus 1876.12
Sardine-Apples!, King of Ninnyvah & Astoria, L.I. 1876.29
Sari 1914.03, 1930.04
Satanella, or, the Power of Love 1863.06, 1883.39
Saturday Night Fever 1999.15
Saw Mill, The, or, a Yankee Trick 1834.03
Say When (Henderson-Koehler) 1934.35
Say When (Perkins-Lief-Harling) 1928.21
Say, Darling 1958.08, 1959.03
Scarlet Pimpernel, The 1997.19, 1999.13
Scheming! 1885.44
School Days 1908.28
School Girl, The (Manchester-Maurice) 1895.44
School Girl, The (Stuart-Taylor) 1904.29
School for Husbands, The (Pickett-Guiterman) 1933.24
School for Husbands, The (Stange-Edwards) 1905.15
Schoolmaster Abroad, The, or, the Frolics of Fitzfoolzleums 1862.06
Sea Cadet, The, or, the Very Merry Mariner 1880.31
Sea King, The 1890.21
Sea Legs 1937.07
Second Little Show, The 1930.25
Secret Garden, The 1991.05
Secret Servants, The 1897.31
See America First 1916.06
See-Saw 1919.23
Seecadet, Der 1879.62
Seeing New York 1906.22
Seeniaya Ptitza 1924.48
Seesaw 1973.06
Selling of the President, The 1972.02
Selwyn's Snapshots of 1921 1921.18
Serenade, The 1897.13, 1900.32, 1930.12
Sergeant Brue 1905.19
Sergeant Kitty 1904.05
Serment d'amour 1887.36
Sesostra 1912.09
Set to Music 1939.07
Seussical 2000.18
Seven Ages, The 1889.46
Seven Brides for Seven Brothers 1982.14
7–11–77 1899.31
Seven Lively Arts 1944.29
Seven Ravens, The 1884.40
Seven Sisters!, The 1860.06
Seven Sons!, The 1861.04
Seven Suabians, The 1890.28
$ 7,000 1867.01
Seventeen 1951.18
1776 1969.06, 1997.15
Seventh Heart, The 1927.18
Seventh Heaven 1955.10
70, Girls, 70 1971.07
Sextet 1974.04
Sgt. Pepper's Lonely Hearts Club Band on the Road 1974.24
Shady Lady 1933.16
Shakespeare's Cabaret 1981.02
Shameen Dhu 1914.05
Shamus O'Brien 1897.03
Shane-na-Lawn 1885.53, 1886.44, 1890.06
Shangri-La 1956.07
Sharlee 1923.42
She 1887.49, 1888.37
She Loves Me 1963.14, 1993.10
She's Come! Jenny's Come! 1850.01
She's My Baby 1928.02
She's a Good Fellow 1919.09
Sheep's Foot!, The 1866.12
Shelter 1973.03
Shenandoah 1975.03, 1989.17
Sherry! 1967.02
Shinbone Alley 1957.05
Ship Ahoy! 1890.44
Shirley MacLaine 1984.06, 1976.07
Sho-Gun, The 1904.37
Shogun: The Musical 1990.17
Shoo-Fly Regiment, The 1907.22
Shoot the Works! 1931.21
Shooting the Chutes 1900.45
Shop Girl, The 1895.32
Show Girl (Gaynor) 1961.01
Show Girl (Gershwin) 1929.27
Show Girl, The, or, the Cap of Fortune (Corliss-Heartz-Barnet) 1902.15
Show Time 1942.24
Show is On, The 1936.31
Show of Wonders, The 1916.23
Showboat 1927.67, 1932.11, 1946.01, 1948.20, 1954.04, 1954.14, 1961.09, 1966.14, 1983.05, 1994.08
Showing Off 1938.03
Shubert Gaieties of 1919, The 1919.16
Shuffle Along (1921) 1921.16
Shuffle Along (1933) 1932.30
Shuffle Along (1952) 1952.08
Shylock, or, the Merchant of Venice Preserved 1857.05, 1867.27
Shylock: A Jerusalem Hearty Joke 1853.05
Siamsa 1976.29
Sicilian Romance, The, or, the Spectre of the Cliffs 1796.02
Sid Caesar & Company: Does Anybody Know What I'm Talking About? 1989.22
Side Show (Krieger-Russell) 1997.17
Side Show, The (George Jenks) 1894.50
Side by Side by Side 1977.05
Sidewalks of New York 1927.48
Sieba and the Seven Ravens 1884.39
Sign in Sidney Brustein's Window, The 1972.01
Silk Stockings 1955.02
Silks and Satins 1920.24
Silver Demon!, The 1872.32
Silver Slipper, The 1902.35
Silver Star, The 1909.28
Silver Swan, The 1929.46
Silverlake, or, a Winter's Tale 1980.04, 1980.25
Simple Simon 1930.08, 1931.08
Simple Simon Simple 1905.47
Simply Heavenly 1957.09
Sinbad (Atteridge-Romberg) 1918.05
Sinbad (Fowler-Rostetter) 1905.10
Sinbad the Sailor! (Lydia Thompson Co.) 1873.14
Sinbad the Sailor, or, the Valley of Diamonds (G.L. Fox) 1865.11
Sinbad, or, the Maid of Balsora (Batchelor-Smith) 1892.29, 1898.16
Sindbad the Sailor, or, the Ungenial Geni and the Little Cabin Boy!! (Lydia-Thompson Co.) 1869.29
Sing Out the News 1938.09
Sing Out, Sweet Land! 1944.32
Sing for Your Supper 1939.19
Sing, Israel, Sing 1967.08
Singin' in the Rain 1985.08
Singin' the Blues 1931.32
Singing Girl, The 1899.34
Singing Rabbi, The 1931.29
Sir Andy De Bootjack 1898.56
Sir Dan O'Pallas, Chief of the Assyrian Jim Jams 1876.14
Sir Harry Lauder 1928.05, 1930.17
Siren, The 1911.27
Sister Mary 1899.35
Sitting Pretty 1924.08
1600 Pennsylvania Avenue 1976.11, 1776 1969.06, 1997.15
66 1868.20
Skating Rink, The 1885.64, 1887.13
Ski-Hi 1908.20
Skipped by the Light of the Moon 1884.15, 1884.56
Sky High 1925.07
Skylark, A 1910.10
Skyscraper 1965.33
Sleeping Beauty and the Beast, The 1901.27
Sleepy Hollow 1948.18
Slim Princess, The 1911.02
Small Wonder 1948.22
Smiff 1881.28
Smile 1986.20
Smile at Me 1935.11
Smiles 1930.39
Smiling Faces 1932.15
Smokey Joe's Cafe, 1995.03
Snake Charmer, The 1881.40
Snapshots of 1921 1921.18
Snow White and the Seven Dwarfs 1979.28
So Long Letty 1916.21
So Long, 174th Street 1976.09
Soap Bubble, A 1886.35
Social Whirl, The 1906.17
Society Circus, A 1905.54
Society Fad, A 1892.56
Soldiers and Sweethearts 1886.39
Some Night! 1918.29
Some Party 1922.16
Somebody's Sweetheart 1918.40
Something More! 1964.35
Something for the Boys 1943.01
Something's Afoot 1976.15
Sometime 1918.30
Somewhere Else 1913.01
Somnambula, La (burlesque by Buckley-Sharpley) 1873.04
Son of Rest, A 1903.20
Song & Dance 1985.12
Song Birds, The 1907.14
Song Writer, The 1928.24
Song of Jacob Zulu, The 1993.04

Song of Norway 1944.21, 1981.21
Song of the Flame 1925.52
Sonnambula, La (burlesque by Byron) 1870.19
Sonny 1921.24
Sons o' Fun 1941.11
Sons o' Guns 1929.44
Sons of Ham 1900.46
Soon 1971.01
Sophie 1963.12
Sophisticated Ladies 1981.06
Sorcerer, The 1879.10, 1879.14, 1882.70, 1892.46, 1915.10
Soul Kiss, The 1908.07
Sound of Music, The 1959.24, 1967.07, 1990.02, 1998.03
South Before the War, The 1894.44
South Pacific 1949.04, 1955.07, 1957.06, 1961.12, 1965.20, 1967.10, 1987.03
Southern Enchantment 1902.38
Southerners, The 1904.21
Sphinx, The 1895.19
Spice of 1922 1922.23
Spider and Fly 1889.47
Spirit of the Air, or, the Enchanted Star, The 1851.05
Spokesong, or, the Common Wheel 1979.07
Spoon River Anthology 1963.19
Sport McAllister, One of the 400 1892.23
Sporting Days 1908.26
Spotless Town 1903.05
Spring Chicken, The (Caryll-Monckton-Ross-Greenbank) 1906.36
Spring Chicken, The (E. Selden) 1898.75
Spring Maid, The 1910.37
Spring is Here 1929.12
Springtime of Youth 1922.40
Squatter Sovereignty 1882.02, 1892.44
Squaw Man's Girl of the Golden West 1904.39, 1906.01
Squonk 2000.02
St. George and the Dragon!, or, the 7 Champions of Christendom 1871.02
St. Louis Woman 1946.08
Stag Party, A, or, a Hero in Spite of Himself 1895.42
Star Gazer, The 1917.30
Star Time 1944.22
Star and Garter (Billy Rose revue) 1942.18
Star and Garter (Bratton-Ford) 1900.52
Stardust 1987.02
Starlight 1892.21, 1893.37
Starlight Express 1987.05
Starmites 1989.09
Stars in Your Eyes 1939.13
Stars on Ice 1942.19
State Fair 1996.04
Steel City 1999.02
Steel Pier 1997.07
Step This Way 1916.09
Stepping Stones 1923.40, 1924.26
Stickiness of Gelatine, The 1902.29
Stop the World - I Want to Get Off 1962.18, 1978.18
Stop! Look! Listen! 1915.31
Story Theatre 1970.16
Strada, La 1969.16
Straight Tip, A 1891.03, 1892.05
Strange Adventures of Jack and the Beanstalk, The 1896.44
Strange Gentleman, The 1839.01
Stranger in New York, A 1897.34
Straw Hat Revue, The 1939.26
Street Corner Symphony 1997.21
Street Scene 1947.02, 1959.08, 1959.17, 1963.15, 1966.02, 1978.23, 1979.27, 1990.08
Street Singer, The (Gilbert-Kempner-Timberg) 1929.32
Street Singer, The (Reid-Colwell) 1904.33
Streets of Paris, The 1939.22
Strider 1979.29
Strike Me Pink 1933.05
Strike Up the Band 1930.02
Strollers, The 1901.13
Struck Gas 1888.28
Struck Oil 1877.28, 1894.32
Strut, Miss Lizzie 1922.22
Stubborn Cinderella, A 1909.02
Student Gypsy, The, or, the Prince of Liederkranz 1963.20
Student King, The 1906.49
Student Prince (in Heidelberg), The 1924.45, 1931.03, 1943.06, 1980.21, 1981.20, 1985.09, 1987.08, 1993.12
Subways are for Sleeping 1961.28
Sue, Dear 1922.24
Sugar 1972.04
Sugar Babies 1979.25
Sugar Hill 1931.47
Sultan of Mocha, The 1880.46
Sultan of Sulu, The 1902.44
Summer Widowers, The 1910.16
Summer Wives 1936.07
Sun Dodgers, The 1912.45
Sun Showers 1923.04
Sun-Kist 1921.17
Sunday in the Park With George 1984.08
Sunny 1925.33
Sunny Days 1928.07, 1928.32
Sunny River 1941.12
Sunset Boulevard 1994.10
Sunshine Girl, The 1913.04
Sunshine of a Paradise Alley, The 1896.15
Superba 1892.59
Superman 1966.06
Supper Club, The 1901.29
Sure Cure, A 1898.61
Susanna, Don't You Cry 1939.21
Suzette (Gutman-Dixon) 1921.38
Suzette (Oscar Weil) 1890.37
Suzi 1914.28
Swan Lake 1998.10
Sweeney Todd - the Demon Barber of Fleet Street 1979.06, 1984.13, 1987.09, 1989.19
Sweeney Todd/Bombastes Furioso 1924.20
Sweet Adeline 1929.31
Sweet Anne Page 1900.54
Sweet Charity 1966.01, 1986.07
Sweet Inniscarra 1897.06
Sweet Little Devil 1924.03
Sweet Marie 1901.24
Sweet and Low 1930.38
Sweetheart Shop, The 1920.29
Sweetheart Time 1926.03
Sweethearts 1913.24, 1929.34, 1947.04
Swell Miss Fitzwell, The 1897.45
Swing It 1937.09
Swing Mikado, The 1939.15
Swing! 1999.24
Swingin' the Dream 1939.29
Swinging on a Star 1995.14
Sybil 1916.01
Syren, The 1862.04
Ta Bouche 1929.14
Tabasco 1894.22
Takarazuka 1989.21
Take Me Along 1959.22, 1985.04
Take a Bow 1944.19
Take a Chance 1932.25
Take it from Me 1919.07
Take the Air 1927.60
Tales of Rigo 1927.26
Talisman, The 1893.21
Talk About Girls 1927.29
Talk of New York, The 1907.57
Tallapoosa, The 1889.52
Tambourines to Glory 1963.27
Tame Cats 1868.29
Tammany, or, the Indian Chief 1794.01
Tangerine 1921.23
Tango Argentino 1985.07, 1999.18
Tango Pasión 1993.08
Tantalizing Tommy 1912.35
Tap Dance Kid, The 1983.21
Tar and the Tartar, The 1891.13
Tata-Toto 1897.08
Tattle Tales 1933.15
Tattooed Man, The 1907.11
Teddy and Alice 1987.19
Telephone Girl, The 1897.54
Telephone, The/The Medium 1947.10, 1948.29, 1950.13
Tell Her the Truth 1932.21
Tell Me More! 1925.14
Temperance Town, A 1893.31
Temptations 1911.18
Tenderfoot, The 1904.09
Tenderloin 1960.19
Terence 1904.02
Texas Steer, A, or, Money Makes the Mare Go 1890.41, 1893.14, 1894.02
Texas, Li'l Darlin' 1949.17
That Girl at the Bijou 1956.11
That's Entertainment 1972.05
The Laughing Husband 1914.04
The Who's Tommy 1993.06
Theatre of the Piccoli 1940.05
There You Are 1932.10
There's a Silver Lining to Every Cloud, or, the Sonnambulist 1859.18
They're Playing Our Song 1979.04
Third Little Show, The 1931.14
13 Daughters 1961.07
This Year of Grace 1928.42
This is the Army 1942.20
This was Burlesque 1965.05, 1981.17
Those Bells 1886.59
Those Were the Days 1990.16
Three Blind Mice! or, Harlequin Tell-Tale Tit 1871.09
Three Cheers 1928.37
Three Dragoons, The 1899.06
3 for Tonight 1955.03
3 from Brooklyn 1992.16
Three Hunchbacks!, The 1871.08
Three Little Girls 1930.15
Three Little Lambs 1899.41
Three Little Maids 1903.22
3 Mus-Ke-Teers, The 1872.30
Three Musketeers, The (Friml) 1928.12, 1984.14
Three Musketeers, The (R.W. Temple) 1921.15
3 of a Kind! 1883.68
Three Romeos, The 1911.42
3 Showers 1920.11
3 Sisters!, The 1866.11

Three Twins 1908.18
Three Waltzes 1937.17
Three Wishes for Jamie 1952.05
Three Wishes, The, or, the Land of the Birds 1908.26
Three of a Kind 1885.10, 1886.05
Three to Make Ready 1946.07
Three's a Crowd 1930.32
Threepenny Opera 1933.07, 1966.19, 1976.10, 1989.24
Thrice Married 1864.13
Thrilby 1895.17
Through the Years 1932.03
Thumbs Up! 1934.42
Thurber Carnival, A 1960.04
Tib, or, the Cat in Crinoline 1863.08
Tick-Tack-Toe 1920.06
Tickets, Please! 1950.09
Tickle Me 1920.27
Tidbits of 1946 1946.15
Tillie's Nightmare 1910.13
Timbale d'Argent, La 1874.12, 1876.28, 1882.67, 1884.55
Timbuktu! 1978.03
Time for Singing, A 1966.09
Time, the Place and the Girl, The 1907.25, 1942.30
Tin Soldier, A 1886.28, 1888.44
Tintypes 1980.27
Tip-Toes 1925.49
Tip-Top 1920.36
Tipperary Christening, A 1901.26
'Tis of Thee 1940.18
Titanic 1997.06
To Live Another Summer - To Pass Another Winter 1971.14
To-Night's the Night 1914.32
Toinette et Son Carabinier 1859.10
Toller Cranston's the Ice Show 1977.09
Tom Jones 1907.51
Tom Moore 1901.15
Tom and Jerry, or, Life in London 1823.01, 1875.03
Tom, Dick and Harry 1905.34
Tom-Tom, the Piper's Son Stole a Pig and Away He Run 1866.31
Tommy Rot 1902.34
Tommy Tune Tonite! 1992.18
Tommy, (The Who's) 1972.08, 1993.06
Tonight at 8:30 1936.29, 1948.11
Tony Bennett and Lena Horne Sing 1974.21
Too Many Girls 1939.27
Too Many Wives 1908.37
Toot Sweet 1919.10
Toot-Toot! 1918.09
Top Banana 1951.23
Top Speed 1929.49
Top o' th' World, The 1907.47
Top-Hole 1924.25
Top-Notchers 1942.14
Topics of 1923 1923.41
Toplitzky of Notre Dame 1946.23
Topsy and Eva 1924.46
Toreador, Le (A. Adam) 1866.25
Toreador, The (Caryll-Monckton-Ross-Greenbank) 1902.01
Touch and Go 1949.12
Tourists in a Pullman Palace Car, The 1879.64, 1880.38, 1882.76
Tourists, The 1906.26
Tovarich 1963.08
Town Lots, or, a Paper City 1888.21
Town Topics 1915.22
Toy Pistol, A 1886.06
Tragédie de Carmen, La 1983.16
Transatlantique Vaudevilles 1889.35
Treasure Girl 1928.43
Tree Grows in Brooklyn, A 1951.14
Treemonisha 1975.19
Trial by Jury 1875.35, 1879.11, 1879.58, 1886.17, 1886.29, 1892.46, 1899.20, 1900.26, 1915.10, 1931.22, 1933.10, 1934.09, 1934.25, 1935.09, 1936.09, 1936.14, 1939.01, 1940.14, 1942.08, 1944.05, 1948.01, 1949.13, 1951.03, 1952.17, 1955.21, 1962.29, 1964.37
Tricks 1973.02
Trifles 1880.30
Trip Around the World!, A 1871.16
Trip to Africa, A (Larkins-Peyton) 1904.38
Trip to Africa, A (von Suppe) 1884.64, 1887.15, 1898.62
Trip to Buffalo, A 1902.11
Trip to Chinatown, A 1891.39, 1894.07, 1894.35
Trip to Coontown, A 1898.22
Trip to Japan, A 1909.20
Trip to Mars, A 1893.29
Trip to the Moon, A 1877.15
Triumph of Love 1997.18
Trois Jeunes Filles Nues 1929.10
Tromb-al-ca-zar, ou Les Criminels dramatiques 1864.03, 1866.30
Trompette 1882.68
Tropical Revue (see also Katharine Dunham Co.) 1943.17, 1944.31
Trouble in Tahiti 1955.05, 1958.09
Truly Blessed: A Musical Celebration of Mahalia Jackson 1990.05
Trumpets of the Lord 1969.10
Tumble In 1919.06
Turned Up 1886.59, 1887.52
Tuxedo 1891.32, 1892.50
12 P.M. 1892.39
Twelve Temptations!, The 1870.05, 1875.10
20th Century Girl, The 1895.04
Twiddle-Twaddle 1906.01
Twinkle, Twinkle 1926.39
Twins 1885.21
Twirly-Whirly 1902.29
Two Bouquets, The 1938.06
Two Doves 1866.20
Two Gentlemen of Verona 1971.18
Two Islands 1907.45
Two Little Brides 1912.17
Two Little Girls in Blue 1921.10
Two Medallions!, The 1882.44
Two Off-Uns, The 1876.07
Two Roses, The 1904.51
Two by Two 1970.19
Two for the Show 1940.03
Two is Company (Briquet-Philipp) 1915.21
Two on the Aisle 1951.19
Two's Company (Duke-Nash) 1952.20
Tycoon, or, Young America in Japan, The 1860.05
Tyrolean, The 1891.30
Tzigane, The 1895.12

U and I 1891.09, 1892.15
Umabatha: The Zulu Macbeth 1997.14
Uncle Celestin 1892.07
Uncle Joe, or, Fritz in a Madhouse 1889.20
Under Cover 1903.26
Under Many Flags 1912.30
Under the Counter 1947.15
Under the Red Globe 1897.09
Unser Fritz, the Bohemian 1884.04
Unsinkable Molly Brown, The 1960.20
Up She Goes 1922.41
Up and Down Broadway 1910.19
Up in Central Park 1945.03, 1947.11
Up in One 1979.11
Up in the Clouds 1922.01
Ups-A-Daisy 1928.35
Upside Down 1888.16
Uptown. . .It's Hot! 1986.02
Utopia, Limited, or, the Flowers of Progress 1894.15
Utter Glory of Morrissey Hall, The 1979.10

Vacation Day 1882.46
Vagabond King, The 1925.32, 1943.08
Valiant Valentine 1866.05
Vamp, The 1955.25
Vanderbilt Cup, The 1906.05, 1907.02
Vanderbilt Revue, The 1930.35
Van Veen, Herman: All of Him 1982.23
Variety, or, the Picture Gallery 1857.03
Vassar Girls 1884.65
Velvet Lady, The 1919.01
Venetian Glass Nephew, The 1931.06
Venetian Romance, A 1904.19
Venus 1882.41
Venus and Adonis 1886.38
Vera Violetta 1911.43
Véronique 1905.46
Very Good Eddie 1915.30, 1975.24
Very Little Faust and Much Marguerite 1897.28
Very Warm for May 1939.28
Via Galactica 1972.25
Vicar of Bray, The 1882.63
Vice Admiral, The 1892.28
Viceroy, The 1900.25
Victor Borge on Broadway 1989.28
Victor, the Blue Stocking 1888.07
Victor/Victoria 1995.15
Vie Parisienne, La 1869.16, 1874.06, 1877.06, 1878.06, 1880.27, 1884.01, 1886.21, 1941.10, 1942.32, 1945.02, 1964.06
Vie!, La 1884.12
Vienna Life 1901.05
Viking, The 1895.11
Village Wedding, A 1892.32
Vintage '60 1960.12
Violoneux, Le 1864.10, 1866.09
Virginia 1937.10
Virginia, or, Ringing the Changes 1883.04
Vision of the Sun, The 1851.06
Viva O'Brien 1941.07
Vivandiere, La 1862.06
Vogues of 1924 1924.06
Voice of McConnell, The 1918.41
Voyage en Chine, Le 1875.01, 1882.73
Voyage en Suisse, Le 1881.35
Voyage of Suzette, The 1893.47
Voyagers in Southern Seas, or, the Children of Captain Grant 1881.15

Waddy Googan 1888.27
Waffles 1903.28
Wait a Minim! 1966.03
Wake Up and Dream 1929.51
Walk With Music 1940.09
Walk a Little Faster 1932.27
Walking Happy 1966.27
Wall Street 1899.29
Wall Street Girl, The 1912.14
Wall, The 1960.18
Waltz Dream, A 1908.06

Wang 1891.11, 1892.22, 1892.33, 1904.17
Wanted, a Family, or, Three Too Many 1862.06
Wanted, a Partner 1884.06
War Bubbles 1898.32
War-Time Wedding, A 1896.43
Wars of the World 1914.19
Watch Your Step 1914.31
Watch on the Rhine, The 1905.12
Water Queen, The 1889.08
Waterman, The, or, the First of August 1858.03, 1959.02
Way to Kenmare, The 1904.46
Wayhighman, The 1897.48
We, Us and Co. (at Mud Springs) 1884.66, 1886.11
Weary Willie Walker 1902.14
Wedding Day, The 1897.17, 1898.27
Wedding Trip, The 1911.47
Wee Willie Winkie 1870.33
Welcome to the Club 1989.07
Well of Romance, The 1930.36
Well-Fed Dora 1884.22
West Point Cadet, The 1904.35
West Side Story 1957.12, 1960.08, 1964.17, 1968.18, 1980.02
What Makes Sammy Run? 1964.05
What's Up 1943.21
What's in a Name? 1920.08
When Claudia Smiles 1914.06
When Dreams Come True 1913.19
When Johnny Comes Marching Home 1902.41, 1917.11
When Sweet Sixteen 1911.31
When We are Forty-One 1905.23
When You Smile 1925.35
Where's Charley? 1948.26, 1951.02, 1966.11, 1974.25
Whirl of New York, The 1921.20
Whirl of Society/A Night With the Pierrots 1912.09
Whirl of the Town, The 1897.26
Whirl of the World, The 1914.01
Whirl-I-Gig 1899.30
White Cat, The (Barnes) 1870.12
White Cat, The (Englander-Smith) 1905.48
White Eagle, The 1927.65
White Elephant, The 1889.31
White Fawn, The 1868.03
White Hen, The 1907.10
White Horse Inn 1936.22
White Lights 1927.53
White Lilacs 1928.26
White Sister, The 1927.22
Who Cares? 1930.23
Who is Who? 1898.08
Who's Who 1938.04
Whoop-Dee-Doo 1903.28
Whoop-Up 1958.20
Whoopee 1928.47, 1979.05
Why Worry? 1918.24
Widow Dooley's Dream 1903.30
Widow Goldstein, The 1897.23
Widow Jones, The 1895.27, 1901.30
Widow, The 1882.33
Wiener Blut 1964.25
Wife Hunters, The 1911.40
Wild Cat, The (Penella-Schrader) 1921.39
Wild Party, The 2000.08
Wild Rose, The (Englander-Smith) 1902.16
Wild Rose, The (Friml-Harbach-Hammerstein) 1926.34
Wild and Wonderful 1971.19
Wildcat (Coleman-Leigh) 1960.22
Wildflower 1923.05
Will Morrissey's Newcomers 1923.23
Will Rogers Follies: A Life in Revue, The 1991.07
William Tell 1870.09
Williams, Andy, With Michel Legrand 1974.20
Wily West, The 1887.30
Wind in the Willows 1985.20
Wine Women and Song (Max Liebman revue) 1942.25
Wine, Women and Song (Schilling-Corbett) 1898.55
Winged Victory 1943.23
Winsome Widow, A 1912.13
Winsome Winnie 1903.38
Wip Wan Winkle 1869.37
Wish You Were Here 1952.10
Witch of the Black Cavern, The, or, the Golden Pills of Magic 1865.09
Without a Name 1870.01
Without the Law 1912.44
Wives 1879.56
Wiz, The 1975.01, 1984.09, 1993.03
Wizard of Oz, The (Arlen-Harburg) 1989.06, 1997.11, 1998.06, 1999.11
Wizard of Oz, The (Tietjens-Sloane) 1903.03, 1904.13, 1904.44
Wizard of the Nile, The 1895.33, 1897.18
Wizard's Tempest, or, the King of the Magical Island, The 1862.05
Wo Die Lerche Singt 1920.46
Woman Haters, The 1912.37
Woman King, The, or The Rainmaker of Syria 1893.32
Woman King, The, or The Royal Prize 1893.32
Woman of the Year 1981.10
Wonder Bar, The 1931.09
Wonder Child, The, or, the Follies of Earth, Air and Sea 1877.20
Wonderful Night, A 1929.39
Wonderful Town 1953.03, 1958.05, 1963.05, 1967.09, 1994.09
Wonderland 1905.44
Woodland 1904.52
Woof, Woof 1929.50
Woollen Stocking, The 1893.36
Words and Music (Hitchcock-Goetz) 1917.35
Words and Music (Sammy Cahn) 1974.10
Working 1978.12
World According to Me, The 1986.21, 1988.11
World of Charles Aznavour, The 1965.30
World of Pleasure, A 1915.26
World's Fair City Directory, The 1893.28
World's Fair, or, Columbia in the Clouds, The 1851.03
World's Fair, or, London in 1851, The 1851.04
Worst Born, The 1897.48
Would-Be Gentleman, The 1946.02
Wrinkles 1885.70
Wrong Man in the Right Place, The 1872.15, 1873.07

Yankee Circus on Mars, A, the Raiders 1905.17
Yankee Consul, The 1904.10, 1905.06
Yankee Doodle Dandy 1898.43
Yankee Girl, The 1910.08
Yankee Prince, The 1908.14
Yankee Princess, The 1922.35
Yankee Tourist, The 1907.27
Ye Legend of Ye Grand Queen Bess! 1867.31
Ye Olden Times 1891.16
Yeah Man 1932.12
Yearling, The 1965.36
Yenuine Yentleman, A 1895.14
Yeomen of the Guard, The, or, the Merryman and His Maid 1888.35, 1915.06, 1933.09, 1933.19, 1934.28, 1935.07, 1936.18, 1939.09, 1944.13, 1948.09, 1955.15, 1964.07, 1965.13, 1968.14
Yes, Yes, Yvette 1927.49
Yip Yip Yaphank 1918.21
Yokel Boy 1939.24
Yon Yonson 1891.46, 1894.12
You Know Me Al! 1918.13
You Never Know 1938.07
You Said It 1931.01
You'll See Stars 1942.35
You're a Good Man, Charlie Brown 1971.11, 1999.03
You're in Love 1917.05
Young Abe Lincoln 1961.11
Young Bacchus, or, Spirits and Water 1857.01
Young Don Juan 1889.53
Young Man, Older Woman 1995.01
Young Rip Van Winkle, A 1876.15
Young Turk, The 1910.07
Your Arms Too Short to Box With God 1976.35, 1980.14, 1982.17
Yours Truly 1927.07, 1928.11
Yours is My Heart 1946.16
Yushny's Seeniaya Ptitza 1924.48
Yushny's The Blue Bird 1924.48
Yvette 1916.12

Z-Seltzer! 1883.56
Zanina, or, the Rover of Cambaye 1881.04
Zara! 1883.07
Zenobia, Queen of Palmyra 1883.49
Ziegfeld Follies of 1922 Summer Edition 1923.20
Ziegfeld Follies of 1907 1907.24
Ziegfeld Follies of 1908 1908.19
Ziegfeld Follies of 1909 1909.13
Ziegfeld Follies of 1910 1910.18
Ziegfeld Follies of 1911 1911.24
Ziegfeld Follies of 1912 1912.38
Ziegfeld Follies of 1913 1913.17
Ziegfeld Follies of 1914 1914.15
Ziegfeld Follies of 1915 1915.15
Ziegfeld Follies of 1916 1916.10
Ziegfeld Follies of 1917 1917.13
Ziegfeld Follies of 1918 1918.19
Ziegfeld Follies of 1919 1919.15
Ziegfeld Follies of 1920 1920.18
Ziegfeld Follies of 1921 1921.21
Ziegfeld Follies of 1922 1922.19
Ziegfeld Follies of 1923 1923.38
Ziegfeld Follies of 1924 1924.18
Ziegfeld Follies of 1924 Fall Edition 1924.18
Ziegfeld Follies of 1925 1925.10
Ziegfeld Follies of 1925 Summer Edition 1925.24
Ziegfeld Follies of 1927 1927.37
Ziegfeld Follies of 1931 1931.19
Ziegfeld Follies of 1933–1934 1934.01
Ziegfeld Follies of 1943 1943.05
Ziegfeld Follies of 1957 1957.01
Ziegfeld's Revue of 1926 1926.18
Ziegfeld Follies of 1936 1936.02
Ziegfeld Follies of 1936–1937 1936.17
Zig-Zag 1888.29, 1889.45
Zig-Zag Alley 1903.01
Zip, or, Point Lynde Light 1877.02
Zizi 1964.39
Zoot Suit 1979.08
Zorba 1968.30, 1983.14
Zulu and the Zayda, The 1965.32

INDEX OF SONGS

Note: All songs which appear in quotation marks in the text have been indexed (for example, "Erbie Fitch's Twitch" or "Which Switch Is the Switch, Miss, for Ipswich?"), including variant titles which appear in parentheses alongside the original title. Thus the song "Merely Marvelous" as it appears in the program for REDHEAD will also appear in the index as "I Feel Merely Marvelous" since its sheet music was published under that title; in the body of the book, it will also appear as "(I Feel) Merely Marvelous." The original SHOW BOAT program contains both "Ol' Man River" and "Old Man River." Generic entries like Song, Specialty, Finale, Dance, Trio are not indexed. Overtures and Entr'actes are not listed in the book, whether or not listed in the program, as they were as often performed as not.

A B C 1900.43
A l'heure ou s'unissent tremblants 1877.32
a la Mode Girl, The 1903.40
A toi j'avais donne ma vie 1884.50
A-1 March 1964.15
A-B-C 1967.16
A-B-Cs of the U.S.A., The 1908.14
A-Flat Polonaise 1928.26
A-L-E 1909.18
A-L-E-X-A-N-D-R-I-A 1904.30
A-m-e-r-i-c-a 1899.04
A-Many Years Ago 1945.08
A-Stage 1972.18
A-Tisket, A-Tasket 1986.02, 1989.16
A. . .My Name is Ellie 1985.03
A.B.C. Song, The 1962.18
A.O.H. March 1880.42, 1882.39
Abadaba Club, The 1929.02
Abandon 1927.45
Abbe's Dream, The 1893.22
Abbondanza 1956.04
Abby's Song 1999.17
ABCs 1962.02
Abduction, The 1965.34
Abdullah's Farewell 1923.34
Abe Lincoln 1938.08
Aber Nit 1904.58
Abide With Me 1987.17
Abie Baby 1968.11
Abomelique's Wives 1860.01
About a Quarter to Nine 1962.17, 1980.20, 1988.08
About Den Adhem 1950.02
About Face 1948.15
About the Middle of the Week 1884.57
About Time 1970.16
About Town 1894.10
Above the Slim Minaret 1900.01
Abracadabra 1944.02
Abraham, Martin and John 1974.09
Absail 1999.02
Absence Makes the Heart Grow Fonder 1900.08, 1902.02
Absent Minded 1972.05
Absent-Minded Girl, The 1901.09
Absinthe Frappe 1904.54, 1911.31, 1924.18
Absolute Don of a Juan, An 1920.37
Absolutely Certain 1920.37
Absolution 1990.17
Absurd Four, The 1903.09
Abundance and Charity 1994.12
Abuse 1975.19
AC/DC 1987.05
Acacias, Des 1892.07
Academic Fugue 1967.14
Academy Rag, The 1912.29
Acceleration Waltz 1964.25
Accelerationenwalzer 1964.25
Accent Makes No Difference in the Language of Love, The 1911.15
Accent Song 1886.34
Accents Melodiques 1955.14
Accentuate the Positive 1997.05
Accident, An 1904.05, 1906.33
According to Dr. Holt 1918.16
According to Mr. Grimes 1928.43
Accordionist, The 1981.04
Accourez a ma boutique! 1883.51
Accourons tous, depechons-nous! 1877.32
Ace in the Hole 1941.08, 1942.11
Ace of Spades 1929.25
Aces Up 1932.10
Ach Louise 1903.38
Aching Heart, The 1898.28
Acid Queen 1993.06
Acid queen, The 1972.08
Acorn in the Meadow 1953.17
Acrobatic, Operatic Quartette 1886.32
Across the broad waters 1868.01
Across the Sands 1879.35
Across the Wide Missouri 1955.13
Act Like a Lady 1968.05
Act to purify our band, An 1898.25
Act, The 1970.07
Acting 1903.02
Active am I 1840.03
Actor's Life, The 1984.14
Actors Who've Seen Better Days, The 1885.29
Actress and a Lady, An 1902.34
Actress hasn't Learned the Lines You'd Like to Hear, The 1979.23
Acts of God 1985.17
Ad, The 1976.20
Ad-dressing of Cats, The 1982.19
Ada With the Golden Hair 1985.02
Ada, My Sweet Potater 1909.10
Adagio 1919.18
Adam 1916.17
Adam and Eve 1908.41, 1913.05, 1935.19
Adam was the Only Lover 1916.25
Adamless Eden, An 1884.60
Add a Little Wiggle 1928.08
Addie's at it Again 1964.44
Addios, Addios 1964.02
Adelaide's Lament 1950.17, 1980.29
Adele 1913.21
Adeline 1902.15
Adieu 1878.05, 1879.42
Adieu c'est dit je m'en vais en voyage 1884.43
Adieu Marquis 1859.17
Adieu to Ballyshannon 2000.01
Adieu, Lorraine, this day is full of sorrow 1887.12
Adios 1904.09
Adios del Soldado, El 1988.15
Adios Hermanos 1998.02
Adios Nonino 1985.07, 1993.08, 1997.13
Adios, Senorita 1909.02
Administration 1958.18
Admirable Admiral, An 1904.28
Admiral 1902.22
Admiral, The 1897.37
Adopt a Pretty Baby 1917.23
Adoption Dance 1966.12
Adorable 1925.25, 1926.23
Adorable Julie 1931.05
Adorable Toreador 1907.33
Adorable You 1928.26
Adoring You 1924.18
Adrift 1956.13
Adrift on a Star 1961.08
Advancement Militaire 1925.25, 1925.48
Advantage of a College Education, The 1905.23
Advantages of Floating in the Middle of the Sea, The 1976.02
Adventure 1960.23
Adventure Never Ends, The 1999.22
Advertising 1907.46, 1923.19
Advertising Man, The 1885.29, 1910.20
Advice 1902.15, 1913.14
Advice to Husbands 1944.16
Advice to Movie Mad Maidens 1927.10
Advice to the Young 1915.04
Aerial Waltz 1904.11
Aeroplane 1911.44
Aesop was a Very Moral Man 1916.08
Aesthetic Dancing 1910.22
Affable, Balding Me 1949.17
Affair to Remember, An 1988.08
Affinity 1906.50
Affluent Society, The 1964.44
Afghanistan 1975.02
Aforesaid Lord Dayrell, The 1887.04
Afraid 1969.08
Afraid of Love 1960.12
Afraid of the Dark 1989.09
Afraid to Go Home at All 1908.39
Africa 1924.13, 1927.63
Africa Burning in the Sun 1988.02
Africa Speaks 1972.19
African Dance 1973.10

African Dip 1921.16
African Shrieks 1931.14
African Whoopee 1929.25
Africana 1929.01, 1934.27
Africana Stomp 1927.32
After a travelling troublesome 1895.29
After All 1978.26
After All These Years 1984.01
After All, I'm Only a Schoolgirl 1929.51
After All, it's Spring 1951.18
After Business Hours 1903.34
After Dinner 1902.29, 1903.28
After Due Consideration 1898.48
After Graduation Day 1947.08
After Hours 1948.30
After Looking for Love 1987.17
After Love 1967.05
After Midnight Dies 2000.08
After Much Debate Internal 1881.37
After My Ship Comes In 1921.08
After Office Hours 1908.10
After the Ball 1891.39, 1893.23, 1927.67, 1946.01, 1966.14, 1983.05, 1994.08
After the Curfew Rings 1924.22
After the Fancy Ball 1901.06
After the Rain - Sunshine 1915.04
After the Show 1900.52
After To-night, Goodbye 1920.35
After Today 1947.06
After Today Gala Polka 1947.06
After Tonight 1940.18
After Vespers 1912.29
After You Alphonse 1902.42
After You're Gone 1916.21
After You've Gone 1975.20, 1989.02
After You, Who? 1980.06
Afternoon of a Faun 1978.26
Afternoon of a Phoney, The 1942.29
Afternoon Tea, An 1904.13, 1904.44, 1914.22
Afterthought, An 1922.29
Afunani Amaphoyisa eSoweto 1988.02
Again 1980.08
Again enfolded within thine arms 1880.04
Again the Night Falls 1972.17
Against the Stream 1938.06
Age of Brass, The 1980.30
Age of Innocence 1922.47
Age of Innocence, The 1929.20
Age tendre et tetes de bois 1966.20
Agent's Lot is Not a Happy One, An 1945.09
Aggie Song, The 1978.13, 1986.03
Aggie's Sewing Machine Song 1936.28
Aggie, Oh Aggie 1970.10
Agincourt Song 1963.03
Agony 1987.18
Ah donnez m'en de la chanson 1963.02, 1965.08
Ah how often have I, sighing 1859.17
Ah is it I? 1902.06
Ah Key Lay 1864.13
Ah Love, Sweet Fragrant Flower 1896.10
Ah m les soirees de province 1929.15
Ah Madame 1929.11
Ah Me! 1894.46
Ah My Children, My Children... 1989.10
Ah My Heart With Fear is Rending 1895.25
Ah the Night Raven's Dismal Voice 1870.15
Ah There 1896.31
Ah Woe is Me 1899.40
Ah Yes 1895.43
Ah! 1958.06
Ah! Ah! Ah! Ah! Pauvre Inigo 1883.51
Ah! Camminare 1962.14
Ah! Che Vedo 1913.36
Ah! Combien de fois, l'ame emue 1885.56
Ah! comme il etait detraque! 1877.32
Ah! compere, le gai festin! 1877.32
Ah! confusion! 1848.04
Ah! Cupid, Meddlesome Boy! Good Bye! 1894.45
Ah! Gallant Soldier 1894.15
Ah! Happy Hour 1868.02
Ah! Heaven's Height has Cracked! 1988.05
Ah! Is she not a beauty? 1884.14
Ah! je vous aime a la folie 1884.43
Ah! let us see 1887.04
Ah! List to Me 1894.45
Ah! Never More Sadly! Now Away 1880.10
Ah! plaignez la misere 1877.32
Ah! Pour moi quelle heureuse chance 1887.35
Ah! que tu connais peu les femmes 1884.43
Ah! Quel bon vin! 1883.51
Ah! quel souper delectable! 1884.43
Ah! vous dirai-je, maman 1933.24
Ah! vraiment! mon pauvre mari! 1877.32
Ah! We Hapless Prima Donnas 1890.39
Ah! yes, as in the play 1859.09
Ah! you can better know, my dear 1855.02
Ah! you have not far 1887.04
Ah, 'Twas Love 1894.08
Ah, Ah, Ah 1922.05
Ah, at Last 1911.47
Ah, che la morte 1880.24
Ah, D'Jakh and D'Jill 1880.47
Ah, Destiny! 1886.15
Ah, Father, how d'ye do? 1880.47
Ah, good morning; how's Mrs. Church warden to-day? 1885.28
Ah, Happy Day 1954.06
Ah, How Capricious 1938.06
Ah, I Laugh 1910.24
Ah, Lady K. Talby 1894.15
Ah, Let Me Be! 1881.22
Ah, Love! 1964.39
Ah, Love, You do Not Know! 1894.28
Ah, May the Red Rose Live Always 1939.21
Ah, Miss 1979.06
Ah, Mosey I am yours for life 1848.03
Ah, Nell, We'll Try to be Precise 1905.46
Ah, never may that faithful heart 1868.01
Ah, never was seen 1868.01
Ah, no man I'll fear 1859.09
Ah, oui, j'etais 1895.26
Ah, Paree! 1977.05
Ah, Paris! 1971.05
Ah, Sweet Mystery of Life 1910.35, 1978.19, 1988.18
Ah, When You've Decided 1888.19
Ah, With Wrath 1881.22
Ah, Yes, I am in Love 1914.09
Ah-wah-ik-to-mani 1890.33
Ahead of the Times 1920.15
Ahi Wela 1912.03
Ai Yi Yi 1947.15
Aiaihea 1912.03
Aid me, Cupid 1882.60
Ain't Broadway Grand 1993.05
Ain't Gonna Rain 1931.11
Ain't Got No 1968.11
Ain't He a Joy? 1965.36
Ain't He Nice and Fat 1884.39
Ain't He Sweet? 1927.31
Ain't it a Shame About Mame 1995.14
Ain't it Awful 1908.09
Ain't it Awful, the Heat? 1947.02
Ain't it Foolish? 1907.14
Ain't it Funny What a Difference Just a Few Drinks Make? 1916.10
Ain't it Funny What a Difference Just a Few Hours Make 1904.10
Ain't it Great to be an Actress 1908.37
Ain't it Sweet 1919.24
Ain't it the Truth 1957.16
Ain't Life Fine 2001.06
Ain't Love Grand 1921.34, 1972.10, 1982.02
Ain't Love Grand? 1927.54
Ain't Love Wonderful 1925.29
Ain't Misbehavin' 1929.23, 1939.29, 1975.22, 1976.04, 1978.09, 1980.10
Ain't No Love 1975.12
Ain't No Mountain High Enough 1976.16
Ain't No Party 1981.29
Ain't Nobody Here But Us Chickens 1992.03, 1995.12
Ain't Puttin' Out Nothin' 1930.19
Ain't She Sweet 1979.24, 1986.06
Ain't too Proud to Beg 1986.02
Ain't We Got Fun 1980.08, 1986.06
Ain't We Got Love 1937.09
Ain't You Ashamed 1962.24
Ain't You Never Been Afraid? 1963.11
Ainsi que vient l'argent 1886.19
Aint'cha Comin' Back Mary Ann to Maryland 1921.16
Aintcha Glad You Got Music 1933.06
Air 1968.11
Air Male 1972.18
Air Minded 1930.11
Air of Violetta, The 1922.37
Air Ship Joy Ride, The 1910.01
Air That I Breath 2000.16
Air, Billy Taylor 1869.42
Airmail Special 1999.24
Airy Fairy Lillian 1895.02
Airy Mary 1904.51
Airy, Fairy Lillian 1893.39
Ajade Papa 1966.03
Akahi Hoi 1912.03
Al Fresco 1945.16
Ala Baba Babies, The 1926.32
Alabama 1909.17
Alabama Blossom, The 1896.49
Alabama Stomp 1926.23, 1927.02
Alabamy 1930.24
Aladdin 1916.23, 1921.07
Aladdin's Daughter 1946.04
Alaiyo 1973.10
Alamo 1906.28
Alarm Clock, The 1899.17
Alas for the Man Without Brains 1903.03, 1904.13, 1904.44
Alas for You 1976.17
Alas! For Me 1890.39
Alas! how quickly 1887.04
Alas! How Sat My Fate 1894.47
Alas! Those chimes so sweetly stealing 1848.04
Alas, a sad and sorry task 1871.19
Alas, Lorraine 1967.02
Alas, the Time is Past 1929.41
Albany 1905.22
Albert Porter 1938.06
Alborea 1992.15
Albumblatt 1944.21
Alcazar 1926.26
Aldermanic Board, The 1885.66
Aldonza 1965.34
Alegrias 1949.07, 1986.17, 1992.15
Alessandro the Wise 1945.04
Alexander 1905.10
Alexander's Bagpipe Band 1912.07
Alexander's Ragtime Band 1946.21, 1988.08, 1989.16
Alexander's Ragtime Wedding Day 1925.18
Alexandria 1919.38
Alexis from Texas 1905.52
Alexis! Doubt me not my loved one! 1879.10
Alf and Alf 1871.16
Algerian Girl 1917.31
Algerian Serenade 1893.40
Algerian Slave Song and Chorus 1903.04
Algy 1896.31, 1904.01, 1909.30
Algy's Simply Awfully Good at Algebra 1903.22
Ali Pacha 1872.10
Alias! I waver to and fro 1888.35
Alibi Baby 1923.27
Alibi Blues 1920.24
Alice Blue Gown 1919.36, 1973.05, 1976.24
Alice in Boogieland 1947.08
Alice in Wonderland 1916.24
Alice is at it Again 1968.19
Alien Song 1970.04
Alike, Alike 1980.09
Alimony 1907.26
Alimony Alley 1915.05
Alimony Blues 1918.11
Alive Again 1900.07
Alive and Kicking 1950.02
Alive to Tell the Tale 1902.06
Alive! 1997.09
Alixe 1873.03
Alkali Ike 1897.33
All a Lie! 1910.05
All Aboard 1883.26, 1904.58, 1906.39, 1913.16, 1914.01, 1929.07
All Aboard for Broadway 1906.11, 1968.07

All Aboard for Dixie 1913.34
All Aboard for Paris 1925.02
All Aboard for the M.G.P. 1880.36, 1883.53
All Aboard for Times Square 1927.60
All All Alone 1910.08
All Alone 1924.09, 1924.44, 1925.22
All Alone I Stand Against the Lot 1877.39
All Alone in a City of Girls 1916.26
All alone in my eerie 1893.02
All Alone Monday 1926.28, 1981.03
All American 1960.12, 1962.18, 1968.06, 1978.18
All American Man 1946.23
All Among the Hay 1873.20
All around is silent 1861.03
All Around the World 1946.04
All Ashore 1920.13
All at Once 1937.04
All at Once You Love Her 1955.27, 1993.16
All Blues 1982.15
All by Myself 1991.04
All by Yourself 1976.03
All Change Places 1922.20
All Choked Up 1972.12
All complications now is ended 1887.04
All Coons Look Alike to Me 1896.52
All Dark People 1937.04
All Day Long 1925.50
All Decked Out 1927.04
All Dressed Up and No Place to Go 1957.17
All Dressed Up in a Tailor-Made 1917.37
All er Nothin' 1943.04
All Eternity 1905.51
All Eyes Look Upon You 1999.22
All for a Girl 1920.33
All for a Green Ribbon 1907.51
All for Glory 1921.01
All for Him 1951.24
All for Joy 1882.39
All for Love 1925.21, 1949.02
All for One 1984.14
All for One and One for All 1928.12
All for the Best 1976.17
All for the Sake of a Girl 1914.30
All for You 1906.35, 1912.12, 1915.24, 1916.09, 1963.08, 2000.18
All Full of Ginger 1915.23
All Gall 1966.32
All Girls are Like a Rainbow 1921.19
All Good Gifts 1976.17
All hail great judge 1875.35
All Hail the Empress 1965.35
All Hail the King 1907.55
All Hail the Queen 1907.01
All Hail to the General 1926.42
All hail to Thee! 1875.19
All Hallowe'en 1912.39
All Hands for an Irish Reel 1911.28
All Hid 1966.15
All Honor Praise 1875.19
All Honor to Charles, Our King 1892.42
All Hope has Flown 1896.41
All I Ask of You 1988.01, 1992.12, 2000.14
All I Care About is Love 1975.14
All I Crave is More of Life 1978.19, 1988.18
All I Need 1972.13, 1979.15
All I Need is One Good Break 1965.17
All I Need is the Girl 1959.13
All I Need Now is the Girl 1991.10
All I Owe Ioway 1996.04
All I Want in the Wide, Wide World is You, Just You 1907.44
All I Want is Just One 1932.04
All I Want is Love 1925.26
All I Want is Ma Chickens 1898.22
All I Want is My Black Baby Back 1975.09
All I Want is You 1906.32
All I Wanted was the Dream 1988.20
All I've Got is Me 1989.25
All I've Got to Get Now is My Man 1940.19
All in a Little Dance 1913.02
All in Fun 1939.28, 1968.03
All in Measure Treading 1871.19
All in the Cause of Economy 1965.14
All in the gentle time of Spring 1887.12
All in the Wearing 1922.43, 1968.07
All is Ended 1880.69
All is Fair 1899.39
All is hushed 1860.01
All is lost 1873.04
All is prepared 1879.10
All is Prepared 1879.72, 1981.01
All is prepared, the Gas is on 1877.23
All is ready 1852.01
All is ready, haste away 1871.10
All is Vanity 1926.23, 1927.02
All is Well in Larchmont 1969.01
All Kinds of People 1955.27
All Lanes Must Reach a Turning 1924.34
All Love Jack 1888.11
All Lovely Art, We Worship at Thy Shrine 1906.18
All Men Have Their Troubles 1900.25
All My Days Till End of Life 1917.24, 1919.20
All My Girls 1906.41
All My Good Mornings 1972.25
All My Heart's Desire 1988.05
All My Life 1918.32, 1976.03
All Nations 1886.45
All Nature Rejoices 1877.20
All Nature's gay 1882.33
All Night 1918.29
All Night Long 1923.46
All night long I've weighed and sifted 1885.28
All of a sudden her Godmama 1862.09
All of Me 1999.24
All of My Dreams 1982.13
All of My Laughter 1969.01
All of My Life 1960.23, 1972.24
All of These and More 1958.01
All of You 1955.02
All on Account of Eliza 1881.07, 1881.16, 1881.17, 1882.20
All Our Friends 1968.07
All Pepped Up 1924.18
All Pull Together 1922.05
All Quiet Along the Potomac, Except the Letter G 1973.08
All Roads Lead to Hollywood 1983.17
All Said the Anchor's Weighed 1879.03
All She Could Say was Oui' 1905.45
All She'd Say was Um Hum 1920.18
All Shook Up 1989.12
All That Glitters 1981.02
All That He'd Want Me to Be 1979.09
All That I Need is a Hallway 1919.18
All That I Want 1920.42
All That Jazz 1975.14, 2000.14
All That Sort of Rot 1897.48
All the bold 1882.63
All the Children in a Row 1984.01
All the Clouds'll Roll Away 1929.27, 1962.17, 1975.22
All the Comforts of Home 1916.21, 1978.10
All the Dearly Beloved 1966.29
All the Documents Must be Signed 1950.05
All the Elks and the Masons 1934.19
All the Girls are Lovely by the Sea 1921.12
All the Girls Have Got a Friend in Me 1917.32
All the Girls Love Me 1906.36
All the guns in town 1882.44
All the King's Horses 1930.32
All the Kings' Horses and Men 1907.08
All the Little Glooms Start Dancing 1920.19
All the Little Ladies Love a Sailor Man 1913.26
All the Little Things in the World are Waiting 1970.12
All the Little Villages 1922.46
All the Livelong Day 1978.12
All the Mothers of the Nation 1933.25
All the news of all the nations 1881.04
All the People on the Levee 1940.01
All the Same to Me 1907.01, 1979.18
All the Stars and Stripes Belong to Me 1908.21
All the Things You Are 1939.28, 1986.01
All the Time 1939.13, 1958.02
All the Wasted Time 1998.21
All the Way 1974.10
All the While 1919.12
All the World is Madly Prancing 1912.24
All the World is Swaying 1918.25
All the World is Wonderful 1922.03
All the World Loves a Lover 1909.14, 1910.20, 1911.30, 1912.01, 1926.33
All the world over 1848.04
All the World to Me 1900.57
All the World's a Stage 1880.42
All the Wrongs You've Done to Me 1924.27
All These Things 1992.06
All Things to One Man 1985.05
All Those Pretty Girls 1970.01
All Those Years 1964.18
All Through the Love of You 1904.28
All Through the Night 1934.36, 1987.15
All to Myself 1922.10
All Washed Up 1919.24
All we seem to agree 1880.04
All who for servants 1878.16
All Work and No Play 1925.35
All Wrapped Up in You 1931.36
All Wrong 1915.17
All Ya Have to do is Wait 1989.29
All Year Round 1924.23
All You Have to do is Stand There 1942.35
All You Need is a Girl 1924.08
All You Need is a Quarter 1960.22
All You Need is a Song 1955.03
All You Need is Love 1977.10
All You Need to be a Star 1920.25
All You Want to do is Dance 1995.14
All Young Girls are Fond of Pleasure 1884.39
All Your Own am I 1911.38
All's Fair in Love and War 1932.06
All's Said, the Anchor's Weighed 1877.25
All's Well 1932.17
All-Girl Band, The 1940.03
All-Out Bugle Call 1942.27
Allaballa Goo-Goo 1912.34
Allah be Praised 1944.15
Allah Guard Thee 1920.34
Allah's Holiday 1915.30
Allay Up 1921.21
Alle sind wir Sunder 1984.05
Allegorical Blues 1922.42
Allegrias 1958.06
Allegro 1947.17
Alleluia 1974.06, 1982.20, 1997.10
Allen's Alcazars 1909.12
Allez Up 1926.13
Allez! Houp La! 1908.16
Allez-Vous-En Go Away 1953.07
Allied High Command, The 1936.28
Allies 1915.24
Alligator, The 1963.21
Allon Account of the Widow 1882.33
Allons 1970.15
Allons! Et point de parasse! 1887.35
Allons! venez ca, la fillette! 1877.32
Allons, il faut en francais 1886.09
Allons, petit serpent 1887.35
Allons, soyez raisonnable 1929.11
Allow Me to Inform You 1899.34
Allume Tes Lampions 1958.06
Alma 1910.26
Alma Mater 1972.12, 1988.12, 1994.07
Alma Redemptoris Mater 1994.08
Almanac Covers, The 1929.29
Almost 1909.03, 1926.22, 1964.44
Almost a Love Song 1995.15
Almost Like Being in Love 1947.07, 1967.11, 1980.26
Almost Paradise 1998.13
Aloha 1916.21, 1930.26, 1972.11
Aloha I Love You 1907.13
Aloha Oe 1912.03
Alone 1896.15, 1927.65, 1952.15, 1972.16
Alone Again Naturally 2000.16
Alone at a Drive-in Movie 1994.07
Alone at a Drive-in-Movie 1972.12
Alone at Last 1913.29, 1916.02
Alone in a Great Big World 1918.29
Alone in the Universe 2000.18
Alone on the Lone Prairie 1937.14
Alone on the Road 1995.04

Alone Together 1932.17, 1972.05
Alone too Long 1954.02
Alone With You 1929.08
Alone, and yet alive 1885.47
Alone, At Last, Alone 1974.03
Along Broadway 1911.42
Along Came Another Little Girl 1917.22
Along Came Bialy 2001.05
Along Came Love 1932.18
Along the Hudson 1918.23, 1919.32
Along the Old Canal 1898.55
Along the Old Lake Trail 1923.47
Along the Rio Grande 1924.47
Along the Road to Love 1924.10
Along the Rocky Road to Dublin 1919.40
Along the Way 1988.08
Along the Way Where Lovers Go 1898.17
Along the Winding Road 1941.12
Along With Me 1946.10
Alors raconte 1966.20
Alors, adieu donc... 1926.49
Alpha to Omega 1938.07
Alpha, Beta, Pi 1933.26
Alphabet Song 1961.07, 1971.02
Alphabet Song and Essence 1900.03
Alpine 1892.31
Alpine Girl, The 1913.30
Alpine Horn, The 1895.38, 1899.34
Also Spake Zarathustra 1999.15
Altdeutscher Liebersreim 1907.37
Alter is prepared, The 1855.06
Alter Nussenboim, Der 1968.22
Although I am a Soldier, I Prefer a Private Life 1902.35
Although I'm so Demure 1903.16
Although of native maids the cream 1894.15
Although she has posed 1895.17
Although your royal summons to appear 1894.15
Always 1925.23, 1987.17
Always Another Girl 1927.34
Always be a Gentleman 1935.17
Always Come Back to You 1908.25
Always do as People Say You Should 1898.60
Always Go While the Goin' is Good 1906.33
Always in My Heart 1930.43
Always Late 1902.44
Always Leave Them Laughing When You Say Goodbye 1903.39, 1907.16
Always Look Cheerful 1896.02
Always Mademoiselle 1969.17
Always Make Allowances for Love 1900.41
Always Marry an April Girl 1973.08
Always Mind Your Sister, Jennie 1893.33
Always on the Job 1925.18
Always Take Mother's Advice 1917.21
Always Tell the Truth 1955.11
Always the Same 1924.36
Always to Espana 1902.01
Always Together 1891.43, 1912.24
Always True to You in My Fashion 1948.32, 1999.19
Always You 1907.37, 1920.01, 1948.15
Always, Always You 1961.10
Am I a Man or a Mouse? 1946.22
Am I a Wife, Widow or Maid? 1908.39
Am I Afraid? 1947.10
Am I Alone? 1881.37, 1938.10
Am I Awake 1882.58
Am I Blue 1953.12
Am I Blue? 1973.14, 1982.12, 1989.02
Am I to Blame? 1917.27
Am I to Wish Her Love 1993.19
Amanzi 2000.05
Amapu 1928.04
Amaryllis 1894.45
Amasalela 1966.03
Amateur Circus 1895.02
Amateur Entertainer, The 1900.41
Amateur Night 1907.14
Amayzing Gertrude 2000.18
Amayzing Mayzie 2000.18
Amazing Grace 1943.10, 1986.02, 1989.12
Amazing journey 1972.08
Amazing Journey 1993.06
Amazon March 1885.08
Amazon March, The 1902.33
Ambassador of Peace 1908.03
Ambassador's March 1908.21
Ambassador's Wooing, The 1879.50
Amber Club, The 1914.01
Ambiguity Girls 1897.32
Ambition 1960.23
Ambitious Animals, The 1904.25
Ambitious Magpie, The 1895.04
Ambivalent Rag 1988.07
Amen Corner 1983.15
Amen Response 1969.10
Ameri-Can-Can, The 1928.40, 1928.45
America 1904.07, 1913.19, 1942.35, 1957.12, 1972.02
AMERICA 1927.43
America First 1915.25
America Loves a Band 1942.29
America Our Heritage 1955.13
America the Beautiful 1980.27
America the Great 1947.19
America's Answer 1919.10
America's Fighting Jack 1917.08
America's Popular Tune 1919.30
American Always Pans Out, An 1886.15
American Beauties 1916.12
American Beauty 1980.27
American Beauty Rose 1926.13, 1989.21
American Beauty Rose, An 1912.46
American Beauty, The 1903.23
American Bolero 1940.02
American Cannes 1948.28
American Couple 1937.13
American Courtship 1913.26
American Dancers 1923.41
American Dream, The 1980.15, 1991.03
American Eagle 1942.20
American Englishman, The 1914.16
American Express, The 1929.45
American Family 1940.19
American Girl in Paris, The 1906.45
American Girl, The 1903.10, 1913.06
American Girls 1895.34, 1904.29
American Heiress, An 1903.41, 1905.29
American Heiress, The 1912.15
American in Israel 1966.21
American in Paris Ballet, An 1999.23
American in Paris, An 1929.27, 2001.07
American Jazz 1922.34
American Jazz, The 1919.39
American League, The 1955.08
American Man on the Moon 1975.04
American Minstrels in Paris, The 1904.31
American Monte Carlo, The 1909.18
American Music 'Tis Better Than Old Parsifal to Me 1905.29
American Patrol 1902.22
American Pie 1982.22, 1997.21
American Plan 1940.21
American Primitive 1949.12
American Ragtime 1908.31, 1982.05
American Ragtime, The 1968.07
American Revue Girls 1926.21
American Serenade 1917.28
American Serio-Comic, The 1898.50
American Thing 1999.12
American Thoroughbred, An 1902.09
American Toast by the Liberty Amazons, An 1884.65
American Trilogy 1978.01
American Tune 1998.11
American Volunteers 1902.22
American Wake 2000.05
American, Oh, Girls? 1903.07
Americanisms 1920.10
Americans are Coming, The 1931.39
Americans are Here, The 1928.37
Ami Francois, c'est jour de fete 1884.50
Amigos Para Siempre 1992.12
Amina, Queen of the Night or the Arab's Dream 1909.11
Ammonia 1898.48
Amo 1913.37
Amoeba's Lament, The 1929.20
Among the Men, Coquets we find 1750.01
Amongst the Village Swains 1855.02
Amor 1982.09
Amorcito Corazon 1988.15
Amorous Esquimaux, The 1904.18
Amorous Goldfish, The 1896.27
Amorous Rose 1917.14
Amorous Star, The 1904.21
Amos Gonna Give You Hell 1972.09
Amour come le notre, Un 1935.19
Amour et Hierarchie 1925.03
Amoureux, Un 1929.13
Amours de Jean-Pierre, Les 1929.05
Amsterdam 1907.63, 1916.26, 1972.16
Amul in a Shtetl 1966.21
Amusing Myself 1924.24
An der schonen blauen Donau 1964.25
An-ti-ci-pa-tion 1917.14
Anameia's Death Scene 1953.10
Anarchists and bootblacks 1886.53
Anastasia Brady 1907.21
Anatevka 1964.27
Anatole of Paris 1939.26
Ancestors Bold 1911.27
Ancestry 1927.20
Anchor's Weigh'd, The 1886.50
Anchored in the Bounding Sea 1882.18
Anchored in the Roadstead 1886.50
Ancient Rules of Observing Etiquette 1913.27
And have I journey'd for a month 1885.47
And now, a long goodbye 1884.14
And the Verdict Was 1892.45
And The World Goes On 1905.26
And Then He Woke Up Father 1896.06
And What do You Think He Said? 1895.19
And... 1975.15
Andalusia Bolero 1946.18
Anelta Sultana Zuleima 1863.06
Anema e Corre 1953.17
Angel 1940.02
Angel Child 1918.38, 1922.23
Angel Face 1919.44
Angel has a Message, An 1999.17
Angel of Innocence, An 1869.43
Angel of Music 1988.01
Angel Rag 1912.36
Angel Town 1920.30
Angel Voices 1905.35
Angel Without Wings 1938.05
Angel! At Last I Find You 1912.10
Angel's Lost 2001.06
Angel's Rink and Social Center 1984.01
Angel, Angel... 1971.17
Angel-Saxons of To-Day 1902.21
Angelette March 1978.13
Angelico 1945.07
Angeline 1939.21
Angelique of the Opera Comique 1911.43
Angels Meet Me at the Crossroads 1955.13
Angels on Your Pillow 1983.20
Angels Sing, And the 1997.05
Angels that around us hover 1848.04
Angels Without Wings 1903.41
Angelus 1870.38, 1913.24
Angelus, The 1897.13, 1906.46, 1910.09, 1930.12, 1947.04
Angle Worm Wiggle 1911.08
Angles 1916.23
Angling 1914.28
Angling by a Babbling Brook 1904.34
Angus Gordon Donald Douglas Ewart John McKee 1911.44
Animal Attraction 1962.04
Animals are Nice 1942.34
Animation 1958.12
Anita is sad 1882.60
Ankle Up to the Alter 1930.18
Ann Aliza 1898.44
Anna 1913.23, 1929.25
Anna in Indiana 1920.33
Anna in Rapture I Come to Thee 1885.41
Anna Lilla 1957.07
Anna Louise of Louisiana 1935.04
Anna of Havana 1916.08

Anna, What's Wrong? 1913.23
Anna, zu Dir ist mein liebster Gang 1885.01
Annabel was Fairest 1902.04
Annabelle Jerome 1911.42
Annabelle Lee 1923.31
Anne of Green Gables 1971.21
Annette 1930.15
Annexation 1907.13
Annie 1924.38, 1977.06
Annie Dear, Good Bye 1869.20
Annie Doesn't Live Here Anymore 1995.14
Annie Laurie 1871.16, 1891.37, 1920.24, 1921.02, 1936.03
Annie Laurie Rag 1924.35
Annie More 1901.08
Annie O' the Banks O' Dee 1866.22, 1866.26
Annie o' the banks O'Dee 1862.06
Annie's Thing 1971.01
Anniversary, The 1973.08
Another Auld Lang Syne 2000.16
Another Autumn 1951.24
Another cheer 1868.01
Another Day 1967.06, 1983.21, 1996.09
Another Girl Who's Just Like Me 1999.17
Another Hundred People 1970.13, 1977.05, 1979.13
Another Life 1980.30, 1983.08
Another Little Coon in Town 1894.34
Another Little Cup of Tea 1960.18
Another Little Girl 1915.07
Another Love Affair 1932.14
Another Memorable Meal 1983.18
Another Memory 1980.08
Another Miracle of Judaism 1992.09
Another Op'nin', Another Show 1948.32, 1999.19
Another Pair of Shoes 1897.55
Another Princely Scheme 1954.13, 1979.22, 1990.20
Another Pyramid 2000.06
Another Situation 1906.44
Another Song About Paris 1988.08
Another Spring 1974.11
Another Suitcase in Another Hall 1979.23, 1992.12
Another Time, Another Place 1961.24
Another Wide River to Cross 1880.32
Anstatt-Dass-Song, Der 1965.04
Answer 1908.22
Answer is No, The 1932.08
Answer Me 1911.18
Answer My Heart 1933.06
Answers That You Don't Expect to Get 1906.14
Antes de la Corrida Del Toro 1922.32
Anthem 1988.09
Anthem of the Common Wheel, The 1979.07
Anthem of the Milk White Flag 1894.37
Anti-Cigarette Society, The 1897.39
Antici-tici-pation 1895.43
Antics of the Comics 1911.26
Antidote of a doting mother, The 1873.05
Antique et fort viel adage, Un 1887.35
Antique Spanish 1917.33
Antiques 1923.07
Antiquity 1980.15
Antoine 1907.38
Antoinette 1901.18, 1914.27
Antonio 1905.48
Antony and Cleopatra 1891.15
Anushka 1922.06
Anvedi Si Che Paciocca 1964.03
Anvil 1880.24
Any Afternoon 1920.32
Any Afternoon About Five 1953.02
Any Bonds for Sale 1938.08
Any Bonds Today 1938.08
Any Dream Will Do 1982.03, 1993.15
Any Friend of Kenny's is a Friend of Mine 1999.14
Any Girl 1918.25, 1921.33
Any Kind of a Daddy Will Do 1919.32
Any Kind of Man 1918.30
Any Kinder Coon 1899.31
Any Little Girl 1907.58
Any Little Girl Will Fall 1923.02
Any Little Melody 1920.19
Any Little Thing 1927.52, 1981.03
Any Little Tune 1926.28
Any Millenniums Today, Lady? 1973.08
Any Moment 1987.18
Any Night on Broadway 1916.11
Any Night on Old Broadway 1921.25
Any Old Iron 1960.17
Any Old Nag at All 1908.21
Any Old Night is a Wonderful Night 1915.07
Any Old Place in Yankee Land is Good Enough for Me 1908.08
Any Old Place With You 1908.07, 1919.14
Any Old Port in a Storm 1909.16
Any Old Thing 1903.16
Any Old Time at All 1906.37, 1907.28, 1918.19, 1923.06
Any Old Time With You 1915.12
Any Old Tree 1904.54
Any Old Tune 1911.45
Any Place I Hang My Hat is Home 1946.08
Any Place the Old Flag Flies 1911.33
Any Place Would be Wonderful With You 1920.18
Any Sort of Girl 1904.03
Any Step 1926.14
Any Time 1927.30
Any Time at All 1910.10
Any Time is Love Time 1921.35
Any Time New York Goes Dry 1919.01
Any Time's Kissing Time 1917.24, 1919.20
Any Time, Any Place, Anywhere 1916.07
Any Way the Wind Blows 1933.16
Anya 1965.35
Anybody's Man Will be My Man 1925.18
Anyone 1981.12
Anyone Can Whistle 1964.15, 1977.05
Anyone Who do's That Can't be so Dumb 1927.05
Anyone Would Love You 1959.11
Anything 1997.18
Anything But Lonely 1990.04
Anything Can Happen 1935.18, 1948.23
Anything Can Happen in New York 1948.04, 1990.09
Anything for Him 1993.09
Anything for You 1962.01
Anything Goes 1934.36, 1978.26, 1987.15, 1995.12
Anything Goes When You Sing Calypso 1947.19
Anything is Possible 1968.06, 1973.02
Anything You Can Do 1946.12, 1966.12, 1999.04
Anything You Liked 1920.14
Anything You Want to do, Dear 1920.38
Anything Your Heart Desires 1928.34
Anytime 1962.17, 1978.01
Anytime, Anywhere, Anyhow 1925.26
Anyway, We've had Fun 1930.39
Anywhere I Wander 1980.29
Anywhere the Wind Blows 1975.09
Anywhere You Are 1974.01
Apache 1995.15
Apache Argentine 1924.47
Apache Argentino, El 1985.07, 1999.18
Apaches, The 1953.07
Apaga La Luz 1970.01
Apalachicola 1995.14
Apassionette 1934.15
Aphrodite 1971.02
Aphrodite Waltz 1919.38
Aphronightie 1919.43
Apollon 1946.21
Apologia 1940.08
Apology 1961.26
Appalachian Spring 2001.04
Appearances Were Against Her 1896.26
Appendectomy 1978.11
Appendectomy II 1978.11
Apperances are Oft Deceitful 1904.51
Applause 1970.09, 1979.13, 1988.20
Apple and the Bough, The 1930.14
Apple Blossom Victory 1978.06
Apple Doesn't Fall Very Far, The 1984.01
Apple for the Teacher, An 1995.14
Apple Jack 1948.23
Apple Mary Maguire 1904.49
Apple Tree, The 1966.18
Apples, Bananas and You 1923.36
Appointments 1973.11
Apres la Guerre 1919.40
Apres les penibles voyages 1887.35
April Blossoms 1923.05
April Face 1952.05
April Fool 1925.17
April in Fairbanks 1956.08
April in Harrisburg 1940.23
April in Paris 1964.02
April in Wisconsin 1981.14
April Showers 1921.34, 1940.10, 1962.17
April Snow 1945.03
April Song 1969.04, 1980.01
Apukad Eros Kezen 1988.09
Aquarius 1968.11
Arab Love Song, The 1908.36
Arab Maid With Midnight Eyes 1927.34
Arabian Fox Trot, The 1917.13
Arabian Nights 1929.28
Araby 1920.02
Araminta to Herself 1951.17
Arbiter's Song 1988.09
Arcadians, The 1902.30
Arcady 1921.34, 1923.12
Arcady is Ever Young 1910.05
Archers' Song 1925.32
Archie 1902.01
Are Then the Vows so Lately Spoken 1891.11
Are We Downhearted, No 1964.28
Are We Strong? 1972.23
Are We Widows, Wives or What? 1912.17
Are You a Man 1974.12
Are You a Single or Married Man? 1906.15
Are You Done, Mr. Dunn 1897.33, 1900.24
Are You Going to Dance? 1912.33
Are You Happy? 1947.10
Are You Havin' Any Fun? 1990.09
Are You Having Any Fun? 1939.25
Are You Insured? 1885.29
Are You Lonesome Tonight? 1978.01, 1989.12
Are You Love? 1931.39
Are You On? 1888.32, 1903.19
Are You Ready, Gyp Watson? 1959.11
Are You Satisfied? 1926.16
Are you sure 1887.44
Are You Sure? 1960.20
Are You the Girl That Dined With Me? 1907.33
Are You There? 1927.08, 1947.10
Are You With It? 1945.18
Areito 1939.18
Aren't We All 1924.04
Aren't You Glad? 1956.04
Aren't You the Girl I Met at Sherry's? 1907.45
Aren't You the Girl I Met at Sherrys? 1907.42
Aren't You Wonderful! 1936.02, 1936.17
Argentina 1922.27
Argentine 1923.03, 1927.19
Argentine Arago, The 1923.10
Argentine Tango 1957.14
Argentines, the Portuguese and Greeks, The 1919.06
Argentines, the Portuguese and the Greeks, The 1919.32
Argufyin' 1927.32
Argument, The 1962.14
Ari's Promise 1971.02
Aria 1948.27, 1966.03, 1993.17
Ariella 1907.52
Arieni 1977.01
Aristocracy 1911.46
Aristocracy, The 1900.59
Aristocratic Annie 1905.43
Arithmetic Dancing Bee 1925.26
Ark Brought to Jerusalem, The 1997.12
Arkansas 1985.06
Arlee 1907.26
Arm in Arm 1963.21
Armadillo Idyll 1966.32
Armadillo, The 1973.08
Armchair Golfer, The, or Whimpers of a Shortchanged Viewer 1973.08
Armored Knight, The 1899.40
Armorer's Song 1896.02, 1896.45
Armorer's Song, The 1929.43, 1944.25
Armors, The 1872.23
Armour 1950.14

Armourer's Song, The 1891.29
Arms of the China Wall 1922.08
Army Air Corps, The 1943.23
Army and Navy Song 1941.09
Army Club Foxtrot, The 1914.22
Army Club, The 1914.22
Army Corps, The 1908.29
Army Directory, The 1909.15
Army Mule Song, The 1952.05
Army of Crooks, The 1916.04
Army of Peace, The 1902.06, 1902.38
Army of the Just, The 1960.19
Army so Grand, The 1890.03
Army Song 1966.19, 1979.07
Army's Made a Man Out of Me, The 1942.20
Around the Clock 1906.40, 1908.02
Around the Town 1907.40, 1914.31, 1916.11, 1920.24
Around the World 1905.27
Around, around, about 1870.15
Arrah' Song 1872.27
Arrest Him 1890.33, 1903.36
Arrest, The 1971.12
Arrival 1982.18
Arrival of Society, The 1923.46
Arrival of Steamboat 1936.22
Arrival of the Amber Empress, The 1916.18
Arrival of the Boom 1916.05
Arrival of the Guests 1910.09, 1922.43
Arrival of the Plot, The 1923.46
Arrival of Tourists 1936.22
Arry and 'Arriet 1911.28
Art 1903.24, 1917.28, 1946.06
Art for Art's Sake 1937.08
Art has No Frontier 1926.14
Art is Calling for Me 1911.38
Art of Conversation 1958.01
Art of Exercising, The 1902.02
Art of Love-Making, The 1900.03
Art of Making Love, The 1896.14
Art of Stimulation, The 1903.40
Art of the Possible, The 1979.23
Art With a Capital A 1910.11
Artful Crocodile, The 1904.24
Arthur 1948.12
Arthur and Martha 1882.39, 1883.26
Arthur in the Afternoon 1977.16
Arthur, Son of Martha 1956.13
Artichauts, Les 1929.13
Article 213 1900.39
Articles of Toilette for a Lady, The 1921.15
Artie 1903.10
Artificial Flowers 1960.19
Artist and His Model, The 1905.40
Artistry in Rhythm 1974.22
Artists and Models 1906.09, 1906.45, 1924.36
Aryans Under the Skin 1942.20
As a Courtier would Please 1875.19
As a Friend 1906.25
As a Troubadour 1925.40
As all alone, now ever day 1859.13
As Along the Street We Wander 1905.46
As Befits My Rank and Station 1904.28
As Birds Greet Morning Skies 1913.01
As Busy as Anyone Can Be 1959.19
As by magic at thy sight, to burst in beauteous, radiant light 1872.10
As Calm as the Ocean 1980.13
As Far as I'm Concerned 1970.19
As good as he ought to be 1882.63
As Good as You 2000.20
As he's looking somewhat pale 1878.16
As I Came Down the Aisle 1914.10
As I Go 1963.27
As I Grow Older 1975.05
As I view now 1859.18, 1873.04
As I vos a Valliking 1857.04
As I was Going Along 1944.32
As I Went Over 1971.20
As if But Yesterday 1890.39
As if We Never Said Goodbye 1994.10
As it Might Have Been 1942.18
As it Should Be 1989.26
As Kipling Says I Learned About Women from Her 1924.24
As Long as He Needs Me 1963.01, 1995.12
As Long as I Have You 1917.04, 1922.28
As Long as I Live 1976.35, 1981.16, 1982.17
As Long as it Pleases the Ladies 1898.47
As Long as Men Love Women 1912.40
As Long as the Wife Don't Know 1923.16
As Long as the World Goes Round 1909.10
As Long as There's a Mother 1959.06
As Long as They on Making 'Em 1924.07
As Long as We're in Love 1928.50
As Long as You're Happy 1991.15
As Love as I Love 1980.10
As of Today 1939.13
As on Moonlit Waves we Ride 1901.17
As on Through the Seasons We Sail 1955.02
As Once I Loved You 1976.08
As One Brother to Another 1933.24
As pure in ray as early day 1855.06
As Simple as That 1961.20
As some day it may happen 1885.47
As the Agent 1898.48
As the Boys Go Marching By 1902.09
As the Butterfly Sips the Roses 1917.30
As the Chairman of the Committee 1931.48
As the Flitting Swallows Fly 1918.26
As the Girls Go 1948.28
As the Prince Waked the Princess 1902.15
As the Sunflower Turns to the Sun 1904.21
As the Years Roll By 1917.28
As They Did in Days of Yore 1896.31
As Time Goes By 1931.36, 1997.01
As Usual 1886.62
As We Go Out Walking 1920.29
As We Leave the Years Behind 1923.36
As We Lie in Languor Lazy 1900.37
As We Peep at the Earth from the Sky 1894.05
As We Sow 1920.45
As We Swing Sweetheart 1905.20
As We Told You 1955.11
As You See Them 1886.15
As You See Us, so are We 1887.05
As You See, I am One of the Army 1887.33
Ascot Gavotte 1956.01, 1993.18
Ashes and Fire 1926.31
Asi Se Baila El Tango 1993.08
Ask Dad 1918.37
Ask Her While the Band is Playing 1908.24, 1909.23
Ask Me Again 1948.18, 1990.14
Ask Papa 1901.19
Ask the Man in the Moon 1891.11
Ask the Stars 1919.29
Ask Us Again 1937.08
Asking for You 1960.23
Aspirations 1901.19
Assassination 1990.17
Assembling of the Two Courts 1906.18
Assembly Dance, The 1959.06
Associated Press 1922.13
Assyrians, The 1984.02
Asterbilts Welcome Home 1899.33
Asthore 1897.49
Astique bien ton fourniment 1884.50
Astoria 1899.12
Astoria Gloria 1978.10
Astronomy 1906.30
Asturias 1949.07
At 0700 Tomorrow 1975.07
At a Fancy Costume Ball 1904.50
At a Grand Hotel 1916.01
At a Reception 1908.18
At an Early Stage of Life 1902.25
At Christmastime 1944.21
At Court 1910.36
At DuPont's 1905.40
At early dawn 1846.01
At Eve 1895.36
At even tide 1884.14
At Gay Raatenbaad 1912.44
At Last 1935.04, 1979.24, 1982.18
At Last has Downtrod Woman 1912.40
At last I find you in 1897.17
At Last it's Love 1940.03
At Last United 1915.20
At last we are alone 1889.10
At Last We are Alone 1907.10
At Last, at Last I Hold You 1908.16
At length I am alone, and here I am at home 1855.03
At Long Last 1939.19
At Long Last Love 1938.07, 1980.06
At Longchamps Today 1929.45
At Lovetime 1930.36
At Madame Regay's 1923.46
At Midnight on My Pillow Lying 1886.30
At My Lady's Feet 1904.01
At My Side 1989.07
At My Time of Life 1900.03, 1976.32
At Night 1903.09, 1913.20
At Night in My Brilliant Salon 1907.19
At Night She Comes Home to Me 1983.19
At night upon the moonlit tide 1859.12
At Night, At Night 1904.52
At Our Tango Tea Last Week 1914.18
At Peace Wid de World 1908.08
At Siesta Time 1917.24, 1919.20
At Sundown 1944.32
At Sunrise 1879.35
At That Colored Jassboray 1920.24
At the 'Alls 1898.17
At the Arrowhead Inn 1910.07
At the Automat 1912.45
At the Bal Masque 1912.39
At the Ball 1914.15, 1922.22, 1988.18
At the Ballet 1975.15, 2001.01
At the Barbecue 1927.68, 1932.12
At the Barber's Ball 1908.22
At the Check Apron Ball 1957.07
At the Edge of the World 2000.05
At the End of the Day 1987.04
At the Ex-Kings Club 1928.03
At the Fair 1927.67, 1946.01, 1966.14, 1979.10, 1983.05
At the Fireplace 1990.16
At the Follies Bergere 1908.36
At the Fountain 1922.01, 1926.11
At the Fox Trot Ball 1915.02
At the Gate of Roses 1925.48
At the Grand Hotel 1989.26
At the Hellrakers 1965.31
At the High Brown Baby's Ball 1919.26
At the Hollywood 1899.29
At the Krazy Kat's Ball 1920.28
At the Mardi Gras 1948.14
At the Matinee 1926.04
At the Met 1951.19
At the Moving Picture Ball 1975.22
At the Music Hall 1904.04
At the Night Races in Paris 1936.02
At the Palace of Boobhamba 1904.40
At the Pan-American 1901.16
At the Party 1906.22, 1925.29, 1926.03
At the Picture Show 1912.45
At the Rail 1940.04
At the Red Rose Cotillion 1948.26, 1974.25
At the Round Table 1927.56, 1943.22
At the Roxy Music Hall 1938.05, 1975.13
At the School-Gate 1932.09
At the Seaside 1903.21
At the Shore 1919.29
At the Signal to Battle 1888.20
At the Spotlight Canteen 1944.14
At the Telephone 1915.22
At the The Dansant 1918.25
At the Toy Shop 1915.27
At the Tree I shall suffer with pleasure 1750.01
At the tree I shall suffer with pleasure 1854.06
At the Tree I Shall Suffer With Pleasure 1957.02
At the Vaudeville Show 1899.22
At Venice, when the moon shone bright 1859.12
At Weddings as a General Rule 1905.46
At West Point 1905.34
At Ye Olde Coffee Shoppe in Cheyenne 1936.26
At Your Service 1926.19
At Your Service, Girls 1915.21
At ze naughty Folies Bergere 1897.39

Athletic Boy 1924.47
Athletic Girls 1899.29
Athletic Prancing 1910.22
Atlantic City 1998.01
Atlantic City Girl, The 1926.14
Atonement 1997.12
Attack of the Banshees 1989.09
Attendez je m'rappell' maint'nant 1886.19
Attends 1935.19
Attends! 1934.32
Attention, pray! 1896.27
Attuck's March, The 1904.26
Au calme plat 1884.43
Au clair de la lune 1933.24
Au Claire de Lune 1947.18
Au Revoir 1930.14, 1967.02
Au revoir 1965.08
Au Revoir Poland-Hello New York! 1964.18
Au Revoir, Cher Baron 1938.07
Au Revoir, Soldier 1945.14
Auction Dance 1913.19
Auction Day 1906.06
Auction Rag 1919.34
Auction Sale 1888.32
Auction, The 1904.55, 1955.03, 1965.33
Auctioneer's Song 1891.29
Auctions 1976.11
Audition 1980.20
Audition Song 1954.06
Audition, The 1993.19
Auditions, The 1960.23
Auf dem Bankerl. . . 1920.46
Auf den berg, es ist schon 1911.28
Auf Weidersehn 1896.10
Auf Wiederseh'n, My Dear 1999.05
Auf Wiedersehen 1908.36, 1983.08
Auf Wiedersehn 1905.27, 1912.42, 1915.18
Auftauchen des Reitenden Boten 1965.04
August Days in Paree 1970.01
Auld Countrie, The 1894.20
Auld lang Syne 1859.01
Auld Lang Syne 1943.23
Auld Robin Grey 1859.01
Aunt Bridget's 1894.31
Aunt Dinah has Blowed De Horn 1975.19
Aunt Jemima 1886.35
Aunt Jemima I'm Comin' Home 1925.18
Aunt Jemima's Big Pound Cake 1895.18
Aunt Susie 1876.04
Auntie Jessie 1986.19
Aupres de Ma Blonde 1981.04
Aupres de vous c'est autre chose 1886.09
Aural Misunderstanding, An 1902.03
Aurora 1903.27
Aurora Blushing Rosily 1913.32
Aurora Borealis 1905.17
Aurora from Aurora, Illinois 1907.47
Aurory Bory Alice 1926.17
Aus ist's mit der Liebe-Ganz ohne Weiber geht die Chose nicht 1984.05
Austrian Patrol 1913.10
Author-Manager am I, An 1894.45
Auto da Fe 1974.06
Auto de Fe 1982.20
Auto Song, The 1907.03
Auto-da-fe 1997.10
Auto-Mo-Biling 1900.52
Autograph Chant 1953.01
Autograph Girls' Song 1903.24
Autograph of You 1932.19
Autographs 1910.12
Automobile Ensemble 1901.13
Automobile Girls, The 1902.42
Automobile Song 1899.38, 1901.06
Automobilia 1915.05
Automobiling 1906.13
Automotivation 1932.19
Autumn 1997.06
Autumn Bells 1945.14
Autumn Carol 1973.07
Autumn Courting, The 1960.05
Autumn Dance of the Hat-Check Girls 1922.42
Autumn in New York 1934.42
Autumn Leaves 1959.15
Autumn Song 1896.15
Autumn Sun 1921.13
Aux iles Hawai 1935.19
Aux Iles Hawaii 1976.16
Avalon 1918.05, 1921.34
Avant de nous mettre en menage 1877.32
'Ave a Glass, won't yer? 1889.54
Ave Maria 1882.39, 1983.03
Ave! My Mother 1881.36
Avec 1964.02, 1965.30, 1973.17
Avec ma voix 1929.15
Avec soin formez chaque lettre 1884.50
Avenue C 1976.34
Avenue Fifth Avenue 1979.13
Avenue of Palms, The 1911.41
Aviation Ballet 1927.60
Avonlea We Love Thee 1971.21
Avos 1990.01
Avreymele Melamed 1971.17
Avril a Paris, En 1964.02
Avril ramene le beaux jours 1877.32
Await Your Love 1928.30
Awake Ma Chile 1903.16
Awake! Awake! 1904.39
Awakened Love 1911.47
Awakening of Bonnie, The 1907.14
Awakening of Galatea, The 1892.19
Away 1952.15
Away Despair 1866.07, 1866.21
Away from Temptation 1963.27
Away from Thee 1914.04
Away from You 1976.08
Away in the Manger 1998.19
Away to Spain 1905.52
Away to the Dungeon Cell 1906.06
Away to the Links 1900.47
Away to the Mountains 1904.28
Away Up in the Sikes 1885.08
Away With Him 1899.40
Away! Away! 1882.60
Away, Away 1900.03
Away, Away! 1868.02
Away, Away! My Heart's on Fire 1879.72, 1981.01
Away, Away, We Sail Today 1905.52
Away, remorse! Compunction, hence! 1887.10
Aweful Battle of the Pekes and Pollicles, The 1982.19
Awful Sad 1930.13
Awfully Awful 1877.23, 1882.28
Awkward Age, The 1917.08
Awkward complication this, An 1898.25
Ay De Mi 1893.16
Ay Mama Tuey 1929.51
Ay Oomps 1912.47
Ay! Cipriano 1926.09, 1926.35
Ay! Que Rico 1917.25
Ayama 1966.03
Aye through the fourth of my husbands 1873.05
Aye, aye, aye 1878.16
Aye, Lye, Lyu Lye 1980.27
Ayikanoni! 1993.04
Ayznban, Der 1990.16
Azabache 1997.13
Azure Te 1992.03

B&O, The 1917.32
B'gosh! 1901.27
B-a-b-e-e 1913.01
B. is the Note 1920.11
B.G. Bigelow, Inc. 1951.15
B.Y.O.B. 1984.15
Baa Baa 1893.35
Baa, Baa, Black Sheep 1905.22
Baba nomana 1993.04
Babbette 1978.02
Babbitt and the Bromide, The 1927.59, 1974.09
Babbling Babette 1923.40
Babes in Arms 1937.04, 1975.13
Babes in the Wood 1915.31, 1928.33, 1975.24
Babes on Broadway 1990.09
Babette 1902.07
Babette of Beaujolais 1913.32
Babette! 1894.29
Babette's Military Dance 1927.43
Babette's Wedding Day 1927.43
Babies in Our Block, The 1879.04
Babies on Our Block 1892.54
Babies on Our Block, The 1879.35, 1883.46
Baby 1904.17, 1926.24, 1947.05
Baby and Nursie 1906.36, 1908.17
Baby Baby 1977.01
Baby Blue 1919.21
Baby Blues 1921.18
Baby Bond, A 1937.13
Baby Boom Boogie Boy 1983.18
Baby Breath 1972.18
Baby Bunting 1923.08
Baby Couldn't Dance 1952.20
Baby Doll 1918.30, 1982.12
Baby Doll Dance 1929.28
Baby Dollie Walk 1921.18
Baby Dolls 1919.43, 1921.19
Baby Dream Your Dream 1966.01
Baby Dreams 1920.42
Baby Elephant Walk 1974.22
Baby Eyes 1914.19
Baby Games 1941.08
Baby Grand 1910.11
Baby I Love You 1985.03
Baby in Love, A 1921.14
Baby in the House 1906.29
Baby Isn't Old Enough to Know 1894.37
Baby Let's Play House 1989.12
Baby Lou 1897.55
Baby Love 1984.15
Baby Mine 1901.13, 1915.20, 1926.19, 1930.34
Baby Moon 1922.08
Baby Number, The 1910.23
Baby on the Shore, The 1898.02
Baby Sister Blues 1920.36
Baby Talk 1910.17
Baby Vampire 1919.10, 1921.25
Baby Vampire Land 1919.16
Baby Vampire, The 1917.02
Baby Walk 1921.04
Baby Wanna Go Bye-Bye With You 1931.05
Baby Wants 1926.19
Baby With the Dimple and the Smile, The 1902.35
Baby Workout 1997.21
Baby You Can Count on Me 1981.07
Baby You Love, The 1953.08
Baby! 1925.14
Baby! Baby! Dance My Darling Baby! 1891.11
Baby! What? 1927.41
Baby's Asleep, Cradle's Gone 1891.32
Baby's Awake Now 1929.12
Baby's Baby 1957.14
Baby's Baby Grand 1925.27
Baby's Best Friend, A 1928.02
Baby's Blue 1927.38
Baby's Doll 1929.28
Baby's Dream 1896.37
Baby's Gone 1909.05
Baby's Smile 1885.03, 1885.50
Baby, Baby 1896.06, 1954.11, 1962.24
Baby, Baby, Baby 1983.19
Baby, be Good 1924.47
Baby, Don't Count on Me 1944.18
Baby, I Could do it for You 1932.12
Baby, I'm Ready Now 1995.01
Baby, it's Cold Outside 1980.29
Baby, Let's Face It 1946.23
Baby, Mrs. Jones, A 1970.03
Baby, My Little Baby 1903.35
Baby, Talk to Me 1960.06
Baby, Who ist Mein Baby 1999.05
Baby, You're a Nasty Little Elf 1869.07
Babykins 1930.05
Bacchanal Rag, The 1912.24
Bacchanale 1919.38, 1921.11, 1958.04, 1963.16
Bacchus' Choruses 1892.31
Baccio, Il 1870.23
Bach, Beethoven and Brahams 1975.13
Bachanol 1926.37
Bachelor Belles, The 1910.34
Bachelor Belles-Bazaar, The 1910.34

Bachelor Days 1911.25
Bachelor Girl and Boy 1916.14
Bachelor Girls 1905.47
Bachelor's Button, A 1917.30
Bachelor's Dance 1972.16
Bachelor's Song 1893.03
Bachelor's Song, A 1913.14
Bachelors and Maids 1902.09
Bacio, Il 1893.36
Back Again 1881.07
Back at the Palace 1950.09
Back at the Seat of Power 1997.16, 1998.08
Back Bay Beat 1943.16
Back from Hollywood 1931.30
Back from Thirty-Six to Twenty-Nine 1912.20
Back Home 1931.29
Back in Business 1999.20
Back in Circulation 1936.30
Back in Circulation Again 1931.21
Back in Show Biz Again 1981.07
Back in the Bars Again 1975.12
Back in the Days of Long Ago 1928.49
Back in the Kitchen 1967.06
Back in Town 1991.03
Back in Your Own Back Yard 1962.17
Back of Life, The 1982.23
Back Out While the Backing Out is Good 1914.14
Back Seat of a Taxi 1932.19
Back to Baltimore 1905.02
Back to Before 1998.01, 2000.16
Back to Broadway 1912.31
Back to Bundling 1942.34
Back to Harrow 1905.27
Back to Killarney 1923.07
Back to Lotusland 1915.22
Back to My Old Home Town 1910.01
Back to Nature 1913.37, 1916.23, 1926.13
Back to Old Broadway 1907.34
Back to Paris 1916.05
Back to School Again 1962.04
Back to School Ballet 1971.21
Back to the Boulevards 1903.10
Back to the Dear Old Trenches 1918.28
Back to the Farm 1943.05
Back to the Parthenon 1956.09
Back to U.S.A. 1905.34
Back to Work 1903.09, 1937.14
Back With a Beat 1978.25
Back Your Fancy 1910.05
Back! Students, Back! 1882.63
Back, Back to Baltimore 1905.10
Back, Back, Back to Akron 1922.42
Back, Back, Back to Baltimore 1904.45
Backlash Blues 1989.12
Backstage Babble 1970.09
Bacon and Greens and a Day of Good Beer 1861.03
Bacorope 1964.39
Bad as They are, We Love These Men 1888.09
Bad Boy 1984.15
Bad Boy and the Good Girl, The 1911.39
Bad Boy from a Good Family, A 1925.23
Bad Breath 1974.03
Bad Chinaman from Shanghai, A 1917.37
Bad Companions 1958.14
Bad Girl 1928.27
Bad Habits 1983.09
Bad Karma 1970.04
Bad Little Boy and Good Little Girl 1922.07
Bad Little Boy With Dancing Legs 1926.37
Bad Luck, I'll Laugh at You 1927.68
Bad Man Number 1927.65
Bad Man Walk, The 1923.01
Bad Sex 1973.14, 1975.12
Bad Timing 1945.20, 1958.21
Bad, Bad Stacker Lee 1940.01
Bad, Glad, Good and Had 1979.15
Badaroma 1948.22
Badmen 1916.06
Bag of Luck, The 1975.19
Bag Pipe 1899.22
Bagdad 1912.39, 1918.05, 1921.38
Bagdad on the Subway 1920.32
Bagels and Yox 1951.20
Baggage Smashers 1879.35
Bagpipe Crazy 1910.19
Bagpipe Serenade, The 1906.37
Bagpipes, The 1953.10
Bah! Bah! 1896.13
Bah! he must think me 1887.04
Bah, Bah, Black Sheep 1907.26
Bahiana 1943.17, 1944.31
Bailonga 1993.08
Baissant les yeux modestement 1877.32
Baiting the Hook 1961.07
Bajour 1964.40
Bake, O Babe 1902.09
Baker's Boy and the Chimney Sweep, The 1914.30
Bal Champete Aux Champs Elysees, Le 1900.49
Bal Chez Madame Mortemouille, Le 1958.18
Bal Petit Bal 1952.09
Bal-a-clan 1869.42
Balada Para Mi Muerte 1985.07, 1999.18
Balada Para Mi Vida 1993.08
Balada Para Un Loco 1993.08
Balalaikas 1943.11
Balaliaka Serenade, The 1947.14
Balcony Scene 1993.17
Balcony Scene, A 1897.32
Balda Para un Loco 1997.13
Baldwin Corners' Brass Band, The 1917.12
Bali Ha'i 1949.04
Balkan Dance 1926.33
Ball at Whitehall, The 1884.57
Ball Begins, The 1923.17
Ball of the Fifty-First, The 1917.27
Ball, The 1976.01, 1976.11, 1989.23, 1990.12
Ballad 1985.15
Ballad for Americans 1939.19
Ballad for Billionaires 1948.22
Ballad in Which Macheath Asks Everyone for Forgiveness 1965.04
Ballad in Which Macheath Begs All Men for Forgiveness 1976.10
Ballad Maker 1966.30
Ballad of a Redneck 1969.03
Ballad of a Social Director 1952.10
Ballad of Belle Boyd, The 1963.22
Ballad of Cananea 1988.15
Ballad of Dependency 1966.19
Ballad of Gangster Joe 1962.23
Ballad of Gracious Living 1976.10
Ballad of Immortal Earnings 1976.10
Ballad of Living in Style 1989.24
Ballad of Mack the Knife 1966.19, 1976.10, 1989.24
Ballad of Mack the Knife, The 1965.04
Ballad of Miss Prim, The 1896.01
Ballad of Pleasant Living, The 1965.04
Ballad of Poor Old John, The 1981.04
Ballad of Return 1996.16
Ballad of Rudolph Reed, The 1966.15
Ballad of Sexual Dependency, The 1965.04
Ballad of Stonewall Jackson, The 1963.22
Ballad of Sweeney Todd, The 1979.06
Ballad of the Billow, The 1881.07
Ballad of the Easy Life 1933.07, 1966.19
Ballad of the Garment Trade 1962.05
Ballad of the Gun 1959.11
Ballad of the Lily of Hell 1977.08
Ballad of the New World 1982.20, 1997.10
Ballad of the Prisoner of Sex 1989.24
Ballad of the Ring 1895.12
Ballad of the Robbers 1938.11
Ballad of the Sad Young Men, The 1959.12
Ballad of the Soldier 1963.09
Ballad to a Brute 1965.01
Ballad to an Absent Friend 1963.03
Ballade 1934.32, 1948.30
Ballade des baladins, La 1966.20
Ballade des Dames du Temps Perdu 1931.06
Ballade of Uncle Sam 1939.19
Ballade von Angenehmen Leben, Die 1965.04
Ballade von der sexuellen Horigkeit, Der 1965.04
Ballade, in der Macheath jedermann Abbitte leistet 1965.04
Ballata Di Rugantino 1964.03
Ballerina 1971.04
Ballerina's Story, The 1947.14
Ballerino, The 1909.07
Ballet Burlesque 1950.12
Ballet Classique 1958.18
Ballet des Perfumes, The 1921.03
Ballet in the Clouds 1944.18
Ballet isn't Ballet Any More, The 1950.09
Ballet Moderne 1958.18
Ballet Moderno 1934.20
Ballet of Flowers, The 1928.03
Ballet of Fruits, The 1905.48
Ballet of Perfumes, The 1921.37
Ballet of Siam, A 1922.34
Ballet of the Four Seasons 1899.19
Ballet of the North Wind 1924.35
Ballet of the Pyramids 1921.02
Ballet, The 1944.18
Ballinasloe 1904.01
Balloon 1938.08
Balloon Girls, The 1916.02
Balloon is Ascending, A 1964.33
Ballooning 1907.18
Balloons 1960.07
Bally Mooney and Biddy McGee 1914.23
Ballyhoo 1932.01, 1946.01
Ballyhooly (Blue Ribbon Army) 1887.29
Ballyhooly Blue Ribbon Army, The 1888.38
Ballyhujah 1932.16
Balmoral Chorus 1902.09
Baltimo' Joe 1978.21
Baltimore Bombashay, The 1910.33
Baltimore Buzz 1921.16, 1978.21
Bamba, La 1979.13, 1988.15, 1990.15
Bambalina 1923.05
Bambazoola 1927.19
Bambo Babies 1925.27
Bamboche! 1962.22
Bamboo Bungalow 1925.04
Bamboo Cage 1954.19
Bamboo Lane 1909.18
Bamboula, The 1921.18
Banana Tree 1954.19
Banana, Banana, Banana 1980.05
Band Began to Play, And the 1901.12, 1901.23
Band Box Girl, The 1907.24
Band Came Back, The 1912.16
Band of Gold 1974.11
Band Played On, And the 1989.16, 1997.01
Band Plays Home Sweet Home, The 1923.21
Band Started Swinging a Song, The 1945.09
Band Wagon, The 1931.31
Band, The 1899.33, 1976.35, 1980.14, 1982.17
Band-Aids 1976.34
Bandana Babies 1928.18
Bandana Ball 1924.44
Bandana Days 1921.16, 1942.13
Bandana Land 1904.54
Bandanaland 1924.27
Bandanna Anna 1923.11
Bandannas on Broadway 1927.27
Bandbox Girl, The 1907.41
Bandoneones 1985.07, 1999.18
Bandstand Boogie 1976.34
Bane of Man, The 1937.03
Bang the Bell Rang 1936.01
Bang! 1999.20
Bang! Bang!! Bang!!! 1921.27
Bang, Bang, Bang 1901.27
Bang, Bang, the Most Harmonious Song 1895.33
Bangaway Isle 1927.58
Banjo Dance 1902.08
Banjo Eyes 1941.13
Banjo Land 1923.39
Banjo Serenade 1905.40
Banjo Serenade, A 1903.16
Banjo That Man Joe Plays, The 1929.51
Banjos 1989.23
Banks of the Wye, The 1915.26
Banquet, The 1927.23
Bar on the Piccola Marina, A 1952.11, 1968.19, 1986.19
Baraka, La 1974.19
Barbara 1961.25

Barbara Allen 1954.11
Barbara Song 1966.19, 1976.10, 1989.24
Barbara-Song 1965.04
Barbarina's Lament 2000.10
Barbary Coast 1930.31
Barbecue, The 1908.35
Barber and His Wife, The 1979.06
Barber of Seville, The 1990.10
Barber Song 1910.03
Barber's Song 1965.34
Barbering Wop of Seville, The 1925.07
Barbers are We 1900.42
Barbiere di Siviglia, Il 1922.06
Barbizon 1911.39
Barca de Guaymas, La 1988.15
Barcarole 1915.23
Barcarole Song 1872.10
Barcarole, The 1923.31
Barcarolle 1974.06
Barcelona 1970.13, 1977.05
Barcelona Girls 1898.17
Barcelone, A 1947.05, 1948.12, 1955.14
Bard and the Beard, The 1952.09
Bare Facts 1979.33
Barefoot 1955.13
Barefoot Gal 1966.30
Barefoot Girl 1930.05
Bargain Day 1898.56, 1905.47
Bargaining 1965.06
Barking Baby Never Bites, A 1940.06
Barley Mow, The 1907.51
Barmaid, The 1898.41
Barmaids are Diviner Than Mermaids 1973.08
Barman's Song, The 1897.20
Barn Dance Schottische 1909.03
Barn Dance, The 1902.08
Barn Door Jig, The 1865.06, 1869.33
Barnaby Beach 1946.07
Barnacle Jim and Binnacle Tim 1900.40
Barney Donohue 1904.15
Barney O'Flynn 1903.31, 1929.48
Barnum and Bailey Rag 1968.07
Barnum and Bailey Rag, The 1914.34
Barnum had the Right Idea 1911.33
Barnyard, The 1974.17, 1981.09
Baron Papouche 1906.36
Baron's Song 1888.39
Baron, the Duchess and the Count, The 1928.46
Baroness Bazooka, The 1958.21, 1977.02
Barque d'Yves, La 1934.32
Barquilleros, Los 1969.11
Barquilleros, The 1969.11
Barrel House 1944.31
Barrel of Beads 1944.27
Barrel Organ, The 1924.48
Barrels of War, The 1970.05
Barrett's Song 1997.06
Barrin'-o'th'-Door,-O 1920.12
Barroom Ballads or Virtue Rides Again 1940.18
Barynya 1977.13
Base Ball 1887.32
Base Ball Girl, The 1911.35
Baseball 1919.26
Baseball Game, The 1971.11
Basement Blues 1944.32
Bashful Chappie, The 1905.37
Bashful Girl, The 1869.06
Bashful Lover, The 1938.06
Bashful Moon, The 1904.18
Bashful Suitor, The 1891.36
Basilia 1917.25
Basin Street Blues 1974.09
Basket, Make a Basket 1945.13
Basketball Song, The 1978.11
Basquette 1955.19
Batata 1970.21
Bateau blanc, Le 1966.20, 1968.21
Bath Room Tenor 1927.27
Bathing Chorus 1887.13
Bathing Girls, The 1900.59, 1909.13
Bathing in the Sea 1898.61
Bathing Lesson, The 1902.08
Bats 1956.13
Battalion of France 1900.34
Battersea Butterfly Shooters, The 1896.48
Battle 1972.09
Battle Cry 1972.11
Battle Cry of Freedom, The 1924.17
Battle Hymn 1989.12
Battle Hymn of the Republic 1955.13, 1975.22, 1990.05
Battle of the Daisies and the Ferns, The 1904.41
Battle of the Genie 1944.18
Battle on the Tiles, The 1904.51
Battle's roar is over, O my love! The 1887.10
Battle, The 1954.13, 1978.22, 1979.22, 1993.17, 1994.04
Battleground Bummer 1975.05
Battlelines 1987.19
Battling Joe 1961.25
Batty 1922.32
Baubles, Bangles and Beads 1953.16, 1978.03, 1999.23
Baxter Avenue 1886.03
Baxter's Party 1926.02
Bay of Bicsay, The 1858.03
Bay of Biscay 1892.29
Bayakhala 1977.01
Bayeza Abangoma 1997.14
Bazaar of the Caravans 1953.16
BBCBC 1964.29
Be a Clown 1999.23
Be a Lion 1975.01
Be a Little Lackadaisical 1932.13
Be a Mess 1949.12
Be a Party at the Party Tonight 1919.22
Be a Performer 1998.15
Be a Performer! 1962.27
Be a Pussycat 1957.05
Be a Santa 1961.28
Be a Spy for Love's Sake 1904.18
Be Aisy 1899.19
Be Anything But a Girl 1989.23
Be Back Soon 1963.01
Be Brave and Wait, I Will Release You 1890.03
Be Calm 1942.26
Be Careful 1921.09
Be Careful of the Hoo-Doo Man 1902.11
Be Careful That He Doesn't Find it Out 1908.37
Be Careful What You Do 1914.15
Be Careful Whom You Kiss 1976.35, 1980.14, 1982.17
Be Careful, it's My Heart 1988.08
Be Clever 1900.41
Be comforted - his downfall I foresee 1895.29
Be Deaf to her Tongue 1787.01
Be Demure 1906.37
Be Glad You're Alive 1944.18
Be Good 1889.24, 1893.42, 1907.24
Be Good and You'll be Happy 1905.09
Be Good or be Gone 1982.04
Be Good to Me 1930.39
Be Good, be Good 1895.27
Be Good, be Good, be Good 1954.16
Be Good, Queen Bess 1923.41
Be Happy 1970.07
Be Happy in Your Dreams 1928.26
Be Happy, Boys, Tonight 1914.27
Be Italian 1982.09
Be Kind to Your Parents 1954.15
Be Like a Bluebird 1934.36
Be Like the Bluebird 1987.15
Be Mine, be Mine 1913.10
Be My Baby 1985.03, 1986.02
Be My Girl 1905.34
Be My Guest 1951.23
Be My Host 1962.03
Be My Little Apple Dumpling 1902.15
Be My Little Baby Bumble Bee 1912.13, 1917.26
Be My Love 1974.10
Be My Mien 1899.34
Be My Sweitzer Bride 1909.05
Be Not Alarmed 1894.08
Be Oh so Careful, Ann 1930.36
Be on Your Own 1982.09
Be Our Guest 1994.04
Be Polite 1905.42
Be Prepared 1997.20
Be Somewhere 1993.19
Be Sure it's Light 1917.05
Be Sweet to Me, Kid 1908.23
Be That Way 1929.06
Be the Secret of My Life 1929.02
Be There 1986.18
Be this mont the brightest 1855.06
Be wise in time, O Phyllis mine 1887.44
Be-Bee 1910.13
Be-In 1968.11
Beach Song, A 1972.17
Beaded Bag, The 1924.29
Beadle, The 1880.18
Beale Street Blues 1919.16, 1919.26
Beans, Beans, Beans 1917.24, 1919.20
Bear Away the Bride 1904.40
Bear Hunt 1965.36
Bear the God of Love Along 1899.39
Beardsley Ballet, The 1959.22
Bearing the Silver Platters 1928.46
Beast and the Beauties, The 1923.33
Beast in You, The 1958.14
Beat Begins, The 1974.05
Beat Behind, A 1993.02
Beat Continues, The 1974.05
Beat Me Daddy Eight to the Bar 1986.06
Beat of a Heart, The 1959.19
Beat Out Dat Rhythm on a Drum 1943.24, 1997.01
Beat the Drum 1877.22
Beatitudes 1976.35, 1980.14, 1982.17
Beatnick Love Affair 1961.18
Beatrice Barefacts 1904.54, 1905.01, 1929.48
Beatrice Little Ballad 1926.17
Beats there a heart? 1840.03
Beau of Georgian Days, The 1897.40
Beau Sabreur, The 1911.47
Beau Sejour, Le 1933.24
Beaucoup 1934.32
Beauteous Queen 1894.37
Beauteous Widow Bohea 1895.08
Beautician Ballet, The 1969.02
Beautiful 1962.01, 1984.08, 1999.22
Beautiful Allelujah Days 1969.15
Beautiful American Girl 1919.16
Beautiful and Damned 1923.17
Beautiful Arizona 1900.38
Beautiful Baby 1924.16, 1925.16, 1926.25
Beautiful Bed 1906.35
Beautiful Booby Prize 1920.36
Beautiful Candy 1961.10
Beautiful Day for a Wedding 1997.17
Beautiful Dream, Come True 1903.09
Beautiful Dreamer 1939.21
Beautiful Dreams 1873.28
Beautiful Dreamtown 1906.48
Beautiful Evening, A 1923.41
Beautiful Eyes 1908.43
Beautiful Faces Need Beautiful Clothes 1920.33
Beautiful Fairy Tales 1901.21
Beautiful Feathers Make Beautiful Birds 1921.18
Beautiful Garden of Girls 1917.13
Beautiful Girl 1977.02, 1985.08
Beautiful Girl, Good-Bye 1917.13
Beautiful Girls 1922.32, 1925.48, 1930.14, 1971.05
Beautiful Girls are Like Opium 1921.02
Beautiful Golden Land 1919.22
Beautiful Human Fly, The 1896.06
Beautiful Island of Girls 1916.10
Beautiful Isle of Repose, The 1906.08
Beautiful Ladies 1922.15
Beautiful Ladies of the Night 1925.48
Beautiful Lady 1918.11
Beautiful Lady in Red 1919.11
Beautiful Lady of the Sea 1917.12
Beautiful Land of Bon-Bon 1905.56
Beautiful Land of Dreams, The 1907.11
Beautiful Lane, The 1965.19
Beautiful Little Baby 1884.37
Beautiful Love 1923.01
Beautiful Maidens are We 1907.01
Beautiful Monte Carlo 1901.17
Beautiful Music 1976.34, 1984.02
Beautiful Night 1870.07, 1918.30, 1934.42

Beautiful Ocean 1911.45
Beautiful People 1985.17
Beautiful People of Denver 1960.20
Beautiful Sea 1925.40
Beautiful Ship from Toyland, The 1912.46
Beautiful Shoulders 1920.23
Beautiful Spain 1907.34
Beautiful Spring 1906.36
Beautiful Through and Through 1972.04
Beautiful Venice 1898.46
Beautiful, Beautiful Girl 1912.38
Beautiful, Beautiful World 1966.18
Beautiful, bountiful Bertie 1895.32
Beautiful, Gay Paree 1897.30
Beautiful, Primitive Indian Girls 1916.06
Beautifying the City 1934.19
Beauty 1930.18
Beauty Adorned 1926.15
Beauty and Beast 1918.05
Beauty and the Beast 1947.14, 1994.04
Beauty Contest, The 1913.31, 1924.18, 1925.10
Beauty in the Movies 1928.17
Beauty is Like a Rose 1920.23
Beauty is Vanity 1926.14
Beauty Lane 1905.42
Beauty of Bath, The 1925.50
Beauty of nature the poets portray, The 1885.63
Beauty School Dropout 1972.12, 1994.07
Beauty That Drives Men Mad, The 1972.04
Beauty Within 1989.09
Beauty's Awakening 1901.27
Beauty's Candy Shop 1921.03
Beauty, My Boy, You are, You Are, A 1894.22
Beaux and the Belles of Bath, The 1919.42
Bebe 1921.34
Because 1974.24
Because He Lives 1995.04
Because He Tole Me So 1903.34
Because He Wears That Hat 1905.34
Because I am a Duke 1904.34
Because I am so Shy 1907.19
Because I Can't Tango 1914.15
Because I Don't Dress Like a Dude 1885.44
Because I Love Thee 1896.50
Because I Love You Dear 1902.35
Because I Love You So 1894.03
Because I'm a Woman 1981.24
Because it Can't Sit Down 1911.07
Because My Mother Told Me So 1888.39
Because of Thee 1882.28
Because of You 1956.02
Because They All Love You 1929.27
Because We are so Innocent, You Know 1898.50
Because You are Just You 1917.13
Because You do Not Know 1918.15
Because You Love the Singer 1923.40
Because You're Beautiful 1928.37
Because You're Different 1919.33
Because You're Mine 1944.28
Because You're You 1945.16
Because You're You! 1906.33
Because, Because 1931.48
Becky from Babylon 1920.47
Becky Miller 1880.51
Bed Time Follies, The 1923.35
Bed, The 1968.11
Bed, Wonderful Bed 1915.07
Bedad, it's for Him That We'll Always Employ 1902.25
Bedalumbo, The 1918.05
Bedecked in Fashion Trim 1893.02
Bedelia 1903.35
Bedtime at the Zoo 1910.21
Bedtime Story, A 1927.23, 1938.08
Bee Buzz'd, The 1892.14
Bee, be My Honey Bee 1903.18
Bee-Deedle Dee-Dum Dey 1921.08
Beecher's Defense 1980.30
Beecher's Processional 1980.30
Beedle 'Em Boo 1921.26
Beedle Um Bee 1924.33
Beek-a-Boo 1885.53
Been a Long Day 1961.22
Beer 1982.08
Beer Barrel Polka 1939.24
Beer is Best 1969.04, 1980.01
Beer That Made Milwaukee Famous, The 1903.04
Beer, Beautiful Beer 1900.41
Bees Among the Clover 1880.42
Beethoven Day 1999.03
Beethoven's Sonata 1922.32
Beetle Race, The 1956.07
Before and After 1903.31, 1929.48, 1961.16
Before and After Taking 1902.08
Before I Gaze at You Again 1960.21, 1980.19, 1993.11
Before I Kiss the World Goodbye 1963.25
Before I Met You 1918.03
Before Lord Dayrell 1887.04
Before our eyes 1896.27
Before the Alter Now I'm Kneeling 1890.33
Before the Barn-door crowing 1750.01
Before the Black Cire Curtain 1934.01
Before the Dawn 1924.40
Before the Moor was master of the hills of old Iberia 1898.25
Before the Morning 1999.22
Before the Parade Passes By 1964.01, 1985.19, 1998.07
Before the Twilight Shadows Change 1898.48
Before these bursting eyes 1855.06
Before You Take a Man 1923.37
Before Your Very Eyes 1974.13
Beg, Borrow or Steal 1960.01
Begat, The 1947.03
Beggar Waltz, The 1931.16
Beggar's Chorus 1903.06
Beggar's Opera 1860.03
Beggars at the Feast 1987.04
Beggars, The 1888.40
Begging the Baby to Sleep 1909.05
Begin the Beguine 1935.14, 1939.16, 1955.19, 1963.10
Beginning of Love 1931.30
Beginning of the End 1975.05
Begone, Sir 1863.04
Beguile, Beguile, With Music Sweet 1907.51
Behave Yourself 1959.01
Behind Milady's Fan 1924.13
Behind My Lady's Fan 1924.36
Behind the Fan 1921.30
Behind the Mask 1927.47
Behind the Scenes 1890.29, 1912.47
Behold 1917.24, 1919.20
Behold before high heaven 1846.01
Behold El Capitan 1896.13
Behold in Me 1880.10
Behold Our Lady Great 1904.36
Behold the Call to Arms 1902.18
Behold the Dove! 1912.40
Behold the Governor 1901.07
Behold the High Executioner 1885.51
Behold the King of Altruia 1905.36
Behold the King of Babylon 1947.10
Behold the Lord High Executioner 1939.15, 1939.17
Behold the Lord High Executioner! 1885.47
Behold the Tomb 1875.19
Behold this, Victor 1859.09
Behold us gathered here to-day 1888.07
Behold Victor 1859.09
Behold! He comes! 1881.25
Bei Nanon ist nicht blos der herrlichste Wein 1885.01
Bei Ninon sich amusiven 1885.01
Bei Ninon sich einzufuhren 1885.01
Beim ersten Mal, wo er sich geschlagen 1885.01
Bein' a Kid 1970.12
Being Alive 1968.01, 1970.13, 1977.05, 1995.12, 1999.20, 2000.16
Being for the Benefit of Mr. Kite 1974.24
Being Good isn't Enough 1967.06
Being With You 1976.09
Bekol Makom 1968.04
Belgium Put the Kibosh on the Kaiser 1964.28
Believe 1971.07, 1997.19
Believe in Yourself 1975.01
Believe it or Not 1930.23
Believe Me 1888.28, 1900.42, 1908.43, 1909.27, 1910.18, 1973.02
Believe Me, Beloved 1920.31
Believe Me, if All Those Enduring Young Charms 1901.15
Believe, me, if all those endearing young charms 1894.36
Belinda on the Telephone 1904.29
Bell Boy, The 1903.09
Bell Buoy, The 1891.32
Bell Chorus 1899.11
Bell Goes Ting-a-Ling-Ling, And the 1897.54
Bell Hop Blues, The 1920.07
Bell Hop, The 1999.12
Bell Trio, The 1879.64
Bella Donna 1948.27
Bella Mia 1918.16
Bellamy Dance, The 1899.19
Belle 1987.05, 1994.04
Belle Boyd's Back in Town 1963.22
Belle Boyd, Where Have You Been? 1963.22
Belle Brandon 1861.04
Belle Conchita, La 1952.04
Belle Francaise, La 1910.15
Belle Helene 1870.01
Belle Histoire D'Amour, La 1981.04
Belle Lizette, La 1908.10
Belle Lulu, La 1915.22
Belle of Avenue A 1902.34, 1902.40, 1922.45
Belle of Avenue A, The 1905.39
Belle of Bald Head Row, The 1907.14
Belle of Bohemia, The 1900.41
Belle of Murray Hill, The 1899.29
Belle of New York, The 1905.42, 1921.20
Belle of Seville 1905.07
Belle of the Ball 1987.02
Belle of the Ball, The 1924.06
Belle of the Barber's Ball, The 1968.07
Belle of the Bathers 1908.17
Belle of the Beach, The 1912.36
Belle of the Dairy Lunch, The 1909.14
Belle of the Silvery Nile 1904.31
Belle of Today, The 1924.06
Belle of Vienne, The 1911.32
Belle Paraisienne, La 1910.29
Belle Paree, La 1912.07
Belle Parisienne, La 1897.39, 1909.24, 1921.20
Belle, a Beau and a Boutonniere, A 1928.07
Belles and Beaux 1911.14
Belles of the Bronx, The 1923.10
Belles of the Tally-Ho Boarding School 1911.25
Belles of Zig-Zag Alley 1903.01
Bellhops, The 1925.45
Bello Ave 'na Donna Dentro Casa, E 1964.03
Bells 1906.45, 1920.18
Bells are Ringing 1956.14
Bells are Ringing, The 1879.63, 1880.39
Bells in the Morning 1906.47
Bells of Hell, The 1964.28
Bells of Shandon 1888.40
Bells of St. Sebastian, The 1982.09
Bells of St. Swithins, The 1929.43
Bells of the Sea 1922.16
Belly Up to the Bar, Boys 1960.20
Belonging 1969.16
Below the Macy-Gimbel Line 1920.42
Belz 1998.11
Bench in the Park 1948.23
Bend before High Heaven 1862.03
Bend of the Road, The 1968.30, 1983.14
Beneath the Moon 1907.37
Beneath the Skies 1894.33
Beneath the Stars 1924.10
Benjamin B. O'Dell 1949.02
Benjamin Calypso 1982.03, 1993.15
Benjamin Franklin 1992.05
Benjamin Partridge, a Person of Parts 1907.51
Benny and the Jets 1982.22
Bensonhurst Gavotte, The 1914.21
Benvenuta 1956.04
Berceuse 1890.19
Bergerac 1973.07
Bergere legere 1933.24
Bergere que je sers, La 1933.24
Berlin on the Spree 1908.25
Berlina, La 1964.03

Bernadette 1998.02
Bernice 1922.22
Berretin 1997.13
Berry-Pickers 1934.32
Berta e Pipinu Cuntamu La Storia, Di 1985.16
Berta Filava 1985.16
Bertha, the Sewing Machine Girl 1937.14
Bertie 1924.38, 1925.10, 1925.24
Bertie the Bounder 1910.21
Beside the Babbling Brook 1923.33
Beside the Star of Glory 1925.06
Bess You is My Woman Now 1958.10, 1974.09
Bess, You is My Woman Now 1935.13, 1983.04, 2001.07
Bessie Clayton 1908.21
Bessie Mae 2000.14
Best Brittany, The 1909.29
Best Christmas of All, The 1998.07
Best Dance I've had Tonight, The 1923.05
Best Dance of All, The 1937.11
Best Friend 2000.08
Best Gold 1960.07
Best I Ever Get is the Worst of It, The 1922.02
Best I Get is 'Much Obliged to You', The 1907.41
Best in the Business, The 1987.14
Best in the Trade, The 1924.22
Best in the World, The 1980.08
Best Little Lover in Town, The 1927.08
Best Little Sweetheart of All, The 1915.17
Best Man Never Gets the Worst of It, The 1918.33
Best Man, The 1982.04
Best Night of My Life, The 1970.09
Best of All Possible Worlds, The 1956.15, 1974.06, 1982.20, 1997.10
Best of Everything, The 1919.12
Best of Good Friends 1922.40
Best of Me, The 1983.17
Best of Times, The 1983.11, 1985.19, 1998.07
Best of What This Country's Got, The 1958.20
Best Queen of All, The 1913.31
Best Songs of All, The 1925.07
Best Thing for You Would be Me, The 1950.15
Best Thing of All, The 1949.16
Best Things in Life are Free, The 1927.41, 1974.26, 1975.22, 1990.09
Best Time of the Day, The 1949.01
Best Toast of All, The 1914.28
Best Waltz of All, The 1915.04
Best Woman in the World, The 1969.11
Best Years of His Life, The 1941.04
Bet on the One You Fancy 1923.47
Betcha by Golly Wow 1997.21
Betcha I Make Good 1942.35
Betrayed 2001.05
Betrothal Kiss, The 1913.14
Betsy Ross 1922.01
Betsy's the Belle of Bathers 1908.17
Better 2001.01
Better & Best 1999.22
Better All the Time 1964.35
Better be Good to Me 1928.30
Better Days 1971.14
Better Far 1969.15
Better Get Out of Here 1948.26, 1974.25
Better Late Than Never 1903.06, 1940.16
Better Not Try It 1930.35
Better Off Dead 2000.16
Better Place to Be 1975.05
Better Than a Dream 2001.03
Better Than Broadway 1980.11
Better Times 1922.30, 1927.53
Betty Lee 1924.47
Betty Lou 1930.29
Betty Martin 1890.23
Betty's Advice 1910.21
Betty, be Good 1920.15
Betty, the One Best Bet 1908.15
Between the Devil and the Deep Blue Sea 1942.11, 1980.10
Between Those Two 1870.38
Between Us All is O'er 1905.46
Between You, Me and the Lamp Post 1940.16
Bevo 1918.21
Beware 1919.29, 1923.37
Beware Brother Beware 1992.03
Beware my hate 1880.24
Beware of an Innocent Maid 1899.29
Beware of Lips That Say, 'Cherie' 1947.13
Beware of Love 1894.08, 1915.33
Beware of the Brigand Bold 1904.03
Beware of the Girl With a Fan 1925.22
Beware of the Rose 1926.09, 1926.35
Beware of the Sirens So Fair 1911.27
Beware you saucy minx 1887.43
Bewitched 1962.17, 1981.16, 1995.12
Bewitched, Bothered and Bewildered 1940.22, 1975.13
Beyond 1999.17
Beyond My Wildest Dreams 1983.01
Beyond the Blue Horizon 1980.08
Beyond the Gates of Paradise 1900.46
Beyond the Sea 2000.07
Beyond the Seas 1895.04
Bhula Weyyanga 1997.14
Bianca 1948.32, 1999.19
Bible Stories 1904.43
Bickering, The 2000.10
Bicycle 1936.03
Bicycle Built for Two 1944.32
Bicycle Built for Two, A 1936.03
Bicycle Girl, The 1895.36
Bicycle Song, The 1964.16
Bid Me Forget 1914.09
Bid Me Goodbye and Go 1889.05
Biddle-be-boo 1919.24
Bidelia 1903.27, 1903.30
Bidin' My Time 1930.31, 1992.02
Bie Mir Bistu Schoen 1990.16
Biff! Bang! 1903.10
Big Ass Rock 2000.15
Big Baby 1979.33
Big Back Yard, The 1945.03, 1947.11
Big Banshee, The 1906.19, 1908.13
Big Beat, The 1974.05
Big Bill 1957.05
Big Black Man 2000.15
Big Bottom Betty 1976.33
Big Boy 1930.24
Big Boy, I Gotta Belong to You 1929.52
Big Brass Band from Brazil, The 1947.20
Big Brass Band, The 1916.07
Big Broad Smile 1942.19
Big Brother 1938.14
Big Brother to Me 1930.05
Big Brown Boo Lo Eyes 1908.22
Big Casino 1921.18
Big Chief Oi, Oi 1908.37
Big Chief Smoke 1908.05
Big City 1949.05, 1982.13
Big Clown Balloons, The 1963.21
Big D 1956.04, 1980.29
Big Department Store, The 1898.56
Big Drum, Little Drum 1919.08
Big Fish, Little Fish 1970.05
Big Four, The 1949.02
Big Future 1972.10
Big Guitar, The 1966.30
Big Hats, The 1908.19
Big Hearted Baby 1928.47
Big Hunk of Love, A 1989.12
Big Indian and Little Maid, The 1904.39
Big Indian and the Little Maid, The 1904.39
Big Indian Chief 1904.04
Big Injun 1905.02
Big Job, A 1993.05
Big Meeting Tonight 1963.13
Big Mole 1949.15, 1972.06
Big Movie Show in the Sky, The 1949.17
Big News! 1998.21
Big Noise from Winnetka 1978.05, 1979.30, 1999.01
Big Offensive 1919.08
Big Old River 1945.08
Big One, A 1965.37
Big Papoose is on the Lose 1930.09
Big Parade, The 1945.09
Big Pound Cake 1902.29
Big Red Shawl, The 1909.10
Big Shoe Act 1888.39
Big Show, The 1918.25
Big Spender 1966.01, 1983.20, 1999.01
Big Time 1956.02, 1974.18
Big Time Buck White Chant 1969.15
Big Time, The 1991.07
Big Town 1944.29
Big Trouble 1967.16
Big, Black Coon, The 1891.14, 1892.06
Big, Black Giant, The 1953.08
Bigger and Better Than Ever 1929.35
Bigger isn't Better 1980.07
Biggest Aspidistra in the World, The 1942.14
Biggest Blame Fool 2000.18
Biggest Thing in My Life, The 1926.04
Bilbao Song, The 1977.08
Bilbo's Song 1966.32
Bile ole possum down 1894.44
Bill 1927.67, 1946.01, 1964.02, 1966.14, 1974.09, 1983.05, 1986.01, 1994.08
Bill and Coo 1911.08, 1920.37
Bill Bailey 1965.05
Bill Bailey, Won't You Please Come Home 1980.27
Bill of Fare, The 1879.35
Bill of Right, The 1940.21
Bill Robinson Walk 1999.06
Bill Simmons 1906.17
Bill's Bounce 1999.24
Billet Doux, A 1900.47
Billet-Doux, A 1901.21
Billeting of the Hussars, The 1929.05
Billie 1928.31, 1968.07
Billie's Blues 1948.13
Billiken Man, The 1909.11
Bills 1918.42
Billy 1904.33
Billy and Furgie 1880.37
Billy Barlow 1862.01
Billy Baxter's Swing Song 1905.51
Billy Gray, U.S.A., O.K. 1903.04
Billy Joe Ju 1969.03
Billy Jones 1894.50
Billy Nubbs, the Poet 1876.11
Billy of the Olden Days 1897.21
Billy Rose Buys the Metropolitan Opera House! 1944.29
Billy the Bubbler 1915.29
Billy, You're off Again 1899.19
Billy-A-Dick 1999.24
Bim-Bam-Bom 1971.17
Bimbo 1904.07
Biminy 1924.18, 1925.10
Bing! Bang! Boom 1888.18
Bingen on the Rhine 1871.16
Bird Ballet, The 1925.25
Bird in a Gilded Cage, A 1980.27
Bird Inside the House 1999.22
Bird of Beauty, The 1862.06
Bird of Paradise 1975.02
Bird of Passage, A 1949.15
Bird Song 1903.36
Bird Talk 1913.33
Bird That Came in Spring, The 1877.25
Bird Upon the Tree 1959.04
Bird Watcher's Song 1947.16
Bird, a Bottle and a Cigarette, A 1898.47
Birdie 1905.36, 1917.03
Birdie, A 1923.47
Birdies 1928.06
Birdies in the Tree, The 1918.02
Birds and Flowers 1872.23
Birds and the Bees, The 1945.03
Birds are Dreaming in the Treetops 1989.10
Birds Fly South, The 1908.43
Birds in the bush 1887.43
Birds in the Sky, The 1984.02
Birds in the Spring 1930.43
Birds in the Trees 1908.25
Birds in the Trees, The 1984.02
Birds of Paradise 1902.22
Birds of Plumage 1923.17
Birds on High 1926.51
Birth of a Chicken, The 1915.16

Birth of a New Revue, The 1923.21
Birth of American Fantasy 1922.01
Birth of Dixie 1929.52
Birth of Passion, The 1910.22
Birth of the Blues 1956.02, 1974.11
Birth of the Blues, The 1926.16, 2000.14
Birth of the Butterfly, The 1910.22, 1929.48
Birth of the Century Girl, The 1916.24
Birthday Card 1941.13
Birthday Ensemble 1914.33
Birthday of Loulou, The 1959.15
Birthday of the Infant, The 1923.31
Birthday on the Beach 1973.08
Birthday Party 1927.59, 1962.27
Birthday Party Song 1903.33
Birthday Party, The 1982.01
Birthday Song 1954.15, 1967.05
Births, Death and the Weather 1985.17
Bit o' Breeze 1920.13
Bit of a Character, A 1965.28
Bit of Diplomacy, A 1902.11
Bit of Earth, A 1991.05
Bit of Opera, A 1916.22, 1920.47
Bit of Optimism, A 1934.18
Bit of Villainy, A 1974.13
Bitch in Heat 1975.02
Bitch is Back, The 1975.12
Bits and Pieces 1975.06
Bitten by Love 1952.08
Bitter Harvest 1946.05
Bivouac Song 1900.50, 1911.47
Bivouac, The 1913.06
Bizarbara's Wedding 1989.09
Black 1970.20
Black 400's Ball, The 1898.22
Black and Blue 1929.23, 1978.09, 1980.10, 1989.02
Black and Tan Fantasy 1989.02
Black and White 1925.17, 1929.27, 1980.07
Black Balloons 1969.15
Black Beauty 1930.13
Black Bottom 2000.08
Black Bottom, The 1926.16
Black Boys 1968.11
Black Butterfly 1997.03
Black Butterfly, The 1909.24
Black Cargo 1927.32
Black Cat Inn, The 1902.06
Black Cat, The 1910.18
Black Crook Galop, The 1866.18
Black Crook Waltes 1866.18
Black Cupids!, The 1876.30
Black Dog Rum 1970.06
Black Domino Polka, The 1866.01
Black Eagles 1927.65
Black Eyes 1942.10
Black Horse Tavern 1934.20
Black is a Moocher 2000.08
Black is the Color of My True Love's Hair 1955.13
Black Maria, O!, The 1887.07
Black Orpheus 1977.09
Black Picture Show 1975.02
Black Rhythm 1936.30
Black Sheep, The 1905.36
Black Spirits and White 1870.15
Black Widow Spider 1992.06
Black Woman 1999.09
Black-Eyed Susans 1921.19
Black-White Calypso 1966.03
Blackberries 1932.08
Blackbird, The 1882.50
Blackbirds 1897.14
Blackbirds are Blue 1930.34
Blackbirds on Parade 1930.34
Blacksheep 1927.64
Blade of Mine 1929.08
Blah! But Not too Blue 1927.15
Blah, Blah, Blah 1983.06, 1999.10
Blah-Blah-Blah-Blah 1937.09
Blake's Own 1890.23
Blame it All on the Girls 1916.21
Blame it All on the Night 1936.27
Blame it on the Summer Night 1986.13
Blame the Weather Man 1907.14
Blame, The 1997.06
Blank Piece of Paper, A 1988.07
Blarney 1909.13
Blarney of Killarney 1911.28
Blarney of Killarney, The 1904.36
Blarney Stone, The 1905.30
Blarney, The 1886.60
Bleeding Moon 1909.10, 1930.16
Bless My Soul 1984.14
Bless the Bohea-Man's Name 1845.01
Bless the Lord 1976.17
Bless This Land 1960.19
Bless You All 1950.19
Bless You, My Children 1995.04
Bless Your Beautiful Hide 1982.14
Bless Your Ever Loving Little Heart 1911.02
Blessings on that reverend land 1868.01
Blest Whitsuntide 1885.63
Bli-Blip 1981.06, 1999.24
Blighty Bound 1919.10
Blind Alleys 1932.19
Blind Date 1944.01, 1999.12
Blind Man Buff 1924.17
Blind Man's Buff 1907.06, 1911.07, 1922.04
Blindman's Buff 1976.33
Bliss Forever Past 1882.64, 1934.17
Blissful Pleasure I Profess, The 1921.01
Blitz-Carmen 1940.04
Bloat 1981.28
Blocks 1959.14
Blonde Blues 1958.01
Blonde That Never Dyes, The 1870.13
Blondes and Brunettes, I Like Them All 1969.11
Blondes, Les 1898.63
Blood Done Signed My Name 1999.09
Blood is Thicker Than Water 1912.40
Blood Money 2000.09
Blood on the Saddle 1931.02
Blood Red Roses 1970.06
Bloodoggling 1935.18
Bloody Mary is the Girl I Love 1949.04
Bloom is Off the Rose, The 1961.27
Bloom of the Apple Tree, The 1905.46
Blooming Lize 1902.20, 1902.42
Blooper Ballet 1994.01
Blossom of My Own 1916.17
Blossom Time 1922.15
Blow Almost Killed Father, The 1896.06
Blow High, Blow Low 1945.05
Blow high, blow low! 1882.75
Blow Hot and Heavy 1927.35
Blow Hot, Blow Cold 1930.42
Blow on Your Piccolo 1912.09
Blow the Bellows 1885.08
Blow the Bellows, Blow 1885.02
Blow the Man Down 1922.21
Blow the Smoke Away 1907.25
Blow Those Blues Away 1929.06
Blow Upon Your Bugles 1908.35
Blow Your Horn 1915.32
Blow, blow the trump, &c 1869.43
Blow, Blow, Blow 1920.33
Blow, Blow, Softly Blow 1891.24
Blow, Gabriel 1932.01
Blow, Gabriel, Blow 1934.36, 1987.15
Blow, Shepherds, Blow! 1963.28
Blowin' in the Wind 1982.22
Blowing Bubbles All Day Long 1922.30
Blowing My Top 1943.20
Blowing the Blues Away 1926.21
Blue 1956.13, 1986.16
Blue Again 1930.35
Blue Alsatian Mountains, The 1881.39
Blue and the Gray, The, or A Mother's Gift to the Country 1897.33
Blue Aspic, The 1978.24
Blue Beard and Eight Wives 1904.22
Blue Bell 1904.14
Blue Bell and the Rose, The 1914.12
Blue Bells of Scotland, The 1889.25
Blue Bird Blues 1922.14
Blue Blondes 1921.02
Blue blood is what we keep alive on 1887.12
Blue Blue 1982.12
Blue Book of Girls, A 1922.11
Blue Bulgarian Band, The 1910.03
Blue Crystal 1984.01
Blue Danube Blues 1921.36
Blue Danube Waltz, The 1964.25
Blue Danube, The 1912.27, 1934.29, 1990.10
Blue Day 1950.06
Blue Days, Black Nights 1990.15
Blue Devils of France, The 1918.19
Blue Eyes 1897.49, 1921.04, 1936.22
Blue Eyes I Dream Of, The 1927.17
Blue Flame 1974.22
Blue Grass 1948.14, 1972.05
Blue Hawaii 1989.12
Blue Holiday 1945.07
Blue Kitten, The 1922.02
Blue Monday 1940.06
Blue Monday Blues 1922.27
Blue Moon 1940.20, 1975.13, 1979.24
Blue Moon of Kentucky 1978.01, 1989.12
Blue Night 1950.12
Blue Ocean Blues 1928.16
Blue Prelude 1942.11, 1985.08
Blue Ribbon Girls, The 1900.41
Blue Room 1975.13
Blue Room, The 1926.07
Blue Shadows 1928.23
Blue Sierras 1954.17
Blue Skies 1926.51, 1952.11, 1992.18
Blue Skies, Gray Skies 1927.47
Blue Suede Shoes 1989.12
Blue Tail Fly 1944.32
Blue Tail Fly, The 1954.08
Blue Turning Gray Over You 1980.10
Blue, Blue, Blue 1933.25
Blue-Eyed Sue 1903.39, 1904.22
Bluebeard's Beard 1930.08, 1931.08
Blueberry Hill 1982.22, 1986.02
Bluebird Song, The 1920.14
Bluebird, The 1923.24
Bluebloods 1993.09
Blues 1917.29, 1949.16, 1953.05, 1953.14, 1956.08
Blues in the Night 1942.10, 1942.18, 1979.24, 1982.12, 1997.05, 1999.24
Blues Man 1999.09
Blues My Naughty Sweetie Gave to Me 1975.09
Blues, The 1954.11
Bluestep 1927.40
Bluezwis 1992.05
Bluff 1904.34, 1907.39, 1928.31
Blunderland 1922.19, 1923.20
Blushing Bride and Groom, The 1917.16
Blushing Bride, The 1884.42, 1886.47, 1888.36
Blushing, Gushing Widow, The 1919.24
Bo Koo 1924.02
Bo Peep 1905.05, 1924.24
Bo-bo-ho-bohoho-bohohoho 1880.40
Bo-Peep 1899.22
Board of Governors 1997.09
Board Walk Crawl, The 1911.34
Boarding School 1880.25
Boarding school girl, The 1884.14
Boardwalk Parade, The 1912.38
Boat from Guaymas, The 1988.15
Boat Race Chorus 1909.28
Boat Sails on Wednesday, A 1909.21
Bob About a Bit 1922.41
Bob and Me 1903.33
Bob Bon Buddy 1909.16
Bob Up Serenely 1881.12
Bob Up Serenely! 1880.69
Bob White 1967.11
Bob-Haired Baby 1926.01
Bob-Haired Bandit 1924.07
Bob-o-link, The 1900.01
Bobbin' Around 1857.07
Bobbing 1901.18
Bobbing Around 1856.01, 1866.06
Bobbing Up and Down 1909.17
Bobby 1907.19
Bobby and Jackie and Jack 1981.27

Bobby and Me 1928.37
Bobby's Nightmare 1928.41
Bobby's Song 2001.01
Bobo's 1977.16
Bodas de Luiz Alonso, Las 1988.15
Body and Soul 1930.32, 1954.11, 1986.02, 1989.02
Body Beautiful, The 1958.01
Body Language 1983.09
Boetie Guitar 1999.12
Boffola 1955.12
Bogie Boo, The 1912.31
Bogie Man, The 1892.29, 1905.17
Boheme, La 1965.30, 1970.01, 1974.19, 1983.03
Bohemia 1900.08, 1903.34, 1912.26, 1916.07
Bohemia Good-Bye 1909.23
Bohemia is the Life for Me 1906.39
Bohemia, Good-Bye 1908.24
Bohemian Artist, The 1899.30
Bohemian Polka 1964.25
Bohmische Polka 1964.25
Bois d'Amour, The 1909.29
Bois de Boulogne, The 1902.20
Bojangles of Harlem 1986.01
Bokhara 1921.06
Bold Banditti, The 1907.59
Bold Brigade, The 1879.15
Bold Dragon, The 1899.06
Bold Dragoon, The 1860.03, 1898.60
Bold Gendarmes' Dance, The 1908.31
Bold Hussars, The 1901.13
Bold Musketeers 1921.15
Bold Pierre 1896.28
Bold Vicious Man 1873.28
Bold-faced ranger 1894.15
Bolerdo d'Amour 1971.05
Bolero 1881.12, 1922.36, 1931.26, 1932.04, 1982.06, 2001.04
Bolero on Rye 1976.09
Bolero, The 1906.07, 1907.07
Bolshie Quartet, The 1924.01
Bom, Bom, Bom 1879.42
Bom-Bom-Beedle-Um-Bo 1924.32
Bombay Bombashay, The 1920.25
Bon Bon Buddie 1908.08
Bon et doux vin de France, Le 1929.11
Bon Jour 1896.28, 1960.20
Bon Jour Monsieur 1897.40
Bon Jour, Marie 1919.21
Bon Soir, Paris 1948.24
Bon Vivant 1964.04
Bon Voyage 1934.36, 1935.03, 1956.15, 1974.06, 1982.20, 1987.15, 1997.10
Bonbonera 1932.19
Bond That Can't be Broken, The 1997.18
Bonds 1970.15
Bonga Boo 1924.30
Bongo on the Congo 1924.08
Bongo, Bongo, Bongo 1947.20
Bongo-Boola 1952.08
Bonita 1927.55
Bonita Cachelti 1905.34
Bonjour Amour 1989.26
Bonjour Follies 1964.22
Bonjour Monsieur 1896.51
Bonjour, Bonsoir 1929.16
Bonjour, General Bombardos 1883.51
Bonne heure, on vous voit mieux, A la 1885.57
Bonne Nuit, Merci 1929.41
Bonnet Shop 1903.33
Bonnie Banks 1939.19
Bonnie Blue Flag 1927.42, 1975.22
Bonnie Briar Bush 1907.14
Bonnie Little Johnnie 1899.12
Bonnie Prince Charlie 1855.01
Bonnie, My Highland Lassie 1908.38
Bons Moments, Les 1970.01
Bonus Blues, The 1922.03
Boo Ra Boo 1902.40, 1908.03
Boo to a Goose 1956.13
Boo-Hoo 1920.12
Boo-Hoo-Hoo 1910.26
Boo-Hoo-Tee-Hee 1908.18
Boo-Ra-Boo 1902.34
Boodle, the Boodle for Me, The 1884.41
Boogie Boo 1910.26
Boogie Boo, The 1909.05
Boogie Shoes 1999.15
Boogie Woogie Bugle Boy 1973.14, 1975.12, 1979.24, 1979.30, 1982.22
Boogie Woogie Bugle Boy of Company B 1999.24
Boogie Woogie Country 1999.24
Boogie-Woogie Bugle Boy 1989.12
Book of Life, The 1972.10
Book Report 1971.11, 1999.03
Book-Maker, The 1892.05
Bookies and Cookies 1925.01
Boola Bola 1912.25
Boola Boo 1917.05
Boola-Boola 1917.17
Boolyvar de Paree, The 1898.63
Boom Chicka Boom 1991.15
Boom Ditty Boom 1971.07
Boom Whee! 1920.45
Boom! 1989.05
Boom, A 1897.52
Boom-Boom 1962.27, 1982.01, 1998.15
Boomerang 1918.35, 1931.31
Boomerang Baby 1967.13, 1968.20
Boomps-a-Daisy 1938.08
Boop-Boop-Poop-a-Doop 1930.09
Boosters 1922.08
Bootblack Quartette 1897.55
Boots 1918.20
Boots and Shoes 1914.32
Boots, The 1990.16
Booze 1973.10
Booze of Auld Lang Syne, The 1923.01
Bored 1969.02
Boring Straight Song 1964.29
Born Again 1963.25, 1979.32
Born All Over Again 1944.27
Born and Bred in Brooklyn 1923.46
Born and Bred in Old Kentucky 1925.01
Born in Puerto Rico 1998.02
Born Lover 1975.06
Born to be Hand-Jive 1972.12
Born to be Together 1990.17
Born to Hand-Jive 1994.07
Borneo 1905.22
Borrow from Me 1912.38
Borscht Belt Buffet 2000.14
Borscht Belt on Broadway 2000.14
Bosom Buddies 1966.10, 1985.19
Bosphorous 1911.12
Boss is Dead, The 1965.30
Boss Tweed 1945.03
Bossa Nova Baby 1989.12
Boston 1931.47
Boston Beguine 1952.09
Boston in the Spring 1938.12
Boston Merger, The 1989.26
Boston Post Road 1928.17
Botany Bay 1886.45, 1886.53
Both Blind and poor dears 1859.14
Both Sides Now 1982.22
Both Sides of the Coin 1985.18
Bottle and a Bird, A 1900.40
Bottle Imp, The 1908.34
Bottle of Canada Dry, A 1925.25, 1925.48
Bottle Song, The 1981.12
Bottle Up a Pretty Girl 1920.22
Bottleneck 1959.11
Bottles 1907.63
Bottom of the Sea, The 1892.29
Bottoms Up 1929.35, 1942.15
Boublitchki 1929.05
Bouboulina 1968.30
Boudior Dolls 1930.06
Bought and Paid For 1914.04
Boukra Fill Mish Mish 1945.17
Boule' Miche 1909.23
Boule' Miche, The 1908.24
Boulevard Glide, The 1909.07
Boulevardiers, The 1904.23
Bounce Me 1926.12
Bounce Me, Brother With a Solid Four 1999.24
Bound No'th Blues 1991.01
Bound to be a Sailor Boy 1866.16, 1867.18
Bounding Brothers of Barbarry, The 1891.46
Bouquet in Bloom, A 1894.37
Bouquet of Fond Memories, A 1929.21
Bouquet of Girls 1922.15
Bouquet, La 1929.16
Bourbon Street Parade 1992.06
Bourgeoise et bourgeois 1877.32
Boutiuque, A la 1884.43
Bow Bow 1938.10
Bow Down Sinners 1936.30
Bow Down! 1895.08
Bow With Air Ceremonious 1899.06
Bow Wow 1870.01
Bow ye Venal Servile Train 1860.03
Bow, Students, Bow! 1882.63
Bow-Legged Sal 1941.12
Bow-Wow 1928.04
Bowed with tribulation 1896.13
Bowery Girls, The 1894.50
Bowery of Today, The 1923.02
Bowery, The 1892.38, 1893.23, 1930.39
Bowl of Roses, A 1907.56
Bowlene 1976.34
Bowler Hat, A 1976.02
Box Office Tells the Story, The 1908.16
Boxing at Shadows 1929.33
Boxing Bout 1930.19
Boy and a Girl, A 1955.14
Boy and Girl 1902.30
Boy and Man 1964.03
Boy for Sale 1963.01
Boy Friend Back Home, The 1929.45
Boy Friend, The 1954.09
Boy from, The 1977.05
Boy Guessed Right the Very First Time, The 1898.46
Boy I Left Behind Me, The 1942.15
Boy I Love, The 1899.19
Boy in the Blue Uniform 1927.03
Boy Like That, A 1957.12, 1977.05
Boy Like You, A 1947.02
Boy Most Likely to Succeed 1956.08
Boy Next Door, The 1989.23, 1999.23
Boy Oh Boy 1976.09
Boy Scouts, The 1913.01
Boy Talk 1965.36
Boy Wanted 1983.06
Boy was Dancing, A 1959.15
Boy With the Fiddle, The 1971.14
Boy With the Violin, The 1913.19
Boy! What Love has Done to Me 1930.31
Boy, a Girl, a Moon, A 1937.06
Boy, I Give You Now 1931.06
Boy, Oh Boy 1980.06
Boys 1913.26
Boys and girls come out to play 1862.02
Boys and Girls Come Out to Play 1971.20
Boys and Girls Like You and Me 1996.04
Boys and Girls of DeVere's, The 1922.43
Boys and the Girls, The 1896.41
Boys Before the Mast, The 1902.21
Boys from the South 1975.04
Boys in Blue 1935.03
Boys in Gray 1927.42
Boys in the Back Room, The 1999.07
Boys in the Backroom, The 1980.29
Boys of the 71st, The 1898.56
Boys of the Empire, The 1898.41
Boys of the Household Brigade 1894.33
Boys of Yankee Land, The 1898.43
Boys Together 1891.14
Boys Who Fight the Flames 1908.09
Boys Will be Boys 1903.02, 1909.07
Boys Will be Boys and Girls Will be Girls 1907.11
Boys, be Proud You're a Usaac 1918.14
Boys, Boys, Boys 1883.04, 1914.06, 1922.18, 1964.44
Boys, The 1985.06
Bracelet Number 1929.28
Bracelets 1927.58
Brad 1946.21
Bradshaw 1901.19
Braes o' Ballachloe 1925.21

Brag and Bluster, The - it's Painful to the Yankee Soul 1912.40
Bragging Song 1921.17
Brahn Boots 1960.17
Braid the raven hair 1885.47, 1885.51
Braid the Raven Hair 1939.15, 1939.17
Brain Wafers 1897.25
Brakeman's Chorus 1888.05
Brand New Day 1979.13
Brand New Day, A 1978.22
Brand New Dress, A 1969.17
Brand New Soldier Tune, A 1912.29
Brand New Start 1994.06
Brand New World 1986.13
Brannigan's Band 1877.05
Bras d'Antonie, Les 1964.39
Brass Band, The 1911.23
Brat, The 1906.15
Brava! Well Done! 1881.36
Brave Blue Coats 1864.12
Brave Deserve the Fair, The 1929.46
Brave Enough for Love 2000.20
Brave Hussar, The 1900.40
Brave Huzzar, The 1914.28
Brave Margot 1958.06
Brave Old City of New York, The 1971.20
Brave Soldier Boy, The 1895.17, 1903.40
Brave Volunteers you must enroll 1864.12
Bravo Antonio! 1917.29
Bravo Bravo 1987.12, 1988.01
Bravo Pour Le Clown 1981.04
Bravo, Bravo 1927.17
Bravo, Bravo, Novelistro 1964.35
Bravo, Giovanni 1962.14
Brazil 1943.02
Brazil Capela 1988.06
Brazilian Jubilee 1915.23
Brazilian Nuts 1942.18
Breachy's Law 1962.14
Bread and Butter and Sugar 1926.02
Bread and Freedom 1986.13
Bread and Gravy 1953.12
Bread Brigade, The 1864.12
Bread, Cheese and Kisses 1897.40, 1917.10
Break into Your Heart 1924.11
Break it Up 1942.29
Break it Up, Cinderella 1940.09
Break That Party 1972.10
Break the News to Mother 1898.61
Break'n th' Rhythm 1929.21
Break-Me-Down, The 1928.34
Break-Neck Quadrille, The 1913.10
Breakaway, The 1908.12
Breakfast 1963.16
Breakfast Dance 1930.06
Breakfast in Bed 1927.01, 1927.68
Breakfast in Harlem 1980.10
Breakin' 'Em Down 1924.27
Breakin' a Leg 1922.22
Breaking into the Movies 1921.17
Breaking the Ice 1947.12
Breaking Up a Rhythm 1933.15
Breath from Bohemia, A 1915.20
Breath of May, The 1894.08
Breathe Soft, Wind of the South 1898.46
Breathing the Air 1974.12
Breeze in the Trees 1919.19
Breeze Kissed Your Hair, The 1931.37
Breeze Off the River 2000.15
Breezes That Blow 1911.05
Breezin' Through Another Day 2000.08
Breezy 1947.20
Brendas 1946.20
Brenton Boat Song 1893.40
Brewster the Millionaire 1907.41
Brickerty-Brackerty-Tootsies 1917.35
Bridal Bevy, The 1914.10
Bridal Chorus 1896.45
Bridal March, The 1887.48
Bridal Moon 1868.03
Bridal Song 1905.53
Bridal Song, The 1895.06
Bridal Veil, The 1887.05, 1920.08
Bride and Groom 1926.36
Bride Bells 1928.37
Bride Sings, The 1967.08
Bride was Dressed in White, The 1928.44
Bride's Song 1903.33
Bride, The 1923.22
Bridegroom and bride 1890.02
Brides and Grooms 1902.03
Bridesmaid's Sextette 1910.21
Bridesmaids 1918.42
Bridesmaids' Chorus 1895.25
Bridge 1908.10
Bridge of Caulaincourt, The 1960.13
Bridge Over the River Kwai 1973.13
Bridge to Nowhere, The 1969.08
Bridget McShane 1921.25
Bridget Salome 1907.24
Brief Encounter 1985.20
Brief Guide to New York, A 1973.08
Brigadoon 1947.07, 1980.26
Brigand Chief 1904.03
Brigands' Chorus, The 1914.09
Bright and Black 1976.11
Bright Champagne 1868.19
Bright College Days 1952.10
Bright Day's Dawning 1916.05
Bright Eyes 1920.33
Bright Lights 1917.01, 1980.15
Bright Morning Star 1915.28
Bright New Day 1993.07
Bright star of love 1898.25
Bright wine and love 1887.43
Bright Young People 1986.19
Brighten Up and be a Little Sunbeam 1948.28
Brightly dawns our wedding day 1885.47, 1885.51
Brighton Beach Rag, The 1912.29
Brindisi 1860.05, 1866.11
Brindle's Farm 1924.21
Bring 'Em Back 1920.39
Bring All the Boys Back Home 1971.18
Bring Along the Camera 1911.11
Bring Along Your Dancing Shoes 1914.22
Bring Back Birdie 1981.07
Bring Back My Blushing Rose 1921.21
Bring Back Nelson Mandela 1988.02
Bring Back That Old Yama Dance to Me 1918.13
Bring Back the Days of Yea and Nay 1987.17
Bring Back Those Wonderful Days 1919.15
Bring Back Tomorrow 1981.14
Bring Back Your Heart to Me 1924.05
Bring Back Your Love 1913.05
Bring Him Home 1987.04, 1997.01, 2000.14
Bring Him My Love Thoughts 1921.14
Bring in 'Da Noise, Bring in 'Da Funk 1996.07
Bring in the prisoner 1896.26
Bring Me a Blonde 1918.14
Bring Me a Radio 1924.32
Bring Me a Rose 1910.05
Bring Me Back My Butterfly 1919.25
Bring Me Back to My Childhood Days 1896.33
Bring Me My Bride 1962.12
Bring Me Roses 1935.19
Bring on the Concubines 1944.16
Bring on the Follies Girls 1931.19
Bring on the Girls 1918.20, 1922.19, 1923.20, 1923.22, 1957.01, 1977.05
Bring on the Men 1997.09
Bring on the Pepper 1922.39
Bring the Brightest of Faces 1888.18
Bring Your Darling Daughter 1961.27
Bringing Up Daughter 1957.14
Brinkley Coon, The 1909.16
Briskly beat the Hollow Drum 1853.01
Britannia Rules the Waves 1928.42, 1937.14
British Maidens 1929.20
British Peer, The 1883.04
British tar is a soaring soul, A 1879.05
British Waiter, The 1884.57
Brittany 1913.20, 1924.32
Briv, A 1970.17
Broad Highway 1924.23
Broad Highway, The 1934.17
Broadcast a Jazz 1924.32
Broadminded 1946.06, 1956.13
Broads Ain't People 1961.21
Broads of Broadway 1926.22
Broadway 1922.03
Broadway at Night 1989.03
Broadway Baby 1971.05, 1977.05
Broadway Battle Cry, The 1924.16
Broadway Beauty Show, The 1897.34
Broadway Belles 1919.13
Broadway Blossom 1945.20
Broadway Blossoms 1958.20, 1958.21
Broadway Blues, The 1920.45
Broadway Boogie Woogie 2001.01
Broadway Butterflies, The 1891.14
Broadway Butterfly 1919.03
Broadway Cabaret, The 1912.02
Broadway Cinderella, A 1920.28
Broadway Coon, The 1899.33
Broadway Favorites 1905.44
Broadway Follies 1981.09
Broadway Girl 1918.13
Broadway Glide, The 1912.38
Broadway in Dahomey 1904.26, 1980.10
Broadway in Paree, A 1914.01
Broadway Indians 1923.38
Broadway isn't Broadway Since They Close at One O'Clock 1917.08
Broadway Lament 1910.10
Broadway Love Song 1949.12
Broadway Mammy 1929.24
Broadway Mammy Blues 1925.20
Broadway Melody 1992.18
Broadway Musical, A 1978.28
Broadway Nights from the Roof Garden 1929.28
Broadway of My Heart, The 1971.09
Broadway Pirates 1921.25
Broadway Reverie 1931.19
Broadway Rhythm 1983.09, 1985.08
Broadway Rose 1923.42
Broadway Sam 1915.12
Broadway School Days 1916.11
Broadway Show, The 1907.42
Broadway Swell and Bowery Bum 1920.27
Broadway Tipperary 1914.34
Broadway to Madrid 1926.23
Broadway Triangle, The 1914.22
Broadway Wedding Bells 1921.27
Broadway Whirl, The 1921.19
Broadway Zoo, The 1962.17
Broadway's Boudoir 1924.33
Broadway's Not a Bad Place After All 1918.19
Broadway, Broadway 1978.28
Broadway, My Street 1971.07
Broadway, My Sweet 1929.27
Broadway, the Heart of the World 1927.46
Broken Blossoms 1919.39
Broken Bus, The 1948.24
Broken Cavalier, The 1884.57
Broken Heart of the Wages of Sin, The 1970.10
Broken Hearted Romeo 1941.07
Broken Hearts 1923.34
Broken Komona, The 1956.08
Broken Nose, The 1871.19
Broken Pianolita, The 1948.24
Broken Rhythm 1926.37
Broken String Blues 1957.09
Broken-Hearted 1927.37
Bronco Busters 1930.31
Bronx Express, The 1927.47
Brook of Haugtussa Cycle, The 1944.21
Brooklyn 1912.44
Brooklyn Baseball Cantata 1940.18, 1942.05
Brooklyn Dodger Strike, The 1981.28
Brooklyn U.S.A. 1945.01
Broom Buy a Broom 1840.03
Broomstick Witches, The 1904.25
Broth of a Boy, A 1914.29
Brother Bill 1903.17
Brother Dear 1877.20
Brother Masons, The 1905.23
Brother new, A 1882.44
Brother the Men 1869.47
Brother Trucker 1978.12

Brother's Lullaby, The 1871.22, 1878.04, 1878.12, 1879.63, 1880.39
Brother, Can You Spare a Dime? 1974.09
Brother, Give Yourself a Shove 1977.08
Brother, My Brother 1999.08
Brother-in-Law Dan 1922.22
Brotherhood of Man 1961.22, 1980.29
Brothers 1919.27, 1928.10
Brothers and Sisters 1908.31
Brothers Came to Egypt, The 1982.03, 1993.15
Brothers in Arms 1905.04
Brothers Vendetto, The 1986.11
Brown 1927.33
Brown Blues 1983.04
Brown Buddies 1930.29
Brown Eyed Girl 1926.27
Brown Eyes 1926.34
Brown Gal 1976.04
Brown October Ale 1944.25
Brown of Colorado 1895.32
Brown Penny 1946.24
Brown Sugar 1932.08
Brown-Skin Gal in the Calico Gown, The 1980.10
Brownies 1896.18
Brush Up Your Shakespeare 1948.32
Brussels 1972.16
Bruta, El 1914.14
Bubble Bubble 1984.10
Bubble Song 1891.20, 1892.31
Bubble, Bubble 1880.10
Bubbles 1903.41, 1913.34, 1919.01, 1924.23
Bubbles in the Wine 1980.29
Bubbles of Bliss 1925.38
Bubbling Brown Sugar 1976.04
Bubbling Spring, The 1912.03
Bucharest 1936.27
Buck in the Bank 1948.15
Buck Up 1917.05
Buck Up to Me 1928.10
Buckets of Gore 1887.43
Buckle Down, Winsocki 1941.06
Bud Among the Roses, A 1922.02
Budapest 1930.20
Buddie Beware 1934.36
Buddie, Beware 1987.15
Buddle-Uddle-Um-Dum 1979.28
Buddy Rose 1927.15
Buddy System, The 1989.29
Buddy's Blues 1977.05, 1989.16, 1999.20
Budget of Up-to-Date Songs 1896.02
Buds and Blossoms 1922.48
Budweiser 1907.24, 1907.34
Buenna Senorita am I, A 1902.29
Buenos Aires 1979.23
Buenos Noches 1866.07, 1866.21
Buffalo Girls 1860.03
Buffalo Nickel Photoplay, Inc. 1998.01
Buffo Song 1875.19
Bugaboo 1922.18
Bugaboo Man, The 1899.41, 1902.29
Buggy Riding 1920.39
Bughouse on the Hudson 1907.12
Bugle Blow 1926.51
Bugle Blues 1927.32, 1928.10
Bugle Call Blues 1922.25
Bugle Horn, The 1878.20
Bugle, The 1963.21
Bugler, The 1891.14
Bui-Doi 1991.03
Build a Nest for Birdie 1906.14
Builders of Dreams 1929.29
Building Going Up 1950.02
Building Up to a Let-Down 1934.40
Buked and Scorned 1966.15
Bulerias 1939.18, 1986.17, 1986.17, 1992.15
Bulgaria Victorious 1947.06
Bull Frog and Coon 1906.06
Bull Frog and the Coon, The 1905.47
Bull Frog and the Dove, The 1910.17
Bull-Frog Ben 1900.55
Bulletin has Just Come In, A 1973.08
Bullfrog Ben 1900.48
Bullfrog Patrol 1919.09
Bulls and Bears 1905.31, 1907.18
Bulls and Bears come get along 1865.03
Bulls and Bears, The 1895.02
Bulls, The 1972.16
Bum Won, The 1959.25
Bum's Opera 1955.27
Bumble Bee and the Butterfly, The 1914.17
Bumble Bee, The 1910.09, 1911.24, 1919.09, 1921.28
Bummers, The 1876.19
Bumpity-Bump 1981.14
Bums 1928.22
Bunch of Bewhiskered Populists, A 1896.26
Bunch of Nonsense, A 1902.42
Bundle of Love 1928.46
Bundle of Nerves 1917.19
Bundling 1941.12
Bungalow for Two, A 1919.24
Bungalow in Quogue 1948.16, 1975.24
Bunk 1926.11
Bunker Hill 1905.09
Bunny Dear 1919.39
Bunny, The 1942.18
Bureau de Tabac, Le 1929.10
Burglar Inn 1922.23
Burglar's Ball, The 1912.44
Burglars 1914.07
Buried Alive in the Mind 1980.13
Burlesque 1955.11
Burlesque Imitations 1908.27
Burlesque of Italian Opera 1880.19
Burlesque Trio 1898.78
Burma Lou 1932.08
Burmah Girl 1906.41
Burmah Moon 1926.22
Burn 'Em Up 1927.11
Burnin' Luv 1991.02
Burning Love 1912.03, 1978.01, 1989.12
Burning to Sing, or Singing to Burn 1922.16
Burning Up the Boulevard 1907.57
Bus from Amarillo 1978.13
Bushel and a Peck, A 1950.17, 1980.29
Busiest Week, The 1916.21
Business is Business 1904.54, 1917.34, 1927.45
Buster's Chums 1905.05
Bustle 1923.31
Bustle! Bustle! 1895.26
Bustopher Jones 1982.19
Busy Bees 1888.44
Busy Bees of DeVere's, The 1922.43
Busy Evening, A 1925.26
Busy Izzy Oo 1903.09
Busy Little Broadway 1907.57
Busy Little Center, A 1927.47
Busy Liz 1899.29
Busy Mr. Bee 1907.47
Busy Night at Lorraine's, A 1991.15
Busy, Busy, Busy 1916.02
But 1960.13
But After the Ball was Over! Then He Made Up for Lost Time 1918.19
But ah, a Dreadful Thought 1880.47
But Alive 1970.09
But can I leave my pretty Hussies 1750.01
But for a little while we part 1886.40
But He Doesn't Know Everything Yet 1887.32
But here! no! yes! 1859.12
But I Could Not Love Thee, Ann, so Much, Loved I Not Honore More 1973.08
But I Rode Some 1991.01
But in Brazil 1922.40
But in the Morning 1917.04
But in the Morning, No! 1939.30
But it Ain't 1905.54
But it's Love 1955.11
But Never Jam Today 1979.18
But Not for Me 1930.31, 1980.09, 1992.02, 1999.10
But Not for You 1917.19
But Not Me 1992.05
But Not Right Now 1987.19
But now again my Spirits sink 1750.01
But Our Charms do Not Stop Quite There 1904.19
But Put Thy Hand in Mine 1921.15
But Still We Smile 1914.25
But That's the Way You Are 1969.17
But the World Goes 'Round 1991.10
But the World Goes Round 1991.04
But there are Things 'tis better not to dwell on 1889.22
But They Didn't 1902.41, 1917.11
But Time Will Tell 1898.03
But Valour the stronger grows 1750.01
But wasn't it an Odd Place to do It 1898.01
But Who Cares? 1927.17
But Why be Afraid? 1947.10
But You Alone 1917.30
But You Can't Believe Them 1919.08
But You Couldn't Hardly Notice it at All 1901.25
But Yours 1959.22, 1985.04
But, Beautiful 1995.14
But, bless my heart 1890.02
But, Colonel Tom 1950.16
But, Mr. Adams 1969.06
But, Oh Beware 1904.01
Butcher, Baker and Candlestickmaker 1930.33
Butcher, Baker, Candle-Stick Maker 1925.17
Butler in the Abbey 1968.02
Butler's Fox Trot, The 1919.34
Butler's Song, The 1976.09
Butler, The 1913.04
Butter and Eggs Baby 1925.44
Buttercup, The 1879.21
Buttercups and Daisies 1893.43, 1899.11
Butterflies 1907.48
Butterflies and Bees, The 1941.12
Butterflies and the Bees, The 1921.28
Butterflies of Fashion 1906.01
Butterfly 1917.30, 1922.18
Butterfly and the Clover 1908.34
Butterfly and the Rose, The 1908.03, 1910.11, 1913.18
Butterfly, Butterfly 1910.36
Butterfly, The 1968.30, 1983.14
Buttermilk Hill 1966.03
Button Me Up the Back 1921.18
Button Up With Esmond 1949.18, 1974.02
Button Up Your Heart 1930.35
Button Up Your Overcoat 1929.03, 1974.26, 1986.06
Buxom Mrs. Bascom, The 1935.18
Buy a Balloon 1896.29
Buy a Bond 1918.14
Buy a Broom 1860.05
Buy a Kiss 1910.24
Buy a Slave 1972.09
Buy a Victory Bond 1974.05
Buy an Extra 1925.35
Buy Her a Box at the Opera 1916.06
Buy it Dear 1857.04
Buy Me Roses 1934.32
Buy my nuts! They're all hot 1888.18
Buy Your Way 1928.06
Buy Yourself a Balloon 1936.31
Buy, Buy, Baby 1911.23, 1914.12
Buy, Buy, Come and Buy 1904.05
Buying a Wedding Present 1960.17
Buzz Mirandy 1921.16, 1922.22
Buzz on Little Busy Bees 1912.17
Buzz, Buzz, or the Life of the Bee 1956.09
Buzzard Song 1976.28, 1983.04
Buzzin' Around 1920.20
By a Piccadilly Cab Stand 1903.21
By a Small Refining Touch 1888.19
By and By 1989.12
By Bacchus 1899.39
By Candlelight 1938.07
By fortune I've been treated 1888.07
By his side 1878.16
By Jove, it is a Pretty Little Slipper! 1894.24
By Lantern Light 1955.01
By Love Undying, Crowned 1901.27
By My Side 1976.17
By My Window I'll be Waiting for You 1918.29
By Myself 1937.16, 1972.05, 1976.32, 1990.06, 1999.23
By Night and Day 1883.12
By Our Bearing so Sedate 1924.45, 1980.21
By sorrow tried severely 1868.01
By Special Appointment 1895.32

By Special Permission of the Copyright Owners, I Love You 1931.05
By Strauss 1936.31
By the Blue Lagoon 1909.24
By the Gallants I am Feted 1900.54
By the Garden Wall 1923.01
By the Gleaming Stars 1846.01, 1862.03
By the Grand Canal 1914.22
By the Honeysuckle Vine 1918.05
By the Light 1852.01
By the Light of the Honeymoon, or Kiss Me and Say You'll be Mine 1905.55
By the Light of the Moon 1924.39
By the Light of the Silvery Moon 1909.15, 1927.12, 1942.35, 1955.03
By the Mississinewa 1943.01
By the Old Oak Tree 1904.31
By the Palmist Tree 1920.13
By the Pyramids 1906.35
By the Sad Luana Shore 1916.09
By the Saskatchewan 1920.04
By the Sea 1944.32, 1968.13, 1979.06
By the Seaside 1905.09, 1906.39
By the Shalimar 1924.16
By the Side of the Mill 1906.33
By the Sweat of Your Brow 1937.09
By the Sword 1999.08
By the Sycamo Tree 1903.23
By the Thicket 1882.75
By the Time This Drink Gets Cold 1998.08
By the Way 1925.50
By This Sweet Token 1900.25
By This Token 1925.39
By Threes 1977.04
By Way of Explanation 1894.47
By Welawela 1930.26
By Wireless 1909.09
By Your Side 1899.04
By-and-By 1902.15, 1907.13, 1922.46
By-Gone Days in Dixie 1909.27
Bye and Bye 1876.14, 1885.08, 1925.31, 1943.10, 1975.13
Bye baby bunting 1862.02
Bye Bye 1913.17
Bye Bye Baby 1919.44, 1974.02
Bye Bye Blackbird 1974.01, 1999.01
Bye Bye Butterfly Lover 1937.16
Bye Bye Love 1977.10
Bye! Bye! On Our Journey 1877.05
Bye, Bye Baby 1949.18, 1995.07
Bye, Bye Barbara 1924.24
Bye, Bye, Baby, Bye, Bye 1882.69, 1888.12
Bye, Bye, Bonnie 1927.05
Bye, Bye, Dreamy Eyes 1907.50
Bye-Bye, Baby 1904.52
Bye-Bye, Baby, Bye-Bye 1886.51, 1891.28
Bye-Bye, Dear Old Broadway 1907.24
Bye-Bye, My Caroline 1907.28
Bye-O-Bye 1882.44
Byebye Babe 1926.20
Bygone Days are Best 1901.08, 1904.43
Bylo Bay 1921.34
Byrd Influence, The 1934.06

C Jam Blues 1997.03
C'est a Hambourg 1981.04
C'est a l'aube 1961.25
C'est affreux, odieux 1878.08
C'est aujord'hui Dimanche 1887.36
C'est aujourd'hui qu'la gros' Germaine 1886.19
C'est Comme Ca 1966.05
C'est de la reclame 1929.16
C'est Defendu 1965.37
C'est du limon 1884.50
C'est elle et son destin la guide 1878.08
C'est fini 1965.30
C'Est Fort la Musique 1955.14
C'est Francois, les bas-bleus 1884.50
C'est gentil quand on y passe 1935.19
C'est la marche de Corneville 1878.08
C'est la vie 1934.19
C'Est La Vie 1955.10
C'est la, c'est la qu'est la richesse 1878.08
C'est Magnifique 1953.07
C'est moi 1896.27
C'est Moi 1960.21, 1980.19, 1993.11
C'est mon livret 1877.32
C'est pas gentil 1929.10
C'est pas la peine 1934.32
C'est Toi 1920.10
C'est toi l'plus beau 1964.22
C'est toujours la meme histoire 1947.18
C'est un char 1929.13
C'est un grave professeur 1885.57
C'est un scandale epouvantable 1884.50
C'est une affaire extraordinaire 1929.11
C'est vous 1927.19
C'est vous que j'aime 1929.44
C'est, je vous le jure, toute une aventure 1885.59
C'etait la petite Niniche! 1885.59
C'etait Moi 1932.04
C'etait mon copain 1966.20, 1968.21
C'mon Folks 1927.67
C'mon Up to Jive Time 1976.04
C-h-a-r-l-e-s-t-o-n 1925.25
C.C. Rider 1978.01
C.D.Q. 1917.32
C.I.A. Men 1970.04
C.O.D. 1913.27
Ca c'est gentil ca c'est pas mal 1929.16
Ca c'est Panam 1964.22
Ca c'est une chose 1929.14
Ca fair passer un moment 1929.13
Ca fait penser un moment 1929.13
Ca ira 1881.25
Ca monte et ca descend 1929.13
Ca Va, Ca Va 1955.14
Ca!... que rien ne nous interrompe! 1885.57
Ca, C'est Sixth Avenue 1934.40
Cab Song, The 1945.11
Cab-Arabian Nights 1916.21
Caballero de gracia 1969.11
Caballito, El 1988.15
Cabanon pres de Toulon, Un 1935.19
Cabaret 1966.24, 1974.01, 1991.10, 1998.04
Cabaret le milleur de la ville, Le 1887.36
Cabaret Siren, The 1914.12
Cabarets 1926.07
Cabby's Serenade, The 1940.07
Cabin Door 1930.34
Cabin in the Sky 1940.17, 1953.12, 1999.23
Cable Car Gripman 1897.26
Caboceers' Choral 1903.08, 1904.26
Cachuca Song 1896.06
Cackle Song 1872.34
Cadava 1985.05
Cadets of Gascony 1899.28
Cadets of St. Cyr, The 1900.34
Cadillac Car 1981.29
Caesar is Wrong 1968.23
Cafe Boheme, The 1924.05
Cafe Chantant, Le 1904.49
Cafe Hoss and Hoss 1891.37
Cafe Man, The 1911.43
Cafetin de Buenos Aires 1993.08
Cage aux Folles, La 1983.11, 1985.19
Cage Aux Folles, La 1998.07
Cahoots 1973.11
Cairo 1916.09
Cake Song, The 1894.29
Cake Walk Jubilee 1896.52
Cake Walk Swell, The 1896.49
Cake-Eaters' Ball, The 1923.47
Cake-Walk Duel, The 1906.48
Cake-Walk, The 1899.35
Cakewalk 1936.31, 1944.31
Cakewalk Strut, The 1927.32
Cakewalk Walk Your Lady 1946.08
Cal Gets By 1968.05
Calandria, La 1988.15
Calcium Moon, The 1910.16
Calcutta 1935.11
Caldonia 1992.03
Calendar of Bacchus 1881.36
Calendar of Love, The 1908.28
Calico Days 1923.33
Calicoquette 1924.16
Californ-i-ay 1986.01
California 1914.16, 1927.45
California Belle 1906.31
California Skies 1926.28
California Sunrise 1908.05
California Sunshine 1923.23
California, Claremont 1908.13
California, Here I Come 1921.34, 1923.12
Calinda, The 1927.38
Calisthenic Song and Dance 1899.11
Calisthenics 1900.46
Call 'Round Again 1904.29
Call Around Again 1914.30
Call Around on Sunday 1906.20
Call for Freedom 1972.17
Call from the Grave 1966.19, 1976.10, 1989.24
Call from the Vatican, A 1982.09
Call in to Her 1970.10
Call it a Dream 1941.12
Call it Applefritters 1949.01
Call it Love 1950.06
Call Me 1994.06
Call Me 'Bill' 1909.11
Call Me Babylove 1971.16
Call Me Back 1970.21
Call Me Irresponsible 1974.10
Call Me Mister 1946.10, 1974.09
Call Me Old-Fashioned, I'm a Broadway Star 1999.14
Call Me Savage 1964.21
Call Me Uncle 1912.46
Call of Broadway, The 1927.58
Call of Life, The 1929.41
Call of Love 1921.07
Call of Love, The 1914.12, 1916.09
Call of the Colors, The 1914.22
Call of the Cozy Little Home, The 1919.07
Call of the Sea 1971.03
Call of the Sea, The 1925.30
Call of the Sixties, The 1919.22
Call of the South, The 1924.44, 1928.18
Call on Me 1915.21
Call on Rag Doll 1917.35
Call Right Here 1914.18
Call the Police 1957.14
Call to Prayer 1969.10
Call to Wander, The 1960.05
Call, The 1960.05
Call-Boy, The 1897.32
Calla Lily Lady 1971.18
Callahan's Gang 1893.36
Caller Herring 1880.34
Calles de Madrid, Las 1969.11
Callie 1904.14
Calling All Stars 1934.39
Calling for Rain 1977.01
Calling You 1995.12
Calling You My Own 1925.04
Calliope 1952.04
Calmon, King of Statues 2000.10
Calvary 1969.10
Calvary Brigade, The 1912.15
Calypso 1999.01
Calypso Isle 1928.14
Calypso Joe 1940.03
Calypso Kitty 1963.16
Calypso Pete 1961.01
Camarades, En 1929.15
Camel Boys, The 1926.32
Camelot 1960.21, 1961.16, 1980.19, 1993.11
Camelot Samba, The 1943.22
Camera Shoot 1928.02
Camerados, All is Clear 1899.06
Camille, Collette, Fifi 1955.10
Camouflage 1919.07
Camp Karefree 1952.10
Camp Meetin' Time 1906.04
Campmeetin' Time 1907.12
Camps Daily Dozen 1922.34
Camptown Races 1939.21, 1944.32, 1955.13
Campus Walk 1929.21
Can a Flower Think 1972.01
Can Anyone See 1945.12

Can Broadway do Without Me? 1929.27
Can Can 1898.38, 1952.04, 1988.08
Can I Believe My Eyes 1882.33
Can I Build My Home in You 1987.17
Can I Find a Toreador 1920.14
Can I Forget You? 1986.01
Can I Forgive Him 1998.02
Can I Let Her Go? 1987.19
Can I survive this overbearing? 1879.05
Can I Survive This Overbearing? 1945.09
Can I? 1997.21
Can it be Love at Last? 1918.26
Can it be Possible? 1964.44
Can it be That I'm in Love 1922.35
Can love be controlled by advice 1854.06
Can Love be controul'd by Advice? 1750.01
Can Macy do Without Me? 1921.06
Can Song, The 1909.27
Can That Boy Foxtrot 1977.05
Can the Cabaret 1917.01
Can the Can-Can 1940.02
Can they not leave us alone 1881.25
Can This be Love 1917.25, 1930.28
Can This be Love? 1922.42
Can We E'er Forget? 1912.34
Can We Stroll With You 1903.09
Can You do This? 1913.01
Can You Feel the Love Tonight 1997.20
Can You Find it in Your Heart? 1998.13
Can You Forget? 1898.47
Can You Hear My Voice? 1971.14
Can You Imagine That? 1961.10
Can You Keep a Secret 1906.17
Can You Sing? 1941.12
Can You Tell 1920.10
Can you tell me? 1882.44
Can You Use Any Money Today? 1950.15
Can you wonder that I am afraid? 1880.40
Can't be Bothered Now 1930.19
Can't Bring Him Back 1897.45
Can't Buy Me Love 1977.10
Can't Get Out of This Mood 1980.29
Can't Get Rid of Me 1932.15
Can't Help Falling in Love 1989.12
Can't Help Lovin' Dat Man 1927.67, 1946.01, 1966.14, 1981.16, 1983.05, 1986.01, 1994.08
Can't I? 1990.06
Can't Leave Now 1981.24
Can't No Grave Hold My Body 1982.17
Can't No Grave Hold My Body Down 1976.35, 1980.14
Can't Nobody do Me Like Jesus 1989.12
Can't Stop the Sea 1945.13
Can't Understand it at All 1897.33
Can't Wait 1996.08
Can't We be Friends? 1929.19
Can't We Get Together? 1929.23
Can't You do a Friend a Favor? 1943.22
Can't You Guess? 1904.43
Can't You Hear Me Calling, Carolina? 1914.21
Can't You Hear Your Country Calling? 1917.13
Can't You Just See Yourself in Love With Me? 1947.16
Can't You See 1918.29, 1964.32
Can't You See I Love You 1909.05
Can't You See I'm in Love 1924.30
Can't You See I'm Lonely 1904.13
Can't you See? 1882.75
Can't You Take My Word 1901.19
Can't You Tell by the Look in His Eyes 1918.29
Can't-Yer-Koon-Jine? 1891.32
Can-Can 1870.07, 1953.07, 1964.22
Can-canola, The 1929.44
Cana 1986.17
Canada at War 1980.13
Canada I Oh 1880.64
Canajoharie 1920.39
Canaro en Paris 1985.07, 1993.08, 1999.18
Canary Cottage 1917.04
Canary's Escape, The 1914.12
Canary, The 1973.08
Canasteros de Triana 1945.10
Cancan Song 1870.08
Cancelling the Bar Mitzvah 1992.09
Cancion de la Flores, La 1941.11
Cancion del Minino 1917.33
Cancion Desesperada 1999.18
Cancion Mexicana 1988.15
Cancion Mixteca 1988.15
Candidate, The 1908.19
Candidates' March 1902.44
Candide 1977.09
Candide's Lament 1982.20, 1997.10
Candle in the Window 1999.08
Candy 1999.24
Candy Jag, The 1919.14
Candy Man 1999.09
Candy Man, The 1974.11, 1974.22, 2000.14
Candyland 1917.22
Canis Minor Bolero Waltz 1975.04
Cannibal King 1895.36
Cannibal Maid, The 1902.03
Cannilaler 1904.41
Cannon rebounding, The 1855.06
Cannon Song 1965.04
Cannon Song, The 1976.10
Canny Canner, The 1905.25
Canons 1997.06
Canterbury Day 1969.04, 1980.01
Cantiamo D'Amore 1999.19
Cantina 1992.15
Cantineer of the Regiment 1900.34
Canto 1993.08
Canto flamenco 1969.11
Cantor for the Sabbath, A 1990.16
Cantor, The 1931.09
Canzone del Monacello 1985.14
Canzone della Zingara 1985.14
Canzonetta 1921.33
Canzoni dei Sette Mariti 1985.14
Canzoni delle Sei Sorelle 1985.14
Caoineadh Chu Chulainn 1996.12, 2000.05
Cap'n Andy's Ballyhoo 1994.08
Cape Cod Chanty 1929.33
Caper, The 1971.07
Capitaine Rene, The 1886.50
Capital Gains 1977.02
Capital H 1912.20
Capital Punishment 1901.13
Capital, excellent, heart-warming wine! 1888.18
Capitan, El 1897.55
Capped Teeth and Caesar Salad 1985.12
Caprice Espagnol 1945.10
Caprice Viennois 1944.28
Captain Bold, The 1882.25, 1894.38
Captain Cholly Chumley of the Guards 1897.42
Captain Cupid 1907.52
Captain D'Arcy 1907.58
Captain Dinklepop 1911.01
Captain Flo 1909.18
Captain from Castille 1977.09
Captain Henry St. James 1958.02
Captain Hook's Waltz 1958.20, 1958.21, 1977.02, 1990.20
Captain Jinks 1944.32
Captain Karl's March 1891.20
Captain Kidd 1913.16
Captain Kidd's Kids 1922.26
Captain Lincoln March, The 1961.11
Captain Mishler 1884.23
Captain of a Ten Day Boat 1982.05
Captain of De Base Ball Nine, De 1885.50
Captain of the Ten-Day Boat 1904.42, 1907.16
Captain Rossiter 1898.17
Captain Terror 1972.02
Captain Valentine's Tango 1936.28
Captain Vane of the Life Guards Pink 1869.47
Captain Walker 1993.06
Captain with His Whiskers 1862.06
Captain with his Whiskers 1864.13, 1890.33
Captain's Song, The 1940.01
Captain, El 1980.27
Captain, Mate and Crew 1937.09
Captain, The 1885.54
Captive and the Bird, The 1883.12
Captive Bird, The 1883.52
Captive Greek Girl 1860.01
Capture of Yaraboo, The 1906.14
Capullito de Aleli 1932.19
Caramba! 1920.09
Cararie Lee 1878.05
Caravan 1981.06, 1999.24
Caravan Moves On, The 1997.12
Caravane, La 1929.13
Caravane, ou La fille de Bedouin, La 1929.13
Cardinal's Guard are We, The 1954.01
Care Free Cairo Town 1921.19
Care's the King of All 1894.08
Care-Free Cairo Town 1919.43
Career Guidance 1957.14
Careful With My Heart 1934.01
Carefully on tiptoe stealing 1879.05
Carefully on Tiptoe Stealing 1879.56, 1945.09
Carefully Taught 1997.01
Careless Love 1940.01, 1954.11, 1966.15
Careless Rhapsody 1942.15, 1975.13
Caress Me, Possess Me Perfume 1958.20
Caresses 1920.41
Caribbean 1935.11
Caribou 1905.07
Carinito 1941.07
Carino Milo 1951.24
Carioca, La 1977.09
Carissima 1903.36, 1906.10, 1929.08
Carlos and Yolanda 1998.02
Carlotta 1944.02
Carlotti's 1920.42
Carlsbad Legend, The 1910.37
Carmela 1927.60
Carmelina 1979.09
Carmen 1898.20, 1930.15, 1998.02
Carmen Girl, The 1911.34
Carmen has Nothing on Me 1927.60
Carmen Jones is Goin' to Jail 1943.24
Carmen the Second 1909.11
Carmena 1902.44
Carmencita 1923.25
Carmenita 1910.34
Carmina 1904.33
Carnegie Hall Pavane 1998.16
Carnival 1896.48, 1909.28, 1934.43, 1943.02
Carnival at Nice 1914.25
Carnival Ballet 1961.10
Carnival Ballet, The 1953.11
Carnival de Venice 1860.05
Carnival de Venise 1880.32
Carnival for Life, A 1912.33
Carnival in Court 1955.12
Carnival is King Tonight 1899.06
Carnival Night 1921.06
Carnival of Roses 1927.03
Carnival of Springtime 1980.21
Carnival of Venice 1929.08
Carnival Song, The 1958.08
Carnival Tango 1954.09
Carnival Time 1924.39, 1924.43
Carnival Times 1919.03
Carnival! Make the Most of Carnival! 1912.33
Carnival, The 1904.54, 1996.08
Carol for New Year's Day, A 1963.28
Carolina 1906.13, 1919.10
Carolina in the Morning 1922.34
Carolina Mammy 1921.34
Carolina Rolling Stone 1987.02
Caroline 1885.03, 1897.01, 1918.32
Caroline Brown 1911.20
Carolita 1932.10
Carosse, La 1961.25
Carosse, Le 1959.15
Carousel 1945.05, 1972.16, 1974.11
Carousel in the Park 1947.11
Carousel Waltz 1993.16
Carpathian National Anthem 1963.29
Carriage Starters' Glide, The 1914.34
Carrie 1988.12
Carrie Barry 1903.03
Carrie! 1925.42
Carried Away 1977.02
Carried Off 1902.37
Carrier Pigeon, The 1906.18

Carrousel in the Park 1945.03
Carry Barry 1904.13, 1904.44
Carry Me Back to Old Virginny 1955.13
Carry On 1930.29, 1936.26, 1976.15, 1986.16
Carry on, Keep Smiling 1930.39
Carry That Weight 1974.24
Carry the News to Mary 1871.12, 1871.16
Cartoonist's Dream 1934.18
Casadh an Sugain 1976.29
Casamagordo, New Mexico 1970.08
Casanova 1936.31
Cascabel, El 1988.15
Case of Rape, A 1964.04
Casey Jones 1944.32 ·
Casey Social Club, The 1878.13
Casey's Dog 1894.10
Cash 1890.26
Cash for Your Trash 1978.09
Cash! 1892.59
Cash, Cash, Cash 1882.74
Casimir and Angeline 1891.46
Casino Girl, The 1900.20, 1901.08
Casino Scrub Women, The 1898.20
Cassie 1979.15
Cassie's Not a Bit Like Mother 1911.01
Castagnette Song 1890.19
Castaways, The 1881.09, 1896.24
Castellana 1949.07
Castle Garden 1966.21
Castle of Dreams 1919.36
Castle on a Cloud 1987.04
Castle Walk 1947.16
Castles in Spain 1893.40, 1907.08
Castles in the Air 1881.24, 1890.16, 1904.54, 1910.11, 1915.02, 1921.08
Castles of the Loire 1975.06
Cat and Fox Song 1938.16
Cat and Mouse 1916.17
Cat Came Back, The 1891.39
Cat Duet 1873.26
Cat's in Our Back Yard, The 1880.42, 1882.39
Cat's in the Cradle 1975.05
Catalina 1937.07
Catamaran 1910.03, 1912.31
Catch 'Em Young, Treat 'Em Rough, Tell 'Em Nothing 1920.21
Catch a Butterfly 1922.36
Catch a Star! 1955.12
Catch Hatch 1943.19
Catch Me 1970.04
Catch Me if You Can 1947.02, 1951.10
Catch My Garter 1968.01
Catch on Fire 1999.09
Catch Our Act 1951.19
Catch Our Act at the Met 1958.20, 1958.21, 1977.02
Catch That on the Corner 1971.13
Catchee Cathcee 1884.14
Catching Up 1923.35
Catfish 1982.04
Catherine the Great 1934.42, 1939.24
Catland 1905.48
Cats 1880.24
Cats on Our Back Fence, The 1886.15
Cats on the Garden Wall 1882.76
Catskills, Hello 1920.04
Caught in the Rain 1929.19
Caught Ole Blue 1940.01
Cause of Civilization, The 1881.11
Cause of the Situation, The 1928.31
Cause of this Confusion, The 1880.47
Cause Uncle Mordecai is so Smart 1968.22
Cause We Got Cake 1939.27, 1975.13
Cause You Won't Play House 1934.06
Caution: Men Cooking 1982.04
Cautivo 1999.18
Cavachok 1934.15
Cavalier 1928.48, 1934.43
Cavalier Americana 1926.21
Cavalier Cat, The 1942.19
Cavalier Song 1904.30
Cavalier, The 1907.48
Cavaliers 1900.12
Cavalla Kings 1999.12
Cavalleria Rusticana 1891.32
Cave-Man and the Cave-Woman, The 1912.40
Cazazza 1922.07
Cazik's land the Spaniard saw, The 1881.04
CC Rider 1989.12
Ce matin je quitte 1884.43
Ce n'est pas tout ca brrr! 1885.56
Ce qu'on dit et ce qu'on pense 1929.16
Cease my heart 1834.03
Cease your Funning 1750.01
Cease your funning 1854.06
Cecelia 1912.20
Cecelia and Amelia 1901.24
Cecil in London Town, The 1904.42, 1907.16
Cecil in London, The 1982.05
Cecily 1927.20
Ceil! quel spectacle imprevu! 1877.32
Ceinture de Chastete 1926.15
Celarius 1860.03
Celebration 1932.17, 1969.02, 1982.15
Celebration of St. Joan the Good 1925.08
Celebration! 1959.19
Celeste 1895.27
Celeste Aida 1966.03
Celestial Emanations 1866.34
Celestine 1914.17
Celina Couldn't Say No 1937.16
Cell Block Tango 1975.14
Cellarer's Toast, The 1902.04
Cellini's Dream 1925.23
Cellini's Plate 1929.22
Cello, The 1953.17
Celos 1993.08, 1999.18
Celui que j'aime est un pioupiou 1885.56
Cent for This and a Cent for That, A 1888.39
Centenarian, The 1932.18
Central Parkish Lawn 1864.12
Cents Vierges, Les 1876.07
Century Girl, The 1916.24
Century of Progress, A 1985.05
Century Promenade, The 1920.23
Century Toddle 1921.02
Ceremonial 1948.24
Ceremonial of the Caliph's Diwan 1953.16
Ceremony of the Sacred Bath 1920.27
Ceremony of Veils 1920.41
Ceremony, The 1991.03
Cerisiers sont blancs, Les 1968.21
Cert'n'y, Lord 1930.10
Certain are we 1886.50
Certain Girl, A 1968.01
Certain Individuals 1952.10
Certain Little Way of Mine, A 1914.26
Certain Something About You, A 1914.07
Certain Sort of Father, A 1911.02
Certainly is the Truth 1923.11
Certainly, Lord 1949.16
Certes!... monsieur doit plaire aux dames! 1885.59
Cervelle, La 1964.39
Cesario's Party 1954.15
Cette nuit, la chose est trop forte 1929.11
Ceylon 1985.18
Cha-No-Yu 1990.17
Chaconne 1978.05
Chacun a son gout 1929.39, 1933.23, 1942.31
Chacun a Son Gout 1954.06
Chain Store Daisy 1937.14
Chair Bottom Dance, The 1927.58
Chairman's Song, The 1983.18
Challenge 1949.01
Challenge Dance 1992.06
Chambermaids 1897.37
Chamois Hunter 1892.31
Champagne 1885.54, 1898.38, 1924.42, 1927.39, 1937.17
Champagne and Kisses 1975.04
Champagne and Laughter 1916.08
Champagne and Terrapin, Vision Darling! 1902.15
Champagne Charlie 1960.17
Champagne Song 1912.36
Champagne the First 1933.23
Champagne Waltz, The 1900.41
Champagne, Le 1885.57
Championship of the World, The 1921.21
Champs Elysees Polka 1952.04
Chances 1971.19
Change in a Home on the Range 1951.05
Change in Me 1994.06
Change in Me, A 1994.04, 1999.16
Change is done, The 1887.04
Change My Luck 1929.52
Change Partners 1920.05
Change You Mind About Me 1933.06
Change Your Act, or Back to the Woods 1942.12
Change Your Luck 1930.19
Change Your Nature 1987.17
Changeable Girls 1918.07
Changes 1980.30
Changing 1973.03
Changing All These Changes 1990.15
Changing of the Guard 1975.05
Changing of the Guards 1931.19
Changing Styles 1918.02
Chanson 1908.40, 1920.23, 1973.13
Chanson d'enfance 1990.04
Chanson de Colonel 1885.57
Chanson de Craonne 1964.28
Chanson de la Bruscambille 1904.22
Chanson des Matelots 1929.10
Chanson du petit bateau 1929.11
Chanson in the Prater, A 1935.17
Chansonette, a 1904.23
Chansonettes 1902.40
Chant D'Amour 1949.01
Chant of the Monks 1929.08
Chant of the Sun Feast 1894.08
Chantant Palpitations 1899.04
Chantey 1969.08, 1986.14
Chantilly Lace 1990.15
Chanty, A 1928.29
Chapeaux, Les 1963.02
Chapel of Love 1975.12, 1979.30, 1984.15, 1985.03
Chaperone, The 1912.42
Chaplin Walk, The 1915.07
Chappies of the Day 1905.07
Chappies' Song 1903.24
Chapter 54, Number 1909 1973.06
Character in Search of a Character, A 1940.04
Characteristic Waltz 1908.14, 1911.33
Characters in the Play 1894.06
Charade 1997.05
Charge is prepar'd, The| The Lawyers are met 1750.01
Charge is prepared, The 1854.06
Charge it to A.R. 1988.20
Charge of the Song Brigade 1919.10
Charge was Prepar'd, The 1957.02
Charge, 1987.19
Charge, Boys, Charge! 1905.36
Charger Good, A 1900.12
Chariot Race Song 1892.20
Charity 1902.07, 1904.55, 1930.12
Charity Bazaar 1899.41, 1901.19
Charity Bazaar, The 1900.08, 1918.25
Charity Box, The 1880.18
Charity charity! 1895.32
Charity Class, The 1924.08
Charity Concert 1979.23
Charity's Soliloquy 1966.01
Charity's Theme 1966.01
Charity's Useful Disguise 1897.37
Charity's Wish 1966.01
Charles Atlas Song 1975.08
Charleston 1923.39, 1925.23, 1945.20, 1964.39, 1977.09, 1980.10, 1981.17, 1989.03
Charleston Blues 1883.26
Charleston Blues, The 1882.79
Charleston Dance, The 1922.44
Charleston Mad 1925.16
Charleston Rag 1975.09, 1978.21, 1980.10
Charleston, Cut Out 1923.11
Charleston, The 1944.32
Charley from That Charleston Dancing School 1925.18
Charley My Boy 1986.06
Charlie 1960.07, 1980.23
Charlie and Algernon 1980.23
Charlie Brown 1890.12, 1995.03

Charlie is My Darling 1866.06
Charlie Welch 1956.02
Charlie's Place 1974.05, 1986.03
Charlie, My Back Door Man 1928.10
Charm 1953.02
Charm School, The 1920.47
Charm Song 2001.01
Charm/My Toreador, The 1926.09, 1926.35
Charmer, The 1891.32
Charmin' Son-of-a-Bitch, The 1969.14
Charmin's Lament 1974.13
Charming 1919.04, 1927.47, 1934.04, 1940.02
Charming Judy Callaghan 1860.03
Charming Ladies 1921.14
Charming Little Actress, The 1898.61
Charming little Broom Girl 1840.03
Charming Weather 1910.05
Charming Women 1925.26
Charming, Charming 1926.50, 1934.34
Charra Dance, The 1927.08
Charreada, La 1988.15
Chartreuse Monks 1883.12
Chase 1987.05
Chase Me Charlie 1986.19
Chase the Devil 1980.05
Chase, The 1911.36, 1923.01, 1947.07, 1971.01, 1976.08, 1980.26, 1981.25, 1984.14
Chasing Henry 1937.07
Chasing Little Rainbows 1923.21
Chasing the Squirrel 1916.21
Chasing the Whos 2000.18
Chastoushki 1922.06
Chat Noire 1955.11
Chattanooga Choo-Choo 1979.24
Chatter 1926.11
Chatter Chatter 1914.31
Chatterbox 1936.07, 1952.04
Chaud, chaud, pour la fete du prince 1885.57
Chauffeur, The 1910.07
Chauffeurs 1904.06
Chaunt of the Monks, The 1893.02
Chauve-Souris of Our Own, A 1922.32
Chauye Souris 1928.42
Chavaleh 1964.27, 1981.18, 1990.18
Chavalillos, Los 1941.11
Chaya 1970.21
Cheating Peddler, The 1900.50
Check it Out! 1997.08
Check Your Troubles 1927.64
Checkmated We 1886.15
Cheek to Cheek 1983.09
Cheeky Kiki 1922.15
Cheer for Kibosh, A 1895.33
Cheer for Simplicitas! 1910.05
Cheer Up 1907.13, 1913.06, 1914.20, 1923.16, 1961.11
Cheer Up Everybody 1905.53
Cheer Up, 'Liza' 1917.16
Cheer Up, Cherries are Ripe 1894.37
Cheer Up, Eat and Grown Thin 1915.21
Cheer Up, My Honey 1910.09
Cheer up, my Sister Dear 1877.20
Cheer, Boys, Cheer 1904.52
Cheer, Girls, Cheer 1924.47
Cheerful Little Earful 1930.38
Cheerily carols the lark Over the cot 1887.10
Cheerio 1925.31, 1928.21
Cheerio My Deerio 1957.05
Cheers for the Hero 1961.08
Cheese Chorus 1907.63
Chef D'Orchestre Est Amoureux, Le 1959.15
Chef d'orchestre est amoureux, Le 1961.25
Chelsea Reach, The 1920.08
Cherchez la Femme 1901.09, 1925.16
Cherie 1889.39
Cherokee Rose 1926.31
Cherries and Plums 1858.03
Cherries are Ripe 1914.20
Cherries Ripe 1905.48
Cherry 1908.12
Cherry Blossom 1982.06
Cherry Blossom Lane 1919.16
Cherry Blossoms 1906.06
Cherry Flower, The 1989.21
Cherry Hill Fusileers, The 1898.43
Cherry in the Glass, The 1907.41
Cherry Pies Ought to be You 1950.20
Chess and Checkers 1957.07
Chess Duet 1896.50
Chess Game, The 1992.09
Chess Hymn 1988.09
Chestnutty Language of Lovers, The 1902.07
Chevalier of the Highway, The 1926.14
Cheyenne 1905.49
Chez les Zoulous 1929.10
Chi Chi 1936.12
Chi-Chi 1913.34
Chi-Ri-Bim 1951.20
Chianti 1918.33
Chic to Cheap 1979.15
Chica Chica Boom Chic 1943.23
Chicago 1904.06, 1921.25, 1940.22, 1986.06
Chicago After Midnight 1975.14
Chicago Bound 1996.07
Chicago Girl, The 1903.06
Chicago Riot Rag, The 1996.07
Chicago Song, Das 1968.13
Chicago Stomp, The 1992.08
Chicago Style 1995.14
Chicago's Great World's Fair 1891.32
Chicago, Illinois 1995.15
Chicas Patas Boogie 1979.08
Chick-a-Pen 1960.20
Chicken 1909.18
Chicken and the Frog, The 1910.10
Chicken Shack Boogie 1992.06
Chicken Thief Man, The 1910.18
Chicken Walk, The 1916.24
Chickens 1922.18
Chico's Revereie 1955.10
Chief Cook and Bottle Washer 1984.01
Chief of Aggregation 1906.08
Chief of Love 1958.08
Chief Rocky Boy 1958.20
Chieftain is found, The 1895.26
Chiffon 1928.27
Chiffon Girl, The 1924.05
Chiffons legers 1929.15
Chiffons! Frou Frous! 1913.18
Child of Erin 1934.41
Child of Heaven! 1993.04
Child of Sympathy 1971.01
Child of the Most High King 1999.09
Child You Are 1967.18
Child, The 1977.01
Childhood Days 1910.26, 1916.14, 1918.37
Childhood Lessons 1915.04
Childhood's Days 1922.36
Childhood's Happiest Moments 1908.28
Children and Art 1984.08
Children in arms not admitted 1867.18
Children of God 2000.20
Children of the Earth 1939.14
Children of the Ritz 1939.07
Children of the Sun 1972.25
Children of the Wind 1986.13
Children Will Listen 1987.18, 1997.01
Children's Chimes 1998.02
Children's Lament 1971.02
Children's Rhymes 1972.13
Children, You Seem Rather Distant to Me 1910.27
Children, Your Line is Dragging 1999.09
Chili Bean 1920.24
Chili-Concarne 1910.16
Chilpericu III 1985.16
Chime In! 1961.26
Chime of the Liberty Bell, The 1908.35
Chimes 1998.02
Chimes of Long Ago, The 1907.01
Chimes of the Chapel 1925.36
Chin Chin 1904.26
Chin Chin, I Love You 1915.25
Chin Up, Ladies 1961.20
Chin, Chin, Chinaman 1896.27
Chin-Chin 1914.23
Chin-Chin Open Your Heart and Let Me In 1914.23
China 1924.24
China Bogie Man 1925.04
China Rose 1925.04
Chinaman, The 1879.64
Chinee Soje-Man 1900.43
Chinese Celebration 1914.34
Chinese Dragon Blues 1919.11
Chinese Fantasy 1920.18
Chinese Finale 1905.42
Chinese Honeymoon, A 1902.19
Chinese Honeymoon, The 1914.23
Chinese Idol, The 1926.23
Chinese Lantern Man 1925.04
Chinese Letter Song 1917.12
Chinese Love Song 1909.09
Chinese Melody 1946.16
Chinese Potentate 1925.04
Chinese Theatre, A 1910.11
Chinese-American Rag 1920.06
Ching a ring a ring 1881.04
Ching Chang 1889.39
Ching Ling Fong 1904.25
Ching-a-ring-a-ree! 1896.27
Ching-Aling-Fling 1920.20
Chingo-Pingo 1946.16
Chink of Gold 1866.11
Chink! Chink! 1900.20
Chink, Chink 1901.08
Chink-Chink, Chink-Chink, Chinyman 1909.27
Chinky China Charleston 1925.40
Chinky Chink 1922.26
Chinkypin 1949.16
Chinquapin Bush 1946.08
Chip Along 1908.21
Chipmunk and the Squirrel, The 1904.21
Chipper China Chaps 1914.23
Chique 1993.08, 1999.18
Chiquette 1924.13
Chiquita 1924.15
Chiquita Banana 1979.24
Chiquitin Trio 1941.02
Chiribim 1968.22
Chiromancy 1956.13
Chirp Chirp 1931.21
Chistu Succedi da Mill'anni 1985.16
Chivalry 1896.27
Chivor Dance 1948.24
Chloe 1918.05, 1931.11
Chloe, I'm Walkin' 1901.25
Chlorophyll Sally 1953.10
Cho'late Bar 1928.10
Choclo, El 1999.18
Choclo, La 1985.07
Chocolate Brown 1921.26
Chocolate Dandies 1924.27
Chocolate Soldier 1910.19
Chocolate Soldier, The 1909.22, 1921.40, 1947.06
Chocounne 1946.21
Choir Practice 1976.20
Cholly 1905.34
Chon Kina 1896.27, 1896.31
Chong 1946.21
Choo Choo Love 1926.12
Choo, Choo, Ch'boogie 1992.03
Choo-Choo Blues 1920.33
Choose a Partner, Please 1923.27
Choose Her in the Morning 1909.07
Choose Your Flowers 1926.30
Choose Your Partner 1951.17
Choosing a Husband's a Delicate Thing 1986.11
Chop Stick Rag 1912.02
Chop Sticks 1889.01, 1922.13
Chop Suey 1958.19
Chopin in E Minor 1975.02
Choral Russe 1946.04
Choro 1944.31
Chorus Girl's Longing, A 1905.35
Chorus Girl's Song, A 1924.35
Chorus of Collective Conscience, The 1958.12
Chorus of Foreigners 1894.38
Chorus of Masqueraders 1899.30
Chorus of Poets 1899.28
Chorus of Saturnalia 1899.39

Chorus of Welcome 1883.12, 1899.39, 1913.04, 1922.40
Chorus of Welcome to Gilfain 1920.09
Chorus of Zaitzeff Brothers, The 1922.06
Chorus Picking Time on Broadway 1926.29
Chosen One, The 1998.19
Chosun is Tangun's Land 1997.16
Chow Down 1997.20
Chow Mein Girls, The 1925.48
Christening Music 1937.11
Christening of a Little Black Coon, The 1898.22
Christening, The 1900.42, 1960.17
Christianity 1972.11
Christine 1960.10
Christine Swanson 1908.11
Christmas 1972.08, 1993.06
Christmas at Hampton Court 1976.08
Christmas Ball, The 1892.59
Christmas Bells 1885.06, 1888.05, 1996.09
Christmas Carol, A 1925.52
Christmas Child 1960.13
Christmas Day in the Cookhouse 1964.28
Christmas Eve Broadcast 1967.02
Christmas Fair Waltz 1903.31
Christmas Fairies 1880.42
Christmas in the Mountains 1998.02
Christmas is Comin' Uptown 1979.32
Christmas is Coming 1971.20
Christmas Night 1924.31
Christmas of All Nations, The 1905.48
Christmas Puppies 1978.11
Christmas Song, The 1998.19
Christmas Together 1994.12
Christmas Waltz, The 1974.10
Christmas-Baby Please Come Home 1985.03
Christmastide Love 1917.35
Christopher 1981.24
Christopher Columbus 1939.29, 1980.10, 1999.01, 2000.07
Christopher Street 1953.03
Christy Girl, The 1909.13
Chromolume #7 1984.08
Chrysanthemum Tea 1976.02
Chrystie Street Brigade, The 1898.56
Chu Chin Chow 1917.13
Chu-Chu-Cars 1906.10
Chuck It! 1926.50
Chunga, La 1949.07
Church Around the Corner, The 1929.04, 1948.16
Church Doors 1983.17
Church in the Dale 1943.10
Church of My Choice 1964.35
Church Parade, The 1905.27
Churning 1944.25
Churning, Churning 1929.43
Chuzi Mama Gwabi Gwabi 1966.03
Ciao, Ciao, Bambino 1987.02
Cicada, The 1988.15
Cider Song, The 1878.16, 1881.41
Cider, Sweet Cider 1876.29
Cigarette 1907.24, 1929.46, 1935.18
Cigarette Land 1924.01
Cigarette Song 1890.19, 1927.14
Cigarettes 1941.09, 1990.16, 1998.11
Cigarettes, Cigars 1931.19
Cigarettes, Les 1953.10
Cigarra, La 1988.15
Cincinnati 1999.22
Cinder Ella 1927.27
Cinderella 1879.38, 1906.35, 1912.48, 1916.20, 1927.09, 1928.14, 1992.10
Cinderella 's Ride 1926.32
Cinderella at the Shoe Store 1909.11
Cinderella Blues 1922.32
Cinderella Brown 1930.09
Cinderella Darling 1961.22
Cinderella Girl 1926.32
Cinderella Lost Her Slipper 1917.03
Cinderella Meets the Prince 1922.26
Cinderella on Broadway 1920.19
Cinderella Song 1894.24
Cinderella Waltz 1912.09
Cinderella Waltz, The 2001.09
Cinderella! You Have Won! 1905.27
Cinderella's Dream 1912.39
Cinders 1923.10
Cindy 1920.19, 1954.11
Cindy I Dreams of You 1900.47
Cinema Blues 1927.18
Cinema in Buenos Aires; July 26, 1952, A 1979.23
Cinema Lorelei 1931.14
Cinematograph 1909.07
Cingnalese Girls 1927.12
Cingoma Chakabaruka 1966.03
Circe, Circe 1954.03
Circle of Life 1997.20
Circle Stomp, The 1996.07
Circle Waltz, The 1981.12
Circle, The 1974.01, 1990.16
Circus Ballet, The 1919.15
Circus Band, The 1907.13
Circus Comes to Town 1919.21
Circus Days 1922.34, 1928.08, 1929.18
Circus in the Moon, The 1916.04
Circus is Coming to Town, The 1918.23
Circus is on Parade, The 1935.15
Circus is Over, The 1957.10
Circus McGurkus, The 2000.18
Circus on Tour, The 2000.18
Circus Queen, The 1908.12
Circus Time 1929.18
Circus Wedding, The 1935.15
Ciribiribin 1974.22
Cirque Francais 1954.15
Citation, The 1968.08
Cities I Love 1903.38
City Called Heaven 1930.10
City Called Heaven - Juba-lee 1952.08
City Chap, The 1925.38
City Grenadiers 1858.04
City Life 1969.03, 1971.20
City Lights 1977.16
City Mouse, Country House 1955.01
City of Angles 1959.14
City on Fire 1979.06
City Theme 1950.16
City, The 1968.07
Ciumachella 1964.03
Ciumachella De Trastevere 1964.03
Civic Song 1945.04
Civilization 1921.23, 1947.20
Civilized People 1961.26
Civilized People, The 1948.24
Clackety-Clack 1938.11
Claim Thou Thine Own 1902.18
Claire de la Lune, Le 1912.07
Clam, The 1973.08
Clam-Bake 1895.36
Clancy 1906.04
Clang Clang 1892.29
Clang Dang the Bell 1960.05
Clang of the Forge, The 1894.46
Clang of the Wooden Shoe 1880.51
Clap Hands 1910.11
Clap Yo' Hands 1926.36, 1990.14, 1999.10
Clap Your Hands 1942.18
Clara 1879.35, 1960.01
Clara Jenkins' Tea 1881.29, 1882.39, 1885.15
Clara Nolan's Ball 1887.23
Clara's Dancing School 1987.14
Clara, Clara 1983.04
Clara, Don't You be Downhearted 1935.13
Claremont 1907.57
Clarence 1976.27
Clarence Levere 1880.25
Clarey Grove Song 1961.11
Class 1902.35, 1975.14, 1991.15, 1993.05
Class Act 1983.21
Classical Blues 1930.09
Classiceccentrique 1913.17
Classifieds 1985.17
Claude Duval 1882.17
Claveles de Espana 1917.33
Clavelitos 1932.19
Clean Out the Corner 1930.21
Clean Platter, The 1973.08
Cleanin' Women 1978.12
Cleaning Up Song 1947.19
Clear Out of This World 1940.07
Clear the Way 1904.52
Clementina's Ditty 1892.07
Clementine 1908.25, 1913.23
Cleopatra 1918.05, 1925.44, 1948.16
Cleopatra had a Jazz Band 1975.09
Cleopatra's a Strawb'ry Blonde 1913.06
Cleopatra's Barge 1926.01
Cleopatra's Nile 1917.24, 1919.20
Cleopatra, We're Fond of You 1928.49
Cleopatterer 1917.17
Clever Detective, The 1914.09
Clever, These Chinese 1930.39
Click Clack goes the Mill! 1880.07
Climb Every Mountain 1959.24, 1998.03, 2000.14
Climb Up the Mountain 1950.20
Climb Up the Social Ladder 1933.25
Climb up, children climb 1894.44
Climb Up, Climb Up 1873.19
Climb Up, Climb Up! or the Mountain Guide 1878.04, 1878.12
Climbers, The 1901.12
Climbin' 1981.14
Climbing Over Rocky Mountain 1879.72, 1981.01
Climbing the Ladder of Love 1907.41, 1919.37
Climbing Up the Ladder of Love 1926.23, 1927.02
Climbing Up the Scale 1923.32
Clinching the Sale 1931.19
Cling a Little Closer 1915.17
Clinging Vine, The 1922.47
Clink Clank 1880.40
Clink! Clank! 1885.58, 1888.13
Clink, Clank 1896.35, 1896.41
Clink, Clink 1898.50
Clip, Clip the Coupons 1923.04
Clochard m'a dit, Un 1965.08
Cloches de corneville, Les 1926.45
Cloches, Les 1947.18, 1968.21
Clock is Striking Ten, The 1913.21
Clock of the Universe, The 1896.15
Clock Song 1908.42, 1920.23
Clock Will Never Strike Again the Hours That Have Passed, The 1896.02
Clockmaker's Song 1903.37
Clog and Grog 1966.27
Clog Dance 1902.29, 1966.30
Clog Dance, The 1986.03
Cloistered from the Noisy City 1933.25
Clorinda 1904.18, 1909.05, 1927.32
Close as Pages in a Book 1945.03
Close Every Door 1982.03, 1992.12, 1993.15
Close Harmony 1964.21
Close Harmony at Detroit 1927.23
Close in Your Arms 1927.45
Close Those Tired Eyes 1891.20
Close to Your Heart 1920.14
Close Upon the Hour 1978.22
Close Your Eyes 1913.21, 1927.36, 1942.11
Close, thou gentle sleep 1880.46
Closing Time 1982.04
Clothes 1921.11, 1978.11
Clothes Make the Soldier Man 1910.20
Clothesline on the Roof, The 1888.15
Cloud Nine 1997.21
Cloudburst 1976.34
Clouds of Love 1923.08
Clouds Roll By 1922.31
Cloudsong Dance 1996.12
Cloudy Morning 1958.12
Clown of London 1961.26
Clown, The 1951.19
Clowns 1897.20
Club Song 1928.49
Clubs and Cudgels 1884.57
Clutching at Shadows 1929.33
Co-Boss 1908.43
Coach has Come, The 1881.36
Coaching to Pelham 1876.07, 1876.09, 1876.10
Coachman's Heart, A 1922.26
Coachmen and Maids 1906.09
Coacoanut Sweet 1957.16

Coal Oil 1925.18
Coalhouse's Demands 1998.01
Coalhouse's Soliloquy 1998.01
Coalition 1985.15
Coat 'o Mine 1919.16
Coax Me 1957.17
Coaxing 1906.30
Coaxing Duet 1885.50
Cobbler and the Flies, The 1902.04
Cobbler's Ghost, The 1898.54
Cobbler's Song, The 1892.20, 1917.24, 1919.20
Cobbler, The 1891.15
Cobblers We 1899.21
Cobweb Man, The 1905.39
Cobweb Waltz Song, The 1892.55
Cobwebs on the Wall 1884.13
Cock Robin 1880.38
Cock-a-Doodle 1896.48
Cock-a-doodle-do 1883.04
Cock-a-Doodle-Doo 1923.31
Cockatoo and the Chimpanzee, The 1903.40
Cockeyed John 1975.05
Cockeyed John, Give Me My Dream 1975.05
Cockeyed Optimist, A 1949.04, 1984.06
Cocktail and a Cherry, A 1905.22
Cocktail Counterpoint 1983.11
Cocktail Hour 1921.07
Cocktail Melody 1926.03
Cocktail of Flowers, A 1918.12
Cocktail Song 1979.07
Cocktail, The 1937.16
Coco 1969.17
Coco-Cola Belle 1913.05
Cocoa Bean Song, The 1961.24
Cocoanut Ball, The 1923.47
Cocoanut Cream Pie 1984.02
Cocoanut Girl, The 1963.29
Coda 1984.01
Coda di Guido 1982.09
Code, The 1955.04
Coefficients of Expansion (a Guide to the Infant Season) 1973.08
Coeur de Ninon, Le 1908.29
Coffee and Cheese 1909.14
Coffee Beer and Whiskey 1982.13
Coffee Break 1961.22
Coffee in a Cardboard Cup 1971.07, 1989.16
Coffee Pot, The 1925.25
Coffee Song 1972.17
Coffee With the Meal 1973.08
Coffee, Black 1996.08
Cohan's Pet Names 1908.31
Cohan's Rag Babe 1908.14
Cohen Owes Me $97 1997.01
Cohen's Yiddisha Band 1912.24
Coin' Thro' the Dye 1892.19
Cois Teallaigh 1976.29
Cokey 1943.17
Cokey's Army 1894.21
Cold and Dead 1956.04
Cold Clear World 1965.02
Cold Comfort 1956.13
Cold Hard Cash 1983.17
Cold-Cream Jar Song 1954.15
Cole Scuttle Blues 1950.02
Colette 1975.12
Collar Cuffs 1886.06
Collection of Blue Notes, A 1909.28
Collective Beauty 1962.02
Colleen Bawn, The 1868.01
Colleen Machree 1915.03
College Boy's Dream, The 1907.44
College Boys 1911.34
College Chums 1906.30
College Days 1903.24, 1905.35, 1905.47, 1908.23, 1912.25, 1926.37
College Drill, The 1892.58
College Girls 1902.24
College is an institute of wonderful utility, A 1886.40
College Man, The 1898.48
College Medely 1909.03
College Military, The 1909.03
College of Hoop-Dee-Doo, The 1900.01
College Pals 1927.39
College Spirit 1919.39
Collegians, The 1925.40
Collegiate Vanitaeaser, The 1928.23
Colombia Calls 1948.24
Colonel and Major 1928.12
Colonel Buffalo Bill 1946.12, 1966.12
Colonel of the Crimson Hussars, The 1916.01
Colonel Peyton is my name 1886.40
Colonel's the Man for Me, The 1894.28
Colonel, The 1899.30
Colonial Chorus 1906.11
Color and Light 1984.08
Color Ballet, The 1925.25
Color Blind 1914.12, 1934.42
Color Line 1943.14
Color Mixing Scheme, The 1914.12
Color Wheel 2001.04
Color Wheel Too 2001.04
Colored Jubilee Singers 1877.05
Colored Lights 1984.01
Colored Spade 1968.11
Colorful 1964.32
Colors of My Life, The 1980.07
Colors of the King, The 1908.43
Colossa, La 1880.38
Colour 1925.50
Columbia 1866.16, 1867.18, 1899.19, 1906.31
Columbia March, The 1892.09
Columbia Won the Race To-day 1881.11
Columbia's Colleen 1905.37
Columbine 1904.18
Columbines' Courtship 1909.11
Columbus and Isabella 1927.19
Columbus Family, The 1894.17
Columbus March 1917.16
Columbus was a Famous Man 1894.38
Columbus Wouldn't Know Columbus Circle as it is To-Day, 1922.08
Comb it genteely 1863.04
Combat 1937.11
Combat Chorus 1899.21
Combat, The 1965.34
Come 1993.09
Come a Little Closer 1971.19
Come Across 1915.05, 1920.21
Come After Breakfast, Bring 'Long Your lunch and Leave 'Fore Supper Time 1911.20
Come again tomorrow night 1864.12
Come All Ye True Bred Irishmen 1897.03
Come Along 1899.30, 1920.18, 1922.19, 1923.20, 1958.04
Come Along Boys 1954.03
Come Along in, the Water's Fine 1907.18
Come Along Little Girls 1916.22
Come Along Mandy 1910.18
Come Along Pretty Girl 1910.03
Come Along to the Ball 1933.23, 1954.06
Come Along to the Carnival 1920.10
Come Along to the Movies 1913.19
Come Along to the Zoo 1907.15
Come Along to Toytown 1918.23
Come Along With Alice 1924.44
Come Along With Me 1953.07
Come Along, Come Along, Come Along 1918.21
Come Along, it's a Trifling Affair 1908.16
Come Along, Little Girl 1918.17
Come Along, Little Girl, Come Along 1914.13
Come Along, Ma Cherie 1911.23
Come Along, My Boys 1906.30
Come Along, My Darlin' 1885.53, 1886.44
Come Along, My Mandy 1910.01, 1930.13
Come along, old fellow 1889.54
Come Along, Pretty Eliza 1906.25
Come Along, Sunshine 1928.28
Come and be Jolly in a moderate way 1869.07
Come and be My Butterfly 1964.01
Come and Bring Your Instruments 1946.22
Come and Cuddle Me 1916.04
Come and Dance With Me 1911.43
Come and Float Me, Freddie Dear 1907.24
Come and Fuss With Me 1916.07
Come and Get Cozy With Me 1955.11
Come and Get These Memories 1984.15
Come and Have a Smile With Me 1907.27
Come and have some luncheon 1879.35
Come and listen now to what I have to say 1886.40
Come and See Our Island 1900.51, 1902.05, 1920.09
Come and Take a Dip in the Sea With Me 1910.16
Come and Take Your Places All 1893.02
Come and Watch the Moon With Me 1913.33
Come at the Call of Love 1926.27
Come away! 1866.11
Come Away, Elves 1866.06
Come Back Sweetheart 1894.27
Come Back to Bohemia 1910.25
Come Back to Erin 1913.07
Come Back to Manistee 1902.44
Come back to me 1882.63
Come Back to Me 1911.43, 1912.09, 1965.31, 1974.01, 1999.23
Come Back to the Old Cabaret 1914.07
Come Back With the Same Look in Your Eyes 1985.12
Come Back, Little Genie 1951.15
Come Back, My Honey Boy, to Me 1900.38
Come Back, Sweet Dreams 1916.14
Come be My Wife 1919.01
Come Boys 1924.45
Come Boys, Let's All be Gay, Boys 1980.21
Come Bustle Lads, about 1852.02
Come Bustle, Little Elves 1861.03
Come Buy My Flowers 1873.19
Come Buy Our Luscious Fruit 1903.04
Come buy, come buy 1880.46
Come Celebrate Our Reforms 1997.16, 1998.08
Come Dance Anyway 1934.32
Come Dance With Me 1918.18, 1980.09
Come day, go day 1873.04
Come Down from the Big Fig Tree 1905.10
Come Down Mister Man in the Moon 1902.15
Come Down Mr. Man in the Moon 1905.35
Come Down My Honey Do 1896.06
Come Down Salomy Jane 1907.24
Come Down to Earth 1910.19
Come Down, Ma Evening Star 1905.42
Come Down, Mrs. Flynn 1891.32
Come Down, My Evenin' Star 1902.29
Come Draw Nigh 1892.20
Come Dream so Bright 1891.29
Come Dreams so Bright 1929.43
Come Drink a Toast to Man and Wife 1905.46
Come Fetch Your Baby Home 1900.38
Come fill every flagon 1864.12
Come fill the Bowl with Sparkling Wine 1866.14
Come Fly With Me 1974.10, 1974.11
Come Follow the Band 1980.07, 1981.08
Come Go, Let's Leave 1870.27
Come Help Yourself to America 1980.17
Come here, Mam'selle 1859.13
Come Hit Your Baby 1929.28
Come hither scholars all! 1878.20
Come hither, every one 1895.29
Come Hither, Eyes 1913.34
Come Home 1947.17, 1993.19
Come in My Mouth 1976.20
Come in to the Tavern 1968.22
Come into the Garden, Maud 1869.47, 1880.42
Come Jolly Bacchus, or Charles of Sweden 1924.20
Come Josephine 1944.32
Come Little Chic 1903.24
Come Little Fishes 1911.38
Come Little Girl, and Tell Me Truly 1902.35
Come Live in My Heart and Pay No Rent 1885.53
Come Live With Me and be My Love 1981.02
Come Look at the Freaks 1997.17
Come Love, Go Love 1900.12
Come mighty Must! 1884.09
Come Miss, Stir Your Stumps 1848.03
Come my dearest 1897.17
Come My Lad and be a Soldier 1918.10
Come My Sweetheart 1912.47
Come On 1923.24
Come on Along 1925.16, 1992.10
Come on and Dance With Me 1919.35
Come on and Kiss Me 1920.17
Come on and Marry Me Honey 1969.04, 1980.01

Come on and Play 1925.01
Come on Children, Let's Sing 1990.05
Come on Down 1976.35, 1980.14, 1982.17
Come on Down to Ragtime Town 1916.15
Come on Down Town 1908.14
Come on Feet do Your Thing 1971.13
Come on Home 1927.30
Come on In 1939.30
Come on in My Kitchen 1999.09
Come on in, the Dancing's Fine 1914.01
Come on in, the Water's Fine 1915.17
Come on Let's Make Whoopee 1928.27
Come on Over Here 1909.05, 1912.37, 1913.20, 1913.20
Come on Possums, Wave Your Gladiola 1999.14
Come on, Baby 1974.11
Come on, Come On 1894.10
Come on, Feet, Let's Go 1924.10
Come on, Let's Step, Step Around 1923.24
Come on, Let's Two Step 1907.14
Come on, Li'l Augie 1946.08
Come on, Play Ball With Me, Dearie 1909.13
Come on, the Music is Fine 1908.13
Come One and All 1905.46
Come One, Come All, and See the Sights 1900.38
Come Out in the Moonlight 1907.58
Come Out of the Kitchen 1917.01
Come Out, Come Out 1997.11
Come Over Eyes 1924.25
Come Over to Deauville 1926.15
Come Play With Me I Have Such a Nice Little Way With Me 1896.31
Come Play Wiz Me 1964.15
Come Rain or Come Shine 1946.08, 1990.09, 1997.05
Come Raising Your Let on Me 1971.13
Come Seven, Come Eleven 1898.12
Come Sir, Will You Join Our Noble Saxon Corps 1980.21
Come Spirit, Come Charm 1991.05
Come Sta 1964.35
Come Summer 1969.07
Come Sunday 1989.02
Come sweet lass 1854.06
Come Sweet Lass 1957.02
Come Take a Dance With Me 1912.31
Come Take a Skate With Me 1906.20
Come Take a Trip in My Airship 1980.27
Come the Bowmen in Lincoln Green 1929.43, 1944.25
Come the Dinner's Waiting 1859.05
Come the Gallants of the Court 1899.28
Come to Africa 1927.33
Come to Arcady 1920.43
Come to Bohemia 1916.07, 1920.28
Come to Colombia 1948.24
Come to Florence 1945.04
Come to Gypsy Land 1917.19
Come to Harlem 1932.12
Come to Lower Falls 1927.29
Come to Me 1961.18, 1987.04
Come to Me Quickly, My Darling 1888.13
Come to Me, Bend to Me 1947.07, 1980.26, 1986.03
Come to Me, My Own 1894.37
Come to me, Sing to me 1894.03
Come to Mee-ow 1957.05
Come to My Garden 1991.05
Come to My Party 1924.38
Come to Paris 1914.12, 1945.04
Come to St. George's 1906.47, 1920.09
Come to St. Thomas's 1928.31
Come to Sunny Spain 1911.38
Come to the Aid of the Party 1934.18
Come to the Ball 1870.27, 1911.39
Come to the Fair 1932.14
Come to the Garden, Maud 1952.11
Come to the Green Wood 1887.05
Come to the heart that is thine 1878.02
Come to the Heart That is Thine 1896.35
Come to the Land of Romance 1918.23
Come to the Sacrifice 1944.16
Come to the Supermarket in Old Peking 1984.10, 1995.12
Come to Trouville 1911.45
Come to Us 1984.14
Come Together 1974.24, 1977.10
Come tous les matins a la confiserie 1884.43
Come Under My Plaidee 1895.41
Come Unto These Yellow Sands 1981.02
Come Up and Have a Cup of Coffee 1943.05
Come Up to My Place 1944.33, 1958.21, 1971.15, 1998.16
Come West, Little Girl, Come West 1928.47, 1979.05
Come What May 1985.20
Come Where My Love Lies Dreaming 1939.21
Come Where Nature Calls 1918.37
Come With Me 1917.25, 1938.14, 1944.16, 1944.18, 1975.13
Come With Me to My Bungalow 1911.33
Come With Me to Paree 1915.22
Come with the gipsy bride 1844.01
Come With the Gypsy Bride 1934.17
Come With Us 1890.12, 1902.29
Come With Welcome 1919.42
Come You Men 1966.09
Come! Shop There! 1890.33
Come, all ye maidens 1893.02
Come, Boys, Come 1897.03
Come, Cavalier 1898.25
Come, Come 1912.36
Come, Come Ye Saints 1955.13
Come, Come, Kerouac! My Generation is Beater Than Yours 1973.08
Come, dear, we will chase 1881.25
Come, dearest Girl 1886.50
Come, farmer small 1878.16
Come, Fill Up a Brimming Flagon 1904.30
Come, Gentle Stranger 1900.34
Come, Hurry Up! 1895.25
Come, Kind Gentlemen 1904.03
Come, Lairds o' the Highland 1894.40
Come, let's all be merry! 1880.07
Come, Little Dearie 1907.39
Come, My Dear 1906.18
Come, My Dear Love 1905.25
Come, My Pretty Maiden 1881.11
Come, Now, My Beauty 1881.22
Come, O Come 1948.14
Come, Oh, Come 1972.05
Come, sweet Lass 1750.01
Come, the Dinner's Waiting 1861.03
Come, the Night Descends 1922.03
Come, Tiny Goldfish to Me 1910.21
Come, Toddle Along 1909.18
Come, Ye Heroes All 1906.18
Come, Youth and Beauty 1892.42
Come-A-Wandering With Me 1961.27
Come-on-a-Good-Life 1972.02
Comediens, Les 1965.30, 1970.01, 1974.19, 1983.03
Comedy Fantasy, A 1924.38
Comedy Tom 1917.22
Comedy Tonight 1962.12, 1977.05, 1989.03
Comedy vs. Tragedy 1890.30
Comes a Birdie Flying 1885.45
Comes a Feeling 1912.37
Comes a train of little ladies 1885.47
Comes a Train of Little Ladies 1939.17
Comes an Exquisite Sensation 1913.37
Comes Love 1939.24
Comes Once in a Lifetime 1961.28
Comes the broken flower 1875.35
Comes the pretty young bride 1888.35
Comes the Revolution 1933.25
Comic Camouflage, A 1918.02
Comic Nursery Rhymes 1876.10
Comic Opera 1900.38
Comic Opera Bandits, The 1902.20
Comic Opera Capsule, A 1905.53
Comical Ditty 1891.32
Comin' Through the Rye 1921.17
Comin' Thru the Rye 1927.01
Coming Home from Meeting 1884.13
Coming Out of the Garden 1928.34
Coming Thro' the Rye 1896.45
Coming Through the Rye 1871.16
Coming Together, Going Together 1971.04, 1976.27
Coming-Out Party Dance, The 1987.19
Comm' tout's les femmes, je suis coquette 1883.51
Command to Love 1928.19, 1934.18
Commanderess-in-Chief, The 1904.54
Comme c'est facile 1926.49
Comme elle danse 1926.49
Comme Il Faut 1997.13
Comme j'aimerais mon mari 1929.16
Comme la fleur qui brille 1884.43
Comme nous passions sur la place 1884.43
Comme Si, Comme Ca 1921.09, 1929.02
Comme une femme 1934.32
Committee 1958.10
Commodore is fast asleep, The 1886.50
Commodore's to mate his daughter, The 1886.50
Common Sense 1946.23
Commuters' Song, The 1948.22
Como la Flor 1926.35
Como le Gusta Me? 1904.22
Compact 1887.33
Compact, The 1879.15, 1914.27
Companions for Me, The 1885.42
Companions of the Bride 1905.44
Companions, I Have Summoned You 1913.32
Company 1970.13, 1977.05
Company Madness 1927.10
Company Promoter this, A 1894.15
Company Way, The 1961.22
Complainte de la Butte, La 1958.06
Complicated Man 1983.18
Compliments 1913.26
Composers' Song, The 1974.09
Composing 1911.46
Comprenez-vous? 1896.44
Compromise 1970.12
Comrad Alonzo 1938.13
Comrade Your Hand 1934.17
Comrade, You Have a Chance Here 1925.06
Comrade, your hands 1844.01
Comrades 1890.29, 1891.26, 1892.05
Comrades and Friends 1846.01
Comrades be Silent 1846.01
Comrades this pledge behold 1846.01
Concarne for Me 1905.52
Concarne Vivandieres, The 1905.52
Concentrate 1923.07
Concentrate a Little on Love 1933.27
Concerning the Insecurity of the Human State 1976.10
Concert, The 1973.06
Concerted Number 1934.17
Concertina 1910.17
Conchita 1923.31, 1932.07
Concrete Shoes 1982.22
Conductor is in Love, The 1959.15, 1961.25
Conductor's Comicalities 1882.76
Coney Island 1930.08, 1931.08
Coney Island Ballet 1942.01
Coney Island Boat 1954.02
Coney Island Hep Cats 1971.15
Coney Island, U.S.A. 1964.44
Coney-by-the-Sea 1937.02, 1946.19
Confession 1931.16, 1972.05
Confession, The 1906.48
Confessional 1975.06
Confessional, The 1970.10
Confidence 1912.01, 1912.16
Confidential 1899.39
Confidential family solicitor 1882.63
Confidential Source 1911.27
Confiding Woman 1897.17
Confirmation 1927.48
Confrontation 1993.17, 1997.09
Confrontation, The 1991.03
Confusion 1975.19
Conga! 1953.03
Congai 1931.39
Congo Love Song 1920.04
Congratulations 1926.33
Congratulations to the Bride and Groom 1990.16
Congress Shall Make No Law 1940.21
Conjuration 1931.06
Conjuror's Forgiven 1975.19
Connemara Christening 1904.44
Connemora Christening 1903.03, 1904.13

Connubial Bliss 1914.27
Connubiality 1962.14
Conondrums 1897.39
Conquering New York 1953.03
Conscience of a Nation, The 1975.07
Consciousness of Innocence, The 1904.55
Consecutive Fifths 1968.19
Conseil de familie ici se reunit, Le 1886.09
Consequences 1904.03, 1910.25
Consider the Rain 1949.16
Consolation 1906.08, 1927.63
Consolation Time 1911.20
Conspiracy Scene, The 1881.25
Conspiracy, The 1905.54
Conspirators 1903.36, 1906.15
Conspirators are We 1905.53
Conspirators Three 1880.10
Conspirators' Chorus 1902.21
Conspirators, The 1903.36, 1937.09
Constancy 1892.45, 1912.03, 1917.18
Constant Lover 1915.26
Constant Lunchers, Constant Diners, Constant Dancers, Constant Kissers 1915.29
Constantinople 1914.14, 1974.06, 1982.20
Constantly 1910.18
Contact 1996.09
Contantly 1910.18
Contenta, La 1886.53
Contented Caterpillar, The 1905.20
Contentment I give you 1887.44
Contest, The 1914.03, 1976.01, 1979.06, 1985.17
Continental Honeymoon 1934.42
Continental, The 1983.09
Contini Submits 1982.09
Continong, The 1879.50, 1898.38
Continuous Performances 1899.40
Contraband Ball, The 1963.22
Contract, The 1973.12
Contrary Mary 1903.17, 1922.29
Contre l'amour y'a rien a faire 1963.02
Contredanse 1933.24
Contribution Box 1907.55
Conundrums 1906.18
Convent Bell, The 1898.46
Convent Bells are Ringing 1925.39
Convent Slept, The 1880.69
Convent Song 1896.28
Convention 1960.12
Convention Bound 1952.09
Conversation Dance 1898.02, 1900.08, 1902.02
Conversation of Strider and the Herd 1979.29
Conversation Piece 1953.03, 1977.05
Conversation Song and Dance 1902.33
Conversation Step, The 1921.32
Conversational Song 1905.22
Conversations 1996.07
Convivial Girl, The 1904.23
Convivial Man 1896.02
Coo Song 1885.08
Coo! 1902.30
Coo-Coo Song 1921.34
Coo-ee 1909.07
Coo-Ee-Doo 1922.14
Coo-oo Coo-oo 1910.03
Cooe-Cooe-Coo 1903.29
Cook and the Bobby, The 1892.19
Cook'd 1884.14
Cookie Chase, The 1964.15
Cookie Cutters 1982.10
Cookin' With Steam 1988.07
Cooking School, The 1889.34
Cool 1957.12, 1966.03
Cool 'Em Off 1926.23, 1927.02
Cool Blues 1974.11
Cool Combo Mambo 1957.14
Cool Credo 1957.14
Cool Off 1928.38
Cool, Cool, Considerate Men 1969.06
Coola Woola 1909.10
Coolest Place in Town, The 1971.13
Coon College 1907.44
Coon Will Follow a Band, A 1903.26
Coon With the Big White Spot, The 1906.05
Coon, the Moon and Octoroon, The 1904.04
Cooney County Fair, The 1922.46
Cooney Spooney Dance, The 1909.28
Coonjine 1905.20, 1940.01
Coonland 1905.22
Coontown Musketeers, The 1894.10
Coontown Quartette 1912.02
Cootch Poor Waunee 1885.06
Copenhagen 1860.05, 1982.12
Copete 1993.08
Coppelia 1929.51
Copper Colored Gal of Mine 1981.16
Copperfield 1981.12
Copulation Round 1965.39
Coquette 1949.18, 1974.02
Coqui, El 1998.02
Coquin du Printemps 1906.36
Cora Angelique 1897.39
Cora Won't You Tell Me That You Love Me Too? 1899.36
Coral Isle 1912.05
Cordalia Malone 1904.15
Corday Waltz, The 1965.39
Cordelia 1904.08
Corduroy Road 1960.22
Corn Beef Hashed 1881.27
Corn on the Macabre 1972.21
Corn Shucking Time 1911.20
Corn Song 1908.08
Corn-Huskers, The 1975.19
Cornelius 1968.21
Corner in My Heart 1918.17
Corner of My Mind 1924.22
Corner of the Sky 1972.22
Cornet Man 1964.11
Coro dei Soldati 1985.14
Coronation 1975.06
Coronation Chorale 1963.29
Coronation March 1891.11, 1904.17
Coronation of the Queen 1929.08
Coronation Rehearsal 1919.04
Coronation, The 1910.25, 1926.34
Corporal Mulcahey 1886.35
Corps de Ballet 1993.19
Corraline 1917.24, 1919.20
Correct 1910.21
Correspondence 1910.04, 1913.36
Correspondence School 1907.30
Correspondence School, The 1912.41
Corrida, La 1966.20
Corrido de Cananea 1988.15
Corsaire I 1977.09
Corsaire II 1977.09
Corsairs Bold 1887.43
Corsica 1907.59
Corsican, The 1912.17
Cortege for a Nobleman 1952.04
Coryphee, The 1911.36
Cosaque, un peu braque, La 1886.09
Cossack Love Song, The 1925.52
Cossack Song, The 1924.48
Costa Polka 1866.18
Coster's 'Oliday, The 1903.23
Cotillion 1921.33
Cotillion, The 1912.09, 1961.07
Cottage for Sale 1991.04
Cottage in the Country 1930.08, 1930.15, 1931.08
Cotton Blossom 1927.67, 1946.01, 1966.14, 1983.05, 1994.08
Cotton Blossom Time 1915.23
Cotton Cloth Ghost, A 1881.11
Cotton Club Stomp 1980.10, 1986.02
Cotton Tail 1981.06
Cotton Time 1924.46
Couches dans le foin 1935.19
Coucous! coucous! 1877.32
Could Be 1952.10
Could I 1894.10
Could I But Tell You 1902.19
Could I ever be false? 1881.25
Could I Fascinate You? 1906.23
Could I Forget 1927.45
Could I Leave You? 1971.05, 1977.05, 1999.20
Could it be Magic 1976.34
Could it be You? 1943.01
Could That Be? 1947.10
Could We Start Again, Please 1971.12
Could You Get Along With Me? 1924.32
Could You Love a Girl Like Me? 1912.13
Could You Love Me? 1907.52
Could You Teach Me? 1919.19
Could You Use Me 1930.31
Could You Use Me? 1992.02
Could'st Thou But Know 1894.24
Could've Been a Ring 1960.05
Couldn't be More in Love 1946.06
Couldn't Keep it to Myself 1982.17
Council Wise are coming here, The 1877.23
Count Me Out 1889.24
Count of Luxembourg, The 1912.33
Count Your Blessings 1944.02, 1948.22
Count Your Money 1923.11
Countdown 1979.13
Counterfeit Deacon, The 1880.37
Countermelody 1960.07
Countess Cathleen, The 2000.05
Countess Dubinsky 1934.01
Countin' Our Chickens 1959.27
Counting the Hours 1924.31
Country Belles 1903.16
Country Club, The 1902.08
Country Gentleman, A 1959.12
Country House 1999.20
Country Lass and a Courtly Dame, A 1908.06
Country Picnic in a Distant Province of Russia, A 1925.03
Country Quadrille 1902.08
Country Store Living 1971.01
Country Suite 1979.10
Country Wife, A 1921.08
Country's in the Very Best of Hands, The 1956.12
Couple of Senseless Censors, A 1924.44
Couplets de charme 1880.58
Couplets-Valse et la Peruvienne 1929.16
Courage 1989.06
Courage Makes a Man 1993.17
Course I Will 1923.05
Course of Nature, The 1938.06
Course of True Love, The 1901.09, 1904.40, 1910.20, 1912.15
Court is Called to Order, The 1906.48
Court is Like a Chessboard, A 1905.48
Court of Louis XIV, The 1933.15
Courting in the Moonlight 1881.11
Courting, The 1961.14
Courtship 1898.73
Courtship de Dance 1915.01
Cousin Kevin 1972.08, 1993.06
Cousins of the Czar 1912.33
Coutiers are ever bowing 1870.20
Cove in Hove 1956.13
Covenant, The 1970.19
Covered Wagon Days 1923.23
Cow and a Plough and a Frau, A 1950.04
Cow Jumped Over the Moon, The 1971.20
Cow's Divertissement 1930.36
Cowboy Potentate 1927.45
Cowboy Song 1936.28, 1979.07
Cowshed Rhapsody 1936.22
Coy Young Maid, A 1905.47
Cozey Corner 1915.20
Cozy Corner 1919.16
Crabbed Age and Youth 1981.02
Crack of the Whip 1904.20
Cradle Duet 1885.50
Cradle of Jazz, The 1948.19
Cradle of the Deep 1926.51
Cradle Will Rock, The 1937.08
Cradled in Thy Arms 1910.36
Cradled upon the heather 1884.14
Cranberry Pickin' 1929.33
Cranes 1982.23
Crap Game Dance, The 1950.17
Crap Game Fugue 1942.03
Crappy Dan De Spo'tin Man 1896.52
Crashing the Golden Gates 1929.26

Crashing Thru 1939.26
Crawlin' King Snake 1999.09
Crazy as a Loon 1940.07
Crazy Elbows 1928.16
Crazy Idea of Love 1932.12
Crazy Night Ballet 1967.16
Crazy Over You 1915.17
Crazy Quilt 1919.16, 1931.13
Crazy Quilt Sextette, The 1931.13
Crazy Rhythm 1928.17
Crazy Strut 1931.32
Crazy Walk 1929.52
Crazy With the Heat 1941.03
Crazy World 1988.07, 1995.15
Crazy, Deaf and Blind 1997.17
Crazyisms 1906.15
Cream of English Youth, The 1970.06
Cream of Mush 1937.14
Cream of the Sky 1907.63
Creation 1920.18
Creation of Man, The 1997.19, 1999.13
Creation, The 1955.13, 1969.10
Credit's Due to Me, The 1900.51, 1902.05
Creditors' Chorus, The 1899.19
Credo 1943.10, 1967.16
Creep, Creep, the World's Asleep 1916.17
Creole Belles 1922.22
Creole Cooning Song 1926.07
Creole Crawl 1927.03
Creole Days 1909.07
Creole Gal 1921.26
Creole Love Call 1980.10, 1999.05
Creole Way, The 1992.08
Crescent Moon 1929.04
Cretonne Girl 1923.21
Crevettes, Les 1929.10
Criada, La 1895.26
Cricket on the Hearth 1887.23, 1889.12, 1913.24
Cricket, The 1890.16
Crickets are Calling, The 1917.17
Cries of London, The 1963.28
Crime 1926.39
Crime of the Century, The 1998.01
Criminal Cried, The 1885.47, 1939.15
Crinoline Days 1922.39
Crinoline Girl 1920.30
Crinoline Girl, The 1914.16
Cripple Creek Bandits, The 1896.18
Crisp Young Chaperone 1891.39, 1894.07, 1894.35
Crispino E. Comare 1922.29
Critic's Blues, The 1919.18
Crocodile Wife 1965.32
Crocodile, The 1904.40
Cronies o' Mine 1930.17
Crooked Path, The 1989.26
Croon Spoon 1937.08
Crooning 1922.22
Croquet Game, The 1907.39
Cross on Over 1972.25
Cross Road Blues 1999.09
Cross the Line 1996.08
Cross the River from Queens 1927.05
Cross Word Puzzles 1929.09
Cross Your Fingers 1929.44
Cross Your Heart 1907.14, 1926.25
Crossing 1991.01
Crossing on the Ferry 1869.42
Crossing Over 1985.06
Crossing the Border 1973.08
Crosstown 1983.21
Crotolos, Los 1917.25
Croupier 1938.04
Crow, The 1968.30, 1983.14
Cruche Casse, La 1892.45
Crucifijo de Piedra, El 1988.15
Crucifix of Stone, The 1988.15
Crucifixion 1953.12, 1969.10
Crucixion, The 1971.12
Cruel Chief 1926.33
Cruel fate why thus p ursuing 1862.09
Cruel Love 1900.16
Cruelty Man, The 1970.10
Cruelty Stomp, The 1989.09
Cruelty to Johnny 1871.16
Cruise of the Boozemobile, The 1912.05
Cruising Home 1905.53
Cruiskeen Lawn 1860.05
Cruiskeen Lawn, The 1899.03
Crunchy Granola Suite 1978.05, 1999.01
Crutch and Toothpick 1879.50
Cry Baby 1923.19, 1923.42, 1982.22
Cry Baby in Town 1911.20
Cry for Us All 1970.10
Cry from the Dungeon 1933.07
Cry Holy 1958.12
Cry Like a Baby 1989.02
Cry Like the Wind 1960.23
Cry Loud 1987.17
Cry Me a River 1999.24
Cry, Baby 1950.02
Cry, Baby, Cry 1889.05
Cry, the Beloved Country 1949.15, 1972.06
Crying because I am so (hic) happy 1885.45
Crying Jane 1916.02
Crying Quartette 1888.05
Crystal Ball, The 1911.44
Crystal Lute, The 1913.06
Crystal Wedding Day 1924.33
Csardas 1954.06
Cuba Girls 1899.31
Cuban Love Song 1979.25
Cuban Slave Lament 1943.17, 1944.31
Cuban Song 1897.42
Cubana 1940.16
Cuckoo 1898.25, 1919.08
Cuckoo Bird, The 1901.13
Cuckoo Club, The 1892.06
Cuckoo Song, The 1880.39
Cuckoo Town 1919.34
Cuckoo, cuckoo goes the clock 1871.10
Cuckoo-Cheena, The 1947.13
Cuddle Me Up 1924.05
Cuddle Up 1923.02, 1926.11, 1946.14, 1947.12
Cuddle Up a Little Closer, Lovey Mine 1908.18
Cuddle Up and Cling to Me 2000.12
Cuddle Up Together 1922.04
Cuddle-Uddle, The 1920.02
Cuesta Abajo 1985.07
Cultural Pursuits 1983.17
Culture Drill 1905.35
Cumparcita, La 1983.09
Cumparista, La 1997.13
Cumparsita, La 1985.07, 1993.08, 1999.18
Cunnilingus Champion of Co. C, The 1976.20
Cup o' Tea, A 1960.17
Cup of China Tea, A 1946.16
Cup of Coffee, a Sandwich and You, A 1925.42
Cup of Tea 1902.21
Cup of Tea, A 1896.50, 1905.19, 1908.16, 1916.01, 1920.31, 1950.01
Cupid 1891.32, 1894.31, 1907.04, 1919.08, 1922.47
Cupid - Sly Little Rascal 1908.30
Cupid and I 1897.13, 1930.12
Cupid and You and I 1907.47
Cupid at the Plaza 1915.07
Cupid Caught Me 1888.38
Cupid has Found My Heart 1904.10
Cupid is a Cruel Master 1912.10, 1912.49
Cupid is King 1895.12
Cupid is the Captain 1902.16
Cupid is the Captain of the Army 1905.27
Cupid Keeps the Love Light Burning 1914.25
Cupid Reigns King 1904.47
Cupid the Conqueror 1911.27
Cupid was an Indian Pickaninny 1909.10
Cupid Will Guide 1899.40
Cupid's Auction Sale 1906.37
Cupid's Biology Book 1956.09
Cupid's Car 1912.35
Cupid's College 1927.20
Cupid's Cure 1904.05
Cupid's Dart 1888.11, 1913.17
Cupid's Fancies 1904.11
Cupid's Flirtation 1912.04
Cupid's Garden 1904.34
Cupid's Gay Bouquet 1907.33
Cupid's Grammar 1905.36
Cupid's Hour 1912.04
Cupid's March 1909.19
Cupid's Mischief 1871.27
Cupid's Mistake 1905.49
Cupid's Private Code 1907.13
Cupid's Ramble 1903.07
Cupid's Rifle Range 1906.25
Cupid's Telephone 1909.04
Cupid's Wedding Bells 1907.62
Cupid's Wireless Telegraph 1910.04
Cupid, Tell Me Why 1911.36
Cupids a Lad 1904.36
Cure for Love, A 1901.27
Cure of Love 1914.07
Cure or Kill 1901.27
Cure, The 1910.37, 1959.27
Cured 1909.17
Curfew Bell has Sounded, The 1911.47
Curfew Shall Not Ring To-Night 1927.09
Curfew Walk, The 1927.19
Curiosity 1921.32, 1924.24, 1980.30
Curiouser and Curiouser 1979.18
Current Events 1978.11
Currier and Ives 1945.03
Curse attends that Woman's Love, A 1750.01
Curse of Cinderella, The 1925.47
Curt, Clear and Concise 1963.29
Cushite Dancde 1929.01
Cushla Agus Machree 1865.06
Custer's Last Charge 1931.02
Custom of Dressing for Dinner, The 1942.30
Custom-Made Maids 1920.37
Customer from Kay's 1903.33
Customer's Always Right, The 1942.11, 1961.18
Cut High, Cut Low 1899.38
Cut In 1930.35
Cut of the Cards 1988.20
Cute Little Beau Called Anna, The 1915.25
Cute Soldier Boy 1918.09
Cutest Little House 1919.41
Cutie 1914.02, 1922.02
Cuttin' a Rug 1941.08
Cynical Owl, The 1909.11
Cynthia Jane 1903.16
Cyrano's Nose 1973.07
Cyrano's Story 1993.17
Czar of the Tenderloin, The 1898.22
Czar, The 1903.08
Czardas 1898.60, 1906.49, 1913.27, 1945.11
Czardos 1885.65

D'Amour 1907.52
D'amour en amour 1934.32
D'Arcy's Aria 2000.01
D'Jakh and D'Jill 1880.47
D'Jakh and I 1880.47
D'ou te vient ce projet morose 1884.43
D'ou vient un pareil tapage 1887.35
D'Une Coquete 1908.16
D. S. O. 1921.12
D.W. Washburn 1995.03
Da Doo Ron Ron 1982.22, 1985.03
Da Doo Run Run 1973.14, 1984.15
Da Nyet, Da Nyet! 1953.10
Da, Da, Daddy Dear 1922.24
Dachau 1940.04
Dad 1985.17
Dad Gum Your Hide Boy 1992.03
Daddy 1919.32, 1979.24
Daddy Buy Me a Bow Wow 1921.25
Daddy Long Legs 1926.01
Daddy was a Railroad Man 1983.20
Daddy Will Not Walking Through the Door 1984.02
Daddy Won't You Please Come Home 1921.16, 1978.21
Daddy Wouldn't Buy Me a Bowwow 1893.11
Daddy, Daddy 1972.07
Daddy, Uncle and Me 1956.02
Daddy, You've Been a Mother to Me 1986.06
Daffodil Time 1909.29
Daffodil, The 1921.34, 1924.04
Daffy 1912.42

Daffy Down Dilly 1903.09
Daggone 1928.34
Dago, de Org' and de Monk, De 1901.25
Dago, The 1900.07
Daily Dozen 1928.41
Daily Dozen, The 1924.47
Daintily Lightly 1908.16
Dainty Dragon Fly 1905.10
Dainty Housemaids We 1906.13
Dainty Little French Maids 1898.44
Dainty Little Girl Like You 1919.19
Dainty Little Ingenue 1904.52
Dainty Little Maid, The 1906.39
Dainty Little Milliner, The 1904.55
Dainty Mignon 1906.10
Dainty Milliners, The 1906.20
Dainty Music Maid, The 1906.30
Dainty Nosegay, A 1924.09
Dainty Saintly Erica 1897.01
Dainty Wisp of a Thistledown 1928.29
Daisy 1917.01
Daisy and the Lark, The 1920.25
Daisy Bell 1892.45, 1979.07
Daisy Chain 1906.30
Daisy Days 1921.25
Daisy Dean 1904.21
Daisy Tell Me Truly 1922.13
Dakota Dick 1899.41
Damages 1965.28
Dame Pique, La 1924.48
Dames 1980.20
Damn Clever, These Chinese 1924.13
Damn it, Janet 2000.17
Damn You, Colonel Tom! 1950.16
Damn-Alot 1961.16
Damned for All Time 1971.12
Damned No Matter How He Turned 1975.07
Damned Ole Jeeter 1943.16
Damsel Who Done All the Dirt, The 1926.07
Damsel, Damsel, Prithee Come Crusading With Me 1916.06
Dan 1906.43
Dan, My Darlin' Dan 1904.46
Dance 1923.32, 1926.07, 1987.14
Dance a Cachucha 1890.02
Dance a Little Closer 1983.08
Dance and Grow Thin 1917.03
Dance Away the Night 1931.19, 1994.08
Dance Away Your Sins 1930.29
Dance Blanche et Noire, La 1905.53
Dance Chant 1997.21
Dance de Maitre de Ballet 1909.13
Dance Different 1924.18
Dance Divertissement 1945.10
Dance Dracula 1912.43
Dance Fever 1926.01
Dance for George 1976.27
Dance from Down Yonder, The 1925.01
Dance Hall Hostess 1931.11, 1953.12
Dance if it Makes You Happy 1983.21
Dance Little Lady 1928.42, 1968.19, 1986.19
Dance Mad 1920.06, 1926.01
Dance Me a Song 1950.03
Dance Me Around 1920.30
Dance Me Good-Bye 1915.20
Dance Me, Darling, Dance Me 1922.24
Dance Montage, The 1978.27
Dance of All Nations 1903.14
Dance of Fate, The 1870.08
Dance of Majorca 1928.26
Dance of Mistakes 1943.02
Dance of Resignation 1979.10
Dance of Sing Ling Foo 1908.20
Dance of Spousal Arousal, The 1989.09
Dance of the Bellhops 1926.19
Dance of the Candle Killers 1964.03
Dance of the Dinosaur 1931.26
Dance of the Fan 1930.23
Dance of the Fisherman 1968.04
Dance of the Flowers, The 1911.28
Dance of the Fortune Wheel, The 1914.01
Dance of the Golden Calf, The 1937.01
Dance of the Grizzly Bear 1910.18
Dance of the Matador 1946.06
Dance of the Midnight Songs, The 1915.27
Dance of the Moods 1931.31
Dance of the Nymphs and Satyrs 1929.43
Dance of the Perfume, The 1913.18
Dance of the Riverwoman 1996.12
Dance of the Robe, The 2000.06
Dance of the Rose, The 1917.05
Dance of the Servants 1918.33
Dance of the Seven Saturnalias, The 1911.23
Dance of the Square Heads 1915.27
Dance of the Temptress 1929.01
Dance of the Wardrobes 1958.18
Dance of the Whirling Wimpus 1958.04
Dance of the Widow, The 1909.13
Dance of Triumph 1987.10
Dance Off the Blues 1920.47
Dance on Friday Night 1900.48, 1900.55
Dance Only With Me 1958.08
Dance Oriental 1915.25
Dance Study, A 1914.22
Dance the Dark Away 1972.25
Dance the Night Away With You 1992.06
Dance to a Dream 1998.02
Dance to the Music 1997.21
Dance We do for Al, The 1931.09
Dance With Me 1910.37, 1915.17, 1916.20, 1917.32, 1923.16, 1925.39, 1940.08, 1961.10, 1983.09, 1995.03, 1997.07
Dance With You 1926.33
Dance Your Troubles Away 1922.39, 1930.37
Dance Your Way to Paradise 1924.25
Dance, Dance, Dance 1870.27, 1912.41, 1917.23, 1921.20, 1927.65, 1930.20
Dance, Gypsy 1934.17
Dance, My Darlings 1935.17
Dance, The 1904.55
Dance: Ten; Looks: Three 1975.15
Danced With a Girl 1999.22
Dancers in Love 1981.06, 1999.24
Dancers of the Cafe Kaboul, The 1926.32
Dances of the Tabarin, The 1908.07
Dancin' 1978.05
Dancin' in the Streets 1986.02
Dancin' Off Third 1981.28
Dancin' to a Jungle Drum 1944.29
Dancing 1885.06, 1904.09, 1924.04, 1964.01, 1998.07
Dancing All the Time 1996.08
Dancing Around the U.S.A. 1915.02
Dancing at the Grand Banquet 1997.16
Dancing at the Wedding 1919.01
Dancing Band, The 1920.40
Dancing Banshee, The 1910.12
Dancing Bear, The 1899.30
Dancing Blues 1924.33
Dancing Blues, The 1920.47
Dancing by Moonlight 1927.13
Dancing Ceremony, The 1908.14
Dancing Colors 1924.36
Dancing Courtship, A 1917.26
Dancing Daily Dozen, The 1923.22
Dancing Dan 1999.01
Dancing Dean, The 1898.17
Dancing Detective, The 1922.43
Dancing Doctor, The 1925.47
Dancing Dollies 1902.08
Dancing Family, The 1917.08
Dancing Fiddler, The 1911.05
Dancing Fool 1932.12
Dancing Fools 1921.20
Dancing Girl 1927.30
Dancing Honeymoon 1922.39, 1923.36
Dancing in the Barn 1884.16, 1884.37
Dancing in the Dark 1923.07, 1931.16, 1932.04, 1972.05, 1991.10, 1992.18, 1999.01, 1999.23
Dancing in the Street 1997.21
Dancing in the Streets 1933.01
Dancing is Everything 1983.21
Dancing is Not a Crime 1998.13
Dancing is not what it used to be 1887.44
Dancing is so Delightful 1908.44
Dancing Jim 1926.15
Dancing Kangaroo, The 1904.34
Dancing Lesson 1944.27
Dancing Lesson, A 1911.39
Dancing Lesson, The 1898.73, 1914.30, 1918.33, 1919.41, 1923.27
Dancing M.D., A 1917.26
Dancing mad 1886.28
Dancing Mad 1888.44, 1914.32, 1923.38
Dancing Maniacs, The 1914.22
Dancing Master, The 1924.06
Dancing Moe 1935.11
Dancing My Worries Away 1922.43
Dancing on a Rainbow 1942.35
Dancing on Your Grave 1994.12
Dancing Our Worries Away 1968.07
Dancing Pirates, The 1916.02
Dancing Romeo, A 1914.01
Dancing Round 1924.23
Dancing School 1918.42
Dancing Shoes 1919.34
Dancing Step Child 1923.31
Dancing Sunbeam 1900.37
Dancing Tambourines 1955.13
Dancing Teacher, The 1914.31
Dancing the Devil Away 1927.12, 1981.03
Dancing the Seasons Away 1921.30
Dancing Time 1924.08, 1924.34, 1925.19
Dancing to Cottillion 1909.28
Dancing to Our Score 1936.02
Dancing Town 1926.14
Dancing Tumble Tom 1920.11
Dancing Turk, The 1897.30
Dancing Up to Date 1892.18, 1892.45
Dancing Wedding 1930.39
Dancing Wedding, The 1911.33
Dancing Will Keep You Young 1917.15
Dancing With Alice 1965.29
Dancing With My Darling 1934.32, 1935.19
Dancing With My Dream 1935.19
Dancing With Tears in Their Eyes 1930.38
Dancing With the Fools 1986.13
Dancing, and I Mean Dancing 1933.06
Dandelion Time 1924.16
Dandies on Parade 1927.67, 1994.08
Dandy 1888.44, 1922.44
Dandy Dan 1899.18, 1904.21, 1925.18
Dandy Night Clerk 1980.17
Dandy Soldier Coon 1900.48
Dandy Sparrow Cops, The 1898.01
Dandy Waiters of the Golden Light 1898.78
Danger Ahead 1921.04
Danger Blues 1999.09
Danger if I Love You 1932.01
Danger in the Dark 1939.22
Dangerous Age, The 1964.21, 1968.23
Dangerous Devil 1926.15
Dangerous Girls, or Our Git Up and Git 1896.44
Dangerous Man from Denver, A 1897.33, 1900.24
Danny by My Side 1891.45
Dans ce beau palais de Delhi 1887.35
Dans des Hottentots 1909.03
Dans la Boule Lumineuse 1926.18
Dans la fumee 1934.32, 1935.19
Dans ma mysterieuse histoire 1878.08
Dans mon pays on cont' l'histoire 1886.09
Dans mon village 1964.02
Dans nos guinguettes de Paris 1887.35
Dansa Ritual del Fuego 1945.10
Danse Arabe 1947.14
Danse des Harlequines, La 1906.39
Danse Parisienne vs. La Americaine, La 1905.03
Danse Russe 1896.31
Dansez Calinda 1999.22
Dansez Princesses 1866.34
Danube so Blue 1914.17, 1934.29
Danza 1993.08
Danza Espanola 1969.11
Danzarin 1985.07, 1999.18
Daphne 1925.40
Daphnis se lamente 1887.36
Dappled Fawn, The 1884.57
Dar'll be Trouble in the Tenderloin Tonight 1897.48
Dar's Somethin' About Yer I Like 1898.69

Darby and Joan 1905.03, 1920.05
Dare I Tell 1873.10
Daring Gibson Girl, The 1929.03
Dark Eyes 1931.11, 1932.04, 1942.23
Dark Eyes am Now a Shinin' for You 1913.22
Dark girl dressed in blue 1864.13
Dark Lantern Flashes 1888.15
Dark Stranger, A 1937.07
Dark Though My Fate May Be 1886.15
Dark Tower 1996.07
Dark Town Strutters Ball 1955.13
Dark-Eyed Eloise 1880.38
Darkest Russia 1924.37
Darkest the Hour 1886.30, 1893.35, 1921.01
Darkey at the Play, The 1876.37
Darkey Cavaliers, De 1901.30
Darkies' Jubilee 1902.22
Darktown Barbecue 1900.40, 1904.21
Darktown is Out To-Night 1898.41
Darktown Poker Club 1922.22
Darktown Poker Club, The 1914.15
Darktown Strutter's Ball 1967.03
Darktown Strutters Ball 1977.09
Darktown Strutters Ball, The 1919.40
Darktown Strutters' Ball 1917.22, 1943.02
Darktown Strutters' Ball, The 1922.25
Darlin' Man 1959.04
Darlin' of New York, The 1969.14
Darling 1918.42, 1920.33
Darling be Careful 1964.22
Darling Good Night 1881.12
Darling I - 1919.31
Darling Little Yum Yum 1897.26
Darling Lou 1902.06
Darling of the Gods 1916.25
Darling Rosalinda 1954.06
Darling's Romance 1979.29
Darling, Darling 1897.03
Darling, Good Night! 1880.69
Darling, I Love You So 1916.14
Darling, Let Me Teach You How to Kiss 1969.04, 1980.01
Darling, My Darling 1899.22
Darlings of Society 1893.30
Darn it, Baby, That's Love 1950.09
Darn Nice Campus, A 1947.17
Darn That Dream 1939.29
Das Lied ist aus 1931.21
Das Lied von Temesvar 1920.46
Das war ein Trunk der uns behagte 1885.01
Das Wasserfall 1884.26
Dashing Cavaliers, The 1888.11
Dashing Little Soldier, The 1888.41
Dashing Militaire 1899.21
Dat Citron Wedding Cake 1880.09
Dat Friend of Mine 1907.32
Dat Gal of Mine 1903.08
Dat Lovin' Touch 1911.12
Dat Ol' Boy 1943.24
Dat's a Plenty 1909.27
Dat's Love 1943.24
Dat's My Girl 1902.09
Dat's Our Man 1943.24
Dat's the Way I Lubs You, Honey Mine 1907.04
Data 1930.40
Data, The 1986.18
Date Tree, The 1913.33
Daughter of Officer Porter, The 1897.14
Daughter of Rosie O'Grady, The 1944.19
Daughter of the Moon am I, A 1903.29
Daughter of the Regiment, The 1905.37
Daughter of Today, The 1898.31
Daughters of a Minister, The 1900.57
Daughters of the Guard 1897.14
Daughters of the Guard, The 1904.29
Daunt yer know? 1889.05
David and Bathsheba 1968.08
David and Lenore 1926.16
David and Michal 1997.12
David Crockett 1926.13
David Kolowitz, the Actor 1976.09
David's Final Hours 1997.12
David's Psalm 1937.01
Davy Jones 1912.05
Dawn 1919.29, 1927.63, 1961.25
Dawn in Florida 1914.21
Dawn is Approaching 1942.33
Dawn of Dreams 1927.07
Dawn of Love 1889.33
Dawn of Love, The 1889.54, 1909.29
Dawn Turns to Morning 1921.13
Dawn, A 1972.18
Dawning, the Dawning, the Shadows Westward Fall 1894.22
Day After Day 1894.52, 1932.17, 1972.05
Day After That, The 1993.09
Day at the Club, A 1923.47
Day Before Spring, The 1945.19
Day Before the Morning After, The 1911.46
Day born of love 1896.27
Day Borrowed from Heaven, A 1960.05
Day by Day 1974.10, 1976.17
Day Dream Bay 1922.13
Day Dreaming 1986.01
Day Dreams 1901.27, 1906.38, 1910.37, 1912.33, 1924.13, 1924.22, 1926.39
Day Dreams of Love 1866.21
Day for the Cat in the Hat, A 2000.18
Day I Met Your Father, The 1968.06
Day I Rode Half Fare, The 1925.01
Day in - Day Out 1997.05
Day in Camp, A 1915.25
Day in Falsettoland, A 1992.09
Day in New York, A 1989.23
Day in the Life, A 1974.24, 1977.10
Day Nigger Wid a White Spot on His Face 1896.05
Day of Joy 1898.48
Day of Love, The 1912.04
Day of the Game, The 1909.03
Day Off, The 1984.08
Day the Snow is Meltin', The 1961.14
Day the Sun Stood Still, The 1999.08
Day Tripper 1977.10
Day We Celebrate, The 1912.02
Day We Greet the New Queen, The 1997.16, 1998.08
Day Will Come, The 1970.17
Day You Came into My Life, The 1985.20
Daybreak 1942.01, 1976.34, 1991.10
Daybreak Express 1986.02, 1989.02
Daylight is Dawning 1903.04
Daylight Love 1864.13
Days Gone By 1924.08, 1963.14
Days Like This I Almost Believe in God 1992.09
Days of Chivalry, The 1917.17
Days of Forty-Nine, The 1904.39
Days of Long Ago 1894.46
Days of Long Ago, The 1897.17
Days of Magic, The 1900.12
Days of My Boyhood 1906.01
Days of Romance, The 1916.07
Days of This Life, The 1972.18
Days of Wine and Roses 1974.22
Days of Wine and Roses, The 1997.05
Days of Youth 1918.35
Days That Used to Be 1920.40
Days when I was young, The 1894.44
Days when we went Typsying in, The 1864.12
Dazzler March, The 1894.16
De Blin' Man Stood on de Road an' Cried 1930.10
De Bo'd of Education 1907.22
De Cards Don't Lie 1943.24
De Dum Dum 1927.19
De la vieille foret discrete 1887.36
De ma refraichir la memoire 1885.56
De Mi Barrio 1999.18
De mon temps 1929.14
De Old Clay Road 1926.31
De Ole Ark's a-Moverin 1930.10
Deacon and the Parrot 1898.38
Deacon Pettigue 1911.29
Deacon Says so, Too, The 1880.37
Dead End 1968.11, 1977.15
Deaf Bertha 1952.04
Dealer, The 1971.20
Dear Algerian Land 1926.32
Dear Bath 1917.27
Dear Beatrice Fairfax 1937.14
Dear Boy 1982.20
Dear Brother 1984.02
Dear Captain, hear me speak 1886.40
Dear Delightful Women 1911.06
Dear Editor 1985.17
Dear English Chappies 1885.31
Dear Eyes That Haunt Me 1927.17
Dear Familiar Faces 1885.03
Dear Felicia 1985.17
Dear Friend 1960.19, 1963.14
Dear Friends and Gentle Hearts 1939.21
Dear friends around me smiling 1863.02
Dear friends, take pity on my lot 1879.10
Dear Girls, Good Bye 1927.50
Dear Golden Days 1896.31
Dear Grandpapa 1886.49
Dear Heart 1908.02, 1974.22
Dear Heart My Heart Sweetheart 1920.25
Dear Home of Mine Goodbye 1926.27
Dear Landlord 1970.16
Dear Little Cafe 1929.41
Dear Little French Grisette, The 1900.39
Dear Little Gad-About 1922.29
Dear Little Games of Guessing 1911.25
Dear Little Girl 1926.36, 1948.16, 1990.14
Dear Little Girl Who is Good, The 1905.57
Dear Little Girlie 1922.38
Dear Little Girls 1906.25
Dear Little Girls of the U.S.A. 1911.14
Dear little Jappy-Jap-Jappy, The 1896.27
Dear Little Pages 1913.10
Dear Little Peter Pan 1923.40
Dear Little Soldiers 1934.34
Dear Little Wise Old Bowery, The 1905.41
Dear Lord and Father of Mankind 1997.09
Dear Love 1907.03, 1965.17
Dear Love, My Love 1921.09
Dear Luzon 1904.26
Dear Mama 1990.16
Dear Mamma 1897.32
Dear Mom 1962.24
Dear Motherland 1908.26
Dear Mr. Schubert 1967.05
Dear Nightingale 1922.06
Dear Old Bells 1894.37
Dear Old Broadway 1899.36, 1904.23, 1906.26
Dear Old Bronx 1917.29
Dear Old College Days 1902.24, 1905.47
Dear Old Crinoline Days 1932.05
Dear Old Dinah 1914.06
Dear Old Dixieland 1905.22
Dear Old Donegal 1955.13
Dear Old Dublin 1917.27
Dear Old Farm, The 1905.41
Dear Old Fashioned Henley 1914.19
Dear Old Fashioned Prison of Mine 1924.08
Dear Old Father 1909.13
Dear Old Father's Knee 1897.48
Dear Old Fighting Boys, The 1915.29
Dear Old Gown 1918.42
Dear Old Heidelberg 1912.44
Dear Old Jersey Home 1903.27
Dear Old London Town 1904.55
Dear Old Manhattan Isle 1904.15
Dear Old Moulin Rouge 1924.13
Dear Old Pal of Mine 1918.10
Dear Old Pals 1889.09, 1889.41, 1890.29, 1905.47
Dear Old Southland 1922.22, 1922.25, 1930.13
Dear Old Story, The 1908.03
Dear Old Syracuse 1938.14, 1975.13
Dear Old White House 1912.30
Dear One 1993.09
Dear Oscar, I am thine alone 1859.09
Dear Papa 1880.47
Dear Sweet Eyes 1921.11
Dear World 1913.19, 1969.05
Dear, Dear Departed 1927.03
Dear, Dear Sisters 1925.21
Dear, Oh Dear 1928.30
Dearest companions 1859.18
Dearest Friends, My Ardent Love 1866.14
Dearest Heart of My Heart 1894.40, 1913.25

Dearest Isabella from Castille 1999.05
Dearest May 1870.01
Dearest Miss Bell 1938.06
Dearest Miss Flo 1938.06
Dearest Papa, I'm Girofla 1877.05
Dearest You're the Nearest to My Heart 1956.02
Dearie 1905.19
Dearly Beloved 1997.05
Death be His Doom 1901.27
Death by Sister Dear 1870.27
Death Message 1966.19
Death of a Comrade, The 1935.16
Death of Absalom 1997.12
Death of Saul, The 1997.12
Death of Swan 1924.48
Death to the Infidel 1914.19
Death to the invader! 1884.09
Death Walk 1990.17
Death's Frontiers are Opened 1950.05
Death's Gointer Lay His Cold, Icy Hands on Me 1930.10
Debutante 1948.27
Debutante, The 1881.36, 1895.34
Decadence 1935.03
Decamp I will to Glory 1858.04
Deceiving Blue Bird 1927.53
December Nights 1980.13
Decent Thing to Do, The 1924.30
Declaration Day 1934.35
Decline and Fall of the Popular Song, The 1953.10
Decorations 1914.07
Decoys 1927.68
Dedicated Teacher, A 1968.06
Dee-lightful is the Word 1961.14
Deed I am about to do, The 1886.40
Deed I Do 1896.02, 1981.16
Deed I do do Blues 1938.19
Deedle-Dee-Dum 1912.14
Deedle-doodle 1949.16
Deeds of Death 1864.22
Deemed of a fisherman's lowly race 1873.05
Deep Blue Sea 1928.10, 1958.12
Deep Blue Sea, The 1925.30
Deep Down Inside 1962.27, 1982.01, 1998.15
Deep Harlem 1929.01
Deep in My Heart 1924.02, 1943.06
Deep in My Heart Dear 1924.45
Deep in My Heart, Dear 1980.21
Deep in Someone's Heart 1923.34
Deep in the Heart 1916.07
Deep in the Heart of Texas 1981.04
Deep in the Night 1971.20
Deep in Your Eyes 1920.40
Deep in Your Heart 1965.29
Deep Night 1942.11
Deep Paradise 1930.37
Deep Purple 1975.12, 1987.02
Deep River 1955.13
Deep Sea Roll 1930.37
Deeper 1920.38
Deeper in the Woods 1975.18, 1976.31
Deer and the Park Avenue Lady, The 1939.28
Defeat We Never Know 1902.43
Defying the Storm 1911.37
Degas Ballet 1932.19
Deja Vu 1978.22
Delia 1902.44
Delighted 1986.16
Delilah Done Me Wrong 1965.37
Delilah's Dilemma 1955.25
Deliver 1929.01
Della and Ella 1904.22
Della, Della, Della 1901.23
Delta Dawn 1973.14, 1975.12
Dem Bones 1940.17
Dem Melech's Sudeh 1968.22
Demain 1973.17
Democracy 1919.04
Democracy's Call 1936.28
Democratic Club Dance 1986.13
Demoiselle sur une balancoire, Une 1961.25
Demon Dance 1895.02
Demon of the Deep, The 1900.34
Demonstration Number 1912.20
Demontrer que par A plus B 1885.56
Demure and Shy 1903.20
Den Kopf jetzt in die Hoh 1885.01
Denied Stone 1987.17
Denishawn 1919.37
Denmark is Still 1976.03
Denn Wovon Lebt Der Mensch? 1965.04
Denny Grady's Hack 1886.03
Denver Police, The 1960.20
Depart 1935.19
Departure 1982.18
Departure, The 1976.01
Depuis ton depart, mon amour 1926.49
Der Alte Cowboy 1999.05
Der Alter Tzigayner 1998.11
Der Blues 1971.10
Der Guten Tag Hop Clop 2001.05
Der Obersteiger 1895.17
Der Onkel Bumba Aus Columba Tanzt Nur Rhumba 1999.05
Der Shimmy 1975.22
Der Wasserfall 1878.15, 1879.64
Derby Ram, The 1924.20
Dere's a Cafe on de Corner 1943.24
Dere's No Hidin' Place Down Dere 1930.10
Derecho Viejo 1997.13
Dernier Pierrot, Le 1984.10
Dervish 1901.19
Des les premiers jours du monde 1884.43
Des petites filles, j'en sais 1885.56
Des que l'age 1929.11
Desdemona 1905.28, 1906.24
Desencuentro 1985.07
Desert Flame, The 1950.19
Desert Island, A 1924.08
Desert Isle 1924.40
Desert Moon 1968.03
Desert Rose 1922.15
Desert Song, The 1926.42, 1946.03, 1987.10
Design for Living 1959.20
Desir 1934.32
Desire 1948.27, 1950.12
Desire Under the Alps 1928.35
Desmond's Dilemma 1971.19
Desormais 1970.01
Despair! Despair! 1864.22
Desperate Ones 1972.16
Destiny 1978.25
Destruction, The 1988.12
Destry has Ridden Again 1940.03
Detective 1911.44
Detectiveland 1991.15
Detectives Bold 1899.21
Detrimental Man, The 1902.35
Deuce, Young Man, The 1913.32
Deutches Weinlied 1966.03
Deutscheland 1907.53
Deutscher Chansons 1962.23
Deutschland 1906.29
Devil and the Deep Blue Sea, The 1917.28
Devil and the Farmer's Wife, The 1944.32
Devil Dog Marines, The 1918.18
Devil in Hell 1975.23
Devil May Care, The 1930.43
Devil Song, The 1954.16
Devil You Know, The 1997.17
Devil's Adventures, The 1898.20
Devil's Cake Walk, The 1907.14
Devil, Devil, Take Yourself Away 1963.27
Devoir d'une femme honnete, Le 1885.57
Devotion 1903.17
Dew d'Andes 1871.08
Dew is on the Flower, The 1876.07
Dew on the Heather, The 1904.49
Dew was on the Rose, The 1946.20
Dewey Blues 1938.19
Dewey March 1898.32
Dewey's Reception 1897.33, 1900.24
Di Pescatore 1873.02
Di Provenza 1869.14
Di Quella Pera 1870.01
Di, Di, Di 1895.02
Dia Que Me Quieras, El 1993.08, 1997.13
Diabolo 1916.23
Diagnosis 1986.16
Dialect Soubrette, The 1901.19
Diamond Finale 1923.41
Diamond in the Rough 1928.44
Diamond King, The 1896.31
Diamond Thief, The 1962.22
Diamonds are a Girl's Best Friend 1949.18, 1974.02, 1995.07
Diamonds in the Starlight 1989.23
Diana 1902.18, 1915.02, 1984.02
Diana's Transformation 1961.08
Diane Is 1964.33
Dianna Lee 1930.34
Diaphanous Diana 1914.12
Diary of a Homecoming Queen 1982.08
Diavolo 1935.15
Dice are Rolling 1979.23
Dick, Dick, the Lamplighter 1924.20
Dickery Dock 1897.19
Dickie 1969.05, 1985.19
Dickie and the Birdie 1895.06
Dickie Birds, The 1886.53
Dickie the King of Dudes 1900.52
Dictator's Song 1938.02
Did He Really Think 1976.01
Did I Ever Really Live? 1969.01
Did You Close Your Eyes? 1957.07
Did You Come Back? 1924.05
Did You Ever Get Stung? 1938.05, 1975.13
Did You Ever Hear Such Topics? 1881.11
Did you ever hear tell of a Jolly Young Waterman 1858.03
Did You Ever Hear That in Turkey? 1910.07
Did You Ever Hear the Blues? 1957.09
Did You Ever See a Dream Walking? 1940.20, 1980.09
Did You Ever See Your King? 1956.09
Did You Ever, etc. 1911.01
Did You Ever? 1880.19
Did You Hear That? 1961.24
Did You Hear What She was Saying 1895.25
Did You Hear? 1971.21
Did You, My Boy, Did You? 1919.37
Diddle Diddle Dumpling 1971.20
Didn't I Tell You 1976.35, 1980.14, 1982.17
Didn't it Happen? 1927.04
Didn't it Rain 1969.10, 1990.05
Didn't My Lord Deliver Daniel 1944.32
Didn't She do it for Love 1976.03
Didn't Yo? 1920.29
Didn't You Believe 1921.36
Didn't Your Mother Tell You Nothing 1941.09
Didoes 1927.20
Die Dorfmusik 1999.05
Die Flabbergast 1973.13
Die Gehemnisse des Teufels 1885.45
Die Greene Koseene 1967.03
Die Herren von Marscillac! Wilkommen meine Herrn! 1885.01
Die Liebe Kommt Die Liebe Geht 1999.05
Die Neue Art 1912.44
Die vogelein singen in dem wald 1911.28
Die Wasserfall 1885.70
Dietes-moi ma mere 1932.04
Different 1972.25, 1987.12
Different Days 1922.07
Different Girl Again, A 1907.41
Different Girls 1906.26
Different Girls on Broadway, The 1906.22
Different Kind of World, A 1971.19
Different Times 1972.07
Different Ways of Proposing 1902.08
Dig, Ye Dagos, Dig 1900.07
Diga Diga Doo 1986.02
Diga, Diga, Do 1928.18
Diga, Digga Do 1980.10
Digits 1975.02
Diguli Que Vengui 1926.09, 1926.35
Dime Ain't Worth a Nickel, A 1978.10
Dime Que Si 1939.18
Diminuendo in Blue 1981.06
Dimple on My Knee, The 1931.48

Dimples 1915.17, 1941.01, 1962.27, 1998.15
Dinah 1901.27, 1908.08, 1910.16, 1913.35, 1917.26, 1923.11, 1923.47, 1927.32, 1953.12, 1980.10, 1986.02
Dinah's Nightmare 1944.18
Dinah's Wedding 1871.16
Ding Dong 1894.40, 1914.14, 1918.21, 1918.34, 1930.02
Ding Dong Bell 1927.04, 1971.20
Ding Dong Dell 1904.54, 1920.35
Ding Dong! The Witch is Dead 1989.06, 1997.11
Ding Dong, Ding Dong 1904.51
Ding Dong, it's Kissing Time 1920.39
Ding Toes 1919.18
Ding, Dong, Ding 1882.44
Ding-a-Ling 1922.11
Ding-Dong 1896.48
Ding-Dong-Ding 1900.57
Dingere Dingale 1966.03
Dinghy 1976.15
Dingle Dangle 1913.01
Dining Out 1908.27
Dining Room Girls 1894.06
Dinkey Arno 1893.43
Dinky Doodle Dicky 1919.02
Dinner Bells 1904.43
Dinner Pail, The 1913.06
Dinner Party, The 1899.17
Dinner Time 1906.29
Dinner, Dinner 1900.57
Dinst, Di 1990.16
Dip in the Ocean, A 1901.25
Dip Me in the Golden Sea 1985.02
Dip to Him Several Times 1892.42
Dip, Dip, Dip 1912.38
Diplomacy 1899.28, 1901.16, 1913.10
Diplomats 1908.03
Dipsey's Comin' Over 1983.21
Dipsey's Vaudeville 1983.21
Dipsy Doodle 1939.29
Direct from Vienna 1961.10
Dirge 1939.19, 1956.13
Dirge for a Soldier 1938.11
Dirty Dig 1928.14
Dirty Dog, The 1950.01
Dirty Hands! Dirty Face! 1921.34, 1923.12, 1995.12
Dirty No Gooder Blues 1982.12
Dirty Old Town 1966.03
Dirty Words 1976.20
Dirty Work 1918.27
Dirtyi Blonde 2000.12
Dis Flower 1943.24
Dis is de Day 1926.31
Dis-Donc 1960.13
Dis-moi jo 1961.25
Disappear 1912.42, 1991.05
Disappointed Love 1913.21
Disco Destiny 1978.25
Disco Duck 1999.15
Disco Inferno 1999.15
Disco Shuffle 1979.15
Disconnected 1988.07
Discontent 1922.03
Discontented Bandits, The 1926.17
Discords 1882.76
Disguise defies a husband's eyes 1888.18
Disguises 1910.03
Disgustingly Rich 1940.06
Dismissal Whistle 1928.17
Disneyland 1986.20
Disperse yourselves near by 1885.28
Dissipated Kitten, The 1903.41
Dissipation 1907.31
Dissolute Mosquito, The 1899.38
Distant Melody 1954.13, 1979.22, 1990.20
Dites oui! 1929.15
Dites-Moi 1949.04
Ditto Ditto 1898.17
Ditty of the Drill 1896.13
Divali Festival, The 1960.10
Dividing the Spoil 1918.27
Divina 1985.07, 1999.18
Divorce 1911.42
Divorce Hunters' Chorus 1900.42
Divorce Song 1896.33
Dix est un chiffre rond 1877.32
Dixiana Rise 1913.34
Dixie 1909.16, 1922.22, 1928.18, 1955.13, 1978.05, 1979.11
Dixie After Dark 1987.02
Dixie Cinderella 1929.23
Dixie Dan 1907.24, 1907.41
Dixie Dreams 1924.37
Dixie isn't Dixie Any More 1939.14
Dixie Jubilee 1919.21
Dixie Love 1912.25, 1912.45
Dixie Moon 1924.27, 1978.21
Dixie Vagabond 1929.25
Dixie Volunteers, The 1917.13
Dixie Wildflowers 1924.37
Dixie's Land 1861.01
Dixie, I Love You 1907.25
Dixieland Band, The 1997.05
Dizzily, Busily 1945.04
Dizzy Feet 1929.49
Dnieper Cossacks, The 1925.03
Do a Little This-do a Little That 1924.32
Do a Revue! 1959.14
Do as You Like 1931.21
Do as You Please 1911.32
Do Buy Some Candy, Sir 1917.14
Do I Do 1986.02
Do I Hear a Waltz? 1965.06, 1999.20
Do I Hear You Saying 'I Love You'? 1928.16
Do I Hear You Saying I Love You? 1975.13
Do I Like Love 1903.22
Do I look any more like Sullivan? 1884.37
Do I Love You 1939.30
Do I Love You Because You're Beautiful? 1993.14, 1993.16, 2001.09
Do I Love You When There's Nothing But 'Yes' in My Eyes 1925.41
Do I or Don't I Blues, The 1925.05
Do It 1924.11
Do it Again 1922.09, 1958.10
Do it Alone 1998.21
Do it for Charity 1927.04
Do it for Me 1917.36, 1976.25
Do it Girl 1970.04
Do it in Two 1960.12
Do it Now 1918.03, 1924.30
Do it the Hard Way 1940.22, 1989.16
Do Listen, Please 1978.07
Do Look at Him! 1918.03
Do Me a Favor 1988.12
Do My Eyes Deceive Me 1937.12
Do Not Harm the Queen 1998.08
Do Not Hesitate to Shoot 1910.03
Do Not Hurry, do Not Worry 1888.19
Do Not Hurt the Queen 1997.16
Do not Jingle 1864.13
Do Not Jump at Your Conclusions 1897.37
Do not mingle 1859.18, 1873.04
Do Not Say Always 1934.32
Do Nothing 'Til You Hear from Me 1981.06
Do Something 1908.23
Do Step the Two Step 1911.27
Do Svedanya 1993.19
Do Tell 1930.18
Do That Thing 1927.58
Do the Swank 1932.19
Do Unto Others 1974.03
Do Wah Diddy 1985.03
Do We? 1971.07
Do What You Do 1929.27
Do What You Like 1931.21
Do What You Wanna Do 1940.17
Do You Believe in Santa Claus? 1905.56
Do You Believe Me 1916.21
Do You Belong to Anyone in Particular? 1911.02
Do You Call That Dancing? 1913.31
Do You Catch On 1892.29
Do You Catch the Idea 1891.40
Do You do the Charleston? 1926.11
Do You Ever Go to Boston 1967.14
Do You Follow Me? 1899.34
Do You Hear the People Sing? 1987.04
Do You Know a Better Way to Make a Living? 1950.19
Do You Know Jesus? 1976.35, 1980.14
Do You Know Mr. Schneider 1908.25
Do You Know Where You're Going To? 1976.16
Do You Know? 1913.32
Do You Like Me Best? 1913.23
Do You Like Tutti-Frutti? 1895.21
Do You Love Me I Wonder? 1925.17
Do You Love Me? 1925.33, 1964.27
Do You Love My Lord? 1943.10
Do You Recall 1937.17
Do You Remember 1982.23
Do You Remember, Love? 1897.40, 1917.10
Do You Remember? 1905.04, 1920.01, 1922.31
Do You See What I See 1988.02
Do you sigh for fame and glory 1892.20
Do You Sigh for Love or Glory? 1893.19
Do you suppose we could wed? 1886.40
Do you think it's alright 1972.08
Do You Think it's Alright 1993.06
Do You Think So? 1888.44
Do You Think That You Have Known Me Long Enough 1903.22
Do You Think the Test, Sir? 1888.34
Do You Wanna Dance? 1975.12, 1979.30, 2000.07
Do You Want to Dance? 1973.14
Do You Want to Go to Heaven 1985.06
Do You Want to Hear the Rest? 1897.01
Do You Want to See Paris? 1929.45
Do You, Don't You, Will You, Won't You 1922.34
Do Your Duty 1975.20
Do, do, Do 1990.14
Do, do, My Huckleberry Do 1894.35
Do, do, My Huckleberry, Do 1894.07
Do, I Dear, I Do 1926.04
Do, Ra, Me 1920.42
Do, Re, Do 1944.33, 1971.15
Do, Re, Mi, Fa, Sol, La, Si, Do 1906.27
Do-do-Do 1926.36
Do-Nuts 1936.12
Do-Re-Mi 1924.46, 1959.24, 1967.12, 1998.03
Doatsey Mae 1978.13
Dock Dance, The 1958.02
Doctor 1922.26
Doctor and Ella 1937.08
Doctor and the Scribe, The 1895.06
Doctor is In, The 1971.11, 1999.03
Doctor Rhythm 1995.14
Doctor Voodoo 1927.33
Doctor's Soliloquy, A 1960.10
Doctor's Song 1891.18
Doctor's, Doctor's 1912.12
Doctor, Doctor, Doctor 1905.07
Doctors Dance, The 1950.01
Documentary 1950.03
Dodo 1927.34
Doe it Catch On? 1883.04
Does He Know? 1954.15
Does it Pay to be a Lady? 1929.37
Does Polly Want Wally 1917.21
Does she love me? 1878.02
Does She Love Me? 1885.58
Does Your Heart Beat for Me? 1987.02
Doesn't Anybody Love Anymore 1976.20
Doesn't Anybody Want Me? 1916.22
Dog 1921.26
Dog Eat Dog 1959.27
Dog Eats Dog 1987.04
Dog is a Man's Best Friend, A 1951.23
Dogalo 1907.55
Doggie in Our Yard, The 1906.25
Doggie Inn 1907.55
Doggies and the Bone, The 1909.29
Doin the Hot-Cha-Cha 1929.24
Doin the New Low Down 1928.18
Doin' it for Sugar 1972.04
Doin' the Chamberlain 1939.22
Doin' the Gorilla 1927.35
Doin' the New Low Down 1980.10
Doin' the Old Yahoo Step 1948.30
Doin' the Production Code 1980.08
Doin' the Shim Sham 1933.27

Doin' the Toledo 1936.30
Doin' the Waltz 1937.12
Doin' What Comes Naturally 1946.12, 1966.12, 1999.04
Doing Good 1966.06
Doing My Bit 1917.23
Doing the Apache 1923.41
Doing the Dumb-bell 1931.31
Doing the High 1971.01
Doing the Latest Rag 1997.06
Doing the New York 1931.19
Doing the Reactionary 1937.14
Doing the Town 1924.22
Doing the Truck 1935.11
Doing Well 1902.40
Dolce Far Niente 1960.20
Doll Dance 1929.48
Doll Dance, The 1935.04
Doll Fantasy, A 1935.17
Doll House, A 1921.37
Doll Song 1930.15
Doll's House 1923.01
Doll's House, A 1956.08
Doll's Lullaby 1888.05
Dollar Bill's the Flag That Rules the World, The 1912.25
Dollar of Our Daddies! 1880.32, 1881.16
Dollar Princesses, The 1909.21
Dollar Sign, The 1908.07
Dollars and Debutantes 1910.04
Dollars as a Wedge 1897.21
Dolls 1961.16
Dolls' Quadrille, The 1887.32
Dolly 1900.16, 1914.07, 1921.10
Dolly Dear 1915.29
Dolly Dimples 1904.15
Dolly Doane 1898.31
Dolly Dollars 1905.29
Dolly from the Follies Bergere 1950.14
Dolly Maxixe, The 1914.01
Dolly Twinkle, The 1918.07
Dolly Varden 1872.14, 1902.03
Dolly With a Dimple on Her Chin 1902.19
Dolly, My Crumpled Horn Cow 1888.40
Dollys and Their Collies, The 1924.32
Dolores 1914.26, 1980.29
Dolores Delago the Toast of Chicago 1979.30
Doly Dimple Song 1902.15
Dom Mauritio 1880.04
Domesticity 1961.26
Domino Chorus 1888.05
Don Jose O'Brien 1941.07
Don Jose of Far Rockaway 1952.10
Don Jose of Sevilla 1897.13, 1930.12
Don Juan 1934.02, 1995.03
Don Medigua, all for thy coming wait 1896.13
Don Medigua, here's your wife 1896.13
Don Pascal de Mesquita 1907.07
Don' Yo' Want to See de Moon? 1920.42
Don't - Don't - Don't 1922.04
Don't Ah Ma Me 1984.01
Don't annoy me, oh! 1864.13
Don't Argify 1904.43
Don't Ask 1926.36
Don't Ask a Lady 1982.01
Don't Ask Me Not to Sing 1933.26, 1986.01
Don't Ask Me Why 1931.21, 1967.13
Don't Bait for Fish You Can't Fry 1955.11
Don't be a Sailor 1916.03
Don't be a Villain 1905.01
Don't be a Woman if You Can 1946.20
Don't be Afraid 1951.14, 1972.04, 1977.08
Don't be Afraid of a Teardrop 1960.23
Don't be Afraid of Romance 1962.20
Don't be Angry 1908.02
Don't be Angry With Me, Darling 1871.12
Don't be Anybody's Moon But Mine 1909.02
Don't be Blue 1922.44
Don't be Cross 1895.17
Don't be Cross With Me 1909.02
Don't be Cruel 1978.01, 1989.12
Don't be Like That 1928.25
Don't be Rash 1910.31
Don't be so Cruel, Ducky Dear! 1894.24
Don't be That Way 1987.02
Don't be What You Ain't 1905.45
Don't Believe a Tale Like That 1900.16
Don't Believe Their Fables 1922.08
Don't Blame it All on Broadway 1913.30
Don't Blame Me 1920.15, 1979.24
Don't Blow That Horn, Gabriel 1940.16
Don't Bother 1961.16
Don't Bother Me, I Can't Cope 1972.13
Don't Butt In 1901.29
Don't Call Her Old 1882.18
Don't Call Them Dearie 1921.09
Don't Care That 1885.54
Don't Choose a Gibson Girl 1909.31
Don't Come too Near 1881.22
Don't Count on It 1988.07
Don't Cry 1956.04
Don't Cry for Me Argentina 1979.23, 1992.12, 1995.12, 2000.14
Don't Cry Out Loud 1979.11
Don't Cry Swanee 1921.34, 1923.12
Don't Cry, Bo Peep 1979.33
Don't Cry, Bo-Peep 1903.31
Don't Destroy the World 1971.14
Don't do Anything 'Till You Hear from Me 1919.14
Don't do It 1929.20
Don't do it Again 2001.01
Don't do the Charleston 1926.18
Don't Ever Leave Me 1929.31
Don't Every be a Poor Relation 1923.44
Don't Fall Asleep 1952.09
Don't Fall in Love With Me 1926.15
Don't Fall Until You've Seen Them All 1920.38
Don't Flirt 1888.34
Don't Forget 1906.04, 1923.37, 1926.25
Don't Forget 127th Street 1964.32
Don't Forget Bandanna Days 1925.18
Don't Forget Me 1908.34, 1925.52
Don't Forget the Beau You Left Behind 1911.05
Don't Forget the Girl from Punxsutawney 1943.16
Don't Forget the Lilac Bush 1947.02
Don't Forget to Dream 1948.23
Don't Forget You're Talking to a Lady 1902.07
Don't Forget Your Etiquette 1928.46
Don't Get Around Much Anymore 1981.06, 1997.03
Don't Get into the Habit of It 1891.18
Don't Give Up the Ship 1957.10
Don't Go 1987.16, 1998.04
Don't Go Away, Monsieur 1937.16
Don't Go in the Water, Daughter 1911.30
Don't Go too Dangerously Nigh 1904.56
Don't Hang Up the Telephone 1983.17
Don't Hang Your Dreams on a Rainbow 1929.26
Don't Have the Baby 1971.18
Don't Hesitate With Me 1914.16
Don't Hold Everything 1928.36
Don't I Love My Lena 1878.04
Don't Judge a Girl by Her Name 1923.37
Don't Know 1889.54
Don't Laugh 1963.13, 1977.05
Don't Leave Me Dangling in the Dust 1970.04
Don't Let Anybody Vamp Your Man 1925.08
Don't Let Him Know You 1956.13
Don't Let it Get You Down 1938.07, 1940.10, 1962.17
Don't Let Me Catch You Falling in Love 1920.35
Don't Let That Moon Get Away 1995.14
Don't Let the Sun Catch You Crying 1992.03
Don't Let's Meet Again 1911.06
Don't Like Goodbyes 1954.19
Don't Listen to Your Heart 1938.01
Don't Look at Me 1917.03, 1971.05
Don't Look at Me That Way 1928.33
Don't Look Back 1963.12
Don't Look Now 1957.14
Don't lose your temper 1880.59
Don't Lose Your Way, Little Boy 1916.18
Don't Make a Move 1964.35
Don't Make Me Laugh 1877.28, 1987.12
Don't Marry Me 1958.19, 1993.16
Don't Mention My Name 1911.23
Don't Mess Around With My Man 1927.32
Don't Mess With Bill 1986.02
Don't Mess With My Man 1992.06
Don't Mind Me 1902.07
Don't Never Look for it Among the Irish 1904.07
Don't Overdo It 1903.16
Don't P-P-Point Them Guns at Me 1961.11
Don't Play That Lovesong Anymore 1981.14
Don't Put it Down 1968.11
Don't Put Me Out of Your Heart 1924.04
Don't Put Your Daughter on the Stage, Mrs. Worthington 1968.19
Don't Quit While You're Ahead 1985.18
Don't Rain on My Parade 1964.11
Don't Say Always 1935.19
Don't Say Good-Bye 1919.41
Don't Scold 1927.20
Don't Sell the Night Short 1941.06
Don't Send Her Away 1894.37
Don't Send Me Back 1924.44
Don't Shake My Tree 1927.07
Don't Shoot the Hooey to Me, Louie 1974.05
Don't Sing Solo 1942.05
Don't Sit Under the Apple Tree 1942.16, 1999.24
Don't Stand too Close to the Picture 1960.01
Don't Start No Arguments With Him 1900.16
Don't Stop 1926.02
Don't Stop Loving Me Now 1922.15
Don't Stop the Carnival 1947.19
Don't Stop, Mr. Jenkinson 1911.18
Don't Tag Along 1922.29
Don't Take Much 1997.08
Don't Take on More Than You Can Do 1942.18
Don't Take Our Charley for the Army 1963.29
Don't Take Your Beau to the Seashore 1911.30
Don't Take Your Troubles to Bed 1924.10
Don't Talk 1950.04
Don't Talk About God 1970.08
Don't Talk to Me of Marriage 1899.34
Don't Teach Me to Swim Alone 1909.02
Don't Tell Mama 1966.24, 1998.04
Don't Tell Me 1956.16, 1978.28, 1984.02
Don't Tell Me it's Bad 1934.35
Don't Tell Me it's Forever 1973.03
Don't Tell My Father 1876.06
Don't Tell tales Out of School 1909.10
Don't Tell Your Folks 1930.08, 1931.08
Don't Tempt Me 1917.02, 1926.27
Don't Tempt Me With My Sister 1965.31
Don't Throw Me Down 1927.53
Don't Throw Me Out of the House, Father 1936.03
Don't Touch My Tomatoes 1964.02
Don't Trust Them 1917.34
Don't Turn Away from Love 1961.18
Don't Turn His Picture to the Wall 1971.09
Don't Turn My Picture to the Wall 1912.26
Don't Turn Your Back 1987.17
Don't Unmask Your Beauty to the Moon 1976.03
Don't Wait 1956.08
Don't Wait 'til it's too Late to See Paris 1956.08
Don't Wake 'Em Up 1928.10
Don't Wake the Baby 1876.37
Don't Wake Them Up too Soon 1945.01
Don't Wanna B N Luv 1995.01
Don't Wanna Write About the South 1950.19
Don't Waste the Moon 1988.12
Don't Whistle so Loud 1904.01
Don't Wish too Hard 1979.11
Don't Worry 1965.33
Don't You Believe Those Eyes 1901.01
Don't You Care 1902.43, 1906.32
Don't You Cheat 1926.20
Don't You Ever Tell I Told You 1908.10
Don't You Ever Think About Me, Dearie? 1912.16
Don't You Feel My Leg 1992.06
Don't You Find the Weather Charming? 1907.51
Don't You Know 1897.39
Don't You Know I Care 1997.03
Don't You Let Nobody Turn You Roun' 1930.10
Don't You Make a Noise 1911.30
Don't You Miss the Train, Boys 1881.09
Don't You Really Think I'll Do? 1914.33
Don't You Remember Sweet Alice Ben Bolt 1895.17
Don't You Remember Those School Days? 1919.22
Don't You Tell 1907.25

Don't You Think I'm Blind! 1876.01
Don't You Think it's Time to Marry? 1906.41
Don't You Think it's Very Nice 1968.24
Don't You Think You'll Miss Me? 1918.26
Don't You Tickle Me 1880.25
Don't You Trifle With Mr, Honey 1894.37
Don't You Want a Paper, Dearie? 1906.37
Don't You Want to Take Me? 1920.04
Don't You Wish That You Were Me? 1905.24
Donde vas con manton de Manila 1969.11
Done Written Down-a My Name 1943.10
Donkey and the Hay, The 1907.06, 1911.27
Donkey Serenade, The 1976.07
Donna 1968.11
Donna e mobile, La 1910.04
Donnet's Color Scheme 1914.12
Donny Did, Donny Didn't 1911.11
Donnybrook 1961.14
Doo-Dab 1925.05
Doo-waa, Doo-wee 1982.10
Doodle Doo Doo 1924.35
Doodle Doodle Wagon's Done Got You at Last, The 1898.67
Doodly, Doodly 1947.10
Dooley's Wedding 1896.14
Dooleys, The 1894.10
Doomed as I am to Marry a Lord 1886.15
Doomed, Doomed, Doomed 1954.03
Door Mats 1924.09
Door of Her Dreams, The 1924.28
Door to Isle Goree, The 1996.07
Doorman at Maxim's, The 1929.05
Doorstep Baby 1931.13
Dope Fiend, The 1910.19
Dopey de Lome 1898.38
Dorkins' Night 1879.32
Dorogoy Dlinoyu 1977.13
Dorothy 1885.06, 1925.48
Dorothy Drew 1895.04
Dorothy Flop 1895.08
Dorrie's Wish 1960.05
Dos Arbolitos 1988.15
Dos Shneider Lid 1968.22
Dost Thou Love Me 1862.06
Dot Boy I Love 1894.32
Dot Leetle Baby Mine 1878.15
Dot's Her Up in de Window 1878.04, 1878.12
Dot's Right 1907.40, 1908.12
Dotlet on the 'i', The 1883.45
Dotting the I 1880.42
Dou Dou 1932.01
Double Fifth Avenue 1927.15
Double Indemnity 1957.01
Double Murder, Double Death 1950.01
Double Order of Chicken, A 1920.06
Double Ring Ceremony 1955.13
Double Soliloquy 1968.02
Double Standard 1958.02
Double Standard, The 1929.20
Double Talk 1989.29
Double Trouble 1980.08
Double, Double 1967.06
Double-Eyed Assassin, A 1900.57
Doubles 1927.10
Doubt Not 1891.36
Doubting Heart That Art To-Day 1894.47
Doubting Love 1892.45
Douce, En 1924.13
Doug's Act 1974.13
Dougal 1910.21
Doughie the Baker 1928.05, 1930.17
Doughnuts 1919.43
Doughnuts and Coffee 1938.01
Doughnuts for Doughboys 1919.08
Dov's Nightmare 1971.02
Dove Dance, The 1917.29
Dove of Peace 1912.40
Dove Song, The 1897.47, 1922.36
Down 1985.05
Down 'Round the 19th Hole 1923.47
Down a Shady Lane 1906.48
Down Among the Pines 1901.23
Down Among the Sugar Cane 1908.08, 1909.16
Down amongst the Dead Men 1862.02
Down Around the River 1921.06
Down at Mammy Jinny's 1911.40
Down at the Bottom of the Sea 1904.47
Down at the Follies Bergere 1908.36
Down at the Gaiety Burlesque 1979.24
Down at the Village 1928.14
Down by the Blue Rio Grande 1905.50
Down by the Country Side 1913.36
Down by the Erie 1920.04
Down by the Erie Canal 1914.34, 1968.07
Down by the Hillside I Met Her 1896.33
Down by the Nile 1919.35
Down by the O-Hi-O 1942.11
Down by the Ocean Stand 1903.28
Down by the Old Mill Stream 1939.29
Down by the River 1900.56, 1975.13
Down by the River Side 1895.34
Down by the Riverside 1980.14, 1982.17
Down by the Sea 1928.16
Down de Lovers' Lane 1900.20, 1901.08
Down East Flapper, The 1922.28
Down Goes the Price of Eggs 1909.31
Down Greenwich Village Way 1922.28
Down Havana Way 1910.15
Down Here in Greenwich Village 1948.16
Down Home 1970.05
Down in a Coal Mine 1872.04
Down in Arkansas 1920.28, 1928.25
Down in Catty Corner 1915.27
Down in Gossip Row 1880.64, 1883.46, 1892.54
Down in My Heart 1888.34
Down in Sparkling Glass 1846.01
Down in the Depths on the 90th Floor 1936.26
Down in the Old Rathskeller 1912.44
Down in the Philippines 1907.22
Down in the Streets 1960.12
Down in the Valley 1949.17
Down Mulberry Bend 1904.47
Down on a County Farm 1925.43
Down on a South Sea Isle 1903.29
Down on MacConnachy Square 1947.07, 1980.26
Down on Pango, Pango Bay 1923.23
Down on That Old Kansas Farm 1920.38
Down on the Banks of the Subway 1919.39
Down on the Brandywine 1904.13, 1904.44
Down on the Delta 1927.36
Down on the Dude Ranch 1940.10
Down on the Farm 1891.03, 1899.41, 1919.41
Down on the Foolish Farm 1908.15
Down on the South Sea Isle 1905.32
Down Once More 1988.01
Down Red Rose Lane 1909.05
Down South 1921.34, 1930.16
Down the Bridal Path of Love 1918.04
Down the Lane With Arabella 1905.48
Down the Line 1901.17
Down the Mother Volga 1925.52
Down the Old Church Aisle 1921.27
Down the Pike 1904.45
Down the Strand 1911.18
Down the Well 1948.15
Down Through the Agents 1942.29
Down to Coney Isle 1896.38
Down to Delaware 1905.42
Down to Earth 1955.11
Down to the Sea 1927.45
Down Went McGinty 1936.03
Down Where the Congo Flows 1902.21
Down Where the Cotton Blossoms Grow 1900.46
Down Where the Jack O'Lanterns Grow 1917.37
Down Where the Morning Glories Twine 1927.13
Down Where the Mortgages Grow 1923.45
Down Where the Ocean Breezes Blow 1902.32
Down Where the Suwanee River Flows 1905.21
Down Where the Tennessee Flows 1913.05
Down Where the Watermelon Grows 1908.43
Down Where the Watermelons Grow 1909.16
Down Where Two Lovers Sat 1903.18
Down With Everyone Who's Up 1933.25
Down With Frye 1937.09
Down With Love 1937.15
Down With Sin 1945.12
Down with the daring slave 1844.01
Down With the Tyrants 1872.23
Down Yonder 1922.22
Down Your Tea 1944.21
Down, Up, Left, Right 1976.25
Downkilty Fair 1908.43
Downy Jail Birds of a Feather 1893.35, 1921.01
Downy Jail-Birds of a Feather 1886.30
Doyna 1934.32
Dozens, The 1971.13
Dr. Blotz 1904.54
Dr. Brock 1960.19
Dr. Crippen 1943.19
Dr. Deathstar 1996.08
Dr. Grouch is Going Away 1913.34
Dr. Jazz 1975.09, 1992.08
Dr. Jekyll and Mr. Hyde 1894.17
Dr. Keley 1942.30
Dr. Lucy 1971.11
Dr. Pepper 1976.34
Dr. Tinkle Tinker 1911.25
Dragon Flight 1971.18
Dragon is coming, The 1864.12
Dramatic Patrol 1899.41
Dramatic Rag, The 1912.16
Drat! The Cat! 1965.29
Draw Near 1883.12
Drawing Lesson, The 1908.10
Dream 1921.24, 1990.09, 1997.05
Dream Babies 1970.20
Dream Boat 1898.31, 1927.45, 1929.08
Dream Days of Seville 1900.47
Dream Drummin' 1974.05
Dream Fantasies 1920.47
Dream for Angela, A 1958.04
Dream Girl 1921.08, 1924.23, 1927.45
Dream Girl Give Back My Dream to Me 1919.35
Dream Girl o' Mine 1914.05
Dream Interpreter 1899.33
Dream is a Wish Your Heart Makes, A 1975.12
Dream Kingdom 1934.15
Dream Love 1908.40, 1911.31, 1911.46
Dream Melody 1910.35, 1922.04, 1929.38
Dream o' Day Jill 1907.51
Dream of Atlanta, The 1998.21
Dream of Demetrios, The 1919.38
Dream of Dreams 1930.36
Dream of Joy 1921.13
Dream of Long Ago, The 1888.25
Dream of Love 1902.24, 1977.09
Dream of Love, The 1862.06
Dream of the Chocolate Soldier 1931.11
Dream of the Phillipines, A 1904.26
Dream of the Reveller, The 1869.47
Dream On 1880.42, 1988.12
Dream on My Princess 1914.33
Dream On, Little Sister 1930.15
Dream on, Little Soldier Boy 1918.21
Dream One Dream of Me 1902.29
Dream Parade 1953.01
Dream Safe With Me 1980.23
Dream Song 1904.35, 1939.30
Dream Sweetheart 1928.28
Dream Toyland 1979.33
Dream Waltz 1913.19
Dream! Dream! 1917.19
Dream! Oh, Dream! 1914.20
Dream, A 1918.19, 1965.35
Dream, The 1890.32, 1967.08, 1989.03
Dreamer With a Penny, A 1949.02
Dreamgirls 1981.29
Dreamily Dream 1899.41
Dreamin' Town 1904.21
Dreaming 1896.45, 1911.06, 1921.33, 1926.21
Dreaming Alone 1922.38
Dreaming by Night 1877.22
Dreaming of Allah 1926.32
Dreaming of Love 1895.25, 1909.15
Dreaming of Mother and Home 1898.63
Dreaming of You 1927.53
Dreaming on the Ohio 1903.01
Dreaming Princess 1911.38
Dreaming, Dreaming 1897.13, 1903.27

Dreamland Dimple, The 1901.18
Dreamless Rest 1897.32
Dreams 1892.06, 1910.29, 1919.41, 1926.06, 1978.27, 1981.29, 1984.14
Dreams Ago 1950.06
Dreams Come True 1945.20
Dreams Don't Die 1992.05
Dreams for Sale 1922.19, 1926.29
Dreams of Delight! 1921.12
Dreams of the Past 1914.16
Dreams of Tomorrow 1921.38
Dreamy Days 1928.04
Dreamy Eyes 1924.42
Dreamy Florence 1919.30
Dreamy Montmartre 1927.15
Dreary, Dreary, Rainy Days 1925.18
Dremlen Feigl 1989.10
Dresden China Belle, The 1920.29
Dresden China Girl, The 1899.41
Dresden China Love Affair, A 1896.45
Dresden China Plate, The 1908.41
Dresden Northwest Mounted, The 1933.01
Dress to Kill 1999.12
Dress, Dress, Dress 1918.20
Dressed in Your Pajamas in the Grand Salon 1997.06
Dressing 1924.06
Dressing Room Echoes 1906.39
Dressing Them Up 1993.09
Drift With Me 1917.02
Drifting 1978.10
Drifting Along With the Tide 1921.22
Drifting On 1920.01
Drigo Serenade 1915.26
Drigo's Polka 1920.33
Drill of the Coquette Corps 1908.42
Drill of the Seventh 1911.33
Drill Song 1961.11
Drill, The 1925.25
Drill, Ye Tarriers, Drill 1888.32, 1888.34
Drink 1944.29
Drink and be Jolly T-Day 1908.30
Drink and be Merry 1913.27
Drink and Let's be Gay 1900.16
Drink of All Nations, The 1902.43
Drink Out the Cold Drinks 1918.32
Drink Some Tea 1917.30
Drink to the Health of This Great Man 1909.30
Drink Up 1906.39
Drink With Me 1907.57
Drink With Me the Night Away 1907.05
Drink With Me to Days Gone By 1987.04
Drink's Song 1966.15
Drink, Drink, Drink 1913.35, 1980.21
Drinkin' Again 1973.14
Drinkin' Shoes 1982.04
Drinking Again 1975.12
Drinking Chorus 1879.15
Drinking Game, The 1964.03
Drinking Song 1869.47, 1881.22, 1885.70, 1896.44, 1896.50, 1905.40, 1924.45, 1925.32, 1930.40, 1932.05, 1968.22
Drinking Song, A 1971.17
Drinking Song, The 1879.64, 1963.20
Drinks of the Day 1897.32
Drittes Dreigroschen-Finale 1965.04
Driving at Night 1996.04
Droit D'Aimer, Le 1981.04
Drole de musique 1964.39
Drop a Nickel in the Slot 1890.03
Drop for me, A 1859.14
Drop in on Me at Luncheon 1905.03
Drop Me a Line 1920.31
Drop Me Off in Harlem 1981.06, 1997.03
Drop Out 1999.02
Drop That Name 1956.14
Drop Your Kerchief 1929.35
Dropsy Cure Weather 1971.16
Drown in the Mantling Glass 1862.03
Drowsily, Dreamily 1901.27
Drowsy Waters, The 1912.03
Drucilla 1914.21
Drug Store Girls 1931.08
Drugstore Scene 1937.08
Drugstore Song, The 1946.10
Drum Dance 1991.04
Drum Major as is a Drum Major, A 1870.33
Drum Major Jimmy 1894.22
Drummed Out 1908.42
Drummin' 1996.07
Drums in My Heart 1932.03
Drums of Kane 1930.26
Drums of the Nations, The 1912.39
Drums, The 1902.41, 1917.11
Drunken Reel 1980.26
Drunken Sailor, The 1922.21
Dry 2000.08
Dry Bones 1955.13, 1963.10
Dry Goods Clerk, The 1871.12
Dub-Derro 1921.18
DuBarry was a Lady 1939.30
Dubbing, The 1965.34
Dublin Boy 1881.39
Dublin Night 1959.04
Dublin Rag, The 1910.22
Dublin Saunter 1963.30
Dublin Town 1960.12
Dublinola 1924.29
Duc de Rivoli 1937.17
Duchess of Central Park, The 1900.40
Duchess of Dreams, The 1916.20
Duchess of Table D'Hote, The 1908.19
Duck Joke, The 1992.17
Duck-Foot Sue 1876.30
Ducks and Geese 1922.04
Ducks Call it Luck, The 1927.39
Dudah 1869.42
Dude All Dude 1972.18
Dudelet in the Front, The 1898.56
Dudes and the Slipper, The 1888.39
Dudes of New York, The 1896.34
Dudu 2000.14
Due Hut Mir Kainer Nit Gezugt 1970.17
Duel!, A Duel!, A 1980.08
Duel, The 1911.11, 1911.12, 1947.18, 1976.33, 1993.17
Duello, The 1941.12
Duet 1925.48, 1979.10, 1990.06
Duet des Domestiques 1929.14
Duet for One 1976.11
Duet of Rachel and Jacob 1937.01
Duetto d'Amore 1985.16
Duetto mamma mamma che bella cosa 1985.14
Dugan Kid Who Lives in Hogan's Alley, The 1896.38
Duke and Duchess hither wend their way, The 1893.02
Duke's Place 1981.06
Dulcinea 1965.34
Dull and Gay 1930.08, 1931.08
Dumb Girl 1931.05
Dumb Luck 1924.27
Dumbells May be Foolish 1924.42
Dumber They Come They Better I Like 'Em, The 1923.47
Dunnerwetter 1910.22
Duo de la Capa 1917.33
Durch die weiten Felder... 1920.46
Dusky Debutante 1938.04
Dusky Lil from Louisville 1898.67
Dusky Love 1928.10
Dusky Maiden 1902.38
Dusky Salome, The 1908.44
Dust Chasers 1924.05
Dust in Your Eyes 1933.20
Dusty Fustchuns 1970.04
Dutch Cadets, The 1900.59
Dutch Comedians 1898.47
Dutch's Song 1976.04
Dutchess of Central Park, The 1902.09
Dutiful Wife, A 1907.48, 1943.09
Dva Kuma 1977.13
Dwarf's Yodel Song 1979.28
Dying Cowboy, The 1938.12
Dying Flamingo, The 1931.09
Dying Swan, The 1916.10, 1937.06
Dynamic 1954.17

'E Didn't Know Exactly What to Say 1899.19
E Didn't Seem to Know Just Wot to Soy 1900.47
E L 'Omo Mio 1964.03
E Oho Te Whaanau 1972.20
E Pare Ra 1972.20
E Street Shuffle 1979.30
E' Nata 1985.14
E-Gypsy-Ann 1923.11
Each Frenchman is surely aware 1888.07
Each Little Jack 1923.04
Each One has a Way of His Own 1907.33
Each Pearl a Thought 1913.29
Each Tomorrow Morning 1969.05
Eadie was a Lady 1932.25
Eager Beaver 1962.03
Eager Hounds, The 1884.57
Eagle and Me, The 1944.23
Eagle high on cloudland soaring 1894.15
Eagle of Battle, The 1868.02
Eagle Rock, The 1914.16
Earl is Crazy 1971.10
Earl was Ahead 1971.10
Early and late, with soldierly gait 1888.07
Early Hours of the Morn 1914.01
Early in the Morning 1866.18, 1926.12, 1992.03
Early to Bed 1943.07
Earth and Other Minor Things, The 1973.12
Earth and the Sky, The 1953.17
Earth Beat 2001.04
Earth is green and fair to see, The 1881.04
Earth, The 1972.18
Ease Along 1921.27
Ease on Down the Road 1975.01
Easier to Love 1983.19
Easiest Way's Always the Best, The 1882.45
East and West Side 1898.61
East Coast Blues 1931.31
East Indian Maid 1919.43
East Lynne 1923.32
East River Hoe Down 1951.19
East River Rhapsody 1981.14
East Side Lil 1905.41
East Side Walk 1905.41
East St. Louis Toodle-O 1930.38
East St. Louis Toodle-Oo 1930.13
East St. Louis Toodle-oo 1989.02
East Wind 1931.39
Easter Greetings 1941.13
Easter Parade 1927.47, 1933.22
Eastern and Western Love 1926.42, 1946.03
Eastern Western Love 1987.10
Easy 1955.11, 1972.15, 1978.05
Easy as Life 2000.06
Easy Boss, The 1897.25
Easy Come, Easy Go 1918.06, 1979.12
Easy Dawson March 1905.26
Easy Does It 1949.12
Easy for You 1986.13
Easy Goin' Man 1970.06
Easy Money 1901.17, 1997.08
Easy Pickins 1921.36
Easy Street 1906.06, 1977.06
Easy Terms 1993.07
Easy to be Hard 1968.11, 2000.16
Easy to be Lonely 1971.10
Easy to Love 1948.13, 1980.06, 1987.15
Easy to Remember 1975.13
Easy to Take 1966.05
Eat a Little Something 1962.05
Eat It 1972.18
Eat Your Nice Lily, Unicorn 1963.16
Ebb and Flow 1900.39
Ebeneezer McAfee III 1964.04
Ebenezer Brown 1905.10
Ebenezer Frye 1907.27
Ebony Rag 1922.22
Eccentricities 1907.04, 1938.03
Eccentrique 1873.29, 1897.19
Echo 1892.31, 1897.19, 1907.01, 1920.12, 1946.20
Echo Duet 1918.18
Echo of a Song, The 1937.06
Echo of My Heart 1908.27
Echo Song 1877.43, 1882.28, 1882.75, 1897.21, 1972.03

Echo Song, The 1895.33
Echo's Answer 1884.11
Echo, The 1902.39
Echoes from Germany 1882.76
Echoes of Harlem 1981.06
Echoes of Yesterday 1939.18
Echoes, The 1870.15
Ecology Waltz 1972.21
Economic Situation, The 1936.02, 1936.17
Economics 1948.25
Economics 1 1937.14
Ecos de Ayer 1939.18
Ed, Did I Hear You? 1886.58
Eddie & Mae 2000.08
Eddie Steady 1923.20
Eddie's Teddy 1975.08, 2000.17
Eddie, be Good 1925.24
Eddy-Mac 1937.06
Edelweiss 1907.10, 1914.26, 1925.08, 1959.24, 1998.03, 2000.14
Edinburgh Rock 1955.19
Edinburgh Wriggle, The 1911.12
Editorial 1985.17
Edna May 1912.02
Educate Your Feet 1929.29
Educated Fool, An 1905.29
Educated Whisk Brooms, The 1922.29
Education 1911.42, 1923.34
Eel, The 1973.08
Eels are a Girl's Best Friend 1972.23
Eenie Meenie Minee Mo 1942.01
Eenie Meenie Minie Mo 1927.13
Eenie Weenie 1917.18
Eeny, Meeny, Miny, Mo 1910.27
Egano D'Galluzzi 1975.23
Egg has Fallen Down, The 1904.47
Egg, Nest and Tree 2000.18
Egg, The 1969.06
Eggs 1986.11
Eglamour 1971.18
Egypt 1903.33
Egypt Land 1902.20
Egyptian 1917.13
Egyptian Dance, The 1921.09
Egyptian Melange 1922.23
Egyptian Rag 1917.23
Eh l'amour 1964.39
Eh Maintenant? 1964.22
Eh quoi! Vous si severe 1887.36
Eh! Bien 1958.06
Eh! Did I Hear You 1885.03
Eh! Did I Hear You? 1894.31
Eh, Did I Hear You? 1890.12, 1890.30
Eh, Eh 1933.15
Eh? Ah? Oh! 1907.41
Ei Ukhnem 1922.06
Eifersuchtsduett, Das 1965.04
Eight Day Week 1972.10
Eight Little Debutantes are We 1906.47
Eight Little Girls 1910.21
Eight Little Nobodys 1921.11
Eighteen Days Ago 1929.35
Eighteen Hundred and Ninety Eight 1948.27
Eighteen Hundred and Sixty One 1910.19
Eighteen-Wheelin' Baby 1982.13
Eighth Day 1972.11
Eileen Asthore 1906.38
Eileen Avourneen 1934.42
Eileen, Alanna, Asthore 1917.07
Eili, Eili 1931.11
Eily Riley 1909.11
Eily, mavourneen 1868.01
Ein hauch, wie von Bluten... 1920.46
Ein Neuer Fruhling Wird In Die Heimat Kommen 1999.05
Eine kleine bombaardonmusik 1966.03
Eine Kleine Fruhlingsweise 1999.05
Einst glaubte ich, als ich noch unschuldig war 1965.04
Einst mals hielt vor dieser Schenke 1885.01
Elaborate Lives 2000.06
Elaine Girl of My Heart 1907.01
Eldorado 1924.06, 1956.15, 1974.06, 1982.20
Eleanor 1922.34
Eleanor Rigby 1977.10
Election Eve 1987.19
Election of the Student King 1906.49
Election Returns 1907.35
Electric Blues 1968.11
Electric Boys, The 1894.06
Electric Dolls 1888.05
Electric Girls, The 1894.06
Electric Light Cadets, The 1901.16
Electric Lights Come to the Village 1943.11
Electric Prophet 1972.18
Electric Signs 1910.02
Electric Waltz Song, The 1884.60
Electricity 1980.27
Elegance 1964.01
Elegant Darky Dan 1900.46
Elegiye Fun Fastrigosso, Di 1968.22
Element of Doubt, An 1957.01
Elements, The 1983.01
Elena 1961.26
Elephant Skid 1918.38, 1919.10
Elephant Song, The 1971.07
Elevation 1911.32
Elevator Gavotte, The 1920.45
Elevator Song 1951.23
Eleven Commandments, The 1972.09
Eleven O'Clock Song 1955.04
Eleventh Commandment, The 1966.05
Eleventh Episode, The 1978.24
Elf King, The 1908.34
Elisabeth 1956.13
Elite Syncopations 1980.27
Eliza Jane 1872.04
Elizabeth 1931.09, 1970.12, 1976.08
Elizabeth I of Chosun 1997.16
Elizabeth's Song 1979.10
Ella 1903.18
Elle a la medaille 1877.32
Elle y venait 1884.43
Ellen Roe 1961.14
Elles sont Jolies 1929.10
Elliot Garfield Grant 1993.02
Elmer's Wedding Day 1940.21
Elopement, The 1880.37, 1903.11
Eloping 1922.13
Elphin Home 1857.03
Elsa is Accused 1906.48
Elsie 1923.08
Emaline 1936.30
Emancipation Day 1875.37
Embassy Burglarious, An 1903.34
Embassy Waltz, The 1956.01, 1993.18
Embrace Me 1931.39
Embraceable You 1930.31, 1942.13, 1980.09, 1992.02, 1999.10, 2001.07
Emdudeni 1977.01
Emelia 1981.24
Emerald City Ballet 1975.01
Emerald, The 1948.24
Emigrants 1906.39
Emigrants' Song 1927.04
Emiment Regent Wang, The 1891.11
Eminent Dr. Fizz, The 1902.18
Emma's Reasons 1997.09
Emmenez-Moi 1970.01, 1974.19
Emmet's Cuckoo Song 1879.63
Emmet's Lullaby 1870.24
Emotions 1997.18
Emperor Hang Chow, The 1902.19
Emperor Jones 1934.06
Emperor Me, The 1974.12
Emperor Song 1963.09
Emperor Waltz 1954.06
Emperor's Lot, An 1895.08
Emperor's Own, The 1900.43
Empire Days 1919.03
Empire Soiree 1980.13
Employment Agency, The 1915.27
Emptiness and Longing 1977.09
Empty Bed Blues 1975.20
Empty Chairs at Empty Tables 1987.04
Empty Hours of Summer Chatter 1912.40
Empty Pockets Filled With Love 1962.20
En bonne mere de famille 1885.56
En ce temps, digne de memorie 1885.56
En frissonnant, je me hasarde... 1885.59
En ma qualite de poete 1886.19
En revenant, apres six mois 1885.59
En Route 1923.47
En Tren Sone 1988.15
Enamorada 1964.02
Enchanted 1926.15
Enchanted Castle 1927.45
Enchanted Guitar, The 1876.11, 1880.32
Enchanted Isle 1927.45
Enchantment 1951.15
Enchantment Passing Through 2000.06
Enchantress of my life 1855.06
Enchantress, The 1952.04
Encore 1982.06
Encounter in the Park 1966.21
End of a Perfect Night, The 1920.15
End of a String 1924.43
End of My Race, The 1970.10
End of the Century Girls 1899.12
End of the News, The 1986.19
End of the Road 1928.05, 1997.21
End of the Road, The 1930.17, 1969.16
End, The 1974.24
End?, The 1961.16
Endgame 1988.09
Endless Journey 2000.05
Endless Night 1997.20
Ends Justify the Means, The 1981.24
Enemy Within, The 1997.12
Energy 1979.07
Enfin, nous voila transportees 1878.08
Engaged to So-and-so 1879.10
Engagement Party, The 1997.09
Engagement Ring 1927.03
Engagement Ring, The 1894.50
Engagement, The 1914.28
Engine of Love 1987.05
Engineer, The 1932.18
England, and Home, Sweet Home 1885.69
English as She Should be Spoke 1898.58
English as You See it on Broadway 1894.37, 1896.02
English Bow, The 1905.55
English Favorite, An 1924.14
English Gentleman, An 1986.12
English Girls 1985.12
English Language, The 1911.29
English Lesson 1934.34
English Lido 1928.42
English Maids 1919.42
English Rose, The 1970.06
English Teacher, An 1960.06
English Version 1898.46
English, by Jove 1885.44
Englishman's Head, The 1948.18
Englishman's Idea of Rag-time, An 1901.16
Englishman's Toast, An 1896.41
Englishman, The 1903.38
Enniscorthy 1889.54
Enough, That's Enough 1907.55
Ensemble 1933.27
Enter Hyacinth 1973.02
Enter! Enter! 1872.23
Enterprise 1978.11
Enterprising Frenchman, The 1907.41
Entrance of Dancers 1921.32
Entrance of Emigrants 1929.51
Entrance of English Visitors 1900.43
Entrance of Hans 1910.24
Entrance of Hilda 1903.36
Entrance of Hussars 1928.03
Entrance of Kow Tow 1905.53
Entrance of Meouma 1908.03
Entrance of the Courtesans 1961.08
Entre 1927.03
Entre Nous 1921.35, 1938.09
Entrerriano, El 1985.07, 1999.18
Envoi 1955.19
Envoy's Duty, An 1900.12
Ephraham Played Upon the Piano 1911.24
Epilogue 1936.31

Epiphany 1979.06
Epitaph 1989.24
Epitaph for Marina 1981.02
Equal Rights 1914.27
Equilibrist, The 1898.22
Erbie Fitch's Twitch 1959.01
Ere I Wed You 1900.39
Ere the Marriage Contract 1882.75
Erewhonia, a Jailer's Song 1956.09
Eros, Eros 1919.38
Erstes Dreigroschen-Finale 1965.04
Erstrahlen die Lichter 1984.05
Es rotelt im Laube 1920.46
Escaped, aye, free at last 1880.54
Eskimo Blues, The 1926.17
Eskimo's Song 1896.33
Esmeralda 1915.17
Esmeralda's Dream 1998.02
Espagnola 1908.40
Espanita 1890.32, 1905.42
Espanola 1949.07
Espanola Antigua 1917.33
Espanola Moderna 1917.33
Espanola Viva 1903.17
Espanole 1922.36
Esquinazo, El 1985.07, 1999.18
Essence 1922.44
Essence of Old Virginia 1885.44
Essie Dear 1876.37
Essie's Vision 1959.01
Est plus de midi, Il 1887.36
Est-ce bien ca? 1929.16
Est-ce que je te demande? 1929.10
Estelle-Por La femme de Narcisse 1892.45
Estellita 1915.24
Esther 1952.20
Estrellita 1931.09
Estrillita 1942.19
Estudiantina 1896.31
Et maintenant 1968.21
Et maintenantuie viendra, Le 1966.20
Et pourtant 1964.02, 1965.30
Et Pourtant 1970.01
Et pourtant, quel reve enchanteur 1877.32
Eternal Flower, The 1926.09, 1926.35
Eternal Sleep 1988.05
Eternal Triangle Blues, The 1917.29
Eternal Youth is Worth a Little Suffering 1994.10
Ethel Levey's Smile Song 1922.17
Ethel's Frolic 1920.39
Ethel, Baby 1956.02
Ethiopia 1908.08
Ethiopian Essence, An 1901.21
Ethiopian Mardi Gras, An 1899.29
Ethiopian Pageant 1980.05
Etiquette 1902.29, 1904.27, 1911.07, 1924.38, 1932.19
Etre 1983.03
Etre adore 1926.49
Eugene O'Neill's Hairy Ape 1922.34
Eugenic Girls 1914.16
Eulalie 1939.21
Eulogy 1975.07
Euphemism 1978.06
Euphoria 1970.04
Euranian Anthem 1926.33
Eureka 1961.08
European Tour, The 1999.04
Ev'ry Boy in Town's My Sweetheart 1928.31
Ev'ry Day Can't be a Sunday 1931.09
Ev'ry Day Comes Something Beautiful 1979.12
Ev'ry Day's a Holiday 1939.30
Ev'ry Hour Brings its Flower 1908.29
Ev'ry Knight Must have a Star 1892.52
Ev'ry Sunday Afternoon 1940.06
Ev'ry Time We Say Goodbye 1944.29
Ev'ry Woman 1978.07
Ev'rybod-ee Who's Anybod'ee 1935.14
Ev'rybody Loves You When You're Asleep 1975.13
Ev'rybody's Gotta be Somewhere 1989.29
Ev'rything I Love 1941.08
Ev'rything I've Got 1942.15
Eva Beware of the City 1979.23
Eva's Final Broadcast 1979.23
Evaristo Carriego, A 1997.13
Eve 1918.12, 1966.18
Eve Cost Adam Just One Bone 1920.33
Eve was Weak, And 1988.12
Evelina 1944.23
Evelyn 1916.04
Evelyn's Bower 1901.15
Evelyn, What do You Say? 1927.56
Even as You and I 1925.22, 1931.36
Even if I Say it Myself 1940.09
Even Me 1990.05
Even Now 1991.10
Even Then 1993.17
Evenin' 1929.25, 1987.02
Evening Bells, The 1922.06, 1924.48
Evening Made for Lovers, An 1993.17
Evening News 1980.17
Evening News! 1881.04
Evening Prayers 1988.12
Evening Star 1934.04
Evening, The 1993.17
Ever After 1987.18
Ever and Ever Mine 1890.33
Ever and Ever Yours 1916.06
Ever be happy 1846.01
Ever be Happy 1862.03, 1866.06
Ever Before Me 1890.39
Ever by Your Side 1918.06
Ever of Thee 1862.06
Ever Ready 1894.47
Ever Since I was a Baby 1954.06
Ever-Loving Bee 1924.18, 1925.10
Everlasting 1951.19, 1984.02
Evermore and a Day 1929.41
Every Animal has its Mate 1927.36
Every Baby is a Sweet Bouquet 1909.05
Every Bee has a Bud of its Own 1918.25
Every Bit of You 1930.37
Every Blossom I See Reminds Me of You 1920.18
Every Body Seemed to be Invited 1907.03
Every Cloud is Silver-Lined 1918.02
Every Coon 1912.20
Every Coon had a Lady Friend But Me 1898.41
Every Day 1912.14, 1922.10, 1927.05, 1974.12
Every Day a Little Death 1973.04
Every Day Another Tune 1979.25
Every Day in Every Way 1922.45
Every Day is a Holiday 1952.13
Every Day is Ladies' Day With Me 1906.33, 1945.16
Every Day Will be Sunday When the Town Goes Dry 1918.33
Every Day, Every Night 1993.17
Every Dog Must Have its Day, and Every Puss Her Afternoon 1902.34
Every Eve 1946.22
Every Fellow Loves a Pretty Girl 1912.36
Every Fellow Wants to Love Me 1907.46
Every Flower has a Melody 1912.45, 1918.04
Every Girl 1921.36
Every Girl I Meet 1910.03
Every Girl in All America 1918.09
Every Girl in Venice 1982.09
Every Girl is Doing Her Bit 1917.29
Every Girl is Like a Weather Glass 1922.33
Every Girl Loves a Uniform 1909.20
Every Girl Must Have a Little Bull 1925.27
Every Girl Wants to Get Married 1962.01
Every Girlie Loves Me But the Girl I Love 1911.25
Every Girlie Wants to be a Sally 1921.18
Every Inch a Lady 1900.52
Every Little Bit 1907.49
Every Little Dog Must Have His Day 1902.36
Every Little Girlie has a Way All Her Own 1919.32
Every Little Miss 1922.14
Every Little Moment has a Meaning All it's Own 1976.07
Every Little Movement has a Meaning All its Own 1910.22
Every Little Note 1925.34
Every Little Object has a History 1906.44
Every Little Something 1905.56
Every Little Thing You Do 1926.18
Every Little While 1916.22, 1928.12
Every Loving Girl 1905.10
Every Man is a Stupid Man 1953.07
Every Movie's a Circus 1994.10
Every Nation has a Broadway of its Own 1920.20
Every Nation has a Flower That it Loves the Best 1912.30
Every Night 1954.15
Every Now and Then 1978.11
Every Once in a While 1959.11
Every Other Heartbeat 1942.29
Every Pretty Girl 1910.13
Every Rose Must Have its Thorn 1891.11, 1895.27
Every Silken Lady has a Touch of Calico 1924.25
Every Small Town Girlie has a Big Town Way 1915.12
Every Star Falls in Love With its Mate 1907.56
Every Story is a Love Story 2000.06
Every Street's a Boulevard in Old New York 1953.01
Every Time I Hear a Band Play 1921.21
Every Time I Meet a Lady 1920.38
Every Time the Music Starts 1980.11
Every Time You Danced With Me 1956.07
Every Year is Leap Year 1912.42
Everybody Brushes By 1910.34
Everybody Calls Me by My Name 1981.25
Everybody Dance 1924.29, 1997.07
Everybody do the Hula 1915.21
Everybody Else's Girl Looks Better to Me Than Mine 1908.40
Everybody Hands Me a Lemon 1906.31
Everybody has His Own Way 1976.35, 1980.14, 1982.17
Everybody has the Right to be Wrong 1965.33, 1974.10
Everybody Hum With Me 1915.33
Everybody is a Star 1982.22
Everybody is Crazy About Dixie 1919.26
Everybody Knows I Love Somebody 1928.03
Everybody Knows Madame Moselle 1914.14
Everybody Knows My Name 1897.25
Everybody Leaves You 1975.09
Everybody Likes You 1961.10
Everybody Love Everybody 1952.10
Everybody Loves a Chicken 1912.43
Everybody Loves a Hero 1990.04
Everybody Loves Louis 1984.08
Everybody Loves My Baby 1986.06, 1989.02
Everybody Loves My Girl 1927.37
Everybody Loves the Blues 2001.04
Everybody Loves to Take a Bow 1953.01
Everybody Means it When They Say Goodbye 1914.01
Everybody Must be Happy 1905.54
Everybody Must Love Someone 1914.06
Everybody Ought to do the Tickle Toe 1976.25
Everybody Ought to Have a Maid 1962.12, 1999.20
Everybody Ought to Know How to do the Tickle Toe 1917.36
Everybody Rag With Me 1914.22
Everybody Rejoice 1975.01
Everybody Says Don't 1964.15, 1977.05
Everybody Shimmies Now 1919.16
Everybody Shout 1927.33
Everybody Sometimes Must Love Someone 1913.17
Everybody Step 1921.30
Everybody Swat the Profiteer 1920.17
Everybody Tells it to Sweeney and Sweeney Tells it to Me 1920.18
Everybody Today is Turning On 1977.04
Everybody Wants to be in Show Business 1955.12
Everybody Wants to do a Musical 1991.15
Everybody Wants to Hold the Baby 1903.063
Everybody Wants to Marry Me 1926.03
Everybody Wonders Why They Love Me? 1918.05
Everybody's Alma Mater 1955.13
Everybody's Awfully Good to Me 1902.01
Everybody's Crazy Part of the Time 1919.44
Everybody's Doin' It 1960.16
Everybody's Doing It 1989.26
Everybody's Girl 1997.07
Everybody's Going to the Devil in New York 1908.28
Everybody's Got 'Em 1976.16
Everybody's Got a Home But Me 1955.27
Everybody's Got Somebody But Me 1920.35
Everybody's Happy in Jimtown 1928.10

Everybody's Happy in Vienna 1914.17
Everybody's Looking for a Sure Thing 1906.01
Everybody's Loved by Someone 1903.39
Everybody's Making it Now 1922.19
Everybody's Rag Time Crazy 1909.18
Everybody's Running 1971.01
Everybody's Strutting Now 1923.08
Everybody's Talking 1982.22
Everyday 1990.15
Everyday a Little Death 1999.20
Everyday I do a Little Something for the Lord 1980.30
Everyone Hates His Parents 1992.09
Everyone He Swear at the Waiter 1918.22
Everyone Here Loves Kelly 1965.01
Everyone in the World is Doing the Charleston 1925.45, 1927.21
Everyone is Beautiful in Someone's Eyes 1923.04
Everyone Knows What Jazz Is 1925.10
Everyone Made Happy 1933.15
Everyone Tells Jason to See a Psychiatrist 1992.09
Everyone Who's "Who's Who" 1956.16
Everyone's Gone to the Moon 1967.13, 1968.20
Everyone's Moving Up Town 1915.02
Everything 1970.15, 1972.05
Everything Beautiful 1961.21, 1965.36
Everything Beautiful Happens at Night 1963.26, 1992.10
Everything But My Man 1933.16
Everything But You 1981.06, 1997.03
Everything Depends on Money 1908.44
Everything Happens to Me 1940.09, 1995.12
Everything has Been so Pleasant Up to Now 1911.14
Everything I do Goes Wrong 1922.12
Everything I've Got 1975.13
Everything in America is Ragtime 1915.25, 1915.32
Everything in the World has a Place 1972.07
Everything in the World I Love 1965.36
Everything is Big in Chicago 1903.38
Everything is Changed 1984.02
Everything is Going Higher 1918.29
Everything is High Nowadays 1907.10
Everything is High Yellow Now 1926.22
Everything is Hunky Dory Down in Honky Tonky Town 1918.23
Everything is Possible in Life 1970.18
Everything is Rosey Now 1918.06
Everything Leads Right Back to Love 1947.08
Everything Looks Rosy and Bright 1917.35
Everything Needs Something 1969.16
Everything Old is New Again 1979.11, 1992.18
Everything Reminds Me of You 1921.16
Everything That Touches You 1980.05
Everything was Perfect 1980.23
Everything Will Happen for the Best 1926.25
Everything You Wrote 1993.17
Everything's All Right 1971.12
Everything's Alright 1992.12, 2000.09
Everything's at Home Except Your Wife 1912.34
Everything's Coming Up Roses 1959.13, 1974.22
Everything's Easy When You Know How 1966.06
Everything's Fine 1992.11
Everything's Going to be All Right 1925.16
Everything's Gonna be Much Worse Next Year 1955.11
Everything's Great 1964.32
Everytime 1941.06
Everytime We Call it Quits 1983.15
Everywhere 1947.15
Evil 1968.13, 1988.05
Evil Eye 1905.56
Evil Hearted Me 1954.11
Evil Weasel 1985.20
Evil-Hearted Man 1945.07
Eviva 1927.50
Evolution 1908.27
Evolution of Dance 1965.05
Evolution of Rag Time, The 1904.22
Evolution of Ragtime 1915.17
Evolution of Ragtime, The 1903.39
Evolution of the Finale, The 1920.08
Evolution Papa 1975.09
Ex-Gigolo 1930.35
Ex-Ray 1923.38
Exactly Like Me 1974.01
Exactly Like You 1930.09, 1979.25
Examination for State Military Service, The 1998.08
Examination Song, The 1980.17
Excelsior 1880.24, 1895.38
Exchange of Lovers 1945.14
Exchanges of Information 1971.04
Excuse for Song and Dance 1931.40
Excuse Me Baby Please, Please if You Don't Mind Baby, Thank You 1988.02
Excuse Me Mr. Moon 1911.13
Excuse Me? Certainly! 1915.08
Excuse My Boldness 1881.22
Excuse My Dust 1926.23
Exercise 1910.12
Exhibition 1909.21
Exhortation 1908.08, 1928.10, 1931.11
Exhortation Theme from Yamekraw Negro Rhapsody 1928.10
Exile's Return, The 1908.43
Exits 1992.17
Exodus, The 1971.02
Exorcism, The 1964.16
Expect Things to Happen 1963.21
Expectant Father 1952.05
Experience 1906.25, 1937.16, 1972.05
Experience Fox-Trot, The 1914.23
Experience One-Step, The 1914.24
Experiment 1997.01
Experiment Degustatory 1973.08
Explanation 1906.10
Explanation I Demand, An 1898.73
Explanations 1919.07
Exploitation Number 1927.10
Expotentisius 1904.43
Express 1986.02
Express Yourself 1965.17
Expressman's Chorus 1888.05
Exquisite Moment 1934.43
Extra Man 1933.15
Extra! 1916.22
Extra! Extra! 1893.46, 1944.16, 1982.05
Extra, Extra 1885.49, 1949.08
Extraordinary 1972.22
Eye of love is keen, The 1868.01
Eye That Never Sleeps, The 1912.43
Eye's delight 1879.38
Eyeful of You 1927.53
Eyes Have a Language 1916.20
Eyes of Black and Eyes of Blue 1900.25
Eyes of Blue 1900.36, 1920.41
Eyes of Love 1927.40
Eyes of the Army 1919.10
Eyes of the Girl I Love, The 1920.31
Eyes of Youth 1920.30
Eyes of Youth See the Truth, The 1917.37
Eyes so Bright 1885.06
Eyes so Dark and Luring 1922.35
Eyes That Came from Ireland, The 1910.06
Eyes That Come from Ireland, The 1906.38
Eyes That Haunt You 1925.06
Eyes That Love 1927.55
Eyesight to the blind 1972.08
Eyesight to the Blind 1993.06

F-A-M-E 1908.31
F.T.P. (Federal Theatre Project) Plowed Under 1937.14
Fables 1922.08
Fabric of Dreams, The 1923.33
Fabulous Feet 1983.21
Facade 1997.09
Face Behind the Mask, The 1914.30
Face in the Crowd, A 1950.14
Face on the Dime, The 1946.10
Faces 1916.11
Faces, Names, Places 1971.01
Fact Can be a Beautiful Thing, A 1968.31
Factory Girls, The/Come Up to My Office 1998.21
Facts of Life 1928.27
Facts of Life Backstage, The 1946.18
Facts, The 1971.21
Faculty Room Scene 1937.08
Fade Out - Fade In 1964.21
Faded Flowers 1925.47
Fading Golden Love Dream 1921.14
Fads 1900.38
Fahrenheit Gesundheit 1973.08
Faint and Wearily 1861.03
Fair American Maid 1898.50
Fair and Warmer Cocktail, The 1916.02
Fair Colonus 1988.05
Fair Columbia 1890.08
Fair Enough 1922.26
Fair Flower of Japan 1909.20
Fair Goddess, Fortune 1889.24
Fair Helen of Sparta 1868.08
Fair Honeymoon 1919.01
Fair Honora 1898.43
Fair is Rose as bright May day 1887.10
Fair Land of Dreaming 1925.02
Fair maid take pity 1893.02
Fair Moon 1945.08, 1945.09
Fair moon, to thee I sing! 1879.05
Fair Phrynette 1901.01
Fair Queen, I beg my suit you'll grant 1863.04
Fair Rosita 1928.29
Fair Trade 1979.12
Fair Warning 1958.01, 1959.11
Fair Weather 1929.50
Fair Weather Friends 1924.04, 1946.06
Fair Weather Sailors 1895.25
Fair, A 1970.17
Fair, The 1934.32
Fair-Haired Boy, The 1888.40
Fairest Flower Divine 1894.37
Fairest Maiden 1881.11
Fairest of earth's attire 1888.18
Fairest of Roses 1904.51
Fairest of the Fair 1906.41
Fairies We 1901.27
Fairies' Chorus 1906.15
Fairies' Lullaby 1900.41
Fairies' Meeting, The 1905.25
Fairies, Fairies Come Forth 1903.21
Fairies, The 1892.14
Fairy Beauty's Queen 1907.05
Fairy Bells 1912.35
Fairy Bells, The 1891.14
Fairy Doll, The 1927.38
Fairy Footsteps 1890.29
Fairy Song 1916.26
Fairy Step 1889.09
Fairy Tale 1925.36
Fairy Tale, A 1886.45, 1941.08, 1990.06
Fairy tale, A 1886.53
Fairy Tales 1897.42, 1919.31, 1920.19, 1924.16
Fairy Whispers 1920.12
Fairyland 1902.41, 1904.47, 1917.11, 1927.01, 1930.08, 1931.08, 1961.10
Fairyland's Daughters 1866.18
Faisons des cornets 1884.43
Faith 1964.44, 1995.04
Faith in Myself 1981.29
Faith, Hope and Charity 1919.09
Faithful Crew, The 1881.07, 1882.20
Faithless 1945.20
Fake Your Way to the Top 1981.29
Fakirs from Fakirsville 1893.16
Falcom, The 1907.08
Falcon in the Dive 1997.19, 1999.13
Fall In 1903.10
Fall not in love 1863.01
Fall of Babylon, The 1968.03
Fall of Man, The 1917.20
Fall of the Leaves, The 1926.15
Fallen Angels 1971.19
Fallen Babies 1925.42
Fallin' 1979.04
Fallin'-Out-of-Love-Rag, The 1971.09
Falling 1952.08, 1990.04, 1995.03
Falling in Love 1909.22, 1931.14, 1947.06
Falling in Love Again 1967.13, 1968.20, 1999.07
Falling in Love With Love 1938.14
Falling in Love With You 1975.13
Falling Off the Wagon 1932.16
Falling Out of Love 1932.15
Falling Out of Love Can be Fun 1949.08

Falling Star 1928.08
Falling Stars 1909.13
False, false woman 1882.60
Fame 1982.15
Fame is Phoney 1934.04
Family 1981.29
Family Brawl, The 1911.15
Family Council, The 1911.47
Family Faces 1919.11
Family Foundling, The 1883.04
Family Fugue 1962.18, 1978.18
Family Ghost, The 1902.15
Family of Man 1975.04
Family Overhead, The 1883.32
Family Pride 1908.43
Family Quarrel, A 1915.22
Family Reputation 1925.45
Family Solicitor, The 1986.12
Family Ties 1988.07
Family Tree, The 1907.62, 1973.05
Family Way, The 1962.05
Family's Ancient Tree, The 1908.06
Famine 1972.09
Famous Black Moguls, The 1898.22
Famous Falls 1923.34
Famous Feet 1980.08
Famous man was Robin Hood, A 1859.01
Famous Men I Have Not Met 1905.49
Fan Club Chant 1955.25
Fan Miss Fannie 1922.22
Fan Tan Fannie 1958.19
Fan, Fan 1964.02
Fanatique de Jazz, Le 1959.15
Fanchon! ah! c'est toi que je revois 1884.50
Fancy Dress 1907.15
Fancy Forgetting 1954.09
Fancy Little Step 1876.32
Fancy Our Meeting 1929.51
Fancy You Fancying Me 1917.29
Fancy! Fancy! 1936.02, 1936.17
Fandango - Bolero 1931.19
Fandango Rag 1910.18
Fandangos 1949.07, 1986.17
Fanfare 1982.20
Fanfarria 1988.15
Fannette 1972.16
Fannie 1925.28
Fanny 1900.01, 1954.15
Fans 1929.22, 1933.20
Fantastic Dream Ballet 1924.42
Far Above You is My Throne 1899.39
Far and Near 1882.75
Far Apart Still You're in My Heart 1918.07
Far Away 1885.03, 1886.62, 1925.52
Far Away and Long Ago 1928.26
Far Away from Home 1963.19
Far away from hostile spying 1888.18
Far Far Away 1885.64
Far Far from Wipers 1964.28
Far from Cohoes 1921.20
Far from Home 1966.09
Far from the Home I Love 1964.27
Far o'er the lake 1868.01
Far Up the Hill 1913.32
Far, Far Away 1908.30, 1938.13
Far, Far Better Way, A 1963.13
Farandol, The 1880.69
Farandole 1882.39
Farandulo Pasa, La 1926.09, 1926.35
Faraway Boy 1960.05
Fare Thee Well 1930.36, 1954.11, 1975.20
Fare thee well, attractive stranger 1882.78
Fare Ye Well 1945.07
Fare You Well 1963.22
Fare-Thee-Well 1896.41
Farewell 1881.11, 1886.45, 1892.42, 1917.32, 1918.27, 1926.42, 1946.03, 1955.19, 1972.03, 1982.01
Farewell Dixieland 1937.09
Farewell Fond Dreams of Love 1907.07
Farewell for Ever 1882.33
Farewell Forever 1877.25, 1879.03
Farewell Forever, Deceitful Old Wretch 1869.07
Farewell Good Angel 2000.20
Farewell Letter 1994.05
Farewell My Lovely 1972.05
Farewell my trimbuilt Wherry, The 1858.03
Farewell Song 1933.07, 1945.04
Farewell to Adrian 1922.36
Farewell to Italy 1893.37
Farewell to old England! 1871.10
Farewell to the King's Highway 1897.40, 1917.10
Farewell to Thee 1912.03
Farewell Waltz, The 1905.03
Farewell, Dear 1924.45
Farewell, farewell 1895.32
Farewell, Farewell 1967.06
Farewell, Fondest and Dearest 1895.08
Farewell, Gents 1880.32, 1881.16
Farewell, Goodbye 1936.28
Farewell, I Go 1905.46
Farewell, Marguerite 1888.28
Farewell, My Eulalie 1939.21
Farewell, my gallant Captain 1848.04
Farewell, My Lovely 1935.12
Farewell, My Own 1945.08, 1945.09
Farewell, my own, Light of my life, farewell! 1879.05
Farewell, Nellie Mine 1904.45
Farewell, O Life 1928.30
Farewell, Old Booth 1871.19
Farewell, Prosperity 1906.44
Farewell, Suzanne 1881.36
Farljandio 1922.19
Farmer 1980.05
Farmer and the Con Gent, The 1897.48
Farmer and the Cowman, The 1943.04
Farmer and the Scarecrow, The 1897.40, 1917.10
Farmer Jacob Lay a-Snoring 1924.45
Farmer Jacob Lay Asnoring 1980.21
Farmer Tan 1982.04
Farmer's Band 1920.02
Farmer's Daughter 1944.23
Farmer's Life, A 1906.48, 1925.02
Farmer's Son 1922.21
Farmerettes, The 1920.02
Farming 1941.08
Farming Life 1919.41
Farming Man, The 1878.02
Farrell Girl, The 1949.02
Farruca 1929.51, 1986.17
Farruca con Zapateado 1958.06
Farruca, La 1939.18
Farvos iz der himl geven nechtn loyter? 1960.18
Farwell Sisters 1863.02
Fascinatin' Rhythm 1988.08
Fascinating Flora 1907.18
Fascinating Girl 1912.13
Fascinating Lady 1926.01
Fascinating Little Man 1871.27
Fascinating Rhythm 1924.43, 1974.09, 1975.22, 1991.10, 1999.10
Fascinating Venus 1904.09, 1908.17
Fascinating Widow, The 1911.30
Fascinating You 1928.23, 1929.26
Fascination 1915.27, 1963.07, 1977.09
Fascination Waltz 1911.26
Fashion Girl, A 1937.15
Fashion Parade, The 1923.10
Fashion Show 1917.23
Fashion Show, The 1915.31
Fashion's Slave, A 1914.22
Fashionable Life 1916.07
Fast and Furious 1931.31
Fast Cars and Fightin' Women 1963.12
Fast Express, The 1913.14
Fast Step Creation, A 1920.31
Fast Steppers 1919.03
Fasten Your Seat Belts 1970.09
Faster and Faster 1917.08
Faster Than Sound 1964.16
Fastest Man in New York 1898.55
Fastrigossa's Lament 1968.22
Fastrigossa's Mame 1968.22
Fat and Forty 1981.06
Fat and Greasy 1978.09
Fat Boy 1896.51
Fat-Fat-Fatima 1921.06
Fatal Chair, The 1890.26
Fatal Curse of Beauty, The 1906.05
Fatal Fascination 1932.17, 1972.05
Fatal Step 1918.02
Fatal Step, The 1886.15, 1887.05
Fatal Wedding, The 1923.17
Fate 1921.27, 1953.16, 1978.03
Fate of the Veiled Mugs, The 1909.27
Fates, Fates, Fates 1894.38
Fates, The 1902.15
Father and Mother 1910.03
Father and Son 1912.01
Father is a Business Man 1910.24
Father Keeps on Doing It 1909.05
Father Knickerbocker 1917.08
Father Malloy 1859.15
Father Never Raised Any Foolish Children 1915.20
Father Nile, Keep Us in Thy Care 1895.33
Father of Little Ninette, The 1862.09
Father of the Bride, The 1966.29
Father of the Queen of Comic Opera 1897.39
Father Penn 1906.40
Father That Wear Rags 1981.02
Father to Son 1992.09
Father Wanted Me to Learn a Trade, And 1915.32
Father's Day 1948.28, 1956.09
Father's joy and pride they are, A 1887.44
Father's Whiskers 1916.05
Father, How Long? 1999.08
Father, Won't You Speak to Sister Mary 1897.34
Father-in-law, son-in-law! 1885.63
Fatherhood Blues 1983.19
Fatherland 1870.26
Fathers and Mothers and You and Me 1984.02
Fathers and Sons 1978.12
Fatima the Fair 1906.39
Fatty 1978.10
Faucett Falls Fancy 1969.07
Faust 1888.44
Faust Up to Date 1913.30
Faust Waltz 1886.28
Favorita 1862.03
Favorita, La 1895.03, 1897.20
Favorite Son 1991.07
Favorite, La 1923.10
Favour 1955.19
Fay of the forest, The 1859.16
Fay Templeton's Woodchuck Song 1903.14
Fe-Fi-Fo-Fum 1888.34
Fear 1949.15, 1964.21, 1972.06
Fear in My Heart 1935.03
Fear No More the Heat of the Sun 1981.02
Fear not, my love 1887.43
Fearless Frank 1980.17
Feast of Lanterns, The 1895.08
Feast of the Lanterns 1927.14
Feast on Me 1972.10
Feasts of the Kubbutz, The 1968.04
Feather Ballet 1902.06
Feather in a Breeze 1931.36
Feather in My Shoe 1969.07
Feather Your Nest 1918.39
February 1942.01
Fede Fede 1986.18
Federn, Dre 1864.13
Fee Fi Fo Fum 1913.33, 1971.20
Fee-Fie-Fo-Fum 1937.10
Feed Me With Love 1913.10
Feel the Rain Fall 1998.21
Feelin' Good 1928.08
Feelin' Loved 1978.10
Feeling Good 1965.19, 1974.22
Feeling Grand 1953.10
Feeling I'm Falling 1928.43
Feeling in Your Heart, A 1927.47
Feeling Lucky Today 1942.01
Feeling We Once Had, The 1975.01
Feelings 1966.18
Feelings You've Got to Hide 1997.17
Feet do Yo' Stuff 1967.06
Feet Don't Fail Me Now 1992.06
Feet on the Sidewalk 1943.14

Felicia 1997.13
Felicida 1964.02
Feline Wisdom 1937.11
Fellatio 101 1976.20
Feller That Looks Like Me, The 1866.22
Fellow Like Me, A 1924.40
Fellow Needs a Girl, A 1947.17
Fellow That Played the Drum, The 1894.21
Fellow Who Might be Galloping, The 1900.51, 1902.05, 1920.09
Fellow Who Might, The 1900.51, 1902.05
Female Drummer, A 1898.78
Feminine Rhythm 1930.20
Femininity 1958.02
Femme de Chambre, The 1897.37
Femme en naissent, A la 1887.35
Femmes 1935.19
Femmes Fatales 1958.18
Fence, The 1982.23
Fencing 1925.23
Fencing Girl, The 1911.29
Fencing Girls, The 1901.25, 1907.24
Fencing Song 1894.28
Fenian Ball, The 1866.26
Ferban 1915.17
Fergus' Dilemma 1983.01
Feria, La 1934.32
Fermons les yeux 1878.08
Fern wie aus vergang'nen Tagen… 1920.46
Ferry boat, The 1887.04
Festa 1917.23
Festa, La 1955.04
Festival 1972.09
Festival Nights 1919.03
Festival of Mourning 1905.53
Festival, The 1948.24
Festive Continong, The 1896.48
Fetch the Cat 1870.20
Fete a Loulou, La 1959.15
Fetes d'Hebe, Les 1933.24
Fetter Mord'che Heist, Der 1968.22
Feudin' and Fightin' 1944.30
Feuds of a nation's strife, The 1844.01
Feuilles Mortes, Les 1959.15
Feux Follets 1978.26
Fever 1983.20, 1999.09
Few Foolish Ideas, A 1898.61
Few Steps in Front of the Curtain, A 1924.37
Fiasco 1969.17
Fickle Finger of Fate 1964.44
Fickle Weather Vane, The 1906.07
Fiddle about 1972.08
Fiddle About 1993.06
Fiddle and I 1899.11, 1901.04
Fiddle Dee Dee 1901.18, 1937.11
Fiddle-dee-dee March 1900.38
Fiddler and the Fighter, The 1964.21
Fiddler Must be Paid, The 1911.07
Fiddlers' Green, The 1969.08
Fidgety Feet 1926.36, 1990.14
Fie on Goodness! 1960.21, 1980.19
Fie Upon You! Fie! 1885.58
Fie, Upon You! Fie! 1878.02
Field and Forest, The 1903.10
Field of Cloth of Gold, The 1976.08
Fiesta 1927.55, 1932.07
Fiesta En Jalisto 1988.15
Fiesta in Madrid 1935.11, 1969.11
Fiesta in Rio 1975.12
Fifer of the Old Drum Corps, The 1902.42
Fifteen Glorious Years 1965.39
Fifteen Minutes 1906.39
Fifteen Minutes a Day 1924.40, 1933.06
Fifth Avenue 1901.12, 1915.27, 1949.01
Fifth Avenue Brigade, The 1908.18, 1908.19
Fifth Avenue Stride, The 1924.16
Fifth Commandment, The 1931.29
Fifth of Beethoven, A 1977.09, 1999.15
Fifty Great Places All in One Place 1981.08
Fifty Million Years Ago 1969.02
Fifty Percent 1978.27
Fifty Ways to Leave Your Lover 1976.32
Fifty-Fifty 1980.27
Fifty-Fifty I'll Fifty-Fifty With You 1919.32
Fifty-Seven Ways to Catch a Man 1904.18
Fifty-Seventh Street 1982.15
Fig Leaf Number 1920.22
Fig Leaves are Falling, The 1969.01
Figaro's Aria 1990.16
Fight at the Marketplace 1997.16
Fight Over Me 1925.30
Fight Song, The 1962.04
Fight Them Like Your Dear Old Dad 1905.34
Fight, The 1964.32, 1969.11
Fighters of Flames are We 1905.25
Fighting for Pharaoh 1972.13
Fighting Kid, The 1908.28
Fighting Man, A 1900.12
Fighting Regiment, The 1910.23
Fights, The 1959.14
Figlia 1985.16
Fiji 1906.04, 1919.03
Fiji Island 1945.07
Fiji Mick 1888.30
Fiji Serenade 1887.29
Filipino Maid, The 1902.05
Fill ev'ry Glass, for Wine inspires us 1750.01
Fill every glass 1854.06
Fill Every Glass 1957.02
Fill High! Drink Deep! 1895.08
Fill in the Words 1979.04
Fill Up Again Warriors 1899.06
Fill up and let us drink 1880.18
Fill up on Champagne and pate de foie gras 1885.45
Fill Up the Loving Cup 1896.41
Fill Up Your Tankards 1903.07
Fill, my jolly Boys 1859.05
Fille de Levy, La 1935.19
Fille de madame Angot, La 1926.47
Fille de Mme. Angot, La 1877.43
Filles qui, la nuit…, Les 1934.32
Filth 1981.07
Fin de Siecle 1929.31
Final Report 1975.07
Final Selection 1987.05
Final Song 1939.23
Final Storm 1991.05
Finale 1948.30
Finaletto 1923.10, 1945.09, 1947.11, 1982.05
Finally 1983.17
Financial Viking, The 1916.14
Financier's Song 1938.02
Find a Good Time 1925.07
Find Me a Hero 1978.11
Find Me a Primitive Man 1929.45, 1975.22
Find Out What They Like and How They Like It 1978.09
Find the Queen, Kill the Fox 1997.16, 1998.08
Find the Right Girl 1922.40
Find Your Own Cricket 1970.21
Find Yourself a Man 1964.11
Finders is Keepers and I Found You 1920.36
Finding a Man Ain't Easy 1995.04
Finding Words for Spring 1965.02
Findjan 1960.18
Fine and Dandy 1930.28
Fine Art of Strip Teasing, The 1936.17
Fine Feathers 1917.23, 1921.25, 1923.21, 1926.37
Fine Old English Gentleman, The 1871.16
Fine Romance, A 1986.01
Fine Strawberries 1911.13
Fine White Horse, A 1991.05
Fine, Thank You, Fine 1969.07
Finer Things, The 2000.20
Finery 1932.06
Finesse 1909.14
Fingers and Toes 1978.10
Fini 1953.17
Finish 1907.46
Finish, The 1898.70
Finishing School 1907.46
Finishing the Hat 1984.08
Finnan Haddie 1929.17
Finnegan's Wake 1866.19
Fioretta 1929.08
Fire and Ice 1989.26
Fire and Mist 1923.04
Fire and Sugar 1993.01, 1995.16, 1998.17
Fire Belles 1911.35
Fire Down Below 1979.30
Fire Ladies' Ball, The 1911.35
Fire on Goodness! 1993.11
Fire on the Bayou 1992.06
Fire Water 1907.07
Fire-Fly 1869.40
Firedance 2000.05
Fireflies 1910.10, 1990.17
Firefly 1916.05
Firefly and the Rose, The 1905.55
Firefly Ballet 1900.07
Firefly, The 1905.40, 1923.08
Fireman's Bride, The 1945.03, 1947.11
Fireman's Flame, The 1937.12
Fireman's Parade, The 1905.26
Fireman's Picnic, The 1909.16
Fireworks 1929.49, 1960.23
Fireworks, The 1938.06
First Act, Second Act, Third Act 1917.36
First and Last 1999.15
First and Only 1907.25
First Blossom Ballet, The 1925.52
First Campaign Song 1969.03
First Class Number One Bum 1970.08
First Class Roster, The 1997.06
First Dance, The 1911.39, 1983.03
First Day of May, The 1917.06
First Final 1987.05
First Gray Hair 1911.46
First I met was a young lieutenant, The 1894.28
First Impression 1937.14
First is Last, The 1924.17
First Kiss of Love 1926.24
First Kiss, The 1907.07
First Lady of the Land, The 1931.21, 1976.11
First Lady, The 1962.20
First Letter 1994.05
First Letter Home 1985.12
First Love 1880.69, 1884.57, 1886.50, 1918.35, 1921.33
First Love Days 1911.35
First Love is the Best Love of All 1915.12
First Man You Remember, The 1990.04
First Mate Martin 1929.31
First Nighters 1917.35
First Nighters, The 1924.07
First Noel, The 1998.19
First Prize at the Fair 1948.14
First Regression 1965.31
First Rose of Summer, The 1919.09
First Spring Day, The 1933.15
First Submarine Boat, The 1902.08
First Thing in the Morning 1932.08
First Thing Monday Mornin' 1970.05
First time at the Looking-Glass, The 1750.01
First Time for Me, The 1930.11
First Time I Spoke of You, The 1957.17
First Time I was Yours in the Dark, The 1950.16
First Time We Rode on the Cars, The 1905.30
First Time, The 1968.30, 1979.30, 1983.14
First We Throw Moe Out 1926.51
First Wench Done Turned White 1896.49
First You Do the Rag, Then You Bombashay, Dat's How de Rag-Time Dance is Done 1899.12
First You Dream 1997.07
First you're born 1894.15
First, Last and Only 1926.06
First, The 1981.28
Firulete, El 1993.08
Fischerine du Kleinere 1888.34
Fish Chorus 1907.55
Fisherman's Prayer 1982.04
Fisherwoman's Song, The 1880.18
Fishes in the Sea, The 1903.22
Fishing 1904.22, 1907.10, 1912.30
Fishing Fleet is Homeward Bound, The 1914.13
Fishing Maidens, The 1894.17
Fishmonger, The 1926.35
Fit as a Fiddle 1985.08
Five Growing Boys 1970.07

Five A.M. 1936.02
Five Daughters 1959.06
Five Dollars a Seat 1904.53
Five Guys Named Moe 1992.03
Five Hundred Million 1936.26
Five Little Haytian Maidens 1899.33
Five Little Piggies 1903.02
Five Lovely Ladies 1969.14
Five Minutes More 1974.10
Five Minutes of Spring 1961.08
Five More Minutes in Bed 1945.18
Five O'Clock 1937.16
Five O'Clock in the Morning 1870.07
Five O'Clock Tea 1906.37, 1925.45
Five O'Clock, Le 1931.14
Five Piece Band 1960.12
Five Profiteers, The 1919.33
Five Shots of Whiskey 1961.02
Five Thousand Francs 1930.43
Five Zeros 1978.02
Five, Six, Seven, Eight...Dance! 1983.09
Five-Foot-Two 1926.02
Five-Leaved Shamrock, The 1872.23
Five-Step 1927.46
Fix Me 1963.27
Fixed for Life 1926.17
Fixin' for a Long, Cold Winter 1951.17
Fixin' to Die Rag 1970.16
Fixing a Hole 1974.24
Fiyou on the Bayou 1992.06
Fizkin and Pickwick 1965.28
Flacton-on-Sea 1914.10
Flag and the Girl I Love, The 1903.20
Flag He Loved, The 1904.54
Flag of My Country 1902.41, 1917.11
Flag of the Union, The 1890.44
Flag of Truce, The 1886.40
Flag, The 1931.16
Flagon of Wine, A 1925.32
Flags of Allies 1918.28
Flahooley 1951.15
Flame of Love 1923.10
Flame of Love, The 1915.04
Flame, The 1965.17
Flamenco 1934.38, 1934.42
Flamenco De Paris 1959.15
Flamenco of Paris 1961.25
Flamenco Song 1969.11
Flaming Agnes 1966.29
Flaming Youth 1927.41, 1948.22
Flaming Youth, 1927 1944.31
Flannel Petticoat al, The 1923.45
Flap-a-Doodle 1926.32
Flapper and the Vamp, The 1921.09
Flapper, The 1922.15
Flappers 1922.19
Flash Bang Wallop 1965.14
Flash of the Skipper's Eyes, The 1902.37
Flat Floot Floogie 1939.29
Flat in Monmartre, A 1928.27
Flat on the Opposite Side, The 1899.19
Flattery 1917.18, 1952.10, 1958.20
Flatulent Ballad, The 1950.01
Fleet's In, The 1997.05
Fleeting 1894.05
Fleeting Honeymoon 1923.07
Fleeting Seasons, The 1892.29
Flesh Failures, The 1968.11
Flesh of My Flesh, Bone of My Bone 1950.16
Fletcher's American Chocolate Choral Society 1930.02
Fleurs que nous admirons, Les 1883.51
Flex-a-Tone 1925.23
Flickers, The 1955.25
Flight of the Air Ship 1910.13
Flights of Fancy 1915.27
Fling him in the briny 1866.16, 1867.18
Flings 1957.07
Flirt 1894.07, 1911.44
Flirtation 1908.03, 1909.19, 1911.47, 1965.05
Flirtation Dance 1920.38, 1926.27
Flirtation Duet 1898.01
Flirtation Fantasies 1919.14
Flirtation on the Beach 1901.25, 1903.11
Flirtation Quartette 1921.03
Flirtation Sextette 1905.35
Flirtation Song 1903.18
Flirting 1905.40, 1907.41, 1912.42, 1915.24, 1920.12
Flirting at St. Moritz 1915.25
Flirting at the Ball 1893.06
Flirting Salesmen, The 1922.43
Flirting With the Bees 1904.11
Flirting With the Man in the Moon 1898.08
Flits Fegelech 1968.22
Flo 1898.02, 1904.24
Float Me Charlie 1905.52
Float Me Down Your Pipeline 1970.04
Floating Down a Moonlight Stream 1918.42
Floating Down the Amazon 1919.21
Floating Down the Nile 1907.22
Floating o'er yon silvery tide 1864.22
Floating Through the Air 1927.11
Floorflushers 1918.36
Floorshow 1975.08
Floorshow/Rose Tint My World 2000.17
Floorwalker, The 1891.14, 1892.06
Floozies 1971.16
Flor de Te 1926.35
Flor del Mal 1926.09, 1926.35
Flora 1898.43, 1902.43
Flora Bella 1916.17
Flora, I am Your Adorer 1901.27
Floradora Slide 1913.18
Floral Wedding, The 1907.11
Floretta 1903.31, 1929.48
Florida by the Sea 1925.45
Florida Mammy 1925.27
Florida Swamp Shimmy, A 1944.31
Florida, the Moon and You 1926.18
Florodora Sextette a la Harlem 1930.24
Florrie 1904.29
Florrie the Flapper 1914.18
Flossie 1924.17
Flotsam and Jetsam 1957.05
Flow on Silver Rhine 1872.06
Flow On, Silver Stream 1866.18
Flow, My Wine 1932.09
Flower Fortune Dance, The 1971.16
Flower Garden Ball 1918.08
Flower Garden Ball, The 1914.06, 1915.25
Flower Garden Girls, The 1918.08
Flower Garden of My Heart 1975.13
Flower Garden of My Heart, The 1940.22
Flower Girl 1880.42
Flower o' th' Heather 1928.05
Flower of Innocence 1877.05
Flower of My Heart 1915.12, 1990.15
Flower of Purity 1870.08, 1870.27
Flower of Sin/Poor Scentless Flower 1926.09, 1926.35
Flower of the Heather 1930.17
Flower of the Woodland 1923.25
Flower Song 1906.20, 1909.20, 1918.35, 1935.02, 1974.12
Flower Song, The 1950.14
Flower Waltz 1947.14
Flowers 1902.20
Flowers and Flowers 1983.20
Flowers in Bloom 1942.26
Flowers ne'er Fading 1887.31
Flowers of Dixie Land, The 1903.28
Flowers of Evil, The 1923.41
Flowers of Spring, The 1885.51
Flowers of the Harem 1897.30
Flowers That Bloom in the Spring 1938.10, 1939.15, 1939.17
Flowers that bloom in the spring, The 1885.47
Flowers, Feathers, Ribbons, Laces 1903.40
Floyd's Guitar Blues 1986.03
Flubby Dub, the Cafe-Man 1917.06
Fluffy Ruffles 1908.27
Flutter, Little Bird 1904.37
Flutterby Baby 1928.23
Fly 1981.16
Fly a Rainbow 1999.17
Fly Away 1979.11
Fly Away, Kite 1907.63
Fly Bird 1955.03
Fly Butterfly 1925.22
Fly by Night 1937.16, 1972.05
Fly Fast, Fond Dove 1892.20
Fly Forth, O Gentle Dove 1938.06
Fly Little Bird 1968.22
Fly Little Heart 1955.12
Fly not yet 1860.05
Fly Song, The 1897.05
Fly to His Arms 1787.01
Fly, The 1973.08
Flying Dutchman 1907.63
Flying High 1910.16, 1930.11
Flying Home 1975.12
Flying Milk and Runaway Plates 1970.20
Fo' de Lawd's Sake, Play a Waltz 1911.02
Foaming Beer 1886.53
Fog and the Grog, The 1961.26
Fogarty 1911.17
Fogarty the Great 1946.04
Foggy, Foggy Dew 1944.32
Fol de Rol 1912.09
Fol-de-iddley-ido! 1905.25
Fol-de-Rol 2001.09
Fol-de-rol-lol 1914.17
Fol-de-rol-rol 1946.24
Folk Songs 1910.37
Folks at Home, The 1950.03
Folks do not much like me here 1881.25
Folks Think I am so Good 1884.39
Folks Who Live on the Hill, The 1986.01
Foll de Broadway 1964.22
Follette 1911.40
Follies Bergere 1982.09
Follies Bergeres 1984.10
Follies Choral Ensemble, The 1934.01
Follies Labiche Overture 1951.13
Follies Minstrels, The 1919.15
Follies Salad, The 1919.15
Follies-Bergere 1955.14
Follow Mamma's Advice 1918.04
Follow Master 1929.07
Follow Me 1904.06, 1910.27, 1914.03, 1914.18, 1916.25, 1918.40, 1925.47, 1960.21, 1980.19, 1993.11
Follow Me Around 1912.31
Follow Me Round 1909.21, 1911.27
Follow Me Up the Stairs 1966.05
Follow Mister Cook 1925.42
Follow Mr. Watteau 1920.03
Follow On 1917.26, 1921.20, 1926.51, 1927.65
Follow the Boys 1918.35
Follow the Cook 1917.04
Follow the Crowd 1904.23, 1914.02
Follow the Drums 1928.03
Follow the Flag 1904.36, 1908.19, 1918.23
Follow the Flag We Love 1925.02
Follow the Fold 1950.17
Follow the Girl 1918.06
Follow the Girls 1944.14
Follow the Girls Around 1917.22
Follow the Good Advice 1907.10
Follow the Guide 1927.07
Follow the Lamb 1970.08
Follow the Leader 1962.24, 1989.25
Follow the Leader Jig 1949.08
Follow the Man from Cook's 1898.46
Follow the Man That Leads the Band 1901.21
Follow the Merry Crowd 1905.10
Follow the Midnight Girl 1913.30
Follow the Minstrel Band 1929.27
Follow the Plow 1908.43
Follow the Rahjah 1925.08
Follow the Rainbow 1971.18
Follow the Yellow Brick Road 1989.06, 1997.11
Follow Through 1927.04
Follow Thru 1929.03
Follow You All Over the World 1922.36
Follow Your Footsteps 1924.10
Follow Your Heart 1955.01
Follow Your Instinct 1985.20
Follow Your Star 1924.36, 1925.23, 2001.01
Follow Your Uncle Dudley 1907.57
Follow, follow 1844.01

Follow, Follow 1907.10
Following in Father's Footsteps 1927.52
Following the Dream 1916.01
Following the Sun Around 1927.08
Folly 1887.13, 1912.08
Fond Love, True Love 1899.40
Fond memory oft 1859.16
Fond of Babies 1920.35
Fond of the Ladies 1912.39
Fond of You 1925.29
Fontaine, La 1933.24
Food for Thought 1948.24, 1966.32
Food, Glorious Food 1963.01
Fool am I, A 1896.41
Fool Dance 1914.34
Fool for Luck 1940.03
Fool is My Brother, A 1888.39
Fool Me 1916.25
Fool on the Hill, The 1977.10
Fool Such as I, A 1978.01
Fool There Was, A 1920.34
Fool's Gold 1966.30
Fool, The 1923.38
Foolin' Ourselves 1959.14
Fooling Around With Love 1931.47
Foolish 1905.45
Foolish Face 1930.25, 1972.05
Foolish Gardener, The 1909.23
Foolish Heart 1943.19
Foolish Little Maiden I 1917.14
Foolish Song, A 1907.24
Foolish Swallow, The 1900.12
Foolish Wedding Bells 1902.44
Foolish Wives 1925.43
Foolishment 1922.24
Foolishness 1905.53, 1912.24, 1915.01
Fools Fall in Love 1940.08, 1995.03
Fools Rush In 1997.05
Football 1904.13
Football Boys and Girls, The 1903.11
Football Girls at Vassar, The 1906.40
Football Girls, The 1904.58
Football Song 1917.17
Footlight Walk 1927.39
Footloose 1998.13
Footman and the Maid, The 1915.22
Footstep 1978.11
Footsteps 1993.02
Footwork 1928.36
For a Boy Like You 1926.22
For a Girl 1894.25
For a Girl Can Love a Sailor 1908.03
For a Girl has Her Living to Make 1913.33
For a Girl Like You 1918.39, 1926.22
For a Good Dog 1973.08
For a Love 1988.15
For a Quarter 1942.18
For a Sight of Old Broadway 1902.43
For all of which I mean that Bridge shall pay 1886.28
For All of Which My Son-in-Law Must Pay 1885.45
For Aye,My Love 1907.51
For Better or for Worse 1915.24
For Better or Worse 1932.13, 1963.25
For Charity's Sake 1906.37
For de Lawd's Sake, Play a Waltz 1912.02
For Ever and for Aye 1894.46, 1899.02
For Every Boy That's Lonely 1911.15
For Every Fish There's a Little Bigger Fish 1957.16
For Every Lover 1913.24
For Every Lover Must Meet His Fate 1947.04
For Foxy has the Brain 1900.50
For Glory and for Love 1904.18
For Goodness Sake Don't Say I Told You 1882.28
For Goodness Sake, Don't Say I Told You 1883.42
For He was a Married Man 1904.18
For he's gone and married Yum-Yum 1885.47, 1885.51
For Her Dear Feet 1875.15
For Home and Ireland 1903.25
For I am Blithe 1938.10
For I Love Only You 1911.02
For I'm a Jolly Postillion 1930.12
For I'm in Love Again 1930.38
For I'm Just I 1911.01
For I'm O'Hooligan 1894.38
For in pleasing the public he 1881.06
For in the field 1897.39
For Ireland 1896.41
For it's Funny How it Goes 1895.25
For Jollity, now let's away 1868.08
For journies when preparing 1859.16
For Jupiter and Greece 1942.15
For lack of gold 1890.33
For Love 1903.06, 1918.26, 1959.04
For love alone 1879.10
For Love I Live Alone 1902.18
For Love of Thee 1906.38
For Love or Money 1956.16
For Mama 1965.30
For Many a Year 1918.27
For Me and My Gal 1917.03, 1955.13
For Me and My Gal' 1967.11
For Me Formidable 1965.30
For me what joy, what happiness 1859.17
For Months and Months and Months 1911.13
For My Mary 1986.13
For My Own 1961.14
For No Good Reason at All 1986.06
For No Reason Whatsoever 1921.17
For No Rhyme or Reason 1938.07
For Old Time's Sake 1907.34
For Old Times' Sake 1927.66
For Once in My Life 1974.11
For Once in Your Life 1968.03
For one day I'm master 1853.02
For Our Sake 1969.01
For Poland 1979.02
For Queen and Country 1925.06
For She's a Jolly Good Fellow 1909.01
For Someone I Love 1929.26
For Sweet Charity 1959.22
For Sweet Charity's Sake 1898.01, 1928.36
For That's What Nobody Knows 1892.42
For the Benefit of Man 1902.03
For the First Time 1961.27
For the Freedom of the C's 1919.16
For the Honor of the Flag 1915.25
For the Life of Me 1946.20
For the Papa 1929.17
For the Rest of My Life 1969.01
For the Sake of Art 1945.12
For the Sake of Humanity 1917.23
For the Sake of Lexington 1939.24
For the twentieth time we'll drink 1897.39
For Thee, My Love 1898.01
For Them 1982.08
For These Little Feet 1870.38
For This 1897.40, 1917.10
For This She Starred Her Eyes With Salt 1931.06
For tho' we've been so long about it 1886.40
For Thy Dea Sake 1890.26
For We're Immensley High-Toned 1886.15
For What Thou Art 1903.21
For You 1889.54, 1904.15, 1965.37
For You and for Me 1930.36
For You and the Girl You Love 1906.01
For You Brother 1972.11
For You Have Twenty-Four 1894.05
For You, Bright Eyes 1910.09
For You, Dear Heart 1913.01
For You, Honey, for You 1904.39
For your indulgence 1884.14
Forbidden Fruit 1889.40, 1914.04, 1922.35, 1966.18
Forbidden Love in Gaul 1966.18
Forbidden Music 1886.53
Forbidden Orchid, The 1948.24
Force and Montana Waltz 1929.20
Fordyce 1930.28
Forehead low, but full of cunning 1866.14
Foreign Cars 1955.12
Foreign Ditties 1902.07
Foreign Vaudevillians, The 1897.48
Foresight 1970.02
Forest Air, The 1903.02
Forest Bird, The 1913.33
Forest Legend, A 1921.38
Forest Loafers 1902.06
Forest Song 1891.29
Forest Song, The 1929.43, 1944.25
Forest Trees, The 1882.18
Forest, Forest 1971.17
Forester's Song, The 1902.04
Forethought! 1918.29
Forever 1924.04, 1966.20, 1967.14
Forever and a Day 1903.14, 1964.16
Forever and Ever 1928.08
Forever Mine 1928.23
Forever Young 1982.22
Forever Yours 1990.12
Forget All Your Books 1930.32
Forget It 1908.30
Forget Me 1960.12
Forget Me Not 1876.32, 1909.19, 1912.03, 1913.01
Forget That Girl, Once and for All 1969.11
Forget Your Troubles 1922.44
Forget-me-not 1885.65
Forget-Me-Nots, The 1900.49
Forgive 1947.06
Forgive and Forget 1911.03, 1914.02
Forgive me, Julia 1859.16
Forgive Us 1923.23
Forgive! 1899.39
Forgiveness 2000.20
Forgotten Dreams 1987.02
Forklifts 1999.02
Forlorn and broken hearted 1859.01
Forlorn Old Maid, The 1882.02
Fors e lui', 'A 1922.37
Forsaken 1932.18
Fortune Favors the Brave 2000.06
Fortune of War, The 1879.15
Fortune Overwhelms Me 1895.25
Fortune Telling 1882.17, 1923.27
Forty Days 1994.05
Forty Eight States 1948.19, 1949.05
Forty Five Minutes from Broadway 1968.07
Forty Forth Street Music Hall March, The 1913.28
Forty Gallant Thieves are We 1899.21
Forty Minutes for Lunch 1943.19
Forty Second Street and Broadway Strut, The 1922.28
Forty-Five Minutes from Broadway 1906.02
Forty-Second Street 1980.09, 1980.20, 1988.08
Forty-Second Street Moon 1924.21
Forward into Tomorrow 1972.07
Forward Joe Soap's Army 1964.28
Forward March 1932.14
Forward March into My Arms 1932.06
Fossil Man, The 1907.26
Fougere 1901.23
Foundling, The 1895.32
Foundlings are we 1895.32
Fountain Fay Protective Institution, Limited, The 1910.37
Fountain Fay, The 1910.37
Fountain in the Garden, The 2001.01
Fountain of Youth, The 1925.38, 1928.49
Fountain, Fairy Water 1905.04
Four and Twenty Little Men 1902.35
Four Aristocrats 1927.07
Four Beauties, The 1891.03
Four Beautiful Birds, The 1925.48
Four Black Dragons 1976.02
Four Characters in Search of an Historian 1924.15
Four Corpses, The 1925.03
Four Doctors, The 1882.28
4-11-44 1885.15, 1889.15, 1895.05
Four fo' Me 1922.22
Four for the Road 1960.07
Four Grecians 1931.36
Four Hundred Girls Ago 1972.25
Four I'm in Love 1927.18
Four Infant Prodigies 1930.18, 1930.33
Four Japanese 1997.16
Four Japanese Merchants 1997.16
Four Jews in a Room Bitching 1992.09
Four Leaf Clovers, The 1926.32
Four Leaved Shamrock, The 1854.04
Four Little Angels of Peace 1937.14
Four Little Girls With a Future and Four Little Girls With a Past 1921.21

Four Little Japs 1896.45
Four Little Mice 1895.19
Four Little Misfits 1955.25
Four Little Songpluggers 1926.13
Four Lunatics, The 1906.13
Four Marys 1954.11
Four Nightingales 1970.07
Four O'Clock Tea 1912.09
Four of Us, The 1968.07
Four Professional Guides 1888.11
Four Seasons of Wedlock, The 1904.47
Four Seasons, The 1907.54
Four Strikes Against Me 1983.21
Four Walls 1927.62
Four Walls and One Dirty Window Blues 1982.12
Four Young People 1939.26
Fourteen Freedoms, The - Calypso 1942.29
Fourth Letter 1994.05
Fourth Light Dragoons, The 1970.06
Fourth of July, The 1900.01, 1987.19
Fourth Telegram, The 1984.02
Foward to Do or Die 1879.64
Fox a poil dur 1948.12
Fox has Left His Lair, The 1925.42
Fox Hunt, The 1966.10
Fox may steal your Hens, Sir, A 1750.01
Fox Trot Military Tune 1918.35
Fox Trot Wedding Day 1915.25
Foyo 1966.03
Fracas at Old Drury 1961.26
Frag' nicht warum ich gehe 1968.20
Frag' Nicht Warum Ich Gehe 1999.07
Fragonard Impression, A 1939.07
Fragrance of the Lehua Wreath 1912.03
Fragrant as their perfume 1881.04
Fragrant Flower 1959.06
Frahngee-Pahnee 1944.29
Fraid Cat 1924.17
Fran and Janie 1982.08
Francais, A la 1882.39
France in arms for war 1881.25
France Will Not Forget 1927.43
France, Glorious France 1902.37
France, La France, La 1973.07
Francie 1941.01
Franco-American Rag 1910.18
Franco-American Ragtime 1909.28
Francois and Cooks 1894.22
Francois! Francois! 1884.50
Frank in the Melting Pot 1980.17
Frank Mills 1968.11
Frank, Frank, Frank 1971.09
Frankfurter Sandwiches 1997.01
Frankie and Johnny 1924.31, 1939.14, 1943.16, 1944.32
Frankie et Johnny 1964.39
Franklin D. Roosevelt Jones 1938.09
Franklin Shephard, Inc. 1981.27
Frantzi Frankenstein 1909.24
Fraternization Ballet 1952.13
Fraternization Song, The 1963.09
Fraught 1941.01, 1942.26
Fred Astaire Affair, The 1967.02
Fred Karno's Army 1964.28
Fred Stone 1908.21
Fred's Farewell 1918.36
Freda 1908.25
Freddy and His Fiddle 1944.21
Freddy, My Love 1972.12, 1994.07
Free 1915.22, 1962.12
Free Again 1977.09
Free and Easy 1974.03, 1975.09
Free and Equal Blues 1945.07
Free as Air 1915.22
Free as the Air 1946.16
Free as the Lark 1882.18
Free at Last 1985.06
Free Etiquette 1910.36
Free for All 1931.28
Free from his fetters grim 1888.35
Free Speech, Free Thought, Free Love 1980.17
Free Trade and a Misty Moon 1917.07
Free, Cute and Size Fourteen 1942.29
Free, Free, Free 1926.30
Freedom 1899.39, 1963.19, 1975.03
Freedom and Ireland 1900.36
Freedom Can be a Most Uncomfortable Thing 1960.10
Freedom is Coming Tomorrow 1988.02
Freedom March 1967.06
Freedom of the Press!, The 1894.28
Freedom of the Press, The 1937.08
Freedom of the Seas, The 1960.13
Freedom Train, The 1963.22
Freedom! 1948.24
Freedom's Child 1999.08
Freedomland 1962.02
Freeze Music 1971.04
Freight 1987.05
Freilekhs, A 1970.17
French Fandango, The 1910.20
French Have a Word for It, The 1939.22
French Lesson 1958.20, 1958.21
French Lesson, The 1924.41, 1977.02, 1997.16
French Maids, The 1905.05
French March 1892.05
French Marching Song 1926.42
French Militaire 1908.31
French Military Marching Song 1946.03, 1987.10
French Pastry Walk, The 1922.10
French Revolution, The 1923.17
French Singing Lesson, The 1884.13
French Soldiers on Leave 1919.10
French Tonic, A 1906.29
French Translation, The 1895.44
French With Tears 1950.02
Frenchie 1918.13
Fresh as a Daisy 1940.19
Freshie, O Freshie 1910.01
Fresno Beauties 1956.04
Freud 1964.44
Friar Larry 1897.32
Friar's Life, A 1895.38
Friday Dancing Class 1948.30
Fridays at Four 2001.01
Friend of Mine, A 1909.14
Friend of the Family 1907.31, 1940.09
Friendliest Thing, The 1964.05
Friendly Chat, A 1932.09
Friendly Enemy 1948.15
Friendly Ghosts 1927.02
Friends 1898.73, 1922.01, 1928.31, 1966.18, 1973.14, 1975.12
Friends Ain't S'posed to Die 1980.13
Friends and Lovers 1928.27
Friends for Life 1988.07, 1992.12
Friends Have to Part 1918.27
Friends of Long Ago 1907.19
Friends That are Good and True 1905.20
Friends to the End 1945.19
Friends, Dear Friends 1898.48
Friends, The 1959.15
Friends, the Best Of 1982.10
Friendship 1895.21, 1916.07, 1922.35, 1924.07, 1930.43, 1939.30, 1987.15
Friendship is a Lovely Thing 1903.16
Friendship That Never Came to Be, A 1977.13
Friendship's Sacred Touch 1906.18
Frightened Chorus 1880.32
Frightened Fawn 1904.18
Friling 1989.10
Frills Upon Their Petticoats 1904.03
Fringe of Society, The 1903.26
Frisco Frizz, The 1911.26
Frisco Melody, The 1916.02
Frisco, The 1912.13
Friska Linda 1902.08
Friskie Linda 1889.41
Frivolity 1907.41, 1916.09
Frivolity Frolics 1951.10
Frocks and Frills 1917.31, 1918.33
Frog and the Owl, The 1905.50
Frog He Lived in a Pond, A 1899.39
Frog Song 1895.27
Frog Song, The 1897.45
Frolic of the Bears, The 1975.19
Frolicking Gods 1922.19, 1923.16
Frolics of Pierrot, The 1907.44
Frolique, La 1895.03
Frollicking 1883.04
From a Different Point of View 1902.37
From a Prison Cell 1960.13
From A to Z 1948.22
From a Trip to the Moon 1886.02
From a Window on the Seine 1952.04
From Across the River 1972.17
From Afar 1976.08
From Africa 1900.20
From an Antique Land 1973.08
From Another World 1940.06, 1975.13
From Atlanta to the Sea 1963.22
From Bagdad We Come 1920.34
From Broadway to Main Street 1923.24
From Cairo, Bagdad, Khorasan 1917.24, 1919.20
From Chambers. . 1880.46
From Cottage to Subway 1924.33
From Courtiers as They Pass 1881.22
From Earth, through Sky, through Air, You fly, you fly, you fly, you fly 1872.10
From Far Peru 1907.15
From Inchigela 1868.01
From la Femme a Papa 1899.38
From Love to Love 1934.32
From Maine to Oregon 1913.06
From Morning Prayer to Sultan 1900.37
From Morning Till Night 1945.17
From My Love Parted 1865.06
From Now On 1919.12, 1929.32, 1938.13
From Now Onward 1948.27
From Now Till Forever 1973.07
From Our Bestiary 1966.32
From Our Sovereign's Wide Dominions 1882.18
From out the darkness of the ages 1887.12
From Peru's majestic mountains 1896.13
From rock to rock 1895.26
From Saturday 'Til Monday 1904.34
From Skowhegan Main, B'gosh 1898.01
From Stopchet to Kolomay 1968.22
From Tango to Taps 1928.19
From the Ankles Down 1985.05
From the Battery to Harlem 1897.26
From the Bottom to the Top 1922.14
From the briny seas comes young Richard 1887.10
From the Chimney to the Cellar 1943.21
From the Circus to the Grand Opera is Only a Step 1905.40
From the distant panorama 1884.09
From the Distant Town of Cadiz 1898.43
From the Earth a Sweetness Rose, And 1950.16
From the Land of Dreams 1908.14
From the Moor, from the Hill 1897.03
From the Philippines We Come 1899.22
From the Plaza to Madison Square 1921.19
From the South Good Will Come 1972.17
From the sunny Spanish shore 1890.02
From the U.S. to the U.S.S.R. 1938.13
From the Valleys and Hills 1844.01
From Then and Now 1919.07
From these Coves could I fly, love 1863.04
From This Day On 1947.07, 1950.06, 1980.26
From This Moment On 1981.16, 1999.01, 1999.19
From Thy Presence 1881.22
From Under Your Hat 1924.17
From Vienna 1939.23
From Where the Scotch Mountains 1903.21
Front Page Expose 1985.17
Front Page News 1937.16
Front! 1900.42
Frontier Politics 1961.11
Frosty the Snowman 1998.19
Frowning castles 1880.54
Frowns 1931.31
Frunze verde 1960.18
Frustration 1934.06, 1971.01
Frutti di mare 1934.43
Fuddle de Duddle 1938.08
Fuga Y Misterio 1993.08
Fugitive from Esquire, A 1940.07
Fugitive from Fifth Avenue, The 1949.01
Fugue 1940.17

Fugue for Four Girls 1970.20
Fugue for Tinhorns 1950.17, 1980.29, 1991.10
Full Blown Roses 1925.31
Full Moon Union, 1st Degree!, The 1893.27
Full Moons, The 1880.09
Fun 1996.08
Fun in the Country 1953.02
Fun Life 1959.12
Fun on a Motor 1902.35
Fun Time 1992.06
Fun to be Fooled 1934.19
Fundamental Character 1948.15
Funeral Dance 1980.26
Funeral Dance, The 1986.03
Funeral Dirge, The 1981.24
Funeral March 1950.10
Funeral March of the Marionettes 1999.06
Funeral Procession 1945.20
Funeral Tango 1972.16
Funky Girl on Motherless Broadway 1971.13
Funky Monkeys 1975.01
Funnies, The 1933.22
Funny 1989.29, 1992.17
Funny Bunny Hug 1944.32
Funny Face 1927.59, 1974.09, 1983.06
Funny Family, The 1902.08
Funny Funeral, A 1965.19
Funny Honey 1975.14
Funny Little Man, A 1897.33, 1900.24
Funny Little Sailor Man 1928.29, 1986.14
Funny Little Something 1918.25
Funny Side of That, The 1897.13, 1930.12
Funny Thing Happened, A 1962.05
Funzapoppin 1949.06
Furs and Frills 1917.21
Further it is from Tipperary, The 1917.29
Furthermore, An' 1928.33
Fussin', Feudin' and Fightin' 1944.30
Future Stars 1942.35
Futurist Girl, The 1914.15
Futurist Rag, The 1920.43
Futurist Twirl, The 1913.26
Futuristic Melody 1921.18
Futuristic Rhythm 1928.50
Fuzzy Wuzzy 1909.05

G-Man 1937.14
G.I. Blues 1989.12
G.I. Jive 1997.05, 1999.24
G.O.P. 1905.03, 1905.33
Ga-Ga 1929.07
Gabey's Comin' 1998.16
Gabie 1899.35, 1902.38, 1963.13
Gabriel 1927.27
Gabriel's Letter 1993.09
Gabrielle 1969.17, 1987.14
Gaby 1916.02
Gaby Glide, The 1911.43, 1912.09
Gaelic Air 1963.30
Gaiety Dance, The 1909.13
Gaiety, The 1965.33
Gaily marches the soldier 1897.17
Gaily Over the Bounding Billows 1904.17
Gaily the Troubadour 1880.24
Gaily, Gaily, Gaily 1890.12
Gaily, the minstrel boy 1859.08
Gainesboro Glide, The 1925.12
Gaite Parisienen 1977.09
Gal With the Hood On 1866.26
Gallagher, Let Her Go 1888.30
Gallant Thunderbomb, The 1881.07, 1882.20
Gallant Would-be-General, A 1900.57
Galli Curci Rag, The 1918.20
Gallo Ciego 1997.13
Gallop, Gallop 1910.09
Gallop, The 1928.48
Gallopin' Dominoes 1926.19
Galloping Cavalree, The 1912.47
Galloping Major 1916.12
Galloping Through the Park 1933.21
Gallous Old Goddess of Greece, The 1910.10
Galop 1904.22
Gamble on Me 1915.12
Gamblers, The 1959.27
Gambling 1929.38
Game of Cards, A 1915.04
Game of Eyes 1914.08
Game of Golf, The 1908.05
Game of Hearts, A 1906.26
Game of Love 1913.24, 1922.18, 1947.04
Game of Love, A 1904.39
Game of Love, The 1901.16, 1956.16
Game of Morra, The 1964.03
Game of Poker, A 1959.27
Game of War, The 1968.24
Game Sports, The 1894.06
Game That Ends With a Kiss, A 1919.02
Game What They're At, The 1877.43
Game, The 1955.08, 1994.01
Games I Play, The 1992.09
Games We Used to Play, The 1904.37
Gamesters and Lawyers are Jugglers alike, The 1750.01
Gang's All Here, The 1931.05
Gangland Chase 1988.20
Gangster Influence, The 1934.06
Gant's Waltz 1978.10
Gantry's Reaction 1970.02
Gap in the Hedge, The 1924.09
Garbage 1969.05
Garcon dansait, Un 1961.25
Garcon, S'il vous plait 1931.48
Garde of Your Dreams, The 1918.19
Garden Gate 1914.18
Garden Guaracha 1970.21
Garden in the Sky 1944.27
Garden in the Sun, A 1970.06
Garden of Beautiful Girls 1928.23
Garden of Birds, The 1914.12
Garden of Dreams 1903.36, 1907.59
Garden of Eden, The 1953.07
Garden of Flowers, The 1912.45
Garden of Girls, The 1912.43
Garden of Kama, The 1923.31
Garden of Love 1923.18, 1924.13
Garden of Love, The 1905.46
Garden of Make Believe 1920.41
Garden of Memories, A 1926.14
Garden of Used to Be, The 1924.32
Garden of Versailles 1947.12
Garden of Yesterday, The 1912.07
Garden of Youth, The 1903.19
Garden Path to Hell, The 1985.18
Garden Sequence 1994.05
Garden That Blooms for You, The 1908.31
Garden, The 1974.23
Gardeners, The 1872.23
Gardens of Paradise 1915.02
Gardiens du palais 1887.35
Garibaldi Band 1919.11
Garlands Bright 1924.45
Garlands Bright With Glowing Flowers 1980.21
Garotin Song 1917.25
Garrison Ball, The 1892.45, 1908.13
Garrotin 1986.17
Garter Song 1867.10, 1869.42
Gary Owen 1978.05
Gary, Indiana 1957.18, 2000.11
Gas Mask 1919.08
Gascony Bred 1984.14
Gashlycrumb Tinies, The 1978.24
Gasman Cometh, The 1966.32
Gasoline Can-Can, The 1985.20
Gassed Last Night 1964.28
Gaston 1994.04
Gastronome, A la 1924.41
Gates of Cairo, The 1920.34
Gates of Heaven, The 1935.04
Gateway of the Temple of Minerva, The 1942.15
Gather Roses While You May 1925.50
Gather the Rose 1927.65
Gather Ye Autographs 1935.14
Gather Ye Rosebuds 1909.19
Gathering of the Clans 1911.44
Gathering of the Clans, The 1910.19
Gathering of the Slaves, The 1917.37
Gathering Shells by the Seashore 1876.14
Gathering Shells on the Seashore 1876.04
Gathering the Myrtle With Mary 1886.44, 1890.06
'Gator and the Coon, The 1905.31
Gaucho Love Song, A 1930.27
Gaudeamus Igitur 1980.21
Gaugin's Shoes 2001.01
Gavotte 1924.45, 1925.31, 1939.30, 1945.14
Gavotte, The 1993.14, 1997.19, 2001.09
Gay and Merry Play, The 1906.40
Gay Bohemi-ah 1895.43
Gay Brazilian 1921.25
Gay Butterfly on the Wheel 1922.15
Gay Butterfly, A 1912.02
Gay Castinets, The 1902.33
Gay Cavalier 1860.05
Gay Cavalier, The 1891.03
Gay Divorcee, The 1904.55
Gay Excursion, A 1913.22
Gay Fleurette 1903.24
Gay Fusilier, The 1907.52
Gay Gendarme, The 1897.37
Gay Georgette 1899.29
Gay Hussar, The 1885.03, 1895.26
Gay Hussars, The 1909.15
Gay Life, The 1914.30
Gay Little Wives 1935.14
Gay Lothario, A 1904.09
Gay New York 1906.10
Gay Nineties 1938.08
Gay Paree 1894.17
Gay Parisienne, The 1896.31
Gay Photographer, The 1880.42, 1882.39
Gay Soldier Boy 1913.21
Gay Soubrettes, The 1898.10
Gay Tom-tit, The 1895.43
Gay Young Farmer, The 1960.17
Gayest Manhattan 1898.01
Gayest Old Sport, The 1897.34
Gayety 1902.02
Gaze on her portrait 1881.04
Gaze on This Face, so Noble 1930.12
Gazooka, The 1936.02, 1936.17
Gee Chee 1926.19
Gee Mom, I Want to Go Home 1943.23
Gee! But This is a Lonesome Town 1908.05
Gee! What a Wonderful Mate You'll Be 1917.16
Gee! Wouldn't That be Great 1904.27
Gee, Ain't I Glad I'm Home 1907.57
Gee, Ain't I Glad I'm Single 1908.38
Gee, But I'd Like to be Bad 1926.29
Gee, But I'd Like to Furnish a Flat for You 1910.16
Gee, But it's Good to be Here 1956.16
Gee, But it's Great to be Alive 1928.37
Gee, But it's Great to be Here 1976.24
Gee, But it's Great to Meet a Girl from Home 1919.40
Gee, But This is a Lonesome Town 1905.55
Gee, But You Look Awfully Good to Me 1908.36
Gee, I Certainly Hate These Trousers 1907.63
Gee, I Wish I had a Girl 1921.20
Gee, I Wish I had Someone to Rock Me in the Cradle of Love 1978.21
Gee, I'm Glad I'm No One Else But Me 1971.21
Gee, I'm so Good it's too Bad 1930.06
Gee, Officer Krupke 1957.12, 2001.04
Gee, We Get Along 1925.35
Gee, You Must be in Love 1924.24
Geht's und verkauft's mei G'wand 1964.25
Geisha 1970.21
Geisha are we 1896.27
Geisha's Lament, The 1926.11
Geisha's Life, A 1896.27
Gem of the Orient 1894.22
Gemissante, La 1933.24
Gems of the Night 1912.42
Gen d'Arms Duet 1873.17
Gendarme 1938.07
Gendarme, The 1937.16
Genealogy 1928.36
General Bingham's Squad 1906.22
General Boom 1904.22
General Boomerang 1898.17
General Election 1834.01
General Four Flush 1903.20

General Hard Tack 1904.20
General has relented, The 1897.17
General Jackson had a Snuff-Box 1857.06
General la corvee est faite! 1883.51
General Sir Hugh M. Trenchard 1980.13
General Siss-Boom-ah 1899.31
General Store 1971.21
General's Gone to a Party, The 1933.25
General's Song, The 1940.17, 1969.03
Generalonely 1970.04
Generosity 1888.44
Genevieve 1870.01, 1879.52, 1898.03
Genius from Bethlehem 1997.12
Gentle Annie 1939.21
Gentle Buffoon, The 1974.12
Gentle Faces 1885.64, 1887.13
Gentle Jenny Gray 1862.06
Gentle Lover 1976.03
Gentle Moon 1914.20
Gentle River 1910.04
Gentle Sighs 1971.01
Gentle Zerlina 1864.13
Gentleman Friend 1948.04
Gentleman is a Dope, The 1947.17, 1993.16
Gentleman Jimmy 1959.25
Gentleman of Leisure 1894.06
Gentleman's Gentleman, A 1909.01, 1965.28, 1968.02
Gentleman, Un 1955.14
Gentlemanly Brigands, The 1911.47
Gentlemen 1910.21, 1923.44
Gentlemen Don't Fall Wildly in Love 1959.06
Gentlemen from Ireland, A 1888.15
Gentlemen of Japan 1933.27
Gentlemen of the Press 1906.02, 1930.05, 1957.17
Gentlemen Prefer Blondes 1925.45, 1926.18, 1926.25, 1949.18, 1995.07
Gentlemen Shoppers 1960.04
Gentlemen, Be Seated 1963.22
Gentlemen, do Not Fight 1886.62
Gentlemen, How Kind 1978.07
Gently 1911.11
Gently the Breeze of Summer 1902.18
Gently, gently, evidently, we are safe so far 1884.09
Genuine Plastic 1972.07
George and Mary 1930.18, 1930.33
George L. 1966.18
Georgia Land 1912.14
Georgia Rose 1921.26
Georgia Shows 'Em How 1975.09
Georgianna Dunn 1906.13
Georgie 1891.39, 1923.07
Georgy 1970.03
Geraniums in the Winder 1945.05
German 5th, The 1877.05
German Cooking 1913.18
German Prince May Wed Me Since, A 1903.21
German Singing Society, The 1898.08
German Swell 1892.31
German Swell, The 1888.30
German Troubles 1894.17
German Warble 1890.29
Germans at the Spa, The 1982.09
Gershwiana 1932.04
Gertie, the Stool Pigeon's Daughter 1942.05
Gertrude Hoffmann Glide, The 1912.43
Geshray of de Vilde Katchke 1951.21
Gesticulate 1953.16, 1978.03
Gesundheit 1892.31
Get a Girlie 1916.23
Get a Load of That 1947.02
Get a Load of This 1926.39
Get a Move On 1913.04
Get Away Boy 1992.08
Get Away for a Day in the Country 1947.16
Get Away from it All 1935.12
Get Away from My Window 1929.18
Get Away, I'm a Married Man 1911.39
Get Away, Young Man 1943.07
Get Back 1974.24, 1977.10
Get Down 1969.15
Get Down Brother, Get Down 1979.32
Get Happy 1930.06, 1951.15, 1984.06
Get Here 1995.12
Get Him on a Moonlight Night 1923.04
Get Him Up 1919.19
Get Hot Foot 1933.16
Get in a Bathing Suit 1923.21
Get Me on That Boat 1980.17
Get Me Out 1952.13
Get Me to the Church on Time 1956.01, 1974.22, 1993.18
Get Next to the Man With a Pull 1901.16
Get on the Merry Go Round 1908.28
Get on With It 1988.15
Get Out and Get Under 1913.30
Get Out of Town 1938.13
Get Ready 1997.21
Get Ready, Eddie 1982.10
Get Rich Quick Wallingford 1912.29
Get the Hook 1911.17
Get the Lady Dressed 1987.12
Get the Money 1905.48
Get Them All Over at Once 1924.31
Get Together 1923.10, 1983.18
Get Up Jack, John Sit Down 1893.46
Get Up on a New Routine 1929.19
Get Up, Jack; John, Sit Down 1885.49
Get Yer Program for de Big Fight 1943.24
Get Your Act Together 1979.32
Get Your Man 1928.14
Get Your Partner for the Barn Dance 1908.27
Get Your Woman 1925.16
Get Yourself a Geisha 1935.12
Gethsemane 1971.12, 1992.12
Gettin' a Man 1959.27
Gettin' Back to Me 1970.03
Gettin' Off 1930.29
Gettin' Ready Rag 1998.01
Gettin' to the Top 1979.15
Gettin' Together 1929.21
Gettin' Up Mornin' 1931.11
Getting Better 1974.24
Getting in the Lifeboat 1997.06
Getting into the Talkies 1929.29
Getting Married Today 1970.13, 1977.05
Getting Oriental Over You 1944.15
Getting Out of Town 1980.20
Getting Tall 1982.09
Getting the Beautiful Girls 1928.23
Getting to Know You 1951.12, 1963.07
Gevald 1968.22
Gevald Aria 1968.22
Ghetto Glide, The 1912.36
Ghetto Life 1972.13
Ghost Ensemble 1923.39
Ghost of a Coon, The 1899.33
Ghost of Deacon Brown, The 1907.22
Ghost of Kelly, The 1910.19
Ghost of Little Egypt, The 1931.34
Ghost of Old Black Joe 1919.26
Ghost of Old Black Joe, The 1928.09
Ghost of the Ukelele, The 1916.23
Ghost Quintette 1912.26
Ghost Recitative 1923.39
Ghost That Never Walked, The 1904.15
Ghost Town 1934.40
Ghosties and Ghoulies and Things That Go Bump in the Night 1989.23
Ghostly Vengeance, We Invoke Thee 1890.03
Ghosts 1917.12
Gianetta 1864.22
Gianina 1919.35
Giannina Mia 1912.46
Giants in the Sky 1987.18
Giava, La 1935.02
Gibson Bathing Girls, The 1907.24
Gibson Coon, The 1908.22
Gibson Girl, The 1906.29, 1906.45
Giddy Up, Giddy Up, Dearie 1913.19
Giddyup Back 1930.28
Gideon Briggs, I Love You 1960.05
Gift Today, A 1962.05
Gigi 1973.12
Gigolette 1925.42
Gigolo 1926.13, 1927.50
Gilbert & Sullivan Blues, The 1945.08
Gilbert and Filbert 1914.18, 1975.22
Gilding the Guild 1925.17
Gilet Raye 1961.25
Gimme Love 1993.09
Gimme Mick 1979.19
Gimme That Old Time Religion 1989.12
Gimme the Shimmy 1950.12
Gimmie a Pigfoot 1975.20, 1980.10
Gimmie Some 1964.32
Gimmie This - Gimme This - Gimme That 1919.19
Gin 2000.08
Gin Rummy, I Love You 1942.19
Gin-Gin-Ginger Boy 1905.56
Gina 1941.01
Ginette 1928.07
Ginger 1912.45, 1915.17, 1917.35, 1922.18, 1923.37
Ginger Brown 1980.10
Ginger Cake and Frosted Cake 1921.20
Gingerbread Bcy, The 1903.27
Gingerbread Doll, The 1898.63
Gingerbrown 1923.39
Gingerena 1923.11
Gingham and Yarn 1986.16
Gingham Girl 1922.28
Gingham Girl, A 1922.28
Gip-Gip 1927.47
Gipsy Song 1897.40, 1917.10
Gipsy Warned Me, The 1922.05
Girl 'n' Girls 'n' Girls 1956.08
Girl and the Gum Tree, The 1888.15
Girl at the Helm, The 1905.03
Girl Behind the Gun, The 1918.28
Girl Behind the Man Behind the Gun, The 1908.03
Girl Belongs to You 1920.19
Girl by the Saskatchewan, The 1911.11
Girl for Each Month of the Year, A 1915.16
Girl for Me, The 1917.31
Girl Friend of the Whirling Dervish, The 1990.09
Girl Friend, The 1926.07, 1974.09, 1975.13
Girl Friends 1970.17
Girl from Broadway, The 1907.04
Girl from Casimo 1923.05
Girl from Everywhere, A 1906.29
Girl from Gay Paree, The 1895.34
Girl from Mars, The 1902.27
Girl from Paree, A 1915.20
Girl from Paris, The 1896.48, 1898.10
Girl from Rector's, The 1917.08
Girl from the Golden West, A 1922.23
Girl from Utah 1914.18
Girl Gets Around, The 1998.13
Girl has a Sailor in Every Port, A 1921.34
Girl He Couldn't Kiss, The 1914.09
Girl He Left Behind Him, The 1904.05
Girl I Can't Forget, The 1912.42, 1918.15
Girl I Knew, The 1909.03
Girl I Know, A 1904.42, 1907.16
Girl I Left in Boston Town, The 1905.20
Girl I Marry, The 1922.01
Girl I Meant to Be, The 1991.05
Girl I Might Have Been, The 1929.20
Girl I Never Met, The 1920.36
Girl I Used to Know, The 1904.02
Girl I Want to Call Wife 1919.33
Girl I Would Have Left Behind, The 1894.51
Girl I'll Call My Sweetheart Must Look Like You, The 1912.06
Girl I'm Gonna Marry, The 1984.15
Girl I've Never Met, The 1923.27
Girl in Blue, The 1903.15
Girl in Every Port 1919.03
Girl in His Arms, The 1958.20
Girl in Pink, The 1911.24
Girl in the Baby-Blue Tights, The 1906.29
Girl in the Clogs and Shawl, The 1914.18
Girl in the Gingham Gown, The 1913.22
Girl in the Mirror, The 1968.13
Girl in the Show, The 1961.01
Girl in the Valley, A 1991.05
Girl in the White Silk Dress, The 1898.41
Girl in the Window, The 1981.14
Girl in Your Arms 1926.03
Girl in Your Arms, A 1921.07

Girl is Like a Book, A 1943.21
Girl is Like Sunshine, A 1923.21
Girl is Nothing But a Rose, A 1897.26
Girl is You, the Boy is Me, The 1926.16
Girl Just Out, The 1904.37
Girl Like Grandma 1921.06
Girl Like You, A 1929.50
Girl May as Well Marry Well, A 1923.13
Girl Meets Boy 1994.10
Girl Next Door, The 1931.28
Girl o' Mine 1918.02
Girl of Greater New York, The 1901.16
Girl of My Dreams, The 1911.25
Girl of My Heart 1918.40
Girl of My Heart, The 1899.39
Girl of the Fan, The 1915.27
Girl of the Golden West, The 1904.39
Girl of the Minute, The 1968.13
Girl of the Moment 1941.04
Girl of the Mystic Star 1985.02
Girl of the Pi Beta Phi 1974.26
Girl of To-Day, The 1914.16
Girl of Tomorrow, The 1925.22
Girl on the Magazine Cover, The 1915.32
Girl on the Police Gazette, The 1942.18
Girl on the Prow, The 1928.29, 1986.14
Girl on the Square 1916.23
Girl She Can't Remain, A 1945.13
Girl That I Admire, The 1880.37
Girl That I Court in My Mind, The 1952.05
Girl That I Marry, The 1946.12, 1966.12, 1999.04
Girl That I'd Call Mine, The 1907.19
Girl That I'll Adore, The 1929.32
Girl That Wins My Heart, The 1916.08
Girl That's Up to Date, The 1894.49
Girl to Remember, A 1964.21
Girl Wanted 1895.03
Girl Who Comes in from the West, The 1903.24
Girl Who Doesn't Ripple When She Bends, A 1943.07
Girl Who Drinks Champagne, The 1917.08
Girl Who is Up to Date, The 1900.41
Girl Who Keeps Me Guessing, The 1920.36
Girl Who Leads the Band, The 1902.02
Girl Who Leads the Fashions, The 1894.31
Girl Who Lived in Montparnasse, The 1961.01
Girl Who Ran Away, The 1894.35
Girl Who Rides the Wheel, The 1895.36
Girl Who Wouldn't Spoon, The 1911.25
Girl With a Brogue, The 1910.05
Girl With a Flame, A 1950.04
Girl With the Banjo Eyes, The 1903.01
Girl With the Changeable Eyes, The 1904.23
Girl With the Clocking on Her Stocking 1909.29
Girl With the Clocks, The 1909.29
Girl with the Golden Switch, The 1870.07
Girl With the Naughty Wink, The 1897.04
Girl With the Paint on Her Face 1938.04
Girl With the Strawberry Mark, The 1898.43
Girl With the Sweet, Long Sigh, The 1902.38
Girl With the Yellow Roses, The 1909.04
Girl Worth the While 1908.20
Girl You Dream About, The 1896.02, 1908.23
Girl You Love, The 1902.03, 1902.35
Girl You Marry 1919.16
Girl You're a Woman 1978.13
Girl, A 1982.23
Girl, a Man, a Night, a Dance, A 1919.27
Girlie 1918.09
Girlie from the Cabaret, The 1915.02
Girlie Girl 1896.18
Girlie With a Bustle 1927.40
Girlie With the Baby Stare, The 1902.23
Girlieland 1911.36
Girlies 1910.26
Girlies are Out of My Life 1915.27
Girlish Laughter 1912.24
Girls 1908.38, 1919.32, 1944.02, 1975.04, 1976.16
Girls & Dogs 1972.16
Girls Against the Boys, The 1959.23
Girls Ahoy! 1993.05
Girls All Around Me 1921.07
Girls Along Fifth Avenue, The 1920.40
Girls and Boys 1905.48, 1959.23
Girls and the Gimmies 1926.24
Girls are Getting Wiser, The 1916.25
Girls are Like a Rainbow 1920.04
Girls are Like the Weather to Me 1919.13
Girls at Maxim's 1964.24
Girls at Maxim's, The 1907.48, 1908.38, 1943.09
Girls Dream of One Thing 1925.26
Girls from DeVere's 1922.43
Girls from the U.S.A. 1904.42, 1907.16
Girls Grow More Wonderful Day by Day 1923.07
Girls Hide Away 1884.42
Girls I'd Like to Love, The 1916.20
Girls I've Met, The 1917.22
Girls I've Never Met 1923.01
Girls in My Address Book 1919.13
Girls Like Me 1961.28
Girls Must Live 1929.39
Girls of Every Land, The 1908.03
Girls of Forty-Nine, The 1906.01
Girls of Gottenberg 1908.25
Girls of Home, Sweet Home, The 1917.12
Girls of Long Ago 1930.05
Girls of My Dreams, The 1920.18
Girls of the Midnight Matinee 1898.55
Girls of the Old Brigade, The 1923.35, 1926.46
Girls of the Pi Beta Phi 1927.41
Girls of the U.S.A. 1906.08
Girls Prepare 1916.23
Girls Were Made for Dancing 1923.21
Girls Were Made to Love and Kiss 1983.12, 1985.11, 1988.14
Girls Who Want to Go Upon the Stage 1909.05
Girls Will be Girls and Boys Will be Boys 1903.39
Girls' Brigade 1928.07
Girls, Girls 1961.02
Girls, Girls, Girls 1903.22, 1908.36, 1920.06, 1922.17
Girls, I am True to All of You 1927.17
Girls, if You Ever Get Married 1916.13, 1916.22
Girls, Just Girls 1906.30
Girls, Keep Your Figures 1911.40
Girls, Pretty Girls 1921.37
Girls, Run Along 1914.02
Girls, The 1924.25, 1941.09
Girls, You are Such Wonderful Things 1916.01
Girly, Girly 1904.41
Girofle-Girofla 1876.04, 1876.05, 1877.05
Git a Horse 1905.17
Git Along, Little Dogies 1931.02
Git on de Boat, Chillun' 1938.06
Gitanillo 1926.09, 1926.35
Gitka's Song, The 1970.19
Give a Little Whistle and I'll be There 1960.22
Give a Little, Get a Little Kiss 1925.08
Give a Little, Get a Little Love 1951.19
Give a Man Enough Rope 1991.07
Give a Viva! 1942.26
Give England Strength 1970.15
Give Him a Welcome Quite Spanish 1907.08
Give Him Back His Job 1919.10
Give Him the Oo-La-La 1939.30
Give Him Your Sympathy 1924.47
Give It 1930.37
Give it All You Got 1958.02
Give it Back to the Indians 1939.27, 1975.13
Give it Love 1952.08
Give it to Me 1976.20
Give Me a Cause 1969.01, 1975.05
Give Me a Good Havana 1911.08
Give Me a Little Cosey Corner 1920.07
Give Me a Man Like That 1930.29
Give Me a Night 1928.21
Give Me a Road 1975.05
Give Me a Roll on a Drum 1933.03
Give Me a Song I Can Whistle 1936.12
Give Me a Star 1971.14
Give Me a Thrill 1924.11
Give Me a Wall 1975.05
Give Me All of You 1916.17
Give Me All the Flowers 1910.30
Give Me All the Money 1984.02
Give Me an Old-Fashioned Girlie 1917.29
Give Me Back My 'Liza 1900.55
Give Me Back My Liza 1900.52
Give Me Death or Victory 1905.33
Give Me Love 1895.43
Give Me Love, Love, Love 1912.47
Give Me My Mammy 1921.34
Give Me One Good Reason 1971.02
Give Me One Hour 1927.65
Give Me Someone 1927.20
Give Me Something in a Uniform of Blue 1913.30
Give Me That Key 1979.10
Give Me That Letter 1920.36
Give Me That Old Soft Shoe 1979.14
Give Me the Moonlight 1918.12, 1919.40
Give Me the Rain 1925.27
Give Me the South All the Time 1919.26
Give Me the Sultan's Harem 1919.18
Give Me the Sunshine 1928.10
Give Me Thy Heart, Love 1906.49
Give Me Wild Trumpets 1936.01
Give Me Your Heart and Give Me Your Hand 1924.46
Give Me Your Love 1932.12
Give Me Your Tired, Your Poor 1949.08, 1955.13
Give My Regards to Broadway 1904.42, 1907.16, 1968.07, 1977.13, 1979.13, 1982.05, 1991.10
Give Paddy But a Chance and He'll Show You What He's Made Of 1890.06
Give Shalom and Sabbath to Jerusalem 1971.14
Give the Devil His Due 1920.41
Give the Doctor the Best in the House 1950.01
Give the Little Kids a Chance 1925.05
Give the Little Lady 1958.14
Give This Little Girl a Hand 1926.50
Give Trouble the Air 1927.38
Give Us a Chance 1915.32
Give Us a Fleet 1908.35
Give Us a Ragtime Tune 1910.34
Give Us Barabbas 1980.14
Give Us Barrabas 1976.35, 1982.17
Give us bread 1846.01
Give us cash! Give us cash! 1893.17
Give Us Power 1988.02
Give Us the Charleston 1925.22
Give Us Your Kind Applause 1914.13
Give Your Heart a Chance to Sing 1948.30
Give Your Heart in June 1925.07
Give, Give 1921.32
Give, Sinbad, Give 1944.18
Give-Away, Give-Away, Banker Man 1973.08
Givers and Getters 1969.03
Giving Life 1976.20
Glad Hand, The 1897.31
Glad I'm from Dixie 1919.26
Glad That You Were Born 1982.14
Glad Tidings 1928.08
Glad to be Back 1948.04
Glad to be Home 1962.20
Glad to be Unhappy 1936.05, 1975.13, 1983.02
Glad to Know Ya 1971.01
Glad, Triumphant Hour 1917.07
Gladys O'Flynn 1905.05
Glamorous Life, The 1973.04
Glass of Beer, A 1908.25
Glass of Fashion 1907.51
Glee Club 1950.03
Glee Club Rehearsal 1971.11, 1999.03
Glee Maiden, The 1890.23
Glenda's Place 1958.20
Glendy Burke 1939.21
Glengall 1897.03
Glide 1999.02
Glide de Luxe, The 1923.12
Gliding 1998.01
Gliding Gondola 1928.23
Gliding Through My Memoree 1958.19
Glimpse of Eden, A 1904.36
Glimpse, A 1902.35
Glimpses of the Moon 1924.11
Glitter and be Gay 1956.15, 1974.06, 1982.20, 1997.10
Glittering Gloria 1904.08
Glittering Gold 1907.26
Globe Trot, The 1921.34
Globe-Trotter, The 1914.12
Gloom and Joy 1922.30

Gloomy Heaven 1934.06
Gloria 1958.01
Gloria Tibi 1972.15
Gloriana 1904.41, 1906.23
Glorie au valeureux Grenicheux 1878.08
Glorifying the Girls 1923.38
Glorious Chase, The 1927.50
Glorious Cheese 1963.16
Glorious Russian 1962.18, 1978.18
Glorious Summer 1903.20
Glory 1902.43, 1922.48, 1972.22, 1999.01
Glory and Liberty 1902.43
Glory Hallelujah 1990.05
Glory Hallelujah Twist 1963.10
Glory of Nations, The 1905.48
Glory of Spring 1929.09
Glory of Spring, The 1929.17
Glory of the Morning Sunshine, The 1925.27
Glory That is Greece, The 1961.08
Glory to Allah 1872.25
Glory! Glory! Glory! 1925.20
Glory, Glory 1966.15
Glory, The 1999.08
Glove Dance 1955.10
Glove, The 1913.07
Gloves 1956.13
Glow of the Cigarette, The 1920.29
Glow Worm 1923.35, 1990.09
Glow-Worm and the Moth, The 1903.07
Glow-Worm, The 1907.41
Gnu, A 1959.20
Go 1888.20
Go 'Way from My Window 1954.11
Go 'Way Mistah Moon 1910.04
Go Ahead and Dance a Little More 1916.03
Go Along! 1875.15
Go and Get Your Partner for the Barn Dance 1908.27
Go as Far as You Like 1909.13
Go Away 1887.13
Go Away from My Window 1967.13
Go Away, Girls, Go Away 1924.21
Go Away, Little Girl - Go Back to School 1911.45
Go Back to Work 1904.01
Go Back Where You Stayed Last Night 1953.12
Go Down to Boston Harbor 1944.30
Go Down to the Cotton Fields 1939.21
Go Down to the River 1945.13
Go Down, Moses 1927.38, 1930.10
Go Easy, Mabel 1922.17
Go Gar Sig Gong-Jue 1914.23
Go Get 'Im 1928.47, 1979.05
Go Holy Ghost 1972.18
Go Home 1997.08
Go Home Ev'ry Once in a While 1928.31
Go Home Train 1964.21
Go in the Best of Health 1973.11
Go into Your Dance 1923.17, 1930.40, 1980.20
Go into Your Trance 1964.16
Go not, happy Day 1878.02
Go on and Marry! 1900.39
Go on and Sell My Suit 1964.25
Go on Your Mission 1910.19
Go on, Write and do Not Scribble 1964.25
Go Places and do Things 1928.38
Go Sit by the Body 1945.13
Go Slow, Johnny 1961.18
Go South 1925.47
Go to Church Sunday 1945.13
Go to Paris or Vienna 1914.04
Go to Sleep 1950.16
Go to Sleep My Little Flower 1989.10
Go to Sleep, My Baby 1915.16
Go to Sleep, Slumber Deep 1929.48
Go to Sleep, Whatever You Are 1966.18
Go to the Mirror 1993.06
Go to the mirror boy 1972.08
Go Visit 1971.07
Go Way from My Window 1968.20
Go West, Young Girl 1918.20
Go where glory waits thee 1864.12
Go Where the Crowd Goes 1904.06
Go, Basest Lord 1884.42
Go, Breaking Heart 1881.37
Go, Go Joseph 1982.03
Go, Go, Go Joseph 1993.15
Go, Go, Go! 1963.16
Go, Little Boat 1918.37
Go, Tyrant, Go 1880.47
Go-A-Head! 1869.29
Go-Getter, The 1925.38
Go-Go Bug 1923.06
Goat, The 1898.25
Gobble Duet, The 1881.21
Goblins 1911.12
God be With You 1969.10
God Bless Africa 1993.04
God Bless America 1997.01, 1998.11
God Bless the Child 1976.04
God Bless the Human Elbow 1964.33
God Bless the Moon 1963.19
God Bless the Woman 1940.19
God Bless Us, Everyone 1994.12
God Could Give Me Anything 1979.18
God Help Us 1980.15
God is an American 1969.03
God is Good 1975.23, 1998.14
God Lead Us Along 1969.10
God of Love 1880.10
God of Love presides, The 1898.25
God of Our Fathers 1955.13
God Only Knows 2000.16
God Said 1972.15
God Said unto Jacob, And 1971.17
God Save the Queen 1871.16
God Shall Wipe All Tears Away 1975.20
God's Country 1937.15
God's Good to the Irish 1927.47
God's Got a Way 1963.27
God's Green World 1945.19
God's Love Can Save 1963.27
God's Trombones 1955.13
God, That's Good! 1979.06
God-Why-Don't-You-Love-Me-Blues, The 1971.05
Goddess of Crystal, The 1928.03
Goddess of Mine 1913.32
Goddess of Rain 1929.23
Goddess of Rector's, The 1905.23
Goden Chains 1878.02
Gods Heard Her Prayer, And the 1990.12
Gods Love Nubia, The 2000.06
Godsons and Grandmothers 1918.28
Godspeed Titanic 1997.06
Goetterdaemmerung 1956.09
Goin' Back in Time 1976.04
Goin' Back to Cucamonga 1979.25
Goin' Back to New Orleans 1979.25
Goin' Courting 1982.14
Goin' Downtown 1981.29
Goin' Gone 1979.32
Goin' on a Hayride 1952.05
Goin' to Die, Goin to Have Some Fun 1907.20
Goin' to the Moon 1955.11
Going Back Home 1945.12
Going Down 1968.11
Going Home 1903.23, 1975.19, 1977.01, 1995.04
Going Home on New Year's Morning 1925.52
Going Home Tomorrow 1978.22
Going Home Train 1946.10
Going Home With My Children 1973.03
Going Home With Nelly After Five 1883.53
Going My Way 1995.14
Going on the War Path 1906.31
Going Over the Bumps 1926.06
Going Rowing 1924.02
Going There 1913.17
Going to Fight the Indians 1908.28
Going to the Ball 1919.42
Going to the Derby 1960.17
Going to the Devil 1954.01
Going to the Market 1884.37
Going to the Opera 1906.48
Going to Town With Me 1931.26
Going Up 1917.36, 1930.22, 1976.25
Going Up in My Aeroplane 1910.17
Going, Going, Gone! 1931.14
Going-Staying 1974.04
Gol-Durn! 1922.46
Gold & Goldberg 2000.08
Gold and Blue and White 1919.42
Gold Bug March, The 1896.30
Gold Cannot Buy 1954.17
Gold Cure Dance 1908.15
Gold Diggers, The 1920.45
Gold Fish 1921.02
Gold! Gold! Gold! 1901.17
Gold, gold is no chimera 1867.18
Gold, gold, is no chimera 1866.16
Gold, Silver and Green 1924.29
Gold, Women and Laughter 1947.13
Golden Age, The 1900.50, 1914.30
Golden Boy 1964.32, 2000.08
Golden Chains 1884.42, 1885.58, 1888.13, 1896.35
Golden Chariot, The 1959.15
Golden Choir, The 1883.32
Golden Crown 1992.06
Golden Days 1919.12, 1924.45, 1943.06, 1980.21
Golden Dream 1891.36
Golden Dream, The 1983.17
Golden Dreams 1926.27
Golden Gate 1928.14
Golden Gates of Happiness 1926.15
Golden Helmet of Mambrino 1965.34
Golden Isle, The 1899.39
Golden Land 1967.05
Golden Land, Golden Life 1978.03
Golden Love 1921.05
Golden Memories of Perfume 1927.62
Golden Moment 1951.17
Golden Net, The 1905.48
Golden Oldie 1981.14
Golden Peri-banou, The 1934.03
Golden Pheasant 1917.31
Golden Pillars of Justice, The 1932.18
Golden Rainbow 1968.03
Golden Ram, The 1970.19
Golden Rod 1929.29
Golden Rules 1903.02
Golden Sails 1907.27
Golden Slumbers 1974.24
Golden Sprite, The 1926.32
Golden Stairs of Love, The 1913.18
Golden Sunshine 1916.26
Golden Trail, The 1923.31
Golden Tresses 1870.13
Golden West, The 1917.08
Goldenhair 2000.01
Goldfarb Variations, The 1974.13
Goldfarb, That's I'm! 1930.31
Goldfinger 1974.11, 1974.22
Goldfish Glide 1927.48
Golf 1903.22, 1924.25
Golf Song 1896.06
Golfing Blues 1923.17
Golfing Love 1928.04
Goliath of Gath 1997.12
Golliwog 1928.09
Golly, Ain't I Wicked 1911.20
Golly, Charlie! 1898.43
Gondola and the Girl, The 1923.26
Gondola Song 1889.24
Gondole a Venise 1964.22
Gondolier Song 1934.43
Gondolier, The 1855.06
Gondoliers' Serenade, The 1892.45
Gondoliers, The 1896.31
Gone 1986.16
Gone Fishing 1976.32
Gone in Sorrow 1966.09
Gone so Long 1988.07
Gone, Gone, Gone 1983.04
Gone, Gone, Gone! 1935.13
Gonna be Another Hot Day 1963.26, 1992.10
Gonna Build a Mountain 1962.18, 1974.11, 1974.22, 1978.18
Goo-Goo 1909.07
Goo-Goo Land 1909.11
Goo-Goo Man, The 1904.25
Gooch's Song 1966.10, 1998.07
Good 'N' Evil 1997.09

Good Advice 1916.01, 1975.19
Good Afternoon, Mr. Jenkins 1900.46
Good and Lasting Piece, A 1869.08
Good and Lucky 1937.10
Good Boy 1928.25, 1968.05
Good Boy Wedding March 1928.25
Good Bye 1892.19
Good Bye Old Friends 1893.10
Good Bye, Becky Cohen 1910.18
Good Bye, Honey Falls 1923.06
Good Bye, Miss Liberty 1909.18
Good Bye, Mr. Ragtime 1908.22
Good Bye, My Tango 1913.17
Good Bye, Sweetheart, Good Bye 1867.10
Good Clean Fun 1960.19
Good Clean Sport 1930.25
Good Day, Yankees! 1902.41
Good Days and Bad Days 1928.28
Good Die Young, The 1888.32
Good Evenin' 1904.21
Good Evening 1908.30, 1989.25
Good Evening - Good Night 1923.01
Good Evening Caroline 1907.31
Good Evening Friends 1931.09
Good Evening, Madame Flora 1947.10
Good Evening, Mr. Man in the Moon 1933.21
Good Evening, Princess 1938.07
Good Fellow, Mine 1926.07
Good Fellows' Club, The 1915.27
Good for You - Bad for Me 1930.11
Good Friends 1970.09
Good Friends Surround Me 1933.03
Good Girls Love Bad Men 1930.42
Good Hand-Organ and a Sidewalk, A 1924.30
Good husband 1859.09
Good Joke, A 1894.17
Good Little Girl and the Bad Little Girl, The 1927.02
Good Little Sunday School Boy, The 1902.07
Good Little Things We Do, The 1918.07
Good Looking Woman 1999.22
Good Luck Comes to Those Who Wait 1892.18
Good Luck, Mr. Flyin' Man 1943.24
Good Luck, Sam! 1918.36
Good Man is Hard to Find, A 1975.20, 1999.06
Good Mornin' 1985.08
Good Mornin', Sistuh! 1983.04
Good Morning 1883.12, 1898.48, 1912.45
Good Morning Blues 1954.11
Good Morning Dearie 1921.36
Good Morning Starshine 1968.11
Good Morning World 1972.21
Good Morning, All 1919.28
Good Morning, Carrie 1900.46, 1930.16
Good morning, dear Vicar 1882.63
Good Morning, Good Day 1963.14
Good Morning, Good Morning 1974.24
Good Morning, Judge 1910.30, 1911.35
Good Morning, Mr. van Pepi 1964.25
Good morrow, good lover! 1882.78
Good morrow, good mother 1882.78
Good News 1927.41, 1974.26
Good News, Bad News 1993.02
Good night 1859.09, 1859.18
Good Night 1866.21, 1873.04, 1880.51, 1886.30, 1895.22, 1900.47, 1902.21, 1904.06, 1907.32, 1914.15, 1921.01, 1924.36, 1966.29
Good Night Angeline 1921.16
Good Night Boat 1920.04, 1975.24
Good Night Finale 1923.38
Good Night Hymn 1969.04
Good Night Ladies 1925.43
Good Night Love 1914.07
Good Night Madrigal 1913.07
Good Night Senior Balthazar 1866.07
Good Night Sweetheart 1931.26
Good night to one and all 1878.02
Good Night! 1881.04
Good Night! Shoo Fly, Don't Bodder Me 1870.20
Good Night, Evangeline 1904.58
Good night, good night, my Lord 1871.10
Good Night, My Beautiful 1939.25
Good Night, My Lady Love 1925.44
Good night, my Lord 1852.01
Good Night, My Own Love 1904.15
Good Night, O Sea 1900.42
Good Night, Sweetheart 1908.18, 1999.05
Good Old Atwater 1917.17
Good Old Bad Old Days, The 1974.22
Good Old Burlesque Show, A 1979.25
Good Old California 1904.42
Good Old Cambria 1908.26
Good Old Circus Band 1912.38
Good Old Days of Yore 1910.09
Good Old Days, The 1931.30, 1948.04, 1966.05
Good Old Days, The - so What? 1939.16
Good Old Egg, A 1928.27
Good Old G.A.R., The 1904.35
Good Old Glory 1897.39
Good Old Levee Days 1914.16
Good old man indeed was he, A 1859.13
Good Old Palmy Days, The 1898.01
Good Old Summer Time, The 1902.33
Good Old U.S.A., The 1903.28
Good Old-Fashioned Way, The 1907.13
Good Ole Girl 1978.13
Good Ole New York 1992.08
Good Pals 1927.55
Good People, Gather Round 1918.27
Good people, gladly 1882.60
Good Ship Caledonia, The 1980.13
Good Ship Honeymoon, The 1916.15
Good Ship Spring 1890.12, 1890.30
Good Sir 1859.09
Good sir, although I sit apart all day 1895.29
Good Thing Going 1981.27, 1999.20
Good Things and Bad Things 1924.21
Good Things in Life, The 1974.22
Good Time Charlie 1969.07
Good Times 1985.15, 1993.09
Good Vibrations 1972.13, 1982.22
Good Wine Needs No Bush 1892.07
Good Young Man That Died 1882.28
Good, Bad, Beautiful Broadway 1919.07
Good, Kind, Jolly Man, The 1905.54
Good-a-Bye, John 1906.33
Good-by, Achmet 1879.35
Good-by, Bridgy 1891.14, 1892.06
Good-by, Cousin Lola 1926.02
Good-by, Little Girl, Good-By 1904.22
Good-Bye 1919.30, 1922.07, 1926.28
Good-Bye - Hello 1919.23
Good-Bye Bill 1918.14
Good-Bye Broadway, Hello France 1917.26
Good-Bye Darling 1877.43
Good-Bye Everybody 1915.08
Good-bye for a Little While 1880.10
Good-Bye France 1918.32
Good-Bye Little Girl, Good-Bye 1901.13
Good-Bye My Emerald Land 1912.06
Good-Bye Old Gal I'm Going Away on the 2:10 Train 1910.22
Good-Bye Sunshine, Hello Moon 1920.10
Good-Bye Sweetheart 1908.12
Good-Bye to Flirtation 1913.04
Good-Bye, Boys 1913.05
Good-Bye, Dear Old Bachelor Days 1916.10
Good-bye, Dear Orpheus 1869.07
Good-Bye, Dinah 1907.47
Good-Bye, Ethiopia 1906.14
Good-Bye, Fedora 1904.44
Good-Bye, Flo 1904.42
Good-Bye, France 1918.18
Good-Bye, Good-Bye 1920.43
Good-Bye, Happy Days 1917.34
Good-Bye, Hiram 1913.22
Good-Bye, Little Girl 1911.29, 1914.14
Good-Bye, Little Rosebud 1923.05
Good-Bye, Maggie Doyle 1905.48
Good-Bye, Molly Brown 1908.44
Good-Bye, Mr. Ragtime 1907.37
Good-Bye, My Darling 1889.41
Good-Bye, My Darling, Good-Bye 1890.29
Good-Bye, My Native Town 1902.25
Good-Bye, New Amsterdam 1900.59
Good-Bye, Old Home 1907.19
Good-Bye, Poor Old Manhattan 1913.16
Good-Bye, Sweet Old Manhattan Isle 1905.28, 1906.24
Good-Bye, Sweetheart 1905.52
Good-Bye, true love 1889.54
Good-Bye, Yankee Doodle 1910.10
Good-Day, Good-Night 1916.17
Good-night 1887.04
Good-Night, Dear 1920.20
Good-Time Flat Blues 1975.09
Good-Time Girl, The 1974.05
Good-Will Movement, The 1944.02
Gooda Monk, The 1889.39
Goodby Charlie 1966.05
Goodbye 1909.20, 1962.27, 1972.19, 1988.02
Goodbye Broadway, Hello France 1917.08
Goodbye Charleston 1926.14
Goodbye Chorus 1891.18
Goodbye Flo 1982.05
Goodbye Forever 1923.13, 1928.40
Goodbye George 1963.14
Goodbye Girls, Hello Yale 1937.02, 1946.19
Goodbye Girls, I'm Through 1914.23, 1922.03
Goodbye Jonah 1937.10
Goodbye Khaki! 1921.12
Goodbye Love 1952.10
Goodbye Main Street 1922.15
Goodbye Old Paint 1931.02
Goodbye Old Year, Welcome New 1908.15
Goodbye Paree 1946.16
Goodbye Saccharine 1979.19
Goodbye Salome 1975.18, 1976.31
Goodbye to All That 1946.20
Goodbye to Blue 1914.12
Goodbye to Dear Old Alaska 1922.32
Goodbye! 2001.05
Goodbye, Au Revoir, Auf Wiedersehn 1936.22
Goodbye, Bargravia 1919.04
Goodbye, Canavaro 1968.30, 1983.14
Goodbye, Darlin' 1956.04
Goodbye, Dear Friend, Goodbye 1951.17
Goodbye, Emil 1988.10
Goodbye, Failure, Goodbye 1967.16
Goodbye, Fedora 1904.13
Goodbye, Lenny! 1926.07
Goodbye, Little Dream, Goodbye 1987.15
Goodbye, London Town 1914.01
Goodbye, Love 1996.09
Goodbye, Miss Liberty 1909.18
Goodbye, My Bachelor 1969.07
Goodbye, My Lady Love 1927.67, 1946.01, 1966.14, 1983.05, 1994.08
Goodbye, My Love 1998.01
Goodbye, Old Girl 1955.08, 1994.01
Goodbye, Sweetheart, Goodbye 1880.42, 1910.04
Goodbye. .ee 1964.28
Goodbyes 1972.18
Goodfellow Days 1925.36
Goodly Little Things We Do, The 1922.48
Goodness Gracious Children 1894.27
Goodness, Ain't You Glad 1915.29
Goodnight 1931.28, 1948.18, 1956.13
Goodnight and Thank You 1979.23
Goodnight Angeline 1978.21
Goodnight Hymn 1980.01
Goodnight is Not Goodbye 1978.27
Goodnight Ladies 1957.18, 2000.11
Goodnight My Someone 1957.18
Goodnight Sweetheart 1930.22
Goodnight to One and All 1885.58, 1888.13
Goodnight, Brother Green 1923.11
Goodnight, Irene 1999.09
Goodnight, Mrs. Astor 1940.03
Goodnight, My Someone 2000.11
Goods, The 2000.15
Goodtime Charley 1975.06
Goodtime Charlie 1954.02
Goody Goody 1983.20
Goody, Goody 1997.05
Googly Gogly Goos 1927.07
Googy-oo 1904.34, 1909.09
Goona Goona 1935.11
Goona' Goona 1932.19
Goona-Goona 1954.03
Goose Girl, The 1906.18

Goose Never be a Peacock 1959.27
Gorgeous 1966.18
Gorgeous Alexander 1928.29, 1986.14
Gospel According to the King, The 1992.17
Gospel of Gabriel Finn, The 1972.25
Gossip 1906.29, 1916.18, 1947.14, 1972.24, 1983.17, 1984.08, 1984.14
Gossip Chorus and March 1901.13
Gossip Polka, The 1945.12
Gossip Song 1906.33
Gossip Song, The 1901.23, 1959.27
Gossip's Chorus 1904.10
Gossipers, The 1902.37
Gossiping 1925.07
Gossiping Housemaids, The 1905.21
Gossips 1928.12
Gossips, The 1948.26, 1974.25
Got a Bran' New Suit 1935.12
Got a Head Like a Rock 1940.01
Got it Again 1930.18
Got No Room for Mr. Gloom 1999.01
Got That Good Time Feelin' 1944.30
Got to be Good Times 1981.29
Got to Get You into My Life 1977.10
Got to Go to Town 1931.40
Got to Have Hips Now 1930.37
Got to It 1916.22
Got Tu Go Disco 1979.15
Got What it Takes 1950.12
Gothic 1929.51
Gott is Gut 1970.08
Gotta Dance 1948.08, 1958.12, 1989.03
Gotta do My Duty 1930.14
Gotta Find a Way to do It 1930.06
Gotta Get de Boat Loaded 1932.12
Gotta Getaway 1984.10
Gotta Go to Town 1980.20
Gotta Live Free 1952.15
Gotta Take a Chance 1980.05
Gottet Got 1900.34
Goualante du Pauvre Jean, La 1958.06, 1981.04
Goulue, La 1952.04
Gout, The 1965.31
Governor Folback! 1884.14
Governor of the State 1906.21
Governor of Villaya, The 1902.01
Governor's Son, The 1901.07, 1906.21
Governor's Song, The 1902.37
Governor's Waltz 1982.20
Governor, The 1907.07
Gown for Each Hour of the Day, A 1906.45
Gowns 1917.18
Gowns, Soft and Clingy 1919.06
Gozinto 1918.08
Grab 1888.32
Grab a Girl 1924.08, 1924.34
Grab Bag, The 1924.35
Grace Connroy 1891.32
Grace Personified 1902.43
Graceful and Fair 1929.46
Graduation 1983.18
Graduation Ball I 1977.09
Graduation Ball II 1977.09
Graduation Ball III 1977.09
Graft 1905.48, 1906.07
Graham's Laugh 1885.50
Grammatical Grievances 1915.26
Granada 1955.13
Granaderos, Los 1969.11
Grand and Glorious Fourth, The 1945.12
Grand Cafe, The 1982.18
Grand Canal 1982.09
Grand Cirque de Provence, Le 1978.22
Grand Guignol, The 1927.02
Grand Hotel 1956.09
Grand Hunting Chorus 1877.43
Grand Imperial Cirque de Paris 1961.10
Grand Jury Jump 1960.07
Grand Knowing You 1963.14
Grand March 1963.22
Grand March of Continentals 1889.46
Grand Mistake, A 1882.44
Grand Old Ivy 1961.22
Grand Old Life 1914.06
Grand Old Rag, The 1906.11
Grand Parade, The 1989.26
Grand Polonaise 1963.08
Grand Prix of Portofino, The 1958.04
Grand Prix, The 1904.39
Grand Waltz, The 1989.26
Grande Boulevards, Les 1959.15
Grande roue, La 1968.21
Grandfather's Clock 1919.33
Grandma 1922.47
Grandma's a Flapper, Too? 1924.30
Grandma's Day 1923.10
Grandmother Told Me So 1883.04
Grandmother's Dress/At the Dance 1926.09, 1926.35
Grandmother's Songs 1899.27
Grandpa 1968.30
Grandpa Guerrila 1942.26
Grandpa is Ashamed 1973.08
Grandpa's Hat 1895.38
Grandpapa 1884.11, 1983.14
Grands boulevards, Les 1961.25
Grant Avenue 1958.19
Grape Dance, The 1914.16
Grapes of Roth 1968.31
Grass Grows Green, The 1974.05
Grass is Always Greener, The 1981.10
Grass Window, The 1917.32
Grasshopper and the Butterfly, The 1891.36
Gratitude 1903.02
Grau Brae Nicht 1926.02
Grave Digger's Song, The 1981.02
Grave Yawns Cold, A 1897.03
Graveyard Mule 1991.01
Graveyard, The 2000.20
Gray Goose, The 1948.18
Grazie Par Niente 1964.35
Grease 'em, squeeze 'em 1865.03
Grease With Cash 1877.43, 1878.20
Greased Lightnin' 1972.12, 1994.07
Great American Opera, The 1952.09
Great Balls of Fire 1982.22, 1989.12
Great Ballyhooly Blue Ribbon Army, The 1888.11
Great Big Bear 1925.52
Great Big Blue Eyed Baby 1909.05
Great Big Blue-Eyed Baby 1912.38
Great Big Girl Like Me, A 1904.39, 1913.07
Great Big Town, Chicago 1975.13, 1989.16
Great Chandelier, The 1939.26
Great Cleopatra Comes 1898.50
Great Come-and-Get-it-Day 1947.03
Great Day 1929.37, 1974.09, 1975.22
Great Dictator and Me, The 1934.20
Great Divide 1975.05
Great Easter Sunday Parade, The 1968.07
Great Four Hundred, The 1890.49
Great Gate in Lovers' Lane, The 1925.48
Great Gettin' Up Mornin' 1933.27, 1943.10
Great I am With a Capital I, The 1907.29
Great If, The 1971.20
Great Indoors, The 1930.40
Great Little Guy 1928.35
Great Lover Tango, The 1973.05
Great Lover, The 1956.09
Great Musicians 1908.34
Great New York Police, The 1922.43
Great News 1988.10
Great Pretender, The 1989.12
Great Ram-Jam, The 1906.39
Great Scotch Sword Dance, The 1888.06
Great Summer Season, The 1889.39
Great Velocipede Song, The 1869.29
Great White Easiest Way, The 1908.24, 1909.23
Great White Father 1970.05
Great White Way 1907.42
Great White Way in China 1925.04
Great White Way Turns Pink, The 1937.14
Great White Way, The 1906.29, 1927.36
Great Wide Open Spaces, The 1924.18
Great Workers for the Cause 1971.21
Great Zampano, The 1969.16
Greatest Battle Song of All, The 1915.27
Greatest Gift, The 1982.10
Greatest Invention, The 1956.08
Greatest Man of All, The 1980.17
Greatest Navy in the World, The 1909.13
Greatest Show on Earth, The 1904.41, 1941.04
Greatest Star of All, The 1994.10
Greatest Team of All 1922.10
Grecian Bend, The 1925.43
Greedy Girl 1949.16
Greek Marine, The 1961.08
Green and Blue 1937.09
Green are the Waving Branches 1881.11
Green Bushes, The 1963.30
Green Carnations 1929.41
Green Corn Dance 1904.13
Green Country, The 1958.12
Green Eyes 1934.01
Green Finch and Linnet Bird 1979.06
Green Grow the Lilacs 1931.02
Green Leaves 1960.18
Green Pants 1971.04, 1976.27
Green Pastures 1930.34
Green River 1920.18
Green Sleeves 1884.57
Green, Chaney, Buster, Slyde 1996.07
Green-Up Time 1948.25
Greenback 1999.08
Greenhorns 1986.13
Greensleeves 1959.20
Greenwich Village 1918.03, 1920.43
Greenwich Village Belle 1917.31
Greenwich Village Carnival, The 1920.28
Greenwich Village Circus Days 1923.31
Greenwich Village Green, The 1925.47
Greenwich Village Nights 1922.32
Greenwich Village Violet 1927.40
Greenwillow Christmas 1960.05
Greet the Old Man With a Smile 1894.22
Greeting 1948.24
Greeting to the King 1892.42
Greetings 1963.20
Greetings, Gates 1940.09
Grenadiers 1905.49
Grenadiers' Marching Song, The 1963.20
Grenadiers, The 1969.11
Gretchen 1907.46
Gretl's Cow 1966.03
Gretna Green 1897.40, 1917.10
Grey Dove, The 1914.23
Grey Musketeers, The 1883.12
Grignan! Nanon! Ist's moglich? 1885.01
Grind, The 1985.05
Gringola 1935.04
Griofle-Grifola 1926.15
Grisbi is le Root of le Evil in Man, Le 1960.13
Grisette 1898.10
Grist for De Mille 1944.01
Grizabella, the Glamour Cat 1982.19
Grogan's Fancy Ball 1897.39
Grogan, the Masher 1885.66, 1889.11
Gros Jean and P'tit Pierre 1898.54
Grosartiga Tanzerinnen 1907.59
Grosse noce, La 1968.21
Grosse Valise, La 1965.37
Grove of Eucalyptus, The 1971.14
Grovel, Grovel 1982.03, 1993.15
Grow Big and Strong, Dear Prince 1997.16, 1998.08
Growing Pains 1945.08, 1951.14
Growltiger's Last Stand 1982.19
Gruntled 1955.12
Guarantees 1964.40
Guard by night, A 1895.26
Guard Marsh 1866.11
Guard My Steps 1866.01
Guard of Israel 1967.08
Guard thee from all emotion 1873.05
Guarda la Bella Tomato 1953.10
Guarded 1927.17
Guardians of the House 1907.05
Guards of Fantasy, The 1926.14
Guardsman, The 1930.33
Guenevere 1960.21, 1980.19, 1993.11
Guess Again 1890.07, 1906.09
Guess I'll Hang My Tears Out to Dry 1974.10

Guess Who I Saw Today? 1952.09
Guests, The 1925.45
Gueuses, Les 1934.32, 1935.19
Guide Me, Guide Me 1877.22
Guides of the Night 1890.23
Guido's Song 1982.09
Guido's Tango 1958.04
Guileless Orphan, The 1881.07
Guillerette 1866.06
Guilt Inside Your Head, The 1991.03
Guilty 1982.15, 1983.18, 1989.07
Guirlande, La 1933.24
Guitar Song 1971.10
Gum Boot Dance 1977.01
Gum Shoe Man, The 1912.16
Gunman, The 1927.07
Guppy The 1973.08
Gus and Sadie Love Song 1937.08
Gus: the Theatre Cat 1982.19
Gustave Gigot's Band 1901.18
Gustave Lorraine 1895.19
Gusto, El 1988.15
Gutter Song, The 1934.06
Guv'ment 1985.06
Guy What Takes His Time, A 2000.12
Guy Who Brought Me, The 1941.06
Guys and Dolls 1950.17, 1980.29, 1991.10
Gwendoline 1935.19
Gwendolyn and Her Mandolin 1906.27
Gwine to Catch a Gig To-Day 1899.33
Gwine to Ketch a Gig 1899.31
Gymnasium Chorus 1907.32
Gypsey Tent, The 1873.28
Gypsies Were Coming, The 1932.09
Gypsies, The 1943.11
Gypsy 1934.15
Gypsy and the Solicitor, The, or the Lawyer's Fortune 1892.08
Gypsy Blues 1921.16, 1922.25
Gypsy Bride 1924.38
Gypsy Dance, A 1963.20
Gypsy Dance, The 1915.04
Gypsy Days 1929.04
Gypsy Girl 1973.02
Gypsy in Me, The 1934.36, 1987.15
Gypsy in My Soul, The 1976.07
Gypsy Jan 1898.60
Gypsy Joe 1928.47
Gypsy Kiss 1911.47
Gypsy Life 1924.23
Gypsy Life, The 1963.20
Gypsy Love 1911.37, 1930.09, 1975.22
Gypsy Love Song 1898.60, 1924.18, 1946.18
Gypsy Maid, The 1902.38, 1903.05
Gypsy Melodies 1918.40
Gypsy of Love 1963.20
Gypsy Rose 1921.38, 1931.05
Gypsy Rover, The 1912.42
Gypsy Song 1911.03, 1917.15
Gypsy Song, The 1923.21
Gypsy Trail, The 1921.10
Gypsy's Good-Night, The 1912.42
Gypsy's Wedding Song, The 1902.16
Gypsy, The 2000.20
Gypsy-Anna 1924.16

H'm, H'm, H'm 1866.14
H-O-K-U-M 1929.24
H. Clark, My Queen 1895.25
H.N.I.C. 1969.15
Ha Ha Song, The 1895.08
Ha! Ha! Ha! 1978.07
Ha! Ha! Ha! Ha! Ha! Ha! 1900.39
Ha! Ha! You are too Late 1895.25
Ha'am Haze 1971.14
Ha, Ha, Ha 1915.02
Habanera 1930.15, 1953.10, 1977.09
Haben Sie Gehoert Das Deutsche Band? 2001.05
Hacienda Garden 1927.45
Had I a Spirit's Wings 1872.06
Had My Pitcher Tooken 1922.23
Had nature only granted 1881.25
Had She Only Let Me Dream an Hour More 1903.20
Haggle, The 1964.40
Hail Bompopka 1904.25
Hail de King of Babylon! 1930.10
Hail Diana 1909.31
Hail Lovely Venice 1873.05
Hail Stonewall Jackson 1927.42
Hail the bride of seventeen summers 1887.10
Hail the Bridegroom 1925.04
Hail the Conquering Hero! 1961.02
Hail the Groom and Hail the Bride 1900.39
Hail the Happy Couple 1933.01
Hail the Hero of Today 1910.23
Hail the King 1930.36
Hail the Rajah 1904.28
Hail the Son of David 1968.08
Hail the Wedding Pair 1911.47
Hail to Aurora 1907.47
Hail to Christmas 1929.48
Hail to Everything Under the Sun 1892.42
Hail to Jove, Our King 1866.11
Hail to Kit Maloney 1889.39
Hail to MacCracken's 1951.23
Hail to Our General 1921.14
Hail to Our King! 1884.58
Hail to Our Noble Guest 1903.10
Hail to Our Queen 1905.25
Hail to Our Queen! 1884.58
Hail to the Baronet 1902.21
Hail to the Beauteous and the Bold 1864.22
Hail to the Beauteous of Flanders 1870.05
Hail to the Bey 1894.38
Hail to the Bride 1911.05
Hail to the Caliph 1899.21
Hail to the Chief 1877.05
Hail to the Daughter 1894.37
Hail to the Deer 1908.43
Hail to the Golden Calf 1916.17
Hail to the Judge 1889.46
Hail to the King 1910.03
Hail to the Magistrate 1905.19
Hail to the Piccadilly Hero 1905.19
Hail to the Princess 1883.66
Hail to the Queen of Beauty 1905.35, 1908.16
Hail to the Sphinx 1968.23
Hail to the Vicar! 1882.63
Hail to Thee, Great Chief 1879.03
Hail to Thee, Great Chief! 1877.25
Hail to Thee, Great Prince 1879.38
Hail to this joyous day 1855.06
Hail U.S.A. 1923.02
Hail! Antonia, Hail! 1899.39
Hail! Hail! 1880.10
Hail! Miss O'Halloran 1905.27
Hail! Oh King of Aragon 1866.16
Hail! Oh, King of Aragon 1867.18
Hail! Our Royal Master 1877.39
Hail! P. Papyrus 1895.19
Hail! The Sacred Cat 1903.20
Hail, Angele, Our Nightingale 1912.33
Hail, Bibinski 1955.02
Hail, Celestial Potentate 1905.03
Hail, Columbia, Happy Land 1894.13
Hail, David 1972.09
Hail, Fame 1902.06
Hail, Gentle Eros 1905.36
Hail, Hail, Hail 1950.20
Hail, Mighty Bashaw 1877.22
Hail, Oh Regent 1895.29
Hail, Our King 1899.06
Hail, the Hero of the Day 1896.48
Hair 1968.11
Hair of the Heir, The 1934.04
Hairpin Harmony 1943.18
Hakuna Matata 1997.20
Halevay Volk Ikh Singl Geven 1990.16
Half a Married Man 1917.20
Half a Moon is Better Than None 1926.29
Half a Sixpence 1965.14
Half Alive 1971.20
Half as Big as Life 1968.31
Half Moon 1926.29
Half Moon! 1920.40
Half of a Couple 1981.07
Half of it Dearie Blues, The 1924.43
Half of it, Dearie, Blues, The 1999.10
Half of Me 1953.12, 1970.03
Half the Battle 1964.33
Half Way to Heaven 1930.35
Half-Caste Woman 1931.19
Half-Past Two 1912.26
Hall of Fame Awaits for Me, The 1925.02
Hall of Fame, The 1902.01
Hall-Way Door, The 1879.04
Hallelujah 1963.16, 1975.22
Hallelujah! 1927.16, 1930.10, 1976.32
Hallelujah, Baby! 1967.06
Hallelujah, I'm a Bum 1944.32
Hallelujah, King Jesus! 1930.10
Hallelujia 1929.52
Hallelujuah to Love 1990.01
Halling 1944.21
Hallow'een 1894.31
Hallowe'en 1910.11
Hallowe'en Tonight 1928.47
Hallowe'en Whoopee Ball 1928.47
Halloween 1926.29, 1996.09
Halloween Ballet 1989.23
Halloweve 1960.05
Halo - Halo - Halo 1929.43
Halted at the Very Gates of Paradise 1980.17
Ham and Eggs 1927.60
Ham Tree Barbecue, The 1905.28, 1906.24
Ham, The 1974.19
Hamba Bhekile 1977.01
Hambone Rhyme 1991.01
Hamburg Waltz 1965.37
Hame o' Mine 1930.17
Hamil's Birthday 1987.12
Hamlet of Fancy, The 1894.45
Hamlet was a Melancholy Dane 1903.04
Hamlet's Ghost 1908.43
Hammacher Schlemmer, I Love You 1972.05
Hammer Ring 1944.32
Hammer Song 1966.03
Hammers Will Go Rap, Rap, Rap, The 1904.10
Hammerstein 1907.14
Hammock in the Blue 1945.17
Hammock Song 1911.23
Hand for the Hog 1985.06
Hand in Hand 1913.26, 1924.10, 1965.35
Hand Me Down That Can o' Beans 1951.24
Hand Me Out a Laugh 1907.47
Hand Me the Wine and the Dice 1990.04
Hand of fate 1895.26
Hand That Rose Over 1870.20
Hand to Hand, Heart to Heart 1890.03, 1894.03
Handful of Keys 1978.09
Handicap, The 1897.04
Handle Me With Care 1907.24, 1907.28
Handle Me With Care, Baby 1909.16
Handle to My Name, A 1904.34
Hands Across the Table 1934.32, 1935.19, 1987.02
Hands All Clean 2001.06
Hands Up 1915.07, 1920.26
Handsomest Man, The 1972.18
Handy Andy 1912.24
Hang a Little Moolah on the Washline 1971.16
Hang on to Me 1924.43, 1999.10
Hang Out the Front Door Key 1907.59
Hang the Mulligan Banner Up 1880.42, 1880.64
Hang Up 1954.02
Hang Up Your Hat on Broadway 1933.15
Hang Your Hat on the Moon 1928.07
Hang Your Sorrows in the Sun 1923.27
Hanging Around Yo Dore 1931.47
Hanging Gardens of Babylon, The 1926.23
Hanging is My Only Sport 1957.02
Hanging Over and Out 1979.15
Hanging Throttlebottom in the Morning 1933.25
Hanging, Hanging, Hanging 1882.18
Hanky Panky 1985.03
Hanky Panky Glide, The 1912.25
Hannah 1906.48
Hannah Dooley 1905.30
Hannah Jackson Greene 1898.78
Hannah's a Hummer 1968.07

Hans Rap 1893.19
Hapless Victims 1873.05
Happiest Girl in the World, The 1961.08
Happiest Hours from the Twilight 1885.06
Happiest Hours of Twilight 1888.30
Happiest House on the Block, The 1955.27
Happiest Moments 1919.23
Happiest Night of His Life, The 1911.07
Happily coupled are we, you see 1887.10
Happily Ever After 1959.26
Happily Ever After After All 1990.06
Happiness 1886.62, 1907.31, 1922.01, 1924.07, 1962.02, 1971.11, 1987.12, 1994.05, 1999.03
Happiness is Jes' a Thing Called Joe 1953.12
Happiness is Just a Thing Called Joe 1945.07, 1999.23
Happiness, joy divine 1859.09
Happy 1923.06, 1925.18, 1927.64, 1928.31, 1930.29, 1989.26
Happy and Free 1882.33
Happy Anniversary 1970.01, 1974.19, 1983.03, 1984.02
Happy Because I'm in Love 1929.37
Happy Birthday 1929.27, 1954.17, 1961.21, 1968.30, 1983.14, 1984.02
Happy Birthday, Josh 1996.08
Happy Birthday, Mrs. J.J. Brown 1960.20
Happy Bride 1925.04
Happy Cigarettes Theme 1987.02
Happy Clown, The 1924.20
Happy Day 1872.23
Happy Day March 1908.07
Happy day, thrice happy day 1892.20
Happy Days 1905.39, 1909.17, 1918.32, 1919.22, 1930.08, 1974.26, 1975.22
Happy Days and Lonely Nights 1930.08
Happy Days are Here Again 1936.03, 1986.06, 1990.05, 1999.05
Happy Days in Dixie 1903.41
Happy Days of Life 1846.01
Happy Days, The 1983.03
Happy End, The 1977.08
Happy Ending 1923.19, 1924.21, 1944.28
Happy Family 1918.28
Happy Family, The 1912.15
Happy Go Lucky 1926.30, 1927.52
Happy go lucky lot are we, A 1881.06
Happy Go-Lucky Days 1924.46
Happy Habit 1954.02
Happy Heaven of Harlem, The 1929.45
Happy Hickory 1981.14
Happy Hobo, The 1917.16
Happy Hoboes 1928.37
Happy Hooligan 1902.09
Happy Hottentots 1916.03
Happy Hunting 1951.15, 1956.16
Happy Hunting Horn 1940.22, 1975.13, 1989.16
Happy in Love 1941.11
Happy in the Morning 1981.10
Happy is the Summer's Day 1905.36
Happy Japan 1896.27
Happy Land 1916.25
Happy Land of Once-Upon-a-Time, The 1908.35
Happy Landing 1930.11
Happy Little Bridesmaids 1890.23
Happy Little Briggs 1876.06
Happy Little Crook 1955.10
Happy Little Kids 1878.20
Happy Little Week-end 1933.21
Happy Man 1972.24
Happy Melody 1924.32, 1926.30
Happy Mother's Day, Mother Earth 1972.21
Happy New Year 1996.09
Happy Prince, The 1924.32
Happy Rickshaw Man 1927.14
Happy sain, across the plain.., A 1885.63
Happy Slumberland 1908.35
Happy Song 1965.37
Happy Song, A 1959.20
Happy Talk 1949.04
Happy the Lot 1884.57
Happy Thoughts 1866.35
Happy Time, The 1968.01
Happy to be Nineteen 1999.12
Happy to Keep His Dinner Warm 1961.22, 1980.29
Happy to Make Your Acquaintance 1956.04
Happy Wanderer, The 1955.13
Happy Wedding Day, A 1919.09
Happy With Winged Feet 1938.10
Happy young heart 1879.10
Happy, Happy Illinois 1903.24
Happy, Happy New Year 1983.08
Happy, Happy, Happy 1988.10
Happy, Noble Outlaw Band, A 1913.33
Happyland 1921.18
Har de News 1876.11
Harbor Girl 1981.04
Harbor of Lost Dreams, The 1909.27
Harbor of My Heart 1927.16
Hard Boiled Egg, A 1897.25
Hard Candy Christmas 1978.13
Hard Day's Night, A 1982.22
Hard Job Being God 1972.09
Hard Life 1911.06
Hard Luck in Society 1912.09
Hard Luck Stories of the Stage 1906.01
Hard Time Blues 1945.07
Hard Times 1894.44, 1926.19
Hard to be a Prince 1986.13
Hard to be Diva 1989.09
Hard to Get Along With 1927.09
Hard to Please 1885.06
Hard to Understand the Ladies 1906.32
Hard-Boiled Herman 1924.28
Hard-Hearted Hannah 1924.13
Hardangerfjord, The 1979.12
Harder They Fall, The 1970.05
Hardly Think I Will 1944.32
Hardware Line 1869.42
Hare Krishna 1968.11
Harem Life 1919.15
Harem on the Loose 1938.08
Hark forward! Hark forward! Away! 1887.44
Hark Hark 1898.56
Hark the trill 1887.04
Hark the Vesper Hymn is Stealing 1873.29
Hark to That Omen 1862.03
Hark to the Chinese 1906.40
Hark to the Scream of the Eagle 1907.50
Hark to the Song of the Night 1950.20
Hark to the Voice of Your Lover 1906.07
Hark! 'Tis the Bugle! 1882.58
Hark! from St. Mungo's Tower 1859.01
Hark! Hark! The dogs do bark. The Witches are coming to town 1869.35
Hark! Love, 'Tis I 1882.33
Hark! The Lark! 1880.19
Hark! The merry marriage bells! 1881.07
Hark! to the Sunset Gun 1881.11
Hark! What was that, sir? 1888.35
Hark, 'Tis the Indian Drum 1870.20
Hark, the Extra Marital Lark 1952.09
Hark, the hour of ten is sounding 1875.35
Hark, the Merry Marriage Bells 1907.51
Harlem 1927.33, 1930.34
Harlem '70 1976.04
Harlem - Time 1976.04
Harlem Dan 1933.06
Harlem Lullaby 1933.15
Harlem Makes Me Feel 1976.04
Harlem Nocturne 1984.15, 1999.24
Harlem Number Man 1938.19
Harlem on My Mind 1979.11
Harlem Rhumbola 1931.11
Harlem Rose 1928.10
Harlem Serenade 1929.27
Harlem Streets 1972.13
Harlem Sweet Harlem 1976.04
Harlem Sweeties 1966.15
Harlem Town 1929.18
Harlem Waltz 1936.17
Harlem Woogie 1938.19
Harlemania 1932.08
Harlequin Hoops, The 1909.11
Harlequin's Doll 1923.38
Harlequinade 1934.06, 1953.17
Harm Him Not 1881.16
Harmless Little Girlie With the Downcast Eye 1896.06
Harmonica Dance 1927.45
Harmony 1921.07, 1924.24, 1946.04, 1962.01
Harmony Boys, The 1937.14
Harp and the piano, etc, The 1859.16
Harp in the Air 1873.28
Harp That Once Thro, The 1892.45
Harp That Once Through Tara's Hall, The 1871.16
Harp That Once, The 1896.31
Harriet Sedley 1967.02
Harriet's Ecdysiastical Delight 1979.05
Harriet's Pavan 1967.02
Harrigan 1908.09, 1968.07
Harry Houdini, Master Escapist 1998.01
Harry, Harry, Won't You Marry Me? 1904.58
Harum-Scarum, The 1911.15
Harvest Moon 1928.26
Harvest Moon, The 1921.09
Harvesters' Song 1919.24
Has Anybody Here Seen Kelly? 1910.01
Has Anybody Seen My Cat? 1901.19
Has Anybody Seen Our Ship? 1986.19
Has Anybody Seen the Waiter? 1916.07
Has Anyone Seen 1897.21
Has Anyone Seen My Bennie? 1973.09
Has Anyone Seen My Mary Ann 1888.34
Has Anyone Seen Our Cat? 1895.17
Has Anyone Seen Our Ship? 1936.29
Has anyone seen the Pytchley Pack? 1882.63
Has Cupid Laid in Wait for You? 1911.31
Has I Let You Down? 1954.19
Hashish 1968.11
Hassan, the Sultan With His Court Approaches 1900.37
Hassidic 1968.04
Hast Thou Been to Mecca? 1920.34
Hasta Manana 1933.15
Haste then to glut my vengeance 1873.05
Haste, love, to me 1859.12
Hasten, Time 1893.19
Hat Like That, A 1939.25
Hat My Father Wore on St. Patrick's Day, The 1909.16
Hat, The 1916.10
Hate Me 1993.17
Hate to Say Goodbye to You 1976.33
Hats 1906.01, 1910.21
Hats Make the Woman 1905.57
Hats Off 1938.12
Hats Off to Ice 1944.20
Hats Off to Me 1891.45
Hattie 1897.34
Haughty Baron, I 1881.16
Haul de Woodpile Down 1887.48
Haul the Woodpile Down 1888.28
Hauled Back Again! 1891.02
Haunted Heart 1948.14
Haunted Hot Spot 1952.20
Haunted Pool, The 1909.31
Haunted Violin, The 1921.27
Haunting Refrain 1932.10
Haut Ecole 1909.07
Haute Couture 1965.33
Hava Nagila 1972.17
Hava Naguila 1962.17, 1964.02
Havana 1921.08, 1926.50, 1950.17
Havana for a Night 1938.08
Havana Made 1911.40
Havana Nights 1922.32
Havanola Roll 1926.04
Have a Dream 1962.04
Have a Good Time, Everybody 1924.27
Have a Heart 1917.01, 1931.26
Have a Little Faith 1997.18
Have a Little Regiment of Our Own 1918.31
Have a Nice Day 1985.19
Have a Restaurant of Your Own 1915.02
Have a Smile With Momus 1910.19
Have I Finally Found My Heart? 1979.32
Have I Got a Girl for You 1970.13, 1976.03
Have I Got a Girl for You? 1999.20
Have I Stayed too Long at the Fair 1959.14
Have I the Right 1980.23
Have I Told You Lately? 1962.05
Have mercy, heaven, it is the hurricane! 1881.04

Have More Than Thou Showest 1981.02
Have settled their troubles at last 1890.12
Have Ye Heard the Brave News 1902.25
Have You Any Little Thing? 1923.06
Have You Ever Been Alone With a King Before? 1968.08
Have You Ever had it Told That Way Before? 1907.07
Have You Ever Heard the German Band? 2001.05
Have You Ever Loved Any Other Girl 1911.13
Have You Ever Seen a Prettier Little Congress? 1970.15
Have you forgot 1880.04
Have You Forgotten Me 1922.45
Have You Forgotten? 1927.03
Have You Got Any Castles, Baby? 1997.05
Have You Heard the News? 1959.06
Have You Heard the Scandal 1915.20
Have You Heard? 1919.42, 1951.05, 1968.08
Have You Met Delilah? 1955.25
Have You Met Miss Jones? 1937.13, 1975.13
Have You Seen Her Lately 1869.42
Have You Seen Him, Did He Pass This Way? 1963.22
Have You Seen My Baby? 1908.15
Have You Seen My Henry Brown 1905.42
Have You Seen the Countess Cindy? 1946.22
Have You Seen the Elephant? 1889.31
Have You Used Soft Soap? 1927.05
Have Yourself a Merry Little Christmas 1979.24, 1989.23, 1999.23
Haven't We Met Before? 1924.09, 1943.16, 1951.10
Havin' a Ball 1938.19
Havin' a Hunch 2000.18
Havin' a Time 1945.20
Havin' a Wonderful Time 1925.18
Having Someone 1987.14
Hawaii 1928.16, 1965.37
Hawaii Ponoi 1912.03
Hawaii's Shore 1930.26
Hawaiian Hula Dance Song 1912.03
Hawaiian Moonlight 1919.26
Hawaiian Night in Dixieland 1922.25
Hawaiian Ritual 1940.18
Hawaiian Shores 1923.10
Hawthorne Buds 1888.28
Hay Ride, The 1907.32
Hay Unos Ojos 1988.15
Hay! Straw! 1928.44
Hay, Hay, Hay 1945.14
Haywire 1934.15
Hazaza 1914.03
Hazel Dell 1861.04
He Ain't in It 1890.07
He Always Comes Home to Me 1983.08
He and She 1938.14, 1975.13
He Blew on His Bugle-E-Oo 1913.18
He Brings Our Score 1884.57
He Came Right Up 1895.25
He Can Cure You of Love 1916.02
He Can Dance 1938.01
He Can do It 1970.05
He can not, must not, shall not 1896.13
He Cert'nly was Good to Me 1897.45, 1898.72
He Certainly has a Soft Spot for Me 1899.35
He Come Down This Morning 1973.10
He Couldn't do a Single Thing Without Me 1900.01
He Couldn't Wink His Eyes 1892.29
He Dangled Me on His Knee 1903.29
He Did it so Politely 1902.07
He Didn't Know Exactly What to Do 1903.10
He Died Good 1960.05
He Doesn't Know 1927.01
He Don't Know Where'e Are 1894.06
He Failed to Underwrite a Happy Home 1923.37
He Flipped, And 1956.08
He Goes to Church on Sunday 1907.15
He Got it in the Ear 1976.03
He had His Rabbit's Foot With Him 1898.47
He had Refinement 1951.14
He has Subdued Her 1912.04
He hasn't a Thing Except Me 1936.02, 1936.17
He is a Bluff 1899.06
He is a man 1894.28
He is a Movie Man 1945.09
He is a Prince 1880.26
He is Gone 1913.10
He is My Bag 1972.19
He is My Steady 1899.30
He is Returning 1880.46
He is saved! 1896.26
He is Sweet, He is Good 1914.22
He is the Bridegroom 1902.19
He is the Prince 1882.18
He is the Type 1925.38
He Just Beats a Tom Tom 1934.39
He knew it! 1889.54
He Knows Milk 1930.02
He Knows Where the Rose is in Bloom 1927.20
He Let Me Live 1990.17
He Lives in You 1997.20
He Look'd at My Sabots 1890.33
He Love - She Loves 1892.42
He Love Me, He Loves Me Not 1907.04
He Loved Her Tender 1888.09
He Loved Me Tender 1909.07
He Loved, He Loves Me Not 1918.15
He Loves and She Loves 1927.59, 1983.06
He Loves Her 1960.10
He Loves Me 1923.04, 1934.06
He Loves Me - He Loves Me Not 1900.51, 1902.05
He Loves to Make Us Laugh 1993.17
He Makes Me Feel I'm Lovely 1961.14
He Man 1928.41
He May be Your Man But He Comes to See Me Sometimes 1980.10
He May be Your Man, But He Comes to See Me Sometimes 1922.25
He May Not Come When You Want Him 1990.05
He Must be Punished 1902.03
He Needs Me Now 1968.03
He Needs You 1961.21
He Never Came Back 1891.02
He never can dance any more 1879.35
He Never Said a Word 1897.17
He Only Comes to See Me Once in a While 1924.37
He Picked it Up and Let it Drop 1894.35
He Plays the Violin 1969.06
He prevents me, 'po my soul 1859.14
He Raised Everybody's Rent But Katies 1920.11
He Says I Must Go 1878.02
He Says She Must Go 1888.13, 1896.35
He Says Yes, She Says No! 1912.46
He Smiles 1972.07
He snores like a thunder storm 1879.35
He Still was There 1866.07, 1866.21
He Takes Me Off His Income Tax 1952.09, 1980.18
He Talks Like a Polly 1885.04
He Talks to Me 1970.12
He Took it in a Good-Natured Way 1896.48
He Tossed a Coin 1970.15
He Tried to Make a Dollar 1947.16
He Tries to be English 1885.42
He Used to be Your Man, But He's My Man Now 1922.25
He Walked Down Piccadilly With a Poppy and a Lily, And 1927.20
He Wanted a Girl 1908.27
He Wanted to Say 1998.01
He Wants to Put the Army in Jail 1975.07
He was a Gentleman 1952.11
He was a Married Man 1900.41
He was a Pal of Mine 1891.43
He was a Wonderful Man 1906.11
He was the Only Man I Ever Loved 1922.15
He was There 1970.02
He was too Good to Me 1975.13
He Went in Like a Lion 1920.24
He Went in Like a Lion and Came Out Like a Lamb 1919.16
He Went to the East 1940.01
He Who Fights and Runs Away 1890.21
He Who Gets Slapped 1927.11
He Who Knows the Way 1983.01
He who shies at such a prize 1882.78
He Will Come Home Again 1976.01
He Will Take Me to His Heart 1912.37
He Will Tonight 1950.04
He Will Understand 1917.05
He Winked at Me 1902.20
He Won't be Happy Till He Gets It 1905.01
He Won't do a Thing to His Opera 1908.16
He Wore a Worried Look 1894.16
He Would Away 1884.42, 1886.47, 1888.36
He Wouldn't Have to Ask Me Twice 1907.06
He Writes a Song 1925.02
He yields! He yields! 1887.10
He' for Me, The 1928.12
He'll Make it Alright 1987.17
He'll Make Me Believe That He's Mine 1983.20
He'll Never be Mine 1971.02
He'll Never Know 1958.20, 1958.21
He'll Understand 1969.10
He's a Bold Rogue 1950.01
He's a Cousin of Mine 1906.27
He's a Dear Old Pet 1914.06
He's a Fan, Fan, Fan 1910.09
He's a Fool 1973.03
He's a Genius 1968.02
He's a Jolly Good Fellow 1906.39
He's a Ladies' Man 1974.26
He's a Man 1972.02
He's a Man of Mystery 1900.42
He's a Man's Man 1929.03
He's a Rebel 1984.15
He's a Rider 1888.34
He's a Right Guy 1943.01, 1998.05
He's a Stew, I'm a Stew 1925.25
He's a Winner 1926.07
He's a Wonder 1976.35, 1980.14
He's A-my Brud 1908.15
He's afraid! Must dissemble 1887.43
He's All That We Need 1981.15
He's as Straight as a Dart 1897.03
He's Back 1968.01
He's Been on the Bottle Since a Baby 1932.18
He's captivated me 1880.40
He's caught at last 1859.16
He's Coming Back 1910.22
He's Coming Home 1916.26
He's Crazy 1911.42
He's English and so Sweet 1886.53
He's found his ideal 1889.10
He's Getting Like His Daddy Every Day 1908.37
He's Goin' Home 1939.13
He's Gone 1903.04, 1906.26
He's Gone Away 1955.13, 1958.12, 1963.19
He's gone| once more I am alone 1859.09
He's Good for Me 1973.06
He's Good for Nothing But Me 1944.01
He's Got the Whole World in His Hands 1955.13, 1976.24, 1990.05
He's Have to Get Under - Get Out and Get Under 1913.05
He's Here 1898.25, 1967.16
He's in Love! 1953.16
He's Just My Ideal 1929.06
He's kiss'd me 1884.60
He's Ma Romeo 1906.13
He's Mine 1928.40, 1928.45
He's Mine, All Mine! 1894.29
He's My Guy 1993.05
He's My Man 1928.17
He's Never too Busy 1970.02
He's No Good 1997.08
He's No king 1892.20
He's no money, so you see 1859.08
He's Not a Well Man 1962.05
He's Not Himself 1933.01
He's on the Police Force Now 1890.03
He's Only Wonderful 1951.15
He's positively crazed 1859.16
He's Safe 1888.36
He's Say Oo-La-La! Wee-Wee, And 1919.163
He's so Fine 1984.15
He's Sure the Boy I Love 1984.15
He's the Hottest Man in Town 1923.47
He's the Man 1953.02
He's the Wizard 1975.01
He's the Wonder of Them All 1911.05
He's Turning Ninety-Four 1880.47
He's under the table 1889.50

He's With My Johnny 1950.01
He's Won! He's Won! Good Night 1880.10
He-Back, She-Back 1922.21
Head in the Clouds 1942.20
Head Over Heels 1886.02, 1918.25
Head Over Heels in Love 1925.38, 1926.29
Headache and Heartache 1951.18
Headin' for a Weddin' 1950.06
Headin' for Harlem 1926.29, 1927.48
Headin' for the Bottom 1955.04
Headin' South 1926.19
Headin' West 1944.20
Headless Dance 1968.19
Heads or Tails 1984.15
Headsman and I, The 1964.03
Heal Their Hearts 1996.12
Health to Dear Mama, A 1938.06
Health to the Lady 1848.04
Hear Dem Bells 1889.12
Hear me swear 1873.04
Hear me swear now 1859.18
Hear Me! 1900.25
Hear Me! Hear Me! 1882.45
Hear Mr, Amelia 1902.01
Hear My Cry 2000.05
Hear My Song of Love 1907.11
Hear the Band 1903.17
Hear the Bell 1917.22
Hear the Gypsies Playing 1936.27
Hear the Hunter's Horn 1906.09
Hear the Trumpet Call 1927.55
Hear Them Bells 1888.42, 1889.25
Hear! Hear! 1900.39, 1955.13
Hear, O Israel! 1931.29
Heard Nobody Pray 1931.11
Heart 1955.08, 1962.17, 1994.01
Heart and Soul 1980.29
Heart Beats 1923.42
Heart bow'd down, The 1844.01
Heart Bow'd Down, The 1934.17
Heart Bowed Down, The 1870.07
Heart Breaker, The 1907.24
Heart Breakin' Joe 1923.39
Heart for Sale, A 1920.04
Heart Full of Love, A 1987.04
Heart has Won the Game, The 1959.06
Heart in Hand 1951.17
Heart is Free, The 1927.03
Heart is Quicker Than the Eye, The 1936.05, 1975.13, 1983.02
Heart of a Rose 1929.28
Heart of Every Girl, The 1941.10
Heart of Mine 1928.12
Heart of My Heart 1891.14, 1916.05, 1917.21
Heart of My Heart I Love You 1899.27
Heart of My Rose, The 1924.35
Heart of Paddy Whack, The 1914.29
Heart of Stone 1958.14
Heart of the Golden West, The 1916.09
Heart of the Rose, The 1915.04
Heart Ride 1955.19
Heart sighs ever to be free, The 1882.60
Heart That Beats for Thee, A 1895.12
Heart That is Still the Same, A 1897.32
Heart That Loves, The 1893.03
Heart That's Free, A 1922.21
Heart to Heart 1909.15, 1916.14
Heart to Let, A 1906.19
Heart's Cry, The 1996.12, 2000.05
Heart's Richest Dower, The 1896.41
Heart, Foolish Heart 1895.06
Heart-to-Heart Talks 1902.21
Heartbeat 1990.15
Heartbeat of the World - Andalucia 2000.05
Heartbreak Hotel 1978.01, 1982.22, 1989.12
Heartbreakers 1920.23
Heartland 2000.05
Hearts Aglow 1949.05
Hearts and Flowers 1936.30
Hearts are Trumps 1911.31
Hearts in Tune 1923.08
Hearts we oft love best 1882.44
Heat is on in Saigon, The 1991.03
Heat Sensation 1983.15
Heat Wave 1933.22, 1980.10
Heathen 1972.11
Heather Belles 1912.07
Heather on the Hill, The 1947.07, 1980.26
Heatherbell 1907.58
Heave Ho! 1890.33
Heaven 1924.46, 1988.12, 1995.12
Heaven Bless Our Home 1944.28
Heaven Help Me 1998.13
Heaven Help My Heart 1988.09
Heaven Help the Sailors on a Night Like This 1967.05
Heaven Hop 1928.33
Heaven in My Arms 1939.28
Heaven Measured You for Me 1914.28
Heaven Must be Missing an Angel 1997.21
Heaven O'er doth shield us with its care and seems to say - Never Despair! 1859.12
Heaven on Earth 1926.36, 1948.23, 1990.14
Heaven on Their Minds 1971.12
Heaven Protect Me! 1959.19
Heaven Sent 1948.15
Heaven Shield the Soldier 1852.01
Heaven Will Protect the Working Girl 1910.13, 1944.32
Heaven's Best Gift 1901.13
Heavenly Body 1920.23
Heavenly Chorus, A 1986.16
Heavenly Days 1930.37
Heavenly Ladies 1914.09
Heavens are Telling 1938.02
Heavy 1981.29
Heavyweight Champ of the World 1965.01
Hebrew Fancy Ball, The 1890.03
Hecate's Call 1870.15
Hector 1917.29
Hee Haw Brigade 1880.42
Heebie Jeebie Dance 1992.06
Heel and Toe 1927.29, 1929.02
Heel and Toe We Always Go 1886.15
Heh Heh, Chuckle, Good Mornin' Sunshine 1971.13
Heia! See the Horseman Come 1978.07
Heia, heia in den Bergen ist mein Heimatland 1984.05
Heigh Ho 1910.20
Heigh Ho for the Feminine Sex 1896.51
Heigh Ho the Gang's All Here 1931.26
Heigh Ho! Lingo Sally 1887.48
Heigh Ho! Which to Choose 1875.15
Heigh Ho, Tra, La, La, La 1942.23
Heigh-Ho 1979.28
Heigh-Ho Cheerio 1928.34
Heigh-Ho, Lackaday! 1925.31
Heil sei der Grafin Delicat 1885.01
Heilige Nacht 1964.28
Heinie Fiftette, The 1919.40
Heiresses, The 1912.15
Heldites, The 1930.23
Helen is Always Willing 1954.03
Helen of Troy 1920.03, 1972.25
Helen of Troy, New York 1923.19
Helen's Hat 1912.16
Hell of a Fix, A 1933.25
Hell of a Hole, A 1933.25
Hell's Finest 1928.49
Heller Jubel 1984.05
Hello 1892.45, 1926.50, 1982.23
Hello Beautiful 1965.08, 1984.10
Hello Bill 1907.27
Hello Cupid, Send Me a Flower 1912.43
Hello Doc 1984.02
Hello Dolly 1965.08
Hello Dolly! 1964.01
Hello Everybody 1981.17
Hello Frisco 1976.25
Hello Frisco I Called You Up to Say Hello 1915.16
Hello Girls 1924.33
Hello Home! 1919.31
Hello Imagination 1920.26
Hello in There 1973.14, 1975.12
Hello is the Way Things Begin 1970.12
Hello Little Girl 1999.20
Hello Ma 1936.01
Hello Ma Baby 1901.28
Hello Miss Knickerbocker 1920.47
Hello Paris 1911.26
Hello People 1909.04
Hello There 1968.11
Hello Twelve, Hello Thirteen, Hello Love 1975.15
Hello Waves 1965.17
Hello Young Lovers 1973.17
Hello Yourself 1928.41
Hello! Good-Bye 1923.07
Hello! Hello! Hello! 1922.19, 1923.20
Hello! Hello! Oh, a Jolly Good Show 1953.10
Hello, Babby 1884.48
Hello, Baby 1884.41
Hello, Beautiful 1932.04, 1947.05
Hello, Broadway 1914.34
Hello, Come Along Girls 1906.47
Hello, Cousin Lola 1926.02
Hello, Dolly 1974.22
Hello, Dolly! 1985.19, 1998.07
Hello, Everybody 1919.34, 1965.05
Hello, Good Morning 1931.48, 1952.07
Hello, Hazel 1953.01
Hello, Hello 1913.02, 1923.03
Hello, Hello There! 1956.14
Hello, Hello, Hello 1918.21, 1951.13
Hello, Hello, Telephone Girlie 1925.30
Hello, Honey 1913.17
Hello, I've Been Looking for You 1916.15
Hello, Little Girl 1987.18
Hello, Little Miss U.S.A. 1914.01
Hello, Little Stranger 1907.32
Hello, Ma Baby 1898.63, 1980.27
Hello, Ma Lulu 1904.56
Hello, Maginnis 1888.42, 1889.25
Hello, Miss Liza Green 1906.40
Hello, Miss Tango 1917.23
Hello, My Dearie 1917.13
Hello, My Lover, Goodbye 1931.42
Hello, People 1920.09
Hello, the Little Birds Have Flown 1925.07
Hello, Tu Tu 1909.11
Hello, Young Lovers 1964.02, 1993.16, 2000.16
Hello, Young Lovers! 1951.12
Hello-Hello 1976.03
Hellz-a-poppin 1938.08
Hellzapoppin Polka 1938.08
Hellzapoppin' Polka, The 1944.30
Help 1972.13, 1977.10
Help Me, Lawd 1950.16
Help the Seamen 1934.20
Help Yourself 1907.13
Help Yourself to Happiness 1931.19
Help! And the Villain Goes to Jail 1909.09
Help, Help, Help 1924.38
Helplessness at Midnight 1988.07
Helter Skelter 1977.10
Hen and the Weather Vane 1908.35
Hence it Don't Make Sense 1944.29
Henchmen are Forgotten 1997.18
Henley on a Summer Day 1914.19
Henny 1903.24
Henny Klein 1905.48
Henrietta Pye 1885.15
Henry Clay 1912.31
Henry Dinkelspiel 1904.58
Henry Ford 1998.01
Henry is Where it's At 1971.01
Henry Street 1964.11
Henry's Dream Theme 1971.01
Henry, Sweet Henry 1967.14
Her Baggage was Checked for Troy 1908.03
Her Bright Shawl 1924.09
Her Bright Smile Haunts Me Still 1865.11
Her Cannonading Eyes 1916.18
Her Dream Man 1947.12
Her Easter Bonnet 1933.22
Her Eyes are Brown 1926.34
Her Eyes Don't Shine Like Diamonds 1894.35, 1895.02
Her Face 1961.10
Her Father's Daughter 1987.19
Her First Can Can 1904.34
Her First Roman 1968.23

Her Front Name was Sally 1898.56
Her Golden Hair was Hanging Down Her Back 1894.31, 1894.51, 1895.32
Her Hair is Black as Licorice 1928.30
Her Is 1954.05
Her Lily-White Hand 1938.06
Her Love is Always the Same 1922.02
Her Majesty 1974.24
Her Memory Brings Me No Regret 1897.52
Her Mother Came Too, And 1923.07, 1975.22
Her Name is Aurora 1993.09
Her Name is Leona 1974.03
Her Name is Mandy 1897.48
Her Pop's a Cop 1939.19
Her Portrait 1906.44
Herald Square Song 1903.05
Here 'Tis 1936.30, 1952.08
Here am I 1929.31
Here am I Broken-Hearted 1927.58
Here and Now 1948.18, 1963.29
Here and There 1935.11
Here are the warriors all ablaze 1895.29
Here at Baiae on the Bay 1899.39
Here at Monte Carlo 1898.17
Here at our post 1880.24
Here at Thy Window, Love 1900.50
Here be Oysters Stewed by Honey 1919.20
Here be Oysters Stewed in Honey 1917.24
Here by the ford we'll wait 1887.04
Here Come the Blues 1955.11
Here Come the Soldiers 1919.04
Here Come Your Men 1966.09
Here Comes De Honey Man 1983.04
Here Comes My Blackbird 1928.18
Here Comes Pansy 1902.43
Here Comes the Bride 1930.09
Here Comes the Groom 1916.20
Here Comes the Kid 1923.22
Here Comes the Ladies 1894.33
Here Comes the Married Men 1916.21
Here Comes the Prince of Wales 1927.11
Here Comes the Showboat 1927.32
Here Comes the Sun 1970.16, 1982.22
Here Comes Tootsi 1915.29
Here ends all artifice and guile 1882.60
Here for the Hearing 1994.06
Here Have I Pitched My Tent 1870.20
Here I Am 1927.31, 1967.14, 1976.16, 1990.06
Here I Come 1958.04
Here I Go Again 1945.18
Here I Stand 1955.03
Here I'll Stay 1948.25
Here in Big Boxes We Bear 1905.04
Here in Cadiz 1894.38
Here in Eden 1966.18
Here in Minipoora 1984.10
Here in My Arms 1925.31, 1975.13
Here in silence 1859.17
Here in the Dark 1927.63
Here in the Moonlight on the Fence 1907.44
Here in the Starlight 1909.03
Here is a case unprecedented 1890.02
Here is a Sword 1930.30
Here is a Tune of a Soldier 1911.47
Here it Comes Again 1906.14
Here it Is 1931.30
Here lies an actor 1888.33
Here on Lords and Ladies Waiting 1921.01
Here on Sunlit Sands 1894.33
Here on the Fence at Doolittle College 1907.44
Here on the Lot 1945.09
Here on the Stoop 1840.03
Here on Who 2000.18
Here She Comes 1928.02
Here She Comes Now 1951.19
Here Take My Heart 1879.06
Here take the sword, King Richard 1869.43
Here There and Everywhere 1921.35
Here They Are 1928.03
Here they come 1896.27
Here They Come 1906.26
Here They Come in Glittering Glory 1902.01
Here Tonight, Tomorrow Where? 1965.35
Here We Are 1914.16
Here We are Again 1965.06
Here we are at risk 1890.02
Here We are in Love 1932.06
Here We are Scrubbing 1911.35
Here We are Sir 1900.39
Here We are Together 1933.15
Here We are Together Again 1925.33
Here We are: Grisettes and Playgirls 1978.07
Here We Come With Rhythmic Measure 1882.18
Here We Go Again 1996.08
Here You Come Again 1978.05
Here You Must Repose 1866.07, 1866.21
Here You See Eight Ladies of Quality 1913.33
Here's a Bale of Cotton for You 1915.02
Here's a Book 1981.12
Here's a Chance for Visitors 1898.17
Here's a Day to be Happy 1930.39
Here's a go! 1863.04
Here's a Hand 1942.15
Here's a Health to His Majesty 1924.20
Here's a Health Unto His Majesty 1963.03
Here's a how-de-do 1885.47
Here's a How-de-do 1939.15, 1939.17
Here's a Kiss 1925.31
Here's a Kiss for Cinderella 1931.48
Here's a man of jollity 1888.35
Here's a Nice to Do 1904.01
Here's a pack 1898.25
Here's a Paradox for Lovers 1907.51
Here's a Song to the Flag 1893.19
Here's a Toast 1936.30
Here's an End to Vacilation 1899.34
Here's Happy Days to You 1903.24
Here's How 1914.27, 1927.50
Here's Howe 1928.17
Here's Love 1963.21
Here's Luck 1944.20
Here's Momma 1972.07
Here's My Plan 2001.06
Here's My Ticket 1889.46
Here's That Rainy Day 1953.11, 1995.14
Here's the Happy Ending 1979.28
Here's Three Times Three 1880.46
Here's to Dear Old Us 1955.04
Here's to Love 1913.04
Here's to My Comrades and Me 1908.40
Here's to Old Champagne 1892.55
Here's to Our Alma Mater 1898.43
Here's to the Bashful Girl of Fifteen 1904.55
Here's to the Bride 1922.13
Here's to the Girl 1908.25
Here's to the Girl of My Heart 1928.47
Here's to the Land We Love, Boys 1914.27
Here's to the Last Girl 1909.31
Here's to the Two of You 1917.36
Here's to Us 1962.27, 1982.01, 1998.15
Here's to You 1934.15
Here's to You, Jack 1927.64
Here's to You, My Sparkling Wine 1915.18
Here's to Your Eyes, Sweetheart 1905.52
Here's to Your Illusions 1951.15
Here's Where I Belong 1968.05, 1989.25
Here, see, we come 1879.38
Here, Steward 1921.10
Hereupon we're both agreed 1888.35
Hermits, The 1925.31
Hernando's Hideaway 1954.05
Hero of the Football Game 1897.33, 1900.24
Heroes 1903.38, 1982.23, 1998.19
Heroes Come Home, The 1954.03
Heroes in the Fall 1939.27
Heroes of Yesterday 1926.15
Heroes That Wear the Blue, The 1905.10
Hesitation Waltz 1957.10
Heut' is heut'! 1920.46
Hey 1967.06
Hey Baby 1981.06, 1999.12
Hey Feller 1983.05
Hey for the Merry Greenwood 1929.43
Hey Good Lookin' 1982.15
Hey Hey Blues 1991.01
Hey Jude 1977.10
Hey Liza it's Me 1991.04
Hey Look at Me 1980.23
Hey Look Me Over 1960.22
Hey Madame 1958.02
Hey Mama 1992.06
Hey Man 1980.05
Hey Nonny Nonny 1932.13
Hey Rube 1898.02, 1928.08
Hey There 1954.05
Hey There, Good Times 1977.04
Hey Yvette 1974.05
Hey! Hey! 1926.07
Hey! Hey! Let 'Er Go! 1924.03
Hey, Big Spender 1976.07
Hey, Feller 1927.67
Hey, Gal! 1942.34
Hey, Girlie 1970.19
Hey, Good Lookin' 1943.01
Hey, Jimmy, Joe, John, Jim, Jack 1961.21
Hey, Little Goats 1998.11
Hey, Look at Me, Mrs. Draba 1978.22
Hey, Love 1963.13
Hey, Mr. Bossman 1944.32
Hey, Nonny, Hey 1928.19
Hey, Nonny, Nonny 1928.19
Hey, Tom Sawyer 2001.06
Hey, Tsigelekh 1998.11
Hey, Why Not! 1972.04
Hey-diddle-diddle! when man is in love 1896.27
Hey...! 1976.03
Hh! Cha! Cha! 1931.37
Hi 1974.04
Hi Boys, Ho Boys 1898.17
Hi Havana! 1946.15
Hi Hi Hi Song 1898.12
Hi Jennie Ho Jennie Johnson 1885.51
Hi There, Buddy 1914.33
Hi Ya Kid 1984.02
Hi Yah 1908.03
Hi! For the Thames on a Summer Day 1896.48
Hi, Hi, Hi! 1861.04
Hi-De-Ho High 1943.07
Hi-Diddle-Diddle 1897.19
Hi-Diddley-Hi-Ti 1893.23
Hi-Diddly-Hi-Ti 1892.38
Hi-Ho, The Hoe-Down Way 1941.11
Hi-Lili Hi-Lo 1974.22
Hiawatha 1903.14
Hiawatha in Fun 1903.09
Hiawatha Songo 1894.08
Hiawatha's Lullaby 1993.01, 1995.16, 1998.17
Hiawatha's Melody of Love 1919.26, 1920.22, 1922.18
Hic Haec Hoc 1964.33
Hic-hiccough Hic-hiccough 1886.24
Hickery Hackery, Jim Jam 1878.02
Hickety, Pickety 1971.20
Hicky Do 1916.23
Hidden Charms 1915.30
Hidden Music 1885.08, 1885.41
Hide and Seek 1904.03, 1911.11, 1911.15
Hier sind alle Anrevwandten 1885.01
High and Dry Let Her Lie 1903.21
High and Low 1931.16, 1972.05
High Art 1916.07
High Ballin' 1940.01
High Class Ladies and Elegant Gentlemen 1973.11
High Finance 1929.19
High Flying Adored 1979.23
High Hat 1927.59, 1983.06, 1999.10
High Heels 1983.21
High Hopes 1974.10
High in the Hills 1924.30
High Infidelity 1956.09
High is Better Than Low 1963.25, 1972.05
High Jerry Ho! 1893.02
High Jinks 1913.34
High Life Down Stairs 1916.20
High Lights 1913.18
High Old Time, A 1903.33
High on a Hill 1926.42, 1946.03, 1987.10
High School All Over Again 1982.08
High Shoes 1933.21
High Society 1898.46, 1998.05

High Steppin' Days 1978.21
High Street, Africa 1925.50
High Up on the Hills 1936.22
High Yaller 1927.07
High Yellow 1926.22
High! High! High! 1909.11
High, High Up in the Clouds 1928.14
High, High, High 1929.17
High-Born Colored Lady 1896.45
High-Class Chaperone 1894.33
High-Toned Lady from Over the Sea, The 1887.05
Highball Syndicate, The 1898.55
Highbrow, Lowbrow 1949.12
Higher and Higher 1975.12, 1976.24, 1982.22, 1984.10
Higher Education, The 1904.39
Higher Ground 1986.02
Higher Than High 1981.24
Highest Judge of All, The 1945.05
Highfalutin Music 1903.24
Highland Kiltie Rag, The 1917.21
Highland lad, my love was born, A 1859.01
Highland Mary 1905.48, 1908.10
Highland Weather 1895.41
Highly Important Fly, A 1905.32
Highly Important Fly, The 1903.29
Highway 57 1982.04
Highway's Call, The 1925.36
Highwayman, The 1897.40, 1915.03, 1917.10
Hiiaka 1961.07
Hija del Carcelero, La 1926.09, 1926.35
Hike 1902.44
Hiko Chorus 1904.37
Hilda 1871.22
Hildebrandt Montrose 1877.11
Hilderbrandt Montrose 1876.31
Hill and Dale 1942.11
Hill of Dreams 1944.21
Hills of Ixtapo, The 1949.15, 1972.06
Hills of Tomorrow, The 1981.27
Himmlisher Vater 1970.08
Hindoo Belle 1905.31
Hindoo Paradise 1907.05
Hindu Hop 1923.16
Hindu Serenade 1943.05
Hinkee Dee 1906.10
Hinkey Dee 1903.18
Hinky Dinky Parlay Voo 1943.23, 1974.09
Hip, Hip, Hurrah! 1909.21
Hip-Hooray for Washington 1969.03
Hippity Hop, The 1925.48
Hippodrome Folks 1914.34
Hippodrome Street Parade, The 1916.15
Hippopotamus, The 1959.20
Hiram Green, Good-Bye 1904.54
Hiram Green/Brown?, Farewell 1905.35
Hiram Skinner's Comb 1922.24
Hire a Guy 1960.07
Hired Girl's Pink Tea, The 1898.03
His and Hers 1955.04
His aspect's not so overpow'ring 1884.14
His Dream is Over 1911.20
His Eye is on the Sparrow 1976.04, 1986.02
His Gift to Me 1990.05
His Heart was True to Poll 1872.11, 1886.53
His Invitation to Love 1932.19
His Legs are Assorted Sizes 1895.27
His Life Hangs on a Chance 1888.19
His Love Makes Me Beautiful 1964.11
His Majesty 1906.15
His Majesty Advances 1906.49
His Old Man 1946.10
His Only Love 1892.08
His Own Little Island 1961.21
His Parents Haven't Seen Him Since 1896.02
His Return 1911.06
His Rocking Horse Ran Away 1995.14
His Rocking Horse Ran Away, And 1995.12
His Spanish Guitar 1926.04
His Wake in the Morning 1890.29
His Work, and Nothing More 1997.09
Hiss for Shame 1903.39
Hiss, Hiss, Hiss 1904.22
Hist! Hist! Hist! 1904.49
Histoire de Thereson, la belle Provencale 1885.56
Historians and Poets 1834.03
Historic Huzzies 1920.43
Historical Histrionics 1935.04
History 1916.26, 1975.06
History Class 1902.34
History Eight to the Bar 1937.14, 1942.26
History is Made at Night 1939.22
History of Three Generations of Chorus Girls, The 1937.17
Hit Enormous 1903.40
Hit in Paris, A 1913.10
Hit it, Lorraine 1971.07
Hit Me With a Hot Note and Watch Me Bounce 1981.06, 1997.03, 1999.24
Hit of the Season, The 1902.34
Hit the Ground Running 1988.07
Hit the Ladies 1980.11
Hit the Ramp 1942.01
Hit the Road Jack 1984.15
Hitch Your Wagon to a Star 1936.06
Hitchy Koo Girl 1918.18
Hitchy's Garden of Roses 1919.25
Hitchykoo 1964.28
Hither as I came 1848.04
Hither He Comes 1895.03
Hither we come 1846.01
Hither we Come 1862.03
Hither, dear Husband, turn your Eyes 1750.01
Hittin' 1996.07
Hittin' the Bottle 1930.22
Hitting on High 1927.64
Hitting the New High 1932.19
Hive of bees, as I've heard say, A 1895.29
Hiya Sucker 1933.16
Ho 1926.42
Ho! 1946.03
Ho! For Africa 1893.50
Ho! For Mulligan Alley 1893.10
Ho! For the Sea 1902.29
Ho! Mollie Grogan 1887.07, 1889.15
Ho! Ye Townsmen 1898.60
Ho, Billy O 1948.25
Ho, Mariners, Ho 1894.22
Hoax and Coax 1904.36
Hobbies 1919.36
Hobo Man, The 1907.04
Hobo Solo Band, The 1903.35
Hobo-Genius Chorus in 4F 1943.11
Hobohemia 1924.32, 1927.09
Hoch! Hoch! Hoch! 1903.28
Hochzeitslied fur armere Leute, Das 1965.04
Hockey, A la 1919.30
Hocus Pocus 1925.27
Hodge Podge 1909.27
Hodge's Country Dance 1885.29
Hoe Down 1949.06, 1969.03
Hoe Ry Die Boere 1966.03
Hoedown 1956.04
Hoedown! 1959.19
Hog Beneath the Skin, The 1959.20
Hogan's Alley 1927.27
Hoggenheimer of Park Lane 1914.10
Hoifzinger 1966.21
Hokey Pokey, The 1998.11
Hoku Loa 1930.26
Hola 1903.38
Hola! 1904.10
Hola! hola! house here 1859.13
Hola! maitre hotelier 1887.36
Hola, Follow, Follow Me 1926.27
Hold 'Em Joe 1953.17
Hold 'em, Joe 1947.19
Hold Fast 1902.09
Hold It! 1948.15
Hold Me 1918.05, 1920.18, 1920.19, 1920.22
Hold Me - Hold Me - Hold Me 1951.19
Hold Me Gently 1975.23
Hold Me in Your Arms 1918.38
Hold Me in Your Loving Arms 1915.16
Hold My Hand 1986.12
Hold On 1991.05
Hold on Abraham 1975.22
Hold on I'm Coming 1997.21
Hold onto Your Hats 1940.10, 1963.12
Hold That Crown 1990.06
Hold That Smile 1943.05
Hold the Lanterns High 1905.03
Hold Tight 1939.29
Hold Tight - Hold Tight 1986.06
Hold Your Hand Out Naughty Boy 1964.28
Hold Your Horses 1905.17, 1933.21
Hold Your Man 1928.27
Hold! hold! 1844.01
Hold! I say! 1881.04
Hold, Monsters! 1879.72, 1981.01
Hold, rash fool, not death but happiness is near! 1892.59
Hold-Up Ensemble 1916.06
Holday Joys 1904.36
Holding Hands 1905.47, 1905.50, 1926.04
Holding Out for a Hero 1998.13
Holding to the Ground 1992.09
Hole in the Wall, The 1896.24
Hole Me Tight 1951.19
Hole-in-One 1982.23
Holiday for Strings 1990.09
Holiday in the Country 1948.28
Holiday in the Market 1906.14
Holiday Number, The 1924.29
Holidays 1911.06, 1989.07
Holidays, The 1924.32
Holka Polka 1925.36
Holler Blue Murder 1947.20
Hollow of My Hand 1922.05
Hollywood and Vine 1939.24, 1949.09
Hollywood Jump, The 1944.19
Hollywood's a Funny Place 1945.09
Hollywood, California 1977.16
Hollywood, Park Avenue and Broadway 1933.05
Holmes and Watson 1965.29
Holy Beauty 1873.05
Holy City, The 1896.15
Holy of Holies 1928.30
Holy Unto the Lord 1940.17
Holy Week 1917.25
Homage to Marat 1965.39
Home 1925.04, 1928.40, 1971.07, 1975.01, 1994.04
Home Again 1898.38, 1907.32, 1916.26, 1925.24, 1959.25, 1962.17
Home Again from a Foreign Shore 1871.16
Home and the Heartland 1996.12
Home Below and Heaven Above 1876.32
Home Blues 1929.27, 1999.10
Home for You, A 1927.65
Home Free All 1970.10
Home from Algeria 1925.02
Home Guards, The 1896.02
Home I loved so, leaving, The 1855.06
Home is Home 1906.19
Home is Where the Heart Is 1912.30, 1948.23
Home Life in New York 1914.31
Home o' Mine 1928.48
Home of My Heart 1925.36
Home on the Range 1931.02
Home Song 1896.11
Home Sweet Heaven 1964.16
Home Sweet Home 1855.01, 1863.02, 1871.15, 1878.04, 1878.12, 1966.03, 1976.01
Home Time in the Old Town 1944.32
Home to Harlem 1933.05
Home Town 1927.29
Home With the Milk in the Morning 1905.22
Home, sweet home 1859.05
Home, Sweet Home 1859.13, 1861.03, 1879.63, 1917.13
Homecoming 1952.15, 2000.05
Homeland 1925.08, 1927.01
Homely, But Clean 1926.46
Homemade Happiness 1922.47
Homer's Pitch 1970.08
Homesick 1983.08, 1995.07
Homesick Blues 1949.18, 1974.02
Homesick Loon, The 1883.04
Homesick Yankee, The 1906.37

Homeward 1965.35
Homeward Bound 1885.58, 1888.13, 1906.37, 1914.31
Homework 1949.08
Hommage Musical 1958.18
Homogenous Cabinet, A 1937.13
Honduras 1924.22
Honest Man 1964.40
Honest Man, An 1899.21
Honestly Sincere 1960.06
Honesty 1930.19
Honey 1903.41, 1915.05, 1923.06, 1979.19
Honey Babe 1907.20
Honey Boy 1903.39
Honey Bun 1949.04, 1993.16, 1997.01
Honey Bunch 1909.09
Honey Dew 1905.31
Honey Does Yer Love Yer Man 1896.37
Honey Gal o' Mine 1943.24
Honey in the Honeycomb 1940.17, 1980.10
Honey Love 1911.31
Honey Man Song 1969.15
Honey O 1894.07, 1894.35
Honey on My Lips 1897.45
Honey Will You Miss Me When I'm Gone 1902.38
Honey You Were Made for Me 1913.16
Honey You'se My Turtle Dove 1898.77
Honey, be Mine 1926.18
Honey, do You Love Me Dearly 1908.20
Honey, Does You Love Your Man 1896.05
Honey, Honey, Honey 1922.21
Honey, I Love You 1922.17
Honey, I'm in Love With You 1925.16
Honey, Love Me All the Time 1905.28, 1906.24
Honey, My Sweet 1903.03
Honey, Send Home for the Money 1902.09
Honey, You'se My Turtle Dove 1899.21
Honey, You've Done Me Wrong 1898.51
Honey-Bun 1924.02
Honey-Love-Moon 1921.38
Honeybunch 1919.32
Honeydew Waltz 1920.31
Honeyland 1911.40
Honeymoon 1955.04
Honeymoon Bells 1909.05
Honeymoon Blues 1924.04
Honeymoon Days 1912.29
Honeymoon Girl, A 1904.29
Honeymoon Hall 1905.25, 1914.07
Honeymoon Home 1923.08
Honeymoon in May 1915.20
Honeymoon Inn 1917.01, 1975.24
Honeymoon is Over 1946.06
Honeymoon is Over, The 1958.01, 1966.29
Honeymoon Land 1918.06, 1918.12
Honeymoon Row 1923.42
Honeymoon Song 1913.26
Honeymoon Trail 1909.31
Honeymoon Trip All Alone, A 1914.10
Honeymoon When Will You Shine for Me? 1921.10
Honeymoon With You 1913.21
Honeymoon, The 1904.36
Honeymooning Blues 1928.06
Honeysuckle and the Bee, The 1901.09
Honeysuckle Rose 1967.13, 1968.20, 1976.04, 1978.09, 1999.07
Honk Kong 1957.14
Honky Tonk Nights 1986.11
Honky Tonk Nights Rag, The 1986.11
Honolulu 1907.13, 1929.26, 1937.08
Honolulu Belles 1899.33
Honolulu Lady 1899.11
Honolulu Lu 1901.23
Honolulu Rag 1910.17
Honolulu Tom Boy 1912.03
Honor and Glory 1889.40, 1925.06
Honor and Homage 1862.03
Honor and Love 1919.42
Honor of Altenstein, The 1909.14
Honor of the Family 1927.47
Honor of Your Name, The 1999.08
Honor System, The 1917.26
Honor the Brave 1909.30
Honor's Hommage 1846.01
Honora Doolin 1906.43
Honorable Mambo 1957.01
Honour and Glory 1921.15
Honours of War, The 1919.42
Honto 1990.17
Hoo-doo-doo-doo-Man, The 1899.21
Hoof! Hoof! 1927.35
Hook and Eye 1893.42
Hook's Tango 1990.20
Hook's Waltz 1954.13, 1979.22
Hooker, The 1971.20
Hookers' Ball, The 1997.08
Hoola Boola, La 1898.22
Hoola, from Coney Isle 1922.22
Hoolah Goolah Stone 1906.39
Hoomalimali 1961.07
Hoop La 1907.04
Hoop-de-Dingle 1959.11
Hoop-Dee-Do 1980.29
Hoopern de dooden do 1864.13
Hoopla, Father Doesn't Care 1912.26
Hoopola 1892.05
Hoops 1931.16
Hooray for Anywhere 1944.30
Hooray for Captain Spalding 1928.38
Hooray for De Yankee Dollar 1957.16
Hooray for George the Third 1954.02
Hooray for Hollywood 1974.09, 1990.09, 1997.05, 1999.01
Hooray for the U.S.A. 1924.03
Hooray for What! 1937.15
Hooray! Hooray! 1882.63
Hooray! Hooray! Oh, happy Fate! 1885.28
Hoosier Way, The 1951.18
Hoot Mon 1917.02
Hoot, Mon 1900.42
Hootch Rhythm 1922.15
Hootin' Owl Trail 1949.17
Hootsatsa 1990.16
Hootspa 1985.15
Hop, a Skip, a Jump, a Look, A 1945.01
Hop, Hop, Hop 1913.33
Hope Ever Smiling 1866.07, 1866.21
Hope for the Best 1946.20
Hope lived, and free from fear, Love sang her roundelay 1893.02
Hope now brightly beaming 1859.09
Hope On 1907.39
Hope Told a Flattering Tale 1924.20
Hope You Come Back 1953.17
Hoppin' the Buck 1927.31
Hopping over muddy crossings 1881.06
Hoppy Poppy Queen 1920.06
Hora Hora 1971.14
Hora Staccato 1955.13
Hora-Galilee 1971.02
Horn, a Horn, A 1851.03
Hornet and the Bee, The 1906.08
Hornpipe Dance 1961.14
Hornpipe Rag, The 1908.44
Horny-Handed Farmers 1897.48
Horoscope 1966.32, 1985.17
Horror-toria, An 1925.47
Horrors 1879.35
Hors d'Oeuvres 1927.38
Horse I used to dry my old clothes on, The 1902.32
Horse Named Bill, A 1963.19
Horse Ride 1980.01
Horse Trot, The 1921.34
Horse, The 1970.20
Horseshoes are Lucky 1949.17
Horton Hears a Who 2000.18
Hosanna 1971.12, 1979.03
Hose Boys 1937.12
Hoshia et Amecha 1971.17
Hoshoryu 1966.03
Hospital, The 1999.08
Hostess With the Mostes' on the Ball, The 1950.15
Hot 1928.35
Hot and Bothered 1929.49, 1986.11
Hot August Night 1978.05
Hot December 1946.13
Hot Dog 1922.45, 1975.24
Hot Dog Buddy 1989.12
Hot Enough for You? 1977.16
Hot Feet 1931.31, 1978.21
Hot Flashes 1985.17
Hot Harlem 1931.47
Hot Heels 1927.31
Hot Honey Rag, The 1999.01
Hot Lover 1971.18
Hot Moonlight 1931.21
Hot Off the Oven 1925.25, 1925.48
Hot Old Time, A 1897.33, 1900.24
Hot Pants 1928.40, 1928.45
Hot Patata, The 1930.40
Hot Patootie 2000.17
Hot Patootie Wedding Night 1929.25
Hot Patootie, Bless My Soul 1975.08
Hot Rhythm 1930.24, 1931.47
Hot Sands 1928.28
Hot Spot 1933.26
Hot Steps 1927.13
Hot Tamale Alley 1895.27, 1896.45, 1897.04
Hot Tamales 1894.21
Hot Time in the Old Town Tonight, A 1980.27
Hot VooDoo 1984.10
Hot Zich Mir Di Shich Zerissn 1989.10
Hot Ziggity 1923.47
Hot, Hot Honey 1927.19
Hot, Hot, Mama 1931.31
Hota 1923.31
Hotcha Chiquita 1934.18
Hotcha Ma Chotch 1930.39
Hotel Astor, The 1906.22
Hotel Caravanserai, The 1897.32
Hotel Clerk, The 1901.09
Hotel Porter, The 1894.06
Hotel Victoria 1993.08
Hothouse on Broadway, The 1904.08
Hotsy Totsy 1927.31
Hotsy Totsy Hats 1929.28
Hottentot Honeymoon 1910.29
Hottentot Potentate 1935.12, 1972.05
Hottest Coon in Dixie 1898.41
Hound Dog 1977.10, 1978.01, 1982.22, 1989.12, 1995.03
Houp-la 1902.21
Hour of Chase, The 1867.10
Hour With You, The 1921.03
Hour? Nay, nay, An 1893.02
Hours creep on apace, the 1879.05
Hours Pass Lightly Away, The 1870.27
House by the Olive Tree, The 1956.09
House Divided, A 1999.08
House I Live In, The 1942.26, 1945.07
House in Algiers 1987.12
House in Town, A 1959.06
House is Haunted, The 1934.01
House is Not the Same Without a Woman, A 1964.03
House Maids, The 1901.25
House of Flowers 1954.19
House of Grass 1972.11
House of lords, The 1897.32
House of Marcus Lycus, The 1962.12
House of the Rising Sun 1954.11
House on Rittenhouse Square 1949.18
House on the Hill 1961.07
House That Hook Built, The 1907.63
House That Jack Built, The 1904.56, 1921.27
House Upon the Hill 1991.05
House Where I was Born, The 1952.04
House With a Little Red Barn, A 1940.03
Houseboat on the Styx, The 1928.49
Household Brigade, The 1885.42
Housetop of Our Own, A 1920.33
How a Monocle Helps the Mind 1904.56
How About a Ball? 1968.24
How About a Boy Like Me? 1930.02
How About a Date? 1946.04
How About It 1931.04
How About It? 1928.21, 1975.13
How About You 1979.24
How About You? 1990.09
How Actresses are Made 1900.20

How are the Boys? 1925.25
How are the Mighty Fallen 1997.12
How are Things in Glocca Morra? 1947.03
How are We to Know 1900.12
How are Ya Since? 1970.10
How are You Greenbacks? 1863.04
How are You, Lady Love? 1926.30
How are you, Old Petroleum? 1865.03
How Awful 1992.11
How Beautiful 1931.48
How Beautiful the Days 1956.04
How Beautifully Blue the Sky 1879.72, 1981.01
How blest must be this country life 1882.60
How Blest We Are 1985.06
How break my word 1887.04
How Can a Lady be Certain? 1924.04
How Can Harry Marry 1898.17
How Can I Call This Home? 1998.21
How Can I Get Rid of Those Blues? 1931.05
How Can I Leave Thee? 1882.76
How Can I Tell Her? 1989.26
How Can I Wait? 1951.24
How Can I Win You Now? 1922.33, 1925.14
How Can I Win? 1993.02
How Can Love Survive? 1959.24, 1998.03
How can they resist me 1888.05
How Can We Bring the Old Folk Round 1938.06
How Can We Swing It? 1939.19
How Can You Describe a Face? 1961.28
How Can You Kiss Those Good Times Goodbye? 1967.02
How Can You Tell an American? 1938.11
How Can You Tell Till You Try 1904.25
How Can You Tell? 1918.18, 1930.36
How Can You Toot? 1909.24
How Cold, Cold, Cold, an Empty Room 1965.32
How Come I'm Born Wid a Hook in My Hand? 1940.01
How Could a Fellow Want More 1936.27
How Could I be so Wrong 1968.03
How Could I Dare to Dream? 1976.01
How Could I Ever Know? 1991.05
How Could I Forget? 1929.27
How Could I Go for You 1930.42
How Could She Love Me Like That? 1920.20
How cruel are the Traytors 1750.01
How d'ya Talk to a Girl? 1966.27
How d'ye Do 1890.23
How D'ye do, Fifth Avenue 1915.25
How D'Ye Do? 1905.55
How D'You Do 1924.01
How D'You do, Goodbye 1914.01
How D'You Do? 1925.42, 1927.04
How Dear is Our Day 1917.24, 1919.20
How Deep is Your Love 1999.15
How Did He Look? 1957.10
How Did I End Up Here? 1988.10
How Did it Get so Late so Early? 1940.23
How Did the Little Bird Know That? 1909.04
How Did the Story End? 1904.09
How Did They Build Titanic? 1997.06
How Did They Know I was an American? 1923.07
How do I Know He Loves Me? 1924.04
How do ye do, Signor Moccoloni? How do you do, Senor Moccolo? 1866.14
How do You Account for That? 1906.07
How do you do 1869.43
How do You Do 1909.21, 1912.17, 1913.01
How do You do It? 1932.16
How do You do, Good-Bye 1915.17
How do You do, Katinka? 1922.45
How do You do, Middle Age? 1963.29
How do You do, Miss Pratt? 1951.18
How do You do, Miss Ragtime? 1912.09
How do You Do? 1913.29, 1925.47
How do You do? How do You Do? 1925.43
How do You Doodle 1923.04
How do You Doodle Do? 1925.26
How do You Follow a Star 1999.17
How do You Get That Way? 1919.44
How do You Know? 1912.09
How do you like the country 1854.04
How do You Like Your Love? 1959.12
How do You Raise a Barn? 1955.01
How do You Say Goodbye 1957.17, 1978.10
How do You Speak to an Angel? 1953.01
How do You Spell Ambassador? 1938.13
How do You Want Me? 1981.25
How do' Do 1913.18
How Does it Start? 1974.04
How Does the Idea Strike You? 1888.28
How dreary to my heart 1848.04
How Engaging, How Exciting 1954.06
How Fair the World 1909.19
How Far a Girl Should Go 1903.10
How Far Can a Lady Go? 1953.11
How Far is too Far? 1982.10
How Fiercely You Dance 1922.36
How Fly Times 1943.21
How Glory Goes 1997.01
How Great Thou Art 1978.01
How Green was My Valley 1966.09
How happy could I be with either 1750.01, 1854.06
How Happy Could This Chappie Be 1905.45
How Happy is the Bride 1932.03
How High Can a Little Bird Fly? 1972.05
How High the Moon 1940.03, 1975.12
How Hogan Paid His Rent 1891.40
How I danced away 1897.17
How I Feel 1970.20
How I have lov'd thee 1859.17
How I Know You 2000.06
How I Love a Pretty Face 1910.37
How I Love Flowers! 1905.36
How I Love My Lou 1897.31
How I Love My Lu 1897.48
How I love my Vangie dear 1880.40
How I Love Your Thingamajig 1984.02
How I Thought I Looked 1904.18
How I Weary 1928.05
How I'd Write a Comic Opera 1903.14
How I've Missed You Mary 1922.31
How is This, Pippo? 1881.22
How it Occurred 1899.19
How Jazz was Born 1928.10, 1975.22
How Laughable it Is 1964.33
How Little Adam Knew 1950.03
How Long Can Love Keep Laughing? 1938.09
How Long has This Been Going On 1928.03, 1999.10
How Long has This Been Going On? 1983.06
How Long Must This Go On? 1994.04
How Long? 1941.07, 1955.27
How Lovely to be a Woman 1960.06
How Low Can a Little Worm Go? 1972.05
How Lucky You Are 2000.18
How many beans make five? 1859.14
How Many Devils? 1999.08
How Many Men? 1992.11
How Many Women 1988.09
How Many Women in the World? 2000.08
How Much I Love You 1943.19
How nice 't would be 1879.35
How Nice for Me 1940.09
How Nice to See You 1990.17
How now, what's the row 1880.46
How oft in fancy have I heard 1859.09
How Sad 1962.03
How say you, maiden, will you wed? 1888.35
How Shall I See Through My Tears? 1988.05
How Soon, Oh Moon? 1961.08
How Strangely Sweet! 1894.24
How sweet in his sleep 1885.63
How Sweet the Moonlight 1880.19
How Sweetly Friendship Binds 1936.28
How Sweetly Simple 1973.02
How the Birds Sing 1885.29
How the First Song was Born 1933.06
How the Girls Adore Me 1928.48
How the Money Change Hands 1960.19
How the Winds Blow 1907.32
How They Treat Us 1883.12
How Time Flies 1927.35
How to (Succeed) 1961.22
How to be a Lass 1896.50
How to be Happy Though Married 1904.49
How to Get in Central Park 1905.22
How to Get on in the Hotel Trade 1980.17
How to Hades, I'm off Slick 1869.07
How to Handle a Woman 1960.21, 1963.02, 1980.19, 1993.11
How to Kill a Man 1960.06
How to kiss 1898.63
How to Make a Pretty Girl 1916.11
How to Pick a Man a Wife 1960.10
How to Raise a Child 2000.18
How to Receive an Invited Guest 1888.39
How to Succeed 1995.05
How to Survive 1966.19
How to Welcome Home Your Hubby 1927.11
How to Win Friends and Influence People 1938.05
How to Write Your Own Schubert Operetta 1953.10
How Vas Dot Poodle 1879.64
How Very Long Ago it Seems 1926.11
How was I to Know 1907.14, 1917.02
How was I to Know? 1975.13
How We Pose 1885.08
How we pose 1885.51
How well you look 1887.04
How Will He Know? 1951.19
How Will I Live from Now On? 1998.08
How Will I Love Now 1997.16
How Wonderful the Peace 1997.12
How Wonderful You Are 1920.11
How Would a City Girl Know 1930.06
How Would You Like it Yourselves 1895.44
How Would You Like to Bounce a Baby on Your Knee? 1916.25
How Would You Like to Spoon With Me? 1905.49
How Would You Like to Take Me Home With You? 1907.44
How Ya Baby 1978.09
How Ya Gonna Keep 'Em Down on the Farm After They've Seen Paree? 1921.16
How Ya Gonna Keep 'Em Down on the Farm? 1974.09
How Ya' Gonna Keep 'Em Down on the Farm After They've Seen Paree? 1919.15
How You Gonna Keep Kool? 1924.16
How you joke 1870.38
How'd You Like to be a Kid? 1921.34, 1923.12
How'd You Like to be My Bow-Wow-Wow 1907.47
How'd You Like to be My Daddy? 1918.05
How'd You Like to be the Shoe Store Man? 1911.18
How'd You Like to Call Me Dearie 1908.37
How'd You Like to Float Me? 1907.24
How'd You Like to Like a Girl Like Me? 1906.34
How'd You Like To? 1927.49
How'dja Like to Love Me? 1980.29
How'dy Do 1904.27
How'ja Like to Take Me Home 1943.20
How'm I Doin'? 1985.15
How's Chances? 1933.22
How's That for I 1870.01
How's Your Health 1940.06
How's Your Uncle? 1931.21
How, Now, Sir 1870.20
Howdy Broadway 1926.50
Howdy Do 1912.31
Howdy Do? 1906.22
Howdy, Mr. Sunshine 1971.09
However Bright 1846.01
Howjadoo 1970.03
Huayno, El 1942.14
Hub Bub 1985.08
Hubby 1922.10
Huckster, The 1886.10
Hudl Mitn Shtrudl 1990.16
Hudl With the Shtrudl 1990.16
Hudson Duster 1927.46
Huggin an' Muggin' 1937.09
Huggin' and Chalkin' 1999.06
Hugh McCue 1896.37
Hugs and Kisses 1926.23, 1927.02
Hula Girl, The 1942.29
Hula Hula, The 1915.32
Hula Shouting Song 1912.03
Hula, Hula, Sailor Man 1924.13
Hula-Lula Girl 1903.35
Hulda's Flirtation Episode 1880.37
Hullabaloo at Thebes 1968.13

Hullo! what's that? 1895.26
Hum a Little Tune 1925.50
Hum Drum Life 1972.18
Human Again 1994.04
Human Band, The 1904.18
Human Canary, The 1906.48
Human Heart, The 1990.12
Human Nature 1915.01
Human Pin-Wheel, The 1909.11
Humble Pie 1971.21
Hummin' to Myself 1931.30
Humming 1961.10
Humoresque 1921.02
Humoresquimos 1922.15
Humorous Ghost, The 1903.36
Humors of a Country Fair 1834.01
Humours of the Bath, The, or Spring's a Coming 1924.20
Humpty and Dumpty 1911.42
Humpty Dumpty 1912.47
Humpty Dumpty Man 1869.43
Humpty-Dumpty 1927.54
Hundred Easy Way to Lose a Man, A 1958.20
Hundred Easy Ways to Lose a Man, A 1958.21, 1977.02
Hundred Million Miracles, A 1958.19
Hundred Years from Now, A 1905.45
Hundred Years from Today, A 1933.27
Hundreds of Girls 1974.18, 1998.07
Hung 1968.11
Hungaria's Hussars 1898.60
Hungaria's Rhythmic Air 1910.36
Hungarian Folk Song 1988.09
Hungry 1968.13
Hungry for Love 1930.24
Hungry Men 1963.26
Hungry Women 1928.47
Hunt Ball Rehearsal 1924.09
Hunt Ball, The 1915.05, 1925.01
Hunt is Up, The 1963.28
Hunt, The 1930.23
Hunted Partridge on the Hill 1997.12
Hunted, The 1946.24
Hunter's Fox-Trot Ball 1916.03
Hunting 1925.32
Hunting Days 1930.05
Hunting for a Happy Little Home in Harlem 1900.07
Hunting Scene 1896.45
Hunting Song 1890.21, 1902.06, 1913.25, 1918.34
Hunting the Fox 1930.08, 1931.08
Huntsman's Home, The 1883.07
Huntsman's Song 1907.01
Huntsman's Song of Love, The 1932.09
Hup an' Downa, A 1938.03
Hurdy Gurdy Girl, The 1907.39
Hurdy Gurdy Man 1899.41, 1906.28
Hurdy Gurdy Man, The 1905.39, 1914.15
Hurdy Gurdy Verdi 1940.21
Hurra for the Bowl 1852.01
Hurra for the road 1852.01
Hurrah for Baffins Bay 1903.03
Hurrah for Bowery Tea 1845.01
Hurrah for Life 1937.11
Hurrah for the Beautiful Golden West 1906.01
Hurrah for the Field 1904.01
Hurrah for the Girls 1897.32
Hurrah for the Great Out-of-Doors 1956.09
Hurrah for the lads of sea! 1871.10
Hurrah for the Minstrel 1876.30
Hurrah for the Road! 1871.10
Hurrah for the sound of the dog's cherry bark 1886.40
Hurrah! for the gipsy tent 1882.17
Hurrah! Hurrah! 1917.11
Hurrah! Hurrah! Pour la Princesse 1886.09
Hurrah! They come 1881.11
Hurrah, for We're in Clover 1898.38
Hurrah, Hurrah and Hurroo for That 1907.59
Hurray for Nicoletti 1945.17
Hurray for Us! 1927.23
Hurroo, Harray, and Hurrah for That 1906.44
Hurry 1956.08, 1972.15
Hurry Back 1970.09
Hurry Boys 1911.07
Hurry Home 1992.03
Hurry Little Children, Sunday Morn! 1893.27
Hurry Now 1918.16
Hurry Up 1889.54
Hurry! It's Lovely Up Here 1965.31
Hurry, Bustle 1907.51
Hurry, Harry 1972.19
Hurry, Little Children 1885.44, 1912.38
Hurry, Little Children, Sunday Morning 1883.53
Husband Cage 1954.19
Husband in Love With His Wife, A 1914.04
Husband's Love, A 1908.06
Husband's Only a Husband, A 1922.35
Husband, Lover and Wife 1931.05
Husband, the Wife and Lover, The 1921.19
Husband-Hunters, The 1899.19
Husbands and Wives 1918.27, 1978.12
Husbands, The 1894.31
Hush 1882.28, 1972.25
Hush Here Comes a Whizzbang 1964.28
Hush Little Girl Don't Cry 1889.46
Hush Look Away 1924.06
Hush Thee, Now, My Babe 1900.08
Hush Yo' Business, Oh Go On 1896.44
Hush Yo' Business, Oh! Go On 1895.02
Hush! Hush! 1876.06, 1918.35
Hush! Hush! Hush! 1882.60, 1912.34
Hush! Hush! These Sounds of Revelry 1870.20
Hush! Not a step 1895.26
Hush! Say Nothing 1896.10
Hush, Hush 1897.21
Hush, Hush! Not a Word 1879.72
Hush, Hush! Not a Word! 1981.01
Hush, Hush, She's Meditating 1905.46
Hush, Hush, Silent Be 1894.22
Hush, I Think I Hear Him 1909.31
Hush, Silence 1895.38
Hush-a-Bye 1895.32
Hush-a-Bye, Bacon 1879.21
Hush-Hush 1938.11
Hushabye Baby 1971.20
Husking Bee, The 1958.08
Husky, Dusky Annabelle 1928.19
Hussar March 1928.03
Hussar's Quadrille 1909.15
Hussars' Song, The 1927.17
Hustle and Bustle Around 1919.41
Hustle, Bustle 1926.39
Hustle, The 1976.07
Hustler has Won, The 1891.40
Hut in Hoboken 1929.19
Huz-zah-zah 2000.14
Huzza 1903.41
Hyacinth 1906.37
Hydrophobia Blues 1926.32
Hygiene 1901.27
Hymen's Engineer 1881.12
Hymen, Hymen 1969.04
Hymenoea, Hymenoea 1875.19
Hymme a l'amour 1964.22
Hymn 1959.04, 1997.06
Hymn for a Sunday Evening 1960.06
Hymn of Betrothal 1944.21
Hymn of the Sacred Hat 1895.26
Hymn to Him 1993.18
Hymn to Him, A 1956.01
Hymn to Hyman 1936.26
Hymn to Hymie 1961.20
Hymn to Peace 1936.28
Hymn to the Sun 1906.46, 1919.39
Hymne a L'Amour 1981.04
Hyphen 1899.12
Hypnotic Kiss, The 1908.18
Hypnotic Waltz 1910.12
Hypnotizing 1916.17
Hypnotizing Moon 1912.08
Hypocrite, The 1904.55
Hysterical Tune 1912.20

I Accuse 1981.14
I Act as If 1983.03
I Admire You Very Much, Mr. Schmidt 1970.08
I Admit 1946.13
I Adore a Certain Party 1904.04
I Adore the American Girl! 1914.20
I Adore You 1927.39
I Ain't Down Yet 1960.20, 1976.24
I Ain't Going to Work No More 1900.55
I Ain't Gonna Give Nobody None o' This Jelly Roll 1992.06
I Ain't Gonna Sin No More 1953.12
I Ain't Got No Shame 1983.04
I Ain't Got Nothin' But the Blues 1997.03
I Ain't Gwine to Work No Mo 1900.48
I Ain't had My Fill 1976.35
I Ain't had No Lovin' in a Long Time 1909.10
I Ain't Married No More 1917.13
I Also Have a Heart 1969.11
I Always Come Back to You 1911.27, 1913.26
I Am 1929.32
I am a Beautiful Wife 1908.01
I am a Court Coquette 1899.28
I am a courtier grave and serious 1890.02
I am a Dago 1899.12
I am a Doll 1897.48
I am a Dumbbell 1921.30
I am a Fascinating Notary 1888.13
I am a Highly Educated Man 1894.37
I am a Judge 1938.10
I am a maiden cold and stately 1884.09
I am a Marvelous Musician 1907.18
I am a Millionaire 1900.42
I am a Minstrel Gay 1885.65
I am a Native Here 1870.07
I am a Poor Unfortunate 1911.08
I am a Practical Brigand, Highwayman 1899.40
I am a Prince 1888.39, 1928.30
I am a Regular Romeo 1905.23
I am a Simple Norman Maid 1897.17
I am a Tom-Boy 1912.35
I am a Waiter at Maxim's 1908.01
I am a Witch 1955.27
I am All A-Blaze 1969.04
I am All Alone 1913.10
I am All Alone, And 1917.01
I am Always Falling in Love With the Other Fellow's Girl 1919.26
I am an American 1940.16
I am an Impressario 1885.41
I am an Indian 1909.19
I am Ashamed That Women are so Simple 1948.32, 1999.19
I am Ashamed to Look the Moon in the Face 1919.18
I am Benoit 1894.28
I am Bulgaria's King 1896.10
I am Captain Jack 1886.53
I am Captured 1927.55
I am Changing 1981.29
I am Chu Chin Chow 1917.24
I am Chu Chin Chow of China 1919.20
I am Cleopatra 1920.03
I am Complete 1877.23
I am Craving for That Kind of Love 1921.16
I am Daguerre 1920.39
I am Don Januario 1880.04
I am Dying 1972.17
I am Easily Assimilated 1956.15, 1974.06, 1982.20
I am Enchanted 1947.14
I am free 1880.18
I am Free 1968.30, 1983.14
I am Gaston 1938.07
I am Going to Follow the Boys 1916.21
I am Going to Like it Here 1958.19
I am Going to Love the Man You're Going to Be 1975.06
I am Happy Here 1945.04
I am here 1880.18
I am here, behold! 1863.06
I am Home 1999.17
I am Hong Kye-Hun 1997.16
I am Ilene 1882.44
I am in Love 1912.33, 1919.27, 1953.07
I am in Love With a Sweet Little Girl 1888.13
I am It 1976.33
I am King Carrot 1872.23
I am King Croesus 1897.21
I am Little Christel 1891.30

I am Lonely for You 1912.05
I am Looking for My Ten 1905.45
I am Looking Here Now, I am Looking There Now 1964.25
I am Loved 1882.33, 1950.20, 1980.06
I am Melpomene 1910.19
I am Mephisto 1870.27
I am No Man 1881.07
I am No Queen 1894.45
I am Not Fancy Free 1882.33
I am Not Interested in Love 1971.18
I am not she 1859.15
I am Not so Different 1916.25
I am Not the Only One 1892.45
I am Only Dreaming 1917.05
I am Only Human After All 1930.18, 1930.33
I am Perfect 1889.36
I am so Eager 1951.22
I am so Easily Assimilated 1997.10
I am so Fair 1907.07
I am so proud 1885.47
I am so Proud 1939.15
I am so sick 1880.04
I am so Volatile 1873.28
I am so Young and You are so Beautiful 1919.02
I am Telling You I am Not Going, And 1981.29
I am the Ballad 1988.15
I am the Boy and I am the Girl 1919.02
I am the Captain of the Pinafore 1879.05, 1945.08
I am the Champion Swimmer 1879.50
I am the God of War 1894.05
I am the great impressario 1881.04
I am the Great Pomposo 1895.25
I am the Janitor 1904.45
I am the Keeper 1902.06
I am the King 1892.42, 1904.47
I am the King of Spain 1848.04
I am the Light 1978.25
I am the Lord Lieutenant 1902.25
I am the Monarch of the Joint 1945.09
I am the monarch of the sea 1879.05
I am the Monarch of the Sea 1945.08
I am the News 1985.17
I am the Pascha 1888.05
I am the Pasha 1903.06, 1919.35
I am the Royal Chancellor 1903.14
I am the Ruler 1895.33
I am the Sheriff of Nottingham 1891.29, 1929.43, 1944.25
I am the Sheriff's faithful man 1887.44
I am the Singer, You are the Song 1933.03
I am the Starlight 1987.05
I am the Sultan 1902.11
I am the Unfortunate Jonathan 1890.39
I am the Very Modern Model of a Modern Major-General 1879.72, 1981.01
I am the Walrus 1977.10
I am Thinking of You 1923.31
I am thy Daughter 1879.38
I am True to All 1916.25
I am trying to remember... 1998.21
I am waiting for thee 1870.44
I am What I Am 1968.08, 1970.08, 1983.11, 1985.19, 1998.07
I am What I Am! 1959.19
I am Your Child 1991.10
I am, I Am 1963.19
I am, I am American 1876.30
I am, Yours Truly 1904.37
I and I 1980.05
I and You, Lovers True 1875.19
I Annex It 1900.34
I Apologize 1932.27, 1952.11
I Arrived in Time to Get It 1899.02
I Asked My Heart 1937.03
I beg your pardon 1840.03
I Beg Your Pardon 1925.31
I Beg Your Pardon, Dear Old Broadway 1911.18
I Believe 1937.09
I Believe Him, And 1910.10
I Believe in God 1972.15
I Believe in Love 1968.11
I Believe in Music 1974.09
I Believe in Takin' a Chance 1963.25
I Believe in You 1961.22, 1980.29
I Believe My Body 1976.20
I Believe My Own Eyes 1993.06
I Believe You 1974.01
I Believed All She Said 1918.16
I Belong Here 1979.02, 1998.07
I Belong to Glasgow 1932.18
I Bow a Glad Good Day 1928.30
I Bring Him Seashells 1973.03
I Bring My Boys Along 1929.04
I Bring My Girls Along 1929.04
I Built a Dream Today (One Day) 1935.17
I built upon a rock 1884.09
I Call Aloud for Thee 1892.20
I Call Upon You Gentlemen 1926.13
I Call You Back to Me 1914.25
I Cam to Your Room 1934.03
I Came as a Cavalier 1891.29
I Came Here 1924.30
I Came to Life 1930.22
I Came to Tan 1983.18
I Came! I Saw! I Fell! 1922.34
I Can 1964.40
I Can Always Find a Little Sunshine in the Y.M.C.A. 1918.21
I Can be Like Grandpa 1943.18
I Can Carry a Tune 1984.02
I Can Cook Too 1944.33, 1971.15, 1998.16
I Can Dance With Everybody But My Wife 1916.01
I Can do That 1975.15
I Can Dream, Can't I? 1938.01, 1988.08
I Can Drink 1912.14
I Can Have it All 1983.18
I Can Hear it Now 1950.19
I Can Hear Music 1985.03
I Can Live Without It 1955.11
I Can Make it Happen 1983.01
I Can Make You a Man 1975.08, 2000.17
I Can Never Go Home Anymore 1984.15
I Can Play This Part 1993.02
I Can Read 2001.06
I Can Say Truly Rural 1909.21
I Can See 1970.12
I Can See Clearly Now 1974.01
I Can Speak Espanol 1927.08
I Can Teach Them! 1962.04
I Can Tell by the Way You Dance, Dear 1915.30
I Can Think of Nothing Else But You, Lou 1904.14
I Can Trust Myself With a Lot of Girls 1918.16
I Can't Afford to Dream 1939.24
I Can't Argue With You 1922.33
I Can't be Bothered Now 1983.06, 1992.02
I Can't be Happy 1926.46
I Can't be in Love 1958.14
I Can't Believe it's True 1928.46
I Can't Believe it's You 1978.10
I Can't Believe That You're in Love With Me 1980.10
I Can't do it Alone 1975.14
I Can't do That Sum 1911.31, 1924.18, 1929.48
I Can't do the Sum 1903.31
I Can't do Without Girls 1915.16
I Can't do Without the Men 1912.31
I Can't Find Another Girl Like You 1905.42
I Can't Forget Your Eyes 1913.29, 1919.11
I Can't Get 'Em Up 1913.06
I Can't Get Along With You 1942.30
I Can't Get Enough 1911.03
I Can't Get into the Quota 1927.11
I Can't Get Over a Girl Like You Loving a Boy Like Me 1927.13
I Can't Get Started With You 1936.02, 1936.17
I Can't Give You Anything But Love 1927.62, 1928.18, 1939.29, 1943.16, 1978.09, 1980.10, 1989.02, 1990.09
I Can't Give You Anything But Love, Baby 1967.13, 1979.25
I Can't Imagine 1890.26
I Can't Love One and All 1918.06
I Can't Make it Out, Can You? 1879.54
I Can't Make My Eyes Behave 1906.45
I Can't Make This Movie 1982.09
I can't refrain from laughing 1896.27
I Can't Remember 1963.22
I Can't Remember the Words 1929.29
I Can't Say No 1943.04
I Can't Say That You're the Only One 1908.25
I Can't Stand Spring 1926.25
I Can't Stand Still 1998.13
I Can't Stay Away 1930.10
I Can't Stay Here by Myself 1943.10
I Can't Stop Lovin' You 1999.09
I Can't Stop Talking 1960.01
I Can't Strip to Brahms 1942.18
I Can't Tell Where They're from When They Dance 1922.27
I Can't Tell You 1980.23
I Can't Think 1928.42
I Can't Think of Nothing in the Wide, Wide World But You 1907.22
I Cani't Say No 1993.16
I canna like ye, gentle sir 1858.03
I Cannot Drink the Old Drinks 1912.44
I Cannot Leave You Now 1918.35
I Cannot Live Without Love 1924.04
I Cannot Live Without Your Love 1936.22
I Cannot Love 1899.39
I Cannot Make Him Jealous 1968.23
I Cannot Marry You All 1907.04
I cannot part with thee 1889.54
I Cannot Play at Love 1902.25
I Cannot Sleep Without Dreaming of You 1920.21
I Cannot Tell what this Love may be 1881.37
I Cannot Understand 1920.07
I Cannot Wait 'til Monday 1907.05
I Capture Every Heart 1885.65
I Care Not for These Ladies 1963.28
I Care Not if the Cup I Hold 1900.37
I Caught You Making Eyes 1904.15
I Certainly Got My Man 1899.29
I Char 1911.06
I Choose You 2001.01
I Chose Right 1983.19
I Come as a Cavalier 1929.43
I Come from Afar 1910.24
I Come from Gascony 1899.28
I Come from Sunny Dixie 1902.34, 1902.40
I Come Out of a Dream 1934.03
I Come Riding 1986.16
I Come! I Come! 1873.19
I Confess 1998.13
I Could be a DuBarry If 1922.21
I Could be Happy 1919.13
I Could be Happy With Either One 1903.07
I Could be Happy With You 1954.09
I Could do a Lot for You 1922.02
I Could do Wonders With You 1930.08
I Could Get Married Today 1951.18
I Could Get Used to Him 1983.21
I Could Give My Heart to You 1907.62
I Could Give Up Anything But You 1929.03
I Could Go Home to a Girl Like You 1915.27
I Could Have Been a Sailor 1979.11
I Could Have Danced All Night 1956.01, 1993.18
I Could Learn to Love You if You'd Only Let Me Try 1907.14
I Could Learn to Love You When You Smile, Smile, Smile 1907.33
I Could Love a Million Girls 1906.23
I Could Love Him 1956.08
I Could Love You if I Tried 1914.32
I Could Really Show You Around 1979.11
I Could Use Five 1906.09
I Could Waltz on Forever With You 1902.41, 1917.11
I Could Write a Book 1940.22, 1975.13, 1989.16
I Couldn't Have Done it Alone 1962.04
I Couldn't Hold My Man 1934.19
I Couldn't Make a Hit With Molly 1907.28
I Couldn't Stand to See My Baby Lose 1899.35
I Cover the Waterfront 1948.13, 1957.10
I Crept into the Crypt and Cried 1993.01
I Dance Along 1938.04
I dare not ask a kiss 1894.03
I Dare Not Love You 1925.39
I Dare to Dream 1953.17
I Dare to Speak of Love to You 1927.17

I Declare I Must Win Him 1892.29
I Depend on You 1980.30
I Detest a Fiesta 1940.19
I Did 1894.51
I Did Feel a Dreadfully Ass 1924.01
I Did It 1999.17
I Did it for Defense 1942.26
I Did it for the Red, White and Blue 1939.14
I Did it My Way 1974.11
I Did Not Know 1934.32
I Didn' Think She'd do It 1895.08
I Didn't Grieve Over Daniel 1923.11
I Didn't Hesitate' Cause I Knew That I was Lost 1918.14
I Didn't Know About You 1997.03
I Didn't Know That it was Loaded 1932.13
I Didn't Know What Time it Was 1939.27, 1975.13
I Didn't Mean No Harm 1905.55
I Didn't Raise My Boy to be a Soldier 1974.09, 1975.22
I Didn't See the Time Go By 1983.03
I Didn't Want Him 1950.02
I Dig You That Way 1965.30
I Disremember Quite Well 1970.04
I Do 1925.29
I do it All by Proxy 1906.18
I do Like Your Eyes 1912.31
I do Miracles 1993.09
I do Not Care What other People Say 1894.22
I do Not Know 1919.42
I do Not Know a Day I Did Not Love You 1970.19
I do Not Mind 1897.32
I do! I Do! 1966.29
I do, He Doesn't 1951.17
I do, I do, I Do! 1907.15
I do, I Will, I Have 1973.08
I do, so there! 1897.39
I do, So, There! 1921.20
I Don't Believe I'll Ever be a Lady 1906.48
I Don't Belong on a Farm 1920.36
I Don't Blame 'Em 1926.24
I Don't Care 1903.33, 1905.40, 1909.13, 1918.27, 1980.27
I Don't Care if the Sun Don't Shine 1989.12
I Don't Care Much 1987.16, 1998.04
I Don't Care to be Your Lady Friend No More 1899.29
I Don't Care What They Say About Me 1945.01
I Don't Care Where They Buried My Body 1940.01
I Don't Get It 1942.18
I Don't Have a Song to Sing 1971.04
I Don't Hear the Ocean 1999.22
I Don't Know 1891.40, 1924.01, 1925.42, 1956.04, 1972.15, 1983.08
I Don't Know Enough About You 1983.20
I Don't Know Her Name Yet 1915.29
I Don't Know His Name 1948.04, 1963.14
I Don't Know How I do it But I Do 1913.24
I Don't Know How to Love Him 1971.12, 1992.12
I Don't Know Nothing About You 1980.29
I Don't Know What You See in Me 1917.34
I Don't Know Where She Got It 1967.06
I Don't Know Why I Trust You But I Do 1976.15
I Don't Know, But I Guess 1906.36
I Don't Laugh at Love Anymore 1920.27
I Don't Like the Sea 1915.12
I Don't Like This Dame 1956.04
I don't like to talk much, but - 1885.45
I Don't Like You 1969.16
I Don't Like Your Family 1907.25
I Don't Love Nobody 1929.18
I Don't Love You 1907.01
I Don't Need Anything But You 1977.06
I Don't Remember That 1903.38
I Don't Remember You 1968.01
I Don't See Where it Comes In 1889.31
I Don't Suppose You Have 1895.08
I Don't Think I'll End it All Today 1957.16
I Don't Think I'll Fall in Love Today 1928.43
I Don't Think I'm in Love 1966.27
I don't think I'm ugly 1863.03
I Don't Wanna Rock 1957.01
I Don't Want a Boy 1981.12
I Don't Want a Little Canoe 1905.41
I Don't Want a Song at Twilight 1927.36
I Don't Want an Auto 1907.24
I Don't Want Any Help 1982.23
I Don't Want Any Wurtzberger 1904.15
I Don't Want Him 1926.12
I Don't Want the Dark 1907.15
I Don't Want the Night to End 1975.12
I Don't Want to be a Lady 1903.39
I Don't Want to be a Man 1942.28
I Don't Want to be a Sailor 1906.04
I Don't Want to be a Soldier 1927.43, 1964.28
I Don't Want to be a Soldier Boy 1910.20
I Don't Want to be in Dixie 1922.19
I Don't Want to be Married 1932.05
I Don't Want to be President if it Means Losing You 1934.39
I Don't Want to be Yo' Lady Fren' No' Mo' 1899.35
I Don't Want to Die 1950.16
I Don't Want to Go Home 1919.44
I Don't Want to Go Over to Vietnam 1975.07
I Don't Want to Know 1969.05, 1985.19, 1998.07
I Don't Want to Marry You 1908.10
I Don't Want to Play in Your Yard 1894.46
I Don't Want to Walk Without You 1980.29
I Don't Want You 1952.15
I Don't Want You to be a 'Sister' to Me 1910.21
I Draw the Line 1993.09
I Dream in the Old Arm-Chair 1894.17
I Dream of a Garden of Sunshine 1924.11
I Dream of a Girl in a Shawl 1929.51
I Dream of Jeannie With the Light Brown Hair 1955.13
I Dream too Much 1986.01
I Dreamed a Dream 1987.04, 1995.12
I Dreamed About Roses 1972.07
I dreamt I dwelt in marble halls 1844.01
I Dreamt I Dwelt in Marble Halls 1934.17
I Dreamt I had Money to Buy a Shawl 1845.01
I Dreamt That I Went to the Grand Opera Ball 1922.30
I Drink from My Heart to You 1900.59
I Dunno Wat, The 1921.17
I Enjoy Being a Girl 1958.19
I Envy the Bird 1897.13, 1930.12
I Fain Would Kiss 1894.07
I Faint! I Die! 1881.36
I Fall in Love too Easily 1974.10
I Fancy You 1906.48
I Faw Down an' Go Boom 1928.47
I Feel a Song Comin' On 1979.25
I Feel a Song Coming On 1967.11
I Feel at Home With You 1927.56, 1943.22
I Feel Good 1975.20
I Feel Grand 1972.07
I Feel Humble 1964.05
I Feel Like a Brother to You 1959.19
I Feel Like I 'm Not Out of Bed 1998.16
I Feel Like I'm Gonna Die Rag 1982.22
I Feel Like I'm Gonna Live Forever 1953.01
I Feel Like I'm Not Out of Bed 1971.15
I Feel Like I'm Not Out of Bed Yet 1944.33
I Feel Like New Year's Eve 1964.35
I Feel My Luck Comin' Down 1946.08
I Feel Pretty 1957.12, 1977.05
I Feel so Good 1975.02
I Feel so Happy 1916.20
I Feel Sorry for the Girl 1959.06
I Feel Sorta - 1934.15
I Feel the Earth Move 1982.22
I Fell Head Over Heels in Love 1926.15, 1926.33
I Fell in Love With Polly 1904.24
I Fell in Love With You 1920.06, 1948.04
I Fly by Night 1989.25
I Follow the Ponies 1927.40
I Forgot the Number of the House 1915.20
I Forgot the Rhyme 1905.34
I Fought Every Step of the Way 1951.23
I Found a Baby on My Door Step 1920.18
I Found a Bit of Paris 1935.19
I Found a Four Leaf Clover 1922.27
I Found a Friend 1929.17
I Found a Million Dollar Baby 1988.08
I Found a Million Dollar Baby in a Five and Ten Cent Store 1931.13
I Found a New Way to Go to Town 2000.12
I Found a Song 1934.04
I Found Love 1981.14
I Found the Answer 1990.05
I Gathered shells from day to day 1869.35
I Gave Her That 1918.05
I Gave My Love a Cherry 1953.10, 1966.03
I Get a Kick Out of You 1934.36, 1987.15, 1995.12
I Get Carried Away 1944.33, 1958.21, 1971.15, 1998.16
I Get Embarrassed 1959.22, 1985.04
I Get Myself Out 1985.05
I Give it Up 1886.06
I Give Myself Away 1930.35
I give the best advice 1868.01
I Go Haywire 1931.26
I Go On 1972.15
I Go so Far With Sophie 1922.15
I Go to Bed 1963.08
I Go to Rio 1979.11
I Go to Rio! 1983.09
I Got a Cookie Jar But No Cookies 1928.34
I Got a Dream to Sleep On 1978.10
I Got a Friend 1980.23
I Got a Gal in Kalamazoo 1988.08, 1999.24
I Got a Marble and a Star 1947.02
I Got a Mule 1945.07
I Got a Name 1981.16
I Got a New Girl 1983.08
I Got a Song 1944.23
I Got Another One 1906.31
I Got Beauty 1950.20
I Got Blues 1961.17
I Got Everything I Want 1964.44
I Got Eyes for a Girl on the Car 1982.02
I Got Him 'Dead' 1898.69
I Got It 1889.23
I Got it Bad 1976.04
I Got it Bad and That Ain't Good 1979.24, 1981.06, 1997.03
I Got Life 1968.11
I Got Lost in His Arms 1946.12, 1966.12, 1999.04
I Got Love 1970.05
I Got Plenty o' Nuttin' 1935.13, 1983.04
I Got Rhythm 1930.31, 1944.32, 1948.13, 1952.11, 1988.08, 1991.10, 1992.02, 1999.10, 1999.23
I Got Something 1941.09
I Got the Beat 1996.07
I Got the Blood 1971.13
I Got the Sun in the Morning 1946.12, 1966.12, 1999.04
I Got You 1991.07
I Got You Babe 1982.22
I Gotcha 1974.01, 1999.01
I Gotta Be 1957.05
I Gotta Have My Moments 1930.43
I Gotta Have You 1959.23
I Gotta Keep Movin' 1972.13
I Gotta Keep My Eye on You 1932.06
I Gotta Right to Sing the Blues 1982.12
I Grovel to Earth 1928.30
I Grovel to Your Cloth 1928.30
I guard the lonely deck for thee 1886.50
I Guess I Love You 1933.21
I Guess I Should be Satisfied 1926.51
I Guess I Talk too Much 1908.35
I Guess I'll Have to Change My Plan 1929.19, 1972.05, 1975.22, 1999.23
I Guess I'll Have to Telegraph My Baby 1897.33, 1900.24
I Guess I'll Have to Telegraphy My Baby 1898.70
I Guess I'll See His Finish Pretty Soon 1897.33, 1900.24
I Guess I'll Take the Train Back Home 1906.04
I Guess I'm More Like Mother Than Like Father 1919.14
I Guess This is Goodbye 1987.18
I had a Ball 1964.44
I had a Dog 1915.18
I had a Little Teevee 1971.20
I Had Fifteen Dollars in My Inside Pocket 1887.23
I had Myself a True Love 1946.08, 1997.05
I had the Craziest Dream 1988.08
I had to Go 1978.11
I had Twins 1938.14

I had Two Dregs 1963.13
I Hail from Cairo 1918.05
I Happen to Like New York 1930.40
I Happened to be There 1898.63
I Hate a Parade 1950.12
I Hate Him 1959.11, 1961.10
I Hate Men 1948.32, 1999.19
I Hate Myself for Falling in Love With You 1930.29
I Hate Myself in the Morning 1946.06
I Hate Spring 1939.12
I Hate the Lovely Women 1920.41
I Hate to Talk About Myself 1926.39
I Hate to Think That You'll Grow Old, Baby 1933.05
I Hate to Wake Up 1904.22
I Hate to Work on Mondays 1908.23
I Hate You 1928.27
I Hate You, Darling 1941.08
I Have a Date 1919.28
I Have a Dream by Night, by Day 1911.38
I Have a Husband 1882.33
I Have a Letter for You 1926.11
I Have a Little Chalet in the Valley 1913.30
I Have a Love 1957.12, 1977.05
I Have a Noble Cock 1969.04, 1980.01
I Have a Pipe 1893.19
I Have a Romantic Head 1876.10
I Have a Run in My Stocking 1932.01
I have a song to sing 1888.35
I Have a Swain in the Army 1893.19
I Have Always Been the Patsy 1916.13
I Have Been a Good Boy 1944.32
I Have Been A-Maying 1895.33
I Have Been Around a Bit 1915.01
I Have Confidence 1998.03
I Have Danced 1997.06
I Have Dreamed 1951.12, 1990.09, 1993.16
I Have Found Them All 1911.03
I have gone too far, I Fear 1859.17
I Have Interviewed the Wide, Wide World 1904.15
I Have Just One Heart for Just One Boy 1918.34
I Have Lived 1974.19
I Have Lost My Little Brown Bear 1908.39, 1909.15
I Have My Doubts 1908.16
I Have My Moments 1928.25
I Have My Own Way 1961.14
I Have No Heart 1894.17
I Have No Words 1993.17
I have often stopped and wondered 1885.63
I Have Room in My Heart 1938.15
I Have Somebody's Heart 1920.19
I Have Something Nice for You 1927.34
I Have the Room Above Her 1986.01, 1994.08
I Have Thought of a Scheme 1904.05
I Have to Tell You 1954.15
I Have What You Want 1970.18
I Have Written a Play 1978.02
I Have You 1925.47
I Haven't Got it Now 1892.29
I Haven't Seen the Little Fellow Since 1913.05
I Haven't Told Him 1906.25
I Hear 1960.22
I Hear America Singing 1978.12
I Hear Bells 1990.09
I Hear Love Call Me 1925.06
I Hear Music 1980.29
I Hear the Soft Note of the Echoing Voice 1881.37
I Heard a Song 1894.17
I Heard Someone Crying 1991.05
I Heard That Tale Before 1913.36
I Honestly Love You 1979.11
I Hope I Get It 1975.15
I Hope I'll Know Better Next Time 1890.21
I Hope it Won't Happen Again 1885.58, 1888.09
I Hope These Few Lines Will Find Thee Well 1898.22
I Huckleberry Me 1985.06
I hurl you defiance 1884.60
I Idolize Ida 1908.17
I in My Chair, And 1970.01, 1974.01, 1974.19, 1983.03
I Introduced 1919.25
I Invented Myself 1964.33
I Jot it Down 1903.07
I Jupiter, I Rex 1950.20
I Just Can't Help Believing 1978.01
I Just Can't Keep My Eyes Off You 1907.55
I Just Can't Wait 1910.10, 1961.28
I Just Can't Wait to be King 1997.20
I Just Couldn't Take it, Baby 1933.27
I Just Dropped In 1897.42
I Just Heard 1964.27
I Just Want Jazz 1919.23
I Just Wanted to Tell You Goodbye 1950.16
I Keep Forgettin' 1995.03
I Keep Telling Myself 1952.13
I Kiss My Hand to Thee 1881.11
I Kiss Your Hand, Madame 1929.07, 1929.28
I Kissed My Girl Goodbye 1944.01
I Knew 'Twould be So 1922.40
I Knew a Private 1960.17
I Knew at First Sight That I Loved You 1902.19
I Knew Her When 1910.16
I Knew Him Before He was Spanish 1930.38
I Knew Him When 1920.21
I Knew I'd Know 1947.08
I knos, I spose, whar de Oil Well flows 1865.03
I Know 1918.07, 1966.18
I Know a Bank 1869.15
I Know a Foul Ball 1933.25
I Know a Girl 1906.47, 1975.14
I Know a Girl Like You 1906.04
I Know a Lassie Out in O-H-I-O 1928.05
I know a youth who loves a little maid 1887.10
I Know and She Knows 1913.29
I Know and You Know 1920.07
I Know Him so Well 1988.09
I know his condition 1885.63
I Know How it Is 1956.04
I Know I Have to Leave Here 1976.35, 1980.14, 1982.17
I Know I'm Nobody 1939.24
I Know I've Been Changed 1999.09
I Know it Can Happen Again 1947.17, 1993.16
I Know it is Only a Dream 1925.02
I Know My Rights 1884.42
I Know Now 1980.20
I Know Now! 1947.10
I Know Someone Loves Me 1925.50
I Know Something 1926.02
I Know That I Love You 1924.22, 1926.03
I Know That I'm in Love 1921.20
I Know That You Know 1926.46
I Know the Feeling 1963.08
I Know the Man 1972.24
I Know the Truth 2000.06
I Know Things Now 1987.18
I Know What I Am 1965.14
I Know What I've Got 1992.03
I Know What Love Is 1879.63, 1880.39
I Know Where I'm Going 1966.03
I Know Where the Flies Go 1921.12
I Know Where There's a Cozy Nook 1945.04
I Know Why Because I'm in Love With You 1919.18
I Know You 1917.19
I Know You by Heart 1941.06
I Know you not! 1882.75
I Know Your Heart 1964.16
I Know Your Husband Very Well 1913.34
I Know Your Kind 1959.11
I Laughed, And 1906.44
I Learned About Women from Her 1920.21, 1922.15
I Leave the World 1975.06
I Left Her on the Beach at Honolulu 1916.10
I Left My Heart at the Stage Door Canteen 1942.20
I Left My Heart in Dixie 1902.11, 1903.24
I Left My Sins Behind Me 1976.35
I Let a Song Go Out of My Heart 1981.06, 1997.03
I Like 'Em Fat Like That 1992.03
I Like 'Em Plump 1911.02
I Like 'Em Wild 1918.17
I Like a Big Town 1923.19
I Like All Girls 1912.17
I Like America 1968.19
I Like Everybody 1956.04, 1980.29
I Like Her and She Speaks Well of Me 1930.25
I Like Him 1965.29
I Like It 1887.01, 1888.06, 1916.25, 1918.28, 1929.50, 1969.01
I Like it Here 1950.04
I Like it Like That 1992.06
I Like It! 1911.11
I Like it, Don't You? 1885.58
I Like it, I Do 1888.38
I Like London 1910.05
I Like New York 1918.23
I Like That 1911.20
I Like the Boys 1916.01, 1918.06, 1927.17
I Like the Company of Men 1965.28
I like the Fox shall grieve 1750.01
I Like the Girls 1925.04
I Like the Likes of You 1934.01
I Like the Look 1971.04, 1976.27
I Like the Military Man 1929.46
I Like the Nose on Your Face 1937.12
I Like Them Just Like You, Little Girl 1908.15
I Like to Go to Strange Places 1936.01
I Like to Have a Flock of Men Around Me 1911.08
I Like to Have a Little Bit On 1911.45
I Like to Have You Call Me Honey 1908.23
I Like to Linger in the Lingerie 1919.07
I Like to Look My Best 1966.30
I Like to Make it Cozy 1927.05
I Like to Play With the Boys 1918.02
I Like to Recognize the Tune 1939.27
I Like to Win 1979.18
I Like What I Do 1981.07
I Like What You Like 1929.37
I Like You 1905.53, 1914.17, 1917.18, 1930.43, 1954.15, 1961.16, 1978.25
I Like You All 1911.06
I Like You as You Are 1928.44
I Like You Too 1907.12
I Like You Very Much 1905.45
I Like You, I Love You, I Want You 1907.23
I Like Your Style 1942.23, 1980.07
I Like Your Way 1905.33
I Likes His Way 1899.35
I Live and Love 1893.24
I Live But in Dreams Alone 1912.49
I Live for You 1974.19
I Live for You Alone 1912.15
I Live I Die for You 1927.55
I Long to be Simple 1927.23
I Lost Everything Losing You 1930.29
I Lost It 1970.10
I Love 'Em All 1981.07
I Love a Cop 1959.25
I Love a Fight 1924.10
I Love a Film Cliche 1980.08
I Love a Girl Who is Made of Stucco 1898.43
I Love a Lassie 1928.05, 1930.17
I love a maid, I love her well 1895.17
I Love a Man in a Uniform 1927.62
I Love a Minstrel Show 1919.15
I Love a Musical Comedy Show 1918.37
I Love a Parade 1942.23
I Love a Piano 1915.32, 1988.08, 1990.09, 1999.01
I Love a Polka So 1936.01
I Love a Young Man Dearly 1880.40
I Love All the Boys in the World 1914.13
I Love America 1923.07
I Love and the World is Mine 1908.06
I love as none can tell 1882.44
I Love Beauty 1920.07
I Love Being Here With You 1983.20
I Love But Thee 1912.03
I Love But You 1909.10
I Love Everyone in This Wide, Wide World 1906.21
I Love Her 1913.05
I Love Her - She Loves Me 1922.15
I Love Her and She Loves Me 1918.38
I Love Her in Spite of All 1894.17
I love her, how I love her 1862.02
I love her, I love her 1840.03
I Love Him 1910.24, 1956.04
I love him - I love him 1875.35
I Love Him Only 1895.43
I Love Him the Rat 1931.28
I Love It 1975.09, 2000.12

I Love Louisa 1931.16
I Love Love 1928.26, 1930.30
I Love Love in New York 1949.01
I Love MacIntosh 1910.21
I Love Mary 1960.17
I Love Me 1922.34
I Love Music 1880.25, 1882.69, 1891.07
I Love My Art 1912.31
I Love My Boo Boo 1972.18
I Love My Father 1971.18
I Love My Honey, Yes I Do 1895.27
I Love My Little Susie 1926.32
I Love My Love 1876.11, 1900.39
I Love My Love Always 1896.50
I Love My Love in the Springtime 1893.30
I Love My Love so Well! 1880.69
I Love My Old Love Still 1888.09
I Love My Wife 1966.29, 1976.11, 1977.04
I Love Nashville 1966.30
I Love New York 1985.12
I Love Only One Girl in the Wide, Wide, Wide World 1903.03
I Love Paris 1953.07, 1998.05
I Love Sinking You 1998.15
I Love That Boy 1945.17
I Love That Girl 1885.42
I Love That Man 1914.15
I Love the Girls 1916.20
I Love the Ground You Walk On 1920.21
I Love the Ladies 1964.33
I Love the Land of Old Black Joe 1920.10
I Love the Lassies I Love Them All 1920.04
I Love the Little Babies 1873.19
I Love the Merry Sunshine 1867.10
I Love the Military 1868.03
I Love the Name of Mary 1911.04
I Love the Ocean 1880.46
I Love the Way We Fell in Love 1938.01
I Love the Woods 1930.08, 1931.08
I Love Thee 1897.48
I Love Thee, Adore Thee 1888.19
I Love Thee, I Adore Thee 1897.13, 1930.12
I Love Them All 1880.18, 1904.06, 1908.02, 1924.04, 1925.39
I Love Them All, Just a Little Bit 1919.40
I Love to be a Sailor 1928.05
I Love to Cry at Weddings 1966.01
I Love to Dance 1915.32, 1920.33, 1922.14, 1926.12, 1978.27, 1983.09
I Love to Dance When I Hear a March 1924.36
I Love to Flutter 1935.11
I Love to Follow a Band 1985.02
I Love to Fox Trot 1920.14
I Love to Go Shopping 1908.36
I Love to Go Swimin' With Wimmin" 1921.06
I Love to Have the Boys Around Me 1914.31
I Love to Hear a Yankee Doodle Tune 1904.22
I Love to Rhyme 1999.10
I Love to Say Hello to the Girls, I Hate to Say Goodbye 1920.25
I Love to See a Red, Red Nose 1851.03
I Love to Sing the Words 1943.14
I Love to Sit and Look at You 1908.27
I Love to Two-Step 1904.43
I Love to Wear That Uniform of Blue 1905.31
I Love What I'm Doing 1949.18, 1974.02, 1995.07
I Love What the Girls Have 1970.20
I Love You 1880.47, 1895.04, 1903.17, 1905.22, 1906.48, 1920.45, 1921.22, 1923.24, 1929.46, 1933.24, 1944.02, 1944.21, 1962.27, 1982.01, 1998.15
I Love You a Little 1919.42
I Love You All the Time 1904.13, 1904.29, 1904.44, 1974.04
I Love You as You Are 1912.42
I Love You Babe, and You Love Me 1900.47
I Love You Because You are You, Dear 1906.04
I Love You But I Like You Even More 1929.20
I Love You Dear, and Only You 1900.59
I Love You Every Hour 1910.29
I Love You for That 1962.24
I Love You in My Dum, Dum, Dumy Way 1906.27
I Love You in Velvet 1906.32
I Love You Just the Same 1914.13, 1927.04
I Love You Madly 1981.06
I Love You More Than Yesterday 1929.07
I Love You My Darling 1924.19, 1932.06
I Love You Only 1903.38
I Love You Samantha 1998.05
I Love You So 1895.06, 1907.48, 1916.12, 1928.27, 1943.09, 1964.24
I Love You so Much Jesus 1976.35, 1980.14, 1982.17
I Love You Then as Now 1903.40
I Love You This Morning 1945.19
I Love You Today 1963.12
I Love You! I Love You! 1902.25
I Love You' Song, The 1974.19
I Love You, Dear 1911.41
I Love You, Dear Tommy 1896.26
I Love You, Dear, I Love But You 1914.20
I Love You, Dolly 1903.06
I Love You, Evaline 1895.38
I Love You, Honey 1931.47
I Love You, I Adore You 1928.26, 1946.18
I Love You, I Love You, I Love You! 1923.05
I Love You, Marina 1914.28
I Love You, My Love, I Do 1898.46
I Love You, Oh! Oh! Oh! 1909.05
I Love Ze Americn Ragtime 1903.16
I Love ze Parisienne 1909.30
I Love, I Adore Her 1894.38
I Love, I Love 1866.07, 1866.21
I Love, I Love Her So 1894.38
I Love, Thou Lovest 1923.07
I Loved 1972.16
I Loved Her Best of All 1924.13
I Loved Her, Too 1947.02
I Loved Him But He Didn't Love Me 1929.51
I Loved Him for He Loved That I Loved 1918.04
I Loved Him, But He Didn't Love Me 1967.11
I Loved You Once in Silence 1960.21, 1980.19, 1993.11
I Loves You Porgy 1974.09
I Loves You, Lady, 'Deed I Do 1904.23
I Loves You, Porgy 1935.13, 1983.04
I Made a Fist 1956.04
I Made It 1987.17
I Made Them Step 1928.04
I Make My Bed Down in Dixieland 1930.23
I Make the Rules 1993.19
I make thee King 1868.02
I Make Up for That in Other Ways 1932.07
I Makes Mine Myself 1920.33
I Married an Angel 1938.05, 1975.13
I Masandieri 1862.06
I May 1926.26
I May be Crazy But I Ain't No Fool 1904.26
I may be princess 1878.16
I May be Small, But I Have Big Ideas 1917.23
I May be This 1893.37
I May be Wrong 1929.32
I May Look Strong But I'm Far from Healthy 1918.04
I May May be Wrong But I Think You're Wonderful 1929.29
I May Never Fall in Love With You 1960.20
I may say without boasting or blowing 1888.07
I May Stay Away a Little Longer 1917.35
I Mean to be a Good Girl Now 1904.01
I Mean to be Married as Soon as I Can 1917.14
I Mean to Introduce it into China 1900.43
I Mean to Say 1930.02
I Mean What I Say 1929.50
I Meant You No Harm 1981.29
I Met a Girl 1956.14
I Met a Jolly Sailor Man 1900.54
I Met Her at the Ball 1893.50
I Met Her at the Metropole But I Lost Her at Jack's 1908.15
I Met You in Pittsburgh, Pa. 1911.34
I Might 1924.01
I Might be Your Once-in-a-While 1919.44, 1947.04
I Might Fall Back on You 1927.67, 1948.20, 1966.14, 1983.05
I Might Say Yes 1917.19
I Miss Him 1972.07
I Miss My Man 1972.23
I Miss You Old Friend 1981.29
I Miss You, My Dear Queen 1997.16, 1998.08
I Missed You 1922.33
I Must Away 1895.08
I Must be Home by Twelve O'Clock 1929.27
I Must be in Love 1928.08, 1982.10
I Must Find Someone 1910.29
I Must Get on That Ship 1997.06
I must go 1887.04
I Must Have a Dinner Coat 1938.04
I Must Have a Lot of Little Girls All 'Round Me 1907.32
I Must Have Been Mistaken 1905.56
I Must Have Her 1979.09
I Must Have My Way 1913.18
I Must Have That Man 1928.18, 1980.10
I Must Love You 1928.30
I Must Marry a Handsome Man 1899.28
I Must Propose to You 1907.15
I Must Waltz 1938.04
I Near the Goal 1881.22
I Need a Garden 1924.19
I Need a Little Sugar in My Bowl 1976.16
I Need Affection 1915.24
I Need All the Help I Can Get 1957.14
I Need New Words 1934.32, 1935.19
I Need Some Cooling Off 1928.02
I Need Someone's Love 1917.09
I Need This One Chance 1985.02
I Need to Know 1997.09
I Need You 1929.18
I Need You Now 1962.17
I Need You So 1929.20
I Never Before Met a Girl Like You 1914.05
I never could, like some girls, smile 1882.60
I Never do Anything Twice 1977.05, 2000.16
I Never do it Now 1907.30
I Never Drink Behind the Bar 1882.79
I Never Felt Better in My Life 1968.06
I Never had a Chance 1961.27
I Never had a Kiss 1912.47
I Never had a Mammy 1924.46
I Never had Such a Time 1903.09
I Never had to Work 1903.34
I Never has Seen Snow 1954.19
I Never Imagined Goodbye 1976.01
I Never Knew 1912.14, 1917.04, 1972.18
I Never Knew His Name 1999.08
I Never Knew What Eyes Could do Till Yours Looked into Mine 1912.13
I Never Know How to Behave When I'm With Girls, Girls, Girls 1910.16
I Never Know When to Say When 1958.14
I Never Laughed in My Life 1953.02
I Never Loved a Love as I Love You 1904.13, 1904.44
I Never Loved a Man as Much as That 1902.29
I Never Loved You 1973.07
I Never Meant to Fall in Love 1960.10
I Never Miss 1920.01
I Never Saw a King Before 1938.15
I Never Tell Tales Out of School 1890.29
I Never Thought 1918.16
I Never Thought I'd Break 1979.11
I Never Tooka Lesson in My Life 1904.49
I Never Want to Go Home Again 1973.12
I Never Want to See You Again 1983.08
I Never Wanted to be a Hero 1971.15
I Never Wanted to Love You 1992.09
I Never was Born 1944.23
I Never was Right in My Life 1906.18
I Never Would Believe It 1905.35
I Once Believed 1989.05
I Once had a Chef 1900.57
I once was a very abandon'd person 1887.10
I once was as meek as a newborn lamb 1887.10
I Once was Wealthy 1886.24
I Only Drink for Friendship's Sake 1910.11
I Only Have Eyes for You 1988.08, 1989.21, 2001.08
I Only Know 1939.12
I Only Know I Love Thee 1898.17
I only mix with Ghosts well-known 1880.18
I Only Wanna Laugh 1969.14
I Only Wish I Knew 1948.19
I Ought to be on the Stage 1933.23

I Ought to Know More About You 1950.14
I Owe it All 1976.15
I Owe Ohio 1963.16
I own I am seducing 1854.04
I Pagliacci 1977.09
I Paused, I Looked, I Fell 1932.19
I Play on My Old Bassoon 1906.49
I Played My Concertina 1915.27
I Plead, Dear Heart 1928.48
I Pledge Allegiance 1938.08
I Praise Sue 1937.09
I Pray Thee Hear Me 1892.20
I Prefer the Cat 1915.22
I Promise I'll be Practically True to You 1928.04
I Promise You 1998.19
I Promise You a Happy Ending 1974.18
I Promised Their Mothers 1954.01
I Put a Spell on You 1999.09
I Put My Hand In 1964.01
I raise an objection to that 1889.54
I Read 1994.05
I Read About it in a Book 1906.13
I Really am so Sleepy 1880.46
I Really Can't Make My Feet Behave 1918.20
I Really Can't Sit Down 1885.15, 1889.18, 1895.05
I Really Don't Know What You Mean 1897.25
I really don't know, do you? 1879.35
I Really Hate to Talk About Myself 1908.15
I Really Like Him 1965.34
I Really Loved You 1980.23
I Remember 1977.05, 1986.13, 1988.01
I Remember Her 1950.01
I Remember How it Was 1983.21
I Remember How Those Boys Could Dance 1988.12
I Remember it Well 1948.25, 1965.08, 1973.12, 1999.23
I Remember Mama 1979.12
I Remember You 1908.25, 1997.05
I Resolve 1963.14
I Rise Again 1978.02
I Said Good Morning 1958.21, 1977.02
I Said Good-Night and You Good-Bye 1894.35
I Said it and I'm Glad 1961.28
I Said No 1942.12
I Said to Love 1960.07
I Said, Oh No 1984.02
I Sail the Airy Blue 1898.55
I Sang This Song 1886.24, 1888.06
I Saved a Waltz for You 1920.32
I saw him but once 1852.01
I saw Him but once 1871.10
I Saw Your Eyes 1931.39
I Say Hello 1959.11
I Say it's Spinach 1932.05
I Say Yes 1966.30
I Say, Flo 1908.14
I See a Man 1973.11
I See by Your Smile 1900.25
I See Her at the Station 1956.04
I see his game 1887.04
I See in Fear you Palpitate 1877.20
I See Something 1964.05
I See the Light 1971.01
I See What I Choose to See 1971.02
I See You But What do You See in Me? 1929.24
I See Your Face Before Me 1937.16, 1972.05
I Sent My Wife to the Thousand Isles 1916.03
I Shall be All Right Now 1918.37
I Shall be Released 1979.30
I Shall Die, Die, Die 1895.03
I shall have 'em 1889.54
I Shall Have to Tell it to Albert, Prince of Wales 1900.08
I Shall Kill You With Love 1964.39
I Shall Love You 1929.01
I Shall Miss You 1965.02
I Shall Never Look at a Pretty Girl Again 1911.41
I Shall Not be Moved 1969.10
I Shall Scream 1963.01
I shipped, d'ye see, in a revenue sloop 1887.10
I Shiver and Shake With Fear 1917.24, 1919.20
I Shot the Works 1931.36
I Should Care 1974.10
I Should Have Been Born a Boy 1912.14
I Should Have Been Offended if My Waist You had not Squeezed 1907.05
I Should Like to Know 1898.63
I Should Like to Know the Reason 1908.41
I Should Rather Like to Try 1899.39
I Should so Love to be a Boy 1906.25
I Should Tell You 1996.09
I Show a Bank 1856.01
I Showed That I Know Something When I Fell in Love With You 1916.21
I Sigh for a Change 1900.38
I Sing a Little Tenor 1902.16
I sing Love's dulcet lay 1882.60
I Sing of Eyes That are Dearer to Me 1889.38
I Sing of Love 1948.32, 1999.19
I Sleep Easier Now 1950.20
I Spit in the Water 1934.32, 1935.19
I Spy 1963.22, 1971.19
I Spy Little Girl 1895.03
I stand at your threshold sighing 1887.44
I Started on a Shoestring 1930.25
I Still Believe 1991.03
I Still Believe in Love 1979.04
I Still Believe in You 1930.08
I Still Can Dream 1922.35
I Still Get Jealous 1947.16, 1989.03
I Still Have Plenty to Learn 1948.18
I Still Look at You That Way 1963.25
I Still Love You 1908.11
I Still See Elisa 1951.24, 1963.02
I Still Suites Me 1986.01
I stole the Prince 1890.02
I Stumbled Over You 1932.15
I Stumbled Over You and Fell in Love 1930.37
I Suddenly Find it Agreeable 1959.06
I Take After Dad 1912.13
I Take After Rip 1930.05
I Talk to the Trees 1951.24
I Talk, You Talk 1985.05
I Tank I Go Home 1938.08
I Thank Heaven 1979.13
I Thank Her for Her Care 1787.01
I Thank You 1925.48
I Think an Awful Lot of You 1907.22
I Think I Oughtn't Auto Anymore 1907.24
I Think I Sees You 1870.20
I Think I Shall Learn, Don't You? 1898.50
I Think I'll Get Wed in th' Summer 1928.05
I Think I'm Gonna Like it Here 1977.06
I Think of You the Whole Year Round 1907.37
I Think She Needs Me 1967.05
I Think She's Absolutely Wonderful 1918.07
I Think so - Don't You? 1888.13
I Think So, Too 1920.30
I Think the Kid Will Do 1984.02
I Think the World of You 1963.13
I Think You're Absolutely Wonderful 1918.07
I Think, I Think 1979.02
I Thought About You 1997.05
I Thought I Wanted Opera 1910.07
I Thought it was You 1930.24
I Thought Wrong 1903.34
I to the World 1981.25
I Told a Friend of Mine 1906.41
I Told You So 1882.18, 1895.25, 1981.10
I Took Another Look 1946.22
I Took My Love to See 'Who's Afraid of Virginia Woolf?' 1963.10
I Took My Time 1986.11
I Took Them All 1906.49
I Took Them Home to Mother 1904.54
I Tremble O'er With Fear 1866.07, 1866.21
I Two Gentlemen of Verona 1971.18
I Understand 1944.33, 1971.15, 1998.16
I Used to Believe in Fairies 1910.06
I Wake at Morning 1928.30
I Walk With Music 1940.09
I Walked Around 1908.03
I Waltz Alone 1989.26
I Waltzed With a Major 1942.10
I Wanna be a Dancin' Man 1978.05, 1988.08, 1999.01
I Wanna be a Producer 2001.05
I Wanna be Bad 1946.24
I Wanna be Good 'n Bad 1951.13
I Wanna be Loved by You 1928.25, 1975.22
I Wanna be Yours 1982.01
I Wanna Dance 1922.22
I Wanna Get Married 1944.14
I Wanna Go Voom Voom Voo 1927.04
I Wanna Hold Your Handel 1964.29
I Wanna Know Your Name 1997.21
I Wanna Love Him so Bad 1985.03
I Wanna Make the World Laugh 1974.18
I Want a Big Butter and Egg Man 1989.02
I Want a Boy 1911.17
I Want a Boy to Love Me 1913.35
I Want a Bungalow 1921.08
I Want a Daddy Who Will Rock Me to Sleep 1919.18
I Want a Determined Boy 1917.36, 1976.25
I Want a Fine Little Steam Yacht 1908.10
I Want a Gibson Man 1908.12
I Want a Girl Just Like the Girl That Married Dear Old Dad 1942.11, 1979.25
I Want a Girl to Call My Own 1926.18
I Want a Home 1921.08
I Want a Kiss 1926.42, 1946.03, 1987.10
I Want a Lily 1920.36
I Want a Little Loving Sometimes 1912.08
I Want a Lonely Romeo 1919.14
I Want a Lot of Girlie Girlies 1910.19
I Want a Loveable Baby 1925.22
I Want a Man 1919.24, 1928.44, 1931.04
I Want a Man Badly Blues 1925.47
I Want a Man Made to Order for Me 1905.49
I Want a Man to Love Me 1909.30
I Want a Man Who's Gentle 1917.27
I Want a Million for You, Dear 1926.30
I Want a Nice Young Man 1894.16
I Want a Pal 1927.07
I Want a Picture of You 1921.27
I Want a Regular Man 1912.14, 1922.17
I Want a Situation 1891.13
I Want a Steam Yacht 1908.10
I Want a Toy Soldier Man 1913.05
I Want a Wife 1910.29
I Want All of the Boys 1916.12
I Want All the World to Know 1915.30
I Want Another Portion of That 1932.07
I Want Another Situation Just Like That 1911.17
I Want Dem Presents Back 1897.56
I Want Him Saved 1912.02
I Want It 1971.04
I Want it All 1907.01, 1983.19
I Want it Just to Happen 1970.12
I Want Jesus to Walk With Me 1940.01
I Want Love 1920.41
I Want My Chicken 1909.10
I Want My Husband When I'm Wed 1918.42
I Want My Little Gob 1919.09
I Want My Lulu 1898.10
I Want My Mama 1940.02
I Want My Rag Time 1906.21
I Want Plenty of You 1928.50
I Want Somebody 1919.11
I Want Someone 1930.14
I Want Someone to Show Me New Yorktown 1908.37
I Want Someone Who's Lonesome 1915.23
I Want Something New to Play With 1911.43, 1912.09
I Want That Man 1930.08
I Want That Star 1916.10
I Want the Boys Around Me 1918.13
I Want the Kind of a Fella 1963.12
I Want the Strolling Good 1913.05
I Want the Whole World to Know I Love You 1907.57
I Want the World to Know 1928.41
I Want Them All to Leave Me Alone 1917.09
I Want to be a Bad Little Boy 1925.36
I Want to be a Ballet Dancer 1924.44
I Want to be a Blooming, Blushing Bride 1920.29
I Want to be a Chaste Woman 1925.16
I Want to be a Christmas present 1998.19
I Want to be a Dancer 1897.54
I Want to be a Drummer Boy 1907.24
I Want to be a Jolly Soldier 1912.46
I Want to be a Lidy 1902.19
I Want to be a Little Frog in a Little Pond 1961.11

I Want to be a Military Man 1900.51, 1902.05, 1920.09
I Want to be a Millionaire 1906.02
I Want to be a Prima Donna 1911.38
I Want to be a Real Lady 1903.08
I Want to be a Romeo 1916.14
I Want to be a Santa Claus 1924.17
I Want to be a Soldier 1898.47
I Want to be a Soldier Boy 1910.20
I Want to be a Soldier Lady 1902.23
I Want to be Bad 1929.03
I Want to be Glorified 1925.20
I Want to be Good But My Eyes Won't Let Me 1916.25
I Want to be Happy 1925.30, 1971.03, 1981.16
I Want to be in Norfolk 1914.22
I Want to be Like Cleo 1919.11
I Want to be Loved 1924.38
I Want to be Loved Like a Leadin' Lady 1907.41
I Want to be Loved Like a Leading Lady 1908.15
I Want to be Merry 1921.13
I Want to be One of the Smart Set 1902.34
I Want to be Popular 1899.39
I Want to be Ready 1930.10
I Want to be Rich 1962.18, 1978.18
I Want to be Seen With You Tonight 1964.11
I Want to be Somebody's Baby 1892.29, 1920.24
I Want to be the Captain 1915.17
I Want to be the Mayor 1985.15
I Want to be There 1924.34, 1927.14
I Want to be Vamped in Georgia 1922.25
I Want to be With You 1964.32
I Want to be Your Wife 1907.63
I Want to Belong 1924.33
I Want to Break into Society 1903.35
I Want to Bring You a Ring 1910.13
I Want to Chisel in on Your Heart 1931.21
I Want to Dance 1924.36, 1934.40
I Want to Dance With You 1925.19
I Want to do a Number With the Boys 1931.13
I Want to Go Back to London 1903.09
I Want to Go Back to Michigan 1952.11
I Want to Go Back to New York 1912.29
I Want to Go Back to the Bottom of the Garden 1946.22
I Want to Go Back to the Boulevard 1905.45, 1906.27
I Want to Go Bye-Bye 1919.02
I Want to Go Home 1916.26, 1918.10, 1924.23, 1938.13, 1964.28, 1974.23, 1996.08
I Want to Go Home Now 1906.30
I Want to Go to City College 1946.23
I Want to Go to Hollywood 1989.26
I Want to Go to Paree, Papa 1903.11
I Want to Go to Paris 1908.36
I Want to Hear a Yankee Doodle Tune 1968.07, 1975.22, 1988.08
I Want to Hold Your Hand 1977.10
I Want to Join the Army 1908.44
I Want to Know 1996.08
I Want to Know Where Tosti Went 1920.33
I Want to Learn How to Jazz Dance 1918.19
I Want to Learn to Dance 1918.15
I Want to Live - I Want to Love 1947.13
I Want to Live as Long as You Love Me 1940.12
I Want to Look Like Lillian Russell 1914.13
I Want to Marry 1918.07, 1920.39
I Want to Marry a Male Quartette 1915.30
I Want to Marry a Man 1900.51, 1907.41
I Want to Marry a Man, I Do 1920.09
I Want to Marry a Military Man 1902.05
I Want to Meet You Some Day in California 1921.17
I Want to Play House With You 1910.22
I Want to Play With the Girls 1936.01
I Want to Pray 1952.15
I Want to Row With the Crew 1987.15
I Want to See More of You 1945.17
I Want to See My Child 1975.19
I Want to See My Ida Hoe in Idaho 1920.36
I Want to See the Happy Man 1904.49
I Want to Share it All With You 1973.11
I Want to Show You Colorland 1920.26
I Want to Sing in Opera 1911.27
I Want to Take You Higher 1997.21
I Want to Tell You a Story 1928.06
I Want to Wed a Soldier Boy 1906.27, 1910.12
I Want Twins 1924.32
I Want Two Husbands 1925.52
I Want What I Want When I Want It 1905.57, 1980.27
I Want Yer, Ma Honey 1895.27
I want yer, ma Honey 1895.32
I Want Yer, Ma Honey 1896.45
I Want You 1907.57, 1920.05, 1922.04, 1974.24
I Want You All to Myself 1929.07
I Want You Baby 1981.29
I Want You for My All Time Girl 1907.52
I Want You Ma' Honey 1906.45
I Want You to be My Baby 1955.13
I Want You to be the First to Know 1962.02
I Want You to Love Me 1930.20
I Want You to Marry Me 1906.33, 1945.16
I Want You, I Need You 2000.12
I Want You, I Need You, I Love You 1989.12
I Wanted to Change Him 1967.06
I Wanted to Come to Broadway 1914.34
I Wants a Loving Man 1904.38
I Wants to be an Actor Lady 1903.05
I was a Deutscher Swell 1878.04
I was a Florodora Baby 1920.18
I was a Gyp in Egypt 1936.12
I was a Hero 1908.10
I was a Pale Young Curate Then 1938.10
I was a Shoo-In 1961.28
I was a Very Good Baby in the Daytime 1918.39
I was Beautiful, And 1969.05
I was Blue - 1925.34
I was Born in Tokio 1888.09
I was Born in Virginia 1968.07
I was Born on a Friday 1905.19
I was Born on the Day Before Yesterday 1975.01
I was Born on the Isle of Man 1914.22
I was Born to Rule 1907.05
I was Born Under a Wand'rin' Star 1951.24
I was But a Little Girl 1872.23
I was Just Going to Ask You About That 1902.02
I was Just Supposing 1906.07
I was Lonely 1918.25
I was Made for Champagne 1988.20
I was Married Once 1908.10
I was Meant for Someone 1925.50
I was Meant for You 1924.01
I was Strolling 1963.30
I was Talking in My Sleep 1894.51
I was the Most Beautiful Blossom 1931.48
I was There 1925.52, 1973.11
I was Walking Round the Ocean 1901.01
I was Wrong 1976.01
I Wash My Hands 1958.20
I welcome you 1886.50
I Went Back Home 1978.11
I Went Home With Michael 1894.37
I Went With Him 1888.39, 1889.09
I Whispered it to the Rose 1915.20
I Whistle a Happy Tune 1951.12
I Who Have Nothing 1995.03
I Will Always Love You, Dear 1910.12
I Will Arise and Go Now 1973.08
I Will be Good 1924.41
I Will be His Wife 1890.03
I Will be Waiting for You 1908.25
I Will Follow Her 1915.12
I Will Follow You 1961.20
I Will Give 1999.22
I Will Give to You 1970.01
I Will Give You All for Love 1911.37
I Will Love You 1999.22
I Will Love You Forever, My Dear 1906.30
I Will Love You, Always Love You 1902.09
I Will Make Things Happen 1975.07
I Will Never Leave You 1997.17
I Will Never See You Again, I Will Never Forget You 1990.01
I Will Not Tell a Soul 1978.11
I will not weep or vainly sigh 1889.10
I Will Return, My Love 1888.15
I Will Set You Free 2000.05
I Will Survive 1982.22
I Will Warm Your Heart 1970.01
I Will, I Won't 1921.08
I Wish 1946.22
I Wish He Knew 1981.12
I Wish I Could Forget You 1994.05
I Wish I Didn't Love Him 1972.07
I Wish I Didn't Love You So 1980.29
I Wish I had a Million 1915.31
I Wish I was a Boy 1954.16
I Wish I was a Boy and I Wish I was a Girl 1909.13
I Wish I was a Queen 1920.42
I Wish I was an Island in an Ocean of Girls 1915.24
I Wish I was Dead 1998.16
I Wish I was in Texas 1938.06
I Wish I was Single Again 1931.02
I Wish I Were a Man 1984.02
I Wish I Were in Love Again 1937.04, 1975.13
I Wish I Were Single Again 1990.16
I Wish it So 1959.04
I Wish it Would Rain Down 1995.01
I Wish That Girls Could Go to War 1918.06
I Wish That I'd Been Born in Borneo 1920.33
I Wish You a Waltz 1978.27
I Wish You Love 1964.22, 1967.13, 1968.20, 1999.07
I Wish You Wouldn't do That 1896.10
I Won't be Home for Dinner 1908.15
I Won't be There 2001.01
I Won't Dance 1980.09, 1986.01, 1999.24
I Won't do Your Washin' Any More 1899.22
I Won't Go Home Until Morning 1907.37
I Won't Grow Up 1954.13, 1979.22, 1990.20
I Won't Let it Happen Again 1968.24
I Won't Let That Happen to Him 1982.23
I Won't Let You Get Away 1974.02
I Won't Play With You Any More 1883.26
I Won't Send Roses 1974.18, 1985.19, 1988.08, 1998.07
I Wonder 1899.28, 1907.51, 1912.41, 1918.11, 1974.04
I Wonder as I Wander 1945.14, 1955.13
I Wonder How I Ever Passed You By 1921.32
I Wonder How it is to Dance With a Boy 1967.14
I Wonder If 1966.09
I Wonder if it's True 1911.43
I Wonder if Love is a Dream 1927.18
I Wonder if She Will Remember 1927.43
I Wonder if the Thing's Worth While 1906.50
I Wonder if They're All True to Me 1908.19
I Wonder if You're Lonely 1909.24
I Wonder What Became of Me 1997.05
I Wonder What Happened to Him? 1968.19
I Wonder What is That Coon's Game 1898.22
I Wonder What is That Coon's Game? 1899.12
I Wonder What She's Thinking of Now 1920.07
I Wonder What the Audience Would Say 1909.19
I Wonder What the King is Doing Tonight? 1960.21, 1980.19, 1993.11
I Wonder What They're Doing Now in Home, Sweet Home 1910.04
I Wonder What's the Matter With My Eyes 1908.39, 1909.15
I Wonder Where I Met You 1912.29
I Wonder Where My Easy Rider's Gone 2000.12
I Wonder Where They'll Go 1908.07
I Wonder Whether I've Loved You All My Life 1918.37
I Wonder Who She Spoons With Now 1915.23
I Wonder Who's Keeping Him Now 1930.38
I Wonder Who's Kissing Her Now 1955.14
I Wonder Who's Kissing Her Now! 1909.31
I Wonder Whom I'll Marry 1913.31
I Wonder Why 1908.27, 1913.37, 1917.02, 1922.31, 1927.50, 1974.10
I Wonder Why She Kept on Saying 'Si Si, Si, Si, Senor' 1918.05
I Wonder Why That Glow-Worm Winks His Eye at Me 1924.15
I Wonder Why You Wander 1945.01
I Wont Say I Will But I Won't Say I Won't 1923.26
I wooed my love 1889.54
I Wore a Tunic When You Wore a Tulip 1964.28
I Would be Your Romeo 1903.14
I Would Die 1959.22, 1985.04
I Would do Anything in the World for You 1906.35
I Would Have Told Thee Long Ago 1895.06
I Would if I Could But I Can't 1987.02

I Would if I Could, But I Can't 1889.31
I Would Like to be Your Pal 1905.55
I Would Like to Correspond With You 1909.18
I Would Like to Flirt With You 1907.62
I Would Like to Fondle You 1926.24
I Would Like to Have a Photograph of You 1905.39
I Would Like to Marry You 1905.49
I Would Like to See the Peaches 1912.01
I Would Love to Have You Love Me 1936.22
I Would Not if I Could 1893.03
I Would Rather be a Lobster Than a Wise Guy 1907.62
I Would Rather Dance a Waltz 1924.22
I Would Tarry 1892.06
I Wouldn't be a Lady if I Could 1898.77
I Wouldn't Bet One Penny 1961.14
I Wouldn't Change a Thing 1976.16
I Wouldn't do Anything Wrong 1897.54
I Wouldn't do That, Would You? 1903.19
I Wouldn't Give That for the Man Who Couldn't Dance 1918.34
I Wouldn't Have had To 1961.21
I Wouldn't Have You Any Other Way 1968.24
I wouldn't in the least object 1886.40
I Wouldn't Like to Tell 1871.12
I Wouldn't Marry You 1961.27
I Wouldn't Mind a Job Like That 1900.52
I Wouldn't Take a Case Like That 1908.35
I Write the Songs 1976.34
I Wrote a Song for You 1936.07
I Wrote the Book 1981.10
I'd Ask No More 1918.37
I'd be a Fool 1931.39
I'd be a Red Hot Mamma 1953.10
I'd be a young girl if I could 1893.02
I'd be Attracted 1985.20
I'd be Crazy to be Crazy Over You 1971.09
I'd be Happy 1929.21
I'd be Happy Anywhere With You 1916.26
I'd be Surprisingly Good for You 1979.23
I'd do Anything 1963.01
I'd do it Again 1965.02
I'd Give My Life for You 1991.03
I'd Gladly Trade 1941.06
I'd Guess You 1908.03
I'd Know It 1963.12
I'd Like a Girl Like You to Like Me 1912.49
I'd Like a Honeymoon With You 1920.05
I'd Like a Lighthouse 1920.04
I'd Like an Introduction to You Dear 1912.45
I'd Like Another Situation Just Like That 1907.59
I'd Like It 1899.40
I'd Like to be a Baby Sitter for a Baby Like You 1949.06
I'd Like to be a Gardener in a Garden of Girls 1925.24
I'd Like to be a Gunner in the Navy 1901.21
I'd Like to be a Monkey in the Zoo 1917.12
I'd Like to be a Quitter, But I Find it Hard to Quit 1915.24
I'd Like to be a Rose 1971.18
I'd Like to be a Soldier 1904.10
I'd Like to be a Soldier, Gay 1912.10
I'd Like to be a Swell! 1869.06
I'd Like to be Liked 1929.49
I'd Like to be Somebody's Baby 1891.21
I'd Like to Bring My Mother 1914.32
I'd Like to Call You Mine 1906.31, 1906.32
I'd Like to Corral a Gal 1925.10
I'd Like to Dunk You in My Coffee 1934.39
I'd Like to Go Halves in That 1904.13
I'd Like to Go on a Honeymoon With You 1911.23
I'd Like to Have a Photograph of That 1899.38
I'd Like to Hide It 1925.31
I'd Like to Know You Better 1974.03
I'd Like to Live Them All 1929.17
I'd Like to Lock You in My Heart 1907.46
I'd Like to Meet Your Father 1907.32
I'd Like to Put You in a Big Glass Case 1924.18
I'd Like to See a Little More of You 1906.45
I'd Like to See It 1905.42
I'd Like to See Them All Together 1909.06
I'd Like to Take You Away 1920.15
I'd Like to Take You Home 1926.07
I'd Like to Teach You the A-B-C of Love 1920.29
I'd Like to Walk With a Pal Like You 1923.08
I'd Like to Wander With Alice in Wonderland 1914.18
I'd Like You to Like Me a Little Bit More 1922.04
I'd Love To 1918.39
I'd Love to be a Lady 1917.07
I'd Love to Waltz Through Life With You 1923.38
I'd Marry You Again 1970.12
I'd Place a Bet 1920.14
I'd Rather be a Chippie Than a Charity Bum 1912.36
I'd Rather be Right 1937.13, 1968.07
I'd Rather Dance Here Than Hereafter 1919.11, 1928.17
I'd Rather Go to Jail 1912.16
I'd Rather Have Nothin' All de Time Than Somethin fo' a Little While 1908.08
I'd Rather Leave While I'm Still in Love 1979.11
I'd Rather Not See You at All Rather Than See You Once in a While 1920.10
I'd Rather Two-Step Than Waltz 1907.28
I'd Rather Two-Step Than Waltz, Bill 1907.18
I'd Rather Wake Up by Myself 1954.02
I'd Sooner be a Has-Been 1907.37
I'd Steal a Star 1926.46
I'd Sure Like to Give it a Shot 1970.08
I'd Write a Song 1933.03
I'll Agree if You'll Agree 1927.23
I'll Always be in Love 1971.16
I'll Always Love Old Dixie 1907.22
I'll Always Love You 1984.02
I'll Always Remember the Song 1988.10
I'll Applaud You With My Feet 1940.07
I'll be a Buoyant Girl 1926.42, 1946.03
I'll be a College Boy's Dear 1917.08
I'll be a Good Little Girl 1905.27
I'll be a Santa Claus to You 1915.16
I'll be a West Point Cadet 1904.35
I'll be Coming Home With a Skate On 1915.32
I'll be Dar 1955.13
I'll be Dictator 1920.13
I'll be Happy Too 1910.07
I'll be Hard to Handle 1933.26, 1986.01
I'll be Here Tomorrow 1979.02, 1998.07
I'll be in My Dixie Home Again Tomorrow 1922.15
I'll be Just the Same 1920.20
I'll be Married to the Music of a Military Band 1908.40
I'll be no submissive wife 1859.15
I'll be No Submissive Wife 1866.17
I'll be Respectable 1959.27
I'll be Seeing You 1938.01, 1957.10, 1979.24, 1988.08, 1991.10, 1999.24
I'll be Sittin' in De Lap o'De Lord 1937.10
I'll be Smiling 1928.07
I'll be There 1914.14, 1919.13, 1920.21, 1930.30, 1982.22, 1983.03
I'll be There - in the Public Square 1903.11
I'll be There in the Public Square 1907.20
I'll be There With Bells On 1906.11
I'll be There With You 1910.15
I'll be True - But I'll be Blue 1933.06
I'll be True to My Honey Boy 1908.22
I'll be True to Thee 1871.27
I'll be True to You 1912.26, 1919.27, 1948.30
I'll be Waiting 1927.17
I'll be Waiting at the Window 1912.26
I'll be With You in Apple Blossom Time 1920.24
I'll be Your Artist and You be My Model 1927.58
I'll be Your Baby Tonight 1970.16
I'll be Your Chanticleer 1910.09
I'll be Your Dewdrop Rosey 1902.08
I'll be Your Honey 1905.05
I'll be Your Lady Love if You'll be My Beau 1905.31
I'll be Your Own Romeo 1916.14
I'll be Your Rainbow 1902.21
I'll be Your Soldier 1924.39
I'll be Your Valentine 1920.28
I'll Bet on Anything But Girls 1922.07
I'll Bet You 1917.36
I'll Betcha That I Getcha 1933.16
I'll Bribe the Stars 1903.37
I'll Build a Bungalow 1922.26
I'll Build a Home in the Jungle 1922.05
I'll Build a Home in the U.S.A. 1915.16
I'll Build a Stairway to Paradise 1922.27, 1974.09, 1984.10, 1990.09, 1999.23
I'll Buy You a Star 1951.14
I'll Can-Can All Day 1937.17
I'll Collaborate With You 1923.05
I'll Come Back to You 1914.01, 1932.03
I'll Cover You 1996.09
I'll Cuddle Up to You 1925.19
I'll Dance My Way into Your Heart 1922.35
I'll do Anything for Love 1929.52
I'll do or Die 1902.18
I'll Dream of That Sweet Co-Ed 1909.03
I'll Dream of You 1903.22, 1922.12
I'll Find a Girl, I'll Find a Boy 1912.43
I'll Find My Love in D-I-X-I-E 1924.27
I'll Follow My Secret Heart 1934.34, 1986.19
I'll Follow the Rule 1893.03
I'll Follow You 1909.09
I'll Forget to Remember the Rest 1908.29
I'll Forget You 1997.19, 1999.13
I'll Get it Back if I Have to Follow Him to the Ends of the Earth 1911.28
I'll Get My Man 1930.11
I'll Get You Yet 1910.18
I'll Get You Yet, Cigarette 1915.23
I'll Give My Love a Ring 1969.04, 1980.01
I'll Give the World to You 1925.44
I'll Give Ye to Next Michaelmas 1897.03
I'll Give You Three Chances to Guess 1891.14
I'll Go Home With Bonnie Jean 1947.07, 1980.26
I'll Go the Route for You 1909.26
I'll Hate to Leave the Boys 1917.14
I'll Have Money to Burn 1896.37
I'll Have My Way 1920.11
I'll Have the Law, I'll Have My Rights 1903.02
I'll Hit a New High 1930.28
I'll Keep a Warm Spot in My Heart for You 1906.14
I'll Keep on Dreaming 1926.27
I'll Know 1950.17
I'll Know Him 1930.11
I'll Lead You Such a Dance 1897.37
I'll Learn Ya 1961.21
I'll Lend You Everything I've Got Except My Wife 1910.18, 1955.19
I'll Love Them All to Death 1928.48
I'll Make a Man of the Man 1966.27
I'll Make a Man of You 1964.28
I'll Make a Ring 'Round Rosie 1910.08
I'll Make an Angel Out of You 1918.20
I'll Make Bubbles 1920.07
I'll Make You Like the Town 1915.27
I'll Marry Him for Love 1913.28
I'll Meet You, Dan 1883.07
I'll Miss You, Old Ireland, God Bless You, Goodbye 1912.06
I'll Name My Dolly for You 1922.13
I'll Ne'er Forget 1882.33
I'll Never be a Soldier 1870.05
I'll Never be Jealous Again 1954.05
I'll Never be Lonely Again 1965.28
I'll Never Complain 1930.36
I'll Never Fall in Love Again 1968.31, 1974.22
I'll Never Forget 1929.20
I'll Never Go There Anymore 1965.01
I'll Never Lay Down Anymore 1967.05
I'll Never Learn 1950.04
I'll Never Leave You 1930.30, 1985.15
I'll Never Make a Frenchman Out of You 1951.13
I'll Never Pass This Way Again 1999.08
I'll Never Ride Again 1868.03
I'll Never Say No 1960.20
I'll Never Smile Again 1974.11, 1979.24
I'll Never Stop Loving You 1974.10
I'll Never Turn Back No Mo' 1943.10
I'll Not Let Love Disparage Marriage 1914.28
I'll Not Marry 1965.31
I'll only Miss Her When I Think of Her 1965.33
I'll Only Miss Him When I Think of Him 1974.10
I'll Pay the Check 1939.13
I'll Peek-a-boo You 1927.14
I'll Pin My Medal on the Girl I Left Behind 1918.19
I'll Produce for You 1934.20
I'll Put a Tax 1900.20
I'll Putcha Pitcha in the Paper 1931.14
I'll Remember Her 1963.29

I'll Remember You 1919.29
I'll Return for You 1921.33
I'll Say I Love You 1921.33
I'll Say I Will 1919.34
I'll Say She Does 1918.05
I'll Say So 1920.01
I'll See You Again 1929.41, 1974.09, 1986.19
I'll See You in C-U-B-A 1919.18
I'll Share it All With You 1946.12, 1999.04
I'll Show Him 1955.01, 1971.21
I'll Show Them All 1963.12
I'll Show You a Wonderful World 1919.43
I'll shut my eyes 1878.16
I'll Shut My Eyes and Think it's You 1902.18
I'll Sing and Dance 1917.24, 1919.20
I'll Sing You a Song 1952.05
I'll Stand Beneath Your Window Tonight and Whistle 1922.23
I'll String Along With You 1989.21
I'll Take an Option on You 1933.15
I'll Take Care of Him 1919.23
I'll Take Care of You 1929.50
I'll Take Care of You, Grandma 1898.45
I'll Take the City 1941.13
I'll Take the Solo 1944.18
I'll Take You All 1914.33
I'll Take You Back to Italy 1917.22
I'll Take You Home Again Kathleen 1980.27
I'll Take You to the Country 1928.27
I'll Talk to Her 1989.05
I'll Teach You How 1907.53
I'll Tell Papa 1938.06
I'll Tell the Man in the Street 1938.05, 1975.13
I'll Tell the World 1918.05, 1921.08, 1922.20, 1952.13
I'll Tell You 1930.15
I'll Tell You a Truth 1966.18
I'll Tell You About My Family 1984.02
I'll Tell You All Someday 1927.26
I'll Think of You 1918.11, 1976.25
I'll Travel the Links With You 1906.20
I'll Treat You Just Like a Sister 1921.32
I'll Try 1959.01
I'll Turn a Little Cog 1947.08
I'll Wait My Love, for Thee 1890.21
I'll Walk Alone 1974.10
I'll Wear the Trousers, Oh! 1880.09, 1893.10
I'm 'Enery the VIII, I Am 1960.17
I'm a Bachelor 1920.32
I'm a Bad Character 1972.10
I'm a Bad, Bad Man 1946.12, 1966.12
I'm a Big Director at Pinafore 1945.09
I'm a Bohemian 1905.40
I'm a Brass Band 1966.01, 1976.07
I'm a Butter Hoarder 1943.18
I'm a Captain Bold and Haughty 1897.26
I'm a Chappie 1885.08
I'm a cherry sweet to taste 1881.04
I'm a Crazy Daffy-Dill 1911.24
I'm a Cuban Girl 1909.04
I'm a Dancing Fool 1920.33
I'm a Dandy Colored Coon 1894.46
I'm a dashing pirate 1887.43
I'm a Devil 1889.34
I'm a Devil With the Ladies 1923.02
I'm a Duchess 1906.47
I'm a Fan 1983.17
I'm a Fascinating Notary 1885.58, 1896.35
I'm a Fickle Maid 1906.29
I'm a Fisher Maiden 1903.29
I'm a Flapper 1923.13
I'm a Fool for You 1928.16
I'm a Fool, Little One 1928.16
I'm a Funny Dame 1956.16
I'm a Giant's Little Baby 1896.41
I'm a Gigolo 1929.51
I'm a Good Old Girl 1957.09
I'm a Great Big Baby 1978.21
I'm a Greenwich Village Chambermaid 1923.04
I'm a Gypsy Blonde 1934.17
I'm a Gypsy Maid 1884.11
I'm a Harum Scarum Boy 1889.46
I'm a High-Toned Genii 1900.01
I'm a Humorist 1899.30
I'm a Hunting Jaguar 1913.31
I'm a Hustler Just the Same 1884.66, 1886.11
I'm a Jolly Little Chap All Round 1888.38
I'm a Jolly Old Tar 1869.07
I'm a Judge of the Modern Society Sort 1894.33
I'm a King With a Capital K 1890.26
I'm a King With a Crown 1892.55
I'm a Lady 1902.24, 1911.45
I'm a Lady, Yes I Am 1894.37
I'm a Lawyer 1906.44
I'm a Leader of Society 1900.25
I'm a Little Bit Fonder of You 1930.05
I'm a Little Blackbird Looking for a Blue Bird 1924.37
I'm a Little Blackbird Looking for a Bluebird 1980.10
I'm a Little English Daisy 1904.04
I'm a Little Lady 1899.21
I'm a Lonesome Little Raindrop 1920.28
I'm a Lonesome Romeo 1912.44
I'm a long-tailed Fish 1877.20
I'm a Loyal Native Son 1978.07
I'm a Man of Reputation 1942.33
I'm a Manicurist 1923.38
I'm a Merry Little Mountain Maid 1884.42, 1886.47, 1888.36
I'm a Merry Maiden 1904.40
I'm a Military Man 1906.47
I'm a Millionaire 1902.33, 1914.32, 1928.31
I'm a Mischievous Girl 1907.39
I'm a Natural Born Hoodoo 1906.31
I'm a Naughty Girl 1899.39
I'm a Nobby Little Swell 1869.07
I'm a nobleman of Mexico 1889.10
I'm a Parish Clerk 1853.01
I'm a Peaceable Party 1904.09
I'm a Person Too 1976.07
I'm a Pinkerton Man 1963.22
I'm a Poor Unhappy Maid 1903.04
I'm a Popular Man 1897.25, 1907.20
I'm a Practical Politician 1898.01
I'm a prim little Puritan maiden 1894.03
I'm a Prince 1900.42
I'm a Real Carnegie Hero 1907.61
I'm a Regular New York Stunner 1860.05
I'm a Respectable Working Girl 1900.38
I'm a Rover of the Sea 1892.29
I'm a Rular 1906.14
I'm a Scion of the House of Highball 1900.47
I'm a Self-Made Nobleman 1899.06
I'm a Sergeant of Police 1905.19
I'm a Simple Author-Manager 1902.15
I'm a Statesman 1914.15
I'm a Stranger Here Myself 1943.19, 1995.12
I'm a Terrible Squaw 1920.18
I'm a Terror to All 1888.40
I'm a Two-Horse Fellow in a One-Horse Town 1908.15
I'm a Vamp from East Broadway 1920.18
I'm a Very Fly Conductor 1895.38
I'm a Very Good Soldier on Land 1904.47
I'm a Waterloo-House Young Man 1881.37
I'm a Woman 1979.09, 1983.20, 1989.02, 1995.03
I'm a Woman of Importance 1905.41
I'm a Wonderful Man in Yonkers 1911.41
I'm a Wonderfully Wicked Woman 1975.05
I'm a Yankee Doodle Dandy 1978.05, 1979.13
I'm A'Tingle, I'm A'Glow 1949.18
I'm About to be a Mother 1931.48
I'm Abu-el-Hassan 1900.37
I'm Afraid 1930.05, 1940.06
I'm Afraid I'm in Love 1944.18
I'm Afraid of the Dark 1934.03
I'm afraid there is somebody looking 1889.54
I'm Afraid to Come Home in the Dark 1908.11
I'm Afraid to Go Home in the Dark 1907.59
I'm Against Rhythm 1937.16
I'm Alive 1971.14
I'm All Ablaze 1980.01
I'm All Alone 1925.04
I'm All for Love 1911.35
I'm All I've Got 1962.14
I'm All O.K. With K. & E. 1909.26
I'm All Right 1899.17, 1910.22
I'm All Smiles 1965.36
I'm All That's Left of the First Pony Ballet 1910.16
I'm All the Way from Gay Paree 1896.48
I'm All Thine 1911.23
I'm All Yours 1950.02
I'm alone 1868.01
I'm Alone 1951.22
I'm Already Gone 1983.15
I'm Always Chasing Rainbows 1918.07, 1976.24
I'm Always Happy When I'm in Your Arms 1932.12
I'm Always Happy With a Crowd of Girls 1918.32
I'm Always Wrong 1966.09
I'm an Actor 1971.04
I'm an American Billionaire 1901.17
I'm an Anaesthetic Dancer 1919.25
I'm an Indian 1918.24
I'm an Indian Too 1946.12, 1966.12
I'm an International Orphan 1935.03
I'm an Ordinary Man 1956.01, 1993.18
I'm as Good as I Ought to Be 1903.04
I'm as sharp as a ferret 1882.63
I'm Atingle, I'm Aglow 1995.07
I'm Awaiting My Love's Return 1887.23
I'm Awfully Strong for You 1907.37, 1908.14
I'm Back in Circulation 1931.26, 1959.01
I'm Bad 1918.24
I'm Beautiful 1961.02
I'm Beginning to See the Light 1981.06, 1997.03
I'm Blue 1944.33, 1971.15
I'm Blue Too 1967.14
I'm Bluff King Hal 1904.30
I'm Born in the Country 1940.01
I'm Breaking Down 1992.09
I'm Breathless 1942.16
I'm Bringing a Red, Red Rose 1928.47, 1979.05
I'm bubbled 1750.01, 1854.06
I'm Bugs Over You 1923.38
I'm Building Up to an Awful Let-Down 1992.18
I'm Built for Speed 1915.20
I'm called little Buttercup 1879.05
I'm Called Little Buttercup 1945.08
I'm Calm 1962.12
I'm Checkin' Home Now 1937.08
I'm Checking Out Goombye 1981.06
I'm cheerful and happy 1880.54
I'm Chock Full of Electricity 1894.05
I'm Columbia, understand 1851.03
I'm Comin' Virginia 1927.32
I'm Coming 'Round to Your Point of View 1981.24
I'm Coming Home 1951.22
I'm Confessing That I Love You 1989.02
I'm Countin' on You 1972.09
I'm Craving for That Kind of Love 1978.21
I'm Crazy Over You 1909.05
I'm Crazy to Go on the Stage 1902.15
I'm Crazy When the Band Begins to Play 1908.39, 1909.15
I'm Cured 1914.15
I'm Descended from Brian Boru 1902.25
I'm Doctor Puff 1878.20
I'm Doin' it for Defense 1997.05
I'm Don Hypolito Lopez Pomposo 1866.07
I'm Dreaming of a Wonderful Night 1915.18
I'm Dreaming While We're Dancing 1935.11
I'm Dying for You 1910.34
I'm Dying to Dance With Oscar 1918.22
I'm Engaged 1972.04
I'm Everybody's Baby 1955.25
I'm Excelsior 1895.38
I'm Falling in Love 1931.09
I'm Falling in Love With Someone 1910.35, 1978.19, 1988.18
I'm Fancy Free 1910.27
I'm Fascinating 1962.04
I'm Feeling Blue 1931.11
I'm Flyin' High 1928.23
I'm Flying 1954.13, 1979.22, 1983.09, 1989.03, 1990.20
I'm Fond of the Girls 1918.22
I'm for You - Eva Tanguay 1905.40
I'm Fraid dis Snap is Most too Good to Last 1899.38
I'm free 1972.08
I'm Free 1993.06, 1998.13
I'm Fresh from the Country 1922.26
I'm from Chicago 1915.18

I'm from Granada 1930.35
I'm from the Court of the Empress Queen 1912.10
I'm Gay 1976.20
I'm Georgie Tree 1898.31
I'm Gettin' so Thirsty 1900.58
I'm Getting 'Long Alright 1989.02
I'm Getting a Big Boy Now 1880.37
I'm Getting More Devilish 1898.61
I'm Getting Myself Ready for You 1930.40, 1998.05
I'm Getting Quite American, Don't You Know 1902.24
I'm Getting Sentimental Over You 1974.22
I'm Getting Tired so I Can Sleep 1942.20
I'm Glad I Waited 1930.39
I'm Glad I'm Leaving 1953.01
I'm Glad I'm Not Methusalem 1903.07
I'm Glad I'm Not Young Anymore 1963.02, 1965.08, 1973.12
I'm Glad I'm Single 1961.27, 1972.05
I'm Glad I'm Spanish 1921.34
I'm Glad My Home is in the States 1911.02
I'm Glad My Wife's in the Country 1914.22
I'm Glad There is You 1981.16
I'm Glad to be Back Again 1920.24
I'm Glad to Get Back to New York 1908.07
I'm Glad to See You Got What You Want 1969.02
I'm Glad You Didn't Know Me 1982.08
I'm Goin' Back 1956.14
I'm Goin' Back to Dixie 1912.09
I'm Goin' South 1921.34, 1923.12
I'm Goin' to Go, Go, Go 1913.35
I'm Goin' to Live Anyhow, 'Til I Die 1980.27
I'm Goin' to Testify 1963.27
I'm Going Away 1909.16, 1913.20
I'm Going Back 1924.19
I'm Going Back to Bottomland 1927.30
I'm Going Back to Carolina 1907.19
I'm Going Back to Dixieland 1903.14
I'm Going Back to Mobile, Alabam 1918.13
I'm Going Crazy With Strauss 1940.04
I'm Going Home 1909.16, 1975.07, 2000.17
I'm Going to be a Conductor 1894.51
I'm Going to be a Marquis 1904.03
I'm Going to be Lonesome 1919.33
I'm Going to be Married Today 1925.21
I'm Going to Change My Man 1903.07
I'm Going to Dance at Your Wedding 1924.47
I'm Going to Find a Girl Someday 1917.17
I'm Going to Join the Musketeers 1921.15
I'm Going to Love, Honor and O'Baby 1920.33
I'm Going to Marry a Nobleman 1908.14
I'm Going to Sit Right Down and Write Myself a Letter 1981.16
I'm Going to Soliloquize 1897.25
I'm Going to the Sea 1909.20
I'm Going to Wait Until the Right One Comes Along 1925.10
I'm Gone Before I Go 1916.10
I'm Gonna 1972.19
I'm Gonna be a Pop 1952.13
I'm Gonna be John Henry 1957.09
I'm Gonna do What the Spirit Say Do 1999.09
I'm Gonna Get Him 1962.20
I'm Gonna Git Down on My Knees 1940.01
I'm Gonna Hit the Numbers Today 1938.19
I'm Gonna Leave Off Wearing My Shoes 1954.19
I'm Gonna Love You Tonight 1999.24
I'm Gonna Make a Fool Out of April 1950.14
I'm Gonna Move 1964.18
I'm Gonna Move to the Outskirts of Town 1945.07
I'm Gonna Sit Right Down and Write Myself a Letter 1978.09
I'm Gonna Take Her Home to Momma 1981.14
I'm Gonna Take My Bimbo Back to the Bamboo Isle 1927.30
I'm Gonna Tell God All My Troubles 1976.04
I'm Gonna Walk Right Up to Her 1965.01
I'm Gonna Wash That Man Right Outa My Hair 1949.04, 1993.16
I'm Good for Nothing But Love 1931.19
I'm Grover 1930.18, 1930.33
I'm Growing Fond of You 1907.46
I'm Gwine to Marry Angeline 1900.48, 1900.55
I'm Happy 1964.03
I'm Harold, I'm Harold 1925.08
I'm Here, Little Girl, I'm Here 1917.01
I'm Hi, I'm Lo 1925.04
I'm Home 1984.02
I'm Honest 1930.19
I'm Hungry for Beautiful Girls 1922.15
I'm Hunkey Dorey 1865.03
I'm in a dreadful state of mind 1864.13
I'm in a Position to Know 1909.12
I'm in League With the Devil 1958.04
I'm in lofe 1878.02
I'm in Lofe 1896.35
I'm in London Again 1965.02
I'm in Love 1926.12, 1929.17, 1929.45
I'm in Love Again 1924.32
I'm in Love With a Soldier Boy 1943.01
I'm in Love With a Wonderful Guy 1949.04, 2000.16
I'm in Love With All the Girls I Know 1909.02
I'm in Love With Miss Logan 1952.09
I'm in Love With One of the Stars 1909.26
I'm in Love With the Beautiful Bugs 1903.29
I'm in Love With Vienna 1975.22
I'm in Love With You 1910.18, 1919.41, 1922.23, 1924.01
I'm in Love! I'm in Love! 1970.15
I'm in Love, Dear 1921.24
I'm in My Glory 1923.47
I'm in Search of a Novelty 1906.23
I'm in the Mood 1940.07
I'm in Wonderland 1924.17
I'm Jotte, the Dressmaker 1916.20
I'm Just a Bit Confused 1956.07
I'm Just a Doorstep Baby 1931.21
I'm Just a Good Man 1918.07
I'm Just a Little Girl from Little Rock 1974.02, 1995.07
I'm Just a Little Indian, Nothing More 1895.25
I'm Just a Little Sparrow 1960.10
I'm Just a Lonesome Vampire 1919.18
I'm Just a Lucky so and So 1997.03
I'm Just a Lucky so-and-So 1981.06
I'm Just About as I Ought to Be 1904.50
I'm Just as Young as I Used to Be 1887.05, 1893.31
I'm Just Crazy 'Bout You 1908.08
I'm Just Looking for a Lonesome Boy 1921.35
I'm Just Out of My Teens 1911.07
I'm Just Simply Full of Jazz 1978.21
I'm Just Taking My Time 1961.28
I'm Just Wild About Harry 1921.16, 1942.13, 1952.08, 1975.22, 1978.21, 1979.13, 1986.06
I'm Keeping Myself Available for You 1979.24
I'm King Ding Dong 1868.03
I'm King of the Shoddy Contractors 1864.12
I'm Knee Deep in Daisies 1925.38
I'm Learning Something Every Day 1908.39, 1909.15
I'm Leavin' Texas 1994.06
I'm Leaving the Bad Girls for Good 1937.06
I'm Leaving You 1997.08
I'm Like a New Broom 1951.14
I'm like a skiff 1854.06
I'm Like a Skiff on the Ocean Toss'd 1957.02
I'm like Skiff on the Ocean tost 1750.01
I'm Like the Bluebird 1964.15
I'm Listenin', Lord 1943.02
I'm Lonely for Only One 1915.05
I'm Lonely When I'm Alone 1919.28
I'm Lookin' for an Angel 1902.27
I'm Looking All Over for You 1924.08
I'm Looking for a Daddy Long Legs 1922.39
I'm Looking for a Girl Like Venus 1914.17
I'm Looking for a Little Girl Who's Looking for a Man 1910.10
I'm Looking for a Man 1979.03
I'm Looking for a Sweetheart 1908.26, 1908.41, 1913.18
I'm Looking for an Angel 1900.58
I'm Looking for an Irish Husband 1913.26
I'm Looking for Someone to Love 1990.15
I'm Looking for Someone's Heart 1915.02
I'm Looking for Something 1981.29
I'm Losing My Heart to Someone 1920.14
I'm Lost 1948.18, 1992.11
I'm Loving 1929.01
I'm Lucky 1902.33
I'm Madame Kapinski 1915.29
I'm Madly in Love With a Dream 1917.14
I'm Making a Bid for Popularity 1898.50, 1899.17
I'm Married Now 1907.10
I'm Married, I'm Single, I'm Divorced and I'm in Love 1918.06
I'm Matthew P. Brady, the Camera Man 1963.22
I'm Me 1959.06
I'm Momm's Pet 1902.32
I'm Monarch Here 1859.11
I'm Neutral 1915.16
I'm Ninety-Eight Pounds of Sweetness 1928.34
I'm No Angel 2000.12
I'm No Butterfly 1925.04
I'm No Stingy Romeo 1908.21
I'm Not a Ladies' Maid 1909.29
I'm Not Alone 1988.12
I'm Not at All in Love 1954.05
I'm Not at Liberty to Tell 1902.08
I'm Not Finished Yet 1966.06
I'm Not in Love 1948.30
I'm Not in Love With You 1921.09
I'm Not Jealous (But I Just Don't Like It) 1918.05
I'm Not Myself 1934.19
I'm Not Myself Tonight 1946.22
I'm Not Particular 1906.22
I'm Not Saying a Word 1993.07
I'm Not so Bright 1948.08
I'm Not That Kind of a Girl 1909.15
I'm Not Through 1972.07
I'm not ugly, I'm not old 1859.16
I'm Not Very Pretty 1890.21
I'm O'Donohue from Nowhere 1884.42
I'm Often at Maxim's 1978.07
I'm Old Enough for a Little Loving 1918.13
I'm Old Enough to Know Better and Young Enough Not to Care 1957.01
I'm Old Enough to Think 1909.14
I'm Old Fashioned 1997.05
I'm Old-Fashioned 1986.01, 1990.09
I'm on a spree, Sir 1868.08
I'm on My Way 1935.13, 1951.24
I'm on My Way to Mandalay 1913.05
I'm on the Lookout 1948.30
I'm on the Water Wagon Now 1903.34
I'm One Little Party 1927.52, 1981.03
I'm One of God's Children 1930.42
I'm One of the Smart Ones 1974.01
I'm One of Your Admirers 1953.11
I'm Only a Girl from the City 1918.22
I'm Only a Little Dutch Girl 1884.11
I'm Only a Poor Little Kid 1918.08
I'm Only a Poor Singing Girl 1898.46
I'm only joking 1893.02
I'm Only the Caddie 1903.22
I'm Only Thinking of Him 1965.34
I'm Only Waiting My Chance 1909.12
I'm Oriental 1920.47
I'm Past My Prime 1956.12
I'm Physical, You're Cultured 1942.29
I'm Pommery Second the King 1892.55
I'm Proud I'm Irish 1896.14
I'm Ready 1966.30
I'm Ready to Begin Again 1979.30
I'm Ready to Quit and be Good 1911.25
I'm Really Not That Way 1932.13
I'm Romantic 1902.01
I'm Running After Nancy 1908.05
I'm Running Wild 1907.31
I'm Satisfied 1922.19
I'm Saving My Kisses 1912.09
I'm Scared of You 1923.06
I'm Seeking the Siegfried 1914.22
I'm Setting My Cap for a Throne 1945.01
I'm Seventeen Come Sunday 1922.21
I'm Seventeen Today 1892.29
I'm Shooting High 1979.25
I'm Shy 1886.35
I'm simple little maid 1889.54
I'm Simply Crazy Over You 1915.17
I'm Simply Full of Jazz 1921.16
I'm Simply Mad About the Boys 1923.10
I'm Singing About a Man 1940.01

I'm Sitting on Top of the World 1925.23, 1962.17, 1986.06
I'm Small 1972.18
I'm Smiling at the Moon That Smiles at You 1912.31
I'm so Busy 1917.01
I'm so Dizzy 1904.24
I'm so Excited 1921.32
I'm so Fond of a Little Bit of Fun 1900.43
I'm so Glad 1975.02
I'm so Happy 1904.15
I'm so Humble 1926.50
I'm so in Love 1934.40
I'm so Lonely 1877.05
I'm so Lonesome 1904.39
I'm so Particular 1908.10
I'm so Sad 1885.06
I'm so Shy 1909.05
I'm so Stylish 1871.17
I'm so Sympathetic 1919.34
I'm so Upset 1902.41
I'm so Weary 1914.12
I'm so Weary of it All 1939.07, 1952.11
I'm Sober 1914.31
I'm Somebody 1981.29
I'm Sorry 1906.29
I'm Sorry Says the Machine 1971.20
I'm Stepping Out of the Picture 1934.39
I'm Stepping Out With Lulu 1927.38
I'm Still Here 1971.05, 1977.05
I'm Still Single 1915.05
I'm Stuck With Love 1959.19
I'm Such a Little Fool 1879.56
I'm Such a Modest Maiden 1906.48
I'm Such a Romantic Girl 1911.36
I'm Sure of Your Love 1945.20
I'm Sure She Said Six-Thirty 1973.08
I'm Sure to Astonish You All 1881.11
I'm Taking the Steps to Russia 1938.13
I'm Talking to My Pal 1989.16
I'm Tellin' the Birds, Tellin' the Bees 1925.01
I'm Telling You, Louie! 1935.03
I'm That Way Over You 1929.44
I'm the Belle of the Ballet 1946.15
I'm the Best if I Know, Says the Queen 1887.32
I'm the Boom, Boom, Boomer 1915.29
I'm the Boy 1897.04, 1905.37, 1956.13
I'm the Bravest Individual 1966.01
I'm the Brother of the Lily of the Valley 1917.23
I'm the Captain 1884.14
I'm the Captain of the Mineola Guards 1908.15
I'm the Cock of the Walk 1910.18
I'm the Daughter of Annie Rooney 1905.25
I'm the Daughter of the Leader of the Band 1897.40
I'm the Doctor 1907.52
I'm the Emperor of Japan 1939.15, 1939.17
I'm the Fellow 1920.14
I'm the Fellow Who Loves You 1935.18
I'm the First Girl 1948.08
I'm the Girl 1950.03
I'm the Greatest Star 1964.11
I'm the Guy 1918.14
I'm the Guy Who Guards the Harem 1919.15
I'm the Heavy-Bearded Villain 1896.26
I'm the Hostess of a Bum Cabaret 1919.18
I'm the Human Brush That Paints the Crimson on Paree 1911.12
I'm the Human Night-Key of New York 1908.07
I'm the King of Bakers 1904.05
I'm the Last of the Red Hot Mamas 1979.25
I'm the Leading Lady 1907.12
I'm the Luckiest Girl Alive 1951.05
I'm the Major Bozo 1925.25
I'm the Man 1898.16, 1906.45
I'm the Manager of the Show 1899.12
I'm the Miller's Daughter 1905.32
I'm the Milliner Monarch of Paris 1905.04
I'm the Most Popular Barber in Town 1942.33
I'm the Old Man in the Moon 1917.26
I'm the One 1924.31
I'm the only one that's left of all the Family 1882.44
I'm the Original Devil 1908.38
I'm the Patsy Bolivar of the World 1913.23
I'm the Princess 1887.32
I'm the Queen of England 1869.42
I'm the Seventh Son of a Seventh Son 1898.48
I'm the Sheriff 1922.44
I'm the Sultan's Vigilant Vizier 1900.37
I'm Thinking of Love 1941.02
I'm Through With Girls 1918.06
I'm Through With Roaming Romeos 1913.34
I'm Throwing a Ball Tonight 1940.19, 1984.10, 1998.05
I'm Thru With War 1927.43
I'm Tickled Pink 1943.18
I'm Tickled Silly 1921.10
I'm Tired 1901.13
I'm Tired of Eatin' in Restaurants 1908.08
I'm Tired of Texas 1948.08
I'm to be a Blushing Bride 1911.30
I'm to be Married Today 1918.03
I'm too Delicate to Work 1882.33
I'm Trying 1920.14
I'm Unlucky 1902.16, 1916.04
I'm Unlucky at Gambling 1929.45
I'm Up in the Air Over You 1921.27
I'm Waiting for You 1915.08, 1925.30
I'm Walkin' the Chalk Line 1933.27
I'm Way Ahead 1973.06
I'm Way Ahead of the Game 1964.04
I'm Wide Awake When I Dream 1931.29
I'm Wild About Horns on Automobiles That Go 'Ta-Ta-Ta-Ta' 1928.47
I'm Wild About Myself 1922.34
I'm Willie Off the Yacht 1896.37
I'm Wise 1907.12
I'm Wishing 1975.12, 1979.28
I'm With You 1931.19, 1964.21
I'm Wondering 1917.09
I'm Worried to Death About That 1904.43
I'm Worse Than Anybody 1962.01
I'm Wrong 1965.30
I'm You 1936.01
I'm Your Girl 1953.08
I'm Your Hootchie Coochie Man 1999.09
I'm Your Man 1948.25
I'm Yours 1930.08, 1931.08
I'se Been A-lookin' for You 1902.40
I'se Coming to Town, Honey 1896.45
I'se Found Yo', Honey, Found Yo', Now be Mine 1899.11
I'se Gwine to Save To' Soul 1901.30
I'se Gwine to Talk 1922.44
I'se Johannes Jerome, oh! oh! 1865.03
I'se Juliet 1906.13
I'se Promoter of the Coon Society 1900.46
I've a Garden in Sweden 1911.13
I've a Little Bit of Scotch in Me 1917.08
I've a Million Reasons Why I Love You 1907.32
I've a most decided notion 1896.13
I've a motion 1884.60
I've a Shooting Box in Scotland 1916.06
I've a Sweetheart in Each Star 1919.18
I've a Very Nasty Temper 1907.07
I've A'ready Started In 1960.20
I've Always Been a Good Old Sport 1909.26
I've Always Been Bad Since I was a Lad 1888.41
I've Always Been Brought Up Polite 1896.05
I've Always Loved You 1955.25
I've an Awful Lot to Learn 1916.06
I've an Inkling 1900.51, 1902.05
I've Been Buked 1990.05
I've Been Decorated 1908.24, 1909.23
I've Been Discharged by Them All 1908.03
I've Been Dreaming of You, Baby 1899.38
I've Been Hoodooed 1895.27
I've Been Invited to a Party 1963.29
I've Been Living With the Blues 1999.09
I've Been Looking for a Girl Like You 1911.42
I've Been Looking for a Perfect Man 1911.38
I've Been Looking for You 1914.17
I've Been Married Once 1909.09
I've Been Sent Back to the First Grade 1971.10
I've Been There and I'm Back 1958.02
I've Been to a Marvelous Party 1939.07, 1952.11
I've Been to America 1913.04
I've Been Told 1908.05
I've Been too Busy 1956.02
I've Been Waiting 1922.03
I've Been Waiting All My Life 1978.27
I've Been Waiting for You All the Time 1919.09
I've Been Wanting You 1923.02
I've Booked the Date 1895.08
I've Brushed My Teeth 1933.25
I've Come Along to Paris 1906.36
I've Come Back to the Fold 1963.27
I've Come Home to Stay 1890.49, 1985.02
I've Come to Wive it Wealthily in Padua 1948.32, 1999.19
I've Confessed to the Breeze 1971.03
I've Danced to Beat the Band 1919.01
I've Fallen Out of Love 1932.15
I've Found the Bluebird 1925.50
I've Found the Girl That I've Been Looking For 1919.22
I've Given My Heart to You, Dear 1917.18
I've Gone Romantic on You 1937.15
I've Got 'Em Standin' in Line 1963.12
I've Got a Baby 1928.35
I've Got a Crush on You 1928.43, 1930.02, 1999.10
I've Got a Date With a Dream 1982.12
I've Got a Feelin' You're Foolin' 1985.08, 1986.06
I've Got a Feeling I'm Falling 1978.09, 1980.10
I've Got a Letter from My Jack 1881.11
I've Got a Little Hubby Now 1905.46
I've Got a Little List 1939.15, 1939.17
I've Got a Lot to Learn About Life 1959.12
I've Got a Molly 1973.11
I've Got a Pair of Swinging Doors That Lead Right into My Heart 1919.02
I've Got a Rainbow 1928.43
I've Got a Rainbow Working for Me 1968.02
I've Got a Right to Sing the Blues 1932.18, 1989.02
I've Got a Sentry 1920.24
I've Got a Sweet Tooth Bothering Me 1916.09
I've Got a Yes Girl 1927.27
I've Got Another Baby 1898.78
I've Got Ants in My Pants 1931.26
I've Got Elgin Watch Movements in My Hips 1975.09
I've Got Enough to Marry You 1916.21
I've Got Everything I Want But You 1914.06
I've Got Five Dollars 1931.04, 1975.13
I've Got Good Common Sense 1907.29, 1907.31
I've Got Harlem on My Mind 1933.22
I've Got Him Now 1914.15
I've Got it All 1978.02
I've Got Me 1946.24, 1948.17
I've Got Money in the Bank 1913.26
I've Got My Captain Working for Me Now 1919.15, 1919.19
I've Got My Fingers Crossed 1978.09
I've Got My Habits On 1921.27
I've Got My Orders 1979.18
I've Got Nothin' to Do 1964.35
I've Got Rhythm 1958.10
I've Got Rings on My Fingers 1909.11
I've Got Some Unfinished Business With You 1941.08
I've Got Somebody Waiting 1919.25
I've Got Something 1975.22
I've Got the Nerve to be in Love 1937.14
I've Got the Nicest Little Home in Dixie 1916.21
I've Got the President's Ear 1948.28
I've Got the Red, White and Blues 1922.03
I've Got the Sun in the Morning 1995.12
I've Got the Words - I've Got the Tune 1931.30
I've Got the World on a String 1984.06
I've Got Them Feelin' too Good Today Blues 1978.05
I've Got Those Runnin' Wild Blues 1922.44
I've Got to be a Rug Cutter 1981.06, 1997.03
I've Got to be Around 1962.20
I've Got to be Good 1928.07
I've Got to be in Love 1937.14
I've Got to be Me 1968.03
I've Got to be There 1933.01
I've Got to Crow 1954.13, 1979.22, 1990.20
I've Got to Dance 1975.24
I've Got to Find a Reason 1961.10
I've Got to Get Hot 1935.18
I've Got to Give Her Her Own Way 1911.03
I've Got to Hand it to You 1941.13
I've Got to Leave You 1919.28

I've Got to Trust You 1972.02
I've Got Troubles of My Own 1900.48, 1900.55
I've Got What it Takes 1932.12
I've Got What it Takes, But it Breaks My Heart to Give it Away 1922.25
I've Got What You Want 1966.18
I've Got You on My Mind 1929.20
I've Got You to Lean On 1964.15
I've Got Your Number 1962.27, 1982.01, 1983.09, 1998.15
I've Gotta be Me 1974.11, 1992.16
I've Gotta Go Back to Texas 1914.31
I've Gotta See a Man About His Daughter 1934.42
I've grasped your scheme 1895.29
I've Grown Accustomed to Her Face 1956.01, 1961.25, 1993.18
I've had It 1986.11
I've Heard it All Before 1975.03
I've Heard so Much About You 1906.07
I've Heard That Before 1911.43
I've Heard That Song Before 1974.10
I've Her Portrait Nex' to My 'Eart 1897.37
I've jibe and joke and quip and crank 1888.35
I've Just Introduced Them 1885.54
I've Just Lost My Teddy Bear 1909.10
I've Just Seen Her 1962.04
I've Known a Lot of Guys 1984.02
I've Laid Him on de Shelf 1900.55
I've Lost Ma Baby 1901.28
I've Lost My Gal 1910.01
I've Lost My Heart 1931.14
I've Lost My Job 1922.21
I've Loved Only Once and the Girl was You 1915.21
I've loved thee long, Louise 1859.09
I've Made a Habit of You 1929.19, 1972.05
I've Never Been in Love Before 1950.17, 1980.29
I've Never Been Kept Waiting 1924.15
I've Never Been Over There 1906.11
I've Never Been to Flushing 1975.12
I've Never Heard About Love 1943.06
I've Never Said I Love You 1969.05
I've no money 1863.03
I've No Patience With a Soldier 1906.32
I've Nothing to Confess 1868.08
I've Nothing to Offer 1934.39
I've Said Good Bye to Broadway 1916.10
I've said it, sir, and law my will must be 1859.09
I've Saved All My Lovin' for You 1916.10
I've seen the battle field 1859.16
I've Shaken Everything I've Got 1920.24
I've Sharpen'd the Sword the Sake of Ould Erin 1897.03
I've songs of every style and fashion 1888.07
I've Still Got My Bite 1980.15
I've Still Got My Health 1940.19
I've struck Ile 1865.03
I've Taken Such a Fancy to You 1912.26
I've Told Every Little Star 1951.22, 1975.22, 1986.01
I've Told My Love 1919.06
I've Trampled All Over 1940.01
I've Travelled by Night and by Day 1894.05
I've Waited All My Life 1922.03
I've Waited Long for Thee 1908.42
I've Waited Long for You, Dear 1914.07
I've Waited, Honey Waited Long for You 1899.11
I've Wandered over many lands 1859.08
I, Don Quixote 1965.34
I, like a Ship in Storms, was tost 1750.01
I, Living I 1939.17
I, Yes Me, That's Who 1970.08
Ice 1989.23
Ice Cream 1947.02, 1971.21
Ice Mazurka 1926.17
Iceman works, The 1898.25
Icemoves 1978.26
Ich bin die fesche Lola 1999.07
Ich bin von Kopf bis Fuss aut Liebe eingestellt 1999.08
Ich brauch keine Professoren 1885.01
Ich Edwin Ronald-Hochzeitstanz-Ja so ein Teufelsweib 1984.05
Ich Liebe Dich 1894.26, 1944.21
Ich such' jetzt da, ich such' jetzt dort 1964.25
Ich warte auf das grosse Wunder-Machen wir's den Schwalben nach 1984.05
Ichabod 1948.18
Ici l'on peche 1935.19
Icicles, The 1931.06
Icy Moon 1989.21
Ida 1912.24
Ida Bell 1903.18
Ida! Sweet as Apple Cider 1919.24
Ida-ho 1904.14
Idaho 1906.40
Ideal Girls, The 1897.04
Idish 1960.18
Idle Colleen, The 1908.43
Idle Dreams 1920.17
Idles of the King 1926.13
Idol and the Maid, The 1903.19
Idol of Eyes 1915.23
Idol of Eyes, The 1915.23
Idyl, The 1879.15
If 1920.43, 1948.18
If 'Tis a Dream? 1890.16
If a Bachelor in Love Should Fall 1917.30
If a Girl isn't Pretty 1964.11
If a Lover is Poor 1866.21
If a Sudden Stroke of Fate 1900.37
If a Table at Rector's Could Talk 1913.17
If a Wish Could Make it So 1920.27
If a Woman is Curious 1882.33
If Adam Hadn't Seen the Apple Tree 1907.22
If all is as you say 1895.29
If All the Moons Were Honeymoons 1909.31
If All the Stars Were Mine 1899.30, 1903.21
If any Wench Venus's Girdle wear 1750.01
If Bill Gillette Could Only See Me Now 1906.21
If Cabby Told Half What He Knows 1900.40
If Central Should Talk in Her Sleep 1915.18
If Dreams Come True 1913.37
If Eve had Left the Apple on the Bough 1917.07
If Ever I Get Up My Irish 1923.37
If Ever I Marry 1902.01
If ever I should have a wife 1859.15
If Ever I Would Leave You 1960.21, 1980.19, 1993.11
If Ever You Want a Favor, Mention Me 1903.18
If Every Day was Sunday 1923.36
If Every Month Were June 1953.17
If Everyone Got What They Wanted 1973.11
If Flowers Could Speak 1924.10
If Flutterby Wins 1961.21
If Girls had Wings 1904.03
If He Knew 1980.21
If He Really Knew Me 1979.04
If He Really Loves Me 1931.01
If He Should Come 1922.04
If He Walked into My Life 1966.10, 1985.19, 1998.07
If He'll Come Back to Me 1927.16
If Hearts But Knew 1902.35
If I Again Would be a Baby 1903.15
If I be Your Best Chance 1966.27
If I Became President 1930.02
If I But Dared 1905.55
If I but dared to tell how much I loved 1859.09
If I But Knew 1902.44
If I But Knew! 1901.25
If I can catch this jolly Jack-Patch 1893.02
If I Can Dream 1989.12
If I Can't Get the Sweetie I Want I Pity the Sweetie I Get 1923.20
If I Can't Have You 1999.15
If I Can't Love Her 1994.04
If I Can't Sell it I'll Keep Sittin' on It 1989.02
If I Could be Beautiful 1980.11
If I Could Only Get a Chance to Cook 1900.42
If I Could Only Get a Decent Sleep 1897.30
If I Could Put You in a Song 1959.12
If I Could Read the Kisses Others Printed on Your Lips 1916.21
If I Could Teach My Teddy Bear to Dance 1908.35
If I Could Trust Me 1985.02
If I Could've Been 1978.12
If I Didn't Have You 1933.06
If I Ever Loved Him 1978.10
If I Fell 1977.10
If I Find the Girl 1915.31
If I Gave You 1964.16
If I Gave You a Rose 1928.04
If I Give Up the Saxophone Will You Come Back to Me? 1928.47
If I had a Beau 1860.03
If I had a Hammer 1966.03
If I had a Little Boy to Love Me 1901.12
If I had a Lover 1927.31
If I had a Million Dollars 1970.20
If I had Any Sense 1992.03
If I had My Druthers 1956.12
If I had Only Met You, Dear 1920.07
If I had the Wings of an Angel 1927.37
If I had You 1904.11, 1999.23
If I had You and You had Me 1924.07
If I Just Think of Her 1910.34
If I Knew 1960.20
If I Liken Thy Shape 1917.24
If I Love Again 1933.21
If I Love You 1955.13
If I Loved You 1945.05, 1993.16, 1997.01
If I Marry the King of France 1904.30
If I Never See You Again 1923.19
If I Never Waltz Again 1945.11
If I Only had a Brain 1984.06, 1989.06, 1997.11
If I Only had a Heart 1989.06, 1997.11
If I Only had a Mustache Like the Kaiser 1903.36
If I Only had a Theatre on Broadway 1904.49
If I Only had the Nerve 1989.06, 1997.11
If I Only had Your Heart 1998.19
If I Only Knew 1949.05
If I Only Knew the Way 1898.17
If I Ruled the World 1965.28
If I Should 1903.14
If I Should Dream of You When Out on the Desert 1911.36
If I Should Lose My Only Girl 1914.14
If I Should Say Good-Bye 1901.23
If I Told You 1923.05
If I was a Boy 1954.16
If I was a Dove 1976.11
If I was a Millionaire 1902.38
If I Were a Bell 1950.17, 1980.29
If I Were a Bird 1889.01
If I Were a Bright Little Star 1903.14
If I Were a Girl Instead 1902.35
If I Were a King 1895.33
If I Were a Man 1995.15
If I Were a Rich Man 1964.27, 1974.22
If I Were an Actress 1903.28
If I Were Anybody Else But Me 1910.35
If I Were Anyone Else But Me 1978.19, 1988.18
If I Were Called Upon to Rule 1897.21
If I Were King of Babylon 1905.27
If I Were King of the Forest 1989.06, 1997.11
If I Were of the Hoi Polloi 1924.04
If I Were on the Stage 1905.57, 1980.27
If I Were Only a Man 1913.28
If I Were Only Mr. Morgan 1903.11
If I Were Only You 1904.45
If I Were Really a King 1896.28
If I Were the Bride of a Soldier 1903.34
If I Were the Governor of Guam 1904.54
If I Were the King of the Forest 2000.14
If I Were the Man 1962.14
If I Were You 1892.57, 1898.69, 1926.51, 1928.02, 1930.42, 1962.04
If I Were You, Love 1930.39
If I Weren't King 1993.14
If I'm Goin' to Die, I'm Goin' to Have Some Fun 1907.20
If I've Got What You Want 1902.06
If in Your Dreams 1894.38
If it Ain't Love 1932.14
If it Feels Good, Let it Ride 1978.05
If it Hadn't Been for Me 1971.21
If it Makes You Happy 1961.16
If it wasn't for My Wife and Family 1917.34
If it wasn't for People 1961.16
If it wasn't for the Irish and the Jews 1912.07
If it wasn't for You There Wouldn't be Me 1999.23
If it Were Easy to Do 1947.20

If it Were True 1916.20
If it's a Dream 1955.10
If it's Good Enough for Lady Astor 1970.21
If it's Love 1934.39, 1946.07
If Jesus Don't Love Ya 1985.04
If Love in a Cottage be All That They Tell 1903.21
If Love Should Come to Me 1927.27
If Love the Virgin's Heart invade 1750.01
If Love Were All 1929.41, 1968.19, 1975.12, 1986.19
If Ma Says No 1904.29
If Menelaus Only Knew It 1944.16
If Momma was Married 1959.13, 1977.05
If Mr. Boston Lawson had His Way 1904.42
If Music and Sweet Poetry Agree 1981.02
If Music be the Food of Love 1981.02
If My Dream Came True 1924.37
If My Friends Could See Me Now 1966.01, 1976.07
If My Man Could do it for Me 1905.33
If My Morning Begins 1976.03
If ninety-nine percent the papers print 1898.25
If No. 1 Met No. 2 1908.17
If Not to You 1976.03
If One Little Girl Loves Me 1912.05
If One of us was You, Dear 1924.15
If Only 1948.27
If Only I Could be a Kid Again 1970.18
If Only I Were a Boy 1901.09
If Only I Were Santa Claus 1909.28
If Only You Cared for Me 1918.09
If Only You Would Take a Tip from Me 1910.09
If our action's stiff and crude 1893.02
If Patriotic Sentiment is wanted 1885.51
If Prayin' Were Horses 1999.08
If Saphir I Choose to Marry 1881.37
If She has Never Loved Before 1969.04, 1980.01
If She Means What I Think She Means 1918.19
If She Walked into My Life 1967.12
If some other sweetheart 1889.10
If somebody there chanced to be 1887.10
If That Ain't Winning a Home, I Don't Know 1897.40
If That Didn't do it, it Can't be Done 1979.15
If That was Love 1957.07
If that's not love - what is? 1896.27
If That's What You Want 1927.55
If the Birds 1966.15
If the Blues Don't Get You 1929.21
If the Fair is not Superfine 1871.19
If the Girl Wants You Never Mind the Color of Her Eyes 1909.01
If the Girlies Could be Soldiers 1915.16
If the Good Die Young 1916.21
If the heart of a man 1854.06
If the Heart of a Man 1957.02
If the Heart of a Man is deprest with Cares 1750.01
If the Man in the Moon was a Coon 1927.12
If the Man in the Moon Would Only Speak 1912.20
If the Morning After Were the Night Before 1912.31
If the Rain's Got to Fall 1965.14
If the Rain's Gotta Fall 1986.03
If the Sergeant Steals Your Rum 1964.28
If the Shoe Fits 1946.22
If the Sweetheart You Love Loves You 1894.05
If the World Were Like the Movies 1992.17
If There be Pardon in your Heart 1881.37
If There is a Lad 1893.19
If There is Someone Lovelier Than You 1934.38, 1972.05
If There Were No More You 1929.03
If There's Any Kind of Crime 1899.40
If There's Love Enough 1971.16
If They Could See Me Now 1984.06
If They Ever Parted Me from You 1918.37
If They Ever Put a Tax on Love 1917.23
If They'd Only Let Poor Adam's Rib Alone 1909.02
If They'd Only Move Old Ireland Over Here 1914.06
If Things Were Only Different 1907.49, 1926.03
If This be Love 1894.21
If This is Glamour! 1949.01
If This is Goodbye 1965.35
If This isn't Love 1947.03
If thus - A Man can die 1750.01
If true his tale 1855.06
If Washington Came to Life 1906.11
If We had had Met Before 1920.05
If We Knew What the Milkman Knows 1907.24
If We Only Could Stop the Old Town Clock 1951.18
If We Only Have Love 1972.16
If We Open Our Eyes 1994.06
If We Part 1904.36
If We Pass Beyond the Portals 1903.21
If We Were on Our Honeymoon 1913.20
If we're weak enough to tarry 1882.78
If well his suit is sped 1887.10
If Wishes Were Horses 1971.20
If Women had Their Way 1905.37
If You and I Should Meet 1893.19
If You are as Good as You Look 1925.38
If You are in Love With a Girl 1926.24
If You Ask Me the Reason 1888.19
If You Ask Me to Advise You 1900.37
If you at an Office solicit your Due 1750.01
If You Believe 1981.16
If You But Knew What I Know 1915.22
If You Can Love Like You Can Dance 1919.44
If You Can't be as Happy as You'd Like to be, be Just as Happy as You Can 1911.38
If You Can't Bring it You've Got to Send It 1925.18
If You Can't Get the Love You Want 1944.27
If You Can't Sing, Dance 1911.23
If You Care 1926.33
If You Could Care for Me 1920.03
If You Could Fancy Me 1911.29
If You Could Only Come With Me 1929.41
If You Could Only See Yourself as Other People Do 1910.12
If You Could Read My Mind 1974.01
If You Could See Her 1966.24, 1998.04
If You Couldn't Change Your Mind 1902.37
If You Didn't Love Me 1936.01
If You do it in the Proper Sort of Way 1898.43
If You do What You Do 1923.47
If You Don't Love Me Why do You Hang Around? 1913.18
If You Don't Mind 1982.13
If you examine human kind 1896.13
If you give me your attention 1884.09
If You Got Music 1957.01
If You Grow Tired, Little Girl 1907.14
If You had Seen 1975.23
If You Hadn't Answered No 1917.35
If You Hadn't But You Did 1958.20, 1958.21, 1977.02
If You Hadn't, But You Did 1951.19
If You Have Troubles, Laugh Them Away 1927.62
If You Haven't Been Vamped by a Brownskin, You Haven't Been Vamped at All 1921.16
If You Haven't Got a Sweetheart 1951.14
If You Haven't Got It 1927.23
If You Knew Susie 1923.47, 1925.01, 1925.07, 1975.22
If You Know What I Mean 1926.17
If You Know What I Think 1927.14
If You Lak-a Me Like I Lak-a You 1989.23
If You Leave 1935.19
If You Like Coffee and I Like Tea 1927.47
If You Like People 1972.02
If You Look Close 1979.19
If You Look in Her Eyes 1917.36, 1976.25
If You Love as I Love 1899.03
If You Love Me 1981.04
If You Love Me Lindy 1904.52
If You Love Me Truly 1897.31
If You Love Me, Marry Me 1912.49
If You Loved Me Truly 1953.07
If You Me as You Say 1876.30
If You Must Make Eyes at Someone 1907.41
If You Only Knew 1917.30
If You Only Knew How Much I Loved You 1906.41
If You Only Know the Way 1918.37
If You Only Know the Way to Pull the Wires 1904.49
If You Only Will 1912.14
If You or I should Tell the Truth 1900.37
If you please 1893.02
If You Propose to Propose 1914.20
If You Said What You Thought 1926.20
If You See a Devil Smash Him 1972.10
If You Should 1896.10
If You Smile at Me 1946.13
If You Take into Your Head 1886.45
If you take into your head 1886.53
If You Think it's Love You're Right 1924.34
If you think that a King 1857.06
If you think that when banded in unity 1894.15
If You Want a Deal With Russia 1943.14
If You Want a Kiss 1894.29
If You Want a Receipt for That Popular Mystery 1881.37
If You Want the Old Batallion 1964.28
If You Want to Break Your Father's Heart 1976.09
If You Want to Die in Bed 1991.03
If you want to know the secret 1889.10
If you want to know who we are 1885.47
If You Want to Know Who We Are 1937.09, 1939.17
If You Were I and I Were You 1902.04
If You Were I, and I Were You 1906.05
If You Were Lost to Me 1906.05
If You Were Mine 1913.23
If You Were Mine Alone 1904.30
If You Were Only Mine 1899.34
If You Were Someone Else 1937.10
If You Were Someone Else and Someone Else Were Only Here 1926.06
If You Were the Only Girl in the World 1916.10
If You Were There With Me 1910.25
If You Were Wondering 1979.11
If you will come to tea 1896.27
If You Will Spare the Time 1903.21
If You Wind Me Up 1970.07
If You Wish to Appear as an Irish Type 1902.25
If you wish to become that delectable creature 1886.40
If You Would Only Come Away 1943.24
If You'd be Happy, Don't Fall in Love 1928.27
If You'll Always Say Yes 1927.34
If You'll be Mine 1948.08
If You'll be My Eve I'll Build an Eden for You 1911.13
If You'll Indulge Us 1978.07
If You'll Just Wait a Little While 1919.41
If You'll Only Say You'll be a Friend of Mine 1910.04
If You'll Put Up With Me 1927.64
If You'll Remember Me 1910.06
If You'll Walk With Me 1907.41
If You're a Friend of Mine 1975.24
If You're Anxious for to Shine 1881.37
If You're Crazy About the Women 1918.12
If You're Fond of Purity 1894.03
If You're in Love, You'll Waltz 1927.08
If you're waking call me early 1862.02
If You've Got a Tambourine Shake it for the Glory of God 1963.27
If You've Never Been Vamped by a Brownskin, You've Never Been Vamped at All 1978.21
If Your Heart's iin the Game 1923.47
If your Life's Moments 1862.04
If Your Shoes Don't Shine 1999.12
If'n 1956.16
If, and, and But 1920.11
Ifs and Ands 1882.20
Ifs and Ans 1881.07
Ignatius McFadden's Debut 1895.17, 1896.26
Ignoble Theft of the Idol's Eyes 1965.29
Ignorance is Bliss 1933.24
Ikey Eisenstein 1896.51
Il Balen 1880.24
Il est precis, il est concis 1877.32
Il Fait Des... 1959.15
Il fait des... le fanatique du jazz 1961.25
Il faut laisser tour esperance 1884.50
Il faut savoir 1965.30
Il faut savoir broyer son coeur 1887.36
Il me grondait, il me brusquait 1877.32
Il parlait d'une voix si tendre 1887.36
Il ramene une belle 1884.43
Il suffit d'un rien 1929.16
Ill Deeds are Seldom Slow 1870.15
Ill Wind 1966.32, 1980.10, 1986.02
Ill-Tempered Clavichord, The 1943.21
Illegitimate Daughter, The 1931.48
Illinois 1963.19
Ills so great, oh! 1863.04
Illusion in White 1931.19
Illusions 1999.07

Illusions! 1884.57
Illustrated Overture 1968.13
Illya, Darling 1967.05
Ilmar's Tomb 1972.25
Ilona 1963.14
Iloveyouiloveyou 1923.05
Ils sont ici! 1877.32
Ils sont tombes 1983.03
Im walde en auf der heiday 1885.44
Image of Me, The 1979.09
Imagination 1905.16, 1916.05, 1928.17, 1995.14
Imaginative Opera 1923.34
Imagine 1937.04, 1975.13, 1982.22, 1984.06, 1991.04
Imagine My Finding You Here 1939.19
Imagine My Frustration 1981.06
Imagine That 1967.02
Imitation Rag, The 1911.24
Imitations 1914.34
Immensikoff 1870.01
Immigration Rose 1979.25
Immolation 1989.09
Immortal Gods 1981.02
Immortality 1999.15
Imp of Montmartre, The 1912.48, 1915.33
Impatient Heat 1979.11
Impatiently we long have waited 1888.07
Impeachment Waltz, The 1969.03
Impecuniosity 1880.24
Imperial Conference, An 1946.13
Imperial Guards' March 1902.44
Important Announcement 1937.11
Important Man, The 1904.34
Imported, Yes We Are 1903.24
Impossible 1962.12, 1993.14, 1993.16, 2001.09
Impossible Dream, The 1965.34, 1967.12, 1974.11, 2000.14
Impossible Eyes 1990.17
Impossible She, The 1955.25
Impressions 1914.16
Impressions and Folk Songs 1962.02
Imprisoned 1898.55
Improvements 1906.48
Improvised Love Song, An 1993.02
In 1988.12
In 2010 1912.24
In a Beauty Shop 1914.13
In a Bungalow 1924.04
In a Bungalow for Two 1912.16
In a Cabaret 1920.35
In a contemplative fashion 1890.02
In a Cosy Little Cottage by the Sea 1907.62
In a Cozy Kitchenette Apartment 1921.30
In a Curio Shop 1921.34
In a Doleful Train 1881.37
In a Dory 1907.49
In a French Girl's Heart 1911.11
In a Garden of Eden for Two 1913.16, 1920.02
In a General Sort of Way 1903.14
In a Gondola With You 1928.09
In a Great Big Way 1928.30, 1928.50
In a Hammock 1905.52, 1909.07
In a Hurry 1915.30
In a Kingdom of Our Own 1919.04
In a Lady-like Way 1908.37
In a Life Boat 1931.29
In a Little French Cafe 1929.05
In a Little Town in California 1984.02
In a Little While 1925.36, 1959.26
In a Little World for Two 1915.24
In a matter of such grave import 1898.25
In a Mellow Tone 1997.03
In a Minute 1892.29
In a Month or Two 1918.11
In a One Night Stand 1903.11, 1907.20
In a Persian Garden 1919.21
In a Poor Little House 1990.16
In a Pretty Little Cottage 1912.38
In a Pretty Little White House of Our Own 1912.38
In a Room 1992.11
In a Sentimental Mood 1981.06, 1989.02
In a Smuggler's Cave 1900.25
In a Studio 1908.15
In a Summer Hotel 1908.44
In a Two by Four 1920.42
In a village once lived a maiden 1888.18
In Amsterdam 1906.29
In an Orem Shtibele 1990.16
In an Oriental Way 1914.23
In an Unconventional Way 1894.38
In and Out 1979.15
In Andrews' Vision 1997.06
In Another Life 1972.01
In Anthem Old 1898.31
In Arabia 1915.27
In Araby With You 1926.32
In Arcady 1915.07
In Armenia 1926.26
In Bad Man's Land 1905.41
In Barcelona 1907.32
In Barcelona Lived a Maid 1894.22
In Battle or Upon Parade 1899.06
In Beautiful Italiano 1914.04
In Between 1951.24
In Bivouac Reposing 1899.28
In Black and White 1904.29
In Bohemia 1900.57, 1906.49, 1907.39
In Bokhara, Miss O'Hara 1921.06
In Bond Street 1913.36
In Bright Array 1905.54
In Bright Mansions Above 1930.10
In Buddy's Eyes 1971.05
In Buffalo 1902.11
In bygone days I had thy love 1887.10
In Cabaret-Land 1917.09
In Califor-n-i-a 1931.04
In California 1924.25
In Central Park 1900.40, 1927.29
In Chichicastenango 1940.21
In Chinatown 1910.19
In Chinatown in Frisco 1926.01
In cities vast of Hindostan 1881.04
In College 1905.39
In Corsica 1914.13
In Court 1898.56
In Dahomey 1898.22, 1927.67, 1946.01
In Darkness Let Me Dwell 1963.28
In Days Gone By 1881.07
In days gone by 1882.20, 1893.02
In Days Gone By 1929.04
In Days of Long Ago 1923.22
In Days Sweet and Olden 1892.08
In Dear Old College Days 1900.59
In Dear Old Fatherland 1904.58
In Dear Old Grandma's Day 1906.09
In Dear Old Grandma's Days 1904.55
In Dear Old London 1898.38, 1899.11
In Disguise 1901.08
In Dreamland 1895.33, 1903.06, 1903.28
In Egern on Tegern See 1951.22
In Endless Waiting Rooms 1950.05
In enterprise of martial kind 1890.02
In Erin's Isle 1917.07
In Every Age 1997.06
In every mental lore 1894.15
In Fair Andalusia 1897.13, 1930.12
In Fair Japan 1920.08
In Far Off Mandalay 1909.27
In Farsovia 1908.01, 1908.38
In Fashions Ring 1889.46
In Florida 1901.21
In Florida Among the Palms 1916.10
In Gardens Where Roses Bloom 1925.02
In Gay Ballyhoo 1903.07
In Gay Ceylon 1904.40
In Gay Japan 1902.15
In Gay Manhattan 1905.52
In Gay Mayfair 1906.47
In Gay New York 1896.18, 1903.23
In Gay Paree 1896.05, 1897.48, 1900.39, 1904.23, 1908.31
In Gay Paris 1900.59
In Gypsy Land 1910.25
In happy moments day by day 1848.04
In Havana 1932.15
In Hennequeville 1922.33
In Here 1997.07
In His Arms 1926.50
In His Care 1969.10
In His Eyes 1997.09
In His Own Time 1983.15
In Honeysuckle Time 1978.21
In Honeysuckle Time When Emaline Said She'd be Mine 1976.04
In Honeysuckle Time When Emmaline Said She'd be Mine 1921.16
In Ireland 1909.12
In Italy 1922.34
In Jail 1908.24, 1926.33
In Japan 1899.35
In Jaunty Suits 1887.31
In Jeddo's City 1860.05
In Lands Unknown 1902.18
In Laughing I Find I Grow Fat 1885.44
In lazy languor 1894.15
In Lisbon Gay 1899.06
In Little Old New York 1925.12
In Little Old New York Not so Long Ago 1920.47
In London Town 1897.40, 1917.10
In Louisiana 1979.25
In Love Again 1924.38
In Love With a Fool 1968.08
In Love With Love 1923.40
In Love With Romance 1948.27
In Love With You 1922.42
In Loving Memory 1964.04
In Loving Time 1911.26
In Marsovia 1907.48, 1943.09
In May 1891.32
In Mayaguez 1998.02
In Me 'Ansom 1896.05
In memory of this day 1878.02
In Merry Merry Way 1912.10
In Michigan 1903.03
In Missouria 1930.29
In Monte Carlo Town 1908.21
In Moonlight Land 1911.14
In My Arms Again 1927.05
In My Birch Canoe With Emmy Lou 1912.44
In My Castle in Sorento 1927.15
In My Curriculum 1904.03
In My Day 1923.44, 1992.08
In My Dixie Dreamland 1923.11
In My Dream of You 1914.08
In My Dreams 1889.22
In My Dreams of You 1910.27
In My Garden 1933.03
In My Garden of Love for 2 1918.13
In My Gondola 1929.08
In My Heart of Hearts I've Always Known 1900.37
In My Homeland 1925.06
In My Life 1987.04
In My Little Red Book 1922.23
In My Looking Glass 1920.21
In My Love Boat 1928.21
In My Merry Oldsmobile 1980.27
In My Museum Now 1900.34
In My New Submarine 1905.45
In My Official Capacity 1902.20
In My Own Home 1908.08
In My Own Lifetime 1970.15
In My Own Little Corner 1993.14, 2001.09
In My Pajamas 1924.19
In My Rickshaw of Bamboo 1905.03
In My War Against Men 1915.27
In my wild mountain valley 1868.01
In My Youth 1882.58
In Napoli 1931.29
In no sweet frame of mind 1887.04
In No Time at All 1964.35
In Normandy 1882.17
In Old Bavaria 2001.05
In Old Ben Franklin's Days 1899.40
In Old Granada 1921.34
In Old Havana Town 1930.20
In Old Japan 1908.03, 1920.10
In Old New York 1904.10, 1905.41, 1945.16
In Old Rangoon 1926.22
In Old Versailles 1918.19
In Old Villanelle 1893.40

In Orcania 1908.42
In Other Respects 1883.65
In Other Words, Seventeen 1939.28
In Our Childhood's Bright Endeavor 1977.08
In Our Cozy Little Cottage of Tomorrow 1945.18
In Our Hands 1986.20
In Our Hide-Away 1962.20
In Our Little Den of Iniquity 1940.22
In Our Little Home, Sweet Home 1917.15
In Our Mountain Bower 1921.23
In Our Parlor on the Third Floor Back 1926.51
In Our Quiet Cloister 1897.13
In our quiet Quaker city 1895.17
In Our Teeny Little Weeny Nest 1948.30
In Our Teeny Little Weeny Nest for Two 1961.01
In Panama 1907.33
In Paris 1907.18, 1908.34
In Paris and in Love 1954.01
In Paris Gay 1899.30
In Peacock Alley 1920.02
In Philadelphia 1899.25, 1907.44, 1909.14
In Pity, Spare Them 1906.30
In Poster-land 1916.07
In Posterland 1900.01
In Praise of Learning 1935.16
In Praise of Police 1956.09
In Praise of Socialism 1935.16
In Praise of Vlasova 1935.16
In Praise of Women 1973.04
In Ragueneau's Cafe 1899.28
In Rangapang 1906.26
In Real Life 1971.09
In Romance Land 1913.18
In Romany 1927.26
In Rose Time 1922.16
In Rotterdam 1906.36
In Ruritania 1925.39
In sailing o'er life's ocean wide 1887.10
In Salem 1919.30
In Sapphire Seas 1912.46
In Sardinia 1925.14
In Search of a Thrill 1915.05
In Seville 1906.36
In Siam 1914.19
In Silence 1902.37
In Society 1912.33
In Society it's Always Dress Parade 1911.41
In Some Little World 1967.14
In Someone Else's Sandals 1968.08
In Spain 1917.34
In Spain our love and sweet romances 1882.60
In Spirit Land 1912.26
In Spite of Puck and Judge 1899.19
In Spotless Town 1902.15, 1903.05
In Stage Land 1902.29
In Sunny Kokomo 1911.45
In Sweet Love Land 1904.23
In Sweet Onion Time 1924.46
In Swell Society 1903.14
In Tammany Hall 1905.41
In That Great Gettin' Up Mornin' 1955.03
In That Great Gettin' Up Morning 1969.10
In the Alps/Swiss Echo Song 1918.18
In the Arms of a Stranger 1969.08
In the Autumn 1924.46
In the Back of a Hack 1948.23
In the Bath 1959.20
In the Bathroom 1930.33
In the Beginning, Woman 1978.03
In the Bright Sunlight 1881.10
In the Carefree Realm of Fancy 1938.15
In the Champs de Mars 1949.18
In the Chest 1909.29
In the Chorus 1904.39
In the Clouds 1930.26
In the Company of Men 1985.04
In the Convent They Didn't Teach Me That 1899.38
In the Convent They Never Taught Me That 1913.24
In the Cool, Cool of the Evening 1997.05
In the Cool, Cool, Cool of the Evening 1989.21
In the Country Where I Come From 1970.06
In the Cradle of Love 1913.17
In the Dark 1916.04, 1926.02
In the Days Gone By 1926.27
In the Days of '49 1908.13
In the Days of My Youth 1957.02
In the Days of my Youth I could bill like a Dove, fa, la, la 1750.01
In the Days of Old 1904.10
In the Days of Wild Romance 1922.10
In the Days When He Came Wooing 1894.29
In the Department Store 1898.78
In the Desert 1966.32
In the Evening 1910.18, 1915.16, 1954.11
In the Evening Time 1903.20
In the French Flip-Flop 1910.29
(In) the French Flip-Flop 1910.29
In the Garden 1910.10, 1975.23, 1989.12
In the Garden of Noor-Ed-Deen 1928.28
In the Garden of Romance 1916.19
In the Garden of the Gods 1905.38
In the Gardens of the King 1926.01
In the Gateway to the Temple of Minerva 1975.13
In the Ghetto 1978.01
In the gipsies' life. . 1844.01
In the gipsy's life you read 1844.01
In the Gloaming 1892.06
In the Golden Dawn 1908.44
In the Golden Long Ago 1911.31
In the Good Old Days 1903.38
In the Good Old Summer Time 1900.38
In the Good Old Summertime 1902.21, 1904.07, 1917.26, 1930.16, 1954.02
In the Gypsy's Life 1934.17
In the Harem 1920.34
In the Harem of the East 1901.09
In the Heart of Spain 1927.35
In the Heart of the Dark 1939.28
In the Heart of the Golden Wine 1911.44
In the Isle of Our Dreams 1906.33
In the Ladies Home Journal 1903.39
In the Land of Lorraine 1915.22
In the Land of Romance 1902.43, 1905.07
In the Land of the Buffalo 1908.02
In the Land of the Free 1911.23
In the Land of Yesterday 1920.25
In the Land Off There 1921.34
In the Latin Quarter 1919.40
In the Light of the Virgin Morning 2000.20
In the Lobby 1949.01
In the Long Run 1927.15
In the Malamute Saloon 1942.18
In the Meantime 1927.41
In the Medieval Ages 1898.17
In the Merry Month of May 1924.48
In the Merry Month of Maybe 1931.13
In the Middle of the Night 1934.38
In the Mood 1973.14, 1974.09, 1975.12, 1978.01, 1982.15, 1999.24
In the Moonlight 1902.01
In the Morning 1897.40, 1904.28, 1923.04, 1946.22, 1962.02
In the Morning by the Bright Light 1879.64
In the Morning of the Year 1890.23
In the Morning When Day is Born 1888.34
In the Movies 1914.18, 1984.06
In the Music Hall Bar When the Curtain is Down 1898.50
In the Night 1963.19
In the Noonday Sun 1934.38
In the Old Neighborhood 1981.03
In the Old Town Hall 1921.21
In the Oven 1909.29
In the Palace Gardens 1920.34
In the Palace of the King 1901.12
In the Pale Moonlight 1903.04
In the Park 1922.04
In the Pink 1948.19
In the Press 1902.34
In the Rattle of the Battle 1930.02
In the Real World 1983.15
In the Ring 1897.20
In the Rough 1923.47
In the Same Old Place 1894.10
In the Same Way I Love You 1925.50
In the Sea 1920.36
In the Shack That Little Flower Built 1908.13
In the Shade of a Sheltering Tree 1924.44
In the Shade of the Alamo 1925.24
In the Shade of the New Apple Tree 1937.15
In the Shadow of the Pyramids 1904.43
In the Shadows 1911.05
In the Sky 1980.13
In the Sky the Stars All Glisten 1989.10
In the Sleeping Line 1978.11
In the Slums of the Town 1923.46
In the Smoke 1934.32, 1935.19
In the South of France 1924.31
In the Spring 1902.18, 1923.36, 1926.25
In the Starlight 1922.18, 1922.35
In the Stars 1931.21
In the State of Matrimony 1918.04
In the Still of the Night 1992.18
In the Stretch 1898.70, 1933.06
In the Summer 1929.49
In the Sunny Old South 1963.22
In the Sunshine of Your Love 1911.04
In the Surf 1907.24
In the Sweet Bye and Bye 1902.42, 1903.05
In the Sweet Spring Time 1904.07
In the Swim 1901.16, 1923.47, 1927.59, 1929.33, 1983.06
In the tromba 1881.04
In the Twi-Twi-Twilight 1907.32
In the Twilight 1927.02
In the U.S.A. 1902.44
In the Used to Be 1926.38
In the Valley of Beautiful Dreams 1913.10
In the Village by the Sea 1929.29
In the Waldorf Halls 1909.26
In the Wine of Our Country 1881.25
In They Go and Out They Come 1924.16
In This Wide, Wide World 1973.12
In This, My Native land 1889.36
In Those Good Old Horsecar Days 1932.13
In Three Quarter Time 1933.01
In Time 1896.50, 1960.01, 1976.08
In time of peace a man engages 1888.18
In Time of Peace Prepare for War 1915.23
In Time to Be 1983.03
In Times Like These 1957.17
In Times of War and Tumults 1936.28
In Tune 1973.06
In Twos 1927.29
In Tyrol 1905.12
In us you see 1878.02
In Us You See 1885.58, 1888.13, 1896.35
In Vacation Time 1905.32
In vain you plead to us, Don't go! 1882.78
In Vanity Fair 1910.34
In Vaudeville 1906.48, 1909.09, 1926.30
In Vienna 1915.30
In Vino Veritas 1968.23
In Waikiki 1939.25
In Wall Street 1899.29
In Waltzing There is Pleasure 1896.50
In Washington 1906.45
In Washington Square 1926.11
In wine that sparkles 1882.44
In woman's heart alone 1880.04
In Yama 1922.22
In Yama Yama Land 1922.16
In Yankee Land 1906.40
In Ylang-Ylang 1902.19
In Your Arms 1911.40
In Your Chapeau 1930.08
In Your Defense 1913.04
In Your Eyes 1973.11
In Your Hands 1971.01
In Your Heart is There No Palpitation? 1882.33
In Your Room 1983.03
In Yucatan 1909.12
In Zanzibar 1902.15, 1904.03
In ze Park 1921.04
In Zulu Land 1926.11
Inauguration Day 1913.18
Inbetween 1946.24
Inca Indian Ritual Dance 1942.14
Incantation 1895.33, 1905.56

Inchworm 1955.13, 1997.01
Incognito 1909.01, 1912.10
Incompatibility 1957.16
Inconsistency 1899.38
Independence Day 1857.03, 1906.09
Independence Day Hora 1961.20
Independent 2001.03
Independent Cadets 1895.34
Indestructible Kate 1929.31
India Rubber Shoe, The 1894.38
India Rubber Shoes 1895.03
Indian Blues 1971.16
Indian Chant 1927.11
Indian Death Song 1894.08
Indian Drum 1876.06
Indian Drum, The 1860.03
Indian Folk Song 1918.09
Indian Fox Trot 1918.09
Indian Girls' Chant 1916.06
Indian Love Call 1924.28
Indian Lullaby 1927.65
Indian Maiden's Lament 1978.02
Indian Maidens' Chorus 1916.06
Indian Moon 1923.06
Indian Prance 1921.32
Indian Prayer 1929.04
Indian Rag, The 1912.14
Indian Suffragette, The 1915.23
Indians Never Lie 1880.10
Indians! 1954.13, 1979.22, 1990.20
Indictment, The 1975.07
Indignation Meeting 1926.32
Indlu Kamalandela 1997.14
Indoor Sports 1915.16, 1919.03
Indu-Chi 1923.22
Industrialization 1996.07
Inevitable, The 1918.08
Infant Incubator, The 1898.43
Infatuation 1937.07
Infelice 1895.08
Influenza Blues 1919.14
Ingane yeZulu! 1993.04
Inherited from My Aunt 1896.51
Inimitably Yours 1951.20
Initials 1968.11
Initiation of Daphne, The 1910.34
Injuns Here We Come 1992.06
Inner Peace 1981.07
Inner Thoughts 1970.09
Innocence 1977.09
Innocent Chorus Girls of Yesterday 1931.04
Innocent City Maid, An 1902.07
Innocent Debutante, The 1906.50
Innocent Eyes 1924.13
Innocent Girls 1920.40
Innocent Ingenue Baby 1922.46
Inoe Threatens King Kojong 1997.16
Inoue Threatens King Kojong 1998.08
Insane Poontang 1971.10
Insect God, The 1978.24
Inseparables, Les 1885.57
Inside Story, The 1931.42
Inside U.S.A. 1948.14
Inspection 1909.21
Inspiration 1924.13, 1924.40, 1928.26, 1958.20, 1958.21, 1977.02
Instead-of Song 1965.04, 1966.19
Instrumental Man, The 1901.21
Insufficient Sweetie 1924.43
Inter-mish-un 1979.15
Interfering Parrot, The 1896.27
Interlude 1946.18, 1960.07
Interlude and Gallop 1979.10
Interlude in a Barber Shop 1935.17
Interlude in Harlem 1942.13
Intermezzo 1925.07
Intermission Talk 1953.08
Internado, El 1993.08
International Merry Widow, The 1908.19
International Rhythm 1930.09
International Vamp 1927.19
International, The 1938.02
Interplay 1945.10
Interpretation in C Minor 1941.03
Interrogative Child, The 1902.07
Interrupted Allegory, The 1910.37
Interrupted Love Song, An 1928.29, 1986.14
Interrupted Love Song, The 1911.47
Interruptions 1914.20
Interview, The 1933.15, 1982.23, 1997.17
Into Society 1925.40
Into the Arena 1888.19
Into the Fire 1997.19, 1999.13
Into the Kitchen Boy 1918.36
Into the Light 1986.18
Into the Night 1945.12
Into the water we go 1878.02
Into the Water We Go 1885.58, 1888.13, 1896.35
Into the Woods 1987.18
Intoxication 1957.01
Intriguers, The 1911.11
Introducin' Mr. Paris 1954.03
Introducing the Futurity Debutante Chorus 1921.06
Introduction Tango 1963.08
Invisible Chorus 1881.16
Invisible Dog 1999.12
Invitation to Love, An 1932.19
Invitation to the Jellicle Ball 1982.19
Invitation to the Wedding 1891.20
Invitation, An 1932.03
Invocation and Instructions to the Audience 1999.20
Invocation of Venus 1902.35
Invocation to Pie 1902.15
Invocation to Venus 1888.20
Invocation, The 1884.42, 1886.47, 1888.36
Inza 1971.09
Iolanthe! From thy dark exile thou art summoned 1882.78
Iole 1913.37
Ionisation 1978.05
Iowa Stubborn 1957.18, 2000.11
Ipi-Tombi 1977.01
Ippleberger, Hirsch and Mayer 1900.16
Irate Pirate am I, An 1928.49
Ireland A! Gra Ma Chree 1901.02
Ireland was Never Like This 1960.10
Ireland, My Land of Dreams 1918.41
Ireland, My Sireland 1917.07
Irene 1919.36, 1973.05, 1976.24
Irene Lorraine 1887.02
Irene Rosensteen 1921.18
Irish and Proud of it, Too 1914.22
Irish are True, The 1891.42
Irish Brigade 1886.60
Irish Cuckoo, The 1896.41
Irish Eyes of Blue 1891.01, 1903.35
Irish Eyes of Love 1914.29
Irish Girl I Love, The 1905.30
Irish Girl, An 1973.05
Irish Have a Great Day To-night, The 1917.07
Irish Jewish Jubilee 1925.05
Irish Jig 1963.28, 1963.30
Irish Jubilee 1927.48
Irish Jubilee, The 1890.30
Irish Lad's Wooing, An 1896.14
Irish Memories 1907.27
Irish Minstrel, The 1888.12
Irish Patriot, The 1896.41
Irish Poker Club, The 1890.29
Irish Potheen 1882.69, 1888.12
Irish Rag, The 1932.14
Irish Refrain, An 1869.43
Irish Rose for Me, An 1924.42
Irish Sheik, The 1924.16
Irish Sidewalk Conversationalists, The 1898.50
Irish Song, The 1952.11
Irish Stew, The 1890.29
Irish Street Singer, An 1897.47
Irish Swell, The 1899.01
Irish Were Egyptians Long Ago, The 1920.10
Irishman's Lilt, An 1903.25
Irishman's Love, An 1891.01
Irishman's Rambles 1869.42
Irishman's Shanty, The 1871.16
Irma la Douce 1976.07
Irma-la-Douce 1960.13
Iron! Iron! Iron! 1913.24
Iron, Iron 1947.04
Irrepressible Yank, The 1904.37
Irresistible 1913.10, 1995.14
Irresistible Tune, The 1906.30
Irving Berlin Melodies, The 1914.34
Is Anybody There? 1969.06
Is Everybody Happy 1906.08
Is Everybody Happy Now? 1927.58
Is Happy, A 1939.15
Is he honest 1859.17
Is He the Only Man in the World 1962.20
Is He Your Son? 1866.07, 1866.21
Is it a Crime? 1956.14
Is it a Dream? 1944.16
Is it Any Wonder? 1924.25, 1925.44
Is it Hard to Guess? 1921.06
Is it Him or is it Me 1948.25
Is it Love 1903.01, 1930.05
Is it Possible? 1939.22
Is it Really Me? 1963.26, 1992.10
Is it Shamus You Seek? 1897.03
Is it the Girl or is it the Gown? 1919.32, 1944.29
Is it the Singer or the Song? 1934.32
Is it the Uniform? 1928.16
Is it Worth While? 1913.21
Is it Yes, or is it No? 1900.40
Is it Your Smile? 1918.40
Is life a boon? 1888.35
Is love a dream 1895.43
Is Marriage a Failure? 1905.53
Is Me 1987.12
Is My Face on Straight? 1908.35
Is No Succor Near 1934.17
Is no succour near at hand? 1844.01
Is Old Man's 'At Won't Fit 'Im 1901.23
Is Rhythm Necessary? 1931.36
Is That All There Is? 1983.20
Is That All? 1914.14
Is That Mr. Riley? 1883.42
Is That My Prince? 1951.14
Is That So! 1923.44
Is the Girl You Married Still the Girl You Love? 1915.08
Is then his Fate decreed, Sir? 1750.01
Is Then His Fate Decreed, Sir? 1957.02
Is There Any Little Thing I Can do for You? 1920.29
Is There Anyone Approachin'? 1902.25
Is There Anything Better Than Dancing? 1991.15
Is This Love at Last? 1913.34
Is This My Town 1971.19
Is This Not a Lovely Spot? 1924.08
Is This the End? 1935.11
Is This What You Call Love? 1994.05
Is This Year Next Year? 1981.28
Is You is or is You Ain't Ma' Baby? 1992.03
Is Your Mama Well 1885.44
Isaac's Equation 1972.25
Isabel 1906.15, 1923.06
Isabel St. Clair 1888.34
Isabella and Romero 1912.04
Isabelle 1965.30, 1970.01, 1974.19, 1983.03
Isabelle St. Clair 1888.27
Isizwe 1988.02
Island in the West Indies 1936.02
Island of Bollamazoo 1986.19
Island of by-and-by, The 1906.14
Island of Love 1902.34
Island of Love, The 1900.51, 1908.03
Island of Roses and Love, The 1912.07
Island that dares to be free, The 1880.46
Island, An 1990.17
Isle d'Amour 1913.17, 1915.12
Isle de Blackwell, The 1878.01
Isle in the West Indies 1936.17
Isle o' Dreams, The 1913.03
Isle of Lillipotu, The 1891.46
Isle of Lost Romance 1917.12
Isle of Love, The 1911.20
Isle of Manasooris 1943.20
Isle of Our Dreams 1945.16
Isle of Tangerine 1921.23
Isle of the Midnight Rainbow 1944.20
Isle of the Phillipines, An 1909.03

Isle of Youth 1918.05
Isms 1960.12
Isn't it a Pity? 1933.01
Isn't it a Funny Thing 1934.18
Isn't it a Lovely View? 1945.17
Isn't it a Pity 1999.10
Isn't it Delicious 1912.42
Isn't it Fun to be in the Movies 1978.06
Isn't it Great to be Married 1915.31, 1975.24
Isn't it June? 1934.35
Isn't it Kinda Fun? 1996.04
Isn't it Lovely to be on the Stage 1904.41
Isn't it Nasty of Papa? 1911.36
Isn't it Remarkable 1933.16
Isn't it Romantic? 1975.13, 1988.08
Isn't it Strange, Snowflakes are Falling 1997.16, 1998.08
Isn't it Swell to Dream 1933.16
Isn't it Wonderful? 1896.48, 1918.37, 1958.04
Isn't She Lovely 1956.08
Isn't That Like a Man 1916.08
Isn't There a Man for Me? 1928.04
Isn't This a Lovely Day? 1980.09
Israel 1970.17
Israel and Saul 1997.12
Israel Israel 1972.17
Israeli Rhapsody 1968.04
Isrulik 1989.10
Issue in Question 1997.18
It 1889.34, 1926.42, 1987.10
It Ain't Etiquette 1939.30, 1941.08
It Ain't Gonna Work! 1981.28
It Ain't Just Me 2001.06
It Ain't Necessarily So 1935.13, 1980.10, 1983.04
It Ain't Us Who Make the Wars 1969.08
It All Belongs to Me 1927.37
It All Comes Out of the Piano 1980.08
It All Depends 1888.20, 1908.41
It All Depends on You 1925.01, 1925.28
It Always Takes Two 1931.05
It Better be Good 1931.16
It Came Out of the Clear Blue Sky 1952.20
It Can All be Explained 1986.18
It Can Happen to Anyone 1941.12
It Can't be Done 1917.02
It Can't be Wrong 1919.28
It Cannot Be! 1890.33
It Could Happen to You 1995.14
It Could Happen, it's Possible 1942.35
It Could Only Happen in the Movies 1941.13
It Couldn't be a Better Day 1955.03
It Couldn't be Done But We Did It 1947.08
It Couldn't Please Me More 1966.24, 1998.04
It Depends on How You Look at Things 1962.02
It Depends on What You're At 1969.04, 1980.01
It Depends Upon the Hair 1906.18
It Does Feel Good to Go to the Bad 1924.06
It doesn't agree with me 1887.43
It Doesn't Cost You Anything to Dream 1945.03
It Don't Mean a Thing if it Ain't Got That Swing 1976.04, 1981.06, 1997.03, 1999.05, 1999.24, 2000.14
It Don't Seem Like the Same Old Smile 1896.02
It don't seem like the same old smile 1896.15
It Feels Good 1953.08
It Fills Me With Distress 1898.55
It Find it Really Better Far 1894.33
It Gets Lonely in the White House 1962.20
It Gets Them All 1918.40
It Goes on and On 1998.21
It had to be You 1924.32, 1983.09, 1999.24
It had to Happen Sometime 1987.14
It Happened 1934.43
It Happens to the Best of Friends 1987.02
It has Reached Me a Lady Named Hubbard 1900.37
It Hurts to be Strong 1988.12
It is a charming girl 1868.01
It is a Most Disagreeable Thing to Do 1903.07
It is Alive 1884.42
It is All for You 1915.02
It is Awful Nice, But it is Awkward 1888.06
It is better to laugh 1873.05
It is Difficult to Shimmer in Society 1900.54
It is Done 1976.03
It is He 1880.69
It is Heaven to Boheme 1915.05
It is I 1913.20
It is my duty 1882.60
It is My Thoughts 1931.06
It is Not Always May 1887.32
It is not love 1879.10
It is Not the End of the World 1979.12
It is Past My Comprehension 1902.25
It is quite a consolation 1882.17
It is really too good to be true 1897.17
It is Safe to Depend on the Irish 1921.13
It is the English 1905.25
It is the Girl, Not the Horse That Wins the Prize 1905.03
It is Their Nature To 1897.37
It is time 1887.04
It is Time Now 1998.21
It is too Bad, Your Time to Waste 1870.27
It is Two Bad Me We Are 1878.20
It is Very Hard to Bring Up Father 1916.17
It is! It is! That child of Song 1864.22
It Isn't Done 1929.45
It isn't Easy 1959.19
It isn't Enough 1965.19
It isn't Hard to Do 1920.42
It Isn't on That We Rely 1889.36
It isn't What You Did 1933.25
It isn't Working 1981.10
It isn't Your Fault 1915.01
It Just had to Happen 1927.04
It Just Occurred to Me 1952.20
It Looks Like Liza 1941.04
It Makes My Love Come Down 1982.12
It Makes No Difference 1972.10
It May be a Good Idea for Joe 1947.17
It May be so, But I Doubt It 1909.28
It may not be - for so the fates decide! 1882.78
It May Rain 1926.13
It Means so Little to You 1931.42
It Might as Well be Her 1966.27
It Might as Well be Spring 1993.16, 1996.04
It Might be an Oomps 1913.26
It Might be an Oomps Sight Worse 1913.26
It Might be Love 1958.04
It Might Have Been 1893.41, 1912.47
It Might Have Been You 1932.06
It Must be Good for Me 1989.05
It Must be Heaven 1929.42
It Must be Love 1905.52, 1906.04, 1920.11, 1925.34
It Must be Me 1956.15
It Must be Now 1889.40
It Must be Religion 1936.12
It Must be So 1956.15, 1974.06, 1982.20, 1997.10
It Must be Spring 1952.05
It Must be You 1922.18
It Must Have Been Svengali in Disguise 1902.16
It Must Have Been the Night 1934.35
It Needs No Poet 1894.45
It Needs Work 1989.29
It Never Can be Love 1978.19
It Never Entered My Mind 1940.06, 1975.13
It Never Troubles Me 1896.31
It Never was You 1938.11, 1995.12
It Never Will Get You a Thing 1924.40
It Never Would've Worked 1983.08
It Never, Never Can be Love 1910.35, 1988.18
It Only Happens When I Dance With You 1983.09, 1988.08
It Only Takes a Moment 1964.01, 1985.19, 1998.07
It Pays to Advertise 1914.34, 1926.25
It Really was a Very Pretty Story 1908.41
It Reminds Me of Home, Sweet Home 1905.22
It Ruined Marc Anthony 1917.04
It Seems Somehow, They Want Me Now 1911.44
It Seems to Me 1894.33
It Seldom Comes True 1919.12
It Should Happen to Me 1941.03
It Showered Again 1886.03
It Sort Makes a Fellow Stop and Think 1919.12
It Sort of Makes a Fellow Stop and Think 1918.37
It Still Belongs to Thee 1894.17
It Takes a Girl to do it Every Time 1892.05, 1892.19
It Takes a Girl to do it, Every Time 1894.25
It Takes a Long Pull to Get There 1935.13, 1983.04
It Takes a Whole Lot of Human Feeling 1972.13
It Takes a Woman 1964.01, 1985.19
It Takes a Woman to Catch a Man 1907.30
It Takes a Woman to Get a Man 1948.28
It Takes an Irishman to Make Love 1916.24
It Takes Nine Tailors to Make a Man 1944.25
It Takes the Cop to Cop the Girls 1908.28
It Takes Two 1987.18
It Thrills! It Thrills! 1914.28
It Used to Be 1963.08
It Wan't Your Fault, it wasn't My Fault 1917.02
It was a Dream 1885.08, 1889.34, 1891.39
It was a Glad Adventure 1954.03
It was a Knight of princely mien 1848.04
It was a Lover and His Lass 1963.28
It was All on Account of Nipper 1918.26
It was Alone 1976.35, 1980.14, 1982.17
It was Destiny 1954.17
It was Different When I Awoke 1898.56
It was Fate 1926.34
It was Fate When I Met You 1921.27
It was Good for Grandma 1944.23
It was Great When it All Began 1975.08
It was indeed a Splendid Sight 1871.19
It was Long Ago 1934.19
It was Many Years Ago 1880.10
It was Marie 1912.37
It was Me 1911.24
It was Meant to Be 1923.19
It was Never Like This 1932.17
It was Nice Knowing You 1944.01
It was Tancred! 1884.14
It was the Dutch 1904.16
It was the Same Old Story 1900.15
It was Written in the Stars 1939.30
It Will All End Up With the Right End Up 1918.18
It Will be Mine 1894.10
It Will be My Day 1970.01
It Will Rain 1934.32
It Will Stand 1992.06
It Will Storm, it Will Rain 1932.09
It Won't be Long 1971.01, 1979.32
It Won't be Long Now 1927.46
It Won't be the Same Old Broadway 1913.18
It Won't Work 1979.15
It Wonders Me 1955.01
It Would be Best if You Would Go Now 1933.23
It Would Happen Anyway 1920.21
It Would Have Been Wonderful 1973.04
It Wouldn't be You 1989.07
It Wouldn't Surprise Me at All 1887.05
It'd be Nice 1974.04
It'll All be the Same a Hundred Years from Now 1960.17
It'll be All Right in a Hundred Years 1949.12
It's a 'Andy Thing to 'Ave About the 'Ouse 1900.16
It's a Beautiful Day Today 1928.47
It's a Beginning 1981.28
It's a Big, Wide Wonderful World 1940.23
It's a Bomb 1910.03
It's a Bore 1973.12
It's a Boy 1896.29, 1972.08, 1975.03, 1991.07, 1993.06
It's a Busy Day 1900.37
It's a Bye-Bye, Pal 1908.23
It's a Chemical Reaction, That's All 1955.02
It's a Clue 1915.17
It's a Cute Little Way of My Own 1916.25
It's a Dangerous Game 1997.09
It's a Deal 1973.10
It's a Different World 1936.02, 1936.17
It's a Dream That Never Comes True 1901.27
It's a Fair Day for a Fair-Day 1908.15
It's a Fairy Tale 1993.19
It's a Far, Far Better Thing 1924.01
It's a Fine Life 1963.01
It's a Fine Old Institution 1953.11
It's a Fish 1966.18
It's a Good Day 1983.20
It's a Good Thing to Have 1896.48

It's a Good Thing, Push it Along 1894.51
It's a Good World After All 1904.29
It's a Grand Night for Singing 1993.16, 1996.04
It's a Great Life 1936.26
It's a Great Life if You Don't Weaken 1922.01
It's a Great Little World 1925.49
It's a Great Sport 1929.03
It's a Great Wild Wonderful World 1949.06
It's a Groove 1968.22
It's a Hard, Hard World for a Man 1918.03
It's a Helluva Way to Run a Love Affair 1955.01
It's a Hit! 1981.27
It's a Jolly Good Thing to be Alive 1905.55
It's a Law 1938.11
It's a Lie 1919.28
It's a Living 1949.02
It's a Long Lane That has No Turning 1911.28
It's a Long Long Time Before Pay Day Comes 'Round 1919.08
It's a Long Time Till Tomorrow 1950.06
It's a Long Way from Broadway to Edinboro Town 1916.02
It's a Long Way to Tiffany's 1918.07
It's a Long Way to Tipperary 1964.28, 1975.22, 1991.04
It's a Long, Long Time 1908.16
It's a Long, Long Way to Tipperary 1914.22, 1914.23
It's a Lovely Day Today 1950.15
It's a Lovely Night on the Hudson River 1937.12
It's a Matter of Opinion After All 1908.10
It's a Maze 1991.05
It's a Mighty Fine Country We Have Here 1941.11
It's a Miracle 1976.34, 1991.10
It's a Most Unusual Day 1974.22
It's a Musical World 1974.22
It's a New King of Thing 1941.11
It's a Nice Cold Morning 1968.24
It's a Nice Night for It 1946.07
It's a Nice Place to Visit 1969.14
It's a Perfect Relationship 1956.14
It's a Pop, Pop, Popular Song 1922.08
It's a Premiere Night 1983.17
It's a Pressing Invitation That I Bring 1903.21
It's a Scandal! It's an Outrage! 1943.04
It's a Simple Little System 1956.14
It's a Sin to Tell a Lie 1978.09
It's a Small, Small World 1920.31
It's a Sure, Sure Sign 1917.01
It's a Sweet Life 1979.33
It's a Very Easy Matter 1920.14
It's a Very Fine World 1915.29
It's a Very Good Scheme if it Works 1884.22
It's a Waste of Time to Worry 1905.26
It's a Way They Have in Chicago 1904.28
It's a Way We Have in Spain 1903.37
It's a Well-Established Fact 1898.48
It's a Windy Day at the Battery 1917.15
It's a Wishing World 1952.05
It's a Woman's World 2000.15
It's a Wonderful Day 1950.16
It's a Wonderful Day to do Nothing 1963.20
It's a Wonderful Spot 1920.13
It's a Wonderful World 1931.39
It's About Magic 1983.01
It's Alive 1886.47, 1888.36
It's All a Matter of Taste 1884.22, 1884.60
It's All A Scheme 1997.16
It's All a Scheme 1998.08
It's All Done by Kindness 1905.27
It's All in Fun 1940.23
It's All in the Book You Know 1905.29
It's All in Your Mind 1960.01
It's All O.K. 1930.21
It's All Over 1981.29
It's All Over But the Shoutin' 1928.36
It's All Over Now 1912.24
It's All Right 1988.02
It's All Right if You Love One Another 1917.35
It's All Right With Me 1927.20, 1953.07, 1956.02, 1998.05
It's All the Same 1965.34
It's All Very Fine and Large 1886.53
It's All Yours 1939.13
It's Allus de Same in Dixie 1904.21
It's Almost Tomorrow 1958.10
It's Alright Now 1987.17
It's Always Going to be That Way 1911.31
It's Always Love 1972.04
It's Always Orange Day in California 1917.04
It's Always Summertime at the Winter Garden 1919.30
It's Amazing, What God Can Do 1990.05
It's an Art 1978.12
It's an Old Spanish Custom 1928.37, 1953.11
It's Awfully Hard to Shop 1903.23
It's awfully nice 1886.53
It's Been a Long, Long Time 1974.10
It's Been a While 1994.06
It's Been a Whole Year 1942.11
It's Best Not to Say too Much About It 1904.11
It's Better Than a Dream 1956.14
It's Better With a Band 1983.09
It's Better With a Union Man 1937.14
It's Bitter News 1897.03
It's Clear that Medieval Art 1881.37
It's Cockney, by Jove 1886.32
It's coming off to-day 1896.27
It's Commencement Day 1929.21
It's De-Lovely 1936.26
It's Delightful Down in Chile 1949.18, 1974.02, 1995.07
It's Delightful to be Married 1906.45, 1980.27
It's Delovely 1987.15
It's Different Now 1919.07
It's Different When You're Full 1885.08
It's Different With Me 1931.01
It's Doom 1958.08
It's Easier for Her 1980.30
It's Easy to Lie to Your Husband 1917.21
It's Easy to Say Hello 1927.04
It's Easy When You Know How 1964.04
It's Edna-Time 1999.14
It's English, You Know 1884.42, 1888.36
It's Enough to Make a Lady Fall in Love 1968.02
It's Enough to Make a Perfect Lady Mad 1904.13, 1904.44
It's Ever My Endeavor 1897.37
It's Every Girl's Ambition 1932.03
It's Finally Happening 1988.02
It's follow my Leader 1877.20
It's Forty Miles from Schenectady to Troy 1896.18
It's Fun to be Free 1942.26
It's Fun to Think 1962.04
It's German dat's so 1885.51
It's Getting Dark on Old Broadway 1922.19, 1923.20
It's Getting Harder to Love You 1988.07
It's Going to be a Pretty Wedding 1907.18
It's Going to be a Very Busy Day 1908.41
It's Going to be Good to be Gone 1979.12
It's Good for You to Exercise Your Mind 1924.15
It's Good to be Alive 1957.07, 1965.32
It's Good to be Back Home 1964.21
It's Good to Fall in Love 1948.12
It's Got to be Love 1936.05, 1975.13, 1983.02
It's Great to be a Doughboy 1927.43
It's Great to be a Wonderful Detective 1913.19
It's Great to be Alive 1932.07, 1933.05, 1949.17
It's Great to be an Actor 1907.14
It's Great to be Crazy 1904.24
It's Great to be Home Again 1938.01
It's Great to be in Love 1919.12, 1931.26
It's Great to be Married 1919.28
It's Great to be Married and Lead a Single Life 1921.23
It's Greek to Me 1918.09
It's Hard to be a Jewish Woman 1970.17
It's Hard to be a Lady 1922.13
It's Hard to be a Lady in a Case Like That 1906.01
It's Hard to Care 1973.03
It's Hard to Find a King Like Me 1906.14
It's hard to lose a Meal 1877.20
It's Hard to Love Somebody When Your Somebody Don't Love You 1908.08
It's hard to speak my heart 1998.21
It's Hard to Tell 1919.12
It's High Time 1949.18, 1974.02, 1995.07
It's High Time I Got the Low Down on You 1936.12
It's Honey All de Time! 1896.37
It's Hot Up Here 1984.08, 1999.20
It's Immaterial to Me 1918.09
It's Impossible 1973.17
It's in His Kiss 1997.21
It's in the Air 1899.02, 1931.13
It's in the Book 1917.02
It's in, it's Out 1926.30
It's Just a Question of Technique 1988.07
It's Just Another New Year's Eve 1976.34
It's Just as Transparent as Glass 1885.65
It's just That Feeling for Home 1923.47
It's Legitimate 1960.23
It's Like 1976.09
It's Like a Beautiful Woman 1956.16
It's Love 1913.21, 1950.14, 1953.03, 1958.20, 1958.21
It's Love! It's Love! 1989.07
It's Lovely When Your Love Loves You 1906.32
It's Magic 1974.10
It's Mardi Gras 1947.13
It's Me 1953.08, 1993.16
It's Me Again 1939.24
It's Mental 1942.23
It's Modernistic 1932.12
It's Money - it's Fame - it's Love 1930.43
It's Money That Makes the World Go Round 1896.05
It's More Fun Than a Picnic 1948.28
It's My Belief 1971.20
It's My Day 1975.05
It's My Nature 1931.42
It's My Neighborhood 1999.15
It's My Opinion 1893.02
It's My Temperament 1919.40
It's Naughty But it's Nice 1871.08
It's Naughty to be Kissed 1907.32
It's Never Quite the Same 1958.02
It's Never too Late 1979.14
It's Never too Late to Fall in Love 1954.09
It's Never too Late to Learn 1910.20
It's New York Town for Mine 1905.42
It's Nice to be a Boy Sometimes 1900.43
It's nice to be somebody's love 1880.24
It's Nice to Get Up in th' Morning 1928.05
It's Nice to Have a Sweetheart 1906.26
It's Nice to Have Some One to Love You 1911.42
It's No Use Crying for the Moon 1907.06
It's Nobody's Business But My Own 1919.15
It's None of My Business 1988.07
It's Not Cricket to Picket 1937.14
It's Not Easy 1961.16
It's Not Irish 1959.04
It's Not Just Christmas 1998.19
It's Not the Proper Thing 1908.30
It's Not the Trick Itself But it's the Tricky Way it's Done 1911.05
It's Not the Weather Cock That Changes, it's the Wind 1898.63
It's Not too Late 1988.10
It's Not What You Say 1919.29
It's Not What You Weigh 1983.09
It's Not Where You Start 1973.06, 1976.07
It's Nothing But a Bubble 1909.13
It's Nothing to do With You 1919.02
It's Now or Never 1989.12
It's Only a Piece of Advice 1908.03
It's Only a Question of Time 1885.41
It's Only a Show 1981.14
It's Only Thirty Years 1953.02
It's Original With Me 1886.59
It's Our Duty to the King 1937.10
It's Our Wedding Day 1918.31
It's Permissible 1912.49
It's Pie 1904.14
It's Pleasant and Delightful 1950.01
It's Possible 1989.05, 2000.18
It's Possible! 2001.09
It's Pretty Soft for Silas 1929.38, 1978.19
It's Pretty Soft for Simon 1910.35
It's Queer What Just a Little Love Will Do 1910.29
It's Quick and Easy 1964.03
It's Quiet on the Potomac Tonight 1963.22
It's Quite Enough to Make Me Weep 1925.17
It's Raining on Prom Night 1972.12, 1994.07
It's She and it's Me 1973.07

It's so Different in London 1905.50
It's so Easy to Fall in Love 1990.15
It's so Nice 1974.03
It's so Nice to be Civilized 1980.15
It's so Simple 1965.02
It's Something You've Got to Get Used To 1888.03
It's Style That Makes the Girl 1910.34
It's Such a Beautiful Day 1974.23
It's Such a Different World 1987.14
It's Super Nice 1966.06
It's Superman 1966.06
It's the Bump 1911.36
It's the Cooks, Not the Looks 1929.17
It's the Custom in Ireland 1893.30
It's the Dancer You Love 1924.22
It's the Darndest Thing 1931.32
It's the Ending of My Day 1979.14
It's the Girl Everytime, it's the Girls 1945.01
It's the Girls 1906.25, 1914.17
It's the Going Home Together 1954.03
It's the Gown That Makes the Gal That Makes the Guy 1952.08
It's the Gown That Makes the Girl 1915.23
It's the Hard-Knock Life 1977.06
It's the Irish 1908.35
It's the Little Things That Count 1916.25
It's the Little Things That Count in Life 1908.41
It's the Nicest Sort of Feeling 1920.37
It's the Nuns 1982.10
It's the Only One for Me 1916.18
It's the Right Time to be Rich 1983.18
It's the Same Old Chow 1918.36
It's the Same Old South 1940.21
It's the Scotch 1918.22
It's the Second Time You Meet That Matters 1958.08
It's the Skirt 1911.05
It's the Strangest Thing 1977.16
It's the Truth in Me 1937.09
It's the Unexpected Happens 1908.16
It's the Weather 1950.03
It's the Witching Hour by the Old Water Tower 1963.22
It's the Women 1918.04
It's Three O'Clock 1934.43
It's Time 1996.08
It's Time for a Cheer-Up Song 1978.28
It's Time for a Love Song 1979.09
It's Time to Go 1993.05
It's Time to Say Aloha 1938.08
It's Today 1966.10, 1985.19, 1998.07
It's too Late 1976.35, 1980.14, 1982.17
It's too Late Now 1909.29
It's Tough to be a Hostess 1927.31
It's understood, I think 1894.15
It's Up to a Cop to Cop a Pretty Maid 1922.08
It's Up to Me 1962.04
It's Up to the Band 1927.37
It's Up to You to do the Rest 1907.04
It's very perplexing 1880.46
It's What Eve Said to Adam 1900.41
It's Wonderful 1918.05, 1926.30
It's Worth While Waiting for Someone Worth While 1918.35
It's You 1921.34, 1957.18, 2000.11
It's You Again 1968.03
It's You for Me 1957.17
It's You I Love 1929.44
It's You I Want 1938.04
It's You I Want to Love Tonight 1934.43
It's You Who Makes Me Young 1969.02
It's Your Carriage That Counts 1921.23
It's Your Fault 1965.29
It's Your Life 1988.07
Italia! Land of Song 1889.40
Italian Band, The 1891.14
Italian Brand, The 1892.06
Italian Joe 1888.27
Italian Man, The 1898.22
Italian Organ Grinder, The 1903.01
Italian Rag 1910.18
Italian Street Song 1910.35, 1978.19, 1988.18
Italian Whirlwind, The 1923.46
Italian, The 1885.35
Italie 1919.31
Italy 1927.38, 1955.04
Itch to be Rich 1963.11
Itoh's Ambition 1997.16
Its and the Whats, The 1884.42
Itzel's Lullaby 1891.13
Ivan loved his Katza well 1885.28
Ivory and Old Gold 1934.01
Ivy and the Oak 1916.14
Ixion March 1885.08
Izicatulo Gumboot Dance, The 1966.03
Izzy Rosenstein 1909.18

J' n'ai pas d'ancetr's dans ma famille 1886.19
J'Ai 1963.16
J'ai danse avec l'amour 1947.18
J'ai de la figure 1884.50
J'ai deux amants 1925.41
J'ai deux amours 1964.02
J'ai Deux Amours 1973.17
J'ai du ciel dans mon chapeau 1948.12
J'ai fait trois fois le tour du Monde 1878.08
J'ai lu dans les saintes ecritures 1929.11
J'ai perdu le tete 1965.30
J'aime d'amour 1929.15
J'aime l'eclat des cours 1887.35
J'aime la femme et je m'en vante 1884.50
J'aime Paris au mois de Mai 1965.30
J'amasse a l'abri des hasards 1886.09
J'attendrai 1964.02
J'avais perdu la tete et ma perruque 1878.08
J'en deduis que je t'aime 1965.30
J'entre comme une reine 1887.36
J'n'ai pas connu 1929.10
J'suis plein d'egards pou la beaute 1885.56
Ja, auf dem Land... 1920.46
Jabberwalky 1926.15
Jack & Jill 1971.04, 1976.27
Jack and Jill 1897.55, 1899.22, 1900.03, 1908.09, 1923.07
Jack be Nimble 1971.20
Jack in the Box 1904.51
Jack is Every Inch a Sailor 1879.06
Jack o' Lantern Joe 1905.25
Jack o' Lantern Man 1902.21
Jack O'Lantern 1901.21
Jack O'Lantern Girl, The 1904.54
Jack O'Lantern Song 1899.27
Jack Roosevelt Robinson 1981.28
Jack's Keep 'Em All Alive-O 1886.45
Jack's the boy 1896.27
Jack-o-Lantern Boogieman, The 1905.51
Jackie 1972.16
Jackie Coogan 1923.25
Jackie, The 1904.37
Jackies of Parade 1902.42
Jackson case, The 1882.63
Jacob and Sons 1982.03, 1993.15
Jacob in Egypt 1982.03, 1993.15
Jacob is Dead 1982.23
Jacob's Ladder 1931.31, 1969.10
Jacques D'Iraq 1956.02
Jade 1927.07
Jaded, Degraded am I 1964.35
Jag of Joy, The 1912.37
Jagrafree 1905.44
Jail Birds 1912.27
Jail-Life Walk 1970.20
Jailer's Daughter, The 1926.09, 1926.35
Jailer, Jailer 1982.18
Jailhouse Rock 1989.12, 1995.03
Jakey Schmidt 1889.31
Jalousie 1978.26
Jamaica is Waiting 1980.05
Jamaica Rum! 1880.69
Jamais d'La Vie 1908.17
Jambalaya on the Bayou 1992.06
Jambes Roses, Les 1958.06
Jamboree Jones 1967.11
Jamboree Jones Jive 1997.05
Jamboree, A 1952.15
James, the Chauffeur 1927.36
Jamie 1970.12
Jamie Dear 1888.05
Jane 1903.31, 1911.07, 1959.06
Jane is a Suffragette 1908.27
Jane Jane 1966.15
Jane, My Pretty Jane 1880.42
January O 1928.05
Japan has Chosen 1998.08
Japan's Choice 1997.16
Japanese and Russians 1905.07
Japanese Baby 1899.11
Japanese Elopement, A 1896.45
Japanese Moon 1927.60
Japanese Sandman, The 1980.08
Japanese Serenade 1927.14
Japanese Umbrella, A 1904.25
Jarabe Tapatio, El 1988.15
Jas o'Mine 1930.13
Jason's Bar Mitzvah 1992.09
Jason's Therapy 1992.09
Jasper's jacket 1887.04
Jasper's Vision 1985.18
Jassamine Lane 1924.27
Java, La 1965.37
Jay, nagy a bay! 1920.46
Jaybird 1940.01
Jays, The 1888.45
Jazz 1927.45, 1948.08
Jazz a la Russe 1924.36
Jazz All Your Troubles Away 1918.42
Jazz Band am the Firstest Aid for Me, A 1918.14
Jazz Blues 1922.22
Jazz Hot, Le 1995.15
Jazz in the Kitchenette 1929.29
Jazz Land 1918.21
Jazz Land Ball 1926.19
Jazz Marimba 1919.03
Jazz Time Came from the South 1924.37
Jazz Up Jasper 1920.02
Jazz Vampire 1919.32
Jazz Wedding, The 1923.41
Jazz Your Troubles Away 1923.39
Jazz, How I Love to Hear It 1918.42
Jazz-a-Muh-Jazz 1918.18
Jazz-Time City 1919.22
Jazza-da-dada 1921.34
Jazzbo Brown 1975.20
Jazzimova 1921.25
Jazzing the Alphabet 1920.19
Jazzmania 1923.21
Jazztime Baby 1924.27
Jazzy-Jazz-Dancing Lesson 1920.05
Je Bois 1998.12
Je cherche apres Titina 1925.05
Je cherche apres Titine 1925.10, 1925.24
Je dis toujours le mot qu'il faut pas dire 1929.15
Je fais tout a contretemps 1929.15
Je l'aime mieux autrement 1929.16
Je lui ai dit 1929.11
Je me suis laisse embouteiller 1929.16
Je me suis longtemps souvenu 1926.49
Je n'ai jamais compris 1929.15
Je n'ai plus rine du ton de la cocotte 1885.59
Je n'en connais pas la fin 1947.18
Je n'sais pas me refuser 1929.13
Je ne la comprends pas 1900.38
Je ne le comprends pas 1897.37
Je ne parle pas Anglais 1918.14
Je ne sais comment faire 1878.08
Je ne sais pas 1919.10
Je ne savais pas 1934.32
Je ne suis plus la Marjolaine 1877.32
Je ne veux pas de vous 1887.35
Je pars 1964.02
Je partirai 1968.21
Je rafraichis! Moi, j'enflamme! 1884.50
Je regardais en l'air 1878.08
Je reviens te chercher 1968.21
Je said que vous etes gentil 1918.31
Je Sais Que Vous Etes Jolie 1960.17
Je sens se fermer ma paupiere 1877.32
Je serais fier, jeune fille 1885.56
Je suis dans les branches 1929.10
Je Suis Gris 1913.35
Je suis malade 1929.10

Je suis perplexe 1884.50
Je suis un bon garcon 1929.15
Je Suis Un Grand Detective 1888.11
Je suis un grande detective 1888.38
Je suis une femme accomplie 1886.09
Je suis venu a pieds 1961.25
Je suis venu simplement te dire bonjour 1929.16
Je T'ai Dans le Peau 1981.04
Je T'Aime 1930.32
Je t'aime - c'est fou 1989.10
Je T'Aime Comme Ca 1965.30
Je t'aime Means I Love You 1926.37
Je t'attends 1966.20, 1968.21
Je t'y prendrais donc toujours 1926.49
Je Te Rechaufferais 1965.30
Je te tuerai d'amour 1964.39
Je vais revoir cette Amelie 1885.56
Je veux, c'est la ma seule loi 1887.36
Je viens de chez le commissaire 1885.59
Je voudrais reveler a la nature 1887.35
Je voue adore 1903.22
Je Vous Aime 1925.05
Je Vous Aime, Milady 1981.14
Je'ne com prom pa Je ne comprends pas 1920.23
Jealous 1926.06
Jealous Moon 1917.13
Jealousy 1985.07, 1997.13
Jealousy Ballet 1954.05
Jealousy Begins at Home 1937.03
Jealousy Duet 1933.07, 1966.19, 1976.10, 1989.24
Jealousy Duet, The 1965.04
Jean 1922.01
Jean and Jacques Were Twins 1896.29
Jean la Princette 1886.33
Jeanette and Her Little Wooden Shoes 1947.04
Jeanette's Showbiz Number 2000.15
Jeannette 1886.30
Jeannie With the Light Brown Hair 1939.21
Jeannie's Packing Up 1947.07, 1980.26
Jeepers Creepers 1939.29, 1988.08, 1997.05
Jekyll's Plea 1997.09
Jellicle Ball 1992.12
Jellicle Ball, The 1982.19
Jellicle Songs for Jellicle Cats 1982.19
Jelly Beans at Walgreen's 1942.35
Jelly Donuts and Chocolate Cake 1980.23
Jelly Fish Song, The 1898.43
Jelly's Jam 1992.08
Jemima Green 1906.15
Jennie Jones 1906.31, 1907.19
Jennie Who Lives in the Dell 1866.35
Jenny 1903.38, 1971.19
Jenny is False 1882.58
Jenny Jones 1860.05
Jenny Lind 1922.32
Jeremiah Obadiah 1971.20
Jeremiah, Blow the Fire 1877.25, 1879.03
Jerezanos 1917.25
Jericho 1928.41
Jerk Song, The 1946.10
Jerome, the Bogey Man 1905.22
Jerry 1955.03
Jerry, My Soldier Boy 1941.08
Jersey Bounce 1999.24
Jersey Walk 1926.29
Jerusalem of Gold 1972.17
Jesce Sole 1985.14
Jessamine 1904.33
Jesse James Glide, The 1914.34
Jesus Christ Superstar 1992.12
Jesus Es Mi Senor 1998.02
Jesus Hi 1972.18
Jesus Remembers When Others Forget 1990.05
Jesus Walked This Lonesome Valley 1955.13
Jet Black Crow 1929.43
Jet Song 1957.12
Jeune Alfred aimait avec droiture, Le 1885.57
Jeune fille dis-moi ton nom 1878.08
Jeunes, filles, selon l'usage 1877.32
Jewel Ballet 1919.03
Jewel of a Duel, A 1950.10
Jewel of Asia, The 1896.27
Jewel Song, The 1923.17
Jewelry 1965.02
Jewels of Pandora, The 1920.08
Jewels of the Follies, The 1921.27
Jig Along, Mr. Jigger 1909.05
Jig Hop 1930.28
Jig Saw Jamboree 1933.15
Jig, The 1963.25
Jigaboo Jig, The 1927.62
Jigaree, The 1915.27
Jiggle Your Feet 1927.15
Jiggs 1925.12
Jijibo, The 1924.03
Jikel' Emaweni 1966.03
Jilted 1931.48
Jilted! 1894.28
Jim 1913.34
Jim Crow 1857.06
Jim Dandy 1934.40
Jim Jam 1896.18
Jim Jam Jems 1920.35
Jim Jam Jumpin' 1986.02
Jim Jam Sailor Superfine 1890.49
Jim, Jam, Jumpin' Jive 1976.04
Jimmie 1920.42
Jimmie and Me 1930.20
Jimmie, the Well-Dressed Man 1929.27
Jimmy 1927.37, 1969.14
Jimmy Jimmy 1983.17
Jimmy on the Chute 1894.33
Jingle Bells 1912.29, 1979.24
Jingle, Jangle, Jingle 1980.29
Jingles and Jokes 1907.14
Jingles, Jokes and Rhymes 1903.39
Jitterbug Waltz, The 1978.09
Jitters 1933.06
Jiu Jitsu 1907.24
Jive Drill 1952.08
Jive Talkin' 1999.15
Jivette Boogie Beat 1985.03
Jo Jo, the Cannibal Kid 1939.14
Jo-Jo Blues 1922.44
Joan of Arc 1920.44
Joan to the Maypole 1924.20
Job Lot, A 1891.14, 1892.18
Jockey Chorus 1888.44
Jockey Chorus, The 1899.19
Jockey's Life for Mine 1924.27
Jockeys Song, The 1883.52
Jocko Homo 1982.22
Jockomo 1992.06
Joe 1978.12
Joe Porter's Car is Seen 1945.09
Joe Worker 1937.08
Joey's Class Act 1963.17
Joey's Tango 1961.15
Joey, Joey, Joey 1956.04
Johann Strauss, Who Made the World Dance 1929.28
Johanna 1979.06, 1984.13, 1989.19
John 19:41 1971.12
John and Mary 1891.43
John Dough 1905.56
John Henry 1931.31
John Paul Jones 1944.14
John Reilly's Always Dry 1881.09
John Would Never do That 1902.32
John, the Gentlemen's Son 1885.54
Johnnie 1923.25
Johnnie, I'll Take You 1904.13
Johnnies of Long Acre Square, The 1900.07
Johnny 1959.04
Johnny and the Puckwudgies 1951.17
Johnny B Goode 1982.22
Johnny B. Goode 1986.02, 1990.15
Johnny be Good 1978.01
Johnny came courting me 1862.06
Johnny Come Follow Me 1917.09
Johnny Cope 1882.50
Johnny Fill Up the Bowl 1870.07
Johnny Get Off the Corner 1903.11
Johnny has Gone 1954.11
Johnny in the Army 1905.12
Johnny is a Hoarder 1942.26
Johnny Mishuga 1962.02
Johnny Morgan 1877.43
Johnny One Note 1975.13
Johnny One-Note 1937.04
Johnny Ride the Sky 1951.17
Johnny Soldier 1966.03
Johnny Strong 1903.41
Johnny Wanamaker 1930.18, 1930.33
Johnny's Dream 1936.28
Johnny's Melody 1936.28
Johnny's Song 1936.28
Johnny, how do you flow? 1865.03
Johnny, wenn Du Geburstag hast 1999.07
Joie and Vasaline 1895.36
Join in Pleasure 1886.30
Join it Right Away 1940.19
Join Our Ranks 1935.03
Join the Army 1975.07
Join the Circus 1980.07
Join the Familee 1915.20
Join the Navy 1919.23, 1927.16
Join Us in a Cup of Tea 1948.30
Join Us in a Little Cup of Tea 1961.01
Joint is Jumpin', The 1978.09, 1979.13
Joke's on Us, The 1941.11
Joker, The 1965.19
Joli Tambour, Le 1922.06
Jollification 1937.09
Jollity Ballet, The 1899.41
Jolly Boys 1892.05
Jolly British Tar 1897.37
Jolly Christmas Party, A 1873.29
Jolly Commodore, The 1890.49
Jolly Convicts and Their Admirers 1898.08
Jolly Good Fellow 1901.07, 1915.01
Jolly Good Time, A 1994.12
Jolly Jack With Hornpipe 1893.43
Jolly Josephine 1898.03
Jolly Jungle Boys 1906.14
Jolly Little Chap All Round, A 1888.11
Jolly Little Japs 1904.29
Jolly Maidens, The 1882.18
Jolly Me 1919.14
Jolly Old Owls, The 1885.49, 1893.46
Jolly Old Potentate, A 1902.18
Jolly Old Tar 1898.47
Jolly Pair, The 1906.49
Jolly Pioneer, The 1883.04
Jolly Students, The 1899.04
Jolly Tars 1905.07
Jolly Tars, The 1929.48
Jolly young Jacks are we 1896.27
Jolly Yourself Along 1905.37
Jolly, jolly huntsmen! 1882.63
Jolly, Rich and Fat 1994.12
Jonah Man 1980.27
Jonah Man, The 1903.08
Jonathan Wild 1886.45
Jones Said I'll be One 1896.37
Jones' Family Friends, The 1928.31
Jonny 1967.13, 1968.20
Jordan 1859.11
Jose, Can't You See! 1932.07
Joseph All the Time 1982.03, 1993.15
Joseph Megamix 1993.15
Joseph Taylor, Jr. 1947.17
Joseph's Coat 1982.03, 1993.15
Joseph's Dreams 1982.03, 1993.15
Joseph, James and John 1900.39
Josephine 1913.04, 1920.23, 1927.01, 1955.02, 1999.12
Josephine My Jo 1900.46
Josephine Waters 1936.31
Josh's Welcome 1996.08
Joshua 1943.21
Joshua Fit de Battle of Jericho 1930.10
Joshua Fit the Battle of Jericho 1955.13
Jota 1949.07
Jota Aragonesa 1939.18
Jota de la Dolores 1958.06
Jota de los Toreros 1866.11
Jour ou la pluie viendra, Le 1966.20, 1968.21
Jour vient de finir, Le 1887.35
Journee est bonne et gaie, La 1885.57

Journey of a Lifetime, The 1990.04
Journey On 1998.01
Journey to Paradise 1939.23
Journey to the Heavyside Layer, The 1982.19
Journey's End 1922.41, 1925.38, 1927.02
Jours meileurs, Les 1968.21
Jours Meilleurs, Les 1966.20
Jousts, The 1960.21, 1980.19, 1993.11
Jove he has gone 1866.11
Jovial Monk, A 1897.41
Joy and Glass 1912.48
Joy and Gloom 1924.29
Joy and Pangs of Motherhood 1926.35
Joy Attend on Erminie 1921.01
Joy Bells 1927.17
Joy Duet, The 1908.29
Joy go with the festive glass 1880.18
Joy is Mine 1928.30
Joy of a Kiss, The 1907.52
Joy of Life, The 1910.05
Joy of That Kiss, The 1912.41
Joy or Strife 1928.48
Joy Ride 1926.04
Joy Ride, A 1911.07
Joy Rules the Day 1902.18
Joy Spreader, The 1925.17
Joy to the King 2000.10
Joy to the lover 1882.60
Joy to the World 1982.22, 1998.19
Joy Town 1917.16
Joy, Ghebers, joy 1859.08
Joy, oh, what Rapture! 1878.20
Joyful Noise 1958.10
Joyful Noise, A 1966.30
Joyful Song, A 1970.17
Joyful Thing, A 1966.27
Joyful Wedding Day, A 1925.21
Joyne Hands 1963.28
Joys of Love, The 1911.03
Joys of the Rustic Dance 1893.35
Juanita 1898.43, 1924.43, 1938.06
Juba Dance 1923.39
Jubilation T. Cornpone 1956.12
Jubilee 1933.06, 1991.01
Jubilee Jim 1870.20
Jubilee Joe 1969.03
Jubilee Melodies 1879.64
Jubilee Stomp 1981.06
Jubilee Today, A 1890.23
Jubilo 1919.09
Judas Dance 1980.14
Judas' Dance 1982.17
Judas' Death 1971.12
Jude's Holler 1969.07
Judgement Day 1999.08
Judgement Day, The 1969.10
Judgement of Paris 1868.08, 1959.20
Judgement of Paris, The 1935.14, 1944.16
Judy 1927.09
Judy Two-Step, The 1910.30
Judy Waltz, The 1910.30
Jug of Wine, A 1945.19
Jugglar 1906.41
Juke Box 1942.05
Juke Box Saturday Night 1942.19
Julia 1906.10
Julia and Donald and Joe 1916.02
Julia Sanderson's Popular Song 1914.18
Julia, jusqu'a cette heure 1929.11
Julianne 1927.45
Julie 1903.04, 1920.41
Julie Dooley 1904.13
Julienne 1897.04
Julius Caesar 1968.06
Jumbalaya 1954.08
Jump Back, Honey 1898.41
Jump for Joy 1980.10, 1993.02
Jump In 1962.14
Jump Jim Crow 1917.15
Jump Shout Boogie 1976.34
Jump Steady 1924.27
Jump, Little Chillun 1951.15
Jumpin at the Woodside 1999.24
Jumpin' at the Woodside 1939.29, 1976.34, 1986.02
Jumpin' Jive, The 1999.24
Jumping Bean, The 1927.08
Jumping from Rock to Rock 1979.18
Jumping Jack 1926.04
Jumping Jacks 1916.24
Jumping Jimminy 1929.32
June 1903.07, 1911.05, 1925.18, 1925.35
June Bells 1920.29
June Bug, The 1920.31
June Days Waltz 1925.26
June is Bustin' Out All Over 1945.05, 1986.03
June is in the Air 1913.26
June Love 1921.09
June Moon 1920.47
June Skies 1890.03
Jung an Jahrent 1885.01
Jungle Bungalow 1922.05
Jungle Chapel, The 1948.24
Jungle Hip Hop 1984.15
Jungle Jamboree 1929.23
Jungle Love 1937.09
Jungle Man, The 1909.07
Jungle Nights in Dixieland 1924.37
Jungle Rhythm 1949.06
Jungle Rose 1927.33
Jungle Shadows 1927.63
Jungle Swing 1937.09
Jungle-Jingle, The 1927.37
Junk Mail 1988.07
Junk Man 1980.29
Junkanoo 1980.05
Jupiter Forbid 1942.15, 1975.13
Jupiter's Levee 1956.09
Jury of His Peers, A 1925.21
Jusqu'la 1896.18
Jusqua La 1894.37
Just 'Cause the Moon was Shinin' 1902.43
Just a Barber Shop Cord 1922.44
Just a Big-Hearted Man 1929.06
Just a Bit Naive 1947.13
Just a Bum 1947.05, 1948.12
Just a Card 1925.47
Just a Closer Walk With Thee 1986.02
Just a Connoisseur 1947.06
Just a Fan 1922.30
Just a Flower from an Old Bouquet 1925.05
Just a Gentle Buck 1902.20
Just a Gentle Touch 1902.20
Just a Gigolo 1979.11, 1986.06
Just a Girl, Just a Boy 1919.24
Just a House 1983.18
Just a Housewife 1978.12
Just a Kiss 1902.37, 1919.34, 1925.04
Just a Kiss Apart 1949.18, 1995.07
Just a Little After Taps 1918.14, 1919.40
Just a Little Bit Behind the Times 1920.35
Just a Little Bit in Love 1917.19
Just a Little Bit More 1939.13
Just a Little Bit of Blarney 1910.04
Just a Little Bit of Jesus Goes a Long Way 1976.35, 1980.14
Just a Little Bit of Lingerie 1911.35
Just a Little Bit of Love 1923.22
Just a Little Blue for You 1929.24
Just a Little Chambermaid 1933.23
Just a Little Ever-Loving Girl 1904.22
Just a Little Gossip 1914.04
Just a Little Joint With a Juke Box 1941.06
Just a Little Laughter 1918.33
Just a Little Line 1919.09
Just a Little Love 1913.17
Just a Little Love Song 1928.19
Just a Little Lump of Sugar for the Bird 1896.18
Just a Little Pent-house and You 1932.10
Just a Little Smile 1927.48
Just a Little Stranger 1927.20
Just a Little Sunshine 1889.05, 1918.35
Just a Little Thing 1928.30
Just a Little Thing Called Rhythm 1925.33
Just a Little Touch of Paris 1919.40
Just a Little White House 1950.19
Just a Little Word Unspoken 1911.39
Just a Lullaby 1923.38
Just a Mile and a Half from Town 1904.07
Just a Minute 1928.34
Just a Moment Ago 1956.16
Just a Play 1909.19
Just a Policeman 1921.12
Just a Pretty Little Home 1923.16
Just a Promise 1934.37
Just a Sister 1930.18
Just a Slip of the Tongue 1918.26
Just a Smile 1920.42
Just a Tiny Cup of Tea 1922.27
Just a Voice to Call Me Dear 1917.20
Just a Wonderful Time 1954.17
Just a word 1882.63
Just Across from Jersey 1883.63, 1893.10
Just Across the River from Queens 1927.05
Just Act Natural 1923.46
Just an Honest Mistake 1961.21
Just an Old Spanish Custom 1932.15
Just an Ordinary Guy 1938.09, 1948.22
Just Another Guy 1956.16
Just Another New Step 1924.17
Just Another Polka 1980.29
Just Another Rhumba 1983.06, 1999.10
Just Another Silly Day 1904.18
Just Answer With a Kiss 1931.29
Just Around the Corner from Easy Street 1919.10
Just as a Rosebud Blossoms 1978.07
Just as Father Used to Do 1911.39
Just as You Are 1912.12
Just Because 1922.13
Just Because He Couldn't Sing 'Love Me and the World is Mine' 1907.41
Just Because it's You 1913.31
Just Begging for Love 1931.21
Just Beyond the Rainbow 1945.18
Just Clothes 1920.23
Just Don't Make No Sense 1971.13
Just Eighteen 1931.28
Just Fancy What is Said 1880.69
Just for a Day 1904.11
Just for a Kiss 1896.48
Just for a Little While 1924.46
Just for a Night 1926.33
Just for Me 1903.07
Just for Once 1959.01
Just for the Ride 1970.03
Just for To-Day 1900.25
Just for Today 1968.23
Just for Tonight 1936.01, 1945.14, 1979.04
Just for You 1911.41
Just Get Out and Walk 1905.29
Just Go to the Movies 1980.08, 1985.19
Just Good Friends 1909.01
Just Got Off th' Chain 1930.17
Just Hello 1936.27
Just Home from College 1907.37
Just How Much I Love You 1907.22
Just Imagine 1919.33, 1927.41, 1974.26
Just in Case 1945.04
Just in Time 1956.14, 1958.20, 1958.21, 1961.25, 1977.02, 1979.14, 1999.23
Just Keep Cool 1900.59
Just Kids 1906.17
Just Laugh 1919.41
Just Lean on Me 1924.47
Just Leave Everything to Me 1985.19
Just Leave it to Bill 1904.22
Just Let Me Look at You 1986.01
Just Like a Doll 1922.40
Just Like a Gypsy 1918.32
Just Like a Man 1952.20
Just Like a Rose 1920.26
Just Like a Woman 1897.31, 1946.19
Just Like Jane 1905.02, 1906.35
Just like Julius Caesar 1853.02
Just Like That 1922.33, 1980.08
Just Like the House That Jack Built 1920.19
Just Like This 1909.14
Just Like You 1912.35, 1921.10
Just Look 1964.03
Just Look Around 1923.45

Just look at all those precious Hussies 1875.19
Just Love 1922.42
Just Lovin' 1926.21
Just Marry the Man and be Merry 1902.41, 1917.11
Just Mention Joe 1934.39
Just Missed the Opening Chorus 1924.19
Just My Luck 1946.04, 1958.01
Just My Style 1905.03
Just My Type 1919.03
Just Off the Chain 1928.05
Just Once Around the Clock 1935.17
Just One Good Time 1921.20
Just One Kiss 1895.21, 1926.28
Just One More 1907.14
Just One More Kiss 1916.12
Just One Night 1983.18
Just One of Those Things 1935.14, 1976.32, 1981.16, 1998.05
Just One Rose 1924.05
Just One Way to Say I Love You 1949.08
Just Plain Jim 1885.69
Just Plant a Kiss 1920.43
Just Say Good-Bye 1920.13
Just Say the Word 1934.20
Just Say You Care 1908.13
Just Snap Your Fingers at Care 1920.28
Just Some One 1908.05
Just Squeeze Me 1981.06
Just Stay Alive 1964.03
Just Strollin' 1940.23
Just Suppose 1921.04, 1929.09
Just Suppose You Loved Me 1909.14
Just Sweet Sixteen 1920.28
Just take a peep 1873.04
Just Take Things as They Come 1904.05
Just Tell Me With Your Eyes 1911.05
Just That You are You 1912.27
Just the Crust 1965.33
Just the One I've Waited For 1914.19
Just the Same 1908.08, 1927.04
Just the same old story 1902.32
Just the Two of Us 1918.32
Just the Way You Are 1955.19
Just Thought I'd Call 1982.13
Just Three Words 1904.51
Just to be a Flower in the Garden of the Lord 1963.27
Just to Know What's Going on in New York Town 1901.21
Just to Pass the Time Away 1898.73
Just Trust in Him 1963.27
Just Two Days Since We Arrived 1898.38
Just Us Two 1890.16
Just We Two 1909.09, 1917.27, 1924.45, 1980.21
Just We Two Dear 1912.36
Just What a Girl Can Do 1918.32
Just When I Thought I had You All to Myself 1927.39
Just Win a Pretty Widow 1915.18
Just You Alone 1918.11
Just You and I and the Baby 1925.16
Just You and I and the Moon 1913.17
Just You and Me 1917.13, 1917.32
Just You Wait 1956.01, 1993.18
Just You Watch My Step 1917.17
Just Your Old Friend 1971.10
Justice 1998.01
Justice Triumphant 1965.29
Justine Johnstone Rag, The 1917.31

K-ra-azy for You 1992.02
K-ra-zy for You 1928.43
K.P. 1919.08
Ka Wahine Akamai 1961.07
Kaddish 1931.29
Kadoola Kadoola Solo 1923.27
Kailua 1921.36
Kaiser Bill 1964.28
Kalamazoo 1908.30
Kalamazoo is No Place for You 1905.32
Kalialani 1972.11
Kalidah Battle 1975.01
Kalimera 1972.23
Kalora's Entrance 1911.02
Kalua Bay 1962.01
Kama Sutra 1968.11
Kama's Garden 1923.31
Kamarinskaya 1922.06
Kamenoi Ostrow 1982.06
Kan the Kaiser 1918.09
Kandahar Isle 1926.37
Kangaroo 1927.38
Kangaroo Hop, The 1912.24
Kangaroo, The 1902.43, 1962.14
Kanonen-Song, Der 1965.04
Kansas City 1943.04, 1993.16, 1995.03
Karanga Tia 1972.20
Karen Yar 1968.04
Karen's Lullaby 1971.02
Karenin's List 1992.11
Karma 1990.17
Karoo-Karoo, how do ye do 1890.03
Karu 1972.20
Kat Cabaret, The 1915.25
Kate Kearney 2000.01
Kate O'Donoghue 1897.05
Kate, Come and Kiss Me 1909.12
Katerina 1904.23
Kathleen Aroon 1913.03
Kathleen Mine 1932.03
Katie 1891.18
Katie and Her Kodak 1904.03
Katie and Tom, or, Love's Helping Hand 1891.32
Katie Clancy 1915.29
Katie Connor 1891.14
Katie Did in Madrid 1946.06
Katie Gray 1908.28
Katie Jonas 1970.02
Katie My Love 1985.05
Katie Rooney 1913.17
Katie was a Business Girl 1907.18
Katie Went to Haiti 1939.30
Katie's Sweet Heart 1889.37
Katie, My Southern Rose 1902.41, 1917.11
Katinka 1915.30, 1922.06, 1923.18, 1923.28, 1924.06, 1925.03
Katinka is Sweet Sixteen 1943.11
Katinka to Eva to Frances 1944.15
Katinka's Unexpected Romance 1922.06
Katrina 1902.15
Katy Malone 1894.36
Katy-did 1913.29, 1975.24
Katydid 1904.41
Katydid, the cricket and the Frog, The 1903.07
Katzenjammer is a Village 1898.56
Kaua i ka Huahuai 1912.03
Kava Ceremony 1972.11
Kawiliwiliwai 1912.03
Kayo Tortoni 1923.38
Kayser do you want to buy a Dog 1870.01
Keb, Sir? Want a Keb? 1901.23
Keep a Fox-Trot for Me 1920.37
Keep a Goin' 1923.19
Keep a Kiss for Me 1925.44
Keep a Taxi Waiting, Dear 1911.18
Keep A-Countin' Eight 1923.46
Keep A-Diggin' 1925.18
Keep Away from Emmaline 1897.56, 1898.50
Keep Away from Rosie 1904.07
Keep Away from the Fellow Who Owns an Automobile 1912.29
Keep Building Your Castles 1925.35
Keep Cool 1907.10
Keep Going 1915.21
Keep it Casual 1942.29
Keep it Confidential 1985.03
Keep it Dark 1877.25, 1879.03, 1903.10, 1921.31
Keep it Gay 1953.08, 2001.05
Keep it Hot 1975.14
Keep it Simple 1958.02
Keep it Under Your Hat 1928.09
Keep it Up 1926.02
Keep Laughing 1940.04
Keep Moving 1915.07, 1915.08, 1923.39, 1934.18
Keep Off the Grass 1902.01, 1917.05, 1972.05
Keep on a Shining, Silvery Moon 1903.18
Keep on Building Castles in the Air 1922.16
Keep on Croonin' a Tune 1925.07
Keep on Dancing 1928.09, 1974.04
Keep on Doing Something 1906.26
Keep on Lovin' 1912.36
Keep on Rollin' 1995.03
Keep on Running 1986.02
Keep on Smilin' 1909.10
Keep on Smiling 1904.52, 1918.30
Keep One Eye on Your Country 1899.02
Keep one thumb and a finger 1857.06
Keep Out of Finnegan's Way 1884.16
Keep Repeating it 1917.14
Keep Romance Alive 1981.03
Keep Shufflin' 1928.10
Keep Smiling and Carry On 1930.39
Keep Smiling at Trouble 1925.01, 1925.23
Keep the Ball A-Rolling 1886.45
Keep the Ball-a-rolling 1886.53
Keep the Golden Gates Wide Open 1895.44
Keep the Home Fires Burning 1964.28
Keep the Love Lamp Burning 1920.15
Keep the Man You've Got 1923.11
Keep the Party Going 1924.22
Keep Them Guessing 1920.15, 1925.35
Keep Them in a Golden Cage 1921.02
Keep Up the Pace 1916.09
Keep Young and Beautiful 1989.21
Keep Your Eye on It 1886.39
Keep Your Eye on the Ball 1921.09, 1923.47
Keep Your Eye on the Red 1980.15
Keep Your Hand on Your Heart 1938.15
Keep Your Head Down, Fritzie Boy 1918.10
Keep Your Nose to the Grindstone 1955.25
Keep Your Sunny Side Up 1974.26
Keep Your Undershirt On 1929.49
Keep Your Weight Down 1920.22
Keep Your Whip in Your Hand 1910.02
Keep-a-Hoppin' 1960.20
Keepin' Out of Mischief Now 1978.09
Keeping Cool With Coolidge 1949.18, 1974.02, 1995.07
Keeping Priglio Company 1937.11
Keepsakes 1923.34, 1946.18
Keewa-Tak-e-Yaka-holo 1920.36
Kelly 1916.09
Kelly's Gone to Kingdom Come! 1909.11
Kemo Kimo 1903.19
Kenosha Canoe 1946.07
Kentucky 1929.01
Kentucky Babe 1904.45, 1980.27
Kentucky Fried Chicken 1976.34
Keokuk Culture Club, The 1905.57
Kept in Suspense 1931.13
Ker-Choo! 1927.42
Kermesse, La 1864.12
Kerry Dances 1942.14
Kettle is Singing, A 1918.16
Key to My Heart 1922.24
Keys of Heaven, The 1923.07
Keys of My Heart, The 1923.07
Keys to Heaven 1926.13
Keys to Your Heart 1930.09
Keystone Glide, The 1915.23
Khanzndl Oyf Shabes, A 1990.16
Khavertes 1970.17
Khonghouse Song 1928.30
Khootorok 1922.37
Khorovod 1895.12
Khosn-Kale mazl-Tov 1990.16
Ki-Ram Wedding March 1902.44
Kic-King, Le 1907.41
Kick Line 1998.04
Kickaboo 1879.03
Kickapoo' 1877.25
Kickin' the Clouds Away 1925.14, 1983.06
Kickin' the Corn Around 1938.12
Kicking Polka, The 1908.42
Kid 1968.03
Kid Days 1903.11, 1907.20, 1922.31
Kid Go! 1996.07
Kid Inside, The 1982.08, 1991.10
Kidder's Reception 1905.53
Kidland 1910.18
Kidnapped 1971.18

Kidnapper, The 1917.22
Kids 1960.06
Kids Game 1993.07
Kids in Hogan's Alley 1896.26
Kig Solomon Knew a Thing of Two 1904.23
Kikerikee 1920.37
Kiki 1925.29
Kiki was a Good Girl 1922.15
Kilimanjaro 1988.02
Kill 1975.07
Killaloe 1888.41
Killarney 1873.10, 1907.28, 1915.03
Killarney's Lakes 2000.01
Killee Kekikako 1876.30
Killer Wants to Go to College 1998.02
Killing Me Softly 2000.14
Killing Time 1990.09
Kim's Charleston 1994.08
Kin of Nur Al-Din, The 1920.34
Kind Conqueror 1876.10
Kind Fortune Smiles To-Day 1904.36
Kind Friends, This Deference 1898.25
Kind Moon Man 1910.13
Kind of Man I Want to Marry, The 1919.41
Kind of Woman 1972.22
Kind sir, you cannot have the heart 1890.02
Kind wishes waft over you 1840.03
Kinda Cute 1929.26
Kinda Dukish 1981.06
Kinda Like You 1932.03
Kindergarten Blues 1922.26
Kindly Pass the Chloroform Along 1905.23
Kindness 1904.31, 1971.20
Kindred Spirits 1971.21
King & Courtesans 1997.16
King Called Cotton 1952.15
King Can do No Wrong, The 1928.03
King Carnival 1916.18
King Edward's Subjects 1903.23
King for a Day 1928.22
King Gilhooly 1899.30
King Hal's Gals 1909.01
King Herod's Song 1971.12
King Kazoo of Kakaroo 1901.17
King Lear Ballet 1964.18
King Neptune 1907.51
King of a South Sea Isle 1912.05
King of autocratic power we, A 1894.15
King of Babyland, The 1909.05
King of Broadway 1917.37
King of Broadway, The 2001.05
King of Effervescence, The 1954.06
King of Glen and Crag 1895.41
King of Hearts 1978.22
King of London 1961.26
King of Man a Woman Needs, The 1965.36
King of Pride Rock 1997.20
King of Ruritania 1897.19
King of the Boulevards 1911.44
King of the King's highway 1882.17
King of the Mosquitos 1890.33
King of the Swells 1885.06
King of the Sword 1928.48
King of Thule 1870.26
King Orders the Drums to be Beaten, The 1922.06, 1925.03
King Polimeniche 1878.02
King Polimenicho 1896.35
King Solomon 1923.16
King Supreme 1868.03
King Though he's pestered with cares, A 1895.29
King's Dilemma 1995.15
King's Favorite, The 1919.30
King's got four acres, The 1883.66
King's Horses, The 1930.38
King's Hunt, The 1963.03, 1963.28
King's Musketeers, The 1899.28
King's Own, The 1902.07
King's Song, The 1893.17, 1968.22
Kingdom for Two, The 1922.15
Kingdom of Dreams 1928.03
Kings of de Policy Shop 1899.31
Kings of the Policy Shop 1899.33
Kings of the Sea, The 1904.30
Kinkajou, The 1927.08
Kinky 1908.08
Kinky Kids Parade, The 1925.48
Kipper, The 1973.08
Kirchner Girls, The 1917.03
Kirmess Punch, The 1884.11
Kiss 'Liza 1896.02
Kiss Affects Me Most of All, A 1916.18
Kiss and a Squeeze in the Moonlight, A 1885.54
Kiss and be Friends 1912.08
Kiss and make it up 1882.44
Kiss at Auction 1916.25
Kiss Before I Go 1928.12
Kiss Burglar, The 1911.35
Kiss Duet 1911.24
Kiss for Cinderella, A 1918.07, 1928.16
Kiss for Each Day in the Week, 1903.14
Kiss from a Red-Headed Miss, A 1922.32
Kiss Her Now 1969.05, 1985.19
Kiss I Must Refuse You, A 1930.27
Kiss in the Dark, A 1896.29, 1922.33, 1923.20
Kiss in the Moonlight 1925.48
Kiss in the Moonlight, A 1925.25
Kiss Invention 1924.24
Kiss Lad and Never Tell 1904.01
Kiss Me 1916.04, 1917.36, 1921.16, 1924.46, 1929.41, 1963.20, 1976.25, 1979.06
Kiss Me Again 1911.31, 1917.26, 1924.18, 1952.11, 1980.27
Kiss Me Again Bebe 1912.17
Kiss Me and 'Tis Day 1912.46
Kiss Me and Kill Me With Love 1955.04
Kiss Me and We'll Both Go Home 1939.12
Kiss Me Good Night, Mother 1862.06
Kiss Me No Kisses 1964.05
Kiss Me Once More 1914.33
Kiss Me Sweet or My Love and I 1888.13
Kiss Me to Sleep 1900.56
Kiss Me! 1927.34
Kiss Me, Dearest, Kiss Me, Do 1911.44
Kiss Me, Honey, Do 1897.56, 1898.50, 1898.72
Kiss Me, Kate 1948.32, 1999.19
Kiss Me, My Love 1910.26
Kiss Me, Sweet 1887.01
Kiss of Love, the 1895.06
Kiss of Romance 1935.19
Kiss of the Spider Woman 1993.09
Kiss Song 1873.17, 1904.06
Kiss the Boys Goodbye 1980.29
Kiss Time 1923.01
Kiss Waltz 1916.26
Kiss Waltz, The 1911.11, 1911.32
Kiss With a Kick, A 1927.35
Kiss You Gave, The 1910.22
Kiss Your Minstrel Boy Good Bye 1908.22
Kiss Your Soldier Boy Au Revoir 1916.22
Kiss, A 1889.08
Kiss, The 1879.32, 1897.19, 1914.12, 1919.07, 1919.28
Kissable Lips 1923.17
Kisses 1904.47, 1905.56, 1919.12
Kisses at Auction 1910.34
Kisses That I Have Missed 1913.02
Kissimee 1920.37
Kissing 1873.10, 1904.47, 1914.20, 1938.06
Kissing Bag, The 1899.30
Kissing Bridge 1886.45
Kissing by Cable 1910.22
Kissing Duet, The 1883.67
Kissing Goes by Favor 1896.35
Kissing in the Rain 1876.11
Kissing in the Starlight 1876.30
Kissing Time 1908.06, 1920.37
Kissing, The 1896.27
Kit 1902.29
Kit Inspection 1921.12
Kitchen Cabaret, The 1912.20
Kitchen Man 1975.20, 1982.12
Kitchen Mechanics' Night Out 1999.24
Kitchen Police 1918.21
Kitchen Range, The 1913.04
Kitchen Sink 1982.23
Kite 1971.11
Kite, The 1999.03
Kitty 1885.08, 1901.27
Kitty Car Ballet 1958.04
Kitty Darlin' 1917.27
Kitty Kat 1923.22
Kitty Kitty 1903.01
Kitty MacKay 1914.16
Kitty More 1898.78
Kitty O'Brien 1897.40, 1917.10
Kitty O'Neill 1907.23
Kitty of Juniper Green 1920.12
Kitty's Kisses 1926.12
Kitty's Not Built That Way 1909.01
Kitty, Please Give Me a Kiss 1909.15
Kitzel Engagement, The 1926.51
Kiyomori 1903.18
Klain Yingeleh 1966.21
Kling-Kling Bird on the Divi-Divi Tree, The 1935.14
Kneedeep in June 1930.22
Knees 1929.42
Knife Grinder, The 1929.05
Knife, The 1889.36
Knight of Alcantara, The 1866.07, 1866.21
Knight of the Mirrors, The 1965.34
Knight of the Woeful Countenance 1965.34
Knights of the Mystic Star 1891.45, 1985.02
Knights of the White Cross 1952.15
Knights on White Horses 1985.04
Knit, Knit, Knit 1917.22
Knitting Chorus 1918.36
Knitting Sextette 1907.63
Knock at the Window To-Night, Love 1884.23
Knock Knock 1997.16
Knock on Wood 1930.06
Knock Three Times 2000.14
Knock Wood 1905.55
Knock'd 'Em in the Old Kent Road 1960.17
Knock, Knock 1965.17
Knock, Knock, Knock 1897.19
Knockers 1988.20
Knocking Bookworms, The 1923.24
Knocking on Wood 1929.32
Knot of Blue, The 1904.54
Knot There's No Untying, The 1902.03
Know Nothing, The 1854.04
Know When to Smile 1928.26
Know Your Business 1972.10
Knowest Thou Those Robes? 1881.22
Knowing When to Leave 1968.31
Ko-Ko 1981.06
Kodak Girl, The 1901.23
Koguette, La 1906.41
Kohala, Welcome 1928.16
Kojong's Imperial Conference 1997.16, 1998.08
Kokohi 1912.03
Kokoraki 1959.20
Kol Nidre 2000.14
Kol Rinah Vishu'ah 1971.17
Kongo Kate 1924.19
Koo-La-Loo 1917.06
Koreru Tsuki 1989.21
Korobeiniki 1977.13
Koroki 1972.20
Kosher Kitty Kelly 1925.19
Kosher Kleagle 1926.21
Kow Tow 1904.25
Kraquette, La 1907.24
Kuiawiak 1943.09
Kukla Katusha 1963.08
Kuli Kuli 1961.07
Kulula 1883.26
Kum Arain in Shenk 1968.22
Kumukahi 1912.03
Kupura Kupika 1966.03
Kuu Home 1912.03
Kwai Sonata, The 1973.13
Kwasa Kusile 1997.14
Kyrie Eleison 1972.24

L'accordeoniste 1947.18
L'Accordeoniste 1981.04
L'Ag'Ya 1944.31, 1950.07

L'Allegra 1871.27
L'amour bon dieu 1983.03
L'amour c'est comme un jour 1965.30
L'amour est un oiseau rebelle 1929.11
L'Amour Sorcier 1934.32
L'Amour Toujours L'Amour 1984.14
L'Amoureuse 1901.25
L'Apres Midi D'Un Boeuf 1939.30
L'apres midi d'un papillon 1926.13
L'Apres-Midi de Gilbert 1956.13
L'autre cote de la rue, De 1947.18
L'aventure est surprenante 1877.32
L'Chayim! 1965.32
L'Elefant Skeed 1919.10
L'Enchaineuse 1926.15
L'Enfant Prodigue 1894.21
L'etoile 1968.21
L'Exposition Universalle 1946.04
L'Heure Bleu 1924.09
L'heure d'or 1926.34
L'Historie de Madame de la Tour 1939.28
L'hotel des amours faciles 1934.32
L'Hotel des amours faciles 1935.19
L'il Gal 1907.22
L'Illusioniste 1955.14
L'important c'est la Rosa 1968.21
L'indolente panthere 1887.35
L'Irlandesa Rosa Dell'Abie 1925.20
L'oiseau de toutes les couleurs 1966.20, 1968.21
L'orange 1966.20
L'Orientale 1955.14
L,-O,-V,-E, Dot Spells Love 1894.32
L-O-V-E 1930.20
L-O-V-E M-O-N-E-Y 1908.37
L.Z. in Quest of His Youth 1964.21
La La La 1962.03
La la la la 1884.14
La Pas Ma La 1896.02
La Plus Belle France 1888.40
La-La-La-La 1895.17
La-Par Micado 1899.11
Label on the Bottle, The 1961.27
Labor Agitator, The 1920.19
Labor Day Parade 1928.10
Labor is the Thing 1937.13
Lace Maker's Song 1923.07
Lace Petticoat 1927.03
Lackaday 1950.10
Lackawanna 1925.01
Lad of My Love, The 1890.44
Lad Who Leads, The 1902.18
Ladder of Roses, The 1915.25
Ladies 1913.04, 1959.11
Ladies and Gentlemen, That's Love 1931.30
Ladies Beware 1908.29, 1934.43
Ladies Beware When the Lights are Low 1911.45
Ladies Cannot sit in Congress 1882.75
Ladies Choice 1921.14
Ladies Choice! 1978.07
Ladies Day 1916.22
Ladies from France 1898.47
Ladies from the Cultured West, The 1922.11
Ladies in Society 1907.15
Ladies in Their Sensitivities 1979.06
Ladies of London 1924.20
Ladies of London and Paris, The 1918.14
Ladies of the Box Office 1925.17
Ladies of the Evening 1938.14
Ladies of the Jury 1928.29
Ladies of the Town 1929.41
Ladies Singin' Their Song, The 1983.19
Ladies Who Lunch, The 1970.13, 1977.05, 1999.20
Ladies Who Sing With the Band, The 1943.07, 1978.09
Ladies' Day 1914.25
Ladies' Day Parade 1907.30
Ladies' Home Companion, A 1927.56
Ladies' Maid, The 1898.17
Ladies' Man, A 1927.41
Ladies' Opinion, The 1950.10
Ladies' Pet, The 1881.36
Ladies' Room 1938.07
Ladies, by your invasion 1881.06
Ladies, Have a Care! 1918.25
Ladies, I am sorry 1897.17
Ladies, The 1910.05, 1913.27, 1917.35
Ladies, We Love You 1908.43
Lads and lasses round about the hop pole trip 1887.44
Lady 1923.13, 1942.01, 1982.15
Lady and Gentleman 1911.06
Lady and the Kick 1897.42
Lady and the Maid, The 1892.14
Lady be Good 1953.12, 1986.02
Lady Bird 1901.13, 1920.12
Lady Bug Song, The 1957.05
Lady Butterfly 1923.01
Lady Do 1927.15
Lady Fair 1882.63, 1923.38, 1926.16
Lady fair, of lineage high, A 1884.09
Lady Fortune 1909.21
Lady has Oomph, The 1940.02
Lady I've Vowed to Wed, The 1916.06
Lady in Ermine 1922.36
Lady in the Moon, The 1900.41
Lady in the Tutti Frutti Hat, The 1988.08
Lady in the Window 1936.27
Lady in Waiting 1932.13, 1958.14
Lady is a Tramp, The 1937.04, 1974.11, 1975.13, 1976.16, 1981.16, 1989.21
Lady is a WAAC, The 1942.26
Lady isn't Looking, The 1972.25
Lady Killer, The 1870.01
Lady Lindy Love 1905.42
Lady Lingerie 1922.24
Lady Luck 1922.47, 1925.49, 1928.37
Lady Luck Smile on Me 1922.41
Lady Luxury 1914.33
Lady Madonna 1977.10
Lady Magnolia 1883.04
Lady Marmalade 1992.06
Lady Mine! 1894.29
Lady Must Live, A 1931.04, 1981.16
Lady Needs a Change, A 1939.13
Lady Needs a Rest, A 1941.08
Lady of Dreams 1922.24
Lady of Mars 1920.19
Lady of My Heart 1925.40
Lady of the Evening 1922.39
Lady of the Fan 1930.35
Lady of the Jury, A 1932.19
Lady of the Lamp, The 1920.47
Lady of the Merry Ha, Ha, The 1903.02
Lady of the Rose 1926.34
Lady of the Slipper, The 1912.39
Lady of the Snow, The 1925.47
Lady on a Tandem Bicycle 1952.04
Lady Osteopath, The 1925.05
Lady Picking Mulberries, The 1889.01
Lady Romance 1917.35
Lady Secretary, The 1907.15
Lady Sings the Blues 1976.16
Lady Sleeps, The 1909.23
Lady St. Heiler 1980.13
Lady Thinks She is Thirty, A 1973.08
Lady wasn't Going That Way, The 1895.43
Lady Whipporwill 1928.28
Lady With a Fan 1981.16
Lady With Money, A 1904.49
Lady With the Tap, The 1935.12
Lady's Choice 1976.33
Lady's in Love With You, The 1980.29
Lady's Maid 1997.06
Lady's Maid, The 1900.43, 1906.41
Lady's Paying, The 1994.10
Lady, The 1940.18
Lady, the Coachman and Cupid, The 1924.48
Lady-Ushers Ball, The 1910.16
Laendler 1959.24
Laertes Coercion 1976.03
Laff 'Em Away 1927.62
Lago de Innamoratti, Il 1964.35
Lagoon Waltz 1964.25
Lagunenwalzer 1964.25
Lagunya 1999.12
Lah De Dah 1880.38
Lak Jeem 1924.28
Lalage Potts, That's Me 1896.05
Lalelani! 1993.04
Lalirette 1966.03
Lalla 1903.17
Lalla Rookh 1879.50
Lambert's Quandry 1972.24
Lambeth Walk, The 1986.12
Lament 1909.27, 1932.19, 1952.04, 1979.23, 1987.18
Lament of Shakespeare, The 1926.23
Lament of the Crusty Dames, The 1906.05
Lament of the Frogs, The 1886.49
Lament of Villagers 1879.15
Lament, A 1886.15
Lamentation 1896.27
Lamp is Low, The 1987.02
Lamp of Love, The 1919.16
Lamp, The 1900.01
Lamp-Posts of Old Broadway, The 1915.25
Lamplight 1934.06
Lamplight Land 1922.15
Lancashire Clog, The 1929.04
Lancashire Lass, A 1882.39
Lancers 1905.19
Lancers, The 1925.43
Lances, The 1904.29
Land and Water 1914.32
Land Beyond the Candle Light, The 1920.19
Land I Love, The 1903.14, 1920.26
Land O'Mine 1922.36
Land of a Thousand Dances 1982.22
Land of Beautiful Dreams, The 1910.26
Land of Betrayal 1971.18
Land of Broken Dreams 1927.13
Land of Butterflies 1920.44
Land of Dancing Pickaninnies 1924.27
Land of Enchantment 1923.03
Land of Fancy, The 1911.37
Land of Going to be, The 1928.33
Land of Golden Dreams 1906.23
Land of Heart's Desire 1898.17
Land of Lace, The 1924.31
Land of Liberty, The 1917.16
Land of Long Ago, The 1924.46
Land of Love and Roses, The 1915.25
Land of Love, The 1894.38, 1909.24
Land of Make Believe 1912.33, 2001.04
Land of Make Believe, The 1904.01
Land of Midnight Son, The 1900.59
Land of Mine 1952.15
Land of My Heart's Desire 1919.13
Land of My Own Romance 1947.04
Land of Opportunities 1946.20
Land of Rockefellera 1942.34
Land of Romance 1905.50, 1926.24
Land of Romance, The 1894.40, 1918.23
Land of Sky Blue Waters 1922.18
Land of the Free, The 1911.02
Land of the Gay Caballero 1930.31
Land of the Midnight Sun, The 1914.26, 1917.19
Land of the Sky, The 1909.02
Land of the Sultan's Dream, The 1911.36
Land of Wot, The 1905.33
Land of Yesteryear, The 1918.08
Land That's Far Away, The 1902.16
Land Where Good Songs Go, The 1917.26
Land Which My Heart Calls Home, The 1907.13
Land You Left Behind, The 1906.20
Land, Ho! 1902.11
Landerirette 1934.32
Landlord at My Door! 1932.15
Landlord, Fill Up! 1883.12
Langenstein in the Spring 1934.04
Language of Flowers 1891.20, 1892.45
Language of Flowers, The 1902.01, 1916.06
Language of Love, The 1903.40
Language of Lovers' Smiles, The 1912.31
Language of Signs 1910.01
Language of the Fan 1917.08
Language Song, The 1960.20
Languanay 1916.22
Languid Man, The 1898.47
Lanky, Yankee Boys in Blue, The 1908.05
Lantern Night 1964.03

Lantern of Love 1926.24
Lapse of Time, A 1922.17
Larceny and Love 1964.04
Lardy Da 1880.42
Large Cold Bottle and a Small Hot Bird, A 1898.50
Larger Than Life 1992.17
Largest Moving Object, The 1997.06
Largo al factotum 1862.02
Lark, The 1927.55, 1988.15
Larry 1907.12
Larry Barry 1900.03
Larry Malone 1877.27
Larry Mulligan 1894.31
Larry O'Brien 1870.20
Lars, Lars 1979.12
Las Vegas 1955.12, 1959.14
Las Vegas, A 1955.14, 1963.02, 1965.08
Lass I Love, The 1901.02
Lass of Richmond Hill 1862.02
Lass that waits for Peter, The 1880.46
Lass Who Loved a Sailor, The 1929.42
Lass With a Lasso, The 1911.45
Lasses Who Live in Glass Houses 1911.05
Lassie 1920.12
Lassies!, The 1890.33
Lasso Duet 1912.04
Lasso Lassie 1905.42
Last 'I Love New York' Song, The 1985.15
Last Blues, The 1976.03
Last Chance Blues, The 1992.08
Last Dance, The 1929.41
Last Drop of Blood 1998.02
Last farewell must now be spoken, The 1888.07
Last Girl is the Best Girl, The 1922.01
Last Girl, The 1997.07
Last Long Mile, The 1918.09, 1944.01
Last Midnight 1987.18
Last Night 1888.44
Last Night of the World, The 1991.03
Last Night on the Back Porch I Loved Her Best of All 1921.34, 1923.18
Last of General Hong, The 1998.08
Last of His Race 1897.21
Last of Hyong Kye-Hun, The 1997.16
Last of the Hogans, The 1891.45
Last of the Knights of old 1894.08
Last One is Best of All, The 1906.27
Last Part of Any Party, The 1919.36
Last Part of Every Party, The 1973.05
Last Rites, The 1992.08
Last Rose of Summer 1929.04
Last Rose of Summer, The 1888.43, 1896.45, 1901.15, 1927.01
Last Round-Up, The 1934.01, 1999.05
Last Summer 1966.03
Last Supper, The 1971.12
Last Thing on His Mind 1924.01
Last Thing You Need, The 1999.12
Last Time I Saw Paris, The 1986.01
Last Time I Saw Richard, The 2000.16
Last Waltz for Dixie 1999.08
Last Waltz I had With You, The 1920.19
Last Waltz, The 1921.14, 1939.19
Last War, The 1938.02
Last Will and Testament 1943.14
Last Word, The 1937.11
Latavia 1926.24
Latavian Chant, The 1926.24
Latchstring is Always Hanging Out for You, The 1899.36
Late Bloomer and Prom Montage 1982.10
Late Count had a Brace of Sons, The 1880.24
Late Hours 1908.08
Late Nite Comic 1987.14
Late, Late Show, The 1960.23
Later 1973.04
Later On 1889.09
Later Than Spring 1961.18
Latest Creation in Girls, The 1909.05
Latest Cure for Ennui, The 1900.38
Latest Sensation in Girls, The 1909.05
Latest Society Pet, The 1911.36
Latest Style, The 1887.31
Latest Thing from Paris, The 1912.46
Latest Thing in Swell Society, The 1903.35
Latigo 1930.27
Latin from Manhattan 1988.08
Latin in Me, The 1940.12
Latin Tune, a Manhattan Moon, and You, A 1940.07
Latin With the Patent Leather Hair 1938.08
Latins Know Him 1940.08
Lattice Room Number, The 1920.17
Lauderbocken 1880.38
Laugh 1935.15
Laugh a Little 1967.18
Laugh and Grow Fat 1921.06
Laugh and Play 1924.06
Laugh and the World Laughs Too 1907.33
Laugh it Off 1923.45
Laugh it Up 1962.20
Laugh Parade, The 1931.40
Laugh the Clouds Away 1928.27
Laugh With a Tear in It, The 1910.06
Laugh Your Blues Away 1926.19
Laugh Your Cares Away 1923.18
Laugh, and the World Laughs With You 1896.02
Laugh, Brothers, Laugh 1864.22
Laugh, Clown, Laugh 1928.08
Laugh, I Thought I'd Die 1959.12
Laugh, The 1919.06
Laughing and Happy am I 1910.36
Laughing at Sorrow 1852.01
Laughing at sorrow, Strangers to fear 1871.10
Laughing Bells 1945.14
Laughing Chorus 1880.32, 1882.33
Laughing Eyes 1907.28
Laughing Eyes of Blue 1888.13, 1896.35
Laughing Farewell, A 1881.16
Laughing Little Almond Eyes 1905.03
Laughing Low, on Tip-Toe 1900.37
Laughing Policeman, The 1979.14
Laughing School, The 1905.54
Laughing Song 1879.03, 1902.33, 1903.29, 1904.20, 1905.32, 1911.32, 1942.31
Laughing Song, The 1895.43, 1898.41
Laughing Stock 1987.05
Laughing Water 1903.39
Laughing Water Ripple 1913.19
Laughing Yodel 1884.65
Laughs 1911.31
Laughter 1904.39
Laughter and Love 1911.46
Laughter, mirth and music gay 1881.04
Laundress, The 1952.04
Laundry Strike, The 1898.10
Laundry Trio 1895.08
Laura 1990.09, 1997.05
Laura Bell 1904.08
Laura DeMaupassant 1953.01
Laura Keene Waltz 1861.04
Laurel Four, The 1905.21
Laurels, The 1988.15
Laurey Makes Up Her Mind 1943.04
Lauterbach 1885.70
Lavender and Old Lace 1922.14
Lavriada 1968.04
Law and Order 1971.20
Law and tradition of the Ladrones, The 1895.26
Law is the true embodiment, The 1882.78
Law Must be Obeyed, The 1915.32
Law of Barataria, The 1894.38
Lawdy Miss Clawdy 1978.01
Lawful Wife of Rustifum, The 1871.19
Lawks John you flatter 1862.06
Lawn as White as Driven Snow 1981.02
Lawn Tennis 1888.43
Lawrence, Massachusetts 1998.01
Lawyer and the Lady's Maid, The 1892.08
Lawyers 1978.28
Lay Me Down 1976.34
Lay of the Cavalier 1894.40
Lay of the Jay, The 1902.03
Lay of the Lute, The 1907.08
Lay Your Bets 1929.50
Lazar's Heroes 1978.11
Lazarus 1998.02
Laziest Girl in Town, The 1967.13, 1968.20, 1999.07
Lazily, Drowsily 1894.38
Lazy 1952.11
Lazy Afternoon 1954.03
Lazy Bill 1898.58
Lazy Levee Loungers 1930.18, 1930.33
Lazy Lulu 1915.29
Lazy Moon 1905.21, 1958.14
Lazybones 1990.09, 1997.05
Lazyland 1907.32
Le Lion et la Souris 1903.40
Le Paradis de Mohamet 1913.18
Lead 'Em On 1925.01
Lead Me to Love 1914.31
Lead on Ebeneezere 1897.26
Lead on, Ebeneezer 1897.54
Leader of a Big Time Band, The 1943.01
Leader of de Company B 1894.21
Leader of Fashion am I 1907.44
Leader of Frocks and Frills, The 1902.19
Leader of the Ball, The 1900.46
Leader of the Band, The 1909.05
Leader of the Colored Aristocracy 1903.08
Leader of the Pack 1979.30, 1984.15, 1985.03
Leaders of the Modern Regime 1926.32
Leading Lady 1900.46, 1990.04
Leading Man 1924.21
Leadville Johnny Brown 1960.20
Leaf in the Wind 1944.15
Leaflets 1937.08
League of Nations 1933.25
League of Nations Depends on Beautiful Clothes, The 1919.43
Leanin' on the Lord 1983.15
Leaning on a Lamppost 1986.12
Leaning on a Shovel 1939.19
Leapfrog 1974.22
Learn How to Laugh 1968.24
Learn to be Lonely 1982.18
Learn to Croon 1931.01
Learn to do the Strut 1923.32
Learn to Sing a Love Song 1927.37
Learn to Smile 1921.32
Learn Your Lessons Well 1976.17
Learned Dr. Pow Wow, The 1897.48
Learned Man 1885.06
Learned man in public is a man of intellect, The 1886.40
Learning to be Silent 1998.13
Learning to Love 1918.35
Lease in My Heart 1931.36
Least That's My Opinion 1946.08
Leave 1935.19
Leave it to Jane 1917.17
Leave it to Katarina 1936.22
Leave it to Levy 1926.51
Leave it to Love 1924.43
Leave it to the Boys in the Navy 1909.03
Leave it to Us, Guv 1965.02
Leave it to Your Milliner 1919.14
Leave Me Alone 1997.17
Leave me, I pray 1859.09
Leave me, leave me 1882.17
Leave the Atom Alone 1957.16
Leave the Whole Business to Me 1886.45, 1886.53
Leave the World Behind 1997.07
Leave Us Let Things Alone Like They Was 1945.01
Leave Well Enough Alone 1958.01
Leavin' Fo' de Promis' Lan' 1935.13
Leavin' for the Promise' Lan' 1983.04
Leavin' Time 1946.08
Leaving's Not the Only Way to Go 1985.06
Lebe is Gut 1965.32
Leben Sie Wohl 1965.35
Leben Zul Colombus 1966.21
Lechaim for All 1968.22
Lecon de piano, La 1947.05, 1965.08
Lee Family, The 1916.10
Lee Shore, The 1890.33
Lees of Old Virginia, The 1969.06
Left All Alone Again Blues 1920.04, 1975.24
Leg It 1928.10
Leg o' Mutton 1987.19

Leg of Nations, The 1920.18
Leg of the Duck, The 1970.10
Legacy, The 1978.02
Legal Heir, The 1976.15
Legalize My Name 1946.08, 1980.10
Leged of the Djin 1907.11
Legend 1908.34
Legend Lives On, The 1978.01
Legend of Black-Eyed Susan Grey, The 1959.19
Legend of Blue Beard, The 1875.19
Legend of Grimm, The 1895.06
Legend of Leda, The 1929.22
Legend of Mackie Messer, The 1933.07
Legend of Niagra, The 1910.23
Legend of the bells 1878.16
Legend of the Bells 1881.41, 1935.02
Legend of the Castle, The 1903.31
Legend of the Chimes, The 1891.29, 1929.43, 1944.25
Legend of the Cyclamen Tree, The 1921.21
Legend of the Donkey, The 1899.06
Legend of the Drums 1923.38
Legend of the Genii 1877.39
Legend of the Islands 1931.19
Legend of the Lily of the Valley, The 1928.42
Legend of the Maguires, The 1904.46
Legend of the Mascots 1881.22
Legend of the Mill 1945.16
Legend of the Mill, The 1906.33
Legend of the Mission Bells 1932.10
Legend of the Mojaves 1906.29
Legend of the Pearls, The 1921.30
Legend of the Rhine, The 1899.04
Legend of the River, The 1895.26
Legend of the Rose 1925.04
Legend of the Sea King, The 1890.21
Legend of the Shirt, The 1924.06
Legend of the Sons of Samson, The 1906.18
Legend of the Stork, The 1900.03
Legend of the Tarantella, The 1900.50
Legend of the Tea Tree, The 1919.39
Legend of the Woodland, The 1923.41
Legend Olden, The 1905.04
Legend Song 1927.14
Legend, The 1920.43, 1944.21
Legendary Eino Fflliikkiinnen, The 1947.08
Legende de Marfa, La 1886.09
Legitiate Coon, The 1905.21
Legitimate 1939.19
Legomania 1925.18
Legs, Legs, Legs 1929.26
Lei Poni Moi 1912.03
Lem and Sue 1939.24
Lemmons 1907.22
Lemon in the Garden of Love, A 1906.36
Lemontech 2001.04
Lemuel 1939.21
Lena 1910.03
Lena, Bring Back My Lena to Me 1910.25
Lend Me a Bob Till Monday 1952.04
Lend Your Ear 1973.17
Lenore 1902.02
Lenox Avenue 1931.09
Leo and Max 2001.05
Leo at Work/What am I Waiting For? 1998.21
Leonora 1911.40
Les Amis 1959.15
Les Halles 1981.14
Less and Less 1979.02
Lesson #8 1984.08
Lesson Book Song 1901.21
Lesson in Acting, A 1901.08
Lesson in Etiquette 1937.14
Lesson in Etiquette, A 1905.03
Lesson in Flirtation, A 1901.13
Lesson in Kissing, A 1902.11, 1906.45
Lesson in Letter Writing 1930.15
Lesson in Love 1908.06
Lesson in Love, A 1911.47, 1914.07, 1920.06
Lesson in Magic Arts, A 1885.65
Lesson in Yiddish, A 1970.18
Lesson With a Fan, A 1901.21
Lesson With the Fan, The 1952.11
Lesson, The 1967.05
Lessons in Love 1911.37
Lessons in Verse 1903.36
Let 'Em Eat Cake 1933.25
Let 'Em Eat Caviar 1933.25
Let a Good Ship be Made Ready 1904.30
Let a Satirist Enumerate a Catalogue of Crimes 1900.37
Let all come who feel despair 1869.43
Let All Obey 1879.64
Let all your doubts take wing 1894.15
Let Antipholus In 1938.14
Let Bygones be Bygones 1914.21
Let Cupid In 1916.11
Let Cutie Cut Your Cuticle 1919.43, 1921.19
Let De Sun Sink Down 1940.01
Let Fate Decide 1932.06
Let Freedom Ring 1991.10, 2000.05
Let Go, Mr. Coon 1904.06
Let Her Down 1905.26
Let Her Go 1917.23
Let Her Go, Gallagher 1886.61
Let him be shot! 1896.26
Let Him Dream 1904.22, 1911.20
Let Him Kick Up His Heels 1965.36
Let it Alone 1906.14
Let it Be 1977.10
Let it be Soon 1919.28
Let it Come Down 1953.03
Let it Go 2000.15
Let it Rain 1925.07
Let it Rain! Let it Pour! I'll be in Virginia in the Morning 1924.35
Let it Ride 1961.21
Let it Snow! Let it Snow! Let it Snow! 1974.10
Let it Snow, Let it Snow, Let it Snow 1998.19
Let Love Go 1926.42, 1946.03
Let Me Awake 1921.31
Let Me Be 1870.42, 1969.07
Let Me be a Friend to You 1928.03
Let Me be a Kid 1978.11
Let Me be Born Again 1933.27
Let Me be Free 1911.36, 1934.43
Let Me be Your Sugar Baby 1979.25
Let Me Build a Nest for You 1910.12
Let Me Come In 1970.20
Let Me Dance 1925.23
Let me draw you a picture 1935.19
Let Me Dream Again 1877.20
Let Me Entertain You 1959.13, 1967.12, 1974.17
Let Me Finish 1985.12
Let Me Go Back 1904.28
Let Me Have a Corner of Your Heart 1918.13
Let Me Introduce You to My Rosie 1923.47
Let me kiss him Yankee Doodle 1864.13
Let Me Live and Stay in Dixie Land 1911.05
Let Me Live and Stay in Dixieland 1911.02
Let Me Live Today 1941.12
Let Me Love You 1966.09, 1990.09
Let Me on That Finger 1882.33
Let Me Put My Arm Around You 1907.28
Let Me Show You Paris 1912.43
Let Me Sing 1905.19
Let Me Sing My Song 1978.28
Let Me Take You for a Ride 1957.09
Let Me Tell You a Little Story 1972.23
Let Music Sound 1902.18
Let My Give All My Love to Thee 1928.44
Let My People Come 1976.20
Let My People Go 1969.10
Let not the soul for sorrows grieve 1844.01
Let Not the World 1863.06
Let Others Boast 1899.40
Let our torches 1878.16
Let Poets sing 1898.25
Let shouts of triumph loud ascending 1881.04
Let the Army Come On 1897.03
Let the Band Play a Pleasing Tune 1903.29, 1905.32
Let the Canakin Clink 1981.02
Let the Church Say Amen 1963.27
Let the Circus Now Appear 1905.54
Let the Devil Take Us 1994.06
Let the Drinks be Served 1977.01
Let the farmer praise his grounds 1868.01
Let the Good Times Roll 1989.12, 1992.03, 1992.06, 1999.06, 1999.09
Let the Healing Begin 1987.17
Let the Lords of Legislation 1880.46
Let the loud glasses cling! 1889.10
Let the Lower Lights be Burning 1958.08
Let the Man Who Makes the Gun 1935.04
Let the Merry Cymbals Sound 1881.37
Let the Music Play 1914.25
Let the music soun 1881.04
Let the mystic Orange flowers 1868.01
Let the Sun of Thine Eyes 1899.28
Let the Sunshine In 1968.11
Let the Trumpets Sound 1905.48
Let the World Begin Again 1971.01
Let Them Go 1901.27
Let There be Light 1986.18
Let Things be Like They Always Was 1947.02
Let Those Who'd Wed 1899.40
Let Us be Jolly as Long as We Can 1903.04
Let us Confess Our Faults 1883.12
Let Us Find a Charming Rendezvous 1912.08
Let us freely have our pleasure 1881.06
Let Us Gaily Sing 1880.59
Let Us Gather at the Goal Line 1946.23
Let Us Gossip of the Latest Court Flirtation 1907.05
Let Us Jolly Be 1896.33
Let Us Keep the Shimmy 1919.16
Let Us Laugh, Let Us Sing 1882.18
Let us leave italy 1864.13
Let us now, with tranquil joy 1877.23
Let Us Play a Polka Dot 1929.31
Let Us Praise 1990.16
Let Us Sing a Song 1980.21
Let Us Stay Where the Crowd Is 1915.29
Let us swear 1886.50
Let us take the Road 1750.01
Let us take the road 1854.06
Let Us Take the Road 1957.02
Let Us Wander in the Orange Grove To-night 1887.48
Let Your Hair Down With a Bang 1938.04
Let's 1966.05
Let's All be Americans 1917.03
Let's All Go Down the Strand 1907.32
Let's All Go Raving Mad 1925.42
Let's All Make Whoopee Tonight 1979.05
Let's All Obey 1885.06, 1887.05
Let's All Sing the Lard Song 1928.37
Let's all speak our minds 1863.01
Let's Away 1899.21, 1902.18
Let's Ball Awhile 1957.09
Let's be Buddies 1940.19, 1980.06
Let's be Happy Now 1927.27
Let's be Lonesome Together 1923.18
Let's be Merry 1907.51
Let's be Strangers Again 1960.01
Let's Begin 1933.26, 1986.01
Let's Believe in the Captain 1975.07
Let's Build a Little Bungalow in Quogue 1917.20
Let's Bungalow 1915.02
Let's Call it a Day 1933.05
Let's Call the Whole Thing Off 1980.09, 1999.10
Let's Comb Beaches 1942.29
Let's Dance 1974.22, 1977.01
Let's Dance a Frailichs 1951.20
Let's Dance and Make Up 1925.35
Let's do and Say We Didn't 1923.47, 1945.17
Let's do It 1928.33, 1968.19, 1986.19
Let's do it, Let's Fall in Love 1928.33
Let's do Something 1937.08
Let's Drink to the Foaming Stein 1905.21
Let's End the Beguine 1944.29
Let's Face It 1941.08
Let's Face the Music and Dance 1992.18
Let's Fetch the Carriage 1959.06
Let's Find Him 1902.06
Let's Fly Away 1930.40
Let's Fly to Meet Our Wives 1876.10
Let's Get Acquainted 1906.34
Let's Get Back to Glamour 1947.15
Let's Get Drunk 1961.16
Let's Get Married 1926.06
Let's Get the Umpire's Goat 1908.19, 1909.13

Let's Get Together 1986.02
Let's Give a Cheer 1928.25
Let's Go 1918.09, 1919.14, 1919.40, 1965.29
Let's Go and Sit on the Piazza 1907.46
Let's Go Back to the Waltz 1962.20
Let's Go Down to the Shop 1918.11
Let's Go Eat Worms in the Garden 1930.28
Let's Go Flying 1991.07
Let's Go Home 1969.17, 1991.15
Let's Go Lovin' 1932.13
Let's Go Out in the Open Air 1931.21
Let's Go to Fairyland 1919.22
Let's Go to Town 1928.10
Let's Go too Far 1944.15
Let's Have a Good Time 1924.13, 1925.35
Let's Have a Love Affair 1926.42
Let's Have a Party 1950.06
Let's Have a Rattling Good Time 1920.47
Let's Have Another Cup of Coffee 1932.05
Let's Have Lunch 1994.10
Let's Hear it for Me 1977.09
Let's Hear it for the Boy 1998.13
Let's Hold Hands 1934.40
Let's Improvise 1961.26
Let's Keep it That Way 1943.20
Let's Kiss and Make Up 1922.41, 1927.59
Let's Laugh and be Merry 1927.43
Let's Make a Little Home for the Old Folks 1887.02
Let's Make a Night of It 1917.06
Let's Make Hey, Hey While the Sun is Shinin' 1929.52
Let's Make it a Night 1980.06
Let's Make it Forever 1952.13
Let's Make Love 1908.37
Let's Make Memories Tonight 1939.24
Let's Make Up 1921.13
Let's Marry 1920.01
Let's Merge 1929.44
Let's Misbehave 1998.05
Let's Not Get Married 1922.33
Let's Not Have a Kissless Day 1916.21
Let's Not Talk About It 1988.10
Let's Not Talk About Love 1941.08
Let's Not Waste a Moment 1961.20
Let's Play Hookey 1922.26
Let's Play Hookie 1918.18
Let's Pretend 1908.07, 1919.37, 1920.21, 1921.06, 1927.20
Let's Pretend We're Free 1920.15
Let's Put it to Music 1938.07
Let's Quietly Steal Away 1885.58, 1888.13, 1896.35
Let's Raise Hell 1931.31
Let's Say Good Night Till it's Morning 1925.33
Let's Say Goodbye 1986.19
Let's Say Goodnight With a Dance 1941.11
Let's scuttle 1887.43
Let's See What Happens 1968.02
Let's Sing Yiddish 1966.21
Let's Sit and Talk About You 1928.50
Let's Steal a Tune from Offenbach 1940.21
Let's Step Out 1929.45
Let's Stroll Along and Sing a Song 1927.04
Let's Swing It 1935.04
Let's Take a Walk Around the Block 1934.19
Let's Take Advantage of Now 1934.35
Let's Take an Old-Fashioned Walk 1907.20, 1949.08
Let's Take Him Home in Triumph 1911.40
Let's take this book before us 1885.28
Let's Talk About the Weather 1936.01
Let's Talk Dirty to the Animals 1979.19
Let's Twist Again 1977.10
Let's Wander Off Nowhere 1907.44
Let's Work Together 1988.09
Let's You and I Just Say Goodbye 1923.46, 1982.05
Let-A-Go Your Heart 1961.07
Letter Boxes Just Placed in New York 1917.03
Letter Chansonette 1904.30
Letter Duet 1916.01, 1930.03, 1952.15
Letter for Roxane, A 1993.17
Letter from Klemnacht 1982.18
Letter from Papa, The 1898.73
Letter Song 1912.27, 1919.41, 1926.41, 1929.39, 1930.03, 1930.15, 1991.05
Letter Song, The 1909.22, 1912.17, 1925.07, 1947.06
Letter to His Dad, A 1891.02
Letter to the Children 1982.18
Letter to the Governor 1998.21
Letter to the President 1935.03
Letter Trio 1916.21
Letter Writing Song 1903.37
Letter You Shouldn't Have Sent, The 1911.25
Letter, A 1970.17
Letter, The 1880.46, 1909.22, 1940.08, 1948.23, 1956.04, 1979.10, 1980.29, 1993.17
Letters 1904.24, 1908.17, 1965.02
Letters from Home 1909.23
Letters That Never Were Written, The 1912.37
Letting Go 1997.09
Levee Along Broadway, The 1915.17
Levee Ladies 1937.09
Levee Land 1922.18
Levee Lou 1928.09
Levi is a Grand Old Name 1913.30
Li'l Augie is a Natural Man 1946.08
Li'l Gal 1930.16
Liable to Catch On 1940.12
Liar's Song, The 1950.10
Liasons 1973.04
Libby 1922.28
Libertad 1861.03
Libertango 1997.13
Liberty 1925.21
Liberty Bell 1918.10
Liberty Girl, The 1900.59
Liberty Hall 1899.19, 1912.15
Liberty Tango 1993.08
Lichtenburg 1950.15
'Licious Meal, A 1876.30
Lick, and a Riff, and a Slow Bounce, A 1943.16
Licorice Lize 1899.29
Lid Fun Der Goldener Paveh, Das 1968.22
Lid Fun Titanic 1998.11
Lida Rose 1957.18, 2000.11
Lido Shores 1929.22
Lido, The 1928.42
Liebchen, mich reisst es 1984.05
Liebe, Liebe Freundlin 1870.27
Lieben Dich 1968.06
Lieber Augustin 1913.23
Liebeslied 1976.10
Liebeslied/Love Song 1965.04
Liebestraum 1924.32
Lied Ist Aus, Das 1968.20
Lied von der Unzulanglichkeit menschichen Strebens, Das 1965.04
Lieutenants of the Lord 1977.08
Life 1972.19
Life All Free from Care 1904.37
Life and Love 1919.01
Life as a Twosome 1928.17, 1928.40, 1928.45
Life Begins 1934.19
Life Begins at City Hall 1934.19
Life Begins at Sweet Sixteen 1935.18
Life Can be Beautiful 1965.01
Life Can be Funny 1973.02
Life Could be a Dream 1982.22
Life Could be so Beautiful 1935.03
Life Does a Man a Favor When it Gives Him Simple Joys 1958.02
Life Does a Man a Favor When it Leads Him Down to the Sea 1958.02
Life Does a Man a Favor When it Puts Him in Paree 1958.02
Life Goes On 1981.16
Life has Just Begun 1915.20
Life in Kansas 1903.03, 1904.13, 1904.44
Life in the Country 1910.04
Life in the Morning 1929.41
Life in the Old Dog Yet 1918.28
Life in the Shop 1966.21
Life in Town 1924.30
Life Is 1968.30, 1983.14
Life is a Carousal 1920.29
Life is a Dance 1983.09
Life is a Dirty Business 1946.18
Life is a Gamble 1921.34
Life is a Game of Bluff 1916.19
Life is a Game of Chance 1912.43
Life is a Game of Checkers 1909.10
Life is a Garden 1914.28
Life is a One-Way Street 1969.14
Life is a Revel 1901.09
Life is a Riddle 1911.36
Life is a See-Saw 1906.44, 1907.59
Life is a Toyshop 1899.25
Life is a Woman 1978.18
Life is Ahead of Me 1987.12
Life is All Sunshine With You 1921.11
Life is But Short at Best 1897.17
Life is Happiness Indeed 1974.06, 1982.20, 1997.10
Life is Just a Bowl of Cherries 1931.30, 1974.26, 1984.06, 1986.06, 1999.01
Life is Just a Joke 1914.33
Life is Just a Merry-Go-Round 1910.17
Life is Like a Punch and Judy Show 1920.36
Life is Like a Toy Balloon 1925.47
Life is Like a Train 1978.02
Life is Lonely 1914.09
Life is Love 1929.02
Life is Love and Laughter 1908.06
Life is Not an Airy Bubble 1903.40
Life is Short, My Dear Friends 1905.46
Life is so Peculiar 1992.03
Life is Such a Stupid Bore 1892.20
Life is too Short 1964.35
Life is too Short to be Wasting Your Time 1904.18
Life is What We Make It 1898.01
Life is What We Make it After All 1910.13
Life itself is at the best 1844.01
Life of a Bold Dragoon, The 1891.46
Life of a Bold Free Lance, The 1903.37
Life of a Nurse, The 1929.07
Life of a Rose, The 1923.17, 1923.18
Life of a Rover, The 1892.52
Life of a Woman, The 1972.07
Life of Love, The 1905.20
Life of Sin 1934.40
Life of the Party, The 1925.47, 1968.01
Life on the Stage 1905.22
Life Oriental 1911.03
Life seems only sunshine 1889.10
Life Support 1996.09
Life Upon the Wicked Stage 1927.67, 1946.01, 1966.14, 1983.05, 1994.08
Life was Pie for the Pioneer 1940.10
Life was Worth While 1920.24
Life Wins 1972.25
Life With Father 1942.15
Life With Harold 2000.15
Life With Rocky, A 1945.20
Life's a Bubble 1895.44
Life's a Bumper 1853.01
Life's a Dance 1917.02, 1937.15
Life's a Dress Parade 1914.01
Life's a Funny Present 1944.27
Life's a Funny Proposition 1904.42, 1982.05
Life's a Game at Best 1917.07
Life's a Game of Cards 1894.31
Life's a Holiday 1970.03
Life's a Masquerade 1905.29
Life's a Race 1919.22
Life's a Tale 1917.20
Life's Highway 1908.33
Life, long life 1840.03
Life, Unbar the Door 1933.24
Lifeline 1976.16, 1979.32
Lifetime Love, A 1964.18
Liffey Waltz, The 1959.04
Lift 'Em Up and Put 'Em Down 1943.24
Lift Him Up 1988.05
Lift Me Up 1988.05
Lift the Cup 1902.21
Lift the Wings 1996.12, 2000.05
Lift Your Eyes to Mine 1916.01
Lift Your Voice Like a Trumpet 1987.17
Liftoff to Love/Ripoff of Love 1991.02
Light 2001.06
Light at the End of the Tunnel 1987.05
Light Fantastic, The 1951.10
Light is My Heart 1910.05

Light My Candle 1996.09
Light of Other Days, The 1887.32
Light of the World 1976.17
Light on My Feet 2001.01
Light One Candle 1969.01
Light Romance 1993.07
Light Sings 1970.20
Light That Lies in Girlish Eyes, The 1906.05
Light That Lies in Woman's Eyes, The 1907.05
Light That Lies in Women's Eyes, The 1908.13
Light Travelin' Man 1959.23
Light Up 1932.06
Light Up My Darkest Night 1998.08
Light, light, your honor 1852.01
Light, Light, your honor 1871.10
Light, Lively and Yiddish 1970.17
Light, The 1986.16
Lightening Bug Song, The 1957.05
Lighthouse and the Boat 1902.21
Lighting the Sabbath Candles 1951.21
Lightly o'er the rippling stream 1881.04
Lightly Row 1889.12
Lightly, Lightly 1888.20, 1919.42
Lightly, Lightly, in the Shifting Shadows 1893.40
Lights and Shadows 1913.18
Lights Come Up, The 1992.17
Lights of Broadway, The 2000.08
Lights of London, The 1981.12
Lights of Long Ago, The 1994.12
Lights of Old Broadway 1927.13
Like a God 1958.19
Like a Lady 1980.15
Like a Leaf Falling in the Breeze 1942.19
Like a Little Ladylike Lady Like You 1927.47
Like a Little Pussy Cat 1958.18
Like a Rolling Stone 1982.22
Like a Shepherdess 1913.37
Like a ship in storms 1854.06
Like a Soldier Fall 1870.23
Like a Splendid Bird 1894.08
Like a Star in the Sky 1934.29
Like a Turk 1877.39, 1878.20
Like a Wandering Minstrel 1927.47
Like a Woman Loves a Man 1956.04, 1980.29
Like a Young Man 1961.20
Like an Arrow from its Quiver Comes My Love to Marry Me 1879.71
Like Everyone Else 1997.17
Like Father Like Son 2000.06
Like Him 1983.21
Like it Was 1981.27, 1999.20
Like June Skies 1890.03
Like Katy Did 1904.33
Like Kelly Did 1898.02
Like Many Girls 1887.33
Like Me Less - Love Me More 1929.26
Like My Own Mother Dear 1906.03
Like Sally 2000.08
Like She Loves Me 1926.46
Like Swallow Flying 1913.21
Like the Breeze Blows 1965.32
Like the Eagles Fly 1978.10
Like the fair flower in its lustre 1854.06
Like the Flower 1926.35
Like the Nymphs of Spring 1925.38
Like You Do 1926.28
Like Yours 1969.01
Like-a-Me, Like-a-You 1926.04
Lil Ole Bitty Pissant Country Place, A 1978.13
Lil, I Like You 1903.24
Lila Tremaine 1964.21
Lilac Domino, The 1914.25
Lilac Time 1928.42
Lilac Wine 1950.03
Lilac, The 1891.20, 1892.31
Lilas 1972.24
Lilas, What Happened to Paris 1972.24
Lili Marlene 1967.13, 1968.20, 1999.07
Lilies of Your Love May Die, The 1898.48
Lillian, Lillian, Lillian 1969.01
Lillie 1929.26
Lilly, The 1907.29
Lily and the Dew, The 1902.15
Lily and the Nightingale, The 1898.60
Lily and the Rose, The 1891.14, 1911.42
Lily Bell Polka 1924.09
Lily Belle May June 1934.42
Lily Done the Zampoughi Every Time I Pulled Her Coattail 1971.13
Lily of Longacre Square, The 1918.18
Lily of the Alley 1986.11
Lily of the Valley 1916.25
Lily White 1905.25
Lily's Eyes 1991.05
Lily's Promenade, The 1903.27
Lily, Oscar 1978.02
Lily, The 1910.19
Lima 1916.06
Lima Beans 1910.15
Limbo Land 1919.06
Limbs of the Law 1927.62
Lime House Nights 1921.19
Limehouse Blues 1924.01, 1945.07, 1999.23
Limehouse Nights 1919.43
Limerick Girls 1902.36
Limerick's Running Yet 1903.26
Limpiabotas 1939.18
Lina, My Lady 1900.40
Linda, Georgina, Marilyn & Me 1976.20
Linda, Look Out de Windah 1902.24
Lindy's 1993.05
Line is Busy, The 1922.13
Line it Out, Mr. Maginnity 1905.22
Line of Duty 1905.19
Line, The 1985.05
Lines in Molly's Hand, The 1910.09
Linger Longer Letty 1919.37
Linger Longer Loo 1895.02
Linger Longer, Lucy 1894.10
Linger Not, Darling 1870.01, 1880.09
Lingerie 1917.34, 1921.03, 1927.68
Link by Link 1994.12
Linnet in the Tree, The 1881.11
Lion and the Lamb, The 1944.18
Lion and the Monk Die Trying, The 1906.14
Lion and the Mouse, The 1902.37, 1903.40
Lion Dance 1976.02
Lion Tamer 1974.13
Lion Tamer, The 1888.44, 1891.46
Lion's Dream 1975.01
Lion's Queen, The 1909.21
Lionnet 1949.16
Lions and Tigers and Bears 1989.06, 1997.11
Lips 1926.20
Lips That Laugh at Love 1929.17
Lips, Lips, Lips 1919.35
Lipstick Traces on a Cigarette 1992.06
Liquid Air 1906.30
Liquid Air Police 1906.30
Liquor Dealer's Dream, The 1977.08
Lisette's a Fresh and Charming Maid 1866.14
List and Learn 1890.02
List to Our Matin Serenade 1895.33
List to the Birds 1887.23
List to the Orders so stern 1875.19
List to the Pleading 1906.39
List to the Wood-Dove Wooing 1888.34
Listen Cosette 1967.02
Listen Lord - A Prayer 1969.10
Listen to Me 1912.08, 1921.23, 1990.15
Listen to Me Men 1897.03
Listen to My Heart Beat 1920.15
Listen to My Love, Dolly 1887.32
Listen to My Prayer 1910.24
Listen to My Tale of Woe 1890.03
Listen to the Anvil 1888.40
Listen to the Beat! 1959.14
Listen to the Big Brass Band 1905.10
Listen to the merry bells 1882.63
Listen to the Mocking Bird 1872.25
Listen to the Night a-Singing 1904.50
Listen to the Nightingale 1883.67
Listen to the Popping of the Corks 1905.42
Listen Well 1895.25
Listen While I Tell You 1895.03
Listen! 1993.04
Listen! Harken, My Lover 1902.25
Listen, Fairies 1866.31
Listen, while I relate the hope of a gipsy's fate 1844.01
Listening 1924.44
Listening on Some Radio 1922.19, 1923.20
Listening to the Radio 1924.21
Listening to You 1993.06
Lites-Camera-Platitude 1964.05
Little Alabama Coon 1895.08
Little Angel Cake 1923.40
Little Annie Rooney 1890.03, 1890.29
Little Baby 1921.20
Little Ball of Golden Thread, The 1872.23
Little Ballerina 1939.23
Little Band of Gold 1899.03
Little Barefoot 1866.26
Little Bear, A 1919.25
Little Bid for Sympathy, A 1916.19
Little Bird 1933.23
Little Bird is Watching All the Time, A 1903.17
Little Bird of Paradise 1908.24
Little Bird on Weary Wing, A 1890.33
Little Bird Told Me So, A 1903.07
Little Bird's Story 1905.38
Little Bird, Little Bird 1965.34
Little Birdie Told Me So, A 1926.50
Little Birdies Learning How to Fly 1897.54
Little Birds Learning to Fly 1897.26
Little Birds of Paradise 1909.23
Little Biscuit 1957.16
Little Bit Delighted With the Weather, A 1939.12
Little Bit in Love, A 1953.03
Little Bit More, A 1922.36, 1979.12
Little Bit O' Jazz, A 1923.19
Little Bit of Atmosphere 1927.04
Little Bit of Blarney, A 1904.22
Little Bit of Cheese, A 1907.63
Little Bit of Constitutional Fun, A 1937.13
Little Bit of Cucumber, A 1960.17
Little Bit of Dinner With a Friend, A 1905.27
Little Bit of Every Nationality, A 1918.05
Little Bit of Good, A 1975.14
Little Bit of Heaven (Sure They Call it Ireland), A 1914.29
Little Bit of Lace, A 1923.44
Little Bit of Love, A 1923.22
Little Bit of Me in You, A 1974.03
Little Bit of Nonsense, A 1916.25
Little Bit of Paint, A 1922.47
Little Bit of Quicksilver, A 1933.06
Little Bit of Ribbon, A 1917.06
Little Bit of Scotch, A 1919.11, 1921.12
Little Bit of Silk, A 1913.26
Little Bit of Spanish, A 1926.04
Little Bit of This, A 1924.30
Little Black Cat, The 1924.33
Little Black Sheep, The 1918.15
Little Blanche Marie 1907.15
Little Blue Book 1922.11
Little Blue Devil, The 1919.34
Little Blue Moon 1906.41
Little Blue Pig, The 1925.08
Little Bo Peep 1920.35
Little Bo-Peep 1899.22, 1900.15, 1929.02
Little Book, The 1920.40
Little Boy 1922.36
Little Boy and Girl 1919.01
Little Boy Blue 1911.44, 1919.16, 1926.02
Little Boy Blue, Come Blow Your Horn 1900.03
Little Boy Blues, The 1948.08
Little Boy for Sale, A 1898.17
Little Boy's Blue 1928.14
Little Boy, Little Boy 1966.15
Little Brains - a Little Talent, A 1955.08, 1994.01
Little Brass Wagon, The 1931.02
Little Bride 1919.39
Little Bride, The 1911.47
Little Brown Hen 1907.47
Little Brown Jug 1979.24
Little Brown Road 1923.33
Little Brunette Soubrette, The 1899.30
Little Bum 1927.48
Little Bunch o' Berries, The 1883.32

Little Bunch of Berries, The 1893.27
Little Bunch of Daisies, A 1906.01
Little Bungalow, A 1925.45, 1927.21
Little Butter-Up 1945.09
Little Butterfly 1923.32
Little by Little 1919.33
Little by Little and Bit by Bit 1916.22
Little Cabaret at Home, A 1913.05
Little Cafe, A 1909.29
Little Champagne for Papa, A 1938.06
Little Change, A 1910.21
Little Chat, A 1944.16
Little Chauffeur, The 1906.05
Little Chicken Fit for Old Broadway, A 1919.06
Little Child Like Me, A 1901.21
Little Chimney Sweep 1907.15
Little China Doll 1909.17
Little China Maid, The 1900.43
Little Chinchilla, The 1895.32
Little Choo-Choo, Gee-Gee, The 1907.22
Little Christmas Tree, The 1891.28, 1894.20
Little Church Around the Corner 1911.07, 1920.44
Little Church Around the Corner, The 1907.18, 1919.35
Little Cinderelatives 1922.27
Little Class of One 1906.29
Little Class of One, A 1904.54, 1918.15
Little Comedy, The 1988.10
Little Cop Number, The 1922.15
Little Coquette 1886.35
Little Corporal, The 1938.15
Little Country Mice 1909.29
Little Country Music, A 1916.19
Little cry, A 1882.44
Little Daffy Pipe Dreams 1901.13
Little Daily Nothings, The 1959.15
Little Daisy with the dimple 1895.43
Little Dancing Jumping Jigger 1911.40
Little Dark Bird 1986.11
Little Darlin' 1978.01
Little Daughter Nell 1893.36
Little Deeds of Kindness 1914.23
Little Devils 1924.05
Little Dickey Birds, The 1899.15
Little Dickey Doubleday 1896.51
Little Difference at Breakfast, A 1915.20
Little do They Know 1977.16
Little Doll, A 1885.08
Little Dollie Dimples - Made a Hit 1907.19
Little Don of Spain, The 1877.43
Little Dottie, Little Tottie 1896.51
Little Dream That Lost its Way, A 1921.06
Little Dreams 1935.19
Little Drops of Water 1923.42
Little Egypt 1995.03
Little Emmaline 1948.27
Little Empress, A 1882.44
Little Eva's Wish 1885.41
Little Fairy in the Home 1920.36
Little Fall of Rain, A 1987.04
Little Farm in Normandie, A 1917.28
Little Farther, A 1908.36
Little Fat Girls 1982.10
Little Fifi 1911.31
Little Fish in a Big Pond, A 1949.08
Little Flat in Soho Square, A 1928.02
Little Flossie Flip 1898.38
Little Flower 1929.08
Little Game of Tennis, A 1948.30
Little Gamins 1943.14
Little Geezer 1931.14
Little Girl 1901.25, 1913.04, 1925.34
Little Girl at Home 1912.39
Little Girl at the Sweet Shop, The 1906.47
Little Girl Blue 1935.15
Little Girl Come Back to Me 1912.37
Little Girl from Illinois, The 1906.20
Little Girl from Little Rock, A 1949.18
Little Girl Goodbye 1950.16
Little Girl I Love You 1911.08
Little Girl in Blue 1907.59
Little Girl in the Night, A 1999.17
Little Girl Like Me, A 1906.20
Little Girl That Couldn't Say No, The 1902.20
Little Girl That's Wise, A 1909.03
Little Girl Up There, The 1908.18
Little Girl You'll Do 1904.29
Little Girl, if You'll be Good 1906.03
Little Girl, Mind How You Go 1913.04
Little Girl, What Have You Done to Me? 1914.20
Little Girls 1977.06
Little Girls Beware of the Sirens 1911.27
Little Girls, Goodbye 1919.27
Little Go Getter 1924.01
Little God of Love 1882.06
Little God of My Heart 1991.03
Little Golden Maid 1912.41
Little goldfinch in her nest, The 1880.18
Little Gossip, A 1965.34
Little Green Leaf in Our Bible, The 1879.68
Little Green Snake 1959.22, 1985.04
Little Grey Home in the West 1913.26
Little Grey House, The 1949.15, 1972.06
Little Hands 1965.35
Little Harlequin, The 1916.20
Little Hedge School, The 1886.52
Little Hero 1989.09
Little House in Soho, A 1928.02
Little Houston Street 1904.54, 1906.29
Little Hunka Love 1932.04
Little Igloo for Two 1926.17
Little in Soldier, A 1886.28
Little Investigation, A 1967.16
Little Italy 1911.05
Little Jack Frost 1942.19
Little Jack Horner 1923.24, 1971.20
Little Japan Lady, A 1908.03
Little Jazz Bird 1924.43, 1999.10
Little Jehu!, The 1889.40
Little Jessie James 1923.24
Little Johnny Duggan 1892.45
Little Johnny Jones 1907.41
Little Kiss, A 1925.21
Little Kleptomaniac, The 1927.36
Little Known Facts 1971.11, 1999.03
Little Lacquer Lady 1928.04
Little Lad 1918.10
Little Lady in Distress 1905.49
Little Lady in the Moon 1910.12
Little Lamb 1959.13, 1977.05
Little Lola Little 1899.41
Little Lotte 1988.01
Little Love But Not for Me, A 1915.26
Little Love, A 1923.44
Little Love, a Little Kiss, A 1913.17
Little M-M-M, A 2000.08
Little Mad'moiselle, The 1895.32
Little Maid of Nicobar, The 1904.25
Little Maid That Couldn't Say No 1902.20
Little Marie 1926.18
Little Mary 1904.08
Little Mary Gardeners, The 1909.11
Little Mary Sue 1969.03
Little Mary Wise 1906.09
Little Maud isn't Meant for You 1915.29
Little Me 1962.27, 1982.01, 1998.15
Little Milliner, The 1903.36
Little Millionaire 1911.33
Little Miss Britten 1962.23
Little Miss Charity 1920.30
Little Miss Melody 1919.02
Little Miss Small Town 1927.15
Little Miss Understood 1914.04
Little Miss Up-to-Date 1908.18
Little Miss Victory Jones 1942.26
Little Miss Wooden Shoes 1907.63
Little Mohee 1944.32
Little Moo-Zoo May 1904.37
Little Moon 1972.02
Little More Cider 1860.05
Little More Cider, A 1882.76
Little More Heart, A 1953.01
Little More Mascara, A 1983.11
Little More Nonsense, A 1916.25
Little More, A 1919.42
Little Mother 1922.12
Little Murad 1907.24
Little Music, A 1986.16
Little Naked Boy, The 1945.04
Little Nest for Two, A 1920.05
Little Nonsense, A 1894.05, 1921.12
Little Old America for Me 1906.37
Little Old Dreamy New York 1929.22
Little Old Lady 1936.31
Little Old New Hampshire 1926.29
Little Old New York 1908.42, 1923.38, 1929.19, 1932.07, 1960.19, 1986.03
Little Old New York is Good Enough for Me 1898.50
Little One 1998.05
Little One's ABC, The 1961.18
Little overdoing it, A 1898.63
Little Peach 1925.08
Little Peach in an Orchard Grew 1888.06
Little Peach, The 1890.03
Little People 1960.01
Little Pet Jockey, The 1872.27
Little Pickaninny from Ole Varginny, The 1885.06
Little Piece of Sugar Cane 1976.31
Little Place of Your Own, A 1924.40
Little Plate of Soup, A 1920.42
Little Pony of Mine 1924.47
Little Poster Maid, The 1899.40
Little Pot of Tea, A 1911.02, 1912.12
Little Priest, A 1979.06
Little Princess 1927.26
Little Privacy, A 1930.33
Little Puck 1888.34
Little Puff of Powder, A 1892.42
Little Racket, The 1892.05
Little Red Book and a Five Cent Bag, A 1912.47
Little Red Hat 1963.26, 1992.10
Little Red Lacquer Cage, The 1922.39
Little Red Riding Hood 1923.40
Little Rover Don't Forget to Come Back Home 1922.15
Little Rumba Numba, A 1941.08
Little Sallie Waters 1886.24, 1888.06
Little Scandal Dolls 1923.18
Little Ships Come Sailing Home 1918.03
Little Shirt My Mother Made for Me, The 1960.17
Little Show 1931.14
Little Side Door, The 1893.27
Little Side Street in Paree, A 1922.23
Little Sister Kissie 1897.39
Little Skipper from Heaven Above, A 1936.26
Little Slut of Six, A 1925.42
Little Smile, a Little Sigh, A 1926.29
Little Soubrette, The 1900.59
Little Spring Melody, A 1999.05
Little Stars Won't Tell, The 1882.82
Little Stockings by the Fire 1880.42, 1882.39
Little Stranger 1927.20
Little Stucco in the Sticks 1932.15
Little Surprise from the Front 1916.15
Little Thing Like a Kiss, A 1913.20
Little Things Mean a Lot 1954.08
Little Things Meant so Much to Me 1950.19
Little Things We Like, The 1942.26
Little Things You do Together, The 1970.13, 1977.05
Little Tin Box 1959.25
Little Tin Soldier 1912.12
Little Tin Soldier and the Little Rag Doll, The 1922.05
Little Tip, The 1903.24
Little Tittle Tattle Tale 1908.28
Little Tommy Murphy 1900.36
Little Tootsie Tripper 1907.44
Little Travelling Music, A 1955.12
Little Trouble, A 1963.13
Little Tsipele 1960.18
Little Tune Go Away 1918.16
Little Wallflowers 1921.13
Little Weather Vane, The 1896.10, 1907.05
Little White House at the End of Honeymoon Lane 1926.29
Little White House With Green Blinds, The 1922.48
Little White Lie, The 1976.11
Little White Lies 1928.21
Little Widow Brown 1902.29
Little Widow Drum, The 1879.37
Little Widow Dunn 1883.46

Little Widow Dunn, The 1892.54
Little Willie Brown 1906.25
Little Woman 1957.14
Little Woman, The 1969.14
Little Women 1916.08, 1928.42
Little World for Two, A 1912.12
Little World of Our Own, A 1916.22
Little Yaller Boy 1897.54
Little Yeller Boy 1897.26
Little Yellow Bird 1905.26
Little Yellow Dog, A 1894.17
Little Yetta's Gonna Get a Man 1947.08
Litvak/Galitsyaner 1990.16
Live a Little 1962.24, 1967.16, 1987.12
Live Alone and Like It 1991.04, 1999.20
Live and Let Live 1953.07
Live for Love 1920.41
Live for the Moment 1981.24
Live for Today 1910.35, 1918.27, 1921.14, 1924.24, 1978.19, 1988.18
Live is a Sandman 1924.25
Live Long Enough 1979.29
Live on the Ocean Wave, A 1871.16
Live Today 1927.15
Live Today - Love Today 1927.15
Live Where You Can 1988.05
Live While You're Here 1923.16
Live, Laugh and Love 1933.16
Live, Laugh, Love 1971.05
Live, My Love, Oh Live 1889.03
Lives of Famous Men, The 1902.43
Living and the Dead, The 2000.01
Living Buddha 1928.30
Living in Sin 1931.28
Living in the Shadows 1995.15
Living Pickles 1902.06
Living Simply 1964.40
Living With a Stranger 1995.01
Living Your Own Life 1902.07
Liza 1922.44, 1929.27, 1930.13, 1956.02, 1962.17, 1975.22, 1980.10
Liza All the Clouds'll Roll Away 1999.23
Liza Ann 1907.15
Liza Crossing the ice 1944.23
Liza Jane 1924.15, 1924.41
Lizette 1914.04
Lizzie Borden 1952.09
Lizzie Green 1908.02
Lizzie's Coming Home 1963.26, 1992.10
Lizzie's Farewell 1877.28
Llamala 1922.23
Lo 'Mir Zingen Yiddish 1966.21
Lo Here the Sabre 1904.22
Lo Que Vendra 1997.13
Lo! Hear the gentle Lark 1880.01
Lo! Hear the Gentle Lark 1921.17
Lo, the awful man approaches 1896.13
Lo, the Notaries 1889.40
Lo-Lo My Lolo Maid 1908.13
Loading Inventory 1997.06
Loads of Love 1962.03
Loathly Bride, The 1954.11
Lobster and the Lady 1903.27
Lobster and the Smelt, The 1904.47
Lobster Crawl 1929.28
Local 1872.34
Local 403 1965.33
Lock of Hair, A 1885.69, 1896.44
Lock Up the Doors 1972.13
Lock-Step, Two-Step Slide 1912.02
Locked Out After Nine 1880.36
Locks 1971.20
Locomotion 1984.15
Locomotive Gallop 1882.76
Lodger 1918.42
Log Cabin Days 1923.39
Logger's Song, The 1969.07
Logic 1919.01
Loidy What is Studyin' for the Stoige, A 1898.50
Loki and Baldur 1982.18
Lola 1904.45, 1905.07, 1913.22
Lola Lo 1923.18
Lola's Ceremony 1987.12
Lolita 1904.33
Lolita, My Love 1929.27
Lolly-Papa 1923.06
Lomir, Loybn 1990.16
London Apprentice 1857.03
London Bus 1964.29
London is a Little Bit of All Right 1963.29, 1986.19
London Johnnies 1925.07
London Pride 1942.14, 1986.19
London Talking Blues 1966.03
London Taps 1916.22
London Town 1923.44, 1928.04
London Town Carol 1995.19, 1997.22, 1998.20, 1999.21, 2000.19
London Underworld 1965.02
Lone Grace, The 1891.32
Lone Star Girl, The 1914.15
Lone, Deserted Maiden, A 1880.40
Lonegan 1912.20
Loneliness of Evening, The 1993.14
Loneliness of War 1977.09
Lonely 1909.31, 1963.29
Lonely at the Top 1978.13
Lonely Boy Blues 1992.08
Lonely Clearing 1965.36
Lonely Day 1991.01
Lonely Girl 1999.12
Lonely Girl, A 1927.29
Lonely Goatherd, The 1959.24, 1998.03
Lonely Heart 1933.22
Lonely Hearts 1921.31
Lonely Hearts' Ball 1930.25
Lonely House 1947.02
Lonely in Town 1915.01
Lonely Lamp, The 1940.16
Lonely Little Melody 1924.18, 1925.10
Lonely Nest, The 1922.33
Lonely Nights 1963.25
Lonely Pickaninny 1932.12
Lonely Room 1943.04
Lonely Town 1944.33, 1958.21, 1971.15, 1977.02, 1998.16
Lonely Women 1947.06
Lonesome 1904.29, 1925.25
Lonesome Cowboy, The 1930.31
Lonesome Little Maid 1904.30
Lonesome Little Tune, A 1917.02
Lonesome Longing Blues 1922.22
Lonesome of the Road 1978.11
Lonesome Romeos 1927.52
Lonesome, it's Lonesome Tonight 1907.25
Long Ago 1895.36, 1899.41, 1923.23, 1940.16, 1965.14, 1982.09
Long Ago and Far Away 1986.01
Long Ago in Alcala 1899.12
Long and Weary Wait 1953.02
Long and Winding Road, The 1974.24, 1977.10
Long as You've Got Your Health 1936.31
Long Before I Knew You 1956.14
Long Distance Love 1995.04
Long Forgotten 1904.36
Long Green Blues 1947.20
Long Green, The 1902.29
Long Island Low Down 1981.03
Long Island Low-Down, The 1928.38
Long Life With Crosses Few 1894.47
Long Live Folly 1903.40
Long Live Leander the True Prince 1870.20
Long Live Prince Lubin 1862.09
Long Live Richard 1892.14
Long Live the King 1907.08, 1914.03
Long Live the Queen 1979.18
Long Long Day, The 1997.12
Long Past Sunset 1984.02
Long Sunday Afternoon 1993.07
Long Tall Sally 1989.12
Long Time Ago, A 1922.38, 1956.04
Long Time No Song 1943.07
Long Time Travelin' 1966.30
Long Years Ago 1881.37
Long, Lean, Lank Letty 1914.21
Long, Lean, Lanky Letty Pepper 1922.14
Long, Long Ago 1924.32
Longer, Longer, Lingerie 1909.13
Longing for You 1914.33, 1927.43
Longshoreman, The 1891.14
Longshoremen's Chanty 1907.27
Lontananza 1932.19
Looey 1903.27
Look and Love is Here 1930.43
Look Around 1991.07
Look Around Your Little World 1968.24
Look at 'Er 1957.07
Look at Me 1894.10, 1990.06
Look at Me When I'm Talking to You 1999.14
Look at Me, I'm Sandra Dee 1972.12, 1994.07
Look at Me, Please 1934.06
Look at That Face 1965.19
Look at the Package They Handed to Me 1912.05
Look at the World and Smile 1927.07
Look at Them 1969.15
Look at Them Doing It 1914.31
Look at Us 1980.15
Look Before You Leap 1917.14, 1918.29, 1934.29
Look Down 1987.04
Look for Small Pleasures 1964.33
Look for the Girl 1921.07
Look for the Happiness Ahead 1971.09
Look for the Men With Potential 1975.07
Look for the Morning Star 1957.09
Look for the Silver Lining 1920.44, 1948.16, 1974.09, 1986.01
Look from the turret, sister dear 1860.01
Look in Her Eyes 1913.23, 1914.07
Look in His Eyes 1917.01, 1917.01
Look in My Heart 1894.36
Look in the Book and See 1902.18
Look in the Looking Glass 1923.18
Look in Your Engagement Book 1927.05
Look it Up in the Dream Book 1901.13
Look Little Girl 1963.21
Look Me Over 1911.26
Look Me Over Carefully and Tell Me Will I Do 1910.18
Look Me Over Closely 1968.20, 1999.07
Look Me Over, Dearie 1911.12
Look Mummy, No Hands 2000.16
Look No Further 1962.03
Look of Love 1985.03
Look on Me 1997.16
Look Out 1939.27
Look Out for Lil 1975.09
Look Out for Mr. Wu 1914.34
Look Out for My Heart 1940.07
Look Out for Number One 1870.07
Look Out for Us Broadway 1924.22
Look Out Sister 1992.03
Look Out! Look Out! Look Out! 1911.03
Look Over There 1983.11
Look Pleasant 1928.37
Look to the Lilies 1970.08
Look to the Mountains 1951.05
Look to the Rainbow 1947.03
Look What Happened to Mabel 1974.18, 1985.19
Look What I Found 1946.13
Look What You've Done 1998.01
Look Where I Am 1963.11
Look Who I am, Surprise! Surprise! 1963.22
Look Who's Alone Now 1991.15
Look Who's Dancing 1951.14
Look Who's Here 1920.07
Look Who's in Love 1959.01
Look-a-Look 1922.01
Lookin' for Love 1997.07
Lookin' Good But Feelin' Bad 1978.09
Lookin' Over from Your Side 1972.13
Looking a Life Through a Rainbow 1929.33
Looking All Over for You 1948.16
Looking Around 1925.50
Looking at You 1929.51
Looking Back 1974.02
Looking for a Boy 1925.49
Looking for a Girl Like You 1911.42
Looking for a Girl My Size 1916.05
Looking for a Man by the Name of Smith 1906.27
Looking for a Needle in a Haystack 1904.29

Looking for a Thrill 1927.09
Looking for Love on Broadway 1995.12
Looks Like Love is Here to Stay 1937.07
Looks Like We Made It 1976.34
Looloo 1927.16
Looney Park 1903.28
Loopin' the Loop 1988.08
Loose Ankles 1929.22
Loose Woman, A 1982.23
Loosen Up 1941.02
Lopsided Bus, A 1955.27
Lord Done Fixed Up My Soul, The 1940.08
Lord Helps Those Who Help Themselves, The 1971.02
Lord I am But a Little Child 1968.08
Lord is Blessing Me, The 1995.04
Lord Knowswho, The 1898.61
Lord Souche's Masque 1963.28
Lord's Prayer 1982.06
Lord's Prayer, The 1988.02
Lord, I Don't Feel Noways Tired 1930.10
Lord, I'm Determined 1990.05
Lord, Oh Have Mercy on Me 1943.10
Lord, You Sure Know How to Make a New Day 1966.30
Lords, it may not be! 1882.78
Lorelei 1906.07, 1927.64, 1928.42, 1974.02
Lorelei on the Rocks 1937.14
Lorelei Waltz, The 1914.30
Lorelei, The 1920.44, 1933.01, 1999.10
Lorena 1975.22
Loretta 1901.13
Lorna's Here 1964.32
Lorraine Serenade 1888.39
Los Amigos, A 1997.13
Los Chucos Suaves 1979.08
Los Laureles 1988.15
Los Olividados 1966.32
Los Sevillanitas 1912.02
Losing My Mind 1971.05, 1977.05, 1991.04
Loss 2001.04
Lost 1946.06, 1948.24, 1979.10
Lost and Found 1989.29
Lost Barber Shop Chord 1926.21
Lost Beat Swing, The 1996.07
Lost Horizon 1956.07
Lost in Darkness 1997.09
Lost in Loveliness 1954.01
Lost in the Stars 1949.15, 1972.06, 1995.12
Lost Pleiad, The 1899.39
Lost Pocketbook, The 1921.02
Lost Step, The 1927.68
Lost Word, The 1977.02
Lot Can Happen in a Day, A 1970.16
Lot of Bull Broadway, A 1927.10
Lot of Livin' to Do, A 1960.06
Lot of Men, A 1984.02
Lots of Good Fish in the Sea 1906.45
Lotta Locomotion 1987.05
Lottie Gibson Specialty 1954.02
Lottie of the Literati 1936.12
Lotus Flower 1922.35, 1923.41
Lotus Flower, The 1927.07
Lotus, The 1907.13
Lou 1910.16
Lou and Sue 1897.34
Lou-Lou 1899.18
Loud and Funny Song, A 1981.25
Loud Let the Bugle Sound 1903.38
Loud your voices raise 1888.18
Loudly I'd like to rejoice 1885.63
Loudly let the trumpet bray 1882.78
Louis is All Right 1907.35
Louis Says 1995.15
Louis XIII Gavotte 1924.02
Louisa 1897.26, 1898.43
Louise 1932.04, 1947.05, 1948.12, 1955.14, 1963.02, 1965.08, 1980.08
Louise Schmidt 1904.23, 1905.10
Louisiana 1912.38, 1916.23, 1926.01
Louisiana Belle 1939.21
Louisiana Elizabeth 1910.08
Louisiana Gals 1944.32
Louisiana Hayride 1932.17, 1972.05
Louisiana Holiday 1947.13
Louisiana Lize 1899.35
Louisiana Lou 1895.32
Louisiana Purchase 1940.08
Lounging at the Waldorf 1978.09
Louwanna 1924.38
Lovable Love 1902.03
Lovable Moon 1919.30
Lovable You 1946.14, 1947.12
Lovce O Songster of the Night 1885.42
Love 1886.40, 1903.02, 1904.05, 1950.03, 1974.22, 1981.16, 1990.09, 1999.23
Love - Just Simply Love 1922.13
Love - Love 1917.21
Love - O - Love 1927.39
Love a Gypsy Knows, The 1921.17
Love Ahoy! 1918.05
Love Ain't Nothin' 2000.08
Love Among the Freaks 1895.08, 1906.17
Love and Archery 1894.17
Love and Beauty 1911.23
Love and I 1940.23
Love and I are Playing 1913.32
Love and Joy 1980.30
Love and Kindness 1956.04
Love and Kisses 1922.28, 1927.19
Love and Kisses 'n' Everything 1926.46
Love and Laughter 1911.06, 1948.27
Love and Law 1888.15
Love and Love Alone 1918.07
Love and Marriage 1974.10
Love and pleasure 1882.60
Love and Rhythm 1933.05
Love and the Automobile 1912.31
Love and the Japanese Plan 1895.32
Love and Victory 1914.07
Love and War 1900.12, 1934.29
Love and Wine 1909.19
Love at First Sight 1892.55, 1913.01, 1941.11
Love at Last 1944.16
Love at Last You Have Found Me 1965.30
Love at Second Sight 1944.18
Love at Sight 1884.62
Love Awakening 1872.23
Love Before Breakfast 1979.09
Love Behind Bars 1989.07
Love Behind the Kitchen Door 1873.10
Love Bird, The 1886.30
Love Birds 1926.14, 1929.35
Love Boat 1919.30
Love Boat, The 1920.18, 1927.58
Love Boats 1930.22
Love Bring Me Summer 1999.22
Love Bug 1923.39
Love by Proxy 1904.55
Love Calls Me 1925.06
Love Came into My Heart 1931.26
Love Came to Me One Day 1900.12
Love Can 1972.19
Love Can't 1975.05
Love Can't Happen 1989.26
Love Can't Say No 1900.59
Love Cannot be Bought 1908.06
Love Changes Everything 1990.04
Love Clock, The 1924.42
Love Come Take Me Again 1963.21
Love Comes A-Stealing 1918.12
Love Comes Like a Butterfly 1920.43
Love Comes Like a Summer Sigh 1886.15, 1890.30
Love Comes Once in a Lifetime 1930.15
Love Comes to Stay 1910.11
Love Comes, Love Goes 1999.05
Love Contagious 1907.14
Love Cottage, The 1924.06
Love Crazy 1979.11
Love Dance, The 1910.22
Love Days 1908.22
Love Dies Hard 1983.15
Love Dreams 1921.35, 1923.46
Love Duet 1933.07, 1977.09, 1989.09
Love Duet I 1992.05
Love Duet II 1992.05
Love Eyes 1958.20
Love Feeds on Hope 1881.37
Love Finds a Way 1922.40
Love Finds the Lonely 1972.24
Love Flew in at the Window 1892.14
Love Flies Everywhere 1916.18
Love for an Hour 1898.73
Love for Sale 1925.32, 1930.40, 1953.12, 1980.10, 1982.15
Love from a Heart of Gold 1961.22
Love Hangover 1976.16
Love has Claimed its Own 1901.08
Love has Come from Lotus Land 1900.43
Love has Come to Live in Our House 1914.21
Love has Driven Me Sane 1971.18
Love has Faded Away 1930.43
Love has Found My Heart 1926.27
Love has Nothing to do With Looks 1952.05
Love has O'ercome Me 1870.08, 1870.27
Love has the Longest Memory of All 1974.22
Love has Wings 1914.03
Love has won 1884.60
Love Held Lightly 1959.27
Love Holds Sway 1916.12
Love I Bear Thee, The 1922.42
Love I Long For, The 1944.27
Love in a Cottage 1924.02
Love in a Home 1956.12
Love in a Tempo 1968.13
Love in an Attic 1897.21
Love in an Orchard 1903.41
Love in Mine Eyes 1899.39
Love in My Breast 1920.34
Love in My Heart 1907.48
Love in the Barnyard 1955.11
Love in the Morning 1984.15
Love in the Ranks 1925.03, 1943.11
Love in the Shadows 1925.48
Love in the Springtime is Not What it Used to Be 1922.03
Love in the Suburbs 1924.16
Love Interest 1918.21
Love Is 1989.05
Love is a Battle 1914.30
Love is a Bubble 1916.23
Love is a Business 1921.23
Love is a Chameleon! 1894.29
Love is a Chance 1964.40
Love is a charm that binds me 1888.07
Love is a Curious Feeling 1908.41
Love is a Dance 1916.17
Love is a Dancer 1936.12
Love is a Dancing Thing 1935.12
Love is a Fancied Dream 1897.21
Love is a Game 1903.06
Love is a Game for Soldiers' 1947.14
Love is a Game of Cards 1920.06
Love is a Jailer 1902.06
Love is a Many Splendored Thing 1982.22
Love is a Peculiarity 1912.14
Love is a Pilgrim 1912.48
Love is a Plaintive Song 1881.37
Love is a Pretty Bubble 1892.42
Love is a queer thing 1889.10
Love is a Race 1911.15
Love is a Random Thing 1946.23
Love is a Riddle 1921.31
Love is a Sickness 1961.01
Love is a Simple Thing 1952.09, 1980.18
Love is a Spell 1898.47
Love is a Story 1894.08
Love is a Story That's Old 1913.32
Love is a Summer's Morning 1914.17
Love is a Traitor 1909.15
Love is a Tyrant 1892.27
Love is a Very Light Thing 1954.15
Love is a Wonderful Feeling 1919.39
Love is a Wonderful Thing 1906.26, 1916.25
Love is All 1923.16
Love is All in All 1905.12
Love is Always Love 1920.08
Love is Always Young 1933.24
Love is an Ailment 1903.14
Love is an Art 1916.08
Love is an Infant 1900.03

Love is Blind 1890.26, 1992.09
Love is Coming Back 1975.04
Love is Divine 1891.20
Love is Elusive 1904.09, 1908.17
Love is Enough 1925.21
Love is Good for You 1962.02
Love is Hell 1958.02
Love is Here to Stay 1999.10
Love is in the Air 1925.14, 1977.05
Love is Just a Fairy Tale 1918.02
Love is Just Around the Corner 1986.06
Love is Just the Same 1902.15
Love is Just the Same Old Game in Every Land 1913.16
Love is King 1904.34, 1908.26, 1922.17
Love is Like a Blushing Rose 1927.05
Love is Like a Butterfly 1915.04
Love is Like a Cigarette 1908.24, 1909.23, 1911.31
Love is Like a Dainty Flower 1895.25
Love is Like a Firefly 1912.46, 1924.09
Love is Like a Little Rubber Band 1911.32
Love is Like a Pinwheel 1924.13
Love is Like a Red, Red Rose 1910.25
Love is Like a Violin 1914.04
Love is Like That 1928.46, 1930.18
Love is Like the Rose 1911.37
Love is Lord 1881.16
Love is Lost 1892.20
Love is Lost, Love is Gone 1977.01
Love is Love Where the Cherry Blossoms Fall 1919.04
Love is Made of Smiles and Tears 1881.04
Love is Merest Folly 1899.34
Love is My Enemy 1945.04
Love is My Friend 1940.22
Love is My Inspiration 1932.18
Love is never blind! 1882.60
Love is Not for a Day 1907.13, 1925.02
Love is Not for a Daytime 1893.16
Love is Not Love 1973.07
Love is Only What You Made, Love 1934.43
Love is Queen of the Sea 1902.21
Love is Quite a Simple Thing 1928.29, 1986.14
Love is Simply Heavenly 1957.09
Love is Spring 1894.45
Love is Such a Cheat 1943.14
Love is Such a Funny Little Feeling 1913.19
Love is Sweeping the Country 1931.48
Love is the Best of All 1915.24
Love is the Bunk 1923.42
Love is the Funniest Thing 1954.01
Love is the Joy of Living 1912.37
Love is the Mountain 1928.47
Love is the Prize 1976.01
Love is the Queen of the Sea 1902.21
Love is the Reason 1915.04, 1951.14
Love is the Sovereign of My Heart 1947.14
Love is the Sun 1928.12
Love is the Tenderest of Themes 1896.45
Love is the Theme of My Dream 1911.30
Love is to All a Dainty Dream 1895.25
Love is Trouble 1952.15
Love is Tyrant so I Bid You Beware 1899.34
Love is Very Different 1917.25
Love is Very Wonderful 1919.22
Love is Victor 1908.03
Love is What I Never Knew 1956.07
Love is Where You Find It 1985.08
Love isn't Everything 1966.29
Love it Hurts so Good 1950.02
Love Land 1913.25
Love Lasts a Day 1926.31
Love laughs at locksmiths 1859.12
Love Laughs at Locksmiths 1904.05
Love Let Me Know 1961.21
Love Letter to Manhattan 1950.19
Love Letters 1899.15, 1899.25, 1916.12, 1929.46
Love Life of a Gondolier, The 1966.03
Love Light in Your Eyes, The 1900.12
Love Like Ours, A 1935.19
Love Lives On 1932.10
Love Long 1947.14
Love Look Away 1958.19
Love Lorn Lilly, The 1900.07
Love Lorn Lobster 1897.09
Love Lost and Found 1879.15
Love Love Love 1947.19
Love Love You Baby 1981.29
Love Lurks Around unknown 1883.66
Love Lust Poem 1976.27
Love Makes Such Fools of Us All 1980.07
Love Makes the World Go 1962.03
Love Makes the World Go Round 1906.44, 1909.17, 1919.35, 1937.02, 1961.10, 1986.12, 2000.16
Love Makes the World Go Round, Boys 1896.28
Love Maketh the Heart a Garden Fair 1907.51
Love Match Test 1889.41
Love May be a Mystery 1916.01
Love May Come Again 1894.08
Love May Come and Love May Go 1902.04
Love Me 1910.26, 1921.08, 1922.44, 1926.46, 1934.27, 1971.18
Love Me and the World is Mine 1905.47
Love Me as You Used to Do 1907.04
Love Me at Twilight 1916.09
Love Me Baby Mine 1909.10
Love Me Best of All 1917.09
Love Me for Old Love's Sake 1894.37
Love Me Forever 1922.42, 1931.40
Love Me in a Viennese Melody 1913.30
Love Me in the Spring 1918.34
Love Me in the Winter 1906.50
Love Me Just a Little Bit 1916.22
Love Me Just Because 1909.02
Love Me Just for Me 1998.19
Love Me Just Like Romeo Loved His Juliet 1909.18
Love Me Like a Real, Real Man 1912.39
Love Me Little, Love Me Long 1891.39, 1902.07
Love Me Lize 1901.04
Love Me Love 1896.51
Love Me More, Love Me Less 1932.08
Love Me or Leave Me 1928.47, 1930.08, 1931.08, 1975.22, 1979.05
Love Me Over Dearie 1911.12
Love Me Tender 1982.22, 1989.12
Love Me Tomorrow 1940.17
Love Me Tonight 1920.32, 1925.32, 1975.13
Love Me While the Lovin' is Good 1913.18
Love Me While the Snow Flakes Fall 1920.33
Love Me While You're Gone 1925.18
Love Me With All Your Heart 1976.32
Love Me, Don't You? 1926.34
Love Me, Honey, Do 1896.02
Love Me, Love Me, Won't You? 1913.33
Love Me, Love My Dog 1905.57, 1915.05, 1949.17
Love Me, Sweetheart Mine 1920.11
Love Me/Don't 1995.03
Love Mill, The 1918.04
Love Mississippi 1972.14
Love Monopoly, The 1916.19
Love Moon 1914.23
Love Must be Blind 1904.37
Love Ne'er Came Nigh' 1894.45
Love Nest, The 1920.38
Love Never Changes 1920.07
Love Never Dies 1911.44
Love Never Goes Away 1982.14
Love Never Went to College 1939.27, 1975.13
Love of a Prince, The 1869.14
Love of Golden Years 1970.18
Love of Long Ago 1922.34
Love of Mine 1919.04
Love of My Life, The 1947.07, 1980.26
Love of the Lorelei, The 1914.30
Love of the Shamrock, The 1879.63
Love or Money 1973.02
Love or Reason 1945.08
Love Parade, The 1931.37
Love Pas de Deux 1969.04
Love Potion #9 1995.03
Love Potion, The 1932.10
Love Power 1972.13
Love Reigns! 1886.15
Love Remains the Same 1896.11
Love Revolution 1977.04
Love Rules the World 1926.24
Love Serves in a Candy Store 1879.03
Love shall guide me 1879.38
Love Sneaks Up on You 1955.10
Love Song 1885.65, 1948.25, 1966.19, 1969.02, 1972.22, 1989.24
Love Song of Montosol 1886.43
Love Song of the Espada 1893.16
Love Song of Today, The 1923.34
Love Song of Yesterday, The 1923.34
Love Song, The 1925.02
Love Songs are Made in the Night 1943.05
Love Spans the World 1922.05
Love Spats 1912.33
Love Spell, The 1913.10
Love Stolen 1975.18, 1976.31
Love Story 1973.17
Love Swept Like a Storm 1952.13
Love Test, The 1922.11
Love That is True 1897.37
Love That Man 1950.19
Love That's Sincere 1911.36
Love the Magician 1896.10
Love the Wife of Your Neighbor 1922.35
Love the World Over is Much the Same 1913.14
Love Thought Garden 1927.45
Love Thoughts 1926.30
Love Through the Ages 1923.22
Love Time 1909.05, 1921.35
Love to Love You Baby 1982.22
Love to Your Heart's Desire 1982.02
Love Today 1923.42
Love Train 1997.21
Love Tunes 1922.23
Love Turned the Light Out 1940.17
Love Unconquerable 1988.05
Love Under the Republicans (or Democrats) 1973.08
Love Up a Tree 1908.13
Love Was 1966.30
Love was Just a Game 1975.23
Love Waves 1911.40
Love Where are You Now 1932.19
Love While You May 1922.40
Love Will Always be the Same 1944.20
Love Will Always Find a Way 1921.06
Love Will Bring You Happiness 1923.11
Love Will Call 1920.25
Love Will Conquer All 1969.04, 1980.01
Love Will Find a Way 1918.27, 1921.16, 1952.08, 1976.04, 1990.09
Love Will Find Out the Way 1959.06
Love Will Find the Way 1890.26
Love Will Find You 1920.09, 1934.29
Love Will Find You Some Day 1925.02
Love will guide 1887.04
Love Will Keep Us Young 1925.44
Love Will Make or Break a Man 1909.26
Love Will See Us Through 1971.05
Love Will Win 1912.26
Love with doubt can never dwell 1881.04
Love Won't Take No for an Answer 1997.18
Love! Love! 1896.27
Love's a Game 1920.09
Love's a Most Exacting Master 1894.47
Love's a Race 1909.21
Love's a Riddle 1939.29
Love's Advent 1901.18
Love's Agony 1928.04
Love's Alphabet 1912.37
Love's Answer 1888.05
Love's Art 1923.37
Love's Awakening 1915.04
Love's Bouquet 1908.27
Love's Call 1926.15
Love's Charming Art 1911.32
Love's Conquests 1911.46
Love's Corporation 1922.24
Love's Cruel Dart 1866.07
Love's Dear Eyes 1894.07
Love's Dream 1888.43
Love's Dream After the Ball 1895.27
Love's Dream is O'er 1897.19
Love's Dream is Over 1908.42
Love's Eternal Song 1907.08
Love's Ever New 1918.11
Love's Fairy Tales 1913.02

Love's Flower is Always Blooming 1913.02
Love's Fond Dream 1912.04
Love's Fragile Flower 1892.27
Love's Golden Day 1905.44
Love's Greatest Plague in Life 1872.10
Love's Happy Dream 1930.15
Love's Hesitation 1914.13
Love's Highway 1922.07
Love's in Need of Love Today 1997.21
Love's in the Air 1926.33
Love's Intense in Tents 1920.25
Love's Language 1907.04
Love's Last Day 1923.03
Love's Last Word 1906.25
Love's Lesson 1906.30, 1911.02
Love's Little Journey 1921.07
Love's Match Test 1889.09, 1890.29
Love's Memories 1883.52
Love's Merry-Go-Round 1907.41
Love's Messenger 1883.52
Love's Misgivings 1904.51
Love's Never Lost 1934.29
Love's Night 1902.41, 1917.11
Love's Not a Science 1883.12
Love's Old Sweet Song 1890.12, 1926.11, 1927.36
Love's Own Call 1917.27
Love's Own Kiss 1913.34
Love's Own Sweet Song 1914.03
Love's Prescription 1897.17, 1907.46
Love's Refrain 1926.24
Love's Revenge 1971.18
Love's Rosy Dream 1891.46
Love's Roundelay 1908.06
Love's Sad Glance 1984.15
Love's Seasons 1883.04
Love's Secret 1907.05
Love's Serenade 1894.37, 1897.34, 1916.12
Love's Sextette, A 1918.36
Love's Sorcery 1911.37
Love's Sweet Lay 1897.55
Love's Telephone 1920.37
Love's the Pleasure 1898.48
Love's Theme 1974.22
Love's Wireless Telephone 1911.17
Love's Young Dream 1901.15, 1902.16, 1924.09
Love, ah love 1895.19
Love, are You Raising Your Head? 1942.34
Love, be sure, finds out the way 1884.60
Love, Come Take Me 1934.40
Love, Don't Turn Away 1963.26, 1992.10
Love, First Love 1895.25
Love, Honour, Happiness 1878.16
Love, I Hear 1962.12
Love, I Will be True 1891.15
Love, I Will Love You Ever 1925.21
Love, is That You? 1971.18
Love, Life and Laughter 1928.42
Love, light of my heart 1898.25
Love, Look Away 1993.16
Love, Look in My Window 1964.01
Love, Love 1881.17, 1918.33
Love, Love, Beautiful Love 1879.32
Love, Love, Love 1881.07, 1882.20, 1904.15, 1905.52, 1907.01, 1907.62, 1909.21, 1918.17, 1920.07, 1922.42, 1955.10, 1967.05
Love, Love, Sweetest Love 1893.46
Love, Mighty Love 1787.01
Love, Now We Nevermore Will Part 1891.29
Love, Nuts and Noodles 1932.16
Love, the Magician 1908.30
Love, unrequited, robs me of my rest 1882.78
Love, What has Given You This Magic Power? 1946.16
Love, You're a Wonderful Game 1903.22
Love-Line 1964.40
Love-Lorn Maid, A 1937.11
Love-Sick 1924.40
Love-Sick Serenade 1961.08
Loveable Irish, The 1961.14
Lovebird 1997.07
Loved One, so Pure and Tender 1905.35
Loveland 1917.05, 1971.05
Loveland Volunteers, The 1906.41
Lovelier Than Ever 1948.26, 1974.25
Lovelight 1905.31, 1908.16, 1910.17
Lovelight in My Eyes, The 1909.05
Lovely 1962.12, 1999.20
Lovely Angeline 1888.06
Lovely Angeline Pretty as a Picture 1884.62
Lovely Bonnabellavita 1895.25
Lovely Corals 1920.12
Lovely Day for a Murder 1940.06
Lovely Day for a Murder, A 1975.13
Lovely Day for a Walk 1903.09
Lovely Day to be Out of Jail, A 1997.08
Lovely Girl, A 1945.20
Lovely Girls of Akbarabad, The 1960.10
Lovely Ladies 1919.39, 1987.04
Lovely Ladies, Kind Gentlemen 1970.21
Lovely Lady 1896.28, 1925.22, 1926.34, 1927.68
Lovely Lady, A 1934.41
Lovely Lassie 1922.45
Lovely Lazy Kind of Day, A 1946.07
Lovely Little Marjorie 1904.35
Lovely Mae 1848.01
Lovely Nancy Brown 1869.20
Lovely Nature, Fare Thee Well 1899.34
Lovely Nell 1886.60
Lovely Night 1880.10
Lovely Night, A 1993.14, 1993.16, 2001.09
Lovely Rita 1974.24
Lovely Sunday Mornin' 1981.14
Lovely to Look At 1986.01
Lovely Trip, A 1914.01
Lovely Wedding, A 1999.22
Lovely You Madly 1997.03
Lovely, Lovely Day 1934.18
Lover 1948.13, 1975.13, 1983.20
Lover and the Bird, The 1882.76
Lover and the Nightingale, The 1872.10
Lover Come Back to Me 1929.02, 1948.13, 1986.14
Lover in Me, The 1957.01
Lover Like a Blind Man 1975.23
Lover Man 1982.12
Lover Man Oh, Where Can You Be? 1948.13
Lover True, A 1900.12
Lover's Frolic, The 1898.20
Lover's Holiday 1932.10
Lover's Lane With You 1922.24
Lover's Roost 1902.40
Lover's Talk 1886.50
Lover, Come Back to Me 1928.29
Lovers of Art 1924.19
Lovers of History 1924.01
Lovers on Christmas Eve 1977.04
Lovers Two Have Sought My Hand 1933.24
Lovers' A.B.C., The 1903.41
Lovers' Lane 1902.15, 1905.34, 1906.23
Lovers' Quarrel 1898.10
Lovers' Quarrel, The 1896.37, 1906.13
Lovers' Talk 1879.03
Loves of May Ann, The 1904.14
Loves of New Orleans 1978.19, 1988.18
Lovesick Blues 1922.22
Lovey 1923.31
Lovey Dove 1922.11
Lovey Dovey 1917.18
Lovey Joe 1910.18
Lovey-Dovey 1934.43
Lovin Al 1978.12
Lovin' is a Lowdown Blues 1992.08
Lovin' Moon 1911.26
Lovin' Off My Mind 1927.05
Lovin' Sam (The Sheik of Alabam') 1922.23
Lovin' Sam the Sheik of Alabam' 1922.44
Lovin' Sam, the Sheik of Alabam' 1922.15
Loving 1910.23
Loving Cup, The 1910.37
Loving Daddy, A 1917.23
Loving Hairdresser, The 1924.48
Loving Her 1993.17
Loving Husband A. 1889.24
Loving is a Habit 1923.42
Loving Time 1909.05, 1927.29
Loving Ways 1910.12
Loving You 1968.06, 1974.12, 1994.05, 1995.03, 1997.01
Loving You the Way I Do 1930.24
Lovingly Yours 1921.07
Low 1982.12
Low Back'd Car, The 1888.12
Low Backed Car, The 1885.53, 1886.44, 1890.06
Low Down Blues 1978.21
Low Down Dance 1930.19
Low sighs the night wind 1877.39
Lowdown Blues 1921.16
Lowdown-Down 2000.08
Lowen-Green Country Club, I Love You 1936.07
Lowlands 1992.11
Lowly peasant girl, A 1868.01
Lowly the lass 1887.04
Lowly we bend in duty 1860.01
Lu-Lu 1920.33
Luana 1930.26
Luana Waltz 1912.03
Lucia de Lammermoor 1904.41, 1927.02
Lucia My Italian Maid 1906.46
Lucidora, surnamed the Fair one 1863.04
Lucidora, the pride of this heart 1863.04
Lucita 1925.23
Luck 1919.37
Luck be a Lady 1950.17, 1980.29, 1991.10
Luck, Luck, Luck 1904.39
Luckiest Man in the World 1933.01
Lucky 1925.26, 1927.12, 1939.19
Lucky Anichino 1975.23
Lucky Bargee 1923.35
Lucky Bird 1927.16
Lucky Boy 1925.45
Lucky in Love 1923.02, 1927.41, 1974.26
Lucky in the Rain 1948.28
Lucky Lindy 1974.09
Lucky little boys and girls 1882.63
Lucky Molina 1993.09
Lucky Pierre 1952.09, 1981.17
Lucky Seven 1930.25
Lucky to be Me 1944.33, 1958.21, 1971.15, 1977.02, 1998.16
Lucky to Me 1930.34
Lucretia 1866.26
Lucy 1901.07
Lucy in the Sky With Diamonds 1974.24, 1977.10
Lucy Lindy Lady 1903.33
Lucy Locket 1971.20
Lucy Long 1862.02
Lucy Lou 1896.44
Lucy Song 1933.07
Lucy's Aria 1989.24
Lucy, Tell Me I'm Your Beau 1898.47
Lud's Wedding 1976.11
Lueur de ces flambeaux, A la 1878.08
Lull'd by waves 1890.33
Lullaby 1883.20, 1893.35, 1907.19, 1913.02, 1919.44, 1921.01, 1926.02, 1927.60, 1938.16, 1940.01, 1944.23, 1946.08, 1947.02, 1950.05, 1956.13, 1959.26, 1963.28, 1988.09, 1989.10, 1997.19
Lullaby for Junior 1946.24
Lullaby for Luis 1978.11
Lullaby from Baby to Baby 1978.11
Lullaby of Broadway 1974.09, 1975.12, 1975.22, 1980.20, 1988.08
Lullaby of the Leaves 1932.14
Lullaby of the Plain 1938.12
Lullaby of the Waves 1892.29
Lullaby, Baby 1963.09
Lullaby, The 1907.14, 1926.09, 1957.05
Lullabye 1886.30, 1983.21
Lullabye of Broadway 1973.14
Lulu 1905.42, 1907.31, 1917.02, 1943.14
Lulu Belle 1926.01
Lulu's Back in Town 1988.08
Lulu's Honeymoon 1903.26
Lum Tum Proper Caper, The 1879.38
Lum-Tum Capah, The 1880.65
Lumbered 1962.18, 1978.18
Luna 1906.31
Luna-Park 1959.15
Lunch is Ready 1906.30
Luncheon Ballad 1968.13
Luncheon Line, The 1910.01

Lunching at the Automat 1932.05
Lupe 1940.18
Lure of the Cape, The 1929.33
Lure of the Night With the Ile de France on the Horizon, The 1929.22
Lure of the Waltz, The 1915.22
Lurline 1896.18
Lush Life 1984.15, 1995.12
Lusty Month of May, The 1960.21, 1980.19, 1993.11
Lute Song 1946.05
Lutie 1904.15
Lydia, the Tattooed Lady 1988.08
Lynching Blues, The 1996.07
Lyre Bird and the Jay, The 1912.25
Lysistrata 1972.23

M'lle. Pirouette 1909.01
M-I-S-S-I-S-S-I-P-P-I 1917.12, 1918.08
M-i-s-s-i-s-s-i-p-p-i 1920.04
M-O-N-E-Y 1908.14
M-O-N-E-Y Spells Money 1901.04
M.A.C.A.R.O.N.I. 1904.15
M.P. Song, The 1919.40
Ma Ann Elizer 1898.41
Ma Belle 1928.12
Ma Belle of the Philippines 1899.22
Ma Blushin' Rosie, Ma Posie Sweet 1900.38
Ma Cherie 1906.45
Ma Curly Headed Baby 1919.26
Ma Ebony Belle 1901.16
Ma Femme 1921.25
Ma Honey Babe 1901.07
Ma Honeysuckle Gal 1917.11
Ma Little One, or Ma Baby 1897.21
Ma Lulu 1896.52, 1897.40
Ma Mere 1931.09
Ma mere l'oye 1929.51
Ma Mome, Ma P'tite Mome 1959.15
Ma perche 1934.20
Ma Petite Cheri 1946.16
Ma Pomme 1947.05
Ma Reguliere 1932.04
Ma Says, Why so Shy 1892.19
Ma Southern Oriole 1905.47
Ma Starlight Queen 1902.24
Ma Tiger Lily 1900.15
Ma' Blushin' Rosie, My Posie Sweet 1912.07
Ma, He's Makin' Eyes at Me 1923.47
Mabel Moore 1900.48
Mac Arthur Park 1977.09, 1979.13
Macaronis We 1904.55
Macavity 1982.19
Machar 1968.04
Machinalement 1929.14
Machine Age 1940.23
Machine Gun 1997.21
Machinen 1966.21
Mack the Knife 1962.17
Mack's Love Song 1897.47
Mack's Lullaby 1899.03
Mack's Serenade 1900.36
Mack's Swing Song 1896.14
MacNamara 1895.04
Macumba 1940.23, 1988.06
Macushla 1911.04, 1912.06
Macushla Asthore 1912.06
Mad 1953.10, 1983.08
Mad About the Boy 1939.07, 1968.19, 1986.19
Mad About You 1927.64
Mad Adventure, A 1884.11
Mad Bombers and Prom Queens 1982.10
Mad Dogs and Englishmen 1931.14, 1968.19, 1986.19
Mad for Art 1968.02
Mad Madrid and the Dance of Danger, The 1910.22
Mad Opera House 1909.13
Mad Rum Below/Escape 1990.17
Mad Sequedilla of Gay Seville, The 1900.54
Madam Angot 1885.44
Madam Venus 1909.13
Madam, with all humility 1863.04
Madame Arcati's Tea Party 1964.16
Madame Arthur 1952.04
Madame Flirt 1854.06
Madame Guillotine 1997.19, 1999.13
Madame is at Home 1938.15
Madame n'est pas la? 1926.49
Madame Rose's Toreadorables 1959.13
Madame Tango's Tango 1954.19
Madame Zuzu 1948.25
Madame, I know all 1859.09
Madcap Princess, A 1904.30
Madcap Zoologist, The 1973.08
Madchen am Fenster, Das 1981.14
Madchenlied 1907.37
Made in the U.S.A. 1915.02
Madeira, M' Dear? 1959.20
Madel guck-Das ist die Liebe 1984.05
Madeleine 1972.16
Madelon 1919.10
Mademoiselle 1908.21
Mademoiselle Cliche de Paris 1969.17
Mademoiselle from Armentieres 1943.23, 1975.22
Mademoiselle from New Rochelle 1930.02
Mademoiselle Lise 1966.20
Mademoiselle Marie 1948.08
Mademoiselle New York 1900.59
Madge's Ballad 1895.44
Madiwa-Madiwa 1977.01
Madman 1993.07
Madness of King Scar, The 1997.20
Madonna Isabella 1975.23
Madrigal 1907.01, 1922.46, 1939.15, 1973.13, 1993.11
Madrigal Blues, The 1981.24
Madrigal, A 1903.36
Madrigale 1985.14
Magdalane, My Southern Queen 1900.48
Magdalena 1948.24
Maggie Flynn 1968.24
Maggie Mooney 1893.30
Maggie Murphy 1893.23
Maggie Murphy's Home 1890.49, 1891.26, 1892.38, 1985.02
Maggie My Own 1896.14
Magic Carpet 1968.23
Magic Frame, The 1894.51
Magic Garden of Love, The 1925.23
Magic Gifts 1937.11
Magic Guitar, The 1881.16
Magic Hour, The 1924.41
Magic in Rhythm 1953.10
Magic Kiss The 1920.35
Magic Kiss, The 1912.36
Magic Knight is Summoned, The 1906.48
Magic Man, The 1905.32
Magic Melody 1928.27
Magic Melody, The 1915.07
Magic Moment 1961.27
Magic Moments 1924.39
Magic Music 1930.08, 1931.08
Magic Nights 1972.04
Magic of Moonlight and Love, The 1925.06
Magic Slipper, The 1866.34
Magic Spell of Love 1930.26
Magic to Do 1972.22
Magic Train, The 1924.08
Magic, Magic 1961.10
Magical Lasso 1988.01
Magical Mystery Tour 1977.10
Magical Things in Life 1964.18
Magician Love 1907.05
Magician of High Degree, A 1895.08
Magnet and the Churn, The 1895.29
Magnet Hung in a Hard-ware Shop, A 1881.37
Magnetic Healing 1980.30
Magnificent Failure 1945.17
Magnolia 1885.06, 1926.19
Magnolia in the Woods 1925.33
Magnolia's Wedding Day 1928.18
Magu'lonne allant a la fontaine 1877.32
Maguires, The 1882.02
Magyar Maid 1906.20
Mah Butterfly 1900.08
Mah Jongg 1924.19
Mah Midnight Lou 1902.02
Maha Roger 1950.09
Maharajah, The 1897.37
Maharanee 1936.02
Mahoneyphone, The 1931.26
Mai Poina oe la'u 1912.03
Maid and the Miller, The 1903.38
Maid and the Officer, The 1897.17
Maid Demure, A 1897.55
Maid from Boston Town, The 1906.15
Maid from Montbijou 1911.27
Maid is like the golden Oar, A 1750.01
Maid Like You, A 1919.16
Maid of Arcadie, The 1906.15
Maid of Beauty, Fond and True 1866.22
Maid of Gold 1923.38
Maid of Honolulu 1912.03
Maid of Jade, The 1926.14
Maid of Mandalay, The 1906.41
Maid of Mesh 1923.32
Maid of my Soul 1877.39
Maid of Sevilla 1910.08
Maid of the Milky Way 1925.23
Maid of the Mill, The 1904.22
Maid of the Witching Eye 1884.57
Maid of Timbuctoo 1903.28
Maid to Order Maid 1919.37
Maid With a Wink in Her Eye, The 1897.32
Maid, The 1990.16
Maid, those bright eyes 1859.18
Maidee Come be My Lady 1902.11
Maiden and the Cavalier, The 1890.23
Maiden and the Jay, The 1903.14
Maiden and the Kissing Bug, The 1904.28
Maiden e'er loves to torment, A 1859.17
Maiden Fair 1925.04, 1950.20
Maiden Fair Awake to Me 1881.27
Maiden fair to see, A 1879.05
Maiden Fair to See, A 1945.08
Maiden I Left in Hong Kong, The 1904.11
Maiden of Gentle Grace 1897.39
Maiden Often Seen, A 1945.09
Maiden Vexed, A 1893.19
Maiden With the Dreamy Eyes 1901.25, 1902.06
Maiden With the Dreamy Eyes, The 1901.25, 1901.29, 1980.27
Maiden's Art, A 1892.42
Maiden's Heart, A 1903.34
Maiden's Sea Trip 1894.31
Maiden, I will ne'er deceive thee 1871.10
Maiden, I'll ne'er deceive thee 1852.01
Maiden, Let Me In 1924.23
Maidens Aquatic 1898.55
Maidens of St. Malo 1890.33
Maidens Tender Glances 1897.55
Maidens Typical of France 1953.07
Maidens we 1882.17
Maidens we, young, blithe and merry 1889.10
Maidie Come be My Lady 1902.11
Maids and Mailmen 1910.11
Maids of Killarney 1905.30
Mail Man, The 1911.08
Mailman Bring Me No More Blues 1990.15
Mailman Must be Mad at Me, The 1923.06
Mailu 1931.19
Maine 1962.03
Maine Will Remember the Maine 1951.17
Mainly a Clogging Main 1880.59
Maint'nant j'ai pris le bel usage 1886.19
Mais Qu'est-ce que J'ai? 1959.15
Mais qu'est-ce que j'ai? 1961.25
Maisie 1901.19
Maison des Lunes 1994.04
Maitre de la Conte, Le 1980.17
Maja de Goya 1917.25
Maja Modernia 1917.25
Majestic Sails at Midnight 1933.22
Major Gilfeather 1881.29, 1883.42, 1885.15, 1895.05
Major Margery 1906.07
Major's Song 1906.41
Major-Domo, The 1925.08
Make 'Em Laugh 1985.08
Make 'Em Pay 1979.11
Make a Friend 1963.08
Make a Fuss of Me 1904.40

Make a Little Sunshine 1978.10
Make a Lot of Noise 1907.20
Make a Miracle 1948.26, 1974.25, 1980.29
Make a New Now, Now! 1989.22
Make a Night of It 1912.04
Make a Quiet Day 1949.16
Make a Wish 1951.13
Make Allowances for Love 1901.25
Make Believe 1926.26, 1964.02, 1986.01, 1986.16, 1990.09, 1994.08
Make Believe You're Happy 1927.68
Make Every Day a Holiday 1924.32
Make Friends 1957.10
Make Hay Little Girl 1919.02
Make His Guess 1915.24
Make it Another Old-Fashioned Please 1940.19
Make it Happen Now 1970.03
Make it New 1982.02
Make it Up 1903.33
Make Love in the Morning 1924.23
Make love to me 1886.50
Make Me 1957.01
Make Our Garden Grow 1956.15, 1974.06, 1982.20
Make Someone Happy 1960.23, 1977.02
Make the Man Love Me 1951.14
Make the Most of Spring 1964.18
Make the People Cry 1953.01
Make Them Hear You 1998.01
Make Up My Heart 1987.05
Make Up Your Mind 1925.02, 1926.27, 1930.09
Make Way 1872.23, 1966.18
Make Way for the Wealthy Widow 1900.57
Make Way for Tomorrow 1983.09, 1986.01
Make With the Feet 1941.13
Make Your Own Sunshine 1906.19
Make Yourself at Home 1917.21
Make-Believe 1904.18
Makes Me so Awfully Wild 1873.28
Makes Our Garden Grow 1997.10
Makin' Whoopee 1962.17, 1979.05, 2000.14
Makin' Whopee 1928.47
Making a Home 1992.09
Making a Venus 1924.23
Making Conversation 1941.12
Making Eyes 1905.22, 1908.21
Making of Woman, The 1904.51
Makulele 1979.03
Malagassy War Song 1883.66
Malaguena 1934.17, 1941.11, 1942.14, 2001.04
Malaguena, La 1879.36, 1879.47
Malecon, El 1998.02
Malguena Salerosa 1988.15
Malkin, My Sweet Spirit 1870.15
Maloney's Leg 1896.52
Mam'selle 1900.20, 1901.08, 1907.12
Mam'selle Fauchette 1904.42, 1907.16
Mam'selle Lucette 1915.21
Mam'zell' non,vous n'et's pas parfaite 1887.36
Mama 1927.20, 1972.24, 1983.20, 1988.02
Mama Always Makes it Better 1979.12
Mama Don't 'Low 1975.20
Mama Don't Allow 1989.12
Mama Says 1998.13
Mama Tembu's Wedding 1977.01
Mama Will Provide 1990.12
Mama's Boarding House 1904.39
Mama's Little Pet 1911.15
Mama's Little Pumpkin Colored Coons 1896.49
Mama, a Rainbow 1970.07
Mama, Don't Get Married 1981.12
Mama, Earl Done Ate the Toothpaste Again 1971.10
Mama, it's Me 1993.09
Mama, La 1983.03
Mama, Laa 1998.12
Mama, Mama, Mama 1971.10
Mamam 1974.09
Mamaw 1982.04
Mamazelle Papazelle 1934.04
Mamba-Java 1961.01
Mame 1966.10, 1967.12, 1985.19, 1998.07
Mame's nign, A 1960.18
Mame, Di 1990.16
Mamenyu Tayere 1990.16
Mamie is Mimi 1949.18, 1974.02, 1995.07
Mamie O'Relly 1898.03
Mamie Reilly 1897.40
Mamie, Come and Kiss Your Honey Boy 1893.49
Mamie, Come Kiss Your Honey Boy 1894.06, 1896.52
Mamma 1998.12
Mamma's Little Joy 1885.42
Mamma, is this thy welcome 1873.05
Mamma, La 1965.30, 1974.19
Mamma, Mamma 1956.04
Mamma, Papa 1900.01
Mamma, What Shall I Do? 1880.19
Mammu's Little Pumpkin-colored Coons 1897.30
Mammy 1923.38, 1927.36, 1953.12
Mammy Songs 1953.17
Mammy's Carbon Copy 1922.38
Mammy's Choc'late Cullud Chile 1924.27
Mammy's Little Baby 1947.13
Mamselle Fifi 1909.05
Mamzell' Marie 1999.22
Man 2000.15
Man About Town 1929.19, 1937.06
Man About Town, The 1897.32, 1908.34
Man About Yonkers 1932.16
Man Among Men, A 1972.11
Man and a Maid, A 1908.40
Man and a Woman, A 1963.26, 1992.10
Man and Shadow 1961.26
Man at Arms, The 1902.04
Man Behind the Club, The 1905.41
Man Behind the Gun, The 1899.41, 1900.01
Man Behind the Scenes, The 1902.20
Man Behind, The 1904.03
Man Bites God 1962.23
Man Burglar, A, Don't Let Him Out 1898.03
Man by the Fountain, The 1956.09
Man Can Have No Choice, A 1961.24
Man Could Go Quite Mad, A 1985.18
Man Doesn't Know, A 1955.08, 1994.01
Man for Sale 1944.23
Man from Conjure Land, The 1908.08
Man from Mexico 1920.41
Man I Love is Here, The 1934.41
Man I Love, The 1910.25, 1911.12, 1974.09, 1974.11, 1990.09, 1991.04, 1999.10
Man I Married, The 1993.05
Man I Never Met, The 1956.07
Man I Used to Be, The 1955.27, 1993.16, 1996.04
Man in My Life, The 1959.27
Man in the Doorway 1971.20
Man in the Moon 1983.21
Man in the Moon has Gone to Rest, The 1878.20
Man in the Moon Might Tell, The 1899.33
Man in the Moon was Looking, The 1877.43
Man in the moon, The 1895.32
Man in the Moon, The 1899.19, 1904.17, 1923.03, 1966.10, 1985.19
Man is a Mistake 1926.20
Man is Faithful Till He's Caught 1913.02
Man is Only a Man, A 1907.10, 1917.37
Man is Such a Schemer from His Childhood 1894.05
Man is the Lord of it All 1921.23
Man Like You, A 1982.09
Man may escape from Rope and Gun 1750.01
Man May Escape from Rope and Gun 1957.02
Man May Know No Voice of Friend, A 1904.01
Man Meant Well, The 1904.54
Man Must Have Something to Live For, A 1964.18
Man Nobody Could Love, The 1988.20
Man o' My Dreams 1925.07
Man of High Degree, A 1930.02
Man of La Mancha 1965.34
Man of Many Names 1876.04
Man of Many Parts, A 1986.11
Man of Spirit, A 1973.02
Man of the Year This Week, The 1951.23
Man on the Box, The 1910.09
Man Overboard 1923.01
Man Say 1973.10
Man She'll Never Meet 1904.37
Man Should Have a Double When He's Single, A 1919.44
Man That Got Away, The 1976.32
Man That Knows it All, The 1884.41
Man that knows it all, The 1884.48
Man That Knows it All, The 1885.03
Man That Leads the Band Leads the Army, The 1905.23
Man That Stole My Luncheon, The 1895.02
Man to Man Talk 1959.26
Man Who Broke the Bank at Monte Carlo, The 1892.45, 1894.46
Man Who Built the Subway, The 1907.24
Man Who has Everything, The 1962.03
Man Who Hypnotized McCarthy, The 1902.21
Man Who Invented Ragtime, The 1899.11
Man Who Made His Life into a Work of Art, The 1980.17
Man Who Owns Broadway, The 1909.26, 1968.07
Man Who Put the Germ in Germany, The 1917.37
Man Who Will Not Love Back, The 1910.02
Man who would woo a fair maid, A 1888.35
Man Who Wrote 'the Vampire' Must Have Known My Wife, The 1914.15
Man Who's Got a Mortgage on the Mint, The 1907.61
Man With a Dream 1955.10
Man With an Elephant on His Hands, A 1891.11
Man With an Elephant on His Hands, The 1904.17
Man With Money, The 1910.15
Man With the Ginger Mustache, The 1976.15
Man With the Tamborine, The 1901.25
Man Worth Fightin' For, A 1981.07
Man You Love, The 1938.06
Man's a Man for a' That, A 1911.31
Man's a Man, A 1911.06
Man's All Right, The 1975.20
Man's Home, A 1952.20
Man, A 1981.25
Man, a Maid, A 1920.32
Man, Man, Fickle Man 1902.44
Man, Man, Man 1904.47, 1917.20, 1921.33
Man, We're Beat 1959.12
Man-O'-Wars Man, The 1892.06
Managed 1963.08
Manager Said, And the 1901.07
Manana 1907.08, 1920.13, 1955.19, 1983.20
Manchester, England 1968.11
Mancipation 1963.22
Manda 1924.27
Mandalay 1910.16, 1921.20
Mandalay Song, The 1977.08
Mandarin Palace on the Grand Concourse, The 1973.11
Mandarin, The 1900.43
Mandarinade 1947.05, 1948.12
Mandy 1901.25, 1907.44, 1918.21, 1919.15, 1922.22, 1922.25, 1942.20, 1946.14, 1947.12, 1976.34, 1991.10
Mandy Lou 1904.21
Mandy Make Up Your Mind 1924.37
Mangos 1957.01
Manhattan 1924.32, 1925.17, 1974.09, 1975.13, 1984.10, 1990.09, 1992.17
Manhattan Lullaby 1932.13
Manhattan Mad 1915.02
Manhattan Madness 1932.05
Manhattan Mary 1927.46
Manhattan Memory 1927.46
Manhattan Nights 1922.32
Manhattan Rhythm Blues 1982.15
Manhattan Showboat 1980.18
Manhattan Walk 1928.25, 1981.03
Manhunt 1998.02
Manicure Girl, The 1911.05
Manicure Maidens, The 1898.70
Manicuring 1925.07
Manisero, El 1931.31
Mannequin 1930.25
Manola 1902.11, 1926.35
Mansion 1971.18
Mansion of Roses, The 1920.23
Manson Trio 1999.01
Mantilla Espanola, La 1917.33
Mantlepiece Tragedy, The 1918.15
Manuel Your Friend 1971.09
Manuelo 1938.12, 1941.11

Many a New Day 1943.04
Many Moons Ago 1959.26
Many the Beasts 1972.23
Many Things that Ought Not to Be 1876.30
Many Ways to Skin a Cat 1964.04
Many Years Ago 1899.01
Many Years Ago I Strode 1902.25
Many years ago, when I was young and charming, A 1879.05
Many Young Men from Now 1968.23
Many, Many Ways to Say Good-By 1904.53
Manzanillo, The 1894.47
Maori 1908.08
Map of Your Heart, The 1999.22
Marabella 1947.19
Maracatu 1950.07
Marathon 1972.16
Marathon Dance, The 1945.20
Marathoners, The 1945.20
Marce du Biable 1880.24
Marceline's Meat Sauce 1907.59
Marcelle 1920.22
March Ahead 1977.08
March Gypsies 1929.04
March No. 1918.35
March of Foreign Commissioners 1910.21
March of the 'Frisco Chinks 1907.16
March of the Allies, The 1900.42
March of the Amazons 1866.18
March of the Bridegrooms 1913.10
March of the City Troops 1897.55
March of the Continentals, The 1917.13
March of the Dwarfs 1944.21
March of the Enchantress 1917.35
March of the Falsettos 1992.09
March of the Flags 1904.15
March of the Frisco Chinks 1904.42
March of the Gladiators 1920.10
March of the Gods, The 1910.10
March of the Guards 1950.10
March of the Heroes 1902.06
March of the King's Amazons 1909.26
March of the Militant Suffragettes 1912.40
March of the Musketeers 1928.12, 1984.14
March of the New York Dailies 1898.01
March of the Newspapers 1897.14
March of the Plumbers 1888.44
March of the Rangers 1927.08
March of the Rice and Old Shoes 1930.14
March of the Royal Amazons 1896.35
March of the Royal Siamese Children 1951.12
March of the States, The 1915.25
March of the Toreadors 1911.18
March of the Toys 1905.55, 1917.26, 1924.18, 1929.48
March of the Trollgers 1944.21
March of the Watch 1893.40
March of the Winkies 1997.11
March of the Wooden Soldiers 1979.33
March of the Yuppies 1985.15
March of Time, The 1930.22
March On 1905.56, 1925.02, 1925.06
March on for Tennessee 1952.15
March On! 1930.10
March to the Gallows 1989.24
March to Zion, The 1937.01
March With Me 1924.01, 1925.42, 1928.02
March, March, March 1978.22
Marche de menilmontant, La 1947.05
Marches des Pompiers 1916.07
Marching 1908.17
Marching Away 1897.40, 1917.10
Marching By 1932.06
Marching Down This Road 1944.32
Marching Song of the Pollicle Dogs, The 1982.19
Marching Through Georgia 1922.25, 1924.37
Marching Through Port Arthur 1904.13
Marchons d'un air conquerant 1883.51
Marchosito 1917.25
Marcia Di Ragazzi 1982.09
Marcus, My Friend 1984.02
Mardi Gras 1954.19
Mardi Gras Day in New Orleans 1935.04
Mardi Gras, The 1909.23
Margaret 1898.10
Margate Sands 1904.08
Margie 1920.33
Margineers, The 1930.09
Margot 1926.42, 1946.03
Marguerite 1887.02, 1893.43, 1894.17
Maria 1934.38, 1938.07, 1957.12, 1959.24, 1962.17, 1993.16, 1998.03, 1998.11, 2000.14
Marian 1926.03
Marian the Librarian 1957.18, 2000.11
Mariana 1922.36, 1926.35
Marianne 1928.29, 1972.07, 1979.02, 1986.14
Marice, La 1947.18
Marie 1909.17, 1997.01
Marie Antoinette 1899.30
Marie Cahill's Congo Love Song 1903.07
Marie from Paree 1907.35
Marie is Tricky 2000.08
Marie Laveau 1992.06
Marie Odile 1915.16
Marie vision, La 1961.25
Marie's Law 1959.25
Marie's Mink Coat 1959.15, 1961.25
Marie, Marie 1908.39, 1967.13, 1968.20
Marie-Vision, La 1959.15
Marieka 1972.16
Mariette 1924.46
Marilyn Monroe 1993.07
Marimba Spiritual 2001.04
Marina 1914.28
Marine's Humn, The 1946.13
Mariner in his barque, The 1848.04
Marineritos, Los 1969.11
Marinesca 1892.52
Marion Lee 1866.19
Marionette Song 1931.43
Marionette Song, The 1910.35
Marionettes 1916.08, 1925.39
Marionettes, The 1915.23
Mariposa, La 1997.13, 1999.18
Marital Infidelity 1961.16
Marital Malignity 1914.04
Marjolaine 1922.04
Marjorie Waltz 1924.21
Mark his approach with thunder 1860.01
Mark His Bright and Flashing Eye 1912.40
Mark of a Man, The 1976.11
Mark Twain 1953.17, 1955.03
Marked Millions 1928.19
Market Day 1925.08
Market Day in the Village 1936.22
Market on Saturday Night 1883.26
Market on Saturday Night, The 1882.79
Market Place, The 1872.23
Marketing, Marketing 1971.01
Marketplace 1997.16
Marlborough Goes to the Wars 1922.06
Marlborough s'en va-t-en guerre 1922.06
Marquis de Boulogne-sur-Mer 1895.44
Marquis is a Good Old Soul, The 1882.33
Marriage 1964.22
Marriage al la Mode 1965.31
Marriage C.O.D. 1922.38
Marriage Game 1905.37
Marriage is a Lottery 1904.09
Marriage is Not What it Used to Be 1913.14
Marriage is Sublime 1903.04
Marriage Knot, The 1919.27
Marriage Market, The 1913.26
Marriage of the Daffodil and the Daisy, The 1903.18
Marriage of the Lily and the Rose, The 1919.22
Marriage Proposal, A 1992.09
Marriage Type Love 1953.08
Marriageable Daughter, A 1880.10
Married 1966.24, 1998.04
Married Couple Seeks Married Couple 1977.04
Married Life 1917.05
Married Life Blues 1923.07
Married Man, A 1965.02
Married Men 1985.12
Married Men and Single Men 1929.03
Married on Michaelmas' Day 1870.44
Marry a Sunshine Girl 1912.45
Marry Me 1914.03, 1984.01
Marry Me a Little 1977.05, 1995.11, 1999.20
Marry Me and See 1916.08
Marry Me Now 1991.07
Marry Me, Terry 1997.17
Marry the Family 1935.03
Marry the Girl Myself 1967.02
Marry the Man Today 1950.17, 1980.29
Marry With Me 1971.16
Marrying for Love 1950.15
Marsch und Palotas 1920.46
Marseilles 1919.03
Marseilles, La 1930.39
Marsellaise, The 1871.16
Marta 1993.09
Martha 1896.45
Martha Spanks the Grand Pianner 1902.19
Martial Music of the Fife and Drum, The 1902.02
Martinete 1986.17
Martinetes 1992.15
Marvelous Dancing 1894.17
Marvelous Fire Machine 1959.22, 1985.04
Marvelous Weekend, A 1976.15
Marvels of Hypnotism, The 1895.17
Marvin at the Psychiatrist 1992.09
Marvin Goes Crazy 1992.09
Mary 1897.56, 1910.21, 1919.41, 1920.38, 1923.27, 1968.07
Mary and Doug 1920.18
Mary and John 1892.05
Mary Ann 1906.30, 1910.19, 1913.27
Mary Ann Malone 1889.05
Mary Ann O'San 1915.05
Mary Ann O'Shea 1917.18
Mary Ann, She's All My Own 1906.20
Mary Ann, Where are You? 1911.42
Mary Black 1901.17
Mary Brown 1917.03
Mary Canary 1904.13, 1904.41
Mary Carey 1908.21, 1911.42
Mary Ellen Brown 1897.26, 1897.54
Mary from Maryland 1903.41
Mary from Tipperary 1904.47
Mary Green 1892.38
Mary had a Lamb That Little Lamb was Me 1915.04
Mary had a Little Lamb 1895.06
Mary has a Little Fair 1927.07
Mary is a Grand Old Name 1906.02
Mary Jane 1899.18, 1902.02
Mary Jane Marie 1897.34
Mary Jane McKane 1923.45
Mary Kelly's Beau 1880.36
Mary Lou 1976.32
Mary Mack 1908.28, 1984.15
Mary Make Believe 1928.42
Mary Margaret's House in the Country 1973.03
Mary Mary 1903.31, 1929.48
Mary McGee 1907.32
Mary to the Market Went 1925.36
Mary was a Housemaid 1899.35
Mary Wise 1907.12
Mary! My Heather Belle 1908.10
Mary's a Grand Old Name 1968.07
Mary's Gone wid' a Coon 1881.47
Mary's Got a Beau 1904.17
Mary's Lamb 1906.26
Mary's Little Lamb 1908.30
Mary, be Wary 1902.24
Mary, Dear! I Miss You Most of All 1926.29
Mary, Get the Supper 1880.25
Mary, Mary 1946.14, 1971.20
Mary, Mary, Quite Contrary 1929.33
Mary, My Prairie Fairy 1906.04
Mary, Queen of Scots 1920.25
Maryland 1896.26
Mascot of the Troop, The 1905.57
Masculinity 1951.17, 1983.11
Masetto's Song 1975.23
Mash Em Up 1980.05
Mash Ethiopia 1980.05
Mash Notes 1926.04
Mashing Eyes 1889.33
Mask, The 1880.04

Masks and Hands 1931.26
Mason and Dixie Blues 1921.25
Mason Cares 1972.02
Mason, The 1978.12
Masque, The 1976.08
Masquerade 1931.26, 1988.01, 1992.12
Masquerade Ball, The 1889.47
Massa's Wedding Night 1887.48
Massa, here be Zanina 1881.04
Massachusetts Mermaid 1948.14
Massacre 1975.07
Masseuse, La 1899.19
Master and Slave 1952.15
Master of the Greatest Art of All, The 1964.35
Master of the House 1987.04
Master! Master! We are ready 1864.22
Matador Terrifico, El 1941.07
Match Makers, The 1914.28
Matchmaker, Matchmaker 1964.27
Matelot 1968.19
Mater Terra 1972.21
Mathilde 1972.16
Matilda 1950.03, 1955.03
Matilda and the Builder 1903.33
Matinee Girls 1900.41
Matinee Idol, The 1909.19
Matinee Maids 1904.54
Matinee, The 1961.16
Mating Time 1923.37
Matrimonial Agent, The 1900.40
Matrimonial Guards, The 1898.48
Matrimonial Handicap, The 1924.03
Matrimonial Mart, The 1913.06
Matrimonial Stomp, The 1956.12
Matrimony 1906.43, 1911.37
Matron of an Hour, The 1880.69
Matron's Good Night's Sleep, A 1919.24
Matruzza Mia 1985.16
Matter of Experience, A 1911.42
Matter of Opinion 1913.21
Matter of Time, A 1963.13
Matters Culinary 1937.11
Maud 1898.50, 1952.11
Maude Adams of the Screen, The 1914.16
Maudie 1901.07, 1904.23
Maui Girl 1912.03
Mauna Kea 1912.03
Maupassant Tells All 1980.17
Maureen 1908.43
Maurice Rag, The 1912.02
Mauricette 1922.12, 1932.19
Mauruf Ballet 1928.14
Mavis 1999.12
Mavourneen 1894.20, 1895.30
Mawrasette 1917.13
Max Jacobs 1978.02
Max the Millionaire 1959.12
Max's Visit 1987.12
Maxford House 1992.17
Maxie 1975.05
Maxim Girl, The 1912.34
Maxim's 1907.48, 1943.09, 1964.24
Maxixe 1944.32
Maxixe-Habanera 1972.24
Maxwell's Silver Hammer 1974.24
May All Our Children Have Rhythm 1943.14
May and September 1921.03
May Breezes 1871.12
May Day in Town 1787.01
May Day is Hey Day 1904.30
May Day Processional 1904.30
May I Have My Gloves 1935.18
May I Return to the Beginning 1982.03
May I Saw That I Love You 1929.44
May I Suggest Romance? 1938.15
May I? 1898.43
May Irwin's Bully Song 1895.27
May it please you, my lud 1875.35
May Moon 1927.01
May Morning in Town 1787.01
May the Best Man Win 1946.04, 1991.15
May the saints above 1881.25
May We Entertain You 1959.13
May you Live and Prosper! 1882.75
May Your Heart Stay Young 1965.32
Maybe 1921.27, 1926.36, 1927.60, 1928.09, 1977.06, 1990.14
Maybe (M-A-Y-B-E) 1918.32
Maybe Baby 1990.15
Maybe He's Kind of Crazy 1956.04
Maybe I Know 1985.03
Maybe I Should Change My Ways 1946.24
Maybe I Will 1927.29, 1927.49
Maybe it's a Bear 1908.28
Maybe it's Me 1926.50
Maybe it's Time for Me 1967.02
Maybe it's You 1927.37
Maybe Means Yes 1928.50
Maybe My Baby Loves Me 1989.26
Maybe So 1928.46
Maybe Some Other Time 1964.05
Maybe the Moon Will Help You Out 1903.31
Maybe They're Magic 1987.18
Maybe This is Love 1928.37
Maybe This Time 1998.04
Maybe Yes or No 1924.05
Maybe You Think I Did 1898.55
Maybe You'll Look Good to Me 1918.35
Maybe, Maybe Not 1993.05
Mayday Song 1989.10
Maydee 1903.29, 1905.32
Mayfair 1927.07
Mayfair Affair 1961.26
Mayflower, I Love You 1925.43
Mayn Alte Heym 1990.16
Mayn Mirl 1998.11
Mayor 1985.15
Mayor of Kankakee, The 1906.20
Mayor of Tokio, The 1903.19, 1905.53
Mayor's Chair, The 1970.10
Mayzie in Palm Beach 2000.18
Maze, The 1980.23
Mazeltov 1979.02
Mazie 1905.56
Mazourka 1930.36
Mazuma 1907.14, 1922.11
Mazurka 1899.34, 1945.14, 1969.11
Mazzari Mazurka 1866.18
McAllister's Four Hundred 1888.15
McCarthy 1886.35
McDonalds 1976.34
McDonnell's Ould Tin Roof 1880.25
McGinty at the Rink 1886.32
McInerney's Farm 1946.23
McIntyres, The 1882.02
McManus 1900.42
McNabb! Who Drives the Cab 1904.31
McNally's Row of Flats 1882.79, 1985.02
McSorley's Trip to Paris 'Cafe Chantants' With Spanish, Scotch and Irish Dances, 1900.38
Me 1918.25, 1926.26, 1994.04
Me an de Minstrel Ban 1904.26
Me and Bessie 1976.27
Me and Jesus 1982.17
Me and Lee 1952.15
Me and Love 1957.14
Me and Marie 1935.14
Me and Martha Ann 1876.05
Me and Mrs. Brown 1902.30
Me and My Arrow 1976.16
Me and My Baby 1975.14
Me and My Bundle 1949.08
Me and My Gal 1986.03
Me and My Girl 1986.12
Me and My Old Man 1884.61
Me and My Old World Charm 1943.07
Me and My Shadow 1967.11, 1975.22, 1976.24, 1986.06
Me and My Town 1964.15
Me and the Elements 1965.01
Me and the Mule 1991.01
Me and the Post 1903.22
Me and You 1918.32
Me for You 1929.42
Me for You Forever 1933.20
Me for You! 1975.13
Me to Me is Me 1908.08
Me Ventura, La 1985.16
Me Welly Poor Old Chinaman 1920.34
Me'ever Lanahar 1972.17
Me, Myself and I 1905.44
Me, the Moonlight and Me 1928.06
Meadow on the Squire's farm 1882.44
Meadow-lark 1945.14
Meadowlark 1992.16, 1995.12
Mean 1959.19, 1964.40
Mean as a Snake 1976.31
Mean Mr. Mustard 1974.24
Mean Ole Lion 1975.01
Mean to Me 1978.09
Mean Woman Blues 1989.12
Measure the Valleys 1973.10
Meat and Potatoes 1962.20
Meat and Vegetables 1927.11
Mechanical Ballet 1930.28
Mechanical Man 1930.21
Mechanical Soldiers 1915.27
Medals on My Chest 1921.12
Medea 2001.04
Medea Tango 1967.05
Media Luz, A 1993.08
Medicine Man, The 1899.33
Medicos 1924.06
Meditation 1975.03
Mediteranee 1971.14
Mediterranean 1985.20
Mediterranean Blue 1905.49
Mediterranean Nights 1924.36
Medley 1869.43
Medley of Song 1916.23
Meerahlah 1946.13
Meeskite 1966.24
Meet Me Again 1888.34
Meet Me at Eight in the Hall 1912.17
Meet Me at the Barber Shop 1907.55
Meet Me at the Fair 1937.10
Meet Me at the Garden Gate 1878.04, 1878.12
Meet Me at the Masquerade 1908.07
Meet Me at the Stage Door To-night 1912.25
Meet Me at the Station 1917.08
Meet Me at the Tabarin 1908.07
Meet Me at Twilight 1906.25
Meet Me Down at Huyler's 1898.43
Meet Me Down on the Corner 1909.09
Meet Me in Rose Time, Rosey 1907.37
Meet Me in Rose Time, Rosie 1908.22
Meet Me in St. Louis 1980.27, 1989.23, 1999.23
Meet Me on the Fence 1905.48
Meet Me Under the Wysteria 1905.23
Meet Me Where the Lanterns Grow 1909.20
Meet Me With Spangles and Bells On 1907.24
Meet Mesalia 1967.02
Meet Miss Blendo 1951.23
Meet My Seester 1970.08
Meet the People 1940.21
Meeting 1967.08
Meeting of Japan's Chosun Policy 1997.16
Meeting on Japan's Chosun Policy 1998.08
Meeting Royalty 1927.54
Meeting Tonight 1988.02
Meg 1981.14
Mehitabel's a House Cat 1957.05
Meilinki Meilchick 1962.18, 1978.18
Mein Blondes Baby 1999.07
Mein freundliches Wirtshaus umvankt ist's Weine 1885.01
Mein Herr 1998.04, 1999.01
Mein kleine Akrobat 1932.17
Mein Shtetele Belz 1962.17
Meine kleine Gruner Kaktus 1999.05
Mejores majeres del mundo, Las 1969.11
Melancholy Baby 1939.29
Melancholy Blues 1922.05
Melancholy Marshmallow, The 1903.07
Melancholy Mary 1894.49
Melancholy Moon Song 1995.16, 1998.17
Melancholy Sunbeam and the Rose, The 1904.15
Melancholy Tale of an Oyster 1885.45
Melancolico 1993.08

Melancolico Buenos Aires 1993.08
Melba Waltz 1918.18
Melenita de Oro 1985.07, 1999.18
Melican Papa 1921.36
Melinda 1965.31
Melindy 1898.55
Melisande 1963.26, 1992.10
Mellow Moon 1922.29
Mellow Sax 1992.06
Melodie purdue 1964.02
Melodies of May 1951.22
Melodies Within My Heart 1928.26
Melodrama 1914.20
Melodrama and Polly's Song 1989.24
Melodramatic Captain, The 1898.17
Melody 1933.03
Melody Dreams 1922.29
Melody in Four F 1941.08
Melody in Sepia 1942.13
Melody Land 1917.16
Melody Lane 1914.21
Melody Man 1912.29
Melody Medley 1927.45
Melody of Dance 1919.35
Melody of Love, The 1911.37
Melody of Parodies, The 1902.17
Melody of the Century, The 1915.23
Melody Triste 1921.31
Melody Will Keep You Young 1916.18
Melt Us 1962.04
Melting Pot, The 1915.27
Members Only 1999.09
Meme sans consulter mon coeur 1878.08
Memoirs 1909.07
Memories 1899.21, 1921.18, 1922.03, 1927.46, 1927.54, 1941.09, 1984.15
Memories of Madison Square Garden 1935.15
Memories of the Past 1920.34
Memories of You 1930.34, 1978.21, 1980.10, 1989.02
Memory 1902.39, 1969.05, 1975.02, 1982.19, 1991.10, 1992.12, 1999.12, 2000.14
Memory of a Happy Moment, A 1990.04
Memphisto is My Name 1870.26
Men 1903.22, 1923.13, 1928.49, 1942.29, 1946.06, 1958.20, 1974.02, 1976.09, 1991.15
Men About Town 1936.29, 1947.13, 1968.19, 1986.19
Men are a Pain in the Neck 1954.17
Men are Ambitious 1903.16
Men Awake 1937.14
Men Grow Older 1922.36
Men in My Life, The 1957.09
Men of China 1946.16
Men of Hades 1928.49
Men of Spain, The 1907.52
Men of the Water-Mark 1949.12
Men Who Have Loved Me, The 1975.23
Men Who Run the Country, The 1959.27
Men! Men! Men! 1911.23
Men, Men, You Foolish Men 1895.38
Menagerie Song 1901.25
Mendelssohn and Liszt 1916.23
Mender of Broken Dreams, The 1925.42
Mendocino Stroll, The 1913.26
Mene Mene Tekel 1937.14
Menlick's Tribute to Queen Tai Tu 1906.14
Menu Song 1982.04
Meow 1922.02
Meow! Meow! Meow! 1912.39
Mercenary Mary 1925.16
Mercenary Mary Ann 1904.25
Merchandisers' Song 1988.09
Merci 1987.12
Merci, Bon Dieu 1975.06
Merci, mes chers amis 1884.43
Mercurial 1956.09
Mercy, Lawd 1950.16
Merely a Matter of Form 1900.59
Merely a Matter of Habit 1900.42
Merely Marvelous 1959.01
Merely Passing Through 1918.20
Mermaid and the Buccaneer, The 1902.39
Mermaid and the Whale, The 1897.17
Mermaid Song 1990.04
Mermaid's Song, The 1870.44
Mermaids 1906.50
Merman's Cave, The 1890.33
Merriest Girl That's Out, The 1869.42
Merrily ring the luncheon bell! 1884.09
Merrily We Roll Along 1981.27, 1999.20
Merrily We Trip the Dainty Measure 1888.39
Merrily We Waltz Along 1934.42
Merrily, Cheerily 1902.18
Merry Bells 1881.16
Merry Cavalier, The 1903.36
Merry Christmas 1926.19, 1941.13, 1998.19
Merry Cricket, The 1891.36
Merry England 1890.23
Merry Go Round, The 1925.12
Merry Little Chop Chop 1913.22
Merry Little Minuet 1953.17
Merry Little Widows, The 1922.08
Merry Maiden and the Jerk, The 1945.09
Merry maiden and the tar, The 1879.05
Merry Maids of Spain 1895.25
Merry Masqueraders, The 1905.21
Merry May 1883.04, 1963.20
Merry Medieval Maid, The 1904.01
Merry Melody, A 1971.17
Merry Miller, The 1894.40, 1913.25
Merry Minstrel Band, The 1905.28, 1906.24
Merry Month of May, The 1911.28
Merry Old Land of Oz, The 1989.06, 1997.11
Merry Tunis 1863.06
Merry Wedding Bells 1891.42
Merry Widow Brown 1911.20
Merry Widow Waltz, The 1964.24, 1974.09
Merry Young Heart 1938.10
Merry, Merry Maidens of the Old Front Row, The 1912.43
Merry, Merry Maids of Spain 1895.25
Merry-Go-Round 1929.46
Mes amis, ju vous remercie 1877.32
Mesdames and Messieurs 1939.30
Mesmerize Magee 1899.12
Message from Mars 1906.10
Message from Roxane, A 1993.17
Message from the Front, A 2000.18
Message from the Land of Love, A 1905.19
Message in a Bottle 1982.22
Message of Spring, The 1904.52
Message of the Cameo, The 1919.18
Message of the Red, Red Rose 1908.30
Message of the Rose 1895.08
Message of the Violet, The 1903.10
Messages I 1981.14
Messages II 1981.14
Messenger 1919.04
Messenger Boy 1918.20
Messenger Boy March, The 1901.19
Messenger Boy, The 1901.19
Messenger Swallow 1876.07
Messin' Around 1929.18
Messin' Round 1929.06
Messing About in Boats 1985.20
Messy Bessy 1992.03
Metamorphosis 1956.13
Metre That Measures the Gas, The 1886.32
Metro 1992.05
Metropolitan Nights 1914.31
Metropolitan Squawk-tette, The 1912.24
Metternich 1929.17
Mexican Bad Men 1941.07
Mexican Blues 1929.01
Mexican Cancion 1988.15
Mexican Serenade 1894.08
Mexicana 1939.18
Mexicana Anna 1905.49
Mexicana, El 1892.23
Mexico 1904.47, 1906.35, 1907.45, 1912.02, 1926.13, 1927.13, 1927.42
Mexiconga, The 1939.25
Mezquita 1958.06
Mgeniso waMgodo waShambini 1966.03
Mi Barrio, De 1985.07
Mi Buenos Aires Querido 1993.08
Mi Chiquita 1927.54
Mi Lady's Dress 1919.03
Mi Noche Triste 1985.07, 1999.18
Mi! Mi! 1934.20
Mi-ya-sa-ma, mi-ya-sa-ma 1885.47
Mia Cara 1924.05
Mia Luna 1925.41
Miami 1925.01, 1925.28, 1956.02
Miami Beach 1989.07
Mice Will Play, The 1907.06
Michael Furey 2000.01
Michael Jordan's Ball 2000.15
Michael McGinnity 1907.56
Michelle 1977.10
Michells Galliard 1963.28
Michigan Water 1992.08
Michu! Michu! 1907.06
Mick Who Sent the Pick, The 1900.08
Mickey 1936.07
Mickey is Gone Away 1867.19
Mickey's Gone Away 1871.20
Microbes 1902.40
Micromaniac, The 1943.05
Mid Shady Groves 1897.55
Midarom Tipatach Hatova 1972.17
Midas Touch, The 1956.14
Middle Age Blues 1981.07
Middle Age Rock & Roll Star 1974.22
Middle Class 1972.16
Middle, The 1973.08
Midgely's Bogie Man, The 1900.03
Midinette, La 1905.04
Midnight - Hot Blood 1976.03
Midnight at the Onyx 1987.02
Midnight Bells 1925.52
Midnight Blue 1936.17
Midnight Cabaret 1919.02, 1925.18
Midnight Cabaret, The 1914.07
Midnight Color Ball, The 1924.36
Midnight Daddy 1927.10
Midnight Deadline Blastoff 1975.04
Midnight Fire Alarm, The 1894.52
Midnight Flirtation 1934.43
Midnight Frolic Glide, The 1915.16
Midnight Frolic Rag, The 1916.10
Midnight Girl at the Midnight Cabaret, The 1914.16
Midnight Girl, The 1914.07
Midnight Kisses 1898.22
Midnight Masquerade 1913.18
Midnight Mass 1976.03
Midnight Matinee 1939.07
Midnight Riding 1980.23
Midnight Serenade, The 1899.35
Midnight Squad, The 1888.27, 1888.34
Midnight Train to Georgia 1997.21, 1998.14
Midnight Waltz 1945.12
Midsummer Maiden 1920.24
Midsummer Night's Dream, A 1924.33
Midsummer Waltz 1915.23
Midsummer's Eve 1944.21
Midtown 1934.18
Midway Flirtation, A 1902.11
Midway Paloma 1894.10
Midway Plaisance 1892.45
Midway Reminders 1902.11
Mighty Dollar, The 1906.40
Mighty Like a Rosenbloom 1921.25
Mighty maiden with a mission 1884.09
Mighty Whitey 1969.15
Mignonette 1906.33, 1915.30, 1945.16
Mikado in Harlem 1933.27
Mikado, The 1919.04, 1938.10, 1939.15, 1939.17
Mike 1941.01
Mike Doolin's Jaunting Car 1905.30
Mike McCarthy's Wake 1902.34
Milady 1989.09
Milady's Boudoir 1919.21
Milady's Toilette Set 1916.25
Milaiya 1923.34
Mild Flirtation, A 1902.42
Mile's End Road 1929.28
Militaire Claribelle and Her Army, La 1899.04
Military Band, The 1903.07
Military Charleston 1926.15

Military Charlie 1902.08
Military Chorus 1890.26
Military Dancing Drill 1930.02
Military Girl, The 1901.25
Military Glide 1919.03
Military Glide, The 1910.19
Military Life 1946.10
Military Maid, The 1906.40
Military Maids 1904.34
Military Man, The 1904.04, 1907.13
Military Mary Ann 1909.24
Military Men I Love 1925.02
Military Model, The 1899.11
Military Mollie 1898.66
Military Mutiny of 1882 1997.16
Military Review 1908.34
Military Stamp 1916.26
Military Wedding of the Nations 1920.02
Military Willie 1906.20
Military, The 2000.18
Milk and Honey 1961.20, 1985.19
Milk Maids Marriage, The 1875.34
Milk Maids, The 1929.43
Milk, Milk, Milk 1941.08
Milkmaid 1971.18
Milkmaid's Song 1891.29, 1935.02
Milkmaid's Song, The 1944.25
Milkmaids of Broadway 1930.21
Milkman's Song 1869.15
Milky Way, The 1926.11
Mill there, The 1859.18
Millefleurs 1948.27
Miller's Cats, The 1902.18
Miller's Son, The 1973.04, 1977.05
Millie 1901.08
Millinery Mannequin, The 1920.39
Million Dollar Ball, The 1912.25
Million Dollar Secret 1999.06
Million Dollar Smile 1945.20
Million Dollars, A 1937.06
Million Eyes, A 1927.19
Million Good Reasons, A 1930.14
Million, A 1906.44
Million, The 1912.38
Millionaire's Daughters 1907.04
Millionaire, The 1920.09
Millions 1987.17
Millions of Tunes 1920.22
Milo You're Just My Style-O 1905.55
Milonga de Mis Amores 1993.08
Milonga del 900 1993.08
Milonga del Tiempo Heroico 1985.07
Milongueando En El '40 1997.13
Milongueando en El 40 1985.07, 1999.18
Milonguero Viejo 1999.18
Milonguita 1985.07, 1999.18
Milord 1981.04
Milord Sir Smith 1897.32
Milord's Waltz, The 1969.11
Milwork 1978.12
Mimetic Doll, The 1906.22
Mimette, My Human Mermaid 1905.36
Mimi 1920.37, 1927.40, 1947.05, 1948.12, 1963.02, 1965.08, 1975.13
Mimi Jazz 1920.37
Mimi La Blonde 1965.08
Mimosa 1926.09, 1926.35
Mina 1907.55
Mind Reader, The 1910.01
Mind Your Own Business 1921.06, 1999.09
Mind Your P's and Q's 1883.66
Minding the Baby 1897.42
Mine 1933.25, 1952.07, 1978.02
Mine Forever Mine 1910.36
Mine Next Monday 1951.14
Mine Song 1983.14
Mine Til Monday 1951.14
Mine was a Marriage of Convenience 1918.19
Mine, All Mine 1900.47, 1907.31
Mine, Oh my love at last 1895.43
Mineola 1964.35
Miner Boy 1931.02
Minerva! Minerva! Oh hear me 1884.09
Minino Song 1917.33
Minnesota 1910.02
Minnesota Strip 1978.11
Minnie 1931.39
Minnie Gavotte 1885.06
Minnie Haha 1926.18
Minnie the Moocher 1963.10
Minnie's Boys 1970.07
Minnie-Ha-Ha 1913.19
Minsky 1937.06
Minsky's Metropolitan Grand Opera 1932.13
Minstrel Band, The 1911.34
Minstrel Boy, The 1896.11
Minstrel Days 1916.03, 1922.16, 1925.45, 1927.13
Minstrel Man 1933.27
Minstrel Man, The 1891.14, 1912.25
Minstrel of Cassel 1864.22
Minstrel Parade 1948.25
Minstrel Parade, The 1912.07, 1914.31
Minstrel Serenade 1919.24
Minstrel Show 1961.17
Minstrel Show, The 1907.41
Minstrel Song 1978.06
Minstrel Take Off, A 1903.09
Minstrel Tune 1912.29
Minstrel, the Jester and I, The 1959.26
Minstrels on Parade 1909.05, 1922.25
Minuet 1908.08, 1928.23
Minuet Blue, Le 1922.02
Minuet of the Minute, The 1924.28
Minuet Velasquez 1924.48
Minuette, The 1923.41
Minute, A la 1920.31
Mio Caro, Il 1876.11
Mio Padre 1929.13
Mir Lebn Eibik 1989.10
Mir Velen Nisht Fasten 1968.22
Mira 1961.10
Miracle cure 1972.08
Miracle Cure 1993.06
Miracle of Judaism 1992.09
Miracle of Miracles 1964.27
Miracle Song 1964.15
Miracles and Mysteries 1999.22
Miraculous Cure, The 1911.47
Miranda 1885.15, 1905.20, 1914.02, 1962.14
Miranda, When We are Made One 1881.29, 1895.05
Mirimba 1920.13
Mirror 1976.20
Mirror Mine 1923.17
Mirror Mirror on the Wall 1971.13
Mirror Never Lies, The 1927.13
Mirror Song 1905.04
Mirror's the Cause of it All, The 1881.09
Mirror, Mirror 1985.17
Mirror, The 1988.01
Mirrors of the Ages 1927.02
Mirua's Audience With the King 1997.16
Mis Amores 1926.35
Mis'ry's Comin' Aroun' 1994.08
Misalliance 1959.20
Miser still is shilling sees, The 1854.06
Miser thus a Shilling sees, The 1750.01
Miserable 1953.10
Miserable With You 1931.16, 1972.05
Misere 1898.32
Misery 1927.67
Misfit Family, The 1906.22
Misfit Soldier, A 1909.15
Misplaced Confidence 1897.19
Miss All You Don't Catch 1957.01
Miss Amorinta Jackson's Promenade 1898.22
Miss Annabelle Lee 1975.22
Miss Blush 1913.04
Miss Boodle and Her Poodle 1910.12
Miss Brady's Piano 1882.02
Miss Brady's Piano Fortay 1880.37, 1882.39
Miss Bubbles 1983.17
Miss Clementina and Her Beau 1901.18
Miss Daisy Gown 1906.22
Miss Dennett 1910.16
Miss Dinah 1902.43
Miss Dooley and Mr. Brown 1921.27
Miss Dorothea Dix 1963.22
Miss Follies 1957.01
Miss Ginger from Jamaica 1907.34
Miss Ginger of Jamaica 1907.24
Miss Hannah from Savannah 1900.46
Miss Harvard of Yale 1899.18
Miss Helen Hunt 1897.34
Miss Hook 1907.63
Miss Hook of Holland 1908.21
Miss Innovation 1915.27
Miss Langley's School for Girls 1943.21
Miss Liberty 1917.16, 1949.08
Miss Logan 1952.09
Miss Lorelei Lee 1974.02
Miss Maloney 1904.41, 1905.31
Miss Margie 1904.06
Miss Marmelstein 1962.05
Miss Mary 1905.38
Miss Mimsey 1936.12
Miss Modesty 1897.40
Miss Nobody from No-Where 1907.06
Miss Pinchin's Boarding School 1902.29
Miss Platt Selects Mate 1949.12
Miss Popularity 1904.41
Miss Susanna from Urbana 1903.14
Miss Turnstiles 1944.33
Miss Turnstiles Ballet 1971.15
Miss Unruly 1919.30
Miss Walker of Kalamazoo 1903.38
Miss Whoozis and Mr. Whatchaname 1923.22
Miss Yankee Doodle 1908.03
Miss You Kiss, A 1955.10
Miss, La 1965.08
Missed America 1968.13
Missing You My Bill 1999.08
Mission Bells 1908.05
Mission Control 1975.04
Mission, The 1998.02
Missionary Maids, The 1912.31
Missionary Man, The 1902.38
Missisppi Dip 1911.08
Mississippi 1929.18, 1944.30, 1999.09
Mississippi Cradle 1922.18
Mississippi Dry 1929.27, 1930.13
Mississippi Joys 1932.12
Mississippi Moan 1929.18
Mississippi, You're a Grand Old Girl 1914.21
Mistah Johnson, Turn Me Loose 1896.52
Mistakes are Apt to Happen 1891.32, 1904.49
Mister Bizzy Rosenstein 1909.18
Mister Cellophane 1975.14
Mister Destiny 1981.14
Mister Dooley 1902.19
Mister Dooley's Geese 1885.02, 1889.18
Mister Drummer Man 1918.11
Mister Love 1916.04
Mister Pat O'Hare 1910.32
Mister Right 1988.18
Mister Soldier Man 1913.22
Mister Washington! Uncle George! 1950.04
Mister You and Missus Me 1927.54
Mistress Muse 1899.41
Misty 1995.14
Mit a Little English 1894.32
Mittel Europa 1942.26
Mitzi's Lullaby 1918.25
Miura's Audience With the King 1998.08
Mix and Mingle 1952.10
Mix-Up Rag, The 1915.26
Mlle. Gelee 1899.12
Mlle. Kek-Kek 1905.40
Mlle. Zizi 1900.41
Mo Tichi-Titi 1903.36
Mo'lasses 1923.06
Moan You Mourners 1975.20
Moanalua 1912.03
Moanin' in the Mornin' 1937.15
Moanin' Low 1929.19, 1954.11
Mob Song, The 1994.04
Mobility on the Midway 1902.11
Mocking Bird 1930.08, 1931.08, 1963.22
Mocking Bird, The 1927.42
Mockowitz, Gogelich, Babblekroit & Svonk 1927.27

Model hasn't Changed, The 1950.12
Model Lodging House Keeper, The 1883.04
Model Married Pair 1912.01
Model of Decorum and Tranquility, A 1988.09
Model of Fashion am I, A 1910.15
Model Toddle, The 1924.36
Model's Complaint, The 1906.10
Model, The 1914.14
Modern Bandit, The 1911.47
Modern Beau Brummel, The 1891.32
Modern Bride 1923.10
Modern Century Girls, The 1897.04
Modern Diplomat, A 1921.38
Modern Drama 1892.29
Modern Florodora Girl 1938.09
Modern Gladiator, The 1900.59
Modern Love 1912.24
Modern Madrigal 1934.06
Modern Maiden's Prayer, The 1917.13
Modern Melody 1916.12
Modern Pirate, The 1903.10
Modern Song, The 1914.24
Modern Spanish 1917.33
Modern Village Blacksmith, The 1921.11
Modernistic 1931.31
Modernistic Moe 1936.02, 1936.17
Modes in Manhattan 1942.01
Modes of the Court so common are grown, The 1750.01
Modest Little Maiden, A 1906.36
Modest Little Model, The 1908.17
Modest Little Thing, A 1926.11
Modest Manicure, The 1907.39
Modest Mazie 1910.29
Modest Meditations on the Here, the Heretofore, and the Hereafter 1973.08
Modest Model Maidens We 1900.47
Moi tout la vie 1929.11
Moi, j'crache dans l'eau 1934.32, 1935.19
Moi, si jetais epoux 1884.43
Mokhibo 1977.01
Molasses to Rum 1969.06
Molecules 1971.01
Moleem Saboo 1885.06
Moleston, El 1993.08
Molinillo Tango, The 1917.33
Moll and Dick 1937.08
Moll and Druggist 1937.08
Moll and Gent 1937.08
Moll's Song 1937.08
Mollie 1896.18
Mollie O 1904.41
Mollie O'Donahue 1929.31
Molly 1885.02, 1898.20, 1920.10, 1924.22, 1969.08
Molly Darling 1922.29
Molly Dear, it's You I'm After 1914.18
Molly Green 1903.08
Molly Malone 1919.30, 1927.47
Molly May 1910.11
Molly O 1906.06
Molly O'Halloran 1905.27
Molly O'Malley 1921.06
Molly O'Reilly 1948.30
Molly on a Trolley 1921.20
Molly the Marchioness 1902.30
Molly, Molly 1921.20
Moment Ago, A 1965.01
Moment de te marier, Au 1887.35
Moment I Looked in Your Eyes, The 1950.09
Moment I Saw You, The 1930.32, 1947.15
Moment is Now 1971.19
Moment Musicale 1921.31
Moment of Peace, A 1918.37
Moment of Truth 1962.02
Moment of Your Love, A 1953.11
Moments in the Woods 1987.18
Moments Musicales 1944.30
Moments of Happiness, The 1982.19
Moments of the Dance, The 1918.25
Momes de la Cloche, Les 1981.04
Momes de la Cloche?, Les 1947.18
Momma, Look Sharp 1969.06
Momma, Momma 1962.05
Mon ami le vent 1935.19
Mon ami mon Judas 1983.03
Mon Ami, My Friend 1936.28
Mon arbre 1966.20
Mon bateau blanc 1964.02
Mon Bijou 1911.27
Mon Bon! 1929.16
Mon bonhomme 1964.39
Mon coeur vous etes le maitre, De 1883.51
Mon Desir 1916.04
Mon Dieu 1981.04
Mon Dieu, mesdames, j'etais prete 1886.09
Mon emouvant amour 1983.03
Mon General 1897.17
Mon Homme 1922.03
Mon homme 1947.18
Mon Homme 1958.06
Mon Legionnaire 1947.18
Mon manege a moi 1961.25
Mon Menage a Moi 1959.15
Mon menage a moi 1964.22
Mon nom est Joquelet 1887.35
Mon pauvre amour 1929.13
Mon petit mari, Cheri, Tous les jours a toi je pense! 1883.51
Mon Petit Tom 1932.04
Mon truc en plumes 1964.39
Mona 1982.04, 2001.01
Mona from Arizona 1954.02
Monastery Bells 1886.32
Monday and Tuesday 1898.78
Money 1901.08, 1907.18, 1942.18, 1998.04
Money Burner, The 1902.43
Money Burns a Hole in My Pocket 1953.01
Money Doesn't Mean a Thing 1924.30
Money isn't Everything 1947.17, 1964.04
Money Isn't What Really Matters 1998.19
Money Kept Rolling in and Out, And the 1979.23
Money Kept Rolling In, And the 1992.12
Money Rings Out Like Freedom, The 1969.17
Money Song, The 1966.24
Money Talks 1912.15
Money to Burn 1897.21, 1965.14
Money Tree, The 1977.16
Money! 1930.40
Money, Beautiful Money 1892.29
Money, Money, Money 1919.12, 1920.38, 1968.02, 1969.15
Mongst the Magnolias 1904.21
Monica 1977.04
Monica, Monica 1947.10
Monk and the Magpie, The 1902.04
Monk and the Maid, The 1897.13
Monkey Around 2000.18
Monkey Doodle 1913.16
Monkey Doodle Doo 1925.45
Monkey in the Mango Tree 1957.16
Monkey Monk, The 1886.28
Monkey See, Monkey Do 1946.05
Monkeys, The 1904.40
Monks of Malabar, The 1900.39
Monks' Quartette, The 1913.24
Monolithic Madness 1988.07
Monotonous 1952.09
Monsieur Beaucaire 1924.33
Monsieur je suis a Boniface 1884.43
Monsieur le Marquis, mon pere 1884.50
Monsieur St. Pierre 1947.18
Monsieur, comment etes-vous chez ma femme 1877.32
Monsieur, monsieur, je vous en prie! 1877.32
Monsoon 1964.05
Montage 1979.23
Montage I 1997.07
Monte Carlo 1894.37
Monte Carlo Boys 1892.45
Monte Carlo Glide, The 1913.30
Monte Carlo Moon 1911.12
Monte Cristo 1919.03
Monte Pincio 1944.21
Monte, the Model 1926.11
Montenegrin Patrol 1903.38
Monterey 1924.47
Monteria, La 1926.09, 1926.35
Montezuma 1906.47, 1912.02
Montezuma's Daughter 1927.08
Month Ago, A 1999.22
Month of Sundays, A 1949.17
Montmart 1953.07
Montmartre 1922.03, 1924.18, 1929.04
Moo Cow 1917.02
Mooche, The 1930.13, 1981.06
Mooching Along 1924.29
Mood Indigo 1978.01, 1981.06, 1997.03
Mood of the Moment 1941.07
Mood You are In, The 1910.09
Moody Blue 1978.01
Moolbarri 1907.15
Moon 1918.03
Moon About Town 1934.01
Moon am Shinin' 1924.46
Moon and I, The 1938.10, 1939.15, 1939.17
Moon and the Owl, The 1901.27
Moon and You and I, The 1927.40
Moon Beams 1907.62
Moon Dances 1978.26
Moon Dear 1905.52
Moon Fell in the River, The 1940.16
Moon Flower 1925.08
Moon has His Eyes on You, The 1905.42
Moon has raised his lamp above, The 1868.01
Moon in My Window 1965.06
Moon is Above, The 1933.24
Moon Like a Silver Window 1987.12
Moon Love 1975.24
Moon Moon 1902.01
Moon of Love 1920.39
Moon of Manakoora, The 1975.12, 1980.29
Moon of My Delight 1928.30
Moon Outside My Window 1963.27
Moon River 1962.17, 1974.22, 1997.05
Moon Shines on the Moonshine, The 1920.33
Moon Song 1939.15
Moon Song, The 1944.18
Moon That was Good Enough for Dad and Mother, The 1922.48
Moon's Shining Cool, The 1930.36
Moon, Dear 1905.54
Moon, Lovely Moon 1912.15
Moon, Moon 1914.33
Moon, Moon, Moon 1905.56, 1910.01
Moon, The 1900.43
Moon, the Wind and the Sea, The 1931.05
Moon-Faced, Starry-Eyed 1947.02
Moon-Man 1924.41
Moon-Music 1943.10
Moonbeams 1906.33, 1918.07, 1919.29, 1927.27, 1945.16
Moondance 2000.07
Mooney Time 1906.34, 1907.45
Moonfall 1985.18
Moonglade 1969.07
Moonglow 1939.29
Mooning 1972.12, 1994.07
Moonland 1939.29
Moonlight 1885.03, 1886.62, 1899.33, 1905.52, 1906.06, 1911.42, 1921.11, 1925.12
Moonlight and Killarney 1882.69
Moonlight and Love 1925.06
Moonlight and Violins 1936.27
Moonlight at Killarney 1889.03
Moonlight Becomes You 1995.14
Moonlight Buggy Ride, A 1905.22
Moonlight Gavotte 1916.05
Moonlight Kiss, The 1887.43
Moonlight Kisses 1923.31
Moonlight Lane 1923.19
Moonlight Madness 1928.22
Moonlight Madonna 1943.02
Moonlight on Notre Dame 1952.04
Moonlight on the Waters 1923.10
Moonlight Passing Through a Window 1988.10
Moonlight Serenade 1891.18, 1897.56, 1898.50, 1974.22, 1987.02
Moonlight Shadows 1882.82
Moonlight Soliloquy 1945.14
Moonlight Song, A 1897.40

Moonlight Waltz 1923.13
Moonlight, You and I 1906.23
Moonshine 1906.43, 1927.08
Moonshine is in the Mountain Still 1919.18
Moonshine Lullaby 1946.12, 1966.12, 1995.12, 1999.04
Moonsong 1993.17
Moonstruck 1910.21, 1975.22
Moorish Bolero 1943.17, 1944.31
Mootching Along at the Cotton Ball 1914.03
Moral Rearmament 1962.02
Morality's a Matter of Geography 1902.43
Morals of a Sailor, The 1920.31
Mordecai Lyons 1882.74
More 1923.18, 1960.12, 1999.20, 2000.08
More and More 1932.10, 1952.13, 1979.02
More Better Go Easy 1972.11
More Dear to Me 1891.11
More Fish 1955.11
More humane Mikado, A 1885.47
More I Cannot Wish You 1950.17, 1980.29
More I See of Men, The 1917.04
More I See of Others, Dear, the Better I Love You, The 1914.27
More I See People, The 1979.18
More I See You, The 1988.08
More Incredible Happenings 1929.51
More Like Their Dad Every Day 1877.43
More Love Than Your Love 1954.02
More new sensation 1884.14
More of the Same 1978.27
More or less 1879.38
More Precious Far 1970.07
More Songs for Our Time 1966.32
More Than a Woman 1999.15
More Than Ever 1999.17
More Than I Like You 1979.11
More Than Just a Friend 1996.04
More Than One Way 1965.33
More Than These 1944.32
More Than We Bargained For 1997.17
More Than You Know 1929.37, 1974.01
More We Dance, The 1926.37
Morelos, Hail 1894.47
Morena, La 1939.18
Moresca 1985.14
Morgenchoral des Peachum, Der 1965.04
Moriah 1910.02
Moritat 1989.24
Moritat von Mackie Messer, Die 1965.04
Moriva 1977.01
Mormon Life, A 1924.34
Mornin's Come 1963.19
Morning 1920.26, 1934.29, 1979.10
Morning Anthem 1966.19
Morning Breakfast 1895.38
Morning Galop, The 1892.08
Morning Glories 1920.31, 1927.13
Morning Glory 1922.45
Morning Glow 1972.22
Morning Hymn 1998.03
Morning in Macedonia 2000.05
Morning in Madrid 1946.06
Morning in Neverland 1979.22
Morning is Breaking 1866.35
Morning is Dawning 1907.29
Morning Mist Spread O'er the Mead, The 1881.11
Morning Music of Montmartre, The 1958.02
Morning of the Dragon, The 1991.03
Morning Prayer 1958.04
Morning Report, The 1997.20
Morning Sky 1906.35
Morning Sun Comes Peeping, The 1879.38
Morning Will Come 1921.34, 1923.12
Mornings at Seven 1940.06
Morocco Dance of Marriage 1946.03
Morocco Drill 1926.37
Morocha, La 1985.07
Morphine Tango 1993.09
Morra, La 1964.03
Mortifying the American Man 1926.22
Mos Scoscious 1992.06
Moscow Belles 1924.09
Moscow Nights 1977.13
Mose Art 1975.02
Moses Andrew Jackson, Goodbye 1906.43
Moses Supposes 1985.08
Moses' Song 1972.09
Mosquito 1938.08
Mosquito and the Midge, The 1904.10
Mosquito Ballet 1922.33
Mosquito Song 1908.19
Mosquito Song, The 1900.58
Mosquitos Frolic, The 1917.26
Most Beautiful Girl in the World, The 1935.15, 1990.09
Most Beautiful Girls in the World, The 1932.18
Most Expensive Statue in the World, The 1949.08
Most Gentlemen Don't Like Love 1938.13
Most Happy Fella, The 1956.04
Most Majestic of Domestic Officials, The 1928.30
Most Omniscient Maid 1913.06
Most potent, grave and reverend Dervish 1881.04
Most Romantic Meeting 1884.42, 1886.47, 1888.36
Most Unlucky Man, A 1902.16
Most Unpopular Potentate, A 1903.04
Motele 1960.18, 1990.16
Moth and the Flame 1915.25, 1921.25
Moth and the Moon, The 1905.29
Moth for My Flames, The 1924.35
Moth Song, The 1957.05
Mother 1916.26, 1927.42, 1942.11, 1983.18
Mother Angel Darling 1973.05
Mother Dear 1891.36, 1919.08
Mother Did 1907.26
Mother Dixie, the Flag and You 1921.18
Mother Doesn't Know 1912.38
Mother Dooley's Geese 1885.08
Mother Earth 1972.21
Mother Eve 1921.22, 1934.18
Mother Give your boy a Buss 1852.01
Mother Goose 1899.22, 1913.24
Mother Grows Younger 1929.42
Mother has Gone Away 1866.06
Mother isn't Getting Any Younger 1937.12, 1946.19
Mother Land 1869.02
Mother Machree 1911.04, 1913.03, 1918.41, 1921.02
Mother Me and the Flag 1923.23
Mother Says I Mustn't 1873.28
Mother Told Me So 1932.17
Mother Will be Pleased 1914.18
Mother's Day 1941.13, 1955.11
Mother's Getting Nervous 1948.25
Mother's Heart, A 1964.18, 1999.17
Mother's Melody, A 1960.18
Mother's Plaid Shawl 1886.10
Mother's Tears, A 1968.22
Mother's the Boss of Our House 1907.24
Mother, give your boy a buss 1871.10
Mother, Mother 1947.10
Mother, Pin a Rose on Me 1906.04
Mother, The 1990.16
Mother, what means those looks so wild? 1868.01
Mother-in-Law 1989.07, 1992.06
Motherhood 1945.14, 1964.01
Motherless Chile 1953.12
Mothers o'Men 1929.04
Mothers of the World, The 1925.23
Mothers' Complaint 1928.42
Mothers' Wedding Dress 1922.48
Motif Lilt 1912.36
Motl Der Opreyter 1998.11
Motor Girl, The 1909.14
Motor Perpetuo 1966.32
Motoring Along the Old Post Road 1918.16
Mots nouveaux, Des 1934.32, 1935.19
Moulin Rouge, Gaity's Treadmill 1898.38
Moulin Rouge, The 1896.05
Mount within this Palanquin 1875.19
Mountain Dew, The 1882.50
Mountain Girl 1972.01
Mountain Greenery 1926.13, 1975.13
Mountain Guide, The 1879.63, 1880.39
Mountain High, Valley Low 1946.05
Mountain maid who Wooeth, The 1862.04
Mountain Maids 1907.10
Mountain Melodies 1886.49
Mountain Moon 1923.37
Mountain Song 1866.19, 1866.22
Mountain Stood Like a Grim Outpost, A 1903.21
Mountaineer's Song 1944.21
Mountains are High, The 1977.01
Mountains Sing Back, And the 1966.09
Mountains, The 1972.18
Mountebank's Song, The 1900.50
Mountebanks, Come Waken from Your Dreaming 1898.48
Mounted Messenger, The 1966.19
Mounties, The 1924.28
Mourir d'aimer 1983.03
Mourners' Chorus 1904.37
Mouse Meets Girl 1944.18
Mouse! Mouse! 1925.42
Mouthful of Kisses, A 1920.23
Mouthfull of Kisses 1919.16
Move On 1894.17, 1984.08
Move on Up a Little Higher 1990.05
Move Over 1914.31
Move Over, New York 1964.40
Move You're Steppin' on My Heart 1981.29
Movement 1919.37
Mover's Life, A 1977.04
Movie Ball, The 1926.28
Movie House in Manhattan 1948.04
Movie in My Mind, The 1991.03
Movie Lesson, The 1922.01
Movie Star Mansions 1978.25
Movies Were Movies 1974.18, 1985.19, 1998.07
Movietone of the Gypsy Song, The 1928.47
Movin' 1951.24
Movin' Out 1981.07
Movin' Uptown Blues, The 2000.08
Moving Day 1931.47
Moving Day in Jungle Town 1909.13
Moving Man, The 1913.05
Moving Picture Baby 1924.44
Moving Picture Glide, The 1914.16
Moving Up in the World 1985.20
Moving Uptown 1976.04, 2000.08
Mozambamba 1941.07
Mozambique 1930.34
Mozart Lincoln 1903.18
Mr. and Mrs. 1922.07, 1925.17, 1926.12
Mr. and Mrs. Jones 1997.21
Mr. and Mrs. Rorer 1924.08
Mr. and Mrs. Sipkin 1925.14
Mr. and Mrs. Smith 1935.14
Mr. and Mrs. Wrong 1944.18
Mr. Andrews' Vision 1997.06
Mr. Banjo Man 1979.24
Mr. Bizzi Izzi Rosenstein 1909.18
Mr. Bojangles 1974.11, 1978.05, 1999.01
Mr. Breezy 1903.23
Mr. Breezy was an Easy Mark 1903.23
Mr. Broadway, U.S.A. 1913.16
Mr. Brown, Miss Dupree 1949.12
Mr. Bugaboo 1904.50
Mr. Burns of New Rochelle 1907.57
Mr. Capra Goes to Town 1940.21
Mr. Clown 1968.24
Mr. Cupid 1906.27, 1927.42
Mr. DeMille 1927.10
Mr. Dolan is Passing Through 1931.04
Mr. Dooley 1903.09
Mr. Earth and His Comet Love 1910.18
Mr. Fezziwig's Annual Christmas Ball 1994.12
Mr. Flynn 1961.14
Mr. Fresh 1898.70
Mr. Goldstone 1974.17
Mr. Goldstone, I Love You 1959.13
Mr. Graffiti 1978.11
Mr. Greed 1997.08
Mr. Grogan, Wake Up 1984.02
Mr. Harris, it's All Over Now! 1980.17
Mr. Henry Jones 1963.12
Mr. Jessel 1930.38
Mr. Jigger 1909.05
Mr. Johnsing's Chowder 1898.43
Mr. Johnson, Good Night 1910.22

Mr. Johnston, You are Knocking Your Own Game 1898.61
Mr. Livingstone 1956.16
Mr. Love Will Get You 1919.11
Mr. Lucky 1974.22
Mr. Mammy Man 1930.19
Mr. Mardi Gras 1992.06
Mr. Mistoffelees 1992.12
Mr. Mistoffolees 1982.19
Mr. Monotony 1989.03
Mr. Moon 1932.01
Mr. New York, Esq. 1897.19
Mr. Nobody Knows a Thing or Two 1900.54
Mr. Othello 1909.09
Mr. Pagliacci 1912.24
Mr. Patrick Henry Must Have Been a Married Man 1916.21
Mr. Peachum's Morning Hymn 1965.04
Mr. Perfect 1998.19
Mr. Rag and I 1917.23
Mr. Right 1948.25, 1954.17, 1997.18
Mr. Scarecrow 1910.29
Mr. Schnoodle 1912.31
Mr. Soldier 1909.01
Mr. Strauss Goes to Boston 1945.12
Mr. Tanner 1975.05
Mr. Tannhauser 1910.29
Mr. Tosti, Good-Bye 1915.02
Mr. Van Dyke from Klondyke 1898.10
Mr. Wagner's Wedding March 1923.21
Mr. Wonderful 1956.02
Mr. Yankee Doodle 1912.43
Mr. Ziegfeld's Idea of Chorus Men 1921.21
Mrs. A 1984.01
Mrs. Brown 1980.05
Mrs. Casey 1910.09
Mrs. Cowslip's Lament 1883.04
Mrs. Dooley on Parade 1902.32
Mrs. Feitelbaum Sees the Dybbuk 1926.17
Mrs. Gowan's Reel 1871.20
Mrs. Grafter's Dinner Party 1912.07
Mrs. Grundy 1909.30
Mrs. Grundy Winked, And 1898.01
Mrs. Higgins' Parlor Floor 1886.60
Mrs. Hoggenheimer of Park Lane 1903.33
Mrs. Krause's Blue-Eyed Baby Boy 1930.11
Mrs. Larry, Tell Me This 1950.01
Mrs. Maloney 1905.22
Mrs. McGowan's Reel 1867.19
Mrs. Melzer Wants the Money Now! 1989.07
Mrs. Mister and Reverend Salvation 1937.08
Mrs. O'Ho 1906.07
Mrs. Patrick Casey's Swell Pink Tea 1898.50
Mrs. Patterson 1954.16
Mrs. Regan's Party 1882.69
Mrs. Reilly's Party 1891.28
Mrs. Robinson 1982.22
Mrs. S.L. Jacobowsky 1979.02, 1998.07
Mrs. Sally Adams 1950.15
Mrs. Wentworth-Brewster 1986.19
Mrs. Worthington 1986.19
Mt. Calvary Baptism Day 1995.04
Mu Lady's Clothes 1917.29
Mu-Cha-Cha 1956.14
Much Obliged to You 1907.34, 1907.41
Much too Soon 1971.04, 1976.27
Muchacha 1931.21
Mud Scow and the Whale, The 1881.12
Muddle Puddle Brakeman, The 1879.50
Muddy Day, The 1883.32
Muddy Water 1985.06
Muffy and the Topsiders 1983.18
Mug Dance 1969.04
Muito Bom 1979.03
Mujer d'en Manelic, La 1926.35
Mujer del Torero, Le 1926.35
Mulberry Springs 1886.52
Mulberry Street 1907.15
Mule's Bewitched, The 1911.28
Mule, he 1878.15
Mulligan Braves, The 1879.68
Mulligan Guard 1985.02
Mulligan's Lament 1893.10
Mulligan's Promises 1880.64
Multi-Millionaires 1901.27
Multiplication Duet 1880.18
Mulunghu Thabu 1927.63
Mum's the word 1882.17
Mum's the Word 1905.32, 1906.32
Mum's the Word, Mr. Moon 1909.27
Mumbo Jumbo 1962.18, 1978.18
Mumm's the Word 1904.43
Mummies, The 1901.19
Mummy, Mummy, Dear 1947.10
Munchkinland 1989.06
Mungojerrie and Rumpleteazer 1982.19
Muniera, La 1949.07
Murder 1914.32, 1921.32
Murder in My Heart 1920.28
Murder in Parkwold 1949.15, 1972.06
Murder, He Says 1980.29
Murder, Murder! 1997.09
Murrayisms 1921.06
Murrel's Gold 2001.06
Muscovite 1910.16
Musette 1933.24
Museum Song 1980.07
Music 1920.02
Music and Laughter 1895.43
Music and the Mirror, The 1975.15, 1976.16
Music Around the World 1935.19
Music Box 1922.04
Music Call, The 1928.26
Music for Madame 1957.01
Music Goes 'Round and 'Round, The 1986.06
Music Hall Song 1979.07
Music Hath Charms 1913.14
Music in My Fingers 1931.42
Music in My Heart 1934.06
Music in the Air 1870.01, 1937.11
Music in the House 1959.04
Music invites us 1873.05
Music Is 1976.33
Music is a Woman 1981.06
Music Lesson, The 1916.24
Music of an Irish Song 1924.25
Music of Home, The 1960.05
Music of Love 1923.25
Music of Love, The 1914.18
Music of the Band, The 1905.55
Music of the Night, The 1988.01, 1992.12, 2000.14
Music of Viol 1910.36
Music That Makes Me Dance, The 1964.11, 1990.09
Music Thrills Me, The 1926.27
Music Went Out of My Life, The 1988.20
Music With Her Silver Sound 1981.02
Music With Meals 1915.05
Music's Message, The 1955.19
Music, Music 1971.01
Music-Hall 1600 1964.29
Musical authority, The 1859.12
Musical Bullfrog, The 1907.07
Musical Chairs 1980.11
Musical Comedy 1924.07
Musical Comedy Maid, The 1907.20
Musical Comedy Man 1968.07
Musical Day 1939.23
Musical Gypsy, The 1905.45
Musical Introduction 1879.03
Musical Lesson, A 1948.18
Musical Mokes, The 1915.23
Musical Moon 1968.07
Musical Moon, The 1911.33
Musical Poker Game 1919.19
Musical Snore, The 1917.05
Musique, La 1958.06, 1964.22
Musketeer Sketch Finale, The 1992.17
Musketeer Sketch Rehearsal, The 1992.17
Musketeer Sketch, The 1992.17
Musketeers 1928.38
Musketeers, The 1899.17, 1901.06
Must be Given to You 1961.02
Must I Remind You 1896.50
Must it be Love? 1964.40
Must We Say Goodbye? 1912.27
Must we then part forever? 1882.76
Must You 1903.03, 1904.13, 1904.44
Mustapha Abdullah Abu Ben Al Raajid 1956.08
Mutual Admiration Society 1956.16
My Heart is Over the Sea, or Maggie's Secret 1924.20
My 62nd Romance 1936.12
My Advice 1919.41
My Affinity 1908.07
My Alamo Love 1904.09
My All Time Girl 1907.52
My Alpine Home 1894.16
My Angeline 1895.33
My Angemima Greene 1902.06
My Ann Elizer 1898.17
My Ann Elizer, the Rag Time Girl 1898.41
My Arab Complex 1934.42
My Arabian Maid 1917.13
My Arms are Open 1928.23
My Arverne Rose 1913.30
My Babe from Boston Town 1930.16
My Baby Elephant 1905.25
My Baby Just Cares for Me 1979.05
My Baby Talk Lady 1926.02
My Baby Talking Girl 1918.20
My Baby That' 'Ate Me 1927.05
My Baby's Arms 1919.15
My Baby's Bored 1949.02
My Bahama Baby 1906.15
My Bajadere 1922.35
My Bandana Land 1908.08
My Bark Canoe 1895.25
My bark which o'er the tide 1855.06
My Beautiful Fragonard Girl 1922.15
My Beautiful Gay Paree 1904.39
My Beautiful Irish Maid 1894.36
My Beautiful Lady 1911.11, 1911.24
My Beautiful Rhinestone Girl 1932.05
My Beautiful Tiger Girl 1919.16
My Bed is Like a Little Boat 1899.35
My Bedouin Girl 1917.08
My Belle 1984.14
My Ben Ali Haggin Girl 1921.30
My best beloved 1878.02
My Best Beloved 1888.13
My Best Girl 1912.31, 1966.10
My Best Love 1993.14
My Best Pal 1928.06
My Best to You 2000.16
My Bibliophile 1918.12
My Big Mistake 1991.07
My Big Moment 1980.09
My Bill has now been read a second time 1882.78
My Bird of Paradise 1930.26
My Black Baby Mine 1895.38
My Black Cloud 1904.18
My Black Dove 1909.05
My Blackbirds are Bluebirds Now 1928.47
My Blanket and Me 1971.11, 1999.03
My Blue Bird's Home Again 1927.46
My Blue Heaven 1927.37, 1944.32, 1967.13, 1968.20
My Blues Melody 1930.29
My Blushing Rose 1906.22
My boat is on the shore 1880.46
My Bobby and I 1901.06
My Body 1997.08
My Bohemian Fashion Girl 1916.25
My Bonnie 1917.17
My Bonnie Conchita 1904.58
My Bonnie, Sweet Bessie, the Maid of Dundee 1898.47
My Boy and I 1923.45
My Boy Friend 1922.26
My boy, you may take it from me 1887.10
My Boy, You're in Society 1896.28
My Boyfriend's Back 1984.15, 1997.21
My boyhood's house 1838.01
My Bridal Day 1919.39
My Bridal Gown 1937.10
My Bridal Rose 1917.16
My Broadway Butterfly 1917.35
My Broadway Chorus Girl 1920.33
My Broncho Boy 1906.04
My Brother Bill 1915.12
My Brother Willie 1926.02
My Brother's Keeper 1971.02

My Brown-Eyed Daisy 1904.27
My Brudder and Me 1948.04
My Buddy 1991.04
My Bungalow Babe 1906.09
My Bus and I 1948.24
My Business Man 1946.22
My Busy Day 1922.38
My Bwanna 1927.63
My Cabin Door 1905.20
My Calicoquette 1924.16
My Caravan 1918.35, 1920.29
My Card 1879.35
My Castilian Girl 1922.15
My Castle in Sorrento 1927.15
My Castle in Spain 1890.23, 1905.01, 1925.50
My Castle in the Air 1916.19
My Castle on the River Nile 1930.16
My Catamaran 1904.54
My Caty Dear 1880.38
My Caveman - My Venus 1923.42
My Charcoal Charmer 1900.47
My Cherokee Rose 1923.07
My Child 1993.07
My Child Will Forgive Me 1998.21
My China Rose 1919.39
My Chum My Dear Old Chum 1921.24
My Cigarette 1907.33
My Cigarette Maid 1908.05
My Cinderella 1907.14
My Cinderella Girl 1913.18
My Cinnamon Tree 1904.40
My City 1973.06, 1985.15
My Clementine 1902.08
My Cleopatra Girl 1914.01
My Climbing Rose 1918.33
My Coal Black Mammy 1922.34
My Combination Girl 1905.25
My Coney Island Queen 1907.23
My Conviction 1968.11
My Cosey Corner Girl 1904.29
My Cosy Little Corner in the Ritz 1919.25
My Cottage in Sunshine Lane 1923.01
My Country 'tis of Thee 1908.28
My Cousin Carus 1909.13, 1909.15
My Cousin in Milwaukee 1933.01, 1999.10
My Creole Girl 1922.44
My Cretonne Girl 1923.21
My Crinoline Girl 1923.08
My Cubist Girl 1913.16
My Cup Runneth Over 1966.29, 1976.32
My Cutey's Due to Two-to-Two To-Day 1926.15
My Dad's Dinner Pail 1883.63, 1893.10
My Daddy Always Taught Me to Share 1985.05
My Daddy is a Dandy 1954.16
My Daffydil 1912.42
My Dahomian Queen 1904.26
My Dainty Dresden Shepherdess 1905.33
My Dandelion 1901.25
My Darlin' Aida 1952.15
My Darlin' Eileen 1953.03
My Darling 1931.26, 1932.18
My Darling I Love You March 1972.18
My Darling, My Darling 1948.26, 1974.25, 1980.29
My Dashing Soldier Boy 1908.16
My Daughter Biddy McFadden 1895.17
My Daughter is Wed to a Friend of Mine 1909.26
My Day 1952.08
My Day of Rest 1950.02
My Dear Bunvenuto 1945.04
My Dear Old Jersey Home 1903.27
My Dear Public 1943.14
My Dear Son 1972.17
My Dear Young Ladies 1881.11
My Dearest Paul 1916.01
My Dearie Dear 1909.12
My Death 1972.16
My Defenses are Down 1946.12, 1966.12, 1999.04
My Delight 1888.32
My Dew Drop Rosy 1904.23
My Diabolo Beau 1908.07
My Diamond Girls 1922.34
My Diamond Horseshoe of Girls 1922.39
My Dixie Anna 1903.09, 1903.20
My Dixie Girl 1907.53
My Dixie Lou 1904.33
My Dixie Queen 1901.23
My Doctor 1925.30
My Dolls 1907.47
My Dream Book of Memories 1943.23
My Dream for Tomorrow 1974.05
My Dream Girl, I Loved You All Along 1924.23
My Dream has Come True 1944.25
My dream is realized 1855.06
My Dream of Dreams 1914.21
My Dream of Love 1883.12, 1909.21
My Dream of Love is You 1919.12, 1921.35
My Dream of You 1896.05
My Dream, Dream Man 1910.30
My Dreams 1928.12
My Duchess of the Long Ago 1918.20
My Dutch Lady 1923.17
My Dynamo 1929.20
My Egyptian Queen 1904.24
My Emmaleen 1903.24
My Eskimo 1907.26
My Estelle 1897.26, 1897.54
My Evaline 1901.12
My Evening Star 1912.07
My excellent friend, Bombardos 1888.18
My Eyes are Fully Open 1981.01
My eyes are fully open to my awful situation 1887.10
My Fair Gitana 1891.13
My Fair Lady 1925.14
My Fair Unknown 1905.29
My Fairy Castle in the Air 1919.20
My Fairy Prince 1913.27
My Fairy Tale 1992.05
My Faithful Heart 1891.13
My Faithful Stradivari 1914.03
My Family Tree 1963.29
My Fannie 1919.12
My Fatal Charm 1954.17
My Fatal Choice Shall Sever 1888.19
My Father 2000.16
My Father Fights for Uncle Sam 1917.11
My Father Said 1934.38
My father! can it be? 1888.07
My Father's Own House 1950.16
My Father's Sword 1917.27
My Father's Wooden Leg 1907.46
My Fatima, My Selim 1877.22
My Favorite Things 1959.24, 1967.07, 1974.22, 1998.03
My Favorite Year 1992.17
My Feet are Firmly Planted on the Ground 1935.03
My Feet Can't Fail Me Now 1992.06
My Filipina Pet 1901.21
My Fire-Fly Lady 1909.11
My First and Only Love 1896.02
My First Love Song 1965.19
My First Love, My Last Love 1930.27
My First Moment 1971.19
My First Promise 1941.06
My first request I'll be confessing 1894.28
My First Smoke 1905.22
My First Solo Flight 1980.13
My First True Love 1904.36
My First Waltz 1946.18
My First Woman 1993.09
My Flag 1914.34
My Flower of the South 1905.35
My Fortune is My Face 1964.21
My Friend 1979.06, 1993.07, 1997.08
My Friend Lebel 1909.15
My Friends! - a Saxon Stranger 1902.25
My Friends, Your Kind Attention 1954.06
My Frivolity Girl 1920.02
My Funny Valentine 1937.04, 1975.13
My Gaby Doll 1923.17
My Gal is Mine Once More 1948.14
My Gal Sal 1901.21, 1903.22
My Galilee 1971.02
My Gallant Boys 1930.32
My Gang 1923.46
My Garden 1969.02
My Garden of Love 1922.42
My Garden of Perfumes 1921.37
My Gasoline Automobile 1904.24
My Gasoline Maid 1906.30
My Gay Golf Girl 1900.47
My Generation 1982.22
My Gentle Young Johnny 1960.19
My Georgia Lady Love 1901.28
My Georgiana 1905.42
My German Rose 1905.12
My Girl 1896.52
My Girl and I 1941.12
My Girl is a Plain Girl 1895.27
My Girl is Just Enough Woman for Me 1959.01
My Girl of Chance 1912.12
My Girl Uses Mineralava That's Why I'm Her Beau 1923.20
My Girl's a Highborn Lady 1927.48
My God is so High 1930.10
My Golden Dream Ship 1922.30
My Golden Girl 1920.05
My Goo-Goo Queen 1903.28
My Grandfather's Muhle 1879.54
My Guiding Star 1910.20
My Guy 1964.39
My Gypsy Sweetheart 1909.30, 1926.09, 1926.35
My Hand is Yours! 1875.15
My Hand Needs Your Hand 1970.01
My hand upon it 1879.21
My Handyman Ain't Handy Anymore 1978.21
My Hannah Lady 1900.52
My Hawaii 1961.07
My Hawaiian Sunrise 1916.24
My Haytian Queen 1909.18
My Heart 1885.58, 1888.13, 1896.35
My Heart Again to Hope Begins 1894.22
My Heart Beats for You 1921.33
My Heart Begins to Thump! Thump! 1930.25
My Heart Belongs to Daddy 1938.13
My Heart Belongs to the U.S.A. 1918.13
My Heart Belongs to You 1929.08
My Heart Controls My Head 1937.17
My Heart is at Thy Feet 1904.40
My heart is broke 1886.53
My Heart is Calling 1922.11, 1931.34
My Heart is Dancing 1937.10
My Heart is Ever Gay 1882.58
My Heart is in the Highlands 1894.40, 1913.25
My Heart is in Thrall to Kitty's Beauty 1897.03
My Heart is Just a Gypsy 1979.05
My Heart is Like a Bird in May 1917.30
My Heart is Like a Violin 1964.21
My Heart is on a Binge Again 1943.20
My Heart is Part of You 1932.17
My Heart is so Full of You 1956.04, 1980.29
My heart is torn asunder 1840.03
My Heart is Unemployed 1938.09
My Heart is Waking 1921.14
My Heart is Weary 1913.07
My Heart is Yours 1934.43
My Heart Leaps Up 1974.18
My Heart Remains With Thee 1876.09, 1876.10
My Heart Stood Still 1927.56, 1943.22, 1975.13, 2000.07
My Heart was so free 1750.01
My heart was so free 1854.06
My Heart was so Free 1957.02, 1957.02
My Heart Will Sail Across the Seas 1922.27
My Heart Won't Say Goodbye 1954.01
My Heart's a Banjo 1931.21
My Heart's an Open Book 1934.15
My Heart's an Open Door 1983.17
My Heart's Darlin' 1952.05
My Heart's Delight 1897.47
My Heart's in the Middle of July 1949.02
My Heart's in the Sunny South 1924.41
My Heart's My Own 1912.10
My Heaven 1928.49
My Heaven With You 1927.65
My Hero 1909.22, 1912.25, 1924.23, 1947.06
My Hideaway 1932.14
My Highbrow Fling 1922.38
My Hindoo Man 1904.54
My Holiday Girl 1918.20

My Holy Prayer 1975.23
My Home is a One Horse Town 1920.18
My Home is in My Shoes 1951.23
My Home Town in Kansas 1923.24
My Home's a Highway 1952.05
My Home's Across the Blue Ridge Mountains 1999.09
My Hometown 1922.22, 1964.05
My Honey Bunch 1903.06
My Honey Nell 1900.49
My Honeysuckle Baby 1908.37
My Honeysuckle Girl 1902.41
My Hong Kong Lady 1903.30
My Honolulu Hula Girl 1912.03
My Honolulu Queen 1899.38
My Honor and My Sword 1903.37
My Hottentot 1906.27
My House 1950.08
My Houseboat Beau 1906.05
My Houseboat on the Harlem 1924.34
My Hula Maid 1915.12
My Hula-Hula Girl 1907.13
My Husband 1909.04
My Husband Makes Movies 1982.09
My Husband Taught Me to be One of the Boys 1898.01
My Husband the Pig 1999.20
My Husband's Dearest Friend 1920.31
My Husband's First Wife 1929.31
My Icy Floe 1926.17
My Idea of Paradise 1911.03
My Idea of Something to Go Home To 1919.44
My Ideal 1905.40, 1930.43
My Indian Family 1960.10
My Indian Maid 1909.10
My Indian Maiden 1904.19
My Indian Summer Moon 1906.09
My Indispensable Girl 1919.31
My Intimate Friend 1902.29
My Intuition 1930.25
My Irish Daisy 1905.41
My Irish Fluffy Ruffles 1907.41
My Irish Gibson Girl 1907.41
My Irish Girl 1907.12, 1910.17
My Irish Maid 1905.30
My Irish Molly O 1905.19
My Irish Romeo 1913.18
My Irish Rosie 1906.25
My Irish Senorita 1912.02
My Isle of Golden Dreams 1918.07
My Jack is a Sailor 1882.82
My Japanee 1910.02
My Japanese Baby 1903.18
My Japanese Cherry Blossom 1901.17
My Jewels 1926.16
My Joe 1943.24
My Josephine 1899.17
My June Love 1921.26
My Jungle Home 1929.52
My Kid 1926.51
My Kimona Queen 1902.40
My Kind of Love 1961.01
My Kind of Night 1948.25
My Kind of Town Chicago Is 1974.10
My King of Love 1920.34
My Kingdom 1898.46
My L'ndy Lou 1955.13
My Lad, 'Tis of Thee 1895.12
My Lady 1895.12, 1904.20, 1920.17, 1926.25, 1927.49
My Lady Bug 1900.52
My Lady Fair 1906.47, 1919.37
My Lady Moon 1904.20
My Lady of Japan 1905.48
My Lady of the Cameo 1920.23, 1922.23
My Lady of the Fan 1922.21
My Lady of the Lamp 1920.47
My Lady of the Manor 1903.37
My Lady of the Nile 1916.10
My Lady of the Telephone 1914.22
My Lady Silhouette 1922.23
My Lady Wine 1908.21
My Lady's Coach has Been Attacked 1907.51
My Lady's Dress 1915.01
My Lady's Fan 1925.12, 1928.50
My Lady's Hand 1937.06
My Lady's Maid 1906.32
My Ladye Faire 1907.52
My Lallapaloosa Girl 1903.19
My Land 1911.04, 1912.06, 1922.08
My Land, My Flag 1915.25
My Landlady 1912.38
My Last Affair 1934.06, 1936.12
My Last Love 1943.21
My Last Thoughts 1888.45
My Late, Late Lady 1957.01
My Life is Love 1918.27
My Linda Love 1903.17
My Lips, My Love, My Soul! 1926.24
My Little 'Rang Outang 1903.20
My Little Baby 1897.39
My Little Bimbo Down on the Bamboo Isle 1920.24
My Little Blarney Stone, or Tipperary Mary Cary 1908.21
My Little Book of Poetry 1921.30
My Little Bronco Queen 1901.16
My Little Buttercup 1905.27
My Little Canoe 1904.29, 1906.04, 1921.32
My Little Castagnet 1946.03
My Little Castagnette 1926.42
My Little China Doll 1904.49
My Little Deutscher Girl 1909.04
My Little Dhudeen 1914.05
My Little Dog has Ego 1950.03
My Little Firefly 1905.40
My Little Fraulein 1905.12
My Little Friend 1913.14
My Little Full-Blown Rose 1922.24
My Little Girl 1993.16
My Little Girl is a Shy Little Girl 1906.47
My Little Girlie 1903.14, 1903.22
My Little Green Cactus 1999.05
My Little Gypsy Maid 1902.16
My Little Havana Made 1911.40
My Little Highland Highball 1919.37
My Little Hindoo Belle 1903.14
My Little Home in Tennessee 1955.19
My Little Hong Kong Baby 1902.19
My Little Irish Rose 1917.07
My Little Japanee 1904.07
My Little Javanese 1919.18
My Little Jungle Queen 1900.55
My Little Lady 1898.41
My Little Lassoo 1905.50
My Little Lost Girl 1960.10
My Little Lotus Flower 1923.17
My Little Love Bird 1903.33
My Little Loving Baby Mine 1918.13
My Little Maid 1924.36
My Little Orang-o-Tang 1904.20
My Little Pet Chicken 1914.15
My Little Piano Man 1929.32
My Little Queen Bee 1914.20
My Little Red Umbrella 1889.41
My Little Room 1979.18
My Little Side Door 1884.13
My Little Simi San 1905.35
My Little Sioux Sue 1905.50
My Little Sunbeam Sue 1905.20
My Little Sunday Girl 1895.38
My Little Tailor Maid 1908.15
My Little Tot's High Chair 1889.37
My Little Woman 1894.31
My Little Yellow Dress 1959.03
My Little Zulu Babe 1900.46
My Log-Fire Girl 1920.10
My Lonesome Louisiana Lady 1905.43
My Long Lost Love, Lenore 1913.21
My Long, Long Ago Girl 1924.32
My Lord and Master 1951.12
My Lord! My Lord! 1878.16
My Lord's a-Writin' All de Time 1930.10
My lord, a suppliant at your feet I kneel 1882.78
My Lords and Ladies 1887.04, 1945.04
My Lou 1911.43
My Loulou 1935.14
My Love 1882.33, 1956.15, 1974.06, 1982.20, 1997.10
My Love and I 1885.58, 1907.07
My Love Bouquet 1923.02
My Love Carries On 1936.07
My Love for You 1988.10
My Love Forevermore 1904.35
My Love I Dare Not Tell Thee 1904.03
My Love is a Blower 1913.06
My Love is a Married Man 1945.19
My Love is a Secret 1917.09
My Love is a Wanderer 1953.17
My Love is all Madness and Folly 1750.01
My love is all my life to me 1894.03
My Love is Fair 1895.38
My Love is Like a Blooming Flower 1912.03
My love is like the lily fair 1889.10
My love is like the red, red rose 1859.01
My Love is on the Way 1954.03
My Love is Young 1936.12
My Love is Yours 1963.20
My Love Must be a Soldier 1890.23
My Love of a Day 1918.26
My Love Parade 1947.05
My Love Serves in a Candy SHop 1877.25
My Love's a Gamblin' Man 1897.07
My Love's so Good 1972.14
My Love, My Own 1897.55
My Love, You Know That I Have Never Used 1931.06
My Loved Home I shall ne'er see more 1868.02
My Loved One 1889.37, 1941.02
My Lover 1927.65
My Lover Must Stay in Bed or He May Catch a Cold 1947.18
My Lover's Gone Off on a Train 1931.02
My Loves 1926.35
My Luck is Changing 1983.21
My Lucky Day 1999.12
My Lucky Lover 1948.18
My Lucky Redskin 1922.26
My Lucky Star 1902.09, 1904.49, 1928.02, 1929.03
My Lulu 1918.35
My Madagascar Maid 1908.17
My Maggie 1889.03
My Magic Lamp 1978.03
My Maker 2000.20
My Mammy 1918.05, 1923.20, 1940.10
My Man 1921.21, 1953.12, 1964.22, 1976.16
My Man is on the Make 1929.42
My Man Rocks Me 1999.09
My Man's Gone Now 1935.13, 1983.04
My Manicure Maids 1920.06
My Margot 1987.10
My Master is Punctual 1879.21
My Matilda 1902.23
My Matrimonial Bon-Bon 1908.03
My Mavourneen 1891.28
My Melody 1922.19, 1923.20
My Melody Man 1929.09
My Memories Started With You 1940.23
My Midnight Frolic Girl 1920.18, 1921.21
My Mindanao Chocolate Soldier 1915.01
My Miracle Man 1914.34
My Miss Mary 1960.19
My Missus 1926.51
My Mobile Gal 1900.41
My Mobile Mandy 1906.08
My Model Girl 1915.18
My Mom 1932.14
My Moonbeam Dream 1908.27
My Morning Glory 1902.02
My Most Intimate Friend 1935.14
My Mother Said 1971.20
My Mother Said 'Don't' 1892.42
My Mother Told Me Not to Trust a Soldier 1928.44
My Mother Would Love You 1940.19
My Mother's Eyes 1979.30
My Mother's Weddin' Day 1947.07
My Motter 1910.05
My Musical Comedy Maiden 1916.02
My Name 1963.01
My Name is Can 1975.04
My name is Fanchette 1880.04
My name is John Wellington Wells 1879.10
My Name is Leda Pearl 1971.10

My Name is Man 1972.13
My Name is Pat O'Hara 1896.41
My Name is Samuel Cooper 1948.25
My Name is Singold 1885.65
My Name is Where the Heather Blooms 1894.40, 1913.25
My Name is Yisrolik 1960.18
My Native Land 1905.20
My Nelie's Blue Eyes 1882.69
My Nellie's Blue Eyes 1885.53, 1886.51, 1887.05, 1888.12, 1891.07
My New Philosophy 1999.03
My New York 1900.20
My Night in Venice 1920.07
My Nightingale 1905.34
My Object All Sublime 1939.17
My Old Banjo 1928.10
My Old Brass Band 1912.05
My Old Country Home 1898.22
My Old Dutch Pipe 1894.32
My Old High Hat 1902.42
My Old High School 1955.13
My Old Hoss 1934.39
My Old Kentucky Home 1879.64, 1920.28, 1939.21
My Old Lady 1908.28
My Old Man 1922.44
My Old New Jersey Home 1921.03
My old spinette 1859.12
My Old Town 1911.28
My Old Virginia Home on the Nile 1940.17
My Old Wife and I 1869.14
My Ole Man 1909.27
My One and Only 1983.06
My One Girl 1928.21
My Only Defense 1998.02
My Only Romance 1946.06
My Orange Blossom Home 1928.37
My Oriental Rose 1912.09
My Own 1906.15, 1925.34
My Own Best Friend 1975.14
My Own Best Love 1898.78
My Own Boy 1906.13
My Own Brass Bed 1960.20
My Own California 1919.11
My Own Cecile 1898.63
My Own Dear Irish Queen 1904.02
My Own Girl 1904.13
My Own Light Infantry 1918.16
My Own Little Girl 1902.30
My own little Pearl 1879.38
My Own Morning 1967.06
My Own Paree 1908.30
My Own Space 1977.16
My Own United States 1902.41, 1917.11
My Own Vienna 1908.29
My own, my native Isle 1869.23
My Oxygen 1877.23
My Pajama Beauty 1902.06
My Paradise 1915.30
My Paramount-Publix-Roxy-Rose 1934.19
My parcels gently bearing 1859.16
My parents were of great gentility 1895.26
My Party 1905.25
My Passion Flower 1927.50
My Peaches and Cream 1912.41
My Pearl's Bowery Girl 1894.31
My Peasant Home 1888.18
My people, who've submitted to the Governor's absurdities 1895.29
My Personal Property 1976.07
My Phantom Loves 1920.19
My Picture in the Papers 1954.03
My Picture of You 1906.09
My Ping Pong Girl 1902.02
My Pipe! 1882.75
My Pirate Lady 1916.03
My Pleasure 1961.07
My Polly is a Peach 1897.04
My Pony Boy 1909.15
My poor Lucy Neal 1873.04
My Poor Wee Lassie 1980.17
My Post Card Girl 1908.39
My Pousse-cafe 1920.01
My Pretty Baby 1885.03
My Pretty Little Family of One 1913.31
My Pretty Rosebud 1905.31
My Prince 1939.27, 1975.13
My Prince Came Riding 1945.11
My Princess Zulu Lou 1901.27
My Propensities are All the Other Way 1897.32
My Queen 1931.09
My Queen of Ping Pong 1902.23
My Queen of the Track 1903.14
My quests no earthly use 1887.04
My Radiant Firefly 1903.14
My Radium Girl 1915.16
My Rag Doll Girl 1903.31
My Raggdydore 1913.05
My Rainbow 1927.62
My Rainbow Beau 1914.22
My Rainbow Bride, or Beautiful Rose Marie 1898.69
My Rainbow Girl 1917.31, 1918.11
My Rainbow Girlie 1923.17
My Real Ideal 1930.20
My Red Letter Day 1936.02
My Regular Girl 1932.04
My Regular Man 1930.19
My Reuben Girlie 1912.24
My Rhapsody 1944.28
My Riviera Rose 1924.36
My Road 1924.30
My Roller Skating Girl 1907.21
My Romance 1935.15
My Rooster 1963.19
My Rose of Memory 1920.24
My Rose of Spain 1927.19
My Roundelay 1885.08
My Rules 1993.02
My Sabots 1905.04
My Sahara Girl 1908.10
My Sahara Rose 1920.10
My Sailor Boy 1901.12, 1907.60
My Sambo 1902.20
My San Domingo Maid 1904.10
My Scarecrow Coon 1905.35
My school is most select 1895.43
My Screen Maid 1921.25
My Senorita 1905.37, 1916.14
My Sent for Me 1906.09
My Sergeant and I 1942.20
My Service Flag 1918.02
My Shaggy Old Polar Bear 1907.47
My Shepherd See 1875.19
My Shining Hour 1979.14, 1997.05
My Ship 1941.04, 1995.12
My Silent Love 1932.14
My Sing Song Girl 1919.22
My Sist' Tetrazin 1909.11
My Sister Bess 1984.02
My Skating Girl 1916.15
My Soldier Boy 1888.34, 1910.30
My Son 1872.34
My Son John 1880.42
My Son the Druggist 1976.09
My Son, the Lawyer 1962.01
My Son, Uphold the Law 1965.29
My Son-in-Law 1946.20
My Song 1931.30
My Sonny Boy 1904.02
My Soul in One Unbroken Sigh 1871.17
My Soul is a Witness 1930.10
My South Car'lina Gal 1900.46
My Southern Belle 1905.49, 1928.19
My Special Friend is in Town 1927.32
My Spies Tell Me 1943.14
My Springtime Thou Art 1921.31
My State 1963.21
My Story Ends That Way 1930.14
My Strongest Suit 2000.06
My Sugar Plum 1925.27
My Sulu Lulu Loo 1902.44
My Sumurun Girl 1976.25
My Sunday Fella 1929.27
My Sunday Girl 1899.19
My Sunflower Sue 1900.47
My Sunny South 1929.26
My Sunny Sunbeam 1907.45
My Sunny Tennessee 1981.03
My Sunshine 1923.42
My Susianah from Louisiana 1898.41
My Sweet 1905.41, 1908.12, 1931.04
My Sweet and Pretty May 1889.10
My Sweet Lord 1973.17, 1984.15
My Sweet Maid 1899.03
My Sweet Moana 1902.38
My Sweet Queen 1901.02
My Sweet Tomorrow 1972.11
My Sweet Wild Rose 1905.33
My Sweet Woman 1982.13
My Sweetest Girl 1897.47
My Sweetheart 1906.45
My Sweetheart 'Tis of Thee 1931.42
My Sweetheart has Her Faults in Plenty 1896.45
My Sweetheart Mamie 1941.09
My sweetheart when a boy 1876.04
My Sweetheart's a Soldier in the Army 1907.22
My Sweetheart's the Man in the Moon 1927.48
My Sweetheart, When I was a Boy 1882.28
My Sweetie's Smile 1921.17
My Sword 1928.12
My Sword and I 1928.12, 1984.14
My Syncopated Gypsy Maid 1906.01
My Syndi-Kate 1905.22
My Tamourine Girl 1919.15
My Tango Queen 1914.13
My Thoughts are Far Away 1885.58
My Thoughts Would Still be With Thee 1898.01
My Time 1980.11
My Time of Day 1950.17
My Toast to You 1911.31
My Tokio Queen 1908.20
My Tonita 1924.05
My Top Sergeant 1944.01
My Toreador 1902.01, 1910.30
My Totem Pole 1907.26
My Town 1968.07
My Treasure 1946.18
My Trilby Maid 1915.12
My Trombone Man 1915.12
My True Heart 1959.04
My True Love is a Shepherdess 1894.40, 1913.25
My Turkey Trotting Boy 1914.10
My Turkish Maid 1910.11
My Type 1985.19
My Unkissed Man 1904.15
My Unknown Someone 1991.07
My Vampire Girl 1918.20
My Very Own 1907.59
My Violin 1920.25
My Vision Girl 1921.16
My Vision in Vermillion 1922.15
My Voodoo Lady 1916.03
My Washy Washy Beau 1908.10
My Way 1965.19, 1978.01, 1989.12
My Way or the Highway 1997.08
My wedded life 1895.29
My Wedding 1929.07
My Wedding Day 1911.03
My Weight in Gold 1964.04
My well-loved lord and guardian dear 1882.78
My White Knight 1957.18, 2000.11
My Wife 1920.47
My Wife - My Man 1917.01
My Wife the Dancer 1977.09
My Wife Will be My Lady 1906.25
My Wife! My Wife 1911.25
My Wife's Gone 1913.22
My Wild Imagination 1953.01
My Wild Irish Rose 1899.01, 1914.05
My Wish 1963.21
My Wooing 1889.02
My Word 1905.03
My Word! Ain't We Carrying On 1918.31
My Word, You do Look Queer 1960.17
My Yankee Doodle Girl 1911.02
My years with sweet contentment bless 1863.03
My Yellow Flower 1948.17
My Yellow Jacket Girl 1913.05
My Yes Girl 1927.27

My Yiddish Colleen 1910.18
My Yiddisha Mammy 1922.15
My Yiddishe Mame 1990.16
My Yokohama Girl 1917.08
My Young Man 1896.26
My Yukon Belle 1904.58
My Zebra Lady Fair 1915.16
My Zoo 1902.01
Myltil and Tyltil 1920.14
Myrella 1912.26
Myron Brown, Farewell 1905.35
Mysterioso 1920.01
Mysterious Kiss, The 1913.10
Mysterious Lady 1954.13, 1977.02, 1979.22
Mysterious Maid 1906.21, 1907.20
Mystery Moon 1930.21
Mystery of History, The 1906.18
Mystery Play, The 1922.43
Mystery Song 1989.02
Mystery Train 1989.12
Mystic Hussars, The 1923.40
Mystic Poet, hear our prayer 1881.37
Mystical Maidens are We 1900.37

N Everything 1918.05
N'est Pas 1898.05
N'fait's pas ca! J'suis tres bonn' fille 1886.19
N'imaginez pas qu'il me coute 1929.11
N.Y.C. 1951.10, 1977.06
Na also schreib' und tu' nicht schmieren 1964.25
Na Botta E Via 1964.03
Nadia 1977.01
Nadjy 1888.45
Nag! Nag! Nag! 1962.18
Naga Saki 1927.62
Nagnu Bekol 1968.04
Najla's Song 1951.15
Naked in Bethesda Fountain 1992.17
Naked Truth, The 1920.28
Name and Day 1893.19
Name it and it's Yours 1939.14
Name of Kelly, The 1922.43
Name of Love, The 1985.18, 1989.07
Name the Day 1920.05
Name's LaGuardia, The 1959.25
Namely You 1956.12
Names I Love to Hear 1922.46
Naming of Cats, The 1982.19
Nana, La 1949.07
Nancy 1896.02, 1902.06, 1910.11
Nancy and I 1897.25
Nancy Brown 1902.16
Nancy Clancy 1904.39
Nancy Hogan's Ball 1897.26
Nancy Hogan's Ball! 1897.54
Nancy Teel 1894.44
Nancy's Farewell 1919.27
Nanette 1919.32, 1931.16, 1952.11
Nanette and Rin Tin Tin 1919.03
Nanking Blues 1920.24
Nanny 1928.05
Nanon Waltz 1885.08
Nanty 1952.09
Nanty Puts Her Hair Up 1952.09
Napenee 1904.28
Napoleon 1861.04, 1909.05, 1917.01, 1934.40, 1957.16
Napoleon Bonaparte 1905.45
Napoleon's a Pastry 1937.15
Naranjo en Flor 1999.18
Narcissus 1980.27
Nargileh 1930.20
Nasty Way He Sez It, The 1891.14
Natacha 1926.23
Natalie 1966.20
Natasha 1972.17, 1980.08
Nathalie 1968.21
Nathan Marching Song 1962.01
Nation is Dying, The 1988.02
Nation's Fate, A 1897.17
National Airs 1918.35
National Guard, The 1890.39
National Hymn 1910.24
National Pastime, The 1981.28
Native Glens 1889.36
Native Plantation Song 1912.03
Native Women 1915.04
Natives 1906.26
Natural Allies 1962.24
Natural Man 1974.01, 1991.04
Nature 1924.21
Nature Class 1905.44
Nature Divine 1915.28
Nature Hunt Ballet 1971.21
Nature Played a Dirty Trick on You 1931.36
Nature's Repose 1896.45
Natuscha 1947.14
Naught's a Naught 1949.16
Naughty Baby 1992.02
Naughty Boy 1910.29, 1929.31
Naughty Boys 1900.03
Naughty Cipriano/That Waltz Espagnol 1926.09, 1926.35
Naughty Continong, The 1894.46
Naughty Cupid 1909.12
Naughty Eyes 1920.19, 1925.35
Naughty Girl 1888.42, 1889.25
Naughty Girl from Paris 1896.49
Naughty Girls 2000.01
Naughty Kid Song 1907.19
Naughty Little Clock, The 1899.06
Naughty Little Fly 1902.21
Naughty Little Lady, O 1907.26
Naughty Little Step 1925.26
Naughty Lola 1967.13, 1968.20
Naughty Marietta 1910.35, 1978.19, 1988.18
Naughty Nineties, The 1927.23
Naughty Nobleman, The 1922.45
Naughty Riquette 1926.26
Naughty Scarecrow, The 1904.23
Naughty Sporty Boys 1894.35
Naughty! Naughty! Naughty! 1916.23
Naughty, Naughty Man 1866.18, 1870.44
Naughty, Naughty Men 1885.29
Naughty-Boy 1927.54
Naughty-Naught 1937.02, 1946.19
Navajo 1903.07
Naval Manoeuvres 1913.26
Naviganti 1880.42
Navy Foxtrot Man, The 1919.09
Navy of To-Day's All Right, The 1917.29
Navy, The 1902.03
Nay, Nay Pauline 1914.17
Nazi Party Pooper 1981.14
Ndinosara Nani? 1966.03
Ne Comptez Pas Sur Moi... Pour Me Montrer Toute Nue 1958.18
Ne dis pas toujours 1934.32, 1935.19
Ne parlez pas de mon courage 1878.08
Ne'er did we such a rascal see 1895.17
Neapoli 1902.08
Neapolitan Jazz 1919.30
Neapolitan Love Song 1915.24
Near Future, The 1919.15
Near Him at Last 1894.47
Near Them 1883.12
Near to You 1955.08, 1994.01
Nearer My God to Thee 1887.02
Nearest and Dearest 1880.69
Nearing the Day 1922.41
Nearly True to You 1922.12
Nearness of You, The 1991.04
Neat to be a Newsboy 1978.12
Neat/Not Neat 1986.18
Neath Italian Skies 1921.34, 1923.12
Neath My Lattice 1900.37
Neath Oriental Skies 1902.11
Neath the Blue Neapolitan Skies 1900.25
Neath the Casement 1920.41
Neath the Cherry Blossom Moon 1927.14
Neath the Old Cherry Tree 1907.53
Neath the Old Palm Tree 1907.33
Neath the Shade of the Old Apple Tree 1922.27
Neath the Southern Moon 1978.19, 1988.18
Neath the Southern Moon for Thee 1910.35
Neath Thy Window 1899.28
Neath Thy Window, Senorita 1903.27
Necessity 1947.03
Nectar for the Gods 1911.07
Need 2000.08
Needles 1926.12
Negotiations at the Grand Banquet 1997.16, 1998.08
Negra, La 1988.15
Negresco 1929.51
Negro Love Song, A 1966.15
Neige 1964.22
Neighborhood 1995.03
Neighborhood Song, The 1964.44
Nell Brinkley Girl, The 1908.19
Nellie After Five 1892.54
Nellie Bly 1946.04
Nellie Kelly 1902.15, 1924.16
Nellie Kelly, I Love You 1922.43, 1968.07
Nellie Kept on Smiling 1896.06
Nellie to Me is a Queen 1894.17
Nellie's Blue Eyes 1885.06
Nelly Bly 1864.13
Nelly Brady 1886.60
Nelson 1980.08, 1985.19
Nena 1926.09, 1926.35
Nenette and Rintintin 1918.33
Nerve 1900.38
Nerves 1986.20
Nervous 1974.04
Nervous Blues 1921.26
Nesting in a New York Tree 1904.42, 1907.16
Nesting Place 1922.04
Nesting Time in Flatbush 1917.06
Nestle by My Side 1907.13
Neuftette 1928.04
Neurotic You and Psychopathic Me 1948.30
Nevada Hoe Down 1954.17
Nevada Moonlight 1931.28
Never 1978.02
Never a Dull Moment 1939.13
Never a Law to Prevent It 1885.08
Never a moment left for leisure 1888.18
Never Again 1900.41, 1912.08, 1915.05, 1927.38, 1939.07, 1965.30, 1997.12
Never Be-Devil the Devil 1961.08
Never Before 1958.20
Never Borrow Trouble 1908.17
Never Breathe a Word of This 1901.07
Never Breathe a Word of This to Mother 1906.21
Never Count Your Chicks Before They're Hatched 1913.26
Never Ending Love 1982.15
Never Felt This Way Before 1953.03
Never for You 1928.29
Never Give Anything Away 1953.07
Never had an Education 1933.03
Never had to Work 1902.35
Never in the Wide, Wide World 1902.04
Never Land 1950.08
Never Let Her Go 1948.18
Never Marry a Dancer 1934.38
Never Marry a Girl With Cold Feet 1907.32
Never Mention Love When We're Alone 1914.30
Never Met a Girl Like You 1923.46
Never Met a Man I Didn't Like 1991.07, 1991.10
Never Mind the Singing - Just Dance, My Dear 1911.41
Never Mind the Why and Wherefore 1945.09
Never mind the why or wherefore 1879.05
Never Mind, Bo-Peep, We Will Find Your Sheep 1929.48
Never More 1919.39
Never More Removing 1787.01
Never Never Land 1958.20, 1958.21, 1977.02, 1988.08
Never Never Land, The 1907.11
Never on Sunday 1962.17, 1967.05
Never Put it in Writing 1985.05
Never Say the Final Journey is at Hand 1989.10
Never Say the World was Made to Cry 1926.14
Never Take a Step too Far 1913.14
Never Take the Horseshoe from the Door 1880.09
Never Talk to Me of Waltzing 1860.05
Never too Late for Love 1954.15
Never Trouble Trouble 1927.20

Never Trust a Soldier Man 1914.22
Never Trust a Virgin 1961.08
Never was There a Girl so Fair 1931.48
Never was There Such a Lover 1909.22
Never Will I Marry 1960.05, 1980.29
Never Worry 1914.17
Never' Becomes 'Today' 1935.16
Never, Never be an Artist 1953.07
Never, Never, Never Fall in Love 1895.25
Never-More 1910.26
Neverland 1954.13, 1979.22, 1983.09, 1990.20
Neverland Waltz 1954.13
Nevermiore 1913.06
Nevermore 1934.34, 1948.15
Nevertheless 1930.22
Nevertheless I'm in Love With You 1981.03
New Belle of New York, The 1898.47
New Argentina, A 1979.23
New Army Unit, Old Army Unit 1998.08
New Art is True Art 1943.19
New Ashmolean Marching Society and Students Conservatory Band, The 1980.29
New Ashmolean Marching Society and Students' Conservatory Band, The 1948.26, 1974.25
New Bully, The 1895.27
New Car 1999.02
New Charleston Ballet 1929.10
New Cook, The 1903.27
New Day 1976.15
New Deal for Christmas, A 1977.06
New Dreams for Old 1958.04
New Era for the Prince 1998.08
New Erminie Waltz 1893.35
New Erminie Waltz Song 1893.35
New Faces 1934.06, 1936.12
New Fangled Preacher Man 1970.05
New Game, The 1925.29
New Hollywood Plots 1955.12
New Hotel, The 1911.45
New Jerusalem 1972.25
New Kind of Rhythm, A 1927.10
New Kind of Two-Step 1908.14
New Leader, The 1912.43
New Leaf 1989.25
New Life on the Planet 1995.04
New Life, A 1997.09
New Look Feeling 1954.17
New Look, The 1948.08, 1949.09
New Love is Old, A 1931.37
New Love, A 1928.17
New Man 1985.05
New March 1894.50
New Me, The 1953.02
New Morning is Dawning in Chosun 1997.16
New Music 1998.01
New New York 1930.25
New Orleans 1922.22
New Orleans Hop Scop Blues 1975.20, 1982.12, 1999.06
New Orleans Jeunesee Doree 1929.38
New Orleans Jeunesse Doree 1910.35, 1978.19
New Pair of Shoes, A 1964.05
New Palm Wine! 1881.04
New Rhythm Ballet 1925.22
New Saucepan, The 1870.38
New Sensation 1934.40
New Sounds 1957.10
New Spring Will Come to the Homeland, A 1999.05
New Sun in the Sky 1931.16, 1972.05
New Town is a Blue Town, A 1954.05
New Waltz, A 1968.13
New Way to Play Tennis, A 1905.28, 1906.24
New Ways to Dream 1994.10
New Woman 1897.21
New Year's Day 1997.17
New Year's Eve 1982.18
New York 1928.31, 1959.12
New York and Chicago 1911.07
New York at Night 1979.13
New York Blues, The 1963.27
New York City Rhythm 1976.34
New York Forever 1903.18
New York Heartbeat 1943.20
New York Hippodrome March, The 1915.25
New York is a Party 1984.15
New York is the Same Old Place 1922.33
New York isn't Such a Bad Old Town 1912.02
New York Laundry Girls, The 1898.10
New York Life 1924.05
New York Lullaby 1979.13
New York Police, The 1895.34
New York Serenade 1928.03
New York Summer, A 1979.13
New York Town 1923.06
New York Town is Full of Strangers 1927.27
New York, New York 1944.33, 1958.21, 1971.15, 1977.02, 1979.13, 1989.03, 1991.04, 1998.16
New York, U.S.A. 1917.25
New York, What's Become of You? 1917.35
New York, What's the Matter With You? 1913.17
New York, You're the Best Town in Europe 1911.24
New York-Paris 1935.19
New Yorker, The 1929.29
New Yorkers 1911.33
New-Fangled Tango, A 1956.16
Newlywed Express 1925.44
Newlyweds 1922.28
Newport by the Sea 1906.10
Newport Dip, The 1904.56
Newport Glide, The 1910.20, 1926.01
News 1928.38
News is most surprising, The 1888.18
News News 1938.19
Newspaper Girl, The 1918.08
Next 1911.05, 1914.12, 1972.16, 1976.02
Next Best Thing to Love 2001.01
Next Big River 1931.02
Next Bigga River I'm Bound to Cross, The 1931.02
Next Dance With You, The 1921.14
Next May be the Right, The 1910.37
Next President's Goin' to be a Coon, The 1897.01
Next Summer in Dear Old New York 1904.39
Next Time I Care, The 1945.14
Next Time it Happens, The 1955.27, 1996.04
Next to Lovin' I Like Fightin' 1975.03
Next to Texas, I Love You 1947.16
Next! 1887.13
Nez Pas 1902.02
Niagra Falls 1921.36
Nibo - Carnival 1945.07
Nic-Nax 1926.22
Niccolo's Piccolo 1903.03, 1904.44
Nice Baby 1925.49
Nice dilemma we have here, A 1875.35
Nice Little Girls and Boys 1907.18
Nice Little Plot for a Play, A 1909.26
Nice People, Nice Talk 1953.03
Nice Place to Visit, A 1931.16
Nice Sweet Kiss, A 1919.19
Nice t' Get Up in th' Morning 1930.17
Nice Ways 1972.04
Nice Work if You Can Get It 1983.06, 1992.02, 1999.10
Nice Young Man 1877.27
Nicest Thing, The 1961.21
Nicholas 1924.01
Nicholas and Alexandra 1977.09
Nick 1941.01
Nick Carter 1902.06
Nickel to My Name, A 1941.13
Nickel Under the Foot 1937.08
Nickel Under Your Foot 1995.12
Nicodemus 1905.33, 1905.34, 1926.46
Nicolo's Piccolo 1904.13
Niece, what do you here? 1881.04
Nigger and the Bee, The 1892.21, 1893.37
Nigger Heaven Blues 1927.36
Night 1934.20, 1934.29
Night After Night 1930.32, 1946.22
Night and Day 1953.10, 1978.26, 1980.06, 1999.05
Night Before the Morning After, The 1937.16
Night Bird is Calling, The 1906.39
Night Birds 1926.33
Night Birds Cooing 1888.05
Night Brigade, The 1912.45
Night Club Nights 1932.01
Night Fever 1999.15
Night Flies By 1951.22
Night Flight 1936.02
Night has spread her pall once more 1888.35
Night Idyl, The 1922.06
Night in June, A 1924.18
Night in the Orient, A 1918.05
Night in the Ukraine, A 1980.08
Night in Venice 1885.08
Night is Dark, The 1882.75
Night it had to End, The 1988.10
Night it Happened, The 1930.14
Night Letter 1971.18
Night Life in Old Manhattan 1914.15
Night Maloney Landed in New York, The 1889.39
Night May be Dark, The 1963.25
Night May Have its Sadness 1924.01
Night of Love 1919.35
Night of Masquerade, A 1927.47
Night of My Nights 1953.16, 1978.03
Night of Screams 1990.17
Night of the Embassy Ball, The 1937.15
Night on Daylights realm encroaches, The 1871.19
Night on Disco Mountain 1999.15
Night People 1959.12
Night Porter, The 1961.25
Night Song 1964.32
Night That Goldman Spoke at Union Square, The 1998.01
Night That Made America Famous, The 1975.05
Night They Drove Old Dixie Down, The 1982.22
Night They Invented Champagne, The 1973.12, 1999.23
Night Time 1906.21
Night Time in Araby 1924.19
Night Time's the Right Time to Spoon With the Girl You Love 1912.16
Night Time, The 1920.21
Night Waltz 1973.04
Night was Alive, The 1997.06
Night was All to Blame, The 1947.13
Night was Made for Love, The 1931.37
Night Watch 1872.23
Night, Night, A Lullaby 1972.17
Night-in-Jail, The 1892.29
Nightcap, A 1880.64
Nightie Parade 1911.30
Nightingale 1906.10, 1998.14
Nightingale and the Rose, The 1892.52, 1907.08, 1922.32
Nightingale and the Star, The 1905.57
Nightingale sigh'd for the moon's bright ray, The 1879.05
Nightingale Song 1891.30, 1892.02
Nightingale Waltz Song 1891.41
Nightingale's Trill 1880.42
Nightingale, Bring Me a Rose 1953.17
Nightingale, The 1855.03, 1877.22, 1891.37, 1922.06
Nightingale, the Moon and I, The 1945.08
Nightlife 1962.04
Nightmare 1974.22
Nightmare Land 1905.52
Nightmare March, The 1907.14
Nightmare, The 1904.13, 1904.44, 1946.06, 2001.01
Nights on Broadway 1999.15
Nightskate 1978.12
Nighttime is No Time for Thinking, The 1945.04
Nightwind 1934.15
Nighty-Night 1925.49
Nigun 1966.21
Nigun Fun Der Megille, Der 1968.22
Nihilists, The 1911.41
Nijigo Novgo Glide 1923.19
Nijinski 1916.10
Nile, The 1926.01
Nimm, Zigeunder, deine Geige-Jaj Mamam, Bruderherz ich kauf mir die Welt 1984.05
Nina 1928.25, 1929.06, 1986.19
Nina Espagnola 1918.30
Nina Rosa 1930.27
Nine 1982.09
Nine Little Missionaries 1920.13
Nine O'Clock 1959.22, 1985.04

Nine Supreme Ball Players 1933.25
Nine to Five 1982.15
Nineteen Hundred and Eight 1924.05
Nineteen Hundred and Eight Life, The 1929.03
Nineteen Hundred and Eighty Seven - Gospel/Hip Hop Rant 1996.07
Nineteen Hundred and Fifty Six - Them Conkheads 1996.07
Nineteen Hundred and Forty Five 1978.25
Nineteen Hundred and Seventy Seven - Blackout 1996.07
Nineteen Hundred and Sixty Seven - Hot Fun 1996.07
Nineteen Hundred and Thirty Four Hot Chocolate Jazz Babies Review, The 1978.28
Nineteen Hundred and Twenty One 1920.47
1999 1986.02
Nineteen Twenty-Seven 1927.29
Ninety Again! 1970.19
Ninety Nine Percent Pure 1927.11
Ninja Raid 1990.17
Ninon was a Naughty Girl 1920.03
Ninon's Father Doesn't Seem to Mind 1904.05
Nippy 1925.50
Nita 1905.20
Nitchevo 1963.08
Niwah Wechi 1999.09
Nix my dolly 1886.53
Nix on the Concertina, Lena 1910.18
Niyayibona Lento Engiyibonayo 1988.02
Nize Baby 1926.18
Nkosi Sikelel' iAfrika 1993.04
Nkosi Sikeleli' Afrika 1988.02
No 1969.07
No Bad News 1975.01
No Better Way to Start a Case 1933.25
No Bird Ever Flew so High He Didn't Have to Light 1904.52
No Birdie Ever Flew so High 1919.33
No Boom Boom 1968.30, 1983.14
No Bottom 1940.01
No Comprenez, No Capish 1933.25
No Contest 1988.09
No Damaged Goods 1913.33
No Discount on That 1884.11
No Doubt I Ought to Try 1911.01
No Encore 1989.26
No Foolin' 1926.18
No for an Answer 1941.01
No Gems, No Roses, No Gentlemen 1946.01
No Good Can Come from Bad 1985.18
No Goodbyes 1974.05
No Hearts for Sale 1925.44
No Heel-Taps 1884.57
No Holds Barred 1982.04
No Home, No Job 1956.04
No I Could Never Forget 1974.19
No Journey's Too Far for a Lover 1913.14
No Lies 1978.13
No Life 1984.08
No Lookin' Back 1940.21
No Love, No Nothin' 1988.08
No Lover for Me 1950.20
No Man 1990.17
No Man is an Island 1955.13
No Man is Worth It 1983.08
No Man Left for Me 1991.07
No Man's Land 1918.05
No Matter What 1994.04
No Matter What Others May Say 1904.17
No Matter Where 1976.33
No Mercy He Need Expect 1892.55
No Moon 1997.06
No More 1964.32, 1987.18, 1989.16, 1993.02
No more can love 1859.16
No More Candy 1963.14
No More Dancing 1926.37
No More Girls for Me 1917.14
No More Mornings 1982.18
No More Rainbows 1983.20
No More Staying Out Late 1911.13
No More Weighted Down by Sorrow 1900.39
No More, No More to Part Forever 1894.47
No mortal power can now avail 1868.02
No Never 1988.05
No News Today 1946.04
No No 1894.05
No Offence 1919.42
No One 1972.18
No One But You 1911.15
No One Cares for Dreams 1947.13
No One has Ever Loved Me 1994.05
No One Here 1882.33
No One in the World Like You 1898.46
No One is Alone 1987.18, 1989.16, 1990.09
No One Knows 1925.38
No One Knows Me 1960.01
No One Knows Who I Am 1997.09
No One Loves a Clown 1921.34
No One Loves Me 1950.01
No One Thinks of Me 1900.57
No One'll Ever Love You 1958.14
No One's Ever Kissed Me 1925.50
No Other Eyes 1923.07
No Other Gal 1920.45
No Other Girl 1924.22
No Other Love 1953.08
No Other Love was Meant for Me 1929.17
No Peace in My Soul 1934.37
No Peach Hangs too High for Him Then No Peach Hangs too High for Me 1905.33
No Place But Home 1975.13
No Place Like London 1979.06
No Place Like This Country 1952.13
No Power on Earth can e'er divide 1750.01
No Power on Earth Can E'er Divide 1957.02
No Questions 1964.35
No Room for Me 1891.32
No Room in My Heart for You 1928.21
No Shoes 1946.01
No Show To-night 1905.44
No Sinners in Jah Yard 1980.05
No Song More Pleasing 1976.08
No Spy am I 1896.41
No Strings 1962.03
No Such Thing as Love 1974.22
No Surprises 1980.23
No Talent 1966.30
No Thank You 1932.19
No Time 1948.22, 1968.05
No Time at All 1972.22
No Time for Love 1949.02
No Trouble at All, it's as Easy as Falling Off a Portable Bar 1973.08
No Turning Back 1999.22
No Two People 1980.29
No Understand 1965.06
No Use Pretending 1936.27
No Way in Hell 1972.11
No Way to Stop It 1959.24, 1998.03
No Wealth Without Labor 1885.66
No Wedding Bells for Her 1904.08
No Wedding Bells for Me 1907.15, 1958.04
No Wonder I'm Blue 1930.42
No Word for Love 1990.17
No Words 1960.12
No! Fate, Why be Defying? 1887.33
No! No! No! 1947.14, 1954.17, 1963.08
No! no! though for a moment 1859.13
No, I am Brave 1981.01
No, I dare not sing 1862.04
No, I Won't 1925.44
No, Mother, No 1942.15
No, No 1921.38
No, No Mam'selle 1947.13
No, No Nanette 1971.03
No, No! - 'Tis You 1880.69
No, No, Nanette 1925.30
No, No, No! 1911.14
No, no, this morning Hardress leaves 1868.01
No, Thank You 1973.07
No, They Can't Song 1976.10
No, You Can't Have My Heart 1938.07
No-One's Tried to Kiss Me 1947.15
Noah 1917.27, 1955.03
Noah Built the Ark 1969.10
Noah Knew a Thing or Two 1906.27
Noah's Ark 1971.14
Noah's Song 1938.02
Noah's Wife had a Wonderful Life 1920.18
Nobby Sport am I, A 1872.14
Nobel Cause of Art, The 1914.01
Nobility 1958.01
Noble's Daughter Loves to Madness, A 1854.05
Nobles of Castilian Birth 1896.13
Nobody 1905.35, 1910.18, 1976.04, 1980.27, 1999.06
Nobody But Fanny 1925.01, 1925.28
Nobody But You 1904.56, 1905.22, 1919.12, 1923.20
Nobody Does it Better 1984.06
Nobody Does it Like Me 1973.06
Nobody Does My Thing 1969.15
Nobody Else But Me 1946.01
Nobody Else But You 1959.23
Nobody Ever Died for Dear Old Rutgers 1947.16
Nobody Ever Pins Me Up 1944.01
Nobody Knows 1888.42, 1889.24, 1889.25, 1893.03, 1922.01
Nobody Knows de Trouble I See 1943.10
Nobody Knows the Answer 1906.27
Nobody Knows the Trouble I've Seen 1963.27, 1975.12
Nobody Knows What We Girls Go Through 1912.44
Nobody Knows You When You're Down and Out 1975.20, 1982.12
Nobody Loves Me 1907.11
Nobody Makes a Pass at Me 1937.14
Nobody Really Do 1979.32
Nobody Seems to Know 1914.15
Nobody Shoots No-One in Canada 1980.13
Nobody Steps on Kafritz 1967.14
Nobody Tells Me How 1978.12
Nobody Throw Those Bull 1958.20
Nobody Told Me 1948.22, 1962.03
Nobody Told Me This 1970.17
Nobody Wants Me 1926.21, 1929.02
Nobody was in Love With Me 1914.01
Nobody Will Remember Him 1983.01
Nobody's Chasing Me 1950.20
Nobody's Ever Gonna Love You 1956.04
Nobody's Gal 1922.22
Nobody's Got Anything on Me 1908.44
Nobody's Heart 1975.13
Nobody's Heart Belongs to Me 1942.15
Nobody's Heart But Mine 1948.28
Nobody's Perfect 1966.29
Nobody's Side 1988.09
Noces Espanolas 1926.11
Noch a glezele tey 1960.18
Nochum, My Son 1990.16
Nocturn, The 1927.19
Nocturna 1999.18
Nocturnal 1939.18
Nocturne 1944.21
Nodding Roses 1915.31, 1975.24
Noi de la Marc 1926.09
Noi de la Mare 1926.35
Nois voii dans labonne ville d'Orleans 1887.36
Noises in the Street 1940.18, 1948.04
Noisy Neighbors 1931.47
Nokhumke, Mayn Zun 1990.16
Nola 1977.09, 1979.14
Non Credo 1972.15
Non je n'ai rien oublie 1983.03
Non, Je Ne Regrette Rien 1981.04
Non, non jamais les hommes 1929.14
Non, nous, vous, n'irez pas 1929.11
None But the Brave Deserve the Fair 1909.02, 1913.37
None of Them's Got Anything on Me 1907.37, 1908.33
None Shall Part Us 1938.10
None shall part us from each other 1882.78
Nonsense 1908.12, 1910.12, 1917.35
Nonsense Rhymes 1869.06
Nonsensical Nonsense 1909.05
Noontide sunshine, warm and glowing 1881.04
Noovo Riche, The 1910.02
Nor That Sort of Girl 1895.22
Nora Maguire 1890.12, 1890.30
Nora Malone Call Me by Phone 1910.08
Nora Ryan 1902.23
Nordraak's Farewell 1944.21
Noreen Mavourneen 1902.36

Normal American Boy 1960.06
Normandy 1892.07, 1924.32, 1959.26
North and South of Today, The 1910.23
North Dakota, South Dakota Moon 1943.20
North Pole, The 1892.55
North Wind Doth Blow, The 1879.64
North, East, G.A.R., South and West 1913.18
North, South, East or West 1905.03
Northbound Train 1999.08
Northern Refrain 1864.12
Northwest Mounted Police, The 1925.25
Norwegian Dance 1944.21
Nose Cone 1962.02
Nose Song 1973.07
Noses 1984.02
Nostalgia 1981.14
Nostalgias 1985.07, 1993.08, 1999.18
Not a Care in the World 1941.13, 1942.12
Not a Day Goes By 1981.27, 1997.01, 2000.16
Not a Drummer 1886.24, 1888.06
Not a ghost at all 1878.16
Not a One Compares With Me 1905.52
Not a Word, Sir! 1877.23
Not Another Day Like This 1980.23
Not Anymore 1973.10
Not as Good as Last Year 1928.22
Not as Simple as I Look 1908.16
Not at Home 1904.01
Not Devotion, but Promotion 1875.19
Not Enough Magic 1984.01
Not Every Day of the Week 1965.17
Not Fade Away 1990.15
Not for a Year, Not for a Day 1925.02
Not for All the Rice in China 1933.22
Not for the Life of Me 1991.04
Not Getting Married Today 1999.20
Not gone yet, I perceive 1859.17
Not Guilty 1959.11
Not Here! Not Here! 1909.21
Not in Business Hours 1923.45
Not Like Other Girls 1904.34
Not Long Ago 1887.33
Not Love 1987.19
Not Me 1966.30, 1991.15, 2000.06
Not Meg 1955.08
Not Mine 1967.06
Not Much 1885.03, 1885.51
Not My Problem 1969.02
Not Now But Later 1913.34
Not Now, But by the Moon 1915.28
Not on Your Nellie 1968.02
Not on Your Tintype 1936.03
Not quite alone! You here! 1885.63
Not Really 1908.10
Not Since Chaplin 1982.09
Not Since Ninevah 1953.16
Not so Fast 1918.02
Not so Long Ago 1925.18
Not That I Care 1931.28
Not That Sort of Person 1910.21
Not the Proper Way to Treat a Lady 1899.35
Not the Sort of Girl I'd Care About 1898.46
Not Tomorrow 1972.24
Not Tonight 1969.01
Not too Young to Get Married 1984.15, 1985.03
Not Wanted on the Voyage 1952.11
Not While I'm Around 1979.06, 1979.13
Not Wife, Nor Maid 1880.69
Not Yet 1900.57, 1918.03
Not Yet, But Soon 1915.20
Notes 1988.01, 1988.01
Nother High Ball 1902.27
Nothin' But Talk 1904.43
Nothin' for Nothin' 1950.04
Nothin' in Common 1963.21
Nothin' Like a Picture Show 1994.06
Nothin' Up 1975.18, 1976.31
Nothing 1975.15
Nothing at All 1914.18, 1955.04
Nothing Beats Chicago 1999.22
Nothing But 1978.25
Nothing But Love 1927.46
Nothing But Nerves 1899.39
Nothing But You 1940.06, 1975.13
Nothing Can Ever Happen in New York 1927.48
Nothing Can Replace a Man 1955.04
Nothing Can Stop Me Now! 1965.19
Nothing Could be Sweeter 1927.16
Nothing Doing 1900.38
Nothing Escapes Me 1918.22
Nothing Ever Happens in Angel's Roost 1954.03
Nothing Ever Troubles Me 1908.19
Nothing from Nothing 1982.22
Nothing has Changed 1992.11
Nothing in Common 1959.19
Nothing is Like it Used to Be 1891.13
Nothing Left But Dreams 1927.11
Nothing Like a Darned Good Cry 1923.46
Nothing Like the City 1998.01
Nothing Like Us 1888.39
Nothing Man Cannot Do 1961.07
Nothing Matters 1945.17
Nothing More 1965.36
Nothing More to Look Forward To 1961.24
Nothing Naughty in a Nightie 1924.29
Nothing New Beneath the Sun 1906.21, 1907.16, 1907.20, 1908.14
Nothing Nicer Than People 1952.10
Nothing of the Sort 1883.26
Nothing on Today 1917.23
Nothing Really Happened 1982.08
Nothing Seems Right, Oh! The World is All Wrong 1917.18
Nothing to Do 1955.19, 1964.03
Nothing to do With Me 1994.12
Nothing to do With You 1900.03
Nothing to Lose 1987.19
Nothing to Wear 1914.15
Nothing too God for the Irish 1894.51
Nothing's Ever Quite Like This 1951.05
Nothing's Missing 1979.03
Nothing's too Bad for Me 1880.59
Nothing's too Good for a Good Little Girl 1916.11
Nothing's Wrong 1927.56
Nothing, Only Love 1978.22
Notice Me 1964.21
Notice Me, Horton 2000.18
Nour revendons de la chapele 1887.36
Nous avons helas! Perdu d'excellents maitres 1878.08
Nous avons vu sur notre routte Des Allemandes pleins de choucroute 1883.51
Nous n'avons pas d'enfant 1983.03
Nous serons toujours heureux 1935.19
Nous sommes consternees 1877.32
Nous sommes pretresses d'Indra 1887.35
Nous sommes un menage a la page 1929.15
Nous voici tous un rendez-vous 1883.51
Nouveau proprietaire, La 1877.32
November Song 1972.04
Novia, La 1964.02
Now 1925.47, 1936.31, 1944.21, 1973.04, 1980.23, 1981.02, 1984.06, 1988.10
Now according to our ancient custom 1887.12
Now across and beyond the deep 1887.12
Now all that we've agreed upon, O- 1895.29
Now and Then 1888.15, 1913.20, 1918.37, 1950.01
Now as Colonel, And 1893.40
Now as you see 1894.36
Now away we will go 1889.10
Now comes our chief 1884.14
Now Comes the Time 1938.08
Now Darker Falls the Night 1882.45
Now Drink a Glass With Me My Friends 1921.15
Now ended in a Panic 1884.60
Now for the Pirates' Lair! 1879.72, 1981.01
Now Give Three Cheers 1938.10
Now harken to my strict command 1884.09
Now he's going away 1879.35
Now He's Got a Beautiful Girl 1916.03
Now His Choice We See 1912.15
Now hope, now fear 1855.01
Now hurrah! Now hurrah! 1887.12
Now I Have Everything 1964.27
Now I Know 1921.21, 1931.34
Now I Know Your Face by Heart 1945.14
Now I Lay Me 1971.20
Now I Lay Me Down to Sleep 1873.10, 1979.32
Now I See It 1980.05
Now I'll get a wife 1880.54
Now I'm Gonna be Bad 1999.09
Now I'm Ready for a Frau 1961.27
Now I'se Got Some Money, Well, I'm Comin' Round 1900.07
Now I've Married a Millionaire 1907.41
Now if you'll excuse me 1882.63
Now is the Month of Maying 1963.28
Now is the South-Wind Blowing 1913.32
Now is the Time 1924.17, 1984.15
Now is the Time to Fall in Love 1986.06
Now is this not Ridiculous? 1881.37
Now it's Fall 1971.09
Now joy is in the air 1895.32
Now let begin 1889.10
Now let the glorious Sun of Joy 1866.18
Now let the royal lieges 1890.02
Now Let the Weeping Cease 1988.05
Now My Season's Here 1975.23
Now One and All 1869.07
Now our King's command fulfilling 1887.12
Now Our Little Game is Ended 1868.03
Now our rivalry is o'er 1863.04
Now take your seats at table spread 1887.44
Now Tell Us We Pray You 1881.37
Now That I've Got it, I Don't Want It 1909.09
Now That I've Got My Strength 1942.15
Now That I've Seen Her 1991.03
Now That You Know Your Way 1897.20
Now That's Tap 1996.07
Now the Carriages All are Waiting 1905.46
Now the Dance of Fate Begins 1870.27
Now the Spell 1884.57
Now the Twilight 1882.75
Now the Vintage Time 1881.22
Now then! Hurry, scurry! 1884.14
Now there's that horrid Milly Jones 1881.06
Now This is the Song of the Devonshire Men 1902.25
Now to Free the Gas Boys 1886.32
Now to Hear the Pilgrims Preaching 1883.12
Now to my lord and king 1887.12
Now to the Banquet we press 1879.10
Now tremble, you traitor 1880.46
Now watch me, while I try to win this lady fair 1889.10
Now We are Glorified 1927.37
Now what would I do if you proved untrue 1895.29
Now When I was a Boy 1886.15
Now with care you must form every letter 1888.07
Now with shouts of joy 1853.02
Now Won't You Come? 1882.75
Now wouldn't you like to rule the roost? 1884.09
Now You has Jazz 1976.32
Now You Know 1981.27
Now You See it, Now You Don't 1938.08
Now You See Me, Now You Don't 1988.20
Now You Talks Mighty Big in the Country 1940.01
Now's the Moment 1982.09
Now's the Time 1967.06
Now, Darling We Must Part 1896.48
Now, Did You Know? 1895.25
Now, Gentlemen and Ladies 1871.19
Now, Here's to the 'Prentices 1903.21
Now, Marie, I prithee hear me 1859.12
Now, Morris 1962.01
Now, now, now 1859.08
Now, O Lips, Say Goodbye 1950.05
Now, Of My Village 1881.22
Now, trumpeters, commence 1881.25
Nowadays 1975.14, 1999.01
Nowhere Man 1974.24, 1977.10
Nowhere to Go But Up 1962.24
Ntaba Zenyuka 1977.01
Nub of the Nation, The 1971.20
Nude Descending a Staircase 1913.37
Nudel, Nudel, Nupp, Nupp 1906.49
Nuit et Jour 1999.05
Nuits blanches 1934.32
Number 12 Train 1954.11
Numberless are the World's Wonders 1988.05
Numbers 1970.20, 1971.20
Nummy Num Num 1894.38

Nunca Tuvo Novio 1985.07
Nunky, darling 1884.14
Nuns Song 1975.23
Nur Temp'rament 1920.46
Nurse Girls and Doctors 1907.12
Nurse, Nurse, Nurse 1914.09
Nursery Clock, The 1923.40
Nursery Fanfare 1918.16
Nursery Melodies 1899.22
Nursery Rhyme Dances 1905.47
Nursery Rhymes 1879.64, 1888.06, 1901.27, 1902.19, 1905.56, 1908.41, 1911.02
Nurses' Chorus 1912.08
Nut Brown Ale 1903.21
Nut Sundae, A 1914.15
Nutcracker Suite, The 1955.13
Nuthin' 1922.03
Nuthin' Like a Celebration 1951.05
Nutmeg Insurance 1945.18
Nuts 1913.04, 1946.06
Nuts Over You 1934.04
NYC Rhythm 1991.10
Nymphs and Satyr 1903.40

O Caspian 1880.46
O Come to Me When Daylight Sets 1860.03
O cruel, cruel, cruel Case 1750.01
O Dry Those Tears 1924.31
O Father, We Regret 1883.12
O Fenihan 1876.30
O for Contracts in I'll go 1861.03
O France, beloved France! 1886.50
O Gabriel, My Best Beloved 1885.58
O Greedy People 2000.10
O Happy Pair, or the load stars 1857.03
O Heart of My Country 1945.14
O Heart! My Lover's Near! 1884.57
O Holy Night 1998.19
O jag' dem Gluck nicht nach 1984.05
O Lovely Home 1894.22
O Lovely Roses 1908.43
O ma maitresse bien aimee 1887.35
O make way for the wise men 1894.15
O Mia Speranza 1908.40
O Misere 1974.06
O Moment of Bliss 1866.14
O Moonlight 1894.47
O Need I Speak 1918.36
O Night! O Day! 1953.10
O Paradise of Love 1917.34
O Picture Charming 1876.30
O Polly, you might have toy'd and kist 1750.01
O Promise Me 1892.45
O rapture, when alone together 1890.02
O Sam! 1929.16
O Sing a Welcome 1894.33
O Sole Mio - Whose Soul are You? 1927.15
O Strange Situation 1905.46
O sunny south 1887.04
O Surprise! 1884.57
O Tell Me, Daisy 1907.01
O Tixo, Tixo, Help Me 1949.15, 1972.06
O What a Row 1879.03
O what Pain it is to part! 1750.01
O why am I moody and sad? 1887.10
O William, sweet William 1882.63
O Woman's Fickle! 1880.69
O! hone a me 1859.01
O! Mystic Moon in Sapphire Sea 1903.19
O' Leo! 1935.12
O'Brien Girl, The 1921.32
O'Dooley's First Five O'Clock Tea 1897.30, 1897.40
O'er Hill and Dale 1892.55
O'er Ocean Gleaming 1890.33
O'er th' Hills tae Ardentinny 1928.05
O'er the Blue Waters 1911.32
O'er the season vernal 1875.35
O'er the Snows 1907.47
O'er Their Young Hearts 1884.57
O'er this Youth once so Painted 1871.19
O'Heigh! 1894.22
O'Reilly 1904.28
O'Reilly's Kettledrum 1891.03
O'Reilly, the Mayor of the Bowery 1905.02
O'Reily, I'm Ashamed of You 1921.21
O'Toole 1921.13
O, April Eyes 1904.25
O, Cherie - La La 1921.12
O, Come My Lou 1907.12
O, Fly Sweet Bird 1892.55
O, Glorious Sun 1904.28
O, Heart of Love 1936.28
O, Kaiser, Dear Kaiser 1910.36
O, Love Divine 1904.23
O, Lovely Maiden 1898.28
O, Lovely Umbrella 1880.19
O, Marie 1916.25
O, Miss Walkaround, Come Walking Out With Me 1963.22
O, My Father! 1880.69
O, Never Trust to Strangers 1908.43
O, shocking sight 1882.63
O, Strange, Oh Sweet Surprise 1894.29
O, Thank You Kindly, My Pretty Dears 1912.40
O, the Picnic in Manassas 1963.22
O, What a Lovely Evening 1969.11
O, What a Pain it is to Part 1957.02
O, What Beauty! 1881.22
O, What Blessings to Receive 1963.27
O, what hopes at their height 1855.06
O, why is my love 1882.63
O, Won't You Shed One Little Tear for Me? 1907.08
O-H-I-O 1920.18
O-o-h, Maybe it's a Robber 1911.25
O.H.M.S. 1964.29
O.I.C. 1910.11
O.I.L. Spells Oil 1920.20
O.K. - 1-A 1942.26
O.K. America 1932.14
O.K. for TV 1951.23
O.K. Two-Step 1913.19
O.P.E.C. Maiden 1981.25
Oahu 1932.19
Oak Leaf Memorial Park 1973.11
Oaken Bucket 1894.44
Oath, Glory of War, The 1889.33
Oath, The 1961.08
Obani Labaya 1997.14
Obedient Mary 1895.42
Object Matrimony 1899.25
Oblige the Ladies 1891.14, 1892.06
Oblivia 1957.17
Obsession 1997.09
Ocarina 1942.30
Ocarina, The 1950.15
Occasional Flight of Fancy 1965.33
Ocean Blues 1920.13
Ocean is Different 1999.22
Ocean of Dreams 1916.05
Ocean Swell 1883.26
Ocean's Fond Caress 1902.21
Ocean, the Ocean, The 1914.28
Oceans of Love 1932.14
Och, the Spalpeen! Let Him Drown 1902.25
Och, thin! 1886.15
Ochone! Far, Oh Far is the Mango Island 1912.40
Ochone, When I Used to be Young! 1897.03
Octette to Bacchus 1903.07
October 1950.01
Octopus Song 1954.15
Octopus, The 1973.08
Odd Lots, Job Lots 1917.15
Odd Moments 1953.12
Odds and Ends of Love, The 1962.24
Ode and Sun Dance 1921.23
Ode de Aphrodite 1909.07
Ode to a Key 1964.35
Ode to Lola 1951.18
Ode to Menelik 1906.14
Ode to Suicide 1982.23
Ode to the Bridge 1965.01
Ode to the Styx 1928.49
Ode to the Sun 1906.14
Ode to Virginity 1981.24
Ode, The 1909.01
Odle De O do 'I Do 1928.06
Odun De 1999.09
Oedipus Rex a la Jazz 1923.41
Of all fates poor maids pursuing 1885.28
Of All Her Sex a Paragon 1911.01
Of all the fine fellows that sail on the sea 1880.04
Of all the Friends in time of Grief 1750.01
Of all the great men of history 1890.44
Of course each Frenchman is aware 1888.07
Of Course I Never Carry Tales 1890.03
Of fairy wand had I the power 1848.04
Of happiness the very pith 1890.02
Of New Pluckt Roses 1883.12
Of the court a Magnate am I 1882.60
Of the Dignified Position 1880.47
Of the People Stomp 1942.26
Of the Stars and Stripes I am Dreaming 1902.41
Of Thee I Sing 1931.48
Of V We Sing 1942.05
Of Viceroys Though We've Had 1902.25
Off for a Sail 1910.22
Off for Atlantic City 1903.01
Off Limits 1997.12
Off on a Week-End Cruise 1937.07
Off the Record 1937.13
Off to Cairo 1901.19
Off to Fairyland 1900.03
Off to Gluckstein 1937.11
Off to Gottenberg 1908.25
Off to Greenwich Village 1924.36
Off to New York 1907.18
Off to Paris 1906.49
Off to Russia 1908.34, 1911.41
Off to See New York 1927.36
Off to Spain 1917.25
Off to the Deacon 1936.12
Off to the Derby 1904.42, 1907.16
Off to the Hunt 1900.03, 1906.13
Off to the Matinee 1911.42
Off to the Races 1985.18
Off to the Wedding 1911.42
Off to Turkey 1903.06
Off to Wimblemere 1924.38
Off We Go 1889.46, 1922.05
Off We Go to Venus 1894.05
Off-Time 1929.23, 1978.09
Office Blues, The 1919.34
Office Hours 1914.31
Officer O'Halley 1885.42
Officers of the 25th 1917.14
Officers of the Calvary 1899.06
Official Resume 1930.02
Oh better for to live and die 1881.06
Oh Boy 1990.15
Oh Bury Me Not on the Lone Prairie 1931.02
Oh Catch Me, Mr. Harris, Cause I'm Falling for You! 1980.17
Oh Could I But His Heart Enslave 1863.06
Oh Cruel Love 1895.44
Oh Dad 1922.13
Oh Darling 1974.24
Oh Days of Yore 1898.72
Oh Dear! It's Not Right! 1933.23
Oh dear! Oh dear! 1878.16
Oh Dear, it Breaks My Heart 1954.06
Oh Doctor 1912.26
Oh Dream of Life 1892.55
Oh Fabulous One in Your Ivory Tower 1941.04
Oh fairest maid beneath the Sun 1860.03
Oh Fatherland 1978.07
Oh Foolish Heart 2000.10
Oh Gee - Oh Joy 1928.03
Oh Girl 1997.21
Oh Glad is the Life of a Sailor at Sea 1904.10
Oh Great God of Power 1968.11
Oh happy fair 1857.03
Oh happy moment 1859.16
Oh Happy We 1974.06, 1982.20, 1997.10
Oh here I am chuck full of woe 1848.03
Oh Honey, My Honey 1894.38
Oh How Happy We Shall Be 1882.58
Oh How I Hate to Get Up in the Morning 1918.19, 1942.20
Oh How Much Good He Does Me 1919.26

Oh How That Man Can Love 1928.23
Oh How You Look in the Light 2000.20
Oh I Want to be Good But My Eyes Won't Let Me 1916.25
Oh is there not one little maid 1881.06
Oh Jesus - it's Time to Take Out the Nags 1979.29
Oh Joy Unbounded 1861.03
Oh joy! Oh rapture! 1884.14
Oh joy, oh rapture unforseen! 1879.05
Oh Lawd, I'm on My Way 1983.04
Oh Little Stars 1983.04
Oh Lonely Heart 1899.03
Oh Love Me Now 1922.42
Oh Lovely Star of Night 1921.15
Oh maid of witching grace 1895.43
Oh Mama Buy Me That 1893.42
Oh Margery 1905.32
Oh Marjorie 1903.29
Oh Me, Oh My, Oh You 1921.10
Oh Mein Papa 1962.17
Oh Mein, Liebchen 1961.27
Oh Mr. Manager tell us of the play 1895.17
Oh My 1898.56
Oh my goodness, here's the nobility! 1895.29
Oh my Heart with Love is beating 1880.24
Oh My Love 1894.38
Oh My! How We Pose 1885.02
Oh My, How We Pose 2000.12
Oh My, Yes 1931.26
Oh Naughty Mr. Bronson 1897.39
Oh no! not in these boots 1870.44
Oh Precious Thought 1913.37
Oh Promise Me 1928.25, 1944.25
Oh promise me by those Bright Eyes 1871.10
Oh Say, Oh Sue 1922.21
Oh Say, Wouldn't it be a Dream 1980.10
Oh Setting Sun, You Bid the World Good-Bye 1902.25
Oh Shenandoah 1966.15
Oh Sun 1979.10
Oh Sunlight of No Light 1988.05
Oh That We Might Fly 1883.12
Oh That We Two Were Maying 1892.45
Oh the Study of Feminine Ways 1978.07
Oh Theobald, Ol Elmer 1929.32
Oh They Call Me Kullman With a Capital K 2000.14
Oh this dolce farniente 1851.03
Oh to be a Movie Star 1966.18
Oh What a Circus 1979.23
Oh what a fund of joy 1895.29
Oh what a horrid crowding 1871.10
Oh what a Lovely Creature 1871.10
Oh What a Lovely War 1964.28
Oh What Delight to be Dancing 1902.07
Oh When I Meet Her in the Fountain 1892.29
Oh Where is the Antidote 1895.04
Oh Why Did He Come 1882.33
Oh Why This Apprehension? 1886.15
Oh Woman in Days of Romance 1904.29
Oh Yes, We are the Chorus 1886.47
Oh yes, we are the Chorus 1888.36
Oh You Beautiful Spring 1912.41
Oh You Chicago, Oh You New York 1911.08
Oh You Circus Day 1912.25
Oh You Crazy Moon 1939.29
Oh You Incense, You Madden Me! 1886.15
Oh You Summertime Romeo 1910.16
Oh You Sweet Old Watcha-May-Call-It 1928.33
Oh You! 1925.40
Oh you've rights 1853.02
Oh! a private buffoon is a lighthearted loon 1888.35
Oh! Argentine 1918.30
Oh! Be Joyful! 1999.08
Oh! Beware! 1882.75
Oh! By Jingo 1919.37
Oh! By Jingo! Oh by Gee, You're the Only Girl for Me 1919.37
Oh! Calcutta! 1971.04, 1976.27
Oh! cruel, cruel case 1854.06
Oh! Dat Low Bridge 1885.66
Oh! dear - Oh! dear! 1881.27
Oh! deep within my inmost heart 1889.10
Oh! Doctor, Doctor 1918.42
Oh! Don't You Tickle Me 1878.04, 1878.12
Oh! fond moment of delight 1859.16
Oh! Friendship 1921.15
Oh! Fudge! 1901.23
Oh! Gee, Oh! Gosh, Oh! Golly I'm in Love 1923.20
Oh! Happy Cat and Bagpipes 1840.03
Oh! Hark, Baby, Hark 1880.09
Oh! He Hit Me in de Nose 1878.12
Oh! He Hit Me in the Nose 1878.04
Oh! Heaven aid me now 1859.18
Oh! Honorka 1912.17
Oh! How I Hate Women 1925.29
Oh! How We Love Our Alma Mater 1926.28
Oh! I Must Go Home To-Night 1909.29
Oh! I'll Greet Him Soft and Slow 1904.01
Oh! If You Were a Girl 1913.36
Oh! It's Nice to Get Money from Home 1918.36
Oh! Joseph 1924.39
Oh! Joy, our chef is sav'd 1884.09
Oh! kaufen sic ein besen 1859.12
Oh! Let me go, you naughty man 1886.40
Oh! Listen to the Band 1898.46
Oh! Love Divine! 1868.08
Oh! love for me 1859.18
Oh! Love sends its Vot'ries on wild expeditions 1834.03
Oh! Mama 1884.28
Oh! Marguerite, my darling 1889.54
Oh! Men of Dark and Dismal Fate 1879.72
Oh! my dummy! 1895.32
Oh! My Poor Moon 1901.07
Oh! No Regular Wife 1881.11
Oh! Oh! Delphine 1912.34
Oh! Oh! Oh! 1908.40
Oh! Osca, Dear! Oh! Osca, Dear 1882.39
Oh! Pa, do let us go 1859.05
Oh! Pa, let us go 1861.03
Oh! Pauline 1915.20
Oh! Polly 1854.06
Oh! Pom-Pom-Pom-Pompadour 1924.39
Oh! ponder well 1854.06
Oh! Pray Don't Speak so Loud 1882.33
Oh! Professor 1923.04
Oh! Rage, Oh! Wild Despair 1846.01
Oh! Sam 1925.43
Oh! She's the Last Rose of Summer 1919.15
Oh! Sonny! 1897.39
Oh! Such a night 1882.44
Oh! That Mitzi 1932.04
Oh! That Yankiana Rag 1908.39, 1909.15
Oh! The World of Peace 1912.40
Oh! Thou Art Fair, My Love 1903.06
Oh! tis charming 1859.13
Oh! Trust My Love 1882.33
Oh! What a Chance to Take 1911.02
Oh! What a Difference in the Morning 1891.13
Oh! What is Woman's Duty 1903.21
Oh! what pleasure 1848.04
Oh! when thus they've bereft me 1855.06
Oh! Where am I? 1866.07, 1866.21
Oh! Where's My Girl? 1882.75
Oh! Who Will be a Queen! 1921.15
Oh! Yes by Day 1834.03
Oh! You Coon 1908.22
Oh! You Girls! 1911.32
Oh! You Sweet Stuff 1918.39
Oh', Dat Watermelon 1890.29
Oh, a bedouin free is the life for me 1895.19
Oh, a Jolly Good Time We Have! Oh, Yes, Das So 1873.19
Oh, Ah! 1888.43
Oh, Alice 1923.41
Oh, Allah 1914.01
Oh, Babe 1921.19
Oh, Baby 1928.08
Oh, Barbara 1880.59
Oh, be Careful of the Crocodile 1906.41
Oh, be Jolly 1909.19
Oh, beautiful land of Spain 1896.13
Oh, Bess, Oh Where's My Bess 1983.04
Oh, Better Far to Live and Die 1879.72, 1981.01
Oh, Black Swan 1947.10
Oh, Boy 1969.01
Oh, Boy Can We Deduct 1939.19
Oh, Boy! 1907.52
Oh, Bride of Mine, Oh Baby Wife 1879.71
Oh, Brother! 1981.25
Oh, Cecilia 1914.02
Oh, Daddy 1926.22
Oh, Daddy, Please! 1917.06
Oh, daughters high and fair 1866.34
Oh, de Lawd Shake de Heaven 1935.13
Oh, de Lawd Shake de Heavens 1983.04
Oh, dear! 1875.19
Oh, Dearie You Must Come Over 1921.19
Oh, Dere's a Somebody Knockin' at De Do 1983.04
Oh, Dinah 1873.04
Oh, Dinah, the Moon am Shining 1897.56
Oh, Diogenes 1938.14, 1975.13
Oh, do Step the Two-Step 1911.27
Oh, Doctor Jesus 1935.13, 1983.04
Oh, don't despair 1859.11
Oh, Don't You See How? 1886.15
Oh, Don't You Tickle Me 1879.63
Oh, Donna Clara 1931.09
Oh, Dr. Sternroyd 1922.04
Oh, Dry the Glistening Tear 1981.01
Oh, False One, You Have Deceived Me! 1879.72, 1981.01
Oh, Fascinating Night 1914.28
Oh, Fifth Avenue 1911.42
Oh, foolish fay 1882.78
Oh, for a cot by a Silvery lake 1852.01
Oh, for a cot by a Silvery Lake 1871.10
Oh, for a Great Idea 1902.34
Oh, for the Life of a Cowboy 1927.48
Oh, Gala Day, Red-Letter Day 1928.30
Oh, Galatea! 1917.31
Oh, Gee! 1969.14
Oh, Gee, Oh Gosh 1922.10
Oh, gentlemen, listen, I pray 1875.35
Oh, George! 1880.59
Oh, Girly-Girly 1879.37
Oh, Give Me the Good Old Days 1937.14
Oh, Go Away 1912.35
Oh, Goodness 1905.36
Oh, Gosh 1928.36
Oh, Gustave 1914.07
Oh, Happy Day 1956.12
Oh, Happy Days 1989.12
Oh, Happy We 1956.15
Oh, Hard is Life for Man and Horse 1979.29
Oh, Have You Met a Man in Debt 1902.25
Oh, He'venly Father 1983.04
Oh, he, Mamma 1885.28
Oh, Heaven 1873.05
Oh, Heigh-Ho! 1906.01
Oh, Help! 1905.19
Oh, Hollow! Hollow! Hollow! 1881.37
Oh, Honey 1895.36
Oh, How Fortunate You Mortals Be 1949.02
Oh, How Happy We'll Be 1928.35
Oh, How I Hate to Get Up in the Morning 1918.21
Oh, How I Long for Someone! 1920.31
Oh, How I Love My Teacher 1906.25
Oh, How I Miss You Blues 1928.35
Oh, How My Heart! 1883.12
Oh, How Near and Yet How Far 1913.26
Oh, How She Can Sing 1919.15
Oh, How Sweet is the Hour of Victory 1904.55
Oh, How That Taxi Got on My Nerves 1910.31
Oh, How the Girls Adore Me 1928.48
Oh, How Warm it is Today 1918.28
Oh, How Would You Like to Pet? 1898.43
Oh, I Can't Sit Down 1935.13, 1983.04
Oh, I have wrought much evil with my spells! 1879.10
Oh, I Must Go Home Tonight 1960.17
Oh, I. Reddick 1894.15
Oh, Innocent Young Thing 1911.08
Oh, is She Dumb? 1922.25
Oh, is There Not One Maiden Breast 1879.72, 1938.10, 1981.01
Oh, it is Indeed a Blessing 1888.19
Oh, it is Such an Unheard-of Proceeding to Marry Her to a Lord 1886.15
Oh, it's Rah! Rah! Rah! 1906.30
Oh, Jesus, Come Dis-a-Way 1943.10
Oh, Joe! 1923.22

Oh, Joe, Hand Around the Beer 1873.19
Oh, Joe, With Your Fiddle and Bow 1907.04
Oh, Johnny, Oh, Johnny, Oh! 1916.25
Oh, Joy 1904.22
Oh, joy unbounded 1875.35
Oh, joyous boon! Oh, mad delight! 1879.10
Oh, Kay 1926.36
Oh, Kay! 1990.14
Oh, Kitty 1904.05
Oh, La, La, La! 1910.01
Oh, Lady 1927.58
Oh, Lady Be Good 1924.43
Oh, Lady be Good 1974.09
Oh, Lady be Good! 1999.10
Oh, Lady! Lady! 1918.03
Oh, light, both beauteous and reliable 1886.40
Oh, Listen to the Band 1899.31
Oh, Lonely One 1945.13
Oh, look here, oh, look dar 1873.04
Oh, Look Who's Here 1906.48
Oh, Love 1880.47
Oh, Love, Airy Like, Fairy Like 1902.20
Oh, luck unequalled 1893.02
Oh, Maiden 1903.38
Oh, maiden rich 1894.15
Oh, Maria 1885.03
Oh, Marie 1907.24
Oh, Marie! 1905.22
Oh, Maritana! 1848.04
Oh, Married Life 1910.27
Oh, Mary, Don't You Weep 1930.10
Oh, Men of Dark and Dismal Fate 1981.01
Oh, Mighty King 1889.34
Oh, Mister Abrams 1908.37
Oh, Mister Postman 1920.29
Oh, Mr. Brown 1907.32
Oh, Mr. Dream Man 1912.09
Oh, Mr. Harris, You're a Naughty Man! 1980.17
Oh, Mr. Johnson 1896.45
Oh, Mr. Jupiter 1910.10
Oh, Mr. Registrar 1907.15
Oh, Mr. Scarecrow Man 1910.29
Oh, Mrs. Lynde! 1971.21
Oh, Mrs.Larry 1950.01
Oh, My Darling, Tilly 1915.28
Oh, My Daughter 1894.33
Oh, My Gal 1890.29
Oh, My Heart 1943.11
Oh, My Lodgings 1892.45
Oh, My Lovin' Brother 1943.10
Oh, My Molly is Waiting for Me 1888.40
Oh, My Mysterious Lady 1958.20, 1958.21
Oh, My! 1917.28
Oh, Naughty, Naughty 1877.39
Oh, never, never, never 1875.35
Oh, now nice 1887.43
Oh, Oh, Baby 1948.17
Oh, Oh, Oh, it's a Lovely War 1921.12
Oh, Paddy Mahon 1857.06
Oh, Papa 1922.17
Oh, Papa and Mama 1993.04
Oh, Papa! 1917.22
Oh, Paris town's the spot for me 1888.07
Oh, Peggy 1927.58
Oh, Please 1926.46, 1959.22, 1985.04
Oh, please you not to go away 1893.02
Oh, please, my dear Miss Tropics! 1881.11
Oh, ponder well! Be not severe 1750.01
Oh, Princess Minutezza 1898.25
Oh, Promise Me 1891.29, 1929.43
Oh, Rash Muezzin! 1893.40
Oh, Rise and Shine 1930.10
Oh, Romeo 1911.42
Oh, Rosalie 1911.01
Oh, Say No More 1907.48
Oh, Say Wouldn't it be a Dream? 1906.08
Oh, Scandal, Infamy 1866.34
Oh, Schneider, How You Vas? 1870.24, 1871.15
Oh, See What She Hangs Out in Our Alley 1922.27
Oh, Senor, Pray 1902.01
Oh, Sergeant Meryll, is it true - 1888.35
Oh, Shrine of Psyche 1902.15
Oh, silent night, thy light and shadows 1887.12
Oh, Silver Moon! 1909.15
Oh, Sky, Goodbye 1952.15
Oh, slumber my darling 1862.02
Oh, smile as thou wert wont to smile 1855.06
Oh, so 'La' Mi 1925.14
Oh, so Happy! 1888.06
Oh, so Nice 1928.43
Oh, Sophia 1894.25
Oh, spare a daughter 1896.13
Oh, Star of Hope 1904.05
Oh, Stars That Form the Milky Way 1898.25
Oh, strange delusion! Oh, wild confusion! 1886.40
Oh, strange indeed is this our parting 1887.12
Oh, Sunlit Sea 1898.48
Oh, Susanna 1955.13
Oh, Susannah 1944.32
Oh, Susey, let us married be 1873.04
Oh, Tender Remembrance 1896.48
Oh, That Beautiful Rag 1910.19
Oh, That Shimmy 1919.19
Oh, That We Two Were Maying 1919.02
Oh, That's the Worst of Girls 1899.38
Oh, the Age in Which We're Living 1902.25
Oh, the Girls 1903.05
Oh, the Heat and the Skeet 1906.48
Oh, the Paying Guests 1903.38
Oh, the rapture unrestrained 1894.15
Oh, the Regatta 1938.06
Oh, the Rio Grande 1936.28
Oh, the Thinks You Can Think! 2000.18
Oh, the Women 1975.22
Oh, There Across the Water 1960.18
Oh, this Gout! 1879.35
Oh, This is Most Ecstatical 1888.19
Oh, This Love 1914.26
Oh, Those Boys 1911.31
Oh, Those Days 1915.02
Oh, Those Jazzing Toes 1922.13
Oh, Those Puritans! 1929.33
Oh, Up! It's Up! 1913.32
Oh, Waiter 1921.38
Oh, Warrior Grim! 1896.13
Oh, We Know 1910.10
Oh, we titti, titti tremble 1877.39
Oh, Whack! 1853.01
Oh, What a Beautiful Baby You Turned Out to Be 1918.18
Oh, What a Beautiful Mornin' 1943.04, 1993.16
Oh, What a Beautiful Morning 1911.07
Oh, What a Beautiful Ocean 1897.45
Oh, What a Bump! 1902.44
Oh, What a Circus 1997.01
Oh, what a day we've had 1879.35
Oh, What a Difference 1892.38
Oh, What a Difference in the Morning 1893.23
Oh, What a Filthy Night Court! 1937.08
Oh, What a Girl 1925.35
Oh, What a Girl! 1919.19
Oh, What a Happy Day 1922.08
Oh, What a Life 1942.27
Oh, What a Little Whopper 1919.28
Oh, What a Lovely Dance 1950.05
Oh, What a Lovely Dream 1901.21
Oh, What a Lovely Night 1960.18
Oh, What a Man 1928.25
Oh, What a Night 1885.69
Oh, What a Nite for a Party 1949.06
Oh, What a Performance! 1988.10
Oh, What a Playmate You Could Make 1926.20
Oh, what a row 1877.25
Oh, What a Row and Rumpus 1897.48
Oh, What a Sad History 1891.14
Oh, what a world this is 1886.53
Oh, What Difference in the Morning! 1891.26
Oh, what fond and fervent love 1873.05
Oh, what full delight 1844.01
Oh, What is Love? 1900.37
Oh, What is the Matter? 1899.40
Oh, What Joy 1889.39
Oh, What Will be the End of It? 1899.39
Oh, What's the Use? 1903.06, 1903.26, 1913.37
Oh, Where is Dancer 1899.25
Oh, who I am, and what I am 1895.19
Oh, will they sell our master up 1896.27
Oh, Willie Boy! 1897.26, 1897.54
Oh, Willie! Don't You Love Me? 1898.43
Oh, Woe is Me 1926.33
Oh, Woman is a Madcap 1877.25
Oh, would some demon power 1894.15
Oh, ye sentinels of order 1881.06
Oh, Yes, We are the Chorus 1884.42
Oh, You Beautiful Doll 1946.21
Oh, You Beautiful Person! 1919.09
Oh, You Bold, Bad Men! 1909.15
Oh, You Chocolate Kid 1909.16
Oh, You Girls! 1917.09
Oh, You John 1914.07, 1914.22
Oh, You Kid 1907.31
Oh, You Lady! 1922.46
Oh, You Lovely Ladies 1916.14
Oh, You Major Scales 1919.28
Oh, You Ridiculous Man 1880.19
Oh, You Sweeties 1917.23
Oh, You Tango 1913.18
Oh, You Wonderful Boy 1968.07, 1982.05
Oh, You Wonderful Girl 1911.33
Oh-Heigh-Ho! 1921.27
Oh-P-p-p-poor Bouchotte 1912.34
Oh:! Dry the Glist'ning Tear 1879.72
Ohe Mama 1885.51, 1921.01
Ohe! ohe! les camarades! 1877.32
Ohf Shabbes 1931.09
Ohio 1953.03, 1958.20, 1958.21, 1977.02, 1997.21
Ohka-No-Zu 1982.06
Oifn Gonickle 1966.21
Oisgetzaichnet 1965.32
Ojos Negros 1993.08
Oka Saka Circus 1946.13
Okay for Sound 1939.13
Oklahoma 1943.04, 2000.14
Ol' Man Mose is Dead 1939.29
Ol' Man River 1927.67, 1940.20, 1946.01, 1966.14, 1967.11, 1974.11, 1975.12, 1983.05, 1986.01, 1994.08
Ol' Pease Puddin' 1970.03
Ola in Her Little Gondola 1927.40
Olayithi 1988.02
Olcott's Irish Serenade 1894.36
Olcott's Lullaby 1899.01
Old age and gout 1859.15
Old are Getting Younger Every Day, The 1915.23
Old Ballet Days, The 1911.23
Old Barn Dance, The 1908.05
Old Barn Floor, The 1887.48, 1985.02
Old Before His Time 1894.21
Old Bill Baker Undertaker 1915.31
Old Black Crow, The 1887.48, 1906.06
Old Black Joe 1920.28, 1922.25, 1929.23
Old Blue Paradise 1915.18
Old Bob 1979.07
Old Boss Barry 1888.27, 1888.34
Old Bowery Pit, The 1882.74
Old Boy Neutral 1915.31, 1975.24
Old Broadway 1906.19
Old Brown Coat 1922.04
Old Buck and Wing, The 1908.23
Old Cabin Home 1883.26
Old Camp Chef, The 1918.14
Old Car 1999.02
Old Chateau, The 1909.29
Old Chisholm Trail 1931.02
Old Clarinet, The 1913.29
Old Court-House Chorus 1902.09
Old Dante' 1999.22
Old Days, The 1897.26, 1897.54
Old Deuteronomy 1982.19
Old Devil Moon 1947.03
Old Dorg Tray 1859.08
Old Dutch Porcelain 1924.48
Old English Cake Walk 1904.29
Old English Folk Song, An 1929.51
Old Enough to Love 1925.31, 1954.02
Old Enough to Marry 1928.06
Old Established Firm 1925.05
Old Fashion Way, The 1918.40
Old Fashioned Cakewalk, An 1922.23

Old Fashioned Flowers 1919.24
Old Fashioned Garden 1923.38
Old Fashioned Girl in a Gingham Gown 1921.34
Old Fashioned Girl, An 1928.22
Old Fashioned Husband 1968.06
Old Fashioned Love 1923.39
Old Fashioned Mother, The 1897.05
Old Fashioned Mothers 1955.04
Old Fashioned Rag 1919.26
Old Fashioned Song 1969.01
Old Fashioned Songs 1903.24
Old Fashioned Sweetheart 1921.25
Old Fashioned Way, The 1974.19, 1983.03
Old Fashioned Wedding 1932.16, 1966.12
Old Father Time 1902.18
Old Feather Bed, The 1882.79
Old Flag Never Touched the Ground, The 1907.22
Old Flame Never Dies, An 1937.10
Old Flames 1921.07
Old Folks 1971.07, 1972.16
Old Friend 1991.04
Old Friends 1907.44, 1981.27, 1988.08, 1991.10, 1999.20
Old Gentleman 1968.23
Old Gentleman's Jazz 1920.19
Old Girl I left behind me 1858.04
Old Glory 1899.30, 1903.27
Old Gray Coat 1999.08
Old Gumbie Cat, The 1982.19
Old Gypsy, The 1998.11
Old Hollywood Custom, An 1933.05
Old Home Week in Maine 1921.37
Old Ireland, you're my darling 1866.11
Old Jay Bird, The 1902.44
Old Jim Canaan's 1993.01, 1998.17
Old Jitterbug 1940.07
Old John Barleycorn 1927.42
Old John Henry 1940.01
Old Jokes' Home, The 1903.30
Old Kentucky Home 1898.22, 1906.08
Old King Cole 1920.19, 1946.14
Old King Mumm Could Make Things Hum 1892.55
Old Lady in the Shoe 1930.20
Old Landmark 1986.02
Old Light, The 1919.21
Old Log Cabin in the Dell 1876.04
Old log Cabin in the Dell, The 1876.30
Old Log Cabin in the Dell, The 1876.32
Old Long John 1966.09
Old Love and Brand New Love 1945.08
Old Love is the True Love, The 1920.11
Old Love Letters 1894.37
Old Love, and the new, The 1888.05
Old love, The 1887.43
Old MacDonald had a Farm 1954.08
Old Maid 1963.26, 1992.10
Old Maid Blues, The 1917.37
Old Maids 1961.07
Old Maids are Willing to Please 1899.40
Old Maids' Dance 1897.21
Old Man Blues 1981.06
Old Man Danube 1945.11
Old Man is a Youth Again, An 1852.05
Old Man Manhattan 1906.17
Old Man Methuselah 1917.04
Old Man Shea 1905.19
Old Man Shouldn't be Born, An 1970.18
Old Man Subway 1933.21
Old Man Woman 1924.28
Old Man's Darling - Young Man's Slave? 1940.08
Old Man's Darling, An 1923.06
Old Man's Song and Dance 1900.46
Old Man, An 1970.19
Old man, I pardon thee 1878.16
Old Meg She was a Gypsy 1962.23
Old Military Canal, The 1965.14
Old Mother Goose 1904.28
Old Music Master, The 1990.09
Old Music Masters, The 1920.19
Old Neighborhood 1891.45
Old Neighborhood, The 1894.49
Old New England Home 1922.46
Old New York 1920.39
Old Noblesse, The 1911.36
Old Oak Tree and the Twining Vine, The 1902.19
Old Oaken Bucket for Mine, The 1904.14
Old Oaken Bucket, The 1887.02
Old Operas in a New Way 1914.31
Old Park Bench, The 1940.07
Old People Gotta 1956.04
Old Plantation 1929.01
Old Potts and Young Potts 1888.34
Old Ramses 1905.56
Old Red Cradle 1887.02
Old Red Gate, The 1924.41
Old Red Hills of Home, The 1998.21
Old Reliable Jokes 1906.27
Old Reuben Blade 1896.02
Old Rhine Wine 1912.30
Old Rip was Flip 1898.55
Old Sam 1960.17
Old Sayin's 1959.04
Old Sea Songs 1914.09
Old Ship of Zion 1990.05
Old Soft Shoe, The 1946.07, 1992.18
Old Soldiers Never Die 1964.28
Old Songs 1924.23
Old Time Song and Dance 1905.20
Old Time Swing 1937.09
Old Time Tune, An 1923.33
Old Times, Good Times 1978.25
Old Town Band, The 1924.18
Old Vienna 1894.10
Old Virginia Reel, The 1923.03
Old Virginia Walkaround 1890.35
Old Waltz, An 1934.32
Old Waltz, The 1940.21
Old War Horse, The 1898.54
Old Woman and Her Pig, The 1869.07
Old Woman Who Lived in a Shoe, The 1903.04
Old Woman's Dream, An 1881.36
Old World Charm 1966.05
Old Wound, An 1993.17
Old Yankee Land for Me 1907.18
Old, old age 1880.59
Old, Old Story, The 1893.16, 1898.43
Old-Fashioned Ballet 1927.11
Old-Fashioned Cakewalk 1914.34
Old-Fashioned Cakewalk, The 1927.32
Old-Fashioned Drama, The 1916.19
Old-Fashioned Garden, An 1919.25
Old-Fashioned Girl 1959.23
Old-Fashioned Girl, An 1925.17
Old-Fashioned Girls 1917.23
Old-Fashioned Glimmer in Your Eye, An 1951.17
Old-Fashioned Groom and an Up-to-Date Bride, An 1915.23
Old-Fashioned Love 1980.10
Old-Fashioned Man is Hard to Find, An 1922.17
Old-Fashioned Rose, An 1903.31
Old-Fashioned Wedding, An 1999.04
Old-Fashioned Wife, An 1917.06
Old-Timer 1940.10
Olden Days, The 1937.17
Older They are the Harder They Fall, The 1918.32
Oldest Established, The 1950.17
Oldest Game in the World, The 1924.01
Oldest Profession, The 1997.08
Oldtime Blues 1921.26
Ole' Ole' 1946.06
Olga from the Volga 1911.43
Olive Oil 1919.20
Olive Tree, The 1953.16
Oliver Twist 1949.09
Oliver! 1963.01
Ologies, The 1883.12
Olvida esa muchacha para siempre 1969.11
Olympia Gavotte 1895.38
Olympian Games, The 1908.35
Olympian Glide, The 1915.02
Olympian Octette 1906.25
Olympics '36 1981.14
Olympics, The 1961.08
Om Mani Padme Hum 1956.07
Omaha 1908.28
Omar 1910.29
Omar Khayyam 1907.11, 1914.16, 1918.02, 1919.34
Ombo 1934.17
Omelet Song, The 1951.05
Omen Bird, The 1948.24
Omi Omai 1903.18
Ominiscient Ostrich, The 1890.26
On a Beautiful Beach 1916.21
On a Beautiful Distant Land 1903.29
On a Beautiful Evening 1923.41
On a Chinese Honeymoon 1903.27
On a Clear Day You Can See Forever 1965.31, 1990.09, 1999.23
On a crust and a handful of pease 1882.17
On a d'la peine 1929.10
On a Day Like This 1959.04
On a Desert Island 1943.22
On a Desert Isle With Thee 1927.56, 1975.13
On a Girl's Hard Life 1969.11
On a Holiday 1923.46
On a Hottentot Honeymoon 1910.29
On a January Morning in Zummersetscheer 1907.51
On a Modern Wedding Day 1914.16
On a Moonlight Night 1923.04
On a Moonlit Night 1920.02
On a Paper and Comb 1905.35
On a Pay Night Evening 1904.44
On a Pony for Two 1927.60
On a Pullman Honeymoon 1908.21
On a Roof in Manhattan 1932.05
On a Saturday Afternoon 1916.20
On a Slow Boat to China 1976.32, 1980.29
On a Starlight Night 1903.23
On a Strike 1905.31
On a Summer's Night 1903.09
On a Sunday by the Sea 1947.16, 1989.03
On a Sunny Afternoon 1914.30
On a Train 1992.11
On a tree by a river 1885.47
On a Wall 1926.22
On a Wonderful Day Like Today 1946.18, 1974.22
On a Yankee Honeymoon 1909.11
On Account of I Love You 1931.34
On an Automobile Honeymoon 1905.28, 1906.24
On and on and On 1933.25
On Any Street 1933.05
On Any Sunday 1998.13
On Atlantic City Beach 1918.23
On Behalf of the Travelling Salesmen 1997.05
On billow rocking 1878.16
On Broadway 1895.04, 1901.12, 1995.03
On Broadway in Dahomey 1903.08
On Broadway in Dahomey Bye and Bye 1904.26
On Cleopatra's Wedding Day 1895.33
On Cupid's Green 1918.05
On Daddy's Back 1903.09
On days gone by we ponder 1859.17
On De Rainbow Road 1891.45
On dit que le Parisien 1884.50
On dit, sans contredit 1878.08
On Double Fifth Avenue 1927.15
On Emancipation Day 1903.08
On guard, strike hard 1887.43
On her fiend accounts 1846.01
On Her Majesty's Service 1964.29
On horseback, I've no fear 1859.16
On Lalawana's Shore 1904.47
On Leave for Love 1942.27
On Love Alone 1934.29
On my heart 1890.33
On My Mind the Whole Night Long 1920.17
On My Nude Ranch With You 1932.13
On My Nuptial Day 1900.25
On My Own 1956.14, 1987.04
On My Way to Love 1962.05
On n'fair pas ca 1929.10
On ne faut pas croire aux serments de femmes 1929.11
On Our Honeymoon 1904.11, 1923.27
On Parade 1913.24, 1935.03, 1947.04
On Probation 1896.10
On Revient de Chantilly 1911.39
On s'en passe 1929.10
On Such a Beautiful Night 1926.03
On Such a Night 1924.04

On Sunday Morning 1897.07
On Ten Square Miles by the Potomac River 1976.11
On That Day 1965.35, 1976.35, 1982.17
On That Day of Days 1970.08
On That Matter No One Budges 1931.48
On the 'Phone 1906.48
On the Atcheson, Topeka and the Santa Fe 1988.08
On the Atchison, Topeka and the Santa Fe 1997.05
On the Avenue 1902.33, 1911.40
On the Balcony of the Casa Rosada 1979.23
On the Banks of the Bronx 1919.27
On the Banks of the Schnitza-Komisski 1920.44
On the Banks of the Wabash Far Away 1920.04
On the Battlefield for My Lord 1990.05
On the Beach 1889.36, 1900.42, 1927.20, 1954.09
On the Beach at Gay Manhattan 1899.29
On the Beach at Narragansett 1897.39
On the Beach at Waiki-ki 1915.32
On the Boardwalk 1910.16
On the Boat 1913.18
On the Border Line 1929.49
On the Boulevard 1903.28
On the Bounding Main 1902.11
On the Bowery 1891.39, 1894.07, 1894.35
On the Brim of Her Old-Fashioned Bonnet 1921.18
On the Campus 1927.41
On the Charts 1971.01
On the Congo 1911.34
On the Corner of the Rue Cambon 1969.17
On the Crest of a Wave 1928.22
On the Day I Marry 1912.48
On the day I was wedded 1890.02
On the Deep Blue Sea 1922.04
On the Dial 1899.39
On the Dummy Line 1897.45
On the Farm 1911.27, 1957.07
On the Fourth of July 1986.13
On the Gay Luneta 1907.22
On the Go 1903.39
On the Golden Trail 1928.44
On the Good Ship Lollipop 1980.08
On the Grand Old Sands 1907.24
On the Grassy Banks of Scheldt 1882.75
On the Ground 1913.36
On the Harlem When the Moon Shines Bright 1889.37
On the Heights of Glentann There's No Voice 1902.25
On the Honeymoon Express 1913.06
On the Lake, or the New Year Festival 1904.40
On the Levee 1928.10, 1932.08
On the Links 1906.10
On the Lonely Lagoon 1914.07
On the Moonlit Swanee 1922.44
On the Mountain 1916.15
On the Other Hand 1934.06
On the Other Side of the Wall 1903.37
On the Parthenon 1956.09
On the Piazza 1907.46
On the Quiet 1912.14
On the Radio 1924.32
On the Right Track 1972.22
On the River Nile 1917.34
On the Riviera 1922.33
On the Road to Calais 1918.05
On the Road to Monterey 1909.10
On the Run 1982.22
On the Runway 1998.14
On the S.S. Bernard Cohn 1965.31
On the Sands of the Negev 1960.18
On the Sea 1886.15
On the Shore at Le Lei Wi 1915.31
On the Shores of Sheepshead Bay 1909.04
On the Side 1903.02
On the Side of the Angels 1959.25
On the Sly 1879.35
On the Stage 1898.61, 1901.09, 1903.37, 1912.07
On the Steps of the Palace 1987.18
On the Street 1993.05, 1996.09
On the Street Where You Live 1956.01, 1993.18
On the Strict Q.T. 1877.23
On the Subway 1966.21
On the Sunny Side of the Street 1930.09, 1979.25, 1990.09
On the Track 1897.40, 1917.10
On the Train of a Wedding Gown 1916.24
On the Twentieth Century 1978.02
On the Washington Train 1924.41
On the Waterfront 1977.09
On the Way to Sloppy Joe's 1946.15
On the Way to Spain 1925.12
On the Willows 1976.17
On the Winning Side 1972.02
On the Yellowstone 1897.33
On the Z-R-3 1925.01
On This Festal Day 1902.18
On This Night of a Thousand Stars 1979.23
On This Rock 1971.20
On this Solemnity 1882.75
On This Wedding Day 1964.18
On Thru the Night 1932.06
On Thy Lattice 1899.40
On to Africa 1933.03
On to Chicago 1894.38
On to Conquer 1915.04
On to Hollywood 1926.29
On to Paris 1887.50, 1903.40, 1930.37
On to Paris a la Automobile 1904.39
On to Petrograd 1916.17
On to the Hall 1886.32
On to Victory 1906.18, 1918.32
On Top 1929.06, 1938.03
On Top of the World 1983.08
On Trial for My Life 1975.07
On Union Square 1886.42
On Wings of Doubt 1918.40
On With the Dance 1914.17, 1920.44, 1925.17, 1930.08, 1931.08
On With the Game 1923.47
On With the Rehearsal 1910.09
On With the Show 1954.17
On y revient tourjours 1895.43
On yonder rock reclining 1864.13
On Your Toes 1936.05, 1936.12, 1952.11, 1975.13, 1983.02
On, admirable art! 1894.15
On, Comrades 1925.39
On, How I Adore Your Name 1966.09
On, on, On 1972.23
On, Students, on! 1882.63
On, Yes! Oh, Yes! 1894.38
Ona Hundred Different Ships 1909.26
Once 1925.14, 1927.59
Once a Fisherman Went to Sea 1912.30
Once a King 1861.03
Once a King there chanced to be 1866.34
Once a Prince there chanced to be, who to marry had a mind 1888.39
Once a Year Day 1954.05
Once Again 1882.39
Once I Loved the Girl Cecelia 1901.24
Once in 2.7 Years 1968.08
Once in a Blue Moon 1923.40, 1927.12
Once in a Lifetime 1928.23, 1962.18, 1974.11, 1974.22, 1978.18
Once in a While 1888.44, 1890.12, 1891.14, 1908.30, 1975.08, 2000.17
Once in Love With Amy 1948.26, 1974.25, 1980.29, 1991.10, 1992.18
Once in September 1927.01
Once in the Highlands 1947.07, 1980.26
Once Knew a Fella 1959.11
Once More to Dream 1907.14
Once More to Find Her 1866.34
Once the Man You Laughed At 1967.18
Once There was a Melody 1971.17
Once Too Often 1904.01
Once Upon a Dream 1997.09
Once Upon a Time 1884.57
Once upon a time 1887.43
Once Upon a Time 1895.25, 1916.19, 1918.29, 1919.35, 1922.47, 1939.12, 1947.14, 1962.04, 1978.11, 1980.06, 1997.01, 1998.05
Once Upon a Time and Long Ago 1958.20, 1958.21
Once Upon a Time Today 1950.15
Once Upon the Natchez Trace 1976.31
Once was Enough for Him 1886.15
Once You Lose Your Heart 1986.12
Once You've Seen a Rainbow 1984.10
Once-in-a-While 1934.38
Onda 9 1993.08
Ondo Takarazuka Koshinkyoku 1989.21
One 1937.03, 1975.15, 1979.13, 2001.01
One - Two - Three 1917.16
One Alone 1926.42, 1946.03, 1987.10
One and One Make One 1906.19
One and Only 1915.04
One auf of de Boys 1878.15
One Baby 1927.09
One Beating a Day 1983.20
One Big Happy Family 1974.03
One Big Union for Two 1937.14
One Boy 1960.06
One Boy's Enough for Me 1927.29
One Brick at a Time 1980.07
One Brief Moment 1939.13
One Bumper at Parting 1860.03
One by One 1978.27, 1997.20
One Candle 1990.17
One Coro Delle Lavandiare 1985.14
One Day 1918.15
One Day a Little Maid 1893.40
One Day in May 1923.08
One Day it Will Come to Pass 1965.39
One day King Papagallo sent a note 1898.25
One Day Margot, or Three to One 1891.36
One Day More 1987.04
One Day We Dance 1960.22
One Day, a Captain Bold 1881.22
One day, the J. LeHay of This town 1895.29
One Dozen Roses 1942.16
One Extraordinary Thing 1979.02
One Feather Tail of Miss Gertrude McFuzz, The 2000.18
One Flag 1971.02
One Flower Grows Alone in Your Garden 1926.42, 1946.03
One Foot, Other Foot 1947.17
One for All 1930.30
One for Another 1896.30
One for My Baby 1997.05
One Fragment of a Moment 1993.17
One Galician Miss 1931.29
One Girl 1923.32
One Girl Boy, The 1921.03
One Girl Man 1928.31
One Girl, The 1907.47, 1928.44, 1929.22
One Golden Hour 1926.34
One Good Boy Gone Wrong 1946.03, 1973.09, 1987.10
One Good Friend 1927.64
One Good Man Gone Wrong 1926.42
One Good Time 1923.10
One Hallow'een 1970.09
One Hand, One Heart 1957.12
One Heart 1933.16
One Heart to Thee 1899.06
One Horse Shay 1858.04
One Hour Ahead of the Posse 1955.12
One Hour Mama 1999.06
One Hour, Sweetheart, With You! 1918.26
One Hundred Easy Ways 1953.03
One Hundred Years from Now 1903.14
One I Love, The 1913.26
One I Love, the Other I Abhor 1902.37
One I Love, Two I Love 1919.14
One I'm Looking For, The 1926.27
One in a Million 1931.36, 1934.15, 1969.14
One in a Million Like You 1912.38
One in the Game of Love 1915.28
One Indispensable Man, The 1938.11
One is a Lonely Number 1950.03, 1952.13
One Kind Word 1959.04
One Kiss 1923.44, 1928.12, 1928.29, 1986.14
One Last Kiss 1960.06
One Last Love Song 1945.11
One Last Waltz 1923.22
One Leg too Few 1973.13
One Life to Live 1941.04
One Little Angry Word 1899.08
One Little Baby 1906.03

One Little Brick at a Time 1970.08
One Little Girl 1913.27, 1925.35
One Little Girl I Know 1899.22
One Little Kiss 1890.23
One Little World Apart 1962.14
One Little Year 1975.06
One Little, Sweet Little Girl 1907.56
One Long Last Look 1964.35
One Look, One Word 1917.19
One Lost Weekend 1988.07
One Love 1929.37, 1930.22
One Love in a Lifetime 1982.16
One Love in My Lifetime 1976.16
One Loving Kiss! 1881.36
One Man 1929.27, 1970.12, 1971.20, 1982.14
One Man Ain't Quite Enough 1954.19
One Man I Need, The 1941.02
One Man in the Moon 1924.04
One Man is Like Another 1924.38
One Meat Ball 1945.07
One Misty Moisty Morning 1971.20
One Moment Alone 1931.37
One moment pray 1878.02, 1887.44
One Moment, Pray 1885.58, 1888.13, 1896.35
One More Angel in Heaven 1982.03, 1993.15
One More Beautiful Song 2001.01
One More Dance 1951.22
One More for the Last One 1970.21
One More Kiss 1971.05
One More Picture Please 1981.29
One More Time 1971.01, 1972.07
One More Walk Around the Garden 1979.09
One Morning in May 1987.02
One Mother Each 1961.02
One Must be Extremely Careful 1933.24
One Nice Little Million 1904.18
One Night 1930.36
One Night in Bangkok 1988.09
One Night in the Rain 1930.21
One Night of Love 1929.22
One Night Only 1905.49, 1981.29
One Night Stands, The 1906.39
One Night With You 1978.01
One Night, One Waltz, One Girl 1919.02
One O'Clock Baby 1925.01, 1925.28
One O'Clock Jump 1982.15
One of a Kind 1970.09, 1989.25
One of the Boys 1904.29, 1912.26, 1920.11, 1981.10
One of the Council placed within my halls 1855.06
One of the Ruins of France 1919.10
One of These Fine Days 1938.09
One of Those Days 1959.14
One of Those Moments 1967.16
One of Those Windows 1927.04
One of Us Should be Two 1926.51
One on One 1971.04
One or Another 1914.09
One Perfect Moment 1956.08
One Person 1969.05
One Piece Blues 1924.42
One Plus One Equals Three 1997.17
One Promise 1965.36
One Rock & Roll too Many 1987.05
One Room 1970.15
One Second of Sex 1931.42
One Side of World 1970.21
One Small Girl 1990.12
One Small Voice 1999.17
One Smile from Thee 1896.10
One Song 1979.28
One Song Glory 1996.09
One Special Man 1996.08
One Step 1983.09
One Step - Two Step 1959.27
One Step at a Time 1988.07
One Step into Love 1915.18
One Step Nearer the Moon 1930.14
One Step to Heaven 1927.68, 1928.21
One Sunny Day 1928.07
One That He Loves Best 1902.15
One That I Loved the Best Gave That to Me, The 1904.05
One Thing Different 1904.34
One Third of a Calendar 1973.08
One Thousand Percent Fahrenheit 1930.24
One Touch of Alchemy 1938.11
One Touch of Loving 1922.12
One Touch of Venus 1943.19
One Touch of Vienna 1945.11
One Track Mind 1944.01, 1945.20
One Two and One Two Three 1924.39
One Two Three 1950.02
One Two Three Four 1915.32
One Umbrella Would be Big Enough for Two 1904.49
One Way of Doing It 1916.08
One Way Street 1926.03
One Way Ticket to Hell 1979.32
One Who Will Understand 1915.30
One Wife 1961.24
One Woman in the World, The 1927.02
One Word from You 1911.38
One Word Led to Another 1950.02
One Word of Kindness 1891.18, 1892.23
One You Love, The 1926.04
One You're Looking For, The 1908.40
One You've Been Waiting For, The 1919.33
One' Fellow's Joy is Another Fellow's Woe 1900.25
One, Two 1971.20
One, Two! 1889.40
One, Two, Button Your Shoe 1995.14
One, two, three 1875.19
One, Two, Three 1884.66, 1886.11, 1897.26, 1908.03, 1918.16
One-Two-Three-Four 1912.03, 1925.25
Ongsay and Anceday 1929.42
Only a Dream of Home 1876.30
Only a Fool 1982.13
Only a Gypsy Maid 1910.36
Only a Heart 1899.41
Only a Hundred Girls in the World for Me 1899.25
Only a Hundred Years Old 1882.18
Only a Kiss 1904.09, 1924.28
Only a Man 1911.08
Only a Rose 1925.32, 1984.14
Only a Slave 1919.20
Only a Smile 1928.48
Only a Story from Fairy Tales 1907.61
Only a Tear 1897.12
Only a Tramp 1885.44
Only a Voice 1911.46
Only a Woman's Heart 1889.39
Only an Eclipse of Love 1888.15
Only an Older Woman 1988.20
Only an Orange Girl 1884.57
Only Another Boy and Girl 1944.29
Only at Night 1992.11
Only Bit of Ireland, The 1911.13
Only Boy, The 1927.29
Only Dance I Know, The 1962.20
Only Dreams 1890.23
Only Fancy 1896.05
Only Fools are Sad 1971.17
Only for Americans 1949.08
Only Game I Would Play, The 1929.46
Only Girl, The 1908.25, 1921.33, 1924.38
Only Home I Know, The 1975.03
Only I and You 1967.08
Only if You Have a Dream 1999.12
Only if You're in Love 1951.23
Only in Dreams 1893.19, 1918.34
Only in My Song 1975.23
Only in the Movies 1993.09
Only in the Play 1898.60
Only Love 1968.30, 1983.14, 1997.19
Only Make Believe 1927.67, 1946.01, 1966.14, 1983.05
Only Man for the Job, The 1974.03
Only Man I Ever Loved, The 1906.45
Only More! 1969.16
Only One 1925.39, 1926.04
Only One for Me, The 1927.58, 1930.27
Only One Girl for Me 1917.15
Only One Hour 1916.04
Only One I Love Is?, The 1909.06
Only One Love Ever Fills the Heart 1921.31
Only One of Anything 1908.24, 1909.23
Only One Waltz 1912.15
Only One, The 1905.44, 1925.29, 1937.17, 1963.08
Only Pair I've Got, The 1985.04
Only Rainbows 1961.02
Only Steal from Thieves 1988.20
Only the Beginning 1981.29
Only the night wind sighs 1895.26
Only Thing That Makes Life Worth Living, The 1902.34
Only think, a Duke and Duchess 1893.02
Only This 1884.65
Only Time of Day, The 1940.04
Only Time Will Tell 1959.11
Only to Love Her 1897.05
Only to You 1914.18
Only Way, The 1914.32
Only With You 1982.09
Only Wounded 1979.11
Only You 1904.13, 1924.11, 1982.09, 1987.05
Only Your Heart Can Tell 1931.29
Only, Only One is You, The 1924.11
Ont une allure charmante, Ils 1929.10
Ontario 1904.30
Onward 1901.27
Onward Christian Soldiers 1938.10
Onward Soldiers 1896.02
Oo La La 1920.21
Oo Wee Bay Bee 1999.12
Oo, How I Love to be Loved by You 1919.12
Oo, How I Love You 1927.29
Oo-La-La 1921.14
Oo-Le-Le 1977.01
Oo-Oo-Oo 1912.41
OO-OOO-OOO, What You do to Me 1951.18
Oof Dah Man, The 1926.19
Oogley, Oogley, Ooo 1909.09
Ooh Poo Pa Doo 1992.06
Ooh! My Feet! 1956.04
Ooh! That Kiss 1931.40
Ooh, do You Love You! 1966.06
Ooh, I'm Thinking 1933.05
Ooh, My Feet! 1980.29
Ooh, What You Said 1940.09
Oolie Girl of Panama 1912.04
Oom Pa Pa Pa 1968.22
Oom-Pah-Pah 1963.01
Oompah, The 1896.52, 1897.40
Ooo-ooo Lena 1912.26
OOOO-EEEE 1968.06
Ootchy-Cootchy 1896.29
Ootsey Totsey 1902.41
Oozey Woozey 1922.12
Oozums 1915.32
Op in the 'Ansom 1904.42, 1907.16
Ope sea, bright rolling sea 1881.04
Opeless ze State of Me 1904.01
Open a New Window 1966.10
Open and Shut Idea 1929.17
Open Book, An 1929.07
Open Door Club 1927.07
Open Gates, The 1896.41
Open Letter 1985.17
Open Sesame 1899.21, 1999.15
Open That Door 1930.19
Open the Council 1890.33
Open the Gates of Madrid 1926.23, 1927.02
Open the shutters wide 1887.04
Open the Window 1971.21
Open the Window, Sam 1981.10
Open Thy Lattice, Love 1939.21
Open Up 1992.06
Open Up the Door 1998.08
Open Up Your Heart 1929.37
Open Your Heart 1920.11, 1923.39, 1988.12
Open Your Heart to Love 1916.18
Open Your Window 1885.03, 1885.50, 1929.17
Opened Up Again 1927.31
Opening 1952.09, 1962.02, 1968.13
Opening Chorus 1923.33
Opening Doors 1981.27
Opening Dream 1991.05
Opening for a Princess, An 1959.26
Opening for Everybody, An 1949.12

Opening Night 1939.19, 2001.05
Opening Number 1946.10
Opening Numbers 1958.10
Opening of Atlantic City 1915.17
Opening of Hat Store 1919.14
Opening of the Ball 1910.35
Opera 1934.20
Opera Ain't Over, The 1981.28
Opera Ball, The 1911.06
Opera Comique 1909.24
Opera of 1860, The 1925.27
Opera Ring 1927.27
Opera, Comic Opera 1919.04
Opera, Opera 1993.17
Opera-Bouffe Cohanesque 1927.47
Operatic Ball, The 1896.49
Operatic Most Emphatic 1899.11
Operatic Mountebanks 1899.21
Operatic Pills 1929.51
Operatic Solution, An 1909.05
Ophelia 1923.07
Opportunity 1916.24, 1922.31
Opportunity! 1959.19
Opposite Sex, The 1937.07
Opposites 1965.33
Opposites are We 1906.49
Optimistic Voices 1973.14, 1997.11
Optimistic Years 1989.06
Opus One 1999.24
Or he or I must die 1879.10
Or Thereabouts 1911.39
Or What Have You? 1929.19
Orang Outang, The 1882.25
Orang-Outgang Song, The 1881.22
Orange Blossoms 1877.22, 1885.06, 1894.06, 1917.23, 1922.33, 1928.07
Orange Fete, The 1909.02
Orange Girl 1915.17
Orange Grove in California, An 1923.32
Oranges 1925.40
Oratorium Salzburgiensis 1940.04
Orb Divine 1899.21
Orbach's, Bloomingdale's, Best & Saks 1969.17
Orchid Ballet, The 1899.19
Orchid, The 1929.28
Orchids 1936.30
Order Wedding Bells for Two 1908.31
Ordinary Couple, An 1959.24
Ordinary Family, An 1990.06
Ordinary Morning 1955.19
Ordinary People 1961.24
Ordinary Town, An 1999.17
Ordinary, Extraordinary Day 1985.17
Ore from a Gold Mine 1946.24
Organ Grinder's Swing 1987.02
Organ Quartette 1903.08
Organdy Days 1924.13
Orgullo Criollo 1985.07, 1993.08
Orgy 1917.08
Orgy, the Temptress 1977.01
Orient 1919.30
Orient Yourself 1989.05
Orienta 1921.10
Oriental Bacchanale, The 1913.05
Oriental Blues 1921.16, 1978.21
Oriental Divertissement 1923.16
Oriental Eyes 1911.34
Oriental Huzzars 1896.45
Oriental Maid, An 1902.11
Oriental March 1897.04
Oriental Memories 1925.23
Oriental Moon 1910.07, 1929.31
Oriental Nights 1926.37
Oriental Plan 1961.07
Oriental Serenade 1921.07
Oriental Slaves are We 1903.04
Oriental Swell, An 1890.03
Oriental Tea Song 1918.25
Orientale Moderne 1932.13
Orientation/Postcard #1 1986.20
Origin of the Coon Song, The 1899.12
Origin of the Tap Dance 1928.22
Original Bowery Boy, The 1898.70
Original Idea, An 1894.22
Original Sneezing Song 1876.01
Original Todd, The 1897.26
Ornamental Baronet, The 1882.17
Ornamental Slaves 1895.44
Orphan in the Storm 1969.02
Orphan is the Girl for Me, An 1924.02
Orphan's Contribution, The 1894.37
Orphan's Drill 1922.13
Orphan, I Am, An 1984.02
Orphan, The 2000.20
Orphans of the Storm 1922.34
Orpheus 1940.21
Orpheus and His Lute 1981.02
Orthodox Fool, An 1962.03
Osbick Bird, The 1978.24
Oshi, Dori 1903.18
Oshkosh 1907.18
Oskaloosa Lou 1905.47
Oskaloosa Pets, The 1915.23
Ossified Man, The 1905.44
Ostend 1901.25
Ostende Nobis Tosca 1978.06
Othello and I had a Cell 1895.17
Other Days 1923.35
Other Fellow's Girl, The 1926.24
Other Fellow, The 1910.22
Other Foot, The 1899.18
Other Generation, The 1958.19
Other Half of Me, The 1964.44
Other Hands, Other Hearts 1954.15
Other One, The 1962.02
Other Page is Missing, The 1899.38
Other Part of Me, The 1983.20
Other People 1980.11
Other Pleasures 1990.04
Other Side of the Sky, The 1972.25
Other Side of the Tracks, The 1962.27, 1982.01, 1998.15
Other Three, The 1968.21
Other Tree, The 1966.20
Otto of Roses 1908.25
Ou donc est notre secretaire? 1884.50
Ouch 1934.04
Oui! Oui! Mademoiselle 1900.55
Oui, j'suis heureux! 1885.57
Oui, mes amis, et vous pouvez m'en croire 1884.50
Oui, Oui!! 1928.46
Oui, si grand'mere entend poursuivre 1885.56
Oui, touchez-la mon cher eleve 1885.57
Ouija Board 1920.45
Ould Dudeen, The 1897.43
Ould Plaid Shawl, The 1908.43
Our Acrobatic Melodramatic Home 1917.37
Our American Colleges 1910.18
Our Ancestors 1918.05
Our Ancient Liberties 1938.11
Our Brave Lancers 1907.58
Our Bridal Night 1927.50
Our Busy Needles Fly 1922.40
Our Canadian Canoe 1911.14
Our Castle of Love 1928.26
Our Cause is the Cause 1903.14
Our Child 1926.19
Our Children 1962.04, 1998.01
Our Chinese Bungalow 1919.39
Our Choir 1880.38
Our chorus is somewhat peculiar 1882.63
Our City of Dreams 1918.37
Our Crown 1935.14
Our Customary Attitude 1898.25
Our Doctor Comes 1907.52
Our Emblem is the Lily 1924.13
Our Emporium 1905.19
Our Fairy Godmamma 1907.06
Our Farm 1910.21
Our Father 1972.15
Our First Kiss 1939.25
Our Floral Queen 1903.10
Our Front Stoop 1892.54
Our Glorious Stripes and Stars 1914.09
Our Goose has a Mint in Her Little Inside 1903.39
Our Great Mikado 1939.15, 1939.17
Our great Mikado, virtuous man 1885.47
Our great pasha 1889.10
Our Health Farm 1919.21
Our hearts are light and free 1880.40
Our Hearts They are Light When Two Hearts Love 1896.29
Our Hebrew Uncles 1891.14, 1892.06
Our Hero 1912.02
Our Home 1938.12
Our Home Sweet Home 1922.31
Our Home Town 1921.21
Our Honeymoon 1914.26
Our Irish Grenadiers 1878.01
Our Jimmy 1969.14
Our Kind of War 1989.05
Our King is Here 1906.48
Our Land of Dreams 1901.06
Our Language of Love 1960.13
Our Last Waltz Together 1937.17
Our Lips are Sealed 1982.22
Our Little Captain 1925.49
Our Little Kingdom 1926.34
Our Little Lady Upstairs 1933.03
Our Little Nest 1918.03
Our Little Secret 1968.31
Our Lodger 1898.41
Our Love has Flown Away 1963.20
Our Love is Here to Stay 1979.24, 1983.09, 1988.08
Our Love, My Love 1974.19
Our Lovely Rose 1923.40
Our Morals are Most Refined 1912.05
Our Nations 1869.26
Our Native Land 1899.34
Our Navy 1890.32
Our Navy Boys Return 1896.45
Our Navy's the Best in the World 1909.20
Our Own Way of Going Along 1927.47
Our Picture Book 1909.05
Our Polly is a Sad Slut 1957.02
Our Polly is a sad Slut! nor heeds what we have taught her 1750.01
Our Presence Still 1846.01
Our Presidents 1920.13
Our Private Love Song 1943.14
Our Private World 1978.02
Our selves, like the Great, to secure a Retreat 1750.01
Our Ship was as Taut as a Vessel Can Be 1894.47
Our situation's trully most abasurd 1886.40
Our Song 1941.07
Our State Fair 1996.04
Our Story Begins 2000.18
Our Story Resumes 2000.18
Our Tale is Told 1900.37
Our Time 1981.27
Our Town 1939.26
Our United Emblem 1902.09
Our Wedding Day 1933.22
Our Welcome Guest 1873.29
Ours 1936.26, 1980.06
Ours is a Happy Home 1894.31
Ours is a Happy Little Home 1894.46
Out for a Racket 1891.39, 1894.07, 1894.35
Out for Blood 1988.12
Out for No Good 1944.14
Out Here on My Own 1982.15
Out in 'Frisco Town 1914.16
Out in a Barnyard 1909.14
Out in No Man's Land 1921.16
Out in the Open Air 1930.32
Out in the Sun 1937.03
Out of a Clear Blue Sky 1930.22
Out of Breath and Scared to Death of You 1930.18, 1930.33
Out of Focus 1966.03
Out of My Dreams 1943.04
Out of my sight 1866.06
Out of Sight, Out of Mind 1950.10, 1962.24
Out of the Blue 1929.31
Out of the Dawn 1979.05
Out of the Swim 1929.33
Out of the Way 1954.01
Out of This World 1965.32, 1997.05
Out of Town Buyers 1927.05

Out on a College Rah! Rah! 1894.49
Out on a Racket 1888.32
Out on the Breezy Morning Air 1905.46
Out on the Loose 1927.08
Out on the Street 1978.11, 1980.15
Out There 1980.07
Out Tonight 1996.09
Out Where the Blues Begin 1928.50
Out Where the Pavement Ends 1924.16
Out With the Boys, The 1903.40
Out, Miss 1859.08
Outdoor Man for My Indoor Sports, An 1928.36
Outlaw Bold, An 1905.55
Outside Looking In 1930.38
Outside of That I Love You 1940.08
Over a Garden Wall 1925.16
Over and Over 1951.13
Over and Over Again 1919.33
Over and over Again 1935.15
Over at the Frankenstein Place 1975.08, 2000.17
Over Here 1929.44, 1963.25, 1974.05
Over hill, over dale, and by mountain 1887.12
Over in Europe 1936.28
Over Sunday 1905.22
Over the Bannister 1989.23
Over the Barley Mow 1882.17
Over the Bright Blue Sea 1938.10, 1945.08
Over the bright blue sea Comes Sir Joseph Porter, K.C.B. 1879.05
Over the clouds and far away! 1866.11
Over the Garden Wall 1882.39, 1927.20
Over the Hill 1975.03
Over the Hills 1895.32, 1966.03
Over the Hills in Monterey 1913.26
Over the Hills to Calabria 1895.31
Over the Moon 1996.09
Over the Moonlit Sea 1904.58
Over the Mountain 1860.03, 1882.69, 1885.53, 1886.51, 1891.07
Over the Mountains 1899.28
Over the Ocean 1913.16
Over the Phone 1922.43
Over the Radio 1924.31
Over the Rainbow 1938.08, 1955.13, 1967.11, 1974.22, 1979.13, 1989.06, 1989.16, 1997.01, 1997.11
Over the River and into the Woods 1962.02
Over the Top 1917.31
Over the Wall 1993.09
Over There 1908.18, 1968.07, 1974.09, 1975.22
Over There and Over Here 1918.27
Over-trained soubrette 1898.38
Overflow 1935.13, 1983.04
Overhead 1992.10
Overhead the Moon is Beaming 1980.21
Overnight 1930.38, 1931.13
Overnight Sensation 1997.17
Overspend 1959.23
Overture 1944.30
Overture Delle Donne 1982.09
Overworked Trumpeter, An 1893.19
Owl and the Thrush, The 1896.30
Owl Song 1928.30
Own Up! 1883.12
Oxenford's March 1963.28
Oxford Bags 1925.42
Oy, a nacht a sheyne 1960.18
Oy, dortn, dortn ibern vaserl 1960.18
Oy, is Dus a Leben! 1942.28
Oyf dem zamd fun negev 1960.18
Oyfn Pripetshik 1990.16, 1998.11
Oysters 1972.25
Oysters, Cockles and Mussels 1954.15
Ozarks are Calling Me Home, The 1936.26
Ozymandias 1972.21

P'raps he will shock us 1890.33
P'raps if you address the lady most politely 1884.09
P'raps you will excuse us stating 1884.14
P'tit air, Un 1965.08
P'tit ferme, un p'tit jardinet, Un 1880.58
P P B B D 1966.32
P.T.O. 1877.39
Pablo 1930.27
Pack Up Your Blues and Smile 1927.49
Pack Up Your Sins and Go to the Devil 1922.39
Pack Up Your Troubles 1964.28
Pack Up Your Troubles in Your Old Kit Bag 1978.05, 1991.04
Pack Your Suitcase With Love 1930.37
Package of Seeds 1915.01
Package of Seeds, A 1917.06
Paddlin' Madelin' Home 1925.33
Paddy and His Pig 1896.41
Paddy and His Sweet Poteen 1888.40
Paddy Duffy's Cart 1882.02, 1882.39
Paddy MacNeil and His Automobile 1963.29
Paddy's Cat 1901.02
Paddy's Nightmare 1955.19
Paddy, Wait Awhile 1891.14, 1892.06
Padlock Your Blues 1928.14
Page a Man for Me 1924.42
Page from Jonathan Swift, A 1934.18
Pageant Song 1971.21
Pages 1928.12
Pages of My Diary 1988.07
Pages Song, The 1879.15
Paging Mr. Sousa 1989.23
Paging Mr. Street 1917.36, 1976.25
Pagliacci 1919.25, 1940.05
Paint 1952.11
Paint a Rainbow 1964.05
Painted emblems of a race 1887.10
Painted Rose 1924.16
Painters and the Rube, The 1904.41
Painting a Vanities Girl 1928.23
Painting Her Portrait 2000.20
Painting My Picture of You 1918.29
Painting Paris 1908.42
Painting the Town 1906.39
Paintings of Clovis Trouille 1971.04, 1976.27
Pair of Dudinettes, The 1886.32
Pair of Ordinary Coons, A 1915.32
Pajama and the Nightie, The 1908.13
Pajama Dance 1948.08
Pajama Game, The 1954.05
Pajama Girlie 1916.23
Pajarillo Embrujado 1939.18
Pak Zich Ain 1989.10
Pal Like You, A 1917.06
Pal-Yat-Chee 1995.16, 1998.17
Palace of Dreams 1930.30, 1934.43
Palace of the Czar, The 1990.16, 2000.14
Palace or Cot 1916.18
Palais Dancers 1955.19
Palais de Glace 1978.26
Pale Moonlight 1897.55
Pale Venetian Moon 1922.45
Palesteena 1920.33
Paletas 1945.11
Palm Beach Baby 1927.38
Palm Beach Girl, The 1917.26
Palm Branches Waving 1902.44
Palm Leaf 1869.14
Palms, The 1888.25, 1889.43, 1890.36
Palmy Days, The 1920.10
Paloma, La 1877.13, 1879.36, 1879.47, 1884.48, 1894.13, 1921.02
Palomino Pal 1965.17
Pals 1922.31, 1925.29
Pals of the Pentagon 1950.02
Pan 1926.11
Pan Handlers, The 1996.07
Panache 1968.02
Panama 1913.17
Panama Pacific Drag 1915.12
Pango Pango 1923.02
Pango Pango Maid 1925.25
Pangs of Unrequited Love, The 1868.02
Panic 1967.16
Panic in Panama 1941.09
Panic's On, The 1930.30
Panisse and Son 1954.15
Pano Muruno, El 1949.07
Pansies on Parade 1931.31
Pansy 1901.19, 1929.21
Pansy Day 1919.02
Pansy Faces 1903.39, 1903.41
Pansy March 1903.39
Panther, The 1973.08
Pantomime 1946.18, 1954.06
Pantomime Baseball 1919.26
Papa 1898.12, 1913.20
Papa Di-Da-Da 1931.11
Papa Knows Best 1970.19
Papa Lewis, Mama Green 1937.14
Papa Likes a Hot Papoose 1929.26
Papa Would Persist in Picking Peaches 1917.26
Papa Wouldn't Care for That 1903.28
Papa's Baby 1888.32
Papa's Baby Girl 1886.35
Papa's Gonna Make it Alright 1975.03
Papa's Got a Job 1939.19
Papa's Little Girl 1892.24
Papa's Popular Boy 1908.42
Papa, Don't Go Out Tonight 1979.25
Papa, Won't You Dance With Me 1974.10
Papa, Won't You Dance With Me? 1947.16
Paper Bag Rag, The 1981.09
Paper Fan, A 1902.19
Paper Hat Brigade, The 1908.28
Paper of Gold 1961.07
Paper of Pins 1963.19
Paper! 1950.03
Papers, The 1929.49
Papillon 1944.21
Papirosin 1998.11
Papirosn 1990.16
Papoose Lullaby, A 1907.49
Pappa, Won't You Dance With Me? 1989.03
Paprica 1915.23
Par Excellence 1870.01, 1871.12
Par le trou de la serrure 1929.16
Par les chemins ombreux 1887.36
Par tour le pays je chemine 1887.35
Para Que Tu Veas 1944.31
Para Que Tu Ver 1943.17
Parachutist, The 1972.17
Parade 1935.03, 1974.06
Parade in Town, A 1964.15
Parade Night 1936.31
Parade of Clowns 1982.23
Parade of Models 1943.20
Parade of the Christmas Dinner 1926.19
Parade of the Wooden Soldiers 1924.18
Parade of the Wooden Soldiers, The 1922.06, 1923.28, 1925.03, 1943.11
Parade, The 1959.22
Paradise 1972.11, 1979.30
Paradise Alley 1895.44, 1921.34, 1924.07
Paradise for Two, A 1918.27
Paradise is Burning Down 1999.22
Paradise Jail Birds 1909.13
Paradise Stolen 1948.27
Paragraphs 1909.21
Parahara, The 1904.40
Paraphrase on Upidee 1895.38
Parasols on Parade 1931.26
Parce Que 1958.06
Parceque 1965.30
Pardon Me if I Stutter 1914.02
Pardon me, madam 1880.18
Pardon My English 1933.01
Pardon My Southern Accent 1997.05
Pardon now the bold Outlaw 1859.01
Pardon Our French 1950.14
Pardon, Ma'am 1963.22
Pardon, The 1892.08
Paree 1907.15, 1935.12, 1937.17, 1938.01, 1952.11
Paree has the Fever Now 1928.09
Paree's a Branch of Broadway 1912.43
Paree, Gay Paree 1911.43
Paree, What Did You do to Me? 1929.45
Parent/Kid Dance 1978.11
Parfum d'Amour 1920.28
Paris 1912.01, 1928.33
Paris at 21 1979.11
Paris boheme 1964.22
Paris by Night 1904.23, 1995.15

Paris Carnival 1906.45
Paris Cuisine 1973.07
Paris Gown 1953.01
Paris Green 1928.09
Paris is a Paradise for Coons 1911.12, 1926.37
Paris is a Spot so Fair 1912.08
Paris is at Her Best in May 1965.30
Paris is Paris Again 1973.12
Paris je t'aime 1965.08
Paris Loves Lovers 1955.02
Paris Makes Me Horny 1995.15
Paris on a Moonlight Night 1903.28
Paris Original 1961.22
Paris Otonal 1993.08
Paris Oui Oui 1955.14
Paris Push, The 1910.15
Paris Se Regarde 1958.06
Paris Sings Again 1946.16
Paris Taught Me Zis 1927.15
Paris Through the Window 2001.01
Paris tu rajeunis 1965.08
Paris Wakes Up and Smiles 1949.08
Paris! Good-Bye! 1913.21
Paris! Paris! 1921.15
Paris, A 1958.06, 1959.15, 1961.25
Paris, France 1951.13
Paris, Oh Festive Land 1913.02
Paris, Paris 1912.49
Paris, Vienna, London, New York 1897.21
Paris? Oh, My! Yes, Dear 1914.03
Parisian Glide 1910.07
Parisian Lover 1933.16
Parisian Nights 1922.32
Parisian Pierrot 1924.01
Parisian Tango 1930.20
Parisian Twist, The 1909.13
Parisian Two-Step 1911.11
Parisiana Roses 1928.09
Parisienne Girl. . ., La 1916.25
Parisienne Grisettes, The 1898.03
Parisienne Mechanical Models 1919.37
Parisienne, A la 1912.49
Parisienne, La 1902.08, 1906.44
Parisiennes, Les 1885.57
Park 1970.12
Park Ave. 1932.19
Park Avenue 1927.27
Park Avenue Strut 1929.09
Park Avenue's Going to Town 1936.01
Parle-moi d'autre chose 1935.19
Parlez-moi d'amour 1934.32, 1935.19
Parlez-moi d'autre chose 1934.32
Parlez-vous Francais? 1990.04
Parlor Games 1911.13
Parlor Match Medley, A 1890.32, 1892.18, 1892.45
Parlor Match, A 1884.48, 1896.31
Parlor Songs 1979.06
Parlour Song, The 1979.07
Parnell's Plight 2000.01
Parodies 1914.34
Parody Man, The 1906.13
Part of Us, A 1990.12
Parted on the Shore 1928.05
Partenza di L'Ambasceria, La 1985.16
Parthenay A 1933.24
Parthenia Took a Fancy to a Coon 1893.37
Particular Marguerite 1909.15
Parting 1984.02
Partis avant qu'on en profite! 1929.11
Partners 1921.32
Partners henceforth you and I 1881.04
Party is in Danger, The 1935.16
Party Line 1929.01
Party of the Second Part, The 1907.26
Party Song 1959.12
Party Talk 1964.35
Party That We're Gonna Have Tomorrow Night, The 1955.27
Party With My Memories, A 1940.04
Party With Our Memories, A 1940.04
Party's on Me, The 1973.06
Party's on the House, The 1965.14
Party's Over Now, The 1939.07, 1952.11, 1986.19
Party's Over, The 1934.40, 1956.14, 1958.20, 1958.21, 1977.02
Party, Party 1981.29
Pas de Deux 1977.09, 1983.08
Pas de Seul 1911.40
Pas Ma La, La 1899.11
Pas Perdus, Les 1955.14
Pas Seul 1904.22, 1924.24
Pas sur la bouche 1929.16
Pass a Little Love Around 1980.15
Pass Around the Apples Once Again 1916.21
Pass Her Along 1976.31
Pass round the wine cup, your glasses be clinking! 1885.63
Pass the Cross to Me 1975.03
Pass the Football 1953.03
Pass the Parting Goblet Round 1852.01
Pass the Wine 1999.17
Passacaglia 1956.13
Passacaglia, A 1972.02
Passant par la Lorraine, En 1933.24
Passatella 1964.03
Passenger's Always Right, The 1961.18, 1986.19
Passing By 1907.41
Passing Fancies 1923.22
Passing of Six Months 1922.01
Passing of the Night, The 1924.04
Passing Show, The 1917.08, 1922.34
Passionate Pilgrim, The 1931.37
. . . Passionement 1929.11
Passionettes 1921.02
Passover 1972.09
Past and Future 1886.30, 1921.01
Past and Present 1915.05
Past appears to me but a dream, The 1844.01
Past is Another Land, The 2000.06
Past, the Present and Future, The 1907.50
Pastels, The 1925.23
Pastime Rag 1980.27
Pastimes 1904.06
Pastry Cooks, The 1921.20
Pat and His Little Brown Mare 1885.02
Pat and His Pipes 1899.27
Pat Malloy 1865.06
Pat McCann 1869.42
Pat Your Feet 1923.06
Patetico 1999.18
Path to Honeymoon Land, The 1914.07
Path to Yesterday, The 1927.54
Pathfinder of Panama, The 1915.25
Pathway of Love, The 1909.10
Patient Angler, The 1882.33
Patient Egg, The 1900.01
Patiently Smiling 1946.16
Patients, for the Use Of 1964.29
Patio Espanol 1969.11
Patriotic Coon, The 1898.61
Patriotic Songs 1953.17
Patron Saints 1982.10
Patrons of the Play 1911.41
Patronymic Name of Smith, The 1877.39
Patsey Bolivar 1903.27
Patsy 1963.12
Patsy and the Horseshoe 1894.09
Patsy Bolivar 1904.41
Patsy Boliver 1918.14
Patter 1922.07
Patter of the Shingle, The 1900.01
Patter Song 1885.08
Patter, Patter, Went the Rain 1885.42
Patterns 1983.19
Patti Waltz, The 1898.41
Paul and Magnolia 1883.04
Paul Arrives 1974.23
Paul Poiret Number 1922.14
Paul Revere's Ride 1955.13
Pauls 1993.02
Pavanne 1903.37
Pavilion of Love, The 1900.34
Pavilion, The 1943.09
Pavlowa Gavotte, The 1914.01
Pavlowa Song 1921.27
Pay Day 1926.19, 1930.27
Pay Day on Levee 1923.39
Pay Day Pauline 1925.30
Pay Heed 1940.17
Pay Me 1927.33
Pay Night 1903.03
Pay the Lawyer 1989.07
Payador 1930.27
Payadora 1993.08, 1997.13
Payday 1951.14
Paying Off 1937.06
Peace and the Diplomat 1938.09
Peace be With You 1897.03
Peace Come to Every Heart 1966.09
Peace in Space 1975.04
Peace Peace 1972.18
Peace Song 1938.02
Peace still smiling, trade is booming 1885.63
Peace Teachers 1975.05
Peace unto this dwelling 1834.03
Peace! Peace! 1902.30
Peace, Brother 1939.29
Peach Blossom Time 1922.30
Peach Girl 1922.45
Peach King, The 1904.18
Peach of a Life, A 1917.17
Peach on the Beach 1971.03
Peaches 1923.124
Peachum's Morning Hymn 1976.10, 1989.24
Peachy 1920.02
Peachy Teacher, The 1902.44
Peacock Alley 1919.13, 1922.31
Peacock Strut 1924.13
Peanut Vendor's Song, The 1931.31
Peanuts and Kisses 1933.21
Pear Tree Quintet 1969.04
Pear Tree Sextet 1980.01
Pearl Maiden, The 1912.05
Pearl of Broadway 1927.12
Pearl of Ceylon, The 1927.12
Pearl of Pekin 1888.09
Pearl of Sweet Ceylon 1904.40
Pearl of the Heart 1895.04
Pearl's a Singer 1995.03
Pearls 1969.05, 1971.18
Pearls of the Orient 1871.08
Pears and Peaches 1972.18
Peasant Girl, The 1915.12
Peasant Queen, The 1926.35
Peasant's Idyll 1992.11
Peculiar Institution, The 1999.08
Peculiar Julia 1904.24
Peculiar State of Affairs 1957.17
Peddlars, The 1872.23
Peddler am I, A 1896.50
Pedestrian Song 1927.46
Pedro the Muleteer 1876.11
Pedro, Ichabod 1948.18
Peek-a-Boo 1882.69, 1882.76, 1886.44, 1886.51, 1889.03, 1890.06, 1891.07, 1905.44, 1909.19, 1919.21
Peekaboo, I Almost See You 1973.08
Peep-Peep 1919.23
Peepin' Tommy 1928.09
Peer Gynt 1944.21
Peering Left and Peering Right 1897.13
Peering Right and Left 1930.12
Peerless Phoebe 1881.07, 1882.20
Peg o' My Dreams 1924.09
Peggy 1904.40, 1919.43
Peggy Blake 1899.41
Peggy Brady 1904.25
Peggy Darlin' 1914.05
Peggy is a New Yorker Now 1904.56
Peggy Machree 1908.43
Peggy O'Moore 1885.53, 1886.44, 1890.06
Peggy of My Heart 1913.17
Peggy Sue 1990.15
Peggy Sue Got Married 1990.15
Peggy's a Creature of Moods 1914.30
Peggy's Leg 1917.27
Peggy, Peggy 1926.50
Pekin Patrol, The 1914.23
Peking Ballet 1984.10

Pela, La 1969.11
Pelea, La 1969.11
Peligro de las Rosas, El 1926.09, 1926.35
Penalty of Love, The 1930.24
Penang-Ourang-Outang, The 1905.48
Pendant que vous dormiez encore 1877.32
Penelope's Hand 1976.01
Pennies from Heaven 1989.16, 1995.14, 1997.01
Penniless Bums 1972.04
Pennsylvania Polka 1943.23
Penny a Tune 1986.13
Penny Candy 1941.01, 1952.09
Penny for Your Thoughts, A 1942.30
Penny in My Pocket 1998.07
Penny Lane 1977.10
Penny Plain, Twopence Colored 1961.26
Pensacola Mooch, The 1910.18
Pensionnaire's Song, The 1892.08
Pensionnaire, Le 1885.57
Penthouse of Your Mind 1975.04
People 1964.11, 1967.03, 1973.17, 1974.22, 1992.16
People Get Hurt 1991.15
People Got to be Free 1982.22
People in Love 1953.02
People in My Head 1995.01
People in My Life 1972.04
People Like Us 2000.08
People Like You 1967.12
People Magazine 1997.08
People of Cyprus 1855.06
People of Taste 1934.06
People Versus Horton the Elephant, The 2000.18
People Watchers, The 1967.14
People Who are Nice 1966.27
People Will Say We're in Love 1943.04
People's Reaction, The 1965.39
Pep 1925.08
Pep it Up 1923.20
Pep Up Your Step 1922.13
Pepe Hillo 1917.25
Pepi! Er? 1964.25
Pepi, He? 1964.25
Pepita 1926.23, 1927.02
Pepper and Salt 1930.21
Pepsi 1976.34
Percolatin' 1930.19
Percussion 1963.16
Percy 1905.33
Percy and Harold 1898.02, 1900.08
Percy With Perseverance 1933.15
Perdido 1980.10, 1981.06
Perennial Debutantes 1936.26
Perfect Cure, The 1862.09
Perfect Day, A 1924.33
Perfect Evening, A 1959.06
Perfect for Each Other 1987.19
Perfect Gentleman, A 1898.47
Perfect Jewels 1917.23
Perfect Lady, A 1907.15
Perfect Little Gentlemen 1890.32, 1892.18, 1892.45
Perfect Love 2000.12
Perfect Lover, A 1920.27
Perfect Models 1930.20
Perfect Song of Love 1921.11
Perfect Strangers 1985.18
Perfect Wreck, A 1893.16
Perfect Year, The 1994.10
Perfect Young Ladies 1954.09
Perfectly Lovely Couple 1965.06
Perfectly Marvelous 1966.24, 1998.04
Perfectly Nice 2000.20
Perfectly Peaceful Person, A 1901.19
Perfectly Terrible, Dear 1908.39
Perfume and Passion 1921.02
Perfume of Love 1920.28
Perhaps 1902.19, 1907.27
Perhaps I Don't 1886.24, 1888.06
Perhaps I Will, Perhaps I Won't 1899.19
Perhaps Love's Dream Will Last Forever 1902.02
Perhaps She's on the Railway 1876.14
Perhaps You May Not Like It 1897.56, 1898.50
Perils of Flirting, The 1872.10
Period Piece 1955.19
Permets qui'ici je te presente 1877.32
Permissable 1913.28
Pernambuco 1948.26, 1974.25
Peron's Latest Flame 1979.23
Perpetual Anticipation 1973.04
Persia 1919.32
Persian Fantasy 1921.06
Persian Love Song 1918.17
Persian Way of Life 1944.15
Personal Appearance 1934.40
Personality 1914.27, 1922.20, 1927.31, 1928.31, 1995.14
Personally Yours 1932.13
Personals 1985.17
Perspective 1963.14
Perspiration 1939.19
Persuasion, The 1960.21
Peruvian Gal-a-Loo, The 1892.23
Pescadero, El 1926.35
Pessimism in the Ate 1893.36
Pessimist, The 1918.08
Pet of the Family 1911.08
Petacal 1948.24
Petals of the Plum Tree, The 1900.43
Petenera 1949.07
Peter Pan 1906.23, 1907.44, 1915.01, 1917.01, 1919.34, 1930.08, 1931.08, 1931.13
Peter Piper 1919.25
Peter's Denial 1971.12
Peter's Journey 1937.04
Peter, Peter 1950.08
Petit amant, Le 1929.14
Petit bout de femme, Un 1929.13
Petit Cafe du coin, Le 1935.17
Petit cafe du coin, Le 1935.19
Petit Caporal, La 1905.04
Petit Caporal, Le 1901.18
Petit ile, La 1935.19
Petit oiseau des iles, Le 1929.13
Petit theatre, Le 1935.19
Petite chanteuese, La 1884.50
Petite soeur il faut secher tes larmes 1887.35
Petite Tonkinese 1906.45
Petits Riens, Les 1959.15
Petticoat High 1959.27
Pettie Mignon 1903.09
Pettin' and Pokin' 1992.03
Petty Crime 1971.19
Peu d'silence, Un. O n'est pas sourd 1886.19
Peuple francais, le politique 1884.50
Pffft! 1958.01
Phalanx of Phidias, The 1894.21
Phantom of the Opera, The 1988.01, 1992.12, 2000.14
Phantom of Your Smile 1917.23
Phantom Patrol 1903.03
Phantom Ship, The 1905.25, 1924.18
Phantom Waltz, The 1920.25
Phantoms of the Ballroom 1924.41
Phantoms, The 1882.75
Pharaoh's Dream Explained 1982.03, 1993.15
Pharaoh's Story 1982.03, 1993.15
Pharaoh's Story, A 1992.12
Phata Phata 1977.01
Phil the Fiddler 1948.04
Philadelphia Drag, The 1911.26, 1912.24
Phillipopolis 1877.22, 1877.25
Phillis have you seen my love 1852.01
Phillis have you seen my love? 1871.10
Philological Waltz 1959.20
Philomel 1919.42
Philomene, the Lazy Girl 1945.07
Philosophic Song and Dance, A 1881.16
Philosophic Tale is Told, The 1898.48
Philosophy 1899.06, 1968.13
Phist. There, Baby 1885.42
Phizzy-Wiz-Wiz 1896.51
Phoebe 1894.31, 1902.07
Phoebe Brown 1909.10
Phoebe Snow 1908.21, 1918.37
Phoebe, Dear, I Love You 1900.42
Phoenix and the Turtle, The 1981.02
Phoney Game, The 1972.10
Phony Ballet, The 1910.16, 1913.18
Phooey 1969.03
Photograph Duet 1880.42
Photograph, The 1880.18
Photography 1910.11
Phrenologist Coon, The 1900.46
Phrenology 1900.51, 1902.05, 1920.09
Physical 1982.15
Physical Culture 1895.21
Physical Culture Girls 1895.03, 1904.06, 1919.21
Physical Fitness 1962.04
Pi in the Sky 1962.02
Pianiste de varsovie, Le 1966.20
Piano du Pauvre, Le 1958.06
Piano Lesson 1957.18, 2000.11
Pianologue 1922.26
Pic et pic et colegram 1929.16
Piccadilly 1981.09
Piccadilly Crawl, The 1906.29
Piccadilly Walk, The 1922.05
Piccaninny Pie 1943.18
Picchi' Chiangi Sta Beddra Rigina 1985.16
Piccolo 1908.06
Pick 'Em Up and Lay 'Em Down 1929.06
Pick a Husband 1914.03
Pick Yourself a Flower 1971.16
Pick Yourself Up 1986.01, 1986.06
Pick-a-Pickaniny 1914.33
Pick-a-Rib 1939.29
Pick-Me-Up! 1959.19
Pick-Pocket Tango 1959.01
Pickalittle Talkalittle 2000.11
Pickalittle, Talkalittle 1957.18
Pickaninnies, The 1898.46
Pickaninny Days 1911.20
Pickaninny Days, The 1909.10
Pickaninny Land 1929.23
Pickaninny Mose 1905.47
Pickaninny Shoes 1921.16
Pickaninny Vamp 1923.11
Pickaninny's Dream 1898.61
Pickaninny's Lullaby, The 1897.45
Pickers are Comin', The 1975.03
Picket Fence 1921.02
Pickin' 'Em Up and Layin' 'Em Down 1916.13
Pickin' Cotton 1928.22
Picking Peaches 1918.30
Pickpocket, The 1971.20
Pickwick Club, The 1903.02
Pickwick's Horse Brigade 1903.02
Pickwickians, The 1965.28
Picnic Club, The 1911.40
Picnic in the Sky 1915.28
Picnic Party With You, A 1923.27
Picnic, The 1971.21
Picture I Want to See, A 1918.03
Picture No Artist Can Paint, A 1900.47
Picture of Happiness, The 1960.19
Picture of Me Without You, A 1935.14
Picture of Mother, A 1891.15
Picture Postcard 1958.10
Picture Show, The 1998.21
Picture That is Turned to the Wall, The 1891.32, 1891.40
Picture That is Turned Toward the Wall, The 1891.15
Picture That is Turned Towards the Wall, The 1891.14
Pictures 1899.21
Pictures in the Smoke 1903.10
Pictures of Home 1888.28, 1890.29
Piddle, Twiddle and Resolve 1969.06
Pidgie Widgie 1922.24
Pie 1904.14, 1923.40
Pie Eyed Piper 1931.36
Pie in the Sky 1931.21
Pie Jesu 1992.12
Piece de Resistance 1948.24
Piece of a Girl, A 1944.01
Piece of Cake 1989.07
Piece of Ground, A 1966.03
Piece of the Action, A 1997.08
Piece of the Pie 1994.06
Piece of the Rainbow, A 1973.11
Pied Piper of Harlem 1935.18
Pied Piper's Can-Can, The 1961.08

Pieniadze 1992.05
Pierre 1903.06, 1925.44
Pierrot 1906.47, 1917.08, 1924.06
Pierrot and Columbine 1895.12
Pierrot and Cupid 1906.25
Pierrot and Pierrette 1928.08, 1929.08
Pierrot Song 1903.37
Pierrot's Ball 1914.20
Pierrotland 1914.10
Piff Paff 1946.18
Piff, Paff Pouf 1890.11
Piff, Paff, Pouff 1868.03
Pig With the Roman Nose, The 1879.71
Pig, The 1973.08
Pigalle 1964.22
Pigeon Run 1975.05
Pigtails and Freckles 1962.20
Pilate and Christ 1971.12
Pilate's Dream 1971.12
Pile-Up, The 1968.13
Pilgrim Fathers, The 1929.20
Pilgrim of Love 1907.08
Pilgrim Riding Music 1969.04
Pilgrims of Love 1947.04
Pilgrims' Procession 1956.15
Pill a Day, A 1925.38
Pill Parade 1960.07
Pill-Box Revue, The 1917.12
Pillar to Post 1967.14
Pillow for His Royal Head, A 1945.01
Pillow Number 1912.47
Pillowing 1990.17
Pills 1972.21
Pilot's Daughter, The 1889.02
Pilot, The 1891.14
Pimlico Malinda 1903.03, 1904.11
Pimp's Ballad 1989.24
Pin Cushion, A 1926.14
Pinafore 1938.10
Pinball wizard 1972.08
Pinball Wizard 1993.06
Pinch and Judy 1922.04
Pinching Myself 1933.06
Pine Cones and Holly Berries 1963.21
Ping Pong 1902.29, 1905.37
Ping-Pong 1902.35
Pining 1928.10
Pink and White 1914.32
Pink Cocktail for a Blue Lady, A 1942.12
Pink Dominos 1877.39
Pink Lady 1931.19
Pink Petty from Peter, A 1907.63
Pinkerton Detective Moon, The 1912.44
Pinkey, My Darling 1898.78
Pinky Panky Poo 1903.01
Pinky, Panky Poo 1902.21
Pinocchio 1938.16
Pinouit 1893.37
Pioneer, The 1956.08
Pious Child, The 1853.03, 1863.02
Pip Pip? Toot Toot 1920.20
Pipe Dreaming 1946.13
Pipe His Blues 1896.31
Pipe in hands 1879.35
Piper o' the Dundee 1920.12
Piper You Must Pay, The 1923.03
Pipes and Grog 1880.46
Pipes of Pan Americana 1943.14
Pipes of Pan are Calling, The 1910.05
Pipes, The 1892.45
Piraeus, My Love 1967.05
Pirate Dance 1928.49
Pirate Jenny 1965.04, 1966.19, 1989.24
Pirate Jenny, The 1933.07
Pirate March 1990.20
Pirate Song 1954.13, 1979.22
Pirate Song, The 1950.08
Pirate Trinity, A 1902.11
Pirate's Doom, The 1908.41
Pirate's Rag 1915.17
Pirates and Quaker Girl 1912.24
Pirates are We 1905.25
Pirates of Penzance 1938.10
Pirates' Prayer 1846.01
Pirelli's Miracle Elixir 1979.06
Pistachio 1948.22
Pistoli Carabi 1897.41
Pit Pat! 1894.28
Pit-a-Pat 1906.41
Pitcher of Beer, The 1879.68, 1883.46, 1892.54
Pitiful Plaint 1869.15
Pitter Patter 1920.32, 1968.24
Pity for one in childhood torn 1844.01
Pity Me 1921.35
Pity My Pitiful Plight 1903.19, 1905.53
Pity the Child 1988.09
Pity the Poor 1976.11
Pity the Poor Millionaire 1937.14
Pity the Sunset 1957.16
Pixie's Entrance 1904.15
Pixley Medley, The 1892.58
Pizarro was a Very Narrow Man 1930.27
Pizza, The 1973.08
Place a Bengaline! 1887.35
Place a la garde-suisse 1884.50
Place Called Alimony Jail, A 1989.07
Place Called Home, A 1994.12
Place in the Country 1928.43
Place Pigalle 1947.05, 1948.12, 1963.02, 1965.08
Places, Everybody 1939.13
Plague of Rats, The 1885.65
Plain Jane 1924.10
Plain Jane Payne 1903.20
Plain Kitty McGuire 1900.41
Plain Mamie O'Hooley 1903.34
Plain Molly O! 1891.28, 1894.20
Plain Ol' Name o' Smith, The 1914.21
Plain Potatoe, The 1887.04
Plain We Live 1955.01
Plaintive, A 1928.48
Plaisir d'amour 1933.24
Plaisir delectable! 1883.51
Plan it by the Planets 1948.24
Planchette, Planchette 1897.17
Planes 1979.11
Planet Shmanet - Wise Up Janet Weiss 2000.17
Planet Shmanet Janet 1975.08
Plank, The 1950.08
Planning 1922.44
Plans A & B 1988.10
Plant You Now, Dig You Later 1940.22
Plantation 1862.06
Plantation Dance 1876.32
Plantation Echoes 1905.07
Plantation in Philadelphia 1950.04
Planter Cafe 1959.15, 1961.25
Plastic Alligator, The 1963.21
Plastic Surgery 1927.64
Platinum Dreams 1978.25
Play 4-11-44 1898.22
Play 7-11-77 1899.31
Play a Little Hindoo 1920.27
Play a Simple Melody 1914.31, 1976.32, 1989.21
Play Ball 1889.39, 1933.25
Play Ball With the Lord 1970.02
Play Boy 1929.42
Play Gypsies 1926.27
Play is the Bunk, The 1934.18
Play Me a Bagpipe Tune 1925.12
Play Me a Country Song 1982.13
Play Me a New Tune 1925.43
Play Me a Tune 1923.02
Play Me a Ukelele 1916.21
Play Me an Old-Time Two-Step 1936.07
Play Me That Tune 1914.32, 1919.11
Play Me the Music 1976.16
Play My Melody 1916.11
Play That Barber Shop Chord 1910.17, 1910.18
Play That Fandango Rag 1909.13
Play the Game 1929.37
Play the Game, Sally 1911.36
Play the Music for Me 1992.08
Play the Queen 1979.03
Play the Queen, or Old Irish Poker 1924.14
Play With Fire 1922.36
Play Without a Bedroom, A 1921.30
Play's the Thing, The 1895.04
Play, Fiddle, Play 1948.13
Play, My Daughter 1934.32
Play, Orchestra, Play 1986.19
Play, Orchestra, Play! 1936.29
Play, Play, Play 1910.15
Play-Fair Man, A 1923.47
Playbill 2000.16
Playground of the Rich Ballet 1971.15
Playhouse in the Sky 1927.48
Playhouse Planned for You, A 1924.10
Playin' 1976.27
Playing da Golden Strings 1897.33
Playing for Position 1982.13
Playing for the Girl 1920.06
Playing the Game 1928.42
Playing the Harpsichord 1931.29
Playland 1906.40, 1908.02
Playmates 1893.43, 1907.12
Plaza 6-9423 1938.09
Plaza Song, The 1983.19
Pleasant Beach House 1959.22
Pleasant Day 1906.31
Pleasant Greeting, A 1924.22
Please 1991.03
Please be Good on Sunday 1956.09
Please be Human 1976.33
Please be Kind 1952.11, 1974.10
Please Don't Keep Me Waiting 1909.03
Please Don't Monkey With Broadway 1992.18
Please Don't Move 1903.06
Please Don't Say There isn't Any Santa Claus 1917.08
Please Don't Stop Him 1999.09
Please Don't Take Away the Girls 1919.16
Please Go Find My Billie-Boy 1911.13
Please Hello 1976.02
Please Learn to Love 1919.31
Please Let Me Tell You 1956.04
Please Let Us Have Our Seance, Madame Flora 1947.10
Please Mr. Postman 1984.15
Please Stay 1968.01
Please Take My Arm 1880.25
Please Tell Me What They Mean 1908.39
Please to make way for us 1882.63
Please to Put That Down 1885.06, 1885.49, 1887.05, 1893.46
Please Turn Your Backs 1912.34
Please Understand 1995.04
Please Yourself 1889.36
Please, Dear Master 1894.05
Please, Oh Please 1910.01
Please, Please 1910.31
Please, Sir, We Want if We May 1905.46
Please, Teacher 1925.26
Pleasure 1922.44
Pleasure and Privilege 1970.15
Pleasure Brigade, The 1908.42
Pleasure of Your Company, The 1976.32
Pleasure Pusher 1979.15
Pleasure's About to be Mine, The 1967.16
Pleasures 1974.12
Pledge of Allegiance 1955.13
Pledge Us Do! 1885.44
Pledge, The 1882.44, 2000.20
Plenty Bambini 1956.04
Plenty More Fish in the Sea 1948.19, 1949.05
Plenty of Pennsylvania 1955.01
Pletty Little Chinee 1900.43
Pleurait, Il 1941.03
Pliney, Come Out in the Moonlight 1909.10
Plot Again, The 1923.46
Plot to Catch a Man In, A 1950.10
Plot, The 1927.47
Plow it All Under 1972.21
Plucking Out the Notes 1888.15
Plum Pudding 1884.39, 1884.41
Plume de Ma Tante, La 1958.18
Plume, The 1872.23
Plundering of the Town, The 1953.11
Plunk, Plunk, Plunk 1922.28
Plus joli reve, Le 1934.32
Pluto Boys, The 1937.14

Pluto's Partner I 1898.48
Plymouth Rock 1921.21
Po Karekare Ana 1972.20
Po' Li'l Black Chile 1926.31
Po' Lil' Frenchie 1940.01
Po, Po, Po 1967.05
Po-lo-ma 1878.05
Poaching 1907.32
Pobre chica, la que tiene que servir 1969.11
Pocahontas 1907.24
Pocapdedious 1973.07
Pocketful of Dreams 1950.12
Pocketful of Miracles 1974.10
Poeme Erotique 1944.21
Poems 1976.02
Poet and Peasant 1942.12
Poetry 1993.17
Poetry and All That Jazz 1960.01
Poetry Competition 1990.17
Poetry in Motion 1944.19
Poetry of Motion, The 1925.14
Poi Ball 1925.23
Point of No Return, The 1988.01
Point Venice 1923.07
Poison Ivy 1995.03
Pokenhatchit Public Protest Committee, The 1981.14
Poker Game 1927.55
Poker Game, The 1981.10, 1999.06
Poker Love 1906.37
Poker Polka 1963.26, 1992.10
Poker Polka, The 1950.14
Polar Bear Strut, The 1926.17
Police Report, A 1834.01
Policeman Song 1881.06
Policeman's Ball, The 1949.08
Policeman's Lot is a Happy One, A 1912.24
Policeman's song 1882.44
Policeman's Song 1938.10
Policemen 1880.59
Policeology 1919.01
Policy Players Ball, The 1899.31
Political Whip, The 1873.10
Politics 1949.17
Politics and Poker 1959.25
Polk Salad Annie 1978.01
Polka 1851.03, 1948.27
Polka Dot, The 1924.08, 1929.29
Polka Dots and Moonbeams 1995.14
Polka, The 1959.27
Polly 1902.08, 1929.02
Polly Believes in Preparedness 1917.01
Polly from Hollywood 1924.44
Polly of Hollywood 1927.10
Polly Poll 1917.16
Polly Pretty Polly 1917.37
Polly Put the Kettle On 1923.47
Polly Wolly Doodle 1944.32
Polly's Lied 1976.10
Polly's Song 1966.19
Polly, will you try me 1859.08
Polly, won't you try me now 1858.04
Pollyanna 1927.20
Polo 1887.32, 1904.03
Polo de Tobalo, El 1992.15
Polonaise 1945.14, 1964.25
Poltergeists 1986.18
Polyglot Trio 1883.04
Polythene Pam 1974.24
Pom-Pom 1916.04
Pomme d'Or 1917.28
Pomme est un fruit plein de seve, La 1878.08
Pomp and Circumstance 1935.12
Pompadour 1933.03
Pompanola 1928.37
Pompeii Restored 1872.23
Pompey's Complaint 1787.01
Poncho De Panther from Brazil 1943.24
Ponies on Parade 1925.48
Pony Boy 1924.47
Poogie Woo 1924.17
Pooh Pooh 1880.47
Pool 1877.22
Pool of Love 1927.34
Pool Room Papa 1929.23
Poontang 1976.20
Poor as a Church Mouse 1944.27
Poor Baby 1970.13
Poor Butterfly 1916.15, 1916.20, 1921.02
Poor Cadets, The 1913.02
Poor Cinderella 1881.11, 1927.09
Poor Cock Robin 1879.64
Poor Everybody Else 1973.06
Poor Florodora Girl 1920.18
Poor Fool, He Makes Me Laugh 1988.01
Poor Irish Minstrel, The 1882.69, 1886.51
Poor Jerusalem 1971.12
Poor Jud 1943.04
Poor Little Country Maid, The 1895.27
Poor Little Fluttering Moths 1901.17
Poor Little Foolish Man 1907.37
Poor little Gipsey, A 1853.01
Poor Little Girl Like Me, A 1908.44
Poor Little Hollywood Star 1962.27, 1998.15
Poor Little Man 1888.18
Poor Little Marie 1926.18
Poor Little Marionette, The 1905.49
Poor Little Mary 1894.38, 1895.02
Poor Little Me 1884.48, 1918.19, 1945.18
Poor Little Person 1967.14
Poor Little Pierrette 1954.09
Poor Little Red Papoose 1904.39
Poor Little Red Pappoose 1906.01
Poor Little Rich Girl 1925.42, 1975.22, 1986.19
Poor Little Rich Girl's Dog 1917.19
Poor Little Rich Little Me 1920.35
Poor Little Ritz Girl 1920.25
Poor Little Shy Little, Demure Little Me 1932.15
Poor Little Wall Flower 1923.07
Poor Man 1948.18
Poor Marat in Your Bathtub Seat 1965.39
Poor Married Man, The 1888.20
Poor O'Hoolihan Held the Fuse 1898.43
Poor Old Dad in New York for the Summer 1909.17
Poor Old Florodora Girl 1920.35
Poor Old King Carrot 1872.23
Poor Old Marat 1965.39
Poor Old Solomon 1910.20
Poor Old World 1923.46
Poor Pierrot 1894.33, 1925.34, 1926.09, 1926.35, 1931.37
Poor Poor Joseph 1982.03, 1993.15
Poor Relations 1889.36
Poor Shepherds We 1900.50
Poor Sister 2000.20
Poor Soldier, The 1860.03
Poor Thing 1979.06
Poor Tied Up Darlin' 1975.18, 1976.31
Poor Uncle Gasazus 1914.13
Poor Unfortunate Sister Anne 1903.04
Poor Wand'ring One 1879.72
Poor Wandering One 1938.10, 1981.01
Poor Wicked Man, The 1881.07
Poor Winter Garden Girl 1920.20
Poor Working Girl, A 1909.12
Poor Workingman 1920.30
Poor young thing 1887.04
Poor, Poor Pharaoh 1982.03, 1993.15
Pop goes his Weasel 1864.13
Pop, Pop, Pop 1898.55
Pop, Pop, Pop! 1900.57
Poppa's Blues 1987.05
Poppies 1960.17, 1997.11
Poppy 1914.15
Poppy Chorus 1903.03, 1904.13, 1904.44
Poppy Dear 1923.27
Poppy Land 1921.19
Poppy the Dream Girl 1925.12
Poppyland 1919.43
Popsey Wopsey 1912.26
Popular Airs, The 1894.51
Popular art of the day, The 1895.43
Popular Girl, A 1910.34
Popular Pauline 1905.44
Popular Pests, The 1919.15
Popular Pop, The 1914.26
Popular Song, A 1910.02, 1922.08
Popular Songs 1906.25
Popular Tune, A 1902.04
Popularity 1922.48, 1924.21, 1968.07, 1986.03
Por Un Amor 1988.15
Porcelain Maid 1922.39
Porgy 1928.18, 1930.34
Port of the World 1931.29
Portenito, El 1999.18
Porter! Porter! 1923.13
Porterology 1925.18
Porto Banos 1920.13
Porto Rico 1911.20
Porto Rico Girls 1899.31
Portofino 1958.04
Portrait Parade 1926.32
Portrait, The 1910.03
Posin' 1980.10
Posing 1910.11
Posing for Venus 1912.34
Possessors of a Magic Art 1875.19
'Possum Chase, De 1899.35
Possum Rag 1911.08
Possum Trot 1929.01
Post Card Beau, A 1911.35
Post Office 1922.48
Postage-Stamp Principality 1956.16
Postcard #2 1986.20
Postcard #3/Dressing Room Scene 1986.20
Poster Diversity 1904.24
Poster Girl 1926.01
Posterity is Just Around the Corner 1931.48
Posterland 1917.31
Posty and a Maid, A 1921.25
Pot Pourri 1919.19
Pot-Pouri 1917.21
Pot-Pourri 1958.06
Potash and Perlmutter Ball, The 1917.37
Potato Bug, The 1917.13
Potato Song, The 1903.02
Potatoes a pound 1880.18
Potekha 1977.13
Potiphar 1982.03, 1992.12, 1993.15
Potpourri 1925.25
Pottawattomie 1939.27
Poules, Les 1965.05
Pour elles, c'est un jour de fete 1883.51
Pour J'en-Ai-Marre 1922.34
Pour la chapelle qu'ono s'apprete 1887.36
Pour le tresor que to nous abandonnes 1878.12
Pour les compter, mes amoureux 1886.19
Pour oh pour the Prowler's whiskey 1881.06
Pour plaire, en nos regouts 1887.36
Pour sortir en tout saison 1929.11
Pour te faire plaisir 1929.15
Pour toi 1929.14
Pour trouver un mari 1929.10
Pour un joyeux repas 1884.43
Pour voir Irma 1887.35
Pour, O Pour the Pirate Sherry 1981.01
Pour, Oh Pour the Pirate Sherry 1879.72
Pourquoi prendre ce front severe 1884.43
Pourquoi rever? 1934.32
Pourquoi vous chagriner 1884.43
Pousse Cafe 1912.13
Poverty Program 1971.20
Poverty Row 1936.06
Poverty's Tears Ebb and Flow 1885.49, 1893.46
Pow Wow Polka, The 1954.13
Pow! Bam! Zonk! 1966.06
Powder My Back 1965.05, 1981.17
Powder Puff 1926.01
Powder Puff Ballet, The 1991.07
Powder Your Nose 1900.56
Power 1982.18
Power behind the throne 1879.35
Power of Gold, The 1878.02
Power of Love 1862.09
Power of Love, The 1863.06, 1870.44, 1881.12
Power of Negative Thinking, The 1956.09
Power of the Human Eye, The 1898.60
Power of the Press, The 1904.55
Powerful Stuff 2000.07
Powers of Goodness 1882.60

Pox Upon the Traitor's Brow, A 1965.29
Practical 1953.02
Practical Patriots, The 1913.27
Practising Up on You 1930.32
Prairie Frolic, A 1918.19
Prairie Mary 1907.53
Praise the Lord and Pass the Ammunition 1980.29
Praises of Cupid, The 1879.38
Prast-Chi - Prast Chi 1925.29
Prater, The 1908.06
Pray 1990.12
Pray Excuse 1910.24
Pray for the Lights to Go Out 1976.04
Pray for the soul's repose 1855.06
Pray Tell Me 1912.04
Pray, Daddy, please to moderate 1859.08
Pray, excuse me 1887.04
Pray, Pretty Maid 1906.49
Pray, Tell Me Why? 1881.22
Prayer 1948.27, 1970.08, 1972.09, 1972.14, 1997.19, 1999.13
Prayer to God 1970.17
Prayer to St. Valentine, A 1907.06
Pre-Eminently Handsome 1890.26
Pre-Historic Man 1912.40
Preach Them Blues 1975.20
Precious Jewels 1920.19
Precious Lord 1990.05
Precious Memories 1989.12
Precision 1958.18
Prefect punctuality, a virtue rare 1888.18
Prehistoric Complaint 1966.32
Preliminary Skirmish 1919.10
Prelude 1969.08
Prelude to a Kiss 1981.06, 1997.03
Preludes, Les 1979.10
Preludio a Francini 1993.08
Preludio del Bandoneon y la Noche 1997.13
Prenez mes roses 1934.32, 1935.19
Preparation Fugue 1986.12
Preparation, The 1969.17
Prepare the Dolls 1910.24
Prepare Ye the Way of the Lord 1976.17
Prepossessing Maid 1904.04
Preposterous 1968.08
Present for Gilbert 1956.13
Presentation of Miss Turnstiles 1998.16
Presentation of Princesses 1953.16
Presenting Clara Spencer 1960.01
Presents for Mrs. Rogers 1991.07
President 1998.01
President am I 1901.27
President Jefferson Sunday Luncheon Party March, The 1976.11
President's Daughter, The 1970.18
Presidente, El 1920.13
Press Conference 1981.29, 1988.09
Press Me to Thee 1912.03
Pretend You're Living 1975.23
Pretending 1909.30
Pretty 1947.19
Pretty am I, so Pretty 1960.18
Pretty Ankle 1923.13
Pretty as a Butterfly 1886.32
Pretty as a Picture 1876.31, 1879.32, 1883.07, 1913.24, 1944.23, 1947.04, 1986.20
Pretty Baby 1914.23, 1916.11
Pretty Baby Doll from Paree 1918.12
Pretty Betsy Brown 1901.25
Pretty Betty, if you love me 1869.43
Pretty Bird 1888.34
Pretty Bobolink 1892.31
Pretty City Girl 1923.07
Pretty Dance is Like a Violin, A 1921.17
Pretty Daughter of Mine 1945.09
Pretty Drummer 1922.06
Pretty Edelweiss 1915.28
Pretty Face 1981.14
Pretty Flowers from Me to You 1923.38
Pretty Girl 1923.37, 1924.11, 1928.23
Pretty Girl is Like a Melody, A 1919.15, 1965.05, 1980.18, 1989.21
Pretty Girl Milking Her Cow 1860.05
Pretty Girl, A 1891.11
Pretty Girl, A Summer Night A 1904.17
Pretty Gitana 1848.04
Pretty Isabella and Her Umbrella 1897.42
Pretty Jemima 1870.01
Pretty Kitty 1957.05
Pretty Lady 1976.02, 1977.05, 1980.20
Pretty Lips 1882.39
Pretty Little Bathers 1902.42
Pretty Little Boys 1880.10
Pretty Little Chichis 1913.10
Pretty Little China Girl 1897.39
Pretty Little Cinderella 1920.02
Pretty Little Dark Blue Eyes 1884.23
Pretty Little Girl Inside, The 1910.19
Pretty Little Girl That I Know 1900.03
Pretty Little Girls Like You 1919.11
Pretty Little Heather Bell 1907.58
Pretty Little Japanese Lady 1908.20
Pretty Little Laundry Girls 1885.29
Pretty Little Maid of Zanzibar, The 1905.35
Pretty Little Maiden on the Screen 1912.30
Pretty Little Mayflower Girl 1916.03
Pretty Little Picture 1962.12
Pretty little Quaker, The 1885.51
Pretty Little Shoe 1881.11
Pretty Little So-and-So 1927.11
Pretty Little Squaw from Utah, The 1904.22
Pretty Little Stranger 1927.09
Pretty Little Sunshine 1911.28
Pretty Lulu Lu 1902.42
Pretty Maid Adelaide 1903.14
Pretty Maid Milking Her Cow 1888.28
Pretty Maid, A 1888.09
Pretty Maiden 1905.36
Pretty Malindy 1923.11
Pretty Milliners, The 1911.12
Pretty Ming Toy 1920.25
Pretty Mollie Shannon She's the Real, Real Thing 1901.25
Pretty Mrs. Smith 1914.21
Pretty Music 1998.21
Pretty New England Pink 1902.21
Pretty Page, My 1869.42
Pretty Pair, The 1873.28
Pretty Part for Me to Play, A 1909.19
Pretty Patty Moss 1938.06
Pretty Peggy 1902.24, 1923.21
Pretty Pin-Up 1978.06
Pretty Polly 1904.31, 1920.02, 1922.40
Pretty Polly Hopkins 1877.25, 1879.03
Pretty Polly Palmer 1896.44
Pretty Polly Primrose 1903.17
Pretty Polly, say 1750.01, 1854.06
Pretty Pond Lillies 1884.48
Pretty Primrose 1906.32
Pretty Punchinello 1909.07
Pretty Soft, Pretty Sweet 1928.10
Pretty Suzette 1897.37
Pretty Things 1924.28
Pretty Tillie, if you Love me 1869.07
Pretty to Walk With 1957.16
Pretty Typewriters, The 1894.17
Pretty Up, Pretty Up, Pretty Baby 1919.26
Pretty Widow, The 1894.07
Pretty Wilhelmina 1877.28
Pretty Woman 1979.06
Pretty Women 1999.20
Pretty Young Widow, The 1891.39, 1894.21, 1894.35
Pretty, Petite and Sweet 1928.34
Prevalent Condition of the Mind, The 1921.06
Priam's Little Congai 1929.20
Pricklepear Bloom, The 1975.18, 1976.31
Pride and Joy 1964.29
Pride and Pet of the Lane, The 1905.21
Pride Goes Before a Fall 1896.41
Pride of the London Stage 1896.24
Priere 1948.12
Priglio Don't Know 1937.11
Prim and Proper 1971.09
Prima Donna 1988.01
Prima Donna Waltz 1855.11
Prima Donna, The 1907.10
Prima Donnas, The 1912.44
Primavera, La 1879.38
Primitive Ebony, The 1932.19
Primrose Path, The 1914.24, 1920.19, 1923.13
Primrose Way, The 1915.12
Prince and Queen 1997.16
Prince and Queen, The 1998.08
Prince Charming 1919.19, 1922.26, 1925.21, 1934.15
Prince here you see, A 1862.08
Prince is a Coming, The 1861.03
Prince is Giving a Ball, The 1993.14, 2001.09
Prince Leander is His Name 1870.20, 1876.06
Prince Leander is My Name 1868.03
Prince of Bohemia, The 1910.04
Prince of Borneo 1906.13
Prince of Borneo, The 1909.07
Prince of Central Park, The 1989.25
Prince of Good Fellows 1903.36
Prince of Humbug, The 1980.07
Prince of My Dreams 1912.40
Prince of Philadelphia, The 1953.10
Prince of Wales, The 1922.34, 1924.31
Prince's Farewell, The 1962.27
Prince's Goodbye, The 1982.01, 1998.15
Princely Scheme, A 1954.13, 1979.22, 1990.20
Princess Beautiful 1922.15
Princess Can't be Found, Sir, The 1912.47
Princess I, A 1896.10
Princess Nicotine 1923.42
Princess of Far Away 1912.39
Princess of Mulberry Bend, The 1899.03
Princess of My Dreams 1921.21
Princess of Pure Delight, The 1941.04
Princess of Trebizonde, The 1895.36
Princess Virtue 1921.11
Princess We Adore, The 1901.27
Princess Who Never Smiled, The 1924.48
Princess Zenobia, La 1936.05, 1983.02
Printemps 1907.10
Priorities 1942.05
Priscilla 1902.29
Prisms 1968.13
Prison in a Prison 1999.22
Prisoner of Love, A 1912.41
Prisoner's Song 1927.37
Prisoner's Song, The 1926.37
Prisoner, Prisoner, Run Along 1918.36
Prisoners in Niggertown 1968.11
Prisoners of Love 2001.05
Prisoners, Stand Up! 1912.40
Prisonniere, La 1927.23
Pristi, sapristi 1878.08
Prithee, Pretty Maiden, Willow, Willow, Waly 1881.37
Private Affair, A 1899.38
Private Conversation 1997.17
Private Dining Room, The 1973.08
Private Parts 1982.10
Private Thoughts 1987.19
Private Tommy Atkins 1894.33, 1894.46, 1900.43
Prize for That, A 1904.03
Probably 1971.10
Problem After Problem 1978.11
Procession, The 1926.09, 1926.35
Processional 1934.43, 1943.10
Processional March 1899.39
Procurer's Ballad, The 1965.04
Prodigal Daughter 1949.02
Prodigal Son, The 1891.27
Profession of a Manicure, The 1906.17
Professional Beauty, A 1883.04
Professional Showbizness Comedy 1992.17
Professions 1897.20
Professor and His Pupil 1905.34
Professor and His Pupil, The 1904.58
Professor and the Students, The 1974.26
Professor Walker and His Solo Symphony 1986.11
Professor Won't You Teach Me All You Know? 1899.38
Progress 1948.25, 1968.05
Progress is the Root of All Evil 1956.12
Progressive Poker Game, The 1898.50
Progressive Poker Party 1905.07
Prohibition 1919.15
Prohibition Ball 1919.08

Prohibition Blues 1918.32
Prologue 1923.17, 1933.27, 1936.31
Promenade 1978.22, 1979.10
Promenade - Havana 1910 1944.31
Promenade Anglais, La 1907.15
Promenade the Esplanade 1927.19
Promenade Walk 1924.36
Promenade Walk at the Beach, The 1925.23
Promenade, A 1938.15
Promenade, The 1983.11
Promise 1937.01
Promise Me a Rose 1959.22, 1985.04
Promise Not to Stand Me Up Again 1927.05
Promise of Living, The 2001.04
Promise of the Future, The 1995.04
Promise of What I Could Be, The 1970.02
Promise Your Kisses 1926.12
Promised Land 1885.50, 1980.05
Promised Land, The 1986.11
Promises 1924.07
Promises, Promises 1968.31
Promoter, The 1899.29
Promoters, The 1900.46
Proper Air, The 1896.48
Proper Gentlemen, A 1965.14
Proper Thing, You Know, The 1889.37
Proper Way to Kiss, The 1903.34
Property Man 1922.03
Prophete, Le 1977.09
Propinquity 1950.02
Proposal Duet 1967.02
Proposal, The 1997.06, 2000.20
Proposals 1910.07, 1919.39
Propriety, prisms and prunes 1882.63
Prosit 1909.14
Prosperity 1915.04
Proteges, The 1921.03
Proud 1976.11
Proud Lady, Have Your Way 1945.09
Proud Little Pages 1918.26
Proud Mary 1982.22, 1986.02, 1997.21
Proud of You 1942.29
Proud, Erstwhile, Upright, Fair 1979.10
Proverbs 1924.10
Prowling 'round the diamond fields 1878.02
Prowling 'Round the Diamond Fields 1885.58, 1888.13, 1896.35
Prudence has Fled 1917.14
Prunella 1914.10
Prunella Mine 1914.15
Przeaprodensky 1918.04
Psalm 23 1997.12
Psalm 8 1997.12
Psalm of Peace, A 1972.09
Psalm, The 1965.34
Psalms, The 1894.52
Psst 1975.01
Psyche 1902.15
Psychedelic Shack 1997.21
Psychiatry Song, The 1936.28
Psychical Society 1908.42
Ptolemy 1968.23
Pua i Mohala 1912.03
Public Enemy #1 1987.15
Public Enemy No. 1 1937.14
Public Enemy Number One 1934.36
Publicity 1904.03
Publish Your Book 1988.07
Puerto Rican Day Parade 1998.02
Puff 1881.36
Puff Puff 1900.38
Puff! Puff! 1898.50
Puff! Puff! Puff! 1906.22
Puff, Puff 1897.30
Puisqu'un heureux hasard 1929.14
Puka Puka Pants 1961.07
Pull Back 1876.32
Pull Down the Blinds 1876.05
Pull it Over 1915.23
Pull the Boat for Eli 1937.02, 1946.19
Pull up 1882.18
Pull Your Strings 1924.36
Pull Yourself Together 1927.35
Pullman Porter's Ball, De 1912.07
Pullman Porter's Lament 1931.11
Pullman Porters on Parade 1933.27
Pullman Porters' Ball, De 1901.17
Pulse of My Heart 1912.06
Pulverize the Kaiser 1968.05
Pump Boys 1982.04
Pump, The 1880.18
Pumping Iron 1987.05
Punalada, La 1985.07, 1999.18
Punch and Judy Get a Divorce 1948.25
Punch and Judy Man 1931.40
Punch Bowl Glide 1912.39
Punch in the Presence of the Passengaire 1877.25
Pure and White is the Lotus 1895.33
Pure in Heart, The 1971.09
Purefoy's Lament 1965.29
Purest Kind of Guy, The 1941.01
Puritan Damsel, A 1893.19
Purity 1917.18
Purity Brigade March 1912.13
Purity Brigade, The 1897.39
Purity Brigadiers, The 1921.20
Purlie 1970.05
Purple and the Brown, The 1947.17
Purple Pansies 1888.05
Purple Rose 1952.20
Pursue the Truth 1997.09
Pursuit 1965.02
Pursuit, The 1905.23
Purty Little Thing, A 1930.06
Push a Button in a Hutton 1948.23
Push Around 1926.51
Push de Button 1981.16
Push Dem Clouds Away 1891.39
Push Ka Pi Shi Pie 1992.03
Push Me Along in My Pushcart 1906.21, 1968.07
Push the Button 1957.16
Push the Jug Around 1897.03
Puss in Boots 1922.29
Pussy and the Bow-Wow 1904.47
Pussy Cat, The 1899.41
Pussy Foot, The 1958.14
Pussyfoot 1920.11
Pussyfoot and Maltese 1920.36
Put 'Em Back 1956.12
Put 'Em in a Box, Tie 'Em With a Ribbon, and Throw 'Em in the Deep Blue Sea 1974.10
Put a Curse on You 1971.13
Put a Lid on It 2000.07
Put a Little Bet Down for Me 1907.57
Put a Little Magic in Your Life 1983.01
Put a Nickel in the Slot 1890.03
Put and Take 1921.26
Put Down Six and Carry Two 1911.31
Put Him Away 1970.19
Put it Away Till Spring 1930.18
Put it Down 1896.05
Put it in the Book 1965.19
Put it Right Here 1975.20
Put Me Among the Girls 1907.44, 1907.46
Put Me in My Little Bed 1871.04, 1985.02
Put Me in My Little Cell 1905.19
Put Me Off at Buffalo 1894.35
Put on a Happy Face 1960.06
Put on a Zoot Suit 1979.08
Put on the Ritz 1924.07
Put on this cap 1861.03
Put on Your Bridal Veil 1886.03
Put on Your Slippers, You're in for the Night 1910.12
Put on Your Sunday Clothes 1964.01, 1979.13, 1985.19, 1998.07
Put Your Arms Around Me 1911.30
Put Your Arms Around Me, Honey 1910.22
Put Your Best Foot Forward, Little Girl 1912.39
Put Your Cares on Ice 1942.19
Put your Head in 1870.27
Put Your Head in, Valiant Soldier 1870.08
Put Your Heart in a Song 1934.35
Put Your Mind Right on It 1929.18
Put Your Old Bandanna On 1924.37
Put Your Troubles in a Candy Box 1925.43
Puttin' it On 1979.15
Puttin' on the Ritz 1924.10, 1942.23, 1989.16, 1992.18
Puttin' Out Roots Again 1979.11
Putting it Together 1984.08, 1999.20
Putting on the Ritz 1928.37
Putty in Your Hands 1967.02
Puzzlement, A 1951.12
Pygmalion and Galatea 1891.13
Pygmalion Roses 1914.34
Pynka Pong 1900.43
Pyramid Lead 1985.17
Pyramids, The 1886.43
Pyramus and Thisbe 1939.29
Pzcherkatrotsky 1920.44

Q.T.U.C.I.M.4.U. (Cutie,, You See I am for You) 1918.04
Qhobosha 1977.01
Qon Qo Qo 1997.14
Qu'ai-jee vu? 1887.36
Qu'as-tu dit?ns ombreux 1887.36
Qu'est-ce que les femmes ont cette annee 1929.13
Qu'il est fier et splendide 1883.51
Qu'on me laisse agir a mon gre 1887.35
Quadalquiver, The 1920.04
Quadrille 1953.07
Quaff the nectar 1894.15
Quai de Bercy 1947.05, 1948.12, 1963.02
Quail on Toast With Pink Champagne 1964.39
Quaint Little House 1924.24
Quaint Toys 1914.23
Quaker Girl, A 1911.39
Quaker Maids, The 1901.21
Quaker Talk 1911.25
Quaker's Meeting 1911.39
Quakertown Cadets, The 1901.07
Qualifications 1932.12
Quality 1998.02
Quality Street 1902.06
Quand il est morte le poete 1966.20
Quand Il Pleut 1999.05
Quand je penetrai dans la cage 1886.09
Quand l'Eternel, au Paradis 1929.11
Quand on a du sens 1929.14
Quand on lui propose une affaire 1878.08
Quand on n'a pas ce que l'on aime 1929.16
Quand on ne dit rien 1929.10
Quand on termine la toilette 1887.36
Quand on veut etre heureux 1929.15
Quand on veut plaire 1929.14
Quand par les verts chemins 1887.36
Quand ton heure sonnera 1929.13
Quand tu m'embrasse 1964.02
Quand une femme a tort 1929.15
Quando, Quando 1964.02
Quanta bella la campagna 1886.49
Quarrel and Part 1918.09
Quarrel Duet 1923.37
Quarrel for Three 1946.24
Quarrel Number 1921.03
Quarrel of Two Dutchwomen, The 1925.03
Quarrel, A 1898.44
Quarrel, The 1908.42, 1910.30, 1912.34, 1912.48
Quarrel-tet 1958.20
Quarreling Coachmen 1904.31
Quarreling Duet 1921.11
Quarrelling Duet 1902.30
Quartet 1979.06, 1991.05
Quartet Erotica 1934.19
Quat-z-arts 1908.42
Quatuor des jeunes filles 1929.10
Que c'est triste Venice 1965.30
Que c'est triste Venise 1974.19, 1983.03
Que Reste-til de Nos Amours 1964.22, 1999.07
Que te importa que no venga 1969.11
Que Voulez Vous 1903.07
Que vous dites 1929.13
Que, hermosa noche me espera! 1969.11
Queen Amang th' Heather 1928.05
Queen at Drury Lane 1961.26
Queen Elizabeth 1926.13
Queen Elizabeth of Chosun 1998.08
Queen Elizabeth's Tea 1928.49

Queen Esther 1942.05
Queen for a Day 1953.17
Queen is Hunted Down, The 1998.08
Queen is Studying French Today, The 1998.08
Queen Min Chased by the Beasts 1997.16
Queen Min's Return 1997.16, 1998.08
Queen of Beauty am I, The 1905.35
Queen of Belle Paree, The 1908.10
Queen of Bohemia 1899.30
Queen of Charcoal Alley, The 1901.28
Queen of Comic Opera 1897.39
Queen of may 1888.05
Queen of Musical Comedy, The 1921.20
Queen of My Dreams 1905.56, 1911.02
Queen of My Heart 1887.44, 1928.12
Queen of Our Hearts 2000.01
Queen of Queens 1926.24
Queen of Society, The 1901.17
Queen of Song 1960.07
Queen of the Alley 1903.01
Queen of the Belles 1889.05
Queen of the Bungalow 1903.23
Queen of the Burlesque Wheel 1963.12
Queen of the Circus Ring 1902.21
Queen of the Comedie Francaise 1903.40
Queen of the Flowers 1886.60
Queen of the Land and Snow 1916.15
Queen of the Magical Islands 1861.01
Queen of the Night 1904.20
Queen of the Nile 1917.16
Queen of the One-Ring Show 1910.02
Queen of the Opera, The 1942.01
Queen of the Phillipine Islands 1900.51
Queen of the Ring 1905.29, 1908.34
Queen of the Sea and Earth 1895.43
Queen of the Song Birds 1877.43
Queen of the Studio 1895.43
Queen of the Vaudevil, a la Anna Held 1898.02
Queen of the Woods 1892.14
Queen of Vanity Fair, The 1911.23
Queen Thou Art 1912.47
Queen's Galliard, The 1963.28
Queen's Game of Chess, The 1880.04
Queen's Presentation 1979.28
Queen's Song, The 1893.17
Queenie was a Blonde 2000.08
Queenie was There With Her Hair in a Braid 1908.25
Queenie's Ballyhoo 1927.67, 1966.14, 1983.05, 1994.08
Queens of Long Ago 1923.41
Queens of Society 1902.21
Queens of the Rose and Gray, The 1898.03
Queer Little Ostrich, The 1902.44
Quejas de Bandoneon 1985.07, 1993.08
Quejas De Bandoneon 1997.13
Quelle noce singuliere 1886.09
Quend en pense 1926.49
Quens on n'en a pas 1929.10
Querida 1926.14
Quest, The 1965.34
Question of Gait, A 1937.11
Question, gentlemen, The 1875.35
Questions 1972.13
Questions and Answers 1983.02
Qui le dites-vous, A 1929.10
Qui, c'est moi, c'est Serpolette 1878.08
Qui, de t'avoir aimee 1983.03
Qui, nous triomphons 1883.51
Qui? 1965.30
Quick Henry, the Flit 1932.15
Quick Service 1918.20
Quiet 1956.15, 1959.26, 1982.20, 1997.10
Quiet Afternoon, A 1923.24
Quiet Evening at Home, A 1915.08
Quiet Girl, A 1953.03, 1958.20, 1958.21
Quiet Land, A 1965.35
Quiet Life, A 1961.14
Quiet Little Home 1889.25
Quiet Little Home, A 1886.61
Quiet Love 1991.04
Quiet Night 1936.05, 1975.13, 1983.02
Quiet Street 1957.05
Quiet Sunday in 1920, A 1908.07
Quiet Thing, A 1965.17, 1974.01
Quintet, The 1990.06
Quintette 1981.29
Quit Kiddin' 1927.07
Quite a Party 1924.03
Quite another story 1870.20
Quite Instinctively 1888.19
Quittin' Time 1940.23, 1972.10
Quixotic is his enterprise 1895.29

R-E-M-O-R-S-E 1902.44
R.S.V.P. 1975.14
Rabbi and the Pupils, The 1924.48
Rabbi's Coming, The 1990.16
Rabbit Chasing 1999.03
Race is Over, The 1925.01
Race of Life, The 1914.20
Race One 1987.05
Race Track Girls, The 1898.08
Race Two 1987.05
Race You to the Top of the Morning 1991.05
Race, The 1926.50
Races, The 1904.14
Rachel 1904.53
Rachel's Song 1938.02
Racin' Form 1946.08
Racing Blues 1920.14
Racing Game, The 1908.26
Racing Quartette, The 1912.37
Racing With the Clock 1954.05
Rackety Boys Song, The 1895.08
Rackety Coo! 1915.30
Rackety Jack 1871.12
Radetsky March 1934.29
Radiance 1922.34
Radio City, I Love You 1942.34
Radio Voices 1924.38
Radium Dance 1904.15
Radium Numbers 1938.19
Radziwill 1930.43
Rafesville, U.S.A. 1960.01
Rafferty 1903.39
Rafferty Bey 1902.11
Raffery's Daughter Kate 1885.06
Raffle Ballet, The 1951.14
Raffles 1940.07
Raft, The 1923.31
Rag Bag Man 1904.41, 1906.40
Rag Doll 1985.08
Rag Doll, The 1920.23, 1921.18
Rag Dolly 1986.16
Rag Lad of Bagdad, The 1918.05
Rag Man, Music Man 1908.21
Rag Me Around 1912.45
Rag of Rags, The 1914.23
Rag Offen the Bush 1956.12
Rag Time College Girl, The 1911.30
Rag Time Dance, The 1898.03
Rag Time Express, The 1913.05
Rag Time Jockey Man, The 1912.24
Rag Time Liz 1898.56
Rag Time Night on Broadway 1900.24
Rag Time Quadrille 1908.22
Rag, The 1993.19
Rag-Time Boxing March, The 1912.43
Rag-Time in Europe 1903.28
Rag-Time Night on Broadway 1897.33
Raggedy Ann 1920.35, 1923.40
Raggedy Man, The 1912.02
Raggedy Rag 1921.21
Ragging the Apache 1916.11
Ragging the Nursery Rhymes 1913.18
Raggy Ragtime Train 1916.25
Rags 1986.13
Rags and Tatters 1929.01, 1930.08, 1931.08
Rags is Royal Raiments 1923.10
Ragtime 1942.18, 1963.12, 1998.01
Ragtime Alphabet, The 1917.12
Ragtime Arabian Nights 1914.01
Ragtime Calisthenics 1916.11
Ragtime Carnival 1915.27
Ragtime Cowboy 1946.21
Ragtime Dance, The 1980.27
Ragtime Dinner Order, The 1915.02
Ragtime Girl, Dat's All 1901.23
Ragtime in the Air 1913.22
Ragtime Melodrama 1915.32
Ragtime Mixes My Brain 1899.11
Ragtime Nightingale 1980.27
Ragtime Opera 1912.25
Ragtime Overtures of Grand Operas 1915.12
Ragtime Pinafore, The 1914.01
Ragtime Pipes of Pan, The 1915.27
Ragtime Razor Brigade 1918.21
Ragtime Regiment, The 1914.15
Ragtime Restaurant, The 1912.41
Ragtime Romeo 1955.25
Ragtime Schottische 1900.46
Ragtime Sextette, The 1912.09
Ragtime Suffragette, The 1913.17
Ragtime Temple Bells 1914.23
Ragtime Terpsichore 1920.05
Ragtime Wedding 1918.38
Ragtime Whirl, The 1914.17
Ragtime Will be Mah Finish 1901.12
Ragtime Yodeling Man 1913.16
Raguenau's Patisserie 1993.17
Rah-Rah-Rah 1898.55
Rahadlakum 1953.16, 1978.03
Railbird 1978.10
Railroad 1906.06
Railroad Fight, The 1959.27
Railroad Guide, The 1887.29
Railroad Smash Up 1870.01
Railroad Song 1870.26
Railroad Woman, The 1988.15
Railroad, The 1872.23
Rain 1924.06, 1924.30, 1990.12
Rain Exorcism 1980.26
Rain Finale 1936.22
Rain in Spain, The 1956.01, 1993.18
Rain in the Face 1907.41
Rain on the Roof 1971.05
Rain or Shine 1904.03, 1928.08
Rain Song 1992.10, 1992.10
Rain Song, The 1963.26
Rainbow 1880.42, 1905.27, 1908.33, 1921.33, 1926.06
Rainbow and Thistle 1907.26
Rainbow Ball 1919.16
Rainbow Ballet, The 1902.06
Rainbow from the U.S.A., A 1918.23
Rainbow Girl 1918.11
Rainbow High 1979.23
Rainbow Logic 1986.18
Rainbow of Girls 1927.37
Rainbow of Jazz 1924.40
Rainbow of Your Smile, The 1926.24
Rainbow Sue 1911.20
Rainbow Tour 1979.23
Rainbow's End 1928.45
Rainbow, The 1895.03
Rainbows 1907.27
Raindrop and the Rose, The 1924.05
Raindrops 1904.34
Raining 1905.27
Raining in My Heart 1990.15
Raining Memories 1952.09
Rainy Afternoon Girls 1924.43
Rainy Afternoons 1920.33
Rainy Day 1924.11
Rainy Day Pal 1927.193
Rainy Day, A 1906.17, 1932.17
Raise a Shout of Joy 1888.20
Raise the Flag of Dixie 1975.03
Raise Them Up Higher 1999.09
Raisin' the Rent 1981.16
Raisin' the Roof 1923.31
Raising a Child 2001.06
Raising Cain 1968.05
Raisins and Almonds 1998.11
Rajah of Bhong, The 1902.30
Rajah of Broadway, The 1908.19
Rakish Young Man With the Whiskers 1944.23
Rally 'Round Me 1930.39
Rally Round the Flag 1978.05

Ram-a-Jam, I Want That Man 1898.38, 1898.67
Ram-a-Jam, or I Want That Man 1897.40
Ramaux, Les 1877.20
Rambler Rose 1917.19, 1922.19, 1923.20
Rampart and bastion gray 1884.14
Rampart Street 1955.13
Ramtah 1919.21
Ran Tin Tin 1923.41
Rancho Mexicano 1925.17
Rang Tang 1927.33
Rangers' Song, The 1927.08, 1927.55
Ransome Guards' Quick-Step 1894.37
Raoul, I've Been There 1988.01
Rap, Rap, Rap 1902.43, 1918.26
Rap, The 1981.29, 1987.05
Rap-Tap-a-Tap 1920.08
Rape of the Sabines, The 1871.18
Rapsodia de Arrabal 1993.08
Rapture! rapture! 1888.35
Raquel 1928.23
Raquel Tango 1928.23
Rara Tonga 1943.17, 1944.31
Rare Anomaly, A 1892.42
Rare Old Mountain Dew 1897.43
Rare Songbirds on Display 1997.17
Rare Wines 1982.18
Rasta Roll Call 1980.05
Rastafari 1980.05
Rastus Johnson, U.S.A. 1906.14
Rastus on Parade 1896.15
Rastus Surely Loves Me Because He Say He Do 1899.19
Rat Row Drag 1930.19
Rat-ta-ta-ta-ci-bum 1901.06
Rat-tat-a-tat 1918.12
Rat-Tat-Tat Song, The 1916.01
Rat-Tat-Tat-Tat 1964.11
Rataplan 1879.21, 1892.08
Rataplan, Rataplan 1875.19, 1883.51
Ratcatcher's Daughter, The 1866.17
Rathskeller Trio, The 1915.02
Rations 1942.30
Rats and Mice and Fish 1982.18
Rattle Chorus 1884.37
Rattle Rattle 1920.23
Raunchy 1963.26, 1992.10
Rave On 1990.15
Raven, The 1923.31
Raving 1903.04
Raving Beauty 1989.23
Ray of Hope, The 1862.04
Ray of Sunlight, A 1880.06
Ray of Sunshine 1922.14
Raymonda 1977.09
Raymonde 1929.10
Raz-Ma-Taz 1918.05
Razzle Dazzle 1890.29, 1975.14, 1999.01
Razzle-Dazzle 1888.34
Re Fa Si 1993.08
RE-7, The 1980.13
Re-fa-si 1985.07, 1999.18
Re-Incarnation 1907.24
Re-Orient Yourself 1989.05
Reach Out 1971.16
Reach Out and Touch 1976.16
Reach Out and Touch Somebody's Hand 1976.24
Reach Right Down 1989.09
Reaching for Someone 1979.05
Reaching for Stars 1948.16
Reaching for the Cake 1900.59
Read 'Em and Weep 1991.10
Read it in the Weekly 1980.30
Read My Sighs 1910.24
Read the answer in the Herald 1885.51
Read the Answer in the Stars 1885.28, 1885.45, 1885.70, 1903.04
Read the Papers Ev'ry Day 1908.35
Read What the Papers Say 1925.22
Read-Head 1915.17
Readin', Writin' and 'Rhythmatic 1942.35
Reading 1980.23
Reading of the Mail 1894.22
Reading, Writing and a Little Bit of Rhythm 1939.22
Reading, Writing, Arithmetic 1904.40
Ready Cash 1955.04
Ready for Work 1924.01
Ready Teddy 1990.15
Ready, Steady Sailor Man, The 1898.17
Ready-Made Sandwich, The 1917.08
Real American Folk Song is a Rag, The 1918.32, 1992.02
Real American Girl, The 1909.03
Real American Tune, A 1928.22
Real Big News 1998.21
Real Coney Island, The 1998.16
Real Emotional Girl 2000.16
Real Estate 1983.18
Real Girls, The 1901.07
Real High Yaller and Sealskin Brown 1929.01
Real Life Lullaby, A 1979.18
Real Live Girl 1962.27, 1982.01, 1991.10, 1998.15
Real Me, The 1962.04
Real Mike Fink, The 1975.18
Real Old Mountain Dew, The 1897.12
Real Slow Drag, A 1975.19
Real Spring Drive, The 1918.16
Real Thing, The 1996.08
Real Town Lady 1904.29
Real Town Lady, A 1903.22
Reality 1946.18
Really and Truly 1928.07
Really Upset 1917.11
Reap What You Sow 1969.10
Reaper's Chorus, The 1913.10
Reason Why, The 1889.46
Rebellious Leg, The 1899.19
Reciprocity 1951.18
Recitado 1993.08
Recitative 1911.40, 1927.03
Recitativo 1982.09
Reckless Baby 1922.44
Reckless Blues 1982.12
Reckless Reddy 1899.26
Recollections 1908.15
Recollections of Gotham 1859.11
Reconciliation 1919.11
Rector Rhythm 1930.24
Recuerdo 1999.18
Red 1989.25
Red and Black 1987.04
Red Ball Express, The 1946.10
Red Baron, The 1971.11, 1999.03
Red Blues, The 1955.02
Red Caps Cappers 1923.39
Red Collar Job 1958.04
Red Cross Girl, The 1910.01
Red Head 1910.16
Red Headed Woman, A 1935.13, 1983.04
Red Hot and Blue Rhythm 1929.44
Red Hot Chicago 1930.11
Red Hot Mama 1963.12
Red Hot Trumpet 1929.12
Red is the Wine 1898.17
Red Ladies, The 1924.33
Red Letter Day 1957.17
Red Mama 1928.47
Red Mikado, The 1937.14
Red Moon 1909.10
Red Moon To-da-lo 1909.10
Red Red Rose 1966.03
Red Riding Hood 1921.11
Red River 1928.49
Red Rose 1919.42
Red Rose and the White, The 1882.63
Red Rover, The 1883.04
Red Scarf, The 1896.15
Red Shoes 1960.07
Red Sky 1906.46
Red Virgin, The 1926.35
Red White and Blues, The 1976.11
Red Wine 1928.29
Red, Hot and Blue 1936.26, 1980.06
Red, Red as the Rose 1919.18
Red, Red Rose 1908.08
Red, the White and the Blue, The 1978.06
Red, White and Blue 1909.21
Red, White and Blue Girl 1903.07
Red, White and Blues 1942.05
Red, White and Maddox Kazoo March 1969.03
Red-Blooded American Boy 1964.44
Red-Hot Mama 1924.13
Reddy Teddy 1978.01
Redecorate 1950.06
Redskinland 1929.23
Reefer Song, The 1978.09
Reel Around the Sun 1996.12, 2000.05
Reel, 1886.53
Reet, Petite and Gone 1992.03
Reflection 1979.10
Reflections 1913.18
Reflections on Ice-Breaking 1973.08
Reform 1960.19
Reform Song, The 1986.11
Refrain, Audacious Scribe 1945.09
Refrain, audacious tar, your suit from pressing 1879.05
Refuse Collectors, The 1977.01
Regal Romp, The 1928.46
Regal Sadness Sits on Me, A 1894.45
Regardez donc quel equipage 1878.08
Regardez la belle prestance 1884.50
Regardez-Moi 1931.39
Regency of the King's Father 1998.08
Regency Rakes 1934.34
Regent and Chinese 1998.08
Regent is Taken to China 1998.08
Reggae Music Got Soul 1980.05
Reggie the Reigning Rage 1898.67
Reggie's Family Tree 1902.15
Regiment Loves the Girls, The 1925.43
Regiment of Frocks and Frills, The 1907.06
Regiment of our Own 1918.31
Regimental Band 1925.08
Regimental Review 1908.44
Regimental Roly Poly Girl, The 1912.44
Regimental Song 1927.65
Registered our marriage vow 1881.04
Regretful Blues 1917.37
Regular Army Man, The 1912.31
Regular Girl, A 1922.07
Regular Guy, A 1923.08
Regular Limited Train, The 1903.24
Regular Parlee-Voo, A 1904.01
Regular William Gillette, A 1901.07
Rehearsal Hall 1934.42
Rehearsal, The 1904.56
Rehearse! 1976.11
Reina del Cortijo, La 1926.35
Reindeer Dance 1926.17
Reiz, reiz, j'en suis heureuse 1886.09
Rejection 1959.12
Rejoice 1970.20
Rejoice, rejoice with me 1886.40
Relatively Simple Affair, A 1958.01
Relax 1952.10
Relax and Enjoy It 1944.18
Relax With Me, Baby 1987.14
Release That Man! 1906.18
Release Yourself 1984.15
Relicario, El 1926.09
Relicaro, El 1926.35
Religion in My Feet 1930.19
Religioso 1934.20
Reluctant Cannibal, The 1959.20
Rely on Our Assistance 1866.14
Remarkable Doctor, A 1904.51
Remarkable Fellow 1955.10
Remarkable People We 1931.42
Rememb'ring You 1925.26
Rememb'wring 1924.46
Remember 1979.03, 1997.01
Remember Always to Give 1984.02
Remember Boy, You're Irish 1886.44
Remember Lizzie 1919.10
Remember Me 1925.02
Remember Me? 1976.07
Remember That Day 1974.12
Remember That I Care 1947.02
Remember the Dancing 1957.14
Remember the Face of Your Driver 1928.40

Remember the Night 1954.17
Remember the Old Continentals 1908.35
Remember the Rose 1920.45, 1921.18
Remember? 1973.04
Remembrance of Love 1898.05
Remind Me 1957.10, 1986.01
Reminiscence 1909.21, 1917.15, 1918.42, 1921.14, 1921.33, 1925.06
Reminiscence, Madame Pompadour 1924.39
Reminiscences 1917.01
Reminiscent Melody, The 1921.27
Reminiscent Rosy-Posy 1915.27
Reminiscing 1952.08
Remorse and dishonor 1848.04
Rendez-vous, The 1884.57
Rendezvous 1921.18, 1933.03
Rendezvous des Artists, Les 1941.03
Rendezvous of Love, The 1925.03
Rendezvous Time in Paris 1939.22
Rendezvous Waltz, The 1918.17
Rene's Song 1881.25
Renew My Mind 1987.17
Renita Reinette 1927.03
Rent 1996.09
Rent a Robot 1972.21
Renzo and Pompea Duet 2000.10
Repent 1978.02
Reporters 1924.07
Reporters, The 1988.09
Reprisal 1930.19
Reprise Sympathetic 1919.34
Reputation 1919.12, 1921.35
Requiem 1969.08, 1973.08
Requiem for Evita 1979.23
Rescue, The 1966.01, 1975.19
Resolutions 1990.17
Resolved 1905.05
Respect 1982.22, 1997.21
Respectability 1959.11
Respectable 1980.30
Respectable Son and His Awful Dad, The 1888.38
Respectable Wife, A 1964.24
Responso 1993.08, 1997.13
Rest Room Rose 1931.13
Reste 1934.32, 1965.30, 1970.01, 1974.19
Reste la 1896.48
Rested Body is a Rested Mind, A 1975.01
Resting 1973.13
Restless 1933.05, 1950.09
Restless Heart 1954.15
Restoration Piece 1952.09
Resurrection Rag 1918.18
Return 1889.09
Return to Sender 1989.12
Return to Warm My Heart Again 1915.28
Return, Oh Holy Dove 1943.10
Return, Return 1988.15
Return, The 1912.01, 1973.08
Returning from the Way 1927.51
Reuben 1926.39
Reuben and Betsy 1904.11
Reuben and Cynthia 1891.39, 1894.07, 1894.35
Reubens on Parade, The 1903.11
Reunion 1982.08
Rev d'Amour 1903.27
Rev. Mr. Barlow, The 1882.63
Reveille 1909.24
Reveille, The 1893.40
Revelation, The 1999.17
Revels of the Jewels, The 1904.39
Revels, The 1899.39
Revenant a Versailles, En 1933.24
Revenge 1920.30, 1962.01, 1966.06
Revenge is Mine 1944.25
Revenge Song 1978.11
Revenge, Revenge 1881.17
Revenge, Revenge! 1881.07
Reverenced name of Mother, The 1866.34
Reviewing the Situation 1963.01
Revival Day 1930.38
Revival, The 1971.10
Revolt, The 1872.23
Revolution 1977.10
Revolutionary Man, The 1909.18
Revolutionary Song 1968.22
Rhapsodie Table d'Hote 1897.37
Rhapsody 1939.12
Rhapsody in Black 1931.11
Rhapsody in Blue 1926.16, 1927.12, 1931.11, 1939.14, 1982.06, 1989.21, 1991.10, 2001.07
Rhapsody of Love 1930.36
Rhapsody, The 1869.43
Rheims Cathedral, The 1927.58
Rhett, Scarlett & Ashley 1940.07
Rhinestones 1927.31
Rhoda and Her Pagoda 1900.43
Rhode Island is Famous for You 1948.14, 1988.08, 1990.09
Rhumba Jake 1943.14
Rhumba Jumps, The 1940.09
Rhyme for Angela 1945.04
Rhymes Have I 1953.16, 1978.03
Rhyming 1922.12
Rhyming for a Dance 1917.30
Rhyming Menu 1993.17
Rhythm 1936.31, 1952.11, 1999.24
Rhythm Feet 1930.19
Rhythm in My Hair 1934.40
Rhythm is a Racket 1937.09
Rhythm is Our Business 1974.10, 1989.02
Rhythm is Red an' White an' Blue, The 1940.18
Rhythm of America 1952.08
Rhythm of Life 1966.01
Rhythm of the Day 1925.25, 1925.48
Rhythm of the Sea 1925.48
Rhythm of the Waves 1929.26
Rhythm on the River 1995.14
Rhythm Songs 1953.17
Ri Ra 2000.05
Ri tooral, looral 1862.02
Ri-fol 1886.45
Ribbon-Pole 1949.07
Ribbons and Bows 1927.37
Ribbons Down My Back 1964.01, 1998.07
Rice and Shoes 1921.10
Rich and Happy 1981.27, 1999.20
Rich Butterfly 1959.23
Rich Coon's Babe, A 1904.26
Rich Is 1970.07
Rich Kids Rag 1998.15
Rich Kids Rag, The 1982.01
Rich Kids' Rag, The 1962.27
Rich Man! Poor Man 1929.12
Rich Man's Frug 1966.01, 1999.01
Rich Man's Son, A 1885.44
Rich Man, Poor Man 1915.01
Rich Man, Poor Man, Beggar Man, Thief 1909.30
Rich or Poor 1930.28
Rich, Rich, Rich 1963.13
Rich, The 1937.08, 1961.10
Richard Bloom, Esq. 1834.03
Richard Carle 1908.21
Richard Carr 1881.07
Richard Crudnut's Charm School 1942.34
Richard Interred 1993.02
Riche, The 1891.39
Richer Than Gold 1911.36
Riches 1975.18, 1976.31
Rickety Crickety 1920.42
Riddle Me This 1932.16
Riddle Song 1954.11, 1971.20
Riddle, The 1997.19, 1999.13
Riddle-Ma-Ree 1907.47
Ride 'Em Cowboys 1929.04
Ride 'em, Cowboy 1949.17
Ride Cowboy Ride 1938.12
Ride Me Around With You, Dearie 1912.43
Ride on a Rainbow, A 1995.07
Ride Out the Storm 1973.06
Ride the Winds 1974.12
Ride Through the Night 1961.28
Ride to the Course, The 1906.05
Ride, Baby, Ride 1978.25
Rider to the Sea 1958.18
Riders to the Stars 1976.34
Ridin' High 1936.26, 1980.06, 1998.05
Ridin' in a Railroad Kerr 1862.06
Ridin' on de Golden Bike 1895.36
Ridin' on the Moon 1946.08
Ridin' the Rails 1936.17
Riding for a Fall 1979.18
Riding in a Motor Car 1907.54
Riding in the Heavenly Rowboat 1894.21
Riding Lesson, The 1909.21
Riding Messenger, The 1965.04
Riding on a Carousel 1964.24
Riding on a Velocipede 1869.07
Riding on the Breeze 1948.17
Riding the Range 1980.17
Riding Through the Mist and Mire 1921.15
Rielera, La 1988.15
Riff Song, The 1926.42, 1946.03, 1987.10
Riff-Raff Rafferty 1915.23
Riffian Ballet, The 1926.29
Rigadoon, The 1902.37
Rigaudon 1944.21
Right 1979.04
Right About Here 1968.13
Right as the Rain 1944.23
Right at the End of It 1930.32
Right at the Start of It 1930.32, 1972.05
Right Boy Comes Along 1922.31
Right Brazilian Girl, The 1916.14
Right Finger of My Left Hand, The 1959.01
Right Girl, The 1916.08, 1971.05
Right Girls 1962.01
Right Hand Man 1970.21
Right Here 1980.18
Right in This Old Town 1905.43
Right Little Girl 1920.35
Right Man, The 1929.28
Right Now 1907.18
Right or Wrong 1929.22
Right Out of Heaven into My Arms 1928.28
Right Place, Right Time 1987.05
Right This Way 1938.01
Right Time, the Right Place, The 1972.24
Right! Left! 1881.36
Right-o 1924.09
Rigo's Last Lullaby 1927.26
Rigodon, The 1903.40
Rigoletto 1935.18, 1955.13
Rigoletto a la Danse 1924.44
Rigoletto Quartette 1920.47
Rin-tin-tin 1925.08
Ring a Ding a Ding Dong Bell 1930.02
Ring a Ding Dong 1876.10
Ring Dat Golden Bell 1885.44
Ring de Banjo 1939.21
Ring dem Wedding Bells 1899.19
Ring forth, ye bells 1879.10
Ring he gave me, The 1859.18
Ring in the Joys 1924.16
Ring Makes the World Go Round, The 1883.04
Ring Me Up in the Morning 1910.17
Ring O' Roses 1909.21
Ring Out the Bells 1965.31
Ring Out the Liberty Bell 1917.08
Ring Out, Glad Bells 1914.13
Ring the Bell 1953.11
Ring the Bells 1894.20, 1895.30
Ring the bells and bang the brasses! 1895.29
Ring the Merry Belles 1945.08
Ring the Merry Bells 1938.10
Ring the Praises Merrily 1898.01
Ring the Wedding Bells 1910.15
Ring Them Bells 1974.01
Ring to the Name of Rose 1968.07
Ring to the Name of Rosie, A 1923.46
Ring Up the Curtain 1942.26
Ring-ting-a-ling on the Telephone 1912.02
Ringalevio 1948.04
Ringing the Chimes 1883.20
Rings of the Sea 1904.30
Rink, The 1984.01
Rinka Tinka Man 1938.04
Rio 1989.07
Rio de Janeiro 1948.21
Rio Rita 1927.08

Riot, The 1964.32
Rip Van Winkle 1901.27, 1945.03, 1947.11
Rise and Shine 1948.21
Rise old Napper 1848.03
Rise Tafari 1980.05
Rise Up and Stand Again 1983.15
Rise Up Jah-Jah Children 1980.05
Rise, People of Chosun 1997.16, 1998.08
Rising early in the morning 1890.02
Rising Star 1937.03
Rising When the Dawn is Gray 1894.40
Rita Cheeta 1971.01
Ritorna a me 1934.20
Ritual Dance 1941.07
Ritual Fire Dance 1946.06
Ritual for Murder 1997.16
River Deep, Mountain High 1985.03
River in the Rain 1985.06
River Jordan 1999.08
River Song 1927.08, 1948.24
River Song, The 1934.03
River Will Sweep You Away, The 1932.19
River!, The River!, The 1895.26
River, Stay 'Way from My Door 1940.20
River, Stay Away from My Door 1942.25
River, The 1989.05
Riverboat Shuffle 1987.02
Riverdance 2000.05
Rivers of Tears 1965.32
Riverside Bus 1926.21
Riverside Drive 1922.24, 1969.14
Riviera 1926.34
Riviera Rage, The 1973.05
Riviera, The 1954.09
Riviere, La 1968.21
Ro-Ro-Rollin' Along 1930.20
Road of Dreams, The 1925.43
Road That Leads Back Home 1918.10
Road That Lies Before, The 1917.01
Road to Anywhere, The 1918.12
Road to Destiny 1919.30
Road to Hampton 1969.07
Road to Heaven 1931.31
Road to Henley, The 1914.19
Road to Home, The 1932.03
Road to Mandalay 1916.05
Road to Morocco 1995.14
Road to Paradise, The 1917.15
Road to Yesterday, The 1907.51
Road Tour, The 1964.32
Road Trip 1999.02
Road You Didn't Take, The 1971.05, 1999.20
Roam on, My Little Gypsy Sweetheart 1927.39
Roamin' in the Gloamin' 1928.05
Roaming in the Gloaming 1930.17
Roaming With Nora 1894.31
Roaming With the Romans 1904.23
Roaring 20's Strike Back, The 1950.19
Roast Beef of old England, The 1862.02
Roavin', A 1922.21
Robber-Baron Minstrel Parade, The 1976.11
Robert E. Lee 1919.21, 1922.25
Robert the Roue 1942.18
Robert the Roue from Reading, Pa. 1939.22
Robert, Alvin, Wendell and Jo Jo 1970.20
Robin 1905.36
Robin Adair 1898.47
Robin and the Rose, The 1900.25
Robin and the Wren, The 1910.12
Robin Hood's Arrest 1905.55
Robin, The 1880.42
Robinson Cruso Thanks You Kindly 1879.03
Robinson Crusoe 1858.04, 1859.08, 1904.41, 1905.45, 1916.03
Rock & Roll Girl 1999.02
Rock 'N' Roll Party Queen 1972.12, 1994.07
Rock and Roll All Night 1982.22
Rock and Roll Music 1982.22
Rock Around the Clock 1977.09, 1982.22
Rock Candy Mountain 1944.32
Rock Island 1957.18, 2000.11
Rock Me in the Cradle of Love 1914.15
Rock Me in Your Loving Arms 1920.19
Rock of Rages 1985.03
Rock the Baby to Sleep 1920.17
Rock'd upon the Billow! 1882.75
Rock, Rock, Rock 1906.27, 1948.28
Rock-a-Buy Baby 1887.02
Rock-a-Bye Baby 1890.36, 1903.31, 1919.26, 1924.44, 1929.48
Rock-a-Bye Baby Dear 1918.16
Rock-a-Bye Your Baby With a Dixie Melody 1918.05, 1967.11
Rock-A-Bye Your Baby With a Dixie Melody 1962.17
Rock-a-Hula Baby 1989.12
Rock-Rock-Rock Let Me Rock in My Old Rocking Chair 1907.30
Rockabye Hamlet 1976.03
Rockabye Your Baby With a Dixie Melody 1997.01, 2000.14
Rocked in the Cradle of Jazz 1949.05
Rocked in the Cradle of the Deep 1952.11
Rocket and the Stick, The 1891.13
Rockin' 1969.07
Rockin' in Rhythm 1932.18, 1981.06
Rockin' Pneumonia 1992.06
Rocking Chair Fleet 1921.07
Rocking the Boat 1981.24
Rocks and Gravel 1966.15
Rocks and Hills, The 1882.33
Rocks in My Bed 1997.03
Rocky Boy Ceremonial 1958.20
Rocky Road to Dublin 1907.04
Rod, Di 1990.16
Rodeo Dreams 1982.13
Rodeo Rider 1982.13
Roderick O'Deyr 1883.53
Roderick O'Dwyer 1880.36
Roderick O'Dwyer! 1893.27
Rodrigo 1977.09
Rogaciano el huapanguero 1988.15
Rogaciano the Singer of Huapangos 1988.15
Roger DeCoverly 1904.55
Rogers, Brothers 1908.21
Rogue lies hid in the wine, A 1897.17
Roi A Fait Battre Tambour, Lle 1966.03
Roll 'Em 1948.15
Roll Along 1918.23
Roll Along, Sadie 1952.20
Roll Call in the Morning, The 1928.49
Roll Dem Bales Along 1930.19
Roll Dem Bones 1897.48
Roll Dem Roly Boly Eyes 1919.24
Roll Jordan 1930.34, 1978.21
Roll Me 1919.33
Roll of the Drum 1928.48
Roll On 1906.50
Roll on, Might Wave 1907.55
Roll on, Mr. Moon 1902.38
Roll on, Silver Moon 1906.13
Roll Out the Hose, Boys 1954.01
Roll Out the Morning 1971.01
Roll Over Beethoven 1977.10
Roll Them Bones 1953.04
Roll Those Eyes 1913.35
Roll Up the Ribbons 1966.29
Roll With the Punches 1986.11
Roll Yer Socks Up 1957.07
Rolland from Holland 1924.07
Rolled into One 1917.06
Roller Rink, A 1887.13
Roller Rinkers 1912.43
Rollicking Band of Pirates We, A 1879.72, 1981.01
Rollicking Blarney O 1906.03
Rollin' in Gold 1964.04
Rollin' on the T.O.B.A. 1999.06
Rolling Chair Song, The 1905.39
Rolling de Bones at Coblenz on de Rhine 1919.08
Rolling Exercise 1918.42
Rolling home! Rolling home! 1886.40
Rolling Stock 1987.05
Rolling Stone 1928.04
Rolling Up the Barcarolle 1920.19
Rolling Waters 1914.14
Rolly Trudum 1954.11
Roly Poly Sam 1904.20
Roly-Poly 1902.19
Roma 1964.03
Roma Nun Fa La Stupida Stasera 1964.03
Romance 1901.08, 1922.12, 1926.42, 1927.14, 1932.19, 1934.43, 1946.03, 1963.20, 1964.24, 1983.19, 1986.17, 1987.10
Romance and Musketeer 1938.11
Romance and Reality 1902.06, 1907.18
Romance in a Dance, The 1927.40
Romance in the Dark 1975.20
Romance is Calling 1934.04
Romance of the Bachelor Bird, The 1904.52
Romance, Romance 1988.10
Romances of Tchaikovsky 1943.11
Romanga 1877.20
Romania 2000.14
Romantic Atmosphere, A 1963.14
Romantic Days 1921.37
Romantic Girl 1912.38
Romantic Knight, A 1920.45
Romantic Notions 1988.10
Romantic You and Sentimental Me 1925.17
Romany 1916.09, 1927.11
Romany Life 1898.60, 1946.18
Romany Rover 1927.53
Romany Rye, The 1888.41
Romanza 1882.45
Romanza Heimweh 1913.27
Romanza? 1945.16
Romba 1929.51
Rome 1962.14, 1968.23
Rome is Burning 1929.20
Romeo 1902.29
Romeo and Juliet 1897.32, 1909.18, 1916.11, 1919.39
Romeo and Juliet in 1888 1888.15
Romeo and Miss Juliet 1909.18
Romeo, Juliet, Johnny and Jane 1924.15
Romeras 1986.17
Romero 1934.32
Roming Around the Town 1904.56
Rondeau de la sorcellerie 1880.58
Roof Garden, The 1892.58
Roof Space 1965.02
Roof Tree 1922.41
Rookie in the Ring 1992.17
Rookombay 1947.19
Room 317 1991.033
Room Enough for Me 1925.22
Room in Bloomsbury, A 1954.09
Room in My Heart 1960.10
Room to be Free 1972.21
Room With a Bath, A 1929.20
Room With a View, A 1928.42, 1968.19, 1986.19
Room Without Windows, A 1964.05
Rooneyisms 1921.06
Roosevelt of Germany 1909.13
Roosevelt, Wilson and Hughes 1916.11
Rooster and the Lark, The 1907.52
Rooster Man 1946.24
Root 1904.11
Root for Riley 1903.11
Rootless 1960.01
Roots of the Tree 1980.05
Rootsie-Pootsie 1912.33
Roping 1930.08, 1931.08
Rory Darlin' 1896.11
Rosa Lee 1894.44
Rosa Rosetta 1905.42, 1910.01
Rosabella 1956.04, 1980.29
Rosabella Clancy 1902.44
Rosalba's Minuet 1931.06
Rosalie 1902.07, 1903.03, 1904.44, 1910.18
Rosalilla of Seville 1913.20
Rosalinda, Love of Mine 1942.31
Rosalynde 1981.02
Rosamund's Dream 1976.31
Rosario 1985.14
Rose 1918.05
Rose and a Lily, A 1902.15
Rose and I, The 1986.18
Rose and the Breeze, The 1903.36
Rose Aria, The 1927.03
Rose Ballet, The 1903.14

Rose Girl Blues, The 1921.03
Rose Girl Waltz 1921.03
Rose in Bloom 1927.20
Rose in the Heather 1937.03
Rose in the Snow 1924.09
Rose is a Rose, A 1950.19
Rose Lovejoy of Paradise Alley 1959.11
Rose Marie 1897.17, 1904.51
Rose of Arizona 1926.13
Rose of Arizona, The 1930.33
Rose of Delight 1926.32
Rose of Delight, The 1926.32
Rose of Iran 1927.34
Rose of Kenmare, The 1904.46
Rose of Killarney, The 1909.16
Rose of Madrid 1924.19
Rose of Old Derry, A 1907.56
Rose of Old Seville 1920.33
Rose of Pyramid Land 1912.25
Rose of Seville 1920.41
Rose of Spain 1920.10, 1921.34
Rose of Stamboul, The 1922.11
Rose of the Morning 1923.17
Rose of the Orient, The 1911.03
Rose of the Rio Grande 1979.24
Rose of the Riviera, The 1903.39
Rose of the Rotisserie 1921.25
Rose of the World 1908.24, 1909.23, 1928.23
Rose of Verdun 1919.10
Rose of Washington Square 1952.11
Rose of Yesterday 1913.02
Rose Song 1882.69, 1891.07
Rose tendre, La 1929.13
Rose tint leaves the sky, The 1898.25
Rose Tint My World 1975.08
Rose tree in full bearing 1859.08
Rose Without a Thorn, A 1904.17
Rose's Greeting, The 1884.22
Rose's Turn 1959.13
Rose, Lucky Rose 1911.38
Rose, Rose, Rose 1903.38
Rose, The 1897.12, 1910.15, 1918.15, 1976.01, 1979.30
Rose-Marie 1921.36, 1924.28
Roseanna 1980.29
Rosebud, The 1869.35
Roseland 1974.04
Rosemarin 1944.28
Rosemary 1912.36, 1921.21, 1927.40, 1961.22
Rosencrantz & Guildenstern Boogie 1976.03
Roses 1917.23
Roses an Butterflies 1910.34
Roses and Lillies 1902.33
Roses and Thorns 1898.01
Roses at the Station 1989.26
Roses Begin With R, Love 1902.07
Roses Bloom for Lovers 1912.15
Roses for the Girl I Love 1903.29
Roses of Picardy 1919.26, 1921.02, 1964.28
Roses of Red 1929.08
Roses Out of Reach 1921.14
Roses Red and White 1902.19
Roses Understand 1927.47
Roses, Lovely Roses 1922.35
Rosetime 1925.22
Rosetime and You 1923.06
Rosetta 1976.04
Rosey is a Gaiety Girl 1895.27
Rosey Posey 1910.18
Rosie 1898.43, 1901.07, 1910.16, 1913.02, 1914.09, 1960.06
Rosie Asthore 1891.01
Rosie Lee 1903.27
Rosie O'Grady 1952.11
Rosie of Palermo 1914.14
Rosie Posie Girls, The 1901.28
Rosie Rossenblott 1915.12
Rosie-Road 1930.37
Rosita 1905.33
Rossignol dans un buisson, Un 1887.36
Rosy 1905.22
Rosy and John 1966.20, 1968.21
Rosy Elixir 1896.37
Rosy morn 1887.43
Rosy Petals We Will Shower 1905.27
Rosy Posy 1922.07
Rothschild and Sons 1970.15
Rotisserie, The 1925.23
Rouge 1956.08
Rough and Ready Man 1982.12
Rough Riders 1897.54, 1898.43
Rough Stuff 1924.01
Rough Times 1961.02
Roulette 1927.45
Roumania 1922.47
Round me still the bells are ringing 1885.63
Round on the End and High in the Middle 1922.12
Round the Corner 1914.32, 1919.28
Round the Operas 1894.51
Round the Operas in Twenty Minutes 1894.21
Round the Town 1902.24
Round-Shouldered Man 1991.05
Round-Up, The 1908.13
Roundabout 1952.20
Rounder, The 1902.11
Rounders' Song, The 1899.25
Roussotte, La 1934.32
Roustabout Song 1928.07
Roustabouts 1923.39, 1929.18
Rout, The 1930.09
Rover of Chambaye, The 1881.04
Roving Gambler, The 1944.32
Row, Row, Row 1912.09, 1912.38, 1920.04, 1964.28
Rowing 1908.26
Rowing Song 1910.17
Roxana 1973.07
Roxane's Confession 1973.17
Roxiana Dooley 1898.43
Roxie 1975.14
Roy's Wife of Aldivalloch 1859.01
Roy, Roy, Tam O'Shanter O'Brien 1900.16
Royal Bangkok Academy, The 1951.12
Royal Blood 1990.17
Royal Crocodile, The 1903.07
Royal Damn Fango, The 1922.20
Royal Garden Blues 1989.02
Royal Honeymoon, A 1902.19
Royal Hussars are We 1905.36
Royal March, The 1937.11
Royal Nonesuch, The 1985.06
Royal Pair are Off To-Day, The 1901.27
Royal Rooster's Ensemble 1902.38
Royal Stores, The 1895.32
Royal Waitresses 1898.55
Royal Wedding, A 1923.17
Royal Whipping Boy, A 1988.18
Royalty 1919.04
Rozhinkes Mit Mandlen 1998.11
Rsecue, The 1997.19
Rub a Dub Dub 1971.20
Rub Your Lamp 1941.08
Rub-a-Dub 1904.34
Rub-a-Dub Your Rabbit's Foot 1929.25
Rubber Heels 1928.40
Rubber Man, The 1899.40
Rubber-Necking Moon 1911.20
Rube Song 1903.39
Rube Wedding 1919.21
Ruben's Holiday 1906.35
Ruben, Tell Your Mandy 1905.17
Rubens on Broadway 1908.15
Rubias y las moreans!, Las 1969.11
Ruby 1987.02
Ruby Baby 1995.03
Rubyiats from the Rubyiat 1920.47
Rue Broadway 1911.26
Rue de la Paix 1926.03
Rue Lepic 1958.06
Rufus Rastus Johnson Brown 1905.34
Rug, Snug 1918.02
Rugantino in the Stocks 1964.03
Ruins of Pompeii, The 1872.23
Ruler of Central Park, The 1898.01
Ruler of the Queen's Navee, The 1945.08
Rulers of the Earth 1909.13
Rules and Regulations 1966.05
Rules of the Asylum, The 1982.23
Rum Below 1990.17
Rum Crowd, The 1893.30
Rum Tum Tiddle 1911.43, 1922.01
Rum Tum Tugger 1982.19
Rum, Rum, Give Us Rum 1877.25, 1879.03
Rum, Tum, Fidele 1912.24
Rum-Nose Ben 1834.03
Rum-Ti-Tiddle 1911.23
Rumania, Rumania 1990.16
Rumba With a Little Jive Mixed In 1943.17, 1944.31
Rumba, La 1930.22
Rumba, The 1930.20
Rumbatism 1931.31
Rumble of the Subway, The 1923.45
Rumble, Rumble, Rumble 1980.29
Rumblin' and a Rollin', A 1998.21
Rumbola 1931.47
Rumors 1992.11
Rumpty Tumpty 1894.38
Rumpty-Foozle Schnoots 1876.01
Rumson 1951.24
Run Along, Little Man 1916.07
Run Along, Mr. Ogre Man 1913.33
Run Away from Home 1938.03
Run Away, Naughty Man 1906.17
Run Between the Raindrops 1983.17
Run for Your Life 1965.33
Run Little Chillun 1943.10
Run Run Runn 1961.21
Run Sinner Run 1969.10
Run to Me, My Love 1949.02
Run, Boy, Run 1902.40
Run, Brudder Possum, Run 1900.40, 1909.10
Run, Brudder Rabbit, Run 1907.22
Run, Indian, Run 1961.11
Run, Injuns 1961.11
Run, Musashi, Run 1974.12
Run, Run, Run Cinderella 1964.04
Run, Sinner, Run 1930.10
Runaround Sue 2000.07
Runaway Colts 1918.09
Runaway Little Girl 1921.09
Runaway Match, A 1911.39
Runaway, A 1899.06
Runnin' 1925.18
Runnin' to Meet the Man 1973.10
Running Around With the Chorus Girls 1916.02
Running Commentary 1955.19
Running Footman, The 1866.34
Running for Jesus 1982.17
Running in Place 1997.07
Runyonland 1950.17
Rushing Ballet, The 1911.34
Russia, the Fatherland 1901.23
Russian and Molokov, The 1988.09
Russian Blues 1925.42
Russian Dervish, The 2000.05
Russian Inn 1924.48
Russian Maidens, The 1906.06
Russian Movie 1993.09
Russian Peasant Girls 1924.48
Russian Shawls 1943.11
Russianata 1928.04
Rustic Ann 1922.16
Rustic Country Inn, A 1988.10
Rustic Rondo 1884.57
Rustic Song 1894.40, 1913.25
Rustic Wedding, The 1875.15
Rustle of Your Bustle 1935.04
Rusty Bell 1990.05
Rusty's Dream Ballet 1981.14
Rusty's Up in the Air 1930.11
Ruth 1972.09
Ruth St. Denis 1917.08
Rutland Bounce, The 1953.01
Rydell Fight Song 1994.07
Rye Whiskey 1931.02

S Wonderful 1927.59, 1975.22, 1983.06, 1999.23
S'a Mechaye 1968.22
S'vet Kumen Der Tog 1970.17
S'Wonderful 1984.06

S-S-S-Something Comes Over Me 1985.20
S.T. 1860 1866.19
S.V.P. 1997.13
Sa Jeunesse 1998.12
Sabbath Prayer 1964.27
Sabbath Song, A 1971.17
Saber Song, The 1926.42, 1946.03
Sabot Dance 1913.24
Sabre Dance 1968.04
Sabre de Mon Pere 1870.23
Sabre of my sire, The 1890.11
Sabre Song, The 1987.10
Sacred Dancing Hula Song 1912.03
Sacred Tree, The 1975.19
Sacrifice 1926.01
Sacrifice of Isaac 1937.01
Sacrifice, The 1971.14
Sad Affair, A 1906.35
Sad and Sordid Saga of Cecilel, The 1997.18
Sad exile on the stranger's shore 1855.06
Sad Experiences 1904.24
Sad Heart of Mine 1886.15
Sad is her lot whom fate selects 1886.40
Sad is that Woman's Lot 1881.37
Sad Predicament, A 1893.16
Sad Tale of the Beauxhommes, The 1990.12
Sad was the Day 1961.14
Sad, Sad World 1907.01
Sadder-But-Wiser Girl, The 1957.18, 2000.11
Sadie 1898.02, 1901.25, 1904.43
Sadie Hawkins Day 1956.12
Sadie, My Lady 1897.26, 1897.30
Sadie, Sadie 1964.11
Sadly I Wait 1903.14
Safe in the Arms of Bill Hart 1920.27
Safe in Your Arms 1932.10
Safe to the bridal home! 1882.60
Safe, Sane and Single 1992.03
Safest o' th' Family 1930.17
Safety in Numbers 1925.26, 1954.09
Saftest o' th' Family 1928.05
Saga of Carmen, The 1943.05
Saga of Haganah, The 1971.02
Saga of Jenny, The 1941.04
Sahara Moon 1927.39
Sahara Twins, The 1910.16
Sahara, Now We're as Dry as You 1919.03
Said Aaron to Moses 1891.141
Said Cupid to me 1880.18
Said I to Myself 1906.47
Sail Away 1916.05, 1961.18, 1982.13, 1986.19, 1988.08
Sail Home 1910.26, 1990.17
Sail on Sweet Universe 1972.21
Sail on the Trail of a Whale, A 1903.29
Sail With Me 1904.25
Sailing 1899.12, 1902.29, 1904.58
Sailing Away 1905.48
Sailing Away o'er the deep blue sea 1887.43
Sailing Away on the Henry Clay 1917.18
Sailing in a Sea-Going Hack 1907.47
Sailing Over the Bright Blue Sea 1898.38
Sailing to the Moon 1892.20
Sailor Boy 1927.36, 1991.04
Sailor Chorus 1892.45
Sailor's a Sweetheart 1925.05
Sailor's Bride, A 1922.40
Sailor's Chantey 1934.36, 1987.15
Sailor's Fling 1916.03
Sailor's Life, A 1900.25
Sailor's Life, The 1902.30
Sailor's Love, A 1880.46
Sailor's Song, A 1897.40
Sailor's Tango, The 1977.08
Sailors Chorus 1891.18
Sailors of St. Hurrah 1904.42
Sailors of the Sea 1963.12
Sailors of the St. Hurrah 1907.16
Sailors on the Town 1944.33, 1989.03
Sailors Sail Away 1923.01
Sailors' Chorus 1891.11
Sailors' Fox Trot Wedding, The 1918.17
Saint Lazare 1952.04
Saint Louis Blues 1945.07
Sainted Mother 1848.04
Saints Go Marchin' In 1992.06
Saints of the Latter Day 1917.09
Sakura/Sakura Gensokyoku 1989.21
Sal's Last Song 1998.02
Salaam 1909.07
Salaam Salaam 1906.39
Salaaming the Rajah 1928.28
Salamaggi's Birthday 1971.13
Sale!, A Sale!, A 1879.03
Sale, a sale, A 1877.25
Sales Lady, The 1904.24
Salesladies' Annual Ball, The 1898.78
Salesmanship 1957.01
Sallie 1906.10
Sallie Mine 1903.09
Sallie Nipp and Jimmie Jones 1898.38
Sallie, Ma Hot Tamale 1901.12
Sally 1900.40, 1902.34, 1902.40, 1920.44, 1979.25, 1980.11
Sally Brown 1885.44, 1922.21
Sally Come Back to the Alley 1921.21
Sally Comes Home 1869.42
Sally Down Our Alley 1917.23
Sally in Our Alley 1857.03
Sally in our alley 1857.03
Sally in Our Alley 1881.39, 1888.28, 1890.12, 1892.36, 1902.23, 1903.01
Sally Simpson 1972.08, 1993.06
Sally, Hot Tamale Alley 1902.21
Sally, the Pride of Dorothy's Alley 1897.04
Salmantina 1949.07
Salome 1953.01, 1994.10
Salome Danced 1979.07
Salomon-Song 1965.04
Salsation 1999.15
Salt Lake City 1917.09
Salt of the Sea 1904.22
Saltarello, The 1964.03
Salute 1902.44
Salute to the King 1913.33
Salute to the Toreador 1911.28
Salvation Army, O!, The 1882.79
Salvation Hymn 1900.07
Salvation Sal 1919.10
Salzburg Puppet Show 1939.23
Sam and Delilah 1930.31
Sam and the Mormon 1884.60
Sam Hall 1931.02
Sam Johnson's Cake Walk 1893.10
Sam Johnson's Colored Cakewalk 1985.02
Sam the Old Accordion Man 1992.18
Sam, Pick Oop Tha' Musket 1960.17
Sam, You Made the Pants too Long 1997.01
Samandoza-we! 1966.03
Samarkand 1917.01
Samba de Roda 1988.06
Sambo 1909.10
Sambo and Dinah 1904.47
Sambo's Banjo 1927.33
Same Old Color Scheme 1973.10
Same Old Crowd, The 1903.06
Same Old Game 1878.20
Same Old Game, The 1877.43, 1906.49, 1915.31
Same Old Girl, The 1906.29
Same Old Love Songs 1927.17
Same Old Me, The 1961.11
Same Old Moon 1904.54, 1927.12, 1929.29
Same Old Moon, The 1907.14
Same Old Places 1920.01
Same Old Song 1917.08
Same Old Stars, Same Old Moon 1920.15
Same Old Story, Nothing New 1899.25
Same Old Story, The 1906.19, 1907.14, 1908.13, 1922.48, 1924.03
Same Old Thing, The 1890.27
Same Old Two, The 1908.24, 1909.23
Same Old Way 1918.35
Same Old Way, The 1923.47
Same One They Picked for Me, The 1913.05
Same Silver Moon, The 1927.42
Same Sort of Girl 1914.18
Same Thing Over Again, The 1897.04
Same Thing, The 1905.51
Same to You, And the 1962.23
Samee Gamee 1900.43
Sammie 1902.21, 1918.20
Sammy 1903.03, 1904.44, 1917.26
Sammy and Topsy 1927.33
Sammy Smug 1878.02, 1885.58, 1888.13, 1896.35
Samoa 1923.25
Samoa Sam, Love Me Some Mo' 1927.40
Samovar the Lawyer 1980.08
Sampson Beauties, The 1986.11
Samson and Delilah 1910.19, 1955.25
Samuel Anoints David 1997.12
Samuel Confronts Saul 1997.12
Samuel Johnson's Cake Walk 1883.63
San 1923.18, 1924.18
San Antoino 1907.12
San Francisco 1974.22
San Francisco Bay 1906.45
San Francisco Fair, The 1915.07
San Pasquale 1964.03
San San Soo 1915.25
San Toy 1924.11
Sand and Sea 1966.20
Sand and Water 2000.16
Sand Flowers 1923.08
Sand in My Shoes 1980.29
Sand Man, The 1905.47
Sand Witches 1921.02
Sandman, The 1906.04
Sandow Girl, The 1907.32
Sands of Time 1953.16, 1978.03
Sandwich for Two 1965.37
Sandwich Man, The 1964.16
Sandwich Men, The 1927.56
Sandy MacDougal 1911.44
Sandy Mahatma Ganghi 1931.26
Sandy-Haired Mary in Our Area 1880.36, 1883.53
Sangalli, La 1869.38
Sans crainte et sans aucun danger 1883.51
Sans Medard je ne pourrais vivre 1886.19
Sans Souci 1951.23
Sans toi 1934.32
Santa Claus 1927.01
Santa Evita 1979.23
Santa Fe 1996.09
Santa Maria March 1896.33
Santa Maria, my joy, my pride 1896.33
Santa Rosa Rose 1909.05
Santero, The 1998.02
Santo Dinero 1949.01
Santo Domingo 1948.30
Saphira 1904.08
Saposhkelekh 1990.16
Sara Lee 1991.04
Sarabande 1982.23
Saracen Song March 1907.27
Sarafina 1988.02
Saragossa Jota 1929.51
Sarah 1999.08
Sarah B 1880.42
Sarah Brown Eyes 1998.01
Sarah from Sahara 1917.34
Sarah of Sahara 1906.40
Sarah, the Sunshine Girl 1934.01
Sarasa 1911.18
Saratoga 1925.38, 1959.27
Sarava 1979.03
Saronita, La 1904.23
Sascha's Got a Girl 1941.03
Sassiest Girl in Town, The 1887.05
Satan Rules 1983.01
Satan's Palace 1922.39
Satanic Strut 1929.50
Satchel and Umbrella Club 1880.32
Satellite Moon 1959.20
Satin and Silk 1955.02
Satin Doll 1981.06, 1986.03, 1990.09, 1997.05
Satin Summer Nights 1998.02
Satisfaction 1982.22
Satisfied With Life 1902.21
Saturday 1921.18

Saturday After Two 1905.19
Saturday Afternoon 1905.19
Saturday Afternoon on Broadway 1914.13
Saturday Afternoon Till Monday Morning 1920.03
Saturday Evening Post 1921.38
Saturday Night 1918.02, 1972.10
Saturday Night at the Rose and Crown 1963.29, 1986.19
Saturday Night Fish Fry 1992.03, 1999.06
Saturday Night in Central Park 1948.04
Saturday Night is the Loneliest Night of the Week 1974.10
Saturday's Child 1948.22
Saturnalia 1969.02
Sauce Diable 1963.25
Saucy Little Sadie 1908.08
Saucy Sparrow, The 1908.16
Sauer Kraut Receipt 1878.04, 1878.12
Saul has Slain His Thousands 1997.12
Sausage King, The 1907.39
Savage I Remain, A 1920.21
Savage Serenade 1933.20
Savannah 1910.01, 1940.17, 1957.16
Savannah Stomp 1929.04
Savannah Sue 1896.24
Savannah's Wedding Day 1957.16
Save a Kiss 1958.14
Save a Kiss for Rainy Weather 1924.15
Save a Little Daylight for Me 1919.14
Save a Little Dram for Me 1920.33
Save a Little Money for a Rainy Day 1906.43
Save it for Me 1903.07
Save Me from Caesar 1968.23
Save the Men 1912.02
Save the People 1976.17
Save the World for Children 1972.21
Save Your Love for Me 1914.15
Saved 1995.03
Saved by the One She Loves 1889.46
Saw Mill River Road 1922.48
Saxophone Man 1924.23
Saxophones 1920.02
Say Au Revoir, Not Good-Bye 1894.37
Say Goodbye to the Freak Show 1997.17
Say it Again 1924.04, 1984.15
Say it isn't So 1988.20
Say it Loud I'm Black and Proud 1982.22
Say it With a Sable 1925.22
Say it With a Smile 1927.20
Say it With a Solitaire 1927.62
Say it With a Ukelele 1923.25
Say it With Gin 1930.40, 1998.05
Say it With Girls 1928.23
Say it With Music 1921.30, 1955.13
Say it With Toes 1927.23
Say it With Your Feet 1929.23
Say No More 1919.42
Say Not Love is a Dream 1912.33
Say So 1928.03
Say So! 1928.03
Say Something Funny 2001.01
Say That You Cannot Forget 1899.06
Say That You Love Me 1928.41
Say the Word 1931.14
Say the Word That Will Make You Mine 1930.24
Say the Words 1976.09
Say to Him 1904.22
Say What I Wanna Hear You Say 1932.07
Say When 1919.44, 1928.21, 1934.35
Say You Love Me, Sue 1899.30
Say You'll be a Friend of Mine 1903.23
Say You'll Stay 1963.08
Say Young Man of Manhattan 1930.39
Say, Darling 1958.08
Say, girl, are you the Miller's bride 1882.60
Say, Sal 1904.41
Scandal 1904.56, 1919.01, 1924.42, 1937.17
Scandal and a Cup of Tea 1924.33
Scandal Club, The 1904.55
Scandal Number 1934.43
Scandal Town 1921.33
Scandal Walk 1920.17
Scandal-monger 1878.16
Scandalous One-Step 1919.13
Scandals in the Air 1915.28
Scanlan's Rose Song 1885.53, 1886.44, 1886.51, 1888.12, 1890.06
Scanlan's Swing Song 1889.03
Scapegoat, The 1885.03
Scapin' 1973.02
Scare Crow 1899.22
Scarecrow 1938.08
Scarecrows 1929.37
Scarem Harem 1938.08
Scarlet Pimpernel, The 1997.19, 1999.13
Scarlet Ribbons 1955.03
Scars, The 1938.11
Scat Song, The 1987.02
Scat With Me 1963.27
Scatterbrain 1995.14
Scatty 1964.29
Scena Delle Ingiuire 1985.14
Scene de Ballet 1944.29
Scenes in New York 1892.19
Scenes that are the brightest 1848.04
Schaffmeister 1896.31
Scheherezade 1930.18, 1951.15, 1977.09
Schemes 1904.37
Scherzo 1944.21, 1944.28
Schlaf Mein Liebling 1999.05
Schneider, How You Vas? Do You Love Me? 1878.04
Schneider, How You Was? 1878.12
Schoe Plattler Tanz 1925.08
Scholar and Soldier, The 1879.15
Schone Isabelle Aus Kastilien 1999.05
Schone Margit. . . 1920.46
Schoner mai, du liebelei, Du 1880.60
School Days 1907.28, 1908.28, 1997.01
School Days! School Days! 1889.18
School Days, School Days 1885.66
School Girls Slept, The 1881.12
School House Blues, The 1921.30
School is Out 1899.22
School of Acting 1907.41
School's Out 1982.22
Schottische 1974.06, 1982.20
Schottiss del Cucu 1917.25
Schrafft's 1948.04
Schrafft's University 1929.29
Schroeder 1971.11, 1999.03
Schwindle Corps, The 1908.30
Sciddle-De-Scow 1929.18
Science 1906.30
Science Fiction 1975.02, 1975.08
Science Fiction Double Feature 2000.17
Scintillating Sophie 2001.01
Scoop 1978.26
Scorpion, The 1999.22
Scotch Boy's Birthday 1942.14
Scotch Highlanders, The 1894.16
Scotch Lassie 1921.21
Scotland Forever 1912.30
Scotland Ye Ken 1908.43
Scots Wha Ha'e wi Wallace bled 1873.10
Scrap 2000.15
Scratch My Back 1956.08
Scream 1977.04
Screw May Twist, The 1938.10
Screwy Little Tune 1931.34
Scrimmage of Life, The 1946.24
Scrub, Scrub, Scrub 1907.39
Scrubwomen's Ballet 1926.21
Scrynatchkielooaw 1978.11
Se Regardant, En 1935.19
Se Saran Rose 1918.18
Sea Chantey 1927.27, 1944.32, 1946.13
Sea Cruise 1992.06
Sea Fever 1959.20
Sea is Calling, The 1919.25
Sea Legs 1925.29
Sea of the Tropics, The 1921.23
Sea Shall Telephone, The 1911.47
Sea Song 1956.13
Sea Song, The 1954.02
Sea, The 1860.05
Sea-Girt Land of My Home 1898.46
Seagull, Starfish, Pebble 1969.16
Sealed Feet 1925.42
Seaman Bold, A 1902.11
Seance Seekers 1896.31
Search and you may find me 1866.34
Search for Wisdom 1978.06
Search the mill! 1882.60
Search throughout the panorama 1884.09
Search, The 1949.15, 1972.06, 2001.09
Searchin' 1995.03
Searchlight Eyes 1905.31
Sears Roebuck 1943.20
Seaside Buccaneer, The 1918.04
Seaside Serenade 1973.08
Seaside Sultan, The 1904.01
Season at the Shore, A 1903.10
Season Ended, The 1932.13
Seasons of Love 1996.09
Seated 'Neath My Family Tree 1923.07
Seaweed 1905.27
Sechaba 1988.02
Second Best 1961.16
Second Campaign Song 1969.03
Second Chance 1997.07
Second Childhood 1928.22
Second City Symphony 1961.17
Second Degree Full Moon Union 1880.36
Second Degree Full Moon Union, The 1883.53
Second Fight, The 1969.11
Second Hand Rose 1921.21
Second Letter 1994.05
Second Letter Home 1985.12
Second Thoughts 1982.08
Second Time Around, The 1974.10
Second Time in Love 1956.07
Second Violin, The 1919.27
Seconde etreinte, La 1929.14
Secrecy 1917.14
Secret in My Life, The 1930.27
Secret Love 1984.15
Secret of Success, The 1937.11
Secret Service Club, The 1919.34
Secret Service, The 1962.20
Secret Singing 1941.01
Secret Society 1903.29
Secret Song 1944.15
Secret Songs 1972.15
Secret Soul 2000.20
Secret, The 1881.16, 1905.03
Secretary is Not a Toy, A 1961.22
Secrets 1914.28
Secrets of the Household 1909.26
Security 1947.16
Seduction, The 1910.22, 1983.02
Seductive Caroline 1909.12
See a Rainbow Arch 1903.21
See America First 1916.05, 1916.06
See at your feet a suppliant one 1844.01
See Her First 1918.39
See here the Happy Couple 1875.19
See Here, My Lads 1881.07
See How it Sparkles 1880.34, 1921.05
See how the Fates their gifts allot 1885.47
See How They Done My Lord 1976.35, 1980.14, 1982.17
See how they glare 1886.53
See Me, Feel Me 1993.06
See No Evil 1929.24, 1970.10
See Saw 1866.31, 1885.64
See Seattle 1963.25
See see, this Stupid Key 1877.22
See That You're Born in Texas 1943.01
See the Blue 1979.10
See the Conquering Hero 1957.02
See the culprit 1848.04
See the Light 1971.07
See the Little Lambkins Play 1929.43, 1944.25
See the merry bunting flying 1895.29
See the mighty dragon comes 1880.59
See the Royal Durbar Palace 1911.28
See the Steamer 1881.04
See Thee and Forget Thee! Never! 1886.30
See What I Mean? 2000.07

See What it Gets You 1964.15
See What the Boys in the Back Room Will Have 1967.13
See What You've Done to Me 1908.39
See where he comes with noble stride 1885.28
See where the Golden Sun 1846.01
See where the Vapors of morn arise 1846.01
See You Around 1972.04
See You in the Funny Papers 1981.10
See Yourselves in the Mirror 1925.46
See! yonder stands our Beauteous Foe 1868.02
See, here comes the King 1863.04
See, see, we saw! 1882.63
See, Sir, See 1873.04
See-Saw 1887.13, 1919.23
Seed of God, The 1948.24, 1948.24
Seeing is Believing 1990.04
Seeing Nellie Home 1917.17
Seeing Paris 1921.11
Seeing Stars 1923.31
Seeing the Sights 1972.07
Seeing the Town in a Yap Wagon 1906.29
Seeing Things 1968.01, 1991.04
Seek the Spy 1909.22, 1947.06
Seek the woman 1887.04
Seems Like Old Times 1955.14
Seena 1976.11
Seerauber-Jenny, Die 1965.04
Seesaw 1973.06
Seguedilla 1890.19
Seguirillas 1992.15
Seguirillas Gitanas 1958.06
Seguiriya 1986.17
Sehan, Onkel Mathieu bringt ein Schweinchen 1885.01
Seidels 1929.17
Seine, La 1964.02
Seise Kinder Yohren 1967.03
Seize Her 1870.20
Seleccion de Milongas 1993.08
Self Made Man 1939.13
Self Made Man, A 1913.27
Self Portrait 2001.01
Self-Expression 1927.11
Self-Made Family, The 1905.29
Self-Made Knight, The 1881.07
Self-made Knight, The 1882.20
Self-Made Maiden, A 1909.21
Self-Made Man, The 1897.48, 1904.58
Selling a Song 1937.06
Selling Gowns 1917.15
Selling Sex 1935.03
Selon le client qui s'avance 1886.09
Semi-Detached 1903.33
Seminole 1902.15, 1904.23
Sempre Boia E 1964.03
Senate in Session 1940.21
Senator's Song, The 1946.10
Senatorial Roll Call, The 1931.48
Send a Boy 1939.12
Send for Me 1920.32, 1930.08, 1931.08
Send for the Militia 1935.03
Send in the Clowns 1973.04, 1976.32, 1977.05, 2000.14
Send Me a Real Girl 1918.29
Send Me a Tender Token 1886.24
Send One Angel Down 1937.10
Send Us Back to the Kitchen 1945.18
Send-Off, The 1968.05
Senor, Senor 1866.07, 1866.21
Senora 1922.18
Senoras de la Noche 1978.11
Senorita 1912.07, 1932.10
Senorita - Senorita 1919.23
Senorita Papeta 1905.34
Sensation 1972.08, 1993.06
Sensible Thing to do, The 1951.17
Sensitivity 1959.26
Sentiment 1924.01
Sentimental Gentleman from Georgia 1987.02
Sentimental Journey 1975.12
Sentimental Me 1924.32, 1975.13
Sentimental Melody 1929.44
Sentimental Moon, The 1910.25
Sentimental Sally 1925.25
Sentimental Sarah 1908.41
Sentimental Silly 1927.27
Sentimental Song and Dance 1919.25
Sentimental Tommy 1910.04, 1911.26
Sentimental Weather 1936.02, 1936.17
Sentry Song 1960.17
Separation Blues 1921.26
September in the Rain 1988.08
September Song 1938.11
September Sunlight 1950.16
Sera Sera Jim 1971.13
Serafina 1913.16
Serdtse 1977.13
Serenade 1880.42, 1880.54, 1895.06, 1896.15, 1896.28, 1902.18, 1910.17, 1912.26, 1917.18, 1918.40, 1920.40, 1921.31, 1922.37, 1922.47, 1924.45, 1925.32, 1929.43, 1929.46, 1930.36, 1975.22
Serenade Blues 1921.16
Serenade Creole 1926.31
Serenade for You 1941.02
Serenade of Achares 1917.33
Serenade of All Nations, The 1898.60
Serenade of Love 1930.27
Serenade of the Blue and the Grey 1899.30
Serenade of the Deceived Pierrot, The 1922.06
Serenade to the Emperor 1936.22
Serenade With Asides 1948.26, 1974.25
Serenade, Madame Pompadour 1924.39
Serenade, The 1899.18, 1907.07, 1916.18, 1930.12, 1944.25
Serenata de Achares 1917.33
Serenity 1997.18
Sergeant Brue 1905.19
Sergeant Hickey of the G.A.R. 1893.36, 1897.43
Sergeant Philip of the Lancers 1912.08
Sergeant Wix 1904.34
Sergeant's Chant 1971.06
Sergeant's Dream 1926.01
Serio-Comic, The 1900.41
Sermon 1972.14, 1995.04
Sermon, The 1960.05
Serpent and the Dove, The 1888.36
Serpent of the Nile, The 1900.07, 1911.29
Serpentina's Garden 2000.10
Serpentine, The 1913.30, 1927.64
Serpuhovsky's Romance 1979.29
Serpuhovsky's Song 1979.29
Servants are we, master is he 1888.07
Servants' Chorus, The 1993.18
Servants' Frolic, The 1923.46
Serve it Only for Two 1919.06
Serve the Caviare 1913.31
Serve Yourself 1982.04
Service for Service 1961.26
Service With a Smile 1934.06
Sesiyahamba 1977.01
Sesqui Centennial Baby, The 1926.14
Sesqui-Centennial 1926.22
Set 'Em Sadie 1923.39
Set it Right 1976.03
Set Me Free 1954.17
Set the Table 1910.24
Setting-Up Exercises 1928.03
Settle Down - We'll Travel 1922.41
Settle Down in a One-Horse Town 1914.31
Settle Down, Travel Around 1922.41
Settling Up the Score 1985.18
Setzen den Fall wir nur 1885.01
Seven Ages of Women 1919.30
Seven and a Half Cents 1954.05, 1973.15
Seven Days 1924.34, 1925.43
Seven Deadly Virtues, The 1960.21, 1980.19, 1993.11
Seven Foreign Envoys 1997.16, 1998.08
Seven Million Crumbs 1956.04
Seven O'Clock in the Evening 1903.21
Seven O'Clock in the Morning 1903.21
Seven Sheep, Four Red Shirts and a Bottle of Gin 1961.24
Seventeen Gun Salute, A 1953.11
1776-1901 1901.16
Seventh Heaven Waltz 1963.20
Seventy Girls, Seventy 1971.07
77 and 83 1888.11
77 & 93 1888.38
Seventy Six Trombones 1991.10, 2000.11
Sevilla 1926.16, 1931.14
Sevillana 1907.08
Sew-Up, The 1964.40
Sex Appeal 1927.29, 1930.20
Sex Delicious 1909.15
Sex Marches On 1940.08
Sextet 1978.02
Sextette - Lucia 1909.13
Sexually Free 1977.04
Sexy Blues 1999.06
Sez I 1961.14
Sez You! Sez I! 1926.25
Sgt. Pepper's Lonely Hearts Club Band 1974.24
Sh! Sh! Shirley! 1927.40
Sh-Boom 1982.22
Sha Shtil 1990.16
Shabes, Shabes, Shabes 1990.16
Shackle Dance 1929.04
Shades of Minstrelsy, The 1929.04
Shades of the Von Spitzenhoffers 1899.04
Shadow Man 1923.35
Shadow of the Moon 1924.08
Shadow of the Sun 1971.20
Shadow Waltz 1980.20
Shadowland 1924.31, 1924.32, 1997.20
Shadows 1914.20, 1916.05, 1936.27
Shadows are Falling 1900.03
Shadows on the Swanee 1995.14
Shadows on the Wall 1931.31
Shady Dan 1932.12
Shady Lady Bird 1941.06
Shady Side of Broadway, The 1906.22
Shaganola 1938.08
Shah 1945.11
Shah! Raise the Dust! 1929.07
Shaindeleh 1966.21
Shake a Leg 1929.21
Shake a Little Hoof 1923.31
Shake a Little Shoe 1927.20
Shake High, Shake Low 1929.06
Shake That Thing 1927.32, 1991.01
Shake Well Before Using 1931.42
Shake Your Bamboo 1932.12
Shake Your Bluesies With Dancing Shoesies 1939.14
Shake Your Duster 1926.19
Shake Your Feet 1923.38
Shake Your Head from Side to Side 1974.10
Shake Yourself Out of Here 1925.25, 1925.48
Shake, Brother! 1927.54
Shake, Rattle and Roll 1989.12
Shakespeare 1968.06
Shakespeare Lied 1967.16
Shakespeare's Epitaph 1981.02
Shakespeare's Garden of Love 1921.25
Shakespearian Rag, The 1915.12
Shakin' at the High School Hop 1972.12, 1994.07
Shakin' the Shakespeare 1932.15
Shaking Hands With the Wind 1969.08
Shaking the Blues Away 1926.37, 1927.37, 1989.21
Shalimar 1924.16
Shall I Compare Thee to a Summer's Day? 1981.02
Shall I Give mine 1875.19
Shall I Sing it Now 1924.16
Shall I Take My Heart and Go? 1958.14
Shall I Tell Him? 1925.06
Shall I Tell You What I Think of You? 1951.12
Shall We Dance 1976.03
Shall We Dance? 1951.12, 1989.03, 1992.02, 1993.16
Shall We Friend? 1972.25
Shall We Join the Ladies 1925.50
Shall We Say Farewell 1961.08
Shalom 1961.20, 1985.19, 1998.07, 2000.14
Shalom L'chaim! 1972.09
Sham, Great Tycoon 1886.15
Shaman Rite for Child Bearing 1998.08
Shaman, The 1997.16
Shamanile 1977.01
Shame on You 1989.05

Shame! Shame! 1844.01
Shamrock Blooms White, The 1894.22
Shamrock of Erin, The 1905.30
Shamrock, The 1880.39
Shandon Belles 1910.04
Shangaane 1977.01
Shanghai Lil 1992.18
Shangri-La 1956.07
Shanty Town Romance 1978.06
Sharlee 1923.42
Sharper Than the Serpent's Fang 1904.17
Shattered Illusions 2000.16
Shauny O'Shay 1948.08
Shav Ain Eleich 1968.04
Shavian Shivers 1930.18, 1930.33
Shayani Izandla 1997.14
She 1974.19, 1983.03
She Alone Could Understand 1920.42
She Always Does Exactly as She's Told 1897.14
She Always Told the Truth 1906.26
She and He 1955.14
She and I Together 1895.30
She Came in Through the Bathroom Window 1974.24
She Came, She Saw, She Canned 1940.10
She Can Love True 1870.20
She Can't Lick Me 1888.05
She Could Shake the Maracas 1939.27, 1975.13
She Did it All Herself 1902.16
She Did the Fandango 1938.06
She Didn't Know 1906.41
She Didn't Know Enough About the Game 1902.35
She Didn't Say 'Yes' 1931.37
She Didn't Say Yes 1986.01
She Didn't Seem to Care 1911.42
She Didn't Understand 1899.25
She Doctor 1975.23
She Doesn't Exist at All 1916.07
She Don't Wanna 1927.37
She Done Him Wrong 1939.14
She Fainted Away in My Arms 1878.04, 1878.12, 1879.63
She Gonna Come Home Wit' Me 1956.04
She Got Him 1941.12
She Hadda Go Back 1963.21
She has No Past 1897.21, 1897.21
She is a Diamond 1979.23
She is My Picnic Girl 1896.02
She is seen 1862.03
She is so Good 1870.27
She is the Belle of New York 1897.39, 1897.39
She is the One Girl 1911.27
She Just Loves Las Vegas 1983.09
She Just Suites Me 1904.46
She Just Suits Me 1905.31
She Just Walks On 1898.38, 1899.19
She Knew a Thing or Two 1908.29
She Knows It 1920.36
She Left Without a Word 1999.17
She Likes Baseball 1968.31
She Lives on Murray Hill 1882.74
She Loved Me, And 1976.20
She Loves Me 1925.35, 1963.14
She Loves Me, She Loves Me Not 1921.37
She Loves Thee 1938.06
She Loves You 1977.10
She Married a Minstrel 1891.32
She May Have Seen Better Days 1927.48
She Never Did the Same Thing Twice 1897.20
She Never Loved a Man as Much as That 1900.41
She Only had a Dollar in Her Purse 1898.56
She Passed My Way 1972.24
She Reads the New York Papers Every Day 1902.40
She Says She's Possessed 1892.42
She Sells Sea Shells 1909.07
She Touched Me 1965.29
She Trimmed Them All so Neatly 1910.34
She Used to Take Me on Her Knee 1898.47, 1902.34
She Walks Like This 1903.16
She Wanted Something to Play With 1896.05
She was a Cau-, She was a Shun 1885.26
She was a Maid of Sweet Simplicit-ee 1898.48
She was Bred in Old Kentucky 1898.66, 1898.70, 1919.16
She was Bred in Old Virginia 1899.23
She was Not Like Other Maidens 1907.27
She was Only a Farmer's Daughter 1919.41
She was Right 1894.35
She was the Miller's Daughter 1903.22
She was There 1997.19, 1999.13
She was Very Dear to Me 1921.23
She wasn't You 1965.31
She will of me a martyr make 1864.12
She Would be a Novelty 1894.17
She'd be Far Better Off With You 1990.04
She'll Do 1902.40
She's a Daisy 1879.09
She's a gal of mine 1869.43
She's a Lady With Money 1905.29
She's a Nut 1978.02
She's a Spectable Married Collud Lady 1898.28
She's a Star 1976.07
She's a Thoroughbred 1898.69
She's a Woman 1993.09
She's Acquitted 1888.13
She's Acquitted, He's Outwitted 1878.02, 1885.58, 1896.35
She's All Right 1903.17, 1904.40
She's an English Girl 1904.29
She's Artistic 1920.29
She's Exciting 1950.04
She's Funny That Way 1928.22
She's Gettin' More Like the White Folks Every Day 1980.27
She's Gone 1916.04, 1997.17
She's Got Everything 1956.08
She's Got That Thing 1998.05
She's Got the Lot 1960.13
She's Got to Go 1987.19
She's Innocent 1921.10
She's Just a Baby 1921.22
She's Just a Little Bit Different from the Others That I Know 1904.37
She's Just Another Girl 1956.16
She's Leaving Home 1974.24
She's Like the Violets Blue 1894.20
She's Ma Daisy 1928.05, 1930.17
She's My Daisy 1908.38
She's My Girl 1897.43, 1903.17
She's My Love 1961.10
She's My Tiger Lily 1900.15
She's No Longer a Gypsy 1970.09
She's Not Thinking of Me 1973.12
She's on File 1985.17
She's on Her Way 1926.32
She's Our Gretel 1985.02
She's Roses 1965.29
She's Salvation Sal 1919.08
She's saved! She's saved! 1878.02
She's Saved! She's Saved! 1885.58, 1888.13, 1896.35
She's Such a Comfort to Me 1929.51
She's Tall, She's Tan, She's Terrific 1980.10
She's Taught Me to Play the Piano 1880.25
She's the Apple of My Eye 1907.39
She's the Image of Her Mother in a Thousand Different Ways 1885.69
She's the Only Girl for Me 1910.12
She's too Far Above Me 1965.14
She's Venus de Milo to Me 1918.31
Sheath Gown in Darktown, The 1908.08
Sheathe the Sword 1896.41
Sheelah, Weave the Spell 1888.40
Sheep Song 1982.20, 1997.10
Sheep's Song 1974.06
Sheer Perfection 1997.12
Sheik of Alabam' Weds a Brown-Skin-Vamp, The 1923.39
Sheik of Araby, The 1922.15
Sheik, The 1922.15
Sheikin Fool 1930.40
Shelling Green Peas 1960.17
Sheltered from the Noonday Glare 1901.19
Sheperdess Interlude, The 1925.03
Shepherd Gavotte, The 1914.22
Shepherd Song, The 1944.16
Shepherd's Delight, The 1963.28
Shepherd's Song 1961.20
Shepherd, The 1937.03
Sheriff's Song 1902.04
Sherry 1967.02
Sheyibone Beis Hamikdosh 1967.03
Sheyn bin ich, sheyn 1960.18
Shh! 1929.50
Shifting of the Sign, The 1898.63
Shifting Sounds 1996.07
Shika, Shika 1954.15
Shilgia 1968.04
Shiloh 1963.22
Shimmering Nile, The 1916.07
Shimmering, Glimmering Nile, The 1918.15
Shimmy - Shaking - Love 1919.34
Shimmy a la Egyptian 1919.30
Shimmy All the Blues Away 1920.06
Shimmy Nods 1920.23
Shimmy Sisters, The 1918.20
Shimmy Town 1919.15
Shimmy Valentine 1920.22
Shinbone Alley 1957.05
Shine 1937.09, 1986.20, 1999.12
Shine 'Em Up! 1927.32
Shine it On 1977.16
Shine on Harvest Moon 1927.12, 1974.01
Shine on Your Shoes, A 1932.17, 1972.05, 1999.23
Shine on, Bright Star 1900.43
Shine on, Harvest Moon 1908.19, 1908.39, 1955.03
Shine on, Little Son 1920.22
Shine on, Right Sunlight 1899.22
Shine on, Silvery Moon 1902.21
Shine, Shine, Shine 1905.47
Ship has Sailed, The 1939.24
Ship I Love, The 1894.17
Ship of Zion 1940.01
Ship Went Sailing, The 1892.19
Ship Without a Sail, A 1929.42, 1975.13
Ship's Concert in the Eighties, A 1934.42
Ship's the Girl for Me, My 1902.03
Shipboard Frolics 1910.13
Shipbuilders' Song, The 1900.50
Shipoopi 1957.18, 2000.11
Shipping News, The 1890.33
Ships in the Night 1916.04
Ships That Pass in the Night 1919.11
Shir Hatan Biem 1968.20
Shir Hattan 1967.13
Shir La Shalom 1972.17
Shirt Song 1882.76
Shirts by Millions 1933.25
Shiver Me Timbers 1975.12, 1979.30
Shivna 1996.12, 2000.05
Shloymele-Malkele 1990.16
Shnyderisher Gezong 1966.21
Sho-Gun of Ka-Choo, The 1904.37
Shoe Shine Boy 1970.17
Shoe-Clap-Platter 1929.46
Shoein' the Mare 1934.19
Shoeless Joe from Hannbal Mo 1999.01
Shoeless Joe from Hannibal Mo 1994.01
Shoeless Joe from Hannibal, Mo 1955.08
Shoemaker Rum 1881.12
Shoener Charley 1877.28
Shoes 1924.36, 1934.40, 1942.34
Shoes of Husband Number One as Worn by Number Two, The 1915.24
Shoes Upon the Table 1993.07
Shogun 1990.17
Sholem Aleichem 1931.29, 1951.20
Shonnie Vas a Nice Young Man 1873.19
Shoo Fly 1869.42
Shoo Fly, don't bodder me 1869.43
Shoo-Fly 1870.07
Shoop Shoop Song, The 1984.15
Shoot Dat Pistol 1927.30
Shooters, The 1880.10
Shooting Craps 1897.07
Shooting Gallery 1940.04
Shooting Show Girls and French Chauffeurs 1911.34
Shooting Star 1920.05, 1992.10
Shooting Star, The 1986.16
Shooting Stars 1925.44, 1985.17
Shop 1917.01

Shop Near By, The 1884.37
Shop Window Girls, The 1908.15
Shopliftin' Clothes 1998.02
Shoppers and Clerks 1904.06
Shoppin' for Clothes 1995.03
Shopping 1901.21, 1903.23, 1905.49, 1907.41, 1908.15, 1910.13, 1915.12, 1920.14
Shopping Around 1952.10
Shopping Glide 1910.13
Shopping in the Orient 1914.23
Shore Leave 1927.16, 1930.26
Short Farewell is Best, A 1917.21
Shortest Day of the Year, The 1938.14, 1975.13
Shortnin' Bread 1980.27
Shosholoza 1977.01
Shot and Shell 1900.03
Shot! Shot! Shot! 1888.28
Should I Speak of Loving You 1976.33
Should I Tell You I Love You? 1946.13
Should Robin at My Window 1883.12
Should You Marry Ma 1898.25
Shoulder Arms 1923.03
Shoulder to Shoulder 1888.18
Shoulders 1931.21
Shout and Feel It 1999.24
Shout High 1885.42
Shout On 1929.18
Shoutin' Sinners 1929.25
Show a Little Pep 1925.44
Show a Little Something New 1918.39
Show Baby, The 1898.25
Show Boat Ballyhoo 1966.14
Show Boat Parade and Ballyhoo 1983.05
Show Boat, The 1927.13
Show Him the Way 1970.02
Show is On, The 1936.31
Show Me 1956.01, 1993.18
Show Me That Special Gene 1972.13
Show Me the Key 1991.05
Show Me the Town 1920.35, 1928.03, 1990.14
Show Me the Way 1917.37
Show Me What You Got 1999.24
Show Must Go On, The 1986.01
Show My Coronet 1898.50
Show of Rice 1918.09
Show Off 1948.22
Show Train 1951.19
Show Us How to do the Fox-Trot 1914.31
Show, Moon and Flower 1989.21
Show, the show, The 1895.32
Showbusiness Nobody Knows, The 1976.20
Showing the Yankees London Town 1908.14
Showman, The 1886.02
Showstoppers 1982.06
Showtime 1948.21
Showtune 1985.19
Shrew, The 1973.08
Shriner's Ballet 1986.03
Shriners' Ballet 1960.06
Shrinking Song 1973.08
Shrug Your Shoulders 1918.02
Shtetl Iz Amereke, A 1998.01
Shtil, di nacht iz oysgeshternt 1960.18
Shtiler, Shtiler 1989.10
Shubert's Serenade 1866.06
Shuffle 1926.51
Shuffle Along 1921.16, 1924.27, 1978.21
Shuffle Off to Buffalo 1980.09, 1980.20
Shuffle Your Feet 1928.18
Shuffle Your Troubles Away 1924.21
Shufflin' Bill 1927.07
Shufflin' Sam 1924.08
Shuffling Shiveree, The 1914.22
Shukh Puster, A 1970.17
Shut Up and Dance 1992.17
Shut Up, Gerald 1981.10
Shver Tsu Zain A Tidene 1970.17
Shy 1959.26
Shy Little Irish Smile 1924.09
Shy Little Violet Blue 1908.42
Shy Strephon 1905.36
Shy Suburban Maid, A 1906.48
Shy widow, The 1882.63
Si ce n'etait qu'une amusette 1929.10
Si dans un beau jour de bataille 1883.51
Si itu savais Maman 1929.14
Si j'avais suivi les voeux de mon pere 1885.59
Si j'etais un petit serpent 1887.35
Si l'Amerique est le plus grand pays du monde 1929.11
Si le prince m'a-t-on conte 1887.35
Si le prince se marie 1887.35
Si maman le veut 1929.13
Si Me Faltas Tu 1973.17
Si petit 1935.19
Si petite 1934.32
Si Si, Senor 1929.37
Si tu pars 1935.19
Si Tu Partais 1981.04
Si vous connaissez la comtesse 1885.59
Si, Si, Senorita 1922.40
Siamsa an Fomhair 1976.29
Siberia 1955.02
Siberian Whirl, The 1911.26
Siciliana 1925.03
Sicillienne, La 1862.03
Sickening Sadness Sits on Me, A 1905.36
Sid, Ol' Kid 1959.22
Sid, Ole Kid 1985.04
Side by Side 1907.47
Side by Side by Side 1970.13, 1977.05
Side by Side by the Seaside 1910.12
Side Show, The 1894.50
Side Street Off Broadway, A 1927.11
Sidestep, The 1978.13
Sidewalk 1921.25
Sidewalk in Paris, A 1934.01
Sidewalk Tree 1973.10
Sidewalks of Cuba 1987.02
Sidewalks of New York 1927.48
Sidewalks of New York, The 1942.16
Siegal Marching Song 1962.01
Siehst du den Mond uber Soho 1965.04
Siempre Flor 1926.09, 1926.35
Siesta Time in San Lucar 1927.08
Sigfreid 1990.10
Sigh by Night 1945.11
Sighing Softly to the River 1879.72, 1981.01
Sighing Song 1882.33
Sighing Swain, The 1886.30
Sights on Broadway 1890.29
Sightseeing in China 1932.12
Sign Here 1951.10, 1965.17
Sign No More Ladies 1963.28
Sign of Love, The 1897.34
Sign of the Honeymoon 1909.17
Signal Lights 1887.29
Signal, The 1925.52
Signalman Dan 1960.17, 1960.17
Signor Gazamma 1900.38
Signor McStinger 1888.09
Signor Monsieur Moldoni 1898.60
Signora Campbell 1979.09
Signora Pandolfi 1962.14
Signs 1903.34, 1907.37
Signs, Omens and Predictions 1888.34
Silas 1901.25
Silas, My Darling 1897.49
Silence 1876.10, 1934.17
Silence of Love 1919.32
Silence! le voici 1887.35
Silence! Silence! 1882.17
Silence, silence! The lady moon 1844.01
Silent Heroes 1878.16
Silent Night 1943.23, 1964.28, 1998.19
Silent Song, The 1880.19
Silent Years, The 1978.06
Silent, the Starry Night 1960.18
Silenzio 1922.45
Silhouette 1927.17
Silhouette Duet 1922.36
Silhouettes Under the Stars 1935.04
Silk 1928.09
Silk Stockings 1926.15, 1955.02
Silken Screen 1914.04
Silks and Satins 1920.47
Silly Ass 1916.12
Silly Billy 1882.39
Silly Bingham Cavalier 1908.01
Silly Boy 1883.32, 1985.02
Silly Cock-a-Doodle-Doo 1911.01
Silly Little Hill 1927.02
Silly Sailors 1904.25
Silly Season, The 1921.10
Silly Song, The 1979.28
Silver Dollar 1987.05
Silver Line, The 1882.63, 1885.26
Silver Moon is Winking, The 1877.22
Silver Ring, The 1913.07
Silver Rose 1980.10
Silver Sails 1934.15
Silver Sea of Love, The 1903.19, 1905.53
Silver Star 1886.53
Silver Star of Love, The 1900.51
Silver Star, The 1886.45, 1909.28
Silver Stars 1922.21
Silver Threads Among the Gold 1918.21, 1924.31
Silver Tree, The 1928.37
Silver Wedding, The 1922.07
Silver Wings 1927.60
Silvered is the Raven Hair 1881.37
Silvers Theme 1971.10
Silverwing 1927.65
Silvery Moon, The 1909.09
Silvery Stars 1876.37
Similar Features 1991.04
Simon Legree 1944.23
Simon the Cellarer 1859.09
Simon Zealotes 1971.12
Simple 1964.15, 1982.09
Simple Ain't Easy 1965.01
Simple as A.B.C. 1863.04
Simple as Bonjour 1959.15
Simple Comme Bonjour 1959.15
Simple days of long ago, The 1886.50
Simple Dimple, A 1904.51
Simple Gifts 2001.04
Simple Girl, A 1909.12
Simple Joys 1972.22
Simple Joys of Maidenhood, The 1960.21, 1980.19, 1993.11
Simple Life 1916.03
Simple Life, The 1905.52, 1926.07
Simple Little Flirts 1891.03
Simple Little Girl, A 1897.39
Simple Little Maid, A 1900.54
Simple Little Sister Mary Green 1901.06
Simple Little Song 1923.35
Simple Little String, A 1897.20
Simple Little Things 1963.26, 1992.10
Simple Little Village Maid 1930.04
Simple Man, A 1979.03
Simple Movie Folk 1945.09
Simple Simon 1900.03, 1971.20
Simple Song, A 1972.15
Simple Spanish Maid 1927.19
Simple Words 1970.21
Simplete 1877.39
Simplified Language 1977.02
Simply Friends 1894.07
Simply Irresistible 2000.07
Simply Looking Around 1914.12
Simpson Sisters, The 1958.22, 1959.01
Since Arrah Wanna Married Barney Carney 1908.11
Since Casey Runs the Flat 1890.07
Since Daddy's Gone Away 1918.08
Since first we parted 1859.16
Since Grandpa Learned to Tango 1914.04
Since Henry Ford Apologized to Me 1927.13
Since Hiram Came Back from the War 1919.41
Since I am Not for Thee 1899.28
Since I am Queen of the Carnival 1900.25
Since I Don't Have You 1994.07
Since I First Met You 1902.44
Since I Met Wonderful You 1918.15
Since I Met You 1916.12
Since I must Swing, - I scorn, I scorn to wince or whine 1750.01
Since I've been in the Army 1862.08
Since Jane Heard a Popular Song 1910.20

Since Laws were made for ev'ry degree 1750.01
Since Laws Were Made for Every Degree 1957.02
Since Ma is Playing Mah Jong 1923.47
Since Maggie Learned to Sing 1890.07
Since Maggie Learned to Skate 1885.64, 1887.13
Since Mother was a Girl 1908.19
Since My Linda's in Da Syn-de-cate 1900.47
Since Nora Brought Her Angora Around 1928.09
Since Sally's in the Ballet 1900.56
Since Sister Nell Heard Paderewski Play 1901.25
Since the Days of Grandmamma 1912.41
Since the Men Have Gone to War 1918.19
Since the Street Cars Have Run on Broadway 1885.44
Since the Time We Met 1967.18
Since To-Day Our Colonel's Mating 1917.14
Since You Came into My Life 1920.32
Since You Said You Loved Me 1912.29
Since You Went Away 1930.24
Since You're Alone 1930.36
Since You're Not Around 1974.05
Sincere 1957.18, 2000.11
Sincerest Form of Flattery, The 1925.47
Sincopated Minuet, The 1922.05
Sing 1926.51, 1929.07
Sing a Christmas Song 1979.32
Sing a Little Jingle 1931.13
Sing a Little Song 1924.45, 1926.30, 1927.59
Sing a Little Tenor 1902.38
Sing a Merry Rondelay 1896.41
Sing a Rhyme of 'Once Upon a Time' 1902.25
Sing a Serenade 1920.26
Sing a Song in the Rain 1929.02
Sing a Song of Sixpence 1912.42
Sing a Tropical Song 1980.29, 1988.08
Sing Alone 1976.03
Sing American Tunes 1933.15
Sing and Dance 1889.54
Sing Boom 1929.07
Sing Cheerily, My Hearty 1892.18, 1892.45
Sing Cheerily, My Hearty a, Yo, Heave Ho 1890.32
Sing Down, Hidery Down 1931.02
Sing for Your Supper 1938.14, 1939.19, 1975.13
Sing Happy 1965.17
Sing Hey for the Aniseseed Bag 1897.48
Sing Hey for the Chaperon 1909.03
Sing Hey, Sing Ho 1904.51
Sing Hi 1976.33
Sing Hopdedoodledoo 1888.19
Sing Israel Sing 1967.08
Sing la La 1868.08
Sing Me a Come-All-Ye Like My Daddy Sang to Me 1908.19
Sing Me a Song of Love 1915.33
Sing Me a Song of Social Significance 1937.14
Sing Me a Song of the South 1928.24
Sing Me Not a Ballad 1945.04
Sing Me Those Pretty Songs Again 1893.30
Sing Me to Sleep With an Old-Fashioned Melody 1915.12
Sing Me to Sleep, Dear Mammy 1921.16
Sing Sing 1923.16
Sing Sing a Song 1976.32
Sing Sing for Sing Sing 1930.40
Sing Sing Sing 1979.13, 1999.01, 2000.07
Sing Sing Tango Tea 1915.17
Sing Something Simple 1930.25
Sing Song Girl 1919.30, 1921.36
Sing Song Lee 1903.38
Sing Sung Sammy 1906.19, 1906.19
Sing Sweet Juanita 1924.35
Sing the Merry 1951.15
Sing the Song of Great Brian 1896.41
Sing to Love 1954.06
Sing to Me, Guitar 1944.02
Sing to Your Dear One 1909.29
Sing Trovatore 1911.12
Sing Your Merriest Songs 1893.19
Sing! 1975.15
Sing! South! Sing! 1952.15
Sing, Birdie, Sing 1866.06
Sing, Darkies, Sing! 1917.11
Sing, O Songster of the Night 1885.42
Sing, pretty maiden, sing 1848.04
Sing, Sing 1964.29
Sing, Sing, Sing 1978.05, 1983.09, 1999.24
Sing, Sing, You Tetrazzini! 1912.41
Sing, You Sinners 1956.02
Sing-a-Long 1982.13
Sing-Bad the Sailor 1898.56
Singer and the Song, The 1912.07
Singer Sang a Song, A 1908.10
Singer's Career, Ha! Ha!, The 1926.24
Singer's Protest 1983.09
Singin' in the Rain 1974.22, 1979.13, 1979.14, 1985.08, 2000.14
Singin' the Blues 1931.32
Singing a Love Song 1928.30
Singing and Dancing 1900.39
Singing Girl, The 1899.34
Singing in Vain for the Moon 1895.21
Singing is the Thing to Make Ye Cheery 1928.05
Singing Lesson 1908.34
Singing lesson, The 1859.16
Singing Lesson, The 1879.15, 1897.13, 1930.12
Singing Models, The 1898.78
Singing Nurses 1925.18
Singing Sensation, The 1999.12
Singing to Baby This Sweet Lullaby 1887.02
Singing to You 1933.21
Singing Tree, The 1948.24
Singing With Someone 1911.40
Single Bird, The 1910.01
Single Day, A 1908.29
Single Dream, A 1983.17
Single I Will Never Be 1882.33
Single Life, A 1979.03
Singspielia 1963.20
Sippi 1928.10
Sir Godfrey 1959.15
Sir Joseph's Berge is Seen 1938.10
Sir Knight and Lady, Listen 1844.01
Sir Middlesex Mashem 1890.23
Sir or Ma'am 1963.29
Sir Oswald Sodde 1966.03
Sir Roger de Coverly 1895.43
Sir Rupert Murgatoryd His leisure and his riches 1887.10
Sir! You Wear a Sword 1904.30
Sir, a secret 1863.04
Sir, you can't refuse me 1864.12
Siren of the Ballet, The 1899.34
Siren of the Tropics 1944.27
Siren Song, The 1948.16
Siren's Song, The 1917.17
Sirens 2000.20
Sirens of Ceylon 1930.20
Sis 1888.43
Sis Hopking 1903.18
Sister 1982.04
Sister Carrie's Song 1995.04
Sister Mary 1888.34
Sister Mary has the Measles 1900.44
Sister Mary Jane's Top Note 1896.48
Sister Susie Glide 1917.29
Sister Susie's Sewing Shirts for Soldiers 1914.22, 1964.28, 1990.09
Sister Susie's Started Syncopation 1915.02
Sisters Gelatine 1898.17
Sisters Giggle, The 1894.38
Sisters Under the Skin 1938.15, 1942.05
Sit Down You're Rockin' the Boat 1980.29
Sit down, 'tis my wish 1855.03
Sit Down, John 1969.06
Sit Down, You're Rockin' the Boat 1950.17
Sit Down, You're Rocking the Boat 1913.30
Sittin' in Clover 1924.24
Sittin' in Ya Ya 1992.06
Sittin' Pretty 1922.14
Sitting Bull 1904.13
Sitting in the Sun 1927.53
Sitting in the Sun Just Wearing a Smile 1929.35
Sitting on a rail 1873.04
Sitting on the Starboard Tack 1905.25
Sitting on Your Status Quo 1937.14
Sitting Over There 1934.40
Sitting Pretty 1924.08
Sitting Watching Jason Play Baseball 1992.09
Sitting, the Lute A-Striking 1893.40
Situation has Quickly Been Changed, The 1998.08
Six Beautiful Maids 1898.02
Six Blocks from the Bridge 1965.01
Six Gun Joe from Cicero 1949.06
Six Lillies of the Valley 1963.29
Six Little Cinderellas 1927.09
Six little Misses 1895.43
Six Little Plays 1926.13
Six Little Sinners 1929.19
Six Little Wives 1900.43
Six Little Wives of the King, The 1916.10
Six Miserable Ruffians, The 1878.02, 1896.35
Six months ago 1882.60
Six Months Out of Every Year 1955.08, 1994.01
Six Palaces 1965.35
Six String Orchestra 1975.05
Six Thirty Monday Morning 1979.11
Six-Times-Six is Thirty-Six 1917.12, 1918.08
Sixes 1879.21
Sixteen Going on Seventeen 1959.24
Sixteen Hundred and Seventeen Broadway 1956.02
Sixteen, Sweet Sixteen 1924.44
Sixty Second Romance 1934.40
Sixty Seconds Ev'ry Minute I Think of You 1922.32
Sizing Up the Girls 1922.38
Skalo-Zwi 1966.03
Skate Boy, The 1912.13
Skateboard Romance 1996.08
Skating 1905.19
Skating Ballet 1926.17
Skating in the Bois 1936.03
Skating Rink, The 1885.64
Skating Song 1906.45
Skeleton Ghost 1927.03
Skeleton Janitor, The 1923.40
Skeletons 1920.12
Skeletons in the Closet 1911.15
Sketch Book 1929.26
Ski Song 1913.30
Ski-ing 1916.14
Skiddle de Scow 1928.10
Skidiskiscatch 1915.30
Skidmore Fancy Ball 1985.02
Skidmore Fancy Ball, The 1883.46, 1892.54
Skidmore Masquerade, The 1880.64
Skidmore's Fancy Ball, The 1879.04
Skids are on Review, The 1879.68
Skids are Out Today, The 1879.37, 1879.64
Skids are Out Tonight, The 1880.64
Skiing at Saks 1938.04
Skimbleshanks 1982.19
Skin and Bones 1969.07
Skinnin' a Cat 1970.05
Skip the Build-Up 1955.04
Skip to My Lou 1931.02, 1975.22, 1989.23, 1999.23
Skipped by the Light of the Moon 1890.12
Skipper 1925.40
Skipping the Skips 1923.47
Skirts are fuller 1887.04
Skit Skat 1932.14
Skull and Bones 1928.43
Sky Girl, The 1927.19
Sky High 1925.07, 1946.04
Sky High Bungalow 1921.18
Sky Rocket 1919.36
Skylark 1997.05
Skylark, The 1855.02, 1855.07, 1911.29
Skyscraper Blues 1949.01
Slander's Whisper 1942.33
Slap Happy 1955.19
Slap My Face 1936.12
Slap That Bass 1990.14, 1992.02
Slash! Dash! Bang! 1907.08
Slaughter on Tenth Avenue 1936.05, 1975.13, 1983.02
Slave Dealer's Song 1900.20
Slave Market, The 1920.34
Slave of Love, The 1924.27
Slave Regina 1955.13
Slave Sale 1892.20
Slave Ship 1929.01
Slave Ships 1996.07

Slave, The 1926.01
Slavery 1916.26
Slavery's Passed Away 1887.48
Slaves of Broadway 1928.14
Slaves of the Demon King 1920.31
Slavlova 1916.23
Sleep Baby Sleep 1932.14
Sleep My Love 1950.05
Sleep on! Snore On! 1910.11
Sleep Peaceful 1946.08
Sleep Sleep 1898.56
Sleep Time, My Honey 1913.17
Sleep You Pretty Creatures 1893.19
Sleep, Baby, Don't Cry 1945.13
Sleep, My Baby, Sleep 1973.03
Sleep, Weary Head 1928.30
Sleep-Tite 1954.05
Sleepin' Bee, A 1954.19
Sleeping Beauty's Dream 1927.34
Sleeping Princess, The 1916.26
Sleepless Nights 1990.14
Sleeptime Lullaby 1945.07
Sleepy Canal, The 1907.63
Sleepy Lagoon 1942.16
Sleepy Little Village 1921.34
Sleepy Man 1975.18, 1976.31, 1995.12
Sleepy Time Down South 1953.12
Sleepy Time Gal 1980.08
Sleepyhead 1926.13
Sleigh Bells May be Wedding Bells 1909.28
Sleigh Ride 1979.13, 1987.02
Sleigh-Bell Quartette 1879.52
Sleighing Song 1895.12
Slice, The 1967.06
Slickens' Pill 1871.17
Slide Some Oil to Me 1975.01
Slide, Boy, Slide 1954.19
Sliding Down a Silver Cloud 1929.22
Slight Case of Ecstasy, A 1946.23
Slight Detail, A 1959.22
Slightly Less Than Wonderful 1943.07
Slightly Perfect 1945.18
Slightly Slightly 1945.18
Sligo 1892.21
Slip into Spring-The Harvest 2000.05
Slip of a Girl 2000.20
Slippery James 1904.54
Slipping Away from You 1987.17
Slippy Sloppy Shoes 1965.37
Slither 1924.38
Slogan Song 1951.23
Sloping Path, The 1914.16
Sloth 1966.32
Slow and Easy Goin' Man 1923.39
Slow Down 1928.27
Slow Movies 1922.05
Slow River 1927.11
Slow Town is a Jazz Town Now 1919.37
Slow Train 1966.32
Slumber Deep 1903.31
Slumber so Gently 1895.25
Slumber Song 1931.28
Slumber! O sentinel 1884.14
Slumber, Mortal! 1882.75
Slumber-On 1902.44
Slumbertown 1911.29
Slumming on the River 1899.19
Slumming Party 1937.14
Sly Cigarette, The 1898.46
Sly Musette, The 1902.37
Sly Old Fox 1906.13
Small Cartel, A 1963.08
Small Craft Warnings 1988.10
Small Fry 1980.29
Small House of Uncle Thomas, The 1951.12, 1989.03
Small Talk 1954.05
Small Town Gal, A 1908.09
Small Town Girl 1920.14
Small World 1959.13
Smart Like That 2001.06
Smart Little Girls 1939.25
Smart People 1928.02
Smart Set 1932.15
Smart Set, The 1899.06, 1904.55
Smart Woman 1961.07
Smartest Girl in Town, The 1895.32
Smash the mirror 1972.08
Smash the Mirror 1993.06
Smashed 1885.51
Smell of Christmas, The 1970.07
Smile 1927.32, 1976.16, 1986.20
Smile (Smile, Smile) 1907.10
Smile a Little Smile for Me 1917.19
Smile and be Merry 1904.51
Smile and Forget 1922.24
Smile at Me 1935.11
Smile Awhile 1951.17
Smile for Me 1953.02
Smile for the Press 1940.09
Smile of the Crocodile 1905.02
Smile On 1925.40
Smile She Means for You, The 1910.22
Smile Thy Sweetest Smile 1876.34
Smile, a Kiss, A 1934.43
Smile, Darn You, Smile! 1927.65
Smile, Please Smile 1905.02
Smile, Smile 1967.06
Smile, Smile, Smile 1911.01, 1916.26
Smiles 1913.24, 1918.20, 1919.40, 1963.13, 1980.27
Smiles, Smiles, Smiles 1902.16
Smiling Hope 1882.33
Smiling Isle, The 1902.44
Smiling Sam 1920.47
Smiling Sambo 1903.33
Smiling Through My Tears 1924.46
Smoke 1918.09
Smoke and Fire 1978.28
Smoke Duet 1999.02
Smoke Get's in Your Eyes 1986.01
Smoke Gets in Your Eyes 1933.26, 1962.17
Smoke Goes Up the Chimney Just the Same, The 1902.40
Smoke Rings 1921.11, 1922.02
Smokey 1954.11
Smokey Joe's Cafe 1995.03
Smokin' Reefers 1932.17
Smoking is clearly annoying 1881.04
Smoking Reefers 1972.05
Smoky Rhythm 1934.06
Smuggler or a Juggler, A 1888.19
Smut Song, The 1994.06
Snag 'Em Blues 1921.26
Snake Charmer's Song 1902.04
Snake in the Grass 1999.01
Snap a Wishbone With Me 1921.02
Snap into It 1927.15
Snap of the Whip, The 1918.29
Snap Out of It 1927.58
Snap Your Fingers 1912.09, 1919.28
Snappy Show in Town 1926.46
Snatched from the Cradle 1917.05
Sneaky Steps 1914.34
Sneeze Time 1907.14
Sneezing Quintette 1904.54
Sneezing Sextette 1906.29
Sneezing Song 1866.34, 1869.47, 1870.01, 1890.26
Sniffle, The 1973.08
Snip, Snip, Snip 1919.09
Sniper 1975.05
Snoop Snoop 1911.46
Snoopy 1971.11, 1999.03
Snoring Song, The 1888.40
Snow Flake 1921.27
Snow-King's Death 1893.03
Snowball Sammy 1904.45
Snowbird Song, The 1965.35
Snowdrops and the Spring 1912.17
Snowflakes and Sweethearts 1965.35
Snowtime 1923.39
Snowy Breasted Pearl, The 1895.30
Snug as a Bug in a Rug 1923.07, 1980.29
Snuggle 1911.08
Snuggle and Dream 1919.06
So am I 1924.43
So are You 1929.27
So Away With Sorrow 1912.17
So Beats My Heart 1955.13
So Beats My Heart for You 1929.32
So Beautiful 1963.16, 1986.16
So Brush Up Your Shakespeare 1999.19
So Did I 1889.41
So Different 1905.30
So do I 1928.07, 1981.24
So Drink a Cup of Cheer 1933.23
So Far 1947.17, 1993.16, 1996.04
So Glad 1943.10
So Glad I Married Her 1988.10
So Glad I'm Here 1969.10
So Got to Him and Say to Him 1881.37
So Happy 1987.18
So He Died, And 1950.01
So I Bid You Beware 1899.34
So I drink off this Bumper. - And now I can stand the Test 1750.01
So I Smile 1913.31
So I Ups to Him 1929.27
So I'll Tell Him 1973.11
So I've Been Told 1906.05
So in Love 1948.32, 1999.19
So it's Kisses You're Craving 1897.03
So Little Time 1972.13
So Lonesome 1931.31
So Long 1944.33
So Long as it isn't Shakespeare 1964.18
So Long as the World Goes Round 1920.37
So Long Baby 1998.16
So Long Bill 1908.05
So Long Bill Take Care of Yourself 1907.27
So Long Dearie 1964.01, 1985.19
So Long Dude 1972.18
So Long for Ever so Long 1934.35
So Long Jazz 1921.04
So Long Letty 1927.13
So Long Mary 1968.07
So Long Pa 1991.07
So Long Sammy 1972.13
So Long, 174th Street 1976.09
So Long, Big Guy 1966.06
So Long, Farewell 1959.24, 1998.03
So Long, Letty 1916.21
So Long, Mary 1906.02
So Long, Sing Song 1904.42, 1907.16
So Low 1934.06
So Mama Says 1895.44
So Many Hours 1965.35
So Much That I Know 1971.01
So Much to do in New York 1985.12
So Much World 1969.07
So Near and Yet so Far 1948.23
So Nice Having You 1948.15
So nimm, mein susser Schatz 1964.25
So Odd a House 1866.21
So Pardon Us 1939.15, 1939.17
So please you, sir 1885.47
So Proud 1965.35
So shy 1886.50
So Small 1934.32, 1935.19
So Stand Back, All You Bullies 1940.01
So Strange a House 1866.07
So Take You a Warning 1896.48
So That's the Way You Like It 1962.23
So There You Are 1926.38
So They Say 1900.25
So This is Havana 1933.15
So this is how you'd have us sue you 1895.29
So This is Love 1923.26
So This is Mexico 1932.07
So This is Paris 1916.11
So This is the States 1925.29
So This is Venice 1923.38
So Very Tender 1894.03
So We Will Sing 1960.17
So What Else is New? 1981.10
So What Goes 1940.16
So What's the Use? 1907.27
So What? 1933.01, 1966.24, 1970.03, 1998.04
So Wie Du 1885.31
So Will You, And 1938.15
So Would I 1928.08

So You Got What You Want 1988.09
So You Wanted to Meet the Wizard 1975.01
So You Will Walk With Me 1934.41
So's Your Old Man 1925.33
So, Long Dearie 1998.07
So, My Dashing Roving Blade 1933.24
So? 1906.19
Soapbox Sillies 1938.01
Sob Song 1881.12
Sobbin Women 1982.14
Social Dance 1982.14
Social Eclat 1903.39
Social Game, The 1920.44
Social Laws 1898.48
Social Observer 1923.47
Social Polkarette, The 1901.18
Social Whirl 1961.26
Social, The 1959.11
Socially Conscious Iron Workers 1965.33
Society 1901.08, 1903.08, 1904.26, 1904.31, 1904.52, 1905.39, 1908.19, 1912.45, 1915.21, 1922.23, 1924.42
Society Blues 1924.29
Society Bud 1923.38
Society Buds 1906.01
Society Circus, The 1910.30
Society Farmerettes, The 1917.26
Society has quite forsaken 1894.15
Society Ladder 1927.52
Society Party 1956.12
Sock Life in the Eye 1972.07
Socrates Jackson 1904.39
Socrates' Song 1938.02
Sodomy 1968.11
Soft be Thy Slumbers 1939.21
Soft in the Moonlight 1926.31
Soft is the Sparrow 1968.05
Soft is the Spring Breeze 1998.08
Soft Lights and Sweet Music 1932.05
Soft Music 1974.05
Soft Shoes 1912.31
Soft to Sensuous Music Swaying 1899.40
Soft, Soft 1895.19
Softly Sleep 1877.20
Softly Stealing Lanterns Gleaming 1902.29
Softly Through the Summer Night 1914.03
Softly, as in a Morning Sunrise 1928.29, 1986.14
Sogno, Il 1890.32
Soirs de Mexique 1929.16
Sol Que Tu Eres, El 1988.15
Solace 1980.27
Sold 1928.28
Soldatskaya 1934.32
Soldier Bold, A 1900.03
Soldier Born, A 1889.54
Soldier Boy 1904.31, 1927.43, 1984.15
Soldier Boy Canteen 1885.06
Soldier Boy's Canteen 1887.05
Soldier Boy's Canteen, A 1885.66, 1889.18
Soldier Boy, The 1908.30
Soldier is the Idol of the Nation, The 1903.07
Soldier knows no other law, The 1882.17
Soldier Men 1917.28
Soldier Needs No Truer Friend, A 1899.40
Soldier of Fortune, A 1900.12, 1904.09
Soldier of Love 1934.42
Soldier of Love am I, A 1900.47, 1905.36
Soldier of My Own, A 1906.32
Soldier Scarcely Ever Feels, A 1894.47
Soldier Stole Her Heart, A 1908.06
Soldier's Chorus 1870.26
Soldier's Dream, A 1942.20
Soldier's Farewell, The 1988.15
Soldier's Gossip 1994.05
Soldier's Life is Never Long, A 1908.40
Soldier's life, A 1844.01
Soldier's Life, A 1886.30, 1892.08, 1904.05, 1909.15, 1911.02
Soldier's Love, A 1908.40
Soldier's Song, The 1933.07
Soldier's Story, The 1902.16
Soldier, Oh Soldier 1963.19
Soldiers 1901.25
Soldiers All 1899.40
Soldiers are Safe, The 1897.03
Soldiers in Love's War 1899.11
Soldiers in the Park, The 1898.46
Soldiers Like You and Me 1928.48
Soldiers of All Nations 1899.06
Soldiers of Bohemia 1912.15
Soldiers of Our Queen, The 1881.37
Soldiers of the Army 1902.35
Soldiers of the Czar 1911.41
Soldiers of the King 1908.14
Soldiers of the Netherlands 1907.63
Soldiers of the Parliament 1897.17
Soldiers of the Stage 1906.21
Soldiers of the Stage, The 1901.07
Soldiers of the Tyrant Emperor 1889.34
Soldiers Prayer 1970.06
Soldiers Return, The 1889.54
Soldiers to the Front 1876.11, 1876.30
Soldiers Tune 1925.04
Soldiers' Chorus 1904.37
Soldiers' March 1952.15
Soldiers' Song 1989.24
Soldiery, The 1904.09
Solea 1992.15
Solea Yel Jaleo, La 1917.25
Soleares 1986.17
Soleares de Triana 1958.06
Soleil, O 1946.21
Solfeggio 1887.05
Solfeggio Company 1885.06
Soliciting Subscriptions 1925.17
Solicitors Song 1965.31
Solid Citizens, The 1887.29
Solid Silver Platform Shoes 1974.13
Soliloquies 1963.29
Soliloquy 1928.44, 1945.05, 1987.04, 1989.16, 1997.01
Solitary Finish, A 1907.46
Solitude 1942.11, 1976.04, 1981.06, 1997.03
Solla Sollew 2000.18
Solo Koko 1903.18
Solo Mio 1921.02
Solo on the Drum, A 1924.40
Solomon 1980.10, 1997.12
Solomon Song 1966.19, 1976.10, 1989.24
Soloquy of the Minister 1929.08
Solution, The 1985.18
Som'thin from Nuthin' 1996.07
Sombrero 1905.22, 1905.52
Sombrero Land 1911.34
Sombrero, El 1960.22
Some Beautiful Day 1903.27
Some Big Something 1920.01
Some Bright Morning 1980.23
Some Cats Know 1995.03
Some Day 1917.28, 1921.03, 1925.32, 1927.33, 1941.03, 1941.03
Some Day I'll Make You Love Me 1921.12
Some Day I'm Gonna Fly 1965.36
Some Day the Sun Will Shine 1921.21
Some Day Waiting Will End 1918.28
Some Day When Dreams Come True 1907.12
Some Day, Some How, Some Where 1918.29
Some Days Everything Goes Wrong 1964.05
Some Days it Seems That it Just Don't Pay to Get Out of Bed 1972.10
Some do, Some Don't 1902.07
Some Enchanted Evening 1949.04, 1993.16
Some Fairy Hand 1866.18
Some Fine Day 1920.04
Some Folks Do 1939.21
Some Girl has Got to Darn His Socks 1915.29
Some Girl is on Your Mind 1929.31
Some Girls 1916.12, 1990.12
Some Girls Can Bake a Pie 1931.48
Some Girls Do 1877.25
Some Have, Some Have Not 1989.26
Some How 1923.25
Some Kind of Man 1970.08
Some Leave to Roam 1860.05
Some Like it Hot 1980.29
Some Like to Hunt 1923.05
Some Little Bug Will Find You Some Day 1915.28
Some Little People 1960.01
Some men, they say, are born to rule 1885.63
Some More Dancing 1923.11
Some Night 1918.29
Some o' Dese Days 1930.10
Some of the Days 1941.09
Some of These Days 1963.02, 1976.04, 1979.25
Some of These Men 1944.32
Some One 1916.19
Some Other Day 1927.53
Some other evening will do just as well 1884.37
Some Other Girl 1919.33
Some Other Time 1919.29, 1944.33, 1971.15, 1977.02, 1989.03
Some Other Times 1998.16
Some Party 1919.09
Some People 1959.13, 1965.08, 1991.04
Some People Make Me Sick 1920.42
Some Say 1882.75, 1990.12
Some seven men form an association 1894.15
Some Sort of Somebody 1915.26, 1975.24
Some Sort of Somebody All the Time 1915.31
Some Sunny Day 1919.12, 1922.22
Some Sweet Days 1923.20
Some Sweet Someone 1928.25
Some Things 1965.32
Some Things are Better Left Unsaid 1896.02
Some Time 1916.20
Some Time Ago 1894.21
Some Time, Some Place, Some Girl 1912.17
Somebody 1896.31, 1896.48, 1900.43, 1900.43, 1900.51, 1920.09, 1969.02
Somebody Did Alright for Herself 1978.27
Somebody Else 1927.07
Somebody Lied to Me 1908.08
Somebody Like Me 1929.25
Somebody Loves Me 1894.50, 1924.19, 1974.09
Somebody New 1980.23
Somebody Older 1997.07
Somebody Ought to be Told 1935.17
Somebody Quite Like You 1929.32
Somebody Somewhere 1980.29
Somebody Told Me 1981.15
Somebody's Arms 1911.06
Somebody's Been 'Round Here Since I've Been Gone 1907.41
Somebody's Coming to See Me Tonight 1939.21
Somebody's Crazy About You 1925.25, 1925.48
Somebody's Dancing With My Girl 1914.22
Somebody's Doin' Somebody All the Time 1973.02
Somebody's Eyes 1913.01, 1920.07, 1998.13
Somebody's Going to Throw a Big Party 1929.45
Somebody's Waiting for Me 1920.32, 1930.17
Somebody, Somewhere 1956.04
Someboy's Sweetheart 1918.40
Someday 1983.21, 1999.08
Someday I'll Find You 1986.19
Someday I'll Walk 1974.12
Someday My Prince Will Come 1979.28
Someday We'll All be Free 1995.01, 1999.09
Someday' is for Suckers 1997.08
Somehow I Never Could Believe 1947.02
Somehow I'd Rather be Good 1926.26
Somehow I've Always Known 1954.17
Somehow it Made Him Think of Home 1902.20
Someone 1922.10, 1926.26, 1927.20, 1951.10
Someone Else is Stepping In 1999.09
Someone Else's Story 1988.09
Someone has Your Number 1918.12
Someone I Used to Know 1912.17
Someone I've Already Found 1970.02
Someone in a Tree 1976.02
Someone in April 1979.09
Someone in the Know 1942.27
Someone is Waiting 1970.13
Someone Just Like You 1916.12
Someone Like Me 1968.08
Someone Like You 1919.44, 1921.09, 1924.10, 1928.49, 1965.06, 1997.09
Someone Loves You After All 1923.47
Someone Must Try 1966.09
Someone Needs Me 1966.29

Someone Nice Like You 1962.18, 1978.18
Someone Stole My Overcoat 1989.10
Someone to Admire, Someone to Adore 1928.19
Someone to Care For 1966.05
Someone to Love 1974.04
Someone to Love You 1929.24
Someone to Watch Over Me 1926.36, 1974.09, 1990.14, 1992.02, 1992.18, 1999.10, 2001.07
Someone Who Believes in You 1924.03
Someone Will Make Me Cry 1923.27
Someone Will Make You Smile 1923.27
Someone Woke Up 1965.06
Someone Wonderful I Missed 1977.04
Someone You Know 1961.11
Someone, Someday, Somewhere 1925.10
Somethin' Ain't Right 1998.21
Somethin' More 1992.08
Somethin' Told Me Not to Trust That Man 1953.12
Something 1908.30, 1909.31, 1912.46
Something About a Uniform 1909.26
Something About Love 1919.11
Something After This Style 1891.03
Something Always Happens When it Shouldn't 1908.40
Something Bad is Happening 1992.09
Something Beautiful 1970.20
Something Better, Something More 1983.21
Something Big 1961.24, 1968.13
Something Burning 1900.57
Something Devilish Wrong 1904.40
Something Doesn't Happen 1970.19
Something for Nothing 1925.01, 1971.16
Something for the Babies 1886.51, 1888.12
Something for the Boys 1943.01
Something Good 1967.07, 1998.03
Something Greater 1970.09
Something Happened 1907.04
Something has Happened 1966.29
Something Holy 1972.02
Something I Dreamed Last Night 1939.25
Something in Here 1922.31
Something in His Eyes 1968.08
Something in My Eye 1942.30
Something in the Air 1986.16
Something in the Air of May 1935.17
Something in the Wind 1953.01
Something is Coming to Tea 1964.16
Something is Wrong in Jerusalem 1976.35, 1980.14, 1982.17
Something Like This 1912.26
Something More 1964.35, 1972.24, 1983.01
Something Must be Done 1979.33
Something New and it's You 1932.19
Something New is in My Heart 1935.17
Something New, Something Different 1985.02
Something Nice and Foolish 1903.09
Something Old, Something New 1927.42
Something or Other Sue 1904.50
Something Pretty 1995.04
Something Seems Tingle Ingleing 1975.22
Something Seems Tingle-Ingle-ing 1913.34
Something Seems to Tell Me 1931.08
Something Somewhere 1970.19
Something Sort of Grandish 1947.03
Something Special 1959.19, 1970.03
Something Tells Me 1927.27, 1964.16
Something Tells Me I'm in Love 1926.06
Something That Money Can't Buy 1918.29
Something There 1994.04
Something to Dance About 1950.15
Something to do With Spring 1986.19
Something to Live For 1929.07, 1964.05, 1981.06, 1997.03
Something to Point To 1978.12
Something to Remember Me By 1995.04
Something to Remember You By 1930.32, 1954.11, 1972.05
Something to Say 1917.17
Something to Sing About 1930.39
Something to Tell 1911.39
Something Very Mysterious 1911.25
Something Very Strange 1961.18
Something was Missing 1977.06
Something Will Turn Up 1981.12
Something Wonderful 1951.12, 1993.16
Something Wonderful Can Happen 1971.19
Something Wrong With Me 1925.26
Something You Don't Expect 1910.18
Something You Lack 1934.06
Something You Never had Before 1961.27
Something's Afoot 1976.15
Something's Always Happening on the River 1958.08
Something's Coming 1957.12, 1962.17, 1977.05
Something's Going to Happen to You 1931.47
Something's Gone Wrong 1975.07
Something's Got to be Done 1916.06, 1922.43
Something's Got to Happen 1933.26
Something's Gotta Give 1989.21, 1997.05
Something's Happened to Rosie 1923.46
Something's Rotten in Denmark 1976.03
Something's Wrong 1881.36
Sometime 1918.30, 1925.47
Sometimes 1920.13, 1925.21, 1978.11
Sometimes - Perhaps 1902.15
Sometimes a Day Goes By 1981.10
Sometimes I Feel Just Like Grandpa 1917.20
Sometimes I Feel Like a Motherless Child 1980.27
Sometimes I'm Happy 1927.16, 1975.22
Sometimes like brinded cats 1870.15
Sometimes the Dream Comes True 1915.21
Sometimes You're Up 1983.20
Somewhere 1906.23, 1908.08, 1910.05, 1918.29, 1956.07, 1957.12, 1963.20, 1977.09, 1986.16
Somewhere Close By 1983.15
Somewhere I Know There's a Girl for Me 1920.21
Somewhere in America 1919.40
Somewhere in Love's Garden 1922.40
Somewhere in Lovers' Land 1925.07
Somewhere in the Heart of a Man 1951.05
Somewhere in the Night 1991.10
Somewhere in the Past 1972.19
Somewhere in the World There's a Little Girl for Me 1906.05
Somewhere is Here 1978.22
Somewhere on Broadway 1917.12
Somewhere There's a Little Bluebird 1961.01
Somewhere There's Some Girl 1919.22
Somewhere There's Someone for Me 1917.32
Somewhere, Someone 1984.02
Sommambula 1860.05
Somnambulistic Melody 1916.10
Somoa Sam 1927.40
Son of a Billionaire 1927.47
Son of a Gun 1977.09
Son of France, A 1919.42
Son of Man 1971.14
Son of the Grenadier, The 1903.40
Son of the Sun, A 1930.26
Sonatina the British 1976.11
Song About Inadequacy, The 1965.04
Song About Love, A 1927.11
Song and Dance 1927.43
Song and Mime of Corday's Arrival in Paris 1965.39
Song Birds Quartette 1923.39
Song for a Banjo Dance 1991.01
Song for Dancing, A 1978.27, 1992.18
Song for Prison, A 1935.16
Song for You, A 1976.32
Song from Mixteca 1988.15
Song from Somewhere, A 1965.35
Song Games 1901.15
Song in the Night 1938.01
Song is You, The 1951.22, 1975.22, 1986.01
Song of a Child Prostitute 1978.11
Song of a Sailor 1922.04
Song of a Summer Night 1956.04
Song of a Yankee Tar, The 1901.21
Song of All Nations 1886.53
Song of All Nations, or She had to Decline 1892.55
Song of Birds, The 1894.15
Song of Brown October Ale 1891.29, 1929.43
Song of Captain Therese, The 1892.08
Song of Chauve-Souris 1943 1943.11
Song of Conundrums 1877.43
Song of Defiance 1944.28
Song of Destiny 1927.26
Song of Frustration, A 1980.17
Song of Futility 1989.24
Song of Galilee 1955.13
Song of Gold, The 1925.52
Song of Greater Britain 1970.06
Song of Hareford 1986.12
Song of Harlem 1929.25
Song of Home 1916.26, 1916.26
Song of Home, The 1905.12
Song of Hope 1977.01
Song of How Mucked Up Things Are 1970.06
Song of India 1957.01
Song of Loretta 1901.13
Song of Love 1921.31, 1924.21, 1927.04, 1959.26
Song of Love, A 1899.39
Song of Love, The 1917.32
Song of Mime of the Glorification of the Beneficiary 1965.39
Song of Miriam 1937.01
Song of Modesty, The 1884.11
Song of Mother Courage 1963.09
Song of My Generation, The 1970.17
Song of My Heart 1934.41
Song of Nations 1904.58
Song of Norway, The 1944.21
Song of Patriotic Prejudice, A 1966.32
Song of Peace, A 1972.17
Song of Priglio, The 1937.11
Song of Reproduction 1959.20
Song of Ruth 1937.01
Song of Solomon 1965.04
Song of Songs, The 1914.17
Song of Sorrento, The 1886.49
Song of Spain 1940.03
Song of Summer Time, The 1902.02
Song of Symbols 1929.26
Song of the Adieu 1879.15
Song of the Aimlessness of Life 1933.07
Song of the Answer, The 1935.16
Song of the Ballad-Mongers 1894.40
Song of the Balloon, The 1958.18
Song of the Banshee, The 1897.03
Song of the Bat, The 1941.01
Song of the Big Shot 1977.08
Song of the Brass Key 1926.42, 1946.03, 1987.10
Song of the Brunette 1886.49
Song of the Bugle 1895.12
Song of the Butterfly, The 1892.08
Song of the Carabine 1894.08
Song of the Carbine 1897.13
Song of the Carbine, The 1930.12
Song of the Chimes 1914.25
Song of the Circus 1891.46
Song of the Claque 1947.14
Song of the Clock 1890.28
Song of the Cocktail 1912.45
Song of the Colonel, The 1899.38
Song of the Cotton Fields 1929.23
Song of the Crusader 1902.04
Song of the Cuckoo Clock, The 1893.19
Song of the Danube, The 1899.34
Song of the Devil, The 1894.29
Song of the Dolls 1910.24
Song of the Drum 1881.22
Song of the Drum Major 1900.20
Song of the Drum, The 1898.54
Song of the Fair Dissenter Lass 1970.06
Song of the Falcon 1902.04
Song of the Fashions 1910.34
Song of the Field 1925.52
Song of the Fields 1943.11
Song of the Flame 1925.52
Song of the Flea 1943.11
Song of the Flea, The 1940.20
Song of the Flint and Steel 1893.19
Song of the Flowering Stein, The 1903.20
Song of the Flowers 1905.54
Song of the Flute 1910.24
Song of the Foreign Legion 1931.30
Song of the Forty-Thieves 1899.21
Song of the Free Lance, The 1906.18
Song of the Goddess 1936.28
Song of the Golden Peacock 1968.22
Song of the Great Capitulation 1963.09

Song of the Great Commander 1892.08
Song of the Great Souls of Earth, The 1963.09
Song of the Grenadier, The 1898.54
Song of the Greutli Mountain, The 1879.54
Song of the Guards 1903.36
Song of the Guns 1936.28
Song of the Hangman 1945.04
Song of the Heart 1909.24
Song of the Herd 1979.29
Song of the Hill 1943.10
Song of the Honeymoon, The 1910.30
Song of the Hours, The 1963.09
Song of the Husbands 1895.06
Song of the Insufficiency of Human Endeavor 1976.10
Song of the Japanese Fisherman, The 1922.21
Song of the Jolly Coachman 1938.16
Song of the King 1951.12, 1982.03, 1993.15
Song of the King, A 1908.14
Song of the Lampoon, The 1898.54
Song of the Little Hunchback 1879.15
Song of the Little Sailor, The 1884.37
Song of the Lonesome Forest 1912.03
Song of the Ma 1959.04
Song of the Malcontents 1969.03
Song of the Mascot 1882.25
Song of the Mascot, The 1882.25
Song of the Matadors 1932.07
Song of the Merry Duchess, The 1883.52
Song of the Mill 1913.36
Song of the Mirror, The 1921.14
Song of the Moonbeams 1929.26
Song of the Mormon 1898.72
Song of the Nightingale 1930.01
Song of the Nightingale, The 1929.29
Song of the Nose 1899.28
Song of the Old West, A 1980.17
Song of the Open Road 1973.08
Song of the Optimist 1895.33
Song of the Outlaw 1902.04
Song of the Peasant 1879.15
Song of the Pictures 1918.36
Song of the Pipe 1905.03
Song of the Poet 1929.48
Song of the Professor 1895.44
Song of the Question, The 1935.16
Song of the Rain 1967.08
Song of the Regiment 1890.23
Song of the Regiment, The 1907.06
Song of the Riffles 1907.26
Song of the Riffs 1926.42
Song of the Rifle, The 1904.39
Song of the Riveter 1929.19
Song of the Roustabouts, The 1935.15
Song of the Sailor 1885.44
Song of the Samovar, The 1920.28
Song of the Sarong 1940.02
Song of the Saucer 1879.52
Song of the Scimitar, The 1917.24, 1919.20
Song of the Sea 1885.51
Song of the Sea, A 1909.07
Song of the Seasons 1870.26
Song of the Shop, The 1895.32
Song of the Silver Blades 1946.14
Song of the Sirens, The 1915.08
Song of the Soldiers 1997.16, 1998.08
Song of the Spokes 1979.07
Song of the Strollers 1901.13
Song of the Sun 1919.25
Song of the Swing 1958.18
Song of the Sword 1879.15
Song of the Sword, The 1900.50, 1902.03
Song of the Tenderloin 1898.20
Song of the Titanic 1998.11
Song of the Trees, The 1918.22
Song of the Troika 1947.14
Song of the Tub 1904.36
Song of the Turnkey 1894.40, 1913.25
Song of the Union, The 1859.06
Song of the Vagabonds 1925.32, 1932.14, 1975.22
Song of the Vendetta, The 1900.50
Song of the Very Vulgar Boatmen, The 1928.04
Song of the WAAC's 1942.23
Song of the Walnut Tree 1968.22
Song of the Watchman's Rattle, The 1900.50
Song of the Weather, A 1959.20
Song of the Wedding Ring 1893.03
Song of the Wise Woman and the Soldier 1963.09
Song of the Witches 1907.29
Song of the Woodman 1936.31, 1948.04
Song of the World, The 1918.22
Song of the Wounded Frenchmen 1936.28
Song of Two Islands 1942.29
Song of Valencia 1949.07
Song of Victory 1927.42
Song of Welcome 1969.04
Song of Yesterday, A 1902.44
Song on the Sand 1983.11, 1985.19, 1998.07
Song That Broke My Heart, The 1891.03
Song that reached my heart, The 1888.05
Song to Sing, A 1972.18
Song Tow 1897.48
Song vom Nein und Ja, Der 1965.04
Song Without Many Words, A 1920.05
Song Without Words 1922.47
Songbird of Melody Lane 1903.04
Songbook 1981.14
Songs for Free, The 1939.25
Songs for the People 1882.79
Songs I Can't Forget 1922.19, 1923.20
Songs My Mother Taught Me 1955.19
Songs of a Pilgrim 1894.37
Songs of Araby 1897.05
Songs of Long Ago, The 1920.17
Songs of Many Nations 1885.45
Songs of the Black Hussars 1922.06
Songs of the Porter 1882.76
Songs of the Times 1882.76
Songs of Yesterday 1912.13
Songs We Hear on the Stage 1894.35
Sonja 1922.34
Sonntag kommt mein Schatz 1920.46
Sonny 1921.24
Sonny Boy 1940.10, 1952.11, 1962.17, 1989.16
Sonny Cunha 1912.03
Sons 1970.15
Sons and Daughters of the Sea 1937.09
Sons Of 1972.16
Sons of Dixie 1999.08
Sons of Every Nation, The 1910.23
Sons of France 1960.13
Sons of Jesse James, The 1922.19
Sons of Old Black Joe, The 1924.27
Sons of the Sea 1945.17
Sont ils gentils ces petits mioches 1886.19
Soon 1930.02, 1964.40, 1971.01, 1973.04, 1975.13, 1983.06, 1999.10
Soon all must obey 1859.09
Soon as I Get Home 1975.01
Soon as we may, off and away! 1882.78
Soon I Will be Done 1990.05
Soon One Morning 1969.10
Soon the Bride 1880.69
Soon the Sun will gae to rest 1859.01
Soon We'll All be Seen Upon the Screen 1918.11
Soon We'll be Upon the Sea 1923.01
Soon You Gonna Leave Me, Joe 1956.04
Sooner or Later 1969.16, 1999.20
Sopha Maria 1897.21
Sophia 1892.19
Sophia! Phia! Phia! 1880.37
Sophie 1926.02
Sophie in New York 1963.12
Sophisticated Lady 1975.22, 1976.04, 1981.06, 1987.02
Sophisticated Swing 1987.02
Sorceress, The 1976.01
Sorrow heaped on thee, The 1855.06
Sorry 1929.18
Sorry for Myself 1958.20
Sorry her lot 1879.05
Sorry Her Lot 1945.08, 1981.01
Sorry I Asked 1991.04
Sorry We Won't 1971.14
Sorry-Grateful 1970.13
Sort o' Lonesome 1927.38
Sotho Girls Dance, The 1977.01
Soubrette's Secret, The 1909.11
Soul 1983.20
Soul Kiss Just for You from Above, The 1908.07
Soul Man 1997.21
Soul Mates 1928.49
Soul of the Harp, The 1923.21
Soul Saving Sadie 1934.01
Sound of Love, The 1986.13
Sound of Money, The 1962.05
Sound of Music, The 1959.24, 1998.03
Sound of Schmaltz, The 1960.07
Sound of the Drum, The 1932.10
Sound of the Rolling Drums 1908.02
Sound of the Sound, The 1920.31
Sounds 1970.20
Sounds from Home 1883.20, 1916.07
Sounds We Love to Hear 1904.36
Sounds While Selling 1963.14
Soup 1917.32
Sour Krout 1873.19
Sourire a la Vie 1973.17
Sous des armures a leur taille 1878.08
Sous le ciel de Paris 1961.25
Sousa Girl, The 1900.08, 1900.16
Soused American Way 1939.26
South America, Take it Away 1946.10
South American Way 1939.22, 1960.07
South Fifth Avenue 1881.09, 1884.16, 1884.37
South Sea Island Blues 1921.23
South Sea Islands According to Broadway, The 1924.14
South Sea Moon 1922.19, 1923.20
South Sea Sweethearts 1922.05
Southearted Men 1974.09
Southern Belles 1932.01
Southern Comfort 1989.07
Southern Hobby, A 1922.25
Southern Melody 1919.23
Southern Nightingale, The 1903.01
Southern Revel 1894.37
Southland 1907.22, 1908.08
Southwind is Calling 1927.03
Souvenez-vous 1885.57
Souvenir 1909.21, 1948.27
Souvenir de cette jeune fille, Le 1886.19
Sow Took the Measles 1963.19
Sow Your Wild Oats Early 1919.44
Spa Music 1982.09
Space Oddity 1982.22
Spain 1918.40, 1929.27, 1930.09
Spain, Beautiful Spain 1903.35, 1904.41
Spain, Spain, Spain 1936.12
Spanglish 1973.06
Spaniard That Blighted My Life, The 1913.05
Spaniard was My Fond Papa, A 1881.25
Spanish 1917.37, 1918.32
Spanish Bolero 1903.03
Spanish Cocktail, A 1921.12
Spanish Coon, The 1904.43
Spanish Dance 1927.45, 1965.37
Spanish Fado 1929.09
Spanish Fandango Rag, The 1910.19
Spanish Fandango, The 1915.12
Spanish Fantasie 1896.31
Spanish Grandee, The 1907.52
Spanish Harlem 1995.03
Spanish Juanita 1924.36
Spanish Love 1911.18, 1911.23, 1920.33, 1920.47, 1923.31, 1924.02, 1927.43, 1927.55
Spanish Love Song, A 1883.52
Spanish Maid 1918.30
Spanish Mantilla, The 1917.33
Spanish Mick, The 1925.34
Spanish Moon 1925.35
Spanish Muleteer Song 1880.19
Spanish Panic 1959.26
Spanish Rose 1960.06
Spanish Senorita, The 1921.03
Spanish Serenade 1905.07
Spanish Shawl, A 1927.19
Spanish Shawl, The 1927.08
Spanish Song 1882.76, 1920.31
Spare a Little Love 1928.04
Spare That Building 1965.33

Spare the Stranger 1880.32
Spark of Life, The 1912.24
Sparkle, My Star 1932.09
Sparkling Champagne 1887.43, 1932.19
Sparkling Eyes 1964.39
Sparkling Moselle 1914.26
Sparkling Rubies from the Rubyiat 1920.47
Sparkling Waters, The 1912.03
Sparks 1880.42, 1972.08, 1993.06
Sparrow and Hippopotamus 1910.03
Sparrow and the Bullfinch, The 1898.17
Spasm, The 1965.31
Speak 1932.08
Speak Easy 1931.05
Speak Low 1903.02, 1943.19
Speak Low, Walls Have Ears 1886.15
Speak to Me of Love 1934.32, 1935.19
Speak to Me of Something Else 1934.32, 1935.19
Speak Without Any Compunction 1923.04
Speak, Only Speak 1876.11, 1877.05
Speak, Sir Captain! 1880.69
Speakeasy 1988.20
Speakeasy Christmas 1988.20
Speaking of Pals 1945.20
Speaking of You 1931.05
Spear Games 1972.11
Special Announcement, A 1962.18
Special Delivery! 1956.04
Special Train, The 1900.34
Specially Made for You 1930.14
Specialty 1923.11
Speed 1923.45
Speed My Arrow 1880.10
Speed of Light 1975.04
Speedy Gonzales 1957.10
Speilman, The 1924.06
Spell is O'er, The 1883.04
Spell of Those Harlem Nights, The 1932.12
Spend It 1926.19
Sphinx of the Desert 1920.10
Sphinx, The 1920.22
Spic and Spanish 1939.27
Spider and the Fly, The 1873.29, 1892.55, 1966.05
Spider and the Lady, The 1953.10
Spider's Web, The 1921.09, 1926.14
Spiel, The 1955.25
Spin Again 1904.04
Spinning a Yarn 1916.03
Spinning Song 1952.11, 1979.07
Spinning Waltz 1884.39
Spinning Wheel 1892.31
Spinning Wheel Song, The 1896.50
Spirit is Moving, The 1972.07
Spirit Level 1999.02
Spirit O Gentil 1860.05
Spirit of '76, The 1935.04
Spirit of America, The 1981.08
Spirit of Capsulanti 1951.15
Spirit of Education, The 1971.20
Spirit of Java 1921.02
Spirit of Mischief, The 1904.51
Spirit of Rhythm 1937.09
Spirit of the Carnival, the 1918.22
Spirit of the Chinese Vase, The 1921.20
Spirit of the Drum, The 1919.39
Spirit of the Good, The 1866.01
Spirit of the Night 1892.42
Spirit of the Radio 1922.29
Spirit of Your Father, The 1995.04
Spirits of the Midnight Spell 1901.27
Splendid Thought! 1875.19
Split Commentaries 2001.04
Spoofing 1906.04
Spook Dance 1910.13
Spooky Nights 1919.32
Spooky Ookum 1919.01
Spoon River 1963.19
Spooning 1906.40
Spoons 1918.13, 1978.11
Spoontime 1906.04
Spoony Croony Tune 1924.13
Spoony Land 1912.14
Spoony Words 1912.16
Sport American, Le 1921.36
Sport and the Crank, The 1896.49
Sport is Sport 1932.15
Sport, The 1918.17
Sporting Duchess, The 1898.03
Sporting Girls 1902.24
Sporting King of Nikobar, The 1904.25
Sporting Man, A 1973.02
Sporting Song 1905.49
Sports 1985.17
Sporty Boys 1919.02
Sposalizio 1956.04, 1980.29
Spotless Town Cadet Trio 1903.05
Spread a Little Sunshine 1972.22
Spread Your Knees 1929.52
Spread Your Love Around 1976.27
Spreadin' Rhythm Around 1978.09
Sprechen sie Deutsch Mein Herr? 1908.25
Sprig of Shillelah 1860.05
Spring 1904.50, 1919.24, 1921.21, 1925.23, 1926.18, 1950.10
Spring Courting, The 1960.05
Spring Dance 1982.14
Spring Dance of the Small-Town Mayors 1922.42
Spring Fever 1922.47, 1934.19
Spring has Come 1950.09
Spring Hat 1901.21
Spring in Autumn 1925.36
Spring in Milwaukee 1937.12
Spring in the City 1968.06
Spring in Vienna 1937.13
Spring is Here 1927.12, 1929.12, 1929.31, 1938.05, 1975.13, 1999.05
Spring is in the Air 1927.27, 1936.06
Spring of Next Year, The 1969.05
Spring Song 1913.14, 1934.06, 1939.29
Spring Time in the Country 1915.12
Spring Time of the Year 1966.30
Spring Tra La 1932.01
Spring Voices 1923.21
Spring Will be a Little Late This Year 1980.29
Spring, Gentle Spring 1873.10
Spring, Spring, Spring 1982.02
Spring, Sweet Spring 1902.41, 1917.11
Spring-Tide 1884.64
Springfield Mountain 1944.32
Springtide 1944.21, 1946.18
Springtime 1922.07, 1924.33, 1926.25, 1937.17
Springtime and a Love Song 1934.18
Springtime Bells 1900.47
Springtime Cometh, The 1951.15
Springtime for Hitler 2001.05
Springtime is in the Air 1937.17
Springtime of Long Ago 1927.48
Sprinkle Me With Diamonds 1921.02
Sprites of earth and air 1879.10
Spunk 1974.04
Spurn not the nobly born 1882.78
Spy Song 1938.02
Spy, The 1917.11
Squab Farm 1918.20
Squabble Song, The 1969.14
Squaw Man 1904.39
Squeak Goes the Fiddle 1883.12
Squeeze Me 1978.09
Squidgulums 1920.02
Srimpi 1932.01
Ssh! - Ssh! - Ssh! 1919.37
St. Bridget 1966.10
St. Cyr's March 1916.12
St. James Infirmary 1931.11, 1933.27, 1965.05
St. Louis Blues 1927.13, 1927.37, 1930.13, 1930.19, 1930.34, 1931.11, 1939.29, 1942.23, 1953.12, 1989.02, 1990.05, 1999.06, 1999.09
St. Patrick's Day 1905.30
St. Pierre 1968.01
Stability 1970.15
Stage and Fashion Hand in Hand, The 1903.40
Stage Door Johnnies 1922.31
Stage Door Number 1912.38
Stage Life 1920.21
Stage Managers' Chorus 1925.17
Stage Society 1923.46
Stain on the Name, A 1978.22
Stair Dance, The 1912.44
Staircase, The 1997.06
Stairway to the Stars 1987.02
Stalacta 1882.77
Stale World and a Pale World, A 1902.37
Stalin wasn't Stallin' 1943.02
Stamboul 1915.30
Stamp Enclosed 1915.22
Stan' Up and Fight 1943.24
Stand Around the Band 1945.08
Stand Back 1902.07
Stand by Me 1995.03
Stand Together 1981.15
Stand Up and Sing for Your Father 1921.19
Stand-Up 1987.14
Standard in a One-Horse Town 1929.28
Standard Watcher, The 1860.03
Standing 1971.10
Standing on the Corner 1956.04, 1980.29
Standing Pat 1905.37
Star 1980.09
Star and Garter Girls 1942.18
Star Dust 1979.14, 1987.02, 1992.18
Star Factory, The 1910.30
Star Gazer 1917.30
Star Girls 1910.16
Star in the Twilight 1928.26
Star Light, Star Bright 1895.33, 1911.31
Star of Destiny 1924.06
Star of Fate 1904.25
Star of Glory, The 1925.06
Star of Hitchy-Koo, The 1920.39
Star of Love 1913.32, 1919.27, 1921.25
Star of My Life 1902.18
Star of My Native Land 1903.03
Star of my soul 1896.27
Star of Stars 1927.35
Star of the North Star State 1947.08
Star of This War, The 1975.07
Star of Zion 1980.05
Star Song 1890.26
Star Spangled Banner 1866.16, 1982.22
Star Spangled Banner, The 1859.16, 1867.18, 1898.32, 1945.07, 1952.11, 1976.11
Star Stepping Stranger Convent 1975.04
Starburst 1975.04
Stardust Waltz, The 1978.27
Starlight 1901.21, 1918.19, 1927.05
Starlight Express 1987.05, 1992.12
Starlight Guards, The 1912.48
Starlight Maid 1907.54
Starlight of Hope 1922.40
Starlight, Starbright 1971.20
Starlit Hour, The 1940.02
Starmites 1989.09
Starry Sky 1932.01
Stars 1914.32, 1987.04
Stars Alone Can Tell, The 1895.08
Stars and Stripes 1927.37
Stars and Stripes Forever 1915.25, 1980.27
Stars and Stripes Forever Waltz 1924.32
Stars and Stripes Forever, The 1978.05
Stars are Shining 1905.25
Stars Fell on Alabama 1987.02
Stars Have Blown My Way 1959.12
Stars in the Service Flag, The 1918.38
Stars in Your Eyes 1940.04
Stars of Broadway 1921.19
Stars of Glory 1972.02
Stars of the Stage 1922.35
Stars of the Vaudeville 1901.04
Stars of Your Eyes 1922.04
Stars on Ice 1942.19
Stars Remain, The 1940.21
Stars Shine Over Us 1880.42
Stars that hear our solemn vow, The 1881.04
Stars With Stripes 1927.23
Stars, Stars, Shining Bright, You May See Future Stars To-Night 1928.22
Stars, Stars, Stars 1996.08
Start Dancing 1946.04
Start Stompin' 1927.09

Start the Ball Rollin' 1946.22
Start the Band 1927.58
Start, The 1898.70, 1909.27
Starting at the Bottom 1930.28
State Farm Insurance 1976.34
Stately American Rose, The 1919.22
Stately Homes of England, The 1939.07, 1986.19
Statement of Policy 1940.21
Station 1982.23
Station Rush 1961.28
Statistics 1971.20
Statue, The 1972.16
Statues 1929.32
Stay 1965.06, 1965.30
Stay a Little Longer 1999.24
Stay a While 1995.03
Stay Away from Louisville Lou 1983.20
Stay Awhile 1920.40
Stay Close to the Music 1995.04
Stay East, Young Man 1938.12
Stay Frederic, Stay! 1981.01
Stay Out of the Moonlight 1933.21
Stay Out, Sammy 1937.14
Stay there if you please 1855.02
Stay Well 1949.15, 1972.06
Stay With Me 1979.30, 1987.18, 1989.29
Stay With Me! 1993.17
Stay With Me, Nora 1982.18
Stay With the Happy People 1950.12
Stay, Bouncer, Stay 1879.21
Stay, Fred'ric, Stay! 1879.72
Stay, or stay 1887.04
Stay, We Must Not lose Our Senses 1879.72, 1981.01
Stay, Won't You Stay 1902.06
Stayin' Alive 1982.22, 1999.15
Staying Young 1959.22, 1985.04
Steady, Boys, Steady 1890.29, 1890.30
Steady, keep together 1882.17
Steady, Steady 1962.14
Steal Away 1882.76, 1943.10
Steal With Style 1976.31
Stealing 1911.06
Steam Heat 1954.05, 1976.07, 1999.01
Steam is on the Beam 1942.29
Steamboat Bill 1916.15
Steamboat Days 1927.30
Steamboat Race 1890.29
Steamboat Whistle, The 1935.12
Steel City 1999.02
Steel Pier 1997.07
Stein Song 1905.42
Steinland 1912.44
Stella 1889.22, 1889.40
Stella Confidanti 1880.42
Stenka Razin 1925.03
Step a Second, A 1927.32
Step Across That Line 1969.15
Step Along With Me 1920.24
Step by Step 1912.40
Step Inside 1920.30
Step into My World 1980.15
Step Lightly, Speak Softly 1882.18
Step on It 1923.17, 1926.03
Step on the Gasoline 1926.02
Step Out in Front 1979.33
Step Right Up 1997.08
Step Sister 1926.01
Step This Way 1914.18, 1916.09, 1919.13, 1946.15
Step to Paris Blues 1928.06
Step to the Rear 1967.16
Step too Far, A 2000.06
Step Up and Pep Up the Party 1928.28
Step, Step Sisters 1925.34
Step, Step, Step 1927.43
Steppin on the Blues 1926.12
Steppin' Along 1933.06
Steppin' Baby 1926.06
Steppin' on It 1930.24
Steppin' to the Bad Side 1981.29
Stepping 1923.22
Stepping Around 1923.27
Stepping on Butterflies 1973.05
Stepping Out 1929.45, 1991.04
Stepping Out To-night 1919.03
Stepping Some 1922.29
Stepping Stones 1923.40
Stepping Stones, The 1909.29
Stepping to the Stars 1975.04
Steps of the Capitol, The 1944.30
Steps Stately 1980.26
Stepsisters' Lament 1993.14, 1993.16, 2001.09
Stepsons of the Revolution 1901.04
Stereophonic Sound 1955.02
Sterling Silver Moon 1918.21
Stetson 1928.47
Stewards' Song 1907.27
Stiboo, Stibee 1894.33
Stick Around 1964.32
Stick Fight 1947.19
Stick to Your Dancing, Mabel 1929.19
Stick to Your Knitting 1923.45
Stiff Upper Lip 1992.02
Still 1997.06
Still Brooding on Their Mad Infatuation 1881.37
Still His Whiskers Grew 1895.03
Still in Love With You 1987.17
Still in the Front Line 1903.39
Still is the Night 1894.10
Still my heart is beating 1852.01
Still Rockin' 1998.13
Still so gently 1873.04
Still the World Rolls on, on, On 1907.05
Stimela Sasezola 1988.02
Stingaree Song 1940.01
Stingaree, The 1963.29
Stingo Stungo 1923.18
Stiochket 1970.18
Stirrup Cup, The 1852.01, 1864.22, 1871.10
Stitch, Stitch 1908.10
Stitching, Stitching 1918.16
Stockings 1904.56
Stokers' Song 1907.27
Stolen Jewels, The 1904.51
Stolen Kisses 1916.14, 1947.14
Stolen Melody, The 1915.02, 1919.18
Stolen Sweets 1920.33
Stomachs and Stomachs 1950.10
Stomp the Blues Away 1986.11
Stompin Em Down 1933.06
Stompin' at the Savoy 1976.04, 1989.02, 1999.24
Stone Bridge at Eight, The 1926.29
Stone the Crows 1982.03, 1993.15
Stonecutter's Song 1895.33
Stonewall Jackson, The 1887.48
Stonewall Moscowitz March 1926.51
Stoopid 1975.05
Stop 1925.18
Stop and Go 1916.10
Stop and Rest Awhile 1921.26
Stop Beating Those Drums 1934.37
Stop Dat Rag 1910.01
Stop Holding Me Back 1950.10
Stop it, Stop It 1914.03
Stop Ladies, Pray! 1981.01
Stop That Dancing 1944.30
Stop Tickling Me 1916.25
Stop Waltz 1919.29
Stop Your Camouflaging With Me 1917.35
Stop! Do Not Go On 1988.05
Stop! In the Name of Love 1986.02
Stop! Look! Listen! 1915.32
Stop, Ladies, Pray! 1879.72
Stop, Look and Listen 1924.23
Stop, Thief 1905.35
Stop, Time 1996.08
Stop, to put an end to everything 1868.01
Stop-Go 1928.06
Stop. Wait. Please 1990.04
Store-Bought Suit 1954.03
Storefront Church 1972.14
Stories 1907.39
Stories Adam Told to Eve 1903.04, 1903.39
Stories Uncle Remus Tells, De 1899.25
Stork Ballet, The 1903.15
Stork Don't Come Around Anymore, The 1929.22
Storm 1991.05
Storm Chorus 1894.29
Storm in My Heart, A 1981.14
Storm, The 1947.14
Stormy Love 1937.03
Stormy Monday Blues 1976.04
Stormy Weather 1945.07, 1953.12, 1974.09, 1976.16, 1980.10, 1981.16, 1981.16, 1986.02, 1999.05
Story Book Days 1907.30
Story Book, The 1900.12
Story Goes On, The 1983.19
Story is Always the Same, The 1892.18
Story of a Kiss, The 1893.37
Story of a Marionette 1911.25
Story of a Sheep, The 1925.21
Story of a Sparrow, The 1915.20
Story of Alice, The 1955.12
Story of Buster, The 1934.40
Story of Chess, The 1988.09
Story of Joseph 1937.01
Story of Lucy and Jessie, The 1971.05
Story of Marie, The 1961.01
Story of Rose, The 1901.15
Story of the Auld Countrie 1891.28
Story of the Carrot, The 1947.08
Story of the Dance 1900.07
Story of the Monkey and the Parrot, The 1903.40
Story of the Paris Night 1924.18
Story of the Rainbow, The 1903.02
Story of the Rose, The 1899.27
Story of the Two Bad Boys 1902.08
Story of the Waltz, The 1920.23
Story of the Wedding March, The 1901.07, 1906.21
Story That Never Grows Old, The 1906.45
Story Vignettes 1953.03
Storybook 1997.19, 1999.13
Stout Boy Wanted 1866.31
Stout Hearted Men 1978.05
Stouthearted Men 1928.29, 1986.14
Stowaway, The 1879.35
Straight 1971.01
Stranded Again 1978.02
Strange adventure! 1888.35
Strange Duet 1961.28
Strange Fruit 1948.13, 1999.09
Strange Interlude 1928.45
Strange Music 1944.21
Strange New Look 1950.03
Strange New World 1968.06
Strange Thing Mystifying 1971.12
Strange Things Happen Every Day 1904.05
Strange, Odd, Queer 1903.07
Stranger 1945.14
Stranger in Paradise 1953.16, 1978.03
Stranger Interlude, A 1929.21
Stranger Than You Dreamt It 1988.01
Strangers in the Night 1975.12
Strapanzoni il Banditto 1866.14
Strauss Waltz 1921.02
Straw Hat in the Rain 1934.39
Straw That Broke the Camel's Back, The 1964.35
Strawberries and Cream 1913.21
Strawberry Festival 1919.37
Strawberry Fields Forever 1974.24, 1977.10
Strawberry Jam 1927.42
Strawberry Roan 1931.02
Streak of Madness 1997.09
Streamlined Pompadour 1941.02
Street Bands 1891.43
Street Scene 1992.08
Street Sermon 1971.20
Street Song 1994.12, 1995.19, 1999.21
Street Sweepers 1977.01
Street Walkers, The 1934.32
Streetcorner Symphony 1984.15
Streets of Cairo, The 1895.27
Streets of Madrid, The 1969.11
Streets of New York, The 1906.33
Streets of Paris, The 1939.22
Streetwalkers, The 1935.19
Strenuous 1905.33
Strephon's a member of Parliament! 1882.78
Strew the Way With Flow'rets Blooming 1895.33
Strict Game, The 1897.32

Strictly Business 1925.29
Strictly Confidential 1937.06
Strictly Honorable 1930.18
Stride La Vampa 1880.24
Stridex 1976.34
Strike 1921.27, 1925.26
Strike Me Pink 1933.05
Strike Out, McCracken 1902.29
Strike Up a Bagpipe Tune 1910.15
Strike Up the Band 1930.02, 1979.24, 1983.06, 1992.18
Strike! 1920.08, 1951.24
Strike, Strike 1899.30
Strike, Strike, Strike 1924.03
Strike, The 1922.41
String 'Em Along 1924.42
String a Ring of Roses 1912.13
String Along With Texas 1927.31
String of Pearls, A 1905.25, 1999.24
Strings are Sighing 1978.07
Strip Flips Hip 1944.14
Strip, The 1974.17
Stroll in the Moonlight, A 1904.22
Stroll With Me 1926.11
Stroller in Dreamland, A 1919.34
Strollers 1914.23
Strollin' Along the Beach 1901.25
Strolling 1903.14, 1904.41, 1905.43, 1925.18, 1976.04
Strolling 'round the Camp With Mary 1918.38
Strolling Along the Boulevard 1898.38
Strolling by the Bay 1887.31
Strolling Chorus 1897.55
Strolling Home 1943.11
Strolling in Society 1901.23
Strolling in the Woodland 1880.59
Strolling on the Sands 1886.52
Strolling Thro' the River 1900.41
Strolling Thru the Park 1938.08
Strolling With the One I Love the Best 1927.42
Strolling, or What Have You? 1925.33
Strong for Girls 1922.18
Stronger Sex, The 1953.11
Strongest Man in the World, The 1966.06
Strongheart 1913.18
Strut Miss Lizzie 1921.21, 1921.26
Strut Your Stuff 1922.18
Strutter, The 1923.02
Strutters' Ball 1944.31
Struttin' Style 1983.04
Struttin' Time 1926.19
Struttinest Strutter, The 1923.13
Strutting the Blues Away 1923.06
Stuck With Each Other 1963.08
Student Life 1980.21
Student's Life 1924.45
Student, The 1872.23
Students Glide 1911.23
Students Marching Song 1980.21
Students of Art are We 1914.14
Students on a Lark 1906.10
Students' Kneipe, The 1906.49
Students' Serenade 1910.30
Studio Musician 1976.34
Study in Black and White, A 1922.34, 1944.19
Study in Pink, A 1904.23
Study in Porcelain, A 1924.29
Study of Legs, A 1925.27
Stupid Boy 1999.12
Stupid Mankind 1885.65
Stupid Mr. Cupid 1908.15
Stuttering Man, The 1898.61
Style 1907.39, 1974.13, 2000.14
Style, Style, Style 1910.10
Su'l Boul'vard 1924.13
Sub-Debs' First Fling 1937.06
Subjected to your heavenly gaze 1894.15
Subterranean Toilers, The 1872.23
Subuhi Sana 1966.03
Suburban, The 1903.14
Suburbio, El 1997.13
Subway Dream 1971.20
Subway Express, The 1907.18
Subway Incident 1961.28
Subway Rider 1980.15
Subway Song 1948.043
Subway Sun, The 1925.17
Subways are for Sleeping 1961.28
Subways Directions 1961.28
Success 1924.07, 1998.01
Success Story 1945.09
Such a Baby 1919.19
Such a Bore 1881.16, 1911.01
Such a Chauffeur 1917.04
Such a Dear Little Man as You 1902.43
Such a getting up stairs 1873.04
Such a Good Looking Boy 1951.20
Such a Little Queen 1919.18
Such a Night 1992.06
Such a Sociable Sort 1966.27
Such a wife to soothe his years 1879.10
Such an Education has My Mary Ann 1878.13, 1985.02
Such conduct is quite sad 1878.16
Such is Fame 1928.28
Such is Life in a Love Song 1923.24
Such return 1859.18
Such return for love 1873.04
Such Stuff as Dreams are Made Of 1940.12
Sudden Lilac 1976.33
Sudden Thrill, The 1953.11
Suddenly 1934.01
Suddenly Love 1980.11
Suddenly the Day Looks Sunny 1976.31
Sue Me 1950.17
Sue, Sue, I Love You 1905.05
Sufficiency 1903.33, 1914.10
Sugar Baby 1919.03
Sugar Baby Bounce, The 1979.24
Sugar Blues 1977.09
Sugar Cane 1930.29
Sugar Foot 1944.01
Sugar Mine 1908.02
Suggestion of 1851, A 1923.21
Suicide Song 1957.05
Suicidio del Femminella, Il 1985.14
Suite for Five Letters 1971.04, 1976.27
Suite of Dances 1989.03
Suits Me Fine 1951.13
Sukey-Sue 1903.20
Sullivan 1908.31
Sullivan's Got a Job 1973.11
Sultan am I 1880.46
Sultan's March, The 1920.34
Sultan's Policy, The 1902.11
Sultana 1918.40
Summer 1979.30
Summer Afternoon 1952.10
Summer Boarders 1907.34
Summer Dresses 1950.19
Summer Girl 1903.14
Summer Girl, The 1898.17, 1900.59, 1910.34
Summer Girls Love, A 1895.25
Summer in Fairview Falls 1955.03
Summer in the City 1982.22
Summer Is 1958.01
Summer is a Comin' In 1942.01
Summer is Over 1962.01
Summer Man, The 1894.51, 1899.29
Summer Night 1916.12
Summer Nights 1927.33, 1971.20, 1972.12, 1994.07
Summer Pastimes 1908.18
Summer Proposals 1903.34
Summer Resort 1888.32
Summer Share 1988.10
Summer Song, A 1891.36
Summer Sports 1915.12
Summer Sweets Shall Bloom Again 1876.10
Summer Time 1928.12, 1935.13
Summer, Summer 1971.18
Summertime 1915.21, 1922.30, 1927.31, 1943.02, 1983.04
Summertime is Summertime 1951.18
Summertime Love 1960.05
Summertime, The 1926.02
Summery Time 1915.17
Sumurun Girl, My 1912.09
Sun About to Rise, The 1929.31
Sun and Moon 1991.03
Sun and Rain 1923.23
Sun Arises, The 1880.10
Sun at My Window, Love at My Door 1955.10
Sun do Move, De 1899.30
Sun Girl 1924.33
Sun has Fallen, The 1947.10
Sun has Got His Hat On, The 1986.12
Sun is Beginning to Crow, The 1961.24
Sun is Down and Over the Town, The 1909.04
Sun is Nigh, The 1920.27
Sun is Rising in Chosun, The 1998.08
Sun Kist Rose 1923.39
Sun on My Face 1972.04
Sun Queen 1974.24
Sun Shines Brighter, The 1917.17
Sun Showers 1923.04
Sun Starts to Shine Again, The 1918.03
Sun That Rose on Thirteen States Now Sets on Forty-Five, The 1905.07
Sun That You Are, The 1988.15
Sun Up 1930.23
Sun Will be Up in the Morning, The 1940.12
Sun Will Shine, The 1929.04
Sun Won't Set, The 1973.04
Sun Worship 1925.04
Sun, the Moon and You, The 1928.42
Sun, whose rays are all a-blaze, The 1885.47
Sun-Girl 1924.33
Sunbeam and the Morning Glory, The 1905.02
Sunbeam of My Heart 1906.03
Sunbeams 1920.26
Sunbonnet Sue 1908.28
Sunday 1958.19, 1984.08
Sunday Afternoon 1926.39, 1998.02
Sunday Beau 1927.54
Sunday Dress Parade, The 1912.49
Sunday in Cicero Falls 1944.23
Sunday in the Park 1937.14
Sunday in the Park With George 1984.08
Sunday Morning 1934.35, 1961.14
Sunday Morning in June 1938.04
Sunday Morning Sunshine 1975.05
Sunday Morning When the Church Bells Ring 1904.07
Sunday Morning, Breakfast Time 1935.14
Sunday Night in New York 1935.04
Sunday Picnic Social, The 1955.03
Sunday's Child 1920.24
Sunday's Not My Day 1970.01
Sunday, Monday or Always 1995.14
Sundown in My Soul 1940.01
Sundown Serenade 1926.19
Sundunga, La 1927.54
Sunflower 1906.34
Sunflower and Lily 1883.42
Sunflower and the Sun, The 1902.06, 1903.41
Sunkissed Land 1918.07
Sunny 1925.33
Sunny Afternoon 1903.01
Sunny California 1944.30
Sunny Disposish 1926.21
Sunny Dixie 1902.40
Sunny River 1941.12
Sunny Riviera, The 1914.25
Sunny Side of Thompson Street, The 1893.36
Sunny Side to Every Situation 1980.20
Sunny Side, The 1869.07
Sunny South 1922.19
Sunny South Sea Islands 1921.22
Sunny Southern Smile 1931.19
Sunny Spain 1927.38
Sunny Sunbeam 1922.05
Sunny, Sunny Moon 1975.04
Sunnyside of You 1927.64
Sunrise 1916.19
Sunrise at the Zoo 1907.33
Sunrise Letter 1994.05
Sunrise on Sunset 1944.15
Sunrise, Sunset 1964.27, 1967.03, 1989.03, 2000.14
Sunset 1885.06, 1972.02, 1978.25
Sunset Boulevard 1994.10

Sunset in Samolo 1968.19
Sunset Tree 1968.02
Sunset, The 1869.42, 1872.23
Sunshine 1925.33, 1949.18, 1973.03
Sunshine Above 1894.10, 1894.33
Sunshine After Rain 1893.16
Sunshine Alley 1918.23
Sunshine and Shadows 1920.18
Sunshine Face 1963.12
Sunshine Girl 1957.07
Sunshine Maxixe, The 1914.13
Sunshine Montage 1995.07
Sunshine of Love 1899.21, 1920.31
Sunshine of Paradise Alley 1896.15
Sunshine of Springtime, The 1911.06
Sunshine of Your Love, The 1982.22
Sunshine Valley 1920.41
Super Heroes 1975.08, 2000.17
Super Singo 1985.17
Super-Sheik 1924.21
Supercalifragilisticexpialidocious 1998.11
Superfluous Relations 1895.32
Superhero Girl 1989.09
Superlative Love 1917.28
Superstar 1971.12, 1973.14
Superstition 1934.18, 1975.19, 1986.02
Supper Chorus 1901.21
Supper Girls, The 1906.25
Supper in the open air, A 1881.04
Supper Out of Doors 1909.05
Supper Time 1933.22
Supper Trio 1950.10
Suppertime 1953.12, 1971.11, 1980.10, 1999.03
Supple Couple 1943.07
Suppose 1905.27
Suppose - I Say, Suppose 1900.37
Suppose a Highwayman You Were 1904.01
Suppose I Darken Your Door 1973.08
Suppose I had Never Met You 1923.24
Suppose We Have a Breakdown 1903.22
Supposing 1924.03
Sur l'ordre de sa hautesse 1887.35
Sur la Plage 1954.09
Sur la plage allons prendre l'air 1885.59
Sur le marche de Corneville 1878.08
Sur le repos du populaire 1884.50
Surabaya Johnny 1977.08, 1995.12
Sure Sign You Really Love Me 1927.39
Sure Thing Baby 1988.20
Sure, Blarney's the Art of Stealing a Heart 1897.48
Surplus Blues 1946.10
Surprise 1958.02, 1972.24, 1975.19
Surprise Party 1938.08
Surprise, Surprise Astounding 1899.40
Surrender 1905.36, 1989.12, 1994.10
Surrender, Surrender 1899.40
Surrey With the Fringe on the Top, The 1993.16
Surrey With the Fringe on Top, The 1943.04, 1981.16
Surrounded by the Girls 1924.13
Survive 1969.02
Susan 1904.08, 1904.34
Susan Anna Anna 1901.25
Susan Belle and the Liza Jane, The 1937.09
Susan Brown from a Country town 1911.12
Susan Simpson, Mary Lou 1899.18
Susanna 1907.31
Susanna and the Elders 1948.17
Susanna, Don't You Cry 1939.21
Susannah's Squeaking Shoes 1923.35, 1925.42, 1952.11
Susceptible Statuette, The 1884.42, 1886.47, 1888.36
Susette 1898.61
Susie 1898.47, 1901.01
Susie Anna 1902.15
Susie McLean 1928.05
Susie Smith from Troy 1897.21, 1898.01
Susie This Coon has Got the Blues 1897.40
Susie Woosie 1902.29
Susie, Mah Sue 1900.07
Susie-Ue 1900.03
Suspicious 1976.15
Suspicious Minds 1978.01, 1989.12
Suttee Procession 1946.13
Suwanee River 1919.13
Suwanee River, The 1917.11
Suwannee River, The 1902.41
Suzanne 1913.29
Suzanne, Suzanne 1912.01
Suzette 1921.38
Suzie Ann 1915.02
Suzie Moon 1972.18
Suzy is a Good Thing 1955.27
Svetlyachok 1977.13
Swallows Fly 1870.20
Swallows, The 1928.02
Swamps of Home, The 1959.26
Swampy River 1930.13
Swan Lake 1948.08, 1993.19
Swanee 1918.05, 1922.08, 1940.10, 1962.17, 1989.10, 2001.07
Swanee Glide 1919.26
Swanee Moon 1952.08
Swanee River 1922.25, 1923.39
Swanee River Blues 1923.38
Swanee Strut 1975.09
Swanee Sway, The 1922.23
Swannee River 1894.44
Swannee River Melody 1926.21, 1927.27
Swannee River Melody, The 1922.08
Sway With Me 1923.01
Swear thou the jury 1875.35
Swearing Chorus 1892.29
Swearing death to all who cave 1866.16, 1867.18
Swede Song 1918.08
Sweeney Todd, Oh Sweeney Todd 1924.20
Sweep Song, The 1851.03
Sweeping the Clouds Away 1932.04
Sweepstakes 1988.07
Sweet Alice 1923.33
Sweet America 1876.19
Sweet Anastasia Brady 1905.19, 1906.20
Sweet and Hot 1931.01
Sweet and Low 1882.76, 1919.26
Sweet and Low Down 1925.49, 1990.09
Sweet and Low-Down 1983.06
Sweet and Pretty 1916.11
Sweet Angeline 1922.22
Sweet Annabel 1891.42
Sweet Arabian Dreams 1924.47
Sweet as Sugar Cane 1929.37
Sweet as You Can Be 1922.02
Sweet Beginning 1965.19
Sweet Betsy from Pike 1975.22
Sweet Blossoms 1938.06
Sweet by and By, The 1910.35, 1978.19
Sweet Bye and Bye 1876.32
Sweet Cactus Rose 1924.47
Sweet Caroline 1978.01
Sweet Charity 1966.01
Sweet Cider 1872.25
Sweet Clarissa 1899.40
Sweet Clear Sun 1974.23
Sweet Cookie 1922.28
Sweet Daisy Stokes 1896.02
Sweet Danger 1961.26
Sweet Dreams 1919.28, 1920.36, 1972.18
Sweet Dreams are Made of This 1984.15
Sweet Dreams, Dear One of Thee 1904.21
Sweet Dudidity 1887.05
Sweet Dudity 1885.06
Sweet Ecstasy 1902.07
Sweet Emerald Isle 1939.21
Sweet Evangeline 1878.02, 1888.13, 1896.35
Sweet Evenin' 1972.01
Sweet Evening Breeze 1927.33
Sweet Eyes 1863.02
Sweet Fool 1934.43
Sweet Georgia Brown 1976.04, 1976.24, 1980.10
Sweet Geraldine 1931.04
Sweet Girl Graduate, The 1906.44, 1907.59
Sweet Girl of My Dreams 1910.06
Sweet Hannah or Alice 1880.46
Sweet Heather Bells 1887.05
Sweet Helen 1944.16
Sweet Henry Loves You 1971.01
Sweet Home Chicago 1999.09
Sweet Inniscarra 1897.05
Sweet is the Perfume of Summer Flowers 1907.54
Sweet Italian Love 1910.19
Sweet Italy 1886.02
Sweet Kentucky Rose, The 1879.68
Sweet Kisses 1919.15
Sweet Kitty 1909.01
Sweet Kitty Bellairs 1910.18
Sweet Kitty Kellairs 1905.23
Sweet Lady 1921.23
Sweet Land Tyrol 1891.20
Sweet Lei Lehua 1912.03
Sweet Liar 1929.02
Sweet Liberty 2000.20
Sweet Little Baby o Mine 1930.19
Sweet Little Devil 1924.03
Sweet Little Mannikin Dolls 1929.09
Sweet Little Rosey Posey 1896.37, 1897.04
Sweet Little Stranger 1920.35, 1932.15
Sweet Lizette, so People Say 1905.46
Sweet Lorraine 1987.02, 2000.07
Sweet Love 1988.15, 1990.15
Sweet Love Arise! 1876.29
Sweet Madness 1933.20
Sweet Maiden 1880.47
Sweet Man of Mine 1922.25
Sweet Marie 1891.15, 1894.16
Sweet Mary Mullane 1896.24
Sweet Memory 1970.03
Sweet Music 1931.16
Sweet Nellie Wood 1903.07
Sweet Nevada 1946.20
Sweet Old Story, The 1896.10
Sweet Old-Fashioned Way 1929.04
Sweet Olive Oil 1917.24
Sweet One 1923.12, 1928.35
Sweet One How My Heart is Yearning 1915.24
Sweet One, Ta Ta 1890.03
Sweet Onion Time in Bermuda 1924.46
Sweet Peter 1925.31
Sweet Popooper 1926.19
Sweet Popularity 1903.11
Sweet Potato 1968.19
Sweet Repose 1894.17
Sweet Rosa Pompetta 1908.42
Sweet Rose of Mexico 1904.23
Sweet Salome 1901.25
Sweet Sano-oo 1904.29
Sweet Saturday 1900.58
Sweet Savannah 1898.66
Sweet Savannah Sue 1929.23
Sweet Senorita 1911.28
Sweet Seventeen 1918.12, 1987.12
Sweet Simplicitas 1910.05
Sweet Sir 1882.75
Sweet Sixteen 1892.05, 1894.29, 1911.47, 1919.15
Sweet Sixty-Five 1937.13
Sweet Sleep, in visions thou dost bring 1859.12
Sweet spirit hear my prayer 1886.40
Sweet Spirit, hear my Prayer 1863.01
Sweet Spirit, Hear my prayer 1870.05
Sweet Summertime 1939.21
Sweet the Birds Were Singing 1898.73
Sweet the song of birds 1878.02
Sweet the Song of Birds 1885.58, 1888.13
Sweet Thing Like Me, A 1985.05
Sweet Thoughts of Home 1904.36
Sweet Thursday 1955.27
Sweet Time 1973.10
Sweet Tokay 1906.20
Sweet Transvestite 1975.08, 2000.17
Sweet William 1899.21, 1938.15, 1957.14
Sweet, a nameless charm, A 1866.34
Sweet, Sweet, Sweet 1974.13
Sweetenheart 1930.08
Sweeter Dan a Sugar Cane 1903.39
Sweeter Than Marmalade 1877.27
Sweeter Than You 1926.39, 1929.49
Sweetest Flower of All 1879.35
Sweetest Flower That Grows in Tennessee, The 1904.07
Sweetest Girl 1921.10
Sweetest Girl in Dixie, The 1904.11, 1904.13, 1904.44
Sweetest Girl, Silly Boy, I Love You 1908.27

Sweetest Love 1885.49, 1985.02
Sweetest Maid of All 1908.06
Sweetest Melody 1920.47
Sweetest of the Roses 1928.35
Sweetest of Williams 1871.16
Sweetest Part of Loving is to Dream, The 1905.33
Sweetest Song in the World, The 1942.14
Sweetest Sounds, The 1962.03, 1962.17, 2001.09
Sweetest Story Ever Told 1894.37
Sweetest Story Ever Told, The 1895.44
Sweetest Words That Ere Were Said, The 1907.30
Sweetheart 1889.39, 1908.29, 1909.22, 1913.06, 1915.21, 1921.38, 1923.03, 1931.08
Sweetheart - -Will You Answer Yes 1921.37
Sweetheart Goodbye 1890.30
Sweetheart Lane 1922.32
Sweetheart Let Us Dance the Boston 1914.06
Sweetheart Love Ne'er Grows Old 1894.37
Sweetheart Lue 1905.05
Sweetheart Mine 1903.27
Sweetheart of All the Words of Love 1900.01
Sweetheart of Mine 1924.42
Sweetheart of My Own, A 1917.22
Sweetheart of Mystery 1923.16
Sweetheart of Our Student Corps 1929.17
Sweetheart of Your Dream, The 1926.24
Sweetheart Shop Wedding, A 1920.29
Sweetheart Shop, The 1920.29
Sweetheart Time 1912.14, 1926.03
Sweetheart Tree, The 1974.22
Sweetheart, Farewell 1923.11
Sweetheart, I Love But Thee 1896.31
Sweetheart, I'm Waiting 1896.13
Sweetheart, if Thou be Nigh! 1884.57
Sweetheart, Let's Go a Walking 1912.30
Sweethearts 1894.38, 1896.06, 1913.24, 1918.07, 1927.08, 1947.04
Sweethearts in Every Town 1905.28, 1906.24
Sweethearts of the Team, The 1939.27
Sweethearts, Wives and Good Fellows 1912.15
Sweetie 1907.34, 1920.39, 1923.20
Sweetie Dear 1906.14
Sweetie Mine 1930.29
Sweetness 1911.20, 1918.13
Sweetness of Love 1938.03
Sweets to the Sweet 1919.14
Swell 1991.15
Swell Girls 1894.37
Swell Song 1877.23
Swell With the Glass in His Eye, The 1885.51
Swell, The 1879.63, 1880.39
Swellest Cullud Lady of Them All, The 1897.34
Swellest Thing in Town, The 1897.30, 1897.40
Swellest Thing, The 1898.78
Swells of the Ocean 1883.04
Swept Away 1961.26
Swift as Dart 1868.02
Swim Out 1884.65, 1886.35
Swimming Master, The 1901.25
Swing Along 1904.26
Swing Low, Sweet Harriet 1943.20
Swing Low, Sweet Chariot 1976.04
Swing Mikado, The 1939.15
Swing on the Corner 1949.06
Swing Shift 1983.17
Swing Song 1918.06, 1963.29, 1963.29
Swing Struck 1939.14
Swing That Music 1986.02
Swing That Swing 1935.14
Swing Wedding 1937.09
Swing With Me 1881.11
Swing Your Bag 1970.10
Swing Your Lady, Mr. Hemingway 1943.05
Swing Your Projects 1961.28
Swing Your Tails 1930.25
Swing! 1953.03
Swing, Brother, Swing 1999.24
Swing, My Petty One, Swing 1902.03
Swing, The 1920.23
Swingaroo Trio, The 1939.26
Swingin' a Dream 1939.29
Swinging 1989.02
Swinging a Dance 1966.30
Swinging in the Lane 1892.19
Swinging on a Gospel Gate 1886.28
Swinging on a Star 1995.14
Swinging on the Gate 1926.02
Swinging Round the Circle 1869.06
Swinging the Bhumba 1942.35
Swinging, Swinging 1888.34
Swings, The 1910.18
Swingy Little Thingy 1933.16
Swirling Snow 1989.21
Swiss Boy 1860.05
Swiss Echo Song 1920.02
Swiss Miss 1924.43
Swiss Mountain Song 1866.26
Swiss Porters 1904.39
Switchblade Bess 1961.01
Switzer's Home, The 1883.07
Switzerland 1913.30
Sword Dance 1980.26
Sword Dance, The 1947.07
Sword in hand, man to man 1880.04
Sword is My Sweetheart True, The 1910.07
Sword of Damocles, The 1975.08, 2000.17
Sword Quadrille, The 1880.59
Sword Song, The 1901.06
Sword, Rose and Cape 1961.10
Swordfight 1976.03
Sylphide, La 1861.06
Sylphides Avec la Bumpe, Les 1942.18
Sylva, ich will nur dich-Ja Madchen gibt es wunderfeine 1984.05
Sylvia the Gibson Girl 1905.27
Sylvie 1955.03
Symbol of Fire 1950.09
Sympathetic Someone 1925.38
Sympathetic Sue 1909.06
Sympathy 1909.22, 1912.46, 1926.03, 1947.06
Sympathy, Tenderness 1997.09, 1997.09
Symphonic Pantomime 1941.12
Symphonic Poem 1923.08
Symphonie des smelles de bois, La 1947.05, 1948.12
Symphony 1971.18
Symphony in Dress 1920.22
Symphony in Smoke, A 1953.10
Symphony Rap 1984.15
Syncopassion 1926.22
Syncopate 1922.29
Syncopated Clock, The 1987.02
Syncopated Cocktail, A 1919.15
Syncopated Harp 1917.04
Syncopated Heart 1920.01
Syncopated Pipes of Pan 1924.32
Syncopated Sandy 1897.45
Syncopated Strain 1923.11
Syncopated Vamp, The 1920.18
Syncopated Walk, The 1914.31
Syncopatia Land 1913.05
Syncopating Baby 1925.24
Syncopation 1915.27
Syncopation Stenos 1921.16
Syndicate Song, The 1961.16
Synergy 1970.04
Syren and Friar, The 1869.14
Syren and the Friar, The 1870.20
Syringa Tree 1922.04
System 1922.38, 1924.03

T & A 1976.16
T Aint Nobody's Biz-ness if I Do 1978.09
T'Ain't Nobody's Bizness if I Do 1975.20
T'Avoir Aimer, De 1970.01
T'es pianiste de Varsovie 1968.21
T'es venu de loin 1966.20
'T' for Texas 1999.09
T'morra', T'morra' 1944.23
T.C.A. Dance 1957.10
T.E.A.M. 1971.11, 1999.03
T.N.D.P.W.A.M. 1982.04
T.S.O.P. 1974.22
Ta bouche 1929.14
Ta Ra Ra 1964.22
Ta Ra Ra Boom De Ay 1929.41
Ta Ta, My Dainty Little Darling 1906.48
Ta Ta, Ol' Bean 1930.06
Ta Voo 1920.47
Ta! Ta! Ma Bonnie Maggie Darlin' 1930.17
Ta, Ta, Old Bean 1931.36
Ta-hoo 1920.47
Ta-Ra-Ra Boom-De-Ay! 1980.27
Ta-ra-ra-boom-de-ay 1892.38, 1893.23
Ta-ra-ra-Boom-de-re 1891.32
Ta-Ta, Little Girl 1911.32
Tablada, La 1993.08, 1997.13
Table Bay 1966.03
Table for Two, A 1917.08
Table Talk 1981.10
Table With a View 1989.26
Tabloid Papers 1926.21
Taboo 1912.05
Tabor and Drum 1893.02
Tabu/Taking Care of the Ladies 2000.08
Tact 1900.51, 1902.05, 1920.09, 1922.02
Tactics 1971.02
Tactless Little Troubadour 1956.09
Taewongun is Taken to China 1997.16
Taewongun's Regency 1997.16
Tafelberg Hotel, The 1999.12
Taffy 1971.20
Tag Day 1922.44
Tahiti 1926.03
Tahiti Sweetie 1926.03
Tail of a Kite, The 1906.39
Tail of a Whale, The 1905.32
Tailor Made 1887.29
Tailor Made Babies 1929.25
Tailor Man, A 1910.36
Tailor Motel Kamzoil, The 1964.27
Tailor's Drinking Song 1968.22
Tailor's Dummy 1905.55
Tailor's Megilla, The 1968.22
Tailor's Song, The 1968.22
Tain't Gwine to be No Rain 1908.08
Tain't Nobody's Bizness 1976.16
Tain't Nobody's Bizness if I Do 1989.02 **see T'a**
Tainted Gold 1905.54
Taisez-Vous 1910.35, 1978.19, 1988.18
Tait Song 1974.26
Takarazuka Forever 1989.21
Takarazuka March 1989.21
Take 'Em to the Door Blues 1925.26
Take a Bow 1944.19
Take a Chance 1923.37
Take a Chance Little Girl and Learn to Dance 1918.34
Take a Chance With Me 1921.02
Take a Crank Letter 1949.17
Take a Day Off, Mary Ann 1891.25, 1891.37, 1891.46
Take a Job 1960.22
Take a Letter to the King 1930.30
Take a Letter, Miss Jones 1993.07
Take a Little Baby Home With You 1925.23
Take a Little One Step 1924.02
Take a Little One-Step 1971.03
Take a Little Perfume 1913.33
Take a Little Sip 1971.16
Take a Little Walk 1925.43
Take a Little Wife 1922.39
Take a Look at Me Now 1910.12, 1921.12
Take a Look at That 1990.06
Take a Maid 1907.30
Take a pair of sparkling eyes 1890.02
Take a Pair of Sparkling Eyes 1938.10
Take a Poem 1942.05
Take a Step With Me 1914.04
Take a Swing With Me 1917.22
Take a Tip from Venus 1909.13
Take a Trip 1992.16
Take a Trip in My Auto 1905.33
Take a Trip to Candyland 1917.22
Take a Trip to Harlem 1930.34
Take a Trip to the Seaside 1910.23
Take a Walk on the Wild Side 1982.22
Take a Walk With Me 1925.02
Take and Take and Take 1937.13
Take Away the Darkening Sky 1997.16
Take Back Your Mink 1950.17, 1980.29
Take Care of This House 1976.11

Take Care, Little Girl, Take Care 1911.24
Take Care, Senor 1906.07
Take Down Dis Letter 1924.27
Take Five 1982.15, 1998.17
Take Good Care of Mother 1894.44
Take Good Care of That Lady 1984.10
Take heed, beware 1887.43
Take Her Away 1901.27
Take Her, My Boy, She's Yours 1905.36
Take Him 1940.22, 1975.13
Take Him Away to the Mountains 1911.01
Take Him to Evaline 1895.38
Take Him to Jail 1925.18
Take Hold the Crutch 1970.20
Take it All Off 1985.19
Take it Away 1952.13
Take it from Me 1913.37, 1915.23, 1919.07
Take it on the Chin 1986.12
Take it Right Back 1982.12
Take it Slow, Joe 1957.16
Take it, My Sweet Darling 1964.25
Take Love 1944.28
Take Love Easy 1946.24
Take Me a Drink of Whiskey 1940.01
Take Me a Ride of Joy 1915.29
Take Me Along 1959.22, 1983.03, 1985.04
Take Me Along With You, Dearie 1911.35
Take Me as I Am 1997.09, 1999.06
Take Me Away 1932.18
Take Me Back 1962.24
Take Me Back to Brooklyn 1898.38
Take Me Back to Herald Square 1901.23
Take Me Back to Manhattan 1930.40
Take Me Back to Paree 1904.14
Take Me Back to Philadelphia, Pa. 1920.06
Take Me Back to Samoa Some More 1923.25
Take Me Back to Texas With You 1951.13
Take Me Back to Tulsa 1999.24
Take Me Dear 1910.37
Take Me Down the Bay 1884.42
Take Me Down to Coney 1921.20
Take Me Down to Coney Island 1896.18, 1897.39
Take Me For - 1913.04
Take Me for a Buggy Ride 1982.12
Take Me for a Honeymoon Ride 1929.31
Take Me Home 1904.25, 1915.27
Take Me Home With You 1914.30, 1976.20
Take Me in Your Arms 1933.21, 1987.02
Take Me or Leave Me 1996.09
Take Me Out to the Ball Game 1998.11
Take Me to That Swanee Shore 1912.43
Take Me to That Tango Tea 1909.05
Take Me to the Chicken Ball 1912.45
Take Me to the Land of Jazz 1919.21
Take Me to the Midnight Cakewalk Ball 1915.12
Take My Advice 1944.16
Take My Bridgework Back to Mother 1938.12
Take My Hand 1972.02
Take My Heart and do With it What You Please 1952.11
Take My Heart With You 1945.01
Take My Mother Home 1955.03
Take now this ring 1873.04
Take Off a Little Bit 1915.32
Take Off the Coat 1950.19
Take Off the Mask 1952.09
Take Off With Us 1999.01
Take Plenty of Shoes 1908.36
Take That 1908.16
Take that and That 1880.47
Take That Look Off Your Face 1985.12
Take That Off, Too 1908.42
Take the "A" Train 1981.06
Take the A Train 1974.22, 1976.04, 1997.03
Take the Air 1927.60
Take the Book 1941.01
Take the Moment 1965.06
Take the Steamer to Nantucket 1945.17
Take the Wheels Off the Wagon 1951.24
Take the Word of a Gentleman 1953.11
Take Them All Away 1925.42
Take Them Both to Death 1890.03
Take Things Easy 1907.11
Take This Little Rosebud 1923.23
Take Those Lips Away 1923.38
Take Thy Way to Earth 1901.27
Take Us 'Round the Island 1912.05
Take Your Black Bottom Out of Here 1927.32
Take Your Hat Off 1972.25
Take Your Pretty Partner to the Ball 1902.30
Take Your Time 1907.31, 1913.23, 1954.17
Take Your Time and Take Your Pick 1955.01
Take Yourself a Trip 1938.07
Take-A-Tour, Congressman 1971.20
Taken by Surprise 1927.20
Taken for a Ride 1931.21
Taken on a foreign tour 1886.40
Takes a Heap O'Love 1922.41
Takin' a Chance on Love 1953.12
Takin' Miss Mary to the Ball 1985.08
Takin' the Light 1979.15
Takin' the Long Way Home 1981.29
Taking a Chance 1897.40
Taking a Chance on Love 1940.17, 1980.10, 1988.08, 1992.18, 1999.23
Taking a Wife 1925.08
Taking Care of You 1968.03
Taking in the Town 1890.49
Taking it Slow 1982.04
Taking My Life Back 1995.01
Taking No Chances 1948.25
Taking Off 1931.34
Taking Off the Robe 1976.27
Taking the Easy Way Out 1972.21
Taking the Subway to Roxy 1928.45
Taku Patu 1972.20
Tale of a Bumble-Bee, The 1902.18
Tale of a Coat, The 1909.22, 1917.21
Tale of a Decent Married Hen 1898.55
Tale of a Mermaid, The 1914.13
Tale of a Monkey, The 1903.19
Tale of a Shirt, The 1925.45
Tale of a Stroll, The 1904.13
Tale of an Oyster, The 1929.45
Tale of the Cassowary, The 1904.13, 1904.44
Tale of the Coat 1947.06
Tale of the Kangaroo, The 1900.59
Tale of the Monkey and the Snake, The 1907.29
Tale of the Red Shirt, The 1904.13
Tale of the Sea-Shell, The 1903.10
Tale of the Tadpole and the Frog 1906.23
Tale of the Tadpole, The 1912.42
Tale of the Tailless Frog, The 1904.28
Tale of the Turtle Dove, The 1904.52
Tale of the Wedding Bell, The 1904.49
Talent 1956.08
Talent is What the Public Wants 1926.16
Tales of Hoffman 1921.02
Tales of Hoffman, The 1926.51
Tales on Ivories 1929.33
Talk 1965.28
Talk About a Busy Little Household 1927.47
Talk About Girls 1927.29
Talk About Time, A 1986.18
Talk About Yo' Luck 1897.42
Talk it Over 1923.24
Talk of the Town, The 1919.36
Talk to Her 1996.08
Talk to Him 1956.02
Talk to Me 1948.04, 1985.17
Talk to Me About Love 1972.18
Talk to Me, Baby 1964.04
Talk to the Animals 1974.22
Talk With My Heel and Toe 1930.05
Talk, Talk, Talk 1902.20, 1919.04
Talkative Toes 1930.32
Talkin' 'Bout Reggae 1980.05
Talkin' Bout You 1959.19
Talkin' in Tongues 1971.16
Talkin' With Your Feet 1956.07
Talking Drummer 1890.29
Talking Picture Show 1981.14
Talking to You 1964.16
Talking to Yourself 1967.06
Tall Dames and Low Comedy 1993.05
Tall Hope 1960.22
Tallahassee 1921.34, 1926.15
Tally Ho 1897.55, 1899.30, 1921.41
Tally Ho, The 1894.49
Tally Jo!!! 1906.17
Tally-Ho 1896.24, 1907.04, 1928.46
Tally-Ho Girls in the Coaching Club 1894.06
Tally-ho! 1868.01
Talons of Time 1972.21
Talor Made Girls 1892.23
Tam 1920.28
Tamamura 1908.20
Tambien yo, tego mi corazoncito 1969.11
Tamboree 1934.04
Tamborina 1925.01
Tamboule 1947.19
Tambourin 1933.24
Tambourine 1947.20
Tambourine Dance 1877.20
Tambourine Song 1893.40
Tambourines to Glory 1963.27
Tammany 1905.03
Tammany Ball, The 1905.41
Tammany Hall 1905.41
Tamos, Le 1970.01
Tampa 1927.27
Tampa Bay 1919.26
Tampico Tap 1927.05
Tampico Tune 1929.25
Tan Manhattan 1980.10
Tandem, A 1912.35
Tangerinamadidge 2001.04
Tangerine 1997.05
Tangi Hia 1972.20
Tangle Footed Monkey Wrench Dance 1913.18
Tanglefoot Trot, The 1919.07
Tanglefoot, The 1919.07
Tangles 1927.20
Tango 1913.04, 1942.01, 1963.29, 1968.13, 1977.09, 1978.26
Tango Ballad 1933.07
Tango Breakfast, The 1914.17
Tango Contest, The 1914.17, 1978.27
Tango del Molinillo, El 1917.33
Tango Dip, The 1914.10
Tango Espagnol 1927.60
Tango Maid, The 1914.10
Tango Melody 1925.45
Tango Rhythms 1934.42
Tango Tragique 1963.14
Tango, The 1995.15
Tango-Ballad 1966.19
Tango-Tango 1978.26
Tango: Maureen 1996.09
Tangoitis 1913.17, 1913.19
Tangoland Tap 1912.01
Tangorilla 1914.15
Tangos 1986.17, 1992.15
Tanguera 1985.07, 1997.13, 1999.18
Tanguillo 1949.07
Tanguillos 1992.15
Tannhauser 1990.10
Tantalizing April 1924.42
Tanz Mit Mir 1961.10
Tanzen mocht' ich-Tausend kleine Engel singen 1984.05
Tap Along With Me 1986.02
Tap Combination, The 1975.15
Tap Dance Drill 1963.22
Tap Tap 1983.21
Tap Tap! 1884.14
Tap Tap, The 1927.31
Tap the Plate 1969.15
Tap the Toe 1925.01
Tap Your Troubles Away 1974.18, 1985.19, 1992.18, 1998.07
Tapahoe Tap, The 1979.05
Tapaholics 1986.11
Tapcopation 1929.18
Tappin' the Barrel 1933.27
Tappin' the Toe 1927.53
Tappin' to the Picnic 1929.01
Tapping at the Window 1866.18
Taps 1928.47, 1930.29
Taquito Militar 1985.07, 1993.08

Tar's Song 1892.18
Tar's Song, The 1891.14
Tarantella 1870.22, 1892.21, 1898.46, 1899.39, 1901.19, 1906.49, 1928.26, 1954.13, 1982.09, 1990.20
Tarantella oi mamma ca mo vene 1985.14
Tarantella Rhythm 1934.20
Taranto 1992.15
Tarantos 1986.17
Tarantula 1952.13
Tarantula, The 1969.11
Tarde del Corpus, La 1926.09
Tarradiddle 1897.32
Tartaglia's Lament 2000.10
Tartar 1925.52
Tartar Legend, A 1928.45
Tartar Song, The 1928.30
Tartarin Now Comes 1893.40
Tartarin, the Terrible 1893.40
Tarts and Flowers 1934.15
Taste 1968.03
Taste of Forever, A 1980.30
Taste of the Sea 1934.42
Tattooed Man, The 1897.42
Tattoos, The 1964.39
Taunting Rusty 1987.05
Tausend kleine Engel singen 1984.05
Tavern Foxtrot 1996.08
Tavern Song 1928.29, 1986.14
Tax the Bachelors 1910.01
Taxi 1975.05, 1996.07, 1997.01
Taxi Dancers' Tango 1988.20
Taxi Drivers Lament 1926.17
Taxicab, The 1908.19
Tbiliso 1977.13
Tchastushky 1924.48
Te Deum 1925.32, 1928.12, 1976.08
Tea 1927.20
Tea and Cake Walk 1903.22
Tea and Toast and Kisses 1880.10
Tea Blossom 1926.35
Tea for Two 1925.30, 1942.10, 1942.16, 1971.03, 1973.13, 1983.09, 1993.01, 1995.16, 1998.17, 1999.05
Tea Garden, The 1923.22
Tea in Chicago 1954.16
Tea in the Orient 1918.33
Tea Kettel Song 1905.12
Tea Kettle, The 1924.06
Tea Leaves 1914.20
Tea Party, The 1918.32, 1969.05, 1985.19
Tea Song 1936.28
Tea Time Tap 1927.52
Tea, Tea, Tea 1904.40
Teach Me Everything You Know 1912.13
Teach Me How 1923.37
Teach Me How to Kiss 1921.20
Teach Me How to Kiss, Dear 1897.39
Teach Me How to Love 1915.32
Teach Me How to Shimmy 1995.03
Teach Me Not to Love You 1997.18
Teach Me to Dance 1923.23
Teach Me to Dance Like Grandma 1928.42, 1968.19
Teach Me to Forget 1911.36
Teach Me to Smile 1915.20
Teach Me Tonight 1974.10, 1991.04
Teach the Young Idea How to Shoot 1904.37
Teach Us the Subtle Art of Kissing 1903.14
Teacher, Teacher! 1919.09
Teachers on Parade 1968.06
Teaching McFadden to Waltz 1910.33
Teacup and a Spoon, A 1920.12
Tear the Town Apart 1972.04
Teas for Two 1947.19
Teasin' Baby 1928.10
Teasing 1911.12
Teasing Mama 1928.10
Tecla's Mood 1945.14
Teddy Bear 1989.12
Teddy Bears 1907.03
Teddy Da Roose 1980.27
Teddy Girl, The 1907.27
Teddy the Jungle Man 1909.05
Teddy Toddle, The 1921.36
Teddy-Bear and the Bee, The 1907.61
Tee Oodle Um Bum Bo 1919.12
Teedelum, Tadelum 1897.25
Teenie, Eenie, Weenie 1914.28
Teeter Totter Tessie 1939.12
Telegrams, the Actor's Great Ball 1876.30
Telegraph Boy, The 1879.64
Telephone Dance, The 1986.03
Telephone Duet 1914.04
Telephone Fighters, The 1899.19
Telephone Girl, The 1897.54, 1917.08
Telephone Girlie 1971.03
Telephone Hour, The 1960.06
Telephone Song 1912.15, 1966.24
Telephone Tango 1956.13
Telephone Your Riskey Issey 1910.18
Telephone, The 1991.03
Telescope, The 1880.46
Television's Tough on Love 1950.09
Tell Her 1956.08, 1966.09, 1973.07
Tell Her in the Springtime 1924.44
Tell Her Now 1993.17
Tell Her While the Waltz is Playing 1922.28
Tell Him 1984.15
Tell him thus the love lingers in the heart 1855.03
Tell Him to Come/Hurry Mateo 1926.09, 1926.35
Tell Him, Rose, That I'll Return 1894.47
Tell it All 1904.54
Tell it All Over Again 1914.27
Tell it Like it Is 1992.06
Tell it to the Marines 1928.16
Tell Me 1902.22, 1904.10, 1917.02, 1919.26, 1925.39, 1999.22
Tell Me a Bedtime Story 1923.32
Tell Me Again 1907.61, 1927.43
Tell Me Again, Sweetheart 1902.04
Tell Me Cigarette 1927.14
Tell Me Daisy 1921.31
Tell Me Honey 1902.02
Tell Me How 1954.17
Tell Me it's Not True 1993.07
Tell Me Jo 1961.25
Tell Me More 1925.14
Tell Me Mother 1932.04
Tell Me Not That You are Forgetting 1925.02
Tell Me on a Sunday 1985.12
Tell Me Ruby, Will You be True? 1895.02
Tell Me Something About Yourself 1932.13
Tell Me the French Word for Squeeze Me 1914.14
Tell Me the Story 1946.07
Tell me true, love 1882.63
Tell Me Truly 1924.07, 1928.23
Tell Me What is Love 1929.41
Tell Me What the Rain is Saying 1971.17
Tell Me What Your Eyes Were Made For 1924.39
Tell Me What's the Matter Lovable Eyes 1922.15
TelL Me Where I Shall Find Him 1900.41
Tell Me Where is Fancy Bred? 1981.02
Tell Me where My Wife has gone 1869.07
Tell Me Who I Was 1982.23
Tell Me Who You Are 1928.35
Tell Me Why 1918.07
Tell Me Why, Why, Why 1904.08
Tell Me With Smiles 1923.12
Tell Me, Crystal Ball 1918.33
Tell Me, Daisy 1886.15, 1920.15
Tell Me, Dusky Maiden 1901.27
Tell me, girl 1878.16
Tell Me, Honey 1892.45
Tell Me, Kind Spirit 1920.06
Tell Me, Little Gypsy 1920.18
Tell Me, Lovers, I Pray 1896.45
Tell Me, Pretty Maiden 1900.51, 1902.05, 1920.09, 1933.21, 1938.09
Tell Me, What This Can Be 1930.43
Tell My Father 1999.08
Tell My Why 1987.02
Tell Sweet Saroyana 1981.25
Tell the Band to Play an Irish Tune 1906.22
Tell the Doc 1927.59
Tell the World I'm Through 1927.52
Tell Them Yer Baby's Comin' to Town 1896.31, 1896.37
Tell Tony and Rosabella Goodbye for Me 1956.04
Tell Us What's the Row 1908.44
Tell Us, Jolly Sailors 1902.29
Tell Us, Pretty Ladies 1900.38
Tell-Tale Eyes 1903.24
Telling Fortunes 1923.03
Temperament 1919.05
Temperamental Dances 1912.47
Temperance Crowd, The 1893.30
Temple Bells 1912.30
Temple of Fortune 1902.42
Temple of Love 1870.38
Temple, The 1971.12
Tempo 1961.17
Tempo Di Gavotte 1913.02
Temporary Widow, The 1913.02
Temporary Wives 1920.37
Temps, Le 1965.30, 1974.19, 1983.03, 1991.04
Tempt Me Not 1939.27
Temptation 1920.15, 1920.27, 1985.08
Temptation Rag 1910.18, 1944.32
Temptation Strut, The 1926.14
Temptation Waltz 1915.20
Temptation, The 1904.36
Ten Cents a Dance 1930.08, 1931.08, 1975.13
Ten Commandments of Love, The 1919.12
Ten Dirty Little Fingers 1918.18
Ten Kopecks 1998.11
Ten Little Bridesmaids 1915.07, 1917.29
Ten Little Gentlemen of Spooney Town 1902.44
Ten Minutes Ago 1993.14, 2001.09
Ten Minutes in Bed 1930.38
Ten O'Clock 1914.07, 1970.17
Ten O'Clock Town 1937.07
Ten Plagues, The 1972.09
Ten Years in the Country 1930.18
Tender Feeling of Heart, A 1787.01
Tender Shepherd 1954.13, 1979.22, 1990.20
Tender Spot, A 1964.05
Tender Trap, The 1974.10
Tenderloin Celebration, The 1960.19
Tenderloin, The 1897.25
Tenderly 1976.32
Tendresse, La 1965.08
Tengu 1974.12
Tennessee 1904.43, 1924.30
Tennessee Dan 1931.04
Tennessee, I Hear You Calling 1914.22
Tennis 1909.21, 1912.25, 1930.23
Tennis Champs 1926.13
Tennis Song 1989.29
Tennis Song, The 1976.33
Tennis Terpsichorean 1921.25
Tennis Tournament 1913.05
Tenor, all singers above, A 1894.15
Tenterfield Saddler 1979.11
Tenth and Greenwich 1971.13
Terence's Farewell to Kathleen 1858.03
Teresa, Little Word 1893.02
Terminate 1975.02
Terminix 1972.02
Terpsichore, the Goddess of Dance 1923.04
Terpsichorean Trifle, A 1898.78
Terrace Duet 1988.09
Terre Haute High 1972.25
Terre, terre, droit devant nous! 1929.11
Terres et des coupons, Des 1929.14
Terrible Man, The 1873.28
Terribly Attractive 1939.13
Terrific Band and a Real Nice Crowd, A 1978.27
Terror, Terror 1895.21
Teru, Teru 1948.24
Terzetto Buffo 1910.22
Tessie, You are the Only, Only, Only 1902.35
Test Song 1892.42
Testament 1933.07
Testimony, The 2001.06
Testing, The 1986.18
Tete a l'ombre, La 1961.25
Tete a Tete 1941.11
Tete a Tete With You, A 1916.25

Tete de roi, La 1963.02
Tetrazzini Family, The 1908.36
Texas 1927.31
Texas Dan 1904.47, 1905.22
Texas has a Whorehouse in It 1978.13
Texas Rangers 1904.09
Texas Rose 1990.15
Texas Stomp 1927.10
Texas Tommy 1911.24
Texas, Barnum & Cohan 1927.31
Texas, Li'l Darlin' 1949.17
Textile Troops, The 1929.20
Tfile Tsu Got 1970.17
Th' Waggle o' th' Kilt 1928.05
Than us you will not find better 1878.16
Thank God 1982.10
Thank God I'm Old 1980.07
Thank Heaven for Little Girls 1963.02, 1965.08, 1973.12
Thank Heaven for You 1972.13
Thank heaven, he's saved 1873.05
Thank the Lord the War is Over 1909.22, 1947.06
Thank You 1972.15
Thank You Father 1930.11
Thank You for the Change in My Life 1990.05
Thank You for Your Invitation, Sir 1978.07
Thank You Madam 1963.14
Thank You so Much 1965.06
Thank You Song, The 1968.24
Thank You, Don't Mention It 1932.15
Thank You, Kind Sir!, Said She 1911.08
Thank You, Ma'am 1966.05
Thank You, Mrs. Butterfield 1950.06
Thank You, No 1972.24
Thank You, North America 1941.11
Thank You, South America 1941.11
Thank Your Lucky Stars and Stripes 1995.14
Thanks a Lot 1972.07
Thanks Awful 1926.21
Thanks for a Darn Nice Time 1928.28
Thanks for a Lousy Evening 1944.14
Thanks for the Francs 1939.22
Thanks for the Memory 1980.08
Thanks to You 1932.01
Thanks, Commodore 1886.50
Thanks, Sweet Jesus! 1970.02
Thanksgiving Dinner, The 1893.30
Thanksgiving Sermon, The 1893.30
That Aeroplane Rag 1911.26
That Ain't Right 1978.09
That Airship of Mine 1917.31
That American Boy of Mine 1923.02
That Awful Bogie Man 1905.56
That Band Did Play 1892.05
That Bandit Man 1910.08
That Barber in Seville 1921.34
That Beautiful Isle of the Sea 1904.30
That Bohemian Rag 1914.16
That Bran' New Gal O' Mine 1923.33
That Brown Skin Flapper 1922.44
That Brownskin Flapper 1922.44
That Certain Feeling 1925.49
That Certain Party 1926.02
That Certain Something 1920.30
That Certain Thing 1929.50
That Chap We Select, And 1888.19
That Charleston Dance 1924.27
That Chop Stick Rag 1909.05
That Deviling Tune 1911.12
That Dirty Old Man 1962.12
That Face 1963.08, 2001.05
That Face! 1951.13
That Fellow Manuelo 1934.38
That Funny Feeling 1895.03
That Gal of Mine 1913.05
That Good Old-Fashioned Cakewalk 1913.18
That Guilty Feeling 1968.08
That Guy 1993.07
That Gypsy Rag 1918.17
That has Nothing to do With You 1919.02
That Hat and Not the Girl 1914.10
That Haunting Melody 1911.43, 1912.24
That Horrid Mosquito 1904.23
That Hypnotizing Rag 1910.08
That is All You Will Know 1888.18
That is All, And 1913.37
That is Art 1913.32
That is Fate 1899.02
That is his way 1885.28
That is Love 1899.04, 1903.03, 1909.30
That is Rock & Roll 1995.03
That is the Life for Me 1913.05
That it Should Come to This 1976.03
That Kind of Man 1922.25
That Ladies Cannot Bathe 1894.33
That Lindy Hop 1930.34
That Little German Band 1918.34
That Little Girl is You 1904.27
That Little Girl is You, And 1911.38
That Little Something 1926.32, 1927.12
That Lovin' Traumerei 1911.13
That Lucky Fellow 1939.28
That Lucky Lady 1939.28
That Man 1904.49
That Man and Woman Thing 1940.23
That Man Over There 1963.21
That May Have Satisfied Grandma 1920.38
That Means Home to Me 1920.33
That Means Nothing to Me 1925.41
That Melody 1908.16
That Minstrel Man 1919.24
That Moment of Moments 1936.02, 1936.17
That Naughty Little Song 1911.38
That Naughty Little, Sporty Little Gay Golf Ball 1899.41
That Naughty Show from Gay Paree 1954.01
That Naughty Waltz 1919.26
That Never Happened in Wall Street 1905.31
That New Gang of Mine 1932.14
That night I'll ne'er forget 1878.16
That Old Black Magic 1956.02, 1979.24, 1997.05
That Old Familiar Ring 1969.14
That Old Featherbed 1985.02
That Old First Love of Mine 1894.35
That Old Hooked Rug 1929.33
That Old Piano 1983.20
That Old Time Crowd 1965.01
That Opera Rag 1910.33
That Ought to Count for Something 1923.37
That Peach-reen-o Phil-a-peen-o Dance 1917.08
That Peculiar Charm 1881.22
That Prelude 1965.35
That Rag-Tag Dance 1914.33
That Ragtime Dinner Band 1913.20
That Really was a Lovely Place for Me 1907.30
That Reminiscent Melody 1920.08
That Rhythm Man 1929.23, 1989.02
That Ring on the Finger 1959.11
That Romance of Mine 1923.02
That Russian Winter 1942.20
That Samson and Delilah Melody 1922.24
That September Night 1927.05
That she is reeling 1875.35
That Slavery is Love 1970.10
That Society Bear 1912.09
That Something Extra Special 1968.02
That Soothing Serenade 1918.20
That Soul Inspiring Sneeze 1911.25
That Spooky Tune 1911.35
That Still Small Voice 1907.22
That Stupid Melody 1927.31
That Sweet Oblivion Drink 1898.73
That Tempting Tango 1914.08
That terrible Jonathan Oscar Wild 1886.53
That Terrible Tune 1940.03
That Terrific Rainbow 1940.22
That Thing I Can't Seem to Forget 1930.28
That Tired Feeling 1930.42
That Touch 1974.12
That Tumble Down Shack in Athlone 1918.41
That Typical, Topical, Tropical Tune 1912.05
That voice! That voice! 1848.04
That was Me 1890.29, 1894.17, 1932.04
That was Yesterday 1961.20
That wasn't All 1908.07
That We're Soldiers No Doubt You Will Guess 1902.25
That Weepy Creepy Feeling 1917.09
That Will Keep Him True to You 1911.15
That Will Serve Her Right 1992.11
That Woman Can't Play No Piano 1983.15
That Wonderful Girl of Mine 1962.17
That Wonderful Melody 1929.41
That Would be Lovely 1909.22, 1947.06
That'll be About All of That 1900.16
That'll be Nice 1886.62
That'll be the Day 1961.08, 1990.15
That'll Show Him 1962.12
That's a Beginning 1968.30, 1983.14
That's a Crime 1960.13
That's a Man Everytime 1950.06
That's a Very Different Thing 1903.22
That's a Very Interesting Question 1971.18
That's a Woman 1989.07
That's a Woman's Way 1919.42
That's About the Size of It 1900.38
That's All 1886.45, 1889.34, 1897.14, 1907.24
That's All He Wants 1920.43
That's All Right 1990.15
That's All Right for McGilligan 1911.12
That's All Right Mama 1989.12
That's All There Is 1923.47
That's an Old Gag With Me 1885.15
That's Art 1905.03
That's as Far as You Can Go 1908.44
That's Broadway 1943.16
That's Called Walking the Dog 1916.11
That's Class 1946.04
That's Easy for a Little Girl to Do 1907.04
That's Enough, Don't You Think? 1892.21
That's Entertainment 1967.11, 1972.05, 1974.22, 1982.06, 1999.23
That's for Me 1996.04
That's for Sure 1951.23
That's Good 1910.17
That's Good - That's Bad 1963.13
That's Good Enough for Me 1967.16
That's Harmony 1911.24
That's Her - That's Her, What Did I Tell Ya? 1925.27
That's Him 1943.19, 1981.25
That's How I Got Treated 1908.16
That's How I Learned to Sing the Blues 1983.20
That's How I Love the Blues 1941.06
That's How it Goes 1951.14
That's How it Is 1970.03
That's How it Starts 1959.22, 1985.04
That's How the Shannon Flows 1912.06
That's How You Jazz 1992.08
That's How Young I Feel 1966.10, 1985.19
That's in My Line 1924.17
That's Love 1958.04
That's Love With a Capitol L 1913.20
That's Me 1921.03
That's My Approach to Love 1943.18
That's My Fella 1950.04
That's My Idea of Love 1900.25
That's My Mammy 1928.22
That's My Man 1927.29
That's My Partner 1985.02
That's Not Cricket 1935.12
That's One Thing a Wizard Can Do 1895.33
That's Peculiar, isn't it? Very 1911.29
That's Religion 1932.12
That's Some Love 1907.57, 1908.31
That's That 1922.38
That's the Kind of a Baby for Me 1917.13
That's the Kind of a Boy for Me 1917.34
That's the Kind of Man You Ought to Marry 1914.17
That's the Kind of Turk I Am 1877.22
That's the Law 1965.28
That's the Lesson I'm Teaching to You 1915.08
That's the Life for Me 1964.18
That's the Life of a Stable Boy 1910.09
That's the Picture I Want to See 1917.26
That's the Place Where Our Flag Shall Fly 1917.05
That's the Time 1906.26
That's the Time When I Miss You 1929.33
That's the Tune 1923.35, 1924.06
That's the Way it Goes 1922.07
That's the Way it Happens 1953.08, 1993.16, 1996.04

That's the Way of a Sailor 1902.15
That's the Way to Treat a Little Doggie 1911.15
That's the Way to Win a Girl 1914.17
That's the Way We do Things in New Yawk 1992.08
That's What a Fellow Does When He's in Love 1908.13
That's What Friends are For 1985.20
That's What Harlem is to Me 1976.04
That's What He Did 1933.25
That's What He Said 1998.21
That's What I Need Tonight 1972.24
That's What I Told Him Last Night 1950.04
That's What I'd Like for Christmas 1965.28
That's What it is to be Young 1965.19
That's What Life is All About 1976.32
That's What Men are For 1918.34
That's What Miracles are All About 1981.16
That's What My Organ Plays 1908.12
That's What Puzzles the Quaker 1880.10
That's What the Bible Say 1976.35
That's What the Dickie Birds Say 1884.66
That's What the Papers Say 1905.37
That's What the Rose Said to Me 1907.24
That's What the Wild Waves are Saying 1892.29
That's What Young Ladies Do 1966.09
That's What, by Gosh! 1896.37
That's Where a Man Fits In 1955.25
That's Where She Sits All Day 1903.03
That's Where the Laugh Comes In! 1873.19
That's Where We Come In 1934.01
That's Why Darkies Were Born 1931.30
That's Why I Never Married 1907.46, 1911.02
That's Why I Want to Go Home 1947.13
That's Why Lots of People Marry 1910.27
That's Why the Danube is Blue 1907.10
That's Why They Call Me Shine 1911.20
That's Why They Call Us Johns 1924.07
That's Why We Misbehave 1929.33
That's Why We're Dancing 1930.09
That's You 1932.19
That's Your Funeral 1963.01
Theatre is a Lady 1952.20
Theatre, the Theatre, The 1993.05
Theatre/Theatre 1972.18
Theatrical Blues, The 1920.08
Theda Bara 1920.19
Their Courage High, You May Defy 1902.25
Their Eyes, their lips, their Busses 1750.01
Their Fathers Fought at Ramillies 1902.25
Their Hearts are Over Here 1917.37
Them There Eyes 1948.13
Them was the Childhood Days 1912.39
Theme from 2001 1978.01
Theme of the Megilla 1968.22
Theme Song, The 1929.19
Then 1925.47, 1936.29
Then All Come Along 1912.34
Then Away We Go 1903.04
Then Came the War 1930.35
Then Comes the Dawning 1922.33
Then Frederic 1981.01
Then He Kissed Me, And 1984.15, 1985.03
Then I am rich 1859.13
Then I may sing and play? 1894.15
Then I Will Live Love for Thee 1894.40
Then I'd be Satisfied With Life 1901.07, 1902.35, 1980.27, 1982.05
Then I'll Have Time for You 1929.03
Then I'll Marry You 1918.40
Then I'm Yours 1951.10
Then Love Began 1920.27
Then Love Me Some Mo 1927.40
Then Off We Go 1896.48
Then one of us 1890.02
Then Say Good Bye! 1894.17
Then Shout Hurrah 1921.40
Then They Winked the Other Eye 1890.29, 1890.30
Then With a Cachuca, Fandango and Bolero 1899.06
Then You Go 1909.21
Then You May Take Me to the Fair 1960.21
Then You Swing, Swing, Swing 1911.23
Then You Were Never in Love 1940.10
Then You Will Know 1926.42, 1946.03
Then you'll remember me 1844.01
Then You're in Love 1924.25
Then, Frederic, let your escort lion-hearted 1879.72
Then, if I Understand Right 1900.39
Then, take me, Clifford 1887.08
Thenardier Waltz of Treachery 1987.04
Theodora 1902.22
Theodore 1907.41
Theophilus 1910.22
Ther's Rhythm in That Heart of Mine 1936.31
There 1956.02
There a Boat Dat's Leavin' Soon for New York 1983.04
There a Boat That's Leavin' Soon for New York 1935.13
There Ain't No Color Line Around the Rainbow 1943.14
There Ain't No Flies on Me 1957.07
There Ain't No Harm in What You Do 1913.19
There Ain't No Love 1930.33
There Ain't No Sweet Man Worth the Salt of My Tears 1929.04
There are 57 Ways to Win a Man 1911.43
There are Bet and Bell 1887.04
There are Brigands in Every Station 1879.71
There are cases 1895.26
There are Days and There are Days 1981.28
There are Fairies at the Bottom of My Garden 1931.14
There are Fairies at the Bottom of Our Garden 1952.11
There are ladies who dwell 1863.04
There are Lots of Things Teacher Does Not Know 1905.50
There are No Girls Like Show Girls 1982.06
There are No Girls Quite Like Show Girls 1980.18
There are Some Eyes 1988.15
There are some things in this wide world 1895.17
There are Some Things We Can Never Forget 1923.44
There are Such Things 1974.09
There are Times 1924.01, 1925.42, 1952.11
There are Tricks in All Trades 1902.43
There are Worse Things I Could Do 1972.12, 1994.07
There are Yanks 1944.01
There But for You Go I 1947.07, 1980.26
There Came a Vision 1911.46
There Comes a Night 1908.15
There Comes a Some Day 1921.03
There Goes My Baby 1995.03
There grew a little flower 'neath a great oak tree 1887.10
There had to be the Waltz 1938.15
There He Goes 1910.13
There He Goes, Mr. Phileas Fogg 1946.13
There I Go Dreaming Again 1932.07
There I'd Be 1945.20
There in the Dark 1969.08
There is a beauty, in the bellow of the blast 1885.47
There is a Birthday 1974.23
There is a flower that bloometh 1848.04
There is a Fountain/it Don't Make Sense 1998.21
There is a Garden in Loveland 1925.06
There is a Girl 1921.33
There is a Santa Claus 1936.12
There is a Soul Mate 1911.36
There is a Star in My Heart 1998.08
There is a Sucker Born Ev'ry Minute 1980.07
There is a Time 1965.30, 1974.01
There is a View... 1997.12
There is Beautiful You Are 1966.09
There is Beauty in the Bellows of the Blast 1939.15
There is Gold Along the Rivers 1907.26
There is Life Everywhere 1924.48
There is More 1983.20
There is More to Love 1990.04
There is no human joy 1855.03, 1855.06
There is No Land Like England 1892.14
There is No Other Way 1976.02
There is No Place Like Home 1908.23
There is no such thing as a Bogie man 1902.32
There is Nothin' Like a Dame 1949.04
There is Nothing too Good for You 1923.18
There is Only One Paris for That 1960.13
There is Somebody Waiting for Me 1928.05
There is Something About You That I Love, Love, Love 1904.22
There is the Key 1904.01
There Isn't Anything That Can't be Cured 1906.30
There isn't One Girl 1924.08
There lived a king, as I've been told 1890.02
There Must be Someone for Me 1944.02
There Must be Something Better Than Love 1950.04
There Must be Something Wrong About My Face 1900.16
There Never was a Baby Like My Baby 1951.19
There Never was a Town Like Paris 1926.37
There Never was a White Hope Whose Christian Name was Cohen 1912.36
There Never was a Woman 1958.14
There Once was a Man 1954.05
There Once was a Small Street Arab 1900.37
There Once was a Time 1886.45
There Once was a Witch 1892.42
There Once was an Owl 1903.37
There Really isn't Any More to Tell 1911.29
There Really Must be Something Nice About Me 1903.22
There she goes with horses prancing 1878.16
There She Is 1982.18, 1997.06
There so Much More 1931.04
There the bells go 1884.14
There was a Fairy Queen 1870.20
There was a Fellow and a Girl 1940.21
There was a Little Man 1971.20
There was a little sailor lad 1888.07
There was a Time 1890.02, 1915.02, 1924.40
There was a Time When on Broadway 1898.50
There was Life, There was Love, There was Laughter 1945.04
There was no ray of light! 1884.14
There was Once a Little Soldier 1902.25
There was Once a Little Village by the Sea 1934.34
There was the Punch 1923.02
There Were Actors Then 1908.07
There When I Need Him 1977.16
There Will be a Girl 1932.15
There Will Never be Another You 1988.08
There You Are 1932.10, 1980.11, 1985.18
There You Have New York Town 1912.24
There'll Always be a Lady Fair 1934.36
There'll Always be an England 1944.29
There'll be a Hot Time in the Old Town To-Night 1896.52, 1897.40
There'll be a Hot Time in the Old Town Tonight 1927.48, 1930.16, 1975.20
There'll be Life, Love and laughter 1945.04
There'll be Lovers as Long as the World Goes Round 1884.41
There'll be Murder Tonight 1895.27
There'll be Some Changes Made 1976.04, 1999.01
There'll be Trouble 1947.02
There'll Have to be Changes Made 1952.15
There'll Never be Another Girl Like Daisy 1917.20
There's "Yes" in the Air 1943.07
There's a Big Cry Baby in the Moon 1908.05
There's a Boat Dat's Leavin' Soon for New York 1958.10
There's a Boat That's Leavin' Soon for New York 1980.10
There's a Brand New Beat in Heaven 1981.07
There's a Brand New Hero 1917.36, 1976.25
There's a Broadway Up in Heaven 1935.11
There's a Certain Kind o' Jingle to My Spurs 1951.05
There's a Chapter 1917.25
There's a Chill in the Air 1934.20
There's a Circus in Town 1969.16
There's a Coach Comin' In 1951.24
There's a Comin' Together 1970.03
There's a Doctor 1993.06
There's a doctor I've found 1972.08
There's a Girl 1991.05
There's a Girl in Havana 1911.35
There's a Great Day Coming, Manana 1940.10
There's a Happy Land 1911.13
There's a Happy Land in the Sky 1943.01
There's a Hill Beyond a Hill 1951.22
There's a Lad That I Know 1896.41
There's a Land in the Silvery Shimmery Moon 1892.55
There's a Legend That is Famous 1889.38
There's a Light in Your Eyes 1918.28
There's a Little Bit of Everything on Broadway 1915.02
There's a Little Fighting Blood in Me 1905.39
There's a little group of isles 1894.15

There's a Little Maid 1904.01
There's a Little Maid I Know 1904.01
There's a Little Street in Heaven Called Broadway 1902.10
There's a Little Street in Heaven They Call Broadway 1903.36
There's a Lobster Left for Me 1901.23
There's a Long Trail 1964.28
There's a Lot of Pretty Little Things in Paris 1913.30
There's a Lovely Crop of Girls This Year 1917.29
There's a man 1878.02
There's a Man 1885.58, 1888.13, 1896.35, 1969.10
There's a Man in My Life 1943.07
There's a Million Little Cupids in the Sky 1978.21
There's a Monster who lives 1864.13
There's a Muddle 1927.20
There's a New Deal on the Way 1973.11
There's a Picture in My Heart 1896.41
There's a Price 1999.17
There's a Rainbow on the Way 1929.44
There's a Rainbow Round My Shoulder 1963.02
There's a Rainbow Waiting for You 1924.09
There's a Romeo for Every Girl I Know 1920.07
There's a Room in My House 1962.01
There's a Small Hotel 1936.05, 1975.13, 1983.02
There's a Strange Fascination About the Stage 1902.34, 1902.40
There's a Stranger in Town 1976.35, 1980.14, 1982.17
There's a Sunbeam for Every Drop of Rain 1921.23
There's a Tender Look in Your Eyes 1920.21
There's a Trace of the War in Everyone's Home 1918.36
There's a Typical Tipperary Over Here 1921.19
There's a Warm Spot in My Heart, Baby 1898.22
There's a Way Out 1920.11
There's a Woman Behind Every Man 1927.05
There's a Yacht Come In 1903.38
There's Always a Girl Who is Waiting 1913.02
There's Always a Seat in the Parlor for You 1882.69
There's Always a Woman 1999.20
There's Always One You Can't Forget 1916.18, 1918.06, 1983.08
There's Always Something Fishy About the French 1934.34
There's Always Something Wrong 1907.22
There's Always the Blues 1995.14
There's an Aeroplane Air About You 1910.25
There's an Eve in Ev'ry Garden 1922.29
There's better days for old Ireland yet 1871.16
There's But One New York 1903.15
There's Gold on the Trees 1973.11
There's Gotta be a Weddin' 1939.29
There's Gotta be Something Better Than This 1966.01
There's History to be Made 1948.18
There's Just a Little Bit of Monkey Still Left in You and Me 1916.25
There's Just One Girl I'd Like to Marry 1907.11
There's Life in the Old Dog Yet 1925.07
There's Life in the Old Folks Yet 1963.20
There's Life in the Old Girl Yet 1924.01, 1925.42
There's Lots of Things You Can do With Two, But Not With Three 1947.08
There's Love in the Heart I Hold 1929.17
There's magic in a flashing eye 1894.28
There's magic music 1878.16
There's Me 1987.05
There's Money in Graft 1911.31
There's More to a Kiss Than the Sound 1919.12
There's More to Life Than Love 1992.11
There's Music in a Kiss 1935.04
There's Music in You 2001.09
There's naught so uncertain 1882.60
There's Never Been Anything Like Us 1983.08
There's No Better Use for Time Than Kissing 1918.16
There's No Business Like Show Business 1946.12, 1966.12, 1999.04
There's No Cure Like Travel 1934.36, 1987.15
There's No Getting Away from You 1948.28
There's No Holding Me 1946.20
There's No Man Like a Snowman 1950.14
There's No one, I'm certain 1895.26
There's No Other Solution 1975.07
There's No Place Like Home 1989.06
There's No Place Like Home for You 1914.03
There's No Place Like Home, When Your Wife has Gone Away 1910.16
There's No Reason in the World 1961.20
There's No School Like Our School 1971.09
There's None so Sweet as Rosalind 1911.31
There's Not a Drop of Blood 1882.45
There's not a sound however light 1855.06
There's Not a Thing I Wouldn't Do 1904.51
There's Not Another Girlie in the World Like You 1907.37
There's Nothin' so Bad for a Woman 1945.05
There's Nothing Better Than Beer 1906.20
There's Nothing But Annoyance 1880.47
There's Nothing Doing in the Old, Old Town 1905.22
There's Nothing Like a Friend 1903.41
There's Nothing Like a Model T 1947.16
There's Nothing Like It 1950.06
There's Nothing Like Marriage for People 1946.20
There's Nothing Like the Life We Sailors Need 1903.04
There's Nothing Like Travel 1946.04
There's Nothing Much More to Say 1904.40
There's Nothing New Under the Sun 1925.50
There's Nothing Nicer Than People 1952.10
There's Nothing so Uncertain as a Dead Sure Thing 1916.18
There's Nothing the Matter With Me 1908.35, 1932.07
There's Nothing too Fine for the Finest 1919.01
There's Nothing Wrong in a Kiss 1930.05
There's Nothing Wrong With Our Values 1961.16
There's Nowhere to Go But Up 1938.11
There's One Born Every Minute 1911.07
There's One Sweetheart I'll Never Forget 1905.33
There's only one girl in the world for me 1895.17
There's Only One Little Girl 1917.34
There's Only One Rose in the Garden of Love 1908.40
There's Only One Thing a Coon Can Do 1915.29
There's Only One Thing to Do 1919.28
There's Only One Who Rules My House 1915.18
There's Ragtime in the Air 1916.10
There's Room Enough for Us 1956.12
There's Something About a Horse 1961.21
There's Something About a Soldier 1942.12
There's Something About Me They Like 1921.10
There's Something About You 1914.22, 1927.17, 1965.28
There's Something About You Dear That Appeals to Me 1916.22
There's Something About You That Appeals to Me 1911.03
There's Something Doing Around My Heart 1906.19
There's Something in That 1929.07
There's Something in the Air 1919.36
There's Something in the Air in Springtime 1914.15
There's Something Irresistible About Me 1921.11
There's Something Missing in the Movies 1915.12
There's Something on My Program 1946.07
There's Something Rather Odd About Augustus 1908.27
There's Something We're Worried About 1933.25
There's sunlight in Heaven 1855.06
There's the Moon 1969.04, 1980.01
There's Trouble 1927.20
There, at the dreamy hour 1887.04
Thereby Hangs a Tail, And 1925.17
Therese 1892.08
Thermodynamic Duo 1966.32
These Amateurs Make Me Sick 1888.05
These are the Good Old Days 1909.16
These Charming People 1925.49
These Colors Will Not Run 1918.07
These Eyes of Mine 1985.05
These Foolish Things Remind Me of You 1982.12
These Four Walls 1970.02
These Little Heads 1882.75
These Little Heads Now Golden 1882.75
These men are all deceivers 1852.01, 1871.10
These to Me are Beautiful People 1931.06
These Tropics 1931.39
These Words May Have Meaning for Thee 1897.55
These Words No Shakespeare Wrote 1890.08
Theses are our sentiments 1898.25
Thespian Art 1896.26
Thessaly 1906.44
They 1979.18
They Ain't Done Right by Our Nell 1940.19
They All Call the Hatter Mad, And 1979.18
They All do It 1877.39
They All Follow Me 1897.39
They All Know Better Now 1898.47
They All Laughed 1980.09
They All Look Alike to Mary 1907.24, 1907.28
They All Look Good When They're Far Away 1911.38
They All Looked at Me 1903.36
They All Love Me 1932.10
They All Made Good 1944.29
They All Need a Little Hot-Cha 1932.07
They All Take After Me 1892.45
They Always Do 1882.33
They Always Follow Me 1908.31
They Always Run a Little Faster 1924.47
They are All After Pott 1901.19
They are Angels Without Wings 1903.16
They are beautiful 1889.10
They are Beautiful 1889.34
They are going 1878.20
They are Hypnotiuized 1903.11
They are Nothing But Girls 1900.34
They are Waiting There for Me 1906.04
They Auto Know Better 1920.24
They Call Her Lovely Mary, the Lily of the West 1893.31
They Call it Dancing 1921.30
They Call Me Pollyana 1921.17
They call me the Belle 1886.53
They Call Me the Belle of New York 1897.39
They Call the Wind Maria 1951.24
They Can't Prohibit Love 1978.06
They Can't Run Off the Reels too Fast for Me 1916.18
They Can't Take That Away from Me 1980.09, 1992.02, 1992.18, 1999.10
They Couldn't Compare to You 1950.20
They Didn't Believe Me 1914.18, 1964.28, 1975.22, 1986.01
They Didn't Want the Likes of Me 1898.38
They do You Much Better at Home 1915.05
They Don't Give You Life at Sixteen 1989.25
They Don't Make 'Em Like That Anymore 1967.16
They Fall in Love 1928.31
They Follow Me Around 1914.31
They Found Me 1913.31
They Gave Me a Medal for That 1902.18
They Go Wild, Simply Wild, Over Me 1973.05
They Handed Me a Lemon 1905.32
They Hardly Know I'm Around 1997.17
They Have Carrie the Bridegroom Off 1905.54
They Hope to Make it a Hit 1925.12
They Keep Coming 1972.13
They Learn About Women from Me 1931.01
They Like Ike 1950.15
They Live in You 1997.20
They Lived to be Loved in Vain 1906.26
They Love It 1922.29
They Love Me 1962.20
They Mean More 1912.13
They Never do That in Our Set 1905.45
They Never Hear What I Say 1983.21
They Never Proved a Thing 1969.14
They Never Tell All What They Know 1893.36
They Never Think About the Man 1910.20
They Notice it so, You Know 1891.32
They Pass by Singing 1935.13, 1983.04
They Pictured Me Like This 1907.05
They Play Those Marches, They Play Those Waltzes 1899.25
They require not words 1881.25
They Satisfy 1926.01
They say 1878.16
They Say 1924.40, 1937.11, 1970.15
They Say He Went to College 1907.34
They Say He Went to College, And 1907.15
They Say I'm Frivolous 1914.10
They Say it's Wonderful 1946.12, 1966.12, 1999.04
They say that I am growing wrinkled 1887.43
They Seek Him Here 1997.19, 1999.13
They Sill Look Good 1925.16
They Stole My Child Away 1870.20

They Talk a Different Language 1949.17
They Were All Doing the Same 1902.16
They Were Irish 1911.26
They Were Only Playing Leapfrog 1964.28
They Will Put Him in a Cell 1900.57
They Won't Know Me 1952.10
They Write the News 1985.17
They'll be Whistling it All Over Town 1917.35
They'll Have to Go 1904.52
They'll Never Take Us Alive 1993.05
They're After Me 1890.32
They're After Us 1890.29
They're All My Boys 1922.43, 1968.07
They're All My Friends 1904.42, 1907.16
They're All Sweeties 1919.15, 1919.16
They're All the Same 1944.28
They're Blaming the Charleston 1925.45
They're Either too Young or too Old 1980.29
They're Getting Away With Murder 1918.34
They're Going into Vaudeville 1901.09
They're Hot Now Up in Iceland 1928.09
They're Jazzing it Up in Heaven 1920.32
They're Looking for Me 1903.38
They're Making Them Wonderful 1920.35
They're Never Gonna Make Me Fight 1968.24
They're Not Doing That This Season 1909.28
They're Off 1933.06
They're on Their Honeymoon 1913.30
They're Playing Our Song 1979.04, 1979.13
They're so Hard to Keep When They're Beautiful 1920.18
They're Taking Him from the Jail 1897.03
They're Waiting for Me 1895.03
They've Completely Camouflaged Me 1918.13
They've Got a Lot to Learn 1963.12
They've Got Me Doing it Too 1916.24
Thief in the Night 1935.12
Thieving Coons 1905.21
Thimbleful 1953.02
Thine Alone 1917.07
Thine own sweet emblem, Princess fair, a rose without a thorn 1872.10
Things 1934.19
Things are Gonna Hum This Summer 1951.18
Things are Looking Up 1992.02
Things are Not What They Used to Be 1903.05
Things are seldom what they seem 1879.05
Things are Seldom What They Seem 1945.08
Things are Very Different Now 1890.21
Things as They Are 1972.01
Things Beyond This Earth 2000.20
Things Get Broken 1972.15
Things I Learned in High School 1982.08
Things I Learned in Jersey 1921.07
Things Left Unsaid 1911.07
Things That Happen Every Day 1907.12
Things That Lovers Say, The 1948.18
Things That We Don't Learn in School 1903.03
Things That Were Made for Love, The 1929.09
Things They Say and the Things They Do, The 1915.21
Things to Remember 1965.19
Things Unfeminine 1912.36
Things We are Not Supposed to Know 1907.11
Things We Did Last Summer, The 1974.10
Things We Pay Money to See 1918.17
Things We Think We Are, The 1968.23
Things You Must Not Do 1917.05
Things You Think are Not the Things You Say, The 1910.20
Think 1960.01
Think Beautiful 1964.44
Think Big 1987.14
Think Big Rich 1971.16
Think How it's Gonna Be 1970.09
Think it Over 1901.18, 1905.55, 1920.05, 1934.38, 1990.15
Think it Over Carefully 1908.144
Think of Me 1988.01, 1992.12
Think of My Reputation 1932.15
Think of Something Else 1966.27
Think of That 1913.37
Think of the Odds 1988.10
Think of the Time I Save 1954.05
Think Spring 1969.07
Think What Might Have Been 1886.45
Think-a-Drink 1942.14
Thinkin' 1955.27
Thinking 1965.06
Thinking Love of The 1888.13
Thinking of Me 1924.27
Thinking of No-One But Me 1986.12
Thinking of You 1925.25, 1926.12, 1927.52, 1981.03
Thinking Out Loud 1934.39
Thinking, love, of thee 1878.02
Thinking, Love, of Thee 1885.58, 1896.35
Thinky, Thanky, Thunk 1910.30
Third Degree Full Moon Union, The 1881.09
Third Letter 1994.05
Third Letter Home 1985.12
Third Thing, The 1935.16
Thirteen Daughters 1961.07
Thirties, The 1964.21
Thirty Five Summers Ago 1943.05
Thirty-One and Up 1925.48
This 'Merry' Christmas 1940.03
This Afternoon at Four 1888.02
This Amazing London Town 1970.15
This and That and the Other 1912.35
This Brave New Land 1978.19
This Can't be Love 1938.14, 1967.11, 1975.13
This Can't Go On 1992.11
This ceremonial our wish displays 1894.15
This Cornucopian Land 1970.10
This Could Go on for Years 1930.02
This Country Lad 1881.22
This Crazy Place 1985.05
This Day of Days 1997.18
This Dear Little Fellow was Cupid 1899.11
This degradation 1852.01
This degradation must I endure 1871.10
This Dream 1965.19
This Funny World 1926.51, 1975.13
This Gay Paree 1913.31
This Goes Up 1928.02
This Green Young Man from Town 1896.50
This had Better be Love 1949.12
This had Better Come to a Stop 1992.09
This Handsome Soldier is too Bold 1912.10
This hateful uniform 1880.04
This heart by woe o'ertaken 1848.04
This heart no more is mine 1861.03
This Heart of Mine 1984.10, 1999.23
This helmet, I suppose, was meant to ward off blows 1884.09
This High Horticultural College 1907.15
This House 1966.29, 1987.19
This insult rude 1881.04
This is a Changing World 1986.19
This is a Darned Fine Funeral 1961.01
This is a Famous Regiment 1870.23
This is a Great Country 1962.20
This is a Night Club 1925.25, 1925.48
This is a practical age 1890.44
This is a Tough Neighborhood 1965.01
This is All Very New to Me 1955.01
This is as Far as I Go 1944.30
This is as Good as it Gets 1993.02
This is Different Dear 1932.13
This is How I Do 1904.37
This is It 1939.13, 1943.05
This is Most Exciting 1898.73
This is My Beloved 1945.18
This is My Beloved, And 1953.16, 1978.03
This is My Busy Day 1913.06
This is My Dance 1925.36
This is My Holiday 1945.19
This is My Kind of Love 1965.35
This is My Lucky Day 1917.21, 1926.16, 1975.22
This is My Night to Howl 1943.22, 1975.13
This is My Wedding Day 1927.15
This is My World 1915.28
This is New 1941.04
This is No Place for a Good Little Girl 1911.29
This is Not a Play by Saroyan 1942.25
This is Not a Song 1934.01
This is Not Over Yet 1998.21
This is our duty plain 1884.09
This is our opportunity - 1895.29
This is Quite a Perfect Night 1956.08
This is Samurai 1990.17
This is so Nice it Must be Illegal 1943.07
This is Someone I Could Love 1972.11
This is Spring 1940.07
This is the Army 1942.20
This is the autumn of our life 1888.35
This is the Best We Ever Struck 1917.09
This is the Day 1919.16
This is the End of the Story 1946.22
This is the Existence 1916.19
This is the Hour 1897.17
This is the Life 1919.23, 1948.25, 1964.32
This is the Life for Me 1914.01
This is the Missus 1931.30
This is the Moment 1997.09
This is the Sign 1956.13
This is the Time 1918.34
This is the Way We Go to School 1971.20
This is thy deed 1844.01
This is What I Call Love 1956.16
This is What I do When I'm Angry 1978.11
This is What it Is 2000.08
This is Where I Came In 1942.01
This is Winter 1940.07
This is Worth Fighting For 1966.03
This isn't a Gentleman's War Anymore 1963.22
This isn't Me 1996.08
This Jesus Must Die 1971.12
This Kind of a Girl 1961.27
This Lady isn't Right for Me 1987.14
This Lady was Your Wife 1882.33
This Little Girl 1920.44
This Little Girl and That 1907.06
This Little Pig Went to Market 1890.16
This Little Yankee 1963.13
This morning bright and early 1881.04
This Much I Know 1956.16
This Must be the Place 1985.05
This Nearly was Mine 1949.04, 1962.17, 1993.16
This New Jerusalem 1997.12
This once my plan succeeding 1859.17
This One Day 1971.16
This One's for You 1976.34
This Really isn't Me 1959.06
This Remarkable Hilarity 1894.05
This Shouldn't Happen to a Man 1949.09
This Sleepy Old Village of Meung 1921.15
This Stewpan Bright and New 1875.15
This Thimble take 1840.03
This Time 1942.20, 1970.21
This Time it's Love 1922.33
This Time it's True Love 1963.29
This Time Next Year 1994.10
This Time of the Year 1947.03
This Time the Dream's on Me 1997.05
This Time Tomorrow 2001.06
This Town I Must Now Shake 1945.09
This was a Real Nice Clambake 1945.05
This was Just Another Day 1951.18
This was the War, What Did it do for Me and You? 1963.22
This Way Out 1941.03
This Week Americans 1965.06
This wine you say 1853.02
This Wine's All Right 1899.38
This Woman 1945.13
This Woman at the Altar 1941.04
This World 1970.20, 1974.06, 1982.20
This World is a Toy Shop 1906.37
This, Victor, I've been told 1859.09
Thistledown 1923.45
Thither the chirping cricket 1870.15
Thither, Thother, Thide of The 1973.07
Tho' Curs May Quali 1918.27
Tho' p'raps I may incur your blame 1882.78
Tho' they may not pursue me 1878.16
Tho' we are worsted 1864.22
Tho' you leave me now in sorrow 1859.01
Thorn, The 1855.01
Thoroughly Modern Millie 1974.10

Thorspring 1982.02
Those 'Come Hither' Eyes 1915.21
Those — 'Shiek-of-Araby' — Blues 1975.09
Those Awful Tattle-Tales 1914.33
Those Canaan Days 1982.03, 1993.15
Those Cats 1881.16
Those College Yells 1908.07
Those Days Gone By 1907.54
Those Days of Long Ago 1904.35, 1913.33
Those days of old 1893.02
Those Dixie Melodies 1919.26
Those Eyes 1911.03
Those Eyes so Tender 1926.33
Those Fat Monkeys 1965.39
Those Girls of Long Ago 1915.05
Those Good Old Minstrel Days 1932.08
Those Great Big Eyes 1901.25
Those Happy Days 1895.25
Those Knowing Nurses 1925.47
Those Magic Changes 1972.12, 1994.07
Those Mammy Boys 1926.11
Those Mammy Singers 1926.11
Those Oriental Blues 1921.08
Those Ragtime Melodies 1912.36
Those Seven League Boots 1913.33
Those Since I Met You Days 1919.44
Those Things Cannot be Explained 1902.16
Those Two Girls and That Boy 1927.66
Those Were Happy Days 1905.50, 1910.34
Those Were the Days 1964.29, 1990.16
Those Were the Good Old Days 1955.08, 1994.01
Those Were the Good Old Times 1899.28
Those Were the Happy Days 1910.16
Those Who Speak 1974.12
Thou art gone from my gaze 1856.01
Thou Art Mine Own One 1898.43
Thou Art the Star 1865.11, 1866.06
Thou chid by the 1861.03
Thou in might supreme 1844.01
Thou Swell 1927.56, 1943.22, 1975.13
Thou to whom my heart was given 1888.07
Thou weenst thy angel she would be - 1885.63
Thou who when Winds 1862.03
Thou, Julia, Thou has Metamorphosed Me 1971.18
Thou, My Beloved Harvest Field 1965.35
Thou, Proteus, Thou has Metamorphosed Me 1971.18
Thou, who canst all depict 1862.04
Though all the world of women fair 1895.43
Though born a man of high degree 1887.44
Though Born in Woods 1868.02
Though every hope be fled 1844.01
Though Hearts We May Secure 1913.22
Though I'm a Little Angel 1975.04
Though I'm but a little fifer now 1888.07
Though in body and in mind 1879.72
Though My Book I Seem to Scan 1881.37
Though so Excellently Wise 1881.37
Though the years have made him mellow 1897.17
Though Tongues May Wag 1938.15
Though We're Rude in Thus Intruding 1910.11
Though You May Choose 1904.01
Though, banished still I dare 1885.63
Thought of staying too long 1896.27
Thought of You, The 1954.15
Thoughtless 1943.16
Thoughts 1919.08, 1969.05, 1985.19
Thoughts of You 1925.48
Thoughts That I Wrote on the Leaves of My Heart, The 1919.06
Thoughts Will Come to Me 1980.21
Thousand and One Arabian Nights, A 1918.05
Thousand Islands Song 1947.20
Thousand Times, A 1927.43
Thousands of Miles 1949.15, 1972.06
Thousands of Trumpets 1982.08
Thousands of Years Ago 1918.34
Three B's, The 1936.05, 1941.06, 1975.13, 1983.02
Three Bad Boys 1869.43
Three Bears, The 1928.25
Three Bells, The 1981.04
Three Boxes of Longs Please 1971.13
Three Brothers 1955.19, 1958.10
Three Cheers for the Union 1930.02
Three Coins in the Fountain 1974.10
Three Cops, The 1899.29
Three Cornered Tune 1980.29
Three from Brooklyn 1992.16
Three Girls in a Boat 1943.21
Three Graces 2000.01
Three Guitars, The 1931.11
Three Huntsmen, The 1922.06
Three in Time 1955.19
Three Jolly Pigeons 2000.01
Three Legs 1972.17
Three Letters 1891.13, 1963.14
Three Little Chaps 1893.43
Three Little Columnists 1932.13
Three Little Debutantes 1939.07
Three Little Fishies 1952.11
Three Little Giggling Girls 1886.62
Three Little Girls 1924.41
Three Little Hairs 1925.50
Three Little Lambs 1899.41
Three Little Maids 1903.22, 1921.19, 1921.31, 1924.06, 1939.17, 1939.22, 1939.22
Three Little Maids from Broadway Town 1927.23
Three Little Maids from School 1885.51, 1885.70, 1928.50, 1933.27, 1938.10, 1939.15
Three little maids from school are we 1885.47
Three Little Marys 1920.23
Three Little Queens of the Silver Screen 1948.30
Three Little Sailors 1969.11
Three Little School-Girls 1928.04
Three Little Sisters 1942.16
Three Love Stories 1906.18
Three Lovers, The 1892.08
Three Loves 1944.21
Three Men in a Boat 1906.27
Three Men on a Date 1941.06
Three Mile Limit Cafe, The 1919.13
Three Million Rupees! 1881.04
Three Musketeers 1930.33
Three Musketeers of Broadway 1920.19
Three Musketeers, The 1925.17
Three New Sports in Town 1890.29
Three Nights Drunk 1963.19
Three O'Clock in the Morning 1921.27
Three of Us, The 1986.18
Three Old Ladies from Hades 1950.01
Three Paradises 1958.02
Three Questions 1946.22
Three R's, The 1937.06
Three Riddles, The 1968.08
Three Rousing Cheers 1942.01
Three Scamps, The 1892.29
Three Ships 1966.09
Three Smart Girls 1939.25
Three Stones to Stand On 1952.15
Three Sunny Rooms 1986.13
3:33 in the Morning 1900.52
Three Thousand Years Ago 1923.10
Three Times a Day 1925.14
Three Trees, The 1919.35
Three Weeks With You 1908.39, 1909.15
Three White Feathers 1939.07, 1968.19, 1986.19
Three Women to Every Man 1901.23
Three years ago 1879.21
Three's a Crowd 1947.14
Three's Company 1955.19
Three-Five-Zero-Zero 1968.11, 1977.15
Thrice Happy the Wooing 1895.25
Thrice Noble is He 1904.30
Thrifty Little Mabel 1911.01
Thrill is Gone, The 1931.30, 1999.09
Thrill Me 1932.16
Thrill of a Kiss, The 1928.48
Thrill of First Love 1992.09
Thrill's All Over Again, The 1935.19
Throttle Throttlebottom 1933.25
Through a Key Hole 1933.22
Through All Eternity 1905.33
Through all my life 1845.01
Through all the employments of life 1854.06
Through All the Employments of Life 1750.01, 1957.02
Through the Bamboo 1925.04
Through the Jungles Strong 1877.25, 1879.03
Through the night 1880.04
Through the Night 1927.64
Through the Parthless Forest Drear 1868.02
Through the woods 1880.54
Through the world thou wilt fly, love 1844.01
Through the Years 1932.03
Through These Portals Pass the Most Beautiful Girls in the World 1935.04
Throw a Petal 1961.07
Throw aside all sorrow 1862.04
Throw Dirt 1953.12
Throw Her in High 1923.18
Throw Him Down, McCloskey 1896.39
Throw it Out the Window 1930.42
Throw Me a Kiss 1922.19, 1923.20
Throw Me a Rose 1916.19
Throw That Girl Around 1999.24
Throw the Anchor Away 1954.02
Throwing a Party 1932.01
Throwing the Bull 1919.01
Thrush and the Star, The 1907.10
Thunder and Lightning 1998.08
Thunder Dance 1927.65
Thunder, The 1987.19
Thunderstorm 2000.05
Thunderstorm Jazz 1923.08
Thurio's Samba 1971.18
Thursday 1939.14
Thursday's My Jonah Day 1907.25
Thus Gamesters United in Friendship are found 1750.01
Thus I stand like the Turk, with his Doxies around 1750.01
Thus love doth bind us firm together 1834.03
Thus Spake Zarathustra 1977.09
Thus the gauntlet down I throw 1859.16
Thus when a good Huswife sees a Rat 1750.01
Thus when the Swallow, seeking Prey 1750.01
Thy Dear Eyes 1891.15
Thy Heart is My Prize 1915.28
Thy Mouth is a Rose 1913.31
Thy Subjects are We 1900.25
Thy Thought, My Thought 1912.04
Thy Will Pardon Me for Wishing 1888.19
Ti Moune 1990.12
Ti Tiro Mai 1972.20
Ti Voglio Bene 1982.09
Tic, Tac 1884.57
Tick Tack Toe 1904.02
Tick Tock 1970.13
Tick, Tick, Tick of the Ticker, The 1922.07
Tick-a-Tack-aTack 1892.29
Tick-a-Tick 1914.28
Tick-Tick 1916.12
Tick-Tock 1977.09
Ticket Speculators, The 1910.19
Ticket to the Promised Land, A 1986.11
Tickets, Please! 1950.09
Ticketyboo 1942.27
Tickle Me 1920.27, 1926.11
Tickling the Ivories 1927.37
Tidbits from the Plays 1902.19
Tiddelee Tot 1924.31
Tiddle De Um, La 1905.47
Tiddle de Winks 1922.21
Tiddly om Pom 1907.41
Tide Pool, The 1955.27
Tie a Red Ribbon on Me 1910.25
Tie a String Around Your Finger 1924.02
Tie Song 1912.35
Tie Your Cares to a Melody 1930.14
Tied to Mother's Apron Strings 1891.32
Tiempos han cambiado, Los 1969.11
Tientos 1986.17
Tiffany Girl 1915.17
Tiffin, Tiffin 1921.20
Tiger in His Lair, The 1897.21
Tiger Lily 1948.14
Tiger Lily-Lou 1924.41
Tiger Love 1910.29
Tiger of Tangaree, The 1892.42
Tiger! Tiger! 1972.21

Tiger, Tiger 1966.18
Tigers' Chorus, The 1883.52
Tight Knit Family, A 1992.09
Tight Rope Walker, The 1902.08
Til the Big Fat Moon Falls Down 1958.20
'Til the Season Comes 'Round Again 1998.19
Till Good Luck Comes My Way 1927.67, 1994.08
Till Him 2001.05
Till I Come Home to You 1918.14
Till I Met You 1929.46
Till My Luck Comes Rolling Along 1922.43
'Till on my venture bold 1887.04
Till the Clouds Roll By 1917.06, 1986.01
Till the Day of My Majority 1903.21
Till the End of Time 1924.05
Till the Liberty Bell Rings Out 1918.10
Till the Light Fades 1890.33
Till the Real Thing Comes Along 1931.11
Till the Volunteers Return 1902.44
Till Then 1969.06
Till There was You 1957.18, 2000.11
Till Tomorrow 1959.25
Till We Meet Again 1877.22, 1894.31
Till We Reach That Day 1998.01
Till You Try 1916.05
Tiller Girls, The 1924.36
Tiller, Foster, Hoffman, Hale and Albertina Rasch 1929.29
Tillie of Longacre Square 1925.27
Tillie Titwillow 1916.03
Tim's Songs and Jokes 1895.44
Time 1958.10, 1979.12
Time After Time 1974.10, 2000.16
Time Ain't Very Long 1927.32
Time and a Half for Overtime 1924.02
Time and Tide 1896.15
Time and Time Again 1935.13, 1942.35
Time Brings About a Change 1972.13
Time for Jukin 1939.24
Time for Love 1926.03
Time for Singing, A 1966.09
Time for Tea 1952.09
Time for the King 1910.03
Time has Changed so Many Customs in the Last Decade 1912.20
Time has come, The 1887.44
Time Heals Everything 1974.18, 1985.19, 1988.08, 1998.07
Time in a Bottle 1997.01
Time is a Gypsy 1934.01
Time is an Ocean 1998.02
Time is Flying 1904.52, 1913.37
Time is Money 1897.25
Time is Not Right, The 1993.04
Time is Now, The 1960.12, 1965.30
Time is Ripe for Loving, The 1976.33
Time is Standing Still 1941.12
Time Marches On 1936.02, 1936.17
Time of Day 1980.29
Time of Dolls is Past, The 1910.24
Time of Our Life, The 1972.21
Time of Your Life 1941.03
Time of Your Life, The 1996.08
Time on My Hands 1930.39
Time Passed Her By 1982.23
Time Stands Still 1948.18
Time Step 1960.07
Time there was when earthly joy 1893.02
Time to Let Go 1968.08
Time to Love, The 1903.39
Time to Sing 1941.09
Time to Take a Drink 1920.31
Time Warp 1975.08
Time Warp, The 2000.17
Time was, when Love and I were well acquainted 1879.10
Time Wasted 1923.23
Time will come, The 1870.20
Time Will Come, The 1894.45
Time Will Tell 1922.31
Time, Oh, Time 1914.03
Time, the Place and the Girl, The 1905.57
Time-Clock Slaves 1923.45
Timely Topics 1898.70
Times are Gettin' Hard, Boys 1963.19
Times Have Changed 1969.11
Times Square 1922.45
Times Square Arguments, The 1915.02
Times Square Ballet 1971.15, 1998.16
Times up to now, to the gate 1877.39
Timid and Graceful 1880.69
Timid Bird 1884.57
Timid Frieda 1972.16
Timing 1985.05
Timothy D. Sullivan Chowder Party, The 1899.19
Tin Gee Gee, The 1900.44
Tin Pan Alley 1953.17
Tin Wedding Whistle 1973.08
Ting Tang Kee 1904.18
Ting-a-Ling 1915.17, 1925.45
Ting-a-Ling Dearie 1963.20
Ting-a-ling-a-ling 1920.37
Ting-a-Ling-a-Ling Ping Pong 1905.37
Tinker Song, The 1944.25
Tinker, Tailor 1907.32
Tinkers' Song, The 1891.29, 1929.43
Tinkle Tune 1923.36
Tinkle-inkle-inkle 1918.12
Tinkle-Tinkle 1929.29
Tiny Room 1948.08
Tiny Touch, A 1913.04
Tip Top Toreador 1920.47
Tip Your Hat 1938.01
Tip Your Hat to Hatty 1919.44
Tip Your Hat to the American Millionairess 1912.15
Tip Your Hat to Uncle Sammy 1905.32
Tip-a-Top 1912.04
Tip-Toe 1919.07
Tip-Toe Tip-Tap 1929.26
Tip-Toes 1925.49
Tip-Top 1920.36
Tipferl aus dem I, Das 1880.60
Tippecanoe 1902.15
Tipperary 1907.34
Tipperary Nora 1906.29
Tippy Tippy Toes 1960.22
Tips 1903.33, 1982.04
Tips of Gay Paree, The 1900.38
Tipsey Song, The 1871.16
Tipsy Swell and the Messenger Boy, The 1908.15
Tiptoe 1911.39
Tira a Campa 1964.03
Tirade, The 1954.03
Tirana, La 1917.25, 1917.33
Tired Business Man, The 1920.01
Tired of it All 1928.41
Tired of Love 1930.25
Tired of the South 1935.11
Tirollallero 1964.03
Tirrallallera 1964.03
'Tis a Glorious Thing to Plot 1888.38
'Tis a gossip too 1887.04
'Tis a Shame I Declare 1860.03
'Tis a Very Ticklish Question 1888.19
Tis an Irish Girl I Love, and She's Just Like You 1912.06
'Tis Astounding 1906.01
Tis Better to Have Loved and Lost Than Never to Have Loved at All 1902.02
Tis Boulotte 1875.19
'Tis done! I am a bride! 1888.35
'Tis Dreadful 1906.01
'Tis Eventide 1897.48
'Tis for a Land of Roses 1888.19
'Tis gone - the past was all a dream 1844.01
'Tis hard to put the hand 1864.13
'Tis He! 1881.36
Tis I Alone Can Tell 1884.28,
'Tis I Alone Can Tell 1885.08
'Tis I! 1884.57
Tis in Vain That I Try to Forget You 1920.15
'Tis Joy to Meet 1882.33
Tis Love 1927.55
'Tis Love has Caused All Mortal Trouble 1881.11
'Tis most perplexing 1888.07
Tis Noon of Tropic Day 1909.04
'Tis Not on Hills 1880.47
'Tis Oanita 1868.02
Tis of Thee 1940.18
Tis Pity, Tis True 1976.03
Tis Sad to Leave 1934.17
'Tis Sad to Leave a Business Grand 1845.01
'Tis sad to leave our fatherland 1844.01
'Tis Sad to Love in Vain 1895.06
'Tis shameful thus to treat you 1877.20
'Tis she! A happy fate 1878.16
'Tis she! Mystery stranger 1888.07
Tis Summer 1912.30
'Tis the Borgia 1873.05
Tis the End 1915.30
'Tis the harp in the air 1848.04
'Tis the Hour 1904.51
Tis the Luck of the Irish 1948.21
'Tis the Spirit Not the Letter 1896.10
'Tis Time 1879.42
'Tis Time to Say Good Night 1880.38
'Tis Twelve, I think 1879.10
'Tis Very Awkward 1882.33
'Tis very hard to choose 1895.26
'Tis Woman that seduces all Mankind 1750.01
'Tis woman that seduces all mankind 1854.06
Tis Woman That Seduces All Mankind 1957.02
Tis You I Love 1902.02
Tisket a Tax It, A 1939.19
Tisket, A-Tasket, A 1997.01
Tit for Tat 1888.28
Tit Willow 1886.11
Tit, Tat, Toe 1876.32
Titina 1924.36, 1925.05, 1925.10, 1925.24
Titled Widows All are We 1894.45
Titles 1908.19
Titsy Bitsy Girl, The 1908.25
Tittle Tattle 1904.55
Titwillow 1939.15, 1939.17
Tizan 1904.17
Tkambuzza 1965.32
TNT 1946.24
To a slow and stately measure 1882.63
To a Small Boy Standing on My Shoes While I am Wearing Them 1973.08
To Adjust is a Must 1957.17
To America 1986.13
To Anacreon in Heav'n 1976.11
To and Fro 1895.08
To Arms 1906.49
To Arms! 1879.15
To Arms! Hear the Cry 1904.50
To arms! To arms! 1886.49
To be a Captain 1997.06
To be a Little Singing Girl 1899.34
To be a Lone Widow 1891.11
To be a Soldier 1983.03
To be Able to Feel 1975.01
To be Alone With You 1964.33
To be an Actor 1907.40, 1908.12
To be Artistic 1967.14
To be Beautiful 1905.02
To be Continued 1910.20
To be or Not to Be 1933.22
To be or Not to be in Love 1955.12
To be Together is the Thing 1919.31
To be Truly Refined 1902.43
To be With Thee 1902.03
To be Worthy of You 1919.36
To bed so soon, Good night 1887.44
To Blazassus 1907.55
To Bring Up a Girl 1909.28
To Call Thee Mine 1903.36
To Day 1899.29
To Death: a Valentine 1956.09
To Die of Love 1974.19
To do What We Like 1938.19
To Drik We Have No Fear 1907.05
To Dwell Beside Us Evermore 1882.18
To Each His Dulcinea 1965.34
To Educate These Young Ladies 1881.11
To Erminie 1886.30
To Every Man His Dreams 1965.34
To Find a Lover 1999.22
To Follow Every Fancy 1916.06

To Get Out of This World Alive 1968.02
To Go Upon the Stage 1945.09
To Have and to Hold 1919.07, 1947.17
To Hear You Say My Name 2001.06
To Heidelberg, Beloved Vision of My Heart 1980.21
To help unhappy commoners 1890.02
To Horse 1944.28
To Hunt the Stag 1881.22
To Keep My Love Alive 1943.22, 1975.13
To Keep You in Your Seats 1921.32
To Know You is to Love You 1928.36
To Life 1964.27
To Live Another Summer, to Pass Another Winter 1971.14
To Live is to Love 1937.17
To London 1913.02
To Look Upon My Love 1961.26
To Love is to Serve 1995.04
To Love You 1919.36
To Make the Boy a Man 1975.06
To Make Them Beautiful Ladies 1922.15
To Make Them Fall 1919.33
To Marry a Millionaire 1901.21
To marry, or not to marry 1898.25
To Me, You're Beautiful 1990.16
To Measure the Darkness 1986.18
To My Daughter 1970.01
To My Judicial Mind 1894.33
To My Love Ever True 1896.50
To My Valentine 1973.08
To My Wife 1954.15
To our flag! 1880.04
To our Governor we sing 1880.04
To Our Homes We'll Go 1906.06
To Our Leafy Haunts We Go 1881.27
To Paradise We'll Gaily Trip 1915.18
To Paris 1913.32
To Pillage and to death 1846.01
To Portsmouth 1963.28
To Prove My Love 1941.07
To Rent, to Let 1913.37
To See Thee 1886.15
To sell my Daughter to a Bird 1877.20
To Sleep 1892.14
To Song and Dance 1886.15
To Spain, said my husband 1895.26
To Spring 1944.21
To Stop a Marriage 1902.20
To Sunlight, Love and Song 1887.33
To te quiero 1917.25
To the Barracks We Have Come 1894.33
To the Beat of the Heart 1934.01
To the Cave Away 1899.21
To the Dead of Family Wars 1978.11
To the End of the World Together 1904.04
To the Fair 1924.34
To the Garden 1969.02
To the Girl You Dance With 1921.33
To the Guard House 1904.05
To the Inn We're Marching 1924.45, 1980.21
To the Island 1903.14
To the King's Court 1864.12
To the Land of Let's Pretend 1914.18
To the Land of My Own Romance 1911.38
To the Market 1848.03
To the Mountain 1857.04
To the mountains away 1838.01
To the One We Love Best 1909.06
To the Paris Exposition 1901.19
To the People 1972.01
To the Public Square Repairing 1875.19
To the Pyramid 1895.33
To the Races 1928.04
To the Regiment We'll Go 1908.29
To the Ship 1954.13
To the Sound of the Pipe and the Roll of the Drum 1903.37
To the Strains of the Wedding March 1911.08
To the Top 1966.30
To thee my Queen 1880.04
To Thee We Cry 1890.19
To thee whose wisdom is the guiding star 1855.06
To This We've Come 1950.05
To Touch the Sky 1971.01, 1972.23
To War! 1938.11
To wed the fairest of Princesses 1890.11
To Whit, to Who 1885.03
To Whit, to Whoo 1886.62
To Whom it May Concern 1938.15
To Whom it May Concern Me 1971.18
To You Ladies 1884.57
To You, Sir Miles 1904.01
To-Day 1904.01
To-Day is the Day 1918.02
To-day we'll dance 1887.04
To-day, To-day 1881.07, 1881.17
To-Morrow 1886.62, 1900.58, 1907.55
To-morrow will be Market Day 1863.03
To-Morrow! 1892.08
To-morrow, To-morrow 1854.05
To-Night's the Night 1902.35, 1911.35, 1914.32
Toast 1919.41
Toast of the Boys at the Post, The 1941.13
Toast of Vienna, The 1935.12
Toast Song 1902.43
Toast to All Colleges, A 1955.13
Toast to Alpha Cholera, A 1947.08
Toast to Michigan, A 1955.13
Toast to the Bride, A 1961.14
Toast to the King of War, A 1908.26
Toast to the Moon, A 1903.19
Toast to the Players, A 1968.22
Toast to Volstead, A 1929.45
Toast to Women's Eyes, A 1915.18
Toast, A 1909.19
Toast, a toast, A 1877.23
Tobacco Blues, The 1950.01
Tobasco March 1894.22
Tobermory 1928.05
Toboggan Slide, The 1887.07
Toby 1947.10
Today 4 U 1996.09
Today at Your House, Tomorrow at Mine 1951.17
Today I am a Glamour Girl 1940.09
Today I is so Happy 1945.13
Today I Met the Boy I'm Gonna Marry 1985.03
Today I Saw a Rose 1969.01
Today is a Day for a Band to Play 1965.29
Today is Spring 1918.25
Today we meet, my baby bride and I 1884.09
Today Will be Yesterday Tomorrow 1944.14
Today's the Day 1974.26
Todder side of Jordan 1873.05
Toddle Along 1925.10, 1925.24
Toddle Go the Girls 1911.01
Toddle Quartette 1921.36
Toddle Top Whirl, The 1921.35
Toddle Trot 1925.27
Toddler's Ball 1918.02
Toddlin' Along 1930.06
Toddling Along 1921.11
Toddling the Todalo 1911.05
Toddy's the Drink for Me 1938.06
Together 1967.11, 1974.17, 1974.26, 1978.02, 1978.28
Together Forever 1966.29
Together, Wherever We Go 1959.13
Togetherness 1960.07, 1962.02
Toi c'est moi 1935.19
Toi qui connais les Hussards de la garde 1922.06
Toi, qui me trouvais autrefois 1887.36
Tokay 1929.41
Tokio 1905.53
Tokio Blues 1924.44
Toledo Glide, The 1910.33
Tom Big Bay 1879.64
Tom Boy, Tom Boy 1910.09
Tom Mahoney 1904.07
Tom Tom 1922.38, 1927.31
Tom, Dick or Harry 1948.32, 1999.19
Tom, Tom 1971.20
Tom, Tom, the Piper's Son 1866.31
Tom, Tom, Toddle 1920.38
Tomi Tomi 1912.03
Tommy 1918.31
Tommy and Me 1903.09
Tommy Atkins 1920.24
Tommy Atkins on a Dress-Parade 1912.46
Tommy Atkins, You're All Right 1908.14
Tommy can you hear me 1972.08
Tommy Can You Hear Me 1993.06
Tommy was a Bad, Bad Boy 1900.08
Tommy Won't You Teach Me How to Tango 1913.36
Tommy's holiday camp 1972.08
Tommy's Holiday Camp 1993.06
Tommy, Tommy 1960.19
Tomorrow 1909.06, 1919.07, 1925.04, 1925.16, 1925.32, 1938.13, 1940.18, 1976.01, 1977.06
Tomorrow Belongs to Me 1966.24, 1998.04
Tomorrow I'm Gonna be Old 1978.10
Tomorrow is a Lovely Day 1940.08
Tomorrow is St. Valentine's Day 1981.02
Tomorrow is the Time 1946.20
Tomorrow Morning 1959.11, 1968.01
Tomorrow Mountain 1946.24
Tomorrow Will be the Same 1970.12
Tomorrow's Another Day 1924.36
Tomtit and the Nightingale, The 1897.17
Ton Grandpere est le soleil 1999.22
Tona 1992.15
Tondelayo 1924.31, 1929.22
Tongo Dance, The 1912.02
Tongola Dance Music 1943.10
Tonight 1931.28, 1933.01, 1957.12, 1962.17, 1974.22, 1991.10
Tonight at Eight 1963.14
Tonight at the Mardi Gras 1940.08
Tonight May Never Come Again 1933.03
Tonight or Never 1930.14, 1931.26, 1941.02
Tonight We Love 1940.16
Tonight You are in Paree 1951.13
Tonight's the Night 1919.01, 1980.11, 1992.02
Tonight's the Night With You 1936.12
Tony Caponi 1911.34
Tony from America 1911.39
Tony Hernandez 1998.02
Tony Sarg 1919.18
Tony the Peddler 1903.37
Tony, Tony, Tony 1927.55
Too a roi-oor a Loi-a 1908.11
Too Bad 1927.36, 1955.02
Too Blue 1927.15
Too Charming 1964.33
Too clever by half 1895.32
Too Close for Comfort 1956.02, 1989.21
Too Darn Hot 1948.32, 1999.19
Too Fresh 1888.44
Too Good for the Average Man 1936.05, 1983.02
Too Good to be Bad 1993.02
Too Good to be True 1928.36
Too Late 1859.09, 1891.36
Too Late, Daddy 1992.08
Too Little Time for Love 1958.04
Too Long from Long Acre Square 1908.31
Too Many Boys 1922.39
Too Many Cooks 1914.10
Too Many Girls 1939.27
Too Many Miles from Broadway 1901.07, 1904.20
Too Many Mirrors 1978.25
Too Many Mornings 1971.05
Too Many Old Ideas 1972.21
Too Many Rings Around Rosie 1925.30, 1971.03
Too Many Tomorrows 1966.01
Too Marvelous for Words 1980.08, 1984.10, 1990.09, 1997.05
Too Much in Love to Care 1994.10
Too Much to Forgive 1972.24
Too Much Trouble 1951.17
Too Much Work 1934.03
Too Much World 1975.05
Too Nice a Day to Go to School 1947.08
Too Particular 1914.32
Too Ra, Loo Ra, Loo Ra, Ly, That's an Irish Lullaby 1914.05
Too Soon 1962.05
Too Tall 1924.33
Too whit, too whoo 1880.18
Too Young to Live 1959.23
Too Young to Love 1922.03

Too, too, Too! 1936.12
Too-Ral-I-Oo-Ral-I-Ay 1910.20
Too-re-loo-re 1917.07
Too-Whoo 1903.40
Toodle 'oo! 1918.33
Toodle Oddle Um 1920.42
Toodle Oo 1923.42
Toodle-oo 1923.45
Toodle-Oo 1927.05
Toodle-oodle-oodle on Your Piccolo 1912.13
Toot Toot Tootsie Goodbye 1962.17
Toot, Toot, the Fog Horn Gay 1910.11
Toot, Toot, Tootsie! Goodbye 1921.34
Toot-Toot! 1918.09
Tooth and Claw 1946.24
Toothache, The 1871.19
Tootle, Tootle 1896.48
Tootsie Wootsie 1913.02
Top Banana 1951.23
Top Banana Ballet 1951.23
Top Hat, White Tie and Tails 1979.13, 1989.16, 1992.18
Top of the Hill, The 1968.30, 1983.14
Top of the Morning, The 1910.08
Top of the Sky 1993.19
Top of the Train 1968.05
Topers Fling Your Glasses Aside 1904.01
Topical Lines and Nursery Rhymes 1888.15
Topics of the Day 1922.38
Topple Down 1929.50
Topsy 2000.07
Topsy Turvy 1919.44
Topsy-Turvy 1899.39
Toque 1986.17
Torch Parade 1934.35
Torch Singer, The 1934.18, 1934.42
Torch Song 1932.05
Torch Song, The 1931.40
Torch Songs 1953.17
Toreador 1905.40
Toreador am I, The 1898.41
Toreador's Song 1902.01
Toreador, Le 1970.01
Toreador, The 1921.28
Toreadors, I see you're ready 1888.18
Torerito 1917.33
Torerito Torerazo 1917.25
Tornado Ballet 1975.01
Torpedo and the Whale, The 1880.69, 1881.16, 1881.17
Torpedo Till 1907.28
Tortured Thomas Cat, The 1904.09
Toscanini Stokowski and Me 1940.07
Tosy and Cosh 1965.31
Tot's Lullaby 1880.21, 1881.10
Totem Tom Tom 1975.22
Totem Tom-Tom 1924.28
Tou Mi Mi 1999.22
Tou-la-ou 1886.33
Touages, Les 1964.39
Touch a Hand 1976.24
Touch and Go 1967.16
Touch Me in the Morning 1976.16
Touch Me With My Clothes On 1979.19
Touch of a Woman's Hand, The 1917.36
Touch of Class, A 1974.10
Touch of Magic 1934.32
Touch of Spring, A 1914.26
Touch of the Irish, A 1989.23
Touch of Your Hand, The 1933.26
Touch Touch 1977.01
Touch-A-Touch-A-Touch Me 2000.17
Touched in the Head and Smitten in the Heart 1937.07
Tough, The 1886.28
Toughest in de Place 1899.33
Toujours 1898.63
Toujours Gai 1957.05
Toujours la Politesse 1909.07
Toujours y love you 1929.15
Tour Must Go On, The 1951.13
Tourists 1916.05
Tourists' March 1880.38, 1882.76
Tourists' Parade 1880.38
Tourists, The 1905.30
Tout cela pour les hommes 1929.11
Tout est bien conclu 1885.56
Tout jamais, A 1965.30
Tout jeune encore 1885.56
Tout Suite 1919.10
Toute a l'heure, A 1964.22
Towards the empyrean heights of every kind of love 1884.09
Tower of Babble 1976.17
Tower of Babel 1992.05
Tower Warders, under orders 1888.35
Town and Country 1897.40
Town and Country Mouse, The 1903.22
Town Crier's Song 1913.25
Town Folks Will be Pleased, The 1900.47
Town Girl, The 1923.35
Town Hall Tonight 1926.07
Town House Maxixe, The 1958.14
Town of It, The 1932.12
Town That Grows Where the Hudson Flows, The 1913.19
Town Topics 1915.23
Townsfolk's Lament, The 1982.14
Toy Clog Dance 1917.26
Toy Dance 1919.03
Toy Monkey, The 1896.27
Toy of Destiny 1924.32
Toy Shoppe, The 1998.19
Toy Soldier 1927.31
Toy Soldiers' March and Military Ball 1903.31
Toy Soldiers, The 1916.24
Toy, The 1896.27
Toyland 1903.31, 1924.18, 1929.48, 1968.13, 1980.27
Toymakers Shop, The 1903.31
Tra Gog Vo In Dein Whole 1978.11
Tra la la 1937.11
Tra La La 1956.13
Tra la la La 1903.14
Tra-la-La 1904.50
Tra-La-La 1907.63
Tra-la-la 1922.10
Tra-la-la, etcetera 1910.31
Tra-la-la-la-la 1925.05
Tra-La-Li 1911.34
Tra-ra-ra Boom-de-ay! 1891.38
Track Down This Murderer 1988.01
Tracks of My Tears, The 1997.21
Tract, The 1909.01
Trade del Corpus, La 1926.35
Trading Solos 1986.18
Tradition 1964.27, 1989.03
Tradition That was Destroyed: Hasidic Medley, The 1971.14
Traffic Island 1964.29
Traftz 1948.04
Tragedy 1999.15
Trail Along 1912.42
Trailing a Shooting Star 1930.30
Trailways Bus 1998.02
Train and the River, The 1958.12
Train du reve, Le 1934.32, 1935.19
Train That Leaves for Town, The 1918.37
Train to Johannesburg 1949.15, 1972.06
Train With the Cushioned Seats, The 1953.02
Train, The 1949.08, 1990.16
Tramp o'er Moss and Fen 1880.24
Tramp, Tramp, Tramp 1910.35, 1978.19, 1988.18
Trample Your Troubles 1928.07
Trampling on Life 1939.26
Tramps and Scamps 1900.37
Tranquilizers 1960.12
Trans-Mag-Ni-Fi-Can-Bam-Dam-U-Ality 1930.16
Transaction, The 1991.03
Transformation 1994.04
Transformation Polka 1866.18
Transformation, The 1997.09, 2001.09
Transplanted Shamrock, A 1896.39
Transport of Delight, A 1959.20
Trasting now to my own invention 1859.17
Trav'lin All Alone 1931.09
Travel the Road of Love 1959.12
Travel, Travel, Little Star 1910.02
Travel, Travel, Travel 1925.40, 1948.24
Travel-On 1927.13
Traveler and the Pie, The 1903.03, 1904.13, 1904.44
Travelin' Blues 1999.06
Traveling Light 1950.17
Traveling Man, The 1887.29
Traveling Show 1963.27
Travellin' 1930.19
Travelling Circus, The 1924.48
Travelling Man 1942.30
Travesty Opera 1919.19
Treason 1942.30
Treasure Hunt, The 1927.12
Treasure Island 1920.39
Treasure Island Trio 1978.12
Treasure of a Girl, A 1912.31
Treasurer's Song, The 1893.17
Treat a Woman Like a Drum 1945.11
Treat Me Nice 1989.12, 1995.03
Treat Me Rough 1930.31
Tree in the Park, A 1926.50
Tree of Life, The 1965.17
Tree That Grows in Brooklyn, A 1944.14
Tree Top Toddle 1929.50
Tree, The 1930.20, 1970.20, 1997.18
Treemonisha in Peril 1975.19
Treemonisha's Bringing Up 1975.19
Treemonisha's Return 1975.19
Trelawney No. 1 1965.31
Trelawny 1899.17
Trembling Lips 1880.51
Tremont Avenue Cruisewear Fashion Show, The 1973.11
Trench Fantasy, A 1918.10
Trenck is My Name 1912.10
Trepak 1947.14
Tres Moutarde 1983.09
Treublich ich stets 1885.01
Trial 1980.14, 1982.17
Trial Before Pilate 1971.12
Trial by Jury 1945.08
Trial of the Rumseller, The 1893.30
Trial Song 1929.46
Trial, The 1952.15, 1960.19
Trials and Tribulations 1978.25
Trials of a Simple Maid 1903.34
Triangle 1927.11
Triangle, The 1915.01
Tribes 1972.09
Tricks 1905.20, 1973.02
Tricks of the Trade 1895.08, 1924.10
Tricky Little Sarah 1897.26, 1897.54
Tried by the Centre Court 1959.20
Trifle Not With Love 1891.36
Trilby O'Farrell 1895.36
Trim Little Phoebe 1881.07, 1882.20
Trim Them All But the One You Love 1925.07
Trina's Song 1992.09
Trink 1953.10
Trink's Narration 1989.09
Trio 1892.08, 1924.20, 1950.16, 1951.24, 1990.17, 1994.05
Trio des Cancans 1929.14
Triomphal 1884.08
Trip Abroad, A 1915.20
Trip Around the Town, A 1896.18
Trip Around the World 1929.50
Trip Doesn't Care at All, A 1949.01
Trip Through My Mind, A 1972.19
Trip to Bermuda, A 1912.46
Trip to Coontown, A 1898.22
Trip to the Library, A 1963.14
Tripartite Intervention and the Atami House Conspiracy 1997.16, 1998.08
Triple Sec 1930.18
Triplets 1937.16, 1972.05, 1999.23
Tripping hither, tripping thither 1882.78
Tripping the Light Fantastic 1952.10
Tritt man bei Ninon an 1885.01
Triumph 1857.06
Triumph March 1903.36
Triumph of Love, The 1915.23
Triumphant Entry of Hans 1910.24

Triumphant Youth 1914.03
Trois Cloches, Les 1981.04
Trois joli's fillettes 1887.36
Trojan Horse, The 1930.08
Trolley Line, The 1905.33
Trolley Song, The 1967.11, 1974.22, 1989.23, 1999.23
Trombone Cholly 1975.20
Trombone Jazz 1918.20
Trooper's Song, The 1894.28
Trooper's the Pride of the Ladies, The 1882.50
Trop, De 1901.21, 1912.46
Tropic Vamps 1921.23
Tropical Moon 1907.28, 1930.24
Tropicana Rhumba 1988.20
Tropics 1944.31, 1946.03
Trot Here and There 1905.46
Trot, Trot, Trot! 1894.28
Trot-i-ty Trot 1909.14
Trottin' to the Fair 1952.05
Trottin' to the Land of Cotton Melodies 1924.37
Trou-Trou-ba-ba-Troubadour 1910.31
Troubadours 1902.18
Trouble 1925.40, 1975.20, 1995.03
Trouble Man 1949.15, 1972.06
Trouble Tree, The 1907.26
Trouble With Women, The 1943.19
Trouble With You, The 1989.07
Trouble's a Bubble 1925.01
Trouble's a Ruler 1973.02
Trouble, Trouble 1944.32
Troubles 1955.03
Troubles of the Reuben and the Maid 1902.24
Troubles With Love 1891.03
Trousse chemise 1974.19
Trousseau Ball, The 1919.06
Trousseau Incomplete, The 1921.06
Trousseau Waltz 1919.06
Trovatore 1896.05
Trovatore, Il 1922.22
Truckers Ball 1936.30
Truckin' 1980.10
Truckin' in My Tails 1935.18
Trudging through the Wet and Dirt 1877.20
True as Steel 1892.29
True Blue 1886.45, 1906.13, 1909.11, 1928.41
True Blue Sal 1919.18
True Daughters of Old Uncle Sam 1897.33, 1900.24
True Hearts 1925.08
True Irish Girl, The 1907.35
True Love 1879.15, 1880.25, 1892.08, 1920.32, 1925.01, 1998.05
True Love from o'er the Sea 1882.75
True Love is Not for a Day 1902.04
True Love Lives But in Our Dreams 1904.05
True Love Must be Single-Hearted 1881.37
True Love Ways 1990.15
True Love Will Find a Way 1914.25
True Romance 1957.05
True to Me 1918.28
True to my troth 1890.33
True to Two 1927.20
Truffaldino's Sausage Shop 2000.10
Truffle Song 1882.70
Truly Blessed 1990.05
Truly Refined 1902.43
Truly, Truly 1896.51
Trumpet Call, The 1892.08
Trumpet's call, The 1882.44
Trumpeteer and the Lover, The 1932.03
Trumpeter, Blow Your Golden Horn 1931.48
Truscalina Brown 1895.03
Truss Dance 1999.02
Trust me 1868.01
Trust Me 1979.15, 1995.15
Trusting Above 1896.50
Truth 1950.10, 1961.02
Truth Cannot be Treason 1975.04
Truth in the Well 1882.75
Truth is so Beautiful 1910.05
Truth Must Come Out Some Day, The 1913.23
Truth Reigns Supreme 1920.26
Truth, The 1879.50, 1962.27
Try a Little Tenderness 1997.21
Try Again 1918.37
Try Again Tomorrow 1928.02
Try Again, Johnnie 1902.30
Try and be Home When the Clock Strikes Nine 1885.69
Try Dancing 1929.49
Try Her Out at Dancing 1928.29
Try Me 1963.14
Try This on Your Pianna, Anna 1911.05
Try to Forget 1931.37
Try to Learn to Love 1928.42
Try to Love Me 1958.08
Try we life long 1890.02
Try, Try Again 1902.40
Trying it On 1910.34
Trying on Dresses 1906.45
Trying to Get the Feeling Again 1991.10
Trysting Tree, The 1884.57, 1909.29
Tschaikowski 1940.12
Tschaikowsky 1941.04
Tschiakowsky 1963.10
Tsen Azeyger 1970.17
Tsen Kopikes 1998.11
Tsin 1920.28
Tsing-la-la 1944.16
Tsipele 1960.18
Tsu Mayn Dor 1970.17
Tu eres ese 1969.11
Tu Me Fais Tourner Ma Tete 1981.04
Tu ne comprends donc rien de rien 1886.09
Tu Reviendras 1950.05
Tu Sais 1932.19
Tu Solo Tu 1988.15
Tu te laisses aller 1965.30
Tu vas m'ecouta 1884.43
Tu Way Pocky Way 1992.06
Tu-Lo-Zo-Lu 1924.31
Tuba Man 1966.03
Tubular Bells 1982.22
Tulip Time 1913.16, 1919.15
Tulip Time in Sing Sing 1948.16
Tulips With Your Color so Bright 1912.30
Tumble El Toro 1919.11
Tumble Inn 1919.30
Tumbrel Song, The 1965.39
Tune in to J O Y 1924.19
Tune They Croon in the U.S.A., The 1915.18
Tune They Plug, The 1920.43
Tune Up 1996.09
Tune You Can't Forget, The 1918.30
Tunes for the Million 1861.04
Tunnel of Love 1997.17
Tunnel of Love Chase 1964.44
Tur i-ad-i-lum, or Santa Claus has Come 1879.68
Turk has the Right Idea, The 1920.07
Turkey and the Turk, The 1900.55
Turkey Gobbler's Ball 1911.24
Turkey Lurkey Time 1968.31
Turkey Trot 1911.13, 1911.17
Turkey Trot, The 1912.29
Turkish Love Song 1910.30
Turkish Trottishness 1913.17
Turn About 1884.57
Turn Around 1978.22
Turn Back, O Man 1976.17
Turn Herbert's Face to the Wall, Mother 1942.14
Turn Me Loose on Broadway 1952.20
Turn My Little Millwheel 1952.04
Turn Not Away 1939.21
Turn Off Your Light, Mr. Moon-Man 1911.13
Turn on the Charm 1945.11
Turn on the Popular Moon 1924.04
Turn on Your Radio 1967.02
Turn on, old Time 1848.04
Turn on, Old Time! 1866.11
Turn Over 1905.22
Turn Over Leaf 1898.56
Turn Those Eyes Away 1904.22, 1904.23
Turn Us Again 1987.17
Turn Your Great Eyes on Me 1896.18
Turn, oh Turn in this Direction 1881.37
Turning 1977.16, 1987.04
Turnkey, The 1896.02
Turnverein Cadets, The 1883.32
Turtle Dove Duet 1890.26
Turtle Doves, The 1871.19
Turtle Song 1954.19
Turtle thus with plaintive crying, The 1750.01
Turtle Thus With Plaintive Crying, The 1957.02
Tus Ojus 1926.35
Tut, Tut 1884.37
Tut, tut, tut! 1884.16
Tutti Fruti 1978.01
Tutti Frutti 1982.22, 1986.02
Tuxedo Girls 1891.32
Tuzzie Marie 1895.21
Twa Sisters O'Binnorie, The 1922.21
Twang of My Rusty Bow 1907.49
'Twas But a Dream 1895.06
'Twas but an impulse 1878.16
Twas Down in the Garden of Eden 1902.41, 1917.11
Twas in a Garden 1914.28
Twas in Hyde Park Beside the Row 1902.25
Twas in September 1914.13
Twas in the Month of June 1920.21
Twas Love All the Day 1903.16
Twas No so Long Ago 1929.31
Twas on a Lovely Eve in June 1944.21
'Twas Over Winding Mountain Roads 1899.06
Twas Pretense 1917.27
'Twas sad when I and Dolly parted 1880.46
'Twas the Rose 1905.36
Twas Twenty-Seven Bells by the Waterbury Watch 1897.37
'Twas Written So 1894.03
'Twas You That Kissed the Pretty Girl 1860.03
Tweedle-dee and Tweedle-dum 1913.32
Tweedledee for President 1933.25
Tweedledum and Tweedledee 1896.48
Tweet Tweet 1926.16
Tweet, Tweet 1924.13
Twelve Days of Christmas, The 1998.19
Twelve Days to Christmas 1963.14
Twelve Hours a Day 1893.19
Twelve Little Heels 1924.31
Twelve o'clock and all is well 1878.02
Twelve O'Clock and All is Well 1888.13, 1944.14
Twelve O'Clock Girl in a Nine O'Clock Town, A 1922.02
Twelve O'Clock, and All is Well 1885.58, 1896.35
Twelve Pretty Wives from Turkey 1903.06
Twelve Rooftops Leaping 1971.20
20th Century Girl, The 1895.38
Twentieth Century Girl, The 1895.04
Twentieth Century Love 1968.07
Twentieth Century Lullaby, The 1919.37
Twentieth Century Rag, The 1914.01
Twenty Fans 1978.13
Twenty Four Hours a Day 1968.03
Twenty Happy Years 1981.07
Twenty Lovesick Maidens We 1881.37
Twenty Miles from Marietta 1998.21
Twenty Million People 1992.17
Twenty One Chateaux 1976.33
Twenty Seven, Rue des Acacias 1935.19
Twenty Tons of T.N.T. 1966.32
Twenty Years Ago 1911.34, 1915.16, 1926.16
Twenty-Eight 1975.07
Twenty-Four Hours of Love 1911.07
Twenty-Four Hours of Lovin' 1978.13
Twenty-Nine Years Ago 1988.07
Twenty-One 1993.06
Twenty-Seven Bells by the Waterbury Watch 1905.10
Twenty-Two Years 1989.26
Twere vain to tell 1892.20
Twice Shy 1966.32
Twickenham Ferry 1880.19
Twickenham School for Girls 1951.05
Twiddle Your Thumbs 1921.33
Twiddley Bits, The 1902.19
Twilight 1888.05, 1922.10, 1922.21, 1926.23
Twilight at Home, Sweet Home 1906.14
Twilight Coterie, The 1880.32
Twilight Glimmers 1860.01
Twilight in Barakeesh 1908.24, 1909.23
Twilight Rose 1924.21

Twilight Song 1919.31
Twilight Voices 1925.39
Twill Never be the Same 1950.10
Twilly of Fifth Avenue 1924.38
Twin Butterflies That Fitfully Fall 1903.21
Twin Duet, The 1897.37
Twin Soliloquies 1949.04
Twinkle 1918.40
Twinkle in Your Eye, A 1938.05
Twinkle in Your Eye, The 1922.28
Twinkle Little Star 1919.28
Twinkle Twinkle 1896.06
Twinkle Twinkle Little Star 1979.18
Twinkle, Twinkle 1880.18, 1917.30, 1926.39
Twinkle, Twinkle, Little Star 1904.23
Twinkling Star 1907.58
Twinkling stars are laughing Love 1869.43
Twist Canotier, Le 1963.02
Twist Her Mind 1976.03
Twist My Arm 1955.12
Twist, The 1982.22
Twisted Every Way 1988.01
Twit, Twit, Twit 1918.20
Twixt Love and Duty 1917.28
Twixt You and Me 1879.50
Two a Day for Keith 1936.05, 1983.02
Two a Day on the Milky Way 1957.01
Two and Four 1999.24
Two and Two 1883.12
Two are Company 1926.26
Two are One 1922.08
Two Bad Men are We 1877.43
Two Big Eyes 1915.26
Two birdies with their feathers 1889.10
Two Bold Bad Men 1898.22
Two Boys 1928.37, 1979.11
Two by Four 1926.03
Two by Two 1970.19
Two Can Play at That Game 1916.01
Two Cockatoos 1911.44
Two Coro Delle Lavandiare 1985.14
Two Dandy Darkies 1914.34
Two Dead Game Sports 1899.18
Two Dolls and the Glory of France, The 1903.40
Two Enemies 1889.09
Two Enemies, The 1889.41
Two Eves, The 1881.36
Two Eyes 1903.07
Two Eyes of Blue 1902.35
Two Eyes of Brown 1903.32
Two Faced Woman 1972.05
Two Faces in the Dark 1959.01
Two Fellows and a Girl 1926.12
Two Gendarmes, The 1904.22
Two Get Together 1934.40
Two Giddy Goats 1909.29
Two Girls from the Chorus 1923.46
Two Guitars 1934.32, 1965.30
Two Happy Gods 1895.26
Two Happy Tadpoles 1916.25
Two Heads 1976.31
Two Heads are Better Than One 1896.29, 1912.45, 1915.21
Two Hearts Beat as One 1906.31, 1908.21
Two Hearts in Gypsy Time 1951.10
Two Hearts Made One 1902.18
Two in a Crowd 1935.19
Two in a Taxi 1940.07
Two in Love 1929.39
Two is Company 1900.57, 1915.22, 1918.39, 1927.34
Two is Company - Three is None 1902.25
Two is Plenty 1908.06
Two Kinsmen 1985.18
Two Ladies 1966.24, 1998.04
Two Ladies and a Man 1936.27
Two Ladies in de Shade of de Banana Tree 1954.19
Two Laughing Irish Eyes 1915.24
Two Letters 1880.19
Two Lips are Roses 1923.08
Two Lips are Waiitng in Tulip Town 1912.16
Two Lips from Georgia 1919.26
Two Little Babes in the Wood 1924.32
Two Little Blue Birds 1925.33
Two Little Cannibal Ladies 1912.40
Two Little Chicks 1902.30
Two Little Dolls 1895.17
Two Little Doves 1903.38
Two Little Girls and a Boy 1923.22
Two Little Girls in Blue 1893.30, 1894.07, 1921.10
Two Little Hearts 1912.15
Two Little Love Bees 1910.37
Two Little Love Birds 1921.06
Two Little Lovebirds 1904.35
Two Little Pals 1923.36
Two Little Ruby Rings 1922.26
Two Little Sausages 1908.25
Two Little Ships 1927.01
Two Little Stars 1926.31
Two Little Tramps from Jail 1886.32
Two Little Trees 1988.15
Two Little Wooden Shoes 1922.23
Two Little Words 1997.07
Two Lives, The 1883.04
Two Lost Souls 1955.08, 1994.01
Two Lovely Black Eyes 1960.17
Two Lovers 1981.24
Two Lovers Once Wooed the Same Maiden 1894.47
Two Loves 1955.19
Two Loving Arms 1927.54
Two Loving Birds 1930.17
Two Make a Home 1923.27
Two Months Have Passed 1882.45
Two Musketeers 1993.17
Two of Us, The 1928.31, 1948.08, 1968.07, 1977.05, 1979.33, 1981.10, 1989.07
Two Old Sports 1894.51
Two People in Love 1983.19
Two Perfect Lovers 1930.20
Two Pictures 1894.07
Two Playhouses, The 1914.34
Two Rivers, The 1881.07, 1882.20
Two Rubes 1920.18
Two Sides of a Story 1894.17
Two Sleepy People 1978.09, 1980.29
Two Thousand and one: Thus Spake Zarathustra 1989.12
Two to One 1919.37
Two Tramps 1892.19
Two Unfortunate Orphans 1931.04
Two wise men, The 1883.66
Two Years in the Making 1958.14
Two's Company 1890.23, 1974.13
Two's Company, Three's a Crowd 1919.35, 1921.35
Two-a-Day 1985.19
Two-Day for Keith 1975.13
Two-Faced Woman 1932.17
Two-Headed Nightingale, The 1908.34
Twould Never Never Do 1884.37
Tycoon March 1886.15
Tyler My Boy 1959.14
Tympany Dance 1927.50
Typewriter Girls, The 1898.08
Typewriter Song, The 1921.37
Typewriting 1909.21
Typical Day, A 1956.12
Typical Mashers, The 1889.37
Typical Opening Chorus, The 1915.02
Typical Self-Made American 1930.02
Typical Topical Tunes 1918.07
Typical tune of Zanzibar, A 1896.13
Typically English 1962.18, 1978.18
Typische Deutsche 1962.18, 1978.18
Tyrolean 1885.03
Tyrolean Duet 1892.45
Tyrolean Maid 1906.49
Tyroliene 1868.08
Tyrolienne 1869.43, 1873.02
Tyup 1922.41
Tzigane Song 1895.12

U Corredu 1985.16
U, Dearie 1909.30
U.N.C.O.U.P.L.E.D. 1987.05
U.S. Black Marines, The 1886.52
U.S. March 1899.12
U.S. Volunteers, The 1904.23
U.S. vs. U.S.S.R. 1988.09
U.S.A. 1903.28, 1904.14
U.S.A. Limited, The 1913.22
Ua Like No a Like 1912.03
Uber die Unsicherheit menschlicher Verhaltnisse 1965.04
Uciekali 1992.05
Udumo Lonke Mbathazeli 1997.14
Ugg-a-Wugg 1954.13, 1979.22
Ugg-aWugg 1990.20
Ugly Chile 1999.06
Uh-Huh, Oh-Yeah! 1958.01
Uh-Oh! 1963.08
Uh-Uh 1924.30
Uia Mai Koia 1972.20
Ukelele Lady 1924.46
Ukelele Lorelei 1925.14
Uking the Uke 1924.33
Ukrainian Song, The 1922.37
Uli, ali ola, e! 1881.04
Ultima Curda, La 1985.07, 1999.18
Ultra Peacock Strut, The 1923.23
Um-Um-Da-Da 1924.46
Umble 1981.12
Umbrellas of Cherbourg, The 1974.20
Umngcwabo 1997.14
Ump-pum Man, The 1903.27
Umpty Umpty Aye 1895.43
Un Garcon Dansait 1959.15
Un Jour Tu Verras 1958.06
Un mari semblable merite 1877.32
Un Mejor Dia Vendra 1978.12
Un Oncore 1904.26
Un par un 1974.19
Un peu d'Amour 1919.12
Un Sale Petit Brouillard 1981.04
Unaccustomed as I Am 1927.23, 1930.33, 1930.37
Unafraid 1965.17
Unbeliever, The 1980.10
Unborn Love, The 1970.05
Uncertainty of Human Conditions, The 1965.04
Unchain the dogs of war 1898.25
Unchained Melody 1955.13, 1997.21
Uncle Chris 1979.12
Uncle Harry 1986.19
Uncle John Tappit 1907.51
Uncle Reilly 1890.49
Uncle Sam 1899.33
Uncle Sam and Columbia 1892.45
Uncle Sam Land 1907.53
Uncle Sam Rag, The 1959.01
Uncle Sam's Best Girl 1907.25
Uncle Sam's Boys in Blue 1900.38
Uncle Sam's Lullaby 1939.24
Uncle Sam's Marines 1904.25
Uncle Says I Musn't, so I Won't 1910.22
Uncle Tom and Old Black Joe 1921.16
Uncle Tom Cabin Blues 1924.46
Uncle Tom Combination, The 1893.10
Uncle Tom's Saloon 1922.16
Uncle Tom's Wedding 1870.38
Uncle-Huck-A-Buck Song, The 1996.07
Und der Deutscher Lied 1894.13
Und nun sagen Sie geschwind 1885.01
Undecided Blues, The 1925.05
Under a Gay Sombrero 1914.19
Under a One-Man Top 1924.03
Under a Panama 1904.13
Under a Spell 1958.04
Under an Oak 1894.45
Under Any Old Flag at All 1907.57
Under Cover 1903.26
Under Fire 1916.02
Under Grecian Skies 1920.03
Under My Umbrella 1925.44
Under Our Lovely Umbrellas 1904.15
Under Separate Cover 2001.01
Under the Bamboo Tree 1902.23, 1902.42, 1903.01, 1917.26, 1946.21, 1980.10, 1989.23, 1999.23
Under the Bargain Tree 1908.07

Under the China Moon 1913.16
Under the Clock at the Astor 1931.13
Under the Clover Moon 1927.19
Under the Deodar 1902.30
Under the Double Eagle 1978.05
Under the Elms at Old New Haven 1901.17
Under the Goo Goo Tree 1904.15
Under the Honeymoon 1908.44
Under the Jessamine 1920.12
Under the Jungle Moon 1907.33
Under the Love Tree 1912.14
Under the Mazuma Tree 1908.12
Under the Midsummer Moon 1927.43
Under the Mistletoe Bough 1902.04, 1903.39
Under the Moon 1919.42
Under the Mulberry Tree 1903.29
Under the Palm Tree Shade 1905.31
Under the pump 1887.44
Under the Ragtime Flag 1912.25
Under the Roller Coaster 1984.01
Under the Ropes 1967.06
Under the Sea 1906.46, 1915.16, 1916.24
Under the Shade of the Palm 1900.51, 1902.05
Under the Shade of the Sheltering Palms 1920.09
Under the Sleeping Volcano 1949.12
Under the Statler Clock 1931.36
Under the Tree 1969.02
Under the Willow She's Sleeping 1939.21
Under the Willow Tree 1917.08
Under the Yum-Yum Tree 1910.12
Under Two Flags 1901.12
Under Wicket 1905.36
Under Your White Stars 1998.11
Under-World, The 1908.42
Underneath a Big Umbrella 1919.14
Underneath a Japanese Moon 1914.15
Underneath it All 1970.07
Underneath the Dixie Moon 1920.10
Underneath the Palms 1922.34
Underneath the Table 1923.22
Understand Don't You See, don't you know 1889.46
Understudy Dance Specialty, The 1926.29
Undertakers' Frolic, The 1899.11
Underture 1972.08
Underworld: an Expose, The 1956.09
Undiscovered Son, The 1978.11
Undo 1972.18
Undressing Girls With My Eyes 1976.09
Une Demoiselle Sur Une Balancoire 1959.15
Une fois seule avec le comte 1885.59
Une Nuit Paris 1913.30
Une servante qui m'importe 1878.08
Unescorted Women 1980.30
Unexpected Song 1985.12, 1992.12
Unexpectedly 1922.25
Unexpressed 2000.16
Unfair 1959.25
Unfaithful One Will Die, The 1977.01
Unfortunate Baron and I 1879.38
Unfortunate Rosie 1928.09
Unhappy 1917.13, 2001.05
UNICEF Song 1960.10
Uniform, The 1937.16
Union Label 1940.21
Union League, The 1933.25
Union Square 1906.19, 1933.25
United Nations 1943.11
United We Stand 1906.07
Universe in Mourning 1972.14
Unlikely Lovers 1992.09
Unlucky Blues 1921.27
Unlucky in Love 1924.44
Unmistakable Sign 1957.14
Unnecessary Town 1956.12
Uno 1923.06, 1925.05, 1985.07, 1993.08, 1999.18
Unofficial Spokesman, The 1930.02
Unprotected Spinster, The 1882.17
Unrequited 1925.21
Unrequited love 1880.46
Unrequited Love 1920.31, 1947.14
Unsuspecting Hearts 1988.12
Untalented Relative, The 1962.02
Unter Daine Vaisse Shteren 1989.10
Unter Dayne Vayse Shtern 1998.11
Unter der Linden 1907.37
Until the Real Thing Comes Along 1974.10
Until the World Needs Me Again 1997.16, 1998.08
Until Then 1908.08
Until Today 1966.30
Until Tomorrow Night 1986.20
Until We Meet Again 1905.44
Until We Say Goodbye 1928.12
Until You Get Somebody Else 1928.47, 1979.05
Until You Say Goodbye 1920.27
Until You Say Yes 1922.31
Unto the Castle Gates I'll Guide You 1877.39
Unto Your Heart 1929.17
Untrue Pigeon, The 1978.11
Unusual Way 1982.09
Unveiling of a Broadway Girl, The 1922.17
Unveiling of the Statue, The 1907.52
Unworthy of Your Love 1999.20
Up Above the Stars 1919.13
Up Among the Chimney Pots 1930.06
Up and at 'Em 1933.25
Up and Down the Boardwalk 1905.23, 1905.37
Up and Down, Over the Town 1907.15
Up Chickamauga Hill 1936.28
Up from the Gutter 1945.03
Up Helm! 1886.50
Up High 1938.08
Up in a Balloon 1869.11, 1909.17
Up in the Air 1919.26
Up in the Clouds 1922.01, 1927.52, 1981.03, 1981.03
Up in the Elevated Railway 1954.01
Up in the Sky 1930.24, 1947.10
Up in the Tenderloin 1894.49
Up on High 1927.36
Up on Our Toes 1923.19
Up on the Hudson Shore 1913.05
Up on the Roof 1900.40
Up She Goes 1922.41
Up the Ladder 1981.12
Up There 1923.44
Up to Date 1889.54
Up to G 1869.40
Up to His Old Tricks 1974.13
Up Where the People Are 1960.20
Up with the banner 1844.01
Up With the Stars 1922.41
Up with the Sun 1864.22
Up! Up! Up! In My Aeroplane 1909.13
Up, Corsairs, have at them 1887.43
Up, Down, Left, Right 1917.36
Up, Up, Help a Fellow Up 1907.49
Up-to-Date Chansonettes, The 1896.34
Up-to-Date Policeman, The 1897.04
Upon a Moonlight Night in May 1946.16
Upon my word, Miss 1893.02
Upon Our Little Farm 1893.19
Upon our sea-girt land 1894.15
Upon Paul's Steeple 1881.11, 1881.27
Upon the sea 1887.43
Upon the Stage Let's Have a Fling 1896.48
Upper Broadway After Dark 1902.24
Upper Crust, The 1922.48
Uprising of the Old Line Units 1997.16
Ups and Downs 1925.06, 1930.20
Ups-a-Daisy 1928.35
Upsi-Daisy 1911.36
Upside Down 1921.33
Upside-Down Thief, The 1965.29
Upstairs 1968.31
Upstairs Over a Speakeasy 1929.24
Uptown 1973.14, 1986.13, 2000.08
Uptown Downtown 1897.54
Urban Renewal 1971.20
Uriah's Fate Sealed 1997.12
Uriti 1962.14
Uriti Kitchen 1962.14
Us on a Bus 1936.07
Usaac 1918.14
Use of French, The 1898.17
Use What You Got 1997.08
Use Your Imagination 1950.20, 1984.10
Use Your Judgement 1921.17
Use Your Noggin 1966.27
Useful Phrases 1961.18, 1968.19
Useless Song 1966.19
Usher 1927.27
Usher from the Mezzanine, The 1964.21
Ushing Ain't the Only Thing We Do 1916.15
Usual Opening Chorus, The 1920.33
Uthando Luphelile 1977.01
Utopia 1927.16
Utsukushiki Nippon 1989.21
Uyamemeza Ungoma 1988.02
Uz-Guz-Goozle-Um 1911.14
V.I.P. 1960.23
Va petite Mousse 1878.08
Va-Pas T'Imaginer 1958.06
Vacation 1982.04
Vacation in the Store 1949.01
Vadinho is Gone 1979.03
Vagabond Boy 1872.34
Vagrant Fancies 1909.15
Vagrant Stream, The 1907.08
Vagrants of Erin, The 1897.12
Vait Sare and hear von little story 1840.03
Val-De-Ri, Val-De-Ra 1955.13
Vale of Dreaming, The 1913.02
Valencia 1926.14
Valentine 1932.04, 1947.05, 1948.12, 1963.02, 1965.08
Valentine for Beecher, A 1980.30
Valentine's Day Card 1941.13
Valet, The 1906.25
Valiant Solders 1870.27
Valking Dat Broadway Down 1870.24
Valley of Dreams 1920.26
Valley of Dreams, The 1920.08
Valley of Elah, The 1997.12
Valley of Hokus Po, The 1904.52
Valley of the Dry Bones 1993.01, 1995.16, 1998.17
Vals de Espana 1948.24
Valse 1909.03, 1972.24
Valse Amoreuse 1931.09
Valse Anglaise 1956.13
Valse au L'Air 1919.06
Valse Julian 1911.30
Valse Milieu 1960.13
Vamos a Bailar 1979.08
Vamp a Little Lady 1918.07, 1919.16
Vamp, The 1919.18
Vampire Dance 1919.03
Vampires, The 1998.02
Vamps, They 1955.25
Van der ershter vet lachn 1960.18
Van Vattel's Vengeance 1882.75
Vandal of Music, The 1936.06
Vanderbilt Cup 1906.05
Vanderdecken 1904.03
Vandyke and Klondyke 1900.40
Vanilla Ice Cream 1963.14
Vaniteaser 1928.23
Vanities 1919.21
Vanities Girls 1924.31
Vanity 1920.13
Vanity Box, The 1922.05
Vanity Drives Them All to Me 1890.26
Variations 1890.23, 1938.08
Variety 1900.20, 1901.08
Varinoe 1906.14
Various Types of Mashers 1898.58
Varsity Drag 1974.26, 1977.09
Varsity Drag, The 1927.41
Varsovienne 1938.06
Vashti's Farewell 1968.22
Vashti's Kloglid 1968.22
Vassar Girl Finds Job 1937.14
Vassar Waiters - Jubilee 1884.65
Vaterland, Oh, Vaterland 1870.08
Vaterland, Vaterland 1870.27
Vaudeville Ain't Dead 1951.19
Vaudeville Duet 1902.21
Vaudeville is Back 1942.10

Vaudeville King, The 1902.29
Vaudevilles, The 1898.56
Vaviandiere's Duet 1888.18
Ve Vas Germans 1900.34
Ve Vouldn't Gonto do It 1938.11
Veda, La 1920.23
Vegetable Love 1954.08
Vegetable Party, The 1898.50
Vegetarian, The 1895.32
Veha'er Eineinu 1971.17
Vei Zu Di Teg 1989.10
Veil of the Temple 1982.17
Velasquez 1928.42
Velocipede, The 1869.42
Ven I Valse 1957.07
Venal Servile Train, Le 1876.06
Venedig, Fair Venedig 1906.01
Venetia 1905.47, 1914.22
Venetian 1923.02
Venetian Carnival, The 1914.22
Venetian Lullaby 1894.31
Venetian Nights 1925.25
Venetian Serenade 1911.28
Venetian Skies 1925.40
Venetian Wedding Moon 1925.27
Venezia and Her Three Lovers 1950.14
Vengeance 1886.50, 1913.02, 1933.23
Vengeance is Mine 1954.06
Vengeance, Vengeance 1863.06
Venice 1930.40
Venice Blue 1965.30
Venice Dressed in Blue 1970.01
Venus and Adonis Suite 1981.02
Venus and Mars 1921.15
Venus Calls and I'll Obey 1914.28
Venus Commands, we will Obey 1868.08
Venus in Ozone Heights 1943.19
Venus Waltz, The 1912.34
Venus, Goddess of Love 1898.48
Ver Der Ershter Vet Lahkn 1990.16
Vera Violetta 1911.43
Verandah Waltz, The 1970.10
Verano Porteno 1985.07, 1993.08, 1999.18
Verdict, The 1975.07
Vereda Tropical 1939.18
Verily, Merrily 1908.29
Verite, La 1926.49
Vermillion Girl, The 1922.15
Veronika, Der lenz ist Da 1999.05
Veronique 1978.02
Versailles 1893.21, 1923.02, 1926.15
Vertigo 1955.11
Very 1965.28
Very Careful, if You Please 1898.17
Very Fond of Living 1894.05
Very Good Girl on Sunday, A 1916.19
Very Latest Thing in Furs, The 1926.11
Very Little Time for Loving Nowadays 1913.26
Very Lonely King, A 1972.09
Very Much in Love 1963.20
Very Necessary You, The 1953.11
Very Next Man, The 1959.25
Very Nice Conduct 1882.45
Very Nice Man, A 1961.10
Very Nice Prince, A 1987.18
Very Old Gag, But it Went, A 1892.20
Very Peculiar 1907.34
Very Proper Town, A 1958.02
Very Proper Week, A 1958.02
Very Soft Shoes 1959.26
Very Special Day, A 1953.08
Very Well Then 1907.10
Very Well, Then 1908.07
Very, Very, Very 1943.19
Verzeih' Papa-Lieben sich zwei Menschenkinder 1984.05
Vesper Bell 1928.12
Vesper Bells 1902.21
Vesper Hymn, The 1870.05
Veteran Guard Cadets 1882.39, 1883.42
Veteran Guard Cadets, The 1881.29
Veteran Guard, The 1876.19
Veteran Guards Cadets, The 1885.15
Vi, Vi! 1906.17
Vi-o-lets 1926.38
Via Galactia 1972.25
Vicar of Bray 1873.28
Vicar of Bray, The 1963.03
Vicomtesse et marquise 1878.08
Victim of the Talkies 1931.19
Victor/Victoria 1995.15
Victoria's Banner 1980.30
Victoria, Victoria 1886.24, 1888.06
Victory 1879.15, 1981.14
Victory Conga 1942.05
Victory March 1925.32
Victory Parade 1943.11
Victory to the Bold 1915.28
Vie Boheme, La 1996.09
Vie en Rose, La 1967.13, 1968.20, 1973.17, 1981.04, 1999.07
Vie Parisienne, La 1921.02
Vienna 1908.06
Vienna Gossip 1937.17
Vienna Life 1964.25
Vienna Nights 1922.32
Vienna Roll 1912.26
Vienna, How D'ye Do 1915.18
Vienna, Vienna 1915.18
Viennese 1926.13
Viennese Women Love to Sing 1964.25
Viennese, A La 1929.46
Viens dans la lumiere 1966.20
Viens dans mes bras 1934.32
Viens danser quand meme 1935.19
Viens danser quand-meme 1934.32
Viens Poupoule 1910.04
Vieux chateau, Le 1935.19
Vilia 1907.48, 1943.09, 1964.24
Villa 1908.01
Villa on a Hill 1989.26
Village Bells 1939.21
Village Blacksmith, The 1894.17
Village Gossip, The 1934.06
Village Maid, The 1904.31
Village Music 1999.05
Village Pines 1925.52
Village Recruits, The 1904.36
Village School and Heinie, The 1905.10
Village Vortex Blues, The 1953.03
Village Well, The 1882.75
Villain Always Gets It, The 1955.04
Villain am I 1878.20
Villain Still Pursued Her, The 1897.25, 1912.09
Villain, you dare! 1868.01
Villains in the Play 1908.14
Villains We See at the Play 1898.08
Villancico 1992.15
Villanella a Ballo vurria addeventare 1985.14
Villanella di Cenerentola 1985.14
Villany is the Matter 1981.12
Ville Inconnue, La 1981.04
Vineyards of Manhattan, The 1929.20
Vingt ans 1947.05
Vintage '51 1975.02
Vintage of Champagne, The 1863.06
Viola comment est Jean 1929.14
Violent Crime 1985.17
Violet 1914.23
Violet Lloyd's Mine Song 1896.27
Violetera, La 1923.26, 1926.09, 1926.35, 1926.37
Violetes 1925.02
Violets 1901.25, 1903.05
Violets and Silverbells 1975.03
Violin Song, The 1916.25
Violincello, The 1907.63
Violins from Nowhere 1950.12
Viper's Drag, The 1978.09
Virgen Roja, La 1926.35
Virgihnia Lee 1914.22
Virgil 1998.02
Virgil and the Warden 1998.02
Virginia 1906.11, 1922.45, 1928.44, 1937.10, 1999.08
Virginia Reel 1904.06, 1929.01
Virginia Skedaddle 1899.21
Virginia, Don't Go too Far 1924.03
Virgins are Like the Fair Flower 1957.02
Virgins are like the fair Flower in its Lustre 1750.01
Virgins Wrapped in Cellophane 1933.20
Virtue Arrivederci 1962.14
Virtue is its Own Reward 1912.01
Virtuoso Great are We 1918.26
Virtuous Gardener, The 1881.07
Virtuous Tailor, The 1882.20
Vision 1977.09
Vision of Hassan, A 1925.27
Vision of the Future, A 1931.29
Vision Song 1946.05
Visions and Voices 1975.06
Visions at Twilight 1918.13
Visions of Love 1911.29
Visions That Pass in the Night 1921.37
Visit from DeGuiche, A 1993.17
Visit Loony Park 1911.34
Visit Panama 1940.19
Visit, A 1993.09
Visiting Rights 1974.04
Visitors Ashore 1934.06
Visitors, The 1922.41
Vita, La 1934.20
Vite, Vite, Vite 1938.13
Vito 1894.31
Viva a Vida 1979.03
Viva Carlu Magnu 1985.16
Viva Count Woolstock 1877.20
Viva for Geneva 1937.15
Viva la Bagatelle 1917.10
Viva la Toreador 1918.40
Viva Mecixo 1988.15
Viva Vitamins 1945.01
Viva Viva La Regina 1985.16
Viva! Let Us Treasure 1894.47
Viva! Viva! Gracious Queen 1882.60
Viva! Viva! Trocadero 1890.33
Viva, Dinah 1873.04
Viva, the Gay Fiesta 1904.10
Vivandiere, The 1893.42
Vivandiers 1897.17
Vive La Bagatelle 1897.40
Vive la Bohemia 1902.20
Vive la Canadienne 1924.28
Vive la Companie 1863.02
Vive La Difference 1968.30
Vive la Difference 1983.14
Vive la France 1984.14
Vive la France! 1917.28
Vive la Liberte 1901.27
Vive la Virtue! 1961.08
Vive le Marquis 1886.30, 1921.01
Vive le Roi 1914.03
Vive Monseigneur! 1887.36
Vivez! 1997.19
Vivi Garibaldi 1880.25
Vivian's Reverie 1945.18
Vivienne the Vivandiere 1903.37
Vivre Contende 1880.24
Vodka 1925.52
Vodka, Vodka 1965.35
Voice Across the Moors, The 2000.20
Voice Calling Me 1918.35
Voice for It, The 1905.44
Voice Foretold, A 1988.05
Voice in My Heart, The 1922.43, 1982.05
Voice l'heure du couvre-feu 1877.32
Voice Mail #1 1996.09
Voice Mail #3 1996.09
Voice Mail #4 1996.09
Voice Mail #5 1996.09
Voice of Bagdad, The 1920.01
Voice of Bygone Days, The 1939.21
Voice of Love, The 1916.08
Voice of My Homeland 1954.06
Voice of the City 1928.25
Voice of the High Sierras 1927.45
Voice of the Mountain Land 1876.05, 1876.14
Voice of the Violet, The 1902.36

Voice With the Smile Wins, The 1917.29
Voices 1969.05, 1985.19
Voices of My Homeland 1933.23
Voices of Youth 1921.11
Voici la minut' deelicate. . 1885.59
Voici la petite chanteuse 1884.50
Voici le Cheese-Knife 1868.05
Voici Madame Grivolin 1887.36
Voila le plus clair de l'affair 1885.56
Vois-tu, j'ai le coeur trop sensible 1877.32
Volare 1987.02
Volga Boat Song 1924.35
Volga Boat Song, The 1924.48
Volga Boatman 1942.16
Volga Boatmen's Song, The 1932.09
Volunteer Fireman, The 1906.48
Volunteers 1904.34
Volunteers, The 1901.19
Volver, Volver 1988.15
Voodoo 1927.33
Voodoo in Haiti 1945.07
Voodoo King, The 1906.08
Voodoo Man 1907.58, 1923.07
Voodoo Night 1947.19
Voodoo of the Zulu Isle 1926.01
Voodoo Pageant 1933.27
Voodoo Venus, The 1888.39
Vordevelle 1918.25
Vote for Lincoln 1961.11
Voting Blues 1950.19
Voting, The 1985.18
Votre femme m'a dit 'je t'aime! 1884.50
Voulez Vous 1920.20
Voulez-vous, Mrs. Yifnif? 1940.21
Vous etes surpris, mes amis 1887.36
Vous ne pouvez la regarder sans rire 1885.56
Vous pouvez, mon cher ami 1886.09
Vous qui voulez des servantes 1878.08
Vous savez ce qu'on dit? 1887.36
Vow, The 2001.06
Voyageur's Song 1919.42
Voyageuse, La 1934.32, 1935.19
Vu Iz Yoysher? 1970.17
Vurria 1932.19

Wa-Hoo 1995.16, 1998.17
Wabash Cannonball 1980.27
Wabash Moon 1927.13
WAC and the Sniper, The 1943.11
Wade in the Water 1990.05
Wading 1909.07
Wading We Go 1901.25
Wages of Sin, The 1951.10, 1985.18
Waggle o' the Kilt 1930.17
Wagon Wheels 1934.01
Wah Wah 1972.18
Wah-Wah 1927.13
Wahzinak's First Letter 1998.02
Wahzinak's Last Letter 1998.02
Wahzinak's Letter 1998.02
Waialae 1912.03
Waikki, I Hear You Calling Me 1922.15
Wail of the Chorus Girl, The 1917.08
Wail of the Tale of the Long Long Trail, The 1919.31
Wail of Their Sweeties 1926.15
Wailana 1912.03
Wait 1935.19, 1971.01, 1979.06
Wait 'Til My Bobby Gets Home 1985.03
Wait 'Til We're Sixty-Five 1965.31
Wait 'Till You See Me in the Morning 1940.09
Wait a Little While 1974.03
Wait for Me 1919.14, 1971.19
Wait for Me Marlena 1974.05
Wait for the Happy Ending 1929.29
Wait for the Little Fairy 1879.38
Wait for the Moon 1924.32
Wait for the Wagon 1854.04, 1980.27
Wait for Tomorrow 1945.14
Wait Til the Clouds Roll By 1884.61
Wait Till I Get on My Robes 1880.24
Wait Till the Cows Come Home 1917.22
Wait Till the Silver Moon Rolls By 1917.35
Wait Till Tomorrow 1917.17
Wait till we see the sweet bye and bye 1893.17
Wait Till You See Her 1942.15, 1975.13, 1990.09
Wait Until My Ship Comes In 1921.34
Wait Until the Sun 1974.23
Wait Until You See My Madeleine 1920.28
Wait! 1934.32
Waiter Girl, The 1906.40
Waiter's Gallop, The 1964.01
Waiter's Song 1885.45
Waiter, the Porter and the Upstairs Maid, The 1940.16
Waiters 1927.17
Waiters' Chorus, The 1893.10
Waiters, The 1906.39
Waiters, The, or Two More to Come 1883.63
Waitin' 1954.19
Waitin' for My Dearie 1947.07, 1980.26
Waitin' for the Evening Train 1963.25
Waitin' Tables 1982.13
Waiting 1920.38, 1992.05
Waiting All the Time for You 1926.04
Waiting Around the Corner 1918.03
Waiting for a Certain Girl 1906.36
Waiting for Charley 1885.06
Waiting for Charlie 1887.05
Waiting for Life 1990.12
Waiting for Me 1898.17, 1907.01, 1912.17
Waiting for the Bride 1907.10
Waiting for the Girls Upstairs 1971.05, 1977.05
Waiting for the Light to Shine 1985.06
Waiting for the Robert E. Lee 1912.09, 1912.29, 1962.17
Waiting for the Sun to Come Out 1920.29
Waiting for the Train 1925.49
Waiting for You 1904.34, 1912.04, 1918.27, 1918.39, 1971.03, 1992.11
Waiting in a Queue 1928.42
Waiting in the Wings 1993.05
Waiting Maid, The 1891.39
Waiting Room 1956.13
Waiting to Ride 1997.07
Waiting, Waiting 1960.22
Wake Me Up a Star 1937.07
Wake Out 1878.04
Wake Out! 1873.19
Wake the Dead 2000.01
Wake Up and Dream 1929.51
Wake Up Father Time 1920.26
Wake Up Little Susie 1982.22
Wake Up! It's Cake Walk Day 1915.23
Wake Up, Little Hepzibah 1913.01
Wake Up, Sleepy Moon 1934.18
Wake Up, Wake Up! 1997.06
Wake, Lady, Wake 1866.07, 1866.21
Wake, The 1952.05
Wake, then, awake! 1895.26
Wake, wake Dinah 1873.04
Wake-Up Sun 1980.15
Wakin' Up the Folks Downstairs 1930.34
Waking Early at Dawn 1868.03
Waking Up Sun 1968.05
Waldorf 1899.12
Waldorf Suite 1992.17
Walk Along John 1871.16
Walk Around 1872.04, 1872.25
Walk Away 1967.16
Walk Down the Avenue With Me 1917.35
Walk Him Up the Stairs 1970.05
Walk into Heaven 1971.16
Walk Like a Sailor 1955.04
Walk On 1963.20
Walk on Gilded Splinters 1992.06
Walk Sweet 1956.07
Walk Tall 1998.14
Walk This Way 1910.01
Walk Together, Children 1930.19
Walk up, walk up 1898.63
Walk up, walk up! 1895.32
Walk, Girls, Walk 1897.03
Walk, Mister, Walk 1903.10, 1904.16, 1905.16
Walk, Walk, Walk 1912.41
Walk, You Sucker, Walk 1901.04
Walker Walk, The 1969.14
Walkin' Along Mindin' My Business 1940.10
Walkin' Sally 1982.15
Walkin' the Track 1926.12
Walking 1905.28, 1906.24, 1999.02
Walking After Midnight 1999.09
Walking Among My Yesterdays 1968.01
Walking Away Whistling 1960.05
Walking Blues 1999.09
Walking by the River 1942.13
Walking Delegate 1911.17
Walking Dogs Around 1926.16
Walking Family, The 1906.39
Walking Happy 1966.27, 1974.10
Walking Home With Angeline 1922.46
Walking Home With Josie 1925.38
Walking in Space 1968.11
Walking in the Starlight 1872.34
Walking Music Store, The 1915.30
Walking My Baby Back Home 1938.19
Walking on a Wire 1911.01
Walking on Air 1931.31
Walking Papers 1977.16
Walking Step Walkover 1915.29
Walking the Deck 1934.20
Walking the Lake 1915.23
Walking Tour, The 1908.10
Walking Walkover, The 1916.07
Walks 1904.07, 1905.29
Walks and Talks 1899.29
Walkure, Die 1990.10
Walkurye 1932.14
Wall Street Blues 1924.11
Wall Street Broker, The 1884.42
Wall Street Reel 1962.02
Wall Street Zoo 1926.30
Walla Walla Boola, The 1963.29
Walla-Walla 1924.17
Wallflower 1911.27, 1924.15, 1984.01
Walter Lee Younger and Son 1973.10
Walter's Dancing School 1897.34
Waltz 1916.05, 1963.12
Waltz and Two-Step 1908.10
Waltz away! Happy day! 1887.12
Waltz by Strauss, A 1964.25
Waltz Caprice 1911.27, 1944.21
Waltz Ensemble 1924.45
Waltz Entrancing 1915.28
Waltz Eternal 1944.21
Waltz Fantasie 1936.27
Waltz for a Ball 1993.14
Waltz for Eva and Che 1979.23
Waltz Huguette 1925.32
Waltz I Heard in a Dream, The 1952.04
Waltz Me Around Again Willie 1980.27
Waltz Me Around Again, Willie 1906.20
Waltz Me Down in the Alley, Sally 1902.15
Waltz Me Up to the Alter, Waiter 1912.16
Waltz of Long Ago, The 1923.32
Waltz of Love, The 1925.10, 1925.24, 1936.22
Waltz of Memory, The 1940.16
Waltz of the Mazy 1897.30
Waltz of the Season 1915.18
Waltz of the Wild, The 1911.40
Waltz Time 1923.01
Waltz Time Girl, The 1912.41
Waltz was Born in Vienna, A 1936.01
Waltz was Made for Lovers, The 1922.35
Waltz With Me 1908.09, 1930.15
Waltz With Me 'Till I'm Dreamy 1908.23
Waltz Without a Kiss, The 1912.17
Waltz, Interlude 1948.27
Waltz, The 1905.50, 1938.03
Waltz, Waltz, Waltz 1904.23
Waltz, You Siren of Melody 1914.09
Waltzing in the Moonlight 1941.09
Waltzing in the Shadow 1963.22
Waltzing in Venice 1952.09
Waltzing is Passing from Land to Land 1921.13
Waltzing Lieutenant, The 1910.18
Waltzing With Jane 1904.15
Walzer von Strauss, A 1964.25

Wanapoo Bay 1930.26
Wand'ring Heart 1934.38
Wand'ring minstrel I, A 1885.47
Wanda 1915.04
Wanderer upon the land and sea, A 1887.12
Wanderer's Serenade, The 1871.22
Wanderer, The 1924.33
Wanderin' 1944.32
Wandering Child 1988.01
Wandering Hero, The 1902.06
Wandering Minstrel, A 1885.51, 1939.15, 1939.17
Wandering Minstrels, The 1894.42
Wandering Musicians 1908.34
Wandering Through Dreamland 1927.13
Wang Dang Doodle 1999.09
Wang Wang Blues 1921.21
Wangishiya U Mabatha 1997.14
Waning Honeymoon, The 1907.25
Wanita Wanna Eat? 1922.34
Wanna Sing a Show Tune 1988.08
Want Ads 1997.21
Wanted, a Fly 1903.06
Wanted: a Cook in a Restaurant 1900.57
Wanting 1986.13
Wanting Things 1968.31
Wanting You 1921.04, 1927.10, 1928.29, 1986.14
War Babies 1970.20
War Echoes 1904.47
War in Heaven, The 1956.09
War is a Bountiful Jade 1900.12
War is a Science 1972.22
War is Hell, But Oh You Jealousy 1911.15
War is War 1925.31
War Song 1938.02
War Song of the Ogallallas 1894.08
War Stamps, Won't You Buy a War Stamp? 1918.20
War! 1904.05
War's Over, Seems We Won, Hooray, The 1967.13
War, The 1979.10
War-Song 1882.45
Warders are ye? 1888.35
Warlords, The 1977.09
Warm All Over 1956.04, 1980.29
Warm and Willing 1979.25
Warm Spring Night 1997.12
Warrior Dance 1924.48
Warrior Prepare 1868.02
Warriors Bold 1894.37
Wart Song, The 1976.03
Warthog, The 1959.20
Wartime Wedding 1974.05
Warum 1999.07
Was Dog a Doughnut 1978.05
Was Ever a Daintier Infant Seen? 1901.27
Was Ever Maid of Spain 1912.40
Was geh'n mich an die Leute 1920.46
Was I Wazir? 1953.16
Was in Frankreich heut gefallt 1885.01
Was ist denn heut wohl fur ein Tag 1885.01
Was it Good for You Too? 1971.04
Was She Prettier Than I? 1964.16
Was there ever, do you think, such a silly 1895.19
Wash Day on the Levee 1894.44
Wash Me in the Water 1964.28
Wash Tub Chorus 1877.39
Wash Tub Rub-sody 1931.11
Wash Tub Song 1887.17
Wash! Wash! Wash! 1901.19
Washboard Ballet 1928.10
Washboard Dance 1897.21
Washing Song 1904.09
Washing Song, The 1979.28
Washing Your Blues Away 1932.08
Washington Post March 1894.16
Washington Square 1920.03, 1923.23, 1950.09
Washington Square Dance 1950.15
Washington Twist, The 1962.20
Washingtons are Doin' Okay, The 1956.08
Washtub Rubsudy 1953.12
Washumlilo 1997.14
Wasn't it a Simply Lovely Wedding? 1959.06
Wasn't it Beautiful While it Lasted 1930.11
Wasn't it Fun? 1989.23
Wasn't it Great? 1928.02
Wasn't it Nice 1926.18
Wasn't it Romantic? 1988.08
Wasp Nest, The 1975.19
Wasserfall, Der 1880.25, 1880.51
Waste of Time to Plan, A 1913.21
Wasted Life Blues 1982.12
Wasting Away 1930.19
Watch always at the lattice 1887.04
Watch Dog Theme 1978.13
Watch Me To-Night in the Torchlight Parade 1903.18
Watch My Baby Walk 1928.23
Watch My Dust 1967.06
Watch on the Rhine, The 1871.16
Watch Out for Claggart 1969.08
Watch the Birdies 1927.03
Watch the Professor 1907.11
Watch the Things You Eat 1918.04
Watch What Happens 1981.16
Watch Your Heart 1973.15
Watching the Clouds Roll By 1928.38
Watchman's Chorus, The 1879.38
Water Cold and Melons Rare 1877.22
Water Front Pastime 1923.46
Water is Wide, The 1963.19
Water Lily 1919.30, 1944.21
Water Mill, The 1880.51
Water Movin' Slow 1945.13
Water Nymphs Galop 1866.18
Water Under the Bridge 1934.01
Water Wears Down the Stone, The 1965.32
Water, Water, Wildflowers 1926.02
Waterfaucet Blues 1984.15
Watermelon and a Pair o' Dice 1918.36
Watermelon Cry 1944.32
Watermelon Party 1901.16
Watermelon Time 1911.20, 1921.25
Waters of March 1997.01
Wathukuthela 1997.14
Watschplattlanz 1966.03
Watson's Lullaby 1998.21
Wave a Hand 1970.02
Wave Crest Waltz, The 1911.40
Wave the Flag 1987.19
Wave the Tartan Plaid 1895.41
Waxworks, Show, The 1889.54
Way Back Home 1955.13
Way Back in 1939 A.D. 1940.09
Way Back to Paradise 1999.22
Way Back When 1979.10
Way Back, The 1997.09
Way Down Blues 1957.05
Way Down Coon Hollow 1894.27
Way Down East 1914.16, 1920.45
Way Down in Colon Town 1907.33
Way Down in Cuba 1912.44
Way Down in Dixieland 1921.26
Way Down in Florida 1905.31
Way Down in Jersey 1906.19
Way Down in Pensacola 1909.04
Way Down in Yucatan 1919.01
Way Down on Honolulu Bay 1915.17
Way Down on the Farm 1907.12
Way Down on the Strand 1907.24
Way Down South 1872.25, 1903.14, 1903.38, 1917.03, 1923.03
Way Down Texas Way 1921.12
Way Down the Ohio 1944.32
Way Down Town 1893.36, 1921.36, 1927.48
Way Down Upon the Suwanee River 1916.03
Way Down Yonder in New Orleans 1922.23, 1939.29
Way Duffy Used to Call, The 1898.02
Way for the Ambassador 1919.42
Way He Arranges His Face, The 1895.08
Way I Do, The 1932.14
Way it's Done, The 1886.33
Way My Ancestors Went, The 1942.27
Way of Trade, The 1907.41
Way Out in Idyho 1931.02
Way Out in Rainbowland 1925.44
Way Out West 1937.04
Way Out West in Jersey 1922.33, 1943.19
Way Out West Where the East Begins 1940.10
Way That Walker Walked Away, The 1901.21
Way Things Are, The 1962.05
Way to do Bomboola, The 1929.25
Way to Jug a Hare, The 1912.04
Way to See Him Home, The 1910.11
Way to the Knife 1893.19
Way to Treat a Lady, The 1897.20
Way to Your Heart, The 1926.11
Way Up North in Dixieland 1943.20
Way We Have in the Army, A 1906.32
Way we live now, The 1884.60
Way We Were, The 1976.32, 1979.19, 1984.15
Way You do the Things You Do, The 1997.21
Way You Look Tonight, The 1986.01
Wayfaring Stranger 1980.27
Ways of the World, The 1957.02
Wayside Flower 1925.08
Wayward Woman 1880.69
We 1969.01
We All Love Our Dear Jack 1905.52
We All Need Love 1974.03, 1992.06
We All Play the Grand Piano 1928.04
We Always Take Them Home 1916.25
We Always Work the Public-Not the Job 1900.59
We are a Band of Gentlemen 1904.28
We are a Daisy Family 1888.39
We are a Gallant Regiment 1904.05
We are Citizens of Rome 1900.38
We are Conspirators 1902.18
We are Cut in Twain 1938.11
We are Dusty Travellers Three 1898.31
We are Engaged in a Sort of Way 1902.44
We are Four Actors 1903.01
We are Four Little Tchin-Tchin Girls 1888.09
We are Four Miserable Ruffians 1888.13
We are Free 1913.02
We are Gay Young American Tars 1894.38
We are Going About Our Labors 1977.01
We are Going to a Party 1954.06
We are Guerillas 1988.02
We are In, And 1972.23
We are Laughing Widows 1911.07
We are Marching Through the Night 1947.06
We are Merry Little Kids 1877.43
We are Not Speaking Now 1919.42
We are Not Strangers 1978.11
We are Off to See Eva 1888.13
We are off to seek for Eva 1878.02
We are Off to Seek for Eva 1885.58, 1896.35
We are One 1972.25, 1985.15
We are Only Poor, Weak Mortals 1910.22
We are Out for a Jolly Good Time, Suzie Anna 1902.33
We are quaking 1882.17
We are Simple Irish Colleens 1896.41
We are so happy 1866.16, 1867.18
We are so Volatile 1873.29
We are sober, we are ready 1880.46
We are Soldiers 1969.10
We are the Band 1899.21
We are the Clerks 1920.09
We are the darlings 1889.10
We are the Duchess' Daughters 1884.42, 1886.47, 1888.36
We are the Fixers 1919.35
We are the Girls in the Chorus 1927.53
We are the Guardians of Beauty 1896.41
We are the Heiresses 1900.34
We are the Horrors of Deadliest Woe 1928.30
We are the Laddies 1906.30
We are the Leon Errol Butlers 1925.25
We are the Men of the Law 1900.42
We are the Ones 1983.17
We are the Priests and Elders 1976.35, 1980.14, 1982.17
We are the Principals 1903.24
We are the Robbers of the Woods 1917.24, 1919.20
We are the Show Girls 1926.23, 1927.02
We are the Six Miserable Ruffians 1885.58
We are the Waiters 1925.25, 1925.48
We are Three Perfect Ladies 1901.17
We are Trying to Support Our Only Mother 1902.15
We are vassals, guard our sov'reigns castles 1885.63
We are Very Wide Awake, the Moon and I 1886.28

We are Villains Double Dyed 1870.20
We are Waiting 1922.31
We are warriors three 1884.09
We are What We Are 1968.05, 1983.11
We Beg to Announce 1925.05
We beg your kind consideration 1896.13
We Believe 1937.11
We Belong to the Johnny Brigade 1895.17
We Belong Together 1951.22, 1995.04
We Beseech Thee 1976.17
We Both Reached for the Gun 1975.14
We Boys and We Girls 1888.34
We Bring Ye Fruits 1917.24, 1919.20
We Came All the Way from Holland 1882.45
We came in Chains 1969.15
We Can All Give Love 1970.02
We Can be Proud 1959.04
We Can do It 2001.05
We Can Make It 1984.01
We Can Never Know 1974.19
We Can Work it Out 1977.10
We Can't be as Good as Last Year 1926.13
We Can't do Without the Men 1912.12
We Cannot Let You Go 1900.34
We cannot see the reason why 1898.25
We Chant a Song of Labor 1913.06
We Clearly Requested a Boy 1971.21
We Come from Dalmatia 1903.04
We Come of Castilian Blood 1904.10
We Come This Way 1897.39
We Come to the Lively Market Square 1900.25
We Come to the Sound of the Drum 1894.40
We Could be Close 1972.04
We Dance 1990.12
We Dance and Sing 1884.58
We Dance the Fancy Dances 1881.16
We Dearly Love Our Teachers 1902.29
We Deserve Each Other 1953.08
We Did it Before, We'll do it Again 1941.13
We Didn't Come Back That Way 1898.55
We disdain thee 1873.04
We do Not Belong Together 1984.08
We do not wish to be abused 1886.40
We do the Dirty Work 1911.33
We Don't do That in Philadelphia 1898.38
We Don't Know Why We Love 1915.28
We Don't Matter at All 1966.06
We Don't Want to Lose You 1964.28
We Drink to You, J.H. Hardy 1938.13
We Dwell in Our Hearts 1989.05
We Fear You Will Not do, Lady Wetherell 1918.11
We Feel Our Man is Definitely You 1947.08
We Fly by Night 1870.15
We Follow the Trail 1928.08
We Forgot the Number of the House 1914.01
We Get Up at 8 A.M. 1900.51, 1902.05
We Go to Church on Sunday 1922.46
We Go to Find the Ring 1904.47
We Go Together 1972.12, 1979.13, 1994.07
We Got a Good Thing Goin' 1983.15
We Got It 1974.05
We Got Us 1968.03
We Gotta Go 1997.08
We Gotta Make it Through the Winter 1982.14
We had a Dream 1997.08
We had a House in France 1947.10
We had to Rehearse 1937.10
We hasten to the rendezvous 1888.18
We Have a Date 1942.05, 1942.26
We have a good party here to-night 1848.03
We Have Come Here Now 1900.43
We Have Come to Invade 1900.37
We Have Come to See 1900.43
We Have Dined 1905.19
We Have Left Pursuit Behind Us 1898.46
We Have Only One Life to Live 1912.08
We Have Presents for the Baby 1893.30
We Have to Die? 1978.11
We Have to Tramp and Tramp and Tramp 1907.54
We Haven't Discovered Him Yet 1900.59
We Haven't Discovered it Yet 1898.54
We Haven't Fought a Battle in Years 1983.01
We Haven't Got a Pot to Cook In 1939.22
We Heard What You Said 1900.08
We Heroes Bold 1857.06
We Hope to See You Again Later On 1889.09
We Hope to See You Later On 1889.41, 1890.29
We Incorporated 1934.20
We Kiss in a Shadow 1993.16
We Kiss in the Shadow 1951.12
We Know it's Wrong to Flirt 1903.10
We Know Reno 1931.42
We Know, Sweetheart, We Know 1912.42
We lack not Village Maids 1875.19
We Like to Play Numbers 1938.19
We Like to Whirl 1915.22
We live in an age of rapidity 1895.17
We Live on Love 1939.22
We Live to Love 1901.07
We Look, and Smile, and Bow, Just So 1890.16
We Love an Old Story 1981.25
We Love to Go to Work 1929.09
We Love Ya, Jimey 1959.01
We Love You Still 1934.29
We Love You, Conrad! 1960.06
We Loved and We Lost, Good-Bye 1917.30
We Made the Doughnuts Over There 1919.15
We Make a Beautiful Pair 1975.03
We Make the Show 1925.07
We Makin' Cash With Sour Mash, No Rickie-Tickie No Licq-ie' Rag, The 1962.24
We Marched Away 1903.39
We May Have to Come to it Yet 1888.39
We May Meet Again 1919.28
We merrily sing, the praise we sing 1886.40
We Met by Chance 1857.03, 1876.06
We Met in Lovers' Lane 1902.03
We Might Play Tiddle de Winks 1928.41
We Must Admit 1883.12
We Must be Off 1878.02, 1885.58, 1888.13, 1896.35
We Must Have a Ball 1976.11
We Must Have It 1928.18
We Must Hooverize 1918.04
We Need a Little Christmas 1966.10, 1985.19, 1998.07
We Need Him 1966.06
We Never Do That in the Orient 1903.06
We Never Sleep 1930.05
We never smile, we never play 1877.23
We no longer gyrate 1882.63
We no more will disagree 1859.17
We Open in Venice 1948.32, 1999.19
We Own a Haunted Castle 1935.19
We Pirates from Weehawken 1926.50
We Prize Most the Things We Miss 1936.22
We quake, we shake 1880.59
We quite understand 1895.26
We Ran Away from School 1924.25
We read that at the hallowed time 1834.03
We Really Ought to be Married 1904.15
We respect the uniform 1890.44
We sail the ocean blue 1879.05
We Sail the Ocean Blue 1945.08
We Sail the Seas 1964.33
We Saw the Swords 1904.01
We Say We'll do a Thing But Then We Don't 1903.06
We Seniors Are 1900.01
We Shall Meet to Part, No Never 1946.08
We Shall Not be Moved 1980.27
We Shall Overcome 1969.10
We Shall Return 1997.16
We Shall Return to the Palace 1998.08
We Shall Rise Again 1997.16, 1998.08
We Share Everything 1997.17
We Should Care 1925.45
We Should Care? 1927.21
We Shreik of Chic 1936.12
We Sing a Jubilee 1907.52
We Sing America 1937.14
We Speak the Same Language 1962.04
We Start Today 1983.19
We Stick to Our Letters 1881.07
We Stopped Them on the Marne 1918.10
We Strive to Win 1912.03
We Take it Just Take it from You 1919.35
We Take Whatever Comes 1972.17
We Tell Him Just What to Do 1908.41
We the Sheppards 1967.08
We Three Kings 1998.19
We Two 1923.13, 1927.63, 1970.18
We Two in an Aeroplane 1908.39, 1909.15
We very much regret to state 1886.40
We Want Our Breakfast 1926.06
We Want Our Money Back 1895.03
We Want to be Simpler 1904.29
We Want to Charleston 1925.22
We Want to Laugh 1917.26
We Want You 1927.52, 1929.49
We Were a Wow 1925.34
We Were Dancing 1936.29, 1986.19, 1989.25, 1992.11
We Were in Love 1921.33
We Were Lucky Together 1942.11
We Were Made to Love 1921.07
We Were Rocking 1999.12
We Were Taught to Walk Demurely 1894.47, 1904.10
We who dwell upon the border 1885.28
We will be merry 1834.03
We Will Fight for Our Land 1988.02
We Will Go, Go All Aglow to Gogo 1911.41
We Will Not Live in a Little Bungalow 1911.02
We Will Ramble 1914.07
We Will Rest Awhile 1975.19
We Will Sail Back Home 1914.13
We Will Trust You as Our Leader 1975.19
We Wish We was in Blighty 1918.31
We Wish You a Pleasant Journey 1915.18
We Won't do a Thing to Mamma's Millions 1900.57
We Won't Forget to Write 1966.30
We won't go home till morning 1861.03
We Won't Let it Happen Here 1938.08
We Won't Take it Back 1948.14, 1972.05
We'd Like to Thank You 1977.06
We'd Rather be Right 1937.14
We'd Rather Dance Than Eat 1927.60
We'll be married, indeed! 1885.63
We'll be the Same 1931.04
We'll be There 1929.44, 1985.02
We'll be Together Again 1975.12
We'll Blow the Jolly Horn 1906.17
We'll Build a Brand New Bamboo bungalow 1925.04
We'll Catch You at Last, Tivolini 1900.25
We'll Dance in the Moonlight 1897.39
We'll Dance the Polka 1933.23
We'll Dance Till Dawn of Day 1916.17
We'll do the Riviera 1922.41
We'll Drift Along 1917.05
We'll Drift Away 1970.01
We'll Drown it in the Bowl 1899.01
We'll Get Along 1929.09
We'll Give a Wonderful Party 1920.38
We'll Go a Long, Long Way Together 1955.13
We'll Go Away Together 1947.02
We'll Go to the Minstrel Show 1910.16
We'll Hang Together 1905.25
We'll Have a Kingdom 1926.34
We'll Have a Model Factory 1923.19
We'll Have a New Home in the Morning 1927.60
We'll have his likeness in a minute 1885.28
We'll Help You Through the Night 1983.17
We'll Hurry to Church and Get Married 1903.25
We'll Impeach Him 1931.48
We'll Just be Two Commuters 1928.34
We'll Keep on Caring 1928.47
We'll Keep the Feast in Pynka Pong 1900.43
We'll Lash Him 1890.29
We'll Live Forever - Year After Year 1989.10
We'll Make a Bet 1920.39
We'll Meet Tomorrow 1997.06
We'll Never Eat 1901.01
We'll Never Grow Old 1921.23
We'll Never Make a Lady Out of You 1907.04
We'll proceed to search for Ada 1895.32
We'll Put for the South 1939.21
We'll Raise the Roof Tonight 1930.16
We'll Sail Sway with Peter 1880.46
We'll See 1917.02
We'll Stand and Die Together 1897.39
We'll Stand by Our Country 1916.15
We'll Swing it Through! 1942.34

We'll Take a Glass Together 1989.26
We'll Take Care of You All 1915.05
We'll Watch for the Blowing Whale 1886.15
We're a Comic Opera Company 1900.07
We're a Home 1968.05
We're a Little Family 1984.02
We're a Party of Gay Serenaders' 1899.06
We're a Philanthropic Couple 1886.30
We're a Scientific Band 1903.19
We're About to Start Big Rehearsin' 1936.26
We're Adding Local Color 1899.25
We're Alive 1959.04
We're all afloat 1879.35
We're All Dodging 1870.01
We're All Good Fellows 1902.20
We're All in the Same Boat 1954.01
We're All in the Swim 1924.42
We're all noddin' 1877.23
We're All of Us Lovely and Young 1902.01
We're All Young Fellows, Bran New 1883.46
We're Almost There 1979.02
We're an Able Bodied Crew 1898.17
We're Awfully Anxious 1894.33
We're Back from Abroad 1898.38
We're Blase 1975.22
We're Bold, Bad Bandits All 1912.10
We're Both on the Stage 1900.51, 1902.05
We're Busy Building Boats 1918.19
We're Butchers and Bakers and Candlestick-Makers 1903.21
We're Calling on Mr. Brooks 1928.36
We're Civilized Now 1900.59
We're Cleaning Up Broadway 1926.18
We're Crooks 1917.26
We're for Love 1952.05
We're Four Jolly Sailormen 1903.21
We're Gathered Here 1918.27
We're Getting Away With It 1919.36, 1973.05
We're Getting on Very Well 1914.18
We're Goin' Around 1975.19
We're Goin' to Have a Barbecue 1897.01
We're Going Abroad 1898.38
We're Going Across 1918.17
We're Going Away 1926.11
We're Going to Balance the Budget 1937.13
We're Going to be Dramatic 1933.20
We're going to call on the Marquis 1896.27
We're Going to Make a Man of You 1912.46
We're Going to Make Boom-Boom 1929.06
We're Gonna be All Right 1965.06
We're Gonna Go to Chicago 1999.22
We're Gonna Have a Good Time 1976.35, 1980.14, 1982.17
We're Gonna Live it Together 1972.02
We're Gonna Make it After All 1985.03
We're Gonna Turn Off Your Juice 1988.07
We're Gonna Work it Out 1981.10
We're Gymnastic 1925.33
We're Having a Baby, My Baby and Me 1941.13
We're Having Our Fling 1943.16
We're Heading for a Wedding 1991.07
We're Here 1930.19
We're Here Because 1924.43
We're Hollandaise 1908.17
We're Home 1959.22, 1985.04
We're in a Salad 1978.06
We're in Love With Dainty, Fair Gavotte 1895.03
We're in the Money 1980.09, 1980.20
We're Indulging in a Frolic 1898.56
We're Jumping into Something 1925.05
We're Just a Pair of Sparrows 1960.10
We're Looking for Marie 1915.20
We're Looking for Something in Peaches 1910.16
We're Men of Brains 1928.30
We're Men of War 1883.12
We're Not Children 1958.02
We're Not Going to Take It 1993.06
We're not gonna take it 1972.08
We're now to have some mystery 1895.32
We're Off 1937.12
We're Off for Budapesth 1914.17
We're Off on a Wonderful Trip 1921.10
We're Off to Feathermore 1935.14
We're Off to Fight the Hun 1980.13
We're Off to India 1921.10
We're Off to See the Wizard 1997.11
We're Okay 1996.09
We're on Our Way 1915.31, 1975.24
We're on Our Way to France 1918.21
We're on Our Way to Hell 1932.06
We're on the Map 1926.39
We're on the Sea 1892.29
We're on the Track 1910.37
We're Perfection Odalisque 1890.03
We're pumping up de Ile 1865.03
We're Recrootin' 1918.14
We're Secret Society Members 1903.29
We're Sharin' Sharon 1970.02
We're so Happy 1917.21
We're Soldiers of the Army 1904.17
We're sorry to delay you 1887.44
We're Still Friends 1977.04
We're Still on the Map 1942.27
We're Supposed to Be 1908.31
We're Sweethearts 1924.05
We're the Berries 1930.34
We're the Doormen of New York 1949.05
We're the Gentlemen of the Harem 1920.41
We're the Girls You Can't Forget 1927.48
We're the Gnomes 1906.26
We're the guard, so you'd best make way for us 1888.07
We're the Handy Dandy Cops 1906.31
We're the lads! 1886.50
We're the Light Brigade 1892.55
We're the Mob Erratic 1899.30
We're the Orchids of the Opera 1908.15
We're the Royal M.D.'s 1907.08
We're True to the College Days 1893.23
We'uns from Dixie 1910.01
We've a Feeling 1908.01
We've a Scheme 1886.15
We've All Been Out on a Tear 1885.44
We've Been Called In 1877.43
We've Been Shopping 1891.11
We've Been Taken In 1908.44
We've Been to Boston Town 1907.22
We've Been to Europe 1912.24
We've Chosen You Lieutenant 1975.07
We've Come for You Ladies 1914.10
We've Come from Court 1906.47
We've Come to an Understanding 1979.11
We've Decided to Stay 1956.07
We've Got a Lot to Learn 1906.07
We've Got Connections 1975.09
We've Got Him 1927.47
We've Got It 1973.06
We've Got Some Work to Do 1916.20
We've Got Something 1920.27
We've Got the Song 1938.09
We've Got the Stage Door Blues 1920.33
We've Got to Build 1922.48
We've Got to Have More 1923.47
We've Got to Put Up With It 1917.29
We've had a Grand Old Time 1927.47
We've just arrived 1875.19
We've Just Begun 1937.14
We've Never Discovered Him Yet 1900.59
We've Painted All the Morning 1912.16
We've reached our destination 1895.43
We've sworn to defend her 1846.01
We've Won 1993.06
We, Us and Our Sweethearts 1876.09, 1876.10
Weak as a Woman 1900.12
Weak Little Women 1910.02
Weaker Sex, The 1926.25, 1928.46
Weal and Woe, The 1882.45
Wealth 1966.18
Wealthy, Shmelthy, as Long as You're Healthy 1987.02
Wear My Ring Around Your Neck 1989.12
Wear the Trousers Oh! 1883.63
Wear Your Sunday Smile 1927.09
Wearers of the Green 1906.38
Wearin' of the Green, The 1908.43
Wearing of the Blue 1957.14
Wearing of the Green, The 1865.06, 1869.33, 1872.27, 1873.20, 1903.25
Weary 1978.21
Weary Feet 1927.32
Weary Near to Dyin' 1967.14
Weary Willie's Wanderings 1899.18
Weather Probabilities 1888.15
Weather Vane, The 1893.40
Weatherbee's Drug Store 1951.18
Weatherman 1924.43
Weave from Your Loom 1914.20
Weave the Fairy Round 1852.01
Weave the Fairy round of pleasure 1871.10
Weave! Weave! 1894.29
Weaving 1907.08
Weaving My Dreams 1922.19, 1923.20
Web of Dreams 1923.07
Webbing 1923.38, 1925.23
Wedded Life 1894.29
Wedding Anthem 1899.38
Wedding Bell, The 1890.16
Wedding Bells 1877.20, 1880.10, 1889.41, 1892.29, 1895.38, 1910.25, 1911.23, 1913.21, 1916.23, 1919.01, 1921.26, 1922.18, 1930.28, 1945.16
Wedding Bells are Calling Me 1915.31, 1975.24
Wedding Bells are Sweetly Ringing 1890.26
Wedding Bells Ring On 1929.37
Wedding Bells Won't Ring Tonight 1898.55
Wedding Bells, The 1899.21, 1909.16
Wedding Blues 1920.32
Wedding Blues, The 1919.06
Wedding by Proxy 1918.42
Wedding by the Sea 1916.23
Wedding Celebration, The 1994.08
Wedding Ceremony, The 1918.11
Wedding Chimes 1925.12
Wedding Chorale 1987.04
Wedding Chorus 1904.37
Wedding Conversation 1979.02
Wedding Dance 1964.27, 1967.08, 1980.26, 1982.14, 1989.03, 1997.19
Wedding Dance, The 1947.07, 1967.03
Wedding Day 1922.18, 1926.01
Wedding day has come at last, The 1868.01
Wedding Day, The 1907.52
Wedding Fete, The 1909.24
Wedding Gifts of Silver 1914.23
Wedding Glide, The 1912.24
Wedding Guests 1911.37
Wedding in the Park 1948.23
Wedding in Troldhaugen 1944.21
Wedding Knell, The 1925.33
Wedding March 1903.22, 1904.40, 1939.29, 1952.05
Wedding March, The 1912.33, 1922.11
Wedding Music 1899.34
Wedding o' Sandy McNab 1928.05
Wedding of a Solid Sender, The 1943.05
Wedding of Fioretta 1929.08
Wedding of Jack and Jill, The 1915.25
Wedding of Luis Alonso, The 1949.07
Wedding of the Blue and Gray 1906.11
Wedding of the Blue and Grey, The 1907.12
Wedding of the Chafing Dish, The 1907.14
Wedding of the Chinee and the Coon, The 1898.20, 1898.22
Wedding of the Dancing Doll, The 1920.26
Wedding of the Lily and the Rose, The 1892.06
Wedding of the Painted Doll, The 1985.08
Wedding of the Reuben and the Maid, The 1901.16
Wedding of the Year 1964.05
Wedding of Words and Music, The 1917.37
Wedding Parade 1958.19
Wedding Parade, The 1930.14
Wedding Procession 1912.30, 1917.24, 1929.25
Wedding Rehearsal 1913.19
Wedding Rehearsal, The 1910.13, 1925.43
Wedding Ring Don't Mean a Thing When You're Married, The 1922.15
Wedding Ring Song, The 1879.15
Wedding Song 1933.07, 1934.06, 1966.19, 1975.08, 1989.24
Wedding Song for Poor People 1965.04

Wedding Song for the Less Well-Off 1976.10
Wedding Song, The 1967.18
Wedding Time 1922.31
Wedding, The 1896.27, 1945.20, 1961.20, 1962.01, 1966.05, 1976.03, 1986.16, 1990.16, 2000.20
Wedding-of-the-Year Blues 1956.16
Wedgewood Maid 1925.27
Wednesday Night Hop 1989.02
Wee Bit of Lace, A 1919.04
Wee Cooper o' Fife, The 1966.03
Wee Deoch-an-Doris 1928.05
Wee Golden Warrior, The 1976.08
Wee Highland Mon 1904.44
Wee-High and Mon 1903.03, 1904.13
Weekend at Hareford, A 1986.12
Weekend Cruise, A 1934.19
Weekend in New England 1976.34
Weekend in the Country, A 1973.04
Weekend, The 1990.06
Weekly Wedding, The 1915.30
Weep No More 1949.01
Weep No More My Baby 1933.20
Weep No More, My Mammy 1921.25
Weeping Willie 1947.05, 1948.12
Weeping Willow Tree 1924.34
Weeping Willow Wept, And the 1906.47
Weight of Love, The 1995.01
Weill Song 1962.23
Weiner Blut 1964.25
Welcome 1903.24, 1955.19, 1963.13, 1963.25, 1972.08, 1989.05, 1993.06, 1998.08
Welcome Fatima 1903.04
Welcome gentry 1887.10
Welcome Hinges 1944.23
Welcome Home 1925.01, 1927.34, 1930.32, 1954.15, 1961.24, 1972.22
Welcome Home Anthem 1963.20
Welcome Home March 1961.11
Welcome Home Miz Adams 1976.11
Welcome Joy! Adieu to sadness! 1879.10
Welcome Mr. Brue 1905.19
Welcome on the Landing Stage 1936.22
Welcome Song 1960.10, 1980.01
Welcome Table 1951.11
Welcome the Bride 1903.27
Welcome the Bridegroom 1889.46
Welcome the present 1844.01
Welcome the strangers! 1885.63
Welcome to a New World 1973.03
Welcome to Brooklyn 1992.17
Welcome to Falsettoland 1992.09
Welcome to Foreign Princes 1903.19
Welcome to Her Party 2000.08
Welcome to His Majesty 1909.01
Welcome to Holiday Inn 1973.06
Welcome to Jerry 1940.19
Welcome to Kanagawa 1976.02
Welcome to Knight and Maiden 1882.17
Welcome to L.A. 1986.16
Welcome to My Party 2000.08
Welcome to Pootzie Van Doyle 1963.29
Welcome to Prince 1924.45
Welcome to Princess 1906.47
Welcome to Sludgepool 1962.18
Welcome to Sludgeville 1978.18
Welcome to Sunvale 1962.18, 1978.18
Welcome to the Kingdom 1979.28
Welcome to the Lovely Bride to Be 1909.04
Welcome to the Moon 1975.04
Welcome to the Queen 1928.12
Welcome to the Theater 1970.09
Welcome To-Night at the Ball 1902.33
Welcome Truth 1920.26
Welcome, Jellie Canvass 1902.21
Welcome, Ladies 1997.16
Welcome, Mr. Anderson 1980.15
Welcome, Mr. Golden! 1970.18
Welcome, Offical Mother-in-Law 1902.19
Welcome, Oloto 1905.53
Welcome, welcome 1897.32
Welcoming the Sabbath 1990.16
Welfare Rag 1975.05
Well All Right 1990.15
Well Beloved, The 1899.34
Well Bred Girl, A 1904.03
Well Fellows, I Guess We're Here 1913.01
Well-informed and well-bred male, A 1895.19
Well Known Fact, A 1966.29
Well of Romance, The 1930.36
Well This is Jolly 1913.29
Well, Did You Evah! 1939.30
Well, Did You Evah? 1998.05
Well, girls! 1890.33
Well, He'd Take Me by the Hand 1897.03
Well, I Said So 1888.41
Well, I'm Not! 1981.07
Well, Well! 1942.34
Well, You See 1931.42
Wells Fargo Wagon 1957.18
Wells Fargo Wagon, The 2000.11
Wendy 1954.13, 1979.22, 1990.20
Wenk 1873.19
Wenn die Shalben 1871.12
Wenn ich auch Philosoph bin 1885.01
Wer ist denn der Mann mit der schonen Frau? 1920.46
Were He a Man 1896.50
Were I Happily Married 1904.55
Were I laid 1854.06
Were I Laid on Greenland Coast 1957.02
Were I laid on Greenland's Coast 1750.01
Were I thy bride 1888.35
Were the Lotus Blossoms Grow 1904.21
Were Thine That Special Face 1948.32, 1999.19
Were you not to Ko-Ko plighted 1885.47
Were You Not to Ko-Ko Plighted 1939.15
Were You Not to Ko-Ko Plighted? 1939.17
Were You There 1969.10
Were You There When They Crucified My Lord? 1976.35
West Country air 1858.04
West Country Lad 1907.51
West End Avenue 1974.13
West End Saga 1964.29
West Point Bugle 1928.03
West Point March 1928.03
West Wind 1943.19
Western People Funny 1951.12
Westphalian Chorale 1997.10
Westward Ho! 1940.02
Wet 1997.07
Wet Day, A 1897.20
Wetona 1921.34
Wha Wha 1921.27
Wha'd You Come to College For? 1931.01
Whaddaye do Sundays, Whaddaye do Mondays, Mary? 1923.27
What - No Dixie? 1933.27
What a Beautiful Baby You Are 1915.23
What a Beautiful Face Will Do 1924.36
What a Blessing 1960.05
What a Case I've Got on You 1930.25
What a Change 1912.49, 1913.28
What a Charming Couple 1961.27
What a Charming, Bright Display 1881.22
What a Country! 1962.04
What a Crazy Way to Spend Sunday 1944.02
What a Day 1974.06, 1982.20, 1982.23, 1997.10
What a Day! 1950.06
What a Delightful Day 1950.02
What a Difference a Uniform Will Make 1918.21
What a Difference When You're Married 1911.07
What a Dreadful Tale 1881.16
What a Dry World This Would Be 1908.16
What a Funny Story 1900.47
What a Game 1998.01
What a Girl 1929.06, 1929.12
What a Good Day is Sunday 1966.09
What a Great Pair We'll Be 1936.26
What a Guy 1985.03, 1993.02
What a Happy Day 1965.36
What a happy meeting this is 1885.28
What a Jamboree 1927.45
What a Joy to be Here 1954.06
What a Life 1925.34
What a Little Moonlight Can Do 1974.11
What a Lovely Creature 1852.01
What a Lovely Day for a Wedding 1947.17
What a Lovely Night 1927.64
What a Man 1969.16
What a Man Can Do 1918.32
What a Man! 1965.19
What a Nice Idea 1971.18
What a Nice Municipal Park 1935.14
What a Night 1933.23
What a Night This is Going to Be 1965.02
What a Party 1966.09
What a Piece of Work is Man 1968.11
What a Position for Me 1919.01
What a Pretty Baby You Are 1942.35
What a Remarkable Age This Is! 1997.06
What a Reward 1993.17
What a Scene of Beauty Glorious 1908.26
What a Scene, What a Joy 1988.09
What a Song Can Do 1955.12
What a Subject to Paint on a Fan 1888.09
What a Thing is Love 1868.03
What a Village Girl Should Know 1924.36
What a Waste 1953.03, 1991.03
What a Way to Make a Living 1951.10
What a Whale of a Difference a Woman Can Make 1927.09
What a Wonderful World 1935.12
What a World This Would Be 1925.22
What About It? 1912.17
What am I Doing Here? 1979.11
What am I Going to do to Make You Love Me? 1910.01
What am I Going to Do? 1927.59
What am I Supposed to Do? 1984.02
What am she, and who's her name? 1873.05
What America Means to Me 1969.03
What an Awful Scandal 1910.29
What an Interesting Vision? 1892.42
What are Names? 1919.42
What are the Basic Things? 1971.14
What are They Doing to Us Now? 1962.05
What are Thou? 1904.36
What are We Coming To? 1912.08
What are We Doing in Egypt? 1968.23
What are We Going to do About It? 1914.14
What are We Going to Do? 1919.16
What are We Gonna do Tonight? 1960.01
What are We Here For 1983.06
What are We Here For? 1928.43
What are You Doing New Year's Eve? 1980.29
What are You Going to do About It? 1983.08
What are You Going to do About Love? 1937.06
What are You Going to do When the Animals are Gone 1917.09
What are You Saying About Me Now? 1974.23
What Became of Me? 1964.32
What Becomes of the Broken-Hearted 1984.15
What Better Time for Love 1979.32
What Can a Fellow Do? 1909.14
What Can a Girl Do? 1927.20
What Can I Do? 1938.06
What Can I Say? 1930.39
What Can I Tell Her 1885.69
What can possibly keep me awake? 1834.01
What Can They See in Dancing? 1925.50
What Can You do With a Man? 1938.14
What Can You Say in a Love Song That hasn't Been Said Before? 1934.19
What Care I? 1925.39
What Care We? 1927.26
What Causes That? 1928.43, 1992.02
What Chance Have I With Love? 1940.08
What Color Eyes do You Love Best? 1904.28
What Could be Better? 1983.19
What Could be Fairer Than That? 1918.32
What Could be Sweeter Than You? 1918.32
What Could I do, But Fall in Love With You? 1930.21
What Could I Do? 1929.06
What could the poor girl do? 1895.32
What D'Ya Say 1927.27
What D'Ya Say? 1928.22
What D'You Mean You Lost Your Dog? 1907.19

What days were those! 1882.17
What delight to roam this great city 1848.03
What Did Annie Laurie Promise? 1924.35
What Did Dey do to My Goil? 1983.20
What Did Eve Give Adam for Christmas? 1916.25
What Did He Get? 1930.24
What Did I Ever See in Him? 1960.06
What Did I Have That I Don't Have 1965.31, 1999.23
What Did I Lose? 1986.16
What Did William Tell? 1927.35
What Difference Does it Make? 1926.04
What do I Care for a Dame? 1963.17, 1976.19, 1989.16
What do I Care? 1893.37, 1918.08
What do I do Now? 1971.16
What do I Have to do to Get My Picture Took? 1949.08
What do I Have to Do? 1972.09
What do I Know? 1952.05
What do I Tell People This Time? 1981.25
What do I Want With Love? 1937.09
What do the Neighbors Say? 1943.18
What do the Simple Folk Do? 1960.21, 1993.11
What do the Simple Folks Do? 1980.19
What do They Say, Dolly Dear? 1913.20
What do We Care? 1931.01, 1957.05
What do We do? We Fly! 1965.06
What do We Have to Hold on To? 1961.16
What do Women Most Desire? 1980.01
What do Women Want? 1969.04
What do You do in the Infantry? 1980.29
What do You Give to a Man Who's had Everything? 1972.04
What do You Have to Do? 1918.30
What do You Say 1963.16
What do You Say? 1924.21, 1927.17
What do You Think About Men? 1950.20
What do You Think I Am? 1941.06
What do You Think My Heart is Made Of? 1934.42
What do You Think of That? 1908.41
What do You Want to Make Those Eyes at Me for When They Don't Mean What They Say, 1916.25
What Does a Lover Pack? 1971.18
What Does He Want of Me? 1965.34
What Does it Mean? 1900.37, 1927.35
What Does it Take to Make You Take to Me? 1995.14
What Does That Dream Mean? 1956.08
What Does the Public Want 1943.20
What Else Can a Gypsy Do? 1912.42
What Ever Happened to Saturday Night 1975.08
What Every Little Girl Should Know 1929.19
What Every Old Girl Should Know 1956.07
What Every Woman Knows 1909.13, 1914.25, 1953.02
What Fools We Mortals Be 1907.59
What funny beds 1889.50
What fury rends his heart 1864.22
What Good Does it Do? 1957.16
What Good is Love? 1937.14
What Good Would the Moon Be? 1947.02
What Great Big Eyes You Have 1932.01
What Great Men Cannot Do 1926.26
What Gudgeons are we Men! 1750.01
What Happened Nobody Knows 1920.25
What Happened to Mary? 1912.45
What Happened to Me Tonight? 1961.24
What Happened to the Old Days? 1984.01
What Happened, What? 1989.05
What Happened? 1944.01
What Happens to Life 1970.20
What has Become of Beauty? 1963.22
What has Become of the Girls I Used to Know? 1910.34
What has happened? What's the matter? 1885.63
What has He Got? 1936.31
What has Made the Movies? 1928.06
What Have I Done? 1930.19, 1931.47, 1985.12, 1997.18
What Have You Been Doing for the Past Ten Years? 1988.07
What Have You Done to Me? 1931.05
What Have You Got to Have? 1932.16
What Have You to Declare 1923.02
What Ho, Mrs. Brisket 1963.29, 1986.19
What Homage of Human Lovers 1899.39
What I Could do Upon the Stage 1910.13
What I Could Have Done Tonight 1980.11
What I Did for Love 1975.15, 1976.16
What I Need 2000.08
What I Say Goes 1962.01
What I Seen Done 1911.32
What I've Always Wanted 1966.06
What if We had Loved Like That, And 1983.19
What in the World 1985.17
What in the World Could Compare to This? 1890.16
What in the World Did You Want? 1964.16
What is a Friend For? 1954.19
What is a Maid to Do 1903.22
What is a Man 1952.01, 1961.15, 1963.17, 1976.19
What is a Man? 1940.22
What is a Poor Girl to Do 1904.05
What is a Woman? 1966.29
What is Done You Can Never Undo 1914.25
What is it I Hear 1868.02
What is It? 1908.25, 1926.07
What is Life - What is Love? 1906.50
What is life? 1882.63
What is Love 1908.40, 1914.31, 1920.02
What is Love? 1881.11, 1895.33
What is That Tune? 1938.07
What is the Army Doing in Soweto? 1988.02
What is the Difference? 1905.36
What is the Good? 1929.04
What is the matter, Peter? 1895.26
What is the spell hath yet effaced 1844.01
What is the Stars? 1959.04
What is There to Say? 1934.01
What is this chant that holds me 1895.19
What is This Feeling in the Air? 1961.28
What is This I See? 1925.21
What is This Old Crow Seeking? 1889.24
What is This Thing Called Love? 1929.51
What is This Vision I See? 1890.03
What it Takes to Make Me Love You - You've Got It 1980.27
What joy breaks forth 1834.03
What Joy in Honey-Mooning 1880.69
What Joy in Honeymooning 1881.12
What joy untold 1887.44
What Keeps a Man Alive? 1965.04
What Keeps Mankind Alive? 1976.10
What Kind of a Boy? 1927.49
What Kind of a Place is This? 1911.12
What Kind of a Wife to Choose 1908.39, 1909.15
What Kind of Fool 1999.15
What Kind of Fool am I? 1962.17, 1962.18, 1974.11, 1974.22, 1978.18
What Kind of Woman 1998.01
What letters have you brought? 1880.18
What Lies Around the Corner 1920.45
What Lips are Made for - Eve Came to Adam's Paradise 1912.40
What Love Means 1902.03
What Makes a Business Man Tired? 1923.19
What Makes a Man 1974.19, 1983.03, 1998.12
What Makes a Man a Man 1991.04
What Makes a Marriage Merry 1968.02
What Makes it Happen? 1966.27
What Makes Me Love Him 1966.18
What Makes the Wild Waves Wild? 1920.36
What Makes the Woman? 1906.47
What Makes You so Wonderful? 1928.25
What Man Dare Say My Truant Heart 1910.02
What May a Lovesick Maiden Do 1904.51
What means these sounds of alarm and dismay 1885.28
What means these words 1855.06
What means this alarm? 1844.01
What Memories 1924.45
What Memories, Sweet Rose 1980.21
What More Can I Say 1992.09
What More do I Need? 1970.18
What Mother Used to Say to Me 1918.22
What New York Swells are coming to! 1869.47
What Next? 1960.07
What noise was that 1887.44
What Noise! 1872.23
What Now My Love 1967.11
What Now My Love? 1964.22
What Now? 1976.08
What of the Night Watchman 1921.12
What Other People Say 1894.22
What Ought We to Do? 1981.01
What Ought We to Do? Gentle Sisters, Say! 1879.72
What Remarkable Things 1907.49
What Says Your Heart 1906.30
What Shall I Do? 1938.07
What Shall We do if the Moon Goes Out? 1920.05
What Shall We do With Him 1898.56
What Shall We Sing? 1918.40
What She Needs 1989.26
What Sort of Wedding is This? 1933.01
What sounds break on the ear? 1844.01
What strange emotion 1859.16
What strange sounds I hear? 1889.10
What Takes My Fancy 1960.22
What the Band Played 1903.06
What the Critics Said 1921.17
What the Devil are You Doing? 1897.03
What the Dickeybirds Say 1893.35
What the Dicky Bird Says 1921.01
What the Dicky Birds Say 1886.30, 1886.30
What the Future Holds 1924.07
What the Girls Will Wear 1923.19
What the Hell 1957.05
What the Hell am I Doing Here? 1974.04
What the Men Will Wear 1924.33
What the Well Dressed Man in Harlem Will Wear 1942.20
What these may be, Utopians all 1894.15
What This Party Needs 1937.14
What Thou See'st When Thou Dost Awake 1981.02
What Thrills Can There Be 1923.38
What vengeance, what fury, within thee doth burn 1859.09
What We Pick Up 1927.36
What We Saw on the Boulevard 1898.38
What We Want and What We Got 1914.01
What Wealth is Here 1909.24
What Well Dressed Humanity Will Wear 1929.33
What Will Become of Me? 1900.37
What Will China Do? 1904.49
What Will Happen Then 1907.18
What Will it Be 1949.16
What Will She Leave Me? 1974.23
What Will the Future Say? 1944.16
What will the Marquis do? 1896.27
What Will We do on a Saturday Night When the Town Goes Dry? 1918.32
What Women and Men Will Wear 1927.58
What would a soldier do 1888.07
What Would I Care 1929.49
What Would I do if I Could Feel 1975.01
What Would I Do? 1992.09
What Would They Say 1897.26
What Would We do Without You 1970.13
What Would You be A-Doing 1902.16
What Would You Do 1905.31
What Would You do for $50,000 1917.01
What Would You do in a Case Like That? 1918.22
What Would You do Without Reggy? 1904.18
What Would You Do? 1932.04, 1966.24, 1970.18, 1998.04
What Would You Say? 1893.16
What You Don't Expect 1902.09
What You Don't Know 1899.41
What You Don't Know About Women 1989.29
What You Don't Know Will do You No Harm 1913.14
What You Don't Know Won't Hurt You 1919.04
What You Go Through 1978.28
What You Gonna Tell Massa Peter When You Meet Him at the Gate 1930.16
What You Need 1989.26
What You Need is a Woman 1985.02
What You Own 1996.09
What You See is What You Get 1985.15
What You Want and What You Get 1905.22, 1911.15
What You Want With Bess? 1935.13, 1983.04
What You Will 1976.33
What! What! What! 1919.39

What'd Yo' do Wid' de Letter Mr. Johnson? 1901.25
What'll I do to McAdoo 1898.03
What'll They Think of Next 1940.09
What's a Girl Supposed to Do 1945.12
What's a Kiss 1904.51
What's a Kiss Among Friends? 1927.16
What's a Maiden 1905.36
What's a Nice Girl Like Her 1971.18
What's a Sailor Got? 1945.17
What's a Show 1951.10
What's A-Gonna be Next? 1921.21
What's Become of the Bowery? 1928.09
What's de matter, Susey? 1873.05
What's Goin' on Here? 1951.24
What's Going on Inside? 1969.16
What's Gonna be Tomorrow 1964.18
What's Gonna Happen to Me 1971.01
What's Good About Good Morning? 1946.19
What's Good for General Bullmoose 1956.12
What's Happening in Lisbon? 1999.05
What's He Like? 1945.17
What's His Name? 1989.23
What's in a Kiss 1885.53, 1886.51, 1888.12
What's in a Kiss? 1891.07
What's in a Name 1950.10
What's in a Name? 1920.08, 1931.29
What's in a Name? Here's What's in a Name, or, I Wonder What Became of John and , 1973.08
What's in it for Me? 1962.05
What's in it for You? 1960.19
What's in Store for You 1925.19
What's it All About? 1902.40, 1922.21
What's it Coming To? 1928.09
What's Mine is Thine 1940.18
What's Mine is Yours 1944.01
What's My Man Gonna be Like? 1930.35
What's New 1995.14
What's New at the Zoo 1960.23
What's New in New York 1944.15
What's New? 1924.10
What's on the Penny 1940.16
What's Out There for Me? 1969.14
What's Passing Here 1884.57
What's Sauce for the Gander is Sauce for the Goose 1911.25
What's she saying 1878.16
What's the Angle 1985.17
What's the Buzz 1971.12
What's the Difference 1931.42
What's the Latest News from Town? 1903.02
What's the Matter 1904.01
What's the Matter With Buffalo? 1964.18
What's the Matter With Ham? 1895.15
What's the Matter With Hannah 1900.15
What's the Matter With Letty? 1919.37
What's the Matter With My Man in the Moon 1904.28
What's the Matter With Our City? 1948.23
What's the Matter With Our Team? 1906.30
What's the Matter With the Moon To-Night? 1902.37
What's the Matter With Women Now? 1920.40
What's the Matter With You? 1916.11
What's the Proletariat? 1933.25
What's the Reason? 1928.14
What's the Use 1909.02, 1982.20
What's the use 1997.10
What's the Use of Dreaming 1908.13
What's the Use of Dreaming? 1906.19
What's the Use of Getting Sober 1992.03
What's the Use of Going to Bed 1911.01
What's the Use of Hanging Around With You? 1930.02
What's the Use of Love? 1903.16
What's the Use of Loving Only One Girl? 1917.32
What's the Use of Moonlight? 1911.36
What's the Use of Talking? 1926.13
What's the Use of Wond'rin' 1945.05
What's the Use? 1907.44, 1918.37, 1924.34, 1956.15
What's the Younger Generation Coming To? 1946.22
What's this rumor? 1884.14
What's to Lose 1959.12
What's Wrong With Me? 1959.15, 1961.24, 1961.25, 1985.08
What's Wrong With Our Love 1987.17
What's Wrong With That? 1986.13
What's Wrong With This Picture? 1925.47
What, Ho! Guards Within 1894.47
What, Marry That Gal! 1898.50
What-a-Ya-Say 1943.18
What-d'ye-say? 1926.29
What? She Your Wife! 1880.69
Whatever 1959.14
Whatever Became of Old Temple 1964.33
Whatever Happened to Melody? 1990.09
Whatever Happened? 1959.14
Whatever has Become of Him? 1884.42
Whatever it is, I've Got It 1928.48
Whatever Lola Wants 1955.08
Whatever Lola Wants Lola Gets 1994.01
Whatever That May Be 1961.08
Whatever the Hue of Your Eyes 1901.08
Whatever Time There Is 1980.23
Whatever Turns You On 1976.20
Whatever's the row? 1884.14
Whats ee I? 1859.18
Whatsoever may be won 1882.75
Wheatless Days 1918.03
Wheel of Fate 1920.19
Wheel the Baby Out 1881.09
Wheels 1928.23
Wheels of a Dream 1998.01
Wheels of Steel 1930.28
When 1950.19, 1990.06
When a Black Man's Blue 1930.29
When a Brother is a Mother to His Sister 1981.14
When a Fella Needs a Friend 1962.24
When a Fellow Loves a Girl 1910.03
When a Fellow Meets a Flapper 1929.02
When a Fellow's on the Level With a Girl That's on the Square 1907.57
When a Felon's Not Engaged in His Employment 1879.72, 1981.01
When a gentleman supposes 1895.29
When a Girl 1918.33
When a Girl Doesn't Know What She Is 1900.34
When a Girl Forgets to Scream 1936.27
When a Girl is Born to be a Lady 1907.27
When a Girl Leads the Band 1910.11
When a Girl's About to Marry 1915.24
When a Good King Reigns 1896.10
When a Good Man Takes to Drink 1945.18
When a Good Soldier 1870.27
When a Hick Chick Meets a City Slicker 1945.17
When a Lady Leads the Band 1902.33
When a Little Farm We Keep 1859.09, 1878.20
When a Lover is Poor 1866.07
When a Maid Comes Knocking at Your Heart 1912.46
When a Maiden is Wooed by a Man 1904.01
When a maiden loves she sits and sighs 1888.35
When a Maiden Must Decide 1942.33
When a Maiden Weds 1891.29, 1929.43, 1944.25
When a Maiden Won't 1907.07
When a maiden's of pure affection 1890.44
When a Man Cries 1972.19
When a man has been a naughty Baronet 1887.10
When a Man is Married 1882.33
When a Man is Single 1916.25
When a Man is Twenty-One 1897.39
When a Man's in Love 1901.18
When a Masculine Stranger Goes By 1894.33
When a merry maiden marries 1890.02
When a Nigger Keeps You Guessing 1897.45
When a Pansy was a Flower 1930.38
When a Pullet is Plump 1917.24
When a Pullet is Plump, it's Tender 1919.20
When a Small own Girl Meets a Small Town Boy 1917.34
When a Wife Gets Fat 1920.07
When a Wife's in her Pout 1750.01
When a Woman Exits Laughing 1920.38
When a Woman has a Baby 1947.02
When a Woman Loves a Man 1982.12
When a Woman Makes Up Her Mind 1995.01
When a wooer goes a-wooing 1888.35
When a Youth and a Maid Pine and Love 1895.38
When Alfred's Friends Their King Forsook 1902.25
When all around in slumber lies 1887.12
When all around our path is dreary 1855.06
When all night long a chap remains 1882.78
When all the world's asleep 1859.15
When am I Going to Meet Your Mother? 1953.17
When an anger spreads his wing 1884.09
When an Englishman Marries a Parisian 1914.22
When an Interfering Person 1900.51
When Another Cherub Songs 1900.54
When Antello Plays the Cello 1911.02
When as sovereign here I reign 1888.18
When ashore 1880.04
When Baya's Raven Tresses 1893.40
When Black Sallie Sings Pagliacci 1919.25
When Bloom the Roses 1895.27
When Britain truly ruled the waves 1882.78
When Broadway and the Bowery Meet 1888.15
When Buffalo Bill and His Wild West Show First Came to Baltimore 1907.55
When Bullets we trade in 1863.01
When but a maid 1894.15
When Caruso Comes to Town 1920.47
When Charlie Plays the Slide Trombone 1902.06
When Ching-a-Lung Hit High 1889.01
When Chloe awakens 1840.03
When Chloe Sings a Song 1899.30, 1912.07
When countryman has a day to himself 1882.20
When Cupid Calls 1916.01
When Cupid Comes a Tapping at the Door 1899.06
When Cupid Entertains 1913.14
When Cupid Hunting Goes 1900.46
When Cupid is the Postman 1908.35
When Dad was Twenty-One 1925.12
When Dancing's a Profession 1919.24
When darkly looms the day 1882.78
When daylight's going 1859.18
When de Reszke Strikes High C 1891.43
When de Wheel Goes Roun' and Roun' 1899.31
When Did I Fall in Love 1959.25
When do We Dance? 1925.49
When Does This Feeling Go Away? 1951.13
When Dreams Come True 1913.19, 1921.27
When Each Day 1918.27
When Enoch, He Knocked, She Knocked Enoch 1894.35
When Ere You Leave 1896.41
When Evening Shadows Fall 1924.32
When Everything is Hunky-Dory 1929.32
When Eyes Like Yours Look into Eyes Like Mine 1908.23
When Eyes Meet Eyes 1902.22
When Eyes Meet Eyes, When Lips Meet Lips 1922.09
When first eighteen 1859.16
When first I heard 1863.01
When First I Put This Uniform On 1881.37
When First I Saw My Lady's Face 1976.33
When first my old, old love I knew 1875.35
When First You Left Our Pirate Fold 1879.72
When Foreign Princes Come to Visit Us 1963.29
When fortune parts 1886.40
When Fortune Smiles 1907.05, 1916.08
When Fred'ric was a Little Lad 1879.72
When Freddy was a little boy 1881.06
When Fredric was a Little Lad 1981.01
When from His Couch Uprising 1888.19
When Gaby Did the Gaby Glide 1913.05
When Gemini Meets Capricorn 1962.05
When gentlemen a-courting go 1859.15
When Gentlemen Disagree 1921.04
When Gentlemen Grew Whiskers and Ladies Grew Old 1927.09
When George Crossed the Delaware 1929.20
When George the Third was King 1869.47, 1903.12
When Girls Command the Army 1908.40
When Grammercy Square was Uptown 1921.04
When Grandma was a Girl 1915.02
When Granny is Elected 1900.03
When Greek Meets Greek 1932.19
When Grown Up Ladies Act Like Babies I've Gotta Love 'Em, That's All 1914.22
When he holds up his Hand arraign'd for his Life 1750.01

When he is here 1879.10
When He Looks at Me 1966.09
When He's Not Near 1903.24
When Hearts are Young 1922.36
When Her Lips Surrender 1923.43
When His Eyes Look into Mine 1911.03
When Husbands go to Crete, you know 1868.08
When I am by Her Side 1900.41
When I am Free to Love 1954.01
When I am Lost 1984.02
When I am Movin' 1987.14
When I am the Chief of Police 1904.56
When I am Twenty-One 1916.20
When I am Yours, Dear 1902.23
When I Behold 1881.22
When I bestow my bosom's store 1895.29
When I Build a Home 1918.32
When I Came to America 1918.12
When I Come Around Again 1965.31
When I Come Back 1882.75
When I Come Out of Here 1904.08
When I Count Three 1907.62
When I Courted Miss Kidd 1866.19
When I Crack My Whip 1927.63
When I Dance Alone 1921.08
When I Dance With the Person I Love 1964.33
When I Discovered You 1914.31
When I do the Highland Fling 1903.39
When I Dream of Annie Laurie 1907.04
When I Drop Around 1904.50
When I Fall in Love 1948.22
When I Feel Like Moving 1972.13
When I Fell in Love 1925.38
When I First Began to Marry, Years Ago 1896.30
When I First Knew You 1916.25
When I first saw Parodi 1851.03
When I First Saw You 1981.29
When I Found My First Gray Hair 1896.33
When I Found You 1920.25
When I Get Back to the U.S.A. 1915.32
When I Get Married 1912.10
When I Get My Name in Lights 1988.20
When I Get Tae Scotland 1930.17
When I Go on the Stage 1928.02
When I Go Out of Doors 1881.37
When I Go Out Walking With My Baby 1996.04
When I Grow too Old to Dream 1997.01
When I Grow Up 1937.14, 1951.05
When I had a Uniform On 1919.25
When I Hear a Syncopated Tune 1918.19
When I Joined the Army 1896.29
When I Leave the World Behind 1914.22
When I Leave Town 1900.51, 1902.05, 1920.09
When I Look at You 1997.19, 1999.13
When I Look in Your Eyes, Mavourneen 1918.41
When I Look into Those Lovey Dovey Eyes 1903.41
When I Look Up 1975.05
When I Love, I Love 1928.36
When I Made the Grade 1924.07
When I March With April in May 1927.30
When I Marry Mister Snow 1945.05
When I Marry My Mary in Maryland 1909.09
When I Meet Love 1921.11
When I Meet MacKaye 1928.05
When I Meet McKaye 1930.17
When I Met You 1896.51
When I Need You Most, You Throws Me Down 1899.12
When I Played Carmen 1914.30
When I Played those Tricks so Charming 1860.03
When I Point My Finger at My Neighbor 1951.05
When I Rise 1980.15
When I Sang My Low C 1902.20
When I Sang Toreador 1909.24
When I Saw Him Last 1928.02
When I Say it's so,it's So 1923.03
When I Say, My Darling 1933.24
When I Show 'Em This 1924.21
When I Sing in Grand Opera 1914.33
When I Sing My High C's 1893.39
When I Step With My Buddy 1922.28
When I Take You All to London 1927.55
When I Think of You 1923.23
When I Took My Jazz Band to the Fatherland 1919.40
When I Used to Lead the Ballet 1916.06
When I Walk Out With You 1919.29
When I Walk With You 1946.24
When I Waltz With You 1910.15, 1922.02
When I Want to Settle Down 1913.18
When I was a Child of Three 1890.26
When I was a childish prattler 1887.12
When I was a Girl Like You 1904.29, 1927.50
When I was a Kid Like You 1908.44
When I was a lad 1879.05
When I was a Lad 1938.10, 1945.09
When I was a Little Cuckoo 1944.29
When I was Born I Weighed Ten Stone 1894.45
When I was Born the Stars Stood Still 1897.39
When I was But a Bounding Boy 1938.06
When I was in the Chorus at the Gaiety 1907.41
When I was King of Bath 1919.42
When I was Single 1944.32
When I was Small 1920.10
When I was Sweet Sixteen 1908.08
When I was Twenty-One 1928.05
When I was young 1881.25
When I was Young 1913.14, 1970.08
When I Wave My Flag 1917.29
When I went to the Bar as a very young man 1882.78
When I Woke up This Morning 1910.22
When I Would Think of You 1910.02
When I Write 1993.17
When I'm 64 1974.24
When I'm a Duchess 1909.14
When I'm a Man Like You 1899.36
When I'm Alone 1963.16
When I'm an Alderman 1903.01
When I'm an American Citizen 1908.28
When I'm are Married 1900.57
When I'm Being Born Again 1965.31
When I'm Blue 1923.11
When I'm by Her Side 1900.55
When I'm by Your Side 1997.17
When I'm in a Quiet Mood 1957.09
When I'm in Love 1963.12
When I'm in Paree 1928.27
When I'm Looking at You 1918.19
When I'm Making Love to You 1917.23
When I'm Near Thee 1894.08
When I'm Not Near the Girl I Love 1947.03
When I'm on Duty 1884.23
When I'm Out With You 1915.32
When I'm the King 1897.19
When I'm Traveling on the Road 1900.07
When I'm Waltzing 1912.44
When I'm Waltzing With You 1911.37
When I'm With the Girls 1921.10
When I'm With You 1905.02, 1906.35
When I've Made Up My Mind to a Thing 1908.03
When I, Good Friends 1938.10
When I, good friends, was called to the bar 1875.35
When in Flanders 1900.54
When in France 1964.24
When in Love 1906.04, 1997.12
When in silence the day is dying 1862.04
When in solitude, I ponder 1859.09
When in the west the day is declining 1887.43
When in Town 1894.33
When Ireland Stands Among the Nations of the World 1917.07
When Irish Eyes are Smiling 1913.03, 1936.03
When Islam First Arose 1900.37
When it Dries 1970.19
When it Ends 2000.08
When it Gets Dark 1925.12
When it Happens to You 1993.19
When it's All Goin' Out and Nothin' Comin' In 1900.46, 1902.23, 1980.27
When it's All Said and Done 1938.13
When it's Apple Blossom Time in Normandy 1912.44
When it's Buzz, Buzz, Buzzin' Time in Bee, Bee, Bee Town 1913.35
When it's Cactus Time in Arizona 1930.31
When it's Raining 1907.01
When it's Sleepy Time Down South 1953.17
When it's Snowing in Hawaii 1923.33
When Jackson Moans on His Saxophone 1916.21
When Johnny Comes Marching Home 1978.05
When Johnny Comes Marching Home from College 1908.21
When Johnny Gets His Gun 1890.03
When June Comes Along With a Song 1923.46
When Knighthood was in Flower 1901.12, 1924.29
When Knights Were Bold 1924.42
When Labor Comes into its Own 1915.20
When Life and I 1890.23
When lightning and dread thunder 1870.15
When Linda Smiles 1904.11
When logs on the ingle (Mill Song) 1887.04
When love and peace are in such bonds united 1885.28
When Love Awakes! 1917.07
When Love Beckoned 1939.30
When Love Begins 1905.20
When Love Comes Stealing In 1915.08
When Love Comes Swinging Along 1934.35
When Love Comes to Your Heart 1920.30
When Love Comes Trip, Trip, Tripping 1922.42
When Love Comes Your Way 1935.14
When Love Goes Astraying 1911.11
When Love is Asleep 1886.30
When Love is Near 1925.36
When Love is There 1910.10
When Love is Waiting 1914.25
When Love is Young 1886.30, 1921.01
When Love Knocked Upon the Door 1920.34
When Love Passes By 1926.09, 1926.35
When Love Sings a Song in Your Heart 1923.21
When Love was Born 1898.01
When Lovely Lady 2000.01
When Lovers are Alone 1902.03
When Mabel Comes into the Room 1974.18
When Mamie, Sweet Mamie's a Bride 1903.26
When managers are fighting 1859.08
When Martha was a Girl 1914.08
When Maudey Wants a Man 1975.05
When McGregor Sings Off Key 1938.08
When Me, Mowgli, Love 1935.14
When Men are Alone 1923.27
When Men are Free 1944.28
When Miss Patricia Salome Dances the Do-La-Palome 1908.10
When Mother Puts the Little Ones to Bed 1887.02
When Mr. Shakespeare Comes to Town 1901.17
When My Baby Goes to Town 1943.01
When My Baby Smiles at Me 1919.18, 1927.37
When My Blue Moon Turns to Gold Again 1978.01
When My Eyes Meet Yours 1927.18
When My Father Sent Me to Ispaham 1900.37
When my Hero in Court appears 1750.01
When My Lady Goes in Quest of Finery 1921.11
When My Little Ship Comes In 1926.04
When My Man Returns 1971.14
When My Violin is Calling 1925.02
When My Wife Returns 1917.21
When Not Engaged in Fighting 1905.46
When O'Donohue Presided at the Grip 1900.07
When Ocean Breezes Blow 1905.53
When Old Glory Floats from Everywhere 1904.28
When Old New York Goes Dry 1917.16
When Once I Get Hold of a Good-Looking He 1894.33
When Our Dinner Hour Comes' Round 1889.37
When our gallant Norman foe 1888.35
When Our Lips in Kisses Met 1902.41, 1917.11
When Our Ship Comes Sailing In 1990.14
When Our Sundays are Blue 1921.03
When our work is done 1882.17
When Pansies Droop and Die 1882.82
When Pavlowa Starts Bucking and Winging 1916.23
When Perrico Plays 1905.44
When Pop was a Little Boy Like Me 1889.12, 1893.31
When Reuben Comes to Town 1900.40
When Roses Fade and Die 1887.31
When Sammy Sang the Marseillaise 1913.34
When Seraphina Plays the Concertina 1901.01
When She Gives Him a Shamrock Bloom 1917.27
When She Walks in the Room 1945.03

When Sist' Tetrazin' Met Cousin Carus 1910.19
When Skies are Bright 1909.19
When Socialism has Full Sway 1900.57
When Soldier Marched 1889.40
When some serious affliction 1896.13
When Somebody Cares 1922.10
When Somebody isn't There 1916.07
When Someone Loves You 1948.30
When Someone Marries Me 1913.10
When Someone Pulls the String 1897.34
When Sousa Comes to Coontown 1903.08
When Sousa Leads the Band 1900.52
When Springtime Comes to My River 1985.20
When Stanislaus Got Married 1995.14
When still the Night, when o'er the Waves 1866.14
When Tetrazzini Sighs High F 1908.21
When Texas Tommy Did the Turkey Trot 1912.36
When That Band Plays 1932.01
When That Somebody Comes 1921.03
When the American Eagle Screams 1904.07
When the Baby Comes 1966.09
When the Band Begins to Play 1914.07
When the Band of Rubensvile Turns Out 1905.39
When the Band Plays Ragtime 1901.29, 1903.34
When the Band Plays the Star-Spangled Banner 1908.37
When the Band Plays Yankee Doodle 1907.28
When the Bell Goes Ting-a-Ling-Ling 1924.41
When the Bell in the Lighthouse Rings, Ding Dong 1930.16
When the Bloom is on the Bottle 1910.10
When the Bo-Tree Blossoms 1927.12
When the Boys Come Home 1944.23
When the Boys Come Home to Tea 1914.32
When the Brass Band Played 1904.14
When the Breeze on High Sang a Lullaby 1943.02
When the Bugles are Calling 1895.33
When the Cat Comes Back 1911.03
When the Cat's Away 1905.28, 1906.24, 1921.06, 1925.05
When the Cat's Away the Mice Will Play 1890.03, 1900.15, 1905.57
When the Cherry Blossoms Fall 1924.39
When the Children are Asleep 1945.05, 1993.16
When the Circus Comes to Town 1903.03, 1908.26
When the Clock in the Tower Strikes Twelve 1882.74, 1893.46
When the Clock is Striking Eight 1880.34
When the Clock Strikes One 1913.19
When the Clock Strikes Two in the Tenderloin 1898.43
When the Colored Band Comes Marching Down the Street 1903.04
When the Colored Regiment Goes Off to War 1915.33
When the Creditor Comes to Call 1914.13
When the Curfew Rings at Nine 1922.48
When the Curtain Falls 1917.36
When the Debbies Go By 1925.14
When the Drum Beat Calls to Glory 1925.02
When the Duchess is Away 1945.04
When the Elves Hold Masquerade 1912.10
When the fair land of Poland 1844.01
When the Fiddler's Bow Begins to Fly 1918.26
When the Foreman Bares His Steel 1879.72, 1981.01
When the Gay Sport 1881.22
When the Girl You Love is Loving You 1908.19
When the Girls Come Back to Town 1902.34
When the Girls Get Wise 1918.18
When the Glasses Clink 1887.31
When the Guards Go Marching By 1911.02
When the Hansom Cab Were Lined Up on the Ranks 1927.02
When the Hawthorne Buds are Springing 1886.60
When the Heart is Light 1904.52
When the heart is young 1902.32
When the Heart is Young 1914.09
When the Honey Moon Stops Shining 1913.05
When the Hurdy Gurdy Plays 1926.06
When the Idle Poor Become the Idle Rich 1947.03
When the Judges Doff the Ermine 1933.25
When the Kaiser's Mother Called Him Little Willie 1918.20
When the Kids Get Married 1966.29
When the Kindly Night has Come 1894.24
When the lads of the village 1859.15
When the Landlord Comes a-Knocking at the Door 1913.27
When the Leaves Came Drifting Down 1898.69
When the Lights are Low 1916.10
When the Little Birds are Sleeping 1913.21
When the loafer shies his fist 1881.06
When the lovely queen of the night 1886.40
When the Madame Goes Away 1915.08
When the Man in the Moon Goes to Sleep 1894.17
When the merry fiddler's tune we hear 1886.40
When the Midnight Choo-Choo Leaves for Alabam 1976.24, 1992.18
When the Minstrels Come to Town 1907.61, 1909.16
When the Mists of the Night 1911.44
When the Moon Comes O'er the Hill 1903.41
When the Moon is in the Sky 1905.25
When the Moon Plays Peek-a-Boo 1908.05
When the Moon Shines Down 1918.12
When the Moon Shines on Broadway 1908.37
When the Moon Shines on the Moonshine 1904.26, 1919.15
When the Moon Slyly Winks in the Night 1914.02
When the Moon With Glory Brightens 1866.19
When the Music Starts to Play 1908.15
When the night wind howls in the chimney cowls 1887.10
When the Nylons Bloom Again 1943.07, 1978.09
When the Old Top Hummed 1911.15
When the One You Care For 1927.09
When the Orchestra Plays 1901.13
When the Orchestra's Playing Your Favorite Waltz 1917.17
When the Organ Plays 1923.34
When the Parlor Clock Strikes 1912.36
When the Party Gives a Party 1945.03
When the Piper Plays 1924.06
When the Power Comes 1976.35, 1980.14, 1982.17
When the Preacher Makes You Mine 1919.21
When the Queen Wakes Up in the Morning 1913.27
When the Red, Red Robin Comes Bob, Bob, Bobbin' Along 1989.16
When the Right Girl Comes Along 1915.29
When the Right Little Girl Comes Along 1905.49
When the Right Man Comes Along 1918.13
When the Right Man Sings Tra La 1911.38
When the Right One Comes Along 1920.18
When the Saints Come Marchin' In 1930.10
When the Saints Go Marching In 1955.03, 1974.09, 1978.01
When the Saxophone is Playing 1917.32
When the Shadows Fall 1918.39, 1924.11
When the Shaker Plays a Cocktail Tune 1926.18
When the Sheets Come Back from the Laundry 1950.06
When the silver moon is beaming 1886.40
When the Simple Peasant 1883.12
When the Snowflakes Fall 1923.21
When the Song of Love is Heard 1908.06
When the Spring is in the Air 1951.22
When the Spring Wakens Everything 1980.21
When the Stars Fall in Love With the Moon 1910.15
When the Statues Come to Life 1921.25
When the Sun Goes Down 1924.05
When the Sun Goes Down in the South 1985.06
When the sun in full splendor 1862.04
When the Sun Kissed the Rose Good-Night 1926.22
When the Sun Meets the Moon in Finale-Land 1930.18
When the Sunset Turns the Ocean's Blue to Gold 1930.16
When the Swallows Return in the Spring 1908.07
When the Tall Man Talks 1958.20
When the Tambourine is Playing 1887.31
When the Teddy Bears Come to Life 1907.61
When the Tenor Married the Soprano and the Alto Married the Bass 1922.48
When the Tide Comes In 1889.39
When the Time is Right 1959.19
When the Troupe Comes Back to Town 1902.23
When the Trumpet in the Cornfield Blows 1886.52
When the Trumpet Sounds to Arms 1905.04
When the Trumpets Sound to Arms 1905.04
When the War is O'er 1898.45
When the War is Over 1943.23
When the Weather's Better 1967.06
When the Wedding Bells are Ringing 1919.27
When the Wedding Bells Ring Out 1923.01
When the Wedding Chimes are Ringing 1922.15
When the Wheel Goes Round 1888.39
When the Whistle Blows 1924.10
When the Wine Gets Cold 1997.16
When the Wintry Moon is Bright 1898.48
When the World was Young 1967.13, 1968.20, 2000.16
When There isn't a Girl About 1906.39, 1908.03
When There's No Light at All 1912.02
When There's No One 1988.12
When There's No One to Love 1920.47
When These Lawyers Don't Deliver 1954.06
When These Uniforms We Got 1897.48
When They Asked Us, And 1964.28
When They do the Dippy Dooliums 1919.24
When They Grow Older 1916.25
When They Start Again 1972.07
When They Start to Yodel Ragtime Songs in Tennessee 1916.21
When They're Beautiful 1919.08
When They're Old Enough to Know Better 1919.15
When Things are Bright and Rosy 1928.38
When Things Come Your Way 1918.39
When Things Go Wrong 1924.17
When this cruel war is over 1864.12
When This Lousy War is Over 1964.28
When this old coat was in the style 1898.25
When Those Mason and Dixon Minstrels Hit Town 1919.26
When Tommy Atkins Marries Dolly Gray 1906.29
When Tommy Atkins Smiles at All the Girls 1914.22
When two days old at most 1895.29
When Two Hearts Love 1893.16
When Two Little Hearts are One 1901.17
When Uncle Sam Rules the Wave 1916.24
When Uncle Sammy Sings the Marseillaise 1906.45
When Upon the Tight-Rope Dancing 1871.19
When Velma Takes the Stand 1975.14
When Villains Ramble Far and Near 1975.19
When was There Ever a Night Like This 1912.24
When We are M-A-double-R-I-E-D 1907.57
When We are Made One 1885.15
When We are Married 1889.34, 1897.39, 1918.29, 1921.20, 1923.44, 1924.02
When We are Married to You and Me 1910.25
When We are Spliced 1926.38
When We Chance to Meet 1889.46
When We Get Our Divorce 1925.33
When we hear the call for battle 1896.13
When We Made the Gallant Charge of Bunker Hill 1908.44
When We Meet Again 1946.10
When We Meet the Mormon 1914.18
When We Were Still Young 1890.39
When We Were Twenty-One 1909.14
When We Were Young 1954.03
When We're Bride and Groom 1926.39
When We're Home on the Range 1943.01
When We're in Love 1946.19
When We're Married 1906.45
When Wed, 'tis good on either side 1871.19
When Whiteman Starts to Play 1924.41
When Will Grown-Ups Grow Up? 1981.07
When Will I be Loved 1982.22
When Will I Learn 1968.06
When Will My Dream Come True 1902.07
When Will You Stand When the Flood Comes? 1998.21
When Woman is the Question 1911.41
When Yankee Doodle Learns to Parlez Vous 1916.25
When Yo' Ain't Got No Money Yo Needn't Come Round 1898.69
When You and I Were Dancing 1924.33
When You and I Were Young Maggie 1909.16
When You and I Were Young, Maggie Blues 1979.25
When you approach the Royal Presence 1895.29
When You are Close to Me 1947.13

When You are Eighteen 1947.08
When You are Found Out 1900.57
When You are Happy 1919.08
When You are in China 1919.39
When You are Married 1894.06
When You are Mine 1902.18, 1919.27
When You are Mine, All Mine 1917.30
When You are Wed to Me 1900.43
When You are Young 1931.39
When You at Last are Mine 1903.10
When You Carry Your Own Suitcase 1963.12
When you censure the Age 1750.01
When You Change Your Name to Mine 1913.06
When You Come Back 1921.41
When You Come Home Again Johnny! 1914.19
When You Come Near Me, I Feel All of a Ooh! 1919.23
When You Come to Think of It 1888.32
When You Dance 1919.23
When You Dance for a King 1993.19
When You Dance With a Certain Girl 1919.33
When You Dance With the Girl You Love 1922.17
When You do the Hinky Dee 1922.43
When You Feel a Little Longing 1918.04
When You Find a Man of Forty 1942.33
When You First Kiss the Last Girl You Love 1909.02
When you first left our prowler gang 1881.06
When You Get to Congress 1927.05
When You Go Down by Miss Jenny's 1946.24
When You Go Out to Dine 1906.19
When You Go to London Town, Gay Paree or Dixie Land 1903.29
When You Got it, Flaunt It 2001.05
When You Grow to be Twenty-One 1916.20
When You Grow Up 1952.15
When You had Left Our Pirate Fold 1981.01
When You Hear Jackson Moan on His Saxophone 1916.21
When You Hear the Wind 1961.07
When You Heart's in the Ring 1924.10
When You Know These Men 1899.25
When You Live in a Furnished Flat 1919.12
When You Live on an Island 1944.27
When You Look in the Eyes of a Mule 1922.22
When You Look in the Heart of a Rose 1918.31
When You Look in Your Looking Glass 1938.08
When You Love 1923.41
When You Love Only One 1934.38
When You Love, Love, Love 1903.03, 1904.13, 1904.44
When You Meet a Man in Chicago 1972.04
When You Run the Show 1983.17
When You Said How do You Do 1912.45
When You Sail for Paris in the Spring 1901.23
When You Say No to Love 1928.09
When You Smile 1920.40, 1925.35
When You Speak of Vamps, Don't Leave Out Caroline 1922.25
When You Steal a Kiss or Two Making Love 1907.41
When You Take a Trip 1906.26
When You Take That Trip Across the Rhine 1918.31
When You Wake Up Dancing 1918.09
When You Walked Out, Somebody Else Walked In 1923.32
When You Waltz With Me 1917.09
When You Want Me 1961.18
When You Wear a 13 Collar 1915.31
When You Wear a Thirteen Collar 1975.24
When You Were All to Me 1904.17
When You Were Shy Eighteen 1902.07
When You Were Sweet Sixteen 1927.48
When You Win a Maiden's Heart 1868.03
When You're a Millionaire 1900.51, 1902.05
When You're All Dressed Up and No Place to Go 1914.13
When You're Away 1912.07, 1912.13, 1914.27
When You're Big 1996.08
When You're Dancing in a Nightie on the Lawn 1920.03
When You're Driving Through the Moonlight 1993.14, 1993.16, 2001.09
When You're Far Away from New York 1963.25
When You're Full of Talk 1916.19
When You're Good to Mama 1975.14
When You're in Love 1897.40, 1905.41, 1918.27, 1924.25
When You're in Love You'll Know 1916.22
When You're in My Arms 1979.04
When You're in Right With the Right Little Girl 1919.35
When You're in Rome 1922.10
When You're on the Stage 1913.20
When You're Pretty and the World is Fair 1945.16
When You're Right, You're Right 1981.10
When You're Safe in Bed at Night 1920.39
When You're Sailing 1908.12
When You're Smiling the Whole World Smiles With You 1930.13, 1965.08
When You're Starring in the Movies 1916.03
When You're Sweet Sixteen 1913.27
When You're Traveling 1913.02
When You've Pampered Your Adipose Tissue 1906.01
When You've Picked Your Basket of Peaches 1917.12
When you've won the battle, let me know 1870.20
When Young at the Bar 1957.02
When Young at the Bar you first taught me to score 1750.01
When Your Ankle Wears the Ball and Chain 1914.27
When Your Boy Becomes a Man 1931.28
When Your Castles Come Tumbling Down 1922.29
When your clothes from your hat to your socks 1893.02
When Your Fortune has Flown 1912.04
When Your Life Seems a Rainy Day 1925.02
When Your Lover has Gone 1986.02
When Your Lover Says Goodbye 1969.17
When Your Pride has had a Tumble 1894.33
When Your Ship Comes Home 1902.39
When Your Troubles Have Started 1980.06
When Yuba Plays the Rhumba on His Tuba 1931.14
When Yuba Plays the Rumba on His Tuba 1999.05
When Yuba Plays the Tuba 1931.14
When Ziegfeld's Follies Hit the Town 1917.37
When Zim Zim Go the Cymbals 1911.01
When-e'er I spoke sarcastic joke 1884.09
Whene'er a Lover only sighs 1859.17
Whenever I Dream 1926.12
Whenever I Think of You 1917.19
Whenever I'm With You 1989.23
Where 1944.32
Where am I Going? 1966.01
Where am I Now? 1985.20
Where am I? 1900.37
Where are the Girls of Yesterday 1969.04, 1980.01
Where are the Girls? 1977.01
Where are the Men? 1934.36
Where are the Old Pals of Yesterday? 1923.33
Where are the Snows? 1966.29
Where are the Songs We Sung? 1986.19
Where are They? 1958.01
Where are Those People Who Did 'Hair'? 1978.11
Where are thou now, my beloved 1878.02
Where are Thou Now, My Beloved? 1896.35
Where are Thou, Illustrious Stranger 1891.46
Where are You Going My Pretty Maid? 1891.11
Where are You Going Wearing That Shawl from Manila? 1969.11
Where are You Going, My Pretty Maid? 1892.21, 1893.37, 1904.17
Where are You Going? 1880.47
Where are You Now That I Need You? 1980.29
Where are You/Where am I? 1988.07
Where are Your Children? 1959.14
Where Art Thou Now, My Beloved 1888.06
Where Art Thou Now, My Lazinski? 1884.22
Where Art Thou, Romeo? 1920.41
Where Balmy Garlic Scents the Air 1880.69
Where Broadway Meets Fifth Avenue 1905.48
Where can he be? 1886.28
Where Can He Be? 1931.16
Where Can I Go from You? 1940.23
Where can my gallant brother 1880.54
Where Can the Baby Be? 1928.02
Where can we get a seamstress 1885.45
Where Can You Take a Girl? 1968.31
Where Credit is Due 1922.42
Where Did it Go 1969.02
Where Did Robinson Crusoe Go With Friday on Saturday Night? 1916.03
Where Did the Bird Hear That? 1912.41
Where Did the Good Times Go? 1974.05
Where Did the Night Go? 1952.10
Where Did the Summer Go To? 1971.21
Where Did We Go Right 2001.05
Where Did We Go? Out 1959.23
Where Did You Get Dem High Heeled Shoes? 1940.01
Where Did You Get That Hat? 1889.05
Where Did You Get Those Irish Eyes? 1917.29
Where Did You Learn to Dance 1983.09
Where do I Go from Here? 1962.17
Where do I Go? 1968.11
Where do Mosquitos Go in the Wintertime? 1920.18
Where do People Go 1978.11
Where do They Come From? 1918.18
Where do They Get Those Guys? 1918.05
Where do You Get Your Greens? 1940.03
Where do You Start 1990.09
Where do You Travel? 1941.06
Where earth is troubled 1846.01
Where East Meets West 1921.22
Where Fate Shall Guide 1907.47
Where Floweth the Wild Mohawk River? 1882.75
Where gentlemen are eaten up with jealousy 1893.02
Where has My Husband Gone Blues 1925.30
Where has Tom Gone? 1956.13
Where has Una Gone? 1914.18
Where Have All the Flowers Gone? 1967.13, 1968.20, 1999.07
Where Have I Been 1968.05
Where have I been? 1889.50
Where Have the Old Timers Gone? 1924.07
Where Have You Been All My Life 1927.35
Where Have You Been All Night? 1947.10
Where Have You Been? 1930.40
Where He Goes We Go Too 1900.39
Where I Live 1999.02
Where I Want to Be 1988.09
Where in the World 1948.21, 1991.05
Where in the World But America 1955.13
Where is he now? 1889.50
Where is Justice? 1970.17
Where is Love? 1900.01, 1944.16, 1963.01
Where is Matthew Going? 1971.21
Where is Me? 1968.13
Where is My Boy? 1923.31
Where is My Homeland? 1940.04
Where is My Little Old New York? 1924.44
Where is My Mommy, Please 1995.04
Where is My Son? 1976.08
Where is now each merry antic? 1871.19
Where is Our Meyer, Where's Himalaya? 1927.51
Where is Respect? 1973.02
Where is She? 1919.24, 1923.18
Where is That Someone for Me? 1955.10
Where is the Beautiful Face? 1920.47
Where is the Clown? 1961.16
Where is the Girl? 1955.11
Where is the Language to Tell? 1917.31
Where is the Life That Late I Led? 1948.32, 1999.19
Where is the Love? 1920.11
Where is the Man I Married? 1964.16
Where is the Man of My Dreams? 1922.27
Where is the Man That is Coming to Marry Me? 1897.03
Where is the plaintiff? 1875.35
Where is the Reason 1976.03
Where is the She for Me 1948.30
Where is the Tribe for Me? 1964.40
Where is the Waltz? 1968.13
Where is the Woman 1882.75
Where is Thy Heart, Oh Brian the Brave? 1896.41
Where Jasmine Flowers are Twining 1902.15
Where Jazz was Born 1928.10
Where Love Grows 1928.48
Where Love Resides 2000.16
Where My Forefathers Died 1906.14
Where Oh Where is My Baby Darlin'? 1976.31

Where or When 1937.04, 1975.13, 1975.22, 1981.16, 1991.10
Where Shall I Find Him? 1961.18
Where shall I take my Bride? 1870.26
Where Shall I Turn? 1939.21
Where Shall We Go 1920.15
Where Shall We Go Tonight? 1922.16
Where the Bamboo Babies Grow 1922.15
Where the Bee lurks 1862.02
Where the Bee Sucks there lurk I 1880.19
Where the Black-Eyed Susans Grow 1916.03, 1916.25, 1952.11
Where the Blue of the Night Meets the Gold of the Day 1976.32
Where the Cotton Blossoms Grow 1918.04
Where the Edelweiss is Blooming 1912.25
Where the Fairest Flowers are Blooming 1903.37
Where the Flag is Waving 1905.50
Where the Ganges Flows 1923.16
Where the Gigantic Ocean Atlantic 1902.01
Where the Honeymoon Alone Can See 1922.02
Where the Hudson River Flows 1925.31
Where the Lances Gleam 1894.08
Where the Lanterns Gleam 1922.12
Where the Morning Glories Grow 1976.32
Where the pocketbook expert is not a snatching 1881.06
Where the Red, Red Roses Grow 1913.05
Where the River Shannon Flows 1907.28
Where the Sparrows and Chippies Parade 1888.27
Where the Sunset Meets the Sea 1928.47
Where the Sweet Magnolia Grows 1887.48
Where the Willow Makes a Shade 1888.15
Where To 1938.08
Where Tomorrow Begins 1920.45
Where was I When They Passed Out the Luck? 1970.07
Where was I? 1966.27
Where was it That We Met 1997.16, 1998.08
Where We Can be in Love 1925.19
Where Were You? 1920.21
Where Were You? Where was I? 1928.31
Where Would I be Without You 1990.09
Where Would You be Without Me? 1965.19
Where Would You Get Your Coat? 1929.45
Where You Are 1930.20, 1944.14, 1946.05, 1963.25, 1993.09
Where You Carved Your Name 1928.22
Where You Go Will I Go 1906.47
Where You Go, I Go 1933.01
Where You Lead 1930.26
Where'd Marilla Come From? 1971.21
Where's (What's Keeping) My Prince Charming? 1931.11
Where's All This Anger Coming From 1993.17
Where's Charley? 1948.26, 1974.25
Where's Mama? 1910.08
Where's My Bess 1935.13, 1942.03
Where's my duck-a-deary? 1893.02
Where's My Happy Ending? 1931.31
Where's My Shoe? 1963.14
Where's My Sweet and Pretty Man? 1920.06
Where's My Wife? 1945.19
Where's North? 1971.18
Where's That Cat? 1876.37
Where's That Rainbow? 1926.50, 1975.13
Where's That Steamboat Going 2001.06
Where's the Boy I Saved for a Rainy Day? 1940.23
Where's the Boy? Here's the Girl! 1928.43
Where's the Bridegroom? 1911.42
Where's the Girl 1997.19
Where's the Girl for Me? 1915.01
Where's the Girl? 1999.13
Where's the Little Boy for Me? 1916.22
Where's the Mate for Me? 1927.67, 1994.08
Where's the Police? 1857.04
Where, Oh Where 1947.10
Where, Oh Where Can I Find Love? 1933.16
Where, Oh, Where 1950.20
Where-Has-My-Hubby-Gone-Blues 1971.03
Where? 1959.04
Whereas 1967.14
Wherefore and the Why, The 1904.55
Wherefore Art Thou Juliet 1936.01
Wherever He Ain't 1974.18, 1985.19
Wherever I May Go 1954.17
Wherever There's Music and Beautiful Girls 1918.07
Wherever They Fly the Flag of Old England 1946.13
Wherever You Are 1927.48
Wherever You Go 1972.09
Which Door? 1966.18
Which is Brown? 1899.08
Which is the Right Life? 1929.51
Which My Sally Didn't Love Me True 1883.04, 1888.11
Which One Shall We Marry? 1906.26
Which Shall I Choose? 1912.09
Which Shall it Be? 1927.64
Which Way do I Go? 1979.03
Which way shall I turn me? - How can I decide? 1750.01
Which Witch? 1953.17
Whichaway'd They Go? 1949.17
Whichness of the Whatness, The 1922.10
Whiffenpoof Song 1974.09
Whiffenpoof Song, The 1943.23
Whiffer's Song 1940.01
While All are Asleep 1917.30
While all the town is sleeping 1884.14
While I' am Waiting 1905.46
While in My Submarine 1905.33
While My Wife's Away 1921.11
While pensive I thought of my love 1860.01
While Strolling Through the Park 1944.32
While the City Sleeps 1964.32
While the Four Winds Blow 1897.40, 1917.10
While There's a Song to Sing 1947.14
While There's Still Time 1972.01
While They Were Dancing Around 1913.05
While this heart 1859.18
While this heart with joy revealing 1873.04
While Wheeling With the Girl You Love 1896.37
While You are Young 1931.01
While You Love Me 1934.29
While You're Thinking 1902.41, 1917.11
Whilst roughest Mountain Tops 1834.03
Whimsical Girl was I, A 1890.23
Whip Dance 1926.18
Whip Dance, The 1986.03
Whip Hand, The 1921.14
Whip, The 1923.46
Whip-poor-Will 1920.44
Whipo-Poor-Wills 1898.55
Whipperwill 1923.06
Whippoorwill Never Again for Me 1911.24
Whippoorwill Waltz, The 1948.16
Whippoorwill, The 1880.24
Whirl of the Opera, The 1914.01
Whirl of the World, The 1914.01
Whirled into Happiness 1925.07
Whirligig 1899.39
Whirligig Stomp, The 1996.07
Whirling Waters, The 1912.03
Whirlwind Trot 1917.01
Whirlwind Whirl, The 1917.32
Whiskerettes 1902.21
Whiskers 1923.31
Whiskers' Dance 1969.08
Whiskey in the Jug 1856.01
Whiskey, You're the Devil 1893.10
Whisper Alone to Me 1894.17
Whisper in My Ear 1920.23
Whisper to Me 1924.38
Whisper Words of Love 1895.25
Whisper Yes or No, Love 1876.05
Whisper, O Whisper Me, Soft in My Ears 1894.41
Whispered Love 1888.39
Whispering Breeze 1902.39
Whispering Song, The 1926.20
Whispering Trees 1926.15
Whist! Sweet Idle Moon 1894.47
Whist! The Boogie Man 1880.09
Whistle 1914.02, 1926.39
Whistle and I'll Come to Meet You 1920.19
Whistle and I'll Come to You 1915.02
Whistle and the Girls Come Running 'Round 1911.45
Whistle as You Walk Out 1907.59
Whistle Away Your Blues 1925.47
Whistle It 1906.33, 1912.14, 1945.16
Whistle When You Walk Out 1906.44
Whistle When You Want Me 1914.33
Whistle When You're Lonely 1908.05, 1910.20
Whistle While You Work 1979.28, 1999.05
Whistle While You Work, Boys 1930.15
Whistle Works, A 1963.20
Whistling Bill 1902.23
Whistling Colored Boy 1896.02
Whistling Cowboy Joe 1913.18
Whistling Dago, The 1894.06
Whistling Dan 1915.01
Whistling Extraordinary 1894.07, 1894.35
Whistling it All Over Town 1921.20
Whistling March, The 1884.60
Whistling Sue 1903.35
Whistling Superlative 1894.37
Whistling Yankee Girl, The 1906.45
White and Brown Girl 1904.40
White and Gold Ballet 1955.10
White and the Pink, The 1938.06
White and the Red, Huzzah!, The 1894.40
White Boys 1968.11
White Cargo 1925.47
White Christmas 1997.01, 1998.11, 1998.19
White Cliffs of Dover, The 1974.09
White Cockade, The 1883.07
White Fete, The 1911.41
White Folks Call it Chanticler, But it's Just Plain Chicken to Me 1910.18
White Grass 1968.20
White Heat 1931.16, 1972.05
White Horse Inn 1936.22
White Horse, The 1970.20
White Lies 1903.10
White Lies, Black Lies 1912.20
White Light Alley 1911.05
White Light Lane 1910.13
White Lights 1927.53
White Lights Were Coming 1929.28
White Lilacs 1928.26
White Man's Hope, The 1912.20
White Rabbit 1982.22
White Rose, Red Rose 1926.15
White Sash, A 1993.17
White Squall, The 1869.14
White Wash 1907.55
White Wild Rose, The 1990.01
White Wings 1936.03
White Wings, They Never Grow Weary 1930.16
White Witch of Jamaica, The 1956.08
Whitehouse Glide, The 1913.18
Whiter Shade of Pale 1982.22
Whitewash Man, The 1909.09
Whither Thou Goest 1966.30
Whizzin Away Along de Track 1943.24
Who 1924.44, 1970.01, 1980.10
Who am I Thinking Of? 1925.04
Who am I? 1926.27, 1950.08, 1987.04, 2000.14
Who are drivers lacking 1878.16
Who are wanting maidens able 1878.16
Who are We Kidding 1963.12
Who are You Now? 1964.11
Who are you, Sir? 1879.21
Who Ate Napoleons With Josephine When Napoleon was Away? 1920.03
Who Bites the Holes in Schweitzer Cheese? 1925.44
Who Broke the Lock? 1999.09
Who Can I Turn To When Nobody Needs Me? 1965.19
Who Can I Turn To? 1974.11, 1974.22
Who can it be? 1882.60
Who Can Tell Where She Dwells? 1894.40
Who Can Tell? 1919.27
Who Can This Be 1930.12
Who Can? You Can? 1961.27
Who Cares 1921.34
Who Cares for a Name 1923.03
Who Cares for Love? 1969.11
Who Cares? 1914.26, 1917.03, 1920.23, 1930.23, 1931.48, 1999.10

Who Carries the Gun? 1918.10
Who Committed the Murder 1933.20
Who Cooks the Bake 1886.52
Who Could Ask for Anything More? 1931.48
Who Couldn't Dance With You? 1989.26
Who dares brave me 1859.09
Who Dat Say Chicken in Dis Crowd? 1898.41
Who Did? 1927.52
Who Did? You Did! 1981.03
Who do You Love, I Hope 1999.04
Who do You Love, I Hope? 1946.12
Who do You Love? 1907.22, 1917.37, 1927.02
Who do You Think You Are? 1947.08, 1975.01
Who Done It? 1950.06
Who Fills the Bill 1964.35
Who Gives a Sou? 1951.13
Who has not heard 1846.01, 1862.03
Who has not heard the Bird of the Air? 1875.06
Who Hit Me? 1948.30
Who is General Staff? 1942.27
Who is he, say, can you tell? 1873.04
Who is He? 1985.05
Who is it Always There? 1956.13
Who is Right? 1890.16
Who is Samuel Cooper? 1948.25
Who is Silvia 1971.18
Who is the Bravest? 1953.01
Who is the Lucky Girl to Be? 1931.48
Who is the Man 1944.32
Who is the woman 1880.04
Who is This Child 1999.17
Who is This Man? 1988.05
Who is This? 1919.42
Who is to Know? 1914.02
Who is Uncle Baggin-dollar? 1887.08
Who is Who 1898.08
Who Killed Cock Robin? 1878.20, 1882.76
Who Killed Nobody 1971.20
Who Knows 1902.41, 1914.29
Who Knows the Way to My Heart? 1964.24
Who Knows What Might Have Been 1961.28
Who Knows Where I'm Goin'? 1963.19
Who Knows? 1917.11, 1945.12, 1962.05
Who Loves Must Dare 1879.50
Who Loves You as I Do? 1926.03
Who Makes the Finest Gingerbread? 1905.25
Who Might You Be? 1894.45
Who Needs the Love of a Woman 1974.03
Who Needs to Dream 1991.10
Who Paid the Rent for Mrs. Rip Van Winkle? 1913.05
Who Paid the Rent for Mrs. Rip Van Winkle? When Rip Van Winkle was Away 1914.10
Who Played Poker With Pocahontas 1919.03
Who Says So 1915.22
Who Says There Ain't No Santa Claus? 1951.15
Who shall be King? 1892.20
Who Shall the Convict Be? 1888.19
Who Started the Rhumba? 1941.13
Who Takes Care of the Cartaker's Daughter While the Caretaker's Taking Care? 1924.43
Who Taught Her Everything 1964.11
Who That Knows How I Love You, Love 1903.21
Who to Love if Not a Stranger? 1970.10
Who Wants a Bad Little Boy? 1925.23
Who Wants Some Milika? 1878.04
Who Wants Some Milka 1873.19
Who Wants to be a Millionaire? 1998.05
Who Wants to Love Spanish Ladies? 1928.44
Who was I? 1973.02
Who was the Last Girl You Called by Her First Name? 1918.39
Who Were You With To-Night 1910.17
Who Will be the Children 1972.18
Who Will be the First to Laugh 1960.18
Who Will be With You When I am Far Away? 1929.27
Who Will Buy? 1963.01
Who Will Love Me as I Am 1997.17
Who Will Take My Place? 1965.30
Who Would a Bachelor Be? 1907.07
Who would be beautiful to be sold? 1887.43
Who Would Have Dreamed 1940.19, 1981.10
Who Would Have Dreamed? 1991.04
Who Would Not be a Soldier's Bride? 1899.06
Who Would've Thought 1993.02
Who Wouldn't 1928.09
Who'd be a Baron? 1879.38
Who'd Ever Think It 1988.09
Who'll Buy Me Violets/The Violet Girl 1926.09
Who'll Buy My Flowers 1904.03
Who'll Buy My Violets/The Violet Girl 1926.35
Who'll Buy My Violets? 1923.26
Who'll Buy? 1949.15
Who'll Help Me Spend My Money? 1898.50
Who'll Mend a Broken Heart? 1926.25
Who's Been Listening to My Heart 1928.38
Who's Been Sitting in My Chair? 1958.14
Who's Doing What to Erwin 1961.21
Who's for the Chase, My Bonnie Hearts 1894.40
Who's Going to Make the Lucky Play? 1899.33
Who's Going to Teach the Children? 1980.15
Who's Gonna be the Winner? 1945.20
Who's Gonna Get You? 1928.08
Who's Got the Pain? 1955.08, 1994.01
Who's It? 1972.18
Who's King Dingdong 1868.03
Who's Sorry Now? 1999.01
Who's That Girl? 1970.09
Who's That Woman? 1971.05
Who's That-a-Calling 1889.41
Who's the Boss 1913.04
Who's the Boy? 1928.21
Who's the Greatest? 1933.25
Who's the Little Girl? 1913.19
Who's the Lucky Fellow? 1924.36
Who's the Thief? 1982.03, 1993.15
Who's the Who? 1925.30
Who's Who 1938.04, 1956.13, 1980.11
Who's Who With You? 1921.10
Who's Who? 1926.03
Who's Your Friend 1904.06
Who's Your Gen'man Frien'? 1906.50
Who's Your Hoosier Friend? 1910.29
Who's Your Little Who-Zis? 1986.06
Who's Zoo in Girl Land 1917.26
Who, Who, Who, Who, Who is She? 1966.18
Who? 1925.33, 1986.01
Who? You! 1926.25
Whoa Bill 1902.09
Whoa Gal 1927.45
Whoa Pagliacci 1923.21
Whoa San 1903.18
Whoa, Bill 1906.04
Whoa, Emma! 1925.43
Whoa-Haw 1975.22
Whoever You Are 1968.31, 1976.09
Whole Loaf, The 1935.16
Whole Lot of Shakin' 1978.01
Whole Lotta Love 1982.22
Whole Lotta Sunlight, A 1973.10
Whole New Board Game, A 1988.09
Whole nickel! A, You have saved my life! 1885.45
Whole Truth, The 1933.25
Whole World Loves, The 1933.03
Whole World's Waitin' to Sing Your Song, The 1992.08
Whole Year Round, The 1908.26
Whom do I love 1886.50
Whoop 'er Up With a Whoop-La 1910.30
Whoop Daddy Ooden Dooden Day 1910.08
Whoop De Dooden Doo 1897.40
Whoop Her Up With a Whoop-La-La! 1908.36
Whoop-De-Dooden-Do 1896.06
Whoop-La-La 1908.31
Whoop-Ti-Ay! 1951.24
Whoopee Ti Yi Yo 1931.02
Whoopem Up 1928.10
Whoopin' and a-Hollerin' 1949.17
Whoopsie 1928.02
Whoopsie Daisy Day 1995.14
Whooshin' Through My Flesh 1971.16
Whos' Christmas Pageant, The 2000.18
Whose Baby are You? 1920.04
Whose Little Angry Man 1973.10
Whose Little Girl are You 1908.41
Whosis Whatsis, The 1925.22
Why 1904.51
Why Adam Sinned 1904.26
Why Ain't I Home? 1930.39
Why Ain't We Free 1952.15
Why Ain't We Got a Dome? 1963.22
Why All This Fuss About Spain? 1922.03
Why am I a Hit With the Ladies? 1925.45
Why am I Blue? 1934.01
Why am I Me 1975.03
Why am I Not Like the Rest of Us Girls? 1895.21
Why am I so Sad 1923.02
Why am I so Sad To-day? 1881.11
Why are All the Girls so Hunrgy? 1909.12
Why are Chickens so High? 1919.26
Why are the Girls so Hungry? 1909.12
Why are They Following Me? 1925.07
Why are We Invited Here? 1915.18
Why be a Hero 1910.17
Why be Afraid to Dance? 1954.15
Why Can't a Girl be a Soldier? 1918.08
Why Can't I Speak? 1968.30, 1983.14
Why Can't I Walk Away? 1968.24
Why Can't I? 1929.12, 1975.13
Why Can't it All be a Dream? 1918.04
Why Can't it Happen Again 1949.02
Why Can't it Happen to Me? 1928.06
Why Can't Me and You? 1980.15
Why Can't the English? 1956.01, 1993.18
Why Can't the World Go and Leave Us Alone? 1983.08
Why Can't They Leave Me Alone? 1992.10
Why Can't This Night Last Forever? 1938.15
Why Can't We All be Nice 1975.06
Why Can't You Behave 1948.32, 1999.19
Why Couldn't We Incorporate? 1930.21
Why D'ya Roll Those Eyes? 1926.21
Why Did He Have to Die? 1976.03
Why Did He Kiss My Heart Awake? 1937.03
Why Did I Choose You? 1965.36
Why did I leave my Country Dear 1868.02
Why Did They Sell Killarney? 1897.33, 1900.24
Why did we Madrid forsaking 1881.04
Why Did We Marry Soldiers? 1926.42, 1946.03, 1987.10
Why Did You do It? 1937.16
Why do Fools Fall in Love 1982.22, 1986.02, 1990.15
Why do I Dream 1869.42
Why do I Love Thee 1898.28
Why do I Love You 1966.14
Why do I Love You? 1925.14, 1927.67, 1946.01, 1983.05, 1986.01, 1994.08
Why do I Weep for Thee? 1870.07
Why do I? 1926.07
Why do Lovers Break Each Others Hearts 1985.03
Why do the Girls 1922.12
Why do the Wrong People Travel? 1961.18, 1986.19
Why do They All Make Love to Me? 1913.23
Why do They All Take the Night Boat to Albany? 1918.05
Why do They Always Say They're the Fair Sex? 1942.27
Why do They Call Me A gibson Girl 1907.15
Why do They Call Me a Gibson Girl? 1906.47
Why do They Die at the End of a Classical Dance? 1922.11
Why do They Make 'Em so Beautiful? 1925.04
Why do They Make Them so Beautiful? 1919.44
Why do We Love Them? 1922.33
Why do Women Have to Call it Love? 1972.24
Why do You Suppose? 1929.42
Why do You Tease Me? 1929.09
Why do You Think I Love You So 1913.37
Why do You Want to Know Why? 1925.45, 1927.21
Why Does a Woman Leave Her Man 1982.13
Why Does it Have to be You? 1955.25
Why Does Love Get in the Way? 1968.19
Why Does the Whole Damn World Adore Me? 1967.02
Why Don't My Baby Write? 1899.35
Why Don't the Band Play? 1900.48, 1900.55
Why Don't They Dance the Polka Anymore? 1914.18
Why Don't They do so Now 1866.22
Why Don't They Leave the Sheik Alone 1924.24
Why Don't They Leave Us Along 1997.08
Why Don't We Live Together 1976.34
Why Don't We? 1929.28
Why don't yo speak for yourself, John? 1894.03

Why Don't You be Nice to Some Young Fellow? 1910.34
Why Don't You do Right? 1983.20
Why Don't You Get a Sweetheart from the Emerald Isle 1911.17
Why Don't You Get a Sweetie? 1920.19
Why Don't You Join the Army? 1890.23
Why Don't You Speak for Yourself, John? 1918.33
Why Don't You Take Out One Little Boy 1906.41
Why Don't You Try 1905.39
Why Don't You Try? 1906.06
Why Don't You? 1907.47, 1920.41
Why Dream? 1934.32
Why Fight This? 1959.27
Why Girls Marry 1902.41
Why Go Anywhere at All? 1961.27
Why God Why? 1991.03
Why Have My Loved Ones Gone? 1939.21
Why Have You Brought Me Here? 1988.01
Why Her? 1957.14
Why Him? 1979.09
Why How Now Madam Flirt 1957.02
Why how now, Madam Flirt? 1750.01
Why I Became a Sailor 1897.40
Why in wild quest 1887.04
Why is It? 1907.52
Why is Love 1925.26
Why is the Ocean so Near the Shore 1914.06
Why is the World so Changed Today? 1926.27
Why is this past believing? 1888.07
Why Me? 1970.19
Why Must I Play the Lady? 1937.10
Why must we always wait? 1894.03
Why Not 1986.16
Why Not for Marriage? 1958.04
Why Not I?, And 1946.07
Why Not Katie? 1955.01
Why Not Me? 1955.11
Why Not, Why Not? 1910.27
Why Paddy is Always Poor 1886.44
Why Should a Little Girl be Lonely? 1925.19
Why should I fear because she chose to roam 1886.40
Why Should I Wake Up? 1966.24
Why Should This a Desert Be? 1981.02
Why Shouldn't I 1935.14
Why Shouldn't I Have You? 1929.45
Why Shouldn't We? 1924.28
Why Shouldn't You Tell Me That? 1912.34
Why Sing of Skies Above? 1937.14
Why so Late 1906.10
Why so Silent 1988.01
Why Take a Girl Down to Coney 1910.18
Why Take a Sandwich to a Banquet 1915.07
Why the Silence? 1945.16
Why They Made Him King 1909.26
Why Throbs this Heart with rapture New 1868.02
Why was I Born on a Farm? 1948.18
Why was I Born? 1929.31, 1975.22, 1986.01
Why was the Sky so Bright Yesterday? 1960.18
Why We Ain't Free 1952.15
Why We Ride the Subway 1920.35
Why We Tell the Story 1990.12
Why Worry 1920.45
Why Worry? 1920.14
Why Would Anyone Want to Get Married? 1966.09
Why Wouldn't I Do? 1929.51
Why, Huntress, Why, wilt thou thy life expose? 1796.01
Why, Mama, Why 1985.05
Why, Oh Why? 1927.16
Why, then, should I - 1882.44
Why-Can't They Song 1989.24
Why? 1929.01, 1929.44, 1963.16, 1976.08
Wick 1991.05
Wicked Man 1898.73
Wicked Old Village of Venice 1929.08
Wicked, Unwholesome, Expensive 1934.40
Wide Open Spaces, The 1954.17
Wide Pants Willie 1925.27
Wide Smile, High Style, That's Me 1987.05
Widow has Ways, A 1906.33
Widow Machtree 1861.04
Widow Magee 1885.06, 1887.05
Widow Nolan's Goat 1882.02
Widow Wood, The 1911.24
Widow's Blues 1922.13
Widow's Weeds 1891.46
Widow's Wile, A 1901.07
Widow, The 1903.10, 1904.55
Widows 1911.12
Wie War's Mal Mit Lissabon 1999.05
Wien, Wien, You're Calling Me 1975.22
Wiener Blut 1964.25
Wiener Frauen singen gern 1964.25
Wife for Each Day in the Week, A 1917.09
Wife of Manelic, The 1926.35
Wife of the Bullfighter, The 1926.35
Wife of Your Own, A 1913.29
Wild 2000.08
Wild About Music 1928.27
Wild and Reckless 1965.29
Wild and Wonderful 1971.19
Wild and Wooley West, The 1897.33
Wild and Woolly West, The 1900.24, 1927.60
Wild Birds Calling 1969.07
Wild Boy 2000.20
Wild Cats 1924.44
Wild Cherry Rag 1910.18
Wild Flowers 1885.44
Wild Flowers and Buttonhole Bouquet 1886.62
Wild Horse Ceremonial Dance 1966.12
Wild Justice, The 1949.15, 1972.06
Wild Man of Borneo 1888.32
Wild Oat Joe 1928.45
Wild Party 2000.08
Wild Romantic Blues 1920.19, 1920.22, 1920.23
Wild Rose 1907.32, 1911.04, 1926.34, 1948.16
Wild Rose, The 1911.31, 1920.44
Wild Time 1999.12
Wild West Pitch Dance 1966.12
Wild Women Don't Have the Blues 1982.12
Wild, Wild Women, The 1917.23
Wildcat 1960.22
Wildfire 1909.10
Wildflower 1923.05
Wilheinderick Strauss 1879.63
Wilheindrick Strauss 1880.39
Wilhelmina 1909.14
Wilkes-Barre P.A. 1963.08
Wilkommen 1966.24, 1998.04
Will Answer All Sincere Replies 1971.04, 1976.27
Will He Ever Return to Me? 1884.66, 1886.11
Will He Ever Smile Again? 1904.47
Will He Like Me? 1963.14
Will He Turn? 1956.09
Will I Ever See Her Again? 1979.28
Will I Ever Tell You 1957.18
Will I Ever Tell You? 2000.11
Will I? 1996.09
Will it All End in Smoke? 1913.20
Will Lifton Lift the Cup? 1903.18
Will o' the Wisp 1908.35, 1914.23
Will O' the Wisp 1923.03
Will o' the Wisp, The 1914.30
Will o' Wisp 1919.14
Will She Come from the East? 1922.39
Will Somebody Tell Me Why? 1898.01
Will they remember me 1855.01
Will We Ever Know Each Other 1981.28
Will You be My Hero, Noble Sir? 1903.34
Will You be My Little Bride? 1904.52
Will You be My Teddy Bear 1906.45
Will You Come Out and Play? 1892.21
Will You Forget 1917.20
Will You Forgive Us 1920.20
Will You Have a Gin Rickey? 1905.35
Will You Love Me Monday Morning as You Did on Friday Night? 1934.19
Will You Love Me When My Flivver is a Wreck? 1916.06
Will You Marry Me? 1923.36, 1955.27
Will You Remember Me 1988.08
Will You Remember Me? 1938.11
Will You Remember Sweet Heart? 1917.15
Will You Remember? 1922.03
Will You Remember? Will You Forget? 1928.35
Will You Sing This Glee With Me 1910.21
Will you so obliging be 1859.16
Will You Still Love Me Tomorrow 1982.22
Will You Still Love Me Tomorrow? 1986.02
Will You Think of Me Tomorrow? 1969.14
Will-a-Mania 1991.07
Will-o'-the Wisp 1892.52
Will-o'-the-Wisp 1942.30
Willful Woman 1898.73
William McKinley High 1948.22
William Tell it to Me 1920.23
William was a Gay Young Sailor 1879.06
William's Song 1983.21
William's sure to be right 1882.17
Willie 1903.18
Willie Off the Yacht 1897.56, 1898.02
Willie was a Gay Boy 1900.51
Willie's Got Another Girl Now 1908.27
Willie's Little Whistle 1934.40
Willing to Learn 1906.35
Willow and the Lily, The 1882.17
Willow Glen 1868.03
Willow Pattern Plate, The 1897.14, 1899.11
Willow Song, The 1981.02
Willow Tit-Willow 1886.24
Willow Tree 1946.05
Willow Weep for Me 1982.12
Willow, Willow, Willow 1961.26
Willy of Piccadilly 1910.05
Willye Wyllie 1899.41
Wilt Thou My True Love Be? 1890.39
Wily Widower, The 1882.63
Wimmens 1916.12
Win for Me 1923.47
Wind Yourself Around Me, Dearie 1907.62
Wind 'Round My Heart 1952.11
Wind in the Willows, The 1985.20
Windflowers 1954.03
Winding of the Yarn, The 1902.39
Winding, Winding, My Love and I 1900.50
Window Cleaners, The 1925.47
Window on the Avenue, A 1949.01
Windows 1992.05
Windy Boys, The 1902.33, 1904.20, 1905.10
Windy City Marmalade 1972.04
Wine Ballet 1919.30
Wine Divine 1901.07
Wine from My Slipper 1941.03
Wine Maid Divine 1911.05
Wine of France 1905.04
Wine of Verzenay 1880.07
Wine of Youth, The 1970.01
Wine Song 1914.04
Wine Song, The 1891.15
Wine's My Only Pleasure 1904.23
Wine, Girls and Gay Paree 1908.01
Wine, Wine 1904.04
Wine, Wine, Wine 1898.43
Wine, Woman and Song 1897.39
Wine, Women and Song 1897.20, 1906.05, 1916.11, 1942.31
Wing a Song in My Heart 1955.13
Wing Lee's Rag-Time Clock 1899.11
Winged Love 1913.32
Winged Victory 1943.23
Wings of Love 1924.25
Wings of the Morning 1930.30, 1932.10
Winifred Wood 1886.45
Wink of His Eye, The 1896.05
Winning 1997.07
Winning a Home 1898.67
Winning Race, The 1918.02
Winning the Prize 1924.10
Wino Will 1971.20
Winona 1927.65
Winsome Widow am I, A 1912.13
Winsome Winnie 1903.38
Winter and Spring 1930.06
Winter and Summer 1969.02
Winter Battle 1990.17
Winter Evening, A 1925.03
Winter in Central Park 1929.31
Winter Nights 1971.20
Winter Song 1963.28

Winter Wonderland 1998.19
Winter's Carnival, A 1892.29
Winter's Here 1971.09
Winter's on the Wing 1991.05
Wintergreen for President 1931.48, 1933.25
Wireless Heart, The 1920.13, 1920.36
Wireless Telephone, The 1906.30
Wireless Way, The 1912.47
Wisconsin 1946.07
Wisdom 1971.20
Wisdom Says 'Festina Lente' 1907.51
Wise Fisherman, The 1910.08
Wise Little Maid of France, The 1897.17
Wise Men Have in All Ages 1885.44
Wise Men in All Ages 1881.22
Wise Old Owl, A 1903.07
Wiseman's Serenaders 1901.04
Wish 1957.17
Wish for a Prince, A 1997.16, 1998.08
Wish I Were Here, or La Vie en Prose 1956.09
Wish Me Luck 1949.12
Wish Them Well 1947.17, 1993.16
Wish You Were Here 1952.10, 1962.17
Wisha Wurra 1961.14
Wishbone Song, The 1951.17
Wishes 1986.18
Wishful Thinking 1966.21, 1984.15
Wishing 1977.01
Wishing and Hoping 1984.15
Wishing Cap, The 1900.41
Wishing Well, The 1898.73
Wishing You Were Somehow Here Again 1988.01, 1992.12
Wistaria My Bride 1904.37
Witch Behind the Moon, The 1903.03
Witch Doctor, The 1953.10
Witches Waining 1882.18
Witches' Brew 1967.06
Witches, The 1904.25
Witchraft 1974.11
With a Big Shillelagh 1902.25
With a Boo 1904.40
With a Glance Demure 1910.36
With a Heart 1898.70
With a Little Bit of Luck 1956.01, 1993.18
With a Little Help from My Friends 1974.24, 1977.10
With a Smile and a Song 1979.28
With a Snap of My Finger 1970.21
With a Song in My Heart 1929.12, 1975.13
With a tear in our voice! 1884.14
With a Twinkle in Her Eye 1912.06
With a Twist of the Wrist 1941.03
With a Wave of My Hand 1946.22
With a Woman You Never Can Tell 1921.09
With All My Heart 1934.29
With All My Heart and Soul 1953.17
With All Proprieties 1902.07
With All the Town in Bright Array 1902.01
With All Your Faults, We Love You Still 1913.14
With anger stern 1895.29
With Anne on My Arm 1983.11
With aspect stern and gloomy stride 1885.47
With banners Waving 1888.34
With brush in hand 1895.43
With Bumpers, Friends, Fill Every Glass 1887.33
With Cat-Like Tread Upon Our Prey We Steal 1981.01
With Cat-Like Tread, Upon Prey We Steal 1879.72
With Cauton Tread 1889.46
With Cracking of Whip and Rattle of Spur 1897.13
With dance, with song 1881.25
With ducal pomp 1890.02
With Ev'ry Heart 1899.06
With Every Breath I Take 1989.29
With Every Star 1944.20
With Fife and Drum 1881.07
With fury deep we burn 1894.15
With Glad Acclaim 1900.39
With heart and with voice 1879.10
With her I will ever 1859.09
With joy abiding, Together gliding 1884.09
With joy in my heart 1878.16
With Joy That is Ecstatical 1914.17
With Keen Anticipation 1900.39
With Laughing Song and Merry Dance 1885.51
With Lowered Head 1914.03
With me you will ever 1859.09
With Militant Stride 1916.18
With Military Pomp 1900.25
With Much Care and Thought 1856.01
With My Sabots 1952.04
With One Look 1994.10
With Papers Duly Signed 1922.11
With Pleasure 1913.06
With Plenty of Money and You 2001.08
With rapture glowing 1848.04
With Red Wine 1928.12
With so Little to be Sure Of 1964.15
With Song and Cheer 1912.10
With splendor auspicious 1896.27
With Stealthy Footsteps Falling 1899.40
With Style 1975.18
With such a dainty dame none can compare 1887.44
With the Boys I Love 1918.29
With the Dawn 1930.27
With the High Dreams of Childhood 1862.04
With the One I Love 1981.12
With This Ring 1967.02
With this treasure I must part 1868.01
With troubled filled and sorrow laden 1857.06
With Type a-Ticking 1918.25
With Tyrolean Fixins 1855.11
With Us Darling 1883.12
With Weary Hearts 1902.19
With wily brain 1894.15
With You 1963.12, 1972.22, 1983.19
With You on My Arm 1983.11
With Your Hand in My Heart 1968.08
Withered Irish Rose 1986.11
Without a Beautiful Girl 1919.32
Without a Caress 1945.01
Without a Companion 1855.01
Without a Girl Like You 1921.04
Without a Mother 1970.18
Without a Shadow of a Doubt 1930.20
Without a Song 1929.37
Without a Sponsor 1943.18
Without a Stitch 1950.01
Without friends 1844.01
Without Him, What's the Band? 1894.37
Without Kissing, Love isn't Love 1920.08
Without Love 1930.11, 1955.02
Without Me 1968.01
Without more ado 1859.15
Without Thinking of You 1927.12
Without You 1904.38, 1913.17, 1918.32, 1934.32, 1941.02, 1956.01, 1991.07, 1993.18, 1996.09
Without You, I'm Nothing 1956.02
Wizard of Wall Street, The 1906.07
Wizard, The 1899.39
Wo, Larry, Wo 1931.02
Wochenend und Sonnenschein 1999.05
Woe is Me 1927.49, 1937.11
Woke Up This Morning 1969.10
Woke Up Today 1973.03
Wolf Song, The 1999.17
Wolf Time 1946.23
Wololo! 1988.02
Woman 1920.01, 1925.43, 1983.14
Woman Against the World 1944.18
Woman Alone, A 1982.18
Woman and a Sword, A 1883.12
Woman and Light 1919.03
Woman for the Man, The 1966.06
Woman Haters' Club Hymn 1912.37
Woman I was Before, The 1960.10
Woman in His Room, The 1948.26, 1974.25
Woman in Love 1967.14
Woman in the Case, The 1904.54
Woman is a Rascal 1945.13
Woman is a Sometime Thing, A 1935.13, 1983.04
Woman is a Woman is a Woman, A 1963.20
Woman is How She Loves, A 1969.17
Woman is Only a Woman, But a Good Cigar is a Smoke, A 1905.29
Woman of Importance, A 1906.04
Woman of Temperament 1913.02
Woman of the wisest wit, The 1884.09
Woman of the Year 1981.10
Woman of the Year, The 1942.27
Woman on the Bus, The 1958.10
Woman on the Run 1973.03
Woman Ought to Know Her Place, A 1982.14
Woman Pays, The 1918.02
Woman Rules the King 1904.30
Woman to Lady 1935.13
Woman Who Lived Up There, The 1947.02
Woman Who Thinks I'm Wonderful, A 1983.08
Woman Wouldn't be a Woman, A 1957.05
Woman's a Wonderful Thing 1908.41
Woman's Dream, A 1910.18
Woman's Dress 1886.30
Woman's Dress, A 1921.01
Woman's Eyes 1908.05 **see women's**
Woman's Hands, A 1972.23
Woman's Heart 1846.01, 1862.03
Woman's heart is like a dove, A 1886.40
Woman's Heart, A 1913.29
Woman's Lot 1888.20
Woman's Love, A 1890.44
Woman's Prerogative, A 1946.08
Woman's Said to be the Fickle Sex 1917.14
Woman's smile 1859.16
Woman's Smile, A 1912.46
Woman's Tact, A 1897.17
Woman's Touch, A 1920.30
Woman's Touch, The 1926.36
Woman's Work 1999.17 **see women's**
Woman's Work is Never Done 1925.52, 1928.40
Woman, How Dare You! 1912.40
Woman, Lovely Woman 1897.13, 1907.30, 1908.21, 1930.12
Woman,s Rights 1880.46
Woman-Woman 1922.04
Women 1904.56, 1907.48, 1908.01, 1918.35, 1935.15, 1964.24, 1969.07
Women All Tell Me, The 1924.20
Women and Men 1974.04
Women Haven't Any Mercy on a Man 1918.28
Women of all ranks and station 1859.16
Women of Valencia 1949.07
Women of Vienna 1988.10
Women Weaving 1948.24
Women's Club Blues 1948.25
Women's Eyes 1910.30
Women's Liberation 1970.18
Women's Will 1882.18
Women's Work 1950.10, 1952.05
Women, The 1943.09
Women, Wine and Jazz 1918.06
Women, Wine and Song 1895.08
Women, Women 1912.49
Women, Women, Women 1946.24
Women, You Women! 1924.40
Wompom, The 1959.20
Won't Go Home Till Morning 1903.18
Won't I Do 1929.50
Won't it be a Lark 1902.01
Won't Some Nice Boy Marry Me? 1918.11
Won't Some One Take Me Home 1910.22
Won't You All Fall in Love With Me? 1920.39
Won't You be My Daddy 1917.08
Won't You be My Girlie? 1906.19
Won't You be My Honey? 1906.31
Won't You be My Little Brown Bear? 1907.22
Won't You be My Lovey Dovey? 1905.20
Won't You be My Playmate? 1908.35
Won't You be My Sweetheart 1894.35
Won't You be My Teddy Bear? 1906.45
Won't You be My Valentine? 1908.35
Won't You Buy a Flower? 1922.15
Won't You Buy? 1907.41, 1916.09
Won't You Change Your Name? 1905.49
Won't You Charleston With Me? 1954.09, 1986.03
Won't You Come Across? 1926.34
Won't You Come and Float Me 1901.25
Won't You Come and Splash Me 1907.18

Won't You Come and Waltz With Me 1913.36
Won't You Come into My Playhouse? 1913.18
Won't You Come to Margate 1896.05
Won't You Come Up to the Table? 1917.30
Won't You Dance? 1914.20
Won't You Fondle Me? 1905.09, 1905.10
Won't You Harmonize With Me 1908.44
Won't You Harmonize With Me? 1908.27
Won't You Help Me Out? 1919.06
Won't You Let Me Carry Your Parcel 1908.27
Won't You Let Me Put My Arms Around You 1906.05
Won't You Let Me Put My Arms Around You? 1906.04
Won't You Let Me Take a Picture of You 1920.33
Won't You Marry Me? 1927.42, 1961.02
Won't You Save That Harem for Me 1919.18
Won't You Say Yes to Me 1907.49
Won't You Smile 1915.08
Won't You Take Me to Paris 1922.40
Won't You Waltz With Me 1911.14
Won't You Waltz With Me? 1914.07
Won't You Waltz? 1906.25
Won't You Write to Me 1917.08
Wonder Child Medley 1877.20
Wonder of You, The 1978.01
Wonder Why 1931.34
Wonder Why? 1951.05
Wonderful 1911.39, 1920.33
Wonderful Cafe Girls 1929.33
Wonderful Cape Cod Girl 1929.33
Wonderful Creature, A 1917.34
Wonderful Dad 1923.40
Wonderful Dance 1923.06
Wonderful Day 1919.33
Wonderful Day Like Today, A 1965.19
Wonderful Days 1915.01
Wonderful Garden of Love 1914.15
Wonderful Girl 1925.27, 1926.46
Wonderful Girl - Wonderful Boy 1920.36
Wonderful Guy, A 1993.16
Wonderful joy our eyes to bless, A 1894.15
Wonderful Kiss 1916.12
Wonderful Magician, The 1899.34
Wonderful Man 1919.29
Wonderful Me 1985.02
Wonderful Music 1963.26, 1992.10
Wonderful Party 1962.01
Wonderful Party, A 1924.43
Wonderful Rhythm 1925.35
Wonderful River, The 1924.11
Wonderful Thing for the King, A 1930.30
Wonderful Thing They Call Love 1914.32
Wonderful Thing We Call Love, The 1922.28
Wonderful Thing, A 1921.05
Wonderful War, A 1920.01
Wonderful Wonderful Day 1982.14
Wonderful World 1911.06
Wonderful Yesterday 1925.35
Wonderful You 1923.01
Wonderful, Marvelous You 1961.02
Wonderin' 1971.21
Wondering Who 1929.33
Wonderland 1907.12, 1922.04
Wonderman 1985.17
Wondrous Midnight Eyes 1921.03
Wood 1930.40
Wood Alcohol Blues 1921.19
Wood Nymph and the River God, The 1900.12
Wood Nymphs, The 1923.40
Wood-Bird's Song, The 1868.02
Woodcutters' Chorus 1882.75
Wooden Shoe Song 1886.35
Wooden Wedding 1943.19
Woodland Wanderings 1944.21
Woodman, Woodman, Spare That Tree 1911.24
Woof 1936.31
Woolly Wild West Show, The 1913.30
Wop Cabaret, The 1915.27
Word is Day, A 1951.23
Word of Love, A 1916.25
Word of the Lord, The 1972.11, 1972.15
Word to Husbands, A 1973.08
Word to Remind You, A 1937.03
Word to the Wise, A 1905.42
Word, The 1879.15
Words and Music 1927.11
Words are in My Heart, The 1989.21
Words are Not Needed Every Day 1917.06
Words Cannot Tell 1896.02
Words He Doesn't Say 1988.10
Words I Never Said, The 1972.07
Words of Love 1990.15
Words of love too loudly spoken 1894.15
Words That Were Never Spoken 1895.04
Words Without Music 1934.42, 1936.02, 1936.17
Words Without Time 1884.42
Words, Music, Cash 1928.26
Words, The 1971.21
Words, Words, Words 1964.40
Work 1969.08
Work Alike 1929.19
Work Eight Hours 1942.30
Work for the Night is Coming 1955.13
Work is Over 1895.44
Workin' it Out 1979.04
Workin' on de Railroad 1940.01
Working and Scrubbing 1895.44
Working for the Pictures 1914.16
Working Girl, The 1913.18
Working in a Coal Mine 1992.06
Workout 1964.32
World After the Death, The 1998.08
World and I, The 1946.18
World Belongs to the Young, The 1969.17
World Dance 1960.04
World forbids it, The 1834.03
World Full of Girls, A 1919.23
World is Beautiful Today, The 1953.01
World is but a broken toy, The 1884.09
World is Comin' to a Start, The 1970.05
World is Dark and Lonely, The 1933.24
World is Full of Loneliness, The 1984.02
World is Full of Villains, The 1945.04
World is Full of Women's Eyes 1910.30
World is in My Arms, The 1940.10
World is Mean, The 1966.19
World is only after all, The 1855.06
World is Waiting for Me, The 1985.20
World is Young Again, The 1944.28
World is Your Balloon, The 1951.15
World Keeps Going Round 1980.15
World Must be Bigger Than an Avenue, The 1973.05
World of a Star, The 1902.16
World of Beauty 1919.03
World of Dreams 1930.06
World of Strangers, A 1950.02
World Outside, The 1956.07
World Owes You This, My Dear, The 1921.35
World Set on Fire by a Black and a Jew, The 1988.07
World Take Me Back 1964.01
World Waiting for Sunrise 1923.02
World Weary 1928.42, 1968.19, 1986.19
World Without End 1972.15
World's Fair, The 1891.14, 1892.45
World's Greatest Show, The 1948.19, 1949.05
World's Inamorata, The 1941.04
World's Worst Women, The 1923.05
Worldly Man, The 1912.01
Worlds Apart 1963.11, 1985.06
Worm Germ, The 1972.25
Worm's Revenge, The 1920.43
Worried 1908.13
Worries 1924.08
Worst is Yet to Come, The 1918.38
Worst Pies in London, The 1979.06
Worst Woman on the Stage, The 1904.58
Worth While Waiting For 1923.04
Wotcher 1960.17
Wotta Night! 1988.12
Would I might be hang'd! 1750.01
Would I might be hanged 1854.06
Would I Might be Hanged 1957.02
Would I Were a Bird 1876.06
Would You 1904.55
Would You Ask? 1896.28
Would You be so Kindly 1940.10
Would You do It? 1906.13
Would You if You Could 1897.54, 1898.43
Would You if You Were I? 1904.28
Would you know the kind of maid 1884.09
Would You Let Me Know? 1956.13
Would You Like a Little Girl Like Me? 1906.49
Would You Like a Sweetheart? 1907.27
Would You Like to Lay Your Head Upon My Pillow? 1965.05
Would You Like to Motor With Mater? 1909.04
Would You Like to Sleep Upon My Pillow? 1921.02
Would You Like to Take a Walk 1930.38
Would You Like to Take a Walk? 1931.13, 1988.08
Would You Love Me? 1917.34
Would You Rather be a Soldier With an Eagle on Your Shoulder, or a Private With , 1918.19
Would You Say No? 1917.34
Would You? 1985.08, 1992.11
Wouldn't it be Loverly 1956.01, 1993.18
Wouldn't it be Nice? 2000.08
Wouldn't it Puzzle You? 1907.07
Wouldn't That be Wonderful 1932.13
Wouldn't You Like to be on Broadway? 1947.02
Wouldn't You Like to Fondle Little Baby? 1894.37
Wouldn't You Like to Learn to Love Me? 1907.01
Wouldn't You? 1925.47
Wound upon thine arm, The 1844.01
Wow-ooh-Wolf! 1944.29
Wow-Yip-Po 1906.50
Wrangle's Infantry 1886.62
Wrap Me in Your Sarape 1941.07
Wrapped in a Ribbon and Tied in a Bow 1947.02
Wreath of Carnations 1912.03
Wreath of Roses 1869.02
Wreath, The 1975.19
Wreathe the Golden Flower 1909.29
Wreck of a Mec 1960.13
Wriggly Rag 1913.16
Write to Marian the Maid 1905.23
Writer Fills the Lowest Niche, A 1945.09
Writer Writes at Night, A 1979.12
Written in the Book of Destiny 1914.33
Written in the Stars 2000.06
Written in Your Hand 1948.27
Wrong 1965.33
Wrong is Never Right 1975.19
Wrong Note Rag 1953.03, 1958.20, 1958.21, 1977.02
Wrong Note Rag, The 1997.01
Wrong Side of the Railroad Tracks, The 1946.24
Wrong Thing at the Right Time, The 1924.30
Wu Chang-Ching and Taewongun 1997.16
Wuggly Ump, The 1978.24
Wunderbar 1948.32, 1999.19
Wunsch' guten Morgen, Herr von Pepi 1964.25
Wyoming Lullaby 1922.22

X9RL-220 1968.13
Xanadu 1965.37, 1972.21
Xhosa Proposition, A 1977.01
Xica da Silva 1988.06
Y Andale 1988.15
Y Como Le Va 1929.01
Y' Can't Win 1959.19
Y'-la 1909.12
Y'All Got It! 1975.01
Y'assou 1968.30, 1983.14
Y'avait un p'tiot matelot 1884.50
Y'up and Away 1907.26
Y-O-U, Dear, Y-O-U 1913.19
Y.M.D. 1911.03
Y.O.U. 1972.18
Ya Chara 1967.05
Ya da la Joie 1945.09
Ya Got Me 1989.03
Ya Got Trouble 1957.18, 1974.11, 1997.01, 2000.11
Ya Gotta Bend Down 1940.01
Ya Gotta Look Out for Yourself 1989.29
Ya-Da-De-Dum-Dum 1919.11
Yaaka Hula Hickey Dula 1916.03
Yacht and the Brig, The 1880.69
Yacht Club Swing 1978.09

Yacht Song 1941.03
Yacht, The 1909.04
Yachting 1910.23
Yada-De-Dum-Dum 1919.11
Yah! Yoh! Yum! 1880.10
Yahoo Step, The 1961.01
Yakety Yak 1995.03
Yale 1919.39
Yaller 1930.32
Yaller Boy and the Moon 1902.01
Yama Yama Man, The 1908.18, 1917.26
Yamaboo 1934.27
Yamboo 1934.37
Yamekraw 1929.18
Yandro 1954.11
Yankee Banners 1899.11
Yankee Boy 1986.13
Yankee Doodle 1909.16, 1914.05, 1929.45, 1932.04
Yankee Doodle Blues 1922.23
Yankee Doodle Boodle 1905.41
Yankee Doodle Boy 1907.16, 1968.07, 1982.05
Yankee Doodle Boy, The 1904.42, 1980.27
Yankee Doodle Boys 1898.28
Yankee Doodle Come to Town 1908.14
Yankee Doodle Coon 1907.55
Yankee Doodle Dance, A 1918.19
Yankee Doodle Dandy 1902.42, 1904.06, 1968.07, 1974.09
Yankee Doodle Disco 1978.05
Yankee Doodle Doings 1901.07
Yankee Doodle Girls 1910.15
Yankee Doodle Girls, The 1899.12
Yankee Doodle Guards, The 1910.20
Yankee Doodle Oo La La 1923.41
Yankee Doodle Parisien 1963.02
Yankee Doodle Yarns 1907.47
Yankee Doodle-Up-to-Date 1905.47
Yankee Doodles are Coming to Town 1979.09
Yankee Girl, The 1903.16, 1910.08
Yankee Jazz 1924.13
Yankee Land 1904.31, 1909.17, 1919.08
Yankee Millionaire, The 1907.27
Yankee Noblemen 1903.19
Yankee Prince Waltz 1908.21
Yankee Romeo, The 1910.12
Yankee Soldier Boy, The 1908.05
Yankee Tourist Girl, The 1903.04
Yankeeland 1907.14
Yankele and Refkele 1931.29
Yankiana Rag 1910.18
Yanks are Coming Again, The 1942.14
Yanks are on the March Again, The 1941.13
Yankyula 1930.26
Yanvalou 1962.22
Yarid, A 1970.17
Yarns 1903.21
Yasni Kozkolai 1963.29
Yatata, Yatata, Yatata 1947.17
Yawcup Heinrich Risender von Dunner und Blitzen Bub 1879.54
Yazoo Rag 1919.26
Ye Lunchtime Follies 1943.22
Ye Olde Hock Shop 1932.08
Ye Spotted Snake 1880.19
Ye Strains of Soft Murmurs 1787.01
Ye Summer Birds 1883.12
Ye Wear 'Em Wid an Air 1904.01
Yea Boys' Let's Have a Time! 1910.08
Yea Ho, My Lads, Heave Ho 1903.18
Yea Ho, My Lads, Heave Oh 1903.18
Year After Year We're Together 1924.19
Year and a Day, A 1905.48
Year from Today, A 1924.08
Year is a Long Time, A 1917.05
Year of the Child, The 1992.09
Years Ago 1901.27
Years are Passing By, The 1994.12, 1998.20
Years Before Us, The 1948.26, 1974.25
Years Touch Not the Heart 1902.41, 1917.11
Yee-ho! Heave-ho! 1885.51
Yeemy Yeemy 1955.25
Yellow Drum 1971.16
Yellow Rose 1894.44
Yenta Power 1978.28
Yer Baby's A-Comin' to Town 1896.18
Yer My Friend, Aintcha? 1957.07
Yerushalaim Shel Zahavi 1972.17
Yerushaliam 1971.02
Yes 1971.07
Yes and No 1925.25, 1932.19
Yes I am Here 1921.15
Yes I Can 1964.32
Yes I see clearly now 1859.09
Yes I'm the Same Little Girl 1903.14
Yes or No 1888.19, 1925.02, 1925.39, 1938.06
Yes Sir, That's My Baby 1974.09, 1986.06
Yes! let me like a Soldier fall 1848.04
Yes! Mistress it's a Pity 1988.02
Yes! that form 1859.18
Yes, 'Tis a Dream 1868.08
Yes, 'Tis the Impressario 1890.39
Yes, Beda, this Beda 1860.01
Yes, He's a Bachelor 1933.25
Yes, I am Brave 1879.72
Yes, I am known as Papyrus 1895.19
Yes, I Love You Honey 1943.16
Yes, I'll be the Little Tycoon 1886.15
Yes, I'll Meet Thee, Dearest 1871.12
Yes, in a Minute 1894.17
Yes, it's Love 1988.10
Yes, Ma'am 1963.27, 1985.05
Yes, Mama 1933.24
Yes, Mr. Baiello 1962.24
Yes, My Darling Daughter 1941.03
Yes, My Heart 1961.10
Yes, No and Nothing at all 1882.75
Yes, of Spain a staunch Grandee 1882.60
Yes, Once Again 1890.21
Yes, she is a darling 1887.43
Yes, Sir, I've Made a Date 1942.34
Yes, Sir, She's My Baby 1944.32
Yes, Sir, That's My Baby 1979.05, 1979.13
Yes, we all will be there 1876.07
Yes, we must part 1859.09
Yes, We've All Seen Sham 1886.15
Yes, Yes 1922.14
Yes, Yes, Yes 1938.07
Yes, Yes, Yvette 1927.49
Yesterday 1913.21, 1919.39, 1955.03, 1973.17, 1977.10
Yesterday and to-day 1882.17
Yesterday and To-Day 1910.31
Yesterday I Left the Earth 1975.04
Yesterday I Loved You 1959.26
Yesterday When I was Young 1970.01, 1974.19, 1981.16, 1983.03
Yesterday, Today and Tomorrow 1994.12
Yesterday, When I was Young 1998.12
Yesterdays 1933.26, 1986.01
Yet I Don't Know, And 1960.17
Yet I Love Her Till I Die, And 1931.02
Yeux brilliants, Les 1964.39
Yeux, Les 1864.13
Yew-ra-liar-ity 1894.06
Yiddish 1960.18, 1970.17
Yiddish International Radio Hour 1990.16
Yiddish Mule Train 1951.21
Yiddisha Butterfly 1916.23
Yidishe Brigades 1989.10
Yip! Yip! 1919.26
Yip, Ahoy, or Adrift on the Old Prairie 1938.09
Yip, I Adee, I Aye 1908.38
Yip-de-addy 1909.11
Yisrolik 1960.18
Yo Ho 1905.52
Yo Ho and a Bottle of Rum 1927.08
Yo Ho for a Jolly Good Sail 1900.59
Yo Ho Ho, The 1961.22
Yo Ho! Yo Ho! 1911.23
Yo Ho, Little Girls, Yo Ho 1902.30
Yo Soy el Corrido 1988.15
Yodel 1880.38, 1921.26
Yodel Blues, The 1949.17
Yodel O 1919.12
Yodel Song 1889.22, 1907.37
Yodel, The 1888.42, 1889.25
Yokahama 1906.06
Yokels' Chorus 1886.45
Yokohama Lullaby 1921.18
Yome, Yome... 1998.11
Yonder in extremis lying 1859.11
Yonder see, sure 'tis she 1871.19
Yoo Hoo Blues, The 1939.12
Yoo-Hoo 1921.34
Yorkshire 1910.21
Yoshke Fort Avek 1990.16
Yoshke's Going Away 1990.16
Yosl Ber 1990.16
Yosl, Yosl 1990.16
You 1930.30, 1970.19, 1979.05
You & Me 1995.15
You Ain't as Warm as You Look 1898.02
You Ain't Gonna Pick Up Where You Left Off 1983.15
You Ain't Gonna Shake Them Feathers No More 1967.06
You Ain't Got No Savoir Faire 1931.04
You Ain't No Astronaut 1971.13
You Ain't One, Two, Three 1898.78
You Ain't Said Nothing Yet 1906.08
You Ain't so Hot 1935.03
You Always Love the Same Girl 1943.22, 1975.13
You Always Talk of Friendship 1930.21
You and I 1886.02, 1891.32, 1897.39, 1897.39, 1904.25, 1904.40, 1912.12, 1913.04, 1915.03, 1923.10, 1924.40, 1988.09
You and I Atta Baby 1921.23
You and I Could be Just Like That 1932.01
You and I in Old Versailles 1923.18
You and I Know 1937.10
You and I Love You and Me 1927.05
You and I, Love 1889.03, 1971.07
You and Me 1902.35
You and Me and P.B. Shelley 1973.08
You and the Night and the Music 1934.38, 1972.05
You Appeal to Me 1927.55, 1950.06
You Are 1968.13
You are a Rose 1931.06
You are a Very Nice Boy 1913.21
You are All I've Wanted 1936.27
You are an Orphan 1881.11
You are Beautiful 1958.19, 1997.01
You are Both Agreed 1928.30
You are for Loving 1989.23
You are Free 1919.27
You are Laughing 1905.46
You are Love 1927.67, 1946.01, 1966.14, 1975.22, 1983.05, 1994.08
You are My Darlin' Bride 1952.15
You are My Day Dream 1929.35
You are My Destiny 1997.16, 1998.08
You are My Downfall 1946.23
You are My Heaven 1928.24
You are My Home 1997.19, 1999.13
You are My Little Cupid 1915.20
You are My Lucky Star 1964.02, 1985.08
You are My Rain-Beau 1922.32
You are My Songs 1934.29
You are My Star, for I Love You 1903.25
You are My Woman 1931.39
You are Never Away 1947.17
You are Not Real 1966.18
You are Not the One for Me 1907.61
You are Not Your Father's Son 1950.16
You are Romance 1943.20
You are Sixteen 1959.24
You are Sixteen, Sixteen Going on Seventeen 1998.03
You are so Beyond 1983.17
You are so Fair 1937.04
You are the King of Chosun 1997.16, 1998.08
You are the Only Girl I'll Ever Care About 1899.29
You are the Only One for Me 1969.11
You are too Beautiful 1975.13
You are What You Feel 1982.03, 1993.15
You are Woman 1964.11
You are You 1965.17
You ask me why 1882.63

You Beautiful so and So 1929.26
You Become Me 1953.02
You Belong to Me 1916.24
You Better Get Outta Town 1988.07
You Better Go Now 1957.10
You Better Min' 1930.10
You Better Mind 1944.32
You Blacksmith, look you here! 1875.15
You Break My Heart 1988.05
You Brought a New Kind of Love to Me 1932.04, 1947.05, 1965.08
You Came Along 1927.54
You Can Always Count on Me 1989.29
You Can Always Explain Things Away 1890.16
You Can Always Find Another Partner 1923.05
You Can be a New Yorker Too! 1985.15
You Can be With Any Girl at All 1986.03
You Can Buy Kisses But You Can't Buy Love 1930.38
You Can Dance 1961.11, 1982.15
You Can Dance With Any Girl at All 1925.30, 1971.03
You Can do Nothing About It 1972.18
You Can Get Up Before Noon Without Being a Square 1971.13
You Can Go as Far as You Like With Me 1911.23
You Can Have Him 1949.08
You Can Have My Husband 1992.06
You Can Have the TV 1991.10
You Can Have Your 'Oh You Kids' But it's a Loving Wife for Mine 1909.28
You Can Make My Life a Bed of Roses 1932.07
You Can Never Go Back 1981.07
You Can Never Tell About a Woman 1906.33
You Can Never Tell About Love 1930.05
You Can Never Tell Till You Try 1904.52
You Can Reach the Sun 1971.19
You Can Read it in My Eyes 1897.37
You Can Sail in My Boat 1905.38
You Can Speak Without Compunction 1923.04
You Can Tell by the Skies 1921.19
You Can Tell That I'm Irish 1916.02
You Can Tell Who We are by the Things That We Have Done 1922.27
You Can Trust Me 1964.05
You Can't Always Get What You Want 1979.30
You Can't Argue 1910.22
You Can't be a Husband Today 1917.32
You Can't Beat It 1930.09
You Can't Beat the Luck of the Irish 1920.26
You Can't Blame a Girl for Dreaming 1923.05
You Can't Blame Your Uncle Sammy 1979.25
You Can't Brush Me Off 1940.08
You Can't Can't Dance 2001.06
You Can't Deny You're Irish 1918.41
You Can't do What My Last Man Did 1927.32
You Can't Experiment on Me 1923.13
You Can't Eye a Shy Baby 1927.15
You Can't Fool a New York Kid 1915.17
You Can't Fool All the People All the Time 1903.07
You Can't Fool the People 1942.05
You Can't Fool Your Dreams 1920.25
You Can't Get a Man With a Gun 1946.12, 1966.12, 1999.04
You Can't Get Ahead 1982.13
You Can't Get Away from Tipperary 1915.02
You Can't Get into Heaven Unless You Have a Jazz Band 1919.30
You Can't Get Over It 1930.10
You Can't Get the Merchandise 1942.01
You Can't Get to Heaven 1997.08
You Can't Go to Heaven 1954.11
You Can't Go Wrong With Us 1914.16
You Can't Keep a Good Girl Down 1920.44
You Can't Keep a Good Man Down 1907.14
You Can't Miss It 1955.01
You Can't Overdo a Good Thing 1952.08
You Can't Pay the Landlord With Love 1911.41
You Can't Play Every Instrument in the Band 1913.04
You Can't Play in Our Yard 1894.21, 1894.31
You Can't Shush Katie 1925.26
You Can't Stop Me from Loving You 1931.11
You Can't Stop Me from Thinking 1914.20
You Can't Stop the Sun from Shining 1927.40
You Can't Take it With You 1950.09
You Can't Take it With You When You Die 1917.21
You Can't Think of Everything 1917.21
You Can't Walk Home from an Aeroplane 1927.39
You Cannot Blame Me for My Spanish Blood 1912.04
You Cannot Drown the Dreamer 1980.30
You Cannot Make Your Shimmy Shake on Ten 1919.15
You Cannot Send Him Away 1947.10
You Click With Me 1938.01
You Could Drive a Person Crazy 1970.13, 1977.05
You Could Never Shame Me 1993.09
You Could Not Please Me More 1979.12
You Couldn't Blame Me for That 1929.49
You Couldn't Get on Without Me, Girls 1904.04
You Cut Up the Clothes in the Closet of My Dreams 1972.10
You Danced With Dynamite 1995.14
You Dear 1907.31, 1927.58
You Deserve a Better Life 1997.17
You Deserve Me 1964.44
You Did It 1956.01, 1993.18
You didn't hear it 1972.08
You Do 1979.03
You do Not Understand 1910.24
You do Something to Me 1929.45, 1980.06, 1999.07
You do-do-do-it Good! 1981.28
You Don't Dance 1944.14
You Don't Have to do it for Me 1970.07
You Don't Have to Know the Language 1995.14
You Don't Know 1912.35, 1918.35, 1963.21
You Don't Know Him 1958.02
You Don't Know Paree 1929.45
You Don't Know This Man 1998.21
You Don't Love Right 1936.17
You Don't Need the Wine to Have a Wonderful Time 1919.15
You Don't See it But it's There 1913.36
You Don't Tell Me 1962.03
You Don't Understand 1978.11
You Don't Want to Play With Me Blues 1954.09
You Done Right 1973.10
You Fell Out of the Sky 1976.15
You Flew Away from the Nest 1924.22
You Forgot Your Gloves 1931.14
You forward hussey 1886.53
You Found Me and I Found You 1918.03
You Fucked Up My Life 1998.02
You Gave Me Your Love 1891.39
You Go to My Head 1975.22, 1992.18
You Go Your Way 1997.05
You Gonna Miss Me 1995.01
You Got Me 1944.33, 1971.15, 1998.16
You Got Me Wrong 1924.31
You Got to Git the Gittin While the Gittin's Good 1978.21
You Got to Keep a' Moving and Dance 1912.38
You Got What Gets 'Em 1923.10
You Gotta be Holdin' Out Five Dollars on Me 1971.13
You Gotta Die Sometime 1992.09
You Gotta do Better Than That 1933.15
You Gotta Get Aut 1960.17
You Gotta Have a Gimmick 1959.13, 1977.05, 1989.03
You Gotta Have Dancing 1978.28
You Gotta Keep Saying 'No' 1945.18
You Gotta Start Each Day With a Song 2000.14
You Have Cast Your Shadow on the Sea 1938.14
You Have Everything 1937.16
You Have Got to Have a Rudder on the Ark 1970.19
You Have it All 1997.12
You Have Made Me Love 1973.07
You Have Me 1908.28
You Have My Heart 1934.20
You have no right 1886.50
You Have to do What You do Do 1945.04
You Have to Get it Out to Get Away 1982.13
You Have to Hand it to Them 1911.26
You Have to Have a Part to Make a Hit 1914.27
You Have to Put a Nightie on Aphrodite 1919.43
You Haven't Changed at All 1945.19
You Haven't Lived Until You've Played the Palace 1961.01
You Help Me 1964.05
You I Like 1979.02, 1998.07
You in Your Room, I in Mine 1927.34
You Interest Me 1982.18
You Irritate Me So 1941.08
You Just Gotta be You 1999.17
You Keep Coming Back Like a Song 1988.08
You Keep Me Hanging On 1982.22
You Kissed Me 1950.04
You Know and I Know and We Both Understand 1915.07
You Know That I Adore You 1900.39
You Know What I Mean 1919.16
You Know What to Do 1922.29
You Know, I Know 1926.39
You Know, Oh Lord 1945.13
You Little Cafe, Good-day 1913.31
You Look Good to Father 1907.14
You Look Much Better Now 1920.10
You Lost That Lovin' Feeling 1978.01
You Lost Your Opportunity 1930.18
You Love Me 1933.20, 1963.08
You love, at least, andc. 1859.16
You Made a Hit With Me 1930.37
You Made Me Love You 1913.05, 1931.19, 1940.10, 1962.17, 1963.02, 1967.11, 1973.05, 1976.24
You Made Me Think You Were in Love 1985.12
You Make it Your Way 1971.20
You Make Me Happy 1997.04
You Marry a Marionette 1978.19, 1988.18
You Marry an Marionette 1910.35
You May be a Bad Man 1920.47
You May be a Whale in Georgia 1928.10
You May be Far Away from Me 1935.12
You May Call Me Phocion 1997.18
You May Have Planted Many a Lily 1925.44
You May Kiss Me Good-Night Dear 1911.26
You May Say 'Yes' Today 1926.26
You May Soar and Search 1892.20
You may talk 1880.18
You May Wander Away 1925.52
You Mean More to Me 1995.19, 1997.22, 1998.20, 1999.21, 2000.19
You Might as Well Pretend 1931.14
You Might as Well Stay on Broadway 1912.38
You Modern Girls 1925.50
You Musn't be Discouraged 1964.21
You Musn't Believe All You Hear 1886.45
You Musn't do That in High Society 1904.55
You Musn't Kick it Around 1940.22, 1983.09, 1989.16
You Must - We Won't 1926.28
You Must be Born With It 1932.05
You Must be Good Girls 1920.15
You Must be Mine, Dear 1910.27
You Must be Part of a Dream 1942.19
You Must Come Over Blues 1925.29, 1926.25
You Must Have Been a Beautiful Baby 1963.02, 1965.08, 1988.08, 1997.05
You Must Have Experience 1913.17
You Must Learn the Latest Dances 1922.28
You Must Meet My Wife 1973.04, 1977.05
You Must Not Cry for Me 1947.10
You Must Not Flirt With Me 1914.32
You Mustn't Kick it Around 1975.13
You Need a Hobby 1962.20
You Need a Man Suzanne 1925.29
You Need Someone 1922.38
You Need Two Souls But One Thought 1922.08
You Needn't Come at All 1911.20
You Needn't Tell Your Mother 1869.44, 1880.17
You Never Can Tell 1914.18, 1919.14, 1920.32, 1929.32
You Never Can Tell About Love 1922.42
You Never Can Tell How a Marriage Will Take 1917.28
You Never Can Tell Until You Try 1912.05
You Never Can Tell What a Kiss Will Do 1900.47
You Never Could Tell We Were Married 1912.24
You Never Give Me Your Money 1974.24
You Never had it so Good 1996.04
You Never Hear a Single Word They're Singing 1926.11
You Never Knew About Me 1917.06
You Never Know 1918.37, 1938.07
You Never Know What Come Next 1945.12

You Never Know What Hit You When it's Love 1950.19
You Never Lose a Little Fish 1895.25
You Never Met a Feller Like Me 1965.28
You Never Saw That Before 1946.04
You Never Say Good Luck on Opening Night 2001.05
You Never Say Yes 1929.12
You Never Told Me That Before We Married 1907.59
You Never Told Me That Before We Were Married 1906.44
You Okay Honey? 1996.09
You Once Were Excess Baggage, Now You'se Only Common Freight 1897.34
You Only You 1988.15
You or No One 1959.27
You Ought to be Here With Me 1985.06
You Ought to Go to Paris 1916.09
You Ought to Hear Olaf Laugh 1929.05
You Ought to Know 1924.27
You Oughta be in Pictures 1934.01
You Oughta Hear Me Sing 1979.11
You Poor Thing 1959.04
You Push it You Way 1971.20
You Rascal, You! 1870.20
You remember 'twas six months ago 1898.25
You Remember Me 1918.42
You Remind Me of My Mother 1922.43
You Remind Me of Someone 1923.10
You Remind Me of You 1970.07
You Rule My World 2000.15
You Said It 1931.01, 1940.19
You Said Something 1917.01
You Saucy Jade 1866.07, 1866.21
You Say - They Say 1970.21
You Say the Nicest Things, Baby 1948.28
You Say You Care 1949.18, 1995.07
You see in me 1896.13
You Send Me 1986.02, 1990.15
You Set My Heart to Music 1961.07
You shall be present at the Prince's Ball 1888.39
You shall be rich and powerful 1889.10
You Shall Drink Miura's Wine 1997.16
You Shall Drink the Wine Offered by Miura 1998.08
You Shall Not Go 1916.04
You Should be Dancin' 1999.15
You Should be Loved 1997.17
You Should be Set to Music 1941.03
You Should Have Married Again 1950.16
You Should Hear Her Whistling 1890.12
You Should Know 1930.19
You should not be long alone 1880.18
You Should See Yourself 1966.01, 1986.07
You Show Some Surprise 1912.40
You Smiled at Me 1926.28
You sometimes think a thing divine 1886.40
You Started Something When You Came Along 1921.10
You Stepped Out of a Dream 1989.21
You Still Have a Long Way to Go 1975.06
You Still Love Me 1971.10
You swear to be good and true 1887.44
You Swear to be Good and True 1888.34
You Sweet so and So 1930.38
You Take an Angel 1875.19
You Talk Just Like My Maw 1943.24
You Teach Me 1922.14
You Think I Got Rhythm 1972.13
You Tickle Me 1921.02
You Told Me That You Loved Me But You Never Told Me Why 1926.11
You Told Me Yo' had Money in the Bank 1899.11
You Told Me You had Money in the Bank 1899.29
You too Can be a Puppet 1951.15
You Took Advantage of Me 1928.16, 1954.12
You Took Me by Surprise 1942.01
You Took My Breath Away 1932.19
You Took Possession of Me 1948.15
You Touched Her 1976.09
You Treacherous Men 1963.11
You Understand 1888.34
You understand? I think I do 1887.10
You Wait and Wait and Wait 1935.17
You Walk With Me 2000.15
You Walked Out 1957.14
You Want Someone to Love You 1907.46
You Want to Lose Your Only Friend? 1988.09
You Was 1949.05
You Wash and I'll Dry 1943.21
You Were Charming 1915.22
You Were Dead, You Know 1956.15, 1974.06, 1982.20, 1997.10
You Were Made for Love 1914.20
You Were Meant for Me 1948.13
You Were Never Lovelier 1997.05
You Were There 1936.29, 1986.19
You Will - Won't You? 1926.32
You Will Forgive 1882.33
You Will Get it Bye and Bye 1894.17
You Will Have to Sing an Irish Song 1908.19
You Will Know When the Time has Arrived 1979.10
You Will Never be Lonely 1961.27
You Will Never Know 1930.06
You Will Not Touch Him 1991.03
You Will Read it in the Papers 1910.17
You Win 1918.42
You Won't be an Orphan for Long 1977.06
You Won't be Happy 1972.19
You Won't do Any Business if You Haven't Got a Band 1904.22, 1904.41
You Would if You Could 1986.12
You Would Say 1979.10
You Wouldn't Fool Me, Would Ya? 1929.03
You'd be Surprised 1919.15, 1919.16, 1919.19
You'd Better Dance 1943.16
You'd Better Go Now 1936.12
You'd Better Love Me 1964.16
You'd Better See America First 1915.12
You'd better stay at Mocha 1880.46
You'd Better Take it Back 1902.07
You'd Like Nebraska 1963.13
You'd Think You Were in Paris 1909.26
You'll be Sorry in the Morning 1904.14
You'll be Surprised 1908.40
You'll Call the Next Love the First 1913.05
You'll Do 1931.01
You'll do it All Over Again 1919.06
You'll Dream of Me 1903.23
You'll Feel Better Then 1908.24, 1909.23
You'll Find a Girl to Please You Here in Town 1898.03, 1898.10
You'll Find Mice 1971.20
You'll Find the Party isn't There 1916.05
You'll Find the Rainbow 1921.13
You'll Get Nothing from Me 1921.07
You'll Get There 1886.28
You'll Have to Change 1989.05
You'll Have to Choose Another Baby Now 1898.22
You'll Have to Find Another Girl 1921.15
You'll Have to Find Out 1919.23
You'll Have to Gallop Some 1916.03
You'll Have to Get Off and Walk 1906.31
You'll Have to Guess 1925.06
You'll Have to Read the Answer in the Stars 1903.04
You'll Have to Stop That Row! 1883.12
You'll Hear a Bell 1989.23
You'll Kill 'Em! 1928.34
You'll Love It 1986.16
You'll Love it in Jail 1985.20
You'll Make an Elegant Butler and I'll Make an Elegant Maid 1963.08
You'll Miss Me When I'm Gone 1898.10
You'll Never be Lonely 1975.12
You'll Never Get a Whimper Out of Me 1919.10
You'll Never Get Away from Me 1959.13
You'll Never Know 1926.25, 1974.10, 1988.08
You'll Never Know a Mother's Love Again 1889.37
You'll Never Know What Love is Until I Love You 1907.44
You'll Never Need a Doctor No Mo 1920.33
You'll Never Walk Alone 1945.05, 1955.13
You'll remember me 1854.04
You'll Remember Me 1870.07, 1934.17
You'll See 1917.27, 1996.09
You'll See a Great Big Beautiful Smile 1927.47
You'll See the Day 1919.16
You'll Surely Have to Guess 1881.10
You'll think e'er many days ensue 1750.01
You'll Think of Someone 1968.31
You're a Bad Influence on Me 1936.26
You're a Builder-Upper 1934.19
You're a Charming Little Maiden 1905.46
You're a Dangerous Girl 1916.03
You're a Good Little Devil 1913.06
You're a Good Man, Charlie Brown 1971.11, 1999.03
You're a Grand Old Flag 1968.07, 1979.13, 1980.27
You're a Hero 1916.18
You're a Liar 1960.22
You're a Little Young for the Job 1984.02
You're a Long, Long Way from America 1961.18
You're a Lovable Lunatic 1973.06
You're a Magician 1935.11
You're a Man 1963.20
You're a Queer One, Julie Jordan 1945.05
You're a Regular Girl 1912.13
You're a Rock 1970.08
You're a Stranger in This Neighborhood 1964.18
You're a Wonderful Girl 1927.43
You're a Young Little Old-Fashioned Girl 1918.07
You're All the World to Me 1926.06, 1929.50
You're Altogether Model Girls 1900.47
You're Another 1877.23
You're as English As 1961.24
You're Asking Me 1934.04
You're at the Music Hall 1980.09, 1982.06
You're Awfully Smart 1942.19
You're Colossal 1955.25
You're Dead 1953.11
You're Delicious 1963.16
You're Devastating 1933.26
You're Driving Me Crazy 1930.39, 1948.13
You're Everywhere 1932.03
You're False 1952.15
You're Far too Near Me 1945.04
You're Getting to be a Habit With Me 1980.20
You're Going to Lose Your Husband 1911.17
You're Gone 1928.24
You're Gonna Dance With Me, Willie 1953.01
You're Gonna Love Tomorrow 1971.05
You're Gwine to Get Somethin' What You Don't Expect 1910.18
You're Here and I'm Here 1914.04
You're in Heidelberg 1924.45
You're in Love 1917.05
You're in Paris 1964.33
You're in the Right Church But the Wrong Pew 1908.08
You're Just a Little Bet Better Than the One I Thought was Best 1914.16
You're Just in Love 1950.15
You're Just the Boy for Me 1908.28, 1920.14
You're Just the Girlie That I Adore 1910.20
You're Just the One I'm Looking For 1906.17
You're Just What I was Warned About 1951.13
You're Lonely and I'm Lonely 1940.08
You're Looking at the Man 1999.22
You're Loving Me 1974.12
You're Lucky to Me 1980.10
You're Mama's 1968.05
You're Mighty Lucky, You Little Ducky 1924.03
You're Mine 1921.33
You're Mine All Mine 1952.13
You're More Than a Name and an Address 1945.01
You're Musical 1969.16
You're My 'So and So' 1927.11
You're My Baby 1912.45
You're My Boy 1914.06, 1947.16
You're My Everything 1931.40, 1932.14, 1988.08
You're My Girl 1909.09, 1947.16, 1974.10
You're My Happy Ending 1924.18
You're My Relaxation 1934.06
You're My Star 1993.05
You're Nearer 1975.13
You're Never Fully Dressed Without a Smile 1977.06
You're Never too Old to Love 1913.17, 1923.45
You're No Brother of Mine 1964.32
You're No Good 1964.05
You're Nobody til Somebody Loves You 2000.07
You're Not Alone 1972.16

You're Not Foolin' Me 1963.26, 1992.10
You're Not the Mayor 1985.15
You're Not the One 1933.16
You're Not the Only Cinder in the Grate 1910.03
You're Not the Only Oyster in the Stew 1995.14
You're Not the Type 1961.27, 1972.05
You're Nothing Without Me 1989.29
You're on My Mind 1941.09
You're on the Right Road 1912.38
You're on Top 1934.36
You're on Very Good Terms With Yourself 1888.19
You're on Your Own 1972.09
You're Only Young Once or Twice 1951.10
You're Perf 1944.14
You're Perfect 1929.07, 1972.07
You're Plenty of a Lady as You Are 1917.27
You're Right, You're Right 1966.27
You're Sensational 1998.05
You're so Beautiful 1918.34
You're so Beautiful That - 1951.23
You're so Different from the Rest 1911.03
You're so Fascinating 1913.20
You're so Indiff'rent 1987.02
You're so Indifferent 1939.14
You're so Much a Part of Me 1953.17
You're so Nice to Me 1927.49
You're so Right for Me 1958.02
You're so Sweet 1923.36
You're Some Girl 1912.14, 1913.17
You're Something to Write Home About 1929.52
You're Talking Rag-Time 1900.16
You're the Better Half of Me 1930.35
You're the Boss 1995.03
You're the Candy 1905.39
You're the Cream in My Coffee 1928.22, 1928.36, 1967.13, 1968.20, 1974.26
You're the Devil in Disguise 1989.12
You're the Fellow the Fortune Teller Told Me All About 1926.30
You're the First Cup of Coffee in the Morning 1948.23
You're the First Thing I Think of in the Morning-and the Last Thing I Think of1927.60
You're the Girl 1916.17
You're the Girl That Sets Me Stuttering 1916.22
You're the Kind of a Girl I Like 1906.13
You're the Lord of Any Manor 1945.01
You're the Nicest Girl I Ever Knew 1911.26
You're the One 1992.06
You're the One I'm For 1968.13
You're the Only One for Me 1907.01, 1914.27, 1918.06, 1918.22
You're the Only One That I Love 1927.30
You're the Reason 1943.18
You're the Sunrise 1930.25
You're the Sweetest Flowers That Grows in Tennessee 1904.07
You're the Sweetest Girl I Know 1906.19
You're the Top 1987.15, 1992.18
You're the Type 1920.27
You're the Very Girl I've Looked For 1918.23
You're Very Like Your Sister, Dear 1911.44
You're Welcome 1967.06
You're welcome, friends 1890.33
You're What I Need 1928.02
You've all drunk cold pizen 1873.05
You've Been a Good Ole Wagon 1975.20
You've Been Kissing the Blarney Stone 1910.34
You've Broken a Fine Woman's Heart 1970.21
You've Built a Fire Down in My Heart 1911.30
You've Come Home 1960.22
You've Got a Friend 1976.32, 1982.22
You've Got a Hold on Me 1943.21
You've Got a Way With You 1928.41
You've Got it All 1942.27
You've Got Me Up a Tree 1928.46
You've Got Mischief in Your Eyes 1919.30
You've Got Possibilities 1966.06
You've Got Something 1936.26
You've Got Something to Say 1960.01
You've Got Something to Sing About 1940.18
You've Got That Kind of a Face 1948.18
You've Got That Thing 1929.45
You've Got the Style and the Smile 1915.23
You've Got to Appease With a Strip Tease 1942.05
You've Got to be a Lady 1963.12
You've Got to be a Little Crazy 1954.01
You've Got to be Carefully Taught 1949.04
You've Got to Dance 1925.05
You've Got to do It 1956.14
You've Got to Go in or Go Under 1918.10
You've Got to Know How to Make Love 1928.49
You've Got to Learn 1965.30, 1970.01, 1974.19, 1983.03
You've Got to Pick a Pocket or Two 1963.01
You've Got to Play Rag-Time 1899.12
You've Got to Sell Yourself 1932.01
You've Got to Surrender 1929.42
You've Got What Gets Me 1990.14
You've Got What I Need 1966.06
You've Got What it Takes 1944.20
You've Hardly Known My Long Enough for That 1901.04
You've Let Yourself Go 1965.30, 1970.01, 1974.19, 1983.03
You've Lied to Me 1904.55
You've Made a Hit With Me 1907.61
You've Made Me Happy Today 1929.32
You've Never Been Loved 1950.12
You've Stolen My Heart 1950.10
You've Stuck Me 1870.20
You've Taken My Blues and Gone 1999.06
You've the Girl I Love 1907.46
You've won these trousers by your trouble 1885.28
You, Dear, You 1907.34
You, Just You 1907.30
You, My Sweetheart Will Have to Be 1917.30
You, You 1911.01
You, You, You 1903.41
You, You, You! 1917.30
You, You, You, Nobody Jes You You 1938.19
You-oo ma Cartol 1929.13
Young 1981.07
Young Agnes 1860.05
Young America 1896.52, 1910.01, 1916.02
Young and American 1986.20
Young and Foolish 1955.01
Young and Healthy 1980.20
Young and the Restless, The 1977.09
Young Black Joe 1928.40
Young Blood 1995.03
Young Cupid 1882.18
Young Fella, You're too Fresh 1876.11
Young Folks and Old Folks 1919.02
Young Girls and Young Men 1938.06
Young Ideas 1935.04
Young Lady a la Mode 1946.18
Young Lady in a Swing, A 1959.15, 1961.25
Young Man Athletic, The 1890.16
Young Man Danube 1945.11
Young Man Despair 1939.15, 1939.17
Young Man in a Shop 1905.19
Young Man With a Horn 1939.19
Young Man With a Reefer 1940.23
Young Man's Fancy, A 1920.08, 1921.27
Young man, despair 1885.47
Young Man, Older Woman 1995.01
Young May Morn 1858.04
Young Men Take a Tip from Me 1916.17
Young Nadir, The 1846.01, 1862.03
Young People 1956.04
Young People Think About Love 1938.11
Young Pretty Girl Like You, A 1968.31
Young Recruit, The 1864.13
Young Rose, The 1896.11
Young Torah Tep was the Boy for Me 1900.01
Young With Him 1972.24
Younger Generation, The 1927.64
Younger Set, The 1927.48, 1929.44
Younger Than Springtime 1949.04
Youngsters of the Navy, The 1912.30
Youp et Youp 1935.19
Your Arms too Short to Box With God 1976.35, 1980.14, 1982.17
Your Auto Ought to Get Girls 1916.11
Your Baby for All the Time 1919.43
Your Cavalcade of Hits Theme 1987.02
Your Daddy's Gone Away 1976.03
Your Daddy's Son 1998.01
Your Disposition is Mine 1928.50
Your Eyes 1926.35, 1928.12, 1996.09
Your Eyes Have Told Me 1923.38
Your Eyes Have Told Me and My Heart has Heard 1912.40
Your Eyes on Yonder Tomb 1875.19
Your Face is so Familiar 1936.12
Your Face is Your Fortune 1943.16
Your Fatal Fascination 1945.17
Your Fault 1987.18
Your Feet's too Big 1978.09
Your frankness no one can deny 1859.16
Your Grace, I am an eligible Count 1880.18
Your Hat and My Hat 1923.32
Your Heart Alone Must Tell 1905.38
Your Highness is Beautiful 1997.16
Your Highness is so Beautiful 1998.08
Your Honeymoon Will Last 1904.37
Your Kiss is Champagne 1918.15
Your Land and My Land 1927.42
Your Life My Little Girl 1897.39
Your Lips 1923.44
Your Lips Say No, But Your Eyes Say Yes 1908.21
Your Love is All I Crave 1929.18
Your Lover Keeps Lifting Me Higher and Higher 1973.14
Your Maiden Hearts 1881.37
Your Majesties 1993.14
Your Mother Wants You Home, Boy 1904.22
Your Mother's Son-in-Law 1933.27
Your Name 1999.22
Your Name Proclaim 1875.19
Your orders have been observed, sir 1888.18
Your orders I am trying to obey 1895.29
Your Orders Shall be Obeyed 1878.20
Your Own 1901.19
Your pardon, friends, I crave 1888.07
Your Photo 1915.30
Your Picture 1915.20
Your Prince was Not so Charming 1934.15
Your Second Wife 1920.31
Your slumbers 1868.01
Your Smiles, Your Tears 1930.27
Your Song 1955.13
Your Time has Come 1890.03
Your Time is Different to Mine 1981.14
Your Type is Coming Back 1933.16
Your Voice I Hear 1919.24
Your Wonderful Lips 1926.09, 1926.35
Your Wonderful U.S.A. 1921.10
Yours for Me and Mine for You 1913.21
Yours is My Heart Alone 1946.16
Yours Sincerely 1929.12
Yours Sincerely U.S.A. 1916.11
Yours Truly 1923.04, 1927.07
Yours, All Yours 1961.02
Yours, Yours, Yours 1969.06
Youth 1912.39, 1914.20
Youth and Love 1870.27
Youth and Spring 1922.40
Youth and Truth 1920.26
Youth of the Heart, The 1959.20
Youth Who Sows, The 1938.06
Youth Will Have its Fling 1927.54
Youth Will Pass too Soon 1870.08
Youth's a Season Made for Joys 1957.02
Youth's the Season made for Joys 1750.01
Yuca Tango, The 1915.05
Yucatana 1941.07
Yugoslavian Washerwomen 1932.09
Yuki Shimaki 1989.21
Yuletide 1948.19
Yuletide Spirit, The 1917.21
Yuletide, Park Avenue 1946.10
Yum Ticky (Ticky Tum Tum) 1961.10
Yum Yum Time 1912.36
Yum, Yum 1888.05
Yum, Yum, Yum 1916.25

Yumba, La 1985.07, 1999.18
Yummie, Yum Yum 1880.37
Yunuen 1939.18
Yussef's Visit 1987.12
Yvonne 1925.48, 1987.14

Zabelle 1907.44
Zambra 1949.07
Zan charisse 1974.17
Zap 1989.25
Zapateado 1992.15
Zaporozhtsi, The 1925.03
Zara 1909.04
Zarita 1891.14
Zarzuelm, La 1932.10
Zatuma 1913.18
Ze English Language 1905.57
Zebekiko 1967.05
Zel-Zel 1904.56
Zemmer, A 1967.03
Zen is When 1960.01
Zenedee 1905.33
Zibuuylle Emasisweni 1988.02
Ziegfeld Follies Rag 1917.13
Ziegfeld Girl, The 1917.34
Ziegfeld Rag, The 1916.02
Ziegfeld Sextette, The 1920.18
Zigeuner 1929.41
Ziguener 1986.19
Zim Boom Ta-Ra 1897.30
Zim Zam Zee 1937.02, 1946.19
Zim-Zim 1916.04
Zimbaba 1977.01
Zing Boom 1888.39
Zing Boom Bah 1918.32
Zing! Went the Strings of My Heart 1934.42
Zing, Faigele, Zing 1967.03
Zinga Zula Man, The 1910.25
Zingaras, The 1912.44
Zip 1926.30, 1940.22, 1975.13
Zita 1927.26
Zither Song 1952.11
Zizi 1912.35
Zizzie Za Zim 1898.38
Zog Nit Keinmol 1989.10
Zongo, My Congo Queen 1904.38
Zoo 1916.23
Zoo Loo 1907.40, 1908.12
Zoo, The 1880.19
Zoological Party 1905.19
Zoom 1963.10
Zubbediya 1978.03
Zuhalterballade, Die 1965.04
Zulu Fifth Avenue 1927.33
Zulu Lou 1924.32
Zulu Love Song 1965.32
Zusammenfugung, Die 1968.13
Zuyder Zee 1907.18
ZuZu and ZaZa 1903.19
Zweiss Dreigroschen-Finale 1965.04

SELECTED INDEX OF PERSONS

Note: All principal performers listed in a musical's program cast list have been indexed here. In order to contain the index size, ensemble or chorus persons have not been indexed, except where they also appear with a given character name, or else if their subsequent fame warrants their inclusion.

A&T Production 1995.09
A'Becket, Mme. 1841.01
A'Dale, Allan 1905.55
A. Roemer and Son 1884.27, 1884.36, 1886.10
A. Uzel and Son 1914.25
Aaron, Adina 2000.03
Aaron, Eric 1982.11
Aaron, Johnny 1872.35
Aaron, Miss 1841.01
Aaron, Myrna 1956.04
Aaron, Paul 1971.07, 1972.05
Aaron, Stephen 1966.15
Aarons, Albert E. 1898.35
Aarons, Alex 1931.32
Aarons, Alex A. 1919.12, 1922.10, 1924.43, 1925.49, 1926.36, 1927.59, 1928.17, 1928.36, 1928.43, 1929.12, 1929.42, 1930.31, 1933.01
Aarons, Alfred E. 1898.38, 1898.56, 1900.16, 1900.44, 1901.18, 1901.21, 1903.17, 1904.49, 1905.55, 1906.20, 1907.21, 1910.29, 1927.50
Aarons, Ruth Hughes 1948.18
Aaronson, Alex 1921.39
Aaronson, Cindy Lynn 1979.20, 1979.27
Aaronson, Irving 1925.05, 1928.33
Aaronson, Max 1918.23
Aaronstein, Martin 1973.08
Aashton, Daisy 1905.30
Abacco, Joe 1901.28
Abarbanell, Lina 1906.49, 1910.22, 1912.47, 1913.09, 1916.17, 1926.30, 1929.46, 1930.36
Abaya, Araby 1985.01
Abbe, Charles 1925.38
Abbey, Edna 1932.26
Abbey, Harold 1934.13
Abbey, Henry B. 1893.45
Abbey, Henry E. 1876.32, 1876.35, 1877.02, 1880.07, 1880.17, 1880.37, 1880.68, 1881.35, 1889.54, 1894.41, 1894.48, 1895.09, 1895.12, 1896.10, 1896.12
Abbey, Maurice 1892.07, 1892.16, 1892.28, 1893.05
Abbey, May 1934.36, 1936.26
Abbot, Marion 1890.43
Abbott, Addie 1870.32, 1870.35
Abbott, Alan 1976.18
Abbott, Bessie 1895.42
Abbott, Betty B, 1948.17
Abbott, Bob 1928.25
Abbott, Bud 1939.22
Abbott, Charles 1871.08, 1883.01, 1883.09, 1883.20, 1888.08, 1901.02, 1909.13, 1970.06
Abbott, Edith 1912.45
Abbott, Eleanor 1924.23
Abbott, George 1915.06, 1918.08, 1935.15, 1936.05, 1938.14, 1939.27, 1940.22, 1941.06, 1941.13, 1942.29, 1944.33, 1945.20, 1947.08, 1947.16, 1948.08, 1948.26, 1949.12, 1950.15, 1951.02, 1951.14, 1953.03, 1953.08, 1954.05, 1954.12, 1955.08, 1957.07, 1957.08, 1959.25, 1959.26, 1960.19, 1961.21, 1962.12, 1962.16, 1964.21, 1965.17, 1965.35, 1966.11, 1967.16, 1968.06, 1969.01, 1973.15, 1974.25, 1976.33, 1983.02, 1989.04, 1994.01
Abbott, Jack 1925.15
Abbott, Jessie 1895.42
Abbott, Joan 1931.30, 1934.18
Abbott, Joey 1979.22
Abbott, John 1906.45, 1917.16, 1918.23, 1922.16
Abbott, Joseph Legrange 1918.36
Abbott, Judith 1976.33
Abbott, Loretta 1973.10
Abbott, Margery 1936.16, 1936.18, 1939.01, 1939.04, 1939.08, 1939.09, 1939.11
Abbott, Marion 1912.26
Abbott, Marjorie 1936.24
Abbott, Merriel 1929.35, 1930.28, 1932.15
Abbott, Mrs. 1851.01, 1851.07
Abbott, Nettie 1884.27
Abbott, Norman 1950.09
Abbott, Patsy 1951.21
Abbott, Ron 1978.21, 1979.05
Abbott, Tom 1962.01, 1963.08, 1964.17, 1976.36, 1980.02, 1981.18
Abbott, Tommy 1957.12
Abby, Maurice 1900.28
ABC, Inc. 2000.12
Abdallah, Abbas Ben 1911.28
Abdullah, Hamadi 1922.30
Abdulov, Alexander 1990.01
Abel, Larry 1974.23
Abel, Marian 1923.14
Abeleda, Tito 1990.17
Abeles, Ed. S. 1901.30
Abeles, Edward 1904.35, 1909.31, 1918.03
Abeles, Edward S. 1897.54, 1899.08, 1903.28
Abelson, R. 1990.16
Abelson, Robert 1990.16
Abene, Michael 1999.23
Abene, Mike 1991.04
Aber, Arline 1930.39
Aber, Charline 1930.39
Aberastain, Judit 1993.08
Aberbach, Jean 1989.12
Aberbach, Julian 1989.12
Aberle, J. 1869.38
Aberle, Jacob 1881.30
Aberlin, Betty 1964.18
Abeytua, Jose 1919.17
Abhann Productions Ltd. 1996.12, 1998.09, 2000.05
Able, Will 1955.01
Able, Will B. 1962.04, 1969.17
Aborn Opera Company 1911.10, 1933.17
Aborn, Mark 1894.11
Aborn, Milton 1902.22, 1911.10, 1925.13, 1926.08, 1929.34, 1929.36, 1929.38, 1929.40, 1929.43, 1929.47, 1929.48, 1930.01, 1930.03, 1930.07, 1930.12, 1930.41, 1931.10, 1931.12, 1931.15, 1931.17, 1931.18, 1931.20, 1931.22, 1931.23, 1931.24, 1931.25, 1931.27, 1931.33, 1931.35, 1931.41, 1931.43, 1931.45, 1932.02, 1933.08, 1933.09, 1933.10, 1933.11, 1933.14, 1933.17, 1933.18, 1933.19
Aborn, Sargent 1911.10
Abott, Bessie 1913.25
Abraham, David 1904.34, 1910.17
Abraham, Edward T. 1885.43
Abraham, F. 1898.56
Abraham, F. Murray 1997.18
Abrahams, D. 1894.18
Abrahams, Dave 1900.03, 1915.24
Abrahams, David 1895.08, 1895.38, 1902.15, 1912.39, 1915.05
Abrahams, Jody J. 1999.12
Abrahams, Jr., David 1915.05
Abrahams, Master 1905.22
Abrahams, Maurice 1913.05, 1913.30, 1914.22, 1927.37, 1964.28
Abrahams, Mr. 1875.03
Abrahao, Roberto 1988.06, 1990.03
Abraho, Roberto 1992.13
Abram, Edward J. 1894.21
Abrams, Alan 1979.03
Abrams, Dave 1907.24, 1908.35, 1916.24
Abrams, David 1902.15, 1904.47, 1906.48, 1909.13
Abrams, Irwin 1926.20
Abrams, Judith Ann 1999.04
Abrams, Lou 1902.05, 1902.10
Abramson, Charles 1934.04
Abramson, Charles H. 1937.06
Abravanel, Maurice 1941.04, 1943.03, 1943.19, 1944.29, 1945.04, 1945.19, 1947.02, 1949.16
Abt, Professor 1884.61
Abuba, Ernest 1976.02
Abud, Charles J. 1890.33
Acayan, Zar 1991.03
Accoe, Will 1904.26
Accooe, Will 1903.08
Accooe, William J. 1899.31, 1899.33, 1900.46, 1900.48, 1901.08, 1901.20, 1901.21
Achard, Ned 1906.02, 1906.42
Achart, Mlle. 1926.47
Acioli, Monica 1992.13
Acker, Dorothy 1928.49
Acker, Mabel 1927.05
Acker, Mitch 1981.24
Ackerley, Messr. 1890.36
Ackerman Brothers 1915.04
Ackerman Studios 1921.11
Ackerman, Bernice 1924.18, 1928.38
Ackerman, Dodd 1911.10
Ackerman, H. 1875.14
Ackerman, Jean 1928.47, 1930.39
Ackerman, Leslie 1974.23
Ackerman, Loni (Zoe) 1968.07, 1971.03, 1976.09
Ackerman, Meyer 1994.01
Ackerman, P. Dodd 1903.20, 1904.23, 1906.13, 1908.18, 1909.05, 1910.09, 1911.10, 1911.15, 1911.25, 1911.38, 1913.10, 1914.22, 1915.11, 1915.16, 1916.03, 1916.11, 1916.25, 1916.26, 1917.10, 1917.21, 1918.12, 1919.07, 1919.14, 1920.30, 1920.45, 1921.06, 1921.23, 1922.08, 1922.10, 1922.17, 1923.10, 1923.24, 1923.37, 1923.40, 1924.08, 1924.26, 1924.40, 1924.47, 1925.30, 1925.34, 1926.07, 1926.24, 1926.39, 1927.09, 1927.43, 1927.49, 1927.50, 1927.54, 1927.66, 1928.28, 1928.34, 1928.41, 1929.23, 1931.34
Ackerman, Robert Allan 1988.20
Ackerman, Sally 1963.25
Ackerman, Virginia 1903.30
Ackermann 1916.09
Ackland, Adelaide 1904.09
Ackman, Alice 1900.07
Acme Olivette Company 1881.14
Acme Sound Partners 2001.01, 2001.03
Aco, Lucas 1946.13, 1947.03
Acosta, Elizabeth 1993.17
Acree, Donald 1985.05
Act III Communications, Inc. 1989.12
Acting Company, The 1975.18, 1976.30
Actman, Irving 1929.26, 1930.24, 1936.01, 1947.05, 1948.12, 1948.18, 1949.01, 1950.02, 1950.17, 1959.23, 1965.15, 1966.13, 1967.09
Actor-Managers, Inc., The 1928.19, 1929.20
Actors' Theatre 1925.09
Acuri, Grace 1937.07
Ada-May 1927.08
Adae, Madge 1900.38
Adahm, J. 1889.26
Adai, D. 1879.23
Adair, Alma 1922.34
Adair, Anne 1907.26
Adair, Eileen 1913.35
Adair, Elsie 1893.34
Adair, Frank 1913.26
Adair, Helen 1909.14
Adair, Janet 1920.47, 1921.34, 1922.34, 1924.35
Adair, Jean 1933.20
Adair, John 1923.03, 1923.25, 1926.33, 1934.01, 1934.18, 1937.08, 1938.10
Adair, Josephine 1920.43, 1922.47, 1923.31
Adair, Kathleen 1905.31
Adair, Marcia 1921.17

Adair, Miss 1861.01
Adair, Mr. 1880.24
Adair, Patrick 1927.02
Adair, Ruth 1922.16
Adair, Ted 1940.06, 1942.23, 1951.21
Adair, Tom 1949.01, 1995.12
Adair, Yvonne 1948.30, 1949.18
Adaire, Josephine 1928.47
Adaire, Rose 1924.40
Adam, Adolphe 1866.25, 1866.27, 1880.22, 1889.26
Adam, Marion 1925.47
Adam, Noelle 1962.03
Adam, Sylvia 1928.47
Adamides, Angela 1950.18
Adamini, Mr. 1895.12
Adams 1887.02
Adams, A. 1895.31
Adams, A.R. 1889.20
Adams, Abbott 1908.17, 1915.01, 1921.19
Adams, Adolph 1917.16
Adams, Alice 1899.18
Adams, Ann 1940.02
Adams, Annie 1886.06, 1889.12, 1890.04
Adams, Beatrice 1905.49
Adams, Bill 1925.44
Adams, Billy 1938.08
Adams, Bob 1903.03, 1903.09, 1904.11, 1904.13, 1906.04, 1906.05
Adams, Bob C. 1915.28
Adams, Charles 1886.13, 1888.43, 1892.57, 1893.31, 1919.30
Adams, Clifford 1931.26
Adams, Corah 1908.43
Adams, D.H. 1881.32
Adams, Dave 1935.15
Adams, David 1982.15
Adams, Dianne 1989.09
Adams, Dick 1992.03
Adams, Donald 1955.15, 1955.16, 1955.18, 1955.20, 1955.22, 1955.23, 1955.24, 1962.25, 1962.28, 1962.30, 1962.31, 1964.36, 1964.38, 1964.41, 1964.42, 1964.43, 1966.22, 1966.23, 1966.25, 1966.26, 1966.28, 1968.25, 1968.26, 1968.27, 1968.28, 1968.29, 1978.17, 1989.15
Adams, Edith 1953.03, 1956.12
Adams, Edna 1903.03
Adams, Edward 1911.35
Adams, Edward B. 1904.58, 1906.10
Adams, Ernest G. 1897.51
Adams, Ernie 1918.09
Adams, Fanny 1889.04
Adams, Florence 1899.36
Adams, Frank 1904.54, 1907.25, 1908.23, 1909.02, 1909.31
Adams, Frank R. 1907.14, 1908.13, 1924.42, 1942.30, 1955.14
Adams, Franklin P. 1922.19, 1923.20, 1924.44
Adams, Franklin Price 1922.42
Adams, G. 1880.21, 1881.10, 1882.82
Adams, Gail 1946.06, 1946.22, 1948.27
Adams, George 1910.23, 1911.28, 1914.19
Adams, George H. 1888.43, 1897.51, 1909.20
Adams, Gertrude 1903.37
Adams, Grimaldi 1875.40
Adams, H. 1888.35, 1889.04, 1892.07, 1902.19
Adams, Hamilton 1886.43
Adams, Harry 1908.20
Adams, Herb 1973.12
Adams, Herbert 1940.02
Adams, Ida 1909.09, 1912.13, 1912.38
Adams, Ida M. 1911.11
Adams, Isabel 1919.06
Adams, J.B. 1998.21, 1999.16
Adams, J.K. 1898.58, 1900.54, 1903.02, 1905.47, 1907.21
Adams, Jack 1961.27, 1968.32
Adams, Jacqueline 1968.13
Adams, James 1906.46
Adams, James R. 1889.47, 1896.40, 1897.51, 1907.54, 1909.20, 1910.23, 1912.30
Adams, Joe 1901.22, 1957.16
Adams, Ken 1959.02
Adams, Kenny 1961.12, 1962.15
Adams, Kevin 2001.01
Adams, Kitty 1897.32
Adams, Laura 1879.38
Adams, Laurette 1929.06, 1932.14
Adams, Lee 1955.12, 1960.06, 1962.04, 1964.32, 1966.06, 1970.09, 1978.28, 1979.13, 1981.07, 1986.03, 1993.05, 1997.01
Adams, Leslie 1933.22
Adams, Lily 1897.51
Adams, Loukmaan 1999.12
Adams, Margaret 1931.03, 1931.37, 1935.14
Adams, Margot 1933.02
Adams, Margret 1934.42
Adams, Marguerite 1898.67, 1942.14
Adams, Mary 1930.20, 1930.37
Adams, Mason 1972.01
Adams, Maude 1889.12, 1890.04
Adams, Melytha 1893.43, 1895.44
Adams, Messr. 1886.36
Adams, Mildred 1905.39
Adams, Minerva 1893.43, 1895.44, 1900.24
Adams, Miss 1872.35, 1903.03
Adams, Mr. 1866.17, 1869.02, 1869.14, 1871.15
Adams, Neile 1953.16
Adams, Nellie 1902.44
Adams, Nick 1896.38, 1898.20, 1898.32, 1905.31, 1907.62
Adams, Paul 1966.07, 1966.14, 1966.31, 1967.04, 1967.09, 1967.17
Adams, R.F. 1889.10
Adams, Ray 1930.32, 1933.26
Adams, Roger 1952.13, 1954.05, 1955.04, 1955.08, 1956.16, 1957.07, 1957.08, 1959.01, 1959.26, 1964.33, 1966.10, 1967.05
Adams, Ruth 1934.13
Adams, S.O. 1879.42
Adams, Sam 1915.02
Adams, Samuel J. 1898.67
Adams, Stanley 1933.16, 1936.31, 1945.01, 1974.09
Adams, Stella 1902.37
Adams, Stephen 1881.39, 1896.15, 1904.22
Adams, Tonina 1897.51
Adams, Tony 1995.15
Adams, Trude 1955.12, 1963.14
Adams, Veola 1908.42
Adams, Violet 1905.49
Adams, Walter 1959.05
Adams, Wiley 1933.20
Adamson, Freddie 1979.14
Adamson, Harold 1930.39, 1931.14, 1931.26, 1931.31, 1931.32, 1941.13, 1942.24, 1948.28, 1988.08
Addell, Helene 1879.54
Adderley, Janet Williams 1987.05
Adderley, Jr., Nat 1979.15
Adderly, Alexander 1934.37
Adderly, Ernest 1934.37
Addie, Mlle. 1870.31
Addington, Ruth 1908.13
Addinsell, Richard 1927.02, 1932.28, 1934.03, 1947.09, 1952.03, 1955.19, 1958.10, 1982.24
Addis, John 1951.16
Addis, Mr. 1836.01
Addison, Bernard 1949.16, 1953.05, 1963.22
Addison, Fanny 1887.49
Addison, John 1956.13
Addison, Larry 1999.09
Addison, Polly 1905.30
Addison, Thomas 1891.02
Addiss, Juss 1942.20
Addy, Wesley 1961.12
Ade, George 1901.04, 1902.44, 1903.24, 1904.37, 1909.03, 1910.02, 1911.02, 1917.17
Adea, Madge 1901.17
Adelaide Festival Center 1996.05
Adelaide, La Petite 1896.06, 1897,26, 1899.12, 1908.13
Adelaide, Miss 1854.01
Adelaide, Mlle. 1921.20
Adeline, Miss 1851.01
Adeline, Mlle. 1852.01
Adelmam, Joseph 1893.47
Adelska, Mlle. 1870.31
Adelson, Lenny 1955.11
Adelson, Leonard 1973.11
Ademy, John 1943.23
Ades, Hawley 1955.13
ADF Enterprises 1999.05
Adiarte, Patrick 1956.03, 1958.19
Adir, Micha 1972.17
Adkins, Clay 1994.07
Adkins, Ted 1954.12
Adlam, Basil 1934.01
Adler 1913.15
Adler Costume Company 1917.10, 1917.14, 1918.42
Adler, Bruce 1979.31, 1981.25, 1990.16, 1992.02, 2000.14
Adler, Celia 1946.17
Adler, Charles 1937.01, 1942.11
Adler, Christopher 1982.23, 1984.06
Adler, Else 1915.28, 1921.09
Adler, Evelyn 1927.26
Adler, Fay 1928.23
Adler, Felix 1914.02, 1916.06
Adler, Hyman 1927.26, 1932.10
Adler, Jerry 1965.29, 1966.09, 1966.32, 1967.13, 1968.20, 1969.05, 1973.13, 1974.10, 1976.05, 1979.12, 1980.19, 1982.13
Adler, Jerry Hilliard 1943.23
Adler, Jr., Jacob P. 1915.22
Adler, Larry 1930.39, 1932.17, 1940.07
Adler, Lou 1975.08, 1979.08
Adler, Luther 1936.28, 1946.17
Adler, Murray 1963.29
Adler, Norma 1980.17
Adler, Richard 1953.17, 1954.05, 1955.08, 1957.08, 1961.24, 1962.17, 1973.15, 1976.07, 1976.08, 1976.33, 1989.04, 1994.01, 1999.01
Adler, Stella 1945.14
Adler, Tom 1928.45
Adler, William 1913.24
Adlmuller, Fred 1984.03
Admins, Ltd. 1968.31, 1969.08
Admire, Jere 1961.18, 1962.16, 1966.24
Adney, Angela 1978.26
Adnitt, Stephen 1999.14
Adoff, Denise 1978.23, 1979.27
Adolfi, Gustav 1879.62, 1880.61, 1880.66, 1882.45, 1886.53
Adolfi, Herr 1879.57, 1880.20, 1883.08, 1883.35
Adolph, Gustav 1889.27
Adolphi, Gustave 1883.44, 1885.09
Adolphus, Adame 1892.24
Adolphus, Theodor 1934.04
Adolphus, Theodore 1947.04
Adonis, Young 1871.18
Adonna, Prymm 1900.45
Adoram, Eliezer 1964.02
Adorci, Blanche 1882.31
Adorci, Miss 1882.36, 1882.37
Adorci, Mlle. 1884.54, 1884.55
Adorci, Mons. 1873.01, 1877.19
Adorcy, Mons. 1875.25, 1875.28, 1875.29, 1877.30
Adore, Renee 1919.19
Adrian 1894.26, 1922.39, 1923.22, 1923.32, 1923.34, 1924.44, 1960.21
Adrian, Diane 1945.18
Adrian, Gilbert 1921.22, 1923.33
Adrian, Henry 1945.17
Adrian, Louis 1953.16, 1954.13
Adrian, Max 1956.15, 1963.03
Adrian, William 1881.13
Adriana, Cora 1876.34
Adriance, William 1918.14
Adrien, Marie 1869.05
Adriene, Mlle. 1877.27
Adrienne 1946.22
Adrienne, Cora 1870.44, 1871.27, 1872.06
Adrienne, Marie 1872.37
Adrienne, Mlle. 1870.44, 1871.27, 1877.29, 1877.31, 1882.67, 1883.27, 1883.30, 1883.34, 1883.41
Adrienne, Mme. 1882.55, 1882.58, 1882.61, 1883.28
Adrover, Lisandro 1997.13
Adshead, Patricia 1981.13
Adventures in Motion Pictures 1998.10
Adzima, Nanzi 1981.03
Aeko, W.B. 1912.03
Aerseth, Arthur E. 1917.18
Affonso, Argemira 1997.13
After Six 1963.28
Afton, Effie 1951.17
Age, Elizabeth 1963.28
Agee, John 1927.10
Ager, Lucille 1919.25
Ager, Milton 1917.16, 1920.08, 1920.23, 1921.27, 1921.34, 1922.15, 1922.23, 1922.44, 1922.45, 1924.13, 1927.37, 1928.08, 1928.47, 1929.29, 1979.24, 1979.25, 1986.06, 1990.05, 1999.05
Aghayan, Ray 1960.12, 1962.17, 1970.09, 1971.15, 1974.02
Agmon, Yaacov 1971.17
Agnes, Mark 1993.17
Agnew, Clairisse 1898.47
Agnew, Claresse 1897.46
Agniel, Marguerite 1922.21
Agnolucci, Mario 1921.24, 1921.35, 1927.63
Agoust, Alfred 1919.22
Agoust, Emil 1913.28
Agoust, Emile 1912.24, 1912.27, 1913.08
Agra, Zuluma 1865.05
Agress, David 1990.09, 1991.04, 1997.12
Agress, Ted 1969.05, 1975.03
Agri, Pablo 1999.18
Aguiar, Edgar 1992.13
Aguirre, Andres 1949.07
Agustin, Julio 1999.01, 2001.03
Ahearn, Charles 1912.43, 1913.35, 1916.15
Ahearn, George 1913.03
Ahearne, Tom 1955.06
Ahern, Gladys 1927.48
Ahern, Pat 1976.29
Ahern, Sean 1976.29
Ahern, Townshend 1921.33
Ahern, Will 1927.48, 1930.08
Ahern, William 1927.48
Aherne, Richard 1951.24
Ahl, Fraulein 1879.62
Ahl, Frl. 1879.57, 1880.20
Ahlberg, Irene 1930.22, 1931.26
Ahlert, Fred 1928.33, 1952.11, 1981.16
Ahlert, Fred E. 1924.01, 1940.16, 1976.32, 1978.09
Ahlquist, Pirkko 1928.12
Ahlstron, Willie 1879.30
Ahmanson Theatre 1992.01, 1995.03
Ahmedo, Master 1911.28
Ahmend, Karl O. 1925.40
Ahrens, Lynn 1990.12, 1992.17, 1994.12, 1995.19, 1996.15, 1997.22, 1998.01, 1998.20, 1999.21, 2000.16, 2000.18, 2000.19
Ahumada, Jose 1961.07, 1962.13, 1963.05
Ai, Tom 1951.24
Aichel, Louise 1910.35, 1912.11
Aidman, Charles 1963.19, 1979.08
Aiken, Carmelyte 1869.34
Aiken, D.M. 1917.06
Aiken, David 1954.01, 1954.18
Aiken, E. 1882.71
Aiken, E.H. 1880.10, 1885.26, 1889.46
Aiken, Ed 1880.65, 1898.38
Aiken, Ed. 1879.35, 1880.06
Aiken, Edward 1880.67, 1880.70, 1883.65, 1889.46, 1900.36, 1903.25
Aiken, Edwin 1882.34
Aiken, Edwin H. 1893.13
Aiken, Frank 1887.48
Aiken, Frank E. 1888.14, 1888.27, 1888.40
Aiken, G.L. 1862.08
Aiken, George 1869.40
Aiken, Messr. 1880.59, 1886.47
Aiken, Michael Blue 1976.09
Aiken, Sol 1888.03, 1897.23, 1898.72
Aikens, Vanoye 1943.17, 1944.31, 1945.13, 1946.21, 1950.07
Ailes, Roger 1972.21
Ailey, Alvin 1954.19, 1957.16, 1972.15
Ailion, Anna 1913.09
Ails, Roscoe 1920.35
Aimee Comedy Company 1884.62, 1886.48, 1886.49
Aimee French Opera Bouffe Company 1873.11, 1873.15, 1873.16
Aimee's French Opera Bouffe Company 1871.26
Aimee, Maria 1875.08
Aimée, Marie 1870.45, 1871.03, 1871.06, 1871.07, 1871.23, 1871.24, 1871.25, 1871.26, 1871.28, 1872.03, 1872.28, 1872.29, 1872.31, 1872.33, 1872.39, 1872.41, 1872.42, 1873.01, 1873.11, 1873.15, 1873.16, 1875.07, 1875.09, 1876.20, 1876.24, 1876.25, 1876.26, 1876.28, 1876.31, 1877.06, 1877.09, 1877.10, 1877.11, 1877.12, 1877.13, 1877.14, 1877.17, 1877.19, 1877.26, 1877.27, 1877.29, 1877.30, 1877.31, 1877.32, 1877.33, 1877.34, 1877.37, 1877.38, 1878.06, 1878.07, 1878.08, 1878.09, 1879.19, 1879.26, 1879.27, 1879.31, 1879.34, 1879.36, 1879.39, 1879.40, 1879.41, 1879.43, 1879.44, 1879.45, 1879.46, 1879.47, 1883.51, 1883.54, 1883.60, 1883.61, 1884.01, 1884.02, 1884.03, 1884.05, 1884.62, 1886.48, 1886.49
Aimee, Mlle. 1883.57
Aimes, Noette 1910.15

Aimes, Paul 1927.10
Ain, Susan 1974.23
Ainscoe, Alice 1904.44
Ainscoe, Miss 1903.03
Ainscoe, Nina 1892.11, 1894.05, 1894.38, 1896.48
Ainscoe, Stubby 1898.50, 1899.30, 1903.03, 1904.13, 1904.44
Ainslee, Winifred 1950.10, 1955.10
Ainsleigh, Lillian 1885.65
Ainsley, Bessie 1884.25
Ainsley, Paul 1971.12
Ainsley, Peter 1936.28
Ainsworth, Edith 1884.19, 1890.19
Aitken 1917.17
Aitken, Bobby 2001.04
Aitken, Messr. 1898.26
Aitken, Spottiswood 1900.28
Akaaboune, Soumaya 1998.14
Akagi, T. 1902.22
Akerley, Messr. 1888.25, 1889.43
Akers, Andra 1980.29
Akers, D. 1975.20
Akers, Karen 1982.09, 1989.26
Aki, Haru 1976.27
Akins, Mary Katherine 1931.46
Akos, Catherine 1954.18
Akramere, Inc. 1919.32
Akselrod, Marcel 1968.21
Akst, Harry 1918.32, 1919.15, 1921.30, 1922.25, 1922.39, 1924.01, 1927.32, 1927.58, 1934.39, 1939.29, 1953.12, 1953.17, 1956.02, 1973.14, 1980.10, 1982.12
Akunyun, Babafumi 1972.06
Alabama Shakespeare Festival 1999.09
Alabama, Young 1911.26
Alabieff-Liszt, Alexander 1943.11
Alain, Frances 1911.40
Alaire, Berenice 1933.26
Alala 1934.16
Alamo, Pablo 1974.14
Alan, Charles 1937.01, 1940.11, 1940.13, 1940.14, 1940.15
Alaves, Lopez 1988.15
Alba, Floriana 1949.07
Albam, Manny 1969.01
Albani, Olga 1928.29
Albano, Gene 1966.31
Albano, Mary Elizabeth 1994.12
Albaugh, H.C. 1881.52
Albee, Fred 1981.17
Albenitz 1927.51
Albeniz, Isaac 1922.21, 1934.32, 1949.07
Alber, Jean 1947.18
Alberghetti, Anna Maria 1961.10
Alberni, Luis 1926.31, 1927.03, 1927.50
Albert 1890.50, 1892.59, 1893.23
Albert, Anthony 1937.15, 1938.15, 1939.13
Albert, Charles 1903.03
Albert, Donnie Ray 1976.28
Albert, Eddie 1938.14, 1949.08
Albert, Ernest 1890.03, 1890.14, 1890.20, 1891.29, 1891.41, 1894.23, 1894.39, 1894.45, 1895.01, 1895.03, 1895.31, 1895.33, 1896.43, 1896.44, 1896.46, 1896.51, 1897.11, 1897.13, 1897.17, 1897.18, 1897.25, 1897.39, 1897.42, 1897.54, 1898.27, 1898.43, 1898.68, 1898.72, 1899.12, 1899.15, 1899.19, 1900.05, 1900.07, 1900.20, 1900.32, 1900.33, 1900.41, 1901.01, 1901.05, 1901.08, 1901.13, 1901.21, 1901.23, 1901.25, 1902.35, 1902.38, 1902.41, 1902.43, 1903.04, 1903.06, 1903.23, 1903.29, 1903.36, 1903.40, 1904.18, 1904.20, 1904.39, 1904.41, 1904.49, 1904.56, 1905.05, 1905.36, 1905.49, 1905.56, 1906.01, 1906.02, 1906.04, 1906.06, 1906.10, 1906.11, 1906.14, 1906.18, 1906.40, 1906.41, 1906.42, 1906.45, 1906.48, 1907.01, 1907.07, 1907.09, 1907.10, 1907.13, 1907.22, 1907.33, 1907.44, 1908.02, 1908.04, 1908.07, 1908.09, 1908.16, 1908.22, 1908.24, 1908.34, 1908.35, 1908.39, 1909.16, 1909.23, 1909.25, 1909.26, 1909.28, 1909.31, 1910.18, 1910.22, 1910.34, 1911.07, 1911.11, 1911.18, 1911.24, 1911.37, 1911.41, 1911.45, 1912.10, 1912.13, 1912.28, 1912.38, 1913.04, 1913.17, 1913.37, 1914.26, 1915.16, 1915.24, 1916.15, 1917.22, 1918.31
Albert, John 1934.35, 1936.22
Albert, Louis 1982.15
Albert, Mary 1880.44, 1880.58, 1881.54
Albert, Messr. 1887.32
Albert, Mr. 1860.03, 1891.33
Albert, Tony 1950.03
Alberta, La Petite 1870.43
Alberta, Laura 1922.38
Albertazzi, Mesdame 1852.05
Albertazzi, Messr. 1852.05
Alberte, Charles S. 1916.03
Alberteri 1898.56
Alberti, Carl J. 1884.22
Albertieri 1902.07
Albertieri, Luigi 1907.47
Albertieri, M. 1901.18
Albertieri, Signor 1912.46
Albertin, M. 1869.08
Albertina, Mlle. 1870.41, 1872.10
Albertine, C. 1976.34
Albertini, Ellen B. 1948.17
Albertini, Rose 1869.38
Alberto, Albert 1918.23, 1920.26, 1921.28, 1922.30
Alberto, Master 1884.61
Alberto, Mlle. 1871.26
Alberts, Bob 1898.64
Alberts, Eunice 1948.31
Albertson, Frank 1951.18
Albertson, Jack 1940.21, 1944.15, 1945.01, 1947.21, 1948.04, 1950.09, 1951.23, 1954.04
Albertson, Kathryn 1959.13
Albery, Donald 1960.13, 1962.23, 1963.01, 1964.45, 1965.23
Albery, Ian 1963.01, 1965.23
Albery, James 1880.18
Albini, Felix 1910.31, 1912.10
Albinoni, Tomasso 1978.26
Albrecht, Herr 1880.66
Albright, Clarence 1936.30
Albright, James 1965.38, 1969.12
Albright, Jessica 1959.02, 1960.06
Albright, Jim 1957.11
Albright, Jimmy 1953.17
Albro, Arthur 1911.37, 1913.28, 1914.33, 1917.15, 1918.20
Albu, Annie 1895.32
Alcantara, Burt 1978.26
Alchourron, Rodolfo 1989.20
Alcorn, Mlle. 1922.34
Alda, Alan 1964.18, 1966.18
Alda, Delyle 1919.15, 1921.04, 1921.18, 1923.18
Alda, DeLyle 1920.18
Alda, Mlle. 1870.45, 1871.06
Alda, Robert 1950.17, 1964.05
Aldema, Gil 1971.17
Alden 1884.59
Alden, Bob 1924.01
Alden, C.J. 1893.17
Alden, Clare 1948.20
Alden, Cyril 1906.06
Alden, Hazel 1919.38
Alden, Hortense 1919.06, 1925.37
Alden, Jane 1928.21, 1929.32, 1931.02, 1931.30
Alden, Jerome 1987.19
Alden, John 1906.12
Alden, Joseph R. 1980.08
Alden, Lynn 1943.03, 1945.04
Alden, Marian 1929.39
Alden, Miles 1999.15
Aldena, Gill 1968.04
Aldene, Judy 1960.08
Alder, Alan 1976.18
Alderfer, Eric 1981.19
Alderman, Jacqualine 1931.29
Alderman, James 1924.06, 1925.02
Alderson, Erville 1916.13
Aldine, Nellie 1880.64
Aldous, Lucette 1976.18
Aldred, Julian 1920.21
Aldredge, Theoni V. 1962.05, 1962.20, 1964.15, 1965.33, 1966.09, 1967.05, 1968.11, 1969.08, 1971.18, 1972.01, 1973.08, 1974.16, 1975.15, 1975.16, 1976.10, 1976.23, 1977.06, 1977.11, 1978.27, 1979.02, 1979.12, 1980.03, 1980.22, 1980.30, 1981.10, 1981.22, 1981.29, 1983.01, 1983.11, 1984.01, 1987.07, 1987.19, 1988.09, 1989.27, 1990.14, 1991.05, 1991.06, 1991.15, 1992.06, 1997.04, 2001.02, 2001.08
Aldredge, Theoni Vachlioti 1959.12
Aldredge, Thomas 1959.12
Aldredge, Tom 1974.25, 1976.08, 1987.18, 1994.05, 1997.15
Aldrich, Alden 1949.17
Aldrich, Charles T. 1901.01, 1914.23, 1915.24, 1917.22, 1918.23
Aldrich, David 1978.24
Aldrich, Gertrude 1914.13
Aldrich, Janet 1989.09
Aldrich, Lillie 1884.29
Aldrich, Louis 1876.12
Aldrich, Margaret 1967.18
Aldrich, Meeka 1928.46
Aldrich, Ray 1902.18
Aldrich, Richard 1939.20
Aldridge, Arthur 1911.21, 1912.18, 1912.21, 1912.22, 1912.23, 1913.08, 1913.11, 1913.12, 1913.13, 1915.06, 1915.09, 1915.10, 1915.12, 1915.13, 1915.14
Aldridge, Theoni V. 1974.09, 1980.07, 1980.20
Aleichem, Sholom 1964.27, 1976.36, 1981.18, 1989.03, 1990.16, 1990.18
Alekseyevtzeva, Mme. 1923.28
Alen, W.W. 1893.06
Alena, Miss 1886.16
Alene, Douglas 1930.42
Aleneff, Messr. 1922.37
Alenikoff, Frances 1964.02
Aleo, Anthony 1949.03
Alers, Yassmin 1998.02
Aletter, Frank 1952.10, 1956.14
Aletter, W. 1905.20
Alex, Jimmy 1953.11, 1954.09
Alex-Cole, Steven 1976.28, 1979.26
Alexa, Mlle. 1898.69
Alexander, Adinah 1998.21
Alexander, Alex 1943.09, 1957.04, 1969.09
Alexander, Alice 1938.01
Alexander, Arthur 1908.22, 1909.16
Alexander, Blanche 1902.36, 1904.02
Alexander, Brandy 1976.20
Alexander, C. 1872.27, 1893.07
Alexander, C.K. 1953.07, 1971.02, 1976.10
Alexander, Carlos 1942.33
Alexander, Charles 1891.36, 1923.21
Alexander, Cheryl 1981.29, 1985.17
Alexander, Cris 1944.33, 1953.03, 1958.05, 1970.19
Alexander, Danny 1949.09
Alexander, David 1952.01, 1953.01, 1955.25
Alexander, Detlev 1998.10
Alexander, Ellen 1968.14
Alexander, G. Keith 1973.17
Alexander, Geraldine 1917.03, 1920.04, 1921.22
Alexander, Gilson 1888.36
Alexander, Gordon 1948.20, 1951.22
Alexander, Guido 1926.38, 1937.08
Alexander, Gus 1906.15, 1928.46, 1931.03
Alexander, Gustav 1897.26
Alexander, Harold 'Ricardo' 1976.34
Alexander, Hi 1930.33, 1936.01
Alexander, James 1893.13, 1894.19, 1946.21
Alexander, Jason 1981.27, 1984.01, 1989.03
Alexander, Jim 1991.13
Alexander, John 1920.08, 1924.27, 1958.16, 1961.05
Alexander, Judy 1962.12
Alexander, K.C. 1957.04
Alexander, Katherine 1919.02
Alexander, Louise 1908.42, 1910.18, 1911.45
Alexander, M. 1886.16
Alexander, Manuel A. 1910.09
Alexander, Mara 1938.04
Alexander, Marian 1908.10
Alexander, Mat. 1894.19
Alexander, Matt 1893.13, 1898.01
Alexander, Max 1928.14
Alexander, Melville 1912.36
Alexander, Messr. 1894.19
Alexander, Michel 1954.19
Alexander, Newton 1922.27, 1923.18, 1924.19, 1925.27, 1926.37
Alexander, Pearle 1897.33
Alexander, Peggy 1939.22, 1941.12
Alexander, Richard Jay 1992.03
Alexander, Richard-Jay 1987.04
Alexander, Rod 1948.14, 1950.06, 1957.05, 1961.07
Alexander, Ron 1978.26
Alexander, Roy 1922.01
Alexander, Sigmund B. 1897.40
Alexander, Stella 1896.05
Alexander, Vada 1925.22, 1927.46, 1929.35
Alexander, Van 1986.02, 1997.01
Alexander, Virginia 1929.04
Alexander, William 1898.20
Alexandra, Emilie 1895.32
Alexandre, Mercia 1992.13
Alexandrine, Dru 1976.05, 1980.30
Alexandrine, Mlle. 1870.44, 1871.27
Alexandrova, Mme. 1929.05
Alexandrowa, Clemence 1871.18
Alexe, Sarina 1896.27
Alexi-Malle, Adam 1997.06
Alexia, Mme. 1897.16
Alf, James 1924.18
Alfasa, Joseph 1967.05, 1968.30
Alfino, Edward 1911.42
Alfiorova, Irena 1990.01
Alfonso, Don 1943.17, 1950.07
Alford, C. 1862.01
Alford, Lamar 1976.17
Alford, Larry 1985.19
Alford, Messr. 1857.04
Alford, Miss 1857.02
Alford, Rodger 1951.11
Alford, Roger 1943.10
Alfred E. Aarons Musical Comedy Company 1900.16
Alfred, Julian 1909.07, 1909.18, 1910.15, 1912.20, 1913.23, 1913.29, 1915.01, 1915.08, 1916.21, 1917.29, 1919.12, 1919.23, 1919.25, 1919.44, 1920.05, 1920.29, 1920.43, 1921.06, 1922.10, 1922.14, 1922.17, 1922.47, 1923.27, 1923.44, 1924.08, 1924.39, 1924.41, 1925.05, 1925.32, 1926.39
Alfred, Mr. 1865.05
Alfred, William 1970.10, 1982.02
Alfredo, Emma 1883.17
Alfredo, James 1883.17
Alger, Joseph 1936.12
Algere, Joseph 1902.14
Algier, Robert 1906.26
Alguerro, Augusto 1964.02
Alhaiza, Messr. 1868.13, 1868.15
Alhert, Fred E. 1919.03
Ali, Bobker Ben 1911.28
Ali, George 1895.03, 1898.63, 1899.21, 1899.30, 1900.38, 1901.17, 1902.16, 1903.18, 1905.05, 1928.30, 1935.03
Ali, H. Ben 1911.10
Ali, Messr. 1898.16
Ali, Mohammed Ben 1925.37
Ali, Muhammad 1969.15
Ali, Salayman 1922.15
Aliabeck 1922.06
Aliabieff 1927.51
Alias 1882.78, 1884.61, 1889.08, 1892.08, 1903.21, 1904.03, 1913.33
Alias, C. 1912.24
Alias, Charles 1886.50, 1886.54, 1902.35
Alias, Mme. 1880.55, 1888.33, 1890.50
Alias, Mme. Charles 1886.54
Alias, Mons. 1880.55, 1888.33, 1890.50
Alice 1968.04
Alice Nielsen Opera Company 1898.60, 1899.34
Alice Oates' English Comic Opera Company 1879.18, 1879.23, 1879.24
Alice Oates' Opera Company 1876.17, 1876.18, 1876.21, 1876.27, 1877.16
Alice, Little 1880.07
Alice, Miss 1857.02
Alicoate, Jack 1925.35
Alison, George 1902.21
Aljoe, Tony 1986.15
Alk, Howard 1961.17
All-Corduroy Production 1968.13
Alla 1977.13
Allan, A. 1840.02
Allan, Betty 1922.41
Allan, Dorothy 1918.03, 1940.16
Allan, Edgar 1934.29
Allan, Edward 1924.38, 1927.16, 1928.37
Allan, Effie 1916.12
Allan, Gene 1969.08
Allan, Jed 1962.04
Allan, Lewis 1945.07, 1948.13
Allan, Mabel 1919.38
Allan, Sean 1964.21, 1965.14
Allan, Steve 1963.12
Allan, Ted 1964.28, 1989.05
Allard, Martine 1983.21
Allau, Jack 1915.31
Allegro, Alfred 1937.11
Allen, A. Hylton 1911.45
Allen, Amelia 1921.14, 1921.35, 1922.39
Allen, Anna 1889.08, 1890.23

Allen, Antoinette 1937.01
Allen, Barbara 1890.50
Allen, Barty 1880.41
Allen, Beatrice 1912.38, 1917.21
Allen, Beatrive 1925.19
Allen, Beau 1982.11
Allen, Bertram 1907.58
Allen, Betty 1926.33, 1933.13, 1936.26, 1939.30, 1944.18, 1954.14, 1974.07, 1974.15, 1975.19
Allen, Betty Lou 1952.06
Allen, Billie 1916.24, 1917.03, 1952.06, 1952.15
Allen, Bob 1979.05
Allen, Bunny 1933.06
Allen, Charles 1887.31
Allen, Clara 1885.45, 1885.52, 1886.37, 1886.43, 1887.12, 1887.18, 1890.21, 1895.24
Allen, Claude 1917.08
Allen, Cliff 1934.06, 1934.40, 1936.12
Allen, Clifford 1967.06
Allen, Crystal 1997.03
Allen, Dave 1981.23
Allen, David 1951.05, 1958.12
Allen, Debbie 1986.07, 1988.12
Allen, Deborah 1973.10
Allen, Don 1947.09
Allen, Dora 1892.55, 1893.20, 1895.07
Allen, E. 1869.15, 1893.34
Allen, Edgar 1903.12, 1911.28, 1935.03
Allen, Edith 1913.24
Allen, Edward 1924.21, 1927.09, 1930.05
Allen, Elizabeth 1961.27, 1965.06, 1967.02
Allen, Eloise 1869.04, 1876.19
Allen, Estelle 1893.34
Allen, Ethan 1896.06, 1897.27
Allen, Ethel 1879.02, 1928.31, 1928.50
Allen, Eva 1900.38, 1901.17, 1902.29, 1903.28
Allen, Fred 1922.34, 1924.06, 1929.02, 1929.19, 1930.32, 1934.01
Allen, George 1893.23
Allen, Georgia 1969.03
Allen, Guy 1989.06
Allen, H.T. 1870.20, 1870.23, 1870.26, 1872.16, 1872.18, 1872.19, 1873.23
Allen, Harriet 1908.34
Allen, Harry 1875.20, 1876.06, 1880.01, 1880.03, 1880.34, 1880.46, 1882.46, 1882.63, 1887.21, 1924.42, 1950.01, 1950.08
Allen, Harry R. 1922.10
Allen, Hazel 1908.33, 1911.05, 1911.35
Allen, Helen 1915.18, 1932.26
Allen, Ian 2000.04
Allen, J. 1904.28
Allen, James 1905.43
Allen, Jay Edward 1979.28
Allen, Joe 1890.25
Allen, Johanna 1933.03
Allen, John 1866.20, 1866.22, 1866.26, 1866.35, 1867.01, 1867.02, 1961.11
Allen, Jonelle 1955.09, 1968.07, 1971.18
Allen, Joseph 1904.28, 1906.19, 1908.18, 1909.19, 1911.41, 1918.37, 1924.34, 1937.13
Allen, Josephine 1896.36, 1897.09, 1897.19, 1897.31, 1897.48, 1898.50, 1899.17, 1900.38
Allen, Josie 1896.05
Allen, June 1950.12
Allen, Kate 1888.17, 1889.39, 1936.28
Allen, Kate B. 1894.06
Allen, Katie 1897.19
Allen, Kirk 1923.43
Allen, Lee 1907.12, 1945.06
Allen, Leslie 1881.15
Allen, Lester 1907.49, 1919.13, 1920.17, 1921.22, 1922.27, 1923.18, 1924.19, 1925.25, 1925.27, 1925.40, 1925.48, 1927.13, 1928.12, 1929.49, 1933.16
Allen, Lewis 1942.05, 1942.26, 1965.14, 1977.06, 1980.13, 1983.06
Allen, Lizzie 1866.19
Allen, Lola 1904.57
Allen, Louise 1885.33, 1886.16, 1887.03, 1888.01, 1888.23, 1889.21, 1889.47, 1891.37, 1893.08, 1902.29, 1916.18, 1917.07, 1918.09, 1918.40, 1920.27, 1922.28
Allen, Mae 1911.32
Allen, Malcolm 1989.11
Allen, Mana 1986.20
Allen, Marc 1970.08
Allen, Marianna 1981.27
Allen, Marie 1901.01, 1902.40, 1904.08
Allen, Mark 1955.04, 1958.01
Allen, Martin 1968.03, 1971.07, 1973.12
Allen, Marty 1962.24, 1964.44
Allen, Maud 1911.33, 1924.13
Allen, May 1911.12
Allen, Messr. 1881.35
Allen, Michael K. 1968.13
Allen, Miss 1882.32, 1882.60, 1883.38, 1904.44
Allen, Mord 1908.08
Allen, Mr. 1854.03, 1854.06, 1854.07, 1855.01, 1855.10, 1876.35
Allen, Mrs. 1834.03
Allen, Mrs. H.T. 1872.18
Allen, Mrs. J.H. 1860.06, 1861.04
Allen, Myrtle 1927.38
Allen, Nellie 1872.16, 1873.23, 1875.20, 1876.06
Allen, Nita 1911.26, 1914.12
Allen, Norman 1965.14
Allen, P. 1881.06
Allen, Paula 1900.33
Allen, Peter 1971.01, 1979.11, 1983.09, 1988.20, 1992.18
Allen, R. 1878.04, 1888.23
Allen, R.A. 1908.07
Allen, Rae 1954.05, 1955.08, 1965.31
Allen, Ralph 1986.11
Allen, Ralph G. 1979.25
Allen, Ray 1887.27, 1888.23, 1889.21, 1889.47, 1891.36, 1893.47, 1897.26, 1949.15
Allen, Raymond 1961.03, 1962.09, 1964.08, 1964.20, 1968.10
Allen, Ricca 1885.33, 1886.41, 1888.10, 1889.08, 1889.50, 1910.19
Allen, Robert 1946.01
Allen, Robert Lee 1918.35, 1924.12, 1926.05, 1931.07
Allen, Ross 1986.16
Allen, Scott 1975.15
Allen, Steve 1993.14, 1995.18
Allen, Sylvia 1944.21
Allen, Thomas 1914.16
Allen, Timothy 1983.04
Allen, Tyress 2000.06
Allen, Vera 1925.20, 1926.17, 1928.19, 1935.12, 1936.31
Allen, Virginia 1913.32
Allen, Vivienne 1941.03, 1942.19
Allen, W. 1881.18
Allen, W.A. 1880.68
Allen, W.H. 1883.47
Allen, W.W. 1878.04, 1878.12, 1879.63, 1880.39, 1882.28
Allen, Walter 1882.57, 1883.37, 1892.55, 1893.20, 1894.22, 1895.07, 1895.19, 1895.33, 1897.18, 1898.34
Allen, William 1881.22, 1893.26
Allen, Woody 1960.07
Aller, John 1986.13
Allers, Franz 1947.07, 1950.01, 1951.24, 1952.15, 1955.01, 1956.01, 1957.13, 1957.15, 1960.21, 1964.23, 1964.24, 1965.22, 1965.24, 1966.12, 1966.14, 1980.19, 1981.19, 1981.26
Allers, Roger 1994.04, 1997.20
Allerton, Maud 1872.14, 1872.36
Alley Theatre 1999.08
Alley, Laura 1988.16
Alleyne, Messr. 1857.02, 1857.03
Alleyne, Miss 1857.01, 1857.02
Alleyne, Mr. 1852.06, 1853.02, 1853.03, 1857.01, 1857.08
Allford, C. 1861.06
Allgood, III, Trey 2001.04
Allien, Emma 1892.47
Allinson, Michael 1969.17, 1984.07
Allison, Bernie 1978.11
Allison, Bessie 1926.31
Allison, C.W. 1882.28, 1887.40
Allison, Charles 1886.39, 1892.17, 1894.13
Allison, Charles W. 1890.44, 1898.27
Allison, Fred 1975.05
Allison, J.M. 1907.47
Allison, James 1893.33
Allison, Jerry 1990.15
Allison, John 1903.20
Allison, L.R. 1884.33
Allison, Lucy 1893.33
Allison, Maud 1903.20
Allison, Mildred 1935.01
Allison, Patti 1978.10
Allison, Polly 1911.26
Allison, Wana 1943.09, 1948.15, 1958.08
Allison, Wanna 1948.25
Allison, Young E. 1894.08
Alliston, Annie 1886.47, 1888.36
Alliston, Lillie 1886.32, 1886.59, 1887.13, 1887.32, 1888.33, 1891.41, 1892.45, 1894.22, 1894.46
Allman, David 1937.13
Allmon, Clint 1978.13
Alloway, Jacqueline 1968.07
Alloy, Al 1943.14, 1943.16, 1943.21, 1948.32, 1952.02, 1960.23
Alloy, Anthony 1971.14, 1972.05, 1973.05, 1974.26
Allsbrook, Bill 1970.09
Allvine, Glendon 1938.10
Allweight, Mr. 1876.03
Allworth, Chris 1904.14
Allworth, Frank 1928.36, 1930.23
Allyn, Edgar S. 1906.39
Allyn, Estelle 1892.29, 1894.14
Allyn, Lillie 1897.04
Allyn, Lon 1893.20
Allyn, Miss 1882.46
Allyn, William 1946.17
Allyne, Lillie 1893.49
Allyne, Miss 1865.01
Allys, Ethel 1926.29
Allyson, June 1938.09, 1941.06
Alma, Kate 1892.06
Alma, Lyda 1947.18
Alma, Richard 1940.04
Almagor, Dan 1968.08, 1971.17, 1972.17
Almanack Theatrical Corporation, The 1929.29
Almeras, Charles 1877.26, 1877.27, 1877.29, 1877.30, 1877.31, 1877.32, 1877.33, 1877.34, 1877.37, 1877.38, 1878.06, 1878.07, 1878.08, 1878.09, 1879.19, 1879.26, 1879.27, 1879.31, 1879.34, 1879.36, 1879.39, 1879.40, 1879.41, 1879.43, 1879.44, 1879.45, 1879.47, 1879.48, 1879.49, 1879.51, 1879.55, 1879.60, 1879.61, 1879.69, 1880.14, 1880.16, 1880.22, 1880.23, 1880.27, 1880.28, 1880.29, 1880.44, 1880.50, 1880.52, 1880.56, 1880.60
Almon, John Paul 1999.17
Almonznino 1969.13
Almy, Brooks 1987.09, 1988.04, 1989.04, 1990.06
Almy, Grace 1900.48
Almy, O.F. 1857.03
Almy, Oscar F. 1857.01, 1857.02, 1857.03, 1859.06, 1859.07, 1859.08
Alny, Mlle. 1926.47, 1926.48
Alny, Sonia 1926.40, 1926.43, 1929.10, 1929.11, 1929.13, 1929.14, 1929.15, 1929.16
Alon, Meir 1968.08
Alonso, Fernando 1938.15, 1939.13
Alonso, Manolo 1974.14
Alonso, Odon 1969.11
Alonzo, Gloria 1902.17
Alpert, Anita 1965.22
Alpert, Herb 1992.08
Alpert, Larry 1951.20, 1961.21
Alpert, Michael 1990.16
Alpert, Millie 1951.20
Alpert, Pauline 1927.13
Alpeter, Greta 1931.07
Alphabet, Madge 1894.38
Alphin, Charles 1908.20
Alphonsine, Mlle. 1866.27, 1875.33, 1877.27, 1877.32, 1877.34, 1877.38, 1878.07, 1878.08, 1879.55, 1879.60
Alphonsine, Mons. 1877.33
Alpine, Jeannette 1908.28
Alpine, Vich 1871.16
Alquist, Pirkko 1930.08
Alsop, M.L. 1889.10
Alston, Barbara 1966.24, 1968.31
Alston, Ladson 1902.38
Alston, Sherwood 1907.24
Alstone 1947.05, 1948.12
Alstone, Louis Poterat 1963.02
Alswang, Ralph 1948.22, 1949.10, 1949.11, 1949.13, 1949.14, 1950.08, 1950.09, 1950.18, 1951.17, 1952.14, 1952.16, 1952.17, 1952.18, 1952.19, 1952.20, 1953.10, 1955.12, 1959.20, 1959.23, 1962.23, 1964.03, 1964.26, 1964.34, 1964.45, 1965.16, 1966.20, 1966.32, 1967.11, 1968.21
Alsworth, Chris. 1906.06
Alt, Natalie 1911.08, 1911.14, 1911.30, 1913.21, 1915.06, 1915.09, 1915.10, 1915.19, 1916.07, 1917.32
Alta, Marian 1925.32
Alten, Bella 1912.19
Alter, Lou 1926.23, 1928.23
Alter, Louis 1926.23, 1927.02, 1927.38, 1928.33, 1930.38, 1930.42, 1931.13, 1933.21, 1980.29
Alter, Melba 1928.26
Alter, Rosalie 1948.25
Alteras, Charles 1880.58
Alters, Elizabeth 1928.20
Alters, Gerald 1953.17, 1961.08, 1962.01, 1976.34, 1981.07
Althea, Blanche 1898.03
Althea, Lillian 1898.03
Altherton, Robert 1958.11
Althoff, Charles 1931.28, 1939.24
Altman 1907.01
Altman, Arthur 1989.21
Altman, Ella 1895.23
Altman, Ruth 1930.26, 1931.12, 1931.15, 1931.27, 1933.10, 1933.11, 1933.17, 1933.18, 1933.19, 1954.09
Altman, Sy 1934.37
Altmann, Adolf 1912.15
Alto, (Bobby) 1992.16
Alton, Bertie 1891.20
Alton, Marjorie 1924.32
Alton, Robert 1924.32, 1933.21, 1934.01, 1934.18, 1934.19, 1934.36, 1934.42, 1935.03, 1936.02, 1936.31, 1937.15, 1937.16, 1938.07, 1938.13, 1939.12, 1939.22, 1939.27, 1939.30, 1940.03, 1940.06, 1940.19, 1940.22, 1941.11, 1942.15, 1942.27, 1943.05, 1943.07, 1944.30, 1952.01, 1953.01, 1953.08, 1955.25
Alton, Royce 1890.12, 1891.14, 1891.20, 1892.06
Altree, Ernest 1909.06
Alvan, Manolo 1974.14
Alvardo, Trini 1978.11
Alvarez, Anita 1940.23, 1943.01, 1944.15, 1945.20, 1947.03, 1949.18, 1955.09, 1960.09
Alvarez, Carmen 1954.05, 1956.12, 1965.36, 1966.18, 1968.30, 1970.08, 1973.05
Alvarez, Julio 1927.15
Alvarez, Leo 1999.21, 2000.19
Alvarez, Pilar 1993.08
Alvarez, Rigoberto Mercado 1988.15
Alvarez, Theresa 1939.19
Alvarez, Tomas 1974.14
Alverado, Domingo 1973.17
Alvers, Zinaida 1943.11
Alves, Clyde 2000.11
Alvin, Farah 1996.17
Alvord, Sinead 1915.25
Alwin, Dolly 1912.34, 1914.30
Alwyn, Dolly 1919.01
Alwyn, Jean 1910.21
Alydon, John 1976.12
Alyn, Glen 1947.15
Alyn, Kirk 1938.04
Alyson, Eydie 1981.18
Alyward, Gertrude 1895.29
Alza, Mlle. 1880.68
Alzado, Pater 1978.27
Amable 1887.27, 1888.01, 1888.23, 1893.45
Amadao, A. 1887.18
Amade, Louis 1968.21
Amadeo, A. 1895.26
Amadeo, Antonio 1887.12, 1888.22
Amado, Jorge 1979.03
Amalli, Mlle. 1869.26
Amami, Yuki 1989.21
Aman, John 1961.12, 1962.20, 1968.02
Amaranth, Elsie 1918.23
Amaranth, Hannah 1919.22
Amaranth, Jennie 1918.23, 1919.22
Amaranth, Mary 1919.22
Amaranth, Tina 1918.23, 1919.22
Amaro, Richard 1989.03, 1989.20
AMAS Musical Theatre 1999.06
Amato, Albert 1935.14, 1937.16
Amaya, Carmen 1942.16
Amber, M.L. 1890.08
Amberg's German Operetta Company 1882.68
Amberg, Bertie 1886.06
Amberg, Charles 1999.05
Amberg, Gustav 1879.57, 1879.62, 1885.01

Amberg, H. 1876.17, 1876.21, 1877.16, 1877.23, 1877.25, 1879.03, 1879.38, 1880.24
Amberg, H.A. 1883.64
Amberg, Harry 1884.66, 1886.11
Amberg, Messr. 1877.22, 1884.42
Amberg, Mr. 1878.20
Ambergh, H. 1877.39
Ambient, Mark 1910.05
Ambler, Jim 1998.13
Ambler, Scott 1998.10
Ambler, William 1948.17, 1949.17
Ambos, Frank 1936.03
Ambos, Franklyn 1936.04, 1936.09, 1936.10, 1936.11
Ambrose, Arthur 1903.18
Ambrose, Billy 1936.06
Ambrose, Frank 1885.53, 1896.14
Ambrose, Franklyn 1934.07, 1934.08, 1936.08
Ambrose, Leona 1892.05, 1905.50
Ambrose, Martin 1961.26, 1963.25, 1966.30, 1967.16
Ambrose, Ruth 1936.06
Amdurs, Sam 1944.33
Ameche, Don 1955.02, 1958.14, 1961.07, 1967.14
Amelie, Mlle. 1879.19, 1879.26, 1879.31, 1879.34, 1879.36, 1879.39, 1879.43, 1879.44, 1879.45, 1879.46, 1879.47, 1879.49, 1880.52, 1880.56
Amelie, Mme. 1880.50
Amend, Karl 1927.35, 1934.17, 1935.11, 1942.30
Amend, Karl O. 1925.16, 1925.25, 1926.03, 1927.05, 1928.10, 1932.30
Amend, Karle O. 1925.48, 1931.34
America Extravaganza Company 1892.29
America, Young 1877.01, 1879.42, 1881.13, 1882.77
America-Italy Society 1985.14, 1985.16
American Allied Arts, Inc. 1927.45
American Dancemachine, Inc. 1986.03
American Express 2000.19
American Music Theatre Festival 1989.20
American National Theatre and Academy 1952.06
American National Theatre and Academy Production 1980.27
American Repertory Theatre, The 1985.06
American Travesty Company 1895.03
Americana, Inc. 1928.45
Amerique, Miss 1930.37
Amerson, Tammy 1994.08
Ames, Alice 1883.65
Ames, Amy 1869.15, 1884.60, 1885.08, 1886.28, 1888.17, 1897.01
Ames, April 1940.08
Ames, Florenz 1917.12, 1920.02, 1923.01, 1923.33, 1924.39, 1925.07, 1926.14, 1928.46, 1929.46, 1930.07, 1930.23, 1931.29, 1931.48, 1933.13, 1933.25, 1937.13, 1942.02, 1942.04, 1942.06, 1942.07, 1942.08, 1942.09, 1944.04, 1944.05, 1944.06, 1944.07, 1944.08, 1944.09, 1944.10, 1944.11, 1944.12, 1944.13, 1950.04, 1952.07
Ames, Genevieve 1927.11
Ames, Gerry 1898.51
Ames, Joseph 1928.25
Ames, Joseph C. 1907.53
Ames, Kenneth 1982.13
Ames, Kenston 1985.02, 1985.20
Ames, Lionel 1952.13
Ames, Louis B. 1958.17
Ames, Mr. 1836.01
Ames, Nancy 1965.18
Ames, Nell 1923.08
Ames, Percy 1906.37, 1908.03, 1909.04, 1911.06, 1916.02, 1918.22
Ames, Percy F. 1904.08, 1905.16
Ames, Winthrop 1916.16, 1926.10, 1926.44, 1927.44, 1927.61
Ames, Wintrop 1927.57
Amfimoff, Messr. 1925.03
Amick, Alan 1977.07
Amiel, Mons. 1885.23
Amies, E. 1922.32
Amihud, Dani 1972.17
Ammon, Richard 1981.19
Ammons, Albert 1944.31, 1945.10
Amonsin, Viraj 1961.12
Amoroso, Jack 1946.05
Amos, Herbert 1907.22
Amos, Keith Lorenzo 1983.15
Amos, Kevin 1999.07
Amos, Ruth 1951.14
Amrani, Hedva 1968.04
Amrose, Lea 1900.47
Amrose, Leona 1892.45
Amsterdam, Morey 1948.21
Amundsen, Monte 1958.15, 1959.04, 1964.18
Amusement Producing Company, Inc., The 1908.16
Amy, Grace 1900.55
Ana Spencer, Inc. 1922.40
Anania, John 1947.04, 1960.10, 1962.27, 1964.18, 1965.33, 1968.03, 1970.09, 1978.04
Anania, Michael 1968.23, 1980.01, 1986.14, 1987.10, 1988.16, 1989.04, 1990.06, 1990.07, 1991.08, 1991.09, 1992.10, 1994.09, 1995.06, 1996.02, 1996.11, 1997.11, 1998.06, 1999.11
Anatarova, Irina Hicks 1931.38
Anatole, Francois 1880.58
Anberg, Charles 1999.05
Anbri, Christiana 1997.04
Anchong, I. 1931.39
Anchutina, Leda 1938.15
Andalman, Jean 1976.27
Andalucia Productions 1992.15
Anden, Mathew 1965.04
Anderman, Maureen 1978.06
Anderon, Leroy 1987.02
Anders, Ann 1937.17
Anders, Darlene 1984.14
Anders, Glenn 1937.17
Anders, Karen 1955.11, 1979.13, 1980.18
Andersen, Virginia 1923.37
Anderson 1945.10, 1955.26
Anderson, Adele 2000.16
Anderson, Adrienne 1976.34, 1979.11, 1983.09, 1991.10
Anderson, Alan 1942.20
Anderson, Albert 1895.41
Anderson, Alfred 1907.22, 1907.29
Anderson, Anne Renee 1948.30
Anderson, Annie 1886.53
Anderson, Arlene 1944.23
Anderson, Arthur 1907.41, 1912.17, 1912.27, 1913.26, 1917.24, 1919.20
Anderson, Audrey 1920.34
Anderson, B. 1877.08
Anderson, B.C. 1879.29
Anderson, Beatrice 1905.29
Anderson, Bette 1945.19
Anderson, Brad 1999.01
Anderson, Carl 1889.47, 1923.24, 1995.02, 1997.03
Anderson, Claire 1944.02
Anderson, D.C. 1871.13
Anderson, David 1970.09
Anderson, Del 1957.07, 1958.14
Anderson, Delbert 1951.24, 1953.03, 1956.16
Anderson, Dolly 1900.34
Anderson, Elizabeth 1993.01
Anderson, Ella 1907.55, 1911.20
Anderson, Elman 1973.06, 1975.22, 1979.13, 1980.09, 1980.18, 1981.14
Anderson, Everett 1944.20
Anderson, F. 1897.15
Anderson, F. Richard 1896.29, 1896.44, 1897.25, 1898.25, 1899.12, 1899.15, 1899.29, 1900.01, 1900.40, 1900.50, 1900.52, 1900.54, 1901.16, 1901.19, 1901.21, 1901.27, 1902.01, 1902.04, 1902.24, 1902.43, 1903.23, 1903.34, 1903.37, 1904.22, 1904.31, 1905.19, 1905.22, 1905.28, 1905.30, 1905.41, 1905.48, 1906.02, 1906.04, 1906.11, 1906.18, 1906.24, 1906.42, 1907.09, 1907.13, 1907.37, 1908.06, 1908.07, 1908.09, 1908.19, 1908.31, 1908.35, 1909.18, 1909.28, 1910.34, 1911.11, 1912.12, 1912.28, 1912.34, 1912.48, 1913.31, 1915.05, 1915.28, 1916.19
Anderson, Frank 1923.04
Anderson, Fred 1992.02
Anderson, G.M. 1907.54, 1917.09, 1920.02
Anderson, Gary 1981.07, 1981.16
Anderson, George 1907.25, 1908.42, 1910.19, 1910.25, 1911.36, 1912.35, 1915.07, 1917.21, 1922.34, 1924.06, 1927.19, 1930.27, 1933.02
Anderson, Gloria 1946.20
Anderson, Gretta 1928.10
Anderson, H. Foster 1927.33
Anderson, Hans Christian 1959.26, 1996.18
Anderson, Harmon 1904.05
Anderson, Harold 1931.36
Anderson, Harry 1924.45, 1925.36, 1931.05
Anderson, Hattie 1883.24
Anderson, Hilding 1908.23, 1911.35, 1912.25, 1912.42, 1912.45, 1913.19, 1915.22, 1918.29, 1919.10, 1919.18, 1920.29, 1922.01, 1922.30, 1923.06, 1923.42, 1924.04, 1924.25, 1924.33, 1925.04, 1925.19, 1925.44, 1925.50, 1927.05, 1927.38, 1928.03, 1928.49, 1930.02, 1930.21, 1930.33, 1937.03, 1940.23, 1947.13
Anderson, Hugh A. 1923.07
Anderson, Ida 1929.21
Anderson, Ivar 1905.16, 1906.16, 1906.37
Anderson, J. 1886.16
Anderson, J.A. 1884.62
Anderson, J.D. 1899.04
Anderson, J.H. 1862.05
Anderson, Jacqueline 1998.10
Anderson, John Murray 1919.18, 1920.08, 1920.28, 1921.27, 1922.32, 1923.07, 1923.31, 1924.32, 1924.44, 1925.31, 1928.50, 1929.29, 1934.01, 1934.18, 1934.19, 1934.42, 1935.15, 1936.02, 1939.12, 1940.03, 1940.23, 1941.12, 1943.05, 1944.30, 1945.04, 1948.23, 1952.09, 1952.20, 1953.17
Anderson, Jonathan 1966.16, 1966.31, 1967.04, 1967.10, 1967.17, 1968.16
Anderson, Judith 1934.03, 1952.03
Anderson, Katherine 1951.17
Anderson, Keith 1989.23
Anderson, Kevin P. 1990.07, 1990.08, 1991.08
Anderson, Lang 1928.23
Anderson, Laura 1935.01
Anderson, Leona 1905.45, 1907.09, 1907.20, 1908.30
Anderson, Leroy 1946.19, 1958.14, 1979.13, 1987.02
Anderson, Lillian 1944.16, 1945.02
Anderson, Louisa 1862.05
Anderson, M.C. 1906.46
Anderson, M.J. 1911.28
Anderson, Madeline 1905.49
Anderson, Madge 1895.07
Anderson, Maxwell 1938.11, 1949.15, 1958.11, 1972.06, 1995.12
Anderson, Messr. 1861.06, 1864.22, 1865.09, 1908.26, 1917.33
Anderson, Mildred 1916.11
Anderson, Mme. 1923.28
Anderson, Mr. 1823.01, 1839.01, 1841.01, 1844.01, 1864.17, 1865.05, 1865.07, 1865.08, 1865.10, 1876.03
Anderson, Myrtl 1943.10
Anderson, Nancy Kathryn 2001.01
Anderson, P. Aug. 1880.17
Anderson, P. Augustus 1881.18
Anderson, P.A. 1876.32, 1876.35, 1877.02
Anderson, Paquita 1943.17, 1944.31
Anderson, Paul 1947.07
Anderson, Paula 1952.15
Anderson, Percy 1888.38, 1890.02, 1890.26, 1891.31, 1891.47, 1892.25, 1893.02, 1893.07, 1893.32, 1894.29, 1895.26, 1895.29, 1895.31, 1896.27, 1896.28, 1897.36, 1897.44, 1898.18, 1898.36, 1898.54, 1899.24, 1899.28, 1900.37, 1902.30, 1905.04, 1907.48, 1911.02, 1912.35, 1917.24, 1919.20, 1919.38, 1919.42, 1920.34, 1934.28, 1934.30, 1934.31, 1936.24
Anderson, Rachel J. 2001.04
Anderson, Richard 1907.57
Anderson, Robert 1950.03, 1951.05
Anderson, S. 1903.25
Anderson, Schneider 1926.23
Anderson, Sonja 1976.05
Anderson, Stephen Lee 1998.02, 1998.13, 2001.06
Anderson, Sybil 1904.08
Anderson, Sydney 1978.28
Anderson, T. Weldon 2000.02
Anderson, Thomas 1934.05, 1971.07, 1972.10
Anderson, Viola 1943.10
Anderson, W. 1904.13
Anderson, Will 1914.07
Anderson, Will R. 1902.35, 1906.41, 1908.05, 1908.25, 1919.07
Anderson-Gunter, Jeffrey 1979.18
Andersson, Benny 1988.09
Anderton, Madeleine 1899.35, 1908.07
Anderton, Madeline 1905.13
Anderton, Miss 1851.06, 1851.07, 1851.08
Andes, Keith 1947.06, 1953.02 1960.22
Andeson, F. Richard 1895.42
Anditzer, Charles J. 1914.09
Andonian, Lucy 1953.16
Andor, Paul 1965.04
Andorci, Blanche 1880.31
Andorci, Madeline 1880.31
Andrada, Dave 1901.04
Andrada, David 1893.08, 1909.17, 1912.02, 1913.32, 1921.03, 1923.15
Andrada, Messr. 1892.12
Andrae, Ruth 1923.38
Andre 1943.17
Andre, Ann 1944.21, 1945.16
Andre, Anthony 1923.43
Andre, Frank 1962.15, 1963.04
Andre, George 1925.01, 1925.28
Andre, Peggy 1930.38
Andrea, Jennie 1953.15, 1955.17, 1958.15, 1959.08, 1959.16, 1959.17
Andreas, Christine 1976.05, 1979.31, 1983.02, 1997.19
Andreas, Otto 1939.23
Andreas, William D. 1898.69
Andreassi, Maria 1950.05
Andree, Mlle. 1885.55, 1885.57, 1885.59, 1885.61, 1886.09, 1886.21
Andree, Mme. 1886.19, 1886.20
Andreopolous, Dennis 1984.15
Andres, Barbara 1969.14, 1970.11, 1975.13, 1976.08, 1983.18
Andres, Juana 1919.17
Andress, Doris 1931.26
Andreu, Helene 1962.08, 1962.11
Andreva, Stella 1946.16
Andrew Bruce/Autograph 1987.04
Andrew, H.E. 1872.16
Andrew, Maud 1925.14
Andrew, Miss 1870.40
Andrew, Thomas 1955.02, 1962.21, 1963.24, 1964.10, 1964.12, 1964.14, 1964.30, 1964.31, 1965.10, 1965.13, 1965.27, 1975.16, 1975.17, 1976.22, 1976.23, 1976.26, 1976.31, 1977.11, 1978.08, 1980.03, 1980.22, 1981.22, 1986.10, 1987.11
Andrews, A. 1838.01, 1844.01, 1848.02u, 1852.03, 1854.02, 1854.04
Andrews, A.G. 1895.17
Andrews, Adora 1919.24, 1924.02, 1932.15
Andrews, Albert G. 1922.04
Andrews, Anita 1914.25
Andrews, Avis 1935.03, 1935.11, 1937.10, 1939.16, 1939.21
Andrews, Billy 1929.01, 1929.21, 1929.25
Andrews, Cameron 1949.17
Andrews, Carrie 1885.26, 1885.41, 1885.63, 1886.47
Andrews, Charlton 1929.08
Andrews, E. 1866.16, 1867.19, 1867.20
Andrews, Edna 1894.11
Andrews, Elizabeth 1881.18
Andrews, Frank 1914.33
Andrews, G. 1879.02
Andrews, George 1863.06, 1863.07
Andrews, George Lee 1973.04, 1978.02, 1983.01, 1988.01, 1990.07, 1991.08
Andrews, Harry 1900.59
Andrews, Herbert 1939.19, 1939.29, 1942.03, 1942.26, 1943.15, 1944.03
Andrews, Inez 1982.17
Andrews, Ismay 1934.37
Andrews, J. 1886.24
Andrews, J.L. 1896.41
Andrews, Jack 1964.18, 1968.03, 1969.14
Andrews, Jennifer Lee 1989.26
Andrews, Jerome 1932.27, 1939.26
Andrews, Julie 1954.09, 1956.01, 1960.21, 1995.15
Andrews, Kathryn 1914.33
Andrews, Kip 1964.33
Andrews, Lillian 1888.08
Andrews, Lillie 1875.10
Andrews, Linda 1970.08
Andrews, Lyle D. 1924.40, 1925.34, 1926.50, 1927.56, 1929.07, 1930.35
Andrews, M. 1871.13
Andrews, Mabel 1901.02
Andrews, Maidie 1934.34, 1939.07
Andrews, Martin 1941.01
Andrews, Maxene 1974.05
Andrews, Miss 1841.01, 1882.16
Andrews, Mme. 1841.01
Andrews, Mr. 1854.05, 1863.01
Andrews, Mrs. W. 1869.27

Andrews, Nancy 1948.21, 1949.12, 1955.01, 1959.04, 1960.10, 1962.27
Andrews, Patty 1974.05
Andrews, Pearl 1899.30
Andrews, Talleur 1905.27
Andrews, W. Talleur 1904.29
Andrews, W.S. 1866.13, 1866.16, 1866.17
Andrews, Walter 1935.08
Andrews, William L. 1932.14
Andreyko, Helena 1976.33, 1979.08, 1993.13
Andrick, Virl 1993.11
Andrietta, Jenette 1906.23
Andrini, Kathy 1979.24
Andriola, Howard 1949.13
Andrisano, Gui 1980.05
Androva, Ada 1916.03
Androw, Alex 1889.08
Andrus, Ebba 1918.01
Anet, Claude 1945.11
Angel 1900.03, 1913.33
Angel, Adrienne 1968.31
Angel, Charles 1926.46
Angel, Lou 1967.06
Angel, Paco 1923.31
Angel, Wilson 1934.41
Angela, Josephine 1904.35, 1906.37
Angela, June 1970.21, 1977.07, 1990.17
Angelbert, Mlle. 1875.33
Angele, Mlle. 1877.06, 1877.13, 1877.19, 1879.48, 1879.49, 1879.60, 1879.61, 1879.69, 1880.14, 1880.16, 1880.23, 1880.27, 1880.28, 1880.29, 1880.56, 1883.51, 1883.54, 1883.55, 1883.57, 1883.61, 1884.01, 1884.05
Angeles, Aimee 1894.37, 1897.34, 1899.36, 1902.19, 1903.39, 1904.18, 1904.39, 1905.20, 1905.44
Angeles, Amiee 1901.17
Angeles, Bert 1905.07, 1930.21
Angeles, Leah 1897.34, 1899.36
Angelescu, Jackie 1996.04, 1999.17
Angeletti, Nita 1973.16
Angelique, Mlle. 1865.02
Angelis, Aimee 1898.50
Angelis, Lear 1898.50
Angelis, Nicholas E. 2001.04
Angelo, Charles 1900.37, 1909.01, 1909.09, 1910.31, 1911.47, 1913.14, 1916.04, 1917.21, 1921.15, 1921.29, 1925.33, 1930.40, 1932.23
Angelo, Dom 1966.05, 1967.05
Angelo, Waldo 1952.08
Angelus, Muriel 1938.14, 1941.12, 1943.07
Anger, Lou 1913.05
Angere, B. 1912.09
Angevine 1907.55
Angiolini, Allessandro 1884.58
Angle, Charles 1931.03
Angle, Robert 1902.33
Anglin, Elizabeth 1907.08
Anglin, Elleen 1907.58
Anglin, Florence 1959.08, 1959.17, 1963.15, 1966.02
Anglund, Robert 1974.26
Angold, Edith 1938.11
Angoletta, Bruno 1932.29, 1934.02, 1940.05
Angus Equities, Inc. 1970.21
Anhalt, Lawrence J. 1925.15
Anholt, Lawrence J. 1927.24
Anita, Paula 1984.09
Anju, Mira 1989.21
Anka, Paul 1974.11, 1989.12, 1990.15
Anker, Charlotte 1980.30
Ankrum, Morris 1938.16
Ann, Edith 1974.17
Anna Spencer, Inc. 1921.19, 1922.01, 1922.13, 1922.28
Anna, Mlle. 1868.31, 1869.01, 1870.44, 1871.06, 1871.07, 1871.27
Annas, John Wesley 1970.04
Anne Geenen Productions, Inc. 1998.22
Annerley, Frederick 1919.02
Annetta, Isrialdi 1871.27
Annie Pixley Company 1892.17
Annis, Marie 1908.27, 1910.11, 1913.26
Annoux 1973.17
Annucci, Lydia 1937.14
Annyenkof, Yury 1931.38
Annyenkoff, G. 1929.05
Ano, Bonnie 1971.09
Ansel, Miss 1889.31
Anson, Ada 1890.25
Anson, Adrian C. 1895.39
Anson, E.A. 1905.25
Anson, G.W. 1872.09, 1872.11, 1897.41
Anson, Miss 1864.22, 1865.05, 1865.08
Anspake, G. 1912.30
Anstey, F. 1888.04, 1888.34, 1890.10, 1943.19
Anta-Goodspeed Production 1965.34
Antell, Miss 1862.02
Anthelme, Mons. 1866.25
Anthony Bradley Farrell Productions 1949.17
Anthony, Brady Farrell 1949.02
Anthony, Dee 1979.11
Anthony, Earle C. 1912.05
Anthony, Edward 1918.36
Anthony, Emmett 1921.26, 1922.44
Anthony, Eugene J. 1983.02
Anthony, Hal 1941.03
Anthony, Jack 1933.21
Anthony, Jill 1934.34
Anthony, John D. 1969.14
Anthony, Joseph 1956.04, 1963.26, 1969.14, 1992.10
Anthony, Kevin 1996.17
Anthony, Leo 1950.14
Anthony, Marc 1998.02
Anthony, Norman 1932.16, 1943.16
Anthony, Philip 1990.15
Anthony, Sal 1952.13, 1959.23
Anthony, Thomas 1973.12
Anthony, William 1899.07
Antier, Benjamin 1886.30, 1888.02, 1889.16, 1889.49, 1893.35, 1897.24, 1898.36, 1899.24, 1903.32, 1921.01
Antigravity, Inc. 1999.24
Antigua, Mons. 1883.55, 1883.59, 1883.61
Antoine, Marie 1875.19, 1875.23, 1875.26
Antoine, Paulette 1915.25, 1917.07
Antoinette, Mlle. 1870.44, 1871.27, 1872.06
Antonia 1970.04
Antonina, Mlle. 1870.44, 1871.27
Antonino, Mlle. 1876.16, 1876.34
Antonio, M. 1865.05
Antonio, Tillie 1883.06
Antony, Jacques 1870.30, 1870.37, 1870.41, 1871.06
Antoon, A.J. 1984.01
Antoon, Jason 2000.07
Anzell, Hy 1946.24
Aoki, Violetta 1928.30
Aouda, Mlle. 1888.23
Apinee, Irene 1962.21
APJAC International 1973.07
Aplon, Boris 1954.04, 1954.07, 1956.15, 1965.35
Apollon, Dave 1940.12
Aponte, Gustavo 1939.18
Apostoleris, Lee 1975.20
Appel, Michael N. 1982.09
Appel, Shulamith 1982.09
Appell, Dave 1977.10
Appell, Don 1961.20
Applebaum, Stan 1986.16
Applebaum, Stanley 1981.07
Appleby, Dorothy 1924.42, 1925.05
Appleby, George 1884.35, 1885.13
Appleby, George S. 1887.21
Applegate, Fred 1998.03
Appler, Walter 1945.14
Appler, Walter F. 1950.11
Appleton, Carrie 1893.01
Appleton, Lewis 1942.19, 1945.14
Appleton, May 1893.04, 1893.22
Aprea, Andrew 1950.04, 1951.15
Aprea, Andy 1948.27
Apt, Sallie 1883.47
Aquateeta, Mlle. 1917.29
Arabanell, Lina 1912.47, 1930.36
Arace, Thomas 1932.05, 1933.02
Arad, Chaya 1972.17
Aragon, Virginia 1896.07
Arai, Messr. 1902.22, 1903.19
Aramini, Auguste 1926.32
Aranda, Estephania 1992.15
Aranha, Ray 1998.21
Arbuckle, Ivan 1912.16, 1918.18, 1928.48, 1930.07
Arbuckle, Messr. 1876.17
Arcall, William 1904.41
Arcaro, Flavia 1906.49, 1907.06, 1909.05, 1909.22, 1910.36, 1911.23, 1912.12, 1912.17, 1917.01, 1919.35, 1922.23, 1925.31, 1927.20, 1929.34, 1929.36
Arcenas, Loy 1990.12, 1998.05
Arch Productions, Inc. 1925.19
Archambauldt, F. 1901.24
Archangelsky, Alexei 1922.06, 1923.28, 1925.03, 1927.51, 1929.05, 1931.38, 1943.11
Archbold, Schellie 1986.11
Archbutt, Gladys 1911.14
Archer, Adele 1894.37, 1895.15, 1896.48, 1899.06, 1901.29, 1902.27, 1903.39, 1913.06, 1914.19
Archer, Anna 1899.26
Archer, Belle 1885.05, 1885.43
Archer, Betty 1925.06
Archer, Cheryl 1948.25
Archer, Claude E. 1918.06
Archer, Donald 1906.41
Archer, E.A. 1887.05, 1888.05
Archer, Edna 1898.46
Archer, Frank 1936.26
Archer, G.A. 1870.01, 1870.14, 1870.18
Archer, George A. 1869.37, 1869.38
Archer, Grace 1897.06
Archer, Harry 1920.32, 1920.41, 1923.24, 1924.07, 1924.40, 1925.34, 1926.39, 1928.34, 1929.24, 1930.38, 1931.21, 1942.11
Archer, Herbert 1885.05, 1885.43, 1886.36, 1892.57
Archer, Herbert R. 1880.31
Archer, Isabelle 1890.49
Archer, J.C. 1875.06
Archer, Jane 1938.06
Archer, Jeri 1945.20
Archer, John 1945.19
Archer, Julie 1988.05
Archer, Laurie 1960.10
Archer, Louis 1896.46
Archer, Lynn 1968.08
Archer, Miss 1861.01
Archer, Mme. 1834.02
Archer, Mrs. 1834.02
Archer, Nicholas 1992.11, 1993.05
Archer, Will 1902.29
Archer, William 1893.24
Archibald, Freddie 1930.10
Archibald, Freddy 1935.01
Archibald, Hazel M. 1922.21
Archibald, J.F. 1913.07
Archibald, John William 1939.12
Archibald, William 1940.03, 1940.23, 1944.30, 1945.13
Archie, Will 1902.06, 1905.55, 1910.16, 1911.35, 1916.22
Archie, Willie 1903.28
Archmere, Ollie 1890.07, 1891.39, 1894.23
Arciero, Jillian 1998.19
Arcuri, Daniela 1993.08
Ard, Ken 1987.05, 1989.20, 1992.08, 1995.03
Ard, Kenneth 1982.19
Arda, Miss 1870.31
Ardao, David 1982.03
Ardath, Fred 1921.37, 1948.20
Ardath, J. 1917.08
Ardell, Florence 1908.07
Ardell, Franklyn 1915.29, 1919.11, 1922.27, 1924.03, 1928.28
Ardell, Jimmy 1930.37
Ardelle, Franklyn 1906.27
Ardelle, Kathlyn 1922.27
Ardelli, Roberto 1926.31
Ardelty, Elly 1948.25
Arden, Del 1936.17
Arden, Doris 1919.32
Arden, Edwin 1912.32
Arden, Elaine 1935.04
Arden, Eve 1934.01, 1935.03, 1936.02, 1939.28, 1940.03, 1941.08
Arden, Gertrude 1900.59
Arden, Helen 1928.01, 1934.38, 1947.02
Arden, Helene 1928.49, 1934.17
Arden, Victor 1924.43, 1925.49, 1926.36, 1927.59, 1928.43, 1929.12, 1939.25
Ardine, Miss 1914.15
Ardine, Ottie 1920.14
Ardisonne, John 1902.35
Arditi, Luigi 1870.23, 1918.18
Arditti, Luigi 1871.10, 1885.08
Ardizone, John 1905.29, 1906.37
Ardizoni, John 1910.04
Ardolino, Emile 1971.04
Arena Stage, The 1979.24, 1980.13, 1980.27
Arenal, Julie 1968.11, 1975.23, 1977.15, 2000.03
Arend, Edna 1905.28
Arent, Arthur 1937.14
Arenzwari-Yushny, A. 1932.09
Arenzwary, V. 1924.48
Arfwedson, Oscar L. 1883.25, 1883.29
Argentinita 1942.14
Argov, Alexander 1971.14
Ari, Robert 2001.03
Ariano, Alan 1990.17, 1991.03
Arians, Elizabeth 1913.29
Arias, Yancey 2000.08
Arigoni, Signor 1878.10
Arington, Mignon 1888.36
Aristides, John 1957.07, 1961.02, 1964.04, 1965.34, 1972.14, 1976.01
Aristophanes 1961.08, 1972.23
Arkell, Flora 1900.59
Arkell, Florence 1908.07
Arkell, Reginald 1925.50, 1926.46
Arkin, Alan 1961.17, 1973.11
Arkin, Juki 1961.20
Arkin, Ted 1940.21
Arkuss, Albert 1943.17
Arkwright, Blanche 1891.02, 1891.39
Arledge, Florence 1924.11, 1925.35
Arlen, Dee 1950.09
Arlen, Harold 1930.06, 1930.22, 1931.01, 1932.18, 1932.20, 1932.24, 1934.19, 1936.31, 1937.15, 1938.08, 1942.10, 1942.11, 1942.18, 1942.23, 1944.23, 1945.07, 1946.08, 1947.01, 1948.04, 1953.12, 1954.19, 1955.13, 1956.02, 1957.16, 1959.27, 1967.11, 1973.14, 1974.09, 1976.16, 1976.32, 1979.24, 1980.10, 1981.16, 1982.12, 1986.02, 1988.08, 1989.02, 1989.06, 1989.16, 1990.09, 1997.01, 1997.05, 1997.11, 1998.06, 1999.05, 1999.11, 1999.23, 1999.24
Arlen, Jerry 1947.01, 1954.19, 1959.27
Arlen, Steve 1970.10
Arlin, Harold 1979.14
Arline, Frances 1889.31
Arling, Albert 1895.07
Arling, Charles 1903.32, 1905.18
Arling, H. 1900.39
Arling, W. 1899.37
Arling, Walter 1894.22
Arling, Wilford 1898.77
Arling, Wilfred 1898.27
Arling, William 1899.19
Arling, Winifred 1898.34
Arlingotn, Jennie 1882.20
Arlington 1920.17
Arlington Company 1918.42
Arlington, Alice 1882.72
Arlington, Arlie 1901.05
Arlington, Bess 1919.10
Arlington, Blanche 1904.38, 1907.55
Arlington, Isabel 1904.14
Arlington, Kathryn 1926.23, 1926.26
Arlington, Madame 1926.23
Arlington, Maggie 1882.56, 1884.20
Arlington, Miss 1882.45
Arlington, Myrtle 1903.04
Arlington, Paul 1912.29, 1922.10, 1923.02, 1923.17
Arlington, Schneider-Anderson 1920.14
Arlington-Mahieu 1925.35
Arlinstaht, Mignon 1899.36
Arlt, Lewis 1981.04
Armand and Barnard 1910.12
Armand, Blanche 1868.26, 1869.03
Armand, Isabella 1867.30
Armand, J.C. 1880.47, 1880.69, 1881.36, 1881.38
Armand, Joseph 1886.40
Armand, Mlle. 1867.05, 1879.19, 1879.26, 1879.27, 1879.31, 1879.34, 1879.36, 1879.39, 1879.43, 1879.44, 1879.45, 1879.46, 1879.47, 1879.48, 1879.51, 1879.55, 1879.60, 1879.61, 1879.69, 1880.16, 1880.23, 1880.27, 1880.28, 1880.29, 1880.52, 1880.58, 1880.60
Armand, Mme. 1869.16, 1869.30, 1880.50
Armande, Mlle. 1866.18, 1869.02
Armbrust, Dick 1955.07
Armbruster, Matt 1905.48
Armbruster, Richard 1958.14, 1960.01, 1963.15, 1965.20, 1966.02
Armbruster, Robert 1926.11
Armen, Rebecca 1982.24
Arment, Gwen 1978.28
Armin, Jeanne 1961.07
Armin, Walter 1915.17, 1919.35, 1926.26, 1928.14, 1929.22, 1932.10, 1933.21, 1934.15, 1934.38, 1938.13, 1939.30, 1946.04
Armini, Auguste 1931.09

Armistead, Diane 1982.18
Armistead, Horace 1947.10, 1948.29, 1949.15, 1949.16, 1950.04, 1950.05, 1952.12, 1953.05, 1953.14, 1960.03, 1962.06, 1966.04, 1966.17, 1974.08, 1975.11
Armitage, Richard 1986.12
Armont, Paul 1922.09, 1922.12
Armour, Steve 1999.24
Arms, Frances 1920.17, 1923.42
Armstead, Joshie Jo 1972.10
Armstrong, Belle 1900.20
Armstrong, Carolyn 1910.03
Armstrong, Cheryl 1974.18
Armstrong, Dorothy 1920.03, 1921.23
Armstrong, Harrison 1897.23
Armstrong, Harry 1902.43, 1904.13, 1907.14
Armstrong, J.H. 1884.23
Armstrong, J.R. 1902.08
Armstrong, J.W. 1882.57
Armstrong, James 1885.67, 1939.21
Armstrong, John A. 1904.18
Armstrong, Karan 1976.26
Armstrong, Lil 1976.04, 1984.15
Armstrong, Louis 1938.08, 1939.29, 1986.02, 1989.02
Armstrong, Margaret 1924.40
Armstrong, Marilyn 1994.09
Armstrong, Nettie 1898.50
Armstrong, Paul 1924.47
Armstrong, Robert 1920.14
Armstrong, V.C. 1907.38
Armstrong, Vanessa Bell 1987.17, 1995.04
Armstrong, W.H. 1905.49
Armstrong, Will 1900.16
Armstrong, Will M. 1895.25
Armstrong, Will Steven 1961.10, 1961.24, 1961.28, 1962.05, 1964.44, 1966.05
Armstrong, William 1897.37, 1898.51
Armstrong, William M. 1896.31
Armus, Sidney 1952.10
Arnal, Mlle. 1870.44
Arnaz, Desi 1939.27
Arnaz, Lucie 1973.07, 1979.04
Arndt, Felix 1979.14
Arne, Thomas 1880.19
Arnell, France 1965.37
Arnell, Patricia 1972.24
Arnengol, Arthur Cuyas 1867.25
Arnett, Chuck 1960.01
Arnett, Kim 1998.18
Arnett, Ray 1945.18
Arnette, Myrtle 1928.49
Arney, Randall 1993.04
Arnheim, Gus 1932.06
Arniostis, Mary 1897.14
Arnnam, Ernestine 1883.50
Arno, Dwight 1972.24
Arno, Louis 1915.32
Arno, Peter 1929.29, 1930.40, 1931.21, 1931.42
Arno, Sig 1944.21, 1964.24
Arnold, Ainsworth 1941.12
Arnold, Alice 1886.47
Arnold, B. 1879.04
Arnold, Barry 1970.18, 1976.04, 1978.01, 1982.03
Arnold, Charles 1884.53
Arnold, Charles E. 1876.16
Arnold, Constable and Company 1892.24
Arnold, Diane 1964.21
Arnold, Dorothy 1920.28, 1922.32
Arnold, Edward 1931.14
Arnold, Eugene P. 1908.24
Arnold, Florine 1882.69, 1917.05
Arnold, Frau 1879.62
Arnold, G.J. 1848.01
Arnold, George Waugh 1899.19
Arnold, Gladys 1905.07
Arnold, Harriet 1920.43
Arnold, Hattie 1875.18, 1880.01, 1880.03, 1902.22, 1903.19, 1905.33, 1906.30, 1911.38, 1913.36
Arnold, Helen 1932.24
Arnold, Henry H. 1942.20
Arnold, Indiola 1902.11, 1906.15
Arnold, J.A. 1868.01, 1868.02, 1868.11
Arnold, James 1932.30
Arnold, Jeanne 1968.01, 1969.17
Arnold, Joseph 1876.03
Arnold, Jr., F.W. 1899.41
Arnold, Ken 1947.04
Arnold, Laura 1917.15, 1923.16
Arnold, Loie 1905.24
Arnold, Lois 1925.11
Arnold, Louise 1922.31
Arnold, Lucille 1925.39, 1926.01, 1927.58
Arnold, Mabel 1901.09
Arnold, Malcolm 1955.19
Arnold, Marjorie 1930.40
Arnold, Marvin 1956.02, 1959.13
Arnold, Max 1885.31, 1891.04
Arnold, Maxine 1944.33
Arnold, May 1915.10
Arnold, Messr. 1885.39
Arnold, Michael 1993.06, 1998.15, 2001.08
Arnold, Miss 1867.07, 1886.36, 1904.13, 1904.44
Arnold, Mons. 1883.48, 1885.33, 1886.16
Arnold, Mrs. J.A. 1868.01, 1868.02
Arnold, Nancy 1928.20
Arnold, Naomi 1900.23, 1900.29, 1900.30, 1903.19
Arnold, Phil 1932.19, 1936.07
Arnold, Phyl 1925.50
Arnold, Richard 1869.35, 1869.43, 1870.04, 1948.04
Arnold, Samuel 1794.01
Arnold, Seth 1931.28, 1950.04
Arnold, Sheila 1953.07
Arnold, Stanley 1948.21
Arnold, Venus 1902.11
Arnold, Verna 1912.44
Arnold, Vernon 1904.13, 1904.44
Arnold, Ward 1928.44, 1932.05
Arnold, William 1905.05, 1908.29
Arnoldoff, Roman 1931.09
Arnone, John 1993.06, 1994.06, 1994.07, 1995.05, 1996.17, 1999.07, 1999.23, 2000.15
Arnot, Jennie 1872.02, 1872.04, 1872.05, 1872.08, 1872.12, 1872.14, 1872.25, 1872.30, 1872.32, 1872.36
Arnott, Jennie 1870.42, 1873.08
Arnott, Jenny 1871.02
Arnott, Louise 1894.27
Arnst, Bobbe 1924.32, 1927.13, 1927.38, 1928.03, 1930.08
Arnt, Charles 1938.11
Arnt, Charlie 1937.17
Aroeste, Joel 1986.16
Arolas, E. 1997.13
Arons, Alex A. 1928.01
Arons, Ellyn 1983.10, 1985.19
Aronson, Abe 1906.46, 1907.54, 1910.23, 1920.47
Aronson, Billy 1996.09
Aronson, Boris 1932.27, 1940.17, 1943.21, 1944.27, 1946.03, 1946.18, 1948.25, 1964.27, 1966.24, 1968.30, 1970.13, 1971.05, 1973.04, 1976.02, 1976.36, 1981.18, 1987.16, 1989.03, 1990.18
Aronson, Frances 1992.09
Aronson, Henry 1989.09, 1989.25, 2000.17
Aronson, Jonathan 1979.05
Aronson, Luann 1992.12
Aronson, Max 1916.15
Aronson, Rudolf 1885.41, 1886.30, 1889.16, 1891.17, 1891.30, 1892.16
Aronson, Rudolph 1883.45, 1884.08, 1885.63, 1886.04, 1887.33, 1887.50, 1888.02, 1888.20, 1888.35, 1889.04, 1889.23, 1889.40, 1889.49, 1890.01, 1890.11, 1890.19, 1890.24, 1890.39, 1891.12, 1891.22, 1892.03, 1892.07, 1892.28, 1893.32, 1896.05, 1897.24, 1901.05
Aronstein, Martin 1967.01, 1967.16, 1968.06, 1968.07, 1968.08, 1968.11, 1968.23, 1968.31, 1969.08, 1969.15, 1969.16, 1970.12, 1971.13, 1972.04, 1972.07, 1972.10, 1972.19, 1972.24, 1973.02, 1973.16, 1974.09, 1976.32, 1978.04, 1978.15, 1979.02, 1980.12, 1998.18
Aroukh, Shymel 1972.17
Arozamena, Amparo 1939.18
Aroztegui, M. 1985.07, 1999.18
Arpino, Gerald 1957.15, 1958.13, 1958.16
Arquette, Lewis 1971.08
Arral, Blanche 1898.72
Arren, Charlotte 1935.04
Arrick, Larry 1991.14
Arrigoni, Messr. 1877.32
Arrigotti, Mons. 1875.07, 1875.08
Arrington, Jr., Joseph 1999.01
Arrington, Nicole 1995.19
Arrogeni, Ferdinand 1875.05
Arroyo 1943.02
Arsenault, Brian 1990.18
Arsene, Mlle. 1868.25, 1868.27, 1868.31, 1869.01, 1869.10
Arsene, Mme. 1870.03
Arshansky, Michael 1953.06, 1953.15
Art at St. Ann's; American Musical Theatre Festival 1999.05
Artega, Amita 1944.19
Artemieva, Ludmilla 1990.01
Arthur Arthur 1903.18
Arthur Shafman International Ltd. 1980.24, 1980.28
Arthur, Adelaide 1886.02
Arthur, Art 1948.15
Arthur, Beatrice 1955.10, 1964.27, 1966.10, 1966.19
Arthur, C.W. 1899.13
Arthur, Carol 1964.16, 1980.16
Arthur, Charles 1897.52, 1898.48
Arthur, Daniel V. 1903.07, 1905.45, 1906.27, 1908.36, 1910.12, 1910.30, 1911.03, 1912.08, 1912.19, 1913.25, 1915.01
Arthur, Donald 1942.19
Arthur, Dorothy 1912.08, 1912.19, 1915.01
Arthur, Ernest 1897.28
Arthur, Florence 1926.11
Arthur, George 1910.21
Arthur, H. 1880.57, 1881.44
Arthur, Harry L. 1899.40
Arthur, Helen 1922.20, 1924.14, 1925.20, 1926.17
Arthur, Helene 1943.06, 1943.12
Arthur, Henry 1938.01
Arthur, Jack 1942.11
Arthur, Jean 1950.08
Arthur, John 1923.08
Arthur, Joseph 1890.35, 1892.01
Arthur, Lee 1905.37, 1918.25
Arthur, Messr. 1902.13
Arthur, Mr. 1863.02, 1902.42
Arthur, Paul 1883.31, 1884.35, 1884.38, 1886.28, 1887.19, 1887.31, 1893.24, 1894.21, 1894.28
Arthur, Perry 1977.15, 1984.14
Arthur, Robert Alan 1961.24
Arthur, Stewart 1940.04
Arthur, Tom 1962.02
Arthurs, George 1906.47, 1908.27, 1909.04, 1909.21, 1910.21, 1911.27
Artiste Management Productions 2000.04
Artists Consultants, Inc. 1976.06
Artists Producers' Corporation 1921.19
Artley, Edith 1929.34, 1929.36
Artois, Mlle. 1866.18
Artressi, J. 1906.46
Artressi, Joe 1905.17
Arts Communications Seoul Company 1998.08
Artus, E. 1894.26
Artz, Elsie 1905.50, 1912.11
Aruba, Ernest 1976.02
Arundel, Frederick 1897.55
Arvold, Mason 1950.02, 1975.09
Aryrs, Christopher 1990.20
Asaf, George 1964.28, 1978.05, 1991.04
Asaf, Michele 1989.09
Asaire, Adele 1922.10
Asburn, James 1906.46
Asbury, Charles A. 1879.28
Asbury, Cleve 1979.22, 1980.02, 1981.07, 1985.02
Asbury, Louisa 1879.28
Ascenzo, Paul J. 1999.10
Asche, Oscar 1917.24, 1919.20, 1920.34
Aschenbeg, Eric P. 1990.11
Ascher, Leo 1916.25
Aschman, Charles 1956.15, 1957.06
Ascott, Mavis 1996.12, 2000.05
Ash, Jeffrey 1993.01, 1995.16, 1998.17, 1999.05
Ash, Russell 1921.39
Ash, Sam 1917.10, 1917.23, 1919.03, 1919.19, 1920.31, 1921.39, 1922.16, 1922.34, 1927.53, 1928.49, 1931.29
Ash, Samuel 1915.29
Ashbaugh, Bessie 1897.20
Ashbrooke, Florence 1891.08, 1897.47
Ashburn, Carroll 1938.14
Ashbury, F. 1865.11, 1866.02
Ashby, Laura 1894.50
Ashcroft, Earl 1943.08
Ashe, Rosemary 1989.01
Asher, Alfred 1895.32
Asher, David 1982.03
Asher, Lawrence 1979.26
Asher, Miss 1872.24
Asher, Tony 1904.50
Asher, William 1896.04
Asher/Frost Management 1988.15
Asherman, Sid 1929.24
Ashford, Nick 1976.16, 1976.24
Ashland, Camila 1968.02, 1973.11
Ashland, Mildred 1905.40
Ashley, Barbara 1948.17, 1950.11, 1950.20
Ashley, Charles 1933.20
Ashley, Christopher 2000.17
Ashley, Clayton 1945.01
Ashley, Edward 1943.23
Ashley, Gene 1934.15, 1942.16
Ashley, George 1975.10
Ashley, J.W. 1915.20
Ashley, Mary Ellen 1992.06, 1999.07
Ashley, Minnie 1899.39, 1900.43, 1902.12, 1902.30
Ashley, Ricky 1999.16
Ashlin, H. 1889.29
Ashlock, Jane 1953.10
Ashlyn 1914.21
Ashlyn, Belle 1905.20, 1908.03, 1915.02
Ashman, Howard 1986.20, 1994.04, 1999.16
Ashmanskas, Brooks 1997.05, 1998.15
Ashmore, Aimee 1902.21
Ashmore, Aimie 1899.36
Ashmore, Amy 1899.26
Ashton, Colleen 1983.08
Ashton, Frederick 1934.05
Ashton, Herbert 1924.29, 1925.23
Ashton, J.L. 1895.41
Ashton, Kate 1879.18
Ashton, Langtry 1900.08, 1903.09
Ashton, Lucy 1905.15
Ashton, Margaret 1898.29
Ashton, Marie 1911.01, 1911.17, 1912.48
Ashton, Miss 1882.46, 1896.44
Ashton, Mr. 1794.01
Ashwander, Donald 1978.26
Ashwell, Ariel 1996.16
Ashwell, Lena 1951.05
Ashwood, Michael 1938.19
Asia 1958.20
Ask, Randl 1995.05
Askam, Perry 1920.47, 1921.31
Askey, Darrell J. 1961.14, 1964.21, 1968.05
Askey, Gil 1976.16, 1981.16
Askin and Mort H. Singer Company, Inc. 1907.25
Askin, Harry 1891.13, 1892.30, 1892.37, 1892.40, 1892.46, 1895.19, 1895.21
Askin, Henry 1892.20
Askin, Perry 1923.15
Askt, Harry 1989.02
Asmus, Harry 1949.01, 1951.16, 1952.01, 1954.01
Aspe, John 1918.23
Aspel, Brad 1996.06, 2001.08
Aspinall, Ruby Greene 1972.06, 1973.09, 1989.18
Aspland, Algernon 1898.57, 1902.41
Asquith, Ruby 1934.29
Asro, Alexander 1938.13
Assante, Armand 1975.23
Associated Artists, Inc. 1928.09
Assoluta, Cerito 1974.12
Astaire, Adele 1917.31, 1918.20, 1919.27, 1921.33, 1922.45, 1924.43, 1927.59, 1930.39, 1931.16
Astaire, Fred 1917.31, 1918.20, 1919.27, 1921.33, 1922.10, 1922.45, 1924.43, 1925.33, 1927.59, 1930.39, 1931.16, 1932.26, 1992.18, 1999.01
Astaire, Lilyan 1932.19
Astar, Ben 1954.12
Astbury, Paul 1993.07
Asteganio, Mlle. 1883.47
Asteggiano, Mlle. 1882.77
Asten, H.R. 1884.46, 1885.68
Astley, Blanche 1897.20
Aston, Margaret 1898.10
Astor, Evelyn 1887.43
Astor, Olivia 1896.48
Astor, Suzanne 1968.13
Astroff, Ed 1918.21
Astrova, Marie 1921.21, 1921.38
Astruc, L. 1883.55
Astruc, Mlle. 1883.60, 1884.43, 1884.52, 1885.23
Astwood, Norman 1938.19
Asya 1964.40
AT&T OnStage 1992.17
Atari, Yona 1971.14
Atchinson-Ely, Edgar 1905.48
Atchison, David 1912.07, 1913.16, 1914.28
Atchison-Ely, Edgar 1902.37, 1904.18, 1904.43, 1908.36, 1911.12
Atchley, Hooper L. 1913.07

Ates, Nejla 1954.15
Ates, Roscoe 1937.07
Athas, Nick 1967.05
Athena, Mlle. 1911.28
Atheneos, Cleo 1933.12
Athens, Arline 1888.36, 1898.02
Athens, Maida 1907.11
Atherton, Alice 1870.13, 1870.19, 1870.21, 1870.35, 1870.42, 1871.01, 1871.02, 1871.05, 1872.02, 1872.04, 1872.05, 1872.08, 1872.12, 1872.14, 1872.25, 1872.26, 1873.12, 1873.14, 1877.23, 1877.25, 1877.39, 1879.33, 1880.06, 1880.10, 1880.42, 1882.03, 1882.39, 1883.26, 1898.41, 1898.58
Atherton, Effie 1925.42
Atherton, Grace 1890.46, 1893.09
Atherton, Margaret 1923.13
Atherton, Millie 1893.05, 1893.09
Atherton, Mitti 1894.40
Atherton, Mittie 1888.11, 1889.36, 1895.24, 1899.39
Atherton, Nancy 1895.39
Atherton, Venie 1924.20
Atherton, William 1972.01
Athon, Robert 1905.34
Atkin, Charles 1938.10, 1955.07
Atkins, Al 1937.13
Atkins, Annie 1879.02
Atkins, Arthur 1942.20
Atkins, Boyd 1992.06
Atkins, Charles 1963.22
Atkins, Cholly 1949.18, 1989.02
Atkins, Eliza 1996.15
Atkins, Forster 1886.14
Atkins, George 1866.18, 1869.07, 1872.13, 1872.25, 1872.30, 1872.32, 1872.36, 1872.38, 1872.40, 1872.43, 1873.10, 1875.06, 1875.11, 1875.15, 1875.20
Atkins, J. 1875.14
Atkins, Joe 1993.07
Atkins, Laurel 1896.06
Atkins, Messr. 1871.18
Atkins, Miss 1862.02, 1866.18, 1870.31, 1882.46
Atkins, Mr. 1855.08, 1855.09, 1857.08
Atkins, Norman 1959.02, 1966.08
Atkins, Norton 1891.26
Atkins, T. 1870.33, 1879.54
Atkins, T.F. 1881.31
Atkins, Tommy 1930.28
Atkins, Tony 1958.01
Atkins, W. 1882.50, 1882.74
Atkins, Win 1980.01
Atkinson's Jolities 1882.80
Atkinson, Amy 1928.28, 1931.45
Atkinson, Arthur 1924.07
Atkinson, Barry 1998.10
Atkinson, Betty 1940.16
Atkinson, Charles 1882.80
Atkinson, David 1954.01, 1955.25, 1956.05, 1957.03, 1958.03, 1958.09, 1959.03, 1960.02, 1972.14
Atkinson, Don 1960.05, 1961.08, 1961.18, 1962.04, 1962.20
Atkinson, E.J. 1879.16
Atkinson, Edith 1897.02
Atkinson, Ella 1884.27, 1887.27, 1894.20
Atkinson, Leo 1949.09
Atkinson, Miss 1883.17, 1883.23
Atkinson, Rena 1896.20
Atkinson, Rowan 1986.15
Atkinson, Sarah 1966.03
Attab, Hamad 1925.37
Attaway, Bill 1955.03
Attaway, Ruth 1954.16
Atteridge, Harold 1907.15, 1910.08, 1910.22, 1911.34, 1911.43, 1912.09, 1912.17, 1912.24, 1912.43, 1913.02, 1913.05, 1913.18, 1914.01, 1914.10, 1914.16, 1914.22, 1915.02, 1915.04, 1915.11, 1915.16, 1915.17, 1915.26, 1915.32, 1916.03, 1916.11, 1916.23, 1917.08, 1917.23, 1917.31, 1918.05, 1918.06, 1918.20, 1919.03, 1919.16, 1919.30, 1919.34, 1920.19, 1920.47, 1921.02, 1921.14, 1921.25, 1921.34, 1922.11, 1922.15, 1922.34, 1923.02, 1923.12, 1923.17, 1923.25, 1923.41, 1924.13, 1924.21, 1924.23, 1924.29, 1924.33, 1925.01, 1925.07, 1925.23, 1925.27, 1925.28, 1926.01, 1926.14, 1926.37, 1927.19, 1927.37, 1928.14, 1929.09, 1931.36, 1934.42
Attles, Joe 1940.01
Attles, Joseph 1953.04, 1961.24, 1963.27, 1965.03, 1976.04
Attwood, J. 1880.46
Attwood, Messr. 1883.31
Attwood, Thomas 1855.01
Atwater, Alice 1906.01
Atwater, Edith 1951.15
Atwater, Janet 1940.02
Atwell, Ben H. 1911.16, 1911.19
Atwell, John 1880.08
Atwell, John B. 1887.02
Atwell, Lester 1965.17
Atwell, Messr. 1867.17
Atwell, Rick 1979.03
Atwell, Roy 1905.45, 1906.27, 1908.21, 1908.29, 1912.46, 1914.04, 1915.27, 1918.37, 1919.12, 1919.27, 1923.19, 1926.21, 1929.29, 1933.05
Atwill, Lionel 1929.08
Atwood, Bob 1961.07
Atwood, C. 1893.07
Atwood, Charles 1883.19, 1893.47
Atwood, Lorena 1907.57, 1912.11
Atwood, Messr. 1882.04, 1882.20, 1883.17
Atwood, Miss 1857.02
Atwood, Persis 1926.40
Atwood, Robert 1957.17
Atwood, W. 1883.19
Atwood, William B. 1899.22
Auber 1852.01, 1860.02, 1862.09, 1867.23, 1892.13
Auber, Daniel 1851.07, 1851.08, 1859.06, 1860.05, 1862.04, 1864.18, 1866.15, 1867.04, 1868.10, 1870.07, 1884.35, 1885.30, 1901.10
Auber, Daniel Francois Esprit 1882.43, 1900.18, 1902.22
Auber, Esprit 1898.33
Auber, Fernande 1891.36
Auber, Louise 1892.29
Auber, Odette 1908.42
Auberjonois, Rene 1969.17, 1973.02, 1979.17, 1989.29
Aubert, Jane 1926.37
Aubert, Jeanne 1930.30, 1931.04, 1931.40, 1932.16
Auble, Larissa 1994.08
Aubret, Maurice 1934.32, 1935.19
Aubrey, Ella 1895.22
Aubrey, Violet 1894.28
Aubrin, Messr. 1882.04
Aubrin, Vincent 1882.04, 1882.20, 1882.25
Auburn, Jayne 1924.43
Auden, W.H. 1938.02
Audran 1884.42, 1886.47, 1888.36, 1894.19, 1899.23
Audran Opera Comique Company 1881.40, 1881.56
Audran Opera Company 1881.34
Audran, Edmond 1880.69, 1881.03, 1881.12, 1881.14, 1881.21, 1881.22, 1881.33, 1881.34, 1881.38, 1881.40, 1881.45, 1881.48, 1881.53, 1881.56, 1882.09, 1882.11, 1882.14, 1882.25, 1882.31, 1882.32, 1882.37, 1882.49, 1882.52, 1882.61, 1883.13, 1883.19, 1883.22, 1883.25, 1883.54, 1884.03, 1884.29, 1884.47, 1885.09, 1885.61, 1886.33, 1886.34, 1886.54, 1887.04, 1887.06, 1887.35, 1887.36, 1887.38, 1891.36, 1891.38, 1892.07, 1892.30, 1892.60, 1897.17, 1897.41, 1898.26, 1898.27, 1899.14, 1900.14, 1909.08, 1926.43
Audran, Edmont 1885.36
Audran, Edmund 1881.16, 1882.39, 1882.47, 1882.72, 1883.26, 1884.28, 1896.21
Audre 1946.07, 1950.04
Audree, Jean 1927.37
Audree, Jeanne 1928.03
Auer, Florence 1925.14, 1932.14
Auer, Mischa 1942.01, 1964.24
Auerbach, Arnold 1946.10, 1948.14, 1950.19, 1957.01
Auerbach, Arthur 1934.39
Auerbach, Boris 1942.28
Aug, Edna 1898.72, 1900.56, 1901.01, 1917.35
Augarde, Adrienne 1905.04, 1908.43, 1909.21, 1912.15
Augins, Charles 1976.20, 1992.03
Augusta, Maria 1990.02
Augusta, Mlle. 1867.25, 1878.03
Augusta, Mrs. 1844.01
Auguste and Cie 1890.50
Auguste Company 1895.20
Auguste, Mme. 1890.33, 1892.10
Auguste, Mons. 1890.33
Augustin Daly Musical Company 1902.30
Augustine, Stephanie 1949.08
Aujac, Mons. 1868.18, 1868.25, 1869.01, 1869.18
Aul, Ronnie 1946.21, 1950.08
Aulino, Tom 1998.16
Aulisi, Joseph G. 1971.20, 1976.03, 1983.17, 1987.06, 1989.03
Aull, Dorothy 1957.05, 1957.14, 1959.26
Ault, Helen 1929.31
Ault, Mary 1931.38
Aumont, Jean Pierre 1963.08
Auracher, Harry 1911.08, 1912.05, 1920.02
Aurcher, Walter 1896.04
Aurelie, Mlle. 1870.44
Aurelle, Mlle. 1871.27
Aurenson, Mons. 1868.13
Aurere, Mons. 1868.27
Auriol, Mlle. 1865.05, 1865.07, 1865.09, 1865.10
Austen, Gerald 1948.21
Austen, Jane 1959.06, 1963.03
Austen, Jerry 1947.08
Austen, Leslie 1937.01
Austen, Phyllis 1925.42
Austin, Anita 1892.49, 1893.01, 1893.22, 1894.40, 1896.12, 1897.46
Austin, Ann 1925.32
Austin, Beth 1979.05, 1980.30
Austin, Charles 1972.26
Austin, Clara 1905.09, 1905.42
Austin, Claude 1938.01, 1938.07
Austin, Cora 1875.11
Austin, Edith 1932.12
Austin, Edward 1912.30
Austin, Elizabeth 1986.16
Austin, Frederic 1928.13
Austin, G. 1886.50
Austin, H.S. 1904.09
Austin, Henrietta 1897.28
Austin, Henry 1941.08
Austin, Ivy 1982.20, 1983.13, 1984.11, 1985.11, 1986.16, 1987.03, 1987.09, 1988.04, 1988.14, 1988.18, 1989.14
Austin, Jennie 1905.09, 1905.42
Austin, John W. 1934.03
Austin, Leslie 1937.06
Austin, Lillian 1900.59
Austin, Lyn 1955.19, 1957.14, 1959.04, 1974.23, 1996.16
Austin, Marguerite 1925.06
Austin, Marie 1942.11
Austin, Michael 2000.03
Austin, N. 1864.23, 1865.04
Austin, Pamela 1958.18
Austin, Patti 1958.11
Austin, Patty 1960.09
Austin, Phyllis 1927.20
Austin, Ralph 1907.47, 1912.43, 1913.33, 1924.36
Austin, Ray 1940.16
Austin, Robert 1904.39, 1944.29
Austin, S. 1992.03
Auston, Mel 1971.04
Australian Ballet Foundation 1976.18
Author, Frank 1893.06
Autry, Herman 1978.09
Avann, Lillian 1903.12
Avant, Lance 1962.17
Avanti, Tony C. 1991.03
Avanzini, Mme. 1890.50
Avedon, S.M. 1907.20
Avedon, Samuel 1906.11, 1907.09, 1908.14
Aveling, Charles 1909.31
Aveling, Claude 1903.33, 1914.10
Aveling, Edward 1915.26
Avenal, Irene 1887.17
Avenall, Irene 1889.14
Aver, Brian 1966.09
Avera, Tom 1971.15, 1981.10
Averell, Florence 1906.36, 1909.12, 1914.16
Averill, Florence 1908.27
Averill, George 1917.28, 1922.16
Averill, Perry 1893.39
Avers, Harry 1925.25
Avery, Arvil 1928.28
Avery, Frances 1909.06
Avery, Harriet 1888.07, 1889.17
Avery, Morris 1913.32
Avery, Phyllis 1937.06, 1943.23
Avery, Val 1962.24, 1964.18
Avery, Vance 1998.04
Avey, West 1920.24
Avian, Bob 1960.08, 1962.24, 1968.31, 1969.17, 1970.13, 1971.05, 1973.06, 1975.15, 1978.27, 1981.29, 1987.07, 1991.03, 1994.10, 1999.20
Avila, Anita 1931.05
Aviv Dancers 1964.02
Avnet, Brian 1974.24
Avon 1915.28, 1916.02
Avrey, Messr. 1929.05
Awan, Adrian 1945.16, 1946.18
Awd, Henry 1912.43
Axe, Martyn 1999.15
Axe, Van 1898.01
Axelrod, Alan 1976.34
Axelrod, David 1968.13, 1971.14
Axelrod, George 1948.22
Axt, William 1919.38
Axt, William P. 1917.27
Axton, Hoyt 1982.22
Axton, Mae Boren 1982.22, 1989.12
Ayer, Jack 1921.12
Ayer, Lewis 1917.07
Ayer, Margaret Hubbard 1902.34, 1902.40, 1903.36
Ayer, Nat D. 1909.05, 1909.13, 1909.25, 1912.14, 1916.10
Ayer, Nathaniel D. 1910.20, 1912.13, 1912.16
Ayers, Catherine 1942.03, 1943.15, 1944.03, 1953.04
Ayers, Christine 1943.05
Ayers, Eileen 1946.22
Ayers, Joseph B. 1868.20, 1869.34, 1869.36, 1869.37, 1869.38, 1870.01, 1870.12, 1870.28, 1870.32, 1870.35, 1870.42, 1871.02, 1872.12
Ayers, Ken 1952.07, 1962.27, 1964.01, 1965.20, 1965.33, 1966.30, 1972.04
Ayers, Kittie 1882.15
Ayers, Laura 1890.04, 1893.31
Ayers, Lemuel 1946.08, 1947.01, 1948.14, 1948.32, 1950.20, 1951.16, 1951.22, 1952.02, 1952.15, 1953.09, 1953.16, 1954.05, 1957.08, 1958.07, 1963.06, 1965.18, 1965.22, 1965.38
Ayers, Paula 1925.15, 1927.63
Ayers-Allen, Phylicia 1975.01
Ayldon, John 1976.13, 1976.14, 1978.14, 1978.15, 1978.16
Ayler, Ethel 1957.16, 1961.24
Aylesworth, Arthur 1922.17, 1929.03
Ayling, Herbert 1908.40
Aylmer, Percyval 1911.25
Aylsworth, Arthur 1912.44
Aylwin, Jean 1911.12
Aymar, Neva 1902.24, 1903.23, 1903.39, 1905.41, 1908.10
Ayr, Michael 1981.04
Ayre, Ivor E. 1921.12
Ayre, Tom 1952.10
Ayres, Charles 1884.19
Ayres, Charlotte 1925.43, 1927.60, 1928.07, 1929.29, 1930.35
Ayres, Christopher 1991.13
Ayres, Joseph B. 1877.08, 1877.20
Ayres, Kate 1882.19
Ayres, Kitty 1882.52
Ayres, Lemuel 1943.04, 1944.21, 1944.23
Ayres, Robert 1924.06
Ayres, Sid M. 1910.17
Ayres, W. 1892.35
Ayrton, Robert 1919.38
Azcona, M. 1999.02
Azenberg, Emanuel 1970.15, 1971.13, 1976.15, 1978.09, 1979.04, 1982.01, 1984.08, 1987.06, 1988.17, 1989.03, 1993.02, 1997.17
Azener, Arthur 1972.19
Azito, Tony 1976.10, 1977.08, 1981.01, 1984.10
Aznarez, Pablo 1999.18
Aznavour, Charles 1958.06, 1964.02, 1965.30, 1968.21, 1970.01, 1974.01, 1974.19, 1981.16, 1983.03, 1998.12
Azova, Ludmilla 1966.04

b and m Productions 1959.19
B. Altman 1913.34, 1914.06
B. Altman and Company 1913.19, 1913.21, 1914.12, 1914.25, 1914.28, 1915.21
Baade, Mabel 1930.08
Baatz, John 1931.24
Baatz, John C. 1931.18
Baba Originals 1962.02

Babas, Barbara Bel 1913.20
Babatunde, Obba 1978.03, 1980.05
Babb, Doris 1927.39
Babb, Kevin 1979.32
Babbett 1875.34
Babbitt, James 1937.06
Babbs, Donna 1966.02
Babbs, Dorothy 1948.30
Babchin, Sol 1937.14
Babcock, Donald 1963.20
Babcock, F.R. 1905.55
Babcock, John 1991.05
Babcock, Karen 1999.11
Babcock, Theodore 1900.58, 1901.15, 1914.21, 1927.07, 1928.11, 1929.49
Babel, Sue 1964.27
Baber, Angele 1918.25
Baber, Vivian 1929.52, 1932.30
Babgy, George 1929.08
Babiar, Steve 1998.06
Babin, Michael 1999.22
Babtunde, Obba 1980.15, 1981.29
Babylon, Guy 2000.06
Baca, Epy 1959.05
Bacall, Lauren 1970.09, 1981.10
Baccarini, D. 1911.16
Bach, Del-Bourree 1997.22, 1998.20, 1999.21, 2000.19
Bach, Frederick 1896.33, 1897.16
Bach, Johan Sebastian 1929.51
Bach, Johann Sebastian 1978.05
Bach, L. Emil 1895.09
Bach, Reginald 1938.10
Bacharach, Burt 1967.13, 1968.20, 1968.31, 1976.16, 1984.15
Bache, Constance 1895.28
Bache, Messr. 1878.05
Bache, Theodore 1946.16
Bachelor 1965.30
Bacher, William 1955.10
Bachich, Annette 1964.24
Bachman, Charles 1903.11
Bachmann, Charles 1904.42
Baci, Agostino 1911.14
Baci, Augustino 1907.08
Baci, Gus 1918.16
Baci, Messr. 1905.22
Bacigalupi, Robert 1975.18
Backman, Carlos 1939.18
Backus, Charles 1879.09, 1880.15, 1881.55, 1882.28
Backus, Charles Salvini 1883.03
Backus, E.Y. 1881.15
Backus, George 1887.08, 1887.17, 1902.41, 1906.27, 1910.12
Backus, P.F. 1884.24
Backus, Richard 1981.26
Baclanova, Olga 1933.20
Bacon, Charles R. 1902.28
Bacon, Dorothy 1928.45
Bacon, Faith 1929.26, 1930.22, 1931.19
Bacon, Gerald 1921.11
Bacon, Glen 1940.23
Bacon, Glenn 1939.26
Bacon, Millar 1906.35
Bacot, Gabrielle 1908.16, 1908.26
Badaloni, Rodolpho 1927.04
Badaloni, Rudolfo 1931.34
Baddeley, Hermione 1969.04
Bade, Annette 1917.35, 1919.38, 1919.43, 1924.06
Bade, Eugenie 1893.25
Badeloni, Rudolf 1926.04
Badii, Enjio 1929.22
Badishy, Shara 1972.17
Bado, Richard 1996.10, 2000.03
Badolato, Bill 1992.01
Badolato, Dean 1979.26
Badoni, Mlle. 1873.10
Badrak, Jim 1990.16
Baer, Abel 1926.38, 1927.15, 1928.22, 1929.05, 1939.16, 1974.09, 1986.06
Baer, Arthur 1925.25, 1925.48, 1926.18, 1928.45
Baer, Bugs 1920.45, 1921.22
Baer, Eddie 1936.30
Baer, Louis 1881.13, 1882.77, 1886.16, 1887.03, 1889.21, 1893.23
Baer, Marion 1981.19
Baerg, Theodore 1985.13, 1986.10, 1987.10, 1987.11
Baerwitz, Samuel 1927.62
Baff, Regina 1971.08
Baffa, Diana 1961.07
Baffa-Brill, Diana 1983.10
Bafunno, Antonio 1918.40, 1920.10, 1921.37, 1924.24
Bagatelle, Mlle. 1876.33
Bagby, George 1928.23
Bageard, Jeanette 1889.09, 1889.41, 1895.18, 1896.18, 1898.20, 1899.19, 1899.29, 1903.10, 1910.32
Bageard, Jeannette 1897.25, 1900.40, 1901.16, 1905.16
Bageard, Jennie 1884.13, 1884.41, 1885.02, 1885.15, 1885.22
Bageard, Mlle. 1869.16
Bageard, Mme. 1870.40
Bageard, Mons. 1876.20, 1877.11, 1877.33
Bages, Frank 1920.44
Bagge, Henry J. 1892.25
Baggett, Bruce 1957.11
Baggetta, Vince 1960.08
Bagioni, Quinto 1957.06
Bagley, Eleanor 1942.05, 1948.04
Bagneris, Vernel 1997.08
Bahler, Tom 1979.13, 1981.08, 1982.06
Bahrer, Messr. 1876.17
Baiano, Valeria 1985.14
Baier, Frank 1985.17
Bail, Ernest 1913.35
Bailey, Adrian 1980.14, 1983.06, 1988.20, 1989.25, 1992.08, 1995.03
Bailey, B. 1867.12
Bailey, Barbara 1946.03
Bailey, Bernard 1983.06
Bailey, Bill 1936.06
Bailey, Buster 1949.16
Bailey, D'Vorah 1997.10
Bailey, Dennis 1985.03
Bailey, Eben Howe 1894.31
Bailey, Edward 1919.08
Bailey, Eve 1934.40
Bailey, Frankie 1894.19, 1894.38, 1896.02, 1896.26, 1896.36, 1897.09, 1897.19, 1897.31, 1897.48, 1898.50, 1899.17, 1899.30, 1900.47, 1901.17, 1902.29, 1903.28, 1905.56, 1907.35, 1912.07
Bailey, Fred 1892.04, 1907.47
Bailey, G. 1868.06
Bailey, George 1896.49
Bailey, Josephine 1884.15
Bailey, Kevin 1999.04
Bailey, Leo 1934.37, 1937.09
Bailey, Marion 1941.03
Bailey, Maureen 1959.23
Bailey, Melissa 1983.17
Bailey, Messr. 1865.11
Bailey, Mr. 1865.01, 1865.07, 1865.08, 1865.09
Bailey, Obie 1983.06, 1997.05
Bailey, Pearl 1946.08, 1950.04, 1950.19, 1954.19, 1967.15, 1975.21
Bailey, Robin 1963.25
Bailey, Shannon 1996.17
Bailey, Todd 1997.05
Bailey, Vera 1919.22
Bailey, William N. 1922.01
Bailey-Britton, Peter 1972.06
Baillo, Consuelo 1919.17
Baily, Franklin 1904.22
Baily, Mr. 1866.02, 1866.28
Bain, Conrad 1956.15, 1958.11, 1963.13
Bainbridge, Clement 1878.14, 1880.17, 1883.40, 1888.07, 1890.47, 1890.48
Bainbridge, Clements 1892.24
Bainbridge, Rolenda 1895.30
Bainbridge, Rolinda 1896.09, 1896.11, 1905.12
Baine, Raymond 1940.19
Baine, Ruth 1903.20, 1905.51, 1907.06
Baines, Dorothy 1906.43
Baines, Shirley 1976.28, 1983.04
Bainter, Fay 1912.04, 1918.15, 1924.23
Baio, Joey 1965.23
Bair, Sarah 1931.17
Baird, Bil 1943.05, 1951.15, 1963.11, 1965.02, 1998.11
Baird, Bobbi 1966.12, 1966.16, 1967.06, 1967.10
Baird, Cora 1943.05, 1951.15, 1963.11
Baird, Elsie 1903.40, 1911.28, 1912.30, 1913.22, 1927.27
Baird, George 1963.11
Baird, Julia 1897.45, 1898.50
Baird, Julie 1896.29
Baird, Messr. 1867.10
Baird, Miss 1886.36
Baird, Quin 1986.07, 1988.20
Baird, Robert 1946.10, 1948.17
Baird, Stewart 1912.49, 1913.02, 1913.37, 1914.30, 1916.01, 1917.19, 1918.35, 1919.16, 1920.19, 1921.03, 1922.12, 1923.43, 1926.41, 1929.33
Bairnsfather, Bruce 1918.31, 1926.38
Baisley, Helen 1955.07, 1957.15, 1958.16
Bajard, Jennie 1885.29
Bakanic, Bob 1951.18, 1962.04
Baker, Alan 1976.31, 1978.08, 1978.23
Baker, B.A. 1869.20
Baker, Belle 1926.51
Baker, Ben A. 1863.01, 1863.02, 1863.03, 1863.04, 1864.16, 1864.18, 1864.19, 1864.20, 1866.06, 1867.13, 1867.14, 1867.15, 1867.16, 1868.08, 1868.16, 1869.14, 1869.34
Baker, Ben. A. 1866.08, 1866.11, 1866.15
Baker, Benjamin A. 1848.01, 1848.03
Baker, Benny 1931.01, 1939.30, 1941.08, 1944.01
Baker, Bert 1910.30
Baker, Bertha Fitzhugh 1934.05
Baker, Billy 1928.09
Baker, Brad 1979.15
Baker, Caroline 1976.13
Baker, Celia 1890.36, 1898.45, 1899.32
Baker, Clara 1884.04, 1884.07, 1886.48, 1886.49
Baker, D.L. 1908.41
Baker, Dale 1976.18
Baker, Dan 1899.36, 1903.24, 1907.24, 1920.36
Baker, Daniel 1893.08, 1895.07, 1895.42, 1896.30, 1899.19, 1915.29
Baker, David 1952.07, 1952.20, 1957.14, 1965.17, 1965.36, 1966.24, 1969.07, 1976.08, 1998.04
Baker, David Aaron 1992.10, 1996.18
Baker, Edward 1912.36
Baker, Edwin 1904.09, 1905.53
Baker, Edythe 1922.07, 1923.02, 1924.13, 1925.01, 1925.28, 1926.02
Baker, Elden 1923.14
Baker, Emily 1879.63
Baker, Emma Mabella 1885.43, 1886.12, 1889.52
Baker, Evelyn 1905.27
Baker, Florence 1879.33, 1880.10, 1887.43
Baker, Florence I. 1879.35, 1880.06, 1880.13
Baker, Frank 1935.12
Baker, G.L. 1903.25
Baker, George 1928.13
Baker, Georgine 1919.02
Baker, Grafton 1900.42, 1900.49, 1900.56, 1902.22
Baker, Gregg 1983.04, 1984.09
Baker, Guelma 1900.30
Baker, Guelma L. 1900.29, 1900.51, 1903.24
Baker, Gulema 1907.45
Baker, Harry E. 1895.40
Baker, Helen 1897.21
Baker, Henry 1965.22
Baker, Herbert 1944.16
Baker, Isaac 1934.37
Baker, J. 1866.28
Baker, Jack 1942.26, 1943.21
Baker, Jennifer 1962.18
Baker, Joan 1941.11
Baker, Joe 1998.13
Baker, John S. 1897.40
Baker, Josephine 1924.27, 1936.02, 1964.02, 1973.17
Baker, Karin 1968.07, 1972.07, 1980.20
Baker, Kenny 1943.19
Baker, Lenny 1977.04
Baker, Lewis 1861.03, 1866.21, 1866.24, 1866.34, 1867.08, 1867.10, 1870.05, 1883.33
Baker, Lilian 1916.07, 1925.39
Baker, Mabella 1893.02, 1897.22, 1898.25, 1900.01, 1904.12, 1906.45, 1908.04, 1911.42
Baker, Mabelle 1908.44
Baker, Mark 1974.06
Baker, Mary 1905.10
Baker, Matthew 1995.19, 1996.15, 1997.22, 1998.20
Baker, May 1893.37, 1896.35, 1899.14, 1900.28, 1901.11
Baker, Messr. 1851.05, 1852.01, 1857.04, 1888.25, 1889.43
Baker, Mildred 1904.29
Baker, Millie 1909.25
Baker, Miss 1888.25, 1889.43, 1890.36
Baker, Mr. 1851.03, 1856.02, 1856.03, 1857.06
Baker, Nat 1908.28
Baker, Nathan 1946.13
Baker, P.F. 1886.35
Baker, Phil 1923.17, 1923.32, 1925.23, 1927.19, 1928.24, 1929.09, 1930.20, 1931.13, 1934.39, 1942.10
Baker, Phyllis 1942.35
Baker, R. Melville 1902.08, 1904.27
Baker, R.M. 1907.49
Baker, Raymond 1982.08
Baker, Robert Michael 1992.04
Baker, Ron 1990.07, 1991.08, 1992.14, 1993.12, 1993.14
Baker, Ronnie B. 1978.25
Baker, Ruth 1965.39
Baker, S. 1898.45
Baker, Sam 1906.46, 1908.26
Baker, Stella 1908.43
Baker, Stephen 1890.36, 1894.52, 1898.45
Baker, Steve 1899.32
Baker, Susan 1962.18
Baker, Suzie 1946.04
Baker, Taft 1998.11
Baker, Terri 1965.20
Baker, Thomas 1856.01, 1857.01, 1857.02, 1857.03, 1859.05, 1859.06, 1859.07, 1860.03, 1860.04, 1860.05, 1860.06, 1861.04, 1862.09, 1863.01, 1863.02, 1863.03, 1863.04, 1863.08, 1863.09, 1863.10, 1864.05, 1864.09, 1864.12, 1864.15, 1864.21, 1866.03, 1868.19, 1870.44, 1873.10, 1876.34, 1879.12, 1881.13, 1882.77, 1886.16, 1887.03, 1889.21, 1892.38, 1893.23, 1894.34, 1896.32
Baker, Thomas E. 1866.18
Baker, Tony 1899.36
Baker, W.S. 1870.40
Baker, William 1897.26, 1936.05
Baker, Willie 1905.10
Bakey, Ed 1966.27
Baklanova, Olga 1925.46, 1925.51
Bakonyi, Karoly 1909.15
Bakos, George 1945.02
Bakst, Len 1919.38
Bakst, Leon 1916.15, 1920.34, 1922.37
Bakula, Scott 1983.17, 1988.10
Bal, Jeanne 1946.18, 1950.06, 1950.15, 1961.27
Balaban, Emanuel 1947.10, 1948.29
Balaban, Nell 2000.20
Balanchine, George 1936.02, 1936.05, 1937.04, 1938.05, 1938.14, 1940.07, 1940.08, 1940.17, 1942.01, 1942.31, 1943.09, 1943.21, 1944.18, 1944.21, 1944.24, 1945.12, 1947.06, 1948.26, 1951.02, 1951.17, 1954.12, 1957.04, 1983.02
Balch, E.F. 1894.37
Baldassari, Mike 1998.04
Balderrama, Michael 1999.15
Baldi, Hugo 1934.41
Baldi, Messr. 1883.48
Baldina, Mmr. 1915.11
Balding, Ivor David 1966.15
Baldiwn, Tallmadge 1895.19
Baldock, Mr. 1836.01
Baldock, Mrs. 1840.02, 1840.03
Baldoni, Gail 1994.09
Baldovi, Laureen 1999.24
Baldridge, Richard 1957.02
Baldwin, A.E. 1921.16
Baldwin, Alice 1913.09
Baldwin, Anita 1917.31
Baldwin, Bob 1933.02
Baldwin, Brooks 1975.18
Baldwin, Carrie 1884.12
Baldwin, Clive 1989.11
Baldwin, Duncan 1938.12
Baldwin, Estelle 1906.33, 1909.07
Baldwin, F. 1897.01
Baldwin, F.W. 1885.65
Baldwin, Franca 1956.08
Baldwin, Frances 1884.27, 1893.07
Baldwin, Frank 1887.43, 1888.32, 1894.37, 1897.01, 1904.33, 1906.34
Baldwin, George 1915.19, 1916.11, 1916.23
Baldwin, J.L. 1898.43
Baldwin, James 1983.15
Baldwin, John 1862.07, 1902.39, 1982.22
Baldwin, Kitty 1904.04, 1912.37
Baldwin, Milton 1904.09
Baldwin, Miss 1917.31

Baldwin, Robert 1926.46
Baldwin, Talmadge 1896.06, 1896.30
Baldwin, William 1898.55
Baldwin, Winnie 1916.21, 1925.16
Balenciaga 1964.02
Bales, William 1939.26
Balesti, Sandra 1969.12
Balestracci, Sandra 1975.16, 1976.23, 1976.26, 1977.11
Balestrino, Richard 1983.11
Balf, Louise 1889.20
Balfe 1859.15, 1915.03
Balfe, Louise 1881.28
Balfe, Michael 1882.13, 1884.33, 1885.32, 1898.39, 1898.76, 1900.22, 1911.10, 1934.17
Balfe, Michael William 1844.01, 1846.01, 1852.03, 1852.04, 1852.06, 1852.07, 1853.04, 1854.02, 1854.03, 1854.07, 1855.05, 1855.06, 1858.03, 1859.03, 1859.15, 1862.02, 1862.03, 1863.06, 1863.07, 1864.04, 1864.19, 1864.20, 1864.21, 1866.10, 1867.07, 1868.12, 1869.41, 1872.17, 1877.35, 1878.03, 1882.64, 1883.39, 1889.28, 1896.16, 1933.17
Balfe, William Michael 1856.04
Balfour, Alfred 1888.38, 1888.41
Balfour, Mary 1919.40
Balfour, William 1919.07, 1922.14, 1927.55, 1929.30, 1929.48, 1930.41, 1933.20, 1934.41
Balgord, Linda 1994.05
Balieff, M. Nikita 1922.06, 1923.28, 1931.38, 1943.11
Balieff, Nikita 1925.03, 1927.51, 1929.05, 1931.38, 1934.32, 1943.11
Balir, Michael 1946.05
Balistreri, Michael 1965.36
Balkan, Glenda 1997.10
Balke,, Bertha 1908.39
Ball, Ambrose 1906.01
Ball, Arthur 1925.22
Ball, Diane 1961.28, 1963.21
Ball, Ernest 1911.04, 1913.03, 1922.19, 1923.20
Ball, Ernest R. 1903.14, 1904.43, 1905.20, 1905.47, 1910.06, 1911.04, 1912.06, 1913.03, 1914.29, 1920.16
Ball, Eva 1914.03
Ball, George 1972.16
Ball, H.F. 1884.44
Ball, Jane 1940.06, 1941.08
Ball, John T. 1896.47
Ball, Lucille 1960.22
Ball, Madelyn 1912.15
Ball, Michael 1990.04
Ball, Olive 1933.04, 1935.13, 1943.10
Ball, Patsy 1927.47
Ball, Samuel C. 1974.12
Ball, W. 1876.04, 1876.09
Ball, William 1876.05, 1876.07, 1876.10, 1876.11, 1876.14, 1876.33, 1877.05, 1888.03, 1961.13
Ballagh, Robert 1996.01, 1996.12, 1998.09, 2000.05
Ballantine, Carl 1972.03
Ballantine, David 1893.30
Ballantine, Lucille 1922.23
Ballard, Bob 1944.20, 1946.14
Ballard, Conoley 1976.31
Ballard, Florence 1946.14
Ballard, Geraldine 1925.37
Ballard, Hank 1982.22
Ballard, Hattie 1888.43
Ballard, John W. 1977.14
Ballard, Kay 1973.11
Ballard, Kaye 1954.03, 1961.10, 1963.05, 1963.16
Ballard, Lee 1951.15
Ballard, Lucinda 1938.15, 1940.06, 1942.19, 1943.14, 1944.32, 1945.08, 1946.01, 1946.12, 1947.02, 1947.06, 1947.17, 1948.20, 1948.25, 1953.11, 1955.02, 1959.24, 1961.27
Ballard, Merlin 1925.37
Ballard, Pat 1929.33, 1931.19, 1955.13
Ballard, Robert 1942.19
Ballard, Roy 1945.02
Ballentine, Lucille 1921.19
Ballew, Julie 1919.16
Ballew, Smith 1932.14
Ballinger, Matthew 1995.19, 1996.15, 1998.03
Ballinger, T.E. 1888.21
Balliot, Lloyd 1924.07
Ballot, Mll. 1882.67
Ballou, Marion 1911.15, 1927.42, 1932.03
Balls, P. 1873.26
Balluch, Fini 1934.18
Balluch, Michael 1934.18
Ballyhoo Productions, Inc. 1932.16
Balmain, Pierre 1964.02, 1980.06
Balno, James 1906.46, 1907.54
Balsam, Mark 1994.01, 2001.03
Balsam, Martin 1950.11, 1962.24
Balser, Barbara 1986.20
Balser, Ronald 1986.20
Balthrop, Carmen 1975.19
Balzer, George 1945.18
Bamberger, Carl 1962.21, 1963.24, 1964.30
Bambic, Gene 1974.03
Bambina, Bonni 1871.27, 1872.06
Bamboschek, Giuseppe 1934.41
Bamer, C. 1876.21
Ban, Akira 1989.21
Bancker, Emily 1887.09
Bancker, Mr. 1823.01
Bancker, Mrs. 1823.01
Bancroft, Anne 1963.09
Bancroft, Clara 1900.50
Bancroft, George 1923.10, 1923.46
Bancroft, Millicent 1928.49
Bancroft, Peggy 1930.05
Bancroft, Penny 1951.18
Banderen, D.B. 1877.02
Bandier, Martin 1982.22
Bane, Paula 1944.29, 1946.10
Banes, Antoine Anatole 1897.08
Banes, Lisa 1998.05
Bang, Charles 1949.17
Bangit, Messr. 1869.29
Bangs, F.C. 1876.12, 1881.31
Bangs, John Kendrick 1904.55, 1906.30, 1923.22, 1928.49
Bank, Maud 1898.08
Bank, Xenia 1944.24, 1952.11
Banke, Herb 1954.15, 1955.07
Banke, Herbert 1958.07
Banke, Richard 1965.22
Banker, Betsy 1889.19
Bankert, Alice 1930.33
Bankey, Chris 1993.05
Bankey, Christopher 1985.15, 1985.19
Bankhardt, Florence 1888.33
Bankoff, Ivan 1914.16, 1920.28, 1935.11
Banks, Ada 1909.27
Banks, Adelaide 1891.21
Banks, Alan 1946.05
Banks, Baby 1928.18, 1928.40
Banks, Diana 1965.22, 1966.16
Banks, E.G. 1888.38
Banks, E.J. 1890.23, 1890.50
Banks, Ernie 1987.17
Banks, Estar 1912.03, 1922.39
Banks, Hugh 1925.01, 1925.28
Banks, Jackie 1988.05
Banks, Jessie 1892.49, 1893.01, 1893.22
Banks, John 1955.15, 1955.18, 1955.20, 1955.21, 1955.23
Banks, Leslie 1949.15
Banks, Matthew A. 2001.04
Banks, Mr. 1866.02, 1866.28, 1868.06, 1871.11
Banks, N. 1867.12
Banks, Vic 1929.08
Bankson, J.W. 1881.32
Bankston, Gary 1995.02
Bann, Billy 1928.09
Banner, Jimmy 1938.04
Banner, John 1886.15, 1939.23
Banner, Veronique 1907.15, 1913.20, 1914.18
Bannerman, Margaret 1942.15
Bannerman, Penryn 1934.34
Banninger, Carole 1978.04
Bannister, Albert 1937.07
Bannister, Barbara 1943.20
Bannister, Frank 1930.37
Bannister, Georgiana 1943.11
Bannister, Harry 1936.03, 1945.14
Bannister, Harry C. 1920.47
Bannister, James 1926.11
Bannister, Mlle. 1888.10, 1888.23
Banome, Nino 1962.14
Bantock, Granville 1894.33
Bantock, Leedham 1894.33, 1897.32, 1907.41, 1909.29
Banton, Travis 1923.22, 1923.26, 1923.41, 1924.40
Bantry, Brian 1997.21
Baptistan, Amelia 1879.02
Baptistan, Mons. 1868.06, 1869.05, 1879.02
Baptiste, Ina 1876.03
Baptiste, Mons. 1865.02
Baptistin, Mons. 1869.34
Baptistine, Mons. 1865.01, 1865.05, 1865.07, 1865.08, 1865.09
Baquerot, Aliane 1999.15
Baragrey, John 1946.17, 1971.16
Barak, Itzik 1972.17
Baral, Vicki 1986.16, 1988.07
Baranco, Phyllis 1899.06
Barandes, Janice 1985.17
Barandes, Martin 1985.17, 1988.12
Barandes, Robert 2001.03
Baranski, Christine 1991.15
Barare, Fraulein 1879.62
Baras, Sara 1992.15
Barath, Ritza B. 1997.12
Baratoff, Leonid 1925.46
Baratt, Watson 1928.15, 1943.06
Baratta, M. 1870.28
Baratti, Signor 1897.29
Baravalle, Richard 1935.14
Baravalle, Victor 1918.42, 1919.41, 1920.41, 1921.11, 1921.27, 1921.36, 1922.45, 1923.10, 1923.33, 1925.38, 1926.32, 1926.41, 1927.67, 1931.37, 1932.22, 1933.26, 1934.34, 1934.38, 1936.22
Baravas, Jose Martinez 1988.15
Baravelle, Victor 1920.04, 1923.40, 1924.18, 1926.09, 1926.51
Barbara, A. 1883.62, 1884.51, 1885.28, 1887.18, 1887.26, 1887.28, 1898.37, 1899.42, 1900.17, 1900.23, 1900.26, 1900.29, 1904.57, 1907.54
Barbara, A.M. 1884.63, 1885.05
Barbara, Angel 1888.22, 1888.24, 1888.26, 1911.28, 1912.30, 1917.16, 1918.23
Barbara, Angel M. 1887.12
Barbara, Angelo 1906.46
Barbara, Marie 1914.33
Barbara, Mr. 1883.45
Barbara, Truly 1946.12, 1948.28
Barbaretto, Burrell 1900.33, 1908.10, 1910.13, 1911.08, 1912.05, 1912.08, 1913.34, 1917.18
Barbarin, Lucien 1990.19
Barbarin, Paul 1992.06
Barbe, Octavie 1901.05
Barbeau, Adrienne 1972.12
Barbeau, Francois 1972.08
Barbee, Richard 1939.13, 1952.03
Barber, Albert 1922.27
Barber, Berni 1921.26
Barber, Carolyn 1907.47, 1908.24
Barber, Dorothy 1924.47, 1925.27, 1926.07, 1928.27
Barber, E. 1848.01
Barber, E.W. 1934.37
Barber, Jean 1983.12, 1985.11, 1985.13, 1986.09, 1988.14, 1991.09
Barber, Joan 1996.08, 1996.15, 1999.21, 2000.19
Barber, Joan Susswein 1992.07
Barber, M. 1848.01
Barber, Red 1981.28
Barber, Samuel 2001.04
Barbera, A. 1884.34
Barberetto, Burrell 1909.12
Barberova, Ann 1929.51
Barbette 1946.13
Barbi, Vincent 1952.13
Barbier 1929.28
Barbier of Paris 1925.23, 1928.46, 1928.48, 1929.06
Barbier, Emmy 1919.21
Barbier, Flora 1905.11
Barbier, George 1919.23, 1922.45
Barbier, Jules 1855.03, 1861.05, 1866.27, 1872.01, 1893.44
Barbier, Willie 1890.23, 1891.41
Barbiere, Paris 1927.01
Barbieri, Bob 1967.10
Barbieri, Francisco A. 1875.24
Barbieri, Francisco Asenjo 1881.24
Barbour, Crimmins and Bryant 1927.66
Barbour, Dave 1983.20
Barbour, Ivy 1910.26
Barbour, James 1927.53, 2000.20
Barbour, Joyce 1925.07, 1928.16, 1929.12, 1930.14
Barbour, Lillian 1905.22
Barbour, Nina 1911.38
Barbour, Virginia 1946.19
Barbretto, Burrell 1912.15
Barcelo, Randy 1971.12, 1974.13, 1974.24, 1975.05, 1978.09, 1978.28, 1985.15, 1988.17
Barcinska, Eva 1944.01
Barckley, Mr. 1875.03
Barclay, Anna 1898.70, 1900.07
Barclay, Annie 1883.47, 1887.17, 1887.46
Barclay, Belle 1893.33
Barclay, Betty 1915.17
Barclay, Bruce 1933.25, 1938.09
Barclay, D. 1872.38
Barclay, Delancey 1881.31
Barclay, Don 1916.10, 1917.13, 1923.06, 1924.32, 1925.44, 1927.27, 1930.27, 1932.20
Barclay, Eddie 1964.02
Barclay, Humphrey 1964.29
Barclay, Jered 1967.01, 1974.04
Barclay, John 1926.10, 1926.44, 1927.44, 1927.57, 1927.61, 1933.23
Barclay, Kelli 1996.04
Barclay, Miss 1915.17
Barclay, Richard 1968.32
Barclay, T. 1870.28, 1870.32
Barclift, Nelson 1941.04, 1942.20, 1946.13
Bard, Ben 1923.02, 1923.41
Bard, Ethel 1907.36
Bard, Marie 1933.17
Bard, Robert 1936.12
Barde, Andre 1916.17, 1920.41, 1928.27, 1929.13, 1929.15, 1929.16
Bardelang, Alfred 1929.44
Bardell, May 1885.26
Bardi, A. 1985.07, 1997.13
Bardin, James 1926.05
Bardine, Jennie 1883.19
Bardini, G. 1894.22
Bardley, James 1873.20
Bardon, Henry 1993.14, 1995.18
Bardsley, John 1914.11
Barefield, Eddie 1953.05
Barer, Marshall 1956.08, 1957.01, 1959.26, 1960.07, 1966.05, 1988.08, 1996.18
Baretta, L. 1867.25
Baretta, Miss 1882.46
Baretta, Mlle. 1869.27, 1870.44, 1873.10, 1882.20
Baretta, Zela 1876.03
Barfoot, Audrey 1951.20
Bargonetti, Steve 1981.16
Barian, Joe 1942.05
Barin, Mlle. 1872.42
Barin, Mme. 1872.41
Barker, A. 1880.46
Barker, A.B. 1879.08
Barker, A.D. 1883.62, 1884.21, 1884.51, 1884.63, 1885.28
Barker, Adela 1898.12
Barker, Adele 1907.01
Barker, Adella 1898.77, 1908.20
Barker, Alan 1976.18
Barker, Albert 1945.08
Barker, Blue Lu 1992.06
Barker, Bradley 1927.27
Barker, Charles 1882.49
Barker, Corinne 1925.30
Barker, Danny 1992.06
Barker, Edith 1901.02, 1903.25
Barker, Eugenie 1898.31
Barker, Eva G. 1878.15
Barker, George 1881.39
Barker, Helen 1903.12
Barker, Irving 1904.25
Barker, Jack 1920.44, 1925.30, 1925.45, 1927.21, 1931.05
Barker, John 1898.45, 1927.55, 1929.03, 1931.16, 1933.02, 1937.17
Barker, Julia 1929.39
Barker, L.W. 1881.30
Barker, Patricia 1951.16
Barker, Richard 1883.52, 1885.47, 1887.10, 1888.20, 1888.35, 1889.04, 1889.24, 1890.03, 1890.26, 1890.43, 1891.31, 1891.36, 1891.47, 1892.17, 1892.25, 1892.29, 1892.60, 1893.02, 1893.07, 1893.35, 1893.39, 1893.47, 1894.28, 1894.29, 1894.41, 1894.48, 1895.04, 1895.08, 1895.16, 1895.22, 1895.25, 1895.26, 1895.42, 1896.05, 1896.25, 1896.28, 1896.45, 1897.17, 1897.36, 1898.54, 1898.73, 1900.37
Barker, Sam 1907.54
Barker, Samuel 1872.06
Barker, Sean 1964.07, 1964.08, 1964.12

Barker, Shirley 1919.18, 1920.45, 1921.10, 1922.02, 1923.01, 1923.06
Barker, Sue 1906.34
Barker, William 1903.08
Barkle, Beatrice 1890.21
Barksdale, Norman 1937.09
Barlab, E.H. 1913.21, 1922.23
Barlow, Anna Marie 1972.24
Barlow, Betty 1922.02
Barlow, Billie 1882.60, 1882.75, 1882.78, 1883.37, 1883.44, 1883.65, 1884.14, 1884.34, 1884.51, 1884.57, 1885.41, 1885.63, 1886.04
Barlow, Charles 1962.02
Barlow, Frank 1888.04
Barlow, Howard 1926.17, 1927.23
Barlow, James 1883.32, 1883.46, 1883.53, 1883.63, 1884.13
Barlow, Miss 1879.72
Barlow, Pam 1974.01
Barlow, Reginald 1904.30
Barlow, Roxane 1991.07, 1995.15, 1998.15, 1999.14
Barlow, Roxanne 2001.02
Barlow, W.A. 1883.63
Barlow, William 1883.32
Barlow, William A. 1883.46, 1883.53, 1884.13
Barmore, W. 1875.21
Barna, Craig 1995.02, 1998.18
Barnabee, Henry Clay 1880.12, 1880.45, 1880.48, 1880.53, 1882.09, 1882.10, 1882.11, 1882.12, 1882.13, 1883.11, 1883.13, 1883.14, 1883.15, 1891.29, 1892.51, 1893.18, 1893.19, 1893.48, 1894.03, 1894.08, 1894.45, 1895.01, 1896.08, 1896.42, 1896.43, 1897.13, 1898.23, 1900.25, 1900.31, 1900.32, 1902.04, 1902.28
Barnabo, Emila 1910.30
Barnard, Charles 1878.21, 1884.66, 1886.11
Barnard, Francis 1957.02
Barnard, G.P. 1871.12, 1871.16, 1879.02, 1881.30
Barnard, George 1884.27
Barnard, Ida 1911.01
Barnard, Mamie 1889.27, 1890.05, 1890.09, 1890.13
Barnard, Messr. 1889.43
Barnard, Mr. 1854.07
Barnard, Mrs. 1854.07
Barnard, Mrs. Charles 1886.02
Barnard, Nellie 1906.03
Barnard, Sophye 1913.02
Barnes 1964.28
Barnes and Jackson 1898.47
Barnes, Billy 1959.14, 1961.16, 1989.23
Barnes, Bob 1982.22
Barnes, Charles 1929.29, 1930.35, 1930.41, 1942.10
Barnes, Cheryl 1974.13
Barnes, Daniel 1928.29
Barnes, Ed. 1885.35
Barnes, Elaine 1980.12
Barnes, Eric 1963.05
Barnes, F. 1887.49
Barnes, F.J. 1909.11, 1910.08
Barnes, Fred J. 1906.19
Barnes, Gregg 1993.14, 1995.06, 1995.18, 1996.02, 1997.11, 1997.17, 1998.06, 1999.11
Barnes, Harry 1884.40, 1895.03
Barnes, Hattie Delaro 1889.44
Barnes, Helen 1915.31, 1916.10, 1917.13, 1918.37
Barnes, Henry 1938.03
Barnes, Irving 1953.04, 1961.07, 1961.13, 1962.07, 1964.19, 1985.20
Barnes, J. 1868.32, 1869.08, 1870.09, 1870.28
Barnes, James 1869.37, 1869.38, 1869.39, 1869.42, 1870.01, 1870.06, 1870.12, 1870.14, 1870.18, 1870.22, 1870.25, 1870.28, 1870.32, 1870.42, 1871.05, 1872.02, 1872.04, 1872.05, 1872.08, 1872.12, 1872.14, 1872.25, 1872.30, 1872.32, 1872.36, 1872.38, 1872.40, 1872.43, 1876.06
Barnes, Johnny 1939.16, 1939.30, 1947.20
Barnes, Kay 1964.19
Barnes, Ken 1976.32
Barnes, Kenneth 1895.30
Barnes, Kennett 1894.20
Barnes, Lois 1943.01
Barnes, Louis F. 1908.35
Barnes, Lucille 1943.01
Barnes, Mae 1925.18, 1930.24, 1954.02
Barnes, Maggie 1879.50
Barnes, May 1927.33, 1928.44
Barnes, Miss 1866.31, 1870.22
Barnes, Mr. 1868.23, 1869.36, 1870.02
Barnes, Muriel 1917.31
Barnes, Paul 1905.49
Barnes, Robalee 1971.12
Barnes, Roy 1943.06, 1943.12
Barnes, Sidney 1879.15, 1880.57, 1880.62, 1881.42, 1881.44, 1881.45, 1884.19, 1884.24
Barnes, Spencer 1931.36
Barnes, Sylvia 1904.48
Barnes, T. Roy 1914.12, 1914.16, 1917.31
Barnes, Violet 1905.41
Barnes, Virginia 1945.14, 1960.01
Barnes, W.A. 1897.52
Barnes, W.R. 1899.38
Barnes, W.S. 1888.37
Barnes, Will 1912.15
Barnes, Will E. 1901.29, 1902.05
Barnes, Will H. 1897.34, 1902.38, 1907.33
Barnes, Will R. 1897.48, 1898.17, 1898.50, 1898.51, 1899.21, 1899.30, 1900.38, 1900.47, 1901.17, 1901.25, 1902.06, 1902.15, 1902.29, 1902.37, 1902.44, 1903.10, 1904.10, 1904.16, 1904.37, 1904.58, 1905.06, 1905.16, 1905.33, 1905.42, 1905.56, 1906.06, 1906.10, 1906.16, 1906.22, 1906.40, 1906.48, 1907.17, 1907.25, 1907.55, 1908.02, 1908.42, 1909.02, 1909.31, 1910.02, 1910.35, 1910.37, 1911.03, 1912.19, 1912.40, 1913.25, 1914.17, 1918.23, 1919.22, 1919.41, 1920.26, 1921.28, 1922.03, 1922.30, 1923.40, 1924.26
Barnes, Willard 1917.16
Barnes, William 1887.06
Barnes, William H. 1919.21
Barnes, William R. 1913.22
Barnes, Wyatt 1906.46
Barnet, D.E. 1897.27
Barnet, Miss 1854.01
Barnet, Mr. 1854.06
Barnet, R.A. 1893.17, 1894.22, 1894.26, 1895.27, 1895.38, 1896.44, 1899.41, 1901.06, 1902.07, 1902.15, 1907.49
Barnet, Ray 1927.65
Barnett, Alice 1879.70, 1879.72, 1885.16, 1885.26, 1885.40, 1895.29, 1896.45
Barnett, Art 1946.12, 1963.17, 1966.07
Barnett, Arthur 1938.18, 1953.10
Barnett, Darrell 1981.13
Barnett, Jack 1946.23
Barnett, Jayne 1978.10
Barnett, John 1854.05
Barnett, Ken 1995.19, 1996.15, 1997.22, 1998.20, 1999.21, 2000.19
Barnett, Lee 1950.08, 1950.19
Barnett, Mary 1933.15, 1968.08
Barnett, Messr. 1846.01
Barnett, Morris 1854.05, 1878.22
Barnett, Mr. 1840.02, 1846.01, 1848.03, 1852.02
Barnett, Mrs. 1840.03, 1852.02
Barnett, Nate 1968.32, 1972.10, 1974.12, 1978.28
Barnett, Robert 1957.03
Barnett, Rose 1902.15
Barnett, Stanley 1971.09
Barnett, Zoe 1913.16, 1914.07, 1914.30, 1920.35, 1921.03, 1921.31
Barnette, Jean 1912.28, 1914.15
Barney 1875.35
Barney, Ariel 1893.25, 1897.36, 1898.54, 1899.24, 1899.28
Barney, Elsie 1903.14
Barney, Jay 1969.01
Barney, John 1927.62
Barney, Marion 1923.43
Barney, Master 1875.34
Barney, Mr. 1869.26
Barney, Sterling 1925.47
Barnhart, Abner 1925.33
Barnhart, Robert 1938.06
Barnolt, Louise 1921.39
Barnstead, Peggy H. 1918.23
Barnum, E.C. 1884.46
Barnum, George W. 1886.44, 1891.15, 1895.27, 1896.52, 1898.48, 1900.47
Barnum, H.B. 1891.44, 1894.43, 1976.35, 1979.18, 1980.14, 1982.17
Barnum, John 1886.50, 1886.54
Barnum, Messr. 1867.17
Barnum, P.T. 1867.32
Barnum, Phineas T. 1861.06, 1862.01, 1862.02, 1862.06, 1864.17, 1864.22, 1865.05, 1865.07, 1865.08, 1865.09, 1865.10
Barnum, Tillie 1894.51
Baron, Al 1925.08, 1937.15, 1940.12
Baron, Albert 1926.42, 1931.08, 1931.40
Baron, Charles 1927.54, 1928.43
Baron, D. 1881.35
Baron, Evalyn 1980.17, 1985.06, 1986.13
Baron, Georgia 1903.03, 1903.31
Baron, Joanne 1976.20
Baron, Julia 1930.14
Baron, Kimberly Beth 2001.04
Baron, Marie 1987.01
Baron, Master 1870.22
Baron, Maurice 1937.10
Baron, Messr. 1881.35
Baron, Miss 1903.03
Baron, Mr. 1911.14
Baron, Paul 1939.18
Baron, Ray 1966.24
Baron, Robert H. 1951.10
Baron, Sandy 1974.01
Baron, Sydney S. 1963.27
Baron, W. 1918.14
Baronova, Irina 1944.14
Baroo, Pat 1974.20
Barova, Marie 1945.12
Barovick, Fred 1947.20
Barr, Betty 1929.33
Barr, Edith 1900.01, 1900.50, 1901.21, 1902.19
Barr, Edna 1927.32
Barr, Georges 1918.34
Barr, Gilbert 1922.34
Barr, H.A. 1898.47
Barr, John 1931.46
Barr, Ken 1946.23
Barr, Lillian 1889.39, 1891.39
Barr, Muriel 1940.02
Barr, Nip 1920.02
Barr, O.H. 1877.24
Barr, Richard 1953.12, 1955.05, 1971.16, 1979.06
Barr, Roseanne 1997.11
Barr, Tom 1920.02
Barraclough, Sydney 1901.25, 1902.05
Barragan, Raul 1943.17
Barrajanos, Danny 1969.09
Barras, Charles M. 1866.18, 1870.44, 1871.27, 1873.10, 1876.34, 1879.12, 1880.08, 1881.13, 1882.77, 1886.16, 1887.03, 1889.21, 1892.38, 1893.23, 1894.34, 1896.32
Barrat, Maxine 1939.12, 1940.23
Barratt, Augustus 1904.55, 1907.06, 1907.49, 1909.19, 1911.39, 1912.31, 1913.04, 1915.19, 1916.26, 1917.01, 1918.12, 1918.20, 1918.35, 1918.42, 1920.08, 1923.07, 1929.46
Barratt, Louise Bascom 1923.17, 1923.25, 1924.36
Barratt, Sheila 1928.14
Barratt, Watson 1918.02, 1918.05, 1918.20, 1918.35, 1918.42, 1919.03, 1919.16, 1919.19, 1919.30, 1920.06, 1920.09, 1920.19, 1921.14, 1921.20, 1921.25, 1921.31, 1921.34, 1922.07, 1922.11, 1922.12, 1922.15, 1922.34, 1922.36, 1922.40, 1923.02, 1923.03, 1923.12, 1923.13, 1923.14, 1923.15, 1923.17, 1923.25, 1923.41, 1924.06, 1924.12, 1924.13, 1924.21, 1924.23, 1924.29, 1924.36, 1924.45, 1925.01, 1925.02, 1925.07, 1925.13, 1925.23, 1925.26, 1925.27, 1925.39, 1925.43, 1926.01, 1926.05, 1926.14, 1926.15, 1926.26, 1926.27, 1926.33, 1926.37, 1927.01, 1927.14, 1927.17, 1927.19, 1927.42, 1927.55, 1927.58, 1927.68, 1928.04, 1928.07, 1928.14, 1928.27, 1928.32, 1928.46, 1928.48, 1929.06, 1929.09, 1929.17, 1929.22, 1929.28, 1929.32, 1929.39, 1930.20, 1930.27, 1930.37, 1930.43, 1931.09, 1931.36, 1932.01, 1932.06, 1932.15, 1934.01, 1934.13, 1934.43, 1937.03, 1937.17, 1938.07, 1938.17, 1940.09, 1941.02, 1943.05, 1943.12, 1943.20, 1945.01, 1947.13, 1948.27, 1956.05, 1957.02, 1959.02, 1959.05, 1962.15
Barratt, Wilson 1899.23, 1930.15
Barrault, Jean-Louis 1964.06
Barre, Albert 1913.29
Barre, Alfred 1904.35
Barre, Ducy 1859.01
Barre, Gabriel 1986.13, 1989.09, 1992.11, 1993.05, 2001.09
Barre, Marguerite 1896.27
Barreca, Christopher 1995.09, 1999.22
Barrere, Jean 1957.08
Barret, Lynn 1961.07
Barret, Raymond 1920.05
Barrett, Alan 1962.29
Barrett, Andrew 1877.07
Barrett, Annie 1888.10
Barrett, Brent 1980.02, 1983.08, 1996.13, 1997.10
Barrett, Charles C. 1903.35
Barrett, Christopher 1972.11, 1977.16
Barrett, Daniel 2000.01
Barrett, Dorothy 1940.02
Barrett, Fenton 1932.23
Barrett, G.H. 1854.03, 1855.01, 1855.02
Barrett, J. Pritchard 1894.18
Barrett, James 1873.12, 1873.14, 1922.22
Barrett, James Lee 1975.03, 1989.17
Barrett, James S. 1924.47, 1925.40, 1927.53
Barrett, Jean 1911.09
Barrett, Joe 1986.16
Barrett, John 1907.14
Barrett, Lorin 1948.17
Barrett, Lorraine 1982.03
Barrett, Louise 1927.68, 1930.06
Barrett, Mace 1958.01, 1959.23, 1964.05, 1989.27
Barrett, Malcolm 1905.17, 1916.07
Barrett, Mary 1868.19
Barrett, Mary Jane 1937.03
Barrett, Messr. 1886.32, 1893.13
Barrett, Michael 1944.29, 1945.11
Barrett, Minnette 1907.37
Barrett, Miss 1886.32, 1886.36
Barrett, Mr. 1852.01, 1857.08, 1859.01
Barrett, Nancy 1965.28
Barrett, Oscar 1880.34, 1894.18
Barrett, Raina 1971.04
Barrett, Reginald 1891.01
Barrett, Sheila 1929.28, 1934.42
Barrett, Sondra 1940.22, 1943.21
Barrett, Tom 1975.11
Barrett, Vicki 1951.15
Barrett, Virginia 1929.09, 1944.30
Barrett, William 1872.06
Barrett, William E. 1970.08
Barretta, Mlle. 1882.20, 1883.23
Barretta, Pauline 1880.07
Barretti, Mlle. 1882.45
Barri, Bebe 1923.36
Barrian, Bill 1968.24
Barrie, Ann 1934.20
Barrie, Barbara 1970.13, 1972.02
Barrie, Charles 1893.30
Barrie, Eleanor 1937.11
Barrie, Fred 1937.01
Barrie, Gracie 1933.05, 1935.18, 1936.31, 1941.03
Barrie, James M. 1921.13, 1950.08, 1953.02, 1954.13, 1979.22, 1989.03, 1990.20, 1991.13, 1998.18
Barrie, Joan 1942.35
Barrie, Lee 1942.05, 1949.06
Barrie, Leslie 1924.07, 1934.36
Barrie, M.V. 1881.16
Barrie, Mira V. 1881.16
Barrie, Mona 1937.10
Barrie, Nigel 1914.04
Barrie, William 1891.46
Barriere, H.B. 1834.03
Barriere, Theodore 1893.01
Barrile, Anthony 1993.06
Barrington, Dede 1944.19
Barrington, Eva 1882.20, 1884.09, 1884.29, 1885.08, 1886.31
Barrington, Lucy 1882.04
Barrington, Rutland 1890.02
Barriscale, Isabel 1896.45
Barrison, Alice 1867.18
Barrison, Lou 1949.06
Barrison, Mabel 1900.51, 1902.29, 1903.31, 1907.14, 1908.13
Barron, Arthur 1920.34
Barron, Bebe 1961.08
Barron, David 1989.19
Barron, Evelyn 1983.21
Barron, Frank 1931.44
Barron, Fred 1920.25
Barron, Georgia 1905.44
Barron, Judith 1934.01

Barron, Louis 1961.08
Barron, May 1931.44
Barron, Sarrah 1998.10
Barron, Ted S. 1904.33
Barrot, G. 1884.43, 1884.54
Barrot, Gabrielle 1884.45, 1884.52
Barrot, L. 1884.43
Barrot, Mlle. 1884.47
Barrow, P.J. 1909.29
Barrowman, John 1999.20
Barrows, Diana 1977.06
Barrows, J.O. 1884.62
Barrows, James O. 1894.39, 1899.08
Barrows, Josephine 1907.61
Barrows, William 1907.30, 1907.61
Barroy, Earl 1921.28
Barroy, Michael 1923.20, 1923.43, 1927.52, 1928.19
Barroy, Michel 1922.19, 1922.20, 1925.20
Barrs, Norman 1961.24, 1965.32
Barruch, Adam 1997.22, 1998.20
Barry 1891.08
Barry and Fay's Comedy Company 1884.19
Barry, Ann 1954.04, 1958.20, 1967.05
Barry, Arthur 1900.37, 1904.30, 1907.07, 1923.26, 1927.17
Barry, B. 1876.19
Barry, B.H. 1985.06, 1989.10, 1989.29, 1992.02, 1992.17, 1995.15
Barry, B.H. (Tango) 1989.20
Barry, Billy 1876.19, 1882.01
Barry, Bobbie 1902.08
Barry, Bobby 1912.20, 1938.08, 1962.16
Barry, C.W. 1869.36, 1869.37, 1869.38, 1869.42, 1870.01, 1870.09, 1886.02
Barry, Carrie 1904.44
Barry, Charles 1899.18, 1903.31, 1905.44, 1908.39
Barry, Charles W. 1870.12
Barry, Claire 1951.21
Barry, Dave 1951.21
Barry, E. 1866.18, 1871.17
Barry, E.F. 1879.02
Barry, Earl 1905.31
Barry, Edward 1879.68, 1882.62
Barry, Edwin 1875.05, 1879.37, 1879.68, 1880.64, 1881.09, 1883.06
Barry, Elaine 1945.03
Barry, F. 1869.27, 1869.32
Barry, Flora 1881.42, 1881.44
Barry, Florence 1887.50, 1890.27, 1891.15
Barry, Frank 1892.04, 1921.27, 1922.14, 1922.41, 1923.47, 1926.24, 1927.15, 1930.23, 1931.21
Barry, Fred 1924.18, 1925.10, 1925.24, 1945.03
Barry, Gene 1937.14, 1942.22, 1942.31, 1943.09, 1946.02, 1950.01, 1950.19, 1983.11
Barry, J. 1900.23, 1900.29
Barry, Jean 1929.51
Barry, Jeff 1973.14, 1975.12, 1979.11, 1979.30, 1982.22, 1984.15, 1985.03, 1986.02
Barry, Jimmy 1922.46, 1923.27
Barry, John 1899.42, 1900.02, 1900.13, 1900.14, 1900.30, 1902.18, 1909.25, 1936.22, 1938.09, 1974.11
Barry, John D. 1900.22
Barry, Jr., Billy 1894.43, 1898.56
Barry, Jr., William 1896.37
Barry, Julian 1957.05
Barry, Kate 1894.18
Barry, Katie 1889.54, 1902.19, 1904.12, 1905.03, 1906.12, 1906.44
Barry, Lee 1955.02, 1961.02
Barry, Leonard 1918.10
Barry, Lydia 1891.08, 1893.30, 1911.34
Barry, Mamie 1882.20
Barry, Merna 1951.21
Barry, Messr. 1852.02
Barry, Miss 1852.02, 1875.05
Barry, Mr. 1852.01, 1852.05, 1856.03, 1869.02, 1869.20
Barry, Mrs. Jimmie 1922.46
Barry, Peter 1940.04, 1940.18, 1948.04
Barry, Philip 1941.05, 1980.06, 1998.05
Barry, Raymond 1977.08, 1979.08
Barry, Richard 1906.09, 1907.12, 1909.06, 1927.47, 1928.31
Barry, Robert 1954.18, 1956.15, 1976.09
Barry, Rod 1965.36, 1968.13, 1968.31
Barry, Roy 1965.36, 1968.24
Barry, Shiel 1872.27
Barry, Thomas 1965.24
Barry, Vivian 1931.48, 1933.13, 1933.25
Barry, W.J. 1919.05
Barry, William 1882.81, 1884.19, 1884.24, 1886.23, 1889.37, 1889.51, 1891.08, 1893.30, 1900.05, 1919.19, 1934.36
Barry, Winifred 1930.21
Barrymore, Chick 1919.26
Barrymore, John 1909.02
Barrymore, Maurice 1876.23, 1887.27, 1892.25
Bars, Jacques 1895.28
Barsch, Delight 1904.36
Barso, Pat 1974.22
Barstar, H.A. 1912.30
Barstar, H.L. 1909.20
Barstow, Mrs. Montague 1999.13
Barstow, Nellie 1890.08
Barstow, Richard 1947.08, 1948.11, 1948.16, 1952.09, 1967.11
Bart, Charles 1919.22
Bart, Jack 1916.15
Bart, Lionel 1963.01, 1965.23, 1969.16, 1984.07, 1995.12
Bart, Roger 1997.12, 1997.18, 1999.03, 2001.05
Barta, Karoly 1961.27
Barte, Leon 1923.07, 1925.23, 1925.27, 1939.26
Bartel, Christine 1961.10, 1968.32
Bartel, Jean 1946.03, 1952.07
Bartell, Bessie 1906.10
Bartell, Eddie 1938.08
Bartell, Mr. 1876.03
Bartelle, Ida 1885.67, 1886.26, 1886.33, 1887.12, 1887.18, 1892.29
Bartels, Joan 1946.10
Bartels, Louis John 1927.52
Bartels, Paul 1941.03
Bartfield, Carl 1932.10
Barth, August 1902.14
Barth, Fred 1927.46
Barth, Nicole 1961.10, 1962.24, 1972.04
Barthel, Louise 1912.23, 1913.08, 1913.11, 1913.12, 1913.13
Barthell, Louise 1912.21
Bartholomae, Philip 1913.19, 1914.20, 1915.30, 1917.31, 1918.02, 1919.18, 1921.23, 1924.32, 1926.12, 1975.24
Bartholomew, Mr. 1864.13
Bartholomew, W. 1875.40
Bartholomew, W.H. 1873.08, 1875.34, 1875.36, 1880.07, 1883.47, 1885.33, 1886.16, 1886.41, 1887.03, 1887.27, 1888.01, 1889.21, 1890.17, 1892.38
Bartholomew, William A. 1869.02, 1869.14
Bartholomew, William H. 1869.20
Barti, Perle 1912.10
Bartik, Otokar 1925.09
Bartine, Jennie 1887.43
Bartine, Miss 1883.23
Bartis, John 1953.01
Bartlemann, Thomas 1878.21
Bartlett, Baby 1915.22
Bartlett, Belle 1900.06, 1900.14, 1900.17
Bartlett, Charles 1971.08
Bartlett, D'Jamin 1975.23
Bartlett, Ella Herbert 1946.18
Bartlett, Guy 1905.21
Bartlett, Guy H. 1903.02
Bartlett, J. 1875.21
Bartlett, Josephine 1891.29, 1892.51, 1893.18, 1893.19, 1893.48, 1894.03, 1894.08, 1894.45, 1895.01, 1896.08, 1896.43, 1897.13, 1898.23, 1900.25, 1900.31, 1900.32, 1902.04, 1902.28, 1903.37, 1904.51, 1904.57, 1905.08, 1905.11, 1905.57, 1907.36, 1908.40
Bartlett, Katherine 1900.20
Bartlett, Kathrin 1901.08
Bartlett, Kathryn 1901.23, 1903.18, 1906.10
Bartlett, Michael 1932.03, 1933.24, 1937.17, 1939.21, 1971.05
Bartlett, Miss 1885.09, 1892.52
Bartlett, Richard 1913.35, 1914.27
Bartlett-Davis, Jessie 1893.48
Bartley, Dallas 1992.03
Bartley, Nalbro 1918.25
Barto, Betty Lou 1948.28
Barto, Dewey 1928.23, 1938.08
Barto, Eddie 1905.31
Bartoletti, Emilia 1893.23
Bartoletti, Malvina 1876.12
Bartolini, Dela 1978.23, 1979.27
Bartolot, A.L. 1931.02
Barton 1884.12, 1886.24, 1886.34
Barton Brothers 1953.04
Barton English Opera Company 1883.39
Barton's Bijou Burlesque and Comedy Company 1886.59
Barton's Bijou Burlesque Company 1886.32, 1886.45
Barton's Bijou Opera Comique Company 1887.06
Barton, Alexander 1990.14
Barton, C.H. 1877.04
Barton, Charles 1882.81
Barton, Charles E. 1906.10
Barton, Daniel 1978.03
Barton, Diane 1972.14
Barton, Donald 1966.11
Barton, Eddie 1951.20
Barton, Edward 1971.12
Barton, Eileen 1947.20
Barton, F. 1881.32
Barton, G. 1851.04
Barton, G.H. 1894.52
Barton, James 1879.64, 1880.47, 1880.69, 1881.37, 1882.06, 1882.63, 1882.66, 1883.24, 1883.39, 1884.06, 1919.30, 1921.14, 1922.11, 1923.13, 1924.29, 1926.18, 1930.38, 1943.16, 1951.24
Barton, John 1963.03
Barton, Joseph 1920.01
Barton, Kathryn 1943.16
Barton, Leonard 1918.19
Barton, Marion 1920.43
Barton, Miss 1881.35, 1886.36
Barton, Mme. 1844.01
Barton, Mr. 1850.01, 1860.06
Barton, Murray 1951.20
Barton, Ned 1915.20
Barton, Nettie 1900.38
Barton, Ottilia 1922.11
Barton, Paul 1951.20
Barton, Ralph 1923.27
Barton, Roxane 1914.24
Barton, Steve 1988.01, 1993.19
Barton, Thomas 1881.31
Barton, Tillie 1919.30
Barton, W. 1891.39, 1894.35
Barton, W.B. 1890.43
Barton, W.T. 1888.32
Barton, William 1897.37
Barton, Zoe Startz 1994.09
Bartow, Art 1964.33
Bartrop, Sybil 1965.37
Bartsch, Hans 1942.17, 1942.21, 1947.06
Bartsch, Rainer H. 1943.12
Bartsch, Rudolf H. 1921.31, 1923.14, 1923.15, 1924.12, 1926.05, 1931.07
Bartuschek, Leo 1915.24, 1916.15
Barty, Billy 1991.11
Barty, Ginia 1929.10, 1929.11, 1929.13, 1929.14, 1929.15, 1929.16
Bartz, Minerva 1920.44
Baruch and Company 1909.28
Baruch, Hugo 1908.27, 1912.09, 1914.02
Baruch, Stephen 1999.24
Baruch, Steve 1997.18, 2001.05
Baruch, Steven 1987.20, 1991.02, 1995.03, 1997.13, 1998.03
Barzin, Leon 1931.06
Barzman, Ben 1940.21
Barzman, Sol 1940.21
Bas, Carlos 1962.20
Bascom, A. 1869.14
Bascom, Nana 1899.13
Bascomb, Arthur W. 1912.27
Bascombe, H.L. 1881.30
Basescu, Elinor 1990.08
Bash, Phyllis 1976.28
Bash, Serena 1965.03
Basher, Mohammed 1925.37
Bashford, Eugenie 1901.29, 1902.05
Basie, Count 1999.24
Basie, William "Count" 1939.29, 1976.34, 1986.02
Basil, Nick 1908.12, 1932.07
Basil, Toni 1979.30
Basile, Charles 1963.17
Basile, Jo 1958.06
Basile, Joe 1964.22
Basile, John 1988.19
Baskerville, Priscilla 1981.06, 1983.04
Baskett, Jimmy 1929.01
Baskette, Billy 1917.08, 1917.26
Baskette, Jimmy 1930.34
Basquette, Lena 1923.07
Basquette, Lina 1923.33, 1924.18, 1925.24, 1927.13
Bass, Bill 1976.27
Bass, Dennis 1977.09
Bass, Emory 1952.02, 1961.15, 1963.17, 1966.11, 1969.06
Bass, George Houston 1991.01
Bass, Jr., Quincey C. 1906.38
Bass, Jr., Quincy C. 1907.56
Bass, Paul 1926.19, 1927.32
Basse, Edward 1917.11, 1918.20, 1924.23, 1926.26
Basset, Jonathan 1962.23
Bassett, Charles 1892.16, 1892.28, 1893.05, 1893.09, 1893.44, 1895.13, 1895.20
Bassett, Charles O. 1890.14, 1890.15, 1890.46, 1896.50, 1898.09
Bassett, Cornelia 1890.46, 1890.47, 1890.48
Bassett, Frank J. 1889.13
Bassett, Jed 1879.52
Bassett, Jr., Harry 1873.03
Bassett, Ralph 1978.23, 1979.27, 1980.21, 1981.20, 1981.21, 1982.20, 1983.13, 1984.11, 1985.13, 1986.04, 1986.08, 1986.09, 1987.03, 1988.04, 1988.18, 1989.14
Bassett, Russell 1880.41, 1907.47
Bassi, A. 1893.02, 1893.07, 1894.14
Bassian, Alexia 1901.06
Bassinson, Kevin 1991.10
Bassler, Sidney 1943.23, 1947.01
Bassman, George 1940.21, 1950.02, 1950.17, 1955.06, 1965.15, 1966.13, 1992.04
Basso, Shirley Ann 1949.06
Bast, Stephanie 1995.19
Bastia 1927.51
Bastia, Jean 1976.16
Bastia, Pascal 1935.19, 1976.16
Bastida, Ramon 1949.07
Bastide, Mons. 1870.41, 1871.07
Bastine, Ronald Cadet 1998.20
Baston, Susan 1968.07
Bastos, Messias 1992.13
Bastos, Soraya 1988.06
Bataeff, Michael 1937.01
Bataten, Edward 1934.05
Batchelder, Fannie 1886.28, 1891.25, 1891.45, 1892.44, 1892.54, 1893.10, 1893.27, 1893.36
Batchelder, Fanny 1893.15
Batchelder, Josie 1884.15
Batchelder, W.H. 1896.28
Batchelder, William H. 1965.18
Batcheler, Fannie 1894.04
Batchelor, W.H. 1892.29, 1895.08, 1897.36, 1898.01, 1898.16, 1899.21, 1900.05
Batchelor, William H. 1902.08
Bate, Dorothy 1926.32
Bate, Tom 1948.27, 1966.11
Bateman, Alice 1878.01
Bateman, Bill 1978.04, 1981.07, 1990.20, 1991.13, 1995.13
Bateman, Harold L. 1868.17, 1868.18, 1868.30, 1868.31, 1869.01
Bateman, Phyllis 1945.16
Bateman, Robert 1984.15
Bateman, Victory 1894.12
Bates, A. 1906.22
Bates, Blanche 1918.10
Bates, C.H. 1900.52
Bates, Charles 1898.18, 1898.46, 1906.09, 1924.13
Bates, Charles A. 1902.08
Bates, Ed 1898.64
Bates, Edna 1912.39, 1916.20, 1917.22, 1918.34, 1920.14
Bates, Eliza L. 1881.31
Bates, G.B. 1886.27
Bates, Granville 1927.50
Bates, Harry 1928.49
Bates, Helen 1902.33
Bates, James 1972.08
Bates, Jeanne 1982.14
Bates, Katherine Lee 1980.27
Bates, Kenneth 1934.06
Bates, Lawson 1958.11
Bates, Lee 1884.10
Bates, Lulu 1950.06, 1951.15, 1957.07, 1962.01
Bates, Marie 1897.47
Bates, Mark 1872.10, 1876.34
Bates, Natalie 1918.22
Bates, Peg Leg 1949.09
Bates, Rawley 1962.18
Bates, Sally 1925.17, 1927.36, 1929.31
Bates, Scotty 1928.41
Bates, Stephen 1999.17

Bates. Thorpe 1922.35
Batho, Kristofer 1996.16
Batie, F.A. 1918.05
Batie, Franklyn 1915.26, 1917.08, 1925.01, 1925.28
Batie, Franklyn A. 1918.05, 1921.34, 1923.12
Batista, Miriam 1932.07
Batista, Wilson E. 1998.10
Batistta, Miriam 1921.20
Batos, Soraya 1988.06
Batt, Bryan 1999.15
Batt, Mike 1992.12
Battaille-Henri 1965.08
Batten, Tom 1970.02, 1974.18, 1978.02, 1981.13, 1986.18
Battista, Miriam 1934.40, 1936.07, 1948.18
Battle, George 1930.16
Battle, Hinton 1975.01, 1981.06, 1983.21, 1991.03
Battle, Kathleen 1975.19
Battle, Lettie 1975.01
Battle, S. 1881.25, 1881.42, 1881.45
Battle, William Edgar 2000.07
Battler, Edgar 1935.18
Battles, George 1927.33, 1928.10
Battles, John 1944.33, 1947.17, 1961.07
Battu, Leon 1864.08, 1868.20, 1869.22, 1875.12
Batutis, Dennis 1981.13
Batwin + Robin Productions, Inc. 1993.06, 1994.06, 1995.05, 1995.14, 1996.07, 2000.17
Batwin + Robin 1999.23
Bauch, Hugo 1905.55
Baudendistel, Robert 1997.09
Baudett, Rose 1911.29
Baudin, Claudine 1949.09
Bauduc, Ray 1978.05, 1979.30, 1999.01
Bauer, Abel 1974.09
Bauer, Adolph 1894.28
Bauer, Alma 1902.02
Bauer, Arthur 1909.15
Bauer, Dorothy 1945.16
Bauer, Erma 1911.18
Bauer, George 1948.30, 1952.03, 1955.19, 1958.10
Bauer, Henry 1898.43
Bauer, Inez 1904.24, 1909.03, 1913.15, 1922.03
Bauer, Irvin S. 1999.06
Bauer, Jack 1927.54
Bauer, Jamie 1953.06
Bauer, Julius 1890.08, 1890.28, 1890.39, 1892.16, 1913.02
Bauer, Kate 1882.31
Bauer, M. 1894.30
Bauer, Miss 1882.36, 1882.37
Bauer, Richard 1975.23
Bauer, Rollin 1941.09
Bauer, Vivian 1948.31
Bauer, William 1946.18
Bauer-Theussl, Franz 1984.03, 1984.04, 1984.05
Bauersmith, Paula 1961.18
Baughman, Renee 1975.15
Baugonetti, Steve 1992.08
Baum, Bernie 1989.12
Baum, Charles 1924.09, 1926.32
Baum, Florence 1951.23
Baum, Frank 1903.03
Baum, Joanne 2001.03
Baum, L. Frank 1904.13, 1904.44, 1975.01, 1984.09, 1989.06, 1993.03, 1997.11, 1998.06, 1999.11
Baum, Louis 1912.31, 1917.26
Baum, Vicki 1989.26
Bauman, Eleanor 1936.22
Bauman, Marie 1884.18
Bauman, Mordecai 1931.46, 1942.26
Bauman, William 1918.21
Baumann, K.T. 1978.04
Baume, J.W. 1901.25
Baumeister, Joseph 1911.13
Baumel, Samuel 1918.17
Baur, Franklyn 1927.37
Bautier, Michele 1987.02
Bautista, Francisco Javier Gonzalez 1988.15
Bavaar, Tony 1951.24, 1953.01
Bavan, Yolande 1972.11, 1979.28, 1995.09
Baverstock, Percy 1924.20
Baviello, Frances 1929.34, 1929.36, 1929.38, 1929.48, 1930.01, 1930.03, 1930.07, 1930.12, 1930.41, 1931.18, 1931.24, 1931.27, 1933.17, 1933.18, 1934.08, 1934.11, 1935.06, 1935.08, 1936.04, 1936.08, 1936.11
Bavier, Frances 1935.16
Baxley, Barbara 1963.14, 1968.30
Baxter, Alan 1934.39, 1934.42, 1935.03, 1943.23, 1957.06
Baxter, Allan 1934.19
Baxter, Carol Ann 1988.20
Baxter, Connie 1942.05, 1945.05
Baxter, Dorothy 1944.32
Baxter, Dwight 1976.20
Baxter, Frank 1889.28, 1889.29
Baxter, George 1926.18, 1937.17, 1943.07, 1947.13
Baxter, George David 1946.17
Baxter, Gladys 1924.09, 1927.04, 1927.14, 1928.15, 1929.17, 1929.34, 1929.39, 1931.07
Baxter, Lloyd 1940.16
Baxter, Maisie 1934.23, 1934.24, 1934.31, 1934.33
Baxter, Margaret 1954.15
Baxter, Marie 1912.13, 1912.38, 1914.30
Baxter, Meryl 1942.19
Baxter, Owen 1913.05
Baxter, Rebecca 1995.18
Baxter, Robin 1995.19, 1996.15, 1997.22, 1998.13
Baxter, Skippy 1942.19, 1947.12, 1948.19, 1949.05
Baxter, Sue 1927.11
Bay, Bob 1941.09
Bay, Howard 1942.11, 1942.27, 1943.01, 1943.09, 1943.19, 1943.24, 1944.14, 1944.21, 1944.24, 1945.03, 1945.06, 1945.11, 1945.14, 1946.01, 1946.02, 1946.09, 1947.11, 1948.20, 1948.24, 1948.28, 1950.12, 1951.15, 1951.19, 1954.04, 1954.14, 1955.09, 1956.06, 1957.18, 1958.13, 1959.10, 1960.09, 1960.18, 1961.09, 1961.15, 1961.20, 1963.17, 1965.21, 1965.34, 1967.04, 1970.10, 1972.14, 1976.01, 1977.12, 1979.10, 1992.07
Bay, Mary 1920.28
Bay, Robert 1942.27, 1943.05, 1943.21, 1946.23
Bayard, Carol 1965.09
Bayard, Jean-Francois 1879.62, 1880.31, 1882.15
Baye, Rose 1926.22
Bayer, Babe 1919.10
Bayer, Carole 1970.03, 1979.04
Bayer, Gary 1978.06
Bayer, Joseph 1927.38
Bayer, Julius 1920.46
Bayer, Lillian 1904.27
Bayer, Patricia 1985.17
Bayer-Schumacher Company 1922.46
Bayes, Nora 1901.16, 1908.19, 1908.39, 1909.13, 1909.25, 1910.01, 1911.13, 1912.44, 1915.02, 1917.37, 1918.32, 1920.05, 1920.45, 1921.18, 1922.38, 1927.12, 1930.13, 1931.19, 1955.03, 1974.01
Bayes, Olive 1931.28
Bayes, Sammy 1969.04, 1972.11, 1973.03, 1974.03, 1976.36
Bayes, Sammy Dallas 1990.18
Bayfield, St. Clair 1908.40, 1910.03, 1910.24
Bayha, Charles 1920.33
Bayle, Pierre 1934.32
Bayle-Silverman, Pierre 1935.19
Bayless, Francis 1898.67
Bayley, T. Haynes 1867.09
Bayley, Thomas Haynes 1875.34
Baylies, Edmund 1961.12
Baylis, Meredith 1949.03, 1953.07, 1954.01
Baylis, Nadine 1978.26
Bayliss, Bertha 1893.40
Bayliss, Gene 1951.13, 1954.17, 1960.06, 1961.10
Bayly, Thomas Haynes 1884.36, 1924.32
Bayne, Mardi 1945.16, 1949.04, 1952.10
Baynes, Eustace 1907.32
Bays, Nora 1917.29
Bazemore, Raymond 1975.19, 1976.28, 1987.10
Bazemore, Raymond H. 1983.04
Bazin, A. 1879.48
Bazin, Francois 1875.01, 1882.73
Bazin, Mlle. 1879.39, 1879.60, 1879.61, 1880.29, 1880.52
Bazzano, Mlle. 1881.32
BB Promotions 1999.24
Beaber, Jack 1969.17
Beach, Albert 1964.22, 1967.13, 1968.20, 1999.07
Beach, Drina 1927.31
Beach, Gary 1976.15, 1981.14, 1983.18, 1994.04, 2001.05
Beach, George 1943.12
Beach, Rex 1924.47
Beach, Richard 1943.23
Beach, Scott 1964.26
Beach, Shannon 1999.15
Beachner, Louis 1970.03, 1974.25, 1984.07
Beacon Theatre Production 1998.19
Beadle, Spofford J. 1975.07
Beahan, Charles 1933.21
Beal, Harrison 1994.04
Beal, John 1941.05, 1952.09, 1987.06
Beal, Royal 1965.18
Beale, Joseph 1938.04
Beale, R.A. 1902.43
Beale, Richard 1898.15, 1898.19, 1898.37
Beale, W.G.F. 1859.13
Beall, C.C. 1918.13
Beall, James 1904.51
Beals, James 1903.37
Beals, Ralph 1905.31
Beam, Alvin 1955.11, 1956.15, 1958.02, 1959.06, 1959.22, 1962.14, 1963.13
Beam, Bob 1944.01
Beam, George 1875.05
Beam, W. Ward 1897.15
Beaman, Genevieve 1892.58
Beamer, Hazel 1925.43
Beamer, Keola 1961.07
Beamer, Nona 1961.07
Beamish, F.L. 1894.35
Bean, Alvin 1952.13, 1953.03
Bean, David 1954.13
Bean, G.A. 1870.07, 1870.15
Bean, Jeffrey 2001.03
Bean, Jr., George A. 1884.26
Bean, Keene 1995.14
Bean, Orestes 1912.32
Bean, Orson 1953.17, 1959.03, 1961.28, 1967.05
Bean, Reathel 1983.18
Beane 1950.07
Beane, F. 1870.26, 1871.18
Beane, Fannie 1871.04, 1873.02, 1891.02
Beane, Fanny 1870.33, 1882.04
Beane, G.A. 1873.02
Beane, George 1870.33, 1871.04
Beane, George A. 1871.18, 1880.21, 1881.10, 1882.82, 1886.13, 1887.02, 1887.42, 1888.25, 1889.43, 1890.36, 1894.37, 1897.34, 1899.15, 1899.35, 1900.48, 1900.55, 1903.24, 1904.04, 1904.24, 1912.34
Beane, Jr., George A. 1888.32, 1891.39, 1894.07, 1894.35
Beane, Mrs. 1861.01
Beane, Reginald 1943.13, 1946.21, 1953.12
Beard, Chuck 1968.18, 1968.32, 1976.09
Beard, Danny 1975.01
Beard, James 1968.17
Beard, Lillian 1903.09
Bearden, Jim 1989.17
Beardsley, C.H. 1906.36
Beardsley, Stella 1903.31, 1906.47, 1910.10, 1911.39
Beart, Guy 1964.39, 1968.04
Beasley, Butterfly 1899.22
Beasley, Carl 1931.02
Beasley, Clarence 1937.10
Beasley, Jennie 1899.22
Beasley, Joyce 1939.14
Beasley, Madeline 1904.16
Beasley, Mayflower 1899.22
Beasley, Russ 1975.24
Beasley, Violetta 1899.22
Beaston, Frank 1925.01, 1927.09
Beatice, Helene 1890.43
Beatles, The 1974.24
Beaton, Betzi 1934.01, 1934.14, 1934.40
Beaton, Cecil 1956.01, 1959.27, 1960.19, 1964.20, 1968.17, 1969.17, 1976.05, 1981.19
Beatrice, Helen 1895.12
Beatrice, Helene 1892.03
Beattie, Brenton 1935.04
Beattie, Herbert 1957.15, 1959.18, 1960.14, 1960.15, 1961.03, 1961.04, 1961.19, 1964.07, 1964.09, 1964.13, 1965.11, 1965.12, 1965.13, 1966.04
Beattie, William 1904.47
Beatts, Anne 1979.19, 1985.03
Beatty, Ethel 1976.04, 1978.21
Beatty, John Lee 1978.09, 1979.05, 1981.03, 1982.02, 1982.08, 1982.24, 1983.19, 1987.20, 1988.17, 1991.02, 1992.01, 1996.14, 1996.18, 1998.13
Beatty, Mrs. S. 1879.66
Beatty, Roberta 1921.36, 1922.45, 1923.10, 1924.09, 1924.45, 1927.55, 1933.26
Beatty, Talley 1937.14, 1944.31, 1946.01, 1948.14, 1969.09, 1971.02, 1976.35, 1979.18, 1980.14, 1982.17
Beaty, Richard 1972.08
Beau Mode Frocks 1927.18
Beaubian, Susan 1986.11, 1987.07
Beaubien, Julia 1914.31, 1915.31
Beauclerc, Jennie 1876.13, 1876.15, 1876.29
Beauclerc, Julia 1876.13, 1876.29
Beaudet, Louisa 1878.22
Beaudet, Louise 1879.15, 1879.19, 1889.36, 1890.14, 1890.50, 1891.12, 1891.22, 1892.42, 1894.47, 1898.68, 1917.34, 1928.26
Beaudet, Mlle. 1879.26, 1879.36, 1879.39, 1879.41, 1879.44, 1879.47, 1879.49, 1879.51, 1879.60, 1880.56
Beaudet, Rose 1882.57, 1883.45, 1883.62, 1884.08, 1885.07, 1885.09, 1885.26, 1885.41, 1885.63, 1886.04, 1886.30, 1890.40, 1891.21, 1894.25, 1896.10, 1896.29, 1898.05
Beaufoy, Simon 2000.15
Beaugard, Mons. 1870.41
Beaugarde, Marie 1910.15
Beaugarde, May 1895.32
Beaugarde, Miss 1895.10
Beauman, Marie 1879.15, 1880.18
Beaumar, Constance 1918.41
Beaumont Studios 1921.26, 1927.30, 1929.25
Beaumont, Ada 1873.12, 1873.14, 1873.17
Beaumont, Alexandre 1883.10, 1883.16, 1883.59
Beaumont, Bertee 1922.28, 1927.10
Beaumont, Emilie 1890.10
Beaumont, Emily 1885.65, 1887.43, 1892.22
Beaumont, Grace 1915.31
Beaumont, J. 1881.26
Beaumont, James 1994.07
Beaumont, Lucy 1917.24
Beaumont, Maud 1881.36
Beaumont, Mlle. 1870.41
Beaumont, Nellie 1875.11, 1880.06, 1880.10, 1880.13, 1896.36, 1897.09, 1897.19, 1897.48, 1900.16, 1903.17, 1904.14, 1907.46
Beaumont, Nelly 1898.50
Beaumont, Ralph 1953.07, 1956.07, 1958.05, 1959.27, 1961.15, 1963.05, 1965.15, 1965.36, 1966.08, 1966.13, 1967.09, 1972.03
Beaumont, Rose 1896.36, 1897.09, 1897.19, 1897.48, 1898.50, 1900.16, 1901.23, 1903.16, 1903.27, 1904.41, 1907.34, 1908.35
Beaumont, Sascha 1920.17, 1925.34, 1926.36
Beaumonte, Bertee 1919.11, 1919.35, 1921.09
Beaupre, Emilie 1900.01
Beauregard, Thomas 1912.44
Beautora, Louise 1918.23
Beauvais, Jeanne 1945.12, 1953.06, 1957.02, 1970.11
Beaux Art Studios 1919.24, 1920.35
Beaux Arts Studios 1921.39, 1922.24, 1923.06
Beauxan, Mons. 1871.07
Beban, George 1903.07, 1905.03, 1905.45, 1906.29, 1907.41, 1908.31, 1912.07, 1913.35
Beban, George E. 1902.11, 1902.42
Bebeto 1988.06
Bebus, M.D. 1873.25
Becaud, Gilbert 1964.02, 1964.22, 1966.20, 1967.11, 1967.13, 1968.20, 1968.21, 1987.12
Becca, Karl 1903.40
Beccardi, Gilda 1911.19
Beccari, T. 1911.16
Becham, Larl 1964.02
Bechdel, Glenn 1995.13
Becher, John 1947.09
Becher, John C. 1957.03, 1962.15, 1963.04, 1966.10, 1974.17, 1983.10
Becher, Thomas 1934.42, 1952.09, 1953.17, 1955.12, 1956.08, 1962.02
Bechet, Sidney 1923.11, 1986.06

Bechtel, Mr. 1891.33, 1892.43
Bechtel, William 1899.34
Beck, Arthur 1959.26, 1963.12
Beck, Barbara 1967.14
Beck, David 1976.09
Beck, Edward 1904.09, 1922.30
Beck, Herr 1882.68
Beck, Jean Waldo 1971.10
Beck, Kittie 1900.45
Beck, Kitty 1892.15
Beck, Larry 1919.13, 1923.23, 1925.34, 1930.14, 1945.14
Beck, Lawrence 1912.02
Beck, Martin 1924.39
Beck, Marvin 1975.02
Beck, Sydney 1963.28
Beck, Vincent 1950.08, 1955.11
Beck, Walter 1932.28
Beck, William 1965.26, 1965.27
Beckelman, Laurie 1996.07
Becker Brothers Studios 1949.06
Becker, Allen 1995.13, 1997.09
Becker, Arthur 1916.23
Becker, Brian 1995.13, 1997.09
Becker, Bruce 1966.24
Becker, Charles 1934.18
Becker, Don 1961.12
Becker, Ed 1955.02, 1956.16, 1958.01, 1958.20, 1960.06, 1962.01, 1965.15, 1966.08, 1966.13, 1969.14, 1971.02, 1975.06
Becker, Farrel 1986.04
Becker, Gerry 1993.04
Becker, John C. 1909.31
Becker, Kitzi 1980.24
Becker, Larry 1986.10, 1987.11
Becker, Lee 1951.12, 1953.17, 1955.10, 1957.12, 1960.19 (see also Theodore, Lee Becker)
Becker, Leslie 2001.09
Becker, Minchen 1890.31, 1891.33, 1892.43, 1894.01
Becker, Peter 1999.05
Becker, Ray 1970.09
Becker, Will H. 1912.20
Becker, William 1912.29
Becker-Grahn, Frau 1866.33
Beckers, Mons. 1868.24, 1868.26, 1869.03, 1869.05, 1869.16, 1869.30
Becket, Marta 1946.01
Becket, Rose 1896.29
Beckett, George 1869.17
Beckett, Gilbert 1892.08, 1882.41
Beckett, Harry 1868.23, 1868.32, 1869.06, 1869.29, 1870.13, 1870.19, 1870.21, 1870.39, 1870.42, 1871.01, 1871.02, 1871.14, 1871.19, 1872.21, 1872.22, 1872.24, 1872.26, 1872.34
Beckett, Margaret 1927.32
Beckett, Marta 1951.14
Beckett, Miss 1893.05
Beckett, Rose 1887.32, 1887.44, 1889.19, 1890.23, 1890.43, 1895.20, 1896.05, 1897.11
Beckett, Samuel 1971.04
Beckham, Billy 1978.10
Beckham, Willard 1974.02, 1976.15
Beckler, Steven 1973.05, 1995.03
Beckman, Al 1951.20
Beckman, Claire 1997.16
Beckman, Donald 1982.20, 1989.14
Becks, Alfred 1866.12
Becks, George 1863.09, 1863.10, 1865.05, 1866.12, 1872.10, 1872.27
Beckwell, Mr. 1836.01
Beckwith, Ellen 1909.07
Beckwith, Linden 1909.11
Beckwith, Reginald 1940.07
Becmann, Edgar 1913.28
Becque, Lucy 1954.18
Beda 1922.34, 1999.05
Beddell, Vera 1890.09
Beddoe, Don 1965.22
Beddoe, Donald 1943.23
Beddow, Margery 1959.01, 1962.16, 1962.27, 1985.20
Bedell, B. 1891.02
Bedell, Vera 1889.34, 1891.35, 1892.02, 1892.13
Bedella, David 1995.02
Bedford Stuyvesant Restoration Corporation 1981.15
Bedford, Beth 1889.12
Bedford, Eugene 1951.05
Bedford, May 1898.56
Bedford, Mr. 1871.22
Bedford, Ronnie 1960.04
Bedin, Ezio 1991.11
Bedini, Jean 1919.21
Bedini, Jehan 1902.42
Bedini, John 1903.18
Bedodw, Margery 1951.19
Bedsow, Len 1963.12
Bee Gees 1999.15
Bee, Messr. 1856.04
Bee, Mr. 1855.09
Beebe, Irving 1918.25, 1920.15, 1920.41, 1922.04, 1924.03, 1925.40
Beebe, Lucius 1936.03
Beebe, M. 1887.27
Beebe, Mary 1880.12, 1880.45, 1885.13, 1886.25
Beebe, Messr. 1864.22
Beech, Arthur 1911.28
Beechele, H.A. 1905.10
Beecher, Marjorie 1943.21
Beecher, Robert I. 1905.53
Beecher, Robert L. 1903.19
Beecher, Rosalba 1884.63, 1885.14, 1885.52
Beecher, Sylvia 1904.23, 1927.18
Beechman, Laurie 1977.06, 1982.03, 1992.12
Beecroft, Victor 1938.10
Beede, Charles H. 1897.56
Beekman, Messr. 1881.04
Beekman, Mr. 1866.15, 1868.04
Beekman, W. 1876.23, 1884.11
Beekman, W.H. 1881.27
Beeler, Virginia 1948.29
Beener, Elaine 1973.10
Beer, Alice 1922.20
Beers, Aaron 1917.16
Beers, Francine 1964.18, 1982.02
Beers, Leo 1920.22, 1920.23, 1926.29
Beerwald, Ben 1916.19, 1917.20, 1918.19
Beerwald, Benjamin 1906.05, 1907.02
Beery, Sr., Noah 1945.03
Beery, Wallace 1907.27
Beery, Wallace F. 1905.50
Beethoven 1884.42, 1886.47, 1888.36, 1894.19, 1899.23, 1940.20, 1963.03
Beethoven, Ludwig 1917.35
Begeard, Jeannette 1907.17
Beggs, Jeanie 1924.20
Beggs, Lee 1928.48, 1931.03
Beggs, Malcolm Lee 1947.11, 1955.10, 1955.25, 1956.02
Begley, Ed A. 1893.49
Begley, Ed. J. 1899.36
Begley, Edward 1899.26, 1906.33, 1913.18, 1917.36
Begley, Edward J. 1892.34
Behar, Joy 1994.13
Behin, Mons. 1879.02
Behman, L.C. 1901.07
Behney, John 1947.09
Behr, A. 1919.18
Behr, Carrie 1884.22, 1886.47, 1887.43, 1888.09, 1889.01, 1905.55
Behr, Miss 1884.42
Behr, Randall 1983.16
Behr, Simon 1994.09
Behrandt, Julius 1928.45
Behrens Costume Company 1920.02
Behrens, Augusta 1912.36
Behrens, Elsie 1930.08
Behrens, S. 1869.41
Behrman, S.N. 1954.15, 1979.02
Beicola 1988.06
Beigelman, Mark 1982.09, 1983.21
Beil, Frl. 1882.68
Beiner, Arthur 1925.05
Beisenhertz, H. 1866.06, 1866.08, 1866.11, 1866.15
Beissenherz, H. 1858.04, 1861.01
Beith, Major 1918.10
Bekefi, Theodore 1927.38
Bekins, Richard 1980.06
Bela, Nicholas 1948.18
Belafonte, Harry 1953.17, 1955.03, 1964.02
Belasco 1897.31
Belasco, David 1891.38, 1897.48, 1901.17, 1917.27, 1929.02, 1929.20
Belasco, Grace 1894.38, 1896.05, 1896.35, 1896.48
Belasco, Grace Wallace 1893.39
Belasco, Henry 1905.15
Belasco, Jacques 1945.17
Belasco, Leon 1955.02, 1956.16
Belaver, Harry 1942.11, 1946.12, 1958.03, 1966.12, 1966.16
Belaver, Lee 1988.04
Belbridge, David 1922.07
Belcher, Frank 1900.11, 1902.25, 1906.48, 1910.10, 1911.31, 1913.24
Belcher, Frank H. 1900.06, 1900.13, 1908.17, 1912.31
Belfort, May 1898.35
Belga, Alice 1910.02
Belga, Alys 1911.13, 1913.31
Belgarde, Adele 1885.46
Belge, Tavie 1918.26
belGeddes, Norman 1921.01, 1922.33, 1924.43, 1925.10, 1925.24, 1925.37, 1927.52, 1937.01, 1940.16
BelGeddes, Norman 1929.45, 1932.17, 1944.29
Belin, Alexander 1972.08
Belin, Charles 1932.22
Belkin, Jeanna 1962.16
Belknap, Katherine 1912.41
Belknap, Stuart 1909.03
Belknap, W.S. 1888.43
Bell, A.H. 1879.20, 1880.26, 1880.57, 1880.62, 1882.18
Bell, Ada 1872.35
Bell, Alex M. 1882.80
Bell, Alex. 1884.59
Bell, Alexander M. 1884.12
Bell, Alice 1925.04
Bell, Anna 1911.22
Bell, Annie 1889.29
Bell, Arthur 1880.62, 1883.58, 1906.41
Bell, Arthur H. 1881.25
Bell, Bessie 1912.31
Bell, Charles W. 1923.08, 1924.07
Bell, Curt 1951.20
Bell, David H. 1990.06
Bell, Derrick 1976.21
Bell, Digby 1881.04, 1881.27, 1882.42, 1882.70, 1883.04, 1883.10, 1883.38, 1883.65, 1884.51, 1884.57, 1885.13, 1885.28, 1887.04, 1887.47, 1888.26, 1889.17, 1890.14, 1890.15, 1890.18, 1890.20, 1891.13, 1892.20, 1893.39, 1894.14, 1894.41, 1894.48, 1903.02, 1915.10
Bell, Digby V. 1880.18, 1880.47, 1880.69
Bell, Emilie 1869.21
Bell, Emily 1890.08
Bell, Emma 1869.11, 1869.25
Bell, F. Gatenby 1912.06
Bell, Florence 1883.02, 1883.17, 1883.19, 1883.23, 1884.34, 1885.05, 1885.41, 1885.63, 1889.40, 1889.49, 1890.19, 1890.24, 1891.12, 1893.32, 1893.39, 1896.26, 1896.36, 1897.09, 1897.28, 1897.48, 1898.50, 1899.30, 1900.38
Bell, Francesca 1961.12
Bell, Francis 1924.35
Bell, Frank 1895.37
Bell, George 1886.16, 1887.03, 1917.24, 1932.22, 1978.03
Bell, Glynis 1975.18, 1993.18
Bell, Harry 1982.15
Bell, Harry B. 1892.58
Bell, Ida 1873.26, 1884.18, 1884.25, 1884.42, 1886.47, 1888.36, 1892.29, 1930.29
Bell, J. Franklin 1918.21
Bell, Jennie 1886.47
Bell, Julia 1872.35, 1873.25
Bell, Katherine 1903.14, 1907.42
Bell, Katie 1870.35
Bell, Kristen 2001.06
Bell, Laura 1883.20
Bell, Laura Joyce 1883.65, 1884.51, 1884.57, 1885.13, 1887.04, 1887.47, 1888.26, 1889.17, 1890.14, 1890.15, 1890.18, 1890.20, 1891.13, 1892.20, 1894.41, 1895.19, 1900.19, 1903.02
Bell, Leslie 1996.04
Bell, Marie 1888.32, 1896.20
Bell, Marion 1947.07
Bell, Marjorie 1946.24
Bell, Marty 2001.01
Bell, Michel 1994.08, 1999.08
Bell, Miss 1836.01, 1851.05, 1869.28, 1883.23
Bell, Mrs. 1851.04, 1854.04
Bell, Norma 1898.77
Bell, Richard 1976.04
Bell, Robert 1999.15
Bell, Robert E. 1894.22
Bell, Ronald 1999.15
Bell, Rose 1868.24, 1869.16
Bell, Service 1943.10
Bell, Steven 1971.12
Bell, Thomas 1926.32, 1997.21
Bell, Tommy 1920.36
Bell, Vanessa 1981.07, 1981.29
Bell, William 1876.30, 1962.07
Bella, Miss 1870.31
Bellac, Mons. 1888.23
Bellaire, Blanche 1917.34
Bellaire, Clarence 1898.59
Bellaire, Florida 1914.09, 1916.18
Bellaire, Retta 1914.09
Bellaire, Rita 1916.18
Bellamore, M. 1875.10
Bellamy, Albert 1881.39
Bellamy, Claxson 1886.30, 1888.02, 1889.16, 1889.25, 1889.49, 1893.35, 1897.24, 1898.36, 1899.24, 1903.32, 1921.01
Bellamy, Don 1993.19
Bellamy, Mr. 1846.01, 1856.02
Belland, Bruce 1980.28
Bellaver, Harry 1933.07
Bellaver, Lee 1978.19, 1981.21, 1990.08, 1991.09
Belle, Catherine 1903.12
Belle, Clara 1895.02
Belle, Marjorie 1946.24
Belle, Minnie 1891.39
Belledna, Alex 1929.21, 1975.20
Bellenda, Alex 1982.12
Belleran, Lisa 1969.16
Belleville, Florence 1903.37
Bellevue, Adrian 1909.20
Bellin, Charles 1979.10
Belline, Dennis 1971.01
Bellinger, Roberta 1926.21
Bellingham, Kate 1890.25
Bellini 1859.18, 1867.11
Bellini, Cal 1968.23
Bellini, Vincenzo 1862.02, 1870.19, 1870.20, 1870.36, 1873.04, 1876.06
Bellis, Richard 1980.12
Bellis, W. Messenger 1927.63
Bellomo, Joe 1965.20
Bellore, Ada 1889.54
Bellote, Peter 1982.22
Bellows, Jean 1936.12
Bellson, Louis 1958.04
Bellville, Clara 1882.04
Bellvue, Adrian 1908.26
Bellwood, Peter 1970.02
Belmar Productions 1974.04
Belmont Operetta Company 1944.17
Belmont, Anna 1899.08
Belmont, Edna 1908.15
Belmont, Frances 1901.06
Belmont, Grace 1901.01, 1902.07, 1903.17, 1904.05, 1905.37
Belmont, Harry 1919.05
Belmont, Harry T. 1913.35
Belmont, May 1889.02
Belmont, Ralf 1918.24
Belmont, Ruth 1907.55
Belmonte, Herman 1928.29
Belmonte, Vicki 1960.06, 1962.04
Belmore, Bertha 1925.24, 1937.10, 1942.15, 1944.28
Belmore, Daisy 1910.21, 1922.04
Belmore, Herbert 1926.30, 1926.38
Belmore, Lionel 1914.07
Belostotsky, Boris 1925.46, 1925.51
Belot, Adolph 1883.06
Belot, Adolphe 1881.02
Belousov, Vladimir 1990.01
Belson, Jerry 1986.20
Belt, Madeline 1930.24, 1933.06
Belton, John 1897.28
Belton, John E. 1895.23, 1897.50
Belton, Lotta 1880.42, 1882.03, 1882.39
Belton, William 1915.17
Belwin Mills Publishing Corporation 1981.06
Belyea, Jeanne 1917.30
Belyskova, Lydia 1925.51
Belzer, Rick 1981.24, 1995.02
Bemis, Messr. 1882.04
Bemister, Florence 1883.64, 1884.09, 1885.26, 1887.21
Bemko, Gregory 1946.02
Ben-Ari, Neal 1987.12, 1988.09
Ben-Moshe, Rafi 1972.17
Ben-Zali, Daniel 1976.33
Benanti, Laura 1998.03, 1999.24
Benatsky, Ralph 1921.14, 1926.33
Benatzky, Ralph 1930.43, 1936.22
Benavente, Joseph 1928.46
Benchley, Robert 1922.42, 1923.32

Benda, G.K. 1924.01, 1925.42
Benda, Marion 1927.08
Benda, Rosel 1931.44
Bendal 1916.01
Bendall 1884.36
Bendel 1914.27, 1918.01, 1919.34, 1920.14, 1922.17
Bendelari, Aneusto 1880.19
Bendell, Alfred 1913.29
Bender, Charles 1927.11
Bender, Dave 1928.34
Bender, Elly 1897.08
Bender, Jack 1979.08
Bender, Milton 1927.11
Bender, Mr. 1893.29
Bender, Peter 1929.31
Bender, Victor 1944.23, 1947.01
Bender, Wesley 1937.03, 1938.07
Bendile, Gideon 1977.01
Bendix, Max 1910.37, 1912.47, 1913.27, 1914.03, 1914.24, 1916.04, 1916.18, 1918.01, 1921.40, 1926.24, 1926.40
Bendix, Theodore 1883.68, 1886.48, 1886.49, 1886.62, 1898.68, 1905.47, 1910.10, 1912.04, 1912.09
Bendsten, France 1919.37
Bendtsen, Franz 1943.08
Bendul, Kristine 1998.16, 1999.24
Benecke, Marc 1979.15
Benedek, Paul 1916.12
Benedetti, Lino 1964.03
Benedetti, Victor 1996.11
Benedetto, Blanca 1897.16
Benedic, Mons. 1877.14, 1877.19
Benedick, L. 1869.18, 1869.19, 1869.22, 1869.24
Benedick, Mons. 1868.07, 1873.11, 1873.15, 1873.16, 1875.25, 1875.28, 1876.24, 1876.25, 1876.26, 1877.10, 1877.11, 1877.13
Benedict 1869.06, 1869.29, 1869.33, 1870.13
Benedict, A. 1871.10
Benedict, Gail 1975.09, 1976.19, 1986.16
Benedict, Grace 1896.01, 1909.07
Benedict, H. 1869.40
Benedict, Julius 1855.03, 1868.01, 1895.13, 1898.06
Benedict, Kingsley 1905.51
Benedict, L. 1867.12
Benedict, Leon 1965.31
Benedict, Lew 1876.05, 1876.07, 1876.09, 1876.10, 1876.11, 1876.14, 1877.03, 1877.05, 1881.19
Benedict, Marie 1916.20
Benedict, Mary 1871.15
Benedict, Messr. 1876.05
Benedict, Mons. 1876.28
Benedict, Mr. 1870.36
Benedict, Paul 2000.11
Benedict, W.W. 1908.03
Benedikt, Eleanor 1937.11
Benedix, Roderich 1933.23
Benenson, Emily 1977.09
Benes, Jara 1936.22
Benesch, Isaac 1928.20
Benet, Stephen Vincent 1939.20, 1944.32, 1959.09, 1982.14
Benet, William Rose 1944.32
Beneteau, Kate 1902.39
Benetti, Carlo 1927.63
Beneux, L.E. 1866.34, 1867.02
Bengal, Richard 1959.06
Bengali, Richard 1944.02
Bengough 1838.01, 1840.02
Bengough, Mr. 1840.04, 1848.01
Benham, Doris 1918.05
Benham, Dorothy 1989.03
Benham, Earl 1909.16, 1911.33, 1918.09, 1918.18, 1919.35, 1920.10, 1922.33, 1923.10, 1923.46
Benham, Earl J. 1905.41, 1906.28
Benham, Earle 1921.07
Benham, Harry 1903.24, 1918.11
Benham, Howell 1914.28
Beni, Charles 1895.03
Beni, George 1898.63
Beni, James 1951.22
Beni, Messr. 1898.16
Beniades, Ted 1953.03, 1958.05, 1960.11, 1963.05, 1964.32, 1968.16, 1969.12
Benichou, Maurice 1983.16
Benington, Charles 1925.31
Benitz, J.J. 1877.36
Benjamin, Edward 1950.08
Benjamin, Elsie 1945.13
Benjamin, Fred 1971.01
Benjamin, Gladys 1912.36
Benjamin, Joe 1970.08
Benjamin, P.J. 1979.03, 1980.23, 1981.06, 1985.20
Benjamin, Paul 1970.04
Benloch, Julian 1917.25, 1917.33
Bennan, John 1894.49
Bennati, Julia 1887.35, 1887.37, 1887.38, 1887.41
Benner, Bill 1936.26, 1938.18
Bennet, Miss 1861.03
Benneteau, Kate 1898.64
Bennett, Al 1928.23
Bennett, Alan 1962.23, 1964.45
Bennett, Alice 1875.39, 1876.19
Bennett, Allen 1906.19
Bennett, Andy 1918.25
Bennett, Arnold 1968.02
Bennett, Bonnell 1931.44
Bennett, Brenda 1936.15, 1936.16, 1936.19, 1936.23, 1936.25
Bennett, C.D. 1887.11, 1889.20
Bennett, Camilla 1883.02
Bennett, Chester 1927.52
Bennett, Dave 1915.07, 1915.20, 1923.34, 1923.36, 1924.28, 1926.32, 1927.02, 1927.36, 1927.50, 1927.63, 1927.68, 1928.37
Bennett, David 1902.16, 1903.34, 1905.19, 1906.25, 1908.30, 1910.10, 1915.30, 1916.22, 1917.09, 1917.17, 1917.34, 1918.07, 1919.29, 1919.43, 1920.15, 1920.25, 1920.32, 1921.07, 1921.08, 1921.09, 1922.38, 1923.05, 1923.16, 1924.01, 1924.06, 1924.21, 1924.23, 1924.25, 1924.34, 1924.47, 1925.25, 1925.33, 1925.38, 1925.40, 1925.48, 1926.23, 1926.46, 1927.06, 1927.12
Bennett, Eloise 1927.68, 1932.12
Bennett, Elsie 1896.27
Bennett, Evelyn 1926.21, 1927.27, 1927.35, 1928.25
Bennett, F. 1878.14, 1879.56
Bennett, Frank 1876.23, 1879.50, 1880.04
Bennett, Fred 1965.31
Bennett, Frederick 1905.17
Bennett, George F. 1903.24
Bennett, Gordon 1928.45
Bennett, Gussie 1904.56
Bennett, Harry 1878.01
Bennett, Harry Gordon 1942.28
Bennett, Helen 1942.15, 1943.07, 1944.15
Bennett, Hugh 1927.60
Bennett, Joe 1928.23, 1964.17
Bennett, John 1928.23
Bennett, Johnstone 1898.78
Bennett, Jordan 1993.17
Bennett, Joseph 1918.04
Bennett, Keith Robert 1990.14, 1992.06
Bennett, Laura 1880.05, 1881.19, 1888.42, 1895.36, 1897.04
Bennett, Lavinia 1880.02, 1880.67
Bennett, Leo 1911.13
Bennett, Libby 1939.27
Bennett, Linda 1964.46, 1967.09
Bennett, Lois 1926.10, 1927.44, 1927.57, 1927.61
Bennett, Lori Aine 1996.08
Bennett, Mabel 1885.08
Bennett, Magda 1927.09
Bennett, Marie 1906.03
Bennett, Mark 1897.38
Bennett, Martin 1898.20
Bennett, Mary 1913.25
Bennett, Matthew 1997.06
Bennett, Meg 1972.12
Bennett, Messr. 1881.04, 1905.54
Bennett, Michael 1961.28, 1963.21, 1966.30, 1967.14, 1968.31, 1969.17, 1970.13, 1971.05, 1973.06, 1973.14, 1975.15, 1978.27, 1981.29, 1987.07
Bennett, Miss 1861.03
Bennett, Mr. 1881.14
Bennett, Patricia Ann 1976.13, 1978.14
Bennett, Pearl 1923.33
Bennett, Reginald 1927.63
Bennett, Richard 1926.46
Bennett, Richard C. 1897.25
Bennett, Robert Russell 1923.05, 1923.31, 1923.40, 1924.02, 1924.08, 1924.18, 1924.26, 1924.28, 1924.41, 1924.43, 1925.10, 1925.24, 1925.33, 1925.38, 1925.52, 1926.25, 1926.32, 1927.12, 1927.67, 1929.31, 1929.42, 1930.31, 1931.04, 1931.16, 1931.32, 1931.37, 1931.40, 1931.48, 1932.05, 1932.07, 1932.17, 1932.22, 1932.25, 1932.26, 1932.27, 1933.01, 1933.02, 1933.13, 1933.21, 1933.26, 1934.04, 1934.19, 1934.29, 1934.35, 1934.36, 1934.38, 1934.40, 1935.03, 1935.04, 1935.12, 1935.14, 1935.17, 1935.18, 1936.02, 1936.17, 1936.26, 1936.31, 1939.28, 1939.30, 1940.08, 1940.12, 1940.19, 1941.06, 1942.27, 1943.01, 1943.04, 1943.16, 1943.24, 1944.01, 1944.02, 1944.18, 1944.28, 1944.29, 1945.06, 1946.01, 1946.07, 1946.09, 1946.12, 1946.13, 1946.22, 1947.01, 1947.03, 1947.04, 1947.13, 1947.17, 1948.14, 1948.16, 1948.20, 1948.23, 1948.32, 1949.02, 1949.04, 1949.17, 1950.03, 1950.06, 1950.20, 1951.12, 1951.14, 1951.16, 1951.22, 1952.02, 1952.04, 1952.05, 1953.09, 1954.02, 1954.04, 1954.14, 1955.07, 1955.09, 1955.27, 1956.01, 1956.03, 1956.05, 1956.06, 1956.14, 1957.01, 1957.06, 1957.07, 1958.03, 1958.19, 1959.01, 1959.04, 1959.24, 1960.09, 1960.11, 1960.21, 1961.07, 1961.08, 1961.12, 1963.18, 1963.25, 1963.29, 1964.20, 1964.23, 1965.18, 1965.20, 1965.31, 1966.12, 1966.16, 1967.04, 1967.07, 1967.10, 1968.16, 1968.17, 1971.16, 1975.13, 1976.05, 1977.07, 1980.19, 1981.19, 1981.26, 1987.03, 1990.02, 1993.14, 1994.08, 1995.18, 1996.05, 1998.03, 2001.09
Bennett, Roy C. 1989.12
Bennett, Rudolph 1963.06
Bennett, Russell 1922.47, 1924.33
Bennett, Seldon 1925.49, 1939.28, 1946.01, 1948.20
Bennett, Stanley 1930.19
Bennett, Suzanne 1926.22, 1927.27
Bennett, Taylor 1907.50
Bennett, Tony 1974.21
Bennett, Venie 1880.59, 1880.65
Bennett, Venie G. 1880.70
Bennett, Virgil 1911.05
Bennett, Wilda 1911.09, 1914.27, 1917.20, 1918.28, 1919.27, 1921.30, 1922.36, 1924.39
Bennett, William 1889.12
Bennington, Whitney 1904.34
Benny, Ben 1922.29, 1924.07
Benny, Jack 1926.14, 1930.22, 1963.07
Bennyhoff, Eric 1997.19
Benois, Alexander 1925.03
Benois, Nicholas 1925.03
Benoit, Denise 1964.06
Benor, Frank 1906.02, 1906.42, 1908.34
Benrimo, J. 1914.33
Benrimo, J.H. 1915.04, 1915.07, 1915.16, 1915.17, 1915.27, 1915.32, 1916.06, 1916.14, 1917.02, 1917.18, 1927.14, 1930.36
Benrimo, J.K. 1916.25
Bensall, Mr. 1852.04
Benschoten, Mr. 1868.19
Benscoten, Mr. 1859.03
Benson, Ada 1978.09
Benson, Albertina 1903.03, 1903.31, 1904.13
Benson, Albertine 1903.03, 1904.44, 1907.17, 1908.35
Benson, B. 1904.44
Benson, Betty 1955.03
Benson, Gloria 1948.15
Benson, Harry 1927.11
Benson, Jerry 1922.23, 1924.01
Benson, Jodi 1986.20, 1989.07, 1992.02
Benson, La Petite 1871.08
Benson, Lucille 1945.19, 1966.27
Benson, Maude 1905.25
Benson, Messr. 1857.03
Benson, Miss 1904.44
Benson, Morgan 1881.09, 1881.29, 1885.15
Benson, Mr. 1857.02
Benson, Peter 1996.04, 1998.15
Benson, R. 1880.21, 1882.82
Benson, Richard 1947.04
Benson, Robby 1970.15
Benson, Robert 1881.10, 1886.13
Benson, Roy 1932.19, 1961.10
Benson, Sally 1945.08, 1951.18, 1989.23
Benson, Susan 1987.01
Bent, Allston 1904.18
Bent, Marion 1902.43, 1921.06
Bent, William G. 1887.28
Benten, Fremont 1907.18
Benthall, Michael 1968.08, 1969.17
Bentley, Carlton 1940.15
Bentley, Carlton H. 1941.01
Bentley, Carol 1995.02, 1999.24
Bentley, Carole 2001.02
Bentley, Eric 1956.09, 1963.09
Bentley, Irene 1895.15, 1897.26, 1898.38, 1898.56, 1899.25, 1900.20, 1900.33, 1900.41, 1901.13, 1902.16, 1903.41, 1906.47, 1908.21
Bentley, J.B. 1852.06
Bentley, John 1972.02, 1972.23
Bentley, Jordan 1951.14, 1953.03, 1958.05
Bentley, Marjorie 1914.23, 1917.20, 1918.37, 1919.12
Bentley, Miriam 1940.11, 1940.13, 1940.15
Bentley, Mr. 1881.57
Bentley, Muriel 1950.15
Bentley, Robert 1918.42, 1919.35, 1930.02
Bentley, Robert Warren 1937.01
Bentley, Ronald 1983.12, 1985.11, 1988.14
Bentley, S.A.L. 1882.72
Bentley, Spencer 1924.38
Bentley, W.H. 1910.07, 1917.19
Bentley, Walter 1886.02
Bentley, Wilmer 1901.13, 1903.16, 1904.21, 1908.05, 1916.25, 1918.34, 1926.03
Bentley, Wilmer H. 1903.41
Benton, Clara 1893.45
Benton, Fremont 1910.32, 1914.07
Benton, J.W. 1870.05
Benton, Joey 1924.31
Benton, Leila 1902.30, 1905.29, 1907.11, 1910.10
Benton, Lelia 1904.03
Benton, Lila 1912.34
Benton, Marguerite 1939.30, 1941.08
Benton, Miss 1870.05
Benton, Robert 1966.06, 1971.04, 1976.27
Bentson, Alice Kraft 1907.03
Benz, Hamilton 1944.17
Benzell, Mimi 1961.20
Benzinger, Suzy 1991.03, 1993.05, 1999.15
Ber, Julien 1882.53, 1882.58
Ber, Mons. 1882.67
Berans, Mesdame 1852.05
Berbard, Dylln 1895.11
Berben, Nella 1897.10
Berberian, Ara 1974.07, 1974.15
Berchman, Leonard 1942.20
Bercien, Theresa 1908.21
Berdahl, Roger 1982.11
Berenger, Messr. 1852.05
Berens, Beatrice 1934.38
Berenson, Beatrice 1934.13
Berenson, M. 1911.36
Berenson, Meyer 1923.43
Bereny, Henri 1911.44
Bereny, Henry 1912.26
Beres, Bertha 1932.10
Beresford Productions, Ltd. 1964.05, 1976.21
Beresford, Douglas 1927.35
Beresford, Evelyn 1933.07
Beresford, F. 1871.27
Beresford, Faie 1898.69
Beresford, Florence 1918.35
Beresford, Frank 1881.31
Beresford, Harry 1897.56
Beresford, Helen 1891.11, 1892.22, 1892.33, 1893.16
Beresford, J. 1872.06
Beretta, Mlle. 1869.08, 1871.27
Berezowski, Barbara 1977.09
Berg, Anna 1913.29, 1917.31
Berg, Barry 1980.11
Berg, Emily 1904.48
Berg, Emma 1880.69, 1883.10, 1895.02, 1897.06
Berg, Frances 1903.09
Berg, Gene 1940.16
Berg, Gertrude 1973.11
Berg, Harold K. 1935.11
Berg, Jimmy 1939.23
Berg, Kittie 1915.32
Berg, Kitty 1919.06
Berg, Leander 1942.20
Berg, Marion 1898.16
Berg, Miss 1883.38, 1917.31
Berg, Sallie 1900.44
Berg, Tony 1979.30
Bergdorf Goodman 1921.24, 1931.34
Bergdorf Goodman and Company 1920.43
Berge, Alphonse 1949.09

Berge, Sallie 1906.05
Bergea, Vesta 1902.11
Bergen, Eugene 1953.05
Bergen, Nella 1898.25, 1898.48, 1904.17, 1904.50, 1906.18, 1907.57, 1910.25
Bergen, Norman 1971.04, 1976.20
Bergen, Polly 1953.17, 1959.06, 2001.02
Berger, Bob 1928.47
Berger, Chris 1891.04
Berger, Mr. 1893.29
Berger, P. 1870.23
Berger, R. 1911.01
Berger, Richard 2001.03
Berger, Savia 1986.09
Berger, Stephen 1982.01, 1994.09
Berger, Susan 1976.30
Bergere, Florence 1906.31
Bergere, Ilon 1909.15
Bergere, Lee 1943.03, 1972.14
Bergere, Rose 1906.31
Bergere, Roy 1927.36
Bergere, Valerie 1932.14, 1933.03
Bergeron, Francois 1998.18
Bergeron, John 1971.10
Bergersen 1955.26
Bergersen, Baldwin 1937.14, 1938.04, 1943.05, 1943.07, 1944.15, 1945.13, 1948.22, 1963.30
Bergersen, Beau 1942.05
Bergersen, Jeanne 1938.04
Bergerson, Baldwin 1940.23, 1946.21
Bergeson, Scott 1980.04, 1980.25, 1981.21, 1982.16, 1982.21, 1983.13, 1985.13, 1986.08, 1988.18, 1993.12
Berget, Paul 1973.07
Bergey, Carol 1963.23, 1964.08, 1964.09, 1964.14, 1968.12
Bergh, Stormy 1938.08
Berghof, Herbert 1939.23, 1940.04, 1949.08
Bergin, Joan 2000.05
Berglund, Michael 1987.05
Bergman Studios 1925.05, 1926.51
Bergman, Alan 1964.35, 1976.32, 1978.27, 1979.19, 1983.09, 1984.15, 1990.09, 1992.18, 1994.13
Bergman, Caryl 1929.31, 1932.03
Bergman, Harry 1905.25
Bergman, Henry 1896.29, 1897.54, 1899.38, 1900.44, 1903.40, 1906.05, 1906.32, 1908.07, 1910.09, 1911.23, 1912.05, 1916.09, 1917.08
Bergman, Ingmar 1973.04, 1990.07, 1991.08
Bergman, Jack 1909.19
Bergman, Marilyn 1964.35, 1976.32, 1978.27, 1979.19, 1983.09, 1984.15, 1990.09, 1992.18, 1994.13
Bergman, Mr. 1793.01
Bergman, R.W. 1931.13
Bergman, Sandahl 1973.12
Bergmann-Nayan Studios 1920.24
Bergquist, Eleanor 1966.27
Berhe, Mlle. 1880.16
Beri, Ben 1941.11
Beri, Beth 1923.07, 1926.18
Berini, Mario 1946.17
Berinstein, Dori 1993.01, 1995.16
Beriozoff, Nicolas 1944.28
Beriza, Marguerite 1915.02
Berk, David 1968.32
Berk, Lew 1918.36
Berke, Dorothea 1932.23
Berkeley, Ballard 1947.15
Berkeley, Busby 1925.36, 1926.34, 1927.56, 1927.65, 1928.16, 1928.23, 1928.25, 1928.44, 1928.50, 1929.09, 1929.22, 1929.28, 1929.32, 1930.06, 1930.09, 1930.38, 1971.03
Berkeley, Buzz 1927.15
Berkeley, Martin 1927.12
Berker, Maidie 1911.43
Berkes, Johnny 1916.03, 1918.05, 1920.47
Berkes, Will 1903.26
Berkley, Charles 1925.37
Berkley, Olive 1884.23
Berkman, John 1969.07, 1969.14, 1970.07, 1971.05, 1971.16, 1972.04, 1972.22, 2001.02
Berkman, Lee 1937.02
Berkowitz, Miss 1857.02
Berkowitz, Sol 1962.24, 1981.21
Berkowsky, Paul B. 1995.14
Berkson, Michael 1966.27
Berl, Herman 1893.06
Berle, Milton 1932.18, 1934.20, 1943.05, 1943.20, 1951.18, 1997.01
Berlein, Anna Mack 1882.74, 1882.79
Berlein, Annie Mack 1883.32, 1904.46
Berlin, Irving 1910.01, 1910.18, 1910.19, 1910.25, 1910.33, 1911.08, 1911.18, 1911.24, 1911.30, 1911.34, 1911.45, 1912.07, 1912.09, 1912.24, 1912.25, 1912.31, 1912.45, 1913.16, 1914.02, 1914.22, 1914.31, 1915.15, 1915.24, 1915.31, 1916.09, 1916.10, 1916.11, 1916.24, 1917.03, 1917.19, 1917.22, 1917.37, 1918.18, 1918.19, 1918.21, 1918.23, 1918.34, 1919.12, 1919.15, 1919.16, 1919.18, 1919.20, 1920.18, 1920.33, 1921.30, 1922.25, 1922.39, 1923.32, 1924.44, 1925.22, 1925.23, 1925.45, 1927.21, 1927.37, 1931.21, 1932.05, 1933.02, 1933.22, 1938.08, 1940.08, 1942.18, 1942.20, 1942.23, 1943.02, 1946.12, 1949.08, 1950.15, 1952.11, 1953.12, 1955.13, 1958.03, 1962.20, 1965.05, 1966.12, 1966.16, 1976.32, 1979.11, 1979.13, 1980.09, 1980.18, 1983.09, 1988.08, 1989.03, 1989.06, 1989.16, 1989.21, 1990.09, 1991.04, 1991.10, 1992.18, 1995.12, 1997.01, 1998.11, 1998.19, 1999.01, 1999.04
Berlind, Roger 1976.08, 1976.33, 1979.24, 1984.01, 1986.06, 1988.17, 1989.03, 1989.29, 1992.04, 1994.05, 1996.06, 1997.07, 1997.08, 1999.19, 2000.08
Berlind, Roger S. 1981.06, 1982.09
Berliner, George 1914.24
Berliner, Rudolf 1911.07
Berlinger, Warren 1946.12, 1978.28
Berlingieri, Osvaldo 1985.07, 1999.18
Berlioz, Hector 1978.26
Berlo, Florence 1917.16
Berlo, Lillian 1917.16
Berlo, Madeline 1917.16
Berlo, Pauline 1917.16
Berlo, Twinnie 1917.16
Berloni, William 1991.15, 1998.06, 1999.11
Berlow, George 1923.04
Berman Costume Company 1959.14
Berman, Gail 1982.03
Berman, Howard A. 1921.31
Berman, L.E. 1908.25
Berman, M. 1963.01, 1965.23
Berman, Norman L. 1979.29
Berman, Shelley 1959.23, 1962.01, 1980.24
Bermejo, Felipe 1988.15
Bermel, Albert 2000.10
Bern, Mina 1966.21, 1967.08, 1970.17, 1990.16
Bernadez, Marcelo 1993.08
Bernal, Barry 1987.05, 1991.03, 1993.02
Bernard 1922.05
Bernard, Ada 1896.25, 1898.27
Bernard, Alice 1922.09
Bernard, Barney 1907.35, 1907.45, 1908.07, 1908.19, 1909.12, 1909.28, 1911.12, 1911.43, 1912.09, 1912.43
Bernard, Ben 1930.28, 1932.08
Bernard, Bob 1948.15, 1949.17, 1959.25, 1963.22
Bernard, C. 1873.08
Bernard, C.B. 1961.10
Bernard, Charles 1981.29
Bernard, Dick 1898.56, 1899.36, 1900.41, 1907.44
Bernard, Dodo 1918.01
Bernard, F. 1899.37
Bernard, Frank 1902.23, 1903.18, 1905.34, 1919.32, 1921.34, 1923.17
Bernard, G.P. 1883.05, 1883.07
Bernard, George 1909.15
Bernard, Hattie 1897.06, 1898.02, 1900.08
Bernard, Ida 1911.36
Bernard, II., Sam 1932.19
Bernard, Jake 1901.28
Bernard, James 1882.04
Bernard, Joe 1955.06
Bernard, Joseph 1956.15
Bernard, Jr., Sam 1934.14
Bernard, Kevin 1995.02
Bernard, Le Clair 1900.44
Bernard, Lester 1907.35, 1907.45, 1928.25
Bernard, Lisette 1869.36, 1869.37
Bernard, Lizette 1870.01, 1870.12, 1870.14
Bernard, Lizzette 1869.42, 1870.09
Bernard, Loraine 1907.07, 1907.49
Bernard, Maison 1914.06
Bernard, Mamie 1885.54, 1890.42
Bernard, Marion 1880.31
Bernard, Messr. 1882.04, 1882.20
Bernard, Mike 1900.56
Bernard, Mr. 1854.03, 1869.02, 1870.20, 1872.19
Bernard, Murray 1912.16
Bernard, Nellie 1900.45
Bernard, Oliver 1955.19
Bernard, Oliver P. 1907.39
Bernard, Peter 1918.31
Bernard, Pierre 1868.01, 1868.11
Bernard, Raymond 1966.20, 1968.21
Bernard, Robert 1944.21
Bernard, Rosalind 1927.04
Bernard, Sam 1888.43, 1896.26, 1896.36, 1897.09, 1897.19, 1897.31, 1897.48, 1898.58, 1898.72, 1899.19, 1900.20, 1900.41, 1901.17, 1902.35, 1903.33, 1905.20, 1906.37, 1908.10, 1910.25, 1912.49, 1913.28, 1914.10, 1916.24, 1920.03, 1921.30, 1923.33, 1927.04
Bernard, Sophye 1911.41, 1917.16
Bernard, Suzanne 1956.08
Bernard, Tristan 1907.46, 1913.31
Bernard, Victor 1896.29
Bernard, Vivian 1894.49
Bernard, Will R. 1892.48, 1892.53
Bernardes, Elaine Garcia Emerson 1992.13
Bernardi, Herschel 1964.40, 1968.30, 1981.18
Bernardi, Mario 1974.16
Bernardi, Roberto 1941.07
Bernardo, Luis 1988.06
Bernaski, Fred 1946.22
Bernauer, Rudolf 1913.23, 1913.36, 1917.15
Bernauer, Rudolph 1909.22, 1910.28, 1921.40, 1930.03, 1931.33, 1934.12, 1942.17, 1947.06
Berners, Lord 1963.03
Berney, William 1948.16
Bernhard, Arnold 1985.02
Bernhard, George 1977.18
Bernhard, Sandra 1998.14
Bernhardt, Don 1982.11
Bernhauser, Rudolf 1922.40
Bernicat, Firmin 1884.37, 1884.48, 1884.50, 1885.44, 1888.07
Bernie, Al 1934.39
Bernie, Ben 1928.17, 1928.50, 1976.04, 1980.10, 1986.06, 1989.06
Bernie, Dick 1942.20, 1948.23, 1949.01, 1965.05
Bernie, Murray 1930.22
Bernier, Buddy 1955.13, 1992.03
Bernier, Daisy 1938.09
Bernier, Estelle 1931.32
Bernier, Peggy 1931.01
Bernis, Alberto 1881.24
Bernstein, Aline 1924.14, 1925.20, 1926.17, 1927.23, 1928.19, 1929.20, 1949.16, 1950.18, 1953.05, 1953.14, 1958.13, 1959.10
Bernstein, Anne L. 1999.07
Bernstein, Dori 1998.17
Bernstein, Douglas 1985.15
Bernstein, Elmer 1954.13, 1967.16, 1983.01
Bernstein, Ira 1968.03, 1970.03, 1978.02, 1979.24
Bernstein, Jeff D. 1892.21, 1893.37, 1905.32, 1908.28
Bernstein, Leonard 1944.33, 1947.21, 1950.08, 1953.03, 1955.05, 1956.15, 1957.12, 1958.05, 1958.09, 1958.21, 1960.08, 1962.17, 1963.05, 1964.17, 1967.09, 1968.18, 1971.15, 1972.15, 1974.06, 1974.09, 1976.11, 1977.02, 1977.05, 1978.26, 1979.13, 1980.02, 1982.20, 1983.13, 1986.08, 1989.03, 1989.06, 1989.14, 1991.10, 1994.09, 1997.01, 1997.10, 1998.11, 1998.16, 2000.07, 2001.04
Bernstein, Lillian 1984.11
Bernstein, Richard 2001.03
Bernstein, Richard N. 1961.11
Bernstein, Robert A. 1955.11
Bernstein, Shirley 1952.15
Bernstein, Sid 1966.30
Berolde, Judith 1890.35, 1892.01, 1903.07
Beron, Elba 1985.07
Beroni, Duicha 1885.01
Beroza, Janet 1979.11, 1991.15
Berr, Georges 1911.11, 1912.28, 1912.34, 1930.43
Berrand, Louise 1948.04
Berrar, Mons. 1876.31
Berre, Charles 1938.02
Berresse, Michael 1990.18, 1994.01, 1996.14, 1999.10, 1999.19
Berri, Beth 1927.13
Berri, J. 1881.35
Berri, Maud Lillian 1898.54
Berri, Maude Lillian 1900.13, 1900.14, 1900.18, 1902.44, 1904.47, 1907.13
Berrian, Lillian 1907.03
Berrian, William 1948.27
Berrick, Milfred 1908.28
Berry, Aimee 1908.03
Berry, Ananias 1930.13, 1931.11
Berry, Audrey 1927.07, 1927.60
Berry, Betty 1943.08
Berry, Chuck 1977.10, 1982.22, 1986.02
Berry, Denny 2000.09
Berry, Dorothy 1911.38, 1913.04
Berry, Eddie 1949.05
Berry, Eric 1954.09, 1972.22
Berry, Jack 1940.18
Berry, James 1931.11
Berry, John 1975.09
Berry, Ken 1959.14, 1961.16
Berry, L. 1999.24
Berry, Lee 1969.12
Berry, Leigh 1973.07
Berry, Leon 1939.29, 1980.10, 1999.01
Berry, Leonard 1935.17
Berry, Lillian 1911.15
Berry, Lynne 1922.26
Berry, Mabel 1911.38
Berry, Marilyn 1957.09
Berry, Mary Sue 1959.02
Berry, Mr. 1864.12, 1864.15
Berry, Robert 1936.01
Berry, T.B. 1864.21
Berry, Warren 1931.11
Berry, William J. 1893.33
Berse, Ellen 1961.20
Bershadsky, Sadie 1937.14
Berson, Beulah 1923.18, 1926.05
Bert, Flo 1921.25
Bertal-Maubon 1924.36, 1925.05, 1925.10
Bertay, Michel 1964.06
Berte, Emile 1929.17
Berte, Heinrich 1912.04, 1921.31, 1923.14, 1923.15, 1924.12, 1926.05, 1931.07, 1943.12
Bertha, Miss 1873.26
Bertha, Mlle. 1867.24, 1868.25, 1873.10
Berthald, Barron 1894.40
Berthat, Mons. 1869.05
Berthe, Madame 1944.19
Berthe, Mlle. 1879.19, 1879.36, 1879.39, 1879.40, 1879.45, 1879.46, 1879.47, 1879.48, 1879.60, 1880.23, 1880.27, 1880.28, 1880.29, 1880.52, 1880.60, 1883.30, 1884.43, 1884.52, 1884.54
Berthe, Mme. 1882.58, 1932.13
Berthon, Mlle. 1871.24
Berthon, Mons. 1871.28, 1872.03, 1872.33, 1872.41, 1872.42, 1873.01
Berti, Michelle 1998.18
Bertil, Guy 1965.37
Bertin, Paris 1929.10, 1929.11, 1929.13, 1929.14, 1929.15, 1929.16
Bertin, Pierre 1964.06
Bertina, Mlle. 1900.53
Bertini, Nina 1887.47, 1892.27
Berton, Charles 1911.18, 1911.26, 1927.45
Berton, Eugene 1947.13
Berton, Phyllis 1899.36
Bertotto, Mlle. 1890.25
Bertoza 1881.32
Bertram, Helen 1890.08, 1891.13, 1893.05, 1893.09, 1894.38, 1895.13, 1897.24, 1900.25, 1900.31, 1900.50, 1903.10, 1905.56, 1907.14, 1932.02, 1932.14
Bertrand, A. 1893.23
Bertrand, Beatrice 1907.10
Bertrand, Claire 1915.31
Bertrand, Dorothy 1904.40, 1905.18, 1906.01
Bertrand, Helen 1908.33
Bertrand, Irma 1911.39
Bertrand, M.A. 1892.38, 1894.34
Beruh, Joseph 1970.08, 1974.13, 1974.17, 1975.05, 1976.17, 1981.09
Berwick, Nellie 1898.15, 1898.28
Besch, Anthony 1964.42, 1966.23, 1968.27
Besche 1888.20, 1889.04, 1890.19
Besche, Lucien 1886.54, 1890.33
Besesti, Mlle. 1876.12
Beson, Ruth 1918.10
Besoyan, Rick 1963.20
Besser, Gedalia 1989.10

Besser, Joe 1941.11, 1946.22
Besserer, Hermione 1902.18
Bessette, Mimi 1982.11
Bessie, Alvah 1925.17
Bessieres, Mlle. 1871.23, 1871.25, 1871.26
Bessieres, Mons. 1871.23, 1871.24, 1871.25, 1871.26
Bessinger, Dorothy 1891.21
Bessinger, Frank 1918.18
Bessinger, Harry 1961.13
Besson, Larry 1931.26
Bessy, Maurice 1978.22
Best, Bettie 1915.01
Best, Ellen 1919.08
Best, Jack 1955.13
Best, Larry 1967.03
Best, Margaret 1920.37
Best, Paul 1941.10, 1942.31, 1945.04, 1945.19, 1947.04, 1955.02
Bestal, Fred 1983.17
Beste, Miss 1890.31, 1894.01
Besterman, Brian 1995.14, 1996.08, 1997.15
Besterman, Doug 2000.11
Besterman, Douglas 1994.01, 1995.07, 1995.19, 1996.15, 1997.12, 1997.22, 1998.20, 1999.01, 1999.21, 2000.18, 2000.19, 2001.05
Bestic, W. 1894.18
Bestor, Vernon 1922.18
Bestor, Vernon E. 1922.18
Besuner, Pearl 1931.46
Beswick, Harry 1913.23
Bethe, David 1934.05
Bethea, David 1943.07
Bethel, Janet 1948.15
Bethel, Pepsi 1961.24
Bethel, Tom 1930.16
Bethel, Virginia 1929.39
Bethell, Anna 1947.22, 1948.01, 1948.02, 1948.03, 1948.06, 1948.07, 1948.09, 1948.10
Bethune, Zina 1956.04
Betove, M. 1929.05
Betrand, A. 1890.50
Bettels, Gussie 1905.31
Bettger, Lyle 1948.25
Betti, H. 1947.05
Betti, Henri 1948.12, 1955.14, 1959.15, 1964.02, 1964.22, 1965.08, 1973.17
Bettinelli, Angelo 1932.19
Bettinson, Rob 1990.15
Bettis, Valerie 1946.24, 1948.14, 1950.06, 1950.19, 1966.05
Betts, Billy 1914.24
Betts, Dorothy 1914.33, 1919.07
Betts, George S. 1900.45
Betts, William 1908.13, 1918.01
Betty, Mlle. 1882.67, 1883.41
Betty, Mme. 1882.55, 1882.61
Betz, Miss 1870.31
Beug, John 1975.08
Beury, James P. 1925.35
Beuvell, Jack 1933.15
Bevan, Alison 1986.04, 1986.10, 1987.11, 1997.07
Bevan, Frank 1938.11, 1944.28
Bevan, Mae 1908.07
Bevans, James 1883.36
Bevans, Philippa 1956.01
Bevel, Charles 1999.09
Beverley, Gaile 1928.16
Beverley, Louise 1872.21
Beverly, Alfred 1876.19, 1877.24
Beverly, Budd 1898.02
Beverly, E.D. 1879.23
Beverly, E.S. 1900.12
Beverly, Gail 1923.23, 1924.13
Beverly, Gaile 1925.43, 1926.25
Beverly, Louise 1872.22
Beverly, Maude 1885.04
Beverly, Mildred 1906.38, 1907.56
Beverly, Mr. 1876.19
Beverly, Richard 1879.24
Beverly, Vera 1895.15
Beverly, W. 1888.41
Beverly, William 1888.38
Bevins, Clem 1907.34
Bevins, Franc C. 1904.41
Bevis, Mrs. 1857.02
Bew, Andy 1972.04
Bew, Andy G. 1969.14
Bewley, Lois 1954.17, 1959.06
Bey, Chief 1973.10
Bey, Marki 1972.06
Bey, Salome 1972.18, 1976.35
Beyer, Enis 1939.22
Beyer, William 1925.20, 1926.17
Bhaskar 1960.10
Bhumibol 1950.12
Biagi, Michael 1992.18
Biagi, Randall 1992.18
Bial, Albert 1884.59, 1884.65, 1885.12, 1885.18, 1885.31, 1885.39, 1885.51, 1885.62, 1886.07, 1886.17, 1886.29, 1886.31, 1886.38, 1886.53, 1889.27, 1889.30, 1889.32, 1889.42, 1889.53, 1890.05, 1890.09, 1890.13, 1890.22, 1890.38, 1890.42, 1890.45, 1891.10, 1891.16, 1891.19, 1891.35, 1892.02, 1892.13, 1892.26, 1892.32, 1892.41, 1892.49, 1893.01, 1893.04, 1893.22, 1893.41, 1897.14
Bial, E. 1924.15
Bial, John 1884.36
Bial, Rudolf 1882.43
Bialik, Ch. N. 1970.17
Bianchi, Nicholas 1960.10
Bianchini, Cledat de la Vigerie 1890.33
Biancifiori, Alfredo 1893.23
Biancifiori, Alberto 1897.27
Bianco, Larry 1964.02
Bianco, Lorenzo 1963.08
Biancofiore, Anne Nicole 1999.15
Biazzi, Miss 1894.21
Bibb, Leon 1946.12, 1966.15, 1968.32
Biber, Colonel Saul 1972.17
Biberman, Abner 1937.01
Biberman, Herbert J. 1931.02
Bibeyran, Mamert 1885.46, 1888.20, 1889.23, 1890.01, 1890.03, 1890.11, 1890.19, 1890.26, 1890.40, 1891.31, 1891.34, 1891.38, 1891.47, 1892.25, 1892.29, 1893.02, 1893.07
Bibeyran, Mimert 1892.55
Bibl, Rudolf 1984.03, 1984.04, 1984.05
Bible, Frances 1956.10
Biblo, Irving 1920.41
Bibo 1875.34
Bibo, Irving 1921.27, 1922.14, 1924.36, 1925.25, 1927.39
Bichel, Ken 1975.23, 1977.04
Bichel, Kenneth 1978.12
Bick, Jack 1915.26
Bickel, George 1904.58, 1908.19, 1909.28, 1910.18, 1912.43, 1919.13, 1920.17, 1921.22, 1924.07, 1927.17
Bickel, George L. 1905.34, 1911.37, 1918.06
Bickel, Margaret 1931.10
Bickell, George 1907.24
Bickerton, Jr., Joseph P. 1913.21
Bickford, Louisa 1883.22
Bicknell, G. 1866.18
Bicknell, Ralph 1897.22, 1901.04
Biddle, Earl 1929.04
Biddle, Nicholas 1895.18
Biddle, Nicholas H. 1903.18
Bidwell, Mr. 1869.43
Bidwell, Patrick 1908.43
Bidwell, Raye 1943.23
Biel, Anne Christine 1983.16
Bienstock, Freddy 1993.10
Bienstock, Miriam 1979.29
Bier, Burt 1961.02, 1961.20, 1962.27, 1965.33, 1966.27
Bier, Stanton 1938.13
Bierko, Craig 2000.11
Bierman, Emil 1901.23, 1904.11, 1910.11
Biermann, Emil 1897.33
Biers, David 1898.34
Bietenkant, L. 1923.14
Big Apple Circus, The 1980.07
Bigard, Albany 1997.03
Bigard, Albany "Barney" 1981.06
Bigby, Dorothy 1942.18
Bigelow, C.A. 1885.36, 1885.37, 1885.38
Bigelow, Charles 1885.34, 1911.32
Bigelow, Charles A. 1896.35, 1896.48, 1897.37, 1898.51, 1901.25, 1902.29, 1904.04, 1904.18, 1904.39, 1906.01, 1906.45, 1908.06, 1908.39, 1909.25, 1910.26
Bigelow, Charles E. 1895.38
Bigelow, Dorothie 1916.06, 1926.46
Bigelow, Joe 1946.06
Bigelow, Lenore 1879.63
Bigelow, Robert 1924.13
Bigelow, Roger 1968.24, 1972.04, 1974.18
Bigelow, Sadie 1880.08
Bigelow, Susan 1978.12, 1986.18, 1987.03
Bigelow, Walter 1926.07
Bigge, Glyn 1892.25
Biggers, Earl Derr 1919.23
Bigley, Isabel 1950.17, 1953.08
Biglin, J. 1879.02
Bihari, Jules 1999.06
Bihin, Monsieur 1862.02
Bijou Burlesque Company 1884.20
Bijou Comic Opera Company 1882.05, 1897.24
Bijou Opera House Company 1882.16, 1882.19, 1882.52
Bikel, Theodore 1959.24, 1964.18, 1966.05
Bilabel, Barbara 1984.04
Bilbao, Antonio 1917.25
Bilby, J.D. 1861.04
Bilby, J.H. 1862.09, 1863.01, 1863.02, 1863.03, 1863.04
Bilby, Mr. 1856.03, 1862.07
Bilby, W.H. 1863.08
Bilchler, J. 1865.01
Bilder, Mr. 1898.53
Bildner, Ida 1938.04
Bilencova, Elizabeth 1937.11
Bilhaud, Paul 1913.34
Bill Nye Comedy Company 1891.27
Bill, Leo 1926.01, 1927.37
Billaud, Paul 1904.35
Biller, Kenneth 1988.07
Billig, Robert 1978.13, 1982.11, 1984.10, 1985.08, 1987.04, 1991.03, 1994.06
Billings, A.D. 1869.46, 1869.47, 1881.31
Billings, C.E. 1902.15
Billings, Cliff 1935.12
Billings, Irene 1949.06
Billings, James 1913.02, 1915.17, 1921.09, 1971.06, 1974.07, 1974.15, 1975.17, 1976.22, 1976.23, 1976.26, 1977.03, 1977.17, 1978.07, 1978.19, 1978.20, 1979.20, 1979.21, 1980.21, 1980.22, 1981.20, 1981.21, 1981.22, 1982.07, 1982.16, 1982.20, 1982.21, 1983.13, 1984.11, 1984.12, 1985.09, 1985.11, 1985.13, 1986.04, 1986.08, 1986.09, 1986.10, 1987.03, 1987.08, 1987.11, 1988.04, 1988.14, 1988.16, 1988.18, 1989.13, 1989.14, 1990.13, 1993.12, 1993.13, 1995.10, 1996.02, 1996.11, 1997.02
Billings, Jeff 1984.16
Billings, Marie 1880.03
Billingsley, Jennifer 1961.10
Billington, F. 1885.47
Billington, Fred 1887.10
Billington, Ken 1972.13, 1975.13, 1976.36, 1977.05, 1978.02, 1978.07, 1978.12, 1978.19, 1978.20, 1979.06, 1979.18, 1979.20, 1979.21, 1979.28, 1980.04, 1980.06, 1980.09, 1980.25, 1980.29, 1981.08, 1981.12, 1981.18, 1981.19, 1982.06, 1982.12, 1982.18, 1982.20, 1983.13, 1984.06, 1984.11, 1984.13, 1984.14, 1985.05, 1986.01, 1986.08, 1987.02, 1987.09, 1987.12, 1987.14, 1989.13, 1989.14, 1989.21, 1989.23, 1990.18, 1992.05, 1993.05, 1993.19, 1995.08, 1995.13, 1996.14, 1997.04, 1997.05, 1997.10, 1998.07, 1998.13
Billon, Louise 1868.03
Billone, Joseph 1981.19
Billy Birch's San Francisco Minstrels 1883.56
Billy, Little 1916.02, 1927.38
Bilous, Vanina 1999.18
Binder, Jay 1998.03
Binder, Roy 1918.18, 1922.30
Bindley, Florence 1904.33, 1905.50, 1906.34
Bines, David 1963.10
Binford, Marguerite 1894.37, 1900.47, 1902.06, 1908.36
Bing, George 1912.24
Binger, James H. 1995.12
Binger, Messr. 1886.36
Bingham 1964.28
Bingham, Amelia 1897.29
Bingham, Bob 1971.12
Bingham, Edward 1903.18
Bingham, F.H. 1880.41
Bingham, George 1919.06
Bingham, J.A. 1911.22
Bingham, Joseph A. 1909.29
Bingham, Leslie 1931.48, 1933.13
Bingham, Mary Alice 1945.04, 1946.07
Bingham, Messr. 1904.13, 1904.44
Bingham, Vincent 1996.07
Binkley, Howell 1993.09, 1995.05, 1998.05, 1998.21, 1999.08, 1999.23, 2000.15
Binkley, Jay 1898.44
Binkow, Aaron 1910.15
Binney, Constance 1918.03, 1924.03
Binns, Frank 1922.31
Binotto, Paul 1981.29, 1984.13
Biondi, Remo 1980.29
Biovannini, Sandro 1964.03
Birabeau, Andre 1927.68
Birbeck, C.J. 1884.26
Birch's San Francisco 1883.66
Birch, Billy 1879.09, 1880.15, 1881.55, 1883.66, 1909.25
Birch, Desdemona 1883.03
Birch, Edna 1900.38, 1901.17, 1902.29, 1907.11, 1908.39
Birch, Fanny 1875.31
Birch, Gertie 1913.36
Birch, Hannah 1875.37, 1875.40, 1876.01, 1876.19
Birch, John 1903.25, 1917.29
Birch, Mr. 1863.07
Birch, Patricia 1956.05, 1957.03, 1958.07, 1958.14, 1960.08, 1970.20, 1971.11, 1972.12, 1973.04, 1974.05, 1974.06, 1976.02, 1976.33, 1977.08, 1978.23, 1979.04, 1979.08, 1979.19, 1979.27, 1982.20, 1983.13, 1984.11, 1984.12, 1985.10, 1986.03, 1986.08, 1986.16, 1987.12, 1989.07, 1989.12, 1989.14, 1990.08, 1990.13, 1992.11, 1993.13, 1995.10, 1997.02, 1997.10, 1998.21, 1999.05
Birch, Peter 1942.17, 1942.21, 1942.22, 1943.08, 1945.05, 1949.18
Birch, Reginald 1894.42
Birch, Walter 1864.18, 1864.19, 1864.20, 1869.41
Bircham, Lily 1903.21
Bircher, Betsy 1988.13
Birchler, J. 1867.12
Birchler, L. 1869.26, 1871.11
Birchler, Louis 1871.09
Birchler, Mr. 1866.02, 1866.28
Birckhead, Muriel 1952.15
Bird, Charles E. 1929.44
Bird, Dorothy 1939.26, 1946.13, 1946.20, 1948.18
Bird, Edward 1930.41
Bird, Ethel M. 1881.22
Bird, Howard 1937.08
Bird, Mary 1877.01, 1879.37, 1879.68, 1880.09, 1880.36, 1880.64, 1881.09, 1881.29, 1882.02
Birdie, Conrad 1981.07
Birdie, William 1923.17
Birdsell, Hattie 1884.27
Birdwood, Judy 1964.29
Birgfeld, A. 1868.25, 1868.27
Birgfeld, Adolph 1868.30, 1868.31, 1869.01, 1869.09, 1869.10, 1869.12, 1869.19
Birgfeld, Adolphe 1867.30
Birkenhead, Susan 1978.12, 1992.08, 1997.18, 1998.05
Birkhead, Muriel 1959.02
Birkle, Carrie 1894.25
Birkmayer, Toni 1929.51
Birmingham, Virginia 1921.19
Birn, Arthur 1930.35
Birney, Estella 1920.43
Birney, Estelle 1923.34
Biro, Lajos 1932.06
Birse, Messr. 1922.06, 1923.28
Birse, Mme. 1922.06, 1923.28, 1925.03, 1927.51, 1929.05
Birsky, Socrates 1953.07
Birth, Patricia 1957.11
Bischoff, Fraulein 1879.62
Bisher, Hamad 1925.37
Bishoff, Joel 1990.02
Bishop 1869.02
Bishop, Adelaide 1943.12, 1945.17, 1948.31, 1953.15, 1954.06, 1959.09
Bishop, Andre 1994.02, 1995.09, 1996.16, 1998.21, 1999.22, 2000.16
Bishop, Andrew 1929.01, 1992.17
Bishop, B. 1886.59
Bishop, Billy 1980.13
Bishop, Bob 1963.14
Bishop, Brigham 1876.31, 1879.32, 1884.62
Bishop, C.B. 1886.45, 1887.06, 1887.14
Bishop, Carole 1968.03, 1968.31
Bishop, Carole Kelly 1975.15
Bishop, Charles B. 1887.13
Bishop, F.A. 1912.12
Bishop, Frankie 1879.30

Bishop, Fred 1912.33, 1917.11, 1927.38
Bishop, Fred A. 1919.07
Bishop, Frederic A. 1911.38
Bishop, Frederick A. 1910.09
Bishop, George 1914.18
Bishop, Henry 1851.01, 1854.01, 1863.09, 1880.01
Bishop, Henry R. 1855.01
Bishop, Joe 1942.11, 1985.08
Bishop, John 1965.09
Bishop, Kenyon 1918.31
Bishop, Lillian 1891.18, 1892.49, 1893.22, 1894.11
Bishop, Linda 1950.12
Bishop, Mesame 1856.04
Bishop, Miss 1851.05
Bishop, Mr. 1857.08, 1859.08
Bishop, Philip 1919.29
Bishop, Randy 1980.05
Bishop, Richard 1951.22, 1955.08
Bishop, Robert 1962.01, 1962.15, 1963.04
Bishop, T. 1852.05
Bishop, W. 1881.33
Bishop, Walter 1999.24
Bisihop, Andre 2000.07
Bising, Harry 1905.53
Bisland, Edward 1919.34
Bissell, Gene P. 1968.13
Bissell, Marian 1958.08, 1959.03
Bissell, Richard 1954.05, 1957.08, 1958.08, 1959.03, 1973.15, 1989.04
Bissell, Whitner 1932.28, 1942.27, 1943.23
Bisset, Messr. 1794.01
Bissett, Esther 1911.01, 1911.17, 1911.45
Bissett, William 1904.45
Bissing, H. 1905.25, 1905.41, 1907.24
Bissing, Harry 1902.24, 1904.31, 1905.30, 1906.02, 1906.42, 1907.37
Bissinger, Paul 1929.19
Bisson 1917.32
Bisson, Alexandre 1892.08, 1920.04
Bistolfi, Gian 1932.29, 1934.02
Bitar, Virginia 1964.07, 1964.10, 1964.12, 1964.13, 1964.14, 1965.10, 1965.11, 1965.12, 1965.13
Bittan, Roy 1972.09
Bittner, Jack 1946.24, 1965.03, 1965.27, 1966.02, 1966.04, 1966.17, 1968.09, 1968.14, 1982.05
Bittner, Julius 1934.29
Bixby, Frank 1910.33
Bixby, Jonathan 1993.03, 1995.13, 1997.21, 1999.05
Bixler, Valerie Leigh 1982.11
Bizard, Henry 1896.48
Bizet 1894.21, 1927.28
Bizet, Georges 1880.35, 1881.47, 1930.15, 1943.24, 1945.06, 1946.09, 1956.06, 1956.11, 1997.01
Bizzaroli, Oreste 1884.58
Bjornson, Maria 1988.01, 1990.04
Blaber, Anne-Marie 1981.21
Black Eyed Susan 1954.08
Black Goat Entertainment 1984.15
Black, Allie 1894.13
Black, Annie 1898.58, 1898.77
Black, Ben 1920.18, 1930.35
Black, Catherine 1907.35
Black, David 1964.29, 1968.07, 1968.11, 1972.03, 1972.23, 1980.17
Black, Don 1983.01, 1985.12, 1990.04, 1992.12, 1994.10
Black, Donald 1927.01, 1935.15, 1938.11
Black, Dr. Frank 1946.06
Black, Eddie 1938.03
Black, Frank 1928.35
Black, Georgie 1898.03
Black, Gertrude 1908.20
Black, Ivy 1929.01
Black, J. Wallace 1899.23
Black, Maurice 1919.25, 1920.39
Black, Miss 1870.31
Black, Nettie 1890.24, 1891.17, 1891.22, 1908.30
Black, Rachel 1998.20
Black, Robin 1979.05
Black, Ruth 1905.43
Black, Sol 1937.13
Black, Violet 1895.41
Black, W. Wallace 1895.18, 1898.05, 1904.21
Black, W.W. 1895.38, 1908.35, 1910.29
Black, Wallace W. 1903.18
Black, Walter 1952.13
Black, William 1897.26, 1901.23, 1972.21
Black, William W. 1899.02, 1903.18, 1906.20, 1907.21
Black, William Wallace 1902.16
Black-Brown, Shirley 1979.32, 1985.03
Blackbirds Productions, Inc. 1931.11
Blackburn, Arlington 1918.18
Blackburn, Clarice 1959.04
Blackburn, Fayne 1967.01
Blackburn, Frank A. 1877.24
Blackburn, Harrison 1930.16, 1931.47
Blackburn, Mark 1919.12
Blackburn, Mary 1918.18, 1918.26, 1919.01
Blackburn, Mary C. 1884.10
Blackburn, Ramon 1941.11
Blackburn, Rhoda 1898.28
Blackburn, Royce 1938.18, 1941.11
Blackburn, Vivian 1898.69, 1910.05, 1911.09
Blackburn, William J. 1890.08
Blackburne, Mary 1918.33
Blackburne, Robert A. 1918.36
Blackey, Don 1954.07
Blackey, Donald 1950.05
Blackman, Charles 1944.17
Blackmore, Willard 1914.24
Blackstone, Gay 1980.12
Blackstone, Harry 1980.12
Blackstone, Milton 1962.17
Blackstone, Nan 1930.18
Blackton, Carlisle 1918.11
Blackton, Jack 1980.09
Blackton, Jay 1941.12, 1943.04, 1947.06, 1948.14, 1949.08, 1950.15, 1951.14, 1952.10, 1954.02, 1956.08, 1956.16, 1958.02, 1959.01, 1961.15, 1961.21, 1962.16, 1962.20, 1963.29, 1966.09, 1967.02, 1968.07, 1969.12, 1970.19, 1976.08, 1979.10, 1979.12, 1979.28, 1979.31
Blackton, Jay S. 1946.12
Blackwell, Carlyle 1943.18
Blackwell, Charles 1954.15, 1971.13, 1983.21
Blackwell, Donald 1930.25, 1930.32, 1936.01
Blackwell, George 1956.15, 1959.19, 1960.06, 1968.23, 1972.04
Blackwell, Harolyn 1997.10
Blackwell, Otis 1982.22, 1989.12
Blackwell, Robert 1990.15
Blacque, Judi 1946.20
Bladd, Marilyn 1954.04, 1954.07
Blades, Edwina 1940.16, 1942.19
Blades, Ruben 1998.02
Blain, Jennifer 1996.15
Blaine, Howard 1947.13, 1947.21
Blaine, Jeffrey 1903.12
Blaine, Terry 1924.08
Blaine, Vivian 1950.17, 1958.08, 1966.13
Blainville, Mlle. 1880.52
Blair, Anthony 1933.07, 1934.39, 1937.01, 1943.07
Blair, Barbara 1931.30, 1932.14
Blair, Charles F. 1903.12
Blair, Edith 1900.48, 1906.32
Blair, Edythe 1900.55
Blair, Ethel 1921.21
Blair, Eugenie 1920.25
Blair, F.B. 1887.08
Blair, Frank 1896.18, 1899.22
Blair, Frank B. 1887.34, 1890.03, 1897.14
Blair, Gertrude 1921.13
Blair, Gladys 1921.25
Blair, Irene 1908.07
Blair, Jack 1936.12, 1938.04, 1941.02, 1954.14
Blair, June 1936.12, 1938.04
Blair, Lucille 1915.04
Blair, Mabel 1893.01
Blair, Maud 1927.66
Blair, Meredith 1996.04
Blair, Michael 1946.05
Blair, O'Donnell 1944.30
Blair, Pam 1972.04
Blair, Pamela 1975.15, 1978.13, 1978.22
Blair, Pauline 1925.27, 1926.11
Blair, Stella 1899.13
Blair, Tony 1933.01
Blair, Walter 1907.14
Blair-Hall, Anthony 2000.18
Blaire, Elaine 1929.49
Blaire, Laine 1926.03, 1926.15, 1927.05, 1929.46, 1930.36, 1931.08
Blaisdel, William 1899.04
Blaisdell, Brad 1976.25
Blaisdell, Geoffrey 1993.17, 1997.09
Blaisdell, J. 1863.07
Blaisdell, J.W. 1863.06, 1865.06, 1866.18
Blaisdell, Miss 1868.04, 1872.22
Blaisdell, Mr. 1862.03
Blaisdell, William 1890.28, 1892.27, 1895.09, 1895.23, 1900.52, 1901.05, 1902.01
Blake, Addie 1870.35
Blake, Agnes 1892.30, 1892.60
Blake, Atta 1939.14
Blake, Bertha 1902.15, 1902.27, 1904.28, 1907.24, 1908.04, 1909.07, 1914.26
Blake, Betty 1931.08
Blake, Beulah 1934.13
Blake, Charles D. 1882.80
Blake, Doris 1944.16, 1945.04
Blake, Eubie 1921.16, 1923.08, 1923.33, 1924.01, 1924.27, 1930.24, 1930.34, 1931.32, 1932.14, 1932.30, 1937.09, 1938.03, 1942.13, 1952.08, 1975.09, 1975.22, 1976.04, 1978.21, 1980.10, 1986.06, 1989.02, 1990.09
Blake, Florence 1908.44
Blake, George 1943.16
Blake, Grace 1900.54
Blake, Harold 1892.37, 1892.40, 1892.46, 1896.08, 1896.51
Blake, Harold C. 1893.35
Blake, Harry M. 1903.40
Blake, Henry 1935.01
Blake, J. 1859.01
Blake, J.W. 1927.48
Blake, James 1936.28
Blake, Josh 1984.02, 1986.13
Blake, Louis 1891.23
Blake, Maggie 1876.03
Blake, Mary 1876.03
Blake, Micah 1891.23
Blake, Mlle. 1868.06
Blake, Mr. 1834.03, 1875.40
Blake, Mrs. W.R. 1851.03, 1861.03
Blake, Nena 1904.28, 1906.04
Blake, Nina 1902.15, 1911.17
Blake, Peggy 1927.08
Blake, Phyllis 1942.09
Blake, Richard H. 1987.19, 1989.25, 1990.02, 1999.15
Blake, Robin 1989.17
Blake, Sydney 1976.09
Blake, T. 1859.01
Blake, W.B. 1855.10
Blake, Winfield 1898.73, 1900.12
Blake, Winifield 1897.17
Blakeley, Bidda 1939.19
Blakeley, James 1904.29, 1906.25, 1908.25, 1914.32
Blakeley, Louise 1928.25
Blakeley, Michelle 1994.07
Blakeley, Mr. 1838.01
Blakeley, T.H. 1834.02
Blakemore, H.D. 1898.77, 1919.24
Blakemore, Harry 1918.10
Blakemore, Herman 1894.38
Blakemore, Michael 1989.29, 1997.08, 1999.19
Blakeney, Jeanette 2000.03
Blakeney, W. 1876.30, 1876.33, 1877.05
Blakey, Maria 1979.30
Blakstone, Nan 1930.06
Blanc, Jeanne 1885.55, 1885.57, 1885.59, 1886.09, 1886.19, 1886.20
Blanc, Marie Lys 1964.39
Blanc, Mel 1990.10
Blanc, Mlle. 1876.28
Blanc, Mme. 1876.20
Blanchard, Alf 1878.22
Blanchard, Arthur 1903.37
Blanchard, Barbara 1968.10
Blanchard, C. 1887.04
Blanchard, E.L. 1873.28, 1875.17, 1876.08, 1890.50
Blanchard, Marna 1916.20
Blanchard, May 1900.47
Blanchard, Miss 1915.17
Blanchard, Nelle 1898.08
Blanchard, Scott 1965.20
Blanchard, Steve 1993.11, 1995.19, 1999.16
Blanche Corelli Opera Company 1884.28, 1884.29, 1884.30, 1884.31
Blanche Roosevelt Comic Opera Company 1880.46
Blanche, Belle 1914.34
Blanche, Francis 1958.18
Blanche, Miss 1884.44
Blanche, Mlle. 1870.44, 1871.27, 1879.39, 1880.52, 1884.43, 1884.54
Blanche, William 1920.18, 1928.22, 1930.42
Blanchet, Peter 1990.08, 1991.08, 1991.09
Blanchette, Messr. 1882.15
Blancke, Gertrude 1898.33
Blancke, Kate 1881.52, 1883.09, 1884.04, 1884.07, 1888.12
Blancke, Katie 1880.39
Blanco, Pierretto 1923.29
Bland, Charles 1880.41
Bland, Edith 1882.63
Bland, H. 1859.01, 1866.34, 1867.08
Bland, Hubert 1945.04, 1956.03
Bland, James 1879.64
Bland, Mr. 1850.01, 1851.04, 1859.02, 1859.04
Bland, Mrs. 1867.08, 1867.10
Bland, Mrs. H. 1866.34
Bland, Nellie 1894.31
Bland, Steven 1981.28
Bland, Trevor 1927.18
Bland, W.F. 1888.10
Blande, W.F. 1895.39
Blandowski, A. 1876.16
Blane, Ralph 1936.12, 1937.15, 1940.08, 1941.06, 1942.01, 1952.05, 1967.11, 1979.24, 1979.25, 1981.16, 1989.23, 1999.23
Blane, Steven 1979.29
Blane, Sue 1975.08
Blaney Harry Clay 1895.02
Blaney, Charles E. 1895.02, 1897.04, 1897.06, 1898.03, 1898.10, 1898.78, 1906.03, 1907.28, 1907.61
Blaney, Norah 1924.01
Blaney, Viola 1924.16
Blanid, Louise 1919.38
Blank, Dorothy Ann 1979.28
Blank, Larry 1979.04, 1979.18, 1980.30, 1981.12, 1987.19
Blank, Paul 1980.10
Blanke, Kate 1879.63
Blankenbuehler, Andy 1999.01, 1999.15
Blankenship, Will 1983.06
Blankfort, Henry 1940.21
Blankfort, Michael 1935.03
Blasetti, Pamela 1987.14
Blasina, Elisa 1867.25
Blaszka, Felix 1964.39
Blatche, Mons. 1887.36
Blatsche, Mons. 1887.35
Blatt, Jerry 1973.02, 1975.12, 1979.30
Blau, Bela 1938.18
Blau, Eric 1972.16, 1981.05
Blau, Renee 1983.17
Blaufoix, Paul 1921.41
Blaufuss, Walter 1918.07
Blausen, Whitney 1974.23, 1976.11
Blauvelt, Lillian 1906.48
Blauville, Mlle. 1880.60
Blaxill, Peter 1967.01
Blaymore, Enid 1980.11
Blazer, Judy 1990.06, 1998.12
Bleasdale, George 1920.26
Blechman, Marcus 1933.24
Bleck, Robert 1937.13
Bledsoe, Jules 1927.67
Bledsoe, Julius 1926.31
Bleecker, Mr. 1848.01
Bleeke, Mark 1999.05
Bleezarde, Gloria 1968.13
Bleichmann, Rudolf 1924.45, 1931.03, 1943.06, 1980.21, 1985.09, 1987.08
Bleiman, Max 1896.29
Blendick, James 1973.07
Blesser, Charles 1881.13, 1882.77, 1883.06, 1884.40, 1885.46, 1885.65
Blesser, Charles M. 1887.03
Blesser, M. 1886.16
Blessing, C. 1881.31
Blessing, Christine 1888.33, 1892.26, 1892.32, 1892.41, 1892.49, 1893.01, 1893.04, 1893.22, 1895.04, 1895.18, 1897.52, 1898.20, 1898.43, 1898.72, 1900.07
Blethen, Joseph 1907.26
Bleu, Barbe 1868.17
Blevins, Michael 1981.07, 1983.21
Blevins, Timothy Robert 1997.12, 2000.03
Bleyer, Archie 1929.09, 1940.21, 1941.06, 1942.29, 1943.07
Blezard, William 1955.19
Blieman, Lillian 1897.46
Bligh, Mae 1927.20
Blinn, Beatrice 1928.24
Blinn, Holbrook 1905.04, 1918.10
Bliss, Fred 1919.26
Bliss, Helena 1944.21, 1946.18, 1954.04, 1954.14

Bliss, Helene 1941.08
Bliss, Imogene 1967.01
Bliss, James A. 1907.33
Bliss, Jane 1912.37
Bliss, Judith 1983.19
Bliss, Lela 1924.28
Bliss, Louise 1911.38
Bliss, Maud 1894.29
Blitzer, Barry 1956.08
Blitzstein, Marc 1930.18, 1935.03, 1937.08, 1937.14, 1941.01, 1942.26, 1947.21, 1949.16, 1950.18, 1953.05, 1953.14, 1958.13, 1959.04, 1959.10, 1960.02, 1962.17, 1966.19, 1976.10, 1989.24, 1992.14, 1995.12
Bloch, Ivan 1980.27, 1983.19, 1989.22
Bloch, Sonny 1989.22
Bloch, Stella 1930.18
Blocher, Walter 1962.15
Block, Alan 1999.09
Block, Bertram 1923.32
Block, Chad 1956.12, 1959.11, 1966.27, 1967.06, 1969.17, 1972.03
Block, Eric 1917.07
Block, Gregory 1978.25
Block, Hal 1941.11
Block, Larry 1994.09
Block, Suzy 1979.27
Block, Vivian 1940.18
Block, Will J. 1895.21, 1897.02, 1904.28, 1906.04
Blodget, Alden S. 1952.04
Blodgett, Kristen 2000.09
Blofson, Richard 1955.09
Blohm, Herr 1883.08, 1883.35
Blomberg, Jan 1966.19
Blome, Adolf 1916.11
Blondeau, Henri 1911.03
Blondelet, Mlle. 1878.18
Blondelet, Mons. 1875.04
Blondelet, Rose 1875.01
Blondell, Edward 1900.53, 1905.07
Blondell, Libbie Arnold 1900.53
Blood, Adele 1918.22
Bloodgood 1905.39
Bloodgood, Fanny 1894.17, 1896.40, 1898.70, 1902.39
Bloodgood, Harry 1884.06
Bloodgood, Linda 1915.03
Bloodgood, Lisle 1903.09
Bloom 1881.24, 1882.05
Bloom, Al 1932.16
Bloom, J. 1894.17
Bloom, J. Michael 1970.02
Bloom, Leo 1965.29
Bloom, Lew 1894.37, 1898.47
Bloom, Lucile 1911.26
Bloom, M.E. 1897.29
Bloom, Rube 1939.14, 1980.10, 1987.02, 1997.05
Bloom, Sol 1903.01
Bloom, Verna 1967.01
Bloom, William 1923.22
Bloomer, Raymond 1911.34, 1911.36, 1912.10
Bloomer, Raymond J. 1910.35
Bloomfield, Ernest 1951.11
Bloomfield, Harry 1945.14
Bloomgarden, Kermit 1956.04, 1957.18, 1960.18, 1961.27, 1962.24, 1964.15, 1967.05, 1972.21
Bloomingdale, Alfred 1941.09, 1943.05, 1943.07, 1944.15
Blore, Eric 1923.26, 1924.01, 1925.42, 1928.17, 1928.46, 1931.42, 1932.26
Blossom, Henry 1902.23, 1903.03, 1905.57, 1906.33, 1907.36, 1908.40, 1909.09, 1911.02, 1912.10, 1912.12, 1912.49, 1913.15, 1913.28, 1914.27, 1915.23, 1916.24, 1917.07, 1917.26, 1918.06, 1919.01, 1920.14, 1924.18, 1929.36, 1934.14, 1945.16, 1952.11, 1980.27
Blossom, Henry M. 1904.10, 1905.06
Blossom, Henry W. 1902.07
Blossom, Ida 1897.11
Blossom, Jr., Henry 1902.40
Blossom, June 1932.17
Blossom, Pinkie 1889.46
Blossom, Roberts 1970.04
Blount, Helon 1956.04, 1965.06, 1969.01, 1971.05, 1981.10
Blow, Evelyn 1888.36
Blow, Leila 1884.22
Blow, Lila 1887.43, 1889.13, 1889.46, 1893.39, 1894.38
Blow, Miss 1884.42
Blow, Sidney 1913.29
Blue, Ben 1928.23, 1939.25
Blue, Harry 1929.26
Blue, John 1918.19
Blue, Peggie 1983.17, 1984.09
Blue, Pete 1982.11
Bluhm, Messr. 1881.35
Blum, Anthony 1957.03
Blum, Ernest 1852.02, 1875.07, 1875.13, 1876.31, 1877.16, 1877.29, 1879.34, 1879.46, 1882.55, 1883.61, 1884.45, 1885.55, 1885.56, 1885.68, 1886.22
Blum, Joel 1976.24, 1994.08, 1997.07, 1997.22
Blum, Leon 1882.43
Blum, Paul C. 1893.43
Blum, Robert 1930.43
Blume, Norman 1916.10
Blume, Norman A. 1911.01, 1911.14, 1914.10
Blume, Robert R. 1981.24, 1989.11
Blumenkrantz, Jeff 1987.03, 1989.24, 1994.01, 1995.05, 2001.01
Blumenthal, A.C. 1932.22
Blumenthal, L. 1907.54
Blumenthal, Oskar 1936.22
Blunkall, E.J. 1941.13
Blunt, Messr. 1852.02
Blunt, Miss 1841.01
Blunt, Mr. 1870.22
Blyar, Hilda 1916.17
Blyden, Larry 1952.10, 1958.19, 1964.04, 1966.18, 1972.03
Blye, Helen 1903.03, 1904.44
Blye, Miss 1903.03, 1904.13, 1904.44
Blye, Rosa 1894.10
Blyer, Archie 1940.02
Blyler, James 1911.24, 1920.23
Blyler, Jimmie 1920.22
Blythe, Coralie 1906.29
Blythe, Frances 1922.30
Blythe, Josephine 1922.05
Blythwood, Geneva 1930.10
Blythwood, Reginald 1930.10
Boa, Kelly 1971.16
Boag, Gil 1929.29
Board, Bill 1898.02
Boardman, C.E. 1886.27
Boardman, Fred W. 1894.37
Boardman, J.F. 1894.37
Boas, Michael 1969.13
Boas, S. 1906.06
Boatner, Adelaide 1957.16
Boaz 1968.04
Bobbie, Walter 1971.09, 1972.12, 1973.02, 1976.25, 1978.06, 1992.04, 1993.16, 1996.14, 1998.13
Bobby Hill, The 1982.17
Bobby, Anne Marie 1984.02, 1986.20
Bobick, James 1995.10, 1996.11, 1996.13
Bobley, Peter A. 1981.28
Bocage, H. 1872.35, 1873.25
Bocage, Henri 1882.26
Bocanha, Luis 1988.06
Boccaccio, Giovanni 1916.08, 1975.23
Boccanfuso, Denise 1996.17
Boccia, Arthur 1974.25, 1976.19, 1976.34
Boccino, Matthew 1941.03
Bochanna, Mlle. 1873.10
Bochell, Ada 1921.30
Bochell, Miss 1870.31
Bocher, Main 1950.15, 1953.03
Bock, Jerry 1955.12, 1956.02, 1958.01, 1959.25, 1960.19, 1962.16, 1963.11, 1963.14, 1964.27, 1966.18, 1970.15, 1976.36, 1981.18, 1986.03, 1989.03, 1989.06, 1989.21, 1990.18, 1993.10
Bock, William E. 1902.43
Bockel, Marie 1884.12, 1884.66, 1887.08
Bockman, George 1947.11
Bockoven, Elizabeth 1944.21
Bodansky, Robert 1909.15, 1911.32, 1912.10, 1912.33, 1930.07
Bodanzky, Robert 1911.37, 1912.48, 1915.27, 1925.07
Boddington, Maurice 1916.18
Bode, A.J. 1901.04
Boden, Harry 1901.19, 1903.03
Boden, Melva 1931.31
Bodenhoff, Janice 1946.01
Bodibe, Matthew 1977.01
Bodin, Duane 1969.06, 1976.36
Bodine, Mark 1980.28
Bodroghy, Adele 1945.14
Boeckell, Marie 1889.45
Boehm, C. 1930.22
Boelen, Carrie 1889.36, 1890.15, 1891.12, 1891.22, 1891.30
Boell, H.B. 1914.25
Boelz, Ed. 1885.01
Boersma, Oliver 1946.23
Boevers, Jessica 1996.06
Boffinger, Hazel 1933.03
Bogaev, Paul 1981.08, 1981.09, 1987.05, 1988.09, 1990.04, 1992.12, 1994.10, 2000.06
Bogan, Karen 1982.03
Bogardus, Stephen 1980.02, 1988.09, 1992.09, 1997.12, 1998.05
Bogarozy and Odierno 1911.10
Bogart, Andrew 1907.07
Bogart, L. 1892.35
Bogart, Master 1857.04, 1857.06
Bogart, Matt 1999.08
Bogart, Miss 1864.02
Bogart, Mr. 1856.02
Bogart, Neil 1981.28
Bogart, Tiffany 1976.36
Bogart, W. 1856.02
Bogdanoff, Rose 1942.11
Bogert, Messr. 1855.10
Boggs, Gail 1972.21, 1974.06
Bogin, Abba 1954.16, 1959.02, 1960.05, 1962.02, 1963.27, 1965.38, 1966.08, 1966.13, 1969.01, 1970.06
Bogue, Kevin 1995.05, 1998.01, 2000.11
Bogyo, Peter 1989.09
Bohachevsky, George 1978.19
Bohanek, James 1997.19
Bohannan, S. 1906.06
Bohannon, M.T. 1922.15, 1922.34
Bohannon, Mr. 1864.13
Bohannon, Mrs. 1866.16
Bohannon, T.H. 1906.39
Bohanon, Messr. 1894.19, 1897.23
Bohdan, Serhij 1974.17
Bohemians, Inc., The 1919.18, 1920.28, 1921.27, 1924.32, 1925.47, 1928.14
Bohlman, Edgar 1931.06
Bohlman, John 1907.19
Bohm, Adolf 1917.26
Bohm, Adolph 1917.26
Bohm, Jack 1919.16
Bohm, John 1917.02
Bohme, Mlle. 1871.18
Bohmer, Ron 1990.18, 1999.13
Bohn, Peanuts 1940.07
Bohnen, Aloys 1916.03
Bohnen, Roman 1936.28
Bohner, Miss 1882.46
Bohnert, Bill 1984.16
Bohrer, Messr. 1877.22
Bohrer, Mr. 1878.20
Bohrer, Theodore 1877.39
Bohrmann, Heinrich 1883.35
Bohrmann-Riegen 1897.53, 1899.05
Boieldieu, Adrien 1853.02
Boileau, Dwight 1951.05
Boinet and Hirsig 1913.01
Bois, Curt 1945.14
Boisselot, Paul 1868.17, 1870.10, 1875.09, 1875.15, 1884.60
Boisson, Mlle. 1883.34
Bojar, Alvin 1964.22, 1974.09
Bojock, Herr 1880.61
Bojock, Reinhold 1879.17
Bokannon, Mrs. 1861.03
Bokee, Mary 1928.20
Bokee, William H. 1880.63
Bolan, Alexis 1938.13
Boland, Clay 1929.22, 1976.07
Boland, Mary 1932.05, 1933.02, 1935.14
Boland, Rita 1917.03
Bolas, T. 1871.17
Bolasni, Saul 1951.17
Bold, Mr. 1867.15
Bold, Richard 1920.02, 1921.06, 1921.27, 1922.27, 1923.18, 1924.19, 1925.27, 1926.37, 1928.04, 1928.23
Bolden, Harry 1933.04
Bolen, Virginia 1939.19, 1940.03
Bolender, Charles 1957.02, 1959.22
Bolender, Todd 1970.10
Boles, John 1925.16, 1926.12, 1943.19
Boles, Viola 1924.17
Boleshavsky, Richard 1928.12
Boleslavsky, Richard 1927.65
Boleslawski, M. 1922.37
Boleslawski, Messr. 1922.37
Boleslawsky, Richard 1923.43, 1925.32
Boley, Ailene 1915.08
Boley, Aline 1910.18
Boley, Arline 1909.13, 1911.24
Boley, May 1898.60, 1902.20, 1904.24, 1907.39, 1911.06, 1911.36, 1913.18, 1914.01, 1916.21, 1918.24, 1919.10, 1919.24, 1921.03, 1923.06, 1924.06, 1924.42, 1925.44, 1935.14
Boleyn, Eleanor 1943.07, 1946.01, 1952.01
Bolger, Jennie 1905.13
Bolger, John F. 1905.09
Bolger, Ray 1926.01, 1926.15, 1929.42, 1931.30, 1934.19, 1936.05, 1940.07, 1942.15, 1946.07, 1948.26, 1951.02, 1969.07
Bolin, Shannon 1954.03, 1955.08, 1963.20
Boll, Patrick 2001.06
Bolotine, Leonid 1963.28
Bolster, Stephen 1968.06, 1970.21
Bolton, Alice 1907.50
Bolton, Cora 1894.37
Bolton, Guy 1915.01, 1915.07, 1915.30, 1916.19, 1917.01, 1917.06, 1917.17, 1917.20, 1917.26, 1918.03, 1918.28, 1918.37, 1919.39, 1920.44, 1921.23, 1922.12, 1922.26, 1923.30, 1924.08, 1924.43, 1925.49, 1926.28, 1926.36, 1927.01, 1927.08, 1927.52, 1928.02, 1928.03, 1929.02, 1929.49, 1930.08, 1930.31, 1931.08, 1934.36, 1940.09, 1940.10, 1944.01, 1944.14, 1947.06, 1948.16, 1955.04, 1965.35, 1975.24, 1981.03, 1986.01, 1987.15, 1990.14, 1992.02
Bolton, Helen 1919.23, 1920.05, 1920.23, 1920.32, 1922.41, 1924.40
Bolton, Howard 1905.21
Bolton, Ira 1928.01
Bolton, John 1997.06, 2000.07
Bolton, Kalmar and Ruby, Ltd. 1929.49
Bolton, Larry 1944.33
Bolton, Lawrence 1939.21
Bolton, Lois 1941.08, 1944.02, 1948.28
Bolwell, Sarah 1892.29
Bolyard, Lewis 1944.21, 1949.08, 1952.01
BoMar, Meta 1910.12
Bomberg, Conrad 1963.09
Bomgardner, Harold E. 1931.03
Bomurwil Productions 1999.08
Bonachevsky, George 1979.20
Bonadio, Renee 1998.06
Bonanni, Luciano 1964.03
Bonanno, S. 1911.16
Bonard Productions 1963.03, 1963.16
Bonay, Armand 1958.01
Bonazzi, Elaine 1965.11, 1965.13, 1980.04, 1984.12, 1991.08, 1991.09
Bonconsiglio, Mlle. 1867.05
Bond, Angela 1995.07
Bond, Annie 1871.09
Bond, Brenda 1927.49, 1928.34
Bond, Christopher 1979.06, 1984.13, 1987.09, 1989.19
Bond, Francine 1953.08, 1962.05
Bond, Frank G. 1928.43
Bond, Fred 1907.18, 1910.32
Bond, Frederic 1906.17
Bond, Grace 1903.03
Bond, Harriet 1897.45
Bond, Harry 1905.34
Bond, Helen 1916.22, 1917.12
Bond, Helene 1915.30
Bond, Jessie 1879.70, 1879.72
Bond, Julie 1993.15
Bond, Lillian 1902.10, 1929.08, 1930.26, 1931.28
Bond, Mary 1876.03
Bond, Miss 1903.03
Bond, Phillip 1975.01
Bond, Ridge 1951.16, 1953.09
Bond, Rollin 1905.47
Bond, Rudy 1967.05
Bond, Ruth 1938.13, 1943.19
Bond, Sally 1941.08
Bond, Sheila 1944.15, 1947.02, 1948.04, 1952.10, 1961.15
Bondoc, Lexine 1996.05, 1999.21
Bonds, Jr., Rufus 1998.21
Boneck, Issye 1922.21
Bonefine, Evelyn 1941.03
Bonehill, Bessie 1893.43
Bonelle, Dick 1972.04
Bonelli, Mlle. 1872.31, 1872.41, 1872.42, 1873.01
Bonelli, William 1909.13, 1910.36, 1925.01, 1925.28

Bonfanti 1879.12
Bonfanti, Maria 1882.52
Bonfanti, Marie 1866.18, 1868.03, 1869.02, 1871.08, 1873.28, 1876.23, 1881.15, 1882.57
Bonfanti, Marietta 1870.44, 1882.49
Bonfanti, Mlle. 1897.29
Bonfiglia, G. 1908.26
Bonfiglio, Signor 1910.23, 1911.12
Bonfils, Helen 1960.04
Bonfils, Helen G. 1961.18, 1963.03, 1963.16
Bonfine, Evelyn 1941.03
Bonham, John 1982.22
Bonheur, Cora 1884.65
Bonheur, Stella 1898.03
Boni, Adele 1873.10, 1877.04
Boni, John A. 1966.08
Boniface, George C. 1866.18, 1869.07, 1870.05, 1871.10, 1883.05, 1883.07, 1893.47
Boniface, Jr., George 1884.63, 1885.67, 1886.28, 1908.30
Boniface, Jr., George C. 1883.65, 1886.37, 1892.17, 1895.06, 1896.45, 1900.16, 1904.49, 1907.15
Boniface, Maggie 1869.07
Boniface, Mrs. George C. 1870.05, 1880.17, 1881.18
Boniface, Peter 1888.01
Boniface, Stella 1877.20, 1885.49, 1885.66
Boning, Charles 1883.66
Bonini, Peggy 1954.10, 1955.17, 1957.15
Bonino, Luigi 1981.13
Bonkovsky, James 1981.27
Bonn, Frank 1897.05, 1899.01, 1900.10
Bonn, Theodore 1935.12
Bonneau, Miss 1870.02
Bonnefous, Jean-Pierre 1978.26
Bonnell, Don 1968.24
Bonnell, June 1908.34
Bonnell, Marian 1927.52
Bonnell, Marion 1931.13
Bonnell, Sam 1943.19
Bonnelli, William 1908.21, 1929.09
Bonner, Beatrice 1898.61
Bonner, Eugene 1931.06
Bonner, Mabel 1897.33
Bonner, Marjorie 1908.04, 1909.13, 1909.25
Bonneville, Bessie 1898.05
Bonney, William E. 1909.15
Bonnington, Keith 1964.37
Bono, Sonny 1982.22
Bonoff, Edward 1918.14
Bonshire, Forrest 1948.25
Bonsiguis, Messr. 1852.05
Bonta, Letitia 1925.47
Bontempelli, G. 1974.19
Bontempo, James 1976.25
Bontemps, Arna 1946.08
Bontrager, Laura 1996.18
Bonus, Ben 1966.21, 1967.08, 1970.17, 1990.16
Bonville, Nace 1900.51, 1905.19, 1907.11, 1920.09, 1927.66
Bonwit, Elise 1924.15, 1926.39
Bonwit, Elsie 1920.25
Bonwitt Teller and Company 1930.37
Bonynge, Leta 1968.17
Boockvor, Steven 1966.24, 1975.07, 1975.22, 1977.06, 1978.12, 1981.28
Booher, Claire 1931.44
Booke, Sorrell 1960.09, 1962.16
Booker Beryl 1948.13
Booker, Billie 1918.03
Booker, George 1937.09
Booker, George A. 1893.33
Booker, Harry 1887.05, 1893.26
Booker, Leonard 1921.15
Booker, Michael C. 1978.04
Booker, Otto 1904.25
Bookman, Kirk 1995.07, 1999.05
Books, C. 1905.06
Books, C.M. 1906.45
Boomer, Eastman 1953.10
Boone, Blanche 1908.26, 1909.20, 1912.30
Boone, Debbie 1982.14
Boone, Debby 1990.02
Boone, John A. 1905.21, 1907.09
Boone, Sherry 1999.22
Boone, Sherry D. 1992.08
Boone, Steve 1982.22
Boor, Frank 1894.15
Boorum, Mattie 1906.01
Boos, Addie 1887.23
Boos, Louis F. 1886.46, 1887.23
Boote, Rosie 1897.32
Booth, Agnes 1876.12
Booth, Anne 1937.10
Booth, Basil 1897.07
Booth, Edwin 1867.29, 1872.27
Booth, Elmer 1912.11
Booth, John 1928.30, 1928.49, 1929.46, 1932.03, 1933.25, 1939.16
Booth, John Hunter 1927.29
Booth, John N. 1935.04
Booth, John Newton 1924.26
Booth, Joyce 1927.27, 1927.35
Booth, Jr., J. 1846.01
Booth, Jr., John 1934.04, 1934.20
Booth, Jr., John N. 1926.07, 1926.24, 1941.07
Booth, Jr., Mrs. 1859.05
Booth, Jr., Mrs. J.B. 1848.03
Booth, Junius Brutus 1892.57
Booth, Marjorie 1921.38
Booth, Mary 1923.12
Booth, May 1880.62, 1881.25, 1881.42, 1881.45
Booth, Miss 1882.23
Booth, Polly 1871.17
Booth, Rachel 1884.16, 1889.39, 1893.06, 1900.28, 1901.19, 1903.06
Booth, Shirley 1945.09, 1951.14, 1954.02, 1959.04, 1970.08
Booth, Sydney 1898.72
Booth-Willoughby 1926.23
Boothe, Earl 1926.06
Boothe, Frederick J. 1990.14
Boothe, Wade 1920.44
Boots, Antoinette 1924.46
Bootz, Erwin 1999.05
Bootz, Sandra 1997.13
Booysen, Junaid 1999.12
Borani, A. 1896.32
Borani, Arthur 1902.08
Borani, H. 1896.32
Borani, Miss 1896.44
Borbridge, Giles 1935.04
Borbus, Alice 1944.24
Borchard, Comte 1864.04, 1864.07, 1864.16, 1864.18, 1864.19, 1864.20
Borde, Albert 1944.14
Bordeau, Francine 1944.22
Bordeaux, Odette 1907.51
Bordeman, Mr. 1883.49
Borden, Ethel 1931.19
Borden, Eugene 1918.31, 1922.09
Borden, Helen 1918.04, 1919.01
Borden, Ivor 1950.14
Borden, John 1959.13
Borden, Johnny 1959.02, 1960.06, 1961.20
Borden, Ray 1951.13
Bordo, Edwin 1977.06
Bordoff, Trudy 1971.16
Bordoni, Irene 1912.43, 1915.25, 1917.12, 1918.18, 1920.03, 1922.09, 1923.26, 1925.41, 1926.41, 1928.33, 1938.15, 1940.08
Borel, Mons. 1879.39, 1879.49, 1880.29, 1880.56
Borel-Clerc, Charles 1932.04
Borelli, A. 1893.43
Boreo, Emil 1926.15
Boreo, Messr. 1922.06
Boretz, Allen 1930.18, 1930.33, 1930.38
Borgars, Mlle. 1867.24
Borge, Victor 1941.03, 1953.13, 1964.34, 1977.14, 1989.28
Borger, Bob 1927.41, 1937.06
Borger, Harriet 1942.21
Borges, Yamil 1987.12
Borghini, Signorina 1911.18
Borgia, Philippe 1932.19
Borgman, C.E. 1881.01
Borgman, Charles E. 1882.24, 1886.05, 1887.08
Borgman, Frank 1955.09
Borhmann-Reigen 1882.71
Borice, Andre 1929.30
Boris, Helen 1897.29
Boris, Ruthanna 1937.15, 1939.26, 1951.19, 1958.03
Boris, Ruthanne 1943.06
Bork, Ferne 1971.12
Born, Walter 1951.22
Borne, Hal 1950.02, 1955.12
Borneman, Albert 1912.47
Borneman, Fred 1906.39
Bornemann, Fred 1883.39, 1891.21
Bornstein, Daryl 1988.19, 1989.25, 1990.09
Borod, Robert L. 1979.18
Borodin, Alexander 1913.05, 1922.21, 1953.16, 1965.22, 1985.13, 1986.09, 1989.21, 1999.23
Borodkin, Herr 1891.21
Borodon, Alexander 1978.03
Boros, Frank J. 1975.07, 1981.02
Borough, Marguerite 1927.26
Borquez, Carlos 1999.18
Borquez, Ines 1999.18
Borracha 1988.06
Borrani, Mr. 1854.03, 1854.07, 1855.01, 1855.02, 1855.04, 1855.05, 1855.06, 1855.07
Borrelli, Jim 1972.12
Borrero, Inez 1912.44
Borrie, Alexandra 1975.05
Borroughs, Don 1920.42
Borrowbody, Mr. 1875.03
Borsa, Signor 1883.48
Borstelmann, Jim 1989.04
Borston, Robert W. 1888.01
Bortnick, Evan 1983.16
Bortselmann, Jim 1996.14
Boruff, John 1935.16
Bos, Jean 1934.32, 1935.19
Bosan, Alonzo 1951.11, 1951.18, 1952.15
Bosberg, Al 1923.32
Bosch, Phillipe 2000.16
Boschell, Ada 1905.39
Boschell, Carrie 1873.19
Bosco, Philip 1961.14, 1970.04
Boscotin, Mons. 1881.46
Boselli, Emy 1955.07
Boshell, Ada 1886.24
Boshell, Louise 1875.32
Bosher, Messr. 1906.05, 1907.02
Bosler, Virginia 1947.01, 1947.07, 1950.20, 1952.09, 1957.03, 1963.04, 1963.06
Bosley, Tom 1959.25, 1962.24, 1968.06, 1994.04
Bosquet, Thierry 1984.12, 1985.10, 1986.10, 1987.11, 1990.13, 1995.10, 1997.02
Boss, Charles E. 1907.34
Boss, Reeder 1934.06
Bossi, Ernestine 1881.15
Bostick, Irene 1930.30
Bostock, Kenneth 1933.24, 1940.09
Boston Comic Opera Company 1882.21, 1882.22, 1882.23, 1942.02
Boston English Opera Company 1882.57
Boston Ideal Opera Company 1880.12, 1880.45, 1882.07, 1882.08, 1882.09, 1882.10, 1882.11, 1882.12, 1882.13, 1883.11, 1883.12, 1883.13, 1883.14, 1883.15, 1888.07
Boston Opera Company 1880.48, 1880.53, 1942.04, 1942.06, 1942.07, 1942.08, 1942.09
Boston Theatre Company 1881.15
Boston, Gretha 1994.08, 1999.09
Boston, Millie 1880.69
Boston, Minnie 1882.49
Boston, Steve 1979.15
Bostonians Opera Company 1897.13
Bostonians, The 1891.29, 1892.51, 1893.18, 1893.19, 1893.48, 1894.03, 1894.08, 1894.45, 1895.01, 1896.42, 1896.43, 1898.23
Bostwick, Barry 1971.01, 1972.12, 1976.30, 1991.15
Bostwick, Herbert 1923.24
Boswell, Gertie 1889.03, 1894.20
Boswell, John 1923.04
Bosworth, Hallam 1922.14
Bosworth, Hobart 1892.14, 1897.20
Bosworth, Jill 1985.09, 1987.08, 1990.02, 1993.12
Botelho, Candido 1940.23
Bothwell, Mary 1926.30
Botkin, Jr., Perry 1979.30
Botsford, George 1910.18, 1912.20, 1912.29
Botsford, L.F. 1906.20
Bottari, Michael 1989.25, 1996.04
Botti, Rose 1904.10, 1905.06
Botto, Louis 1956.08
Botto, Mabel 1908.33
Bottomley, Roland 1920.12, 1922.35, 1932.26
Bottomly, Roland 1913.35
Bottoms, John 1971.18
Boublil, Alain 1987.04, 1991.03, 1995.12, 1997.01
Boucher, Ron 1976.31, 1978.08
Boucheron, Maxime 1891.38
Bouchet, Daniel 1993.08
Bouchier, R.B. 1883.06
Bouciault, Dion 1882.75
Boucicault, Aubrey 1895.06, 1895.21, 1895.31, 1896.22, 1898.63, 1898.77, 1904.39, 1906.05
Boucicault, Dion 1854.04, 1859.11, 1865.06, 1867.17, 1868.01, 1869.33, 1872.27, 1873.20, 1889.38, 1895.13, 1898.06, 1903.25
Boucicault, Mrs. Dion 1872.27
Boucicault, Ruth Holt 1908.40
Boucree, Gladys 1939.15
Boudinot, Annie 1879.10
Boudinot, F. 1887.44
Boudinot, Frank 1887.21
Boudinot, Franklin 1886.40, 1887.15
Boudinot, Mlle. 1867.24, 1868.25
Boudinot, Mr. 1862.03, 1862.04
Boudinot, Mrs. 1866.10, 1872.20
Boudray, Leon 1890.25
Boudreau, Robin 1981.01
Boudwin, Barbara 1944.21
Bouffes Parisiennes 1878.18
Bouie, John 1951.11, 1955.09, 1957.09, 1958.03
Bouillon, Jo 1964.02
Boulais, Adele 1920.05
Boulais, Monica 1925.11
Boulanger, Daniel 1978.22
Boulard, Mme. 1844.01
Boulard, Mr. 1841.01
Boulden, Alice 1925.27, 1926.37, 1928.36, 1929.42, 1930.28
Boulden, Howard 1924.47
Bouley, Frank 1954.13, 1965.36, 1966.24, 1979.09, 1981.19
Bouleyn, Kathryn 1980.21
Boulia, William 1927.66
Boullard, Marius 1885.59, 1886.19
Boulton, Milo 1957.17, 1965.21, 1967.14
Bouman, Frank 1908.09
Bouquett, Tamara Tunie 1990.14
Bourbon, Jose 1978.19, 1979.20
Bourgeois, Ancient 1887.27
Bourget, Ernest 1864.03, 1866.30
Bourgoin, Mons. 1868.24, 1868.26, 1869.16, 1869.30
Bourguignon, Guy 1947.18
Bourke, Walter 1976.18
Bourman, Anatole 1922.37
Bourman, Messr. 1922.37
Bourman, Michele 1978.12
Bourn, William 1912.14
Bourne, Matthew 1998.10
Bourneuf, Philip 1937.12, 1939.12, 1949.08, 1959.05
Bourneuf, Phillip 1943.23
Bourneuf, Stephen 1981.25, 1987.07, 1988.20, 1989.25
Bouroff, Kita 1973.09, 1979.09, 1989.18
Bourtayre, Henri 1955.14
Bousquet, Louis 1919.10
Bousquet, Thierry 1993.13
Boustead, Margaret 1907.43, 1908.32
Bouton, Mabel 1894.38, 1896.51, 1898.12, 1898.77
Bouton, Mabelle 1894.26
Bouton, Madeline 1901.09
Bouton, May 1906.36
Boutte, Duane 1994.02
Boutwell, Jack 1904.24
Boutwell, Neva 1907.38
Bouvard, A. 1879.49, 1880.14, 1880.16, 1880.22, 1880.29, 1880.56
Bouvard, Mlle. 1879.51, 1879.55, 1879.60, 1879.61, 1879.69, 1880.23, 1880.27
Bouvard, Mons. 1879.49, 1879.51, 1879.55, 1879.60, 1879.61, 1879.69, 1880.14, 1880.16, 1880.22, 1880.23, 1880.27, 1880.28, 1880.29, 1880.56
Bouvier, Adine 1898.48, 1899.39, 1900.57, 1902.30
Bouvier, G.W. 1883.33, 1887.34
Bouvier, H. 1908.04
Bouvier, Yvonne 1939.22
Bova, Joe 1959.26
Bova, Joseph 1963.13, 1980.20
Bove, Joseph 1921.30
Bove, Mark 1980.02, 1997.08
Bovill, C.H. 1906.25, 1908.25, 1908.27, 1911.45
Bovinet, Gordon 1982.18
Bow, Dorothy 1928.28
Bow, Lila 1900.03
Bowab, John 1966.01, 1966.10, 1968.24, 1969.01, 1983.10

Bowan, Sibyl 1935.04, 1959.06, 1961.14, 1965.21, 1968.24, 1969.14
Bowden, Charles 1953.12, 1955.05
Bowden, Joyce Leigh 1982.22
Bowdin, Rae 1914.20, 1916.03, 1924.03
Bowdoin, H.L. 1906.46
Bowe, Morton 1942.02, 1942.04, 1942.06, 1942.07, 1942.09, 1949.10, 1949.11, 1949.13, 1949.14
Bowe, Stella 1909.14
Bowen, Agnes 1886.26, 1886.33, 1886.43
Bowen, Andrea 1998.03, 2000.20
Bowen, Beatrice 1907.55
Bowen, Edward 1900.55
Bowen, Elgie 1900.43, 1902.12, 1907.42, 1909.19, 1910.37
Bowen, Fred 1868.05
Bowen, Graham 1996.08
Bowen, H. 1918.21
Bowen, James 1895.36
Bowen, Kate 1890.50
Bowen, Minnie 1895.35
Bowen, Steven D. 1995.12
Bowen, Will 1986.15
Bower, Beverly 1956.09, 1958.15, 1959.16, 1959.21
Bower, Edward 1920.02
Bower, Edward P. 1920.11
Bower, F. 1888.41
Bower, Jay 1962.02
Bower, William 1946.03
Bowerman, Joe 1995.07
Bowers, Arthur 1882.64
Bowers, Bill 1997.19
Bowers, C. 1877.04
Bowers, Charles 1936.31
Bowers, Charles B. 1901.09
Bowers, Charles H. 1897.36, 1898.36, 1898.54, 1899.24, 1899.28, 1900.34, 1903.16, 1903.41
Bowers, Clent 1981.28, 1985.02, 1996.08
Bowers, E. 1910.17
Bowers, Edward 1916.03
Bowers, Frederick V. 1900.52, 1902.27, 1906.24, 1908.37, 1910.07
Bowers, H. Clent 1993.03
Bowers, J.H. 1869.31
Bowers, Jane 1930.23
Bowers, Jordan 1963.12
Bowers, Josephine 1912.32
Bowers, Kenneth 1941.06
Bowers, Kenny 1946.12
Bowers, May 1879.50, 1880.04
Bowers, Miss 1908.19
Bowers, Nellie 1887.05
Bowers, Robert Hood 1903.34, 1904.24, 1905.23, 1906.05, 1906.36, 1907.02, 1907.39, 1907.46, 1908.17, 1909.03, 1909.04, 1909.28, 1910.37, 1911.17, 1911.18, 1911.23, 1912.15, 1913.32, 1914.27, 1915.31, 1917.26, 1919.14, 1919.15, 1920.33, 1926.10, 1927.20, 1934.14
Bowers, Vining 1864.13, 1868.03, 1870.34, 1876.16, 1877.07
Bowers, Viola 1915.32
Bowers, Violet 1911.12
Bowers, William 1942.03
Bowes, A.G. 1928.45
Bowes, Martha 1918.25
Bowes, Mr. 1851.08
Bowhan, Sibylla 1922.11, 1923.37, 1930.23
Bowie, Buster 1930.19, 1930.24
Bowie, David 1982.22
Bowie, Pat 1993.04
Bowin, Lynn 1960.06
Bowkett, Sidney 1906.12
Bowlen, Bert 1919.22, 1922.16
Bowler, Annie Kemp 1873.18
Bowler, Brookhouse 1858.03, 1872.17
Bowler, G. 1882.42
Bowler, Richard 1943.15, 1944.03, 1958.11
Bowles, Anthony 1956.13
Bowles, Belle 1888.39
Bowles, Frank 1876.05
Bowles, George 1895.03, 1899.22
Bowles, Matt 1999.21
Bowles, Paul 1941.05
Bowling, Tom 1880.46
Bowman Productions, Inc. 1972.07
Bowman, Betty 1929.09
Bowman, Carrie 1901.17, 1902.29, 1906.37, 1908.31, 1911.25
Bowman, Dolores 1950.16
Bowman, E.W. 1907.51
Bowman, Elmer 1900.46
Bowman, F. 1887.08
Bowman, Fred 1885.10
Bowman, Fred A. 1883.33
Bowman, Fred. 1883.68, 1886.05
Bowman, Grace 1924.13, 1927.19, 1929.04
Bowman, Hazel 1926.23
Bowman, Jeremy 1934.03
Bowman, Joan 1951.18
Bowman, Messr. 1879.23, 1882.04
Bowman, Patricia 1934.01, 1934.39, 1937.10, 1944.28
Bowman, Polly 1912.34, 1914.26, 1918.11
Bowman, Rob 1990.06
Bowman, Sibylla 1924.42
Bowman, Thomas 1946.01
Bowman, Tom 1948.15
Bowmann, Herr 1879.17, 1879.22
Bown, Paul 1881.11
Bown, W. Paul 1881.21, 1886.60
Bown, William Paul 1881.04, 1883.22, 1885.62, 1886.07, 1888.15
Bowron, George 1880.37, 1891.40
Bowron, W.L. 1880.38, 1881.28
Bowron, William Lloyd 1889.35, 1890.41
Bowser, Charles 1879.53, 1881.08, 1887.49, 1888.37, 1893.38, 1905.15, 1905.24
Bowson, George 1881.31
Bowyer, F. 1896.48
Bowyer, Fred 1897.40
Bowyer, Frederick 1889.54
Box, William 1961.16
Boxer, B.S. 1883.06
Boxwell, James 1937.09
Boxwill, James 1933.04
Boxwill, James Thomas 1933.27
Boyar, Monica 1961.07
Boyce, Bonnie 1917.11
Boyce, Burke 1927.36
Boyd, Alice 1875.10
Boyd, Andrew 1877.15
Boyd, Anna 1885.35, 1885.42, 1885.44, 1886.53, 1888.13, 1888.29, 1889.45, 1891.39, 1894.07, 1895.08, 1904.01, 1906.26, 1907.07, 1907.35, 1910.10, 1910.22
Boyd, Annie 1885.65
Boyd, Annie Errol 1893.47
Boyd, D'Ambrose 1998.06, 2000.19
Boyd, Edith 1946.06
Boyd, Elena 1946.06
Boyd, Elisse 1952.09, 1956.08
Boyd, Ethel 1917.19
Boyd, Gregory 1999.08
Boyd, Henrietta 1938.04
Boyd, Howard 1951.05
Boyd, James 1972.08
Boyd, Jennie 1881.36, 1881.38
Boyd, Julianne 1978.21, 1980.30
Boyd, Michael 1982.11
Boyd, Mildred 1946.06
Boyd, Miss 1877.39, 1892.20
Boyd, Mr. 1863.10, 1864.15
Boyd, Nellie 1876.02, 1879.04, 1900.59
Boyd, Patrick 1994.07
Boyd, Robert 1897.55
Boyd, Suzanne 1907.01
Boyd, Sydney 1945.18
Boyd, Thomas 1966.27
Boyd, Tom 1979.25
Boyd, Wayne 1964.46
Boyd-Jones, Ernest 1900.51, 1902.05, 1905.13, 1920.09
Boyden, Peter 1979.05
Boye, Aenny 1911.28
Boyer, Blanche 1891.01, 1898.08
Boyer, Carol 1934.13
Boyer, Claude 1902.37
Boyer, Josephine 1946.15
Boyer, Lucienne 1934.32, 1935.19
Boyer, Martha 1934.13
Boyer, Patricia 1948.27
Boyer, Rosalie 1902.07
Boyesen, May Stevens 1897.15
Boylan, Anna Marie 1962.20
Boylan, Arthur 1923.25
Boylan, Jennie 1905.49
Boylan, Rose 1923.25
Boyle, Ada 1880.63
Boyle, Charles H. 1899.09
Boyle, F.M. 1904.57
Boyle, Francis D. 1894.45
Boyle, Francis J. 1905.54, 1909.22, 1915.04, 1917.24
Boyle, Frank 1903.37, 1904.51, 1905.08, 1905.11
Boyle, Frank N. 1907.09
Boyle, J.F. 1896.42, 1898.42
Boyle, J.H. 1901.06
Boyle, Jack 1916.11, 1940.21
Boyle, James 1915.32
Boyle, John 1914.20, 1915.11, 1916.02, 1926.18, 1926.24, 1927.04, 1927.31, 1927.66, 1929.06, 1929.09, 1929.49, 1931.13, 1932.20
Boyle, Johnny 1931.21
Boyle, Robert Ott 1982.24
Boyll, Lawrence 1965.35
Boynton, Wesley 1926.17
Boys, Mr. 1864.12
Boyt, Aline 1904.18
Boyt, John 1946.17, 1954.04, 1954.06, 1954.07, 1954.14
Boyton, Miss 1885.09
Bozan, Alonzo 1933.06
Bozano, Enzo 1916.15
Bozardt, Victor 1904.22, 1927.01
Bozardt, Victor H. 1911.07
Bozart, Victor 1907.39
Boze, Billie 1943.20
Bozeman, Beverlee 1948.14
Bozyk, Max 1966.21, 1967.08
Bozyk, Rizel 1970.17
Bozyk, Rose 1966.21
Bozza, Fausto 1927.28
Braatz, Mickey 1933.20
Brabant, Mons. 1868.07, 1869.01, 1870.41, 1871.07
Brabin, C. 1904.03
Brabyn, Joseph 1883.39
Bracchitta, Jim 1989.27
Bracciani, Mr. 1852.06
Bracelo, Randy 1972.18
Bracey, Sidney 1900.37
Brack, Paul 1928.08, 1930.28
Bracken, Eddie 1939.27, 1957.05, 1960.01, 1970.12, 1978.04
Brackett, Helen 1894.38, 1896.41, 1897.26, 1898.69
Brackett, Kevin 1991.10
Brackett, Paul B. 1897.15
Brackman, Jacob 1978.22
Brackney, Bonnie 1991.07
Brackney, Tom 1991.07
Bracy, Mr. 1841.01
Bracy, Philip H. 1905.04
Bracy, Sidney 1912.19, 1913.25
Brad, J. 1873.26
Bradbury, J.H. 1891.44, 1893.26, 1894.43, 1896.40
Bradbury, J.W. 1880.49
Bradbury, James 1911.26, 1917.01, 1924.43
Bradbury, James H. 1906.45, 1908.09
Bradbury, Jessie 1897.56, 1910.37, 1912.40
Bradbury, Jr., James 1918.01
Bradbury, Lane 1959.13
Bradbury, Walter 1926.12
Bradbury, William L. 1975.22
Bradcome, Vinnie 1905.25, 1907.37, 1910.09
Braddock, Lisette 1929.34
Braden, Edward A. 1897.33, 1900.24
Bradfield, W. Louis 1894.33, 1897.32
Bradford, Alex 1969.09, 1972.13, 1976.35, 1980.14, 1982.17
Bradford, Billy 1927.38, 1928.31
Bradford, Bob 1895.14
Bradford, Charles 1893.14, 1894.02, 1896.02
Bradford, Dick 1963.09
Bradford, Edith 1900.39, 1909.22, 1910.28, 1913.21
Bradford, Grace 1913.09
Bradford, Laura 1904.32, 1907.43, 1908.32
Bradford, Marshall 1928.30
Bradford, Perry 1921.26, 1922.25, 1927.32, 1928.10, 1929.18
Bradford, Roark 1930.10, 1935.01, 1940.01, 1951.11
Bradford, Ted 1928.23
Bradley, A.D. 1862.05, 1869.40, 1869.44
Bradley, Arthur 1934.40
Bradley, Bill 1947.17, 1948.25, 1949.08
Bradley, Brad 1996.15, 1997.22, 1999.04
Bradley, Brian 1994.07
Bradley, Brown 1965.18
Bradley, Charles 1900.19, 1908.34
Bradley, Edward H. 1898.06
Bradley, Everett 1999.24
Bradley, Frank 1917.27
Bradley, H.B. 1878.14, 1880.17, 1881.18
Bradley, Harry 1886.59
Bradley, Harry B. 1896.39
Bradley, Harry C. 1913.21, 1930.26
Bradley, J. 1873.20, 1873.27, 1875.31
Bradley, Jacque 1907.02
Bradley, James 1872.07, 1873.22, 1873.27, 1875.34, 1875.35, 1875.36, 1875.37, 1875.38, 1875.40, 1876.01, 1876.13, 1876.15, 1876.22, 1876.29, 1877.01
Bradley, Jean 1953.11
Bradley, Jessie 1925.39
Bradley, Leonora 1882.18, 1887.08
Bradley, Lizzie 1885.08
Bradley, M. 1878.01, 1880.36, 1881.29, 1882.02, 1882.50, 1882.74, 1882.79, 1883.32, 1883.46, 1883.53, 1883.63, 1884.13, 1884.41, 1885.02, 1885.22
Bradley, M.J. 1885.49, 1885.66, 1886.03, 1886.42, 1886.52, 1887.07, 1887.16, 1887.39, 1887.45, 1887.48
Bradley, Marilyn 1955.27
Bradley, Marion 1948.27
Bradley, May 1901.17
Bradley, Michael 1877.24, 1878.01, 1878.13, 1878.17, 1879.04, 1879.37, 1879.68, 1880.09, 1880.64, 1881.09, 1885.15
Bradley, Michael J. 1887.48
Bradley, Miss 1897.41
Bradley, Mr. 1876.19, 1895.10
Bradley, Oscar 1922.36, 1924.23, 1924.45, 1925.23, 1926.42, 1927.08, 1930.08, 1930.42, 1931.19, 1931.39, 1932.11, 1934.04
Bradley, Pauline 1901.17
Bradley, Thomas 1905.53, 1922.38
Bradley, Vincent 1898.22
Bradley, Wallace 1938.03
Bradley, Wilber 1946.21
Bradley, Wilbert 1950.07
Bradley, William 1894.27
Bradley, Willie 1923.36
Bradley, Wilson 1940.17
Bradon, Thea 1959.02
Bradshaw, Al 1888.15
Bradshaw, Blanche 1869.27, 1869.32, 1870.07
Bradshaw, C.H. 1881.18, 1883.40, 1884.46, 1885.68
Bradshaw, Charles 1905.29
Bradshaw, Charles H. 1889.05, 1892.19
Bradshaw, Dawn 1962.29
Bradshaw, Messr. 1846.01
Bradshaw, Mollie 1889.10
Bradshaw, Mr. 1846.01, 1852.02, 1858.04, 1861.01
Bradshaw, Mrs. 1869.44, 1870.07
Bradshaw, S. 1860.02, 1865.01, 1865.11, 1866.02
Bradshaw, T. 1999.24
Bradstreet, L.W. 1888.31
Brady, Agnes 1920.28
Brady, Alice 1911.06, 1911.21, 1912.18, 1912.21, 1912.22, 1912.23, 1915.12, 1915.13, 1915.14, 1921.33, 1923.13
Brady, Anthony 1950.04
Brady, Arthur 1933.07
Brady, Bee 1924.12
Brady, Bernadine 1923.09
Brady, Bessie 1908.08, 1909.27
Brady, Florence 1926.23
Brady, James 1923.33
Brady, James Jay 1889.34, 1894.17
Brady, Jimy 1922.30
Brady, Jr., William A. 1929.19, 1930.25
Brady, Jud 1908.44
Brady, June 1950.02
Brady, Leo 1942.27
Brady, Loretta 1916.07
Brady, N.F. 1897.12
Brady, Olive 1927.13, 1928.47, 1930.31
Brady, Patrick 1997.18
Brady, Patrick S. 1999.01, 2001.05
Brady, Patrick Scott 1991.15, 1996.08
Brady, Patti 1944.21
Brady, Ruth 1942.15
Brady, Scott 1959.11
Brady, W.K. 1933.21
Brady, William 1913.33
Brady, William A. 1892.23, 1899.36, 1900.15, 1902.08, 1904.27, 1906.22, 1910.14, 1911.06, 1911.21, 1912.18, 1912.21, 1912.22, 1912.23, 1913.08, 1913.11, 1913.12, 1915.06, 1915.09, 1915.10, 1915.12, 1915.13, 1915.14, 1926.12, 1934.40
Brady, William S. 1929.46

Brae, Bonnie 1951.18
Braff, Ruby 1955.27
Brag, Mons. 1869.03, 1869.16, 1869.30, 1871.23, 1873.16
Bragdon, Guy 1923.36
Bragdon, Helen 1955.11
Bragg, John 1929.07
Braggins, Nellie 1893.40, 1894.05, 1897.50
Braggiotti, Francesca 1930.35
Braggiotti, Mario 1930.35, 1932.04
Braggiotti, S. Herbert 1928.48
Braggiotti, Stiano 1942.01
Bragin, Teddy 1986.13
Braham, Alma 1915.01
Braham, Belle 1888.22
Braham, D. 1879.02
Braham, Dave 1875.14, 1878.13, 1880.32, 1884.42, 1885.08, 1894.19, 1898.70, 1899.23
Braham, David 1869.07, 1872.34, 1873.20, 1873.22, 1873.27, 1873.29, 1875.31, 1875.34, 1875.35, 1875.36, 1875.37, 1875.38, 1875.40, 1876.01, 1876.19, 1876.31, 1877.11, 1877.24, 1878.01, 1878.13, 1878.17, 1879.04, 1879.35, 1879.37, 1879.64, 1879.68, 1880.09, 1880.15, 1880.35, 1880.36, 1880.42, 1880.64, 1881.09, 1881.29, 1882.02, 1882.39, 1882.50, 1882.74, 1882.79, 1883.26, 1883.32, 1883.46, 1883.53, 1883.63, 1884.13, 1884.16, 1884.37, 1884.41, 1884.48, 1885.02, 1885.15, 1885.22, 1885.44, 1885.49, 1885.66, 1886.03, 1886.42, 1886.47, 1886.52, 1887.05, 1887.07, 1887.16, 1887.39, 1887.45, 1887.48, 1888.08, 1888.14, 1888.27, 1888.36, 1888.40, 1889.07, 1889.11, 1889.15, 1889.18, 1889.24, 1890.49, 1891.25, 1891.27, 1891.37, 1891.45, 1891.46, 1892.44, 1892.54, 1893.10, 1893.15, 1893.23, 1893.27, 1893.36, 1893.42, 1893.46, 1894.04, 1894.49, 1895.05, 1896.24, 1896.38, 1897.05, 1897.43, 1985.02, 2000.12
Braham, George 1903.26
Braham, George F. 1885.29, 1896.24, 1897.12
Braham, H. 1882.80, 1894.52, 1898.45, 1899.32
Braham, Harry 1879.06, 1880.42, 1884.16, 1884.37, 1892.58, 1895.39, 1904.05, 1905.26
Braham, Harry S. 1879.01
Braham, John 1882.48, 1886.55, 1886.57, 1890.03, 1894.15, 1898.70, 1910.04
Braham, John J. 1886.24, 1886.32, 1887.33, 1887.43, 1887.50, 1888.06, 1889.16, 1889.46, 1890.43, 1895.38, 1898.05, 1898.41, 1899.21, 1899.36, 1900.19, 1902.12, 1906.50
Braham, Jr., Dave 1892.54, 1893.10, 1893.46, 1896.24, 1897.43
Braham, Jr., David 1893.27, 1893.36, 1894.04, 1894.49, 1895.05
Braham, L. 1881.55
Braham, Leonora 1879.71, 1880.46
Braham, Lionel 1919.20, 1920.34
Braham, Mr. 1892.04
Braham, Philip 1905.48, 1923.36, 1924.01, 1925.42, 1925.50, 1999.23
Braham, Phillip 1926.46
Braham, Professor 1884.61
Braham, Rose 1897.43
Brahams, Johannes 1921.03
Brahms, Caryl 1977.05
Brahms, Johannes 1922.21
Brainard, Ralph 1913.25, 1922.30, 1924.30, 1930.07
Brainard, William 1925.19
Braine, Robert 1924.25
Brainerd, Mary Bella Beale 1886.33
Brainin, Jerome 1942.18
Braisted, Harry 1898.66, 1898.70, 1919.16
Braithwaite, Clara 1904.29
Braley, Berton 1918.09, 1926.23
Brambell, Wilfrid 1965.01
Brambilla, Signora 1883.48
Bramble, Mark 1979.02, 1980.20, 1984.14, 2001.08
Bramlett, Bonnie 1973.14
Bramley, Raymond 1931.39, 1960.19
Brammer, Julius 1914.04, 1916.14, 1921.14, 1922.11, 1922.35, 1926.27, 1927.17, 1928.15, 1986.06
Brancato, Rosemarie 1944.28
Branch, Billy 1939.22
Branch, Gretchen 1934.37
Branch, Rooney 1934.37
Branche, Gretchen 1933.27
Branciard, Mlle. 1876.26
Branciard, Mons. 1876.24, 1876.26
Branciart, Mlle. 1877.11, 1877.13, 1877.19
Branciart, Mons. 1877.06, 1877.13, 1877.14, 1877.19
Brand, A. 1889.28
Brand, Deane 1894.18
Brand, Georgiana 1938.16
Brand, Gibby 1982.01
Brand, Herman 1899.42, 1900.06, 1908.25
Brand, John 1881.04, 1881.11, 1881.21, 1890.19, 1892.42, 1894.11, 1896.28, 1897.36, 1898.54
Brand, John E. 1886.40, 1887.44, 1889.04, 1889.23, 1889.40, 1889.49, 1895.26, 1899.28
Brand, Max 1959.11
Brand, Mr. 1852.04, 1887.10, 1891.33
Brand, Mrs. 1872.17
Brand, Oscar 1966.30, 1968.06
Brand, Phoebe 1936.28
Brand, Robert 1971.17
Brand, William 1922.34
Brandeaux, Pal'mere 1930.14, 1931.34
Brandeaux, Pal'Mere 1930.20, 1930.37
Brandeis, Odna 1927.23
Brandell, Elizabeth 1909.07
Brandell, Josephine 1909.29, 1912.27
Branden, Ethel 1921.31
Brander, Arthur 1927.18, 1927.24
Brander, John 1907.30
Brander, Margot 1941.11, 1944.30
Brandes, E. 1893.24
Brandfon, Joe 1927.43
Brandin, Walter 1955.10
Brandis, Marie 1896.07
Brandl, Johann 1895.35
Brandle, Ella 1908.13
Brando, Marlon 1946.17
Brandon, Barbie 1996.10
Brandon, Billy 1965.23, 1968.07
Brandon, Charles 1898.59
Brandon, Dorothy 1902.32
Brandon, Edith 1883.10, 1886.50, 1886.54
Brandon, Ethel 1884.39, 1885.53, 1916.26
Brandon, Florence 1888.33
Brandon, Florene 1888.33
Brandon, Francis 1914.24
Brandon, Johnny 1978.21
Brandon, Olga 1884.39, 1885.21, 1885.45, 1885.52, 1886.16, 1893.24
Brandon, Peter 1952.03
Brandon, Thomas H. 1930.16
Brandon, Winnie 1913.10
Brandow, Jerry 1939.29
Brandow, Russell 1902.38
Brandram, Rosina 1879.72
Brandt, Eddie 1929.50
Brandt, Edward 1930.32
Brandt, Edwin 1897.47, 1899.03, 1899.27, 1900.36
Brandt, Helga 1940.16, 1946.14, 1947.12
Brandt, Helge 1942.19
Brandt, Inga 1946.14
Brandt, Inge 1940.16, 1942.19, 1947.12
Brandt, James 1988.20
Brandt, Jerry 1979.15
Brandt, Lizzie 1881.13
Brandt, Noah 1897.27
Brandt, Sophie 1908.06, 1908.16, 1910.24
Brandt, William 1911.47, 1924.47
Brandzel, Robert 1974.12, 1977.12
Branen, Jeff T. 1901.13, 1906.04, 1908.08, 1914.22
Branford, Bert 1903.03
Branham, David 1891.26
Brani, Cecile 1895.28
Branigan, Andrew 1911.17
Branigan, J. 1884.13
Brannerd, Mons. 1876.31
Brannick, Eckert 1900.53
Brannick, Heck 1900.53
Brannigan, A. 1912.13
Brannigan, Bernard 1976.29
Brannigan, Robert P. 1974.09
Brannon, Jerry 1942.16
Brannum, Hugh 1955.13
Brannum, Lumpy 1955.13
Branscombe, Dora 1891.24
Branscombe, Maud 1876.13, 1876.15, 1876.29
Branscombe, Maude 1879.14
Branscombe, Mr. 1884.59
Branscombe, W.L. 1905.27
Bransombe, Messr. 1886.36
Branson, Miss 1886.57
Branson, Phil 1886.57, 1906.30, 1908.40, 1914.22
Branson, Philip 1882.05, 1888.09, 1889.01, 1896.25, 1910.27
Brant, Jack 1919.40
Brantford, Bert 1901.19
Brantley, Marion 1937.09
Branton, Allen 1998.14
Branum, Virginia 1929.01
Branz, Cecilia 1931.15
Branz, Celia 1925.25
Brash, Marion 1965.04
Brasica, John 1953.01
Brasill, Daniel 1891.37, 1893.08
Brasington, Alan 1983.01, 1986.18
Brasno, Richard 1942.27
Brassea, Bill 1986.12
Brassens, Georges 1958.06
Brassine, Mons. 1887.37
Brastoff, Sascha 1943.23
Braswell, Charles 1960.04, 1960.22, 1961.18, 1963.13, 1966.10, 1970.13
Bratt, George 1924.14, 1925.20, 1927.23, 1928.19
Bratt, Max 1920.46
Bratton, Jack 1895.24, 1912.16
Bratton, John 1907.41, 1907.42
Bratton, John W. 1894.07, 1894.35, 1896.05, 1896.15, 1896.37, 1897.26, 1897.30, 1900.47, 1900.52, 1900.59, 1901.21, 1902.01, 1902.15, 1902.19, 1902.40, 1903.34, 1904.18, 1904.29, 1904.43, 1905.05, 1905.19, 1905.20, 1905.25, 1909.05, 1925.42
Braun, Betty 1919.25
Braun, Clayton 1925.37
Braun, Elsie 1913.10
Braun, Eugene 1936.22, 1942.19, 1944.20, 1946.14, 1947.12, 1948.19, 1949.05
Braun, Freda 1910.21
Braun, Harvey 1946.22
Braun, Patricia 1982.23
Braun, Ralph 1980.16, 1981.12
Braun, Roger 1968.07
Braun, Sam 1927.19
Braunneck, Alfa 1898.10
Braunneck, Carrie 1898.10
Braunstein, Alan 1971.12, 1984.07
Bravelle, Victor 1926.35
Bravo, Luis 1997.13
Braxton, Brenda 1979.18, 1988.20, 1995.03
Braxton, Brenda B. 1992.08
Braxton, George 1921.26
Bray, Adele 1889.05, 1889.37
Bray, Florence 1952.11
Bray, Stephen 1976.25
Bray, Virginia 1880.21
Bray, Will H. 1878.04, 1878.12, 1879.64, 1880.38, 1890.41, 1893.14, 1894.02, 1897.01, 1902.41, 1903.26
Brayford, Frank 1921.12
Brayton, Jude 1921.41
Brazelton, Conni Marie 1987.17
Brazil, W. 1908.22
Brazil, Walter 1915.11, 1916.02
Brealond, Toney 1971.13
Breannan, Jay 1927.19
Breau, Louis 1922.19, 1923.36
Breaux, Marc 1948.32, 1950.16, 1955.12, 1956.12, 1959.11, 1960.23, 1961.28, 1970.07, 1970.21
Brecher, Kenneth S. 1979.08
Brechner, Eti 1972.17
Brecho 1988.06
Brecht, Bertolt 1933.07, 1935.16, 1962.17, 1963.09, 1965.04, 1966.19, 1976.10, 1977.08, 1989.24, 1995.12
Brecht, Stefan 1975.10
Bredel, Maud 1902.02
Bredschneider, Willy 1913.36, 1917.15
Bree, Chester 1928.44, 1929.42, 1932.14
Bree, Chet 1934.36
Bree, Chett 1938.13
Breedlove, Comer W. 1903.12
Breedlove, Geena 1997.20
Breedon, Arnold 1881.07
Breem, David 1931.08
Breen, Catherine 1918.23
Breen, David 1927.21
Breen, Grace 1917.07
Breen, Harry 1910.17
Breen, Inez 1918.23
Breen, John 1918.23
Breen, Kathleen 1913.32
Breen, Mabel 1907.27
Breen, Margaret 1925.39, 1926.15, 1926.50, 1931.08
Breen, Mr. 1863.01
Breen, Nellie 1918.23, 1922.34, 1923.37, 1925.16, 1925.40, 1926.42
Breen, Red 1949.06
Breen, Robert 1938.18, 1953.04
Breffort, Alexandre 1960.13
Breger, Peter 1994.01
Bregman, Vocco 1962.17
Bregnazzi, Marie 1899.21
Bregvadze, Nani 1977.13
Breisach, Paul 1942.32, 1948.31
Breitenbach, Robert 1890.31, 1892.43, 1893.29, 1894.01, 1894.30, 1896.34, 1897.35, 1898.53
Breitenfeld, Emil 1918.09, 1922.19, 1923.20
Breiter, John Stuart 1942.35
Brel, Jacques 1972.16, 1974.11, 1981.05
Bremer, Walter 1928.08
Bremers, Beverly Ann 1970.20
Bremmer, Clark 1931.01
Brenan, W. 1888.40, 1889.07
Brendel, Al 1920.19
Brendel, El 1921.25
Brengle, George 1893.43
Brennan, A. St. John 1910.24
Brennan, B. 1913.10
Brennan, Dan 1922.18
Brennan, E. 1918.23
Brennan, Ed. 1906.10
Brennan, Eileen 1963.18, 1963.20, 1964.01
Brennan, Emma 1898.63
Brennan, Florence 1904.56
Brennan, George 1900.10, 1901.02, 1902.36, 1904.02, 1905.38, 1906.38, 1907.56, 1910.06, 1912.06
Brennan, George M. 1894.20, 1894.32
Brennan, H.R. 1884.10
Brennan, J. Keirn 1912.06, 1914.29, 1920.16, 1927.58, 1929.06, 1929.17, 1929.22, 1929.28, 1930.26
Brennan, J.A. 1924.46
Brennan, J.H. 1927.14
Brennan, James 1921.38, 1974.26, 1975.13, 1976.09, 1982.01, 1985.20
Brennan, James A. 1922.34
Brennan, Jay 1918.19, 1920.28, 1922.32, 1924.33, 1925.23, 1929.08
Brennan, Joe 1917.26
Brennan, John 1889.11, 1889.15, 1892.54, 1893.27, 1893.36, 1896.24
Brennan, John E. 1906.22
Brennan, Joseph 1892.58
Brennan, Keirn 1928.48
Brennan, Lilla 1907.23
Brennan, Maureen 1974.06, 1976.25, 1982.05, 1987.02
Brennan, May 1910.13, 1911.40
Brennan, Messr. 1894.04
Brennan, Nan 1911.05, 1911.35
Brennan, Nan J. 1909.11, 1916.09
Brennan, Nora 1980.19
Brennan, Stanley 1922.23
Brennan, T.F. 1871.13, 1872.27
Brennan, Thomas F. 1882.81
Brennan, Walter 1928.48
Brennen, T.E. 1884.19
Brenner, Bonny 1930.33
Brenner, Dorothy 1909.02, 1911.40
Brenner, Marie 1902.26
Brenner, Ruth 1929.19
Brenner, S.M. 1907.07
Brenner, Sophie 1919.41, 1920.13
Brenner, Yul 1976.01
Brennir, Albert 1875.19, 1875.23, 1875.26
Brent, Earl 1985.08
Brent, Eva 1873.04, 1873.05
Brent, Romney 1925.17, 1926.13, 1929.19, 1942.01
Brentano, Felix 1941.10, 1942.21, 1942.31, 1942.32, 1943.09, 1944.24, 1945.02, 1945.12, 1947.06, 1957.04
Brentano, Lowell 1938.15
Brentte, Gerard 1967.14, 1972.04
Bresee, R.A. 1889.29
Breslau, Bobbie 1923.24
Breslaw, Bobbie 1924.03, 1926.03, 1926.32
Breslin, Tom 1980.11
Breslin, Tommy 1971.07, 1974.26, 1981.13
Bresnahan, Shannon 1985.13

Bressler, Jerry 1992.03
Breton y Hernandez, Tomas 1949.07
Breton, J. Robert 1972.05
Breton, Mlle. 1868.26, 1869.05
Breton, Robert 1944.30
Breton, Tomas 1969.11
Bretschneider, Carl 1925.02
Brett, Miss 1796.01, 1796.02
Bretton, Elise 1969.06
Breuer, Ernest 1912.36, 1923.20
Breuer, Kurt 1929.17
Breuer, Lee 1988.05
Breuler, Robert 1993.04
Breuning, Georgie 1888.05
Brevarde, J.G. 1884.41
Brevarde, James 1885.02, 1885.15, 1885.22
Brevarde, James G. 1886.42, 1886.52, 1887.07
Brevoor, Anna 1883.26
Brevort, Kate 1875.21
Brew, H.E. 1886.59
Brewer, F. 1887.28
Brewer, James 1978.19, 1978.23
Brewer, John H. 1923.10
Brewer, Sherri 'Peaches' 1967.15
Brewer-Moore, Cathy 1973.06
Brewers, James R. 1910.20
Brewster, Betty 1913.21, 1916.06
Brewster, Bobby 1918.03
Brewster, Clarence 1898.69
Brewster, George 1877.24
Brewster, Henrietta 1924.09
Brewster, John 1925.37
Brewster, Pat 1944.30
Brewster, Ralph 1940.09
Bri, Browley 1992.03
Brian, Antony 1934.34
Brian, Donald 1901.29, 1902.05, 1902.10, 1904.42, 1906.02, 1906.42, 1907.48, 1909.21, 1911.27, 1913.26, 1914.18, 1915.18, 1916.01, 1917.28, 1918.28, 1919.31, 1921.40, 1922.41, 1931.27, 1934.12, 1939.28
Brian, Michael 1985.06
Briansky, Oleg 1951.14
Briant, Paul 1916.15
Briant, Roger 1966.24, 1968.18
Briant, Walter 1916.15
Brianza, Carlotta 1884.39
Briar, Suzanne 1990.04
Briault, Denise 1946.14
Brice, Carol 1958.13, 1959.10, 1959.27, 1961.09, 1961.13, 1962.07, 1963.22, 1964.19, 1965.03, 1967.04, 1971.16, 1976.28
Brice, Elizabeth 1906.17, 1908.10, 1908.29, 1909.14, 1910.01, 1911.02, 1911.05, 1912.13, 1912.35, 1913.17, 1914.31, 1917.26, 1917.35, 1919.10, 1920.20
Brice, Eugene 1961.13, 1962.07, 1965.03
Brice, Fannie 1913.05, 1916.10, 1918.24, 1920.18, 1921.21, 1923.38, 1924.44, 1929.08, 1930.38, 1931.13, 1934.01, 1936.02, 1936.17
Brice, Fanny 1910.18, 1911.24, 1917.13
Brice, Jonathan 1939.21
Brice, Lew 1913.18, 1914.16, 1915.02, 1916.09, 1926.21, 1931.13
Brice, Lilly 1872.07, 1873.27
Brice, Margery 1920.20
Brice, Monty C. 1944.19
Brick, Billy 1875.40
Brick, Eva 1923.35
Brickhill, Joan 1989.23
Bricohi 1881.32
Bricusse, Leslie 1962.17, 1962.18, 1965.19, 1965.28, 1974.11, 1974.22, 1978.18, 1995.15, 1997.09
Bride, Messr. 1852.01
Bridge, Andrew 1984.07, 1988.01, 1990.04, 1992.03, 1993.15, 1994.10, 1999.01, 1999.15
Bridge, Betsy 1956.04
Bridgeland, Thomas 1892.14
Bridgeman 1884.36
Bridgeman, J. 1864.22
Bridges, Deborah Lynn 1976.35, 1979.32
Bridges, Kenneth 1970.02, 1970.15, 1975.06
Bridges, Madelyne 1979.07
Bridges, Scott 1998.18
Bridgewater, Dee Dee 1975.01, 1979.24
Bridgman, Mr. 1861.06, 1862.01, 1862.02
Bridou, Lucienne 1962.12
Bridwell, Thom 1986.02
Brier, Bill 1965.03
Brier, John 1872.21
Briere, Claire 1926.40, 1926.43
Briere, Mlle. 1926.45, 1926.47, 1926.48
Brierly, Bertha A. 1898.45
Briess, Fred 1946.16
Brigate, Edward 1982.22
Briggs, Bunny 1945.18, 1989.02
Briggs, Clare 1923.25
Briggs, Jean 1934.06
Briggs, John R. 1982.13
Briggs, Matt 1944.23, 1947.01
Briggs, Mr. 1848.03
Briggs, Tom 1996.04, 2001.09
Brigham, Alice 1891.02
Brigham, Constance 1946.02, 1955.05, 1957.02
Brighenti, Messr. 1883.48
Brighenti, Signor 1883.48
Brighouse, Harold 1966.27
Bright, Charles 1880.55
Bright, Chester 1926.08
Bright, Ione 1937.11
Bright, John 1881.31
Bright, Lee 1924.12
Bright, Martha 1908.01
Bright, Messr. 1904.44
Bright, Michael 1985.20
Bright, Miss 1871.11
Bright, Patricia 1942.35, 1950.09
Bright, Richard S. 1978.06
Bright, Tom 1882.80
Brightman, Julian 1990.20, 1991.13, 1995.13
Brightman, Sarah 1988.01
Brightman, Stanley 1914.32, 1923.36
Brighton, Charles 1894.35
Brighton, Georgie 1891.41
Brighton, Hilda 1925.42
Briglio, Nick 1905.26
Brilhante, Patricia 1940.21
Brill, Charles 1950.08
Brill, E.S. 1908.27
Brill, Edwin S. 1898.77
Brill, Fran 1969.03
Brill, King 1948.20
Brill, Klaus 1940.04
Brill, Leighton K. 1928.44, 1930.42, 1931.31
Brill, Marty 1964.18
Brill, Robert 1998.04
Brilliant, Paul 1864.02
Brin, Celia 1971.12
Brink, Lillie 1900.49
Brink, Lilly 1898.34, 1899.15, 1900.56, 1901.12, 1902.06, 1903.18
Brink, Robert 1942.19, 1944.18
Brink, Yvonne 1978.26
Brinker, Lynn 1960.05
Brinkhurst, Frank 1892.27
Brinkley, Grace 1928.14, 1928.26, 1929.09, 1930.11, 1931.42, 1931.48
Brinkley, H.W. 1885.42, 1889.20
Brinkley, Howell 1994.07, 1996.17
Brinkley, Mark 1976.18
Brinkley, Vic 1899.26
Brinkman, Edward 1957.04
Brinkworth, W.H. 1872.25
Brinkworth, William H. 1870.28, 1870.31, 1870.32, 1870.40, 1871.05, 1872.02, 1872.04, 1872.05, 1872.08, 1872.12, 1872.14, 1872.30, 1872.36, 1872.38, 1872.40, 1872.43
Brinsley, Harry 1889.05
Brinsley, Henry 1893.30
Brinsley, J.S. 1887.11
Brinsley, Richard 1905.15
Brinson, Philip 1951.11
Brinton, Florence 1925.37
Briot, Mlle. 1868.26, 1869.03, 1869.05, 1869.16, 1870.45, 1871.03, 1871.06, 1871.07, 1871.26
Briot, Mme. 1870.03
Briquet, Jean 1910.26, 1913.21, 1914.07, 1915.19, 1915.21
Brisbane, Ruth 1985.05
Brisbin, Gloria 1981.21
Briscoe, Fannie 1896.05, 1897.40, 1898.12, 1899.06
Briscoe, Fanny 1898.60
Briscoe, Murray 1942.25
Briscoe, Ray 1888.31, 1894.49
Brisebois, Danielle 1976.31, 1977.06
Brisky, Gaston 1999.18
Brisky, Socrates 1958.20
Brislin, Lauretta 1934.12
Brisson, Carl 1936.27
Brisson, Frederick 1954.05, 1955.08, 1957.07, 1969.17, 1976.09, 1983.08
Brisson, Mlle. 1870.44, 1871.27
Brist, Mlle. 1871.23
Bristoe, Ray 1885.66, 1886.03
Bristol, Messr. 1851.05
Bristoll, Mr. 1851.03
Bristow, George F. 1855.03, 1855.04, 1855.05, 1855.06, 1855.07, 1855.08, 1855.09
Bristow, Nora 1962.13
Brite, Betty 1939.31
Brito, Adrian 1989.20
Britt, Jacqueline 1970.07
Britta, Mlle. 1911.18
Brittan, Robert 1973.10
Britten, Benjamin 1948.31, 1950.18
Britten, William 1939.19
Britton, Dorothy 1929.26, 1930.22
Britton, Edith 1928.49
Britton, Ethel 1931.05, 1932.23
Britton, Florence 1939.07
Britton, Frank 1931.19
Britton, George 1946.18
Britton, Jeff 1970.20
Britton, Joe 1899.31
Britton, Milt 1931.19
Britton, Minnie 1901.09
Britton, Pamela 1947.07
Britton, Sadie 1899.31
Britz, John R. 1916.13
Broad, Jay 1969.03
Broad, Lois 1969.03
Broad, Mr. 1823.01
Broadbent, Aida 1945.16, 1946.03, 1946.18
Broadbent, Lynn 1962.15
Broadbent, Lynne 1953.09, 1959.11
Broadcloth, G. 1867.12
Broadhurst and Currie 1903.20, 1905.33, 1906.35
Broadhurst, Cecil 1951.05
Broadhurst, George 1907.29, 1907.30, 1918.22
Broadhurst, George H. 1903.07, 1905.33
Broadhurst, Janet 1961.19
Broadhurst, Jeffrey 1999.23
Broadhurst, Jeffrey Lee 1989.03, 1992.02
Broadhurst, Miss 1796.01, 1796.02
Broadnax, Edward 1933.04
Broadway Fund, The 1993.19
Broadway in Concert, Inc. 1992.12
Broadway Theatre Opera Company 1897.50, 1899.06
Brobyn, Virginia 1974.08
Broccolini, J.C. 1887.43
Broccolini, Signor 1882.66, 1886.25, 1886.55, 1886.57
Brock, Art 1904.27
Brock, Arthur 1898.31
Brock, Frances 1939.17
Brock, Jerry 1974.09
Brock, Mesdame 1852.05
Brockbank, Harrison 1910.10, 1911.38, 1913.10, 1914.11, 1918.10, 1918.30, 1919.27, 1921.14, 1923.03, 1925.02, 1928.12, 1933.03
Brockman, James 1917.37, 1928.47
Brockmeyer, W.C. 1897.53, 1898.04, 1898.15
Brockmeyer, W.E. 1898.14, 1898.30
Brocksmith, Roy 1976.10, 1984.14
Brockway, Mr. 1869.17, 1869.28
Brockway, W.H. 1868.14, 1870.08, 1870.11, 1870.16, 1870.17, 1885.53, 1886.44, 1886.51
Brockway, William 1868.33
Brockway, William H. 1866.32, 1866.35, 1867.21, 1868.05, 1868.21
Brocolini, C. 1884.09
Brocolini, Signor 1879.70, 1879.72, 1882.21, 1882.23
Brodbelt, Florence 1913.20
Brode, David B. 1987.18, 1992.04
Brode, Herman 1880.34, 1892.37
Broder, J. Scott 1989.22
Broderick, Diana 1982.11
Broderick, Edna 1910.03, 1912.48
Broderick, George 1886.12, 1888.35, 1893.02, 1895.15, 1897.22, 1898.15, 1904.12, 1986.11
Broderick, George H. 1885.43, 1889.16
Broderick, George L. 1894.42
Broderick, H. 1870.01
Broderick, Helen 1923.33, 1925.05, 1926.46, 1929.45, 1931.16, 1932.18, 1933.22
Broderick, James 1953.02, 1998.19
Broderick, Johnny 1935.04
Broderick, Lillian 1920.18, 1938.03
Broderick, Matthew 1995.05, 2001.05
Broderick, R.W. 1890.25
Broderick, Robert 1889.41, 1895.25, 1899.28, 1903.32, 1905.03, 1908.29
Broderick, William 1892.52, 1893.35, 1896.50, 1897.24, 1898.05, 1898.39, 1898.40, 1898.42, 1900.47, 1902.01, 1903.32
Broderip, Messr. 1869.37
Broderson, Margaret 1964.20
Broderson, Moishe 1967.08
Brodie, Ann 1942.11
Brodin, Helena 1966.19
Brodnax, Margaret 1920.34
Brodszky, Nicholas 1974.10
Brody, Bonnie 1962.04, 1962.18
Brody, Lee 1931.21, 1934.40, 1939.22, 1939.26
Brody, Leonore 1930.01
Brody, Max 1913.26, 1916.01
Brody, Miska 1916.19
Broeck, Mary Ten 1904.50
Broeck, May Ten 1880.05, 1881.17, 1881.19, 1883.02, 1894.21, 1899.02, 1899.19
Brogan, Hal 1928.19, 1929.20
Brogan, Messr. 1861.06
Brogan, Mr. 1863.10
Brogan, Patricia 1963.30
Brogger, Ivar 1993.07
Brogsdale, Walter 1928.34, 1929.18, 1930.29, 1932.12
Brohn, Bill 1975.13, 1978.03, 1978.22, 1980.26, 1983.17, 1984.10
Brohn, William D. 1966.14, 1985.20, 1989.03, 1991.03, 1991.05, 1992.02, 1992.10, 1993.19, 1994.02, 1994.08
Brohn, William David 1998.01, 1998.05, 1999.23
Broich, Madame 1918.31
Brokaw, Charles 1934.29, 1935.14
Bromberg, J. Edward 1946.23
Bromley, Leslie 1969.04
Bronell, Mildred 1915.27
Brongo, Laurie 1985.15
Bronner, C. 1922.15
Bronner, Cleveland 1920.23, 1920.47, 1921.02, 1922.15
Bronskill, Reginald 1989.17
Bronson, Aileen 1917.31
Bronson, Aleen 1917.31
Bronson, E. 1881.32
Bronson, Edna 1903.29
Bronson, James 1952.03
Bronson, Miss 1886.36
Bronson, Percey 1916.21
Bronson, Percy 1907.30, 1907.59
Bronson, Walter 1878.15, 1880.51
Bronson, Yank 1930.19
Bronson-Howard, George 1912.24, 1912.43
Bronte, C. 1872.23, 1872.35
Bronte, Charlotte 2000.20
Bronte, Mae 1910.23
Bronzini, A. 1911.19
Brooderick, Helen 1907.24
Brook's Uniform Company 1915.29
Brook, Clifford 1918.22
Brook, Harold Ten 1930.26
Brook, Leonard 1968.32
Brook, Mazy 1899.33
Brook, Mesdame 1852.01
Brook, Peter 1954.19, 1960.13, 1965.39, 1983.16
Brook, Sara 1971.02, 1972.13, 1972.19, 1972.24, 1973.09, 1978.26, 1989.18
Brook, Sidney 1922.38
Brookbank, Harrison 1930.21
Brooke, Claude 1886.41, 1896.29
Brooke, Clifford 1918.02, 1918.26, 1918.33, 1921.04, 1929.08, 1934.15
Brooke, Francis 1896.47
Brooke, J. Clifford 1919.35, 1920.05
Brooke, John 1931.34
Brooke, Mamie 1908.33
Brooke, Percy 1894.39
Brooke, Tom 1966.02
Brooke, Tyler 1915.05, 1915.28, 1916.22, 1919.44, 1920.39
Brooke, Virginia 1881.11
Brooker, Gary 1982.22
Brookes, Alice 1871.15
Brookes, G. 1862.01
Brookes, George 1869.31
Brookfield, Charles 1894.25
Brookfield, Charles H.E. 1906.47
Brookins, Fred 1948.20
Brooklyn Academy of Music Next Wave Festival 1988.05

Brooklyn Calcium Light Company 1887.28
Brookmeyer, Bob 1958.12
Brooks 1921.38, 1929.47, 1930.21, 1930.23, 1931.06, 1931.27, 1931.35, 1931.41, 1931.43, 1931.45, 1932.02, 1932.12, 1933.06, 1933.16, 1933.18, 1933.23, 1937.07
Brooks and Dingwall 1908.43
Brooks Company 1925.04
Brooks Costume Company 1924.37, 1926.06, 1926.12, 1926.23, 1926.26, 1926.36, 1927.02, 1927.53, 1928.01, 1928.09, 1929.01, 1929.35, 1929.45, 1935.05, 1935.06, 1935.07, 1935.08, 1935.09, 1935.10, 1938.02, 1938.10
Brooks Marjorie 1925.35
Brooks Theatrical Costumers 1921.28
Brooks Uniform Company 1918.40, 1919.08, 1919.25, 1919.27, 1920.02, 1920.14, 1922.32, 1925.09, 1926.41
Brooks, A.R. 1876.16
Brooks, Alan 1909.02
Brooks, Arthur 1920.35, 1922.27
Brooks, Arthur D. 1914.17
Brooks, Beatrice 1967.01
Brooks, Blanche 1903.06
Brooks, C.M. 1907.24
Brooks, Catherine 1932.30, 1933.06
Brooks, Cliff 1896.49
Brooks, David 1944.23, 1947.07, 1955.05, 1962.20, 1970.12, 1981.13
Brooks, Donald 1962.03, 1964.21, 1965.17, 1965.31, 1968.31, 1970.07, 1974.26, 1975.22, 1977.02, 1977.14, 1979.01, 1979.09, 1983.08
Brooks, Eleanor 1905.33
Brooks, Eleanore 1927.58
Brooks, Ellanore 1906.49
Brooks, Ellis 1888.15
Brooks, Etta 1884.59
Brooks, Evelyn 1942.14, 1942.29, 1942.34
Brooks, Flo 1926.16
Brooks, Florence 1904.41, 1907.34
Brooks, Francis 1975.10
Brooks, G. 1861.06, 1862.02
Brooks, G.H. 1896.05
Brooks, Georgia 1905.33
Brooks, Georgie 1906.49
Brooks, Glenn 1973.10
Brooks, Gwendolyn 1966.15, 1999.06
Brooks, Harry 1896.01, 1921.18, 1929.23, 1939.29, 1975.22, 1978.09, 1980.10, 1989.02
Brooks, Harvey 1918.13, 2000.12
Brooks, Hawley 1912.11
Brooks, Helen 1902.24
Brooks, Howard 1942.20
Brooks, Ida 1896.05, 1897.25
Brooks, Inc. 1930.29
Brooks, Irving 1909.05, 1915.28, 1917.25
Brooks, Jack 1924.32
Brooks, Jeff 1978.06, 1991.06, 1991.15, 1999.16
Brooks, John 1875.05
Brooks, Joseph 1894.39, 1901.27, 1903.39, 1905.25
Brooks, Laurie 1888.39
Brooks, Lawrence 1944.21, 1948.27, 1952.13, 1965.35
Brooks, Lewis 1957.04
Brooks, Louise 1929.08
Brooks, Marjorie 1924.01, 1929.51
Brooks, Mary 1931.36
Brooks, Matt 1939.25, 1940.10, 1948.04, 1948.15
Brooks, Maude 1930.21
Brooks, May 1918.32
Brooks, Mel 1957.05, 1962.04, 2001.05
Brooks, Melvin 1952.09
Brooks, Messr. 1869.07, 1883.04, 1883.52
Brooks, Miss 1869.43, 1881.04
Brooks, Mme. 1841.01
Brooks, Myra C. 1898.75
Brooks, Phyllis 1940.19
Brooks, Sharon 1976.35, 1984.09
Brooks, Sharon K. 1979.18
Brooks, Shelton 1919.40, 1922.25, 1924.37, 1930.29, 1943.02, 1949.09, 1953.12, 1955.13, 1963.02, 1967.03, 1976.04, 1979.25, 2000.12
Brooks, Sheoton 1917.22
Brooks, Sinclair 1936.30
Brooks, Tyler 1913.29
Brooks, Una 1915.12, 1915.14, 1915.23
Brooks, Virginia Fox 1918.05, 1918.20
Brooks, Walter 1917.34, 1918.06, 1919.32, 1921.16, 1922.44, 1923.06, 1923.08, 1923.24, 1923.37, 1924.10, 1924.40, 1925.44, 1927.10, 1927.53, 1927.64, 1932.30
Brooks-Bell, Lillian 1880.47
Brooks-Hunt, Ida 1904.52
Brooks-Mahieu 1923.10, 1923.16, 1923.23, 1923.31
Brooks-Mahieu Company 1923.08, 1923.46
Brooks-Mahieu Costume Company 1923.40, 1924.10, 1924.26
Broome, John 1962.18
Broomfield, Leroy 1923.11
Broones, Martin 1924.33, 1927.13
Brophy, John 1948.28
Brophy, Sallie 1954.13
Broschi, Karl 1890.40
Brosi, Elsa 1882.76
Brosi, Frl. 1883.08
Brosi, L. 1883.49
Broske, Octavia 1910.13, 1911.26, 1912.34, 1914.14, 1914.26, 1919.14
Brossecola, Coka 1958.18
Brosset, Colette 1958.18, 1965.37
Brosten, Harve 1988.10
Brother 1914.25
Brothers, Claire 1973.14
Brothers, Martin 1961.10, 1968.32
Brotherson, Eric 1943.03, 1943.14, 1949.18, 1964.23, 1975.22
Brotherson, Lez 1998.10
Brotherton, Bob 1971.19
Brotherton, George C. 1886.15
Brouard, Andre 1919.42
Brough, Lionel 1886.50, 1886.54
Brough, Mr. 1836.01
Brough, Robert 1859.05, 1859.06
Brough, Robert B. 1867.29
Brough, Sidney 1886.50, 1886.54
Brough, William 1859.05, 1859.06, 1868.32, 1869.08, 1869.25, 1870.11, 1876.30
Brougham, Ethel 1899.39
Brougham, Harry 1885.52
Brougham, Henry 1885.67
Brougham, John 1848.02, 1851.02, 1851.03, 1851.05, 1853.01, 1855.11, 1856.02, 1856.03, 1857.08, 1859.14, 1863.10, 1866.13, 1866.16, 1866.17, 1867.18, 1867.20, 1868.04, 1868.22, 1869.04, 1869.13, 1869.15, 1870.34, 1871.13, 1872.23, 1872.35, 1873.03, 1876.23, 1876.35, 1878.22, 1881.18
Brougham, Mrs. John 1848.02
Broughton, H. 1870.43
Broughton, J.H. 1870.39
Broughton, Madeline 1903.09
Broughton, Mamie 1884.34
Broughton, Mr. 1870.39, 1871.19
Broughton, Philip 1930.06
Brouillette, Eli J. 1905.41
Broun, Heywood 1922.42, 1924.15, 1931.21
Broun, Jeremy 1964.20
Broussard, Mary 1944.24, 1946.13
Brousseau, James 1987.18, 1989.23
Broussolle, Jean 1964.02, 1968.21
Brower, Frank 1865.03
Brower, Jay 1960.07, 1964.18
Brower, Olive 1920.28
Brower, Robert 1880.51, 1881.24
Brower, Walter 1920.19
Brown, A. Seymour 1905.22, 1907.13, 1909.05, 1909.13, 1909.25, 1910.20, 1912.14, 1912.16, 1912.38, 1914.15, 1915.24, 1923.16, 1924.32, 1925.47, 1927.05, 1927.14, 1928.45
Brown, Ada 1930.29, 1945.08
Brown, Agnes Cain 1907.26
Brown, Agnes Caine 1907.08
Brown, Al W. 1913.02, 1913.05
Brown, Albert W. 1913.18
Brown, Alex 1897.07, 1984.15
Brown, Alfred 1920.36
Brown, Alice 1884.46, 1922.22, 1923.11
Brown, Ann 1996.18, 1998.03, 2000.11
Brown, Ann Whitlow 2001.06
Brown, Anne 1935.13, 1937.14, 1942.03
Brown, Anthony 1940.01, 1942.11
Brown, Arnold 1927.16
Brown, Arthur 1924.18, 1925.10, 1925.31
Brown, Arthur William 1924.36
Brown, Arvin 1979.07
Brown, B. 1859.05, 1859.07
Brown, Barry 1983.11, 1989.27, 1991.06
Brown, Barry M. 1974.17, 1978.25
Brown, Ben 1992.08
Brown, Betty 1916.14
Brown, Bill 1925.29, 1927.64, 1928.19
Brown, Billings 1948.22
Brown, Billy 1920.36
Brown, Blair 1976.10, 2000.01
Brown, Bly 1916.11, 1917.31
Brown, Bob 1963.11
Brown, Burton 1923.26
Brown, Calvin 1928.21
Brown, Candy 1975.14, 1985.05
Brown, Cassie 1901.20
Brown, Chamberlain 1932.14
Brown, Charles 1868.14, 1870.17, 1881.26, 1911.01, 1911.14, 1911.45, 1913.06, 1915.08, 1918.12, 1918.35, 1921.19, 1922.18, 1924.06, 1924.25, 1928.01, 1930.15
Brown, Charles D. 1935.03
Brown, Charles H. 1905.47
Brown, Charles P. 1888.43
Brown, Charlie 1919.23
Brown, Charnele Dozier 1988.02
Brown, Chester 1918.40
Brown, Craig 1974.17
Brown, Daisy 1896.46, 1909.10
Brown, Danial Jerod 1999.15
Brown, Daniel 1976.01
Brown, Dave 1980.17
Brown, Deborah K. 1978.03
Brown, Dempsey 1899.23
Brown, Donald 1934.35
Brown, Doris 1945.06, 1946.09
Brown, Dorothy 1922.39, 1924.33, 1926.03
Brown, Dorothy E. 1926.22
Brown, Dun 1866.13
Brown, E. 1879.28
Brown, E.P. 1894.37
Brown, Earl 1977.16
Brown, Eddy 1919.24
Brown, Edgar 1930.29
Brown, Eleanor 1914.22, 1915.02, 1915.11, 1915.26, 1916.03, 1916.23
Brown, Elmer 1924.33, 1925.33
Brown, Ernest 1952.02, 1965.18
Brown, Evelyn 1929.48
Brown, Fannie 1862.08
Brown, Fleta Ian 1908.07
Brown, Flo 1933.06
Brown, Forman 1936.12, 1945.16, 1947.14, 1964.24, 1976.01
Brown, Frank 1909.10
Brown, Fred 1920.36
Brown, G. 1879.04
Brown, G.B. 1896.49
Brown, Garfield 1924.07
Brown, Garrett M. 1979.05
Brown, George 1898.22, 1901.20, 1935.01, 1999.15
Brown, George Francis 1927.36
Brown, Georgia 1963.01, 1979.09, 1987.12, 1989.24
Brown, Georgie 1922.38
Brown, Georginna 1922.32
Brown, Ginger 1980.10
Brown, Graham 1975.02
Brown, H. 1873.18
Brown, H.A. 1880.48
Brown, H.W. 1882.76
Brown, Hal 1929.25
Brown, Harold 1923.43
Brown, Harold R. 1954.06
Brown, Harry 1881.21, 1881.33, 1882.63, 1882.66, 1882.80, 1885.08, 1888.11, 1889.19, 1889.29, 1893.11, 1894.47, 1897.13, 1899.29, 1899.36, 1900.12, 1903.07, 1903.18, 1903.23, 1904.43, 1920.36
Brown, Harvey 1956.11
Brown, Haskell 1932.01
Brown, Hattie 1882.07, 1882.09, 1883.13
Brown, Hattie A. 1883.11, 1883.12, 1883.15
Brown, Helen 1927.37
Brown, Henry 1902.04
Brown, Honey 1928.10
Brown, Ida 1932.30
Brown, Isabelle 1942.25
Brown, J. 1875.40
Brown, J. Albert 1906.40
Brown, J. Mardo 1924.27, 1930.16, 1930.42, 1933.06, 1946.08
Brown, J.B. 1875.05, 1884.10
Brown, J.E. 1880.37
Brown, J.M. 1879.06
Brown, Jack 1964.33, 1972.11
Brown, James 1982.22
Brown, James B. 1927.27
Brown, Jane 1907.58
Brown, Jason Robert 1998.21
Brown, Jean 1922.31
Brown, Jeb 1981.07
Brown, Jessica 1917.37, 1919.08, 1920.13, 1920.19, 1920.22, 1920.23, 1921.02
Brown, Jessica Leigh 2001.02
Brown, Jessie 1907.26
Brown, Joe E. 1920.35, 1923.31, 1924.47, 1925.29, 1926.39, 1951.17, 1961.09
Brown, Johnny 1964.32
Brown, Joseph 1930.24
Brown, Joyce 1970.05, 1972.25, 1973.10, 1973.15, 1975.09, 1981.28
Brown, Jr., Newton 1890.44
Brown, Jr., Oscar 1969.15
Brown, Julia 1876.13
Brown, Julius Richard 1980.14, 1982.17
Brown, Ka-Ron 1982.22
Brown, Kay 1961.02
Brown, Kelly 1960.07, 1962.05, 1965.18
Brown, Kenneth 1931.44
Brown, L. Slade 1960.06, 1962.04
Brown, Larry 1976.16
Brown, Larry W. 1999.06
Brown, Leon E. 1917.32
Brown, Leonard D. 1978.11
Brown, Leonore 1931.44
Brown, Les 1975.12
Brown, Lester 1898.43, 1908.23
Brown, Lester W. 1898.28
Brown, Lew 1910.22, 1919.37, 1919.40, 1920.24, 1920.28, 1921.34, 1923.18, 1924.01, 1925.01, 1925.22, 1925.28, 1926.16, 1927.04, 1927.41, 1927.46, 1928.22, 1928.36, 1928.37, 1929.03, 1929.35, 1930.11, 1931.30, 1932.07, 1933.05, 1934.39, 1937.09, 1939.24, 1939.25, 1940.10, 1941.03, 1942.16, 1952.11, 1956.02, 1962.17, 1967.13, 1968.20, 1974.11, 1974.26, 1975.22, 1984.06, 1986.06, 1989.16, 1990.09, 1999.01, 1999.24
Brown, Lewis 1967.01, 1991.01
Brown, Lillian 1924.37
Brown, Lillyan 1952.02
Brown, Lillyn 1949.16
Brown, Lisa 1978.13
Brown, Lorenzo W. 1918.36
Brown, Lorna 1978.26
Brown, Louis 1919.05
Brown, Louise 1925.11, 1925.29, 1926.18, 1928.44, 1929.07, 1929.50
Brown, Lucy 1953.05
Brown, M. 1885.68
Brown, Marion 1942.20
Brown, Marjorie 1937.11
Brown, Martin 1908.18, 1909.14, 1909.29, 1910.19, 1910.25, 1911.32, 1912.09, 1912.27, 1913.17, 1914.34, 1928.33
Brown, Martin G. 1907.10, 1907.24
Brown, Mary 1930.33
Brown, Master 1870.22
Brown, Maude 1911.45
Brown, Maudie 1910.04
Brown, Max 1959.11, 1975.06, 1975.24
Brown, Max J. 1970.07, 1970.08
Brown, Maxine 1917.29, 1919.31, 1922.24, 1924.04
Brown, Melville 1905.34
Brown, Messr. 1853.01, 1903.36, 1905.22
Brown, Michael 1952.09, 1956.08, 1972.07, 1986.14
Brown, Mildred 1924.03, 1924.17, 1925.18
Brown, Miss 1862.02, 1866.18, 1869.08, 1869.36, 1870.02, 1870.31, 1871.11, 1886.36, 1917.31
Brown, Mollie 1887.49, 1888.37
Brown, Mr. 1852.04, 1859.06, 1860.03, 1860.04, 1862.07, 1864.22, 1867.23, 1869.26, 1892.43
Brown, Mrs. Sedley 1863.02, 1863.04, 1863.09, 1863.10, 1864.05, 1864.06, 1864.09, 1864.12, 1864.15, 1867.22, 1867.23, 1867.26, 1867.27, 1869.28
Brown, Nacio Herb 1940.02, 1964.02, 1979.14, 1983.09, 1985.08, 1986.06, 1989.21, 1992.18
Brown, Nat 1903.05
Brown, Nellie 1912.24
Brown, Nicholas 1902.09
Brown, Norma 1909.11, 1917.28, 1921.08
Brown, P.L. 1983.05

Brown, Patricia 1981.21
Brown, Patrika 1972.09, 1975.23
Brown, Paul 1956.01
Brown, Paula Anita 1984.09
Brown, Pearl 1907.29, 1907.31
Brown, Peggy 1921.25
Brown, Pendleton 1971.01, 1972.01
Brown, Peter 1974.24, 1982.22
Brown, Phil 1938.18
Brown, Porter Emerson 1906.12
Brown, R.A. 1905.23
Brown, R.G. 1962.02
Brown, Ralph 1939.14, 1989.02
Brown, Raquel C. 1991.03
Brown, Raymond A. 1905.26
Brown, Richard 1901.29, 1918.17
Brown, Robert 1869.28, 1911.25, 1952.03
Brown, Roger 1966.13, 1967.10
Brown, Rosa 1939.17
Brown, Rosalind 1998.13
Brown, Rose 1907.55, 1943.14
Brown, Rowland 1942.11
Brown, Russ 1928.35, 1930.11, 1940.10, 1941.07, 1945.09, 1947.11, 1955.08
Brown, Russell 1918.13
Brown, Ruth 1983.15, 1989.02
Brown, S. 1857.03
Brown, Samuel 1879.42
Brown, Sandra 1994.02
Brown, Sarah 1929.39
Brown, Seymour 1905.48, 1908.19, 1910.12, 1912.07, 1927.05
Brown, Sharon 1968.24
Brown, Sherman 1921.09
Brown, Sid 1911.24
Brown, Slade 1966.30, 1981.07, 1984.01
Brown, Steve 1979.29
Brown, Susaye 1931.32, 1932.08
Brown, Susie 1898.17
Brown, T. Allston 1885.21, 1886.48, 1886.49
Brown, T.A. 1906.31
Brown, Theo. M. 1889.05
Brown, Theodore 1895.35, 1899.35
Brown, Tom 1898.22, 1909.27, 1920.36, 1956.15
Brown, Troy 1939.29, 1940.09
Brown, Vanessa 1989.08
Brown, Verne 1920.36
Brown, Vida 1948.25
Brown, W. 1892.35, 1901.24
Brown, W. Earl 1989.12
Brown, W. Eaton 1885.68
Brown, W.D. 1877.15
Brown, W.H. 1899.05
Brown, W.P. 1883.31, 1904.01
Brown, Walter 1892.37, 1898.67, 1954.14
Brown, Walter P. 1955.09, 1956.06, 1958.03, 1962.16, 1965.20, 1965.33, 1967.15, 1973.10
Brown, Warren 1955.27
Brown, Warren J. 1955.07, 1956.16, 1962.20
Brown, Will P. 1892.45, 1896.48, 1898.51
Brown, William 1894.13, 1894.42, 1898.60
Brown, William Eaton 1882.57
Brown, William F. 1968.13, 1975.01, 1978.28, 1984.09, 1993.03
Brown, William H. 1888.27
Brown, William Maynardier 1895.19
Brown, William P. 1891.15, 1894.46, 1901.15, 1903.25
Brown, William Potter 1896.31
Brown, William Scott 1988.01
Brown, William Yates 1935.12
Brown, Zack 1983.02
Brown, Zoe 1974.04
Browne, Bothwell 1911.29
Browne, Earle 1905.26
Browne, Edward 1943.03
Browne, Edwin 1886.60
Browne, Florence 1918.25, 1920.28, 1922.23
Browne, Francis 1875.21, 1882.62
Browne, G. Byron 1885.47
Browne, G.F. 1860.06, 1867.20
Browne, George H. 1890.50
Browne, Harry 1911.29
Browne, Harry C. 1918.03, 1919.28, 1922.16
Browne, Hattie A. 1883.14
Browne, Irene 1934.34, 1963.29
Browne, J. Albert 1914.08, 1919.11, 1921.07
Browne, J.H. 1878.05, 1885.21
Browne, J.S. 1839.01
Browne, John H. 1884.10
Browne, Leslie 1993.19, 1996.13
Browne, Lew 1922.15
Browne, Lewis Allen 1924.42
Browne, Louisa 1864.06
Browne, Mesdame 1856.04
Browne, Miss 1896.44
Browne, Mrs. G. 1864.12
Browne, R.A. 1905.49
Browne, Raymond A. 1901.13, 1902.01
Browne, Richard 1979.28
Browne, Robert M. 1980.30
Browne, Roscoe Lee 1966.15, 1983.06
Browne, Tom 1891.24, 1901.06
Browne, W.M. 1899.41
Browne, Walter 1892.40, 1910.11, 1911.09
Browne, William H. 1923.43
Brownel, Louise 1919.39
Brownell, Bobby 1959.13
Brownell, John C. 1906.28
Brownfoot, Andrew 1970.11
Brownfoot, Margaret 1970.11
Brownie 1921.26
Browning 1908.28
Browning, Edith 1911.04, 1913.03
Browning, Edna 1879.65, 1879.67
Browning, Eleanor 1905.03, 1905.38
Browning, Harry 1905.14
Browning, Ivan H. 1924.27
Browning, Joe 1921.02
Browning, Kirk 1959.07
Browning, L.W. 1886.49
Browning, Miss 1881.03, 1881.14, 1882.37
Browning, Sara 1879.65, 1879.67
Browning, Susan 1970.13, 1973.03, 1975.06, 1985.06, 1994.09
Browning, W.L. 1886.48
Browning, William E. 1926.28
Brownlee, John 1943.08, 1979.29
Brownlow, Wallace 1904.36, 1905.08, 1905.11
Brox, Dagmar 1921.30, 1923.32, 1924.44, 1925.45
Brox, Kathlyn 1921.30, 1923.32, 1924.44, 1925.45
Brox, Lorraine 1921.30, 1923.32, 1924.44, 1925.45
Broze, N. 1873.26
Brozini, A. 1911.16
Bruant, Aristede 1952.04
Brubaker, Robert 1978.19, 1978.23, 1979.20, 1979.27, 1980.21, 1981.20, 1982.16, 1983.13, 1984.11, 1985.09, 1985.13, 1986.04, 1986.09, 1987.03, 1987.08, 1987.10, 1988.04
Brubette, Esther 1902.27
Bruccaini, Mr. 1864.09
Bruce, Andrew 1988.09, 1991.03, 1999.20
Bruce, Betty 1938.14, 1940.07, 1941.09, 1943.01, 1945.03, 1947.11
Bruce, Carol 1940.08, 1942.23, 1946.01, 1948.20, 1949.01, 1961.15, 1965.06, 1967.14
Bruce, Dan 1908.23
Bruce, Dorothy 1921.20, 1922.34, 1923.02
Bruce, Eddie 1935.11, 1947.03, 1955.09, 1960.09, 1988.20
Bruce, Edwin 1964.18
Bruce, Florence 1918.07
Bruce, Geraldine 1909.08
Bruce, Ida 1879.50
Bruce, Jack 1982.22
Bruce, Lloyd 1919.10
Bruce, Mae 1893.24
Bruce, Michael 1982.22
Bruce, Mr. 1857.08, 1865.04
Bruce, Nigel 1937.10, 1938.10
Bruce, Richard 1920.21
Bruce, Shelley 1977.06
Bruce, Vince 1991.07
Bruce, Virginia 1931.04
Bruce, Wilma 1919.10
Bruciani, Mr. 1863.10
Brucianni, Mr. 1864.12
Bruck, Arnold 1983.17
Brucken, Hugo 1931.09
Bruckner, Larry 1968.02
Bruder, Patsy 1959.13
Brudno, Abraham 1998.11
Brueler, Robert 1994.02
Bruenig, Mureil 1947.04
Bruening, George 1885.06, 1887.05
Brugger, George 1916.04
Brugiere, Emil 1904.50
Brugmann, Herr 1866.33, 1897.08
Brummel, David 1973.15, 1976.33, 2001.03
Brun, Alfred 1863.07
Brun, George L. 1902.44
Brunaux, Mons. 1871.18
Brunck, Von 1888.29, 1889.45
Brundage, Miss 1823.01
Brune, Gabrielle 1938.06
Brune, Phoebe 1925.52
Bruneau, Phillip 1963.12
Bruneau, Ralph 1983.18
Brunelle, Louise 1908.25, 1912.15
Brunelle, Maggie 1873.26
Brunelle, Margaret 1914.07
Bruner, Cecil 1925.14
Bruner, Jerome 1920.45
Brunet, Mons. 1868.30, 1869.01, 1869.24, 1870.41, 1870.45
Brunette, Esther 1902.06, 1909.09, 1910.05
Bruning, Albert 1895.14
Bruning, Alfred 1949.16
Bruning, Mary Ann 1964.02
Brunjes, Hank 1953.17, 1957.12
Brunk, Vena 1904.09
Brunn, Francis 1967.11
Brunner, M.A. 1986.02
Bruno, A.J. 1887.30
Bruno, Amelia 1911.16
Bruno, Augustus 1884.18
Bruno, Augustus J. 1879.64, 1880.32, 1880.35
Bruno, Chris 1898.32, 1899.36
Bruno, Christopher 1897.52
Bruno, George 1944.17
Bruno, Gus 1886.11, 1888.05, 1891.16, 1891.19, 1891.35, 1892.15, 1896.01, 1904.11
Bruno, Jean 1960.01, 1962.01, 1970.07, 1974.02
Bruno, Jr., Gus 1891.19
Bruno, Messr. 1875.39
Bruno, Mr. 1876.19
Bruno, Will H. 1907.60
Brunot, Mons. 1870.37
Bruns, Jack 1927.16, 1928.03, 1930.11, 1931.05
Bruns, Julia 1915.25
Bruns, Mr. 1836.01
Bruns, Philip 1959.16, 1960.02, 1970.06, 1972.23
Brunskill 1914.32
Brunswick 1880.22
Brunswick, Earl 1916.26
Brunswick, Leo 1907.54
Brunton Studios 1924.15
Brunton, John 1921.30
Brunton, Mr. 1852.01, 1869.23
Brunton, R. 1897.28
Brunton, Rita 1888.27
Brunton, Robert 1914.21
Brusch, John S. 1909.25
Brush, Bob 1981.28
Brush, John S. 1908.39
Brusher, Betty 1948.24
Brushingham, Marcia 1975.22, 1980.16
Brusie, Judson D. 1908.05
Bruskin, Perry 1942.05, 1946.24, 1948.04
Brustein, Robert 1985.06
Bruton, Mr. 1869.06
Brutone, J. 1870.34, 1872.11
Brutone, J.W. 1869.06, 1869.33, 1869.40, 1869.44, 1870.19, 1870.21, 1870.24, 1871.10, 1871.15, 1872.27, 1873.10, 1873.28
Brutone, Julia 1886.02
Brutone, Mrs. J. 1871.10
Brutone, Mrs. Julia 1871.15
Brutone, W. 1870.13, 1880.08
Bruzovna, Halina 1923.14
Bryan 1904.22
Bryan, Al 1927.19
Bryan, Alfred 1903.04, 1911.30, 1912.14, 1913.05, 1913.17, 1914.11, 1915.02, 1916.25, 1917.01, 1917.23, 1918.05, 1918.37, 1919.02, 1919.03, 1919.16, 1919.26, 1919.30, 1920.03, 1920.10, 1920.22, 1920.23, 1920.47, 1921.02, 1922.12, 1922.15, 1931.19, 1974.09, 1975.22
Bryan, Arthur Q. 1990.10
Bryan, Buddy 1965.22
Bryan, Darlene 1979.08
Bryan, Don 1937.16
Bryan, Francis 1914.33
Bryan, Frank 1905.22
Bryan, Frank D. 1904.06
Bryan, Frederick 1980.10
Bryan, Geoffrey 1961.02
Bryan, Gertrude 1911.44, 1924.08
Bryan, Jack 1955.09
Bryan, Jennie Stetson 1890.10
Bryan, Kenneth 1982.03, 1984.02
Bryan, Lettie 1898.77, 1900.35
Bryan, Miss 1841.01
Bryan, Norman 1918.09
Bryan, Phyllis 1922.05
Bryan, Tom 1920.45
Bryan, Vincent 1901.27, 1902.16, 1902.24, 1903.03, 1903.05, 1904.13, 1904.29, 1904.44, 1904.58, 1905.03, 1905.16, 1905.23, 1905.33, 1905.44, 1906.30, 1906.45, 1907.15, 1907.24, 1907.41, 1908.04, 1908.10, 1908.24, 1908.25, 1908.28, 1908.42, 1910.02, 1910.18, 1911.18, 1911.24
Bryan, Vincent P. 1900.56, 1980.27
Bryan, Virginia 1940.21
Bryan, Wayne 1974.26, 1975.13
Bryan, William Jennings 1925.17
Bryant, Ben 1966.05
Bryant, Boudleaux 1977.10, 1982.22, 1990.15
Bryant, C.B. 1888.27, 1888.40
Bryant, Charles 1897.04, 1936.27
Bryant, Dan 1869.33
Bryant, David 1914.24, 1987.04, 1994.08
Bryant, Faule 1972.20
Bryant, Felice 1977.10, 1982.22, 1990.15
Bryant, Frances 1923.16
Bryant, Francis 1900.55
Bryant, Francis J. 1895.27, 1897.40, 1898.67
Bryant, Glenn 1943.24, 1945.06, 1946.09
Bryant, Gordon 1931.02
Bryant, Hugh 1956.13, 1957.16
Bryant, John 1914.33
Bryant, Joyce 1965.03
Bryant, Lucile 1903.03
Bryant, Marie 1946.24, 1967.15
Bryant, Miss 1903.03
Bryant, Nana 1926.34, 1927.56, 1932.23
Bryant, Teresa 1911.22
Bryant, Theresa 1907.58
Bryant, Willie 1945.07
Bryce, Edward 1950.11
Bryce, Edward S. 1947.21
Bryce, Josephine 1924.40
Bryce-Gemmel, Mme. 1895.19
Bryde, Edgar 1912.17
Bryden, Eugene 1946.11, 1946.22
Bryer, John 1871.14, 1871.19, 1872.22, 1872.24, 1872.26, 1872.34, 1873.12, 1873.14
Brymer 1933.20
Brymm, J. Tim 1906.14
Brymm, James T. 1900.46, 1906.06, 1907.31, 1911.20
Brymn, T. 1976.16
Brymn, Tim 1921.26, 1922.44
Bryne, Barbara 1984.08
Bryne, James 1898.64
Bryner, Vera 1950.05
Brynner, Kathy Lee 1985.01
Brynner, Yul 1946.05, 1951.12, 1976.01, 1977.07, 1985.01
Bryson, Arthur 1925.40, 1929.50, 1930.24
Bryson, Claiborne 1930.22
Bryson, Ralph 1923.39
Bryton, Georgie 1896.19, 1896.21
Bubbles, John 1931.19, 1945.06, 1946.09, 1967.11
Bubbles, John W. 1930.34, 1935.13, 1937.10, 1943.13, 1980.10
Bubier, Walter 1894.52
Bubrosa, Marje 2000.20
Bucalossi, Ernest 1903.33
Bucalossi, Procida 1882.60
Bucchino, John 2000.16
Bucci, Mark 1958.09, 1962.02
Buch, C.B. 1877.35
Buchan, Michael 1976.14, 1978.16
Buchanan Miss 1870.34
Buchanan, Aleen 1950.06
Buchanan, Donald 1909.24, 1910.03, 1911.46, 1912.47
Buchanan, Harry 1914.24
Buchanan, Jack 1923.36, 1924.01, 1925.42, 1929.51, 1937.16
Buchanan, Lee 1914.33
Buchannan, Robert 1908.03
Buchbinder, Bernard 1912.33, 1930.07
Buchbinder, Bernhard 1910.36
Buchbinder, Willner 1930.07
Bucheister, H. 1886.39
Buchheister 1883.08, 1883.44
Buchheister, Charles 1882.68
Buchheister, Herr 1880.61, 1880.66
Buchheister, Joseph 1882.45
Buchholtz, Fred 1982.04

Buchner, Pavlowna 1885.01
Buck, Bernice 1914.13
Buck, C. 1876.36
Buck, Dennis 1986.19
Buck, Dudley 1880.54
Buck, Ford 1931.19, 1945.06, 1946.09
Buck, Ford L. 1935.13, 1937.10
Buck, Ford Lee 1943.13
Buck, Gene 1913.17, 1914.06, 1914.13, 1914.15, 1915.15, 1916.10, 1917.13, 1918.19, 1919.15, 1919.16, 1920.10, 1920.18, 1921.21, 1921.22, 1922.19, 1923.20, 1923.38, 1924.18, 1925.10, 1925.24, 1926.18, 1927.07, 1927.60, 1928.11, 1931.19, 1976.25
Buck, Helen 1934.35
Buck, Inez 1908.37
Buck, Jr., Fred C. 1928.41
Buck, K. 1880.03
Buck, Mr. 1863.06
Buck, Nell Roy 1922.23
Buck, Pearl S. 1960.10
Buck, Richard H. 1980.27
Buckhannan, Jack 1998.10
Buckhantz, Allan A. 1959.19
Buckheister, J. 1883.64
Buckingham, Mr. 1882.32, 1882.38
Buckland, Wildred 1892.14
Buckland, Wilfred 1891.05, 1893.25
Buckles, Ann 1956.02, 1957.08
Buckley, Andrew M. 1904.53
Buckley, Anna 1898.05
Buckley, Annie 1891.45, 1892.44, 1892.54, 1893.10, 1893.15, 1906.27, 1911.13
Buckley, Bert 1896.11, 1901.02
Buckley, Betty 1982.19, 1985.18, 1988.12, 1997.18
Buckley, Dennis 1971.12
Buckley, Dorothy 1920.17
Buckley, E.J. 1885.33
Buckley, Ed. J. 1880.41
Buckley, Emerson 1961.19, 1963.22
Buckley, F.T.S. 1905.31
Buckley, G. Swaine 1871.17, 1873.04, 1873.05
Buckley, Gerard 1976.29
Buckley, Harry 1899.18
Buckley, J. 1883.23
Buckley, James 1889.47, 1919.34
Buckley, Jennie 1901.02
Buckley, Joe 1879.04, 1880.09, 1883.23
Buckley, Jos. 1880.36
Buckley, Joseph 1879.37, 1880.64, 1883.02, 1883.17, 1883.19
Buckley, Kate 1906.05
Buckley, Kay 1948.16
Buckley, Madeline 1907.12
Buckley, Mary 1926.33
Buckley, Messr. 1882.20
Buckley, Nellie 1888.20
Buckley, Richard 1961.02
Buckley, Robert 1963.15
Buckley, Robert A. 1978.04, 1983.05, 1992.11
Bucklin, Bella 1900.15
Bucklin, Belle 1897.02, 1897.42
Buckner, Blanche 1904.25
Buckner, Clay 1993.01, 1995.16, 1998.17
Buckridge, Gladys 1919.03
Buckstone, J.B. 1855.07, 1871.19
Buckstone, John Baldwin 1853.03, 1863.02, 1867.19, 1872.18
Buckstone, John C. 1893.13
Budd, James 1915.20
Budd, Norman 1944.24, 1957.04
Buddeke, Kate 1994.02
Budworth, F. 1875.03
Budworth, Frank 1879.10, 1882.50, 1883.02, 1883.17, 1883.19, 1883.23
Budworth, Little 1875.03
Buechner, Edward 1898.34
Buehler, Camille 1908.36
Buell Scenic Studios 1932.08
Buell, Bill 1981.28, 1989.07, 1993.06
Buell, Juliet 1927.24
Buell, Mabel 1924.10, 1937.07
Buell, Mabel A. 1919.32, 1933.27, 1936.07, 1939.14
Buery, James 1924.11
Bufano, Remo 1932.28, 1944.33, 1947.09
Buffalino, Frances 1966.14
Buffalo Bills, The 1957.18, 1965.21
Buffaloe, Katharine 1981.12, 1982.03
Buffery, Anthony 1964.29
Buffett, Kenneth 1943.21
Buffett, Kenny 1944.30, 1948.15
Buffman, Zev 1979.22
Buffy, Vito 1984.07
Bufman, Zev 1960.12 1967.01, 1969.15, 1970.16, 1971.08, 1979.31, 1980.02, 1980.26, 1981.25, 1981.28, 1982.03, 1983.20, 1985.17, 1985.19
Bufort, Annie 1879.42
Bugatch, Samuel 1967.03
Bugos, Keith 1998.19
Buie, John 1956.06, 1958.03
Buimi, Adele 1876.03
Buislay, Adolphe 1866.12
Buislay, Auguste 1866.12
Buislay, Etienne 1866.12
Buislay, Grenet 1866.12
Buislay, Joaquin 1866.12
Buislay, Julio 1866.12
Buislay, Justin 1866.12
Buissert, Mons. 1875.21
Buisson, Mlle. 1882.67, 1883.27, 1883.28, 1883.30, 1883.41, 1883.51, 1883.54, 1883.55, 1883.57, 1883.59, 1883.60, 1884.02, 1884.03, 1884.05
Buisson, Mme. 1882.53
Buissonneau, Paul 1947.18
Buka, Donald 1944.16
Bulak, Cindi 1969.14
Bulanchin, G. 1929.05
Bulger 1922.17
Bulger, Harry 1891.37, 1893.08, 1895.18, 1897.07, 1899.11, 1899.29, 1901.04, 1901.12, 1901.27, 1903.39, 1904.52, 1905.23, 1906.30, 1916.02
Bulger, Jr., Harry 1917.10
Bulkley, Fannie 1896.29
Bull, John 1926.38, 1963.28
Bull, Peter 1965.28
Bullard, Buff 1931.08
Bullard, Gene 1966.04
Bullens, Cynthia 1972.23
Bullis, Muriel 1949.17
Bulloch, Mr. 1857.02
Bullock, Donna 2001.01
Bullock, H. Ridgely 1979.10, 1979.32
Bullock, Harry 1892.04
Bullock, J. 1866.03
Bullock, Leslie K. 1979.32
Bullock, Mary 1862.05
Bullock, Tom 1879.10
Bullock, Turner 1935.03, 1939.19
Bullock, W. 1864.21
Bullock, Walter 1950.06
Bullock, Wesley 2001.04
Bullock, William 1878.02, 1879.01
Bulmash, Jay S. 1988.10
Buloff, Joseph 1943.04
Bulwer-Lytton, Edward 1883.62, 1884.51, 1887.26, 1898.30, 1899.42, 1913.08
Bulwer-Lytton, G.E.L. 1871.10
Bunbee, Messr. 1856.02
Bunce, Alan 1957.14
Bunchu, Tessie 1907.08
Bundonis, Al 1998.08
Bundsmann, Anton 1936.12
Bundy, George 1896.04
Bunim, Shmuel 1968.22
Bunker, Eleanor 1936.12
Bunker, Ralph 1915.19, 1924.33, 1926.20, 1937.17, 1942.29, 1943.07, 1951.24
Bunn, Alfred 1844.01, 1846.01, 1848.04, 1852.03, 1852.04, 1852.06, 1852.07, 1853.04, 1854.02, 1854.03, 1854.07, 1855.05, 1855.06, 1858.03, 1859.03, 1862.03, 1864.04, 1864.19, 1867.07, 1868.12, 1869.41, 1872.17, 1877.35, 1878.03, 1882.13, 1882.64, 1884.33, 1885.32, 1889.28, 1896.16, 1898.39, 1898.76, 1900.13, 1900.22, 1911.10, 1933.17, 1934.17
Bunn, David Alan 1999.06
Bunnell, Jane 1985.11
Bunner, H.C. 1884.34
Bunney, John 1895.15
Bunny, John 1905.26, 1907.51, 1908.27, 1909.30
Bunny, John H. 1900.15
Bunt, George 1968.17, 1968.24, 1970.07, 1978.28
Bunte, Edna 1928.12
Bunting, Edward 1918.14
Bunting, Frank 1912.32
Buntrock, Stephen R. 2000.20
Bunyea, Nimon 1929.46
Burani, Michelette 1925.09
Burani, Paul 1884.50, 1888.07, 1893.21, 1910.22
Burba, Blake 1996.09
Burbage, C.J. 1884.24
Burbank, Edith 1898.77
Burbank, Juno 1891.38, 1894.21
Burbank, Mary 1871.15
Burbank, Messr. 1893.13
Burbank, Sam 1911.02, 1914.31, 1916.20, 1919.40, 1920.13
Burbank, Samuel 1912.39
Burbeck, Frank 1891.28
Burbridge, Ed 1980.05
Burbridge, Edward 1967.01, 1969.15, 1991.01
Burby, Charlotte 1891.14
Burby, Gordon 1927.56, 1938.02
Burby, Jane 1896.24, 1897.45, 1898.69, 1900.48, 1904.43, 1909.18, 1918.11
Burch, Billy 1882.28
Burch, Dick 1905.31
Burch, Edwin 1907.63, 1913.26
Burch, Shelly 1978.18, 1982.09
Burcher, Harry B. 1902.35, 1906.47, 1913.36
Burchinal, Frederick 1979.26
Burckley, Arthur 1917.20, 1929.36
Burckly, Arthur 1919.36, 1924.24
Burcky, Mr. 1882.41
Burd, Edna 1902.25
Burdell, Hattie 1903.18
Burdell, Sadie 1903.18
Burden, Mr. 1866.02, 1866.28
Burden, S. 1867.12
Burden, Tommy 1989.12
Burdett, Florence 1907.51, 1911.22
Burdett, Jane 1913.09
Burdick, David 1991.13
Burdick, Greta 1905.19
Burdick, Richard 1942.20
Burdoni, Irene 1926.41
Burgard, Mons. 1875.04
Burge, Gregg 1981.06, 1985.12, 1990.14
Burge, Wendy 1977.09
Burger, John 1940.16
Burges, Paul 1870.20, 1872.19
Burgess, Anthony 1973.07
Burgess, Cool 1870.08
Burgess, Dorothy 1927.05
Burgess, Emma 1879.33, 1879.35, 1880.06, 1880.59, 1880.65, 1880.70
Burgess, Fred 1904.48
Burgess, Gilbert 1891.36, 1895.31
Burgess, Grover 1926.17, 1936.28
Burgess, J.W. 1871.13
Burgess, Joan 1932.26
Burgess, Kendall 1926.26
Burgess, Kitty 1891.18
Burgess, Lee 1931.06
Burgess, Marjorie 1919.42
Burgess, Mary 1963.22, 1963.23, 1964.07, 1964.09, 1964.12, 1964.13, 1964.14, 1965.11, 1965.12, 1965.13, 1968.12, 1968.14, 1968.15
Burgette, Gladys 1922.42, 1923.07
Burgoyne, Olga 1933.04
Burgoyne, Ollie 1899.33
Burgstaller, Fritzi 1927.17
Burk Brothers 1887.30
Burk, Bobby 1934.14
Burk, Carolyn 1915.17
Burk, J.O. 1879.63, 1880.39
Burk, Major 1886.39
Burk, Maude 1920.46
Burk, Messr. 1876.19
Burk, Miss 1870.02, 1915.17
Burk, Mr. 1864.02, 1894.01
Burk, Robert 1932.19
Burka, Ellen 1977.09
Burke, Agnes 1887.32
Burke, Aileen 1894.15, 1894.47
Burke, Aleen 1896.12
Burke, Alice 1896.27
Burke, Billie 1924.38, 1934.01, 1936.02, 1936.17
Burke, Billy 1893.47
Burke, Brian 1999.02
Burke, Carolyn 1914.33, 1915.17
Burke, Charles 1888.21, 1891.41, 1898.28, 1907.23
Burke, Charles A. 1893.34, 1895.42
Burke, Charles B. 1898.78
Burke, Dan 1887.45, 1887.48, 1888.14, 1889.15, 1890.49, 1891.25, 1891.45, 1892.44, 1892.54, 1893.15, 1893.27, 1893.36, 1893.46, 1894.04, 1894.49
Burke, Daniel 1888.27, 1888.40, 1889.07, 1889.11
Burke, Edgar 1936.17
Burke, Edwin 1923.32
Burke, F. Bond 1903.26
Burke, Georgia 1940.17, 1953.04
Burke, Ione 1860.04, 1860.05, 1861.04, 1862.05, 1862.09, 1863.01, 1863.04, 1863.08
Burke, Irving 1995.12
Burke, J. 1869.33
Burke, James 1887.48, 1888.14, 1888.27, 1888.40, 1889.07, 1889.11, 1889.15, 1889.18, 1890.49, 1891.25, 1891.45, 1892.44, 1892.54, 1893.15, 1893.27, 1893.36, 1894.49, 1895.05
Burke, Joe 1925.23, 1928.23, 1936.17
Burke, John 1887.45
Burke, John J. 1895.08
Burke, John T. 1881.31, 1887.51, 1896.39
Burke, Johnny 1939.29, 1942.23, 1946.04, 1953.11, 1961.14, 1989.16, 1992.03, 1995.14, 1997.01
Burke, Joseph 1928.23, 1974.26
Burke, Jr., Thomas 1925.36
Burke, Karen 1973.10
Burke, Katherine 1927.08, 1928.03, 1928.47, 1930.39
Burke, L. 1872.10
Burke, Lee 1937.12
Burke, Liam 2000.11
Burke, Lottie 1898.10, 1899.13, 1902.32
Burke, Louis 1914.25, 1989.23
Burke, Mae 1927.31
Burke, Major 1881.07, 1882.23
Burke, Marie 1922.15, 1922.36, 1934.29
Burke, Marion 1951.23
Burke, Maude 1898.40
Burke, Maurice 1945.03
Burke, Melville 1927.66
Burke, Michele 1952.05, 1953.03, 1957.14, 1970.18
Burke, Millicent 1890.50
Burke, Miss 1859.11, 1860.03
Burke, Mr. 1855.11, 1866.05, 1867.18, 1869.29, 1887.39
Burke, P.J. 1915.03
Burke, Peter 1956.06
Burke, Robert 1929.39
Burke, Sheila 1929.09
Burke, Sonny 1950.02
Burke, Tom 1923.02, 1924.33, 1925.13, 1926.08, 1927.03
Burke, Virginia 1940.18
Burke, Walter 1927.31, 1937.11, 1944.27, 1945.03, 1947.11, 1952.05
Burke, Willi 1978.02, 1982.18
Burke, William 1891.41
Burke, William H. 1942.19, 1944.20, 1946.14, 1947.12, 1948.19, 1949.05, 1949.06
Burkes, Audrey 1942.35
Burkey 1882.06
Burkhard, Paul 1962.17
Burkhardt, Addison 1903.14, 1905.32, 1906.04, 1906.29, 1906.41, 1908.07, 1908.21, 1908.39
Burkhardt, Bob 1949.18
Burkhardt, Gerry 1978.13, 1992.02, 1994.06
Burkhardt, Messr. 1886.36
Burkhart, Addison 1910.18
Burkhart, Lillian 1895.35
Burks, Donnie 1968.11
Burks, Edgar 1930.10
Burks, Hattie 1915.17, 1917.09, 1920.42
Burks, Jo Lynn 1990.15
Burleigh, Alston 1933.04
Burleigh, Jack 1933.21
Burles, George 1955.10
Burley, Douglas 1928.40
Burley, Duglas 1928.45
Burley, Jack 1922.30, 1930.28
Burlingame, Lloyd 1965.39, 1972.25
Burmester, Leo 1986.16, 1987.04, 1999.08
Burn, Jonathan 1965.39
Burnaby, David 1914.32
Burnand, F.C. 1868.23, 1869.21, 1869.28, 1869.43, 1870.02, 1870.06, 1872.05, 1872.07, 1872.11, 1872.14, 1872.24, 1872.36, 1879.64, 1884.44, 1885.18, 1886.31, 1891.36, 1892.08, 1892.60, 1934.22, 1936.20, 1939.05, 1948.05, 1951.08
Burnand, Francis C. 1879.21
Burnap, Wilder Luke 1977.08
Burnard, F.C. 1885.08
Burnard, Francis C. 1895.26
Burnege, Mabel 1912.27
Burnell, Billy 1942.25

Burnell, Buster 1942.25
Burnell, Lotta 1933.07
Burnell, Marie 1903.03
Burnell, Miss 1904.13
Burnet, Mons. 1870.30
Burnett 1884.61
Burnett, Brevard 1922.22, 1929.25
Burnett, C. 1861.04, 1862.05
Burnett, Carol 1959.26, 1964.21, 1999.20
Burnett, Connie 1961.07
Burnett, Ernie 1939.29
Burnett, Frances Hodgson 1991.05
Burnett, J.G. 1857.01, 1860.04, 1860.05, 1860.06, 1861.04, 1865.06, 1866.16, 1866.18
Burnett, J.H. 1877.24, 1879.11
Burnett, James G. 1862.05
Burnett, James H. 1879.07
Burnett, John H. 1877.24
Burnett, Jonathan H. 1879.59, 1882.44
Burnett, Leslie 1919.43
Burnett, Martha 1939.25, 1942.15, 1945.03
Burnett, Miss 1867.07, 1872.06
Burnett, Mr. 1859.05, 1859.06
Burnett, Uarda 1921.05, 1921.13
Burney, Fanny 1963.03
Burney, Steve 1980.17
Burnham 1891.02
Burnham, C.D. 1905.43
Burnham, Florence 1911.22
Burnham, Harry 1919.07
Burnham, Hattie 1875.21
Burnham, Lillian 1898.34
Burnham, Lucille Vera 1901.18
Burnham, Messr. 1879.56
Burnham, Mons. 1879.50
Burnham, N. 1881.11
Burnham, N.S. 1881.27, 1883.42, 1885.04, 1886.25, 1886.55, 1886.57, 1889.40, 1889.49, 1891.38, 1893.41
Burnham, Nicholas 1896.06, 1897.54, 1906.32
Burnham, Nick 1899.37, 1902.22, 1916.19
Burnham, Sophie 1904.45
Burnhand, F.C. 1944.07
Burnley, Martine 1917.35
Burns, Arthur 1963.11
Burns, Barbara 1979.19
Burns, Barry 1960.08, 1964.17
Burns, Bill 1962.04, 1999.01
Burns, Bobbie 1898.63, 1899.37
Burns, Bobby 1897.26, 1901.01, 1901.21
Burns, Catherine 1970.04
Burns, Charles 1861.06, 1862.01, 1864.17, 1864.22
Burns, Dan 1918.13
Burns, Dave 1932.05
Burns, David 1943.14, 1945.20, 1948.04, 1948.23, 1950.02, 1950.20, 1952.20, 1955.12, 1957.18, 1960.23, 1962.12, 1964.01, 1970.21
Burns, Eileen 1933.20
Burns, Eleanor 1900.20, 1900.33
Burns, Frances 1917.17
Burns, George 1917.11
Burns, Harry 1923.21, 1944.30
Burns, John 1904.14
Burns, Karla 1983.05
Burns, Lillian 1905.27
Burns, Maryann 1966.24
Burns, Messr. 1867.10, 1869.26, 1886.36
Burns, Mr. 1848.01
Burns, Nat 1948.27, 1952.02
Burns, Paul 1922.14, 1923.06
Burns, Paul E. 1917.37, 1918.32
Burns, Peter J. 1942.20
Burns, Ralph 1957.14, 1962.03, 1962.27, 1963.13, 1964.11, 1964.21, 1964.32, 1964.35, 1965.06, 1966.01, 1967.05, 1968.02, 1970.07, 1971.03, 1972.22, 1973.05, 1975.14, 1977.16, 1978.05, 1979.04, 1981.07, 1986.06, 1986.07, 1991.04, 1996.14, 1999.01
Burns, Reese 1966.07
Burns, Robert 1873.10, 1903.31, 1909.13, 1966.03
Burns, Robert D. 1928.12
Burns, Sam 1908.03
Burns, T.H. 1887.52
Burns, Teddy 1905.42, 1908.33
Burns, Tessie 1902.26
Burns, Thomas H. 1885.46, 1886.48, 1886.49
Burnside, Isabelle 1905.40
Burnside, Kathryn 1926.32
Burnside, R.H. 1895.17, 1898.27, 1900.57, 1902.25, 1903.38, 1903.41, 1904.05, 1904.55, 1905.03, 1905.36, 1905.49, 1905.52, 1905.55, 1906.07, 1906.17, 1906.26, 1906.32, 1907.05, 1907.18, 1907.42, 1908.26, 1908.41, 1909.20, 1910.23, 1911.23, 1911.31, 1911.42, 1912.02, 1912.39, 1912.40, 1914.13, 1914.17, 1914.23, 1914.31, 1915.24, 1915.31, 1916.15, 1917.11, 1917.16, 1917.22, 1918.23, 1919.22, 1919.41, 1920.13, 1920.26, 1920.36, 1921.28, 1922.16, 1922.30, 1923.33, 1923.40, 1924.26, 1924.39, 1925.04, 1925.38, 1926.32, 1928.37, 1929.37, 1932.15, 1933.21, 1934.14, 1935.05, 1935.06, 1935.07, 1935.08, 1935.09, 1935.10, 1940.09, 1942.02, 1942.04, 1942.06, 1942.07, 1942.08, 1942.09, 1944.04, 1944.05, 1944.06, 1944.07, 1944.08, 1944.09, 1944.10, 1944.11, 1944.12, 1944.13, 1944.25
Burnside, Richard 1902.37
Burnson, George 1946.03
Burnton, G.W. 1877.24
Burpee, Louise 1905.44, 1908.04
Burpee, Madge 1902.18, 1904.10, 1905.06, 1905.44
Burr, Bessie 1902.32, 1903.30
Burr, Charles 1975.22, 1976.01
Burr, Courtney 1932.27
Burr, Donald 1930.33, 1932.27, 1940.09, 1942.32, 1946.02, 1958.03, 1965.33, 1967.02
Burr, Henry 1921.19
Burr, Hillyer 1896.01
Burr, John 1922.21
Burr, Mary 1951.24
Burr, Raymond 1941.03
Burr, Robert 1947.21, 1957.02, 1964.40, 1971.19
Burr, S.J. 1852.05
Burrage, Alice 1931.04, 1933.25
Burrell, Deborah 1979.32, 1980.15, 1981.29
Burrell, Fred 1967.05
Burrell, James 1938.18
Burrell, John 1950.08
Burrell, Kenny 1960.06
Burrell, Pamela 1979.29, 1993.19, 1997.19
Burrell, Teresa 1986.11
Burrell, Terry 1978.21, 1995.14
Burrell-Cleveland, Deborah 1992.06
Burress, Brances 1913.25
Burress, William 1897.45, 1898.58, 1900.03, 1900.56, 1901.12, 1902.19, 1904.54, 1907.14, 1910.06, 1910.16, 1910.37, 1914.17, 1919.41, 1920.13
Burridge 1882.06, 1892.59, 1893.23
Burridge, Walter 1883.04, 1883.06, 1883.37, 1883.39, 1887.44, 1889.46, 1895.31, 1896.29, 1897.13, 1897.17, 1898.12, 1898.16, 1898.27, 1898.34, 1898.44, 1898.77, 1899.06, 1899.07, 1899.15, 1900.32, 1902.18, 1902.30, 1902.44, 1903.03, 1903.10, 1903.24, 1904.10, 1904.13, 1904.37, 1904.44, 1904.52, 1905.06, 1905.16, 1905.26, 1906.16, 1906.30, 1906.49, 1907.33, 1907.48, 1907.51, 1909.15, 1909.19, 1911.09, 1911.42, 1912.12, 1912.37
Burridge, Walter W. 1898.73, 1907.27
Burrill, Bennett 1947.02
Burris, Glenn 1950.11
Burris, James 1911.20
Burris, James Henry 1910.18
Burris, Jim 1980.27
Burroughs, Charles R. 1892.49, 1893.04, 1893.22
Burroughs, Charles T. 1893.01
Burroughs, Don 1922.09
Burroughs, Hazel 1900.08
Burroughs, James 1923.14
Burroughs, Joe 1920.08
Burroughs, Judyth 1949.01
Burroughs, Mark 2001.04
Burroughs, Miss 1886.36
Burroughs, Mrs. 1864.07, 1864.19
Burroughs, Mrs. M.E. 1864.16, 1864.20
Burroughs, Venie 1884.22, 1884.60
Burrows, Abe 1950.17, 1951.13, 1951.19, 1952.05, 1953.07, 1955.02, 1955.06, 1956.16, 1958.08, 1959.03, 1959.06, 1961.22, 1962.13, 1964.05, 1965.15, 1966.07, 1966.13, 1976.21, 1981.13, 1992.04, 1995.05
Burrows, Ann 1922.08
Burrows, Arthur 1903.19
Burrows, B. 1886.50
Burrows, Charles 1906.37, 1910.25, 1914.10, 1918.02, 1932.05
Burrows, Charles K. 1909.24
Burrows, Charles R. 1908.27
Burrows, Ida 1894.39
Burrows, Joe 1922.21, 1923.23
Burrows, Kevin M. 1999.16
Burrows, Mme. 1844.01
Burrows, Vinie 1951.11, 1954.16
Burry, Solen 1947.08
Burry, Sollen 1943.16
Bursk, Sybil 1924.40
Bursky, Jay 1978.13
Burson, Letha 1929.37
Burstein, Danny 1995.11
Burstein, Lillian 1971.14
Burstein, Lonnie 1973.02
Burstein, Mike 1968.22
Burstein, Pesach 1968.22
Burston, Bud 1955.12
Burston, Buddy 1943.05
Burt, Benjamin Hapgood 1902.07, 1902.35, 1903.34, 1903.39, 1904.29, 1905.19, 1905.27, 1905.45, 1905.55, 1906.27, 1907.27, 1907.41, 1908.39, 1910.17, 1910.32, 1914.13, 1915.08, 1915.24, 1916.20, 1917.08, 1917.16, 1917.22, 1918.34, 1919.12, 1919.30, 1921.23
Burt, Ed 1877.24, 1878.01, 1878.13, 1879.04, 1880.36, 1880.64
Burt, Edward 1878.17, 1879.37, 1879.68, 1880.09, 1881.09, 1881.29, 1882.02, 1882.74, 1882.79, 1883.32, 1885.15, 1885.22
Burt, Fannie 1871.10
Burt, Fanny 1875.03
Burt, Fanny L. 1876.19
Burt, Flo 1920.19
Burt, Frederic 1923.08
Burt, H.J. 1876.19, 1879.05
Burt, Hapgood 1912.14
Burt, Harriet 1903.06, 1903.27, 1905.56, 1907.25, 1908.24, 1912.01, 1912.31
Burt, Hilda 1923.27
Burt, John 1989.09
Burt, Laura 1884.12, 1885.31, 1885.51, 1885.62, 1886.07, 1886.31, 1889.02, 1890.35, 1897.23, 1898.72, 1901.12
Burt, Mae 1898.52
Burt, Master 1865.02
Burt, Messr. 1879.04
Burt, Mr. 1868.06, 1871.11, 1876.19
Burt, Nellie 1891.40
Burt, Sadie 1913.18
Burtnett, Paul 1917.14
Burton, Alice 1922.27
Burton, Audrey 1916.19
Burton, Bob 1929.37
Burton, Bud 1945.01
Burton, Carl 1904.05
Burton, Carlton 1898.61
Burton, Carrie 1878.03, 1880.18, 1881.07, 1881.37, 1882.17, 1882.51, 1884.14, 1889.22
Burton, Charles 1903.09
Burton, Charles P. 1905.07
Burton, Christine 1929.20
Burton, Clara 1919.20
Burton, Daisy 1914.21, 1918.04
Burton, David 1924.34
Burton, E.A. 1888.21
Burton, Edward 1879.15, 1880.31
Burton, Eleanor 1900.28
Burton, Florence 1880.31
Burton, Frederick 1915.32, 1918.07, 1926.31
Burton, George 1949.09
Burton, Herbert 1906.43
Burton, Herschell 1969.15
Burton, Irving 1989.05
Burton, Janet 1906.45, 1909.25
Burton, John 1926.21
Burton, Kate 1982.24, 1983.18, 1995.11
Burton, Kenneth 1929.33
Burton, Lily 1927.39
Burton, Lizzie 1880.45, 1880.48, 1882.07, 1882.08, 1882.09, 1882.10, 1882.11, 1882.12, 1882.13, 1883.11, 1883.12, 1883.13, 1883.14, 1883.15
Burton, Mariam 1943.10
Burton, Martin 1923.41
Burton, May 1901.26
Burton, Michael 2001.06
Burton, Micky 1930.18
Burton, Miriam 1946.21, 1950.07, 1951.11, 1953.04, 1954.19
Burton, Mrs. 1853.05
Burton, Nat 1974.09
Burton, R.M. 1881.13
Burton, Richard 1907.61, 1960.21, 1980.19
Burton, Robert 1933.25, 1934.40, 1936.12, 1939.26
Burton, S.M. 1881.02
Burton, Sarah 1939.07, 1948.11
Burton, T.H. 1902.20
Burton, Thomas 1928.40
Burton, Tiny 1891.28
Burton, Tom 1912.16, 1926.21, 1927.27, 1928.45
Burton, W.E. 1841.01, 1872.06, 1884.27
Burton, W.H. 1894.20, 1897.05
Burton, Will E. 1888.15
Burton, William 1850.01
Burton, William E. 1851.04, 1853.05, 1854.04, 1854.05, 1857.08
Burts, Miss 1864.22
Burtson, Bud 1943.20
Burtsyn, Mike 1993.05
Buruss, Monica 1976.34
Burvill, Alice 1877.23
Burville, Alice 1877.22, 1877.25, 1877.39, 1881.07, 1881.37
Burwell, Cliff 1987.02
Burwell, Clifford 2000.07
Burwell, Evelyn 1935.01
Bury, John 1964.28, 1970.15, 1972.25
Buryl, Red 1976.01
Busby, Albert 1899.34, 1911.47
Busby, Earl 1928.01, 1928.27, 1930.31, 1933.01, 1934.36, 1938.04
Busby, Georgia 1897.05
Busby, Mrs. Bill 1918.31
Busch, Betty Ann 1947.04
Busch, Bobby 1941.03
Busch, Robert 1952.15
Buscher, Dorothy 1906.49
Bush Lubin and Freisinger 1910.15
Bush, Anita 1909.27, 1937.09
Bush, Frank 1882.28, 1896.03
Bush, Georgie 1894.13
Bush, Joe 1942.20
Bush, Ronald 1969.03
Bushkin, Beatrice 1959.27
Bushkin, Joe 1976.32, 1995.14
Bushman, Frank X. 1908.42
Bushong, Alice 1894.27
Busia, Akosua 1991.01
Buske, Bill 1969.14
Busley, Jessie 1934.29
Busnach, Paul 1888.23
Busnach, William 1880.28
Buss, John 1890.50
Buss, John G. 1894.17
Busse, Henry 1921.21, 1928.21
Bussert, Anna 1909.15, 1912.04
Bussert, Meg 1980.16, 1980.26, 1981.26
Busto, Julia 1975.10
Butcher, George 1983.15
Butcher, IV., Howard 1972.21
Butin, Messr. 1906.11, 1907.09
Butler, A.C. 1896.44
Butler, Alexander C. 1896.04
Butler, Alice 1884.25, 1893.21, 1893.41
Butler, Ann 1924.16, 1929.04
Butler, Artie 1983.20, 1991.10
Butler, Bill 1950.05, 1952.12, 1954.18, 1990.15
Butler, Billy 1932.12, 1945.07, 1946.21
Butler, Bobby 1988.05
Butler, C.W. 1875.20, 1876.35
Butler, Charles 1881.38, 1902.34, 1908.03
Butler, Charles W. 1900.15, 1908.34, 1911.30
Butler, Dan 1920.36
Butler, Etta 1899.36, 1901.09, 1901.21
Butler, Eva 1893.30, 1895.34
Butler, Fred J. 1892.58, 1894.20
Butler, H. 1868.19, 1871.14, 1872.26, 1875.14
Butler, H.L. 1899.07, 1899.20
Butler, Henry 1973.09, 1989.18
Butler, J.H. 1870.36
Butler, Jean 1996.01, 1996.12, 1998.09, 2000.04, 2000.05
Butler, John 1888.08, 1950.05, 1952.12, 1953.05, 1953.06, 1953.14, 1953.15, 1956.10, 1962.01, 1963.16
Butler, Joseph Campbell 1971.01
Butler, Jr., Sam 1988.05
Butler, Laura 1903.32, 1904.35, 1907.51

Butler, Leslie 1975.01
Butler, Mark Anthony 1978.11
Butler, Messr. 1867.01
Butler, Michael 1968.11, 1977.15, 1980.05
Butler, Miss 1883.17, 1883.23
Butler, Mr. 1872.24
Butler, Nellie 1895.39, 1896.02, 1897.34, 1897.49, 1898.56, 1905.05, 1908.27
Butler, Rhoda 1974.06, 1975.06, 1982.20, 1983.13, 1986.08, 1989.14
Butler, Richard W. 1888.38
Butler, Robert 1880.07
Butler, Sitara 1882.15
Butler, T.B. 1889.05
Butler, Todd 1968.17
Butler, Trevor 1925.50
Butler, W. 1866.32
Butler, William 1873.05, 1906.10
Butler, William H. 1867.21
Butron, Grace 1894.36
Butron, Tim 1894.36
Butterfield, Everett 1924.05
Butterfield, J.A. 1909.16
Butters, Fred E. 1887.11
Butters, William 1899.11
Butterworth, Charles 1926.21, 1927.35, 1928.25, 1929.31, 1932.17, 1942.27
Butterworth, Paul 1931.08
Butterworth, Walter 1948.18
Buttignol, Val 1947.13
Button, Dick 1957.06
Button, Jeanne 1975.18, 1976.30, 1989.12
Buttons, "Red" 1948.15
Buttons, Red 1943.23, 1947.08, 1995.08
Buttykay, Akos 1916.04
Butzow, W. 1924.48
Buwen, John 1963.10
Buzzell, E. 1893.42
Buzzell, Eddie 1919.15, 1920.33, 1922.28, 1924.22, 1926.03, 1926.42, 1928.25, 1929.07
Buzzi, Ruth 1966.01
Byam, John 1920.22, 1920.23, 1922.15, 1924.38, 1927.05, 1929.04, 1929.22
Byant, Miss 1881.11
Byatt, Irene 1967.10
Bybell, Patricia 1947.17, 1950.02
Byck, Lehman 1926.21, 1927.36, 1933.21
Bye, George 1931.46
Byers, Bill 1959.15, 1963.16, 1975.15, 1976.32, 1978.18, 1979.13, 1980.29, 1981.09, 1982.18, 1983.09, 1985.05, 1986.20, 1989.29, 1991.07, 1993.02, 1995.15
Byers, Gladys 1912.03
Byers, H.D. 1891.46
Byers, Hale 1919.30
Byers, Henri 1970.01
Byers, Karen 1995.02
Byers, Lavender 1906.03
Byers, Margaret 1927.27, 1929.48, 1930.41
Byers, Michael 1985.20
Byers, Ralph 1985.06, 2000.11
Byers-Blackwell, Karen 1997.04
Byrd Foundation, Inc., The 1975.10
Byrd, A.D. 1906.08
Byrd, Carolyn 1976.04
Byrd, Debra 1976.34, 1984.02, 1984.15, 1989.08, 1991.10
Byrd, Evelyn 1897.54
Byrd, Joe 1925.18, 1930.10, 1931.32, 1936.30, 1939.14, 1942.13
Byrd, John 1944.23, 1947.01
Byrd, Joseph 1934.37
Byrd, Josephine 1930.10
Byrd, Jr., Joe 1929.33
Byrd, Sam 1940.01
Byrd, William 1963.28
Byrde, Edye 1976.21
Byrk, Hugo 1910.03
Byrn, Robert 1943.22, 1945.05, 1947.17, 1948.25, 1949.15
Byrnbriar, Eddie 1933.15
Byrne, Alfred 1893.47
Byrne, Andrew 1891.24, 1895.40, 1898.64, 1918.23, 1922.30
Byrne, Arnold 1917.16
Byrne, Barbara 1987.18
Byrne, C.A. 1870.03, 1894.05, 1897.21
Byrne, Charles A. 1897.21
Byrne, Charles Alfred 1888.09, 1888.45, 1889.01, 1889.44, 1890.16, 1892.11, 1892.55, 1893.20, 1893.39, 1894.05, 1898.12, 1898.34
Byrne, Gaylea 1965.21
Byrne, George 1927.48
Byrne, Gypsy 1928.34
Byrne, Helen 1891.24
Byrne, Helena 1905.04
Byrne, Helene 1895.40, 1898.64
Byrne, J. Edmund 1937.07
Byrne, Jack 1933.21
Byrne, James 1895.40, 1917.16, 1918.23, 1922.30
Byrne, John 1917.16, 1917.22, 1918.23
Byrne, John F. 1891.24, 1895.40, 1898.64, 1922.30
Byrne, John H. 1881.39
Byrne, John H.W. 1901.03
Byrne, Matthew 1891.24
Byrne, Matthew F. 1994.12
Byrne, Messr. 1851.07
Byrne, Mr. 1841.01, 1851.06
Byrne, Norma 1928.01
Byrne, Richard 1991.09, 1991.12
Byrne, Susie 1878.01
Byrnes, Albert 1914.06
Byrnes, Dolly 1922.16
Byrnes, James 1917.29
Byrnes, John J. 1918.17
Byrnes, Kevin 1975.10
Byrnes, Maureen 1965.37
Byrns, Harold 1945.19
Byron 1869.07, 1869.46
Byron, A.S. 1927.03, 1927.31
Byron, Ada 1884.17
Byron, Alfred 1887.43
Byron, Annie 1869.06
Byron, Betty 1929.48, 1930.41
Byron, Carla 1904.03
Byron, Delma 1945.03
Byron, Eva 1891.20, 1902.39
Byron, Frank 1923.02
Byron, Franklyn 1924.13
Byron, George 1936.12
Byron, Grace 1914.33
Byron, H.J. 1864.09, 1864.13, 1870.35, 1878.20, 1890.24
Byron, Helen 1891.44, 1893.50, 1897.15, 1901.14, 1903.03
Byron, Henrietta 1891.44, 1893.50, 1922.31
Byron, Henry J. 1867.13, 1867.22, 1867.23, 1867.26, 1869.11, 1869.17, 1869.27, 1869.32, 1869.47, 1870.19, 1870.36, 1871.19, 1872.12, 1873.18, 1873.19, 1881.31
Byron, Jack 1946.12
Byron, Lord 1876.12
Byron, Lorna 1945.16
Byron, Milton 1878.12
Byron, Susan 1882.74
Byron, Susie 1880.64, 1881.09, 1882.02, 1882.50, 1882.79

C. Itoh and Company, Ltd. 1990.18
C.A. Chizzola and Company 1872.28, 1872.29, 1872.31, 1872.33, 1872.39, 1872.41, 1872.42, 1873.01
C.D. Hess Acme Opera Company 1882.31, 1882.33, 1882.36, 1882.37, 1882.40
C.D. Hess Opera Company 1877.35, 1877.36
Cabal, Mlle. 1870.44, 1871.27
Caballero 1949.07
Caballero, Christophe 1989.03
Caballero, Manuel Fernandez 1919.17
Caballero, Ramon 1963.18
Caballos, Larry 1925.01
Cabanne, Mimi 1950.04
Cabello, Emilio 1932.29
Cabin, Mr. 1852.04
Cable, Christopher 1977.18
Cable, Florence 1909.11, 1912.09, 1912.24
Cable, Stanley 1928.40
Cabot, Tony 1950.03
Caccia, Roger 1958.18
Cacciola-Morales, Keith 1990.08
Cacoyannis, Michael 1972.23, 1983.14
Caddick, David 1985.12, 1987.05, 1988.01, 1991.03, 1994.10, 1999.20
Caddigan, Jack 1919.18
Caddock, Earle 1925.37
Cade, Jack 1867.01
Cadeau, Noe 1882.61, 1883.28, 1883.34
Cadet, E. Mani 2000.03
Cadic, Mlle. 1868.13, 1869.01
Cadicamo, E. 1985.07, 1999.18
Cadiff, Andrew 1988.07
Cadix, Mlle. 1868.18, 1869.10
Cadiz, Nina 1895.43
Cadiz, Trizie 1905.47
Cadman, Ethel 1911.42
Cadwalladar, Lyn 1882.63
Cadwalladr, Llewellyn 1882.75, 1882.78
Cadwalladr, Lyn 1881.37, 1882.17
Cady, David 1981.27
Caesar, Arthur 1924.32, 1926.23
Caesar, Irving 1918.05, 1919.02, 1919.11, 1919.12, 1919.26, 1920.33, 1920.37, 1921.04, 1921.10, 1922.05, 1922.15, 1922.21, 1922.23, 1922.32, 1923.02, 1923.27, 1923.31, 1924.32, 1924.47, 1925.30, 1925.39, 1925.42, 1926.03, 1926.18, 1926.51, 1927.01, 1927.29, 1927.49, 1928.17, 1928.40, 1928.45, 1928.47, 1929.02, 1929.35, 1930.05, 1930.06, 1930.27, 1931.09, 1931.30, 1932.24, 1933.03, 1933.16, 1934.32, 1934.42, 1936.22, 1940.10, 1942.10, 1943.14, 1962.17, 1971.03, 1975.22, 1979.11, 1981.16, 1986.03, 1986.06, 1989.10, 1993.01, 1995.16, 1998.17, 1999.05, 2001.07
Caesar, James 1942.19, 1944.20, 1946.14, 1947.12
Caesar, Shirley 1995.04
Caesar, Sid 1948.04, 1962.27, 1989.22
Cafferty, Nat K. 1901.21, 1904.03
Cafferty, Nat. K. 1904.53
Caffey, Marion J. 1985.15, 1997.21
Caffrey and Wilson 1872.34
Caffrey, J.W. 1885.06
Caffrey, O'Brien 1868.06
Cagney, James 1928.19, 1929.20
Cagwin, Jack 1919.26
Cahill, Alfred 1906.26
Cahill, Ed 1908.43
Cahill, James 1967.01, 1989.29
Cahill, Julie 1914.25
Cahill, Marie 1888.05, 1888.44, 1889.37, 1895.38, 1896.30, 1898.17, 1900.52, 1902.16, 1902.23, 1903.07, 1904.54, 1905.45, 1906.27, 1908.36, 1910.30, 1911.21, 1912.08, 1915.01, 1927.27, 1930.40
Cahill, Mr. 1869.29
Cahill, W.B. 1870.19, 1870.35, 1870.42, 1871.05, 1873.12, 1873.14, 1873.17, 1873.28, 1875.39
Cahill, William 1906.27, 1912.16
Cahill, William B. 1870.13, 1870.21, 1878.05, 1878.20, 1879.03
Cahn, C. 1918.21
Cahn, David 1977.18, 1983.11
Cahn, Larry 1980.16, 1987.15
Cahn, Melvin Stanley 1931.26
Cahn, Sammy 1947.16, 1952.11, 1952.20, 1965.33, 1966.27, 1970.08, 1974.10, 1974.11, 1980.09, 1980.10, 1980.18, 1982.06, 1986.03, 1989.02, 1989.03, 1990.16, 1991.04, 1998.19
Cahn, William 1946.23
Cahoon, Kevin 1997.20, 2000.17
Cain, Billy 1924.37
Cain, J.E. 1900.08
Cain, Jess 1902.02
Cain, John 1902.26
Cain, John E. 1895.08
Cain, Sibol 1943.24, 1945.06, 1946.09
Cain, Viola 1912.08, 1912.48, 1913.26, 1917.20
Caine, Georgia 1896.29, 1898.05, 1898.38, 1899.12, 1899.29, 1900.50, 1901.19, 1902.23, 1903.24, 1904.37, 1905.49, 1906.37, 1907.63, 1909.14, 1910.31, 1911.42, 1913.09, 1913.21, 1915.21, 1918.37, 1920.38, 1921.32, 1922.43, 1924.30, 1930.39
Caine, Jess 1904.24, 1905.53
Caine, William 1906.47
Caird, John 1987.04, 2000.20
Caird, Lawrence 1897.32
Cairns, Angus 1947.09, 1950.10, 1971.01
Caits, Harry 1925.23
Caits, Joseph 1925.23, 1928.35
Caits, Louis 1928.35
Calabrese, Maria 1991.07, 1993.06, 1995.05
Calabresi, Messr. 1868.13, 1868.15
Calame, Madame 1898.34
Calamia, Marc 1999.01
Calbes, Eleanor 1965.20, 1968.16, 1970.21
Calcott, A. 1890.23
Caldarella 1985.07
Caldarella, J. 1999.18
Calder, Alexander 1950.01
Calder, Crane 1946.24, 1947.17, 1950.06, 1951.18, 1955.01, 1955.10
Calder, Jeffrey 1981.19
Calder, King 1951.18
Calderon, Ian 1975.07, 1978.03
Caldicott, Alfred J. 1890.33
Caldron, C. 1907.54
Calducci, Jean 1905.03
Calduel, Lorenzo 1924.27, 1928.09, 1937.09
Caldwell, Al 1894.27
Caldwell, Ann 1924.33
Caldwell, Anna 1891.09, 1898.61, 1905.19, 1905.55, 1906.17, 1907.47
Caldwell, Anne 1906.17, 1912.39, 1914.06, 1914.23, 1916.04, 1916.22, 1917.22, 1918.34, 1919.09, 1919.11, 1920.04, 1920.29, 1920.36, 1920.39, 1920.44, 1921.36, 1922.04, 1922.45, 1923.30, 1923.40, 1924.09, 1924.26, 1924.41, 1925.38, 1926.32, 1926.46, 1927.07, 1927.12, 1927.60, 1928.11, 1928.37, 1975.24
Caldwell, Annie 1876.21, 1882.15, 1882.71
Caldwell, E.J. 1910.09
Caldwell, Ella 1876.17, 1876.18, 1876.21, 1877.16, 1884.30
Caldwell, F.W. 1897.56
Caldwell, G. 1873.21
Caldwell, George 1879.65, 1879.67
Caldwell, Gisela 1973.16
Caldwell, Gladys 1913.11, 1915.06, 1915.09, 1915.10, 1915.14, 1920.13, 1920.36, 1921.34
Caldwell, H. 1873.18
Caldwell, James 1905.25
Caldwell, Lorenzo 1932.12, 1937.09
Caldwell, Meta 1896.44
Caldwell, Miss 1877.39, 1883.38, 1896.44
Caldwell, Mr. 1866.21, 1866.24, 1870.39, 1870.43, 1876.16
Caldwell, Mrs. 1872.20
Caldwell, Nance 1912.03
Caldwell, Neal 1930.33
Caldwell, Orville R. 1920.34
Caldwell, Sandra 1990.15
Cale, Bennett 1989.09
Cale, David 1981.19
Cale, William 1904.48, 1907.35
Cale, William J. 1903.23
Caleb, John 1981.19
Calef, Emma 1883.67, 1886.47, 1888.36
Calef, Jennie 1879.33, 1879.35, 1880.06, 1880.10, 1880.13, 1880.40, 1882.34
Calef, Jessie 1879.33, 1879.35, 1880.06, 1880.13, 1880.40, 1883.64
Calef, Lillian 1882.48
Calef, May 1880.48, 1880.53, 1882.07, 1882.08, 1882.09, 1882.10, 1882.11, 1882.12, 1882.13
Calendrelli, Jorge 1999.23
Caleraft, Mr. 1841.01
Caley, Dorothy 1940.16, 1942.19
Caley, Hazel 1940.16, 1942.19
Calgary, Andre 1948.21
Calgary, Steve 1948.21
Calhoun, Bill 1948.32
Calhoun, Charles 1989.12
Calhoun, Jeff 1982.14, 1991.07, 1992.18, 1994.06, 1994.07, 1996.17, 1999.04, 2001.03
Calhoun, Kirtland 1900.15
Calhoun, William 1949.08
Calice, M. 1880.62
Calice, Myron 1879.25, 1880.35, 1882.82, 1901.15, 1904.46
California Opera Company 1889.10
Calin, Mickey 1954.09, 1955.12, 1957.12
Calkins, Florence 1932.13
Calkins, J.T. 1907.43
Calkins, Jess 1908.32
Call, Catherine 1905.33
Call, John 1944.23, 1947.01, 1955.27, 1963.01, 1965.28, 1966.09
Calla, Miss 1855.06, 1855.08
Callaghan, Frank 1910.09
Callaghan, Huri 1972.20
Callaghan, John 1938.08
Callaghan, Matekino 1972.20
Callahan, Bill 1943.01, 1944.02, 1946.10, 1952.20
Callahan, Bob 1926.03
Callahan, Charles 1919.04
Callahan, Charles E. 1894.27
Callahan, Clark 1948.28
Callahan, Dennis 1983.11

Callahan, Dick 1888.11
Callahan, Ethel 1916.10
Callahan, Florine 1938.14
Callahan, George 1907.52, 1909.14, 1917.27
Callahan, George R. 1901.14
Callahan, George W. 1910.24, 1911.46, 1919.12
Callahan, J. 1884.29
Callahan, J. Will 1918.20, 1980.27
Callahan, J.F. 1888.27
Callahan, J.T. 1888.40
Callahan, James 1888.11, 1900.33
Callahan, James F. 1892.34, 1893.49, 1897.40, 1898.45
Callahan, John 1938.08
Callahan, Mabel 1914.31
Callahan, Marie 1921.36, 1923.38, 1928.29
Callahan, R.E. 1888.27, 1888.40
Callahan, Will 1919.40
Callahan, William 1976.25
Callam, Alexander 1931.03
Callam, J. Paul 1905.55
Callan, Chris 1973.09, 1989.18
Callan, Christopher 1976.36
Callan, James 1882.01
Callan, Jane 1918.11
Callan, John 1882.01, 1891.18
Callan, Josephine 1947.17
Callan, Paul 1927.45
Callas, Demetri 1989.27
Callaway, Ann Hampton 1999.24
Callaway, Anna 1880.26
Callaway, Annie 1880.62
Callaway, Bessie 1888.19
Callaway, Liz 1981.27, 1983.19, 1984.14
Callen, Chris 1989.25
Calley, Robert 1916.21, 1922.36, 1924.45
Calligne, T. 1867.12, 1868.06
Callish, Betty 1914.04
Callner, Marty 1998.14
Callot 1912.38
Callot, Paris 1926.49
Calloway, Annie 1882.57
Calloway, Bessie 1887.12, 1887.18
Calloway, Cab 1953.04, 1963.10, 1967.15, 1973.15, 1976.04, 1986.02, 1987.02, 1999.24
Calloway, Chris 1967.15, 1973.15
Calloway, Mayme 1896.46
Calloway, Northern J. 1970.20
Callum, Lola Ann 1992.06
Calm, Alex 1927.48
Calmer, Virginia 1923.02
Calthrop, Donald 1926.15
Calthrop, Gladys E. 1928.42, 1929.41, 1934.34, 1936.29, 1939.07
Calud, Annette 1991.03
Calvan, Joe 1946.10, 1951.14
Calvert, Carter 1999.09
Calvert, Charles 1876.12
Calvert, Margaret 1908.03
Calvert, Maud 1900.07
Calvert, Nelly 1875.39
Calvert, Patricia 1935.17
Calvet, Maude 1900.44
Calveyra, Pedro 1997.13
Calvi, Gerard 1958.18, 1965.37
Calvin, David 1943.23
Calvin, Henry 1947.06, 1948.16, 1950.01, 1953.16, 1965.22
Calvin, William 1911.09
Calvo, Pilar 1949.07
Calyo, Hannibal 1868.13, 1868.15, 1868.24, 1868.26, 1869.03, 1869.16, 1869.30, 1869.35, 1870.03, 1875.02, 1879.02
Calyo, Hannibal W. 1869.05, 1871.25, 1871.26, 1875.07, 1875.25, 1875.27, 1875.28, 1875.29, 1875.30, 1875.33, 1880.44
Calzado, Messr. 1917.33
Camacho, Chucha 1939.18
Camais, Adele 1882.57
Camara, Fraulein 1879.62, 1880.66
Cambeilh, Paul 1962.03
Cambell, Douglas 1938.02
Camber, Susan 1968.06
Camboa, Marcello 1965.37
Cambon, Mons. 1868.26
Cambridge Drama Festival 1957.02
Cambridge Theatre Company, Ltd., The 1981.14
Cambridge, Ed 1981.15
Cambridge, Godfrey 1958.11, 1967.18
Camerano, Signor 1884.39
Cameron Mackintosh, Inc. 1985.12
Cameron Mackintosh/Shubert Organization Production 1985.12
Cameron, Alice 1895.22
Cameron, Annie 1889.36, 1890.47, 1890.48, 1896.41, 1897.24, 1902.12, 1903.38
Cameron, Blanche 1880.59
Cameron, Bruce 1988.11, 1989.22, 1990.11, 1994.03, 1994.13
Cameron, Bruce D. 1986.21
Cameron, Cecil 1905.04
Cameron, Daisy King 1907.19
Cameron, Donald 1932.28
Cameron, Dora 1907.58
Cameron, Doris 1908.10, 1908.21, 1908.42, 1911.34, 1911.43, 1912.09
Cameron, Dorothy 1915.22, 1916.21
Cameron, Edith 1897.44
Cameron, Edward 1884.51, 1884.57
Cameron, Elsie 1885.47, 1887.10
Cameron, Frances 1903.29, 1907.48, 1912.17, 1912.33, 1916.21, 1917.09, 1918.30, 1919.14, 1920.41
Cameron, George A. 1903.04
Cameron, Grace 1900.25, 1900.31, 1900.32, 1900.50, 1903.07, 1904.15, 1907.19, 1908.41
Cameron, Hugh 1904.23, 1912.25, 1913.30, 1917.04, 1920.03, 1921.11, 1921.30, 1923.32, 1925.52, 1927.62, 1930.08, 1932.16, 1934.15, 1934.42, 1936.17, 1939.30
Cameron, Irene 1905.19
Cameron, Irene L. 1901.08
Cameron, J. 1885.14
Cameron, Jack 1930.41
Cameron, James 1904.35, 1928.42
Cameron, John 1964.29, 1987.04, 1993.15
Cameron, Kathryn 1948.16
Cameron, Kay 1996.04
Cameron, L. William 1895.41
Cameron, Lawrence 1917.10
Cameron, Lorna 1972.08
Cameron, Madeline 1915.22, 1916.21, 1924.47, 1926.30, 1926.51, 1927.16, 1929.03
Cameron, Madge 1966.05
Cameron, Marlene 1946.12, 1948.28
Cameron, Messr. 1882.04
Cameron, Miss 1878.14, 1886.32, 1886.36
Cameron, Mme. 1898.01
Cameron, Nellie 1889.02, 1906.10
Cameron, Phyllis 1931.05, 1933.16, 1936.01, 1950.09
Cameron, Rudolf 1924.08
Cameron, Rudolph 1927.05
Cameron, Vera 1902.43, 1905.55
Cameron, Violet 1886.50, 1886.54
Cameron, W.M. 1882.14
Cameron, William 1892.36, 1892.56, 1893.28, 1894.10, 1894.21, 1896.51, 1897.15, 1897.39, 1898.68, 1899.37, 1900.05, 1900.34, 1901.09, 1901.23, 1903.06, 1903.18, 1908.24, 1908.41, 1919.44, 1923.08, 1925.12
Cameron, Yukona 1930.25
Camilla, Mlle. 1870.44, 1871.27
Camille D'Arville Comic Opera Company 1894.05
Camillo, Marvin 1967.10, 1969.09
Camiolo, Joseph 1946.05
Camis, Aida 1879.42
Cammeron, Miss 1882.23
Cammeyer, A.D. 1903.33
Cammeyer, Alfred D. 1898.46
Cammeyer, J. 1884.31
Cammeyer, Jerry 1879.59
Cammis, Mlle. 1886.16
Camoens, Mr. 1854.03
Camp, (Hamid) Hamilton 1964.26, 1965.01, 1965.31, 1970.16, 1971.08
Camp, Grace 1914.11, 1914.19
Camp, Samantha 1997.16
Camp, Sara 1929.43
Camp, Shep 1919.02, 1921.03, 1924.17, 1927.43, 1927.55, 1928.01
Camp, Wallace 1917.09
Campana, Joyce 1986.14, 1987.10, 1988.14, 1988.16, 1989.04
Campanella, Frank 1962.24, 1965.15, 1966.13
Campanella, Joseph 1963.13
Campanella, Stephen 1998.16, 1999.23, 2001.02
Campanile, Festa 1964.03
Campano, Janet 1965.36
Campbell, A. Allan 1908.42
Campbell, Alan 1994.10
Campbell, Alexander 1935.13
Campbell, Alice 1897.28, 1898.25, 1898.52, 1902.30, 1903.14
Campbell, Allan 1905.49, 1927.67, 1932.11
Campbell, Arthur 1926.31, 1930.21, 1931.19
Campbell, Bartley 1879.06, 1882.69, 1885.46, 1891.28
Campbell, Bessie 1898.02
Campbell, Bill 1989.06
Campbell, Brittany Alexander 1999.21
Campbell, C.J. 1879.42, 1879.71, 1882.06, 1902.02
Campbell, Camelia 1937.11
Campbell, Catherine 1998.13
Campbell, Charles 1889.40, 1890.39, 1894.14, 1897.24, 1898.15, 1898.40, 1898.42, 1908.16, 1938.13
Campbell, Charles J. 1881.41, 1882.42, 1882.47, 1882.51, 1882.70, 1883.04, 1883.10, 1889.16, 1889.49, 1892.17, 1894.28, 1895.22, 1905.53, 1906.20, 1907.21, 1909.14
Campbell, Clara 1875.11
Campbell, Claudia 1951.14
Campbell, Colin 1916.18, 1918.31, 1922.04, 1922.35, 1923.35, 1924.24, 1925.01, 1925.28, 1934.41
Campbell, Craig 1909.19, 1911.23, 1912.46, 1917.31, 1927.24, 1931.24
Campbell, David 1986.11
Campbell, Dean 1948.08, 1951.23, 1953.01
Campbell, Delia Lee 1902.26
Campbell, Dick 1940.17
Campbell, Donald 1927.64, 1930.43
Campbell, Douglas 1963.28
Campbell, Edith 1929.03
Campbell, Elaine 1971.21
Campbell, Elison 1892.03
Campbell, Eric 1916.04
Campbell, Flo 1924.36
Campbell, Florence 1911.15
Campbell, Francis 1895.31
Campbell, Frank 1907.19
Campbell, Frank J. 1884.48
Campbell, G.F. 1893.34
Campbell, George 1886.24, 1889.46, 1920.25
Campbell, George F. 1886.45, 1893.34, 1895.38, 1897.26, 1898.05
Campbell, George W. 1896.20
Campbell, Georgia 1903.37
Campbell, Graeme 1984.07
Campbell, Helen D. 1888.07
Campbell, Henry 1892.04
Campbell, Irma 1920.11
Campbell, J. Kenneth 1973.07
Campbell, J.C. 1868.21
Campbell, J.K. 1871.12, 1871.16
Campbell, James 1930.22
Campbell, Jimmy 1931.26, 1997.21, 1999.23
Campbell, Joan 1976.26
Campbell, John 1939.19
Campbell, Louise 1894.24
Campbell, Lulu 1880.65, 1882.34, 1885.26
Campbell, Martha 1881.44
Campbell, Mattie 1881.45
Campbell, Maude 1903.09, 1907.62
Campbell, Messr. 1881.11, 1883.31, 1888.36
Campbell, Minnie 1897.24
Campbell, Mr. 1856.02, 1865.08, 1865.09, 1883.66
Campbell, Norman 1971.21
Campbell, Pat 1955.05, 1960,14, 1960.15
Campbell, Patton 1959.18, 1961.02, 1961.03, 1961.04, 1961.06, 1961.19, 1961.23, 1962.04, 1962.09, 1962.10, 1962.19, 1963.23, 1964.08, 1964.09, 1965.09, 1965.11, 1965.34, 1966.03, 1968.09, 1968.10, 1968.12, 1972.14, 1974.07, 1974.15, 1975.17, 1976.22, 1976.26, 1977.03, 1977.12, 1977.17, 1980.21, 1981.20, 1985.09, 1987.08, 1992.07, 1993.12
Campbell, Paul 1945.11
Campbell, Peggy 1944.32, 1947.01
Campbell, Percy 1921.12
Campbell, Raymond 1927.30
Campbell, Robert 1905.21, 1920.37
Campbell, Rod 1998.01
Campbell, S.C. 1864.04, 1864.07, 1864.16, 1864.18, 1864.19, 1864.20, 1866.10, 1866.14, 1867.03, 1867.04, 1867.06, 1867.07, 1868.01, 1868.09, 1868.10, 1868.11, 1868.12
Campbell, S.G. 1868.02
Campbell, Sande 1972.21
Campbell, Shawn 1966.30
Campbell, Susan 1967.10
Campbell, Violet 1876.06
Campbell, Virginia 1934.40
Campbell, Walter 1926.19, 1932.12
Campbell, William 1990.19
Campbell, Winifred 1934.34
Campbell-Walker, Edith 1923.10
Campeggi, L. 1911.16
Campeggi, Luigi 1911.19
Campiglio, P.F. 1891.23
Campion, Annie 1869.11, 1869.17, 1869.25, 1869.28
Campion, Thomas 1963.28
Campo, Julius 1930.43
Campobello, Eurico 1884.33, 1884.38
Campora, Giancarlo 1990.03
Canada, Jan 1958.03
Canadian National Musical Theatre 1971.21
Canaro, F. 1985.07, 1997.13
Canarutto, Angelo 1934.02, 1940.05
Canary, David 1961.08
Canary, Thomas 1893.39, 1894.14, 1894.21, 1895.04, 1895.06, 1895.18, 1896.06, 1896.18, 1896.30, 1896.51, 1898.28
Canby, A.H. 1889.24, 1890.26, 1891.47, 1893.35, 1894.29, 1896.28, 1919.41
Canby, Al H. 1895.26
Canby, Miss 1866.28
Cancilla, Elaine 1959.25, 1961.22, 1965.17, 1966.01, 1970.10
Candee, Jr., Charles E. 1892.21, 1905.40, 1911.46
Candlish, Forbes 1995.02
Canduit, J. 1900.57
Canduit, J.P. 1895.09
Canepa, E. 1911.16
Canepa, Elvira 1911.19
Canepa, Guiseppe 1911.16, 1911.19
Canetti, Jacques 1959.15, 1961.25
Caney, C.E. 1904.47
Caney, R. 1901.27, 1903.39, 1904.47, 1905.48
Caney, Robert 1897.03
Canfield, Eugene 1888.44, 1889.12, 1890.04, 1893.31, 1897.49, 1898.78
Canfield, John 1887.13
Canissa, Pauline 1882.54
Cannar, Jennie 1905.28
Cannefax, Charles 1924.36
Canning, Effie I. 1887.02, 1890.36
Canning, Heather 1965.39
Canning, James 1972.12
Cannold, Sammi Rose 1998.17
Cannon, Alice 1971.06
Cannon, Bert 1906.06
Cannon, Beth 1935.11
Cannon, Cedric C. 1993.11
Cannon, Elida 1879.66
Cannon, Grace 1899.22
Cannon, Gracie 1899.23
Cannon, Hughie 1904.43, 1965.05, 1980.27
Cannon, J.C. 1887.11
Cannon, Maureen 1941.06, 1943.18, 1945.03, 1947.11
Cannon, Reuben 1987.17
Cannon, Thomas 1931.44
Cano, Charles 1905.09
Canoll, Mr. 1856.02
Canonge, Mlle. 1879.19, 1879.27
Canonico, Gerard 2000.19
Canova, Ann 1939.24
Canova, Anne 1934.39
Canova, Diana 1995.11
Canova, Juda 1939.24
Canova, Judy 1934.39, 1936.02
Canova, Leon 1926.46
Canova, Pete 1934.39
Canova, Peter 1908.40
Canova, Pietro 1913.06
Canova, Zeke 1934.39, 1939.24
Cansino, Eduardo 1916.25, 1917.23, 1920.13
Cansino, Elisa 1916.25, 1917.23, 1920.13
Canter, Harry 1930.24
Cantor, Arthur 1963.11, 1963.28, 1964.26, 1965.37, 1977.02, 1986.01, 1986.15, 1987.05
Cantor, Charles 1897.46
Cantor, Eddie 1917.13, 1918.19, 1919.15, 1920.18, 1920.33, 1922.15, 1923.20, 1923.38, 1924.01, 1927.37, 1928.47, 1929.26, 1930.06, 1941.13, 1946.04
Cantor, John 1897.46
Cantor, Lew 1923.04
Cantor, Mrs. 1838.01

Cantorale, Hermanos 1988.15
Cantrell, Roger 1983.16
Cantrelle, Grace 1928.49
Cantrelle, Mlle. 1872.33, 1872.42, 1873.01, 1873.11, 1875.08
Cantrelle, Mme. 1872.41
Cantu, Jr., Jesus 2001.04
Cantwell, John 1908.15, 1930.23
Canty, Fay 1932.30
Canty, Marietta 1933.04
Cantzen, Conrad 1925.37
Canyon Productions 1969.16
Cape Playhouse 1929.33
Cape, Vandy 1934.40
Capehart, Charles 1924.05
Capel, Gertrude 1889.54
Capel, Miss 1851.01
Capelini, Eugenie 1879.42
Capelini, Mlle. 1879.42
Capers, Virginia 1959.27, 1973.10
Capes, Michael 1979.26
Capitaine, Alcide 1893.47
Capital Cities/ABC, Inc. 1990.12, 1994.05
Caples, Martha 1934.06, 1936.12, 1939.12
Capo, Bobby 1946.21
Capobianco, Tito 1969.11, 1978.07, 1978.20, 1979.21, 1989.13
Capon, Ruby 1898.27
Capone, Clifford 1976.15
Capote, Truman 1954.19, 1971.16
Capoul, Victor 1879.48, 1879.49, 1879.51, 1879.55, 1879.61, 1879.69, 1880.14, 1880.16, 1880.22, 1880.56, 1883.30
Capp, Al 1956.12
Capp, James 1952.05, 1952.13
Capp, Madeline 1951.10
Cappa, Messr. 1882.34
Cappallini, Eugenia 1884.18
Cappelini, Eugene 1880.63
Cappelini, Mlle. 1880.08, 1883.06
Cappella, M. 1926.14
Cappellini, Mons. 1889.08
Cappellini, Signora 1883.48
Capps, Kendall 1925.47, 1929.06, 1931.01
Cappy, Ted 1946.23, 1949.01, 1951.19, 1952.05
Capri, Dick 1991.14
Capri, Henry 1945.03
Capri, Rena 1889.33
Capron, Robert 1916.25, 1931.41, 1931.43, 1931.45, 1932.10
Capti, Dick 1991.14
Cara, Irene 1968.24, 1970.20, 1972.25, 1979.15
Carabella, Angela 1947.13
Carabuena, Philipp Lee 1994.02
Caracolillo, Maria 1958.06
Caracolillo, Rosa 1958.06
Caradimas, Lana 1973.09, 1989.18
Caralp, Mons. 1869.03, 1872.39, 1873.01
Caramba 1932.29, 1934.02, 1940.05
Carare, Michel 1893.44
Carber, D.B. 1902.42
Carbon, H.W. 1892.07
Carbone, A. 1917.10
Carbone, Silvio 1911.19
Carbone, Vincent 1946.22
Carbrey, Douglas 1915.22
Carbrey, John 1915.22
Carby, Fanny 1964.28
Card, June 1963.22
Card, Virginia 1942.32
Cardell, Edith 1928.01
Cardell, Marion 1928.01
Cardelli, Giovanni 1948.31
Cardellini, Emilio 1932.29
Carden, James 1869.33
Carder, Floyd 1926.46
Carder, Tom 1982.03
Cardiff, James 1902.09
Cardin, Pierre 1990.01
Cardinal, Arthur 1919.03, 1920.19, 1926.16, 1928.22, 1929.35, 1930.42
Cardiner, Reginald 1935.12
Cardini, John 1934.41
Cardon, C.F. 1906.40
Cardon, Jean 1964.39
Cardona, Debra 1997.22, 1998.20, 1999.21
Cardona, Milton 1998.02
Cardoni 1870.05
Cardoni, Gerald 1953.16
Cardownie, Jessie 1905.35, 1907.19, 1911.08
Cardownie, Phoebe 1907.19
Cardoza, Mr. 1881.40
Careca, Ana 1992.13
Careme, Mons. 1873.01
Caress, Bill 1917.16
Caress, William 1917.22
Caret, Paul 1926.01
Carew, Beryl 1940.21
Carew, D.J. 1918.23
Carew, Dan 1917.16
Carewe Edwin 1907.56
Carewe-Carvel, Virginia 1913.32
Carey, A.J. 1923.02
Carey, Addison 1924.27, 1930.29, 1932.30
Carey, Ann 1931.24, 1931.33, 1931.35, 1931.43
Carey, Bessie 1916.07
Carey, Cecile 1936.26
Carey, Claiborne 1960.01
Carey, David 1970.17, 1987.06
Carey, Eleanor 1888.10
Carey, Frank 1972.10
Carey, Henry 1881.39, 1902.23, 1903.01
Carey, James 1904.48
Carey, Jodina Rosario 2001.04
Carey, Joseph 1907.42, 1908.06, 1908.20, 1908.24, 1910.07, 1911.11, 1912.28
Carey, Joyce 1936.29
Carey, Macdonald 1941.04
Carey, Madison 1916.18
Carey, Mary 1924.31
Carey, Michael 1910.33
Carey, Polly 1886.58
Carfrae, Doug 1976.33
Carhart, Georgia 1900.16
Carhart, J.L. 1881.32
Caridi, Carmine 1968.32
Caridi, Tony 1941.08
Carine, Martha 1904.40
Carini, F.J. 1886.31
Cariou, Len 1970.09, 1973.04, 1979.06, 1983.08, 1987.19
Carl, Barry 1979.20, 1979.27, 1980.21, 1981.20
Carl, Marjie 1896.27
Carl, Richard 1904.24
Carl, Tom 1883.13
Carland, Louis 1875.05
Carlberg, Louis 1885.30
Carle Amusement Company 1904.24
Carle, Alice 1886.25, 1886.55, 1886.57, 1890.27
Carle, Carlo 1869.02, 1869.14
Carle, Cynthia 1982.08
Carle, Emma 1869.02, 1869.14, 1869.20
Carle, Mons. 1869.06
Carle, Richard 1893.06, 1893.49, 1895.38, 1896.06, 1896.18, 1897.25, 1898.28, 1898.43, 1898.56, 1898.58, 1899.26, 1899.29, 1899.39, 1900.16, 1901.18, 1904.09, 1904.24, 1905.53, 1906.36, 1907.39, 1908.17, 1909.12, 1911.08, 1912.26, 1913.20, 1915.01, 1916.02, 1917.35, 1921.19, 1923.16, 1930.40
Carle, William 1898.22
Carlebach, Shlomo 1972.17
Carleen, Ellen 1947.02
Carleton English Opera Company 1885.07, 1885.09
Carleton's Opera Company 1896.20
Carleton, Adelaide 1880.47
Carleton, Alice 1932.16, 1932.24, 1935.18
Carleton, Arthur 1895.07, 1897.42, 1898.34
Carleton, Carle 1919.36, 1923.09
Carleton, George 1935.13
Carleton, Jack 1913.05
Carleton, Jr., William P. 1906.44
Carleton, Lillian 1908.03
Carleton, Minnie 1890.12, 1890.30, 1896.01
Carleton, Popert 1896.20
Carleton, Propert 1893.21, 1893.35
Carleton, W.P. 1900.05, 1901.09, 1903.38
Carleton, W.T. 1882.14, 1885.09, 1885.41, 1892.60, 1893.02, 1898.15, 1899.24, 1904.03, 1904.55, 1908.29, 1910.04
Carleton, Will 1889.12, 1890.04
Carleton, Will C. 1895.27
Carleton, Will P. 1907.59
Carleton, William 1879.63, 1880.39, 1881.52, 1882.81, 1884.07, 1886.23, 1888.44, 1889.51, 1892.12
Carleton, William P. 1895.10, 1907.11, 1910.05, 1912.14, 1916.13
Carleton, William Probert 1900.34
Carleton, William T. 1881.14, 1881.37, 1882.17, 1882.45, 1882.60, 1882.75, 1882.78, 1883.62, 1884.08, 1885.07, 1893.07, 1895.13, 1896.20, 1896.22, 1899.41, 1927.55
Carley, Marion 1949.16
Carlibach, Rabbi 1971.14
Carlier, Mons. 1880.28, 1880.44, 1880.50, 1881.50, 1881.54
Carlin, Bob 1903.05
Carlin, Cynthia 1935.11
Carline, Miss 1866.16
Carlington, Miss 1886.32, 1886.36
Carlisle, Blanche 1898.26, 1898.46
Carlisle, Crissie 1898.28, 1899.25
Carlisle, Cryssie 1894.21
Carlisle, Florence 1891.09, 1891.36, 1892.60, 1893.07, 1895.18, 1900.34, 1901.06
Carlisle, George 1887.12
Carlisle, Gertie 1905.25, 1907.11
Carlisle, Gerty 1900.03
Carlisle, Jessie 1894.21, 1896.06, 1897.25
Carlisle, Katherine 1898.13, 1898.48
Carlisle, Kevin 1957.14, 1958.02, 1959.01, 1962.16, 1967.06, 1968.01, 1980.12, 1991.10
Carlisle, Kitty 1933.23, 1936.22, 1937.17, 1940.09, 1948.31, 1956.05
Carlisle, Leonora 1901.06
Carlisle, Louise 1896.13
Carlisle, Lyda 1915.21
Carlisle, Mae 1906.01
Carlisle, Marion 1934.13
Carlisle, Mary 1889.15, 1889.18
Carlisle, May 1888.27, 1888.40, 1889.11, 1911.28
Carlisle, R.C. 1912.30
Carlisle, Una Mae 1942.13
Carllsmith, Lillian 1895.26
Carlo Studios 1932.10
Carlo, Don 1966.02, 1978.19, 1978.23, 1979.20, 1979.27
Carlo, Monte 1921.23, 1923.08, 1924.05, 1924.24, 1924.42, 1925.44, 1926.23, 1928.49, 1930.21, 1947.13
Carlo, Signor 1851.06
Carlous, A. 1892.59
Carlson, Deborah 1981.13
Carlson, Eugenie 1949.06
Carlson, Philip 1974.23
Carlson, Richard 1939.13
Carlson, Robert 1947.09
Carlson, Robert Eric 1947.03
Carlson, Sally Ann 1962.24
Carlson, Stanley 1942.32, 1944.26, 1946.24, 1950.11, 1951.15, 1952.15, 1954.04, 1954.06, 1954.07, 1958.02
Carlson, Thomas 1904.58
Carlson, Violet 1924.45, 1927.01, 1927.24, 1927.55, 1928.48, 1934.15
Carlstedt, Claudia 1895.33, 1896.45, 1897.26, 1897.42
Carlstedt, Viola 1902.16, 1902.23
Carlstedt, Xenia 1892.29
Carlton, Arthur C. 1893.20
Carlton, Bessie 1884.12
Carlton, Carle 1921.23, 1924.07, 1927.03
Carlton, Dean 1938.13
Carlton, Edwina 1879.15
Carlton, Evelyn 1912.38, 1913.17
Carlton, F. 1888.23
Carlton, Marion 1898.29
Carlton, Pauline 1918.04
Carlton, Sam 1942.35
Carlton, Sydney 1898.17
Carlton, Thelma 1920.45, 1925.23
Carlton, Upert 1917.29
Carlton, William 1884.19
Carlton, William P. 1916.25
Carlyle, Charles 1885.67
Carlyle, Chrissie 1898.20
Carlyle, Cora 1897.09
Carlyle, Crissie 1893.04, 1893.22, 1894.28, 1895.04, 1897.02, 1898.38, 1898.56
Carlyle, Frank 1885.68
Carlyle, G. 1888.35
Carlyle, George 1887.18, 1887.26
Carlyle, Grace 1925.02
Carlyle, Louise 1952.07
Carlyle, Marie 1888.16, 1889.20, 1890.43
Carlyle, Meta 1934.18
Carlysle, Crissie 1901.21
Carman, C. 1868.22
Carman, L. 1867.19, 1867.20, 1868.22
Carman, La Petite 1851.01
Carman, Mesdame 1852.01, 1852.05, 1856.04
Carman, Miss 1855.11, 1867.19, 1867.20
Carman, Mrs. A. 1851.08
Carmelim, The 1968.04
Carmello, Carolee 1988.09, 1989.29, 1992.09, 1998.21, 1999.13
Carmen, Carl 1932.14
Carmen, Eric 1998.13
Carmen, Kitty 1914.30
Carmen, Lillian 1890.29, 1935.04
Carmen, Mae 1912.28, 1917.20, 1918.16
Carmen, May 1914.15, 1916.10
Carmen, Mlle. 1869.01
Carmical, Robert 2001.04
Carmichael, Estrella 1904.10
Carmichael, Hoagy 1936.31, 1940.09, 1953.12, 1978.09, 1979.14, 1980.29, 1987.02, 1989.21, 1990.09, 1991.04, 1992.18, 1997.05, 1999.24
Carmina, Rudolfo 1884.58
Carminati, Tullio 1932.22, 1938.15
Carmody, Eileen 1927.01
Carmody, James 1912.43
Carmody, Vivian 1927.02
Carmontel, Hattie 1919.20
Carnaby, Floyd 1936.22
Carnahan, Kirsti 1983.19, 1993.09
Carne, Judy 1970.11
Carnegie, Hail 1944.17
Carnegie, Hattie 1926.36, 1941.04, 1943.03, 1948.11
Carnegie, Rollo 1905.53
Carnelia, Craig 1978.12, 1982.08, 1991.10
Carney, Alan 1954.15
Carney, Art 1965.17
Carney, Grace 1961.14, 1978.10
Carney, Harry 1980.10, 1981.06
Carney, Kay 1974.23
Carney, Mary 1928.44
Carnovsky, Morris 1936.28, 1962.01
Carns 1908.08
Caro, Eva Perez 1939.18
Caro, Mlle. 1882.67, 1883.27, 1883.30, 1883.34, 1884.43, 1884.45, 1884.47, 1884.50, 1884.52, 1884.54, 1884.55, 1885.23, 1885.55, 1885.56, 1885.57, 1885.59, 1885.60, 1885.61, 1886.08, 1886.09, 1886.18, 1886.21, 1886.22
Caro, Mme. 1882.55, 1882.58, 1882.61, 1883.28, 1886.19
Carol, Nita 1939.31
Carol, Sylvia 1925.26, 1928.14
Carol, Tito 1929.09
Carola, Edith 1937.05
Carole, Trudy 1962.04
Caroli, Mlle. 1887.35, 1887.36
Caroline Richings Bernard English Opera Company 1869.41
Caroline Richings English Comic Opera Company 1866.10
Caroline Richings English Opera Company 1867.03, 1867.04, 1867.06, 1867.07, 1867.09, 1868.09, 1868.11, 1868.12
Caroline Richings Opera Company 1863.07, 1868.10
Caroline, Miss 1869.43
Caroline, Mlle. 1871.27, 1872.06, 1873.10
Carolton, James 1899.04
Caroly, Mlle. 1887.37
Caron, Alphons 1884.65
Caron, Edward 1899.04
Caron, George 1884.65
Caron, Joseph 1869.27
Caron, Mr. 1869.20
Caron, Sally 1884.65
Caron, W. 1869.20
Carosi, Mauro 1985.14
Carow, Joseph 1959.26, 1965.21
Carpani, Ricardo 1993.08
Carpenter, A. 1880.07
Carpenter, A.S. 1869.40
Carpenter, Carleton 1946.07, 1953.17
Carpenter, Constance 1926.36, 1927.56, 1931.14, 1934.43
Carpenter, Edward Childs 1933.03
Carpenter, Eugene 1870.21
Carpenter, Frederick 1929.29
Carpenter, Imogen 1942.23, 1943.05
Carpenter, Irving 1920.04
Carpenter, Irving J. 1914.31
Carpenter, Jean 1930.35
Carpenter, John 1992.04
Carpenter, Larry 1976.03, 1989.09
Carpenter, Lloyd 1916.06
Carpenter, Messr. 1856.01
Carpenter, Miss 1841.01
Carpenter, Mr. 1856.02
Carpenter, Mrs. 1856.01

Carpenter, Ruth 1891.27
Carpenter, Thelma 1945.08, 1948.14, 1952.08, 1955.04
Carpenter, W. 1873.08, 1873.10, 1880.07
Carpenter, W.B. 1871.02
Carpenter, William B. 1870.42, 1872.04, 1872.05, 1872.08, 1872.25
Carpentier, Curtis 1924.27
Carper, Constance 1918.16
Carpeza, Messr. 1881.02
Carpezat 1881.32
Carpezat, Mons. 1889.08
Carpezzat 1888.23
Carpin, Mons. 1877.19
Carpinello, James 1999.15
Carpizal 1885.65
Carr, Alexander 1907.42
Carr, Allan 1983.11
Carr, Andrew 1931.36
Carr, Anna 1901.27
Carr, Benjamin 1796.01
Carr, Betty 1954.15, 1957.10
Carr, Buddy 1925.25
Carr, Catherine 1980.07
Carr, Eddie 1922.08
Carr, Edward 1886.17
Carr, Edwin 1878.22, 1886.10
Carr, Elmo 1931.02
Carr, Ernest 1917.21
Carr, F. Osmond 1895.02, 1895.03, 1897.32
Carr, F.D. 1897.15
Carr, George H. 1902.27
Carr, Gretta 1901.02
Carr, Helen 1919.22
Carr, J.P. 1876.34
Carr, Jack 1933.04, 1934.37, 1935.13, 1942.03, 1943.24, 1945.06, 1946.09
Carr, James W. 1938.13
Carr, Jessie 1907.11
Carr, Jimmie 1929.30
Carr, Jimmy 1929.24
Carr, Joan 1933.24
Carr, Josephine 1906.03
Carr, Kenneth 1968.18
Carr, Lawrence 1954.02, 1956.07, 1959.01, 1960.09, 1963.13, 1966.01, 1966.10, 1969.01
Carr, Louise 1931.36
Carr, Madge 1891.34
Carr, Marie 1892.26, 1892.32, 1892.41, 1892.49, 1893.01, 1893.04, 1893.22
Carr, Mary 1866.13, 1873.25
Carr, Mary Ann 1939.07
Carr, Maurice 1936.22
Carr, Nat 1917.08
Carr, Olive 1906.03, 1911.40
Carr, Osmond 1895.29
Carr, Percy 1919.42, 1921.15
Carr, Sadie 1913.35
Carr, Samuel 1942.20
Carr, Tottie 1899.01, 1900.10, 1901.02, 1902.36
Carr, Vinnie 1884.58
Carr, W. 1889.24
Carr-Shaw, Lucy 1897.03
Carradine, John 1962.12
Carradine, Keith 1991.07
Carrafa, John 2000.12
Carragher, Bernard 1983.06
Carranti, Ugo 1911.19
Carras, Nicholas 1959.19
Carrasco, Gustavo 1932.19
Carrasco, Manuela 1986.17
Carre, Albert 1893.05
Carre, Fabrice 1886.43
Carre, Genny 1929.05
Carre, Jr., Michel 1891.05
Carre, Michael 1868.20, 1869.22
Carre, Michel 1855.03, 1861.05, 1863.05, 1864.08, 1866.27, 1867.30, 1870.38, 1872.01, 1875.12, 1875.15, 1875.27, 1879.20, 1882.43, 1884.18, 1893.25, 1900.30, 1916.16, 1920.41, 1925.09
Carrel, Judd 1934.03
Carreno 1969.11
Carreno, Lillian 1911.28
Carretero, Angel 1934.32
Carrette, Florence 1905.30
Carrick, Hartley 1919.20
Carrie, Little 1867.32, 1880.07
Carrie, May 1899.30
Carrier, Dora 1900.59
Carrier, Mabel 1903.14, 1904.35
Carrier, Mons. 1868.24, 1868.26, 1869.03, 1869.05, 1869.16, 1869.30
Carriere, Berthold 1987.01
Carriere, Jean-Claude 1983.16
Carriere, Mons. 1869.05
Carriker, Terry 1982.06
Carrillo, Leo 1915.05
Carrillo, Violeta 1949.07
Carrington, Alex 1976.28
Carrington, Alice 1912.26, 1915.01
Carrington, Bruce 1931.42
Carrington, Ella 1888.33
Carrington, Evelyn 1910.20
Carrington, Evelyn Carter 1912.08, 1914.20
Carrington, Helen 1924.10, 1924.34, 1926.25, 1928.17, 1931.16, 1932.17
Carrington, John 1898.52, 1898.71
Carrington, Katherine 1930.33, 1932.05, 1932.22, 1937.01
Carrington, M. 1881.38
Carrington, Mary 1900.06, 1900.13
Carrington, Miss 1881.03
Carrington, Nell 1918.20, 1922.15
Carrington, Paul 1973.10
Carrington, Reginald 1903.40
Carritte, Nita 1897.53, 1898.04, 1898.14
Carrol, J. 1907.54
Carrol, Jane 1922.35
Carrol, Joyce 1947.02
Carrol, Kelly 1977.18
Carrol, William F. 1907.10
Carroll, Adam 1928.46, 1929.19, 1936.05, 1937.04, 1942.35
Carroll, Albert 1922.20, 1922.42, 1924.14, 1925.20, 1926.17, 1927.23, 1928.19, 1929.20, 1930.18, 1930.33, 1931.19, 1932.20, 1944.29
Carroll, Art 1951.14
Carroll, Barbara 1953.08
Carroll, Bert 1989.12
Carroll, Bryant 1998.13
Carroll, Carroll 1930.18, 1930.33
Carroll, Clara 1917.31, 1918.22, 1920.13, 1920.20
Carroll, Clare 1922.16
Carroll, Danny 1957.18, 1965.17, 1968.07, 1980.20
Carroll, David-James 1975.13, 1981.25, 1982.14, 1985.20, 1988.09, 1989.26
Carroll, Diahann 1954.19, 1962.03
Carroll, Dick 1871.18
Carroll, Dorothy 1929.26
Carroll, Earl 1912.02, 1912.24, 1913.16, 1913.17, 1914.21, 1916.17, 1916.21, 1917.04, 1918.04, 1919.03, 1922.21, 1923.21, 1924.31, 1925.25, 1925.40, 1925.48, 1926.23, 1927.02, 1928.23, 1929.08, 1929.20, 1929.26, 1930.22, 1931.26, 1932.18, 1933.20, 1935.04, 1940.02
Carroll, Eddie 1871.18, 1989.11
Carroll, Edw. H. 1895.21
Carroll, Edward H. 1897.28
Carroll, Edwin 1899.06
Carroll, Edwin H. 1891.41
Carroll, Eleanor 1922.20
Carroll, Frank 1959.04
Carroll, Garrett 1914.33
Carroll, George 1903.22, 1906.32
Carroll, Georgia 1940.08
Carroll, Gladys 1912.37
Carroll, Harry 1910.18, 1912.14, 1914.10, 1914.16, 1914.22, 1915.02, 1916.10, 1918.07, 1919.34, 1920.18, 1920.28, 1921.21, 1976.24
Carroll, Helen 1937.10, 1939.16
Carroll, Helena 1963.01, 1965.28, 1970.03
Carroll, Irene 1930.33
Carroll, Irv 1951.20
Carroll, Isabel 1900.35
Carroll, Isabelle 1902.05
Carroll, J. 1893.30, 1917.31
Carroll, J.C. 1878.13
Carroll, J.P. 1892.23
Carroll, J.W. 1876.32, 1876.35, 1877.02
Carroll, James 1860.01, 1888.36, 1890.10, 1893.30, 1898.38
Carroll, James A. 1891.41
Carroll, Jane 1917.17, 1919.18, 1920.18, 1921.33, 1922.07, 1923.44, 1924.22, 1925.23, 1925.32
Carroll, Jean 1917.31, 1918.22, 1923.13, 1927.62, 1935.11
Carroll, Joan 1940.19
Carroll, Joe 1934.35
Carroll, John 1908.34
Carroll, John W. 1881.18
Carroll, Joseph 1904.54
Carroll, Joseph J. 1898.67
Carroll, Joyce 1949.13
Carroll, Jr., Richard F. 1895.21, 1897.02
Carroll, June 1934.06, 1942.34, 1946.22, 1952.09, 1956.08, 1957.10, 1962.02, 1968.13, 1980.18
Carroll, Ken 1950.06
Carroll, Lambert 1931.36
Carroll, Leo G. 1935.17, 1938.06
Carroll, Lewis 1932.28, 1947.09, 1969.09, 1979.18, 1982.24
Carroll, Louis 1898.55
Carroll, Lynn 1966.12
Carroll, Marcelle 1919.08
Carroll, Marie 1917.06, 1919.05, 1920.05, 1921.35, 1936.31
Carroll, Mary 1913.25, 1945.17
Carroll, Mathew 1891.41
Carroll, Miss 1917.31
Carroll, Mollie 1918.31
Carroll, Mr. 1855.10
Carroll, Nancy 1925.43
Carroll, Pat 1931.11, 1955.12
Carroll, Penny 1948.15
Carroll, Philip 1989.24
Carroll, Phyllis 1933.21
Carroll, R.M. 1868.28, 1871.18, 1873.27
Carroll, Renee 1943.16
Carroll, Richard 1891.09, 1892.15
Carroll, Richard F. 1886.32, 1886.60, 1889.23, 1890.01, 1890.11, 1890.19, 1893.21, 1894.40, 1895.21, 1896.41, 1897.02, 1897.28, 1898.12, 1898.31, 1898.72, 1899.06, 1902.23, 1904.01, 1904.24, 1905.43, 1906.15, 1906.47, 1908.42, 1925.12
Carroll, Rita 1883.65, 1884.21, 1884.60, 1885.26, 1886.47, 1888.36
Carroll, Robert 1947.14
Carroll, Ronn 1966.12, 1966.16, 1967.04, 1967.09, 1982.13, 1984.01, 1989.27, 1991.06, 1992.02, 1994.06, 1995.05, 1997.07, 1999.04
Carroll, Sidney 1957.10
Carroll, Terry 1931.04, 1932.14
Carroll, Vinnette 1969.09, 1969.10, 1972.13, 1976.35, 1979.18, 1980.14, 1982.17
Carroll, W.F. 1906.39
Carroll, William 1882.04, 1944.21
Carroll, William F. 1903.30
Carroll-Kerker Opera Company 1897.02
Carron, Elisabeth 1958.13, 1959.08, 1959.10, 1959.17, 1963.15, 1966.04
Carron, Elizabeth 1954.18
Carron, M. 1864.23, 1865.02, 1865.04
Carrow, Joey 1967.04
Carrubba, Philip 1982.03
Carruthers, Ben 1997.03
Carruthers, Edna 1912.49
Carruthers, Mabel 1924.13
Carry, Louis 1979.28, 1980.18, 1997.11
Carse, Roland 1898.63
Carson, Adele 1904.19, 1904.29, 1906.45, 1907.24
Carson, Alexander 1955.25
Carson, Catherine 1904.44
Carson, Daisy 1904.44
Carson, Doris 1928.40, 1930.02, 1930.26, 1931.37, 1936.05
Carson, E. 1881.16
Carson, Emma 1880.24, 1881.16, 1883.38, 1883.58, 1884.20
Carson, Grace 1926.07
Carson, Harry F. 1892.59
Carson, Henry 1935.19
Carson, Jack 1952.07
Carson, James 1873.18
Carson, James B. 1908.15, 1908.36, 1909.14, 1910.19, 1910.30, 1911.29, 1911.34, 1911.43, 1912.41, 1917.34, 1920.21, 1923.24, 1923.34
Carson, Jeanie 1970.06
Carson, Jeannie 1960.09
Carson, Jim 1927.65
Carson, Lillian 1937.06
Carson, Maxine 1928.07
Carson, Mindy 1957.06, 1958.01, 1959.03
Carson, Trudy 1968.13
Carson, Violet 1929.31, 1930.20, 1937.06
Carson, William 1955.10
Carss, Edith 1891.34
Carswell, Ben 1927.16
Carswell, Benn 1930.08
Carten, Kenneth 1936.29, 1939.07
Carten, Sabrina Elayne 2000.03
Carter 1887.23
Carter, A.G. 1882.54
Carter, Alyce 1940.01
Carter, Annie 1891.02
Carter, B. 1876.19
Carter, Barrington 1926.19
Carter, Benny 1980.10, 1983.20
Carter, Bert 1898.77
Carter, Betty 1918.42
Carter, Bill 1957.17, 1959.06
Carter, Billy 1876.19
Carter, Bobby John 1989.27, 1991.06
Carter, C.C. 1955.03
Carter, Caitlin 1993.05, 1995.15, 1996.14, 1999.24, 2001.03
Carter, Carvel 1961.10
Carter, Charlene 1962.01
Carter, Charles 1899.32, 1904.32
Carter, Charles J. 1897.23
Carter, Charlotte 1913.31
Carter, Desmond 1914.32, 1929.51, 1932.23, 1934.29, 1992.02
Carter, Dixie 1964.24, 1965.24, 1974.04, 1976.19
Carter, Donald C. 1979.31
Carter, Dorothy 1898.03, 1899.13, 1905.21
Carter, Earl 1934.37
Carter, Frank 1914.22, 1916.03, 1917.23, 1918.19, 1919.23
Carter, Gertrude 1905.42
Carter, Glenn 2000.09
Carter, Gregory Scott 1991.07
Carter, Harry 1885.46, 1901.14
Carter, Helen E.H. 1881.22
Carter, Henry 1895.03
Carter, Herbert 1900.01, 1906.15
Carter, Irving 1925.01
Carter, J. Patrick 1961.09
Carter, J.B. 1870.08, 1870.11, 1870.38, 1871.12, 1871.16
Carter, Jack 1931.32, 1956.02
Carter, James 1946.14, 1947.12
Carter, Janice 1939.30
Carter, Janis 1939.30
Carter, Jimmy L. 1988.05
Carter, Joey 1962.02
Carter, John 1955.10
Carter, Katie 1894.52
Carter, Lavaida 1932.30
Carter, Lawrence J. 1907.60
Carter, Lincoln J. 1907.60, 1914.22, 1917.31
Carter, Lou 1881.38
Carter, Louise 1908.15
Carter, Louise Leslie 1891.38
Carter, Lucie 1911.46
Carter, Lulu 1881.36
Carter, Mabel 1939.15
Carter, Maggie 1943.10
Carter, Marion 1945.02
Carter, Maud 1896.27
Carter, Maude 1897.44
Carter, Mesdame 1856.04
Carter, Miss 1852.01
Carter, Nell 1971.01, 1978.09, 1980.10, 1988.17, 1997.04
Carter, Paul 1950.18
Carter, R. Peyton 1902.40
Carter, Ralph 1972.18, 1973.10
Carter, Rex 1921.14
Carter, Robert Peyton 1907.30
Carter, Roland 1893.49, 1895.27, 1896.52, 1898.69, 1899.35, 1900.48, 1900.55, 1902.37, 1904.43, 1907.07
Carter, Ronald 1897.45
Carter, Rosanna 1981.15
Carter, Shirley 1958.11
Carter, Stanley 1898.66, 1898.70, 1911.41, 1919.16
Carter, Terry 1954.16, 1955.09, 1961.24
Carter, Vicki 1978.21
Carter, William 1899.02
Carter-Waddell, Joan 1927.04, 1927.43, 1929.19, 1931.06, 1932.13
Carthay 1943.12
Carthay, Dan 1934.18
Carthe, Dan 1931.26
Cartier, Deidre 1970.06
Cartier, Jacques 1927.36, 1927.63, 1934.01
Cartier, Jeanne 1916.06
Cartier, John 1962.26
Cartier, Robert 1926.40
Cartlitch, J.P. 1852.04
Cartmell, Charles 1918.18
Cartmell, Charles A. 1903.35

Cartwell, Charles 1908.09
Cartwright, Bruce 1946.13
Cartwright, Mindy 1989.03
Cartwright, Peggy 1932.20
Carty, J.F. 1918.23
Carty, James 1916.15, 1917.16, 1926.16, 1928.22
Carty, James F. 1923.33
Carty, Jim 1924.19, 1925.22, 1929.35
Caruel, Mlle. 1866.29
Carugati, Thea 1932.29, 1934.02
Carus, Emma 1900.49, 1900.56, 1901.12, 1902.06, 1902.21, 1903.18, 1904.03, 1904.52, 1905.23, 1907.24, 1910.01, 1910.19, 1911.40
Caruso, Joseph 1950.04
Caruso, Thomas 2001.02
Carvalho, Nilze 1988.06
Carver, Brent 1993.09, 1998.21
Carver, Charles 1925.32, 1928.48, 1930.07
Carver, Jack 1933.01
Carver, Jody 1954.08
Carver, John 1963.04
Carver, Mr. 1855.11
Carver, Ronny 1942.35
Carvil, Henry 1926.38
Carville, Marjorie 1921.25
Carwin, James 1929.40
Cary, Claiborne 1957.07
Cary, Clara 1878.11
Cary, Miss 1867.15
Caryl, Jeanne 1980.19, 1981.26
Caryl, William 1919.05, 1924.25, 1929.50, 1932.01
Caryle, Marie 1895.35, 1896.15
Caryll, Ivan 1888.11, 1888.38, 1890.50, 1891.36, 1891.41, 1892.60, 1894.38, 1895.03, 1895.32, 1896.48, 1897.20, 1898.05, 1898.29, 1898.46, 1899.35, 1900.28, 1900.52, 1900.56, 1901.18, 1901.19, 1902.01, 1902.19, 1902.35, 1903.33, 1905.04, 1905.49, 1906.25, 1906.36, 1907.15, 1908.06, 1908.25, 1910.21, 1911.01, 1911.11, 1911.24, 1912.28, 1912.34, 1913.31, 1914.10, 1914.23, 1914.26, 1917.22, 1918.28, 1918.34, 1920.04, 1920.36, 1920.37, 1922.03, 1922.12, 1931.19
Caryll, Primrose 1920.37, 1922.16, 1923.40, 1924.26, 1926.32
Carzley, Mr. 1894.18
Casaboni, Therese 1886.26
Casale, Glenn 1998.18
Casanova, Emeeta 1933.21
Casanova, Giacomo 1931.06
Casastana, Joseph 1946.23
Casati, Catarina 1879.42
Casavant, Louis 1892.01, 1895.33, 1897.18, 1898.54, 1899.42, 1900.04, 1900.06, 1900.09, 1900.11, 1900.13, 1900.17, 1900.18, 1900.21, 1900.22, 1900.23, 1900.26, 1900.27, 1900.30, 1900.50, 1903.36, 1907.08, 1909.31, 1911.23, 1915.23, 1917.20, 1925.08, 1927.42, 1929.50
Casazza, Veloz 1943.02
Casazza, Yolanda 1929.09
Cascelles, Clare 1906.47
Case, Allen 1957.06, 1967.06
Case, Anita 1927.40, 1929.22
Case, Edith True 1954.02
Case, Evelyn 1942.30
Case, Helen 1907.02, 1924.46
Case, Messr. 1834.02
Case, Paul T. 1906.04
Case, Richard 1951.22
Case, Ronald 1989.25, 1996.04
Case, Virginia 1928.25
Casella, Max 1997.20, 2000.11
Casey, Charles E. 1907.56
Casey, Daniel 1924.35
Casey, Eileen 1964.17, 1972.04
Casey, Frank 1883.56, 1891.14, 1897.26, 1904.17, 1905.36
Casey, Harry 1999.15
Casey, James F. 1904.06
Casey, John 1875.10
Casey, Kenneth 1945.03, 1976.04, 1980.10, 1989.06
Casey, Kittye 1926.02
Casey, Michael 1980.18, 1981.08, 1982.06, 1984.10
Casey, Peter 1997.16, 1998.08
Casey, Stuart 1931.09, 1933.24, 1943.22
Casey, Taggart 1947.21
Casey, Teddy 1945.03
Casey, Thomas 1888.32, 1888.34
Casey, Warren 1972.12, 1994.07, 1996.17
Cash, Charles 1963.15
Cash, Messr. 1875.40
Cash, Nat 1929.21, 1930.24
Casher, Izidor 1942.28
Casher, Jennie 1942.28
Cashin, E. 1867.20, 1868.22
Cashin, Mr. 1867.19
Cashman, Nellie 1990.16
Caskey, Marilyn 1979.10
Caskie, Jean 1900.16
Caskie, Jeanne 1900.49, 1900.59
Casler, Richard 1965.35, 1969.03
Casling, LeRoy 1906.46
Casmore, Vic 1920.27, 1923.01, 1927.07, 1928.11
Casmore, Victor 1907.40, 1908.12, 1930.27, 1934.13, 1935.17
Casnoff, Philip 1988.09, 1990.01, 1990.17
Cason, Barbara 1967.01
Cason, Yvette 1997.03
Cason, Yvette Louise 1987.07
Casper, Colonel 1930.05
Cass, Bradley 1928.40
Cass, Byrle 1954.17
Cass, Gil 1947.13
Cass, Lee 1956.04, 1959.02, 1960.05, 1964.08, 1964.31, 1965.09, 1965.11, 1965.12, 1966.08
Cass, Maurice 1913.31, 1916.19, 1919.12
Cass, Peggy 1949.12, 1960.04
Cassade, Cora 1881.03
Cassady, James 1897.43
Cassard, Frances 1944.33
Cassati, Mlle. 1880.08
Cassavant, Louis 1908.34, 1922.08
Cassel, Aline 1906.14
Cassel, Sid 1940.10
Cassel, Walter 1938.15, 1939.13, 1940.23, 1946.03, 1959.09
Cassell, Vinnie 1892.08, 1892.10
Casselle, Anna 1903.01
Casselle, Lizzie 1894.27
Casselli, Senor 1873.02
Casselli, Signor 1871.18
Casselli, Tom 1882.15, 1882.16, 1882.19
Cassels, John 1964.29
Cassenelli, Miss 1896.44
Cassidy, Cora 1872.35, 1873.24, 1873.26
Cassidy, David 1969.01
Cassidy, Ellen 1917.35
Cassidy, Florence 1916.08
Cassidy, G. 1889.10
Cassidy, George 1944.32
Cassidy, H.A. 1893.35
Cassidy, Jack 1946.13, 1947.14, 1948.14, 1948.22, 1950.02, 1952.10, 1956.07, 1957.02, 1963.14, 1964.21, 1966.06, 1968.24
Cassidy, James 1896.24
Cassidy, Joe 1998.20, 1999.21, 2000.19
Cassidy, John 1945.04
Cassidy, Margaret 1912.44
Cassidy, Marjorie 1916.24
Cassidy, Patrick 1985.03
Cassidy, Tim 1974.26, 1979.13, 1987.07
Cassilly, Richard 1954.18
Cassin, Stephen 1900.46
Cassin, Stephen B. 1901.08
Cassin, Steve B. 1906.40, 1908.02
Cassini, Irene 1912.46, 1913.09
Cassini, Oleg 1948.28
Cassmore, Judy 1964.21
Cassmore, Victor 1906.43
Castalloo, Frl. 1879.22
Castan, Maria 1949.07
Castel Bert and Dodge 1894.22
Castel, Messr. 1875.27, 1877.31
Castel, Mons. 1875.25, 1875.28, 1875.30, 1877.26, 1877.29, 1878.06, 1878.07, 1878.08, 1878.09
Castel, Nico 1966.02, 1968.15, 1969.11, 1974.08, 1978.23, 1982.21
Castel, Vernon 1907.41
Castel-Bert 1896.10, 1907.01, 1907.42, 1908.10, 1908.28, 1909.23, 1910.08
Castel-Bert, E. 1900.12
Castel-Bert, Mme. 1906.48, 1907.44, 1908.16
Casteldo, Ida 1879.65, 1879.67
Castella, Bob 1959.15, 1961.25
Castellan, Nino T. DeJesus 1875.22
Castellano, Wally 1937.14
Castellanos, Julio 1939.18
Castellanos, P. 1999.18
Castelli, Bertrand 1968.11
Castelli, Victor 1989.03
Castello, John 1948.17, 1948.32
Castello, Lita 1903.07
Castello, Mr. 1864.17
Castilla, Cuates 1939.18
Castillo 1948.14, 1958.14
Castillo, C. 1985.07
Castillo, Nicandro 1988.15
Castle and Harvey 1905.22, 1911.15
Castle Square Opera Company, The 1897.53, 1898.04, 1898.06, 1898.07, 1898.09, 1898.14, 1898.15, 1898.16, 1898.19, 1898.21, 1898.24, 1898.30, 1898.33, 1898.37, 1898.39, 1898.40, 1898.42, 1898.49, 1898.52, 1898.57, 1898.62, 1898.65, 1898.71, 1898.74, 1898.76, 1899.05, 1899.07, 1899.10, 1899.14, 1899.16, 1899.20, 1899.42, 1900.02, 1900.04, 1900.06, 1900.09, 1900.11, 1900.13, 1900.14, 1900.17, 1900.18, 1900.21, 1900.22, 1900.23, 1900.26, 1900.27, 1900.29, 1900.30
Castle, Edgerton 1917.27
Castle, Gene 1959.13, 1964.16, 1968.07
Castle, Irene 1913.04, 1914.31, 1917.26, 1947.16
Castle, James 1899.41
Castle, John 1970.03
Castle, Joyce 1962.08, 1983.12, 1985.10, 1985.13, 1986.04, 1987.09, 1990.08, 1991.12, 1995.10
Castle, Nick 1948.23
Castle, Paul 1942.19, 1944.20, 1946.14, 1947.12, 1948.19, 1949.05
Castle, Roy 1965.28
Castle, Vernon 1906.29, 1908.21, 1909.11, 1909.30, 1910.16, 1911.05, 1912.39, 1913.04, 1914.31, 1947.16
Castle, William 1864.04, 1864.07, 1864.16, 1864.18, 1864.19, 1864.20, 1866.07, 1866.10, 1867.03, 1867.04, 1867.06, 1867.07, 1868.01, 1868.02, 1868.09, 1868.10, 1868.11, 1868.12, 1877.35, 1877.36, 1879.30, 1881.05, 1882.33, 1886.04, 1922.47, 1924.02, 1926.06, 1928.33, 1940.09
Castle, William E. 1923.36, 1924.41
Castleman, William 1893.05, 1893.09, 1894.45
Castler, Dan 1918.21
Castles, Dolly 1912.37, 1913.02
Castles, Lynn 1980.12
Castles, Miss 1856.01
Castleton, Kate 1876.15, 1876.22, 1880.35, 1882.28, 1883.42, 1886.01
Castleton, Robert 1921.27
Castling, Harry 1914.18
Casto, Jean 1940.22, 1945.05
Castor, Alan 1890.25
Castree, Paul 1994.07, 1998.13, 1999.15
Castriotta, S. 1985.07, 1999.18
Castro, Carlos 1949.07
Castro, Luis 1993.08, 1997.13
Castro, Sebastian 1949.07
Casucci, Leonello 1979.11, 1986.06
Catal, Frank 1950.18
Catania, Claudia 1992.01
Catanzaro, Tony 1966.16
Catapano, Luciano 1985.14
Catchem, Messr. 1861.01
Catenhusen, Ernest 1894.29
Catenhusen, Ernst 1882.45, 1882.71, 1883.44, 1883.58, 1883.64, 1884.14
Cater, Messr. 1887.10
Cates, Demo 1990.15
Cates, Joseph 1963.19, 1968.23, 1970.02
Cates, Madlyn 1967.01
Cathcart, Mae 1927.39
Cathcart, Minnie 1895.43
Cathcart, Mr. 1876.16
Catherine Lewis Comic Opera Company 1883.25, 1883.29
Cathey, Reg. E. 2000.10
Cation, Kathryn 1975.10
Catlett, Mary Jo 1964.01, 1969.04, 1972.07, 1972.23, 1973.15, 1982.13
Catlett, Sidney 1945.10
Catlett, Walter 1916.21, 1918.06, 1920.44, 1922.39, 1923.30, 1924.34, 1924.43, 1927.12, 1928.43
Catlett, Walter L. 1917.13
Catlin, Don 1929.48
Catlin, Donald 1929.34, 1929.47
Catlin, E.N. 1871.17
Catlin, George 1899.33, 1903.08, 1904.26, 1906.14, 1908.08
Catlin, Margie 1905.31
Cato, Minto 1930.34, 1940.01
Caton, Edward 1944.27, 1946.04
Catspaw, Mr. 1871.11
Cattanio, Lorenzo 1884.58
Cattell, W.A. 1892.35
Catteneo, Hank 1991.04
Catusi, James 1963.09
Cauble, Becky 1921.23
Cauble, Rebekah 1925.44
Caudrey, Peggy 1913.23
Cauffman, F.G. 1883.15
Cauffman, Frank G. 1882.54
Caughan, Edward 1978.19
Caughley, Mme. 1899.25
Cauldwell, E. 1870.36, 1872.35
Cauldwell, Miss 1881.14
Caulfield, Joan 1942.29
Caully, Zachary 1930.27, 1931.03
Caupolican, Chief 1928.47
Causins, Constant 1870.37
Cauto, Joseph 1900.28, 1900.43, 1902.12
Cava, Frank 1988.20, 1989.20
Cavadore, Hazel 1927.28
Cavadore, Joseph 1927.28
Cavalcanti, Waldir 1988.06
Cavaliere, Al 1973.09, 1975.21, 1989.18
Cavaliere, Felix 1982.22
Cavallaro, Michael 1953.07, 1962.13
Cavalli, Rina 1924.20
Cavallori, Mlle. 1911.18
Cavanagh, J.W. 1895.27
Cavanagh, John 1996.12
Cavanagh, M.J. 1891.43
Cavanagh, Thomas 1989.17
Cavanaugh, Alice 1922.24, 1924.17
Cavanaugh, Bernard 1927.05
Cavanaugh, Evelyn 1917.09, 1918.15, 1920.05, 1920.37, 1921.06, 1923.05, 1923.13, 1926.07
Cavanaugh, Hobart 1919.36, 1932.21, 1948.28
Cavanaugh, J.H. 1891.14
Cavanaugh, James 1890.12, 1890.30, 2000.07
Cavanaugh, James H. 1897.30
Cavanaugh, Lucille 1915.15
Cavanaugh, Robert D. 1987.19
Cavanaugh, Ruth 1942.26
Cavanaugh, Slim 1929.26, 1931.02
Cavander, Kenneth 1975.23
Cavanna, Elise 1925.10, 1925.24
Cavara, Lucita 1926.37
Cavari, Perry 1999.01
Cave, A. 1871.25, 1871.26
Cave, Miss 1867.13, 1867.16
Cavedore, Joseph 1927.28
Cavenagh, J.W. 1895.27
Cavender, Leona 1869.27, 1869.32
Cavendish, Lester 1870.07
Cavendish, Maude 1884.21
Cavendish, Milly 1866.18
Caveness, Pamela 1948.20
Caverly's Great English Folly Company 1880.05
Caverly, Anne 1896.27
Caverly, Charles 1902.10
Caverly, Frank 1912.29
Caverly, R.B. 1880.05
Cavett, Dick 1986.03, 2000.17
Cavis, Belle 1887.04
Cawlo, Ann 1978.23, 1979.27
Cawthorn, Herbert 1907.27
Cawthorn, Joseph 1897.29, 1897.55, 1898.60, 1899.25, 1899.34, 1903.39, 1905.41, 1906.18, 1907.46, 1908.35, 1910.17, 1911.02, 1913.04, 1914.18, 1915.18, 1916.01, 1917.19, 1918.34, 1920.40, 1922.02, 1925.33
Cawthorn, Le Petite 1870.31
Cawthorn, Susie Forrester 1907.27
Cawthorne, Herbert 1899.35, 1899.37, 1901.09, 1903.04, 1904.25, 1908.30
Cawthorne, Joseph 1901.27
Cawthorne, Miss 1870.31
Cayla, Alphonse 1870.30
Cayla, Mlle. 1871.26
Cayla, Mons. 1870.41, 1871.07, 1871.23
Caymmi, Dorival 1942.18, 1955.26
Cazauran, A.R. 1881.32
Cazden, Norman 1941.01
Cazelle, Florence 1929.34, 1929.36
Cazentre, Albert 1937.01
Cea, Patrick 1981.21

Cearcy, Darlesia 1993.02
Ceballos, Arturo 1988.15
Ceballos, Hilarion 1904.47, 1912.24
Ceballos, Larry 1919.21, 1921.38, 1923.04, 1923.07, 1923.31, 1924.04, 1924.22, 1924.32, 1925.47, 1926.03, 1926.15, 1926.21, 1929.45
Ceballos, Rene 1982.19, 1989.20
Ceballos, Rene M. 1995.09
Ceballos, Rosalie 1904.47, 1912.24
Cecil, Arthur 1886.45
Cecil, Mildred 1905.29
Cecil, Nora 1901.27
Cecil, Sylvia 1936.13, 1936.16, 1936.18, 1936.21, 1936.23, 1936.24
Cecill, Ron 1955.11, 1955.25
Cecill, Ronald 1953.17, 1954.15
Cee, Joey 1991.13
Ceeley, Leonard 1927.50, 1928.15, 1930.27, 1934.13
Ceiley, Leonard 1924.02
Celada, Raul 1947.16, 1948.08
Cele, Baby 1988.02
Celeste, Marie 1893.08, 1893.39, 1894.28, 1897.25, 1897.27, 1898.16, 1898.24, 1899.22, 1900.28, 1900.43, 1902.12
Celeste, Miss 1852.01, 1872.35
Celeste, Mona 1920.28
Celete, Mona 1919.33
Cella, Sam 1918.38
Cella, Susan 1986.12
Celli, Frank 1885.63, 1898.26
Cellier, Aldred 1882.60
Cellier, Alfred 1879.70, 1879.72, 1880.18, 1880.46, 1881.07, 1881.36, 1881.38, 1882.06, 1882.75, 1882.78, 1886.45, 1886.62, 1887.44, 1890.50, 1891.41, 1893.02, 1895.20, 1898.57
Cellier, Frank 1926.41
Cellier, Mr. 1879.06
Celliger, Alfred 1882.60
Cenicola, Johnny 2000.19
Cennicola, Johnny 1999.21
Center Theatre Group 1975.20, 1992.01, 1995.03
Center Theatre Group (of Los Angeles) 1979.08
Center, E.C. 1898.28, 1899.12
Centracco, Cookie 2000.02
Cerbi 1884.34
Cerbi, George W. 1890.21
Cerbi, Mamie 1886.25, 1888.39
Cerbi, Miss 1884.42
Cercone, Janis 1979.11
Cerdan, Esteban 1929.30
Cerf, Bennett 1941.01
Cerise, Vivian 1898.75
Cernovitch, Nicholas 1972.08
Cerow, Vincent 1957.09
Certio, Rosa 1865.04
Cerullo, Jonathan 1988.20, 1992.11
Cerullo, Jonathan Stuart 1999.05
Cervallo 1902.03, 1902.31
Cervantes 1844.01, 1868.30
Cervantes, Miguel de 1965.34
Cervantes, Miguel y 1923.43
Cervantes, y Saavedra Miguel De 1972.14
Cerveris, Michael 1993.06
Cervila, Jr., Antonio 1999.18
Cesar, Lori 1971.09
Cesario, Michael J. 1980.11
Cessna, Robert 1964.45
Cetin, Oezlem 2000.12
Cetti, W.S. 1904.41
Cetti, William 1902.26
Cezanne, Jackie 1946.13
Chabeau, Ray 1976.24
Chabelman, Martha 1893.07
Chadbourne, Mortimer 1926.12
Chadel, Georges 1910.24
Chadman, Christopher 1970.15, 1972.22, 1975.14, 1976.03, 1976.19, 1976.20, 1978.05, 1982.07, 1982.21, 1983.01, 1986.06, 1988.08, 1988.19, 1990.09, 1992.04
Chadwick, Cyril 1907.58, 1911.01, 1911.22, 1915.08, 1916.12, 1916.26, 1918.15, 1934.43
Chadwick, George W. 1894.22
Chadwick, George Whitefield 1911.09
Chadwick, Ida May 1924.07
Chadwick, Samuel 1896.28, 1897.36, 1898.54
Chadwick, Thomas 1929.31, 1931.39
Chadwick, W. 1899.41
Chaffee, George 1944.16
Chafkin, Fred-Nil-Dora 1968.04
Chaflin, Paul 1917.26
Chaiken, Fay 1967.01
Chaiken, Joel 1988.04
Chailee, J.T. 1910.33
Chailee, Joseph 1903.18
Chaille, Henri 1899.25
Chaille, J.T. 1912.12
Chaillee, J.T. 1894.29, 1898.54, 1903.37
Chaillee, Joseph 1898.36, 1899.24, 1903.18
Chaillee, Joseph T. 1896.28, 1897.36
Chain, Dell 1921.17
Chain, Mme. 1876.31
Chakraband 1950.12
Chalain 1875.21, 1877.04, 1882.62, 1885.33, 1886.41
Chalains 1876.36
Chales Brothers 1905.42
Chalfant, Lucille 1922.32
Chaliapine, Lydia 1934.32
Chalif, Louis 1934.41
Challee, William 1927.23, 1936.28
Challenger, Rudy 1963.27
Challis, Bennett 1937.01
Challis, Edith 1870.04, 1872.10
Challis, William 1937.03
Challoniet, Mary 1888.04
Chalmer, Cary 1981.24
Chalmers, Donald 1913.01
Chalmers, Lionel 1920.34, 1922.35
Chalmers, Thomas 1937.01
Chalmers, William 1937.06
Chalzel, Leo 1936.27, 1937.15
Chalzell, Leo 1935.14
Chamberlain, Ada 1886.31, 1886.38, 1890.22, 1890.38
Chamberlain, Andrea 1998.15
Chamberlain, Effie 1892.19, 1892.45
Chamberlain, Ida 1890.13
Chamberlain, Ida Hoyt 1927.45
Chamberlain, John 1875.05
Chamberlain, Jr., Charles 1862.08
Chamberlain, Miss 1823.01
Chamberlain, Nelse 1892.19
Chamberlain, Nelsy 1895.18, 1897.26
Chamberlain, Peggy 1928.17
Chamberlain, Richard 1993.18
Chamberlain, W.E. 1904.32
Chamberlain, Winthrop 1916.14
Chamberlaine, Ada 1888.39
Chamberlin, Frank 1939.21
Chamberlin, Kevin 1997.18, 2000.12, 2000.18
Chamberlin, Peggy 1927.37
Chamberlin, Riley C. 1910.33
Chamberlyn, A.H. 1900.34, 1901.06, 1901.09, 1902.21
Chambers, Carol 1978.13
Chambers, Craig 1978.13, 1982.11
Chambers, David 1978.06
Chambers, Ernest 1961.01
Chambers, Ernie 1989.08
Chambers, Gertie 1930.19
Chambers, H. Kellett 1911.46
Chambers, Howard 1904.30, 1905.57, 1906.26, 1907.36, 1911.04
Chambers, Kitty 1911.46
Chambers, Marguerite 1873.25, 1873.26
Chambers, Marie 1915.20
Chambers, Marion 1923.27, 1929.44
Chambers, Mr. 1855.06, 1855.07, 1855.08, 1855.09
Chambers, Norma 1947.02
Chambers, Peter 1931.16, 1931.37, 1939.21
Chambers, Ralph 1942.11, 1946.01, 1950.15, 1954.05
Chambers, Ralph W. 1957.08
Chambers, Robert W. 1913.37
Chambers, William 1938.15
Chaminade 1913.07
Champion, Gower 1939.22, 1942.01, 1942.27, 1948.22, 1948.30, 1951.13, 1955.03, 1960.06, 1961.10, 1964.01, 1964.16, 1966.29, 1967.15, 1968.01, 1968.32, 1972.04, 1973.05, 1974.18, 1975.21, 1976.03, 1978.04, 1978.28, 1980.20, 1986.03, 1995.13, 2001.08
Champion, Marge 1955.03, 1983.09, 2001.02
Champlain Productions, Ltd. 1976.03
Champnes, L. 1881.38
Champness, Ethel 1880.49
Champney, C. 1884.25
Champneys, E. 1881.03
Champneys, Ethel 1879.15
Champneys, Miss 1881.41
Chamption, Bonnie 1982.11
Chan, David Shoichi 1987.12
Chan, Donald 1987.16
Chan, Eric 1990.17, 1991.03
Chan, Eric Y.L. 1987.15
Chan, Peter 1958.19
Chance, Anna 1898.02, 1904.14, 1905.43
Chance, George T. 1912.26
Chandler, Anna 1911.08
Chandler, Byron 1910.11, 1911.46
Chandler, Carol 1946.20
Chandler, Costella 1894.52
Chandler, Douglas 1948.15
Chandler, F. 1902.40
Chandler, Jamie Beth 1987.05, 1993.02
Chandler, Julia 1931.28
Chandler, Leah 1973.16
Chandler, Mary 1929.09
Chandler, Maud M. 1895.27
Chandler, Maude 1896.29
Chandler, Mr. 1856.01
Chandler, Perdita 1945.04
Chandler, Richard 1969.02
Chandler, Stan 1987.16
Chandler, Wilfred 1913.20
Chandler, William 1936.12
Chandler-Torns, Jamie 1993.19
Chandon, Daniel 1891.34
Chanel 1923.26
Chanel, Lili 1981.17
Chaney, David 1972.05, 1997.09
Chaney, Jan 1958.04
Chaney, Lon 1989.02
Chaney, Stewart 1936.12, 1941.12, 1942.01, 1944.18, 1944.30, 1945.12, 1948.16, 1950.06, 1951.18
Chanfrau, F.S. 1848.01, 1848.03, 1857.04
Chanfrau, Mrs. 1864.13
Chanfrau, Mrs. F.S. 1860.03, 1860.05, 1861.04, 1863.06
Chang, Betsy 1994.12
Chang, John 1996.05
Chang, Tisa 1970.21
Channing, Carol 1941.01, 1948.30, 1949.18, 1955.25, 1961.01, 1964.01, 1974.02, 1978.04, 1979.25, 1995.13
Chansky, Dorothy 1976.27
Chantal, Mons. 1875.01, 1875.04
Chanz, La 1995.11
Chapa, Marina 1991.03
Chapel, C.M. 1904.54, 1908.07
Chapel, Edward 1947.01
Chapell, Alyce 1937.03
Chapell, George 1931.39
Chapelle, Alyce 1938.17
Chapelle, Chappy 1922.25
Chapelle, P.A. 1868.20
Chapelle, Rose 1882.66
Chaperon 1893.45
Chapi, Ruperto 1969.11
Chapin, Alice 1918.41
Chapin, Billy 1952.05
Chapin, Brian 1963.25, 1965.28
Chapin, Carl 1939.19
Chapin, Frederick 1895.24, 1907.23
Chapin, Harry 1975.05, 1997.01
Chapin, Lee 1912.43
Chapin, Margery 1921.21
Chapin, Schuyler G. 1972.15
Chapin, Stephen 1975.05
Chapin, Tom 1975.05
Chapine 1912.04
Chaplin, Charles 1976.16
Chaplin, Clive 1986.01
Chaplin, George 1862.05
Chaplin, George D. 1862.08, 1875.16, 1890.35, 1892.01
Chaplin, Saul 1952.11, 1958.21, 1974.10, 1977.02, 1980.10, 1989.02, 1990.16
Chaplin, Sydney 1956.14, 1961.28, 1964.11
Chaplow, Rene 1915.26
Chapman, Alan 1980.28
Chapman, Arthur 1889.54
Chapman, Bert 1927.67
Chapman, Beth Nielson 2000.16
Chapman, Blanche 1866.12, 1880.31, 1881.34, 1881.40, 1895.37, 1898.34, 1899.21, 1902.44, 1906.05, 1907.02
Chapman, Catherine 1926.16
Chapman, Charles 1909.06
Chapman, Christopher 1968.01
Chapman, Cliff 1946.13
Chapman, David 1969.03, 1971.01, 1973.08, 1974.09, 1974.13, 1981.28, 1982.13, 1983.14, 1984.15, 1987.16
Chapman, Dixie 1887.43
Chapman, E. 1870.19, 1870.21, 1872.23, 1872.35, 1873.03, 1875.10, 1875.17, 1876.08
Chapman, E.T. 1875.21
Chapman, Ed 1879.38, 1880.24, 1880.34, 1881.33, 1883.50, 1894.19
Chapman, Ed. 1879.15, 1880.40
Chapman, Edward 1877.20, 1882.51, 1896.35, 1896.48, 1898.17, 1899.23
Chapman, Edwin 1892.11, 1894.38
Chapman, Ela 1877.23
Chapman, Ella 1877.22, 1877.25, 1877.39, 1879.38, 1880.24, 1896.05
Chapman, F. 1866.34, 1867.08, 1872.23, 1872.35, 1873.03
Chapman, F.B. 1868.16
Chapman, F.C. 1910.24
Chapman, G. 1869.33
Chapman, Gary 1986.06
Chapman, George 1903.02
Chapman, Graham 1964.29
Chapman, Harry 1879.08
Chapman, J. 2000.07
Chapman, Jessie 1904.45
Chapman, Julia 1877.16
Chapman, Messr. 1867.10
Chapman, Miss 1861.06, 1862.02, 1869.23
Chapman, Mr. 1861.06, 1866.21, 1866.24, 1867.10, 1872.23
Chapman, Mrs. H. 1868.04
Chapman, Mrs. Harry 1876.17, 1876.18, 1876.21
Chapman, Mrs. T.S. 1834.02
Chapman, Sandy 1907.12
Chapman, T. 1870.13, 1870.19
Chapman, Thomas 1875.32, 1877.20
Chapman, Tomes 1935.17, 1936.27
Chapman, Tracy Nicole 1993.06, 1997.20, 2000.11
Chapman, William 1956.15, 1958.17, 1959.08, 1959.17, 1960.05, 1960.15, 1961.04, 1961.06, 1961.12, 1961.23, 1962.06, 1962.09, 1962.10, 1964.08, 1964.10, 1964.13, 1965.09, 1965.10, 1965.12, 1966.02, 1968.09, 1968.15, 1978.23, 1979.27
Chappel, Ed 1949.08
Chappel, Sid 1896.32
Chappel, Vickie D. 1980.15
Chappell, Delos 1934.03
Chappell, Edward 1904.01
Chappell, Fred 1969.03
Chappell, George S. 1916.07
Chappell, W.H. 1899.33
Chappelle, Chappie 1929.01
Chappelle, Chappy 1923.11, 1931.47
Chappelle, Charles 1881.32, 1885.33, 1905.52
Chappelle, Frederic 1922.05
Chappelle, Rose 1879.20, 1879.25, 1881.07, 1881.37, 1882.06
Chappelle, W.H. 1904.26, 1908.08
Chaput, Isabel 1999.18
Chapuy, Effie 1892.08, 1892.10, 1892.29, 1893.09, 1894.07
Charbonneau, Patricia 1978.23
Chard, Dorothea 1925.17, 1926.13, 1927.27, 1927.36
Chard, Kate 1894.18
Chardieno, Rajah 1940.17
Charell, Erik 1936.22, 1939.29
Charig, Phil 1924.32, 1927.49, 1930.38, 1943.20, 1944.14, 1955.12
Charig, Philip 1926.21, 1927.35, 1927.49, 1927.54, 1929.02, 1929.51, 1930.32, 1931.21, 1931.34
Charise, Andre 1935.12
Charisse, Rita 1965.37
Charisse, Zan 1974.17
Charkouie, Azeada 1926.37
Charlap, Mark 1954.13, 1990.20
Charlap, Mark (Moose) 1979.22, 1983.09, 1991.13
Charlap, Moose 1958.20, 1961.02, 1965.01, 1989.03, 1998.18
Charles B. Cochran 1929.41
Charles Christie Company 1926.38, 1937.07
Charles E. Blaney Amusement Company 1905.21, 1906.03
Charles H. Yale Studios 1905.39
Charles Kelman Productions 1998.03
Charles Teichner Studios 1928.09
Charles W. Thomas' Company 1893.31
Charles, Allen 1935.01
Charles, C. 1877.04
Charles, D.E. 1917.17

Charles, David 1993.10
Charles, Ernest 1928.23, 1929.35
Charles, Frances 1947.07
Charles, G. 1870.01, 1870.09
Charles, G.C. 1869.33, 1869.36, 1869.42, 1870.12, 1870.22, 1870.25, 1870.28, 1870.32, 1871.01, 1871.02, 1872.25, 1872.27, 1872.30, 1872.32, 1872.36, 1872.38, 1872.40, 1872.43, 1877.04
Charles, George 1869.38
Charles, George C. 1869.37, 1871.05, 1877.15
Charles, Irwin 1946.07
Charles, J. 1886.48
Charles, J.M. 1870.07, 1870.15
Charles, Jacques 1921.21, 1924.18, 1947.18, 1953.12, 1958.06, 1964.22
Charles, John 1935.01
Charles, John Wood 1912.30
Charles, Jymie 1976.21
Charles, Keith 1969.02
Charles, Lee 1958.11
Charles, Lewis 1946.24
Charles, Lilian 1915.23
Charles, Mack 1894.44
Charles, Master 1879.38, 1885.49
Charles, Messr. 1844.01
Charles, Miss M. 1852.02
Charles, Mme. 1870.03
Charles, Mr. 1869.02, 1869.14, 1870.02
Charles, Mrs. Samuel 1899.27
Charles, Paul 1965.01, 1966.30, 1969.16
Charles, Percy 1890.02
Charles, R.G. 1882.32
Charles, Ray 1947.03, 1983.20
Charles, Richard 1946.03
Charles, S. 1884.25
Charles, Vicki 1941.12
Charles, Walter 1990.04, 1992.10, 1994.12
Charles, Zachary A. 1943.19, 1951.23
Charleston, Helen 1936.07
Charleston, John F. 1876.05
Charleston, Milton 1935.04, 1936.06, 1941.11, 1949.09
Charlesworth, Tom 1953.16
Charleton, Bowen 1938.04
Charlie, Dashing 1894.44
Charlie, Master 1885.22
Charlot, Andre 1924.01, 1925.42, 1927.02
Charlotte, Miss 1870.31, 1895.40
Charlotte, Mlle. 1921.28
Charlotte, Mme. 1870.26
Charlotte, Mons. 1868.13
Charlottetown Festival 1971.21
Charlton, Richard 1956.13
Charlton, T.C. 1989.09
Charmettes, Jules 1911.45
Charmoli, Tony 1948.04, 1955.04, 1960.17, 1962.17, 1976.07, 1981.10
Charnay, Lynne 1962.01
Charney, Eva 1977.15
Charnin, Martin 1957.12, 1959.23, 1960.08, 1963.13, 1969.16, 1970.19, 1973.08, 1974.09, 1977.06, 1979.12, 1981.16, 1981.28, 1989.22, 1997.04
Charnley, Michael 1948.14
Charriere, Mons. 1868.26, 1869.03
Charron, Jessie 1896.03
Charson, Mons. 1881.50, 1881.53
Charter, Herbert 1888.09
Charteris, Ivan 1905.25
Charters, Spencer 1923.13, 1924.38, 1927.29, 1928.47
Charters, Ted 1921.12
Chartok, S.M. 1934.07, 1934.08, 1934.09, 1934.10, 1934.11, 1936.04, 1936.08, 1936.09, 1936.10, 1936.11, 1949.10, 1949.11, 1949.13, 1949.14, 1952.14, 1952.16, 1952.17, 1952.18, 1952.19
Chartwell Communications, Inc. 1981.23
Chase, A.E. 1881.15
Chase, Alice 1906.23, 1911.39
Chase, Annie 1888.08
Chase, Anthony 1999.05
Chase, Arlene 1917.17
Chase, Arline 1915.30, 1919.09, 1920.04
Chase, Bob 1925.24
Chase, Chaz 1925.24, 1930.42, 1934.20, 1941.09
Chase, Colin 1920.02
Chase, David 1996.06, 1997.17, 1997.19, 1998.15, 1999.13, 2000.11, 2000.18, 2001.02
Chase, Diana 1930.26
Chase, Dollie 1885.28
Chase, Dolly 1881.38, 1891.11, 1892.22
Chase, E.H. 1879.28, 1883.40
Chase, Edna 1906.26, 1908.01, 1908.39, 1909.13, 1912.07, 1912.44, 1915.28, 1917.03
Chase, Emma 1896.15
Chase, Erma 1927.03, 1927.20
Chase, Florence 1892.20
Chase, Frances 1920.37
Chase, Grace 1891.15
Chase, H.D. 1890.21
Chase, Harry E. 1888.27
Chase, Harry L. 1898.49, 1898.52, 1898.57, 1898.62, 1898.65, 1898.71, 1898.76, 1899.07
Chase, Ilka 1934.38, 1940.07
Chase, L. Everett 1989.23
Chase, Lonnie 1989.23
Chase, Marion 1897.50, 1905.11, 1905.29, 1907.07
Chase, Miss 1889.31, 1892.52
Chase, Mr. 1892.20
Chase, Norman 1971.06
Chase, Paula Leggett 1994.01
Chase, Pauline 1899.25, 1900.34, 1901.06, 1901.21, 1910.21
Chase, Rita 1885.08
Chase, Sera 1972.20
Chase, Stephen 1947.17
Chase, Toni 1933.03
Chase, William P. 1914.14
Chasemore, A. 1886.45
Chasemore, Arthur 1890.03
Chasen, Dave 1924.31, 1925.25, 1928.08, 1930.28, 1933.21
Chason, Cornelia 1932.06
Chassaigne, Francis 1884.14, 1886.37, 1887.22, 1888.20, 1888.45, 1889.04, 1890.19, 1900.17
Chasson, Mons. 1882.35
Chastain, Don 1962.03, 1966.06, 1983.08, 1998.21
Chatelaine, Stella 1911.24, 1913.17, 1914.15
Chatham, Etta 1897.38
Chatinere 1890.24, 1893.05
Chatrian, Alexandre 1893.03
Chatterson, J.H. 1870.20, 1872.17, 1872.19
Chatterson, Messr. 1864.22
Chatterton, J.H. 1870.23
Chatterton, Jack 1894.47
Chatterton, Ruth 1924.41
Chatton, Sidney 1938.08
Chaucer, Geoffrey 1969.04, 1980.01
Chaviano, Hernando 1974.14
Chawner, Richard 1906.25
Chawner, Robert 1902.30
Chayes, Joel 1967.08
Chayres, Nestor 1945.10
Chazal, Mireille 1965.37
Chazin, Judith 1958.14
Cheatam, Kitty 1892.14
Cheatham, Kitty 1888.02
Checchi, Eugene 1900.06
Checco, Al 1948.30, 1952.13
Chechile, Dana 1998.20
Check, Jean 1983.15
Chedister, America 1923.07
Cheeney, George C. 1895.03
Cheesman, Frank 1898.38
Cheesman, W.M. 1907.27
Cheetham, Everett 1931.02
Cheffer, Ch. 1970.17
Chein, Julian 1934.40
Chekhov, Anton 1980.08
Chekle, Edouard 1959.15, 1961.25
Chekoff, Anton 1922.06
Chellis, Matthew 1995.10, 1997.02
Chelmsford, Miss 1870.05
Chelsea Producing Corporation 1923.07
Chelsea Theatre Center 1974.06, 1977.08, 1979.29
Chelsi, Larry 1954.03
Chen, Lynn 1987.03
Chen, Tina 1984.01
Chenat, Leon 1865.05, 1865.07, 1865.08
Chenault, L.E. 1907.29
Chenault, Lawrence E. 1896.49
Chenaval, Mildred 1938.13
Cheney, Charles 1895.40
Cheney, Ed 1931.40
Cheng, Chun-Tao 1951.24
Cheng, Kam 1991.03
Chenkin, Victor 1924.48
Chenkina, M. 1932.09
Chenoweth, Kristen 1997.07
Chenoweth, Kristin 1999.03
Cheremeteff, Dmitry 1964.24
Cheret, J. 1888.10
Cheri, Rose 1866.18
Cherie, Adelaide 1880.63
Cherin, Robert 1975.21
Cheris, Adelaide 1883.06
Cherry, Donna 1991.10
Cherry, Dorothy 1980.06, 1991.05
Cherry, Francis H. 1925.36
Cherry, James 1893.43, 1898.02, 1900.40, 1901.16, 1902.24, 1903.23, 1905.17, 1905.54, 1918.24
Cherry, Joetta 1968.05
Cherry, John 1921.38, 1922.48, 1926.22, 1929.43, 1930.12, 1930.23, 1932.02, 1933.24, 1934.07, 1934.08, 1934.09, 1934.10, 1937.13, 1941.07, 1942.21, 1943.22, 1944.28
Cherry, Paul 1970.12
Cherry, T. 1865.11, 1866.02
Cherry, Vivian 1946.01
Cherry, Wendell 1991.05
Cherrye, James C. 1891.15
Chertok, Kenneth 1955.02
Chesley, Herbert D. 1887.19
Chesley, Kate 1892.59
Chesmond, Dorothy 1914.04
Chesneau, Rose 1890.10
Chesney, Charles 1929.17, 1929.39, 1931.03
Chesney, Jayne 1924.08
Chessneam, Rose 1887.03
Chester, Albert 1931.47
Chester, Alfred 1929.21
Chester, Alma 1924.10
Chester, Blanche 1887.31
Chester, Eddie 1927.58
Chester, Elizabeth 1928.33
Chester, May 1888.20
Chester, Miss 1903.32
Chester, Rachel 1928.16
Chester, Shirley 1957.02, 1962.08, 1962.10, 1962.11
Cheston, Helen 1900.47, 1904.28, 1905.03
Chetwynd, Ross 1949.03
Chevalet, E. 1866.09
Chevalet, Emile 1882.59
Chevalier, Albert 1889.54
Chevalier, Maurice 1930.13, 1932.04, 1947.05, 1948.12, 1955.14, 1963.02, 1965.08
Chevalt, Emile 1864.10
Cheviot, Henri 1895.22
Cheviot, J.C. 1891.37, 1897.29
Cheviot, Jack 1911.28
Cheviot, James 1918.23
Cheviot, John 1912.30
Chew, Bruce 1982.05
Chew, King Lan 1935.19
Chew, Ray 1979.15
Chez Routon 1924.05
Chiampi 1949.06
Chiang, Dawn 1979.08, 1990.07, 1991.08, 1993.08
Chiari, Walter 1961.27
Chiasson, Gilles 1996.09, 1997.19, 1999.08
Chicas, Roy 1996.17
Chichester, Helen 1901.19, 1902.34, 1902.40
Chidley, Messr. 1886.54
Chidley, Sydney 1892.31, 1895.15
Chief Bearpaw 1981.09
Chiesa, Norberto 1978.26
Chiffarelli, Albert 1924.16
Chihara, Paul 1981.06, 1990.17
Chila, Doreen 1998.18
Child, Alan 1933.23
Child, Marilyn 1968.13
Childers, Michael 1971.04
Childs, Clare 1888.19, 1888.22, 1888.26
Childs, Eddie 1925.50
Childs, Gilbert 1911.27
Childs, Hannah Lee 1938.18
Childs, Harry 1916.04
Childs, J.H. 1914.21
Childs, Jeanette 1911.15
Childs, Kristen 1985.19
Childs, Lee 1935.17
Childs, Messr. 1885.14, 1885.52
Childs, Nathaniel 1880.10, 1880.42, 1880.67, 1882.03, 1882.39
Childs, S. Russell 1888.18
Childs, Terri B. 1997.04
Childs, Timothy 1997.04
Chilters, Nellie 1904.45
Chilton, Charles 1964.28
Chilton, Dorothy 1927.27, 1936.12
Chilvers, Hugh 1897.46, 1898.77, 1899.39, 1917.28, 1919.24, 1920.32, 1923.27, 1926.27, 1928.15, 1928.48, 1929.37
Chilvers, Thomas 1898.77
Chilvers, Thomas H. 1902.02
Chiment, Marie Anne 1992.05
Chinese-American Importing Company, Inc. 1925.04
Ching, William 1947.17
Chinn, Lori 1970.21
Chip, Sam 1905.44
Chipman, A.Z. 1883.05, 1883.07
Chipman, Story 1909.29, 1910.34
Chipmonck 1975.08, 1979.30
Chippendale, F. 1877.24
Chippendale, Mary 1921.41
Chippendale, Mr. 1853.01
Chiriaeff, Ludmilla 1972.08
Chisholm, Robert 1927.63, 1929.31, 1930.26, 1933.07, 1938.06, 1938.10, 1939.21, 1940.06, 1941.02, 1943.12, 1943.22, 1944.33, 1945.20, 1946.20, 1950.19
Chismar, Nancy Louise 1980.02
Chisnell, Newton 1884.62, 1886.48, 1886.49, 1888.06, 1888.11, 1890.41, 1893.14, 1894.02, 1895.14
Chita 1988.06
Chitjian, Howard 1973.12
Chitos, Richard 1958.01
Chitten, C. 1890.50
Chitten, Concettina 1893.20
Chitten, V. 1890.50
Chitten, Vincenzina 1891.41
Chittick, Joyce 1996.08, 1998.04, 2000.18
Chivot, Heni 1890.33, 1898.07
Chivot, Henri 1869.05, 1871.24, 1872.42, 1876.10, 1879.31, 1879.43, 1880.44, 1880.49, 1880.69, 1881.03, 1881.14, 1881.21, 1881.22, 1881.33, 1881.34, 1881.36, 1881.38, 1881.40, 1881.45, 1881.46, 1881.48, 1881.53, 1881.54, 1881.56, 1882.09, 1882.11, 1882.14, 1882.25, 1882.31, 1882.32, 1882.37, 1882.47, 1882.49, 1882.52, 1882.61, 1882.72, 1883.13, 1883.19, 1883.22, 1883.25, 1883.41, 1883.51, 1883.54, 1883.55, 1884.02, 1884.03, 1884.28, 1884.29, 1884.47, 1884.52, 1885.07, 1885.09, 1885.20, 1885.61, 1887.06, 1887.35, 1887.38, 1888.09, 1888.18, 1889.01, 1889.40, 1889.44, 1891.36, 1892.10, 1892.11, 1892.30, 1892.60, 1893.47, 1896.21, 1897.17, 1898.27, 1899.14, 1900.14, 1909.08, 1926.43
Chivot, M. 1901.09
Chivot, Mons. 1890.37
Chizzola, C.A. 1873.11, 1873.15, 1873.16, 1875.01, 1875.02, 1875.04, 1875.07, 1875.08, 1875.09, 1875.13, 1875.25, 1875.27, 1875.28, 1875.29, 1875.30, 1875.33
Chmiel, Mark 1987.15
Cho, Irene 1989.03
Choder, Jill 1975.23
Chodorov, Edward 1960.10
Chodorov, Jerome 1950.02, 1953.03, 1954.01, 1958.05, 1963.05, 1964.44, 1967.09, 1994.09
Choi, Hye-Young 1977.07
Choi, Hyung O. 1997.16, 1998.08
Choi, Joohee 1996.05
Choi, Mu Yeol 1997.16
Choi, Young Jae 1998.08
Chol, Messr. 1864.01, 1864.03, 1864.08, 1864.11
Chol, Mons. 1866.30
Chon, S. Sydney 1918.16
Chong, Ah 1927.16
Chong, Rae Dawn 1990.14
Choos, George 1923.36, 1928.41
Chopin 1940.20, 1945.14
Chopin, F. 1976.34
Chopin, Frederic 1922.06, 1928.26, 1934.32, 1945.14, 1956.11
Chopin, Mons. 1867.24, 1868.24, 1869.03, 1869.30
Choquet, Mlle. 1880.44, 1880.52, 1880.60, 1881.54
Chorister, G. 1872.11
Chorlton, Joan 1955.19
Chorpenning, Ruth 1930.18, 1930.33, 1931.02
Chosnyk, William 1931.02
Chotzinoff, Samuel 1958.17
Choulfleuri, Mons. 1869.19

Chrisdie, C. 1871.08
Chrisdie, Charles 1900.36, 1903.12
Chrisdie, Mme. 1897.29
Chrispijn, Ron 1982.23
Chrissie, Ed 1892.34, 1896.03
Christakos, Jerry 1993.09
Christen, Robert 1993.04
Christenberry, Jr., Charles W. 1954.17
Christenson, Irving 1903.03
Christerson, Irving 1903.03
Christian, Charles 1999.24
Christian, Irving 1904.44
Christian, Irving H. 1904.13
Christian, John 1937.11
Christian, Messr. 1904.13
Christian, Mlle. 1898.38
Christian, Robert 1981.04
Christiani, Emil 1891.33
Christiani, Mr. 1890.31, 1894.01
Christiansen, Harold 1934.29
Christiansen, Lew 1934.29, 1941.05
Christianson, Bob 1979.19
Christie and Company 1918.31
Christie, Audrey 1933.16, 1938.05, 1941.13, 1946.06
Christie, Earle 1932.18
Christie, George 1922.32, 1924.32, 1929.29
Christie, George Stuart 1912.34
Christie, Jennie 1881.06, 1882.04, 1882.20, 1883.01, 1883.09, 1883.46, 1883.53, 1883.63, 1884.13
Christie, Ken 1937.10
Christie, Le Petite 1870.31
Christie, Marie 1903.28, 1904.49
Christie, Maurice 1931.07
Christine, Bobette 1933.26
Christine, Henri 1898.47, 1910.20, 1932.04, 1963.02, 1965.08
Christine, Lilly 1950.12
Christine, Mlle. 1859.06
Christine, P.H. 1906.45, 1908.04, 1915.01, 1918.31
Christman, Rick 1981.20
Christmas, David 1975.24
Christopher, Edward 1943.24, 1945.06, 1946.09
Christopher, Gavin 1983.09
Christopher, Tony 1995.02, 1997.09
Christos, Marianna 1979.21
Christrup, Carl 1882.72
Christrup, Charles 1875.11, 1875.15, 1875.20, 1883.06
Christrup, K. 1882.57
Christy, D. 1884.13
Christy, Dorothy 1929.03
Christy, Eileen 1965.24
Christy, Eleanor 1912.38
Christy, Eleanore 1914.24
Christy, Estelle 1907.42
Christy, George 1866.22, 1866.32
Christy, Lew 1916.18, 1924.10, 1926.18, 1927.43
Christy, Lewis 1920.09
Christy, Louis 1919.11
Christy, Messr. 1882.37
Christy, Thomas A. 1885.30
Chryst, Gary 1980.04, 1980.25
Chrystal, Peter 1879.07
Chrysty, Molly 1914.20
Chubb, Mr. 1844.01
Chuck London Media/Stuart Werner 1987.20
Chudiakoff, A. 1924.48
Chueca, Federico 1969.11
Chueca, Frederico 1949.07
Chun, Anne 1997.16
Chunayev, Boris 1990.01
Chung, Hazel 1956.03
Chunn, M. 1999.02
Church, Charles 1896.52, 1899.35, 1900.48, 1900.55, 1904.43
Church, George 1936.02, 1936.05, 1938.14, 1940.10, 1943.04, 1954.12, 1958.07, 1963.06, 1963.17, 1963.26
Church, Harden 1928.48, 1934.15
Church, Joe 2000.10
Church, John 1902.14, 1903.01
Church, Joseph 1993.06, 1997.20, 1999.10
Church, Lottie 1886.31
Church, Sandra 1959.13
Churchill, Frank 1979.28, 1999.05
Churchill, Larry 1975.12
Churchill, Stewart 1942.20
Chute, B.J. 1960.05
Chute, Paul J. 1902.15
Chwatt, Richard 1983.21
Ciampa, John 1950.14
Cianelli, Edward 1924.28
Ciannelli, Edouard 1920.01
Ciannelli, Eduardo 1930.04
Ciappa, Mlle. 1879.42
Cibelli, Jr., Aldred 1953.09
Cibelli, Renato 1956.16, 1961.20, 1965.34, 1972.14, 1977.12
Ciceri, Charles 1794.01, 1796.01, 1796.03
Ciemietcka, Josephine 1883.39
Cifala, Jo-Ann 1979.05
Cifarelli, D. 1918.17
Cilento, Wayne 1975.15, 1980.29, 1983.19, 1985.19, 1986.06, 1993.06, 1995.05, 1997.05, 2000.06
Cimber, Alphonse 1953.10
Cimberg, Jesse M. 1943.06
Cimino, Leonardo 1950.11
Cinko, Paula 1974.26
Cinton, Harry 1915.29
Cintron, Monique 1987.12
Cinty Pritzker, Inc. 1985.08
Cioffi, Janice 1947.04
Cionnaith, Paula Nic 1996.12, 1998.09
Circle in the Square 1969.10, 1974.25, 1976.19, 1979.07, 1988.13, 1989.10, 1989.19, 1992.11
Circle Production Company 1908.15
Cirker and Robbins 1925.18, 1930.23, 1930.26, 1930.42
Cirker, Ira 1943.23
Cissel, Chuck 1975.15
Cistone, Danny 1989.27, 1991.06
Citarella, Joseph A. 1981.21, 1992.14, 1996.11
Citti, Gertrude 1884.60, 1886.35
Citti, Miss 1882.23
City Center 55th Street Theatre Foundation, Inc. 1989.01
City Center Acting Company 1973.16
City Rhythm Band, The 1976.34
Ciulla, A.C. 1987.05, 1998.13
Civic Light Opera Company 1931.10, 1931.12, 1931.15, 1931.17, 1931.18, 1931.20, 1931.22, 1931.23, 1931.24, 1931.25, 1931.27, 1931.33, 1931.35, 1931.41, 1931.43, 1931.45, 1932.02, 1933.08, 1933.09, 1933.10, 1933.11, 1933.14, 1933.19
Civic Repertory Theatre 1929.20, 1932.28
Claflin, Josie 1897.33, 1910.06, 1917.07
Claggette, Helen 1912.24
Clahane, Jack 1907.53
Clahane, John 1904.53
Claiborne, Lillian 1896.31
Clair, Al 1927.08
Clair, Herbert 1920.07, 1922.27
Clair, Joseph 1882.23, 1887.04
Clair, Louise 1905.19
Clairbol 1913.07
Claire 1894.14
Claire, Athalie 1889.28, 1889.29
Claire, Attalie 1891.36, 1898.49, 1898.57, 1900.19, 1900.49
Claire, Bernice 1934.12
Claire, Charles 1875.18
Claire, Dorothy 1932.05, 1969.14
Claire, Eileen 1911.08
Claire, Gladys 1897.21, 1904.27, 1908.21
Claire, Helen 1941.12
Claire, Ina 1911.39, 1914.33, 1915.15, 1916.10
Claire, Joseph 1890.17, 1893.02
Claire, Ludie 1955.02
Claire, Marion 1934.29
Claire, Messr. 1869.07
Claire, Mildred 1900.40, 1904.56, 1905.37
Claire, Rosalie 1924.32, 1927.53, 1928.07
Claire, Stella 1954.09
Claire, Teddy 1925.23
Claire, Will 1931.29
Claire, Willis 1918.17, 1942.27
Claire, Wyn 1929.51
Clairon, Laura 1927.67, 1932.11
Clairon, Papa 1979.02
Clairville 1866.29, 1872.42, 1873.11, 1873.18, 1875.02, 1875.28, 1876.10, 1876.17, 1876.26, 1877.27, 1877.39, 1879.48, 1883.30, 1883.57, 1884.54, 1885.19, 1885.38, 1887.37, 1890.22, 1890.24, 1902.13, 1925.51, 1926.45, 1926.47
Clairville, Charles 1884.43
Clairville, Miss 1870.05
Clampett, Robert 1990.10
Clancey, Laura 1878.16
Clancey, Mlle. 1875.04
Clancy, Carrie 1876.21
Clancy, Miss 1876.18
Clancy, Thaddeus 1950.10
Clancy, Tom 1959.04
Clancy, Venie 1875.20, 1876.17, 1876.18, 1876.21, 1876.27, 1877.15, 1879.01, 1879.53
Clancy, Venie G. 1875.15, 1879.06
Clanton, Ralph 1946.05
Clapp, A. 1867.12
Clapton, Eric 1982.22
Clara, Mlle. 1870.44, 1871.27, 1876.26, 1877.06
Clara, Mrs. 1844.01
Clarabel, F. 1870.05
Clarance, Lloyd 1884.61
Clare, Ethel 1885.13
Clare, F. 1887.49, 1898.45
Clare, Fred 1894.52, 1898.45, 1899.32, 1907.43, 1908.32
Clare, George 1879.18, 1879.23, 1887.32
Clare, Gloria 1928.49, 1936.26, 1939.13
Clare, Grace 1879.08
Clare, Henry 1887.15
Clare, J. 1875.14, 1877.22, 1877.23
Clare, J.S. 1893.23
Clare, John 1885.21
Clare, Joseph 1877.25, 1880.34, 1881.43, 1884.09, 1884.34, 1884.64, 1885.11, 1885.48, 1886.12, 1886.40, 1886.44, 1887.12, 1887.28, 1887.47, 1890.08, 1890.16, 1890.37, 1890.40, 1891.13, 1893.07, 1893.47, 1897.53, 1898.04, 1898.06
Clare, Joseph D. 1889.50, 1890.25
Clare, Messr. 1879.23
Clare, Sidney 1921.02, 1921.25, 1924.01, 1925.47, 1932.18, 1975.22, 1980.08
Clarence, Ed. 1886.07
Clarence, Little 1870.31
Clarence, Lizzie 1879.02
Clarence, Master 1871.16
Clarendon, Dot 1889.12, 1890.04, 1891.01, 1891.28, 1894.20, 1895.30, 1896.09, 1896.11
Clarendon, Hal 1894.39
Clarendon, Hal. 1887.40
Clarendon, J. Hayden 1906.16, 1907.17
Clarendon, Katherine 1912.06
Clarens, Sallie 1884.65
Clarenze, Frederick 1904.14
Clarenze, James 1897.15
Claret, Gaston 1934.32, 1935.19
Clarey, Cynthia 1983.16
Clarges, Verner 1884.61, 1905.38
Claribel 1881.39, 1886.02
Clarion, Laura 1930.28
Clarissa 1946.03
Clark Marguerite 1910.03
Clark, A. 1875.31
Clark, A.L. 1911.22
Clark, Addie 1918.04
Clark, Adelaide 1916.15
Clark, Alexander 1886.32, 1890.43, 1894.19, 1895.17, 1896.51, 1898.17, 1899.22, 1899.36, 1901.18, 1902.06, 1902.10, 1902.21, 1903.14, 1904.25, 1906.49, 1908.29, 1911.23, 1915.08, 1915.23, 1918.33, 1919.09, 1921.01, 1925.06, 1926.06, 1927.24, 1937.02, 1959.03, 1961.15, 1962.15, 1964.46, 1965.18, 1966.31, 1967.17
Clark, Austin 1916.22, 1917.06, 1928.25
Clark, Bert 1915.02, 1918.27
Clark, Bertha 1908.08
Clark, Bessie 1888.05
Clark, Billy 1919.08, 1919.33
Clark, Bobby 1919.21, 1922.39, 1923.32, 1924.44, 1926.28, 1930.02, 1931.42, 1932.27, 1934.42, 1936.17, 1939.22, 1942.18, 1944.02, 1946.02, 1947.04, 1948.28, 1950.12, 1979.24, 1979.25
Clark, Bonnie 1900.41
Clark, Bryan 1978.06
Clark, Budd 1931.04
Clark, Buddy 1943.16
Clark, C. 1892.35
Clark, C.J. 1893.08
Clark, C.W. 1891.46
Clark, Carl 1959.05
Clark, Carolyn 1961.27
Clark, Charles Dow 1904.52, 1906.05, 1907.02, 1914.34, 1917.37
Clark, Charles H. 1884.51, 1894.52, 1898.45, 1904.32, 1907.43, 1908.32
Clark, Cheryl 1975.14
Clark, Claudia 1907.11, 1912.01
Clark, Connie 1944.24
Clark, Cumberland 1925.50
Clark, Cuthbert 1908.07
Clark, David J. 1908.25
Clark, Dick 1982.22
Clark, Dollie 1892.02, 1892.13
Clark, Dolly 1890.13, 1890.38, 1890.42, 1891.35, 1892.26, 1892.32
Clark, Donald 1941.12
Clark, Dorothy 1920.36, 1921.24
Clark, Dort 1953.03, 1956.14, 1961.12, 1961.21, 1962.16
Clark, Dwayne 2000.03
Clark, E.A. 1907.51, 1909.20
Clark, Eddie 1910.29
Clark, Edgar 1919.19
Clark, Edward 1903.09, 1912.02, 1917.05, 1917.21, 1919.19, 1920.14, 1920.30, 1922.07, 1923.10, 1924.07
Clark, Edward H. 1902.26
Clark, Edwin A. 1908.26, 1910.23
Clark, Eliza Atkins 1995.19
Clark, Emily 1890.50
Clark, Emma 1904.13, 1904.44
Clark, Erminie 1910.17, 1911.11
Clark, Esq., Robert Edwin 1950.12
Clark, Ethel 1931.12, 1931.23, 1931.24, 1931.35
Clark, Etta 1880.63
Clark, Eugene 1880.01, 1880.03, 1881.07, 1894.52
Clark, Eva 1921.17, 1922.21, 1923.45, 1924.39
Clark, F. 1866.18, 1870.44
Clark, Frances 1905.51
Clark, Frank 1932.02
Clark, G. 1848.01, 1885.14
Clark, G. Davison 1925.16, 1929.08
Clark, G. Thomas 1999.04
Clark, Gage 1938.15
Clark, George 1889.45, 1905.10
Clark, George R. 1904.32
Clark, Gertie 1887.12
Clark, Gilbert 1923.07, 1923.32
Clark, Gladys 1916.09, 1917.08
Clark, Gordon 1931.42
Clark, Grace Gayler 1890.32
Clark, Grace Gaylor 1906.05
Clark, H.A. 1895.18
Clark, Harriet 1941.03
Clark, Harry 1923.13, 1936.12, 1943.19, 1946.10, 1948.32, 1952.10
Clark, Harry Corson 1908.21
Clark, Hattie 1898.77
Clark, Helen 1907.12, 1919.12
Clark, Henry Savile 1884.60
Clark, Herbert 1927.66
Clark, Hilda 1895.25, 1896.42, 1897.50
Clark, Hughie L. 1918.21
Clark, Ida 1898.37
Clark, J. 1864.16, 1864.20
Clark, Jack J. 1905.47
Clark, James 1978.23, 1980.04, 1980.25, 1985.13, 1986.09, 1988.04
Clark, Jenie 1879.42
Clark, Jennie 1879.03
Clark, Jessie 1895.16
Clark, Jinx 1948.19, 1949.05
Clark, John 1879.70, 1879.72, 1887.25, 1934.43
Clark, John W. 1888.31
Clark, Joseph 1907.62, 1909.31, 1910.32, 1922.31
Clark, Josh 1982.24
Clark, Keith 1932.18
Clark, Kenneth 1905.22
Clark, Kenneth S. 1905.22, 1906.37, 1908.07, 1909.05, 1910.08
Clark, Leona 1884.14, 1885.65, 1886.37
Clark, Les 1933.15
Clark, Lillian Cleeves 1878.05
Clark, Lillion 1936.27
Clark, Little 1870.31
Clark, Lizzie 1886.47
Clark, Louise 1916.09
Clark, Lucile Gilbert 1923.02
Clark, Lyle 1944.33
Clark, Mabel 1898.05, 1898.28
Clark, Mae 1927.46
Clark, Marguerite 1902.16, 1903.02, 1903.18, 1905.36, 1908.41, 1909.07

Clark, Marilyn 1975.22
Clark, May 1880.26
Clark, Messr. 1861.03, 1883.31
Clark, Miss 1872.22, 1873.24, 1877.39, 1903.03, 1904.13, 1904.44, 1908.19
Clark, Mr. 1861.03
Clark, Nevin 1918.31
Clark, Norman 1930.25
Clark, Oliver 1964.33
Clark, Patrice 1922.45, 1923.44
Clark, Patricia 1921.36, 1924.43
Clark, Peggy 1938.12, 1944.33, 1945.20, 1946.24, 1947.07, 1947.16, 1948.25, 1948.31, 1949.12, 1949.18, 1950.10, 1950.19, 1951.24, 1952.01, 1952.07, 1953.02, 1953.03, 1953.16, 1954.13, 1955.01, 1956.02, 1956.08, 1956.14, 1957.03, 1957.04, 1957.06, 1957.08, 1957.11, 1958.03, 1958.05, 1958.07, 1958.08, 1958.19, 1959.03, 1959.04, 1959.14, 1960.06, 1960.20, 1961.01, 1961.18, 1962.17, 1963.04, 1963.05, 1963.06, 1963.17, 1963.18, 1963.29, 1964.40, 1964.46, 1965.15, 1965.18, 1965.20, 1965.38, 1966.07, 1966.08, 1966.11, 1967.04, 1967.07, 1967.09, 1967.17, 1968.02, 1969.14, 1980.11
Clark, Peter 1932.18
Clark, Rachel May 1926.42
Clark, Randy 1989.11
Clark, Richard 1939.21
Clark, Robert E. 1908.40
Clark, Ron 1986.21, 1988.11
Clark, Rudy 1984.15, 1997.21
Clark, Samuel 1891.08
Clark, Sterling 1960.08, 1961.27, 1964.15, 1965.01, 1965.14
Clark, Sumner 1893.14, 1894.02
Clark, Sylvia 1911.12, 1919.25
Clark, Thomas 1896.38
Clark, Tom 1993.02, 1997.17, 2000.15, 2000.20
Clark, Valerie 1918.04
Clark, Victoria 1992.04, 1993.16, 1995.05
Clark, Viola 1911.39
Clark, Violet 1890.50
Clark, Virginia 1919.33, 1920.35
Clark, W.H. 1885.07, 1888.18, 1909.20, 1910.23
Clark, Wallie 1894.42, 1894.52
Clark, Wally 1905.47
Clark, Wilfred 1928.50
Clark, William H. 1907.54
Clark, Willis 1899.29
Clarke 1910.21
Clarke, A.H. 1888.13
Clarke, Alexander 1894.38, 1900.19, 1901.29
Clarke, Annie M. 1892.57
Clarke, Arthur F. 1895.33, 1897.18
Clarke, Bill 1999.17
Clarke, C. Al. 1904.14
Clarke, C.V. 1900.57
Clarke, C.W. 1866.01, 1866.05
Clarke, Campbell 1875.11
Clarke, Charles 1938.18
Clarke, Charles S. 1938.18
Clarke, Claudia 1909.12
Clarke, Della 1905.51
Clarke, Dolly 1892.41
Clarke, Donald 1948.31, 1949.16
Clarke, Douglas 1963.12
Clarke, Edwin A. 1905.54, 1906.46, 1907.54
Clarke, Emma 1903.03
Clarke, Ethel 1931.10, 1931.25, 1933.08
Clarke, Eugene 1878.16, 1879.05, 1880.31, 1880.46, 1881.43, 1882.34, 1883.22, 1883.31, 1898.72
Clarke, Eva 1922.46
Clarke, F.C. 1892.59
Clarke, Frank 1915.06
Clarke, G. 1863.07, 1875.18, 1892.04
Clarke, G.H. 1863.10
Clarke, Gage 1895.39, 1931.06
Clarke, George 1892.14
Clarke, George H. 1864.15
Clarke, Gertie 1885.28, 1885.67, 1888.24, 1888.26, 1895.21
Clarke, Gertrude 1885.52
Clarke, Gilbert 1924.44
Clarke, Gordon 1939.19
Clarke, Gordon B. 1958.08, 1959.03, 1965.36
Clarke, Grace 1880.62
Clarke, Grant 1911.24, 1912.01, 1912.14, 1912.31, 1913.05, 1913.30, 1915.16, 1916.03, 1916.25, 1917.37, 1920.10, 1920.24, 1920.33, 1921.18, 1921.21, 1921.34, 1923.12, 1923.20, 1924.37, 1953.12, 1973.14, 1980.10, 1982.12, 1989.02, 1995.12
Clarke, H. 1889.36
Clarke, Hamilton 1886.45, 1888.38
Clarke, Harry 1882.76, 1907.11, 1909.03, 1911.41, 1912.35, 1917.05, 1918.15, 1918.32, 1918.34, 1919.05, 1919.14, 1921.08, 1924.42, 1925.04, 1930.23, 1932.01, 1932.06, 1932.15
Clarke, Harry C. 1889.31
Clarke, Harry Corson 1909.24, 1922.07
Clarke, Hazel Kirke 1899.22
Clarke, Helen 1915.07, 1917.02, 1918.37
Clarke, Henry 1951.16
Clarke, Henry Corson 1904.34
Clarke, Herbert 1894.27
Clarke, Hope 1960.08, 1967.06, 1972.13, 1985.05, 1992.08
Clarke, Hughie 1931.01
Clarke, J. 1864.18
Clarke, J.H. 1861.06, 1862.01, 1862.02
Clarke, James 1870.08, 1870.11
Clarke, Jennie 1873.25
Clarke, Jerry 1924.37
Clarke, John 1919.42, 1921.21, 1923.15, 1924.23, 1925.39, 1928.12, 1932.23, 1938.14, 1940.22, 1942.29
Clarke, John Lee 1904.43
Clarke, Kenneth S. 1907.41
Clarke, Lawrence 1934.04
Clarke, Leona 1887.24, 1888.34, 1890.14, 1890.20, 1890.23
Clarke, Lexie 1908.11
Clarke, Lulu Belle 1950.04
Clarke, Marguerite 1901.23
Clarke, May 1880.62
Clarke, Miss 1867.19, 1867.20, 1868.22, 1871.14, 1872.09
Clarke, Mr. 1840.04
Clarke, Myers 1885.42
Clarke, N.B. 1851.07, 1859.01
Clarke, Patrice 1917.06
Clarke, Patricia 1921.10, 1932.23
Clarke, Payne 1895.13
Clarke, Ray 1938.04, 1939.24
Clarke, Raymond 1918.14
Clarke, Richard 1890.02
Clarke, Robert 1909.15, 1939.21, 1943.24, 1945.06, 1946.09
Clarke, Rose 1900.16
Clarke, Stanley 1918.23
Clarke, Sylvia 1910.19
Clarke, T.J. 1903.36
Clarke, Thatcher 1961.27, 1962.14
Clarke, Vera 1928.49
Clarke, Victor 1907.27, 1946.12, 1948.25
Clarke, W.H. 1890.18, 1896.16, 1906.46, 1911.28
Clarke, Wilfred 1898.46, 1900.43, 1919.34
Clarke, William H. 1899.06, 1908.26
Clarkson, John 1976.05
Clary, Miss 1881.04
Clary, Robert 1952.09, 1955.10
Clary, Wilton 1946.03, 1950.16, 1952.05
Clasis, Mlle. 1913.28
Classic Presentations, Ltd. 1969.04
Classon, Jack 1930.31
Clater, Robert 1987.07
Clatworthy, David 1966.17
Claude, Toby 1900.05, 1900.34, 1901.09, 1901.29, 1902.05, 1904.50
Claudio, Joseph 1946.03
Claudius, Dane 1919.22
Claudius, Mons. 1883.55, 1884.52, 1884.54
Clausen, Alf 1972.21
Claussen, Joy 1961.08
Claveau, Sharon 1978.19
Clavell, James 1990.17
Clavelle, Emma 1882.44
Clavery, Roderick 1954.19
Clawson, Barbara 1943.18
Clawson, Doris 1943.18
Clawson, Dorothy 1943.18
Claxton, Irving 1901.21
Claxton, Joyce 1939.31
Claxton, William 1972.02
Clay, Annie 1898.60
Clay, Bertha 1927.02
Clay, Dorothy 1918.04
Clay, Eddy 1944.31, 1946.21, 1950.07
Clay, Edwin 1943.04, 1948.32
Clay, Frederic 1879.71, 1880.18, 1883.52
Clay, Frederick 1878.22
Clay, James 1911.25
Clay, James Frederic 1897.05
Clay, Louise 1967.01
Clay, Paul 1996.09
Clayborn, Miss 1892.52
Clayburgh, Jill 1970.15, 1972.22
Claypoole, Edward B. 1908.10, 1910.20
Claypoole, Milton E. 1918.14
Clayson, Rodman 1992.13
Clayton, Alice 1875.14
Clayton, B. 1976.34
Clayton, Bessie 1891.15, 1894.35, 1896.02, 1898.50, 1899.17, 1899.30, 1901.17, 1902.29, 1904.54, 1908.01, 1909.13, 1912.44, 1913.18
Clayton, Beth 1996.10
Clayton, Estelle 1879.50, 1880.04, 1895.11
Clayton, Ethel 1918.12
Clayton, Evelyn 1926.38
Clayton, Frank 1892.41, 1908.33
Clayton, Fred 1892.46
Clayton, Gilbert 1889.44, 1890.26, 1891.31, 1891.47, 1893.39, 1895.11, 1895.42, 1900.42, 1901.06, 1901.09, 1902.21, 1903.03, 1903.34, 1905.19, 1907.11, 1910.27, 1911.38, 1913.15, 1913.32, 1914.28, 1916.07, 1916.17, 1918.26
Clayton, Herbert 1900.37, 1930.20
Clayton, J. 1903.03
Clayton, Jan 1945.05, 1946.01, 1956.03
Clayton, Joe 1930.28
Clayton, Joseph 1927.64
Clayton, Josephine 1903.03, 1904.13, 1904.44
Clayton, Lawrence 1992.06, 1995.02, 1996.18, 1999.08, 2001.03
Clayton, Lew 1916.23
Clayton, Lou 1918.20, 1930.40
Clayton, M. 1903.03
Clayton, Marie 1903.03, 1904.44
Clayton, Marion 1951.05
Clayton, Mary 1904.03, 1905.19
Clayton, Pat 1928.06, 1930.04
Clayton, Philip 1987.05, 1990.04
Clayton, Richard 1950.14
Clayton, Ruth 1934.29, 1941.07
Clayton, Stanley 1990.15
Clayton, Viola 1904.35
Cleale, Lewis 1995.14, 1996.18
Clear, Charles 1918.06
Cleary, Louise 1896.42, 1897.13
Cleary, Mena 1893.48, 1894.03, 1894.45, 1895.01
Cleary, Michael 1928.23, 1931.13, 1931.14
Cleary, Michael H. 1930.35, 1931.21, 1932.13, 1936.01, 1937.07
Cleary, Thomas C. 1898.75
Cleary, William J. 1928.21
Cleave, Van 1943.21
Cleaver, Jennie 1864.22
Cleaver, Lillian 1888.13, 1889.13
Cleaver, Robin 1983.01
Cleaves, Ardelle 1920.25
Cleese, John 1964.29, 1965.14, 1976.06
Cleeve, Van 1944.14
Cleland, Thomas J. 1905.49
Clemande, J. 1929.10
Clemandh, C. 1929.13, 1929.14
Clemandh, J. 1929.11, 1929.15, 1929.16
Clemandl, Julian 1926.40
Clemence, Miss 1870.31
Clemence, Richard 1959.08, 1959.17
Clemens, Frankie 1879.02
Clemens, Gertrude 1926.46
Clemens, Joy 1960.15
Clemens, LeRoy 1921.04
Clemens, Richard 1945.17
Clement, Clay 1928.03, 1947.16
Clement, Frank 1902.05, 1920.09
Clement, Frank A. 1900.51
Clement, Joan 1923.19, 1925.33, 1927.12, 1928.02, 1930.32
Clement, Laura 1886.34, 1887.49, 1888.37, 1891.38, 1892.60, 1893.02, 1893.07, 1907.13
Clement, Maris 1978.28, 1981.12, 1982.01, 1983.13
Clemente, Dan 1999.02
Clemente, Francesco 1996.10
Clemente, Rene 1982.13, 1982.19
Clementine, Mlle. 1868.24, 1868.26, 1869.03
Clements 1971.03
Clements Joy 1968.15
Clements, Beatrice 1898.26, 1898.46, 1899.41
Clements, C. 1895.29
Clements, Clay 1930.27
Clements, Dolly 1920.25
Clements, Dudley 1929.22, 1930.02, 1931.42, 1931.48, 1933.13, 1933.25, 1934.15, 1934.20, 1941.12, 1944.21
Clements, Florence 1908.02
Clements, Hal 1905.39
Clements, Hazel 1917.05, 1921.32
Clements, Joy 1959.08, 1959.17, 1960.11, 1961.04, 1961.05, 1961.19, 1962.10, 1962.11, 1962.19, 1963.15, 1963.18, 1968.10
Clements, L.D. 1963.15, 1963.18, 1966.02
Clements, Otis 1973.05
Clements, William H. 1980.23
Clemmons, Dave 1997.19, 1999.08
Clemons, Evelyn 1900.59
Clemons, Gertrude 1924.40
Clemons, James 1915.02, 1916.11, 1917.23, 1920.28, 1924.32
Clemson, J. Osborne 1927.45
Clemson, John 1927.05
Clemson, John Osborne 1928.49
Clemson, Osborne 1895.26, 1904.04, 1917.10
Clennett, George 1903.39
Clennett, George C. 1907.61
Clerc, B. 1947.05
Clerc, Borel 1924.18
Clerc, Le 1962.22
Clerget, Paul 1916.16
Clerise, Ethal 1898.75
Clerk, Clive 1975.15
Clermont, Frl. 1882.68
Clether, Brenda 1934.34
Cleveir, Linda 1887.02
Cleveland, Albert 1903.03
Cleveland, Bessie 1886.33, 1887.15, 1887.21, 1889.31, 1889.47, 1890.34, 1891.43, 1892.36, 1892.52, 1893.35
Cleveland, Camille 1889.41, 1892.23, 897.30
Cleveland, Carol 1976.06
Cleveland, Del 1930.25
Cleveland, Delancey 1937.11
Cleveland, H.L. 1886.44
Cleveland, Jean 1944.02
Cleveland, John 1941.03, 1952.09
Cleveland, Messr. 1904.13, 1904.44
Cleveland, Mr. 1796.01, 1796.02
Cleveland, Mrs. 1796.02
Cleveland, Pat 1976.20
Cleveland, Phyllis 1924.38, 1925.14, 1925.38, 1927.21
Clevely, Messr. 1852.05
Cleverly, Messr. 1851.01, 1854.01
Clewis, Cullen 1927.03
Clidd, George 1928.32
Cliefden, Emma 1883.05, 1883.07
Cliento, Osvaldo 1993.08
Cliff, Laddie 1911.18
Cliffe, H. Cooper 1911.09, 1934.41
Clifford, Al 1937.01
Clifford, Alice 1903.17
Clifford, Bessie 1902.11, 1905.34, 1905.50, 1908.27, 1911.35, 1921.02
Clifford, Billy 1897.40, 1905.09
Clifford, Billy S. 1898.67, 1905.32
Clifford, George 1920.42, 1922.32
Clifford, Harry 1899.25
Clifford, J.H. 1864.17
Clifford, Jack 1912.13, 1922.48, 1937.06
Clifford, Jenny 1869.31
Clifford, Kathleen 1907.05, 1907.18, 1907.47, 1911.18, 1911.43, 1912.09, 1912.13
Clifford, Larry 1919.26
Clifford, Lillian 1915.18
Clifford, Louise 1927.61
Clifford, Marie 1913.33
Clifford, Messr. 1876.35
Clifford, Minnie 1890.50
Clifford, Miss 1872.22, 1872.35
Clifford, Mr. 1880.25
Clifford, Nelson 1936.22
Clifford, R.C. 1879.12
Clifford, Ross 1908.25
Clifford, Thomas E. 1896.15
Clifford, William 1898.67
Clift, Alice 1959.19
Clift, Anna Mae 1920.28
Clift, Montgomery 1935.14
Clifton, Ada 1861.03, 1884.21
Clifton, Eileen 1934.34

Clifton, Fred 1879.70, 1879.72, 1884.36, 1884.64, 1885.16, 1885.21, 1886.14, 1889.36, 1890.46, 1892.20
Clifton, Frederick 1888.18, 1897.29
Clifton, Genevieve 1897.48
Clifton, Genevive 1896.36
Clifton, Gladys 1916.22, 1918.22
Clifton, H. 1877.15
Clifton, Harry 1938.02
Clifton, Harry D. 1877.04
Clifton, Herbert 1914.15
Clifton, Jennie 1892.22
Clifton, John 1987.06
Clifton, Maisie 1924.32
Clifton, Marie 1880.43
Clifton, Marion P. 1888.08
Clifton, Maude 1884.40
Clifton, Miss 1857.03, 1883.17, 1883.23, 1897.09
Clifton, Nellie 1881.14
Clifton, W.F. 1882.62, 1886.16, 1890.17
Clifton, William 1909.05, 1912.28, 1918.11
Clifton-Allen, Lynne 1979.18
Climan, Tamar 1997.04
Cline, Eddie 1911.17
Cline, Edward 1944.30
Cline, Emma 1870.39, 1872.10
Cline, Fred 1964.21, 1965.14
Cline, Maggie 1894.09, 1896.39, 1898.10
Cline, Minnie 1901.08
Cline, Mr. 1852.02, 1860.03, 1861.03
Clinkscales, J.T. 1988.05
Clinton, C.R. 1870.08, 1870.11, 1876.05, 1876.07, 1876.10, 1876.14, 1876.30, 1876.33, 1877.05
Clinton, Eileen 1918.04
Clinton, Estele 1887.43
Clinton, Estelle 1892.04
Clinton, Fraunces 1902.39
Clinton, Jack 1907.62
Clinton, Katherine 1898.46
Clinton, Larry 1939.29
Clinton, Lillie 1902.39
Clinton, Margaret 1934.37
Clinton, Miss 1859.11, 1860.03, 1883.58
Clinton, T.C. 1888.30
Clinton, Walter 1910.17
Clive, David 1959.03
Clive, Helen C. 1927.08
Clive, Madeleine 1943.01, 1956.16
Clive, Minnie 1879.10
Clive, Mr. 1872.23
Cloak, Beatrice 1918.05
Clod, Messr. 1861.01
Clodoche, Messr. 1869.29
Clogg, Halley 1911.25
Cloney, E.J. 1884.09
Clooney, Rosemary 1976.32
Close, Charles 1905.41
Close, Del 1959.12
Close, Glenn 1976.08, 1980.07, 1994.10
Closser, Louise 1895.30, 1896.09
Clough, Inez 1896.46, 1924.27
Clouser, James 1962.15
Clovelly, Cecil 1919.02, 1929.33
Clover, Carroll 1896.32
Clovis, Hal 1927.12
Clow, James 1993.07
Clower, Messr. 1861.03
Clowes, Eugene 1899.22
Cloy, Robert C. 1927.43
Clucas, Carroll C. 1909.14
Cluett, H.E. 1905.54, 1906.46
Cluett, H.S. 1907.54
Cluett, Harry 1909.20, 1914.19
Cluett, Harry E. 1905.17, 1908.26, 1912.30
Clurman, Harold 1955.27
Clustine, Ivan 1916.15
Clute, Chester 1927.11
Clutsam, G.A. 1934.29
Clutsam, G.H. 1919.26
Cluxton, Walter A. 1904.50
Clyde, Ivy 1904.36
Clyde, James 1908.39
Clyde, June 1937.15, 1941.13
Clymas, Sari 1957.17, 1961.28
Coal, C. 1873.26
Coast, John 1924.45
Coate, Gwendoline 1903.17, 1912.37
Coates, Eric 1936.22, 1942.16
Coates, Florence Earl 1908.06
Coates, Jefferson 1946.17
Coates, John 1894.15, 1895.43
Coates, Norman 1985.17, 1989.25
Coates, Sherman 1896.04
Coates, Wendy 1997.11, 1998.06, 1999.11
Coats, William Alan 1998.18
Cobb and Edwards 1906.29
Cobb, Arthur 1905.51
Cobb, B.F. 1881.16
Cobb, Daniel 1944.27
Cobb, F.H. 1886.10
Cobb, George L. 1913.34, 1915.03
Cobb, Ira 1946.16
Cobb, Irwin S. 1908.03
Cobb, Jane 1919.06
Cobb, John S. 1955.11
Cobb, Jr., Henry Ives 1917.01
Cobb, Lee J. 1935.16, 1936.28, 1943.23
Cobb, Margaret 1907.58, 1908.03
Cobb, Mrs. 1881.16
Cobb, Will 1904.44, 1906.20, 1907.21
Cobb, Will D. 1899.29, 1899.35, 1901.13, 1901.29, 1903.03, 1903.04, 1904.03, 1904.13, 1904.43, 1904.52, 1906.29, 1906.45, 1907.24, 1907.41, 1907.42, 1907.44, 1908.04, 1908.15, 1908.28, 1908.36, 1908.38, 1909.11, 1910.18, 1913.17, 1922.09, 1942.35, 1980.27, 1997.01
Cobb, Will H. 1902.15
Cobham, Edward 1928.32
Cobian, J.C. 1985.07, 1999.18
Cobin, Jennie 1898.26
Coburn, Charles 1918.31, 1920.11, 1926.38
Coburn, David 1999.15
Coburn, George 1908.16
Coburn, Gladys 1922.01
Coburn, J. 1865.01, 1865.11, 1866.02, 1867.12
Coburn, Mr. 1859.08
Coburn, Mrs. Charles 1918.31, 1920.11
Coburn, Richard 1918.07
Coca, Imogene 1925.35, 1930.18, 1930.33, 1931.21, 1932.17, 1934.06, 1934.40, 1936.12, 1938.04, 1939.26, 1940.23, 1945.10, 1978.02, 1979.05
Coccia, Aurelia 1900.41
Coccia, Aurelio 1906.39
Cochran, Alice 1927.64
Cochran, Ann 1927.64, 1930.23
Cochran, C.A. 1892.35
Cochran, C.B. 1929.51
Cochran, Charles B. 1920.03, 1928.42, 1934.34
Cochran, Dorcas 1940.02
Cochran, E.F. 1907.43, 1908.32
Cochran, Gifford 1933.07
Cochran, J. 1892.35
Cochrane, James 1938.16, 1985.18
Cochrane, June 1925.17, 1926.07
Cochrane, Roy 1918.41, 1926.38
Cochrane, Steve 1988.06, 1999.11
Cochren, Felix E. 1981.15, 1983.15
Coco, James 1968.05, 1982.01
Coconut Grove Playhouse 1993.08
Coda, Frank 1964.28
Codori, Joseph 1962.16
Cody, Ethel May 1955.01
Cody, J. 1889.20
Cody, J.W. 1910.17
Cody, James W. 1925.48
Cody, Jennifer 2000.18
Cody, Kathy 1963.21
Cody, Lewis J. 1907.28
Cody, Louis J. 1914.01
Cody, M.J. 1887.11
Cody, Martin 1883.09
Cody, Martin J. 1878.12, 1883.20, 1884.04, 1884.07
Cody, Pat 1974.17
Coe, E.D. 1899.13
Coe, Ed 1901.22
Coe, Fred 1970.03
Coe, George 1964.05, 1966.10, 1970.13, 1978.02
Coe, Heidi 1979.28
Coe, Isabelle 1880.21, 1881.10, 1882.82, 1886.28, 1888.44, 1889.12, 1894.37
Coe, Jerry 1929.29
Coe, John 1969.16
Coe, John A. 1977.08
Coe, Kelvin 1976.18
Coe, Peter 1963.01, 1965.23, 1965.28, 1984.07
Coedes, Auguste 1882.26
Coes 1875.31, 1875.34
Coes, G.H. 1875.35
Coes, George 1872.13
Coes, George H. 1870.27, 1875.31, 1875.34, 1875.35, 1875.36, 1875.37, 1875.38, 1883.56
Coes, Messr. 1875.31
Coffee, J. 1882.02
Coffee, John 1880.64
Coffee, P. 1880.09
Coffey, Charles 1852.06, 1882.50, 1882.79, 1883.32, 1883.46, 1883.53, 1883.63, 1884.13, 1884.41, 1885.02, 1885.15, 1885.22, 1885.49, 1885.66, 1886.03, 1886.42, 1886.52, 1887.07, 1887.16, 1887.39, 1887.45, 1888.14, 1888.27, 1888.40, 1889.07, 1889.11, 1889.15, 1889.18, 1890.49, 1891.45, 1892.54, 1893.10, 1893.15, 1893.27, 1893.36, 1894.04, 1894.49, 1896.24
Coffin, C. Hayden 1892.25, 1892.60, 1893.02, 1893.07
Coffin, Estelle 1907.15
Coffin, Harry 1893.12
Coffin, Maurice 1930.24
Coffman, Eileen 1946.20
Cogan, David 1980.05
Cogan, Gussie 1893.05, 1894.34
Cogan, Miss 1887.32
Cogan, Mme. 1890.50
Cogan, Susan 1966.13
Coggswell, W.J. 1877.02
Coghill, Nevill 1969.04, 1980.01
Coghlan, Charles F. 1876.23
Coghlan, Eily 1884.09
Coghlan, James 1930.25
Coghlan, James J. 1930.35
Coghlan, Rosalind 1910.33
Coghlan, Rose 1872.24
Cogley, Edward F. 1902.43
Cogley, J. 1898.43
Cognaird, Theodore 1852.02
Cogniard Brothers 1886.36
Cogniard, Freres 1866.12
Cogniard, Theodore 1854.05
Cogswell, W.G. 1880.54
Cogswell, W.J. 1876.32, 1876.35, 1880.69
Cohan, George 1938.16
Cohan, George M. 1895.27, 1897.04, 1898.61, 1898.70, 1900.24, 1901.07, 1902.35, 1903.11, 1903.39, 1904.22, 1904.42, 1905.14, 1906.02, 1906.11, 1906.21, 1906.42, 1907.09, 1907.16, 1907.20, 1907.57, 1908.09, 1908.14, 1908.22, 1908.31, 1909.16, 1909.26, 1911.33, 1911.41, 1911.43, 1912.11, 1912.26, 1914.13, 1914.34, 1916.02, 1917.36, 1917.37, 1918.36, 1918.41, 1919.04, 1919.40, 1920.04, 1920.38, 1921.32, 1922.43, 1923.46, 1927.47, 1928.31, 1930.19, 1937.13, 1963.02, 1968.07, 1974.09, 1975.22, 1977.13, 1978.05, 1979.13, 1980.27, 1982.05, 1986.03, 1988.08, 1991.10
Cohan, Helen F. 1903.11, 1904.42, 1906.11, 1906.21, 1907.09, 1907.20, 1908.14, 1911.33
Cohan, Jerry J. 1901.07, 1903.11, 1904.42, 1906.11, 1906.21, 1907.09, 1907.20, 1908.14, 1911.33
Cohan, Josephine 1904.31, 1908.14
Cohan, Josie 1903.11
Cohan, Jr., George M. 1912.11
Cohan, Mary 1968.07
Cohan, Mary Anne 1953.07
Cohan, Robert 1956.07, 1978.26
Cohan, William 1908.03, 1916.19
Cohen, Alexander H. 1942.05, 1943.16, 1951.13, 1951.17, 1959.20, 1960.16, 1961.25, 1962.23, 1963.02, 1964.03, 1964.34, 1964.45, 1965.02, 1965.08, 1965.16, 1966.09, 1966.32, 1967.13, 1968.20, 1969.05, 1973.13, 1974.10, 1979.12, 1980.08, 1983.16, 1994.13
Cohen, Allen 1979.10, 1985.04
Cohen, Arthur 1946.13
Cohen, Benjamin 1897.29
Cohen, F. 1894.13
Cohen, Fanny 1885.06
Cohen, George 1880.02, 1887.43, 1889.13
Cohen, Harold 1945.01
Cohen, J.M. 1918.38
Cohen, Jamie 1981.21, 1989.03
Cohen, Jason Steven 1981.01, 1984.02, 1985.18
Cohen, Jay David 1978.11
Cohen, Jay J. 1978.21, 1981.15
Cohen, Jr., Wilbur 1935.01
Cohen, Julie 1981.07
Cohen, Kittie 1884.12
Cohen, Lawrence D. 1988.12
Cohen, Leo K. 1990.14
Cohen, Lynn 1978.23
Cohen, Martin 1955.25
Cohen, Martin B. 1960.10
Cohen, Messr. 1879.01
Cohen, Michael 1968.13
Cohen, Miss 1844.01, 1846.01
Cohen, Mons. 1879.06
Cohen, Myron 1973.01
Cohen, N.D. 1918.36
Cohen, Phoebe 1896.48
Cohen, Robert D. 1918.17
Cohen, S.A. 1979.15
Cohen, Sally 1891.15, 1895.27, 1896.52, 1897.40
Cohen, Sharleen Cooper 1997.21
Cohen, Steven A. 1988.03
Cohen, Ted 1948.17
Cohen, Walter 1960.10
Cohenour, Patti 1982.18, 1985.18, 1988.01, 1998.03
Cohn, Al 1973.10, 1974.09, 1981.06
Cohn, F. 1890.08
Cohn, Max 1923.37
Cohn, Nik 1999.15
Cohn, Paul 1899.36
Cohna, George H. 1905.14
Cohoen, Kate 1872.35
Coid, Marshall 1986.13, 1989.10
Coigne, Edna 1924.10
Coini, Jacques 1910.24, 1910.35, 1916.07
Coit, Sam 1925.29
Cokas, Nick 1996.18
Coke, Peter 1971.07
Colacino, Dick 1959.05
Colagrande, M. 1911.16
Colaneri, Joseph 1983.12, 1984.11, 1984.12, 1985.09, 1985.10, 1985.11, 1985.13, 1986.04, 1986.08, 1986.09, 1986.14, 1987.08, 1987.10, 1987.11, 1988.04, 1988.14, 1988.16, 1988.18, 1989.04, 1990.02, 1990.08, 1990.13, 1991.09, 1991.12, 1992.10, 1992.14, 1993.12, 1993.13, 1993.14, 1994.09, 1995.10, 1995.18, 1996.11, 1996.13
Colavecchia, Franco 1975.19
Colbert, Estelle 1906.34
Colbert, Helen 1953.04
Colburn, Anna Mae 1931.45
Colburn, Miss 1852.02
Colby, Betty 1955.11, 1963.12
Colby, Evelyn 1949.04
Colby, Jack 1930.42
Colby, Marion 1940.21, 1946.23, 1954.05
Colby, Mildred 1917.35
Coldren, Clarence 1909.08
Coldwell, Julia 1898.34
Cole, Arthur 1928.46
Cole, Austin 1929.21
Cole, Belle 1880.54, 1881.26, 1882.45
Cole, Billy 1930.19
Cole, Bob 1893.37, 1900.40, 1900.46, 1900.48, 1902.06, 1902.10, 1902.42, 1903.01, 1903.04, 1903.07, 1903.28, 1904.22, 1904.47, 1904.56, 1906.27, 1907.22, 1908.39, 1909.10, 1909.25, 1917.26, 1920.04, 1980.10, 1980.27, 1989.23, 1999.23
Cole, Bobby 1967.11
Cole, Caren 1990.15
Cole, Carol 1951.18, 1975.02
Cole, Carter 1971.11
Cole, Cole 1900.55
Cole, Cosy 1943.24
Cole, Cozy 1948.13, 1956.06
Cole, Dennis 1963.04, 1963.06, 1964.46, 1966.31, 1967.17
Cole, Doris 1945.07
Cole, Edith 1889.01
Cole, Ella 1904.38
Cole, Fletcher 1901.20
Cole, Frances 1929.04
Cole, Fred 1890.17
Cole, Gene 1907.11, 1913.26, 1915.18
Cole, Gertrude 1924.11
Cole, J. 1872.06
Cole, Jack 1934.15, 1934.42, 1935.17, 1942.12, 1943.01, 1943.05, 1944.15, 1948.24, 1950.02, 1953.16, 1957.16, 1961.14, 1961.26, 1962.12, 1964.04, 1965.22, 1965.34, 1972.14
Cole, John F. 1872.10

Cole, Kay 1971.12, 1974.24, 1975.15
Cole, Lena 1885.35
Cole, Lena W. 1885.42
Cole, Lester 1926.50
Cole, Louis 1927.30
Cole, Michael 1990.08
Cole, Morris 1907.38
Cole, Muriel 1942.11
Cole, Nat King 1978.09
Cole, Newton 1986.03
Cole, Nora 1982.17, 1998.16
Cole, Norma 1891.41
Cole, Robert 1898.22, 1899.12, 1899.31, 1899.35, 1901.25, 1901.27, 1901.29, 1902.23, 1903.15, 1903.39, 1903.41, 1904.04
Cole, Robert A. 1899.35
Cole, Ruby 1934.37
Cole, Saidee 1866.34, 1867.10
Cole, Saidie 1867.08
Cole, T. Kelly 1896.43
Cole, Thornton 1900.52
Cole, Tom 1929.21
Cole, Vera Bayles 1921.34, 1923.12
Cole, Walter 1895.36
Coleman, A.J. 1902.39
Coleman, Carole 1947.16
Coleman, Charles 1931.44, 1932.05, 1944.03, 1975.01, 1978.03, 1980.06, 1982.12, 1984.09
Coleman, Clara 1903.12
Coleman, Cy 1953.17, 1960.22, 1962.27, 1966.01, 1973.06, 1974.11, 1976.07, 1977.02, 1977.04, 1978.02, 1980.07, 1981.08, 1982.01, 1983.09, 1983.20, 1984.06, 1986.07, 1989.07, 1989.29, 1991.07, 1991.10, 1997.08, 1998.15, 1999.01
Coleman, Dan 1902.02, 1904.11, 1907.53
Coleman, Desiree 1986.06
Coleman, E. 1867.20, 1869.17, 1869.47
Coleman, Ed J. 1904.19
Coleman, Ed. 1871.04
Coleman, Edward 1869.34, 1869.40
Coleman, Emil 1942.16
Coleman, Frank 1965.22
Coleman, Frazer 1932.14
Coleman, Gilbert 1910.21
Coleman, Gladys 1908.34
Coleman, H. 1868.22
Coleman, Harry 1920.37, 1923.35
Coleman, Herbert 1946.08, 1949.15
Coleman, Jane 1967.10
Coleman, Jim 1983.10, 1986.14, 1987.08, 1987.10, 1988.16
Coleman, Joey 1973.17, 1975.12
Coleman, John 1890.26, 1891.31, 1891.47, 1933.12, 1955.05
Coleman, John A. 1891.32, 1892.50, 1893.50
Coleman, Kitty 1886.10, 1896.11, 1897.05, 1926.33, 1928.44, 1929.37
Coleman, Leo 1947.10, 1948.29, 1950.13
Coleman, Lillian 1898.18, 1899.04, 1903.10, 1903.23, 1904.47, 1905.55
Coleman, Margret 1973.15, 1977.12
Coleman, Marie 1880.03, 1882.07, 1882.08, 1882.09, 1883.12, 1883.13
Coleman, Marilyn 1987.17, 1991.01
Coleman, Marilyn B. 1971.13
Coleman, Nancy 1941.05
Coleman, Oliver 1946.09
Coleman, Rich 1883.02
Coleman, Sarah 1975.09
Coleman, Shepard 1963.20, 1964.01, 1964.28, 1967.14
Coleman, Ted 1907.61, 1919.07, 1924.11
Coleman, Warren 1935.13, 1942.03, 1943.15, 1944.03, 1949.15
Coleman, Yvonne 1946.08
Coleman-Jackson, Desiree 1995.04
Coles, (Charles) Honi 1949.18, 1980.10
Coles, Charles "Honi" 1983.06, 1992.18
Coles, Joyce 1932.23, 1935.02
Coles, Miss 1883.16
Colet, Betty 1925.35
Colette 1973.12
Coletti, Augustus 1903.02, 1904.17
Coletti, Frank 1930.39, 1934.15
Coley, Thomas 1939.29
Colgan, Casey 1998.06, 1999.11
Colias, Jim 1989.28
Colin, Paul 1929.51
Colin, Saul 1942.33
Colitti, Rik 1976.10
Colker, Jerry 1988.07
Coll, Ivonne 1995.09
Coll, Owen 1930.40, 1932.27, 1950.15
Coll, Ricky 1959.13
Collard, Avalon 1938.10
Collard, Henry 1872.37
Collazo, Bobby 1964.02
Colleano, Con 1942.24
Collenette, Beatrice 1920.43
Collenette, Joan 1945.14
Colleti, Frank 1928.47
Collett, Irene 1942.11
Collett, Richard 1955.07
Collette, Estelle 1920.24
Collette, Mildred 1930.22, 1931.19
Collette, Ruth 1930.22, 1931.19
Collette, Toni 2000.08
Colletti, G. 1892.33
Collier, A.W. 1892.35
Collier, Dan 1898.58
Collier, E. 1869.40, 1870.19, 1870.21
Collier, E.K. 1870.44, 1871.15, 1871.27, 1873.08, 1873.10, 1873.28, 1876.12, 1877.07
Collier, Florence 1918.22
Collier, Frederick 1901.03
Collier, Harry 1875.19, 1875.23, 1875.26
Collier, Helena 1891.37, 1893.08
Collier, J.W. 1862.03, 1862.07
Collier, Kitty 1893.08
Collier, Lizzie Hudson 1891.27, 1894.39
Collier, Louise Allen 1906.29
Collier, Naomi 1956.10, 1957.13, 1957.15, 1958.09, 1958.11
Collier, William 1890.07, 1890.34, 1891.02, 1891.37, 1893.08, 1902.29, 1911.17, 1912.07, 1914.34, 1920.17, 1920.27, 1920.32, 1921.30, 1923.21, 1923.33, 1924.30, 1926.03, 1926.34, 1927.27
Collier, Willie 1891.37, 1921.30
Colligan, Billy 1921.34, 1923.12
Colligan, Walter 1913.03, 1914.05, 1914.29
Collignon, Harry 1904.45
Colling, Sam 1894.34
Collingborne, Miss 1841.01
Collinge, Patricia 1908.42, 1911.09
Collings, W.H. 1880.51, 1884.15, 1884.56
Collings, William H. 1879.12
Collins 1917.17, 1918.40
Collins, A. 1883.37, 1900.02
Collins, A.W. 1900.23
Collins, Arthur 1901.27, 1903.04, 1903.39, 1904.47, 1905.48, 1913.33
Collins, Augustus 1882.48
Collins, B. 1918.21
Collins, Ben 1889.06
Collins, Blanche 1925.52, 1937.08, 1965.31, 1968.17
Collins, C.E. 1885.69
Collins, Charles 1873.28, 1906.25, 1930.05, 1932.15, 1934.35, 1937.07, 1945.16, 1973.03
Collins, Charles M. 1891.28
Collins, Courtney 1919.06
Collins, Dorothy 1971.05
Collins, Ed 1962.05
Collins, Ed. 1892.04
Collins, Ernest 1911.26
Collins, Frank 1920.41, 1928.42, 1929.51
Collins, G. Pat 1931.28
Collins, Gene 1922.31, 1927.64
Collins, George 1905.25
Collins, George Eaton 1907.08
Collins, Guy 1916.11, 1918.01, 1920.41
Collins, Harry 1897.18, 1902.07, 1917.09, 1917.21, 1917.27, 1917.36, 1918.03, 1918.04, 1918.33, 1918.37, 1922.28
Collins, Iris 1938.03
Collins, J. 1869.25, 1869.38, 1869.39, 1869.42
Collins, J. Palmer 1896.14
Collins, Jack 1959.22, 1969.14
Collins, James 1869.37, 1870.01, 1899.09, 1925.12
Collins, James J. 1905.31
Collins, Janet 1950.20
Collins, Jennie 1897.21
Collins, Jim 1938.08
Collins, John 1852.01, 1871.10, 1948.13
Collins, Jose 1911.43, 1912.09, 1912.27, 1913.17, 1914.16, 1914.28, 1915.27
Collins, Judy 2000.16
Collins, Kate 1869.31
Collins, Larry 1973.14, 1975.12
Collins, Laurel Lynn 1994.06
Collins, Lella 1893.37
Collins, Lester 1888.31
Collins, Lillian 1898.58, 1901.16, 1905.30
Collins, Lillie 1897.15, 1900.48, 1902.05, 1902.10, 1902.24
Collins, Lilly 1900.56
Collins, Lily 1897.55, 1904.03
Collins, Lottie 1914.10
Collins, M.H. 1911.26
Collins, M.T. 1918.36
Collins, Madeline 1925.06
Collins, Mary 1930.39
Collins, Master 1884.26
Collins, Maude 1898.64
Collins, Melville 1900.12
Collins, Melville S. 1905.40
Collins, Messr. 1869.28, 1869.36
Collins, Milt 1927.11
Collins, Miriam 1914.24, 1918.37, 1920.12
Collins, Miss 1870.31
Collins, Mr. 1860.03, 1860.04, 1870.02
Collins, Nellie 1886.42
Collins, P.A. 1891.15
Collins, Palmer 1894.20
Collins, Pat 1976.10, 1978.09, 1978.18, 1978.22, 1983.19, 1988.17, 1996.18
Collins, Radley 1935.17
Collins, Regina 1897.15, 1897.55
Collins, Robert 1938.10, 1938.18
Collins, Rose 1900.45
Collins, Russell 1936.28, 1945.05, 1950.11
Collins, Ruth 1918.16
Collins, Sam 1892.38, 1898.75, 1901.08, 1908.21, 1910.05
Collins, Samuel 1893.20, 1902.12
Collins, Sim 1908.35
Collins, Thomas 1899.15
Collins, Tom 1894.42, 1899.25, 1900.33, 1902.29, 1903.18, 1903.29, 1907.03, 1907.63, 1910.05, 1931.43
Collins, Ulric B. 1899.36
Collins, Una 1964.28
Collins, W.B. 1898.78
Collins, William 1899.09, 1915.23
Collins, Willie 1903.20
Collis, Florence 1890.08
Collis, James 1871.12
Collmer, Frl. 1897.08
Collodi, Carlo 1938.16
Collyer, Dan 1881.06, 1881.12, 1882.04, 1882.20, 1883.02, 1883.23, 1885.29, 1885.49, 1885.66, 1886.03, 1886.42, 1886.52, 1887.07, 1887.16, 1887.39, 1887.45, 1887.48, 1888.14, 1892.44, 1892.54, 1893.10, 1893.39, 1896.24, 1899.38, 1903.26, 1914.02, 1917.17
Collyer, David 1947.17, 1948.25, 1949.08, 1950.11, 1950.14, 1953.07, 1955.10, 1959.25, 1961.22
Collyer, Manning J. 1883.66
Collyer, Messr. 1893.13
Colman, Booth 1948.11
Colman, Charles 1943.15, 1952.06
Colman, Messr. 1844.01
Colodner, Joel 1973.16
Cologrande, Maria 1911.19
Colombara, Medea 1931.09
Colombini, Willy 1964.03
Colon, Aberano 1893.17
Colon, Mme. 1871.25
Colonne, E. 1868.25, 1868.27, 1868.30, 1868.31, 1869.01, 1869.10, 1869.18, 1869.19, 1869.22, 1869.24
Colson, C. David 1970.05
Colson, Kevin 1990.04
Colson, Miss 1868.03
Colston 1971.03
Colston, Percy 1926.19
Colston, Robert 1980.20, 1990.14
Colt, Alvin 1944.33, 1946.13, 1947.08, 1947.14, 1950.17, 1951.23, 1954.03, 1954.15, 1955.06, 1955.09, 1955.27, 1956.05, 1956.12, 1957.14, 1957.17, 1958.08, 1959.03, 1959.06, 1959.11, 1960.05, 1960.10, 1960.22, 1961.07, 1963.21, 1964.07, 1964.35, 1965.13, 1967.14, 1968.03, 1968.14, 1972.04, 1974.02, 1981.09, 1989.03, 1994.13
Colt, Ethel 1952.03
Colt, Ethel Barrymore 1931.30, 1971.05
Colt, Joseph S. 1900.51
Colt, Phyllis 1940.12
Coltellacci, Giulio 1964.03
Colton, Chevi 1979.02
Colton, John 1944.27
Colton, Thomas 1918.23, 1919.22
Colton, Tommy 1915.24, 1917.16, 1918.23
Colton, Tomy 1922.30
Columbia Artists 1999.10
Columbia Artists Theatricals Corporation 1980.12
Columbia Pictures Stage Productions, Inc. 1983.01
Columbia Theatrical Enterprises, Inc. 1964.39
Columbo, A.C. 1920.28
Columbo, Patti 1998.18
Columbus, Charles 1918.03, 1923.32, 1926.46, 1929.08, 1930.37, 1937.03
Colvan, Zeke 1911.26, 1917.08, 1927.37, 1927.67, 1930.08, 1931.08
Colville Opera Burlesque Company 1878.20, 1879.03, 1879.38, 1880.24
Colville, Charles 1879.38
Colville, J.M. 1885.50, 1888.23
Colville, Samuel 1866.06, 1866.08, 1866.11, 1866.15, 1873.12, 1873.14, 1873.17, 1876.17, 1876.18, 1876.21, 1876.27, 1877.16, 1877.22, 1877.23, 1878.20, 1879.03, 1879.38, 1881.31, 1884.53
Colvin, Kathryn 1901.27
Colwell Worth 1923.25
Colwell, Maud 1904.33
Colwell, Victor 1904.33
Colyer, Austin 1966.07, 1967.04, 1968.24
Comacho, Leu 1954.19
Coman, Morgan 1910.32
Comboy, Miss 1917.31
Comden, Betty 1944.33, 1945.20, 1951.19, 1953.03, 1954.13, 1956.14, 1958.05, 1958.08, 1958.21, 1959.03, 1960.23, 1961.25, 1961.28, 1963.05, 1964.21, 1967.06, 1967.09, 1970.09, 1971.15, 1974.02, 1977.02, 1978.02, 1979.13, 1979.14, 1979.22, 1982.18, 1983.09, 1985.08, 1988.08, 1989.03, 1989.06, 1990.20, 1991.07, 1991.10, 1991.13, 1994.09, 1997.01, 1998.16, 1998.18, 1999.23, 2001.03
Comee, Lillie 1884.34
Comelli 1895.28, 1897.03, 1897.20, 1898.29, 1901.27, 1903.04, 1903.39, 1905.48, 1912.33, 1913.20, 1913.36
Comelli, A. 1894.41, 1906.49
Comer, Imogene 1896.36
Comer, Lawrence 1909.17
Comer, Sybil 1930.27
Comerford, Elsie 1914.33
Comerford, Gladys 1920.26, 1922.30
Comerford, Mary 1918.01
Comfort, Jane 1994.05
Comfort, Marion 1916.08
Comfort, Vaughn 1909.16
Comley-Barton Opera Company 1881.38
Comley-James Barton Company 1880.69
Committed Artists Production, A 1988.02
Commodore, Edna 1933.04
Comont, Mme. 1916.03
Comopton, Alan 2001.04
Complex IV 1973.11
Compton, Betty 1924.06, 1925.38, 1926.21, 1926.36, 1927.59, 1928.36, 1929.45
Compton, Fay 1914.32
Compton, Frank 1905.27
Compton, Gardner 1971.04, 1976.27
Compton, John 1883.16
Compton, June Lynn 1967.02
Compton, W.H. 1882.49
Comstock, Alex 1891.18
Comstock, David 1990.07, 1990.08
Comstock, E. Ray 1917.24, 1919.20
Comstock, F. Ray 1908.08, 1909.07, 1909.27, 1913.33, 1915.07, 1916.22, 1917.06, 1917.17, 1917.27, 1918.01, 1918.03, 1918.27, 1918.37, 1919.38, 1919.39, 1920.22, 1920.34, 1920.41, 1922.06, 1923.28, 1924.08, 1925.03, 1925.46, 1925.51, 1927.51
Comstock, Frances 1934.19, 1939.12, 1940.03, 1942.17
Comstock, Frances Marion 1934.13
Comstock, G.L. 1875.14
Comstock, Irene 1888.25
Comstock, Josephine 1900.08
Comstock, Jr., A.C. 1883.66
Comstock, Laura 1901.28
Comstock, Nanette 1887.29, 1891.28
Comstock, Ray 1915.04
Comstock-Elliott Company 1916.22, 1917.06
Comtois, George 1965.31
Comyns, Lillian 1897.29

Conant, Homer 1916.06, 1916.11, 1916.14, 1916.23, 1916.25, 1917.15, 1917.23, 1917.31, 1918.05, 1918.40, 1919.16, 1919.29, 1919.30, 1920.01, 1920.03, 1920.06, 1920.19, 1920.23
Conant, Jessie 1898.09
Conant, Messr. 1895.44
Conaway, Charles 1957.01, 1966.05
Conaway, Jeff 1985.17
Conaway, Jr., Charles 1944.14
Concert Productions International 1989.12
Conche, Robert 1930.09
Concheta 1988.06
Concordi, Messr. 1881.02
Concors, Arthur 1894.22, 1895.07, 1895.18
Conde, Felisa 1953.15
Condell, H.A. 1944.26, 1945.15, 1946.11, 1946.16, 1950.16, 1961.04, 1964.13, 1965.12
Condon, Catherine 1900.13
Condon, Dennis 1989.11
Condon, Eva 1926.07, 1940.06
Condon, Hamilton 1921.27, 1922.21
Condon, Kate 1902.25, 1905.52, 1912.23, 1913.08, 1913.11, 1913.13, 1917.24
Condon, Mary 1904.48
Condon, Max 1942.19
Condon, Miss 1879.02
Condos, Frank 1930.22
Condos, Harry 1930.22
Condos, Steve 1948.23, 1958.08, 1972.04
Cone, Michael 1980.26, 1986.13, 1995.19
Conforti, Donna 1966.12, 1966.16
Conforti, Gino 1962.01, 1963.14, 1964.27, 1965.34
Conforti, Tony 1981.24
Congdon, James 1967.16, 1980.20, 1983.19
Congrove, Douglas 1922.24
Conkey, Aida 1932.05
Conkey, Thomas 1913.24, 1916.08, 1916.18, 1917.25, 1918.26, 1922.46
Conkley, Sally 1926.40
Conklin, Cathy 1953.09, 1956.01
Conklin, Charles 1933.25
Conklin, Grace 1908.03
Conklin, Harold W. 1925.17
Conklin, Helen 1889.53
Conklin, John 1963.27, 1974.02, 1976.08, 1982.07, 1982.21
Conklin, Peggy 1929.19
Conkwright, Anna 1910.27
Conlan, Francis X. 1918.37
Conlan, Frank 1926.14, 1933.05
Conlan, Joseph 1901.26
Conlan, Joseph E. 1896.38
Conlan, William J. 1900.35
Conlee, John Ellison 2000.15
Conley, 'Hi Wilberforce' 1950.12
Conley, H.L. 1895.44
Conley, Harry 1965.05
Conley, Harry J. 1929.28
Conley, Jay 1934.13
Conley, John 1897.22
Conley, Larry 1991.04
Conley, Ruth 1922.32, 1924.22
Conley, William 1908.20
Conley, William H. 1906.31
Conliffe, Florence 1885.04
Conlow, Peter 1948.28, 1951.10, 1951.17, 1952.05, 1956.08, 1957.14, 1959.22
Conloy, J.C. 1901.10
Conly, J.E. 1881.21, 1881.33, 1901.11
Conn, Chester 1962.17
Conn, Didi 1999.21, 2000.10
Conn, Harry 1931.30
Connaught, Brian 1942.29
Connaughty, J. 1866.31
Conne, Lillian 1913.18
Connell, E.L. 1884.18
Connell, Edward 1879.18, 1879.23, 1879.24, 1880.01, 1880.03, 1880.55, 1881.03, 1881.41, 1882.51, 1882.64, 1882.65, 1883.52, 1884.30, 1884.32, 1884.33, 1884.35, 1889.28, 1889.29
Connell, Edward L. 1884.28
Connell, Gordon 1961.28, 1964.01, 1972.23, 1984.02, 1985.06
Connell, Gregory 1979.11
Connell, Jane 1956.08, 1965.29, 1966.10, 1969.05, 1972.23, 1983.10, 1986.12, 1992.02, 2001.06
Connell, Maurice 1885.32
Connell, Mr. 1883.44
Connell, Tim 1991.15
Connell, Tom 1932.10
Connell, William 1881.05
Connelley, Ed. J. 1885.54
Connelly 1875.05
Connelly, Arthur 1897.55, 1899.22
Connelly, Bobby 1929.27, 1929.44
Connelly, David 1993.04
Connelly, Dolly 1913.16, 1921.07
Connelly, E.J. 1887.32
Connelly, Edward 1906.39
Connelly, Edward J. 1898.63, 1903.37, 1906.01
Connelly, John 1894.06
Connelly, Marc 1915.24, 1921.01, 1922.42, 1923.19, 1924.15, 1924.30, 1928.21, 1930.10, 1930.25, 1931.14, 1935.01, 1935.12, 1938.06, 1938.18, 1951.11
Connelly, Marcus C. 1916.18
Connelly, Messr. 1875.18
Connelly, Michael 1869.06, 1869.29, 1870.21, 1873.08, 1873.10, 1873.14, 1884.21, 1886.54
Connelly, Miss 1892.29
Connelly, Reg 1930.22, 1931.26, 1997.21, 1999.23
Connelly, Sadie 1891.46, 1894.12
Conner, Bardell 1976.21
Conner, Glen 1909.04
Conner, Richard 1904.26
Conner, T.W. 1901.19
Connerly, Mr. 1869.26
Conners, Frank 1887.11, 1907.33
Conners, James 1916.03
Connick, Jr., Harry 1990.19
Connoll, E. 1883.49
Connolly, Bobby 1920.39, 1926.12, 1926.29, 1927.09, 1927.41, 1927.59, 1928.43, 1929.03, 1929.12, 1930.11, 1930.30, 1931.04, 1931.19, 1931.28, 1931.39, 1932.07, 1932.16, 1932.25, 1933.03, 1934.01
Connolly, Charles 1928.29
Connolly, David 1989.17
Connolly, Dolly 1917.08
Connolly, Don 1934.15
Connolly, E.J. 1900.05
Connolly, Edw. J. 1909.21
Connolly, Edward J. 1906.01
Connolly, John 1933.07
Connolly, John H. 1895.27
Connolly, Marc 1934.38
Connolly, Michael 1868.23, 1868.32, 1870.02, 1870.13, 1870.19, 1870.35, 1870.42, 1871.01, 1871.02, 1871.14, 1872.21, 1872.22, 1872.24, 1872.26, 1872.37, 1873.28, 1877.22, 1877.23, 1877.25, 1877.39, 1885.08, 1886.50, 1981.12
Connolly, Mr. 1870.07, 1870.15, 1872.35
Connolly, P. 1871.17, 1872.06
Connolly, Robert 1926.42
Connolly, Sadie 1895.14, 1906.28
Connop, Herbert 1912.37
Connor, Bar Dell 1983.06
Connor, Dean B. 1894.26
Connor, Della 1905.19, 1915.07
Connor, Edgar 1909.10, 1912.36
Connor, Elsie 1929.08
Connor, Frank 1925.11
Connor, George H. 1878.19
Connor, Jim 1961.12, 1965.28
Connor, Kaye 1946.18
Connor, Kittie 1895.38
Connor, Minnie 1882.48
Connor, Miss 1854.04
Connor, Peggy 1925.42
Connor, Philip 1903.02, 1903.36
Connor, Thelma 1922.19, 1923.20, 1926.18
Connor, Thomas 1942.14
Connor, Tommie 1967.13, 1968.20, 1999.07
Connor, Velma 1922.19, 1923.20, 1926.18
Connor, W.F. 1883.48
Connors and Bennetti 1927.11
Connors, Frank 1904.47
Connors, Jack 1919.04, 1924.17, 1926.22, 1927.45
Connors, Messr. 1894.19
Connors, Richard 1899.33, 1900.46, 1903.08
Connors, Vivian 1920.08
Connors, W. 1898.34
Connorty, Lyn 1954.09
Conolly, Patricia 1998.03
Conoly, Marybeth 1930.32
Conor, H.J. 1884.16, 1884.37
Conor, Harry 1888.34, 1890.10, 1891.39, 1894.07, 1894.35, 1896.02, 1897.34, 1901.01, 1902.20, 1902.40, 1903.16, 1910.36, 1911.01, 1912.08, 1912.13, 1914.06, 1914.33, 1915.27, 1918.12
Conover, Jack 1940.12
Conover, Mrs. 1852.06
Conover, Stuart 1896.31
Conover, Theresa Maxwell 1920.31
Conover, W. 1848.01
Conquest, Arthur 1904.47
Conquest, George 1880.34
Conquest, Jr., George 1880.34
Conquest, Laura 1880.34
Conquest, Lila 1904.10, 1905.06
Conrad, Arthur 1906.36, 1910.09, 1911.40
Conrad, Barbara Smith 1964.19
Conrad, Con 1920.33, 1921.18, 1921.34, 1923.12, 1923.31, 1923.47, 1924.01, 1924.04, 1924.36, 1924.47, 1925.01, 1925.16, 1925.28, 1926.12, 1926.21, 1927.60, 1928.10, 1953.12, 1983.09
Conrad, Constance 1965.04
Conrad, Eddie 1924.33, 1925.27, 1927.04
Conrad, Eddy 1928.28
Conrad, Edith 1904.24
Conrad, Eugene 1924.25, 1929.50, 1930.22, 1932.18, 1933.20, 1934.20, 1935.04, 1936.06, 1944.30
Conrad, Eugene J. 1924.25
Conrad, Harriett 1972.04, 1977.12
Conrad, Jane 1918.32
Conrad, Johnny 1951.20
Conrad, Karen 1943.18
Conrad, M. 1891.12
Conrad, Marion 1964.22
Conrad, William 1891.17, 1892.03, 1892.16
Conradi, Ignace 1891.20, 1892.31
Conradi, Ignatz 1885.51
Conradi, Margie 1937.06
Conradi, William 1891.22
Conreid's Comic Opera Company 1890.08
Conreid, Hans 1953.07
Conreid, Heinrich 1890.08, 1890.39, 1891.30, 1892.07
Conreid, Herman 1883.08
Conreid, Miss 1879.70
Conried, Hans 1971.07
Conried, Heinrich 1883.35, 1884.40, 1885.41, 1885.63, 1886.04, 1890.08, 1891.12, 1892.03, 1892.16, 1897.08
Conron, Marie 1881.03, 1883.16, 1883.21, 1885.11
Conron, Miss 1886.32
Conrow, Jonathan 1975.22
Conroy, Allen 1952.09
Conroy, Annie 1891.18
Conroy, Artie 1942.18
Conroy, Dave 1903.05
Conroy, Ella 1892.21
Conroy, Frank 1913.18, 1915.05
Conroy, James 1887.05
Conroy, Jarlath 1989.10
Conroy, John 1904.07, 1904.31, 1905.30, 1906.21, 1907.57
Conroy, Miss 1875.05
Conroy, Thom 1942.11
Conroy-Ward, James 1976.13
Consoer, Diane 1954.17, 1959.16
Consoer, Dianne 1957.13, 1957.15, 1958.15, 1959.21
Consoll, Miss 1866.18
Constance, Beatrice 1888.30, 1920.43
Constance, E. 1904.46
Constant, Connie 1944.01
Constant, Lucille 1929.46
Constant, Marius 1983.16
Constant, Yvonne 1958.18, 1961.27
Constantin, Jean 1955.14, 1959.15, 1961.25, 1964.39
Constantine, A. 1883.20
Constantine, Miss 1888.33
Constantine, Signor 1869.08
Constantine, W.J. 1912.03
Conte, Carlo 1935.17
Conte, Carlos 1923.07, 1923.31, 1926.01
Conte, Carol 1968.03, 1969.14
Conte, John 1947.17, 1950.04, 1954.07
Content, Marjorie 1924.14
Conterno, Signor 1875.21
Contet, Henri 1959.15, 1961.25, 1981.04
Conti, Louisa 1916.03
Conti, Louise 1918.20
Conti, Messr. 1883.48
Conti, Nina 1884.40
Conti, Signor 1883.48
Continer, Anthony 1934.37
Contracts International, Ltd. 1990.15
Contreras, Jose 1975.19
Contreras, Ray 1978.11
Contursi, P. 1985.07, 1999.18
Convere, Lila 1896.27, 1897.44
Convere, Marienne 1894.47
Convers, Mr. 1852.06
Convers, Philip 1925.47
Converse, F. 1865.03
Converse, Frank B. 1884.62
Converse, Harry 1929.24
Converse, Harry E. 1905.56
Converse, Hugh 1897.33
Converse, Leighton 1926.38
Converse, Mr. 1859.03
Conville, Frank 1955.04
Convy, Bert 1959.14, 1960.12, 1962.24, 1963.16, 1964.27, 1966.24
Conway, Bert 1941.01
Conway, Bill 1940.09
Conway, C. 1917.03
Conway, Carl 1949.17
Conway, Curt 1936.28, 1941.01, 1942.05
Conway, Diane 1967.15
Conway, Evelyn 1914.23, 1915.31, 1916.10, 1916.24, 1917.03, 1917.22
Conway, F. 1851.07
Conway, Fawn 1912.13, 1912.48, 1919.03
Conway, Frank 1888.11, 1891.37, 1894.13, 1902.07, 1903.34
Conway, Fred 1959.02
Conway, Hart 1879.21, 1879.50, 1879.56, 1880.04, 1881.24, 1889.12
Conway, Leo 1924.31
Conway, Lizziey 1897.38
Conway, Louise 1892.22, 1892.33
Conway, Mamie 1891.40
Conway, Marianne 1883.10
Conway, Marie 1930.08
Conway, Maude 1891.11
Conway, Minnie 1875.21
Conway, Mme. 1834.02
Conway, Morgan 1936.07
Conway, Mr. 1851.01, 1854.01
Conway, Peggy 1925.17, 1927.16
Conway, Russel 1942.11
Conway, Shirl 1955.01
Conway, Timothy 1918.10
Conwell, Mary 1902.24, 1904.30
Conwell, May 1904.19
Conwell, O'Kane 1915.28, 1916.07, 1916.18, 1919.44, 1920.04, 1920.13, 1920.39
Conwell, Virginia 1948.25, 1949.08
Conwit, Phil 1939.19
Conyers, Addie 1889.54
Conyers, Mr. 1852.03
Conyngham, Mary 1900.37
Coogan, Gussie 1890.23
Coogan, Jack 1975.09
Cook and Fields 1920.17
Cook, Abbie Mitchell 1900.46, 1908.08
Cook, Adelaide 1875.21
Cook, Alice 1896.29
Cook, Anna E. 1900.46
Cook, Arthur 1887.23, 1888.31
Cook, Augustus 1884.53, 1897.20, 1904.02
Cook, Aynsley 1858.03
Cook, Barbara 1951.15, 1953.09, 1954.07, 1955.01, 1956.15, 1957.11, 1957.18, 1960.11, 1961.27, 1963.14, 1964.35, 1966.14, 1971.16, 1987.06
Cook, Candace 1972.07
Cook, Carole 1980.20
Cook, Caroline 1898.77
Cook, Cecil 1903.33
Cook, Charles 1944.14, 1950.01, 1952.02, 1965.18
Cook, Charles "Cookie" 1980.10
Cook, Charles Emerson 1900.03, 1903.36, 1907.08
Cook, Charles L. 1941.07, 1942.01
Cook, Christine 1904.27
Cook, Clyde 1919.22
Cook, Edith Miller 1904.02
Cook, Ethel 1921.15
Cook, F.N. 1861.06
Cook, Frank 1949.06
Cook, Frederick 1860.06
Cook, Furneaux 1879.70, 1879.72

Cook, George 1955.21, 1955.22, 1962.25, 1962.28, 1962.29, 1962.30, 1964.37, 1964.38, 1964.41, 1964.42, 1964.43, 1966.22, 1966.23, 1966.25, 1966.26, 1968.25, 1968.27, 1968.28, 1978.17, 1989.15
Cook, Gerald 1954.11
Cook, Geraldine 1900.35
Cook, Gloria 1936.07
Cook, Gordon 1967.10, 1967.17, 1968.08
Cook, Howard A. 1918.10
Cook, J. 1864.23
Cook, J.A. 1882.62, 1885.33
Cook, James 1911.26, 1979.22
Cook, James F. 1908.44, 1909.14
Cook, Jill 1980.29, 1983.06
Cook, Joe 1923.21, 1924.31, 1925.48, 1928.08, 1930.28, 1933.21, 1940.16, 1979.28
Cook, John 1961.09
Cook, John H. 1903.08
Cook, Joseph 1919.25
Cook, Jr., Elisha 1926.02
Cook, Jr., Joe 1936.06, 1942.20
Cook, Louise 1914.21, 1915.30, 1916.22, 1933.06
Cook, Marie 1916.24, 1918.11, 1919.22, 1920.25
Cook, Messr. 1868.23, 1870.02
Cook, Millie 1871.19, 1872.13, 1873.08, 1875.19, 1875.23, 1875.26, 1875.37, 1875.38, 1875.40, 1876.01
Cook, Milly 1872.37
Cook, Miss 1873.26, 1897.41, 1917.03
Cook, Mr. 1869.45
Cook, Mrs. 1857.07
Cook, Nellie 1871.14
Cook, Olga 1919.30, 1921.02, 1921.31, 1924.29
Cook, Ollie 1899.21
Cook, Pearl 1913.35
Cook, Peter 1962.23, 1964.45, 1966.15, 1973.13
Cook, Phil 1922.29, 1924.10, 1925.35
Cook, Philip 1951.16, 1955.10
Cook, Pierre 1995.04
Cook, Ralph 1930.09
Cook, Ray 1946.22, 1951.15, 1977.05, 1981.14
Cook, Roderick 1963.29, 1968.19, 1981.10, 1986.19
Cook, Rosa 1888.25, 1889.43, 1893.06, 1896.18
Cook, Rose 1869.08
Cook, Victor Trent 1989.09, 1995.03, 1997.21, 2001.09
Cook, Will A. 1922.44
Cook, Will Marion 1898.41, 1899.33, 1900.20, 1901.08, 1901.23, 1902.16, 1903.08, 1903.41, 1904.21, 1904.43, 1906.14, 1908.08, 1908.36, 1910.18, 1910.30, 1927.32, 1953.12
Cook, William 1927.29
Cook, William Marion 1904.26
Cooke, Anna 1899.33
Cooke, Arthur 1888.31
Cooke, Charles 1940.01, 1940.17, 1944.27
Cooke, Charles C. 1941.11
Cooke, Charles E. 1952.08
Cooke, Charles L. 1930.29, 1932.12, 1933.16, 1939.17, 1940.23, 1941.13, 1946.07, 1954.09, 1970.11
Cooke, Edmund Vance 1897.39, 1898.47
Cooke, Emerson 1898.31
Cooke, Harold 1940.03
Cooke, J. 1853.05, 1854.04, 1855.10, 1857.05, 1857.07
Cooke, J.P. 1870.01, 1870.14, 1870.40, 1871.02, 1878.14
Cooke, Jeanette 1916.22
Cooke, Jeannette 1917.06, 1919.05
Cooke, John 1859.08, 1860.01, 1862.03
Cooke, John B. 1917.07
Cooke, John T. 1864.13
Cooke, Johnny 1924.31
Cooke, Jonathan P. 1867.17
Cooke, L.C. 1986.02
Cooke, M. 1854.04
Cooke, Malcolm 1983.17
Cooke, Martin 1945.14
Cooke, Master 1878.14
Cooke, Messr. 1851.01
Cooke, Mildred 1907.01
Cooke, Miss 1841.01, 1851.04
Cooke, Mrs. 1854.04
Cooke, P. 1880.17
Cooke, Rosa 1866.04, 1879.64, 1881.43, 1882.21, 1882.22, 1882.23, 1882.43, 1882.46, 1884.18, 1887.19, 1887.43, 1892.17, 1895.11, 1896.18, 1897.54
Cooke, Rosina 1897.51
Cooke, Sally 1974.17, 1981.05
Cooke, Sam 1990.15
Cooks, Charlie 1943.20
Cooks, Lee Roy 1975.12
Cooksey, Curtis 1925.37, 1943.08
Cookson, Peter 1953.07, 1958.05
Cooley, Dennis 1971.12, 1974.25
Cooley, Eddie 1983.20, 1999.09
Cooley, Florence 1894.23
Cooley, Lillian 1894.13, 1895.38, 1897.02, 1897.52
Cooley, William 1905.14
Coolidge, Beulah 1898.28
Coolidge, Buelah 1898.56
Coolidge, Philip 1944.32, 1947.08, 1950.11, 1953.16
Coolman, C. DeWitt 1908.18
Coolman, DeWitt 1912.02, 1914.31
Coolman, DeWitt C. 1910.20, 1912.44, 1913.16
Coolman, Dewitt C. 1914.12
Coombs, Frank 1910.24
Coombs, Frank T. 1972.21
Coombs, J. Parker 1907.54, 1908.26, 1909.20, 1918.23
Coombs, J.P. 1906.46, 1916.15, 1917.16
Coombs, Kristi 1983.17
Coombs, Louis 1919.28
Coombs, Parker 1904.10
Coombs, Richard 1917.10
Coomes, Frank 1904.22
Cooney, Kevin 1994.06
Cooney, M.A. 1877.36
Cooney, Ray 1977.01
Cooper, Adam 1998.10
Cooper, Alice 1881.36, 1982.22
Cooper, Anita 1957.02
Cooper, Anthony Kemble 1964.04
Cooper, Ashley 1924.46, 1931.32
Cooper, Beatrice 1902.33
Cooper, Bigelow 1904.33, 1906.34
Cooper, Bud 1924.13
Cooper, Carrie 1905.31
Cooper, Catherine 1905.03, 1907.63
Cooper, Chuck 1983.15, 1997.08
Cooper, Claude 1906.33, 1910.02
Cooper, Edwin 1939.19
Cooper, Fred 1882.20, 1882.25, 1936.01
Cooper, Gene 1968.31, 1972.04
Cooper, George 1876.31, 1879.32, 1884.62, 1906.03, 1909.16
Cooper, George W. 1923.11, 1928.18
Cooper, Harry 1910.35, 1912.25, 1913.30
Cooper, Helmar Augustus 1990.14
Cooper, Horace 1945.20, 1948.26, 1951.02
Cooper, Hy 1945.17
Cooper, Irving 1929.25
Cooper, Irwin 1951.10
Cooper, James 1881.28, 1905.37, 1934.37
Cooper, Jane 1898.47, 1935.18
Cooper, Jerry 1940.12
Cooper, Jimmie 1929.25
Cooper, Joe 1912.25, 1913.06
Cooper, John W. 1930.16
Cooper, Katherine 1904.04
Cooper, Kevin 1999.09
Cooper, Laura 1972.26
Cooper, Lew 1913.06, 1918.32, 1919.19, 1943.10
Cooper, Lillian Kemble 1919.25, 1920.04
Cooper, Lou 1942.05, 1942.26
Cooper, Madeline 1907.31
Cooper, Marilyn 1956.02, 1957.03, 1959.13, 1962.05, 1967.06, 1968.03, 1970.19, 1971.15, 1981.10
Cooper, Mary 1943.23
Cooper, Maurice 1939.15
Cooper, Max 1927.02, 1994.13
Cooper, Melville 1935.14, 1943.09, 1944.16, 1945.04, 1946.18, 1950.11, 1951.13, 1957.04
Cooper, Messr. 1882.04, 1882.20, 1886.19, 1886.20
Cooper, Millie 1880.63
Cooper, Miss 1841.01, 1881.07
Cooper, Mons. 1885.55, 1885.56, 1885.57, 1885.59, 1885.61, 1886.08, 1886.09, 1886.21
Cooper, Pamela 1985.03
Cooper, Peggy 1969.16, 1970.15, 1975.06
Cooper, Percy 1882.57
Cooper, Percy F. 1881.45
Cooper, Percy J. 1881.42, 1881.44
Cooper, Rex 1954.02
Cooper, Richard 1921.16
Cooper, Robert 1949.18
Cooper, Robert M. 1976.04
Cooper, Roy 1969.04
Cooper, Saralou 1960.05
Cooper, Scott 1904.35, 1905.26
Cooper, Sheila 1987.16
Cooper, Terrence 1999.06
Cooper, Tex 1920.27, 1931.02
Cooper, Theodore 1949.17
Cooper-Hecht, Gail 1987.14, 1990.16
Coopersmith, James 1966.18
Coopersmith, Jerome 1965.02
Coor, E. 1870.35
Coote, Bert 1885.68
Coote, Charles 1886.36, 1886.59, 1887.25, 1887.52, 1894.25, 1895.42
Coote, Henry 1904.57, 1905.08, 1905.11, 1905.22, 1906.49, 1907.17, 1907.58, 1909.08, 1923.09
Coote, Lucy 1892.17
Coote, Robert 1956.01, 1960.21, 1976.05
Coots, Clayton 1957.17
Coots, Fred 1930.05, 1992.18
Coots, J. Fred 1921.27, 1921.42, 1922.23, 1922.31, 1923.13, 1924.13, 1924.36, 1925.11, 1925.23, 1925.26, 1925.27, 1925.43, 1926.01, 1926.15, 1926.37, 1927.53, 1928.06, 1928.22, 1929.44, 1975.22, 1980.10, 1981.16
Coover, Rex 1932.15
Cope, Harry 1881.31
Copeland, Andrew 1931.47
Copeland, George 1925.09
Copeland, Jane 1951.14, 1952.15
Copeland, Joan 1964.35, 1970.19, 1976.19
Copeland, Les 1912.29, 1917.13
Copeland, Martha 1929.50
Copeland, Nick 1933.15
Copeland, Virginia 1954.18
Copeland, William 1940.21
Copello, Carlos 1999.18
Copes, Johana 1999.18
Copes, Juan Carlos 1962.02, 1985.07, 1999.18
Copin, George 1881.31
Copinger, Inc. 1922.41
Copland, Aaron 2001.04
Coplen, Yorke 1931.01
Coppe, Carlo 1895.08
Coppel, Alec 1958.02
Coppin, Grace 1937.12
Coppini, Ettore 1883.48, 1884.39, 1887.27
Coppola, Anton 1952.09, 1954.09, 1962.14, 1964.03, 1964.20, 1965.20, 1966.07, 1968.17
Coppola, William 1961.09, 1961.13
Coppola, William J. 1965.31
Coquatrix, Bruno 1964.02, 1968.04, 1973.17
Coquerelle, Rene 1958.06
Coraglia, Mlle. 1875.07
Coral, Tito 1927.19, 1932.07, 1939.18, 1948.27
Coram, Ralph 1926.01
Corbeil, Claude 1982.07
Corbett, Andrew 1998.10
Corbett, Charlotte 1907.15
Corbett, Dan 1927.04
Corbett, Edward 1893.33, 1898.55
Corbett, James J. 1899.36, 1917.23
Corbett, Jim 1962.02
Corbett, Leonora 1946.20
Corbin, Edw. 1893.14, 1894.02
Corbin, Frederick 1907.27
Corbley, James F. 1903.26
Corbley, James H. 1903.26
Corby, Don 1961.12
Corby, Donald 1960.08
Corby, Joseph 1964.17, 1967.05
Corcoran, Bill 1993.05
Corcoran, Jack 1914.34
Corcoran, Jane 1926.12
Corcoran, Josephine 1879.15
Corcoran, Teri 1979.05
Corday, Diana 1942.21, 1945.09
Corday, Genise 1922.31
Corday, Mary 1922.31
Corday, Ottilie 1923.42
Corday, Peggy 1944.16
Cordelia, Mme. 1896.04
Cordell, Christopher 1997.22
Cordell, Sandyl 1955.25
Corden, Juliette 1894.40, 1895.24
Corder, Leeta 1923.37, 1926.05
Corder, Paul 1966.02
Cordes, Fred A. 1908.43
Cordes, Miriam 1908.43
Cordner, Blaine 1926.28, 1928.41, 1929.20, 1929.27, 1944.23
Cordoba, Daniel 1949.07
Cordon, Juliette 1893.05
Cordon, Lillian 1904.32
Cordon, Norman 1947.02
Cordova, Richard 1996.16
Cordova, Victoria 1941.07, 1946.13, 1947.13
Cordrey, Peggy 1943.07
Corduner, Allan 1997.06
Cordy, Henry 1965.04
Core, Natalie 1959.27
Corelli, Blanche 1879.07, 1879.11, 1880.63, 1884.28, 1884.29, 1884.30, 1884.31
Corelli, Carlo 1951.22
Corey, Arthur 1922.01
Corey, Irwin 1942.34, 1948.23, 1950.01, 1951.15
Corey, Madison 1893.31, 1895.39, 1897.49, 1917.32
Corey, Wendell 1944.01
Corhan, Michel 1947.09
Corin, J.P. 1906.34
Corin, Joel P. 1908.27, 1910.10
Corinne 1888.11, 1904.49
Corio, Ann 1965.05, 1981.17
Cork, Frank 1937.07
Cork, J. Frank 1921.06, 1922.40, 1925.43
Corkrey, Colleen 1960.01
Corlett, Irene 1919.11, 1942.15, 1943.18
Corlette, Ethel 1887.34, 1889.06
Corley, Nick 1993.10, 1994.12, 1995.19, 1996.15, 1999.21, 2000.19
Corliss, E.W. 1902.07
Corliss, Edward W. 1899.41, 1901.06, 1902.15
Corliss, William 1899.40, 1902.18
Corliss, William H. 1896.45
Corliss, William S. 1897.50, 1903.38
Cormack, L. Shannon 1918.10
Corman, Paul A. 1976.36
Cormelli 1913.26
Cormican, Peter 2001.02
Cormon, Adolphe 1878.01
Cormon, Eugene 1869.24, 1876.07, 1877.12, 1878.09, 1882.29
Cormon, Jules 1884.18, 1900.30
Cornalba, Adele 1879.42, 1880.08, 1880.63, 1882.45, 1883.47, 1884.27, 1885.46, 1887.32, 1890.50
Cornalba, Mlle. 1880.41, 1881.02
Cornejo, Rudolfo 1955.27
Cornelious, E. Clayton 2000.11
Cornelis, Marcel 1958.06
Cornelius, Chip 1983.14
Cornell, Frank 1919.14
Cornell, Grace 1932.19
Cornell, L. 1873.21
Cornell, Michael 1990.07
Cornell, Nord 1943.12
Cornell, Olive 1920.18
Cornell, Peggy 1928.07, 1928.46, 1929.32, 1933.22
Cornell, W.W. 1882.31
Cornett, Barbara 1961.11
Cornett, Stanley 1987.08
Corney, Arthur 1884.44
Cornforth, Annie 1869.35, 1870.04
Cornil 1882.62, 1886.41
Cornil, Mons. 1875.21
Cornish, Edith 1885.26
Corns, W.J. 1894.12
Cornu, Dean 1936.01
Cornu, Louis F. 1893.40
Cornu, Louis J. 1888.15
Cornwall, Ardon 1937.10, 1937.16
Cornwell, Ardon 1939.29
Cornwell, Dean 1923.25, 1924.36
Cornwell, Eric 1998.11
Cornwell, O'Kane 1920.36
Corona, Sandro 1934.06
Corray, Percy 1909.01
Corray, Robert 1909.01
Correia, Don 1980.29, 1982.01, 1983.09, 1985.08
Correra, Emilio Arrieta y 1881.24
Corri, Haydn 1875.19
Corrigan, John F. 1894.06, 1906.46
Corrigan, Mary Ann 1964.04
Corrigan, Nancy 1927.16

Corrigan, Richard 1960.08
Corrish, Lester 1912.01
Corrister, Messr. 1868.16
Corrister, Mr. 1867.15, 1867.16
Corrister, W. 1867.17, 1868.08
Corrister, W.D. 1865.03
Corrister, William D. 1871.12, 1871.16
Corry, Pittman 1944.15, 1945.01
Corsaro, Frank 1975.19, 1979.05, 1980.15, 1985.13, 1986.09
Corsaut, John 1982.18
Corsell, Henry 1928.25
Corsi, Adelaide 1946.13
Cort, Harry L. 1918.39, 1919.33, 1920.35, 1922.08, 1923.06, 1923.42, 1925.04, 1927.10, 1934.04
Cort, Irene 1938.19
Cort, John 1907.26, 1912.04, 1912.42, 1912.47, 1913.06, 1913.35, 1915.08, 1915.23, 1916.08, 1916.17, 1917.34, 1918.26, 1918.33, 1918.39, 1919.24, 1919.33, 1920.35, 1921.39, 1923.42
Cort, Muriel 1922.05
Cortelezzi, Louis 1979.11
Cortelyou, Sadie 1885.04
Cortelyou, Winthrop 1927.34
Cortes, Armand 1901.19, 1906.37, 1908.40
Cortes, Cece 1994.02
Cortes, Jose 1986.17
Cortese, Dominic 1955.10
Cortez, Armand 1944.22
Cortez, Armond 1905.20
Cortez, Billie 1928.18, 1929.25
Cortez, Don 1929.32, 1938.13, 1940.08, 1945.17
Cortez, John 1933.01
Cortez, M. 1902.24
Cortez, Stephen 1920.47, 1930.27
Corthell, Herbert 1905.48, 1911.06, 1913.18, 1914.08, 1916.05, 1917.04, 1919.06, 1919.32, 1922.08, 1923.41, 1925.23, 1925.32
Corthell, Hubert 1904.27
Corti, Jesse 1987.04
Corti, Jim 1974.06, 1998.01
Cortis, Mme. 1931.38
Cortland, Helene 1885.31
Cortland, Marjorie 1908.21
Cortland, Rosa 1880.55
Cortlandt, Xesia 1887.43
Corto, Diana 1961.07, 1962.18, 1968.23
Corvalan, Juan 1993.08
Corvera, Lucita 1924.36, 1926.15
Corwey, Ferry 1920.26, 1921.28, 1937.15
Corwin, Arlene 1959.12
Corwin, Norman 1942.05
Cory, Joan 1964.11
Coryphees, Mlle. 1872.06, 1872.10
Cosby, John 1935.05, 1935.07, 1935.08, 1935.10
Cosden, Robert 1956.15
Cosgraye, J.G. 1892.27
Cosgrove 1891.02, 1894.16
Cosgrove, Mytrle 1905.18
Coslow, Sam 1921.34, 1922.34, 1924.36, 1924.46, 1927.39, 1956.02, 1984.10
Cosma, Joseph 1959.15
Cosmos, Jean 1961.25
Cosmowska, L. 1924.48
Coss, E.C. 1878.10
Cossa, Dominic 1974.16, 1980.03, 1980.21, 1981.20, 1981.22, 1984.12
Cossart, Ernest 1908.25, 1934.29
Cossart, Valerie 1948.11
Cossette, Pierre 1991.07, 1992.18, 1997.19, 1999.08
Costa, Davide 1866.18, 1868.03, 1868.06, 1868.18, 1869.26, 1870.05, 1870.30, 1870.44, 1871.27
Costa, Giuseppe 1932.29, 1934.02
Costa, Madame 1866.18, 1868.03
Costa, Mme. 1868.06, 1869.26
Costa, Nelaci 1992.13
Costa, Richard 1995.07
Costa, Signor 1870.04
Costa-Greenspon, Muriel 1963.15, 1963.23, 1964.13, 1965.07, 1965.09, 1965.11, 1965.12, 1965.26, 1966.02, 1968.09, 1968.12, 1969.11, 1974.08, 1975.11, 1975.17, 1976.22, 1977.03, 1977.17, 1980.21, 1980.25, 1981.20, 1981.21, 1982.07, 1982.20, 1983.13, 1984.11, 1985.09, 1986.08, 1986.14, 1987.03, 1987.08, 1988.04, 1988.16, 1989.14, 1993.12
Costabile, David 1997.06
Costallos, Suzanne 1983.14, 1999.15
Costanza, Peter 1965.28, 1968.17
Costanzo, Anthony Roth 1995.19
Costar, Miss 1863.02
Costellanos, J. 1906.47
Costello, Ambrose 1939.13
Costello, Amby 1933.20
Costello, Andy 1932.18
Costello, Bartley 1912.06
Costello, Bartley C. 1902.43, 1903.14, 1904.03, 1911.04
Costello, Diosa 1939.27, 1941.03
Costello, Don 1933.02
Costello, Edward 1918.17
Costello, J.R. 1890.50
Costello, Lou 1939.22
Costello, Miss 1904.13
Costenyra, Miss 1872.35
Costigan, James 1963.16
Costignero, Miss 1873.24
Costin, Bill 1955.04
Costley, Guy 1976.11
Coston, Rex 1947.21
Cote, Emile 1927.12, 1927.48
Cothran, Dorothy 1947.01
Cothran, Robert 1986.11
Cotlow, Marilyn 1947.10
Cotrelly, Mathilde 1885.14, 1885.52
Cotsirilos, Stephanie 1982.09
Cotsworth, Staats 1972.06
Cotta, G. 1876.21
Cotta, Messr. 1876.17
Cotta, Mr. 1890.31, 1891.33, 1894.01
Cottam, Kent 1973.09, 1989.18
Cotte, Julie 1898.42
Cottee, Evelyn 1905.04
Cotter, Anna Marie 1930.33
Cotter, Nora 1911.40
Cotton, Fred 1943.23
Cotton, Idalene 1895.37, 1899.37, 1900.07, 1901.23
Cotton, Messr. 1856.04
Cotton, R.F. 1895.17, 1897.23
Cotton, Robert F. 1890.28, 1899.15
Cottrell, Harry 1887.05
Cottrell, William 1894.44, 1969.07
Cottrelly, Mathilda 1903.40
Cottrelly, Mathilde 1879.57, 1879.62, 1880.20, 1880.61, 1880.66, 1882.71, 1883.45, 1883.62, 1884.08, 1884.14, 1884.51, 1884.57, 1885.05, 1885.28, 1885.45, 1885.67, 1886.26, 1886.33, 1886.43, 1887.12, 1887.18, 1887.22, 1887.24, 1887.47, 1888.19, 1888.24, 1888.26, 1889.17, 1889.22, 1890.28, 1893.28, 1894.19, 1896.25, 1897.46, 1901.14
Cotty, Eileen 1919.02
Couacevich, Nicholas 1962.17
Couch, Lucy 1883.04
Coudray, Clara 1892.07, 1892.16
Coudray, Miss 1892.07
Coudray, Peggy 1937.08, 1939.19
Coudy, Douglas 1945.09
Couelite, Mons. 1871.28
Cougat, Xavier 1927.19
Cough, Mr. 1869.13
Coughlan, Bruce 1996.18
Coughlan, H. 1918.15
Coughley, Belle 1901.04
Coughlin, Bruce 1982.08, 1996.05, 1997.18, 1998.03, 1998.16, 1999.04, 2000.08
Coughlin, James 1933.20
Coughlin, Kevin 1956.03
Couldock, Miss 1860.06
Coullet, Rhonda 1976.30
Coulombel, Genevieve 1958.18
Coult, Carol 1939.19
Coulter, Charles 1883.65
Coulter, Dorothy 1928.45
Coulter, Frazer 1891.28, 1913.19, 1918.01
Coulter, Kay 1954.12
Coulter, Ned 1981.19
Countryman, William 1969.08
Coupe, Diane 1962.24, 1963.25, 1964.11, 1965.37, 1966.10
Coupe, Walter 1919.41, 1920.13, 1921.05
Courage, A.M. 1949.09
Coursen, Frieda 1920.46
Courson, Robert 1983.07, 1989.22
Court, Belle 1906.24
Courtain, Harry 1881.03
Courtaine, Harry 1888.34
Courtaine, Mrs. Harry 1885.21
Courtenay, Maud 1895.20
Courtes, Mons. 1893.25
Courtland, Jerome 1951.15
Courtleigh, William 1906.27, 1922.16
Courtneidge, Charles 1925.50
Courtneidge, Cicely 1925.50, 1947.15
Courtneidge, Robert 1905.55, 1907.32, 1907.51
Courtney, Ada 1893.07
Courtney, Aida 1891.38
Courtney, Anna 1899.04
Courtney, Bill 1977.09
Courtney, C.C. 1971.10
Courtney, Charles 1899.19
Courtney, Dennis 1979.22
Courtney, Edith 1894.15
Courtney, Edna 1884.21, 1884.40
Courtney, G. 1898.43
Courtney, George 1896.48
Courtney, Inez 1921.04, 1926.34, 1927.41, 1929.02, 1929.12, 1931.04, 1933.21
Courtney, Jack 1977.09, 1978.26
Courtney, Mabel 1901.09
Courtney, Mabelle 1907.01
Courtney, Marguerite 1963.25
Courtney, Marion 1922.27
Courtney, Maud 1901.04
Courtney, Maybelle 1902.27
Courtney, Minerva 1900.35, 1901.08, 1902.24, 1903.23, 1924.16
Courtney, Neil 1923.17
Courtney, Perqueta 1925.34, 1926.39, 1927.64
Courtney, Ragan 1971.10
Courtney, Sheila 1920.08
Courtney, William 1880.18, 1918.27
Courtright, William 1876.33
Courtwright, Billy 1877.03
Courtwright, William 1877.05, 1880.35
Cousens, Lenora 1896.01
Cousin Joe Maphis 1954.08
Cousin, Tome 2000.07
Cousins, Derek 1969.04
Cousins, Fred W. 1906.26
Cousins, Michael 1986.10, 1986.14, 1987.10, 1987.11, 1988.16
Cousins, Virgie 1921.26
Couteur, Julie 1886.50, 1886.54
Couturier 1964.28
Covan, Willie 1924.37, 1925.14
Covarrubias, Miguel 1925.17
Coveney, Howard 1887.49
Coventry, Gerald 1886.17, 1895.03, 1897.46, 1902.19, 1903.14, 1904.12
Coventry, Gerard 1904.15
Coventry, Julia 1875.39
Cover, H.B. 1902.38
Covera, Lucita 1924.06
Coverdale, Minerva 1906.01, 1911.26, 1915.02, 1919.01
Coverly, Robert 1895.23
Coverly, Roger D. 1903.28
Coverra, Leslie 1911.24
Covert, Bruce 1936.26
Covert, Don 1951.23
Covey, Edna 1926.18
Covey, Marion 1947.02
Coville, Samuel 1880.24
Covington, Robert 1918.14
Covington, Zellah 1919.44
Cowan, Edie 1968.07, 1977.06
Cowan, Edwardyne 1993.18
Cowan, Grant 1971.11
Cowan, Harry 1910.07
Cowan, Helen 1930.07
Cowan, Irv 1983.20
Cowan, Jerome 1933.22, 1957.17, 1958.08
Cowan, Lillian 1930.19
Cowan, Marge 1983.20
Cowan, Marianne 1936.03
Cowan, Robert 1898.47
Cowan, Rubey 1919.26
Cowan, Tom 1926.22
Coward, Edward Fales 1899.36
Coward, Noël 1924.01, 1925.42, 1928.42, 1929.20, 1929.29, 1929.41, 1931.14, 1931.19, 1934.13, 1934.34, 1936.29, 1939.07, 1942.14, 1948.11, 1952.11, 1961.18, 1963.29, 1964.16, 1968.19, 1974.09, 1975.12, 1975.22, 1986.19, 1988.08, 1989.06
Cowdery, J.T. 1897.11
Cowdery, Messr. 1897.03
Cowdery, Richard 1938.11
Cowell, Joseph 1823.01
Cowell, Sydney 1876.23
Cowell, Virginia 1949.08
Cowen, Frederick 1893.04
Cowherd, Jon C. 1999.24
Cowie, Margaret 1972.06
Cowl, Jane 1932.03
Cowl, Martin 1932.03
Cowles, Albert 1907.02, 1927.15
Cowles, Chandler 1946.10, 1947.10, 1947.21, 1948.22, 1948.29, 1950.05, 1950.13, 1952.07, 1954.18, 1960.02
Cowles, Eugene 1891.29, 1892.51, 1893.18, 1893.19, 1893.48, 1894.03, 1894.08, 1894.45, 1895.01, 1896.08, 1896.42, 1896.43, 1897.13, 1898.23, 1899.34, 1903.37, 1906.27, 1908.36, 1909.23, 1911.21, 1912.18, 1912.21, 1912.22, 1912.23, 1914.11, 1919.20
Cowles, Eugeneh W. 1898.60
Cowles, Frances 1926.17, 1928.19
Cowley, Mr. 1841.01
Cowley, William 1968.25, 1968.26, 1968.27, 1968.28, 1968.29, 1976.12, 1976.14
Cowper, A. 1881.20
Cox, Adele 1905.55
Cox, Catherine 1976.33, 1979.05, 1983.19, 1986.19, 1998.13
Cox, Conway 1868.20, 1869.07
Cox, Eddie 1919.34
Cox, Fred 1912.30
Cox, Gertrude "Baby" 1933.06
Cox, Harry 1872.09, 1872.11
Cox, Hazel 1906.02, 1908.28, 1910.10, 1911.13, 1911.29, 1913.18, 1915.08, 1915.28, 1919.30
Cox, Hazell 1918.05
Cox, Ida 1982.12
Cox, India 1930.01
Cox, J. 1881.32
Cox, Jimmy 1975.20, 1982.12
Cox, Louise 1887.24, 1918.07
Cox, Mabel 1907.06
Cox, Nellie 1885.28
Cox, Palmer 1894.42
Cox, Ray 1911.12, 1911.35, 1912.36, 1974.02
Cox, Richard 1972.01, 1978.25
Cox, Samuel P. 1888.04, 1888.34, 1890.10
Cox, Susie 1887.18
Cox, Tony 1993.17
Cox, Veanne 1986.20, 1995.11
Cox, Wally 1950.03
Cox, Wilbur 1917.11, 1920.11
Cox, William 1976.33, 1978.10
Cox, Wilma 1932.13, 1933.05
Coy, Johnny 1949.01
Coye, Guenn 1891.34
Coye, Jean 1891.34
Coyle, E. 1872.02, 1872.04, 1872.08
Coyle, E.C. 1872.36
Coyle, Elizabeth 1919.22, 1922.05
Coyle, Hugh 1890.25
Coyle, Jack 1927.39
Coyle, James 1937.11
Coyle, John 1960.06, 1963.17
Coyle, Julia 1882.15
Coyle, Mary 1930.08
Coyle, Wally 1927.41, 1929.29, 1930.32, 1945.03, 1947.11
Coyler, Austin 1966.11, 1967.09, 1976.19, 1985.08
Coyne, Helen 1905.40
Coyne, Helene 1922.28
Coyne, Jeanne 1945.18
Coyne, Joe 1905.20
Coyne, Joseph 1897.30, 1900.52, 1901.04, 1902.01, 1903.23, 1904.56, 1906.17, 1906.32
Coyne, Phoebe 1900.44, 1901.18, 1901.27, 1904.55, 1907.58
Cozzi, Esther 1911.19
Crabtree, Don 1959.11, 1961.08, 1962.01, 1963.12, 1963.26, 1964.32, 1966.05, 1980.20
Crabtree, J.A. 1883.40
Crabtree, Lotta 1864.14, 1867.19, 1867.20, 1868.04, 1868.19, 1868.22, 1869.40, 1869.44, 1870.34, 1871.13, 1871.20, 1871.21, 1876.32, 1876.35, 1877.02, 1878.14, 1880.17, 1881.18, 1883.40, 1884.46, 1885.68
Crabtree, Paul 1949.17
Cracraft, Tom Adrian 1933.16, 1937.11
Craddock, Earle 1924.22
Craddock, Ethel 1895.10
Craddock, Louis 1930.16
Craetive Management Ltd. 2000.04

Craft, Helen 1934.14
Craft, Morton 1964.02
Craft, Mr. 1860.01
Craft, Selma 1964.02
Craft, Sylvia 1911.28
Craft, Tom 1997.13
Crafts, Charles 1924.15
Crage, Herr 1910.18
Craig, Alex 1913.22
Craig, Alice 1938.14
Craig, Althe 1896.27
Craig, Amanda 1923.11
Craig, Betsy 1980.26
Craig, Brad 1962.17
Craig, C.G. 1880.08
Craig, Charles G. 1918.42
Craig, Dagmar 1957.09
Craig, David 1952.07, 1957.14
Craig, Dick 1948.19, 1949.05
Craig, Donald 1977.06
Craig, George 1922.07
Craig, Helen 1936.12, 1946.05
Craig, J. 1896.44
Craig, Jack 1975.21, 1978.04
Craig, Jerry 1949.18, 1953.01
Craig, Joel 1961.28, 1962.24, 1973.07, 1975.24
Craig, John 1892.14, 1956.16, 1965.27
Craig, Jr., Richy 1926.28, 1932.13
Craig, Jr., Ritchie 1926.11
Craig, Lillie 1886.45
Craig, Lucretia 1922.41, 1923.27
Craig, Mabel 1886.45, 1886.59
Craig, Noel 1976.25, 1983.08
Craig, Ollie 1900.28
Craig, R. 1974.19
Craig, Richard 1941.11, 1946.14, 1947.12
Craig, Ritchy 1924.34
Craig, Robert 1872.23
Craig, Thomas 1956.08
Craig, Tobie 1901.12
Craig, Virginia 1963.13, 1970.08
Craig, Walter 1929.33
Craigen, Maida 1886.27
Craigin, Jerrie 1931.08
Craik, Robert 1925.32
Crain, Jon 1953.06, 1956.09, 1956.10, 1958.15, 1962.11, 1962.21, 1964.31, 1965.25
Crain, Stephen 1979.31, 1981.28, 1982.13
Craine, W.C. 1904.38
Cramer, Augustus 1895.29, 1898.17
Cramer, Blanche 1900.20
Cramer, Floyd 1979.16
Cramer, Miss 1884.42
Cramer, Mrs. 1853.03
Cramer, Richard 1919.31, 1923.43
Crampton, Howard 1906.03
Crampton, Ruth 1943.24
Crand, Miss 1866.28
Crandall, Burr 1938.10
Crandall, Catherine 1927.35
Crandall, Elizabeth 1928.50, 1930.07, 1930.12, 1934.13
Crandall, Gail 1905.30
Crandall, Harry 1905.43
Crandall, Victoria 1948.21
Crandell, Elizabeth 1934.43
Crane 1879.06
Crane, A. Wilbur 1904.18, 1905.05
Crane, Alan 1928.35
Crane, Bettymae 1938.08
Crane, Beverly 1938.08
Crane, Cliff 1934.18
Crane, Cora 1881.22
Crane, Dean 1953.17, 1954.15, 1959.05, 1961.10, 1965.38, 1968.32
Crane, Donald 1916.08
Crane, Frank 1875.06, 1880.07, 1894.13
Crane, Frank H. 1898.17
Crane, H.O. 1899.21
Crane, Harold 1907.06, 1907.49, 1910.04, 1911.34, 1912.45, 1919.02, 1923.12, 1925.31, 1929.09, 1932.23
Crane, Harold C. 1901.19
Crane, Irving 1939.19
Crane, Jeanne 1915.01
Crane, Jessie 1914.18, 1915.01
Crane, Jimmy 1962.17
Crane, John 1894.22
Crane, Louise 1894.40
Crane, Raymond 1921.29
Crane, Raymond C. 1922.47
Crane, Rita 1928.35, 1929.08
Crane, S. 1879.01
Crane, S.M. 1877.21
Crane, Seth 1897.11
Crane, Seth M. 1881.22, 1885.03, 1891.47, 1893.03
Crane, Thurston 1936.26
Crane, W. 1885.65
Crane, W.H. 1873.18, 1873.21, 1873.23, 1876.35, 1886.16
Crane, William 1865.11, 1866.02, 1866.28, 1867.12, 1868.06, 1869.31, 1870.26, 1883.06, 1884.40, 1885.46, 1897.29
Crane, William B. 1872.30
Crane, William H. 1872.16, 1872.18, 1872.20, 1872.36, 1876.16, 1894.39
Cranfield, Miss 1866.02
Cranko, John 1956.13
Crankshaw, Edward 1938.02
Cranshaw, Bob 1981.16, 1983.03
Cranston, Gladys 1922.30
Cranston, Robin 1977.09
Cranston, Toller 1977.09
Cranton, Hal 1952.13
Crao, Mme. 1886.20
Crapo 1891.13
Crapo, Harry 1914.03
Craske, Edith 1890.50, 1891.41
Craswell, Gary 1971.21
Crater, Alene 1910.02
Crater, Aline 1906.33
Crater, Allene 1895.08, 1896.31, 1897.28, 1898.32, 1902.07, 1904.13, 1904.44, 1912.39, 1917.22
Crater, Arline 1897.52
Craufurd, Kent 1913.14
Cravat, Noel 1937.01, 1937.16, 1939.16, 1941.02
Cravath, Martin 1932.26
Craven, Alfred 1914.32
Craven, Archie 1898.38
Craven, Edward 1905.55, 1906.17, 1907.18, 1938.15
Craven, Ella 1894.34
Craven, Frank 1916.22, 1917.36, 1920.04, 1920.13, 1922.41, 1926.39, 1975.24
Craven, Hawes 1890.02, 1894.18, 1894.41
Craven, J.T. 1881.21, 1881.33
Craven, John 1888.17
Craven, John T. 1881.15, 1893.14, 1894.02
Craven, Robin 1951.12
Craven, Sally 1940.12
Craven, Sidney 1895.14
Craven, Tom 1904.14
Craven, Walter S. 1903.21
Cravens, Pierce 1996.15, 2001.06
Craver, Sidney 1894.12
Crawford 1894.47
Crawford and Simpson 1899.22
Crawford, Alvin 1990.15
Crawford, Archie 1895.04
Crawford, Bessie 1914.16
Crawford, Boyd 1939.29
Crawford, C. 1892.29
Crawford, Cheryl 1940.05, 1942.03, 1943.15, 1943.19, 1944.03, 1947.07, 1947.09, 1948.17, 1948.25, 1949.16, 1950.10, 1951.15, 1951.24, 1963.09, 1963.25, 1969.02
Crawford, Clarisse 1949.16
Crawford, Clifford 1915.04
Crawford, Clifton 1901.06, 1901.21, 1902.07, 1902.08, 1902.16, 1903.06, 1903.39, 1906.22, 1908.18, 1911.39, 1912.31, 1915.04, 1915.26, 1916.11, 1916.26, 1918.12, 1918.34
Crawford, Clyde 1912.03, 1916.01
Crawford, E. 1892.29
Crawford, E. Albert 1918.13
Crawford, E.H. 1914.33
Crawford, Edith 1894.13
Crawford, Edna Archer 1931.29
Crawford, Edward 1913.24
Crawford, Ellen 1982.10
Crawford, Harry 1886.52, 1924.16
Crawford, James 1992.06
Crawford, Jared 1996.07
Crawford, Jerry 1962.07
Crawford, John 1911.47
Crawford, Joseph 1953.04, 1960.10, 1961.13, 1962.16
Crawford, Kathryn 1930.40
Crawford, Lester 1912.02, 1925.05, 1929.45, 1932.18
Crawford, Lester J. 1911.08
Crawford, Lew 1932.08
Crawford, Margaret 1904.36, 1913.22
Crawford, Marion 1927.22
Crawford, Michael 1988.01, 1992.12
Crawford, Mrs. 1881.39
Crawford, Nan 1924.21
Crawford, Nancy 1904.13
Crawford, Nellie 1913.35, 1919.35
Crawford, Regina 1918.12
Crawford, Robert 1943.23
Crawford, Roberta 1886.36
Crawford, Traverse 1945.08
Crawley, Milton 1928.18
Crawley, Sayre 1932.28
Crayon 1948.21
Creamer, Henry 1916.21, 1917.13, 1918.05, 1920.11, 1921.21, 1921.26, 1922.16, 1922.19, 1922.22, 1922.23, 1922.25, 1923.11, 1923.20, 1924.13, 1924.21, 1925.27, 1926.23, 1927.02, 1927.38, 1928.10, 1929.01, 1930.13, 1975.20, 1975.22, 1989.02
Creamer, Henry S. 1907.55
Crean, Patrick 1973.07
Creash, Bob 1961.25
Creatore, Luigi 1968.24, 1989.12
Crecelius, Albert 1911.03
Creco, William 1923.16
Creed, Kay 1969.11
Creed, Linda 1997.21
Creedon, Richard 1979.28
Creighiton, Bertha 1922.48
Creighton, Georgia 1964.15, 1965.33
Creighton, Maude 1900.16
Creighton, Pat 1955.27, 1956.12
Cremieux, H. 1872.35, 1873.25
Cremieux, Hector 1861.02, 1866.33, 1867.05, 1868.13, 1868.26, 1868.31, 1869.10, 1870.26, 1870.27, 1870.30, 1871.26, 1872.31, 1872.41, 1875.07, 1875.08, 1875.13, 1875.33, 1876.31, 1877.16, 1877.19, 1877.29, 1877.37, 1879.34, 1879.46, 1879.60, 1882.55, 1883.61, 1883.65, 1884.45, 1886.22, 1897.28, 1900.06, 1956.09
Cremieux, Henri 1866.12
Cremin, Susan 1991.06
Creole Producing Company 1922.22
Cressey, Harry 1922.15
Cresson, James 1959.22, 1963.13, 1965.17, 1975.14, 1978.02
Cressy, Will M. 1894.52, 1898.45
Crew-Jones, F. 1906.47
Crews, Laura Hope 1924.23
Crews, Lyndon 1943.06
Crichton, Don 1953.01
Crichton, Kyle 1935.03
Crichton, Madge 1903.22, 1906.32
Crickets, The 1979.16
Crigler, Lynn 1975.03, 1976.25, 1979.05, 1981.03, 1982.05, 1985.04
Crimans, Will C. 1917.17
Crinkle, Nym 1887.14
Crinkley, Richmond 1980.27
Crior, Jesse 1942.13
Cripe, Michael 1995.15
Cripps, Florence 1916.20, 1917.03, 1917.12, 1918.19
Cripps, H.A. 1881.07, 1881.15, 1881.38, 1882.63, 1882.66, 1884.06, 1884.51, 1887.47, 1888.19, 1888.22, 1891.11, 1892.22, 1892.33, 1892.47, 1893.16, 1894.24, 1896.13, 1897.10, 1898.13, 1898.48
Cripps, H.C. 1884.08
Cripps, Herbert 1915.06, 1915.09, 1915.10, 1915.12, 1915.13, 1915.14
Cripps, Herbert A. 1873.12, 1884.14, 1886.37, 1887.04, 1887.26, 1887.28, 1888.24, 1889.22
Cripps, Mr. 1873.14
Crips, Florence 1919.01
Criqui, A.J. 1902.33
Criqui, Major 1908.01
Crisa, Tino 1939.31
Criscuolo, Louis 1972.19
Crisham, Wally 1925.29, 1929.31, 1930.06
Crisp, Donald 1908.14, 1911.33
Crispi, Ida 1906.23
Crissy, Miss 1884.11
Criste, Mirla 1991.03
Cristiani, Belmonte 1942.20
Criswell, Kim 1981.28, 1983.19, 1987.02, 1989.24
Critcherson, Sam 1921.34, 1929.49
Critcherson, Samuel 1918.35
Critchet, Messr. 1862.02
Criterion Productions, Inc. 1923.11
Crittenden, Jean 1928.19
Crittenden, T.D. 1907.51
Crittendon, Jean 1926.13
Crivello, Anthony 1985.17, 1987.04, 1993.09, 1999.22
Croce, Jim 1997.01
Croche 1889.08
Crochet, Laurie 1987.16
Crocker, Alfred 1916.03
Crocker, Donald 1948.27
Crocker, Stan 1999.25
Crocker, Viola 1869.21
Croffut, W.A. 1880.54
Crofoot, Alan 1965.23
Crofoot, Cayle 1977.16
Crofoot, Leonard John 1973.12, 1980.07, 1985.05
Croft, Irma 1908.05
Croft, Mabel 1905.31, 1907.11, 1907.46
Croft, Millie 1884.58
Croft, Paddy 2000.01
Croft, Walter 1915.27, 1919.11, 1919.36
Crofut, Pete 1888.43
Croisille, Nicole 1964.22
Croker, Mrs. B.M. 1904.02
Croker-King, Charles 1928.26
Crolins, H. 1876.35
Crolius, J. 1881.06
Croll, Don 1971.15
Crolla, Henri 1959.15, 1961.25
Crom, Rick 1993.02
Crombie, Laura 1948.07
Cromer, Allan 1926.38
Cromer, Harold 1939.30, 1943.07, 1986.03
Crommette, Jessie 1914.29
Crompton, Maude 1913.33
Crompton, Miss 1869.31, 1921.42
Crompton, Nanci 1953.17
Crompton, W.H. 1879.10
Cromwell, David 1978.06, 1997.19, 1999.13
Cromwell, Irene 1903.31
Cromwell, John 1926.12, 1946.19
Crone, John 1917.08, 1919.30, 1927.04
Cronin, Christopher 1999.25
Cronin, Dan 1980.30
Cronin, J.F. 1902.05
Cronin, Jack 1923.43, 1926.18
Cronin, Jackie 1966.18
Cronin, John 1927.04
Cronin, T. 1880.09
Cronin, T.J. 1888.28, 1890.37, 1893.39
Cronin, Tim 1892.15
Cronin, Timothy 1879.37, 1981.21
Cronkhite, W.H. 1893.50
Cronkhite, W.H.A. 1892.50
Crook, John 1887.04, 1896.06, 1898.41, 1898.58
Crook, John P. 1865.06
Crook, Mervin 1979.20, 1980.21, 1981.20, 1983.12, 1985.11, 1985.13, 1986.09
Crook, Messr. 1881.35
Crooker, A. 1910.17
Crooker, Earl 1932.01, 1932.27, 1936.01
Crooker, Earle 1927.64, 1929.19, 1931.14, 1934.42, 1938.15
Crooks, Leeroy 1973.17
Cropper, Harriette 1905.48
Cropper, Roy 1921.31, 1923.14, 1923.38, 1927.13, 1929.38, 1929.40, 1929.43, 1929.47, 1930.01, 1930.03, 1930.07, 1930.12, 1931.27, 1931.33, 1931.35, 1931.41, 1931.43, 1931.45, 1932.10, 1933.08, 1933.09, 1933.10, 1933.11, 1933.14, 1933.17, 1933.18, 1933.19, 1934.07, 1934.08, 1934.09, 1934.10, 1934.11, 1936.04, 1936.08, 1936.09, 1936.10, 1936.11, 1936.31, 1938.17, 1943.12
Crosbie, C. 1869.13
Crosbie, Flora 1909.08, 1909.14, 1912.28, 1914.02, 1914.26, 1915.28
Crosby, B.J. 1995.03
Crosby, Bing 1976.32, 1987.02
Crosby, Bob 1978.05, 1979.30, 1999.01
Crosby, Florence 1901.12
Crosby, Harry 1917.07
Crosby, Henry 1927.64, 1931.09
Crosby, III., Harry 1976.32
Crosby, Kathryn 1976.32, 1996.04
Crosby, Kim 1985.19, 1987.18
Crosby, Mary-Frances 1976.32
Crosby, Miriam 1927.68
Crosby, Mr. 1796.03
Crosby, Nathaniel 1976.32

Crosby, Oma 1907.31
Crosby, Phoebe 1923.34
Crosby, W.C. 1879.16
Crosby, Wagner 1905.21
Crosby, Warner 1903.09, 1905.21
Crosby, Warren 1925.47
Crosley, Harry 1930.09
Cross, Alan 1944.19
Cross, Beverley 1965.14
Cross, Glen 1987.19
Cross, James A. 1942.20
Cross, Jules 1925.43
Cross, Julian 1872.11, 1872.23, 1872.35, 1873.03
Cross, Lulu 1894.52
Cross, Murphy 1976.19
Cross, Richard 1958.17, 1959.07
Cross, Roderic 1931.46
Cross, Ruth 1930.23
Cross, Sam 1929.18, 1930.19
Cross, Walter 1925.32, 1927.65
Cross, Wellington 1909.14, 1912.14, 1913.18, 1913.29, 1915.22, 1916.22, 1917.35, 1919.33, 1925.30
Crossan, Blanche 1918.01
Crosse, Julian 1872.09
Crossen, J.F. 1877.01
Crossen, J.S. 1873.20, 1873.22, 1873.27
Crossen, James F. 1877.24, 1878.01
Crossen, Miss 1869.29
Crossin, J.F. 1876.22
Crossin, James F. 1875.31, 1875.34, 1875.35, 1875.36, 1875.37, 1875.38, 1875.40, 1876.01, 1876.22, 1876.29
Crossland, Maggie 1894.33
Crossland, Marjorie 1946.12
Crossland, Maud 1905.13
Crossland, Maude 1905.49
Crossley 1875.35
Crossley, Charlotte 1971.12, 1973.14, 1975.12
Crossley, Karen 1975.24
Crossley, Mae 1897.30
Crossley, Messr. 1875.37, 1876.34
Crossman, Bert 1912.37
Crossman, D.F. 1905.42
Crossman, Edgar 1886.60
Crosson, J.F. 1873.27
Crosson, Joanna 1966.08
Crossroads Theatre Company 1999.09
Crossy, John Stewart 1880.01, 1880.03
Croswell, Anne 1963.08, 1968.08
Crothers, Rachel 1914.29
Crothers, Sam 1978.02, 1985.05, 1985.15, 1987.12, 1989.26, 1991.07, 1997.08
Crotty, Edward 1985.01
Crouch, Annie 1898.59
Crough, Ethan 1999.11
Crouse, Charles J. 1880.11, 1883.33
Crouse, Russel 1931.05, 1933.21, 1934.36, 1936.26, 1937.15, 1950.15, 1956.16, 1959.24, 1962.21, 1967.07, 1987.15, 1990.02, 1998.03
Crouse, Timothy 1987.15
Crouta, Mr. 1846.01
Crovini, Jennie 1902.26
Crow, J. 1867.12
Crowder, Bob 1976.04
Crowder, Jack 1967.15
Crowder, Mae 1921.26
Crowder, Robert 1961.24
Crowe, Deborah 1976.25
Crowe, Gordon 1972.05
Crowell, Evelyn 1929.08
Crowell, Floy 1894.27
Crowley, Ann 1951.18, 1976.33
Crowley, Bob 1994.02, 1998.02, 1999.20, 2000.06
Crowley, Dick 1960.06
Crowley, Morgan 1996.12
Crowley, Ty 1983.17
Crowley, William 1931.40, 1976.13
Crowningshield, Keith 1989.26
Crox, Elvia 1889.12, 1890.16, 1892.06, 1892.55, 1893.20, 1894.22
Crox-Seabrooke, Elvia 1897.55
Croxson, L.H. 1896.01, 1898.45
Croxson, Louis 1898.45
Croxson, Louis H. 1899.32
Croy, Homer 1930.37
Croyden, Ltd. 1917.28, 1918.37
Croydon, Ltd. 1917.21, 1918.11, 1918.28, 1918.30, 1919.01, 1919.12
Croyle, Dorothy 1927.02, 1928.50
Crozier, Emmett 1929.04
Crozier, Eric 1950.18
Crudup, Arthur 1989.12, 1990.15
Cruger, Dox 1892.50
Cruger, Louis 1937.11
Cruger, Randolph 1893.50
Cruikshank, Holly 1999.01, 2000.07
Crumb, Ann 1990.04, 1992.11
Crumbley, Walter 1924.37, 1929.21, 1937.09
Crume, Camilla 1918.29
Crumit, Frank 1920.15, 1920.28, 1921.23, 1923.33, 1926.25, 1927.49, 1928.01, 1938.15
Crump, George E. 1892.34
Crumpton, Master 1916.20
Crumpton, Ruth 1946.09
Crutchfield, Buddy 1980.18, 1992.01
Cruz, Francis J. 1991.03
Cryer, David 1964.21, 1969.07, 1971.02, 1972.15, 1973.09, 1989.18
Cryer, Gretchen 1962.27, 1973.03
Csaszar, Luu Ann 1980.18
CTM Productions 1998.17, 1999.09
Cubitt, Clara 1901.02
Cucchiara, Tony 1985.16
Cuccioli, Robert 1997.09
Cucksey, Frank 1941.03
Cuddy, Margaret 1948.17, 1964.20
Cuden, Steve 1997.09
Cuervo, Alma 1982.08, 1989.10
Cuervo, Marcelo 1999.18
Cuff, Sharon 1978.03
Cui, Cesar 1923.29
Cuillo, Bob 1997.05
Cuillo, Nicole Michelle 1997.05
Cuk, Andrew 1987.03
Cuka, Frances 1984.07
Culberson, Gail 1952.15
Culbert, Messr. 1859.08
Culbert, Samuel 1875.05
Culbreath, Lloyd 1983.21, 1986.11
Culkin, Philip 1924.21
Cullen, Countee 1946.08
Cullen, David 1982.19, 1985.12, 1987.05, 1988.01, 1990.04, 1990.17, 1992.12, 1994.10, 1998.10
Cullen, Donald 1964.45
Cullen, Edward 1947.07
Cullen, Frank 1929.08
Cullen, John 1897.38
Cullen, Lillian 1917.17, 1919.40
Cullen, Myra 1920.17, 1921.22, 1922.27
Cullen, Raymond 1924.39
Cullen, Sadie F. 1898.45
Cullen, Terry 1972.04
Culleton, Edmund 1918.17
Culley, Fred 1955.13
Cullimore, Gwyeth 1948.03, 1948.09, 1948.10
Cullimore, Gwyneth 1948.01, 1948.07
Cullinan, Hellen 1910.11
Cullington, William 1890.41, 1893.31, 1896.05
Culliton, Joseph 1987.03
Culliver, Karen 1983.05, 1989.23
Cullman, Joan 1979.09, 1981.25, 1984.01
Culloo, Billy 1927.17, 1930.40
Culloo, William 1932.27
Cullum, John 1960.21, 1965.31, 1975.03, 1978.02, 1989.17
Cullum, Ridgewell 1908.25
Culshaw, Eileen 1930.09
Culver, Carol 1970.11
Culvert, Grace 1921.35
Cumberbatch, Scott Owen 2000.19
Cumby, Billy 1930.10, 1935.01, 1938.19
Cumming, Addie 1884.16
Cumming, Adelaide 1915.32
Cumming, Alan 1998.04
Cumming, Don 1933.15, 1941.03
Cummings, Claudia 1990.02
Cummings, Georgie 1914.28
Cummings, Julia 1909.07
Cummings, Marie 1903.12
Cummings, Maude 1901.27
Cummings, Minnie 1878.21, 1878.22
Cummings, Patrick 1963.21, 1970.02
Cummings, Ralph Waldo 1947.03
Cummings, Richard 1889.16
Cummings, Robert 1922.08, 1933.20, 1934.01
Cummings, Roy 1918.18, 1923.17, 1923.41
Cummings, Vicki 1937.06
Cummings, Vickie 1942.30
Cummings, Victoria 1931.42
Cummins, Jane 1990.08
Cumpson, John R. 1895.41, 1898.03
Cumpsty, Michael 1997.15, 2001.08
Cundy, H.M. 1918.13
Cuney, Warren 1945.07
Cuningham, Davis 1954.18
Cunnard, William 1882.45
Cunneff, Joseph 1945.17
Cunningham, A.G. 1897.03
Cunningham, Arthur 1897.41, 1898.11, 1898.36, 1898.48, 1900.28, 1904.35, 1904.49, 1904.57, 1905.08, 1905.11, 1910.14, 1911.12, 1911.47, 1912.22, 1912.23, 1913.08, 1913.11, 1913.12, 1913.13, 1913.23, 1916.24, 1917.03, 1917.11, 1917.26, 1920.39, 1927.42, 1930.05
Cunningham, Beau 1948.17
Cunningham, Billy 1981.24
Cunningham, C.T. 1908.04
Cunningham, Cecil 1913.01, 1913.13, 1913.29, 1914.09, 1914.22, 1919.18, 1919.39
Cunningham, Davis 1939.13, 1941.04
Cunningham, G.D. 1898.44
Cunningham, George 1945.16
Cunningham, H. 1867.12, 1870.15
Cunningham, H.C. 1870.07
Cunningham, Jo Ann 1989.23, 1992.11
Cunningham, John 1902.37, 1904.35, 1963.13, 1968.30, 1970.13, 1992.11, 1997.06
Cunningham, Johnny 2000.04
Cunningham, Leon 1925.32, 1927.65
Cunningham, M. 1917.05, 1921.32
Cunningham, Mary 1918.22, 1919.35
Cunningham, Messr. 1861.06
Cunningham, Michael 1920.25
Cunningham, Mr. 1840.02, 1840.03, 1840.04, 1862.02
Cunningham, Nikola 1923.25
Cunningham, Paul 1940.16
Cunningham, Robert 1919.42
Cunningham, Roland 1904.51
Cunningham, Ronnie 1941.13, 1945.11
Cunningham, Roy 1923.17
Cunningham, Sarah 1965.32
Cunningham, Vinson 1973.17, 1975.12
Cunningham, William D. 1978.03
Cunningham, Zamah 1944.25, 1957.02
Cunnington, Dr. 1862.03, 1863.07
Cunnington, Mr. 1846.01
Cuplan, Mons. 1885.23
Cuppia, Billie 1909.30, 1910.16
Curdy, James 1896.38
Cureau, Mlle. 1875.33
Curelop, Shepard 1946.19
Curet, Raoul 1961.01
Curiel, Gonzalo 1938.08
Curillo, Mlle. 1882.45
Curl, Kathryn 1931.35
Curlee, Karen 1980.12, 1994.08
Curless, John 1996.05, 1998.03
Curley, Pete 1900.45
Curley, Peter 1898.20, 1899.29, 1910.09
Curley, Wilma 1957.12, 1962.05, 1964.17
Curlier, Mons. 1880.27
Curnock, Richard 1964.28
Curran, Brennen 1948.24
Curran, Frank 1922.21
Curran, Homer 1944.21, 1948.11, 1981.21
Curran, J.B. 1866.11, 1866.15, 1868.20, 1869.35
Curran, James 1915.31, 1923.15, 1929.07
Curran, John P. 1891.03, 1892.05, 1894.16
Curran, Michael 1907.35, 1907.45
Curran, Mike 1908.33
Curran, Sean 2000.01
Curren, Messr. 1919.33
Currens, Stephen 1978.24
Currie, Jack 1951.05
Currie, W.H. 1893.31, 1898.47
Currie, William H. 1897.01
Currier, B. 1893.41
Currier, Elsie 1905.07
Currier, Frank 1886.45, 1896.15
Currier, Terrence P. 1994.01
Curry, Diane 1978.23, 1979.27
Curry, Elda 1908.41, 1910.12
Curry, Jack 1937.06
Curry, John 1978.26, 1980.26
Curry, Jon Brent 1996.13
Curry, Kenneth 1925.40
Curry, Michael 1997.20
Curry, Randolph 1895.18, 1896.51, 1897.26, 1898.43, 1898.63, 1900.01, 1900.54
Curry, Richard 1956.02
Curry, Roberta 1927.65
Curry, Rosa 1997.07
Curry, Rose 1907.56, 1910.06
Curry, Samuel 1892.15
Curry, Steve 1959.13, 1960.10, 1961.07, 1962.05, 1964.17, 1968.11
Curry, Tim 1975.08, 1992.17
Curt, Fred 1982.14
Curti, Alfredo 1911.18
Curti, Carlos 1905.47
Curti, Franz 1898.11
Curtin, Cindy 1973.14
Curtin, Phyllis 1955.17, 1957.13
Curtin, Saranne 1998.10
Curtis, Alice 1900.38
Curtis, Allan 1902.02
Curtis, Ann 1986.12, 1997.09
Curtis, Arthur 1904.14
Curtis, Billy 1934.36
Curtis, Cecelia 1891.36
Curtis, Celia 1891.18
Curtis, Edith 1892.59
Curtis, Edwin H. 1903.12
Curtis, F. 1873.19
Curtis, Frank 1873.24
Curtis, Harry 1968.32
Curtis, Hope 1888.29, 1889.34, 1892.29
Curtis, J. 1889.51
Curtis, Josephine 1934.21, 1936.16
Curtis, Julie 1903.15
Curtis, June 1983.17
Curtis, Keene 1970.15, 1972.25
Curtis, Laura 1887.43
Curtis, Lola 1914.23, 1917.22
Curtis, M.B. 1896.01, 1896.51
Curtis, Mamie 1888.34, 1890.10
Curtis, Mann 1953.17
Curtis, Miss 1896.44
Curtis, Myron 1964.20, 1976.36
Curtis, Norman 1928.43
Curtis, Richard 1986.15
Curtis, Rita 1907.19
Curtis, S.J. 1894.05
Curtis, Sam 1919.19
Curtis, W.J. 1911.13
Curtis-Hall, Vondie 1981.29
Curtiss, Julia 1905.30
Curtiss, Willard 1906.17, 1908.18
Curtsinger, Gene 1948.24
Curty, Gene 1975.07
Curzon 1920.22
Curzon, Frank 1911.06, 1911.14
Curzon, George 1914.25
Curzon, Helen 1904.18
Curzon, Zaina 1912.38
Curzon, Zaini 1911.26
Cusack, Margaret 1990.08
Cusanelli, Joe 1953.07
Cusanelli, Joseph 1981.13
Cuscuna, Lisa Podgur 2000.20
Cushing and Masakazu Shibaoka Broadway Pacific 1992.09
Cushing, C.C.S. 1914.03
Cushing, C.S. 1930.04
Cushing, Catherine Chisholm 1918.33, 1920.12, 1922.04, 1924.46
Cushing, R.F. 1908.03
Cushing, T.M. 1928.20
Cushing, William 1894.37
Cushman, Asa 1869.17, 1869.21, 1870.07
Cushman, Charlotte 1841.01, 1867.29
Cushman, Dan 1958.20
Cushman, Edwin 1914.08
Cushman, Frank 1883.56, 1884.59, 1884.65, 1888.17
Cushman, James 1925.31, 1930.42
Cushman, John 1894.46
Cushman, Miss 1884.11
Cushman, Nancy 1962.27, 1965.33
Cushman, Wilbur 1924.46
Cusick, Kristoffer 1999.15
Cutell, Lou 1961.11, 1966.07
Cuthbert, May 1893.07, 1896.29, 1897.17, 1897.48, 1898.50, 1899.30
Cuthbert, Miss 1892.60
Cuthbert, Mr. 1848.03, 1879.70
Cuthbert, T. 1880.46
Cutler, Ben 1928.08, 1937.01, 1937.12
Cutler, Edward 1905.37, 1907.42, 1911.34, 1911.43, 1912.09, 1912.24, 1913.36
Cutler, Jeff 1970.04
Cutler, Jon 1981.26, 1987.19
Cutler, Messr. 1881.29
Cutler, Mr. 1873.25
Cutler, R. 1867.32, 1870.33, 1871.04
Cutler, R.J. 1886.10

Cutler, Robert 1864.17, 1864.22, 1868.06, 1869.26, 1876.03, 1876.23, 1877.21, 1878.17, 1879.04, 1879.68, 1880.04, 1880.09, 1880.36, 1880.64, 1881.09, 1896.44
Cutler, Robert F. 1939.12
Cutler, Robert J. 1873.26, 1875.32, 1884.58, 1890.49, 1891.25
Cutler, Roy 1904.35
Cutner, Solly 1918.21
Cutrer, Victor 1939.07
Cutro, Nicholas 2000.15
Cutten, Rudolf 1917.17
Cutter, F. 1882.18
Cutter, Helen 1922.21
Cutter, Messr. 1855.10
Cutter, Mr. 1854.01, 1854.07, 1855.01
Cutter, Murray 1935.15
Cutter, Roy 1898.20
Cutter, Royal 1912.10, 1914.14, 1921.08, 1922.04, 1923.43, 1927.65
Cutter, Samuel P. 1890.29
Cutting, Ernest 1923.24, 1924.40, 1925.34, 1926.07, 1928.21, 1929.50
Cuttler, Byron 1945.13, 1946.21
Cutts, Roderick 1961.26
Cutty, Thomas 1905.21
Cuvillier, Charles 1914.25, 1916.17, 1920.41
Cuyas, Arturo 1881.24
Cuzzoni, Dino 1988.06
Cypher, Jon 1965.34, 1967.02, 1969.17, 1996.08
Cypkin, Diane 1970.17
Czaja, C. Sager 1930.39
Czajka, Mariusz 1992.05
Czaroulch 1922.06
Czarovich, Fizchok 1923.28
Czatkowska, Miss 1890.31
Czettel, Ladislas 1942.31, 1944.16, 1945.02
Czibulka, Alfons 1885.63, 1889.17, 1889.34
Czitron, Rose 1937.14

D'Agostino, Antonella 1985.14
D'Alesandro, Joseph 1979.16
D'Allessandro, Aldo 1935.02
D'Allot, Chrisie 1914.25
D'Alroy, Phoebe 1890.50
D'Alton, Mlle 1896.07
D'Amato, Anthony 1972.12
D'Amato, Ernest 1924.32, 1944.30
d'Amboise, Charlotte 1985.12, 1988.12, 1989.03, 1995.11
d'Amboise, Christopher 1985.12
D'Amboise, Jacques 1957.05
D'Ambricourt, Adrienne 1922.09
D'Amico, Susi Cecchi 1986.06
D'Amur, Hene 1933.21
D'Ancona, Miranda 1972.24
d'Ancourt, Grenet 1914.26
D'Andrea, Carole 1957.12
D'Andrea, Cecile 1922.23, 1924.11
D'Angelo, Beverly 1976.03
D'Angerio, Joseph 1979.09
D'Anguera, Cora 1897.21
D'Antonakis, Fleury 1965.06
D'Arc, Victor 1976.03
D'Arcy, Alexander 1946.16
D'Arcy, Belle 1896.27, 1900.02, 1900.04, 1900.06, 1900.11, 1900.21, 1900.23
D'Arcy, John 1906.01
D'Arcy, Lynn 1905.03, 1905.30, 1906.29
D'Arcy, Mary 1984.08, 1985.08
d'Arcy, Max 1912.49
D'Arcy, Murray 1907.27, 1911.08, 1915.01
D'Arcy, Richard 1944.33, 1946.22, 1948.08, 1948.23, 1949.02, 1961.01
D'Arle, Yvonne 1926.27, 1928.12
D'Armand, Isabelle 1901.06
D'Armond, Frank 1934.20
D'Armond, Isabel 1907.46, 1908.23
D'Armond, Isabelle 1901.23
D'Armonde, Isabelle 1904.22
D'Arnell, Nydia 1924.46, 1925.43, 1926.08, 1926.30, 1927.63
d'Artois, Armand 1885.01, 1885.41, 1892.03, 1898.15, 1900.23
D'Arvigne, Grace 1899.21
D'Arville, Camille 1888.18, 1890.24, 1892.30, 1892.51, 1893.18, 1893.19, 1894.05, 1895.06, 1895.16, 1896.33, 1897.02, 1907.05
D'Arville, Colette 1928.17
D'Arville, Jeannette 1904.33
D'Attili, Maria 1948.29
D'Auban, Ernest 1901.27, 1903.04, 1903.39, 1904.47, 1905.48, 1913.33
D'Auban, John 1890.33, 1892.10, 1895.29, 1895.43
D'Aube, Belle 1915.28
D'Aubrey, Diane 1914.14
D'Auinoy, Countess 1855.10
D'Autry, Ioma 1905.50
d'Egville, Herve 1890.33
D'Elia, Chet 1975.07, 1992.07
D'Elmar, Camille 1880.43, 1880.49
D'Emanuele-Sanders, Cara 1998.19
D'Ennery 1886.26
d'Ennery, Adolph 1886.41
d'Ennery, Adolphe 1848.04, 1855.04, 1864.07, 1864.16, 1867.03, 1868.09, 1875.21, 1877.04, 1881.30, 1881.31, 1881.32, 1882.62, 1884.38, 1885.33, 1890.17, 1893.21
D'Ennery, Adolphe 1876.07, 1880.41, 1881.15
d'Ennery, Adolphe Philippe 1900.13
d'Ennery, Adolphe Phillippe 1898.19
D'Ennery, Eugene 1878.01
d'Ennery, Michael 1892.35
D'Estere, Mabel 1909.01
D'Hardelot, Guy 1952.11
D'Harville, Madeline 1911.45, 1912.02
D'Herlys, Semone 1916.24, 1917.26
D'Honau, Dorothy 1956.02, 1959.26, 1962.13, 1962.24, 1963.17, 1968.32
D'Honau, Lillian 1955.12, 1956.12, 1961.15, 1962.13, 1962.24
D'Honau, Marilyn 1957.12, 1959.13, 1962.13, 1963.17, 1978.22
D'Lugoff, Art 1989.22
d'Orsay, Cora 1920.37
D'Orsay, Fifi 1971.05
D'Orsay, Larence 1926.38
D'Orsay, Lawrence 1884.53, 1895.43, 1907.58, 1908.39, 1909.25, 1912.09, 1913.16, 1914.10, 1916.03, 1918.05, 1927.65
D'Orsay, Redford 1904.18
D'Orselle, Saberye 1902.28
D'Orso, Wisa 1957.01, 1962.20
D'Oyly Carte Opera Company 1879.70, 1879.72, 1887.10, 1888.35, 1894.15, 1934.21, 1934.22, 1934.23, 1934.24, 1934.25, 1934.26, 1934.27, 1934.28, 1934.30, 1934.31, 1934.33, 1936.13, 1936.14, 1936.15, 1936.16, 1936.18, 1936.19, 1936.20, 1936.21, 1936.23, 1936.24, 1936.25, 1939.01, 1939.02, 1939.03, 1939.04, 1939.05, 1939.06, 1939.08, 1939.09, 1939.11, 1947.22, 1948.01, 1948.02, 1948.03, 1948.06, 1948.07, 1948.09, 1948.10, 1951.01, 1951.03, 1951.04, 1951.06, 1951.07, 1951.08, 1951.09, 1955.15, 1955.16, 1955.18, 1955.20, 1955.21, 1955.22, 1955.23, 1955.24, 1962.25, 1962.26, 1962.28, 1962.29, 1962.30, 1962.31
D'Oyly Carte Opera Trust, Inc. 1978.16
D'Oyly Carte Opera Trust, Ltd. 1964.36, 1964.37, 1964.38, 1964.41, 1964.42, 1964.43, 1966.22, 1966.23, 1966.25, 1966.26, 1966.28, 1968.25, 1968.26, 1968.27, 1968.28, 1968.29, 1976.12, 1976.13, 1976.14, 1978.14, 1978.15, 1978.17
D'Oyly Carte, Bridget 1966.22, 1966.23, 1966.25, 1966.26, 1966.28, 1968.25, 1968.26, 1968.27, 1968.28, 1968.29, 1976.12, 1976.13, 1976.14, 1978.14, 1978.15, 1978.16, 1978.17
D'Oyly Carte, R. 1881.36, 1885.13, 1886.57
D'Oyly Carte, Richard 1880.69, 1881.07, 1881.38, 1885.43, 1885.47, 1886.12, 1886.25, 1886.55, 1890.02, 1899.16, 1900.27, 1900.37, 1910.14, 1912.23, 1913.11, 1915.09, 1925.13, 1927.45, 1931.10, 1931.25, 1933.08, 1934.07, 1935.05, 1936.04, 1936.13, 1940.13, 1942.04, 1959.18, 1961.03, 1974.15, 1976.12, 1978.15, 1984.13, 1985.10, 1990.13, 1993.13, 1995.10, 1997.02
D'Smith, L. 1880.49
D'Soyer, Ida 1870.20, 1872.19
D'Sylva, Allan 1931.01
D.W. Truss and Company 1895.25
Dabbs, Orens 1947.11
Dabdoub, Jack 1951.24, 1952.15, 1956.16, 1963.13, 1965.35, 1966.12, 1966.16, 1968.23, 1969.17, 1972.14, 1980.26, 1994.08
Dabney, Ford 1910.18, 1911.20, 1915.07, 1927.33
Dabney, Ford T. 1937.09
Daboll, Fanny 1885.29, 1902.11
Daboll, W.S. 1883.68, 1885.10, 1885.29, 1886.05, 1886.30
Daboll, William S. 1888.02
Dachshund, George W. 1909.31
DaCosta, Linda 1896.06, 1899.06, 1902.18
DaCosta, Morton 1955.01, 1957.18, 1959.27, 1960.18, 1968.24, 1975.22
daCosta, Raie 1930.09
DaCosta, Theodora Linda 1882.75
Dacre, Annie 1898.08
Dacre, Harry 1892.45, 1979.07
Dade, Charles 1878.22, 1886.44, 1890.06, 1895.35
Dade, Charles R. 1889.03
daDona Geralda, Marquinho 1988.06
Dae, Muriel 1917.08
Dafora, Asata 1934.16
Dagand, Henry 1930.37
DaGeralda, Marquinho 1992.13
Daggett, Larry 1998.01
Daggett, Messr. 1886.36
Dagmar, Alexandra 1926.05, 1928.15
Dagmar, Camille 1896.01
Dagnan, W.J. 1884.41, 1885.02
Dagnie, Sigrid 1940.06
Dagoni 1875.21, 1882.62, 1885.33, 1886.41
Dagwell, Annie 1897.16, 1897.29
Dagwell, Natalie 1912.13, 1912.38, 1916.15
Dah, Oof 1926.19
Dahl, Arlene 1945.12
Dahl, Cyrena 1920.28
Dahl, Joyce 1964.20
Dahl, Kris 1917.16
Dahl, Magda 1908.06
Dahlman, Lou 1942.35
Dahm, Marie 1923.38
Dahm-Petersen, Adolph 1896.07
Daian, Henry 1889.16
Daigle, Kenneth M. 1990.18
Dailey, Agnes 1902.15
Dailey, Ambrose 1898.54
Dailey, Dannul 1986.03, 1989.12
Dailey, Joe 1894.43, 1896.40
Dailey, Jr., Dan 1939.13
Dailey, Mae 1929.24
Dailey, Margaret 1924.06
Dailey, Mr. 1855.08
Dailey, Peter F. 1891.03, 1892.05, 1893.06, 1893.49, 1895.34, 1896.37, 1897.48, 1898.50, 1899.17, 1899.30, 1900.47, 1902.29, 1903.28, 1904.22, 1904.56, 1905.52, 1906.29, 1908.01
Dailey, Robert 1908.31, 1912.29
Dailey, Robert F. 1907.02
Dailey, Robert L. 1902.15, 1910.01
Daily, Frederick 1890.40
Daily, Peter F. 1897.31
Daily, Willis 1953.04
Dainton, Marie 1900.41
Dair, Betty 1929.09, 1932.06
Daisey, Annie 1879.02
Daish, Sid 1925.48
Daisy 1981.26
Daisy, Annie 1884.27
Daisy, T. 1867.12
Daks, Nicholas 1930.36
Dalamater, Bruce 1905.15
Dalamatoff, Michael 1943.11
Dalberg, Camille 1919.31
Dalberg, Louise 1925.52
Dalberg, Lucile 1915.32
Dalby, Albert 1907.02
Dalby, Alfred 1907.39, 1921.30, 1922.39
Dalby, Matthew 1998.10
Dale, Amy 1906.36
Dale, Ann 1922.13
Dale, Anne 1901.04
Dale, Bertie 1901.11, 1905.47
Dale, Charles 1918.24, 1919.30, 1921.20, 1926.23, 1927.48, 1936.07, 1939.16, 1942.16, 1943.16
Dale, Clamma 1976.28
Dale, Evelyn 1908.04
Dale, Frank N. 1898.66
Dale, Gertrude 1909.25
Dale, Glen 1924.04, 1926.42, 1927.62
Dale, Grover 1956.12, 1957.12, 1960.05, 1961.18, 1963.06, 1965.14, 1969.08, 1973.06, 1973.11, 1974.13, 1988.07, 1989.03
Dale, H. 1880.62, 1907.54
Dale, H.S. 1884.32, 1884.33
Dale, Harry 1881.25, 1881.42, 1881.45, 1884.38, 1894.03, 1896.42, 1896.43, 1897.13, 1900.25, 1900.31, 1900.32, 1902.04, 1906.46, 1908.26, 1909.20, 1910.23, 1911.28, 1914.19
Dale, Henry 1902.15
Dale, Jim 1980.07, 1997.10
Dale, John 1921.37
Dale, Johnnie 1931.05
Dale, Johnny 1920.24
Dale, June 1897.24, 1897.28, 1899.21
Dale, Kate 1897.30
Dale, Laurence 1983.16
Dale, Lenn 1948.25
Dale, Louise 1919.14, 1920.24
Dale, Margaret 1918.03, 1919.02, 1923.10, 1928.03, 1930.23, 1941.04, 1943.03
Dale, Marian 1925.48, 1926.21, 1927.27
Dale, Maryon 1932.19
Dale, Miss 1882.46, 1917.31
Dale, Mr. 1863.10
Dale, Myrtle 1905.43
Dale, Naomi 1910.09
Dale, Nonie 1934.15
Dale, Norma 1920.24
Dale, Reba 1913.14
Dale, Robert 1920.24
Dale, Sunny 1927.13, 1929.49
Dale, Thomas 1928.29
Dale, William 1895.40, 1898.64, 1918.21
Daley, Bob 1956.04, 1959.05, 1964.32, 1974.02
Daley, C. 1868.23
Daley, Cass 1936.17
Daley, Edward 1900.36
Daley, Frank 1929.37
Daley, George 1973.11
Daley, Jack 1927.67, 1932.07, 1932.11, 1946.01
Daley, James 1919.03
Daley, Jerome 1923.05, 1926.34, 1927.16, 1933.03
Daley, Lillian 1918.04
Daley, M.C. 1869.08
Daley, R.F. 1997.19
Daley, Timothy 1922.36
Dalgeish, Trudy 1999.02
Dalhart, Vernon 1914.11
Dall, Evelyn 1935.03
Dall, Harry 1880.57
Dalland, Dorothy 1911.24
Dallapozza, Adolph 1984.03
Dallas, J.J. 1894.15
Dallavo, John 1931.31
Dallen, Mons. 1893.25
Dallerup, Ellen 1915.24, 1916.15
Dallimeur, Mrs. 1868.11
Dallin, Jacques 1941.03
Dallry, Miss 1862.02
Dally, Francoise 1958.18
Dalmatoff, Messr. 1922.06, 1923.28, 1925.03, 1929.05
Dalmatoff, Michael 1931.09
Dalmores, Aimee 1914.22
Dalnert, D. 1912.09
DalPorto, Lita 1952.03
Dalrymple, Jean 1957.02, 1957.03, 1957.04, 1957.06, 1957.11, 1958.03, 1958.05, 1958.07, 1959.02, 1959.03, 1959.05, 1960.09, 1960.11, 1961.09, 1961.12, 1961.13, 1961.15, 1962.13, 1962.15, 1962.16, 1963.04, 1963.05, 1963.06, 1963.17, 1963.18, 1964.17, 1964.19, 1964.20, 1964.46, 1965.15, 1965.20, 1965.21, 1966.07, 1966.08, 1966.11, 1966.13, 1966.31, 1967.04, 1967.07, 1967.09, 1967.17, 1968.16, 1968.17, 1968.32
Dalrymple, Margaret 1907.48
Dalton, Charles 1927.66, 1938.03
Dalton, Claire 1946.14, 1947.12
Dalton, Doris 1951.18
Dalton, Dorothy 1919.38
Dalton, Fred 1927.08
Dalton, Harry 1881.02
Dalton, J.F. 1882.14, 1892.27
Dalton, J.T. 1892.03
Dalton, James F. 1881.57
Dalton, Kathie 1966.24
Dalton, Myra 1903.18, 1904.24
Dalton, Nancy 1968.18, 1969.14
Dalton, Peter 1964.28
Dalton, Verna 1911.15
Daltrey, Roger 1972.08

Daltry, Faith 1955.01
Daltry, Joseph 1940.11
Daltry, Joseph S. 1940.11, 1940.13, 1940.14, 1940.15
Daltry, Roger 1998.20
Daly, Agnes 1895.21
Daly, Ambrose 1902.07
Daly, Arnold 1903.41, 1923.22
Daly, Augustin 1870.16, 1872.23, 1872.35, 1873.03, 1873.11, 1873.15, 1873.16, 1873.25, 1873.26, 1875.18, 1876.09, 1876.23, 1877.21, 1879.50, 1879.56, 1880.04, 1881.04, 1881.11, 1882.26, 1884.11, 1891.05, 1892.14, 1893.25, 1894.33, 1895.10, 1895.28, 1896.27, 1897.20, 1897.44, 1898.11, 1898.18, 1898.26, 1898.29, 1898.46, 1907.58
Daly, C. 1887.04
Daly, Dan 1891.43, 1892.36, 1892.56, 1893.34, 1894.10, 1895.04, 1895.18, 1895.35, 1896.06, 1897.26, 1897.39, 1898.68, 1899.25, 1900.34, 1901.23
Daly, Daniel 1888.16
Daly, Frank 1938.02
Daly, H.F. 1860.06, 1861.04, 1863.01, 1863.02, 1863.03, 1863.08
Daly, J.V. 1870.05
Daly, James 1900.12, 1920.19
Daly, Jerome 1927.10
Daly, John 1893.50
Daly, John P. 1908.11
Daly, Joseph M. 1909.06
Daly, Josie 1902.02, 1909.06
Daly, Katherine 1911.24
Daly, Lee 1929.34, 1929.36, 1934.07, 1934.08, 1934.09, 1934.10, 1934.11
Daly, Lizzie 1895.18
Daly, Lizzie Derious 1888.16, 1891.04
Daly, Lucy 1891.39, 1893.39, 1894.14, 1894.21, 1898.02, 1900.08, 1902.02, 1906.09, 1907.12, 1909.06
Daly, M.C. 1867.25, 1868.32, 1870.05, 1877.21, 1883.05, 1883.07, 1887.17, 1887.46
Daly, Maggie 1891.39
Daly, Messr. 1864.13, 1882.20
Daly, Minnie 1898.66
Daly, Mr. 1862.03
Daly, Nellie 1897.06, 1903.31, 1904.47, 1905.23
Daly, Orlando 1925.41
Daly, Patricia 1973.12
Daly, Phil 1928.25
Daly, Philomena 1976.29
Daly, Sally 1905.19, 1913.30
Daly, Thomas A. 1882.76, 1888.16
Daly, Thomas D. 1891.37, 1893.08, 1905.17
Daly, Thomas J. 1905.54
Daly, Thy 1920.15
Daly, Timothy 1921.14
Daly, Tyne 1989.27, 1991.06
Daly, Vinie 1904.21, 1907.09
Daly, W. 1869.33, 1869.40
Daly, W.H. 1885.05, 1885.14, 1886.39
Daly, William 1915.16, 1919.09, 1919.27, 1920.37, 1921.33, 1922.10, 1922.35, 1922.46, 1923.01, 1923.07, 1923.21, 1923.44, 1924.19, 1924.43, 1925.14, 1925.22, 1925.49, 1926.16, 1926.36, 1928.03, 1928.22, 1929.27, 1929.35, 1931.48, 1932.03, 1932.25, 1933.01, 1933.13, 1933.25
Daly, William H. 1885.28, 1886.15, 1887.14, 1890.27
Daly, William J. 1916.20
Daly, William M. 1917.12, 1918.23
Dam, H.J.W. 1894.41
Dam, Harry J.W. 1895.32
Damakude, Thuli 1987.12
Daman, John 1987.19
Damane, David Aaron 1998.20
daMangueira, Ledinha 1988.06
Damansky, A. 1932.09
Damari, Shoshana 1973.01
Dambrun, Mlle. 1866.29
Dame, Beverly 1947.10, 1948.29
Damian, Grace 1895.28
Damita, Lily 1929.44, 1932.24
Damman, George 1927.35
Damon, Bertie 1888.04
Damon, Cathryn 1954.02, 1955.25, 1957.05, 1962.01, 1964.04, 1965.17, 1969.07
Damon, Lisa 1967.10
Damon, Stuart 1959.06, 1960.07, 1965.06
Damrosch, Leopoldine 1930.18
Damrosch, Walter 1912.40
Damur, Hene 1938.05
Dan, Yoel 1969.13
Dana, Dick 1948.28, 1950.12
Dana, Dick 'Gabby' 1950.12
Dana, Dwight 1915.26, 1917.09
Dana, F. Mitchell 1986.19
Dana, Frederic 1897.40
Dana, Frederick 1897.30
Dana, Leora 1974.23
Dana, Lizzie 1879.35, 1880.06
Dana, Marie Dana 1937.13
Dana, Natasha 1937.16, 1939.13
Dana, Nathalie 1912.36
Dana, Newton 1886.02
Dana, Nick 1955.11
Dana, Paul 1896.01
Dana, Rosa 1882.21
Dana, Rose 1879.35, 1880.02, 1880.40
Danby, Charles 1888.38, 1888.41, 1889.54, 1896.06, 1900.16, 1900.34
Danby, Frank 1894.15
Dance, Bill 1970.10
Dance, C. 1834.02
Dance, George 1896.06, 1896.48, 1898.05, 1898.28, 1898.41, 1898.58, 1901.18, 1902.19, 1904.12
Danceny, Robert 1908.36
Dancer, Earl 1921.26, 1927.32, 1936.30
Dancing Duchess Company 1914.17
Dancrey, Ann 1913.18
Dando, Howard 1974.24
Dandridge, Dorothy 1939.29
Dandridge, Etta 1939.29
Dandridge, Putney 1930.29
Dandridge, Vivian 1939.29
Dandy, Jess 1899.36, 1905.16, 1906.16, 1907.17, 1908.30, 1911.35
Dane, Clemence 1934.03, 1952.03
Dane, Daisy 1882.80
Dane, Faith 1946.04, 1959.13
Dane, Paul 1926.38
Dane, Rita 1916.04
Danek, Michael 1981.12
Danelle, John 1972.01
Danesi, Natali 1934.38
Danforth, Charles 1886.17
Danforth, E. Howard 1886.17, 1886.29
Danforth, May 1884.22, 1885.58, 1887.43
Danforth, Will 1897.42, 1899.40, 1913.21
Danforth, William 1896.19, 1902.07, 1903.04, 1904.10, 1905.06, 1905.36, 1910.03, 1910.14, 1911.13, 1911.42, 1912.26, 1914.30, 1915.06, 1915.09, 1915.10, 1915.12, 1915.19, 1916.07, 1918.06, 1918.27, 1921.31, 1925.13, 1925.39, 1926.08, 1927.24, 1928.49, 1929.43, 1931.10, 1931.12, 1931.15, 1931.17, 1931.18, 1931.22, 1931.23, 1931.24, 1931.25, 1932.02, 1933.08, 1933.09, 1933.10, 1933.11, 1933.14, 1933.18, 1933.19, 1934.07, 1934.08, 1934.09, 1934.10, 1934.11, 1935.05, 1935.06, 1935.07, 1935.08, 1935.09, 1935.10, 1936.04, 1936.08, 1936.09, 1936.10
Dangerfield and Street 1897.02
Dangerfield, F. 1890.07, 1890.34
Dangerfield, Fred 1892.29, 1894.10, 1895.16, 1899.21
Dangerfield, Frederick 1895.08, 1896.30, 1896.45, 1897.26
Dangerfield, Rodney 1988.03
Dangler, Anita 1973.07
Dangon, Mons. 1882.73
Dangon, V. 1881.51
Daniderff, Leo 1924.36, 1925.05, 1925.10, 1925.24
Daniecki, John 1992.14
Daniel, Billie Lynn 1961.13
Daniel, Billy 1941.08
Daniel, Gary 1979.22
Daniel, Lee 1903.12
Daniel, Lenny 1999.11
Daniel, Leslie 1969.17
Daniel, Mlle. 1883.59, 1883.60, 1883.61, 1884.01, 1884.43, 1884.45, 1884.47
Daniel, Tom 1902.03
Daniele, Diana 1996.11
Daniele, Graciela 1964.05, 1968.05, 1968.31, 1969.17, 1971.05, 1975.14, 1978.06, 1978.12, 1978.19, 1979.12, 1979.20, 1979.26, 1981.01, 1983.14, 1984.01, 1985.18, 1989.20, 1990.12, 1993.02, 1995.09, 1998.01, 1999.04
Daniele, Graciele 1999.22
Danieley, Jason 1997.10
Danieli, Fred 1946.10
Daniell, Edith 1906.45, 1908.04
Danielle, Martha 1966.14, 1967.10, 1976.08
Danielli, Fred 1948.26
Danielli, Isa 1985.14
Daniels, Barbara 1984.03
Daniels, Billy 1945.08, 1964.32, 1975.21
Daniels, Bus 1925.37
Daniels, C. 1879.52
Daniels, Carrie 1881.23, 1881.47, 1893.24
Daniels, Danny 1941.06, 1945.20, 1947.02, 1948.04, 1962.04, 1964.16, 1966.12, 1966.16, 1966.27, 1979.12, 1983.21, 1986.03
Daniels, David 1955.01
Daniels, Dennis 1976.08, 1978.18, 1993.02
Daniels, Douglas 1935.12
Daniels, Edgar 1957.07, 1960.09
Daniels, Eleanor 1917.27, 1919.12
Daniels, Florence 1913.35
Daniels, Frank 1882.80, 1884.16, 1884.37, 1888.04, 1888.34, 1890.10, 1895.33, 1897.18, 1897.42, 1899.40, 1902.07, 1903.34, 1905.19, 1907.11, 1907.63, 1909.29, 1912.44
Daniels, George 1905.09
Daniels, Grace 1917.14, 1917.15, 1919.02
Daniels, Howard 1938.08
Daniels, J.W. 1886.15
Daniels, Jimmie 1942.13
Daniels, John 1913.25
Daniels, Leon 1952.13
Daniels, Lorraine Dulcie 1978.14, 1978.18
Daniels, M.W. 1902.15
Daniels, Marc 1940.04, 1957.14
Daniels, Marguerite 1920.45
Daniels, Mark 1943.23
Daniels, Miss 1908.19
Daniels, Ruth 1925.37
Daniels, Sharon 1979.26
Daniels, Stan 1976.09
Daniels, Ted 1927.67, 1940.19
Daniels, Wilber 1935.12
Daniels, William 1965.31, 1969.06
Danielson, Mr. 1870.04
Daniely, Jason 2000.15
Danilova, Alexandra 1934.29, 1958.02
Danjou, Jeanne 1924.17
Danks, H.P. 1918.21
Danks, Mr. 1866.07
Dankworth, E. 1884.41
Dankworth, Miss 1882.32
Danley, Carrie 1886.31
Dann, Larry 1964.28
Dannenberg, Louis 1913.17
Danner, Blythe 2001.02
Danner, Branden 1984.07
Danner, Dorothy 1978.27, 1983.05
Danner, Harry 1964.40
Dano, Edward 1922.41
Dano, Paul Franklin 1995.19, 1997.22
Dano, Royal 1947.03, 1952.05
Danoff, Sid 1962.17
Dansby, William 1984.13
Danser, Herr 1880.66
Dansicker, Michael 1981.04
Dansky, David 1992.18
Dantas, Patricia 1992.13
Dantchenko, Vladmir Nemirovitch 1925.46, 1925.51
Dante, Nicholas 1975.15
Dante, Nikolas 1972.24
Dante, Ron 1969.08, 1978.09, 1982.01
Dante, Shura 1927.38
Danton, E. 1897.53, 1898.15
Danton, Eugene 1900.29
Dantuono, Michael 1981.13, 1983.14, 1984.14
Dantzler, Rex 1920.08
Danvers, J. 1875.35
Danvers, James 1876.02, 1876.16
Danvers, W.H. 1865.05, 1865.06
Danze, F. 1870.07
Danzig, Evelyn 1955.03
Daray, Gabriel 1923.38
Darby, Charles 1877.17
Darby, Myrna 1927.08, 1928.47
Darby, Phil 1925.39
Darby, Phillip 1924.11
Darby, Prudence 1976.21
Darbyshire, Michael 1965.28
Darce, H.E. 1892.23
Darce, Peter 1976.32
Darcel, Denise 1950.14
Darcey, A.T. 1904.20
Darcey, M. 1929.10
Darcey, Maurice 1902.41
Darci 1915.21
Darcier, Lakme 1904.29
Darcy, C.H. 1882.67
Darcy, Charles 1877.06, 1877.09, 1877.10, 1877.11, 1877.12, 1877.13, 1877.14, 1877.18, 1877.19, 1877.26, 1877.27, 1877.29, 1877.30, 1877.31, 1877.32, 1877.33, 1877.34, 1877.37, 1877.38, 1878.06, 1878.07, 1878.08, 1878.09, 1879.19, 1879.27, 1879.31, 1882.53, 1882.55, 1882.58, 1882.61, 1882.73
Darcy, Don 1943.15, 1944.03
Darcy, Frank 1886.15
Darcy, Jacques 1929.29
Darcy, Maurice 1897.42, 1904.15, 1905.30, 1907.03, 1917.11, 1922.33
Darcy, Messr. 1875.27
Darcy, Mlle. 1859.10
Darcy, Mons. 1875.25, 1875.28, 1875.30, 1875.33
Darcy, Pattie 1985.03
Dardashi, David 1972.17
Darden, Michael 1960.09
Darden, Severn 1961.17
Dardignac, Mons. 1868.18, 1869.19
Dare Brothers 1886.07
Dare, Ada 1889.33, 1889.47, 1890.43, 1891.14, 1892.60, 1893.02, 1893.07, 1894.10, 1894.14, 1894.48, 1895.09, 1896.02, 1896.30, 1897.39
Dare, Al 1925.24
Dare, Albert 1924.31
Dare, Beryle 1905.41
Dare, Danny 1923.13, 1927.52, 1929.19, 1929.31, 1930.38, 1931.01, 1933.15, 1940.21
Dare, Dorothy 1931.04, 1931.42, 1932.19, 1933.05, 1934.14
Dare, Grace 1902.11
Dare, Hope 1933.03
Dare, Jeanne 1917.35
Dare, Madeline 1921.08
Dare, Robert G. 1971.07
Dare, Thelma 1953.16
Dare, Thomas 1889.47
Dare, Tommy 1888.01
Darel, Bertha 1902.41
Darewski, Herman 1911.02, 1914.22, 1918.31, 1920.03, 1924.01, 1964.28
Darewski, Hermann 1990.09
Darewski, Jr., Herman E. 1907.32
Darewski, Max 1916.22, 1923.35
Darian, Anita 1960.11, 1961.09, 1963.18, 1965.07, 1965.26, 1968.16
Darien, Marie 1884.65
Darion, Joe 1957.05, 1965.34, 1967.05, 1967.12, 1968.22, 1972.14, 1974.11, 1977.12, 1992.07
Dark, Mlle. 1873.10
Darle, Yvonne 1918.12
Darley, Brian 1913.03
Darley, Herbert 1901.19
Darley, T.S. 1883.37
Darlia, J. 1870.41, 1871.03, 1871.06
Darlia, L. 1870.37, 1870.41, 1870.45, 1871.03, 1871.06
Darlia, T. 1870.37
Darling, Al. T. 1906.01
Darling, Alfred 1910.36, 1912.15
Darling, Beatrice 1921.03
Darling, Candy 1979.05, 1981.29
Darling, Denver 1992.03
Darling, Edward I. 1882.18, 1887.14
Darling, Edward Irving 1895.11
Darling, Elizabeth 1921.03
Darling, Erik 1958.12
Darling, Frank 1907.17, 1908.17, 1908.39, 1909.25, 1910.18, 1912.38, 1913.17, 1915.15, 1916.10, 1917.13, 1918.19, 1919.15
Darling, Frank N. 1902.18, 1904.10, 1905.06, 1912.13, 1914.15
Darling, George M. 1903.30
Darling, Hattie 1916.11, 1920.06
Darling, James 1901.13
Darling, Jean 1945.05
Darling, Jennifer 1967.16, 1968.24
Darling, Mae 1904.10, 1905.06
Darling, Miss 1905.25
Darling, Robert 1964.29
Darlington, Beatrice 1898.77
Darlington, Bill 1979.30

Darnay, Toni 1973.11
Darnell, Delle 1920.02
Darnell, Rick 1999.09
Darnell, Robert 1961.11, 1972.02, 1972.19
Darnley, Herbert 1904.34
Darnutzer, Don 1999.09
DaRocha, Iris 1992.13
Daron, Mons. 1868.25, 1868.27
Darr, Deborah 1982.20, 1984.11, 1986.08, 1987.03, 1989.14
Darrah, James 1995.13
Darrell, Frederic 1884.46, 1886.32, 1888.18
Darrell, Frederick 1886.39
Darrell, Gertrude 1908.29
Darrell, Lyda 1893.49
Darrell, Robert 1930.41
Darrell, Rupert 1929.48
Darren, John 1959.05
Darrenkamp, John 1974.08, 1975.11
Darrieux, Danielle 1969.17, 1972.24
Darrington, Frances 1904.12
Darsey, Herbert 1925.50
Darville, Evelyn 1927.50
Darwin, Cress 1976.27
Daryl, Ruth 1887.30
Darys, Jeanne 1914.27
Dash, Calvin 1951.11, 1952.06, 1952.15
Dash, Irwin 1979.25
Dash, Julian 1974.09
Dashiel, R.K. 1887.50
Dashiell, Willard 1927.64, 1935.15
Dashwood, Violet 1886.50
daSilva, Daniel 1927.43
DaSilva, Harold 1960.01
daSilva, Howard 1932.28, 1937.08, 1947.21
DaSilva, Howard 1943.04, 1959.25, 1960.02, 1965.32, 1969.06
Dass, Mlle. 1884.43, 1884.45, 1884.52, 1884.55, 1885.23, 1887.37
Dassin, Jules 1948.24, 1952.20, 1967.05
Daste, Marie-Helene 1964.06
Datcher, Irene 1976.21
Dates, C. Oliver 1888.05
Datz, Lisa 2000.15
Daube, Belle 1908.43
Daube, Harda 1917.24
Daubenas, Joseph 1959.05
Daubigny, Lloyd 1892.14
Daubl, Betti 1884.40
Dauche, Arthur 1913.26
Daufy, Jose 1929.10, 1929.11, 1929.13, 1929.15, 1929.16
Daugherty, Don 1989.02
Daugherty, George 1990.10
Daugherty, Joseph 1992.17
Daughn, Delphie 1920.24
Daum, Margaret 1935.05, 1935.06, 1935.07, 1935.08, 1935.10, 1936.10
Dauntless, Mr. 1867.15
Dauscha, Wolfgang 1984.04, 1984.05
Dauvray, Helen 1895.04
Davalis, Messr. 1877.31
Davalis, Mlle. 1875.01
Davalis, Mons. 1873.11, 1875.02, 1875.25, 1875.30, 1876.20, 1876.25, 1876.26, 1876.28, 1876.31, 1877.09, 1877.10, 1877.11, 1877.12, 1877.19, 1877.26, 1877.27, 1877.29, 1877.33, 1878.07, 1878.09
Daveau, I. 1875.17, 1876.08
Daven, Lillian 1908.26
Davenny, Hollis 1923.14, 1931.03
Davenort, Eva 1901.25, 1904.10
Davenport, A.H. 1857.05, 1861.03, 1862.07, 1864.13, 1871.22, 1872.13
Davenport, Clara 1883.65, 1886.47
Davenport, E.L. 1862.03, 1862.04
Davenport, Edgar L. 1885.46
Davenport, Eva 1889.40, 1889.49, 1890.24, 1890.39, 1891.12, 1891.17, 1891.22, 1892.03, 1892.27, 1892.42, 1894.11, 1894.28, 1896.50, 1897.11, 1897.25, 1897.37, 1898.51, 1899.38, 1905.06, 1905.44, 1909.04, 1909.30, 1911.32, 1912.18, 1913.04, 1921.06
Davenport, Frank 1866.31, 1869.31, 1927.14
Davenport, G. 1915.05
Davenport, G.C. 1866.06
Davenport, George 1864.17
Davenport, George C. 1880.25, 1881.28
Davenport, Harry 1879.29, 1890.49, 1891.25, 1893.32, 1893.47, 1895.21, 1897.39, 1899.15, 1899.25, 1900.33, 1901.01, 1901.21, 1902.21, 1903.33, 1904.54, 1912.31, 1914.03, 1914.17
Davenport, Horace G. 1914.26
Davenport, J.W. 1891.46
Davenport, Jeremy 1990.19
Davenport, John 1999.09
Davenport, Johnny 1983.20
Davenport, Lew 1887.31
Davenport, Marie 1896.50
Davenport, Milla 1923.19
Davenport, Miss 1865.05, 1865.07, 1865.10, 1877.15, 1884.42, 1886.32
Davenport, Mr. 1860.01
Davenport, Mrs. L.W. 1857.08
Davenport, Nellie 1866.31, 1872.14
Davenport, Nelly 1869.31
Davenport, Pembroke 1940.16, 1940.23, 1941.11, 1945.10, 1945.13, 1946.01, 1947.04, 1948.08, 1948.16, 1948.32, 1950.20, 1953.01, 1960.11, 1961.07, 1961.26, 1962.17, 1963.17, 1963.18, 1964.44, 1965.18, 1965.38, 1966.11
Davenport, Ruth 1890.50, 1892.04, 1893.22, 1893.41
Davenport, Vic 1887.31
Davey, Lizzie 1867.17, 1868.08
Davey, Messr. 1877.15
Davey, Mrs. 1867.14
Davey, Mrs. T.W. 1867.13
Davey, Shaun 2000.01
Davi 1969.13
David 1964.28, 1968.04
David Henderson and Company 1887.32
David Strong Warner, Inc. 1992.04, 1992.08
David, Av 1972.17
David, Clifford 1960.22, 1965.31, 1966.30, 1993.15
David, Crawford 1969.06
David, Fingleton 1897.20
David, Frank 1886.36, 1887.05, 1887.19, 1887.43, 1889.19, 1893.40, 1898.78
David, Hal 1968.31, 1976.16, 1984.15, 1989.21
David, Jim 1994.06
David, Keith 1992.08
David, Lee 1923.38, 1927.31, 1929.22, 1929.28
David, Mack 1943.16, 1968.21, 1973.11, 1975.12, 1981.04, 1981.06, 1989.12, 1997.03, 1999.24
David, Michael 1974.06, 1977.08, 1982.04, 1987.18, 1988.05, 1991.05, 1995.05, 1998.11, 1998.13
David, Mons. 1882.61
David, Ross 1892.25
David, Strong, Warner, Inc. 1993.06
David, Thomas 1905.38
David, William 1945.20, 1947.16, 1950.15, 1954.05, 1957.08
David, Worton 1909.21, 1910.21, 1911.27, 1914.18, 1915.07, 1916.22, 1918.10, 1920.41
Davidenko, Grigori 1977.13
Davidge, D. Scot 1982.14
Davidge, Helen 1899.23
Davidge, Jr., W. 1870.05
Davidge, Jr., William 1879.42, 1880.63, 1881.03
Davidge, Mr. 1859.01, 1859.02, 1859.06, 1859.07
Davidge, W. 1851.01, 1852.01, 1852.05, 1854.01, 1855.01, 1855.02, 1859.04, 1863.09, 1863.10, 1864.09, 1864.12, 1864.15, 1876.23
Davidge, W.P. 1854.06
Davidge, William 1879.05, 1879.50, 1879.56
Davidoff, Messr. 1922.06, 1925.03
Davidow, Ed 1922.46
Davidow, Popella 1924.48
Davids, R. 1893.41
Davidson and Francis 1885.46
Davidson, Abbott 1903.30
Davidson, Alexander 1895.03
Davidson, Bunty 1915.17
Davidson, Dore 1883.47, 1903.31
Davidson, Dorothy 1908.21
Davidson, E. 1887.27
Davidson, Emmet 1880.08, 1881.02
Davidson, Emmett 1883.06
Davidson, Gordon 1972.15, 1979.08, 1995.03, 1999.20
Davidson, I. 1880.08
Davidson, Ian 1999.14
Davidson, Isadore 1881.31
Davidson, Jo 1924.14
Davidson, John 1964.04, 1965.38, 1996.04
Davidson, Ken 1942.16
Davidson, Lorraine 1976.20
Davidson, Miss 1871.11, 1915.17
Davidson, Pauline 1890.40
Davidson, Richard M. 1989.10
Davidson, Sue 1948.16
Davidson, W.B. 1921.09
Davies, Andrew 1980.17
Davies, Arthur 1943.03
Davies, Ben 1928.45
Davies, Brian 1959.24, 1962.12, 2000.01
Davies, Charlotte 1912.30
Davies, Dennis Russell 1996.10
Davies, E.D. 1872.37, 1873.10
Davies, Ethel 1913.31, 1917.03
Davies, Fanille 1925.06
Davies, Gary-Michael 1983.17
Davies, H. Reese 1883.43
Davies, H.R. 1884.53, 1884.54
Davies, Harry 1900.06, 1900.30, 1901.14, 1904.27, 1918.17
Davies, Howard 1981.04, 1993.18
Davies, Irving 1955.19, 1986.01
Davies, Joan 1989.01
Davies, Lilian 1926.33
Davies, Maitland 1909.23, 1910.16
Davies, Margaret 1920.28, 1923.21, 1924.31
Davies, Maria Thompson 1918.42
Davies, Marion 1915.31, 1916.10, 1916.20, 1917.06, 1917.26, 1917.35, 1920.10
Davies, Paul Hyde 1915.19
Davies, Reine 1903.06, 1903.16, 1903.27, 1904.21, 1917.04
Davies, Robert 1911.21
Davies, Rosa 1917.03
Davies, Rose 1897.20
Davies, Spencer 1961.16
Davies, Stephen 1981.04
Davies, Valentine 1963.21
Davies, Vincent 1880.42
Davila, Diana 1971.18, 1976.01
Davin, Paul 1929.34, 1932.20
Davine, W.M. 1880.68
Davis 1965.30
Davis and Cooke 1901.22
Davis and Keogh 1898.66
Davis, A. 1918.23
Davis, Addie 1883.52
Davis, Al 1922.44
Davis, Albert 1907.23
Davis, Albert C. 1914.26
Davis, Alberta 1906.23
Davis, Amon 1923.11, 1929.21, 1930.16, 1930.24, 1932.08
Davis, Audrey 1932.03
Davis, Belle 1896.46, 1899.08, 1899.31
Davis, Benjamin O. 1925.12
Davis, Benny 1917.08, 1917.26, 1919.18, 1920.33, 1922.23, 1927.58, 1929.26, 1929.44, 1930.05, 1944.19, 1956.02, 1980.10, 1981.16
Davis, Bertha 1898.25
Davis, Berton 1947.13
Davis, Bessie McCoy 1917.26, 1919.18, 1919.43
Davis, Bette 1952.20
Davis, Betti 1938.17
Davis, Betty 1932.06
Davis, Bill 1992.03
Davis, Blevins 1944.28, 1953.04
Davis, Bob 1942.26
Davis, Boyd 1925.37, 1930.43, 1932.15
Davis, Brian 1931.01, 1934.13
Davis, Bruce Anthony 1986.06, 1994.01, 1996.14
Davis, Bus 1948.23
Davis, Buster 1948.28, 1951.13, 1953.17, 1956.14, 1959.06, 1960.23, 1964.11, 1964.21, 1964.35, 1965.14, 1967.06, 1968.02, 1970.08, 1971.03, 1974.02, 1975.09, 1975.13, 1976.15, 1980.06, 1986.20
Davis, C.M. 1934.37
Davis, C.T. 1926.38
Davis, Charles 1898.08, 1921.16, 1926.19, 1926.42, 1927.33, 1928.03, 1930.29
Davis, Charles L. 1888.31
Davis, Charlie 1924.27, 1932.30, 1982.12
Davis, Charlotte 1924.24
Davis, Cherry 1955.08, 1963.01
Davis, Christopher 1993.03
Davis, Christopher F. 1996.15, 1997.22, 1998.16
Davis, Clifton 1971.18
Davis, Clive 1982.08, 1985.03
Davis, Colin 1906.19, 1911.26
Davis, Collin 1904.53, 1908.12, 1908.13, 1910.09
Davis, D. 1929.21
Davis, Dani 1998.19
Davis, Diane 1942.34
Davis, Donna 1978.10
Davis, Dori 1956.15, 1960.06
Davis, Dorothy 1935.11
Davis, Dru 1979.13
Davis, Drusilla 1957.07
Davis, Duane 1979.32
Davis, Eddie 1939.25, 1940.10, 1941.11, 1942.12, 1944.14, 1955.04
Davis, Edith 1932.21
Davis, Edward 1938.19
Davis, Edward H. 1986.11
Davis, Elsie 1899.29, 1900.40, 1901.16, 1906.29
Davis, Emil 1916.15
Davis, Ethel 1921.02, 1924.32
Davis, Florence 1889.44
Davis, Frank 1891.01, 1920.02, 1929.18, 1929.52, 1955.13
Davis, Fred 1948.32
Davis, Garry 1946.07, 1950.19
Davis, George 1916.15, 1918.23, 1921.28, 1945.20, 1992.06
Davis, George D. 1893.27, 1893.36
Davis, Georgiana 1875.11
Davis, Gussie L. 1895.27
Davis, H.C. 1894.22
Davis, H.H. 1866.01, 1866.04, 1866.05
Davis, Hal 1982.22, 1997.21
Davis, Harriet 1905.21
Davis, Harris 1963.24, 1964.07, 1965.13, 1968.14, 1978.08, 1978.19, 1978.23, 1979.20, 1979.27, 1980.21, 1981.20, 1985.13, 1986.09, 1986.14, 1988.16, 1990.08, 1991.09
Davis, Harry 1880.37, 1916.22, 1962.14
Davis, Hazel 1939.15
Davis, Helene 1908.44
Davis, Henrietta Elizabeth 1983.04
Davis, Henry 1923.15, 1930.19, 1935.13, 1942.03, 1943.15, 1944.03
Davis, Hubert 1925.31
Davis, Inaya Jafan 1993.03
Davis, Ivan L. 1897.38
Davis, J. 1884.41, 1886.03, 1970.01, 1974.19
Davis, J. Charles 1890.16, 1890.37, 1890.40
Davis, J. Gunnis 1910.05
Davis, J.R. 1871.08
Davis, J.S. 1889.20
Davis, Jack 1933.01
Davis, James 1914.09, 1914.19, 1930.19
Davis, Jean 1944.09
Davis, Jeff 1974.01, 1974.12, 1985.13, 1986.09, 1990.06, 1992.10, 1992.14, 1993.14, 1994.09, 1995.18, 1996.11, 1997.03
Davis, Jeffrey Bryan 1985.01
Davis, Jessie Bartlett 1885.07, 1885.09, 1891.29, 1892.51, 1893.19, 1893.48, 1894.03, 1894.45, 1895.01, 1896.08, 1896.42, 1896.43, 1897.13, 1898.23, 1903.32
Davis, Jimmie 1933.06
Davis, Jimmy 1948.13, 1982.12
Davis, Joe 1885.15, 1885.22, 1887.16, 1960.13, 1967.13, 1968.20, 1978.14
Davis, John 1918.23, 1979.15
Davis, John H. 1894.52, 1903.28
Davis, Johnny 1916.15, 1917.16
Davis, Joseph 1885.02, 1885.49, 1886.42, 1886.52, 1887.07, 1893.30, 1903.26
Davis, Josephine 1907.62
Davis, Jr., Sammy 1956.02, 1964.32, 1974.11, 1978.18
Davis, Kate 1883.11, 1883.12, 1884.12, 1884.58, 1888.44, 1889.51, 1890.12, 1891.14, 1891.38, 1893.01, 1893.13, 1893.32, 1895.15
Davis, Keith 1978.02
Davis, Kery 1997.03
Davis, Kevin 1988.05
Davis, Kishna 2000.03
Davis, L. 1881.24
Davis, Lanier 1956.12, 1959.11, 1959.27, 1961.22, 1966.03, 1968.03
Davis, Lee 1924.32, 1944.14
Davis, Leo 1918.23
Davis, Lillian 1917.35
Davis, Lindsay W. 1983.09, 1985.18, 1990.07, 1991.08, 1992.10
Davis, Lorri 1968.11

Davis, Lou 1921.37, 1922.38, 1928.22
Davis, Luther 1941.03, 1952.09, 1953.16, 1965.22, 1978.03, 1985.13, 1986.09, 1989.26
Davis, Luther B. 1938.04
Davis, Mac 1974.09
Davis, Mack 1923.36, 1941.03
Davis, Maggie 1899.33, 1900.46, 1906.14, 1908.08, 1909.27
Davis, Maria 1880.13, 1911.01
Davis, Mary 1903.02, 1942.32
Davis, Mary Bond 1988.07, 1992.08, 1999.22
Davis, Maude 1939.26, 1940.07
Davis, Maureen 1987.18
Davis, Maybelle 1898.61
Davis, Messr. 1886.36, 1893.30
Davis, Meyer 1943.10, 1945.09
Davis, Michael 1959.02, 1960.01, 1960.04, 1966.01, 1966.18, 1969.05, 1970.08, 1981.09, 1986.07, 1986.13, 1994.13
Davis, Michael Rees 1988.14, 1988.16, 1988.18, 1990.07, 1993.12
Davis, Mina 1918.27
Davis, Miss 1750.01, 1896.44, 1921.42
Davis, Mr. 1851.06, 1852.04, 1864.17, 1866.02, 1866.16, 1866.28, 1892.24
Davis, Myra 1892.45
Davis, Myron P. 1903.36
Davis, Nancy 1946.05
Davis, Nellie 1880.43
Davis, Osceola 1973.09, 1989.18
Davis, Ossie 1951.11, 1957.16, 1965.32, 1970.05, 1972.26
Davis, Owen 1901.22, 1905.51, 1907.54, 1928.47, 1929.07, 1929.12, 1937.10, 1979.05
Davis, Patti 1967.16
Davis, Paul 1999.02
Davis, Pearl 1908.33
Davis, Peggy 1921.21
Davis, Peter 1932.20, 1989.29
Davis, Phyllis 1916.04
Davis, Pike 1930.29, 1931.11
Davis, Prentiss 1936.26
Davis, Randy 1998.18
Davis, Richard 1966.07
Davis, Richard B. 1794.01
Davis, Richard Harding 1907.27, 1920.13
Davis, Rita 1897.20
Davis, Robert 1940.21
Davis, Robert Hobart 1903.14
Davis, Rodger 1931.13
Davis, Roger 1910.21, 1912.24, 1921.33, 1922.45, 1930.38
Davis, Roland 1897.45
Davis, Rookie 1929.01
Davis, Sam 1901.20
Davis, Saul 1942.05
Davis, Sr., Sammy 1956.02
Davis, Stephen 1914.29
Davis, Thomas H. 1891.40, 1894.12, 1894.51, 1896.03, 1898.70
Davis, Virginia 1946.10
Davis, W.H.H. 1879.28
Davis, Walder 1936.30
Davis, Will 1947.09
Davis, William 1908.23, 1910.03, 1926.01
Davis, William O. 1943.10, 1951.11
Davis, William S. 1906.19
Davis, Winifred 1934.34
Davison, Abbott 1903.19, 1904.41
Davison, Jack 1962.13, 1965.21, 1966.10
Davison, Peter J. 2000.09
Davison, Robert 1944.21, 1945.19, 1946.13, 1946.17
Davitaya, Teimuraz 1977.13
Davolis, Mons. 1877.06
Davy, Gloria 1952.15
Davy, John 1855.01
Daw, Mae 1923.30, 1924.18
Daw, Tom 1912.11
Dawd, Tommy 1914.19
Dawe, Patrick 1905.48
Dawe, Virginia 1930.21
Dawes, G. 1852.07
Dawn, Dorothy 1927.20
Dawn, Eleanor 1922.28, 1922.47, 1925.30, 1926.28, 1941.03
Dawn, Elliott 1878.05
Dawn, Gloria 1924.02, 1924.07, 1924.18
Dawn, Hazel 1911.11, 1912.28, 1913.31, 1914.30, 1916.24, 1923.33, 1924.16, 1926.14
Dawn, Isabel 1925.48
Dawn, Jr., Hazel 1948.27
Dawn, Thera 1927.45
Dawson, Anne 1940.11, 1940.15
Dawson, Curt 1982.24
Dawson, Dan 1908.02, 1911.28, 1914.19, 1919.08
Dawson, Daniel 1914.11
Dawson, Ella 1896.49
Dawson, George 1897.04
Dawson, Georgia 1914.33
Dawson, Jenny 1888.38
Dawson, John 1934.37
Dawson, Joseph 1905.47
Dawson, Kate 1997.22, 2000.19
Dawson, Madge 1905.19
Dawson, Mark 1916.15, 1942.15, 1947.04, 1947.16, 1950.06, 1953.08, 1955.04, 1957.07, 1959.25
Dawson, Rudolph 1930.16
Day W.H. 1886.26
Day, Ben 1877.01
Day, C. 1901.06
Day, Carita 1906.08, 1907.55
Day, Connie 1973.11, 1990.06
Day, Diana 1926.39
Day, Dorothy 1929.45
Day, E. Marie 1916.12
Day, Edith 1916.04, 1916.25, 1917.36, 1919.36, 1922.33, 1923.05
Day, Edmund 1902.02
Day, Eugene 1927.40
Day, F.H. 1926.38
Day, Frederick 1910.21, 1911.05, 1911.12
Day, Genevieve 1904.19
Day, George 1950.14
Day, George W. 1898.70, 1911.24
Day, Harry 1947.03
Day, Ida 1908.08, 1909.27
Day, J. 1868.22
Day, J.A. 1892.25
Day, John B. 1891.34
Day, Juliette 1911.09, 1914.23, 1917.20, 1918.37, 1923.42, 1926.04
Day, June 1951.05
Day, Marie 1971.21
Day, Marie Louise 1890.32, 1891.21
Day, Marilyn 1946.22, 1948.22, 1952.02
Day, Marion 1892.31
Day, Mary Louise 1894.42
Day, May 1912.34, 1915.28
Day, Miss 1851.04, 1867.19
Day, Olive 1905.19
Day, Richard 1979.28
Day, Sonny 1954.08
Day, W.H. 1891.18
Day, Wilfred 1899.33
Day, William H. 1890.44, 1891.34
Daye, Bobby 1987.07, 1993.03
Daye, Dorothy 1927.11
Daye, Margaret 1927.11
Daye, Ruth 1938.13
Dayne, Elinor 1909.14, 1909.25
Dayne, Helen 1886.27
Dayne, Marie 1928.06
Days, Maya 2000.09
Dayton, A. 1883.16
Dayton, Anna 1884.12
Dayton, Annie 1882.41, 1883.52, 1885.63
Dayton, Frank H. 1889.20
Dayton, Fred Erving 1924.36
Dayton, G.W. 1883.64
Dayton, George 1868.04, 1870.30, 1870.41, 1871.06, 1872.10, 1872.35, 1873.03, 1888.11
Dayton, George W. 1870.05, 1872.23, 1882.70, 1882.75, 1883.21, 1883.38, 1883.39, 1883.58, 1884.21
Dayton, Helena Smith 1923.25, 1924.36
Dazey, Charles T. 1896.42, 1925.01, 1925.28, 1933.06
Dazian 1881.24, 1886.30, 1889.02, 1890.27, 1892.17, 1892.59, 1894.28, 1894.48, 1895.42, 1896.02, 1898.46, 1900.39, 1901.06, 1902.01, 1903.12, 1903.29, 1905.17, 1907.32, 1907.63, 1909.23, 1910.21, 1911.27, 1911.31, 1915.19, 1915.28, 1916.01, 1917.12, 1917.26, 1918.27
Dazian, Henry 1881.14, 1881.41, 1881.57, 1882.06, 1882.51, 1882.63, 1882.70, 1883.04, 1884.12, 1884.25, 1884.34, 1884.59, 1887.32, 1887.33, 1887.49, 1888.20, 1888.35, 1889.04, 1889.23, 1890.01, 1890.08, 1891.13, 1892.20, 1893.50, 1896.46
Dazian, Messr. 1907.36
Dazian, Mlle. 1905.57, 1907.46
Dazian, Mme 1894.13
Dazian, W. 1881.06, 1886.44, 1895.22
Dazian, William 1892.29
Dazians 1932.24
Dazie, La Belle 1905.05, 1905.23
Dazie, Mlle. 1907.24, 1908.19, 1911.12, 1912.27, 1915.02
Dazieri, Vincent 1937.14
Ddu, Bryn Celli 1990.09
de Alarcon, Pedro A. 1893.39
De Belleville, Frederic 1911.09
de Billemont, Jean-Jacques 1885.33, 1886.41
de Castelan, J. 1875.24
de Debillemont, Jean-Jacques 1875.21, 1877.04, 1882.62
de Felcourt, Mlle. 1867.24
de Forges, Pittaud 1868.20
de Francesco, G.V. 1875.03
De Francesco, Marie 1869.38
De Francesco, Marietta 1875.03
De Francesco, Rachel 1869.38
de Francesco, Rachel 1875.03
de Gillert, Theodora 1882.62
de Grimm, Baron 1891.13
de Grimm, C. 1885.41
de la Calle, J. 1985.07
De la Calle, J. 1999.18
De La Harpe 1879.06
De La Harpe, J.A. 1876.03
De La Harpe, Joseph 1873.03, 1873.11, 1873.19, 1873.26
de la Harpe, Joseph 1889.37, 1889.51
De la Harpe, Messr. 1877.32
de la Renta, Oscar 2000.16
de la Rosa, Oscar 1964.02
de laCroiz, Elsa 1938.15
de laFontaine, Gerard 1939.29
de laJeroma, Carmen 1992.15
de laJoaquina, Pepe 1992.15
De LaPena, George 1993.19
de laTour, Evelyn 1928.04
de Lavigerie, Draner 1883.48
de Lestrac, M. 1881.46, 1881.48
de Lestrac, Messr. 1881.49, 1881.50, 1881.51, 1881.53, 1881.54
De Lestrac, Messr. 1882.35
De Lestrac, Mons. 1882.29
de Leuven, Adolphe 1880.22
de Levita, Robin 1998.11, 1998.13
de Locle, Camille 1869.19
de losReyes, Imelda 1991.03
de Masson, Paul 1976.18
de Mille, Agnes 1939.29, 1943.04, 1943.19, 1944.23, 1945.05, 1947.01, 1947.07, 1947.17, 1948.31, 1949.03, 1949.18, 1950.10, 1950.20, 1951.16, 1951.24, 1953.09, 1954.01, 1954.07, 1957.03, 1957.11, 1958.07, 1958.14, 1959.04, 1961.24, 1962.15, 1963.04, 1963.06, 1963.26, 1964.46, 1965.24, 1965.38, 1966.31, 1967.17, 1969.07, 1969.12, 1979.31, 1980.26, 1992.10, 1994.02
de Mille, Agnes George 1937.15
de Morny, Duc 1872.18, 1873.23, 1876.11
de Morny, Le Duc 1869.12
de Planard, Francois-Antoine Eugene 1880.14
De Quercy, Mons. 1875.04
de Quercy, Mons. 1875.28
de Rialp, F. 1881.24
de Rille, Laurent 1880.58
de Ruyther, Julie 1882.70, 1883.45
de Saint Georges, J.H. Vernoy 1846.01
de Saint-Albin, Albert 1877.19, 1883.34, 1885.25, 1885.60
de Saint-George, Jules-Henri Vernoy 1877.35
de Saint-Georges, J.H. Vernoy 1852.03, 1852.04, 1854.02, 1854.07, 1862.03, 1863.07
de Saint-Georges, Jules-Henri Vernoy 1852.07, 1853.04, 1854.03, 1855.05, 1858.03, 1859.03, 1864.04, 1864.19, 1867.07, 1868.12, 1869.41, 1872.17, 1889.28
de Saint-Georges, Jules-Henry Vernoy 1844.01
de Sante, Leonilde 1881.15
de Smith, Louis 1893.17
de St. Remy, Mons. 1876.11
de Surmont, Mons. 1866.27
deAbravanel, Maurice 1938.11
Deacan, Annie 1879.03
Deacon, Addie 1877.25
Deacon, Annie 1877.39, 1878.20, 1879.38, 1880.24
Deacon, Miss 1877.22
Deady, John 1890.41, 1893.14, 1894.02
Deady, Mary 1976.29
Deagle, Tessie 1897.12
Deagon, Arthur 1902.18, 1903.24, 1907.25, 1908.19, 1909.13, 1912.40, 1914.15, 1915.24, 1922.43, 1924.28
Deagon, Grace 1920.19
Deal, Borden 1966.30
deAlarcon, Pedro 1934.38
Dealey, Kathleen 1905.13
deAlmeida, Antonio 1982.07
Dealy, Mae 1910.19
Dealy, May 1912.24, 1914.22, 1921.20
Dean, Barbara 1920.44
Dean, Benjamin 1875.05
Dean, Bert 1904.44
Dean, Charlotte 1888.10
Dean, Donna 1896.44
Dean, Doug 1998.19
Dean, Douglas 1942.11
Dean, Dudley S. 1943.23
Dean, Elsie 1879.03, 1879.38, 1880.24
Dean, Gerri 1970.20, 1975.20
Dean, Hortense 1891.24
Dean, J. 1984.15
Dean, J.C. 1894.13
Dean, Jacque 1965.29, 1985.08
Dean, Jo Ann 1940.16
Dean, John 1934.21, 1934.22, 1934.28, 1934.30, 1934.31, 1934.33, 1936.15, 1936.16, 1936.20, 1936.23, 1936.24, 1936.25, 1939.02, 1939.04, 1939.05, 1939.09, 1939.11
Dean, Julia 1919.35
Dean, Laura 1983.18
Dean, Lucia 1866.01
Dean, Madge 1899.15, 1899.36, 1900.16
Dean, Martha 1918.32
Dean, Maysie 1939.01, 1939.02, 1939.03, 1939.04, 1939.08
Dean, Michael-Pierre 1981.25
Dean, Miss 1886.32, 1896.44, 1897.14, 1904.13, 1904.44
Dean, Nina 1934.29, 1935.05, 1935.06
Dean, Rita 1903.37, 1905.17, 1905.54
Dean, Roger 1997.05
Dean, Sadie 1892.55, 1893.20
Dean, Shannon 1938.10, 1944.30, 1950.12
Dean, Sidney 1938.08
Dean, Syd 1938.08
Dean, W.J. 1897.05
Dean, Will J. 1904.33
DeAnchoriz, Alba 1914.24
DeAnda, Peter 1965.32
Deane, B. 1865.06, 1866.31, 1869.31
Deane, B.J. 1871.17
Deane, Ben 1890.35
Deane, Berna 1927.55
Deane, Bobby 1923.30
Deane, Daisy 1900.44
Deane, Douglas 1945.20, 1948.26, 1950.17, 1954.09
Deane, Elsie 1880.34
Deane, Ethel 1907.16
Deane, George 1908.36
Deane, Gussie 1894.19
Deane, Jeane 1930.23
Deane, Lonnie 1899.18, 1900.45
Deane, Lucia 1866.04, 1866.05, 1866.06
Deane, Madge 1899.36
Deane, Maggie 1892.24
Deane, Sidney 1904.01
Deane, Sydney 1900.51, 1902.37, 1903.17
Deane, Toby 1954.17
Deane, Vera 1938.18, 1941.03
Deane, Winnie 1888.29
DeAngelis, Freddie 1888.22
DeAngelis, Jefferson 1885.04, 1885.08, 1886.11, 1887.18, 1887.22, 1887.24, 1887.28, 1887.47, 1888.19, 1888.22, 1888.24, 1888.26, 1889.17, 1889.22, 1890.39, 1891.12, 1891.17, 1891.22, 1891.30, 1892.07, 1892.16, 1892.28, 1892.47, 1894.21, 1894.28, 1895.12, 1895.22, 1896.25, 1897.17, 1898.27, 1898.73, 1900.57, 1905.03, 1907.07, 1907.42, 1909.07, 1910.14, 1912.05, 1913.07, 1913.25, 1917.08, 1917.10
deAngelis, Jefferson 1921.29, 1922.16, 1926.40
Deans, Jonathan 1994.01, 1995.02, 1997.10, 1997.12, 1997.21, 1998.01, 1998.21, 1999.01, 1999.16, 2000.11, 2000.18, 2001.02
Dearborn Theatre Management, The 1904.09
Dearborn, Bettina 1956.03
deArco, Alfredo 1957.06

DeArco, Delphino 1961.07, 1961.12
Dearden, Audrey 1952.17, 1952.19
Dearduff, F.S. 1900.12
Dearduff, Frank 1903.07, 1903.20, 1905.33
Dearing, Judy 1975.02, 1990.12, 1995.14
Dearing, Samuel 1892.26
Dearinger, Kevin Lane 1976.05
DeArmas, Juan 1998.19
DeArmond, Isabel 1909.07
Deas, Ella 1907.55
Deas, Lawrence 1907.55, 1921.16, 1930.19, 1943.17
Deasy, Ann 1950.10
Deaton, Ralph 1992.08
Deaves, Ada 1885.06, 1886.11, 1895.08, 1897.19, 1900.59, 1905.36, 1908.41
Deaves, Harry 1888.45
Deaves, Lillie 1894.37
Deaves, Rillie 1884.37, 1885.06, 1888.04
Deayton, Angus 1986.15
DeBabian, Mabel 1885.08
DeBall, Alf 1906.02, 1906.42
DeBall, Alfred 1907.24, 1909.07
DeBar, Benedict 1845.01
DeBar, Mr. 1846.01
DeBar, Mrs. C. 1859.06, 1859.07
DeBarclay, H. 1872.10
deBeauplan, Arthur 1889.26
deBebeduoro, Tome 1988.06
deBeck, Billy 1923.25
deBecker, Harold 1911.06, 1918.41, 1926.20
deBecker, Nesta 1911.04
deBeer, Gerrit 1965.28, 1967.05, 1973.15, 1989.26
DeBeer, Gerrit 1968.30
Debeer, Mons. 1875.01
DeBeer, Mons. 1875.08, 1875.09
DeBeers, Clara 1908.07
DeBell, Bill 1963.10
deBella, Richard 1958.01
DeBenedictis, Richard 1964.21, 1964.40, 1965.06, 1966.12, 1966.14, 1966.16, 1972.03
Debenham, Cicely 1923.35
deBethel, David 1955.19
deBethel, Joan 1955.19
deBetrand, Julia 1884.60
DeBevoise, J. 1885.65
deBieville 1891.30
deBilbao, Antonio 1917.33
Debillement, Mons. 1881.15
deBillemont, Jean-Jacques 1890.17
Debillemont, Mons. 1892.35
Deblinde, Mlle. 1879.19, 1879.26, 1879.27, 1879.36, 1879.44, 1879.47
DeBoer, Ed 1982.23
DeBold, L.J. 1912.05
Debonay, A.J. 1872.05, 1872.08, 1872.12, 1872.14, 1872.36
deBonay, J. 1869.39
DeBonay, J. 1869.42
Debonay, J. 1869.45, 1870.01, 1870.06, 1872.25, 1872.30, 1872.32, 1872.36
Debonay, J.L. 1870.12, 1870.14, 1870.33, 1871.04
Debonay, John 1872.38, 1872.40, 1872.43
DeBoney, A.J. 1869.37
Deboney, J. 1869.08
DeBoney, J. 1869.38
Deboney, Messr. 1868.23, 1870.02
DeBoney, Messr. 1869.36
Debonnay, Mr. 1871.18
deBori, Riana 1935.11
deBouvier, Simone 1925.08
Debow, Miss 1892.29
DeBray, Harold 1900.14, 1900.21, 1900.23, 1900.26, 1900.27, 1900.30
Debray, J. 1879.48
Debray, Mlle. 1879.39
deBrett, Diane 1946.05, 1959.05
Debreuil, Signor 1861.05
deBries, Magda 1926.23
DeBrille 1879.50
deBroca, Philippe 1978.22
deBrocq, E.L. 1922.04
Debrussy 1979.14
DeBurgh, Shirley 1961.07
Debussey, Agatha 1920.44, 1923.30
Debussy, Claude 1922.21, 1929.05, 1978.26
deCaillavet, Gatson 1913.20
DeCamp, Edward 1919.12
deCardi, Laura 1923.45
deCardoba, Pedro 1915.01
Decareau, Dick 1995.07
DeCarlo, Yvonne 1971.05
DeCaro, J. 1985.07
Decart, M. 1929.10
deCart, Mr. 1929.13
Decart, Mr. 1929.15
Decaye 1947.18, 1981.04
deCervantes, La Gitanilla Miguel de 1900.22
DeCeunynck, Robert 1980.04, 1980.25
Dechamp, June 1900.58
Dechamps, Mons. 1873.11
DeChazza, Pepe 1963.14
Decker, A.W. 1883.47
Decker, C. 1876.21
Decker, C.N. 1877.16, 1879.18, 1879.23
Decker, Edith 1905.33, 1906.05, 1907.02, 1908.04, 1908.39, 1909.04, 1910.36, 1911.40, 1912.15, 1915.29, 1921.10
Decker, Elma 1918.32, 1921.07
Decker, Elsie 1922.35
Decker, Hugh H. 1905.43
Decker, J. 1887.16, 1888.40, 1889.07
Decker, Jay 1887.45
Decker, John 1887.48, 1888.27, 1889.11, 1889.15, 1889.18, 1890.49, 1891.25, 1891.45, 1892.54, 1893.15, 1893.27, 1893.36, 1893.46, 1894.04
Decker, John H. 1887.07
Decker, Marceline 1965.34, 1977.12, 1992.07
Decker, Messr. 1879.23
Decker, Mr. 1867.18, 1887.39
Decker, N. 1866.16, 1866.17, 1871.13, 1871.20, 1871.21
Decker, Nelson 1872.27, 1881.35
Decker, Paul 1903.06, 1903.33, 1904.21, 1915.19
deClairmont, Blanche 1890.29
deClue, Dorothy 1926.22
deCordova, Fred 1943.05
DeCormier, Robert 1960.18, 1961.08, 1961.20, 1963.26
deCorodoba, Rosa 1925.36
Decosta, Fannie 1894.13
DeCosta, Harry 1918.20, 1923.22
deCosta, Harry 1924.01
DeCosta, Leon 1918.13, 1919.32
deCosta, Leon 1925.19, 1926.20
DeCosta, Viola 1906.23
deCosta, Viola 1907.35
deCoteau, Bert 1973.02
deCottons, Victor 1900.34
deCourville, Albert 1922.05
Decre, Mlle. 1868.13
Decre, Mons. 1868.13, 1868.27, 1869.10, 1869.19, 1869.24
DeCristo, Al 1987.12
deCroisset, Francois 1922.33
DeDeyn, Severin 1908.13
DeDio, Harry 1969.11
Dedovitch, Messr. 1927.51, 1929.05
Dee, Anthony 1979.11
Dee, George 1902.19
Dee, Paula 1946.22
Dee, Pauline 1928.49, 1930.21
Dee, Sheila 1960.01
Dee, Sylvia 1947.08
Deeder, Dorothy 1926.21, 1927.27, 1927.53
Deei, Kale 1956.07
Deel, Sandra 1948.08, 1949.04, 1955.07
Deems, Mickey 1950.02, 1960.12, 1962.27
Deene, Marie 1900.33
Deer, Joe 1986.03, 1986.04, 1991.12
Deer, Princess White 1919.25, 1920.36
Deer, White 1922.35, 1927.12
Deerin, Oliver 1923.07
Deering, Belle 1884.21, 1884.66
Deering, Diane 1963.26
Deering, E. 1881.16
Deering, Eleanor 1878.20, 1879.03, 1880.32, 1881.16
Deering, Gladyce 1929.50
Deering, Jane 1943.07, 1946.07
Deering, Olive 1937.01, 1941.01, 1943.23
Deering, Patricia 1941.04
Deering, Rosemary 1930.09, 1930.20
Deery, Alfred 1911.46
Dees, Rick 1999.15
deFalla 1949.07
deFalla, Manuel 1945.10
deFay, Jack 1924.13
deFelcourt, Mlle. 1868.07, 1868.27
DeFilippe, Dora 1903.21
deFilippo, Jacy 1994.12
deFlers, Robert 1913.20
DeFoe, Daniel 1869.23, 1880.13
Defoe, Daniel 1877.25, 1879.03
DeForest, Anthea 1963.15, 1965.07
DeForest, Jim 1919.21
deForest, Marie 1940.21
deForest, Maude 1929.52
deForest, Muriel 1920.09, 1922.15
DeForest, Patsie 1919.08
DeForrest, Charles 1868.04, 1868.23, 1868.32
DeForrest, Hal 1907.02
DeForrest, Mr. 1863.06
DeForrest, Muriel 1920.22, 1920.23
DeForrest, S.G. 1879.54
DeFossez, A.J. 1881.34
Defossez, A.J. 1881.40, 1881.56
Defossez, Mme. 1885.35
DeFoye, Jeanne 1908.04
Defrang, Mlle. 1875.07
DeFrankie, Sylvia 1920.07
DeFrece, Lauri 1914.32
DeGange, Anny 1983.12
deGanon, Camille 1989.03, 1991.12
Degeiter, P. 1938.02
deGerald, Guy 1924.01, 1925.50
DeGerde, Oliver 1918.31
deGergorio, Felice 1927.28
DeGez, J. 1887.03
DeGez, John 1886.16, 1887.27, 1897.23
DeGillert, Theodora 1883.06
deGillert, Theodore 1884.40
Degnell, Thomas 1885.34
DeGoruche, Mme. 1848.03
DeGraff, Dolores 1903.13
DeGraff, Georgia 1903.13
deGranada, Rose 1918.40
deGrandy, Miguel 1974.14
DeGrasse, Nellie 1907.21, 1910.13, 1913.16
deGraves, Bernardine 1923.30
Degraw, H. 1894.13
DeGray, Sid 1895.02
deGray, Sidney 1898.17
DeGray, Sidney 1900.44
deGray, Sydney 1898.05
DeGray, V. 1898.61
DeGrazia, Elizabeth 2000.20
DeGregorio, Felice 1917.24, 1919.20
DeGresac, Fred 1911.38, 1911.47
deGresac, Fred 1913.10, 1913.24, 1917.34, 1922.33, 1929.34, 1947.04
DeGrey 1903.19
DeGrey, Sidney 1905.20
DeGrey, Sydney 1899.23, 1904.34
deGrey, Sydney 1902.27, 1906.44
deGrignan, Juliette 1893.38
DeGrim, C. 1891.18
Degrimm, Baron 1892.29
DeGrimm, Baron C. 1890.21, 1892.42
DeGrimm, C. 1884.40, 1890.11, 1890.39, 1890.43, 1891.14, 1891.15
DeGrimme, Baron 1894.06
deGroat, Andrew 1975.10
DeGross, Lillian 1895.36
deGrouche, Mons. 1857.04, 1857.06
DeGrue, Marie 1902.07
deGuzman, Josie 1992.04
deGuzman, Jossie 1978.11, 1979.09
deHaas, Darius 1999.10, 1999.22
deHartog, Jan 1966.29
DeHaven, Carter 1903.28, 1905.29, 1908.42, 1908.43, 1910.27, 1910.32, 1912.25, 1913.16, 1917.09
DeHaven, Charles 1913.18, 1918.30
DeHaven, Flora Parker 1913.16
deHaven, Gloria 1955.10
deHierapolis, Leo 1925.13
Dehn, Mura 1932.19
Dehncke, H. 1894.30
Dehneke, Mr. 1892.43
DeHon, Billie 1916.11
deHorn, Ernest 1888.22
Dehorn, Herr 1882.68
Deice, C. 1862.01
Deign, Peter 1959.05
Deissler, Mike 1992.05
Deit, Edmond 1911.18
Deitch, Belle M. 1989.25
Deitch, Burttress 1921.31, 1923.14
Deitch, Kathy 1998.13
Deitrich, Gary 1980.25
Deitz, Howard 1927.27
Deitz, Messr. 1886.32
deJari, M. 1925.25, 1925.48, 1926.23
DeJean, Michelle 1995.02
deJerz, Gitanos 1992.15
Dejonge, Mr. 1844.01
deKarlo, Sergio 1944.02
Dekker, Thomas 1963.28
DeKnight, Jimmy 1982.22
deKnight, Rene 1945.08
deKock, Paul 1886.36
Dekova, Margit 1945.12
deKoven Opera Company 1912.19
deKoven, Jean 1933.07
DeKoven, Reginald 1887.47, 1891.29, 1892.45, 1892.51, 1892.52, 1893.18, 1893.19, 1893.40, 1893.48, 1894.40, 1895.01
deKoven, Reginald 1895.12, 1895.24, 1895.27, 1897.48, 1903.36, 1911.47, 1912.19, 1929.43, 1932.02, 1944.25
DeKoven, Reginald 1896.02, 1896.08, 1896.37, 1896.45, 1897.50, 1898.04, 1898.23, 1899.06, 1899.19, 1899.38, 1900.07, 1900.31, 1900.50, 1901.25, 1902.04, 1902.28, 1903.27, 1905.36, 1906.49, 1907.52, 1908.34, 1909.07, 1913.25, 1913.27, 1917.10
deKoven, Roger 1937.01
DeKoven, Roger 1964.11, 1979.29
DeKoven-Smith Opera Company 1896.45
Del Campo, A. 1886.48, 1886.49
Del Corso, Geralyn 1999.24
Del-Mely, Mme. 1893.41
Del-Mely, Mons. 1893.41
deLa Passardiere, Guy 1966.05
dela Vega, Ricardo 1969.11
DeLacey, Jennie 1868.03
Delacour, Alfred 1875.01, 1880.61, 1882.73, 1883.44, 1883.45, 1884.63, 1887.33, 1887.41, 1888.22, 1912.08
Delacour, Clairville 1887.33
DeLacy, Jennie 1871.13
deLacy, V. 1888.20
Delafield, Helen 1893.01
DeLaFontaine, Mlle. 1877.32
Delafosse, Mons. 1887.35, 1887.36, 1887.37
Delahoussaye, Dayne 2001.04
Delair, Suzy 1964.06
Delamanning, Mr. 1881.04
Delamarcie, M. 1926.43, 1926.45, 1926.47, 1926.48
Delamarcie, Messr. 1926.47
Delamonte, Miro 1900.13
Delamotta, Miro 1897.46, 1902.27
Delamotte, Miro 1900.14, 1900.23, 1900.26
Delancey, Jere 1937.04
Deland, Annie 1872.23, 1872.35, 1873.03, 1873.19, 1877.07, 1884.24, 1886.60
Deland, Georgie 1898.74, 1898.76
Deland, Helen 1876.35, 1877.02
Delaney and Meynet 1925.50
Delaney, B. 1886.10
Delaney, Barry 1910.13
Delaney, Geraldine 1955.02
Delaney, Jere 1923.09, 1925.16
Delaney, Martin 1911.47
Delaney, Patsey 1923.04
DeLange, Eddie 1939.29, 1942.11, 1976.04, 1997.03, 1999.24
DeLange, Jean 1896.26
DeLange, Louis 1879.13, 1879.66, 1886.32, 1890.43, 1896.05
deLange, Louis 1897.48, 1898.77, 1899.22
DeLange, Louis 1900.54
Delano, Allen 1936.01
Delano, Dickie 1883.52
Delano, Fannie 1886.23
Delano, Jeppe 1886.23
Delano, Lee 1989.22
Delano, Marion 1963.14
Delano, Sue 1993.18
Delanoe, Pierre 1967.13, 1968.20, 1968.21
Delany, Patsy 1921.06, 1923.46
deLaPaz, Pauline 1903.21
DeLaPaz, Ray 1998.02
DeLaPena, George 1983.02, 1995.09
Delapenha, Denise 1971.12
Delaporte, Michel 1859.10
deLappe, Gemze 1951.12, 1951.24, 1958.07, 1959.04, 1962.15, 1964.46, 1965.24, 1965.38, 1966.31, 1967.17, 1969.12, 1978.24, 1979.31, 1986.03, 1996.13
DeLaria, Lea 1998.16, 2000.17
Delaro, Elma 1880.01, 1880.03, 1880.55, 1881.08, 1882.15, 1882.16, 1884.21, 1884.28, 1886.15, 1886.40, 1889.04, 1889.24, 1890.21
Delaro, Hattie 1886.24, 1887.31, 1888.04, 1888.18, 1889.19, 1892.29, 1899.36, 1900.16, 1903.31
Delaro, Miss 1881.07
Delarova, Eugenia 1942.01
deLaval, Mario 1949.03

deLavallade, Carmen 1954.19
DeLavallade, Carmen 1963.13
DeLaValle, Jean 1919.02
Delavan, Mr. 1869.43
Delavault, Helele 1983.16
deLavigerie, Cledat 1883.48
Delavigne, Mme. 1882.55, 1882.58, 1882.61
delBondio, J.H. 1938.15, 1947.06
delBondio, John H. 1932.13
Delbridge, Edwin 1927.42, 1934.20, 1934.36
Delby, Alfred 1920.24
delCampo, Rudy 1958.05
DelCorral, Victor 1974.14
delDrego, George 1930.20
delDrigo, George 1929.49
DelDuca, Jr., Lennie 1981.24
deLee, Lillian 1906.48
Delehante, Dhenise 1931.27, 1931.41
Delehante, Dhoris 1931.35, 1931.43
Delehanty, Messr. 1872.40, 1872.43
deLeo, Don 1932.19, 1945.20
deLeon, Bobby 1929.52
deLeon, Carlos 1974.14
DeLeon, Inez 1879.59
deLeon, Michael 1949.04
deLeon, Noel 1949.04
Deleon, R. 1970.01
DeLeon, Thomas Cooper 1870.07
deLeon, Walter 1923.13, 1924.02, 1924.37, 1926.06, 1928.41
Delerue, Georges 1982.23
Delery-Whedon, Susan 1978.19, 1978.20, 1978.23, 1979.20, 1979.21, 1979.27, 1984.11
Delest, Mlle. 1885.55, 1885.56, 1885.57, 1885.60, 1885.61, 1886.21
Deleste, Mlle. 1886.08, 1886.22
DeLestrac, Messr. 1882.30
DeLestrac, Mlle. 1882.30
Delettre, Jean 1934.32, 1935.19, 1987.02
deLeuven, Adolphe 1889.26
Delevan 1870.04
Delevan, Annie 1893.32
DeLevita, Robin 1993.17, 1995.15
Delf, Harry 1914.07, 1916.02, 1918.11, 1918.29, 1919.18, 1920.42, 1923.04, 1926.23
Delfino, E. 1985.07, 1999.18
Delfont, Bernard 1962.18, 1965.28, 1973.13
Delgado, Gustavo 1949.07
Delgado, Louis 1929.42, 1930.39
Delgado, Miguel 1979.08
Delgardo, Louis 1932.07
Delgatto, Marc Stephen 1984.02
Delgleish, Trudy 1999.02
Delgmann, Frl. 1879.22
Delia, Mrs. 1844.01
deLiagre, Jr., Alfred 1954.03, 1961.24, 1983.02
Deliane, Mlle. 1902.13
Delibes, Leo 1922.21, 1929.51
Deliere, Blanche 1898.56
Delievre, Leo 1934.32
deLignamare, Willie 1921.11
Deligne, H. 1866.23, 1866.25, 1866.27, 1866.29, 1866.30
Deligne, Mons. 1866.29, 1869.16
deLille, Lola 1927.52
DeLillies, Virginia 1919.14
deLima, C.A. 1917.25, 1920.30
Delina, Mlle. 1884.43
deLind van Wijngaarden, Lydia 1966.19
Delinge, Mons. 1869.30
deLisle, Leon 1904.03
Delius, Robert 1899.40
deLiva, Terry 1959.02
Dell'Isola, Salvatore 1947.17, 1949.04, 1953.08, 1954.12, 1955.04, 1955.27, 1958.19
Dell, Betty 1934.35
Dell, Billie 1925.50
Dell, Claudia 1925.27, 1927.37, 1928.03
Dell, Delano 1922.45, 1923.41
Dell, Dorothy 1931.19, 1933.15
Dell, Gabe 1950.09
Dell, Gabriel 1955.04, 1962.13, 1963.05, 1964.15
Dell, Josie 1883.18
Della Fox Comic Opera Company 1894.28, 1895.22
della Sorte, Joseph 1967.10
Della, Helene 1885.01
Dellett, George 1911.43
Delli, Ceil 1961.20
Dellinger, Rudolf 1886.26
Dellinger, Rudolph 1887.12, 1888.24, 1888.39
Dellorto, Carl 1915.02
DelMaestro, Lorna 1953.11, 1955.11
Delmaning, Florence 1880.05
Delmanning Brothers 1887.30
Delmar, Belle 1911.39
Delmar, Elaine 1986.01
Delmar, Ethel 1915.05, 1917.20, 1918.11, 1919.13, 1920.17
Delmar, Florence 1917.20, 1918.28
Delmar, Frank 1934.18, 1934.42
Delmar, Grace 1908.40
Delmar, Harry 1927.62, 1944.14
Delmar, Jean 1883.52, 1888.21
Delmar, John 1934.18, 1934.42
delMar, Josephine 1940.21
Delmar, Kenny 1949.17
Delmar, M. 1875.20
delMar, Norman 1950.18
Delmar, Ruby 1905.46
Delmar, Thomas 1917.17
delMarga, Rita 1926.03
Delmas, Mlle. 1875.07, 1875.08
Delmet, Paul 1952.04
Delmont, Ethel 1880.55
Delmont, Gene 1921.25, 1923.22
Delmont, Isobel 1902.30
Delmonte, E. 1881.30
DelMonte, George 1957.15, 1959.08, 1959.17, 1960.02, 1962.13
Delmore, Connie 1890.43
Delmore, Elinore 1907.17
Delmore, Herbert 1923.43, 1925.32
Delmore, Ralph 1883.40, 1886.02
Deloff, Walter 1927.26
DeLon, Jack 1956.15
deLon, Jack 1957.02, 1958.01, 1959.02, 1959.08, 1966.08
DeLon, Jack 1962.01, 1963.25, 1965.15, 1966.02, 1966.31
DeLong, George 1901.19
deLong, George 1904.50
DeLonton, Natalie 1907.24
deLoraine, Alfred 1922.15
Delorme, F. 1881.49, 1881.50, 1881.54
Delorme, Harry 1881.47, 1882.66, 1883.26
DeLorme, Harry 1882.32, 1882.72
Delorme, L. 1875.19, 1875.23, 1875.26
Delorme, Mlle. 1879.41, 1879.48, 1879.49, 1879.55, 1880.23, 1880.28, 1880.52, 1880.56, 1883.51, 1883.55, 1883.57, 1883.59, 1883.61, 1885.23, 1886.09, 1886.22
Delorme, Mme. 1880.44, 1884.45, 1884.50, 1884.52, 1884.54, 1885.55, 1885.56, 1885.59, 1886.19, 1886.20
DeLorme, Pauline 1914.28
Delournay, Mlle. 1882.67, 1883.30, 1883.41, 1883.55, 1883.57, 1883.59, 1883.60, 1883.61, 1884.01
Delournay, Mme. 1882.55, 1882.58, 1883.28
deLova, Muriel 1931.08
deLoville, Aljan 1937.04
Delphine, Anna 1930.33
Delphine, Mlle. 1869.10
DelPuente, Joseph 1917.01
delRigo, George 1932.01
Delrita, Eone 1895.28
delRivero, Nydia 1974.14
DelRosario, Andrea 1957.06
DelRossi, Angelo 1998.06, 1999.11
Delroy Irene 1920.02
Delroy, Dollie 1884.46, 1889.01
Delroy, Dolly 1885.63, 1886.43, 1887.14, 1898.42
Delroy, Irene 1923.31, 1924.06, 1924.15, 1925.47, 1927.37, 1928.17, 1929.03, 1929.49
Delsener, Ron 1973.14, 1974.01, 1975.12, 1979.11, 1979.19, 1979.30, 1983.03, 1988.08, 1988.19, 1989.16, 1990.09, 1998.12
Delsenerslater/SFX Entertainment 1998.12
delSolar, Alberto 1993.08
Delting, Renee 1919.35
Deltwyn, A.C. 1893.23
DeLuca, John 1999.23
DeLuce, Florence 1900.21, 1900.26
deLuce, Virginia 1952.09
Delugg, Milton 1980.29
DeLuise, Dom 1963.20
DeLuisi, Louise 1881.39
deLussan, Zelie 1888.07
deLuz, Trudy 1949.08
Delval, Helene 1866.18
delVal, Jean 1929.45
Delval, Rose 1866.18
Delves, Nellie 1898.72
Delworth, George 1922.27
DeLyle, Dorothy 1891.18
DeLyon, Mlle. 1899.31
DeLyons, Frank 1907.22
deLys, Derna 1948.29, 1950.13
Delysia, Alice 1923.41
Delza, Sophia 1928.19
deMagnus, Louis 1946.03
DeMain, John 1976.28, 1980.02, 1983.05, 2000.03
DeMain, John J. 1978.04
deMalita, Anna Maria 1921.02
DeManby, Alfred 1915.18
deMangus, Louis 1947.04
DeMar, Carrie 1894.17, 1906.22, 1907.14
DeMar, Fleurette 1902.08, 1904.23, 1906.22
deMar, Ramsey 1921.06
deMarco, Antonio 1925.45, 1930.31, 1932.07
deMarco, Don 1988.08
deMarco, Michael 1953.07, 1954.15, 1959.05
deMarco, Nina 1925.45
deMarco, Renee 1930.31, 1932.07, 1940.12
DeMarco, Ronnie 1972.07
deMarco, Sally 1941.13, 1944.22
deMarco, Tony 1940.12, 1941.13, 1944.22
deMarcos, Anthony 1924.19
deMarcos, Antonio 1927.21
deMarcos, Nina 1924.19, 1927.21
Demare, L. 1985.07
Demarest and Lohmuller, Inc. 1929.50
Demarest, Frances 1909.31, 1910.22, 1911.37, 1913.28, 1914.04, 1914.16, 1915.11, 1915.17, 1916.11, 1916.14, 1917.14, 1917.21, 1919.04
Demarest, William 1920.24, 1929.26, 1929.50, 1931.26
deMaris, Aida 1927.07
DeMaris, Merrill 1979.28
deMarquis, Marie 1914.21
DeMart, Carrie 1902.08
deMartin, Imelda 1953.17, 1956.01, 1957.06, 1959.13, 1959.23
DeMartin, Imelda 1956.01, 1958.14, 1963.25, 1964.46
Demas, Carole 1972.12
DeMatthews, F. 1918.21
DeMay, Sally 1967.16, 1971.07
DeMayo, Margarita Flora 1920.13
deMayo, Peter 1954.03
Dembrun, Mlle. 1867.05
Demby-Cain, Michael 1986.11, 1995.15
deMel, Marcia Labios 1992.13
deMenil, Francois 1982.08
Demetriou, Claude 1992.03
DeMetrius, Claude 1989.12
deMette, Stella 1932.14
deMeyer, Aileen 1926.01
deMeyer, Baron 1920.02
deMilhau, Louis 1942.20
deMille, Agnes 1986.03, 1986.04, 1991.12, 1996.13
Demilt 1862.03, 1862.04, 1863.06, 1863.07
Demilt, Messr. 1875.35
DeMilt, Mr. 1851.05
Demilt, Mr. 1855.11, 1865.04
Demilt, W. 1856.02
Demilt, W.W. 1869.04, 1869.13
deMin, Jacqueline 1964.39
Deming, Will 1916.22, 1922.09
Deming, Will J. 1922.17
Demmigar, John 1942.03
Demmler, Gertrude 1926.22
Demmler, Maxine 1926.22
deMonde, Belle 1924.16
deMonde, Delores 1930.20
DeMone, Richard 1981.17
Demont, Billy 1930.16
DeMora, Bob 1973.14
deMora, Robert 1985.03
DeMorest, G.V. 1879.25
Demorest, Mr. 1879.14
deMott, William 1924.37
Demoz, Leelai 1993.04
Dempsey, George 1903.01
Dempsey, Jackie 2000.02
Dempsey, James E. 1942.11
Dempsey, Jerome 1985.18
Dempsey, Laura 1880.08
Dempsey, Louisa 1880.41
Dempsey, Louise 1880.05, 1881.13, 1884.17, 1886.38, 1888.21, 1889.42, 1892.59, 1903.01, 1911.17
Dempsey, Mark 1972.06
Dempsey, Peggy 1919.26
Dempsey, Thomas J. 1891.42
Dempspey, John J. 1912.12
Dempster, Jennifer 1986.03
Dempster, Monroe 1873.05
Dempster, Robert 1908.29, 1910.03, 1911.46
Demsond, Maggie 1869.43
Denby, Edwin 1938.11
Denda, Elena 1969.11
Denda, Gigi 1978.07, 1989.13
Dene, Daisy 1905.14
Denecke, Mr. 1890.31
Denehy, Anna May 1929.39
DenEnde, Joop Van 1995.15
Denese, Dorothy 1927.67, 1932.11
Dengate, Dennis 1944.24, 1945.12
Denger, Grace 1878.22
Denham 1869.27
Denham and Lundy 1866.24
Denham, A.H. 1880.41, 1881.02, 1881.13, 1881.32, 1882.62, 1883.06, 1885.33, 1886.16, 1887.03, 1888.01
Denham, Bessie 1904.03
Denham, F. 1856.02, 1856.03
Denham, George 1869.34
Denham, George W. 1881.34, 1881.40, 1885.30, 1885.32, 1903.31
Denham, J. 1867.17, 1869.20
Denham, J.C. 1869.35, 1870.04
Denham, John 1881.31, 1881.43
Denham, Johnny 1869.28
Denham, Miss 1859.11, 1862.03
Denham, Mr. 1856.02, 1856.03, 1869.43
Denham, O.H. 1884.39
Denier, Tony 1864.06, 1864.17, 1864.22, 1865.05, 1865.07, 1865.08, 1865.09, 1865.10, 1871.09, 1871.11
Denin, E. 1881.11
Denin, G. 1881.11
Denin, Georgie 1894.42
Denio, Laura 1898.52
Denis, Carol 1984.09
Denis, George 1961.01
Denise, Diane 1942.10
Denise, Patricia 1950.14
Denisova, Alexandra 1944.28
Denizon, Jean-Paul 1983.16
Denman, Jeffrey 1997.05
Denman, Jeffry 2001.05
Dennan, Georgie 1885.63
Dennay, Albert A. 1908.40
Denne, Lon 1922.21
Dennee, Charles 1900.03, 1902.21
Dennehy, Dennis 1972.11, 1975.07, 1987.14
Dennen, Barry 1971.12
Dennery, H. 1868.18, 1868.25, 1868.27, 1868.30, 1868.31, 1869.01, 1869.09, 1869.10, 1869.12
Dennes, Eileen 1916.20
Denni, Lucien 1925.05, 1926.30
Denniker, Paul 1976.04
Dennin, Georgie 1888.02, 1888.20, 1889.23, 1889.40, 1889.49, 1893.32, 1893.39, 1894.14
Dennin, K. 1881.04
Dennin, Miss 1846.01
Dennin, Susan 1846.01, 1848.03
Denning, Dorothy 1892.26, 1892.32, 1892.41, 1893.01, 1893.04, 1893.22
Denning, Frank 1945.01
Denning, Katherina 1903.09
Denning, Kathryn 1903.09
Dennis, Carol 1997.21
Dennis, Dorothy 1942.34
Dennis, Estelle 1928.20
Dennis, John 1950.08, 1954.02, 1955.01
Dennis, Matt 1995.12
Dennis, Nick 1936.05
Dennis, Patrick 1962.27, 1966.10, 1982.01, 1983.10, 1998.15
Dennis, Paul 1944.26
Dennis, Phillip 1991.10
Dennis, Ray 1938.07, 1939.07
Dennis, Richard 1950.16
Dennis, Robert 1971.04, 1976.27
Dennis, Ronald 1975.15, 1983.06
Dennis, Shirley 1944.22
Dennis, Tiramate 1972.20
Dennis, Winifred 1895.10
Dennison, Annabelle 1913.10
Dennison, E. 1872.10, 1873.08
Dennison, John 1958.11
Dennison, Loretta 1934.01
Dennison, Mac 1965.05
Dennison, Mark 1888.28

Dennison, Messr. 1864.13
Dennison, Mr. 1845.01, 1846.01, 1864.13
Dennison, Roy 1908.27
Denniston, Leslie 1980.06, 1981.12
Denny, Doreen 1934.21, 1934.25, 1934.31
Denny, Harry 1927.39
Denny, J. 1990.15
Denny, Jr., George V. 1926.38
Denny, Reginald 1919.30
Denny, W.H. 1905.49, 1909.07, 1909.15
deNobili, Lilla 1958.18
DeNoel, Miss 1881.41
DeNovelis, A. 1904.21
DeNovelis, Antonio 1882.43, 1882.46
DeNovellis, A. 1897.50, 1898.36, 1900.07, 1900.50, 1901.13, 1902.43, 1904.30, 1906.47, 1910.28, 1913.14, 1916.05
deNovellis, A. 1917.11
DeNovellis, Antonio 1881.14, 1882.64, 1882.65, 1883.49, 1884.34, 1884.51, 1885.14, 1885.45, 1885.52, 1886.26, 1886.33, 1886.37, 1886.43, 1887.18, 1887.44, 1888.18, 1889.24, 1890.26, 1891.31, 1893.35, 1894.40, 1899.06, 1899.25, 1900.20, 1901.08, 1905.29, 1908.16, 1908.43, 1909.22, 1912.10
deNovellis, Antonio 1884.57, 1885.13, 1885.28, 1885.67, 1895.26, 1896.45, 1907.52
DeNoville, Carrie 1915.17, 1918.22
DeNoyer, Edward 1911.34
Densen, Irwin 1975.17, 1976.22, 1976.31, 1977.03, 1977.17, 1978.08, 1979.27
Denslow, W.W. 1905.25
Dent, Nellie Graham 1924.25
Dentler, Helen 1916.07
Dentling, Renee 1920.19
Denton, Herbert 1912.36
Denton, Herbert E. 1908.37
Denton, Ray 1938.03
Dentsu, Inc. 1992.08
Denver Center 1983.05
Denver, Margaret 1910.02
deOca, Montes 1966.08
dePach, Maurice 1932.05, 1933.02
dePackh, Henry 1904.39
dePackh, Maurice 1918.18, 1920.08, 1920.18, 1921.21, 1921.24, 1921.30, 1921.37, 1922.03, 1922.28, 1922.29, 1922.48, 1923.07, 1923.32, 1924.19, 1924.30, 1924.44, 1925.22, 1925.45, 1926.03, 1926.07, 1926.12, 1926.16, 1926.32, 1927.05, 1927.09, 1927.21, 1927.38, 1927.46, 1927.54, 1928.03, 1928.28, 1928.41, 1928.50, 1929.29, 1929.35, 1930.21, 1931.19, 1932.24, 1938.01
dePackh, Meurice 1938.07
dePaolo, Dan 1945.09
dePaolo, Daniel 1943.06, 1946.13
DePass, Paul 1979.16, 1979.31, 1980.26, 1981.25, 1983.21, 1991.13
dePaul, Gene 1955.11, 1956.12, 1974.10, 1982.14, 1991.04
dePaul, Justine 1929.33
dePaur, Leonard 1940.01, 1941.07, 1943.23
Depaur, Leonard 1956.06
dePauw, Bille 1942.19
DePena, Valerie 1992.07
dePeri, Panchita 1964.39
Depeuty, Charles 1864.03
Depew, Freda 1893.49, 1895.34
Depew, H. 1880.62
Depew, P.O. 1898.30, 1898.42
Depew, Pete 1907.38
dePinna, Connie 1935.14, 1937.17
DePol, Henry 1867.25
DePol, John 1867.25
dePolanco, Nunez 1934.38
dePont, Donald 1906.37
dePoumeyrac, Jane 1929.10, 1929.11, 1929.13, 1929.14, 1929.15, 1929.16
dePoyster, Paul 1944.21
Depp, Harry 1907.46, 1911.11, 1913.31
Depp, Olive 1910.34, 1911.11
Deppe, Lois 1929.37, 1930.37, 1931.31
DeQuercy, Mons. 1875.01, 1875.02
deQuercy, Mons. 1875.25, 1875.30, 1875.33
DeRango, Harry 1904.35
Deransart, Edouard 1892.32
Derbas, Frank 1952.02
Derbeneva, Tatiana 1990.01
Dere, Ann 1941.07
deReeder, Pierce 1920.25
deReeder, Pierre 1928.26, 1929.32, 1931.03
Dereeder, Pierre 1934.13
deReeder, Pierre 1938.17, 1943.12
Derefinko, Rod 1967.01, 1969.02
DeReu, Minnie 1893.44, 1897.11
deRex, Billie 1924.32
deRhona, Linda 1871.09, 1871.11
Deriberpres, Emma 1875.28, 1875.29
Derickson, Charles 1919.18, 1920.08, 1924.07
DeRigney, Lillian 1902.05
DeRigney, Louise 1902.16, 1903.15, 1905.49, 1907.42
Derious, George W. 1888.16
Derman, L. 1910.24
Derman, Louis 1913.08
Dermody, Edward 1898.55
Dermond, Mlle. 1887.36
Dermont, Mlle. 1887.37
Derny, Madge 1919.30
deRoche, Rene 1930.35
deRochemont, Ben 1964.39
DeRocher, Albert 1906.34
deRosa, Josephine 1872.06, 1876.36
DeRosa, Josephine 1877.04, 1877.15
deRosa, Judith 1974.08
DeRosa, Judith 1975.11, 1976.31, 1978.08
DeRosa, Mlle. 1868.18, 1880.08, 1880.41, 1881.02, 1882.77, 1885.33, 1886.16
deRosa, Mlle. 1872.10
DeRosa, Vera 1910.35, 1912.46
deRose, Peter 1934.01, 1940.02, 1940.16, 1953.12
DeRose, Peter 1975.12, 1987.02
DeRosen 1879.12
deRoss, Frank 1940.19
deRouge, Wilbur 1922.34
deRoze, Georges 1934.32
Derpa, Mlle. 1871.18
Derr, Frank 1918.16
Derr, Richard 1955.01
Derretta, Lottie 1880.31
Derrian, Margaret 1907.03
Derrick, Fred 1927.17
Derrick, Joseph 1885.21
Derricks, Cleavant 1977.15, 1979.18, 1980.14, 1981.29, 1986.06, 1987.07
Derricks, Marguerite 2001.01
Derricks-Carroll, Clinton 1976.35
Derro, John 1948.22
DeRue, Minnie 1881.36, 1881.38, 1885.14, 1890.46, 1890.47, 1890.48
deRugeris, Joseph 1978.07, 1978.20, 1979.21, 1989.13
deRuyther, Julie 1882.19, 1883.18, 1883.21, 1883.58, 1884.14
Derval, Paul 1964.22
Derwent, Clarence 1925.09, 1927.26, 1928.12, 1946.05, 1946.18, 1959.05
des Jardins, Lang 1966.07
Des Moulins, Messr. 1796.01
Desailly, Jean 1964.06
deSaint-Albin, Albert 1891.47
deSaint-George, Jules-Henri Vernoy 1898.39, 1898.76
deSaint-Georges, Jules-Henri Vernoy 1896.16, 1900.22
DeSal, Frank 1967.16, 1969.01, 1981.07, 1983.14
deSalomko, Serge 1910.20
DeSantis, John 1978.28
deSaussure, Bessie 1938.19
DeSaussure, Celetine 1979.18
Desca, Eve 1934.41
Deschamp, June 1897.16
Deschamps, Mlle. 1872.33, 1872.42, 1873.01, 1873.11
Deschamps, Mme. 1872.41
Deschamps, Mons. 1873.15
deSchmidt, Louis 1892.04
Desclauzas, Marie 1868.26, 1869.03, 1869.16
Desclauzas, Mlle. 1869.05, 1869.30
Desclos, Mons. 1887.37
Descourcelles, Rose 1904.51
deSegonzac, Daisy 1928.21
DeSellem, Elaine 1904.57, 1905.08
Desenfants, Mlle. 1868.18
Desha, Mlle. 1922.11
Deshays, Raymond 1939.31
Deshe, A. (Pashanel) 1990.18
DeShields, Andre 1973.14, 1975.01, 1975.12, 1978.09, 1984.15, 1987.02, 1988.17, 1993.03, 1997.03, 1997.21, 2000.15
Deshon, Florence 1913.04
Deshon, Frank 1885.34, 1885.36, 1885.37, 1885.38, 1901.14
DeSilke, V.M. 1896.05, 1898.69
DeSilva, Buddy G. 1919.12
deSilva, Clarence 1928.03
deSilva, Nancy 1926.38
DeSilveria, Messr. 1856.04
DeSilveria, Mr. 1857.05
deSimone, Roberto 1985.14
DeSio, Al 1968.08, 1968.30, 1969.17
DeSio, Alfred 1961.14, 1961.26
Desiree, Adele 1876.26, 1877.09, 1877.19, 1877.26, 1877.27, 1877.29, 1877.31, 1877.33, 1877.38
Desiree, Mlle. 1870.22
Desjardins, Peter 1941.07
Deslandes, P. 1880.28
Deslys, Gaby 1911.34, 1911.43, 1913.05, 1914.10, 1915.31
DeSmith, L. 1876.17, 1876.21, 1877.16, 1879.38, 1880.24
deSmith, L. 1877.39
DeSmith, Louis 1894.26, 1896.35
DeSmith, Messr. 1879.03
DeSmith, Mons. 1877.33
DeSmith, Mr. 1875.26, 1878.20
Desmond, Alma 1890.21, 1892.55, 1897.06
Desmond, Belle 1903.41
Desmond, Denny 1955.12
Desmond, Eugene 1897.17, 1898.27
Desmond, Fannie 1882.77
Desmond, Florence 1928.42, 1946.22
Desmond, Gladys 1909.01
Desmond, Johnny 1958.08
Desmond, Laurie 1914.32
Desmond, Maggie 1869.17, 1869.29, 1869.35, 1870.04
Desmond, Mary 1913.07
Desmond, Miss 1903.36
Desmond, Mona 1901.17, 1903.36, 1918.31
Desmond, Olma 1898.50
Desmond, Paul 1998.17
Desmond, Paula 1902.27, 1906.33
Desmore, Mercedes 1924.20
DeSolla, Mr. 1869.29
deSoria, Charles 1905.54
DeSoria, Charles 1910.09
deSoria, Fenita 1924.12
deSoria, Finita 1917.34, 1921.32
DeSousa, May 1904.12, 1909.31, 1910.10, 1913.23
deSousa, May 1915.21
DeSouza, Mauricio 1992.13
DeSouza, May 1904.13
DeSoyer, Ida 1870.23
Despo 1967.05, 1973.04
Dessau, Paul 1963.09
Dessault, Nancy 1959.18
Dessez, Paul 1935.11
Dessyllas, Pantelis 1984.03, 1984.04, 1984.05
Destazio, Brian 1976.01
Destine, Jean Leon 1946.21, 1953.10
deSurra, John 1942.33
Desvallieres, Maurice 1897.54, 1912.01
DeSylva, B.G. 1999.01
DeSylva, Buddy 1921.18, 1921.19, 1921.21, 1921.34, 1922.09, 1922.23, 1922.27, 1922.33, 1922.35, 1923.12, 1923.18, 1923.20, 1923.26, 1923.30, 1923.33, 1924.01, 1924.03, 1924.19, 1925.01, 1925.22, 1925.23, 1925.27, 1925.28, 1925.29, 1926.16, 1926.25, 1927.41, 1927.46, 1928.22, 1928.36, 1928.37, 1929.03, 1929.35, 1930.11, 1932.25, 1939.30, 1940.08, 1940.19, 1952.11, 1956.02, 1962.17, 1967.13, 1968.20, 1974.09, 1974.11, 1974.26, 1975.22, 1983.06, 1984.06, 1984.10, 1986.01, 1986.06, 1989.16, 1990.09
DeSylva, Buddy G. 1918.05, 1918.06, 1918.19, 1919.02, 1919.43, 1920.28, 1920.44, 1924.44, 1925.07, 1925.27, 1940.10, 1999.23
deTarr, Seiza 1986.05
Detchon, Adelaide 1880.12
Deter, Mlle. 1902.13
Detering, Frank 1911.11, 1912.28, 1912.33, 1912.48, 1913.17
Dethloff, Lottie 1905.40
deTisne, Raoul 1929.44, 1930.30, 1931.04
Detling, Rene 1914.25
Detloff, Henry 1913.18
DeTreville, Yvonne 1897.11
DeTroia, Garet 1968.18
Detts 1922.21
deTuscan, Bella 1940.07
deTuscan, Joanna 1940.07
Detweiler, Lowell 1989.09
Deuel, Dorothy 1926.14
Deuel, Eleanor 1926.14
Deuel, J.P. 1872.27
Deulin, Mlle. 1861.06, 1862.01
Deulin, Mme. 1859.11
Deuschateau, Netta 1931.19
Deusing, William C. 1898.60
Deutsch, Adolph 1931.42, 1933.01, 1933.22, 1935.15
Deutsch, Helen 1961.10, 1968.32
Deuvil, T. 1887.27
Deval, Jacques 1963.08
Deval, Lucile 1904.45
Devalis, Mons. 1875.28, 1878.06
DeVamper, Dane 1891.03
deVan, Sylvia 1959.17
deVarenne, Ninon 1906.35
deVarney, Emile J. 1916.16
DeVarny, E.J. 1908.36
deVarny, Emile 1919.35
deVassey, Count 1916.08
DeVassey, T. 1908.42
deVassey, Thomas 1899.28
DeVassey, Thomas 1915.25
deVaultier, Richard 1946.09
deVaux, Baron Voruz 1917.19
Deveau, Chick 1919.40
Deveau, J. 1876.23
DeVecchi, Antony 1963.08, 1965.01, 1965.34, 1968.03, 1977.12
deVega, Miguel 1960.08
Deventhal, Theodore 1902.22
Devera, Emilie 1898.44
Deveraux, Emily 1884.24
Devere, Ada 1866.34
Devere, C. 1864.23, 1865.02
DeVere, Daisy 1907.11
deVere, Elise 1903.36
DeVere, Fred 1889.08
DeVere, Frederick 1888.10, 1888.23
deVere, Frisco 1922.35
DeVere, G.V. 1894.39
Devere, George F. 1873.19
DeVere, George F. 1873.19, 1873.24, 1876.16, 1894.39
DeVere, Ida 1867.08
Devere, Ida 1876.03
DeVere, Ida 1876.16
Devere, Kittie 1911.18
Devere, Kitty 1921.32
DeVere, Lillian 1903.03, 1904.13, 1904.44
Devere, Lillian 1905.44, 1906.29, 1917.02
DeVere, M. 1904.13
DeVere, Mabel 1903.03
DeVere, Master 1872.35
Devere, May 1897.07
Devere, Messr. 1871.12
Devere, Mildred 1904.03
Devere, Miss 1881.03, 1892.29
Devere, Nanne 1892.60
DeVere, Nannie 1893.07
Devere, Nellie 1876.16, 1884.21
deVere, Stephen 1895.30
Devere, William 1885.44, 1896.02, 1898.47
Devereaux, Adele 1920.47
Devereaux, Emily 1884.19
Devereaux, Mae 1920.47
Deverell, John 1913.31, 1925.41
Devereux, Messr. 1866.20
Deverille, Louise 1875.10
Deverna, W. 1857.01, 1857.02
Deverna, W.E. 1870.05
Deverna, William 1873.08, 1873.10, 1873.28
DeVerna, William E. 1897.29
DeVert, Ivana 1991.11
DeVeulle, Reginald 1908.42
Devi, Anjali 1960.10
Devi, Regina 1922.21
DeVielle, Zoe 1885.28, 1885.52, 1885.67, 1886.26, 1886.43, 1887.18, 1887.32
deVielle, Zoe 1886.33
Deville, M.G. 1899.04
deVilliers, Mai 1902.35
Devine, Barry 1929.30
Devine, Ella 1901.05
Devine, Erick 1989.22, 2000.18
Devine, Lillian R. 1927.40
Devine, Loretta 1978.28, 1979.32, 1981.29, 1984.10, 1986.06
Devine, Michael 1970.16
Devine, Tom 1928.42
deViney, Grace 1925.11
Devins, John 1903.28
DeVito, Christine 1995.13, 1998.06
Devitt, Tiah 1927.39
DeVittorio, Giuseppe 1985.14

Devlin, Bert 1908.41
Devlin, Edward 1910.18
Devlin, H. 1904.13, 1904.44
Devlin, Helen 1941.08
Devlin, John 1969.08
Devlin, Jon 1982.15
Devlin, Messr. 1904.13, 1904.44
Devlin, Sandra 1953.11, 1955.27, 1961.21
DeVoe, Helene 1898.34
Devoe, Kittie 1877.24
Devoe, Margaret 1875.40
Devoe, Marjorie 1926.43
DeVoe, Mesame 1856.04
deVoe, Mlle. 1926.45
DeVoie, Bessie 1902.15, 1903.04, 1904.31, 1907.32
deVoie, Bessie 1905.30
DeVol, Gordon 1973.12
Devoll, George 1899.40
Devoll, George E. 1895.31
Devon, Larry 1968.17
DeVore, Nell 1903.13
Devorin, Ruth 1949.03
Devotions, B. 1979.13
Devotions, Sheila 1979.13
Devoy, Clara 1878.01
Devoy, Emmet 1895.44
DeVoy, Gilbert 1901.06
Devoy, Josie 1878.01
DeVoy, Josie 1886.58
Devoy, Kate 1871.02, 1876.19, 1878.17
deVries, Beppie 1929.47
deVries, Henri 1916.23
DeVries, Michael 1991.05, 1995.13
deVries, Peter 1952.09, 1952.20
DeVries, Peter 1968.13
Dew, Edward 1945.16, 1946.22
DeWalden, T.B. 1871.04
Dewar, John 1987.04
deWeale, Emma 1923.09
deWeerth, Ernest 1927.23
Dewey, Earl 1903.03, 1904.13
Dewey, Earle S. 1927.10, 1930.14
Dewey, Frances 1925.11, 1931.21, 1934.06
Dewey, J.A. 1885.49
Dewey, John 1905.07
Dewey, Luella 1889.50
Dewey, Lulu 1905.07
Dewey, Messr. 1903.03
Dewey, William 1904.38
DeWilborn, Mlle. 1866.08
deWit, Jacqueline 1952.03
deWitt, Camilla 1946.12
DeWitt, David 1997.16
deWitt, Fay 1950.14, 1951.15
DeWitt, Fay 1960.12, 1963.06
DeWitt, Frances 1920.33
DeWitt, Francis 1911.08, 1919.15
deWitt, Francis 1927.20
deWitt, Frank 1930.08, 1931.08
DeWitt, Grace 1886.42
Dewitt, H.C. 1886.59
DeWitt, H.C. 1887.13, 1887.14, 1888.28
DeWitt, Harry 1886.59
DeWitt, Harry C. 1887.06
DeWitt, Josie 1893.26, 1897.07, 1897.19, 1899.11
deWitt, Josie 1898.35
DeWitt, Miss 1869.36
DeWitt, Mlle. 1883.51, 1883.54, 1883.55, 1883.57, 1883.59, 1883.60, 1883.61, 1884.01, 1884.02, 1884.03, 1884.05, 1885.55, 1885.56, 1885.57, 1885.59, 1885.60, 1885.61, 1886.08, 1886.09, 1886.18, 1886.21, 1886.22
DeWitt, Mme. 1886.19, 1886.20
DeWitt, Venie 1893.26
deWitte, Daisy 1921.17
DeWolf 1911.44
DeWolf Hopper Comic Opera Company 1896.13, 1897.10
DeWolf Hopper Company 1893.16
DeWolf Hopper Opera Bouffe Company 1890.16
DeWolf Hopper Opera Company 1891.11, 1892.22, 1892.33, 1892.47, 1898.48, 1903.02
DeWolf, David 1904.11
DeWolf, Laurier 1905.31
DeWolf, Lillian 1891.41, 1898.59
DeWolf, Linton 1905.31
DeWolf, Wachner and Company 1913.06
DeWolf, Wolf 1916.12
DeWolfe Wachner Company 1916.04
deWolfe, Billy 1953.17, 1957.01
DeWolfe, Billy 1966.07
DeWolfe, David 1909.06
DeWolfe, Drina 1902.34, 1902.40
deWolfe, Elsie 1915.07, 1916.22
DeWolfe, Elsie 1915.30
DeWolfe, F. 1908.40, 1909.03
DeWolfe, Frederica 1907.30
DeWolfe, Linton 1907.62
DeWolfe, Mme. 1907.44
DeWolfe, Wachner and Company 1909.09, 1912.47
DeWolfe, Ward 1916.26, 1917.21
Dews, Carl 1930.01, 1930.07, 1930.12
Dexter, Alan 1965.21
Dexter, Brina 1961.02
Dexter, Joan 1942.26
Dexter, John 1965.06, 1989.24
Dexter, Lida 1894.37
Dexter, Rose 1936.12
Deykarhanova, Mme. 1922.06, 1925.03, 1927.51, 1929.05
Deyle, John 1998.13
Deyo, Blanche 1895.38, 1902.30, 1904.40, 1906.07, 1906.17, 1906.36, 1907.49
Deyo, George W. 1886.44, 1886.51, 1897.47, 1899.27, 1900.36, 1901.15, 1904.46
Deyo, Mlle. 1896.48
DeYoung, Dennis 1995.02
deYoung, Hallie 1913.14
DeYoung, Mabel 1911.34
DeYoung, Marie 1917.16
deYoung, Marie 1922.30
deZamora, Jose 1923.44
deZarn, Teresa 1989.24
DeZarn, Teresa 1991.05
Dezina, Kate 1982.09
Dezina, Kathe 1975.06
deZulueta, Pedro 1913.26
DG Producciones 1999.18
Dhery, Robert 1958.18, 1965.37
Di Renzo, Raul 1999.18
Diakonova, Mlle. 1931.38
Diamant, Sherry Lynn 1968.18
Diamond, Carlena 1923.21
Diamond, Charles 1911.25
Diamond, Edward P. 1928.23
Diamond, Etta 1903.03
Diamond, G. 1913.37
Diamond, Harold 1941.07
Diamond, Hugh 1941.07
Diamond, I.A.L. 1950.02, 1955.12, 1968.31, 1972.04
Diamond, Jack 1946.15, 1948.32, 1950.08
Diamond, James 1909.23
Diamond, Jim 1929.07
Diamond, Lee 1992.06
Diamond, Libbian 1900.44
Diamond, Libbie 1902.29
Diamond, Louis 1929.48
Diamond, Marguerite 1899.01, 1900.10
Diamond, Maurice 1915.26, 1921.18
Diamond, Miss 1903.03, 1904.13, 1904.44
Diamond, Muni 1939.19
Diamond, Neil 1978.05, 1999.01
Diamond, Tom 1941.07, 2000.02
Diani, E. 1867.25
Diani, Ermesilda 1867.25
Diani, Mlle. 1872.37
Dianina, Mme. 1922.06, 1923.28
Diard, Fatimah 1889.19
Diard, William 1961.04, 1961.05, 1962.10, 1962.11, 1962.19, 1963.23, 1964.09, 1965.11, 1965.12
Diaz, Hector 1981.09
Diaz, Justino 1987.03
Diaz, Leandro 1919.17
Diaz, Natascia A. 1998.02, 2000.18
Dibdin 1859.15
Dibdin-Pitt, George 1979.06, 1984.13, 1987.09, 1989.19
Dibrook, Marie 1903.25
DiChiera, David 1979.26
Dick Clark, Inc. 1982.22
Dick, Henry 1940.07
Dick, Richard 1941.06
Dickason, Cynthia 1975.18
Dickens, Angie 1902.26
Dickens, Bertha 1898.34
Dickens, C. Stafford 1961.18
Dickens, Charles 1839.01, 1851.02, 1867.20, 1868.04, 1868.22, 1870.34, 1871.13, 1873.29, 1876.35, 1877.01, 1878.10, 1880.17, 1881.18, 1902.03, 1902.31, 1903.02, 1963.01, 1965.23, 1965.28, 1979.32, 1981.12, 1984.07, 1985.18, 1994.12, 1995.19, 1996.15, 1997.22, 1998.20, 1999.21, 2000.19
Dickens, Dean 1934.11
Dickens, Deane 1933.14
Dickens, Dene 1929.40, 1929.47, 1929.48, 1930.01, 1930.41, 1931.17, 1931.20, 1931.27, 1935.10, 1936.04, 1936.08, 1936.10, 1936.11
Dickens, Hamp 1964.17
Dickens, John 1932.08, 1938.18
Dickens, John W. 1879.68
Dickens, Lottie 1894.18
Dickens, Matthew 1987.07
Dicker, Charlotte 1971.20, 1978.22
Dickerman, Daisy 1905.31
Dickerman, Goodwal 1903.24
Dickerson, Berchard 1909.11
Dickerson, Glenda 1980.05
Dickerson, James L. 1893.03
Dickerson, Jennie 1914.09, 1915.19
Dickerson, Jenny 1895.25, 1895.44
Dickerson, Nathaniel 1947.03
Dickerson, Wyatt 1976.09
Dickey, Annamary 1944.28, 1945.09, 1947.17
Dickey, Paul 1915.25, 1924.28, 1927.06, 1927.07, 1927.66, 1928.11
Dickinson, Harold 1940.09
Dickinson, Homer 1920.19
Dickson 1891.18
Dickson, Artells 1943.08
Dickson, Belle 1884.56
Dickson, Charles 1888.31, 1895.18, 1895.35, 1896.06, 1896.48, 1897.54, 1899.15, 1906.05, 1908.18, 1910.09, 1917.18
Dickson, Charles S. 1881.28, 1890.37
Dickson, Curtis 1976.28
Dickson, Dorothy 1917.06, 1917.13, 1918.02, 1918.16, 1919.04, 1919.43, 1920.12
Dickson, Edgar 1914.18
Dickson, Emma 1917.16
Dickson, Georgie 1880.47, 1885.63, 1886.04, 1893.03
Dickson, H. Nelson 1918.16
Dickson, Harry 1889.33
Dickson, Marian 1924.08
Dickson, Maude 1889.33
Dickson, Messr. 1883.04, 1883.52, 1887.25, 1887.48
Dickson, Mr. 1875.10
Dickson, Muriel 1934.21, 1934.24, 1934.26, 1934.28, 1934.31, 1934.33
Dickson, Stephen 1981.21
Dickstein, Sol 1970.17
DiDia, Maria 1978.28
diDio, Marietta 1907.15
Didjah, Belle 1934.17, 1951.22
Diehl, Charles 1893.24, 1896.02
Diehl, Crandall 1949.18, 1952.07, 1954.03, 1955.01, 1956.01, 1976.05, 1981.19
Diehl, Jr., Bill 1969.03
Diem, Charles J. 1907.28
Diener, Joan 1948.22, 1953.16, 1965.34, 1970.10, 1972.14, 1976.01
Dierking, Sharon 1966.27
Diers, Daniel 1918.23
Diers, Dippy 1915.24, 1916.15, 1917.16, 1938.08, 1944.30
Diers, Eugene 1917.16
Diers, Jr., T.C. 1906.01
Diers, T.C. 1906.01
Dieter, George 1932.22
Dieter, Georgina 1931.18, 1931.20, 1931.41, 1931.45, 1936.11
Dietl, Fritz 1940.16, 1942.19, 1946.14, 1947.12
Dietl, Marta 1942.19
Dietrich, Bill E. 1997.09
Dietrich, Dena 1968.05
Dietrich, Elizabeth 1995.18
Dietrich, Gary 1980.03, 1980.04, 1980.22, 1981.21, 1981.22, 1982.20, 1983.13, 1984.11, 1986.08, 1989.14
Dietrich, James 1926.11
Dietrich, Janette 1921.34
Dietrich, Jeanette 1920.47
Dietrich, Marlene 1967.13, 1968.20
Dietrich, Mr. 1879.21
Dietrich, W.C. 1868.01, 1868.02
Dietrich, W.G. 1867.07
Dietrich, W.H. 1867.03, 1867.04, 1867.06, 1867.09
Dietrich, William G. 1878.03
Dietrichstein, Leo 1913.34
Dietrick, Carrie M. 1886.15
Dietschy, Veronique 1983.16
Dietz, Carl 1918.24
Dietz, Ella 1872.23, 1872.35
Dietz, Harry 1894.13, 1895.11
Dietz, Harry C. 1889.34
Dietz, Howard 1922.42, 1923.27, 1924.34, 1929.19, 1929.20, 1930.06, 1930.25, 1930.32, 1930.33, 1931.16, 1932.17, 1934.38, 1935.12, 1936.31, 1937.16, 1940.07, 1944.01, 1944.27, 1948.14, 1952.11, 1954.11, 1957.01, 1961.27, 1963.25, 1967.11, 1972.05, 1975.22, 1976.32, 1982.06, 1988.08, 1989.06, 1990.09, 1990.14, 1991.10, 1992.18, 1999.01, 1999.23
Dietz, Susan 1988.07
Dieu, Nicole 1964.39
DiFalco, Diego 1997.13
Diffen, Ray 1976.01
diGaetano, Adam 1943.13
diGaetano, Jane 1943.13
diGatano, Adam 1931.40, 1944.14
diGatano, Amelia 1931.40
diGatano, Jayne 1944.14
Digby Bell Opera Company 1892.20
Digby, L. 1879.08
diGenova, Eddy 1946.04, 1946.13
diGerlando, Maria 1954.18, 1960.03
Digges, Dudley 1925.17
Diggett, Betty 1920.43
Diggs, John 1950.16
Diggs, Mabel 1933.04
Diggs, Taye 1994.02, 1996.09
DiGiovanni, Constance 1961.07
DiGiuseppe, Enrico 1965.07, 1968.10, 1976.31
diGiuseppe, Enrico 1978.08
Dignimont Aaron 1958.18
DiGrazio, Randy 1973.12
Dijmos, George 1933.26
Dika, Juliette 1906.33, 1908.42, 1912.15
Dill, George 1924.25
Dill, George V. 1927.42
Dill, Max M. 1908.05
Dill, Mollie 1907.22, 1909.10
Dill, Mr. 1906.29
Dillabough, F.G. 1908.27
Dillard, Bill 1946.24
Dillard, Pierre 1951.11
Dillard, William 1943.24, 1945.08, 1949.16, 1951.11, 1952.08, 1952.15, 1953.05, 1953.14, 1964.19
Dille, Marjorie 1931.39, 1933.03, 1933.07
Dillea, Herbert 1896.02, 1898.08, 1900.08, 1902.02
Dillehay, Kaylyn 1980.01
Dilley, Dorothy 1923.32, 1926.12, 1927.20, 1927.60
Dillingham, Charles 1904.30, 1905.57, 1906.33, 1907.11, 1907.36, 1907.46, 1908.40, 1909.03, 1909.09, 1910.02, 1910.20, 1910.27, 1911.02, 1912.02, 1914.23, 1914.31, 1915.24, 1915.25, 1915.31, 1916.15, 1916.20, 1916.24, 1917.03, 1917.16, 1917.22, 1917.33, 1918.23, 1918.34, 1919.09, 1919.22, 1919.27, 1919.40, 1920.04, 1920.13, 1920.26, 1920.36, 1920.40, 1921.28, 1921.33, 1921.36, 1922.30, 1922.45, 1923.29, 1923.33, 1923.40, 1923.44, 1924.26, 1924.39, 1925.05, 1925.33, 1925.38, 1926.32, 1926.46, 1927.12, 1927.48, 1928.02, 1928.37, 1930.05, 1930.13, 1932.04
Dillingham, Charles B. 1903.34, 1903.37, 1904.51, 1904.57, 1905.08, 1905.11, 1905.19, 1905.29, 1912.39, 1917.26, 1934.06
Dillingham, Mabel 1903.30
Dillman, Hugh 1918.17
Dillon, Ben F. 1897.21
Dillon, Ben T. 1903.01, 1908.05
Dillon, Benjamin J. 1897.54
Dillon, Conway 1922.41
Dillon, Denny 1974.17, 1983.06
Dillon, Florence 1915.01
Dillon, Harry 1894.07, 1894.35, 1896.03, 1907.46
Dillon, Herbert 1902.02
Dillon, Isabelle 1900.37
Dillon, J.J. 1907.56
Dillon, Jay 1920.33
Dillon, John 1894.07, 1894.35, 1896.03, 1905.43

Dillon, Joseph 1915.17, 1917.07
Dillon, Melinda 1971.08
Dillon, Mr. 1861.04
Dillon, Mrs. 1861.04
Dillon, R.J. 1889.12
Dillon, Richard H. 1893.31
Dillon, Richard J. 1890.04, 1897.47, 1901.15, 1906.38
Dillon, Sandy 1982.22
Dillon, Sara 1948.20, 1951.23
Dillon, Thomas 1943.23
Dillon, William 1929.46, 1942.11, 1979.25
Dilly, Erin 2001.02
Dilson, John H. 1927.66
Dilthy, Minnie 1884.12
diLucca, Dino 1954.19
Dilworth, Gordon 1941.12, 1944.16, 1944.24, 1945.15, 1951.24, 1956.01, 1965.17, 1965.31, 1966.27
Dilworth, Hubert 1944.23, 1947.01
Dilworth, Hugh 1953.04, 1957.16
DiMartino, Giuseppe 1985.16
DiMeo, Donna 1989.03
Dimey, Bernard 1964.39
DiMilano, Sormani 1974.14
Dimino, Richard 1982.15
Dimond, William 1863.09
DiMucci, Dion 2000.07
Dinehart, Allan 1926.21, 1927.27
Dingbat, James 1923.11
Dingenary, Gene 1972.24
Dingeon, Helen 1876.23, 1881.41
Dingeon, Helene 1879.32, 1880.11, 1889.10
Dingle, Charles 1949.08
Dingle, Tom 1911.24, 1911.45, 1914.34, 1921.06, 1923.04, 1923.46
Dino, Peter 1978.01
Dino, Ralph 1995.03
Dinsmore, Laura 1887.05
Dinsmore, Zephie 1880.48, 1882.07, 1882.08, 1882.09, 1882.10, 1883.11, 1883.12, 1883.13, 1883.14
DioGuardi, Joseph 1983.17
Dion, Hector 1904.32
Dior, Christian 1964.02
diPaolo, Dante 1949.17
DiPasquale, Frank 1983.11, 1991.05
Dippel, Andreas 1914.25, 1918.04
Dippell Opera Comique Company 1914.25
Director, Henry 1956.04
Dirks, Rudolph 1900.53
Dirkson, Sherman 1937.09, 1938.16
Discepolo, E.S. 1985.07, 1999.18
Dishy, Bob 1960.07, 1962.13, 1965.17
Disipio, Fred 1982.22
Diskins, Messr. 1904.13, 1904.44
Display Stage Lighting Company 1929.25
Distin, Samuel 1871.04
Ditrichstein, Leo 1895.42, 1896.10, 1914.06
Ditt, Josie 1894.19, 1894.38
Dittebrandt, Mr. 1891.33
Dittman, Dean 1978.02
Dittmar, Leopold K. 1889.27
Diveny, Mary 1999.07
Dix, Beulah Marie 1924.23
Dix, Frank 1913.33
Dix, Franklin J. 1927.68
Dix, Georgie 1905.17
Dix, Lillian 1906.43
Dix, Mae 1932.14
Dix, Richard 1983.05
Dix, Rollo 1926.31
Dix, Tommy 1941.06
Dixey, Harry E. 1878.02, 1883.52
Dixey, Helen 1902.19
Dixey, Henry 1917.24
Dixey, Henry E. 1877.21, 1879.33, 1879.35, 1880.06, 1880.10, 1880.13, 1880.59, 1880.65, 1880.67, 1880.70, 1882.34, 1883.22, 1883.31, 1883.64, 1884.42, 1886.47, 1887.31, 1887.43, 1888.09, 1888.36, 1889.01, 1889.44, 1889.46, 1892.30, 1892.37, 1892.40, 1892.46, 1893.13, 1894.19, 1896.22, 1896.35, 1897.14, 1897.19, 1898.36, 1899.23, 1900.59, 1911.21
Dixey, Henry F. 1880.48, 1880.53
Dixey, Jr., Henry E. 1892.40, 1892.46
Dixey, Mabel 1898.05
Dixie, H.F. 1880.12
Dixon, Adeele 1937.16
Dixon, Artells 1946.04
Dixon, Beryl 1955.18, 1955.20, 1955.24
Dixon, Bob 1959.01, 1961.02, 1961.10
Dixon, Catherine 1927.39
Dixon, Christopher 1983.09
Dixon, Clara 1880.62, 1882.57
Dixon, Daisy 1898.28, 1898.38, 1898.56
Dixon, Dorothy 1930.35, 1931.30
Dixon, Ed 1984.14, 1993.17, 1997.19
Dixon, Emmie V. 1892.29
Dixon, F. 1882.17
Dixon, Fred 1880.26, 1880.46, 1881.42, 1881.44, 1882.57, 1882.64, 1882.72, 1894.45
Dixon, Gale 1969.17
Dixon, Harland 1913.05, 1914.22, 1915.31, 1916.24, 1918.34, 1921.36, 1923.38, 1923.47, 1926.36, 1927.46, 1928.44, 1929.49, 1951.14
Dixon, Harriet 1927.39
Dixon, Harry 1930.35, 1931.30
Dixon, Henry 1881.03
Dixon, Irene 1917.32
Dixon, J.B. 1880.15
Dixon, James 1899.09
Dixon, Jerry 1990.12, 1992.03
Dixon, John C. 1893.46
Dixon, Lee 1940.06, 1943.04
Dixon, Luther 1984.15
Dixon, MacIntyre 1971.08, 1974.05, 1982.24, 1989.24
Dixon, Madeline 1883.67
Dixon, Marion 1919.35
Dixon, Messr. 1886.36
Dixon, Miss 1903.03
Dixon, Mort 1927.62, 1930.38, 1931.13, 1931.40, 1932.14, 1940.20, 1942.25, 1974.01, 1980.20, 1988.08, 1999.01, 2001.08
Dixon, Mr. 1885.07
Dixon, Rae 1903.03
Dixon, Robert 1946.12, 1948.23, 1948.30, 1952.10
Dixon, Roy 1921.38
Dixon, T.B. 1880.15
Dixon, Walter 1898.22, 1901.20, 1904.21
Dixon, William 1888.31, 1888.43
Dixon, Willie 1999.09
Dixson, Harry 1894.08
Djaoui, Andre 1997.12
Djeli, Sahary 1915.26
Djimos, George 1926.34, 1929.31, 1930.26
DL Theatrical Productions, Inc. 1978.01
Dlamini, Busi 1977.01
Dlamini, Dumisani 1988.02
Dlamini, Khumbuzile 1988.02
Dlamini, Lindiwe 1988.02
Dlamini, Ntomb'khona 1988.02
DLT Entertainment 1999.05
Dlugos, Gregory J. 1987.14
Dmitri, Richard 1972.23
Dneproff, Ivan 1927.01
Dniestroff, Messr. 1922.37
Doane, Frank 1898.63, 1900.44, 1900.49, 1900.56, 1901.12, 1902.06, 1902.37, 1904.52, 1906.04, 1907.42, 1909.07, 1910.24, 1912.34, 1914.26, 1915.05, 1918.08, 1918.28, 1919.14, 1920.37, 1922.35, 1923.06, 1924.05, 1924.41, 1925.38, 1926.07, 1928.02
Doane, Lillian 1880.05
Doane, Melanie 1990.15
Dobbs, George 1923.36, 1925.26, 1926.01, 1928.15, 1928.48, 1929.28, 1937.03
Dobert, Frank 1931.39, 1932.22
Dobie, Edgar 1994.10, 1998.02
Dobie, Paul 1991.03, 1993.06
Dobos, Viola 1930.09
Dobrinin, N. 1932.09
Dobrinine, M. 1924.48
Dobrinor, Daisy 1904.19
Dobson, Eleanor 1905.28
Dobson, Frank 1923.01, 1924.13, 1933.02
Dobson, James 1945.04
Dobson, John 1905.28
Dobson, Margaret 1955.16, 1955.20, 1955.21, 1955.24
Dobson, W.T. 1886.35
Dobuzhinsky, M. 1929.05
Dobuzhinsky, Mstislaff Vererianovitch 1927.51
Dobuzhinsky, R. 1927.51
Doche, Marie 1866.18
Docherty, Peter 1977.05
Dockery, Adam 1905.52
Dockery, Leslie 1978.21, 1999.06
Dockstader, Lew 1889.52, 1922.16
Dockstader, Lou 1888.15
Doctor, Bernadette 1973.17
Doctor, Doretha 1975.12
Doctor, Dorthea 1973.17
Doctor, J. 1899.11
Doctorow, E.L. 1998.01
Dodd, Clare 1930.39
Dodd, H.W. 1889.19
Dodd, Harry 1895.13, 1897.39
Dodd, Henry W. 1890.50
Dodd, John 1971.20
Dodd, Judy 1990.18
Dodd, Patricia 1978.26
Dodd, Rory 1976.03
Dodd, Tom 1926.22
Doddridge, Elizabeth 1905.29
Dodds, Jack 1953.16
Dodds, Malcolm 1981.06
Doddsworth, Edna 1913.21
Dodge 1911.13
Dodge and Castle 1911.30, 1912.01, 1912.08, 1912.15, 1912.20, 1912.37, 1912.49, 1913.14, 1913.24, 1913.27, 1913.28, 1913.32, 1914.08, 1914.27, 1915.01, 1916.11, 1916.18, 1917.09, 1917.11, 1917.28, 1918.22, 1918.32, 1919.02, 1919.09, 1919.34, 1920.13, 1920.32, 1920.37, 1920.40
Dodge and Castle Studio 1920.02
Dodge, Anne Bacon 1932.19
Dodge, Beth 1929.22
Dodge, Betty 1929.22
Dodge, Charles F. 1899.28
Dodge, D. Frank 1890.49, 1891.25, 1891.45, 1892.44, 1892.54, 1893.15, 1893.27, 1893.39, 1893.46, 1894.04, 1894.14, 1894.21, 1894.40, 1894.47, 1894.49, 1895.04, 1895.05, 1895.24, 1895.44, 1896.06, 1896.18, 1896.41, 1896.48, 1896.51, 1897.26, 1897.37, 1897.39, 1897.54, 1898.03, 1898.05, 1898.12, 1898.20, 1898.28, 1898.43, 1898.51, 1898.63, 1898.68, 1898.72, 1899.02, 1899.19, 1899.21, 1899.25, 1899.38, 1900.05, 1900.07, 1900.16, 1900.20, 1900.33, 1900.34, 1900.41, 1900.42, 1900.54, 1900.57, 1901.05, 1901.08, 1901.09, 1901.13, 1901.23, 1902.16, 1902.19, 1902.21, 1902.23, 1902.40, 1902.41, 1903.02, 1903.06, 1903.14, 1903.16, 1903.18, 1903.27, 1903.38, 1904.05, 1904.12, 1904.21, 1904.24, 1904.55, 1904.56, 1905.03, 1905.33, 1905.49, 1907.30, 1907.59, 1909.17, 1910.29, 1910.37, 1911.08, 1911.13
Dodge, Frank 1899.36, 1902.34, 1908.15
Dodge, George E. 1892.23
Dodge, Gilbert 1956.11
Dodge, J. Frank 1905.53, 1908.28
Dodge, Jacqueline 1947.16
Dodge, Jerry 1960.06, 1963.26, 1964.01, 1968.07, 1973.09, 1974.18, 1989.18
Dodge, Marcia Milgrom 1988.04
Dodge, Marion 1928.12, 1930.08
Dodge, Miles 1929.22
Dodge, Ray 1910.19, 1911.12, 1913.29
Dodge, Roger 1922.21, 1923.25
Dodge, Roger Pryor 1930.38
Dodge, Wendell Phillips 1924.20, 1924.48
Dodger Endemol Productions 1997.06, 1998.13
Dodger Endemol Theatrical Productions 1997.15
Dodger Endemol Theatricals 1997.01, 1998.05, 1998.11, 1998.20, 1999.21
Dodger Management Group 1996.18, 1997.06
Dodger Productions 1982.04, 1985.06, 1988.05, 1991.05, 1992.04, 1993.06, 1994.12, 1995.05, 1995.19, 1996.05, 1996.06, 1996.15, 1996.18, 1997.22
Dodger Theatricals 2000.11, 2001.04, 2001.08
Dods, John 1994.04, 1999.16
Dodson, A.E. 1895.32, 1907.32
Dodson, Charles 1929.44
Dodson, laMott 1940.07
Dodson, St. Clair 1930.24
Dodsworth, Betty 1918.15, 1918.26
Dodsworth, Edna 1907.32
Dodworth, C. 1856.03
Dodworth, Harvey B. 1863.06, 1863.07, 1865.06, 1866.18
Dody, Dan 1906.40
Doe, Joe 1907.34
Doerge, Craig 1981.16
Doerge, Ida 1897.26, 1900.05, 1903.03, 1906.29
Doerge, Minna 1904.13, 1904.44
Doerge, Miss 1903.03, 1904.13, 1904.44
Doggett, Norma 1954.15, 1956.14
Doherty, Barbara 1960.06
Doherty, Dennis 1975.04
Doherty, Don 1964.15
Doherty, James J. 1917.16, 1919.25
Doherty, Kathleen 1965.01
Doherty, Lillian 1905.53
Doherty, Lindy 1951.23
Doherty, Madeleine 2001.05
Doherty, Mae 1914.30
Doherty, Moya 1996.01, 1996.12, 1998.09, 2000.05
Dohn, Robert 1929.44
Dohoerty, Mae 1908.07
Dohrman, W. 1883.52
Dokes, Joseph 1899.09
Dokuchitz, Jonathan 1993.06, 1995.11, 1997.05
Dolan, Bobby 1931.39, 1932.17
Dolan, Don 1967.10
Dolan, Edward 1928.25
Dolan, Frank 1942.11
Dolan, George 1902.43
Dolan, James F. 1898.03, 1898.66
Dolan, Joseph P. 1908.39
Dolan, Judith 1981.27, 1982.03, 1982.20, 1983.13, 1984.11, 1986.08, 1989.14, 1997.10, 1998.21
Dolan, Peggy 1920.17, 1922.27, 1928.48
Dolan, Robert 1930.30, 1934.01, 1935.17, 1936.27
Dolan, Robert Emmett 1937.15, 1938.13, 1939.28, 1940.08, 1949.17, 1959.04, 1964.04, 1969.17
Dolan, Roger 1907.47
Dolaro, Genevieve 1900.38, 1901.17, 1920.34
Dolaro, Hattie 1882.72, 1884.09
Dolaro, Selina 1880.43, 1880.49, 1881.14, 1881.34, 1881.40, 1881.56, 1882.47, 1882.52, 1882.60, 1882.75, 1883.52
Dold, Karl Heinz 1984.05
Dolf, John 1981.13, 1983.11
Dolin, Anton 1927.02, 1930.09, 1940.09, 1944.29
Dolin, Gerald 1935.11
Dolin, Gerry 1948.26
Dolinoff, M. 1931.38
Doll, Charles 1912.44
Doll, Lauren 2000.02
Doll, Roy 1928.23
Dollar, William 1938.15, 1952.06
Dollarrd, Clara 1906.42
Dollis, Theodore 1992.06
Dolliver, Dick 1920.08
Dolliver, Mr. 1906.29
Dolliver, R.M. 1911.31, 1914.06, 1914.17
Dolliver, Richard 1904.39, 1905.46
Dolliver, Richard M. 1908.24
Dollman, Master 1896.11
Dolly, Jennie 1910.20, 1912.13, 1924.32
Dolly, Jenny 1911.24
Dolly, Rose 1910.20, 1913.17
Dolly, Rosie 1912.13, 1924.32
Dolly, Rosika 1911.24
Dolly, Roszika 1912.27, 1913.23
Dolly, Rozsika 1913.08, 1914.34
Dolly, Yancsi 1912.27, 1913.05
Dolman, Dorothy 1924.01
Dolore, Mlle. 1917.26
Dolores, Rose 1918.19
Dolores, Zitelka 1917.26
Dolph, Jack 1955.13
Dombi, Fraulein 1879.62
Dombrovsky 1881.32
Dombrowski, Jacques 1964.39
Dome Production, A 1981.12
Dome/Cutler-Herman Production, A 1980.19, 1981.19, 1981.26
Domenico, Michael 1952.09
Dominiguez, Phil 1995.02
Domino, Antoine 1982.22
Domislavski, M. 1916.15
Domnitz, William 1969.03
Dompierre, Ellen 1907.26
Don, Carl 1940.04
Don, D.L. 1889.46, 1893.34, 1895.38, 1897.26, 1898.05, 1898.43, 1898.68, 1900.41, 1901.13, 1903.18, 1905.22, 1910.03, 1912.36
Don, David L. 1906.33
Don, Emma 1890.25
Don, Jennie 1880.05
Don, Lady 1867.10
Don, Lula 1890.25
Don, Messr. 1888.36

Dona, A. 1976.07
Donaggio 1973.17
Donaghey, Steven 1976.34
Donaghy, Harry 1927.43, 1928.03
Donaghy, Karen 1972.20
Donah, Paul 1927.06, 1932.22
Donahue, Alice 1926.32
Donahue, J. 1908.26
Donahue, Jack 1919.44, 1922.29, 1924.30, 1925.33, 1928.03, 1929.44, 1930.30, 1940.19
Donahue, Joe 1928.40
Donahue, John 1892.19, 1893.26, 1902.32, 1904.52, 1928.14, 1931.28
Donahue, Jr., Theodore P. 1980.17
Donahue, May 1910.19
Donahue, Robert 1970.02
Donahue, Vincent J. 1959.24, 1963.25
Donahue, Walter 1951.16
Donald, Campbell 1902.28, 1904.57, 1905.08, 1905.11
Donald, Donald K. 1985.07, 1986.16, 1986.17, 1989.02, 1993.08
Donald, Frew 1937.06
Donaldi, Maria 1980.21, 1981.20
Donaldson, Arthur 1898.46, 1900.54, 1903.10, 1904.16, 1905.16, 1906.16, 1906.41, 1939.19
Donaldson, Drew 1890.01, 1890.19, 1890.24, 1891.30, 1892.03, 1894.23, 1895.15, 1895.23, 1896.25, 1896.50, 1900.23
Donaldson, Ethel 1908.01, 1908.39
Donaldson, Frew 1890.11
Donaldson, George 1904.14
Donaldson, John 1937.06
Donaldson, Lyn 1915.23
Donaldson, Miss 1881.04, 1904.13
Donaldson, Norma 1961.08, 1976.21
Donaldson, Peggy 1904.44
Donaldson, W. 1869.14
Donaldson, Walter 1919.11, 1919.15, 1920.10, 1920.24, 1920.33, 1921.34, 1922.15, 1922.34, 1923.20, 1924.15, 1925.01, 1925.27, 1925.48, 1926.03, 1927.37, 1928.47, 1930.08, 1930.39, 1931.08, 1931.19, 1932.14, 1940.10, 1944.19, 1944.32, 1947.05, 1948.13, 1962.17, 1965.08, 1967.13, 1968.20, 1974.09, 1975.22, 1979.05, 1984.10, 1986.06, 1989.06, 1992.18, 1995.16, 1997.05, 1998.17
Donaldson, Will 1919.26, 1926.12
Donaldson, William 1962.23, 1964.45
Donalson, Miss 1904.44
Donatella, Joe 1936.01
Donatella, Joseph 1932.24
Donath, Ludwig 1963.14
Donatien, Messr. 1864.01, 1864.03, 1864.08, 1864.11
Donatien, Mme. 1864.01, 1864.03, 1864.08, 1864.11
Donatien, Mons. 1864.10
Dondlinger, Mary Jo 1989.19, 1992.11
Donegan, Francis X. 1924.22, 1925.38, 1926.07
Donegan, Nellie 1908.04
Donell, Eva 1882.04
Donelle, Marie 1888.34
Donelson, Mr. 1857.01
Donen, Stanley 1940.22, 1985.08, 1993.19
Doner, Joe 1911.01
Doner, Joseph 1895.03, 1899.21
Doner, Kitty 1914.22, 1916.03, 1918.05, 1923.02
Doner, Maurice 1942.35
Doner, Nellie 1913.22, 1914.19, 1917.16
Doner, Rose 1923.02
Doner, Ted 1923.02, 1924.13, 1927.17
Dones, Don 1989.05
Doney, Randy 1961.26
Donhowe, Gwyda 1978.28
Donida, Carlo 1995.03
Donizetti 1859.15, 1859.17, 1880.35, 1990.10
Donizetti, Gaetano 1860.05, 1869.11, 1873.02, 1873.05, 1880.33, 1881.47, 1882.28, 1890.30, 1896.46, 1912.09
Donkin, Eric 1987.01
Donlan, Yolande 1940.02
Donlevy, Brian 1927.16, 1928.44, 1934.19
Donlin, Mike 1911.17
Donn, Berta 1921.18, 1923.04, 1924.41, 1925.26, 1927.42, 1932.10, 1932.21, 1934.38
Donn, Marion 1912.11
Donna, Jennie 1902.09
Donne, Berta 1921.24
Donnell, Ena 1882.20
Donnellan, Sean 1996.13
Donnelly 1911.24
Donnelly, Arthur 1921.02
Donnelly, Carrie 1884.12
Donnelly, Donal 1989.10
Donnelly, Dorothy 1916.17, 1918.12, 1921.31, 1923.14, 1923.15, 1923.27, 1924.12, 1924.45, 1926.02, 1926.05, 1927.42, 1927.50, 1931.03, 1931.07, 1938.17, 1943.06, 1943.12, 1975.22, 1980.21, 1981.20, 1985.09, 1987.08, 1993.12
Donnelly, H. Grattan 1888.17, 1889.06, 1889.09, 1889.39, 1889.41, 1890.29, 1890.44, 1891.44, 1893.26, 1894.43, 1895.15, 1896.40, 1896.47
Donnelly, Henry V. 1885.64, 1886.39, 1888.17, 1889.06, 1889.39, 1894.06, 1896.44, 1905.13, 1906.05
Donnelly, J. 1878.10
Donnelly, J. Ed. 1895.40
Donnelly, J.S. 1906.02, 1906.42
Donnelly, Jack 1919.30
Donnelly, James 1924.16
Donnelly, Jamie 1965.17, 1968.07, 1975.08, 1975.13
Donnelly, Jimmy 1938.03
Donnelly, John 1884.32, 1884.33, 1884.35, 1884.38, 1909.30
Donnelly, Ken 1980.11
Donnelly, Leo 1911.34, 1915.20, 1925.01, 1925.28, 1927.53
Donnelly, Mamie 1893.12
Donnelly, Mr. 1869.07
Donnelly, Ruth 1917.36, 1920.03
Donnelly, T.L. 1866.11, 1866.15, 1867.13, 1867.14, 1867.15, 1867.16, 1867.17, 1876.34
Donnelly, Theodore 1953.05
Donnelly, Tom 1870.16, 1876.09
Donnelly, W.J. 1881.52, 1883.01, 1883.09, 1883.20
Donnelly, W.T. 1890.40
Donner, Diamond 1904.18, 1905.22, 1906.19
Donner, Dorothy 1903.41
Donner, Vyvyan 1926.42
Donniker, Jonathan P. 1870.36
Donoghue, Kitty 1903.15
Donoghue, Tim 1992.12
Donohew, Edna May 1904.33
Donohue, Jack 1920.18, 1931.31, 1932.01, 1933.16, 1944.29, 1945.18, 1951.23, 1952.07, 1956.02, 1957.17
Donohue, Jiggs 1906.46
Donohue, Joseph 1897.09, 1981.15
Donohue, May 1895.18, 1899.09, 1904.43, 1906.43
Donohue, Pat 1949.18
Donohue, Red 1942.16
Donohue, Vincent J. 1955.05
Donohue, William F. 1927.60
Donovan, John F. 1904.33
Donovan, Linda 1963.25, 1971.09
Donovan, Louise 1912.26, 1914.18
Donovan, M.F. 1879.66
Donovan, Marcella 1925.47
Donovan, Mlle. 1873.22
Donovan, Peter 1914.06
Donovan, W.H. 1905.10
Donovan, Walter 1942.16
Donovan, Warde 1946.23, 1954.02, 1957.04, 1959.27
Donsch, Karl 1984.03, 1984.04
Donskoy, P. 1924.48
Donsu, H.L. 1933.07
Donsu, J.C. 1931.39
Dontzoff, Nicholas 1943.11
Dooley, Gordon 1917.35, 1919.03, 1925.22, 1926.29, 1928.23
Dooley, J. Francis 1921.02
Dooley, Johnny 1917.08, 1918.39, 1919.15, 1920.21, 1921.09, 1922.45, 1923.18, 1924.16, 1927.02
Dooley, Larry 1894.17
Dooley, Ray 1917.35, 1918.18, 1919.15, 1920.18, 1921.21, 1922.45, 1923.33, 1925.10, 1925.24, 1926.18, 1927.48, 1928.23, 1934.42
Dooley, William 1917.35, 1919.03
Dooling, Katherine 1904.33
Doolittle, Forest 1908.13
Doolittle, James A. 1961.01, 1964.25
Doolittle, John 1979.24
Doonan, Tony 1965.37
doPandeiro, Gerson 1988.06
DoPandeiro, Ray 1992.13
Doran, E. 1881.30
Doran, John 1900.37, 1920.34
Dorati, Antal 1941.10, 1945.02
Dore, Aleta 1919.02
Dore, Daniel 1903.27, 1906.20, 1907.21, 1911.18
Dore, Demaris 1928.16
Dore, Gladys 1922.38
Dore, Gustave 1869.47
Dore, J. 1891.36, 1894.14
Dore, Jean 1892.60, 1893.07
Dore, Katharine 1998.10
Dore, Lynne 1930.06
Dore, Nonie 1902.19
Dore, Richard 1917.09, 1918.15, 1920.05, 1923.13
Dore, Robert 1911.12
Dore, Thea 1928.37
Doree, Betty 1933.15
Doreen, Lillian 1907.45
Dorel, Esther 1875.04
Doremus, Gertrude 1903.34, 1907.11, 1908.40
Doremus, Mrs. Charles A. 1891.21
DoRepenique, Marcio 1992.13
doRepinique, Miguel 1988.06
Dorfman, Andrew 1982.22
Dorfman, Nat 1931.11, 1939.14
Dorfman, Nat N. 1930.09, 1933.27
Dorgan, Messr. 1889.01
Dorgan, Theo 1996.01, 1996.12, 1998.09
Dorge, Ida 1906.29
Dori, Adriana 1931.09
Doria, Mons. 1878.18
Doria, Vera 1916.21
Dorian, Bob 1998.06
Dorian, Ray 1949.06, 1953.03, 1954.15
Dorin, F. 1965.30, 1970.01, 1974.19
Doriva, Tamara 1934.38
Dorlia, Mlle. 1871.23, 1871.25, 1871.26, 1871.28
Dorly, Leah 1969.13
Dorman, Edna 1908.05
Dormann, Felix 1908.06, 1912.15, 1916.17, 1916.25
Dormonde, George 1947.18
Dormonde, Tim 1947.18
Dorn, Evelyn 1918.37
Dorn, Patricia 1932.27
Dornberger, Charles 1923.18
Dorne, Phyllis 1952.01, 1955.11, 1955.25
Dorney, Joseph R. 1923.42
Dornfold, W. 1922.03
Dorning, Charles 1939.06, 1947.22, 1948.01, 1948.03, 1948.06, 1948.07, 1948.10
Doro, Mariana 1965.29
Doro, Marie 1902.43, 1906.25, 1912.18
Dorr, Dorothy 1903.14
Dorr, Lester 1927.13, 1928.29
Dorr, Marion 1919.14
Dorrego, Don Pedro 1871.12
Dorrian, William 1918.30
Dorriani, William 1920.27
Dorrichon, Messr. 1884.11
Dorrin, John 1957.03, 1957.14, 1959.02, 1964.05, 1964.21, 1965.24, 1966.12, 1966.16, 1967.04, 1968.08
Dorrington, F. 1875.14, 1875.19, 1877.22, 1877.23, 1877.25, 1880.34, 1882.48, 1884.21, 1885.28, 1885.45, 1885.52, 1886.26
Dorris, Joe 1936.06
Dorris, Sue 1952.15
Dorsay, Edmund 1946.18
Dorsay, Mlle. 1883.41, 1883.60
Dorsay, Mme. 1882.53, 1882.58, 1882.73
Dorsch, Ad 1894.37
Dorsch, Madaline 1903.13
Dorsell, Sabery 1912.30
Dorsell, Sabrey 1911.28
Dorsell, Sabry 1910.23
Dorsey, Abner 1934.05
Dorsey, Don 1981.08
Dorsey, Jimmy 1981.16
Dorsey, Lee 1992.06
Dorsey, Sandra 1971.15
Dorsey, Thomas A. 1990.05
Dorst, Mlle. 1889.47
Dose, Louise 1923.17
DosReis, Ana Paula 1992.13
Doss, Dean 1964.21
Dossert, Frank G. 1910.10
Dossett, John 2001.06
Doswell, Fannie 1890.45
Dot, Baby 1920.44
Doti, Paul R. 1917.11
Dotson, Deborah 1983.17
Doty, Charles 1901.22, 1906.17
Doty, Charles W. 1898.77
Doty, David 1994.06
Doty, Helen 1923.08
Dotzman, Matthew 1999.16
Doubinsky, Messr. 1922.06
Double Quartette 1887.02
Doubledenee, Signor 1854.01
Doubrovsky, Georges 1943.11
Doucet, Catherine Calhoun 1925.08
Doucet, Paul 1927.43
Douchet, Messr. 1902.13
Doud, Frank 1885.07, 1885.09, 1888.08
Doud, Katy 1870.36
Doud, Kitty 1870.39
Doud, Oliver 1878.12, 1879.63, 1880.39
Dougal, Alberta 1926.31
Dougal, Claude 1925.37
Dougall, Bernard 1933.26, 1986.01
Dougherty, George 1909.24
Dougherty, Highey 1883.66
Dougherty, Hughey 1883.66, 1891.32, 1892.50
Dougherty, J.J. 1904.48
Dougherty, J.P. 1984.14
Dougherty, James F. 1902.38
Dougherty, Lee 1898.61
Dougherty, Lillian 1899.13
Douglas, Alice 1862.08
Douglas, Annie 1878.04
Douglas, Bertie 1906.31
Douglas, Betty 1942.01
Douglas, Bill 1949.05
Douglas, Bob 1942.15, 1945.11
Douglas, Byron 1890.40
Douglas, Charles Noel 1904.29, 1905.01, 1907.04
Douglas, Clara 1880.62, 1881.25, 1881.42
Douglas, Dan 1927.14
Douglas, Don 1935.14
Douglas, Donald 1927.08
Douglas, Duddie 1891.08
Douglas, Edward 1925.07
Douglas, Elsie 1919.32
Douglas, Emmet 1926.08
Douglas, Florence 1908.44, 1911.43
Douglas, Frankie 1906.36
Douglas, Fred 1903.08
Douglas, G.B. 1870.05
Douglas, Gertrude 1904.08, 1905.13, 1905.55, 1909.29
Douglas, Gladys 1932.08
Douglas, H. 1878.04
Douglas, Hal 1983.05
Douglas, Helen 1892.45, 1895.03
Douglas, J.L. 1879.16
Douglas, Jay 2000.15
Douglas, Johanna 1966.10
Douglas, John E. 1921.01
Douglas, Larry 1943.21, 1946.06, 1948.15, 1948.21, 1951.12, 1963.21, 1968.23, 1969.14
Douglas, Laura 1939.07
Douglas, Louis 1927.32
Douglas, Mabel 1905.07
Douglas, Malcolm 1894.42
Douglas, Mary 1936.07
Douglas, May 1885.34, 1885.36, 1885.37, 1885.38
Douglas, Melvyn 1946.10, 1959.04
Douglas, Milton 1933.03, 1936.07
Douglas, Miss 1861.06, 1862.01, 1862.02, 1866.28, 1911.34
Douglas, Nellie 1890.01
Douglas, Norma 1957.14
Douglas, Pi 1975.01
Douglas, Robert 1942.30
Douglas, Ronnie 1970.10
Douglas, Suzanne 1913.09, 1989.24
Douglas, Walter 1923.37
Douglas, William 1948.19
Douglas, Winston 1938.19
Douglass, Anna 1892.58
Douglass, Annie 1887.17, 1887.46
Douglass, Barbara 1905.09
Douglass, Charles Noel 1905.20
Douglass, Clara 1880.26, 1881.45, 1882.49
Douglass, Dudie 1887.29
Douglass, Fred 1899.33
Douglass, Larry 1957.08
Douglass, Margaret 1944.23

Douglass, Milton 1928.25
Douglass, Nancy 1944.23
Douglass, Nellie 1892.22
Douglass, Pi 1971.12
Douglass, Stephen 1949.03, 1951.13, 1954.03, 1955.08, 1957.17, 1963.26, 1966.14
Douras, Ethel 1912.36
Douste, Jeanne 1895.28
Douthitt, Wilfrid 1914.25
Dova, Ben 1928.14, 1939.22
Dova, Nina 1970.15, 1979.29
Dove, Alfred L. 1984.09
Dove, Johnnie 1925.27
Dove, Julius 1920.01
Dove, Marie 1928.10
Dovel, Ken 1978.23
Dovel, Kenn 1976.31, 1978.08, 1978.19
Dovel, Lynn 1967.10
Dovey, Alice 1909.02, 1909.30, 1910.16, 1911.11, 1912.28, 1914.02, 1914.26, 1915.07, 1915.16, 1915.30
Dovey, Ethel 1910.26
Dovey, Mark 1987.16
Dow, Ada 1879.18, 1879.24
Dow, Anna Gardner 1878.03
Dow, Bruce 2000.20
Dow, Pamela 1943.12
Dow, Philip 1882.77
Dowd, Harrison 1941.02, 1956.05
Dowd, Kitty 1871.15
Dowd, Mel 1960.21
Dowd, Mlle. 1967.07, 1972.24
Dowd, Mr. 1882.71
Dowdy, Helen 1935.13, 1942.03, 1943.10, 1943.17, 1944.31, 1946.01, 1948.20, 1953.04, 1954.16, 1965.03
Dowe, Juliue F. 1910.24
Dowe, Julius 1910.35
Dowell, Saxie 1952.11
Dowland, John 1963.28
Dowlen, Glenn 1962.06, 1962.07, 1963.15, 1964.07, 1964.31, 1965.13
Dowley, Harry N. 1890.27
Dowling and Griffiths 1918.34
Dowling, Bertha 1890.08, 1898.56, 1901.04, 1904.23, 1905.07
Dowling, Doris 1942.29, 1942.34
Dowling, Eddie 1919.01, 1919.15, 1922.31, 1925.11, 1926.29, 1927.48, 1934.42, 1939.18, 1948.23
Dowling, Edward 1921.27
Dowling, Edward D. 1936.17
Dowling, Edward Duryea 1937.16, 1938.08, 1939.22, 1940.07, 1941.11, 1952.11
Dowling, George 1911.40
Dowling, Henry 1927.48
Dowling, Jr., Eddie 1925.14
Dowling, M. 1897.09
Dowling, M.L. 1896.48, 1897.37, 1898.05, 1901.05
Dowling, Marian 1925.48
Dowling, Mary L. 1895.38
Dowling, Mme. 1896.26, 1897.21, 1899.22, 1905.07, 1905.17
Dowling, Mrs. 1904.23
Dowling, Mrs. M. 1896.36
Dowling, S.M. 1853.03
Dowling, Vernon 1929.20
Dowlings, George 1909.30
Downe, Cubby 1978.26
Downe, Jr., Edward R. 1976.08, 1976.33
Downer, Herb 1973.10
Downer, Stephen West 1947.21
Downes, David 2000.05
Downey, Catherine Marie 2000.19
Downey, Gertrude 1938.03
Downey, Morton 1927.66
Downey, Norman 1938.02
Downey, Tom 1903.13
Downie, Barbara 1948.17
Downing, Al 1929.03, 1930.42, 1931.04, 1931.28, 1938.08, 1940.19, 1946.06
Downing, Andrea 1946.01
Downing, Evelyn 1919.10
Downing, Robert 1958.08
Downing, Teresa 1899.26
Downs, Charles H. 1927.27
Downs, Frederic 1959.25
Downs, Geraldine 1926.30
Downs, Jason 1894.12
Downs, Jean 1918.01
Downs, Johnny 1933.05, 1945.18, 1948.15
Downs, Leslie-May 1972.08
Downs, M. 1887.11
Dox, Charles 1900.34, 1901.08, 1906.33
Dox, Charles L. 1896.18, 1896.51, 1897.26, 1899.19
Doxie, Devona 1935.17
Doyle, Buddy 1923.25
Doyle, Charles 1927.30, 1930.14
Doyle, Corinne 1939.16
Doyle, David 1960.01, 1963.21, 1967.10
Doyle, Ella 1901.08
Doyle, Florence 1895.09
Doyle, George 1883.06
Doyle, Gertrude 1918.05
Doyle, J.W. 1925.08
Doyle, Jack 2000.11
Doyle, James 1910.15, 1913.05, 1914.22, 1915.31, 1916.24, 1918.34, 1923.05
Doyle, James G. 1909.25
Doyle, James J. 1902.14, 1902.33
Doyle, Lee H. 1976.25
Doyle, Michael 1940.21
Doyle, Miriam 1918.27
Doyle, Miss 1878.14, 1895.03
Doyle, Richard 1878.17, 1879.68, 1880.64, 1881.09
Doyle, Sir Arthur Conan 1965.02
Doyle, W.L. 1911.22
Doyle, W.T. 1883.42
Doyle, William 1913.31
Doyle, William E. 1907.09
Doyne, Florence 1894.41
Dozier, Lamont 1982.22, 1984.15, 1986.02
Draak, Tom 1931.48, 1933.13
Drabinsky, Garth 1978.28, 1993.09, 1994.08, 1997.10, 1998.01
Drae, Elsie 1895.43
Dragonette, Jessica 1925.25, 1926.17
Drahosch, Peter 1984.04, 1984.05
Drake, Alfred 1935.07, 1937.04, 1938.06, 1939.12, 1939.26, 1940.03, 1943.04, 1944.32, 1946.24, 1947.21, 1948.32, 1950.11, 1951.17, 1953.16, 1961.26, 1964.03, 1965.22, 1973.12
Drake, Alice 1943.12
Drake, Charles 1897.12
Drake, Diana 1954.04, 1954.17
Drake, Donna 1975.15, 1985.20, 1998.06, 1999.11
Drake, Edwin 1930.27
Drake, Ervin 1943.20, 1964.05, 1968.23, 1980.10, 1981.06
Drake, George 1947.07
Drake, Henry 1938.19
Drake, Josephine 1908.27, 1923.17, 1928.27
Drake, Leslie 1900.32
Drake, Marty 1940.10, 1943.20, 1951.20
Drake, Milton 1982.12
Drake, Ronald 1970.06
Drake, Susan 1900.33, 1902.35
Drake, Susie 1899.15, 1899.25, 1900.20
Drake, Tony 1956.15
Drake, William A. 1937.01
Drake, Wilma 1942.11
Drakeley, Ray 1948.18
Dramatic Publishing Company 1975.19
Dranciard, Mme. 1876.31
Drange, Emily 1920.44
Draper, Jessie 1929.29, 1935.04
Draper, Joesf 1945.14
Draper, Kate 1980.08
Draper, Louise 1898.18
Draper, Paul 1934.42, 1942.10, 1963.22
Draper, Sanders 1939.07
Draper, Sedgewick 1915.30
Drasin, Tamara 1927.11, 1931.13, 1931.28, 1938.13
Dratch, Sam 1937.14
Drauer, Mons. 1869.05
Draw, Inez 1927.33
Drayson, Danny 1936.06, 1948.23
Drayton, Blanche 1895.23
Drayton, Cisco 1995.04
Drayton, Henri 1859.09, 1859.12, 1859.13, 1859.15, 1859.16, 1859.17, 1859.18, 1872.17
Drayton, Henry 1869.41
Drayton, Messr. 1883.31
Drayton, Mrs. Henri 1859.09, 1859.12, 1859.13, 1859.15, 1859.16, 1859.17, 1859.18
Drayton, Mrs. Henry 1869.41
Drayton, Thaddius 1922.44
Drayton, Thelma 1969.09
Dregely, Gabor 1923.26
Dreher, Minnie 1889.01
Dreher, Virginia 1884.11
Dreisbach, Bill 1978.11, 1982.04, 1984.15
Drejac, Jean 1961.25, 1964.39, 1965.08
Dremann, Janis 1938.05
Drenova, Felicia 1925.39
Drescher, Otto 1927.39
Dresser, Edward 1905.15
Dresser, Louise 1906.29, 1907.41, 1908.25, 1909.09, 1910.12, 1912.43, 1914.34, 1917.01, 1918.16
Dresser, Paul 1897.33, 1898.66, 1902.06, 1904.22, 1920.04
Dressler, Eric 1927.66
Dressler, Florence 1901.17
Dressler, Marie 1892.25, 1893.39, 1894.14, 1895.06, 1895.42, 1896.06, 1897.40, 1898.28, 1898.38, 1898.63, 1899.19, 1900.58, 1901.12, 1902.06, 1902.27, 1904.39, 1906.01, 1909.12, 1910.13, 1912.44, 1913.07, 1916.24, 1920.47, 1923.02
Dreufys, Max 1905.49
Drew, Ada May 1886.39
Drew, Adine 1887.04
Drew, Alex 1926.05
Drew, Andre 1943.17, 1944.31
Drew, C.H. 1879.03
Drew, Charles 1870.26, 1894.42, 1896.17, 1907.11
Drew, Charles H. 1872.16, 1872.18, 1872.19, 1876.17, 1876.18, 1876.21, 1876.27, 1877.16, 1878.20, 1884.25, 1884.37, 1890.24, 1894.42, 1897.22, 1898.25, 1900.01, 1901.05
Drew, Don 1934.13
Drew, Dorothy 1891.18, 1892.24, 1895.37, 1897.26
Drew, Ettie 1903.09
Drew, Frank 1864.05, 1864.09, 1864.12, 1878.22, 1879.06
Drew, Georgiana 1876.23
Drew, H.J. 1869.05
Drew, Henry 1868.07
Drew, John 1879.50, 1879.56, 1884.11, 1892.14, 1962.04, 1963.12, 1968.32
Drew, Leona 1907.02
Drew, Lowell B. 1919.13
Drew, Luella 1900.59
Drew, M. 1881.09
Drew, M.F. 1881.29, 1882.02, 1882.50, 1882.74, 1882.79, 1883.32
Drew, Master 1848.01
Drew, Maurice 1887.27, 1890.17, 1896.24, 1904.48, 1914.05
Drew, Maurice F. 1888.15
Drew, Miss 1861.06, 1883.47
Drew, Mr. 1857.04, 1869.16
Drew, Mrs. Sidney 1897.19
Drew, Sidney 1895.04, 1897.19
Drew, T. 1884.27
Drew, Will N. 1905.34
Drewes, Glenn 1999.01
Drewes, Russell W. 1943.23
Drews, Elsie 1908.27
Drexel, Corinne 1909.25
Dreyer, Billy 1920.06
Dreyer, Dave 1919.19, 1927.62, 1962.17, 1963.02, 1967.11, 1975.22, 1986.06
Dreyer, David 1918.20
Dreyer, Laura 1920.06
Dreyfus, Max 1904.34, 1913.05
Dreyfuss, Henry 1927.36, 1928.36, 1930.28, 1931.05, 1931.21, 1931.37, 1933.05
Driggs, Grace 1928.48
Drigo, Riccardo 1915.25
Drischell, Ralph 1970.04
Driscoll, Clara 1906.07
Driscoll, Fannie 1919.32
Driscoll, J.F. 1882.48, 1884.21, 1885.28, 1885.45, 1885.52, 1886.26, 1888.19
Driscoll, Loren 1957.13, 1958.13, 1958.15, 1959.04, 1959.10
Driscoll, Marian 1919.32
Driscoll, Peggy 1931.08
Driscoll, Ralph 1976.10
Drisin, David 1975.19
Drislane, Jack 1908.11
Drivas, Robert 1982.01, 1983.20
Driver, Don 1952.05, 1952.13, 1954.04
Driver, Donald 1967.01, 1981.09, 1981.25
Driver, Donn 1951.14, 1954.17, 1955.09
Driver, John 1974.05, 1974.12, 1981.02, 1987.19, 1990.17
Driver, Kip 2001.09
Drivet, C. 1866.09, 1866.23, 1866.25, 1866.27, 1866.29, 1866.30
Drix, Walter 1939.23
Drolet, Kitty 1911.28
Drollet, David 1926.01
Dror, Liat 1989.10
Drotar, Gregory 1973.12
Drotos, Ron 1995.14
Drouet, Robert 1913.07
Drover, Dorothy 1934.34
Drucker, Mort 1957.17
Drum, Dorothy 1929.09, 1930.20, 1933.02, 1933.21
Drum, Leonard 1967.01, 1979.05
Drumheller, C. 1911.10
Drummond, David 1972.08
Drummond, Jack 1954.05, 1960.01
Drummond-Grant, Ann 1936.14, 1936.16, 1936.19, 1936.24, 1936.25, 1955.15, 1955.16, 1955.18, 1955.20, 1955.22, 1955.23, 1955.24
Drury Lane Company of America 1913.33
Drury, Carl 1915.23
Drury, Carrie 1884.12, 1884.21
Drury, Charles 1920.09, 1923.18, 1926.01, 1927.60, 1930.38, 1931.13, 1935.12, 1939.25, 1946.04
Drury, Charles H. 1925.11
Drury, Hazel 1927.63
Drury, John 1904.18
Drury, Maude 1922.03
Dryden, Helen 1914.31, 1919.39
Dryden, Wheeler 1937.03, 1937.17, 1938.17
Dryer, Dave 1999.01
Dryer, Derek 1990.08
Dryer, Jerome Jay 1982.10
Dryis, Renee 1908.40
Drylie, Pat 1956.01
Drylie, Patricia 1954.12
dseCordova, Fred 1940.07
Dtover, F. 1877.02
Du Mare, Annetta 1880.42
Duane, Jerry 1945.18
Duane, Michael 1943.23
Duane, William 1873.18, 1919.41
Duart, Carl 1932.15
Duarte, Desiree 1999.24
DuBard, Rayfield 1952.06
DuBarry, Frances 1907.06
Dubarry, Gwen 1911.47
DuBarry, Harriet 1907.06, 1916.07
Dubarry, Harriet 1914.30
Duberman, Martin 1971.01
Dubey, Matt 1956.08, 1956.16, 1976.24
Dubin, Al 1912.06, 1925.42, 1927.53, 1927.60, 1939.22, 1940.07, 1942.18, 1957.10, 1962.17, 1973.14, 1974.09, 1975.12, 1975.22, 1976.07, 1979.25, 1980.09, 1980.20, 1988.08, 1989.21, 1992.18, 1997.01, 2001.08
Dubinsky, Vladimir 1927.66
Dubois, Camille 1871.14, 1871.19, 1872.21, 1872.24, 1872.34, 1873.12, 1873.14, 1873.17
DuBois, Camille 1872.22, 1872.26
Dubois, Gladys 2000.12
Dubois, James 1912.16
DuBois, Jeannette 1964.32
DuBois, Lona 1900.58
Dubois, Miss 1892.07
Dubois, Mlle. 1872.01, 1872.03
DuBoise, Grace 1912.38
Dubouchet, Mlle. 1875.07
Dubouchet, Mons. 1875.07
Dubov, Stephen 1979.26
Dubreuil, Ernest 1884.50, 1888.07
Dubro, Bette 1952.15
Dubrow, Marsha 1999.05
Dubuis, Charles 1916.16
Duca, Lennie Del 1977.18
Ducharme, Marc 1907.15
Duchateau, Eme 1882.71
Duchateau, Emma 1879.18, 1879.23, 1880.06, 1880.13, 1880.65, 1880.70, 1881.34, 1881.56, 1882.28, 1884.60
DuChateau, Emma 1886.36
Duchateau, Juliet 1884.25
Duchateau, Laura 1881.40
DuChateau, Miss 1886.36
Duchateau, Mons. 1887.37
Duchene, Maria 1910.35
Duchesne, E. 1866.19
Duchesne, Mlle. 1867.24

Duchesne, Mons. 1867.24, 1868.07, 1868.18, 1868.25, 1868.27, 1868.30, 1869.10, 1869.12, 1869.19, 1870.03, 1870.45, 1871.03, 1871.07, 1871.23, 1871.24, 1871.25, 1871.26, 1871.28, 1872.03, 1872.28, 1872.29, 1872.31, 1872.33, 1872.42, 1873.01, 1873.11, 1873.15, 1873.16
Duchworth, Mesdame 1852.05
Duck 1964.02
Duck, Roy 1918.17
Duckat, Lipman 1940.19
Duckens, Dorceal 1975.19
Ducker, L.H. 1893.39
Ducker, Maud 1894.14
Duckling, Jenny-Lynn 1997.17
Duckworth, Dortha 1960.05, 1963.01, 1965.17
Duckworth, Miss 1855.10
duClos, Danielle 1990.04
duClos, Deanna 1990.04
Duclos, Jeanne 1868.18
Duclos, Marie 1866.18
Duclos, Mlle. 1868.30, 1869.10, 1869.19, 1869.24
Duclos, Mons. 1883.55
DuCoe, Tedde 1897.21
DuCoe, Teddie 1898.28
Ducos, Frl. 1897.08
Ducos, M. 1883.41
Ducos, Mons. 1882.73, 1883.27, 1883.28, 1883.30, 1883.34, 1883.51, 1883.54, 1883.57, 1883.60, 1884.01, 1884.02, 1884.03, 1884.05, 1884.43, 1884.47, 1884.49, 1884.50, 1884.52, 1884.54
Ducret, Mauricette 1932.19
Ducro, Messr. 1892.27
Ducrow, Mr. 1895.42
Ducrow, Tot 1898.34
Ducrow, Tote 1892.06
Ducy-Barre, Mlle. 1851.02
Duda, Andrea 1969.14
Duda, Kevin 2001.09
Duda, Matthew 1980.23
Duddy, Lyn 1950.09
Dudley Buck Opera Company 1880.54
Dudley, Alice 1934.15, 1934.42, 1935.17, 1940.09, 1942.27
Dudley, Bernard 1926.15, 1926.23
Dudley, Bide 1917.29, 1919.08, 1919.28, 1920.26, 1922.24, 1926.04, 1927.05
Dudley, Bronson 1939.07, 1939.26
Dudley, C.E. 1894.27
Dudley, Daisy 1895.02, 1906.09
Dudley, Ethel 1907.06
Dudley, Grace 1903.33
Dudley, Harry 1905.28
Dudley, Helen 1913.20
Dudley, Jane 1932.19
Dudley, John 1893.02, 1894.28, 1895.22, 1900.57, 1902.25, 1906.32, 1919.29, 1939.03, 1939.08, 1946.11
Dudley, John E. 1891.47, 1892.60, 1893.47
Dudley, K. 1866.01
Dudley, Ninon 1912.27
Dudley, Renee 1963.26
Dudley, S.H. 1911.20
Duel, Miss 1863.01
Duel, Mr. 1863.01, 1863.02
Duell, H. 1866.16
Duell, Mr. 1866.16, 1866.17
Duell, William 1967.05, 1976.10, 1996.06
Duenweg, Robert 1931.05
Duenweg, Robert L. 1927.16
Duerr, Donald 1951.14
Duers, Toussaint 1930.24
Dueth, Leonie 1894.24, 1900.40
Duey, Philip 1927.15
Dufac, M. 1926.45, 1926.48
duFaye, Grace 1929.26
Duff Opera Company 1893.05
Duff, C. 1881.03
Duff, J.C. 1890.50, 1895.31, 1900.43, 1902.30, 1907.06, 1928.13
Duff, James C. 1877.26, 1877.27, 1879.05, 1879.15, 1879.21, 1883.16, 1883.21, 1884.18, 1884.64, 1885.11, 1885.16, 1885.48, 1886.40, 1887.15, 1887.20, 1887.21, 1887.44, 1889.36, 1890.14, 1890.15, 1890.18, 1890.20, 1893.05, 1893.09, 1897.03, 1897.11
Duff, John C. 1904.40
Duff, John J. 1884.31
Duff, Michael 1985.17
Duff-Gordon, Lady 1916.10, 1917.13, 1917.26, 1919.15, 1920.18
Duffey, J. Humbird 1912.15, 1914.03, 1926.44, 1927.61
Duffey, John H. 1904.36
Duffey, John Humbird 1921.40
Duffey, Patrick J.P. 1997.22
Duffield, Blanche 1911.10, 1912.10, 1912.21, 1912.22, 1913.08, 1914.03
Duffield, Brainerd 1946.13
Duffield, H.S. 1877.04
Duffield, Harry S. 1879.12
Duffield, S.B. 1867.25, 1871.10, 1872.10
Duffin, Matt 1929.29, 1935.04
Dufford, Dean 1991.09
Duffy, Carolyn 1917.30
Duffy, Clarence 1888.06
Duffy, Eileen 1974.20
Duffy, Elsie 1931.05, 1931.36
Duffy, Gordon 1959.19
Duffy, Henry 1947.14
Duffy, Humbird 1930.04
Duffy, J. Humbird 1921.15, 1926.10, 1927.44, 1927.57
Duffy, James 1912.27, 1918.38
Duffy, James C. 1912.43
Duffy, Jimmie 1922.19
Duffy, Jimmy 1923.21, 1925.25, 1925.48, 1929.24
Duflocq, Louis 1869.04, 1869.13, 1870.05, 1872.23, 1872.35, 1873.03, 1873.26, 1879.50, 1879.56
Dufour, Mons. 1892.32
Dufranne, Georges 1921.29
DuFreHouston, Ethel 1913.24, 1919.08
DuFrene, May 1903.03, 1904.13
DuFrene, Miss 1903.03, 1904.13
Dufy, Colin 1971.16
Dufy, E. 1974.20
Dugan, Bill 1922.38
Dugan, Charles 1893.02
Dugan, Jack 1929.07
Dugan, Leo 1928.44
Dugan, Yung Kid Battling 1917.29
Dugen, Shaun 1997.14
Duggan, J.F. 1859.12
Duggan, Karen 2001.04
Duggan, Louis 1918.14
Duggan, Maggie 1882.25, 1882.32, 1882.38, 1882.41
Duggan, Mary 1890.02
Duggan, Mr. 1838.01, 1841.01
Duggan, Norman 1931.38
Duggan, Thomas 1920.24
duGuary, Babette 1928.31
Duguay, Brian 1986.03, 1998.04
Duhamel, Mlle. 1868.13
DuHeld, Alice 1898.03
DuHeld, Blanche 1898.03
DuHeld, Georgia 1898.03
DuHeld, Lillian 1898.03
duHeron, Helen 1903.28
duHoffmann, Karl 1999.15
Duhrtal, Alain 1935.19
Duke of Iron 1947.19
Duke, Betty 1926.01
Duke, Bill 1971.13
Duke, Paul 1942.19, 1953.10
Duke, Peter 1983.17
Duke, Robert 1946.22
Duke, Vernon 1930.18, 1930.32, 1930.33, 1931.21, 1932.20, 1932.27, 1934.01, 1934.42, 1936.02, 1936.17, 1936.31, 1940.07, 1940.16, 1940.17, 1941.13, 1942.01, 1942.12, 1944.01, 1944.27, 1952.20, 1953.12, 1964.02, 1980.10, 1982.12, 1988.08, 1992.18, 1999.23
Dukelan, George W. 1891.32, 1892.50
Dukes, Ashley 1926.41
Dukore, Phyllis 1970.09
Dulaine, Pierre 1989.26
Dulany, Dean B. 1903.36
Dulany, Miss 1864.17, 1866.28
Dull, Harry 1900.24
Dulo, Jane 1945.18
duLocke, Camille 2000.06
Dulzell, Paul 1918.15
Dumakude, Thuli 1997.14
Dumanoir, Philippe 1848.04, 1855.04, 1864.07, 1864.16, 1867.03, 1868.09, 1879.62, 1880.31, 1882.15, 1884.38, 1886.26
Dumanoir, Philippe Francois 1898.19, 1900.13
Dumaresq, William 1984.02
Dumas, Alex 1873.12
Dumas, Alexandre 1870.19, 1901.06, 1919.27, 1921.15, 1928.12, 1961.26, 1984.14
Dumas, Francez 1931.29
Dumas, Mal 1930.24
Dumbrille, Douglass R. 1925.39, 1928.12, 1930.30
Dumke, Ralph 1942.15, 1943.09, 1944.16, 1944.27, 1945.12, 1946.01
Dumond, Joseof 1903.15
Dumond, Mlle. 1903.15
Dumont, Andre 1923.38
Dumont, Audre 1926.31
Dumont, Charles 1981.04
Dumont, Daisy 1909.29
Dumont, Dorothy 1915.18
Dumont, Ed 1962.14
Dumont, Frank 1881.55, 1883.56, 1894.06, 1902.09
Dumont, Harry 1918.24
Dumont, Margaret 1922.17, 1923.46, 1925.45, 1927.21, 1928.38, 1932.21
Dumont, Marie 1905.39
Dumont, Meri 1903.09
Dumont, Merle 1904.25
Dumont, Paul 1969.17
Dumpere, Lydia 1907.08
Duna, Steffi 1933.07
Dunaeff, Alex 1946.10
Dunaevsky, I. 1977.13
Dunar, Leon 1933.25
Dunaway, Faye 1982.02
Dunbar, Ann 1948.18
Dunbar, Annie 1888.10, 1888.23
Dunbar, Barbara 1904.29, 1909.01
Dunbar, Brooks 1947.21
Dunbar, Dixie 1934.19, 1939.24
Dunbar, Dorothy 1904.29
Dunbar, E.C. 1882.20
Dunbar, Ella 1882.77
Dunbar, Errol 1903.37
Dunbar, F.E. 1886.10
Dunbar, Florence 1893.34
Dunbar, Helen 1890.50, 1894.11, 1897.48, 1898.50, 1899.17, 1899.30
Dunbar, Lillie 1897.21
Dunbar, Madge 1897.21
Dunbar, Miss 1897.09
Dunbar, Mlle. 1888.10, 1888.23
Dunbar, Paul Laurence 1898.41, 1901.08, 1903.08, 1907.22, 1966.15
Dunbar, Paul Lawrence 1914.29
Dunbar, R.N. 1886.15, 1889.10
Dunbar, Robert 1892.55, 1893.21, 1898.68
Dunbar, Ronald 1974.11
Dunbar, William 1896.01
Duncan, Andrew 1961.17
Duncan, Anna 1925.37
Duncan, Augustin 1946.05
Duncan, Betsy 1916.25
Duncan, C.H. 1879.14
Duncan, Cleone 1971.21
Duncan, Danny 1949.09
Duncan, Doris 1924.17
Duncan, Dorothy 1931.27
Duncan, Emily 1877.22, 1877.23, 1877.25, 1877.39
Duncan, George W. 1912.30
Duncan, H. 1907.53
Duncan, Harold 1936.12
Duncan, Harry 1904.45, 1938.16, 1959.09
Duncan, Ina 1921.16, 1923.39, 1930.24, 1931.47, 1933.27, 1936.30
Duncan, Isadora 1896.27
Duncan, Jeff 1957.14
Duncan, Jessie 1914.14
Duncan, Laura 1930.24, 1933.27, 1939.07, 1940.18
Duncan, Laura Marie 2000.15
Duncan, Ronald 1948.31
Duncan, Rosetta 1917.23, 1919.09, 1920.36, 1924.46, 1936.12
Duncan, Sammy 1929.26
Duncan, Sandy 1965.21, 1966.31, 1967.04, 1967.07, 1969.04, 1970.11, 1979.22, 1983.09
Duncan, Stuart 1976.17
Duncan, Todd 1935.13, 1940.17, 1942.03, 1943.15, 1949.15
Duncan, Tommy 1999.24
Duncan, Vivian 1917.23, 1919.09, 1920.36, 1924.46, 1936.12
Duncan, William Carey 1923.45, 1927.29
Duncan, William Cary 1913.10, 1917.09, 1918.26, 1919.04, 1920.11, 1921.03, 1922.02, 1922.29, 1924.42, 1927.49, 1928.07, 1928.32, 1929.37
Duncan, Willis 1939.27
Duncan-Gibbs, Mamie 1989.20, 1992.08, 1996.14
Dunckley, Mary 1927.68
Dundas, Clementine 1910.02
Dundy, Elmer S. 1905.17, 1905.54
Dunfee, Josephine 1913.12
Dunfee, Nora 1971.17
Dungan, C.W. 1885.14, 1885.52, 1887.21, 1893.47
Dungan, Charles 1882.15, 1882.49, 1891.36, 1892.60, 1894.28, 1895.22, 1900.57, 1902.25
Dungan, Charles W. 1882.16, 1884.12, 1884.20, 1884.57, 1885.13, 1886.26, 1887.15, 1887.28, 1888.24, 1888.26, 1889.17, 1889.22, 1906.32
Dungan, Joseph 1976.10
Dungan, R.N. 1884.48
Dunham, Christine 1997.22, 1998.20, 1999.21, 2000.19
Dunham, Clarke 1970.20, 1973.09, 1976.04, 1982.20, 1983.13, 1984.11, 1985.05, 1986.08, 1987.14, 1989.14, 1989.18, 1997.10
Dunham, Curtis 1914.33
Dunham, George 1903.32
Dunham, Hazel 1902.26
Dunham, Katherine 1937.14, 1940.17, 1943.17, 1944.31, 1945.07, 1945.10, 1945.13, 1946.21, 1950.07, 1955.26, 1962.22, 1986.03
Dunham, Miss 1871.04
Dunham, Ronald 1975.01
Dunham, William 1914.16
Dunhills, The 1963.10
Dunkel, Eugene 1934.40, 1935.05, 1935.06, 1935.07, 1935.08, 1935.09, 1935.10, 1937.02, 1937.12, 1939.10
Dunkel, Eugene B. 1938.12
Dunlap, Bert 1916.03, 1917.37, 1918.41
Dunlap, Edith 1900.45
Dunlap, Florence 1943.19, 1954.15, 1956.16
Dunlap, George 1892.11
Dunlap, Helen 1901.04
Dunlap, Maurice Pratt 1902.44
Dunlap, R. 1908.38
Dunlap, Robert 1908.01
Dunlap, William 1796.01, 1796.03
Dunlay, Will 1899.26
Dunlay, William 1896.18, 1897.26
Dunleavy, William M. 1889.51
Dunlevy, J.S. 1903.40
Dunlevy, William M. 1889.37, 1898.63
Dunlop, Christopher 1981.11
Dunlop, Frances 1919.34
Dunlop, Frank 1980.19, 1981.26
Dunmire, Donna 1999.22
Dunmore, Eveleen 1904.12
Dunn, Annie 1897.38
Dunn, Arthur 1879.30, 1882.48, 1890.03, 1895.38, 1898.69, 1899.29
Dunn, Charles 1961.26
Dunn, Colleen 1988.20, 1991.07, 1997.04, 2001.02
Dunn, Edward 1913.37
Dunn, Edward Delaney 1921.13, 1921.14, 1923.03, 1923.13, 1928.48
Dunn, Elaine 1953.17, 1955.12, 1963.17
Dunn, Emma 1897.56, 1921.24
Dunn, F.E. 1902.29
Dunn, Geoffrey 1976.26
Dunn, Henry 1900.53, 1924.31, 1944.19
Dunn, Irene 1925.38
Dunn, J. Colville 1927.19, 1938.13
Dunn, J.C. 1866.13, 1866.16, 1866.17, 1867.13, 1867.14, 1867.16, 1867.17, 1868.08
Dunn, James 1852.07, 1856.03, 1862.03, 1862.04, 1878.14, 1880.08, 1940.19
Dunn, James C. 1856.02, 1868.16, 1869.25, 1869.28, 1881.24
Dunn, James Joseph 1918.33
Dunn, Jennie 1879.30, 1882.48
Dunn, John 1870.13, 1870.19
Dunn, John P. 1901.03
Dunn, Johnny 1921.26, 1922.25
Dunn, Joseph 1918.25
Dunn, Josephine 1932.25
Dunn, Julia E. 1875.06
Dunn, Kate 1868.16, 1869.21

Dunn, Kathy 1959.24
Dunn, Katie 1869.25
Dunn, Mignon 1954.18, 1956.09
Dunn, Miss 1866.13, 1867.13, 1867.16, 1869.28
Dunn, Mr. 1851.02, 1851.03, 1851.05
Dunn, Mrs. 1851.05, 1856.02, 1858.03
Dunn, Patricia 1953.16
Dunn, Patrick 2000.19
Dunn, Ralph 1927.18, 1954.05, 1959.19, 1960.19
Dunn, Richard 1936.16, 1936.20, 1939.08, 1948.02, 1948.03, 1948.05, 1948.07, 1948.09
Dunn, Robert 1972.10
Dunn, Sally Mae 1994.06
Dunn, Sally Mae. 2001.02
Dunn, Thomas 1895.17
Dunn, Vera 1913.23, 1918.33, 1934.36
Dunn, W.J. 1918.36
Dunn, William 1916.11
Dunne, Colin 1996.01, 1996.12, 1998.09, 2000.04, 2000.05
Dunne, Irene 1922.47, 1927.07, 1928.02, 1928.27
Dunne, James 1981.13
Dunne, Jno. W. 1872.27
Dunne, John 1906.38, 1907.56
Dunne, John W. 1900.51
Dunnie, J.F. 1866.20
Dunnie, Mr. 1866.26
Dunning, Alice 1869.07, 1869.46
Dunning, Philip 1915.32, 1918.17
Dunnington, Steve 1984.14
Dunnock, Mildred 1946.05
Dunphy, Elizabeth 1904.33
Dunscombe, Annie 1880.43
Dunsmuir, Eleanor 1928.32
Dunsmuir, Helen 1928.07
Dunsmuire, John 1905.36
Dunsmure, John 1900.25, 1900.31, 1900.32, 1904.55, 1907.13, 1910.07, 1910.10, 1910.28, 1911.44, 1918.40, 1920.31, 1921.40, 1925.02, 1928.43, 1930.03, 1934.12, 1934.17
Dunstan, Cliff 1940.22, 1942.29, 1946.12, 1950.04
Dunstan, Clifford 1938.14
Dunstan, George W. 1912.30
Dunston, George 1913.27
Duntiere, Victor 1962.13, 1965.20
Dunton, Ethel 1929.28
Dunton, John 1904.18
Duo Art Productions, Inc. 1927.31
Duo, Arenera 1911.18
duPage, Richard 1938.04
Duparc, Florence 1875.25, 1875.27, 1875.29, 1875.30, 1876.20, 1876.28, 1876.31, 1877.06, 1877.12, 1877.13, 1877.14, 1877.18, 1877.26, 1877.29, 1877.30, 1877.31, 1877.32, 1877.33, 1877.38, 1878.06, 1878.07, 1878.09
Duparc, L. 1879.36, 1879.40, 1879.47, 1880.16
Duparc, Louise 1879.19, 1879.26, 1879.39, 1879.44, 1880.52
Duparc, Mlle. 1879.45, 1879.46, 1879.48, 1879.60, 1880.23, 1880.27, 1880.28, 1881.50, 1881.51, 1882.30, 1882.35, 1883.41
Duparc, Mme. 1880.50, 1883.28
Duparc, Mons. 1877.17
Dupeuty, Charles 1866.30
Dupin, Mlle. 1881.48, 1881.51, 1881.53, 1882.30, 1882.35
Dupin, Mons. 1881.48, 1881.50
Duplan, E. 1881.48, 1881.49, 1881.50, 1881.51, 1881.54, 1882.29, 1882.30, 1882.35, 1884.55
Duplan, Messr. 1875.27, 1877.31, 1879.26, 1880.28, 1885.20
Duplan, Mons. 1873.11, 1873.16, 1875.01, 1875.02, 1875.25, 1875.28, 1875.29, 1875.30, 1875.33, 1876.20, 1876.25, 1876.28, 1877.06, 1877.09, 1877.10, 1877.11, 1877.12, 1877.13, 1877.14, 1877.17, 1877.19, 1877.26, 1877.27, 1877.30, 1877.32, 1877.33, 1877.37, 1877.38, 1878.06, 1878.07, 1878.08, 1878.09, 1879.27, 1879.31, 1879.34, 1879.36, 1879.39, 1879.40, 1879.43, 1879.44, 1879.45, 1879.46, 1879.47, 1879.48, 1879.49, 1879.51, 1879.55, 1879.60, 1879.69, 1880.16, 1880.22, 1880.27, 1880.29, 1880.44, 1880.50, 1880.52, 1880.56, 1880.58, 1880.60, 1882.53, 1882.55, 1882.58, 1882.61, 1882.67, 1883.27, 1883.28, 1883.30, 1883.34, 1883.41, 1883.51, 1883.54, 1883.55, 1883.57, 1883.59, 1883.60, 1883.61, 1884.01, 1884.43, 1884.45, 1884.47, 1884.49, 1884.52, 1884.54, 1885.17
Dupler, Ranolds 1938.09
Duplessis, Mlle. 1877.27, 1877.31, 1877.32, 1877.34, 1877.38, 1878.07
duPlessis, Rene 1930.32, 1933.26
Duplessy, Mlle. 1878.08
Dupont, Helen 1897.54
Dupont, Heloise 1898.20
Dupont, Jacques 1965.37
duPont, Monsieur 1931.05
duPont, Paul 1936.28, 1942.03, 1942.26, 1942.30, 1943.15, 1943.19, 1944.03, 1957.03, 1957.04
Dupont, Paul 1942.17, 1942.19
DuPont, William 1917.16
Duport 1881.50, 1883.12
Duprato, Jules 1869.19
Dupre, Betty 1925.11
Dupre, Ernest 1884.43
Dupre, Fanny 1901.17
DuPre, Lynette G. 1990.05
Dupree, Frank 1892.27, 1907.61, 1927.43
DuPree, Marie 1908.44
Dupree, Minnie 1886.62, 1891.27
DuPree, William 1956.06, 1963.15, 1966.02
Dupuis, Eugene 1905.53
Dupuis, Jose 1885.60, 1885.61, 1886.18, 1886.19, 1886.20
Dupuis, Marie 1907.49
Dupuis, Mons. 1879.19, 1879.26, 1879.27, 1879.31, 1879.36, 1879.39, 1879.40, 1879.41, 1879.43, 1879.44, 1879.45, 1879.46, 1879.47, 1879.48, 1879.49, 1879.61, 1879.69, 1880.29, 1880.56, 1885.55, 1885.56, 1885.57, 1885.59, 1886.08, 1886.09, 1886.21
Dupuy, Ellen 1876.16
Duquan, Doreese 1961.13, 1962.07
Duquesnay, Ann 1984.09, 1992.08, 1996.07
Duquette. Ton, 1960.21
Duran, Darryl 1954.13
Duran, Lwo 1927.28
Duran, Marcela 1997.13
Duran, Michael 2000.11
Durand and Company 1878.18
Durand, A. 1883.51, 1883.54, 1883.55, 1883.57, 1883.59, 1883.60, 1883.61, 1887.35, 1887.36, 1887.37, 1887.38, 1887.41, 1894.30, 1896.34
Durand, Aurelie 1905.12
Durand, B. 1999.24
Durand, Beverly 1999.24
Durand, Charles 1858.03
Durand, Edouard 1906.45, 1908.04, 1908.27, 1910.26, 1914.07, 1919.31, 1922.09, 1925.08
Durand, Edward 1915.29
Durand, Elsie 1886.37
Durand, Juliette 1968.30
Durand, Mr. 1794.01, 1890.31, 1891.33, 1892.43, 1893.29, 1894.01
Durand, Rosalie 1856.01
Durando, Miss 1886.31
Durang, Chris 1978.06
Durang, Messr. 1794.01, 1796.01, 1796.02
Durang, Miss C. 1823.01
Durang, Miss I. 1823.01
Durang, Mrs. 1796.01
Durango, Pepita 1949.07
Durant, Al 1942.11
Durant, Bessie 1912.12
Durant, C.W. 1887.14
Durant, Florence 1881.22
Durant, Jack 1929.35, 1931.26, 1940.22, 1945.17, 1963.17
Durant, Kevin Serge 2001.06
Durant, Mr. 1853.01, 1853.03
Durant, Paul 1946.16
Durante, Jimmie 1921.27, 1929.27
Durante, Jimmy 1930.40, 1933.05, 1935.15, 1936.26, 1939.13, 1940.07
Durante, Vito 1963.05, 1964.40, 1967.09, 1968.19
Durasova, Nina 1925.51
Duray, Elizabeth 1928.11
Durden, Tommy 1982.22
Durdy, R. 1871.09
Durel, Joseph 1891.23
Durfee, Duke 1993.17
Durflocq, Louis 1880.04
Durham, Eddie 2000.07
Durham, Messr. 1889.01
Durham, Sidney 1894.11
Durie, Mr. 1823.01
Durie, Mrs. 1834.02
During, Herr 1882.68
Durkee, Dorothy 1944.02
Durkin, Lillian 1920.10
Durkin, Master 1926.08
Durning, Charles 1965.29, 1966.05, 1968.01
Duroe, Joel 1926.07
DuRoy, Lizzie 1893.34
Durrenberger, Jack 1954.08
Durrence, Betty 1945.14
Durrence, Bettye 1946.10
Durston, David 1943.23
Duru, Alfred 1869.05, 1871.24, 1872.42, 1876.10, 1879.31, 1879.43, 1880.44, 1880.49, 1880.69, 1881.03, 1881.14, 1881.21, 1881.22, 1881.33, 1881.34, 1881.36, 1881.38, 1881.45, 1881.46, 1881.48, 1881.53, 1881.54, 1881.56, 1882.09, 1882.11, 1882.14, 1882.25, 1882.31, 1882.32, 1882.37, 1882.47, 1882.49, 1882.52, 1882.61, 1882.72, 1883.13, 1883.19, 1883.22, 1883.25, 1883.41, 1883.51, 1883.54, 1883.55, 1884.02, 1884.03, 1884.28, 1884.29, 1884.47, 1884.52, 1885.07, 1885.09, 1885.20, 1885.61, 1887.06, 1887.35, 1887.38, 1888.09, 1888.18, 1889.01, 1889.40, 1889.44, 1890.33, 1891.36, 1892.10, 1892.11, 1892.30, 1892.60, 1893.47, 1895.22, 1896.21, 1897.17, 1898.07, 1898.27, 1899.14, 1900.14, 1909.08, 1926.43
Duru, Mons. 1890.37
Durya, Julie 1899.23
Duryea, Amelia 1884.27
Duryea, May 1893.39, 1894.14, 1898.56
DuSauld, Gabrielle 1881.02
DuSauld, Miss 1876.23
Duschesne, Mons. 1872.39
Dusenberry, Vincent 1910.03
Dusenheimer, Mlle. 1873.22
Dushock, Dorothy 1953.17, 1961.15, 1963.17
DuShon, Jean 1982.12
DuSouchet, H.A. 1912.02
duSouchet, Henry A. 1897.45
Dussault, Nancy 1959.08, 1959.17, 1960.02, 1960.14, 1960.23, 1964.40, 1966.31, 1967.04
Dustan, R.J. 1884.46, 1887.46, 1891.27
Dutheld, Kenneth 1923.35
Duthers, Lou 1929.45
Dutton, Ed 1960.08
Dutton, Henri 1888.01
Dutton, J. 1887.27
Dutton, Laura Deane 1942.34
Dutton, Miss 1869.29
Duval, Alexandre 1866.23
Duval, Annette 1900.59
Duval, Edna 1922.12
Duval, Franca 1958.17
Duval, Gabrielle 1938.16
Duval, Georges 1905.46, 1906.36, 1907.06
Duval, Helen 1904.25
Duval, J.A. 1879.28
Duval, Jose 1957.04
Duval, Josephine 1925.43
Duval, Paulette 1923.38
Duval, Viola 1920.35
Duval, Violet 1906.05, 1922.12
Duvalis, Mons. 1875.04
Duvall, William 1964.24
Duvernay, W. 1870.44
Dvonch, Frederick 1949.03, 1950.04, 1951.12, 1955.06, 1955.07, 1955.09, 1956.03, 1956.05, 1957.06, 1957.08, 1957.17, 1958.03, 1958.07, 1959.06, 1959.24, 1965.06, 1967.07
Dvorak, Anton 1999.05
Dvorkin, Ellie 1998.19
Dvorovenko, Irina 1995.18
Dvorsky, George 1982.11, 1983.17, 1991.12, 1993.14, 1994.05, 1995.07, 1995.18
Dvorsky, Peter 1973.16, 1975.18
Dwelley, Trish 1964.21
Dwight, Mabel 1909.20, 1910.23
Dwight, Marquita 1900.54
Dwyer, Allys 1927.52
Dwyer, Bill 1949.04
Dwyer, Daisy 1898.77, 1901.05
Dwyer, Edward 1875.10
Dwyer, Emil 1915.15
Dwyer, Ethel 1903.12
Dwyer, George 1909.15
Dwyer, Hugh 1915.06
Dwyer, John 1926.22
Dwyer, John T. 1927.09, 1929.49, 1931.01
Dwyer, Leo 1919.39
Dwyer, Michael 1895.32
Dwyer, Phil 1915.15, 1919.15, 1921.21, 1938.16
Dwyer, Terrence 1995.05
Dybas, James 1965.06, 1968.07, 1976.02, 1997.19
Dye, H. 1887.14
Dyer, Ada 1984.09
Dyer, Bertie 1895.34
Dyer, Bill 1976.16
Dyer, George 1996.11, 1996.13
Dyer, Henry 1903.18, 1913.05
Dyer, James H. 1886.28
Dyer, John 1933.15
Dyer, Mansel 1936.18, 1939.09
Dyer, Mell 1894.13
Dyer, Sammy 1939.15
Dyer, William 1960.07
Dyett, Walter F. 1906.15
Dylan, Bob 1970.16, 1979.30, 1982.22
Dyllyn, Bernard 1888.03, 1889.09, 1890.12, 1894.06, 1897.33, 1913.17
Dyllyn, J. Bernard 1900.24, 1904.42, 1905.49, 1914.15
Dyllyn, J.B. 1885.35
Dyllyn, John B. 1917.37
Dymmock, Dorine 1894.43
Dyott, Miss 1844.01
Dyott, Mr. 1851.01
Dyott, Mrs. John 1844.01
Dyrenforth, James 1922.48, 1931.13, 1931.34
Dyring, H.T. 1881.06, 1881.39
Dys, Deanna 1988.20, 1999.15
Dyson, Hal 1925.26
Dyson, Ronald 1968.11
Dyson, Wynn 1936.23, 1939.11
Dyszel, William 1987.03

E. Nussbaum and Company 1920.02
E.B. Dunkel Studios 1942.17
Eads, Dollie 1908.16
Eads, Paul 1981.01
Eady, Joseph 1946.08
Eagan, Daisy 2000.01
Eagan, Gladys 1907.49
Eagan, Irene 1893.36, 1893.46
Eagan, Lucille 1903.18
Eagan, Michael 1980.06
Eagan, Raymond B. 1925.36
Eagan, Rene 1893.27
Eagan, Susan 1979.27
Eagen, James 1927.40
Eagen, Lucille 1905.44
Eager, Edward 1944.18, 1944.32, 1950.11, 1963.22, 1964.03
Eager, Johnny 1945.17
Eagle, Henry Red 1916.06
Eagle, Oscar 1918.30, 1918.42, 1919.28, 1919.34, 1920.11, 1920.42, 1922.04, 1922.13, 1923.05, 1924.42, 1924.46, 1925.35, 1925.36, 1925.45, 1926.04, 1927.21, 1927.45, 1928.38, 1928.49
Eales, Margaret 1964.36
Eames, Cece 1943.16
Eames, Ernest 1940.11, 1940.14
Eames, Howard 1926.50
Eames, Miss 1856.01
Eardon, John 1955.17
Earl, Erminie 1900.34
Earl, Florence 1897.49
Earl, Harry 1899.23, 1903.35
Earl, Marcelle 1917.22
Earl, Mary 1922.16
Earl, Maude 1905.39, 1906.23
Earl, Tilly 1872.22, 1872.24, 1872.26, 1873.12
Earl, V. 1908.21
Earl, Virginia 1889.09, 1889.41, 1898.46, 1901.01
Earl, Wheeler 1904.21
Earl, William 1924.35
Earlcott, Gladys 1919.20
Earle, Agnes 1886.31
Earle, Arthur 1890.08, 1896.37
Earle, Carla 1980.10, 1984.09
Earle, Charles 1896.50
Earle, Dottie 1998.16, 2001.02

Earle, Ed. C. 1903.09
Earle, Edward 1980.11, 1980.23
Earle, Ermine 1903.06
Earle, Erminei 1898.28
Earle, Erminie 1898.20, 1906.01
Earle, Evelyn 1920.31
Earle, Florence 1921.08, 1927.29, 1928.50, 1932.16, 1934.36
Earle, Fred 1905.27
Earle, George 1905.30
Earle, Harry 1887.42, 1888.25, 1889.43, 1890.36, 1895.38, 1897.26, 1898.05, 1898.70
Earle, Jane 1947.03
Earle, John 1933.02
Earle, Lawrence 1902.30
Earle, Mabel 1893.31
Earle, Marie 1911.26
Earle, Marion 1918.25
Earle, Marion A. 1889.37
Earle, Mattie 1878.12, 1880.37, 1882.50, 1882.74, 1884.40, 1884.54, 1891.15
Earle, Messr. 1870.02, 1888.25, 1890.36
Earle, Miss 1869.07, 1870.09, 1883.37
Earle, Ronald Hamilton 1912.42
Earle, Rosa 1903.37
Earle, Rose 1903.04, 1903.15, 1904.30
Earle, Tilly 1871.14, 1872.21, 1872.34, 1873.14, 1873.17
Earle, Vashti 1899.02
Earle, Virginia 1895.18, 1895.31, 1896.06, 1896.18, 1896.30, 1897.20, 1897.44, 1898.26, 1898.29, 1900.20, 1900.41, 1901.23, 1901.29, 1902.05, 1904.05, 1904.56, 1905.22
Early, Gertrude 1919.41
Early, James 1884.09
Early, John W. 1900.08
Earnest, Arthur 1906.20
Earnest, Arthur T. 1900.25, 1900.31, 1900.50
Easley, Bill 1992.08
Easley, Byron 1990.14
Easley, Richert 1983.04
Eason, Myles 1964.20
East Egg Entertainment 2001.01
East, Erin 1999.24
East, Mark 1967.10
East, Virginia Clark 1982.15
Easterbrook, Randall 1977.15
Eastham, Dickinson 1949.04
Eastman, Constance 1906.33, 1909.03, 1910.02
Eastman, Fred 1894.18
Eastman, Glenn 1911.26
Eastman, Gretchen 1916.05, 1917.32, 1921.27
Eastman, H.C. 1914.19
Eastman, Julia 1901.16, 1902.24, 1903.23, 1905.30
Eastman, Julie 1912.28, 1918.11
Eastman, L.A. 1880.63
Eastman, Marjorie 1904.24
Eastman, W. 1885.33
Eastmond, Barry 1981.15
Easton, Bob 1936.06
Easton, L. 1895.08
Easton, Lee 1897.28
Easton, Sheena 1992.07
Easton, Sidney 1930.16, 1953.12
Eastwood, Charles 1896.47
Eastwood, Gini 1972.09
Eaton, Adelaide 1884.46, 1885.68, 1887.51
Eaton, Charles 1922.23, 1927.12
Eaton, Doris 1920.18, 1924.22, 1927.66, 1928.28
Eaton, Elwyn 1924.20
Eaton, Evelyn 1932.11
Eaton, Ewing 1924.36
Eaton, Howard 1978.14
Eaton, John 1932.02, 1936.08, 1936.09, 1936.10, 1936.11
Eaton, Mary 1916.25, 1917.31, 1919.04, 1920.18, 1921.21, 1922.19, 1923.20, 1927.12, 1927.52
Eaton, Pearl 1920.06, 1925.25, 1925.38, 1926.32, 1927.20, 1927.36, 1928.02
Eaton, Sally 1968.11
Eaton, Timothy 1978.23, 1979.27
Eaton, Trevor McQueen 1999.04
Eaves 1879.56, 1880.10, 1880.55, 1881.21, 1881.43, 1882.19, 1882.32, 1882.38, 1882.45, 1884.17, 1884.25, 1885.43, 1896.21, 1903.20, 1906.14, 1907.25, 1908.01, 1908.05, 1908.23, 1918.10, 1921.15, 1921.30, 1921.38, 1930.36, 1930.37, 1931.10, 1931.12, 1931.22, 1931.23, 1931.25, 1931.31, 1931.44, 1932.10, 1934.07, 1934.08, 1934.09, 1934.10, 1934.11, 1934.17, 1937.02, 1939.10
Eaves and Company 1896.46
Eaves Company 1912.32
Eaves Costume 1925.08
Eaves Costume Company 1889.19, 1889.26, 1895.17, 1895.20, 1905.36, 1905.45, 1917.37, 1928.11, 1928.38, 1942.21
Eaves Theatrical Costumes 1921.28
Eaves Uniform Company 1926.41
Eaves, A.J. 1875.20
Eaves, C.A. 1894.24
Eaves, Colin 1900.43, 1905.18
Eaves, Dashiell 1998.03, 2000.01
Eaves, H.J. 1875.18, 1880.54, 1881.03, 1882.26, 1883.64
Eaves, J.H. 1880.04, 1880.18, 1881.04
Eaves, Mme. 1897.28
Ebarb, Cheryl 1982.11
Ebb, Fred 1960.07, 1965.17, 1966.24, 1968.01, 1968.30, 1971.07, 1974.01, 1975.14, 1976.07, 1977.16, 1981.10, 1982.06, 1983.14, 1984.01, 1986.03, 1987.16, 1988.08, 1989.16, 1991.04, 1991.10, 1993.09, 1996.14, 1997.07, 1998.04, 1999.01, 1999.23
Eben, Al 1937.14
Eberle, E. 1862.08, 1870.39
Eberle, E.A. 1864.13, 1867.22, 1867.23, 1867.26, 1867.27, 1867.31, 1870.43, 1885.49
Eberle, Eleanor 1938.09, 1941.04
Eberle, Eugene 1870.36, 1870.39
Eberle, Eugene F. 1880.54, 1881.24
Eberle, Mrs. E.A. 1907.30
Eberle, William 1893.21
Ebers, Fritz 1939.23
Ebersole, Christine 1979.31, 1980.19, 1985.02, 2001.08
Ebert, Franz 1890.31, 1891.33, 1892.43, 1893.29, 1894.01, 1894.30, 1897.35, 1898.53, 1903.40, 1904.39
Ebert, Franze 1896.34
Ebert, Fraulein 1866.33
Ebert, George 1935.07
Ebert, Messr. 1892.12
Ebert, Thomas 1896.16, 1896.17, 1896.19, 1896.21, 1896.22
Ebert-Lau, Elise 1898.53
Eberts, Carrie 1879.38
Ebner, George 1907.25
Ebner, Jacques 1965.37
Ebo, Evelyn 1993.03
Ebsen, Buddy 1932.17, 1934.01, 1939.24, 1946.01
Ebsen, Vilma 1932.17, 1934.01, 1937.16
Eburne, Maude 1918.34, 1920.40, 1921.35, 1923.01, 1928.37, 1929.37
Eby, Helyn 1920.24
Eby-rock, Helyn 1926.29
Echard, Flora 1883.22, 1890.30
Echard, Minnie 1885.28, 1887.12, 1895.24
Echardt, M. 1885.14
Echart, Minnie 1887.18
Echegaray, Miguel 1919.17
Echort, Fred 1894.13
Eck, Marsha L. 1969.10, 1973.11
Eckart, Jean 1954.03, 1955.08, 1956.12, 1957.14, 1958.01, 1959.25, 1959.26, 1961.08, 1961.21, 1962.16, 1963.14, 1963.21, 1964.15, 1964.21, 1965.17, 1965.32, 1966.10, 1967.06, 1968.06, 1968.24, 1969.01, 1983.10
Eckart, William 1954.03, 1955.08, 1956.12, 1957.14, 1958.01, 1959.25, 1959.26, 1961.08, 1961.21, 1962.16, 1963.14, 1963.21, 1964.15, 1964.21, 1965.17, 1965.32, 1966.10, 1967.06, 1968.06, 1968.24, 1969.01, 1983.10
Eckert, Carl 1918.18, 1920.02
Eckert, Maybelle 1900.53
Eckert, T. Wilmot 1880.38, 1895.02, 1897.06
Eckhard, May 1890.21
Eckhardt, E. 1890.08
Eckhardt, H. 1869.04, 1869.13
Eckhardt, Herr 1867.13, 1867.14, 1867.15
Eckhardt, Lizzie 1869.15
Eckhardt, Mrs. H. 1869.04
Eckhardt, Professor 1867.31
Eckhart, Janis 1982.16
Eckhart, Lois 1928.22, 1933.03
Eckles, Lew 1933.20, 1940.10, 1942.11, 1942.27, 1945.18
Eckles, Robert 1940.11, 1940.13, 1940.15, 1944.04, 1944.05, 1944.06, 1944.07, 1944.08, 1944.09, 1944.10, 1944.12, 1944.13, 1949.10, 1949.11, 1949.13, 1949.14, 1952.14, 1952.16, 1952.17, 1952.18, 1952.19, 1957.11
Eckley, Dan 1942.26, 1943.16, 1944.02, 1944.15
Eckstein, Don 1971.09
Eckstein, Ernest 1890.40
Eckstein, George 1959.14
Eckstein, Paul S. 1991.01
Eckstein, William 1920.10
Eckstine, Billy 1976.04
Eckstrom, Carl 1921.04
Eckstrom, Clara 1912.26, 1913.20, 1914.18, 1915.18
Ecton, Robert 1929.25, 1942.03
Eda-Young, Barbara 1970.04
Eddie, Master 1873.08
Eddinger, Lawrence 1911.39
Eddinger, Lorle 1898.71, 1899.14
Eddinger, Neil 1985.09, 1987.08, 1988.04, 1988.18, 1990.08
Eddington, Grace 1910.05
Eddleman, Jack 1957.05, 1958.02, 1963.13, 1963.29, 1964.20, 1964.28, 1974.07, 1974.15, 1975.17, 1976.22, 1976.26, 1977.03, 1977.17, 1979.20
Eddy, E. 1851.08, 1859.01, 1859.02, 1859.03, 1859.04
Eddy, Eddie 1941.03
Ede, Diana 1964.21
Edel 1893.23, 1894.38
Edel of Paris 1910.17
Edel, Alfred 1893.45
Edel, Alfredo 1892.38, 1894.34, 1905.20, 1905.54, 1906.46, 1907.54, 1908.19, 1908.24, 1908.26, 1908.27, 1909.13, 1910.23
Edel, M. Alfredo 1905.17
Edelka, Mlle. 1869.26
Edell, Ruth 1935.11
Edelman, Gregg 1987.16, 1989.29, 1992.11, 1994.05, 1997.15
Edelman, H. 1910.21
Edelman, Herbert 1964.40
Edelman, Randy 1976.34
Edelstein, Ray 1971.04
Edem, Earl 1932.22
Eden, Beatrice 1946.16
Eden, Blanche 1887.43
Eden, Paul 1959.05, 1962.16
Edens, Roger 1932.25, 1958.21, 1977.02, 1985.08
Eder, Linda 1997.09
Edeson, Charles 1886.49
Edeson, Elinor 1927.25
Edeson, George 1881.32, 1883.06, 1897.22
Edeson, George R. 1879.42, 1881.32, 1882.62, 1883.06, 1885.33, 1888.15, 1894.25
Edeson, Messr. 1857.04
Edeson, Mr. 1857.06
Edgar, George 1879.10
Edgar, Lou 1888.19, 1888.22, 1888.24
Edgar, Louise 1886.39, 1888.07, 1889.17, 1890.16, 1891.11
Edgar, Prince 1884.61
Edgard, Messr. 1863.05, 1864.01, 1864.03, 1864.08, 1864.11
Edgard, Mlle. 1872.03
Edgard, Mons. 1858.01, 1858.02, 1864.10, 1866.23, 1866.29, 1866.30, 1868.13, 1868.18, 1869.01, 1870.03, 1871.03, 1871.07, 1871.23, 1871.24, 1871.25, 1871.26, 1871.28, 1872.03
Edge, J. 1859.06
Edge, J.G. 1859.06
Edgecomb, Chris 1999.08
Edgerton, C. 1884.34
Edgerton, Effie 1883.65
Edgerton, Frank 1884.44
Edgerton, Jeff 1998.21
Edgerton, Kate 1871.14
Edgerton, William 1883.47
Edgewood Organization, The 1977.14, 1990.20
Edinburgh, Zitta 1937.14
Edington, May 1971.03
Edison Electric Light Company 1883.48
Ediss, Connie 1895.32, 1907.41, 1910.05, 1913.36, 1914.28
Edley, Zaida Coles 1981.15
Edloe 1972.25
Edlund, Eric 1996.10
Edmead, Wendy 1975.01, 1978.18, 1981.08, 1982.06, 1982.19
Edmond, Grace 1907.04, 1912.34, 1918.29
Edmond, May Florine 1907.04
Edmonds, C.J. 1869.47
Edmonds, Charles 1921.27
Edmonds, Christopher 1984.02
Edmonds, E.C. 1896.16, 1898.39
Edmonds, Kenneth 1997.21
Edmonds, Louis 1956.15
Edmonds, Martha 1911.26
Edmonds, Mitchell 1969.03
Edmonds, Mrs. C. 1868.06
Edmonds, Mrs. Charles 1892.01
Edmonds, R. 1898.62
Edmonds, Shepard N. 1980.27
Edmondson, Annie 1876.32
Edmondson, Janet 1880.62
Edmondston, Janet 1881.25
Edmonson, Miss 1879.02
Edmonson, William 1929.01
Edmund Enterprises, Inc. 1926.04
Edmund, Lada 1960.06
Edmunds, C. 1869.13
Edmunds, E. 1869.15
Edmunds, E.C. 1898.30
Edmunds, Kate 1980.23
Edmunds, Leslie 1891.04
Edmunds, Victor 1926.21, 1927.27
Edmunds, W. 1879.56
Edmunds, Walter 1879.50, 1880.04
Edmunds, William 1910.07, 1934.20
Edna, Dame 1999.14
Edney, Florence 1912.31, 1914.06, 1919.09, 1926.27, 1928.33
Ednor, Chick 1924.43
Edouin, Julia 1880.42
Edouin, May 1900.51
Edouin, W. 1870.23
Edouin, Willie 1870.23, 1870.35, 1870.42, 1871.01, 1871.02, 1871.14, 1871.19, 1872.21, 1872.22, 1872.24, 1872.26, 1872.34, 1873.12, 1873.14, 1873.17, 1877.22, 1877.23, 1877.25, 1877.39, 1879.33, 1879.35, 1880.06, 1880.10, 1880.13, 1880.42, 1880.70, 1882.03, 1882.39, 1883.26, 1900.51
Edson, Jerome 1982.03
Edson, Marjory 1970.07
Eduardo, Elsa 1923.31
Edward E. Rice's Big Burlesque Company 1894.19
Edward E. Rice's Opera Comique Company 1881.43
Edward G. Unitt and Wickes 1906.33, 1906.38, 1906.41, 1907.57, 1907.58, 1907.63, 1908.27, 1908.31, 1908.34, 1909.07, 1910.17, 1911.04, 1911.24, 1912.13, 1912.34
Edward H. Harvey's Comic Opera Company 1879.14
Edward Sundquist Studios 1930.29
Edward, May 1897.48
Edward, Mons. 1876.20
Edward, Mrs. Seidle 1903.03
Edward-Stevens, Michael 1981.28
Edwardes, Fanny 1882.60
Edwardes, Felix 1924.43
Edwardes, George 1888.38, 1888.41, 1895.29, 1895.32, 1895.43, 1903.22, 1903.33, 1905.04, 1905.46, 1910.22
Edwardes, Paula 1897.11, 1897.39, 1898.46, 1900.28, 1902.15, 1902.21, 1907.01
Edwardes, Peggy 1902.21
Edwardine, Vera 1903.22
Edwards, Al 1897.38
Edwards, Alan 1917.02, 1920.45, 1921.18, 1922.28, 1923.27, 1924.43, 1926.39, 1927.47, 1928.37, 1930.08
Edwards, Andy 1999.15
Edwards, Annie Joe 1975.09
Edwards, Anthony 1959.05
Edwards, Ben 1938.02, 1970.05, 1972.26
Edwards, Blake 1995.15
Edwards, Blanche 1878.17
Edwards, Bobby 1918.08, 1930.23
Edwards, Brandt 1975.15
Edwards, Burt 1985.01
Edwards, C. 1884.51
Edwards, C.F. 1903.13
Edwards, C.N. 1882.01
Edwards, Carlo 1914.24, 1914.30
Edwards, Carrie 1899.30
Edwards, Charles 1903.18, 1920.37

Edwards, Cliff 1921.25, 1924.43, 1925.33, 1927.37, 1935.18
Edwards, Cynthia 1988.14
Edwards, D. 1881.30
Edwards, Duncan 1999.08, 2001.09
Edwards, E. Snitz 1890.43
Edwards, E.K. 1914.26
Edwards, Earl 1940.17
Edwards, Ed. Schnitz 1890.27
Edwards, Eddie 1906.31
Edwards, Edith 1885.52, 1889.23
Edwards, Elsie 1937.06
Edwards, Emelie 1884.48
Edwards, Eugene 1964.19, 1980.15
Edwards, Fannie 1890.47, 1890.48, 1892.37
Edwards, Fanny 1889.36, 1890.23, 1892.46
Edwards, Frank 1899.34, 1902.42
Edwards, G. 1892.35
Edwards, Gale 2000.09
Edwards, George 1885.22, 1894.33, 1917.34
Edwards, Germaine 1984.09, 1987.07
Edwards, Gerome 1910.06
Edwards, Gloria 1971.13
Edwards, Gus 1899.29, 1899.35, 1900.47, 1901.13, 1901.29, 1902.15, 1903.03, 1903.04, 1904.03, 1904.04, 1904.13, 1904.22, 1904.29, 1904.43, 1904.44, 1905.03, 1905.23, 1905.37, 1906.20, 1906.29, 1906.41, 1906.45, 1907.15, 1907.21, 1907.24, 1907.28, 1907.44, 1907.47, 1908.04, 1908.15, 1908.28, 1908.39, 1909.13, 1909.25, 1910.17, 1910.18, 1914.16, 1922.09, 1927.12, 1932.06, 1936.06, 1955.03, 1980.27, 1997.01
Edwards, Gwilym 1904.09
Edwards, Gwilyn 1910.23, 1911.28, 1912.30
Edwards, H. 1879.23
Edwards, Harry 1884.21
Edwards, Harry B. 1891.23
Edwards, Irving 1926.15, 1927.02
Edwards, Jack 1917.29, 1926.13, 1927.27, 1934.04, 1935.14
Edwards, James 1982.22
Edwards, Jane 1876.13
Edwards, Jeane 1908.11
Edwards, Joan 1940.16, 1950.09
Edwards, John 1904.26, 1950.14
Edwards, Julian 1889.19, 1889.36, 1890.14, 1890.15, 1890.18, 1890.20, 1890.23, 1890.46, 1890.47, 1890.48, 1892.20, 1892.30, 1892.46, 1892.57, 1893.03, 1893.44, 1894.14, 1895.06, 1895.19, 1896.10, 1896.41, 1897.17, 1898.27, 1898.40, 1898.73, 1900.12, 1902.03, 1902.31, 1902.41, 1904.36, 1905.15, 1906.20, 1907.05, 1907.07, 1907.21, 1908.16, 1909.14, 1909.24, 1910.11, 1917.11
Edwards, K.A. 1891.24
Edwards, Kate 1859.08
Edwards, Kathleen 1932.22
Edwards, Kent 1942.34, 1944.21
Edwards, Lee 1945.02, 1945.12
Edwards, Leo 1900.53, 1905.37, 1907.42, 1910.15, 1912.38, 1913.17, 1915.02, 1915.11, 1915.17, 1916.10, 1917.13, 1920.18, 1920.23, 1921.20, 1921.21, 1923.38, 1924.44, 1925.39, 1936.06, 1942.35
Edwards, Lew 1938.03
Edwards, Lizzie 1869.44, 1875.34, 1878.17, 1879.04
Edwards, Lou 1921.02, 1921.25
Edwards, Mae 1900.47
Edwards, Marcelle 1932.18
Edwards, Margaret 1919.24
Edwards, Mattie 1904.26, 1907.50
Edwards, Maurice 1950.01, 1954.03, 1957.02, 1964.27
Edwards, May 1898.50, 1899.17
Edwards, Messr. 1878.13, 1879.56
Edwards, Michael 1987.02
Edwards, Miss 1869.40
Edwards, Mons. 1879.50
Edwards, Mr. 1855.08, 1857.06, 1864.12, 1875.37
Edwards, Naz 1992.11
Edwards, Nealy 1915.22
Edwards, Nita 1923.29
Edwards, Norman 1962.17
Edwards, Paddy 1965.02
Edwards, Paula 1893.27, 1893.36, 1896.21, 1896.40, 1897.26
Edwards, Pauline 1892.54, 1893.10
Edwards, Penny 1943.05, 1944.30, 1946.06
Edwards, Phil 1999.15
Edwards, Randall 1988.20
Edwards, Robert 1919.18
Edwards, Robert W. 1904.23
Edwards, Rod 1993.07
Edwards, Ronnie 1950.09
Edwards, S. Gordon 1893.45
Edwards, Sam 1908.10, 1916.06
Edwards, Samuel 1897.20, 1898.31, 1899.15
Edwards, Sara 1922.30
Edwards, Sarah 1921.11, 1925.13, 1927.47, 1931.24
Edwards, Sarah M. 1927.24
Edwards, Sherman 1937.14, 1961.07, 1969.06, 1997.15
Edwards, Snitz 1890.44, 1894.42, 1896.02, 1897.52, 1900.03, 1900.16, 1900.49, 1902.35, 1912.37, 1913.34
Edwards, Stewart 1928.44
Edwards, T. 1869.44, 1872.10
Edwards, T.F. 1865.05
Edwards, T.L. 1865.09
Edwards, Thelma 1927.54
Edwards, Thomas 1961.12
Edwards, Tommy 1898.67
Edwards, Urolin 1908.26
Edwards, Virginia 1944.02
Edwards, W.A. 1882.57
Edwards, Welsh 1866.06, 1867.13, 1867.14, 1867.16, 1867.17, 1868.08, 1868.16, 1872.13, 1875.06, 1875.11, 1875.14, 1875.31, 1875.34, 1875.35, 1875.36, 1875.37, 1877.24, 1878.13, 1878.17, 1879.68, 1880.09, 1881.41, 1882.77, 1883.43
Edwards, Zella 1926.30
Edwards-Adams Theatrical, Inc. 1995.15
Edwardy, Gerome 1898.17
Edwin Cleary's French Company 1893.25
Edwin H. Morris and Company 1967.16
Edwin, C.E. 1875.14
Edwin, Cecelia 1920.35
Edwin, Lena 1869.07
Edwin, Lina 1867.22, 1867.23, 1867.26, 1867.27, 1867.31, 1869.46, 1870.13, 1870.19, 1870.36, 1870.39, 1870.43
Edwin, Rober 1945.20
Edwin, Walter 1923.46, 1926.24
Edwin, William 1840.02, 1840.03, 1840.04
Eeber, Alton 1918.12
Effron, David 1975.17, 1981.22
Effron, Howard 1974.09
Effron, Howard P. 1981.24
Efimovskaya, Mme. 1927.51
Egan, Daisy 1991.05
Egan, Frank 1894.26
Egan, George 1916.25, 1917.19, 1918.34
Egan, Jack 1917.13, 1937.11
Egan, Jefferson 1902.30
Egan, John 1923.27
Egan, John Treacy 1997.09
Egan, Lucille 1900.14, 1903.32
Egan, Miss 1903.32
Egan, Pierce 1823.01
Egan, Ray 1935.04
Egan, Raymond B. 1919.10, 1919.14, 1924.15, 1928.47, 1935.04, 1976.32, 1980.08, 1986.06
Egan, Renee 1898.20
Egan, Renie 1893.10
Egan, Seamus 2000.04
Egan, Susan 1994.04, 1997.18
Egan, Sylvia 1900.14
Egar, Vallie 1893.30, 1894.39
Egbert, Jane 1927.55
Egbert, Nannie 1869.46, 1869.47, 1870.05
Egberts, T.F. 1877.24
Egelston, Penny 1964.21
Egen, Non 1932.19
Egerton, Evelyn 1918.27
Egerton, Kate 1871.19
Egerton, Lucy 1868.03
Egerton, Maud 1875.19
Egerton, Maude 1875.23
Eggenton, Joseph 1906.35
Eggers, Ursula 1978.07, 1978.20, 1979.21, 1989.13
Eggert, Marta 1940.06
Eggerth, Marta 1943.09, 1944.24, 1945.14, 1957.04
Eggett, Charles 1912.02
Eggleston, Marjorie 1924.08
Eggleton, Edward 1885.29
Egi, Stanford 1987.15
Egleson, Polly 1884.27
Eglevsky, Andre 1938.15
Eglevsky, Marina 1980.26
Egli, Miss 1883.17, 1883.23
Egnos, Bertha 1977.01
Ehara, Mary 1966.24
Eheman, Joan 1957.11
Ehinger, Jim 1999.09
Ehler, Ernest 1927.65
Ehlers, Stephen 1989.06
Ehrendt, E. 1894.30
Ehrenworth, Adam 1990.20
Ehrhardt, Peter M. 1976.25
Ehrich Brothers 1897.21
Ehrle, John 1933.02
Ehrle, John W. 1930.28
Ehrler, Anita 1985.19
Ehrlich, Aimee 1908.35
Ehrlich, Beth 1898.69
Ehrlich, Frl. 1882.68
Ehrlich, Sam 1907.44, 1917.23
Eich, Stephen 1993.04, 1998.02
Eichberg, Julius 1866.07, 1866.14, 1866.19, 1866.21, 1866.24, 1867.06, 1868.11, 1882.46
Eichberg, Richard 1942.21
Eichel, Paul 1964.21, 1967.04, 1968.02, 1970.08, 1971.01, 1975.09
Eichelberger, Ethyl 1989.24
Eichenberger, Rebecdca 1994.02
Eichiman, W.H. 1883.12
Eichler, Alan 1978.03
Eichorn, Nancy 1997.03
Eichorn, William 1981.20, 1982.16, 1983.12
Eiferman, George 1976.24
Eigenberg, Julie Anne 1989.10
Eigenthumer, Herr 1880.61
Eiger, Walter 1944.27, 1958.02
Eigsti, Karl 1972.12, 1976.06, 1978.21, 1982.03, 1983.15
Eikenberry, Jill 1980.30
Eillson, Elaine 1889.46
Eilson, Elaine 1893.11
Einedshofer, Julius 1916.15
Einhorn, Hy 1973.01
Einodshofer, Julius 1899.02, 1915.24
Eis, Alice 1905.44
Eisele, Lou 1944.14, 1945.01, 1945.17, 1946.14, 1947.12, 1947.19, 1948.27
Eisenberg, Avner 1989.10
Eisenberg, Emanuel 1935.03, 1937.14
Eisenberg, Franny 1979.30
Eisenberg, Jack 1952.03
Eisenberg, Ned 2000.10
Eisenberg, Rafe 1940.21
Eisenhauer, Peggy 1989.12, 1989.20, 1991.14, 1992.18, 1994.06, 1994.12, 1995.15, 1995.19, 1996.07, 1996.15, 1997.21, 1997.22, 1998.01, 1998.04, 1998.20, 1999.10, 1999.21, 1999.22, 2000.08, 2000.19, 2000.20
Eisenstadt, Maurice 1962.15, 1963.04, 1964.46, 1967.17
Eising, George 1925.11
Eisler, Chuck 1974.09
Eisler, David 1981.21, 1982.20, 1984.11, 1985.10, 1986.04, 1986.08, 1989.14, 1991.12
Eisler, Hans 1935.16
Eisner, Frl. 1883.08
Eisner, Joseph 1910.23
Eissing, Cecile 1890.21, 1890.26, 1891.31, 1891.47, 1894.47
Eissing, Ida 1887.04, 1889.24, 1890.21
Eissing, Louise 1898.40, 1898.42
Eissung, Cecile 1893.35
Eissung, Miss 1882.36
Ekmirg, W.H. 1893.03
Elaine, Mabel 1915.22, 1916.23, 1919.26, 1922.18
Elaine, Mildred 1910.15, 1912.09
Elaine, Sybil 1935.15
Elam, E. Louise 1897.16
Elba, Marie 1895.28
elBakkar, Mohammed 1954.15
Elbaum, Ruth 1937.14
Elbel, Louis 1955.13
Elbert, Charles 1915.15
Elbert, Tracy 1909.29, 1915.08
Elberton, Ethel 1901.12
Elberts, Carolyn 1899.29
Elberts, Carrie 1899.12
Elberts, Cary 1879.03
Elberts, Mr. 1875.06
Elberts, R. 1872.10
Elbew, Grace 1925.47
Elbey, Charles 1929.04
Elbon, Annie 1882.49
Elbon, Jennei 1882.49
Elbon, Miss 1882.45
Elborne, Daniel 1999.17
Eldee, Lillian 1905.46
Elden, Alice 1914.33
Elder 1875.35
Elder, Althea 1938.05, 1944.01, 1945.20, 1946.07
Elder, Clinton 1892.08, 1892.10, 1894.15, 1895.16, 1896.28, 1897.36, 1898.36, 1899.07, 1899.10, 1899.14, 1899.16, 1899.20, 1899.24, 1900.14
Elder, David 1996.18, 1997.06
Elder, Eldon 1954.01, 1955.05, 1957.05, 1964.03, 1968.22, 1976.33, 1979.17
Elder, Judith 1936.03
Elder, Messr. 1875.37, 1876.34
Eldon, Vincent 1891.46
Eldred, Mike 1995.02, 1999.08
Eldredge, Lillian 1904.10
Eldredge, Lynn 1931.03
Eldrid, Gordon 1899.11
Eldridge, Billy 1896.46
Eldridge, Edith 1902.21
Eldridge, Elaine 1938.16
Eldridge, Evelyn 1927.39
Eldridge, Florence 1918.16
Eldridge, H.E. 1925.31
Eldridge, Lillie 1869.08, 1870.36, 1871.04, 1891.43, 1903.26
Eldridge, Louise 1885.21
Eldridge, Mrs. 1867.18
Eldridge, Press 1886.17, 1886.29, 1886.31, 1886.38
Eleanor, Peggy 1916.11
Eleanori, F. 1911.16
Electric Factory Concerts 1999.09, 2000.04
Elena, Mlle. 1861.05
Eleonari, Fausto 1911.19
Eleonore, Miss 1870.31
Elese, Mlle. 1882.01
Eley, Helen 1923.36
Eley, Jean 1955.13
Eley, Lou 1955.13
Eley, Stephanie 1981.29, 1983.06
Eley, Wallace 1958.04
Elfers, John 1892.34
Elg, Taina 1970.08, 1974.25, 1979.10, 1982.09
Elgar, Anne 1964.13, 1964.31, 1965.09, 1965.10, 1965.12, 1965.25, 1965.27, 1966.02
Elgart, Larry 1976.34
Elgart, Les 1976.34
Elgin, Claire 1923.21
Elhai, Robert 1997.20
Elias, Albert 1897.56
Elias, Alix 1971.18
Elias, Bert V. 1921.29
Elias, Rosalind 1984.13, 1992.14
Elias, Sylvia 1921.11
Elic, Josip 1965.01
Eline, J. Frank 1894.06
Elinore, Kate 1903.35, 1910.35, 1911.34
Elinore, May 1903.35
Elinson, Izzy 1941.13
Elio, Donna 1974.17
Elio, Donna Marie 1981.27, 1986.20, 1989.03
Eliot, John 1938.13, 1940.08
Eliot, T.S. 1982.19, 1991.10, 1992.12
Eliran, Ron 1973.01
Elis, Melville 1909.30
Elisa, Mlle. 1867.25
Elisabeth Marbury-Ray Comstock Company 1915.30
Eliscu, Edward 1927.27, 1929.07, 1929.29, 1929.32, 1929.37, 1930.06, 1930.18, 1930.35, 1930.38, 1931.14, 1931.36, 1932.01, 1932.06, 1933.15, 1937.03, 1940.21, 1942.26, 1974.01, 1974.09, 1975.22
Elise, Miss 1869.43
Elise, Mlle. 1866.18, 1872.10, 1873.10, 1878.10, 1883.47
Elisheva 1969.13
Elizonda, J.F. 1917.25
Elizondo, Minerva 1988.15
Eljas, Anders 1988.09, 1988.12
Elkas, Edward 1892.03
Elkin, Paul M. 1979.05
Elkins, Doug 1998.22
Elkins, Henry 1903.18

Elkins, Hillard 1964.32, 1970.15, 1976.27, 1978.18
Elkins, Jeanne 1938.15
Elkins, W.C. 1899.33, 1906.14
Elkins, William 1896.46, 1904.26
Ellain, Lesitta 1879.08
Elledge, David 1989.26
Ellen, Mary 1942.31
Ellen, Mlle. 1885.55, 1885.59
Ellen, Sandy 1965.29, 1967.05
Ellenwood, Kelly 2000.19
Eller, Giole 1924.18
Eller, John 1879.53, 1884.42, 1885.21, 1886.47, 1888.36, 1894.19, 1899.23
Eller, Miss 1887.19
Ellerton 1964.28
Ellfeldt, William 1952.05
Ellias, Sylvia 1918.19
Elliman, Yvonne 1971.12
Ellin, David 1968.06, 1970.17
Ellinger, Desire 1927.14
Ellinger, Desiree 1926.34, 1927.34
Ellingham, Mr. 1865.02
Ellingham, R. 1864.23
Ellington, Duke 1930.13, 1930.38, 1942.11, 1945.07, 1946.24, 1954.11, 1966.05, 1975.22, 1976.04, 1979.24, 1980.10, 1981.06, 1986.02, 1986.03, 1987.02, 1989.02, 1990.09, 1997.03, 1997.05, 1999.05, 1999.06, 1999.24
Ellington, Ed 1931.01
Ellington, Mercedes 1963.05, 1963.17, 1975.05, 1979.02, 1980.06, 1980.10, 1986.02, 1997.03
Ellington, Mercer 1981.06
Ellington, Mr. 1860.01
Ellins, Jim 1918.17
Elliot, Marc 1984.10
Elliot, Maurice 1906.02, 1906.42
Elliot, Rose Marie 1945.04
Elliott, Anna 1884.61
Elliott, Arthur 1918.31
Elliott, Audrey 1937.06
Elliott, Beth 1923.25, 1925.27
Elliott, Bill 1999.24
Elliott, Bob 1970.14
Elliott, Dick 1959.19
Elliott, Dickson 1913.04, 1914.18
Elliott, Don 1960.04, 1963.16
Elliott, Elizabeth 1904.07
Elliott, Elsie 1928.32
Elliott, Eugene 1913.25
Elliott, G.F. 1875.18
Elliott, George 1908.20
Elliott, Gladys 1920.15
Elliott, Grace 1921.35, 1923.43
Elliott, J. 1913.32
Elliott, Jack 1959.25, 1962.16, 1962.20, 1963.14
Elliott, James 1884.61
Elliott, James E. 1898.66
Elliott, James W. 1926.24
Elliott, Jane 1913.27, 1918.32, 1994.02
Elliott, Jessie 1905.51, 1950.02
Elliott, John 1943.23
Elliott, Katie 1884.61
Elliott, Leonard 1938.01, 1945.11, 1946.02, 1961.27
Elliott, Lottie 1885.39
Elliott, Louise 1904.49
Elliott, Marianna 1997.03
Elliott, Mattie 1884.61
Elliott, Maude 1903.20
Elliott, Maurice 1907.57, 1934.36
Elliott, Maxine 1893.47, 1938.02
Elliott, Miss 1886.32, 1910.12
Elliott, Patricia 1973.04
Elliott, Patrick 1976.34
Elliott, Paul 1990.15
Elliott, Pauline 1902.19
Elliott, Polly 1884.61
Elliott, Professor 1884.61
Elliott, Rand 1946.02
Elliott, Robert 1911.22
Elliott, Rose Marie 1943.03
Elliott, Ross 1942.20
Elliott, Scott 1993.05
Elliott, Shawn 1981.05, 1989.29, 1999.22
Elliott, Sophie 1894.33
Elliott, Stephen 1967.01, 1970.03
Elliott, T.H. 1872.20
Elliott, Thomas 1884.61, 1899.04, 1984.15
Elliott, Valleaux 1912.35
Elliott, Vance 1928.08, 1931.39, 1933.25
Elliott, W. 1880.34
Elliott, Walter 1937.01
Elliott, William 1880.59, 1911.11, 1914.24, 1916.22, 1917.06, 1917.17, 1917.24, 1917.27, 1918.01, 1918.03, 1918.27, 1918.37, 1919.20, 1920.22, 1978.09, 1981.01, 1988.17
Elliott, Zo 1964.28
Ellis 1935.19
Ellis, A. 1905.43
Ellis, Al 1914.06
Ellis, Anita 1958.19
Ellis, Antonia 1988.07
Ellis, Bob 1963.22
Ellis, C.T. 1886.62
Ellis, Celie 1886.33, 1887.18, 1887.22, 1887.24, 1887.32, 1892.01
Ellis, Charles 1927.67, 1932.11, 1932.28
Ellis, Charles E. 1883.17
Ellis, Charles T. 1883.17
Ellis, Chris 1986.12
Ellis, Diane 1930.06
Ellis, Don 2001.04
Ellis, Elaine 1942.21
Ellis, Eleanor 1885.08
Ellis, Evelyn 1945.07
Ellis, F. 1866.18
Ellis, Florence 1876.02, 1876.36, 1877.04, 1877.15, 1878.02, 1879.15, 1880.01, 1880.03, 1895.15
Ellis, Frank 1884.48
Ellis, Georgia 1933.03
Ellis, Glen 1913.32
Ellis, H. Wayne 1886.60
Ellis, H.M. 1876.36
Ellis, H.W. 1876.02
Ellis, Harold 1906.41
Ellis, Harry 1914.31
Ellis, Helene 1950.16
Ellis, Jacqueline 1945.16
Ellis, James 1927.42
Ellis, Jessie 1909.27
Ellis, Joan 1978.13
Ellis, Kathleen 1945.16
Ellis, Larry 1971.09
Ellis, Lavinia 1901.20
Ellis, Lucille 1943.17, 1944.31, 1945.13, 1946.21, 1950.07
Ellis, Mabel 1906.02, 1929.39
Ellis, Madge 1893.50
Ellis, Marge 1944.15, 1954.09
Ellis, Mary 1924.28
Ellis, Maurice 1930.29, 1931.31, 1939.17, 1940.17, 1943.07, 1951.18
Ellis, Melville 1899.35, 1902.01, 1902.16, 1902.19, 1902.35, 1903.23, 1905.41, 1906.29, 1907.15, 1907.42, 1907.56, 1908.21, 1908.29, 1908.30, 1909.11, 1909.24, 1909.29, 1910.01, 1910.03, 1910.04, 1910.13, 1910.14, 1910.16, 1910.19, 1910.25, 1910.36, 1911.06, 1911.12, 1911.32, 1911.34, 1911.36, 1911.43, 1912.09, 1912.18, 1912.24, 1912.27, 1912.43, 1912.49, 1913.02, 1913.05, 1913.08, 1913.09, 1913.12, 1913.13, 1913.16, 1913.18, 1913.23, 1913.28, 1913.29, 1914.01, 1914.07, 1914.10, 1914.16, 1914.21, 1914.22, 1914.24, 1915.02, 1915.04, 1915.20, 1915.25, 1915.30, 1916.06, 1918.01
Ellis, Messr. 1861.03, 1869.44
Ellis, Michael 1947.03, 1951.17, 1952.20
Ellis, Miss 1903.32
Ellis, Peggy 1918.15, 1929.33
Ellis, Phil 1938.08
Ellis, Philip 1934.37
Ellis, Ray 1964.21
Ellis, Renee Gina 1993.03
Ellis, Roy 1927.62
Ellis, S. 1872.10
Ellis, Sally 1934.37
Ellis, Sam 1972.13
Ellis, Scott 1980.11, 1984.01, 1990.07, 1991.08, 1992.10, 1993.10, 1995.11, 1997.07, 1997.15, 2001.06
Ellis, Sheila 1972.14, 1976.35, 1979.18, 1980.14, 1981.29
Ellis, Sidney 1905.12
Ellis, Sidney R. 1886.44, 1886.51, 1891.20, 1892.31, 1895.41, 1902.39, 1905.12
Ellis, Sydney R. 1899.04
Ellis, Toni 1933.27
Ellis, Vivian 1925.50, 1930.38, 1936.22
Ellison, Ben 2000.12
Ellison, Edith 1892.29
Ellison, Elaine 1890.50
Ellison, George 1920.09
Ellison, Jon 1976.12, 1976.13, 1976.14, 1978.15, 1978.16
Ellison, Margie 1938.19
Ellison, Mary 1921.05
Ellison, Maude 1898.75
Ellison, Nancy 1989.24
Ellison, Sidney 1910.25, 1910.36
Ellison, Sydney 1895.43, 1905.46, 1912.31, 1914.25
Ellison, Todd 2000.08, 2001.01, 2001.08
Elliston, Jennie 1887.32
Ellkors, Edward 1902.23
Ellott, Paul 1999.12
Ellsner, Joseph 1915.24, 1916.15
Ellsperman, Jean 1951.22
Ellstein, Abraham 1950.06, 1998.11
Ellston, Maude 1898.55
Ellsworth, Dorothy 1918.08
Ellsworth, Eugene 1897.01, 1903.07
Ellsworth, Florence 1899.33, 1900.46
Ellsworth, Grace 1917.04, 1920.23, 1921.06, 1923.13
Ellsworth, Harry 1923.13
Ellsworth, Helen 1915.31
Ellsworth, Hugh 1935.11
Ellsworth, Ursula 1918.33
Elma, Lillian 1892.18
Elma, Sophie 1873.27
Elman, Esta 1937.10
Elman, Ziggy 1997.05
Elmendorf, Allie 1879.59
Elmendorf, Maud 1879.59
Elmendorf, W. Clarence 1879.59
Elmer, Frank N. 1889.51
Elmer, Michael 1949.02
Elmo, Monte 1905.48, 1906.18
Elmore, Florence 1918.05, 1918.20, 1920.28, 1921.20
Elmore, Howard 1929.01
Elmore, Jennie 1907.60
Elmore, Julia 1886.28
Elmore, Lillian 1891.38
Elmore, Lucille 1923.40, 1924.26
Elmore, Marion 1877.22, 1877.23, 1877.25, 1877.39, 1878.20, 1879.03, 1879.33, 1879.35, 1880.06, 1880.10, 1880.13, 1880.59, 1880.65, 1880.67, 1880.70, 1882.03, 1885.46, 1886.28
Elmore, Steve 1963.05, 1963.25, 1964.21, 1965.01, 1970.13, 1973.08
Elmslie, Kenward 1971.16
Eloise, Mlle. 1885.46
elPipa, Antonio 1992.15
ElRey, Claire 1916.15
ElRey, Zoe 1916.15
Elrod, John 2001.04
Elsass, Jeffrey 1998.18
Elsbach, Eduard 1885.01, 1885.27
Else, Bertha 1900.45
Else, Mlle. 1877.20
Elsegood, Jim 1946.07
Elsie, Connie 1889.42
Elsie, May 1918.03
Elsie, Mlle. 1882.06
Elsner, Edward 1911.46, 1927.18, 1927.34
Elsner, Emma 1882.31, 1882.40
Elsner, Joseph 1914.19, 1918.23, 1919.22
Elson, Anita 1916.02
Elson, Charles 1949.16, 1951.21, 1958.17, 1958.18, 1959.06, 1960.22
Elston, Robert 1963.19
Eltinge, Julian 1908.22, 1914.08, 1915.20
Eltinge, Julian Dalton 1904.34
Elton, Ben 1986.15
Elton, Edmund 1920.14, 1926.42, 1928.36
Elton, Eleanor 1896.33, 1897.21, 1897.54
Elton, Ernest A. 1910.21
Elton, George 1924.01
Elton, Jane 1903.26
Elton, Miss 1848.01
Elton, W. 1875.14
Elton, William 1974.09
Elvidge, June 1914.16, 1920.21
Elvin, Harry 1899.09, 1900.24
Elward, James 1955.09
Ely Alfred S. 1903.37
Ely, Edgar 1891.38
Ely, Edgar Atchison 1909.08, 1910.31, 1918.05
Ely, Helen 1915.11
Elyk, F.K. 1884.22
Elzy, Ruby 1931.31, 1935.13, 1940.01, 1942.03
Emanuel, N.B. 1901.24
Emanuel, Terrence 1975.21
Embree, Louise Eissing 1890.10
Embry, Dorothy 1930.19, 1933.06
Emden, H. 1894.18, 1903.04
Emden, Henry 1881.07, 1903.39, 1904.47, 1905.48, 1913.33
Emeline, Petite 1859.05
Emelli, Regina 1889.53
Emens 1889.02, 1907.11
Emens and Unitt 1905.04, 1905.29
Emens, Hawley 1887.49
Emens, Homer 1885.40, 1887.02, 1887.44, 1887.49, 1889.43, 1892.20, 1892.24, 1894.29, 1898.36, 1899.24, 1900.01, 1902.03, 1902.31, 1902.41, 1903.31, 1903.33, 1903.34, 1903.37, 1904.15, 1904.19, 1904.30, 1904.51, 1905.01, 1905.57, 1906.29, 1906.33, 1906.38, 1906.41, 1907.08, 1907.33, 1907.36, 1907.43, 1907.46, 1907.56, 1908.03, 1908.05, 1908.06, 1908.32, 1908.40, 1909.03, 1909.09, 1910.02, 1910.05, 1910.15, 1910.27, 1911.04, 1911.27, 1912.04, 1912.26, 1912.34, 1912.39, 1913.04, 1914.21, 1914.23, 1915.20, 1915.24, 1916.01, 1916.20, 1917.19, 1917.22, 1919.08
Emens, Homer F. 1887.29, 1888.15, 1889.12, 1890.04, 1890.21, 1890.26, 1890.35, 1890.36, 1891.28, 1891.31, 1891.43, 1892.01, 1892.38, 1892.56, 1893.14, 1893.23, 1893.35, 1894.20, 1894.34, 1894.46, 1894.52, 1895.30, 1895.31, 1896.15, 1896.25, 1897.05, 1898.45, 1899.32, 1912.19, 1913.03, 1913.06, 1913.26, 1915.23
Emer, Michel 1947.18
Emer. M. 1981.04
Emerald, Alice 1910.15
Emerald, Connie 1926.26
Emerald, May 1910.15
Emerald, Nellie 1903.21, 1904.05
Emerick, George E. 1900.45
Emerlie, Mlle. 1868.26
Emerson, Adelaide 1891.38
Emerson, C.W. 1908.03
Emerson, Charles 1903.37
Emerson, Frank 1967.01
Emerson, Fred 1910.17
Emerson, Hope 1932.15, 1942.22, 1947.02
Emerson, Ida 1898.63, 1901.28, 1905.42, 1906.19, 1980.27
Emerson, John 1914.08, 1930.06
Emerson, Lillian 1932.21, 1934.35
Emerson, Mamie 1898.41, 1899.33, 1906.08
Emerson, Maud 1889.13, 1899.36
Emerson, Maude 1887.43
Emerson, Mort 1894.51
Emerson, Rita 1892.24, 1894.46, 1895.34
Emery, Edward 1921.15, 1927.41, 1931.28
Emery, Edwin T. 1913.09, 1914.10, 1920.07, 1927.43
Emery, Gilbert 1928.21
Emery, Glen 1898.75
Emery, Jeanette 1895.26
Emery, Josephine 1917.24
Emery, Karl 1969.03
Emery, Katherine 1938.18
Emery, Louie 1920.12
Emery, Mac 1920.18
Emery, May 1907.24, 1908.04
Emery, Pollie 1903.22
Emery, Rick 1980.11
Emery, Ted 2000.10
Emesz, Magdalena 1984.04
Emett, Harry W. 1888.18
Emhan, Inc. 1979.26, 1980.29
Emick, Jarrod 1994.01, 2000.17
Emile, Mons. 1869.03, 1880.44, 1881.54, 1883.41
Emilie Melville Opera Company 1882.16
Emilie, Mlle. 1888.39
Emilius, Messr. 1844.01
Emily, Mlle. 1873.10
Emler, Ernestine 1911.13
Emma Abbott Grand English Opera Company 1881.05
Emma, Mlle. 1871.08, 1871.18
Emmanuel, Donna 1977.08
Emmanuel, Ivor 1951.03, 1966.09
Emmer, Irwin 1920.03
Emmerich, Robert 1992.03
Emmerson, Dorothy 1968.06
Emmet, Gracie 1886.35
Emmet, J.K. 1894.09

Emmet, Joseph K. 1870.24, 1871.15, 1871.22, 1873.19, 1873.24, 1878.04, 1878.12, 1879.63, 1881.52, 1883.01, 1883.09, 1883.20, 1884.04, 1884.07, 1887.11, 1889.20, 1892.12, 1893.12
Emmet, Jr., J.K. 1893.12, 1893.38
Emmet, Katherine 1906.50
Emmet, Miss 1884.44
Emmett, Harry W. 1891.18
Emmett, Joseph K. 1880.39
Emmett, Jr., J.K. 1894.09
Emmonds, Charles 1894.51
Emmonds, Julia 1894.51
Emmons, Beverly 1975.10, 1975.12, 1980.05, 1980.08, 1981.04, 1982.01, 1982.08, 1983.18, 1988.08, 1988.19, 1992.06, 1994.05, 1995.09, 1997.09, 1999.04
Emmons, Don 1959.13
Emmons, Grace 1905.11, 1905.25, 1908.03, 1911.47
Emmons, Lotta 1907.60
Emmons, Mae 1897.42, 1899.40
Emmons, Sadie 1897.18, 1899.40, 1904.13, 1904.44, 1905.44, 1908.04
Emmy, Carlton 1929.26
Emon, H.D. 1876.34
Emond, Laura 1928.19
Emonts, Ann 1979.32, 1981.25
Emory, Mae 1900.18
Emory, May 1900.14, 1910.10, 1912.15, 1913.27
Emory, Miss 1908.19
Emory, Richard 1935.01
Empire Producing Corporation 1920.37
Empire State Instituite for the Performing Arts 1986.16
Empress, Marie 1913.31
Emrek, Jack 1957.03, 1958.03
Emsden, H. 1901.27
Endemol Theater Productions, Inc. 1995.15
Endicott, Carrie 1883.13
Endicott, Harry 1969.16
Endicott, Louise 1894.42
Endor, Chick 1925.33, 1926.18, 1931.19
Endress, Annie 1881.15
Endrey, Eugene 1930.04
Enelow, Yettanda 1962.01
Enfield, John 1875.10
Enfield, Messr. 1886.36
Engalitcheff, Nikolas 1931.09
Engebretsen, Ollie 1950.15
Engel, Arthur J. 1911.02
Engel, Bruce 1986.13
Engel, Carl H. 1911.01
Engel, David 1983.11, 2000.18
Engel, Julius 1875.12
Engel, Lehman 1936.28, 1937.08, 1937.11, 1938.18, 1946.10, 1949.10, 1949.11, 1949.13, 1949.14, 1950.02, 1950.05, 1950.11, 1950.19, 1952.14, 1952.16, 1952.17, 1952.18, 1952.19, 1953.03, 1954.15, 1956.07, 1956.12, 1957.16, 1958.05, 1958.14, 1959.11, 1959.22, 1960.02, 1960.23, 1962.05, 1963.05, 1963.16, 1964.05, 1964.40, 1965.37, 1973.09, 1975.22
Engel, Lew 1907.61
Engel, Philip 1884.13
Engel, Scotty 1955.01, 1955.27
Engelberger, Willy 1999.05
Engelhard, Cecil 1903.21
Engelhardt, Wally 1968.06
Engelhart, Helen 1890.08
Engelheart, Cecil 1904.03
Engelke, L. 1859.18
Engelman, Arnold 1997.08
Engelman, Mayys 1899.23
Engels, Philip 1886.03
England, Daisy 1881.35
England, Hal 1957.02
England, M. 1907.54
England, Paul 1948.26, 1951.02
Englander, Ludwig 1883.35, 1884.40, 1885.11, 1893.30, 1894.21, 1894.22, 1895.04, 1895.16, 1896.25, 1896.28, 1897.14, 1897.25, 1897.36, 1898.54, 1899.02, 1899.15, 1899.19, 1899.25, 1899.37, 1900.20, 1900.33, 1900.34, 1900.39, 1900.41, 1901.08, 1901.13, 1901.23, 1902.16, 1902.23, 1903.06, 1903.34, 1903.41, 1904.30, 1904.51, 1905.48, 1906.37, 1907.42, 1908.39, 1909.25, 1910.18, 1914.14, 1927.04
Englander, Miss 1884.64
Englander, Otto 1979.28
Englander, Roger 1962.06
Engle, Arthur 1904.18
Engle, Fannie 1894.06
Englefield, Violet 1918.12, 1918.20, 1920.47, 1925.07
Engler, James 1943.23
Engler, Jr., John 1868.06
Englert, John 1936.31
English Comic Opera Company 1866.07, 1866.14, 1866.19
English Opera Company 1872.17, 1889.28, 1889.29
English, Anna 1957.09, 1963.27
English, Cory 1991.06, 1994.01, 1995.13, 1996.06
English, Drake 1998.18
English, Ellia 1984.15
English, Floyd 1923.30
English, Genora 1937.09, 1939.19
English, Granville 1928.04
English, Jane 1897.26, 1897.42, 1897.54, 1899.15
English, Joan 1931.05
English, Kay 1926.18, 1927.08, 1931.19
English, Lillian 1905.55
English, Scott 1976.34
English, William M. 1899.31
Englund, George H. 1957.03
Englund, Patricia 1978.10
Englund, Richard 1960.05
Engran, Marvin 1984.09
Engstrom, John 1973.15
Engstrom, Jon 1975.24
Engum, Silas 1945.09
Enklewitz, Abel 1957.09
Ennis, LeVerne 1879.59
Ennis, Luce 1959.24, 1959.26, 1964.24
Eno, Harry 1963.09
Eno, Terry 1969.04, 1974.26, 1989.25
Enos, A. 1870.05
Enos, A.G. 1872.35, 1873.03, 1873.26
Enos, G.F. 1872.23
Enos, Mr. 1873.25
Enright, Flora 1900.12
Enright, Florence 1919.29
Enriquez, David 1990.18
Ensemble Company 1979.24
Ensign, Herman Lee 1897.46
Ensor, Ernest C. 1925.50
Ensslen, Dick 1964.40, 1966.08, 1967.10, 1969.04, 1973.09, 1977.06, 1979.12, 1989.18
Enten, Boni 1975.08, 1976.19
Enters, Anita 1922.21
Enters, Marjorie 1932.19
Enters, Warren 1975.23
Entertainment Group, The 1988.20
Entwistle, John 1972.08, 1993.06
Envel and Stobitzer 1918.04
Enz, George 1936.02
Epailly, Jules 1921.11, 1926.05, 1927.68, 1931.39, 1932.07, 1934.41, 1937.16, 1938.15
Eparaima, Cecilia 1972.20
Eparaima, Richard 1972.20
Ephraim, Lee 1947.15
Eppens, Phil 1937.02
Epperly, Verna 1948.27
Epperson, Brandon J. 2001.04
Epps, April 1978.01
Epps, Sheldon 1982.12, 1997.03
Epstein, Alvin 1960.07, 1962.03, 1989.24
Epstein, Dasha 1976.15, 1978.09, 1988.10, 1988.17
Epstein, Diane 1979.05
Epstein, I.L. 1938.16
Epstein, Judy 1979.31
Epstein, Laura 1975.10
Epstein, Matin 1998.19
Equity Library Theatre Production, An 1980.01
Erani Corporation, The 1968.19
Erasme, Joelle 1976.20
Erckmann, Emile 1893.03
Erdman, Ernie 1921.34, 1962.17
Erdman, Jean 1971.18
Erdmann, Frl. 1883.08
Erens, Joseph 1943.05, 1943.16
Ergotti, Herman 1930.28
Erhardt, Peter M. 1979.05
Eric, Caja 1930.08
Eric, Sven 1915.23
Erick, Sven 1913.32
Ericksen, Eddie 1955.13, 1961.14, 1961.26, 1968.08
Erickson, Art 1949.05
Erickson, Jean 1908.16
Erickson, Julius 1892.48
Erickson, Knute 1906.15, 1916.13
Erickson, Leif 1940.06
Erickson, Mitchell 1986.15
Erickson, Philip 1966.04, 1966.17
Ericson, Eric 1942.27
Ericson, Melvin 1939.15
Ericson, Richard 1985.20
Erikson, Bo G. 1983.19
Erlanger Productions, Inc. 1931.16
Erlanger, A.L. 1896.44, 1913.31, 1919.42, 1926.30
Erlanger, Abe 1912.48, 1916.19
Erlanger, Abe L. 1906.24, 1915.28, 1919.01
Erlanger, Abraham 1903.39, 1927.37
Erlanger, Abraham L. 1893.42, 1894.42, 1897.25, 1898.25, 1899.12, 1899.29, 1900.01, 1900.25, 1900.31, 1900.32, 1900.40, 1900.50, 1901.16, 1901.21, 1901.27, 1902.04, 1902.24, 1902.43, 1903.04, 1903.23, 1904.22, 1904.31, 1904.47, 1904.56, 1905.22, 1905.25, 1905.28, 1905.30, 1905.41, 1905.46, 1905.48, 1906.02, 1906.18, 1906.36, 1906.42, 1907.13, 1907.37, 1908.35, 1909.08, 1909.18, 1909.28, 1910.07, 1910.34, 1911.11, 1912.12, 1912.28, 1912.33, 1912.34, 1914.26, 1915.05, 1917.20, 1917.25, 1918.11, 1918.28, 1920.16, 1921.10, 1921.37, 1922.35, 1924.35, 1925.50, 1926.29
Erlanger, Alene 1927.36
Erlanger, Winnie 1902.09
Erle, Marian 1887.52
Erlich, Martha 1916.09
Erlynne, Roydon 1894.27
Ermesilda, Mlle. 1867.25
Ermides, Peter C. 1997.12
Ermoloff, George 1943.08
Ermoloff, Messr. 1925.03
Ernest, Harry 1888.42, 1889.25, 1891.18, 1892.06, 1893.33
Ernest, Henry 1895.18
Ernest, L. 1867.12
Ernest, Messr. 1888.42
Ernestine, Mlle. 1864.17
Ernie, Val 1941.09
Ernst Marischka 1999.05
Ernst, Leila 1939.27, 1940.22, 1946.22
Errett, Geoffrey 1936.26
Errickson, Julius 1892.53
Errico, Melissa 1992.11, 1993.18, 1998.05
Erritt, Geoffrey 1936.26
Errol, George 1905.14
Errol, Kathleen 1922.35
Errol, Leon 1911.24, 1912.13, 1912.38, 1913.17, 1914.15, 1915.15, 1916.24, 1917.03, 1917.12, 1917.35, 1918.18, 1920.44, 1921.11, 1921.18, 1922.02, 1923.30, 1925.08, 1927.07, 1928.11, 1929.08
Erroll, George 1899.13
Erroll, Kathleen 1915.23
Errolle, Martha 1941.02
Errolle, Marthe 1946.20
Errolle, Ralph 1910.37, 1927.01
Errolovitch, Leon 1916.24
Ershova, Mme. 1922.06, 1923.28, 1925.03, 1927.51, 1929.05
Ersi, Elsa 1924.04
Erskine, Anna 1937.12
Erskine, Dick 1930.28
Erskine, John 1931.46
Erskine, Julian 2000.05
Erte 1922.27, 1922.32, 1922.34, 1923.18, 1923.38, 1923.41, 1924.19, 1925.22, 1925.23, 1926.01, 1926.16, 1927.46, 1928.22, 1929.22, 1929.35, 1939.31, 1958.18, 1991.11
Ertheiler, Harry 1897.40
Ervin, James A. 1993.03
Ervin, John 1941.13
Erwin, Barbara 1977.06, 1989.27, 1991.06
Erwin, Frank 1927.55
Erwin, Ralph 1929.07, 1929.28, 1931.01
Erwin, Ramona 1943.17, 1944.31
Erwin, Stuart 1950.06
Esai, Mlle. 1868.13
Esami, Musu 1934.16
Escamilla, Alicia 1930.10
Escamillo 1922.18
Escariz, Emilina 1966.14
Esched, Irith 1972.17
Escobar, Conchita 1949.07
Escobedo, Idlefonso Moya 1988.15
Escott, Lucy 1858.03, 1859.01, 1859.02, 1859.03, 1886.32, 1887.06, 1887.52, 1894.38, 1897.48, 1898.50
Escott, Miss 1886.32, 1886.36
Escudero, Vicente 1934.32
Esdale, Charles 1919.23, 1929.02
Esher, Jim 1982.17
Eshet, David 1990.16
Eskeli, Dick 1955.25
Eskew, Doug 1990.05, 1992.03
Eskew, Jack 1979.13
Eskow, Jerome 1964.18
Esmond, Annie 1905.27, 1907.46, 1915.25
Esmond, Harry 1929.31
Esmond, Henry V. 1905.23
Esmond, Mercita 1912.26
Esmonde 1926.22
Esmonde Costume Studios 1928.09
Esmone, Charlotte 1925.14
Espantoza, Lucille 1879.15
Esparza, Raul 2000.17
Esparza, Roberta Delgado 1979.08
Espero, Sidonie 1917.27, 1917.30, 1918.27, 1920.14
Espinosa, Clarence 1968.24
Espinoza, Brandon 1996.08
Espinoza, Carmen 1908.17
Esposito, Giancarlo 1968.24, 1972.06, 1973.06, 1981.27, 1987.17
Esposito, H.Y.V. 1999.18
Esposito, Mark 1989.03
Esposito, Michele 1908.43
Esposito, Vincent 1968.24
Essen, Abdul 1934.16
Essen, Viola 1949.01
Essenova, Viola 1942.22
Essig, Dorothy 1932.21
Essing, Cecile 1887.04
Essler, Fred 1939.23
Essley, Charmine 1921.35
Establishment Theatre Company, Inc., The 1966.15
Estabrook, Howard 1907.44, 1915.25
Estasen, Ana 1934.40
Estavo, Eliana 1988.06, 1992.13
Estcourt, Kate 1883.39
Estee, Adlyn 1901.04
Estelle, A. 1876.02
Estephe, Mlle. 1869.16, 1878.18, 1879.39
Esterbrook, Randall 1980.11
Esterel, Jacques 1958.18
Estes, Michael 1979.22
Estevan, J. 1914.02
Esteve, Charles 1870.30, 1870.37, 1870.41, 1871.07
Esteve, Mlle. 1879.55, 1879.60, 1880.16, 1880.27, 1880.29
Estevez, Aramis 1985.06
Estevez, Luis 1962.02
Estey, SuEllen 1989.19
Esther, Mlle. 1877.13
Esthere, Mlle. 1877.06
Estiot, Messr. 1883.28, 1884.45, 1886.19, 1886.20
Estiot, Mlle. 1883.59, 1884.43
Estiot, Mons. 1884.49, 1884.50, 1884.52, 1884.54, 1884.55, 1885.23, 1885.55, 1885.56, 1885.57, 1885.59, 1885.60, 1886.09, 1886.18, 1886.21, 1886.22
Estner, Robert 1982.20, 1989.14
Estoclet, David 1911.09
Estol, Helen 1973.14
Estore, Louise 1885.45
Estrada, LaRosa 1945.13, 1946.21
Estradere, Mlle. 1879.19, 1879.26, 1879.27, 1879.31, 1879.34, 1879.36, 1879.39, 1879.40, 1879.43, 1879.44, 1879.45, 1879.46, 1879.47, 1879.48, 1879.49, 1879.51, 1879.55, 1879.60, 1879.61, 1880.16, 1880.29, 1880.52, 1880.56, 1880.58, 1880.60
Estradere, Mme. 1880.44, 1880.50, 1881.54
Estrin, Melvyn J. 1982.03
Estwick, Pat 1972.14
etCie, Idare 1929.51
Ethane, Arleen 1949.17
Ethel, Kate 1881.24, 1881.28, 1884.34, 1885.05, 1885.13, 1885.28, 1885.45, 1885.52, 1885.67, 1886.33, 1886.37, 1892.55
Etheria, Mlle. 1880.34
Etheridge, Dorothy 1947.14, 1950.19, 1951.19, 1954.03, 1956.03, 1956.05, 1957.03, 1957.08, 1957.11

Etheridge, Eleanor 1930.28, 1932.26
Etheridge, Helen 1929.48
Etheridge, Victor 1930.35, 1931.01
Etherington, Arthur 1894.14, 1896.30, 1899.25
Etherton, Sadie 1906.23
Etting, Ruth 1927.37, 1928.47, 1930.06, 1930.08, 1931.19
Ettinger, Heidi 1997.18, 1998.03, 2001.06
Ettinger, Lotta 1898.28
Ettlin, Emilietta 1978.07, 1989.13, 1996.02
Ettlinger, Don 1972.24
Eubanks, Joseph S. 1983.04
Eugene O'Neill Memorial Theatre Center 1982.09
Eugene, Larry 1905.21
Eugene, Max 1896.41, 1898.19
Eugene, Max C. 1904.34, 1905.49, 1913.05
Eugene, Mons. 1876.26
Eugenia, Mlle. 1867.25
Eugenie, Mlle. 1870.44, 1871.27
Eula, Joe 1978.26, 1979.15
Eulalie, Gertrude 1904.19
Eumicke, H. 1897.08
Eunice, Master 1877.20
Eunice, W. 1870.15, 1889.25
Eunice, William 1888.01, 1893.47
Europe, James Reece 1903.39
Europe, James Reese 1904.22, 1907.22, 1909.10, 1915.07, 1978.21, 1980.27
Eustace, Edna 1930.23
Eustice, Fred 1909.17
Eustis, Belle 1882.20
Eustis, Fred 1884.60, 1884.66, 1899.40, 1902.07
Eustis, Fred J. 1883.42, 1884.25, 1888.39, 1890.03, 1893.45, 1895.03, 1895.22, 1896.25, 1897.28, 1900.03, 1904.09
Eustis, Frederick 1884.66, 1899.22
Eustis, Frederick J. 1898.72
Evain, Mr. 1852.04
Evan, Robert 1997.09
Evanko, Ed 1969.04, 1976.08
Evans and Company 1898.03
Evans, Agnes 1892.02, 1892.13
Evans, Al 1937.12, 1938.12
Evans, Albert 1995.06, 1996.02
Evans, Alice 1888.32, 1893.14, 1894.02, 1895.39, 1968.08
Evans, Arthur 1899.42, 1900.14, 1900.23, 1900.29, 1907.25
Evans, Beverly 1961.05, 1962.08, 1962.10, 1962.11, 1962.19, 1963.22, 1964.12, 1964.14, 1964.30, 1964.31, 1965.25, 1965.27, 1966.02, 1966.04, 1966.17
Evans, Bob 1948.15
Evans, Bobby 1939.14
Evans, Bonnie 1953.16, 1955.10, 1956.12
Evans, Bruce 1938.10, 1939.28, 1944.30
Evans, Byrdeatta 1925.27, 1925.39
Evans, C.J. 1905.27
Evans, Charles 1890.32, 1892.18, 1892.45, 1930.42
Evans, Charles E. 1884.48, 1890.32, 1892.18, 1896.31, 1896.45, 1904.37, 1913.07
Evans, Claire Louise 1948.28
Evans, Clem 1904.41
Evans, Constance 1923.23
Evans, Damon 1972.06, 1972.25
Evans, Dan 1907.21
Evans, David 1962.12, 1979.31, 1982.18, 1983.11, 1990.14, 1999.22, 2001.03
Evans, Edith 1952.12
Evans, Edyth 1933.15
Evans, Eleanor 1951.01, 1951.03, 1951.04, 1951.06, 1951.07
Evans, Erna 1903.03
Evans, Eva 1890.21
Evans, F. 1868.04
Evans, Flora 1897.04
Evans, Frank 1869.38, 1898.46
Evans, Frank C. 1907.34
Evans, G. 1871.14, 1872.24
Evans, George 1866.05, 1867.24, 1871.19, 1872.21, 1900.38, 1902.21, 1902.40, 1904.07, 1908.22, 1908.43, 1909.16, 1917.26, 1921.14, 1980.27
Evans, Greek 1917.07, 1918.09, 1924.12, 1924.45, 1925.52, 1927.07, 1927.45, 1927.60, 1929.17, 1929.43, 1930.12, 1931.39
Evans, Griffith P. 1898.08
Evans, Gwyllum 1965.24
Evans, H. 1871.11
Evans, H.A. 1907.58
Evans, Harry 1907.21, 1908.28, 1928.28, 1936.01
Evans, Harvey 1964.15, 1968.07, 1970.11, 1971.05, 1974.04, 1997.19, 1999.13
Evans, Helena Phillips 1926.30
Evans, Herbert 1938.19
Evans, J.H. 1862.08
Evans, Jack 1913.08, 1913.23, 1914.16
Evans, Jane 1935.14
Evans, Joseph 1921.24, 1980.21, 1981.22, 1982.16
Evans, Karen 1978.11
Evans, Key 1979.24
Evans, Leigh 1959.19
Evans, Leon 1981.07, 1986.02
Evans, Lloyd 1968.09, 1974.16, 1975.16, 1976.23, 1976.26, 1977.03, 1977.11, 1977.17, 1980.03, 1980.22, 1981.22, 1986.10, 1987.11
Evans, Louise 1917.20
Evans, Lyle 1926.42, 1928.29
Evans, Margie 1927.58, 1941.08
Evans, Mary Alice 1945.03
Evans, Mattie 1899.33
Evans, Maurice 1960.19
Evans, Messr. 1868.19
Evans, Michael 1927.65
Evans, Michele 1965.22
Evans, Miss 1870.05, 1903.03
Evans, Morley 1948.18
Evans, Mr. 1859.06, 1859.07, 1862.05, 1863.10, 1866.18, 1892.20, 1922.20
Evans, Murray 1917.08, 1917.37, 1922.30, 1930.28
Evans, Neal 1934.36
Evans, Neil 1922.36, 1932.14
Evans, Nicholas 1992.06
Evans, Noreen 1987.16
Evans, Ollie 1896.37
Evans, Pearl 1905.06
Evans, Persie 1897.21
Evans, Ray 1941.11, 1958.02, 1961.21, 1979.25
Evans, Read 1989.21
Evans, Rex 1933.07, 1948.27, 1949.18
Evans, Robert 1886.11, 1890.10, 1893.34, 1941.03, 1957.18
Evans, Robert A. 1902.01
Evans, Rose 1871.15
Evans, Saditha 1898.72
Evans, Scott 1984.11, 1986.08
Evans, Sticks 1953.05, 1957.09
Evans, Sylvan 1945.02
Evans, Tellula 1888.37
Evans, Tempe 1918.26
Evans, Thomas 1863.10, 1897.07, 1898.47, 1900.58, 1901.23
Evans, Timothy Leigh 1999.05
Evans, Vicky 1998.10
Evans, Virginia 1912.25, 1913.30
Evans, Warwick 1993.07
Evans, Wilbur 1942.21, 1942.22, 1942.32, 1944.02, 1945.03, 1954.02
Evans, Will J. 1918.23
Evans, William 1892.27
Evans, William A. 1912.32, 1924.20
Evans, William Kendall 1908.31
Evans, William Thomas 1997.19
Evanthea, Miss 1926.01
Evarde, J. 1880.54
Evarts, Harold 1918.12
Eveleen, Messr. 1882.04
Evely, Edith 1893.38
Evelyn, A.J. 1905.04
Evelyn, Carlotta 1880.41
Evelyn, Fay 1920.09
Evelyne, Annie 1886.31
Even, Jean 1969.01
Everall and Wallach Costume Department 1911.31
Everall, Harry J. 1911.31
Everard, George 1904.34
Everard, Mr. 1839.01, 1845.01
Evercott, M. 1859.08
Everest, Nellie 1879.29
Everett, Alice 1875.31
Everett, Ed 1890.21
Everett, Edward 1897.50, 1900.50, 1902.43
Everett, Elsie 1889.54
Everett, Eugene 1904.47
Everett, Frances 1937.09
Everett, George 1921.41
Everett, L.H. 1860.01
Everett, Mary 1866.08, 1868.16
Everett, Miss 1859.06, 1860.06, 1862.09, 1872.10, 1875.36
Everett, Pamela 1992.02, 1994.06, 1996.06
Everett, Sonny 1996.04
Everett, Sophie 1927.01
Everett, Tanya 1964.27
Everett, Timmy 1954.12, 1955.08
Everett, William 1918.06
Everham, J.B. 1884.24
Everhart, Rex 1960.19, 1965.33, 1967.16, 1978.12, 1981.10, 1986.13, 1987.15
Everitt, Tracy 1960.06
Everle, Clark 1879.63
Everleigh, Adele 1882.04
Everleigh, Edith 1880.63
Everleigh, Kate 1877.22, 1877.23, 1877.25, 1877.39, 1878.20, 1879.03, 1880.24
Everleigh, Pearl 1880.46, 1880.63
Everlie, Edith 1879.25, 1879.42
Everlie, Pearl 1879.25, 1879.42
Everly, Jack 1978.04, 1983.05, 1993.02, 1995.13
Everly, Phil 1982.22
Everly, Will 1911.20
Evers, George 1902.10
Evers, Joseph 1905.31
Evers, Larry 1945.05
Evers, Messr. 1823.01
Evers, Miss 1864.22
Evers, Mr. 1834.02
Evers, Nancy 1974.18
Eversfield, Harry 1895.43
Everson, Isabelle 1879.50, 1879.56
Everson, Nina 1879.42
Everton, Ethel 1900.42
Everton, Paul 1899.01, 1900.10, 1901.02, 1923.47, 1927.12, 1927.56, 1930.35, 1934.36
Everton, T. 1870.39
Everts, Herold 1915.27
Eves Costume Company 1918.14
Evesson, Isabel 1882.26
Evesson, Isabelle 1880.04
Evesson, Miss 1881.04
Evett, Robert 1913.20, 1914.28
Evill, William 1925.31
Eville, William 1916.04, 1923.26
Evins, Donny Ray 1989.11
Evrard, Marcelle 1926.40
Evrard, Mlle. 1926.45, 1926.47
Ewart, Philip 1966.31
Ewell, Lois 1906.02, 1906.48, 1907.48, 1910.28
Ewell, Tom 1941.05, 1941.12, 1948.22, 1960.04
Ewing, Bert 1907.33
Ewing, Billy 1925.18
Ewing, Gerald 1921.15
Ewing, Gordon 1956.01
Ewing, Marjorie 1947.20, 1948.31
Ewing, Max 1927.23, 1928.19, 1929.20
Ewing, Sherman 1947.20, 1948.31
Expert, Mme. 1883.28
Express, B.T. 1986.02
Exton, Valerie 1951.05
Eyck, Matie Ten 1909.14
Eyck, Melissa Ten 1910.19, 1912.09, 1912.17, 1917.04
Eyck, Ten 1916.08, 1922.01, 1936.27
Eyck, Weily 1916.08
Eyen, Tom 1981.29, 1987.07
Eyre, Marjorie 1933.11, 1934.21, 1934.23, 1934.26, 1934.27, 1934.28, 1934.30, 1934.31, 1934.33, 1936.13, 1936.15, 1936.16, 1936.18, 1936.21, 1936.23, 1936.24, 1936.25, 1939.02, 1939.03, 1939.04, 1939.08, 1939.09, 1939.11
Eyre, Richard 1964.29
Eysler, Edmund 1905.20, 1909.19, 1911.19, 1911.43, 1912.37, 1914.04, 1915.17
Eythe, William 1948.30, 1950.11, 1950.20
Eytinge, Pearl 1876.16, 1892.24
Eytinge, Rose 1869.33
Eytinge, Walter 1881.31, 1884.39
Eyton, Frank 1930.32, 1939.22, 1954.11, 1986.02, 1989.02
Ezier, Carrie 1902.09
Ezralow, Daniel 2000.10

F. Ray Comstock, Inc. 1907.18
F. Shoultz and Company 1904.09
F.W.M. Producing Group 1985.12
Fabares, Nanette 1940.21
Faber, F.W. 1908.16
Faber, Ruth 1938.08
Faber, Thomas W. 1908.16
Fabian, Robert 1980.17
Fabian, Warren 1908.41
Fabiani, Joel 1964.45
Fabiono, Lioto 1908.33
Fables, Helen 1924.16
Fables, William 1905.17, 1907.26
Fabray, Claretta 1958.11
Fabray, Jaro 1934.40
Fabray, Nanette 1941.08, 1943.14, 1944.01, 1947.01, 1947.16, 1948.25, 1950.04, 1951.13, 1962.20
Fabregas, Manolo 1963.18
Fabretti, Giorgio 1964.03
Fabris, Amanda 1893.35
Fabrizi, Aldo 1964.03
Fadeuilhe, Andre 1929.10, 1929.11, 1929.13, 1929.14, 1929.15, 1929.16
Faery, Irene 1927.31
Faffael, John J. 1893.09
Fafter, Frank 1904.34
Fagan, Alan 1916.20, 1919.27
Fagan, Allen 1921.11, 1922.42
Fagan, Barney 1886.10, 1890.30, 1891.18, 1892.23, 1894.21, 1899.11, 1903.25, 1904.18, 1911.24, 1927.48
Fagan, Garth 1997.20
Fagan, James B. 1900.36
Fagan, Joan 1958.05, 1959.01, 1961.14
Fagan, Scott 1971.01
Fagan, Sybil Sanderson 1928.05
Fagan, Vincent F. 1946.23
Faggen, Edith 1931.34
Fagin, Annetta 1901.20
Fagin, Gary S. 1979.24
Fago, Jack 1934.13
Fahey, Joseph 1883.62
Fahnestock, Jessie 1892.29
Faiarbairn, Bessie 1887.04
Faibisy 1916.11, 1916.22, 1916.26, 1917.02, 1917.06, 1918.09
Faibisy and Paul Arlington, Inc. 1918.07
Faibisy, Madame 1918.25, 1919.23
Faibsey 1916.03, 1917.26
Fain, Matty 1927.10
Fain, Sam E. 1941.11
Fain, Sammy 1925.07, 1928.47, 1929.05, 1931.30, 1931.36, 1938.01, 1938.08, 1939.14, 1939.25, 1940.12, 1942.24, 1946.23, 1947.05, 1950.02, 1950.12, 1951.15, 1955.04, 1955.12, 1957.01, 1957.10, 1960.10, 1964.35, 1965.08, 1979.24, 1982.22, 1987.02, 1988.08, 1990.09, 1991.10, 1999.24
Fair, Daisy 1905.43
Fair, Dorothy 1903.09
Fair, Florence 1925.27, 1938.14
Fair, Frankie 1892.12
Fair, Joseph 1966.17
Fair, Miss 1865.01
Fair, Nancy 1919.19
Fair, Thelma 1902.41, 1904.34, 1905.20
Fairbairn, Bessie 1898.07, 1898.14, 1898.15, 1898.16, 1898.19, 1898.21, 1898.24, 1898.33, 1898.37, 1898.40, 1898.42, 1899.23
Fairbairn, Polly 1885.34, 1885.36, 1885.37, 1885.38
Fairbank, Ida 1891.09
Fairbank, Josie 1891.09
Fairbank, Spring 1975.24
Fairbanks, Douglas 1905.03
Fairbanks, E.B. 1866.20, 1866.22, 1866.26
Fairbanks, Ethel 1913.07
Fairbanks, Ida 1896.35
Fairbanks, Jack 1911.07
Fairbanks, John 1912.34
Fairbanks, Josephine 1896.35
Fairbanks, Josie 1896.48
Fairbanks, Madeleine 1918.19, 1919.15, 1924.33, 1925.16, 1926.36, 1927.64
Fairbanks, Madeline 1917.13, 1921.10, 1922.39, 1926.16, 1927.35
Fairbanks, Marion 1917.13, 1918.19, 1919.15, 1921.10, 1922.39, 1924.35, 1926.16, 1926.36
Fairbanks, Marjorie 1907.51
Fairbanks, Miss 1892.20
Fairbanks, Nola 1947.12, 1948.19, 1949.05
Fairbrother, Alfred 1908.39, 1909.25
Fairchild, Andrew 1923.11
Fairchild, C. Willard 1924.36
Fairchild, Charlotte 1962.20
Fairchild, Donna 1931.29

Fairchild, Edgar 1922.27, 1925.40, 1926.25, 1927.11, 1927.37, 1928.28, 1932.27, 1934.39, 1936.01, 1936.05, 1937.04
Fairchild, George 1937.08, 1941.01
Fairchild, Jackson 1929.08, 1929.31
Fairchild, Robert 1901.25
Fairchild, Robert D. 1903.03
Fairchild, S. 1881.45
Fairclough, Thomas 1918.38
Fairfax, Virginia 1883.18
Fairhurst, Nana 1898.25
Fairleigh, Harry 1901.08, 1902.23, 1904.10, 1904.52, 1905.20, 1907.47, 1907.52, 1908.06, 1910.28, 1912.08, 1912.31, 1914.11
Fairman, Derek 1937.07, 1942.20
Fairmont, Alan 1978.25
Fairweather, H.F. 1882.33, 1882.37, 1883.65
Fais, Charles C. 1921.01
Faison, George 1972.13, 1972.25, 1975.01, 1976.11, 1981.14, 1983.04, 1993.03
Faison, Sandy 1977.06, 1980.23, 1982.08
Faith, Christine 1978.25
Faithful, Doris 1918.34
Faku, Dorcas 1977.01
Falabella, John 1980.06, 1980.29, 1982.12, 1987.06, 1990.19, 1993.08
Falana, Lola 1964.32, 1975.09
Falank, Shannon 1995.02
Falco, Anthony 1962.04, 1962.20, 1964.33, 1965.17, 1979.13
Falcone 1965.30
Falcone, Marc 1987.07
Falcone, Rina 1952.13, 1956.02
Falconer, Edmund 1863.06, 1864.20, 1864.21, 1866.10, 1868.19, 1869.40, 1883.39
Falconer, Edward 1867.31
Falconer, Helen 1912.39, 1914.23, 1917.22
Falconer, I. 1917.03
Falconer, M. 1917.03
Falconer, Mary 1966.12, 1966.16
Falk, Eleanor 1897.01, 1901.24
Falk, Ella 1894.31
Falk, Henri 1925.41
Falk, Sawyer 1957.05
Falk, W.F. 1891.09, 1894.22
Falk, Willy 1983.17, 1991.03, 1992.12
Falke, S. 1919.43
Falkenburg, Jinx 1940.10
Falkenhain, Patricia 1979.10
Falkenstein, Eric 2000.02
Falkman, Carl Johan 1983.16
Fall, Leo 1909.21, 1910.27, 1911.27, 1913.20, 1913.23, 1922.11, 1924.39
Fall, Richard 1909.21, 1936.22
Falla, Dolly 1934.42
Falla, Holly 1934.42
Fallet, Marcel 1938.03
Fallon, Eva 1906.49, 1907.27, 1909.19, 1910.20, 1910.29, 1910.34, 1913.10, 1913.33, 1914.07, 1915.23, 1918.40
Fallon, Larry 1972.11, 1973.06, 1973.11, 1981.24, 1983.20
Fallon, Lucille 1901.16
Fallon, Robert 1976.24
Falls, Arlene 1904.25, 1907.59
Falls, C.B. 1923.25
Falls, Charles B. 1919.18
Falls, Marie 1904.48
Falls, Robert 2000.06
Falugi, Mlle. 1888.23
Falzone, Peter 1965.36
Fambro, Frankie 1939.15
Family Affair Enterprises, Inc. 1979.16
Fanchionette, Marie 1910.13
Fanchon and Marco 1921.17
Fanchonetti, Marie 1915.19
Fancis, Alfred 1918.04
Fancohn, Miss 1921.17
Fancourt, Darrell 1934.22, 1934.23, 1934.24, 1934.26, 1934.27, 1934.28, 1934.30, 1934.31, 1934.33, 1936.13, 1936.15, 1936.18, 1936.19, 1936.21, 1936.23, 1936.24, 1936.25, 1939.02, 1939.03, 1939.04, 1939.06, 1939.09, 1939.11, 1947.22, 1948.02, 1948.06, 1948.09, 1948.10, 1951.01, 1951.04, 1951.09
Fancy, Richard 1985.08
Fane, Caryl 1948.07, 1951.06
Fane, Julian 1901.25
Fanetti, Ruddi 1974.14
Fang, Charlie 1934.36
Fann, Al 1964.19
Fanning, Lotta 1927.07, 1928.11
Fanning, Richard 1912.07
Fant, Roy 1927.38, 1960.19
Fantus, Felix 1909.12
FAO Schwartz 1996.08
Fara, Peter 1946.10
Faraker, Lois 1976.17
Farbeau, William 1899.21
Farber, Connie 1908.18
Farber, Constance 1918.05, 1920.28
Farber, Donald C. 1992.05
Farber, Irene 1918.05, 1920.28
Farber, Malka 1946.24
Farber, Mitch 1979.13, 1981.08
Farber, Paul 1931.44
Farber, Sandy 1963.20, 1971.09
Farbman, Abel 1963.08
Farceurs, Les 1950.12
Fardo, Signor 1883.48
Fargo, Olive 1912.36
Fargue, Annie 1982.22
Faria, Arthur 1970.11, 1972.04, 1975.13, 1978.09, 1981.09, 1981.16, 1988.17
Faricy, Robert 1927.67, 1932.11
Farina, Carissa 1998.20
Farina, Michael J. 1990.18, 1993.18
Fariss, William 1938.15
Farjeon, Bert 1927.23
Farjeon, Eleanor 1938.06
Farjeon, Herbert 1912.03, 1938.06, 1952.09, 1953.17, 1960.07
Farkas, Jonathan 1983.06, 1983.11, 1984.01, 1985.05, 1986.06, 1988.20
Farkas, Karl 1931.09, 1938.07, 1943.09, 1944.24, 1945.11, 1946.16
Farkoa, Maurice 1895.43, 1903.22, 1906.48, 1912.27, 1914.32, 1915.25
Farley, Bonnie 1908.41
Farley, Edward 1986.06
Farley, Frederick 1947.15
Farley, J.J. 1988.05
Farley, Jack 1918.21
Farley, James 1903.01
Farley, John 1866.21, 1866.24
Farley, Mary 1927.46
Farley, Sadie L. 1900.08
Farlow, Earl 1916.14
Farm, Tekla 1904.36
Farmer, Elisabeth 1966.04
Farmer, Florence 1911.22
Farnac, Paul 1913.08
Farneau, Emily 1880.43
Farney, Evelyn 1942.25
Farnham, Hilda 1930.19
Farnie, H.B. 1884.12, 1884.20, 1884.57, 1886.32, 1886.37, 1886.50, 1887.04, 1887.22, 1890.33, 1892.10, 1893.04, 1896.20, 1898.07, 1900.17, 1931.41, 1941.10
Farnie, Henry 1880.69
Farnie, Henry B. 1869.02, 1869.06, 1869.07, 1869.29, 1869.46, 1870.21, 1870.26, 1871.01, 1871.10, 1871.14, 1872.22, 1875.15, 1877.22, 1877.23, 1877.25, 1877.39, 1879.03, 1879.20, 1881.36, 1881.38, 1881.41, 1882.06, 1882.59, 1882.75, 1884.14, 1886.54, 1901.11
Farnsworth, Dudley 1919.06
Farnsworth, Frances 1934.38
Farnsworth, Ralph 1954.05
Farnsworth, Robert 1937.08
Farnum, Dustin 1899.01, 1900.10
Farnum, Frank 1929.24
Farnum, Franklyn 1913.01
Farnum, Harry 1907.60
Farnum, Hilda 1929.52
Farnum, M. 1901.03
Farnum, Sally J. 1919.25
Farnum, William 1921.01
Farnworth, Don 1948.18, 1957.05, 1960.06
Farnworth, Ralph 1956.04, 1964.40, 1976.19
Faroane, Signor 1883.48
Farone, Dominick 1980.21
Farquhar, Marian 1945.02
Farquhar, Marion 1941.10, 1942.32
Farr, Chris 1979.22
Farr, Cynthia 1927.38
Farr, Frances 1909.25
Farr, Kimberly 1972.21, 1976.25, 1980.06
Farrall, Marie 1876.03
Farrance, Lulu 1890.21
Farrar, Charles R. 1887.02, 1887.42
Farrar, F. 1880.41
Farrar, Matthew 1943.19
Farrar, Messr. 1852.01
Farrar, Tony 1942.34
Farrel, Frank 1869.31
Farrell, Alice 1907.56, 1910.06, 1911.04, 1912.06
Farrell, Aniko 1974.02
Farrell, Anthony Brady 1952.01, 1953.01, 1954.01, 1955.04
Farrell, Baby 1942.27
Farrell, Billy 1894.52
Farrell, C.L. 1884.40
Farrell, Charles 1931.19
Farrell, Edna 1904.08
Farrell, Frank 1944.25
Farrell, Fred F. 1903.06
Farrell, Isabel 1959.05
Farrell, Isabelle 1960.07, 1961.07, 1978.22
Farrell, J.H. 1885.42
Farrell, James 1936.17, 1941.13
Farrell, Kevin 1978.28, 1981.08, 1981.09, 1990.20, 1991.13
Farrell, Leila 1886.32
Farrell, Lelia 1886.45, 1886.59, 1887.06
Farrell, Leslie 1991.12
Farrell, M. 1873.26
Farrell, Margaret 1912.47
Farrell, Marguerite 1905.30, 1913.06, 1916.09, 1919.16
Farrell, Marie 1921.13
Farrell, Richard 1926.24, 1927.12
Farrell, Robert 1927.18
Farrell, Shellie 1949.01, 1962.14, 1963.05, 1963.17, 1964.11
Farrell, Tom Riis 1997.15
Farrell, Tommy 1947.08
Farrell, Tony 1888.15
Farrell, Walter 1961.02
Farren 1883.38
Farren, Jack 1968.06
Farren, Miss 1854.04
Farren, Mrs. 1836.01
Farren, Nellie 1888.41
Farren, Nelly 1888.38
Farren, R.E. 1875.18
Farren, Richard 1866.21, 1866.24, 1875.05
Farrer, Joyce 1955.23
Farri, G. 1911.16, 1911.19
Farri, Virginia 1911.19
Farrington, Adele 1891.37, 1893.08, 1900.34, 1900.58
Farrington, Albert 1900.50, 1902.20, 1904.53
Farrington, Florence 1896.06
Farrington, Frank 1896.18, 1901.23, 1907.05, 1908.29, 1910.32, 1912.27, 1913.23, 1917.20, 1919.41
Farrington, Mark 1943.09
Farrington, Nina 1891.34, 1891.41, 1892.16, 1893.13, 1893.32, 1895.04, 1901.12, 1901.29, 1902.06
Farrington, Ralph 1980.14
Farrington, Stuart N. 1929.08
Farris, Dolores 1926.46
Farrll, Lizzie 1894.52
Farron, T.J. 1886.35
Farrow, Claude 1934.34
Farrow, Edward 1927.30
Farthing, Kuini 1972.20
Farwell, Ada 1882.50, 1882.74, 1882.79, 1883.32, 1883.46, 1883.53, 1883.63, 1884.13, 1884.41, 1885.02, 1885.22, 1885.49, 1885.66, 1886.03, 1887.16
Farwell, Addie 1875.39, 1876.03, 1881.30, 1885.15
Farwell, C.L. 1875.03
Farwell, Charles L. 1881.30
Farwell, Henry 1906.03
Farwell, Jonathan 1985.01
Fashion Productions 1923.22
Faske, Paul 1983.17
Fasman, Barry 1983.09
Faso, Laurie 1976.17
Faso, Nina 1975.08, 1976.17, 1978.12
Fassett, Edna 1905.57
Fassett, Jay 1925.21, 1926.11, 1927.26, 1927.65
Fassit, Messr. 1876.35
Fast, Irving 1915.23
Fata, Wesley 1985.17
Fatima 1896.07
Fatta, James 1983.08
Faucett, Marie 1895.32
Faucherard, W.H. 1893.44
Faugno, Rick 1991.07
Faulkner, Helen 1912.15
Faulkner, Kelley 1990.08
Faulkner, May 1908.03
Faulkner, Virginia 1940.23
Faulkner, Worth 1923.34
Faulkner, Worthe 1917.27, 1922.04, 1924.41, 1926.29
Faull, Eileen 1953.05
Faun, Florence 1927.11
Faure 1877.20
Faure, Jean Baptiste 1888.25, 1889.43, 1890.36
Fauss, M. Michael 1990.20, 1991.13
Faust 1939.20
Faust, Allen 1979.13
Faust, Dr. 1931.05
Faust, George 1910.29
Faust, George W. 1887.50
Faust, Gilberta 1924.09
Faust, Henry 1931.44
Faust, Lotta 1896.15, 1900.20, 1901.06, 1901.21, 1904.13, 1904.44, 1905.44, 1907.10, 1907.41, 1908.21, 1909.11
Faust, Lottie 1900.33
Faust, Tim 1907.61
Faustin 1879.72
Faustine, Mlle. 1867.24, 1869.30
Fauvell, Tim 1996.04
Faver, Annette 1880.18
Favor, Alfred C. 1884.26
Favor, Ed. M. 1884.26
Favor, Edward 1921.15
Favor, Edward F. 1907.52
Favor, Edward M. 1890.44, 1891.21, 1893.17, 1894.26, 1895.20, 1906.41, 1907.18, 1908.42, 1909.08, 1909.12
Favor, Wash. 1885.35
Fawcett, Eric 1925.42
Fawcett, George 1890.35, 1910.33
Fawcett, George D. 1887.49
Fawcett, H. 1866.13
Fawcett, John 1918.36
Fawcett, Owen 1869.07, 1873.03
Fawsitt, Amy 1876.23
Fax, Reuben 1897.15
Fay 1891.08
Fay, Barry 1884.24
Fay, Bert 1931.05
Fay, Culprit 1884.59
Fay, David 1997.09
Fay, Elfie 1900.16, 1904.21, 1905.39
Fay, Frank 1918.02, 1918.20, 1919.19, 1920.35, 1922.08, 1922.21, 1923.25, 1927.62, 1933.15, 1939.16, 1943.13
Fay, Hugh 1882.01, 1882.81, 1884.19, 1886.02, 1886.23, 1889.37, 1889.51, 1909.12
Fay, Joseph 1885.14, 1893.44, 1902.01, 1928.41
Fay, Joseph C. 1886.55, 1886.57, 1890.14, 1890.20, 1890.23, 1890.46, 1890.47, 1890.48, 1896.01, 1900.28
Fay, Messr. 1876.19
Fay, Mildred 1908.07
Fay, Mr. 1883.45
Fay, Olive 1929.50
Fay, Theodore S. 1836.01
Fay, Tom 1979.07, 1981.27, 1983.14, 1984.01, 1985.05, 1987.15, 1988.07, 1990.14, 1994.01, 1996.18
Fay, Vivian 1930.22, 1932.24, 1933.03
Fay, William 1933.20
Faye 1929.24
Faye, Alice 1974.26
Faye, Berenice 1908.28
Faye, Denise 1985.12, 1992.04, 1993.02, 1995.09, 1996.14
Faye, Frances 1943.20
Faye, Herbie 1942.25, 1951.23
Faye, Joey 1938.09, 1944.15, 1946.06, 1946.15, 1947.16, 1951.23, 1962.27, 1965.15, 1971.07, 1985.05
Faye, Lucie 1875.27, 1875.28, 1875.30
Faye, Messr. 1864.01, 1864.03, 1864.08, 1864.11
Faye, Pascale 1995.15, 1996.18, 2000.07
Fayot, Gertrude 1911.39
Fazah, Adib 1985.09
Fazakas, Franz 1963.11
Fazan, Eleanor 1962.23, 1964.45, 1993.17
Fazer, Messr. 1881.14
Fazio, Anthony 1937.14
Fazioli, Billy 1920.10
Feagan, Leslie 1987.15, 1992.04
Fearl, Clifford 1951.15, 1955.07, 1956.16, 1964.33, 1966.10, 1969.05, 1969.14, 1976.05, 1981.19

Fearnley, John 1953.02, 1956.03, 1957.06, 1957.11, 1958.07, 1960.11, 1961.12, 1962.15, 1962.17, 1963.04, 1963.06, 1963.18, 1964.19, 1964.46, 1965.18, 1965.38, 1967.07, 1968.16, 1969.12, 1975.13
Fears, Peggy 1917.01, 1926.18, 1927.13, 1932.22
Feaster, Carl 1982.22
Feaster, Gwendolyn 1924.27
Feathers, Leslie 1907.53
Featherstone, A. 1881.24
Featherstone, E. 1881.11
Featherstone, George 1904.40
Featherstone, Kevin 1967.04
Featherstone, Miss 1881.04
Fechheimer, Richard 1919.40
Fechheimer, Richard B. 1918.14
Fechner, Antonia 1926.01
Fechner, Antonina 1931.09
Fechner, Mme. 1922.06, 1923.28, 1925.03
Feday, Suzanne 1918.10
Feder 1936.12, 1938.02, 1939.19, 1940.10, 1952.05, 1954.09, 1955.10, 1956.01, 1958.14, 1960.05, 1960.21, 1964.20, 1965.31, 1966.31, 1968.16, 1968.17, 1968.32
Feder, Abe 1934.05, 1934.39, 1937.08, 1943.23, 1975.06, 1975.09, 1979.09
Feder, Julie 1869.23
Federici, F. 1885.47, 1887.10
Feeley, A.K. 1884.62
Feeley, Gertrude 1921.36
Feeney, James E. 1906.49
Feeney, Patrick 1884.44
Fehl, Walter 1930.28
Fehlhaber, Fred R. 1965.35
Feiber, Matt 1918.21
Feiden, Robert 1982.08
Feiffer, Jules 1966.18, 1971.04, 1976.27
Feig, Jonathan 1978.11
Feigay, Paul 1944.33, 1945.20
Fein, Irving 1963.07
Fein, Lupin 1932.01
Fein, Maurice M. 1927.26
Fein, Richard 1981.21
Feinberg, Marty 1986.11
Feiner, Herman 1930.15
Feiner, Leonard 1914.04
Feingold, Michael 1977.08, 1989.24
Feinstein, Martin 1972.15
Feinstein, Michael 1983.06, 1988.08, 1988.19, 1990.09
Feirce, Louis 1905.51
Feist, Felix 1904.13
Feist, Felix E. 1907.14
Feist, Felix F. 1908.27, 1910.10
Feist, Frances 1939.14, 1939.24
Feist, Gene 1993.10, 1993.16
Feist, Ruth 1946.10
Feitner, Dora 1888.26
Feitner, L. 1880.46
Feitner, Miss 1882.37
Fekaris, Dino 1982.22
Felch, Stanley 1878.03, 1889.10
Feld Ballet, The 1981.21
Feld, Eliot 1981.21
Feld, Irvin 1980.07, 1984.14
Feld, Kenneth 1980.07, 1984.14, 1993.01, 1995.16, 1996.08
Feld, Morey 1944.29
Felder, Clarence 1969.03
Felder, Hershey 2001.07
Felder, Raoul Lionel 1999.25
Feldkamp, Walter 1934.06
Feldman, Al 1989.16
Feldman, Bob 1984.15
Feldman, Gladys 1913.34, 1914.15, 1916.10, 1918.19
Feldman, Jack 1989.08, 1991.10
Feldman, Lawrence 1987.06
Feldman, Robert 1997.21
Feldman, Shellie 1967.01
Feldman, Susan 1999.05
Feldman, Tillie 1937.14
Feldshuh, Tovah 1973.07, 1975.13, 1979.03
Feldstein, Mark 1983.21
Feliciano, Alberto 1946.16
Felicita, Bedon 1871.27, 1872.06
Felix 1891.41
Felix, Hugo 1910.22, 1911.39, 1912.35, 1916.04, 1920.12, 1920.29, 1922.04, 1923.43, 1924.09
Felix, Mr. 1893.29
Felix, Seymour 1908.21, 1923.04, 1924.25, 1924.29, 1924.33, 1924.36, 1925.01, 1925.07, 1925.26, 1925.28, 1926.01, 1926.02, 1926.26, 1926.37, 1926.50, 1927.16, 1928.03, 1928.47, 1930.08, 1931.08, 1933.05
Fell, Mesdame 1852.05
Fell, Mess 1852.01
Fellegi, Theresa 1925.06
Fellini, Federico 1966.01, 1969.16, 1982.09, 1986.07
Fellner and Dreyfuss 1911.42
Fellon, Mae 1902.19
Fellow, O. 1885.51
Fellows, Blanche 1942.34
Fellows, Don 1949.04, 1955.07
Fellows, Edith 1947.13
Fellows, Susan 1962.15
Fels, James 1962.07
Fels, Marion 1962.05
Felton, H. 1879.04
Felton, Jr., Francis 1927.18
Felton, Selma 1945.12
Felty, David Michael 1999.08
Femistre, T.H. 1889.51
Fendel, Messr. 1861.03
Fender, Harry 1918.06, 1919.16, 1920.09, 1921.14, 1923.16, 1925.08
Fender, Henry 1922.36
Fenderson, Alonzo 1922.44, 1930.10
Fenderson, Reginald 1930.10, 1935.01
Fenholt, Jeff 1971.12
Fenley, Corporal 1919.10
Fenn, Jean 1953.15
Fenn, Messr. 1919.33
Fenn, Otto 1907.54
Fennell, Bessie 1909.25, 1912.38
Fennell, Lois 1906.36
Fennelly, Parker 1925.40, 1966.31
Fennessey, J.J. 1902.04
Fennessy, William 1900.53
Fenning, Stephen 1971.11
Fenno, A.W. 1852.01, 1864.14, 1871.13, 1871.20, 1871.21, 1872.27
Fentelle, Harry 1907.04
Fenton, Edna 1919.41, 1920.13
Fenton, Edwin 1875.05
Fenton, Frank 1934.41
Fenton, G. 1871.04
Fenton, J. 1865.05, 1865.07
Fenton, James 1987.04
Fenton, John C. 1899.03, 1900.36, 1909.06
Fenton, Josephine 1893.26
Fenton, Julia 1868.06, 1870.33, 1881.13
Fenton, M. 1908.02
Fenton, Mabel 1889.51, 1890.30, 1894.06, 1896.26, 1896.36, 1897.09, 1897.19, 1897.31, 1897.48, 1898.50, 1899.17, 1899.30, 1900.49, 1900.56, 1903.28, 1906.17, 1908.01
Fenton, Maud 1892.24, 1893.32
Fenton, Miss 1864.22, 1865.01, 1865.05, 1866.02, 1866.31, 1869.31, 1892.52
Fenton, S. 1865.07
Fenton, Sarah 1868.06, 1870.33
Fenton, William 1935.01
Fenwick, Don 1972.06
Fenwick, Fred 1921.12
Fenwick, Genevieve 1907.01
Fenwick, Harry 1891.42
Fenwick, Harry W. 1893.30
Fenwick, John 1971.21
Fenwick, Messr. 1867.10
Ferago, Eugene 1925.02
Feranda, Fredda 1934.37
Ferario, Messr. 1888.10
Ferario, Sig. 1879.12
Feraudo, Vincent A. 1979.29
Ferber, Edna 1927.67, 1932.11, 1946.01, 1948.20, 1954.04, 1954.14, 1959.27, 1961.09, 1966.14, 1983.05, 1994.08
Ferdely, Miss 1890.31, 1894.01
Ferden, Bruce 1973.12
Ferenz, Mr. 1890.31, 1891.33
Ferenzo, Mischa 1926.01
Feretti, Marie 1890.40
Ferguson, Allyn 1960.12
Ferguson, Bill 1948.22
Ferguson, Daniel 1905.07
Ferguson, Dave 1927.10
Ferguson, Dick 1938.03
Ferguson, Elsie 1901.21, 1905.29
Ferguson, George 1927.12
Ferguson, Harry 1937.09
Ferguson, Helen 1947.02, 1963.27
Ferguson, Hilda 1922.39, 1923.38, 1924.18, 1927.07
Ferguson, Jean 1924.09
Ferguson, Jesse Tyler 1998.16
Ferguson, Kate 1885.42
Ferguson, Laura 1933.09, 1933.19, 1934.07, 1934.08, 1934.10
Ferguson, Lynnda 1981.07
Ferguson, Marguerite 1906.16
Ferguson, Mary Jane 1962.04
Ferguson, Mattie 1884.20, 1884.48, 1886.06, 1887.09, 1888.15, 1889.03, 1889.14, 1889.48, 1890.06, 1891.06, 1891.07
Ferguson, Maynard 2001.04
Ferguson, Myrtle 1924.46
Ferguson, Robert V. 1891.20, 1892.31, 1895.41, 1912.06
Ferguson, Rose 1908.33
Ferguson, Sandy 1912.30
Ferguson, Sheer 1938.03
Ferguson, Stanley 1910.23, 1911.28, 1914.19, 1916.15, 1917.16
Ferguson, Stephen 1894.42
Ferguson, W.J. 1883.18, 1885.42, 1897.23, 1908.40, 1919.28
Ferguson, William 1948.18, 1949.04
Ferland, Danielle 1984.08, 1987.18, 1990.07, 1991.08
Ferlger, Alvin 1970.04
Fern, Harry 1918.09
Fern, Harry S. 1910.17, 1911.31
Fern, Vera 1939.27
Fernand, Messr. 1884.11
Fernandez, Bijou 1886.06, 1937.13
Fernandez, Drisco 1999.15
Fernandez, E.L. 1912.41
Fernandez, J. 1943.02
Fernandez, Jose 1939.18, 1970.20
Fernandez, Paco 1949.07
Fernandez, Stacia 2001.06
Fernando, Miller 1898.28
Ferner, Rhoda 1902.05
Ferns, Nellie 1927.13
Ferrall, Gina 1998.03, 2000.20
Ferrandou, Don W. 1919.20
Ferrante, John 1970.10
Ferrar, Fred 1901.10
Ferrara, Andy 1990.20, 1991.13
Ferrara, Johnny 1928.27
Ferrard, Buddy 1959.03
Ferrari, Gustave 1917.24, 1919.20
Ferraro, Buddy 1946.06
Ferrat, Jean 1964.39, 1982.23
Ferre, Cliff 1950.03
Ferre, Leo 1958.06, 1959.15, 1961.25
Ferreira, Jose Roberto 1988.06
Ferrell, Andy 1980.01, 1983.13
Ferrell, Elizabeth 1996.13
Ferren, Bran 1982.22, 1984.08, 1989.12
Ferrer, Amperito 1915.01
Ferrer, H. 1985.07, 1997.13, 1999.18
Ferrer, Jose 1941.09, 1958.02, 1959.04, 1963.29, 1979.09
Ferrer, Richard 1974.03
Ferrera, Darryl 1992.07
Ferrers, Mme. 1841.01
Ferri, Ron 1979.15
Ferrier, Pat 1957.07, 1959.01
Ferrier, Paul 1880.16, 1881.49, 1881.50, 1883.12, 1886.43
Ferrier, Robert 1987.08, 1988.14, 1990.08
Ferris, Evelyn 1918.16
Ferris, Geoffrey 1984.07
Ferris, Peggy 1948.18
Ferris, Rene 1892.24
Ferris, Tom 1912.17
Ferry, Mabel 1912.10, 1922.48, 1923.16
Ferry, Stephen 1953.16
Ferry, Will 1937.15
Ferry, William 1894.44, 1931.08
Ferry, William J. 1930.08
Fertel, Morris 1912.30
Fervous 1920.22
Fesco, Michael 1959.05, 1962.02
Fessenden, W.H. 1880.12, 1882.08, 1882.09, 1884.57
Fessler, Walter 1879.54, 1885.53
Festival of Two Worlds 1976.35
Fetherston, Edward 1924.17
Fetherstone, Eddie 1921.41
Fette, Emma 1911.28
Fette, Emme 1912.30
Fetter, Ted 1930.25, 1931.14, 1935.14, 1936.06, 1936.31, 1937.02, 1937.12, 1938.12, 1939.10, 1946.19, 1948.04, 1953.12, 1980.10, 1988.08, 1999.23
Fetter, Theodore 1930.18
Feuer, Cy 1948.26, 1950.17, 1951.02, 1953.07, 1954.09, 1955.02, 1958.20, 1961.22, 1962.27, 1965.33, 1966.27, 1977.16, 1979.12
Feuhrer, Lillie 1909.04
Feuhrer, Robbie 1909.04
Feuhrer, Robert 1912.27
Feuillet, Octave 1858.01
Feval, Paul 1887.27
Fevrier, Henri 1919.38
Feydeau, Georges 1899.30, 1912.26
Feyder, J. 1953.11
Feyhe, B. 1999.24
Feyti, Robert 1947.04
Ffolkes, David 1947.07, 1948.18, 1948.26, 1949.01, 1950.10, 1951.02, 1951.15, 1951.18
Fialkov, Max 1963.12
Fibich 1943.02
Fibich, Felix 1966.21, 1967.08, 1970.17
Fichandler, Max 1911.10
Fichmam, Joel S. 1976.04
Fickett, Homer 1934.39, 1936.12
Fiddes, Josephine 1869.33
Fiddler, Harry 1906.08, 1932.12
Fidler, Harry 1896.46
Fidora, Cav. R. 1923.29
Fiebach, Fraulein 1879.62
Fiebach, Frl. 1879.57
Field, Ada B. 1923.46
Field, Al. G. 1896.49
Field, B. 1893.34
Field, Ben 1907.58
Field, Bessie 1893.34
Field, Billy 1983.09
Field, Blanche 1913.34
Field, Carol 1955.12
Field, Emma 1895.14
Field, George B. 1904.13, 1904.44
Field, Grace 1903.31, 1904.54, 1906.25, 1911.13, 1912.41, 1913.23, 1916.08, 1918.15
Field, Kate 1880.19
Field, Leta 1904.44
Field, May 1907.11
Field, Messr. 1903.03
Field, R.M. 1884.37, 1884.48, 1885.44, 1886.27
Field, Robert 1943.09, 1944.25, 1945.03, 1945.19
Field, Robert S. 2000.07
Field, Ron 1953.11, 1962.24, 1964.18, 1966.14, 1966.24, 1968.30, 1970.09, 1971.15, 1978.22, 1983.09, 1986.03, 1986.13, 1987.16
Field, Ruth 1906.29
Fielder, Adele 1918.04
Fielder, Frances 1918.04
Fielder, Ronald 1930.22
Fielderhof, John 1914.25
Fielding, Adele 1887.39
Fielding, Edward 1898.38, 1918.41
Fielding, Harold 1965.14
Fielding, Henry 1907.51
Fielding, Jerry 1962.17
Fielding, Katie 1884.27
Fielding, Maggie 1884.19, 1896.24, 1901.15, 1903.25, 1907.56
Fielding, Marjery 1935.15, 1938.01, 1942.10, 1944.19
Fielding, Marjorie 1940.23
Fielding, May 1879.50, 1880.04, 1881.04, 1881.11, 1882.26, 1884.11
Fielding, Miss 1859.11
Fielding, Mr. 1866.08, 1869.20
Fielding, Mrs. 1862.09
Fielding, W.T. 1876.19
Fieldng, Mr. 1859.01
Fields Stock Company 1904.54
Fields, Ada 1921.22, 1921.37, 1922.19, 1923.20
Fields, Al 1903.14, 1923.23
Fields, Amelia 1902.25, 1903.21
Fields, Arthur 1912.14
Fields, Benny 1928.14, 1944.22
Fields, Bertha A. 1921.09
Fields, Chip 1975.21, 1987.17
Fields, Clare 1982.11
Fields, Cora 1903.09
Fields, Donald 1922.44

Fields, Dorothy 1927.62, 1928.18, 1930.09, 1930.35, 1931.11, 1931.21, 1931.32, 1939.13, 1939.29, 1940.04, 1941.08, 1943.01, 1943.16, 1944.02, 1945.03, 1946.12, 1947.11, 1950.04, 1951.14, 1954.02, 1957.10, 1958.03, 1959.01, 1966.01, 1966.12, 1966.16, 1967.11, 1967.13, 1973.06, 1976.07, 1978.09, 1979.24, 1979.25, 1980.10, 1983.20, 1984.06, 1986.01, 1986.02, 1986.06, 1986.07, 1989.02, 1990.09, 1999.01, 1999.04, 1999.24
Fields, Ed 1924.35
Fields, Eddie 1922.22
Fields, Fannie 1898.03
Fields, Florence 1930.10, 1935.01
Fields, George 1904.13, 1904.23
Fields, Gracie 1942.14
Fields, Harry 1905.39
Fields, Herb 1951.23, 1955.04, 1956.02, 1957.07, 1964.04, 1969.14
Fields, Herbert 1917.26, 1919.14, 1925.17, 1925.31, 1926.07, 1926.13, 1926.50, 1927.16, 1927.56, 1928.16, 1928.30, 1928.50, 1929.45, 1930.40, 1931.04, 1933.01, 1939.30, 1940.19, 1941.08, 1943.01, 1943.22, 1944.02, 1945.03, 1946.12, 1947.11, 1950.04, 1954.02, 1958.03, 1959.01, 1961.09, 1966.12, 1966.16, 1999.04
Fields, J. Joseph 1885.42
Fields, Joan 1951.23
Fields, Joe 1905.07, 1905.32, 1971.13
Fields, John J. 1882.01
Fields, Johnny 1928.49
Fields, Joseph 1918.17, 1949.18, 1953.03, 1954.01, 1958.05, 1958.19, 1963.05, 1967.09, 1974.02, 1994.09, 1995.07
Fields, Jr., John 1899.18
Fields, Julius 1965.22
Fields, Lew 1897.09, 1901.17, 1903.28, 1904.04, 1904.54, 1906.29, 1907.41, 1908.21, 1909.11, 1909.23, 1909.30, 1910.01, 1910.04, 1910.08, 1910.13, 1910.16, 1910.19, 1911.05, 1911.34, 1911.35, 1911.40, 1912.07, 1912.25, 1912.44, 1912.45, 1913.16, 1913.28, 1916.09, 1917.26, 1919.14, 1920.25, 1921.04, 1921.18, 1923.31, 1924.32, 1926.07, 1926.50, 1927.16, 1927.56, 1928.16, 1928.30, 1928.50, 1930.35
Fields, Lew M. 1896.26, 1896.36, 1897.19, 1897.31, 1897.48, 1898.50, 1899.17, 1899.30, 1900.38, 1902.29
Fields, Lynn 1965.01
Fields, Mrs. 1904.40
Fields, Nat 1905.39, 1910.01, 1912.45, 1913.16
Fields, Peter 1948.24
Fields, Richard 1973.03
Fields, Ricki 1951.20
Fields, Robert 1967.01
Fields, Sally 1923.02
Fields, Sandie 1968.24
Fields, Sol 1898.50, 1904.23, 1905.07
Fields, Stanley 1911.41
Fields, Thor 1980.19, 1981.26
Fields, W.C. 1905.28, 1906.24, 1915.15, 1916.10, 1917.13, 1918.19, 1920.18, 1921.21, 1922.27, 1923.27, 1925.10, 1925.24, 1928.23, 1930.42
Fierce, Mr. 1867.15
Fierman, Jack 1974.20
Fierson, Andrew 1959.17, 1965.03
Fierstein, Harvey 1983.11, 1988.20
Fifer, Albert 1922.08
Fifer, Jean 1922.08
Fifer, Ruth 1922.08
Fifth Avenue Productions 1987.18, 1988.05
Fifth Avenue Theatre Musical Company 1899.41
Fifty Fifth Street Dance Theatre Foundation, I 1986.03
Figman, Max 1880.40, 1882.39, 1884.28, 1884.29, 1888.10, 1890.39, 1891.12, 1891.17, 1891.22, 1892.03, 1892.24, 1893.11, 1893.47, 1896.30, 1903.36, 1907.26, 1925.32, 1928.29, 1930.36, 1932.23
Figman, Oscar 1898.32, 1898.78, 1917.34, 1919.37, 1924.09, 1924.39, 1926.33, 1928.46
Figman, Oscar L. 1897.40
Figman, Rose 1892.05, 1892.24, 1893.40, 1896.30
Filber, Louis 1887.16, 1887.39, 1888.14
Filhart, Tammie 1968.01
Filho, Chico 1992.13
Filiato, Phillip 1972.24
Filiberto, J. deDios 1997.13, 1999.18
Filiberto, J. DeDios 1985.07
Filkins, Grace 1886.43, 1894.21, 1905.15
Filkins, Shellie 1946.10
Fill, Albert I. 1970.01
Filler, A. 1881.35, 1883.39
Fillery 1882.75
Filley, Dolly 1911.05
Fillmore, Clyde 1939.27
Fillmore, Nellie 1914.06, 1919.09, 1924.41
Fillott, Messr. 1889.24
Filmore, Clyde 1932.05
Filmore, Ethel 1908.27
Finch, Flora 1907.61
Finch, M.L. 1868.08, 1868.16
Finch, Pat 1954.15, 1957.06
Finch, Patricia 1958.07, 1965.18
Finch, Richard 1999.15
Finchely 1919.23
Finchette, M. 1873.26
Finchette, Mme. 1876.23
Finchley 1916.22, 1917.17, 1918.02, 1918.26, 1919.36, 1920.11, 1920.30, 1920.38, 1924.02
Finck, David 1988.08, 1988.19
Finck, Herman 1911.05, 1912.04, 1914.18, 1915.25, 1915.28, 1922.03, 1964.28, 1975.22
Findlay, Agnes 1899.38, 1900.15
Findlay, Denise 1948.02, 1948.03, 1948.07
Findlay, John 1891.28, 1914.27
Findlay, Mrs. John 1920.04
Findlay, Raymond 1899.13
Findley, Raymond 1898.10
Fine, Larry 1929.22, 1939.25
Fine, Miriam 1925.23
Fine, Sylvia 1939.26, 1941.08
Fine, Vivian 1933.12
Fingleton, D.J. 1894.39
Fingleton, Dan J. 1895.30, 1896.09
Fingleton, Daniel 1896.11
Finigan, Bill 1979.24
Finin, Charles 1927.47
Fink, David 1990.09
Fink, Henry 1912.36
Fink, Winship 1913.26, 1915.18
Finke, Lewis 1880.49
Finkel, Barry 1997.17, 1998.05
Finkel, Elliot 1988.08, 1989.22
Finkel, Fyvush 1981.18
Finkel, Ian 1988.08, 1988.19, 1990.09
Finkel, Joshua 1993.09
Finkelstein, Joan 1986.13
Finkle, David 1968.08, 1972.19
Finklehoffe, Fred 1943.13
Finklehoffe, Fred F. 1942.24, 1955.04
Finklehoffe, Fred H. 1939.14
Finlay, Genevieve 1902.30, 1904.40, 1911.22
Finlay, Raymond 1890.41, 1897.04
Finlay, Vera 1910.09, 1911.35
Finlayson, Flora 1891.29, 1892.40, 1892.46, 1893.18, 1895.12, 1896.16, 1896.19, 1896.21, 1896.22
Finlayson, Fora 1896.17
Finlayson, Richard 1939.19
Finletter, Gretchen Damrosch 1930.18
Finley, Agnes 1906.44
Finley, Edward 1924.08
Finley, Felicia 1997.08
Finley, Gracie 1971.21
Finley, Margie 1925.27, 1926.01, 1926.37, 1933.21
Finley, Marjorie 1928.07
Finley, Muriel 1928.47
Finley, Murrel 1927.37
Finley, Raymond 1902.32
Finn, Elfin 1924.10
Finn, Frank 1945.12
Finn, Irving S. 1922.04
Finn, J.H. 1883.64, 1885.58
Finn, James 1888.13
Finn, Lizzie 1882.02, 1882.50, 1883.32, 1883.46, 1883.63, 1884.13, 1884.41, 1885.02
Finn, Miss 1870.31
Finn, Robyn 1977.06
Finn, Terry 1981.27
Finn, Tim 1999.02
Finn, William 1989.20, 1992.09
Finnell, Carrie 1942.18
Finneran, Katie 1992.17
Finnerty, Mary Sue 1975.13
Finney, Jameson Lee 1905.15
Finney, Mary 1951.13, 1956.16, 1959.06
Finnigan, Bill 1951.23
Finocchio, John 1978.01
Finton, Miss 1865.01
Fiordellisi, Angelina 1983.14
Fiore, Frank 1929.08
Fiore, Mark 2000.16
Fiore, Roland 1948.27
Fiorentino, Imero 1975.05
Fiorillo, Elisa 1984.14
Fiorini, Lando 1964.03
Fiorito, John 1991.09
Fiorito, Ted 1919.16, 1986.06
FioRito, Ted 1928.08, 1962.17
Firman, Anita 1926.39
Firman, Annie 1869.15
Firmin, Annie 1869.04, 1870.28, 1870.32, 1870.42, 1871.02
First Japanese Manufacturing and Trading Company 1885.48
First, Harry 1904.45, 1912.29
Firth, Elizabeth 1905.04, 1911.27
Firth, Tazeena 1979.23, 1982.18
Fisch, Bertha 1889.44
Fisch, Bertie 1884.42, 1888.09, 1889.01
Fischer, Alice 1890.40, 1904.15, 1905.15, 1908.03, 1916.09, 1927.55, 1928.50
Fischer, Bob 1918.17
Fischer, Clifford C. 1939.31, 1942.10, 1942.12, 1942.14, 1942.23, 1947.18
Fischer, Doris 1937.10
Fischer, Henrietta 1879.15
Fischer, Howard 1937.02, 1937.12, 1960.22, 1967.04
Fischer, J.B. 1883.62
Fischer, Jane 1951.15
Fischer, Joseph C. 1907.21
Fischer, Loretta 1942.10, 1944.19
Fischer, Martin 1990.09
Fischer, Robert 1922.33
Fischer, Robert A. 1887.27
Fischer, Robert C. 1929.31, 1934.29, 1935.17
Fischoff, George 1970.03
Fiser, Don 1927.31, 1945.12
Fiset, Adelaide 1918.25
Fish, Marguerite 1882.48, 1888.39, 1890.07
Fish, Stephen D. 1991.14
Fishelson, Bob 1937.04
Fisher 1913.33
Fisher and Berman 1922.05
Fisher and Company 1905.53
Fisher Theatre Foundation, The 1980.23, 1981.25
Fisher, Alex 1933.05, 1936.17, 1946.02
Fisher, Alfred 1904.56, 1905.28, 1906.24, 1909.18, 1912.34
Fisher, Alice 1906.04
Fisher, Bruce 1982.22
Fisher, C. 1868.22, 1869.14
Fisher, Carl 1975.12
Fisher, Charles 1868.19, 1876.23, 1877.15, 1879.50, 1879.56, 1880.04, 1884.11
Fisher, Charles E. 1883.47
Fisher, Chic 1924.27
Fisher, Clara 1852.06, 1853.04, 1854.02, 1869.15, 1870.02, 1870.06, 1875.11, 1875.15, 1875.20, 1878.19
Fisher, David (Dudu) 2000.14
Fisher, E.O. 1881.40
Fisher, Eddie 1962.17, 1967.12
Fisher, Edward 1937.01
Fisher, Frank 1889.45
Fisher, Fred 1907.18, 1908.15, 1913.05, 1913.17, 1914.11, 1917.23, 1920.10, 1922.15, 1925.23, 1927.12, 1929.04, 1930.08, 1930.38, 1931.19, 1956.11, 1973.05, 1978.09, 1986.06
Fisher, George 1952.15
Fisher, Grace 1903.02, 1907.58, 1916.23, 1918.04, 1919.04
Fisher, H.A. 1878.13, 1879.04, 1880.09
Fisher, H.D. 1876.34
Fisher, Harry 1878.13, 1879.37, 1880.36, 1880.64, 1881.09, 1881.29, 1882.02, 1882.74, 1883.63, 1884.41, 1885.02, 1885.15, 1885.22, 1885.49, 1885.66, 1886.03, 1886.42, 1886.52, 1887.07, 1887.39, 1888.27, 1888.40, 1889.11, 1889.15, 1889.18, 1890.49, 1891.25, 1891.45, 1892.44, 1892.54, 1893.10, 1893.15, 1893.36, 1893.46, 1894.04, 1894.49, 1902.39, 1903.26, 1904.54, 1906.29, 1909.11, 1911.12, 1911.45, 1912.45, 1914.16, 1915.11, 1918.03
Fisher, Harry A. 1877.24, 1878.17, 1879.04, 1879.68, 1880.09, 1882.50, 1882.79, 1883.32, 1883.46, 1883.53, 1884.13, 1887.16, 1887.45, 1887.48, 1888.14, 1889.07, 1893.27, 1895.05, 1896.24, 1897.43
Fisher, Harry E. 1898.67
Fisher, Harry H. 1905.12
Fisher, Harry S. 1907.28
Fisher, Irving 1916.24, 1917.03, 1917.13, 1917.37, 1918.32, 1920.44, 1924.18, 1925.10, 1925.24, 1926.18, 1928.11, 1928.27
Fisher, J.H. 1875.18
Fisher, J.J. 1897.30
Fisher, J.W. 1979.09
Fisher, Jack 1925.40
Fisher, Jacqueline 1949.04
Fisher, Jennie 1876.35, 1882.81, 1884.66
Fisher, John 1834.02, 1882.77
Fisher, John C. 1900.51, 1902.05, 1902.35, 1903.21, 1904.03, 1904.08, 1905.13, 1905.18, 1905.55, 1906.44, 1914.30
Fisher, John Irving 1923.23
Fisher, Jules 1963.19, 1963.22, 1963.23, 1963.24, 1964.15, 1964.16, 1964.30, 1965.06, 1965.14, 1965.27, 1965.28, 1965.36, 1966.15, 1966.19, 1967.10, 1968.04, 1968.05, 1968.11, 1969.04, 1969.10, 1970.02, 1970.07, 1971.01, 1971.03, 1971.11, 1971.12, 1972.22, 1972.23, 1973.06, 1973.11, 1974.01, 1974.24, 1975.04, 1975.14, 1976.03, 1977.10, 1977.15, 1978.05, 1982.22, 1983.11, 1984.01, 1985.12, 1986.06, 1986.13, 1988.15, 1988.20, 1989.12, 1989.20, 1989.26, 1991.07, 1991.15, 1992.08, 1992.17, 1992.18, 1994.06, 1994.12, 1995.09, 1995.15, 1995.19, 1996.07, 1996.15, 1997.21, 1997.22, 1998.01, 1998.20, 1999.21, 1999.22, 2000.08, 2000.19, 2000.20
Fisher, Kurt 1996.09
Fisher, Linda 1975.23
Fisher, Lola 1952.15, 1954.02, 1956.01, 1962.16
Fisher, M. Anthony 1985.06, 1987.18
Fisher, Mark 1930.13, 1965.08, 1989.11
Fisher, Marvin 1958.12
Fisher, Max 1927.60
Fisher, May 1904.44
Fisher, Messr. 1879.04
Fisher, Mildred 1918.03
Fisher, Miss 1841.01, 1860.02, 1879.12, 1881.37, 1884.39, 1886.16, 1889.21, 1890.50, 1900.43, 1904.13, 1904.44, 1905.18
Fisher, Mme. 1914.32
Fisher, Mr. 1856.02
Fisher, Nelle 1948.04, 1951.10
Fisher, Nellie 1944.33
Fisher, Orville 1920.10
Fisher, Paula 1987.18
Fisher, Paula Heil 1994.01
Fisher, Peggy 1942.35
Fisher, Perkins 1899.15
Fisher, Rick 1998.10
Fisher, Rob 1995.18, 1996.14
Fisher, Robert 1886.17, 1887.17, 1896.30, 1970.07, 1978.06, 1982.05
Fisher, S. 1872.08
Fisher, Sallie 1905.19, 1906.30, 1907.11, 1907.59, 1909.02, 1912.01, 1912.11, 1912.37, 1912.48, 1914.31, 1921.05
Fisher, Sally 1902.43
Fisher, Sam 1895.18
Fisher, Samuel 1895.04
Fisher, Stuart 1914.33
Fisher, Susie 1904.22
Fisher, William 1971.02
Fishko, Robert S. 1976.27
Fisk, Florence 1908.40
Fisk, James 1868.25
Fisk, Jr., James 1868.30, 1868.31, 1869.01, 1869.09, 1869.10, 1869.12, 1869.18, 1869.19, 1869.22, 1869.24, 1870.05, 1870.30, 1870.37, 1870.41, 1870.45, 1871.03, 1871.06, 1871.07, 1871.08
Fisk, Louise 1943.14
Fisk, Mr. 1854.01
Fiske, George 1904.25
Fiske, Helen 1889.26

Fiske, Kate Woods 1932.14
Fiske, Linnet 1903.20
Fiske, M.W. 1869.43, 1870.04, 1870.12, 1870.20, 1870.23, 1872.10, 1872.19, 1872.37, 1878.16, 1880.34, 1882.72
Fiske, Marion 1873.02, 1876.22, 1876.36, 1879.12, 1880.35, 1881.47, 1888.16
Fiske, Miss 1877.15
Fiske, Moses W. 1870.09, 1870.32
Fiss, Thomas Michael 2000.15
Fissinger, Virginia 1917.14, 1917.23, 1919.03
Fitch, Betty 1924.31
Fitch, Clyde 1893.11, 1901.17, 1919.34, 1925.29, 1927.42
Fitch, Dorothy 1914.33
Fitch, Ella 1904.09
Fitch, Harry 1900.42
Fitch, Robert 1964.20, 1965.17, 1968.31, 1969.17, 1974.02, 1974.18, 1977.06, 1982.10
Fitch, T.L. 1873.04
Fitsgibbons, Dorothy 1928.21
Fitts, Dudley 1988.05
Fitz, A.H. 1898.66
Fitz, Albert H. 1899.35, 1903.39
Fitz, Charles 1899.19, 1900.49, 1903.36
Fitz, E.B. 1885.44, 1889.34
Fitz-Gerald, O.S. 1897.55
Fitzallen, William 1875.10
Fitzball, Edward 1848.04, 1852.01, 1855.04, 1864.07, 1864.16, 1867.03, 1868.09, 1884.38, 1898.19, 1900.13
Fitzgerald, A. 1870.34
Fitzgerald, Alex 1870.44
Fitzgerald, Alex. 1869.33
Fitzgerald, Alice 1879.16
Fitzgerald, Aubrey 1905.46
Fitzgerald, Cissy 1894.33
Fitzgerald, Clarice Swan 1987.19
Fitzgerald, Dan 1908.43
Fitzgerald, Ella 1986.02, 1989.16, 1997.01
Fitzgerald, F. Richard 1986.17
Fitzgerald, George 1926.38
Fitzgerald, George F. 1927.27
Fitzgerald, Geraldine 1926.30
Fitzgerald, Gilbert 1903.26, 1904.53
Fitzgerald, J. 1875.21
Fitzgerald, John 1976.29
Fitzgerald, Kathy 1995.14, 2001.05
Fitzgerald, Lillian 1906.01, 1920.10, 1922.15, 1924.24, 1932.20, 1945.07
Fitzgerald, Miss 1839.01
Fitzgerald, Neil 1942.21, 1958.11
Fitzgerald, Peter 1981.24, 1983.11, 1983.15, 1985.19, 1986.13, 1987.19, 1988.03, 1988.06, 1988.10, 1988.20, 1989.24, 1989.27, 1989.29, 1990.05, 1990.18, 1990.20, 1991.06, 1991.07, 1991.13, 1991.14, 1991.15, 1992.06, 1992.09, 1993.18, 1995.13, 1995.15, 1997.05, 1997.08, 1998.07, 1999.14, 1999.24, 2001.08
Fitzgerald, Peter J. 1998.02, 1999.07, 1999.23
Fitzgerald, Richard 2000.17, 2001.08
Fitzgerald, Robert 1988.05
Fitzgerald, T. Richard 1977.07, 1979.18, 1979.22, 1980.20, 1980.26, 1981.25, 1982.10, 1983.05, 1983.14, 1983.17, 1991.02, 1991.11, 1994.04, 1995.07, 1995.14, 1997.04
Fitzgerald, W. 1877.15
Fitzgerald, W.H. 1876.36, 1877.04, 1881.24, 1884.18, 1885.41, 1885.63, 1896.16, 1896.19, 1896.21, 1896.22, 1897.13, 1898.23
Fitzgerald, Will H. 1902.04
Fitzgerald, William H. 1883.37, 1883.44, 1885.11, 1885.29, 1886.04, 1900.25, 1900.32
Fitzgerald. W.H. 1900.31
Fitzgibbon, Dave 1929.51, 1932.27
Fitzgibbon, Dorothy 1931.14, 1932.27
Fitzhugh, Anna 1903.03, 1904.13, 1904.50, 1905.19
Fitzhugh, Ellen 1985.05
Fitzhugh, Ida 1889.24, 1891.32, 1892.50, 1895.22, 1911.38, 1925.11
Fitzhugh, John 1912.31
Fitzhugh, Louise 1983.21
Fitzhugh, Marie 1903.03
Fitzhugh, Venita 1911.38, 1913.16, 1913.26, 1914.04, 1914.18, 1915.26
Fitziu, Anna 1926.22
Fitzmaurice, Michael 1942.17, 1942.21
Fitzpatrick, Allen 1995.07, 1997.19, 2001.08
Fitzpatrick, David S. 1979.16
Fitzpatrick, Edmund 1923.14, 1924.23
Fitzpatrick, J.H. 1888.10
Fitzpatrick, John 1977.02
Fitzpatrick, Lynn 1976.05
Fitzpatrick, M.J. 1912.14
Fitzpatrick, Margaret 1892.36, 1892.56, 1895.37, 1897.34, 1901.02
Fitzpatrick, Marybeth 1951.22
Fitzpatrick, Paul 1950.04
Fitzpatrick, Thomas 1923.10
Fitzpatrick, Tom 1921.33
Fitzroy, Emily 1914.33
Fitzroy, J.L. 1902.15
Fitzroy, L.C. 1900.50
Fitzroy, Louis 1905.19
Fitzroy, Mr. 1875.10
Fitzsimmons, J. 1878.17, 1882.02
Fitzsimmons, James 1879.37, 1880.36, 1880.64, 1881.09, 1882.50, 1882.74, 1883.46, 1883.53
Fitzsimmons, Joseph 1879.04, 1907.24
Fitzsimmons, Robert 1972.02
Fitzsimons, James 1883.32
Fitzwilliam, Edward 1855.07
Fitzwilliams, Nina 1901.27
Five Blind Boys of Alabama 1988.05
Fjellman, Richard 1950.15
Fjorde, Grace 1917.10
Flack, Nanette 1908.26, 1909.20, 1910.23, 1917.11, 1917.25, 1920.26, 1922.16, 1922.30, 1926.02, 1929.30
Flack, W.E. 1898.64, 1903.01
Flageolet, Messr. 1869.29
Flagg, C. 1881.04
Flagg, Clara 1881.11
Flagg, Georgine 1879.50, 1880.04, 1881.11
Flagg, James Montgomery 1923.25, 1924.36
Flagg, Minnie 1883.65, 1884.12
Flagg, Miss 1881.04
Flagg, Tom 1994.06
Flaherty, Hugh 1906.15
Flaherty, Hughey 1906.15
Flaherty, Hughie 1907.39
Flaherty, Jack 1930.28
Flaherty, Stephen 1990.12, 1992.17, 1998.01, 2000.16, 2000.18
Flaiano, Ennio 1966.01, 1969.16, 1982.09, 1986.07
Flake, Frank 1883.22
Flam, Dorothy 1916.26
Flanagan, Celine 1951.14
Flanagan, D.J. 1907.01
Flanagan, Ed 1923.17
Flanagan, Edward 1915.22
Flanagan, Edward J. 1902.44
Flanders, Dolores 1936.27
Flanders, Michael 1959.20, 1966.32
Flanigam, Louisa 1991.12
Flanigen, Betty 1930.41
Flaningam, Louisa 1969.04, 1979.26, 1982.13
Flannery, Cornelia 1863.10, 1864.05, 1864.06, 1864.09, 1864.12, 1864.15
Flannery, Gary 1984.06
Flannery, George 1880.34
Flannery, Georgianna 1859.08
Flannery, Miss 1869.04, 1869.13
Flannery, Mr. 1856.04, 1857.05, 1857.07
Flanry, T. 1855.11
Flash, Lady 1976.34
Flatau, Dorota 1924.01
Flate, John-Michael 1989.09
Flatley, Michael 1996.01, 1996.12, 1998.09, 2000.05
Flatt, Ernest 1964.21, 1966.06, 1974.02, 1979.25, 1986.11
Flatt, Lester 1954.08
Flavelle, Edgar 1904.06
Flavelle, Robert 1954.03
Flavin, Aileen 1906.22
Flavin, M.C. 1904.10, 1905.06
Flavin, Margaret 1908.11
Flavin, Tim 1979.26, 1983.14
Flaxman, John 1968.24, 1972.02
Fleason, Neville 1920.24
Fleccia, Annetta 1884.27
Fleer, Harry 1946.23
Fleeson, Neville 1920.14, 1922.28, 1927.05, 1929.29, 1938.04
Fleetwood, Tom 1965.36
Fleischer, Prof. 1888.45
Fleischer, Randall Craig 1995.10, 1997.02
Fleischman, Mark 1959.05
Fleming, A. 1871.27
Fleming, A.W. 1900.02, 1905.20, 1911.01
Fleming, Blanche 1926.13, 1927.27, 1927.65
Fleming, Bud 1960.06
Fleming, Carroll 1905.17, 1906.46, 1911.12, 1911.28, 1912.30
Fleming, Eugene 1992.06, 1993.03, 1995.14, 1997.21, 1999.01
Fleming, Fred 1928.19, 1929.20
Fleming, Fred T. 1923.04
Fleming, George 1917.16
Fleming, Gus 1970.04
Fleming, John 1906.46, 1907.54, 1908.26, 1952.15
Fleming, John P. 1980.10
Fleming, Johnny 1914.19
Fleming, Jr., Tony 1943.24, 1945.06
Fleming, Juanita 1984.09
Fleming, Louis 1951.05
Fleming, Madge 1891.18
Fleming, Marion 1885.03
Fleming, Robert 1929.07, 1948.20
Fleming, Ruth Ann 1952.15
Fleming, Suzanne 1927.46
Fleming, Una 1919.01, 1920.29, 1920.45
Fleming, W.J. 1869.38, 1875.05, 1884.27, 1892.35
Fleming, W.M. 1862.08
Flemming, A.W. 1911.22
Flemming, Carol 1963.08, 1964.02, 1964.24, 1965.31, 1967.06
Flemming, Claude 1906.32, 1912.27, 1914.21, 1915.21, 1916.03
Flemming, John 1942.05
Fleron, William 1892.24
Flers, P.L. 1923.33
Fless, Scott 1980.30
Fletcher, Allen 1961.06, 1961.23, 1962.09, 1964.07, 1964.08, 1965.13, 1968.09, 1968.10, 1968.14
Fletcher, Bill 1963.20
Fletcher, Bramwell 1953.02
Fletcher, Charles 1885.64, 1887.13, 1909.31
Fletcher, Clinton "Dusty" 1931.31
Fletcher, Dan 1986.03, 1987.15
Fletcher, Dorothy 1930.33
Fletcher, Dusty 1929.25
Fletcher, Jack 1958.05, 1962.13, 1964.33, 1965.29, 1966.30, 1967.09, 1968.17, 1969.04, 1972.23, 1974.02, 1979.25
Fletcher, Joe 1927.39
Fletcher, Juanita 1913.14, 1917.11, 1917.27, 1919.27, 1920.30
Fletcher, Lawrence 1947.17
Fletcher, Lillian 1885.64, 1887.13
Fletcher, Lizzie 1885.50
Fletcher, Messr. 1851.02, 1851.05, 1868.06
Fletcher, Mr. 1852.07
Fletcher, Neil 1928.09
Fletcher, Pauline 1897.56
Fletcher, Percy 1917.24
Fletcher, Percy E. 1919.20, 1920.34
Fletcher, Raymond 1964.28
Fletcher, Robert 1953.06, 1953.15, 1954.10, 1955.17, 1956.10, 1957.02, 1961.08, 1961.22, 1962.01, 1962.24, 1962.27, 1964.04, 1964.16, 1966.27, 1970.10, 1971.06, 1982.14, 1983.07, 1985.08
Fletcher, Ron 1951.23
Fletcher, Ronald 1946.05
Fletcher, Susann 1982.11, 1989.03, 1993.02
Fletcher, Tempy 1956.02
Fletcher, Tom 1942.13, 1946.21
Fletcher, William 1885.64, 1887.13
Fleurette 1895.17
Fleury, Mme. 1866.09
Fleury, Mons. 1866.09
Fleury, Mrs. 1868.07
Fleury, Vanni 1947.18
Flick, Joseph R. 1918.36
Flick, Pat C. 1940.12
Flick, Patsy 1934.39
Flicker, Theodore J. 1959.12
Fliege, Madeline 1915.01
Flindt, Albertine 1883.48
Flinn, Denny Martin 1976.19
Flinn, Marjorie 1939.08
Flint, Douglas 1897.20, 1898.29, 1898.37, 1898.39, 1898.42, 1898.63, 1904.34
Flint, Ella 1892.47
Flint, James 1918.10
Flint, Mlle. 1883.48
Flint, Mr. 1836.01
Flippen, J.C. 1926.14
Flippen, Jay C. 1925.26, 1926.02, 1927.31, 1930.25, 1944.19
Flockton, C.P. 1884.32
Floetman, Lucille 1945.19
Flohr, Henry 1880.07
Flood, J.W. 1891.01
Flood, Marie 1910.19
Flood, Messr. 1863.07
Flood, Peter 1973.03
Flora, Mildred 1909.20, 1911.28, 1912.30
Flora, Millie 1864.02, 1876.03
Flora, Mlle. 1876.03
Florede, Nellie 1902.24
Florell, Walter 1943.09, 1944.24, 1945.12, 1946.24
Florence, Bertie 1891.22, 1891.30
Florence, Evelyn 1902.16
Florence, F. 1872.06
Florence, Freda 1908.12
Florence, Grace 1896.12
Florence, Irwin 1896.05
Florence, Mabel 1896.03, 1900.48, 1900.55
Florence, Marguerite 1909.05
Florence, Miss 1854.04, 1855.04, 1872.09, 1882.60
Florence, Mlle. 1875.29
Florence, Mr. 1862.09, 1863.01, 1863.02, 1864.04, 1864.07, 1869.13, 1869.45
Florence, Mrs. W.J. 1859.08, 1864.13, 1869.08
Florence, N.S. 1887.27
Florence, T. 1870.01, 1872.06
Florence, W.J. 1859.08, 1864.13, 1869.08, 1879.53
Florence, Winifred 1902.20
Florentine, Carlos 1884.31
Flores, E.C. 1985.07, 1999.18
Flores, Marissa 1939.18
Flores, Paul 1963.18, 1968.16
Florestano, Joseph 1944.23
Florian, Karl 1934.18
Florianne, Mme. 1923.38
Florin, L.M. 1881.26
Floring, Florence 1890.03
Florio, Caryl 1879.30, 1887.19, 1895.11
Florman, Irving 1943.11
Flourants, Mr. 1859.08
Flower, Belle 1931.15
Flower, Carol 1922.45
Flower, Chris 1980.28
Flower, R. 1913.37
Flowerdew, Elena 1895.10
Flowers, Martha 1952.06, 1961.13
Flowers, Michael 1984.06
Flowers, Ramon 1998.10
Flowerton, Consuelo 1921.21, 1933.25
Floyd, Bella 1881.26
Floyd, Charles 1918.23
Floyd, Edna 1900.32
Floyd, Estelle 1926.19, 1927.67, 1932.11
Floyd, George W. 1887.52
Floyd, J.S. 1906.03
Floyd, Kenneth 2000.03
Floyd, Marie 1887.27
Floyd, Mr. 1859.08
Floyd, Mrs. 1859.08, 1864.13
Floyd, Paul 1921.16, 1929.18
Floyd, Paul C. 1923.39
Floyd, Sara 1946.01, 1948.20, 1954.04, 1954.14
Floyd, Sarah 1961.09
Floyd, Tony 1987.19
Floyd, W.R. 1880.34
Floyd, Walter 1903.01
Fludd, III., Quitman 1975.09, 1978.02
Fludd, Quitman 1972.11
Flushing, Loretta 1923.24
Flyeman, Rose 1931.14
Flying by Foy 1979.22
Flying Karamazov Brothers, The 1986.05, 1994.11, 1998.22
Flynn, Charles 1904.39
Flynn, Charles E. 1903.05, 1903.30
Flynn, Eddie 1919.26
Flynn, Elinor 1934.40, 1937.11
Flynn, Hazel 1930.32
Flynn, J. Lee 1996.04
Flynn, James D. 1899.18
Flynn, Jimmy 1921.26
Flynn, Joe 1894.34
Flynn, John 1892.54, 1893.27, 1893.36, 1894.49, 1895.05, 1920.02
Flynn, John H. 1908.38, 1909.11
Flynn, Joseph 1955.10
Flynn, Kathleen 1903.03
Flynn, Kitty 1912.29, 1922.07, 1922.31
Flynn, Lawrence 1899.41
Flynn, Lillian 1894.04

Flynn, Lillie 1893.10, 1893.27, 1893.36, 1893.46
Flynn, Marie 1912.36, 1913.19, 1917.05, 1919.01
Flynn, Martha 1947.14, 1952.15, 1957.18
Flynn, Maurice 1884.26, 1885.35
Flynn, Messr. 1894.04
Flynn, Miss 1840.02, 1840.03, 1903.03
Flynn, Mr. 1836.01
Flynn, Mrs. 1836.01, 1846.01
Flynn, Patrick 1977.15
Flynn, Radley 1934.21, 1934.26, 1934.27, 1934.30, 1934.31, 1936.13, 1936.16, 1936.21, 1936.24, 1936.25, 1939.03, 1939.06, 1939.08, 1948.01, 1948.06, 1948.07, 1948.09, 1951.03, 1951.04, 1951.06, 1952.14, 1952.17, 1952.18
Flynn, Ralph 1955.10
Flynn, Robert 1911.36, 1917.16
Flynn, Ruth 1930.36
Flynn, Tom 1898.70, 1993.06, 1995.05
Foard, Merwin 1983.10, 1997.15
Fodor, Joleen 1963.20
Foederer, Ernest 1990.07
Fogarty, Alex 1938.07
Fogarty, Alexander 1929.33, 1936.12
Fogarty, John J. 1902.44
Fogel, Al 1969.13
Fogelberg, Dan 2000.16
Fogelson, E.E. 1963.28
Fogerty, John 1997.21
Fogerty, John C. 1982.22, 1986.02
Fois, Georges 1926.40
Foix, Georges 1929.10, 1929.11, 1929.13, 1929.14, 1929.15, 1929.16
Foix, M. 1926.45, 1926.47, 1926.48
Foix, M. Georges 1926.43
Fokina, Vera 1921.28
Fokine 1922.19
Fokine, Leon 1935.02
Fokine, Michel 1919.38, 1920.34, 1921.03, 1921.28, 1922.19, 1923.20, 1924.03
Foldes, Lew 1945.05
Folds, Lou 1947.12
Foley, Brian 1977.09
Foley, Charlotte 1956.02
Foley, Chotzi 1959.13
Foley, Cynthia 1924.26, 1926.32, 1928.37
Foley, E.M. 1914.12
Foley, Ellen 1977.15
Foley, John 1982.04
Foley, Kate 1881.47, 1884.06, 1885.08, 1886.46
Foley, Ken 1948.18
Foley, L.B. 1902.43
Foley, Lew 1900.07
Foley, Lou 1900.49
Foley, Louis 1900.42
Foley, Louis B. 1904.31, 1906.28
Foley, M. 1873.26, 1880.09, 1880.36, 1880.64, 1881.29, 1882.02, 1882.74, 1882.79, 1883.32, 1883.46, 1883.53, 1883.63, 1884.13, 1884.41, 1885.02
Foley, Michael 1879.37, 1880.64, 1881.09
Folger Theatre Group 1980.23
Folger, Avis 1899.22, 1899.25
Follansbee, Oliver 1908.29
Follett, Benjamin 1896.45
Follett, Miss 1866.02
Follette, Mazie 1899.06, 1900.38, 1901.09, 1901.29, 1902.05, 1907.35
Follies, Dorothy 1908.39
Follis, Dorothy 1912.15, 1920.31
Follis, Nellie 1900.59, 1902.20, 1902.43
Follis, Thomas 1905.21
Follwell, J. 1866.02
Follwell, S. 1866.02
Folsom, Agnes 1885.14, 1885.26, 1885.41, 1885.63, 1886.04, 1886.30
Folsom, Bobby 1925.25
Folsom, Carrie 1880.68
Folsom, Cora 1902.11
Folsom, Elsie 1863.09
Folsom, Frances 1905.30, 1911.26
Folsom, Miss 1880.68
Folsome, Agnes 1884.34
Folts, Barbara 1989.27, 1991.06
Foltz, Virginia 1900.38, 1901.17, 1903.31
Folugi, Mlle. 1888.10
Fonda, Henry 1934.06
Fonda, Jeanne 1925.33, 1927.12
Fontaine, Betty 1935.11
Fontaine, Evan Burrows 1920.10
Fontaine, Gene 1935.11
Fontaine, Luther 1978.03, 1981.28
Fontaine, Robert L. 1968.01
Fontan, Jack 1949.04
Fontana, D.J. 1978.01
Fontana, Franco 1988.06, 1990.03, 1992.13
Fontana, Georges 1925.33, 1925.38, 1930.09
Fontana, Mlle. 1868.03
Fontanel, Mlle. 1868.24
Fontanna, Georges 1928.42
Fontenoy, M. 1947.05
Fonteny, Albert 1888.20, 1889.04
Fonteyn, Margot 1976.18
Fooshee, Gladys 1922.18
Fooshee, Sybil 1922.18
Foot, Katharine Lucille 1897.14
Foot, Mr. 1823.01
Foote, Barrington 1907.15
Foote, Dick 1952.05
Foote, Gene 1966.01, 1968.03, 1972.22, 1975.14
Foote, Horton 1952.20
Foote, McClough West 1868.06
Foran, Dick 1943.22
Foran, William 1919.18, 1925.40, 1938.10
Forbes, Ada 1884.40
Forbes, Allan 1914.09
Forbes, Austin 1888.10
Forbes, Ben 1920.21
Forbes, Brenda 1939.12, 1940.03, 1946.07, 1968.02, 1976.05
Forbes, Donna Liggitt 1972.19
Forbes, Edward 1937.11
Forbes, Esther 1969.07
Forbes, Evelyn 1898.08
Forbes, H.R. 1895.35
Forbes, Harold 1907.09, 1908.31, 1911.25
Forbes, Harry 1917.17
Forbes, Hazel 1928.03, 1930.08
Forbes, James 1912.32
Forbes, Jean 1916.03
Forbes, Kathryn 1979.12
Forbes, Kenneth 1943.23, 1946.19
Forbes, Mamie 1896.35, 1898.05, 1898.51, 1900.47
Forbes, Michael 1933.25, 1938.13
Forbes, Ralph 1924.41
Forcen, Ida 1902.38
Ford Uniform Company 1913.19, 1922.31, 1922.40, 1923.02
Ford's Miniature Pinafore Company 1879.29
Ford's Theatre 1990.05
Ford's Theatre Production, A 1976.35
Ford, Anna 1908.36, 1910.12, 1910.30
Ford, Archie 1931.01
Ford, Barbara 1954.04
Ford, Bickie 1920.22
Ford, Chip 1975.03
Ford, Clebert 1971.13, 1991.01
Ford, Constance 1958.08
Ford, Corey 1930.32, 1932.17, 1933.21
Ford, Darrian C. 1996.04
Ford, David 1969.06
Ford, Earl 1903.12
Ford, Edward E. 1920.08
Ford, Ethel 1916.22
Ford, Etna 1894.31
Ford, Frances 1933.21
Ford, Frank 1967.02
Ford, Gene 1921.22
Ford, George 1913.18, 1923.17, 1925.31
Ford, Harry 1925.31
Ford, Helen 1920.01, 1920.29, 1922.10, 1922.28, 1923.19, 1924.22, 1925.31, 1926.50, 1928.30, 1933.23, 1938.15
Ford, Hugh 1906.05, 1907.02, 1910.33, 1922.45
Ford, J.L. 1885.51, 1886.07
Ford, J.M. 1880.41
Ford, James T. 1922.28
Ford, Jay 1931.04
Ford, Jean 1958.14
Ford, John 1901.12, 1901.29, 1902.06, 1957.07, 1961.21
Ford, Johnny 1906.13, 1919.06, 1927.54
Ford, Karen 1972.06
Ford, Kittie 1883.65
Ford, Kitty 1887.43
Ford, Lena Guilbert 1964.28
Ford, Mabel 1916.11
Ford, Marion 1908.30, 1911.18, 1917.32
Ford, Marjorie 1938.17
Ford, May 1890.44
Ford, Mr. 1841.01
Ford, Nancy 1973.03
Ford, Nellie 1913.09
Ford, Paul 1958.20, 1960.04, 1989.16, 1997.01, 1998.11
Ford, Phil 1981.17
Ford, Richard 1924.09, 1928.19
Ford, Robert F. 1927.50
Ford, Ruth 1939.29, 1971.16
Ford, S.H. 1899.20
Ford, Spence 1981.12, 1983.01
Ford, Steven 1987.17
Ford, Sylvia 1921.06
Ford, Tom 1925.25, 1926.23
Ford, W.J. 1906.45, 1909.26
Ford, Walter 1894.35, 1896.05, 1896.37, 1900.47, 1900.52
Ford, Walter H. 1890.44, 1894.07, 1894.38, 1896.15, 1897.26, 1897.30, 1901.21
Ford, William 1911.33, 1912.11
Ford, William T. 1912.48
Ford-Wallace American-English Opera Company 1885.30, 1885.32
Forde, Dolly 1904.02
Forde, Enid 1905.49
Forde, Ethel 1917.06
Forde, Eugenie 1904.02
Forde, Hal 1913.21, 1915.02, 1916.14, 1917.06, 1920.31, 1922.29, 1924.33, 1927.20, 1928.49, 1929.39, 1931.27, 1931.33, 1933.22, 1935.18, 1936.06
Forde, Harold 1911.38
Forde, Harold H. 1913.10
Forde, Larry 1979.15
Forde, Stanley 1909.26, 1917.10, 1920.35, 1922.31, 1924.42, 1925.13, 1926.24
Forde, Stanley G. 1912.01
Forde, Stanley H. 1903.21, 1904.03, 1904.52, 1907.57, 1918.32, 1919.12, 1919.29
Forde, Stanley L. 1907.01
Fordin, Wolff 1905.35
Fording, Lillie 1890.50
Fordyce, George 1919.27
Forella, Ronn 1965.21, 1971.19
Foreman, C. Edgar 1891.32
Foreman, Charles E. 1906.10, 1908.02
Foreman, Lorraine 1994.08
Foreman, Richard 1976.10
Forest, M. 1879.04
Forest, Mildred 1903.37
Forest, Miss 1877.15
Forest, Mr. Phyllys 1888.08
Forestieri, Marcel 1981.07
Forgie, Hugh 1942.16
Forkins, Marty 1930.29
Forlow, Ted 1972.14, 1977.12, 1986.18, 1992.07
Forman, Ada 1919.18, 1921.02
Forman, Hilda 1931.04
Forman, Kathie 1958.01
Forman, Lou 1942.10, 1942.23, 1943.13
Forman, Louise 1931.04
Forman, Maxine 1931.04
Forman, Sands W. 1897.27
Formes, Carl 1887.18, 1888.24, 1894.21, 1937.01
Formes, Jr., Karl 1892.55, 1893.20, 1895.07, 1898.34
Formilli, C. 1903.39, 1913.33
Foronda, Joseph 1990.17
Forrest, A.H. 1876.12, 1877.08
Forrest, Almira 1900.28, 1900.50
Forrest, Almyra 1905.16, 1905.56
Forrest, Arthur 1905.15, 1911.38
Forrest, Capitola 1880.05, 1881.17, 1881.19
Forrest, Carrie 1894.18
Forrest, Edwin 1867.29
Forrest, George 1914.33, 1944.21, 1946.18, 1948.24, 1953.16, 1961.26, 1965.22, 1965.35, 1978.03, 1981.21, 1985.13, 1986.09, 1989.26, 1999.23
Forrest, Ingrid 1947.15
Forrest, James 1898.38
Forrest, June 1938.15, 1940.16
Forrest, Marguerite 1923.43
Forrest, Mary 1910.04, 1951.20
Forrest, Maude 1906.43
Forrest, Messr. 1886.16
Forrest, Mildred 1902.07
Forrest, Miss 1866.28, 1869.06, 1893.06
Forrest, Paul 1969.14, 1981.28
Forrest, Sam 1918.41, 1919.04, 1920.14, 1920.38, 1922.39, 1923.32, 1927.47, 1927.50, 1928.31
Forrest, Samuel M. 1893.30
Forrest, Steve 1958.01
Forrest, Undine 1953.11, 1955.12
Forrest, William 1903.11
Forrestal, Josephine 1963.30
Forrester, B.E. 1904.33, 1905.31, 1906.34, 1907.62
Forrester, George 1875.05
Forrester, Jack 1923.02, 1925.29
Forrester, Mr. 1875.05
Forrester, Mrs. William 1880.24
Forrester, N. 1863.10
Forrester, Sid H. 1902.15
Forrester, Susie 1899.37, 1904.25
Forrester, W. 1875.35, 1877.25, 1883.52
Forrester, William 1875.19, 1875.23, 1875.26, 1877.23, 1879.01, 1879.06, 1881.16
Forsberg, Edwin 1921.32, 1927.29
Forsberg, Harold 1871.13, 1876.35, 1887.27
Forsburg, Edwin 1924.21
Forsburg, Harold 1885.46
Forshaw, Robert Pierpont 1942.33
Forssen, David 1966.12, 1966.16
Forsslund, Amy 1904.40
Forste, Allegra 1987.03
Forste, Allegra Victoria 1988.04, 1990.08
Forster, E.M. 1963.03
Forster, John 1986.18
Forster, Kate 1882.78, 1885.47, 1887.10
Forster, Margaret 1970.03
Forster, Miss 1882.60
Forstmann, Ted 1997.19, 1999.13
Forstner, Josef 1984.05
Forsyeth, Harry 1919.26
Forsyth, Bruce 1979.14
Forsyth, Charles 1926.11
Forsyth, Dorothy 1934.29
Forsyth, Ed 1983.17
Forsyth, Ethel 1909.01
Forsyth, Hattie 1908.07, 1908.42
Forsyth, Millicent 1909.01
Forsyth, Peggy 1912.35
Forsythe, Ethel 1905.04
Forsythe, Harriet 1907.42
Forsythe, Hattie 1906.47
Forsythe, Henderson 1992.10
Forsythe, Melba 1932.23
Fort, Gertrude 1889.05, 1892.34, 1895.34, 1908.02
Fort, Sylvilla 1943.17
Fort, Syvilla 1944.31, 1946.21
Forte, Rose M. 1889.02
Fortescque, George K. 1900.43, 1905.18
Fortescue, George 1893.34
Fortescue, George K. 1875.35, 1876.01, 1876.29, 1879.01, 1879.06, 1880.02, 1882.34, 1883.42, 1887.01, 1888.13, 1890.50, 1896.01, 1896.05, 1897.39, 1900.05, 1900.35
Fortescue, Jessie 1879.06
Fortescue, Miss 1870.05
Fortescue, Viola 1893.34, 1896.01
Fortesque, George 1907.06
Fortesque, George K. 1880.40, 1884.22, 1885.58, 1896.35, 1902.12
Fortesque, Miss 1867.29
Fortie, Eggie 1886.52
Fortier, Bob 1953.08
Fortier, Robert 1952.01
Fortis, John 1944.20, 1946.14, 1947.12
Fortner, Herr 1866.33
Fortner, Keith 1998.20, 1999.21
Fortnum, Thomas 1906.22
Fortuna, Jane 1899.30
Fortune, John 1937.09
Fortune, Thomas 1908.20
Fortus, Daniel 1970.07, 1973.11
44 Productions 1991.14
Forwood, Luke 1905.27
Fosburgh, Mr. 1864.15
Fosdick, Eugene 1920.28
Foss, Harlan 1975.04, 1978.07, 1978.19, 1978.20, 1979.20, 1979.21, 1979.27, 1980.04, 1980.21, 1980.22, 1980.25, 1989.13, 1990.08, 1996.02
Foss, John 1936.30
Fosse 1927.28
Fosse, Bob 1950.03, 1954.05, 1955.08, 1956.14, 1957.07, 1957.08, 1957.14, 1959.01, 1961.02, 1961.15, 1961.22, 1962.27, 1963.17, 1966.01, 1966.07, 1972.22, 1973.15, 1974.01, 1975.14, 1976.07, 1978.05, 1982.01, 1986.06, 1986.07, 1996.14, 1999.01
Fostelle, Charles 1888.06, 1900.38
Foster 1955.26
Foster, A. 1914.14
Foster, Ada 1879.02
Foster, Allan 1924.34

Foster, Allan K. 1914.14, 1914.30, 1915.22, 1915.27, 1916.03, 1916.11, 1916.14, 1916.23, 1916.25, 1917.08, 1917.14, 1917.15, 1917.23, 1917.31, 1918.02, 1918.30, 1918.42, 1919.03, 1919.16, 1919.26, 1919.30, 1919.35, 1920.02, 1920.09, 1920.19, 1920.22, 1920.40, 1921.14, 1921.20, 1921.25, 1921.34, 1922.01, 1922.10, 1922.11, 1922.15, 1922.18, 1922.23, 1922.31, 1922.34, 1922.36, 1922.40, 1923.12, 1923.17, 1925.11, 1927.17, 1932.06, 1933.06, 1935.15
Foster, Allen K. 1906.04
Foster, Anna 1872.10
Foster, Arthur T. 1896.05
Foster, Beno 1966.12, 1966.16
Foster, Bruce 1978.01
Foster, C. 1846.01, 1865.11, 1866.02, 1877.25, 1879.03
Foster, Charles 1871.17, 1879.02, 1879.54, 1880.01, 1885.68, 1907.31, 1907.55, 1919.20, 1924.37
Foster, Clairborne 1914.20, 1915.20
Foster, Donald 1930.31, 1952.07
Foster, Duane Martin 1998.01, 2000.03
Foster, E.P. 1907.51
Foster, Elene 1907.25
Foster, Elizabeth 1953.04
Foster, Florence 1875.10, 1893.12, 1940.12
Foster, Frances 1991.01
Foster, Francis 1875.10
Foster, Francis R. 1875.10
Foster, Frank 1883.43
Foster, Franklin 1908.24
Foster, G.A. 1882.69
Foster, Gae 1938.08
Foster, George 1952.20
Foster, Gloria 1966.15
Foster, H.B. 1913.32
Foster, Hernandez 1866.18, 1868.03
Foster, Hunter 1994.07, 1998.13
Foster, J. 1846.01, 1865.04, 1871.10
Foster, John 1864.23, 1913.22, 1914.11
Foster, Joseph 1841.01
Foster, Joseph C. 1870.05, 1872.10, 1875.06, 1875.10
Foster, Josie 1889.50
Foster, Judy 1961.11
Foster, Leesa 1961.13, 1962.07
Foster, Lillian 1909.14
Foster, Llora 1927.37
Foster, Louise 1912.47
Foster, Marie 1948.26, 1960.05
Foster, Mary C. 1866.28
Foster, Master 1841.01
Foster, Maude 1875.11
Foster, Messr. 1852.05
Foster, Miss 1852.01, 1895.12
Foster, Mme. 1841.01
Foster, Mr. 1846.01, 1865.02, 1867.18, 1870.19
Foster, Nancy 1962.21
Foster, Oliver 1929.25, 1935.01
Foster, Phil 1951.21
Foster, Roxie 1946.21
Foster, Royal 1935.04, 1949.09
Foster, Stephen 1871.27, 1879.64, 1902.41, 1939.21, 1944.32, 1955.13
Foster, Sutton 1997.04
Foster, W.H. 1888.07
Foster, Warren 1926.05
Foster, William 1906.14
Fotopoulos, Mark 1980.02, 1985.02, 1986.13
Foudray, Messr. 1883.17
Fougere, Esther 1911.26
Fougere, Eugenie 1899.37
Foulk, Archie 1929.28
Foulkes, Cathy 1978.26
Fountain, Clarence 1988.05
Fountaine, William E. 1930.29
Fouquet, Jeanne 1883.59, 1884.01, 1884.03
Fouquet, Mlle. 1883.61
Four Star Stage Lighting 1972.20
Four, Melodee 1932.12
Four, Wilmor 1987.19
Fournier, George 1894.41
Fournier, Louis 1916.16
Fouse, Jr., Thomas Jefferson 1976.35
Fowell, Miss 1866.31
Fowler, A.N.C. 1907.11
Fowler, Addison 1924.02
Fowler, Anita 1907.43
Fowler, Anita L. 1904.32, 1907.43, 1908.32
Fowler, Arlene B. 1983.19
Fowler, Beth 1970.02, 1973.04, 1979.22, 1983.19, 1985.04, 1987.19, 1989.19, 1994.04, 2001.03
Fowler, Bruce 1997.20
Fowler, Charles 1931.04, 1933.25, 1934.19
Fowler, Edesse 1907.60
Fowler, Edwin 1906.23, 1942.31
Fowler, Gene 1969.14
Fowler, John 1889.31, 1902.14, 1904.20, 1905.10
Fowler, Julia 1999.04
Fowler, Lemuel 1980.10
Fowler, Robert 1987.07, 1997.07
Fowler, Robert H. 1995.02, 1999.16, 2001.05
Fowler, Rose 1903.09
Fowler, Scott 1989.03, 1991.12, 1993.05, 1993.19, 1999.24
Fowler, Steve 1987.05
Fowles, Glenys 1974.07, 1974.15, 1976.22, 1978.07, 1989.13
Fowley, Walter 1917.09
Fownes, Henry 1968.23
Fox and Perla 1992.11
Fox and Shaffer 1885.33
Fox and Vincent 1900.48
Fox George L. 1858.04
Fox Searchlight Pictures 2000.15
Fox Theatricals 1999.03
Fox, Al 1920.17, 1927.40
Fox, Alan 1928.35
Fox, Bernard 1989.29, 2000.02
Fox, Bertram 1911.38
Fox, Bobby 2000.04
Fox, C.D. 1882.39
Fox, C.K. 1864.17, 1871.18, 1873.02
Fox, Charles 1884.39, 1884.44, 1981.16
Fox, Charles K. 1860.02, 1861.01, 1864.06, 1864.17, 1865.01, 1865.05, 1865.07, 1865.08, 1865.09, 1865.10, 1866.02, 1866.28, 1867.12, 1868.06, 1869.26, 1870.15, 1871.09, 1871.11, 1873.26
Fox, Della 1890.08, 1890.16, 1891.11, 1892.22, 1892.33, 1892.47, 1893.16, 1894.28, 1895.22, 1897.17, 1898.27, 1898.77, 1900.40, 1904.35
Fox, Dorothy 1935.14, 1938.09
Fox, Dorothy Kennedy 1934.06
Fox, Dulce 1937.08
Fox, Earl 1914.22
Fox, Earl A. 1921.11
Fox, Edna 1941.08
Fox, Fontaine 1923.25
Fox, Franklyn 1934.15, 1937.15, 1941.09, 1943.07, 1945.05
Fox, Frederick 1937.06, 1942.25, 1948.04, 1961.17, 1965.37
Fox, G.L. 1873.25, 1878.10
Fox, George 1907.49
Fox, George L. 1860.02, 1861.01, 1864.06, 1865.01, 1865.11, 1866.02, 1866.28, 1867.12, 1868.06, 1869.26, 1870.07, 1870.15, 1870.26, 1870.33, 1871.04, 1871.18, 1873.02, 1873.26, 1875.32
Fox, Gladys 1913.35
Fox, Harry 1912.24, 1913.05, 1915.02, 1915.31, 1918.07, 1924.15, 1925.22
Fox, Hattie A. 1873.10
Fox, Helen 1919.14, 1921.20, 1923.02
Fox, Irene 1937.14
Fox, J. 1880.09
Fox, Jack 1921.24
Fox, James 1877.07, 1879.37, 1880.36, 1880.64, 1881.09, 1881.29, 1882.02, 1882.79, 1883.32, 1883.46, 1884.41, 1885.02, 1885.15, 1885.22, 1885.49, 1885.66, 1886.03, 1900.42, 1908.16, 1915.22
Fox, James E. 1887.15
Fox, Janet 1934.40, 1940.06, 1967.02
Fox, Jay 1981.18
Fox, Jimmie 1918.17, 1919.16
Fox, Jimmy 1916.23, 1933.21
Fox, John 1901.28
Fox, John C. 1897.19
Fox, Kate Fraser 1875.21
Fox, Kevin 1990.15
Fox, L. 1852.02
Fox, Lilly 1890.16
Fox, Louise 1879.02, 1881.03, 1885.62
Fox, Louise A. 1884.26
Fox, Manheim 1981.06
Fox, Maxine 1972.12, 1974.05
Fox, Messr. 1879.04, 1879.37, 1884.23
Fox, Miss 1881.07
Fox, Mr. 1875.03
Fox, Nancy 1982.14
Fox, Nellie 1866.03
Fox, Ray Errol 1972.01
Fox, Rick 1993.07
Fox, Robert 1980.19, 1988.09
Fox, Stephen 1986.04, 1991.12
Fox, Thomas 1991.06
Fox, Virginia 1927.57, 1927.61
Fox, Ward 1922.42
Fox, William 1912.29
Fox-Geig, Nick 2000.02
Foxcroft, Gene 1910.19
Foxworth, Julius 1921.26
Foy 1986.16, 1989.03, 1990.20, 1991.13, 1993.01, 1993.06, 1993.19, 1994.12, 1995.16, 1995.19, 1996.15, 1997.22, 1998.06, 1998.17, 1998.20, 1999.11, 1999.21, 2000.19
Foy, Bertha 1880.26
Foy, Bryan 1919.12
Foy, Constance 1884.60
Foy, Eddie 1895.03, 1899.21, 1902.16, 1903.04, 1904.15, 1905.49, 1907.15, 1908.44, 1910.19, 1912.02, 1957.17
Foy, Edwin 1886.62, 1888.39, 1890.03, 1898.63, 1901.13
Foy, Gloria 1920.08, 1922.41, 1924.15, 1924.47, 1927.17
Foy, Ida 1879.07
Foy, Jr., Eddie 1930.05, 1930.39, 1931.37, 1935.12, 1937.06, 1945.16, 1954.05, 1961.14
Foy, Kenneth 1989.27, 1990.14, 1991.06, 1997.04, 1998.07, 1999.14
Foy, Magda 1910.06
Foye, Hope 1950.03, 1951.11
Foyer, Bernie 1951.18
Fraboni, Angelo 1995.15, 1997.05, 2000.15
Fraboni, Angelo H. 1989.03
Fracaswell, Hyman 1990.14
Frachon, Joseph 1947.18
Fracini, E.M. 1997.13
Fracks, Mr. 1851.08
Fraction, Edward 1939.15
Fradel, Miss 1870.22
Fradkin, Leslie 1977.10
Fraer, Louise 1925.39
Fragna, A. 1955.13
Fragson, H. 1898.63
Frail, Horace 1873.04, 1873.05, 1878.02, 1879.01, 1879.38, 1880.24, 1880.40, 1883.64, 1883.67
Frail, Messr. 1873.05, 1884.42, 1886.47
Fraiser, Sudworth 1926.15
Fraizer, Bernice 1978.01
Frame, David 1998.10
Frame, Milton 1927.13
Franc, Jacqueline 1939.30
France, F. 1857.04, 1860.02
France, Master 1855.09
France, Messr. 1855.06, 1857.04
France, Miss 1855.05, 1855.07, 1855.08
France, Mr. 1854.06, 1855.01, 1855.08, 1857.06, 1864.12
France, Mrs. 1854.06, 1855.01, 1857.04, 1860.02, 1861.06, 1862.02
France, Nancy 1898.15
France, Nicole 1949.18
France, R. 1862.01, 1864.22
France, R.G. 1864.07
France, Richard 1951.18, 1952.10, 1954.02, 1956.05, 1957.08, 1958.03, 1959.23, 1961.09, 1962.16, 1963.06, 1964.05, 1965.38, 1967.09, 1968.32
France, Rosa 1861.06, 1862.02, 1890.34, 1891.04, 1891.37
France, Shirley 1876.34
France, Suzanne 1963.21, 1964.33
Frances 1912.35, 1915.19, 1915.27, 1922.14, 1923.16, 1925.30
Frances Company 1911.30
Frances, Corinne 1913.18
Frances, Fannie 1879.63, 1880.39
Frances, Haline 1936.06
Frances, Inc. 1914.03, 1916.04, 1917.01, 1920.43, 1923.34
Frances, Kathleen 1934.23, 1934.24, 1934.25, 1934.27, 1934.28, 1934.30, 1934.31, 1934.33
Frances, Madame 1918.25
Frances, Miss 1861.04
Frances, Mme. 1910.31, 1924.38, 1925.08
Frances, Winifred 1906.40
Francesca, Anita 1916.08, 1917.32
Francesca, Estelle 1916.08
Franchetti, Aldo 1927.28
Franchi, Leon 1896.26
Franchi, Michele 1963.08
Franchi, Sergio 1965.06
Franchonette, Miss 1901.19
Francies and Company 1926.24
Francillon, Inc. 1927.48, 1928.02
Francine, Anne 1954.02, 1978.28, 1979.28, 1983.10, 1987.15
Francioli, A. 1894.47, 1895.16, 1896.07, 1897.02, 1897.26
Francioli, Augusto 1893.39, 1893.47, 1894.14, 1894.21
Francioli, Signor 1895.04, 1896.18, 1897.39, 1897.54, 1898.20, 1898.68, 1900.05
Franciosa, Massimo 1964.03
Francis 1915.17
Francis Leon's Minstrels and Burlesque Opera Troupe 1867.11, 1876.04, 1876.05, 1876.07, 1876.10, 1876.11, 1876.30, 1876.33, 1877.03, 1877.05
Francis Leon's Minstrels and Burlesque Troupe 1876.14
Francis Wilson and Company 1889.24, 1890.26, 1891.31, 1897.36
Francis Wilson Comic Opera Company 1891.47
Francis Wilson Company 1895.26, 1899.24
Francis Wilson Opera Company 1898.54, 1899.28
Francis, Adele 1897.15, 1899.23
Francis, Allan 1980.06
Francis, Alma 1911.11, 1912.48, 1913.31
Francis, Arthur 1920.29, 1921.10, 1922.05, 1922.10, 1922.27, 1923.33
Francis, Carl 1927.48, 1928.31
Francis, Carl D. 1927.31
Francis, Cassie 1884.27
Francis, Charles 1918.10, 1951.12
Francis, Dick 1928.42
Francis, Dorothy 1921.29, 1925.02, 1925.33
Francis, Emily 1898.77, 1900.57, 1902.29, 1903.28, 1906.25, 1907.32, 1913.20
Francis, Emma 1897.06, 1900.24, 1900.40, 1901.16, 1902.24, 1903.39, 1905.05
Francis, Eva 1904.52, 1906.01, 1908.07, 1908.19, 1908.39, 1909.09, 1910.08, 1918.28
Francis, Evelyn 1906.42
Francis, Floyd E. 1906.02, 1906.42
Francis, Gayle 1999.05
Francis, George 1929.21
Francis, Harry K. 1906.04
Francis, Helen 1916.22
Francis, Ida 1882.46
Francis, Isabel C. 1912.47
Francis, James 1897.12, 1902.35
Francis, Joseph 1879.50
Francis, Jr., William 1914.18
Francis, Jr., William T. 1913.04
Francis, Kate 1880.07, 1882.46, 1892.34
Francis, Katie 1884.27
Francis, Larry 1919.19
Francis, Lulu 1878.13
Francis, Mary 1935.01
Francis, Maud 1897.15, 1899.23
Francis, Maude 1900.07
Francis, May 1905.04
Francis, Messr. 1879.03, 1887.48
Francis, Mme. 1910.22, 1912.01, 1912.37, 1916.15, 1919.15, 1920.38, 1921.23, 1923.47
Francis, Mons. 1866.29, 1866.30, 1868.18, 1868.31, 1869.01, 1869.30, 1870.03
Francis, Mr. 1865.11
Francis, Nick 1965.05
Francis, Noel 1926.18, 1927.08
Francis, Pauline 1909.21
Francis, Richard 1890.35, 1892.01
Francis, Stacy 1997.21, 1998.13
Francis, Stephen 1928.43
Francis, Sybil 1900.18
Francis, W.T. 1889.54, 1894.17, 1895.17, 1899.21, 1902.29, 1903.28, 1905.20, 1907.63, 1908.25, 1909.01, 1909.08, 1909.21, 1910.21, 1912.07
Francis, William 1915.18, 1916.01
Francis, William T. 1897.19, 1898.48, 1898.77, 1900.57, 1902.15, 1903.28, 1904.29, 1905.27, 1906.25, 1907.32, 1908.27
Francis, Winifred 1908.02
Francis-Robertson, James 1924.22
Francisco, Edith 1898.38
Francisco, Elena 1868.18

Francisco, Mlle. 1868.18
Franck, Nelly 1939.23, 1940.04
Franck, Rose 1888.39, 1890.03
Franck, V. 1856.01
Franck, Virginia 1926.32, 1928.43
Francks, Don 1965.01
Franco, Abel 1979.08
Franco, Tony 1957.01
Francois, Carrie 1888.43, 1889.31
Francois, Claude 1974.11
Francois, Daniel 1898.33
Francois, Ryan 1999.24
Franey, Agnes 1930.08
Frangipane, Ronald 1969.08
Frank Daniels Opera Company 1895.33, 1897.18
Frank Enterprises 1976.21
Frank L. Perley Opera Company 1904.19
Frank McKee's Comedy Company 1895.39
Frank McKee's Musical Comedy Company 1896.02
Frank Productions, Inc. 1957.18, 1960.05, 1961.22, 1966.03, 1969.04
Frank Sanger's Company 1892.53
Frank Smith and Company 1882.78
Frank Williams' Company 1892.39
Frank, Aldo 1974.19, 1983.03
Frank, Alexander 1918.22, 1922.34, 1924.36
Frank, Alexander F. 1918.07
Frank, Allan 1938.16
Frank, Amy 1922.12, 1923.21
Frank, Arlyne 1950.18
Frank, Art 1927.13
Frank, Bernard 1965.35
Frank, Charles 1928.05
Frank, Chris 1993.01, 1995.16, 1998.17
Frank, David 1959.08, 1973.02, 1974.04
Frank, Dick 1978.25
Frank, Dorothy 1959.26, 1972.07
Frank, Dottie 1968.13
Frank, Doug 1983.17
Frank, Earl 1924.22
Frank, Herbert 1911.12
Frank, Howard 1946.01, 1948.20
Frank, Jacob 1929.24
Frank, Larry 1971.09
Frank, Mary 1885.67
Frank, Melvin 1940.07, 1956.12, 1979.09
Frank, Neal 1927.01
Frank, Paul 1923.21
Frank, Perry 1944.17
Frank, R.M. 1909.15
Frank, Sherman 1961.02, 1966.05
Frank, Stephen 1996.13
Frank, Tillie 1887.18, 1887.24, 1887.28, 1888.19, 1888.26
Frank, Yasha 1938.16
Frank, Zella 1898.28, 1899.19, 1899.25, 1900.33, 1900.35, 1900.41, 1900.58
Frankau, Edla 1925.20, 1926.17, 1928.19, 1929.20
Frankau, Edna 1927.23
Frankau, Ethel 1927.23
Frankau, Joseph 1893.31, 1896.02, 1896.33
Franke, Earle Payne 1922.32
Frankel, Ben 1947.15
Frankel, Eddie 1920.06
Frankel, Fannie 1902.32
Frankel, G. 1895.14
Frankel, Gene 1972.06, 1975.05
Frankel, Gus 1888.05, 1891.15
Frankel, Gustave 1885.45
Frankel, Jennifer 1998.16
Frankel, Jerry 1997.09, 1999.03, 1999.10
Frankel, Julius 1937.14
Frankel, Kenneth 1979.07
Frankel, Leo 1913.08, 1921.04
Frankel, Richard 1987.20, 1991.02, 1995.03, 1997.13, 1997.18, 1998.03, 1999.12, 1999.24, 2001.05
Frankel, Scott 1989.03, 1992.09
Franken, Stephen 1959.03
Frankenstein, Adolph 1904.45
Frankie, Sylviade 1915.28
Frankiss, Harry 1919.42
Frankle, Louise 1875.11
Franklin Malvin F. 1917.09
Franklin Simon and Company 1924.23
Franklin, A.G. 1905.33
Franklin, Annie 1882.69
Franklin, Ben 1924.29, 1926.02
Franklin, Bessie 1907.47, 1909.14
Franklin, Blanche 1880.07, 1920.02
Franklin, Bonnie 1970.09
Franklin, C.J. 1878.10
Franklin, Charlotte 1998.19
Franklin, Daniel 1967.08
Franklin, E. 1908.21
Franklin, Edgar S. 1920.30
Franklin, Eva 1939.23
Franklin, Gertrude 1882.21, 1882.22
Franklin, H.L. 1875.31
Franklin, Harold B. 1934.32, 1934.34, 1934.38
Franklin, Irene 1904.38, 1907.15, 1910.16, 1915.16, 1917.08, 1921.27, 1929.31
Franklin, J. 1870.44
Franklin, J.C. 1876.03, 1876.34
Franklin, J.O. 1871.08
Franklin, Kate 1900.12
Franklin, Kathleen 1901.05, 1901.08
Franklin, L. 1908.21
Franklin, Lidija 1947.07, 1948.31, 1954.06, 1957.03
Franklin, Louis 1899.04, 1906.41, 1908.21, 1911.40
Franklin, Louisa 1875.40, 1876.01
Franklin, Louise 1875.34, 1875.35, 1875.36, 1875.38, 1876.01
Franklin, Lyda 1908.33
Franklin, Lydia 1902.32
Franklin, M. 1881.13
Franklin, Malvin 1911.40, 1913.16
Franklin, Malvin F. 1921.18
Franklin, Malvin M. 1914.25
Franklin, Marie 1901.05
Franklin, Martha 1897.06, 1900.05
Franklin, Maud 1895.28
Franklin, May 1905.40
Franklin, Melvin M. 1919.14
Franklin, Michael 1970.15
Franklin, Miriam 1941.08
Franklin, Miss 1862.02
Franklin, Nancy 1948.30, 1952.10, 1980.23
Franklin, Nony 1945.16, 1947.04
Franklin, P. 1908.21
Franklin, Pearl 1923.46
Franklin, Robert 1952.17
Franklin, Roger 1955.25, 1960.08, 1969.04
Franklin, Sid 1906.40
Franklin, Tony 1981.29
Franklin, Wilberforce 1895.28
Franklin, William 1939.15, 1944.03, 1945.13
Franklyn, Bessie 1910.27
Franklyn, Beth 1914.05
Franklyn, C. 1898.07
Franklyn, Estelle 1901.09
Franklyn, Frankie 1888.17
Franklyn, Leonard 1934.05
Franklyn, Lottie 1911.26
Franklyn, Louis 1910.09
Franklyn, Marie 1905.44
Franklyn, Milt 1990.10
Franklyn, R. 1908.10
Franklyn, Walter 1931.27
Franko, Miss 1894.21
Franko, Nathan 1895.23
Franko, Paula 1887.47
Franks, A.S. 1883.47
Franks, Florrie 1903.09
Franks, Laurie 1965.35, 1979.10, 1984.02
Franks, M. 1900.53
Franks, Messr. 1855.01
Franks, Will E. 1904.06
Franks, Wilson 1903.09
Frann, Mary 1971.08
Franosch, A. 1879.65, 1879.67
Franosch, Herr 1879.22
Fransisco, Julian 1878.21
Franton, Clara 1897.25, 1901.16
Franton, F. 1893.39
Franton, Florence 1891.09, 1891.36, 1892.60, 1893.07, 1893.32, 1893.39, 1893.47
Franton, Grace 1897.26, 1898.28
Franz, Donald 1997.20
Franz, Joy 1965.15, 1972.23, 1980.11, 1987.18
Franz, Robert 1996.04
Franza, Joan 1924.06
Franzell, Carlotta 1943.24, 1945.06
Franzioni, Mlle. 1888.01
Franzos, Leslie 1961.27, 1963.26, 1965.01, 1967.02, 1967.17
Frary, Julia 1911.02
Frary, Mrs. 1848.02
Fraser E. Lovat 1895.43
Fraser, Alison 1988.10, 1991.05
Fraser, Ann 1962.15, 1963.04
Fraser, Claud Lovat 1928.13
Fraser, Denise 1998.14
Fraser, Don 1977.09
Fraser, Douglass 1995.02
Fraser, Dudsworth 1931.15
Fraser, E. Lovat 1895.43, 1904.08
Fraser, E. Lovatt 1902.40
Fraser, Edith 1907.01
Fraser, Elisabeth 1943.23
Fraser, George 1951.05
Fraser, Helen 1895.10
Fraser, Henry 1879.15
Fraser, Ian 1962.18, 1974.22, 1978.18, 1995.15
Fraser, J. Edward 1903.22
Fraser, Jane 1940.22
Fraser, John Arthur 1901.14
Fraser, Margaret 1895.10, 1905.27
Fraser, Marie 1940.01
Fraser, Robert 1875.32, 1876.03, 1878.10, 1880.07, 1880.68, 1887.25, 1888.04, 1888.34, 1889.47, 1890.27
Fraser, Ronald 1965.37
Fraser, Vivienne 1907.26
Fraser-Simipson, Harold 1918.27
Frasier, Sudworth 1925.15
Fratantoni, Diane 1993.10
Fratti, Mario 1982.09
Fratus, Estelle 1929.26
Frawley, James 1964.15
Frawley, Mark 1981.07
Frawley, Paul 1917.29, 1919.08, 1920.11, 1920.37, 1921.30, 1923.19, 1923.30, 1925.33, 1927.04, 1927.46, 1928.43, 1929.49, 1931.42
Frawley, Peggy 1927.07, 1928.11
Frawley, T. Daniel 1914.21
Frawley, T.D. 1887.02
Frawley, William 1925.34, 1927.05, 1927.29, 1928.02, 1928.17, 1929.44, 1932.21
Fray, Jacques 1930.35, 1932.04
Fray, Rona 1925.37
Frayer, John 1962.17
Frazee and Lederer Costume Department 1911.08
Frazee and Lederer's Costume Department 1911.07
Frazee, H.H. 1910.22, 1911.07, 1911.08, 1912.01, 1913.32, 1913.37, 1918.32, 1925.30, 1927.49
Frazee, Marian 1925.43
Frazer, Bessie 1885.28, 1885.67
Frazer, Grenoldo 1975.21
Frazer, H.W. 1885.28, 1885.52, 1885.67
Frazer, J.J. 1853.04, 1854.02
Frazer, James 1895.10
Frazer, Jane 1938.09
Frazer, Mr. 1844.01
Frazer, Robert 1892.21, 1893.37, 1894.13
Frazer, Wesley 1938.03
Frazier, Awilda 1943.10
Frazier, Michael 1981.16, 1982.23, 1985.05, 1988.07, 1992.16
Frazser, Messr. 1882.37
Frean, Robin 1978.25
Frear, F.H. 1881.38, 1882.06
Frear, Fred 1882.54, 1891.13, 1896.50, 1897.27, 1900.54, 1902.22, 1902.44, 1905.53, 1906.26, 1907.48, 1909.19, 1913.25
Frear, Fred H. 1882.47
Freary, Ricardo 1873.22
Frechette, Marilyn 1949.08
Frechheimer, Richard 1918.34
Freddy, Petite 1889.35
Frederic, Helen 1925.39
Frederic, Joe 1941.07
Frederic, Joseph 1936.17
Frederic, Mons. 1851.04
Frederic, Mr. 1850.01, 1854.04
Frederick, Helena 1898.73, 1902.25, 1904.09
Frederick, Jean 1924.36
Frederick, John 1946.23
Frederick, Kate 1942.18
Frederick, Maude 1900.07
Frederick, Pauline 1903.21, 1904.54
Frederick, Vicki 1970.07, 1973.07
Frederick, William 1910.35
Fredericks Studios 1932.12
Fredericks, Arline 1919.29
Fredericks, C.S. 1897.41
Fredericks, Charles 1922.22, 1946.01, 1947.14
Fredericks, Chester 1924.31, 1925.40, 1926.37
Fredericks, David 1982.05
Fredericks, George 1884.46, 1885.68, 1916.02, 1927.64
Fredericks, Lydia 1945.03, 1946.01, 1954.01
Fredericks, Lydia S. 1964.11
Fredericks, Mr. 1851.06, 1855.06, 1855.07
Fredericks, Norman 1959.06
Fredericks, Pauline 1902.24
Fredericks, Richard 1961.05, 1961.06, 1961.23, 1962.06, 1962.07, 1962.08, 1963.22, 1964.31, 1965.09, 1968.10, 1976.22, 1980.22
Fredericks, Rita 1966.15, 1975.23
Fredericks, Rose 1905.44
Fredhoven, Hans 1929.08
Fredricks, Anna 1918.29
Fredricksen, Erik 1973.07
Fredrik, Burry 1971.19, 1980.01
Freeborn, Cass 1905.27
Freeborn, Cassius 1904.19, 1904.23, 1906.23, 1909.24, 1914.05, 1920.39
Freeborn, Cassius M. 1919.25
Freeborn, Pat 1955.24
Freed, Arthur 1920.24, 1964.02, 1979.14, 1983.09, 1984.10, 1985.08, 1986.06, 1992.18, 1999.23
Freed, Bert 1943.19, 1945.04, 1945.19
Freed, Fred 1955.14, 1963.02, 1965.08
Freed, Les 1965.17, 1966.06, 1976.01
Freed, Ralph 1955.19, 1979.24, 1990.09
Freed, Sam 1974.06
Freedhoven, John 1938.15
Freedley, Vinton 1919.41, 1922.10, 1923.08, 1924.43, 1925.49, 1926.36, 1927.59, 1928.01, 1928.17, 1928.36, 1928.43, 1929.12, 1929.42, 1930.31, 1931.32, 1933.01, 1934.36, 1936.26, 1938.13, 1940.17, 1941.08, 1944.01, 1945.08, 1950.06
Freedman, Bob 1981.16
Freedman, Caesar 1926.51
Freedman, David 1926.51, 1930.38, 1931.13, 1934.01, 1934.19, 1936.02, 1936.17, 1936.22, 1936.31
Freedman, Gerald 1961.27, 1963.11, 1964.17, 1966.09, 1968.11, 1971.01, 1974.16, 1975.16, 1975.18, 1976.23, 1976.30, 1977.11, 1978.19, 1979.02, 1980.02, 1980.03, 1980.22, 1981.21, 1981.22, 1986.04, 1986.10, 1987.03, 1987.11, 1991.12
Freedman, Lester 1945.05
Freedman, Robert 1973.10
Freedman, Robert L. 2001.09
Freedman, Robert M. 1974.21, 1978.06, 1978.28, 1981.08
Freeland, Miss 1920.44
Freeland, Mr. 1844.01
Freeman, Adele 1919.35
Freeman, Arny 1963.13, 1964.05, 1970.07, 1978.12, 1979.24
Freeman, Bobby 1973.14, 1975.12, 1979.30, 2000.07
Freeman, Bud 1960.01
Freeman, Caroll 1982.21
Freeman, Carroll 1990.13
Freeman, Charles K. 1944.21
Freeman, Cheryl 1993.06, 1997.03, 1999.08
Freeman, Christopher 1998.10
Freeman, Clara 1898.22, 1900.46, 1901.20
Freeman, Clare 1915.23
Freeman, Damita Jo 1978.25
Freeman, Elisabeth 1921.41
Freeman, Elizabeth 1977.09
Freeman, Grace 1897.02, 1897.17, 1897.34, 1898.58, 1899.01, 1900.40, 1901.16, 1902.30, 1903.33, 1911.22
Freeman, H. Lawrence 1906.08, 1907.29
Freeman, Howard 1938.11, 1941.05, 1941.12, 1952.07, 1963.13
Freeman, Irving 1942.35
Freeman, Isabel 1868.04
Freeman, Isabella 1862.08
Freeman, J. 1869.20, 1869.27, 1869.32
Freeman, James 1873.08
Freeman, John 1914.16
Freeman, Jonathan 1978.25, 1993.10, 1995.05, 1998.16, 2001.08
Freeman, Jr., Al 1970.08
Freeman, K. Todd 1993.04
Freeman, Kathleen 2000.15
Freeman, Mark 1917.16
Freeman, Max 1883.65, 1884.12, 1884.20, 1886.30, 1887.33, 1887.50, 1888.02, 1889.23, 1889.40, 1890.01, 1890.11, 1890.16, 1890.40, 1891.17, 1891.22, 1892.08, 1892.52, 1893.21, 1894.14, 1894.40, 1894.47, 1895.06, 1895.09, 1895.12, 1895.21, 1896.10, 1896.12, 1896.30, 1896.33, 1897.24, 1897.50,

1898.70, 1898.77, 1899.22, 1899.24, 1899.25, 1900.07, 1900.33, 1900.54, 1903.16, 1904.36, 1904.49, 1904.57, 1905.11, 1910.32
Freeman, Mazie 1905.31
Freeman, Millie 1926.05, 1931.07
Freeman, Morgan 1967.15, 1988.05
Freeman, Mr. 1869.14
Freeman, Pauline 1898.22, 1900.46, 1901.20, 1902.38
Freeman, Stan 1964.44, 1968.20, 1970.21, 1988.19, 1990.09
Freeman, Stu 1972.09
Freeman, Virginia 1980.23
Freeman, W. 1906.47
Freeman, W.S. 1908.03
Freeman, Yvette 1976.20
Freer, Fred H. 1885.58
Freer, Herbert 1904.30
Freer, William H. 1899.18
Frees, John 1893.06, 1897.40, 1900.36
Frees, Jr., John 1900.36
Freese, Della 1904.07
Freeth, J.W. 1873.26
Freeth, Lulu 1883.65
Freeth, Miss 1883.17, 1883.23
Freeze, Jeffrey Lane 1998.10
Freeze, L. 1908.22
Freeze, W. 1908.22
Frehrmann, Max 1892.59
Freibus, Florida 1932.28, 1947.09, 1982.24
Freigh, Benny 1979.28
Freirichs, Garret 2000.12
Freisinger 1911.44, 1916.04, 1917.11, 1917.12
Freisinger, E.L. 1914.25
Freisinger, E.S. 1905.53, 1907.24, 1908.19, 1921.29
Freisinger, Mme. 1902.01, 1902.18, 1902.28, 1903.21, 1904.05, 1904.25, 1904.41, 1904.42, 1907.16, 1907.62, 1908.21, 1916.15, 1916.20, 1917.16, 1925.06
Freitag 1950.07, 1955.26
Freitag, Dorothea 1957.10, 1963.08, 1968.08, 1968.30, 1969.05, 1970.02, 1971.07, 1971.15, 1973.09, 1973.10, 1978.22, 1979.22, 1989.18
Freitag, Dorothy 1948.30
Freleng, Friz 1990.10
Frelich, W.B. 1869.31
Freligh, William B. 1875.05
Fremont, Alfred 1889.38
Fremont, Lottie 1907.41
French, Aileen 1917.31
French, Arthur 1971.13, 1991.01
French, Bert 1908.21, 1918.22, 1918.27, 1918.33, 1919.06, 1919.28, 1919.34, 1920.14, 1920.27, 1920.42, 1921.04, 1921.07, 1921.19, 1921.23, 1921.30, 1922.04, 1922.13, 1922.41, 1922.48, 1923.08, 1923.19, 1924.02, 1924.05
French, Briggs 1913.24
French, Charles K. 1903.41
French, Edwin 1880.15, 1881.55, 1898.41
French, Florence 1888.30
French, Georgie 1898.15
French, Harold 1925.50
French, Harry W. 1881.04
French, Helene 1912.14
French, Henri 1922.28
French, Henry 1894.46
French, Henry T. 1893.02, 1893.47, 1894.09
French, Honore 1906.47
French, Hugh 1939.07
French, Jack 1974.01, 1984.06
French, James 1939.25
French, Janet 1904.24
French, Joseph 1903.25
French, Jr., Charles 1894.46
French, Kate 1880.54, 1880.69, 1884.04, 1884.07
French, Laverne 1943.17
French, LaVerne 1946.01, 1948.20
French, Leslie 1938.06
French, Levern 1949.15
French, Lillie 1880.43
French, Mamie 1876.06
French, Minnie 1892.18, 1892.45, 1896.31
French, Mr. 1852.03
French, Paulina 1917.28
French, Peggy 1942.12
French, Percy 1925.31
French, R.T. 1877.04
French, Rick 1949.01
French, T. Henry 1891.36, 1892.60
French, T.H. 1893.07
French-American Opera Comique 1926.40, 1926.43, 1926.45, 1926.47, 1926.48
Frenche, Little 1870.31
Frenche, Miss 1870.31
Frenchmen Productions, Inc. 1999.06
Freni, Rosemarie 1978.23, 1979.27
Frenor, James 1882.71, 1897.53, 1899.05
Frenyear, Mabel 1903.31
Freschi, Bob 1973.05, 1977.06, 1982.01, 1992.01
Fresco, Michael 1960.07
Frescott, Norman 1926.23, 1927.02
Freshwater, Kim 1986.03, 1987.14
Freslinger, Mme. 1893.05
Fresnay, Pierre 1934.34
Frett, Kenneth 1974.12
Fretwell, Elbert 1914.09
Freund, Julius 1914.02
Freund, Kim 1968.01
Frew, Charles 1886.62, 1889.38
Frewen, Bessie 1911.12
Frewen, Patricia 1917.27, 1918.27
Frey, Edward 1937.09
Frey, Fran 1927.41, 1928.47, 1950.14
Frey, Gloria 1930.04
Frey, Hugo 1907.15, 1908.01, 1908.38, 1909.31, 1910.26, 1911.09, 1917.34, 1926.20, 1927.02
Frey, Jeanne 1966.13, 1968.18
Frey, Leonard 1964.27
Frey, Nathaniel 1947.08, 1947.16, 1949.12, 1950.15, 1951.14, 1953.03, 1954.12, 1955.08, 1958.14, 1959.25, 1963.14, 1968.06
Frey, William (Christopher) 1987.05
Freydberg, James B. 1983.19, 1993.01, 1995.16, 1996.08, 1998.17
Friberg, Carl 1968.13
Friday, Betsy 1981.07, 1991.05
Friebus, Theodore 1905.52
Fried, Howard 1959.08, 1960.02, 1963.15, 1974.16
Fried, Martin 1929.33
Friedberg, Billy 1952.20
Friedberg, William 1951.19
Friede, Kenneth 1930.37
Friedeck, Ray 1996.15, 1997.22
Frieder, Sol 1965.04, 1966.24
Friedheim-Kremer, Aloys 1916.16
Friedland, Abe 1907.12
Friedland, Abraham 1902.43
Friedland, Anatol 1909.11, 1911.40, 1912.43, 1918.09
Friedland, Anatole 1916.25, 1917.23
Friedland, Charles 1906.42
Friedlander, Emil 1927.46
Friedlander, Sylvia 1970.17
Friedlander, William 1922.15
Friedlander, William B. 1920.02, 1920.32, 1924.04, 1925.16, 1927.04, 1927.39, 1930.14, 1931.34, 1942.30
Friedlich, Kate 1943.04, 1946.10, 1948.22, 1951.10
Friedman, Arthur 1948.17
Friedman, Charles 1935.16, 1937.14, 1938.09, 1939.23, 1940.01, 1943.24, 1945.06, 1946.09, 1947.02, 1952.15
Friedman, David 1979.03, 1982.03, 1994.04, 1999.16
Friedman, Gary William 1970.20, 1972.01, 1978.25
Friedman, Howard 1971.13
Friedman, John 1938.04
Friedman, Leo 1901.13, 1903.14, 1907.01
Friedman, Leonard 1977.02
Friedman, Lewis 1977.14
Friedman, Louis 1921.14
Friedman, Max 1982.22
Friedman, Murray 1942.25
Friedman, Nate 1971.09
Friedman, Pater 1981.04
Friedman, Peter 1998.01
Friedman, Phil 1986.07
Friedman, Sol 1922.20, 1922.42
Friedman, Stephen R. 1976.25, 1977.06, 1978.12
Friedman-Gartner 1956.11
Friedrich, Herr 1882.68
Friedson, Adam 1999.09, 1999.14
Friedson, David 1999.09, 1999.14
Friel, Jack 1973.10
Friend, Cliff 1920.19, 1922.38, 1923.12, 1924.35, 1925.01, 1927.04, 1928.47, 1929.35, 1931.26, 1932.24
Friend, Henry 1915.20
Friend, Hilary 1923.11
Friend, Howard 1918.21
Friend, Irma 1929.30
Friend, Jack 1948.26
Friend, Robert 1971.17
Friend, William 1906.09, 1927.10
Frierson, Andrea 1963.15, 1990.12
Frierson, Andrew 1959.08, 1959.10, 1961.09, 1963.15
Frierson, Butler Andrew 1958.13
Frierson, George 1926.13
Frierson-Toney, Andrea 1999.22
Fries, Catherine 1982.10
Fries, Gerald 1958.05
Fries, K.T. 1969.09
Friese, Annie 1888.08
Friesen, Rick 1976.36
Frife, Rose 1900.07
Friganza, Bessie 1907.42
Friganza, Trixie 1892.20, 1892.30, 1892.37, 1892.40, 1894.05, 1897.41, 1900.33, 1900.41, 1902.20, 1904.16, 1906.01, 1907.15, 1908.31, 1912.24, 1915.22, 1917.04, 1929.29
Frillman, H.W. 1879.09, 1880.15, 1881.55, 1887.49, 1888.37, 1891.32, 1892.50, 1893.50, 1894.52, 1896.15
Friml, Rudolf 1912.46, 1913.34, 1915.04, 1915.29, 1917.05, 1917.27, 1918.30, 1918.33, 1919.06, 1919.28, 1921.09, 1921.21, 1922.02, 1923.10, 1923.13, 1923.38, 1924.28, 1925.10, 1925.32, 1926.18, 1926.34, 1927.65, 1928.12, 1930.06, 1930.42, 1931.45, 1934.43, 1943.08, 1975.22, 1976.07, 1984.14
Friml, Rudolph 1927.06, 1930.26
Frings, Ketti 1966.27, 1978.10
Fripp, B.A. 1925.37
Friquet, Jules 1907.28
Frisby, Kenneth 2001.04
Frisch, Letitia 1882.65, 1883.22
Frisch, Richard 1964.21, 1987.12
Frisch, W. 1919.37
Frischberg, Dave 1988.08
Frischer, Herr 1897.08
Frisco, Al 1929.21
Frisco, Eddie 1928.34
Frisco, Joe 1918.19, 1928.23
Friske, Nicholas 1891.44
Frist, Don 1928.31
Fritch, Letitia 1886.04
Fritsch, Hugo 1885.63
Fritts, Marguerite L. 1917.32
Fritz Schoultz and Company 1899.42, 1900.02, 1900.06, 1900.29
Fritz, Anna Mae 1930.10, 1935.01
Fritz, Edwin 1881.39
Fritze, Herr 1879.57
Fritzi Scheff Opera Company 1913.15
Frizzell, Genevieve 1943.23
Froeba, Frank 1999.24
Froehlich, Rico 1956.04, 1959.04, 1959.19, 1961.27, 1962.14, 1962.24, 1963.25, 1964.35
Froelich, Florence 1926.11
Frohman, Alice 1931.30
Frohman, Bert 1942.11
Frohman, Charles 1886.06, 1891.38, 1893.11, 1895.29, 1895.32, 1895.43, 1897.32, 1898.63, 1900.37, 1901.01, 1903.22, 1903.33, 1904.01, 1904.29, 1905.20, 1905.27, 1906.25, 1906.37, 1907.32, 1907.63, 1908.25, 1908.27, 1909.01, 1909.21, 1910.05, 1910.21, 1911.27, 1912.26, 1913.04, 1913.20, 1913.26, 1914.04, 1914.18, 1915.18, 1916.01, 1917.19, 1923.26, 1925.41
Frohman, Daniel 1900.28, 1900.43, 1902.12, 1902.18
Frohoff, Joseph 1905.29, 1907.05, 1917.16, 1918.23, 1919.22, 1922.30
Froisart, George 1884.21
Frolich, Herr 1883.35
Frolisch, John 1907.51
Froman, Jane 1934.01, 1942.16, 1943.20
Froman, Valentin 1951.16
Fromant, Mons. 1868.26
Frome, Milton 1949.02
Fromkes, Harry 1951.11
Fromm, Jane 1940.07
Fromont 1877.04, 1877.15, 1893.45
Fromont, Mons. 1869.05
Frondaie, Pierre 1919.38
Fronsioli, Georgia 1905.42
Frontai, Jean 1932.26
Frontiere, Dominic 1983.20
Frontiere, Georgia 1983.20
Froom, A. 1897.16
Froom, Albert 1895.08, 1905.52, 1906.26, 1908.07, 1910.23, 1912.30, 1914.19, 1917.16, 1918.23, 1919.22, 1927.43, 1928.31
Froom, Charles 1922.13, 1928.48
Froome, Albert 1899.29, 1909.13, 1911.28, 1913.22
Froome, Alfred 1908.19
Frost, Alice 1931.02
Frost, Edith 1911.05
Frost, Jack 1920.36, 1921.19, 1924.16, 1979.25
Frost, John 1996.05
Frost, Sebastian 1999.12
Frost, Sue 1995.07
Frost, Thomas 1895.35
Frost, Tom 1896.13, 1898.13
Frothingham, G.B. 1873.05
Frothingham, George 1880.12, 1880.45, 1880.48, 1880.53, 1882.07, 1882.08, 1882.09, 1882.10, 1882.11, 1882.12, 1882.13, 1883.11, 1883.12, 1883.13, 1883.14, 1883.15, 1891.29, 1892.51, 1893.18, 1893.19, 1893.48, 1894.03, 1895.01, 1896.08, 1897.13, 1898.23, 1900.32
Frothingham, George B. 1873.04, 1894.08, 1894.45, 1896.43, 1900.25, 1900.31, 1902.04, 1902.28, 1912.19
Froude, John 1868.03
Fruehauf, Messr. 1892.43
Fruehauf, Mr. 1893.29
Fruge, Romain 2000.15
Fry, E. 1886.02
Fry, Mr. 1851.01
Fry, Ray 1947.21, 1970.04
Fry, Stephen 1986.12
Fryatt, John 1955.15, 1955.20, 1955.21
Fryberg 1999.05
Frye, Ben 1960.10
Frye, Charles 1913.21
Frye, David 1987.03, 1987.10, 1988.16, 1990.08, 1991.09
Frye, Dwight 1924.08, 1989.05
Frye, Ed 1920.06
Frye, G. Clayton 1919.24
Frye, Gilbert 1943.23
Frye, Hal 1951.22
Frye, Lawrence 1900.12
Fryer, Randall 1928.44
Fryer, Robert 1951.14, 1953.03, 1954.02, 1956.07, 1959.01, 1959.27, 1960.09, 1963.13, 1966.01, 1966.10, 1975.14, 1978.02, 1979.06, 1981.27, 1982.18
Frymire, Jack 1968.12
Frymire, Virginia 1968.12
Ftitgerald, Lillian 1908.38
Fubler, Renaye 1961.24
Fubler, Vaughn 1961.24
Fuchs, Isidor 1894.41
Fuchs, Jason 1994.12, 1995.19, 1996.15
Fuchs, Peter Paul 1956.11
Fuehrer, Robert 1909.30
Fuentes, Ruben 1988.15
Fuerst, Eugene 1933.13
Fuerst, Jim 1962.02
Fuery, James A. 1901.23
Fuguet, Alphonse 1902.07
Fuguet, Daisy 1907.01
Fuguet, Daisy R. 1903.36
Fuhrman, Debbi 1993.14, 1995.18
Fuji Television Network, Inc. 1996.08
Fujii, Timm 1976.02, 1989.05
Fujikawa, Jerry 1966.06
Fujima, Eiken 1989.21
Fujimoto, Haruki 1976.02
Fulco, Giovanni 1935.02
Fulco, John 1932.07
Fuld, Miss 1917.31
Fulda, Ludwig 1914.27, 1934.14
Fuller, Bobby 1931.15
Fuller, Carrie 1880.05
Fuller, Charles A. 1903.39
Fuller, Charles P. 1898.66
Fuller, David 1991.08
Fuller, Dean 1953.02, 1956.08, 1957.01, 1959.26, 1996.18
Fuller, Dolores 1989.12
Fuller, Edward 1937.08, 1939.19
Fuller, George 1900.49
Fuller, H. 1878.04

Fuller, Harrison 1933.09, 1933.19
Fuller, Ida 1914.19
Fuller, James 1930.10, 1935.01, 1951.11
Fuller, L. 1881.38
Fuller, Larry 1957.11, 1961.26, 1962.14, 1964.11, 1970.06, 1972.05, 1978.02, 1979.06, 1979.23, 1980.04, 1980.25, 1981.27, 1982.18, 1984.10, 1984.13, 1987.09
Fuller, Lew 1908.23
Fuller, Loie 1886.45, 1886.59, 1887.13, 1887.14, 1887.32, 1887.49, 1889.29, 1892.07, 1893.24
Fuller, Lorenzo 1946.08, 1947.03, 1948.32, 1953.10
Fuller, Marion 1915.32
Fuller, Mart 1902.32
Fuller, Mart M. 1898.61
Fuller, Miss 1882.23
Fuller, Mollie 1882.21, 1884.42, 1885.58, 1886.47, 1889.41, 1890.29, 1894.17
Fuller, Molly 1895.04, 1896.30, 1900.15
Fuller, Penny 1961.12, 1970.09, 1976.08
Fuller, Richard 1911.09
Fuller, Robert 1885.02
Fuller, Rosalind 1920.08, 1921.27, 1922.21
Fuller, William 1917.26
Fuller-Golden, Mart 1919.03
Fullerton, Lew 1910.01, 1915.30
Fullerton, Nell 1887.07, 1887.16
Fulling, Edna 1926.21
Fullum, Clay 1970.15, 1971.20, 1972.11, 1973.07, 1976.28, 1978.06
Fulton, Bobby 1929.33
Fulton, Chandos 1879.10
Fulton, Charles 1918.11, 1918.29
Fulton, E.L. 1893.07
Fulton, Emily 1903.03, 1904.13, 1905.44
Fulton, J. Robert 1920.30
Fulton, Maud 1906.23
Fulton, Maude 1906.50, 1907.15, 1908.03, 1909.09
Fulton, Miss 1903.03
Fulton, R.E. 1875.10
Fulton, Rolfe 1892.27
Fulton, Thomas 1912.41
Fulton, Turnour 1892.27
Fulton, Webster C. 1890.21
Fuma, Andre 1961.01
Funami, Zelda 1977.01
Fuqua, J.C. 1966.05
Furber, Douglas 1920.41, 1923.36, 1924.01, 1925.42, 1928.02, 1929.02, 1929.51, 1986.12, 1999.23
Furber, Ed. 1901.20
Furery, G. 1883.62
Furey, J.A. 1881.26, 1882.17, 1882.60, 1884.08, 1884.34, 1884.57, 1885.13, 1885.28, 1886.04, 1888.02, 1888.20, 1889.23, 1890.01, 1890.11, 1890.19, 1892.07, 1892.52, 1894.14, 1896.18, 1897.26, 1898.43, 1899.19, 1900.20, 1904.05
Furey, James 1901.13, 1903.18
Furey, James A. 1884.51, 1892.16, 1898.20, 1900.33, 1900.41
Furle, Wallace 1929.20
Furlong, Frank 1915.25
Furman, Ariel 1968.22
Furman, Phil 1921.27
Furmansky, Abbie 1993.13
Furniss, Dorothy 1908.07
Furr, Teri 1989.27, 1991.06
Furry, E. 1886.30
Furry, James 1885.63
Furse, Roger 1965.28
Fursman, Leslie 1890.40
Furst, Tim 1998.22
Furst, Timothy Daniel 1983.07, 1986.05
Furst, W.W. 1883.33, 1893.20, 1895.43
Furst, William 1888.37, 1891.38, 1893.39, 1894.28, 1895.22, 1898.12, 1900.37
Furst, William W. 1887.49, 1892.55, 1898.34
Furstner, Miss 1894.21
Furtado, Ernie 1957.14
Furth, George 1963.13, 1970.13, 1977.16, 1981.27, 1995.11
Furth, Seymour 1904.13, 1905.20, 1906.45, 1907.15, 1907.24, 1907.34, 1907.41, 1907.42, 1908.10, 1908.21, 1909.24, 1911.24, 1915.15, 1922.23, 1925.12
Furze, John 1854.01, 1854.07, 1855.01, 1855.02, 1856.01
Furze, Miss 1854.07
Futral, Elizabeth 1992.14
Futrelle, Virginia 1920.26, 1922.16, 1922.30
Fyerson, Florence 1999.11
Fyfe, Jim 1988.20
Fyffe, C.J. 1883.36
Fyffe, Will 1932.18
Fyleman, Rose 1952.11
Fyre, Dwight 1970.10
Fysher, Nilson 1913.17

G.W. Hunt 1877.28
Gabel, Martin 1965.02
Gabel, Messr. 1872.31, 1902.13
Gabel, Mons. 1868.26, 1869.03
Gabet, Charles 1877.36, 1878.08, 1878.16, 1879.24, 1879.27, 1879.40, 1880.50, 1881.05, 1881.41, 1881.51, 1882.08, 1882.36, 1882.58, 1883.60, 1884.32, 1885.19, 1885.38, 1889.29, 1896.20, 1898.74, 1900.09, 1902.13, 1926.45, 1931.41
Gabet, Clairville 1877.36, 1878.08, 1878.16, 1879.24, 1879.27, 1879.40, 1880.50, 1881.05, 1881.41, 1881.51, 1882.36, 1882.58, 1883.60, 1884.32, 1889.29, 1896.20, 1898.74, 1900.09
Gable, June 1974.06
Gabler, Milt 1997.03
Gabler, Milton 1992.03
Gabowitz, Martin 1944.31
Gabriel, Frank 1900.16
Gabriel, Gloria 1961.07
Gabriel, Ida 1912.28
Gabriel, James 1906.46
Gabriel, Master 1901.24, 1905.05, 1908.35, 1922.14
Gabriel, Max 1894.30, 1898.35, 1898.38, 1898.56
Gabrielle, Belle 1880.68
Gabrielle, Ida 1902.16, 1903.06, 1903.34, 1905.19, 1907.26, 1910.34, 1911.11
Gabrielle, Mlle. 1873.10, 1884.43, 1884.47, 1884.50, 1884.55
Gabrielle, Pearl 1907.26
Gabrielson, Frank 1934.17, 1934.19, 1935.03, 1936.01
Gabrilov, Alexander 1925.47
Gaby, Frank 1923.23, 1924.36, 1926.37, 1929.28
Gaby, Yvonna 1926.40
Gade, J. 1985.07, 1999.18
Gade, Jacob 1997.13
Gade, Niels 1978.26
Gae, Nadine 1939.12, 1940.03, 1943.05, 1947.20
Gaebler, Mary 1980.16
Gaff, Billy 1981.24
Gaffne, Yolande 1953.10
Gaffney, Lauren 1990.02
Gaffney, Robert 1960.06
Gaffney, W.V. 1897.29
Gage, Erford 1938.02
Gage, Gary 1969.03, 1976.15
Gage, Mr. 1866.18
Gage, Nedra 1909.12
Gagel, Frederic 1890.43
Gagel, Frederick 1889.41, 1890.29, 1891.32, 1895.07, 1897.55, 1899.22
Gagel, Fritz 1885.50
Gagen, Frank 1929.12, 1929.32, 1934.40
Gaggs, Thomas H. 1888.42
Gagnon, Chick 1938.04
Gagnon, Roland 1973.16, 1976.11, 1977.08
Gahnz, Craig 1990.18
Gaiety Comic Opera Company 1885.26, 1885.40
Gaiety Theatre Company, Ltd. 1906.36
Gaige, Crosby 1937.01
Gaige, Russell 1957.03
Gaige, Trueman 1934.13
Gaige, Truman 1929.39, 1931.07, 1934.43, 1937.17, 1938.07, 1953.16, 1959.27, 1965.22, 1973.12
Gaillard, Alice 1888.24, 1889.10, 1897.22
Gaillard, F. 1887.20
Gaillard, Francis 1886.34, 1888.19, 1889.10, 1909.01, 1915.32
Gaillard, Marion 1929.10, 1929.13, 1929.14, 1929.15, 1929.16
Gaillard, Mme. 1913.15
Gaillard, Mons. 1884.43, 1884.47, 1884.49, 1884.50, 1884.52, 1885.23, 1885.61
Gaillard, Mr. 1897.22
Gaillard, Slim 1939.29
Gaily, Grace 1892.15
Gain, Richard 1959.06
Gaines, Angie 1893.49
Gaines, Beverly 1956.04
Gaines, Boyd 1993.10, 1995.11, 2000.07
Gaines, David 1980.19
Gaines, Davis 1986.14
Gaines, Irene 1904.38
Gaines, John 1927.01
Gaines, Lee 1945.08, 1981.06
Gaines, Leslie "Bubba" 1980.10
Gaines, Marjorie 1930.21
Gaines, Muriel 1946.15
Gaines, Reg E. 1996.07
Gaines, Rosemary 1956.01
Gaines, Sonny Jim 1991.01
Gainey, Andrew 1948.31
Gainina, Ai-Gul 1976.18
Gairabetoff, Messr. 1929.05
Gaites, Joseph 1905.40
Gaites, Joseph M. 1899.13, 1908.18, 1910.09, 1911.15, 1911.25, 1911.38, 1913.10, 1919.07, 1922.01
Gaither, David 1926.38
Gaither, Gant 1955.10
Gaithers, Lita 1999.09
Gaithright, Margaret 1962.05
Gaity Company 1888.38
Gajda, Lisa 1999.01
Gal, Nir Ben 1989.10
Galagher, Charles E. 1926.08, 1927.65, 1929.43, 1930.12, 1934.41
Galahoff, Basil 1936.05, 1938.15, 1939.13
Galan, Esperanza 1974.16, 1975.16, 1976.23, 1977.11, 1978.19, 1979.20, 1980.03, 1980.22, 1981.22, 1982.16, 1983.12, 1985.11, 1985.13, 1986.09, 1986.10, 1986.14, 1987.11, 1988.14, 1988.16, 1988.18, 1991.09
Galanta, Katherine 1917.24
Galantich, Tom 1989.29
Galasso, Michael 1975.10
Galati, Frank 1998.01, 2000.18
Galbraith, Ruth 1907.38
Galbreath, Sally 1929.34
Galde, Anthony 1989.25, 1999.08
Gale 1884.12, 1884.17
Gale, Andy 1986.13, 1997.17
Gale, Catherine 1962.04
Gale, Charles 1927.48
Gale, Charlotte 1898.10
Gale, Eddie 1938.07
Gale, Edwin 1938.07
Gale, George W. 1887.13
Gale, Gregory 1999.05
Gale, Jane 1930.11
Gale, Jean 1930.11
Gale, Joan 1930.11
Gale, June 1930.11
Gale, Lotta 1895.12
Gale, Martha 1929.48
Gale, Nita 1934.37
Gale, Roberta 1927.11
Gale, Sandra 1931.14
Gale, Sherry 1926.30
Gale, Shirley 1938.10
Gale, Victory 1902.44
Gale, Walter 1878.11, 1880.21, 1881.10, 1882.82, 1886.13, 1887.02, 1887.42, 1888.25, 1889.43, 1890.36, 1894.52, 1904.32
Gale, William 1886.34
Galer, Lillian 1916.22
Galey, Grace 1892.21
Gali, Gali 1948.21
Galiber, Doris 1961.07
Galinde, R.P. 1907.42
Galindo, Ramon 1983.01, 1989.03
Galjour, Warren 1951.22, 1953.03, 1963.05
Gall, Robert 1965.30, 1974.19, 1983.03
Gall, Tami 1972.17
Gallagher 1883.47
Gallagher, Betty 1926.30, 1930.30
Gallagher, Charles 1911.10, 1912.10
Gallagher, Charles E. 1929.40
Gallagher, Dan 1943.08, 1944.23
Gallagher, David 1994.12
Gallagher, Dick 1995.12, 2000.16
Gallagher, Ed 1922.19, 1923.20
Gallagher, Edward 1912.15, 1920.02
Gallagher, Frank 1929.48
Gallagher, Gina 1988.09
Gallagher, Helen 1945.12, 1945.20, 1947.07, 1947.16, 1949.12, 1951.13, 1952.01, 1953.01, 1955.06, 1955.09, 1957.03, 1958.04, 1958.07, 1966.01, 1970.10, 1971.03
Gallagher, Ida 1879.29
Gallagher, Joe 2001.06
Gallagher, Juliana 1947.02
Gallagher, M. 1888.45
Gallagher, M.J. 1884.16
Gallagher, Maggie 1886.23
Gallagher, Matt 1891.16
Gallagher, May 1875.18
Gallagher, Michael 1976.25, 1978.28
Gallagher, Peter 1982.18, 1992.04
Gallagher, Richard 1922.41, 1924.21, 1924.41, 1925.38, 1927.12
Gallagher, Robert 1951.19, 1954.04, 1954.14
Gallagher, Skeet 1922.01
Gallaudet, John 1931.05, 1931.42
Gallaudet, John B. 1925.35
Gallaway, Edward 1935.17
Galleti, E. 1911.19
Galletti, Annetta 1862.03, 1863.06, 1863.07
Galli, Augusto 1932.29, 1934.02, 1940.05
Galli, Nino 1934.02
Galliand, Miss 1881.04
Gallico, Paul 1961.10, 1968.32
Gallier, Miss 1926.01
Gallimore, Catherine 1923.38, 1926.01, 1927.58
Gallimore, Katherine 1931.05
Gallimore, Peggy 1926.16
Gallis, Paul 1993.17
Gallo, David 1998.15, 1999.03
Gallo, Little Norma 1919.10
Gallo, Norma 1920.19, 1926.28
Gallo, Paul 1980.27, 1985.18, 1986.20, 1987.15, 1989.29, 1992.02, 1992.04, 1996.06, 1996.08, 1997.06, 1997.18, 1998.03, 1998.16, 1999.08, 2000.17, 2001.08
Gallois 1915.21
Gallop, Sammy 1949.02, 1990.09
Gallot, Messr. 1844.01
Gallot, Mrs. 1844.01
Galloway, Edward 1938.09
Galloway, Goodie 1927.14
Galloway, J. 1883.29
Galloway, James T. 1888.08, 1890.32, 1892.18, 1892.45, 1896.31
Galloway, Jane 1982.05
Galloway, Katherine 1916.08, 1918.22
Galloway, Leata 1968.11, 1971.01, 1976.03, 1984.02
Galloway, Louise 1904.14, 1926.06
Galloway, Messr. 1861.03, 1882.34
Galloway, Selby 1926.15
Galloway, Tod B. 1943.23
Gallup, Sammy 1953.17
Gallus, Robert 1998.05
Galon, Jack 1916.25
Galpen, William 1917.12
Galperin, Mikhail 1925.46, 1925.51
Galston, Phil 1976.34
Galton, Blanche 1868.20, 1870.39, 1870.43, 1872.20, 1879.05
Galton, C.P. 1913.36
Galton, Joseph 1909.04
Galton, Joseph P. 1913.08, 1914.10, 1914.16
Galton, Susan 1868.20, 1872.10
Galton, Susan Pyne 1868.20
Galuback, Helen 1938.16
Galuten, Albhy 1999.15
Galvan, Gil 1941.07
Galvez, Lorenzo 1992.15
Galvin, Gene 1946.05, 1959.05
Gama, Philip 1977.01
Gamache, Laurie 1993.19
Gambacorta, Leo 1980.10
Gamble, Glenn 1920.41
Gamble, Kenneth 1997.21
Gambles, Eva A. 1897.33
Gamboa, Marcelo 1968.32, 1970.11
Gambogi, Mons. 1869.16, 1869.30
Gamboji, Mons. 1869.05
Gameron, Charles 1894.13
Games, Albert 1879.28
Gamet, Steve 1968.11
Gamez, Carmen 1949.07
Gamlin, Douglas 1955.19
Gammage, Florence 1902.07
Gammage, William 1908.39
Gammon, William 1969.03, 1976.28
Gamo, Formiguinha 1992.13
Gampel, Chris 1963.29
Ganay, Lydia Pinkus 1969.13, 1973.01
Gandell, Linda 1972.04
Gandolfi, Alfredo 1935.02
Ganeau, Wilda 1927.40

Ganes, Margery 1905.28
Ganes, Marjory 1907.26
Ganley, Mary 1943.05
Gannaway, Lynne 1974.06, 1979.29
Ganne, Louis 1911.03, 1911.16
Ganne, M. Louis 1910.24
Gannon, Belle 1926.30
Gannon, James 1957.11, 1957.18, 1961.14
Gannon, Joe 1989.08
Gannon, Kim 1951.18
Gannon, Mary 1856.04
Gannzman, Mr. 1868.06
Ganor, Warwick 1897.46
Gans, Danny 1995.17
Gans, George 1894.26, 1896.35
Gansert, Jack 1943.11, 1944.24, 1945.11
Gant, Henry 1907.22
Gant, Mabel 1926.19
Ganthony, Richard 1901.17
Gantillon 1885.05
Gantvoort, Carl 1912.19, 1913.09, 1913.37, 1916.04, 1917.20, 1918.27, 1918.35
Gantvoort, Herman 1929.46
Gantzberg, Martha 1920.46
Ganun, John 1994.01
Gany, Lydia Pincus 1971.14
Ganz, Al 1941.11
Ganzer, Johnn 1982.03
Garat, Henri 1926.01
Garaventz, Georges 1983.03
Garbayo, Joaquin Gaztambide y 1881.24
Garber, Victor 1979.06, 1982.01, 1994.01
Garbit 1875.04
Garbit, James 1885.66
Garboat, M. 1925.37
Garces, John 1963.18
Garchery, Gaston 1929.10, 1929.13, 1929.15, 1929.16
Garcia, Bob 2000.04
Garcia, Graciela 1993.08
Garcia, Luisa 1949.07
Garcia, Nino 1969.11
Garcia, Rita 1928.08
Garcia, Ruben 1934.42
Garcia, Victor Cardenas 1988.15
Garde, Betty 1943.04, 1958.07, 1963.06
Gardeen, Gertrude 1929.01
Gardel 1985.07
Gardel, C. 1997.13
Gardell, Tony 1945.20, 1950.17, 1955.02, 1958.20, 1960.10, 1962.16
Gardella, Tess 1927.67, 1932.11
Gardella, Theresa 1921.22
Gardella, Toni-Ann 1978.07, 1978.19, 1978.20, 1979.20, 1979.21, 1989.13, 1996.02
Gardella, Veronica 1993.08
Garden, E.W. 1895.43
Garden, Louis 1942.33
Gardener, Darcy 1946.10
Gardener, Messr. 1854.04
Gardenier, Ed 1902.24, 1903.23, 1904.31, 1907.33, 1907.47
Gardenier, Ed. 1901.16
Gardenier, Edward 1908.28
Gardet, M. 1929.10
Gardie, Madame 1796.01
Gardiner, Arline 1919.07, 1926.21
Gardiner, C.R. 1888.43
Gardiner, E. Gertrude 1884.60
Gardiner, Edgar 1919.07, 1924.11, 1926.21, 1927.35, 1928.08
Gardiner, Edith 1913.34
Gardiner, Elizabeth 1908.44
Gardiner, Evelyn 1936.13, 1936.16, 1936.18, 1936.19, 1936.21, 1936.23, 1936.24, 1936.25, 1939.02, 1939.03, 1939.04, 1939.08, 1939.09, 1939.11
Gardiner, Frank 1926.36, 1928.01
Gardiner, Helen 1919.07
Gardiner, Helene 1925.33
Gardiner, James W. 1945.18, 1955.01
Gardiner, Jimmy 1943.07
Gardiner, Joshua 1972.20
Gardiner, May 1900.08
Gardiner, Reginald 1935.12, 1936.31, 1952.11, 1964.20
Gardiner, Vincent 1938.04
Gardner 1883.47
Gardner, A. 1881.14
Gardner, Ada 1900.35
Gardner, Amelia 1894.29, 1918.07
Gardner, Amy 1889.44
Gardner, Andy 1900.35
Gardner, Ann 1969.04
Gardner, Annie 1881.03
Gardner, Bert 1918.28, 1926.02, 1927.19
Gardner, Callie T. 1892.15
Gardner, Charles 1894.46
Gardner, Charles A. 1879.38, 1880.24, 1886.56, 1891.20, 1892.31
Gardner, Dan 1896.38
Gardner, David 1921.02
Gardner, Dick 1896.38
Gardner, E. 1882.41
Gardner, Elizabeth 1908.21
Gardner, Ella 1902.42
Gardner, Evelyn 1936.15
Gardner, Frank 1892.15
Gardner, Frank L. 1886.02
Gardner, Garold 1959.02, 1960.01
Gardner, Gertrude 1885.08
Gardner, Horace M. 1919.23
Gardner, Jack 1896.38, 1900.35, 1906.47, 1907.57, 1908.14, 1908.27, 1910.22
Gardner, Jack E. 1909.22
Gardner, Jake 1983.16
Gardner, Jeff 1997.19
Gardner, Joan 1923.30
Gardner, Kitty 1898.34
Gardner, L. 1881.14
Gardner, Louise 1904.09
Gardner, Lynn 1943.21
Gardner, M. 1881.38
Gardner, Messr. 1878.05
Gardner, Mr. 1848.04, 1883.49
Gardner, Patricia 1945.16
Gardner, Rita 1962.01, 1963.17
Gardner, Rose 1931.44
Gardner, Sammy 1936.30
Gardner, Tony 1971.12
Gardner, Will 1892.15
Gardner, William 1982.10
Gardy 1888.23, 1893.45
Garen, James 1905.09
Garey, James R. 1907.28
Garfield, David 1970.15
Garfield, F. 1902.15
Garfield, Frank 1904.03
Garfield, Gil 1979.30
Garfield, Jules 1936.28
Garfield, Matt 1996.04
Garfield, Randy 1962.01
Garfinkel, Judith 1981.21
Garfinkle, Louis 1973.11
Gargan, Edward 1927.10, 1932.05
Gari, Brian 1987.14
Garinei, Pietro 1964.03
Garing, A.J. 1919.22, 1920.26, 1921.28, 1922.30
Garlan, Ann 1942.05
Garland's Burlesque and Comedy Company 1867.22, 1867.23, 1867.26, 1867.27, 1867.29, 1867.31
Garland, C.H. 1867.22, 1867.23, 1867.26, 1867.27, 1867.29, 1867.31
Garland, Charles 1927.18, 1930.37, 1931.36
Garland, Gene 1895.39
Garland, Geoff 1973.07, 1982.24
Garland, Jacki 1968.01
Garland, Jamil K. 1980.14, 1982.17
Garland, Joe 1973.14, 1974.09, 1975.12, 1999.24
Garland, Judy 1967.11
Garland, Marc 1987.20
Garland, Patricia 1975.15
Garlick, David 1984.07
Garn, Jack 1927.36, 1927.40
Garneau, Lois 1902.25
Garnell, Grant 1945.15
Garnella, Bob 1882.01, 1882.77
Garnella, Dick 1882.01, 1882.77
Garnella, Richard 1888.03, 1899.17
Garnella, Robert 1888.03
Garner, Andre 1999.22
Garner, Andrew 2000.11
Garner, Erroll 1995.14
Garner, Jay 1969.03, 1975.06, 1978.13, 1995.13
Garner, Luvenia 1983.04
Garner, Martin 1973.11
Garner, Mitzi 1934.15
Garner, Mitzie 1932.26
Garner, Paul 1931.05
Garner, Ward 1946.10, 1948.18
Garnett, Chip 1974.06, 1976.04
Garnett, David 1990.04
Garon, Pauline 1919.14, 1919.31
Garr, Eddie 1933.05, 1934.42, 1942.21
Garr, Ginna 1965.15
Garr, Nicholas 1989.03
Garreau, Claude 1952.08
Garrene, William 1889.02
Garret, Harrison 1917.11
Garrett, Becky 1980.12
Garrett, Betty 1942.05, 1942.26, 1943.01, 1944.01, 1944.30, 1946.10, 1960.01, 1963.19, 1989.23, 2001.02
Garrett, Frank 1880.01, 1880.03
Garrett, Harrison 1912.31
Garrett, James 1926.46
Garrett, Joy 1971.20
Garrett, Kelly 1972.21, 1974.10, 1975.05
Garrett, Lloyd 1920.17, 1920.24, 1921.22, 1924.11, 1926.16
Garrett, Louise 1908.34
Garrett, Maggie 1891.03
Garrett, Russell 1999.13
Garrett, Tom 1980.16, 1982.06
Garrette, Elsa 1917.11
Garretty, Minnie 1900.38
Garretty, Sissie 1900.38
Garrick Burlesque Company 1895.17
Garrick, Bell 1897.04
Garrick, Beulah 1959.04, 1981.12
Garrick, Cecilia 1898.46
Garrick, David 1898.11
Garrick, Helena Collier 1912.07, 1912.44
Garrick, John 1932.01
Garrick, M.J. 1899.13
Garrick, Richard 1911.17
Garrick, Yvonne 1918.08
Garrison, Anne 1923.41
Garrison, Arthur 1960.09
Garrison, David 1978.06, 1980.08, 2001.03
Garrison, Gregory 1989.03
Garrison, Jon 1987.08
Garrison, Messr. 1895.44
Garry Van Egmond 1999.02
Garry, Ian 1966.27
Gars, Mindy 1981.21
Garson, Betty 1924.17
Garson, John 1965.04
Garson, Marion 1903.39, 1906.37, 1909.12
Garstin, Herbert 1937.10
Garth, Caswell 1934.29
Garth, III., John 1946.12
Garth, John 1935.13, 1942.03
Gartlan, George T. 1906.50
Garuffi, Carlo 1935.02
Garuffi, Maria 1935.02
Garvarentz, Georges 1963.02, 1964.02, 1965.08, 1965.30, 1974.19
Garver, Martha 1904.03
Garvey, Miss 1848.01
Garvie, Eddie 1905.55, 1907.01, 1918.39, 1920.15, 1932.15
Garvie, Edward 1894.06, 1894.37, 1897.01, 1900.47, 1904.24, 1908.25, 1909.29, 1910.10, 1911.30, 1913.19, 1918.09, 1929.32
Gary, Bill 1943.02
Gary, Cora 1926.31
Gary, George Branson 1977.03
Gary, Harold 1941.03, 1946.17, 1961.21, 1967.05, 1976.19
Gary, Romain 1987.12
Gary, Ted 1939.13, 1940.09, 1941.03
Gary, Willard 1940.03
Garza, Ronald 1987.05
Garza, Troy 1979.15
Garzon, Gustavo 1949.07
Gase, Leslie 1913.37
Gaskill, Clarence 1922.08, 1925.25, 1925.48, 1928.47, 1929.24, 1963.10, 1980.10
Gaskin, George 1891.15
Gaskin, Leonard 1955.05
Gaskins, Pauline 1929.24, 1931.42
Gasman, Ira 1997.08
Gaspar, Eddie 1960.08
Gaspar, Marie 1920.08
Gasparinetti, Trudi 1959.05
Gasparo, John B. 1910.06
Gasparo, Marion 1911.04
Gasper, Eddie 1962.27, 1966.01, 1969.01
Gassner, Florence 1959.12
Gast, Florence 1921.03
Gaste, Loulou 1959.15
Gastineau 1877.39
Gastineau, Clairville 1880.58
Gastineau, Octave 1880.58
Gaston, B. 1884.41
Gaston, Billy 1905.55, 1907.24, 1908.05, 1912.36, 1927.62
Gaston, George 1879.14, 1881.38, 1882.42, 1882.47, 1882.52, 1882.71, 1883.18, 1883.24, 1884.30, 1884.31, 1899.06, 1918.30
Gaston, Ken 1971.02, 1972.11
Gaston, Lydia 1993.19
Gaston, Penny 1962.14
Gaston, Walter 1901.20
Gaston, William 1909.23
Gatchell and Neufeld, Ltd. 1987.05
Gatchell, Jr., R. Tyler 1974.24, 1979.23, 1982.19, 1984.07, 1985.12
Gatchell, Tyler 1971.12, 1988.09
Gately, David 1979.20
Gates and E.A. Morange 1900.19
Gates and Morange 1895.21, 1899.29, 1899.31, 1900.16, 1901.04, 1903.26, 1904.20, 1904.55, 1905.10, 1905.11, 1905.45, 1906.05, 1906.27, 1909.02, 1909.31, 1910.08, 1910.12, 1911.13, 1912.19, 1913.19, 1913.25, 1915.24, 1918.25, 1922.19, 1922.45, 1923.20, 1923.47, 1924.07, 1924.18, 1928.44, 1930.36
Gates, Aaron 1927.30
Gates, Dorothy 1919.22, 1922.30
Gates, Earl 1919.24
Gates, Frank 1898.77, 1899.40, 1900.01, 1905.33, 1906.40, 1907.30, 1907.62, 1908.02, 1908.34, 1913.17, 1914.20, 1916.06, 1919.08, 1919.23, 1920.11, 1921.36
Gates, Frank E. 1895.03, 1895.21, 1898.55, 1899.06, 1903.07, 1905.03, 1906.33, 1907.02, 1907.08, 1907.18, 1908.07, 1908.36, 1911.13, 1923.05, 1923.45, 1924.28, 1926.51, 1927.06, 1929.31, 1929.37
Gates, George S. 1893.49
Gates, Lewis 1908.07
Gates, Ruth 1948.20
Gateson, Marjorie 1913.31, 1915.28, 1917.01, 1918.12, 1918.35, 1919.16, 1920.30, 1921.03, 1921.33, 1922.10, 1923.01, 1924.03, 1926.20, 1927.20, 1947.04, 1954.04
Gathright, Margaret 1961.26
Gatinaeu, Mlle. 1883.57
Gatineau, Mlle. 1883.30, 1884.01, 1884.43, 1884.54, 1884.55
Gatineau, Mme. 1883.28
Gatts, George M. 1925.19, 1943.02
Gauder, George L. 1918.38
Gaudin, Kevin Michael 1999.24
Gaudio, Gino 1982.14
Gaudreau, Hazel 1924.11
Gaugain, Marie 1876.36, 1877.04, 1877.15
Gaugain, Mlle. 1870.41
Gaughan, John 1984.16, 1994.04, 1999.16
Gaul, Franz 1884.40, 1890.08
Gauld, Carlton 1944.26
Gault, Warner 1919.18, 1921.19
Gaumont, Irving 1952.08
Gaunt, Messr. 1883.17, 1883.23
Gaunt, P.B. 1883.19
Gaunt, Percy 1888.32, 1888.44, 1889.12, 1891.39, 1893.23, 1894.07, 1894.35, 1894.37, 1895.14
Gaunt, Richard 1896.25
Gaunt, William 1899.30
Gaunt, William G. 1899.06
Gaus, Robert 1969.06
Gausins, Constant 1870.30, 1870.41, 1870.45, 1871.03, 1871.06, 1871.07
Gaut, Louis 1918.21
Gauthier, Donat 1924.21
Gauthier, Juliette 1926.17
Gauthier, Katherine 1929.20
Gauthron, Bernard 1965.37
Gautier, Dick 1960.06
Gautier, Leonard 1943.13
Gautier, Mlle. 1888.39
Gautier, Rose 1894.43
Gautier, Theophile 1956.11
Gauvin, J.A. 1929.10, 1929.11, 1929.13, 1929.14, 1929.15, 1929.16
Gavant, Mons. 1879.19, 1879.39, 1879.49, 1879.51, 1879.61, 1880.29, 1880.56
Gavant, Monsieur 1888.01
Gavarentz, Georges 1970.01
Gavault, Paul 1900.34
Gavaut, Messr. 1879.26, 1879.44
Gavin, Gene 1957.05, 1961.15, 1961.18, 1962.14, 1962.27
Gavin, Jerry 1976.34

Gavin, Kevin 1976.34
Gavin, Tommy 1936.22
Gavito, Carlos 1997.13
Gavon, Igors 1961.10, 1964.01, 1967.01, 1972.04, 1975.22, 1979.29
Gawger, Jennie 1877.20
Gaxton, William 1922.39, 1924.33, 1927.56, 1929.45, 1931.48, 1933.13, 1933.25, 1934.36, 1936.22, 1938.13, 1940.08, 1942.12, 1945.09, 1946.04
Gay, Alden 1920.28, 1921.27, 1923.22, 1923.44, 1925.31
Gay, Byron 1918.07, 1919.18, 1923.19
Gay, C. 1868.06
Gay, Charles 1920.43
Gay, Charles A. 1910.33
Gay, Dorothy 1925.19
Gay, Irene 1867.32
Gay, J. 1867.12
Gay, John 1750.01, 1854.06, 1855.08, 1859.04, 1928.13, 1933.07, 1946.24, 1957.02, 1965.04, 1973.16
Gay, Katherine 1897.24
Gay, Lawrence 1902.39
Gay, Maisie 1911.39, 1916.01, 1922.05
Gay, Messr. 1865.11
Gay, Miss 1867.13, 1867.14, 1867.15, 1868.06, 1876.03, 1920.35
Gay, Mr. 1866.02
Gay, Nadine 1940.19
Gay, Noel 1927.02, 1930.38, 1942.12, 1986.12
Gay, Sophie 1866.23, 1869.19
Gaye, Gregory 1932.03
Gaye, Marvin 1997.21
Gayer, Echlin 1918.26
Gayer, Echlin P. 1905.37
Gayer, Joseph 1990.13
Gayle, Marvin 1986.02
Gaylen, Diana 1937.03, 1938.05
Gayler, Charles 1857.04, 1862.05, 1865.03, 1870.24, 1871.15, 1871.22, 1873.24, 1887.11
Gayler, Grace 1894.16
Gayler, Mollie 1893.22
Gaylor, Bobby 1899.36, 1900.15, 1903.03
Gaylor, Charles 1867.18
Gaylor, James 1922.23, 1925.37
Gaylor, May 1892.23
Gaylor, Minnie 1898.12, 1898.50
Gaylor, Mollie 1898.12
Gaylor, Mr. 1851.03
Gaylor, Robert 1892.23
Gaylord, Al E. 1908.09
Gaylord, Janet 1947.20, 1963.12
Gaylord, Willie 1878.10
Gaynes, Edmund 1958.01
Gaynes, George 1952.12, 1953.03, 1957.02, 1959.18, 1961.03, 1961.05, 1961.19, 1962.06, 1962.08, 1962.10, 1962.11, 1962.13, 1964.07, 1964.09, 1964.12, 1964.14, 1965.11, 1965.13, 1973.12
Gaynes, Kathy 1945.17
Gaynes, Kim 1945.17
Gaynor, Charles 1948.30, 1961.01, 1973.05
Gaynor, Gay 1943.18
Gaynor, Jane 1978.09
Gaythorne, Pamela 1912.03
Gaze, Heino 1965.08
Gaze, Leslie 1909.09, 1910.10
Gear, Louella 1942.27
Gear, Luella 1917.02, 1923.08, 1923.27, 1926.25, 1928.04, 1928.35, 1932.26, 1934.19, 1936.05, 1939.22, 1941.03, 1948.27
Gearhart, Livingston 1955.13
Geary, Arthur 1913.02, 1917.14, 1917.30, 1918.23, 1919.22, 1920.26, 1926.27, 1928.15
Geary, Gil 1896.49
Geary, J.J. 1891.41
Geary, Joyce 1955.11
Geary, Messr. 1852.01
Geary, Mina 1866.19
Geary, Mr. 1851.08
Geary, Steve 2000.07
GeBauer, Gene 1972.04
Gebe 1982.23
Geber, Mr. 1893.29
Gebert, Gus 1891.18
Gebest, Charles 1899.11, 1907.16, 1909.26
Gebest, Charles J. 1901.07, 1903.11, 1904.42, 1906.11, 1906.21, 1907.09, 1907.57, 1908.09, 1908.14, 1908.31, 1910.17, 1911.41, 1912.11, 1914.13, 1914.34, 1916.02, 1917.37, 1920.38, 1921.32, 1922.43, 1923.46, 1927.47, 1928.31
Gebhardt, George 1946.17
Gebirtig, M. 1990.16
Gebirtig, Mordecai 1966.21, 1998.11
Geddes, Carre 1869.06
Geddes, Ida 1869.35
Geddis, Ralph 1927.23
Gedge, James 1983.05
Gedney, Judge 1884.59
Gedney, William 1919.38
Gee, Lottie 1921.16, 1924.27
Gee, Simone 1989.05
Geer, Will 1937.08, 1938.09, 1947.21, 1963.26
Geery, Messr. 1852.05
Geery, William 1940.11
Geffen, David 1982.19
Geffner, Deborah 1976.19
Gehlert, Gerald 1928.48
Gehm, Charlene 1980.02
Gehring, Dean 1940.13
Gehrue, Daisy 1901.04
Gehrue, Mayme 1900.03, 1900.20, 1900.49, 1900.56, 1901.12, 1901.17, 1906.13, 1910.29, 1912.08
Geiber, Milt 1918.21
Geier, Jack 1919.34
Geiger, Henry 1925.17
Geiger, Sigrid 1959.05
Geisel, Theodore 2000.18
Geiser, Maxine 1941.01
Geiss, Tony 1962.02, 1968.13
Geistinger, Marie 1882.68
Gelb, Jody 1993.06
Gelb, Sandra 1993.13
Gelbart, Larry 1961.02, 1972.03, 1989.03, 1989.29, 1996.06
Gelbtrunk, Adam 1936.22
Geld, Gary 1970.05, 1972.26, 1975.03, 1978.10, 1989.17
Gelder, George 1897.45
Geleznova, Katia 1944.16, 1954.01, 1954.12, 1963.08
Gelfer, Steven 1974.17, 1979.05, 1982.19
Gelikhovsky, Messr. 1929.05
Gelikhovsky, Mme. 1929.05
Gelke, Becky 1978.13
Gellert, Marie 1902.02
Gelli, Cesare 1964.03
Gelman, Sandra 1937.14
Gemigani, Sam 1978.02
Gemignani, Paul 1976.02, 1976.33, 1977.05, 1979.06, 1981.27, 1982.18, 1984.01, 1984.08, 1984.13, 1985.05, 1985.09, 1986.04, 1986.09, 1986.20, 1987.03, 1987.09, 1988.07, 1989.03, 1990.07, 1991.08, 1991.12, 1992.02, 1992.10, 1994.05, 1994.12, 1995.19, 1996.08, 1996.15, 1997.15, 1997.22, 1998.05, 1998.20, 1999.19, 1999.21, 2000.19, 2001.06
Gemp, Robert 1901.24
Gems, Pam 1981.04, 1999.07
Gendell, Gary 1969.14, 1975.14
Gendron, Lyn 1982.15
Gene and Jeanne 1929.23
Gene, Adeline 1908.07
Gene, Alexander 1909.28
Genee, Adeline 1909.28, 1910.34
Genee, Alexander 1908.07
Genee, Richard 1879.22, 1879.25, 1879.57, 1879.65, 1879.67, 1880.04, 1880.20, 1880.26, 1880.31, 1880.48, 1880.57, 1880.62, 1880.66, 1881.04, 1881.25, 1881.42, 1881.44, 1882.07, 1882.15, 1882.16, 1882.45, 1882.57, 1882.65, 1882.71, 1883.08, 1883.11, 1883.41, 1883.55, 1883.62, 1884.08, 1884.18, 1884.51, 1884.52, 1884.64, 1885.01, 1885.05, 1885.08, 1885.11, 1885.14, 1885.41, 1885.52, 1885.63, 1886.36, 1887.15, 1887.20, 1887.26, 1887.41, 1888.26, 1889.17, 1889.22, 1892.03, 1892.28, 1897.53, 1898.15, 1898.30, 1898.49, 1898.62, 1899.05, 1899.42, 1900.02, 1900.23, 1900.30, 1904.57, 1905.11, 1912.27, 1913.08, 1931.44, 1932.23, 1933.23, 1953.06, 1953.15, 1954.06, 1954.10, 1955.17, 1956.10, 1957.13, 1958.15, 1959.16, 1964.31, 1965.25, 1974.16, 1975.16, 1976.23, 1977.11, 1980.03, 1980.22, 1981.22, 1984.03, 1986.10, 1987.11
Genest, Edmond 1980.30
Geneva, Alice 1935.01
Geneva, Florence 1912.34
Genevieve 1962.13
Genevieve, Mme. 1925.35
Gennaro, Liza 1992.01, 1996.18
Gennaro, Peter 1950.17, 1954.05, 1955.10, 1956.14, 1957.12, 1959.25, 1960.08, 1960.20, 1962.20, 1964.17, 1964.40, 1969.14, 1973.05, 1977.06, 1979.09, 1980.02, 1982.01, 1985.08, 1989.03, 1989.24, 1997.04
Gennell, Hettie 1887.03
Gennert, Henry 1928.45
Genni, Gwynne 1925.05
Genot, Mons. 1868.24, 1868.26, 1869.03, 1869.16, 1870.03, 1875.02, 1875.04, 1875.08
Genovese, Gen 1952.13
Gensler, Lewis 1922.38, 1924.30, 1925.01, 1925.23, 1932.16
Gensler, Lewis E. 1922.42, 1923.31, 1925.29, 1926.25, 1928.35, 1930.28, 1931.05, 1986.06
Gentile, Nick 1955.07
Gentle, A. 1900.41
Gentle, Alice 1910.24, 1912.08, 1912.49
Gentles, Avril 1972.23, 1983.05
Gentner, Norma 1945.04
Gentry, James B. 1894.38
Gentry, James E. 1891.37, 1893.08
Gentry, Joseph 1962.04, 1966.06
Gentry, Ken 2001.09
Gentry, Michael 1962.04, 1966.06
Gentry, Minnie 1971.13
Genty, Mary 1981.11
Genty, Philippe 1981.11
Genus, Karl 1958.04
Geoffrey, Doug 1938.08
Geoffreys, Minnie 1887.05
Geoffreys, Stephen 1984.02
Geoffroy, Coralie 1875.04, 1875.13, 1875.25, 1875.28, 1875.29, 1875.30, 1875.33
George Conquest Pantomine and Burlesque Company 1880.34
George MacFarlane Productions, Inc. 1926.06
George Street Playhouse 1995.14
George Thatcher's Minstrels 1891.32
George W. Dayton and Sons 1882.78, 1883.16, 1883.42
George, Ben 1989.26, 1993.18
George, Betty 1948.23, 1955.04
George, Byron 1878.19
George, Carl H. 1908.23
George, Carolyn 1954.12, 1957.05
George, Charles 1922.17
George, D. 1999.24
George, Don 1938.08, 1981.06, 1997.03
George, Doris 1927.35
George, Fred 1907.38, 1908.33
George, George B. 1919.31
George, George W. 1964.33, 1972.25
George, H. 1868.19, 1884.58
George, Hal 1983.14
George, Helen 1945.15
George, Irene 1910.10
George, J.W. 1881.30
George, Jeffry 1978.13
George, John 1956.03
George, Joseph 1901.05, 1903.16
George, Kathleen 1923.43
George, L. 1884.41
George, Lovette 1994.02, 1999.22
George, Marie 1893.20, 1897.26, 1897.26, 1897.39, 1898.43, 1898.72, 1899.15, 1899.25, 1901.13
George, Marion 1913.29
George, Martha 1908.16
George, Master 1868.06, 1868.18, 1885.49
George, Messr. 1852.01
George, Miss 1915.17
George, Nancy 1750.01
George, Philip 1945.02
George, Phyllis 1927.35
George, Ray 1921.08
George, Russel 1948.18
George, Russell 1947.02
George, Walter 1944.13
George, Yvonne 1922.32, 1926.01
George, Zelma 1950.13
George-Jacquin, Mr. 1891.18
Georges, M. 1929.10
Georgi, James 1915.27
Georgi, Lucie 1904.35
Georgia, Little 1878.12
Georgianna, Miss 1865.05
Georgianna, Mlle. 1865.07, 1865.08
Georgiou, Vilma 1952.12
Gepp, Edward 1917.37
Gerace, Julia 1957.06
Geraci, Paul 1989.27, 1991.06
Geraghty, Bob 1929.26, 1931.26
Gerald, Ara 1926.14
Gerald, Catherine 1891.14, 1892.06
Gerald, Charles 1968.02
Gerald, Florence 1909.31
Gerald, Jack 1942.26
Gerald, John 1940.16
Gerald, May 1919.22
Gerald, Mesdame 1852.05
Gerald, Nita 1879.38, 1880.05
Geram, Mons. 1892.53
Gerard, Anne-Marie 1989.25
Gerard, Ben 1970.14
Gerard, Bettina 1891.23, 1903.19
Gerard, Danny 1986.18
Gerard, Douglas 1932.27
Gerard, Eddie 1924.22
Gerard, Elaine 1927.11
Gerard, Frank 1906.31
Gerard, Geraldine 1911.18
Gerard, Gil 1983.15
Gerard, Grand 1917.25
Gerard, James 1944.04, 1944.06, 1944.08, 1944.13
Gerard, Lucy 1912.09
Gerard, Messr. 1879.51, 1880.60, 1882.55, 1883.28
Gerard, Miss 1899.37, 1904.13, 1904.44
Gerard, Mons. 1875.25, 1875.28, 1875.29, 1876.20, 1876.28, 1877.11, 1877.14, 1877.26, 1877.29, 1877.30, 1877.33, 1878.06, 1879.49, 1879.55, 1879.60, 1879.69, 1880.14, 1880.16, 1880.27, 1880.56, 1883.27, 1883.54, 1883.55, 1883.57, 1883.60, 1883.61, 1884.01, 1884.02, 1884.03, 1884.47
Gerard, Philippe 1961.25, 1964.22
Gerard, Richard H. 1902.08
Gerard, Rolf 1952.11, 1960.13, 1963.08
Gerard, Sadie 1900.33
Gerard, Saida 1940.18
Gerard, Will 1983.17
Gerarde, Aimee 1900.52
Geraud, Rene 1888.11
Geray, Steve 1939.31
Gerber, Alex 1919.08, 1919.18, 1919.35, 1920.18, 1920.25, 1920.47, 1921.18, 1921.19, 1922.11, 1922.15, 1924.29
Gerber, Bill 1973.08
Gerber, Billie 1929.29
Gerber, Ella 1965.03
Gerber, Hugo 1895.38
Gerber, Jonathan S. 1985.17
Gerber, Ludwig 1962.22
Gerber, Miss 1869.08
Gerber, Tony 1996.09
Gerbidon, Marcel 1922.09, 1922.12
Gerdes, Heather Lea 1980.02
Gerdes, Wilfred 1902.09, 1903.18
Gere, Richard 1971.01
Gereaux, Bettie 1918.03
Gerebeuck, Mons. 1870.03
Gerentes, Miss 1877.39
Gergely, Eliz 1916.26, 1931.03
Gergley, Elsie 1913.34
Gergory, Frank L. 1914.16
Gerhardi, George 1932.22
Gerhart, Michael 1993.18
Gerken, Carolyn 1926.22
Gerlach, H. 1986.02
Gerlach, Robert 1976.15
Germain, E. 1868.06
Germain, G. 1868.06
Germain, Mons. 1885.55, 1885.56, 1885.57, 1885.59, 1885.60, 1885.61, 1886.09, 1886.18, 1886.21
Germain, P. 1868.06
Germaina, Florece 1893.12
Germaine, A. 1870.36
Germaine, D. 1885.42
Germaine, Dorothy 1916.20
Germaine, E. 1870.43
Germaine, George 1904.58
Germaine, Katherine 1898.34
Germaine, Miss 1864.22, 1870.23
Germaine, S. 1870.36, 1870.43
Germaine, Sarah 1870.15
German, Arthur 1880.55
German, Edward 1902.25, 1903.21, 1907.51

Germon, Effie 1869.04, 1869.13, 1869.15, 1892.48, 1894.36, 1896.09, 1896.11, 1897.20
Germon, G.C. 1885.65
Germon, George 1875.32
Germon, Mr. 1862.03, 1862.04
Germon, Mrs. 1859.01, 1859.02, 1859.04
Germond, Pearl 1918.05
Germonde, Perle 1920.09, 1923.02
Gerold, Hermann 1885.01
Gerome, Elsie 1885.68, 1888.11
Gerome, Gerald 1902.25
Geroux, Marion 1889.46
Gerrard, Alfred 1919.01, 1920.38, 1922.31, 1924.47
Gerrard, Jay 1924.10
Gerrish, Paul 1933.20
Gerrish, Sylvia 1882.03, 1882.39, 1886.39, 1887.25, 1887.33, 1887.50, 1888.20, 1888.35, 1889.04, 1889.23, 1889.40, 1889.49, 1892.07
Gerrits, Paul 1940.23
Gerroll, Daniel 1998.05
Gerry, David 1929.08
Gerry, J.J. 1892.38, 1893.23
Gerry, Roger 1940.19
Gersene, Georges D. 1942.30
Gersham, Herbert 1905.41
Gershe, Leonard 1950.02, 1959.11
Gershenson, M. 1970.17
Gershenson, Sue Anne 1984.08
Gershovsky, Varon 1989.29
Gershovsky, Yaron 1999.24
Gershwin, Arthur 1945.01
Gershwin, Frances 1927.27, 1928.40
Gershwin, George 1918.32, 1919.02, 1919.11, 1919.12, 1919.43, 1920.17, 1920.29, 1920.33, 1921.04, 1921.18, 1921.19, 1921.22, 1922.09, 1922.10, 1922.23, 1922.27, 1922.46, 1923.02, 1923.18, 1923.26, 1923.31, 1924.03, 1924.19, 1924.43, 1925.49, 1925.52, 1926.21, 1926.36, 1927.12, 1927.59, 1928.01, 1928.03, 1928.43, 1929.27, 1930.02, 1930.06, 1930.13, 1930.31, 1931.11, 1931.48, 1932.24, 1933.01, 1933.13, 1933.25, 1935.13, 1935.19, 1936.31, 1939.14, 1940.10, 1942.03, 1942.13, 1942.23, 1943.15, 1944.03, 1944.32, 1952.07, 1952.11, 1953.04, 1953.12, 1956.02, 1958.10, 1961.13, 1962.07, 1962.17, 1963.02, 1964.19, 1965.03, 1965.08, 1974.09, 1974.11, 1975.22, 1976.28, 1979.24, 1980.09, 1982.06, 1983.04, 1983.06, 1983.09, 1984.10, 1986.02, 1988.08, 1989.06, 1989.10, 1989.21, 1990.09, 1991.04, 1991.10, 1992.02, 1992.18, 1999.10, 1999.23, 2000.03, 2001.07
Gershwin, Ira 1918.32, 1920.29, 1921.10, 1922.05, 1922.10, 1923.33, 1924.30, 1924.43, 1925.14, 1925.29, 1925.49, 1926.21, 1926.36, 1927.59, 1928.01, 1928.03, 1928.43, 1929.27, 1930.02, 1930.06, 1930.13, 1930.18, 1930.31, 1930.33, 1930.38, 1931.13, 1931.21, 1931.48, 1933.01, 1933.13, 1933.25, 1934.19, 1935.13, 1936.02, 1936.17, 1936.31, 1941.04, 1942.03, 1942.13, 1943.03, 1943.15, 1944.03, 1944.32, 1945.04, 1946.20, 1952.07, 1952.11, 1953.04, 1953.12, 1956.02, 1962.07, 1962.17, 1963.10, 1964.19, 1965.03, 1974.09, 1974.11, 1975.22, 1976.28, 1976.32, 1979.24, 1980.09, 1983.04, 1983.06, 1983.09, 1984.10, 1986.01, 1988.08, 1989.06, 1990.09, 1990.14, 1991.04, 1991.10, 1992.02, 1992.18, 1995.12, 1999.10, 1999.23, 2000.03, 2001.07
Gerson, Hal 1948.30
Gerson, May 1907.32
Gerstacker, Franz 1984.03, 1984.04
Gerstad, John 1969.07, 1969.12
Gersten, Bernard 1968.11, 1971.18, 1975.02, 1975.15, 1976.10, 1978.11, 1978.27, 1983.04, 1983.09, 1986.05, 1987.15, 1988.02, 1991.01, 1992.17, 1994.02, 1995.09, 1996.16, 1998.21, 1999.22, 2000.07, 2000.16
Gersten, Berta 1963.12
Gerstenberger, Emil 1922.40, 1924.36, 1924.45, 1925.01, 1925.08, 1925.23, 1925.27, 1925.28, 1925.31, 1925.39, 1926.18, 1927.03, 1927.50, 1927.55, 1928.03, 1928.29, 1928.46, 1929.09, 1929.17, 1943.20
Gerstman, Felix G. 1964.02, 1964.25
Gervais, Blanche 1919.25
Gervais, M. 1902.13
Gervais, Mlle. 1877.04
Gervais, Mme. 1868.26, 1883.06
Gervaise, A. 1885.14
Gervaise, Edward 1887.31
Gervaise, Gussie 1899.23
Gervass, Mme. 1886.16
Gervault, Paul 1912.35
Geshwin, Ira 1923.26
Gesmar, Charles 1974.13
Gesner, Clark 1968.13, 1971.11, 1979.10, 1999.03
Gest, Madge 1911.22
Gest, Morris 1909.07, 1912.43, 1913.33, 1915.04, 1917.17, 1917.24, 1917.27, 1918.01, 1918.27, 1919.20, 1919.38, 1919.39, 1919.43, 1920.22, 1920.34, 1920.41, 1922.06, 1923.28, 1924.08, 1925.03, 1925.46, 1925.51, 1927.51, 1929.05, 1931.09, 1931.38
Getchell, Sadie 1875.15, 1875.20
Getchell, Sallie 1875.11
Gethins, Mildred 1932.23
Getke, Richard 1975.16, 1976.23, 1977.11
Geto, Al 1942.05, 1942.26
Gettelfinger, Sara 2000.18
Getter, Philip M. 1980.08
Getz, C.S. 1861.03
Getz, Charles 1894.42
Getz, Charles S. 1877.07, 1881.15, 1892.38, 1893.23, 1894.34
Getz, J.S. 1892.38, 1893.23, 1894.34
Getz, Mara 1988.07
Getz, Stuart 1964.33
Getze, Tilda 1939.07
Geva, Tamara 1927.51, 1928.47, 1930.32, 1932.17, 1936.05
Gevault, Paul 1903.34
Geyans, Jon 1952.12
Geyer, Siegfried 1938.07
Geyer, Steve 1996.17
Ghapman, Graham 1976.06
Ghelfi, Chris 1999.10, 1999.15
Gherzi, Mlle. 1877.11
Gherzi, Mons. 1877.33
Gherzi, Sophie 1875.25, 1875.29, 1875.33, 1876.24, 1876.25, 1876.26, 1876.28, 1877.06, 1877.09, 1877.10, 1877.19, 1877.26, 1877.27, 1877.30, 1877.31, 1877.32, 1877.34, 1877.38, 1878.06, 1878.07, 1878.08
Gherzie, Sophie 1877.13
Gherzy, Mlle. 1873.11, 1873.16
Gherzy, Mme. 1873.15
Gherzy, Sophie 1875.28
Ghezzi, Paul 1927.37
Ghigi, Renato 1964.03
Ghislanzoni, Antonio 1952.15, 2000.06
Ghor, Mr. 1855.08
Ghostley, Alice 1952.09, 1955.05, 1956.07, 1960.04, 1963.22
Giacosa, Giuseppe 1996.09
Giagni, D.J. 1985.02, 1987.19
Giaimo, Michael 1990.10
Giambattista, Anne Marie 1982.15
Giangi, D.J. 1983.21
Giannitto, Anthony 1927.31
Gianono, Joseph 1985.19, 1988.10, 1988.19
Giant, Bill 1989.12
Giasi, John 1938.02
Giavassi, Emilia 1873.10
Gibb, Barry 1982.22, 1999.15
Gibb, Maurice 1982.22, 1999.15
Gibb, Robin 1982.22, 1999.15
Gibbens, Bill 1970.06
Gibbens, Gertrude 1906.36
Gibbons, Addie 1903.26
Gibbons, Carroll 1931.13
Gibbons, Charles 1880.15
Gibbons, Edythe 1903.09
Gibbons, Elsie 1903.21
Gibbons, Frank 1903.09, 1907.40, 1908.12
Gibbons, George 1879.15
Gibbons, Gertrude 1908.16
Gibbons, J. Frank 1903.36
Gibbons, Messr. 1886.32
Gibbons, Orlando 1963.03
Gibbons, Waxey 1963.11
Gibbs, E. Payton 1918.15
Gibbs, Ethel 1900.45
Gibbs, Fred 1898.02
Gibbs, Lloyd G. 1898.22, 1908.08
Gibbs, Miss 1892.29
Gibbs, Mr. 1908.15
Gibbs, Musette 1899.18
Gibbs, Nancy 1921.20, 1923.25, 1924.36, 1926.22
Gibbs, Robert Paton 1905.33, 1908.10, 1908.39, 1921.31, 1927.63
Gibbs, Ron 1999.11
Gibbs, Ruth 1940.01
Gibbs, Sheila 1978.11, 1990.12
Gibney, Charles 1927.12, 1928.49
Gibney, William 1914.30
Gibson, Alexander 1913.32
Gibson, Arthur V. 1898.20, 1905.30
Gibson, Bessie 1911.13
Gibson, Bessie Evelyn 1903.27
Gibson, Buddy 1974.24
Gibson, Charles 1903.12, 1906.25
Gibson, Charles Dana 1924.36
Gibson, Darren 1998.16
Gibson, David Warren 1986.07
Gibson, Dessa 1907.10
Gibson, Don 1979.16, 1999.09
Gibson, Dorothy 1907.32
Gibson, Edith 1935.08
Gibson, Enid 1907.32
Gibson, Fred 1903.03, 1904.13, 1904.44
Gibson, Geneva 1903.03
Gibson, Genevra 1903.03
Gibson, George 1901.29
Gibson, Glenn 1960.08
Gibson, Henry 1907.14
Gibson, J.C. 1898.33
Gibson, J.G. 1899.05
Gibson, Jo 1949.17
Gibson, John 1912.48, 1914.19
Gibson, Judy 1972.06
Gibson, Karen 1976.05, 1979.10, 1980.30
Gibson, Leonard 1939.07
Gibson, Mabel 1914.18, 1915.18
Gibson, Madeline 1928.42
Gibson, Margaret 1943.03, 1946.20
Gibson, Marie 1952.05, 1952.13
Gibson, Mary 1895.15, 1899.26
Gibson, Melissa 1999.02
Gibson, Michael 1974.05, 1975.04, 1979.13, 1980.09, 1980.18, 1980.30, 1981.10, 1983.06, 1984.01, 1984.10, 1987.12, 1987.15, 1987.16, 1988.07, 1989.05, 1989.23, 1992.04, 1993.09, 1993.16, 1997.07, 1998.04, 1999.17
Gibson, Michel 1999.03
Gibson, Millard 1944.27
Gibson, Miss 1898.50
Gibson, Pollie 1900.33
Gibson, Robert A. 1955.15, 1955.16, 1955.18, 1955.20, 1955.21, 1955.22, 1955.23, 1955.24
Gibson, Scott 1961.13, 1962.07
Gibson, Sidney 1938.08
Gibson, Tanya 1984.09
Gibson, Virginia 1956.16
Gibson, William 1964.32, 1973.06, 1986.16
Gibson, William L. 1915.26
Gibson, Wynne 1925.35
Giddens, Darrell 1974.11
Gideon, Melvile 1911.43
Gideon, Melville 1908.19, 1908.36, 1908.39, 1909.07, 1909.24, 1909.25, 1910.19, 1911.34, 1918.31, 1920.03, 1923.36, 1928.04
Giebel, Adam 1980.27
Gierasch, Stefan 1945.20, 1959.24
Gierette, Mlle. 1869.30
Giersberg, Max 1934.04
Giersdorf, Elvira 1927.38, 1928.28, 1928.50
Giersdorf, Irene 1927.38, 1928.28, 1928.50
Giersdorf, Rae 1927.38, 1928.28, 1928.50
Giesel, Louis 1894.09
Giesenschlag, Russell 1982.14
Gieser, Harold 1921.06
Gietz, E. Ray 1906.17
Gietz, Gordon 1993.12
Giffen, R.L. 1907.49
Gifford, Ada 1902.32, 1903.30
Gifford, George 1918.23
Gifford, Gordon 1943.14
Gifford, Harry 1909.07, 1911.32, 1912.44, 1914.01, 1930.13
Gifford, Jack 1928.47
Gifford, Julia 1902.41, 1917.11
Gifford, Kathie Lee 1999.20
Gifford, Louise 1926.10, 1926.44, 1927.57
Gifford, Mr. 1884.27
Giffort, Mabel 1864.15
Giftos, Elaine 1968.13
Giglio, Alexander 1927.22
Giglio, Clememt 1927.22
Gignoux, Regis 1928.06
Giguere, Eddie 1898.08
Gil, Chuco Martinez 1988.15
Gilad, Ami 1966.21, 1967.08, 1968.04
Gilb, Melinda 1985.08
Gilbart, Larry 1962.12
Gilbers, Mrs. G.H. 1864.21
Gilbert and Sullivan Company 1927.44
Gilbert and Sullivan Opera Company, The 1926.44, 1944.04, 1944.05, 1944.06, 1944.07, 1944.08, 1944.09, 1944.10, 1944.11, 1944.12, 1944.13
Gilbert Clark, Inc. 1921.33, 1923.19
Gilbert, Alan 1945.20, 1947.03, 1949.04, 1951.14, 1956.04, 1981.19
Gilbert, Alice 1889.33
Gilbert, Allie 1891.18, 1894.34, 1899.17, 1899.30, 1900.38
Gilbert, Argyle 1899.01, 1900.10
Gilbert, B. 1900.03
Gilbert, Barbara 1983.19
Gilbert, Beatrice 1904.13
Gilbert, Benjamin Thorne 1916.12
Gilbert, Bert 1914.09
Gilbert, Bessie 1892.23
Gilbert, Billy 1945.16, 1947.06, 1948.16, 1952.13
Gilbert, Bob 1923.17, 1928.28
Gilbert, C. Allen 1924.36
Gilbert, Charles R. 1899.01, 1900.10
Gilbert, David 1979.17
Gilbert, Dolly 1928.22
Gilbert, Dorothy 1918.25
Gilbert, Earl 1931.05
Gilbert, Edward 1939.26, 1940.23, 1942.34, 1944.24, 1946.14, 1946.22, 1946.23, 1947.12, 1948.15, 1949.02
Gilbert, Edwin 1930.35, 1936.12, 1936.17, 1938.07
Gilbert, Edythe 1911.07
Gilbert, Emma 1887.08, 1888.28
Gilbert, Franklin 1948.30, 1953.02
Gilbert, Fred 1892.45, 1894.46
Gilbert, G.H. 1876.23, 1881.11
Gilbert, George 1873.19, 1873.24, 1956.02, 1958.08, 1959.06
Gilbert, Gerald 1923.40
Gilbert, Gloria 1927.52, 1932.16, 1939.22, 1941.13, 1949.06, 1963.10
Gilbert, Grace 1911.35
Gilbert, Harry 1867.32, 1927.24
Gilbert, Harry F. 1912.43
Gilbert, Helen 1903.13
Gilbert, J. Charles 1930.07
Gilbert, J.L. 1880.42, 1898.47
Gilbert, James A. 1882.23
Gilbert, Jean 1913.29, 1914.02, 1914.22, 1915.08, 1922.36, 1926.33, 1928.48, 1932.06
Gilbert, Jody 1946.22
Gilbert, Jody S. 1938.04
Gilbert, John 1851.08, 1862.04, 1875.39, 1882.56, 1884.06
Gilbert, John Charles 1931.07
Gilbert, John D. 1886.01, 1892.29, 1895.03
Gilbert, Katie 1889.16, 1890.18
Gilbert, L. Wolfe 1912.09, 1912.29, 1912.43, 1914.25, 1916.24, 1916.25, 1917.23, 1919.19, 1929.05, 1931.29, 1931.31, 1974.09
Gilbert, Larry 1945.12
Gilbert, Lauren 1947.02
Gilbert, Lawrence 1944.32
Gilbert, Lisa 1933.20
Gilbert, Louis 1940.01
Gilbert, M.B. 1901.06, 1902.07
Gilbert, Marjorie 1927.02
Gilbert, Maud 1897.09, 1899.21, 1899.36
Gilbert, Maude 1896.26, 1896.36
Gilbert, Mercedes 1927.03, 1929.25, 1930.10, 1935.01, 1945.13
Gilbert, Miss 1904.13
Gilbert, Mons. 1868.13
Gilbert, Mrs. G.H. 1868.04, 1884.11, 1891.05
Gilbert, Myrtle 1907.07, 1912.25, 1913.30
Gilbert, Nealey 1981.13
Gilbert, Pierre 1947.05, 1948.12
Gilbert, Ray 1975.21
Gilbert, Robert 1920.47, 1936.22, 1943.09, 1957.04
Gilbert, Ruth 1908.33

Gilbert, Tony 1989.19
Gilbert, W.S. 1895.29, 1945.08, 1960.14, 1960.15
Gilbert, Walter 1915.18, 1916.01, 1937.01
Gilbert, William 1880.45, 1880.53, 1882.16, 1882.26, 1884.11, 1890.23, 1892.14, 1900.11
Gilbert, William S. 1875.35, 1879.05, 1879.06, 1879.07, 1879.08, 1879.09, 1879.10, 1879.11, 1879.13, 1879.14, 1879.16, 1879.17, 1879.28, 1879.29, 1879.30, 1879.58, 1879.59, 1879.64, 1879.66, 1879.70, 1879.71, 1879.72,
Gilbert, William S. (*cont.*) 1880.12, 1880.18, 1881.19, 1881.37, 1881.43, 1881.57, 1882.10, 1882.12, 1882.19, 1882.21, 1882.22, 1882.38, 1882.40, 1882.41, 1882.42, 1882.48, 1882.54, 1882.70, 1882.78, 1883.14, 1883.15, 1883.21, 1883.24, 1883.26, 1884.09, 1884.30, 1884.31, 1884.37, 1885.04, 1885.13, 1885.16, 1885.34, 1885.37, 1885.43, 1885.47, 1885.48, 1885.70, 1886.12, 1886.17, 1886.25, 1886.29, 1886.55, 1886.57, 1887.10, 1887.21, 1887.25, 1887.29, 1888.35, 1889.23, 1890.01, 1890.02, 1890.14, 1890.15, 1890.18, 1890.20, 1890.46, 1890.47, 1890.48, 1891.32, 1892.37, 1892.40, 1892.46, 1893.02, 1893.09, 1894.15, 1894.23, 1896.17, 1896.19, 1896.22, 1898.09, 1898.21, 1898.26, 1898.29, 1898.42, 1898.52, 1898.65, 1898.71, 1899.07, 1899.16, 1899.20, 1900.04, 1900.21, 1900.26, 1900.27, 1902.22, 1905.22, 1910.14, 1911.21, 1912.18, 1912.21, 1912.22, 1912.23, 1913.11, 1913.12, 1913.13, 1914.11, 1915.06, 1915.09, 1915.10, 1915.12, 1915.13, 1915.14, 1918.23, 1925.13, 1925.15, 1926.08, 1926.10, 1926.44, 1927.24, 1927.25, 1927.44, 1927.57, 1927.61, 1928.20, 1931.10, 1931.12, 1931.15, 1931.17, 1931.18, 1931.20, 1931.22, 1931.23, 1931.24, 1931.25, 1933.08, 1933.09, 1933.10, 1933.11, 1933.14, 1933.18, 1933.19, 1934.07, 1934.08, 1934.09, 1934.10, 1934.11, 1934.21, 1934.23, 1934.24, 1934.25, 1934.26, 1934.27, 1934.28, 1934.30, 1934.31, 1934.33, 1935.05, 1935.06, 1935.07, 1935.08, 1935.09, 1935.10, 1936.04, 1936.08, 1936.09, 1936.10, 1936.11, 1936.13, 1936.14, 1936.15, 1936.16, 1936.18, 1936.19, 1936.21, 1936.23, 1936.24, 1936.25, 1938.10, 1939.01, 1939.02, 1939.03, 1939.04, 1939.06, 1939.08, 1939.09, 1939.11, 1939.15, 1939.17, 1940.11, 1940.13, 1940.14, 1940.15, 1942.02, 1942.04, 1942.06, 1942.07, 1942.08, 1942.09, 1944.04, 1944.05, 1944.06, 1944.08, 1944.09, 1944.10, 1944.11, 1944.12, 1944.13, 1945.09, 1946.11, 1947.22, 1948.01, 1948.02, 1948.03, 1948.06, 1948.07, 1948.09, 1948.10, 1949.10, 1949.11, 1949.13, 1949.14, 1951.01, 1951.03, 1951.04, 1951.06, 1951.07, 1951.09, 1952.14, 1952.16, 1952.17, 1952.18, 1952.19, 1955.15, 1955.16, 1955.18, 1955.20, 1955.21, 1955.22, 1955.23, 1955.24, 1959.18, 1961.03, 1961.04, 1961.05, 1961.06, 1961.19, 1961.23, 1962.08, 1962.09, 1962.10, 1962.11, 1962.19, 1962.25, 1962.26, 1962.28, 1962.29, 1962.30, 1962.31, 1963.23, 1964.07, 1964.08, 1964.09, 1964.10, 1964.12, 1964.13, 1964.14, 1964.36, 1964.37, 1964.38, 1964.41, 1964.42, 1964.43, 1965.09, 1965.10, 1965.11, 1965.12, 1965.13, 1966.22, 1966.23, 1966.25, 1966.26, 1966.28, 1968.09, 1968.10, 1968.12, 1968.14, 1968.15, 1968.25, 1968.26, 1968.27, 1968.28, 1968.29, 1974.07, 1974.15, 1975.17, 1976.12, 1976.13, 1976.14, 1976.22, 1977.03, 1977.17, 1978.14, 1978.15, 1978.16, 1978.17, 1981.01, 1984.12, 1985.10, 1987.01, 1989.01, 1989.15, 1990.13, 1993.13, 1995.10, 1996.11, 1997.02
Gilbert, Willie 1950.09, 1961.22, 1963.13, 1966.07, 1995.05
Gilbert, Wolfe 1962.17, 1964.28
Gilbert, Zack 1899.21
Gilberte, Clarice 1911.38
Gilboa, Ilan 1972.17
Gilbret, Jean 1912.01
Gilcher, Edwin 1930.18, 1930.33
Gilchrist, Jack 1938.01
Gilchrist, Newton R. 1993.11, 1996.04
Gilday, Alfred 1922.34
Gilday, Charles 1882.04
Gilday, George 1925.01, 1925.28, 1929.09
Gildea, Agnes 1914.13, 1918.41
Gildea, Mary 1907.09
Gilder, Frank 1880.19
Gildersleeve, J.R. 1881.24
Gildin, Leon H. 1969.13
Gile, Bill 1975.24, 1976.25, 1982.16
Giler, Bernie 1945.17
Giles, Archie 1902.12
Giles, Carrie 1926.31
Giles, E.T. 1902.15
Giles, Edward 1906.23
Giles, Edward B. 1905.21
Giles, Evelyn 1946.12
Giles, Nancy 1985.15
Giles, Ray 1929.25
Gilette, Viola 1913.33
Gilfether, Daniel 1887.46, 1894.36, 1895.30, 1896.09, 1896.11, 1897.05, 1899.01, 1900.10, 1901.02, 1903.25
Gilfoil, Harry 1891.39, 1894.07, 1894.35, 1897.34, 1901.13, 1901.21, 1910.08, 1912.14, 1913.18
Gilford, Jack 1940.21, 1950.02, 1959.26, 1962.12, 1966.24, 1971.03
Gilford, Madeline Lee 1986.13
Gilford, Marcia 1962.27
Gilford, Michael 1955.09
Gilford/Freeley 1999.05
Gilkey, Stanley 1939.12, 1940.03, 1946.07, 1953.17
Gilkyson, Terry 1999.07
Gill, Bob 1977.10, 1982.22
Gill, C.C. 1931.32
Gill, Charles 1930.19
Gill, Dorothy 1934.21, 1934.23, 1934.24, 1934.26, 1934.27, 1934.28, 1934.30, 1934.31, 1934.33
Gill, Edith 1906.34
Gill, Eijah 1982.17
Gill, Elijah 1980.14
Gill, Frank 1920.31, 1921.30
Gill, Geula 1968.04, 1969.13
Gill, Jack 1981.14
Gill, Mason 1898.47
Gill, Milton 1936.22
Gill, Peri 1982.18
Gill, Ray 1981.28
Gill, Teri 1976.25
Gill, William 1878.20, 1879.03, 1879.35, 1880.06, 1880.32, 1881.16, 1882.56, 1884.42, 1884.53, 1884.62, 1885.04, 1886.06, 1886.24, 1886.32, 1886.47, 1886.48, 1887.40, 1888.06, 1889.46, 1889.47, 1890.27, 1893.13, 1893.30, 1894.13, 1894.19, 1895.44, 1897.49, 1899.23, 1901.06, 1904.48
Gill, William B. 1888.36, 1892.58
Gill, William S. 1903.26
Gill, William T. 1879.38
Gille, Philippe 1882.75, 1883.29
Gillelspie, Marion 1918.31
Gillen, Frank 1914.06
Gilles, Napoleon 1867.22, 1867.23, 1867.26, 1867.27, 1867.29, 1867.31
Gillespie, Arthur 1900.08, 1902.02, 1905.49, 1905.53, 1906.19, 1908.13
Gillespie, Arthur J. 1912.04
Gillespie, Ben 1962.15, 1963.04, 1963.06, 1964.46, 1965.18
Gillespie, Edward C. 1905.43
Gillespie, F.M. 1923.14, 1923.15, 1924.12
Gillespie, Frank M. 1921.31, 1923.03, 1929.37
Gillespie, Haven 1932.18, 1975.22, 1992.18
Gillespie, Henry A. 1904.54
Gillespie, Marian 1927.40
Gillespie, Paul 1976.20
Gillespie, Robert 1980.17
Gillet, E. 1868.06
Gillet, Mlle. 1902.13
Gillett, Eric Michael 1999.19
Gillett, Maud 1903.18
Gillette, Anita 1961.10, 1962.04, 1962.20, 1965.01, 1965.15, 1969.14
Gillette, Bobby 1931.21
Gillette, Charles 1979.13
Gillette, Florence 1882.41
Gillette, Lorenzo 1918.36
Gillette, Myrtle 1910.10
Gillette, Penn 2000.13
Gillette, Priscilla 1949.16, 1950.20, 1953.05, 1954.03
Gillette, Ray 1888.43
Gillette, Ruth 1925.27, 1930.41, 1971.07
Gillette, Viola 1901.27, 1903.39, 1909.07, 1912.18, 1912.21, 1912.22, 1913.08, 1913.12, 1913.13, 1913.23, 1923.03, 1925.04, 1926.06
Gillette, William 1887.49, 1888.37, 1897.31, 1919.32, 1922.16
Gilliam, Harry 1906.08
Gilliam, Paula Hutter 1987.02
Gilliam, Terry 1976.06
Gillies, Archie 1900.42
Gilliland, Helen 1928.48
Gillin, Phil 1974.03
Gillingham, Joan 1939.06, 1947.22, 1948.02, 1948.03, 1948.06, 1948.07, 1948.09, 1948.10, 1951.01, 1951.04, 1951.06, 1951.07, 1951.09
Gillingwater, Claude 1897.04, 1905.57, 1907.36, 1910.02, 1910.27, 1913.15
Gillis, Roland 1938.19
Gillis, Stephen 1913.02
Gillis, Verna 1969.09
Gillman, Mabelle 1898.29
Gillmore, Margalo 1954.13, 1961.18
Gillmore, Ruth 1922.42
Gillmore, Stuart 1915.30
Gillon, Marion 1929.39
Gillon, William 1884.64, 1897.27
Gillow, J. 1892.46
Gillow, Pollie 1882.75
Gillow, W. 1882.32, 1882.60, 1882.75
Gillow, W.T. 1882.38
Gillow, William 1882.42, 1882.49, 1885.11
Gilman and Benstein 1922.28
Gilman Company 1923.08, 1923.23
Gilman, A.C. 1912.43
Gilman, Ada 1886.01, 1912.11
Gilman, Carlotta 1893.45
Gilman, D. 1924.42
Gilman, Elise 1890.27
Gilman, Julian 1914.16
Gilman, Lotta 1891.23
Gilman, Mabel 1897.20, 1898.46, 1899.15, 1899.25
Gilman, Mabelle 1896.27, 1898.18, 1900.20, 1902.06, 1902.37
Gilman, Mme. 1921.06, 1922.44
Gilman, Nellie 1914.16
Gilman, Sondra 1981.06
Gilman, Toni 1942.29, 1944.14
Gilmar, Miss 1863.01
Gilmer, Jennie 1867.27, 1867.29, 1870.20, 1872.19
Gilmer, Jenny 1866.06, 1867.31
Gilmer, Miss 1863.02
Gilmore 1883.47
Gilmore, Barney 1896.38
Gilmore, Barney F. 1896.38
Gilmore, Billie 1922.30
Gilmore, Charles 1912.38, 1913.17
Gilmore, Douglas 1933.21, 1943.08
Gilmore, E.G. 1880.08, 1881.31, 1884.40, 1885.46, 1890.50, 1891.41
Gilmore, E.R. 1881.41
Gilmore, Ed. 1903.09
Gilmore, Eleanor 1929.48, 1930.41, 1931.20, 1931.25, 1934.11, 1935.07, 1935.08
Gilmore, Ethel 1906.45
Gilmore, Flora 1902.26
Gilmore, Helen 1893.20, 1911.28, 1912.30
Gilmore, Janette 1925.48, 1926.36
Gilmore, Jeanette 1923.17, 1925.25
Gilmore, Jeannette 1925.40
Gilmore, Judy 1927.39
Gilmore, Kittie 1894.50
Gilmore, Mary 1912.26
Gilmore, Paul 1897.05, 1929.30
Gilmore, Ray 1907.03
Gilmore, W. 1886.28
Gilmore, W.G. 1888.04
Gilmore, W.H. 1921.13, 1922.09, 1922.46, 1923.26, 1924.21, 1925.41
Gilmore, W.L. 1921.05
Gilmore, William 1885.11
Gilmore, William H. 1926.41, 1928.33
Gilmore, William J. 1890.21
Gilmour, Alice 1898.44
Gilmour, Boyd J. 1900.45
Gilmour, David 1982.22
Gilner, Margaret 1928.20
Gilpatrick, Betty 1946.10
Gilpin, Charles 1907.29, 1907.31
Gilpin, Phil 1906.46, 1917.16, 1918.23
Gilrain, Winifred 1914.16
Gilraine, Winifred 1908.17
Gilroy, Ella 1901.17, 1903.03, 1904.13, 1904.44
Gilroy, Etta 1896.02, 1896.52
Gilroy, John 1891.04, 1891.44, 1896.02, 1896.29, 1898.38, 1900.05, 1901.21, 1902.16, 1903.18
Gilroy, John H. 1893.20
Gilroy, Mamie 1891.32, 1893.14, 1897.15, 1900.16, 1900.56, 1901.12
Gilroy, Miss 1903.03
Gilson, Blanche 1903.24
Gilson, George 1889.46
Gilson, George B. 1891.41
Gilson, Gertie 1898.66
Gilson, Lottie 1896.26, 1897.09
Gilson, Messr. 1884.42, 1886.47
Gilson, Miss 1897.04
Gilson, Molly 1908.33
Gilvert, Ada Vanden 1897.05
Gimbel, Harriet 1920.28
Gimbel, Harriette 1922.32, 1923.25
Gimbel, Norman 1958.20, 1961.02, 1981.16
Gimber, Messr. 1851.05
Gimber, Miss 1859.11, 1860.03
Gimenez 1969.11
Gimenez y Bellido, Geronimo 1949.07
Gindin, David 1946.02
Ginet, Mons. 1885.55, 1885.56, 1885.60, 1886.08, 1886.21
Ginet, Paul 1885.59, 1886.09, 1886.18
Gingles, Keith 1946.03
Gingold, Charlotte 1970.18
Gingold, Hermione 1953.17, 1959.06, 1960.07, 1973.04
Ginn, Sophie 1960.02
Ginnes, Abraham S. 1961.21
Ginnett, Frank 1922.30
Ginnett, Poppy 1922.30
Ginnette, Frank 1922.30
Ginot, Mons. 1869.30
Ginsburg, Ned 1999.23
Ginto, Leonora 1897.37
Ginzburg, Kalman 1968.08
Ginzler, Robert 1958.02, 1959.13, 1959.23, 1960.06, 1960.13, 1960.22, 1961.02, 1961.14, 1961.22, 1962.01, 1962.04, 1962.14, 1962.24, 1966.07, 1974.17, 1989.27, 1991.06, 1995.05
Ginzler, Seymour 1956.16
Giombetti, Karen 1979.26, 1983.14, 1985.18
Giordano, Gus 1952.10
Giorgi, L. 1911.16
Giorgione, Ganine 1994.06
Giorza, Paolo 1869.38
Giovani, Mlle. 1868.18
Giovanni, Don 1934.02
Giovanni, Prince 1904.20
Giovonelli, Rosa 1940.05
Gipple, Tom 1905.47
Gipson, J. Derek 2001.04
Giradeau, Charles H. 1918.14
Giradot, Etienne 1900.16
Giradoux, Jean 1969.05
Girard, Alfred 1920.02
Girard, Andre 1964.06
Girard, Belle 1881.14
Girard, Dixie 1916.15
Girard, E. 1882.04
Girard, Ed 1882.04
Girard, Eddie 1886.01, 1888.17, 1889.06, 1889.39, 1896.44, 1898.38, 1900.19, 1925.38
Girard, Edgar F. 1884.46
Girard, Edward 1882.04, 1883.66, 1894.06
Girard, Emil 1875.40
Girard, Fanny 1884.27
Girard, Frank 1881.06, 1881.12, 1882.04, 1882.20, 1883.02, 1883.17, 1883.19, 1883.23
Girard, Gilbert 1897.33
Girard, Harry 1902.31, 1907.26
Girard, Henry 1900.43
Girard, Inez 1909.08
Girard, Isabel 1938.15
Girard, Julian 1875.40, 1884.27
Girard, Kate 1877.07, 1883.47
Girard, Lewis 1875.40
Girard, Lois 1942.26
Girard, Messr. 1879.46, 1882.04
Girard, Miss 1884.42

Girard, Mons. 1876.25, 1876.26, 1877.06, 1877.09, 1877.10, 1877.19, 1877.27, 1877.32, 1878.07, 1879.41, 1879.45, 1880.29, 1882.67, 1883.30, 1883.34, 1883.41, 1883.59, 1884.45, 1884.49, 1884.52, 1884.54, 1884.55, 1885.23, 1885.59, 1885.60, 1886.09, 1886.21, 1886.22
Girard, Oscar 1892.11, 1895.24, 1898.04, 1898.07, 1898.15, 1898.16, 1898.19, 1898.21, 1898.24, 1898.40
Girard, Paulette 1954.09
Girard, Pearl 1907.26
Girard, Victorine 1884.12
Girard, William 1882.04
Girardet, Etienne 1921.10
Girardin, Berthe 1875.02
Girardot, Etienne 1903.12, 1919.38, 1925.37, 1927.27
Giraud, Claude 1964.39
Giraud, Hubert 1961.25, 1964.02
Giraud, Mons. 1883.41
Girlando, Paul J. 1934.17
Girolmo, David 1997.10
Gironetti, E. 1911.19
Giroux, Larry 1972.24
Giroux, Marion 1888.36, 1897.45
Giroux, Maude 1889.34
Giroux, Miss 1886.47
Girrebeuk, Mons. 1870.41
Girvan, Edith 1908.30
Girvin, Edith 1904.03
Gish, Lillian 1965.35, 1975.22
Gisiko, Alexis 1892.24
Gissentanner, Joyce 1951.11
Gitlin, Murray 1954.03, 1960.11
Gitlitz, Murray 1928.40
Giuffre, Joe 1989.06
Giulivo, Lello 1985.14
Giuran, John 1921.14
Giuseppe, Signor 1871.10
Giusti, Roy 1923.21
Given, Cud 1889.31
Givot, George 1929.26, 1932.20, 1933.01, 1944.02, 1958.05, 1960.23
Glad, Gladys 1927.08, 1928.03, 1928.47, 1931.19
Gladdings, Helen 1920.20
Glade, Anthony 1997.12
Glade, Carol 1961.21
Gladings, Helen 1917.16
Gladke, Peter 1949.02, 1962.13
Gladstone, Beatrice 1909.25
Glaenzer, Doris 1929.33
Glaenzer, Marion 1929.33
Glanville, Maxwell 1957.09, 1964.32
Glanzberg, Norbert 1959.15
Glanzberg, Norman 1961.25
Glanzburg, Constantin 1964.22
Glanze, F. 1875.10
Glasca, Ada 1890.08
Glaser, C.J.M. 1909.28
Glaser, Darel 1970.10, 1976.01
Glaser, Lulu 1893.35, 1894.29, 1895.26, 1896.28, 1897.36, 1898.36, 1898.54, 1899.24, 1899.28, 1900.54, 1901.09, 1902.03, 1902.31, 1904.30, 1905.29, 1907.37, 1908.01, 1908.29, 1910.36
Glaser, Pese 1901.02
Glaser, Thomas 1995.03
Glaser, William 1907.37
Glasgow, Isobel 1945.03
Glass, Frank 1957.16, 1961.24
Glass, G. Clennett 1912.34
Glass, Jeralyn 1981.19
Glass, Mary Ellen 1946.12
Glass, Montague 1917.25, 1918.23, 1922.42
Glasser, Stanley 1966.03
Glassey, Rick 1984.16
Glassford, Andrew 1866.31
Glassford, David 1913.03, 1914.05, 1920.12
Glassford, Eliza 1866.31, 1877.24
Glassford, Jessie 1884.20
Glassford, Kate 1866.31, 1879.02
Glassford, Walter 1875.10
Glassman, Stephen 1969.08
Glassman, William 1963.08, 1965.21, 1969.07
Glassmeyer, Steve 1998.19
Glavin, Stephen 1985.18
Glayton, H. 1901.03
Glaze, Gary 1974.07, 1974.15, 1974.16, 1975.16, 1975.17, 1976.22, 1976.23
Glazener, Janet 1985.19
Glazer, Benjamin F. 1945.05, 1949.03, 1954.07, 1957.11, 1965.24, 1966.31, 1994.02
Glazer, Herman 1945.03
Glazier, Marie 1904.28
Glazounov 1924.32
Glazunoff, Alexander Constantinovitch 1927.51
Glazunov, Alexander 1919.38, 1922.21
Gleason, Ellen 1954.04
Gleason, Greta 1909.08
Gleason, Gretta 1908.07
Gleason, Helen 1929.24, 1937.03, 1941.02, 1942.17, 1942.21
Gleason, Jack 1940.07, 1974.05
Gleason, Jackie 1943.20, 1944.14, 1949.01, 1959.22
Gleason, James 1928.08
Gleason, James A. 1914.21
Gleason, Joanna 1977.04, 1987.18, 1991.15
Gleason, John 1965.37, 1970.04, 1970.19, 1971.09, 1973.15, 1974.02, 1975.21, 1976.05, 1976.06, 1976.16, 1976.18, 1976.20, 1978.10, 1978.25, 1981.23, 1984.12, 1985.10, 1990.13, 1993.13, 1995.10, 1997.02
Gleason, Mary 1919.05
Gleason, Thomas 1936.02, 1949.04, 1954.02
Gleason, Tom 1954.15
Gleason, William R. 1913.03
Gleckler, Robert 1929.42, 1932.07, 1932.25
Gledhill, Mr. 1857.08, 1858.03, 1860.04, 1862.03, 1863.10, 1866.16, 1866.17
Gleeman, Millicent 1919.29
Gleerich Productins, Inc. 1921.07
Gleicher, Bonnie 2000.20
Glen, Hazel 1923.40, 1924.26, 1927.65
Glen, Messr. 1867.10
Glendinning, Ernest 1913.05, 1915.08, 1921.24, 1924.04, 1924.25
Glendinning, John 1910.32
Glenn, Alice 1964.21
Glenn, Carrie 1938.10
Glenn, Florence 1910.33
Glenn, Frank 1898.70
Glenn, J.W. 1865.03
Glenn, John 1933.12
Glenn, Nettie 1907.22
Glenn, Roy 1964.32
Glenn, S.W. 1872.27
Glenn, Samuel 1876.16
Glenn, Vivian 1925.14
Glenn, Wilfred 1944.25
Glenn-Smith, Michael 1969.02
Glenne, Daphne 1911.39
Glenney, T.H. 1865.05, 1865.06, 1885.54
Glennon, Albertine 1906.46
Glennon, Tom 1947.16
Glenny, T.H. 1881.35
Glenroy, Thomas 1904.06
Glenville, Peter 1959.22, 1963.08
Glenville, Shaun 1921.13
Gleson, Messr. 1841.01
Glick, Ben 1929.52
Glick, Mari 1999.24
Glickman, Will 1948.14, 1948.30, 1950.02, 1955.01, 1956.02, 1958.01
Gliddon, Helen 1893.26
Glimer, Jenny 1867.16
Glinka, Mikhail 1922.06
Glisson, James Y. 1892.18
Globe Electric Company 1906.21
Globe Lighting Company 1909.05
Glockner, Eleanor 1989.29, 1992.04, 1994.04
Glogau, Jack 1913.16
Gloria, Adelaide 1923.46
Gloria, Albert 1923.46
Glose, Augusta 1901.21
Glosford, A. 1878.22
Glosz, Rosemary 1901.05, 1904.54
Glovatski, Nikolai 1919.38
Glove, Julia 1894.10
Glove, Marie 1889.52
Glover, Amelia 1890.07, 1890.34, 1891.43, 1892.36, 1892.56, 1893.28, 1894.10
Glover, Bill 1960.09
Glover, Bruce 1963.09
Glover, Cyd 1989.02
Glover, Doreen 1927.02, 1928.02, 1929.06
Glover, Grace 1926.15
Glover, Harry 1925.02
Glover, Howard 1868.03, 1869.08, 1869.17, 1869.21, 1869.25
Glover, Ida 1879.35
Glover, J.M. 1886.02, 1901.27, 1903.39, 1904.47, 1913.33
Glover, Joe 1944.14, 1945.18, 1950.15, 1951.14, 1956.08, 1956.16, 1957.01, 1958.02, 1961.07
Glover, John 1972.02
Glover, Joseph 1937.15, 1944.27, 1946.22
Glover, Jr., Alden 1917.06
Glover, Julia 1895.36, 1899.36
Glover, Julie 1899.23
Glover, Lillie 1883.65
Glover, Lottie 1888.13
Glover, Louis N. 1887.34
Glover, Marie 1882.05, 1889.16, 1890.27
Glover, Marion 1916.11
Glover, Ralph 1925.28, 1928.30, 1930.40, 1934.29, 1937.13, 1945.19, 1947.14
Glover, Russell G. 1878.21
Glover, Savion 1989.02, 1992.08, 1996.07
Gloves, W.F. 1895.08
Glovina, Ameah 1887.43
Glucas, Carroll 1928.50
Gluck 1940.20
Gluck, M. Senia 1925.25, 1927.34
Gluck, Sandore 1937.15
Gluck, Senia 1922.21, 1923.21, 1924.31
Gluck, Wally 1927.43
Gluckman, Leon 1966.03
Glukoff, Sigmund 1931.35
Glushak, Joanna 1986.13, 1991.08, 1991.09
Glvoer, Miss 1877.15
Glyn, Eleanor 1928.18
Glyn, J. Ryder 1908.29
Glyn, Trevor 1929.41
Glynde, Rita 1929.29
Glynn, Carlin 1978.13, 1982.11
Glynn, Celia 1925.50
Glynn, J. Rider 1906.17
Glynn, Rita 2000.20
Glynn, William 1912.01
Gmelch, Gertrude 1912.15
Gnito, Leonora 1899.06
Gnojewski, Stephen 1996.17
Goatcher 1891.17
Goatcher and Young 1890.11
Goatcher, Phil 1880.37
Goatcher, Phil H. 1881.18
Goatcher, Phil. 1888.19
Goatcher, Philip 1877.04, 1881.14, 1881.22, 1882.60, 1883.38, 1883.45, 1883.58, 1884.21, 1884.39, 1884.63, 1885.28, 1885.45, 1885.52, 1887.25, 1887.28, 1888.25, 1889.20, 1889.24
Goatcher, Philip W. 1875.18, 1880.47, 1881.03, 1886.26
Goatcher, W.P. 1877.15
Goatleg 1971.10
Gobel, George 1961.21
Gobel, Wood 1909.30
Goberman, Max 1944.33, 1945.14, 1945.20, 1948.26, 1951.14, 1957.12, 1959.09, 1961.20
Goburn, Gladys 1917.26
Goby, Mons. 1868.24, 1868.26
Gochman, Len 1966.07, 1967.04
Godard, Charles 1932.19
Godard, Lucile 1922.24
Goday, Marie 1894.31
Godbold, Ida M. 1906.01
Godchaud, P. 1882.45
Godchaux 1882.06
Godchaux, P. 1882.70, 1882.71, 1883.04, 1883.39, 1883.47, 1883.65, 1884.09, 1884.18, 1884.22, 1884.42
Goddard, Charles W. 1915.25
Goddard, Gary 1997.09
Goddard, George 1894.37
Goddard, Malcolm 1965.39
Goddard, Mark 1977.16
Goddard, Neville 1930.37
Goddard, Pauline 1947.14, 1949.18
Goddard, Warren 1937.08
Goddard, Willoughby 1963.01
Godfrey, Arthur 1946.07
Godfrey, Bertram 1902.36
Godfrey, Carrie 1883.26, 1884.22, 1884.25, 1884.42, 1885.08, 1889.10, 1900.21, 1900.26, 1900.29
Godfrey, D.S. 1892.58
Godfrey, Dorothy 1911.26, 1912.38, 1916.11, 1919.11
Godfrey, Fred 1914.01, 1921.12
Godfrey, Ilene 1951.05
Godfrey, Isidore 1934.21, 1934.22, 1934.23, 1934.24, 1934.25, 1934.26, 1934.27, 1934.28, 1934.30, 1934.31, 1934.33, 1936.13, 1936.14, 1936.15, 1936.16, 1936.18, 1936.19, 1936.20, 1936.21, 1936.23, 1936.24, 1936.25, 1939.01, 1939.02, 1939.03, 1939.04, 1939.05, 1939.06, 1939.08, 1939.09, 1939.11, 1947.22, 1948.01, 1948.02, 1948.03, 1948.06, 1948.07, 1948.09, 1948.10, 1951.01, 1951.03, 1951.04, 1951.06, 1951.07, 1955.15, 1955.16, 1955.18, 1955.20, 1955.21, 1955.22, 1955.23, 1955.24, 1962.25, 1962.26, 1962.28, 1962.29, 1962.30, 1962.31, 1964.36, 1964.37, 1964.38, 1964.41, 1964.42, 1964.43, 1966.22, 1966.23, 1966.25, 1966.26, 1966.28
Godfrey, Jeff 1914.22
Godfrey, John 1917.29
Godfrey, Lynnie 1978.21
Godfrey, Vaughan 1924.11
Godfrey, Vaughn 1922.01, 1924.30, 1928.26, 1932.10, 1934.17
Godin, Emmerich 1964.25
Godin, Messr. 1902.13
Godineaux, Edgar 1999.24
Godino, Stephanie 1985.13, 1986.04, 1986.09, 1991.09, 1991.12, 1993.14, 1995.18
Godkin, Dwight 1939.13
Godkin, Paul 1946.24, 1947.16, 1948.17, 1953.02
Godowsky, Leopold 1921.18
Godoy, Jose F. 1875.24
Godoy, Marie 1896.44
Godoy, Marina 1896.01
Godquick, Mr. 1861.01
Godreau, Miguel 1969.05, 1978.03
Godwin, Doris 1907.03
Godwin, Mary 1946.02
Godwin, Rack Howard 1952.11
Godwin, Richard 1992.02
Goe, Bernie 1926.04
Goeddertz, Charles 1972.11
Goegtlin 1880.43
Goehr, Rudolf 1946.17
Goehr, Rudolph 1950.01
Goell, Julie 1989.10
Goell, Kermit 1999.06
Goely, Guy 1989.17
Goeppinger, Susan 1969.16
Goering, Hal 1986.06
Goerner, Selma 1891.33, 1892.43, 1894.30, 1896.34, 1897.35, 1898.53, 1904.20
Goethe 1867.28
Goettler, Charles A. 1898.25
Goetz, Coleman 1914.22
Goetz, E. Ray 1905.49, 1906.32, 1907.15, 1907.24, 1907.41, 1907.42, 1908.39, 1909.07, 1909.13, 1909.25, 1910.04, 1910.12, 1910.18, 1911.05, 1911.26, 1911.30, 1911.34, 1911.35, 1912.07, 1912.25, 1912.44, 1912.45, 1913.16, 1913.30, 1914.31, 1915.16, 1915.20, 1916.03, 1916.09, 1917.03, 1917.12, 1917.35, 1918.06, 1918.18, 1920.03, 1920.23, 1921.18, 1922.09, 1922.27, 1923.18, 1923.26, 1923.38, 1925.41, 1926.09, 1926.35, 1926.41, 1928.33, 1929.45, 1930.40, 1955.13, 1975.09, 2000.12
Goetz, Inez 1933.02
Goetz, Ray 1967.11
Goetzl Theatrical Enterprises, Inc. 1921.03
Goetzl, Anselm 1912.15, 1914.25, 1919.04, 1919.38, 1921.03, 1921.28
Goetzl, Robert A. 1929.39
Goff, Charles 1968.17, 1985.18, 1993.19, 1996.04
Goff, Gerry 1930.02
Goff, Herbert 1919.40, 1922.03, 1925.39
Goff, Winfred 1897.39
Goffin, Gerry 1976.16, 1982.22, 1984.15, 1986.02
Goffin, Morris 1927.36
Goffin, Peter 1948.09, 1955.15, 1955.18, 1955.23, 1962.25, 1962.26, 1962.28, 1962.29, 1962.30, 1962.31, 1964.36, 1964.37, 1964.38, 1964.41, 1964.43, 1966.22, 1966.23, 1966.25, 1966.26, 1966.28, 1968.25, 1968.26, 1968.27, 1968.28, 1968.29, 1976.13, 1978.18
Goffredo 1900.06
Goggin, J. Ed. 1898.08
Gogin, J.W. 1873.24

Gogliano 1943.17, 1946.21, 1950.07
Gogliano, Vadico 1950.07
Gogotzky, N. 1924.48, 1932.09
Gohman, Don 1972.24
Goines, Baby 1932.08
Goins, Baby 1927.32, 1930.24, 1931.31
Goins, Bobby 1927.32
Goland, Arnold 1963.20, 1964.05, 1968.05, 1971.09, 1990.14
Gold, Al 1931.21
Gold, Annabelle 1955.27
Gold, Belle 1898.03, 1905.28, 1906.24
Gold, David 1957.14, 1960.05, 1962.27, 1965.29, 1966.01, 1968.06, 1983.02
Gold, Ernest 1968.08
Gold, Joe 1919.16
Gold, Julie 1995.12
Gold, Leon 1942.28
Gold, Mervin 1955.02
Gold, Michael E. 1997.04
Gold, Robert Alan 1969.02
Gold, Wally 1989.12
Gold, Zisha 1968.22
Goldberg, Dave 1929.20
Goldberg, David 1928.26
Goldberg, Diane 1961.20, 1970.18
Goldberg, Harry 1929.08
Goldberg, Jerry 1970.11, 1973.11
Goldberg, Leonard J. 1971.02, 1972.11
Goldberg, Mark 2001.03
Goldberg, Norbert 1990.12
Goldberg, Rube 1923.25, 1923.31, 1924.36, 1925.27, 1929.29, 1936.01
Goldberg, Stan 1970.20
Goldberg, Stan J. 1974.05
Goldberg, Steven 1990.10
Goldblatt 1968.04
Goldblatt, Hanan 1971.14
Goldblum, Jeff 1981.14
Goldby, Derek 1968.23
Goldeck, Rosita 1896.23
Golden, Annie 1977.15, 1985.03, 1998.16, 2000.15
Golden, August 1929.01
Golden, Bella 1873.24
Golden, Earnest 1919.18, 1921.19, 1921.27
Golden, Eathel 1905.31
Golden, Emily 1983.16
Golden, Ernest 1918.08
Golden, Ernie 1916.22, 1928.23, 1930.20
Golden, George Fuller 1901.29
Golden, Grace 1890.19, 1890.24, 1890.39, 1891.12, 1891.17, 1892.03, 1892.52, 1895.23, 1896.41, 1897.53, 1898.04, 1898.06, 1898.14, 1898.15, 1898.19, 1898.21, 1898.39
Golden, H. 1873.26
Golden, Irena 1904.14
Golden, J.G. 1873.03
Golden, Jay 1936.06
Golden, Joe 1978.01
Golden, John 1910.17, 1910.30, 1912.13, 1912.26, 1913.04, 1914.23, 1916.01, 1916.03, 1916.15, 1916.20
Golden, John L. 1896.37, 1896.44, 1900.58, 1907.46, 1909.09, 1909.15, 1910.13, 1910.20, 1911.02, 1912.02, 1915.24, 1915.26, 1916.22, 1917.16, 1918.23, 1922.03
Golden, Louise 1955.12
Golden, Margaret McFeeley 2000.20
Golden, Martin 1872.23, 1872.35, 1873.19, 1873.24
Golden, Mr. 1873.03
Golden, Ray 1940.21, 1943.05, 1950.02, 1955.12, 1972.21
Golden, Richard 1877.21, 1879.01, 1879.06, 1880.02, 1881.36, 1881.41, 1882.14, 1882.45, 1885.07, 1885.09, 1887.31, 1888.13, 1894.11, 1898.60, 1900.12, 1906.26
Golden, Roslyn 1936.06
Golden, Ruth 1985.11, 1986.08, 1988.14
Golden, Webster 1950.02
Goldenberg, Billy 1961.21, 1976.16, 1978.27, 1983.09
Goldenberg, Samuel 1937.01
Goldenberg, William 1960.16, 1963.26, 1964.16, 1967.14, 1992.10, 1992.18, 1994.13
Goldenthal, Elliot 1996.16, 2000.10
Goldfaden, Abraham 1998.11
Goldfinch, Mrs. 1905.15
Goldgram, Henri 1965.30
Goldie, Beatrice 1895.11, 1897.14
Goldie, Jack 1938.12
Goldin, Al 1964.11
Goldin, Ricky Paull 1994.07
Golding Studios 1921.38
Golding, Edward 1934.08, 1934.09, 1934.10, 1934.11
Golding, Lucy 1895.43
Golding, Richard 1963.03
Golding, Stephen 1936.03
Goldman, Byron 1958.17, 1970.07, 1975.06, 1975.24, 1989.03
Goldman, Gloria 1976.20
Goldman, Harold 1930.18
Goldman, Herbert G. 1920.33
Goldman, James 1962.01, 1971.05, 2001.02
Goldman, Louis S. 1970.06
Goldman, Nina 1998.10, 2000.07
Goldman, Robert 1959.06
Goldman, Sherwin M. 1976.28, 1979.26, 1983.04
Goldman, William 1962.01
Goldmark, George 1885.63
Goldmark, Leo 1883.44
Goldner, Charles 1954.01
Goldoni, Carlo 1897.13, 1950.11
Goldpen, Mr. 1873.26
Goldrich, P.C. 1883.63, 1884.13, 1887.16, 1887.45
Goldrich, Peter 1881.17, 1881.19, 1885.49, 1885.66, 1886.03, 1886.42, 1886.52, 1887.07, 1887.16, 1887.39, 1887.45, 1887.48, 1888.14, 1888.27, 1888.40, 1889.07, 1889.11, 1889.15, 1889.18, 1890.49
Goldrich, Peter C. 1883.46, 1883.53
Goldrick, Patrick 1934.40
Goldsboro, Bobby 1979.30
Goldsmith, Bea 1942.05
Goldsmith, Eleanor 1947.03, 1948.14, 1949.17
Goldsmith, Gerald 1970.10
Goldsmith, Gertrude 1939.26
Goldsmith, Harvey 2000.04
Goldsmith, Herb 1994.11, 1997.04
Goldsmith, Herb Productions 1999.07
Goldsmith, Lee 1960.07, 1974.04
Goldsmith, Lillian 1906.34
Goldsmith, Merwin 1970.07, 1976.08, 1979.24, 1993.05
Goldsmith, Oliver 1796.03, 1904.51
Goldstein, Chuck 1940.09
Goldstein, Eugene 1937.14
Goldstein, Gerald 1984.15, 1997.21
Goldstein, Hyman 1937.14
Goldstein, Jerold 1993.05
Goldstein, Jerome 1951.20
Goldstein, Jess 1980.23, 1980.27, 1992.01
Goldstein, Joel 1983.15
Goldstein, Miss 1921.42
Goldstein, Mlle. 1882.30
Goldstein, Nat 1919.12
Goldstein, Smulik 1966.21
Goldston, Messr. 1854.01
Goldstone, Nat 1944.23, 1947.01
Goldsworthy, John 1911.08, 1916.06, 1917.19, 1919.04, 1930.15
Goldsworthy, John E. 1910.11
Goldsworthy, John H. 1914.02, 1914.17, 1916.14, 1928.48
Goldthwaite, Dora 1875.21, 1876.12
Goldthwaite, Fred 1879.15
Goldthwaite, Jennie 1891.27, 1892.24, 1895.25
Goldwasser, Lawrence L. 1939.22
Goler, Lauren 1980.30, 1982.03, 1986.20, 1987.14
Goler-Kosarin, Lauren 1999.16
Golkin, Jeffrey 1968.01
Goll, Wanda 1928.50
Golman, Daniel A. 1982.10
Golomb, Sheldon 1964.44
Golonka, Arlene 1959.22
Golovanova, Tamara 1977.13
Gomer, Hortense 1875.29
Gomer, Mlle. 1872.03
Gomersal, Mrs. William 1866.21, 1866.34, 1867.10
Gomersal, William 1866.21, 1866.24, 1866.34, 1867.08
Gomez, Armour 1982.15
Gomez, Beryl 1902.44
Gomez, Catalina 1894.18
Gomez, Georgia 1909.27
Gomez, Marie 1896.47
Gomez, Mike 1979.08
Gomez, Tommy 1943.17, 1944.31, 1945.13, 1946.24, 1951.12
Gomez, Tony 1961.10
Gomez, Vincente 1939.18, 1943.02
Gomila, Myrna Lynn 1998.02
Gon, Zamira 1946.17
Gondell, Harris 1947.08
Gondinet, Edmond 1885.60
Gondra, Arthur 1944.02
Gone, Lillian 1913.18
Gong, Michael Gregory 1997.08
Gontacharoff, Messr. 1922.06
Gontcharova, Natalia 1931.38
Gonzales, David 1987.01
Gonzales, Eddie 1974.14
Gonzales, Ernesto 1954.18
Gonzales, Guillermo 1972.08
Gonzales, Lou 1973.06
Gonzales, Maggie 1882.75
Gonzales, Max 1921.39
Gonzales, Miss 1881.35
Gonzales, Mr. 1858.03, 1867.18
Gonzalez, A. 1999.24
Gonzalez, Aldrin 1999.24
Gonzalez, Ernesto 1974.12
Gonzalez, Lou 1977.04, 1978.21, 1980.05
Gonzalez, Maria 1992.15
Gonzalez, Mr. 1852.03
Gonzalez, Natividad Santiago 1988.15
Gonzalez, Ruben Oscar 1999.18
Gonzalez, Sophie 1881.38
Gooch, May 1900.06, 1900.54
Gooch, Trevor Lee 2001.04
Good, Charles 1907.38
Good, Dan 1887.43
Good, Jack 1930.37, 1932.05, 1933.02, 1936.31
Good, Miles 1998.18
Goodal, Will 1920.02
Goodall, Elizabeth 1911.18, 1915.27, 1917.30
Goodall, Howard 1986.15
Goodall, Kate 1878.21
Goodall, Violet 1898.29, 1898.46
Goodchild, Tim 1989.01, 1992.03
Goode, Charles J. 1904.05
Goode, Herbert 1931.21
Goode, Jack 1946.03, 1946.18, 1948.16
Goode, Jimmy 1921.12
Goode, Richard 1972.02
Goodell, A.W. 1921.41
Goodell, Danzi 1926.32
Goodelle, Neila 1930.33, 1934.14
Goodelle, Niela 1936.01
Gooderowe, Joseph 1900.43
Goodfriend, Linda 1974.26
Goodfriend, Oscar 1906.31
Goodhart, Al 1932.27, 1952.11, 1985.08
Goodhart, Ernest 1928.48, 1944.14
Goodheart, Al 1999.05
Goodheart, Ernest 1938.17
Goodhue, Helen 1928.41, 1929.50
Goodier, Henry 1951.06
Gooding, Casey Marshall 2001.04
Gooding, E.D. 1872.07, 1875.39
Gooding, Geraldine 1935.01
Gooding, H.G. 1883.47
Gooding, Sally 1934.18
Goodis, Marvin 1966.13, 1967.09
Goodjohn, Arlouine 1945.19, 1948.17
Goodlake, Richard H. 1964.20
Goodman, A. 1925.50
Goodman, Al 1920.19, 1930.11, 1930.40, 1931.14, 1931.16, 1931.30, 1932.07, 1932.17, 1932.24, 1933.03, 1933.05, 1934.19, 1934.39, 1934.43, 1935.12, 1939.13, 1939.24, 1940.06, 1940.10
Goodman, Alfred 1917.04, 1919.37, 1920.47, 1921.02, 1921.14, 1921.20, 1921.25, 1921.34, 1922.11, 1922.23, 1922.34, 1922.36, 1923.02, 1923.03, 1923.12, 1923.13, 1923.17, 1923.25, 1923.41, 1924.06, 1924.13, 1924.21, 1924.29, 1924.36, 1925.01, 1925.02, 1925.07, 1925.13, 1925.23, 1925.26, 1925.27, 1925.28, 1925.39, 1926.14, 1926.15, 1926.18, 1926.26, 1927.01, 1927.14, 1927.17, 1927.41, 1928.29, 1929.03, 1930.30, 1931.04
Goodman, Arthur 1928.18
Goodman, Baby 1879.29
Goodman, Benny 1939.29, 1944.29, 1975.12, 1976.04, 1987.02, 1989.02, 1999.24, 2000.07
Goodman, Bergdorf 1924.02
Goodman, Bob 1971.19
Goodman, Davis 1924.46
Goodman, Dody 1952.15, 1953.03, 1962.16, 1974.02
Goodman, Dolores 1949.08
Goodman, Edward 1928.40, 1937.11
Goodman, Edward T. 1925.21
Goodman, Frank 1920.07
Goodman, George 1952.06
Goodman, Gordon 1955.13
Goodman, Harold 1934.06
Goodman, J.S. 1866.08, 1866.11, 1866.15
Goodman, John 1985.06
Goodman, Jules Eckert 1918.24
Goodman, Lee 1950.03, 1951.10, 1953.11, 1966.07, 1976.09
Goodman, Leonard 1934.34
Goodman, Mr. 1868.04
Goodman, Philip 1923.27, 1924.34, 1926.28, 1927.52, 1928.44
Goodman, Robyn 2001.01
Goodman, Sam 1907.35
Goodman, Susan 1984.14, 1985.18, 1987.04
Goodman, Tommy 1955.02
Goodner, Lillian 1921.26
Goodness, Joel 1992.02
Goodrich, C. 1860.03, 1860.04, 1860.05
Goodrich, Edena 1905.20
Goodrich, Edna 1903.14, 1903.40
Goodrich, Frances 1927.66, 1931.36, 1982.14
Goodrich, Mamie 1905.05
Goodrich, Messr. 1860.06
Goodrich, Mr. 1860.04
Goodridge, Ted 1975.21
Goodrow, Garry 1964.26
Goodrum, Randy 1998.19
Goodson, Ann 1976.06
Goodspeed Opera House 1975.03, 1975.24, 1976.15, 1976.25, 1981.03, 1982.05, 1985.02, 1985.04, 1990.14, 1992.01, 1995.07, 1995.14
Goodspeed, Don 1990.04
Goodwin, Aileen 1905.19
Goodwin, Charles 1886.10
Goodwin, Cheever 1880.42
Goodwin, Deidre 2000.17
Goodwin, Dora 1905.40
Goodwin, Doris 1910.07, 1910.31, 1946.24
Goodwin, E.D. 1893.23
Goodwin, E.F. 1886.45, 1887.06, 1887.52
Goodwin, E.K. 1894.34
Goodwin, Ed. F. 1886.59
Goodwin, Edward F. 1885.64, 1887.13, 1887.14
Goodwin, F. 1879.25, 1879.67
Goodwin, Frank 1871.14
Goodwin, Frank L. 1889.31
Goodwin, Fred 1928.45
Goodwin, George 1929.22
Goodwin, Gloria 1917.02, 1918.42
Goodwin, Harry 1918.24
Goodwin, J. Cheever 1876.18, 1876.21, 1877.21, 1878.02, 1878.19, 1879.01, 1880.02, 1880.40, 1884.21, 1885.58, 1887.01, 1887.24, 1887.28, 1888.13, 1889.13, 1890.26, 1890.43, 1891.11, 1891.31, 1891.36, 1891.47, 1892.04, 1892.22, 1892.33, 1893.07, 1893.16, 1894.24, 1894.28, 1894.29, 1895.08, 1895.16, 1895.22, 1896.29, 1896.35, 1897.11, 1898.12, 1899.21, 1899.36, 1900.19, 1900.34, 1900.39, 1900.40, 1901.27, 1902.24, 1903.04, 1904.17
Goodwin, Joe 1918.10, 1920.28, 1920.35, 1922.05, 1922.15, 1926.22, 1930.13, 1965.08
Goodwin, John 1934.06
Goodwin, Jr., Nat C. 1877.21, 1881.27
Goodwin, Karen Walter 1988.05
Goodwin, Kate 1880.43, 1880.63
Goodwin, Kia Joy 1998.02
Goodwin, Louise 1905.47
Goodwin, Maud 1886.24
Goodwin, Michael 1972.24, 1973.07
Goodwin, Mr. 1866.02, 1866.28, 1872.24, 1872.26
Goodwin, Myra 1882.81
Goodwin, Nat C. 1879.53, 1881.08, 1885.64, 1886.45, 1886.59, 1887.06, 1887.13, 1887.14, 1887.52
Goodwin, Nate 1921.24
Goodwin, Russell 1953.05, 1953.14, 1954.07, 1954.18, 1956.04, 1957.18, 1961.27, 1965.21
Goodwin, Ruth 1928.22, 1930.14
Goodwin, T. 1867.12

Goodwin, T.G. 1897.29
Goody, Ray 1946.13
Goodyear, Cris 1951.10
Goodyear, Dottie 1900.07
Goold, Ned 1990.19
Goolsby, Byrd 1912.25, 1916.26
Goor, Carolyn 1989.03
Gorbatcheff, Nadine 1958.18
Gorbea, Carlos 1974.06, 1992.15
Gorcey, Bernard 1907.51, 1918.40, 1920.01, 1925.52, 1927.14
Gordan, Mel 1965.20
Gorden, Grace 1900.08
Gorden, Irene 1908.33
Gordon, Ada 1906.41, 1908.21
Gordon, Adele 1905.44
Gordon, Alex 1968.05
Gordon, Alice 1895.28, 1910.25, 1914.10, 1921.09
Gordon, Allan S. 1996.09
Gordon, Amy 1879.33, 1879.35, 1880.32, 1882.18, 1883.64, 1883.67
Gordon, Annabelle 1908.36
Gordon, Archibald 1891.18
Gordon, Barbara 1952.11
Gordon, Barry H. 1980.11
Gordon, Bert 1921.22, 1940.10
Gordon, Bob 1926.03
Gordon, Bruce 1937.12, 1962.24
Gordon, C.H. 1876.05, 1876.07, 1876.09, 1876.10, 1876.11, 1876.14
Gordon, Carl 1908.01, 1908.34, 1910.13, 1971.13
Gordon, Caroline 1905.28
Gordon, Carolyn 1897.44, 1898.26, 1898.29, 1898.46, 1900.28, 1900.43, 1906.24
Gordon, Charles H. 1876.04
Gordon, Clark 1952.01
Gordon, Cliff 1905.42, 1910.15
Gordon, Diana 1921.21, 1922.27
Gordon, Edith 1950.13
Gordon, Edward 1890.49
Gordon, Elaine 1908.07, 1952.10
Gordon, Eleanor 1919.01, 1919.34
Gordon, Elsie 1917.04, 1918.07, 1918.22
Gordon, Ethele 1901.18
Gordon, F. 1870.05
Gordon, Frances 1900.43, 1904.43, 1905.45, 1909.26, 1912.28
Gordon, Francesca 1898.29, 1898.46, 1908.07
Gordon, Gary 1954.03
Gordon, Gavin 1924.38
Gordon, George 1934.15
Gordon, Georgie 1894.10
Gordon, Gerald 1912.04
Gordon, Grant 1967.07
Gordon, Guy 1957.03
Gordon, Harold 1902.28, 1908.31, 1944.17, 1956.02
Gordon, Harold E. 1957.05
Gordon, Harry 1928.07, 1928.32
Gordon, Hayes 1943.04, 1943.23, 1947.07, 1948.18, 1948.22
Gordon, Helen 1900.35, 1902.04, 1932.24
Gordon, Herr Al 1932.24
Gordon, Irving 1942.18, 1981.06, 1997.03
Gordon, J. 1867.07
Gordon, Jack 1908.21
Gordon, James McRobbie 1934.21, 1934.22, 1934.23, 1934.24, 1934.25, 1934.26, 1934.27, 1934.28, 1934.30, 1934.31, 1934.33
Gordon, Jeanne 1944.33
Gordon, John 1971.11
Gordon, Judith 1978.06, 1980.07, 1992.06
Gordon, Kitty 1905.46, 1909.24, 1910.26, 1911.12, 1911.38, 1915.26
Gordon, Kurt 1920.46
Gordon, Lawrence 1986.20
Gordon, Leo 1916.06
Gordon, Leon 1921.04
Gordon, Lillian 1930.09
Gordon, Lola 1903.03, 1904.13, 1904.44
Gordon, Lolita 1906.01
Gordon, Lolo 1904.13
Gordon, Louise 1885.26
Gordon, Mack 1930.43, 1931.19, 1931.31, 1931.36, 1932.06, 1932.15, 1933.05, 1940.20, 1943.23, 1979.24, 1980.09, 1982.12, 1983.09, 1988.08, 1999.24
Gordon, Mackenzie 1902.35
Gordon, Marvin 1958.03, 1958.07, 1966.05
Gordon, Maude Turner 1913.06, 1918.42, 1923.08, 1925.01, 1925.28
Gordon, Max 1930.32, 1931.16, 1931.37, 1932.17, 1933.26, 1934.29, 1935.14, 1938.09, 1939.28, 1941.12, 1945.04, 1945.09, 1946.20
Gordon, May 1888.27, 1888.40
Gordon, Michael 1953.02
Gordon, Miss 1884.11, 1903.03, 1904.13, 1904.44
Gordon, Noel 1904.40, 1945.11, 1950.19
Gordon, Paul 2000.20
Gordon, Peggy 1976.17
Gordon, Philip 1941.03
Gordon, Phyllis 1910.19
Gordon, Richard 1930.09
Gordon, Richard H. 1945.05
Gordon, Robert 1887.16, 1887.45, 1887.48, 1932.14
Gordon, Robert H. 1932.28, 1937.14, 1939.19, 1942.26, 1942.33, 1943.21, 1944.15, 1946.10, 1948.14, 1950.02
Gordon, Robert J. 1891.18
Gordon, Roland 1922.30
Gordon, Roy 1917.01, 1920.29, 1928.48, 1930.30, 1935.17
Gordon, Ruth 1927.68, 1929.07
Gordon, Suzette 1919.38
Gordon, Taylor 1931.21, 1932.26
Gordon, Valerie 1992.02
Gordon, Vera 1918.24
Gordon, Virginia 1946.20
Gordon, W.C. 1911.18
Gordon, Waxey 1933.05
Gordon, William 1930.26
Gordon, William C. 1914.19, 1926.10, 1926.44, 1927.44, 1927.57, 1927.61, 1930.03, 1931.10, 1931.12, 1931.17
Gordon, William G. 1914.11
Gordon, Withald 1920.03
Gordy, Berry 1982.22
Gore, Altovise 1961.24
Gore, Christopher 1972.25
Gore, Edward 1902.01, 1903.40, 1904.08, 1904.40, 1905.13
Gore, Mabel 1930.14, 1934.03
Gore, Michael 1988.12
Gorelik, Mordecai 1935.16
Gorenflo, Marie 1873.20, 1873.27, 1875.31, 1875.34, 1875.35, 1875.36, 1875.37, 1875.38, 1875.40, 1876.01, 1876.13, 1876.15, 1876.22, 1876.29, 1877.01, 1878.01, 1879.68, 1880.09, 1881.29, 1882.02, 1883.32, 1883.53, 1883.63, 1884.13, 1884.41, 1885.02, 1885.15, 1885.22, 1892.44, 1892.54, 1893.10, 1893.36
Gorenflo, Miss 1893.27
Gorey, Edward 1978.24
Gorey, Lou 1920.28
Gorgas, Alice 1929.01
Gorgioni, Al 1976.34
Gorham, George H. 1990.06
Gorham, Robert 1928.19
Gorim, Pauline 1929.31
Gorin, Igor 1942.33
Goring-Thomas 1913.07
Gorki, Maxim 1935.16
Gorlizki, Ili 1971.14
Gorman 1876.01
Gorman's Philadelphia Church Choir Company 1879.13, 1879.66
Gorman, Billy 1920.33
Gorman, D. 1883.42
Gorman, Eddie 1920.33
Gorman, Edward 1891.25, 1892.44, 1893.27, 1893.36, 1893.46, 1894.49, 1926.24
Gorman, Emma 1911.24
Gorman, Freddie 1984.15
Gorman, George 1903.35, 1904.18, 1910.13, 1913.37
Gorman, James 1883.66, 1903.01, 1903.11, 1904.53, 1905.05, 1906.09, 1908.14, 1908.22, 1911.33, 1911.41, 1912.05, 1914.34, 1917.37
Gorman, John E. 1904.18, 1910.13
Gorman, Messr. 1893.13, 1894.04
Gorman, Michael 1981.12, 1985.02
Gorman, Mme. 1890.50
Gorman, Pat 1983.01, 1987.15
Gorman, Richard 1891.03, 1892.05, 1898.01, 1904.46
Gorman, Robert 1961.28, 1965.14, 1967.16, 1970.02
Gorman, Ross 1925.25, 1979.24
Gorman, Trisha 1993.10
Gorme, Eydie 1968.03
Gormley, Ruth 1929.28
Gorner, Selma 1890.31
Gorney, A.J. 1923.17
Gorney, Jay 1924.01, 1924.25, 1924.32, 1924.33, 1924.36, 1925.25, 1925.48, 1926.03, 1927.09, 1927.27, 1929.26, 1930.22, 1930.33, 1931.19, 1931.21, 1932.20, 1940.21, 1942.26, 1948.23, 1949.12, 1952.11, 1961.08, 1974.09
Gorniak, Edyta 1992.05
Gorodetsky, Messr. 1922.06, 1923.28, 1925.03, 1927.51, 1929.05
Gorostiza, Celestino 1939.18
Gorrill, Maggy 1975.09, 1979.22
Gorrin, John 1974.12
Gorrin, Michael 1959.24
Gorsey, Renee 1965.20, 1966.07
Gorshin, Frank 1969.14
Gorshuniova, Galina 1925.51
Gorski, Virginia 1945.20, 1948.08, 1949.01
Gorss, Desmond 1979.10
Gory, Gene 1931.19
Goshal, Kumar 1927.63
Goslar, Lotte 1938.04, 1939.23, 1940.04
Gosling, Pat 1966.24
Gosmen, Thomas 1886.06
Gosnell, Evelyn 1925.41
Gosnova, Florentine 1923.38, 1924.38, 1925.08, 1926.29
Goss, Ed 1879.04, 1880.36
Goss, Edward 1880.09, 1880.64, 1881.09, 1881.29, 1882.02
Goss, Julia 1968.28, 1976.12, 1976.13, 1978.15, 1978.17
Goss, Messr. 1879.37
Goss, Ray 1942.20
Goss, Robert 1964.24, 1965.36
Gossett, Lou (Louis) 1958.11, 1963.27, 1964.32, 1965.32
Gossman, Gertrude M. 1928.20
Gossman, Thomas 1887.49
Goth, Trudy 1946.16
Gotham City Gates 1999.24
Gotham, Jerry 1964.21
Gothard, Lawrence 1907.60
Gotshalks, Jury 1962.21
Gott, Tom 1921.06
Gottehrer, Richard 1984.15, 1997.21
Gottesfeld, Charles 1943.14
Gotthold, C.F. 1895.30
Gotthold, Charles 1888.10, 1896.11, 1904.54, 1928.03
Gotthold, Charles F. 1894.36, 1896.09
Gotthold, J. Newton 1884.23
Gotthold, J.N. 1881.31
Gotthold, Kate 1906.43
Gotthold, Newton 1888.10
Gottler, Archie 1914.22, 1918.19, 1920.33, 1928.25
Gottlieb, John 2001.07
Gottlieb, Myron I. 1993.09, 1994.08, 1998.01
Gottlieb, William B. 1897.21
Gottschalk, Fredinand 1903.41, 1904.08
Gottschalk, L.F. 1899.40
Gottschalk, Louis 1880.19, 1916.24
Gottschalk, Louis F. 1896.02, 1901.19, 1901.21, 1902.01, 1903.36, 1904.40, 1905.56, 1906.37, 1906.48, 1907.48, 1909.30, 1911.23, 1911.37, 1912.01
Gottschall, Ruth 1982.11, 1987.16, 1988.20, 1989.25, 1993.02
Goudreault, Zeph 1899.04
Goudvis, Helena 1944.01
Gouge, E.H. 1880.25
Gougenheim, Adelaide 1851.01, 1851.06, 1854.01, 1855.01, 1859.05, 1859.06, 1859.07
Gougenheim, Joey 1859.07
Gougenheim, Josephine 1851.01, 1851.06, 1854.01, 1854.06, 1855.01, 1859.05, 1859.06
Gougeon, Mons. 1868.13
Gough, F. 1869.04, 1869.15
Gough, Lloyd 1941.01
Gough, Rita 1888.36
Gough, William H. 1902.36
Goukovsky, Messr. 1927.51
Goula, Juan 1881.24
Gould, Berni 1942.15, 1942.26
Gould, Bert 1927.12
Gould, Billy 1914.21
Gould, Carrie 1885.31, 1885.62
Gould, Chuck 1949.06
Gould, Dave 1928.41, 1929.20, 1930.25, 1930.28, 1931.05, 1931.14, 1932.13, 1938.09
Gould, Elliott 1957.17, 1958.08, 1959.03, 1962.05, 1965.29
Gould, Gordon 1979.29
Gould, Herbert 1931.41
Gould, Heywood 1971.09
Gould, Howard 1934.37
Gould, Jay 1920.06, 1921.19, 1922.29, 1923.41, 1924.10
Gould, Julia 1851.02, 1851.03, 1851.05, 1852.01, 1853.02, 1853.03, 1857.01, 1857.02, 1857.03
Gould, Kelly 1922.05
Gould, Louise 1897.48, 1904.53
Gould, Mamie 1900.38
Gould, Marissa 1999.21
Gould, Martin 1982.14
Gould, Mesdame 1852.05
Gould, Miss 1882.23
Gould, Morton 1934.03, 1940.16, 1942.26, 1945.10, 1945.20, 1950.04, 1958.21, 1989.03
Gould, Peter David 1994.10
Gould, Rita 1914.15, 1919.38
Gould, Sam 1924.19
Gould, Sandra 1934.06
Gould, William 1891.40, 1899.26, 1899.37, 1900.07, 1900.56, 1901.23, 1902.24, 1903.14, 1904.21, 1907.44
Goulden, Harold 1921.11
Goulding, Ray 1970.14
Gouldson, Mr. 1851.08
Goulet, Robert 1960.21, 1968.01, 1993.11
Goullaud, Louis S. 1891.08
Goulston, Andre 1962.23, 1964.03, 1964.29, 1964.45, 1968.06
Gounder, Jill B. 1995.02
Gounod 1894.21, 1923.25
Gounod, Charles 1864.13, 1867.28, 1893.04, 1893.44, 1999.06
Gour, Betty 1953.09
Gouraud, Jackson 1898.28, 1898.43, 1899.12, 1901.23
Gouraud, Powers 1901.23, 1926.37
Gouraud, Yvonne 1917.08, 1918.12
Gourlay, J. 1859.08
Gourlay, Jennie 1864.04
Gourlay, John 1879.32, 1880.11, 1880.59, 1880.65, 1880.67, 1880.70, 1882.24, 1884.15, 1884.56, 1897.37
Gourlay, Messr. 1844.01
Gourlay, Miss 1855.09, 1858.04
Gourlay, Mr. 1851.04, 1852.01, 1854.04, 1866.01, 1866.04, 1866.05, 1882.59
Gouroud, Powers 1929.22
Gouthiere, Mlle. 1879.40
Gouthure, Mlle. 1879.39
Gover, Lucy 1904.07
Governor, George 1964.21
Gowans, "Brad" 1944.31, 1950.07
Gowans, Brad 1946.21
Gowing, Almerin 1921.08
Gowraud, Jackson 1902.40
Goyeneche, R. 1985.07, 1999.18
Goyeneche, Roberto 1985.07
Goz, Harry 1964.40, 1970.19, 1988.09
Goz, Michael 1992.04, 1997.12
Gozzi, Carlo 2000.10
Graae, Jason 1982.10, 1987.02, 1993.16
Grabber, Ariel 1989.09
Grabem, Messr. 1861.01
Grable, Betty 1939.30
Grace Cameron Opera Company 1907.19
Grace VanStuddiford Amusement Company 1908.34
Grace, Barbara 1926.25
Grace, Buster 1940.16, 1942.19, 1946.14, 1947.12, 1948.19, 1949.05
Grace, Edmond 1884.44
Grace, Eileen 1923.43
Grace, Frank 1916.03, 1918.05, 1920.47
Grace, George A. 1893.14, 1894.02
Grace, John 1880.08
Grace, Michael 1953.17
Grace, Nikolas 1989.01
Grace, Steven 1999.02
Grace, Thomas 1947.09
Grace, Timothy 1945.08
Gracey, Spencer 1892.29, 1893.45
Gracie, Sally 1942.26
Grad, Lottie 1907.31
Grad, Peter N. 1970.07, 1972.19
Grade, Lord 1981.27, 1987.05

Graden, David 1979.10
Gradl, Christine 1982.10
Gradwell, A. 1879.18, 1887.43
Gradwell, Alex 1879.23
Gradwell, Messr. 1879.23
Grady, Al 1915.24
Grady, Alfred 1909.05
Grady, Blanche 1945.01
Grady, Chester 1922.03
Grady, Lottie 1907.29, 1909.27
Grady, Morris 1876.19
Grady, T.J. 1884.19
Grady, Thomas J. 1891.02, 1894.13, 1903.20
Graeber, Betty 1957.06
Graee, Mr. 1855.01
Graey, James R. 1907.61
Graf, Herbert 1944.16
Graf, James M. 1930.21
Graf, Jenny 1937.05
Graf, Walter 1945.04
Graff, Ellen 1962.03
Graff, Florie 1901.11
Graff, George 1913.03
Graff, Ilene 1977.04
Graff, J. 1879.14
Graff, Jr., George 1910.06, 1911.04, 1913.03, 1914.05
Graff, Lillian 1987.10, 1989.04
Graff, Mr. 1855.08
Graff, Randy 1979.03, 1989.29, 1998.05, 2001.01
Graff, Renee 1932.19
Graff, Todd 1983.19
Graffman, Goran 1966.19
Graft, J. 1876.13
Graft, James 1875.37
Grafton, Gloria 1930.25, 1935.15
Grafton, Maud 1890.40
Grahal, Fernando 1965.34, 1972.14
Graham, Ann 1939.30, 1940.19, 1942.16
Graham, Anne 1939.07
Graham, Arnold 2000.14
Graham, Arthur 1963.15
Graham, B.R. 1893.38
Graham, Beatrice 1938.04
Graham, Bessie 1903.06, 1906.05
Graham, Bette 1957.14, 1959.01
Graham, Carrie 1899.09, 1903.18, 1905.52
Graham, Charles 1876.02, 1877.01, 1877.12, 1877.19, 1877.39, 1878.04, 1879.09, 1881.40, 1889.36, 1889.39, 1891.15, 1891.32, 1891.40, 1893.08, 1893.30, 1893.33, 1894.07, 1897.52
Graham, Charles E. 1896.32
Graham, Chele 1957.08
Graham, D.K. 1893.03
Graham, Deborah 1988.10
Graham, Donna 1977.06
Graham, E. 1885.14
Graham, Edna 1884.21
Graham, Edward 1920.28, 1928.23
Graham, Effie 1914.22
Graham, Elsie 1886.01
Graham, Ernest 1907.01
Graham, Evelyn 1905.17
Graham, Faye 1930.14, 1931.34
Graham, Fred 1913.31, 1948.32
Graham, Frederic 1917.17, 1920.38
Graham, Frederick 1918.37, 1919.23, 1922.41, 1925.08, 1936.22
Graham, George 1840.02, 1840.03, 1840.04, 1911.36
Graham, George M. 1909.29
Graham, Gwendolyn 1924.37
Graham, H. Gordon 1939.19
Graham, Harry 1916.01, 1918.27, 1922.36, 1925.07, 1926.33, 1930.38
Graham, Herbert 1893.11
Graham, Howard 1891.03, 1892.05, 1892.34, 1894.16, 1897.52
Graham, Irvin 1936.12, 1938.04, 1940.23, 1941.03, 1942.25, 1956.08, 1957.10
Graham, James 1916.15
Graham, Jennie 1899.22
Graham, Jessie 1908.32, 1928.49, 1935.17
Graham, John 1975.24
Graham, Joseph 1892.01, 1904.35, 1925.47
Graham, June 1946.20, 1948.23, 1949.02, 1953.02, 1956.03
Graham, Kate 1906.05
Graham, Kitty 1912.28
Graham, L. 1870.11
Graham, Larry 1984.15
Graham, Laura 1864.22
Graham, Lillian 1908.21, 1911.23
Graham, Martha 1923.31
Graham, Matt 1886.27
Graham, Messr. 1888.42
Graham, Miss 1869.43, 1889.09
Graham, Mr. 1867.19, 1872.09, 1881.14
Graham, Nathan Lee 2000.08
Graham, Paul 1931.43
Graham, R.E. 1879.18, 1879.23, 1879.24, 1879.38, 1880.24, 1881.23, 1882.56, 1885.03, 1885.50, 1886.15, 1888.39, 1896.19, 1898.77, 1900.51, 1907.48, 1912.15, 1914.23
Graham, R.J. 1888.42, 1889.25, 1892.06
Graham, Rachael 1989.23
Graham, Richard 1893.33, 1959.27, 1970.08
Graham, Richard J. 1891.18
Graham, Robert 1908.34
Graham, Robert E. 1884.06, 1897.14, 1906.32
Graham, Ronald 1937.10, 1938.14, 1939.30, 1942.01, 1942.15, 1944.18
Graham, Ronny 1952.09, 1956.08, 1957.10, 1961.21, 1962.02, 1962.14, 1964.35, 1968.13
Graham, Rose 1878.12, 1880.39
Graham, Roze 1879.63
Graham, Stephen 1980.13
Graham, T. 1867.20
Graham, Vivian 1905.27
Graham-Dent, Nellie 1919.02, 1919.28, 1922.13
Grahame, George 1922.35
Grahame, Gerald 1980.03
Grahame, Kenneth 1985.20
Grahame, Nellie 1880.43
Grahame-Johnstone, Anne 1966.26
Grahame-Johnstone, Janet 1966.26
Grahame-Smith, Evelyn 1910.30
Grahl, Arthur 1954.12
Grahme, Evelyn 1913.10
Grain, F. 1836.01
Grain, R. Corney 1886.45
Grain, Robert 1866.06, 1866.08, 1866.11, 1866.15, 1868.20, 1868.23, 1868.32, 1869.08, 1869.38
Grainger, Porter 1925.18, 1930.24, 1930.29, 1931.31, 1932.12, 1975.20, 1976.16, 1978.09, 1989.02, 1999.06
Gramlich, David 1988.18
Gramm, Donald 1953.06, 1953.15, 1954.06, 1954.10
Grammer, Sidney 1934.34
Grammis, Adam 1982.06
Gramnotina, Mme. 1927.51
Gran, Albert 1910.03
Grana, Maria 1985.07, 1999.18
Granada, Carmen 1918.40
Granados 1949.07
Granados, Georgina 1974.14
Granafei, Dolores 1939.26
Granat, Arny 1999.25
Granat, Frank 1964.33
Granat, Harvey 1974.10
Granat, Louis M. 1900.35
Granata, Dona 1976.11
Grand Ballets Canadiens, Les 1972.08
Grand, Murray 1952.09, 1956.08, 1968.13
Grandais, M. 1926.45, 1926.47, 1926.48
Grandais, M. Georges 1926.43
Grandall, Constance 1936.06
Grande, George 1934.06
Graner, LeBlanc 1876.29
Graner, Marjorie 1961.15
Grange, Eugene 1880.28, 1896.29
Granger 1879.12
Granger and Kennedy 1877.04
Granger, Farley 1959.06, 1960.11, 1962.15
Granger, Maude 1877.07, 1895.35, 1903.33
Granger, Michael 1964.27
Granger, Seth 1987.19
Granger, Thomas 1883.46, 1883.53, 1883.63, 1884.13, 1896.24
Granger, Tom 1897.43
Granger, Tommy 1883.02
Granichstadten, Bruno 1912.15
Granitzer, L. 1885.67
Granlund, Niles T. 1926.11
Grannum, Karen 1976.04
Granoff, Perry B. 1987.06
Grant 1891.02, 1894.16
Grant, Al 1903.07
Grant, Alfred 1891.02, 1895.02
Grant, Bert 1904.38, 1912.07, 1912.14, 1912.38, 1913.30, 1915.16, 1916.09, 1919.02, 1919.40, 1920.19, 1923.41
Grant, Bertha 1904.38
Grant, Billy 1922.16
Grant, Brian 1978.26
Grant, Cameron 1944.21
Grant, Cary 1922.30, 1927.63, 1929.06, 1929.39, 1931.34
Grant, Charles 1919.14, 1920.18, 1921.30, 1922.39, 1923.32, 1924.33, 1926.18, 1927.38
Grant, Charles N. 1912.02, 1916.13, 1916.22, 1917.19, 1924.43
Grant, Dolores 1930.08
Grant, Douglas 1968.24, 1970.20
Grant, E. 1883.45
Grant, E.D. 1881.40
Grant, E.S. 1881.56, 1882.05, 1882.16, 1882.52, 1883.38, 1883.64, 1883.65, 1886.34, 1887.19
Grant, Ed S. 1883.10
Grant, Edith 1939.13
Grant, Eva 1971.16
Grant, Faye 1985.08
Grant, Frances 1920.15, 1920.27, 1922.26
Grant, Francis 1918.07
Grant, Fred 1905.09
Grant, Gertrude 1906.05, 1909.30, 1910.34
Grant, Gretchen 1921.32
Grant, Helen 1905.31
Grant, Henry 1909.10
Grant, J. 1866.20
Grant, J. Lloyd 1976.04
Grant, J.L. 1907.55
Grant, James 1898.17, 1902.43, 1905.22, 1905.46, 1913.16, 1916.23, 1919.30, 1928.14
Grant, James F. 1900.58
Grant, Jane 1904.24
Grant, Jeanne 1976.36
Grant, John 1927.41
Grant, Karen 1966.08
Grant, Katherine 1914.33
Grant, Keith Lee 1999.22
Grant, Lackaye 1925.37
Grant, Laurence 1914.01
Grant, Lauretta 1914.33
Grant, Lawrence 1910.05, 1916.05
Grant, Lawrence. 1914.19
Grant, Lottie 1871.02
Grant, Louis 1895.18
Grant, Mabel 1930.19
Grant, Malcolm 1985.13
Grant, Mary 1905.04, 1944.02, 1944.29, 1945.11, 1945.14
Grant, Maxwell 1957.01, 1960.12
Grant, May 1906.01
Grant, Messr. 1905.22, 1908.25
Grant, Micki 1963.27, 1972.13, 1976.35, 1978.12, 1980.14, 1980.15, 1982.17, 1984.15
Grant, Mr. 1860.01
Grant, Richard 1904.21
Grant, Robert 1958.05
Grant, Sean 1987.05, 1989.25, 1993.02
Grant, Sidney 1912.24
Grant, Sterling 1929.01, 1929.18, 1930.19
Grant, Sydney 1894.42, 1910.11, 1913.02, 1913.18, 1914.21, 1916.21, 1919.28, 1923.42, 1924.17, 1945.12
Grant, Ted 1922.02
Grant, William 1908.20, 1922.16
Granval, Jean-Pierre 1964.06
Granville, Bernard 1912.38, 1914.01, 1914.16, 1914.22, 1915.15, 1916.10, 1919.34, 1919.43, 1920.18, 1922.08, 1923.06, 1926.24
Granville, Ella 1884.27
Granville, Eva 1886.06
Granville, Evelyn 1885.63
Granville, Gertie 1881.29, 1882.02, 1882.50, 1882.74, 1882.79, 1883.46, 1883.53, 1883.63
Granville, Homer 1903.33
Granville, Joseph 1940.06
Granville, May 1888.04
Granville, Miss 1886.36
Granville, Sydney 1934.21, 1934.23, 1934.24, 1934.25, 1934.27, 1934.28, 1934.30, 1934.31, 1936.13, 1936.14, 1936.15, 1936.16, 1936.18, 1936.19, 1936.24, 1936.25, 1939.02, 1939.03, 1939.04, 1939.08, 1939.09
Granville, Taylor 1900.44, 1905.25
Granz, Norman 1959.15, 1961.25
Grapewin, Charles E. 1905.43
Grapewin, Charley 1904.14, 1908.11
Graphenreed, Timothy 1975.01, 1979.32, 1981.14, 1984.09, 1985.03, 1993.03
Graser, Shirley 1956.02
Grassby, Bertram 1909.04
Grasses, Kate 1901.20
Grassi, Enzo 1937.14
Grassi, V. 1923.29
Grattan, Emma 1869.06, 1869.27, 1869.32, 1872.25, 1872.30, 1872.32, 1872.36, 1872.38, 1872.40, 1872.43, 1885.21
Grattan, Mrs. H.P. 1855.08, 1857.02, 1863.06
Grattan, V. 1863.10
Gratton, Muriel 1938.15
Grau, Jacob 1868.24, 1868.26, 1869.05, 1869.16, 1869.30
Grau, Joseph 1869.03
Grau, Jules 1884.28, 1884.29, 1884.30, 1884.31
Grau, Maurice 1877.37
Grau, Maurice 1875.01, 1875.02, 1875.04, 1875.07, 1875.08, 1875.09, 1875.13, 1875.25, 1875.27, 1875.28, 1875.29, 1875.30, 1875.33, 1876.26, 1876.31, 1877.09, 1877.10, 1877.11, 1877.12, 1877.14, 1877.17, 1877.18, 1877.19, 1877.29, 1877.30, 1877.31, 1877.32, 1877.33, 1877.34, 1877.38, 1879.44, 1879.46, 1880.14, 1883.61, 1884.01, 1884.02, 1884.03, 1884.05, 1884.62, 1885.17, 1885.19, 1885.20, 1885.55, 1885.56, 1885.57, 1885.59, 1885.60, 1885.61, 1886.08, 1886.09, 1886.18, 1886.19, 1886.20, 1886.21, 1886.22, 1887.35, 1887.36, 1887.37, 1887.38, 1887.41, 1888.15, 1889.54, 1893.45, 1894.41, 1894.48, 1895.09, 1895.12, 1896.10, 1896.12
Grau, Robert 1893.24
Graus, Frank 1911.28
Graus, Isabel 1911.28
Grauss, Carrie 1891.20, 1892.31
Grauss, Frank 1891.20, 1892.31
Grauya, Ted 1934.32
Gravenstein, A. 1881.46, 1881.48, 1881.49, 1881.50, 1881.51, 1881.53, 1881.54, 1882.29, 1882.30, 1882.35
Graver, J. Adams 1876.19
Graver, J.A. 1873.20, 1873.22, 1873.27, 1875.31, 1876.19
Graver, Mr. 1876.19
Graves, C.L. 1877.20
Graves, Douglas 1912.32
Graves, George 1907.06
Graves, Julie 1989.27
Graves, Katherine 1954.15
Graves, Kia 1990.02
Graves, Leonard 1951.12, 1956.03
Graves, Margie 1888.27
Graves, Pauline 1896.25
Graves, Phillip 1968.23
Graves, Rupert 1923.43
Graves, Russell 1932.12
Graves, Tom 1913.31, 1915.07
Graves, Virgie 1886.32
Graves, Yolanda 1986.11
Graveson, Jan 1993.07
Gravier, Ernest 1864.01, 1864.03, 1864.08, 1864.11
Gravitte, Debbie Shapiro 1993.05
Gray Maud 1896.52
Gray, Adrienne 1944.32, 1945.11
Gray, Alexander 1922.19, 1923.20, 1925.14, 1926.15, 1940.01, 1943.12
Gray, Anthony J. 1892.34
Gray, B. 1876.19
Gray, Bee Ho 1922.18
Gray, Bessie 1881.12, 1882.04, 1882.20, 1911.26, 1919.05
Gray, Billy 1876.19, 1877.24, 1878.01, 1878.13, 1878.17, 1879.04, 1879.37, 1879.68, 1880.09
Gray, Carl C. 1930.14
Gray, Charles 1907.34, 1971.12
Gray, Charles S. 1875.12
Gray, Christian 1965.33
Gray, Dolle 1925.21
Gray, Dolores 1944.29, 1945.18, 1951.19, 1953.11, 1959.11, 1967.02
Gray, Don 1960.09
Gray, Dorothy 1894.16, 1962.22
Gray, Eddie 1923.39
Gray, Edith 1885.31
Gray, Elsie 1892.38
Gray, Evelyn 1889.47, 1902.32
Gray, Frank 1929.19

Gray, George Branson 1974.15
Gray, Georgy 1884.60
Gray, Gilda 1919.16, 1921.18, 1922.19, 1923.20
Gray, Grace 1900.59, 1934.06
Gray, Gracie 1898.61
Gray, Gussie 1902.32
Gray, Harold 1977.06, 1997.04
Gray, Helen 1927.18, 1930.06, 1930.25, 1933.26, 1935.19, 1936.27
Gray, Jack 1929.31
Gray, Jane 1887.40
Gray, Janie 1884.29
Gray, Jerri 1956.02
Gray, Jerry 1999.24
Gray, John 1926.39, 1980.13
Gray, John T. 1898.60
Gray, Jr., Gordon 1972.13
Gray, Kevin 1989.05, 2000.09
Gray, L. Michael 1982.17
Gray, Laura 1889.50
Gray, Lawrence 1931.40
Gray, Len 1927.30
Gray, Leslie 1944.03
Gray, Lulu 1931.08
Gray, Madeline 1930.14
Gray, Margery 1960.05, 1963.08
Gray, Mary 1886.11, 1888.03, 1888.45
Gray, Maude 1911.35
Gray, Maurice 1877.06
Gray, Mellie 1883.47
Gray, Michael 1976.35
Gray, Millie 1897.29
Gray, Minnie 1876.36
Gray, Miss 1857.01, 1870.31, 1871.11, 1881.06, 1882.46, 1884.42, 1886.36
Gray, Mr. 1841.01, 1869.04, 1869.13
Gray, Neil 1875.05, 1879.02, 1897.29
Gray, Norman 1938.10
Gray, Oliver 1961.26
Gray, Richard 1951.19
Gray, Rita 1905.37
Gray, Roger 1908.16, 1919.04, 1923.24, 1924.33, 1924.40, 1926.22, 1927.16, 1928.21, 1929.04, 1932.24
Gray, Ruth 1922.24
Gray, Stella 1898.50
Gray, Stokely 1957.07, 1964.20, 1967.09, 1968.17
Gray, T.J. 1921.30
Gray, Thomas J. 1915.22, 1917.09, 1921.19
Gray, Timothy 1964.16, 1971.06, 1974.26
Gray, Violet 1921.24
Gray, Wilhelmina 1957.09
Gray, William 1879.37, 1879.68, 1880.09, 1880.36, 1880.64, 1881.29, 1882.02, 1882.50, 1882.74
Gray, Willie 1906.43
Gray-Stewart Musical Company 1911.22
Grayam, Penny 1958.03
Grayson, Helen 1879.15, 1881.22, 1882.25
Grayson-Norcross Opera Company 1881.22
Grayu, Maurice 1877.13
Graziani, Itzchak 1968.04
Grazzini, Mons. 1875.28, 1875.29
Grean, Robin 1971.12, 1973.14, 1975.12
Greanin, Leon 1943.11
Greatrex, Newman 1928.04
Greaves, Danielle 1994.08
Greaves, William 1947.03, 1949.15
Greaza, Walter N. 1937.07
Grebenetsky, Messr. 1929.05
Greek Theatre Association 1964.25
Greel, Muriel 1928.25
Green, Adolph 1944.33, 1945.20, 1951.19, 1953.03, 1954.13, 1956.14, 1958.05, 1958.08, 1958.21, 1959.03, 1960.23, 1961.25, 1961.28, 1963.05, 1964.21, 1967.06, 1967.09, 1970.09, 1971.15, 1974.02, 1977.02, 1978.02, 1979.13, 1979.14, 1979.22, 1982.18, 1983.09, 1985.08, 1988.08, 1989.03, 1989.06, 1990.20, 1991.07, 1991.10, 1991.13, 1994.09, 1997.01, 1998.16, 1998.18, 1999.23, 2001.03
Green, Al 1982.17
Green, Alan 1947.20
Green, Aline 1928.16
Green, Amanda 1994.09
Green, Andrea 1982.01
Green, Bella 1867.18
Green, Belle 1870.31
Green, Billie 1932.26
Green, Bradley Kerr 2001.04
Green, Brian Lane 1989.09
Green, Bud 1919.16, 1920.07, 1928.33, 1931.13, 1933.16, 1939.29, 1975.12
Green, Burt 1910.16
Green, Burton 1915.16, 1917.08, 1918.20, 1920.01, 1921.27
Green, C. 1869.44
Green, C.H. 1883.37
Green, Colton 1993.09, 1998.01
Green, Cora 1921.26, 1922.22, 1924.37, 1938.19
Green, Daisy 1903.38, 1908.19, 1909.04
Green, David 1987.19, 1989.04
Green, Del 1966.07, 1967.05
Green, Denis 1948.32
Green, Diana 1983.03
Green, Doe Doe 1922.44
Green, Donald 1947.01
Green, Doris 1920.28
Green, Eddie 1929.23, 1932.08, 1939.17, 1975.20, 1999.06
Green, Elizabeth 1995.13
Green, Ella 1875.11
Green, Erma 1907.02
Green, Ethel 1905.22, 1909.23, 1910.12, 1911.15
Green, Ettie 1892.31
Green, Fanni 1991.01
Green, Florence 1984.15
Green, Forrest 1955.02
Green, Frank 1922.12, 1923.41, 1946.08, 1956.14, 1957.12, 1959.27
Green, Frank W. 1880.43
Green, G. 1869.40
Green, Gary 1945.14
Green, Gerald 1964.35
Green, Gladys 1925.37
Green, H.F. 1957.07, 1959.25, 1962.24
Green, Harry 1918.21
Green, Herman 1939.29
Green, Howard J. 1925.17
Green, Irving 1931.03
Green, J. Ed 1906.08, 1907.29, 1907.31
Green, Jack 1923.18
Green, Jackie 1942.35
Green, James 1937.09
Green, James F. 1899.04
Green, Jane 1920.22, 1920.23, 1923.33, 1925.47
Green, Jess 1966.14
Green, John W. 1931.42
Green, Johnny 1930.08, 1930.25, 1930.32, 1931.08, 1933.20, 1942.15, 1942.24, 1942.29, 1948.13, 1954.11, 1957.10, 1986.02, 1989.02
Green, Jonathan 1978.07, 1978.23, 1979.27, 1982.07, 1983.12, 1987.11, 1988.04, 1989.13, 1990.08, 1993.12, 1993.14, 1996.02
Green, Jr., Isaac 1947.13
Green, Lawrence 1925.50
Green, Le Petite 1870.31
Green, Leroy 1999.15
Green, Lil 1975.20
Green, Lillian 1895.11, 1895.17, 1901.06
Green, Margaret 1920.37
Green, Marion 1919.42, 1921.39, 1922.11, 1923.31, 1924.38, 1926.08, 1932.23, 1937.13, 1945.04
Green, Martin 1898.64
Green, Martyn 1934.21, 1934.22, 1934.23, 1934.24, 1934.26, 1934.27, 1934.28, 1934.30, 1934.31, 1934.33, 1936.13, 1936.15, 1936.16, 1936.18, 1936.19, 1936.21, 1936.23, 1936.24, 1936.25, 1939.02, 1939.03, 1939.04, 1939.06, 1939.08, 1939.09, 1939.11, 1947.22, 1948.02, 1948.03, 1948.06, 1948.07, 1948.09, 1948.10, 1951.01, 1951.04, 1951.06, 1951.07, 1951.09, 1952.14, 1952.16, 1952.17, 1952.18, 1952.19, 1956.07, 1969.04
Green, Messr. 1841.01, 1919.33
Green, Mildred 1929.32
Green, Milicent 1935.16
Green, Miss 1869.07, 1917.31
Green, Mitzi 1937.04, 1940.09, 1942.26, 1945.20
Green, Morris 1920.28, 1921.27, 1922.32, 1923.31, 1924.22, 1924.32, 1925.47, 1928.08, 1928.13, 1930.28, 1931.05, 1932.21, 1932.23
Green, Mort 1952.20
Green, Mr. 1841.01
Green, Natalye 1946.16, 1949.13
Green, Nathalie 1910.02
Green, Norma 1941.01
Green, Paul 1936.28, 1971.06
Green, Penny Ann 1960.06
Green, Phil 1953.17, 1956.08
Green, Robert 1869.02, 1869.14
Green, Rodney 1975.01
Green, Ronald 1916.18
Green, Rose 1906.21
Green, Rosie 1907.57, 1908.31, 1909.13, 1910.18, 1921.20
Green, Ruby 1939.07
Green, Sadie 1926.23
Green, Sam 1928.45
Green, Schuyler 1921.10
Green, Solomon Earl 1954.19
Green, Teddy 1965.02, 1968.02
Green, Theresa 1952.15
Green, Thomas 1898.35
Green, Tom 1897.27, 1926.33
Green, W.R. 1885.70
Green, William 1914.16, 1924.05
Greenac, Alex 1920.46
Greenbank, Harry 1894.33, 1895.10, 1895.43, 1896.27, 1896.31, 1896.36, 1897.20, 1897.44, 1898.17, 1898.18, 1898.29, 1898.46, 1899.35, 1899.39, 1900.28, 1900.43, 1902.12, 1902.19, 1905.18
Greenbank, Henry 1913.09, 1931.35
Greenbank, Percy 1896.27, 1901.19, 1902.01, 1902.30, 1902.35, 1903.22, 1903.33, 1904.01, 1904.04, 1904.40, 1905.46, 1905.49, 1906.32, 1906.36, 1906.41, 1907.06, 1907.15, 1909.29, 1910.21, 1911.22, 1911.39, 1912.26, 1914.18, 1914.32, 1915.18, 1919.02, 1989.16
Greenbaum, Fritz 1930.04
Greenberg, Edward 1964.23, 1964.24, 1965.22, 1965.24
Greenberg, Mitchell 1981.13, 1983.17, 1986.18, 1989.24, 1993.05
Greenberg, Steven A. 1980.07
Greenblatt, Kenneth D. 1982.09, 1983.06, 1983.11, 1983.14, 1983.19, 1984.01, 1985.05, 1985.19, 1989.26, 1991.14, 1996.08
Greenblatt, Sandra 1989.26, 1991.14
Greenburg, Dan 1967.18, 1971.04, 1976.27
Greene 1964.28
Greene, Angela 1943.07
Greene, Billy M. 1924.24, 1938.12
Greene, Blanche 1877.21
Greene, Brad 1938.01
Greene, Clay M. 1877.28, 1887.51, 1890.03, 1894.03, 1894.28, 1896.39, 1897.25, 1899.15, 1899.36, 1899.37, 1900.15, 1900.19, 1902.35
Greene, Daisy 1900.51, 1902.35, 1907.42, 1908.10
Greene, Ellen 1976.10
Greene, Evie 1905.04
Greene, Frank 1905.04, 1905.18, 1905.22, 1921.11, 1923.02, 1924.28, 1927.14, 1927.68, 1934.04
Greene, Fred 1923.33
Greene, Gladys 1894.25
Greene, H.H. 1905.12
Greene, Harriet 1978.23, 1979.27
Greene, Harry C. 1928.34
Greene, Herbert 1944.33, 1948.22, 1950.01, 1950.17, 1951.02, 1951.19, 1955.02, 1955.06, 1956.04, 1956.14, 1957.18, 1959.27, 1960.20, 1961.27, 1962.24, 1964.15, 1965.21
Greene, Herman 1939.15
Greene, J.H. 1880.68
Greene, Jeanne 1926.11, 1926.41
Greene, Jo 1992.03
Greene, Joseph 1905.50
Greene, Kim Morgan 1999.01
Greene, Margie 1940.10
Greene, Mary-Pat 1974.06
Greene, Milton 1955.12, 1958.01, 1960.07, 1962.03, 1964.27, 1970.15, 1976.36, 1981.18, 1990.18
Greene, Miss 1870.31
Greene, Mr. 1846.01
Greene, Ruby 1931.31
Greene, Sam 1944.32, 1957.14, 1958.14, 1962.01, 1964.33
Greene, Schuyler 1915.07, 1915.20, 1915.30, 1916.13, 1916.22, 1917.01, 1917.19, 1918.32, 1975.24
Greene, Sidney 1936.17
Greene, Stanley 1957.09
Greene, Thomas Evans 1896.07
Greene, Tom 1897.17, 1898.27, 1938.08
Greene, William 1965.09, 1965.12, 1965.13
Greener, Dorothy 1951.10
Greenfield, Debra 1981.24
Greenfield, Ida 1875.39
Greenfield, Lillian 1922.21
Greenfield, Rose 1942.28
Greenhalgh, Edward 1964.04
Greenlaw, Gene 1935.15
Greenlaw, Rupert 1916.04
Greenlaw, William 1914.15
Greenleaf, Augusta 1906.33
Greenleaf, Mace 1905.38
Greenleaf, Raymond 1947.09
Greenlee, R. Eddie 1922.44
Greenough, Walter 1931.06
Greensfelder, J.S. 1882.16
Greensfelder, Joseph 1882.19, 1889.10
Greensfelder, Joseph S. 1881.34, 1881.40, 1881.56, 1882.05, 1882.42, 1882.47, 1882.52, 1882.71, 1883.25, 1883.29, 1895.25
Greenstreet, Sydney 1915.26, 1918.11, 1920.43, 1923.34, 1928.06, 1933.26
Greenville, Miss 1881.40
Greenwald, Gean 1929.08
Greenwald, Joseph 1936.27
Greenwald, Raymond J. 1986.19, 1989.07
Greenwald, Robert 1975.20
Greenway, T. 1937.11
Greenwell, Gean 1946.11
Greenwich, Ellie 1973.14, 1975.12, 1979.30, 1982.22, 1984.15, 1985.03, 1986.02
Greenwood, Barratt 1918.02
Greenwood, Barrett 1919.32, 1921.06, 1922.18, 1922.43, 1924.30
Greenwood, Charlotte 1912.24, 1913.02, 1913.18, 1914.21, 1916.21, 1919.37, 1922.14, 1922.39, 1924.33, 1927.13, 1950.20
Greenwood, Clarice C. 1914.21
Greenwood, Jane 1965.14, 1968.08, 1971.07, 1972.05, 1993.10, 1994.05, 1996.18, 1997.19, 1998.05, 1999.13, 2000.01
Greenwood, John 1956.06
Greenwood, Leslie 1895.32
Greenwood, Lottie 1907.33
Greer, A. 1896.19
Greer, Howard 1922.32, 1923.31
Greer, Jesse 1920.24, 1926.23, 1927.02, 1927.13, 1927.17, 1927.31, 1927.62, 1927.68, 1928.21, 1928.23, 1933.16
Greer, Justin 2000.18
Greer, Leslie 1908.33
Greer, Marlyn 1956.04
Greer, Norris 1956.04
Greer, Simeon 1934.17
Greer, Will 1955.25
Greet, Madge 1894.41, 1895.43, 1904.29, 1905.27
Greeter, Arthur 1920.32
Gregg, Bud 1950.03
Gregg, Irene 1908.33
Gregg, John 1928.10
Gregg, Julie 1968.01
Gregg, Mitchell 1951.22, 1958.08, 1959.03, 1962.03
Gregg, Mitchell M. 1956.16
Gregg, Norma 1927.38
Gregg, Valency 1950.03
Greggory, David 1940.04, 1940.16, 1940.18, 1942.26
Gregoire, Cecile 1879.27, 1879.40, 1881.46, 1882.29, 1882.30
Gregoire, Messr. 1886.20
Gregoire, Mlle. 1879.45, 1879.46, 1879.51, 1879.55, 1880.14, 1880.23, 1880.27, 1880.28, 1880.29, 1886.21
Gregoire, Mme. 1886.19
Gregoire, Mons. 1885.55, 1885.56, 1885.57, 1885.59, 1885.60, 1886.08, 1886.09, 1886.18, 1886.22
Gregori, Elsa 1893.20
Gregori, Miss 1886.36
Gregorie, Alan 1990.16
Gregory, Andre 1959.05
Gregory, Annie 1884.27
Gregory, Cynthia 1980.03, 1980.22
Gregory, David 1937.14, 1939.23, 1948.04
Gregory, Dick 1962.17
Gregory, Don 1980.19, 1981.12, 1981.19, 1981.26, 1995.08
Gregory, Fred 1916.15
Gregory, George 1907.32
Gregory, Georgie 1886.31

Gregory, Gilbert 1888.36, 1890.10, 1894.19, 1895.42, 1896.18, 1899.11, 1899.26, 1899.37, 1900.07, 1900.35, 1901.06, 1904.25, 1905.56, 1906.30, 1908.31
Gregory, Gillian 1986.12
Gregory, Heathe 1904.36
Gregory, James 1928.08
Gregory, Jay 1966.09, 1970.06
Gregory, Jno. E. 1895.11
Gregory, John 1947.15
Gregory, Josie 1884.22, 1884.25, 1889.27, 1889.30, 1889.53, 1890.05, 1890.09, 1890.13, 1890.22, 1890.38, 1890.42, 1890.45, 1891.10, 1891.19, 1891.35
Gregory, K.W. 1891.24
Gregory, Michael Scott 1987.05, 1989.03
Gregory, Paul 1927.63, 1928.47, 1930.39, 1955.03
Gregory, Rupert 1914.16
Gregory, S.J. 1875.21
Gregory, W.R. 1875.06
Gregson, George 1928.13
Gregson, Hartley 1927.25
Gregson, Richard 1973.07
Gregus, Lubitza Luba 1989.22
Gregus, Peter 2000.07
Greif, Michael 1995.05, 1996.09
Greig, Algernon 1916.06
Greig, Edvard 1894.26
Greig, Grace 1989.06
Greig, Robert 1928.15, 1938.15
Greiner, Heinrich 1880.61, 1880.66
Greinert, Herman 1898.20
Gremaud, Mlle. 1871.06
Grenek, Gino 1998.10
Grenelle, Helen 1923.43, 1927.65, 1934.41
Grener, Mrs. 1864.12
Grenet, Elisco 1929.51
Grenet, Mlle. 1872.28, 1872.42
Grenet, Mme. 1872.41
Grenfell, Joyce 1955.19, 1958.10
Grenfell, Katy 1994.07, 1997.08
Grennell, Ben F. 1906.27
Grenus, Arthur 1890.17
Grenville, Claire 1904.33, 1905.35, 1918.11, 1923.04, 1925.06, 1925.26, 1948.28
Grenville, Marie 1884.25
Gres, Francoise 1964.22
Gresh, Lorraine 1940.02
Gresham, Alice 1882.75
Gresham, Edith 1937.03, 1961.02
Gresham, Grace 1902.30
Gresham, Herbert 1883.50, 1884.42, 1886.47, 1888.36, 1889.46, 1892.14, 1897.20, 1897.44, 1898.18, 1898.26, 1898.29, 1898.46, 1899.35, 1901.19, 1901.21, 1902.01, 1902.04, 1902.43, 1903.04, 1903.23, 1903.39, 1904.22, 1904.31, 1904.47, 1904.56, 1905.19, 1905.22, 1905.25, 1905.28, 1905.30, 1905.48, 1906.18, 1906.21, 1906.24, 1907.13, 1907.24, 1908.06, 1908.07, 1908.19, 1908.35, 1909.08, 1909.13, 1909.28, 1910.07, 1911.11, 1912.28, 1912.33, 1912.34, 1912.48, 1913.14, 1913.31, 1914.02, 1915.05, 1915.28, 1916.19, 1917.20, 1918.11, 1919.12
Gresham, Messr. 1867.10
Greshoff, A. 1922.42
Greshoff, Tony 1908.19, 1914.26, 1915.05, 1918.11, 1919.44, 1920.21, 1920.29, 1921.37, 1922.35, 1924.27
Gress, Louis 1920.33, 1922.15, 1923.47, 1925.10, 1925.24, 1927.04, 1927.29, 1928.28, 1931.01, 1937.06
Gretchaninoff 1922.06
Gretsjaninov, Alexsandr 1922.06
Grevain, Alice 1886.07
Grevatt, Bonnie 1952.18
Grever, Marie 1941.07
Greville, Jessie 1879.42, 1880.30
Greville, Mary 1907.02
Grevin 1879.42, 1880.63
Grew, Burt 1925.40
Grew, William A. 1925.25, 1925.40, 1925.48, 1926.23
Grey, Alan 1987.02
Grey, Alexander 1924.38, 1926.26
Grey, Alice 1883.36
Grey, Annabel 1921.15
Grey, Anthony 1937.11
Grey, Bessie 1881.06, 1882.25, 1882.38, 1888.44
Grey, Brad 1998.02
Grey, C. 1881.30
Grey, Clara 1877.39
Grey, Clifford 1916.10, 1920.37, 1920.44, 1922.12, 1923.01, 1923.30, 1924.06, 1924.21, 1924.36, 1924.38, 1925.07, 1925.10, 1925.23, 1925.26, 1925.27, 1925.43, 1926.01, 1926.14, 1926.15, 1926.33, 1926.37, 1927.01, 1927.16, 1927.20, 1928.04, 1928.06, 1928.07, 1928.12, 1928.32, 1928.35, 1929.04, 1929.28, 1930.39, 1947.05, 1948.16, 1975.22, 1976.32, 1984.14
Grey, Dappy 1900.38
Grey, Ethel 1892.31, 1901.06
Grey, Frank 1927.64
Grey, Frank H. 1922.24, 1926.04
Grey, Gabriel 1919.26
Grey, Gillian 1963.24
Grey, H. 1982.12
Grey, Jennie 1882.04, 1882.20
Grey, Joel 1966.24, 1968.07, 1975.06, 1979.02, 1980.04, 1987.16, 1996.14
Grey, June 1910.27
Grey, Lillian 1907.06
Grey, Lilly 1884.25
Grey, Madeline 1922.24, 1926.04, 1927.26, 1927.45, 1928.34, 1928.50, 1929.50
Grey, Mary 1945.04, 1946.12
Grey, Master 1868.06
Grey, Maud 1906.22
Grey, Maude 1915.05
Grey, Minerva 1919.44, 1920.21
Grey, Miss 1869.08, 1877.22, 1879.02, 1883.23
Grey, Nicholas 1926.15
Grey, Phyllis 1906.45
Grey, Ruth 1900.48
Grey, Stanley 1881.55
Grey, Stella 1899.30
Grey, Sylvia 1888.38, 1888.41
Grey, Thomas J. 1920.28, 1921.30
Grey, William 1881.09
Grey, William Daniel 1977.18
Grey, Yvonne 1928.03, 1929.03, 1930.30
Greybrook, Ethel 1889.20
Gribben, Marie 1905.40
Gribbin, Marie Louise 1907.54
Gribble, Harry 1918.13
Gribble, Harry Wagstaff 1923.25, 1923.41, 1924.36, 1925.23, 1925.26, 1926.01, 1930.43
Gribbon, Mabel 1902.19
Gribbon, Marie Louise 1904.12, 1906.46
Grice, Brian 1992.08
Grider, Paula 1995.07
Griebe, Mr. 1896.34
Griebe, Mrs. 1896.34, 1897.35
Grieg, Algernon 1917.07, 1917.17
Grieg, Babs 1925.35
Grieg, Eduard 1922.21
Grieg, Evelyn 1917.06
Grier, David Alan 1981.28
Gries, Edvard 1981.21
Grieve, Frederick 1933.09, 1933.19
Grifasi, Joe 1979.24, 1985.18
Griffies, Ethel 1949.08
Griffin, Arthur 1935.04
Griffin, Benjamin Taber 2001.04
Griffin, Bernard 1946.12
Griffin, Bessie 1962.22
Griffin, Denise 1952.10
Griffin, Donald 1991.01
Griffin, E.J. 1912.02
Griffin, G.H. 1876.03
Griffin, G.W.G. 1868.14
Griffin, G.W.H. 1868.05, 1868.21, 1875.39, 1876.19, 1877.24
Griffin, George 1878.01
Griffin, Gerald 1885.51, 1898.06
Griffin, John 1891.15
Griffin, John D. 1896.15
Griffin, Josephine 1942.32, 1943.09
Griffin, Martin 1919.26
Griffin, Mr. 1876.19
Griffin, Olney 1890.41, 1893.14, 1894.02
Griffin, Peter 1906.35
Griffin, Peter V. 1907.24
Griffin, Terri 1980.10
Griffin, Victor 1941.09, 1942.27, 1943.05, 1971.05
Griffin, Wee 1929.34, 1929.38, 1929.48, 1930.01, 1930.03, 1930.07, 1930.12
Griffin, Winifred Wee 1931.29
Griffis, William 1960.02, 1963.21, 1969.12, 1969.14, 1970.10, 1974.05, 1976.08
Griffith, A. 1876.13
Griffith, Andy 1959.11
Griffith, Anegline 1877.01
Griffith, Angela 1875.31
Griffith, Angeline 1876.15, 1877.01
Griffith, Billy 1945.16
Griffith, David 1976.26
Griffith, Dawn 1895.31, 1896.06
Griffith, E.H. 1892.38, 1893.23
Griffith, Eadie 1952.11
Griffith, Eleanor 1919.34, 1920.25, 1921.14, 1922.40
Griffith, Fred 1947.12
Griffith, G.W.H. 1875.39
Griffith, Harry 1909.20
Griffith, Herbert 1934.29
Griffith, Herman 1997.21
Griffith, Kay 1945.03
Griffith, Linda 1940.19
Griffith, Louise 1888.39
Griffith, Margie 1903.03
Griffith, Miss 1875.35, 1882.37, 1903.03
Griffith, Mlle. 1888.39
Griffith, Mme. 1844.01
Griffith, Peter 1947.02
Griffith, Robert 1941.06
Griffith, Robert E. 1954.05, 1955.08, 1957.07, 1957.12, 1959.25, 1960.08, 1960.19
Griffith, Thomas 1981.28
Griffith, Viola 1925.27
Griffith, William 1928.30, 1929.07, 1929.29, 1934.06
Griffith, William M. 1926.13, 1929.29, 1931.14
Griffith, William N. 1882.41
Griffiths, A. 1875.40
Griffiths, Angela 1875.23, 1878.17
Griffiths, E. 1873.24
Griffiths, G.H. 1873.19
Griffiths, George 1873.24
Griffiths, H. 1881.38
Griffiths, Harry 1915.24
Griffiths, Helen 1881.03
Griffiths, Kate 1882.31
Griffiths, Katherine 1895.13
Griffiths, Katie 1880.03
Griffiths, Louisa 1879.02
Griffiths, May 1907.06
Griffiths, Miss 1877.15, 1882.46
Griffiths, Neville 1951.01, 1951.04, 1951.09, 1955.16, 1955.18, 1955.22
Grififn, Gerald 1868.01
Grififn, Merv 1955.09
Grigas, John 1966.06, 1971.05
Griggs, Jessie 1931.44
Griggs, Robyn 1992.05
Grignon, Louise 1904.09
Grigolates, The Seven 1896.07
Grigolatis, Mlle. 1904.47
Grigsby, Kimberly 1999.03
Grilikhes, Michael M. 1989.06
Grilley, Don 1962.05
Grillo, M. 1911.19
Grillo, N. 1911.16
Grimaldi, Dennis 1992.06
Grimaldi, John 1999.06
Grimaldi, Lorrie 1915.29
Grimaldi, Marie 1929.36, 1931.05
Grimball, Elizabeth B. 1927.36
Grimes, Jerry 1982.22
Grimes, Jr., Rollin 1927.42
Grimes, Mary 1938.18
Grimes, Rollin 1915.01, 1917.02, 1922.26
Grimes, Tammy 1960.02, 1960.20, 1964.16, 1965.31, 1975.22, 1980.20
Grimes, Taryn 1985.04
Grimes, Thomas 1905.02
Grimke, W.H. 1898.60
Grimke, William H. 1901.24
Grimm, Brothers 1870.13, 1905.44
Grimm, Jacob 1987.18
Grimm, Jakob 1895.28
Grimm, Lores 1906.48, 1908.09
Grimm, Wilhelm 1895.28, 1987.18
Grimwood, Herbert 1920.34
Grinage, Raphael 1970.16
Grinbank, Daniel 1999.18
Grindell, Grace 1905.30
Grindell, Malcolm 1913.16
Grindelli, S. 1927.22
Grinnage, Jack 1961.16
Grinnel, B. 1918.38
Grinnell, Annie 1882.34
Grinnell, Ben 1919.21
Grinnell, Ben F. 1886.36, 1891.44, 1896.40, 1902.42
Grinnell, Benjamin F. 1887.05, 1893.26, 1905.17
Grinnell, Frank 1934.13
Grinnell, Hattie 1886.36, 1888.01, 1889.08
Grinnell, Malcolm 1912.07
Gripit, Messr. 1869.29
Grisar 1859.09
Grisel, Louis R. 1906.02, 1906.42
Grishin, Natasha 1966.07
Griska, Susan 1946.11
Grisman, Sam H. 1923.11, 1927.29, 1936.27, 1937.08
Grisman, Samuel 1929.01
Grismer, Joseph R. 1900.15
Griso, Frank 1966.09
Grissette, Jennifer 1981.21
Grist, Reri 1950.16, 1956.06, 1957.05
Griswold, Gertrude 1887.12
Griswold, Grace 1905.26, 1906.05, 1907.02, 1908.38
Griswold, Russell 1913.04, 1914.09, 1914.18
Grivel, Mlle. 1883.27
Grivel, Mons. 1882.53, 1882.55, 1882.58, 1883.30, 1883.34, 1883.41
Grizzard, George 1968.19
Gro, Josephine 1891.27
Groag, Edward 1946.16
Grobe, Edouard 1927.17
Grobe, Edourd 1928.47
Grobokoratal, Messr. 1922.06
Grod, Fred 1921.24
Groday, Doris 1931.28
Grody, Donald 1997.09
Grody, Gordon 1975.07
Grody, Svetlana McLee 1981.19
Groenendaal, Cris 1983.12, 1983.13, 1984.08, 1984.13, 1985.09, 1986.04, 1986.09, 1987.03, 1987.08, 1987.09, 1987.10, 1988.01, 1994.05, 1996.06
Groener, Harry 1979.31, 1981.25, 1982.08, 1982.19, 1985.02, 1992.02
Groenewold, Chris 2000.02
Grof, Vicki 1976.26
Grofe, Ferde 1927.37, 1933.27, 1939.14
Grogan, Norman A. 1961.05, 1961.09, 1961.13, 1962.06, 1962.07, 1962.11, 1962.16
Grogan, Oscar 1931.01
Grollnek, Jerry 1974.20, 1974.22, 1976.24
Grolnick, Don 1973.14
Grom, Frank 1911.17, 1913.10
Groneberg, Master 1883.32
Gronemann, Sammy 1968.08
Groniec, Katarzyna 1992.05
Groody, Helen 1922.08, 1922.48
Groody, Louise 1915.28, 1918.09, 1918.26, 1920.04, 1921.36, 1923.44, 1925.30, 1927.16
Groome, Edith 1939.19
Gropman, David 1979.24, 1980.13, 1981.16
Gros, Bessie 1917.20
Gros, Ernest 1892.52, 1893.05, 1893.32, 1894.24, 1894.28, 1895.11, 1895.29, 1895.32, 1896.13, 1896.51, 1897.11, 1898.13, 1899.15, 1899.40, 1899.41, 1900.01, 1900.40, 1900.43, 1900.50, 1901.01, 1901.16, 1902.01, 1902.04, 1902.24, 1902.28, 1903.23, 1903.33, 1904.29, 1904.31, 1905.18, 1905.20, 1905.27, 1905.28, 1905.30, 1905.57, 1906.24, 1906.25, 1906.37, 1907.32, 1909.21, 1912.03, 1912.12, 1913.01, 1914.03, 1923.33, 1923.44
Gros, Ernest M. 1893.16, 1895.25, 1896.25, 1897.10, 1897.20, 1897.39, 1898.25, 1898.29, 1898.48, 1898.73, 1900.05, 1911.44
Grosberg, Gertrude 1914.25
Groscup, Marie 1948.24, 1950.02
Grose, Andrew 1989.03
Groset, Vera 1919.19
Gross, Annie 1889.52
Gross, Arnold 1973.11, 1979.25, 1981.27
Gross, Bessie 1912.33, 1914.15
Gross, Edward 1946.08
Gross, Hans 1891.33
Gross, Irving 1915.28
Gross, Lee 1920.26
Gross, Messr. 1879.04, 1883.44
Gross, Milt 1940.21
Gross, Nelson L. 1946.21
Gross, Rick 1976.34
Gross, Robert 1916.15, 1949.09

Gross, Shelly 1967.02, 1968.04, 1974.02, 1974.19, 1974.21, 1976.34, 1977.07, 1979.14, 1981.07, 1984.06, 1989.28, 1993.11
Gross, Ted 1997.22
Gross, Todd 1998.20
Gross, Walter 1976.32
Grosse, Messr. 1852.01
Grosse, Vera 1919.05
Grosser, Maurice 1934.05, 1952.06, 1996.10
Grosset, Vera 1920.33
Grossi, A. 1865.05, 1865.07, 1865.08, 1865.09, 1867.08, 1867.12, 1870.12
Grossi, M. 1866.05
Grossi, M.A. 1864.17
Grossi, Mons. 1866.02, 1866.12, 1866.28
Grossi, Signor 1866.34
Grossman, Bernard 1919.37
Grossman, Hal 1963.12
Grossman, Henry 1989.26
Grossman, Herbert 1958.17, 1959.07, 1964.13, 1965.19, 1965.29, 1966.27, 1970.10, 1972.24
Grossman, Hertha 1942.19
Grossman, Larry 1970.07, 1975.06, 1980.29, 1982.18, 1984.06, 1985.05
Grossmith, Ed 1915.20
Grossmith, George 1910.21, 1913.36, 1914.32, 1930.30, 1930.43
Grossmith, Jr., George 1880.19, 1895.32, 1902.01, 1904.29, 1906.25, 1906.36, 1908.25, 1908.27, 1909.04, 1909.21, 1911.11, 1911.45
Grossmith, Lawrence 1906.29, 1915.07, 1916.17, 1917.02, 1931.37
Grosso, Guy 1965.37
Grosvenor, Joseph 1854.06
Grosvenor, Lucie D. 1976.04
Grosvenor, May 1886.43, 1888.04, 1890.01
Grosvenor, Mr. 1854.01, 1856.02, 1859.01, 1859.08
Grosz, Marty 1978.09
Grothusen, Fraulein 1879.62
Grounds, Peter 1972.02
Group Theatre, The 1936.28
Group V Ltd., Production, A 1967.11
Grousseau, Miss 1881.03
Grousseaux, J. 1881.38
Grout, James 1965.14
Grouya, Ted 1934.32, 1935.19
Grove, Betty Ann 1968.07, 1979.12, 1983.02
Grove, Jessica 1997.11, 1998.06, 1999.11
Grove, Jill 1996.10
Grover 1892.59
Grover, Arthur 1911.12
Grover, Eleanora 1923.07
Grover, Grace 1884.21
Grover, Jane 1908.24, 1909.30, 1910.16
Grover, Leonard 1867.03, 1867.04, 1867.06, 1867.07, 1867.09, 1869.02, 1869.14, 1869.20, 1869.27, 1869.32, 1883.36, 1884.17
Grover, Stanley 1951.18, 1952.10, 1956.15, 1961.07, 1961.12, 1961.21, 1962.20, 1967.04, 1968.16, 1973.09, 1989.18
Groves, Billy 1915.32
Groves, Charles 1880.40
Groves, Charlotte 1902.44
Groves, Evelyn 1928.12
Grovini, Jennie 1894.17
Grow, James 1948.17
Grubb, Ellen 1919.42
Grubb, L. 1883.42
Grubb, Lillian 1887.33, 1887.50
Grubb, Lillie 1884.42, 1886.47, 1887.06, 1887.13, 1887.14
Gruber, Franz 1890.31, 1894.01, 1943.23
Gruber, Lee 1974.02
Gruber, Michael 1991.03, 1997.11, 1999.24
Grubman, Patty 1978.22, 1989.26
Gruchala, Zosia 1947.02
Grudeff, Marian 1965.02
Gruelle, Johnny 1986.16
Gruenberg, Louis 1919.24, 1931.46
Gruenewald, Thomas 1985.04
Gruenwald, Alfred 1945.12
Gruet, Allan 1970.15
Gruette, Ruth 1938.04
Grumble, Albert 1913.17
Grunbaum, Alfred 1911.32
Grunbaum, Fritz 1909.21, 1914.03
Grunbaum, Patti 1978.05
Grundman, Clare 1948.30, 1952.20, 1955.19, 1961.01, 1965.29
Grundy, Bill 1965.05
Grundy, George 1914.18, 1915.18
Grundy, Sydney 1882.63
Grundy, Will 1911.20
Grundy, William 1924.27
Grunewald, Fraulein 1879.62, 1880.66
Grünwald, Alfred 1914.04, 1916.14, 1921.14, 1922.11, 1922.35, 1926.27, 1927.17, 1928.15
Grunwell, Charles 1949.15
Grupper, Adam 2000.08
Grusin, Dave 1983.20
Grusso, Don 1958.05
Gruzinsky, Peter 1977.13
Gryce, Elaine 1897.29
Gschmeidler, Ernst 1883.64, 1885.01
Guadobina, Yelizaveta 1925.51
Guard, Audrey 1944.21
Guard, Sully 1899.21
Guard, W.C. 1898.30
Guardino, Harry 1964.15, 1981.10
Guare, John 1971.18, 1981.06, 1999.19
Guarnera, Michael 1995.02
Guarnieri, John 1963.10
Gubeli, Mesdame 1852.01
Guber, Lee 1961.08, 1967.02, 1968.04, 1974.19, 1974.21, 1976.34, 1977.07, 1979.14, 1981.07, 1984.06, 1986.13
Guckenimi, Signor 1876.07
Gudrun, Elna 1926.15
Guelis, Jean 1945.04
Guelis, John 1944.16
Guelpli, Gabrielle 1932.22
Guenther, Felix 1946.16
Guenther, Skeet 1955.04
Guerard, Roland 1944.21, 1947.07
Guererri, Giovanni 1929.08
Gueretti, Mlle. 1868.26, 1869.16, 1869.30
Guerin, Archie 1902.16
Guerin, Gaston 1911.45
Gueringhelli, Mlle. 1888.39
Guerite, Laura 1904.34, 1907.15, 1907.42, 1908.44, 1909.17, 1910.32
Guerman, Mme. 1929.05
Guernoy, Mons. 1887.35, 1887.37
Guernsey 1868.04
Guernsey, L. 1876.02
Guernsey, Levi 1866.11, 1869.08, 1884.27
Guerra, Enrique 1999.18
Guerra, M. Salvator 1885.61
Guerra, Mlle. 1871.26
Guerra, Nicola 1892.38
Guerra, Robert 1972.24, 1980.18, 1981.08
Guerra, Salvator 1881.57, 1885.55, 1885.56, 1885.57, 1885.59, 1885.60, 1886.08, 1886.09
Guerra, Salvatore 1886.18, 1886.19, 1886.20, 1886.21, 1886.22
Guerra, Signor 1882.42
Guerrero, Lalo 1979.08, 1988.15
Guerzi, Sophie 1876.31, 1877.29
Guerzy, Mlle. 1875.01
Guess, Alvaleta 1995.14
Guest, Clifford 1950.12
Guest, Frederick 1903.12, 1912.32
Guetary, Georges 1950.04, 1958.04
Guettel, Adam 1997.01
Gueymard, Blanche 1876.20, 1876.24, 1876.26, 1876.28, 1877.06, 1877.10, 1877.11, 1877.14, 1877.26, 1877.29, 1877.30, 1877.31, 1877.33, 1877.34, 1878.06, 1878.07
Gueymard, Mlle. 1876.25, 1877.19
Guffroy, Mons. 1867.24
Guffroy, V. 1868.07, 1868.17
Gugleotti, Vincent 1948.25
Guhl, Edwin 1933.21
Guhlke, Antoinette 1948.30
Guiberson, W.P. 1889.09
Guiberson, William 1886.12
Guiberson, William P. 1892.17
Guida, Maria 1978.22, 1981.01
Guida, Mlle. 1917.24, 1919.20
Guidall, George 1970.18
Guidi, Agostino 1940.05
Guidi, L. 1911.16
Guidi, Ludovico 1911.19
Guidion, Charles 1915.27
Guidon, Charles 1915.04
Guidon, Mons. 1868.25, 1868.27, 1869.01, 1869.10, 1869.12
Guidry, Bonnie 1971.10
Guiffre, Jimmy 1958.12, 1959.15
Guigesse, Ada 1906.14
Guigley, Herb 1939.29
Guignard, Lisa 1974.26, 1981.19
Guigo, Jean 1959.15, 1961.25
Guilbert, Ann 1959.14
Guilbert, Warburton 1934.06
Guilbert, Yvette 1952.04
Guild, Art 1954.08
Guild, Lurelle 1924.36
Guile, Helen 1961.09, 1962.08, 1962.21, 1963.15, 1963.24, 1964.10, 1964.13, 1964.14, 1964.30, 1965.10, 1965.11, 1965.12, 1965.27, 1968.15
Guilford, Nanette 1934.15
Guilford, Willor 1938.19
Guilfoyle, J. 1920.06
Guillard, Fred J. 1907.60
Guillaume, H.B. 1908.08
Guillaume, Michel 1981.11
Guillaume, Mlle. 1887.36
Guillaume, Robert 1960.09, 1961.24, 1963.27, 1964.19, 1972.26, 1974.09, 1976.21
Guillemaud, Marcel 1911.11, 1912.28, 1912.34
Guillemot, Mme. 1870.03
Guillome, Mme. 1929.05
Guilmette, J.L. 1885.64
Guinan, Texas 1913.33, 1927.31
Guintini, Camile 1918.23
Guintini, Poppy 1918.23
Guion, Harry 1872.07, 1883.63, 1887.16, 1889.07, 1889.11
Guion, Jr., Harry 1886.42, 1886.52, 1887.07, 1889.15, 1889.18
Guion, Master 1882.74, 1882.79, 1883.32, 1883.46
Guion, Netta 1886.15
Guion, Raymond 1928.21
Guiot, Mlle. 1871.26
Guiot, Mons. 1872.03
Guiran, John 1921.02
Guise, Florence 1905.55
Guise, Henry 1885.30
Guise, R.W. 1892.19, 1892.45
Guise, Richard 1897.24, 1898.56
Guise, T.A. 1884.14
Guise, T.S. 1881.40, 1889.26
Guise, Thomas 1883.58, 1891.21, 1894.24
Guise, Thomas S. 1896.13, 1897.10, 1898.13
Guiseppe, Mlle. 1866.18
Guiterman, Arthur 1933.24
Guiterrez, Gerald 1992.01
Guiterson, Waldemar 1944.22
Guitierrez, Lolina 1974.14
Guito, Leonora 1897.13
Guitreau, Christian 1964.39
Guitry, Sacha 1925.41, 1926.41, 1926.49
Guittard, Laurence 1973.04, 1975.13, 1979.31, 1990.02
Gulack, Max 1976.10, 1988.10
Gulager, Miriam 1957.06
Gulick, Joseph A. 1883.66
Gulland, Donald 1910.17
Gullard, Gene 1966.17
Gumble, Albert 1907.41, 1909.28, 1918.05, 1920.02, 1922.18
Gumble, Arthur 1907.58
Gumperz, William J. 1972.07
Gunas, Gary 1993.06, 1997.09, 1999.08, 2000.18
Gunderman, Claire 1957.17
Gunderman, David 1990.06
Gunderman, May 1904.13
Gunderman, Miss 1904.13
Gunhus, Eric 2001.05
Gunn, Archie 1899.06, 1899.40, 1900.16, 1900.34, 1901.09, 1901.25, 1902.21, 1903.16, 1903.27, 1904.05, 1904.07, 1904.24, 1904.52, 1905.31, 1905.54, 1905.56, 1906.30, 1907.47
Gunn, Bill 1975.02
Gunn, George 1918.38
Gunn, John 1895.29
Gunn, Moses 1966.15
Gunn, Nellie 1894.18
Gunn, Nicholas 1985.18
Gunn, Thomas 1927.67, 1932.11
Gunnersen, Mickey 1954.01
Gunning, Eva 1900.59
Gunning, Louise 1898.47, 1899.29, 1903.02, 1903.34, 1904.36, 1907.10, 1907.51, 1908.30, 1911.21, 1913.06
Gunning, W.B. 1895.05
Gunning, W.H. 1892.21
Gunsky, M. 1912.36
Gunter, A.C. 1887.17, 1887.46
Gunter, Archibald Clavering 1883.18, 1886.01, 1886.27, 1892.17
Gunter, Arthur 1989.12
Gunther, Archibald C. 1888.04, 1888.34, 1890.10
Gunther, Archibald Clavering 1911.41
Gunther, E.J. 1904.11
Gunther, Florence 1927.20
Gunther, Frederick 1911.12
Gunther, George C. 1912.32
Gunther, Helen 1919.20
Gunther, John 1948.14
Gunther, Miss 1916.10
Gunther, Ted 1960.08
Gunther, Virginia 1911.26
Gunther, Walter 1905.31
Gunthier, Virginia 1913.18
Gunton, Bob 1978.12, 1978.22, 1979.23, 1987.12, 1988.04, 1989.19
Guri, Hayim 1971.14
Gurland, Patrick 1981.19
Gurner, Mrs. 1834.02
Gurnett, Irene 1892.35
Gurnett, Ursula 1896.18, 1897.26, 1898.25
Gurnett, Ursulla 1899.34
Gurney, Dennis 1930.01
Gurney, Edmund 1918.25
Gurney, Frank J. 1896.05
Gurney, John 1939.20
Gurney, Kate 1879.07, 1881.28, 1882.41
Gurney, Priscilla 1929.04, 1930.14
Gurnsey, Levi 1868.23, 1868.32
Gurnsey, Messr. 1855.10
Gurst, Lee 1976.34
Gurwin, Danny 1999.13
Guske, William 1967.06
Gusmao, Wellington 1992.13
Guss, Jonathan 1985.09, 1987.03, 1987.08, 1988.14, 1988.18, 1990.08, 1991.09, 1991.12, 1993.12
Guss, Louis 1963.09, 1965.17
Gussie, Miss 1876.18
Gustafson, Bob 2000.06
Gustafson, Gloria 1958.13
Gustafson, Karen 1965.37, 1967.05, 1972.06, 1973.08, 1975.04, 1978.22
Gustin, Harriet 1923.17
Gustine, Harriet 1923.02
Gutcheon, Jeffrey 1978.09, 1988.17
Guterson, Waldemar 1946.03
Guterson, Walter 1942.24
Guthrie, David 1972.07, 1973.15
Guthrie, Emma 1880.46, 1882.52, 1883.04, 1883.18
Guthrie, Francesca 1880.57, 1882.26, 1883.31
Guthrie, Joseph 1911.03
Guthrie, Mercedes 1922.21
Guthrie, Tyrone 1956.15
Gutierrez, Carmen 1956.15, 1957.05
Gutierrez, Gerald 1982.02, 1982.05, 1996.18
Gutierrez, Jose 1961.20, 1963.04
Gutierrez, Rafael 1939.18
Gutman, Arthur 1912.27, 1920.45, 1922.39, 1923.22, 1927.37, 1929.25, 1936.06
Gutman, Arthur H. 1916.12, 1919.33, 1921.38, 1924.15
Gutrick, Tinka 1986.03, 1986.04, 1989.12
Guttman, Arthur 1918.38
Guy, Barrington 1929.52, 1934.37, 1936.30
Guy, Bart L. 1905.21
Guy, Bessie 1933.04, 1943.10
Guy, Edna 1931.31
Guy, George 1866.22, 1866.26, 1866.35, 1867.21, 1868.14, 1868.21, 1870.38
Guy, Jasmine 1984.09, 1985.03, 1996.17
Guy, Messr. 1885.20
Guy, Mons. 1883.51, 1883.55, 1883.57, 1883.59, 1884.01, 1884.03, 1884.05, 1884.43, 1884.49, 1884.50, 1884.52, 1884.54, 1885.17
Guy, Nora 1909.21
Guy, Richard 1972.15
Guy, Rosa 1990.12
Guy, W. 1867.21, 1868.14
Guy, Willie 1866.22, 1866.26, 1866.35
Guyer, Charles 1895.18, 1897.06, 1902.15, 1902.27, 1903.31
Guyer, May 1905.51
Guyon, L.N. 1879.65, 1879.67
Guys, Sheila 1945.08
Guyse, Sheila 1949.15
Guyves, Noel 1961.01
Guzman, Pauline 1907.17
Guzman, Suzanna 1996.10
Gwillim, Jack 1971.02, 1972.06, 1981.19
Gwinnette, Harry 1872.37
Gwynette, Harry 1873.08, 1881.32, 1907.57

Gwynne, Fred 1963.21, 1978.10
Gwynne, Georgia 1928.49, 1929.39
Gwynne, Harold 1922.07
Gwynnette, Harry 1873.10
Gyarmathy, Michel 1964.22
Gyngell, Paul 1988.12
Gynt, Kaj 1927.33
Gyse, Alisa 1986.02, 1987.07

H. Bissing and Company 1903.39, 1904.47
H. Jaeckel and Sons, Inc. 1926.41
H. Mahieu and Company 1918.26, 1918.39, 1919.24, 1922.28
H. Mahieu Company 1919.11, 1920.35
H. Mahieu Costumes, Inc. 1928.10
H. Mahieu, Inc. 1930.14
H. Robert Law Studios 1912.14, 1916.25, 1917.07, 1917.29, 1917.34, 1919.12, 1919.25, 1920.17, 1922.01, 1922.13, 1922.19, 1922.23, 1922.29, 1922.43, 1923.18, 1923.20
H.B. Mahn's Comic Opera Company 1880.26, 1881.25, 1881.42, 1881.44, 1881.45
H.B. Mahn's English Comic Opera Company 1880.62
H.B. Mahn's English Opera Company 1880.57
H.L. Bateman's Opera Bouffe Company 1867.24, 1867.30
H.M. Tennent, Ltd. 1977.05
Haager, Cordelia 1912.43
Haakon, Paul 1933.23, 1934.43, 1935.12, 1936.31, 1937.15, 1944.02
Haals, Ione Anne 1935.08
Haas, Amelia 1960.06, 1964.01
Haas, Dolly 1959.05
Haas, Helen A. 1922.08
Haas, Hugo 1948.24
Haase, Oscar 1914.09
Habach, Otto 1925.52
Habbema, Eddy 1993.17
Habelman 1881.32
Habelman, Mabel 1898.55
Habelman, Martha 1892.60, 1894.14, 1895.09, 1895.18, 1896.12, 1898.38
Habens, Heather 1998.10
Haber, Bill 1997.15, 1997.19, 1998.05
Haber, Louis 1939.14
Haberman, Linda 1983.11, 1992.04
Habunek, Vlado 1969.04
Hache, Ferd T. 1871.23
Hache, Julie 1870.37, 1870.41, 1870.45, 1871.03, 1871.06, 1871.07, 1871.25, 1871.26
Hache, Mlle. 1871.28
Hache, T. 1871.26
Hache, T. Julie 1871.23
Hack, Moe 1938.16
Hack, Monroe B. 1945.07
Hack, Morton 1948.04
Hackady, Hal 1955.11, 1968.13, 1970.07, 1972.24, 1975.06, 1987.19
Hackeny, Pauline 1906.08
Hacker, Phil M. 1905.35
Hacker, Sander 1976.21, 1977.01
Hacket, Joan 1970.12
Hackett, Albert 1928.47, 1931.36, 1982.14
Hackett, Buddy 1964.44, 1967.12
Hackett, Dolly 1916.11, 1917.03, 1920.47, 1922.15
Hackett, Edward 1944.29
Hackett, Hal 1953.16
Hackett, Jeanne 1927.62
Hackett, Jeannette 1943.18
Hackett, Miss 1862.05
Hackett, Raymond 1922.48
Hackett, Walter 1918.22
Hackforth, Norman 1952.11
Hackins, Dick 1931.05
Hackler, Blake 2001.06
Hadary, Jonathan 1989.27, 1991.06
Hadaway, Mr. 1861.06, 1862.01
Hadaway, Thomas 1898.46, 1899.41
Hadaway, Tom 1901.19, 1909.05, 1912.04
Hadden, Amie 1900.35
Hadden, Frances 1951.05
Haddock, H.C. 1905.12
Haddon, Amy 1902.26
Hadebe, Congo 1988.02
Hadfield, Patricia 1948.03
Hadjidakis, Manos 1962.17, 1967.05, 1990.16
Hadley, Hap 1920.28
Hadley, Henry K. 1903.07
Hadley, James 2000.19
Hadley, Jerry 1981.22, 1985.09
Hadley, Joe 1908.21
Hadley, Joseph 1917.06
Hadley, Louis D. 1898.27
Hadley, Peggy 1957.06
Hadobas, Paul 1997.09
Hadreas, Jimmy 1930.28
Haedrick, F.W. 1879.29
Haefner, Susan 1996.04
Haege, Jeana 1989.27, 1991.06
Haenschen, Walter 1926.17, 1926.18
Haenschen, Walter Gustave 1914.15
Haeusserman, Michael 1965.04
Haffner, Carl 1879.57, 1885.14, 1885.52, 1900.02, 1912.27, 1953.06, 1953.15, 1954.06, 1954.10, 1955.17, 1956.10, 1957.13, 1958.15, 1959.16, 1964.31, 1965.25, 1974.16, 1975.16, 1976.23, 1977.11, 1980.03, 1980.22, 1981.22, 1984.03, 1986.10, 1987.11
Haffner, Karl 1933.23
Hafid, Ali 1968.30
Hafleigh 1908.19
Haft, Simone Genatt 1998.03
Hagan, Charles 1888.43, 1894.42
Hagan, J.F. 1885.65, 1886.60
Hagan, Joe 1872.43
Hagan, Mr. 1869.34
Hagan, Oliver 1926.26
Hagan, Will J. 1903.09
Hagan, William J. 1896.38
Hagar, Mr. 1922.20
Hagar, Sammy 1998.13
Hageman, Alice 1903.24, 1906.15, 1906.29
Hageman, Maurice 1906.10
Hagen, Bert 1904.39
Hagen, Claude 1896.44
Hagen, Earle 1984.15, 1999.24
Hagen, Hans 1964.25
Hagen, John Milton 1927.40
Hager, Clyde 1934.18
Hager, Frederick 1903.39
Hager, Linda Rae 1962.04
Hager, Louis Busch 1982.04, 1988.05
Hager, Ring 1920.10
Hagerman, Maurice 1906.06
Hagert, Mr. 1841.01
Haggard, H. Rider 1887.49, 1888.37
Haggard, Ida 1888.39
Haggart, Bob 1978.05, 1979.30, 1999.01
Haggart, Bobby 1944.14
Haggart, John 1927.23
Haggart, Robert 1995.14
Haggart, Stephen 1934.03
Hagger, Emma 1882.40, 1884.23, 1887.09
Haggerty, Fan 1918.25
Haggerty, George 1928.41, 1929.50, 1931.01
Haggerty, Miss 1841.01
Haggin, Ali Ben 1924.18, 1925.10, 1925.24
Haggin, Ben Ali 1920.18, 1921.21, 1923.20, 1923.38, 1926.18
Haggott, John 1945.04
Hagins, Marshall 1983.10
Hagler, Stan 1955.11
Hagman, Larry 1959.12
Hagner, Jack 1911.01, 1915.23
Hague, Albert 1950.03, 1955.01, 1959.01, 1959.23, 1964.18, 1969.01
Hague, J.W. 1890.04, 1893.38, 1894.36, 1895.30, 1896.09
Hague, Octavia 1908.44
Hahn, Henry 1868.20, 1869.08
Hahn, Messr. 1895.35
Hahn, Pauline 1948.28
Hahn, Philip 1910.35
Hahn, Reynaldo 1926.41, 1926.49
Haid, Charles 1976.17
Haig, Alex. 1892.56, 1893.28
Haig, Alexander 1892.36, 1894.10
Haig, Emma 1916.10, 1917.26, 1921.30, 1922.46, 1923.46, 1925.14
Haigh, Henry 1869.41
Haight, Beckie 1894.25
Haight, Becky 1892.19
Haight, Jr., George 1929.04
Haight, Reba 1897.22
Hail, William 1950.15
Hailes, Vioal 1926.43
Haimes, Todd 1993.10, 1993.16, 1995.11, 1997.15, 1998.15, 2001.02
Hain, Charles 1940.16
Hain, Horace 1898.20
Hain, Horace J. 1913.10
Hain, William 1932.23, 1933.26
Haines, A. Larry 1968.31
Haines, Carrie 1872.34
Haines, Fred 1902.08
Haines, H.E. 1905.55
Haines, Helen 1924.09
Haines, Herbert E. 1905.27
Haines, Howard 1981.27
Haines, J.T. 1838.01
Haines, Jessie 1898.20
Haines, Jim 1989.05
Haines, Louis 1906.18
Haines, Miss 1869.43
Haines, Mr. 1841.01
Haines, Nat C. 1930.37
Haines, Tillie 1893.37
Haines, W.G. 1942.14
Haines, Will E. 1913.20
Hair, Horace 1898.43
Hair, Roy Newton 1903.12
Hairston, Jacqueline 1952.15
Hairston, Jester 1930.37
Haizlip, Melissa 1992.08
Hajek, Michael 2000.03
Hajos, Karl 1925.06, 1928.26
Hajos, Mitzi 1911.12, 1916.04, 1918.25, 1920.43, 1923.34, 1926.26, 1928.06, 1930.04
Hajos, Mizzi 1913.27, 1914.03
Hakohen, Hanna 1971.17
Halare, Vera 1922.14
Halasz, Andreij 1964.25
Halasz, Laszlo 1944.26, 1945.15, 1946.11
Halberg, Ray 1932.16
Halberstadt, Charles L. 1894.27
Halbert, Ruth 1903.02
Hald, Iris 1930.37
Haldane, Harry M. 1959.19
Hale, Alan 1918.16, 1919.14
Hale, Betty 1920.04, 1923.46
Hale, Betty Hope 1918.07
Hale, Birdie M. 1975.21
Hale, Bobby 1916.15
Hale, C. 1868.04, 1869.13
Hale, Charles 1860.01, 1862.05, 1869.15, 1937.01
Hale, Chester 1921.30, 1924.09, 1924.33, 1924.41, 1927.54, 1927.62, 1927.68, 1928.14, 1928.46, 1928.48, 1928.49, 1929.17, 1929.22, 1929.28, 1929.39, 1933.20, 1937.03, 1937.17, 1941.07
Hale, Claire 1946.24
Hale, Corky 1979.11
Hale, Dorothy 1925.12
Hale, Edward 1927.36
Hale, Elinor 1898.61, 1899.09
Hale, Elizabeth 1976.36
Hale, Frank 1915.08, 1916.04
Hale, George 1920.22, 1920.23, 1929.42, 1930.02, 1930.31, 1930.40, 1931.26, 1931.48, 1933.13, 1936.26, 1940.10, 1942.01, 1952.08
Hale, Georgie 1922.15, 1923.46, 1924.32, 1925.05, 1925.45, 1927.05, 1933.01
Hale, Grace 1946.06
Hale, Harry 1941.03
Hale, Helen 1903.24, 1904.52, 1906.30, 1907.27
Hale, John 1930.22, 1932.18
Hale, Louise Closser 1915.32, 1928.33
Hale, Marion 1912.38
Hale, Mr. 1853.01
Hale, Mrs. 1853.01, 1853.03, 1855.08
Hale, Richard 1919.38, 1931.02, 1939.20, 1939.21, 1943.03
Hale, Robert 1968.10, 1968.14
Hale, Ruth 1920.25, 1931.06
Hale, Walter 1903.12
Hale, William 1929.49
Halee, Royal 1925.47
Halel, Ali 1925.37
Hales, N. St.Clair 1926.38
Halet, Laurant 1924.18
Halevi, Asaf 1967.08
Halevy 1945.06, 1946.09
Halévy, Ludovic 1867.24, 1868.07, 1868.08, 1868.15, 1868.16, 1868.18, 1868.24, 1868.25, 1868.27, 1868.31, 1869.01, 1869.16, 1869.18, 1870.03, 1870.11, 1870.40, 1870.41, 1870.45, 1871.03, 1871.07, 1871.23, 1871.25, 1871.26, 1871.28, 1872.03, 1872.20, 1872.28, 1872.29, 1872.33, 1872.39, 1873.01, 1873.15, 1873.16, 1873.21, 1875.19, 1875.22, 1875.23, 1876.24, 1876.25, 1876.27, 1876.30, 1877.06, 1877.10, 1877.13, 1877.14, 1877.30, 1877.31, 1877.34, 1877.38, 1878.06, 1878.07, 1878.14, 1879.15, 1879.18, 1879.19, 1879.36, 1879.39, 1879.45, 1879.47, 1879.51, 1879.55, 1879.57, 1879.61, 1879.69, 1880.27, 1880.28, 1880.52, 1880.60, 1882.35, 1882.68, 1883.27, 1883.65, 1884.01, 1884.05, 1884.20, 1884.34, 1885.14, 1885.52, 1886.08, 1886.18, 1886.19, 1886.20, 1886.21, 1887.50, 1889.23, 1890.01, 1890.11, 1891.17, 1894.48, 1895.09, 1896.12, 1899.10, 1900.02, 1900.06, 1912.27, 1925.46, 1926.48, 1929.39, 1933.23, 1941.10, 1942.32, 1945.02, 1953.06, 1953.15, 1954.06, 1954.10, 1955.17, 1956.06, 1956.09, 1956.10, 1957.13, 1958.15, 1959.16, 1964.06, 1964.31, 1965.25, 1974.16, 1975.16, 1976.23, 1976.26, 1977.11, 1980.03, 1980.22, 1981.22, 1982.07, 1982.21, 1983.16, 1984.03, 1986.10, 1987.11
Halevy, Ludwig 1943.24
Haley Jack 1940.06
Haley, Bernice 1917.09, 1919.30
Haley, Bill 1989.12
Haley, Doris 1953.10
Haley, Ed 1944.32
Haley, Grace 1917.09, 1919.30
Haley, Jack 1924.15, 1925.27, 1926.37, 1929.03, 1931.28, 1932.25, 1942.24, 1948.14
Haley, Jr., Jack 1999.23
Haley, Lucile 1917.09
Haley, Lucille 1919.30
Haley, Mabel 1917.09, 1919.30
Haley, Morris 1882.01
Haley, Mr. 1869.34
Haley, William 1878.12
Half Brothers, The 1963.07
Halfss, Al 1963.07
Halfss, Roberto 1963.07
Halicey, Lloyd 1923.18
Halicka, Alice 1938.05
Haliday, Bryant 1957.10
Hall Dorothy 1930.11
Hall Glen 1917.27
Hall, A. 1882.32
Hall, A.H. 1885.05
Hall, Adalade 1923.39
Hall, Adelaide 1926.19, 1928.18, 1930.29, 1957.16, 1980.10
Hall, Al 1959.15, 1961.25
Hall, Al K. 1924.31
Hall, Albert 1905.21, 1971.13, 1975.02
Hall, Albertina 1879.18, 1879.23
Hall, Alex 1923.21, 1927.02
Hall, Alexandra 1904.39
Hall, Alfred 1919.12
Hall, Anna 1907.51, 1911.15
Hall, Annetta 1881.38, 1887.24
Hall, Annette 1882.71, 1884.34, 1884.57, 1885.28, 1885.45, 1885.52, 1886.43, 1887.18
Hall, Annie 1882.50, 1883.32, 1883.46, 1883.53, 1883.63, 1884.13, 1884.41, 1885.02, 1885.15, 1885.22, 1885.49, 1885.66, 1886.03, 1886.42, 1887.07, 1887.16
Hall, Anthony Blair 1997.22, 1998.20
Hall, Artie 1908.33, 1911.35
Hall, Ben 1990.15
Hall, Bettina 1927.44, 1927.57, 1927.61, 1929.19, 1930.43, 1931.37, 1934.14, 1934.36, 1939.20, 1939.21
Hall, Cardell 1976.35
Hall, Carl 1971.20, 1984.09, 1990.05
Hall, Carlyle 1969.07, 1970.10
Hall, Carol 1978.13, 1982.11, 1986.03, 1994.06
Hall, Charles 1892.11, 1908.08, 1918.11, 1918.29, 1979.28
Hall, Cliff 1931.19, 1963.21, 1967.02
Hall, Cliff "Charlie" 1933.01
Hall, Clyde 1911.26
Hall, Daisy 1887.29
Hall, Daniel 1907.49
Hall, Delores 1971.20, 1972.18, 1975.05, 1976.35, 1978.13, 1982.11
Hall, Dennis Michael 1998.20, 1999.21
Hall, Donald 1895.10, 1907.32, 1908.40, 1910.27, 1911.22, 1912.35
Hall, Ed 1965.32
Hall, Edmund 1949.17, 1955.10, 1961.25
Hall, Edward 1904.06
Hall, Elaine 1911.39
Hall, Eleanor 1944.15
Hall, Esther 1933.04

Hall, Eunice 1928.11
Hall, Fannie 1881.43, 1882.21, 1882.23
Hall, Frantz 1990.14
Hall, Fred 1889.23, 1921.10, 1921.34
Hall, Frederick 1920.32
Hall, G.W. 1876.19
Hall, George 1898.20, 1908.02, 1946.10, 1948.30, 1949.12, 1996.13
Hall, George F. 1894.27, 1894.51
Hall, Glenn 1913.32
Hall, Grayson 1961.28, 1977.08
Hall, Gus 1907.55
Hall, Gustavus 1881.38, 1887.25
Hall, Gustavus F. 1876.21, 1881.43
Hall, H. 1856.01
Hall, Harrison 1931.34
Hall, Harry 1857.04, 1857.06
Hall, Hedley 1921.15
Hall, Herbert 1931.04
Hall, Howard 1907.38, 1908.17
Hall, Iris 1922.22
Hall, Isobel 1900.28, 1900.43, 1902.12, 1903.38, 1904.16, 1905.52
Hall, Jack 1914.30, 1923.17
Hall, Jane 1905.49, 1906.37, 1908.07, 1908.27, 1913.21
Hall, Jean 1909.21
Hall, Jefferson 1903.19
Hall, Jessie Mae 1902.17
Hall, Jim 1958.12, 1959.15, 1961.25
Hall, John L. 1870.35, 1870.43
Hall, John R. 1930.28
Hall, John T. 1908.42
Hall, Josephine 1889.41, 1896.48, 1898.56, 1900.16, 1900.44, 1900.57, 1901.18, 1903.17, 1927.33, 1928.10
Hall, Josie 1885.26, 1885.40, 1885.58, 1887.31, 1897.26, 1898.38
Hall, Juanita 1944.32, 1946.08, 1947.02, 1949.04, 1954.19, 1957.06, 1958.19
Hall, Judson 1936.28
Hall, Judson Best 1938.18
Hall, Kate 1939.14
Hall, Katherine 1932.27
Hall, L. 1890.01
Hall, L.J. 1901.04
Hall, L.M. 1883.62, 1884.34, 1884.51, 1885.28, 1885.45, 1885.52, 1885.67
Hall, La Tanya 1998.20, 1999.21, 2000.19
Hall, Laura Nelson 1911.09
Hall, Leonne 1946.24
Hall, Lillie 1869.07, 1869.45, 1870.02, 1870.06, 1870.32, 1870.42, 1872.07, 1884.48, 1885.44
Hall, Lizzie 1870.28
Hall, Mamie 1889.47
Hall, Margaret 1964.16, 1966.10
Hall, Marie 1920.31
Hall, Marilyn 1992.08
Hall, Marshall 1917.26
Hall, Mary Porter 1992.06
Hall, Mary V. 1910.33
Hall, Mesdame 1856.04
Hall, Messr. 1879.23, 1882.04, 1882.20, 1883.31
Hall, Mike 1999.01
Hall, Mills 1878.02, 1879.18, 1879.23, 1879.24, 1880.46, 1883.22
Hall, Minerva 1905.29
Hall, Miss 1879.14, 1881.07, 1881.14
Hall, Morrison D. 1908.40
Hall, Mr. 1876.19, 1884.40
Hall, Mrs. John L. 1870.43
Hall, Natalie 1930.15, 1932.03, 1932.22, 1934.43, 1938.10, 1998.03
Hall, Nellie 1881.22
Hall, Owen 1894.33, 1895.10, 1895.43, 1896.27, 1897.44, 1898.18, 1900.51, 1902.05, 1902.35, 1903.33, 1904.03, 1905.13, 1905.19, 1906.25, 1913.09, 1914.10, 1920.09, 1931.35, 1933.21
Hall, Pamela 1969.05, 1972.03
Hall, Patricia 1943.05, 1966.12, 1966.16
Hall, Patti 1947.13
Hall, Pauline 1879.18, 1879.23, 1879.24, 1880.06, 1880.10, 1880.13, 1880.40, 1881.41, 1881.57, 1882.14, 1882.49, 1882.54, 1883.65, 1884.20, 1884.40, 1884.60, 1885.08, 1885.41, 1885.63, 1886.04, 1886.30, 1888.02, 1889.40, 1889.49, 1892.42, 1894.11, 1898.36, 1912.19, 1913.09, 1917.26, 1918.19, 1919.27, 1920.36, 1921.36, 1923.44
Hall, Peter 1972.25
Hall, Peter J. 1979.08
Hall, Phil 1982.13
Hall, R. 1873.20, 1873.27
Hall, R.M. 1873.22
Hall, Randy 1953.08
Hall, Richard 1916.07
Hall, Robert 1880.36, 1880.64, 1881.09, 1881.29, 1882.02
Hall, Roy 1934.34
Hall, Sidney 1919.28
Hall, Spaulding 1921.36
Hall, Stafford 1905.55
Hall, Sterling 1950.04
Hall, Steve 1981.24, 1992.10
Hall, Teddy 1938.08, 1943.16
Hall, Terry 1982.22
Hall, Thomas 1994.01, 1997.03, 2000.15
Hall, Thurston 1914.27, 1917.01, 1922.09, 1929.45
Hall, Vivian 1930.20
Hall, Wilbur 1931.40
Hall, Willard 1927.10
Hall, William 1898.64
Hall, William D. 1906.08
Hallahan, W. Anson 1918.13
Hallam, Grace 1920.15
Hallam, Henry 1888.02, 1888.20, 1888.35, 1889.04, 1889.23, 1890.01, 1890.11, 1890.19, 1890.24, 1893.02, 1893.07, 1896.01, 1897.21, 1898.59
Hallam, Jr., Mrs. Lewis 1796.01
Hallam, Lewis 1794.01, 1796.01, 1796.02
Hallam, Mrs. Lewis 1793.01, 1794.01
Hallaran, Desmond 1936.12
Hallderson, Birger 1943.08
Halle 1877.32
Halle, Charles 1877.04
Halleck, Agnes 1879.18, 1879.23
Hallee 1875.21, 1882.62, 1885.33, 1886.41
Hallee, Royal 1922.47
Hallen, Fred 1883.23, 1889.09, 1889.41, 1890.29
Hallen, Frederick 1894.17, 1896.30, 1900.15
Haller, Herman 1923.03
Haller, Hermann 1932.04
Haller, Tobias 1978.24
Hallett, Jack 1979.24, 1981.28
Halley, Beryl 1924.18, 1925.10, 1925.24, 1926.11, 1927.43, 1928.23
Halley, Jr., Ben 1978.06
Halley, R.H. 1870.27
Halley, Richard 1884.53
Halley, Sharon 1988.14, 1988.16, 1993.14, 1995.06, 1995.18, 1996.02
Halliday, Andrew 1867.10, 1869.42
Halliday, Bud 1922.22
Halliday, Buzz 1957.05, 1959.23
Halliday, Frances 1921.31, 1927.43, 1932.05
Halliday, Francis 1923.36
Halliday, Gordon 1975.03
Halliday, Grace 1899.33
Halliday, Heller 1954.13
Halliday, Hildegarde 1925.17, 1926.13, 1930.18, 1934.06, 1941.03, 1948.27
Halliday, Johnny 1964.39
Halliday, Richard 1954.13, 1959.24, 1963.25
Halliday, Robert 1923.13, 1924.46, 1925.36, 1925.49, 1926.42, 1928.29, 1930.30, 1934.14, 1934.43, 1936.22, 1952.05
Halliday, Will 1906.39
Halliday, William 1902.09, 1910.09
Halligan, T.J. 1952.01, 1956.02, 1961.02
Halligan, Tom 1945.16
Halligan, William 1927.13
Halligan, William J. 1914.31
Halliwell, Joseph 1889.33
Hallman, Ella 1947.22
Hallmark Entertainment 1997.19, 1998.19
Hallock, Agnes 1880.35, 1882.28, 1891.32
Hallock, Carol 1965.22
Hallor, Edith 1917.03, 1917.13, 1917.17, 1920.33
Hallor, Edith Kingdon 1915.04
Halloran, Jr., William A. 1918.13
Halloran, Tommy 1958.01
Hallow, John 1964.04, 1978.27, 1979.13
Halloway, Robert 1925.37
Halloway, Sterling 1946.03
Halls, Violet 1903.16, 1903.34
Hallstead, Byron 1919.23
Halman, Ella 1939.06, 1939.08, 1948.02, 1948.03, 1948.06, 1948.07, 1948.09, 1948.10, 1951.01, 1951.04, 1951.06, 1951.07, 1951.09, 1952.14, 1952.16, 1952.18, 1952.19
Halmi, Jr., Robert 1997.15, 1998.03, 1998.19
Halouze, Edouard 1942.23
Halperin, Nan 1922.15, 1923.24
Halperin, Sandra 1975.18
Halpern, Mortimer 1990.05
Halpern, Morty 1944.32
Halpern, S. 1892.35
Halpin, Ellen 1960.01, 1961.15, 1964.11
Halpin, Hebe 1921.36
Halpin, Helen 1955.12
Halpin, Luke 1959.22
Halpin, S. 1875.05
Halpren, Helen 1920.43
Halpren, Suzanne 1903.14, 1905.41
Halsey, Minnie 1899.39
Halstead, Byron 1920.19, 1944.02
Halstead, Edgar 1900.07, 1901.12, 1902.06, 1903.17, 1909.03, 1910.20, 1912.11
Halstead, Miss 1872.22
Halston 1977.16
Halton, Charles 1903.28, 1906.17, 1923.43
Halton, J.E. 1895.23
Halton, Marie 1887.44, 1889.40, 1890.19, 1890.24, 1896.33, 1974.02
Halton, P.W. 1882.17, 1885.47, 1887.10
Halton, W.P. 1881.37
Halvers, Hulda 1896.38, 1899.18, 1903.31, 1905.44
Halvorsen, Charles 1892.12
Ham, Fred P. 1887.09
Hama, Larry 1976.02
Hamberg, Perke 1927.25
Hambleton, John 1937.13, 1938.05, 1938.09, 1939.13, 1940.01
Hambleton, T. Edward 1954.03, 1959.26
Hamblin, Harry 1882.48, 1883.62
Hamblin, T.S. 1836.01, 1848.04
Hamblin, Thomas S. 1851.08, 1852.07
Hambro, Leonid 1964.34
Hamburg, Anna 1863.05, 1864.01, 1864.03, 1864.08, 1864.11
Hamburger, F. 1918.21
Hamburger, Jay 1976.17
Hamer, Gerald 1933.07
Hamer, Janet 1944.21
Hamer, Nigel 1989.17
Hamil, John 1944.01
Hamill, Fred J. 1899.36
Hamill, John 1944.17, 1944.28, 1946.11
Hamill, Kathryn 1927.12
Hamill, Kay 1930.25
Hamill, Mark 1985.02
Hamilton, A. 1871.01
Hamilton, Ada 1880.03
Hamilton, Adelaide 1888.33
Hamilton, Aileen 1924.35
Hamilton, Alice 1887.18
Hamilton, Alma 1975.10
Hamilton, Andy 1928.27
Hamilton, Arthur 1999.24
Hamilton, Audrey 1910.11
Hamilton, Barbara 1931.08, 1951.10
Hamilton, Beatrice 1892.55, 1893.26, 1896.35, 1897.28, 1898.34, 1898.38
Hamilton, Belle 1895.35
Hamilton, Ben 'Spike' 1950.12
Hamilton, Betty 1918.07, 1933.01
Hamilton, Bob 1956.08, 1957.17
Hamilton, Burton 1918.13
Hamilton, Caroline 1891.29, 1895.01
Hamilton, Carroll 1906.10
Hamilton, Cosmo 1905.27, 1906.47, 1907.46, 1916.17, 1917.30, 1920.02
Hamilton, Dave 1943.14
Hamilton, David 1985.10
Hamilton, Douglas 1985.09, 1986.08, 1987.08
Hamilton, Edgar 1922.28
Hamilton, Effie 1901.29, 1902.05, 1902.10
Hamilton, Elise 1908.39, 1909.13, 1909.25, 1912.38, 1915.05
Hamilton, Elsie 1910.18, 1911.45, 1912.07
Hamilton, Eric 1967.07, 1968.16
Hamilton, Estelle 1898.67
Hamilton, Ethel 1912.10
Hamilton, Evelyn 1893.34
Hamilton, Florence 1889.38
Hamilton, Frank 1967.06, 1980.26
Hamilton, G. 1875.21
Hamilton, Gary 1967.07
Hamilton, Gene 1915.27
Hamilton, Gertrude 1918.27
Hamilton, Gloria 1947.06, 1948.30, 1951.17
Hamilton, Gordon 1951.19, 1952.15
Hamilton, Grace 1891.13, 1891.32, 1892.50, 1894.42, 1921.39, 1922.40, 1923.25
Hamilton, Harry 1914.09
Hamilton, Henry 1894.33, 1894.46, 1899.39, 1904.29, 1905.04, 1905.46, 1907.06, 1952.13, 1953.02, 1953.08
Hamilton, Irene 1884.21
Hamilton, J. 1888.01
Hamilton, James 1923.17, 1926.04, 1969.14, 1979.15
Hamilton, Joe 1919.26
Hamilton, John 1912.26, 1915.32, 1927.13, 1928.40, 1929.42
Hamilton, Laura 1912.09, 1913.18, 1914.17, 1915.05, 1916.09, 1917.29, 1918.11, 1927.09
Hamilton, Lavinia 1957.16
Hamilton, Lawrence 1984.09, 1986.02, 1997.03
Hamilton, Lillian 1888.03
Hamilton, Louise 1894.27, 1912.32
Hamilton, Lynn 1963.27
Hamilton, Mahlon 1914.06
Hamilton, Margaret 1905.40, 1958.03, 1958.14, 1966.14, 1969.07, 1969.12
Hamilton, Marian 1927.38
Hamilton, Marie 1914.25
Hamilton, Marilyn 1973.10
Hamilton, Marion 1923.01, 1928.31
Hamilton, May 1895.38, 1896.35, 1896.48, 1899.36
Hamilton, Messr. 1881.11, 1881.27, 1884.11, 1911.18
Hamilton, Miss 1870.13
Hamilton, Mitzi 1978.22
Hamilton, Mons. 1868.07, 1868.18, 1869.01, 1869.24
Hamilton, Morris 1926.23, 1927.02, 1927.36, 1928.23, 1929.19, 1931.14
Hamilton, Mr. 1852.07, 1873.25
Hamilton, Mrs. 1794.01
Hamilton, N. 1885.14
Hamilton, Nancy 1934.06, 1936.12, 1939.12, 1940.03, 1942.27, 1946.07, 1975.12, 1979.14, 1992.18
Hamilton, Ona 1918.22, 1923.33
Hamilton, Ord 1930.20, 1975.22
Hamilton, Patrick 1982.11, 1987.14
Hamilton, Peter 1944.01, 1944.17, 1944.32, 1947.20, 1955.19, 1960.01
Hamilton, R. 1868.06
Hamilton, Reed 1928.33
Hamilton, Robert 1910.09
Hamilton, Robert L. 1918.36
Hamilton, Roger 1970.15, 1972.22
Hamilton, Ross 1921.12
Hamilton, T. Edward 1948.17
Hamilton, Thalie 1929.39
Hamilton, Theodore 1868.19, 1870.44, 1875.18
Hamilton, Thomas 1933.22
Hamilton, W. Franklin 1904.25
Hamilton, W.F. 1904.42
Hamilton, W.H. 1873.26, 1875.03, 1879.20, 1879.25, 1883.21, 1883.24, 1883.39, 1887.31, 1893.09, 1896.20
Hamilton, William 1879.71, 1880.46, 1881.07, 1881.36, 1882.17, 1882.21, 1882.23, 1883.03, 1887.44
Hamilton, William H. 1884.57, 1885.48, 1893.05
Hamlin's Farce Comedy Company 1891.04
Hamlin, Amy 1913.07
Hamlin, Anna 1931.44
Hamlin, Fred R. 1903.03, 1903.31, 1904.13, 1904.44, 1904.54, 1905.01
Hamlin, Harry L. 1891.04
Hamlin, Jeff 1983.01
Hamlin, Miss 1886.32
Hamlin, Pearl 1903.35
Hamlisch, Marvin 1967.14, 1968.03, 1970.07, 1973.06, 1974.01, 1975.15, 1976.16, 1976.32, 1979.04, 1979.11, 1979.19, 1984.06, 1984.15, 1986.20, 1993.02, 1999.23, 2001.01
Hamm, Minna 1922.30
Hammer, Arthur 1979.08
Hammer, Benjamin 1963.09
Hammer, Donald 1943.23
Hammer, Jack 1982.22, 1989.12
Hammer, Maribel 1956.01
Hammer, Tessie 1918.04
Hammer, Vernon 1937.16
Hammerlee, Pat 1948.25
Hammerlee, Patricia 1950.15, 1952.09, 1955.10, 1955.25
Hammernic, W.J. 1906.28
Hammerschlag, Peter 1939.23

Hammerstein, Arthur 1912.46, 1913.09, 1913.34, 1915.29, 1917.05, 1917.21, 1918.30, 1918.40, 1919.06, 1920.01, 1920.27, 1920.42, 1922.02, 1922.26, 1923.05, 1923.35, 1923.45, 1924.28, 1925.52, 1926.34, 1927.06, 1927.63, 1928.25, 1929.02, 1929.31, 1930.26, 1930.42, 1956.02
Hammerstein, Elaine 1913.34
Hammerstein, I., Oscar 1910.24
Hammerstein, II, Oscar 2000.16, 2001.09
Hammerstein, II., Oscar 1917.21, 1920.01, 1920.27, 1920.42, 1922.26, 1922.38, 1923.35, 1924.15, 1924.28, 1925.33, 1925.52, 1926.34, 1926.42, 1927.06, 1927.63, 1927.67, 1928.25, 1928.29, 1928.44, 1929.31, 1930.42, 1931.05, 1931.28, 1931.39, 1932.11, 1932.22, 1935.17, 1938.08, 1938.10, 1939.28, 1940.20, 1941.12, 1942.22, 1943.04, 1943.24, 1944.17, 1945.05, 1945.06, 1946.01, 1946.03, 1946.09, 1946.12, 1947.17, 1948.13, 1948.20, 1949.03, 1949.04, 1951.12, 1951.16, 1951.22, 1953.08, 1953.09, 1954.04, 1954.07, 1954.14, 1955.07, 1955.13, 1955.27, 1956.03, 1956.06, 1957.06, 1957.11, 1958.07, 1958.19, 1959.24, 1960.11, 1961.09, 1961.12, 1962.17, 1963.06, 1963.18, 1964.02, 1964.23, 1965.20, 1965.24, 1965.38, 1966.14, 1966.31, 1967.07, 1967.10, 1967.11, 1967.12, 1968.16, 1969.12, 1973.09, 1973.17, 1974.09, 1974.11, 1975.12, 1975.22, 1977.07, 1978.05, 1979.31, 1981.16, 1983.05, 1984.06, 1985.01, 1986.01, 1986.03, 1986.14, 1987.03, 1987.10, 1988.16, 1989.03, 1989.06, 1989.16, 1989.18, 1990.02, 1990.09, 1993.14, 1993.16, 1994.02, 1994.08, 1995.18, 1996.04, 1996.05, 1997.01, 1998.03
Hammerstein, James 1965.20, 1990.02, 1996.04
Hammerstein, Oscar 1893.21, 1893.41, 1896.07, 1896.33, 1897.16, 1897.21, 1897.41, 1898.32, 1901.24, 1902.13, 1903.15, 1910.35, 1923.05, 1923.45
Hammerstein, Reginald 1928.25, 1929.31, 1930.42, 1951.22, 1955.04
Hammerstein, Stella 1908.14, 1908.31, 1911.09
Hammerstein, Ted 1931.21
Hammerstein, Theodore J. 1930.35, 1933.16
Hammerstein, William 1954.04, 1954.06, 1954.07, 1954.14, 1955.07, 1955.09, 1956.03, 1956.05, 1956.06, 1979.31
Hammet, Dashiell 1991.15
Hammil, John 1976.27, 1978.25
Hammill, Harry 1937.01
Hammond, Albert 2000.16
Hammond, Blair 1962.24, 1963.25, 1964.11
Hammond, Blake 1998.16, 1999.19, 2000.11
Hammond, C. 1881.18
Hammond, Earl 1959.04
Hammond, F. 1900.12
Hammond, Frank 1904.04
Hammond, Frank H. 1898.20
Hammond, George 1904.26
Hammond, Grace 1910.15
Hammond, John 1879.12
Hammond, Jr., John Henry 1941.01
Hammond, Laurens 1923.38
Hammond, Messr. 1794.01, 1865.01
Hammond, Mr. 1871.22, 1883.44
Hammond, Percy 1909.24
Hammond, Peul 1937.01
Hammond, Thomas 1950.11
Hammond, Victor 1925.37
Hammond, Virginia 1919.06, 1943.23
Hammons, Shannon 2000.07
Hamner, Teresa 1911.28
Hamp, Charles 1918.14
Hampden, Burford 1922.31, 1925.11
Hampden, Charles 1916.01
Hample, Stuart 1972.02
Hampshire, W.F. 1881.56
Hampshire, W.H. 1883.39
Hampshire, W.P. 1881.40, 1882.28, 1883.24
Hampshire, Walt 1884.36
Hampshire, Walter 1883.52, 1884.18
Hampton, Alf 1889.31, 1890.07, 1890.34, 1891.04, 1892.39
Hampton, Alf M. 1887.29, 1888.32
Hampton, Alfred M. 1889.34
Hampton, Christopher 1994.10
Hampton, Earl 1927.59
Hampton, Ethel 1932.26, 1936.05
Hampton, Hope 1927.50
Hampton, Jennifer 1999.16
Hampton, Lionel 1939.29, 1975.12
Hampton, Max 1959.19
Hampton, May 1898.09
Hampton, Myra 1924.08
Hampton, P.G. 1899.31
Hampton, P.H. 1899.31
Hampton, Pete 1896.49, 1903.08
Hampton, Peter 1900.46
Hampton, Stewart 1928.39
Hampton, T. 1867.18
Hanafin, Patricia 1976.29
Hanak, Christine 1999.08
Hanan, Stephen 1981.01, 1982.19, 1990.20
Hanayagi, Hagi 1989.21
Hanayagi, Yoshijiro 1989.21
Hanbury, Edith 1915.20
Hance, Mable 1906.34
Hance, Michael 1997.19
Hanchett, Julia 1880.17, 1881.18
Hanchett, Mr. 1855.01
Hancock, Carolyn 1925.17, 1926.13
Hancock, James S. 1942.14
Hancock, Raymond 1913.25
Hancock, Thomas 1939.09, 1948.07, 1948.09, 1951.06
Hand, Carl 1907.34
Hand, Herman 1922.06
Hand, Hilda 1916.08
Handel, Benjamin Raymond 2001.04
Handers, Thomas 1917.34
Handford, Edwin 1911.20
Handler, Henry 1999.25
Handler, Jimmy 1901.03
Handley, Alan 1937.02, 1937.12
Handley, Allen 1934.06
Handley, J.W. 1890.23
Handman, Lou 1920.10, 1989.12
Handrow, Sally 1889.27
Hands, Charles E. 1910.22
Hands, Terry 1988.12
Handsue, F. 1885.67
Handwerger, Roshi 1983.10
Handy, John 1973.02
Handy, Maurice 1913.03
Handy, Violet 1906.36
Handy, W.C. 1919.16, 1919.26, 1927.13, 1927.37, 1930.13, 1930.19, 1931.11, 1939.29, 1942.23, 1944.32, 1945.07, 1953.12, 1954.11, 1966.15, 1989.02, 1990.05, 1999.06, 1999.09
Handy, William 1905.21
Handy, Wyer Owens 1940.01
Handyside, Clarence 1904.51
Handysides, Clarence 1904.55, 1907.02
Handzlik, Anna 1940.11
Handzlik, Jean 1946.06, 1947.14, 1948.18, 1949.02, 1949.10, 1949.11, 1949.14, 1950.11, 1954.07, 1954.14, 1957.07
Hanegan, Ernest 1902.23, 1903.27
Hanemann, H.W. 1930.06
Haness, Abigale 1975.08
Haney, Carol 1954.05, 1958.19, 1962.14, 1963.14, 1964.11, 1986.03, 1999.01
Haney, Felix 1887.34, 1902.40, 1905.17, 1905.54, 1906.18, 1912.47, 1913.22
Haney, Lee 1899.04
Haney, Sonja 1972.03
Hanford, Charles B. 1912.32
Hanford, Edward 1897.20
Hanford, Ford 1920.28
Hanighen, Bernard 1946.05, 1947.06, 1959.05, 1967.11, 1982.12
Hanighen, Bernie 1997.05
Haniola, Mlle. 1869.26
Hankenson, Craig 1980.26
Hanker, Mr. 1841.01
Hankerson, Barry 1987.17
Hankin, Larry 1964.26
Hankins, J. 1864.23
Hankinson, Jeffrey 1998.15
Hanlan, T. 1883.37
Hanley, Charles 1906.06
Hanley, Del 1960.01
Hanley, Don 1900.53
Hanley, Ed 1955.04
Hanley, Eddie 1951.23
Hanley, Ellen 1946.12, 1947.08, 1952.20, 1959.06, 1959.25
Hanley, Ema 1887.31
Hanley, Emma 1885.26, 1885.41, 1885.63, 1886.04, 1886.47, 1888.34, 1891.03, 1892.05, 1892.28
Hanley, Felix 1911.28
Hanley, J.G. 1868.19
Hanley, Jack 1921.28
Hanley, James 1916.03, 1916.12, 1917.13, 1920.28, 1920.35, 1921.21, 1922.05, 1924.13, 1924.18, 1924.19, 1924.21, 1924.44, 1925.27, 1926.18, 1926.25, 1926.29, 1927.48, 1927.60, 1929.24, 1952.11
Hanley, James F. 1921.22, 1922.05, 1922.14, 1922.15, 1922.19, 1922.23, 1923.18, 1925.01, 1925.28, 1934.01, 1934.42
Hanley, John F. 1890.03
Hanley, Josie 1884.32
Hanley, Lottie 1886.47
Hanley, M.W. 1882.27
Hanley, Martin W. 1881.23, 1885.29
Hanley, Matt 1910.12, 1917.25, 1924.24, 1926.20
Hanley, Matthew 1925.06
Hanley, May 1887.43, 1888.36, 1889.01, 1892.03
Hanley, Miss 1883.38
Hanley, Patrick 1912.44
Hanlon Brothers 1892.59
Hanlon, Alice 1921.01
Hanlon, Bert 1917.12, 1918.08, 1920.04, 1922.12, 1930.25
Hanlon, Burt 1919.13
Hanlon, George 1913.18, 1928.23, 1937.15
Hanlon, Harry 1908.23
Hanlon, Helen 1926.38
Hanlon, Leddy 1938.03
Hanlon, Robinson 1860.01
Hanlon, Stemsky 1938.03
Hanlon, Toma 1888.43, 1890.27, 1894.37, 1904.23, 1907.23
Hanlon, William 1889.02
Hanlon, Wong 1938.03
Hanlon, Zoyara 1860.01
Hanlon-Lees, Alfred 1881.35
Hanlon-Lees, Edward 1881.35
Hanlon-Lees, Frederick 1881.35
Hanlon-Lees, George 1881.35
Hanlon-Lees, William 1881.35
Hanlons, The 1889.02
Hann, W.A. 1924.27
Hann, Walter 1876.12, 1907.06
Hanna, Betty 1932.14
Hanna, E.J. 1899.32
Hanna, Edward J. 1904.32
Hanna, G. 1877.04
Hanna, Joseph A. 1904.32
Hanna, Lisa 1995.07
Hanna, Phil 1950.10
Hanna, Roland 1968.19
Hanna, William A. 1926.11
Hannafin, Dan 1957.06
Hannafin, Daniel P. 1958.05, 1961.12, 1963.04, 1963.06, 1964.46, 1965.17, 1965.38
Hannah, Ned 1989.27, 1993.02, 1998.15
Hannam 1913.33
Hannan 1968.04
Hannan, Chick 1931.02
Hannan, Peggy 1931.02
Hannaux, Luc-Michel 1972.08
Hanneford, George 1939.16
Hanneford, Poodles 1927.17, 1935.15
Hannibal Calyo and Sons 1867.25
Hanning, Dorothy 1965.20
Hanning, Geraldine 1981.25
Hannons, Evelyn 1933.25
Hannum, T. 2001.04
Hannum, Zuruby 1865.05
Hanon, C.P. 1893.47
Hans, J. 1880.62
Hans, Joseph 1881.25
Hansberry, Lorraine 1972.01, 1973.10
Hanschman, A. 1908.34
Hanschmann, Anton 1911.37
Hanscombe, Harry 1904.02
Hansel, Emil 1904.33
Hansel, Messr. 1876.19
Hanseler, Frau 1897.08
Hansell, Ingeborg 1922.32
Hanselman, Messr. 1880.69
Hansen, Elizabeth 1982.10
Hansen, Ellen 1967.04
Hansen, Hans 1938.13
Hansen, Harold 1927.25
Hansen, John 1972.03
Hansen, Joseph 1964.02
Hansen, Kai 1934.15
Hansen, Kaji 1931.03
Hansen, Larry 1983.05, 1992.11
Hansen, Louise 1931.36
Hansen, Randy 1983.05
Hansen, Ronn 1970.07
Hansen, William 1947.07
Hanshue, Frank 1888.07
Hanson, Alice 1894.31
Hanson, Aune 1930.23
Hanson, Ed 1891.18
Hanson, Edward 1892.06, 1893.33
Hanson, Frank 1882.01, 1907.54, 1909.20, 1911.28, 1912.30
Hanson, Gladys 1920.34
Hanson, J. 1906.46
Hanson, John T. 1894.50
Hanson, Tripp 1992.02, 1992.18
Hanta, Morey 1915.03
Hanton, Charles 1923.43
Hantoot, Mustapha 1925.37
Hanwood, Fanny 1872.14, 1872.36
Hanzel, Carol 1966.14, 1968.18
Hapgood, Benjamin 1900.38, 1915.27, 1925.40
Hapgood, Emile 1923.43
Harada, Ann 2000.18
Harada, Ernest 1976.02
Harak, Buddy 1928.36
Haraldson, Marian 1962.20, 1963.29, 1964.24, 1965.29, 1981.10
Haran, Mary-Cleere 1979.24
Harary, Franz 1998.01
Harbach, Otto 1917.26, 1917.27, 1917.36, 1919.06, 1920.27, 1920.38, 1920.42, 1921.09, 1921.32, 1922.02, 1922.29, 1923.05, 1923.07, 1923.47, 1924.28, 1924.47, 1925.30, 1925.33, 1926.12, 1926.32, 1926.34, 1926.42, 1926.46, 1927.06, 1927.12, 1927.63, 1928.25, 1930.27, 1931.37, 1931.45, 1933.26, 1936.27, 1946.03, 1962.17, 1971.03, 1973.09, 1975.22, 1976.07, 1976.25, 1981.03, 1986.01, 1986.03, 1987.10, 1989.18
Harbach, Otto A. 1919.28
Harben, Hubert 1907.58
Harbison, Georginna Brown 1923.07
Harbord, Carl 1934.34
Harbright, Mr. 1841.01
Harburg, E.Y. 1929.26, 1930.08, 1930.18, 1930.22, 1930.33, 1930.35, 1931.08, 1931.13, 1931.19, 1931.21, 1932.16, 1932.20, 1932.27, 1934.01, 1934.06, 1934.19, 1934.32, 1936.31, 1937.15, 1938.08, 1940.10, 1944.23, 1945.07, 1947.01, 1947.03, 1948.04, 1951.15, 1952.11, 1953.12, 1955.09, 1955.13, 1957.16, 1960.09, 1961.08, 1962.17, 1964.02, 1967.04, 1967.11, 1968.02, 1973.14, 1974.09, 1981.16, 1983.09, 1986.01, 1988.08, 1989.06, 1989.16, 1990.09, 1997.01, 1997.11, 1998.06, 1999.11, 1999.23
Harcourt, Elizabeth 1917.30
Harcourt, Ellyn 1919.02
Harcourt, George 1917.30, 1927.54
Harcourt, Jack 1931.01
Harcourt, Marie 1875.11, 1923.02
Harcourt, Messr. 1857.03
Harcourt, Mr. 1855.10, 1857.02
Harcourt, Roy 2001.03
Harcourt, William K. 1908.40
Hardeen, Theo 1938.08
Harden, Dan 1936.01, 1938.07, 1941.04
Harden, John 1898.64
Hardenberg, Frank 1873.25
Hardenburg, Helena 1887.23
Harder, James 1975.24
Hardesty, Leslie 1980.14
Hardie, James M. 1888.30
Hardie, Marcella 1924.11
Hardie, S.R. 1887.18
Hardie, Thomas 1912.40
Hardin, Charles 1990.15
Hardin, Rae 1944.19
Harding, Annette 1927.67
Harding, Bessie 1869.29
Harding, John 1907.33
Harding, Miss 1796.01
Harding, Muriel 1948.10, 1951.04, 1951.06, 1951.09, 1955.15, 1955.16, 1955.20, 1955.22
Harding, Phyllis 1928.42, 1934.34

Hardinge, Emma 1855.10
Hardlow, Edith 1913.20
Hardman, J. 1884.41
Hardman, Leo 1900.45
Hards, Ira 1922.38, 1922.47, 1923.34, 1924.02, 1927.53, 1936.07
Hardt, Mignon 1903.27
Hardt-Warden, Bruno 1925.07, 1930.15
Hardwick, Cheryl 1978.22
Hardwick, Dana 1937.04
Hardwick, Mark 1982.04
Hardwick, Paul 1963.03
Hardy 1875.04
Hardy, Al 1925.24
Hardy, Doris 1918.01
Hardy, Jay 1996.08
Hardy, Joseph 1970.14, 1971.11, 1973.12
Hardy, Jr., William 1976.35
Hardy, Jr., William-Keebler 1980.14
Hardy, Leo 1898.75
Hardy, Mark 1992.12
Hardy, Michele 1963.22, 1965.14
Hardy, S.B. 1916.10
Hardy, Sam 1917.20, 1918.34
Hardy, Sam B. 1915.23, 1916.10
Hardy, Timothy 1965.39
Hare, Betty 1936.29
Hare, Ernest 1909.04, 1910.19, 1911.34, 1911.43, 1912.09, 1912.24, 1915.04, 1915.11, 1916.23
Hare, Mr. 1855.11
Hared, Ygal 1968.04, 1969.13
Harell, Gordon Lowry 1978.05
Hargate, Bill 1979.22, 1979.31, 1984.16
Harger, Burt 1927.27, 1928.34, 1943.07
Harger, Gary 1975.03
Harger, Messr. 1928.34
Hargrave, Miss 1886.42
Hargrave, Roy 1944.01
Hargrave, William 1933.15, 1934.20
Hargraves, Adele 1932.12
Hargraves, Albert 1905.09
Hargreaves, William 1905.26, 1909.29
Hargreeve, Miss 1841.01
Hari, Otto 1939.26
Harice, Pauline 1903.30
Haring, Forrest C. 1932.13
Harington, Nancy 1993.01
Hariton, Gerry 1986.16, 1988.07
Hark, Norma 1919.32
Harkaway, Harry 1877.39
Harker, Joseph 1894.41, 1897.03, 1899.39, 1901.19, 1905.46, 1907.06, 1913.33, 1914.32, 1917.24, 1919.20, 1919.38, 1920.34, 1948.06, 1951.03, 1951.04, 1955.21, 1955.22, 1964.38, 1968.25, 1976.14, 1978.16
Harker, Paul 1948.06, 1955.22
Harker, Phil 1914.32, 1917.24, 1919.20, 1919.38, 1951.03, 1951.04, 1955.21, 1964.38, 1968.25, 1976.14, 1978.16
Harker, Philip 1920.34
Harkins, D.H. 1879.07, 1879.11, 1879.20, 1879.25
Harkins, Dolla 1925.14
Harkins, Jim 1929.24
Harkins, John 1963.09
Harkins, W.S. 1880.25, 1888.23, 1890.41
Harkins, William S. 1888.37
Harkness Organization, The 1976.09
Harkness, Sam 1980.05, 1984.09
Harkrider, John 1927.67, 1928.12, 1930.08, 1930.39, 1931.08, 1931.19, 1932.11, 1941.08
Harkrider, John W. 1926.18, 1927.08, 1927.37, 1928.03, 1928.47, 1929.27, 1932.22
Harlam, Macy 1905.38, 1908.36
Harlan, Macy 1893.47, 1913.07
Harlan, Otis 1887.29, 1888.32, 1892.09, 1893.50, 1894.22, 1896.02, 1898.47, 1900.07, 1900.52, 1901.01, 1906.05, 1906.48, 1908.04, 1909.17, 1911.18, 1911.44, 1914.17
Harland, Ada 1868.23, 1868.32, 1869.45, 1870.02, 1870.06, 1870.14, 1871.01, 1871.02, 1871.04
Harland, Miss 1881.35
Harlekyn U.S.A. Company 1982.23
Harlem Productions, Inc. 1925.18
Harless, Betty 1958.02
Harley, Claire 1888.21
Harley, Eve 1947.11
Harley, John F. 1896.50, 1898.01
Harley, Margot 1975.18, 1976.30, 1982.02
Harling, Frank 1926.31, 1956.02
Harling, W. Frank 1923.19, 1980.08
Harling, W. Franke 1924.33, 1928.21
Harloff, Benjamin W. 2001.04
Harlow, Lou 1902.27
Harlow, Lou M. 1898.77
Harlow, Maude 1901.01
Harlow, Miss 1899.36
Harlow, Ralph 1909.26
Harlow, Richard 1892.04, 1893.17, 1894.26
Harlowe, Beatrice 1925.12
Harlowe, Louise 1896.45
Harlowe, Ralph 1911.41
Harman, Barry 1988.10
Harman, Messr. 1881.11, 1881.27
Harman, Miss 1882.37
Harman, Paul 1987.04, 1988.09, 1997.10
Harman, Victor 1879.15
Harmathy, Sandar 1917.15
Harmer, C.H. 1883.05
Harmon, April 1925.50
Harmon, Erv 1959.13
Harmon, Florrie 1894.18
Harmon, George 1881.32
Harmon, Gwen 1953.08, 1957.05
Harmon, Josephine 1911.37, 1921.06
Harmon, Lucille 1921.17
Harmon, Mary 1951.23, 1954.02, 1954.16
Harmon, Miss 1881.14
Harmon, Muriel 1909.07
Harmon, Wynn 2000.03
Harmony, Gladys 1929.18
Harmony, Olive 1929.18
Harmony, Pearl 1929.18
Harms, Carl 1963.11
Harms, Virginia 1905.51
Harn, William 1928.42
Harnden, Red 1929.07
Harnden, Richie 1908.08
Harnden, Ritchie 1908.10
Harndoff, Mons. 1866.09
Harner, Bud 1989.08
Harney, Ben 1896.52, 1975.19, 1981.29
Harnick, Jay 1953.17, 1961.11
Harnick, Sheldon 1952.09, 1952.20, 1953.17, 1958.01, 1958.04, 1959.25, 1960.19, 1962.16, 1963.11, 1963.14, 1964.27, 1966.18, 1967.03, 1970.15, 1974.09, 1976.08, 1976.36, 1978.07, 1978.20, 1979.21, 1981.18, 1983.17, 1986.03, 1989.03, 1989.06, 1989.13, 1990.18, 1993.10, 1993.17
Harnish, Mayme 1900.58
Harnley, Leslie 1962.22
Harold L. Bateman's Opera Bouffe Company 1868.18, 1868.25, 1868.27
Harold L. Bateman's Parisian Opera Company 1868.07
Harold, Arthur 1882.54
Harold, Donald 1879.33, 1879.35, 1880.06, 1880.10, 1880.13, 1880.59, 1880.65, 1880.67, 1880.70, 1883.05, 1883.07, 1906.09
Harold, George 1925.39
Harold, J. 1923.03
Harold, Jennie 1881.52
Harold, Maggie 1879.56
Harold, Mr. 1882.06
Harold, Robert 1905.48
Harold, Stuart 1886.57, 1887.06, 1887.14, 1894.47
Harper, Alice 1928.48
Harper, Andrew 1910.13, 1916.11, 1917.23
Harper, Barbara 1967.15
Harper, Belle 1896.45, 1898.11, 1898.18, 1898.26, 1898.46, 1902.04
Harper, Brenda 1888.33
Harper, Dolores 1944.31, 1946.21, 1950.07, 1954.19
Harper, Fred 1926.15, 1927.14, 1928.01
Harper, Herbert 1940.09
Harper, J.W. 1975.18
Harper, Jean 1938.16
Harper, Ken 1975.01
Harper, Leonard 1929.23, 1942.13
Harper, Lillian 1896.32
Harper, Mary 1920.29
Harper, Mary Louise 1936.06
Harper, Messr. 1875.39, 1877.22
Harper, Mr. 1878.20
Harper, Otis 1921.36
Harper, Robert 1927.01
Harper, Samantha 1971.04
Harper, Sherrill 1974.02
Harper, Tom 1873.27
Harper, Valerie 1959.22, 1961.28, 1971.08
Harper, W.H. 1877.39
Harper, Wally 1969.08, 1970.13, 1973.05, 1974.09, 1976.09, 1979.02, 1980.08, 1980.26, 1982.09, 1983.06, 1983.09, 1983.17, 1984.14, 1987.06, 1989.06, 1989.26, 1992.17, 1992.18, 1994.06, 1995.11
Harper, William 1916.11
Harpur, W.H. 1879.03
Harr, Warren 1949.03
Harrell, Bobby 1941.06
Harrell, Gordon Lowry 1971.20, 1974.24, 1976.03, 1983.11, 1984.14, 1985.05, 1986.06, 1987.19, 1989.29, 1991.15, 1993.19, 1995.07, 1997.08, 1999.01
Harrigan, Charles 1957.09
Harrigan, Dorothy I. 1922.16
Harrigan, E. 1876.19
Harrigan, Edward 1873.20, 1873.22, 1873.27, 1875.14, 1876.19, 1876.31, 1877.11, 1877.24, 1878.01, 1878.13, 1878.17, 1879.04, 1879.35, 1879.37, 1879.64, 1879.68, 1880.09, 1880.15, 1880.35, 1880.36, 1880.42, 1880.64, 1881.09, 1881.29, 1882.02, 1882.39, 1882.50, 1882.74, 1882.79, 1883.26, 1883.32, 1883.46, 1883.53, 1883.63, 1884.13, 1884.16, 1884.37, 1884.41, 1884.48, 1885.02, 1885.08, 1885.15, 1885.22, 1885.29, 1885.44, 1885.49, 1885.66, 1886.03, 1886.42, 1886.52, 1887.07, 1887.16, 1887.39, 1887.45, 1887.48, 1888.14, 1888.27, 1888.40, 1889.07, 1889.11, 1889.15, 1889.18, 1889.24, 1890.49, 1891.25, 1891.26, 1891.37, 1891.45, 1891.46, 1892.44, 1892.54, 1893.10, 1893.15, 1893.27, 1893.42, 1893.46, 1894.04, 1894.49, 1895.05, 1896.24, 1897.12, 1897.43, 1903.26, 1985.02, 2000.12
Harrigan, James 1897.07, 1906.31
Harrigan, Jr., Edward 1895.05
Harriman, Alfred 1917.13
Harriman, Josephine 1912.12, 1914.04
Harrington, C.J. 1904.42, 1907.16
Harrington, Charlene 1983.02
Harrington, Edward 1893.36
Harrington, Frank 1927.06
Harrington, Hamtree 1921.26, 1922.22, 1924.37, 1928.18, 1930.19, 1932.01, 1933.22, 1939.14, 1952.08
Harrington, Harry 1909.30
Harrington, Helen 1887.32, 1891.44, 1895.15
Harrington, J.P. 1901.25
Harrington, John 1921.12
Harrington, John C. 1881.39
Harrington, Joseph 1900.49, 1900.56
Harrington, Nancy 1995.16, 1998.17
Harrington, Nettie 1884.25, 1889.01, 1894.38
Harrington, Pat 1940.19, 1942.18, 1950.15
Harrington, Rita 1899.10
Harrington, Robert 1909.02, 1954.13
Harrington, Ruth 1919.06
Harrington, Wendall 1979.11, 1981.14, 1984.02, 1991.07, 1991.14, 1993.06, 1994.12, 1995.11, 1995.19
Harrington, Wendall K. 1996.15, 1997.07, 1997.22, 1998.01, 1998.20, 1999.08, 1999.20, 1999.21, 2000.19
Harrington, Wendell K. 1998.02
Harrington, William 1881.39
Harris and Woods 1904.41
Harris Associates, Inc. 1968.24, 1969.01
Harris Margaret 1983.15
Harris Opera Company 1885.34, 1885.36, 1885.37, 1885.38
Harris, A. 1864.12, 1868.02
Harris, A.A. 1881.39
Harris, A.G. 1892.35
Harris, Albert 1987.02
Harris, Alice 1916.02, 1932.08
Harris, Amelia 1870.36, 2000.19
Harris, Amilie 1866.03, 1869.46
Harris, Anita 1884.24, 1885.69
Harris, Anneta 1883.50
Harris, Arthur 1953.10, 1972.07, 1980.09, 1980.18
Harris, Artie 1998.13
Harris, Augustos 1897.03
Harris, Augustus 1863.06, 1864.20, 1864.21, 1866.10, 1883.39, 1895.28
Harris, Averell 1902.16, 1940.22, 1942.29
Harris, Barbara 1961.17, 1963.09, 1965.31, 1966.18
Harris, Beatrice 1903.25
Harris, Ben 1923.11
Harris, Bert D. 1904.18
Harris, Billy 1959.13
Harris, Bobby 1901.28
Harris, Brenda 1960.05
Harris, Bud 1934.40, 1936.12
Harris, Charlene 1950.19, 1979.18
Harris, Charles 1881.07, 1881.36, 1881.37, 1882.17, 1882.60, 1882.75, 1882.78, 1888.38, 1894.15
Harris, Charles K. 1891.39, 1893.23, 1894.17, 1898.61, 1946.01, 1994.08
Harris, Charles L. 1885.04, 1886.12
Harris, Charlise 1976.04
Harris, Clarence 1943.10
Harris, Clifford 1906.25, 1912.26, 1916.22, 1917.29
Harris, Cora 1892.24
Harris, D.L. 1875.38
Harris, Daisy 1899.33
Harris, Daniel 1936.27
Harris, Dede 1999.24, 2000.11
Harris, Donald 1939.06, 1947.16, 1948.06, 1951.01, 1951.03, 1951.04, 1951.09, 1975.20
Harris, Donny 1948.28
Harris, Dooney 1872.35
Harris, Duncan 1914.24, 1918.01
Harris, Earl 1904.38
Harris, Ed 1899.33
Harris, Edna M. 1930.10, 1935.01
Harris, Edna Mae 1943.10
Harris, Elaine 1969.03
Harris, Elmer 1914.21, 1916.21, 1917.04
Harris, Erona 1945.06, 1946.09
Harris, F. Clifford 1905.27, 1918.27
Harris, Frances 1906.29
Harris, Frank 1980.17
Harris, G.H. 1871.13
Harris, Gary 1971.20, 1973.11, 1974.04, 1975.04, 1979.29, 1982.15, 1987.02
Harris, Gavin 1907.59
Harris, Grace 1873.22
Harris, H.B. 1896.37
Harris, H.H. 1898.12
Harris, Harvey 1997.09
Harris, Hazel 1927.68, 1929.50, 1930.20
Harris, Henry B. 1897.40, 1910.10, 1911.18, 1911.26, 1911.39, 1912.31
Harris, Holly 1947.01, 1948.25, 1952.02
Harris, Hope 1999.08
Harris, Howard 1948.21
Harris, Ida 1901.20, 1911.26
Harris, J. 1873.26
Harris, J.W. 1896.35
Harris, James 1905.44, 1928.45
Harris, James Berton 1974.03
Harris, James C. 1912.43
Harris, Jean 1945.14
Harris, Jed 1929.20, 1945.07
Harris, Jeff 1961.12
Harris, Jeremiah J. 1990.17
Harris, Jimmy 1976.34
Harris, Joe W. 1884.25, 1897.46
Harris, Jonathan 1946.17, 1953.01
Harris, Joseph 1911.25, 1916.07
Harris, Joseph P. 1963.08, 1963.11, 1966.01, 1966.10, 1968.03, 1969.01, 1970.03, 1974.19, 1974.21, 1978.02, 1979.05, 1979.24, 1982.18, 1986.07, 1990.17
Harris, Jr., William 1910.10, 1924.23
Harris, Julie 1947.09, 1965.33
Harris, Kelly 1972.20
Harris, Kent 1995.03
Harris, L.W. 1871.17
Harris, Laura 1903.35, 1908.09, 1918.18, 1985.20
Harris, Lawrence 1934.40, 1936.12
Harris, Lenore P. 1900.44
Harris, Leonore 1900.19, 1901.01
Harris, LeRoy 1935.11
Harris, Lew 1939.25
Harris, Lillian 1904.03, 1908.10
Harris, Lloyd 1932.27, 1971.07
Harris, Louise 1885.53
Harris, Lowell 1957.12, 1970.06
Harris, Lulu 1897.26
Harris, Mabel Josephine 1916.08
Harris, Maggie 1898.67
Harris, Marcia 1913.16
Harris, Marion 1927.07
Harris, May 1908.07, 1910.10
Harris, Messr. 1844.01, 1879.23
Harris, Miss 1864.09

Harris, Mitchell 1935.17
Harris, Mr. 1851.01, 1851.06, 1867.25
Harris, Nat 1907.54, 1909.20, 1910.23
Harris, Nat W. 1907.54, 1908.26
Harris, Netousha 1998.20
Harris, Niki 1980.08, 1983.06, 1994.06
Harris, Ralph 1929.21
Harris, Raymond C. 1984.09
Harris, Richard 1981.26
Harris, Robert H. 1948.08, 1964.04
Harris, Ruth 1944.26
Harris, S.A. 1905.29
Harris, Sadie 1905.45
Harris, Saidie 1907.57
Harris, Sam 1908.22, 1908.31, 1909.16, 1911.33, 1911.41, 1912.11, 1914.13, 1914.34, 1917.36, 1917.37, 1918.41, 1919.04, 1994.07, 1997.08
Harris, Sam H. 1904.42, 1906.02, 1906.11, 1906.21, 1906.42, 1907.09, 1907.16, 1907.20, 1907.57, 1908.09, 1908.14, 1909.26, 1916.02, 1920.14, 1921.30, 1922.39, 1923.32, 1924.44, 1925.45, 1927.21, 1928.38, 1931.48, 1932.05, 1933.02, 1933.13, 1933.22, 1933.25, 1935.14, 1937.13, 1941.04, 1943.03
Harris, Sara Lou 1952.08
Harris, Schrode 1913.33
Harris, Scott 1993.05
Harris, Sidney 1905.29
Harris, Skip 1982.24
Harris, Sydney 1905.18
Harris, Sydney A. 1903.29
Harris, Sylvia 1963.08, 1966.01, 1966.10
Harris, Ted 1969.03
Harris, Thomas 1903.35
Harris, Tom 1972.12
Harris, Val 1911.24
Harris, W. 1906.46
Harris, Walter 1968.11
Harris, William 1888.16, 1891.03, 1891.26, 1892.05, 1893.49, 1893.50, 1895.27, 1895.34, 1896.52, 1897.30, 1897.40, 1897.47, 1899.03, 1903.25, 1964.19
Harris, William H. 1977.09
Harris, Winifred 1919.04, 1922.31, 1923.24, 1925.26, 1927.48, 1934.19
Harrison's English Opera Troupe 1864.04, 1864.07
Harrison, Al 1920.26
Harrison, Alice 1868.06, 1869.02, 1869.14, 1869.20, 1869.27, 1869.35, 1869.43, 1870.04, 1870.25, 1870.28, 1870.32, 1871.01, 1871.02, 1871.05, 1881.23, 1882.27, 1885.08, 1885.43, 1886.36, 1890.34
Harrison, Alma 1914.02, 1914.18
Harrison, Andrew 1999.02
Harrison, Arnold 1867.03, 1867.04, 1867.06, 1868.09, 1868.10, 1868.11, 1868.12
Harrison, Bertram 1919.06, 1922.17, 1923.19, 1924.47, 1928.21, 1928.43, 1931.32, 1934.35, 1937.07
Harrison, Beth 1905.30, 1912.33
Harrison, E. 1875.18
Harrison, Edward 1930.22
Harrison, Frank 1926.31
Harrison, Gabriel 1864.04, 1864.07
Harrison, George 1970.16, 1973.17, 1977.10, 1982.22, 1984.15
Harrison, Gertrude 1915.17, 1918.15
Harrison, Gregory 1997.07, 2001.02
Harrison, Hindie 1883.31, 1884.22, 1884.25, 1885.26, 1885.58
Harrison, Hindle 1887.01
Harrison, Howard 1999.12, 1999.20
Harrison, Jr., Edward 1894.49
Harrison, Juan 1924.37
Harrison, K. 1870.12
Harrison, Lee 1889.31, 1890.03, 1892.55, 1894.21, 1895.18, 1896.18, 1897.26, 1898.20, 1898.28, 1898.43, 1899.17, 1899.26, 1899.29, 1900.40, 1901.17, 1902.24, 1903.23, 1904.56, 1906.01, 1908.07, 1908.19, 1909.28, 1911.12, 1911.23
Harrison, Lewis 1877.20
Harrison, Llewellen 1987.17
Harrison, Louis 1876.34, 1879.33, 1879.35, 1880.06, 1880.10, 1880.13, 1880.70, 1881.23, 1882.27, 1884.15, 1884.56, 1887.43, 1888.09, 1889.01, 1889.44, 1891.36, 1891.43, 1891.44, 1892.08, 1892.36, 1892.55, 1892.60, 1893.02, 1893.07, 1893.20, 1893.28, 1893.39, 1893.47, 1894.05, 1895.36, 1895.42, 1896.29, 1897.26, 1898.34, 1898.72, 1899.02, 1899.19, 1899.35, 1900.07, 1900.42, 1900.55, 1900.56, 1901.12, 1902.06, 1903.37, 1904.51, 1904.57, 1905.11, 1905.22, 1907.18, 1908.34, 1910.25, 1917.22, 1918.34, 1920.36, 1924.39, 1925.33, 1930.22
Harrison, Madeline 1912.35, 1912.45
Harrison, Mae 1906.35
Harrison, Margaret 1908.40
Harrison, Mark 1908.29
Harrison, May 1905.33
Harrison, Messr. 1856.04
Harrison, Michael 1967.09
Harrison, Miss 1881.07, 1882.23, 1915.17
Harrison, Mr. 1855.11, 1856.04
Harrison, Muriel 1921.36, 1931.08
Harrison, Patrick 1967.01
Harrison, Ray 1940.18, 1944.33, 1946.19, 1947.17, 1948.04, 1950.20, 1955.17, 1956.05, 1958.04, 1960.07, 1963.20
Harrison, Rex 1956.01, 1981.19
Harrison, Richard B. 1930.10, 1935.01
Harrison, Robert 1912.03, 1937.01, 1952.03
Harrison, Ruth 1933.05, 1936.17, 1946.02
Harrison, Sadie 1898.50
Harrison, Sam 1884.15, 1884.56, 1886.39
Harrison, Samuel 1871.19
Harrison, Seth 1971.07
Harrison, Stafford 1980.05
Harrison, Stanley 1920.03, 1927.17, 1930.20, 1930.40, 1933.24
Harrison, W.B. 1865.05, 1865.09, 1865.10, 1899.04
Harrison, William 1854.03, 1854.06, 1854.07, 1855.01, 1855.02, 1855.03, 1855.04, 1855.05, 1855.06, 1855.07, 1855.08, 1855.09
Harrison, Zelda 1866.07, 1866.10, 1867.03, 1867.04, 1867.06, 1868.09, 1868.10, 1868.11, 1868.12
Harriton, Maria 1945.20
Harrod, James 1914.25
Harrold, Jack 1955.25, 1958.16, 1959.16, 1959.17, 1959.21, 1960.02, 1960.03, 1962.21, 1963.15, 1963.24, 1964.02, 1964.30, 1965.27, 1980.03, 1980.04, 1980.21, 1980.22, 1980.25, 1981.20, 1981.22, 1982.07, 1982.16, 1982.20, 1983.12, 1983.13, 1984.11, 1985.09, 1985.10, 1985.11, 1986.08, 1986.09, 1986.10, 1986.14, 1987.08, 1987.11, 1989.14
Harrold, John 1944.24, 1945.12, 1945.15
Harrold, Lizzie 1877.21, 1881.22
Harrold, Maggie 1881.04
Harrold, Merle 1929.20
Harrold, Orville 1907.05, 1910.35, 1915.24, 1925.36
Harrold, Patti 1922.48, 1925.01, 1925.36
Harron, Donald 1971.21
Harrow, Bruce 1972.11
Harry Collins, Inc. 1919.28
Harry, Jackee 1978.28
Harry, Nettie 1937.14
Harshaw, Cee-Cee 1992.08
Hart, A. 1886.45
Hart, Al 1901.29, 1912.26
Hart, Albert 1886.24, 1891.03, 1892.05, 1894.16, 1898.25, 1900.20, 1901.08, 1902.05, 1902.16, 1903.16, 1903.41, 1904.21, 1904.49, 1904.57, 1905.17, 1906.18, 1908.01, 1908.38, 1909.21, 1911.37, 1912.20, 1913.33, 1914.11
Hart, Annie 1927.67, 1932.11
Hart, Bernice 1920.24, 1921.34
Hart, Billy 1898.50
Hart, Bret 1876.14
Hart, Charles 1944.32, 1953.09, 1988.01, 1990.04, 1992.12
Hart, Dan 1885.29, 1892.29
Hart, Daniel 1884.48
Hart, Daniel F. 1891.10
Hart, Daniel J. 1892.39
Hart, David Earl 1994.08
Hart, Dolores 1934.06
Hart, Edith 1904.41
Hart, Elizabeth 1911.20
Hart, Enid 1883.23
Hart, Flo 1912.38, 1915.31, 1916.24, 1917.26, 1917.35
Hart, Frances 1926.01
Hart, Frank 1913.02
Hart, George V. 1908.36
Hart, Gussie 1896.24, 1897.45
Hart, Irene 1920.24, 1921.34
Hart, J. 1892.08
Hart, Jack 1980.12
Hart, Jerry 1896.39, 1912.45
Hart, Joe 1889.09, 1889.41, 1890.29, 1994.06
Hart, John 1875.39
Hart, John C. 1907.12, 1907.23
Hart, Joseph 1889.41, 1890.29, 1891.46, 1893.42, 1894.12, 1894.17, 1897.38, 1902.08, 1904.27, 1906.22, 1907.14
Hart, Josh 1872.07, 1873.20, 1873.22, 1873.27, 1875.14, 1875.31, 1875.34, 1875.35, 1875.36, 1875.37, 1875.38, 1875.40, 1876.01, 1876.13, 1876.15, 1876.22, 1876.29, 1877.01
Hart, Josie 1898.61
Hart, Jr., John N. 1978.21, 1980.30, 1995.05
Hart, Kathryn 1919.16
Hart, Libbie 1900.35
Hart, Lilly 1905.22
Hart, Lily 1902.24, 1905.28
Hart, Linda 1979.30, 1987.15, 1989.22
Hart, Lorenz 1919.14, 1923.19, 1925.17, 1925.26, 1925.31, 1926.07, 1926.13, 1926.50, 1926.51, 1927.56, 1928.02, 1928.16, 1928.30, 1929.07, 1929.12, 1929.42, 1930.08, 1930.33, 1931.04, 1931.08, 1931.13, 1935.15, 1936.05, 1936.31, 1937.04, 1937.13, 1938.05, 1938.14, 1939.27, 1940.06, 1940.20, 1940.22, 1942.15, 1943.22, 1947.05, 1952.01, 1952.11, 1954.12, 1955.13, 1957.10, 1961.15, 1962.17, 1963.02, 1963.17, 1965.08, 1967.11, 1968.07, 1974.09, 1974.11, 1975.13, 1975.22, 1976.16, 1976.19, 1979.24, 1981.16, 1983.02, 1983.09, 1983.20, 1988.08, 1989.06, 1989.16, 1989.21, 1990.09, 1991.10, 1995.12
Hart, Lorenz M. 1920.25
Hart, Lori 1995.14
Hart, Louis 1908.35
Hart, Mable 1949.15
Hart, Margie 1942.25
Hart, Mark 1897.07, 1905.41, 1906.19, 1912.29
Hart, Mary Ella 1930.10
Hart, Max 1919.29, 1952.02
Hart, Melissa 1970.03
Hart, Messr. 1846.01, 1851.01, 1854.01
Hart, Minnie 1915.32
Hart, Miss 1851.05, 1916.10
Hart, Moss 1930.14, 1932.05, 1933.02, 1933.22, 1934.29, 1935.14, 1936.31, 1937.13, 1938.09, 1941.04, 1943.03, 1943.23, 1944.29, 1948.14, 1949.08, 1956.01, 1960.21, 1964.20, 1967.02, 1968.17, 1976.05, 1980.19, 1981.27, 1993.11
Hart, Murray 1920.35
Hart, Paul E. 1981.18
Hart, Peggy 1923.23
Hart, Percy 1900.41
Hart, Robert 1864.02
Hart, Rose 1903.41
Hart, Stan 1979.13, 1980.09, 1980.18
Hart, T. 1876.19
Hart, Teddy 1938.14, 1942.22, 1943.19, 1946.19
Hart, Thomas A. 1929.22
Hart, Timothy Eric 1997.19
Hart, Toni 1944.23
Hart, Tony 1873.20, 1873.22, 1875.14, 1876.19, 1877.24, 1878.01, 1878.13, 1878.17, 1879.04, 1879.37, 1879.68, 1880.09, 1880.36, 1880.64, 1881.09, 1881.29, 1882.02, 1882.50, 1882.74, 1882.79, 1883.32, 1883.46, 1883.53, 1883.63, 1884.13, 1884.41, 1885.02, 1885.15, 1885.22, 1886.06, 1886.40, 1886.60, 1901.04, 1908.11
Hart, Violet 1905.37
Hart, Vivian 1925.25, 1925.48, 1926.27, 1927.03, 1927.25, 1929.46, 1930.01, 1930.03, 1931.17, 1931.18, 1931.20, 1931.33, 1931.41, 1932.02, 1933.09, 1933.14, 1934.07, 1934.08, 1934.09, 1934.10, 1934.11, 1935.05, 1935.06, 1935.07, 1935.08, 1935.09, 1936.04, 1936.08, 1936.09, 1936.11
Hart, William 1904.41, 1930.16
Hart., Jr., Joseph 1917.29
Hartberg, A. 1891.21
Hartberg, Carl 1890.23, 1895.19, 1897.18, 1902.20, 1905.29
Hartberg, F. 1889.36
Harte, Marion 1903.34
Harten, James 1879.07, 1879.11
Hartford Stage Company 1982.08
Hartford, Lucia 1895.44, 1905.40
Hartford, Mazie 1907.26
Hartig, Herbert 1962.02
Harting, Olga 1913.09
Hartla, Ethela 1912.44
Hartland, Mr. 1865.04
Hartley, Amy 1896.45, 1898.07
Hartley, Arthur 1913.16, 1919.37, 1928.17, 1930.23
Hartley, Ben 1998.10
Hartley, Jack 1943.01
Hartley, Jan 1998.15
Hartley, Miss 1895.03
Hartley, Mlle. 1892.32
Hartley, Rae 1918.05
Hartley, Ray 1915.32
Hartley, Richard 1975.08, 2000.17
Hartley, Susan 1983.06
Hartman, Annie 1882.36
Hartman, Charles 1918.03
Hartman, Dan 1979.13
Hartman, David 1964.01, 1965.36
Hartman, Elek 1978.10
Hartman, Ferris 1890.08, 1891.23, 1897.41, 1897.46, 1899.19, 1899.37, 1925.29, 1928.43
Hartman, Grace 1932.16, 1936.26, 1938.07, 1942.12, 1942.14, 1947.20, 1949.02, 1950.09
Hartman, Gretchen 1913.24
Hartman, Marian 1908.07, 1908.21
Hartman, Minnie 1879.65, 1879.67
Hartman, Miss 1870.31, 1881.14, 1882.37
Hartman, Paul 1932.16, 1936.26, 1938.07, 1942.12, 1942.14, 1947.20, 1949.02, 1950.09, 1952.07, 1957.08
Hartman, Pauline 1879.65, 1879.67
Hartman, Susan 1956.02
Hartman, Warren 1998.19
Hartmann, Charles 1916.22
Hartmann, Frl. 1880.66
Hartmann, Jeanne 1875.28
Hartmann, Ronnie 1949.17
Hartnell, Norman 1928.42
Hartner, Frl. 1897.08
Hartnett, D.F. 1879.54
Harton, James 1879.25
Harton, Messr. 1881.35
Hartsell, Harold 1889.20, 1891.46, 1911.17
Hartt, Sherle 1940.18
Hartung, Billy 1997.17, 1998.13, 1999.23
Hartung, Elsa 1903.15
Hartwell, Julie 1937.12
Hartwell, Merle 1919.33
Hartwig, Mr. 1897.35
Harty, Frank 1949.06
Harty, Patricia 1959.25, 1961.18
Harty, Thomas 1931.36
Harty, Tom 1932.16
Harty, Veola 1913.20
Hartz, Belle 1890.26, 1891.31
Hartz, Mattie 1913.14
Hartz, Miss 1892.53
Harum, Avind 1965.02, 1968.18
Harum, Eivind 1981.10
Harum, Tim 1963.12
Harvath, Julia 1943.08
Harve, George 1922.22
Harven, Jane 1952.13
Harvey Company 1879.16
Harvey, Alex 1973.14, 1975.12
Harvey, Amy 1882.51
Harvey, Claire 1942.35
Harvey, Clarence 1892.55, 1902.15, 1902.30, 1906.20, 1907.21, 1910.13, 1911.34, 1911.43, 1912.09, 1912.24, 1914.07, 1915.21, 1916.14, 1921.14, 1921.25, 1929.47, 1931.09, 1933.21
Harvey, Colin 1943.06
Harvey, Edythe 1898.66
Harvey, Elsie 1902.11
Harvey, Eugene 1883.10
Harvey, F. 1897.56
Harvey, Fletcher 1918.41
Harvey, Georgette 1923.39, 1932.08, 1935.13, 1942.03, 1943.15, 1944.03, 1949.15
Harvey, Georgia 1910.26, 1914.26
Harvey, J. Clarence 1900.58, 1907.42, 1917.20, 1919.12

Harvey, J.J. 1904.45
Harvey, James 1964.23
Harvey, James Clarence 1889.26
Harvey, Jane 1950.19
Harvey, John 1875.19, 1961.26, 1963.08, 1963.13, 1963.26
Harvey, Joseph 1892.59
Harvey, Ken 1951.23, 1957.17
Harvey, Kenneth 1955.27
Harvey, Lottie 1914.30
Harvey, M.J. Clarence 1898.28
Harvey, Maria 1879.14
Harvey, Marie 1879.14
Harvey, Marion 1941.08
Harvey, Maud 1891.19, 1892.26, 1892.32, 1898.66
Harvey, Maude 1890.22, 1892.49, 1893.01
Harvey, Messr. 1834.02
Harvey, Michael 1943.23, 1971.16, 1977.08, 1981.28
Harvey, Miss 1872.14
Harvey, Morris 1923.35, 1925.42, 1926.15
Harvey, Owen 1917.30
Harvey, Pauline 1884.65
Harvey, Peter 1970.12, 1971.06, 1975.02, 1975.08, 1975.10
Harvey, Richard 1948.17
Harvey, Robert 1940.01, 1943.10
Harvey, Robert H. 1938.18
Harvey, Roslyn 1932.19, 1942.05, 1942.26
Harvey, Russell 1931.29
Harvey, Thelma 1924.31
Harvey, W.M. 1911.38
Harvey, Walter 1924.16, 1925.19, 1927.20, 1927.29, 1927.53
Harvey, Walter H. 1913.10
Harvey, Willard 1898.72
Harwell, George 1961.14, 1961.26
Harwick, Marion 1929.20
Harwood, Harry 1891.38
Harwood, James 1951.10
Harwood, John 1917.30, 1922.12, 1922.40, 1923.07, 1925.49, 1926.07, 1926.28, 1926.36, 1927.08, 1927.52, 1928.28, 1929.02, 1929.49, 1931.01, 1965.39
Harwood, Marybly 1946.22
Harwood, William C. 1983.04
Hasbrook, Ethelberta 1927.64
Hasbrook, G.F. 1885.67
Hasbrouck, Fannie 1916.09
Hascall, Alice 1919.10
Hascall, Lon 1919.10, 1919.30, 1922.11, 1924.16, 1927.13, 1927.35, 1929.49
Hasegawa, I. 1903.19
Hash, Burl 1974.06
Hashimoto, Kazuakira 1989.21
Haskell, H. 1884.28
Haskell, Helen 1974.09
Haskell, Jack 1925.23, 1925.52, 1926.07, 1927.13, 1927.52, 1928.04, 1928.30, 1928.36, 1929.02, 1930.35, 1932.03, 1962.20
Haskell, Jimmie 1975.12, 1978.25
Haskell, Loney 1905.42
Haskin, Harold 1936.05
Haskins, Charles 1918.01
Haskins, James 1983.17
Haslam, Isabel 1896.06
Haslam, J. 1884.40
Haslam, Jno. 1889.08
Haslam, John 1883.48, 1888.10
Haslam, Maud 1882.71, 1887.52
Haslam, Messr. 1883.48
Haslam, Miss 1882.46
Haslam, Mlle. 1888.10, 1888.23
Haslem, Bert 1895.10
Haslem, E.H. 1889.54
Haslem, Heralda 1876.03
Hassa, E. 1879.25
Hassall, Christopher 1976.18
Hassan, John 1907.51
Hassan, Rita 1947.09
Hasselberg, D. 1887.18
Hasselberger, Cararie 1873.26
Hassell, Gene 1908.26
Hassell, George 1915.16, 1915.32, 1916.14, 1917.02, 1918.20, 1919.02, 1919.16, 1920.09, 1922.34, 1923.17, 1924.29, 1924.45, 1926.27, 1927.17, 1928.04, 1928.30, 1928.50, 1930.20, 1931.03
Hassell, Virginia 1927.17
Hassen, Ismut 1925.37
Hasserly, Kate 1875.39
Hasson, Thomas 1960.08
Hasson, William 1926.24
Hastie, Messr. 1882.04, 1882.20, 1883.17, 1883.23
Hastings, A.H. 1870.24, 1871.15, 1871.22
Hastings, Alice 1879.38, 1883.43
Hastings, Beatrice 1902.27
Hastings, Bill 1979.26, 1986.13
Hastings, Florence 1887.07, 1887.16
Hastings, Frederick 1913.07
Hastings, Hal 1950.09, 1954.05, 1955.08, 1957.07, 1959.25, 1959.26, 1960.19, 1969.16
Hastings, Harold 1951.23, 1953.11, 1962.12, 1963.14, 1965.02, 1965.17, 1965.35, 1966.06, 1966.24, 1968.30, 1970.13, 1971.05, 1972.02, 1973.04
Hastings, John 1934.37, 1995.12, 2000.16
Hastings, Laura 1925.02
Hastings, Lou 1894.13
Hastings, Miss 1886.42
Hastings, Pat 1933.25
Hastings, Patty 1926.39
Hastings, Philip 1890.07
Hastings, Robert 1913.05
Hastings, Vesta Dora 1891.21
Hasty, Effie 1902.44
Haswell, Lena 1889.05
Haswell, Percy 1892.14, 1922.16
Haswell, William 1887.06
Hatch Stella 1880.48
Hatch, Alonzo 1879.58, 1880.04, 1881.34, 1881.57, 1882.14, 1883.22, 1884.30, 1884.31
Hatch, David 1964.29
Hatch, Frank 1904.39, 1926.12
Hatch, Kate 1875.11
Hatch, William 1897.02
Hatch, William Riley 1900.59, 1906.04
Hatcher, Jessie 1891.02, 1894.16
Hatcher, Mary 1949.17
Hateley, Linzi 1988.12
Hatfield, Kate 1884.25, 1884.32, 1884.33, 1884.38
Hatfield, Katherine 1919.34
Hatfield, Kathryn 1919.43
Hatfield, Lansing 1937.10, 1939.20, 1939.21, 1944.27
Hatfield, Messr. 1869.35
Hathaway, A. 1858.04
Hathaway, Clara 1905.23
Hathaway, Donny 1999.09
Hathaway, Dorothy 1925.07, 1925.47
Hathaway, Lillian 1907.28
Hathaway, V. 1903.25
Hatley, Tim 2000.04
Hatten, Lennie 1942.05
Hatter, J. 1869.02
Hatter, W.H. 1885.64, 1886.61, 1888.42, 1889.25
Hatter, Will H. 1899.14, 1899.16
Hatter, William 1896.02
Hattie, Little 1880.07
Hatton 1859.15
Hatton, Anne Julia 1793.01, 1794.01
Hatton, Bradford 1932.15, 1951.23
Hatton, Ella 1882.76, 1906.05, 1907.02
Hatton, John 1859.09
Hatvany, Lili 1941.02
Haubell, Felcitas 1906.24
Haubrich, Frau 1882.68
Hauerbach, Otto 1910.22, 1911.15, 1911.25, 1911.30, 1912.46, 1913.34, 1914.08, 1914.28, 1915.29, 1917.05
Hauerbach, Otto A. 1908.18, 1910.09
Hauff, Hugo 1939.23
Haug, Betsy 1968.31, 1979.11
Haughton, J. 1888.23
Haulit, Messr. 1869.29
Hauman, Elizabeth 1903.04
Hauman, Lillian 1922.30
Hauman, Lonie 1903.04
Hauman, Lorette 1922.30
Haun, Mary 1922.26
Hauptman, William 1985.06
Hauptmann, Elisabeth 1933.07, 1977.08
Haurie, Vin 1882.49
Hausam, Wiley 1996.07, 2000.08
Hausdorf, Hattie 1937.14
Hausen, Roy 1972.06
Hauser, Alexis 1975.16
Hauser, Carl 1885.51, 1886.07, 1886.53
Hauser, Frank 1971.16
Hauser, Franklin 1934.41
Hausman, Elaine 1975.18, 1980.26
Hausman, John 1975.18
Hausmann, Ron 1959.25
Haussain, Mohammed 1923.16
Hauten, A.V. 1878.19
Hautonville, Mrs. 1852.02
Havala, Lily 2000.19
Havel, Arthur 1928.34, 1929.22
Havel, Clara 1893.23, 1900.03, 1903.04
Havel, Morton 1928.34, 1929.22
Havel, Tommy 1928.34
Haven, Sidney 1884.60, 1885.08
Havenport, Eva 1900.57
Havens, E. 1880.34
Havens, Ernest 1901.02
Havens, Hattie 1898.15
Havens, John 1903.07
Havens, John C. 1997.07
Havens, William 1902.43
Havercroft, Lorraine 1951.24, 1953.08
Haverly's Mastodon Minstrels 1883.66
Haverly's Opera Company 1881.57, 1882.14
Haverly, Burt 1890.10, 1890.34, 1891.43, 1895.11
Haverly, J.H. 1879.64, 1881.28, 1881.31, 1881.57, 1883.66
Haverstick, Madame 1921.28
Haverstick, Mme. 1923.02, 1924.25
Haverstock, Madame 1920.19
Haverty, D. 1912.01
Havez, Jean 1911.24, 1911.34, 1914.15
Havez, Jean C. 1897.45, 1898.72, 1899.12, 1899.22, 1900.58, 1910.18, 1912.29, 1955.19
Havez, Lou 1914.16
Haviland, Augusta 1917.06
Haviland, Courtney 1886.01
Haviland, E. 1864.22
Haviland, James 1878.05
Haviland, Kenneth 1925.40
Haviland, Marguerite 1899.29
Haviland, Mr. 1856.02, 1861.06, 1862.01, 1862.02
Havner, Fred J. 1887.30
Havoc, June 1936.27, 1940.22, 1944.02, 1944.27, 1945.20
Havrilla, Al 1925.08
Havrilla, Alois 1925.39
Havron, Mr. 1870.24, 1871.15
Hawes, Janey 1927.40
Hawes, Mary Margaret 1927.40
Hawk, White 1925.37
Hawkes, Al 1903.36
Hawkes, Albert 1926.17
Hawkin, Tim 1999.11
Hawkins, Bill 1922.02
Hawkins, C.B. 1882.44, 1882.69, 1889.34
Hawkins, Charles 1938.03
Hawkins, Charles B. 1898.61
Hawkins, Doug 1941.13
Hawkins, Douglas 1939.30
Hawkins, Edward 1950.07
Hawkins, Edwin 1989.12
Hawkins, Florence 1905.07
Hawkins, George W. 1879.28
Hawkins, Harris 1953.09
Hawkins, Hoyt 1978.01
Hawkins, Ira 1978.03, 1986.11, 1987.12
Hawkins, Iria 1913.33
Hawkins, Jay 1999.09
Hawkins, Jesse 1946.21
Hawkins, John 1969.04, 1980.01
Hawkins, Jr., John F. 1927.56, 1928.30
Hawkins, Judine 1987.14
Hawkins, June 1943.24, 1945.06, 1946.08
Hawkins, Lew 1897.09, 1900.49
Hawkins, Micah 1834.03
Hawkins, Norman 1973.17
Hawkins, Norman P. 1975.12
Hawkins, Patricia 1971.04
Hawkins, Roy 1999.09
Hawkins, Sid 1928.07
Hawkins, Sidney 1929.24
Hawkins, Stanley 1902.15, 1903.36, 1904.55, 1905.33
Hawkins, T.J. 1882.44, 1882.56, 1884.53, 1887.40
Hawkins, Tim 1994.12, 1995.19, 1996.15, 1997.11, 1997.19, 1997.22, 1998.06, 1998.13, 1998.20, 1999.13, 1999.21
Hawkins, Walter Carpenter 1883.66
Hawley, Andros 1904.34
Hawley, Charles R. 1895.01, 1896.42, 1897.13
Hawley, George 1894.06
Hawley, Georgie 1885.66, 1896.51
Hawley, Hughson 1881.04, 1881.28, 1881.31, 1881.40, 1882.05, 1882.17, 1885.48, 1886.40, 1887.02, 1887.10, 1887.29, 1887.44, 1892.25
Hawley, Ida 1898.46, 1899.41, 1900.42, 1903.37, 1904.51, 1904.57, 1905.08, 1905.11, 1905.25, 1907.30
Hawley, J. 1902.01
Hawley, Jennie 1898.60, 1899.34, 1900.47, 1902.01
Hawley, Kay 1927.65
Hawley, Martha 1998.03, 2000.11
Hawley, Monte 1929.25, 1932.08
Hawley, Monty 1942.13
Hawley, Peter 1926.26
Hawley, Walter 1897.04
Hawley, William 1905.17, 1930.14
Hawley, William R. 1907.54
Hawly, Alma 1915.32
Hawman, Lizette 1904.15
Hawman, Louise 1904.15
Haworth, Jill 1966.24
Haworth, Joe 2001.04
Haworth, Vinton 1932.14
Hawthorne, Albert 1924.31
Hawthorne, Albert F. 1931.05
Hawthorne, C.J. 1869.04, 1869.13
Hawthorne, Charles 1857.03, 1894.20
Hawthorne, Charles J. 1857.01, 1857.03
Hawthorne, Gordon 1927.40
Hawthorne, Hilda 1897.38
Hawthorne, Irene 1944.32
Hawthorne, Jim 1949.04, 1957.04
Hawthorne, Lillian 1889.36, 1890.48, 1892.40, 1893.19, 1894.08, 1895.03
Hawthorne, Lola 1892.40, 1894.08, 1895.03
Hawthorne, Mabel 1902.32
Hawthorne, Mr. 1857.02
Hawthorne, Nellie 1892.19, 1898.41, 1899.11
Hawthorne, Una 1929.20
Hawtrey, G.P. 1896.31
Hay, Bessie 1924.29
Hay, Eddie 1919.40
Hay, Edgar L. 1912.39
Hay, Edgar Lee 1914.23
Hay, Ian 1918.10
Hay, Joan 1923.17
Hay, Mary 1920.44, 1922.04, 1923.45, 1925.33, 1928.43
Hay, Tracy 1924.29
Hayakawa, Sessue 1927.28
Hayama, Kiyomi 1989.21
Hayden 1907.61, 1909.17
Hayden and Company 1911.30
Hayden and Rowley and Bush and Heiland 1904.20
Hayden, Betty 1930.41
Hayden, Blanche 1872.23, 1891.32, 1892.50, 1893.50
Hayden, Carl 1911.02
Hayden, Cissie 1920.26
Hayden, Eugenie 1906.03
Hayden, F. 1905.07
Hayden, Frank 1888.11, 1899.22, 1905.10, 1906.10, 1907.34
Hayden, George E. 1882.04, 1882.23, 1884.21, 1892.30
Hayden, Gladys 1896.38
Hayden, Joe 1896.52, 1897.40, 1980.27
Hayden, John 1927.09, 1937.16
Hayden, Joseph 1975.20
Hayden, Martin 1892.27, 1905.04, 1910.27
Hayden, Melissa 1948.25
Hayden, Messr. 1887.25
Hayden, Michael 1994.02
Hayden, Mr. 1836.01
Hayden, Mrs. W.R. 1870.23
Hayden, Robert 1947.14
Hayden, Sophie (Schwab) 1992.01
Hayden, Thomas F. 1900.41
Hayden, W.B. 1870.23
Hayden, W.R. 1870.20, 1872.19
Haydn 1884.42, 1886.47, 1888.36, 1894.19, 1899.23
Haydn, Carl 1905.36, 1911.37
Haydn, Richard 1939.07, 1940.03
Haydock, John 1912.30
Haydon, Martin 1906.25, 1907.56, 1908.40, 1915.23
Haydon, W. 1881.22
Hayes, Alfred 1938.08, 1940.18, 1942.05
Hayes, Bill 1953.08, 1967.17
Hayes, Billie 1956.08
Hayes, Catherine 1913.01, 1928.12
Hayes, Catherine J. 1904.34

Hayes, Christopher 1918.36, 1919.20
Hayes, Clancy 1999.06
Hayes, Collington 1930.10
Hayes, Donald 1930.16
Hayes, Edward 1901.26, 1903.20, 1932.22, 1943.05
Hayes, Every 1972.14, 1972.26
Hayes, Florence 1900.59, 1902.06
Hayes, Frances 1934.29
Hayes, Frank 1903.31, 1906.49
Hayes, Gardner 1972.12
Hayes, George 1896.48, 1898.05, 1931.38
Hayes, Georgie 1930.37
Hayes, Grace 1922.45, 1926.15, 1927.19, 1930.42, 1932.01
Hayes, Harry 1900.24
Hayes, Helen 1909.30, 1910.16, 1911.35
Hayes, Henry 1881.03
Hayes, Irene 1917.26, 1918.04
Hayes, J.E. 1866.18
Hayes, Jack 1897.28, 1995.05, 1997.07, 2000.07
Hayes, James E. 1863.06, 1863.09, 1863.10, 1864.05, 1864.12, 1864.15, 1864.21, 1868.06, 1869.26, 1870.07, 1870.15, 1870.20, 1870.23, 1870.26, 1870.33, 1871.04, 1871.18, 1872.19, 1872.31, 1872.33, 1872.34, 1873.02
Hayes, Janet 1955.01, 1955.08, 1964.15
Hayes, Jerome 1904.29, 1907.56
Hayes, Joseph 1866.03, 1871.04
Hayes, Jr., Isaac 1997.21
Hayes, Katherine 1925.32
Hayes, Leo 1905.32
Hayes, Lorey 1981.15
Hayes, Messr. 1857.02, 1857.03
Hayes, Michael 1996.02
Hayes, Milton 1975.22
Hayes, Mimi 1925.32, 1928.42
Hayes, Mr. 1854.06, 1855.07, 1855.08, 1855.09, 1857.01, 1857.08, 1858.03, 1862.05
Hayes, Myrtle 1927.38
Hayes, Peter Lind 1943.23, 1948.23
Hayes, Prudence 1938.04
Hayes, Richard 1959.12, 1963.16
Hayes, Roland 1993.03
Hayes, Tommy 1928.42
Hayes, W. 1859.11, 1860.03, 1860.04, 1860.05
Hayes, William 1949.06
Hayes, William P. 1904.06
Hayes, William T. 1931.02
Hayeson, Jimmy 1971.13
Hayman, Al 1887.49, 1888.37, 1895.29, 1895.32, 1895.43, 1897.32
Hayman, Clifford 1952.20
Hayman, Coreania 1946.09
Hayman, Joe 1924.32
Hayman, Lillian 1957.05, 1961.24, 1964.19, 1967.06, 1971.07, 1975.09
Hayme, Messr. 1879.47
Hayme, Mons. 1877.27, 1877.30, 1877.32, 1877.33, 1877.34, 1877.37, 1877.38, 1878.06, 1878.07, 1878.08, 1879.19, 1879.26, 1879.27, 1879.34, 1879.36, 1879.39, 1879.44, 1879.45
Haymer, Johnny 1956.08
Haymes, Mons. 1879.40
Hayne, Charles 1911.09
Hayne, Horace 1899.25, 1900.33
Hayne, Messr. 1877.31
Haynes, Daniel L. 1927.33, 1930.10, 1935.01
Haynes, Edward 1976.25
Haynes, George 1896.18
Haynes, Herman 1898.07
Haynes, Jessie 1897.25
Haynes, John 1929.37
Haynes, John Emerson 1927.50
Haynes, Lawrence 1954.04
Haynes, M.P. 1894.05
Haynes, Olivetta 1903.24
Haynes, Robin 1993.07
Haynes, Tiger 1956.08, 1960.09, 1964.21, 1965.18, 1967.04, 1973.15, 1975.01, 1978.28, 1979.32
Hays, Alfred 1888.20, 1889.04
Hays, Audrey 1960.08
Hays, David 1960.02, 1962.01, 1962.03, 1965.29, 1970.19, 1978.25
Hays, Davie 1981.07
Hays, Laurence 1944.17
Hays, Lee 1966.03
Hays, Rex David 1978.10, 1978.22, 1980.30, 1981.10, 1988.04, 1989.26
Hays, Warren 1962.04
Hayseed Productions, Inc. 1922.46
Haythe, Sean 1997.22
Hayton, Lennie 1981.16
Hayward, Bridget 1990.04
Hayward, Fanny 1873.26
Hayward, Ina 1920.47, 1923.22, 1927.47, 1928.31, 1932.14
Hayward, Leland 1949.04, 1950.15, 1952.10, 1959.13, 1959.24, 1962.20
Hayward, Leonard 1972.06
Hayward, Thomas 1944.26, 1959.16
Haywood, Billie 1934.06, 1934.40, 1936.12
Haywood, Emma 1858.03
Haywood, Fannie 1890.08
Haywood, Frances 1964.19, 1966.14
Haywood, J. 1873.18
Haywood, Nancy 1963.16, 1965.28
Hazard, Dick 1986.20
Hazard, Richard 1979.04
Haze, Ralf Paul 1982.17
Hazel, Dorothy 1940.16
Hazell, Rupert 1922.05
Hazeltine, L. 1905.13
Hazeltine, William 1896.27
Hazelton, George C. 1919.38
Hazelton, Ida 1888.45
Hazelton, Ruth 1920.22, 1921.25
Hazelwood, Michael 2000.16
Hazleton, F. 1885.14
Hazlett, Darren M. 2001.04
Hazlett, Madeline 1904.35
Hazlitt, Frederick 1948.24
Hazzard, Jack 1918.28, 1931.21
Hazzard, John 1912.42
Hazzard, John E. 1904.10, 1904.23, 1905.06, 1906.43, 1907.39, 1908.25, 1910.20, 1911.23, 1911.36, 1914.25, 1915.30, 1916.19, 1916.22, 1919.12, 1920.04, 1921.23, 1922.10, 1922.32, 1923.44, 1924.24, 1926.08, 1928.49, 1933.23, 1975.24
Heacock, Kent A. 1990.07, 1990.08, 1991.08
Head, Cloyd 1925.37
Head, Helaine 1976.28, 1981.04, 1983.04
Head, Josephine 1922.21
Headley, G.L. 1945.17
Headley, George L. 1945.17
Headley, Heather 1997.20, 2000.06
Heagney, William 1932.10
Heald, Anthony 1987.15
Heald, Louise 1911.04
Heale, Timothy 1977.01
Healey, Dan 1915.26
Healey, Eunice 1940.03
Healey, H.S. 1888.30
Healey, Harry 1884.26
Healey, Harry S. 1888.30
Healey, S. 1890.50
Healy, Betty 1925.25, 1927.19
Healy, Bruce 1927.66
Healy, Cathleen 1924.29
Healy, Dan 1923.16, 1924.10, 1926.51, 1927.37, 1928.25, 1929.50, 1942.20
Healy, Daniel 1920.29
Healy, Danny 1918.21
Healy, Eileen 1929.04, 1929.26
Healy, Eunice 1930.31, 1931.40, 1934.42, 1940.10, 1942.29
Healy, F.H. 1918.36
Healy, Florence 1927.31
Healy, J.R. 1869.33, 1870.05, 1872.10
Healy, Joseph 1891.25
Healy, Joseph F. 1897.12
Healy, Martin 1900.24
Healy, Mary 1942.27, 1946.13
Healy, Ted 1925.25, 1927.19, 1929.22, 1931.05, 1931.13
Healy, William 1916.11
Heaney, Ned Jouyce 1924.44
Heap, Yvette 1945.04
Heard, Erika L. 1993.04
Heard, James 1918.31
Hearn, David 1904.18
Hearn, Fred 1949.08
Hearn, George 1966.09, 1979.12, 1982.18, 1989.10, 1989.23, 1994.10, 1999.20
Hearn, Harry 1905.37
Hearn, Lew 1914.28, 1915.22, 1920.23, 1922.15, 1923.38, 1924.13, 1929.04, 1939.24
Hearn, Mlle. 1876.36
Hearn, Roma 1971.21
Hearn, Sam 1922.23, 1925.16, 1925.47, 1928.25
Hearne, Affie 1881.13
Hearne, Nan C. 1922.05, 1928.42
Hearne, Sam 1915.11
Hearne, Walter P. 1912.37
Hearshen, Ira 1986.18
Heartz, H.L. 1899.41, 1901.06, 1902.07, 1902.15, 1904.09, 1907.39, 1908.17, 1909.12
Heasley, Tim 2001.04
Heaslip, Liam 1976.29
Heaslip, Pierce 1976.29
Heaslip, Sean 1976.29
Heaston, Nicole 1996.10
Heater, Claude 1951.23
Heath, A. Claire 1906.02, 1906.42
Heath, A.C. 1908.38
Heath, Babs 1943.09, 1944.24, 1945.12
Heath, Belle 1903.18
Heath, Bob 1973.07
Heath, Bruce 1975.09, 1981.06, 1992.06
Heath, D. Michael 1987.05
Heath, Dody 1951.14
Heath, E.P. 1914.03, 1930.04
Heath, Eileen 1972.08
Heath, Frankie 1919.30, 1922.32
Heath, George 1890.40, 1897.44, 1901.19
Heath, Grayce 1930.36
Heath, Hy 1992.03
Heath, J.K. 1916.23
Heath, John 1946.02
Heath, Sigrid 1979.12
Heath, T.K. 1905.28, 1906.24
Heath, Thomas 1909.18, 1922.18
Heath, Thomas K. 1919.26
Heatham, Josephine 1937.08
Heathcote, Kate 1871.14, 1871.19, 1872.16
Heathen, Boyd 1945.04
Heather, Alfred 1928.13, 1929.30
Heatherton, Joey 1959.24
Heatherton, Ray 1930.18, 1937.04
Heaton, Harold 1926.41
Heavens, Peggy 1928.09
Heawood, John 1954.09, 1955.19, 1957.02
Hebb, Bobby 1974.01
Heberden, Mary 1933.07
Hebert, Eve 1951.23
Hebert, Rich 1982.22
Hecht, Albert 1925.21
Hecht, Ben 1935.15, 1944.29, 1946.17, 1953.01, 1978.02
Hecht, Don 1999.09
Hecht, Frl. 1883.08, 1883.35
Hecht, Harold 1928.19, 1939.19
Hecht, Herb 1950.09
Hecht, Joshua 1956.09, 1958.13, 1959.09, 1959.10, 1960.02, 1960.03
Hecht, Manfred 1943.05
Hecht, Marie Armstrong 1930.15
Hecht, Paul 1969.06, 1970.15
Hecht, Rosa Prindle 1922.21
Hecht, Summit L. 1897.40
Hecht, Zoltan 1922.21
Hechter, Frl. 1898.38
Heck, F. Stanton 1898.54, 1906.45, 1908.04, 1908.39, 1909.28, 1910.34, 1913.31
Heck, F.S. 1898.07, 1898.30, 1899.28
Heck, J.H. 1902.39
Heck, Ludwig 1900.53
Heckart, Eileen 1961.15, 1962.01
Heckel, Jean-Louis 1981.11
Hecken, Frl. 1879.22
Heckert, M. 1888.32
Heckert, M.L. 1893.08, 1906.06, 1906.10, 1906.40
Heckert, Michael 1905.10
Heckinger, Clif 1926.20, 1930.07
Heckinger, Cliff 1924.21, 1928.49, 1932.22
Heckinger, Clifford 1910.32
Heckler, Grace 1900.38, 1901.17, 1904.44
Heckler, Lillian 1900.38, 1901.17
Heckler, Miss 1904.44
Hector, Frank 1923.35
Hector, Louis 1928.12
Hector, Terry 1999.12
Hedge, Albert 1914.09
Hedge, Ray 1932.14
Hedges, Florence 1922.01
Hedin, Edna 1931.36
Hedley, Charles 1930.15, 1932.14
Hedlund, F. 1887.26
Hedlund, Fred. 1888.22, 1888.24
Hedlung, F. 1887.18
Hedrick, Ronny 1967.09
Hedvig, Hulda 1932.26
Hedwig, Ula 1984.15
Heed, Helen 1929.30
Heege, Gus 1891.46, 1894.12, 1895.14
Heelan, Will 1903.39, 1904.22, 1907.15, 1907.41, 1908.10, 1909.24
Heeley, Desmond 1973.07, 1976.18, 1980.19, 1981.26, 1986.04, 1987.03, 1991.12, 1996.13
Heenan, James 1923.45
Hefer, Hayim 1971.14
Hefferan, Miss 1883.06
Hefferman, Ed 1891.14
Hefferman, Mike 1910.23
Heffernan, John 1970.05, 1982.24
Heflin, Marta 1971.01
Heft, Robert 1921.09
Hegeman, Alice 1909.25, 1910.18, 1911.11, 1912.28, 1914.20, 1920.08
Hegeman, E. 1886.04
Hegeman, J. 1905.56
Hegeman, Maurice 1908.39, 1909.13, 1909.25, 1910.18, 1911.11, 1912.28
Heggins, Amy 1994.06, 1995.15, 1997.05, 1998.16, 2001.02
Hegierski, Kathleen 1978.23, 1979.27, 1980.25
Hegira, Anne 1969.16
Hegobura, Loulou 1926.01
Hegt, Beatrice 1931.46
Heider, Fred 1917.13
Heidt, Winifred 1954.07
Heifner, Jack 1985.03
Heigh, Helen 1942.11
Heigle, Mr. 1854.04
Heikin, Nancy 1981.01
Heilbrunn, David 1913.08
Heilge, George 1851.04, 1853.05, 1855.06, 1861.06, 1862.01, 1864.17, 1864.22, 1865.10, 1866.34, 1867.32, 1880.01
Heilig, Anton 1898.38
Heilig, O. 1885.41, 1885.63
Heilig, Otto 1887.43, 1900.41
Heilweil, David 1950.13, 1951.10
Heim, Eddie 1956.14
Heimann, Mr. 1896.34
Heimberger, Paul 1937.09
Hein, Silvio 1903.07, 1905.45, 1906.27, 1906.43, 1907.24, 1908.36, 1910.08, 1910.12, 1910.30, 1911.03, 1911.21, 1911.34, 1911.45, 1912.05, 1912.14, 1913.19, 1914.13, 1914.20, 1914.24, 1915.27, 1916.20, 1916.22, 1917.09, 1917.21, 1917.34, 1918.01, 1918.22, 1920.07, 1920.13, 1920.36, 1922.16
Heindl, Anton 1902.44, 1905.41, 1906.18, 1907.44, 1908.01, 1908.34, 1910.27, 1910.30, 1911.22, 1911.42, 1912.12, 1912.33, 1913.31, 1914.26, 1918.09, 1919.28, 1920.13, 1921.30, 1922.16, 1922.41, 1925.32, 1927.65
Heinds, Miss 1872.35
Heine, Heinrich 1901.25
Heineman, Eda 1950.04
Heineman, George 1885.46
Heineman, Victor 1984.16
Heinemann, Eda 1951.13
Heinemann, George 1886.49, 1892.59
Heinemann, Helen 1914.11
Heinemann, Waldo 1911.18
Heinfling, Martin 1983.11, 1986.13
Heinly, Althea 1929.27, 1930.05
Heinman, Henry 1894.38
Heinneman, Messr. 1876.35
Heinrich, W. 1875.12
Heinroth, Theodore 1914.30
Heins, Helen 1906.01
Heinsohn, Elisa 1988.01
Heinzman, Otto M. 1894.27
Heisey, George 1888.37
Heisey, Jane 1946.16
Heisey, Mark E. 1906.17
Heisey, Mart E. 1891.42, 1897.21
Heisler, Jack 1914.30, 1920.27, 1920.42, 1925.47, 1927.64, 1928.09
Heister 1882.06
Heister, George 1851.01, 1851.06, 1851.07, 1852.01, 1852.05, 1854.01, 1854.07, 1855.01, 1855.02, 1855.10, 1871.27, 1872.06, 1872.11, 1872.23, 1872.35, 1873.03, 1873.26, 1877.07, 1878.14, 1879.63, 1880.07, 1880.17, 1880.21, 1881.31, 1883.52
Heit, Sally-Jane 1978.27
Heitzman, Michael 1999.24

Helburn, Theresa 1941.05, 1943.04, 1944.32, 1945.05, 1947.17, 1949.03, 1950.04, 1951.16
Held, Anna 1896.31, 1897.41, 1899.38, 1903.40, 1904.39, 1906.45, 1908.04, 1908.39, 1909.25, 1910.18, 1913.35, 1916.25, 1980.27
Held, Jr., John 1925.10, 1925.24, 1926.21, 1928.40, 1928.45
Held, Lillian 1946.16
Held, Ludwig 1885.45, 1887.28, 1891.30
Held, Muki 1978.26
Held, Peter 1957.06
Held, Robert C. 1956.16
Held, Wilbur 1904.45
Helder, Fred 1921.42
Helder, Ruby 1915.02
Heldman, Dianna 1995.10
Helen 1921.07
Helen Price, Inc. 1918.15
Helene, Mlle. 1862.03, 1866.18, 1870.44, 1871.27
Helene, Patrice 1951.20
Helevy, Ludovic 1864.11
Helf, J. Fred 1903.39, 1904.22, 1905.55, 1906.32, 1980.27
Helgren, Mari 1932.11
Helie, Louis 1908.10
Helier, LeMaistre 1890.02
Hellberg, Heinz 1984.04
Helle, Estelle 1927.23
Heller, Adam 1995.15
Heller, Andre 1991.11
Heller, Barbara 1960.12
Heller, Buck 1964.32
Heller, Don 1959.12
Heller, George 1925.20, 1926.17, 1927.23, 1928.19, 1929.20, 1933.07
Heller, Helen 1922.31
Heller, Jackie 1939.24
Heller, Jayne 1955.27
Heller, Marc 1990.02
Heller, Randee 1972.19
Hellerman, Fred 1968.13
Hellerman, Michael 1970.11
Hellinger, Mark 1931.19, 1932.07
Hellman, Frances 1937.01
Hellman, Jerome 1989.24
Hellman, Lillian 1941.01, 1949.16, 1953.05, 1953.14, 1956.15, 1958.13, 1959.10, 1974.06, 1982.20, 1983.13, 1984.11, 1986.08, 1989.14, 1992.14
Hellman, Mr. 1893.29
Hellmesberger, Jr., Joseph 1891.12
Helm, Mornay D. 1920.28
Helm, Morney D. 1921.27
Helm, Richard 1983.09
Helmers, June 1969.12, 1971.06, 1973.02
Helmore, Tom 1945.19
Helms, Alan 1961.18
Helmund, Meyer 1927.28
Helmych, Charles 1884.15, 1884.56
Helou, Victor R. 1964.11, 1964.35, 1965.18
Helper, Stephen 1995.03
Helpmann, Robert 1976.18
Helpmann, Sir Robert 1972.11
Helston, Dollie 1898.44
Helston, Gussie 1898.44
Helston, Kitty 1898.44
Helton, Melanie 1979.26
Helton, Percy 1913.32, 1927.64, 1930.23, 1931.21, 1937.02
Helvecio, Ilson 1992.13
Helwad, Dale 1982.02
Hemdale, Ltd. 1973.13
Hemenway, Harry 1904.11
Hemery, Emile 1882.26
Hemmer, Carl 1921.32, 1925.31, 1927.01, 1927.35
Hemmer, Edward 1937.08
Hemmi, Aida 1903.17, 1903.27
Hemming, Alfred 1917.30
Hemming, Violet 1908.27
Hemmingway, Frank 1926.33
Hemphill, A. Marcus 1981.15
Hemple, S. 1862.05
Hemple, S.A. 1879.42
Hempstead, Messr. 1854.04
Hempstone, Olga 1911.32, 1912.24, 1912.38, 1913.29, 1914.22, 1915.11, 1915.26, 1919.16
Hemsley, Estelle 1954.16
Hemsley, Jr., Gilbert V. 1972.15, 1973.07, 1976.28, 1976.35, 1977.04, 1978.23, 1979.01, 1979.25, 1979.26, 1979.27, 1979.32, 1980.21, 1981.20, 1981.21, 1982.07, 1982.16, 1982.21, 1983.04, 1983.12, 1985.09, 1985.11, 1987.08, 1990.08, 1993.12
Hemsley, Sherman 1969.09, 1970.05, 1972.26
Hemsley, Winston DeWitt 1967.06, 1967.15, 1976.03
Hendee, Edith 1898.73, 1900.25, 1900.31
Hendee, Harold F. 1906.25
Hendel, Helena 1968.04
Henderson, A. 1881.28, 1882.72
Henderson, Adolph 1932.30, 1943.10
Henderson, Al 1882.15
Henderson, Albert 1882.51, 1946.02
Henderson, Alex 1871.14, 1871.19
Henderson, Alex. 1873.12, 1873.14
Henderson, Alexander 1875.19, 1875.23, 1875.26, 1877.22, 1877.23, 1877.25, 1883.21
Henderson, Arthur 1942.02
Henderson, Bart 1947.09
Henderson, Brooke 1999.02
Henderson, C.L. 1921.25
Henderson, Charles 1927.05, 1927.65, 1929.33, 1931.01, 1935.15, 1943.08, 1949.09, 1955.13
Henderson, Charlie 1942.11
Henderson, David 1892.29, 1895.08, 1899.21, 1900.44
Henderson, Don 1963.22, 1965.07, 1965.18, 1965.26, 1968.14, 1976.31, 1978.08, 1979.27, 1990.08
Henderson, Douglas 1946.24
Henderson, Fletcher 1939.29
Henderson, Florence 1952.10, 1953.09, 1954.15, 1963.29, 1967.10
Henderson, Frances 1944.30
Henderson, Graham J. 1886.49
Henderson, Harry 1897.50
Henderson, Horace 1939.29
Henderson, Horton 1944.02
Henderson, Isabel 1934.17
Henderson, J. 1867.18
Henderson, Jack 1902.40, 1906.26, 1906.44, 1908.23, 1910.16, 1911.07, 1912.28, 1912.40, 1914.14, 1914.26
Henderson, Jesse 1890.26, 1891.31, 1891.47
Henderson, Joe 1922.22
Henderson, John 1904.01
Henderson, Jr., Luther 1958.19
Henderson, Katherine 1927.30
Henderson, Lucius 1927.01
Henderson, Luther 1960.23, 1962.14, 1963.13, 1964.11, 1964.44, 1967.06, 1968.03, 1970.05, 1971.03, 1971.19, 1972.05, 1972.26, 1974.26, 1975.09, 1975.13, 1976.09, 1978.09, 1980.06, 1981.16, 1981.28, 1986.03, 1988.17, 1989.02, 1992.08, 1997.03
Henderson, Marcia 1950.08
Henderson, Mark 1986.15
Henderson, Master Arthur 1944.06
Henderson, Melanie 1970.20
Henderson, Michael 2000.07
Henderson, Miss 1881.38, 1884.17, 1884.59, 1920.44
Henderson, Mr. 1852.04
Henderson, Nellie 1871.01, 1871.02
Henderson, Peter 1886.24
Henderson, Ray 1925.01, 1925.22, 1925.23, 1925.28, 1926.16, 1927.41, 1927.46, 1928.22, 1928.36, 1928.37, 1929.03, 1929.35, 1930.11, 1931.30, 1932.07, 1933.05, 1934.35, 1935.18, 1940.10, 1943.05, 1952.11, 1956.02, 1961.16, 1962.17, 1967.13, 1968.20, 1974.01, 1974.11, 1974.26, 1975.22, 1984.06, 1986.06, 1989.16, 1990.09, 1999.01
Henderson, Robert 1974.06
Henderson, Rose 1932.12
Henderson, Skitch 1963.15
Henderson, Slim 1927.30
Henderson, Spencer 1974.01
Henderson, Suzanne 1989.26
Henderson, W. 1867.32
Henderson, W.J. 1884.34
Henderson, William 1878.10, 1879.58, 1879.67, 1879.71, 1894.25
Henderson, William J. 1887.12, 1888.24, 1888.39
Hendesron, Charles 1935.12
Hendler, Hirschel 1913.35
Hendra, Tony 1964.29
Hendricks, A.H. 1908.35
Hendricks, Ben 1912.47, 1917.35, 1918.09, 1918.35, 1926.02
Hendricks, Ben. 1887.40
Hendricks, Carol 1953.01
Hendricks, Floyd 1998.10
Hendricks, John 1902.22, 1904.25, 1910.02, 1911.41, 1913.13, 1914.34, 1916.02, 1917.16, 1919.41, 1920.13, 1920.21, 1922.16, 1922.24, 1934.17
Hendricks, John B. 1901.16
Hendricks, Jon 1976.34, 1992.03
Hendrickson, Benjamin 1973.16, 1979.29
Hendrickson, Stephen 1971.19
Hendrix, Jim 1982.22
Hendrix, Jimi 1997.21
Hendrix, Leslie 2000.11
Hendrix, Manda 1905.12
Hendrix, Pauline 1915.18
Hendy, Jacqueline 2001.02
Hendy, John 1904.08
Heneker, David 1965.14, 1986.03
Henely, Edward J. 1884.44
Henely, Helen Bertram 1896.08
Henery, George K. 1902.20, 1905.40
Henessey, Guy 1888.17
Hengler, Flo 1907.33, 1910.02
Hengler, Flora 1902.34, 1903.14, 1904.08, 1904.40
Hengler, Florence 1895.38, 1901.27
Hengler, May 1901.27, 1902.34, 1903.14, 1904.08, 1904.40, 1907.33, 1910.02
Hengler, Messr. 1872.40, 1872.43
Hengler, T.M. 1881.07, 1882.23
Hengler, Thomas 1881.04
Henie, Sonja 1940.16, 1942.19, 1944.20, 1946.14, 1947.12, 1948.19, 1949.05
Henig, Andi 1984.07, 1985.06
Henley, Edward J. 1884.44, 1895.15
Henley, Jack 1931.26
Henley, Ken 1976.08, 1980.19, 1981.26, 1983.10
Henley, Rosina 1911.01
Hennequin and Delacour 1914.32
Hennequin, Alfred 1885.56, 1885.57, 1885.59, 1899.38, 1912.08
Hennequin, Maurice 1895.35, 1899.25, 1900.33, 1909.01, 1912.49, 1913.34, 1918.28, 1926.36, 1926.46, 1928.07, 1928.32, 1929.11
Henner, Marilu 1974.05, 1976.19
Hennessey, Bill 1973.14, 1975.12
Hennessey, J.A. 1880.02
Hennessey, May 1910.17
Hennessy, Francis X. 1917.07
Hennessy, Frank 1909.14
Hennessy, Gus 1886.28, 1897.01
Hennessy, Jill 1990.15
Hennessy, Mae 1914.30
Hennessy, May 1911.11, 1915.15
Hennessy, W. 1871.27
Henning, Debby 1983.01, 1984.16
Henning, Doug 1974.13, 1983.01, 1984.16
Henning, Henriette 1939.26
Henning, Hilda 1898.46
Henning, Leo 1921.18, 1925.12, 1927.47, 1932.19
Hennings, Dora 1883.49
Hennings, J.W. 1872.35
Hennings, John 1900.53
Hennings, Mamie 1900.53
Hennings, Sr., John 1900.53
Henri Bendel 1913.15, 1914.04, 1917.19, 1918.02, 1918.22, 1920.42, 1923.47
Henri, F. 1921.19
Henri, M. 1929.10
Henri, Marc 1924.01, 1929.51
Henrichs, J.B. 1898.60
Henriette, Miss 1870.31
Henriette, Mlle. 1878.18
Henrion, Poly 1875.12, 1876.33, 1882.54
Henriot, Mons. 1880.28
Henrique, Messr. 1844.01
Henriques, Baby 1892.12
Henriques, Estelle 1896.31
Henriques, Winston George 1954.19
Henritze, Bette 1968.05, 1974.05
Henry C. Miner and Brooks 1896.29
Henry Dazian and Son 1885.46
Henry E. Dixey's Adonis Company 1888.36
Henry E. Dixey's Opera Company 1892.30, 1892.37, 1892.40, 1892.46
Henry W. 1866.03
Henry W. Savage, Inc. 1923.34, 1924.02
Henry, Ada 1908.29
Henry, Ann 1956.08
Henry, Brian 1990.18
Henry, C. 1865.03, 1879.54
Henry, Cynthia 1982.17
Henry, D. 1883.06
Henry, Eleanor 1915.18, 1917.37, 1919.14, 1919.37
Henry, Elenor 1915.01
Henry, Emma 1879.13, 1879.66, 1887.25
Henry, F. 1880.69
Henry, Emmaline 1960.12
Henry, George 1878.14, 1880.37, 1881.18, 1894.07, 1922.28
Henry, Grace 1926.23, 1927.02, 1927.36, 1928.23, 1929.08, 1929.19, 1931.14
Henry, H.C. 1886.10
Henry, Hank 1942.20, 1952.02
Henry, Helen 1935.16
Henry, Ida 1992.02
Henry, J. 1975.20
Henry, J.J. 1882.77
Henry, J.M. 1869.46
Henry, Jack 1910.17
Henry, Jack F. 1911.01
Henry, John 1793.01, 1794.01, 1872.16, 1905.34, 1927.17
Henry, Josephine 1862.03
Henry, Judith 1983.15
Henry, Louis 1894.27
Henry, M. 1865.05, 1865.07
Henry, Margaret 1914.13
Henry, Marion 1899.31
Henry, Master 1850.01, 1879.05, 1885.16, 1897.03
Henry, Miss 1854.07, 1855.05, 1866.05
Henry, Mr. 1848.01, 1851.04, 1861.04, 1869.43, 1879.07
Henry, Mrs. 1848.01, 1851.04, 1854.06, 1858.04
Henry, Ora 1907.55
Henry, P. 1880.41
Henry, Pat 1928.23
Henry, Patrick 1925.11
Henry, Petit 1859.05
Henry, R.M. 1881.02
Henry, Ralph 1932.12
Henry, Richard 1888.38, 1920.34
Henry, S. 1943.02
Henry, S.R. 1920.30
Henry, Stanley 1915.04
Henry, Thomas R. 1905.10
Henry, Victor 1923.14
Henry, Vincent 1943.08, 1965.22
Henry, W. 1864.12, 1864.21, 1868.06, 1873.28
Henry, William 1863.10, 1864.15, 1870.07, 1884.53, 1889.24
Henryal, Marc 1959.15
Hensel, Howard 1976.31, 1977.17, 1978.07, 1978.20, 1979.20, 1983.16, 1989.13, 1996.02
Hensel, Karen 1979.08
Hensell, Marie 1894.27
Henshall, Ruthie 1999.20
Henshaw, John E. 1880.05, 1881.17, 1881.19, 1883.02, 1894.21, 1899.02, 1899.19, 1904.50, 1909.30, 1922.16
Henshaw, John H. 1883.02
Henshaw, Venie 1900.49
Henshaw, Vernie 1889.37
Henshaw, Vinnie 1905.42
Hensley, Dale 1987.15
Henson, Gladys 1939.07
Henson, John 1956.04
Henson, Leslie 1914.32
Henson, Robert 1964.11
Heom, Mlle. 1888.23
Hepari, Dawn 1972.20
Hepburn, Betsy 1966.02
Hepburn, James 1928.42
Hepburn, Katherine 1969.17
Hepburn, Philip 1949.16, 1950.08, 1951.11
Hepburne, Mr. 1836.01
Hepner, Louise Willis 1900.12
Hepps, Mr. 1877.06, 1877.09, 1877.10, 1877.11, 1877.12, 1877.13, 1877.14, 1877.17
Her Own Grand English Burlesque Company 1888.33
Herald, Burgundian 1925.32
Herbaux, Yvette 1929.10, 1929.14, 1929.16
Herbeaux, Yvette 1929.13
Herbert, A.P. 1983.12, 1985.12, 1988.14
Herbert, Ada 1870.36
Herbert, C.F. 1880.51, 1891.24
Herbert, Don 1963.07

Herbert, Dora 1870.39
Herbert, Elsbeth 1925.37
Herbert, Emily 1876.03
Herbert, Eugene 1908.16
Herbert, Evelyn 1923.40, 1925.02, 1925.39, 1926.15, 1927.42, 1928.29, 1930.30, 1933.03, 1934.13
Herbert, Florence 1932.19
Herbert, Frances 1890.40
Herbert, Frank 1917.22, 1921.28
Herbert, Fred 1961.14, 1969.17
Herbert, Gene 1943.16
Herbert, George 1902.26, 1902.34
Herbert, George M. 1892.25
Herbert, George W. 1885.46
Herbert, H.M. 1898.64
Herbert, Henry 1926.38
Herbert, Hugh 1927.10
Herbert, J.W. 1885.43, 1886.25, 1886.55, 1886.57, 1891.38, 1895.08
Herbert, James 1898.29
Herbert, Jean 1930.24, 1934.42
Herbert, Jocelyn 1989.24
Herbert, John 1848.03, 1965.21, 1966.24
Herbert, Joseph 1893.40, 1894.23, 1894.40, 1895.12, 1896.12, 1896.26, 1896.29, 1896.36, 1897.09, 1897.19, 1898.18, 1898.26, 1898.35, 1900.33, 1902.34, 1902.40, 1904.54, 1906.07, 1906.17, 1910.03, 1910.14, 1910.31, 1911.14, 1911.36, 1912.10, 1915.27, 1916.20, 1920.31, 1921.30, 1922.24, 1927.49, 1930.09
Herbert, Joseph W. 1888.09, 1889.01, 1890.08, 1890.50, 1895.17, 1896.10, 1896.48, 1898.17, 1898.38, 1898.56, 1898.60, 1899.34, 1901.25, 1902.23, 1903.36, 1903.40, 1904.35, 1906.29, 1907.15, 1907.18, 1907.47, 1908.06, 1908.33, 1909.07, 1912.41, 1913.05, 1913.29, 1915.07
Herbert, Jr., Joseph 1906.29, 1907.42, 1910.20, 1917.29, 1921.23
Herbert, Jr., Joseph W. 1904.33, 1914.13
Herbert, Lila 1966.02, 1978.08, 1978.19, 1978.23, 1979.27, 1990.08
Herbert, Lillian 1911.17
Herbert, M.L. 1891.37
Herbert, Manuel D. 1955.25
Herbert, Marc 1882.06
Herbert, Marion 1870.05
Herbert, Mr. 1852.02
Herbert, N. 1894.18
Herbert, Paul K. 1922.32
Herbert, Ralph 1942.31, 1945.02, 1965.04
Herbert, Ralph J. 1916.26
Herbert, Rich 1997.08
Herbert, Robin 1975.24
Herbert, Sidney 1891.05
Herbert, Tait 1873.25
Herbert, Thomas 1914.24, 1925.40
Herbert, Tim 1944.14
Herbert, Victor 1894.45, 1895.33, 1896.30, 1896.43, 1897.13, 1897.18, 1897.42, 1898.60, 1899.28, 1899.34, 1899.40, 1900.25, 1900.32, 1903.31, 1903.37, 1904.54, 1905.01, 1905.22, 1905.29, 1905.44, 1905.57, 1906.33, 1906.48, 1907.11, 1907.14, 1907.36, 1908.24, 1908.35, 1908.40, 1909.23, 1909.30, 1910.35, 1911.02, 1911.31, 1911.36, 1911.38, 1912.39, 1913.15, 1913.24, 1913.32, 1914.27, 1914.30, 1915.23, 1916.24, 1917.07, 1917.13, 1917.26, 1917.28, 1919.01, 1919.15, 1919.44, 1920.05, 1920.18, 1920.21, 1920.44, 1921.21, 1922.19, 1922.33, 1923.20, 1923.30, 1923.38, 1924.15, 1924.18, 1924.23, 1925.10, 1929.34, 1929.36, 1929.38, 1929.40, 1929.48, 1930.06, 1930.12, 1930.41, 1931.11, 1931.43, 1934.14, 1934.17, 1945.16, 1946.18, 1947.04, 1952.11, 1978.19, 1979.20, 1980.27, 1988.18
Herbert, Victoria 1921.22
Herbert, William 1880.18, 1883.44, 1885.41, 1894.32
Herbert., Jr., Joseph W. 1905.50
Herberth, Hans 1939.23
Herblin, David 1927.07
Herbst, Jeffrey 1990.06
Herczeg, Geza 1931.09, 1945.12
Herdicks, G.W. 1908.12
Heredia, Wilson Jermaine 1996.09
Hereford, Kathryn 1928.37, 1930.05, 1930.39
Herendeen, Fred 1918.18, 1930.21, 1937.06
Herendeen, Frederick 1916.12, 1934.04
Herendeen, Helen 1921.14, 1923.41
Herendeen, Hope 1923.02
Herford, Beatrice 1918.08, 1920.08
Herford, Oliver 1909.19, 1921.27
Herg, Eric 1964.25
Herget, Bob 1948.30, 1951.10, 1956.16, 1962.01, 1964.35
Heritage, Clarence 1884.19, 1895.39
Herk, I.H. 1942.25
Herlein, Lillian 1909.23, 1911.35
Herlick, Edith 1944.25
Herlick, Jety 1963.14
Herlie, Eileen 1959.22, 1962.04
Hermalyn, Joy 1993.17, 1994.12, 1995.19, 1996.15, 1997.22, 1998.20
Herman Oppenheimer Company, Inc., The 1907.03
Herman, Al 1919.18, 1921.27
Herman, Chester 1929.09, 1929.48, 1935.17
Herman, Cynthia 1973.16
Herman, Dorothy 1917.35
Herman, George 1922.30, 1923.40, 1924.26, 1926.32, 1936.17
Herman, Gilbert 1943.23
Herman, Helene 1926.04
Herman, Henry 1899.03
Herman, Ian 1999.24
Herman, Jerry 1960.07, 1961.20, 1964.01, 1965.08, 1966.10, 1967.12, 1967.15, 1969.05, 1974.09, 1974.18, 1975.21, 1978.04, 1979.02, 1979.13, 1980.08, 1983.10, 1983.11, 1985.19, 1988.08, 1992.18, 1995.13, 1998.07
Herman, John 1963.13
Herman, John F. 1960.09
Herman, Lores 1906.28
Herman, M. 1892.19, 1903.25
Herman, Messr. 1851.01, 1854.01
Herman, Milton C. 1926.22
Herman, Miss 1917.31
Herman, Mme. 1907.27, 1907.51
Herman, Rober 1959.03
Herman, Selma 1895.41
Herman, Simon P. 1954.02
Herman, Steve 1981.26
Herman, William 1906.27, 1907.51
Hermann, Ann 1945.03
Hermann, Bernard 1932.20
Hermann, George 1916.15
Hermann, M. 1900.36
Hermann, Maurice 1899.27
Hermann, Mme. 1907.48
Hermann, Sam 1923.21
Hermany, Garda 1965.21
Hermany, Richard 1963.12
Hermany, Roma 1965.21
Hermsden, Harry 1929.40
Hermsen, Harry 1912.02, 1914.13, 1914.25, 1919.41, 1927.45, 1928.49
Hern, May 1922.05
Hernan, John 1889.18
Hernandez, A.M. 1870.23
Hernandez, Arthur 1881.39
Hernandez, Hen 1944.02
Hernandez, Irene 1887.29, 1892.23
Hernandez, Jr., Freddy 2001.04
Hernandez, Juan 1939.29
Hernandez, Juano 1931.31
Hernandez, Louis 1960.10
Hernandez, Oscar 1998.02
Hernandez, Philip 1993.09, 1998.02
Hernandez, Ricardo 1996.07
Hernandez, Riccardo 1998.21, 2001.03
Hernandez, Vivian 1961.07, 1961.12
Hernberg, Herr 1883.08
Herndon, Bill 1978.23, 1979.27
Herndon, John 1889.15
Herndon, Richard 1924.09, 1925.37, 1926.21, 1927.27
Herndon, Richard G. 1920.30, 1922.21, 1932.19
Herndon, T.J. 1889.12
Herndon, Thomas J. 1890.04
Herne, A. 1868.06
Herne, John 1877.15
Herne, Julie 1905.26
Herne, Master 1863.07
Herne, Miss 1863.07
Hernon, John 1888.14, 1888.27, 1888.40, 1889.07, 1889.11
Hero, Maria 1965.15, 1965.20, 1966.11, 1968.32
Herold, Don 1941.03
Herold, Knox 1927.27
Herold, Louis Joseph Ferdinand 1880.14
Heron, Eddie 1904.46, 1907.08
Heron, Edward 1908.41
Heron, Edward J. 1898.51, 1901.15
Heron, Matilda 1858.04
Herrand, March 1947.18
Herrera, John 1985.18, 1988.09, 1990.17, 1997.15, 2001.06
Herrera, Lorenzo 1950.16
Herrera, Roberto 1999.18
Herrett, Emery J. 1927.54
Herrick, Jack 1993.01, 1995.16, 1998.17
Herrick, Landon 1930.18, 1932.28
Herriman, George 1923.25
Herring, Fanny 1858.04, 1860.02, 1865.11, 1869.31, 1869.43
Herring, Miss 1851.08, 1870.02
Herring, Mrs. 1836.01
Herring, Robert 1939.30
Herrmann, A. 1889.35
Herrmann, Carl 1883.08, 1883.35
Herrmann, Harry 1950.09
Herrmann, Keith 1980.30, 1988.10
Herrmann, M. 1887.05, 1901.15
Herrmann, Werner 1937.05
Herron, Bertie 1903.18
Herron, Daniel 1998.06
Herron, Randy 1973.02
Herrup, Leo 1918.36
Herschel, Clement 1894.03, 1900.41
Herschell, Clem 1889.36
Herschell, Clement 1894.08
Herschfield, Harry 1924.36
Hersee, C. 1872.35
Hersee, Charles 1873.08
Hersee, Clive 1872.23
Hersee, Rose 1872.23
Hersey, David 1979.23, 1981.27, 1982.19, 1987.04, 1987.05, 1988.09, 1991.03
Hersey, Louise 1920.15
Hersey, Miss 1872.35
Hershey, June 1981.04
Hershfield, Harry 1923.25, 1931.26
Hershfield, Max 1912.17
Hershkowitz, J. 1921.19
Hershon, Milton 1985.01
Herson, Marian 1928.08
Herston, Jester 1955.03
Hertel, H. 1929.17
Hertelle, Buddy 1938.07
Hertz, Otto 1945.02
Hertz, Ralph 1930.14, 1950.01
Hertz, Ross 1960.08
Hertzfeld, Hetty 1900.37
Hervaux, Yvette 1929.15
Herve 1859.10, 1869.03, 1870.26, 1870.27, 1870.30, 1872.41, 1875.08, 1875.15, 1875.33, 1877.19, 1877.37, 1879.60, 1884.46, 1885.55, 1885.56, 1885.57, 1885.68, 1886.09, 1886.19, 1887.05, 1899.38
Herve, Emily 1901.08
Herve, Florimond 1897.28
Herve, Paul 1910.26, 1913.21, 1914.07, 1915.19, 1915.21
Hervey, Adele 1927.40
Hervey, Lord 1963.03
Hervey, Owen 1916.26
Herwig, A.E. 1891.24
Hery, C.W. 1890.40
Herz, Carl 1896.07
Herz, Henrik 1893.44
Herz, Herr 1879.62
Herz, R.C. 1907.37
Herz, Ralph 1910.22, 1911.15, 1912.36, 1914.01, 1914.14, 1915.16, 1915.32, 1917.18, 1919.03, 1920.01
Herz, Ralph C. 1905.29, 1907.10, 1908.07
Herzer, Ludwig 1937.03, 1946.16
Herzer, Martin 1971.14
Herzig, Sig 1930.35, 1931.21, 1932.16, 1932.20, 1944.23, 1947.01
Herzig, Sigmund 1931.31
Herzl, Robert 1984.04, 1984.05
Herzog, Jonathan C. 1996.04
Herzog, Jr., Arthur 1976.04
Hess, Alexia 1989.03
Hess, C.D. 1877.35, 1877.36, 1881.14, 1887.40
Hess, Cliff 1916.09, 1917.37
Hess, Elizabeth 1905.24
Hess, Florence 1897.21
Hess, Frances 1928.16
Hess, Hannah 1909.30
Hess, Joan 2001.03
Hess, Nancy 1989.03, 1993.02
Hess, Nellie 1890.22
Hess, Rhea 1909.30
Hess, Rodger 1981.03, 1985.03, 1989.12, 1992.08, 1997.04, 1997.15
Hess, Seymour 1894.21
Hess, Seymour G. 1891.09
Hesse, Alfred 1919.02
Hesse, Lulu 1886.39, 1888.39, 1893.21
Hessong, Charles 1904.22, 1906.45, 1908.04, 1910.18, 1911.24
Hessong, W. 1909.13
Hester, Florence 1934.05
Hester, George 2001.04
Hester, Tom 1960.01
Hethart, W. 1897.26
Hetherington, Hugh 1989.01
Hethert, Mr. 1892.11
Hettinger, Donald 1976.33
Hettler, Edna 1918.03, 1919.06
Heuberger, Richard 1912.08
Heuchling, Peter 1982.10
Heuer, George 1885.50
Heuett, E.J. 1927.47
Heughan, William 1931.44
Heuhn, Clara 1905.25
Heuhn, Stella 1905.25
Heuman, Barbara 1976.15
Heumann, Mr. 1896.23
Heusel, Emil 1878.17, 1879.04, 1881.29, 1883.46, 1883.53, 1883.63, 1884.13, 1885.15, 1885.22, 1888.05, 1902.24, 1903.33
Heusel, Emile 1888.30
Heusel, Master 1878.13
Heustis, Carolyn Minerva 1899.02
Hevonpaa, Sulo 1931.48, 1933.13
Hewer, John 1954.09
Hewett, Christopher 1955.11, 1956.01, 1959.06, 1960.07, 1961.26, 1966.11, 1967.07, 1968.16, 1976.33
Hewett, H.S. 1886.33
Hewett, Peggy 1969.14, 1980.08
Hewitt, Alan 1950.15
Hewitt, David 1988.05
Hewitt, Edmund 1947.21
Hewitt, Frankie 1976.35, 1990.05
Hewitt, Georgia 1920.15
Hewitt, Georgianna 1922.08
Hewitt, H.S. 1884.42
Hewitt, James 1794.01, 1796.01, 1834.03
Hewitt, Robert 1965.32
Hewitt, Tom 2000.17
Hewlett, Roger 1941.06
Hewlitt, Queenie 1905.29
Hewsel, Emil 1898.55
Hexter Productions, Inc. 1963.27
Heyden, Melissa 1948.25
Heyden, Pauline 1870.20, 1872.19
Heydt, Louis Jean 1931.34
Heyer, Bill 1953.01
Heyer, Grace 1905.04
Heyer, Rosemarie 1969.17
Heyland, Michael 1976.12, 1976.13, 1976.14, 1978.14
Heyman, Edward 1930.25, 1930.32, 1931.26, 1931.42, 1932.03, 1932.14, 1932.18, 1933.20, 1934.01, 1934.15, 1936.12, 1936.17, 1948.13, 1950.14, 1954.11, 1957.10, 1967.13, 1968.20, 1985.08, 1986.02, 1989.02
Heymann, Henry 1963.22, 1964.31, 1965.25
Heyward, Dorothy 1930.14, 1935.13, 1942.03, 1943.15, 1944.03, 1953.04, 1961.13, 1962.07, 1964.19, 1965.03, 1976.28, 1983.04, 2000.03
Heyward, duBose 1935.13, 1942.03, 1943.15, 1944.03, 1945.07
Heyward, DuBose 1953.04, 1961.13, 1962.07, 1964.19, 1965.03, 1974.09, 1976.28, 1983.04, 2000.03, 2001.07
Heywood, C. 1868.14
Heywood, Chester D. 1926.13
Heywood, Donald 1927.30, 1927.32, 1929.52, 1930.16, 1930.24, 1932.08, 1934.37, 1936.30
Heywood, Fanny 1873.25
Heywood, Messr. 1888.36
Heywood, Miss 1858.03, 1859.03, 1859.04
Heywood, Nellie 1883.47
Hezera, Mae 1897.21
Hiatt, Teri 1982.15
Hibbard, David 1996.18, 2001.01

Hibbard, Edna 1918.16, 1919.06, 1922.09, 1922.38
Hibbard, S. 1873.26
Hibbart, Thomas 1892.27
Hibbert, Edward 1982.24, 2000.10
Hibbert, Geoffrey 1954.09
Hibbler, Al 1981.06
Hibiki, Mito 1989.21
Hickey J.C. 1897.05
Hickey, Ed 1926.51
Hickey, Eddie 1921.25, 1923.22
Hickey, J.C. 1899.01
Hickey, John Benjamin 1998.04
Hickey, John J. 1941.07
Hickey, Jr., John 1929.24
Hickey, Louise 1979.31, 1987.10, 1988.07, 1989.03
Hickey, May 1909.25
Hickey, S.M. 1882.81
Hickey, William 1958.01
Hickman, Alfred 1902.34, 1903.07, 1903.34, 1905.19, 1906.26, 1906.50, 1907.15, 1907.33, 1920.30
Hickman, Art 1920.18, 1939.29
Hickman, Darryl 1966.11, 1968.07
Hickman, George 1934.06
Hickman, James 1962.05
Hickman, Leo 1992.03
Hickman, R.N. 1889.20
Hickman, Robert 1903.40
Hickok, John 1998.21, 2000.06
Hicks and Brooks 1903.04
Hicks, Bert 1943.23
Hicks, David 1964.19, 1968.14
Hicks, Frederick 1891.46
Hicks, Julian 1901.27, 1905.46
Hicks, Kenneth 1975.19
Hicks, Leonard 1946.19
Hicks, Leslie 1983.01
Hicks, Malcolm 1917.13, 1923.43
Hicks, Messr. 1897.23
Hicks, Munson 1975.23
Hicks, Nettie 1869.46, 1869.47
Hicks, Rodney 1996.09, 2000.09
Hicks, Russell 1934.04
Hicks, Seymour 1894.18, 1895.32, 1898.46, 1900.28, 1904.04, 1905.27, 1905.49
Hicks, Shauna 1989.23
Hicks, Sue 1932.27
Hickson 1919.29
Hickson's 1915.07
Hickson, Inc. 1915.23, 1919.11
Hickson, Joseph 1923.02
Hickson, New York 1921.11
Hicley, Florence 1887.18
Hidago, Allen 1997.10
Hidden, Ira 1918.14
Hider, Ruth M. 1965.13
Hidey, Hal 1960.01
Hield, Jr., W. 1848.03
Hiester, Messr. 1841.01
Hiffart, Mme. 1844.01
Hiffert, Miss 1851.08
Higgins, Billy 1923.11, 1976.04, 1999.01
Higgins, Bob 1918.21
Higgins, Daniel 1927.27
Higgins, David 1925.43
Higgins, James 1965.32
Higgins, Janet 1998.18
Higgins, Janet Kay 1990.20, 1991.13
Higgins, Joel 1975.03, 1976.33, 1978.10
Higgins, Kinzie 1909.09
Higgins, Messr. 1870.19
Higgins, Minnie 1909.05
Higgins, Mr. 1859.04
Higgins, Peter 1931.28, 1935.04
Higgins, Robert 1922.48
Higgins, W.S. 1866.01, 1866.04, 1866.05
Higginsen, Vy 1995.04
Higginson, Andrew 1906.25, 1916.18
Higginson, Polly 1882.77
Higgs, Mme. 1841.01
High John Productions 1969.15
High Willows, The 1968.04
High, John 1946.05
Hight, Lizzie 1891.24
Hight, Pearl 1926.46, 1930.05
Highton, Sylvia 1923.13
Hightower, Loren 1952.13, 1958.14, 1960.09, 1963.04, 1963.06, 1963.26, 1965.18
Hightower, Robert 1942.15
Hightowery, William 1942.15
Hiha, Lena 1972.20
Hijo and Company 1875.22, 1875.24
Hiken, Gerald 1959.12, 1964.04, 1979.29
Hiken, Nat 1949.01, 1951.19, 1952.20
Hikuroa, Christine 1972.20
Hilaire Mahieu and Company 1915.01
Hilbert, Jane 1914.27
Hilbok, Bruce 1978.11
Hilbon, Leona 1899.30, 1900.38, 1901.17
Hilda, Irene 1942.30
Hildebrand, F. 1881.39
Hildebrand, Richard 1955.07
Hildebrande, G. 1873.02
Hildegarde 1942.12
Hildesley, Charles 1898.31, 1899.06
Hildreth, E. 1848.03
Hilferty, Susan 1995.05, 1998.22, 2000.12
Hilfiger, Ally 1999.17
Hilgenberg, Katherine 1965.24
Hill, Alexander 1933.06, 1989.02
Hill, Annabelle 1948.32
Hill, Annie 1900.08
Hill, Arthur 1903.03, 1904.13, 1904.44, 1907.47, 1909.13, 1910.20, 1915.11, 1917.16, 1917.37, 1918.23, 1919.22, 1964.35
Hill, Barre 1932.14, 1932.24
Hill, Barton 1886.49
Hill, Bette Cerf 1993.04
Hill, Billy 1934.01, 1999.05
Hill, Bobby 1972.13, 1976.35
Hill, C. Wesley 1921.16, 1923.39
Hill, Charles 1935.01
Hill, Clay 1916.10, 1917.13, 1918.19, 1920.29
Hill, Dorothy 1951.14, 1951.24, 1952.20
Hill, Drina 1934.15
Hill, Dule 1996.07
Hill, Eloise 1950.07
Hill, Erin 1998.04
Hill, Eunice 1899.36
Hill, F.L. 1887.43, 1889.44
Hill, Frank 1903.18, 1904.17, 1923.13
Hill, Frank G. 1903.06
Hill, Fred 1909.17, 1910.13
Hill, Frederick 1897.14
Hill, Genevieve 1893.21, 1897.21
Hill, George 1951.11
Hill, George Roy 1960.05, 1967.14
Hill, Glynn 1952.19
Hill, Graham 1909.04
Hill, Gus 1897.38, 1902.09, 1902.33, 1902.38, 1902.42, 1903.05, 1908.02, 1925.12
Hill, Harry M. 1905.14
Hill, Howard 1932.30
Hill, Inga 1935.17
Hill, J. Leubrie 1904.26, 1906.08, 1908.08, 1909.27, 1911.26, 1913.17, 1914.15
Hill, J.M. 1886.14, 1886.46, 1887.23
Hill, James Leubrie 1903.08
Hill, Jane 1851.04
Hill, Jesse 1992.06
Hill, Joe 1944.32, 1961.28
Hill, John 1904.38
Hill, Katherine 1914.22
Hill, Kittie 1888.29, 1915.26
Hill, Kitty 1889.47, 1915.11
Hill, Laura 1912.43
Hill, Leubrie 1915.11, 1915.26
Hill, Linda Lee 1936.07
Hill, Louisa 1884.25
Hill, Louise 1884.59, 1884.65
Hill, Mabel 1914.22, 1928.22
Hill, Maria 1870.33
Hill, May 1882.38
Hill, Messr. 1856.04, 1868.13, 1868.15, 1880.12, 1881.15, 1889.01
Hill, Miss 1841.01
Hill, Mr. 1836.01, 1851.01, 1851.06, 1864.12, 1866.16, 1866.17, 1867.07, 1867.18
Hill, Mrs. 1883.39
Hill, Paul 1935.11
Hill, Phyllis 1943.21, 1944.16
Hill, Pickaninny 1927.32
Hill, Professor 1883.45, 1883.58
Hill, R.H. 1904.48
Hill, Ralston 1961.11, 1965.24
Hill, Richard 1969.04, 1980.01
Hill, Robert Lee 1917.24
Hill, Ronald 1942.14
Hill, Rosena M. 1999.22
Hill, Ruby 1946.08
Hill, Russell 1907.62
Hill, Stella 1905.43
Hill, Stephanie 1965.17
Hill, Steve 1946.17
Hill, Strap 1905.21
Hill, Viola 1939.15
Hill, W.F. 1866.19
Hill, W.J. 1868.32, 1869.06, 1869.29
Hill, Warren F. 1901.03
Hill, Wesley 1930.10
Hill, Westley 1925.18
Hill, Z.Z. 1999.09
Hillaire, Marcel 1955.02
Hillarde, Helen 1916.08
Hillary, Lucy 1944.24, 1948.16, 1957.04
Hillbon, Leona 1900.38
Hillebrand, Fred 1919.07, 1921.03, 1923.10, 1928.04, 1929.09
Hiller, Frederic 1898.11
Hiller, J. Sebastian 1901.12, 1902.30, 1903.21, 1906.04, 1911.01
Hiller, J.S. 1887.15, 1887.21, 1891.11, 1892.22, 1892.33, 1892.47, 1893.16, 1896.13, 1897.10, 1906.40, 1908.02
Hiller, John S. 1890.28, 1894.24
Hiller, John Sebastian 1902.35, 1904.15
Hiller, Sebastian 1897.44, 1898.18, 1898.26, 1898.29, 1898.46
Hilley, Ron 1987.03, 1991.09, 1993.12, 1994.09, 1996.13
Hilliam, B.C. 1919.31, 1919.40, 1921.11
Hilliard, B. 1901.03
Hilliard, Bob 1947.20, 1950.12, 1953.01
Hilliard, H. 1861.01, 1865.06, 1866.12
Hilliard, H.S. 1885.26, 1885.40
Hilliard, Harry 1885.11, 1885.16, 1887.19, 1887.25, 1890.37, 1914.06
Hilliard, Harry S. 1885.48
Hilliard, Jack 1951.21
Hilliard, Ken 1987.19
Hilliard, Lawrence 1904.05
Hilliard, Louida 1904.52
Hilliard, Louise 1890.08
Hilliard, Mack 1943.18
Hilliard, Mae 1907.34
Hilliard, Mollie 1892.47
Hilliard, Molly 1890.08
Hilliard, Mr. 1871.15, 1871.22
Hilliard, Robert 1886.59, 1890.35, 1892.01
Hilliard, Walter 1927.27
Hillias, Peg 1950.08
Hillibrand, Fred 1939.16
Hillier, Claire 1918.16
Hilliger, Miss 1881.07
Hilliges, Miss 1880.69
Hillis, O. Kane 1894.20
Hillman, C.H. 1903.21
Hillman, George 1897.30
Hillmer, Leann 1978.23
Hillner, Bert 1946.18
Hillner, John 1992.02, 1995.11, 1998.13
Hills, Alice 1902.34, 1902.40, 1908.34, 1919.07
Hills, Margaret 1956.09
Hills, Trevor 1955.16, 1955.20, 1955.21, 1955.22
Hillyar, Gertrude 1889.54
Hillyard, C. 1869.04
Hillyard, H. 1855.04, 1855.05, 1855.06, 1855.07, 1855.09, 1856.02, 1866.16, 1871.19
Hillyard, J. 1871.14
Hillyard, John 1876.29
Hillyard, Mr. 1844.01
Hilson, Mme. 1841.01
Hilt, Ferdinand 1948.24, 1952.13, 1953.07, 1962.01, 1962.13, 1966.11
Hilton, Dora 1920.06
Hilton, H. 1890.08
Hilton, Harry 1890.29
Hilton, Hattie 1900.35
Hilton, Helen 1905.44, 1911.13
Hilton, Hugh 1893.12
Hilton, James 1956.07
Hilton, Juno 1898.27
Hilton, Lola 1912.38, 1917.29
Hilton, Louise 1900.15
Hilton, Marie 1888.34, 1890.10, 1897.52, 1902.15
Hilton, Merrill 1949.17
Hilton, Miss 1872.24
Hilton, T. 1883.18
Hilyard, C. 1869.13
Himan, Al 1893.42
Himan, Alberto 1894.21, 1894.35
Himes, Ross 1924.46, 1927.37, 1928.17
Hinchley, Miss 1881.04
Hinckings, Mr. 1836.01
Hinckley, Allen C. 1902.04, 1902.28
Hinckley, E. 1879.50
Hinckley, Emily 1879.15
Hinckley, Emma 1879.56, 1881.11, 1885.68
Hinckley, Sallie 1866.12
Hinckley, Sallie A. 1866.34, 1867.08
Hind, Gary 1999.12
Hind, Messr. 1851.07
Hind, Miss 1870.34
Hind, Mr. 1851.01, 1852.01, 1864.13
Hind, Mrs. A. 1862.07, 1863.02, 1871.10
Hind, T. 1867.20, 1868.22
Hind, T.J. 1864.21, 1866.03, 1868.19
Hinde, Frank 1880.49
Hindle, Winnifred 1947.15
Hindley, Thomas 1882.41
Hindley, Thomas W. 1896.15
Hindman, James 1989.29, 1999.13
Hindmarsh, Jean 1962.26, 1962.28, 1962.30
Hinds, Esther 1976.28
Hindsley, Charles 1964.12, 1964.13
Hindus, Milton 1940.04
Hine, Harry 1889.09, 1889.41, 1890.29
Hineman, George 1879.08
Hines, Altonell 1934.05, 1952.06
Hines, Babe 1950.03, 1955.11
Hines, Earl 1976.04
Hines, Elizabeth 1916.08, 1919.23, 1921.06, 1921.32, 1922.43, 1924.21, 1925.26
Hines, Gabriel 1924.12
Hines, Gregory 1954.01, 1978.21, 1979.32, 1980.10, 1981.06, 1992.08
Hines, Harold 1935.01
Hines, Harry 1920.24, 1939.16
Hines, J. 1894.13
Hines, Jack 1924.36
Hines, Jackson 1916.01, 1917.27, 1918.27
Hines, John 1908.28
Hines, Johnnie 1909.11
Hines, Jr., Jesse K. 1881.18
Hines, Laurene 1939.14
Hines, Maurice 1954.01, 1978.21, 1981.07, 1986.02
Hines, Mimi 1996.17
Hines, Patrick 1969.04, 1973.07
Hines, William E. 1885.42
Hingle, Pat 1972.02, 1997.15
Hingston, Leota 1909.14
Hingston, Sean Martin 1999.24, 2000.07
Hinkley, Del 1967.02, 1971.01
Hinley, Clara 1870.31
Hinnant, Bill 1971.09
Hinshaw, William 1914.11
Hinton, Charles M. 1913.33, 1919.02
Hinton, Esselene 1932.12
Hipp, Paul 1990.15
Hirch, Louis A. 1908.21
Hirigaray, M. 1926.40, 1926.43, 1926.45, 1926.47
Hirose, George 1936.04, 1961.07
Hirsch, Bernice 1919.37
Hirsch, Caroline 1986.15
Hirsch, Emil 1938.16
Hirsch, Fluffer 1971.20
Hirsch, Freda 1914.15
Hirsch, Gene 1932.20
Hirsch, Gregory Allen 1992.07
Hirsch, Hilda 1914.15, 1917.26
Hirsch, Irving 1928.24
Hirsch, Louis 1911.32, 1915.15, 1921.32, 1922.32, 1924.47
Hirsch, Louis A. 1907.42, 1908.07, 1908.10, 1908.39, 1909.24, 1910.19, 1910.25, 1911.34, 1911.43, 1912.09, 1912.17, 1912.24, 1915.28, 1916.10, 1917.32, 1917.36, 1918.11, 1918.19, 1918.37, 1919.23, 1920.38, 1922.19, 1923.20, 1923.31, 1976.25
Hirsch, Walter 1923.12, 1981.16, 1986.06
Hirschberg, H.J. 1890.04
Hirschfeld, Abe 1989.25, 1996.03
Hirschfeld, Al 1959.20
Hirschfeld, Max 1894.11, 1902.20, 1904.54, 1905.01, 1912.40, 1915.07, 1916.22, 1917.06, 1918.03, 1920.31, 1921.29, 1922.48, 1925.06, 1925.15, 1926.08, 1927.24, 1930.41
Hirschfeld, Susan 1989.09
Hirschfield, Max 1889.13, 1902.23, 1903.06, 1903.31, 1906.33, 1908.35, 1915.30, 1918.37, 1919.29, 1938.02
Hirschhorn, Joel 1974.19, 1977.09, 1981.12, 1982.14
Hirschmann, Henri 1912.09
Hirshhorn, Naomi Caryl 1963.19
Hirshman, Col. John J. 1947.19
Hirson, Roger O. 1966.27, 1972.22
Hirst, Bessie 1903.09

Hirst, George 1919.32, 1925.19, 1928.37, 1932.06, 1938.10, 1943.22, 1945.09, 1952.02
Hirst, George S. 1922.03, 1927.21
Hitchcock, Raymond 1894.31, 1895.34, 1896.52, 1897.53, 1898.06, 1898.07, 1898.16, 1898.21, 1898.24, 1898.30, 1898.42, 1898.49, 1898.52, 1898.57, 1898.62, 1898.65, 1899.10, 1899.14, 1899.16, 1899.41, 1900.30, 1900.48, 1900.59, 1901.05, 1902.18, 1904.10, 1905.06, 1905.26, 1907.27, 1909.08, 1909.26, 1911.41, 1914.13, 1916.20, 1917.12, 1917.33, 1917.35, 1918.06, 1918.18, 1919.25, 1920.39, 1921.21, 1922.21, 1924.33
Hite, Mabel 1904.19, 1908.15, 1911.17
Hittemans, Paul 1870.30, 1870.37, 1870.41, 1870.45, 1871.06
Hitz, Alex 1997.18
Hitz, Elsie 1914.20
Hively, Bessie 1905.40
Hixon, Butler 1944.23
Hixon, Edna 1904.12, 1906.23, 1906.37
Hixon, Hal 1920.22, 1920.23
Hixson, Opal 1923.08
Hlatshwayo, Sam 1977.01
Hlela, Betty-Boo 1977.01
Hlengwa, Lindiwe 1988.02
Hlengwa, Zandile 1988.02
HMT Associates 1976.07
Ho, Wai Ching 1969.09
Hoag, Ethel 1900.59
Hoag, George 1925.20, 1926.17, 1927.23, 1928.19
Hoare, Douglas 1913.29
Hoback, James 1983.16
Hoban, Molly 1942.26
Hoban, Stella 1912.12, 1912.34, 1915.05, 1916.11, 1920.04, 1923.19
Hobard, Rick 1971.19
Hobart, George V. 1897.15, 1900.07, 1900.42, 1900.44, 1900.47, 1900.49, 1900.56, 1900.58, 1901.12, 1901.21, 1901.23, 1902.06, 1902.10, 1902.16, 1902.23, 1903.18, 1903.23, 1903.27, 1903.39, 1904.31, 1904.43, 1905.17, 1905.28, 1905.30, 1905.43, 1905.45, 1906.04, 1906.24, 1906.43, 1907.14, 1908.01, 1908.11, 1908.38, 1909.09, 1909.30, 1910.08, 1910.17, 1910.20, 1910.26, 1911.13, 1911.24, 1911.31, 1912.02, 1912.20, 1912.37, 1913.17, 1914.15, 1914.24, 1916.10, 1917.13, 1918.01, 1919.25, 1919.26, 1919.31, 1920.18, 1920.37, 1921.24, 1921.30, 1922.14, 1922.16, 1922.32, 1922.39
Hobart, Margot 1901.08, 1904.19
Hobart, W. 1912.12
Hobart, W.L. 1903.41
Hobart, William 1915.18
Hobart, William L. 1912.33
Hobbs, J. 1880.62
Hobbs, John 1881.45
Hobbs, Robert 1924.01, 1927.01, 1929.30, 1930.09
Hobper, Herr 1870.26
Hobson, I.M. 1983.08
Hobson, Ida 1898.46
Hobson, James 1966.08, 1970.21
Hobson, Maud 1894.33, 1897.32, 1903.22
Hobson, May 1906.47
Hobson, Richard 2000.03
Hoby, Marie 1884.27
Hoch, Theodore 1889.53
Hocher, Barbara 1974.08, 1975.11
Hochman, Larry 1982.10, 1987.14, 1988.19, 1999.10, 2000.20, 2001.01
Hockey, Milton 1925.17
Hocking, Leah 1997.09, 2000.08
Hockman, Shari 1925.23
Hockstader, Miss 1870.31
Hoctor, Harriet 1924.46, 1927.38, 1928.12, 1930.08, 1931.08, 1932.18, 1933.21, 1936.02
Hoctor, Robin 1972.04
Hodapp, Ann 1980.17
Hodd, Daniel 1996.16
Hodd, Daniel James 1997.12
Hodes, Bernard 1982.14
Hodes, Gloria 1970.02, 1986.12
Hodes, Stuart 1950.16, 1951.24, 1958.03, 1959.06, 1959.26, 1961.20, 1963.12
Hodgdon, Alice 1888.44
Hodgdon, Dana 1965.14
Hodge, Eddie 1929.44, 1945.20, 1948.08
Hodge, Edwin 1925.49, 1927.59
Hodge, Martha 1941.05
Hodge, William T. 1905.48, 1906.48
Hodges, Ann 1962.03, 1972.11
Hodges, Barclay 1955.10
Hodges, Eddie 1942.11, 1957.18
Hodges, Elijah 1943.10, 1943.24, 1945.06, 1946.09
Hodges, F. 1857.04
Hodges, Frank 1893.21
Hodges, George J. 1999.24
Hodges, Joe 1899.33, 1901.20
Hodges, Johnnie 1981.06
Hodges, Johnny 1980.10, 1997.03
Hodges, Joy 1937.13, 1944.18, 1946.04
Hodges, Miss 1866.18
Hodges, Mitchell 1939.22
Hodges, T. 1856.02
Hodgkins, Gene 1912.36
Hodgkins, W.F. 1934.33
Hodgkinson, John 1794.01, 1796.01, 1796.02, 1796.03
Hodgkinson, Mrs. John 1794.01, 1796.01, 1796.03
Hodgson, Claire 1919.35, 1923.13
Hodgson, Miss 1892.07
Hodgson, Red 1986.06
Hodo, David 1976.19
Hodo, Mr. 1865.04
Hodson, Georgina 1855.11
Hodson, William 1903.20
Hoe, Yank 1889.33
Hoebee, Mark 1991.15
Hoefer, Anita 1965.04
Hoeffle, Thelma 1914.16
Hoeffler, Charles E. 1977.10
Hoefler, Charles E. 1969.14, 1980.15
Hoekstra, Jerry 1919.40
Hoel, Edson 1959.10
Hoeller, Harald A. 1964.25
Hoemburg, Hans 1995.15
Hoerlein, Lillian 1906.10
Hoermanson, Hjalmar 1939.16
Hoestetter, Paula 1987.10
Hoey, Dennis 1926.33, 1937.10
Hoey, Evelyn 1928.11, 1930.35, 1932.27
Hoey, George 1885.69, 1901.09
Hoey, Herbert 1915.30, 1921.21, 1925.11
Hoey, Iris 1914.32
Hoey, James F. 1893.17
Hoey, John 1898.31
Hoey, Loyd 1903.21
Hoey, William 1884.48, 1890.32, 1892.18, 1892.45, 1896.31
Hoey, William F. 1894.46
Hofe, Nandl 1891.30
Hofele, F. 1865.01, 1865.11, 1866.02, 1866.28, 1867.12
Hofele, F.W. 1879.02
Hofele, Ferdinand W. 1875.05, 1879.54, 1879.65
Hofer, Carl 1891.30, 1892.31
Hoff, Alex 1972.24
Hoff, Christian 1993.06
Hoff, Edwin 1885.45, 1885.52, 1887.26, 1887.47
Hoff, Edwin C. 1897.29
Hoff, Edwin W. 1885.28, 1885.67, 1886.26, 1887.04, 1887.18, 1891.29, 1893.18, 1893.19, 1894.03
Hoff, Emily 1907.14
Hoff, Fred 1923.03, 1924.05, 1932.10, 1934.17, 1943.06
Hoff, Fred R. 1905.12
Hoff, Henry 1902.42
Hoff, Louise 1960.07
Hoff, Vanda 1921.10
Hoffa, Portland 1929.19, 1930.32
Hoffenstein, Samuel 1932.26
Hoffman, "Think a Drink" 1939.22, 1944.19
Hoffman, A.W. 1878.02, 1881.13, 1882.77, 1883.48, 1884.40, 1886.16, 1887.03, 1887.27, 1889.21, 1891.41, 1893.23
Hoffman, Aaron 1905.31, 1905.34, 1905.39, 1907.33, 1907.53, 1907.62, 1909.05, 1910.07, 1910.18, 1912.16, 1924.22
Hoffman, Aaron S. 1903.07, 1905.32
Hoffman, Al 1932.27, 1952.11, 1975.12, 1985.08, 1999.05
Hoffman, Anna 1910.30
Hoffman, Annette 1929.45, 1936.07
Hoffman, Armin 1959.14, 1965.16
Hoffman, Bena 1901.17, 1903.28, 1912.12, 1915.23
Hoffman, Bern 1950.17, 1956.12
Hoffman, Cecilia 1913.24
Hoffman, Charles 1896.03
Hoffman, Clarence 1953.07
Hoffman, Constance 2000.10
Hoffman, Dorothy 1927.11
Hoffman, Emma 1879.04
Hoffman, Ferdi 1945.04, 1955.10
Hoffman, Fred 1867.21
Hoffman, George 1943.23
Hoffman, Gertrude 1903.27, 1904.45, 1904.58, 1905.03, 1905.23, 1905.33, 1905.34, 1905.45, 1906.30, 1907.20, 1907.24, 1917.03, 1923.38, 1926.01
Hoffman, Gertrude May 1903.15
Hoffman, Guy 1904.30
Hoffman, H.G. 1899.41
Hoffman, Henry 1889.24
Hoffman, Hilda 1907.61
Hoffman, Jane 1940.18, 1941.03, 1943.19, 1963.09
Hoffman, Jay K. 1966.19
Hoffman, Jr., Max 1922.38, 1926.37, 1929.31, 1930.42
Hoffman, Laura 1914.28
Hoffman, Llora 1919.16, 1920.19, 1923.02, 1923.41, 1925.23
Hoffman, Lola 1904.04
Hoffman, Marjorie 1932.14
Hoffman, Matthew 1996.15
Hoffman, Max 1901.04, 1903.18, 1903.23, 1903.27, 1904.58, 1905.30, 1907.24, 1907.33, 1908.04, 1910.07, 1925.29, 1927.19
Hoffman, Messr. 1844.01, 1911.18
Hoffman, Miss 1863.01, 1863.02, 1863.04
Hoffman, Mollie 1901.17
Hoffman, Mr. 1852.06
Hoffman, Naomi 1966.21
Hoffman, Otto 1909.17
Hoffman, Otto F. 1910.37
Hoffman, Patricia 1965.35
Hoffman, Pauline 1926.51
Hoffman, Philip 1982.08, 1983.19, 1987.18, 1997.19
Hoffman, Rena 1911.26
Hoffman, Theodore 1921.34
Hoffman, Think-a-Drink 1942.14
Hoffmann, A.W. 1892.38, 1894.34
Hoffmann, Aaron 1912.29
Hoffmann, Charles B. 1894.30
Hoffmann, Gertrude 1906.45, 1912.43, 1925.23, 1927.19
Hoffmann, Harry 1904.39
Hoffmann, Herr 1883.08
Hoffmann, Jr., Max 1933.16
Hoffmann, Max 1903.18, 1904.31, 1906.45, 1912.43, 1916.24
Hoffmann, Sr., Max 1933.16
Hoffmann, W.W. 1885.65
Hofmann, Oscar 1920.46
Hofschueler, Frl. 1883.48
Hofschuler, Frl. 1883.48
Hofsis, Jack 1980.21, 1981.20, 1982.07, 1985.09, 1987.08, 1993.12
Hofsiss, Jack 1976.34
Hogan, Celeste 1977.18
Hogan, Dick 1943.23
Hogan, Edmund 1902.36
Hogan, Edward 1925.17, 1926.13
Hogan, Ernest 1896.02, 1896.52, 1898.41, 1899.11, 1900.46, 1900.55, 1902.38, 1906.08, 1907.55
Hogan, G. 1883.66
Hogan, H. 1871.13, 1883.66
Hogan, Harry 1876.12
Hogan, J. 1868.19, 1875.35
Hogan, John 1868.05, 1875.19, 1875.23, 1875.26, 1886.40
Hogan, John P. 1896.15
Hogan, Julia 1875.35, 1876.02
Hogan, Larry 1929.32
Hogan, Lavinia 1877.25, 1877.39
Hogan, Mr. 1866.16, 1866.17
Hogan, Sheila 1946.01, 1948.20
Hogan, Vincent 1876.02, 1876.16, 1878.03, 1879.11, 1879.25, 1880.26, 1880.57, 1880.62, 1881.25, 1881.42, 1881.44, 1881.45, 1882.46, 1882.65, 1884.59, 1885.12, 1886.17, 1886.53
Hoganas, Bende 1964.22
Hoganas, Egon 1964.22
Hoganas, Les 1964.22
Hogarth, Lionel 1900.52, 1904.40, 1913.14
Hogarty, John E. 1891.46
Hogg, Ian 1965.39
Hogsander, Arne 1966.19
Hogue, Bill 1948.23
Hogue, Roland 1925.07
Hogue, William 1950.01, 1950.11
Hoh, Dick 1963.20
Hoha, Hal 1938.01
Hohenwart, Eugene 1915.17
Hoiby, Lee 1959.09
Hoier, Thomas 1948.32
Hoier, Tom 1948.18
Hoins, Jack 1922.34
Hoisington, Eric A. 1989.03
Hoist, Eduard 1897.46
Hoistit, Messr. 1869.29
Hoit, Michael 1977.15
Holbein, Ida 1901.26
Holbook, Al 1913.23
Holbrook, A. 1896.10, 1903.37
Holbrook, A.H. 1909.18
Holbrook, A.M. 1889.36, 1895.23, 1898.12, 1898.54, 1899.28, 1901.13, 1904.51, 1908.34, 1912.42
Holbrook, A.W. 1892.28
Holbrook, Al 1897.15, 1897.24, 1902.31, 1903.34, 1904.19, 1905.29, 1906.27, 1906.48, 1907.36, 1907.37, 1907.52, 1909.22, 1910.20, 1910.27, 1910.28, 1912.05, 1912.10
Holbrook, Al E. 1902.03
Holbrook, Al M. 1902.41, 1904.50, 1906.01, 1908.03
Holbrook, Al. 1895.20, 1912.16
Holbrook, Al. M. 1900.39
Holbrook, Alfred 1892.07
Holbrook, Alice 1895.26, 1898.31
Holbrook, Bessie 1905.29, 1907.11
Holbrook, Billy 1920.39
Holbrook, D. 1876.22
Holbrook, Florence 1894.17, 1908.07, 1910.09
Holbrook, H. 1890.39
Holbrook, Harry 1925.36, 1928.34, 1929.44, 1930.30, 1931.42
Holbrook, Miss 1892.07
Holbrook, W.M. 1914.31
Holbrook, William 1917.12, 1918.18, 1922.30, 1923.33, 1924.03, 1925.05, 1927.38, 1929.04, 1929.29, 1930.05, 1930.23, 1930.33, 1931.36, 1943.22
Holcenberg, David 2000.18
Holcomb, M. 1872.04
Holcomb, Marion 1871.02
Holcomb, Maron 1872.08
Holcomb, Maud 1872.12
Holcomb, Willard 1904.58, 1905.42, 1906.31
Holcombe, Marie 1870.35
Holcombe, Marion 1870.42, 1914.24, 1918.01
Holden, Bertha 1888.36
Holden, J. Maurice 1906.13
Holden, Jessie 1888.36
Holden, John 1919.08
Holden, Kitty 1896.47
Holden, Louise 1945.03, 1947.11
Holden, Mamie 1896.47
Holden, Maurice 1891.01
Holden, Minnie 1889.21
Holden, Richard 1940.04
Holden, William 1923.13, 1927.68
Holder 1868.03
Holder, Don 1991.10
Holder, Donald 1996.16, 1997.20, 2000.10, 2001.03
Holder, Geoffrey 1954.19, 1964.02, 1975.01, 1978.03, 1982.06
Holding, John 1889.06
Holdridge, Lee 1966.30, 1968.06, 1986.18
Holdsworth, Mr. 1876.19
Holdsworth, S. 1875.39, 1876.03
Holdsworth, Sam 1876.19
Holdsworth, Samuel 1881.06
Hole, Jonathan 1932.14
Holgage, Ron 1999.04
Holgate, Danny 1972.13, 1974.03, 1976.04, 1976.21, 1978.21, 1980.09, 1980.15
Holgate, Ron 1979.02, 1980.11, 1999.19
Holgate, Ronald 1961.20, 1962.12, 1969.06
Holiday, Billie 1948.13, 1976.16
Holiday, Bob 1959.25, 1966.06
Holiday, Hope 1956.12
Holiday, Joy 1984.10
Holiday, Melanie 1984.04
Holiday, Ron 1984.10

Holiner, Mann 1926.37, 1928.27, 1928.46, 1928.48, 1929.06, 1930.09, 1931.11, 1932.13, 1933.27, 1953.12
Holk, Agnese 1886.39
Holkmann, Loretta 1983.04
Hollaender, Victor 1897.35, 1915.08
Holland, Alfred 1879.06, 1879.58, 1879.71
Holland, Alva 1905.41
Holland, Arthur 1921.12
Holland, Betsy 1951.23, 1953.01
Holland, Betty Lou 1946.10
Holland, Brian 1984.15, 1986.02
Holland, Bryant 1982.22
Holland, Charles 1943.10
Holland, Chauncey 1903.04
Holland, Dennis 1980.16
Holland, Dorothy 1980.30
Holland, E.M. 1875.14
Holland, Eddie 1982.22, 1984.15, 1986.02
Holland, Edwin 1895.39
Holland, Estelle 1900.45
Holland, F.W. 1886.58
Holland, Frank W. 1887.32, 1889.34, 1890.30, 1891.14, 1892.06
Holland, G. 1856.04
Holland, George 1859.11, 1867.19, 1868.19, 1906.46, 1908.26
Holland, Gilbert 1928.10, 1931.31
Holland, Herman 1913.32
Holland, Jack 1924.46
Holland, Joseph 1939.29
Holland, Leila 1889.34
Holland, Leland 1951.05
Holland, Lyndsie 1976.12, 1976.13, 1976.14
Holland, Maurice 1921.35, 1922.04, 1922.24, 1925.26, 1928.07, 1928.26, 1930.07
Holland, Messr. 1883.17, 1883.23, 1892.06
Holland, Mildred 1927.26
Holland, Miss 1881.03, 1881.35
Holland, Mme. 1889.34
Holland, Mr. 1858.04, 1883.66
Holland, T. 1886.42, 1887.07
Holland, Tim 1886.52
Holland, V. 1886.57
Hollander, E. 1910.24
Hollander, Frederick 1967.13, 1968.20, 1980.29, 1999.07
Hollander, Friedrich 1999.05
Hollander, Irma 1943.14
Hollander, Victor 1891.33, 1910.18, 1912.36, 1915.08
Hollenbeck, Bertha 1900.08
Holler, Dick 1974.09
Holley, Bertha 1922.45
Holliday, Billie 1976.04
Holliday, David 1969.17, 1976.33, 1980.29, 1992.07
Holliday, Harry 1885.21, 1902.07
Holliday, Jennifer 1981.29
Holliday, Jennifer-Yvette 1980.14
Holliday, Judy 1956.14, 1963.13
Holliday, Mark 1977.12
Holliday, Peter 1939.30
Hollihan, M.J. 1892.22
Holliman, W. 1882.62, 1885.33
Hollingsworth, G. 1887.04
Hollingsworth, Grace 1885.67, 1886.26
Hollingsworth, Indus 1936.12
Hollins, Frank 1905.39, 1908.14
Hollins, Hilda 1892.20, 1892.30, 1893.50, 1895.06, 1895.20, 1896.44, 1899.23, 1900.57, 1904.15, 1905.40, 1907.05
Hollins, Mabel 1904.15, 1906.20, 1906.25, 1907.21, 1908.25
Hollins, Maud 1892.20, 1892.37, 1895.06, 1895.20, 1898.73, 1900.39
Hollins, Maude 1896.44
Hollis, George 1907.58
Hollis, J.B. 1910.17
Hollis, John 1896.24
Hollis, Lillian 1902.22
Hollis, Marnee 1993.18
Hollis, Tommy 1998.01, 2001.06
Hollister, Louise 1901.30, 1903.36
Hollister, Sarah 1905.48
Hollnad, George 1907.54
Holloman, Charlotte 1950.16, 1952.15
Holloway, Bob 1962.13, 1992.18
Holloway, David 1975.16, 1976.26, 1977.11
Holloway, Dennis 1955.19
Holloway, Joan 1956.07
Holloway, Julian 1993.18
Holloway, Miss 1841.01
Holloway, Robert 1962.16
Holloway, Stanley 1956.01, 1960.17
Holloway, Sterling 1925.17, 1926.13, 1930.18, 1930.33
Holls, Violet 1901.06, 1902.37, 1905.49
Holly, Bertha 1904.51, 1904.57, 1905.08, 1905.11, 1905.57, 1907.36, 1912.26, 1913.15
Holly, Buddy 1990.15
Holly, Charles 1893.09, 1915.17
Holly, Ellen 1966.15
Holly, William 1919.38
Hollywell, Marie 1917.34, 1918.25
Hollywood Theatre Alliance, The 1940.21
Hollywood, Clara 1896.27, 1899.28
Hollywood, Jimmy 1938.08
Holm, Celeste 1943.04, 1944.23, 1979.10
Holm, Hanya 1948.17, 1948.32, 1950.11, 1950.20, 1952.02, 1952.15, 1954.03, 1956.01, 1956.05, 1960.10, 1964.20, 1965.18, 1965.35, 1968.17, 1976.05, 1981.19
Holm, John Cecil 1941.06, 1941.13, 1947.04, 1961.21, 1962.20
Holm, Klaus 1954.03, 1960.11, 1961.14, 1964.28, 1966.03
Holman, Alfred 1862.06
Holman, Benjamin 1862.06
Holman, Bill 1983.20
Holman, Elizabeth 1925.17
Holman, George 1851.04, 1854.04, 1855.06, 1855.07
Holman, Georgie 1906.34
Holman, Harriet 1854.04
Holman, Julia 1862.06
Holman, Libby 1927.27, 1929.04, 1930.32, 1934.38, 1938.07, 1954.11
Holman, Lola 1969.09
Holman, Messr. 1844.01
Holman, Mr. 1850.01, 1855.05, 1857.08, 1884.40
Holman, Mrs. 1823.01, 1855.07, 1857.08
Holman, Mrs. George 1851.04
Holman, Sallie 1862.06
Holman, Valentine 1908.44
Holmann, Gene 1953.02
Holmes, B.B. 1865.05
Holmes, Ben 1926.37, 1930.37
Holmes, Bernice 1898.30
Holmes, Betty 1928.45
Holmes, Brenda 1974.02
Holmes, E.B. 1865.06, 1866.18, 1868.03, 1870.36, 1870.39, 1878.04
Holmes, E.G. 1879.25
Holmes, F. 1912.05
Holmes, F.W. 1908.03
Holmes, Florence 1908.36
Holmes, Frank 1907.07, 1913.05, 1916.03, 1918.05, 1921.34, 1923.12, 1925.28
Holmes, George 1941.12
Holmes, George E. 1888.07
Holmes, Jack 1960.07, 1962.02, 1971.09, 1971.11
Holmes, Jake 1976.34
Holmes, Jered 1972.05
Holmes, Jr. Matthew 1879.42
Holmes, Madeleine 1948.27
Holmes, Matthew 1878.15, 1880.31
Holmes, Maurine 1933.21
Holmes, Maynard 1937.08
Holmes, Messr. 1879.23
Holmes, Millie 1930.19
Holmes, Miss 1857.07, 1886.36
Holmes, Mr. 1857.05, 1857.07
Holmes, Mrs. E.B. 1871.17
Holmes, Peggy Anne 1938.18
Holmes, Peter 1949.18, 1959.26
Holmes, Ralph 1939.24
Holmes, Rapley 1919.41, 1921.07, 1922.11
Holmes, Raymond 1879.53, 1881.56
Holmes, Roy 1940.21
Holmes, Rupert 1976.34, 1985.18, 1989.06
Holmes, Scott 1984.01, 1986.01, 1994.06
Holmes, T. 1905.55
Holmes, Taylor 1909.11, 1911.18, 1913.01, 1922.12, 1926.30, 1934.35, 1937.13, 1945.11
Holmes, Violet 1899.15, 1979.13, 1980.09, 1981.08, 1982.06, 1983.09
Holmes, Virgil 1908.40
Holmes, W.F. 1879.18
Holmlan, Libby 1928.44
Holms, Violet 1980.18
Holofcener, Larry 1955.12, 1956.02, 1989.21
Holse, Glenn 1959.14, 1962.17
Holst, Edward 1887.31
Holstein, Al. H. 1902.39
Holstein, Al. T. 1905.12
Holston, William 1864.21
Holt, Ada 1911.22
Holt, Adele 1914.24
Holt, Bernard 1904.08
Holt, Bland 1875.39
Holt, Calvin 1955.12
Holt, Ednah 1983.03
Holt, Elise 1869.17
Holt, Elsie 1869.11, 1869.21
Holt, Ethelyne 1936.26, 1943.09
Holt, Fred 1939.19
Holt, Fritz 1974.17, 1975.12, 1978.25, 1980.29, 1983.11
Holt, Henry 1909.24, 1910.19, 1910.25, 1913.15
Holt, Henry M. 1912.49, 1913.28
Holt, Janice Lorraine 1994.07
Holt, Jean 1923.15
Holt, Minnie 1876.34
Holt, Mlle. 1876.36
Holt, Natalie 1913.16
Holt, Paul 1998.14
Holt, Rebecca 1995.05
Holt, Ruth 1897.20
Holt, Sophie 1893.32
Holt, Stacey Todd 2000.07
Holt, Sylvia 1898.66
Holt, Vivian 1919.26, 1920.22, 1920.23, 1922.18
Holt, Will 1969.07, 1970.20, 1975.20, 1976.33, 1978.25
Holte, Sylvia 1896.06, 1896.18
Holton, Mary C. 1982.01
Holtum, Christian 1922.47
Holtz, Lew 1915.26
Holtz, Lou 1919.13, 1920.17, 1921.22, 1923.02, 1925.14, 1927.46, 1931.01, 1934.39, 1942.10, 1944.22
Holtzmeyer, Genee 1883.65
Holtzmeyer, Genie 1883.26
Holtzmeyer-Rosenfeld, Genie 1884.22
Holwerk, Otis 1931.35
Holy Modal Rounders, The 1970.04
Holy, B. 1879.04
Holzer, Adela 1972.18, 1975.19
Holzer, Jane 1979.15
Holzer, Peter 1972.18
Holzman, Ben F. 1929.35
Holzmayer, Silvia 1964.25
Homan, Alfred 1952.01, 1952.02
Homan, Libby 1929.19
Homann, Charloatte 1931.42
Homans, Blanche 1902.27
Homberg, Terri 1985.19
Home, Charles 1893.26
Home, William 1931.38
Homer 1954.03, 1976.01
Homer, Ben 1975.12
Homer, C. Welch 1916.12
Homer, Charles 1937.01
Homer, Charles Welsh 1919.07
Homer, Dorothy 1910.29
Homer, J. 1935.01
Homfrey, Gladys 1895.43, 1912.33, 1914.32
Hominuke, Janet 1977.09
Hominuke, Mark 1977.09
Hona, Eva 1972.20
Honeckman, Henry 1972.03
Honey, Dorothy 1914.33
Honey, George 1894.41, 1894.48, 1895.09, 1895.32, 1896.45, 1897.24, 1897.37, 1898.51, 1901.19, 1902.24, 1903.17
Honey, Laura 1859.07
Honeycutt, Jr., Donnis 1979.15
Honeymoon, R. 1870.33
Honeywood, H.H. 1871.04
Hong, Arabella 1958.19
Honheimer, Ray 1930.37
Honig, Howard 1970.15
Honneaux, Marie 1876.03
Honor, Miss 1841.01
Honrath, Donald 1934.06
Hontabat, Marcelle 1912.44
Hood, Ann 1964.38, 1964.43, 1966.25, 1966.26, 1966.28
Hood, Basil 1896.01, 1896.05, 1897.37, 1898.51, 1900.37, 1902.25, 1903.21, 1906.47, 1907.51, 1908.25, 1912.33, 1930.07
Hood, Jane Adelaide 1906.31
Hood, Marion 1888.38, 1888.41
Hood, Mark 2001.04
Hood, Messr. 1867.25
Hood, Mrs. 1855.09
Hooey, Evelyn 1929.45
Hook, Anna 1892.33
Hook, Nina Warner 1960.07
Hook, Walter 1965.35
Hooker, Brian 1921.09, 1921.21, 1922.04, 1922.46, 1925.21, 1925.32, 1926.41, 1927.65, 1932.03, 1932.14, 1934.41, 1943.08, 1975.22
Hooker, Charles 1902.16
Hooker, John Lee 1999.09
Hooks, David 1954.03, 1970.02
Hooks, Robert 1967.06
Hooley, Rob 1885.49
Hooley, Robert 1883.66
Hoomer, Charles 1934.41
Hoon, Barbara 1989.03
Hoope, J. 1900.49
Hoope, Mme. 1890.50
Hooper, Claire 1921.20, 1928.07, 1930.37
Hooper, Cricket 1998.17
Hooper, H. 1913.06
Hooper, J.W. 1894.15
Hooper, Lee 1968.30, 1972.06
Hooper, Lewis 1900.51, 1902.05, 1902.34, 1902.40, 1904.40, 1906.04, 1907.30, 1920.09
Hooper, Oren 1899.04
Hoopes, Isabella 1953.03, 1958.05, 1959.27, 1961.09
Hooter, Mr. 1863.04
Hoots, Verenetta 1928.32
Hoover, Legotie 1919.35
Hoover, Peggy 1928.41
Hoover, William 1893.47
Hope, Anthony 1925.39
Hope, Arthur 1894.33, 1897.32
Hope, Bob 1927.48, 1928.35, 1932.16, 1933.26, 1934.35, 1936.02, 1936.26
Hope, Cecil 1894.33
Hope, Edward 1926.13, 1930.33
Hope, Faith 1931.02
Hope, Florence 1921.08
Hope, Flossie 1905.05, 1905.20, 1906.37, 1907.32, 1913.04
Hope, Francis 1900.56
Hope, Frank 1921.07
Hope, Gloria 1940.06
Hope, Lester 1927.48
Hope, Peggy 1921.27
Hope, Stephen 1982.03, 1997.19
Hope, Vida 1954.09
Hopes, Messr. 1851.05
Hopf, Herr 1879.17, 1879.22
Hopf, Max 1879.17
Hopgood, Miss 1873.24
Hopgood, Rose 1869.27
Hopkin, Jacob Mark 1983.05, 1983.10
Hopkins, Angus 1940.21
Hopkins, Arthur 1926.31
Hopkins, Benjamin 1899.11
Hopkins, Carlos 1902.02
Hopkins, Charles 1938.02
Hopkins, Clement 1898.11
Hopkins, David 1989.10
Hopkins, Ethel 1912.43, 1913.18, 1917.16
Hopkins, Hattie 1906.14, 1909.27
Hopkins, Ken 1950.12
Hopkins, Linda 1970.05, 1971.20, 1975.20, 1989.02
Hopkins, Maureen 1962.24, 1968.32
Hopkins, May 1904.40, 1908.15, 1908.39, 1909.29, 1910.02, 1913.07, 1917.32
Hopkins, Miriam 1923.24, 1927.66
Hopkins, Peggy 1917.13
Hopkins, Rober 1937.08
Hopkins, Ryan 1996.05, 1998.03
Hopkins, Violet 1909.04
Hopp, F.A. 1902.29
Hopp, Julius 1883.35
Hoppe, Carl 1932.20
Hoppe, Vera 1925.02
Hopper, Baron 1949.06
Hopper, C. Harrie 1884.46
Hopper, Charles 1892.52, 1893.32
Hopper, Charles H. 1893.50
Hopper, DeWolf 1882.50, 1885.14, 1885.28, 1885.45, 1885.52, 1885.67, 1886.26, 1886.33, 1886.37, 1886.43, 1887.12, 1887.18, 1887.22, 1887.24, 1887.26, 1887.28, 1887.47, 1888.19, 1888.22, 1888.24, 1888.26, 1889.17, 1889.22, 1890.16, 1891.11, 1892.22, 1892.33, 1892.47, 1893.16, 1894.24, 1896.13, 1897.10, 1898.13, 1898.48, 1900.38, 1901.17, 1903.02, 1904.17, 1905.36,

1908.41, 1910.12, 1911.21, 1912.18, 1912.21, 1912.22, 1912.23, 1913.08, 1913.11, 1913.12, 1913.13, 1913.23, 1913.33, 1915.06, 1915.09, 1915.10, 1915.12, 1915.13, 1915.14, 1917.08, 1918.23, 1921.01, 1921.18, 1922.16, 1928.26
Hopper, Edna Wallace 1894.24, 1897.10, 1898.13, 1900.01, 1900.51, 1902.35, 1906.29, 1908.09, 1911.08, 1918.02
Hopper, Irma 1928.21
Hopping, Irene 1913.04, 1913.26, 1914.30
Hopps, Stuart 1989.01
Hopwood, Aubrey 1898.46, 1900.28, 1900.52
Hopwood, Avery 1898.46, 1910.30, 1913.01, 1919.06, 1923.26, 1925.41, 1937.07
Horan, Bill 1949.17
Horan, E. 1872.16, 1882.71
Horan, Ed 1876.21, 1885.09
Horan, Ed. 1876.17, 1876.18, 1877.16, 1879.18
Horan, Ed. W. 1876.27
Horan, Edward 1872.18, 1873.18, 1873.21, 1873.23, 1879.23, 1879.24, 1922.05, 1930.35
Horan, Edward A. 1934.04
Horan, James 1887.50, 1888.32, 1893.14, 1894.02, 1898.31, 1898.55, 1899.22, 1900.07
Horan, James F. 1890.41, 1894.02
Horan, Mary 1929.44
Horan, Messr. 1879.23
Horase 1961.28
Horchow, Roger 1992.02, 1999.19
Horchus, Karl L. 1902.15
Horda, Dorian 1999.05
Horgan, Marie 1914.09, 1914.11, 1915.06, 1915.09, 1915.10, 1915.12, 1915.13, 1915.14, 1916.05
Horgan, Patrick 1959.01, 1965.02
Horii, Tina 1990.17
Horiuchi, Gen 1985.12
Hormby, Marie 1888.17
Horn, Angela 1995.10, 1996.11, 1997.02
Horn, Arthur 1947.07
Horn, Bob 1976.34
Horn, Christine 1943.03
Horn, Eph 1873.27
Horn, Frank 1927.17, 1928.26, 1930.27
Horn, Frank E. 1923.15
Horn, Frau 1880.20
Horn, Harald 1963.08
Horn, Kate 1852.01
Horn, Lena 1939.14
Horn, Roderick 1984.07
Horn, Thelka 1939.13
Horn, Van 1903.02, 1904.57
Hornaday, Frank 1941.02, 1943.06
Hornby, Marie 1889.06
Hornby, Mattie 1890.03
Horncastle, Henry 1839.01, 1855.04
Horncastle, James Henry 1840.03, 1840.04
Horncastle, Mr. 1838.01, 1855.02, 1855.05, 1855.06, 1855.08, 1855.09
Horne, C. Morton 1911.01, 1911.44, 1912.36, 1913.15
Horne, Geoffrey 1981.27
Horne, James 1909.19
Horne, Lena 1957.16, 1974.21, 1981.16
Horne, Marie 1909.29, 1918.01
Horne, Messr. 1851.01
Horne, Nat 1956.06, 1957.16, 1959.27, 1960.09, 1963.12, 1968.08, 1968.30, 1970.09
Horne, R. Morton 1914.15
Horne, Terry 1930.20
Horne, William 1942.20, 1944.16, 1944.26
Horner, Cara 1995.19, 1996.15
Horner, Carrie 1979.12
Horner, Harry 1937.01, 1941.04, 1941.08, 1941.13, 1942.18, 1943.03, 1943.23, 1953.01
Horner, Louise 1907.38
Horner, Paul 1983.20
Horner, Richard 1964.16, 1970.15, 1975.13, 1976.03
Horner, Sidney H. 1889.50, 1890.25
Horner, Wilma 1941.03
Hornez, Andre 1955.14, 1964.02, 1973.17
Hornick, Ethel 1898.18, 1898.26, 1898.29
Hornick, Harry 1933.07
Hornig, Alice 1902.09
Hornsbee, Leonard 1913.36
Hornsby, Hubert 1907.25
Hornsey, Leonard 1914.10
Hornung, Richard 1985.17
Horosko, Marian 1949.01
Horowitz, J. Ronald 1979.22
Horowitz, Jeffrey 2000.10
Horowitz, Jimmy 1981.24
Horowitz, Lawrence 1999.09
Horrigan, Patrick 1973.17
Horrocks, Esther 1960.01
Horse, Chief Eagle 1919.25
Horsefall, Te kani 1972.20
Horsley, Gus 1927.32
Horstmann, Del 1955.08, 1959.02, 1959.25, 1962.16, 1963.21, 1969.12, 1969.14
Hortense, Mlle. 1870.44, 1871.27, 1875.33
Horter, Max 1882.76, 1884.66, 1886.11, 1888.03
Horton, Alfred 1881.02
Horton, Asata Dafora 1934.16
Horton, Claude 1960.11
Horton, Edward Everett 1965.24
Horton, Frank 1927.66
Horton, H.H. 1891.01
Horton, Heloise 1903.18
Horton, James I. 1894.27
Horton, Jeanette 1908.03, 1908.42, 1910.10, 1912.10, 1914.02
Horton, John 1979.07, 1999.19
Horton, Julian 1897.02
Horton, Lottie 1876.03
Horton, Mr. 1854.06, 1854.07, 1921.42
Horton, Robert 1963.26
Horton, Roy 1954.08
Horton, Vaughn 1992.03
Horton, W.E. 1898.10
Horton, Walter 1914.08
Horton, Walter G. 1905.21
Horvath, James 1981.13, 1982.14
Horvath, Jan 1986.07, 1988.01, 1989.24
Horvath, Juliu 1974.16, 1975.16, 1976.23, 1977.11
Horwitt, Arnold B. 1937.14, 1945.18, 1948.04, 1948.14, 1952.20, 1955.01, 1959.23
Horwitz, Charles 1900.52, 1902.27, 1908.37
Horwitz, David 1974.06, 1978.02, 1981.12
Horwitz, J.J. 1909.21, 1913.04
Horwitz, Murray 1978.09, 1984.15, 1988.17
Hosbein, James 1977.06
Hoschna, Karl 1905.50, 1907.04, 1908.18, 1909.28, 1910.09, 1910.20, 1910.22, 1911.08, 1911.15, 1911.25, 1911.30, 1912.14, 1917.26, 1976.07, 1980.27
Hoschna, Karl L. 1900.07
Hosdez, Julie 1875.27, 1875.29, 1875.30, 1875.33
Hosford, Maud 1914.29
Hoshko, John 1989.25, 1995.07
Hoshour, Robert 1982.19, 1988.10
Hosie, Bill 1971.21
Hosier, Beverly 1938.13, 1945.20, 1948.30, 1952.03
Hoskins, Charles 1901.11, 1903.03, 1904.13, 1904.44
Hoskins, Messr. 1903.03, 1904.13, 1904.44
Hoskins, Sheldon B. 1943.24, 1945.06, 1946.09
Hosmer, Alice 1880.26, 1882.27, 1882.39, 1886.24, 1892.55, 1894.24, 1896.13, 1897.10, 1898.13, 1899.15, 1909.19
Hosmer, Lucius 1898.31, 1907.08
Host, Agnes 1983.16
Hoster, Henry 1906.43
Hostetter, Messr. 1886.36
Hostetter, Paula 1985.09, 1987.03, 1987.08, 1988.18, 1989.04, 1993.12, 1994.09
Hostettler, Andy 1975.06, 1980.16
Hoston, Jewel 1968.24
Hotchkiss, Mary 1922.13
Hotchkiss, Miss 1882.23
Hotchner, A.E. 1989.07
Hotopp, Michael J. 1976.35, 1979.16, 1979.31, 1980.26, 1981.25, 1983.21, 1991.04, 1991.13
Hotto, Harry 1872.13, 1873.08, 1895.37
Hotton, Donald 1959.05, 1963.09
Hoty, Dee 1981.03, 1989.29, 1991.07, 1994.06, 1998.13
Hoty, Tony 1989.27
Houck, Edna 1911.22
Houck, Jr., Ted 1980.01
Houck, Miss 1910.12
Houdin, Mons. 1868.27
Houdina, Mary Jane 1971.05, 1974.04, 1986.18
Houdini, Harry 1917.16, 1918.23
Hough, Lotty 1856.01, 1860.06, 1861.04
Hough, Mrs. 1854.04
Hough, Will M. 1904.54, 1907.14, 1907.25, 1908.13, 1908.23, 1909.02, 1909.31, 1920.32, 1942.30, 1955.14
Hough, William M. 1915.08
Hougham, Jill 1958.18
Houghton, Genevieve 1920.33
Houghton, Norris 1954.03, 1959.26
Hould-Ward, Ann 1984.08, 1987.18, 1992.09, 1994.04, 1997.05, 1999.16
Hould-Ward, Anne 1998.15
Houlihan, M.J. 1892.33
Houlle, Francoise 1958.06
Houloose, Jean 1947.17
House of Lanvin 1964.02
House, Billy 1928.27, 1933.20, 1948.20
House, Charles 1893.17, 1894.06, 1896.31
House, E.H. 1865.06, 1867.17, 1869.33, 1872.27, 1873.20, 1903.25
House, Jane 1954.15
Houseboat on the Styx, Inc., The 1928.49
Houseman, John 1934.05, 1937.08, 1939.20, 1941.05, 1946.05, 1959.09, 1973.16, 1976.30, 1982.02
Houser, Georgie 1888.08
Housley, Matt 1906.08, 1909.27
Hously, Angelo 1908.08
Hously, Matt 1908.08
Houssian, Mohammed 1925.37
Houston Grand Opera 1975.19, 1978.04, 1983.05
Houston, Bill 1936.26
Houston, Elizabeth 1932.05, 1936.01, 1942.21, 1944.17
Houston, Ethel 1915.04
Houston, Ethel Dufre 1912.10
Houston, George 1928.30, 1929.08, 1931.06, 1933.03, 1934.15, 1934.41
Houston, Gil 1947.21
Houston, Grace 1943.21, 1944.20, 1945.03, 1946.10, 1947.11, 1949.05, 1950.05
Houston, James P. 1928.47
Houston, Josephine 1934.19
Houston, Lee 1923.04
Houston, Lucie 1904.49
Houston, Tom 1930.15
Houston, William 1936.01
Hovell, W.E. 1913.37
Hoven, Johanne 1939.13
Hovenden, Peggy 1934.06, 1934.40
Hover, William 1895.16
Hoving, Lucas 1946.24, 1948.31, 1959.24
Hovis, Larry 1960.07, 1978.13
Howard Hall Amusement Company 1907.38
Howard, A. 1915.05
Howard, Adele 1925.02
Howard, Alan 1953.02
Howard, Alice 1900.48
Howard, Anna 1902.26, 1915.28
Howard, Annie 1879.37, 1879.68, 1880.09
Howard, Barron 1954.08
Howard, Bart 1953.17, 1990.09
Howard, Benjamin 1901.13, 1904.12
Howard, Bert 1905.47
Howard, Bessie 1897.36, 1899.28
Howard, Blanche 1887.30, 1890.21, 1891.26, 1897.21, 1905.43
Howard, Blanche M. 1892.09
Howard, Bob 1943.07
Howard, Bronson 1879.56, 1882.24, 1883.33
Howard, Bruce 1934.05, 1946.10
Howard, C. 1859.05, 1862.02
Howard, Charles 1857.04, 1877.20, 1883.38, 1894.44, 1904.11, 1905.42, 1907.56, 1919.25, 1924.13, 1929.08, 1944.23
Howard, Cheryl 1983.08
Howard, Chip 1886.53
Howard, Clute 1880.63
Howard, Clyde 1886.50
Howard, Curley 1939.25
Howard, Don 1929.26
Howard, Dos 1908.07
Howard, E. 1879.14
Howard, E.M. 1871.04
Howard, Edna 1923.24
Howard, Edward 1897.38, 1999.09
Howard, Ellen 1934.40
Howard, Elton 1945.16
Howard, Emma 1886.61, 1888.42, 1889.25
Howard, Estelle 1921.24
Howard, Esther 1920.29, 1923.05, 1925.14, 1925.33, 1927.35, 1928.29
Howard, Eugene 1912.24, 1914.01, 1915.11, 1916.23, 1918.20, 1920.47, 1922.34, 1925.07, 1926.16, 1928.22, 1929.35, 1931.30, 1932.16, 1932.24, 1934.01, 1935.18, 1936.31, 1939.25, 1941.03
Howard, F. 1876.30, 1882.15
Howard, F.K. 1879.06
Howard, F.M. 1882.18
Howard, Frank 1875.15, 1883.10, 1884.12, 1885.28, 1887.05, 1893.06
Howard, Frederic 1893.17
Howard, G. 1852.06, 1876.34
Howard, G.C. 1866.28, 1869.26
Howard, Garland 1930.19
Howard, George 1884.42, 1905.20
Howard, George H. 1886.47
Howard, George W. 1880.06, 1880.10, 1880.13, 1880.59, 1880.65, 1880.67, 1880.70, 1882.27, 1888.36, 1889.46, 1894.46, 1895.37, 1896.39
Howard, Graeme 1972.21
Howard, Gus 1931.28, 1931.39
Howard, H.C. 1931.03
Howard, H.H. 1881.26
Howard, Harry 1929.22, 1945.11
Howard, Harvey 1927.24
Howard, Helga 1902.16, 1903.04
Howard, II., Tulane 1976.20
Howard, Jack 1933.21, 1941.09, 1947.11
Howard, James 1932.24
Howard, Jan 1951.20
Howard, Jean 1897.51
Howard, Jerry 1962.04
Howard, Jim 1952.01, 1952.02
Howard, Joanna 1995.19
Howard, Joe 1904.13, 1942.30, 1976.09
Howard, John 1953.01
Howard, Jordon 1959.02, 1960.05
Howard, Joseph E. 1895.27, 1898.63, 1901.28, 1904.54, 1906.19, 1907.14, 1907.25, 1908.13, 1908.23, 1909.02, 1909.31, 1955.14, 1980.27, 1994.08
Howard, Josephine 1910.05
Howard, Karen 1983.19
Howard, Ken 1968.31, 1969.06, 1973.06, 1976.11
Howard, Kisha 1998.05
Howard, Larry 1954.02
Howard, Laurent 1892.34
Howard, Leah 1999.02
Howard, Lee 1959.22, 1960.06
Howard, Lillie 1887.43
Howard, Louise 1875.15
Howard, Madeline 1912.38, 1914.24
Howard, Marc 1978.06, 1979.06, 1979.10
Howard, Marcella 1938.05
Howard, May 1889.30, 1889.32, 1895.18
Howard, Mel 1985.07, 1986.17, 1989.02, 1991.11, 1993.08
Howard, Melvin 1943.24
Howard, Messr. 1864.13, 1882.34
Howard, Miss 1869.43, 1879.14, 1881.04, 1889.31
Howard, Moe 1939.25
Howard, Mr. 1851.04, 1852.03
Howard, Mrs. 1872.06
Howard, Mrs. Charles 1857.04, 1857.06
Howard, Nellie 1880.04, 1881.11, 1883.18
Howard, Nelly 1882.34, 1883.04
Howard, Noel 1992.03
Howard, Norah 1948.11, 1951.22
Howard, Paul 1929.03
Howard, Peter 1958.08, 1958.21, 1961.10, 1961.28, 1962.05, 1963.21, 1964.01, 1965.19, 1967.15, 1967.16, 1968.23, 1968.32, 1969.06, 1969.16, 1970.07, 1971.02, 1973.02, 1975.14, 1977.06, 1978.04, 1979.02, 1980.07, 1983.06, 1983.08, 1983.19, 1983.21, 1985.02, 1986.01, 1986.18, 1989.04, 1991.04, 1992.02, 1992.10, 1994.13, 1995.13, 1995.14, 1996.14, 1997.15, 1999.11, 1999.23
Howard, Philip 1891.24
Howard, Rita 1924.16
Howard, Robert 1957.18, 1961.28, 1964.11
Howard, Robin 1958.12
Howard, Rollin 1872.05, 1872.08, 1872.12, 1872.14
Howard, Shafter 1906.15
Howard, Shemp 1927.19, 1929.22
Howard, Sidney 1894.41, 1894.48, 1923.43, 1946.05, 1956.04, 1959.02, 1959.05, 1966.08, 1979.26, 1991.09, 1992.01
Howard, Stephen 1903.32

Howard, T.C. 1871.10
Howard, Tao 1905.25
Howard, Tom 1923.31, 1924.37, 1925.47, 1928.08, 1930.39, 1931.05, 1934.18
Howard, William 1885.33, 1890.17, 1920.07, 1924.16
Howard, Willie 1912.24, 1914.01, 1915.11, 1916.23, 1918.20, 1920.47, 1922.34, 1925.07, 1926.16, 1928.22, 1929.35, 1930.31, 1931.30, 1932.16, 1932.24, 1934.01, 1935.18, 1936.31, 1939.25, 1941.03, 1942.10, 1943.14, 1948.16
Howard. F. 1882.16
Howarde, Mr. 1852.04
Howden, Philip 1905.55
Howe, Beattie 1888.33
Howe, Bob 1977.05
Howe, Clara 1880.31
Howe, E.T. 1907.16
Howe, Edith 1895.04
Howe, Edward 1907.25
Howe, Fannie 1880.31
Howe, Frank 1905.43
Howe, Gary 1960.06
Howe, Henry 1938.08
Howe, Howard 1900.53
Howe, Jessie 1912.34
Howe, John 1905.09
Howe, Julia Ward 1955.13, 1975.22, 1990.05
Howe, Junius 1897.55, 1899.22
Howe, Katherine 1888.17, 1889.39
Howe, Katherine B. 1890.43, 1891.04
Howe, Laura 1892.12
Howe, Leo 1916.22
Howe, Linda 1961.20, 1965.24
Howe, Mabelle 1900.58
Howe, Mabelle Wallace 1896.06
Howe, Messr. 1882.34
Howe, Miss 1860.03, 1877.39, 1896.44
Howe, Mlle. 1871.18
Howe, W.R. 1897.55
Howe, William 1897.05
Howell 1892.38, 1893.23, 1894.34
Howell, Bert 1930.16
Howell, Billy 1946.13
Howell, Bobbie 1943.09
Howell, Edward 1919.38
Howell, Elizabeth 1955.08, 1959.24, 1965.35
Howell, Gail Cook 1998.06, 1999.11
Howell, Harry 1928.01, 1945.17
Howell, Helen 1927.27, 1928.34
Howell, Herman 1969.09
Howell, Ida 1887.43
Howell, James 1938.03
Howell, John Daggett 1948.31
Howell, Lawrence 1904.03
Howell, Lillian 1913.28
Howell, Lottice 1926.31, 1927.05
Howell, Mabel 1909.12
Howell, Miss 1857.01
Howell, Mr. 1865.05
Howell, Pearl 1924.10
Howell, Raynor 1947.04
Howell, Sarah 1857.04
Howell, Stephen 1995.18
Howell, Thomas 1949.01
Howell, Virginia 1927.49
Howell, William 1938.18, 1941.03
Howells, Reby 1963.21, 1965.14, 1968.24
Hower, Frank 1928.41
Howes, Bobby 1960.09
Howes, Carrol 1937.01
Howes, John 1949.06
Howes, Sally Ann 1961.24, 1962.15, 1963.04, 1964.05, 1990.07, 1991.08, 1993.14, 1995.18, 2000.01
Howig, Gustave 1895.29
Howitt, Bella 1871.08
Howitt, Belle 1870.02, 1870.07, 1872.02, 1872.04, 1872.05, 1872.08, 1872.12, 1872.14, 1872.25, 1872.30, 1872.40, 1872.43, 1878.05, 1879.12
Howkins, James 1927.53, 1930.06
Howland, Alice 1944.26
Howland, Beth 1964.16, 1968.02, 1970.13
Howland, E.W. 1886.60
Howland, J. 1873.26
Howland, J.B. 1866.28, 1867.12, 1868.06, 1869.26
Howland, J.H. 1873.25, 1873.26, 1881.02, 1881.20
Howland, Jason 1997.09, 1999.08, 1999.13
Howland, Jobyna 1900.58, 1901.19, 1903.38, 1905.28, 1912.24, 1915.32, 1918.06
Howland, Katherine 1903.31, 1908.16, 1908.24
Howland, Kathryn 1901.11, 1901.17
Howland, Kathryne 1905.44
Howland, Kitty 1906.33
Howland, Olin 1913.08, 1913.16, 1917.17, 1919.09, 1919.37, 1920.08, 1921.10, 1922.13, 1922.46, 1923.05, 1927.63, 1930.18
Howland, W.A. 1894.08
Howlett, Lloyd 1940.01
Howlett, Stanley 1921.05
Howson English Opera Company 1872.20
Howson, Albert 1917.24, 1919.20, 1923.12
Howson, Albert S. 1912.24
Howson, Celia 1869.39
Howson, Emma 1869.41, 1870.40, 1871.10, 1872.17, 1872.20, 1872.23, 1872.35, 1881.21, 1882.14
Howson, Frank 1881.21, 1929.30
Howson, Frank A. 1872.16, 1872.18, 1872.19, 1872.20, 1873.18, 1873.21, 1873.23
Howson, John 1872.20, 1876.17, 1876.18, 1876.21, 1876.27, 1877.16, 1880.47, 1880.69, 1881.36, 1881.38, 1882.06, 1882.42, 1882.70, 1883.04, 1883.10, 1883.38, 1884.21
Howson, John J. 1869.39
Hoxit, Linda 1982.14
Hoxworth, Mary Ann 1954.16
Hoy, Anna 1917.22
Hoy, Marietta 1917.22
Hoy, Mary 1917.22
Hoye, Vonnie 1910.18
Hoyem, Robert 1959.04
Hoyer, Roy 1917.12, 1920.36, 1923.40, 1924.26, 1928.46, 1929.09
Hoyle, Geoff 1997.20
Hoylen, Anthony 1985.17
Hoym, Frau 1866.33
Hoysradt, John 1936.02, 1944.15
Hoyt 1888.18, 1894.14
Hoyt and McKee's Comedy Company 1894.37
Hoyt, Andrew J. 1889.40
Hoyt, Charles 1912.13, 1916.22
Hoyt, Charles H. 1883.26, 1884.16, 1884.37, 1884.48, 1886.28, 1886.40, 1887.29, 1888.32, 1888.44, 1889.12, 1890.04, 1890.32, 1890.41, 1891.39, 1892.18, 1892.45, 1893.14, 1893.31, 1894.02, 1894.07, 1894.35, 1894.37, 1895.39, 1896.02, 1896.31, 1897.01, 1897.34, 1898.47, 1918.32
Hoyt, Edith 1888.39, 1891.24
Hoyt, Estella 1888.29, 1897.24
Hoyt, Estelle 1899.21
Hoyt, H. 1885.05
Hoyt, H.E. 1879.63, 1880.07, 1883.48
Hoyt, Harriet 1935.01
Hoyt, Henry 1880.37, 1881.35, 1884.14, 1884.25, 1884.34, 1884.57, 1885.41, 1886.37, 1891.36, 1892.28, 1892.60, 1896.35
Hoyt, Henry E. 1877.20, 1880.17, 1880.55, 1881.03, 1881.22, 1881.41, 1885.14, 1886.04, 1886.30, 1886.50, 1887.33, 1887.50, 1888.02, 1888.18, 1888.20, 1889.04, 1889.16, 1889.23, 1889.40, 1889.49, 1890.01, 1890.24, 1890.26, 1891.12, 1891.22, 1891.30, 1891.31, 1892.03, 1892.07, 1892.14, 1892.16, 1892.17, 1892.55, 1893.07, 1893.20, 1894.22, 1894.40, 1894.48, 1895.09, 1895.12, 1895.24, 1895.38, 1896.10, 1896.12, 1896.27, 1896.28, 1897.20, 1897.36, 1897.45, 1898.11, 1898.29, 1898.46, 1899.19, 1899.21, 1899.35, 1899.41, 1900.07, 1900.39, 1900.43, 1902.30, 1903.32, 1905.18
Hoyt, Henry M. 1890.03
Hoyt, Henry T. 1897.44, 1898.18
Hoyt, Howard 1955.04
Hoyt, John 1953.02
Hoyt, Jr., J.Q. 1879.65
Hoyt, Kate 1884.32
Hoyt, Leo 1931.09
Hoyt, Leonard B. 1906.19
Hoyt, Lon 1982.22, 1983.19, 1997.21
Hoyt, Messr. 1885.63, 1886.36, 1886.54
Hoyt, Nellie 1884.41
Hoyt, Peggy 1921.29, 1922.47
Hoyt, Stella 1894.05
Hoyt, Vonnie 1904.15, 1906.01
Hsu, Emily 1997.17, 2001.03
Hsu, Mark 1976.02
Hsu, Y.Y. 1931.39
HTG Productions 2001.07
Huara, Helba 1927.19
Huard, Jeffrey 1993.09, 1994.08
Huata, Bernadette 1972.20
Huata, Hemi 1972.20
Huata, Ngamoni 1972.20
Huata, Paraire 1972.20
Hubart, M. 1916.15
Hubbard, A.J. 1880.48, 1882.07, 1882.11, 1882.12, 1882.13, 1883.11, 1883.12, 1883.14
Hubbard, Alma 1943.15, 1944.03
Hubbard, Alma L. 1951.11
Hubbard, Anna 1894.52
Hubbard, Bruce 1983.05
Hubbard, Bruce A. 1978.03
Hubbard, Elizabeth 1966.09, 1979.12, 1983.08
Hubbard, J.B. 1931.02
Hubbard, Jugh J. 1980.30
Hubbard, Karen 1975.21
Hubbard, Marjorie 1928.18
Hubbard, Valeska 1934.41
Hubbell, Raymond 1903.14, 1905.03, 1905.55, 1906.07, 1906.29, 1906.44, 1907.59, 1909.11, 1909.28, 1910.01, 1910.34, 1911.24, 1911.42, 1912.12, 1912.13, 1912.38, 1913.17, 1914.15, 1915.05, 1915.24, 1916.07, 1916.15, 1916.20, 1916.22, 1917.13, 1917.16, 1918.15, 1918.18, 1918.23, 1919.05, 1919.22, 1919.41, 1920.26, 1921.24, 1922.16, 1922.30, 1923.20, 1923.33, 1924.18, 1924.33, 1925.05, 1925.10, 1925.24, 1927.07, 1928.11, 1928.37
Hubbell, Walter 1883.47
Huber, Jeremiah Todd 2001.04
Huber, Kim 1999.22
Huber, Paul 1927.05, 1930.30, 1930.40, 1938.18
Huber, Rose 1913.28
Hubert of Paris 1925.02
Hubert, Frank 1924.20, 1939.22, 1942.18
Hubert, Fritz 1934.20
Hubert, Irene 1931.35
Hubert, Janet L. 1981.28, 1982.19
Hubert, Jean 1929.26, 1934.20, 1939.22, 1942.18
Hubert, Rene 1964.24
Hubner, Frau 1866.33
Hubon, Cora 1889.51
Huchet, Mme. 1875.25, 1875.27, 1875.28, 1875.29, 1875.30, 1875.33
Hudak, Julia 1927.28
Hudd, Daisy 1915.05
Huddart, John F. 1885.41
Huddleston, David 1981.28
Huddleston, Floyd 1952.08
Huddleston, Jessie 1895.28
Huddleston, John L. 1907.19
Hudes, Watty 1900.48
Hudgins, Johnny 1924.27, 1925.18, 1930.24
Hudgins, Marilyn 1978.04, 1989.25
Hudson Productions Company, Inc. 1922.17
Hudson Shad 1999.05
Hudson, Anna 1907.26
Hudson, Don 1933.25
Hudson, Eliza S. 1888.08
Hudson, Geraldine 1942.18
Hudson, Harry 1904.29, 1906.23
Hudson, Helen 1923.18, 1924.19, 1925.22, 1941.03
Hudson, James 1852.06, 1853.04
Hudson, Jr., Alfred 1906.23
Hudson, Judith 1980.28
Hudson, Lillian 1901.27, 1902.43, 1904.56, 1905.22, 1907.08
Hudson, Mr. 1852.03, 1852.04
Hudson, Muriel 1916.17
Hudson, R. 1902.15
Hudson, Ray 1935.04, 1942.18
Hudson, Richard 1997.20
Hudson, Roland 1929.09
Hudson, Sunshine 1935.04
Hudson, Teddie 1919.01
Hudson, Teddy 1910.17, 1911.11, 1912.28, 1914.26, 1915.05, 1915.28, 1916.07, 1916.19, 1917.12, 1924.30
Hudson, Travis 1961.11, 1962.02, 1966.05, 1975.24, 1979.02
Hudson, Virginia Tyler 1907.03
Hudson, W.A. 1880.26
Hudson, Walter 1984.02
Hudson, Will 1939.29, 1940.16, 1987.02
Huebner, C. 1875.21
Huebner, F.C. 1883.09
Huehn, Julius 1931.46
Hueist, Charles 1883.44
Huelsman, Marilyn Kay 1993.18
Huerting, Elsa 1903.04
Huesel, Emil 1892.54
Huestis, Belle 1882.04
Huey, Richard 1941.12, 1944.23
Huff, Betty 1948.24
Huff, Carrie 1931.47
Huff, F.W. 1879.13
Huff, Forest 1913.28, 1914.33
Huff, Forrest 1905.28, 1909.17, 1912.04, 1912.27, 1914.10, 1918.05, 1921.34, 1923.12, 1927.65, 1930.12
Huff, Leon 1997.21
Huffine, Charles 1946.10
Huffman, Cady 1991.07, 2001.05
Huffman, Chet 1918.01
Huffman, J.C. 1894.12, 1895.14, 1907.10, 1907.41, 1908.10, 1908.21, 1908.29, 1911.12, 1911.32, 1911.35, 1911.36, 1912.09, 1912.17, 1913.02, 1913.23, 1913.29, 1914.16, 1914.20, 1914.22, 1914.24, 1915.02, 1915.04, 1915.11, 1915.26, 1916.03, 1916.11, 1916.23, 1917.08, 1917.14, 1917.23, 1917.31, 1918.01, 1918.05, 1918.06, 1918.12, 1918.20, 1919.03, 1919.16, 1919.30, 1919.35, 1920.02, 1920.19, 1920.33, 1920.47, 1921.14, 1921.31, 1921.34, 1922.11, 1922.15, 1922.34, 1922.40, 1923.02, 1923.12, 1923.14, 1923.15, 1923.17, 1923.41, 1924.12, 1924.23, 1924.29, 1924.45, 1925.01, 1925.26, 1925.39, 1926.01, 1926.05, 1926.15, 1926.27, 1926.33, 1926.37, 1927.17, 1927.42, 1927.55, 1927.58, 1927.68, 1928.14, 1928.15, 1930.27, 1932.06
Huffman, Rosanna 1965.14
Huffman, Ted 1990.02
Huffmann, J.C. 1926.14
Hufford, Nick 1938.03
Huffstodt, Karen 1983.12
Hugel, Herb 1979.18
Huget, Mons. 1882.61
Hugh, Jimmy 1939.29
Hughes, Adelaide 1915.22
Hughes, Allen Lee 1990.12, 1991.01
Hughes, Anthony 1918.09, 1919.03, 1924.47, 1930.08
Hughes, Arthur 1936.12, 1967.16
Hughes, B.B. 1876.16
Hughes, Barnard 1967.16
Hughes, Beatrice 1917.03, 1917.22
Hughes, Billy 1930.22
Hughes, C.A. 1913.08
Hughes, Carolyn 1933.04
Hughes, D.B. 1885.46, 1888.33
Hughes, Dick 1947.11
Hughes, Dickson 1960.07
Hughes, Edith 1921.15
Hughes, Esther 1851.04
Hughes, Florence 1905.14
Hughes, Hughie 1884.44
Hughes, J. Early 1906.43
Hughes, J.J. 1919.03, 1927.03
Hughes, J.M. 1864.17
Hughes, Jack 1927.52
Hughes, James 1905.13, 1915.06
Hughes, Jennie 1870.19, 1870.21, 1872.07, 1873.22, 1873.27, 1875.31, 1875.40, 1876.22, 1876.29, 1877.15, 1880.55, 1882.17, 1882.51, 1882.63, 1882.66, 1883.31, 1883.67
Hughes, John 1923.37
Hughes, Johnny 1915.22, 1921.20
Hughes, Julie 1973.03
Hughes, Langston 1937.14, 1947.02, 1950.16, 1957.09, 1959.08, 1959.17, 1963.15, 1963.27, 1966.02, 1966.15, 1978.23, 1979.27, 1989.12, 1990.08, 1991.01, 1999.06
Hughes, Leila 1912.17, 1913.14, 1914.09, 1914.12, 1915.08
Hughes, Lizzie 1886.14
Hughes, M. 1884.64
Hughes, Maritn A. 2001.04
Hughes, Mary 1898.02
Hughes, Master 1865.09
Hughes, Messr. 1861.06, 1870.19, 1886.36
Hughes, Michaela K. 1983.02, 1983.10
Hughes, Mick 1989.01
Hughes, Mildred 1948.28, 1950.09, 1955.11
Hughes, Miss 1870.13

Hughes, Mme. 1897.30
Hughes, Nellie 1897.42
Hughes, P. 1887.27
Hughes, Professor 1880.43
Hughes, R. 1852.02
Hughes, Ray 1925.25
Hughes, Revella 1923.39, 1929.25, 1930.24
Hughes, Rhetta 1972.10, 1979.15, 1983.15, 1987.07
Hughes, Richard 1868.05, 1946.03
Hughes, Robert 1945.16
Hughes, Rupert 1895.23, 1902.27, 1902.34, 1902.40, 1918.09
Hughes, Stanley 1918.13
Hughes, T. Penry 1936.14, 1939.01, 1939.08
Hughes, William 1880.35, 1881.47
Hugill, Randy 1980.01
Hugnes, J.J. 1910.19
Hugo Baruch and Cie. 1909.22, 1910.28, 1912.10
Hugo Baruch and Company 1897.29
Hugo, Victor 1873.05, 1886.26, 1888.41, 1987.04
Huguely, Jay 1982.13
Huguet, Mons. 1882.53, 1883.28
Huist 1883.62
Hujer, Flower 1942.15, 1944.01
Hulbert, Jack 1924.01, 1925.50, 1947.15
Hulen, Harold 1919.19
Hulett, Otto 1928.19, 1929.20, 1930.18, 1930.33
Hulicius, Otto 1925.20, 1926.17, 1927.23
Hull, Alizon 1979.27
Hull, Arthur Stuart 1917.36
Hull, Camilla 1938.18
Hull, J. Warren 1925.02
Hull, Warren 1927.42, 1928.08
Hull, Weslyn 1921.29
Hulson, Messr. 1868.06
Hultman, Robert L. 1965.01, 1968.32, 1972.24
Hultman, Rune 1943.23
Humans, Maria 1941.03
Humason, Sally 1926.13, 1930.18, 1930.33
Humbert, Eugene 1884.50, 1888.07
Hume, Edward 1908.13
Hume, Edward W. 1893.27, 1893.36, 1893.46
Hume, Elaine 1948.20
Hume, Marylou 1982.14
Hume, Nancy 1987.19
Hume, Thomas 1945.20
Humerson, A.S. 1911.11, 1912.28
Humes, Helen 1999.06
Hummel, Mark 1981.07, 1981.28, 1983.01, 1983.09, 1984.14, 1985.19, 1988.20, 1992.04, 1992.18, 1993.02, 2001.03
Hummel, Miss 1882.45, 1882.60
Hummel, S. 1883.44
Hummel, Sophie 1880.34, 1880.57, 1881.03, 1883.16, 1883.39, 1883.52, 1884.06, 1884.31, 1884.36, 1884.59, 1885.29, 1885.51, 1885.62
Hummell, Miss 1881.07
Humperdinck, Engelbert 1895.28
Humphrey, Cavada 1948.28
Humphrey, Dick 1955.02
Humphrey, Doris 1933.04, 1933.24, 1944.32, 1950.16
Humphrey, F.S. 1912.33
Humphrey, Fred W. 1869.23
Humphrey, George L. 1901.01
Humphrey, John 1879.25, 1879.67
Humphrey, Joseph M. 1880.63
Humphrey, Orral 1898.61
Humphrey, Richard 1956.09
Humphrey, William 1889.12
Humphreys, Dorothy 1925.35, 1927.27, 1928.49, 1929.19
Humphreys, Dorotny Loring 1927.05
Humphreys, Gillian 1964.36, 1964.41, 1964.42
Humphreys, H.W. 1899.34
Humphreys, Harry 1908.42, 1911.25
Humphreys, Joseph 1894.24, 1899.03
Humphreys, Kalita 1941.08
Humphreys, Pauline 1901.20
Humphries, Barry 1963.01, 1999.14
Humphries, Dorothy 1930.35
Humphries, H.R. 1879.08, 1879.14, 1879.58, 1879.71, 1881.26
Humphries, H.W. 1869.23
Humphries, Joseph 1899.27, 1900.36
Humphries, Julie 1947.17
Humphries, Kalita 1938.18
Humphries, Ruth 1907.41
Humphry, Ola 1899.35
Hun, Ben 1894.52
Hundley, John 1925.34, 1926.07, 1928.34, 1929.02, 1929.12, 1929.42, 1932.27
Hunger, Gigi 1984.09
Hunn, Ben 1902.38
Hunn, Mrs. Ben 1902.38
Hunnerwell, Clyde 1913.19
Hunnewell, Clyde 1907.25, 1922.42, 1923.19
Hunsberger, Herbert 1978.19, 1978.20, 1978.23, 1979.21, 1979.27, 1980.21, 1981.20
Hunsen, Mr. 1875.03
Hunster, Lewis 1899.33
Hunt, Bradford 1922.47
Hunt, Constance 1913.04
Hunt, Don 1979.14
Hunt, Doug 1966.08
Hunt, Edward 1959.03
Hunt, Edward A. 1938.08, 1939.26
Hunt, Elizabeth 1924.12
Hunt, Ella 1883.36
Hunt, Estelle 1926.22, 1929.50
Hunt, F.H. 1882.45
Hunt, G.W. 1888.38
Hunt, Grady 1961.16
Hunt, Ida Brooks 1908.24, 1909.22, 1929.43
Hunt, J. Homer 1906.50
Hunt, Jay 1881.23, 1885.46, 1885.65
Hunt, Lillie 1883.22
Hunt, Lois 1952.13
Hunt, Lulu 1933.04
Hunt, Marie 1931.09
Hunt, Master 1879.38
Hunt, Messr. 1851.05
Hunt, Minnie 1897.32
Hunt, Mlle. 1873.10
Hunt, Mr. 1851.03
Hunt, Peter 1963.27, 1965.22, 1965.24, 1966.12, 1966.16, 1968.18, 1968.19, 1969.06, 1970.03, 1997.19
Hunt, Peter H. 1975.06
Hunt, R.W. 1905.57, 1907.36
Hunt, Ray 1927.46
Hunt, Richard 1892.39
Hunt, Tina 1905.50
Hunter, Alberta 1930.19, 1982.12
Hunter, Alison McLellan 1931.36, 1932.01
Hunter, Anne 1938.12
Hunter, Archie 1892.53
Hunter, Bessie 1879.42
Hunter, Charles A. 1909.10
Hunter, Clara 1894.36
Hunter, Colin 1926.38
Hunter, Cornelia 1905.09
Hunter, Diana 1959.22, 1963.12
Hunter, Eddie 1923.11, 1926.19, 1933.27
Hunter, Edna 1898.46, 1900.01, 1900.50, 1901.21, 1910.17, 1912.02, 1914.26
Hunter, Florence 1928.16
Hunter, Frank 1902.44
Hunter, Frederick 1947.09
Hunter, G. Harrison 1907.09
Hunter, George 1934.15
Hunter, Gigi 1984.09
Hunter, Glenn 1929.12
Hunter, Hal 1945.18
Hunter, Harry 1875.40, 1877.21, 1878.02, 1879.01, 1880.02, 1880.40, 1882.39, 1923.11
Hunter, Henry 1879.06
Hunter, I. 1986.02
Hunter, Ian McLellan 1964.04
Hunter, Ivy Jo 1997.21
Hunter, Jacquelyn 1922.26
Hunter, James 1907.39, 1922.09
Hunter, JoAnn M. 1989.03, 1990.17, 1991.03, 1997.07
Hunter, Kenneth 1911.06
Hunter, Laurie Ann 1992.14
Hunter, Leslye 1960.10
Hunter, Louise 1927.63
Hunter, Marie 1882.17, 1883.33
Hunter, Mark 1962.18
Hunter, Mary 1945.13, 1948.17, 1950.06, 1954.13
Hunter, Messr. 1864.22
Hunter, Mr. 1864.17, 1865.05, 1872.24
Hunter, Nina 1923.11
Hunter, Oliver 1918.38
Hunter, Raymond 1923.01
Hunter, Robert 1961.01
Hunter, Scott 1959.25
Hunter, Tim 1999.10, 2001.09
Hunter, Timothy 1997.11, 1998.06
Hunter, Walt 1966.12, 1966.16, 1975.07
Hunter, William Gregg 1982.22
Hunting, Dorothy 1904.31
Hunting, John 1900.24
Hunting, Louis 1900.24
Hunting, Mollie 1900.24
Hunting, Mons. 1879.50
Hunting, Mr. 1879.56
Hunting, P. 1879.50
Hunting, Russell 1892.38
Hunting, Tony 1913.18
Huntington, Agnes 1890.33, 1892.08, 1892.10
Huntington, Bessie 1891.02
Huntington, Grace 1896.05
Huntington, Mae 1900.06, 1900.23
Huntington, Martier-Raymond 1965.05
Huntington, May 1899.42
Huntington, Rex 1965.05, 1981.17
Huntington, Van 1899.11, 1900.59
Huntley, Barbara 1903.22, 1909.01
Huntley, Fred 1903.21
Huntley, G.P. 1903.22, 1909.01, 1920.39, 1924.30
Huntley, Hugh 1928.24
Huntley, Jack 1936.07
Huntley, Jobe 1963.27
Huntley, Jr., G.P. 1928.42, 1932.26
Huntley, Marian 1935.17
Huntley, Messr. 1893.13
Huntley, Miss 1851.05
Huntley, Mr. 1887.10
Huntley, P. 1924.09
Huntley, Raymond 1931.06
Huntly, Fred W. 1905.18
Hupfeld, Herman 1926.15, 1927.38, 1929.19, 1930.25, 1931.14, 1931.36, 1932.13, 1932.20, 1932.24, 1936.31, 1950.03, 1957.01, 1997.01, 1999.05
Hupfield, Herman 1933.20
Hurd, Alex 1940.16, 1942.19
Hurd, Denny 1972.25
Hurd, Earl 1979.28
Hurd, George 1921.32
Hurd, Jane 1924.11
Hurd, Miss 1873.26
Hurd, W.S. 1882.62
Hurd, William S. 1885.33, 1890.17
Hurd-Sharlein, Adrienne 1989.20
Hurdle, Lawrence 1942.34
Hurgon, Austen 1907.63, 1911.01, 1914.32
Hurgon, Austin 1909.01, 1911.02
Hurlburt, Gladys 1940.06
Hurlburt, Jackie 1924.33
Hurlbut, Jackie 1929.06
Hurlbut, William J. 1911.13
Hurleigh, Franclyn 1891.46
Hurley, Arthur 1926.42
Hurley, Catherine 1976.29
Hurley, Edward 1930.24
Hurley, J. 1858.03, 1866.16, 1868.08, 1869.13
Hurley, J. Albert 1934.07, 1934.08, 1934.09, 1934.10, 1934.11, 1936.04, 1936.08, 1936.09, 1936.10, 1936.11
Hurley, Julia 1923.14
Hurley, Laurel 1953.06, 1954.04, 1954.10, 1954.14
Hurley, Messr. 1868.16
Hurley, Mr. 1857.08, 1860.03, 1860.05, 1863.07, 1866.17, 1867.15, 1867.16, 1869.04, 1869.34, 1872.09
Hurley, Oliver 1976.29
Hurley, W.J. 1869.15
Hurly, Mr. 1860.04
Hurman, Annie 1899.36
Hurok, Sol 1932.09, 1932.29, 1937.05, 1943.17, 1944.31, 1949.07, 1950.07, 1955.26, 1962.25, 1962.26, 1962.28, 1962.29, 1962.30, 1962.31, 1964.06, 1964.29, 1964.36, 1964.37, 1964.38, 1964.41, 1964.42, 1964.43, 1966.22, 1966.23, 1966.26, 1966.28, 1968.25, 1968.26, 1968.27, 1968.28, 1968.29, 1972.15
Hurst, Catherine 1912.14
Hurst, David 1988.09
Hurst, Dorothy 1925.50
Hurst, Frank 1921.25
Hurst, Howard 1989.17, 1990.05
Hurst, James 1956.12, 1961.18
Hurst, Katherine 1916.22, 1917.06
Hurst, Lou 1945.18
Hurst, Manola Mada 1904.03
Hurst, Sophie 1989.17, 1990.05
Hurst, Vera 1929.33
Hurt, Jo 1947.21
Hurtig and Seamon 1907.55
Hurtig, Jules 1900.46, 1903.08, 1904.26, 1904.58, 1905.42, 1906.08
Hurwitt, Lawrence 1974.04
Hurwitz, Stan 1974.26
Husel, Emil 1880.36, 1880.64, 1881.09, 1882.02, 1884.41, 1885.02, 1892.44
Husel, Master 1879.68, 1880.09
Husk, Harry 1908.03
Husmann, Ron 1959.25, 1960.19, 1962.04, 1970.21, 1971.15, 1981.13
Hussein, Ahmed 1981.25
Hussey, James 1916.11, 1921.25
Hussey, Jimmy 1921.25, 1922.23, 1923.22, 1925.05, 1926.51
Hussey, John 1965.39
Hussey, St. George 1889.05
Hussung, Will 1955.04, 1968.03
Huston, Carla 1965.04
Huston, Jon 1971.01
Huston, Josephine 1932.18, 1933.01, 1933.07
Huston, Philip 1938.12
Huston, Walter 1938.11
Hutch, Willie 1982.22
Hutcherson, Abbi 1998.21
Hutcherson, LeVern 1945.06, 1946.09, 1953.04
Hutcheson, David 1929.44, 1931.28
Hutchings, Alice 1880.38
Hutchings, Edith 1898.29
Hutchins 1911.17
Hutchins, Brice 1934.01
Hutchins, Colleen 1953.17
Hutchins, Edith 1898.46, 1900.39, 1903.03, 1903.39
Hutchins, Harriet 1934.18
Hutchins, Mr. 1859.03
Hutchinson, Ann 1945.11, 1945.20, 1947.03
Hutchinson, Art 1962.15, 1963.04
Hutchinson, Catherine 1902.15
Hutchinson, Denis 1997.14
Hutchinson, E.S. 1921.19
Hutchinson, Ed 1915.17
Hutchinson, Edward 1916.06, 1917.26, 1918.02, 1920.07
Hutchinson, Ernest 1891.02
Hutchinson, Josephine 1932.28
Hutchinson, Kathryn 1905.25, 1906.37, 1907.46
Hutchinson, Mary 1926.24
Hutchison, Chad 1990.20
Hutchison, Edward 1902.21, 1903.03
Hutchison, Jim 1954.05, 1956.16
Huth, Maud 1897.40, 1898.67
Huther, Mrs. 1868.23, 1868.32
Huthinson, Mark Michael 1993.07
Hutner, Rosalynd 1934.29
Hutson, David 1998.22
Hutson, Eric 1948.07, 1986.12
Hutton, Betty 1940.03, 1940.19
Hutton, Bill 1982.03
Hutton, Timothy 1995.03
Huxhold, Kristin 1998.20, 1999.21
Huxley, Carroll 1959.26
Huyler, Frank 1932.14
Hwang, David Henry 2000.06
Hyams, John 1897.34, 1900.41, 1901.18, 1901.27, 1904.15, 1914.17
Hyams, Paul 1981.27
Hyatt, Betty 1963.05
Hyatt, Edan 1918.25
Hyatt, F. Stuart 1902.25, 1903.36
Hyatt, John Kenneth 1937.10
Hyatt, Stuart 1900.37, 1901.29, 1902.05, 1902.10
Hybelmann, Martha 1898.34
Hyde Walter 1886.02
Hyde, Alexander 1918.17
Hyde, Blanche 1910.36
Hyde, Bruce 1969.04
Hyde, Frances 1925.17
Hyde, Harry 1894.17, 1907.48, 1909.19
Hyde, Helen 1916.26
Hyde, Henry 1902.34, 1902.40
Hyde, J.W. 1898.66
Hyde, James 1893.33, 1903.35
Hyde, Lottie 1889.05, 1889.34
Hyde, Miss 1873.03
Hyde, Nettie 1909.30
Hyde, Raymond Newton 1917.07
Hyde, T. 1868.06
Hyde, Victor 1908.27, 1909.30, 1910.36
Hyde, Walter 1912.19

Hydes, Watty 1883.26, 1891.14, 1892.18, 1892.19, 1894.13, 1896.50, 1898.69, 1899.35, 1900.55, 1903.34, 1905.19, 1907.37, 1908.04, 1910.05, 1912.28
Hye, Melvin 1893.32
Hyem, Constance 1904.29
Hyem, Dorothy 1890.50
Hyers, Frank 1940.19
Hylan, Donald 1921.30
Hyland, Gus 1930.25
Hyland, Katherine 1905.49
Hyland, Lily 1924.14, 1925.20, 1926.17, 1928.19
Hyland, Lily M. 1922.20
Hylands, Fred 1893.37, 1905.35
Hylands, Marie 1904.07, 1905.35
Hyldoft, Joan 1946.14, 1947.12
Hyle, Therese 1931.27
Hylton, Evelyn 1939.22
Hylton, Jack 1958.18, 1964.03
Hylton, Kate 1939.22
Hylton, Margo 1939.22
Hyman, Dick 1975.09, 1979.25, 1980.10
Hyman, Joseph M. 1948.04
Hyman, Larry 1976.25, 1981.07
Hyman, Phyllis 1981.06
Hyman, Rob 2000.16
Hyman, Robert 1982.03
Hyman, Sarah Ellis 1927.18
Hymes, John 1905.39
Hymes, Virginia 1983.04
Hynd, Ghretta 1988.05
Hynd, Ronald 1976.18
Hynes, Elizabeth 1979.20, 1980.04, 1981.20, 1982.16, 1984.12, 1985.09
Hynes, Harry 1911.25
Hynes, James 1878.17, 1879.04
Hyperion Theatricals 2000.06
Hyrt, Nell 1940.04
Hyson, Carl 1917.06, 1917.13, 1918.02, 1918.16, 1919.04, 1919.43, 1920.12, 1920.37
Hyson, Ray 1952.10, 1954.02, 1955.01, 1961.11
Hytner, Nicholas 1991.03, 1994.02

I.W. Norcross Opera Company 1882.45
Iacovelli, John 1998.18
Iannucci, Michael P. 1965.05, 1981.17
Iauco, Dianne 1985.10
Ibrahim, Mohammid 1931.09
Ibsen, Henrik 1924.15, 1982.18
Icarus Productions 1977.06
Ida, Miss 1887.40
Ida, Mlle. 1869.26, 1870.31
Ide, Leonard 1926.38
Ideal Extravaganza Company 1890.03
Ideal, Amelie 1934.15
Idle, Eric 1976.06, 2000.18
Igarashi, Linda 1990.17
Iglesias, Franco 1969.11
Igoe, Grace 1903.03
Igoe, Miss 1903.03
Ijaky, Josef 1970.17
Ikeda, Thomas 1987.03, 1992.17
Ilan 1968.04
Ilanit 1968.04
Ileo, J. 1969.11
Illes, Mary 1997.07
Illica, Luigi 1996.09
Illman, Margaret 1993.19
Illo, Frank 1926.19
Ilma, Alfred 1925.41
Ilo, Angelique 2000.07
Imagination Company, Ltd., An 1994.11
Imai, Noaji 1989.21
Imano, H.M. 1892.20
Imano, R.S. 1884.64
Imano, Signor 1884.36
Imbimbo, Ines 1911.19
Imero Fiorentino Associates 1975.05
Imeson, A.B. 1929.51
Imfrey, Clara 1879.65, 1879.67
Imhof, Roger 1923.07
Immerman, Connie 1929.23
Immerman, George 1929.23
Immerman, Joseph 1900.58
Imperato, Arthur 1934.36
Imperato, Carlo 1978.11
Imperia, Lina 1912.09
Imperial Burlesque Company 1887.32
Imperial Opera Company 1891.23
Imree, Miss 1872.22
Imrie, James 1873.08
Imrie, Mr. 1872.24
Ince, Emma Jones 1889.46
Ince, J.E. 1878.05
Ince, John 1892.25
Ince, John E. 1880.25, 1888.34
Ince, Jr., John C. 1900.36
Ince, Lionel 1952.02
Ince, Lottie 1881.26
Ince, Miss 1841.01
Inch, Minnie 1894.18
Inch, Reuben 1894.18
Incomes Company, Ltd., The 1977.05
Incoronato, Anna 1985.14
Incrocci, Agenore 1986.06
Industrial FX Productions, Inc. 1990.10
Inescourt, Frieda 1926.41
Ing, Alvin 1976.02
Ingalls, James 1984.02
Ingalls, Phil 1947.20, 1950.09
Inge, Clara 1905.30
Inge, Matthew 1976.36
Ingersoll, Robert G. 1895.18
Ingersoll, William 1905.45, 1918.01, 1920.40
Ingham, Barrie 1981.12, 1981.26, 1997.09
Ingham, Eleanor 1905.31
Ingham, Esther 1917.34, 1918.39
Inghram, Rose 1942.15, 1944.16, 1945.14, 1946.07, 1951.02
Ingle, Charles 1889.54
Inglefield, Violet 1920.20
Inglis, Jack 1929.24
Inglis, Johnny 1907.61
Inglis, William 1957.02
Ingliss, Jack 1920.20
Ingman, Nick 1996.01, 1996.12, 1998.09, 2000.05
Ingoldsby, Charles 1904.32, 1907.43, 1908.32
Ingraham, Herbert 1909.28
Ingram, Georgia 1925.44, 1926.21, 1927.27
Ingram, Lawaune 1943.17, 1944.31, 1945.13, 1946.21
Ingram, Marguerite 1923.43
Ingram, Michael 1979.03, 1997.09
Ingram, Michael H. 1994.12, 1995.19, 1996.15
Ingram, Milroy 1951.11
Ingram, Rex 1938.09, 1940.17, 1946.08, 1961.24
Ingram, Roger 1990.19
Ingram, Tad 1979.29, 1992.01, 1993.19, 1998.21
Ingre, Tonia 1930.35
Ingster, Peter 1989.17
Ink and Pasteboard 1890.42
Inman, W. Clay 1923.41
Inneo, Anthony 1973.07
Innes, James H. 1887.43
Innes, John 1884.30
Innes, K. Craig 1988.20
Innes, Messr. 1882.34
Innes, Neil 1976.06
Inness, Addie 1888.39
Innez, Albert 1921.21
Innez, Frank 1921.21
Innis, Frank 1930.28
Innvar, Christopher 1995.15
Insardi, Nicholas J. 1945.02
Insull, Sigrid 1980.01
INTAR Hispanic American Arts Center 1995.09
Integrity Designworks 2001.09
Inter-State Amusement Company, Inc., The 1908.06
Introdpdi, Josie 1875.23
Intropidi, Ethel 1928.06, 1937.04
Intropodi, Ethel 1904.19, 1905.30, 1908.29
Intropodi, F. 1879.59, 1885.07, 1885.09
Intropodi, Fred 1879.52, 1882.04, 1882.20, 1883.17, 1883.23, 1886.39
Intropodi, Frederic 1889.26
Intropodi, Frederick 1896.01
Intropodi, Josephine 1899.28
Intropodi, Josie 1895.37, 1899.05, 1900.50, 1900.54, 1904.19, 1905.30, 1908.29, 1911.31, 1914.04, 1914.14, 1916.08, 1916.19, 1917.28, 1918.26, 1920.15, 1922.14, 1922.31, 1925.11, 1926.29
Invernezzi, Mlle. 1868.18
Iracledes, Vasilis 1983.13, 1984.11, 1985.13, 1986.08, 1986.09
Irby, Iva 1912.16
Iredale, F. 1879.50
Iredale, Jane 1985.20
Ireland, Robert 1895.41
Ireland, Young 1891.01
Irie, Kaoru 1989.21
Irion, Yolanda Mero 1945.02
Irivng, Georgie 1903.20
Irivng, Washington 1893.19
Irma, Mlle. 1868.18, 1868.30, 1868.31, 1869.01, 1869.22, 1869.24
Irons, Willoughby 1922.21
Irosch, Irjana 1984.04
Irschick, Fraulein 1866.33
Irvin, May 1910.33
Irvin, Rae 1906.37
Irvine, Ila 1894.36
Irvine, Mabel 1895.21
Irving, Alicia 1997.17
Irving, Carl 1886.30, 1887.18, 1887.24, 1887.28
Irving, Daisie 1916.23
Irving, Daisy 1916.23
Irving, Dorothy 1921.33, 1925.05
Irving, Fenner 1925.42
Irving, Frank W. 1878.11
Irving, George 1959.10
Irving, George S. 1943.04, 1946.10, 1949.01, 1949.18, 1952.20, 1953.08, 1956.14, 1957.02, 1957.05, 1958.13, 1962.14, 1963.08, 1965.04, 1965.35, 1966.02, 1968.01, 1973.05, 1976.09, 1979.12, 1981.12, 1983.02, 1986.12, 1993.14, 1995.18, 1996.02
Irving, Henrietta 1875.10, 1881.14
Irving, Henry 1886.59
Irving, Irma 1921.33, 1923.44, 1925.05, 1926.46
Irving, Isabel 1891.05
Irving, J. Edwin 1876.16
Irving, J.E. 1864.14
Irving, Jane 1943.03
Irving, John 1958.11
Irving, Joseph 1869.23
Irving, Jules 1970.04
Irving, Julia 1882.20
Irving, Margaret 1917.22, 1922.39, 1925.16, 1926.42, 1928.38, 1939.22, 1940.10, 1943.18
Irving, Miss 1863.01, 1883.16
Irving, Mrs. J. 1869.23
Irving, Nellei 1882.49
Irving, Paul 1917.30, 1919.39, 1920.41
Irving, Richard 1942.20
Irving, Robert 1896.49, 1929.39, 1959.18, 1960.14, 1960.15, 1961.03, 1961.06
Irving, Stephen 1932.27
Irving, Washington 1852.05, 1875.06, 1882.75, 1907.08
Irwin, Bill 1983.09, 1993.01, 1995.16, 1998.17
Irwin, Charles 1927.38, 1929.04, 1945.03
Irwin, David 1916.15
Irwin, Deedy 1957.07, 1959.25
Irwin, Flo 1897.14
Irwin, Flora 1881.06, 1881.12, 1882.04, 1882.20, 1883.02, 1883.17, 1883.19, 1883.23, 1887.06, 1890.34, 1891.26, 1892.09, 1896.37
Irwin, Florence 1895.17
Irwin, Fred 1904.48
Irwin, Harry 1924.16
Irwin, Holly 1990.20
Irwin, Jack 1958.03
Irwin, May 1881.06, 1881.12, 1882.04, 1882.20, 1883.02, 1883.17, 1883.19, 1884.11, 1890.34, 1891.26, 1892.09, 1893.11, 1893.49, 1894.06, 1895.27, 1896.52, 1897.45, 1898.69, 1899.35, 1900.48, 1900.55, 1901.30, 1904.43, 1906.43, 1922.42
Irwin, Mr. 1872.26
Irwin, Mrs. 1887.03
Irwin, Mrs. Selden 1884.39, 1886.16
Irwin, Mrs. Seldon 1892.38
Irwin, Rea 1923.25
Irwin, Smiley W. 1923.43
Irwin, Wallace 1907.27, 1908.03, 1908.27, 1912.40
Irwin, Will 1929.20, 1930.25, 1930.32, 1930.38, 1931.14, 1932.13, 1934.40, 1935.03, 1935.04, 1936.22, 1936.31, 1938.09, 1939.07, 1940.23, 1941.11, 1942.18, 1943.21, 1944.14, 1945.18, 1946.05, 1946.22, 1949.17, 1958.04, 1959.05
Irwin, William 1929.20
Isaac, Gerald 1983.12, 1986.14, 1988.16
Isaacs, Edith S. 1922.32
Isaacs, Florence 1881.35
Isaacs, Pamela 1997.08
Isabella, Mlle. 1871.27, 1872.06
Iscove, Rob 1979.22, 1981.12
Iscove, Robert 1967.14
Isenburg, Edna 1941.11
Ish, Kathryn 1964.26
Isham, Edwin 1895.33
Isham, Frederick 1923.07, 1932.21
Isham, Frederick S. 1927.49
Isham, John W. 1896.46, 1899.31
Ishay, Galia 1971.17
Ishee, Suzanne 1983.10
Isherwood, Christopher 1966.24, 1987.16, 1998.04
Isherwood, Fanny 1848.03
Isherwood, H. 1868.19, 1871.14, 1871.19, 1872.21, 1875.01, 1877.22
Isherwood, Henry 1852.03, 1853.04, 1855.11, 1856.04, 1857.05, 1857.07, 1859.14
Isherwood, Mrs. 1851.06
Isherwood, Mrs. H. 1841.01
Ishida, Masaya 1989.21
Ishihama, Hideo 1989.21
Ishii, Leslie 1990.17
Ishikawa 1946.13
Ishikawa, Naoki 2001.04
Isiano, Juan Manuel Biurquis 1988.15
Ismaeloff, Sergei 1945.14
Isquith, Louis 1929.18
Isquith, Louis I. 1924.10
Israel, Roger Lee 1999.15
Israel, Walter 1945.16
Israel, William 1918.17
Istomina, Anna 1945.02
Itamar 1967.08
Ito, Genji 1976.02
Ito, Michio 1920.08, 1927.14, 1927.44
Ito, Robert 1967.10
Itow, Candace 1978.07, 1978.19, 1978.20, 1979.20, 1979.21, 1982.16, 1983.12, 1985.11, 1985.13, 1986.09, 1988.14, 1989.13, 1996.02
Itow, Michio 1922.21, 1923.31, 1925.37
Itow, Yuji 1922.21, 1925.37
Ittner, Ella 1898.45
Itzel, Adam 1891.32
Itzel, Jr., Adam 1891.13
Ivan, Charles 1935.01
Ivan, Rosalind 1938.10
Ivanova, Cladia 1922.30
Ivel, Jeannette 1899.21, 1900.28
Ivel, Marion 1898.71
Ivell, Marion 1898.39
Iven, Lo 1930.36
Ivers, Eileen 1996.12
Iversen, Marya 1945.04
Iverson and Henneage 1921.10
Iverson, Adele 1886.47
Ives, Burl 1938.14, 1942.20, 1944.32, 1951.24, 1954.04
Ives, George 1902.02, 1959.19
Ives, Jeremy 1962.01
Ives, Mr. 1879.09
Ivey, Cornell 1993.03
Ivey, Dana 1984.08
Ivey, Judith 1981.04, 2001.02
Ivor-Szinnyey, Stephen 1919.04
Ivory-Davis, Delores 1976.28
Iwamatsu, Sala 1991.03
Izmailov, Ivan 1931.39, 1938.13
Izobell, Alistair 1999.12
Izquierdo, Raul 1949.07

J.B. DeBeauvais and Son 1890.35
J.B. Debeauvais and Son 1892.01
J.C. Associates 1983.19
J.C. Duff Comic Opera Company 1890.14, 1890.15, 1890.18, 1890.20, 1890.46, 1890.47, 1890.48
J.C. Duff Opera Company 1889.36, 1893.09
J.C. Duff's Opera Company 1894.23
J.H. Haverly's Grand English Opera Company 1879.30
J.H. Lester and Company 1891.01
J.H. Renie Opera Comique Company 1882.38
J.M. Gidding and Company 1915.27, 1919.25
J.M. Giddings and Company 1917.09
J.M. Hill's Opera Company 1892.52
J.S. Crossy's American Comic Opera Company 1880.01, 1880.03
Jabara, Paul 1968.11, 1983.09
Jablonski, Peter 1987.02
Jablow, Lisa 1990.08
Jacchia, Paul 1932.14, 1939.19
Jack's of Hollywood Productions 1955.03
Jack, J.H. 1868.04, 1871.10

Jack, John 1884.39
Jack, Mary 1883.63, 1884.13, 1884.41, 1885.02, 1885.49, 1886.52, 1887.07, 1887.16
Jack, Mrs. 1883.32
Jacka, Jeremy 1989.01
Jackel, Paul 1991.05, 1997.22
Jackin, Henri 1928.03
Jacklin, Charles 1899.11
Jacklow, Ben 1923.13
Jackman, Hope 1963.01
Jackness, Andrew 1988.08, 1988.19, 1997.19, 1999.13
Jacks of Hollywood 1965.05
Jacks, Leopold 1909.22, 1910.28, 1921.40, 1930.03
Jackson, "Poppa" Charlie 1991.01
Jackson, A.W. 1861.03
Jackson, Adolph 1897.47, 1906.43
Jackson, Alfred 1927.04
Jackson, Alice 1897.45
Jackson, Anna 1939.07
Jackson, Anna L. 1887.43
Jackson, Annie 1888.03
Jackson, Arthur 1916.12, 1918.19, 1919.13, 1920.17, 1920.33, 1921.22, 1922.10, 1924.43
Jackson, Arthur J. 1919.12
Jackson, Bee 1899.42
Jackson, Bessie 1880.26
Jackson, Bonita 1975.09
Jackson, Brady 1933.27
Jackson, Bryan 2000.03
Jackson, C. 1903.32
Jackson, Calvin 1942.10
Jackson, Carrie 1883.31, 1885.28, 1885.52, 1885.67, 1886.14
Jackson, Charles 1897.45, 1898.58, 1907.18
Jackson, Charlie 1927.32
Jackson, Columbus 1929.01
Jackson, Crawford 1927.33, 1928.18, 1930.34
Jackson, Daisy 1897.32
Jackson, David 1983.06, 1989.26
Jackson, Delle 1893.06, 1895.36
Jackson, Dorothea 1938.01
Jackson, E.A. 1934.37
Jackson, Ed. 1904.38
Jackson, Eddie 1930.40
Jackson, Edward 1938.08
Jackson, Ernestine 1973.10, 1976.21
Jackson, Ethel 1898.38, 1898.63, 1900.03, 1900.19, 1901.05, 1906.41, 1907.48, 1930.29
Jackson, Ethel Shannon 1932.18
Jackson, Evelyn 1908.40
Jackson, F.R. 1886.06
Jackson, Frank 1919.08, 1937.09
Jackson, Frank R. 1893.49
Jackson, Fred 1919.01, 1921.10, 1922.10
Jackson, G.W. 1866.22, 1866.26, 1866.35
Jackson, Gary 1982.22, 1984.10, 1994.09
Jackson, Gary Lee 1973.14, 1975.12, 1976.24
Jackson, George 1904.03, 1939.15
Jackson, George B. 1903.21, 1905.50
Jackson, George Russell 1884.64
Jackson, Glenda 1965.39
Jackson, Harriet 1942.03, 1943.15, 1944.03, 1945.08, 1945.13
Jackson, Harry 1870.13, 1870.19, 1870.36, 1910.23, 1911.28, 1912.30, 1914.19, 1939.27
Jackson, Harry L. 1913.22
Jackson, Howard 1931.01, 1931.14, 1931.19, 1931.30, 1933.15, 1943.05
Jackson, Irving 1915.32, 1918.03, 1921.36
Jackson, Jennie 1898.55
Jackson, Jerry 1982.14
Jackson, Joe 1915.02, 1917.03, 1920.26
Jackson, John P. 1890.08, 1890.39, 1892.28
Jackson, Joseph 1889.06, 1890.07, 1890.34, 1891.43, 1892.36, 1892.56, 1894.10
Jackson, Josephine 1927.33
Jackson, Jr., Joe 1947.12
Jackson, June 1898.41
Jackson, Keisha 1995.01
Jackson, Leonard 1972.06, 1991.01
Jackson, Lidell 1976.35
Jackson, Lila 1953.16
Jackson, Lonny 1944.33
Jackson, Lorna Doone 1929.43, 1930.12
Jackson, Mahalia 1990.05
Jackson, Marge 1944.15
Jackson, Margie 1942.26
Jackson, Martin J. 1898.56
Jackson, Mary 1903.03
Jackson, Mesdame 1852.01
Jackson, Messr. 1866.20
Jackson, Millie 1995.01
Jackson, Minnie 1869.11, 1869.17, 1869.21, 1869.25, 1869.28, 1872.13
Jackson, Miss 1869.26, 1869.36, 1870.02, 1870.09, 1870.22, 1870.35, 1879.65, 1879.67, 1886.36, 1903.03
Jackson, Mr. 1836.01, 1846.01, 1857.02
Jackson, Myrtis 1938.10
Jackson, Nagle 1979.10
Jackson, Nkosane 2000.03
Jackson, Patty Ann 1953.08
Jackson, Phyllis 1922.21
Jackson, R. 1901.24
Jackson, Reggie 1978.28
Jackson, Richard 1945.16
Jackson, Richardena 1944.31, 1946.21
Jackson, Robert 1973.10, 1979.32
Jackson, Rufus E. 1982.17
Jackson, Stewart 1916.14
Jackson, Susan 1968.25, 1968.26, 1968.29
Jackson, T.E. 1867.32, 1869.20
Jackson, T.J. 1885.03
Jackson, Thomas 1897.47, 1899.03, 1900.36
Jackson, Thomas E. 1883.68, 1885.10, 1886.05, 1899.27, 1903.25, 1904.46, 1919.39
Jackson, Tina 1884.37
Jackson, Tod 1962.24, 1972.07
Jackson, Van 1930.19
Jackson, Veda 1983.17
Jackson, Viola 1904.38
Jackson, Virgie 1875.15
Jackson, Wallace 1919.38
Jackson, Walter 1896.49
Jackson, Warren 1918.18, 1943.13
Jackson, William 1906.06, 1910.12
Jackson, Zaidee 1927.33
Jacob, Abe 1971.12, 1972.22, 1972.23, 1973.07, 1974.24, 1975.08, 1975.09, 1975.14, 1975.15, 1976.03, 1976.06, 1977.10, 1977.15, 1977.16, 1978.03, 1978.05, 1978.28, 1979.08, 1979.19, 1979.23, 1980.14, 1981.09, 1981.10, 1982.05, 1982.14, 1983.01, 1985.03, 1986.06, 1986.16, 1987.14, 1989.02, 1990.01, 1990.02, 1990.07, 1991.08, 1991.09, 1991.12, 1992.10, 1993.03, 1993.14, 1994.09, 1995.06, 1995.18, 1996.02, 1996.13, 1999.10
Jacob, Bill 1969.14
Jacob, Patti 1969.14
Jacob, Steven 1981.27
Jacobi, A. 1870.30
Jacobi, G. 1888.10
Jacobi, Georges 1889.08, 1889.33
Jacobi, Georgio 1895.08
Jacobi, Lou 1964.21
Jacobi, M. 1892.38, 1893.23, 1894.34
Jacobi, Victor 1913.26, 1916.01, 1917.19, 1918.19, 1919.27, 1920.40, 1921.32, 1932.19
Jacobs, Al 1962.17
Jacobs, Angela 1927.47
Jacobs, Craig 1993.18
Jacobs, Edward T. 1980.07
Jacobs, H. 1868.19
Jacobs, Harvey 1981.08
Jacobs, Ira 1922.12, 1924.10, 1924.31, 1925.16, 1926.26
Jacobs, Jack 1882.48
Jacobs, Jacob 1970.18, 1990.16, 1998.11
Jacobs, Jesse 1950.16
Jacobs, Jim 1972.12, 1994.07, 1996.17
Jacobs, Max 1965.32
Jacobs, Miss 1844.01
Jacobs, Mr. 1871.15
Jacobs, Rusty 1979.22
Jacobs, Sally 1965.39
Jacobs, Sander 1989.26
Jacobs, Steven 1966.27
Jacobs, Will 1972.21
Jacobsen, John 1974.23
Jacobson 1884.11
Jacobson, Benno 1910.22
Jacobson, C. 1894.18
Jacobson, Dan 1965.32
Jacobson, Eduard 1885.45
Jacobson, Gela 1979.08
Jacobson, Henrietta 1970.18, 1971.07
Jacobson, Hy 1951.20
Jacobson, Hymie 1990.16
Jacobson, Irving 1965.34, 1972.14
Jacobson, Leopold 1908.06, 1917.14, 1926.33, 1931.33, 1934.12, 1942.17, 1947.06
Jacobson, Louis 1898.44
Jacobson, Mamie 1884.27
Jacobson, Mme. 1844.01
Jacobson, Steven 1980.02
Jacobson, Vernon 1928.08
Jacobson, W. 1894.18
Jacoby 1870.03
Jacoby, Coleman 1957.01
Jacoby, Elliot 1944.33, 1948.21
Jacoby, Elliott 1946.04, 1946.07
Jacoby, Josephine 1910.14, 1911.12, 1912.21, 1914.11
Jacoby, Mark 1986.07, 1994.08, 1998.01
Jacoby, Scott 1968.03, 1970.10
Jacomo, Claudia 1988.06
Jacoves, Felix 1925.17, 1926.13
Jacox, Martin 1988.05
Jacqueline, Mme. 1905.57
Jacqueline, Olive 1918.16
Jacquemont, Raymond 1943.06
Jacquemot, Ray 1947.13
Jacques, A. 1876.12
Jacques, Andrew 1884.36
Jacques, Charles 1922.03
Jacques, Miss 1883.16
Jacques, Nita 1925.14, 1926.28
Jacquet, H. Maurice 1929.46, 1930.36
Jaeger, Bertha 1890.31, 1891.33, 1892.43, 1893.29, 1894.01, 1894.30, 1896.34, 1898.53
Jaeger, Harry A. 1908.32
Jaffe, Charles 1964.17
Jaffe, Moe 1929.09, 1929.22, 1929.28
Jaffe, Sam 1925.17, 1927.36
Jaffee, Lynne 1937.14
Jaffee, Moe 1932.01, 1976.07
Jaffee, Sam 1937.01
Jaffray, Laura 1911.14, 1911.22
Jafollo, Thomas 1938.13
Jageman, Walter 1939.29
Jagemann, Walter 1935.18, 1939.24
Jager, Susan 1954.10
Jagger, Dean 1938.18
Jagger, Mick 1979.30, 1982.22
Jago, Messr. 1750.01
Jahan, Marine 1997.19
Jaillet, Lorraine 1930.39
Jaime, Adolphe 1870.26, 1870.27, 1870.30, 1872.41, 1875.08, 1875.33, 1876.28, 1877.37, 1879.60, 1882.67, 1884.55, 1897.28, 1906.36
Jaimes, Ray 1958.02
Jaimes, Raymond 1961.21
JaJuan, Kimberly 1997.12, 1999.22
Jaketic, Gary 1980.19
Jakobi, Anita 1940.10
Jakobowski, Edward 1886.30, 1887.23, 1888.02, 1889.16, 1889.25, 1889.36, 1889.49, 1893.35, 1894.29, 1894.41, 1897.24, 1898.36, 1899.24, 1903.32, 1903.38, 1921.01
Jakobs, Ned 1928.49
Jali, Promise S'thembile 1997.14
Jallais, Armand 1877.18
Jam Theatricals 1999.25
Jamal, Sati 1971.13
Jamblan 1935.19
Jambone, M. 1868.06
Jame, Paul 1930.28
Jamerson, Clifford 1975.12
Jamerson, Thomas 1974.07, 1976.23, 1980.21, 1981.20, 1982.16, 1983.12
James A. Oates Comic Opera Company 1870.26
James C. Duff Comic Opera Company 1888.18
James Evans and Company 1937.10
James McCreery and Company 1886.40
James Scanlan's Boston Miniature Ideal Opera Company 1882.48
James, A. 1880.30
James, Albert 1890.33, 1892.08, 1892.10, 1915.28
James, Alex 1926.23
James, Alf P. 1927.08
James, Alfred 1892.48, 1892.53, 1925.08
James, Alfred P. 1920.44, 1923.30, 1930.08
James, Aphie 1934.29
James, Bob 1972.02
James, Brian D'Arcy 1994.02
James, Brian d'Arcy 1997.06
James, Cairns 1895.29
James, Clark 1975.07
James, Daisy 1910.26
James, Dan 1944.23, 1947.01
James, Dorothea 1927.62, 1930.30, 1931.28
James, Eddie 1964.04, 1965.22
James, Edna 1934.03
James, Elmore 1982.17
James, Emerony 1900.59
James, Frankie 1919.21, 1923.23, 1925.01, 1925.28
James, Fritz 1888.33
James, G.T. 1877.04
James, George E. 1883.50
James, Gladys 1921.25
James, H. 1999.24
James, Hal 1965.34, 1967.06, 1969.07, 1972.14
James, Harry 1897.04, 1898.03, 1916.21, 1922.14, 1981.06, 1997.03
James, Henry 1914.21, 1972.24
James, Horace 1921.24
James, Ida 1944.30, 1945.08
James, Jacqueline 1949.17
James, Jessica 1982.01
James, John 1901.30
James, Joseph 1949.15, 1951.18, 1953.04, 1956.06, 1965.03
James, Jr. 1866.15
James, Julia 1910.21
James, Laura 1879.67
James, Leavitt 1903.34, 1905.19, 1909.03, 1912.02, 1915.25, 1917.26
James, LeRoy 1937.04
James, Lester 1965.31
James, Lilith 1944.23, 1947.01
James, Linda 1980.14, 1982.17
James, Lisa 1962.12
James, Lithgow 1881.34, 1882.78, 1883.37
James, Marcia 1947.04
James, Mark 1989.12
James, Mary 1888.39
James, Messr. 1856.04, 1864.22
James, Millie 1925.26
James, Miss 1856.01, 1862.02, 1870.21
James, Mr. 1855.11, 1866.06, 1868.04, 1875.40, 1887.10
James, Murphy 1966.06
James, Nikki M. 2001.06
James, Olga 1956.02, 1958.11
James, Paul 1928.21, 1929.19, 1930.06, 1930.18, 1930.33
James, Philip 1920.05
James, Polly 1965.14
James, Rian 1980.20, 2001.08
James, Spencer 1946.13
James, Stephen 1979.24, 1980.08
James, Sunshine 1908.35
James, Terry 1981.26
James, Toni-Leslie 1992.08, 1995.09, 1998.13, 1999.22, 2000.08
James, True S. 1918.24
James, W. 1866.08, 1866.11, 1882.37
James, Walter 1902.43
James, William 1906.45, 1907.08, 1968.17, 1968.24, 1976.05, 1980.19, 1981.26
Jameson, Joyce 1959.14, 1961.16
Jameson, Ralph 1937.01
Jamesworth, Alfred 1932.05
Jamieson, Carrie 1876.15, 1876.22, 1877.01
Jamieson, House 1925.17
Jamieson, James 1950.10, 1957.03, 1962.15, 1963.04, 1964.46, 1980.26, 1986.04, 1991.12
Jamieson, Mrs. W.L. 1864.22
Jamieson, W.L. 1861.06, 1862.01, 1864.22, 1865.06
Jamin-Bartlett, D. 1973.04
Jamison, Frank E. 1885.50
Jamison, J. 1895.29
Jamison, James 1947.07
Jamison, Judith 1981.06
Jamison, Marshall 1946.19, 1954.02
Jampolis, Neil Peter 1971.10, 1971.14, 1971.19, 1972.13, 1974.20, 1974.22, 1977.14, 1986.18, 1986.21, 1988.11, 1989.02, 1989.22, 1990.02, 1990.11, 1993.11, 1994.03, 1996.03, 1997.21
Jane, Mary 1920.42, 1924.32, 1925.14, 1925.38, 1926.18, 1927.47, 1928.47
Jane, Sara 1931.40
Janek, James 1980.14, 1984.09
Janes, Alan 1990.15
Janet E. Fox, Inc. 1916.12
Janette, R.P. 1909.06
Janeway, Ashley 1985.13, 1986.09, 1988.14
Jang, Eun Soo 1998.08

Jani, Robert F. 1979.13, 1979.28, 1980.09, 1980.18, 1981.08, 1982.06
Janice, Dorotohy 1924.29
Janier, Mr. 1872.24
Janik, Ada 1980.11
Janik, Nina 1968.32
Janis, Beverly 1947.02, 1949.10, 1949.11, 1949.14
Janis, Elsie 1906.05, 1907.02, 1907.46, 1909.03, 1911.02, 1912.02, 1912.39, 1915.25, 1915.30, 1916.24, 1919.40, 1922.03, 1925.05, 1934.06, 1939.16, 1975.24
Janis, Percy 1905.23, 1906.05, 1907.02
Janis, Vivian 1934.01
Janiver, Emma 1916.18, 1916.22
Janki, Devavand N. 1997.17
Jannath, Heba 1930.24
Janney, Leon 1935.03, 1965.01
Janney, Russell 1922.04, 1923.43, 1925.32, 1927.65, 1934.41, 1943.08
Jannings, Orrin 1936.28
Jannsen, Bernard 1936.26
Janov, Janet 1937.01
Janowski, Robert 1992.05
Jans, Alaric 1982.10
Jans, Harry 1927.31, 1928.14, 1930.09, 1930.26
Jans, Tom 1979.30
Jansen, Jim 1980.30
Jansen, Marie 1880.47, 1880.69, 1881.36, 1881.38, 1882.06, 1882.63, 1882.66, 1882.78, 1883.24, 1883.39, 1883.58, 1885.28, 1885.67, 1888.02, 1888.20, 1889.24, 1890.26, 1891.31, 1891.47, 1893.42, 1895.35, 1897.56
Jansley, Jerry 1943.05
Janssen, B.H. 1890.07, 1891.42
Janssen, Werner 1921.35, 1922.14, 1923.01, 1924.33, 1925.10, 1925.24, 1926.22, 1928.27, 1929.06
Jansson, Ulf Hakan 1966.19
Janswick, Henry 1919.40
January, Lois 1939.24, 1941.09
Janus, Billy 1921.34
Janusz, Thom 1971.19
Janvert, Paul 1932.22
Janvier, Emma 1896.29, 1897.46, 1906.36, 1908.09, 1908.39, 1909.28, 1921.10, 1922.29, 1923.27
Janvier, Janie 1955.08
Japan Satellite Broadcasting 1991.07, 1992.01
Jaquet, Frank 1945.16
Jarahal 1930.16
Jarbea, Miss 1880.68
Jarbeau, Minnie 1905.14
Jarbeau, Vernona 1878.21, 1879.05, 1879.58, 1879.67, 1879.71, 1880.02, 1880.40, 1881.07, 1881.43, 1882.22, 1882.23, 1882.66, 1883.16, 1883.21, 1883.31, 1884.39, 1885.40, 1885.48, 1892.21, 1893.37
Jarboe, Jennie 1894.43
Jarboe, Minnie 1896.50
Jardon, Dorothy 1903.29, 1908.15, 1910.09, 1910.22, 1911.12, 1911.34, 1911.47, 1913.30, 1914.17, 1914.26
Jared, Bob 1990.10
Jari, De 1923.22
Jarman, Nellie 1870.05
Jarmon, Rene 1961.26
Jarnac, Dorothy 1948.23, 1950.09
Jarnagin, Jerry 1929.31
Jarno, George 1910.36
Jaroff, J. 1932.09
Jarolslow, Lori Ada 1981.18
Jaroslow, Ruth 1976.36, 1981.18, 1990.18
Jarosz, Judith 1990.07, 1991.08
Jarrard, Miss 1868.06
Jarratt, David 1967.10
Jarratt, Howard 1952.15
Jarratt, William 1906.37
Jarred, Joseph 1989.11
Jarret, Jr., Danie 1913.07
Jarrett 1876.12
Jarrett, Art 1940.09
Jarrett, Arthur 1906.38, 1907.56, 1911.04
Jarrett, Daniel 1888.31, 1905.38, 1906.38, 1907.56, 1911.04
Jarrett, Dorothy 1927.68
Jarrett, Henry 1866.18, 1868.03, 1869.02, 1869.06, 1869.14, 1869.20, 1869.27, 1869.29, 1869.32, 1869.33, 1869.35, 1869.40, 1869.43, 1869.44, 1870.04, 1870.13, 1870.19, 1870.21, 1870.44, 1871.10, 1871.15, 1871.22, 1871.27, 1872.06, 1872.09, 1872.11, 1872.37, 1873.08, 1873.10, 1873.28, 1877.07
Jarrett, Henry C. 1862.03, 1862.04, 1880.35, 1880.55, 1881.47
Jarrett, Jerry 1990.18
Jarrman, Sunshine 1925.23
Jarrott, John 1908.14
Jarvis, Frank 1926.15
Jarvis, Graham 1975.08
Jarvis, J.H. 1881.14
Jarvis, John Barlow 1998.19
Jarvis, Louise 1943.07, 1944.15
Jarvis, Lucy 1990.01
Jarvis, Mr. 1871.15
Jarvis, Scott 1968.05
Jarvis, Sidney 1900.39, 1912.13, 1917.28
Jarvis, Sydney 1909.03, 1911.09, 1911.33, 1914.34, 1917.37, 1919.03
Jason, Adele 1915.16
Jason, Bert 1929.26
Jason, Bill 1961.07
Jason, Isabelle 1912.24
Jason, Larry 1925.37, 1929.45
Jason, Michael 1971.01, 1971.12
Jason, Mitchell 1964.21, 1968.02, 1973.02, 1973.11, 1976.09, 1989.26
Jason, Sylvia 1914.30, 1916.25, 1917.23
Jason, Ysobelle 1911.26
Jasper, Miss 1881.11
Jaubert, Jean-Louis 1947.18
Jaurs, R.L. 1876.35
Jausse, Mlle. 1871.25
Javello, Wilhelm 1884.58
Javits, Joan 1961.11, 1963.08
Javitts, Joan 1952.08
Javorsky, K. 1932.09
Jaw, Miss 1865.01
Jaworski, Antoni 1978.20, 1979.21
Jaxson, Frankie 1938.19
Jay, Brian 1989.23
Jay, David 1972.06
Jay, Don 1973.10
Jay, Ivy 1901.08
Jay, Mary 1987.19
Jay, Roger 1976.10
Jay, Stephen 1988.07
Jay-Alexander, Richard 1979.08, 1991.03
Jay-Thorpe 1932.21
Jayne, Estelle 1934.39, 1935.18
Jayne, Nancy 1927.40
Jayson, Vernon 1932.05
Jbara, Gregory 1994.01, 1995.15
Jean, Myvanwy 1979.12
Jean, Thomas 1926.01
Jeane, Ira 1925.06
Jeanette, Gertrude 1949.15
Jeanette, Mlle. 1871.27
Jeanmaire, Zizi 1964.39, 1981.13
Jeanmarie 1954.01
Jeanne, Ida 1913.02
Jeanne, Laura 1980.30
Jeanne, Mlle. 1870.44, 1871.27
Jeannette, Mlle. 1870.44, 1872.06, 1873.10
Jeans, Edna 1905.49
Jeans, Ronald 1924.01, 1925.42, 1925.50, 1927.02, 1929.29, 1929.51, 1930.18, 1934.42
Jedd, Gerry 1952.03
Jeff Satkin, Inc. 1981.17
Jefferson de Angelis Opera Company 1902.25
Jefferson DeAngelis Comic Opera Company 1896.25
Jefferson DeAngelis Opera Company, The 1898.73, 1907.07
Jefferson, C.B. 1893.42, 1894.42
Jefferson, Catherine 1900.07
Jefferson, Cornelia 1857.01, 1860.03, 1860.05
Jefferson, Joe 1867.29
Jefferson, Joseph 1796.01, 1796.02, 1859.11, 1860.03, 1860.04, 1860.05, 1869.37, 1870.32
Jefferson, Lauretta 1943.20, 1944.01
Jefferson, Loretta 1943.14
Jefferson, Miss 1857.02
Jefferson, Norman 1920.11
Jefferson, Tavia Rivee 1997.22
Jefferson, Tavis Rivee 1998.20
Jefferson, William 1900.48, 1900.55, 1905.27
Jefferson, William Winter 1920.11
Jeffrey, Carl 1955.12, 1956.01
Jeffrey, Howard 1960.08, 1970.03
Jeffrey, J. Wesley 1923.39
Jeffrey, Mr. 1887.10
Jeffrey, Terry Mike 1989.12
Jeffreys, Alan 1957.01, 1960.12
Jeffreys, Anne 1947.02, 1948.27, 1952.05, 1965.22
Jeffreys, Miss 1870.05
Jeffreys-Goodfriend, Ida 1905.15
Jeffries 1964.28
Jeffries, James J. 1899.36, 1956.12
Jeffries, Jay 1987.02
Jeffries, Messr. 1850.01, 1859.08
Jeffries, Mr. 1855.11, 1859.08, 1862.05
Jeffs, Rebecca 1999.02
Jellison, John 1983.19, 1984.08, 1985.20, 1991.15, 1998.02, 1998.16
Jemima, Aunt 1921.22, 1927.67
Jenack, John 1979.07
Jenbach, Bela 1910.31, 1914.25, 1915.17, 1917.20, 1983.12, 1984.05, 1985.12, 1988.14
Jencks, Frederick 1931.44
Jendell, Gary 1966.12, 1966.16
Jenkins 1927.66, 1934.36, 1937.06
Jenkins Gowns 1960.04
Jenkins, Alan 1996.17
Jenkins, Allen 1943.01
Jenkins, Allen C. 1920.09
Jenkins, Athalie 1918.31
Jenkins, Bette 1959.02, 1963.08, 1965.01
Jenkins, Capathia 1999.08
Jenkins, Carol 1991.02
Jenkins, Daniel 1996.08
Jenkins, Daniel H. 1985.06
Jenkins, David 1972.08, 1975.13, 1980.21, 1981.04, 1981.20, 1981.21, 1985.09, 1987.02, 1987.08, 1988.04, 1989.07, 1993.12, 2000.01
Jenkins, Gene 1954.08
Jenkins, George 1938.19, 1943.07, 1944.02, 1944.15, 1945.08, 1945.18, 1948.11, 1949.15, 1952.05, 1955.04, 1957.04, 1957.15, 1957.17, 1958.03, 1961.07, 1962.21, 1963.24, 1963.25, 1964.30, 1965.27
Jenkins, Gordon 1936.31, 1942.11, 1949.01, 1962.17, 1982.12, 1983.20, 1985.08
Jenkins, J. Harry 1927.53
Jenkins, Jesse 1888.44, 1889.12
Jenkins, Oliver 1883.43
Jenkins, Walter 1908.34
Jenkins, Warren E. 1979.05
Jenkins, Wesley 1907.22, 1909.10
Jenkle, J. 1880.03
Jenks, Frederic 1931.44
Jenks, George G. 1984.50
Jenks, Harry 1900.53
Jenn, Myvanwy 1964.28
Jenner, Julie 1935.12
Jennery, Trixie 1919.03, 1920.10
Jenness, Edith 1885.04
Jennesse, Edith 1886.55, 1886.57
Jennie, Little 1880.07
Jennie, Miss 1879.29
Jennie, Mlle. 1871.27
Jennings, Arthur 1907.04
Jennings, Belle 1887.04
Jennings, David 1996.18
Jennings, Don 1978.27, 1979.09
Jennings, Florence 1908.03
Jennings, Fred 1924.27
Jennings, George 1893.14, 1894.02
Jennings, J.W. 1872.23, 1873.03, 1875.14
Jennings, John 1892.56
Jennings, John W. 1873.24, 1875.21, 1876.16, 1890.07
Jennings, Kathy 1975.21
Jennings, Ken 1979.06, 1985.15, 1989.26, 1994.12, 1995.19, 1996.15, 1997.17, 1998.20, 2000.19
Jennings, Mae 1918.41
Jennings, Mary 1964.07, 1964.12, 1965.07, 1965.11, 1965.13, 1965.26
Jennings, Messr. 1864.13
Jennings, Mr. 1875.10
Jennings, Nellie 1885.67
Jennings, P. O'Malley 1910.29, 1915.28
Jennings, Patricia 1949.17
Jennings, Percival 1906.04
Jennings, Percy 1902.36
Jennings, Robert 1954.02
Jennings, W.A. 1896.44
Jennings, Waylon 1979.16
Jennings, Will 1976.34, 1991.10
Jenny, Mlle. 1870.44
Jenoure, Aida 1887.10, 1888.33, 1889.44, 1890.50
Jens, Salome 1968.08
Jensen, Carol Lee 1962.20
Jensen, John 1973.07
Jensen, Paul 1929.20
Jensen, Robert 1993.19
Jensen, Scott 1930.28
Jensen, Tina Marie 1930.23
Jentes, Harry 1925.25, 1925.48
Jeong, Young Joo 1998.08
Jeong, Young Ju 1997.16
Jephson, Edward 1924.20, 1924.43
Jepson, Agnes 1917.03
Jepson, E.O. 1875.15, 1875.20
Jepson, Eugene 1892.14, 1901.16, 1902.24
Jepson, Eugene O. 1878.11, 1880.21, 1881.10
Jepson, J.J. 1971.09, 1989.26
Jericho, Herr 1883.08
Jermon, Irene 1903.19
Jerome, Adele 1937.14, 1942.05
Jerome, Ben 1901.29, 1902.16, 1903.41, 1904.25, 1905.19, 1912.45, 1926.25, 1927.49
Jerome, Ben M. 1900.16, 1902.20, 1903.04, 1903.18, 1904.28, 1904.47, 1908.21, 1908.44, 1909.14, 1910.25, 1915.08
Jerome, Charles 1893.43, 1895.02, 1921.11
Jerome, Clara Belle 1904.04, 1905.19
Jerome, Ed 1931.16, 1933.26
Jerome, Edwin 1898.59, 1910.15
Jerome, Elmer 1903.35
Jerome, Florence Nugent 1913.17
Jerome, Helen 1959.06
Jerome, Jerome K. 1918.11
Jerome, M.K. 1919.16
Jerome, Messr. 1882.04, 1882.20, 1883.17, 1883.23
Jerome, Nat S. 1927.47
Jerome, Richard 1933.05, 1936.17
Jerome, Timothy 1970.15, 1981.14, 1986.12, 1989.26
Jerome, Vera 1892.52
Jerome, William 1891.02, 1892.05, 1892.45, 1893.43, 1894.31, 1894.50, 1900.52, 1901.13, 1901.17, 1901.27, 1902.15, 1902.16, 1902.19, 1903.04, 1903.12, 1903.27, 1903.30, 1903.35, 1903.39, 1904.08, 1904.15, 1905.19, 1905.22, 1905.28, 1905.41, 1905.48, 1905.52, 1906.20, 1906.24, 1906.25, 1906.37, 1907.21, 1907.24, 1907.27, 1907.28, 1907.37, 1907.42, 1908.10, 1908.19, 1908.31, 1908.33, 1908.39, 1909.16, 1909.18, 1909.25, 1909.28, 1910.08, 1910.19, 1910.20, 1911.30, 1912.02, 1912.07, 1912.09, 1912.13, 1912.31, 1912.38, 1913.05, 1913.17, 1914.06, 1915.16, 1915.24, 1916.04, 1916.09, 1916.20, 1917.16, 1918.23, 1919.26, 1920.04, 1922.11, 1964.28
Jerrold, D. 1867.12
Jerrold, Mr. 1865.07, 1865.09, 1866.02, 1866.28
Jerry, Philip 1989.20
Jersey, Myrtle 1911.46
Jeschek, Wolfgang 1984.04
Jeslo Productions 1999.24
Jesmer, Helene 1920.28
Jessel, George 1919.16, 1923.17, 1923.19, 1930.38, 1941.09, 1942.24, 1943.10
Jessel, Georgie 1923.17
Jessel, Leon 1922.06, 1923.28, 1943.11
Jessel, Ray 1988.08, 1990.09
Jessel, Raymond 1965.02, 1979.12
Jessop, George 1889.48
Jessop, George H. 1884.62, 1885.04, 1886.48, 1889.03, 1891.06, 1891.28, 1894.20, 1894.36, 1896.09, 1896.14, 1897.03, 1904.01
Jessup, George H. 1882.28, 1895.30
Jessup, Stanley 1907.35, 1921.10, 1927.55, 1930.27, 1942.27
Jessye, Eva 1934.05, 1935.13, 1942.03, 1943.15, 1944.03, 1945.08, 1953.04, 1958.11
Jeter, Michael 1989.26
Jethro, Phil 1971.12
Jett, Joan 2000.17
Jewell, Clara Alene 1897.46
Jewell, James 1951.10, 1953.17
Jewell, Martin 1965.22
Jewell, Violet 1898.20, 1900.01, 1900.38, 1901.17, 1901.21, 1909.25
Jewett, Ethel 1900.38, 1907.35
Jewett, J. 1884.40
Jewish Repertory Theatre Production, A 1989.05

Jezek, Jarolslav 1938.04
Jiggets, Yvonne 1951.11
Jiggetts, Shelby 1996.07
Jillana 1959.11
Jillette, Penn 1987.20, 1991.02
Jillian, Ann 1979.25
Jillson, Joyce 1965.19, 1965.37
Jim, Marion 1956.03, 1974.12
Jimenez, Fernando 1993.08
Jimenez, May 1887.42
Jimenez, Tai 1998.16
Jimnolds 1923.19
Jines, Henry 1926.19, 1937.09
Jingo 1903.09
Jinja 1960.10
Jiranek, David 1982.02, 1998.17
Jo, Lisa 1963.18
Jo, Patti 1972.26
Jo-Ann, Ebony 1991.01, 1993.03
Joachim, Andrew 1925.23
Joanna, Mlle. 1873.10
Joaquin, Master 1866.12
Jobe, Andy 1994.12
Jobe, Lindsay 1994.12
Jobim, Antonio Carlos 1997.01
Jobson, E.C. 1890.32, 1893.50
Jocelyn, Folett 1894.05
Jocelyn, Follett 1894.38
Jocelyn, Gwennllyan 1914.20
Jocelyn, Hazel 1908.27
Jocelyn, Jarvis 1904.39, 1906.01
Jocelyn, Mildred 1944.28, 1945.18
Jocelyn, Sylvia 1922.39
Jochim, Ande 1923.17
Jochim, Andrew 1924.29
Jochim, Andy 1928.12
Jochim, Anthony 1919.03, 1920.47
Jockers, Bob 1976.20
Jockin, Henry 1927.43
Joe, Little 1922.21
Joe, Montego 1961.24
Joel, Dan 1975.06
Joelson, Lynn 1952.01
Joelson, Suzanne 1978.26
Joerder, Norbert 1993.11
Joffe, Bob 1930.29
Joffrey, Robert 1957.13, 1957.15, 1958.13, 1959.08, 1959.09, 1959.10, 1959.17
Jofsiss, Jack 1982.21
Johann, Cameron 1982.09
Johann, Dallas 1968.01, 1968.24
Johann, Zita 1925.20
Johannsen, Sigurd 1928.26
Johansen, Mary 1981.27
Johanson, Don 1992.08, 1994.06
Johanson, Robert 1980.01, 1986.14, 1987.09, 1987.10, 1988.16, 1993.14, 1995.06, 1995.18, 1996.02, 1997.11, 1998.06, 1999.11
John A. Stevens' Comic Opera Company 1882.18
John Annunziato Production, A 1981.24
John Blushkin Quartet 1976.32
John F. Kennedy Center 1972.06, 1972.15, 1976.01, 1976.36, 1978.03, 1979.17, 1980.02, 1980.23, 1981.25, 1982.05, 1983.05, 1983.08, 1985.04, 1986.16, 1987.04, 1988.07, 1992.04, 1993.06, 1995.05, 1996.05
John F. Kennedy Center for the Performing Arts 2000.11
John Hart Associates, Inc. 1985.03
John R. Rogers Comedy Company 1882.56
John Stetson's Opera Bouffe Company 1878.19
John W. Isham Company 1898.55
John W. Norton and Company 1888.39, 1890.03
John Wanamaker 1905.57
John Young Studio 1915.27
John, Alf. 1890.17
John, Elton 1975.12, 1982.22, 1997.20, 2000.06
John, Graham 1923.35, 1924.33, 1925.50, 1929.32, 1930.05
John, Leslie 1946.05
John, Little 1905.55
John, Master 1868.06
John, Michael 1976.08
John, Theodore 1896.06
John, Tom 1968.07, 1971.09, 1972.02
John, Tom H. 1975.01, 1976.21, 1983.09, 1983.17, 1983.20
Johnakins-Kirk 1989.02
Johnk, Catherine 1943.20
Johnnie, Little 1880.07
Johnny Mann Singers, The 1963.10
Johnosn, J. Rosamund 1909.25
Johns, Al 1903.09, 1904.26, 1904.43, 1908.08, 1909.27
Johns, Barter 1895.32, 1905.04
Johns, Baxter 1893.24
Johns, Brooke 1923.07, 1923.38, 1927.04
Johns, Clay 1971.06
Johns, Eva 1890.01, 1890.19, 1890.24, 1891.30
Johns, Florence 1918.09
Johns, Glynis 1973.04
Johns, H.D. 1905.35
Johns, Kenneth 1934.17
Johns, Kurt 1988.09
Johns, M.S. 1882.62, 1885.33, 1890.17
Johns, Martin 1986.12
Johns, Mr. 1855.11
Johns, R. 1897.53
Johns, Romaine 1932.30
Johns, Stuart H. 1878.19
Johns, W. Barter 1885.10
Johns, W.B. 1881.32, 1885.50, 1901.03
Johns, W.S. 1894.47
Johnson 1989.02
Johnson, Alan 1958.05, 1960.08, 1962.03, 1964.15, 1965.24, 1976.07, 1976.09, 1981.28, 1984.06, 1988.20
Johnson, Albert 1918.23, 1933.22, 1934.01, 1934.19, 1934.29, 1934.38, 1935.15, 1937.16, 1938.07, 1938.13, 1939.25, 1940.01, 1941.03, 1943.14, 1944.32, 1945.17, 1950.14, 1952.07, 1952.08
Johnson, Albert R. 1930.32, 1931.16, 1932.05, 1932.20, 1933.02, 1933.25, 1938.15
Johnson, Alice 1888.09, 1893.11, 1894.42, 1898.77
Johnson, Alice E. 1888.29
Johnson, Allan 1992.18
Johnson, Anita 2000.03
Johnson, Ann 1931.41, 1931.43, 1961.21
Johnson, Annie 1876.13, 1877.01
Johnson, Annie Lewis 1888.30
Johnson, Arnold 1928.14, 1929.26, 1933.15, 1987.02
Johnson, Arte 1997.10
Johnson, Ben 1914.24, 1964.04
Johnson, Benny 1937.09
Johnson, Bernard 1962.16, 1965.31, 1971.13, 1972.10, 1973.10, 1976.04, 1976.21, 1978.21
Johnson, Betty 1985.04
Johnson, Bill 1907.29, 1940.23, 1941.13, 1943.01, 1945.19
Johnson, Billy 1898.22, 1899.12, 1899.35, 1902.06, 1903.39
Johnson, Bob 1942.13
Johnson, Bobby 1938.04, 1952.02
Johnson, Bruce 1976.34
Johnson, Buster 1921.21
Johnson, C. Rosamond 1900.40, 1903.07
Johnson, Carroll 1889.38, 1891.42
Johnson, Catharine 1938.08
Johnson, Catherine 1941.11, 1944.30
Johnson, Charles 1888.45, 1895.03, 1896.49, 1899.31
Johnson, Charles G. 1933.20
Johnson, Charles H. 1905.10
Johnson, Charlie 1978.09
Johnson, Chic 1923.20, 1938.08, 1941.11, 1942.27, 1944.30, 1949.06, 1950.14
Johnson, Chickie 1950.14
Johnson, Choo Choo 1943.07
Johnson, Christine 1938.15, 1945.05, 1949.03
Johnson, Clemontien 1889.47
Johnson, Cora 1975.19
Johnson, Danny 1993.04
Johnson, David Cale 1981.19, 1982.18
Johnson, David Lawrence 1984.02
Johnson, Dorothy 1928.45, 1934.03, 1938.10, 1946.24
Johnson, Doug 1982.04, 1991.05, 1995.05, 1998.11, 1998.13
Johnson, E. 1866.16, 1999.24
Johnson, Eddie 1940.21
Johnson, Edward 1908.06
Johnson, Elaine 1965.31
Johnson, Enotris 1989.12
Johnson, Eric 1986.12, 1988.09
Johnson, Ethel 1904.09, 1905.25, 1906.33, 1910.02, 1910.30, 1911.05
Johnson, Fannie 1894.05
Johnson, Fanny 1888.17, 1892.60
Johnson, Frank 1899.33, 1910.22, 1922.30
Johnson, Frank M. 1900.48
Johnson, Frank W. 1900.55
Johnson, Fred 1903.26
Johnson, Freddie 1925.18
Johnson, G. 1875.03, 1997.21
Johnson, George 1872.10, 1875.06, 1875.10, 1907.12, 1907.25
Johnson, George A.D. 1895.41, 1899.04
Johnson, George W. 1881.30, 1909.16
Johnson, Gertrude 1883.40, 1922.25, 1924.15, 1927.29
Johnson, Gil 1943.18
Johnson, Greer 1951.10, 1954.16
Johnson, Hall 1930.10, 1933.04, 1935.01, 1943.10, 1945.07, 1951.11, 1955.03
Johnson, Hannah 1873.26
Johnson, Harry 1912.33
Johnson, Haven 1934.06, 1936.12
Johnson, Heidi Karol 1998.06
Johnson, Henry 1910.18
Johnson, Henry M. 1912.28
Johnson, Howard 1914.22, 1916.25, 1919.44, 1921.23, 1924.07, 1927.03, 1933.15, 1936.06, 1937.02, 1939.10, 1942.11, 1975.22
Johnson, Hugh 1944.16
Johnson, Ida 1952.06, 1952.15
Johnson, Imogen 1888.19
Johnson, J. 1859.08, 1866.02, 1866.28, 1870.26, 1870.33, 1871.04, 1877.15, 1877.22
Johnson, J. Lewis 1927.67, 1930.16, 1930.19, 1931.47, 1932.11
Johnson, J. Louis 1939.21, 1940.17
Johnson, J. Rosamond 1899.35, 1900.46, 1900.48, 1900.55, 1901.25, 1901.29, 1902.06, 1902.42, 1903.04, 1903.28, 1903.39, 1903.41, 1931.31
Johnson, J. Rosamund 1896.46, 1901.27, 1902.23, 1903.01, 1903.15, 1904.22, 1904.47, 1906.14, 1906.27, 1907.22, 1908.08, 1909.10, 1909.27, 1911.13, 1911.26, 1928.40, 1930.29, 1930.34, 1931.11, 1935.13, 1939.14, 1940.17, 1942.03, 1989.23
Johnson, J.A. 1868.06, 1869.26, 1871.18, 1872.34, 1873.12, 1873.14, 1873.18
Johnson, J.C. 1930.19, 1930.29, 1931.09, 1975.20, 1978.09
Johnson, J.P. 1869.34
Johnson, J.W. 1980.27
Johnson, James 1879.09, 1880.15, 1881.55, 1898.02, 1906.39, 1918.23
Johnson, James C. 1927.32
Johnson, James P. 1923.39, 1927.38, 1928.10, 1930.22, 1938.19, 1943.16, 1944.32, 1980.10
Johnson, James W. 1904.47
Johnson, James Weldon 1900.40, 1900.46, 1900.48, 1900.55, 1903.07, 1903.39, 1904.56, 1906.14, 1907.22, 1908.08, 1911.13, 1955.13, 1969.10, 1980.27
Johnson, Jeff 1981.08
Johnson, Jeremy 1977.01
Johnson, Jimmie 1929.18
Johnson, Jimmy 1926.23, 1927.02, 1929.18, 1931.47
Johnson, Joe 1946.07
Johnson, John 1796.01, 1796.02, 1904.43
Johnson, Johnson B. 1936.12
Johnson, Josi 1942.11
Johnson, Jr., J. 1865.11, 1867.12
Johnson, Jr., Mel 1978.02, 1978.21, 1984.01, 1986.06
Johnson, Jube 1896.46
Johnson, Julianna 1879.37
Johnson, Julie 1931.21, 1997.10
Johnson, June 1949.06, 1950.14
Johnson, Justine 1973.11
Johnson, L. 1870.35
Johnson, Lawrence 1898.59
Johnson, Lawrence E. 1937.07
Johnson, Lawson 1955.15
Johnson, Lilly 1882.04, 1882.20
Johnson, Linda 1989.06
Johnson, Louis 1952.06, 1961.24, 1970.05, 1972.06, 1972.26, 1975.19, 1979.13, 1997.03
Johnson, Lucille 1936.26
Johnson, M. 1876.35
Johnson, M.D. 1891.24
Johnson, M.M. 1904.03
Johnson, Mabel 1929.50
Johnson, Madison 1896.49
Johnson, Major 1906.48, 1917.16
Johnson, Marian Page 1926.13
Johnson, Mary Lea 1978.02, 1979.06, 1982.18, 1985.05, 1985.15, 1987.12, 1989.26
Johnson, Merilyn J. 1982.11
Johnson, Messr. 1834.02, 1870.22, 1875.39, 1883.23, 1886.54
Johnson, Miss 1823.01, 1841.01, 1852.01, 1870.22, 1871.14, 1872.26, 1876.15, 1877.01, 1884.42
Johnson, Mister 1944.28
Johnson, Mme. 1841.01
Johnson, Mr. 1834.02, 1839.01, 1840.01, 1848.03, 1869.13, 1869.34, 1872.09, 1875.03, 1882.11, 1882.12, 1882.13
Johnson, Myra 1940.01
Johnson, Naomi 1925.24, 1928.12, 1928.23, 1930.20
Johnson, Nora 1903.20, 1967.14
Johnson, Norman 1992.06
Johnson, Nuggie 1927.30
Johnson, Nunnally 1931.21, 1946.20, 1967.14
Johnson, Olivia 1959.05
Johnson, Orrin 1894.39, 1921.35
Johnson, Otto 1909.18, 1916.23
Johnson, Otto F. 1905.28, 1906.24
Johnson, Patricia 1951.16, 1996.02
Johnson, Pauline 1892.47
Johnson, Pete 1945.10
Johnson, Philander 1896.06, 1920.37
Johnson, Ray 1887.39, 1930.05, 1930.31, 1934.36
Johnson, Reginald Vel 1979.18
Johnson, Richard 1963.28
Johnson, Rida 1910.06, 1929.38
Johnson, Robert 1928.39, 1936.12
Johnson, Robert L. 1999.09
Johnson, Rokey 1911.41, 1914.31
Johnson, Rosamond 1904.04
Johnson, Rosamund 1904.56, 1908.39, 1917.26, 1920.04, 1999.23
Johnson, Ruth 1928.18
Johnson, Sabel 1904.22
Johnson, Sallie 1894.11
Johnson, Spoder 1905.09
Johnson, Stacy J. 2001.04
Johnson, Stretch 1936.12
Johnson, Susan 1950.10, 1952.13, 1956.04, 1958.02, 1958.20, 1961.14
Johnson, Sy 1982.12, 1989.02
Johnson, T. 1870.07
Johnson, T.B. 1860.06
Johnson, Tilly 1882.20
Johnson, Tina 1987.03, 1993.10, 1996.04
Johnson, Tommi 1982.17, 1986.02
Johnson, Troy Britton 1994.06
Johnson, Van 1936.12, 1939.27, 1940.22
Johnson, Virginia 1944.02
Johnson, W. 1909.13
Johnson, W.T. 1883.07, 1884.23
Johnson, Walter 1925.07, 1927.58, 1929.32, 1932.01, 1943.06, 1943.12
Johnson, Weldon 1901.27
Johnson, William 1883.05, 1925.32, 1955.27
Johnson, Willie 1943.02
Johnson, Wini 1942.13
Johnson, Winnie 1936.12
Johnson-White, Carolyn 1988.05
Johnsonn 1880.37
Johnsrud, Harold 1932.20, 1935.03, 1937.01
Johnston, Al. 1901.28
Johnston, Alfred Cheney 1937.07
Johnston, Alice 1890.03
Johnston, Amy 1897.16
Johnston, Anna 1904.50
Johnston, Annie 1876.22
Johnston, Arthur 1923.32, 1924.37, 1924.44, 1927.21, 1927.38, 1928.03, 1928.50, 1929.25, 1980.10, 1989.16, 1995.14, 1997.01
Johnston, Barney 1959.27, 1960.09, 1962.14, 1964.20, 1964.21
Johnston, Carrie 1890.03
Johnston, Daisy 1903.18
Johnston, Donald 1978.28, 1979.18, 1980.20, 1980.30, 1981.12, 1983.17, 1990.14, 2001.08
Johnston, Dorothy 1932.22
Johnston, Edith 1895.28
Johnston, Eve 1928.11
Johnston, Fannie 1889.39, 1900.51
Johnston, Fanny 1889.06, 1891.36, 1893.07
Johnston, Fred 1907.27
Johnston, Grace 1931.28
Johnston, H. 1882.50
Johnston, J. 1877.23, 1877.25
Johnston, Jane 1960.02

Johnston, Joan 1945.16
Johnston, Johnny 1951.14
Johnston, Justine 1966.07, 1971.05, 1978.10, 1986.12
Johnston, Mabel 1923.04, 1924.04, 1924.35, 1924.44, 1927.02, 1927.46, 1927.47, 1928.38, 1929.37
Johnston, Mabel E. 1923.24, 1925.05, 1927.07, 1927.12, 1927.35, 1928.11, 1928.23, 1928.28
Johnston, Mack 1909.30
Johnston, Mary 1870.33
Johnston, Meredithi 1938.18
Johnston, Mr. 1851.04
Johnston, Mrs. T.B. 1857.01, 1857.02
Johnston, Nancy 1991.05
Johnston, Norman 1926.05
Johnston, Owen 1990.17
Johnston, R. 1875.18
Johnston, Robert 1877.01, 1882.69
Johnston, Roy M. 1942.21
Johnston, S. 1864.14
Johnston, T. 1854.04
Johnston, T.B. 1851.04, 1853.05, 1856.01, 1857.01, 1857.02, 1857.03, 1857.04, 1857.06, 1859.11
Johnstone and Hartford 1904.47
Johnstone, Alexander 1891.20, 1911.46, 1912.47, 1914.12, 1918.26
Johnstone, Alyce 1926.29
Johnstone, Anna Hill 1949.15, 1958.30
Johnstone, Gordon 1927.43
Johnstone, H. 1865.01
Johnstone, Jane 1942.26
Johnstone, Justine 1914.31, 1915.15, 1915.31, 1916.10, 1916.20, 1917.06, 1917.31
Johnstone, Lucy Jane 1906.41
Johnstone, Mabel 1925.10, 1925.24
Johnstone, Mary 1911.04
Johnstone, Tom 1920.02, 1922.01, 1922.29, 1924.10, 1924.11, 1925.35
Johnstone, W.B. 1911.46
Johnstone, Wesley 1896.01, 1898.25
Johnstone, Will 1923.25, 1924.36
Johnstone, Will B. 1912.47, 1914.12, 1919.07, 1922.01, 1924.11
Johnstone, William 1926.13, 1927.36
Jokai, Mor 1886.04, 1898.14, 1944.26, 1945.15
Jolie, Danielle 1999.15
Jolivet, Messr. 1879.46, 1879.47
Jolivet, Mlle. 1879.36, 1879.47
Jolivet, Mons. 1877.19, 1877.27, 1877.29, 1878.07, 1879.19, 1879.34, 1879.39, 1879.41, 1879.45
Jolivet, Tyrone 1983.04
Jolley, James 1927.04, 1927.27, 1933.24
Jolley, Nick 1979.31
Jollie, Fleur 1866.18
Jollie, June 1952.03
Jolly, Ed. S. 1900.45
Jolly, James 1926.38
Jolly, Russ 1990.15
Jolly, Winnie 1900.45
Jolson Theatre Musical Comedy Company 1930.01
Jolson's Musical Theatre Company 1929.48
Jolson's Theatre Musical Comedy Company 1929.34, 1929.36, 1929.38, 1929.40, 1929.43, 1929.47, 1930.03, 1930.07, 1930.12
Jolson, Al 1911.12, 1911.43, 1912.09, 1913.05, 1914.22, 1916.03, 1918.05, 1921.34, 1923.12, 1925.01, 1925.23, 1925.28, 1927.62, 1931.09, 1940.10, 1952.11, 1962.17, 1963.02, 1967.11, 1975.22, 1976.26, 1986.06, 1989.16, 1995.12, 1999.01
Jolson, Harry 1911.34
Joly 1877.13
Joly, Mlle. 1877.06, 1877.27, 1877.32, 1877.38
Jon, Lori 1953.01
Jonas, Edouard 1926.41, 1926.49
Jonas, Emil 1875.30
Jonas, Mr. 1863.10
Jonas, Nicholas 2000.19
Jonason, Louisa 1984.12
Jonathan, John 1968.17
Jonathan, Marc 1999.07
Jonay, Roberta 1947.17
Jones and Son 1905.21
Jones, A.L. 1920.28, 1921.27, 1922.32, 1923.31, 1924.22, 1924.32, 1925.47, 1928.08, 1928.13
Jones, Ada 1889.05, 1890.30, 1891.15
Jones, Alan 1930.32, 1933.26
Jones, Alexander 1937.09, 1937.11
Jones, Allan 1931.44, 1934.13, 1942.17, 1944.01
Jones, Anne 1959.26
Jones, Arthur 1952.13
Jones, Benny 1909.10
Jones, Bill 1944.01, 1982.22
Jones, Bob 1975.18
Jones, Bobby 1912.43, 1912.45, 1915.11, 1919.26
Jones, Brenda Elaine 1976.16
Jones, Broadway 1930.34, 1931.47
Jones, Byron 1924.37, 1927.33, 1928.10
Jones, C. 1884.34
Jones, C.H. 1882.45, 1885.45, 1888.19, 1888.26, 1892.20
Jones, Candy 1945.14, 1977.09
Jones, Carl 1945.08
Jones, Carol 1952.15
Jones, Ceinwen 1951.06
Jones, Charles 1885.28, 1885.67, 1887.12, 1892.30, 1927.24
Jones, Charles H. 1885.45, 1886.26, 1886.33, 1886.43, 1887.18, 1887.28, 1888.22, 1890.21, 1891.13, 1898.33, 1898.37, 1902.18, 1906.44
Jones, Charlotte 1952.13, 1966.10, 1967.16, 1971.06
Jones, Cheryl 1981.21
Jones, Christine 2000.10
Jones, Chuck 1990.10
Jones, Clarence 1914.06
Jones, Cliff 1976.03
Jones, D. Bradley 1977.18
Jones, Dale 1928.34, 1965.21
Jones, Dave 1936.05
Jones, Davey 1930.25
Jones, David 1938.05, 1963.01
Jones, Dean 1970.13, 1986.18
Jones, Denis 1994.07, 1998.15, 2000.15
Jones, Disley 1964.42, 1966.23, 1968.27, 1976.12, 1978.15
Jones, Don 1981.02, 1983.21
Jones, E. 1867.08
Jones, E. Forrest 1892.20
Jones, Earl 1906.43, 1980.10
Jones, Earl C. 1906.08, 1906.14, 1906.45
Jones, Earle C. 1910.01, 1914.15
Jones, Edward 1890.50
Jones, Eleanor 1944.23, 1946.22
Jones, Ellis O. 1930.35
Jones, Emma 1880.25
Jones, Evan 1934.34
Jones, F. 1870.26
Jones, F.C. 1896.40
Jones, F.V. 1879.06
Jones, Frank 1894.25, 1904.06, 1929.09
Jones, Frankie 1891.46
Jones, Fred 1914.02, 1956.15
Jones, Freddie 1965.39
Jones, Frederick 1925.29
Jones, G. 1879.02
Jones, Gareth 1978.14
Jones, Gattison 1920.35, 1922.23, 1928.32, 1928.46
Jones, Genie 1880.24
Jones, George 1936.03, 1940.01
Jones, Gertie 1888.19
Jones, Grace 1916.10
Jones, Gussie 1899.35, 1900.48
Jones, Gwen 1944.21
Jones, H.L. 1876.35
Jones, Hank 1957.14
Jones, Henry 1947.09
Jones, Herber 1882.31
Jones, Herbert 1882.33, 1882.36, 1906.03
Jones, III., Frederick 1923.07
Jones, Isham 1924.32, 1925.50, 1983.09, 1997.01, 1999.24, 2000.16
Jones, J. 1889.10
Jones, J.F. 1876.30
Jones, J.H. 1870.20, 1870.23, 1872.16, 1872.18, 1872.19, 1872.20, 1873.18, 1873.21, 1873.23, 1876.27, 1877.16
Jones, J.P. 1879.42
Jones, James 1884.27
Jones, James Earl 1966.15
Jones, James H. 1876.17, 1876.18, 1876.21
Jones, Jannie 2000.15
Jones, Jay Aubrey 1995.05
Jones, Jen 1980.16
Jones, John Christopher 1993.02, 2001.06
Jones, John Price 1920.32, 1921.36, 1923.44, 1925.44, 1927.13, 1927.41, 1929.07
Jones, John Randolph 1965.32
Jones, Josie 1927.22
Jones, Jr., George 1924.27, 1932.30
Jones, Judd 1963.27, 1967.10
Jones, Jumel 1951.11
Jones, Katie 1906.14, 1908.08, 1909.27
Jones, Kitty 1975.09
Jones, Lauren 1964.33, 1971.13
Jones, Lavine 1900.46
Jones, Leilani 1985.05
Jones, Lena N. 1890.36, 1894.52
Jones, Leroy 1990.19
Jones, Leslie 1913.35
Jones, Leslie Julian 1953.17
Jones, Louis Weslyn 1899.36
Jones, M. Howard 1911.14
Jones, Mabelle 1909.15
Jones, Maggie 1879.28
Jones, Maria 1889.54
Jones, Mark 1965.39
Jones, Marshall 2000.19
Jones, Martin 1936.12
Jones, Maxine 1937.09
Jones, Messr. 1846.01, 1856.02, 1869.28, 1882.04, 1882.20, 1885.14, 1885.52, 1892.06
Jones, Miss 1841.01, 1862.01, 1867.10, 1868.06, 1879.02, 1879.04
Jones, Mme. 1841.01
Jones, Mr. 1836.01, 1841.01, 1846.01, 1855.04, 1855.05, 1859.03, 1860.01, 1860.03, 1866.28, 1869.15, 1869.26, 1872.24, 1875.03, 1875.05, 1875.40, 1876.16
Jones, Mr. T.C. 1957.10
Jones, Mrs. 1839.01, 1840.01, 1865.05
Jones, Mrs. W.G. 1852.02, 1879.54, 1886.44
Jones, N. 1878.13
Jones, N.D. 1878.19, 1880.07
Jones, Nat T. 1884.58
Jones, Nathaniel 1964.44
Jones, Neil F. 1966.18, 1968.31
Jones, Nellie 1877.24, 1878.01, 1878.13, 1879.04
Jones, Olive 1933.23
Jones, Oscar 1907.39
Jones, Owen 1913.04, 1914.30
Jones, Patricia 1947.20
Jones, Pattie Darcy 1995.03
Jones, Paul 1925.17, 1928.23
Jones, Paulette Ellen 1971.20
Jones, Peggy Ann 1962.25, 1962.26, 1962.28, 1964.41, 1964.42, 1964.43, 1966.22, 1966.23, 1966.25, 1966.28, 1968.26, 1968.27, 1968.28, 1968.29, 1978.17, 1989.15
Jones, Philip 1926.13
Jones, Quincy 1979.13
Jones, R. 1881.35
Jones, R.J. 1848.03
Jones, Ralph H. 1914.24
Jones, Randolph 1899.41
Jones, Ras 1907.31
Jones, Reed 1979.22, 1979.27, 1980.02, 1981.08, 1982.13, 1982.19
Jones, Reina 1912.36
Jones, Richard 1934.40, 1997.06, 1999.06
Jones, Richard J. 1895.27
Jones, Robert 1860.06
Jones, Robert Earl 1988.05, 1991.01
Jones, Robert Edmond 1913.05, 1944.01, 1946.05, 1959.05
Jones, Robert Edmund 1918.36, 1930.10, 1935.01, 1938.18, 1939.20, 1939.21, 1944.16, 1951.11
Jones, Roland 1935.01
Jones, Roy L. 1987.07
Jones, Sabra 1982.24
Jones, Sam 1930.29
Jones, Sanford R. 2001.04
Jones, Shirley 1957.02, 1968.24
Jones, Shirley Yvonne 1976.16
Jones, Sidney 1894.33, 1895.02, 1895.10, 1895.43, 1896.27, 1896.31, 1896.36, 1897.44, 1898.18, 1899.39, 1900.43, 1902.12, 1904.01, 1904.03, 1905.18, 1910.03, 1913.09, 1931.35, 1932.29
Jones, Spike 1998.17
Jones, Starr 1925.17, 1927.17, 1930.31
Jones, Starr West 1937.01
Jones, Stephen 1919.15, 1919.25, 1920.10, 1920.18, 1920.33, 1921.10, 1921.21, 1921.30, 1921.36, 1922.28, 1922.45, 1923.01, 1923.07, 1923.27, 1924.15, 1924.21, 1924.30, 1924.43, 1924.44, 1925.29, 1925.45, 1926.03, 1927.16, 1927.21, 1927.29, 1927.38, 1927.49, 1928.50, 1929.37, 1932.25, 1945.09
Jones, Stephen P. 1928.49
Jones, Steve 1922.39, 1923.32, 1924.18, 1925.10, 1925.24, 1926.18
Jones, Steven 1988.10
Jones, Strappy 1925.40
Jones, Sydney 1914.18, 1915.18
Jones, T.C. 1945.17, 1956.08
Jones, T.J. 1991.01
Jones, T.L. 1927.53
Jones, Terry 1976.06
Jones, Thomas 1979.15
Jones, Thompson 1899.33
Jones, Todd 1970.10
Jones, Tom 1929.06, 1930.18, 1930.33, 1930.37, 1931.36, 1935.18, 1939.16, 1963.26, 1966.29, 1969.02, 1976.32, 1992.10
Jones, Valorie Denise 1976.16
Jones, Vanessa A. 1995.02
Jones, Virgil 1992.08
Jones, W. 1883.52
Jones, W.G. 1871.17, 1875.05
Jones, W.L. 1899.01
Jones, W.W. 1915.28
Jones, Walter 1892.06, 1893.17, 1894.26, 1895.38, 1896.06, 1896.18, 1897.25, 1898.20, 1898.28, 1898.43, 1899.19, 1901.04, 1902.20, 1907.49, 1908.38, 1913.29, 1918.16
Jones, Walter F. 1922.28
Jones, Walton 1979.24
Jones, Warren 1943.03
Jones, Will 1892.47
Jones, William 1880.68, 1895.30, 1897.05, 1907.56, 1910.06, 1943.24
Jones, William J. 1894.20
Jones, William L. 1900.10
Jones-Bey, Elmira 1946.24
Jongerius, Gerard 1982.23
Jongeyans, George 1950.05, 1950.20
Jonka, Mlle. 1869.26
Jonns, Birl 1965.24
Jonsen, Pauline 1888.24
Jonson, Bill 1951.17
Jonson, Clara 1856.01
Jonson, Jane 1937.11
Jonson, William 1952.06, 1961.03, 1961.04, 1961.05, 1961.06, 1961.09, 1961.13, 1962.08, 1962.09, 1962.10, 1962.11, 1962.19, 1963.15, 1963.23, 1964.14, 1964.19, 1964.46
Jooss, Kurt 1942.02
Joplin, Carol 1965.20
Joplin, Scott 1975.19, 1980.27
Joray, Peter 1929.33
Jorbeau, Vernona 1893.37
Jordan, Al 1928.49
Jordan, Bert 1920.36, 1923.40, 1924.26
Jordan, Charles E. 1926.38
Jordan, Claudia 1944.23
Jordan, Dorothy 1926.13, 1928.43
Jordan, Earl 1928.20
Jordan, Emily 1903.30
Jordan, Frances 1917.22
Jordan, G.H. 1878.04
Jordan, Glenn 1953.15, 1954.06, 1957.15
Jordan, H.C. 1851.08
Jordan, Harry 1864.14
Jordan, Irene 1944.32
Jordan, J.B. 1898.43
Jordan, Jack 1973.17
Jordan, Jackson 1945.01, 1945.09
Jordan, Jessie 1900.20, 1901.06
Jordan, Joe 1906.08, 1907.22, 1907.31, 1908.08, 1910.18, 1915.02, 1922.22, 1927.30, 1929.01, 1930.29, 1931.19, 1931.31, 1935.11, 1980.10
Jordan, John 1961.26
Jordan, Joseph 1933.27, 1937.07
Jordan, Jr., Jack 1941.06
Jordan, Jules 1897.34, 1898.47
Jordan, Lillian 1927.10
Jordan, Louis 1992.03, 1999.06
Jordan, Lulu 1876.34, 1880.17, 1881.18, 1883.40
Jordan, Lynda 1959.21, 1962.21, 1963.24
Jordan, M.J. 1881.15
Jordan, Marc 1962.27, 1964.11, 1966.18, 1968.02, 1968.23, 1973.15, 1976.15, 1976.33, 1979.09

Jordan, Marguerite 1902.38
Jordan, Mary 1926.13
Jordan, May 1889.51, 1892.06
Jordan, Miss 1870.05
Jordan, Mr. 1851.04, 1868.04
Jordan, Mrs. Harry 1879.12
Jordan, Nellie 1894.25
Jordan, Paul 1961.26
Jordan, Tenita 1981.29
Jordan, Trevor 1976.16, 1976.24
Jordan, W. 1886.28, 1888.44, 1892.35
Jordan, W.H. 1887.29
Jordan, Will 1960.06
Jordan, William 1927.20
Jordanaires, The 1978.01
Jordon, Dorothy 1927.59
Jordon, Jessie 1898.77
Jordon, Shirley 1931.32
Jordon, Will 1978.01
Jorensen, Nels 1958.13
Jorgens, Linda 1968.03
Jorgensen, Nels 1958.13
Jory, Jon 1973.02
Jose, Edouard 1897.52, 1898.51
Jose, M. 1929.10
Jose, R.J. 1893.50, 1894.52
Jose, Richard J. 1891.32, 1892.50, 1896.15
Josef, Carl 1890.31, 1894.01
Josef, William 1972.08
Josefsberg, David 1996.17
Josefson, Johannes 1923.31
Joseph 1912.09, 1915.17, 1917.31, 1918.06, 1920.07, 1922.09, 1922.14, 1926.01, 1928.04
Joseph E. Howard Amusement Company 1908.13
Joseph Papp Public Theatre 2000.08
Joseph Papp Public Theatre/NY Shakespeare Festival 1996.08, 1998.16
Joseph Physioc and Company 1902.40
Joseph Physioc Studio 1919.11
Joseph Wickes Studio 1922.43, 1922.48
Joseph's of New York 1929.06
Joseph, Carl 1892.43
Joseph, Catrice 2000.18
Joseph, Edmund 1927.10
Joseph, Irene 1925.37
Joseph, Irving 1981.14
Joseph, Jackie 1959.14, 1961.16
Joseph, Leonard 1991.03
Joseph, Messr. 1844.01, 1892.43
Joseph, Peter 1966.30
Joseph, Robert 1936.28
Joseph, Robert L. 1952.15
Joseph, Stephen M. 1970.20
Josephine, Lois 1912.14, 1913.18, 1913.29, 1915.22, 1916.22, 1921.09
Josephine, Miss 1852.01, 1852.05, 1866.18
Josephine, Mlle. 1871.27, 1872.06, 1872.10
Josephs 1915.27
Josephs, Harry 1870.36, 1870.39, 1876.02, 1877.21, 1878.02, 1878.19
Josephs, L. 1883.06
Josephs, Miss 1865.01
Josephs, Therese 1918.31
Josette, Mme. 1927.64
Josey, Vilma 1941.11
Joslin, D. 1894.13
Joslin, Howard 1950.14
Joslyn, Allen 1920.28
Joslyn, B.F. 1888.02, 1890.26, 1891.31, 1891.47
Joslyn, Benjamin F. 1889.24
Joslyn, Betsy 1982.18, 1998.05
Josti 1884.28
Jouard, Messr. 1877.31, 1879.26, 1879.44, 1879.46
Jouard, Mons. 1877.26, 1877.27, 1877.30, 1877.32, 1877.33, 1877.34, 1877.38, 1878.07, 1878.08, 1878.09, 1879.19, 1879.27, 1879.31, 1879.36, 1879.39, 1879.40, 1879.41, 1879.43, 1879.45, 1879.47, 1879.48, 1879.49, 1879.51, 1879.55, 1879.61, 1879.69, 1880.14, 1880.22, 1880.23, 1880.29, 1880.56
Joubert, Joseph 1990.05
Joukovitch, Messr. 1923.28
Jourard, Messr. 1880.28
Jourdan, Julia 1876.16
Jourist, Messr. 1922.06
Journet, Marcel 1942.22
Jousse, Juliette 1870.37, 1871.06
Jousse, Mlle. 1870.45, 1871.03, 1871.26
Jousse, Mme. 1870.41
Jovovich, Scott 1989.03, 1999.01
Joy, Carol 1956.06
Joy, James Leonard 1985.04, 1990.20, 1991.13, 1992.14, 1996.04, 1997.03
Joy, John 1967.16, 1969.01
Joy, Mildred 1924.11
Joy, Miss 1841.01
Joy, Nicholas 1927.01, 1932.22, 1958.11
Joyce 1862.03, 1863.07
Joyce, Adrian 1923.11
Joyce, Carol 1925.35
Joyce, Carol Leavy 2000.05
Joyce, Dorothea 1974.23
Joyce, Eddy 1883.02
Joyce, Edith 1897.42
Joyce, Elaine 1972.04
Joyce, Gussie 1899.36
Joyce, Jack 1906.01, 1949.06
Joyce, James 2000.01
Joyce, Janice 1933.24
Joyce, Jennie 1889.27, 1889.30, 1889.32, 1889.42, 1889.53, 1890.05, 1890.09, 1890.13, 1890.22, 1890.38, 1890.42, 1891.10, 1891.19, 1891.35, 1892.02, 1892.13
Joyce, Laura 1872.37, 1873.08, 1878.16, 1879.30, 1880.01, 1880.03, 1881.04, 1881.11, 1882.42, 1882.70, 1883.04, 1883.10, 1883.38
Joyce, Lee 1944.15, 1944.30
Joyce, Louise 1922.35, 1930.36
Joyce, Milo 1903.18, 1906.37
Joyce, Mylo 1899.19
Joyce, Ned 1909.14
Joyce, Paul 1929.46
Joyce, Peggy Hopkins 1923.21
Joyce, Phyllis 1923.35
Joyce, Robert 1976.03
Joyce, Talbot 1890.28
Joyce, Thomas 1872.27, 1922.30
Joyce, Thomas H. 1898.43, 1898.55
Joyce-Bell, Laura 1887.26, 1887.28
Jozefowicz, Janusz 1992.05
Juanas, Paco 1973.17
Juarez, Juanita 1942.29
Judah, Catherine 1940.11, 1940.13, 1944.04, 1944.06, 1944.08, 1944.09, 1944.10, 1944.11, 1944.12, 1944.13, 1946.11
Judah, Percie 1906.34
Judd, Carl 1916.04, 1921.20, 1927.52
Judd, Carl C. 1913.20
Judd, Rebecca 1991.05
Jude, Patrick 1977.18, 1979.15, 1980.23, 1981.24, 1985.17
Judels, Charles 1902.11, 1903.17, 1904.53, 1909.30, 1910.16, 1911.02, 1912.38, 1913.35, 1915.07, 1916.09, 1916.22, 1917.14, 1917.23, 1918.25, 1920.38, 1922.10, 1923.05, 1925.27, 1926.01, 1926.15, 1926.37, 1927.19, 1927.58, 1947.13
Judels, May 1940.16, 1942.19, 1944.20, 1946.14, 1947.12, 1948.19, 1949.05
Judge, Count Wellington 1977.01
Judge, Eddie 1904.11, 1909.06
Judge, Eddy 1902.02
Judge, Jack 1914.22, 1914.23, 1942.24, 1964.28, 1975.22, 1991.04
Judic, Anna 1885.55, 1885.56, 1885.57, 1885.59, 1885.60, 1885.61, 1886.08, 1886.09, 1886.18, 1886.19, 1886.20, 1886.21, 1886.22
Judson, Alice 1898.48, 1900.07, 1904.01, 1907.06
Judson, Charles 1919.26
Judson, Helen 1925.37
Judson, Helen G. 1898.04
Judson, James 1947.11
Judson, Lester 1955.11
Judy, James 1995.19, 1996.15, 1997.19, 1999.21, 2000.19
Juhnke, Mr. 1897.35
Juhre, Albert 1896.51, 1899.05, 1899.10, 1902.18, 1904.10
Juignet, Messr. 1863.05
Juignet, Mons. 1859.10, 1878.18
Juignet, Mr. 1863.05
Juignet, P. 1866.09, 1866.23, 1866.25, 1866.27, 1866.29, 1866.30
Juignet, Paul 1868.24, 1868.26, 1869.03, 1869.05, 1869.16, 1869.30, 1882.43, 1882.46
Jujamcyn Theatres 1979.09, 1979.24, 1983.06, 1984.01, 1987.18, 1989.26, 1989.29, 1991.05, 1992.04, 1992.08, 1993.18, 1993.19, 1994.07, 1994.11, 1995.03, 1995.12, 1996.06, 1996.17, 1997.04, 1997.18, 1998.03, 1999.08, 1999.24
Jujamcyn Theatres Interamerica, Inc. 1997.13
Jukes, Bernard 1930.04, 1930.39
Jule Styne Organization 1959.06
Jules, Charles 1919.19
Jules, M. 1929.10
Julia, Miss 1864.23, 1865.02, 1865.04
Julia, Raul 1971.18, 1972.25, 1974.25, 1976.10, 1982.09, 1992.07
Julian, Alexander 1990.19
Julian, Don 1930.17
Julian, Mr. 1891.26
Julian, Ruth 1907.06
Julian-Jones, Leslie 1956.08
Juliani, Mlle. 1868.07
Juliano, John 1951.12
Julie, Mme. 1917.27
Julien, A. 1871.23
Julien, Albert 1871.25
Julien, Jay 1964.29, 1980.15
Julien, Marie 1875.29
Julien, Mlle. 1871.26, 1872.03, 1872.33, 1872.42, 1875.04, 1875.33, 1877.32
Julien, Mons. 1871.28, 1872.03, 1872.28, 1872.39, 1872.41, 1872.42, 1873.11, 1873.15, 1873.16, 1875.28
Julien, Mr. 1870.22
Juliet 1924.19
Juliet, Miss 1916.02
Juliette, Mlle. 1858.01
Julius, Anita 1908.33
June 1929.02
June, Roma 1916.06, 1917.23, 1918.29
Jung, Mr. 1890.31, 1894.01
Junger, Esther 1934.19, 1935.03, 1940.18
Junior, John 1910.33
Junker, Conrad 1885.27
Junker, Herr 1882.68
Junod, Betty 1931.39
Junor, Kenneth 1905.31
Jupyeat, C. 1898.07
Jurgens, Claus 1965.04
Jurgens, Dick 1942.16
Jurgens, Mina 1902.11
Jurist, Irma 1948.15, 1950.02, 1951.10
Jurist, Messr. 1922.06
Jurman, Karl 1994.06
Jurmann, Walter 1999.05
Jury, A. 1896.12
Jury, Paul 1990.15
Just Because, Inc. 1922.13
Just, Helen 1878.11
Justice, June 1925.35
Justice, W.C. 1905.18
Justin, Dorothy 1927.27
Juteau, Messr. 1879.46, 1880.28
Juteau, Mlle. 1872.28, 1872.39, 1873.01, 1873.11, 1873.15
Juteau, Mme. 1872.33, 1872.41, 1872.42
Juteau, Mons. 1872.28, 1872.29, 1872.31, 1872.33, 1872.39, 1872.41, 1872.42, 1873.01, 1873.11, 1873.15, 1873.16, 1879.26, 1879.27, 1879.31, 1879.34, 1879.36, 1879.40, 1879.41, 1879.43, 1879.44, 1879.45, 1879.47, 1879.48, 1879.60, 1880.16, 1880.23, 1880.27, 1880.29
Juvelier, Aaron 1958.18
Jwara, Martin 1997.14

Kabatchnik, Amnon 1968.22
Kabler, James 1983.17
Kaczorowski, Peter 1993.10, 1995.11, 1997.07, 1999.19, 2000.07, 2000.11, 2001.05
Kadelburg, Gustav 1936.22
Kademova, Bessie 1926.03
Kaden, Eileen 1995.02
Kadison, Harry 1937.14
Kadison, Philip 1949.01
Kadokawa, Haruki 1989.24, 1990.17
Kadous, Raphael 1925.37
Kaempfert, Bert 1975.12
Kaestner, William 1909.19
Kagan, Richard 1985.03, 1986.20, 1993.02
Kahal, Irving 1927.39, 1928.47, 1929.26, 1931.36, 1938.01, 1940.12, 1941.11, 1957.10, 1965.08, 1979.24, 1988.08, 1991.10, 1999.24
Kahal-Norman, Irving 1947.05
Kahl, Howard 1963.13, 1964.21, 1965.21, 1965.35, 1966.24, 1970.09
Kahn and Bowman 1924.05
Kahn, Amtullah 1981.17
Kahn, Ben 1978.02, 1978.24
Kahn, Carl 1904.22, 1909.23
Kahn, Gary 1989.29
Kahn, Gus 1914.22, 1917.18, 1918.05, 1918.07, 1919.19, 1921.34, 1922.15, 1922.34, 1924.32, 1924.46, 1925.36, 1925.48, 1926.12, 1928.47, 1929.27, 1930.08, 1930.13, 1931.08, 1931.11, 1944.32, 1956.02, 1962.17, 1974.09, 1975.22, 1976.32, 1979.05, 1980.08, 1983.09, 1986.01, 1986.06, 1989.06, 1989.21, 1992.02, 1999.10, 1999.23, 1999.24
Kahn, Harold 1936.07
Kahn, Jeannette 1919.35
Kahn, Jr., E.J. 1985.02
Kahn, Judy 1973.04
Kahn, Leo 1942.12
Kahn, Madame 1917.31
Kahn, Madeline 1968.13, 1970.19, 1978.02
Kahn, Michael 1968.05, 1983.05
Kahn, Mme. 1916.09, 1916.11, 1916.26, 1917.14, 1918.02
Kahn, Mr. 1890.31, 1891.33, 1892.43, 1893.29, 1894.01
Kahn, Roger Wolfe 1928.17, 1928.40, 1928.45, 1930.06
Kahn, Theodore 1930.29, 1931.47
Kahn, Victor 1911.44
Kahn, Walt 1922.21
Kahu, Rongo 1972.20
Kaiawe, S.M. 1912.03
Kaier, Edna 1926.43
Kailimai, Henry 1915.30, 1915.31
Kain, Paul 1898.43
Kaina, Jimmy 1973.14
Kainer, Ludwig 1924.18, 1925.24
Kairoff, Leon 1930.09
Kaise 1964.28
Kaiser, George 1980.04, 1980.25
Kaiser, Norma 1950.15, 1955.06
Kal Amend Studio 1923.23
Kalama, Sylvester 1912.03
Kalan, Aroon 1991.11
Kalan, Charles 1968.30
Kalba, Taras 1979.20, 1980.03, 1980.22, 1981.20, 1981.22
Kalbfuss, K. 1932.01
Kalcheim, Lee 1972.19
Kaldenberg, Keith 1954.18, 1955.27, 1956.04, 1958.16, 1959.02, 1959.08, 1959.09, 1959.17, 1960.02, 1962.10, 1964.18
Kales, Arthur F. 1912.05
Kales, Elisabeth 1984.03, 1984.05
Kalet, Mlle. 1926.45
Kaley, Charles 1927.02
Kalfin, Robert 1974.06, 1977.08, 1979.29, 1990.05
Kaliban, Bob 1961.02, 1964.33
Kaliban, Robert 1961.22
Kalich, Jacob 1942.28
Kalil-Ogly 1930.27
Kalioujny, Alexandre 1954.01
Kalish, Larry 1980.15
Kalisz, Armand 1907.46, 1918.15
Kaliz, Arman 1922.23
Kalkanis, Harry 1967.05
Kalkhurst, Eric 1928.33
Kallen, Lucille 1950.02, 1950.09
Kallini, Joseph 1938.13
Kallman, Dick 1951.18
Kálmán, Emmerich 1909.15, 1914.03, 1916.19, 1916.26, 1917.20, 1922.35, 1926.27, 1927.17, 1927.63, 1928.15, 1930.04, 1945.11, 1975.22, 1984.05
Kalmanov, H. 1970.18
Kalmar, Bert 1917.35, 1920.18, 1920.33, 1921.18, 1922.15, 1922.32, 1923.19, 1923.32, 1923.33, 1924.22, 1924.44, 1925.05, 1925.36, 1925.42, 1925.47, 1926.03, 1926.23, 1926.28, 1926.32, 1926.39, 1927.12, 1927.52, 1928.02, 1928.25, 1928.38, 1929.49, 1941.09, 1975.22, 1981.03, 1999.01
Kalusky, Yakov 1972.17
Kaman, Brian 1980.02, 1983.13
Kamaroff, George 1945.01
Kamaroff, Georges F. 1943.20
Kamarova, Natalie 1943.20, 1945.01
Kamdin, Dorothy 1930.36
Kamel, Stanley 1978.25
Kamen, J.J. 1962.17
Kamen, Justin Bartholomew 1994.12
Kamen, Michael 1980.05
Kamernitsky, Dmitry 1925.46, 1925.51

Kamman, Effie 1898.02
Kammerer, Harry 1903.01
Kammerer, Henry 1895.40, 1898.64
Kammerer, William 1889.28
Kammerlee, Carrie 1882.09
Kammerlee, G. 1882.07, 1882.09, 1882.11, 1882.13, 1898.45
Kammerlee, Gus 1880.12, 1880.48, 1880.53, 1882.12, 1887.02, 1887.42, 1888.25, 1889.43, 1890.36, 1898.45, 1899.32, 1904.32, 1907.43, 1908.32
Kamo, Professor 1917.29
Kamp, Charles 1911.22
Kamp, Lena 1900.59
Kamp, Tana 1927.67, 1932.11
Kamph, Ita 1904.03
Kanagawa, Kennedy 1998.20, 1999.21
Kanapoff, Fishl 1990.16
Kanavan, Dani 1971.17
Kandaky, Mme. 1927.51
Kandel, Aben 1931.09
Kandel, Lenore 1976.27
Kandel, Paul 1993.06, 1995.19, 1996.15, 1997.22, 1998.20, 1999.21, 2000.09, 2000.19
Kander, John 1959.13, 1960.13, 1962.01, 1965.17, 1966.24, 1968.01, 1968.30, 1971.07, 1974.01, 1974.17, 1975.14, 1977.16, 1981.10, 1982.06, 1983.14, 1984.01, 1986.03, 1987.16, 1988.08, 1989.16, 1989.27, 1991.04, 1991.06, 1991.10, 1993.09, 1996.14, 1997.07, 1998.04, 1999.01, 1999.23
Kane, Allegro 1957.09
Kane, Andrea 1996.16
Kane, Brad 1993.10
Kane, Clarence 1937.11
Kane, Donna 1989.23
Kane, Dorothy 1929.39, 1930.41
Kane, Edward 1937.01, 1938.15, 1939.13, 1948.31
Kane, Frank 1943.23
Kane, Gail 1912.06
Kane, Helen 1927.19, 1928.25, 1933.16
Kane, Irene 1960.19
Kane, J. 1873.05
Kane, James 1900.34
Kane, Jim 1908.15
Kane, Joe 1903.18, 1906.28
Kane, John 1926.30, 1927.64, 1930.30, 1948.15, 1997.11, 1998.06, 1999.11
Kane, Joseph 1896.38, 1898.68, 1899.25, 1903.18, 1904.31, 1905.25, 1907.33, 1911.05
Kane, Karol 1929.24
Kane, Lida 1927.09
Kane, Lottie 1872.14, 1872.36
Kane, Mickey 1938.16
Kane, Whitford 1922.20, 1925.20
Kanengeiser, Anne 1998.01
Kanin, Fay 1961.27, 1985.05
Kanin, Garson 1960.23, 1964.11
Kanin, Michael 1961.27, 1981.10
Kanin, Myer 1932.08
Kanrich, Albert M. 1907.49
Kansas, Jeri 1980.20
Kantor, Kenneth 1979.02, 1980.26, 1983.10, 1987.10, 1988.16, 1992.04
Kantor, Mary 1989.20
Kantrowitz, Jason 1989.09, 1999.14
Kapellmeister, Herr 1880.61
Kaper, Bronislaw 1945.14
Kapetan, Peter 1982.03
Kaplan, Hyman 1937.14
Kaplan, Isabel deWitt 1906.30
Kaplan, Joan 1968.10
Kaplan, Jonathan 1992.09
Kaplan, Mitchell 1998.14
Kaplin, Stephen 1996.16, 1999.05
Kapon, Michael B. 1976.30
Kapp, David 1961.14
Kapp, Peter 1988.08
Kapp, Richard 1987.19
Kappelar, Alfred 1898.72
Kappeler, Alfred 1910.05, 1911.17, 1911.42, 1918.07, 1925.04, 1937.17
Kar, Eileen 1889.46
Karabanova, Mme. 1922.06, 1923.28, 1925.03, 1927.51, 1929.05
Karachentsev, Nikolai 1990.01
Karapetian, Lauren 1970.16
Karaty, Tommy 1966.05, 1966.10
Karavaeff, Simeon 1927.38, 1927.60, 1943.11
Karbacz, Kelly 1990.02
Karbi, Ras 1980.05
Karby, R.I. 1883.43
Karcher, Jack 1976.05, 1979.02
Karczykowski, Richard 1984.04
Kardana 1999.04
Kardana Productions, Inc. 1992.04, 1993.06, 1995.05, 1996.14
Kardana-Swinsky Productions 1999.12, 2000.11
Kardon, Helen 1962.02
Karel, Charles 1968.03, 1969.05, 1983.14
Karels, Harvey 1929.29
Karen, Lynda 1983.05
Kari, Magda 1939.22
Karinsky, Irene 1939.31
Karkalits, Patti 1955.27
Karl O. Amend Studios 1924.04
Karl, Eileen 1893.17, 1894.26
Karl, Robert 1955.06, 1958.20
Karl, Tom 1880.45, 1880.48, 1880.53, 1882.07, 1882.08, 1882.10, 1882.11, 1882.12, 1882.13, 1882.65, 1883.11, 1883.12, 1883.15, 1891.29, 1892.51, 1893.18, 1893.19, 1893.48, 1894.03, 1894.08, 1896.08
Karle, Amalia 1899.21
Karle, George 1943.08
Karle, Theo 1929.08
Karlick, Gerd 1999.05
Karlin, Josephine 1907.11, 1909.30
Karloff, Boris 1950.08
Karlsson, Gert 1964.22
Karlton, Sylvia 1947.17
Karlweis, Oscar 1942.31
Karm, Michael 1970.19
Karm, Mickey 1965.20, 1967.10
Karman, Werner 1964.25
Karmon Histadruth Ballet, The 1968.04
Karmon, Jonathan 1968.04, 1969.13, 1971.14, 1973.01
Karmstedt, Mr. 1883.62
Karna, Bob 1923.38
Karner, Chris 1959.26
Karner, Christine 1944.32, 1951.10
Karnilova, Maria 1946.10, 1949.08, 1952.20, 1957.02, 1959.13, 1962.14, 1964.27, 1968.30, 1973.12, 1981.07, 1981.18, 1993.14
Karpe, Curt 1909.26, 1918.13
Karpe, Curtis 1918.33, 1921.41, 1930.21
Karr, Darwin 1906.34
Karr, Dennis 1974.17
Karr, Harold 1956.08, 1956.16, 1976.24
Karr, James 1959.03
Karr, Joan 1927.35
Karr, Mary 1904.27
Karr, Patti 1956.14, 1958.01, 1959.01, 1959.26, 1962.02, 1970.08, 1972.07, 1972.23, 1978.28, 1979.15, 1980.11, 1993.18
Karrol, Dorothy 1946.16
Karroll, Dorothy 1946.22
Karroll, Virginia 1899.40
Karson, Nat 1934.39, 1938.01, 1939.17, 1940.07, 1941.09, 1943.22, 1946.04, 1948.17
Kartavin, Leon 1925.06
Karyl, Iris 1942.35
Karyle, Ann 1929.44
Kasakoff, Sam 1953.04
Kasdan, Michael 1971.16
Kase, Donald Walter 1983.04
Kasha, Al 1974.19, 1977.09, 1981.12, 1982.14
Kasha, Lawrence 1963.14, 1964.11, 1964.40, 1966.14, 1970.09, 1970.21, 1971.20, 1973.06, 1981.10, 1982.14, 1985.08
Kashner, David 1955.25
Kasia 1945.07
Kaslan Productions 1982.14
Kasman, Mort 1972.02
Kasmer, Miss 1884.11
Kasper, John 1948.19, 1949.05
Kass, Alan 1968.03, 1972.04
Kass, Jerome 1978.27
Kassel, Art 1924.35
Kassoff, Russell 1991.04, 1998.12, 1999.23
Kasten, Sam 1942.28
Kasten, Sonia 1934.18
Kaster, Miss 1863.01
Kastner, Peter 1974.03
Kasznar, Kurt 1937.01, 1941.03, 1955.10, 1959.24, 1965.04
Katarina, Mlle. 1872.10
Katchaturian, Aram 1968.04
Katheryn Arlington, Inc. 1927.02
Katiska, Mlle. 1869.26, 1870.31
Katrine, Mlle. 1862.03, 1863.06, 1863.07
Katsaros, Doug 1976.03, 1989.07, 1997.08, 1998.13, 2000.17
Katscher, Robert 1931.09, 1938.07
Katsulas, Andreas 1983.16
Kattwinkel, Susan 1881.06
Kattwinkel, Walter 1946.22
Katz, Arthur 1985.06
Katz, Bill 1981.06, 1990.15
Katz, Mickey 1951.21, 1967.03
Katz, Natasha 1986.11, 1989.27, 1990.17, 1990.20, 1991.06, 1991.13, 1993.16, 1993.18, 1994.04, 1996.04, 1997.19, 1998.02, 1999.13, 1999.16, 2000.06, 2000.18
Katzboeck, Rudolf 1984.05
Katzell, William R. 1947.03, 1948.30, 1950.02
Katzka, Emil 1952.01
Katzka, Gabriel 1962.23, 1964.45
Katzman, Louis 1925.16, 1925.45, 1927.21, 1927.37, 1927.38, 1927.40, 1927.53, 1931.34, 1942.30
Katzska, Gabriel 1965.02
Kau, Andrew 1977.01
Kau-Lee, Valerie 1986.20
Kauahi, Norman Wendall 1988.20
Kauffman, C. 1884.63, 1885.14
Kauffman, Charles 1885.28, 1885.52
Kauffman, Charles F. 1888.31
Kauffman, John 1906.11
Kauffman, Messr. 1883.58
Kauffmann, Christian 1988.20
Kauflin, Jack 1961.11
Kaufman Costume Company 1911.31
Kaufman, Alan 1975.18
Kaufman, Alvin 1932.19
Kaufman, Charles W. 1912.37
Kaufman, Don 1973.11
Kaufman, Eric H. 1989.27
Kaufman, Frances 1918.16
Kaufman, Frederick 1927.14, 1927.55
Kaufman, George S. 1922.32, 1922.42, 1923.19, 1923.32, 1924.15, 1924.30, 1925.45, 1927.21, 1928.38, 1929.19, 1930.02, 1931.16, 1931.48, 1932.05, 1932.17, 1933.02, 1933.13, 1933.25, 1937.13, 1938.09, 1944.29, 1945.09, 1946.20, 1950.17, 1952.07, 1955.02, 1967.02, 1981.27
Kaufman, Harry 1939.26, 1941.11, 1942.27, 1944.30
Kaufman, Harry A. 1943.05
Kaufman, Harry Alvin 1940.07
Kaufman, Irving 1918.24, 1947.02
Kaufman, Joseph 1906.01, 1908.18
Kaufman, Martin R. 1989.26
Kaufman, Mildred 1932.19
Kaufman, Minnie 1919.22
Kaufman, Mr. 1882.71, 1883.45
Kaufman, Rebecca 1902.35
Kaufman, Rose 1937.14
Kaufman, S. Jay 1920.08, 1939.22, 1940.07
Kaufman, S. Kay 1924.15
Kaufman, S.J. 1940.07
Kauser, Kim 1984.01
Kautizky 1881.32
Kautsky and Rottonara 1914.25
Kautsky, Herr 1890.50
Kautzenbach, Arthur 1917.07
Kautzenbach, Arthur F. 1914.33
Kava, Caroline 1976.10
Kavan, Albia 1939.26
Kavanagh, Eily 1885.26
Kavanagh, John 1996.01, 1998.09
Kavanagh, Joseph A. 1889.51
Kavanagh, Lila 1888.36
Kavanagh, Mary 1876.03
Kavanagh, Messr. 1844.01, 1886.32
Kavanagh, Stan 1936.02, 1936.17
Kavanaugh, Messr. 1927.33
Kavanaugh, Ray 1928.23, 1929.26, 1930.22, 1931.26, 1932.18, 1933.20, 1935.04, 1936.12, 1939.12, 1940.03, 1940.23, 1944.19, 1945.11
Kavanaugh, Ray M. 1946.07
Kawala, A. 1912.03
Kawalek, Nancy 1979.29
Kawamura, Betty 1973.14
Kay, Arthur 1937.15, 1944.21, 1946.18, 1948.24, 1953.16, 1965.22
Kay, Billy 1949.06, 1950.14
Kay, Hershy 1944.33, 1954.03, 1956.15, 1959.04, 1959.26, 1961.08, 1961.20, 1963.26, 1964.18, 1965.01, 1965.29, 1968.08, 1969.17, 1971.15, 1974.06, 1975.15, 1975.22, 1976.11, 1976.33, 1978.02, 1978.19, 1979.09, 1979.23, 1980.07, 1982.20, 1983.13, 1984.11, 1986.08, 1989.14, 1992.10, 1997.10
Kay, Honey 1920.08
Kay, Katharine 1896.12
Kay, Lisan 1946.05
Kay, Marlene 1965.20
Kay, Mildred 1921.31
Kay, Stanley 1986.02
Kaye, A.P. 1928.03, 1935.15
Kaye, Alma 1944.32
Kaye, Benjamin M. 1925.17, 1926.13, 1930.18, 1930.33
Kaye, Beryl 1955.19
Kaye, Buddy 1948.21, 1983.03
Kaye, Danny 1939.26, 1941.04, 1941.08, 1963.10, 1970.19
Kaye, Florence 1989.12
Kaye, Fred 1894.33, 1905.27
Kaye, Gina 1964.23, 1964.44
Kaye, Gloria 1959.02, 1959.05, 1964.17
Kaye, Hershy 1950.08
Kaye, Irene 1949.09
Kaye, Jim 1955.11
Kaye, Joel 1951.21
Kaye, Judy 1978.02, 1981.14, 1981.25, 1988.01, 1989.04, 1996.13, 1998.01
Kaye, Lionel 1941.11
Kaye, Nora 1935.02, 1939.13, 1952.20
Kaye, Paul 1943.23
Kaye, Paula 1946.01
Kaye, Robert 1963.05, 1965.17, 1968.24
Kaye, Ronna 1982.10
Kaye, Sidney 1963.10
Kaye, Sparky 1952.02
Kaye, Stubby 1950.17, 1956.12, 1974.26, 1985.05
Kaye, Tina 1965.05
Kaye, Tom 1983.17
Kaye, Toni 1986.11
Kaye, V. Ann 1932.11
Kayne, E.M. 1870.27, 1871.16, 1889.05
Kays, Alan 1978.08, 1978.20, 1978.23, 1979.21, 1979.27, 1983.12
Kayser, Joseph 1923.22
Kayworth, Leo 1955.10
Kaz, Aysa 1927.65
Kazan, Elia 1936.28, 1943.19, 1948.25
Kazan, Lainie 1961.08, 1962.14, 1964.11, 1992.17
Kazantzakis, Nikos 1968.30, 1983.14
Kazantzeva, Nadezhda 1977.13
Kazda, Patrick 1946.14
Kazounoff, Berenece 1932.01, 1940.04
Kazounoff, Berenice 1937.14
Kazounoff, Bernece 1936.01
Kazuko Hillyer International 1984.03, 1984.04, 1984.05
Keagy, Grace 1975.06, 1979.02, 1979.09, 1980.11, 1981.10
Kealty, Mayme 1898.05
Kealy, Kenny 1961.02, 1964.35
Kean, Betty 1932.24, 1941.03, 1955.04
Kean, E. 1881.35
Kean, Jane 1943.07, 1945.17, 1955.04, 1957.08, 1961.09
Kean, Norman 1975.20, 1975.23, 1976.27, 1978.28
Kean, Thomas 1750.01, 1884.04
Keane, Audrey 1946.01
Keane, Dillie 2000.16
Keane, George 1947.07
Keane, John 1987.01
Keane, Lew 1922.25
Keane, Martin 1954.03
Keane, Robert Emmet 1917.32
Keane, Robert Emmett 1914.16, 1917.09, 1918.25, 1929.31, 1933.02, 1934.14
Keane, Teri 1943.08, 1943.18
Keans, Allen 1927.59
Kearley, Harry 1918.05
Kearney, Eileen 1908.42, 1909.07, 1909.29, 1913.04
Kearney, Jack 1924.30
Kearney, James 1890.40, 1897.43, 1924.47
Kearney, John 1918.05, 1923.16, 1924.30, 1926.04, 1927.07, 1928.11
Kearney, John H. 1896.04
Kearney, John L. 1912.01
Kearney, John R. 1943.23
Kearney, M. 1893.27
Kearney, M.J. 1896.40, 1897.43
Kearney, Michael 1892.54, 1893.36, 1894.04

Kearney, Mildred 1903.38
Kearney, Mr. 1893.15
Kearney, Ty 1948.18
Kearney, Tyrone 1936.05
Kearns, Allen 1914.20, 1919.08, 1920.27, 1921.23, 1923.01, 1923.24, 1925.16, 1925.49, 1926.51, 1928.17, 1928.50, 1930.31
Kearns, Allyn 1920.08
Kearns, Daniel F. 1995.16, 1996.08
Kearns, Jack 1921.34, 1922.34, 1924.47
Kearns, John 1919.03, 1920.19
Kearns, Thomas K. 1898.17
Kearny, John 1944.01
Keast, Paul 1925.02
Keast, Raymond 1947.17
Keathley, Adriana 1960.01
Keating, B.J. 1949.17, 1951.23, 1953.01
Keating, Barry 1989.09
Keating, Fred 1929.29, 1930.06, 1946.16, 1960.03
Keaton, Diane 1968.11
Keats, Mildred 1920.32, 1921.34, 1923.12, 1923.36, 1924.24, 1928.32
Keay, Nancy 1917.16
Keck, Charles 1918.14
Keck, Gladys 1927.60
Keck, John William 1979.13, 1979.28, 1980.09
Kedrova, Lila 1983.14
Kee, High 1888.09
Keefe, Frank 1882.48
Keefe, George 1911.40
Keefe, John 1896.18, 1897.15, 1898.02, 1902.08, 1903.17
Keefe, John H. 1894.26
Keefe, Jonathan 1907.20, 1908.15, 1911.29
Keefe, Matt 1916.15
Keegan, Arthur 1947.09
Keegan, Fran 1949.18
Keegan, Robert 1967.01
Keegan, Ted 1989.19
Keel, Howard 1957.11, 1959.27, 1972.24
Keeler, Joseph W. 1888.43
Keeler, Kate 1910.22
Keeler, Madam 1924.46
Keeler, Madame 1917.04
Keeler, Marion 1927.65
Keeler, Ora 1916.07
Keeler, Ruby 1927.05, 1927.12, 1927.48, 1971.03
Keeling, Lucyle 1929.34, 1929.36
Keen, Elizabeth 1973.16
Keen, Keith 1990.18
Keen, Malcolm 1952.05
Keen, Master 1884.61
Keenan, Annetta 1875.11
Keenan, Frank J. 1891.08, 1894.37, 1897.01
Keenan, Harry G. 1924.40
Keenan, Joan 1945.05, 1950.04
Keenan, Thomas 1917.16
Keenan-Bolger, Andrew 1999.21, 2000.18
Keendon, John 1923.09
Keene, Aggie 1872.04, 1872.30, 1872.36, 1872.43
Keene, Christopher 1974.08, 1975.11
Keene, Dick 1924.16, 1927.48, 1929.12
Keene, Elizabeth 1922.26, 1923.45
Keene, Josephine 1950.16
Keene, Laura 1853.03, 1856.01, 1857.01, 1857.02, 1857.03, 1859.05, 1859.06, 1859.07, 1860.04, 1860.06, 1861.04, 1862.09, 1863.08
Keene, Lew 1924.37
Keene, Louis 1925.18
Keene, Margaret 1922.26, 1923.45
Keene, Mary 1881.28
Keene, Mattie 1897.49, 1923.03, 1927.42
Keene, Richard 1926.02, 1934.14
Keene, Richard W. 1921.30
Keene, Rose 1875.19, 1875.23, 1875.26, 1875.35
Keene, S.W. 1883.37, 1889.06
Keene, Samuel 1909.24
Keene, Samuel W. 1883.37
Keene, T.W. 1869.38, 1870.12, 1870.18, 1870.22, 1870.28, 1871.01, 1871.02, 1871.05, 1872.02, 1872.14
Keene, Theodora 1918.31
Keene, W. 1870.25
Keener, Suzanne 1924.09
Keepa, Sonny 1972.20
Keeshon, Grace 1916.11, 1918.05, 1919.03, 1919.30, 1920.19, 1920.47, 1921.20, 1921.34
Keezel, Florence 1942.09, 1944.09
Kegley, Kermit 1963.06
Kehoe, Annie 1893.10
Kehoe, M. 1884.53
Kehr, Don 1984.02
Kehr, Donnie 1993.06
Kehrig, Diana 1968.09, 1974.16, 1976.23, 1976.31, 1977.03, 1977.17
Keifert, Mr. 1921.38
Keil, Mary 1989.09
Keiler, Lizzie 1882.05
Keill, Agnes 1897.21
Keim, Adelaide 1904.02
Keim, Betty Lou 1949.17
Keimes, Messr. 1851.01, 1852.01, 1852.05, 1854.01, 1855.01
Keinz, Leah 1906.10
Keirn, Judy 1960.06
Keiser, Robert A. 1898.28, 1899.36
Keita, Keita 1972.03
Keith, A.L. 1925.41
Keith, Diane 1949.03
Keith, Eugene 1917.01
Keith, Gertrude 1936.03
Keith, Isham 1937.02, 1937.12
Keith, Kenneth 1922.23, 1922.26
Keith, Lawrence 1964.16
Keith, Lester 1906.44
Keith, Lester W. 1907.18
Keith, Paul 1983.05
Keith, Roberta 1962.12
Keith, Roydon 1913.37, 1915.21
Keith, Sally 1942.23
Kelcy, Frances 1903.05
Kelcy, Kate 1903.05
Kelcy, Nelly 1903.05
Keldkakmp, Walter 1927.05
Kelety, Julia 1919.08, 1920.01, 1921.10, 1927.43
Kelety, Julie 1951.22
Kelk, Jackie 1935.14, 1953.08
Kellam 1914.21
Kellam, William 1920.12
Kellan, William 1897.07
Kellar, Andrew 1932.10
Kellar, Arthur 1927.65
Kellar, Frank 1917.12
Kellar, Jack 1919.14
Kellar, Marie 1905.20
Kellard, Bill 1993.01, 1995.16, 1998.17
Kellaway, Cecil 1960.05
Kelleher, Alfred 1872.20
Kelleher, Louis 1888.33
Kelleher, Sue 1905.44
Kelleher, Susie 1902.30, 1903.31
Kellems, Happy 1949.06
Keller, Agnes 1900.35
Keller, Alma 1924.12
Keller, Dorothy 1944.14, 1948.23
Keller, Elana 1946.01
Keller, Evelyn 1947.10, 1948.29, 1950.13
Keller, Frl. 1879.22
Keller, Hiram 1968.11
Keller, Jeff 1974.06, 1976.36, 1979.24, 1983.08, 1988.01, 1994.12
Keller, Judith 1966.14
Keller, Jules 1889.42
Keller, Marie 1906.30
Keller, Mario 1927.14
Keller, Sheldon 1979.09
Keller, William 1914.06
Kellerd, John E. 1893.24, 1908.36
Kellerman, Alice 1931.05
Kellerman, Annette 1911.43
Kellett, Maud 1905.21
Kellett, Robert 1987.15
Kelley, Barry 1943.04
Kelley, Bob A. 1901.20
Kelley, Bunty 1947.07, 1948.31
Kelley, C.L. 1914.31
Kelley, Charles B. 1882.34
Kelley, Charles L. 1912.02
Kelley, D.A. 1873.20, 1873.22
Kelley, Daniel 1888.44
Kelley, Edgar Stillman 1927.28
Kelley, Eithel 1912.15
Kelley, Ethel 1912.13
Kelley, Frank 1907.30, 1908.20, 1909.07
Kelley, Georgia 1903.04
Kelley, Harry 1912.13
Kelley, Jack 1929.32
Kelley, Lew 1909.06
Kelley, Louise 1911.11, 1912.28, 1914.07, 1914.27, 1920.07
Kelley, Marie 1928.27
Kelley, Maude Alice 1907.23
Kelley, Messr. 1882.34
Kelley, Norman 1952.12, 1956.09, 1958.17, 1959.07, 1959.09, 1959.18, 1960.14, 1961.03, 1961.05, 1961.19, 1961.23, 1962.06, 1962.11, 1962.19, 1963.23, 1964.07, 1964.09, 1964.12, 1965.09, 1965.11, 1965.13
Kelley, Orry 1929.32, 1929.39
Kelley, Peter 1952.20
Kelley, Ronald 1976.31, 1990.08
Kellin, Mike 1955.04, 1955.27, 1963.09
Kellino, Master 1865.08, 1865.10
Kellner, Murray 1943.16
Kellogg, Cal Stewart 1976.31, 1978.08
Kellogg, Clara Louise 1861.05
Kellogg, Dell 1887.25
Kellogg, Fanny 1870.03
Kellogg, Florence 1883.23, 1884.27
Kellogg, Florence D. 1883.17, 1883.19, 1883.23
Kellogg, Helen 1884.27
Kellogg, Louise 1870.03
Kellogg, Lynn 1968.11
Kellogg, Marie 1889.29
Kellogg, Marjorie 1974.25, 1978.13, 1979.07
Kellogg, Marjorie Bradley 1982.11
Kellogg, Mary Ann 1985.08
Kellogg, Miss 1870.02
Kellogg, Paul 2000.03
Kellogg, Peter 1992.11
Kellogg, Shirley 1908.39, 1910.02, 1911.42, 1912.24
Kellogg, Viola 1901.27, 1904.40, 1909.04
Kelloski, Hary 1916.24
Kelly 1884.12
Kelly and Leon's Minstrels 1867.21, 1868.05, 1868.21
Kelly, Al 1941.03, 1943.14, 1948.21
Kelly, Alice 1898.10
Kelly, Allan 1916.04, 1917.17
Kelly, Ann 1926.39
Kelly, Anne 1916.22
Kelly, B.F. 1902.33, 1904.20
Kelly, Bessie 1915.30
Kelly, Billy 1924.25
Kelly, Clyde 1934.13
Kelly, D.A. 1873.22, 1876.13, 1876.22, 1877.01
Kelly, Daren 1981.10, 1987.03
Kelly, David Patrick 1974.24, 1978.12, 1982.08
Kelly, Dennis 1994.01
Kelly, E.A. 1883.42
Kelly, E.H. 1910.04
Kelly, E.T. 1892.04
Kelly, Edgar S. 1889.01
Kelly, Edgar Stillman 1892.42
Kelly, Edith 1908.25, 1909.04, 1922.05
Kelly, Edward A. 1883.65, 1887.13
Kelly, Edwin 1862.06, 1866.20, 1866.22, 1866.26, 1866.32, 1866.35, 1867.01, 1867.02, 1867.11, 1867.21, 1867.28, 1868.05, 1868.14, 1868.28, 1868.29, 1868.33, 1870.08, 1870.10, 1870.11, 1870.16, 1870.27, 1870.29, 1870.38, 1871.12, 1871.16, 1876.04, 1876.05, 1876.07, 1876.09, 1876.10, 1876.11, 1876.14, 1876.30, 1876.33, 1877.03, 1877.05
Kelly, Eithel 1902.06, 1904.29, 1908.27, 1910.05
Kelly, Ella 1885.52, 1885.67
Kelly, Emmet 1940.07
Kelly, Ethel 1923.30
Kelly, Ethel Amorita 1913.17, 1914.16
Kelly, Eugene 1905.44
Kelly, Eva 1898.03, 1898.10, 1899.25, 1903.22, 1909.01
Kelly, F. 1856.01
Kelly, Frank 1898.77
Kelly, Frank M. 1907.08
Kelly, Fred 1942.20, 1971.05
Kelly, Frederic N. 1948.27
Kelly, Frederick 1893.40, 1897.12
Kelly, Gene 1938.13, 1939.12, 1940.22, 1941.06, 1958.19, 1985.08
Kelly, George 1905.23, 1923.31, 1927.38, 1942.11
Kelly, Georgia 1901.12, 1902.06, 1902.23, 1906.04
Kelly, Georgie 1905.02, 1911.15
Kelly, Glen 1983.08, 1994.04, 1994.12, 1995.19, 1996.15, 1997.07, 1997.22, 1998.05, 1998.20, 1999.16, 1999.21, 2000.19, 2001.05
Kelly, Gregory 1908.28
Kelly, H. 1867.01
Kelly, H. Daniel 1898.68
Kelly, H.W. 1898.02
Kelly, Harry 1888.39, 1891.09, 1895.04, 1896.30, 1898.38, 1899.26, 1899.36, 1901.01, 1901.19, 1902.43, 1903.17, 1904.22, 1904.54, 1906.15, 1906.20, 1907.21, 1908.35, 1909.13, 1910.29, 1911.01, 1914.31, 1916.24, 1917.26, 1918.07, 1918.19, 1919.19, 1920.23, 1922.40, 1923.25, 1926.03, 1927.07
Kelly, J.J. 1876.13, 1876.22
Kelly, J.W. 1896.39, 1917.14
Kelly, Jack 1915.32, 1916.14, 1928.14
Kelly, James 1875.03
Kelly, James J. 1892.32
Kelly, James T. 1892.02, 1892.13, 1892.26, 1892.41, 1896.37, 1898.03, 1898.10, 1899.13, 1900.59
Kelly, Jamie 1914.06
Kelly, Jean 1987.18
Kelly, Jen 1996.01, 1996.12, 1998.09
Kelly, Joe 1897.06, 1898.08, 1902.02, 1903.13
Kelly, John 1899.19, 2000.01
Kelly, John T. 1886.10, 1887.30, 1889.09, 1889.41, 1891.09, 1895.04, 1895.18, 1896.02, 1896.26, 1896.31, 1896.36, 1897.09, 1897.19, 1897.31, 1897.48, 1898.50, 1898.69, 1899.17, 1899.30, 1900.38, 1901.17, 1902.29, 1903.28, 1911.17, 1912.07
Kelly, Jonathan 1976.18
Kelly, K. 1873.26
Kelly, K.C. 1978.13
Kelly, Kitty 1921.20, 1923.10, 1923.45, 1926.46, 1930.21
Kelly, Kristen Lee 1996.09, 2000.17
Kelly, Louise 1917.18, 1939.19
Kelly, M.A. 1902.06
Kelly, Mabel 1916.11
Kelly, Malachi 1902.10
Kelly, Margot 1916.16, 1920.09
Kelly, Mark M. 1981.21
Kelly, Mary Pat 1999.17
Kelly, Master 1856.01
Kelly, Maude Alice 1902.02, 1902.37
Kelly, Maurice 1937.16, 1938.13
Kelly, May 1938.02
Kelly, Messr. 1876.33
Kelly, Michael 1999.17
Kelly, Mickey 1999.17
Kelly, Mike 1888.44
Kelly, Mme. 1897.28
Kelly, Mr. 1896.02, 1898.29
Kelly, Mrs. 1896.19
Kelly, Neil 1917.37
Kelly, Nell 1928.35, 1929.06, 1929.32
Kelly, Nona 1912.03
Kelly, Norman 1962.08, 1964.14
Kelly, Orrin 1927.43
Kelly, Orry 1927.31, 1929.06, 1929.17, 1929.32, 1929.35, 1930.27
Kelly, P.J. 1958.20
Kelly, Pat 1963.08
Kelly, Patricia 1968.05
Kelly, Patsy 1927.62, 1928.37, 1929.26, 1930.22, 1931.09, 1932.17, 1971.03, 1973.05
Kelly, Paul 1930.06, 1999.24
Kelly, Paul Austin 1988.14, 1992.14, 1993.13
Kelly, Paula 1964.35, 1971.08
Kelly, Rachael 1978.11
Kelly, Renee 1911.45
Kelly, Robert 1898.26, 1900.52, 1922.25
Kelly, Robert A. 1898.22, 1906.08, 1907.55
Kelly, Ronald 1990.07, 1991.08
Kelly, Rose 1903.13
Kelly, Spencer 1894.41
Kelly, Terry 1944.14
Kelly, Therese 1926.39
Kelly, Thomas 1872.23, 1876.23, 1877.21
Kelly, Thomas J. 1873.26
Kelly, Tom 1911.17
Kelly, Tresha 1966.24
Kelly, Vivian 1925.32
Kelly, W.C. 1903.34
Kelly, W.J. 1911.24
Kelly, Walter 1925.02
Kelly, Walter C. 1914.01, 1916.23, 1929.37
Kelman, Charles 1997.18
Kelman, Charles D. 1981.13
Kelo, Carralo 1925.24, 1926.14

Kelo, Charles 1925.24, 1926.14
Kelsee, F. 1904.13
Kelsey, B. 1964.28
Kelsey, Carleton 1925.07, 1927.31, 1927.64
Kelsey, Lizzie 1869.02, 1869.06, 1869.43, 1870.04, 1872.37, 1873.10, 1876.06, 1876.13, 1876.15, 1876.29, 1877.01
Kelsey, Louis 1930.10
Kelsey, Miss 1873.26
Kelso, Harry 1919.21
Kelso, James 1924.16, 1940.19
Kelso, Joe 1919.21
Kelso, Lee 1923.13
Kelso, Louis 1899.34, 1900.50, 1902.16, 1904.56
Kelso, Maym 1902.21
Kelso, Mayme 1890.34, 1891.43, 1894.10, 1900.07, 1907.39, 1908.06, 1911.18
Kelso, Vernon 1927.50
Kelton, Gene 1959.26, 1963.21, 1964.21, 1970.09
Kelton, Pert 1925.33, 1927.52, 1932.23, 1940.23, 1957.18, 1960.05
Kelvin, Walter 1952.15, 1953.03, 1955.02, 1963.05
Kemarskaya, Nadiezhda 1925.46, 1925.51
Kemball, Charles 1884.29, 1884.31
Kemball, Colin 1964.28
Kemble, Adelaide M. 1877.20
Kemble, C.W. 1873.24
Kemble, Frankie 1884.21, 1889.13
Kemble, John 1905.48, 1906.44, 1907.18
Kemble, Keith 1905.48
Kemmerling, Warren 1955.27
Kemp, Alice 1875.20
Kemp, Alice M. 1875.11
Kemp, Annie 1866.18
Kemp, David 1906.31
Kemp, Emme 1976.04
Kemp, Tony 2000.04
Kemp, Will 1998.10
Kemper, Charles 1936.12, 1938.07
Kemper, Dave 1908.08
Kemple-Cooper, Anthony 1947.04
Kempner, Brenda 1965.39
Kempner, David 1911.40
Kempner, Dolores 1953.11
Kempner, Nicholas 1927.35, 1929.32, 1930.32
Kempner, Nick 1932.27
Kempner, Nicklas 1929.37
Kempner, Niclas 1925.30
Kempner-Hochstadt, Max 1923.03
Kenann, John 1898.64
Kendall, Dickie 1915.32
Kendall, Edwin F. 1913.03
Kendall, Ezra F. 1884.66, 1886.11
Kendall, Harry 1927.54
Kendall, Henry 1925.41
Kendall, Jo 1964.29
Kendall, Kuy 1915.30, 1918.21, 1919.16, 1920.31, 1922.08, 1923.42
Kendall, Lottie 1907.45, 1907.59, 1908.20
Kendall, Miss 1903.03, 1904.13, 1904.44
Kendall, Pat 1926.14
Kendall, Terry 1926.14
Kendall, Tichie 1894.52
Kendall, Trent Armand 1999.11
Kendall, Virginia 1903.03, 1904.13, 1904.44
Kendall, William 1937.16
Kendis, James 1906.29, 1913.06, 1925.26
Kendler, Lorelei 1927.38
Kendrick, Anna 1998.05
Kendrick, F.M. 1889.05
Kendrick, Frank M. 1893.06, 1903.25
Kendrick, Murray 1931.44
Kendrick, Rexford 1913.37
Kenin, Jean 1926.16
Kenna, Messr. 1794.01
Kenna, Mrs. 1794.01
Kennebel, Charles 1903.01
Kennebel, Frank 1903.01
Kennedy 1879.12
Kennedy, Alice 1928.48
Kennedy, Andrew 1918.13
Kennedy, Bettie 1897.28
Kennedy, Bill 1965.18
Kennedy, Bob 1945.17
Kennedy, Brian 2000.05
Kennedy, Charles 1924.03
Kennedy, Clayton 1903.39
Kennedy, Don 1950.06
Kennedy, E. John 1921.01
Kennedy, E.J. 1918.10
Kennedy, Frances 1908.18, 1909.29, 1912.41
Kennedy, Frank 1907.40, 1908.12
Kennedy, Georgia 1960.01
Kennedy, Harold 1932.14, 1942.20
Kennedy, Harry 1881.55, 1893.30, 1894.37
Kennedy, Jack 1923.04, 1927.41
Kennedy, Jay 1979.13, 1981.08
Kennedy, Jimmy 1955.13, 1979.07
Kennedy, John 1907.24, 1929.50, 1943.20, 1944.02, 1945.03, 1946.02, 1947.04, 1947.11, 1947.20, 1957.01
Kennedy, John A. 1938.18
Kennedy, John P. 1901.19, 1902.43, 1905.31
Kennedy, Joseph 1928.31
Kennedy, Louise 1901.26
Kennedy, M.A. 1873.25, 1884.39, 1891.38, 1896.29
Kennedy, Mack 1920.43
Kennedy, Madge 1923.27
Kennedy, Margaret Upshur 1934.16
Kennedy, Mat 1912.16
Kennedy, Matt 1926.22
Kennedy, Matthew 1904.53
Kennedy, May 1904.25
Kennedy, Memay 1902.44
Kennedy, P.A. 1902.09
Kennedy, Ray 1997.05
Kennedy, Sandy 1951.12
Kennedy, Steve C. 2000.06
Kennedy, Steve Canyon 1993.06, 1993.17, 1994.02, 1995.05, 1996.08, 1997.06
Kennedy, Steven C. 2001.05
Kennedy, Tara 1979.12
Kennedy, Thomas C. 1936.28
Kennedy, Tom 1951.05
Kennedy, Tony 1894.50, 1901.26
Kennedy, Will J. 1912.20
Kennedy, William 1963.04, 1984.16
Kennedy, Zetti 1898.65, 1898.71, 1902.41
Kennedy, Zettie 1898.74
Kennedy-Fox, Dorothy 1934.40
Kennel, Louis 1927.15
Kennelly, Don 1929.24
Kennelly, Francis 1933.07
Kenner, Chris 1982.22, 1992.06
Kenneth-John Productions 1983.14, 1983.19, 1984.01, 1985.19
Kenneth-Mark Productions 1983.06
Kennett, Karl 1898.38
Kenney, Charles Horace 1888.33
Kenney, Charles L. 1890.11, 1891.17, 1899.10
Kenney, Charles Lamb 1883.38, 1883.58, 1894.11, 1894.48
Kenney, Ed 1956.07, 1958.19, 1961.07
Kenney, Elba 1902.05
Kenney, Kay 1941.03
Kenney, Sharyn 1952.15
Kennick, T. 1866.18
Kennington, Pat 1976.29
Kennon-Wilson, James 1967.15
Kenny, Charles 1932.19, 1976.32
Kenny, Elba 1902.16
Kenny, J.C. 1880.05
Kenny, Jack 1988.18, 1990.18
Kenny, James C. 1876.23
Kenny, Nick 1976.32, 1981.06, 1997.03
Kenny, Sean 1962.18, 1963.01, 1965.19, 1965.23, 1965.28, 1984.07
Kenny, Stella 1894.02
Kenny, Talbot 1938.03
Kenny, Thomas 1944.29
Kenny, Tom 2000.04
Keno, Joe 1908.28, 1921.20
Keno, Joseph 1911.05
Kensett, James 1884.17
Kensmoe, Jeff 1991.08
Kent, Allegra 1957.05
Kent, Arthur 1938.05
Kent, Billy 1905.39, 1907.24, 1907.63, 1918.09
Kent, Carl 1940.18, 1941.03, 1944.21, 1945.10
kent, Charles 1886.27
Kent, Charlotte 1929.19, 1930.38, 1931.13, 1936.01, 1939.19
Kent, Craufurd 1910.21, 1911.11, 1912.28, 1913.21
Kent, Crawfurd 1916.12
Kent, Dorothy 1896.14, 1906.05
Kent, Edgar 1924.14, 1924.39, 1925.20, 1948.26
Kent, Eleanor 1912.42
Kent, F. 1869.02
Kent, F.M. 1857.03
Kent, Guy 1961.21
Kent, J. Stapleton 1907.58
Kent, Lennie 1943.18
Kent, Leonard 1939.29
Kent, Livingstone 1879.14
Kent, Lucille 1920.21
Kent, M. 1869.02
Kent, Michael 1958.18
Kent, Mildred 1924.17, 1927.18
Kent, Mr. 1823.01
Kent, Nimmie 1883.02
Kent, Roberta 1989.08, 1991.10
Kent, Rockwell 1916.07
Kent, Sandra 1965.32
Kent, Stapleton 1936.03, 1941.03
Kent, Walter 1936.17, 1939.24, 1942.26, 1951.18, 1974.09
Kent, William 1918.32, 1918.40, 1919.16, 1920.32, 1921.36, 1923.36, 1924.28, 1927.59, 1928.35, 1930.31, 1932.01
Kenting, Jodell 1965.26
Kenward, Edith 1892.25
Kenway, Albert 1918.31
Kenway, G.F. 1867.20
Kenway, Mr. 1867.19
Kenworth, Messr. 1883.17
Kenworth, T.H. 1883.19
Kenworthy, F.H. 1885.64
Kenworthy, Frank 1892.11
Kenworthy, Messr. 1883.23
Kenwright, Bill 1993.07
Kenyon, Charles 1906.37
Kenyon, Doris 1915.23
Kenyon, Ethel 1930.02
Kenyon, Laura 1971.15, 1972.14, 1982.09
Kenyon, Leslie 1912.12, 1912.37, 1913.02
Kenyon, Nancy 1946.01
Kenyon, Neal 1971.09
Keough, Miss 1858.04, 1859.01, 1859.03, 1859.04
Keough, W.M. 1885.35
Keough, William 1890.32, 1892.23, 1892.45, 1895.34, 1896.31, 1901.07, 1903.11, 1907.20
Keough, William T. 1894.51, 1896.03, 1898.70
Keppel, Messr. 1864.22
Keppler, Jesse 1908.28
Ker, Paul 1914.07, 1921.31
Kerber, Randy 1979.30
Kerby, Paul 1942.31
Kercheval, Ken 1961.11, 1968.05
Kerker, Gustav 1897.54, 1898.68, 1902.19, 1904.55, 1906.17, 1906.29, 1907.10, 1912.17, 1921.20
Kerker, Gustave 1883.08, 1883.65, 1884.12, 1884.20, 1884.32, 1884.33, 1884.35, 1884.38, 1885.30, 1885.32, 1888.09, 1889.01, 1889.23, 1889.44, 1890.01, 1890.11, 1890.16, 1890.19, 1890.24, 1890.39, 1891.12, 1891.17, 1891.22, 1891.30, 1892.03, 1892.07, 1892.11, 1892.16, 1892.52, 1892.56, 1893.05, 1893.09, 1893.21, 1893.32, 1893.39, 1894.05, 1894.19, 1894.26, 1894.38, 1895.21, 1895.31, 1896.06, 1896.18, 1896.30, 1896.44, 1896.51, 1897.26, 1897.39, 1897.40, 1897.46, 1898.20, 1898.28, 1898.43, 1899.19, 1900.05, 1901.01, 1902.43, 1903.16, 1903.38, 1904.12, 1904.51, 1905.40, 1905.52, 1906.26, 1907.18, 1907.30, 1908.07, 1917.26, 1922.16
Kerker, Gustave A. 1880.26, 1880.62, 1881.25, 1881.42, 1881.44, 1881.45, 1883.35, 1886.32, 1886.45, 1886.59, 1887.06, 1887.13, 1887.14, 1887.43, 1897.02
Kerker, Gustavus 1885.58
Kerman, Shep 1977.10
Kerman, Sheppard 1958.07, 1973.06, 1978.25
Kermoyan, Kalem 1954.01
Kermoyan, Michael 1958.20, 1959.19, 1961.08, 1963.08, 1964.23, 1964.35, 1965.35, 1966.31, 1968.16, 1973.09, 1977.07, 1989.18
Kern, George D. 1904.34
Kern, J. 1913.06
Kern, Jerome 1904.04, 1905.27, 1905.49, 1906.25, 1906.32, 1907.15, 1907.18, 1907.32, 1908.25, 1908.27, 1909.01, 1909.21, 1909.24, 1910.03, 1910.20, 1910.21, 1911.05, 1911.12, 1911.13, 1911.24, 1911.27, 1911.32, 1912.08, 1912.13, 1912.26, 1912.27, 1912.37, 1913.20, 1913.26, 1914.04, 1914.07, 1914.32, 1915.01, 1915.05, 1915.07, 1915.08, 1915.20, 1915.25, 1915.30, 1916.10, 1916.19, 1916.22, 1917.01, 1917.02, 1917.06, 1917.13, 1917.17, 1917.20, 1917.26, 1918.03, 1918.09, 1918.16, 1918.25, 1918.34, 1919.09, 1920.04, 1920.39, 1920.44, 1921.36, 1922.45, 1923.30, 1923.40, 1924.08, 1924.26, 1924.34, 1925.33, 1925.38, 1926.32, 1927.12, 1927.67, 1929.31, 1931.37, 1932.11, 1932.22, 1933.26, 1939.28, 1940.20, 1946.01, 1948.16, 1948.20, 1951.22, 1954.04, 1954.14, 1957.10, 1961.09, 1964.02, 1964.28, 1966.14, 1967.11, 1974.09, 1974.11, 1975.12, 1975.22, 1975.24, 1981.16, 1983.05, 1983.09, 1986.01, 1986.06, 1990.09, 1994.08, 1997.05
Kern, Jerome D. 1905.55, 1906.37, 1908.06, 1912.41, 1913.29, 1914.18, 1915.18
Kernan, David 1977.05, 1986.01
Kernell 1875.37
Kernell, Bill 1919.40
Kernell, Harry 1875.31, 1875.34, 1875.36, 1875.37, 1875.40, 1876.01, 1883.02, 1910.17
Kernell, John 1883.02, 1891.40, 1894.51, 1896.36
Kernell, William B. 1918.14, 1918.34, 1919.40, 1926.02
Kerner, Evelyn 1917.35
Kerner, George 1916.15
Kerner, Mme. 1916.17, 1918.33
Kerner, Norberto 1995.09
Kerner, R. 1917.34
Kerns, Frank 1873.20, 1873.22
Kerns, R.F. 1875.40
Kerns, Rhoda 1955.12
Kerns, Robert 1959.18, 1960.02
Keroul, Henri 1892.07, 1913.29
Kerper, Mitch 1979.15
Kerr, Alvin 1937.04
Kerr, Betty 1935.17
Kerr, C. Herbert 1903.04, 1907.19
Kerr, C.H. 1905.35
Kerr, C.V. 1914.17
Kerr, Donald 1917.08, 1919.34, 1920.25, 1921.17, 1921.27
Kerr, E.A. 1891.24
Kerr, Ed. A. 1899.18
Kerr, Elizabeth 1961.02
Kerr, Geoffrey 1930.06
Kerr, George W. 1891.24, 1903.05
Kerr, Goff 1927.46
Kerr, Herbert 1913.06, 1913.28, 1914.07, 1915.17
Kerr, Ione 1904.49
Kerr, Jean 1949.12, 1953.17, 1958.14
Kerr, Mr. 1899.18
Kerr, Nancy 1971.21
Kerr, Richard 1976.34, 1991.10
Kerr, Walter 1942.27, 1944.32, 1949.12, 1958.14
Kerrigan, J.M. 1921.05, 1925.21
Kerrigan, Kathleen 1911.09
Kerrigan, Messr. 1892.12
Kerruish, W.D. 1895.23
Kerry, Anne 1989.24
Kerry, Lee 1947.13
Kerschell, William 1926.32, 1928.37, 1930.05
Kersey, Robin 1985.19, 1986.11
Kersey, Ron 1999.15
Kershaw, Craig 1930.42
Kershaw, Whitney 1982.19
Kershaw, William 1928.12
Kersley, Belva Don 1904.08
Kert, Larry 1950.09, 1953.17, 1957.12, 1960.08, 1962.01, 1969.16, 1974.09, 1975.22, 1986.13
Kerwan, Kathryn 1911.34
Kerwin, Susie 1906.41
Kerwin, Winnie 1926.22, 1927.27
Kerz, Leo 1947.13, 1954.17, 1956.09, 1956.10, 1957.13
Kerza, Ygal 1969.13
Kerzman, Robert 1979.03, 1980.13, 1982.13, 1983.03, 1983.07
Kesler, Lew 1929.04, 1938.04, 1940.19, 1944.02, 1947.11, 1955.11
Kesner, Adele 1906.24
Kessler, C.K. 1917.16
Kessler, Jr., William H. 1989.07
Kessler, Lew 1943.01, 1946.18
Kessler, Richard 1927.34
Kessler, Woody 1963.25, 1966.29
Kessler, Zale 1959.12, 1969.05, 1970.02
Kessner, Adele 1902.02
Kessner, Rose 1899.04, 1924.17, 1939.16

Keston, Felix 1886.54
Ketcham, Roy 1931.02
Ketchum, Dave 1961.16
Ketchum, E.A. 1886.49
Ketchum, G.F. 1869.33, 1872.23, 1873.03
Ketchum, G.K. 1872.35
Ketchum, George 1870.15
Ketchum, George F. 1866.07, 1866.14, 1869.06, 1869.29, 1870.07
Ketchum, George K. 1866.14
Ketchum, Mr. 1875.03
Ketelby, Albert 1942.12
Kett, J. Ward 1905.45
Ketteler, Don 1981.01
Kettell, Miss 1873.26
Kettler, Charles 1894.17
Keustner, Charles 1953.14
Kevin, Gene 1955.27
Kevin, Ilsa 1942.34
Kevinson, Keith 1997.04
Kevoian, Peter 1983.14, 1988.01
Kewene, Rachel 1972.20
Key, Benny 1999.06
Key, Gustave 1899.25
Key, James Barton 1895.15
Key, Leonard 1952.01
Keyes, Bert 1979.18
Keyes, Bessie 1900.35
Keyes, Betty 1931.29
Keyes, Daniel 1960.10, 1965.02, 1974.03, 1978.10, 1980.23
Keyes, Donald 1947.09
Keyes, Evelyn 1928.10
Keyes, Frances 1947.13
Keyes, Harriet 1904.33
Keyes, Harriette 1905.50
Keyes, Harry 1888.13
Keyes, James 1982.22
Keyes, Jr., Joe 1972.10
Keyes, Marta 1926.13
Keyes, Ralph 1982.08
Keys, Nelson 1923.35
Keys, Willa 1906.38
Keyser 1865.11, 1866.02, 1866.28, 1867.12
Keyser, Henry 1850.01
Keyser, M. 1851.04
Keyser, Messr. 1841.01
Keyser, Mr. 1851.04, 1869.31
Keyser, Robert Mann 1992.10
Kezer, Glenn 1956.01, 1964.21, 1976.10
Khalaf, Ramzi 1994.12
Kharklin, Hortense 1938.15
Khojoolalla 1881.04
Khoury, Pamela 1981.25, 1989.03
Khoutieff, Jeannine 1979.29
Khumalo, Leleti 1988.02
Khumalo, Nellie 1977.01
Khumalo, Siboniso 1988.02
Khuzwayo, Mhlathi 1988.02
Kiallmark 1887.02
Kibbee, Roland 1976.01
Kibble, Mark 1995.04
Kibbutz, Judith 1967.08
Kibler, Belva 1948.31
Kibrig, Joan 1961.11
Kid, Jenny 1875.02, 1875.04
Kid, Mlle. 1875.29, 1876.20
Kidd, Billy 1989.08
Kidd, Kathleen 1929.20
Kidd, Michael 1947.03, 1948.15, 1948.25, 1950.04, 1950.17, 1953.07, 1955.06, 1955.09, 1956.12, 1959.11, 1960.09, 1960.22, 1961.28, 1963.21, 1964.33, 1965.33, 1970.15, 1973.07, 1974.26, 1980.16, 1986.03, 1993.02
Kidder, E. 1869.40
Kidder, Edward E. 1883.68, 1885.10, 1886.05, 1891.42, 1905.26
Kidder, George M. 1892.35
Kidder, Hugh 1927.10, 1927.26
Kidder, Messr. 1870.19
Kidston, Fanny 1912.24
Kief, Garry 1991.10
Kief, Garry C. 1989.08
Kiefert 1917.15
Kiefert, Carl 1897.52, 1920.31
Kieffert, Carl 1924.05
Kiepelback, Messr. 1852.01
Kiepura, Jan 1943.09, 1944.24, 1945.14, 1957.04
Kier, Harvey 1946.16
Kier, Mary 1900.43, 1902.12
Kierman, Frank 1940.11, 1940.13, 1940.15
Kiernan, James 1888.36
Kiernan, James A. 1898.01
Kiernan, Nora 1888.36
Kiernan, Robert 1968.11
Kiernan, Thomas 1888.36, 1890.10, 1898.01, 1899.23
Kiernnan, Thomas A. 1905.13
Kierns, Thomas 1896.48
Kierns, Thomas F. 1896.35, 1898.05
Kies, Patricia 1993.11
Kieva, Maria 1926.01
Kikabidze, Vakhtang 1977.13
Kikuchi, Lynn 1956.03, 1957.06
Kikuchi, Susan 1989.03, 1996.05
Kilcoyne, May 1905.47
Kildahl, John 1980.30
Kildare, Dan 1919.40
Kilday, Frank 1882.62, 1883.06
Kilday, Master 1877.28
Kiley, Richard 1953.16, 1959.01, 1962.03, 1964.44, 1965.34, 1968.23, 1972.14, 1977.12
Kilgallen, Dorothy 1944.18
Kilgore, John 1989.09
Kilgour, Joseph 1905.15
Kilgren, Cheryl 1959.26
Killalea, J. Edward 1914.29
Killcoyne, Kathleen 1940.11
Kille, F.E. 1885.33
Killeen, Fred. 1908.40
Killeen, Madelyn 1925.48, 1927.29
Killiam Collection 1974.18
Killiam, Paul 1946.19
Killion, Jeff 1957.07, 1964.15, 1972.14
Killmer, Nancy 1975.06, 1976.09, 1982.24
Kilmer, Dorene 1954.12
Kilpatrick, Empress 1976.20
Kilpatrick, James 1921.24
Kilpatrick, Mrs. W.I. 1890.36
Kilpatrick, Thomas 1930.16
Kilrain, W.A. 1894.42
Kilroy and Britton 1907.50
Kilty, Jack 1940.16, 1942.19, 1948.04
Kim, Cholsu 1990.17
Kim, Do Kyung 1997.16
Kim, Hae Shik 1972.08
Kim, Hak Jun 1997.16
Kim, Hak Muk 1998.08
Kim, He Jung 1997.16
Kim, Hee Gab 1997.16, 1998.08
Kim, Helen 1925.37
Kim, Ho Jin 1997.16
Kim, Hyun Dong 1997.16, 1998.08
Kim, Hyun Sook 1997.16, 1998.08
Kim, Ki Young 1997.16, 1998.08
Kim, Kwang Lim 1997.16, 1998.08
Kim, Mara 1950.01
Kim, Min Soo 1998.08
Kim, Nin Soo 1997.16
Kim, Randall Duk 1996.05
Kim, Sung Ki 1997.16, 1998.08
Kim, Taewon 1996.05, 1997.16
Kim, Taewon Yi 1998.08
Kim, Willa 1940.16, 1945.18, 1946.06, 1970.04, 1972.23, 1975.06, 1978.05, 1981.06, 1985.12, 1988.20, 1991.07, 1992.18, 1994.07, 1995.15, 1996.17
Kim, Wonjung 1997.16, 1998.08
Kim, Young Hwan 1997.16, 1998.08
Kimako 1979.32
Kimball Opera-Comique Company 1894.13
Kimball, Charles 1884.30
Kimball, Charles H. 1882.18
Kimball, Frank 1935.11
Kimball, Grace 1901.21, 1903.03, 1903.36, 1910.34, 1913.18
Kimball, Jennie 1888.06, 1888.11, 1894.13
Kimball, Lillian 1906.34
Kimball, Marie 1888.25, 1889.43, 1890.36, 1894.52, 1898.45, 1899.32
Kimball, Robert 1980.10
Kimball, Starra 1895.02
Kimball, Virginia 1888.06, 1888.11
Kimball, Wendy 1986.13
Kimber, Kathryn 1940.03
Kimber, Kay 1942.15
Kimberly, Robert 1947.13
Kimbrough, Charles 1970.13, 1984.08
Kimbrough, Fred 1960.01
Kimmel, Alan 1971.11, 1972.21
Kimmel, Gretchen 1936.06
Kimmins, Kenneth 1969.01
Kinburn, Bella 1937.14
Kincade, Mr. 1860.01
Kind, Roslyn 1992.16
Kinder, W. 1898.34
Kindgren, Karen 1950.11
Kindley, Jeffrey 1982.08
Kinetograph Company 1906.05, 1907.02
King 1975.22
King and Company 1908.28
King DeLoss 1879.54
King Street Production, A 1983.06
King World Productions 1998.02
King's Head Theatre Club 1980.17
King, A.L. 1884.64
King, Adrienne 1908.27
King, Alan 1965.15, 1970.09
King, Allyn 1916.10, 1917.13, 1918.19, 1923.04, 1924.04, 1925.40
King, Alonzo 1918.17
King, Alta 1920.44
King, Armand 1909.26
King, Belle 1898.22, 1904.38
King, Ben E. 1995.03
King, Bertha 1896.01
King, Beula 1937.07
King, Bradley Clayton 1978.13
King, Calvin M. 1918.14
King, Carl 1899.28, 1900.40
King, Carlotta 1931.44
King, Carol 1943.20
King, Carole 1976.32, 1982.22, 1984.15, 1986.02
King, Charles 1908.21, 1911.02, 1911.05, 1912.13, 1913.09, 1913.18, 1914.31, 1917.26, 1919.02, 1921.08, 1921.22, 1922.43, 1924.16, 1926.18, 1927.16, 1928.16, 1930.40, 1937.07
King, Clarence 1897.07
King, Clement 1897.28
King, Daisy 1900.54
King, David 1975.22
King, De Los 1881.52
King, DeLoss 1884.23, 1885.69
King, Dennis 1924.28, 1925.32, 1928.12, 1932.11, 1937.03, 1938.05, 1951.22, 1956.07
King, Donna 1978.13, 1981.13, 1982.19
King, Ed 1882.02, 1883.32, 1884.41
King, Edith 1937.03, 1946.02, 1959.27, 1960.22
King, Eleanor 1933.12
King, Elizabeth 1903.26
King, Ellen 1919.08
King, Emily 1872.06
King, Emma 1898.04, 1898.16, 1898.21, 1898.37, 1898.49, 1899.16, 1907.19
King, Eugene W. 1934.41
King, Everett 1982.02
King, Frances R. 1899.36
King, Frances Rockefeller 1904.18
King, Frank 1897.53, 1898.04, 1898.06, 1898.07, 1898.09, 1898.14, 1898.15, 1898.16, 1898.19, 1898.21, 1898.24, 1898.30, 1898.33, 1898.37, 1898.39, 1898.40, 1898.42, 1898.49, 1898.52, 1898.57, 1898.62, 1898.65, 1898.71, 1898.74, 1898.76, 1899.05, 1902.33, 1927.55, 1928.44
King, Geoffrey 1931.38
King, Ginny 1980.20
King, Gordon 1942.35
King, Grace 1910.10
King, Harry 1926.03
King, Hattie 1881.22
King, Henrietta 1923.09
King, J. 1871.09
King, J.C. 1913.03
King, Jane 1922.14
King, Jessie 1893.07
King, John 1908.22, 1909.16
King, John C. 1934.36
King, John L. 1927.55
King, John M. 1951.22
King, John Michael 1951.17, 1956.01, 1965.35, 1977.07, 1979.09
King, Jr., Dennis 1947.21
King, Jr., Woodie 1987.17
King, Kenneth 1967.13, 1968.20
King, Larry L. 1978.13, 1982.11, 1994.06
King, Leslie 1925.44
King, Lottie 1893.07
King, Louise 1882.04
King, Lulu 1933.04
King, Lulu B. 1943.10
King, M.F. 1872.06
King, Mabel 1972.10, 1975.01, 1980.15
King, Margaret 1905.55
King, Marie 1917.17
King, Marjorie 1940.11, 1944.26
King, Martha 1945.01, 1959.27
King, Mary 1922.14
King, Mary Mable 1967.15
King, Mazie 1906.39, 1908.21, 1911.05, 1913.20
King, Merle D. 1975.22
King, Messr. 1834.02, 1841.01, 1844.01, 1889.01
King, Michael 1952.07, 1953.08, 1963.11
King, Michael E. 1979.28
King, Miss 1841.01, 1867.16, 1877.15
King, Mollie 1913.18, 1919.02, 1921.04
King, Mr. 1794.01, 1796.01, 1841.01, 1862.07
King, Mrs. 1794.01
King, Nancy 1954.01
King, Nellie 1898.34, 1908.21, 1913.29, 1919.02, 1923.32
King, Oliver 1975.09
King, Patsi 1959.26, 1963.12
King, Paul 1948.29, 1950.13
King, Paul L. 1993.14, 1994.09
King, Pete 1941.03
King, Peter 1900.52
King, Peter W. 1910.10
King, Phil 1946.13
King, Philip 1941.03
King, Ray 1929.28
King, Raymond 1996.07
King, Robert A. 1962.17
King, Robert Woolf 1935.17
King, Rosalie 1933.04, 1943.10, 1946.21, 1950.07, 1963.27
King, Rose 1927.38, 1927.60, 1934.42, 1936.31, 1941.09
King, Rufus 1933.20
King, Shirley 1911.03
King, Stephen 1988.12
King, Stoddard 1964.28
King, Tessie 1894.14
King, W. 1870.39
King, Wanza 1961.13, 1962.07, 1964.19
King, Woodie 1980.05
Kingdon, Frank 1918.42, 1920.44, 1923.30, 1924.38, 1925.16, 1926.20, 1927.48, 1929.03, 1933.20
Kingdon, Hazel 1910.30, 1912.08
Kingdon, Patrick 1947.08
Kingi, Tangiwai 1972.20
Kingman, Dan 1969.11, 1978.19, 1978.23
Kingsbury, Audrey 1902.25
Kingsbury, Carol 1929.08
Kingsbury, Jacob 1925.37
Kingsford, Walter 1914.24, 1944.21
Kingsland, Charles 1907.51
Kingsley, A.S. 1894.23, 1895.19
Kingsley, Eleanore 1965.22
Kingsley, Eugene 1946.23
Kingsley, Evelyn 1968.22
Kingsley, Gershon 1958.18, 1960.12, 1964.02, 1964.18, 1968.08, 1969.09
Kingsley, Gretchen 1989.19
Kingsley, Hal 1937.01
Kingsley, Henry 1891.20
Kingsley, Herbert 1945.07
Kingsley, J.W. 1896.17
Kingsley, Miss 1920.44
Kingsley, Patti 1947.13
Kingsley, Percy 1891.01, 1891.24
Kingstead, Helen 1931.38
Kingston, Kay 1955.12
Kingston, Mindel 1910.18
Kingston, Natalie 1920.33
Kinley, William 1920.19
Kinleyside, Donald 1925.02
Kinne, Robert 1942.20
Kinney, J.A. 1879.10
Kinney, Ray 1938.08
Kinnir, Anna L. 1892.15
Kinoy, Ernest 1964.40, 1968.03
Kinross, Mr. 1872.17
Kinser-Lau, Patrick 1976.02, 1978.18
Kinsley, Dorothy 1982.14
Kinslow, E.S. 1907.18
Kinter, Richard 1967.01
Kinter, Roddy 2000.03
Kipness, Joseph 1943.16, 1947.16, 1958.18, 1964.44, 1965.37, 1970.09, 1971.20, 1973.06, 1976.03, 1977.04, 1978.22
Kippen, Manart 1929.45, 1934.04
Kirafly, Haniola 1869.26
Kiralfy, Arnold 1873.10, 1875.21, 1876.36, 1877.04, 1877.15, 1880.08, 1880.41, 1881.02, 1881.32, 1882.62, 1883.48, 1885.33, 1886.41, 1887.27, 1888.01, 1899.22

Kiralfy, Bolossy 1869.26, 1870.31, 1871.18, 1873.10, 1875.21, 1876.36, 1877.04, 1877.15, 1879.12, 1879.42, 1880.08, 1880.41, 1880.63, 1881.02, 1881.13, 1881.32, 1882.62, 1882.77, 1883.06, 1883.48, 1884.39, 1884.44, 1885.33, 1885.65, 1886.16, 1886.41, 1887.03, 1888.10, 1888.23, 1889.08, 1889.33, 1890.17
Kiralfy, Emilie 1871.18, 1873.10, 1875.21
Kiralfy, Grimaldi 1870.31
Kiralfy, Haniola 1870.31, 1871.18, 1873.10, 1875.21
Kiralfy, Imre 1869.26, 1870.31, 1871.18, 1873.10, 1875.21, 1876.36, 1877.04, 1877.15, 1879.12, 1879.42, 1880.08, 1880.41, 1880.63, 1881.02, 1881.13, 1881.32, 1882.62, 1882.77, 1883.06, 1883.48, 1884.39, 1884.44, 1885.33, 1885.65, 1886.16, 1886.41, 1887.03, 1887.27, 1888.01, 1889.21, 1890.17, 1893.45
Kiralfy, Kati 1873.10
Kiralfy, Katie 1871.18, 1875.21
Kiralfy, M.E. 1873.26
Kiralfy, Mme. 1873.26
Kirby, Christopher R. 1999.01
Kirby, Florence 1884.44
Kirby, John Mason 1976.15
Kirby, Langford 1907.32
Kirby, Maurice Brown 1909.15
Kirby, Max 1929.41
Kirby, Sadie 1888.02, 1890.07, 1891.26, 1892.09, 1894.35, 1896.51, 1898.17
Kirchback, Wolfgang 1898.11
Kirchner, Lisa 1984.02
Kirchner, Mr. 1917.03
Kirchner, Paul 1875.12
Kirchner, Raphael 1916.24
Kirchner, Ray 1954.02
Kiriushkin, Natalia 1977.13
Kiriushkin, Oleg 1977.13
Kirk, Alan 1959.05
Kirk, Alyson 1985.04
Kirk, Beverly 1938.15
Kirk, Blanche 1904.32
Kirk, Bonnie 1982.16, 1982.20, 1983.13, 1989.14
Kirk, Charles 1918.14
Kirk, Charlotte 1978.26
Kirk, Frank 1896.49
Kirk, George 1930.27, 1931.37, 1932.17, 1933.25, 1934.38
Kirk, Jimmy 1921.25
Kirk, John 1939.21
Kirk, Keith Byron 1996.15
Kirk, Keith byron 1999.08
Kirk, Kelby 1986.03
Kirk, L. 1881.38
Kirk, Lillian 1898.34
Kirk, Lisa 1947.17, 1948.32, 1974.18
Kirk, M. 1881.03
Kirk, Mr. 1869.31
Kirk, Patrick 1948.24
Kirk, Richard 1955.13
Kirk, Roger 1996.05, 2000.09, 2001.08
Kirk, Sally 1961.21
Kirk, Van 1940.18
Kirk, William 1987.09
Kirk. William F. 1911.44
Kirkbride, Bradford 1921.11, 1922.24
Kirke, Charles 1888.45, 1890.27, 1892.21, 1894.13, 1895.11, 1896.06, 1896.18, 1897.25, 1898.28, 1899.26, 1900.07
Kirke, Hazel 1911.40, 1912.44, 1913.24, 1916.05, 1918.26, 1919.19
Kirkeby, Ed 1978.09
Kirkham, Sam 1950.02, 1957.06, 1957.08, 1957.11, 1960.03, 1960.11, 1963.18, 1965.20, 1967.01, 1968.16, 1969.12
Kirkland, Alexander 1948.17
Kirkland, Hardee 1891.06, 1891.07
Kirkland, Jack 1936.27
Kirkland, Jean 1928.11
Kirkland, Leroy 1976.34
Kirkland, M. 1881.11
Kirkland, Miss 1881.04
Kirkley, Donald 1928.20
Kirkpatrick, Ethel 1904.09
Kirkpatrick, Lindsay 1954.15
Kirkpatrick, Sam 1985.20
Kirkpatrick, Shane 2001.03
Kirkwood, James 1975.15
Kirkwood, Jim 1963.05
Kirkwood, Jimmy 1950.03
Kirkwood, Josephine 1901.07, 1906.37
Kirland, Robert W. 1944.28
Kirner, George 1912.13
Kirov, Ivan 1941.11
Kirsch, Carolyn 1969.17, 1975.15
Kirsch, Dolly 1895.10
Kirshbaum, Miss 1870.31
Kirstein, Lincoln 1941.01, 1954.18
Kirsten 1999.05
Kirsten, Dorothy 1938.15, 1944.17
Kirtland, Louise 1932.21, 1933.16, 1934.14, 1949.01, 1950.02, 1963.08, 1983.10
Kirtley, Leonard 1911.12, 1912.30
Kirwan, Susie 1904.45
Kirwin, Edward 1888.31
Kirwin, Susie 1880.63
Kiser, Franklin 1964.33
Kiser, Jane 1944.16
Kiser, S.E. 1903.24
Kiser, Terry 1973.03
Kish, Mitzi 1928.15
Kishon, E. 1967.08
Kiss, Teddy 1950.14
Kisselev, Andrei 2000.05
Kissinger, Brittny 1997.04
Kitchell, Iva 1956.11
Kitchen, Heather 1998.05
Kitchen, May 1921.08
Kitchen, May Cory 1922.02, 1924.10
Kitson, James 1934.01
Kitson, Max 1950.12
Kitt, Eartha 1945.13, 1946.21, 1952.09, 1954.16, 1957.05, 1978.03, 1998.06, 2001.09
Kitt, Ertha 2000.08
Kittask, Avo 1987.01
Kitteridge, Louise 1898.46
Kittredge, C. Harry 1899.15
Kitts, W.P. 1892.35
Kitwack, Ned C. 1948.23
Kitzinger, Fritz 1939.20
Kiviat, Yetta 1917.29
Kiviat, Yvette 1920.15
Kiviette 1919.03, 1920.24, 1923.19, 1923.33, 1923.36, 1924.03, 1924.16, 1924.27, 1924.34, 1924.43, 1925.29, 1925.49, 1927.41, 1927.59, 1928.17, 1928.18, 1928.35, 1928.36, 1928.43, 1929.03, 1929.07, 1929.12, 1929.42, 1929.49, 1930.06, 1930.31, 1930.32, 1931.01, 1931.16, 1931.21, 1931.28, 1931.32, 1931.37, 1931.42, 1932.05, 1932.24, 1932.25, 1932.27, 1933.02, 1933.05, 1933.25, 1933.26, 1934.01, 1934.19, 1937.16, 1944.01
Kiviniemi, Brigitta 1964.24
Kiwa, Lila 1939.18
Kiyo, Emma 1916.15
Kjeldsen, Ingeborg 1965.22
Kjellson, Ingvar 1966.19
Kladitis, Manny 1983.10, 1985.01, 1992.07, 1995.07, 1995.13, 1998.07, 1999.10, 1999.15
Klaer, Adele 1923.25
Klages, Ray 1926.23, 1927.02, 1928.23
Klages, Raymond 1920.10, 1922.31, 1925.11, 1926.23, 1927.02, 1927.17, 1927.68, 1928.21, 1931.26
Klages, Raymond W. 1921.27
Klapper, Ian D. 1990.08, 1991.08
Klare, Kathryn 1898.70
Klaris, Harvey J. 1982.09, 1983.21
Klatz 1990.15
Klatzkin, Philip 1902.05
Klausen, Ray 1994.13
Klausner, Terri 1979.23, 1981.06
Klausner, Willette 1999.12
Klaussen-Koch, Mrs. 1898.53
Klavun, Walter 1958.08, 1964.05
Klaw and Erlanger 1904.30, 1905.19
Klaw and Erlanger Costume Company 1906.21, 1908.22, 1908.39, 1909.25, 1909.26, 1911.41
Klaw and Erlanger Costume Department 1908.43
Klaw and Erlanger Costuming Company 1908.17
Klaw and Erlanger's Costume Company 1908.14
Klaw, Joseph 1917.20, 1918.29
Klaw, Marc 1893.42, 1894.42, 1896.44, 1897.25, 1898.25, 1899.12, 1899.29, 1900.01, 1900.25, 1900.31, 1900.32, 1900.40, 1900.50, 1901.16, 1901.21, 1901.27, 1902.04, 1902.24, 1902.43, 1903.04, 1903.23, 1903.39, 1904.22, 1904.31, 1904.47, 1904.56, 1905.22, 1905.25, 1905.28, 1905.30, 1905.41, 1905.46, 1905.48, 1906.02, 1906.18, 1906.24, 1906.36, 1906.42, 1907.13, 1907.37, 1908.35, 1909.08, 1909.18, 1909.28, 1910.07, 1910.34, 1911.11, 1912.12, 1912.28, 1912.34, 1912.48, 1913.31, 1914.26, 1915.05, 1915.28, 1916.19, 1917.25, 1918.11, 1918.28, 1919.01
Klaw, Marcus 1912.33
Klawans, Bernard 1932.22
Kleban, Edward 1975.15, 1976.16, 2001.01
Klebba, Martin 1997.11, 1998.06, 1999.11
Klebs, Mr. 1855.08, 1870.36, 1870.43
Kleeman, Paul 1924.09, 1924.45
Kleigl 1905.42
Kleigl Brothers 1904.54, 1905.44, 1906.21, 1906.22, 1907.33, 1908.24, 1909.05
Klein, A. 1883.08
Klein, A.A. 1908.13
Klein, Al 1919.16
Klein, Albert 1885.53, 1887.11
Klein, Alexander 1884.64, 1885.11
Klein, Alfred 1879.30, 1884.14, 1884.63, 1885.63, 1886.04, 1886.37, 1887.18, 1887.22, 1887.24, 1888.19, 1888.22, 1890.16, 1891.11, 1892.22, 1892.33, 1892.47, 1893.16, 1894.24, 1896.13, 1897.10, 1898.13, 1898.48
Klein, Alisa 1996.17
Klein, Arthur 1911.39, 1915.28, 1918.40, 1946.15, 1950.09, 1953.10
Klein, Arthur A. 1906.34
Klein, Charles 1895.35, 1895.37, 1896.13, 1897.10, 1898.13, 1898.48, 1900.57, 1903.02, 1903.36, 1915.20, 1922.14
Klein, Christopher 1971.06
Klein, Criag 1990.19
Klein, Emily 1998.21
Klein, Evelyn 1930.27
Klein, Harry 1919.16
Klein, Hermann 1903.02
Klein, I.W. 1966.01
Klein, J.C. 1917.32
Klein, James 1925.02
Klein, John 1944.27
Klein, Joseph 1971.06, 1972.14, 1974.05, 1982.06
Klein, Lou 1913.06, 1914.06
Klein, Lulu 1892.58
Klein, Manuel 1903.02, 1903.41, 1905.17, 1905.54, 1906.30, 1906.46, 1907.47, 1907.54, 1908.26, 1908.41, 1909.20, 1910.06, 1910.23, 1911.12, 1911.28, 1912.30, 1913.22, 1913.33, 1914.11, 1914.19, 1918.10, 1921.08
Klein, Messr. 1861.02
Klein, Moritz 1896.34
Klein, Norman 1968.13
Klein, Paul 1960.07
Klein, Reid 1965.14, 1967.07, 1968.02
Klein, Robert 1966.18, 1968.13, 1979.04, 1988.13
Klein, Sally 1981.27
Klein, Sophie 1890.31, 1891.33, 1894.01
Kleinecke, August 1911.30, 1912.45, 1914.14, 1914.20, 1915.20, 1926.22
Kleinecke, Gus 1907.57, 1921.23
Kleink, Herr 1866.33
Kleinman, Alex 1910.07
Kleinman, Harry 1910.07
Kleinman, Marlena 1962.08, 1962.09, 1962.11, 1963.23, 1964.08, 1964.09, 1964.10, 1964.12, 1964.14, 1965.09, 1965.10, 1965.11
Kleinman, Michael 1982.09, 1983.21
Kleinman, Sy 1955.12
Kleinsinger, George 1940.18, 1942.05, 1957.05
Klemperer, Werner 1987.16, 1990.02
Klen, Manuel 1907.47
Klendon, John 1912.11, 1926.28
Klendor, Jack 1911.33
Kletter, Max 1967.03
Klewer, Dorothy 1917.12, 1917.26
Klick, Mary 1954.08
Kliegl Brothers 1906.05, 1907.02, 1908.12, 1910.09, 1912.03, 1913.21
Klien, Franklin 1936.30
Klimczewska, Violetta 1992.05
Kline, Bertha 1880.68
Kline, Devra 1955.02
Kline, Dollie 1888.44
Kline, Gustave H. 1891.20
Kline, Izidore 1879.65, 1879.67
Kline, J.C. 1882.18
Kline, J.H. 1921.15
Kline, John 1877.24, 1928.12
Kline, Kevin 1973.16, 1975.18, 1978.02, 1981.01
Kline, L. 1878.05
Kline, Libbie 1878.12
Kline, Linda 2001.01
Kline, Miss 1880.68
Kline, Stephanie 1970.16
Kline, William 1914.33
Klineke, Gus 1926.11
Kling, Bernard 1903.13
Kling, Helen 1924.05
Kling, Henri 1902.22
Klingel, Miss 1910.12
Klinger, Pam 1993.06, 1999.16
Klingman, Mark 1973.14, 1975.12
Klint, George 1895.41
Klne, Gustave H. 1892.31
Klohe, Hans-Werner 1998.10
Klores, Dan 1998.02
Kloss, Leo 1887.10
Klotz, Florence 1957.06, 1957.11, 1958.03, 1958.07, 1966.06, 1971.05, 1973.04, 1976.02, 1977.05, 1978.02, 1978.26, 1982.18, 1983.20, 1985.05, 1985.19, 1986.13, 1987.12, 1989.29, 1993.09, 1994.08
Kloznisky, Frl. 1883.08
Klugman, Israel 1972.17
Klugman, Jack 1959.13
Kmeck, George 1983.02
Knabenshue, Harry 1930.41
Knaiz, Judith 1972.05
Knapp, Bridget 1961.09
Knapp, Charles 1887.50, 1911.03
Knapp, Dorothy 1923.21, 1924.18, 1925.10, 1925.24, 1925.48, 1926.23, 1928.23, 1929.08, 1931.28
Knapp, Eleanore 1965.34, 1972.14
Knapp, Ella 1885.67
Knapp, Emilie 1900.12
Knapp, Essie 1902.10
Knapp, Frank 1890.36, 1894.52, 1898.45, 1899.32, 1904.32, 1907.43, 1908.32
Knapp, Josephine 1885.52, 1887.12, 1887.26, 1887.28, 1887.47, 1888.22, 1888.24, 1888.26, 1889.17, 1889.22, 1890.28, 1891.13, 1892.20, 1894.11, 1899.24, 1899.28
Knapp, Josie 1886.26, 1886.33, 1886.37, 1886.43
Knapp, Kenneth 1949.03
Knapp, Marjorie 1940.12, 1942.18
Knapp, Miss 1870.05
Knapp, Mrs. A. 1870.30
Knapp, Orville 1929.24
Knapp, Sadie 1902.05
Knauer, Ian 1996.04
Knauer, Max 1892.11, 1902.37
Kneale, Beatrice 1927.25
Kneass, Master 1834.02
Kneass, Messr. 1844.01
Kneass, Mr. 1844.01
Kneass, Nelson 1884.27, 1895.17
Knee, Allan 1987.14
Kneebone, Tom 1968.19
Kneeland, Frank 1924.45
Kneitel, Harriet 1915.32
Knell, Anna 1898.72
Knepler, Paul 1932.23, 1937.17, 1982.16, 1983.12, 1985.12, 1988.14
Knick Knacks, Inc. 1926.22
Knickerbocke, Herr 1864.23
Kniffen, Chase 1998.18
Knight, D. 1899.37
Knight, Dorothy 1918.10
Knight, E.B. 1889.49, 1890.21, 1900.07, 1901.05, 1903.06
Knight, E.G. 1893.35, 1899.24
Knight, E.N. 1898.09, 1898.14, 1898.24, 1898.76
Knight, Ed 1894.28
Knight, Ed G. 1898.16
Knight, Edward 1895.16, 1895.22, 1896.25
Knight, Emory 1955.09
Knight, Eric 1983.12
Knight, Fannie 1884.58, 1887.45
Knight, Fanny 1883.52
Knight, Felix 1940.16, 1942.21, 1942.33
Knight, Florence 1897.46
Knight, Frederic M. 1897.18

Knight, Frederick 1908.13
Knight, Fuzzy 1927.02, 1928.17, 1929.04
Knight, George 1927.36
Knight, George J. 1883.47
Knight, George S. 1875.39, 1877.07, 1877.21, 1878.02, 1878.15, 1880.51, 1885.03, 1886.62
Knight, Gillian 1962.25, 1962.26, 1962.28, 1962.30, 1962.31, 1964.36, 1964.38, 1964.41, 1964.42, 1964.43
Knight, Harlan 1904.07
Knight, Hilda 1930.40, 1933.03, 1937.06
Knight, Jack 1967.09, 1967.10
Knight, Jacqueline 1927.36, 1927.40
Knight, John Philip 1952.11
Knight, Joseph 1930.41
Knight, Josie 1879.18, 1884.21, 1890.21
Knight, June 1932.07, 1932.25, 1935.14, 1946.02, 1947.04
Knight, Lavinia 1931.44
Knight, Lloyd 1949.17
Knight, Margaret 1900.52, 1902.08, 1902.27
Knight, Miss 1882.23, 1896.44
Knight, Mme. 1841.01
Knight, Mr. 1870.15
Knight, Mrs. 1844.01
Knight, Mrs. George S. 1878.15, 1880.51, 1885.03, 1886.62
Knight, Patricia 1937.07
Knight, Percival 1909.01, 1909.21, 1909.24, 1910.03, 1910.05, 1911.39, 1913.26, 1916.22, 1918.10, 1918.31, 1919.27
Knight, Raymond 1935.12
Knight, Tanya 1941.07
Knight, Walter 1916.16
Knight, William 1971.04, 1976.27
Knighton, Nan 1997.19, 1999.13, 1999.15
Knights, Frederick 1898.34
Knill, Milo 1891.40
Knilling, Anthony 1927.16, 1928.16
Knipper, Lev 1943.11
Knisely, George 1926.17
Knittel, Wolfgang 1972.16
Knoblock, Edward 1928.04, 1953.16, 1965.22, 1978.03, 1985.13, 1986.09
Knoch, Ernest 1921.15
Knoch, Ernst 1920.46
Knoche, Bradley 1919.40, 1922.03
Knollenberg, Richard 1906.41
Knorr, G.T.R. 1879.66
Knorr, Herr 1866.33
Knott, Clara 1894.51, 1900.36
Know, J. Armory 1890.06
Knowles, Allen 1946.22, 1949.08, 1960.06
Knowles, Almon 1906.07, 1906.39
Knowles, C.E. 1887.02
Knowles, Christopher 1975.10
Knowles, Edwin 1899.41
Knowles, Edwin F. 1876.12
Knowles, George 1893.41
Knowles, Harry 1873.26
Knowles, Howard 1902.14, 1902.33
Knowles, Lillian 1896.01
Knowles, Mabel 1891.41
Knowles, Marie 1885.34
Knowles, Mr. 1867.15
Knowles, Nettie 1899.18
Knowles, Priscilla 1932.14
Knowles, R.J. 1903.34
Knowlton, Alice 1903.07
Knowlton, Arthur 1933.06
Knowlton, Dora 1879.50, 1879.56
Knowlton, Georgie 1880.63
Knowlton, Maude 1903.26, 1912.14
Knowlton, Miss 1885.65
Knowlton, Sarah 1998.16
Knox, Andrew 1926.18
Knox, Bessie 1893.09
Knox, Collie 1924.01
Knox, J. Armory 1885.53, 1886.44
Knox, Joseph J. 1879.13, 1879.66
Knox, Richard 1950.08
Knox, Teddy 1922.05, 1922.19, 1923.20
Knox, Tommy 1946.10
Knox, Villa 1891.12, 1891.22, 1892.07, 1892.28, 1893.09, 1894.19, 1894.28, 1898.49, 1898.62, 1898.74, 1901.14
Knudson, Kurt 1982.02, 1984.08, 1985.04
Knyght-Smith, Douglas 1995.01
Kobart, Ruth 1955.27, 1958.17, 1959.08, 1959.17, 1960.02, 1960.03, 1960.14, 1961.03, 1961.22, 1962.12, 1963.15, 1965.38, 1966.02
Kobayashi, Kohei 1989.21
Kobbe, Philip 1930.22
Kobbe, Phillip 1926.11
Kobeleff, Constance 1932.19
Kobeleff, Constantin 1920.19
Kobeleff, Vadie 1920.19
Kober, Arthur 1941.01, 1952.10
Koch, David 1989.04, 1997.09
Koch, Edward I. 1985.15
Koch, Henry 1885.65
Koch, Mlle. 1870.44, 1871.27
Koch, Mr. 1890.31, 1891.33, 1894.01
Koch, Richard 1930.27
Kochanski, Steve 1950.14
Kochetovsky, Messr. 1922.06
Kodama, Al 1989.21
Koeck, Karl 1924.38
Koegh, William 1906.21
Koehler, A. 1894.30
Koehler, Miss 1890.31, 1892.43, 1893.29
Koehler, Ted 1930.06, 1930.22, 1932.18, 1932.24, 1934.35, 1942.11, 1942.23, 1945.07, 1953.12, 1974.09, 1976.16, 1978.09, 1979.25, 1980.10, 1981.16, 1982.12, 1986.02, 1989.02, 1999.05
Koenig, Henry J. 1905.47
Koenig, John 1940.22, 1942.20
Koenig, Marie 1885.41
Koepler, Mrs. 1894.01
Koerber, Miss 1893.29
Koetter, Stella 1899.28
Koeugh, William T. 1891.40
Koffee, Dorothy 1917.35
Kogan, Borris 1942.30
Kogan, Jack 1926.07
Kogan, Maurice 1955.02
Kogan, S. 1929.05
Kogema, Y. 1902.22
Koger, Georges 1964.02, 1973.17
Kohan, Buz 1984.06
Kohan, Lynn-Rose 1955.09
Kohana, Princess 1927.63
Kohler, Harry 1938.03
Kohler, Howard 1879.66
Kohler, Leonora 1917.03
Kohler, Marion 1944.33
Kohlman, Leon 1901.29
Kohlmar, Lee 1925.26
Kohlmar, Leon 1900.58
Kohlmer, Leon 1902.06
Kohne, Wayne 1926.21
Kohnie, W.H. 1885.58
Kohrs, Karl 1936.26
Koiransky, A. 1922.06, 1923.28
Kokic, Kazimir 1948.31, 1949.08, 1949.18
Kokich, Kasimir 1956.14, 1960.06
Kokich, Kazimir 1955.27, 1959.01
Kokin, Mabel 1922.31
Kola, Horace 1928.09
Kolb and Dill 1908.05
Kolb, Alexandra 2001.09
Kolb, C. William 1908.05
Kolb, Florence 1911.03
Kolb, Mina 1961.17
Kolb, Nat 1905.43, 1907.39
Koldovski, Gustav 1904.50
Kole, Bob 1953.17, 1956.02
Kole, Robert 1953.03
Kolins, Howard 2000.19
Kolinski, Joseph 1983.08, 1984.02, 1984.14, 1987.04, 1994.12
Kolitz, Zvi 1968.08, 1968.22
Kolk, Stanley 1958.09
Kolk, Walter Scott 1927.60
Koller, Dagmar 1964.25, 1984.03
Kolletz, Charles 1875.07, 1875.08
Kollhammer, Eveline 1964.25
Kollins, King 1897.45
Kollmar, Richard 1938.11, 1939.27, 1941.03, 1942.15, 1943.07, 1944.18, 1945.18, 1955.01, 1958.01
Kollo, Walter 1913.20, 1913.36, 1917.15, 1921.13, 1922.40, 1928.33, 1930.15
Kolman, Ossy 1984.03
Kolo, Fred 1990.05
Koloc, Bonnie 1984.02
Kolomuku, W.K. 1912.03
Kolpe 1967.13, 1968.20
Koltai, Ralph 1988.12, 1993.18
Komac 1983.17
Komack, Jimmie 1955.08
Kombrink, Ilona 1959.07
Komisarjevskaia, Mme. 1922.06
Komisarjevskaya, Mme. 1923.28, 1931.38
Komisarjevsky 1934.38
Komisarjevsky, Theodore 1931.38
Komisarshevskaya, Mme. 1927.51
Komissarjevska, Mme. 1929.05
Komlossy, F. 1891.33
Kommissarjevskaya, Mme. 1925.03
Komolossy, Franz 1890.31, 1894.01
Komolova, Valentina 1990.01
Kompe, C. 1880.68
Kon, H. 1967.08
Kondo, Naoe 1925.37
Kondraiteff, Messr. 1927.51
Konecky, Isobel Robins 1980.23
Konig, Frl. 1883.35
Konig, Marie 1880.61, 1880.66
Koning 1890.22, 1890.24
Koning, Victor 1873.11, 1873.18, 1875.02, 1875.28, 1876.17, 1876.26, 1877.27, 1879.48, 1880.03, 1883.30, 1883.57, 1884.54, 1887.37, 1925.51, 1926.47
Konnen, Catherine 1902.02
Kononovich, Vladimir 1977.13
Konopka, Albin 1977.05
Konopka, Kenneth 1943.15, 1944.03
Konradt, Mlle. 1889.08
Konroth, Helena 1888.10
Konroth, Henrietta 1888.10
Konroth, Mlle. 1888.23
Konstam, Phyllis 1951.05
Konyot, Marin 1991.11
Konyot, Marion 1950.14
Konyot, Robert 1950.14, 1991.11
Konzal, Jack 1959.22
Kook, Nannie 1864.22
Kookoolis, Martinez 1971.01
Kopernak, Galina 1925.09
Kopfstein, Jacques 1931.26
Kopit, Alan S. 2001.03
Kopit, Arthur 1982.09, 1998.05
Kopp, Norma 1897.42, 1899.40, 1903.04
Kopp, William G. 1907.56
Koppelman, Charles 1982.22
Koppitz, Charles 1861.03, 1867.27
Koppmeier, Keith 1976.08
Korabel, Faz 1963.11
Koran, S. 1927.51
Korbich, Eddie 1989.19, 1994.02
Korda, Nina 1946.24
Kordek, Jinny 1974.17
Koretzky, Mme. 1923.28
Korey, Alexandra 1978.04, 1981.01
Korey, Alix 1993.05, 1993.14, 1995.18
Korff, Arnold 1936.22
Korhler, Leonore 1917.26
Korn, Mr. 1897.35
Kornau, Adelaide 1908.25
Kornau, Adele 1912.12
Kornay, Adelaide 1905.37
Kornblum, I.B. 1921.04
Korngold, Eric Wolfgang 1934.29, 1942.31, 1944.16
Kornicki, Kevin 2000.02
Koro, Yama 1934.16
Korogodsky, Mikhail 1976.26, 1977.03
Korthaze, Richard 1965.33, 1966.27, 1972.22, 1975.14, 1985.04, 1987.15
Kortkam, Moreland 1948.21
Kortman, Cynthia 1999.10
Korzina, Galina 1977.13
Kosai Studios 1927.28
Kosarin, Michael 1985.15, 1991.05, 1994.04, 1997.12, 1997.18, 1999.16
Kosarin, Oscar 1952.01, 1953.01, 1956.02, 1958.02, 1964.35, 1966.01, 1968.01, 1969.04, 1970.12, 1971.07
Kosciusko, Robert 1903.12
Kosco, Marie 1928.14
Kosis, Tom 1997.19, 1999.13
Koski, Fraun 1922.39
Kosloff, Alex 1918.05
Kosloff, Alexis 1915.11, 1916.23, 1917.24, 1918.35, 1919.20, 1920.22, 1920.33, 1923.41, 1925.02, 1925.27, 1925.33
Kosloff, Ira 1989.12
Kosloff, Theodor 1915.11
Kosloff, Theodore 1912.24, 1913.05, 1915.02, 1915.04, 1915.16, 1915.26, 1916.06, 1930.39
Koslow, Ira 1988.15
Koslow, Pamela 1992.08, 2000.20
Kosman, Louis 1962.16, 1962.20, 1965.01
Kosmowskaja, L. 1932.09
Kosmowskaja, P. 1932.09
Kosmowskaya, L. 1924.48
Kossuth, Ilka 1900.49
Kosta, Hilda 1933.07
Kosta, Miss 1923.03
Kosta, Tessa 1914.13, 1917.24, 1919.04, 1920.12, 1921.11, 1921.40, 1922.11, 1923.03, 1924.42, 1925.15, 1925.52, 1929.40
Kostal, Irwin 1950.12, 1957.05, 1957.12, 1959.25, 1960.08, 1960.19, 1961.18, 1961.24, 1962.12, 1962.16, 1964.17, 1968.18, 1972.03, 1973.12, 1976.08, 1980.02, 1981.12, 1982.14
Kostelanetz, Andre 1932.17
Koster and Bial 1898.01, 1898.35, 1898.38, 1898.56
Koster and Bial's 1900.19
Koster, Albert 1884.36
Koster, Dorothy 1940.12
Koster, John 1884.59, 1884.65, 1885.12, 1885.18, 1885.31, 1885.39, 1885.51, 1885.62, 1886.07, 1886.17, 1886.29, 1886.31, 1886.38, 1886.53, 1889.27, 1889.30, 1889.32, 1889.42, 1889.53, 1890.05, 1890.09, 1890.13, 1890.22, 1890.38, 1890.42, 1890.45, 1891.10, 1891.16, 1891.19, 1891.35, 1892.02, 1892.13, 1892.26, 1892.32, 1892.41, 1892.49, 1893.01, 1893.04, 1893.22, 1893.41, 1897.14
Koster, Miss 1863.04
Kotchetovsky 1924.29
Kotchetovsky, Mme. 1922.06
Kotek, Fred 1923.43
Kotshetovsky, Mr. 1922.06, 1923.28
Kottke, David 1979.03
Kotto, Yaphet 1965.32
Koud, William 1925.12
Koun, Nellie 1918.18
Koun, Sara 1918.18
Kouns, Nellie 1920.02, 1928.05
Kouns, Sara 1920.02, 1928.05
Kourkoulos, Nikos 1967.05
Kousnezoff, Maria 1922.37
Kouzoff, Messr. 1922.37
Kova, Marija 1962.06, 1962.19
Kovac, Jan 1952.02
Kovach, Nora 1960.07, 1965.25, 1965.27
Kovesy, Frl. 1882.68
Kowa, Maria 1964.25
Kowal, James 1989.20
Kowalski, George W. 1918.14
Kowley, J. Henry 1906.13
Koyke, Hizi 1931.10, 1931.25, 1931.35, 1933.08, 1934.07
Kozlova, Valentina 1996.15
Kozma, Tibor 1947.09
Kraatz, Curt 1908.29, 1928.35
Kraber, Garrit 1927.40
Kraber, Tony 1936.28, 1938.12, 1938.18, 1964.04
Krach, Bill 1952.03
Krach, William 1949.18, 1956.01, 1964.20
Krachmalnick, Samuel 1954.18, 1956.15, 1958.13, 1959.08, 1959.10, 1959.17, 1959.19
Kraemer, Jean 1953.07
Kraemmer, Hans 1984.04
Krafft, Frl. 1879.57
Kraft, Beatrice 1944.15, 1944.27, 1953.16, 1965.22
Kraft, Charles 1943.07
Kraft, Edna 1916.07
Kraft, Eveleyne 1944.15
Kraft, H.S. 1932.07
Kraft, Helen 1914.27
Kraft, Hy 1951.23, 1964.18
Kraft, Jack 1920.20, 1923.22
Kraft, Martin 1946.07, 1948.15
Krahn, Meta 1937.05
Krakaner, Prof. 1867.32
Krakeur, Richard 1942.27
Krakeur, Richard W. 1924.21
Krakowski, Jane 1987.05, 1989.26, 1995.11, 1996.18
Krall, Heidi 1950.03
Kramarevsky, Alex 1987.19
Kramarich, Irene 1956.09
Kramarr, Elena 1945.02
Kramer, Alex 1992.03, 1995.12
Kramer, Alex C. 1999.24
Kramer, Alma 1898.47
Kramer, Arthur 1937.14
Kramer, August 1880.59
Kramer, Augustus 1898.05
Kramer, Clair 1931.28, 1939.20, 1943.18
Kramer, Clark 1936.27
Kramer, Dave 1942.35
Kramer, David 1999.12

Kramer, Edward B. 1908.35
Kramer, Henry 1880.06, 1880.41, 1880.70
Kramer, Ida 1911.12
Kramer, Jonathan 1968.11
Kramer, Lou 1974.05
Kramer, Mark 1948.25, 1949.15
Kramer, Marsha 1979.22
Kramer, Mary Burke 1995.14
Kramer, Messr. 1880.59, 1884.42
Kramer, Renaye 1999.12
Kramer, Sam 1944.30
Kramer, Searle 1940.21
Kramer, Terry Allen 1974.26, 1977.04, 1978.24, 1979.25, 1986.12, 1991.15, 1993.15
Kramer, Wilhelm 1880.61, 1880.66
Kramer, Winnie 1900.47
Kramm, Joseph 1932.28
Krane, David 1979.09, 1985.20, 1986.11, 1989.19, 1993.09, 1993.10, 1994.01, 1994.08, 1995.15, 1996.08, 1998.01, 1998.04, 1998.15, 1999.23, 2000.11, 2001.06
Krane, Peter 1977.06
Kranendonk, Leonard 1955.13
Krantz, G. 1906.37
Krasker, Tommy 1992.02
Krasnoff, Serge 1932.27
Krasnoff, Syuleen 1930.36
Krasnopolsky, Urey 1955.05
Krasny, Diana 1964.15
Krass, Michael 1999.03
Krassner, Brad 1997.09
Kraus, Milt 1958.18
Kraus, Philip 1973.03
Kraus, Samuel 1971.14
Krause, Albert 1889.34, 1905.03, 1906.41, 1910.34, 1912.36
Krause, Christian 1880.25, 1881.47
Krause, Fritz 1893.29
Krause, Mr. 1898.53
Krause, Richard 1962.07, 1962.08, 1962.11, 1962.21, 1963.22, 1963.24, 1964.07, 1964.10, 1964.14, 1964.30, 1965.07, 1965.10, 1965.11, 1965.13, 1965.26, 1965.27
Kraushaar, Arnold A. 1920.43
Kraushaar, Janice 1931.46
Krauss, Charlotte 1940.04
Krauss, Marvin A. 1967.02, 1983.01, 1983.11, 1986.13, 1987.07, 1987.13, 1988.10, 1988.20, 1989.12, 1989.26
Krausse, A. 1898.73
Krausse, Albert 1891.23, 1894.20, 1894.36, 1895.30, 1896.09, 1896.11, 1897.05, 1900.01, 1900.54, 1907.47, 1910.12
Krauter, Marvin 1955.27
Krauth, William A. 1920.06
Kravat, Jerry 1985.15, 1987.06
Kravitt, Harold 1927.14, 1942.33
Krawford, Gary 1966.05, 1968.06, 1968.30
Krebill, Dorothy 1954.18, 1956.15
Krebs, Beatrice 1959.08, 1959.17, 1961.04, 1961.06
Krebs, Blanche 1926.30, 1927.05
Krebs, Celia 1937.06
Krebs, David 1977.10, 1982.01, 1982.05
Krebs, Eric 1918.13, 1999.09
Krebs, T. 1870.39
Kreckow, Paul 1921.28
Kreger, Matthew A. 1996.10
Kreig, Frank 1943.21, 1944.14
Kreighoff, Bertha 1903.31
Kreis, Robert 1981.26
Kreisel, Betty Colburn 1949.09
Kreisler, Fritz 1919.27, 1922.21, 1934.32, 1940.04, 1944.28, 1999.05
Kreissig, Hans 1882.14, 1884.30, 1884.31
Kreitzberg, Danny 1982.11
Kreling, John 1889.10
Krell, Frances 1952.01
Krell, Stan 1958.18
Krellberg, Sherman S. 1964.02
Kremer, August 1880.65, 1899.36
Kremer, Isa 1932.09
Kremer, Messr. 1879.23
Kremer, Mons. 1875.25, 1875.29
Kremer, us 1887.43
Kremm, L. 1901.13
Kren, Jean 1900.47
Krenn, Leopold 1898.72
Krensi, Messr. 1852.05
Krenz, Frank 1992.12, 1998.19
Kresa, Helmy 1933.22, 1946.12, 1949.08
Kresley, Ed 1960.06, 1962.04
Kresley, Edmond 1986.03
Kressen, Sam 1968.03
Kressyn, Miriam 1970.17
Kreste, Mary 1952.12
Kretzmer, Herbert 1965.30, 1970.01, 1974.19, 1981.16, 1983.03, 1987.04, 1995.12, 1997.01, 1998.12
Kreueder, Peter 1999.07
Kreuger, Anna 1864.19
Kreuger, Annie 1866.34
Kreuger, Charles 1888.25
Kreuger, Messr. 1888.25
Kreutzberg, Herr 1879.62
Krevoff, Sam 1930.38
Krider, Edna 1976.35
Kriefall, Hans 1995.02
Krieger, Henry 1981.29, 1983.21, 1987.07, 1997.17
Krieger, Lee 1949.01, 1959.01
Krieger, Mitchell 1981.22, 1983.13
Kriese, Gladys 1961.05, 1961.06, 1961.19, 1961.23, 1962.09, 1962.10, 1962.11
Krilling, Messr. 1861.02
Krimer, G. 1892.17
Krimsky, Jerrold 1933.07, 1936.03, 1937.02, 1937.12, 1938.12, 1939.10, 1946.19
Krimsky, John 1936.03, 1937.02, 1937.12, 1938.12, 1939.10, 1956.13
Kripska, Dania 1943.11
Krischner, Karen 1915.04
Kristen, Eric 1945.04, 1950.20
Kristen, Erik 1945.19, 1949.08, 1957.08, 1961.02
Kristen, Ilene 1972.12, 1985.15
Kristen, Robert 1964.40
Kristien, Dale 1983.05
Kristin, Karen 1969.04
Kristopher, Andrei 1944.20
Kristy, Carol 1972.21
Kristy, Gloria 1959.13, 1962.12
Krivett, Rita 1927.39
Krivit, Harry 1928.45
Krivoshei, David 1971.14
Krivoutz, V. 1929.05
Krlgarin, T.S. 1952.08
Kroeger, Barry 1956.07
Kroener, Helen 1920.03
Krofft, Sid 1949.05
Krohe, Rose 1894.16, 1901.08
Krohm, Amy 1876.03
Krohn, Fred 1999.25
Krok, Loren 1989.23
Kroll, Bernice 1951.10
Kroll, Louis 1918.04, 1924.42, 1929.34, 1929.36, 1929.38, 1929.40, 1929.43, 1929.47, 1929.48, 1930.03, 1930.07, 1930.12, 1930.15, 1931.27, 1931.41, 1931.43, 1931.45, 1935.06, 1935.07, 1935.08, 1935.09, 1935.10, 1942.02, 1942.04, 1942.06, 1942.07, 1942.08, 1942.09, 1944.04, 1944.05, 1944.06, 1944.07, 1944.08, 1944.09, 1944.10, 1944.11, 1944.12, 1944.13
Kroll, Mark 1957.01
Kroll, Ronnie 1963.21
Krone, W.A. 1894.42
Kroner, Helen 1915.29, 1916.19
Kroner, John 1980.01
Krones, Fred H. 1982.12, 1994.01, 1997.03, 2001.03
Krongold, Susan 1975.10
Kronkite, Walter 1995.05
Kronold, Selma 1900.06
Kronyack, Nick 1914.16, 1914.22
Kroon, Carol 1963.17
Kroonder, Hans 1964.39
Kropp, H.R. 1877.21
Kropp, John 1879.01, 1880.02
Kross, Ronald 1969.06
Krouse, H.S. 1912.04
Krueger, Dana 1979.20
Krueger, Martin 1895.08
Krug, Alicia 1953.02
Kruger, Anna 1864.20, 1864.21
Kruger, Eloise 1892.59, 1895.15
Kruger, George 1927.40
Kruger, Jacques 1877.20, 1878.10, 1880.42, 1882.04, 1882.20, 1883.02, 1883.17, 1883.19, 1883.23, 1884.12, 1884.20, 1886.14, 1888.21, 1890.35, 1892.42, 1894.10, 1895.15, 1895.27, 1896.52, 1897.40, 1898.38, 1900.48, 1900.55, 1906.05, 1907.02, 1907.39, 1910.18
Kruger, Martin 1892.29
Kruger, Messr. 1889.43, 1890.36
Kruger, Mlle. 1871.27, 1872.06
Kruger, Ottilie 1946.19
Krula, Renate 1984.04
Krumm, Stella 1900.43
Krumschmidt, E.A. 1950.15
Krupa, Gene 1980.29
Krupa, Olek 1992.05
Krupska, Dania 1951.18, 1953.07, 1954.01, 1956.04, 1959.02, 1961.08, 1961.09, 1962.16, 1964.03, 1968.23, 1976.08
Kruschen, Jack 1962.05
Kruschke, Gerhard 1989.17
Krutova, Nadiezhda 1925.51
Kruvi, Hovav 1968.04
Krygar, Ruth 1929.25
Kryl, Bob 1949.08
Krynicki, George 1988.10
Kubala, Michael 1982.06, 1983.17, 1989.03, 1992.02, 1996.14
Kubert, Anya 1938.16
Kubiak, Wiktor 1992.05
Kuchar, Erich 1984.04
Kudeyarova, Larisa 1977.13
Kudisch, Marc 1998.05, 1999.13, 2000.08, 2001.03
Kudo, Daini 1964.39
Kuebler, John 1935.15
Kuehn, Robert 1963.28
Kuester, John 1906.41
Kuestner, Charles 1952.12, 1953.05, 1954.04, 1954.14
Kughn, Richard 1986.18
Kuhler, Edna 1927.28
Kuhlman, Kim 1982.15
Kuhlman, Ron 1975.15
Kuhlmann, Rosemary 1951.17
Kuhn, Jeffrey 1998.01
Kuhn, John 1958.17
Kuhn, Joseph A. 1881.43, 1882.34
Kuhn, Judy 1985.18, 1986.13, 1988.09, 1993.10, 1997.12
Kuhn, Katherine 1943.02, 1947.12, 1948.19, 1949.05
Kuhn, Kathryn 1943.20, 1945.09, 1946.22
Kuhn, Mr. 1892.43
Kuhn, Walt 1922.21, 1922.42, 1923.31, 1927.27
Kuhnly, Fred 1942.30
Kuhr, Gail 1956.02, 1957.17
Kuhse, Frl. 1879.17, 1879.22
Kukutai, Karu 1972.20
Kuley, Hattie 1890.03
Kuller, Sid 1940.21, 1943.05, 1950.02, 1956.02, 1999.24
Kully, Mlle. 1888.23
Kulok, Peter 1993.17
Kuluva, Will 1940.10
Kumerfelt, Dora 1914.19
Kumi-Kimball, Christina 1978.28
Kumin, Ron 1996.04
Kummer, Clare 1903.07, 1903.33, 1904.26, 1905.19, 1905.20, 1906.25, 1907.51, 1907.59, 1912.08, 1914.02, 1915.01, 1921.05, 1923.44, 1924.38, 1924.39, 1937.17
Kummer, Clare V. 1910.27
Kummer, Frederic Arnold 1919.35, 1920.05
Kummer, Herr 1879.17, 1879.22
Kummer, Martin 1969.04
Kumon, Ken 1989.21
Kun, Ladislas 1926.13
Kuney, Scott 1981.07
Kunii, Masahiro 1990.17
Kunisch, C. 1901.15
Kunkel, Karyl 1927.06
Kunneke, Eduard 1923.03
Kunneke, Edward 1925.02, 1925.43
Kunz-Baker, Bertha 1937.01
Kunze, Emily 1893.07
Kupferman, Meyer 1965.32
Kupperman, Alvin 1970.07
Kuramoto, Dan 1979.08
Kurdock, Marybeth 1971.15
Kurer, Vilma 1940.04
Kurkamp, John 1904.14
Kurlan, David 1937.01, 1950.08, 1952.13
Kurland, Jerry 1963.10, 1981.17
Kurnitz, Harry 1963.29
Kurnitz, Julie 1970.07, 1978.24
Kursky, Nikolai 1925.46
Kurtman 1912.26
Kurton, Peggy 1921.36
Kurtz, John Henry 1981.24
Kurtz, Manny 1981.06
Kurtz, Marie 1870.44
Kurtz, Swoosie 1978.06
Kurz, Friedrich 1988.12
Kuselbach, Messr. 1852.05
Kusell, Daniel 1922.28, 1927.29, 1928.28
Kushibiki, Messr. 1902.22, 1903.19
Kushiki, Messr. 1925.13
Kushnier, Jeremy 1998.13
Kusik, Larry 1967.12
Kusmiak, Eugene 1946.05, 1952.14, 1952.16, 1952.17, 1952.18, 1952.19
Kusner, Jon 1999.06
Kussel, Daniel 1927.04
Kussel, Maurice L. 1934.39
Kuster, Frl. 1879.17, 1879.22, 1880.61
Kuttner, A. 1894.30
Kuttner, Alfred J. 1899.04
Kutton, Kay 1939.30
Kutzreba, Joseph S. 1975.07
Kux, Bill 1993.05
Kuzak, Andzia 1942.32
Kuznetsov, Villor 1990.01
Kuznetsov, Vladimir 1990.01
Kwartin, Paul 1941.01, 1942.32
Kwartz, Bertha 1968.04, 1969.13
Kya-Hill, Robert 1962.16
Kyle, Bessie 1905.30
Kyle, Billy 1950.02
Kyle, Daisy 1903.09
Kyle, Ethel 1880.18
Kyle, George 1884.22, 1888.29, 1889.45
Kyle, George W. 1888.19
Kyle, Joe 1968.13
Kyle, Kitty 1911.26, 1912.24
Kyme 1986.11, 1990.14
Kynock, May 1931.44
Kynock, Messr. 1876.34
Kynock, Peter 1875.32
Kyodo Tokyo, Inc. 1996.08
Kyte, E.M. 1918.17
Kyte, Mary 1980.27, 1986.20

L'Allemand, Pauline 1889.28, 1891.22
L'Estelle, Eleanor 1910.15
L'Estrange, Jean 1913.35
La Comete, Messr. 1869.29
La Moss 1900.34
La Verde, Belle 1888.45
La Zingaro 1865.10
LaBarre, Dede 1999.01
LaBeau, Jeannette 1905.34
Labeille, Daniel 1954.15
LaBelle, Patti 1982.17
Labey, Ken 1997.19
Labiche, Eugene 1875.01, 1882.73
Labis, Raoul 1926.49
LaBostrie, D. 1982.22, 1986.02
Labostrie, Dorothy 1992.06
LaBourdette, Katie 1989.11
LaBoy, Elsie 1909.30
LaBrecque, Doug 1994.08
Labriola, A. 1935.04
Labriola, Gary 1999.23
Labriola, Tony 1941.07
LaBrujere, Mlle. 1885.65
LaCause, Sebastian 1999.23, 2000.17
Laceby, Arthur 1910.21, 1912.15, 1915.32
Lacelles, Sara 1882.44
Lacey, Florence 1978.04, 1979.02, 1995.13, 1998.07
Lacey, Franklin 1957.18, 1965.21, 1980.16, 1988.04, 2000.11
Lacey, Helene 1898.58
Lacey, Milton 1933.04
Lacey, Miss 1881.38
laChamp, Adrienne 1927.40
LaChance, Manette 1982.14
LaChance, Steven 1981.13
LaChanze 1990.12
Lachaume, Aime 1893.25, 1901.09, 1901.21
Lachere, Marie 1899.21, 1899.26
Lachere, Mary 1904.03
LaChiusa, John 1999.22
LaChiusa, Michael John 1995.09, 2000.08
Lack, Madeline 1894.10
Lackaday, Messr. 1834.02
Lackaye, Emilyn 1905.05
Lackaye, Emmalyn 1906.15
Lackaye, James 1890.40, 1898.28
Lackaye, William 1886.23
Lackaye, Wilton 1887.49, 1890.40, 1902.29
Lackey, Bessie 1893.42
Lackey, Herndon 1980.19, 1985.18, 1993.09, 1998.21
Lackland, Ben 1933.20, 1944.01, 1956.03, 1956.05

Laclaire, Ida 1891.11
Lacome, Paul 1884.43, 1887.33, 1896.31
LaCroix, Arda 1904.33
Lacroix, Arda 1909.19
LaCroix, Emile 1902.36
Lacroix, Mlle. 1866.18
LaCross, Arline 1909.07
LaCrosse, Arline 1906.01
LaCrosse, Bob 1959.02, 1959.25, 1962.01, 1965.36, 1966.14
LaCrosse, Jeanne 1905.52
laCurto, James 1942.11
Lacy, D. 1878.03
Lacy, D.L. 1888.30
Lacy, Daniel 1886.23
Lacy, E. 1868.06
Lacy, Ernest 1899.03
Lacy, F. 1868.06
Lacy, Frank 1868.06, 1869.26, 1911.09
Lacy, Harry 1879.50, 1879.56, 1881.04, 1881.11
Lacy, Helena 1898.69
Lacy, Rophino 1864.18, 1867.04, 1868.10
Lacy, Terry 1985.13, 1986.04, 1986.09, 1986.14, 1987.03, 1988.16
Laczko, Brian J. 1997.05
Ladd, Eleanor 1920.37
Ladd, Hank 1942.23, 1947.20, 1949.01
Ladd, Ivanelle 1921.17
Ladd, Rob 1993.01, 1995.16, 1998.17
Ladd, Tom 1945.17
Ladd, William 1924.09, 1924.33, 1925.47
Ladden, Cassidy 1997.04, 1999.04
Laddis, Frank 1908.41
laDeaux, Elyse 1928.32
Ladella, Chester 1918.23
Ladella, George 1918.23
laDella, Pete 1930.08, 1931.08
Ladella, Peter 1916.15
Ladella, Tony 1916.15
Ladella, W.G. 1916.15
Ladella, Will 1918.23
laDelPipa, Juana 1992.15
Laderoute, Joseph 1944.16
Ladman, Jeff 1997.03
Ladoux, Emile 1931.39
Lady Duff Gordon 1915.15, 1919.11
Lafaille, Michael 1982.23
LaFanu, Joseph Sheridan 1897.03
Lafarge, Guy 1964.02
LaFaye, George 1958.06
LaFaye, Michael 1958.06
Lafayette, J. 1903.34
Lafferty, Mamie 1905.31
Lafferty, William 1911.41
Laffey, Bruce 1952.02
Lafoie, Miss 1852.01
LaFond, Phyllis 1900.38, 1905.20
Lafont, M. 1869.38
Lafontaine, Mlle. 1875.08
LaFontaine, Mlle. 1877.38, 1878.07, 1878.08
LaFontaine, Mme. 1868.05
Laforest, G. 1870.05
LaForest, Mrs. 1846.01
LaForrest, Charles 1869.08, 1869.36, 1869.37, 1869.38, 1870.01, 1870.12, 1870.28, 1870.32, 1870.35, 1870.42, 1871.02, 1872.04, 1872.05, 1872.08, 1872.12, 1872.25, 1872.30, 1872.36, 1872.38
Lafose, Frank 1898.64
LaFosse, Robert 1980.21, 1989.03, 1996.13
LaFrance, Doris 1914.28
LaFranconi, Terry 1941.07
laGallienne, Eva 1947.09
LaGallienne, Richard 1910.06
LaGarete, Miss 1897.14
Lage, Norman 1987.04
Lagidze, Revaz 1977.13
Lagier, Roger 1961.01
Lagomarsino, Ron 1992.17
LaGrande, Charlotte 1915.23
laGranna, Louis 1930.37
LaGrassa, C. 1873.18
Lagriffoul, Mons. 1867.24, 1867.30, 1868.07, 1868.18, 1868.25, 1868.27, 1868.30, 1869.01, 1869.09, 1869.10, 1869.12, 1869.24
LaGuardia, Francesca 1990.08
LaGuardia, Midge 1971.06
LaGue, Mildred 1918.05, 1920.47
LaGuerre, Irma-Estel 1985.01, 1996.16
LaGuerre, Yvonne 1896.35
Laguzzi, Viviana 1993.08
Lagye 1883.41
Lagye, A. 1882.61, 1882.73, 1883.27, 1883.30, 1883.51, 1883.54, 1883.55, 1883.57, 1883.59, 1883.60, 1883.61, 1884.01, 1884.03, 1884.05, 1884.43, 1884.45, 1884.47, 1884.49, 1884.50, 1884.52, 1884.54, 1884.55, 1885.19, 1885.25
Lagye, M.A. 1885.23
Lagye, Mons. 1882.53, 1882.55, 1882.58, 1882.67, 1884.02
Lagye, Mr. 1883.28
LaHarpe, De 1893.30
LaHarte, Rosa 1911.28
LaHarte, Rose 1905.54, 1906.46, 1907.54
Laharte, Rose 1916.12
laHarte, Rose 1926.04
LaHarte, Rosessie 1903.29
Lahiri, Sarat 1925.37
Lahiri, Saret 1922.21
Lahr, Bert 1927.62, 1928.36, 1930.11, 1932.07, 1932.24, 1934.19, 1935.18, 1936.31, 1939.30, 1944.29, 1948.04, 1951.19, 1959.23, 1964.04
Lahr, Marybeth 1969.04
Lai, Francis 1964.39, 1973.17
Laible, George 1902.33, 1905.10
Laidlaw, Messr. 1868.06
Laidlaw, Robert 1907.61
Laidlaw, W.S. 1896.05
Laidlow, Messr. 1871.11
Lail, Barbara 1974.26
Laimbeer, Fifi 1929.45
Laine, Cleo 1985.18
Laine, Fannia 1928.18
Laine, Frankie 1975.12
Laing, Hugh 1945.19
Laing, Stewart 1997.06
Laird, Ernest 1949.08
Laird, George 1928.09
Laird, Gladys 1926.13
Laird, Marvin 1965.33, 1966.11, 1968.01, 1970.03, 1981.09, 1981.25, 1991.04, 1999.04
Laird, Mignon 1930.23
Laird, W.S. 1889.25, 1893.34
Lait, Jack 1922.23, 1927.13
LaJolla Playhouse, The 1985.06, 1995.05
laJoy, Fred 1921.26
Lake, Amy 1905.23, 1907.02
Lake, Arthur 1876.11
Lake, Georgie 1890.41
Lake, Gladys 1928.11
Lake, Harriette 1931.04, 1931.36, 1933.13
Lake, Julia 1897.21
Lake, M.L. 1923.46
Lake, Marie 1967.06
Lake, Mike 1927.47, 1928.31
Lake, Thoral 1919.20
Lakier, Gail 1977.01
Laktionov, Nikolai 1977.13
Lalaew, Antonina 1928.03
Lally, Janet 1945.03, 1947.11
Lally, Joan 1945.03
Lally, Joanne 1947.11
Lalor, Edward 1938.16
Lalor, F.S. 1905.52
Lalor, Frank 1897.33, 1900.24, 1902.15, 1904.04, 1904.34, 1905.52, 1909.09, 1910.34, 1911.11, 1912.28, 1913.37, 1914.26, 1915.31, 1916.18, 1917.09, 1917.18, 1921.38, 1928.27, 1929.32, 1932.02
Lalor, Helen 1911.14
Lalska, Edward 1911.15
Lam, Miss 1877.39
Lam, Zoie 1989.05
Lama, Serge 1976.07
Lamagna, Giani 1985.14
laMance, Eleanor 1932.02
LaManna, Janine 1999.24, 2000.18
LaManna, Raphael 1983.14
LaManna, Signor 1852.03, 1853.04, 1854.02, 1854.03, 1854.06, 1854.07, 1855.01, 1855.02, 1855.11, 1856.04, 1863.10
Lamant, Mons. 1884.01
Lamar, Al 1905.05
Lamar, Al. 1903.20
LaMar, Albert 1901.24
LaMar, Dorothy 1904.07, 1905.34
laMar, Dorothy 1923.09
Lamar, Frances 1902.22
Lamar, George 1909.15, 1931.19
Lamar, Lee 1893.47, 1894.42
LaMar, Marguerite 1893.21, 1894.17
LaMar, Marie 1909.25
laMarr, Henry 1935.15
LaMarr, Moses 1953.04, 1957.05
LaMartine, Frank 1895.40
LaMartine, Joe 1895.40
Lamas, Fernando 1956.16
Lamb, Arthur 1903.18
Lamb, Arthur J. 1892.59, 1898.63, 1903.29, 1905.32, 1907.19, 1980.27
Lamb, Charles 1889.37, 1889.51, 1891.08
Lamb, E. 1863.07, 1868.19, 1870.25
Lamb, Edward 1863.06
Lamb, Frank E. 1881.08, 1884.62
Lamb, George 1926.38
Lamb, Gil 1939.31, 1940.10, 1948.18, 1971.07
Lamb, Gwendoline 1920.43
Lamb, J. Kathleen 1995.02
Lamb, J.W. 1904.38
Lamb, Joseph F. 1980.27
Lamb, Mary Ann 1987.05, 1989.03, 1993.02, 1996.06, 1996.14, 2000.18
Lamb, May Ann 1999.01
Lamb, Mr. 1823.01, 1851.08
Lamb, P. 1870.44
Lamb, Sybil 1952.10, 1955.01
Lamb, Wayne 1946.16, 1948.04
Lambard, Richard 1902.34
Lambart, Ernest 1906.01, 1907.06, 1908.24, 1909.04, 1910.21, 1911.23, 1914.14, 1921.18, 1934.18
Lambart, Harry 1912.15
Lambart, Richard 1902.40, 1934.29
Lambele, Mlle. 1868.18, 1868.25
Lambelet, N. 1898.63
Lambelet, Napoleon 1896.27, 1899.35
Lambelle, Aline 1868.13, 1868.15, 1868.31
Lambelle, Mlle. 1868.30
Lambert, Ainsley 1926.07
Lambert, Beverly 1986.04, 1990.07, 1991.08
Lambert, Charlotte 1905.07
Lambert, Dave 1976.34
Lambert, David 1945.18
Lambert, Dora 1899.22
Lambert, Edward 1946.22
Lambert, Edward J. 1934.20, 1935.11, 1945.12
Lambert, Ernest 1903.33, 1912.42
Lambert, Frank 1895.43, 1922.19, 1923.20, 1924.18, 1925.10, 1925.24, 1925.31
Lambert, George 1903.26
Lambert, Gloria 1960.08, 1967.05
Lambert, Happy 1922.30
Lambert, Harry 1918.29
Lambert, Hugh 1953.01, 1955.25, 1957.01, 1961.22, 1966.07
Lambert, Jack 1919.22, 1920.26, 1942.11, 1942.27
Lambert, John 1923.40, 1924.26, 1926.32, 1928.37
Lambert, Josephine 1948.25
Lambert, Juliet 1989.23, 1992.12, 1994.05
Lambert, Marie 1926.11
Lambert, Marion 1882.32, 1882.38, 1882.42
Lambert, Mark 1973.04
Lambert, Maud 1905.13, 1910.16, 1912.02
Lambert, Maude 1899.05, 1899.07, 1899.10, 1900.06, 1900.11, 1900.13, 1900.17, 1900.18, 1900.22, 1900.23, 1900.27, 1900.30, 1902.41, 1905.22, 1905.48, 1905.55, 1908.05, 1915.02
Lambert, Messr. 1926.32
Lambert, Mlle. 1870.44, 1871.27, 1902.13
Lambert, Nora 1900.43, 1902.12
Lambert, Olga 1897.55, 1899.22
Lambert, Oscar 1913.03
Lambert, Richard 1902.16, 1930.42
Lambert, Robert 1989.27, 1991.06
Lambert, Sally 1978.19, 1978.23, 1979.20, 1979.27
Lambert, Sammy 1947.11, 1948.15, 1949.02, 1951.18
Lambert, Sarony 1900.43, 1902.12, 1907.06, 1908.25
Lambert, Waverly 1934.40
Lamberti, Michael 1940.02
Lamberti, Prof. 1942.18
Lamberts, Heath 1994.04, 1996.18
Lamberts, Jennifer 1997.05
Lambet, Ernest 1928.08
Lamborn, Theresa 1879.38, 1880.24
Lambrinos, Ted 1961.27
Lambrinos, Vassili 1968.30
Lambrose, George 1947.14
Lamee, Margaret 1981.28
LaMirada Theatre for the Performing Arts 1998.18
Lamm, Mario 1953.16
Lamoine, Emma 1905.37
Lamont, Clara 1891.37
Lamont, Elsie 1923.23
Lamont, Helen 1886.57
Lamont, Jennie 1902.42, 1905.10, 1908.43, 1912.06, 1913.03, 1914.05, 1914.29
Lamont, John C. 1919.07
Lamont, Lina 1985.08
Lamont, Louis 1906.45, 1908.04
Lamont, Michael 1965.06
Lamont, Miki 1960.11, 1961.07
Lamont, Robert 1953.16, 1965.22
Lamont, Robin 1976.17, 1978.12
LaMont, William 1888.04
Lamontagne, Susan 1999.01
LaMora, Miss 1905.57
laMore, Harry 1937.15
Lamos, Mark 1973.07, 1999.10
LaMoss, E. 1886.27
LaMoss, Edward 1903.24, 1904.10, 1904.52, 1905.06
LaMotta, Jake 1965.15
LaMotta, John 1968.08, 1968.30
Lamoureux, Robert 1955.14
Lamp, Eric 1983.11
Lamparella, Gina 2000.20
Lampe, Dell 1934.18
Lampe, J. Bodewait 1920.47
Lampe, J. Bodewalt 1919.16, 1919.30, 1920.31
Lampe, J. Dell 1922.15, 1922.18
Lampell, Millard 1960.18
Lampert, Rachel 1968.18
Lampert, Virginia 1891.40
Lampert, Zohra 1963.09, 1972.01
Lamphier and Buhler 1899.11
Lampl, Carl 1948.21
Lampp, Kittie 1897.38
Lamprey, L. 1901.08
Lamprey, Peggy Hagen 1974.03
Lams, Jeff 1999.08, 1999.12
Lamson, Albert 1911.15, 1915.25
Lamson, Harry 1888.28
Lan, David 1989.10
Lanagan, M. 1870.19
Lanagan, Mr. 1875.05
Lancaster, Dick 1927.62
Lancaster, Dorothy 1909.25
Lancaster, John 1899.08
Lancaster, Lillian 1880.34
Lancaster, Lucie 1963.29, 1964.40, 1967.16, 1971.07
Lance, Herb J. 1999.09
Lancelot, Hubert 1947.18
Lancer, Mr. 1868.04
Lancetti, E. 1911.19
Lanchbery, John 1976.18
Lanchmere, Lola 1894.52
Lancier, Virginia 1919.10
Land, Belle 1869.06, 1870.04
Land, David 1971.12, 1979.23, 1982.03
Land, Elizabeth Ward 1999.13
Land, Grover 1907.53
Land, Ken 1995.15, 1997.19, 1999.13
Landau, Emily 1985.06
Landau, Irving 1944.16, 1944.27, 1945.02, 1945.14
Landau, Tina 2001.03
Landay, David S. 1981.10, 1982.14
Landek, Violetta 1966.11
Lander, Annie 1885.66, 1886.03
Lander, David 2000.12
Lander, Frank 1895.41
Lander, Harry 1912.29
Lander, Henrietta 1890.40
Lander, Jeff 1993.19
Lander, Toccoa 1937.11
Landers, Dorothy 1914.30
Landers, Mabel 1915.18
Landers, Matt 1978.12
Landers, Minnie 1896.25
Landers, Mr. 1856.04, 1857.05, 1857.07
Landers, Pearl 1901.27
Landes, Francine 1985.18
Landes, Minnie 1892.55, 1895.04
Landesman, Fran 1959.12
Landesman, Heidi 1985.06, 1987.18, 1991.05, 1993.19, 1995.03
Landesman, Jay 1959.12
Landesman, Rocco 1982.04, 1985.06, 1987.18, 1991.05, 1995.05, 1995.12, 1998.11, 1998.13, 2001.05
Landfield, Timothy 1995.11, 1998.03
Landi, Elaine 1963.21
Landi, Jami 1962.16, 1962.24

Landi, Mara 1953.11, 1954.05, 1956.16, 1957.07, 1959.25, 1961.22, 1963.21, 1966.24, 1969.01, 1987.16
Landie, C.E. 1896.08, 1896.42
Landin, Nils 1944.24
Landis, Carole 1945.01
Landis, Jeanette 1965.39
Landis, Jessie Royce 1944.26
Landis, Lynn 2001.05
Landloff 1906.45
Landloff and Millet 1877.32
Landmark Entertainment Group 1995.02
Landolf, Mons. 1883.06
Landolff 1877.26, 1887.35, 1887.36, 1887.37, 1887.38, 1887.41, 1889.21, 1908.04, 1910.24, 1911.44
Landolff of Paris
Landolff, Messr. 1879.19
Landolff, Mons. 1890.17
Landolff, Mr. 1880.44
Landolph 1891.41
Landon, Daniel 1974.23
Landon, Joseph 1988.20
Landon, Margaret 1951.12, 1956.03, 1960.11, 1963.18, 1964.23, 1968.16, 1977.07, 1985.01, 1989.03, 1996.05
Landor, Annie 1887.39
Landor, Neville 1935.12, 1938.17
Landorf 1909.15
Landorff 1912.09
Landres, Simm 1969.08
Landrieu, Nelson Roberto 1995.09
Landron, Jack 1972.19, 1975.09
Landrum, Bill 1962.04
Landrum, Kinny 1981.24
Landry, Carole 1972.08
Landry, Cy 1929.12, 1930.38
Landry, Glenda 1971.21
Landry, Monsieur 1869.12, 1869.19
Landy, Doris 1921.09
Lane 1869.35
Lane, Abbe 1958.02
Lane, Agnes Rose 1896.02
Lane, Alice 1900.35
Lane, Allie 1881.38
Lane, Annie 1905.40
Lane, Betty D. 1976.28
Lane, Beverly 1942.10
Lane, Bobby 1937.04, 1941.03, 1944.02
Lane, Bradley F. 1927.55
Lane, Burton 1930.20, 1930.32, 1931.14, 1931.26, 1931.32, 1932.20, 1940.10, 1944.30, 1947.03, 1955.09, 1960.09, 1962.17, 1965.31, 1967.04, 1974.01, 1979.09, 1979.24, 1980.29, 1990.09, 1999.23
Lane, Casmo 1912.37
Lane, Charles 1904.43, 1906.50
Lane, Clara 1884.37, 1887.43, 1895.12, 1899.21, 1900.30
Lane, Constance 1929.03
Lane, Doreen 1948.18
Lane, Drury 1937.10
Lane, E.G. 1897.51
Lane, Edith 1948.27, 1955.07
Lane, Eleanor 1884.56
Lane, Elen 1947.02
Lane, Elmira 1922.11, 1926.42
Lane, Frank 1889.12, 1890.04, 1897.01
Lane, George 1945.03, 1947.11
Lane, George C. 1923.11
Lane, Georie 1918.17
Lane, Gerald 1907.48
Lane, Gloria 1950.05, 1952.12, 1954.18
Lane, Harry 1901.10, 1901.11, 1904.19, 1905.40, 1907.27, 1914.24
Lane, Harry J. 1918.01
Lane, James 1940.22, 1942.29, 1947.08, 1948.08, 1948.26, 1951.02
Lane, James C. 1911.13, 1917.29
Lane, Jennifer 1990.08
Lane, Jody 1959.13, 1965.20
Lane, John 1898.59
Lane, John E. 1898.59
Lane, Joy 1957.14
Lane, Judy 1930.27
Lane, Julia 1924.09, 1929.17
Lane, Karen 1942.19
Lane, Kenneth 1959.02
Lane, Laura 1900.35
Lane, Leotabel 1929.48
Lane, Lillian 1928.06, 1929.28
Lane, Lupino 1920.41, 1924.18, 1925.13
Lane, M.S. 1873.18
Lane, Marguerite 1906.02, 1906.42, 1908.07
Lane, Margy 1926.20
Lane, Marjorie 1913.05, 1922.43, 1923.46, 1927.47, 1928.31
Lane, Marjory 1913.29
Lane, Mark 1903.19
Lane, Mary 1920.08
Lane, Midgie 1931.31
Lane, Miss 1904.13, 1904.44
Lane, Nancy 1975.15
Lane, Nathan 1983.01, 1985.20, 1992.04, 1996.06, 2001.05
Lane, Nellie 1904.13, 1904.44
Lane, Nicholas 2001.04
Lane, Ralph 1945.01
Lane, Richard 1928.16, 1930.35, 1935.18
Lane, Rosemary 1941.06
Lane, Stewart F. 1979.02, 1980.02, 1981.10, 1981.13, 1983.11, 1990.06, 1991.07, 1993.02, 1997.15, 1999.23
Lane, Sylvia 1948.18
Lane, Thomas W. 1907.03
Lane, Walter 1920.34
Lane-Plescia, Gillian 1993.04
Lanergan, J.W. 1880.37
Laney, Ben 1966.12, 1966.16, 1967.09, 1969.14, 1970.08
Laney, Flora 1935.17
Lang's Comedy Comiques 1885.44
Lang, Andrew 1937.11
Lang, Arthur 1926.12, 1926.29
Lang, Augusta 1911.41
Lang, Barbara 1966.18, 1973.04, 1976.09, 1976.30, 1982.18, 1983.10
Lang, C.F. 1885.04
Lang, Charles 1878.03, 1881.03, 1889.16
Lang, Charles F. 1880.01, 1880.03, 1880.54, 1884.09, 1890.08, 1896.01
Lang, Edward 1891.15
Lang, Edwin R. 1885.44
Lang, Eric 1975.04
Lang, Gertrude 1922.34, 1923.14, 1927.43, 1929.17
Lang, Gussie 1879.15, 1879.56
Lang, Harold 1945.12, 1946.07, 1948.08, 1948.32, 1951.13, 1952.01, 1956.07, 1957.01, 1962.05
Lang, Harry 1920.43, 1923.18
Lang, Jeanie 1930.42
Lang, Lester 1938.02
Lang, Lise 1983.17
Lang, Maria 1976.18
Lang, Michael 1999.16
Lang, Mrs. 1794.01
Lang, P.M. 1884.28
Lang, Pearl 1945.05, 1949.12
Lang, Peter 1891.29, 1892.51, 1893.18, 1893.19, 1893.48, 1894.03, 1894.45, 1895.01, 1896.28, 1897.36, 1899.28, 1920.14, 1922.48, 1931.28
Lang, Peter M. 1895.26, 1898.56
Lang, Phil 1951.02
Lang, Philip J. 1942.26, 1945.20, 1946.12, 1947.08, 1947.16, 1948.16, 1948.26, 1950.04, 1951.13, 1951.19, 1952.20, 1953.07, 1954.15, 1955.01, 1956.01, 1956.07, 1956.12, 1957.07, 1957.16, 1958.02, 1958.03, 1958.04, 1958.14, 1958.20, 1959.01, 1959.11, 1959.22, 1959.27, 1960.10, 1960.21, 1961.10, 1961.28, 1962.13, 1962.20, 1963.08, 1963.25, 1964.01, 1964.20, 1964.33, 1964.44, 1965.19, 1966.10, 1966.11, 1966.29, 1967.02, 1967.15, 1967.16, 1968.07, 1968.17, 1968.24, 1968.32, 1969.05, 1970.09, 1970.21, 1971.02, 1972.04, 1972.24, 1973.07, 1974.02, 1974.18, 1974.26, 1975.22, 1976.05, 1977.06, 1979.02, 1979.12, 1979.13, 1979.28, 1980.09, 1980.18, 1980.19, 1980.20, 1980.23, 1981.07, 1981.13, 1981.19, 1981.26, 1983.10, 1983.20, 1985.04, 1995.13, 1997.04, 2001.08
Lang, Samuel 1935.04
Lang, William A. 1885.44
Langan, David 1993.12
Langan, Kate 1982.16
Langan, Vincent 1925.36, 1925.44
Langan, William 1927.25
Langdale, Reginald 1900.51
Langdon, Adelaide 1885.63
Langdon, Adele 1885.41
Langdon, Allan 1932.03
Langdon, Anna 1885.02, 1887.07
Langdon, Annie 1882.50, 1882.74, 1883.32, 1883.46, 1883.53, 1883.63, 1884.13, 1884.41, 1885.15, 1885.49, 1885.66, 1886.03, 1886.42, 1886.52, 1887.16, 1887.39, 1887.45, 1888.14, 1889.11
Langdon, Cecil 1920.35
Langdon, Dick 1939.24
Langdon, Donald 1973.13
Langdon, Dorothy 1912.34
Langdon, Ethel 1892.04
Langdon, Grace 1892.26, 1893.22, 1916.11, 1918.05
Langdon, H.A. 1894.39
Langdon, Harry 1920.35
Langdon, Julia 1887.11
Langdon, Kate 1883.32, 1883.46, 1883.53, 1883.63, 1884.13, 1884.41, 1885.02, 1885.15, 1885.22, 1885.49, 1885.66, 1886.03, 1886.42, 1887.07, 1887.16, 1887.39, 1887.45, 1888.14
Langdon, Margaret 1912.35
Langdon, Marian 1886.32
Langdon, Marion 1896.20, 1900.40
Langdon, Mary 1882.50
Langdon, Messr. 1859.08
Langdon, Miss 1886.32
Langdon, R.P. 1880.41
Langdon, Ruth 1905.49
Lange, Arthur 1914.22, 1920.08, 1920.30, 1921.07, 1923.19, 1923.21, 1923.22, 1927.48
Lange, Charles F. 1878.16
Lange, Elsie 1919.14, 1919.34
Lange, Johnny 1990.05, 1992.03
Lange, Juliette 1911.46
Lange, Miss 1892.43
Langella, Frank 2000.19
Langenbach, Mr. 1870.36
Langer, Hedwig 1927.31
Langer, Siegfried 1931.35, 1931.43, 1931.45
Langergan, Messr. 1854.01
Langford, Bonnie 1974.17
Langford, Frances 1931.42
Langford, Gordon 1962.18
Langford, James 1935.18
Langhart, Chris 1979.15
Langhofer, Vladanka 1964.39
Langhorne, J. Vickery 1899.23
Langlen, Paula 1926.10, 1926.44, 1927.57, 1927.61
Langler, Marie 1880.68
Langley, Frank 1872.25
Langley, Georgie 1870.24
Langley, Josie 1883.68, 1885.10, 1886.05
Langley, Leland H. 1895.10
Langley, Miss 1881.41, 1882.60
Langley, Noel 1989.06, 1997.11, 1998.06, 1999.11
Langley, Stuart 1941.06, 1943.01, 1943.23
Langley, Walter H. 1896.45
Langlois, Louise 1870.44
Langlois, Michael 1991.09
Langlois, Sylvain 1904.05, 1905.53, 1906.36, 1907.39
Langner, Christine 1981.07, 1982.19
Langner, Lawrence 1921.23, 1933.23, 1933.24, 1941.05, 1943.04, 1944.32, 1945.05, 1947.17, 1949.03, 1950.04, 1951.16
Langner, Philip 1996.04
Langolis, Michael 1991.09
Langstaff, A.M. 1904.19, 1905.25, 1909.18
Langstaff, Alfred 1906.24
Langton, Addie 1886.47
Langton, Nellie 1889.54
Langtry, Lionel 1921.15
Langweed, Lillian 1902.26
Langworthy, Norma 1996.04
Lani, Shawni 1932.19
Lanier, Jane 1987.15, 1989.03, 1999.01
Lanier, Sidney 1966.32
laNier, Vanita 1926.51
Lanin, Paul 1927.38
Lankas, Gene 1929.23
Lankston, John 1961.15, 1961.26, 1963.17, 1964.11, 1968.12, 1968.14, 1968.15, 1975.11, 1976.26, 1978.07, 1980.21, 1980.25, 1981.20, 1982.20, 1983.13, 1984.11, 1984.13, 1985.11, 1985.13, 1986.08, 1986.09, 1986.14, 1987.09, 1988.14, 1988.16, 1988.18, 1989.13, 1989.14, 1991.09, 1993.14, 1994.09, 1995.18, 1996.02
Lannan, Nina 2000.10
Lanner, Kathi 1873.08, 1875.03, 1875.06, 1875.10
Lanner, Katti 1893.21
Lanner, Margaret 1879.56
Lannier, Kathi 1872.37
Lannin, Paul 1921.10, 1922.10, 1924.43, 1926.22, 1927.16, 1927.37, 1929.37, 1930.39
Lannin, Paul J. 1928.17
Lanning, Don 1930.23
Lanning, Eva 1905.07
Lanning, Jerry 1966.10, 1974.04, 1974.25, 1976.05, 1992.11, 1997.15
Lanning, Michael 1999.08
Lanoe, J. Liquel 1908.14
Lanouette 1881.11, 1881.27, 1881.35
Lanouette, T.W. 1879.05
Lans, R.J. 1902.39
Lansbury, Angela 1964.15, 1966.10, 1969.05, 1974.17, 1979.06, 1983.10
Lansbury, Edgar 1970.08, 1974.13, 1974.17, 1975.05, 1976.17, 1981.09
Lansford, Jeanne 1910.16
Lansing, Charlotte 1931.39, 1932.02, 1938.17
Lansing, Everett 1913.03
Lansing, John 1972.01
Lansing, Mr. 1875.05
Lansing, W. 1875.05
Lanswell, Joe 1899.26
Lanteau, William 1956.12
Lanti, Al 1955.08, 1962.14, 1965.29, 1966.27
Lanton, Frank 1887.29
Lantz, Robert 1959.12, 1961.26
Lanvin 1934.34
Lanvin, Helen 1942.02, 1942.04, 1942.06, 1942.07, 1942.09
Lanvin, Jean 1926.49
Lanvin, Jeanne 1928.33, 1934.32
Lanyon, Wilma 1928.20, 1929.20
Lapaugh, N.C. 1864.09
LaPearl, Harry 1912.30, 1913.22, 1914.11
laPenna, James 1927.53
laPenner, James 1926.03
Lapidus, Ted 1983.03
LaPierie, Marguerite 1913.02
LaPierre, Adele 1912.38
Lapin, Jerome M. 1972.17
Lapin, Regina A. 1972.17
Lapine, James 1984.08, 1987.18, 1992.09, 1994.05, 2000.12
LaPoint, Annetta 1864.02
Lapointe, Carlotta 1867.25
laPorta, Sal 1942.35
Laporte, Hilda 1891.40
Laporte, Mr. 1857.05
Laporte, Rose 1891.40
Lapotaire, Jane 1981.04
LaPrade, Jan 1963.17, 1964.01
LaPrade, M. 1918.27
LaPrise, Roland 1998.11
Lapue, Andre 1923.33
Lapue, Maurice 1927.60, 1930.02
laPue, Maurice 1928.23, 1930.37, 1930.40
Larabee, Louise 1949.03, 1966.31
Lardas, Steven 1976.24
Lardinois, Clara 1898.72
Lardner, Jr., James 1953.01
Lardner, Jr., Ring 1964.04, 1981.10
Lardner, Ring 1915.30, 1917.13, 1918.32, 1922.19, 1922.42, 1930.06, 1930.39
laRedd, Cora 1928.21, 1929.18, 1930.19
Laren, Messr. 1871.27
Large, Graham 1976.07
Large, Norman 1979.27, 1980.03, 1980.04, 1980.22, 1980.25, 1981.22
Large, Norman A. 1982.18
Larici, Miriam 1997.13
Larimer, Bob 1979.18
Larin, Manon 1972.08
Larios, Paloma 1949.07
laRiviere, Lucien 1926.01, 1927.40, 1932.19
Larkell, Nellie 1880.08
Larkell, Nelly 1872.43
Larkelle, Nellie 1873.18, 1873.21, 1875.20, 1878.19, 1882.77
Larkin, C.R. 1905.52
Larkin, Joan 1934.40
Larkin, Peter 1954.13, 1956.07, 1956.08, 1958.14, 1959.06, 1960.05, 1960.22, 1962.24, 1978.05, 1981.09, 1983.18, 1984.01, 1986.06
Larkins, Ellis 1966.05
Larkins, Helen 1916.07
Larkins, John 1904.38
Larner, Elizabeth 1984.07, 1986.12

LaRocco, Jody 1966.08
laRoche, Mary 1944.30
LaRose, Harry 1890.09
Larranaga, Carmen 1929.33
Larregla 1949.07
Larrimore, Francine 1918.30
Larrimore, Martha 1954.03
Larsen, Caitlin 1987.16
Larsen, Liz 1981.18, 1989.09
Larsen, Ray 1981.04
Larsen, Robert R. 1989.07
Larsen, William 1965.14, 1969.05
Larson in Paris 1963.02
Larson, Jonathan 1996.09
Larson, Linda 1968.07
Larson, Lisby 1981.03
Larson, Liz 1992.01
Larson, Niels Bjorn 1937.05
Larson, Peter 1982.10, 1983.06
Larson, Peter M. 1976.15
Larson, Stuart 1989.23
LaRue, Dorothy 1918.22
LaRue, Eugene 1905.21
LaRue, Grace 1906.26, 1906.41, 1907.24, 1908.19, 1910.11, 1910.31, 1911.46, 1917.12
laRue, Grace 1922.39
Larue, Grace 1928.14
laRue, John 1930.16
laRue, Martha Escoe 1949.05
Laruelle, Mlle. 1868.25
Larvy, M. 1968.04
Lary, Messr. 1885.20
Lary, Mons. 1883.51, 1883.54, 1883.55, 1883.57, 1883.59, 1883.60, 1883.61, 1884.01, 1884.02, 1884.03, 1884.05, 1884.45, 1884.47, 1884.49, 1884.50, 1884.52, 1884.54, 1885.17, 1885.23
LaSalle Theatre Company 1904.28
LaSalle, Denise 1999.09
laSalle, Gay 1927.11
Lascelles, Eme 1881.36, 1881.38, 1883.25, 1883.29, 1884.25, 1884.40
Lascelles, Emily 1880.31
Lascelles, Emma 1881.38, 1882.06
Lascelles, Kendrew 1966.03, 1980.05
Lascelles, Miss 1910.12
Lascelles, Nanette 1893.40
Lascelles, Sara 1879.06, 1879.50, 1879.56, 1880.04, 1881.03, 1882.44
Lasco, Morry 1992.03
Lascoe, Henry 1950.15, 1953.03, 1955.02, 1961.10
LaSelva, Vincent 1965.07, 1966.04
Laser Media 1979.22, 1986.18
Lash, Lee 1909.14
Lash, Roland 1931.44
LaShan, Ada 1918.23
LaShelle, Kirk 1895.33, 1897.18
LaShelle, Kirke 1897.42, 1899.40, 1900.12, 1902.07
Lashly, Messr. 1923.21
LaShure, Burt 1905.31
Laska, Edward 1905.49, 1906.31
Laskey, Charles 1938.05, 1940.08
Lasky, Jesse 1908.15, 1911.26
Lasky, Jesse L. 1911.18
Lasser, Louise 1967.14
Lassie, Inc. 1920.12
Lassiter, Franc 1929.29
Lassiter, Mildred 1940.01
Lassiter, Warren 1929.29
Laster, Marty 1982.11
Laszlo, Aladar 1993.10
Laszlo, Halasz 1942.33
Laszlo, Miklos 1963.14, 1993.10
Lataine, Patti 1898.02
Latebe, Florence 1887.43
Latell, Alfred 1904.20, 1905.55, 1915.16, 1916.02, 1942.27
Latell, Blanche 1907.34, 1926.46
Latendorf, Walter 1934.18
Latessa, Dick 1968.06, 1971.05, 1986.13, 1991.07, 1994.01
Latham, Cynthia 1916.01, 1959.01, 1970.03
Latham, Florence 1905.19
Latham, Fred C. 1923.13
Latham, Fred G. 1903.37, 1904.51, 1905.57, 1906.33, 1907.36, 1908.40, 1909.03, 1909.09, 1910.20, 1910.27, 1913.15, 1913.32, 1914.27, 1915.23, 1916.01, 1917.07, 1917.28, 1918.34, 1919.09, 1919.27, 1920.04, 1920.40, 1922.35, 1922.45, 1923.03, 1923.44, 1924.08, 1925.02, 1925.07, 1926.26, 1926.30
Latham, Frederick 1913.24
Latham, Frederick G. 1911.38, 1911.41, 1912.46
Latham, Leslie 1972.04
Latham, Shirley 1920.37
Latham, W.H. 1834.02
Lathan, John 1998.02
Lathram, Elizabeth 1976.17
Lathrop, Alton 1972.14, 1976.04
Lathrop, Dorothy 1896.32
Lathrop, G.P. 1884.40
Lathrop, Helen 1903.07, 1905.48
Lathrop, Jack 1937.16
Lathrop, Louisa 1904.21
Latimer, John 1936.03
Latimer, Webster 1990.08
Latitmore, Jonita 1996.10
Latone, Belle 1897.21
Latorre 1949.07
laTorre, Charles 1932.07, 1939.22, 1940.08
Latouche, Jean-Treville 1936.03
Latouche, John 1937.14, 1939.19, 1939.23, 1940.17, 1941.13, 1942.01, 1942.12, 1942.26, 1944.28, 1945.14, 1946.24, 1948.17, 1953.12, 1954.03, 1955.25, 1956.15, 1974.06, 1980.10, 1982.20, 1983.13, 1984.11, 1986.08, 1988.08, 1989.14, 1997.10
Latouche, Jonathan 1999.23
Latour, C. 1885.65
laTour, Charlotte 1924.32
Latour, Doris 1900.37
laTour, Evelyn 1930.18
LaTour, Katharine 1900.45
LaTourneaux, Robert 1967.05
Latsch, Robert 1911.03
Latta, Lee 1897.42
Latte, Alfred 1921.42
Latten, Helen 1912.37
Latterner, Charles 1940.13
Lattuada, Emma 1940.05
Lau, Elise 1893.29, 1894.30
Lau, Elsie 1896.34, 1897.35
Lauder, Harry 1930.17
Lauder, Sirne 1928.05
Lauer, Marion 1949.17
Lauer, Sadie 1900.51, 1903.14
Laufer, Murray 1971.21
Laugenbach, Mons. 1870.39
Laughlin, Anna 1900.35, 1900.41, 1901.23, 1903.03, 1904.13, 1904.44, 1906.15, 1907.47, 1912.20, 1914.06
Laughlin, Catherine 1931.05
Laughlin, Catheryn 1939.29
Laughlin, Harry 1911.26
Laughlin, Jack 1908.21
Laughlin, Jane 1966.27
Laughrin, J.A. 1882.07
Laumer, Edith 1943.14
Laun, Elna 1959.22
Laun, Louis 1948.22
Launcelot, C. 1889.02
Launchmere, Lola 1899.33, 1901.20
Launders, Percy 1930.32
Lauper, Cyndi 2000.16
Laura, Miss 1868.06
Laurell, Kay 1914.15, 1915.15, 1918.19
Lauren, Elaine 1927.11
Lauren, Lilyan 1927.11
Laurence Rivers, Inc. 1935.01, 1936.22
Laurence, Arthur 1903.40
Laurence, Baby 1973.17
Laurence, Charles 1939.31
Laurence, Georgia 1899.12
Laurence, Georgie 1921.24
Laurence, J. 1887.14
Laurence, Jeanne 1926.25
Laurence, Larry 1946.13, 1951.19, 1954.02
Laurence, Lenore 1927.39
Laurence, Lionel E. 1901.29
Laurence, Mons. 1879.50
Laurence, Paula 1939.19, 1943.01, 1943.19, 1946.06, 1950.11, 1956.09, 1957.02
Laurence, Pauline 1932.20
Laurenson, Diana 1982.15, 1989.20
Laurent, A. 1868.06, 1869.26
Laurent, Ada 1883.47, 1886.49
Laurent, Charles 1929.05
Laurent, Henri 1875.15, 1876.17, 1876.18, 1876.21, 1876.27, 1877.16, 1879.05, 1880.63, 1881.43, 1882.21, 1882.23, 1882.32, 1883.25, 1883.29, 1894.10
Laurent, Henry 1879.07, 1879.11, 1895.36
Laurent, Mlle. 1868.06, 1870.44
Laurentis, Mlle. 1866.23, 1866.27, 1866.30, 1867.05
Laurents, Arthur 1957.12, 1959.13, 1960.08, 1962.05, 1964.15, 1964.17, 1965.06, 1967.06, 1968.18, 1974.17, 1980.02, 1983.11, 1989.03, 1989.27, 1991.06, 1991.15
Laurenz, P. 1985.07, 1997.13
Laurenzo, M. 1929.10
Laurenzo, Mr. 1929.15
Lauret, Armand 1927.18
Laurey, S.W. 1881.28, 1882.69
Laureys 1869.33, 1869.40
Laureys and Auguste and Company 1871.27
Laureys, C. 1871.10
Laureys, J.W. 1870.44
Laureys, Mr. 1870.04, 1870.13
Laureys, S.W. 1868.03, 1869.02, 1869.06, 1869.27, 1869.29, 1869.35, 1869.43
Lauri, Charles 1869.35, 1872.23, 1872.35
Lauri, Ed 1899.36
Lauri, George 1890.37
Lauri, Harry 1869.35, 1872.35
Lauri, Henri 1872.23
Lauri, John 1869.35, 1872.23, 1872.34, 1872.35
Lauri, Jr., Charles 1872.23
Lauri, Mme. 1869.35, 1872.35
Laurie, Joe 1917.31
Laurie, Jr., Joe 1924.10
Laurie, St. John 1934.34
Laurie, Virginia 1895.31
Laurini, Peter 1951.16, 1953.09
Laury, T. 1867.12
Lautencin, M. 1868.20
Lautner, Joe 1952.09, 1953.08
Lautner, Maurice 1993.03
Lautrec, Toulouse 1941.03
Laval, Maria 1925.39
Laval, Marie 1927.14
LaVallay, Charles 1898.78
laValle, Babs 1930.09
LaValy, Charles R. 1897.04
laVarre, Frank 1940.12
LaVarre, Madelon 1920.22, 1920.23
Lavarre, Marie 1915.22, 1916.23
laVarre, Paul 1940.12
Lavedan, Henri 1899.17, 1903.28
laVella, Gertrude 1925.12
Lavelle, Calixe 1882.33
Lavelle, Marie 1909.25
LaVelle, Miriam 1941.12
laVelle, Miriam 1942.12
Lavender, George 1916.03
Lavenia, Alice 1872.43
Lavenia, Miss 1872.14, 1872.36
laVer, James 1939.22
Lavera, Jeanie 1931.05
LaVerde, Belle 1891.18, 1892.23
LaVerde, Lillie 1886.53, 1889.53
Laverdet 1924.01
Laverenz, Mary Gail 1968.01
Laverne, Florence 1898.38
laVerne, French 1948.20
laVerne, Lupton 1939.27
laVerni, Marie 1929.30
Laverty, John 1945.18, 1947.08, 1949.18, 1951.13, 1951.23
Laverty, Johnny 1956.08
Laverty, W. 1898.54
Laverty, W.A. 1894.29
Laverty, William 1896.28, 1897.36, 1899.28, 1903.32
Lavery, James 1964.35
Lavie, Aric 1971.14
LaVie, Pauline 1908.33
Lavie, Raul 1985.07, 1999.18
Lavigne, Anna 1901.03
Lavigne, Maurice 1903.33, 1911.10, 1933.17
Lavigne, May 1896.35, 1896.48, 1898.38
Lavigne, Miss 1873.26
Lavin, Julian C. 1901.07
Lavin, Linda 1962.01, 1965.31, 1966.06
Lavine, Audrey 1986.13
Lavine, Clara 1890.08, 1892.27, 1899.04
Lavine, Edward 1883.47
Lavine, Gertrude 1875.21, 1882.62
LaVine, Louis 1909.06
LaVine, W. Robert 1968.24, 1969.14, 1976.05
Lavine, William 1895.04
Lavine, William S. 1894.22
Lavis, Camille 1908.16
LaVista, Nancy 1997.05
laVonne, Helen 1923.22, 1923.36
Lavonne, Lillian 1916.22, 1917.06
LaVorgna, Bill 1991.04, 1999.23
Lavrova, Vera 1924.13
Law 1908.29
Law Studios 1918.39, 1919.13, 1920.07
Law, Evelyn 1921.10, 1922.19, 1923.20, 1924.18, 1925.08, 1926.51, 1928.14
Law, Fred 1907.40, 1908.12
Law, H. Robert 1906.22, 1908.21, 1909.07, 1909.24, 1910.10, 1910.25, 1910.31, 1910.36, 1911.03, 1911.06, 1911.21, 1911.29, 1911.32, 1911.34, 1911.39, 1911.47, 1912.09, 1912.18, 1912.21, 1912.22, 1912.23, 1912.31, 1912.40, 1913.08, 1913.11, 1913.12, 1913.13, 1913.16, 1913.18, 1913.23, 1914.01, 1914.06, 1914.10, 1914.17, 1914.22, 1914.28, 1915.02, 1915.11, 1915.16, 1915.22, 1915.26, 1916.03, 1916.08, 1917.16, 1918.07, 1918.18, 1920.25, 1920.26, 1921.08, 1921.10, 1924.16, 1925.19
Law, Harry 1913.04, 1914.18
Law, Jenny Lou 1948.30, 1953.02, 1957.02
Law, Lindsey 2000.15
Law, Lyndon 1910.02
Law, Mary Kate 1989.09
Law, Messr. 1890.36
Law, Mildred 1939.27, 1943.20
Law, Miss 1864.17, 1864.22, 1865.01, 1866.02
Law, Mr. 1866.18
Law, Richard 1999.05
Law, Robert 1914.16, 1917.11, 1923.04
Law, Tom 1887.42, 1888.25, 1889.43, 1890.36
Law, Tommy 1926.13
Law, Walter 1910.09
Law-Gisiko, Alex 1898.63
Lawes, John W. 1896.01
Lawford, Betty 1940.09
Lawford, Ernest 1926.10, 1926.44, 1928.26
Lawhead, Mark 1975.04
Lawing, Skip 1979.29
Lawler, Anderson 1950.06
Lawler, Charles 1892.19
Lawler, Daniel 1915.03
Lawler, Marvin 1934.06, 1936.17
Lawless, Sue 1981.03
Lawley, Cooper 1925.02
Lawley, Lynda 1971.10
Lawlor, Anderson 1957.14
Lawlor, Andrew J. 1920.11
Lawlor, C.B. 1927.48
Lawlor, Charles B. 1890.30, 1894.17
Lawlor, James Reed 1951.10
Lawlor, Jr., Andrew 1925.31
Lawlor, Mary 1922.34, 1923.46, 1924.38, 1925.30, 1926.25, 1927.41, 1928.28, 1928.50, 1931.01
Lawlor, Terry 1933.25, 1936.31
Lawlor, Thomas 1966.23, 1966.26, 1968.25, 1968.27, 1968.29, 1989.01, 1989.15
Lawner, Mordecai 1986.13
Lawnhurst, Vee 1936.07, 1936.17
Lawrence Rivers, Inc. 1930.10
Lawrence, Al 1907.19
Lawrence, Alfred J. 1930.13
Lawrence, Alfred S. 1911.32
Lawrence, Anita 1902.17, 1903.30
Lawrence, Arthur R. 1907.58
Lawrence, Atkins 1877.07
Lawrence, Bea 1951.24
Lawrence, Bert 1909.24, 1910.25, 1940.21
Lawrence, Beth 1983.17
Lawrence, Betty 1925.23
Lawrence, Bob 1935.15, 1938.14, 1941.12
Lawrence, Brian 1945.02
Lawrence, Burke 1989.17
Lawrence, Carol 1952.09, 1955.07, 1956.07, 1957.01, 1959.27, 1960.08, 1961.28
Lawrence, Carolyn 1895.35
Lawrence, Charles 1918.14, 1919.40, 1923.19, 1927.34, 1927.55, 1929.17, 1929.25, 1930.06, 1930.21, 1933.02, 1938.09, 1942.12
Lawrence, Charles W. 1920.40
Lawrence, Charlie 1922.03
Lawrence, David 1933.25, 1935.03
Lawrence, Eddie 1956.14, 1965.01, 1967.02
Lawrence, Edmund 1893.35, 1898.36, 1899.24, 1899.41, 1904.55, 1909.09
Lawrence, Edna 1901.08
Lawrence, Edwin 1926.15

Lawrence, Elliot 1960.06, 1961.22, 1963.21, 1964.32, 1966.18, 1968.03, 1969.16, 1970.03, 1972.04, 1974.09
Lawrence, Emily 1882.42
Lawrence, Emma 1889.04, 1889.23, 1889.49
Lawrence, Ethel 1908.03
Lawrence, Fred 1938.18
Lawrence, Frederic 1867.10, 1869.42
Lawrence, George 1904.54, 1953.09
Lawrence, Georgie 1897.30, 1900.47, 1902.23, 1907.30, 1910.04
Lawrence, Gertrude 1924.01, 1925.42, 1926.36, 1928.43, 1930.09, 1936.29, 1941.04, 1943.03, 1948.11, 1951.12
Lawrence, Henry 1946.10, 1961.09, 1961.18, 1964.20, 1966.07, 1967.09, 1967.17, 1969.14
Lawrence, Howard 1899.40
Lawrence, J. 1881.11
Lawrence, Jack 1942.16, 1951.17, 1957.01, 1964.44, 1976.32, 1981.16, 2000.07
Lawrence, Jane 1911.43, 1943.04, 1948.14, 1948.26
Lawrence, Jerome 1948.08, 1956.07, 1966.10, 1969.05, 1983.10
Lawrence, Joseph 1927.36
Lawrence, Josie 1901.08
Lawrence, Kitty 1897.26
Lawrence, Leo 1887.43
Lawrence, Leon 1938.01
Lawrence, Les 1972.16
Lawrence, Lester 1943.05
Lawrence, Lionel 1892.24, 1897.39, 1899.26, 1900.05, 1906.23
Lawrence, Lionel E. 1900.56
Lawrence, Lynn 1940.12
Lawrence, Mabel 1902.32
Lawrence, Madge 1904.23, 1920.35
Lawrence, Mal Z. 1991.14, 1997.10, 2000.14
Lawrence, Mark 1948.22
Lawrence, Mary 1887.11
Lawrence, Messr. 1879.56
Lawrence, Mildred 1903.12
Lawrence, Miriam 1898.36, 1899.24, 1961.09, 1961.12
Lawrence, Miss 1879.71, 1881.07, 1882.23
Lawrence, Mr. 1881.04
Lawrence, Norman 1940.02, 1940.21, 1944.27
Lawrence, Pauline 1933.12, 1934.19
Lawrence, Peter 1950.08, 1950.18, 1957.05, 1993.02, 1994.10
Lawrence, Reginald 1950.20
Lawrence, Sharon 1987.16, 1990.18
Lawrence, Stephanie 1993.07
Lawrence, Steve 1964.05, 1968.03
Lawrence, Susannah 1926.38
Lawrence, Vera 1912.36
Lawrence, Vera Brodsky 1975.19
Lawrence, Vincent 1927.64, 1928.43
Lawrence, Vivian 1913.28
Lawrence, W.A. 1897.29
Lawrence, Walter 1906.30, 1907.39, 1908.21, 1912.17, 1912.37, 1912.48
Lawrence, Walter A. 1900.12
Lawrence, Walter N. 1906.50
Lawrence, William 1904.41
Lawrence, Yvette 1991.15
Lawrenson, John 1963.03
Lawrie, Ted 1948.17
Laws, Debra 1999.09
Laws, Eloise 1999.09
Laws, Jerry 1943.15, 1944.03, 1947.03, 1953.04, 1960.09, 1961.13, 1965.03, 1967.04
Lawson, Arthur 1947.01
Lawson, Christyne 1957.16
Lawson, Claude 1926.19, 1929.25
Lawson, David 1974.17
Lawson, Elsie 1918.33, 1919.09
Lawson, G. 1855.05
Lawson, Kate 1938.10, 1940.21
Lawson, Kate Drain 1930.18, 1930.33, 1934.05
Lawson, L.N. 1907.49
Lawson, Marcia 1913.14
Lawson, Mark 1893.17, 1915.16, 1915.24, 1916.15, 1917.16, 1918.23, 1919.41, 1920.13, 1920.26, 1922.03, 1922.30
Lawson, Messr. 1854.04, 1855.06, 1855.07
Lawson, Miss 1870.15
Lawson, Mr. 1853.05, 1855.04, 1857.08
Lawson, R.E. 1884.53
Lawson, Roger 1967.15
Lawson, Sid 1946.10, 1948.15, 1949.08
Lawson, Sidney 1945.14
Lawton, Frank 1887.09, 1894.37
Lawton, Lillian 1905.49
Lawton, Lillie 1899.35, 1905.13
Lawton, Louise 1900.39, 1901.13
Lawton, Peggy 1904.56
Lawton, Thais 1926.24
Lax, Miriam 1925.39, 1926.01
Laxton, Ann 1935.18
Lay, Ann 1947.13
Lay, Dilys 1954.09
Lay, Edward 1931.44
Laye, Evelyn 1929.41, 1937.16
Laye, Gilbert 1904.01
Laylin, Arthur C. 1913.03
Laymann, Si 1924.05
Layne, Rickie 1951.20
Layton, Joe 1953.03, 1959.24, 1959.26, 1960.19, 1961.18, 1962.03, 1963.29, 1964.35, 1965.29, 1967.02, 1967.10, 1968.07, 1969.05, 1970.19, 1975.12, 1976.16, 1978.25, 1980.07, 1981.07, 1981.10, 1982.22, 1984.14, 1985.02, 1986.03, 1990.19
Layton, Turner 1916.21, 1917.13, 1918.05, 1920.11, 1921.21, 1921.26, 1922.16, 1922.19, 1922.22, 1922.23, 1922.25, 1923.20, 1930.13, 1975.20, 1989.02
Lazar, Alice 1909.07
Lazar, Reina 1912.04
Lazard, Desiree 1906.02
Lazareff, Ivan 1925.09
Lazarev, Vladimir 1943.11
Lazarin, Louis 1926.21
Lazaro, V. Sanchiz 1921.39
Lazaron, Harold 1946.16
Lazaroni, Bhen 1972.25
LaZarre, Jerry 1955.27
Lazarro, Jr., Nat 1930.21
Lazarus, Emma 1949.08, 1955.13
Lazarus, Frank 1980.08
Lazarus, Milton 1931.21, 1944.21, 1945.16, 1964.24, 1981.21
Lazarus, Roy 1956.04, 1959.02
Lazarus, Sidney 1924.37
Lazell, Kathryn 1938.09, 1941.03, 1944.14
Lazell, Kay 1929.19
Lazo, Agustin 1939.18
Le Bret, Herr 1897.08
Lea, Bruce 1973.05, 1976.24
Lea, Emilie 1912.15, 1913.34, 1914.33, 1918.04, 1918.33, 1921.06
Lea, Emily 1911.18, 1919.02, 1919.44
Lea, Flora 1923.41, 1924.36
Leabo, Loi 1962.15, 1963.04, 1963.06, 1965.38
Leach, Albert 1883.47
Leach, Archie 1922.30, 1927.63, 1929.06, 1929.39, 1931.34
Leach, C.A. 1892.35
Leach, Edna 1904.13, 1904.44
Leach, John C. 1888.09, 1889.01, 1889.44, 1897.33
Leach, Lillian 1887.07, 1887.16
Leach, Lulu 1887.07, 1887.16
Leach, Marjorie 1929.17, 1948.28, 1971.07
Leach, Marjory 1924.13, 1944.02
Leach, Messr. 1844.01
Leach, Miss 1904.13, 1904.44
Leach, Mr. 1851.03, 1851.05, 1852.03, 1857.04, 1857.06
Leach, Percy 1909.31
Leach, Percy F. 1908.43, 1912.26
Leach, Stephen 1851.02, 1853.04
Leach, Wilford 1981.01, 1984.02, 1985.18
Leacock, Bubblesette 1937.10
Leader, James 1897.32
Leaf, Sven 1980.21
Leahey, James 1888.31
Leahey, William 1888.31
Leahy, Edward 1895.39, 1905.29
Leahy, J. 1905.29
Leahy, James 1886.36, 1892.01, 1905.29
Leahy, James A. 1889.52, 1895.39, 1896.39
Leahy, Messr. 1886.36
Leak, W.H. 1864.20
Leal, Felilpe Valdez 1988.15
LeaLestina, Bessie 1914.29
Leali, Brad 1990.19
Leaman, Isabel 1899.08
Leamy, Deborah 1999.01
Lean, Cecil 1902.02, 1908.07, 1910.09, 1913.02, 1915.17, 1917.26, 1920.07, 1922.07, 1924.13, 1927.35, 1931.36
Leando, J. 1905.17
Leap, Tommy 1963.18
Lear, Howard 1955.07, 1955.09
Learock, Gilberti 1895.02, 1897.06, 1900.45
Learock, Henri 1881.57
Learwood, Beatrice 1908.01
Leary, David 1981.04
Leary, Gilda 1918.41, 1923.02
Leary, Helen 1932.19
Leary, J.F. 1900.52
Leary, Jennie 1896.40
Leary, Lottie 1896.40
Leary, Nolan 1932.19
Leary, Thomas 1920.34
Leary, Thomas C. 1902.43, 1904.37, 1906.49
Leary, W.H. 1886.58, 1888.30
Leary, Willy 1888.40
Leason, D. 1875.21
Leatherlungs, Jennie 1875.36
Leatherwood, Messr. 1875.34
Leatta, Mlle. 1880.68
Leavel, Beth 1992.02, 1999.08, 2001.08
Leavenworth, Ben K. 1929.20
Leaver, Grace 1880.43
Leavitt and Grossman 1908.23
Leavitt, Abe 1906.31
Leavitt, Charles 1946.05
Leavitt, Doug 1943.12
Leavitt, Douglas 1919.07, 1921.08, 1928.32, 1938.17
Leavitt, Douglass 1926.37
Leavitt, Fred 1883.36
Leavitt, Gerard 1953.17
Leavitt, M.B. 1880.43, 1881.17, 1881.19, 1888.33, 1889.47
Leavitt, Michael 1997.09, 1999.03
LeBaron, Louise 1904.51, 1904.57, 1905.11, 1905.57
LeBaron, William 1910.20, 1911.26, 1914.12, 1917.28, 1919.27, 1920.40
leBaron, William 1921.33, 1922.35, 1924.04
Lebedeff, A. 1990.16
Leber, Steven 1977.10, 1982.01, 1982.05
leBerthon, Helena 1943.12
leBerthon, Helene 1943.06, 1945.01
Lebish, Louis 1995.03
Leblang, Tillie 1932.21, 1932.23
Lebo, M. 1997.20
LeBoeuf, Madeline 1906.02, 1906.42
LeBowitz, Jack 1918.01
Lebowitz-Nowak, Dov 1994.09
Lebowsky, Stanley 1958.20, 1960.13, 1962.01, 1963.08, 1965.14, 1970.02, 1971.02, 1972.22, 1975.14, 1977.16, 1979.24, 1980.18, 1981.13, 1981.14, 1982.06, 1982.19, 1985.08, 1986.12
Lebowsky, Stanley R. 1999.01
LeBrandt, Joseph 1905.09, 1905.32
LeBrasse, J.O. 1889.14, 1889.48, 1890.06, 1891.06, 1891.07, 1891.28, 1894.20
leBreton, Flora 1928.04, 1928.16, 1931.29, 1931.37, 1933.24
LeBreton, Louise 1905.08
LeBron, Rafael 1974.14
LeBrun, Addie 1861.06, 1862.01, 1862.02, 1864.22
Lebrun, Emma 1861.06
LeBrun, Emma 1862.01, 1862.02
LeBrun, Marie 1876.13
LeBrun, Miss 1862.02, 1863.07, 1870.34
LeBrun, Mrs. 1848.01
LeBrun, William 1913.17
LeBrunn, George 1893.23
LeBrunn, Leo 1901.25
Leca, Carlos 1992.13
Lecaire, Ida 1892.22
Lecat, Jean-Guy 1983.16
Lecesne, James 1984.10
leClair, Blanche 1929.37
LeClair, Francesca 1908.16
LeClair, Harry 1885.31, 1885.39, 1885.51, 1892.26
LeClair, Henry 1885.18, 1885.31, 1965.17, 1967.09, 1969.06
LeClair, Maggie 1904.06
LeClair, Zuida 1901.03
LeClaire, Emma 1881.39
LeClaire, George 1880.42
Leclaire, Ida 1892.33
LeClaire, Miss 1868.03
Leclerc, Arthur 1882.51
Leclerc, J. 1926.49
Leclerc, Messr. 1879.23
Leclerc, Mlle. 1880.28
Leclerc, Mons. 1875.25, 1876.20, 1880.27, 1880.29, 1880.52
Leclercq, Charles 1879.50, 1879.56, 1880.04, 1881.04, 1881.11, 1881.27, 1891.05, 1892.14
Leclere, Mons. 1876.25, 1876.31, 1877.06, 1877.10, 1877.11
LeClerq, Arthur 1882.72
Leclerq, Charles 1873.25
LeClerq, Florence 1894.18
LeClerq, George 1884.44
Lecocq 1880.35
Lecocq, Charles 1869.05, 1871.24, 1872.42, 1873.11, 1873.18, 1875.02, 1875.04, 1875.11, 1875.26, 1875.28, 1876.07, 1876.10, 1876.17, 1876.20, 1876.21, 1876.26, 1877.09, 1877.11, 1877.26, 1877.27, 1877.32, 1877.33, 1878.18, 1879.15, 1879.18, 1879.19, 1879.23, 1879.26, 1879.39, 1879.41, 1879.44, 1879.48, 1879.49, 1879.50, 1879.56, 1880.03, 1880.29, 1880.33, 1880.52, 1880.56, 1881.47, 1881.49, 1882.06, 1882.28, 1882.30, 1882.68, 1883.10, 1883.16, 1883.28, 1883.29, 1883.30, 1883.34, 1883.51, 1883.57, 1883.59, 1884.34, 1884.54, 1885.17, 1885.23, 1885.24, 1885.25, 1885.60, 1886.19, 1887.37, 1887.50, 1888.09, 1888.18, 1889.01, 1889.24, 1889.44, 1890.22, 1892.11, 1893.04, 1893.07, 1894.14, 1896.12, 1905.08, 1925.51, 1926.40, 1926.47
Lecoq, Charles 1890.24
leCount, Muriel 1926.16
Lecourt, Mlle. 1876.25, 1877.10
Lecroix, Messr. 1864.13
Lecuona, Ernesto 1934.17, 1943.02, 1946.21, 1990.16, 2001.04
Lecuyer, C. 1873.11, 1873.15
Lecuyer, Messr. 1872.31
Lecuyer, Mons. 1872.29, 1872.33, 1872.39, 1872.41, 1872.42, 1873.01, 1873.15, 1873.16
Ledbetter, Heddie 1955.03
Ledbetter, Huddie 1999.09
Ledbetter, William 1964.13, 1964.14, 1964.30, 1965.07, 1965.09, 1965.12, 1965.13, 1965.25, 1965.26, 1965.27, 1968.09, 1968.12, 1974.08, 1975.11, 1975.17, 1976.22, 1976.31, 1977.03, 1978.07, 1978.08, 1978.20, 1978.23, 1979.21, 1979.27, 1981.20, 1982.07, 1982.16, 1982.20, 1982.21, 1983.12, 1983.13, 1984.11, 1984.13, 1985.09, 1985.11, 1985.13, 1986.04, 1986.08, 1986.09, 1987.08, 1987.09, 1987.10, 1988.04, 1988.18, 1989.04, 1989.13, 1989.14, 1990.02, 1990.08, 1991.09, 1991.12, 1993.12, 1994.09, 1996.02, 1996.13
Ledbury, H. 1889.24
Ledbury, Mr. 1884.40
Lederer's Costume Department 1912.20
Lederer, Charles 1952.05, 1953.16, 1965.22, 1978.03, 1985.13, 1986.09
Lederer, Didi 1937.05
Lederer, George 1896.06, 1900.33, 1906.04, 1910.22
Lederer, George V. 1903.18
Lederer, George W. 1884.22, 1886.36, 1891.09, 1893.20, 1893.39, 1894.14, 1894.21, 1895.04, 1895.06, 1895.18, 1896.18, 1896.30, 1896.51, 1897.26, 1897.39, 1897.54, 1898.20, 1898.28, 1898.36, 1898.43, 1898.68, 1898.72, 1899.02, 1899.15, 1899.19, 1899.25, 1899.37, 1900.05, 1900.20, 1900.35, 1900.41, 1901.08, 1901.13, 1901.23, 1902.16, 1902.20, 1902.23, 1903.06, 1903.16, 1903.27, 1904.21, 1911.07, 1911.08, 1912.20, 1912.36, 1914.14, 1919.44, 1920.21
Lederer, Peppi 1930.06
Ledner, Sam 1927.46
leDuc, Edward 1939.19
Leduc, Mons. 1867.24, 1867.30, 1868.07, 1868.25, 1868.27, 1868.30, 1868.31, 1869.01, 1869.09, 1869.10, 1869.12
LeDuc, Teddy 1912.04
Lee 1859.15
Lee Lash and Company 1909.31
Lee Lash Company 1910.34
Lee Lash Studio 1902.38, 1905.10, 1906.18, 1911.08, 1911.10, 1919.21
Lee Lash Studios 1910.11, 1910.17, 1910.19, 1911.45, 1913.23, 1913.29, 1915.22

Lee, A. 1890.02
Lee, Ada 1877.25, 1877.39, 1878.20, 1879.03, 1879.38, 1880.24, 1880.59, 1880.65
Lee, Addie 1886.34, 1887.43
Lee, Adelle 1881.26
Lee, Agnes 1873.25, 1873.26
Lee, Al 1933.20
Lee, Alfred 1931.14
Lee, Allen 1935.04
Lee, Amy 1879.42, 1881.24, 1882.44, 1882.80, 1884.39, 1885.49, 1885.66, 1886.03, 1886.42, 1886.52, 1887.07, 1887.16, 1887.39, 1887.45, 1887.48
Lee, Andrew 1899.08
Lee, Ann 1941.04, 1943.03
Lee, Annie 1856.01, 1878.19, 1881.02
Lee, Arthur 1905.37
Lee, Baayork 1951.12, 1958.19, 1962.14, 1962.20, 1968.31, 1975.15, 1983.06
Lee, Beatrice 1925.30
Lee, Bernice 1931.36, 1932.27
Lee, Bert 1911.13, 1914.18, 1917.29, 1918.23, 1924.01, 1925.50, 1926.26, 1932.21, 1964.28
Lee, Bessie 1895.26
Lee, Betty Mae 1942.35
Lee, Big 1970.21
Lee, Bill 1966.15
Lee, Bob 1923.39
Lee, Bobby 1976.17
Lee, Buddy 1927.36
Lee, C.Y. 1958.19
Lee, Carol 1949.17, 1951.13
Lee, Caroline 1866.03
Lee, Craig 1913.37
Lee, Darren 1990.17, 1991.03, 1995.15, 1999.19, 2000.18
Lee, Don 1928.45
Lee, Donald 1925.39
Lee, Dorothy 1906.42, 1928.41
Lee, Dra 1927.35
Lee, Earle 1925.39
Lee, Ellen 1986.02
Lee, Emilie 1915.16
Lee, Eugene 1972.18, 1974.06, 1979.06, 1979.19, 1981.27, 1984.13, 1987.09, 1994.08, 1998.01, 2000.18
Lee, Fannie 1873.28
Lee, Flora 1867.18, 1868.06, 1869.26, 1870.26, 1870.33, 1871.04, 1871.18, 1878.02, 1878.19, 1881.02, 1881.13
Lee, Florence 1918.32, 1930.10, 1935.01
Lee, Floyd 1876.03
Lee, Frances 1897.16, 1898.32
Lee, Francis 1901.24
Lee, Franne 1972.18, 1974.06, 1979.06, 1979.19, 1981.14, 1982.22, 1984.13, 1987.09, 1993.11
Lee, Fred M. 1894.32
Lee, G.S. 1856.04
Lee, George 1965.02
Lee, Gypsy Rose 1932.07, 1933.03, 1936.17, 1939.22, 1942.18, 1959.13, 1974.17, 1989.27, 1991.06
Lee, H.A. 1877.24
Lee, Harriette 1923.04
Lee, Hee Hwan 1998.08
Lee, Hee Jung 1997.16, 1998.08
Lee, Helen 1914.20, 1918.02, 1931.30
Lee, Helouise 1904.49
Lee, Henrietta 1896.19, 1896.47, 1908.17
Lee, Henry 1892.31
Lee, High 1889.01
Lee, Ida 1876.34, 1877.39
Lee, Irving 1912.36
Lee, Irving Allen 1974.12, 1976.03, 1978.28, 1986.07
Lee, J. 2001.04
Lee, Jack 1932.06, 1969.01, 1971.09, 1973.05, 1979.22, 1983.06, 1989.26, 1991.15, 1993.18
Lee, Jackie 1944.21
Lee, Jae Hwan 1997.16
Lee, Jae Woo 1976.02, 1977.07, 1985.01
Lee, James 1893.17, 1894.26, 1896.03, 1896.35, 1898.05, 1902.26, 1902.32, 1911.28
Lee, James F. 1900.07
Lee, James S. 1895.21, 1897.02
Lee, Jennie 1871.27, 1872.06, 1872.11
Lee, Jennifer 1999.07
Lee, Jennifer Paulson 1992.10
Lee, Jimmy 1905.50
Lee, Joan 1926.01
Lee, John 1929.52, 1933.06
Lee, Johnny 1942.13
Lee, Jon 1958.19
Lee, Joseph 1899.19
Lee, Joy 1991.01
Lee, Kathryn 1944.16, 1944.30, 1945.18, 1947.17, 1948.28, 1953.02
Lee, Kenneth 1889.05, 1897.19, 1897.31
Lee, Kyoung Woo 1998.08
Lee, Laura 1884.36, 1889.53, 1928.14, 1929.22, 1929.28
Lee, Lawrence 1920.43
Lee, Lela 1912.26
Lee, Leonard 1989.12, 1992.06
Lee, Lester 1927.62, 1929.24, 1942.01, 1942.18, 1942.23, 1943.05, 1943.23, 1949.02
Lee, Lillian 1886.51, 1906.48, 1907.24, 1908.19, 1909.11, 1911.05, 1911.40, 1912.39, 1919.36, 1923.10
Lee, Lillie 1886.44
Lee, Linda Talcott 1999.16
Lee, Lois 1947.16
Lee, Lora 1992.03
Lee, Lovey 1924.09, 1924.34, 1924.41, 1925.49
Lee, Lulu 1906.10
Lee, M. 1883.16
Lee, Mable 1952.08
Lee, Margaret 1928.10, 1929.03, 1930.32, 1932.05, 1933.02, 1934.38
Lee, Margerite 1931.47
Lee, Marie 1902.32
Lee, Marion 1903.02
Lee, Mary 1908.25
Lee, Mattie 1889.02
Lee, Messr. 1796.01, 1796.02, 1924.13, 1924.23, 1924.29, 1927.17, 1928.15
Lee, Michael K. 2000.09
Lee, Michele 1962.14, 1973.06
Lee, Ming Cho 1963.09, 1966.09, 1968.05, 1968.11, 1969.08, 1969.16, 1971.18, 1978.10, 1979.02
Lee, Mulford 1934.37
Lee, Myra 1926.05
Lee, Ora 1944.31
Lee, Orlanda 1931.02
Lee, Paula 1924.17
Lee, Peggy 1983.20
Lee, Phoebe 1921.22
Lee, Pinky 1942.25
Lee, Ray 1932.19
Lee, Rebecca 1943.05
Lee, Richard 1902.34, 1902.40, 1911.09, 1926.01, 1927.55, 1929.06
Lee, Richard L. 1907.63
Lee, Robert 1924.29
Lee, Robert E. 1948.08, 1956.07, 1966.10, 1969.05, 1983.10
Lee, Robyn 1983.01
Lee, Ronald 1960.09
Lee, Ronnie 1955.01, 1956.02
Lee, Rosa 1881.17, 1881.19, 1885.18, 1885.31, 1886.29, 1886.31, 1886.38, 1927.64
Lee, Rose 1879.42
Lee, Russell 1931.31
Lee, Ruth 1922.35
Lee, Sallie 1896.49
Lee, Sally 1960.01, 1961.21, 1962.24, 1965.14
Lee, Sam 1909.16, 1927.52, 1929.09, 1931.05
Lee, Samantha Robyn 1996.08
Lee, Sammy 1912.46, 1918.21, 1920.30, 1922.28, 1923.21, 1923.32, 1923.45, 1924.03, 1924.30, 1924.31, 1924.43, 1925.29, 1925.30, 1925.45, 1925.49, 1926.25, 1926.28, 1926.36, 1926.51, 1927.08, 1927.21, 1927.29, 1927.37, 1927.49, 1927.67, 1928.01, 1928.17, 1928.28, 1929.07, 1931.13, 1931.32
Lee, Samuel 1924.35
Lee, Sang Ryul 1997.16, 1998.08
Lee, Simon 2000.09
Lee, Sondra 1947.16, 1954.13, 1959.08, 1959.17, 1963.15, 1964.01, 1966.02
Lee, Spencer 1992.03
Lee, Su Mun 1997.16, 1998.08
Lee, Sung Ho 1998.08
Lee, Sung Hoon 1998.08
Lee, Sylvan 1926.26
Lee, Thelma 1938.09, 1976.36
Lee, Tom 1940.08, 1940.09
Lee, Tomy 1940.16
Lee, V.H. 1902.16
Lee, Valerie 1963.21
Lee, Vernon 1905.17
Lee, Vernon H. 1903.41
Lee, Virginia 1918.12, 1918.30
Lee, Will 1936.28, 1959.26, 1961.10, 1973.14
Lee, Willard 1892.38, 1896.01
Lee, William A. 1944.02
Lee, Woo Jong 1997.16, 1998.08
Leece, Mary 1882.81
Leech, Al 1904.27, 1906.22, 1910.01, 1911.35
Leech, Ed 1919.07
Leech, Edward 1909.15, 1910.21
Leech, Lloyd Thomas 1953.05, 1953.14, 1953.15, 1954.06, 1954.10, 1955.17
Leech, Messr. 1908.25
Leeder, Miss 1854.01
Leedom, Edna 1923.38, 1924.18, 1925.24, 1926.18, 1927.68
Leeds, Adelaide 1898.03
Leeds, Andrew Harrison 1992.09
Leeds, Dorothy 1917.03, 1918.19, 1920.09
Leeds, Harry 1911.34
Leeds, Jo Anne 1961.07, 1962.18
Leeds, Lyda Sue 1936.31
Leeds, Michael 1976.19, 1995.14
Leeds, Peter 1979.25
Leeds, Phil 1942.05, 1942.26, 1951.13, 1953.07, 1960.10, 1962.24, 1963.05, 1963.12, 1972.19
Leeds, Sandy 1960.08
Leeman, George 1944.14
Leeming, Artie 1919.14, 1927.62
Leerburger, Jeff S. 1884.25
Lees, Carol 1979.24
Lees, Gene 1965.30, 1970.01, 1974.01
Leeson, Dan 1860.06
Leet, Marjorie 1925.10, 1926.32
Leet, William 1975.02
Lefebre, Hans 1940.04
leFebvre, Edouard 1921.36
LeFevre, Adam 1998.13
Lefevre, Jean 1958.18
LeFevre, Johnnie 1898.08
Lefevre, Mons. 1867.24, 1867.30, 1868.07, 1868.26, 1869.03, 1869.05
Lefferson, L.R. 1908.16
Leffingwell, M.W. 1851.08, 1854.06, 1855.01, 1866.06, 1866.08, 1866.11, 1866.15, 1867.22, 1867.23, 1867.26, 1867.27, 1867.29, 1867.31, 1869.27, 1869.32, 1870.18, 1872.37
Leffingwell, Mrs. 1851.08, 1867.22, 1867.26, 1870.36, 1870.39
Leffingwell, Mrs. M.W. 1867.23, 1867.27, 1867.29, 1867.31
Leffler, Ben 1924.17
Leffler-Bratton Company 1909.05, 1912.16
Lefkowitch, Henry 1998.11
Lefort, Bernard 1983.16
Lefort, Cecile 1884.45, 1884.47, 1884.49, 1884.52, 1884.54, 1884.55, 1885.17, 1885.19, 1885.20
LeFrak, Francine 1982.09, 1983.06, 1985.03
Lefranc, R. 1895.43
Leftwich, Alexander 1923.22, 1924.06, 1925.01, 1925.07, 1925.23, 1925.28, 1926.01, 1927.16, 1927.56, 1927.60, 1928.08, 1928.16, 1928.24, 1928.30, 1928.50, 1929.12, 1929.19, 1930.02, 1930.31, 1930.38, 1931.14, 1932.13, 1937.06
Leftwich, Helen 1937.06
Leftwich, Jr., Alexander 1929.46
LeGalliene, Richard 1906.38
LeGallienne, Eva 1919.40. 1982.24
leGallienne, Eva 1932.28, 1939.16
Legg, Master 1867.12
Leggett, Paula 1992.02
Leginska, Ethel 1931.44
leGon, Jeni 1936.30, 1943.07
Legrand, Michel 1964.39, 1974.20, 1981.16
leGrand, Phyllis 1922.33
LeGrant, David 1953.09
Legras, Jacques 1958.18
Legro, Dianne 1976.20
leGroh, Dandy 1924.35
leGroh, Handy 1924.35
leGroh, Pansy 1924.35
Legros, Messr. 1877.31
Legros, Mlle. 1870.41, 1871.03, 1871.06
Legros, Mons. 1870.41, 1870.45, 1871.06, 1871.07, 1877.27, 1877.30, 1877.34, 1877.38, 1878.06
LeGue, Mildred 1918.30
LeGuere, George 1907.37
Leguillou, Lisa 1993.06, 1995.09
Lehac, Ned 1931.14, 1939.19
Lehack, Ned 1942.05
Lehak, Ned 1930.06, 1930.18, 1930.33, 1930.38
Lehár, Franz 1907.48, 1908.01, 1911.37, 1912.13, 1912.33, 1912.48, 1913.02, 1914.09, 1915.27, 1916.10, 1917.30, 1920.46, 1921.29, 1925.42, 1929.47, 1930.07, 1931.27, 1937.03, 1942.21, 1943.09, 1944.24, 1946.16, 1957.04, 1957.15, 1958.16, 1959.21, 1962.21, 1963.24, 1964.24, 1964.30, 1965.27, 1974.09, 1974.14, 1975.22, 1976.18, 1978.07, 1978.20, 1979.21, 1982.16, 1983.12, 1984.04, 1985.11, 1985.12, 1988.14, 1989.13, 1995.06, 1996.02
leHardin, Maria 1934.32
Lehassen, Raise 1925.37
Lehay, Edward 1904.35
LeHay, John 1895.29, 1900.37, 1905.46
Lehedder, Mactar 1925.37
Lehew, Stephen 1975.13, 1980.26
Lehman, Bert 1893.05, 1893.09
Lehman, Bertha 1890.46
Lehman, Henry 1914.01
Lehman, Jeanne 1975.22, 1998.03
Lehman, Kenny 1979.15
Lehman, Louise 1900.15
Lehman, M. 1865.04
Lehman, Mlle. 1871.27, 1872.06
Lehman, Mrs. 1865.04
Lehman, O. 1885.63
Lehman, Samuel 1906.31, 1911.43, 1912.09, 1912.24, 1919.26
Lehmann, Liza 1905.19, 1931.14, 1952.11
Lehmann, Mr. 1883.44
Lehmann-Haupt, Miriam 1966.24
Lehmkuhl, Terry 1990.17
Lehn, Norma 1941.06
Lehne, John 1963.16
Lehnhardt, C. 1884.40
Lehr, Leroy 1992.14
Lehrain, George C. 1925.43, 1927.57
Lehrer, Scott 1990.12, 1992.17, 1996.14, 1999.17, 2000.01
Lehrian, George C. 1927.44, 1927.61
Lei, Jon 1950.07
Leib, Dick 1980.11
Leibbee, Arthur 1895.23
Leiber, Jerry 1979.30, 1995.03
Leibman, Harriet 1927.02
Leicester, Amy 1907.26, 1912.49, 1913.28, 1914.07
Leicester, Maud 1886.34
Leicester, Maude 1886.45
Leidal, Marie 1947.21, 1948.25
Leidy, Harriet 1911.26, 1914.31
Leigh, Alice 1890.35, 1893.20
Leigh, Barbara 1956.02
Leigh, Caro Gordon 1900.15
Leigh, Carol 1954.02
Leigh, Caroline 1896.29
Leigh, Carolyn 1954.13, 1957.01, 1960.22, 1962.27, 1967.16, 1974.11, 1979.22, 1982.01, 1983.09, 1989.03, 1990.09, 1990.20, 1991.10, 1991.13, 1998.15, 1998.18
Leigh, Clara 1862.09
Leigh, Clifford 1912.32
Leigh, Courtney 1999.17
Leigh, Dorma 1913.36
Leigh, Eleanor 1919.35
Leigh, Fred W. 1905.27, 1909.11
Leigh, Grace 1906.45, 1907.24, 1908.19, 1913.31, 1915.19
Leigh, Henry 1877.15
Leigh, Henry S. 1879.25, 1879.65
Leigh, Kelly 1958.08, 1959.03
Leigh, Laura 1863.08
Leigh, Leona 1907.04
Leigh, Leslie 1909.20, 1911.18, 1915.24
Leigh, Lois 1919.13, 1919.35, 1920.04
Leigh, Messr. 1750.01
Leigh, Miss 1750.01
Leigh, Mitch 1965.34, 1967.12, 1970.10, 1972.14, 1974.11, 1976.01, 1977.12, 1979.03, 1983.10, 1985.01, 1989.05, 1992.07, 1993.05, 1999.10
Leigh, Philip 1905.03, 1906.26, 1907.33
Leigh, Rowland 1927.02, 1932.23, 1932.27, 1934.43, 1937.17, 1938.07, 1940.09, 1941.02, 1948.27
Leigh, Susanna 1873.26
Leigh, T.J. 1866.13
Leigh, Valerie 1982.11
Leigh, Vivian 1963.08

Leigh, W.H. 1877.39
Leighs, Mr. 1866.16
Leight, Warren 1985.15
Leighton, Bert 1916.15
Leighton, Betty 1973.07
Leighton, Daisy 1903.14
Leighton, David 1982.20, 1982.21, 1989.14
Leighton, Frank 1916.15
Leighton, Harry 1891.40
Leighton, Isabel 1925.16, 1926.27, 1926.33, 1929.02
Leighton, Louise 1877.08, 1880.49
Leighton, Minnie 1889.37
Leighton, Rose 1877.25, 1879.01, 1879.06, 1879.38, 1880.24, 1880.57, 1880.62, 1881.25, 1881.42, 1881.44, 1881.45, 1883.62, 1884.32, 1884.33, 1884.35, 1884.38, 1885.13, 1886.45, 1886.59, 1887.44, 1888.18, 1889.19, 1890.16, 1891.09, 1893.07, 1895.21, 1897.02, 1897.41, 1898.49, 1898.57, 1898.62, 1898.65
Lein, Sandra 1967.06
Leinsdorf, Erich 1956.09, 1956.10
Leinwand, Shirley 1964.18
Leip, Hans 1967.13, 1968.20, 1999.07
Leiser, Henry 1942.33
Leister, Georgia 1872.36
Leitche, Helen 1939.16
Leith, Maud 1885.06
Leith, Patricia 1946.13
Lejeune, Nina 1891.38
Lekosky, P. 1905.41
Lekosky, Pincus 1905.22
Leland, Flora 1870.05
Leland, Jennie 1888.15
Leland, John 1894.13
Leland, Walter 1897.03
LeLang, Christine 1903.13
Lelik, Elena 1932.09
Lellman, Albert 1896.33
Lellman, Mr. 1882.71
Lelmonier, Tom 1900.46
LeLoka, Tsidii 1997.20, 2000.05
Lemac, Linda 1979.13, 1980.18, 1981.08, 1982.06
LeMack, Thomas 1883.66, 1890.12, 1890.30, 1891.14, 1891.43, 1892.06, 1892.18, 1894.06, 1895.38, 1896.14, 1896.24, 1897.47
LeMack, Tom 1897.30
LeMaire, Charles 1918.38, 1919.40, 1920.27, 1920.33. 1924.08
leMaire, Charles 1922.03, 1922.11, 1922.19, 1922.26, 1922.43, 1923.05, 1923.20, 1923.32, 1923.42, 1923.45, 1924.06, 1924.09, 1924.18, 1924.21, 1924.28, 1924.29, 1924.33, 1924.35, 1924.41, 1924.47, 1925.25, 1925.34, 1925.45, 1925.47, 1925.48, 1926.23, 1926.28, 1926.39, 1927.02, 1927.06, 1927.13, 1927.21, 1927.32, 1927.50, 1927.52, 1927.55, 1927.60, 1927.68, 1928.08, 1928.22, 1928.29, 1928.37, 1928.41, 1928.44, 1928.50, 1929.04, 1929.08, 1929.29, 1929.31, 1929.35, 1929.44, 1930.02, 1930.05, 1930.11, 1930.22, 1930.26, 1930.28, 1930.30, 1930.40, 1930.42, 1931.04, 1931.09, 1931.11, 1931.21, 1931.26, 1931.30, 1931.39, 1931.48, 1932.07, 1932.24, 1932.25, 1933.03, 1933.05, 1933.13, 1933.27, 1934.01, 1934.35, 1935.18, 1938.07, 1939.25
Lemaire, Charles 1926.03, 1926.51
LeMaire, George 1913.18, 1920.33
Lemaire, George 1915.05, 1919.15, 1924.23
leMaire, George 1921.22, 1925.27
leMaire, Georgie 1926.03
leMaire, Rufus 1922.46, 1923.19, 1924.47, 1925.27, 1926.03, 1927.13
leMaire, Rufus R. 1924.21
Leman, Mr. 1863.07, 1864.17
Lemanski, Thomas 1981.21
Lemar, Al. 1903.20
LeMar, Trixie 1911.34
Lemarchand, Henry 1964.02
leMarie, Charles 1923.27
Lemarque, Francis 1952.09, 1959.15, 1961.25
Lemasney, Blanche 1904.28
leMassena, William 1948.14, 1958.03, 1959.01
LeMassena, William 1961.02, 1967.17, 1969.07
Lemay, Emmie 1896.07
Lemay, Kate 1896.07
Lemay, Maurice 1972.08
Lemay, Nellie 1896.07
Lembach, Cornelius 1905.37
Lembeck, Harvey 1957.06, 1958.07
Lemberg, Steven 1984.15
leMeau, Ann 1922.41
Lemee, Diane 1916.07
Lemenager, Nancy 1995.05, 1997.05
Lemery, J.R. 1910.07
Lemeunier 1893.45
Lemmon, Gertrude 1923.21, 1925.40
Lemmon, Shirley 1974.10
Lemoine, Fred 1969.17
Lemoine, Mlle. 1868.18
Lemon, Marguerite 1895.31, 1898.11, 1898.18, 1899.06
LeMone, Franc V. 1904.04
Lemonier, Tom 1902.08, 1903.08, 1904.26, 1905.20, 1906.08, 1908.08
Lemonopoulos, Harry 1967.05
LeMont, Lillian 1888.39
LeMoyne, Cleo 1912.14
LeMoyne, Judith 1903.13
Lemoyne, Ralph 1904.54
LeMoyne, Sarah Cowell 1911.09
LeMoyne, W.J. 1897.11
Lemsky, Mitchell 1991.03
Lencioni, Louis 1879.65, 1879.67
Lenclud, Mlle. 1911.18
Leng, Lois 1935.03
Lengsfelder, Hans 1980.10, 1981.06
Lengyel, Melchior 1923.43, 1955.02
Lenhardt, Mary 1943.23
Lenharr, Ida 1898.03, 1898.66
Lenhart, Arnold 1935.12
Lenihan, Burton 1913.01
Lenihan, Liam 1959.04
Lenn, Robert 1948.17, 1949.01, 1953.01, 1957.18, 1958.20, 1961.12, 1964.16, 1968.16
Lennard, Horace 1894.18
Lennart, Isobel 1964.11
Lennen, Emmet 1906.31
Lennert, Herr 1866.33
Lennon, Joe 1930.35
Lennon, John 1971.04, 1973.17, 1974.24, 1976.27, 1977.10, 1982.22, 1984.06, 1991.04
Lennon, Nester 1892.38
Lennon, Nestor 1893.23
Lennon, Robert Emmett 1908.14
Lennon, Russell 1907.07, 1912.16
Lennox, Adelaide 1873.25, 1873.26
Lennox, Annie 1984.15
Lennox, Beatrice 1897.26
Lennox, F.L. 1880.69
Lennox, F.W. 1880.47
Lennox, Fred 1882.16, 1883.25, 1883.29, 1891.31, 1891.47, 1892.30, 1892.37, 1892.40, 1892.46, 1898.05, 1911.42, 1919.06, 1923.44, 1925.38
Lennox, Fred W. 1881.40, 1881.56, 1882.05, 1882.15, 1882.19
Lennox, Jean 1905.40
Lennox, Jr., Fred 1895.25
Lennox, Mary 1991.05
Lennox, Miss 1895.03
Lennox, Sr., Walter 1880.37, 1887.02, 1887.42, 1896.15
Lennox, W.S. 1862.03
Lennox, Walter 1862.09, 1863.01, 1863.04, 1872.06, 1876.02
Lennox, William 1919.32
Lenny, Jack 1927.27
Lenoir, F. 1880.66
Lenoir, Helen 1881.37, 1882.17, 1882.60, 1882.75, 1882.78
Lenoir, Herr 1879.57, 1879.62, 1880.20, 1882.68
Lenoir, Jean 1934.32, 1935.19
leNoire, Rosetta 1939.17
LeNoire, Rosetta 1955.09, 1958.11, 1959.11, 1961.12, 1963.12, 1963.27, 1964.44, 1966.14, 1972.06, 1976.04, 1999.06
Lenox Arts Center/Music-Theatre Performing Group 1974.23
Lenox, Adriane 1999.10, 1999.19
Lenox, Emma 1900.20
Lenox, Fred 1904.04, 1927.12
Lenox, Jean 1905.26, 1907.18, 1980.27
Lenox, Sr., Walter 1888.25, 1889.43, 1890.36
Lenters, Howard 1945.20, 1947.16
Lenton, Frank 1889.47
Lenton, John 1889.47
Lentz, Frau 1880.66
Lentz, Julie 1881.48, 1881.50, 1881.51, 1881.53
Lenya, Lotte 1937.01, 1945.04, 1966.19, 1966.24
Lenz, Dean 1977.14
Lenzberg, Jules 1931.34
Lenzberg, Julius 1919.13
Leo Delibes 1893.01
Leo, Frank 1903.03, 1905.19, 1909.04
Leo, J. 1868.03, 1869.33, 1881.31
Leo, John 1873.28, 1879.12, 1880.08, 1881.02
Leo, Mme. 1893.44
Leo, Tom 1904.45
Leon, Anna 1903.03
Leon, C.L. 1875.18
Leon, Daisy 1906.05, 1907.02, 1912.05
Leon, Dorothy 1972.12
Leon, Dwight 1984.09
Leon, E.W. 1887.14
Leon, F.A. 1886.25, 1890.02
Leon, Feliz 1965.32
Leon, Francis 1862.06, 1866.20, 1866.22, 1866.26, 1866.32, 1866.35, 1867.01, 1867.02, 1867.11, 1867.21, 1867.28, 1868.05, 1868.14, 1868.21, 1868.28, 1868.29, 1868.33, 1870.08, 1870.10, 1870.11, 1870.16, 1870.17, 1870.27, 1870.29, 1870.38, 1871.12, 1871.16, 1876.04, 1876.05, 1876.07, 1876.09, 1876.10, 1876.11, 1876.14, 1876.30, 1876.33, 1877.03, 1877.05, 1883.56, 1884.59, 1884.65
Leon, Frederic A. 1897.52
Leon, Frederick A. 1897.37
Leon, James 1962.13, 1963.05
Leon, Joseph 1880.68, 1955.27, 1964.24
Leon, Josephine 1888.39
Leon, Lillian 1905.56, 1906.41
Leon, Margaret 1900.52
Leon, Marguerite 1897.17, 1899.06
Leon, Miss 1892.07, 1903.03
Leon, Mme. 1887.10
Leon, Tania 1984.02
Léon, Victor 1897.08, 1901.05, 1907.48, 1910.27, 1912.08, 1914.09, 1916.26, 1921.29, 1929.47, 1931.27, 1942.21, 1943.09, 1944.24, 1946.16, 1957.04, 1957.15, 1958.16, 1959.21, 1962.21, 1963.24, 1964.24, 1964.25, 1964.30, 1965.27, 1974.14, 1976.18, 1978.07, 1978.20, 1979.21, 1982.16, 1983.12, 1984.04, 1985.11, 1988.14, 1989.13, 1995.06, 1996.02
Leonard, Agnes 1924.31
Leonard, Anne 1903.25, 1906.34
Leonard, Benny 1918.21, 1923.02
Leonard, Billie 1931.01, 1934.15
Leonard, Dave 1943.16
Leonard, David 1927.26, 1943.18, 1944.02
Leonard, David A. 1937.01
Leonard, Eddie 1904.21, 1905.22, 1908.22, 1919.24
Leonard, Edmund 1928.20
Leonard, Eliot 1929.33
Leonard, Elona 1903.18, 1905.30
Leonard, Flora 1897.16
Leonard, Frank 1935.18
Leonard, Frankie 1894.40
Leonard, Freda 1919.16
Leonard, George 1910.36, 1928.34, 1942.22
Leonard, Grace 1898.66
Leonard, Harry 1904.28, 1911.26
Leonard, Herbert 1909.31
Leonard, J. Elliott 1934.35, 1935.03
Leonard, J.B. 1903.13
Leonard, J.E. 1935.03
Leonard, J.F. 1902.09
Leonard, J.W. 1867.19, 1867.20, 1868.22
Leonard, John F. 1896.38, 1906.39
Leonard, Julia 1885.49
Leonard, Leon 1917.34
Leonard, Lu 1957.15, 1961.08, 1961.27, 1962.14, 1965.29
Leonard, Messr. 1796.01, 1796.02
Leonard, Michael 1965.36, 1967.18, 1972.12, 1989.06
Leonard, P.A. 1921.23
Leonard, Parker 1913.08
Leonard, Patricia 1976.12, 1976.14, 1978.14, 1978.15, 1978.16, 1978.18
Leonard, Patrick A. 1934.15
Leonard, Queenie 1928.42
Leonard, Richard 1974.10
Leonard, Robert 1925.19, 1929.45, 1936.26
Leonard, Susanne 1894.41, 1894.48, 1896.51
Leonard, Susie 1895.09
Leonard, Suzanne 1891.36, 1896.12
Leonard, Tom 1888.08
Leonard, W.J. 1868.19
Leonard, W.L. 1875.14
Leonard, William 1903.38
Leonard-Boyne, Eva 1923.26
Leonardi, Leon 1926.27, 1944.23, 1946.08, 1946.23
Leonardo, R. 1882.77
Leonardos, Urylee 1943.24, 1945.06, 1946.09, 1951.15, 1952.08, 1953.04, 1956.14, 1961.20, 1963.12, 1973.09, 1989.18
Leoncavallo 1894.21, 1898.24
Leone, Fran 1960.01
Leone, Henri 1882.31, 1882.40, 1883.65
Leone, Henry 1904.04, 1904.28, 1913.15
Leone, Jenkins P. 1924.43
Leone, Lizzie 1888.27, 1888.40, 1889.11, 1889.15, 1889.18, 1890.24
Leone, Maud 1919.24
Leonetti, Adrienne 1979.26
Leong, David 1994.02, 1995.11, 1999.08
Leonhart, Jay 1983.20
Leoni, Eva 1920.46
Leoni, Henri 1885.65, 1889.16, 1890.01, 1890.24, 1891.30, 1893.05, 1893.09, 1894.38, 1900.19, 1908.04, 1912.47
Leoni, Henry 1886.39, 1887.33, 1887.50, 1889.23, 1890.11, 1890.19, 1892.07, 1892.16, 1892.28, 1892.52, 1894.05, 1897.02, 1897.37, 1906.45, 1918.26
Leoni, Lizzie 1892.07
Leoni, Mr. 1890.31, 1891.33, 1894.01
Leonidas, Professor 1897.14
Leonidoff, Leon 1930.06, 1937.10, 1940.16, 1944.32
Leonie, Mlle. 1870.44, 1871.27
Leonora, Lily 1918.31
Leontine, Clara 1873.08
Leontine, Miss 1882.46
Leontine, Mlle. 1871.27, 1872.06, 1873.10, 1882.77
Leontowich, Mme. 1922.37
Leonx, Sr., Walter 1890.36
Leopold, Frederick 1891.26
Leopold, John 1891.26
Leopold, Joseph 1891.26
Leopold, Lewis 1891.26
Leopold, Willie 1891.26
Leopoldi, Hermann 1945.19
Leotine, Mlle. 1870.44
LePage, Roger 1964.33, 1965.28
Lepel, Ivy 1880.46
LePera 1985.07
Lepera, A. 1997.13
Lepere, William H. 1894.47
lePique, Gene 1927.68
Leporska, Zoya 1971.15, 1973.15, 1976.07, 1981.07
Leporsky, Zoya 1944.17
Lepoukhin, Messr. 1927.51
Lepri, Amalia 1881.24, 1882.46, 1882.49, 1882.52
Lepri, G. 1882.43, 1882.49, 1882.52
Lepri, Giovanni 1881.24
Lepri, Signor 1882.46
Leps, Anthony F. 2001.04
Lerch, Georgia 1928.22
Lerefolo, Ari 1977.01
Lerit, Sharon 1960.06
Lerman, Oscar 1955.25
Lerman, Oscar S. 1960.10
Lerner, Alan Jay 1943.21, 1945.19, 1947.07, 1948.25, 1950.10, 1951.24, 1956.01, 1957.03, 1960.21, 1961.25, 1962.15, 1963.02, 1963.04, 1964.20, 1964.46, 1965.08, 1965.31, 1967.11, 1967.17, 1968.17, 1969.17, 1973.12, 1973.17, 1974.01, 1974.09, 1976.05, 1976.11, 1979.09, 1980.19, 1980.26, 1981.19, 1981.26, 1983.08, 1986.03, 1986.04, 1987.19, 1990.09, 1991.12, 1993.11, 1993.18, 1996.13, 1999.23
Lerner, Ina 1951.20
Lerner, Irving 1946.13
Lerner, Sam 1943.14, 1948.15
Lerner, Sammy 1936.22, 1999.07
Lerner, Samuel 1930.20
Leroux, Gaston 1988.01
Leroux, Helene 1881.49
LeRoux, Madeleine 1972.23
Leroux, Mlle. 1883.30
Leroux, Pearl 1890.45

Leroux, Xavier 1926.01
Leroux-Bouvard, Mlle. 1880.14, 1880.22
LeRoy, Alan 1951.19
Leroy, Dawn 1902.11
LeRoy, Grace 1914.22
leRoy, Hal 1931.05, 1931.19, 1934.42, 1942.27
Leroy, Hal 1933.05, 1939.27
LeRoy, Ken 1962.05, 1963.18
Leroy, Ken 1981.18
leRoy, Kenneth 1945.04
LeRoy, Kenneth 1950.15
Leroy, Lew 1913.04
Leroy, Lilian 1913.20
Leroy, Lillian 1906.42
LeRoy, Lillian 1907.32
Leroy, Lizzie 1883.39
LeRoy, M. 1893.34
LeRoy, Marian 1893.34
leRoy, Martin 1928.28, 1936.22
Leroy, Martin 1931.48, 1933.13, 1933.25
Leroy, Mary 1923.42
LeRoy, Maud 1911.07
LeRoy, Maude 1900.59, 1907.32
leRoy, Milton 1928.19, 1931.19, 1932.16
Leroy, Mlle. 1879.19, 1879.26, 1879.44
leRoy, Myrtle 1925.35
Leroy, Nat 1925.12
Leroy, Pamela 1922.05
LeRoy, Servais 1898.35
LeRoy, Victor 1906.37, 1908.27, 1910.21, 1913.20, 1915.21, 1916.04
Leroy, Victor 1918.27
LeRoy, Walter 1908.31
Lertora, Joseph 1914.20, 1917.36, 1918.33, 1919.17, 1920.29, 1923.19, 1925.08, 1926.39, 1928.21, 1929.39, 1931.07, 1932.10
Lertora, Joseph R. 1915.23
Lesage, Mlle. 1870.41, 1870.45, 1871.06
Lesan, David 1935.03, 1936.01, 1939.19
Lesard, Parker 1914.16
LeSawyer, Mary 1959.08, 1959.17, 1962.06
Lescaut, Bianca 1893.21
Lescot, Mlle. 1883.51, 1883.54, 1883.57, 1883.59, 1883.60, 1883.61, 1884.01, 1884.02, 1884.03, 1884.05, 1884.45, 1884.55
Lescott, Mlle. 1883.55
Lesdernier, Mrs. 1856.01
Lesenger, Jay 1981.21, 1990.08
Leser, Robert 1947.09
Leser, Tina 1946.20
leSeyeux, Jean 1939.22, 1940.02, 1942.23
Lesguillon 1885.01, 1885.41, 1892.03
Lesguilon 1900.23
Leska, Elene 1913.01
Lesko, John 1963.25, 1965.33, 1966.29, 1968.24, 1974.09, 1975.22, 1976.09, 1977.07, 1979.10, 1980.20, 1984.07, 2001.08
Lesko, Jr., John 1948.17
Leslay, Charlote 1903.18
Leslay, Charlotte 1904.22, 1910.26, 1912.01
Leslie 1868.28
Leslie Fannie 1897.14
Leslie, Alice 1909.25
Leslie, Anna 1904.13, 1904.44
Leslie, Annie 1886.40, 1902.29
Leslie, Beatrice 1893.32
Leslie, Bert 1908.27, 1910.21, 1910.35, 1911.05, 1915.22
Leslie, Blanche 1890.50
Leslie, Bob 1956.02, 1957.01
Leslie, Claire 1905.19
Leslie, Connie 1889.30, 1889.32
Leslie, Cora 1899.25
Leslie, Doree 1927.46, 1930.08
Leslie, Earl 1924.13
Leslie, Eddie 1924.31, 1932.19
Leslie, Edgar 1913.05, 1913.06, 1913.30, 1914.22, 1916.03, 1916.20, 1917.03, 1917.13, 1917.35, 1921.34, 1923.12, 1923.20, 1936.17, 1955.13, 1967.11, 1979.24, 1995.12
Leslie, Edna 1918.41
Leslie, Elizabeth 1895.35
Leslie, Ellen 1947.01
Leslie, Emma 1887.45, 1888.14, 1899.26
Leslie, Eva 1899.11
Leslie, Fannie 1872.21, 1872.24, 1872.34
Leslie, Fanny 1872.22, 1872.26
Leslie, Florence 1901.26
Leslie, Frances 1909.25, 1912.38
Leslie, Frank 1924.31, 1927.53
Leslie, Fred 1888.41, 1913.23, 1914.22, 1924.01, 1926.03
Leslie, Frederick 1881.36, 1882.06, 1883.62, 1884.08, 1888.38
Leslie, George 1876.30, 1897.38
Leslie, George W. 1910.26
Leslie, Gladys 1898.67, 1900.23
Leslie, Grace 1884.25, 1903.13
Leslie, H.J. 1890.50
Leslie, Helen 1886.24, 1886.34, 1887.29
Leslie, Henry J. 1886.45, 1887.44, 1888.38, 1890.50, 1895.20
Leslie, Henry John 1891.41
Leslie, J. Frank 1923.21
Leslie, J.J. 1885.42
Leslie, Jack 1916.22, 1932.06, 1945.11
Leslie, John 1943.03, 1956.16
Leslie, Joseph 1903.11, 1904.42, 1906.11, 1907.09, 1907.20
Leslie, Kathryn 1902.26
Leslie, Larry 1957.01
Leslie, Larry B. 1956.02
Leslie, Lew 1922.25, 1924.15, 1924.37, 1928.18, 1930.09, 1930.34, 1931.11, 1933.27, 1939.14, 1980.10
Leslie, Lillie 1912.49
Leslie, Lorayne 1913.31, 1914.23
Leslie, Lorraine 1909.25
Leslie, Lulu 1896.38
Leslie, M. 1908.19
Leslie, May 1902.29, 1905.44, 1906.29, 1907.24, 1908.04, 1912.12, 1912.38, 1913.17, 1914.15, 1916.24, 1917.26
Leslie, Messr. 1857.03
Leslie, Michael 1977.15
Leslie, Michelle 1996.08
Leslie, Miss 1887.45, 1896.44, 1904.13, 1904.44
Leslie, Paula 1912.11
Leslie, Pauline 1872.21
Leslie, Rose 1907.03, 1907.32, 1911.07, 1912.11
Leslie, Stacia 1906.29, 1907.24
Leslie, Sylvia 1934.34
Leslie, Tunnie 1899.40
Lesoir, George 1892.14, 1898.29, 1898.46, 1900.28
LeSoir, George 1904.40, 1907.49
leSoir, George 1922.02, 1939.29
leSoir, Jack 1928.23
Lespinasse, Mlle. 1902.13
Less, Robert 1937.13
Lessac, Arthur 1944.32
Lessack, Arthur 1937.14, 1939.23
Lesser, Amy 1900.47, 1904.01, 1904.18
Lesser, Arthur 1947.05, 1948.12, 1949.01, 1951.19, 1958.06, 1964.22, 1965.37
Lesser, Gene 1973.16
Lesser, Lou 1921.32
Lessey, George 1935.04, 1935.13, 1939.21
Lessey, George A. 1907.56
Lessey, George E. 1906.38
Lessiems, Mark 1884.22
Lessing, Edith Maada 1912.25
Lessing, Florence 1944.01, 1953.16
Lessing, Madge 1890.13, 1890.22, 1890.38, 1890.42, 1890.45, 1891.10, 1891.16, 1891.19, 1891.35, 1892.02, 1892.13, 1892.26, 1892.32, 1892.41, 1892.49, 1893.01, 1893.04, 1894.21, 1896.18, 1896.44, 1897.26, 1898.43, 1898.72, 1900.03, 1900.33, 1900.39, 1903.32, 1904.17, 1915.05, 1921.01
Lessing, Mme. 1895.35
Lessner, George 1941.02, 1945.12, 1948.18
Lester, Al 1905.21
Lester, Amy 1923.14
Lester, Annie 1893.07
Lester, Bernard 1892.27
Lester, Carrie 1879.42
Lester, Charles 1916.01
Lester, Clare 1880.46
Lester, Dorothy 1900.34, 1901.09, 1901.21
Lester, Dottie 1968.32
Lester, Edward 1923.01, 1930.15
Lester, Edwin 1870.27, 1876.04, 1876.05, 1876.07, 1876.09, 1876.10, 1876.14, 1876.30, 1876.33, 1877.05, 1944.21, 1946.18, 1948.24, 1953.16, 1964.24, 1973.12, 1981.21
Lester, Florence 1906.38, 1907.37
Lester, Frank 1889.21
Lester, Gladys 1899.21
Lester, Harry B. 1905.24, 1907.62
Lester, Harry E. 1900.45
Lester, Hugh 1980.23
Lester, Ida 1882.49
Lester, Jennie 1878.01
Lester, Jerry 1940.02, 1942.29, 1944.01
Lester, Kate 1894.10
Lester, Lida Holden 1891.01
Lester, Lillian 1899.15
Lester, Loraine 1908.28
Lester, Lorraine 1948.18
Lester, Louise 1883.52, 1884.18, 1884.59, 1885.62, 1886.07, 1886.17
Lester, Marion 1888.27, 1888.40
Lester, Messr. 1861.03, 1876.04, 1876.05, 1876.33
Lester, Miss 1872.35, 1883.17, 1883.23, 1886.36
Lester, Mr. 1855.11, 1856.04
Lester, Sonny 1965.05
Lester, Todd 1980.02, 1983.01, 1987.05
Lester, W. 1881.06
Lester, William 1881.06, 1928.20
Lestina, Bessie Lea 1897.12
Lestocq, George 1905.19
LeStrange, Joe 1908.22
LeStrange, Mons. 1884.10
Lestue, Mlle. 1883.60
leTang, Henry 1943.14, 1944.18
LeTang, Henry 1952.08, 1978.21, 1981.06, 1987.02, 1989.02
Letchworth, Eileen 1958.08
Letelier, Mlle. 1877.11
Letellier, Mlle. 1876.25, 1877.09, 1877.10, 1877.13, 1877.14, 1877.19, 1878.18
Leterrier 1898.12
Leterrier, Eugene 1875.04, 1875.11, 1875.26, 1875.29, 1875.38, 1876.20, 1876.21, 1877.09, 1877.11, 1877.26, 1877.32, 1877.33, 1878.18, 1879.23, 1879.26, 1879.41, 1879.44, 1879.49, 1880.29, 1880.56, 1882.06, 1882.30, 1883.28, 1884.14, 1885.17, 1885.23, 1885.24, 1886.37, 1887.22, 1887.24, 1889.24, 1890.26, 1891.31, 1894.14, 1896.28, 1897.36, 1900.17, 1905.08, 1926.40
Lethbridge, Alice 1886.50, 1886.54
Letournier, Anais 1876.36
Letowt, Marle 1959.13
Lett, Robert 1901.10, 1903.29, 1907.46
Letta, Joelle 1996.17
Letters, Will 1910.01
Lettich, M. William 1977.13
Letzinger, George 1862.03, 1862.04, 1863.07
Leutze, Theo. 1880.41
Leuyllemn, Marie 1905.55
Levan, Martin 1982.19, 1985.12, 1987.05, 1988.01, 1988.12, 1990.04, 1992.12, 1993.09, 1993.15, 1994.08, 1994.10
Levanion, G. 1881.30
Levans, Daniel 1978.23
Levant, Harry 1930.09, 1938.14, 1939.27, 1940.22, 1943.14, 1944.02, 1945.17, 1946.13, 1947.15
Levant, Harry S. 1947.04
Levant, Oscar 1930.05
Levasseur, F. 1870.05
Levasseur, Mme. 1864.01, 1864.03, 1864.08, 1864.11
Levastre 1888.23
Levaux, Mme. 1876.31
Leve, Charles 1897.43
Leve, Sam 1942.29, 1955.13, 1963.07, 1964.18
Leve, Samuel 1940.11, 1940.13, 1940.14, 1940.15, 1952.13
Levean, Florence 1877.20
Leveen, Raymond 1941.07
Levelle, Estelle 1923.10
Levelle, Fatelle 1923.25
Levene, Sam 1950.17, 1961.21, 1964.18
Levenson, Jay 1938.08
Levenson, Jeanine 1991.05
Levenson, Lew 1929.07, 1929.19
Leventhal, Jules J. 1945.11
Leventhal, Julius J. 1946.17
Lever, F.C. 1881.18
Leverde, Belle 1892.39
Levere, Joseph 1906.11, 1907.09
Levere, Messr. 1851.04
Levere, Mr. 1848.01, 1850.01, 1855.11, 1856.04, 1857.05, 1857.07
Levering, Kate 2000.11, 2001.08
Levering, Nancy 1972.24
Levey, Adele 1890.32, 1892.18
Levey, Carlotta 1890.32
Levey, Emma 1896.06, 1897.30, 1897.54, 1898.77, 1899.15
Levey, Ethel 1901.07, 1903.11, 1904.42, 1906.11, 1906.21, 1908.10, 1911.18, 1922.17, 1941.12, 1945.11
Levey, Florence 1889.54
Levey, Harold 1918.25, 1922.47, 1923.34, 1924.41, 1925.47, 1926.06, 1927.68, 1937.17
Levey, Harold A. 1918.25, 1920.43
Levey, J.H. 1936.30
Levey, Lotta 1892.18
Levey, May 1892.18
Levey, May Lillian 1890.32
Levey, W.C. 1886.02
Levi, Gavri 1968.04, 1969.13, 1973.01
Levi, Maurice 1893.39, 1894.38, 1895.02, 1896.44, 1897.07, 1897.21, 1899.12, 1899.29, 1900.40, 1901.16, 1901.27, 1902.24, 1904.39, 1906.01, 1908.07, 1908.19, 1909.13, 1910.18, 1911.18, 1911.24
Levi, Morris 1898.28
Levia, Adelina 1911.19
Levian, Harry 1912.37
Levick, Gustavus 1884.40, 1885.41
Levick, Messr. 1857.04
Levick, Milnes 1860.06, 1861.04, 1863.08, 1864.22, 1867.32
LeVie, Louis 1918.27
Levigne, May 1893.49, 1896.05
Levigne, Miss 1892.53
Levin, Herman 1940.11, 1940.13, 1940.14, 1940.15, 1946.10, 1949.18, 1950.19, 1956.01, 1973.02, 1976.05
Levin, Ira 1965.29
Levin, Jane 1965.38
Levin, Kathy 1989.27, 1991.06
Levin, Michael 1970.04
Levin, Pete 1988.19
Levin, Sylvan 1954.01, 1959.05
Levin-Townsend Enterprises, Inc. 1968.24, 1969.01
Levine, Andrea 1972.23
Levine, Bill 1972.16
Levine, Daniel 1992.11
Levine, Elias 1937.14
Levine, Elliot 1967.04
Levine, Florence 1924.14
Levine, Fred 1912.30
Levine, G.V. 1894.11
Levine, Herman 1963.29, 1970.18, 1970.21
Levine, Ilana 1999.03
Levine, Johanna 1970.14
Levine, Joseph E. 1965.01, 1966.15
Levine, Joseph I. 1958.14, 1959.20, 1970.14
Levine, Julia 1899.26
Levine, Marc 1989.08
LeVine, Marilynn 1986.17, 1989.02
Levine, Maurice 1949.15, 1951.15, 1951.22, 1952.07, 1952.13, 1953.02, 1957.05, 1957.14, 1979.09
Levine, Rhoda 1961.11, 1971.16, 1972.01
Levine, Richard 1991.06
Levine, Sam 1942.28
Levinge, May 1891.11
Levings, Nigel 1996.05
Levinsky, Walt 1975.23
Levinson, Borra 1929.31
Levinson, Fred 1980.29
Levinson, J.J. 1927.34
Levinson, Larry 1998.19
Levinson, Leonard L. 1945.12
Levinson, Leonard Louis 1944.28
Levinson, Richard 1983.01
Levinson, Yefim 1977.13
Levis, Patrick 1996.08
Levison, Jay 1941.11
Levister, Alonzo 1968.13
Levitt, Barry 1991.14, 1995.14
Levkova, Sonja 1971.05
Levy, Abe 1906.31
Levy, Abraham 1919.28
Levy, Al 1937.14
Levy, Arnold 1973.08
Levy, Bert 1918.23, 1919.22, 1921.28
Levy, Charles 1939.15
Levy, David 1997.03
Levy, Emma 1895.18, 1897.02, 1900.44
Levy, Florence 1893.24
Levy, Harold 1927.68
Levy, Harriet Newman 1999.12
Levy, Henry 1918.17
Levy, Jacques 1971.04, 1976.27, 1983.18
Levy, Julia C. 2001.02

Levy, Lorie Cowen 1999.24, 2000.11
Levy, Mark 1989.12
Levy, Morris 1982.22, 1986.02, 1990.15
Levy, Mr. 1871.08
Levy, Newman 1925.17, 1926.13, 1929.19, 1930.18, 1930.33, 1934.06, 1934.18
Levy, Norman 1927.27
Levy, Parke 1938.01, 1940.07, 1940.09
Levy, Sol 1919.26
Levy, Steven M. 1999.14
Levy, Ted L. 1992.08
Levy, W.C. 1873.28
Lew Fields, Inc. 1914.28
Lewellyn, Harry 1911.06, 1923.43
Lewenstein, Oscar 1980.17
Lewers, William 1894.39
Lewin, B.N. 1921.15
Lewin, Ben 1916.04
Lewin, Jamie 1970.18
Lewin, John 1970.06
Lewin, Lionel H. 1882.39
Lewine, Richard 1934.40, 1936.03, 1936.06, 1937.02, 1937.12, 1938.12, 1939.10, 1940.18, 1946.19, 1948.04, 1959.23, 1970.08, 1975.13
Lewis and MacCoughtry 1900.55
Lewis and Macoughtry 1900.42
Lewis Maxine 1927.38
Lewis, A.J. 1872.30
Lewis, Abby 1971.07
Lewis, Ada 1890.49, 1891.25, 1891.45, 1892.44, 1892.54, 1893.10, 1893.15, 1893.49, 1895.27, 1896.52, 1898.38, 1899.29, 1901.29, 1902.06, 1905.41, 1906.17, 1907.18, 1908.10, 1909.30, 1910.16, 1911.18, 1912.07, 1913.05, 1914.17, 1915.30, 1917.23, 1918.39, 1920.04, 1921.36, 1923.44
Lewis, Adair 1984.13
Lewis, Al 1903.28, 1906.06, 1955.13, 1982.22, 1986.02, 1986.06
Lewis, Albert 1940.17, 1941.13, 1952.05, 1959.08, 1959.17, 1963.15
Lewis, Alexander 1928.16
Lewis, Allan 1999.09
Lewis, Annie 1887.23, 1889.41, 1890.29, 1891.46, 1894.16, 1895.16
Lewis, Arthur 1952.05
Lewis, Ben 1933.20
Lewis, Bernie 1905.21
Lewis, Bob 1936.28
Lewis, Bobo 1978.12
Lewis, Boncellia 1981.28
Lewis, Brenda 1945.15, 1948.31, 1949.16, 1953.05, 1953.14, 1954.01, 1958.13, 1959.10, 1964.18
Lewis, C.M. 1872.06
Lewis, Carol Jean 1979.03
Lewis, Carrington 1946.08, 1965.03
Lewis, Catherine 1878.16, 1879.50, 1879.56, 1880.04, 1880.55, 1880.69, 1881.36, 1881.38, 1882.06, 1882.72, 1883.25, 1883.29, 1883.44, 1895.15, 1896.24, 1898.26, 1898.29, 1898.46, 1900.34, 1901.09, 1902.23
Lewis, Clarence 1992.06
Lewis, Constance 1883.29
Lewis, Darryl 1999.02
Lewis, Dave 1900.33, 1900.58, 1901.18, 1904.28, 1906.04, 1906.19, 1907.24, 1908.21
Lewis, David 1964.29
Lewis, Dolly 1922.28
Lewis, E.W. 1900.59
Lewis, Ed 1972.19
Lewis, Edwina 1978.13, 1991.01
Lewis, Ellen 1870.39, 1872.04
Lewis, Elsie 1918.03
Lewis, Emma 1870.39, 1873.29, 1876.16, 1897.01
Lewis, Flo 1920.06, 1925.01, 1925.28, 1926.39
Lewis, Frank 1876.19, 1908.27
Lewis, Fred Irving 1941.08
Lewis, Frederick 1924.39
Lewis, Frederick G. 1934.03
Lewis, G. 1873.20, 1875.35
Lewis, Garrett 1959.06
Lewis, Garry Q. 1980.14, 1993.03
Lewis, Gary Q. 1979.18
Lewis, George 1875.40, 1884.13, 1885.22
Lewis, George W. 1891.32, 1892.50, 1908.22
Lewis, Gertrude 1900.44, 1901.29
Lewis, Guy 1904.33
Lewis, Gwen 1918.31
Lewis, Gwenn 1965.02
Lewis, H. 1841.01, 1875.18
Lewis, Hallam 1793.01
Lewis, Harold 1924.17
Lewis, Harry 1943.23
Lewis, Hazel 1910.34, 1912.38, 1914.23, 1915.31, 1916.10, 1916.24
Lewis, Henry 1875.18, 1912.29, 1916.25, 1917.23, 1919.16, 1920.02
Lewis, Horace 1895.41
Lewis, Ida 1899.12
Lewis, Inez 1902.33
Lewis, Isobel 1875.26
Lewis, Ivan 1934.37
Lewis, J. 1860.02, 1864.17, 1865.01, 1865.11, 1866.02, 1866.28, 1872.07, 1873.22, 1884.41
Lewis, J.A. 1882.50
Lewis, J.F. 1868.06
Lewis, J.L. 1867.12, 1869.26, 1870.15
Lewis, J.R. 1879.54
Lewis, James 1866.03, 1869.11, 1869.17, 1869.21, 1876.23, 1881.04, 1881.11, 1881.27, 1884.11
Lewis, Jean 1865.05, 1865.07, 1865.08
Lewis, Jeffreys 1905.26, 1913.29
Lewis, Jenifer 1979.32, 1982.22
Lewis, Jennie L. 1898.01
Lewis, Jesse 1912.38
Lewis, Jessie 1920.21
Lewis, Jim 1989.20, 1995.09
Lewis, Joe E. 1938.01, 1942.01
Lewis, John 1938.01
Lewis, John H. 1901.03
Lewis, John Richard 1985.06
Lewis, Joseph 1960.08
Lewis, Joseph D. 1955.05
Lewis, Jr., Alde 1983.06, 1986.06
Lewis, Jr., William 1931.14
Lewis, Jr., William M. 1930.25
Lewis, Kathryn 1940.15
Lewis, Ken Krashner 2000.13
Lewis, L. 1877.01
Lewis, Laura May 1974.12
Lewis, Lee 1960.08, 2000.10
Lewis, Lelia 1901.27
Lewis, Lillian 1897.23
Lewis, Little Ferdie 1930.29
Lewis, Loney 1959.13
Lewis, M. 1865.03, 1875.03
Lewis, Mable Sanford 1945.13
Lewis, Marcia 1986.13, 1987.12, 1990.18, 1994.07, 1996.14
Lewis, Martin 1945.14
Lewis, Mary 1920.28, 1921.21, 1922.19, 1923.20, 1927.13, 1945.13, 1946.21
Lewis, May 1905.49
Lewis, Meade Lux 1943.17, 1944.31
Lewis, Mesdame 1852.05
Lewis, Messr. 1841.01
Lewis, Michael 1965.31, 1968.02
Lewis, Michael J. 1973.07
Lewis, Minard 1852.04, 1859.05, 1861.04, 1862.09, 1863.04, 1863.08, 1866.34, 1868.06, 1868.18, 1869.06, 1872.23
Lewis, Minard. 1868.07
Lewis, Minnie 1873.27
Lewis, Miss 1852.01, 1869.06, 1869.08, 1869.29
Lewis, Mitchell 1912.10
Lewis, Monica 1942.11
Lewis, Morgan 1934.06, 1937.02, 1937.12, 1939.10, 1939.12, 1940.03, 1946.07, 1975.12, 1979.14, 1992.18
Lewis, Mort 1936.12, 1938.04, 1940.07
Lewis, Mr. 1836.01, 1852.04, 1864.02
Lewis, Mrs. 1875.40
Lewis, Nadine 1967.07, 1971.06
Lewis, Nat 1917.09, 1918.18, 1919.11
Lewis, Nellie 1872.02, 1872.05, 1872.08, 1872.12
Lewis, Nettie 1907.29, 1907.31
Lewis, Norm 1993.06, 1997.17, 2000.08
Lewis, R.J. 1872.02, 1872.04, 1872.05, 1872.08, 1872.12, 1872.14, 1872.25, 1872.32, 1872.36, 1872.40, 1872.43, 1876.06
Lewis, Ralph 1904.30, 1942.34
Lewis, Ripple 1957.07
Lewis, Robert 1888.31, 1933.25, 1947.07, 1949.16, 1950.10, 1953.05, 1953.14, 1957.16, 1961.24, 1964.04, 1965.31
Lewis, Roger 1942.16
Lewis, Ron 1974.01, 1976.24, 1977.16
Lewis, Ruby 1908.01, 1908.39, 1911.11, 1912.38, 1914.15, 1920.21
Lewis, Russell 1946.03, 1948.11
Lewis, Ruth Virginia 1937.01
Lewis, Sam 1916.25, 1918.05, 1922.25, 1923.20, 1924.01, 1925.01, 1925.23, 1927.15, 1927.32, 1927.37, 1928.08, 1929.07, 1929.28, 1935.04, 1938.16, 1953.12, 1962.17, 1967.11, 1974.09, 1980.10, 1986.02
Lewis, Sam M. 1906.04, 1911.13, 1911.30, 1912.31, 1916.03, 1916.09, 1917.08, 1919.02, 1919.03, 1919.15, 1938.08, 1939.29, 1940.10, 1997.01
Lewis, Samuel L. 1986.06
Lewis, Samuel W. 1986.06
Lewis, Scott 1948.15
Lewis, Shannon 1999.01
Lewis, Shelton 1949.18
Lewis, Sinclair 1970.02
Lewis, St. John 1899.08, 1899.19, 1900.56, 1901.12, 1901.29, 1901.30, 1902.05, 1902.06
Lewis, Sydney 1973.10
Lewis, Ted 1919.18, 1921.27, 1927.13, 1927.37, 1927.58
Lewis, Thomas 1887.31, 1893.50, 1894.52
Lewis, Tillie 1872.14, 1872.36
Lewis, Tilly 1872.43
Lewis, Tom 1891.32, 1892.50, 1904.42, 1907.16, 1907.44, 1908.14, 1911.33, 1913.04, 1913.34, 1916.08, 1916.23, 1917.08, 1919.03, 1922.07, 1923.19, 1924.18, 1925.10
Lewis, Vicki 1982.10, 1985.20, 1994.01
Lewis, W.D. 1891.39
Lewis, Walter 1927.32, 1935.15
Lewis, Willa 1896.49
Lewis, William 1896.49, 1957.15
Lewis, William J. 1922.23
Lewis-Evans, Kecia 1990.12
Lewisohn, Irene 1922.20, 1925.20, 1926.17
Lewisohn, Ludwig 1937.01
Ley, Benton 1923.38, 1924.32
Leybourne, George 1931.14
Leydecker, Arthur 1918.17
Leyden, Leo 1968.02, 1970.15, 1986.12
Leyden, Norman 1968.05
Leyden, William H. 1891.20
Leyerle, William 1973.09, 1989.18
Leygand, Mlle. 1877.29
Leyland, James E. 1896.04
Leyland, Norma 1930.27
Leyle, William 1906.11, 1907.09, 1907.57, 1908.14
Leyman, Randolph 1928.12
Leyton, Helen 1884.11
Leyton, Marie 1891.41
Leyton, May 1889.26
Leyton, Rose 1877.39
Leyton, Sonya 1923.14
Leyva, Laura 1979.08
Li, Chao 1958.19
Liable, George 1902.14
Liadoff 1923.28
Liandre, Lil 1937.01
Libbey, Aldrich 1893.21, 1897.21
Libbey, J. Aldrich 1890.08, 1891.14
Libbon, Robert P. 1991.02
Libby, Dee 1957.01
Libby, Emma 1880.25
Libby, J. Aldrich 1894.17
Libby, James 1930.36
Liberman, Bill 1974.01
Libert, Estelle 1904.28
Libertella, Jose 1993.08
Libertini, Richard 1971.08
Liberto, Don 1942.15, 1944.01, 1946.12, 1946.22, 1948.08
Libidins, D. 1924.48, 1932.09
Libin, Andrea Clark 1989.10
Libin, Paul 1969.10, 1974.25, 1976.19, 1979.07, 1988.13, 1989.10, 1989.19, 1992.11, 1995.12
Libman, Lillian 1978.14, 1978.15, 1978.16, 1978.17
Libowitzky, Hervig 1986.18
Libuse, Frank 1941.11, 1944.30
Libussa, Fraulein 1879.62
Licenstein, Messr. 1907.36
Lichine, David 1942.29, 1944.28, 1945.14
Licht, Ronald 1983.19
Lichtefeld, Michael 1989.19, 1995.07, 1998.03
Lichtenfeld, Izhack 1972.17
Lichtenstein 1919.27
Lichtenstein Millinery Company 1921.33
Lichtenstein's, Fifth Avenue 1920.40
Lichtenstein, Miss 1848.04
Lichter, Anna 1903.10
Lichter, James 1905.34
Lichter, Paul 1978.01
Lichtman, Nat 1940.18
Liddell, Beatrice 1903.04, 1904.15
Liddiard, Fanny 1892.48, 1892.53
Liddy, James R. 1923.25, 1925.07
Lidums, Zanza 1966.19
Lieb, Beatrice 1886.41, 1902.08
Lieb, Dick 1992.18, 1997.05
Lieb, Francis 1912.42, 1921.01, 1922.12
Lieb, Francis K. 1913.32
Lieb, Lora 1906.20, 1907.21, 1909.26
Lieb, Mani 1990.16
Lieber, Jerry 1977.10, 1978.05, 1982.22, 1983.20, 1989.12
Liebersman, H. 1942.28
Liebert, Dick 1943.16
Liebert, Edward 1910.33
Liebgold, Leon 1970.17
Liebler and Company 1903.26, 1906.05, 1907.02, 1910.33, 1911.01, 1911.17
Liebler, Theodore 1903.26
Liebling, Howard 1974.19
Liebling, Leonard 1910.36, 1911.43, 1913.06
Liebling, William 1927.27
Liebman, Harriet 1925.43
Liebman, Max 1936.01, 1939.26, 1941.03, 1941.08, 1942.25, 1948.04, 1950.02, 1950.09, 1961.17
Liebmann, Walter 1906.23
Lieder, Rose 1937.12
Liederman, Susan 1993.04
Lief, Max 1928.14, 1928.21, 1928.27, 1929.09, 1929.20, 1931.13, 1931.14, 1931.21, 1932.13, 1936.01
Lief, Nat 1936.01
Lief, Nathaniel 1928.14, 1928.21, 1928.27, 1929.09, 1929.20, 1931.13, 1931.14, 1931.21, 1932.13
Lien, Evanna 1959.24
Liesegang, Adolph 1892.40, 1892.46, 1897.53, 1898.04, 1898.06, 1898.07, 1898.09, 1898.14, 1898.15, 1898.16, 1898.19, 1898.21, 1898.24, 1898.30, 1898.37, 1898.39, 1898.40, 1898.42, 1898.49, 1898.52, 1898.57, 1898.62, 1898.65, 1898.71, 1898.74, 1898.76, 1899.05, 1899.07, 1899.10, 1899.16, 1899.20, 1905.16
Liesegang, Aldoph 1899.14
Liferman, Georges 1959.15, 1961.25
Liff, Samuel 1964.20, 1965.19, 1965.39, 1967.16, 1968.01, 1968.17, 1968.31, 1973.02
Liff, Spencer 1996.08
Lifshey, Karen 1999.10
Lifshey, O. 1920.10
Liftin, Robert I. 1970.08
Liggins, S.J. 1896.46
Lightfoot, Gordon 1974.01
Lightfoot, J.E. 1906.14, 1909.27
Lightfoot, James 1904.26, 1911.20, 1940.01
Lightfoot, James E. 1908.08
Lightner, Claude 1908.37
Lightner, Claudius A. 1903.35
Lightner, Fred 1954.17
Lightner, Thea 1922.27, 1923.18, 1924.19
Lightner, Winnie 1922.27, 1923.18, 1924.19, 1925.27, 1926.37, 1927.62
Lightning, Mr. 1873.26
Ligon, K.C. 1992.10, 1997.15
Ligon, Kevin 1997.15
Liker, George 1960.08
Lila Clay's Music and Dramatic Company 1884.60
Lilford, Henry 1893.11
Lili 1929.25
Liliana, Lili 1970.17
Liliputians, Ergotti 1917.04
Lillard, James A. 1930.29, 1939.17
Lilley, Barbara 1976.14, 1978.14, 1978.16
Lilley, Edward Clark 1927.66, 1930.09, 1930.11, 1937.10
Lilley, Edward Clarke 1930.23, 1930.30, 1931.19, 1931.42, 1932.07, 1934.01, 1934.42, 1935.04, 1936.02, 1936.17, 1936.31, 1939.12, 1940.23, 1945.17, 1955.04
Lilley, Joseph 1940.10, 1946.04
Lilley, Joseph J. 1980.29

Lillford, Harry 1910.02, 1911.13, 1924.08
Lillian Russell Comic Opera Company 1894.48
Lillian Russell Opera Comique Company 1891.36, 1892.60, 1893.02, 1893.07
Lillian Russell Opera Comique Organization 1893.39, 1894.14
Lillian Russell Opera Company 1895.09, 1895.12, 1896.10, 1896.12, 1896.51
Lillian Russell-Della Fox-Jeff DeAngelis Comic Opera 1897.17, 1898.27
Lillian, La Petite 1880.12
Lillian, Lily 1909.20
Lillian, Little 1880.53, 1887.11
Lilliard, James A. 1927.30
Lillie, Beatrice 1924.01, 1925.42, 1926.46, 1928.02, 1928.42, 1931.14, 1932.27, 1935.12, 1936.31, 1939.07, 1944.29, 1948.14, 1952.11, 1957.01, 1964.16
Lillie, La Petite 1870.31
Lillie, Miss 1870.31
Lillie, Muriel 1923.35, 1925.42, 1952.11
Lilling, Bill 1948.32
Lilling, William 1924.12, 1933.01, 1938.13, 1941.08
Lillite, William 1920.09
Lilly, Paul 1947.02
Lillywhite, Mr. 1852.01
Lillywhite, Mrs. 1851.02
Lilo 1953.07, 1966.05
Lily Turner Attractions 1981.05
Limat, Mlle. 1875.08
Limb, Sidney 1931.30
Limer, B. 1873.02
Limon, Jose 1933.12, 1933.26, 1940.07, 1942.31
Lina, Trio 1939.18
Lince, John W. 1890.27
Linck, Mary 1900.06
Lincke, Paul 1907.41, 1908.07, 1909.11, 1910.10, 1990.09
Lincoln Center Theatre 2000.16
Lincoln Center Theatre Company 1996.16, 1998.21, 1999.09, 1999.22, 2000.07
Lincoln, Arthur 1945.14
Lincoln, Corinne 1906.24
Lincoln, Dell 1890.25
Lincoln, Georgie 1886.47, 1887.06
Lincoln, Lorna 1922.30
Lincoln, Miss 1882.45
Lind, Betty 1938.04
Lind, Christina 1938.09
Lind, Clara 1885.65
Lind, Della 1939.22, 1947.14
Lind, Gloria 1947.04, 1954.06
Lind, Helen 1929.19
Lind, Homer 1902.41, 1905.56
Lind, Ida 1876.03
Lind, Jenny 1875.36
Lind, Karl 1873.26
Lind, Letty 1888.38, 1888.41
Lind, Norman 1936.01, 1936.26
Lind, Ostrid 1946.12
Lind, Paula 1927.65, 1934.41
Lind, Stefan 1956.06
Lind-Oquendo, Abraham 1976.28
Lindahl, Stanley 1925.17
Lindau, C. 1901.13
Lindau, Carl 1898.72, 1911.44
Lindau, Karl 1909.19, 1912.37
Lindauer, August 1929.08
Linde, Denis 1989.12
Linde, Iris 1946.07
Lindeman, Edith 1954.08
Lindeman, Lillie B. 1893.30
Linden, Bert 1934.41
Linden, Ellika 1966.19
Linden, Hal 1964.35, 1967.05, 1968.06, 1970.15, 1972.01, 1973.15, 1997.22
Linden, Joyce 1916.19
Linden, Lilla 1891.03
Linden, Lillie 1892.24
Linden, Margaret 1918.25, 1923.26
Linden, Master 1880.35
Linden, Robert 1940.16, 1966.01, 1968.19
Linden, Rosa 1883.17
Lindenberg, Paul 1939.23, 1940.04
Linder, Barbara 1966.14
Linder, D. Scott 1977.09
Linder, Helene 1897.35
Linder, Herr 1897.08
Linder, Jack 1936.07
Linder, Mark 1936.07
Linder, Seymour 1936.07
Linderman, Ed 1976.15
Linderman, Minert H. 1893.30
Lindfors, Viveca 1963.17
Lindgren, Robert 1954.12, 1955.01
Lindholm, Herbert 1921.41
Lindholm, Robert 1932.27, 1934.39
Lindinger, Hugo 1964.25
Lindley, Don 1925.25, 1925.48
Lindley, Donald 1925.25, 1925.48
Lindley, Florence 1908.16
Lindley, Kathleen 1918.11
Lindner, Helen 1902.14
Lindner, Helene 1898.53
Lindner, Mr. 1898.53
Lindo, F. Newton 1900.57, 1906.05, 1907.02, 1912.28
Lindo, Newton 1911.11
Lindon, Lois 1931.02
Lindsay, A. 1880.51
Lindsay, Carmen 1961.09
Lindsay, Claudia 1965.03
Lindsay, Earl 1920.24, 1924.16, 1925.43, 1925.49, 1926.14, 1927.05, 1927.48, 1927.55, 1928.35, 1930.42
Lindsay, Frank 1954.13
Lindsay, Grace 1907.32
Lindsay, Howard 1922.42, 1932.26, 1934.36, 1936.26, 1937.15, 1950.15, 1956.16, 1959.24, 1962.20, 1967.07, 1987.15, 1990.02, 1998.03
Lindsay, James 1935.01
Lindsay, Kevin 1970.20
Lindsay, Oscar 1896.49
Lindsay, Robert 1986.12
Lindsay, Walter C. 1906.19
Lindsey, Bert 2000.03
Lindsey, Earl 1927.58, 1930.26
Lindsey, George 1962.04
Lindsey, Kathleen 1985.17
Lindsey, Lee 1959.12
Lindsey, Mort 1964.40
Lindstrom, Carl 1972.03
Lindsy, Earl 1925.27
Lindup, David 1962.18
Lines, Harry 1978.26
Ling, Henry 1908.33
Ling, Jack Mei 1953.16
Ling, Richard 1896.17
Ling, Richie 1891.30, 1895.09, 1896.10, 1896.12, 1899.34, 1902.21, 1903.21, 1903.37, 1904.35, 1904.50, 1904.57, 1905.08, 1905.11, 1917.24, 1920.10, 1921.24, 1934.29
Ling, Ritchie 1907.07
Lingard, Dickie 1869.07, 1869.46, 1869.47
Lingard, George 1865.05, 1868.08, 1868.16, 1869.34
Lingard, Georgie 1893.49, 1897.04
Lingard, J.W. 1858.04, 1861.01, 1866.31
Lingard, James W. 1860.02
Lingard, Mr. 1856.02
Lingard, Nellie 1883.20
Lingard, William Horace 1869.07, 1869.46, 1869.47, 1879.10
Lingen, Henri 1919.25, 1920.39
Linhart, Buzzy 1973.14, 1975.12
Linhart, Joe 1967.06
Liniva Productions, Inc. 1985.20
Link, Adolf 1882.68
Link, Adolph 1916.17, 1924.45, 1931.03
Link, Billy 1901.12, 1901.29
Link, Carl 1919.38, 1920.34
Link, Harry 1978.09, 1980.10, 1982.12
Link, Herr 1897.08
Link, Peter 1971.10, 1972.23, 1978.22
Link, William 1983.01
Linkey, Harry 1906.22, 1907.23
Linkous, Ray 2001.04
Linley, Margaret 1931.46
Linn, Bambi 1943.04, 1945.05, 1947.09, 1948.16, 1950.06, 1954.07, 1957.11, 1962.05, 1982.24
Linn, Ben 1916.21, 1923.03
Linn, Betty 1920.28
Linn, Ralph 1945.05, 1953.08, 1956.12
Linn, Rexford 1908.33
Linn-Baker, Mark 1983.18, 1996.06
Linne, Hans S. 1904.54, 1906.29, 1910.22, 1911.08, 1912.20, 1912.35
Linne, Ragna 1886.39
Linnenkamp, Ernest 1926.11
Linning, S. 1985.07, 1999.18
Linscott, Hubert 1918.14
Linsk, Lester 1966.27
Linthicum, Lotta 1919.28, 1927.04
Linton, Betty Hyatt 1961.15, 1962.13, 1963.17, 1966.07, 1967.04, 1967.09, 1968.24
Linton, Bill 1960.01, 1962.01
Linton, Harry 1901.21, 1902.16, 1903.30
Linton, Mayne 1919.38
Linton, Stoney 1884.48
Linville, Albert 1950.15, 1951.14, 1953.03, 1955.08, 1961.21
Linwood, Miss 1886.32
Linyard, Catharine 1896.18
Linyard, Catherine 1890.12, 1890.30, 1894.22, 1896.51, 1897.26, 1899.19
Linyard, Freda 1906.01, 1906.29, 1908.07
Linz, Joe 1940.16
Lion, Margo 1989.24, 1991.05, 1992.08, 1997.18
Lionel Productions, Inc. 1927.18
Lionel, Stanley 1998.11
Liorat, Armand 1888.20, 1889.04, 1897.11
LiPari, Marjorie 1968.11
Lipkin, Seymour 1958.15
Lipkowska, Lydia 1921.29
Lipman, A.S. 1884.39, 1904.43
Lipman, Clara 1895.11, 1896.48, 1897.54
Lipman, David 1992.17, 1993.05
Lipman, Joseph 1978.18
Lipman, Milton 1894.32
Lippa, Andrew 1999.03, 2001.09
Lippe, Juliette 1915.11, 1916.17
Lipper, Jr., Arthur 1934.20
Lippincott 1883.65
Lippincott, Annie 1889.26
Lippincott, Miss 1870.13
Lippincott, Mr. 1882.71
Lippincott, William 1899.09
Lippman, Arthur 1935.19
Lippman, Jennie 1891.18
Lippman, Sidney 1947.08
Lippmann, Arthur 1931.36
Lippy, Earl 1958.20
Lipscott, Alan 1940.07, 1940.09
Lipscott, Allen 1938.01
Lipshutz, Jack L. 1928.41
Lipsky, Lisa 1971.02
Lipson, Arthur 1905.51, 1911.18, 1911.31, 1914.12, 1914.28, 1918.16, 1924.34, 1925.44, 1926.21, 1927.27, 1928.38
Lipson, Clifford 1971.12
Lipson, Lauren 1979.28
Lipson, Mary Ann 1974.26
Lipson, Paul 1953.11, 1955.25, 1962.16, 1964.27, 1976.36, 1981.18
Lipson, Philip 1885.22
Lipson, Stella 1897.24
Lipton, Ann 1941.10
Lipton, Blanche 1910.24, 1910.35
Lipton, Celia 1953.02, 1953.17, 1996.04
Lipton, Dan 1911.13, 1915.07
Lipton, George 1944.25, 1945.15, 1946.12, 1949.16, 1957.04, 1961.07
Lipton, James 1962.24, 1967.02, 1979.01
Lipyeat, Lillian 1896.27, 1898.16, 1898.39, 1898.42, 1904.30
Lisa, Luba 1961.10, 1962.05, 1964.44
Lisanby, Charles 1982.06
Lisboa, Claudia 1992.13
Lisbourne, John 1883.50
Lisbourne, Thomas 1883.50
Lischiner, Leon 1941.10
Lischner, Rose 1961.20
Lishner, Leon 1950.05, 1953.05, 1953.14, 1954.18
Lisle, H.D. 1869.38
Lisle, Sylvia 1902.19
Liss, Richard 1989.17
Lissek, Leon 1965.39
Lissit, Benjamin 1911.11, 1912.28
List, Emanuel 1916.15
Liste, Margaret 1927.68
Lister, Dorothy 1968.05
Lister, Lance 1929.51
Lister, Laurier 1955.19, 1958.20
Lister, Marquita 2000.03
Listerino, Herbert 1928.10
Liston, Hudson 1876.34, 1893.12
Liszt, Franz 1922.06, 1978.26, 1979.10, 1990.10
Litanny, Danny 1971.17
Litch, Messr. 1844.01
Litchfeld, Michael 1991.05
Litel, John B. 1919.36
Lithgow, John 1979.07
Lithgow, Stewart 1898.44
Litke, Allen 1971.15
Litomy, Leslie 1936.03, 1937.02, 1937.12, 1938.09, 1947.21, 1950.11
Litt, Jacob 1891.46, 1894.12, 1895.14
Littau, Frank 1932.24
Littau, Joseph 1940.09, 1941.02, 1943.24, 1945.05, 1948.25, 1952.05
Littell, Mrs. 1855.10
Litten, Jim 1975.07, 1975.13
Little, Alfred 1921.13
Little, Beatrice 1917.31
Little, Bill 1921.18
Little, Cleavon 1970.05
Little, D.C. 1862.07
Little, Edwetta 1978.18
Little, Eric 1925.50
Little, Eugene 1973.10, 1975.01
Little, Florence 1902.22, 1903.11, 1906.13, 1930.41
Little, Frank 1866.18
Little, George A. 1922.34, 1930.29
Little, James 1941.11
Little, Joseph 1907.08
Little, Julian 1914.24
Little, Mallie 1900.53
Little, Marion 1907.63
Little, Miss 1917.31
Little, Roger 1919.03, 1920.19, 1922.27
Little, Tara 1996.01, 1996.12, 1998.09
Little, Todd 1995.14
Little, William 1913.05
Littlefield, C.W. 1890.09
Littlefield, Carl 1949.06
Littlefield, Catherine 1940.10, 1940.16, 1941.03, 1942.19, 1944.14, 1944.20, 1945.04, 1946.14, 1947.04, 1947.12, 1948.19, 1949.05, 1949.06
Littlefield, Dorothee 1943.08
Littlefield, Dorothie 1944.20, 1944.21, 1946.14, 1947.12, 1948.19, 1949.05
Littlefield, Emma 1906.42, 1907.57, 1911.07
Littlefield, James 1942.19, 1944.20, 1946.14, 1947.12
Littlefield, Nick 1965.22
Littlejohn, Dorothy 1938.18
Littlewood, Joan 1964.28
Litvin, Mark 1998.16
Litwin, Burton L. 1981.06, 1987.02
Litz, Katherine 1948.17
Litzsinger, Sarah E. 1984.07
Lively, Bob 1928.07, 1928.32, 1930.11
Lively, Delee 1995.03
Lively, Robert 1932.14
Livent 1992.12
Livent (U.S.), Inc. 1993.09, 1994.08
Livent, Inc. 1997.10, 1998.21, 1999.01
Liverati, Mesdame 1852.01
Liverati, Messr. 1852.01
Livesey, Emma 1884.04, 1884.07
Livesey, Mamie 1884.04
Livevent, Inc. 1998.01
Livingston, Alice King 1890.41
Livingston, Bertha 1884.46
Livingston, Billi 1933.16, 1934.19, 1934.39, 1935.03, 1935.04, 1938.04
Livingston, Billie 1935.05, 1935.06, 1935.07, 1935.08, 1935.09, 1935.10, 1936.04, 1936.08, 1936.09, 1936.10, 1936.11
Livingston, Billy 1939.16, 1943.01, 1944.30, 1946.14, 1947.12, 1948.19, 1949.02, 1949.05
Livingston, Carrie 1891.18, 1892.21
Livingston, Charles 1879.12
Livingston, Dorothy 1927.39
Livingston, E. 1871.13
Livingston, Eleanor 1918.25, 1920.43
Livingston, Fod 1928.50
Livingston, Frank 1888.16
Livingston, Fud 1940.17
Livingston, G.L. 1884.27
Livingston, Henrietta 1929.09
Livingston, Jay 1958.02, 1961.21, 1979.24, 1979.25
Livingston, Jeanne H. 1974.05
Livingston, Jerry 1943.16, 1973.11, 1975.12
Livingston, Kate 1881.40, 1881.56, 1882.15
Livingston, L. 1884.10
Livingston, May 1879.64, 1880.65
Livingston, Paul 1904.45
Livingston, Pearl 1899.21
Livingston, Robert H. 1970.20, 1972.02
Livingston, Robert L. 1965.01
Livingstone, Bertha 1884.25
Livingstone, Dorothy 1899.35
Livingstone, May 1880.59
Livingstone, Stella 1891.34

Livitz, Barbara 1986.20
Liy, Ellen 1937.05
Lizette, Mlle. 1873.10
Lizie, Miss 1870.31
Lizst, Franz 1880.19, 1940.05
Lizzie Cummins, Inc. 1917.09
Llana, Jose 1996.05, 1997.21
Llayton, Joe 1960.05
Llewellyn, Dorothy 1929.33
Llewellyn, Richard 1966.09
Llewellyn, Will 1904.45
Llewllyn, William 1907.53
Lloyd, Alan 1975.10
Lloyd, Albert S. 1915.26
Lloyd, Ann 1948.20
Lloyd, Annie 1889.51, 1902.42
Lloyd, Arthur 1882.39
Lloyd, B. 1914.12
Lloyd, C. Balfour 1917.05, 1918.33
Lloyd, Christopher 1969.03, 1977.08
Lloyd, Clara 1887.05, 1912.24
Lloyd, David 1957.13
Lloyd, Doris 1916.23
Lloyd, Ethel 1904.05, 1904.24, 1905.53
Lloyd, Evans 1901.13, 1908.08
Lloyd, Florence 1894.33, 1897.32
Lloyd, Frances 1903.12
Lloyd, Frank 1928.39, 1929.18
Lloyd, Frank W. 1905.24
Lloyd, George 1939.12, 1940.18
Lloyd, Henry 1932.19, 1934.14
Lloyd, Jack 1906.40, 1908.02, 1973.05
Lloyd, John Robert 1946.05, 1949.12, 1955.11, 1960.17
Lloyd, Linda 1981.29
Lloyd, Lisbeth 1987.08
Lloyd, Louise 1900.20, 1901.08
Lloyd, Marie 1890.42
Lloyd, Mr. 1863.07
Lloyd, Natalie 1990.14, 1996.04
Lloyd, Norman 1938.18, 1954.03
Lloyd, Paula 1957.04, 1959.22
Lloyd, Ray 1916.08
Lloyd, Robert 1965.39
Lloyd, Ruth 1911.17
Lloyd, Virginia 1925.43
Lloyd, William 1880.55
Lloyd-Jones, Betti 1968.27, 1989.15, 1993.13
Lo, Randon 1982.03
Loader, Josephine 1972.20
Loadwick, Frederick 1940.11
Loane, Josie 1882.62, 1884.23, 1885.69
Loane, Mary 1967.02
Loasby, Alice 1907.26
Lobato, Julian 1875.24
Lobato, Nina Carmen 1875.22
Lobel, Adrianne 1983.06, 1994.05, 1998.16
Lobell, Marc 1928.19
Lobenhofer, Lee 1990.17
Lober, David 1953.03
Lober, Greb 1953.17
Loblov, Bela 1935.17
Locarro, Joe 1993.02, 1998.01
Locatelli, Mille. 1884.39
Locher, Robert 1921.27, 1923.07
Locher, Robert E. 1917.12, 1920.08, 1920.28, 1925.21, 1929.29
Lockard, Barbara 1958.16
Lockaway, Gertrude 1948.17
Locke, Anna 1928.36
Locke, Carolina 1900.52
Locke, Caroline 1906.17
Locke, Carrie 1900.28
Locke, Charles E. 1890.16, 1890.37, 1890.40
Locke, Charles O. 1930.37
Locke, David R. 1906.01
Locke, E.A. 1876.32, 1876.35, 1877.02, 1878.19, 1880.41, 1889.31
Locke, Edward 1903.12, 1927.55
Locke, Fred 1935.12
Locke, Harry 1928.36
Locke, J.P. 1885.04
Locke, Mary Susan 1959.24
Locke, Matthew 1870.15
Locke, Messr. 1882.15
Locke, Ralph 1924.10, 1932.20
Locke, Sam 1940.18, 1942.26, 1946.15, 1955.25
Locke, Sam D. 1942.05
Locke, Samuel 1939.26
Locke-Elliott, Sumner 1953.17
Lockery, Leslie J. 1992.18
Lockett, Angela 1998.21
Lockett, Jimmy 1992.12
Lockett, Lou 1917.37
Lockford, Naro 1922.11
Lockford, Zita 1922.11, 1922.36
Lockhart, Calvin 1980.05
Lockhart, Dorothy 1912.11
Lockhart, Eugene 1917.20, 1923.25
Lockhart, Gene 1926.11, 1937.10
Lockhart, Helen 1928.34
Lockhart, Warren 1971.11
Lockin, Danny 1964.17
Lockley, Michael 1993.12
Lockname, Clement 1896.50
Lockroy 1869.24, 1877.12, 1878.09, 1882.29
Lockwood, Bee 1924.36
Lockwood, C.G. 1865.03
Lockwood, Gladys 1904.03, 1905.13
Lockwood, Gussie 1876.03
Lockwood, Miss 1876.03
Lockwood, Ruth 1928.32, 1938.17
Lockwood, Ruth Mary 1921.08
Lodella, Will 1906.48
Loder, Charles A. 1897.38
Loder, E.J. 1859.09
Loder, Edward 1851.02
Loder, George 1839.01, 1840.01, 1840.04, 1851.02, 1851.03, 1851.05
Loder, Mrs. George 1851.02
Lodge, Ben 1891.44, 1893.40, 1896.21, 1897.21, 1897.46
Lodge, Henry 1944.32
Lodge, John 1941.02
Lodge, Muriel 1919.14, 1920.09
Loe, Clarence 1940.02
Loe, Herr 1879.62
Loe, M. 1883.44
Loe, Mme. 1884.18, 1884.64, 1886.04, 1886.30, 1887.50, 1888.20, 1888.35, 1889.04, 1889.16, 1889.23, 1889.40, 1890.01, 1891.12, 1891.17, 1891.22, 1891.30, 1892.03, 1892.07, 1892.16, 1892.28, 1893.05, 1894.24
Loeb, Charles 1987.06
Loeb, D.S. 1894.22, 1895.07
Loeb, Frankie 1899.30, 1902.29
Loeb, John Jacob 1931.26, 1933.20, 1955.14, 1979.14
Loeb, Philip 1925.17, 1926.12, 1926.13, 1927.27, 1928.30, 1930.18, 1930.33, 1931.16, 1932.17, 1933.25, 1934.19, 1935.03, 1938.09, 1939.29, 1944.29
Loeb, William 1976.32
Loebell, Marc 1925.20, 1926.17, 1927.23, 1928.19, 1929.20
Loebell, Mark 1919.38
Loehr, Matt 2001.05
Loesch, F. 1889.03
Loesch, George 1877.20, 1880.32, 1880.35, 1888.07, 1888.12, 1889.14, 1889.48, 1890.06, 1891.06, 1891.07, 1891.28
Loesch, George A. 1883.39
Loesch, George E. 1883.39
Loesser, Emily 1990.02
Loesser, Frank 1936.01, 1942.12, 1947.05, 1948.26, 1950.17, 1951.02, 1955.06, 1955.13, 1956.04, 1959.02, 1960.05, 1961.22, 1965.15, 1966.07, 1966.08, 1966.11, 1966.13, 1967.13, 1974.25, 1975.12, 1976.21, 1976.32, 1978.09, 1979.26, 1980.29, 1988.08, 1990.16, 1991.09, 1991.10, 1992.01, 1992.04, 1992.18, 1995.05, 1997.01, 1999.07
Loesser, Lynn 1956.04
Loew, E.M. 1943.20
Loewe, Edmund 1896.23
Loewe, Frederick 1936.01, 1938.15, 1943.21, 1945.19, 1947.07, 1950.10, 1951.24, 1956.01, 1957.03, 1960.21, 1961.25, 1962.15, 1963.02, 1963.04, 1964.20, 1964.46, 1965.08, 1967.11, 1967.17, 1968.17, 1973.12, 1973.17, 1974.09, 1976.05, 1980.19, 1980.26, 1981.19, 1981.26, 1986.03, 1986.04, 1991.12, 1993.11, 1993.18, 1996.13, 1999.01, 1999.23
Loewinger, Guggi 1984.03
Loff, Jeanette 1931.28
Lofman, Carl O. 1983.19
Lofsnes, Martin 1998.10
Loft, Phyllis 1927.02
Loftin, Robert 1988.07
Loftis, Linda 1964.28
Lofton, Michael 1992.14
Loftus, Cecilia 1906.48, 1907.58
Loftus, Cissie 1898.69, 1899.35, 1900.14, 1900.48, 1900.55
Loftus, Gladys 1916.10
Loftus, Kitty 1899.37
Loftus, Marie 1884.44
Loftus, Walter 1895.40
Logan, A. 1869.36
Logan, Alice 1868.23, 1869.08, 1869.39, 1870.01, 1881.10, 1886.13
Logan, Ella 1934.39, 1939.25, 1941.11, 1942.24, 1947.03
Logan, Frederic K. 1900.57
Logan, Frederick K. 1902.25
Logan, Frederick Knight 1910.06, 1911.04, 1912.06
Logan, George 1918.31
Logan, Gladys 1917.35
Logan, Grace 1868.23, 1879.50, 1879.56
Logan, Hugh 1895.10
Logan, Joseph 1886.42
Logan, Joseph H. 1885.49, 1885.66
Logan, Joshua 1938.05, 1938.11, 1939.13, 1940.03, 1940.06, 1942.15, 1942.20, 1946.12, 1949.04, 1952.10, 1954.15, 1955.07, 1957.06, 1961.12, 1962.04, 1962.20, 1965.20, 1967.10, 1970.08, 1987.03
Logan, Kate 1868.32, 1869.08
Logan, Michael 1965.28
Logan, Nedda Harrigan 1985.02
Logan, Olive 1878.14
Logan, Paul 1895.16
Logan, Ron 1994.04
Logan, Stacey 1992.02, 1994.04, 1997.10
Logan, Stanley 1923.26, 1928.48, 1929.17, 1929.28
Logan, Tony 1876.03
Loggins, Kenny 1998.13
Logheder, Luigi R. 1887.05
Logue, Elizabeth 1950.10, 1951.15
Lohmann, A. 1885.69
Lohmuller, Bernard 1924.31, 1925.25, 1925.40, 1925.48, 1926.23, 1927.02, 1927.35, 1928.23, 1929.26, 1929.50
Lohner, Fritz 1946.16, 1982.16, 1999.05
Lohner-Beda, Fritz 1917.30, 1931.09, 1937.03
Lohr, L. 1918.21
Loibl, Frl. 1897.08
Loiret, Eugene 1859.10
Lokos, Allan 1965.28
Lomakina, Mme. 1922.06
Loman, Hal 1951.23, 1956.02
Lomas, Sallie 1905.13
Lomas, Tom 1935.15
Lomax, Allan 1966.15
Lomax, Betty 1926.22
Lomax, Dodson 1888.08
Lomax, John A. 1999.09
Lomax, Lawrence 1937.09
Lomax, Rosemary 1939.07
Lomax, Terry 1963.01
Lombard, Leda 1932.14
Lombard, Michael 1991.15
Lombard, Peter 1961.10
Lombard, Thomas C. 1880.19
Lombardi, Robert 1964.06
Lombardo, Carlo 1935.02
Lombardo, Carmen 1932.24, 1955.14, 1979.14
Lombardo, Sal 1964.40
Lomeka, Michael 1998.20, 1999.21
LoMier, Charles 1903.09, 1908.12
LoMier, Helen 1903.09, 1908.12
LoMonaco, Thomas 1981.25
Lomonier, Tom 1899.33
London Burlesque Combination 1869.25, 1869.28
London, Amy Jane 1989.29
London, Barbara 1959.13
London, Bobby 1977.18
London, David 1927.47, 1928.31, 1929.33, 1959.11, 1959.25, 1961.20
London, Louis 1912.17
London, Zach 1995.19
London, Zachary 1991.09
Londoner, Dorothy Jane 1916.02
Londorini, Signor 1876.07
Lone, Robert 1962.04, 1968.13
Lonergan, Arthur 1945.16
Lonergan, John 1929.33, 1933.15, 1934.15
Lonergan, John E. 1930.33, 1930.35
Lonergan, Jr., Lester 1935.16, 1942.11
Lonergan, Lenore 1950.02, 1952.07
Lonergan, Lester 1894.27
Long, Avon 1936.30, 1939.28, 1942.03, 1943.15, 1944.03, 1945.08, 1945.13, 1946.24, 1951.11, 1952.08, 1954.16, 1963.22, 1965.03, 1972.10, 1976.04
Long, Bob 1936.05
Long, Brenda 1959.27
Long, C. 1864.12
Long, Charles 1864.15
Long, Fay 1937.06
Long, Frank 1898.64
Long, Harry 1927.07
Long, Helen 1920.31
Long, J.N. 1879.64, 1880.38, 1882.76, 1886.01
Long, J.P. 1915.07, 1921.12, 1964.28
Long, Jodi Kim 1962.24
Long, Johnny Lee 1930.24, 1932.08
Long, Joseph 1934.15
Long, Jr., Nick 1924.02, 1926.46, 1928.02, 1929.32, 1932.03, 1934.35, 1940.08
Long, Jr., Walter B. 1938.13
Long, Lily 1926.15
Long, Morey 1902.11
Long, Natalie 1930.24, 1932.08
Long, Nick 1884.12, 1895.37, 1899.37, 1900.07, 1901.23, 1904.43, 1943.20
Long, Nigel 1999.02
Long, Ray 1943.05, 1949.17
Long, Richie 1935.14
Long, Robert 1934.43
Long, Sadie 1902.26, 1904.49
Long, Sally 1922.27
Long, Sarah 1876.35
Long, Shorty 1956.04
Long, Tamara 1974.02
Long, Verna 1935.18, 1937.06
Long, Violet 1907.38
Long, Walter 1888.36, 1890.10, 1940.12, 1944.14, 1946.23
Long, William Ivey 1979.24, 1982.09, 1983.21, 1986.20, 1988.07, 1989.07, 1992.02, 1992.04, 1994.12, 1995.03, 1995.11, 1995.19, 1996.08, 1996.14, 1996.15, 1997.07, 1997.12, 1997.15, 1997.22, 1998.04, 1998.20, 1999.04, 1999.08, 1999.21, 1999.24, 2000.07, 2000.11, 2000.18, 2000.19, 2001.05
Long, Zola 1967.01
Longbottom, Robert 1997.17, 1997.19, 1999.13
Longfellow 1887.01
Longfellow, Henry Wadsworth 1880.10
Longley, Marie 1880.07
Longmore, Marie 1869.23, 1870.07, 1870.15, 1870.35, 1870.42
Longstreet, Stephen 1947.16, 1989.03
Longworth, D.G. 1884.18, 1886.06
Lonnen, E.J. 1889.54
Lonsdale, Frederic 1923.38
Lonsdale, Frederick 1911.06, 1911.14, 1916.20, 1918.27, 1919.42, 1922.36, 1926.33
Lonsdale, Harold 1909.01, 1910.21
Lontin, Mlle. 1884.40
Loo, Richard 1949.04
Loomis, Amelia 1925.18
Loomis, Clarence 1939.21
Loomis, Joe 1937.09
Loomis, Joe E. 1927.27
Loomis, Madge 1918.23
Loomis, Maxine 1932.24
Loomis, Nellie 1897.26
Loomis, Virginia 1932.24
Loos, Anita 1930.06, 1949.18, 1974.02, 1995.07
Loose, Harry 1939.28
Loowrie, Jeanette 1902.27
Lope, Lita 1932.19
Loper, Don 1939.12, 1940.23
Loper, Edward 1902.32
Lopez, Carlos 1930.35, 1994.07, 1994.09, 1999.04
Lopez, Carmen 1917.25, 1917.33, 1919.17
Lopez, Francis 1955.14
Lopez, Guido 1981.09
Lopez, Jose 1988.15
Lopez, Lillian 1976.04
Lopez, Mara 1941.07
Lopez, Maria Luisa 1939.18
Lopez, Matilde 1921.39
Lopez, Miss 1862.02
Lopez, Pilar 1942.14
Lopez, Priscilla 1972.23, 1975.15, 1980.08
Lopez, Vincent 1921.06, 1924.32, 1928.23
Lopez, Zenia 1949.07
Lopokova, Lydia 1912.39, 1915.05, 1921.03
Lopouhin, Peter 1938.13

Loquasto, Santo 1978.18, 1978.22, 1978.26, 1979.03, 1985.08, 1989.26, 1993.02, 1998.01, 1999.01
Loraine, Alice 1897.26
Loraine, Emma 1878.04
Loraine, Karol 1945.19
Loraine, Miss 1883.06
Loraine, Natalie 1926.30
Loraine, Oscar 1924.16
Loraine, William 1921.19
Lorance, Milton 1927.11
Lorber, Martha 1919.20, 1920.34, 1921.23, 1922.19, 1923.20, 1924.18, 1925.10, 1926.41
Lorber, Samuel 1931.34
Lorca, Roberto 1969.11
Lorco, Roberta 1973.17
Lord and Taylor 1902.19, 1903.11, 1904.42, 1905.57, 1906.27, 1907.34, 1907.36, 1908.36, 1909.17, 1910.05, 1910.12, 1910.21, 1911.27, 1911.41, 1912.26, 1913.04, 1928.21
Lord, Bob 1953.09
Lord, Bruce 1945.03
Lord, Helen 1898.68, 1902.07, 1903.14
Lord, Leonard 1930.23
Lord, Mindret 1929.51, 1934.06, 1936.12
Lord, Philip 1925.35, 1926.13, 1931.28, 1931.42, 1932.06
Lord, Sylvia 1962.02
Lorear, Larri N. 1930.24
Loredo, Armando 1938.16
Loree, Elena 1926.22
Loreit, Messr. 1869.29
Lorella, Colie 1922.30
Lorella, Coly 1917.22
Lorellas, The Great 1878.05
Lorendo, Cam 1975.06
Lorenz, Doris 1957.17
Lorenz, Frank 1895.40, 1898.64
Lorenz, Fred 1939.23, 1940.04
Lorenz, Hermine 1885.01
Lorenz, John 1909.14, 1911.26
Lorenz, John A. 1943.16
Lorenz, M.H. 1899.34
Lorenz, Mart 1908.13
Lorenz, Paul 1935.11
Lorenz, Robert 1944.33
Lorenze, Mercedes 1918.06
Lorenzo, Ange 1980.08
Lorenzo, Katrini 1884.58
Lorenzo, Mr. 1929.11
Loreto, Richard 1974.12, 1982.15
Lorett, Adelaide 1916.15
Loretta, Dee 1920.42
Loretta, Mariette 1916.15
Lorette, Mariette 1915.24
Lorick, Robert 1983.21
Lorimer, J. 1918.23
Lorimer, Myrtle 1906.03
Lorimer, Robert 1969.09
Lorimer, Thomas 1945.03
Lorin 1964.02
Loring, Anita 1927.20
Loring, August 1931.35
Loring, Bonita 1897.04
Loring, Bonnie Bonita 1899.18
Loring, Edith 1879.35
Loring, Estelle 1945.19, 1947.21, 1948.14
Loring, Eugene 1939.20, 1943.24, 1945.06, 1946.09, 1952.05, 1952.13, 1955.02
Loring, Gus 1944.13
Loring, L.J. 1883.68, 1885.10, 1886.05
Loring, Louisa 1879.38, 1880.24
Loring, Louise 1880.34
Loring, Michael 1938.04, 1938.09
Loring, Norman 1926.41
Lorman, Ron 1988.05
Lorne, Marion 1950.03
Lorner, James 1928.45
Lorrain, Andree 1939.31
Lorrain, Cecil 1897.04
Lorrain, Percy 1887.23
Lorraine 1879.12
Lorraine, Andree 1898.05
Lorraine, Belle 1898.02, 1900.08
Lorraine, Betty 1946.10
Lorraine, Cecil 1898.40
Lorraine, Claire 1916.18
Lorraine, Emma 1878.19
Lorraine, Ethel 1917.16
Lorraine, Gaby 1920.47
Lorraine, Hattie 1907.10, 1908.21, 1909.24
Lorraine, Hatty 1907.32
Lorraine, Lena 1891.36
Lorraine, Lillian 1908.39, 1909.13, 1910.18, 1911.24, 1912.02, 1912.38, 1918.19, 1919.34, 1922.02
Lorraine, Lina 1881.22
Lorraine, Natalie 1926.22
Lorraine, Oscar 1925.25
Lorraine, Ted 1915.17, 1917.31, 1918.42, 1919.16, 1920.22, 1920.23, 1921.02, 1921.14
Lorraine, William 1902.11, 1903.24, 1905.52, 1910.08, 1912.14
Lorraine-Holt, Janice 1992.08
Lorrane, Lillian 1917.29
Lorrimer, Lou 1917.16
Lorrimer, William 1916.15
Lortel, Lucille 1988.02
Lorwin, Liza 1988.05
Losch, Lee 1922.30
Losch, Tilly 1928.42, 1929.51, 1931.05, 1931.16
Loseby, Constance 1886.50, 1886.54
Losee, Frank 1883.43, 1885.46
Losee, Harry 1934.18, 1935.12, 1936.31
Losey, Jana 2000.02
Losk, Diana 1986.03
Lossky, Vladimir 1925.46, 1925.51
Lota, Remo 1947.02
Lothian, C.E. 1885.69
Lothian, Jr., Napier 1881.21, 1890.50, 1891.13, 1892.20, 1892.30, 1893.50, 1895.33, 1897.18
Lothian, Miss 1861.03
Lothian, Napier 1868.03, 1869.11, 1872.11, 1881.07
Loti, Sylvia 1910.35
Lotito, Mark 1992.01, 1995.15, 1999.22
Loton, Jennie 1882.49
Lott, Harry 1902.03
Lott, Michael 1986.03
Lott, Myra 1936.06
Lotta 1885.68
Lotta, Miss 1867.29
Lottie, Little 1887.25
Lotto, Fred 1884.40, 1895.35
Lotty and Brice 1922.28
Lou, Cindy 1997.04
Loubet, Phoebe 1905.44, 1908.36
Loud, David 1981.27, 1993.10, 1995.11, 1997.07, 1998.01, 2001.01
Loud, Ed 1934.15
Loudon, Dorothy 1962.24, 1968.19, 1969.01, 1977.06, 1978.27, 1985.19, 1994.13
Loughborough, William 1981.16
Loughlin, Jack 1909.29
Loughrane, Basil 1925.19
Loughrey, J.B. 1907.32, 1908.25
Loughrin, J.A. 1882.09, 1883.11, 1883.12, 1883.13
Louiguy 1955.14, 1961.25, 1963.02, 1965.08, 1968.20, 1973.17, 1981.04, 1999.07
Louire, Miles 1976.34
Louis and Macaughtry 1900.48
Louis, A. 1875.31
Louis, Andy 1902.21, 1903.01
Louis, Eugene 1956.16
Louis, F. 1871.11
Louis, Jean 1871.09
Louis, Kim 1999.12
Louis, Master 1879.07
Louis, Maud 1905.51
Louis, Mr. 1869.26
Louis, Willard 1912.31, 1915.16
Louis, Willard S. 1905.51
Louise Beaudet Opera Bouffe Company 1894.47
Louise, Emily 1921.42
Louise, Ivy 1904.29
Louise, Marie 1959.08, 1959.17
Louise, Mary 1956.06, 1958.11, 1962.16, 1963.21, 1966.18, 1975.21
Louise, Merle 1970.13, 1979.06, 1987.18, 1993.09
Louise, Mlle. 1868.18, 1870.44, 1871.27, 1872.33, 1875.33, 1879.36, 1879.39, 1879.47, 1879.55, 1880.52, 1884.43, 1888.10
Louise, Rose 1932.07, 1933.03
Louise, Tina 1952.20, 1953.17, 1956.12, 1964.21
Louiselle, Bryan 1995.08, 1997.05
Loukin, Messr. 1923.28
Lounsberry, James 1921.05
Lounsbery, James 1915.30, 1918.02
Louther, William 1964.21
Louw, Allan 1965.36, 1967.01
Louys, Pierre 1919.38
Love, Andy 1937.16
Love, Darlene 1985.03, 1988.12
Love, Dorothy 1949.17, 1953.01
Love, Edmund G. 1961.28
Love, Ellen 1929.33, 1943.04, 1944.32
Love, Geoff 1990.05
Love, James K. 1930.16
Love, Kermit 1937.02, 1937.12, 1943.19, 1946.19
Love, Kimara 1978.23
Love, Mabel 1895.29
Love, Margaret 1906.05, 1925.21
Love, Mike 1982.22
Love, Mr. 1852.04
Love, Mrs. Valentine 1869.02
Love, Pee Wee 1991.01
Love, Ralph 1924.37
Love, Valentine 1869.02
Loveday, Louie 1894.18
Lovejoy, Alec 1923.11
Lovejoy, Alex 1930.19, 1936.30
Lovejoy, Bertha 1884.58, 1896.42, 1897.13, 1900.32
Lovelace, Alice 1897.21
Lovelace, Edith 1897.21
Lovelace, Fanny 1870.05
Lovelace, Henrietta 1940.01
Lovelace, Kamara 1979.27
Lovelace, N. 1900.49
Lovell, A. 1879.50
Lovell, Jane 1903.18, 1905.28, 1906.24
Lovell, Katherine H. 1917.16
Lovell, Susan 1953.08
Lovelle, Louise 1933.06
Lovelock, V. 1885.67
Lover 1859.15
Lover, Samuel 1885.53, 1886.44, 1890.06, 1917.26
Loveridge, Marguerite 1909.08
Lovesee, George 1941.13
Lovett, Beresford 1927.04
Lovett, C.E. 1868.06
Lovett, Dylan 1997.12
Lovett, Josephine 1899.03, 1899.27, 1900.36, 1901.15
Lovett, Marcus 1987.04, 1997.12
Lovette, Alice 1885.68
Loving, Keith 1976.34
Loving, Max 1987.12
Lovitz, John B. 1908.21
Lovreiglio, Chavalier 1927.22
Low, Betty 1946.20, 1950.06, 1959.04
Low, Carl 1979.17
Low, Frieda 1920.46
Low, William H. 1908.37
Lowande, Oscar 1927.17
Lowe, Alan 1928.30
Lowe, Allen 1902.21, 1904.25, 1907.03
Lowe, Bernie 1989.12
Lowe, Charles 1961.01
Lowe, David 1947.21, 1948.16
Lowe, Donna 1978.18
Lowe, Edith 1906.39, 1913.28
Lowe, Herry Shaw 1958.19
Lowe, Isabel 1918.20
Lowe, Isabelle 1918.42
Lowe, Jackie 1983.21, 1985.20
Lowe, Joan 1962.01, 1964.11
Lowe, John 1919.12, 1920.22, 1920.23, 1921.02
Lowe, John V. 1921.14, 1922.11, 1923.22, 1924.06
Lowe, Marvin 2000.03
Lowe, Milton 1946.16
Lowe, Ralph 1951.02
Lowe, Robert 1898.69, 1937.11
Lowe, Roslyn 1949.04
Lowe, Roslynd 1952.10
Lowe, Ruth 1974.11, 1979.24
Lowe, Van 1925.25, 1925.48, 1926.11
Lowe, W. 1891.41
Lowell, Allan 1946.13, 1947.14
Lowell, Estella 1880.13
Lowell, Ethel 1899.36
Lowell, Helen 1883.24, 1883.39, 1883.65, 1884.06, 1885.64, 1891.15, 1912.41, 1916.13, 1917.32, 1927.38
Lowell, Helene 1891.46
Lowell, Marten 1942.19
Lowell, Mollie 1910.21
Lowens, Curt 1965.04
Lowenstein, David 1989.03, 1995.19, 1996.15, 1997.15
Lowenworth, Ann 1923.17
Lowery, Mae 1898.47
Lowery, May 1900.52
Lowery, Melvin 1976.26, 1977.11
Lowey, Marilyn 1986.18, 1990.19
Lowitz, John 1908.08
Lowitz, John B. 1904.30, 1904.43, 1908.10
Lowitz, W.W. 1892.17
Lownie, Den 1910.17
Lowrey, Arthur 1889.02
Lowrey, Gwendolyn 1915.21
Lowrie, Arthur 1916.20
Lowrie, Jeanette 1906.18, 1919.23
Lowrie, Jeannette 1904.03, 1918.04
Lowrie, Nettie 1889.37, 1889.51
Lowrie, Renee 1924.46
Lowry, Ed "Scooter" 1936.06
Lowry, Hazel 1908.09
Lowry, June 1904.28
Lowry, Terence 1914.24
Lowther, Hugh Cecil 1886.50, 1886.54
Lowther, William C. 1898.67
Lozier, Lionel 1908.39, 1909.25
Lozito, Allan 1976.20
Lubar, Cynthia 1975.10
Lube, Dr. 1880.61
Lube, Frau 1879.62, 1880.20, 1880.66
Lube, Frl. 1880.61
Lube, Herr 1879.57, 1879.62, 1880.20, 1880.61, 1880.66, 1883.35
Lube, J. 1883.44
Lube, Max 1880.66, 1885.01, 1885.27, 1890.01, 1890.11, 1890.19, 1890.24
Lube, Mme. 1883.44
Lubell, Lily 1922.20, 1924.14, 1925.20, 1926.17, 1927.23, 1928.19
Lubin 1914.23
Lubin, Harry 1931.29
Lubin, Joe 1982.22, 1986.02
Lubin, Miss 1881.41
Lubin, Mme. 1907.42
Lublov, Bela 1936.27
Lubovitch, Lar 1987.18, 1993.19, 1996.05, 1998.05
Lubritsky, David 1942.28
Luby, Edna 1903.37, 1907.24
Luby, Roger 1981.28
Lucas, Clarence 1908.43
Lucas, Craig 1975.03
Lucas, Daisy 1900.33, 1903.18, 1907.26
Lucas, Doug 1971.12, 1977.18
Lucas, Harry 1928.18
Lucas, Helene 1901.21
Lucas, Jamilah 1984.06
Lucas, Jane 1973.09, 1989.18
Lucas, Joan 1977.18
Lucas, Jonathan 1948.22, 1949.12, 1952.07, 1954.03, 1959.06, 1960.12
Lucas, Lauren 1972.03
Lucas, Mary 1923.10, 1927.09
Lucas, May 1894.33
Lucas, Mira 1878.21
Lucas, Nick 1926.03, 1949.09
Lucas, Philip 1965.15, 1965.20, 1967.10
Lucas, Roxie 1982.11, 1985.02
Lucas, Rupert 1928.44
Lucas, Sam 1907.22, 1909.10
Luce, Alexis 1924.42
Luce, Clair 1924.34, 1924.44
Luce, Claire 1926.18, 1927.37, 1932.26
Luce, Edna 1921.06
Luce, Ted 1947.20, 1950.09
Lucelle, Fannie 1872.34
Lucette, Madeleine 1881.07, 1887.20, 1888.19
Lucette, Madeline 1882.70, 1883.38, 1885.63, 1887.15
Lucey, Leola 1911.07, 1916.05
Lucia, Victor 1967.15
Lucien, Messr. 1867.05
Lucien, Mons. 1866.29
Lucier, Fred 1898.75
Lucier, Mlle. 1875.28
Lucile 1911.13, 1912.47, 1914.33, 1915.19, 1917.18, 1917.36, 1919.08
Lucile, Ltd. 1911.08, 1916.16, 1917.37, 1918.02, 1919.36
Lucille 1911.17, 1916.24, 1918.16, 1918.30
Lucille, Ltd. 1911.39, 1911.42, 1922.17
Lucior, Luce 1929.10
Luck, Harry 1912.38
Lucke, Lydia 1930.41
Lucker, Bruce 1997.03
Lucker, Leo 1957.11, 1958.03
Luckett, Edith 1914.29
Luckey, Susan 1959.22
Luckman, D.G. 1892.19

Luckstone, Harry 1890.04, 1893.31, 1896.02, 1897.28, 1898.25, 1899.20, 1900.26
Luckstone, J. 1896.33
Luckstone, Minnie 1887.02, 1887.42, 1888.25, 1889.43, 1890.36, 1894.52
Luckstone, Miss 1890.36
Lucy Escott Opera Troupe 1858.03
Lucy, Arnold 1927.49
Lucy, Chapin 1882.27
Lucyk, Michael 1947.04
Lucyor, Luce 1929.15, 1929.16
Ludd, Patricia 1981.21
Luders, Gustav 1898.16, 1899.11, 1899.29, 1900.59, 1902.18, 1903.10, 1903.40, 1904.16, 1904.37, 1904.52, 1905.16, 1905.54, 1906.16, 1907.13, 1907.17, 1908.30, 1909.03, 1910.02, 1912.42, 1913.01, 1930.01
Ludgin, Chester 1957.13, 1958.15, 1958.16, 1959.07, 1959.16, 1959.17, 1959.21, 1960.03, 1987.08
Ludington, Helen 1898.45, 1899.32
Ludlam, Miss 1852.02
Ludlow, Ben 1937.02, 1937.12, 1938.12, 1939.10, 1946.10
Ludlow, E.B. 1886.39
Ludlow, Jennie 1886.17
Ludlow, Jr., Ben 1950.11
Ludlow, Patrick 1929.41
Ludlow, Wandah 1907.50
Ludmila, Anna 1920.36
Ludmilla, Anna 1924.32
Ludovic, Mons. 1875.25, 1875.28, 1875.29, 1875.30, 1875.33
Ludvinsky, Sholom 1965.32
Ludwig Zwieback and Brother 1914.25
Ludwig, Arthur 1924.28
Ludwig, George 1932.22
Ludwig, James E. 1906.23
Ludwig, Joseph 1896.14
Ludwig, Ken 1992.02, 2001.06
Ludwig, Mr. 1897.35
Lueck, Mr. 1891.33, 1892.43, 1893.29, 1894.01
Luescher, Mark A. 1910.37, 1911.13, 1912.15, 1913.24, 1913.27
Luft, Joe 1967.11
Luft, Loran 1967.11
Luft, Sid 1967.11
Luft, Uriel G. 1972.08
Luftig, Hal 1991.05, 1992.08, 1997.03, 1998.05, 1999.04, 2000.18
Lugenbeal, Carol Jo 1974.25, 1978.02
Lugosi, Bela 1925.37, 1933.20
Lui, Va 1884.40
Lui, Wonci 1956.03
Luiken, Carol 1976.31, 1978.08
Luis, Pepe 1919.17
Luisa, Mlle. 1866.12
Luisi, James 1966.01, 1968.30
Luisidi, Mlle. 1866.18
Lukas, Paul 1950.15
Lukcso, David 1981.21
Luke, G.B. 1897.38
Luke, Keye 1958.19
Luke, Messr. 1866.08
Luker, Rebecca 1988.01, 1991.05, 1994.08, 1996.13, 1998.03, 2000.11
Luketas, R. 1927.10
Lukie, Annie 1885.26, 1885.58
Lull, Dorothy 1928.23
Lully, Jean Baptiste 1946.02
Lulu Glaser and Company 1900.54
Lulu, Emily 1881.39
Lum, Alvin 1970.21, 1971.18, 1989.05, 1989.29
Lum, Frances 1880.65
Lum, James 1912.44
Luman, Carl 1948.17
Lumb, Geoffrey 1950.15, 1963.01
Lumbard, Dirk 1980.07, 1983.02, 1998.06, 1999.11
Lumet, Baruch 1937.01
Lumet, Sidney 1937.01, 1962.24
Lumpkin, Bruce 1989.26
Lumpkin, Patricia 1978.03
Lumsden, D. Mack 1901.21
Lumsden, D.M. 1903.41, 1905.28
Luna y Carne, Pablo 1949.07
Luna, Barbara 1949.04
Luna, Jovita 1985.07, 1999.18
Lunceford, Jimmy 1974.10, 1989.02
Lund, Alan 1971.21
Lund, Art 1956.04, 1959.02, 1961.14, 1962.16, 1963.12, 1966.08
Lund, Dian 1951.20
Lund, Herb 1930.42
Lund, Hettice 1900.37
Lund, John 1903.37, 1904.51, 1904.57, 1905.11, 1905.57, 1907.36, 1908.40, 1910.14, 1912.37, 1912.49, 1913.15, 1913.23, 1914.21, 1942.34, 1943.07
Lund, Karen 1944.21
Lund, Lee 1968.18
Lund, Marie 1942.34
Lundberg, Elizabeth 1996.15, 1997.22
Lundborg, Arne 1936.01
Lundell, Kert 1971.01, 1971.13, 1972.10, 1975.05, 1976.11, 1989.17
Lundell, Kert F. 1976.03
Lundgreen, Margo 1960.04
Lundon, Mary 1942.09, 1944.08, 1944.09, 1944.10, 1944.11, 1944.12
Lundquist Scenic Studio 1917.05
Lundy, J. 1866.05
Lundy, J.H. 1885.47
Lundy, John 1868.25, 1868.27, 1871.27
Lundy, John D. 1868.07
Luneska, Gene 1904.12, 1908.34, 1909.25
Lunick, Olga 1946.01, 1948.17
Lupino, Barry 1916.03, 1927.55, 1928.48, 1929.48
Lupino, Jr., Barry 1929.48
Lupino, Stanley 1926.26, 1927.01
Lupo, Eugenia 1867.25, 1872.37
Lupo, Giovanni 1867.25
Lupo, Mlle. 1870.41
LuPone, Patti 1973.16, 1975.18, 1978.12, 1979.23, 1984.07, 1987.15, 1995.12
LuPone, Robert 1968.18, 1968.19, 1974.13, 1975.15, 1987.14
Lupton, LaVerne 1942.18
Lupue, Maurice 1922.21
Luquet, M. 1929.10
Lurch, Tilly 1873.26
Lurenz, Betty 1989.11
Lurie, Carol 1978.02, 1980.30, 1982.18, 1983.10
Lurie, Victor 1975.19
Lurio, Don 1954.13
Lusby, Vernon 1948.15, 1957.18, 1961.21, 1962.15, 1963.04, 1963.06, 1963.26, 1965.21, 1969.02, 1969.07
Lusk, Milton 1914.17, 1921.28
Lusk, Milton W. 1906.36, 1908.31
Luskin, Jean 1982.03
Lussa, Raymond 1980.16
Lussier, Laura 1922.09
Lustberg, Arch 1972.13
Lustik, Marlena 1966.05
Lusuaradi, Mlle. 1872.10
Lutgenhorst, Manuel 1980.04, 1980.25
Luther, Clyde 1903.09
Luther, Doug 1951.23
Luther, Douglas 1948.28
Luther, Frank 1943.20
Luther, Harry H. 1907.49
Luther, Jane 1938.04
Luther, Jean 1938.04
Lutie, Miss 1929.51
Lutken, David M. 1999.08
Luttrell, Helen 1914.08
Lutyens, Edith 1947.10, 1948.29
Lutz, Clarence 1909.02, 1917.06
Lutz, Henry 1914.15
Lutz, Meyer 1879.50, 1884.44, 1888.11, 1888.38, 1888.41, 1889.54, 1903.33
Lutz, Myer 1899.21
Lutz, W. Meyer 1886.45, 1888.11, 1888.38
Lutz, William 1967.10
Lutzkmeyer 1881.32
Lux, Lillian 1968.22
Luxemburg 1977.17
Luxemburg, Leslie 1978.19, 1979.20
Luz, Franc 1979.05
Luzzi, A.E. 1908.36
Lyberopoulo, Notty 1907.14
Lycan, Bryan 1924.43, 1925.32
Lyday, Paul 1948.15
Lydecker, George 1907.17, 1907.33, 1909.26, 1912.08, 1912.26, 1915.07, 1917.25
Lyden, F. 1897.29
Lydia Thompson Company 1871.14, 1877.22, 1877.23, 1877.25
Lydia Thompson Troupe 1870.35, 1872.21, 1872.24
Lydia Thompson's Burlesque Company 1872.22, 1872.26, 1872.34
Lydia Thompson's Burlesque Troupe 1870.42
Lydiard, Bob 1971.06
Lydiard, Robert 1978.04
Lydiate, Annie 1917.02
Lydiate, Maude 1921.35, 1922.28
Lyding, Elsie 1918.41
Lyding, George 1914.29
Lydon, Jimmy 1938.09
Lydon, Ormond 1938.18
Lydwig, George 1918.41
Lydy, Beth 1915.27, 1916.09, 1916.14, 1916.26, 1918.11
Lyford, Nettie 1890.26, 1891.31, 1891.47, 1894.38, 1897.14, 1899.30
Lykens, William 1890.27
Lykens, William L. 1888.08, 1895.11
Lyle, Carl 1915.07, 1917.06
Lyle, Cora 1885.54
Lyle, Daisy 1906.24
Lyle, E.H. 1910.05
Lyle, Edna 1895.22, 1896.05, 1896.45
Lyle, Frances 1928.22
Lyle, Henry 1927.17
Lyle, Herbert 1927.17
Lyle, Jack 1906.06
Lyle, Jocelyn 1928.35
Lyle, Leslie 1900.08
Lyle, Miss 1869.04
Lyle, Nonette 1912.12
Lyle, Richard 1885.54, 1961.26, 1965.18
Lyle-Cortenay, Maude 1900.44
Lyles, Aubrey 1907.31, 1912.36, 1921.16, 1926.14, 1927.33, 1928.10, 1929.37, 1931.47, 1999.06
Lyles, Aubrey L. 1907.55, 1923.39
Lyman, Abe 1976.32
Lyman, Clifford 1908.37
Lyman, Debra 1972.04, 1976.05
Lyman, Ethel 1901.05
Lyman, Francis 1929.17, 1932.14
Lyman, George 1902.43, 1906.27, 1909.14, 1912.27
Lyman, James 1885.36
Lyman, Jimmy 1929.32
Lymon, Frank 1982.22, 1986.02, 1990.15
Lyn, Donna 1960.10
Lyn, Susan 1960.11
Lynam, A. 1890.08
Lynch, Anita 1963.15
Lynch, Bessie 1890.03
Lynch, Charles H. 1904.15
Lynch, Doreen 1925.50
Lynch, Florence 1907.61
Lynch, Frank 1913.35, 1929.24
Lynch, George 1909.30, 1924.24
Lynch, George R. 1912.26, 1920.07
Lynch, Gertrude 1907.61
Lynch, Hal 1963.19
Lynch, J. 1869.33
Lynch, Jack 1920.39
Lynch, Jamie 1906.39
Lynch, Jr., Edward J. 1979.16
Lynch, Kitty 1901.05
Lynch, Lester 2000.03
Lynch, Lori 1996.17
Lynch, Louise 1934.06
Lynch, Matt 1894.07, 1894.35
Lynch, Messr. 1880.43
Lynch, Michael 1989.03
Lynch, Nancy 1955.10
Lynch, Nellie 1895.08, 1896.44, 1900.01, 1900.52, 1905.56, 1910.01
Lynch, Regina 1907.61
Lynch, Rosalie 1907.61
Lynch, Teddy 1934.40
Lynch, Thomas 1992.17, 2000.07, 2000.11
Lynch, Thomas L. 1999.24
Lynch, Tom 1980.27
Lynd, Helen 1928.08, 1928.44, 1931.26, 1936.01
Lynd, Helene 1927.49
Lynd, John 1888.15
Lynd, Mme. 1896.46
Lyndal, Percy 1910.09
Lynde, Joseph 1889.19, 1896.16, 1896.17, 1896.19, 1896.21
Lynde, Laura 1900.56
Lynde, Paul 1952.09, 1956.08, 1960.06, 1962.02
Lyndeck, Edmund 1943.05, 1969.06, 1979.06, 1982.18, 1983.01, 1987.18
Lynden, Frank 1897.24, 1897.55, 1899.22
Lynds, John 1948.26, 1951.02
Lyndwood, Miss 1869.29
Lynehan, J.E. 1908.31
Lynes, Kristi 1993.10, 1995.05
Lyng, Nora Mae 1985.20, 1987.16
Lynn, Agnes 1908.28
Lynn, Bert 1935.04
Lynn, Betty Ann 1946.20
Lynn, Billy 1917.30, 1945.17
Lynn, Elaine 1955.01, 1958.03
Lynn, Eleanor 1939.29
Lynn, Eve 1950.02
Lynn, George 1896.37
Lynn, Harold 1900.12
Lynn, Henri 1893.33
Lynn, Jim 1966.12, 1966.16
Lynn, Joe 1981.29
Lynn, Jonathan 1964.29, 1981.14
Lynn, Judy 1951.23
Lynn, Leni 1949.02
Lynn, Mabel 1902.29, 1903.28
Lynn, Mara 1957.07, 1958.01, 1962.13
Lynn, Maryan 1927.68
Lynn, Neva 1930.08
Lynn, Robert 1927.53
Lynn, Rosamund 1976.19
Lynn, Tobie 1964.17
Lynn, William 1941.05, 1943.01
Lynn-Thomas, Derrick 1950.13, 1951.10
Lynne, Ada 1948.15
Lynne, Ann 1940.02
Lynne, Carol 1928.09, 1942.19, 1944.20
Lynne, Ethel 1929.34, 1929.48, 1930.41
Lynne, Georgia 1920.37
Lynne, Gillian 1965.19, 1965.28, 1967.16, 1982.19, 1988.01, 1990.04
Lynne, Harry 1851.02, 1851.05
Lynne, Henry 1851.03
Lynne, Jessie 1920.37
Lynne, Josie 1890.03
Lynne, Kathleen 1883.67, 1885.08
Lynne, Kitty 1965.05
Lynne, Lotta 1894.36
Lynne, Michael 1983.10
Lynne, Mimi 1943.16
Lynne, Miss 1882.60
Lynne, Olivce 1888.39
Lynne, Phyllis 1946.23
Lynnier, George 1907.55
Lynton, Daisy 1889.35
Lynton, Ethel 1879.02, 1879.64
Lynton, Everett 1925.50
Lyon, Annabelle 1938.15, 1945.05, 1959.04
Lyon, Damon 1897.40, 1902.12
Lyon, Elsa 1913.10
Lyon, Esther 1925.36
Lyon, Ezra 1879.65, 1879.67
Lyon, Frances 1890.50
Lyon, Frank 1922.42
Lyon, Frank A. 1893.31
Lyon, Fred 1925.22, 1926.16, 1929.35, 1934.35
Lyon, Frederic 1923.33
Lyon, Hattie 1871.02
Lyon, Kimberly 1998.15
Lyon, M.D. 1923.35
Lyon, May G. 1906.34
Lyon, Milton 1954.04, 1954.14
Lyon, Miss 1870.02
Lyon, Peter 1908.26
Lyon, Robert 1944.23
Lyon, Wanda 1917.08, 1917.30, 1924.39, 1927.04, 1931.09
Lyons, A.L. 1891.21
Lyons, Adolph 1931.29
Lyons, Arthur 1922.22
Lyons, Bernard 1909.15, 1910.13
Lyons, Collette 1939.25, 1943.20, 1946.01
Lyons, E.D. 1895.17
Lyons, Edmond D. 1889.20
Lyons, Essie 1900.32, 1905.22
Lyons, Esther 1887.52, 1901.21, 1903.41
Lyons, Etta 1888.27, 1888.40, 1891.18
Lyons, Fred 1924.19
Lyons, George 1942.35
Lyons, Harry S. 1881.39
Lyons, Helen 1919.06, 1921.03, 1924.44, 1932.05
Lyons, James 1945.02
Lyons, Joan 1925.26
Lyons, Joe 1923.31, 1925.47, 1928.08, 1930.28, 1930.39, 1942.18
Lyons, John 1923.34
Lyons, John L. 1921.41
Lyons, Joseph 1939.22
Lyons, Julius J. 1884.22, 1885.08, 1885.41, 1888.19, 1892.47
Lyons, Laura 1888.27, 1888.40
Lyons, Mary 1976.29
Lyons, Miss 1864.23, 1892.07

Lyons, Nettie 1905.31, 1907.35
Lyons, Tobie 1904.33
Lyons, Toby 1909.12, 1909.18
Lyons, Wanda 1916.03
Lyons, William 1906.34
Lyric Opera Company, The 1940.11, 1940.13, 1940.14, 1940.15
Lysat, Walter 1912.05
Lysinger, Pat 1971.03, 1976.25
Lyster, Fred 1851.05, 1852.06, 1853.02, 1853.03, 1854.02, 1870.40, 1873.29, 1891.38, 1892.07
Lyster, Georgie 1872.43
Lyster, Messr. 1852.01, 1852.05, 1853.01, 1855.01
Lyster, Miss 1851.05
Lyster, Mr. 1851.02, 1851.03, 1852.01, 1852.03
Lytell, Bert 1941.04
Lytell, Blanche 1934.04
Lytell, Florence 1885.34
Lytell, W.H. 1876.36, 1877.04, 1877.15, 1879.16, 1881.02, 1881.13, 1887.27, 1890.17, 1897.21, 1898.01, 1898.31
Lytell, William 1897.29
Lythgoe, David 1902.07, 1902.16
Lythgoe, David H. 1897.52
Lythgow, David 1904.34
Lytle, Ethel 1911.26
Lytle, Marian 1919.08
Lytle, Marjorie 1919.08
Lyttleton, Trevor 1980.08
Lytton, Edward Bulwer 1852.01, 1871.04
Lytton, Emily 1893.12, 1893.38, 1894.09
Lytton, Frances 1886.50
Lytton, Henry 1886.54
Lytton, Margie 1897.26
Lytton, Miss 1892.12
Lytton, Ruby 1897.38

M'Donald, James 1873.22
M'Kenzie, Messr. 1796.02
M.B. Leavitt English Opera Burlesque Company 1880.49
M.M.G. Arena Prodouctions 1989.06
M2 Entertaiment 1982.12
Ma, Jason 1989.05, 1989.25, 1990.17, 1991.03, 2001.09
Maar, Graham 1927.28
Maas, James 1890.39, 1891.12, 1892.03
Maas, Peggy Ayn 1992.02
Mab, Queen 1904.20, 1905.10
Mabee, Ruth 1918.39
Mabel, Little 1886.10
Maberly, Miss 1848.01
Mabie, Dorothea 1927.20
Mable, Ilai 1904.44
Mable, Miss 1904.44
Mabley, Jackie 1932.08, 1939.29
Mabley, Jackie "Moms" 1931.31
Mac 1992.13
Mac, Charles 1923.02, 1924.13
Mac, Little 1866.31, 1866.35
Macaire, Robert 1889.16, 1921.01
MacAleese, Richard 1928.49
Macaleese, Richard 1929.42
Macalush, Crysta 1993.06
Macao 1991.11
Macart, W.H. 1899.11, 1900.49, 1907.13
Macart, William 1905.48
MacArthur, C.E. 1911.25
MacArthur, Charles 1935.15, 1978.02
MacArthur, Claude 1920.37, 1922.31, 1928.34
MacArthur, Claude E. 1917.21
Macarthy, F.J. 1883.11, 1883.12
Macarthy, Harry 1975.22
Macarthy, Marian 1854.04, 1860.01
Macarthy, Mlle. 1873.22
Macarthy, Mr. 1854.04
Macaulay, Joseph 1923.34, 1924.44, 1926.34, 1927.25, 1927.34, 1927.55, 1928.12, 1930.26, 1931.12, 1931.15, 1931.17, 1931.20, 1931.22, 1931.23, 1932.05, 1933.23, 1934.38, 1937.01, 1937.13, 1938.15, 1941.08, 1946.18, 1949.10, 1949.11, 1949.14, 1952.14, 1952.16, 1952.18, 1952.19, 1964.11
MacAvoy, Daniel 1900.56
MacAvoy, James 1896.06
MacBoyle, Darl 1910.17, 1915.27, 1916.26, 1918.23, 1919.15
MacBride, Edith 1908.31, 1913.35
MacBride, Edith Ethel 1906.29, 1909.23
Maccari, Hilda 1890.03
Maccari, Ida 1888.39
MacCarthy, Vincent 1910.04
MacClaskie, Alden 1912.48
MacClellan, Robert 1920.26
MacCloy, June 1928.22, 1932.07
MacColl, Ewan 1966.03
MacColl, James 1934.19, 1935.12, 1939.27, 1942.20, 1945.14, 1946.06
MacCollin, A.F. 1901.05
MacCollin, A.W.F. 1890.37, 1898.09, 1898.14, 1898.15, 1898.16, 1898.19, 1898.30, 1898.39, 1898.40, 1898.42, 1900.02, 1900.04, 1900.09, 1900.11, 1900.13, 1900.14, 1900.17, 1900.18, 1900.21, 1900.22, 1900.27, 1900.29, 1900.30
MacCollins, A.W.F. 1900.23
MacComber, Ken 1928.18
MacConnell, Harry I. 1902.15
MacConnell, Harry T. 1900.20, 1900.35, 1900.41, 1900.47, 1901.08, 1901.13, 1901.21
MacCormick, Langdon 1917.13
MacCracken, James 1952.13
MacDermott, G.H. 1875.19, 1875.23, 1875.26, 1875.35, 1875.36, 1875.37, 1875.38, 1876.01
MacDermott, G.M. 1875.38, 1875.40
MacDermott, Galt 1968.11, 1971.18, 1972.18, 1972.25, 1977.15, 1984.02, 2000.16
MacDermott, Marc 1908.43
MacDevitt, Brian 1997.17
MacDonagh, Donagh 1950.01
MacDonald and Sullivan 1904.50
MacDonald, Ann 1924.14
Macdonald, Ballard 1909.11, 1910.10, 1910.18, 1912.25, 1912.26, 1917.13, 1918.38, 1920.18, 1920.28, 1920.35, 1921.06, 1921.21, 1921.22, 1922.05, 1922.06, 1922.14, 1923.18, 1923.36, 1924.19, 1925.27, 1926.03, 1926.18, 1927.13, 1927.31, 1927.39, 1934.01
MacDonald, Ballard 1921.03, 1927.40, 1927.62, 1930.24, 1930.38, 1934.42, 1952.11
MacDonald, Barbara 1933.05
MacDonald, Bernard 1911.31
MacDonald, Brian 1928.23, 1968.24
Macdonald, Brian 1987.01
MacDonald, Charles 1900.36, 1905.41, 1912.41
MacDonald, Charles F. 1904.56
MacDonald, Christie 1893.35, 1894.29, 1895.19, 1895.26, 1896.28, 1898.25, 1899.19, 1899.37, 1900.12, 1900.34, 1900.47, 1902.01, 1904.04, 1904.37, 1906.07, 1906.47, 1907.63, 1910.04, 1910.14, 1910.37, 1913.24, 1920.09
MacDonald, Cordelia 1919.12
MacDonald, Dave 1982.22
MacDonald, Dinnie 1918.17
MacDonald, Donald 1912.41, 1914.20, 1918.09, 1919.11, 1923.07, 1938.12
Macdonald, Donald 1913.19, 1915.16, 1916.08, 1916.18, 1917.01
MacDonald, Dorothy 1932.14
MacDonald, Earl 1964.46
MacDonald, Gertrude 1929.07
MacDonald, Glen 1911.35
MacDonald, Harl 1943.17
MacDonald, Helen 1922.32
MacDonald, Hugh 1964.29
MacDonald, James 1935.16
Macdonald, James F. 1893.37
MacDonald, James F. 1903.19
MacDonald, Jeanette 1923.34, 1927.49, 1928.07, 1928.46, 1929.06
MacDonald, Jeannette 1925.49
MacDonald, Jet 1946.12, 1946.24, 1951.10
MacDonald, L.T. 1897.39
MacDonald, Loretta 1906.29
MacDonald, Margaret 1891.44, 1893.26
Macdonald, Margaret 1900.19
MacDonald, Marguerite 1894.07
MacDonald, Maxie 1912.49
MacDonald, Miss 1892.20, 1892.29
MacDonald, Mr. 1884.40
MacDonald, Ruth 1937.17
MacDonald, Viola 1902.26
MacDonald, Vivian 1912.38
MacDonald, W.H. 1879.15, 1880.45, 1882.07, 1882.08, 1882.09, 1882.10, 1882.11, 1882.12, 1882.13, 1883.12, 1891.29, 1892.51, 1893.18, 1893.48, 1894.03, 1894.08, 1894.45, 1895.01, 1896.08, 1896.43, 1898.23, 1902.04, 1904.49
Macdonald, W.H. 1893.18, 1893.19
MacDonald, William H. 1896.42, 1897.13, 1900.25, 1900.31, 1900.32, 1902.28
Macdonald-Rouse, Heather 1966.03
MacDonnell, Kyle 1946.20, 1948.04, 1949.12
Macdonough, F. 1881.11
MacDonough, Glen 1893.40, 1893.42, 1895.27, 1896.30, 1897.38, 1898.58, 1898.69, 1899.35, 1900.01, 1900.48, 1901.05, 1901.23, 1903.03, 1903.31, 1904.13, 1904.44, 1904.54, 1905.01, 1905.44, 1906.29, 1908.24, 1909.11, 1909.23, 1910.01, 1911.05, 1912.48, 1914.02, 1915.05, 1916.07, 1917.12, 1918.15, 1919.05, 1920.03, 1920.39, 1924.18, 1929.48, 1930.07, 1980.27
Macdonough, Glen 1910.16, 1912.33
Macdonough, Harry 1881.27, 1882.26, 1883.62, 1884.14, 1885.45, 1886.37, 1887.22, 1887.24, 1887.28, 1887.47, 1889.24, 1890.26, 1890.39, 1891.12, 1891.22, 1891.30, 1892.16, 1892.28, 1892.42, 1894.05, 1894.38, 1895.16, 1897.50, 1902.43, 1907.52, 1911.03, 1911.37, 1913.14, 1913.32
MacDonough, Harry 1892.07, 1897.26, 1898.73, 1900.50, 1904.19, 1905.19, 1905.25, 1907.01
Macdonough, J. 1881.04
MacDonough, James M. 1900.55
Macdonough, John E. 1870.26
MacDonough, Jr., Harry 1910.19
Macdonough, Jr., Harry 1913.14
MacDonough, Thomas B. 1881.31
Mace, Alyce 1946.01, 1948.20
Mace, Fred W. 1904.12
Mace, Hartwell 1976.28
Mace, James W. 1888.05
Mace, Jed 1953.04
Mace, Paul 1970.20, 1979.08
Mace, Sterling 1948.04
Mace, Susie 1889.50, 1891.02
Macedonough, Harry 1891.17
MacElhern, James 1915.28
Macey, Gertrude 1939.12
Macey, Viola 1905.31
MacFadden, James 1947.07
MacFarlane, George 1909.07, 1913.08, 1913.11, 1913.13, 1913.23, 1914.07, 1915.13, 1916.19, 1922.40, 1926.06
MacFarlane, George G. 1912.22
MacFarlane, George J. 1903.29, 1911.21, 1912.18, 1912.21, 1912.23, 1913.12
MacGahan, Nora 1900.30
MacGaskill, Duncan 1957.03
MacGeachey, Cora 1911.05, 1911.35, 1911.40, 1923.33, 1924.26
MacGeachy, Charles 1885.06, 1892.55
MacGeachy, Cora 1907.44, 1910.09, 1911.47, 1912.14, 1912.25, 1912.44, 1912.45, 1913.22, 1913.30, 1914.15, 1914.30, 1914.34, 1915.05, 1915.22, 1915.28, 1916.02, 1916.10, 1916.24, 1917.26, 1918.05, 1919.14, 1920.09, 1920.19, 1920.25, 1920.47, 1921.30, 1921.37, 1922.15, 1922.19, 1923.40, 1923.44, 1923.46, 1927.47
MacGiehan, Niel 1887.47
MacGill, Casey 1999.24
MacGill, Moyna 1954.09
MacGillivray, David 2000.07
MacGowran, Jack 1959.04
MacGrath, Leueen 1955.02, 1959.05
MacGreachy, Cora 1929.35
MacGregor, Edgar 1918.15, 1918.28, 1919.01, 1919.13, 1920.35, 1921.06, 1922.28, 1922.46, 1923.08, 1924.03, 1924.16, 1925.06, 1925.29, 1926.29, 1927.05, 1927.15, 1927.48, 1927.59, 1929.03, 1929.08, 1931.26, 1932.07, 1932.18, 1932.25, 1940.08, 1940.10, 1940.19, 1941.08, 1943.14, 1946.04, 1947.13
MacGregor, Edgar J. 1920.29, 1923.16, 1927.41, 1928.23, 1928.35, 1929.07, 1929.26
MacGregor, Edward 1932.03, 1939.30
MacGregor, Knight 1926.05
MacGregor, Rae 1944.14, 1946.10
Macguire, R. Reid 1923.21
MacGunigle, Robert 1932.27
Mache, P. 1885.64, 1887.13
Macheu 1927.45
Machin, Antonio 1931.13
Machiner, Mme. 1885.65
Machiner, Mons. 1885.65
Machiz, Herbert 1959.08, 1959.17, 1963.15, 1966.02
Macht, Stephen 1972.23
MacInnes, John 1997.07
MacInnis, John 1990.08
MacIntyre, Marguerite 2000.20
MacIntyre, R. 1886.24
Mack and Mahieu 1914.19
Mack, Andrew 1891.14, 1892.06, 1894.31, 1894.32, 1896.02, 1896.14, 1897.45, 1897.47, 1899.03, 1899.27, 1900.36, 1901.15, 1903.25, 1904.46, 1910.04, 1910.14, 1929.50
Mack, Annie 1877.24, 1878.01, 1878.17, 1879.04, 1879.37, 1879.68, 1880.09, 1880.36, 1880.64, 1881.09, 1881.29, 1882.02
Mack, Bertha 1906.45, 1908.04
Mack, Betty 1921.06
Mack, Bobby 1898.66
Mack, C.O. 1902.14
Mack, Catherine 1917.17
Mack, Cecil 1899.33, 1900.46, 1902.16, 1903.08, 1904.21, 1906.27, 1908.08, 1911.20, 1923.39, 1930.34, 1931.11, 1937.09, 1944.32, 1980.10
Mack, Charles 1916.11, 1920.18, 1924.32, 1926.18, 1926.23, 1927.02, 1998.11
Mack, Dan W. 1906.10
Mack, E. 1877.08
Mack, E.H. 1886.35
Mack, E.J. 1876.34
Mack, Ed 1894.13, 1897.45
Mack, Edward 1893.36, 1893.46, 1894.04, 1896.24
Mack, Edward J. 1893.27
Mack, Ernest 1908.11
Mack, F. 1875.18
Mack, George C. 1917.18
Mack, George E. 1904.05, 1906.44, 1911.14, 1911.22, 1911.41, 1914.13, 1916.01, 1917.19, 1918.34, 1920.13, 1924.08, 1925.04, 1925.36, 1927.45, 1931.48, 1933.13, 1933.25, 1934.36, 1937.04, 1938.13, 1942.12
Mack, Georgie 1902.08, 1907.62, 1910.12, 1913.06, 1920.07
Mack, Harry 1883.23, 1888.04, 1888.34, 1942.26
Mack, Helen 1925.20
Mack, Henry 1915.04, 1915.16
Mack, Hugh 1885.35, 1890.32, 1892.23, 1892.45, 1895.34, 1896.31, 1901.07, 1903.11, 1908.31
Mack, James 1869.14, 1899.18, 1915.05, 1916.15, 1917.08, 1924.31, 1933.15
Mack, James W. 1876.29
Mack, Joe 1902.33, 1903.30, 1904.41, 1923.37
Mack, John A. 1876.16, 1879.02
Mack, Johnny 1942.29, 1944.19
Mack, Joseph E. 1902.14
Mack, Lavinia 1927.33
Mack, Leo 1928.44
Mack, Lizzy 1996.08
Mack, Marie 1922.30
Mack, Messr. 1872.40, 1872.43
Mack, Miss 1871.22
Mack, Mr. 1852.02, 1869.02
Mack, O.C. 1909.28
Mack, Ollie 1900.45, 1925.12
Mack, Pete 1889.39
Mack, Richard 1897.51
Mack, Robert 1887.05, 1895.15, 1902.17, 2000.03
Mack, Ronald 1984.15
Mack, Russell 1920.01, 1920.13, 1921.34, 1922.17, 1922.28, 1924.40, 1927.29
Mack, Steve 1978.25
Mack, Tommy 1925.24
Mack, Violet 1909.15
Mack, W. Andrew 1890.12, 1890.30, 1891.14
Mack, W.A. 1890.12
Mack, W.F. 1892.29
Mack, W.H. 1887.01, 1891.44, 1905.56
Mack, W.S.K. 1892.39
Mack, Will J. 1885.54
Mack, Willard 1916.13, 1921.21
Mack, William 1887.29, 1910.35
Mack, William B. 1922.16
Mack, William F. 1888.32, 1890.07, 1890.34, 1893.28, 1894.10, 1896.02
Mack, William Hugh 1917.34

Mack, William Kellar 1899.09
Mack, William Keller 1900.24
Mack-Berlien, Annie 1893.30
Mackay Production Company 1914.12
MacKay, Bruce 1957.05
Mackay, Bruce 1957.14
MacKay, Bruce 1958.02, 1959.02, 1959.19, 1960.05, 1961.14, 1968.23, 1969.06
Mackay, Edward 1911.09
Mackay, Erica 1923.09
Mackay, Eunice 1909.25, 1910.34, 1912.34
MacKay, Eunice 1914.18
Mackay, F.F. 1887.49
Mackay, George E. 1937.04
MacKay, Harper 1973.12
Mackay, J. 1875.21
Mackay, J.A. 1872.23
Mackay, John 1879.63, 1880.59
Mackay, John A. 1878.15, 1880.65, 1880.67, 1880.70, 1882.03, 1883.42, 1885.04, 1885.21, 1885.58, 1887.31
Mackay, Margery 1927.38
Mackay, Minnie 1889.53, 1890.13
Mackay, Mr. 1872.23
MacKay, Phoebe 1954.09
Mackay, Rita 1928.42
Mackay, Thomas 1899.03
Mackay, William 1897.50
Mackaye, Dorothea 1919.23
Mackaye, Dorothy 1918.25, 1924.28, 1925.52
Mackaye, Phoebe 1952.03
Mackeben, Theo 1932.23
MacKenna, Edwin 1932.14
Mackenzie, Alice 1927.09, 1929.46, 1930.03
MacKenzie, Alice 1928.49
Mackenzie, Archie 1887.17
Mackenzie, Bishop J. 1927.38
Mackenzie, D. 1878.10
MacKenzie, Eva 1906.46
MacKenzie, Eva 1908.26
MacKenzie, Flora 1971.21
Mackenzie, George 1891.22, 1892.16, 1892.28, 1892.52, 1894.41, 1895.09
Mackenzie, George H. 1892.07
Mackenzie, Jamie 1993.18
Mackenzie, Joseph 1927.38
MacKenzie, Kenneth 1949.03
Mackenzie, Len 1979.24
MacKenzie, Margaret 1908.40, 1910.21
Mackenzie, May 1902.29, 1908.19
Mackenzie, Wendy Leigh 1978.25, 1982.22
Mackenzie, Will 1963.05, 1964.46, 1965.14
MacKenzie, Will 1974.09
Mackey, Alice 1906.08
Mackey, Bill 1976.01
Mackey, Eunice 1909.13, 1911.11
Mackey, Julie 1889.05
Mackey, Putiputi 1972.20
Mackey, William 1872.16
Mackid, Mary 1909.21
Mackie, Bob 1971.15, 1974.02, 1976.24, 1978.25, 1979.13, 1994.06, 1999.20, 1999.23
Mackie, David 1978.14, 1978.15, 1978.16, 1978.17
Mackie, Florence 1914.20
Mackie, J.B. 1886.06
Mackie, James B. 1894.50
Mackin, Dennis 1894.17
Mackinder, Lionel 1908.25
Mackinlay, Clyde 1908.39
Mackintosh, Cameron 1977.05, 1982.19, 1984.07, 1987.04, 1988.01, 1991.03, 1992.03, 1994.02, 1998.10, 1999.20
Mackintosh, Louise 1902.37, 1919.41, 1922.16
Mackintosh, Robert 1952.10, 1953.12, 1954.09, 1955.02, 1956.02, 1966.10, 1967.02, 1967.16, 1969.01, 1974.17, 1983.10
Mackintosh, Woods 1978.11
Mackle, Jane 1946.16
Macklin, Albert 1912.37, 1983.18
Macklin, Cecil 1983.09
Macklyn, Frederick 1919.38
Macklyn, Fritz 1911.06
MacLaine, George S. 1976.07
MacLaine, Shirley 1954.05, 1976.07, 1984.06
MacLaren, Donald 1904.17
MacLaren, Ian 1913.17
Maclaren, Ian 1925.20, 1926.17
MacLaren, June 1947.11
MacLean, Christie 1895.41
MacLean, R.D. 1912.32
MacLean, Ross 1931.30
MacLean, Ted 1927.59
MacLeish, Elizabeth 1977.01
MacLellan, Lilias 1947.11
MacLeod, Mary 1999.01
MacMahon, Aline 1922.20, 1925.23
Macmahon, Aline 1924.14
MacMichael, Florence 1944.33
MacMillan, Donald 1916.07
Macmillan, Frankie 1891.18
MacMillan, Kenneth 1978.26
MacMillan, Sir Kenneth 1994.02
MacMillan, Thomas 1929.09
MacMillan, Violet 1910.17
MacMurray, Fred 1930.32, 1933.26
MacMurrough, Dermot 1911.04
MacNair, Susan 1978.27
MacNamara, Edward J. 1931.21
MacNamara, George W. 1908.40
Macnamee, Jean 1905.40
MacNaughton, Harry 1924.17
MacNaughton, Virginia 1931.08
MacNeil, Cornell 1947.04, 1950.05
MacNeil, Dorothy 1952.14, 1953.14
MacNeill, Katherine 1895.23
MacNichol, Katie 2000.10
MacNichol, L.H. 1885.30
MacNichol, Lizzie 1894.40, 1895.21, 1897.53, 1899.05, 1899.16
Macnichol, Lizzie 1895.24, 1898.07, 1898.09, 1898.14, 1898.39, 1898.49, 1898.52, 1898.57, 1898.62, 1898.76, 1899.07, 1899.10, 1899.20
Macnichol, W.F. 1887.46
MacNicol, Josephine 1922.32
MacNicoll, Josephine 1919.25
Macomber, Ken 1929.23, 1929.25, 1929.50, 1930.34, 1931.11, 1932.12, 1933.27, 1939.14, 1947.19
Macon, Sara 1943.21
MacPherson, Jeannie 1934.06
MacPherson, R.C. 1937.09
MacQueen, James 1916.23
Macquinn, W.E. 1902.03, 1911.02, 1914.23
Macquinn, William 1917.22
MacQuinn, William E. 1900.12, 1906.29, 1907.41, 1920.36
Macquinn, William E. 1904.36, 1909.09
Macrae, Arthur 1947.15, 1953.17
MacRae, Gordon 1946.07
MacRae, Heather 1968.05, 1992.09
MacRae, Sheila 1965.15
Macready, George 1933.24
Macready, J.J. 1887.51
Macreery, Wallace 1879.58, 1879.72, 1881.25, 1882.15, 1882.19, 1883.21
Macrery, Wallace 1891.23
MacShane, Anita 1979.18, 1980.14, 1982.17
MacSweeney, J.P. 1905.56, 1906.34
MacSweeney, J.W. 1885.34
MacSweeny, J.P. 1885.36, 1885.37
MacSwiney, Paul 1889.38
MacTammany, Ruth 1919.11
Macurdy, John 1959.08, 1959.17, 1960.02, 1961.06, 1961.23
MacVae, Cynthia 1926.46
MacVeigh, Earl 1946.02
MacVeigh, Earle 1935.17, 1936.05, 1947.11, 1949.10, 1949.11, 1949.13, 1949.14
Macveigh, Earle 1953.16
MacVeigh, Earle 1965.22
MacWatters, Arthur 1908.21
MacWatters, Virginia 1942.31, 1945.12, 1946.11
Macy, Carlton 1918.02, 1930.31
Macy, Cora 1895.37
Macy, Gertrude 1940.03
Macy, Stanley 1885.06, 1887.05, 1888.05, 1888.30
Mad Auguste and Company 1891.41
Mad Musicians 1992.06
MaDan, Chester 1944.13
Madden, Donald 1959.06
Madden, Edward 1903.07, 1903.20, 1903.32, 1905.27, 1907.33, 1907.62, 1908.05, 1908.15, 1908.21, 1908.27, 1908.44, 1909.13, 1909.24, 1909.25, 1910.15, 1910.18, 1910.22, 1910.25, 1911.12, 1911.43, 1911.44, 1912.13, 1912.14, 1912.26, 1915.20, 1920.20, 1927.12, 1942.35, 1955.03
Madden, Edward J. 1909.11
Madden, Jeanne 1938.11
Madden, Joe 1949.06
Madden, Joseph 1917.29
Madden, Ronald 1983.16
Maddern, Dorothy 1891.11
Maddern, Emma 1888.15
Maddern, John 1913.10
Maddern, Lizzie 1871.22
Maddern, Mary 1867.22, 1867.23, 1867.27, 1867.29
Maddern, Merle 1939.21
Maddern, Minnie 1871.15, 1871.22
Maddern, Richard 1890.03
Maddern, Sallie 1894.07
Maddern, William J. 1907.50
Maddock, Charles B. 1919.29
Maddox, Al. W. 1904.14
Maddox, Lou 1948.27
Maddox, Miss 1872.35
Maddox, Richard C. 1907.50
Maddox, Sallie 1869.02, 1869.14
Maddox, Sally 1869.20
Maddux, Emma 1872.07
Madeira, Dasheill 1898.19
Madeira, Dashiell 1898.21, 1898.33
Madeira, Marcia 1980.16, 1982.09, 1983.06, 1983.17
Madeira, Paul 1981.16
Mader, Arnott 1959.05
Madero, Ralph 1980.15
Madigan, Franc 1894.13
Madison Square Garden 1994.12, 1995.19
Madison Square Garden Enterprises 1989.12
Madison Square Garden Productions 1973.01, 1998.13
Madison Square Productions 1999.11
Madison, C. 1895.39
Madison, Connie 1919.08
Madison, Constance 1921.09
Madison, Ellen 1961.20, 1978.10
Madison, George 1911.47
Madison, Harry 1908.44
Madison, Lillie 1890.08, 1892.24, 1900.33
Madison, Lilly 1891.02
Madison, Louise 1933.27
Madison, Mauri 1917.35
Madison, Ronnie 1927.14
Madison, Rosalind 1943.08
Madison, Stella 1892.11, 1898.52, 1900.01
Madjette, Claire 1926.24
Madsen, Harold 1928.34
Madson, Ethel 1946.06
Madurga, Gonzalo 1979.09
Mae, Elsie 1923.02
Mae, Lida 1925.43
Maeader, Frank 1883.68
Maeder 1884.57, 1887.19, 1887.42, 1887.49, 1888.23, 1889.02, 1891.06, 1891.41
Maeder and Schaeffer 1890.21, 1890.40
Maeder, Frank 1879.32, 1880.11, 1881.01, 1882.24, 1883.33, 1883.68, 1885.10, 1886.05, 1887.34
Maeder, Fred 1869.40, 1869.44
Maeder, Fred D. 1892.21, 1893.37
Maeder, Fred G. 1869.08, 1884.23, 1888.04, 1888.34
Maeder, Gaspard 1856.02, 1865.03, 1875.01, 1879.32, 1880.07, 1881.31, 1885.05, 1885.46
Maeder, J. 1862.03
Maeder, J.G. 1863.04
Maeder, James G. 1855.11, 1866.13
Maeder, James Gaspard 1852.05
Maeder, Maria 1865.06
Maeder, Messr. 1885.63
Maeder, Mr. 1862.04
Maeder, Mrs. 1866.01, 1866.05
Maeder, Mrs. J. 1862.04
Maegher, T.F. 1878.17
Maehl, Lillie 1889.09, 1889.41
Maen, Norman 1961.14, 1978.26
Maerins, Mme. 1891.41
Maerschert, M. 1898.43
Maertens, Mme. 1890.50
Maffit, James 1869.02, 1869.14
Maffit, James F. 1888.13, 1892.04
Maffit, James S. 1864.02, 1869.20, 1878.19
Maffitt, Brian 1989.10
Maffitt, James 1885.58
Maffitt, James S. 1873.08, 1875.31, 1875.34, 1880.07, 1880.68, 1883.47, 1887.01, 1893.40
Maflin, A.W. 1871.09, 1871.11, 1872.16, 1872.19, 1876.17, 1876.18, 1876.21, 1876.27, 1877.16, 1878.20, 1879.03, 1879.38, 1880.24, 1880.34, 1882.28, 1882.49, 1882.70, 1883.04, 1883.38, 1883.45, 1883.58, 1884.14, 1884.22, 1884.63, 1885.14, 1885.28, 1885.52, 1885.67, 1886.30, 1888.02, 1888.20, 1889.23, 1889.40, 1889.49, 1890.19, 1890.24, 1892.07, 1892.16, 1894.42, 1896.01, 1898.16
Maflin, Jr., A.W. 1884.63
Magallanes, Nicholas 1947.14
Magee, Ed. 1895.39
Magee, Eddie 1894.31
Magee, Jack 1918.08
Magee, Patrick 1965.39
Magee, Robert 1892.27
Magee, Sherry 1932.13
Magelssen, Ralph 1934.29, 1937.17, 1941.10
Magelsson, Ralph 1937.03, 1939.21
Magerald, Mlle. 1880.68
Mages, Libby Adler 1982.10, 1999.24
Maggart, Brandon 1965.01, 1968.13, 1970.09, 1974.02, 1980.11
Maggioni, Ettore 1938.16
Magic Promotions and Theatricals 1995.02
Magic Promotions, Inc. 1989.12
Magicworks 1999.10
Magid, Deborah 1980.19
Magid, Larry 1986.02, 1999.14, 2000.04
Magid, Paul 1994.11, 1998.22
Magid, Paul David 1983.07, 1986.05
Magidson, Herb 1928.23, 1928.24, 1930.35, 1931.30, 1932.24, 1939.25, 1942.12, 1942.24, 1950.12, 1953.12
Magidson, Herman 1943.06
Magill, Gertrude 1888.23
Magill, J.B. 1871.08
Magill, Wallace 1929.08
Magin, Frank 1909.02
Maginley, B. 1870.44, 1872.37
Maginley, Ben 1869.02, 1869.14, 1870.07
Maginn, Bonnie 1897.48, 1898.50, 1899.17, 1899.30, 1900.38, 1901.17, 1902.29, 1903.04, 1904.39, 1906.01
Maginness, Mlle. 1873.22
Maginnis, Molly 1983.05
Magis, George 1928.44, 1929.20, 1929.31, 1931.37
Magis, Oscar 1929.45
Magiver, Tommy 1894.12
Magliani, Teresina 1893.47
Magna, Helen 1949.06
Magnani 1881.13, 1881.32, 1885.65, 1886.16, 1887.03
Magnani, Cav. 1884.39, 1887.27
Magnani, G. 1890.17
Magnani, Messr. 1888.10
Magnes, Alex 1927.11
Magness, Marilyn 1990.20, 1991.13
Magni, G. 1927.22
Magnin, Michele 1939.31
Magnini 1885.33, 1888.23, 1889.08
Magnus, Elva 1922.03
Magnuson, Merilee 1982.11, 1983.06, 1985.02
Magoon, Jr., Eaton 1961.07, 1972.11
Magrath, Charles 1928.13
Magraw, Margaret 1905.12
Magruder, Augusta 1919.38
Magruder, James 1997.18
Maguinnis, D.J. 1881.15
Maguire, Ciaran 2000.04
Maguire, George 1980.01
Maguire, Michael 1987.04, 1990.07, 1991.08
Maguire, Mlle. 1873.22
Maguire, Peter H. 1903.35
Maguire, Reid 1923.42
Maguire, Sylvester 1907.33
Maguire, Thomas 1888.21
Maguire, William Anthony 1929.27
Mahaffey, Valerie 1976.08, 1980.17
Mahan, Frances 1923.32
Mahan, Jack 1920.18
Maher, Albert 1896.47
Maher, Bernard 1936.18
Maher, James N. 1970.02
Maher, Jim 1959.25, 1959.26
Maher, Joseph 1979.07
Maher, Thomas 1987.03
Mahieu 1920.07, 1922.17, 1927.26, 1927.31, 1928.34, 1931.47, 1942.23, 1943.18
Mahieu and Company 1916.11, 1920.02
Mahieu Costume Company 1927.39
Mahieu Costumers, Inc. 1927.66
Mahieu, Brooks 1924.11
Mahiu and Lanzilott 1916.07
Mahl, Lori Ann 1989.27, 1991.06, 1995.13
Mahler, Albert 1936.22
Mahler, Fritz 1944.28

Mahler, Mona 1916.11
Mahlmann, Jean 1993.11
Mahmed, J. 1882.62
Mahn, H.B. 1881.42, 1881.44, 1881.45
Mahned, H.A. 1883.06
Mahon, Daniel 1983.10
Mahon, Kimberly 1991.05
Mahon, Kristen 1989.27, 1991.06
Mahon, Lizzie 1869.04
Mahone, Andrew 1881.31
Mahoney, Arthur 1930.38
Mahoney, Billie 1961.15
Mahoney, F.X. 1933.20
Mahoney, Francis 1946.01
Mahoney, Francis X. 1920.47, 1923.17, 1927.67, 1932.11
Mahoney, Harry 1887.43
Mahoney, J.F. 1918.23
Mahoney, Jack 1918.13, 1964.28
Mahoney, Jack F. 1918.23
Mahoney, Kathleen 1921.32
Mahoney, Trish 1972.03
Mahoney, Will 1922.34, 1924.19, 1927.60, 1929.26, 1931.26, 1955.09
Mahoney-Bennett, Kathy 1981.25
Mahony, Sean 1986.13
Mahony-Bennett, Kathleen 1987.15
Mahr, Ida 1890.31, 1891.33, 1892.43, 1893.29, 1894.01, 1894.30
Mai, Edith 1884.21, 1888.20, 1889.04
Mai-Lan 1960.10
Maide, Miss 1920.44
Maier, Barbara 1963.15
Maier, Marcia 1946.22
Maier, Tommy 1949.17
Maillard, Aime 1869.24
Maillard, Carol Lynn 1979.32, 1980.15
Maillart, Aime 1882.29
Maillart, Aimee 1877.12, 1878.09
Maillet, Mlle. 1864.10
Maillet, Mme. 1864.01, 1864.03, 1864.08, 1864.11
Maillon, Lelia 1907.02
Main, Laurie 1959.06
Main, Marjorie 1932.22
Main, Norman 1978.10
Maina, A. 1885.67, 1886.33, 1887.04
Maina, M. 1887.18
Mainbocher 1943.19, 1946.20, 1954.11, 1959.24
Maine, Bruno 1942.19, 1944.20, 1947.12, 1948.19, 1949.05, 1951.20
Maine, Lenoir 1902.32
Maingy, Guy 1908.25
Mainland, Louise 1925.37
Mair, Alexander 1884.18
Mairs, Miss 1857.01
Mairs, Stella 1857.03
Mais, Michele 1979.08, 1987.12
Maisell, Joe 1979.15, 1981.05
Maison Andre Sherri 1919.11
Maison Berkovitz 1914.03
Maison Blum 1911.39
Maison Lucile 1914.32
Maison Simone 1927.66
Maison, Alice 1921.11
Maison, Gil 1942.18, 1948.21
Maitlan, Amie 1879.67
Maitland, Arthur 1914.05
Maitland, Clara 1879.25
Maitland, Dexter 1965.05, 1981.17
Maitland, Dick 1973.06
Maitland, Emma 1929.18, 1930.19, 1931.31
Maitland, Gertrude 1919.09, 1923.01
Maitland, Lena 1905.46, 1928.13
Maitland, Michael 1966.10, 1970.15
Maitland, Richard 1956.12
Maitland, William 1899.39
Majer, Joseph 1927.65, 1943.08
Majeroni, George 1907.47
Majeroni, Georgio 1911.34
Majeroni, Giorgio 1907.05
Majilton, Caroline 1883.50
Majilton, Carrie 1873.29
Majilton, Charles 1873.29
Majilton, Frank 1873.29, 1883.50
Majilton, Marie 1873.29
Major, Aja 1986.03, 1987.14
Major, Carrick 1912.04
Major, Charles 1904.30
Major, Leon 1968.15
Major, Little 1906.29
Major, Miss 1896.44
Major, W. 1875.06
Majoroni, George 1909.14
Makalif, Edmond 1919.18
Makalif, Edmund 1915.29, 1919.11
Makarenko, Daniel 1934.20, 1936.07
Makarova, Natalia 1983.02
Makeba 1966.03
Makeba, Miriam 1990.16
Maker, Jessie 1924.16
Makin, Charles 1879.05, 1879.21
Mako 1976.02
Makter, Beine 1925.37
Malaguti, R. 1992.13
Malaidy, James C. 1915.32
Malakoff, Messr. 1922.06
Malambos, Los 1981.09
Malamet, Marsha 1979.11
Malamude, Yetta 1925.37
Malas, Spiro 1961.03, 1961.04, 1962.08, 1962.09, 1962.10, 1962.19, 1962.21, 1963.23, 1964.30, 1969.12, 1974.16, 1975.16, 1976.23, 1981.22, 1982.21, 1992.01
Malbin, Elaine 1949.10, 1949.11, 1949.13, 1952.15, 1953.06
Malchien, Richard 1899.01, 1900.10, 1901.02, 1905.38, 1921.01
Malcles, Jean-Denis 1964.06
Malcolm, Christopher 2000.17
Malcolm, Florine 1893.45
Malcolm, John 1905.46, 1966.09
Malcolm, Margaret 1906.15, 1910.09
Malcolm, Russell 1893.02
Malcolm-Smith, George 1945.18
Malden, Karl 1943.23
Malekos, Nick 1968.24
Malenfant, Lloyd 1971.21
Malette, Mr. 1870.40
Maley, Denman 1902.42, 1907.41, 1909.11, 1911.35, 1912.45, 1914.07, 1916.07, 1918.15, 1919.05, 1922.42, 1923.31
Maley, Eda 1906.40
Maley, Marty 1918.38
Maley, Stephen 1898.69, 1900.19, 1900.47, 1903.03, 1904.13, 1911.05, 1913.16, 1917.06
Maley, Steve 1896.02
Malfitano, Catherine 1976.31, 1978.08, 1978.23, 1979.27
Malia, V. 1911.16
Malie, Thomas 1929.27
Malina, Luba 1944.02, 1945.11
Malina, Robert 1971.13
Malinou, Selma 1962.04
Malkin, Seth 1996.15, 1997.10
Mallandaine, W.E. 1873.12
Mallard H. Frane's Sons 1929.01
Mallard, David E. 1989.19
Mallen, Dave 1927.31, 1936.31, 1951.16
Malley, Victor 1905.43
Malley, William L. 1891.08, 1893.30
Malli, Blanche 1911.39
Mallia, Henry 1919.22
Mallia, Maud 1917.16
Mallia, Maude 1919.22
Mallicoat, Jean Marie 2001.04
Mallina, Trudy 1930.07
Mallinson, H.R. 1923.22
Mallison, H.R. 1919.08
Mallory, Ed 1899.33
Mallory, Frank 1899.33
Mallory, Victoria 1971.05, 1973.04
Mallow, Tom 1980.14, 1984.09
Malloy, Dana 1938.02
Malloy, Francetta 1924.26, 1925.43, 1930.35, 1931.04, 1932.20, 1942.23
Malloy, Judy 1997.17, 1999.17
Malloy, William 1893.38
Malm, Mia 1986.20
Malmane, G. 1881.11
Malmasha, Ludovico 1866.22
Malmberg, G. 1866.28, 1867.12
Malmberg, Kathy 1977.09
Malmsha, L. 1869.35
Malmsha, Ludovico 1866.20, 1866.26, 1866.32, 1866.35, 1867.01, 1867.02, 1867.11, 1867.21, 1868.25, 1868.27, 1869.20, 1869.27
Malmude, Seymour 1937.11
Malneck, Matt 1980.29, 1983.20, 1987.02, 1997.05
Malo, Gina 1931.05
Malonam, Natalie 1925.47
Malone, Bettye 1969.03, 1975.22
Malone, Dale 1963.08, 1966.13
Malone, Edgar 1904.33
Malone, Elizabeth 1946.12
Malone, Geraldine 1906.18, 1908.06, 1909.04
Malone, Howard 1946.10
Malone, J.A.E. 1898.29, 1909.21, 1911.39, 1913.04, 1914.18, 1915.18, 1918.27, 1919.42
Malone, J.E.A. 1897.20, 1897.32, 1904.29, 1907.06, 1908.25
Malone, John 1888.10, 1891.34
Malone, Kay 1955.12
Malone, Kitty 1959.02
Malone, Mike 1980.05
Malone, Russell 1990.19
Maloney, James A. 1885.68
Maloney, Joseph 1912.41
Maloney, May 1908.42, 1910.10, 1911.35
Maloney, Patty 1991.11
Maloney, Russell 1948.18
Malory, Sir Thomas 1963.03
Malotte, Hay 1982.06
Malstrom, Gustava 1931.03
Maltby, H.F. 1921.27
Maltby, Jacquey 1989.29
Maltby, Jr., Richard 1968.13, 1978.09, 1983.09, 1983.19, 1985.12, 1988.17, 1990.09, 1991.03, 1991.15, 1996.08, 1999.01
Maltin, Bernard 1929.25, 1931.19
Maltz, Maxwell 1945.01
Malvenna, Mlle. 1879.56
Malvern, Miss 1875.05
Malvey, Con 1889.45
Malvey, Master 1884.26
Malvin, Arthur 1979.24, 1979.25
Malvina, M. 1881.46
Malvina, Madame 1900.01
Malvina, Miss 1879.50
Malvina, Mlle. 1876.16, 1880.04, 1880.52, 1880.58, 1880.60, 1881.48, 1881.50, 1881.51, 1881.53, 1882.26, 1882.30, 1882.35
Malvina, Mme. 1880.44, 1880.50, 1881.11, 1881.54, 1884.11, 1899.29, 1900.50
Malvino, Mlle. 1876.34
Malz, Herr 1882.68
Mambazo, Ladysmith Black 1993.04
Mameluch, Robert 1924.17
Mamert, Bibeyran 1881.15
Mamet, Liane 1924.10, 1924.40
Mamie, Little 1886.02
Mamlet, Alexandra 1938.16
Mamoulian, Rouben 1935.13, 1944.27, 1945.05, 1946.08, 1949.03, 1949.15, 1950.04, 1951.16, 1953.09, 1958.07, 1965.38, 1966.31, 1969.12
Man, Christopher 1964.35
Mana-Zucca 1925.17
Management Three Productions, Ltd. 1969.04
Manara, Mr. 1882.65
Manatt, Fred 1920.31, 1930.11, 1931.30
Manatt, Frederick 1917.28, 1934.35
Manatt, Frederick B. 1933.03, 1939.25
Manatt, Georgia 1917.29, 1919.07
Manchester, George 1895.44
Manchester, Mary 1966.14
Manchester, Melissa 1978.05
Mancina, Mark 1997.20
Mancini, Henry 1962.17, 1974.22, 1995.15, 1997.05
Mancuso, Sam 1989.17
Mandan, Robert 1968.24, 1970.09, 1988.07
Mandel, Frank 1912.47, 1914.27, 1920.07, 1920.27, 1920.38, 1920.42, 1921.32, 1922.38, 1924.03, 1925.29, 1925.30, 1926.42, 1927.41, 1928.29, 1928.50, 1929.03, 1931.04, 1931.28, 1931.39, 1934.14, 1935.17, 1942.22, 1944.17, 1946.03, 1971.03, 1974.26, 1986.14, 1988.16
Mandel, Joe 1921.21, 1923.31
Mandel, John 1979.13
Mandel, Johnny 1983.20, 1988.19, 1990.09
Mandel, Rose 1929.36
Mandel, William 1921.21, 1923.31
Mandell, Michael 1994.12
Mandell, Rick 1967.18, 1970.06, 1971.15
Mandevile, William 1895.11
Mandeville, Alicia 1866.34
Mandeville, Butler 1908.11
Mandeville, Frank A. 1905.38
Mandeville, Jane 1899.40, 1902.44, 1903.28
Mandeville, W.C. 1887.31
Mandeville, William C. 1902.44
Mandia, John 1970.10
Mandjgaladze, Alexander 1977.13
Mandracchia, Charles 1987.03, 1989.26, 2000.03
Manfred, Louise 1881.57
Manfredi, Nino 1964.03
Manfredini, Harry 1982.13
Mangasarian, Christine 1914.13
Manger, Itzik 1966.21, 1967.08, 1968.22, 1990.16
Mangione, Chuck 2001.04
Manhattan Rhythm Kings 1992.02
Manhattan Theatre Club 1978.09
Manhatters Company, The 1927.36
Manheim, Ralph 1976.10
Manilow, Barry 1973.14, 1975.12, 1976.34, 1989.08, 1991.10
Manim, Mannie 1988.02, 1997.14
Maning, John 1887.27
Maning, Maude 1892.60
Manion, Lucille 1920.15
Manisoff, M. 1936.03
Mank, Mme. 1912.15
Mankes, Karen 1982.22
Mankiewicz, Herman 1924.15
Mankiewicz, Herman J. 1925.47
Mankiewicz, Joseph 1970.09
Mankiewicz, Tom 1970.03
Mankowitz, Wolf 1965.28
Manley, C.M. 1870.14, 1870.28, 1870.32, 1870.35, 1871.02, 1871.17
Manley, Iris 1946.01
Manley, Jack 1907.12
Manley, James 1907.24
Manley, John 1909.06
Manley, Mark 1994.06
Manley, Master 1870.22
Manley, Mildred 1924.13
Manley, Miti 1925.04
Manley, Mitti 1923.42
Manley, Mr. 1873.25
Manley, T. 1870.01
Manley, W.H. 1880.34
Manly, C. 1873.26
Manly, C.M. 1870.40, 1871.01
Mann, A.L. 1891.46
Mann, Alison 1985.02
Mann, Allan 1932.20
Mann, Andrea 1948.16
Mann, Barry 1978.05, 1984.15, 1995.03
Mann, Bertha 1914.06
Mann, Billy 1926.18
Mann, Clara 1903.13
Mann, Daniel 1937.14, 1951.24
Mann, David 1947.20
Mann, Edith Audrey 1931.44
Mann, Edward 1983.15
Mann, Elaine 1930.08
Mann, Ethel 1944.32
Mann, Frances 1920.28, 1929.29
Mann, Friedericke 1964.25
Mann, George 1928.23, 1938.08
Mann, Harry 1884.48, 1888.12
Mann, Heinrich 1966.05
Mann, Howard 1968.03
Mann, III., Fred C. 1986.07
Mann, Jack 1941.09, 1973.04, 1974.17, 1976.02, 1977.05, 1978.12, 1978.26, 1979.02, 1979.06, 1980.04, 1980.25, 1980.27, 1981.04, 1981.27, 1982.09, 1982.18, 1982.24, 1983.19, 1983.21, 1984.07, 1985.20, 1986.11, 1986.18
Mann, Jack 'Peanuts' 1950.12
Mann, Jean 1918.25
Mann, Jerry 1951.16
Mann, Joan 1938.15, 1945.20, 1946.20, 1948.14, 1948.22, 1950.09, 1952.07
Mann, Johnny 1963.10
Mann, Jonathan 1989.10
Mann, Kal 1977.10, 1989.12
Mann, Lew 1927.62
Mann, Lili 1934.41
Mann, Lloyd 1925.12
Mann, Louis 1895.18, 1896.48, 1897.54, 1903.28, 1907.10, 1921.20
Mann, Martin 1922.41
Mann, Michael 1944.16, 1947.06, 1959.08, 1959.17
Mann, Mildred 1920.28
Mann, Miss 1841.01
Mann, Nancy 1944.16
Mann, Nat D. 1896.48, 1901.30, 1902.01, 1902.44, 1905.49, 1905.55
Mann, O. 1903.25
Mann, P.J. 1976.01
Mann, Pat 1930.39, 1932.11
Mann, Paul 1936.28, 1938.08

Mann, Philip 1922.20, 1925.20
Mann, Rheta 1887.05
Mann, Rita 1891.23
Mann, Sam 1912.43, 1931.48
Mann, Stuart 1964.23, 1965.15
Mann, Terrence 1986.13, 1987.04, 1994.04, 1995.19, 1997.19
Mann, Terrence V. 1980.07, 1982.19
Mann, Theodore 1965.32, 1969.10, 1974.25, 1976.19, 1979.07, 1988.13, 1989.10, 1989.19, 1992.11
Mann, W.D. 1890.32, 1892.18, 1894.46, 1896.45
Mannat, Fred 1934.01
Mannat, Frederick B. 1927.49
Mannering, Moya 1912.26, 1913.26
Manners, Charles 1892.53, 1905.31
Manners, Dorothy 1926.22
Manners, Ginger 1938.09
Manners, Hilda 1927.27
Manners, J. Hartley 1907.58, 1909.24, 1910.04, 1918.10, 1924.09, 1932.26
Manners, Jane 1927.47, 1928.46, 1930.20
Manners, Jayne 1942.15, 1943.16, 1944.15
Manners, Jos. 1855.10
Manners, Josephine 1857.01, 1857.03, 1857.05, 1857.07
Manners, Loraine 1943.12
Manners, Margaret 1926.16, 1928.22, 1929.08
Manners, Mildred 1911.32
Manners, Miss 1857.02
Manners, Zeke 1943.23
Mannes, Marya 1929.19, 1950.03
Manning, Alice 1924.06
Manning, Ambrose 1934.29
Manning, Catherine 1917.30
Manning, Charles 1917.31
Manning, David 1938.16, 1946.17, 1966.12, 1966.16
Manning, Doncharles 1979.03
Manning, Fletcher 1880.62
Manning, Frank 1904.06
Manning, Frankie 1989.02, 1997.03
Manning, Hallie 1921.19, 1924.07
Manning, Hope 1939.21
Manning, Irene 1945.19
Manning, Jack 1919.03, 1919.35, 1947.09, 1958.08, 1965.06
Manning, James H. 1893.30, 1901.07, 1903.11, 1906.02, 1906.42, 1907.20
Manning, Joanne 2000.07
Manning, John 1890.17
Manning, Katharine 1933.12
Manning, Katheryn 1903.20
Manning, Mae 1918.12
Manning, Margaret 1903.26
Manning, Maybelle 1927.48
Manning, Messr. 1893.30
Manning, Mildred 1908.35, 1910.04, 1912.34, 1914.22, 1932.23
Manning, Monroe 1946.16
Manning, Rena 1918.12, 1921.14, 1922.16
Manning, Rick 1988.20, 1992.07, 1993.02
Manning, Robert 1920.08
Manning, Ruth 1973.11
Manning, Sam 1947.19
Manning, Samuel L. 1947.19
Manning, W.J. 1895.10
Mannings, Allan 1956.08
Mannion, Elizabeth 1959.08
Mannis, Sandra 1973.09, 1989.18
Manno, Dana 1978.21
Mannstadt, Wilhelm 1889.17
Manocherian, Jennifer 1994.01, 2000.20
Manoff, Dinah 1985.03
Manola, Adelaide 1903.26
Manola, Marion 1886.30, 1887.18, 1887.22, 1887.24, 1887.26, 1887.28, 1887.47, 1888.22, 1888.24, 1888.26, 1889.17, 1889.22, 1890.16, 1892.57, 1893.03
Manola-Mason Company 1892.57, 1893.03
Manola-Mason, Marion 1892.25
Manon, Sylvia 1951.13
Manor, Joseph 1897.12
Manor, Lela 1931.21
Manor, Lila 1931.21
Manos, Christopher B. 1993.03
Manos, Dean 1979.06
Manos, Judy 1979.06
Manosalvas, Alfonso 1969.11
Manrico, H. 1882.65
Mansa, Cobra 1988.06
Mansa, Cobrinha 1992.13
Mansager, Jack 2001.04
Manser, Dave 1912.17
Mansey, Miss 1872.35
Mansfield, Ada 1893.32
Mansfield, Alice 1873.12, 1873.14, 1889.20
Mansfield, Eleanor 1907.63
Mansfield, Gertrude 1895.27, 1897.31, 1897.48
Mansfield, H. 1907.54
Mansfield, Herbert 1908.26, 1909.20, 1910.23
Mansfield, Laurie 1990.15
Mansfield, Martha 1918.19
Mansfield, Messr. 1903.03
Mansfield, Miss 1904.44
Mansfield, Richard 1882.60, 1882.75, 1884.12, 1885.11, 1886.27, 1895.31
Mansfield, Robert A. 1897.25
Mansfield, Sidney 1898.47
Mansfield, Vicki 1963.14
Mansfield, William 1905.07
Manson, Alan 1942.20, 1946.10
Manson, Allison R. 1979.32
Manson, Eddy 1946.15
Manson, Mary 1929.28
Manson, Nita 1909.08
Mansour, Achille 1881.50, 1883.12
Mansouri, Lofti 1984.12, 1985.10, 1990.13
Mansouri, Lotfi 1997.02
Mansur, Susan 1978.13, 1994.01
Mansz, W.J. 1889.40
Mantel, Selma 1908.01
Mantell, Anna 1891.30
Mantell, Dot 1919.26
Mantell, George 1923.09
Mantell, Joe 1952.13
Mantell, Trixie 1908.12
Mantia, (Buddy) 1992.16
Mantilla, Rosecita 1908.33
Mantilla, Rosita 1914.12
Mantinan, Alejandra 1993.08
Manton, Kevitt 1926.04
Manton, Stephen 1963.03
Mantova, Mme. 1922.30
Manuel 1988.15
Manuel, Barbara 1925.13
Manuel, Luis 1979.08
Manuel, Vida 1927.27
Manulis, Martin 1946.06
Manuscript Productions 1983.19
Manville, Lorraine 1922.02, 1924.10, 1944.28
Manvini, Grace 1938.15
Manz, William J. 1891.22
Manzanero, Armando 1973.17
Manzantinita, Doloretes 1917.25
Manzella, Fred 1965.33
Manzone, Lena 1890.03
Manzoni, Mlle. 1888.39
Manzoni, Mme. 1890.50
Manzotti, Luigi 1883.48, 1900.19
Manzotti, Signor 1887.27
Mao, Freddy 1976.02
Maple, Audrey 1912.46, 1916.08, 1917.18, 1917.28, 1919.03, 1924.42, 1926.26, 1927.50, 1928.07, 1928.32, 1928.46, 1929.32
Mapleton, Agnes 1875.21, 1882.62
Maquaire, M. 1926.47
Maquinn, William 1902.41
Maquot, Flo 1908.33
Mara, Alma 1920.12
Mara, Angela 1992.13
Mara, Frank 1887.02, 1887.42, 1888.25, 1889.43, 1890.36, 1894.52, 1896.15
Mara, Master 1896.15
Mara, Miss 1896.15
Mara, Mrs. Frank 1896.15
Marable, Ed 1878.14
Maraenco, Romualdo 1883.48
Maraes, Sonia Regnia 1992.13
Marage, Mons. 1868.18
Maran, George 1940.10
Marand, Patricia 1952.10, 1966.06
Marano, Marguerite 1928.11
Marascolo, John 1990.15
Marat, Mons. 1869.22, 1869.24
Maratrat, Alain 1983.16
Maravell, Melissa 1994.09
Maravilha, Nilton 1992.13
Marba, James 1892.38
Marba, Jo Smith 1903.11, 1905.53, 1907.20
Marba, Joe Smith 1907.57
Marba, Joseph S. 1914.08
Marbe, Fay 1919.01, 1919.35, 1922.12, 1923.41
Marble Arch Productions 1980.06
Marble, Blanche 1906.03
Marble, Carolyn 1986.16
Marble, Dan 1912.37, 1916.22, 1924.24
Marble, Ed 1875.16, 1880.17, 1881.03, 1891.32, 1892.50
Marble, Edward 1884.17, 1891.32
Marble, Grace 1906.03
Marble, John 1886.48, 1886.49, 1911.18
Marble, John S. 1894.37
Marble, Queenie 1906.03
Marble, Scott 1885.03, 1886.58, 1889.10, 1890.12, 1890.30, 1894.31
Marbot, Rolf 1999.05
Marburg, G.W. 1894.39
Marbury, Elisabeth 1915.07, 1916.06, 1917.02, 1918.02, 1928.21
Marbury, Elizabeth 1922.37
Marc Henri and Laverdt 1928.42
Marc Piven, Inc. 1982.01
Marcarie, Laura 1997.13
Marcas, Mons. 1872.29, 1872.33, 1872.39, 1872.41, 1872.42, 1873.01
Marceau, Yvonne 1989.26
Marcel, Arthur 1890.02
Marcel, Inez 1906.24
Marcel, Jean 1911.26
Marcel, Melba 1932.10
Marcel, Ted 1929.24
Marcelle, Inez 1906.23
Marcelle, Jeannette 1905.32
Marcelle, Melba 1929.30
Marcelle, Mlle. 1914.21
Marcelli, Louise 1899.01, 1900.10, 1901.02
Marcelli, Rino 1985.14
Marcellus, G.W. 1870.05
Marcellus, Scott 1985.01, 1987.17
Marcey, Therese 1881.05
March, Alexander 1948.08
March, Eve 1969.17
March, George 1960.08
March, Iva 1961.10
March, Joseph Moncure 2000.08
March, Ursula 1902.22
Marchal, Miss 1882.46
Marchand, Colette 1951.19
Marchand, Messr. 1879.46, 1882.35
Marchand, Mons. 1879.45, 1880.29, 1880.50, 1880.52
Marchand, Nancy 1993.14
Marchand, Susan 1978.24
Marchant, Claude 1943.17, 1944.31, 1946.01, 1947.19, 1950.07
Marchant, Mr. 1854.05
Marchante, Marion 1930.27
Marche, Helen 1918.12
Marchesi, Clotilda 1871.27, 1872.06
Marchetti, F. 1896.41, 1898.17
Marchetti, Filiberto 1895.08, 1899.21
Marchetti, H. 1898.17
Marchetti, Signor 1896.06
Marci, Blanche 1916.15
Marciona, Anthony 1974.17
Marck, Georges 1916.15
Marck, Yvonne 1916.15
Marco, Caterina 1888.19
Marco, Claude 1888.30
Marco, Maria 1917.25, 1917.33
Marco, Mr. 1921.17
Marco, Pepita 1949.07
Marco, Professor 1888.30
Marco, Sano 1931.15, 1931.18, 1931.24, 1931.27, 1931.35
Marcon, Barbara 1961.21, 1962.24
Marcovicci, Andrea 1972.24
Marcu, Remus 1981.21
Marcuco, R. 1884.39
Marcum, Brian J. 1999.10, 1999.15
Marcum, Kevin 1976.05, 1987.04
Marcus, B. 1918.21
Marcus, D. Frank 1929.25
Marcus, Daniel 1997.15, 1998.20, 1999.21, 2000.19
Marcus, James A. 1907.28
Marcus, Lynne 1954.01
Marcus, Toni 1963.07
Marcy, C.H. 1879.15
Marcy, Everett 1934.06, 1936.12, 1938.04, 1940.23, 1957.10
Marcy, George 1951.23, 1955.08, 1961.10, 1967.09
Marden, Mrs. 1861.01
Marden, W. 1871.17
Mardirosian, Tom 1992.17
Mardo, Al 1949.09
Mare, Pietro 1884.58
Marean, Maud 1898.49
Marechal, Mauree 1881.15
Mareikura, Gabrielle 1972.20
Marenco, Romauldo 1900.19
Maresca, Ernest 2000.07
Maret, John 1925.27
Maret, Joyce 1967.10, 1969.04
Maretzek, Max 1876.16, 1877.01, 1879.07, 1879.11, 1879.17, 1879.20, 1880.55, 1895.11
Mareuil, J. 1974.19
Mareuil, Jacques 1959.15, 1961.25, 1963.02
Marewa, M. 1932.09
Marfield, Dwight 1945.19
Margaret 1974.26
Margaret Dorothy 1922.39
Margarita, Tamiris 1924.44
Margelssen, Ralph 1942.20
Margetson, Arthur 1922.34, 1923.02, 1928.33, 1946.13, 1946.20
Margio, R. 1911.16
Margolies, Abe 1968.08
Margoshes, Steve 2000.06
Margoshes, Steven 1983.17, 1985.06, 1986.15, 1990.17, 1993.06, 1994.07, 1995.03, 1996.17
Margot, Louise 1896.41
Marguerite and Strauss 1928.09, 1929.18, 1930.37
Marguerite, laPetite 1921.02
Marguerite, Mlle. 1868.07, 1868.27, 1879.19, 1879.36, 1879.39, 1879.40, 1879.47, 1880.52, 1920.31, 1921.30
Marhler, Messr. 1854.01
Mari, Dolores 1959.08, 1959.17, 1963.15, 1966.02
Mari, Theresa 1955.07
Mari-Touchnoff, Messr. 1925.03
Maria, Helen 1924.29
Maria, Mlle. 1867.05
Maria, Olga 1988.06
Mariachi Vargas deTecalitlan 1988.15
Mariano, Patti 1961.18, 1968.07, 1986.13
Maricle, Marijane 1951.24, 1960.06
Marie Aimee's French Opera Bouffe Company 1876.24, 1876.25, 1876.26, 1876.28, 1876.31, 1877.26, 1877.27, 1877.29, 1877.30, 1877.31, 1877.32, 1877.33, 1877.34, 1877.37, 1877.38, 1878.06, 1878.07, 1878.08, 1878.09
Marie, Jean 1992.02
Marie, Julienne 1958.20, 1964.04, 1965.06, 1980.23
Marie, Mlle. 1866.18, 1868.31, 1870.44, 1871.27, 1872.10, 1873.10, 1876.26, 1883.54, 1886.21
Marie, Mons. 1871.18
Marie, N. 1882.73
Marie, Paola 1879.48, 1879.51, 1879.55, 1879.60, 1879.61, 1879.69, 1880.16, 1880.23, 1880.27, 1880.28, 1880.29, 1880.44, 1880.50, 1880.52, 1880.56, 1880.58, 1880.60, 1881.46, 1881.48, 1881.49, 1881.50, 1881.51, 1881.53, 1881.54, 1882.30, 1882.35
Marie, Rose 1951.23
Mariebriot, Mlle. 1868.24
Mariette, Auguste 1952.15
Marievsky, Joseph 1926.18
Marievsky, Messr. 1922.06, 1923.28, 1925.03
Mariewa, M. 1924.48
Marin, Guillermo 1949.07
Marinaro, Francesca 1935.02
Marine, Joe 1955.13
Marineau, Barbara 1995.19, 1999.16
Marinetti, Ignacio 1897.45
Marini, Elma 1875.15
Marino, Frank 1934.20
Marinoff, Fania 1922.08
Marinoff, Judith 1999.24
Marinos, Peter 1983.14, 1991.05, 1998.08, 2001.05
Mario, Al 1928.34
Mario, Berthe 1877.31, 1877.37
Mario, Mlle. 1877.33
Mario, Paul 1945.12
Marion, Ben 1922.40
Marion, Dave 1907.51
Marion, David 1891.39, 1896.45, 1913.01

Marion, Floyd 1927.29
Marion, Frances 1934.13
Marion, George 1889.52, 1899.38, 1900.34, 1901.25, 1903.02, 1903.10, 1903.24, 1904.10, 1904.16, 1904.39, 1904.52, 1905.06, 1905.16, 1905.26, 1906.16, 1906.30, 1906.49, 1907.17, 1907.27, 1907.48, 1908.10, 1908.15, 1908.24, 1908.36, 1909.02, 1909.15, 1909.19, 1910.37, 1911.09, 1911.18, 1911.30, 1911.37, 1912.01, 1912.15, 1912.35, 1912.37, 1913.06, 1913.10, 1913.27, 1914.03, 1914.09, 1914.28, 1914.30, 1916.04, 1916.08, 1916.18, 1917.07,
Marion, George (*cont.*) 1917.32, 1918.24, 1918.25, 1920.03, 1921.21, 1921.23, 1921.29, 1922.16, 1928.26, 1928.46, 1929.06
Marion, George F. 1892.09, 1896.04, 1899.12, 1904.37, 1908.23
Marion, Harry S. 1898.41
Marion, John 1889.30, 1889.32, 1889.53, 1890.09
Marion, Jr., George 1939.27, 1942.29, 1943.07, 1944.15, 1945.11, 1946.23, 1978.09
Marion, Leslie 1898.44, 1915.32
Marion, Marie 1936.22
Marion, Messr. 1892.53
Marion, Millie 1888.33
Marion, Miss 1886.47, 1892.52
Marion, Mlle. 1922.23
Marion, Paul 1937.01
Marion, Rosa 1884.34
Marion, Rose 1882.46, 1885.05, 1885.28
Marion, Sam 1892.48, 1892.53, 1896.45, 1897.30, 1903.14, 1903.20, 1904.37, 1904.39, 1904.41, 1904.52, 1905.17, 1905.33, 1906.01
Marion, Samuel 1896.45
Marion, Sidney 1918.13
Maris, Dorothy 1938.01
Maris, Mons. 1887.35, 1887.36
Maris, Stella 1889.03
Marischka, Ernst 1934.29
Marisse, Ann 1964.18
Maritn, Lea 1897.16
Maritn, Sam 1907.12
Maritn, Tom 1889.34
Marius, C.D. 1894.22
Marius, Mons. 1893.03
Marivaux, Pierre 1997.18
Mark Taper Forum 1999.20
Mark Taper Forum Production, A 1970.16, 1979.08
Mark, Christopher 1994.12
Mark, Flip 1958.03
Mark, Laurence 1996.08
Mark, Michael 1977.04
Mark, Tamara 1982.16, 1983.02
Mark, Zane 1996.07, 2000.15
Markam, Genevieve 1922.26
Markarian, Alicia Helen 1968.30
Markel, Cecil 1916.22
Marker, Preshy 1962.12
Marker, Thornton 1952.15
Markert, Russell 1928.22, 1928.34, 1931.42, 1932.24, 1934.35, 1935.18
Markert, Russell E. 1928.08, 1928.38, 1928.40, 1928.45, 1929.24
Markey, Enid 1926.20, 1938.06, 1954.16
Markey, Frances 1929.44, 1930.30
Markey, Francis 1931.39
Markey, Frank 1903.01
Markey, Irene 1913.18
Markey, Shauna 1999.11
Markham, Alexis 1885.41
Markham, Dewey 1930.24, 1932.08
Markham, Dewey "Pigmeat" 1939.14
Markham, Frank 1915.18, 1916.01
Markham, Geraldine 1923.33
Markham, Lillian 1890.32, 1891.04, 1892.18, 1892.45, 1894.37
Markham, Monte 1973.05
Markham, Pauline 1868.23, 1869.06, 1869.29, 1869.35, 1870.13, 1870.19, 1870.21, 1870.35, 1870.44, 1872.02, 1872.04, 1872.05, 1872.08, 1872.12, 1872.14, 1872.25, 1872.30, 1872.32, 1872.36, 1872.38, 1872.40, 1873.10, 1881.13, 1881.24, 1889.47
Markinson, Martin 1979.05, 1992.06, 2001.07
Markle, Cecile 1917.26
Markley, Dan 1994.01
Markley, Edna 1875.31, 1875.34
Marko, Robert 1941.03
Markoff, Messr. 1922.37
Markoff, Michael 1923.02
Markoff, Olga 1930.35, 1930.37
Markova, Alicia 1944.29
Markovitz, Herr 1879.62
Markowitz, David 1975.18
Markowitz, Richard 1962.22
Markowitz, Roy 1978.25
Marks, Ben 1936.07
Marks, Charles 1904.24, 1906.36, 1907.39, 1908.17, 1909.12
Marks, Clarence 1909.16, 1921.06
Marks, David 1932.28
Marks, Emmaretta 1968.11
Marks, Esther 1904.07
Marks, Gerald 1934.42, 1935.04, 1936.22, 1943.14, 1948.15, 1999.24
Marks, Hugo 1902.02
Marks, I.W. 1999.08
Marks, Jennifer 1964.36, 1964.43, 1966.22, 1966.25
Marks, Joe 1941.09
Marks, Joe E. 1942.27, 1944.23, 1947.01, 1950.08, 1954.13, 1956.12, 1965.17, 1967.05
Marks, Joel 1897.23
Marks, Loretta 1923.21
Marks, Lynda Sue 1972.23
Marks, Maurice 1928.08, 1934.20
Marks, Maurice E. 1914.13
Marks, Messr. 1750.01, 1881.35
Marks, Ogden 1897.12
Marks, Robert 1917.05, 1917.21, 1918.09, 1918.16, 1918.39, 1919.33, 1920.01, 1920.35
Marks, Robert A. 1908.20
Marks, Sylvia 1942.05
Marks, W.D. 1880.54, 1881.06
Marks, Walter 1964.40, 1968.03, 1974.11, 1981.09, 1992.16
Markush, Fred 1987.02
Markwell, Robert 1916.01
Marlan, Miss 1851.05
Marlay, Andrew 1986.14, 1988.04, 1988.16, 1988.18
Marlay, Andrew B. 1979.29, 1990.05
Marlborough, Helen 1889.13, 1895.04, 1896.06, 1898.38, 1898.56, 1905.29
Marlborough, Lillian 1897.33
Marlene, Joy 1955.10
Marley, James 1957.05
Marley, Lenni 1899.09
Marlin, Glenn 1942.18
Marlo, Maria 1950.05, 1952.12, 1954.18, 1960.03, 1962.06
Marlo, Mary 1951.16, 1953.09
Marlo, Micki 1957.01
Marlow, Dorothy 1903.20
Marlow, Mary 1941.09
Marlow, Mrs. Owen 1887.02
Marlow, Raymond 1927.31
Marlow, Virginia 1887.02
Marlowe, Albertine 1917.26, 1918.16
Marlowe, Arthur 1932.10
Marlowe, Babe 1919.06
Marlowe, Bessie 1898.75
Marlowe, Dorothy 1903.04, 1904.15, 1905.18
Marlowe, Edith 1895.14
Marlowe, Eva 1903.04, 1910.13
Marlowe, Evelyn 1904.15
Marlowe, Frank 1946.23
Marlowe, Geneva 1922.05
Marlowe, Gloria 1955.01
Marlowe, Harry 1910.21
Marlowe, Helen 1911.18
Marlowe, Hugh 1943.03
Marlowe, J.C. 1901.21, 1905.44
Marlowe, James C. 1905.55, 1908.09, 1909.02, 1916.02, 1918.29, 1919.09, 1920.38, 1922.17, 1922.47
Marlowe, Jonathan 1948.28
Marlowe, Julie 1953.11
Marlowe, Marion 1959.24
Marlowe, Martha 1900.33
Marlowe, Mary 1925.12, 1926.26
Marlowe, Mr. 1863.02, 1863.04
Marlowe, Mrs. Owen 1861.04, 1878.11, 1881.24
Marlowe, Norma 1948.28
Marlowe, Norma Jane 1947.03
Marlowe, Owen 1861.04, 1875.21
Marlowe, Raymond 1924.45
Marlowe, Selma 1936.06
Marlowe, Vivian 1925.02, 1927.20
Marlyn, Isabel 1937.11
Marmorstein, Louis 1931.29
Marmoulian, Rouben 1943.04
Marnay, Eddy 1959.15, 1961.25
Marne Productions, Inc. 1919.08
Marolda, Diva 1905.33
Marone, Terry 1964.20
Maronek, James 1982.10
Marouani, Felix 1968.21
Maroze, Mario 1968.24
Marquardt, F. 1894.30
Marques, David 1999.10, 2001.06
Marquette 1900.03
Marquette, Chris 1995.19
Marquette, Christopher 1997.22
Marquette, Miss 1871.15, 1872.06
Marquez, Gabriel Garcia 1995.09
Marquez, Luis 1949.07
Marquez, Veronica 1911.40
Marquis Family, The 1963.10
Marquis, Don 1957.05
Marquise, Mercia 1930.34
Marquise, Veronica 1919.19
Marquisini, Zoie 1883.17
Marr, Beth 1900.28
Marr, John 1894.21
Marr, Richard 1976.09
Marr, Trude 1922.39
Marracci, Livia 1930.09
Marre, Albert 1953.16, 1956.07, 1961.20, 1965.34, 1970.10, 1972.14, 1976.01, 1977.12, 1989.05, 1992.07
Marrenner, Alice 1909.08
Marrin, W. 1875.39, 1876.03
Marriner, Gregg 1980.01
Marriott, Fanny 1888.38, 1888.41
Marriott, James 1870.19
Marriott, John 1951.11
Marriott, Polly 1898.38
Marriott, T.A. 1880.69
Marriott, W. 1892.42
Marritt, Larry 1968.03
Marron, John 1897.12
Marrow, Esther 1979.32
Marrow, Macklin 1933.07, 1934.03, 1952.03
Marrow, Queen Esther 1990.05
Marryett, Elsie 1914.11
Mars 1894.28
Mars Theatrical Productions 1999.24
Mars, Anthony 1897.54, 1899.25, 1910.32
Mars, Antony 1900.33, 1909.01, 1912.01
Mars, Leo 1905.57, 1907.36, 1908.39
Mars, Lucien 1964.39
Mars, Oralla 1911.37
Marschante, Marian 1927.53
Marschante, Marion 1927.04, 1927.54
Marsden, Adelaide 1902.09, 1903.05
Marsden, Beri 1903.09
Marsden, Beryl 1911.07
Marsden, Edward R. 1889.03, 1889.14
Marsden, F. 1870.18
Marsden, Frank 1906.02, 1906.42
Marsden, Fred 1870.01, 1870.14, 1870.39, 1883.07, 1883.40, 1883.43, 1889.14, 1891.07, 1896.11
Marsden, Frederick 1878.15, 1880.51
Marsden, Freduel 1876.32
Marsden, Messr. 1868.23, 1869.36, 1870.02
Marsden, Millie 1890.33, 1892.08, 1892.10
Marsden, Mr. 1869.45
Marsden, Richard 1893.07, 1904.22
Marsdon, F. 1893.48, 1894.03, 1894.08
Marsee, Susanne 1979.20, 1981.21, 1982.16, 1982.21, 1983.12, 1985.11, 1986.09, 1987.08, 1988.18, 1990.07, 1990.08, 1991.08, 1991.09
Marsh, Berkley 1954.09
Marsh, Bernard J. 1986.06
Marsh, C. Leland 1920.06
Marsh, Caren 1948.23
Marsh, Cora 1894.49
Marsh, Edwin 1944.09
Marsh, Emma 1896.35
Marsh, Eva 1905.06
Marsh, Frederick Percy 1887.09
Marsh, Harry 1877.24
Marsh, Helena 1925.47
Marsh, Howard 1917.32, 1920.28, 1921.31, 1924.12, 1924.45, 1927.14, 1927.67, 1930.36, 1931.10, 1931.12, 1931.15, 1931.17, 1931.18, 1931.20, 1931.22, 1931.23, 1931.25, 1932.02, 1935.05, 1935.06, 1935.07, 1935.08, 1935.09, 1935.10
Marsh, Ida 1890.44
Marsh, Joe 1995.13, 1997.09
Marsh, Mary 1925.17, 1927.36
Marsh, Mr. 1852.02
Marsh, Myrtle 1909.25
Marsh, Nellei 1898.28
Marsh, Nelly 1898.60
Marsh, R. 1899.21
Marsh, Reginald 1923.43, 1929.29
Marsh, Sy 1974.11
Marsh, Vera 1931.04, 1931.28, 1931.39
Marshak, Larry 1978.01
Marshal, Henry I. 1917.26
Marshall Field and Company 1904.09, 1905.53
Marshall, "Red" 1942.30, 1950.12
Marshall, Albert J. 1903.41
Marshall, Allie 1905.21
Marshall, Alphonso 1954.19
Marshall, Amelia 1985.02
Marshall, Anthony D. 1982.24
Marshall, Armina 1950.04
Marshall, Assota 1946.01, 1948.20
Marshall, Austin 1937.13
Marshall, Betty 1920.17, 1920.42
Marshall, Boyd 1918.25, 1920.43, 1923.34, 1927.66, 1930.04
Marshall, Don 1942.35, 1945.04
Marshall, Donna Lee 1992.12, 1994.12, 1996.08, 1998.13, 2001.06
Marshall, E.A. 1851.01, 1851.06, 1851.07, 1852.01, 1852.05, 1854.01, 1854.03, 1854.06, 1854.07, 1855.01, 1855.02, 1855.10
Marshall, E.G. 1973.08
Marshall, Earl W. 1914.11
Marshall, Edward 1886.50, 1886.54, 1928.48, 1939.20
Marshall, Eileene 1912.31
Marshall, Everett 1931.30, 1933.03, 1934.01, 1934.39, 1938.17, 1943.06
Marshall, Frederick 1877.22, 1877.23, 1877.25, 1877.39
Marshall, Fredye 1943.10, 1943.24, 1945.06, 1946.09, 1952.15
Marshall, Garry 1974.26
Marshall, Gary DeWitt 1993.04
Marshall, George 1932.01, 1933.02
Marshall, Harry B. 1902.11, 1904.23
Marshall, Henry 1911.24, 1914.06, 1918.18
Marshall, Henry I. 1911.02, 1912.13, 1912.14, 1913.35, 1920.36, 2000.12
Marshall, Herbert 1967.18
Marshall, Iris 1940.12
Marshall, J.C. 1894.05
Marshall, J.R. 1907.55
Marshall, Jack 1902.11
Marshall, James 1925.39, 1927.14, 1930.23, 1944.32
Marshall, James R. 1921.38, 1924.05
Marshall, Jay 1948.25, 1950.06, 1957.01
Marshall, John 1893.14, 1894.02, 1923.31
Marshall, Jr., Frank J. 1930.21
Marshall, Kathleen 1994.01, 1995.14, 1997.15, 1999.19, 2000.18, 2001.02
Marshall, Ken 1980.02
Marshall, Larry 1971.20, 1976.03, 1976.28, 1978.28, 1979.32, 1981.25, 1983.04, 1986.06, 1989.24, 1997.03
Marshall, Lee 1931.31, 1997.09
Marshall, Lee D. 1995.13
Marshall, Leona 1909.10
Marshall, Lillian 1904.04
Marshall, Madeline 1897.21, 1897.33, 1898.75, 1908.35
Marshall, Madelyn 1906.20, 1906.48, 1910.29
Marshall, Maithe 1945.06
Marshall, Marilyn 1965.05
Marshall, Marion 1896.27
Marshall, Mat 1907.29, 1907.31
Marshall, Michelle 1979.02
Marshall, Minnie 1880.43, 1880.49, 1961.24
Marshall, Mort 1948.22, 1949.18, 1952.07, 1959.13, 1962.04, 1962.27, 1966.11, 1970.07
Marshall, Pat 1942.35, 1943.21, 1944.20, 1956.02
Marshall, Patricia 1945.19
Marshall, Pauline 1902.32
Marshall, Percy 1895.10, 1895.43
Marshall, Peter L. 1965.33
Marshall, Polly 1860.06
Marshall, Red 1940.23
Marshall, Rob 1983.14, 1985.18, 1993.09, 1993.10, 1994.01, 1995.11, 1995.15, 1996.06, 1998.04, 2000.18

Marshall, Robert 1928.46, 1942.33, 1946.15, 1998.15
Marshall, Sherry 1922.39
Marshall, Sid 1972.06, 1975.05
Marshall, Tina 1951.11
Marshall, Tully 1891.34
Marshall, Virginia 1908.10, 1908.39, 1909.13, 1909.25
Marshall, Wendell 1958.08
Marshall, Will Sharpe 1973.04
Marshall, William 1926.07, 1943.23, 1949.15, 1950.08, 1951.11
Marshall, Winnie 1891.23
Marshalls 2001.09
Marshe, Vera 1932.16, 1935.03
Marshton, Miss 1881.38
Marsland, James 1966.28, 1968.26
Marston 1905.22
Marston, E.W. 1875.05, 1878.05
Marston, F.M. 1898.56
Marston, Fred 1886.51, 1888.12, 1897.27
Marston, Fred M. 1896.41
Marston, Gladys 1923.41
Marston, Henry 1898.36
Marston, Joseph 1899.15
Marston, Lawrence 1897.23, 1922.01
Marston, Madge 1907.51
Marston, Margaret 1902.23
Marston, Richard 1866.18, 1868.03, 1869.04, 1869.07, 1869.13, 1870.05, 1870.30, 1870.41, 1872.10, 1875.04, 1877.28, 1886.02, 1888.20, 1889.04, 1890.01, 1891.47, 1892.37, 1892.40, 1893.17, 1893.19, 1893.35, 1893.39, 1893.47, 1894.26, 1894.29, 1894.38, 1895.22, 1895.26, 1895.42, 1896.28, 1897.15, 1897.36, 1898.34, 1898.54, 1899.06, 1899.24, 1899.28, 1899.38, 1899.40, 1904.56, 1905.19
Marston, Roso 1897.29
Marston, Theodore 1911.18
Marston, Vivian 1905.51
Marston, W.E. 1876.16
Martal, Isaye 1878.08
Martal, Mlle. 1877.27
Martan, Nita 1925.04, 1925.35
Martel, Annie 1888.43
Martel, Gene 1933.12, 1935.12
Martel, Michel 1966.03
Martel, Remi 1938.04, 1941.03, 1942.26, 1943.01, 1948.23
Martel, Tom 1972.09
Martell 1894.44
Martell, Annie 1892.21, 1894.06, 1903.09, 1904.07
Martell, Fred 1948.19, 1949.05
Marten, Gretchen 1871.18
Marten, Mme. 1871.18, 1882.59
Marten, Mons. 1871.18
Martens, Carl 1890.21
Martens, Clara 1930.01
Martens, Elsa 1898.41
Martens, George 1907.58
Martens, Lora Jeanne 1980.30
Martens, Mme. 1887.44, 1888.18, 1889.36, 1890.23
Martens, Mr. 1890.23
Marthe, Mlle. 1876.24, 1876.25, 1876.26, 1877.10, 1877.13, 1877.14, 1877.19, 1884.43, 1884.47
Marti, Fernando 1949.07
Marti, Frank 1956.02
Martin 1933.15
Martin, A. 1873.22
Martin, Al 1921.20
Martin, Alexis 1990.08
Martin, Alice 1911.04
Martin, Amy 1900.37
Martin, Andrea 1992.17, 1997.10
Martin, Angela 1968.07
Martin, Barney 1962.04, 1966.02, 1975.14
Martin, Barry L. 1965.37
Martin, Bernard 1921.41
Martin, Beulah 1901.17, 1905.46
Martin, Bob 1947.16
Martin, Buzzy 1950.08
Martin, Charles 1888.08
Martin, Charles G. 1954.17
Martin, Christopher 1989.17
Martin, Claire 1920.39
Martin, David 1957.09
Martin, Delores 1952.08, 1956.05, 1956.06
Martin, Dorothy 1926.39, 1930.23
Martin, Douglas 1934.37
Martin, Easthope 1932.14
Martin, Edith 1928.28
Martin, Eileen 1998.09, 2000.05
Martin, Elliott 1949.17, 1985.02, 1993.10
Martin, Erin 1962.02, 1964.17
Martin, Ernest 1954.09
Martin, Ernest H. 1948.26, 1950.17, 1951.02, 1953.07, 1955.02, 1958.20, 1961.22, 1962.27, 1965.33, 1966.27, 1977.16
Martin, Ethel 1924.41, 1952.01, 1953.16, 1963.17, 1972.02
Martin, Etta Baker 1894.36, 1895.30, 1896.09, 1897.05, 1899.01, 1900.10, 1901.02
Martin, Eugene 1942.35, 1946.22
Martin, Evelyn 1923.22, 1924.07
Martin, Fay 1936.07
Martin, Florence 1908.27, 1912.01, 1913.15, 1924.46
Martin, Frank 1919.30
Martin, Freddy 1940.16
Martin, George 1894.34, 1895.13, 1952.01, 1953.11, 1956.16, 1957.17, 1961.26, 1963.17
Martin, George E. 1897.49
Martin, George N. 1985.18
Martin, Georges Andre 1935.19, 1947.18
Martin, Glenn 1983.05
Martin, Greta 1989.03
Martin, Harry 1888.08
Martin, Helen 1937.06, 1970.05, 1972.26, 1973.10
Martin, Helene 1907.61
Martin, Herbert 1965.36, 1989.06
Martin, Howard 1951.14
Martin, Hugh 1937.15, 1939.12, 1939.22, 1939.27, 1939.30, 1940.08, 1940.17, 1940.22, 1941.06, 1942.01, 1947.08, 1947.16, 1948.08, 1948.23, 1948.28, 1949.18, 1951.13, 1951.23, 1953.01, 1964.16, 1967.11, 1974.02, 1974.26, 1979.24, 1979.25, 1981.16, 1988.08, 1989.03, 1989.23, 1999.23
Martin, I.A. 1908.33
Martin, J. 1880.15
Martin, J.J. 1899.40, 1902.04
Martin, James 1980.19
Martin, Jay 1943.05, 1945.12, 1946.14
Martin, Jesse L. 1996.09
Martin, John 1794.01, 1876.05, 1906.03, 1961.09, 1962.16, 1971.05, 1979.13
Martin, John A. 1883.56
Martin, John E. 1796.03
Martin, Johnny 1876.04, 1876.30
Martin, Joyce 1976.36, 1981.18
Martin, June 1927.39
Martin, L.J. 1883.06
Martin, Larry 1944.02
Martin, Lee Hobbs 1906.35
Martin, Leila 1950.12, 1951.19, 1952.10, 1955.06, 1970.15, 1988.01
Martin, Les 1963.14
Martin, Lewis 1933.24
Martin, Louise 1883.65
Martin, Luke 1891.28, 1894.36, 1895.30, 1896.09, 1896.11, 1897.05, 1899.01, 1900.10, 1901.02, 1903.25, 1904.01, 1904.46
Martin, M. 1883.56, 1887.38, 1887.41
Martin, Maria 1996.12
Martin, Marion 1936.12
Martin, Mary 1938.13, 1943.19, 1946.05, 1949.04, 1954.13, 1959.24, 1963.25, 1966.29
Martin, Master 1871.27, 1872.06, 1875.39, 1876.03, 1885.15, 1885.22
Martin, May 1937.14
Martin, Melissa 1990.08
Martin, Michael X. 1994.12, 1995.19, 1996.15, 1997.15, 1999.19
Martin, Millicent 1954.09, 1977.05, 1978.22
Martin, Milton 1933.04
Martin, Miss 1865.01
Martin, Mons. 1844.01, 1887.35, 1887.36, 1887.37
Martin, Monsieur 1844.01
Martin, Mr. 1793.01, 1794.01, 1852.03, 1863.01, 1865.05, 1868.03
Martin, Nicholas 1982.24
Martin, Norman 1955.12, 1960.07
Martin, Norman L. 1971.07, 1973.11
Martin, Olivia 1934.12
Martin, Owen 1938.14, 1943.04, 1951.16, 1953.09, 1958.07
Martin, Paul 1928.41
Martin, Perry 1949.06
Martin, Porte Saint 1877.04
Martin, Randy 1977.18
Martin, Rea 1916.13
Martin, Robert 1887.29, 1888.11, 1888.38, 1888.41
Martin, Robert J. 1889.54
Martin, Roberta 1990.05
Martin, Ross 1953.01, 1957.05
Martin, Ruth 1953.06, 1953.15, 1954.06, 1954.10, 1955.17, 1956.10, 1957.13, 1958.15, 1959.16, 1964.31, 1965.25, 1974.16, 1975.16, 1976.23, 1977.11, 1980.03, 1980.22, 1981.22, 1982.07, 1982.21, 1986.10, 1987.11
Martin, Sara 1927.30
Martin, Stacey 1999.15
Martin, Ted 1969.03
Martin, Theodore 1911.41
Martin, Thomas 1953.06, 1953.15, 1954.06, 1954.10, 1955.17, 1956.10, 1957.13, 1958.15, 1959.16, 1964.31, 1965.25, 1974.16, 1975.16, 1976.23, 1977.11, 1980.03, 1980.22, 1981.22, 1982.07, 1982.21, 1986.10, 1987.11
Martin, Thomas P. 1953.06, 1953.15, 1954.10, 1956.10, 1968.10
Martin, Tom 1887.32, 1888.39, 1889.34, 1928.25
Martin, Virgie 1900.41
Martin, Virginia 1954.05, 1955.04, 1956.08, 1958.08, 1961.22, 1962.27, 1979.09
Martin, Vivian 1927.43
Martin, Walter 1939.23, 1940.04
Martin, William 1873.10, 1905.26, 1975.07
Martin, Yvette Laura 1985.01
Martina, Mlle. 1901.27
Martindale, James 1954.07
Martindel, Edward 1906.07, 1907.26, 1910.35, 1911.47, 1913.10, 1915.01, 1917.07, 1919.02, 1919.34
Martindell, Edward 1902.31, 1903.21, 1908.16
Martindell, Edward B. 1904.37, 1906.30
Martine, Angie 1875.10
Martine, Miss 1852.02
Martine, Stella 1905.16, 1905.54
Martineau, Frank W. 1900.54
Martineau, Sadie 1877.01
Martineau, Sydney 1912.11
Martinet, Eugene 1921.31
Martinet, Francoise 1958.13, 1958.16
Martinette, Albert 1889.21
Martinette, Gene 1920.47
Martinetti, Albert 1880.68, 1883.47, 1888.01
Martinetti, Ignacio 1870.22, 1878.11, 1880.21, 1881.10, 1882.82, 1886.13, 1888.34, 1890.07, 1890.34, 1891.26, 1892.09, 1893.08, 1893.42, 1898.69, 1900.07, 1900.42, 1900.55, 1904.03, 1906.47, 1907.41, 1908.15, 1910.22, 1913.34, 1919.19, 1922.36
Martinetti, Ignatio 1904.19, 1929.45
Martinetti, J. 1880.68
Martinetti, Julien 1876.03
Martinetti, Louis 1901.22
Martinetti, Messr. 1892.27
Martinetti, Mlle. 1865.01, 1866.02, 1866.28, 1867.12, 1867.13, 1867.14, 1867.15, 1867.16
Martinetti, Mons. 1876.03
Martinetti, Pauline 1869.05, 1880.68
Martinetti, W. Julian 1880.68
Martinez, Dickie 1896.17
Martinez, Elena 1894.05
Martinez, Enrique 1959.04
Martinez, Federico Torres 1988.15
Martinez, Francisco 1875.24
Martinez, Isadore 1878.03
Martinez, L. 1898.42
Martinez, Lillian 1890.37
Martinez, Nino Francisco 1875.22
Martinez, Pepe 1988.15
Martinez, Ricardo Caballero y 1881.24
Martinez, Richard 2000.10
Martinez, Teresa 1949.07
Martinez, Tony 1957.16, 1977.12, 1992.07
Martini Richard 1980.14
Martini, Clara 1905.18
Martini, Richard 1999.09, 1999.14
Martini, William 1890.03
Martino, Fernando 1964.03
Martino, Mark 1981.25
Martino, Nina 1895.10
Martinoli, Carlos 1976.32
Martinot, Sadie 1876.15, 1885.41, 1893.47, 1896.22, 1897.34
Martins, Frank 1919.24
Martins, Peter 1978.26, 1983.02, 1985.12
Martinson, Art 1964.20
Martner, Master 1888.04
Martorano, Michael 1981.21, 1984.11
Martos, Ferenc 1916.19
Martos, Frank 1916.01
Martos, Franz 1913.26, 1914.28, 1930.30
Martrit, Minna 1907.32, 1913.32
Martson, Lawrence 1927.43
Martson, Richard 1896.30
Martyn, Edward 1911.39, 1934.41
Martyn, Evelyn 1921.25
Martyn, Kathlene 1923.30, 1924.34, 1924.43
Martyn, Marjorie May 1928.50
Martyne, Agnes 1895.26, 1896.28
Martz, Hattie 1900.17
Martz, Mattie 1900.09, 1900.11, 1900.14, 1900.22, 1900.23, 1900.27, 1900.29, 1900.30, 1904.25
Marvel, Frank 1937.08
Marvell, Holt 1982.12
Marvenga, Ilsa 1923.20
Marvenga, Ilse 1924.45, 1929.38, 1931.43, 1931.45, 1932.10
Marvil, Billy 1932.16
Marvin Productions, Inc. 1982.10
Marvin, Ada 1888.43
Marvin, Anthony 1936.22
Marvin, Doris 1917.14
Marvin, Helen 1897.03, 1897.11, 1898.72, 1899.36, 1902.30
Marvin, Johnny 1926.29
Marvin, Mel 1970.09, 1972.11, 1978.06, 1980.27, 1999.10
Marvin, Roy 1922.47
Marvin, Virginia 1933.24
Marwick, Dudley 1925.39, 1927.25
Marwick, Irma 1918.25, 1918.39, 1920.35, 1923.08
Marwick, Niobe 1918.25
Marwig, Carl 1895.44, 1896.44, 1897.20, 1897.25, 1897.50, 1898.25, 1898.29, 1899.12, 1899.15, 1899.19, 1900.07, 1900.42, 1900.49, 1900.56, 1902.06, 1902.27, 1903.16
Marwig, Charles 1894.42
Marwig, Herr 1892.14
Marwig, Olga 1917.04
Marwood, T. 1884.15
Marx, Arthur 1924.11, 1970.07
Marx, Chico 1925.45, 1927.21, 1928.38, 1944.19
Marx, Grocho 1970.07
Marx, Groucho 1925.45, 1927.21, 1928.38, 1930.32
Marx, Harpo 1925.45, 1927.21, 1928.38
Marx, Herbert 1924.11
Marx, Jules H. 1924.11
Marx, Leonard 1924.11
Marx, Max 1908.08, 1908.22, 1909.26, 1916.02, 1917.36, 1917.37
Marx, Mr. 1890.31, 1894.01
Marx, Peter 1999.04
Marx, Zeppo 1925.45, 1927.21, 1928.38
Mary-Brown, Katherine 1979.29
Marze, Addie 1910.03
Marzetti, Mlle. 1863.06, 1863.07
Marzetti, Mons. 1863.06
Marzorati, Jodi 1983.17
Marzullo, Steve 1990.12
Mascagni 1894.21
Mascagni, Pietro 1898.09
Mascagno, Ernesto 1876.12
Mascagno, Eva 1928.26
Mascagno, Signor 1877.15
Mascarina, Mlle. 1877.15
Mascarini, Mlle. 1876.12
Mascher, Mary 1934.15
Maschi, Rosina 1884.58
Maschwitz, Eric 1960.07, 1982.12
Masciarelli, Sylvio 1941.11
Masckey, N. 1903.25
Mascolo, Joseph 1970.04
Masekela, Barbara 1965.32
Masekela, Hugh 1988.02
Masella, Arthur 1983.13, 1984.11, 1984.13, 1986.08, 1987.09, 1988.04
Masella, Joni 1982.03, 1985.19
Maseng, Don 1971.17
Masenheimer, David 1997.17, 1999.13
Masi, Margaretta 1906.02, 1907.15
Masiell, Joe 1969.05, 1972.07, 1972.16
Maskell, Nellie 1902.17, 1905.21
Maskell, Ray 1891.28

Maslansky, Harris 1982.08
Maslin, Isabel 1882.15
Maslova, Lisa 1946.05
Maslow, Sophie 1954.10
Mason 1887.02
Mason, Adelaide 1912.07, 1912.44, 1914.28
Mason, Bertha E. 1898.45
Mason, Bertha Estelle 1899.32
Mason, Buck 1998.18
Mason, Cameron 1975.15
Mason, Charles 1879.12, 1889.03, 1889.48, 1890.06, 1891.06, 1893.42
Mason, Charles A. 1897.06, 1898.08, 1902.17, 1911.24, 1912.39
Mason, Dan 1902.17, 1906.10
Mason, Daniel 1887.01
Mason, Delia 1903.22
Mason, Delil 1906.32
Mason, Earl 1934.13
Mason, Edgar 1941.07
Mason, Edith 1889.52, 1898.30, 1898.33, 1898.37
Mason, Edythe 1917.28
Mason, Elizabeth 1926.21
Mason, Eric 1966.06
Mason, Fay 1957.07
Mason, Frank 1908.12
Mason, Henry 1892.34
Mason, Isabelle 1926.21
Mason, J. 1875.34
Mason, J.B. 1887.52
Mason, J.L. 1882.62
Mason, Jack 1904.20, 1907.18, 1910.07, 1910.15, 1910.17, 1911.23, 1911.24, 1911.30, 1911.44, 1912.29, 1914.07, 1914.10, 1914.16, 1914.20, 1914.22, 1915.02, 1915.04, 1915.11, 1915.16, 1915.26, 1916.01, 1916.09, 1916.25, 1916.26, 1917.19, 1917.37, 1918.05, 1918.12, 1918.20, 1918.35, 1918.38, 1919.08, 1919.14, 1920.22, 1920.23, 1920.33, 1921.02, 1921.14, 1922.07, 1922.24, 1922.36, 1924.07, 1924.13, 1924.30, 1926.27, 1927.42, 1927.47, 1928.15, 1937.09
Mason, Jackie 1986.21, 1988.11, 1990.11, 1994.03, 1996.03, 1999.25
Mason, James 1883.47, 2001.04
Mason, Jane 1961.02
Mason, John 1892.57, 1893.03, 1927.30, 1929.01, 1929.25, 1930.29, 1933.27, 1934.37
Mason, Joseph L. 1883.06
Mason, Karen 1982.13
Mason, Kate 1879.02
Mason, Kay 1931.47
Mason, Kitty 1910.21, 1934.05
Mason, Lowell 1998.21
Mason, Luba 1995.05, 1998.02
Mason, Margaret 1917.06
Mason, Marguerite 1916.22
Mason, Marilyn 1967.16
Mason, Marilyne 1963.06, 1969.01
Mason, Marissa 1960.06, 1961.14
Mason, Marlyn 1963.15
Mason, Martha 1923.02, 1924.45, 1926.33, 1932.03
Mason, Martin 1924.13
Mason, Mary 1930.19, 1933.06
Mason, Melissa 1932.24, 1936.22, 1941.02, 1942.27
Mason, Messr. 1856.04, 1870.02, 1881.35
Mason, Mike 1954.15
Mason, Miss 1871.11
Mason, Mr. 1869.31
Mason, Nan 1980.18
Mason, Norma 1929.33
Mason, P.C. 1904.28
Mason, Pauline 1925.08, 1926.29
Mason, Post 1901.11
Mason, Ralph 1968.25, 1968.26, 1968.29
Mason, Ray 1953.11, 1954.01, 1955.04, 1959.11, 1961.22
Mason, Reginald 1918.03
Mason, Richard 1973.14
Mason, Robert 1938.19
Mason, Ruth 1942.25
Mason, Snippy 1921.16, 1922.44, 1926.19
Mason, Virginia 1962.18, 1978.14
Mason, W.C. 1911.25
Mason, W.H. 1873.26
Mason, W.J. 1897.47, 1899.03, 1899.27
Mason, William 1877.08, 1922.31, 1925.11
Mason, William D. 1896.14
Mason, Ysobel 1927.27
Masondo, Lawrence 1997.14
Masoner, Gene 1975.03, 1978.10
Masque Sound 1972.20
Mass, La 1886.34
Massa, Steve 1982.24
Masse, Miss 1859.08
Masse, Victor 1855.03, 1861.05, 1866.27, 1872.01
Massel, Paul 1987.01
Massen, L.F. 1879.25
Massen, Miss 1869.41
Massenet, Jules 1940.05
Masser, Michael 1976.16
Massett, Stephen H. 1869.42
Massey, Blanche 1894.33
Massey, Daniel 1963.14, 1973.12
Massey, Guy 1926.37, 1927.37
Massey, Ilona 1943.05
Massey, J.W. 1890.40
Massey, Kenya U. 1999.10
Massey, Olive 1916.07
Massey, Rose 1869.08, 1870.04, 1875.16
Massey, William 1867.08
Massi, Bernice 1955.25, 1960.01, 1962.03, 1964.05
Massine, Leonide 1929.50, 1944.16, 1945.02
Massinger, Charles 1924.36, 1929.34
Massoni, Miss 1892.14
Mast, Charles 1914.23, 1920.36, 1925.08, 1928.37, 1930.05
Mast, L.H. 1905.12
Mastantuono/Palumbo 2000.02
Mastelle, Helen 1939.21
Masten, Fritz 1986.09
Masteroff, Joe 1963.14, 1966.24, 1971.07, 1987.16, 1993.10, 1998.04
Masters, David 1976.36, 1990.18
Masters, Edgar Lee 1963.19
Masters, Eleanor 1919.41, 1920.13
Masters, Frank 1921.25, 1924.23, 1927.47
Masters, Frankie 1995.14
Masters, Grace 1923.23
Masters, Harry 1920.20, 1923.22
Masters, Johnny 1942.10
Masters, Kittie 1888.31
Masterson, Carroll 1960.01, 1960.07, 1962.02, 1964.40
Masterson, Debora 1978.18
Masterson, Harris 1960.01, 1960.07, 1962.02, 1964.40
Masterson, Jeannine 1956.14, 1959.27, 1960.06
Masterson, Mary Stuart 1982.24
Masterson, Peter 1978.13, 1982.11, 1994.06
Masterson, Valerie 1964.36, 1964.41, 1966.22, 1966.23, 1968.25, 1968.27, 1968.28, 1978.17, 1989.15
Mastice, Catherine 1947.10
Mastin, Will 1956.02
Mastrantonio, Mary 1981.12, 1981.25
Mastrantonio, Mary Elizabeth 1984.02
Mastrocola, Frank 1984.01, 1987.05
Mastrone, Frank 1996.08, 1997.09, 1999.15
Masullo, Tony 1966.21
Mata, Meta 1939.26
Matalon, Vivian 1980.26, 1983.21
Matalon, Zack 1960.12
Matassa, Cosmo 1992.06
Matcus, Charlie 1991.13
Mathe, Mlle. 1877.09
Mather, Charles C. 1922.19, 1923.20
Mathers, Jack 1961.07
Mathes, Martha 1956.04
Mathews 1908.15, 1919.08
Mathews, A.S. 1880.07
Mathews, Bert 1928.38
Mathews, Carmen 1951.17, 1965.36, 1968.08, 1969.05, 1972.24, 1981.12
Mathews, Charles 1834.01
Mathews, Christine 1956.03, 1961.15
Mathews, Edward 1918.25
Mathews, Ezra 1904.48, 1907.40
Mathews, Frances Aymar 1903.12
Mathews, George 1960.23, 1966.09, 1966.30
Mathews, Irene S. 1919.18
Mathews, J. Cleneay 1904.47
Mathews, J. Sherrie 1891.37, 1893.08, 1899.29, 1901.04
Mathews, Jimmy 1979.25
Mathews, John 1939.07
Mathews, Joyce 1941.09, 1949.01
Mathews, Jr., William H. 1914.11
Mathews, Julia 1875.19, 1875.23, 1875.26, 1875.34, 1875.36, 1875.37, 1875.38
Mathews, Julian 1897.07
Mathews, Junius 1922.20
Mathews, Mary 1933.27
Mathews, Mary Jo 1932.26
Mathews, Michael 1914.18
Mathews, Miss 1875.36
Mathews, Mr. 1851.01, 1875.03
Mathews, P.J. 1913.22
Mathews, Peggy 1920.28
Mathews, W.H. 1907.24, 1908.34, 1917.12, 1922.04, 1922.30
Mathews, William H. 1928.23, 1929.08
Mathey, Maria 1904.44
Mathey, Marie 1904.13, 1904.44
Mathey, Merle 1904.13
Mathias, Philip 1955.06
Mathieu, Adelina 1883.39
Mathieu, William 1961.17
Mathilde, Mlle. 1867.24, 1868.07, 1868.18, 1868.25, 1868.31, 1869.01, 1869.10, 1876.26, 1877.06, 1877.13
Mathis, Bonnie 1964.01
Mathis, Claude 1981.17
Mathis, June 1911.30
Mathis, Lee 1979.08
Mathis, Sherry 1976.33
Mathis, Stanley Wayne 1990.14, 1992.08, 1997.20, 1999.03, 1999.19
Mathison, A.E. 1925.18
Mathon, A. 1985.07, 1999.18
Mathues, Craig 1939.25
Matier, Frank 1918.18
Matis, Jack 1942.35
Matisse, Nana 1939.26
Matlock, B.L. 1876.12
Matlock, Harry 1945.03
Matlock, Norman 1971.18
Matlock, Ruth 1927.03
Matlovsky, Samuel 1957.03, 1963.09
Matlowsky, Samuel 1953.04
Matons, William 1933.12, 1938.18
Matos, Valeria 1992.13
Matosich, Jr., Fred 1993.10
Matray, Ernst 1950.14
Matray, Maria 1950.14
Matsey, Jeff 1993.12, 1993.13
Matsios, Christine 1948.24, 1950.17
Matson, Jill 1996.08
Matson, Vera 1982.22, 1989.12
Matsumoto, Paul 1991.03
Matsumoto, Yuri 1989.21
Matsusaka, Tom 1974.12, 1976.02
Matsuyama, Saeka 1998.11
Matta 1934.16
Mattaliano, Marc 1979.27
Mattei, Tito 1888.11
Mattern, Katherine 1939.23, 1940.04
Mattern, Kitty 1942.12
Matteson, Ruth 1939.12, 1943.09, 1945.12, 1946.20
Matthaei, Konrad 1961.07, 1968.07
Matthau, Walter 1950.11, 1955.06
Matthew, Jack 1956.12
Matthews 1908.21, 1913.27, 1918.25
Matthews, A. 1873.26
Matthews, Anderson 1975.18
Matthews, Art 1964.33, 1966.10
Matthews, Artie 1980.27
Matthews, Babe 1936.30
Matthews, Bert 1930.14, 1930.41, 1951.24
Matthews, Billy 1960.01, 1961.07, 1965.18
Matthews, Brian 1981.12
Matthews, Denese 1990.15
Matthews, E. 1904.01
Matthews, Eddie 1936.30
Matthews, Edward 1934.05, 1935.13, 1942.03, 1943.15, 1944.03, 1952.06
Matthews, Ellen 1954.15
Matthews, Evelyn 1891.18
Matthews, Ezra 1908.12
Matthews, Fred 1889.19
Matthews, Gerald 1944.21
Matthews, Gerry 1965.31
Matthews, Hale 1978.24, 1980.06
Matthews, Homer 1879.42
Matthews, Inez 1943.10, 1945.06, 1949.15, 1952.06
Matthews, J. Sherrie 1897.07, 1899.11
Matthews, Jessie 1929.51
Matthews, Jon 1978.11
Matthews, Joy Lynn 1999.22
Matthews, Joyce 1940.10
Matthews, Jr., W.H. 1913.32
Matthews, Junius 1924.14, 1925.20, 1927.23, 1929.20
Matthews, Lester 1946.03
Matthews, Mary Jo 1933.25
Matthews, Matty 1901.03
Matthews, Messr. 1846.01
Matthews, Mr. 1846.01, 1851.06, 1851.07, 1851.08, 1852.05, 1854.01
Matthews, Neal 1978.01
Matthews, Roger 1921.16
Matthews, Sherrie 1895.18
Matthews, Tony 1942.15, 1999.09
Matthews, W. 1912.46
Matthews, W.H. 1908.19, 1909.13, 1910.18, 1911.24, 1918.15
Matthews, William H. 1907.41, 1907.44, 1910.10, 1910.29, 1914.15, 1915.08, 1915.24, 1917.16, 1918.23, 1920.21, 1922.08, 1922.42, 1929.46
Matthews, William Henry 1910.11, 1913.30, 1914.30, 1916.24, 1924.41
Matthews, William J. 1908.01
Matthews, Y. Yvonne 1983.04
Matthewson, Eleanor 1914.30
Matthias, Sean 1999.07
Matthiessen, Ruth 1891.34
Matthison, A. 1869.04
Matthison, Arthur 1869.15, 1871.27, 1872.06
Mattice, Wallace 1927.42
Mattina, Vincenzo 1935.02
Mattingly, H. 1929.21
Mattingly, Hendricks 1930.24
Mattioli, Louis 1977.15, 1996.04
Mattison, Johnny 1937.07
Mattoli, Mario 1935.02
Mattox, Allen E. 1918.14
Mattox, Harold 1946.20
Mattox, Jean 1958.08, 1959.03
Mattox, Matt 1948.24, 1953.11, 1955.25, 1957.03, 1958.08, 1959.03, 1959.26, 1963.25, 1964.05
Mattson, Eric 1945.05, 1949.03
Mature, Victor 1941.04
Matus, Kalmanc 1918.24
Matz, Agnes 1905.04
Matz, Jerry 1987.12, 1989.10, 1990.18
Matz, Peter 1957.16, 1958.20, 1960.01, 1961.18, 1962.03, 1967.06, 1979.13, 1984.16, 1989.26, 1992.11, 1992.18, 1994.06, 1999.23
Matzenauer, Adrienne 1934.19
Maubourg, Jeanne 1914.25
Maubury, Charles 1883.05, 1883.07
Mauceri, John 1974.06, 1978.19, 1978.23, 1979.20, 1979.27, 1982.20, 1983.02, 1984.11, 1985.12, 1986.08, 1989.14, 1997.10
Maud Daniel Opera Company 1901.10, 1901.11
Maud, Bonnie 1908.36
Maud, Margery 1968.17
Maude, Margery 1964.20
Mauder, Mons. 1889.08
Mauer, Gary 1992.12
Mauge, Baby 1883.34
Mauge, Mons. 1882.29, 1883.41
Maugham, Dora 1943.18
Maugham, Somerset 1944.27
Maughan, Dora 1930.28
Maul, Paul 1926.14
Mauldin, Randolph 1983.14
Maule, Michael 1946.12, 1948.25, 1957.04, 1958.07, 1964.30, 1964.31
Maule-Cole, Cecile 1929.41
Maultsby, Carl 1980.15
Mauras, Joseph 1881.49, 1882.29
Maure, Lillian 1904.04
Mauree, Leta 1945.14
Maurel, C. 1881.24
Maurel, Louisa 1880.31
Maurel, Mme. Victor 1913.10
Maurel, Pauline 1881.05
Maurelli, Edward 1927.48
Maurens, William 1888.23
Maurer, Emil 1963.11
Maurer, Harry R. 1920.35
Maurer, Michael 1962.24, 1984.05, 1986.18
Maurer, Miss 1892.43
Maurer, Rose 1903.09
Mauresette, Mlle. 1917.26
Mauret, Virginie 1929.48, 1930.41
Maurette, Marcelle 1965.35
Mauri, Mlle. 1877.04, 1877.15
Maurice Grau's Famous French Opera Company 1885.23, 1885.24, 1885.25

Maurice Grau's French Opera Bouffe Company 1879.19, 1879.26, 1879.27, 1879.31, 1879.34, 1879.36, 1884.43, 1884.45, 1884.47, 1884.49, 1884.50, 1884.52, 1884.54, 1884.55,
Maurice Grau's French Opera Company 1879.39, 1879.40, 1879.41, 1879.43, 1879.45, 1879.47, 1879.48, 1879.49, 1879.51, 1879.55, 1879.60, 1879.61, 1879.69, 1880.16, 1880.22, 1880.23, 1880.27, 1880.28, 1880.29, 1880.44, 1880.50, 1880.52, 1880.56, 1880.58, 1880.60, 1881.46, 1881.48, 1881.49, 1881.50, 1881.51, 1881.53, 1881.54, 1882.29, 1882.30, 1882.35, 1882.53, 1882.55, 1882.61, 1882.67, 1882.73, 1883.27, 1883.28, 1883.30, 1883.34, 1883.41, 1883.51, 1883.54, 1883.55, 1883.57, 1883.59, 1883.60,
Maurice Grau's New French Opera Company 1882.58
Maurice, Albert 1895.44
Maurice, Eugene 1906.37
Maurice, Louie 1897.47, 1898.58, 1902.39
Maurice, May 1905.51
Maurice, Mlle. 1868.26
Maurice, Mons. 1911.45, 1912.02
Maurice, Monsieur 1915.16, 1932.19
Maurice, Mr. 1912.43
Maurice, V. 1869.30
Maurice, Victoria 1869.16
Maurier, J. 1880.29
Maurier, P. 1880.29
Mauries, Mlle. 1879.36
Mauriez, F. 1878.08, 1879.27, 1879.40, 1880.14
Mauriez, Mlle. 1879.47
Mauriez, Mons. 1877.27, 1877.33, 1879.48, 1879.49, 1879.55, 1880.16, 1880.56
Mauro, Ernie 1958.18
Mauro, Vince 1979.11
Mauro, Wilson 1988.06, 1990.03, 1992.13
Maury, Jessie 1904.25
Maury, Richard 1956.08, 1962.02
Maury, Richard F. 1948.22
Maury, Stella 1901.16, 1902.24, 1904.25
Maussey, Ida 1889.02
Maussey, William 1906.31
Mauvel, Camm 1891.11, 1892.22, 1892.33, 1892.47, 1893.16, 1897.27
Mauzens, Frederic 1918.34
Mavana, France 1997.14
Maveroffer, Amalia 1892.38
Mavimbela, Thandani 1988.02
Mavoides, Peter 1979.14
Mawin Productions, Inc. 1932.30
Mawson, Edward R. 1889.48, 1890.06
Mawson, Elizabeth 1971.21
Max and Mahieu 1910.30, 1911.17, 1912.04, 1912.08, 1912.09, 1912.21, 1912.22, 1912.23, 1913.11, 1913.24, 1914.06, 1914.13
Maxim, John 1965.37
Maximilian, Professor 1870.33
Maximo, Lucia Helena 1988.06
Maxner 1906.19
Maxon, Richard 1968.17, 1972.04, 1981.26
Maxson, Ray 1921.19
Maxwell, Alfred 1914.33
Maxwell, Arthur 1943.05, 1945.01, 1948.30, 1950.02, 1953.08
Maxwell, Barry 1890.41, 1891.18, 1911.09
Maxwell, Box 1964.05
Maxwell, Chris 1909.05
Maxwell, Eddie 1998.17
Maxwell, Edwin 1918.24
Maxwell, Elsa 1938.04
Maxwell, F. 1887.27
Maxwell, Frank 1938.18, 1953.02, 1955.07, 1958.05
Maxwell, G. 1870.05
Maxwell, James 1872.06
Maxwell, Jan 1998.03
Maxwell, Jerry 1931.03
Maxwell, John 1926.11, 1929.29
Maxwell, Jr., Robert E. 1966.08
Maxwell, Miss 1879.56
Maxwell, Mitchell 1982.12, 1994.01, 1997.03, 2001.03
Maxwell, Mr. 1863.02, 1909.07
Maxwell, Pauline 1921.35
Maxwell, Rosalie 1961.24
Maxwell, Rose 1972.20
Maxwell, Terry 1972.20
Maxwell, Tom 2000.07
Maxwell, Vera 1908.44, 1911.24, 1914.17, 1916.24, 1917.03, 1917.26
Maxwell, Victoria 1994.01, 1997.03, 2001.03
Maxwell, William 1906.09, 1916.15
May Irwin Company 1897.45
May, Ada 1888.33
May, Aileen 1899.35
May, Ailleen 1898.69
May, Alice 1883.39, 1884.63, 1891.44, 1897.46
May, Angela 1903.21
May, Annetta 1892.08
May, Beverly 1982.02
May, Billy 1981.08, 1983.20
May, Bonnie 1901.14
May, Carrie 1898.12, 1899.06, 1900.38
May, Charles 1959.19
May, Dorothy 1930.41
May, Edna 1897.39, 1898.68, 1900.05, 1901.01, 1904.29, 1905.27
May, Elaine 1960.16
May, Eleanor 1903.09
May, Elsa 1898.09
May, Flo 1912.25, 1913.30
May, Florence 1900.33
May, Frank 1929.04
May, H.H. 1905.18
May, Helen 1913.21
May, Henrietta 1880.26
May, Ida Bowdoin 1884.17
May, James 1946.09, 1966.21
May, Jane 1901.01, 1904.29, 1905.27
May, Jessie 1900.56, 1901.12
May, June 1907.53
May, Leah 1924.05
May, Lilly 1954.08
May, Marguerite 1908.40, 1918.27
May, Marion 1891.20
May, Marjorie 1925.39
May, Marty 1940.09, 1941.06, 1943.20, 1946.12, 1949.06, 1950.14
May, Miss 1880.69
May, Mr. 1865.01
May, N. 1886.40
May, Olga 1903.41
May, Olive 1923.37, 1928.09, 1930.23
May, Phila 1896.01
May, Rose 1876.16
May, Samuel 1869.07, 1869.46, 1872.21, 1873.12, 1873.14, 1875.19
May, Theo 1894.41
May, W. 1904.03
May, William 1983.17
Maya, Teresa 1934.32
Mayake, Kiki 1989.24
Maybaum, Robert F. 1973.17
Maybaun, Edith 1924.46
Maybe, Florence 1902.27
Maybel, Clara 1880.43
Maybrick, Michael 1881.39
Maybury, Carol 1925.23
Maye, Carolyn 1948.25, 1954.15
Maye, Charlotte 1943.07
Maye, Edythe 1928.41
Maye, Fred 1928.35
Mayehoff, Eddie 1944.28, 1945.10
Mayer, Adolphe 1924.24
Mayer, Al 1921.16
Mayer, Cecile 1904.34
Mayer, Charles 1976.36
Mayer, Clementine 1964.25
Mayer, Daisy 1891.08
Mayer, Edwin Justus 1945.04
Mayer, Ella 1945.09
Mayer, Fred M. 1887.51
Mayer, Harry 1969.14
Mayer, Hy. 1908.26, 1911.09
Mayer, Joseph 1930.26
Mayer, Lisa 1999.16
Mayer, Marcus R. 1890.33, 1892.08, 1892.10
Mayer, Margery 1948.29
Mayer, Michael 1997.18, 1999.03
Mayer, Miss 1896.44
Mayer, Mlle. 1871.18
Mayer, Pieter 1921.23
Mayer, Ray 1930.22, 1933.15, 1939.28, 1940.08, 1941.13
Mayer, Tess 1915.30, 1917.17, 1919.01, 1920.42, 1922.05
Mayer, Timothy S. 1983.06
Mayerhofer Company 1895.15
Mayeroffer, Amelia 1897.27
Mayers, Lloyd 1981.06
Mayerson, Frederic H. 1985.06, 1987.18, 1991.05, 1995.03, 2001.05
Mayerson, Rhoda 1991.05, 1995.03, 2001.05
Mayes, Doris 1952.06
Mayes, Sally 1989.07, 1993.10
Mayfair, Mitzi 1931.19, 1932.25, 1934.39, 1936.31
Mayfield, Carline 1917.03
Mayfield, Cleo 1913.02, 1915.17, 1917.26, 1920.07, 1922.07, 1924.13, 1927.35
Mayfield, Julian 1949.15
Mayfield, Katherine 1938.15
Mayfield, Kathryn 1937.07, 1939.13
Mayfield, Menlo 1927.40
Mayfield, Percy 1984.15
Mayforth, Leland 1956.07
Mayhew, Billy 1978.09
Mayhew, Eva 1897.04
Mayhew, John 1892.45
Mayhew, Kate 1906.05, 1907.02, 1920.34
Mayhew, Katie 1875.06
Mayhew, Stella 1904.18, 1904.53, 1905.22, 1905.41, 1910.01, 1911.12, 1911.43, 1912.09, 1915.26, 1927.03, 1927.16, 1930.37
Mayland, R.H. 1891.18
Mayle, Brian 2001.04
Maylon, Joseph 1906.32
Maynard, Charles A. 1912.27
Maynard, Clinton 1894.12
Maynard, Dorothy 1902.12, 1903.36, 1913.06, 1916.14, 1920.37
Maynard, Edwin 1908.23
Maynard, Emily 1876.35, 1880.05
Maynard, Eugeneie 1883.44
Maynard, Eugenie 1880.18, 1884.12, 1885.63, 1888.20, 1892.33
Maynard, Fannie 1884.58
Maynard, Frederick 1908.32
Maynard, Gaylord 1981.09
Maynard, Hattie 1883.65
Maynard, Helen 1902.12
Maynard, Henry 1889.21
Maynard, Jennie 1879.25, 1906.34
Maynard, Miss 1881.07, 1883.16, 1903.36
Maynard, Nevada 1906.02
Maynard, Orivalle 1923.15
Maynard, Richard 1990.08
Maynard, Ruth 1963.01
Mayne, Christine 1895.43
Mayne, Earl 1927.65
Mayne, Frank 1901.15, 1904.39, 1907.24, 1908.21, 1917.35, 1920.03, 1922.46
Mayne, Leslie 1901.19, 1902.01, 1906.36, 1907.15, 1910.21
Mayne, Nellie 1905.19
Mayo, Don 1945.19, 1946.22, 1948.32, 1996.15, 1999.21
Mayo, Edna 1908.01
Mayo, Eleanor 1893.44
Mayo, Flo 1939.16
Mayo, Fred 1918.05
Mayo, George 1888.04, 1920.06
Mayo, Gertrude 1900.07
Mayo, Harry 1921.06, 1922.26
Mayo, Leslie 1905.19
Mayo, Margaret 1912.14, 1918.16
Mayo, Martha 1921.09
Mayo, Sam 1921.12
Mayo, Virginia 1941.13
Mayo, Will 1888.43
Mayo, Win 1955.02, 1959.02
Mayon, John 1891.25, 1891.45, 1892.54, 1893.15, 1893.27, 1893.36, 1894.49, 1895.05, 1897.50, 1898.34, 1900.42, 1900.49, 1905.25, 1906.25
Mayon, Ruth 1926.14, 1927.41
Mayoral, Elsa Maria 1999.18
Mayoral, Hector 1999.18
Mayorga, Emelia 1875.24
Mayorga, Nina Emilia 1875.22
Mayro, Jacqueline 1959.13, 1971.02
Mays, Gayle 1925.47
Mays, George 1921.30
Mays, Tristin 1999.21
Maytorena, Catalina 1949.07
Maywood, Caroline 1917.08
Mazard, Salome 1992.02
Mazelle, Belle 1922.11
Mazey, Duane F. 1976.20
Mazier, Eddie 1919.24, 1938.03
Mazilier 1844.01
Mazin, Stan 1966.11
Mazini, Khalil Oglou 1932.01
Mazone, Lea 1888.39
Mazurette, Hortense 1905.53, 1907.05
Mazuz, Robert 1923.16
Mazzanovich 1881.37
Mazzanovich, J. 1881.32, 1886.37
Mazzanovich, John 1882.48, 1882.60, 1883.65, 1884.14, 1884.57
Mazzanovich, Jonathan 1885.41
Mazzantini, Luigi 1884.40
Mazzello, Mary 1990.02
Mazzeo, Roger 1998.02
Mazzeri, G. 1869.08
Mazzeri, Giovana 1866.18
Mazzeri, L. 1869.08
Mazzeri, Louisa 1866.18
Mazzeri, Louise 1872.10
Mazzeri, Mlle. 1868.18, 1870.41
Mazzie, Marin 1994.05, 1998.01, 1999.19
Mazzini, Herb 1964.33
Mazzini, Pietro 1918.18
Mazzini, Signor 1861.05
Mbalo, Jabu 1977.01
Mbambo, Nonhlanhla 1988.02
MCA Music Entertainment Group 1987.05
MCA, Inc. 1971.12
MCA/Universal 1939.19, 1994.06
McAdee, Dudley 1906.06
McAfee, Diane 1965.17
McAllen, Kathleen Rowe 1982.03, 1984.02, 1990.04
McAlliste, R.E. 1889.37
McAllister, Blue 1928.18, 1930.34, 1931.11, 1933.27
McAllister, Paul 1898.46, 1918.21
McAllister, Phosa 1876.34
McAllister, R.E. 1891.08
McAllister, Rich 1906.40, 1908.02
McAnally, Brian 1983.10
McAndrews, J.W. 1876.11, 1876.30, 1877.05
McAndrews, Messr. 1876.14, 1876.30
McAndrews, R.L. 1907.15
McAnuff, Des 1982.04, 1985.06, 1991.05, 1993.06, 1995.05, 1998.11, 1998.13
McArdle, Andrea 1977.06, 1987.05, 1996.04, 1999.16
McArdle, J.J. 1897.12
McArdle, James 1962.15
McArdle, John 1913.36
McArt, Jan 1989.25
McArthur, Edwin 1946.01
McArthur, Neil 1992.03
McArtney, James 1879.25
McAssey, Michael 1987.14
McAteer, Kathryn 1985.15, 1986.18
McAuliffe, Jere 1914.10, 1920.30
McAuliffe, Jerre 1926.29
McAuliffe, Jerry 1912.05
McAuliffe, Nicholas 1976.29
McAvin, Andy 1980.19, 1981.26
McAvoy, Annie 1873.05
McAvoy, Dan 1902.06, 1902.23, 1903.04, 1905.02, 1906.04
McAvoy, Daniel 1900.56, 1901.12
McAvoy, Fred 1873.05
McAvoy, John 1926.29
McAvoy, Regina 1904.12
McBain, Allison 1917.02
McBane, Ralph 1937.08
McBoyle, Daniel 1918.23
McBoyle, Darl 1922.05
McBride, Edith Ethel 1907.41
McBride, Irene 1934.42
McBride, Michele 1987.03, 1988.14, 1990.02, 1990.13, 1991.09, 1991.12, 1993.12
McBride, Patricia 1986.10, 1987.11
McBridge, Michel 1985.13
McBroom, Amanda 1979.30
McCabe, Bernice 1919.36, 1922.48
McCabe, Ellen 1980.11
McCabe, Felix F. 1913.35
McCabe, Frank 1893.23
McCabe, George 1905.51
McCabe, J.D. 1891.24
McCabe, James 1920.31
McCabe, James C. 1896.37, 1919.30
McCabe, Lake 1922.41
McCabe, May 1911.29
McCaffrey 1872.16, 1884.27
McCaffrey, D.J. 1906.46
McCall, Dave 1903.26
McCall, Janet 1972.16, 1973.07, 1979.12
McCall, Lizzie 1878.02, 1901.13, 1904.14
McCall, Martri 1984.15
McCalliom, Joseph 1926.11
McCallion, Jimmie 1927.07, 1928.11
McCallion, Joseph 1924.09
McCallon, Joe 1927.64
McCallum, Martin 1987.04, 1991.03, 1998.10

McCallum, Sandy 1969.03
McCalum, Martin 1999.20
McCandless, Stanley 1944.28
McCann, Elizabeth I. 1981.04, 1985.03
McCann, Elizabeth Ireland 1991.15
McCann, Frances 1942.31, 1943.08, 1947.06
McCann, Geraldine 1888.36, 1889.46, 1891.39, 1894.35, 1895.42
McCann, J.R. 1882.69
McCann, Jack 1934.40
McCann, James R. 1924.30
McCann, Miss 1886.57
McCarey, Leo 1988.08
McCarroll, Earl 1980.01
McCarron, Charles 1916.03, 1975.09
McCarry, Charles E. 1992.16
McCart, A.T. 1883.43
McCart. W.H. 1903.39
McCarthy, Agnes 1914.23
McCarthy, Alicia 1920.07
McCarthy, Carolyn Kim 2000.20
McCarthy, Charles 1892.54, 1893.10, 1894.04
McCarthy, Charles F. 1884.66, 1891.45, 1892.44, 1893.15, 1893.27, 1893.36, 1894.49, 1895.05, 1905.30, 1906.22, 1910.04
McCarthy, Dan 1886.10, 1904.48
McCarthy, Dorothy 1922.39, 1925.22, 1926.16, 1929.07
McCarthy, F.J. 1907.48
McCarthy, Jeff 1997.17
McCarthy, John 1898.70, 1943.06, 1976.29
McCarthy, Joseph 1910.33, 1912.14, 1913.05, 1916.25, 1917.23, 1918.07, 1918.23, 1919.04, 1919.15, 1920.18, 1920.41, 1921.19, 1922.41, 1922.48, 1923.09, 1923.38, 1923.47, 1928.28, 1931.19, 1940.10, 1953.17, 1962.17, 1963.02, 1967.11, 1973.05, 1976.24
McCarthy, Joseph J. 1924.18, 1925.10
McCarthy, Jr., Joe 1958.12
McCarthy, Jr., Joseph 1953.17
McCarthy, Justin 1925.32, 1943.08
McCarthy, Justin Huntly 1913.32, 1934.41
McCarthy, Kevin 1943.23
McCarthy, Margaret 1926.16, 1929.07
McCarthy, Mary 1920.07, 1971.05
McCarthy, May 1913.27
McCarthy, Messr. 1883.58, 1890.02
McCarthy, Michael 1987.19
McCarthy, Mr. 1883.45
McCarthy, Myles 1909.31, 1916.24
McCarthy, Nellie 1898.70
McCarthy, Robert E. 1975.08
McCarthy, W.J. 1908.18, 1908.34, 1910.02, 1915.29, 1929.47, 1929.48
McCarthy, William 1928.02
McCarthy, William J. 1913.27, 1926.39, 1929.34, 1929.36, 1929.38, 1929.40, 1929.43, 1933.23, 1935.15, 1950.04
McCartney, Jesse 1998.20
McCartney, O.H. 1908.03
McCartney, Paul 1973.17, 1974.24, 1977.10, 1982.22
McCarty, Dan 1896.24
McCarty, Joseph 1919.36, 1927.08
McCarty, Lawrence 1892.38, 1893.23, 1894.34, 1912.39
McCarty, Mary 1948.18, 1948.22, 1949.08, 1950.19, 1975.14
McCarty, Messr. 1882.20
McCarty, Michael 1978.22, 1984.07, 1989.19, 2001.08
McCarty, Mike 1970.04
McCarty, Paul 1920.35
McCarty, Robert J. 1960.06
McCary, Albert 1948.20
McCatty, Mary Frances 1994.06
McCaul, Sorcha 2000.04
McCauley, Jack 1931.05, 1932.13, 1936.31, 1943.05, 1944.32, 1947.16, 1949.18
McCauley, John 1900.58, 1927.16, 1929.19, 1936.31, 1939.22, 1940.07, 1942.27
McCauley, Judith 1969.12, 1973.06, 1997.11, 1998.06, 1999.11
McCauliffe, James C. 1898.06
McCaull Comic Opera Company 1883.38
McCaull Opera Comique Company 1882.71, 1883.45, 1884.08, 1884.14, 1884.34, 1884.57, 1885.13, 1885.14, 1885.28, 1886.26, 1886.33, 1886.37, 1886.43, 1887.04, 1887.12, 1887.26, 1887.28
McCaull Opera Company 1882.42, 1882.51, 1882.70, 1883.04, 1883.10, 1883.58, 1883.62, 1884.51, 1884.63, 1885.05, 1885.52, 1885.67, 1887.18, 1887.22, 1887.24, 1887.47, 1888.19, 1888.22, 1888.24, 1888.26, 1889.17, 1889.22, 1890.28
McCaull, John 1883.04, 1885.45, 1885.52, 1890.39
McCaull, John A. 1880.46, 1881.40, 1882.05, 1882.16, 1882.19, 1882.42, 1882.51, 1882.52, 1882.70, 1882.71, 1883.10, 1883.18, 1883.38, 1883.45, 1883.58, 1883.62, 1884.08, 1884.14, 1884.34, 1884.51, 1884.57, 1885.05, 1885.13, 1885.14, 1885.28, 1885.67, 1886.26, 1886.33, 1886.37, 1886.43, 1887.04, 1887.18, 1887.24, 1887.26, 1887.28, 1887.47, 1888.19, 1888.22, 1888.24, 1888.26, 1889.17, 1889.22, 1890.28
McCaull, Joseph A. 1884.63, 1887.12
McCay, Neal 1897.44, 1906.33, 1914.12
McCay, Neil 1896.27, 1897.20, 1898.18, 1898.29
McChesney, Ernest 1930.30, 1947.06, 1954.10, 1956.10, 1957.13, 1958.13, 1958.15, 1959.10, 1959.16
McClain, Billy 1896.49, 1902.38
McClain, C. 1896.49
McClain, Cordelia 1894.44, 1902.38
McClain, George 1911.20
McClain, Marcia 1974.25
McClain, Saundra 1979.32
McClain, William 1896.04
McClane, Walt 1930.10
McClannahan, Charles 1995.04
McClannin, R.F. 1888.08
McClarney, Pat 1945.17
McClary, William 1976.33
McClaskie, Alden 1904.50
McCleary, R.C. 1903.04, 1905.55
McCleery and Terraine 1912.27
McCleery, R. 1913.33
McCleery, R.C. 1901.27, 1903.39, 1904.47, 1905.48
McClellan, Bob 1918.05
McClellan, C.M.S. 1911.11, 1912.28
McClellan, Frankie 1871.22
McClellan, George B. 1898.20
McClellan, Jack 1927.15
McClellan, Miss 1872.16
McClellan, Robert 1919.02, 1922.30
McClelland, Charles 1890.27
McClelland, Donald 1949.08
McClelland, Kay 1987.18, 1989.29, 1994.09
McClelland, Reed 1927.40, 1928.46, 1934.06
McClelland, Stanley 1927.12
McClendon, Afi 1990.12
McClendon, Rose 1926.31
McClennon, George 1932.30
McClintic, Guthrie 1952.03, 1954.16
McClintock, Marjorie 1919.37
McClintock, Poley 1955.13
McCllough, James 1879.37
McClory, Nora 1911.39
McCloskey, Anita 1915.18
McCloskey, Charles H. 1907.38
McCloskey, J. 1860.02, 1865.01, 1865.11
McCloskey, J.B. 1867.23, 1867.26, 1867.27, 1867.31
McCloskey, John 1907.63, 1910.26, 1911.47
McCloskey, Mr. 1859.01, 1859.03, 1859.04
McClosky, J. 1869.31, 1871.08
McCloud, Leslie 1931.43, 1931.45
McCloud, Myrtle 1911.39
McCloud, Wesley 1929.38
McCloy, F.M. 1891.21
McClure, Bob 1963.13, 1963.21
McClure, Edna 1903.18, 1904.03, 1904.50, 1906.26
McClure, John 1911.36, 1976.11, 1979.09, 1981.12, 1981.19, 1981.26, 1983.08
McClure, Linda 1974.02
McClure, Olive 1926.01, 1928.40, 1929.04
McClure, Robert 1956.12
McClure, Spike 1989.10
McClusky, Jack 1930.28
McColgan, John 1996.01, 1996.12, 1998.09, 2000.05
McColl, James 1942.20
McCollin, A.W.F. 1881.07, 1881.43, 1882.21, 1882.23, 1890.46, 1890.47, 1890.48, 1892.24
McCollough, Walter 1898.44
McCollum, H.H. 1923.43, 1934.41
McCollum, Kevin 1994.01, 1996.09
McComas, Carroll 1904.19, 1905.25, 1913.26, 1918.03
McComb, Alice 1915.06, 1915.09, 1915.10, 1915.12, 1915.13, 1915.14
McComb, John 1871.04
McComb, Malcolm 1930.38, 1932.13
McConahay, Liz 2000.15
McCone, George S. 1908.03
McConkey, Joel 1949.17
McConkie, Ruth 1928.19
McConnachie, Morton 1925.14
McConnell, Barney 1907.25
McConnell, Harry T. 1900.47
McConnell, Lulu 1920.25, 1921.18, 1922.19, 1924.29, 1925.23, 1926.50, 1928.28, 1930.35, 1932.16
McConnell, Lynda 1987.07
McConnell, Marie 1919.35
McConnell, Regina 1983.04
McConnell, Ty 1969.05
McConnell, W.A. 1900.58
McConnell, William A. 1891.04
McConny, Norman 1939.14
McConrad, Guthrie 1936.06
McCook, John 1964.17
McCoole, John 1876.16
McCord, Caroline 1904.18
McCord, J.C. 1948.14, 1948.22, 1950.06, 1951.19, 1957.02
McCord, Jonas 1979.16
McCord, Lisa Merrill 1993.18
McCord, Mary 1921.13
McCord, Nancy 1932.14, 1933.02, 1934.04, 1935.17, 1939.20
McCord, Walter 1931.44
McCormack, Dani 1976.24
McCormack, Edward J. 1904.46
McCormack, Erik J. 2001.06
McCormack, Frank 1914.24, 1916.09, 1917.24
McCormack, Gerald 1947.09
McCormack, James 1906.48
McCormack, Jay Carlton 1921.40
McCormack, John 1937.11
McCormack, Langdon 1937.15
McCormack, Laverta 1926.16
McCormack, Michael 1928.19
McCormack, Miss 1871.14
McCormack, Oliver T. 1921.39
McCormack, Owen 1897.55
McCormack, Pearl 1929.01, 1929.21
McCormack, W.A. 1895.18
McCormack, Will A. 1898.43
McCormick Amusement Company 1921.26
McCormick, Andrew 1899.06
McCormick, Andrew A. 1897.50
McCormick, E. 1862.02
McCormick, Frank 1915.30
McCormick, LaVerta 1928.22
McCormick, M. 1881.30
McCormick, Michael 1993.09, 1997.15, 1999.22
McCormick, Miss 1862.02
McCormick, Mlle. 1852.01
McCormick, Myron 1949.04, 1955.05
McCormick, O.F. 1892.01
McCormick, Oliver T. 1924.12, 1926.05
McCormick, Owen J. 1900.50
McCormick, T.B. 1908.16
McCormick, Thomas 1909.30
McCormick, Thomas B. 1908.16
McCormick, Veronica 1961.07
McCormick, W.A. 1889.30, 1897.26
McCormick, Will A. 1899.19, 1901.06, 1911.07
McCorvey, Everett 1983.04
McCowan, John J. 1904.58
McCown, Ellen 1951.18, 1960.05
McCown, Marjorie 1989.04, 1990.08
McCoy, Bessie 1903.40, 1904.57, 1905.17, 1906.36, 1908.18, 1910.20, 1911.24
McCoy, Eleanor 1975.01, 1978.03
McCoy, Frank 1930.28, 1931.05
McCoy, Gerald 1915.03
McCoy, Jack 1913.02
McCoy, Jean 1943.23
McCoy, Joe 1983.20
McCoy, Julia 1900.58
McCoy, Kerry 1989.11
McCoy, Lizzie 1903.28
McCoy, Mary 1929.39, 1938.17
McCoy, Nellie 1903.28, 1903.40, 1905.49, 1909.28, 1911.38, 1913.24
Mccoy, Nellie 1904.55
McCoy, Paul 1918.14
McCoy, R. 1992.03
McCoy, Thomas P. 1990.20, 1991.13
McCoy, Winston 1923.25
McCoy-Rigby Entertainment Production, A 1990.20
McCracken, Joan 1943.04, 1944.23, 1945.20, 1950.03, 1953.08
McCrady, Tucker 1993.11
McCrane, Paul 1954.09, 1982.02
McCrany, A.L. 1882.69
McCraw, Charles 1963.04, 1963.06, 1964.46
McCraw, Charles B. 1962.15
McCreadie, Sandi 1969.14
McCready, Kevin 1979.22, 1981.13, 1982.14
McCready, Kevin Neil 1999.19
McCreary, Bud 1952.11
McCree, Bobby 1921.20
McCree, Johnny 1921.20
McCree, Junie 1901.29, 1902.06, 1902.16, 1903.18, 1904.05, 1904.21, 1905.55, 1907.15, 1908.23, 1910.08, 1910.19, 1910.22, 1911.07, 1912.20
McCree, Maxa 1921.20
McCreery, Mr. 1882.71
McCreery, Wallace 1883.16, 1884.09
McCreery, Wayman C. 1882.05
McCue, Frank 1905.34, 1942.18
McCulloh, Barbara 1998.18
McCullough, Carl 1909.18, 1917.04
McCullough, E.J. 1883.36
McCullough, F. 1912.15
McCullough, Frank 1906.23
McCullough, J. 1880.64, 1882.02, 1882.74, 1882.79, 1883.32, 1883.46, 1883.53, 1883.63, 1884.13, 1884.41, 1885.22, 1887.16, 1887.45
McCullough, James 1882.50, 1885.02, 1885.15, 1885.49, 1885.66, 1886.03, 1886.42, 1886.52, 1887.07, 1887.39, 1887.48, 1888.27, 1888.40, 1889.07, 1889.11, 1890.49, 1891.25, 1891.45, 1892.54, 1893.15, 1893.27, 1893.36, 1893.46, 1894.04, 1894.49, 1895.05, 1896.24, 1903.26
McCullough, James H. 1889.15
McCullough, John 1878.13, 1880.09
McCullough, Mark 2000.09
McCullough, Messr. 1881.29
McCullough, Miss 1877.39
McCullough, Mr. 1889.18
McCullough, Paul 1919.21, 1922.39, 1923.32, 1924.44, 1926.28, 1930.02, 1931.42, 1932.27, 1934.42
McCullum, H.H. 1925.32
McCully, William 1947.17
McCune, Rod 1999.24, 2001.02
McCurdy, George 1902.30, 1904.40
McCurdy, Jane 1924.17
McCurn, George 'Ooppee' 1972.10
McCurry, Carolyn 1976.30
McCurry, John 1953.04, 1960.09, 1967.04
McCutcheon, Barbara 1948.15, 1948.25
McCutcheon, Bill 1956.08, 1987.15
McCutcheon, John T. 1902.44
McCutcheon, Jr., Wallace 1912.48
McCutcheon, Sherry 1951.18, 1956.02, 1959.02, 1961.09
McCutcheon, Wallace 1908.25, 1911.02, 1911.23, 1914.17, 1925.25, 1925.48
McDaniel 1989.02
McDaniel, David 1956.14, 1963.10
McDaniel, John 1994.07, 1995.12, 1996.17, 1999.04
McDaniel, Keith 1985.03, 1993.09
McDaniel, William 1951.11, 1952.08
McDaniels, William 1905.44
McDargh, Harry 1892.23
McDermott, G.H. 1875.40
McDermott, George 1909.19
McDermott, J. 1912.13
McDermott, Loretta 1918.08
McDermott, Sandy 1899.11
McDermott, Sean 1987.05, 1991.03
McDermott, William 1950.13
McDevitt, Ruth 1948.18
McDonal, Mary 1928.12
McDonald 1873.22
McDonald, A.A. 1905.18
McDonald, Alexander 1940.17
McDonald, Allan 1918.35
McDonald, Annette R. 1985.17
McDonald, Annie 1879.59
McDonald, Audra 1998.01, 1999.22
McDonald, Audra Ann 1994.02
McDonald, Ballard 1935.18
McDonald, Bill 1959.22, 1961.02, 1962.01
McDonald, C.P. 1903.24, 1907.58

McDonald, C.T. 1880.49
McDonald, Charles 1895.07
McDonald, Charles M. 1892.12, 1904.07, 1906.19
McDonald, Chip 1971.10
McDonald, Country Joe 1970.16
McDonald, Daniel 1997.07, 1998.05
McDonald, David 1997.17
McDonald, Earl 1937.03, 1937.17, 1945.01, 1967.17
McDonald, Edna 1882.20
McDonald, Gerald 1913.05
McDonald, Gertrude 1923.33, 1923.44, 1925.49, 1926.46, 1927.59, 1928.43, 1931.14
McDonald, Grace 1937.04, 1939.12, 1939.28
McDonald, Helen 1923.33, 1925.05
McDonald, J.F. 1897.38
McDonald, J.R. 1918.13
McDonald, J.T. 1989.08
McDonald, James 1876.03, 1898.59, 1976.15
McDonald, James F. 1897.54
McDonald, Jet 1948.15
McDonald, Joe 1982.22
McDonald, Joyce 1966.14, 1967.10
McDonald, Katherine 1911.12
McDonald, Kirk 1998.21, 1999.13
McDonald, Lafayette 1900.05
McDonald, Lee 1999.02
McDonald, Loretta 1908.01
McDonald, Marcia K. 1993.17
McDonald, Margaret 1894.35, 1895.17, 1897.46, 1898.43, 1898.72, 1899.36
McDonald, Marie 1905.30
McDonald, Mary 1918.22, 1920.44, 1923.30, 1928.49
McDonald, Maxie 1913.15
McDonald, Maybelle 1913.22
McDonald, Midget 1876.03
McDonald, Monique 2000.03
McDonald, P.J. 1897.07
McDonald, Quentin H. 1985.17
McDonald, R. 1879.15
McDonald, Ray 1937.04, 1943.23, 1946.20
McDonald, Sadie 1889.51, 1890.30, 1891.14, 1892.38, 1895.03, 1895.42
McDonald, Saidee 1889.37
McDonald, T. Bernard 1907.24
McDonald, T.B. 1932.07
McDonald, Tanny 1992.07
McDonald, Viola 1905.21
McDonald, William 1900.32, 1963.22
McDonnell, Arch. 1884.12
McDonnell, Austine 1940.03
McDonnell, Mary 1944.15, 1946.07
McDonnell, Tom 1942.20
McDonogh, Miss 1856.01
McDonough, Barney 1888.05, 1888.30
McDonough, Glen 1908.41, 1918.18, 1921.18, 1930.41
McDonough, H. 1884.63
McDonough, J.F. 1908.03
McDonough, James 1900.48
McDonough, Joe 1989.06
McDonough, John E. 1870.05
McDonough, Justin 1967.06, 1967.10
McDonough, Marty 1980.30
McDonough, Miss 1856.02
McDonough, Mr. 1883.45
McDonough, Stephen 1985.04
McDouall, Messr. 1854.01
McDouall, Mr. 1854.06, 1854.07, 1857.02
McDouall, Mrs. S.E. 1871.13
McDougall, Gregory 1946.13
McDougall, H. 1857.01
McDowall, Roddy 1960.21 1997.22
McDowell, A.E. 1887.15
McDowell, Alfred 1885.70
McDowell, Harry 1891.23
McDowell, John 1927.58
McDowell, Ralph 1931.44
McDowell, Robin 1980.12
McDowell, Violet 1943.10
McDuffie, Alvin 1980.05
McDuffie, Laura 1971.19
McDuffie, Tom 1945.05
McEachran, Michael 1998.15
McElhanh, Tom 1960.09
McElhany, Tom 1947.03
McElroy, Jackie 1955.27
McElroy, James 1886.24
McElroy, Michael 1992.06, 1993.06, 1997.21, 2000.08
McElwane, James 1989.09
McEnnis, Pat 1960.06, 1966.07
McEnroe, Robert 1961.14
McEvilly, Burton 1935.13
McEvoy, Fred 1873.04
McEvoy, J.P. 1925.10, 1925.24, 1926.18, 1926.21, 1927.35, 1928.40, 1928.45, 1929.27, 1932.20, 1939.13
McEvoy, Mrs. Fred 1873.04
McEvoy, Rennie 1932.20, 1939.13
McEwan, Belle 1921.18
McEwen, Frank 1911.25
McEwen, Walter 1895.32
McFadden, Gene 1981.15
McFadden, Harry 1898.10
McFadden, James 1945.03, 1950.10
McFaddin, Theresa 1976.16
McFarland, Agnes 1890.02
McFarland, Beulah 1921.10
McFarland, Gary 1971.14
McFarland, Nan 1959.24
McFarland, Phil 1903.05
McFarland, Robert 1980.04, 1980.25
McFarland, William 1935.01
McFerrin, Robert 1949.15, 1951.11
McGaffney, Charles 1908.05
McGahan, Nora 1900.17
McGahen, B. 1901.25
McGahen, Benjamin 1903.36
McGann, Michael John 1997.04
McGarne, Thomas J. 1903.25
McGarvey, Bert 1919.24
McGavin, Darren 1964.23
McGeachey, Cora 1911.28
McGeachy, Cora 1909.05, 1909.17, 1912.07, 1919.30, 1922.30, 1922.38, 1923.18, 1923.20, 1927.60
McGee, Charles L. 1913.04
McGee, Frank 1951.05
McGee, J. 1868.19, 1868.22
McGee, Truly 1939.17, 1942.23, 1942.25, 1943.16
McGeorge, Nancy 1965.20
McGhee, Brownie 1957.09, 1999.09
McGhee, Charles 1908.20
McGhee, John 1898.33
McGhie, Charles 1913.24
McGhie, John 1896.29, 1898.54, 1899.24, 1899.28, 1903.32, 1904.37, 1906.30, 1907.27, 1908.24, 1911.06, 1913.37, 1914.09, 1914.17, 1915.01, 1915.29, 1917.05, 1917.17, 1918.27
McGieghan, Neil 1887.12
McGiehan, C.D. 1894.15
McGiehan, Neil 1887.04
McGill, Aline 1921.04, 1921.37, 1923.01, 1924.02
McGill, Bruce 1983.06
McGill, M. 1891.36, 1892.60
McGill, Messr. 1886.36
McGill, Mollie 1893.07
McGill, Molly 1895.18
McGillan, Jim 1960.09
McGillin, Howard 1985.18, 1987.15, 1993.10
McGinity, Marie 1892.39
McGinley, Phyllis 1948.22
McGinn, Francis D. 1915.25
McGinn, Frank 1917.06
McGinn, Walter 1968.05, 1969.04
McGinnis, Donald 1930.40
McGinniss, F. 1908.22
McGinniss, Joe 1972.02
McGinty, Derrick 1997.11
McGinty, Ted 1944.30
McGiven, W.H. 1884.19
McGiveney, Michael 1980.28, 1984.16
McGiveney, Owen 1949.09
McGiver, John 1960.04
McGlennon, Felix 1890.29, 1891.13, 1891.26, 1892.05, 1893.23, 1894.31, 1894.51, 1895.32
McGlinn, John 1996.11, 1996.13
McGonigal, William 1897.12
McGonigle, William 1889.48
McGough, Roger 1985.20
McGourty, Patricia 1981.01, 1982.04, 1983.18, 1985.06
McGovern, Dennis 1978.24
McGovern, J.P. 1890.08
McGovern, J.T. 1884.58
McGovern, John 1925.17, 1926.13
McGovern, Maureen 1989.24
McGowan, Adair 1965.35
McGowan, Charles 1997.05
McGowan, Jack 1919.07, 1919.34, 1920.38, 1922.11, 1922.27, 1923.46, 1927.66, 1932.18, 1933.01, 1933.05, 1934.35
McGowan, John 1928.36, 1929.29, 1929.42, 1930.11, 1930.31, 1931.32, 1933.05, 1992.02
McGowan, John J. 1912.04
McGowan, Louis 1887.43, 1902.15
McGrain, Myrtle 1903.31, 1904.40, 1905.19
McGranary, Al 1952.07
McGrane, Paul 1938.04, 1942.19, 1947.12
McGrane, T.J. 1889.02, 1912.48
McGrath, Don 1975.07
McGrath, Emmanuel 1997.14
McGrath, James 1895.36
McGrath, Joe 1962.14, 1966.08, 1967.16, 1969.01, 1969.14, 1973.13, 1979.26
McGrath, Joseph 1961.26, 1969.14
McGrath, Katherine 2000.11
McGrath, Mark 1982.01
McGrath, Matthew 1978.12, 1979.27
McGrath, Michael 1995.14, 1998.15
McGrath, Mollie 1908.44, 1909.11
McGrath, Molly 1906.37, 1908.25
McGrath, Patricia 1929.04
McGrath, William 1891.01
McGraw, Bill 1947.20
McGraw, Charles 1963.04
McGraw, Jock 1927.65, 1928.16
McGreevey, Anne 1981.14
McGreevey, Annie 1974.13
McGregor, Donald 1897.37
McGregor, Edgar 1926.25
McGregor, Eugene 1906.02, 1906.42, 1923.36
McGregor, G.W. 1930.36
McGregor, Messr. 1869.37
McGregor, Rae 1942.30
McGregor-Stewart, Kate 1978.06
McGucken, Albert 1896.33, 1902.41
McGuckin, Albert 1895.31, 1897.17, 1898.27, 1899.34, 1904.55, 1907.07
McGuigan, William 1934.34
McGuire, Betty 1955.01, 1958.02
McGuire, Biff 1948.04, 1949.04, 1950.03, 1959.19, 1960.01, 1960.09
McGuire, Dorothy 1939.29
McGuire, Florence 1917.06, 1918.37, 1922.05, 1922.21
McGuire, Francis 1905.39
McGuire, Joseph 1891.37
McGuire, Mitchell 1971.04
McGuire, Paul C. 1964.23, 1965.24, 1966.12, 1966.16, 1966.31, 1969.12
McGuire, Tom 1898.41
McGuire, William Anthony 1920.02, 1923.47, 1924.18, 1926.51, 1928.03, 1928.12, 1928.47, 1929.27, 1930.05, 1930.39, 1979.05, 1984.14
McGuirk, Frederick 1926.31
McGurk, Michael 2000.11
McGurn, Mr. 1895.12
McGurn, Ned 1928.44, 1932.18, 1933.20, 1933.25, 1936.12, 1937.13, 1938.09, 1939.19
McGushion, Dorothy 1928.27
McGushion, Gertrude 1928.27
McGutcheon, Jeffrey 1978.09
McHale, Duke 1930.30, 1936.02, 1937.04, 1945.18
McHale, Gannon 1998.03
McHattie, Stephen 1989.10
McHenry, Carrie 1879.38, 1880.24, 1880.37
McHenry, Charles 1915.03
McHenry, Don 1954.15, 1959.11, 1963.08
McHenry, Nellie 1875.16, 1879.32, 1880.11, 1881.01, 1882.24, 1883.33, 1883.68, 1885.10, 1886.05, 1887.08, 1887.34, 1891.44, 1893.26, 1894.43, 1895.36, 1896.47, 1911.39
McHenry, Tillie 1879.63, 1880.39, 1888.05
McHorter, Evelyn 1923.10, 1923.38, 1923.47, 1927.60
McHorter, Evlyn 1924.10
McHugh, Augustin 1921.08
McHugh, David 1892.04
McHugh, Frank 1927.66, 1967.04
McHugh, James 1939.22, 1940.07
McHugh, Jimmy 1921.34, 1922.23, 1923.12, 1925.07, 1927.62, 1928.18, 1928.50, 1930.09, 1930.35, 1931.11, 1931.21, 1931.32, 1943.16, 1947.05, 1948.28, 1967.13, 1974.09, 1978.09, 1979.24, 1979.25, 1980.10, 1980.29, 1986.01, 1986.02, 1988.08, 1989.02, 1990.09
McHugh, Joanne 1998.15
Mchunu, Linda 1988.02
Mchunu, Mary-Anne Busi 1997.14
McIlmoyle, Jean 1898.01
McIlmoyne, Jean 1897.01
McIlvain 1904.41
McIlvaine 1899.04, 1902.39
McIlvaine, Thomas 1891.21, 1905.23
McIlvaine, Thomas J. 1890.16
McIlvane, Thomas 1901.07
McIlwaine, Janet 1918.16, 1919.01
McInerney, Bernie 1982.02
McIntire, Fannie 1888.32
McIntosh, Elaine 1921.13
McIntosh, Hattie 1903.08, 1904.26, 1906.14, 1908.08, 1909.27
McIntosh, Nancy 1895.29, 1897.20, 1897.44
McIntyre, Charles 1996.03
McIntyre, Dianne 1991.01
McIntyre, Fanny 1890.04
McIntyre, Frank 1912.34, 1919.39, 1924.08, 1925.47, 1926.25, 1928.07, 1929.06
McIntyre, Gerry 1987.15, 1990.12
McIntyre, Harry 1911.25
McIntyre, James 1905.28, 1906.24, 1909.18, 1916.23, 1919.26, 1922.18
McIntyre, Jo 1908.18
McIntyre, Leila 1903.39, 1904.22, 1914.17
McIntyre, Maud 1890.15, 1892.30
McIntyre, Maude 1890.20
McIntyre, Messr. 1888.36
McIntyre, Miss 1886.32
McIntyre, Molly 1917.02
McIntyre, N. 1869.33
McIntyre, Robert 1886.45, 1893.14, 1894.02
McIntyre, Stephen 1989.17
McKay, Beatrice 1907.32, 1908.38
McKay, Brian 1985.05
McKay, Bruce 1917.13
McKay, Don 1951.23, 1964.17
McKay, Frederic 1916.13
McKay, Frederick 1912.14, 1914.06
McKay, George 1905.44, 1908.15, 1914.15, 1920.14, 1921.18, 1929.04
McKay, James 1931.08
McKay, Jocelyn 1969.01
McKay, Kay 1925.37, 1930.20, 1930.43
McKay, Louis 1976.24
McKay, Neil 1977.01
McKay, Roy 1989.17
McKay, Scott 1957.03, 1964.46
McKay, Winsor 1908.35
McKaye, Adelee 1897.26
McKayle, Donald 1950.19, 1954.10, 1959.01, 1964.32, 1966.09, 1968.08, 1973.10, 1975.09, 1981.06, 1999.09
McKechnie, Donna 1961.22, 1968.06, 1968.31, 1970.13, 1971.15, 1974.09, 1975.15, 1996.04
McKee, Alex 1928.08
McKee, Andy 1881.39
McKee, Donald 1950.10
McKee, Frank 1888.44, 1894.02, 1894.35, 1894.37, 1897.01, 1900.47, 1900.52, 1906.45, 1907.07, 1908.06, 1908.24
McKee, Franklin 1897.34, 1898.47
McKee, Harry 1903.19, 1922.40
McKee, John 1906.34, 1919.23, 1920.43, 1921.35
McKee, Joseph 1985.09, 1985.10, 1986.14, 1987.08, 1987.09, 1987.11, 1988.16, 1988.18, 1990.13, 1993.12, 1993.13, 1995.10, 1996.11, 1997.02
McKee, Lonette 1981.28, 1983.05, 1994.08
McKee, Margaret 1922.39
McKee, May 1900.45
McKee, Richard 1976.26, 1977.03, 1977.11, 1977.17, 1978.19, 1980.03, 1984.12, 1985.13, 1986.10, 1986.14, 1988.04, 1988.14, 1990.13, 1993.13, 1995.10, 1997.02
McKee, Tom 1944.30
McKeever, Jacquelyn 1958.02, 1963.05
McKeiver, Foley 1868.14
McKellen, Jr., Gordon 1977.09
McKelvey, William 1929.18
McKendrick, Josephine 1934.29
McKenna, Boots 1926.11, 1931.05, 1934.20, 1935.04, 1945.01
McKenna, Harry 1915.30
McKenna, Herschel 1997.17
McKenna, Janice 1997.17
McKenna, John H. 1919.23
McKenna, Philip C. 1963.14
McKenna, Roger 1917.07
McKenna, William 1910.01, 1916.05
McKenna, William J. 1906.43, 1907.40, 1908.12

McKenney, Chick 1930.19
McKenney, Ruth 1953.03
McKensie, Constance 1927.29
McKenzie, Alice 1922.16
McKenzie, Allen 1928.01
McKenzie, Beatrice 1898.63, 1902.17
McKenzie, Charles 1909.27
McKenzie, E. 1907.54
McKenzie, Fay 1940.21
McKenzie, Herbert 1914.08
McKenzie, J.M. 1922.45
McKenzie, Julia 1999.20
McKenzie, Julie N. 1977.05
McKenzie, May 1900.38, 1904.39
McKenzie, May M. 1901.17
McKeon, Joe 1931.05
McKeon, Joey 1933.21
McKeon, Joseph H. 1912.27
McKever, Joseph 1901.26
McKey, Beatrice 1906.22
McKimmey, Ray E. 1918.17
McKimson, Robert 1990.10
McKinley, Andrew 1950.05
McKinley, Barbara 1976.25
McKinley, Clyde 1905.06
McKinley, Joseph 1888.13
McKinley, Mary 1972.21
McKinley, Phililp William 1987.10
McKinley, Roy 1935.01
McKinney, John 1980.27, 1985.02
McKinney, Margaret 1902.18, 1905.18
McKinney, Mina Mae 1928.18
McKinney, Morris 1935.01
McKinney, Nina Mae 1932.16
McKinney, Ruth 1958.05, 1963.05, 1967.09, 1994.09
McKinney, Thomas 1973.14
McKinzie, Virginia 1979.32
McKissick, Stanford 1930.16
McKneely, Jerry 1995.03
McKneely, Joey 1987.05, 1987.12, 1989.03, 1993.10, 1997.08, 2000.08
McKnight, Messr. 1796.01, 1796.02
McKnight, Sharon 1989.09
McKnight, Thomas 1925.35, 1930.18, 1930.33, 1938.04
McKnight, Tom 1938.08, 1939.22
McKnight, Violet 1912.28
McLaglen, Denise 1959.13
McLain, Ellen 1981.19
McLain, John 1979.07, 1983.02
McLain, Jonathan 1993.03
McLain, Minor 1920.09
McLain, Weston F. 1907.04
McLaren, Conrad 1998.01
McLaren, Donald 1904.30, 1909.03
McLaren, Jack 1921.12
McLaren, Tay 1982.12
McLaughlin, B.J. 1871.09, 1871.11
McLaughlin, George 1898.64
McLaughlin, J. 1906.01, 1982.01
McLaughlin, J.C. 1879.18
McLaughlin, John 1889.38
McLaughlin, Joseph C. 1879.23
McLaughlin, W.F. 1887.04
McLaughlin, W.H. 1890.18
McLaughlin, W.J. 1886.37, 1892.37
McLaughlin, William 1889.36, 1890.14, 1890.15, 1890.20, 1892.46, 1893.44, 1896.19, 1896.22
McLaughlin, William H. 1894.40, 1895.24
McLaughlin, William J. 1890.46, 1890.47, 1890.48, 1892.40
McLaurin, Billy 1929.18
McLean, Ann 1980.12
McLean, Billy 1894.44
McLean, Catherine 1889.36
McLean, Charles 1921.12
McLean, Don 1982.22, 1997.21
McLean, Doreen 1957.14
McLean, Douglas 1987.01
McLean, J.H. 1904.10
McLean, Marian 1902.44
McLean, Messr. 1867.17
McLean, Miss 1866.18
McLean, Rae 1959.22, 1961.21
McLean, Tony 1999.16
McLean, Willard 1928.18
McLee, Svetlana 1953.08
McLellan, C.M.S. 1892.42, 1897.39, 1898.68, 1900.05, 1911.01, 1911.24, 1913.31, 1915.28, 1920.04
McLellan, E.G. 1907.32
McLellan, G.M.S. 1912.34
McLellan, George B. 1892.42, 1894.11, 1897.54, 1898.36, 1898.43, 1898.68, 1898.72, 1924.06
McLellan, Harry 1900.19
McLellan, W. 1922.45
McLennan, Oliver 1928.03
McLennan, Rod 1956.01
McLennan, Rodney 1936.02, 1942.11, 1943.21
McLeod, Allison 1977.14
McLeod, Billy 1928.14
McLeod, Grace 1904.20
McLeod, Lane 1922.03
McLeod, Leslie 1929.40, 1932.27
McLeod, Marilyn 1976.16
McLeod, Mary 1877.39
McLeod, Mercer 1965.14
McLeod, Raymond Jaramillo 1997.09
McLerie, Allyn 1948.26, 1949.08
Mclerie, Allyn 1951.02
McLerie, Allyn Ann 1960.08, 1961.12, 1963.16, 1966.14
McLernon, Pamela 1981.12, 1987.19
McLoughlin, Charles 1937.13
McLusky, Graham 1990.15
McMahon, Coyal 1943.15, 1944.03
McMahon, Edward 1943.23
McMahon, Frazer 1929.17, 1931.03
McMahon, Helen 1915.26, 1921.18
McMahon, Horace 1958.08
McMahon, Jere 1943.16, 1943.22, 1944.29
McMahon, Jim-Patrick 1975.07
McMahon, Katie 1996.12, 1998.09
McMahon, Miss 1909.13
McMahon, Tom 1908.18
McMahon, Vincent 1956.05
McManus, C.A. 1871.10
McManus, Carrie 1918.04, 1918.25
McManus, George 1906.31, 1909.05, 1912.16, 1925.12
McManus, John 1926.12, 1929.28, 1930.23, 1931.28, 1931.40, 1934.01, 1934.20, 1936.02, 1936.29, 1938.07, 1939.07, 1939.22, 1940.07, 1940.12, 1941.11, 1942.27, 1943.05, 1944.30
McManus, John L. 1921.08, 1922.03, 1924.07, 1924.47, 1925.26, 1926.03, 1927.13, 1927.62, 1928.07, 1928.48
McManus, Joseph 1914.24
McManus, May 1914.24, 1918.01
McManus, Mr. 1881.55
McMartin, John 1961.02, 1966.01, 1971.05, 1980.06, 1994.08, 1998.05
McMein, Neysa 1919.25
McMichael, George 1939.16
McMichael, Joe 1939.16
McMichael, Lewis 1925.20, 1926.17, 1937.11
McMichael, Ted 1939.16
McMichaels, William A. 1918.14
McMillan, James 1956.06
McMillan, Jim 1957.06, 1961.12, 1967.04
McMillan, Larry 1975.24, 1979.05
McMillan, Lida 1896.14, 1908.27
McMillan, Richard 1987.01
McMillan, Violet 1904.53, 1910.07
McMillen, Lida 1891.42
McMillen, Violet 1907.25
McMillian, Larry 1981.03
McMinn, Jack 1957.06, 1962.20
McMinn, Mari 1977.06
McMoon, Cosme 1946.02
McMullen, Ken 1994.12, 1995.19
McMullen, Kenneth 1997.22, 1998.20, 1999.21, 2000.19
McMurray, William 1877.04, 1882.79, 1883.32, 1883.46, 1883.53, 1883.63, 1884.41, 1885.02
McMurrough, Dermont 1912.06
McNabb, Anna 1902.11, 1905.47, 1907.49
McNabb, Barry 1988.01
McNabb, Maureen 1966.14
McNair, Barbara 1958.01, 1973.15
McNair, Cecil T. 1930.10
McNair, Robert 1889.03, 1889.14, 1889.48, 1890.06, 1891.06, 1891.07
McNally, Edward 1964.05
McNally, John J. 1880.40, 1880.42, 1880.59, 1882.39, 1888.16, 1891.03, 1891.26, 1892.05, 1892.09, 1893.06, 1893.49, 1895.27, 1895.34, 1896.37, 1896.52, 1897.30, 1897.40, 1899.12, 1899.29, 1900.40, 1900.52, 1901.16, 1901.27, 1901.30, 1902.24, 1903.04, 1903.23, 1903.39, 1904.22, 1904.31, 1904.47, 1904.56, 1905.22, 1905.41, 1907.37, 1908.27, 1909.18
McNally, Jr., John J. 1931.26
McNally, T. 1866.20, 1866.22, 1866.26, 1866.32, 1866.35, 1867.01, 1867.02, 1867.11
McNally, Terrence 1968.05, 1984.01, 1993.09, 1998.01, 2000.15
McNamara, Betty 1957.06
McNamara, Edward J. 1933.21
McNamara, Mary 1980.12
McNamara, Maureen 1993.05
McNamara, Pat 1988.20
McNamara, Rosemary 1966.08
McNamara, Ted 1922.48
McNamara, Teddy 1922.41, 1923.36
McNamara, Tom 1929.24
McNamee, Robert 1965.23
McNaughton, Charles 1913.20, 1917.14, 1918.31, 1924.10, 1926.38
McNaughton, Harry 1923.41, 1924.29, 1927.04, 1927.20, 1927.37, 1930.06, 1934.39
McNaughton, Steve 1982.03
McNaughton, Tom 1910.37, 1913.24, 1914.28, 1915.05, 1916.04, 1919.35, 1919.36
McNaughton, Virginia 1930.08
McNeal, Neal 1913.33
McNeal, William 1919.38
McNeel, Betty 1913.25
McNeel, Sally 1902.43, 1904.10, 1905.06
McNeel, Satie 1899.32
McNeeley, Gale 1973.07
McNeely, Anna 1982.05, 1982.19, 1989.27, 1991.06
McNeil, Claudia 1957.09, 1968.23
McNeil, Fannie 1886.53
McNeil, Fanny 1879.50, 1885.08
McNeil, Joe 1976.34
McNeil, Justin 1977.10
McNeil, Lillian 1919.21
McNeil, Lily 1925.07
McNeil, Lonnie 1972.26, 1976.04, 1978.21
McNeil, Neil 1904.19, 1904.22, 1905.47, 1907.14, 1907.49, 1911.44
McNeil, Seppie 1903.04, 1904.15
McNeill, Fanny 1879.56
McNeill, Neil 1898.17
McNeill, Rex 1976.18
McNeill, William 1919.38
McNelis, Neil 1965.22, 1966.14
McNellis, Frank 1927.52
McNesbit, Mr. 1852.06
McNevins, Charles 1901.04
McNicol, J.E. 1884.62
McNish, Frank E. 1901.22
McNish, Jr., Frank 1906.11, 1906.21, 1907.09, 1907.20
McNiven, J. 1886.44
McNulty, Dorothy 1925.07, 1926.03, 1926.14, 1932.13, 1932.27
McNulty, John 1937.11
McNulty, June 1934.06
McNulty, Marguerite 1919.32
McNulty, Nellie 1897.55
McOwen, Bernard 1927.29
McPhail, Lindsay 1923.18, 1924.18
McPherson, Fred S. 1922.30
McPherson, H. 1889.28
McPherson, Lieutenant 1919.10
McPherson, R.C. 1904.21, 1904.43, 1906.14, 1906.27, 1908.08
McPherson, Richard C. 1900.46
McPherson, Saundra 1967.06
McPhillips, Tom 1986.02
McQuade, Mary 1932.22
McQuaid, J.H. 1896.45
McQuaid, J.M. 1900.03
McQuaid, James 1900.20
McQueen, Armelia 1978.09, 1983.09, 1985.02, 1988.17
McQueen, Butterflyn 1939.29
McQueen, Simon 1970.11
McQueen, Sterling 1976.21
McQuillan, Paul 1990.15
McQuinn, Robert 1914.31, 1915.24, 1915.31, 1916.15, 1917.02, 1917.04, 1917.16, 1918.23, 1922.30, 1923.40, 1924.26
McQuinn, William E. 1912.39
McRae, Bruce 1923.26
McRae, Calvin 1976.25, 1980.16
McRae, Charles 1949.15
McRae, Charles A. 1957.09
McRae, Floyd F. 1982.22
McRae, Mr. 1857.08
McRobbie, Peter 1985.18
McRobie, William 1905.14
McShane, Charley 1887.05
McShane, Tommy 1887.05
McSorley, Jack 1919.29
McSorley, Miss 1882.23
McSpadden, Becky 1974.06
McSwain, Monica 1995.09
McSweeney, George 1938.02
McSweeney, J.P. 1891.14, 1908.13
McSweeny, J.P. 1885.38
McTernan, Master 1897.15
McTyre, Robert 1994.04
McVayne, Ruth 1952.15
McVeigh, John 1900.45, 1904.27, 1905.23, 1907.47, 1996.10
Mcveigh, John 1904.47
McVey, Anne 1990.20, 1991.13
McVey, Beth 1988.01
McVey, Pat 1948.15
McVicker, Julius 1910.36
McVicker, Sarah 1897.23, 1897.54, 1900.33, 1919.44
McVine, Olive 1906.38
McWade, Edward 1893.03
McWade, John 1893.35
McWade, John E. 1885.16, 1885.40, 1890.29
McWade, John T. 1885.26
McWade, R. 1868.19
McWade, Robert 1867.25, 1892.57, 1893.03
McWaters, Arthur 1910.18
McWatters, Arthur 1912.20
McWatters, W.O. 1938.02
McWherter, Joe 1962.04
McWhinney, Michael 1962.02, 1968.13
McWhorter, George 1966.14
McWilliams, Albert 1937.11
McWilliams, Caroline 1975.23
McWilliams, Paulette 1979.30
McWilliams, Ralph 1953.17, 1963.12
Meacham, F.W. 1902.22
Mead, George 1942.33, 1944.26, 1945.15
Mead, Lew 2001.06
Mead, Lewis 1980.30, 1985.15, 1995.08, 1996.05
Mead, Messr. 1886.36
Mead, Mildred 1902.06
Mead, Miss 1892.07
Mead, Shepherd 1961.22, 1966.07, 1995.05
Mead, Sue Belle 1905.24
Meade, Ada 1904.51, 1904.57, 1905.08, 1905.11, 1905.57, 1913.34, 1915.26, 1918.28, 1923.08
Meade, Ade 1917.19
Meade, Claire 1943.21
Meade, J.A. 1872.08, 1872.35, 1873.03, 1877.07, 1879.23, 1879.24
Meade, James 1872.35
Meade, James A. 1872.23, 1879.18, 1879.24, 1880.43, 1880.49
Meade, James H. 1879.13, 1879.66
Meade, Mary Louise 1944.01
Meade, Mildred 1896.45, 1898.15, 1900.34, 1903.28
Meade, Norman 1982.22
Meade, Tommy 1916.13
Meader and Schaeffer 1890.27, 1890.28
Meader, George 1931.37, 1933.23, 1934.14, 1945.16
Meader, William 1933.16
Meadows, Arlene 1987.01
Meadows, Christine 1988.18
Meadows, Kristen 1980.17
Meadows, Michael 1971.12
Meagher, G.H. 1880.41
Meagher, Thomas Francis 1879.42, 1880.63
Meakins, Charles 1907.48, 1911.44, 1913.29, 1914.03, 1916.19, 1918.22, 1919.23, 1927.06
Mealey, John 1877.24, 1878.13, 1878.17, 1879.04, 1879.37, 1879.68, 1880.64, 1925.32, 1927.65, 1934.41
Mealey, Joseph 1886.15
Mealey, Mr. 1909.13
Mealing, Miss 1848.01
Mealy, Jack 1937.08
Meaney, Lottie 1931.31
Means, Waneta 1919.25
Means, William K. 1918.38
Meany, Patrick 1947.13
Mears, Ben S. 1906.40
Mears, Elizabeth 1927.09

Mears, John Henry 1919.18, 1919.43, 1921.19, 1927.09
Mears, Miss 1886.32
Mears, Paul 1935.11
Mears, Poppy 1935.11
Mears, Stanard 1918.13, 1926.02
Meat Loaf 1975.08, 1976.03
Meauberts, Messr. 1861.02
Meazza, Michela 1998.10
Mebus, Gus 1901.04
Mecchi, Irene 1997.20
Meco 1979.13
Mecusker, Inez 1897.15
Medcraft, Russell 1921.24, 1925.47, 1941.08
Medeeyum, Amelia 1883.33
Mederick, Mons. 1868.13
Medeyum, Amelia 1882.24
Medford, Kay 1951.24, 1953.17, 1955.11, 1957.11, 1960.06, 1963.17, 1964.11
Media House Production, A 1976.04
Media Innovations 1989.11
Medica, Leon 1971.10
Medie, Miriam 1918.11
Medin, Harriet 1981.19
Medina, Aixa M. Rosario 1995.15
Medina, Benigno 1942.14
Medina, Louisa H. 1836.01
Medina, Mlle. 1870.44, 1871.27
Medinger, Kate 1888.30
Medjuck, Joe 1983.01
Medley, Lottie 1900.58, 1907.16
Medlin, Janet 1947.04
Medoff, Sam 1945.17
Medrano, Roberta 1924.15
Medwin, Charles 1888.38, 1888.41
Mee, Rose 1900.45
Meech, Clifford W. 1905.42
Meech, George T. 1913.26, 1914.24, 1918.01
Meeh, Gregory 1993.06, 1993.17, 1994.01, 1996.08, 1997.09, 2001.09
Meehan, Aileen 1924.22, 1925.26, 1926.12
Meehan, Danny 1958.20, 1964.11
Meehan, Frank 1896.14, 1918.17
Meehan, Ginger 1930.18, 1930.33
Meehan, Harry 1896.14, 1905.23, 1908.33, 1936.03, 1937.02, 1937.12, 1938.11, 1945.03, 1947.11
Meehan, John 1921.22, 1923.46, 1924.22, 1976.18
Meehan, Jr., John 1927.29, 1942.31, 1944.16
Meehan, Sarah 1884.27
Meehan, Thomas 1977.06, 1979.12, 1993.05, 1997.04, 2001.05
Meehan, William E. 1907.16
Meek, Deanne 1997.02
Meek, Donald 1917.36, 1919.29, 1927.50
Meek, Frederick 1902.18
Meek, Kate 1877.02
Meek, William 1928.25
Meeker, George 1895.15, 1905.10, 1927.09
Meeker, Jess 1951.18
Meeker, Jesse 1950.15
Meeker, Maybelle 1909.11
Meeker, Willie 1905.10
Meers, Thelma 1932.08
Meffert, Emmy 1885.01
Megley, Macklin 1922.29, 1936.27, 1938.04
Megna, John 1960.05
Megrew, Janet 1920.13
Megvinet-Ukhutsesi, Tiemuraz 1977.13
Mehan, Dodd 1931.06
Mehl, Brynar 1966.12, 1966.16, 1969.12
Mehl, Charlene 1963.08, 1964.21
Mehlinger, Artie 1913.18, 1915.16, 1919.26
Meibach, Ina Lea 1984.14
Meier, Johanna 1974.16, 1975.16, 1976.23, 1977.11, 1978.20
Meiggs, H.B. 1894.42
Meighan, James 1927.42
Meighan, T.W. 1857.04, 1857.06
Meilhac 1945.06, 1946.09
Meilhac, Henri 1867.24, 1868.07, 1868.08, 1868.15, 1868.18, 1868.24, 1868.25, 1868.27, 1869.01, 1869.16, 1869.18, 1870.03, 1870.40, 1870.41, 1870.45, 1871.03, 1871.07, 1871.23, 1871.25, 1871.28, 1872.03, 1872.20, 1872.28, 1872.29, 1872.33, 1872.39, 1873.01, 1873.15, 1873.16, 1873.21, 1875.19, 1875.22, 1875.23, 1876.24, 1876.25, 1876.27, 1877.06, 1877.10, 1877.13, 1877.14, 1877.30, 1877.31, 1877.34, 1877.38, 1878.06, 1878.07, 1878.14, 1879.15, 1879.18, 1879.19, 1879.36, 1879.39, 1879.45, 1879.47, 1879.51, 1879.55, 1879.57, 1879.61, 1879.69, 1880.27, 1880.52, 1880.60, 1882.35, 1882.68, 1882.75, 1883.27, 1884.01, 1884.05, 1884.20, 1884.34, 1884.46, 1885.14, 1885.52, 1885.55, 1885.68, 1886.08, 1886.09, 1886.18, 1886.19, 1886.20, 1886.21, 1887.50, 1889.23, 1890.01, 1890.11, 1891.17, 1894.48, 1895.09, 1896.12, 1899.10, 1899.38, 1900.02, 1907.48, 1912.27, 1921.29, 1925.46, 1926.48, 1929.39, 1929.47, 1931.27, 1933.23, 1941.10, 1942.21, 1942.32, 1943.09, 1943.24, 1944.24, 1945.02, 1953.06, 1953.15, 1954.06, 1954.10, 1955.17, 1956.06, 1956.10, 1957.04, 1957.13, 1958.15, 1959.16, 1962.21, 1964.06, 1964.30, 1964.31, 1965.25, 1965.27, 1974.14, 1974.16, 1975.16, 1976.23, 1976.26, 1977.11, 1978.07, 1978.20, 1979.21, 1980.03, 1980.22, 1981.22, 1982.07, 1982.21, 1983.16, 1984.03, 1984.04, 1985.11, 1986.10, 1987.11, 1988.14
Meir, Golda 1971.17
Meisel, Bella 1990.16
Meisel, Will 1999.05
Meiser, Edith 1925.17, 1926.13, 1926.50, 1930.18, 1941.08, 1944.02, 1960.20
Meisler, Bess 1981.18
Meisner, Sanford 1925.17, 1936.28
Meiss, Edwin 1936.12
Meissener, Nell 1900.37
Meisslinger, Louise 1895.28
Meister, Barbara 1960.14, 1960.15, 1959.18, 1961.03, 1961.05, 1966.08, 1966.13
Meister, Fred 1964.25
Meister, Mirzl 1892.31
Meister, Mrs., Toni 1898.53
Meister, Toni 1890.31, 1891.33, 1892.43, 1893.29, 1894.01, 1894.30, 1897.35
Mejia, Carlos 1927.55
Mekka, Eddie 1975.07
Melancon, Corinne 1993.18, 1996.15
Melanie, Mlle. 1862.05
Melbane, May 1902.32
Melbourne, Ada 1876.36
Melbourne, Lillian 1891.18
Melbourne, Madge 1903.20, 1908.03, 1908.27
Melbourne, Richard 1915.17
Melburn, Arline 1927.01
Mele, Louise 1924.42
Melendez, Guadalupe 1917.16
Melendy, E.G. 1907.21
Melesville 1866.27, 1882.45, 1884.08
Melfi, Leonard 1971.04, 1976.27
Melford, Austin 1923.36, 1928.04
Melford, Mark 1886.59, 1887.52
Meli, Gloria 1949.04
Melihac, Henri 1868.16
Melin, Florence 1889.04
Melino, Van J. 1922.01
Melius, Nancy 1989.27, 1991.06
Mella, Fred 1947.18
Mella, Signora 1898.38
Mellen, Dan H. 1903.09
Meller, Harro 1952.08
Meller, Raquel 1926.09, 1926.35
Meller, Tina 1929.51
Melles, Sadie 1910.11, 1912.15
Mellette, Helen 1920.47
Mellette, Rosalie 1920.47
Mellin, Florence 1888.20
Mellini, D. 1894.30
Mellish, Fuller 1924.45, 1926.34, 1927.42
Mellish, Harold 1926.50
Mellish, Jr., Fuller 1926.50, 1928.16
Mellish, Mary 1925.06
Mellner, Frl. 1882.68
Mello, Albert 1966.29, 1970.21
Mellon, Edward 1918.14
Mellon, James J. 1980.02
Mellor, James 1965.39
Mellor, Tom 1911.32, 1912.44, 1930.13
Mellow, Stephen 1968.06
Melmoth, Mrs. 1793.01, 1796.01
Melnick, Daniel 1946.21, 1965.01
Melnotte, K. 1871.18
Melnotte, Katie 1870.33
Melody, Charles 1917.16, 1918.23
Melody, Deanna 1966.12, 1966.16
Melotti, Joe 1989.08
Melrose, Ada 1885.35, 1892.15, 1892.59
Melrose, Bert 1933.14
Melrose, Frank 1895.40, 1897.29
Melrose, Howard 1975.09
Melrose, John 1895.40
Melrose, Kitty 1909.21
Melrose, Ron 1997.09, 1997.19, 1999.13
Melrose, Ronald 1977.16, 1979.28, 1980.09, 1980.29, 1981.10, 1983.17, 1987.16
Melrose, Wally 1895.40
Melrose, Walter 1939.29, 1982.12, 1992.08
Mels, Fred 1924.18
Mels, Irving 1920.47, 1921.31
Melton, A. 1879.04
Melton, Katherine 1906.42
Meltzer, Andrew 1979.26, 1980.21
Melville, A.E. 1904.18
Melville, Alan 1952.09, 1953.17, 1960.07
Melville, Belle 1881.02, 1881.13
Melville, Bert 1919.31, 1921.24
Melville, Bert D. 1914.04
Melville, Emelie 1877.35, 1882.15
Melville, Emilie 1866.13, 1866.16, 1866.17, 1877.36, 1882.16
Melville, Frank 1905.17, 1906.46, 1908.26
Melville, Frederick 1896.32
Melville, George 1906.46, 1908.26, 1910.23
Melville, George D. 1889.50, 1890.25, 1891.41, 1899.04
Melville, Herman 1969.08
Melville, Janet 1907.03
Melville, Julia 1864.02
Melville, June 1952.09
Melville, Lloyd 1897.29
Melville, Messr. 1861.03, 1882.04, 1882.20
Melville, Miss 1855.11
Melville, Mrs. George D. 1890.25
Melville, Nellie 1922.30
Melville, Rose 1899.11
Melvin, Crissie 1924.11
Melvin, Joseph 1948.04
Melvin, Louise 1885.16
Melvin, Mabel 1904.14
Melvin, Maureen 1955.15, 1955.20, 1955.24
Melvin, Murray 1964.28
Melvin, Robert 1978.28
Melvine, Mable 1908.12
Melvyn, Miss 1860.06
Memoli, Leon 1997.03
Menahemi, Elis 1972.17
Menard, Mark 1998.06, 1998.10, 1999.11, 1999.20, 2000.20
Menard, Raymond 1984.13
Mence, Len 1926.34, 1927.63, 1929.31, 1937.17, 1939.28, 1951.12
Mence, Leonard 1937.01
Menchen Electrical Company 1904.41
Menchen, Joseph 1900.12, 1902.15, 1903.36, 1904.15, 1904.20, 1905.15, 1906.10
Menchen, Joseph C. 1902.19
Mencher, Murray 1935.04
Menching, Joseph 1902.38
Mende, William 1938.15, 1946.10, 1948.18
Mendel, Herr 1883.08
Mendelsohn, Daniel 1941.05
Mendelsohn, Edward 1921.30
Mendelsohn, Jack 1942.20
Mendelsohn, Joseph 1923.15
Mendelssohn 1862.09, 1880.55
Mendelssohn, Felix 1939.29
Mendelvitch, Rodion 1915.11
Mendes, John 1942.20
Mendes, Sam 1998.04
Mendez, Julio 1946.21
Mendez, Lucila 1923.24
Mendez, Lucilla 1924.40
Mendez, Lucille 1925.34
Mendez, Philipo 1943.02
Mendick, Charles 1941.01
Mendizabal, R. 1985.07, 1999.18
Mendoza, Arturo 1988.15
Mendoza, Claudia 1993.08, 1997.13
Mendoza, David 1940.16, 1942.19, 1944.20, 1946.14, 1947.12, 1948.19, 1949.05
Mendoza, Fred 1887.05, 1891.41
Mendoza, Norma 1915.29
Mendum, Georgie Drew 1908.23, 1910.20, 1915.08
Menefee, Pete 1975.20, 1984.06
Menendez, Carlos 1964.02
Menendez, Rosendo Gali 1974.14
Menette, Ada 1890.25
Meng, Constance 1964.04
Menges, Herr 1879.62
Menken, Alan 1994.04, 1994.12, 1995.19, 1996.15, 1997.12, 1997.22, 1998.20, 1999.16, 1999.21, 2000.19
Menlin, Ving 1943.18
Mennier, Louise-Marie 1994.08
Menotti, Gian-Carlo 1947.10, 1948.29, 1950.05, 1950.13, 1952.12, 1954.18, 1958.17, 1959.07, 1960.03, 1962.06, 1965.07, 1965.26, 1966.04, 1966.17, 1974.08, 1975.11, 1976.31, 1978.08
Menowitz, Fred 1970.02
Menteer, Gary 1970.21, 1974.26
Menter, Mack 1891.40
Mention, Michael 1964.39
Menton, Olive 1907.41
Mentzer, Abigail 1993.14
Menz, Clifford 1935.17
Menzel, Idina 1996.09
Menzeli, Lola 1920.46
Menzelli, Elizabeth 1876.16, 1880.07
Menzelli, Helen 1876.16
Menzelli, Helene 1878.03
Menzies, Angus 1939.07
Menzies, Lee 1999.12
Menzies, Lillian 1893.27, 1893.36, 1896.35
Menzies, Pony 1900.35
Meo, Julie 1928.13
Meola, Tony 1986.01, 1986.15, 1987.15, 1990.17, 1992.04, 1993.10, 1993.16, 1993.19, 1994.06, 1994.12, 1995.03, 1995.09, 1995.11, 1995.19, 1996.05, 1996.06, 1996.15, 1996.16, 1997.07, 1997.20, 1997.22, 1998.03, 1998.05, 1998.13, 1998.20, 1999.19, 1999.21, 2000.08, 2000.19
Meorz, Otto C.A. 1914.17
Merande, Doro 1965.21
Merano, Cora 1929.25
Mercado, Hector 1977.12
Mercado, Hector Jaime 1972.14, 1975.09, 1976.35, 1982.19
Mercedes 1938.04
Mercedes, E. 1927.62
Mercenary, Mary 1904.25
Mercer, Beryl 1922.42
Mercer, Frances 1939.28, 1943.01
Mercer, Johnny 1930.18, 1930.33, 1932.20, 1939.14, 1939.29, 1940.09, 1940.16, 1942.10, 1942.18, 1942.24, 1946.08, 1949.17, 1951.23, 1956.02, 1956.12, 1959.27, 1962.17, 1963.02, 1964.04, 1965.08, 1967.11, 1967.13, 1968.20, 1973.14, 1974.09, 1975.12, 1976.32, 1978.05, 1979.14, 1979.24, 1980.08, 1980.20, 1981.06, 1982.12, 1982.14, 1983.20, 1984.10, 1986.01, 1986.03, 1988.08, 1989.06, 1989.21, 1990.09, 1992.18, 1997.05, 1999.01, 1999.06, 1999.24, 2000.16, 2001.08
Mercer, Mabel 1908.27, 1950.05, 1952.12, 1960.03, 1962.06, 1966.04, 1966.17, 1974.08, 1975.11
Mercer, Marian 1962.02, 1968.31, 1978.18
Mercer, Ruby 1931.46, 1936.27, 1941.10, 1942.22
Mercer, Vera 1918.05
Mercer, Will 1904.21
Merchant, Jan 1978.13
Mercier, G.W. 1996.16
Mercier, Rene 1927.39
Mercoolova 1958.20
Mercoolova, Asia 1958.02
Mercouri, Melina 1967.05, 1972.23
Merdith, H. 1868.22
Meredith, Ann 1911.24
Meredith, Burgess 1932.28, 1933.07, 1950.01, 1960.04
Meredith, F.S. 1876.35
Meredith, Gene 1938.08
Meredith, Harry 1880.41, 1881.02, 1894.36
Meredith, Hoyt 1928.14, 1929.28
Meredith, J.C. 1902.38
Meredith, Jane 1912.03
Meredith, Lee 1980.11
Meredith, Letta 1894.21, 1894.34
Meredith, Lottie 1896.46
Meredith, Lucille 1886.12
Meredith, Madeline 1929.28
Meredith, Maude 1901.22
Meredith, Morley 1960.10
Meredith, Pearl 1898.41
Meredith, Suzanne 1946.18
Meredith, William 1921.24
Merediz, Olga 1984.02
Mergenthaler, D.J. 1984.16
Merian, Leon 1955.02
Meriden, Messr. 1879.56
Merighi, G. 1911.16
Merighi, Guiseppe 1911.19

Merimée, Prosper 1869.01, 1871.03, 1871.23, 1872.28, 1873.16, 1876.25, 1877.10, 1878.07, 1879.51, 1883.27, 1886.20, 1925.46, 1926.48, 1943.24, 1945.06, 1946.09, 1956.06, 1983.16
Mering, Constance 1927.08, 1928.35
Meritt, George 1883.53
Merivale, Clara 1880.45
Merjan, Barbara 1987.16
Merkel, Louis 1902.33, 1904.20, 1905.10
Merkel, Ludwig 1893.29, 1894.30, 1896.34
Merkel, Mr. 1894.01
Merkel, Una 1959.22
Merkert, Russell 1950.06
Merket, D.W. 1908.03
Merkin, Robby 1989.12, 1990.06
Merkle, Louis 1902.14, 1911.40
Merkt, Marilyn 1945.05
Merkyl, John 1918.30, 1922.46
Merkyl, Wilmuth 1913.23, 1914.03, 1914.30
Merle, M. 1887.38, 1887.41
Merle, M.V. 1884.47
Merle, Margaret 1924.12, 1925.23, 1927.42, 1929.28
Merle, Margarete 1930.06
Merle, Messr. 1882.30
Merle, Mlle. 1880.58
Merle, Mons. 1887.35, 1887.36, 1887.37
Merle, Pauline 1880.50, 1880.52, 1881.50, 1881.53
Merle, Sandi 1992.16
Merle, V. 1880.44, 1880.50, 1880.52, 1880.58, 1880.60, 1881.46, 1881.48, 1881.49, 1881.50, 1881.51, 1881.53, 1881.54, 1882.29, 1882.30, 1882.35, 1883.51, 1883.54, 1883.55, 1883.57, 1883.59, 1883.60, 1883.61, 1884.01, 1884.02, 1884.03, 1884.05, 1884.43, 1884.45, 1884.49, 1884.50, 1884.54, 1884.55, 1885.19, 1885.25, 1885.55, 1885.56, 1885.57, 1885.59, 1886.08, 1886.09, 1886.18, 1886.19, 1886.20, 1886.21, 1886.22
Merley, Heinz 1929.17
Merlin, Frank 1933.04, 1934.20, 1935.11, 1937.09
Merlin, Frank S. 1926.24
Merlin, Joanna 1964.27, 1973.03
Merlin, Ving 1944.15, 1945.01
Merlino, Joe 1921.41
Merlo, Guillermo 1997.13
Merloff, Diane 1945.04
Merly, Mlle. 1882.30
Merly, Mons. 1881.50, 1882.29
Mermaid Theatre 1977.05
Merman, Ethel 1930.31, 1931.30, 1932.25, 1934.36, 1936.26, 1939.13, 1939.30, 1940.19, 1943.01, 1946.12, 1950.15, 1956.16, 1959.13, 1964.01, 1966.12, 1966.16
Merman, Ruth 1948.23
Merner, George 1971.21
Mero-Irion, Yolanda 1943.09, 1944.16, 1944.24
Merode, Jean 1922.13
Merola, G. 1913.09, 1915.04
Merola, Gaetano 1910.35, 1912.46, 1914.28, 1915.27, 1915.28, 1916.14, 1917.14, 1917.30
Meron, Neil 1979.11
Merrett, Miss 1870.34
Merriam, Eve 1971.20
Merrian, Miss 1881.14, 1882.37
Merrick, David 1954.15, 1957.16, 1958.17, 1958.18, 1959.11, 1959.13, 1959.22, 1960.12, 1960.13, 1960.23, 1961.10, 1961.28, 1962.05, 1962.18, 1963.01, 1963.26, 1964.01, 1964.04, 1964.28, 1965.19, 1965.23, 1965.28, 1965.39, 1966.29, 1967.15, 1967.16, 1968.01, 1968.31, 1972.04, 1974.18, 1975.24, 1980.20, 1990.14, 1996.04
Merrick, Dr. Walt 1992.03
Merrick, Joseph 1900.40
Merrick, Mahlon 1963.07
Merrick, May 1893.42
Merrick, Mike 1980.19, 1981.12, 1981.19, 1981.26
Merrifield, Don 1909.02, 1915.03
Merril, Dorrit 1947.18
Merrilees, Jessie 1894.46
Merrill, Alice 1907.20
Merrill, Bessilee 1909.14
Merrill, Bill 1975.07, 1982.12
Merrill, Blanche 1912.38, 1915.02, 1915.11, 1915.17, 1916.10, 1917.03, 1917.13, 1919.08, 1919.16, 1920.18, 1921.21, 1921.27, 1923.07, 1923.38, 1924.44, 1925.05, 1925.25, 1925.48
Merrill, Bob 1957.07, 1959.22, 1961.10, 1964.11, 1967.03, 1967.14, 1968.32, 1972.04, 1973.17, 1985.04, 1988.08, 1990.09, 1992.16, 1993.19, 2000.16
Merrill, Dina 1983.02
Merrill, Edith 1886.47, 1888.36, 1889.46, 1890.29, 1892.29, 1897.09, 1897.48
Merrill, Ellen 1940.15, 1941.01
Merrill, Flora E. 1917.16
Merrill, Gary 1942.20, 1943.23
Merrill, George E. 1875.15, 1875.20
Merrill, Gertrude 1905.33
Merrill, Howard 1958.02
Merrill, Joan 1942.10
Merrill, L.B. 1896.42
Merrill, Lola 1908.31
Merrill, Louis G. 1918.36
Merrill, Marian 1907.12
Merrill, Marion 1909.06
Merrill, Martha 1932.19
Merrill, Mary 1939.19
Merrill, Ray 1943.23
Merrill, Rita 1902.09
Merrill, Scott 1955.10, 1959.08, 1966.19
Merrillees, Carrie 1894.46
Merrillees, Edith 1894.46
Merriman, Dan 1959.08, 1959.17, 1959.21, 1960.02, 1960.03, 1972.11
Merriman, Henrietta 1919.10
Merriman, Leo 1906.06, 1918.15, 1919.05
Merriman, Margaret 1918.11
Merriman, Robert 1919.20
Merrimore, Joy 1945.08
Merrit, Gordon 1928.25
Merrit, Harriet 1905.13
Merritt, George 1880.64, 1881.09, 1881.29, 1882.02, 1882.50, 1882.74, 1882.79, 1883.32, 1883.46, 1883.63, 1884.13, 1884.41, 1885.02, 1885.15, 1885.22, 1885.29, 1885.49, 1885.66, 1886.03, 1886.42, 1886.52, 1887.07, 1887.16, 1887.39, 1887.45, 1887.48, 1888.14, 1888.27, 1888.40, 1889.07, 1889.11, 1889.15, 1889.18, 1890.49, 1891.25, 1891.45, 1892.44, 1892.54, 1893.10, 1893.15, 1893.27, 1893.36, 1893.46, 1894.04, 1894.49, 1895.05, 1896.24, 1897.43, 1903.26, 1997.09
Merritt, George Robert 1976.28, 1983.04
Merritt, Harriet 1907.42
Merritt, J.H. 1875.11
Merritt, Jack 1917.06
Merritt, John 1876.21
Merritt, Larry 1962.24, 1971.15
Merritt, Messr. 1876.17
Merritt, Miss 1881.35
Merritt, Myra 1976.28
Merritt, Pauline 1873.18, 1873.21
Merritt, Peggy 1910.19
Merritt, Theresa 1969.10, 1991.01
Merritt, W. 1880.64, 1881.29, 1884.41, 1885.49
Merritt, William 1882.02, 1882.50, 1882.79, 1883.32, 1883.46, 1883.63, 1884.13, 1885.02, 1885.66, 1886.03, 1886.42, 1886.52, 1887.07, 1887.45
Merritt, William H. 1882.74
Merritte, Theresa 1945.06, 1946.09
Merrod, Gertie 1916.12
Merry and Simmonds 1880.08
Merry, Alice 1863.02, 1863.04
Merry, Annie 1866.06
Merry, Harley 1879.12, 1881.02, 1881.13, 1882.70, 1882.71, 1883.06, 1883.47, 1883.48, 1883.58, 1883.62, 1883.65, 1884.12, 1884.17, 1884.23, 1884.34, 1884.36, 1885.41, 1885.47, 1886.16, 1886.24, 1886.34, 1886.39, 1886.45, 1886.59, 1887.03, 1887.06, 1887.13, 1887.14, 1887.27, 1888.18, 1889.08, 1889.46, 1890.17, 1891.15, 1891.36, 1892.38, 1892.60, 1893.39, 1894.34, 1903.12
Merryman, Thomas 1920.34
Mershon, Bernice 1911.03, 1925.15, 1927.25, 1929.36, 1929.45
Mershon, Henry 1928.45
Mershon, Miles 1920.47
Merson, Billy 1913.05
Mertens, Elsie 1903.03
Mertens, Katie 1884.22
Mertens, Miss 1884.42
Mertimer, Messr. 1906.05, 1907.02
Merton, Florence 1881.06
Merton, W. 1880.46
Mertz, Paul 1928.41
Merville, Lena 1880.65, 1880.67, 1886.06, 1887.32, 1889.06, 1890.12, 1890.21, 1909.18
Merville, Lina 1877.22, 1877.23, 1877.39, 1878.20, 1879.03, 1879.33, 1879.35, 1880.06, 1880.10, 1880.13, 1880.59
Merville, P.F. 1890.39
Meschke, Michael 1966.19
Meshkoff, Janice 1959.12
Meshonek, June 1961.10
Meskill, Jack 1931.26
Meskill, Katherine 1943.05
Mesmer, Adelaide 1919.20
Mesrobian, Robert 1956.15
Mess, Suzanne 1982.16, 1983.12, 1985.11, 1987.10, 1988.14, 1990.02
Messager, Andre 1884.37, 1884.48, 1884.50, 1885.44, 1887.24, 1888.07, 1893.05, 1905.46, 1907.06, 1919.42, 1925.41, 1926.49, 1929.11
Messel, Oliver 1928.42, 1929.51, 1954.19, 1973.12
Messenger, Andre 1899.12
Messenger, Irene 1910.29
Messinger, Hugel Gene 1979.18
Messner, Marie 1906.05
Messr. Vantine and Company 1885.48
Mestayer, Harry 1902.36, 1932.22, 1934.43, 1937.17
Mestayer, L.J. 1864.22, 1872.25
Mestayer, Louis 1868.32, 1869.08, 1869.20, 1869.27, 1869.32, 1869.35, 1869.43, 1870.04, 1870.09, 1870.14, 1870.18, 1870.28, 1875.03
Mestayer, Louis J. 1871.05, 1872.30, 1872.32, 1872.38, 1872.40, 1872.43, 1875.18
Mestayer, Mr. 1868.23
Mestayer, W.A. 1866.04, 1879.33, 1888.03, 1888.45
Mestayer, William A. 1879.35, 1879.64, 1880.38, 1882.76, 1884.06, 1884.21, 1884.66, 1886.11, 1890.50
Mestelle, Helen 1939.21
Mestepes, Eugene 1882.59
Meta, Frl. 1880.20
Metaxa, Georges 1931.37, 1934.38
Metcalf, Arthur 1913.26
Metcalf, E.S. 1896.39
Metcalf, Edward 1910.37
Metcalf, Eva 1924.37
Metcalf, Miss 1884.42
Metcalf, William 1958.09, 1961.03, 1961.05, 1961.19, 1962.11, 1968.15
Metcalfe, E.S. 1895.39
Metcalfe, Edward 1914.13, 1924.11
Metcalfe, Edward F. 1899.34
Metcalfe, Jane 1976.12, 1976.13, 1978.15
Metcalfe, W. 1911.39
Metchik, Zetta 1913.09
Metespes, E. 1866.09
Metespes, Eugene 1864.10
Meth, Max 1927.58, 1928.14, 1929.22, 1930.20, 1930.27, 1931.14, 1932.16, 1932.25, 1934.35, 1934.40, 1935.03, 1938.01, 1938.09, 1940.17, 1941.08, 1943.16, 1943.20, 1944.01, 1944.18, 1945.03, 1946.24, 1948.28, 1950.06, 1955.10, 1957.01, 1960.09, 1968.22
Meth, Mex 1952.01
Methot, Mayo 1928.24, 1929.37
Methot, Minnie 1904.50
Methven, Billy 1912.02
Methven, Florence 1918.31
Methven, Grace 1912.02
Methven, Jeanette 1912.02
Methven, Jeannetta 1921.23
Methven, Jennetta 1917.30
Metkiff, G.F. 1867.25
Metkiff, George 1869.40, 1869.44
Metra, Olivier 1886.54
Metropolitan Opera, The 1979.17
Metropolitan Theatrical Entertainment, Inc. 1995.15
Metsch, Herr 1882.68
Mette, Jack 1962.20, 1966.30
Mettenleiter 1915.11
Metter, Jeff 1998.19
Mettke, Dorothy 1920.46
Mettlar, Emma 1879.08
Mettler, Emma 1878.16
Metz, George 1892.31
Metz, Janet 1999.22
Metz, Lucius 1920.09, 1921.13, 1921.31, 1923.15, 1924.45
Metz, Steve 1974.24
Metz, Theodore A. 1889.34
Metz, Theodore H. 1896.52, 1897.40, 1980.27
Metz, Theodore M. 1975.20
Metzetti, Charles 1916.15
Metzgar, Andrew 1879.35, 1880.06, 1880.13
Metzgar, Messr. 1882.34
Metzger, A. 1878.02
Metzger, Andrew 1879.33, 1880.10, 1880.65, 1880.67, 1880.70, 1883.65
Metzger, Ann 1936.06
Metzger, David 1997.20
Metzger, Messr. 1886.47
Metzger, Rita 1959.17, 1961.08, 1963.08, 1965.35, 1966.08, 1972.14, 1978.19, 1978.23, 1979.27, 1981.20, 1981.21, 1988.04, 1990.08, 1991.09
Metzl, Lothar 1939.23, 1940.04
Metzler, Lawrence 1971.18, 1974.14
Mews, Peter 1971.21
Mexican Juvenile Opera Company 1875.22
Meyakos, Esther 1921.37
Meyakos, Florence 1921.37
Meyakos, George 1921.37
Meybohm, Herman A. 1906.13
Meyder, Carl 1881.35
Meyer, Ann 1925.15
Meyer, Bernie 1961.02
Meyer, Charles 1891.13, 1896.50, 1899.42, 1900.30, 1914.09
Meyer, Charles W. 1889.45, 1902.18, 1918.29
Meyer, Craig 1991.10
Meyer, Craig A. 1989.23
Meyer, Douglas 2001.05
Meyer, Douglas L. 1999.24
Meyer, Edith 1907.24
Meyer, Elsie 1921.15
Meyer, Florence 1937.01
Meyer, Franz 1882.68
Meyer, Fred 1901.13
Meyer, Frl. 1883.08
Meyer, George 1916.25, 1921.18, 1922.25
Meyer, George W. 1912.16, 1912.31, 1916.03, 1917.03, 1919.26, 1924.37, 1955.13, 1967.11, 1974.09, 1980.10
Meyer, H.H. 1910.05
Meyer, Harry 1933.16
Meyer, Harry H. 1907.48
Meyer, Herman 1928.23
Meyer, Irwin 1976.25, 1977.06, 1978.12
Meyer, Joe 1927.20
Meyer, Joseph 1921.34, 1922.21, 1923.12, 1923.36, 1924.01, 1925.01, 1925.27, 1925.28, 1925.42, 1926.03, 1927.54, 1928.17, 1929.07, 1929.51, 1930.14, 1930.38, 1931.21, 1934.01, 1935.12, 1936.12, 1936.17, 1943.23, 1952.08, 1975.22, 1980.29, 1992.03
Meyer, Marcus 1890.32
Meyer, Marie 1889.29
Meyer, Mesdame 1852.05
Meyer, Mr. 1852.04, 1854.02, 1854.07, 1898.53
Meyer, O. 1880.66
Meyer, Otto 1885.01
Meyer, Pauline 1991.01
Meyer, Pieter 1920.03
Meyer, Stan 1994.04
Meyer, Stanley A. 1999.16
Meyer, Taro 1983.14
Meyer-Forster, Wilhelm 1924.45, 1931.03, 1943.06, 1980.21, 1985.09, 1987.08
Meyerbee 1862.09
Meyerbeer, Giacomo 1893.04
Meyerovich, Alvin 1981.18
Meyerowitz, David 1967.03
Meyerowitz, Jan 1950.16
Meyers 1921.07
Meyers, A.B. 1898.45
Meyers, Al 1941.11
Meyers, Annie 1886.37, 1887.04, 1887.47, 1888.22, 1890.21, 1890.28, 1891.13, 1891.30, 1892.07, 1892.16, 1892.28, 1894.41, 1896.01
Meyers, Busby 1992.03
Meyers, Charles 1892.20, 1900.02, 1900.09, 1900.14, 1900.17, 1900.18, 1900.21, 1900.29
Meyers, Charles W. 1910.37, 1913.08
Meyers, Eddy 1918.16

Meyers, Ernest 1935.12
Meyers, Frank 1917.28
Meyers, Grace 1902.22
Meyers, Henry 1930.16
Meyers, Isabelle 1907.32
Meyers, Jeanine 1999.15
Meyers, Jennie 1906.24
Meyers, Jerry 1965.22
Meyers, Jo 1930.18
Meyers, Joseph E. 1931.09
Meyers, Julian 1900.07
Meyers, Lanny 1968.13
Meyers, Louise 1907.51, 1912.49, 1913.28, 1914.15, 1920.14
Meyers, Messr. 1852.05
Meyers, Pee Wee 1920.28
Meyers, Richard 1929.32
Meyers, Timothy 1972.12
Meyers, Vera 1918.04
Meynall, Percy 1881.35
Meynell, Louis 1895.21
Mezieres, J. 1876.24, 1876.25, 1876.28, 1877.06, 1877.09, 1877.10, 1877.13, 1877.14, 1877.26, 1877.30, 1877.31, 1877.32, 1877.34, 1877.37, 1877.38, 1878.06, 1878.07, 1878.08, 1879.26, 1879.27, 1879.31, 1879.36, 1879.39, 1879.40, 1879.41, 1879.43, 1879.44, 1879.45, 1879.47, 1879.48, 1879.51, 1879.55, 1879.61, 1879.69, 1880.16, 1880.27, 1880.29, 1880.44, 1880.50, 1880.58, 1880.60, 1881.46, 1881.48, 1881.49, 1881.51, 1881.53, 1881.54, 1882.30, 1882.35, 1882.58, 1882.61, 1882.67, 1882.73, 1883.27, 1883.28, 1883.30, 1883.34, 1883.51, 1883.54, 1883.57, 1883.60, 1884.01, 1884.02, 1884.03, 1884.05, 1884.43, 1884.47, 1884.50, 1884.54, 1884.55, 1885.17, 1885.19
Mezieres, Messr. 1879.26, 1879.34, 1879.36, 1880.28, 1885.20
Mezieres, Mons. 1879.46, 1885.55, 1885.56, 1885.57, 1885.59, 1885.60, 1885.61, 1886.08, 1886.18, 1886.19, 1886.20, 1886.21, 1887.35, 1887.36
Mezzacappa, Matthew 1994.12
Mezzio, John 2001.09
Mgwazi, Mafika 1997.14
Mhlongo, Ndaba 1988.02
Miaco, Steve 1917.16
Miallet, Mons. 1878.18
Micacchion, Al 1979.05, 1982.05
Miceli, Peter 1950.04
Michael 1968.04
Michael, Margaret 1919.32
Michael, Messr. 1852.05
Michael, Paul 1958.20, 1961.07, 1963.08, 1964.21, 1971.06, 1976.33
Michael, Steven 1980.07
Michaelis, Hulda 1885.01
Michaelis, Lisa 1985.17
Michaelis, Robert 1907.10, 1907.36, 1922.33
Michaels, Bert 1965.02, 1965.37, 1966.24, 1969.04, 1972.04, 1974.18
Michaels, Brian 1990.07, 1991.08
Michaels, Dan C. 1930.16, 1934.37
Michaels, Devon 1986.13
Michaels, Edwin 1926.25, 1938.16
Michaels, Frankie 1966.10
Michaels, Frl. 1883.08
Michaels, Halden 1995.13
Michaels, Jackie 1942.35
Michaels, John 1992.16
Michaels, Laura 1970.20, 1971.12, 1972.21
Michaels, Marilyn 1991.14
Michaels, Patricia 1969.04, 1983.17
Michaels, Sidney 1964.33, 1975.06
Michaels, Steve 1992.16
Michaels, Tanis 1986.07
Michaels, William M. 1918.14
Michalski, John 1978.24
Michel, Carolyn 1989.22
Michel, Frank 1921.08
Michel, Henry 1949.04, 1954.15
Michel, Jerane 1959.26
Michel, Leonard 1934.34
Michel, Lillian 1927.29
Michel, Werner 1939.23, 1940.04
Michele, Lea 1998.01
Michele, Linda 1979.26, 1987.10
Michelena, F. 1892.52
Michelena, Kate 1895.13, 1897.22, 1898.01, 1899.39
Michelena, Vera 1906.26, 1907.52, 1908.03, 1910.27, 1914.15, 1915.22, 1917.34, 1919.07, 1921.21, 1921.35
Micheline, Josephine 1869.38
Michell, Lillian 1925.49
Michells, Ivan 1884.10
Michelotti, Angelo 1964.03
Michels, Kim 1970.15
Michels, Lorne 1979.19
Michels, Madame 1876.35
Michels, Stephanie 1997.08, 2000.07
Michels, Walter 1924.18
Michener, James A. 1949.04, 1955.07, 1957.06, 1961.12, 1965.20, 1967.10, 1987.03
Michi 1954.17
Michigan Opera Theatre 1979.26
Michilos 1927.28
Michon, Joe 1930.06
Michon, Michel 1943.11
Michon, Pete 1930.06
Mickelson, Jerry 1999.25
Mickens, Ernest 1937.09
Mickens, Viola 1935.01
Mickles, Jacqueline 1953.17
Micone, Ed 1990.19, 1991.04
Micone, Jr., Edward J. 1999.23, 2000.04
Micunis, Gordon 1962.08, 1964.14
Middlemas, Robert 1919.31, 1927.13
Middleton, Carle V. 1918.14
Middleton, Edwin 1906.50
Middleton, George 1888.27, 1893.12, 1929.02
Middleton, Louise 1900.35, 1901.21
Middleton, Miss 1897.14
Middleton, Ray 1938.11, 1943.23, 1946.12, 1948.25, 1965.20, 1965.34
Middleton, Raymond 1931.46, 1933.26, 1939.25
Middleton, Tony 1964.19, 1971.01
Midgeley 1896.44
Midgeley, Maud 1892.59
Midgely, Sager 1900.03, 1919.12
Midgette, Monique 1999.08
Midgette, Monique L. 2000.18
Midgley, Raymond 1923.35, 1924.42, 1925.35, 1927.27, 1928.48
Midgley, Sager 1905.25, 1907.13
Midler, Bette 1973.14, 1975.12, 1979.30
Miele, Elizabeth 1954.17
Mielziner, Jo 1929.19, 1930.25, 1930.38, 1931.14, 1931.48, 1932.13, 1932.26, 1933.13, 1933.23, 1935.14, 1936.05, 1938.05, 1938.09, 1938.11, 1938.14, 1939.13, 1939.27, 1940.06, 1940.22, 1941.06, 1942.15, 1945.04, 1945.05, 1945.09, 1945.13, 1946.12, 1947.02, 1947.03, 1947.06, 1947.08, 1947.17, 1948.18, 1949.03, 1949.04, 1950.03, 1950.17, 1951.12, 1951.14, 1951.23, 1952.10, 1953.07, 1953.08, 1954.02, 1954.15, 1955.02, 1955.06, 1955.07, 1955.27, 1956.03, 1956.04, 1956.16, 1957.06, 1958.02, 1958.20, 1959.02, 1959.13, 1960.10, 1960.11, 1961.12, 1962.04, 1962.13, 1962.20, 1963.18, 1965.15, 1965.20, 1966.08, 1966.13, 1969.06, 1970.03, 1970.08, 1989.03
Miers, Lee 1904.07
Mierse, Freda 1928.47
Mierse, Frieda 1930.08, 1931.08, 1931.40
Migan, Paul 1950.17, 1955.06
Migenes, Julia 1964.27, 1965.26, 1966.17
Migley, Fanny 1906.18
Miglietta, John 1982.24
Miglinio, D. 1918.21
Migniani, Armand 1974.20
Mignini, Carolyn 1973.02, 1980.27
Miguel, Mayumi 2000.07
Miguel, Pablo 1942.14
Mihailovakaya, Olga 1922.30
Miki, Minoru 2001.04
Miklaszewska, Agata 1992.05
Miklaszewska, Maryna 1992.05
Miko, Joyce 1963.22
Milan, Frank 1963.04
Milan, Joe 1949.08, 1950.17, 1952.10, 1954.09, 1961.15
Milan, Joseph 1949.08
Milana, Vincent Duke 1979.08
Milani, Linda 1983.05
Milasch, Robert 1919.08
Milbro Productions 1984.01
Milburn, Amos 1992.06
Milburn, Ann 1924.25, 1925.07, 1927.14
Milburn, Ellsworth 1964.26
Milburn, Grace 1901.08
Milburn, Mary 1918.39, 1919.44, 1920.21, 1921.21, 1922.29, 1926.03, 1926.37
Milburn, Rob 1993.04
Milchan, Arnon 1980.15
Miles, Ben J. 1888.13, 1892.04
Miles, Benjamin J. 1887.01
Miles, Carlotta 1924.11
Miles, Casey 1998.18
Miles, David 1979.26, 1981.19, 1983.10
Miles, Dilys 1937.06
Miles, Emily 1913.16, 1917.08, 1918.20, 1920.47, 1922.34, 1925.07
Miles, Julia 1848.03
Miles, Maralyn 1968.32
Miles, Mr. 1866.18
Miles, Muriel 1918.19
Miles, Myra 1895.19
Miles, Patrick 1891.01
Miles, R.E.J. 1879.18, 1879.23, 1879.24
Miles, R.F. 1875.18
Miles, Robert 1886.32
Miles, Robert E.J. 1884.12, 1884.20, 1886.24, 1886.34, 1886.45, 1886.59, 1887.06
Miles, Roland 1954.04
Miles, Ross 1968.02, 1975.06
Miles, Sarah 1995.11, 1995.15
Miles, Terrin 1964.32
Miles, William 1930.25
Miles, William B. 1930.25, 1930.32
Miley, Bubber 1930.13, 1930.38, 1989.02
Miley, Kathryn 1920.35, 1925.04
Miley, Kittie 1896.40
Miley, William 1933.24
Milford, Bliss 1909.09
Milford, Jim 1981.07, 1984.01
Milford, Kim 1975.08, 1976.03
Milford, Penelope 1975.03
Milgrim 1922.09, 1922.17, 1922.41, 1923.02, 1924.23, 1926.04, 1926.12, 1927.49, 1928.16
Milgrim Brothers 1919.08
Milgrims 1925.08, 1925.30
Milhaud, Darius 1935.19
Milheim, Don 1940.02
Milholland, Bruce 1978.02
Milie, William 1957.17
Milk, Harvey 1971.20
Milke, Happy 1916.15
Millar, Betty 1916.07
Millar, Dan 1894.52
Millar, Gertie 1908.25
Millar, Harold D. 1919.12
Millar, Jack H. 1905.27
Millar, Jean 1907.49
Millar, Ronald 1974.11
Millar, Virginia 1942.12
Millard, Emma 1896.16
Millard, Ethel 1904.58, 1911.15, 1912.34
Millard, Jack 1936.22
Millard, Jennie 1889.50
Millard, Julia 1902.30, 1904.40, 1905.18
Millard, Laura 1896.16, 1898.56, 1899.05, 1899.16
Millard, Lauretta 1886.36
Millard, Marie 1892.33, 1892.47, 1895.19, 1896.50, 1897.01
Millard, Maurice 1949.06, 1950.14
Millars, Ariel 1928.25
Millaud, Albert 1875.25, 1877.17, 1882.53, 1884.46, 1884.49, 1885.55, 1885.56, 1885.57, 1885.59, 1885.68, 1886.09, 1886.19, 1886.50, 1895.35, 1899.38
Millen, Dave 2001.04
Miller 1899.03
Miller Brothers 1889.50, 1890.25
Miller Marilyn 1928.03
Miller, Ada 1891.11
Miller, Agnes Heron 1913.03
Miller, Alice Duer 1924.41, 1925.26, 1933.26
Miller, Ambrose 1885.14
Miller, Amy 1982.10
Miller, Ann 1939.25, 1946.06, 1979.25
Miller, Annie 1901.17
Miller, Arthur 1890.44, 1893.34, 1902.05, 1902.10, 1903.32, 1969.03
Miller, Arthur E. 1892.42
Miller, Arthur England 1873.12
Miller, Arthur F. 1900.35
Miller, Ashley 1903.12
Miller, Austin 1915.32
Miller, Belle 1922.35
Miller, Benjamin 1947.08
Miller, Beth 1928.09
Miller, Bill 1975.08
Miller, Billy 1896.49, 1899.31
Miller, Bob 1971.19
Miller, Bryan 1976.20
Miller, Buzz 1952.01, 1952.20, 1953.08, 1954.05, 1959.01, 1962.14, 1963.13, 1964.11, 1986.03
Miller, Charles 1890.40, 1893.09, 1893.44, 1915.08, 1922.30, 1928.49, 1940.21
Miller, Christie 1876.06, 1883.46, 1883.53
Miller, Court 1981.28
Miller, Craig 1980.07, 1981.03, 1985.04, 1985.20, 1988.10, 1990.14, 1992.01
Miller, D.W. 1867.25
Miller, Dan 1990.19
Miller, Darleigh 1981.12
Miller, Dick 1966.06
Miller, Dora 1884.65
Miller, Dorothy 1918.12
Miller, Duke 1928.40
Miller, Duquesne 1928.21
Miller, E. Flournoy 1927.33
Miller, Eddie 1919.30, 1960.08
Miller, Edith 1893.07, 1897.20
Miller, Edward 1897.04, 1919.10, 1963.20
Miller, Edward A. 1926.03
Miller, Elaine 1943.16
Miller, Emma 1886.43, 1888.19, 1888.24, 1888.26
Miller, Eric 1985.13, 1986.09
Miller, Ernest 1921.34
Miller, Everett 1930.18, 1930.33
Miller, F.E. 1978.21
Miller, Fanny 1880.31
Miller, Flourney 1930.34, 1931.47
Miller, Flournoy 1907.31, 1912.36, 1921.16, 1926.14, 1928.10, 1929.37, 1932.30, 1942.13, 1952.08, 1999.06
Miller, Flournoy E. 1907.55, 1923.39, 1932.30
Miller, Frank 1907.18, 1919.40, 1922.03, 1931.26
Miller, Fred 1959.22, 1964.23, 1965.23, 1987.06
Miller, Freda 1951.15
Miller, Frederick 1882.44
Miller, Gene 1999.08
Miller, Gertrude 1904.38
Miller, Gilbert 1919.42, 1928.33, 1929.20, 1955.14, 1981.09
Miller, Gladys 1918.42, 1919.11, 1919.36, 1924.05, 1925.44
Miller, Glenn 1979.24, 1987.02
Miller, Grady 1921.11
Miller, Gregory 1981.15
Miller, Gwendolyn 1988.20
Miller, H. Heron 1907.42
Miller, Hannah 1885.45
Miller, Harry 1917.21, 1919.10, 1929.46, 1938.16
Miller, Hazel 1919.38
Miller, Helen 1971.20
Miller, Henry 1893.11, 1900.25, 1900.31, 1902.16, 1911.04, 1913.03, 1914.05, 1914.29, 1924.41
Miller, Irvin C. 1921.26, 1922.44
Miller, J. 1881.18
Miller, J.D. 1908.23
Miller, J.E. 1883.12, 1883.13, 1896.42, 1905.50
Miller, Jack 1931.02
Miller, James 1918.18, 1919.13, 1920.17, 1921.22, 1923.18, 1924.19, 1926.16
Miller, James E. 1881.22, 1894.45, 1896.43, 1897.13, 1900.25, 1900.31, 1900.32, 1915.03
Miller, Jane E. 1914.25
Miller, Jerry 1950.04
Miller, Joe E. 1920.35
Miller, John 1899.30, 1915.05, 1916.15, 1917.08, 1924.31, 1977.04
Miller, John C. 1904.39
Miller, Jon 1993.07
Miller, Jonathan 1962.23, 1964.45
Miller, Joseph 1916.08, 1918.26, 1925.32
Miller, Joseph E. 1904.12, 1906.32
Miller, Jr., Denzil A. 1977.15
Miller, Jr., Fred 1890.44, 1893.34
Miller, Kathryn 1898.45
Miller, Kellis 1963.22, 1964.31, 1965.03, 1965.25
Miller, Lara Jill 1980.16
Miller, Lawrence 1982.09, 1985.13, 1986.09, 1991.14
Miller, Lew 1902.02
Miller, Linda 1975.02
Miller, Lizzie 1885.63

Miller, Lorraine 1948.24
Miller, Lou 1890.42, 1904.11
Miller, Louis 1892.05, 1893.34, 1896.01
Miller, Louis E. 1926.27, 1928.15
Miller, Louise 1890.38
Miller, Mabel 1901.05
Miller, Margaret 1925.35
Miller, Margo 1927.20
Miller, Marian 1942.25
Miller, Marie 1898.63
Miller, Marie Louise 1909.08
Miller, Marilyn 1915.11, 1918.19, 1919.15, 1920.44, 1923.30, 1925.33, 1930.39, 1933.22, 1934.40
Miller, Marilyn Suzanne 1979.19
Miller, Marilynn 1914.16, 1916.23, 1918.12
Miller, Marion 1903.12, 1912.08
Miller, Martha 1881.30
Miller, Maud 1885.04
Miller, Max 1881.30, 1891.02, 1894.16
Miller, Meri 1954.04, 1956.04
Miller, Messr. 1794.01, 1852.05
Miller, Michael 1970.04
Miller, Michael G. 1991.14
Miller, Midgie 1920.35, 1922.23, 1927.10, 1929.24, 1930.24
Miller, Minnie 1884.22, 1886.47, 1888.36, 1889.46
Miller, Miriam 1921.25, 1921.36
Miller, Miss 1852.02, 1884.42
Miller, Mitch 1968.05
Miller, Mr. 1796.03, 1841.01, 1855.08, 1855.09
Miller, Mrs. 1794.01
Miller, Myrtle 1927.11, 1927.27
Miller, Olivette 1934.37
Miller, Patsy Ruth 1947.14
Miller, Paula 1936.28
Miller, Peggie 1883.01
Miller, Peggy 1883.09
Miller, Phil R. 1901.20
Miller, Prince 1906.32
Miller, Professor 1893.33
Miller, Quintard 1922.44
Miller, Ray 1920.10, 1934.15, 1935.15
Miller, Raymond 1937.01
Miller, Renard 1982.22
Miller, Reverend Earl F. 1988.05
Miller, Richard 1967.09
Miller, Richard A. 1972.13
Miller, Richard G. 1980.24, 1980.28, 1981.02
Miller, Robert 1935.16
Miller, Roger 1985.06
Miller, Ron 1976.16
Miller, Rosamund 1912.36
Miller, Sam 1897.04
Miller, Sebastian 1889.53
Miller, Sharon 1973.15
Miller, Stan 1974.01, 1975.12
Miller, Susan 1940.02, 1942.29, 1943.02
Miller, Sylvia 1930.33
Miller, Taps 1932.30, 1939.14
Miller, Thomas 1903.06
Miller, Tod 1968.05, 1969.04
Miller, Tommy 1931.01
Miller, Verna 1908.13
Miller, Virginia 1943.05
Miller, W. 1883.63
Miller, W. Christie 1879.63, 1880.39, 1881.52
Miller, William 1927.13
Miller, William C. 1883.01, 1883.09
Miller, William H. 1895.40
Miller, William Henry 1912.06, 1920.16
Miller, William R. 1966.31
Miller, Woods 1931.26, 1933.20, 1934.18, 1935.12
Miller, Wynne 1960.04, 1960.19
Millership, Florrie 1920.38
Millet 1875.04
Millet, Georges 1892.07
Millet, Messr. 1879.19
Millet, Mons. 1875.07, 1880.44, 1880.52, 1880.60, 1881.53, 1881.54, 1882.35, 1882.53, 1883.27, 1883.30, 1883.55, 1883.57, 1883.59, 1884.03
Millet, Tully 1934.15
Milletaire, Carl 1948.24
Millett 1877.35, 1877.36
Millette, Belle 1902.32
Millette, Nellie 1902.32
Millham, Margot 1933.21
Millhollin, James 1959.27
Milli, Villi 1931.08, 1933.20
Millian, Max 1899.13
Milliard, Miss 1886.36
Milligan, Byron 1942.05, 1943.03, 1947.01
Milliken, Messr. 1909.13
Milliken, Robert 1910.19, 1911.06, 1911.32, 1911.36
Milliken, Sandol 1898.18, 1901.21, 1902.21
Millikin, Robert 1913.08
Milliman, Grace 1936.12
Millington, Gertrude 1904.28
Millis, Arthur 1917.34
Millis, Nannon 1947.14
Millison, William 1931.36
Millman, Bird 1916.10
Millman, Gabriel 1998.20
Millman, L'estrange 1929.33
Millns, Jim 1977.09
Millocker, Carl 1882.16, 1883.62, 1884.16, 1885.05, 1885.11, 1885.28, 1885.29, 1885.45, 1885.67, 1885.70, 1886.36, 1886.54, 1887.18, 1887.20, 1890.28, 1890.39, 1892.16, 1892.28, 1898.30, 1898.37, 1900.29, 1913.08
Millocker, Karl 1883.08, 1884.51, 1885.27, 1887.26, 1932.23
Millon, Mille. 1884.39
Mills, A.J. 1921.12
Mills, Alice 1898.46
Mills, Annette 1934.32, 1938.08
Mills, Berta 1908.17, 1908.42
Mills, Bertha 1907.39
Mills, Bessie 1906.05
Mills, Billy 1922.44, 1927.32, 1932.12
Mills, Carley 1941.08, 1955.11
Mills, Erie 1982.20, 1986.08, 1989.14
Mills, Eva 1879.05, 1879.58
Mills, Evelyn 1937.13
Mills, Fanny 1872.36, 1872.43
Mills, Florence 1919.36, 1922.25, 1924.37
Mills, Frank 1918.17
Mills, Frederick W. 1911.30
Mills, Georganna 1980.02
Mills, Gloria 1972.03
Mills, Grant 1930.23
Mills, Gus 1891.40
Mills, Harry 1884.16, 1885.44, 1886.34, 1893.11
Mills, Horace 1888.41
Mills, Irving 1939.29, 1942.11, 1963.10, 1974.09, 1975.22, 1976.04, 1981.06, 1987.02, 1989.02, 1997.03, 1999.05, 1999.24
Mills, Jack 1937.13
Mills, James 1883.42
Mills, Jeannette 1905.47
Mills, Jerry 1902.38, 1907.29, 1907.31, 1928.10
Mills, Julia 1910.17, 1911.15, 1915.30
Mills, Kerry 1896.15, 1903.41, 1980.27, 1989.23, 1999.23
Mills, Marion 1906.22, 1908.17, 1909.03
Mills, Miss 1896.44
Mills, R.J. 1872.40
Mills, Richard 1960.11
Mills, Ruth 1920.47, 1921.14
Mills, Saxonia 1989.26
Mills, Stephanie 1968.24, 1975.01, 1984.09, 1993.03
Mills, Steve 1965.05, 1971.07
Mills, W.J. 1876.03
Mills, Warren 1937.13
Millspaugh, Basil 1902.44, 1904.10, 1905.06
Millward, Edith 1905.22
Millward, H.S. 1894.46
Millward, Jessie 1910.32
Millward, Marie 1899.35
Millwood, Victor 1893.47
Milman, George 1977.15
Milne, Gwendolyn 1929.44
Milner, Raynard 1975.12
Milner, Ron 1987.17
Milnes, Sherrill 1966.04
Milo and Roger 1981.09, 1991.11
Milo, Robert 1920.20
Milo, Vic 1906.31
Milon, Mlle. 1883.48
Milons, Mr. 1851.08
Milot, J. 1866.13
Milstead, Alma 1931.46
Milstein, Fredric 1962.06
Milton, Agnes 1895.27, 1896.37, 1897.40
Milton, B. 1910.24
Milton, Bernard 1918.23
Milton, Billy 1928.42, 1934.40
Milton, Burt 1945.17
Milton, C. 1881.11, 1881.27
Milton, Clara 1877.04
Milton, E. 1867.19, 1867.20, 1868.22
Milton, Edna 1978.13
Milton, Emily 1857.05, 1857.07
Milton, Frank 1944.33, 1946.22, 1950.01, 1950.20, 1956.14
Milton, George 1935.01
Milton, Maud 1905.27
Milton, Robert 1915.01, 1915.20, 1915.25, 1918.03, 1918.37, 1919.39, 1925.26, 1926.50, 1927.25, 1934.41, 1939.16, 1941.07
Milton, T. 1868.19
Milton, Vernon 1908.15
Milward, Edith 1904.56
Mimmo, Harry 1953.17
Min, Ja-young 1997.16
Minami, Roger 1977.16, 1989.21
Minard, Fern 1906.02
Minard, Gordon 1971.06
Minart, Mons. 1886.08, 1886.18, 1886.21
Minat, Mons. 1886.21
Minchin, C. 1879.29
Mindell, Fania 1935.16
Minehart, Glory 1924.46
Minehart, Murray 1922.36, 1926.18
Minelly, Leontine 1875.01, 1875.02, 1875.04, 1875.13
Mineo, John 1967.14, 1968.07, 1971.15, 1972.04, 1972.22, 1974.05, 1983.14, 1989.12, 1989.20, 1996.14
Miner, Bob 1982.22
Miner, Craig 1912.03
Miner, Jason 1989.27
Miner, John 1976.22, 1983.04
Miner, Modesta 1898.28
Miner, Raymond 1973.14
Miner, Raynard 1976.24, 1984.10
Miner, Sadie 1898.78
Miner, Worthington 1934.38, 1936.05
Minerva, Bertha 1884.27
Mines, Madeleine 1976.26, 1977.03, 1980.21, 1981.20, 1981.21, 1985.09, 1985.13, 1986.09, 1987.08, 1988.18, 1993.12
Minetti, Ada 1893.23
Minevitch, Borrah 1925.33, 1928.25, 1930.38
Miniature Operetta Company 1879.59
Minich, Peter 1984.03
Minichiello, Michael 2000.02
Minim, Messr. 1862.02
Minjer, Harold 1925.20, 1926.17
Minjir, Harold 1928.19
Mink, Frances 1914.33
Mink, Janice 1966.24
Mink, Louise 1912.20, 1912.41, 1919.05, 1919.37
Minkoff, Frank 1968.13
Minkus, Barbara 1968.06
Minnegerode, Meade 1943.23
Minnehan, James 1914.06
Minnelli, Liza 1965.17, 1974.01, 1977.16, 1984.01, 1991.04, 1999.23
Minnelli, Vincent 1936.17, 1999.23
Minnelli, Vincente 1930.22, 1930.34, 1931.26, 1932.18, 1932.23, 1935.12, 1936.02, 1936.31, 1937.15, 1939.28, 1950.03
Minnevitch, Borrah 1925.05
Minnick, H. 1892.35
Minnie Palmer Opera Company 1890.37
Minnie, Little 1878.04
Minnie, Miss 1870.31
Minnie, Petite 1872.09
Minoff, Tammy 1991.07, 1993.02
Minor, Kiki 1964.20, 1968.17
Minor, Robert 1976.17
Minskoff, Jerome 1973.05, 1978.22, 1981.13, 1983.08, 1983.17, 1984.14, 1986.06, 1986.07
Minskoff, Lee 1978.22
Minster, Robert 1904.29
Minter, Calire 1947.01
Minton, Augustus 1913.37, 1919.16, 1922.45
Minton, Gus 1914.31, 1916.24, 1917.13, 1918.19, 1920.36
Minton, Mr. 1867.19
Minturn, Harry 1939.15
Minturn, Marie 1898.34
Minty, Mado 1913.28
Mintz, Alan 1986.18
Mintz, Eli 1973.11
Mintz, Etta 1905.24
Mintz, J. Louis 1906.47
Mintz, Melanie 1985.03
Mintz, Nat L. 1937.01
Mintz, Thalma 1970.18
Mintzer, William 1973.10, 1978.06, 1978.21
Minucci, Ulpio 1957.01
Mio, Tesore 1934.15
Mir, Willi 1927.51
Mira, Lotta 1871.14, 1871.19
Mirabella, Joan 1983.12, 1985.11, 1985.13, 1986.09, 1988.14, 1991.09, 1991.12
Miraeva, Mme. 1922.37
Mirais, Josef 1946.15
Mirammu 1934.16
Miramuna, Miss 1925.13
Mirand, Sol. 1893.22
Miranda, Carmen 1939.22, 1941.11
Miranda, D. 1859.01, 1859.02, 1859.03, 1859.04
Miranda, Evan H. 1978.11
Miranda, John 1965.23
Miranda, Lotta 1897.06
Miranda, Mario A. Santiago 1988.15
Mirande, Yves 1922.02, 1923.44, 1929.10, 1929.14
Mirandoli, Sol 1892.02, 1892.41
Mirandoli, Sol. 1892.13, 1892.27
Mirchener, Harold 1948.17
Mireille 1935.19, 1959.15, 1961.25, 1965.08
Mirella, Mlle. 1896.35
Miroff, Seymour 1971.12
Miron, J.C. 1894.29, 1898.43
Miron, Joseph 1904.19, 1908.03
Miron, Joseph C. 1888.07, 1890.21, 1891.43, 1892.36, 1892.56, 1895.26, 1896.28, 1899.02, 1899.19, 1900.12, 1900.34, 1902.20, 1903.38, 1904.15, 1904.28, 1907.07, 1908.16, 1911.02, 1911.08
Miron, Joseph Charles 1897.36
Mirr, Dorothy 1954.04
Mirras, Diana 1975.09
Mirvish, David 1987.01, 1990.15
Mirvish, Ed 1987.01
Mirybel, Mlle. 1885.55, 1885.57, 1885.60, 1885.61, 1886.09, 1886.18, 1886.21
Mirybel, Mme. 1886.19, 1886.20
Mirybell, Mlle. 1885.59
Mirzl, Rose 1891.20
Mischka, Anna 1869.41
Misgen, Florence 1928.14
Mishka, Olga 1919.06
Mishkin, Chase 1999.14, 2000.12, 2001.01
Misita, Michael 1971.05
Misita, Mike 1970.09
Miskel, Caroline 1893.31
Miskel, Sarah 1897.01
Miskel-Hoyt, Caroline 1897.01
Miskell, Brad 1985.18
Misner, Susan 1996.06, 1997.05
Misraki, Paul 1961.25
Miss Emma 1925.09
Mistretta, Sal 1978.02
Mitchel, Ella 1984.09
Mitchell, Abbie 1904.21, 1909.10, 1935.13
Mitchell, Ada 1905.53, 1911.15
Mitchell, Adrian 1965.39, 1967.01, 1981.04
Mitchell, Adrienne 1888.28
Mitchell, Agnes 1880.45
Mitchell, Arthur 1952.06, 1954.19, 1956.05, 1956.06, 1957.05, 1968.19
Mitchell, B. 1893.41
Mitchell, Barry 1943.23
Mitchell, Brian 1988.07, 1990.14
Mitchell, Brian Stokes 1998.01, 1999.19
Mitchell, Byron 1957.14, 1963.08
Mitchell, Carrie 1885.67
Mitchell, Charles 1894.12, 1910.02, 1912.07, 1912.13, 1916.09, 1920.13, 1927.12
Mitchell, Charles E. 1904.44
Mitchell, Charlie 1919.14
Mitchell, Cuyler 1908.44
Mitchell, David 1969.11, 1977.04, 1977.06, 1978.12, 1979.12, 1980.07, 1981.07, 1981.13, 1983.08, 1983.11, 1985.02, 1988.20, 1992.06, 1993.05, 1997.05
Mitchell, Dodson 1907.37, 1920.14
Mitchell, Doris 1901.17, 1902.29, 1903.31, 1905.44
Mitchell, Earle 1926.42, 1928.29
Mitchell, Edna 1901.22, 1906.35
Mitchell, Ella 1993.03
Mitchell, Esther 1905.18, 1922.20, 1924.14, 1925.20
Mitchell, Evelyn 1906.01, 1907.01, 1909.29
Mitchell, Ewing 1944.21
Mitchell, Fanny Todd 1928.46, 1929.06, 1929.17, 1929.39
Mitchell, Frank 1929.35, 1931.26
Mitchell, Fred 1940.01

Mitchell, Geneva 1927.07, 1927.60
Mitchell, George 1869.08, 1942.21, 1942.22, 1943.12, 1944.17
Mitchell, George D. 1942.11
Mitchell, Georges 1910.24
Mitchell, Gladys 1900.59
Mitchell, Gloria 1944.31, 1946.21
Mitchell, Gregory 1981.21, 1983.01, 1985.12, 1989.20, 1992.07, 1995.09, 1997.07
Mitchell, Harry 1884.10, 1905.17
Mitchell, Henry W. 1886.41
Mitchell, Irving 1949.18
Mitchell, J. 1876.06
Mitchell, Jacqueline 1962.31
Mitchell, James 1945.20, 1947.07, 1951.24, 1957.11, 1959.06, 1961.10, 1969.07, 1974.18
Mitchell, Jerry 1983.02, 1989.03, 1994.07, 1996.17, 1997.09, 1999.03, 2000.15, 2000.17
Mitchell, Jessie 1896.04
Mitchell, John Cameron 1991.05
Mitchell, John W. 1896.02
Mitchell, Joni 1982.22, 2000.16
Mitchell, Joseph 1891.26, 1892.09, 1964.40
Mitchell, Joseph E. 1925.47
Mitchell, Julia 1925.18
Mitchell, Julian 1873.10, 1883.26, 1886.40, 1887.29, 1890.41, 1891.26, 1891.32, 1891.39, 1892.05, 1892.09, 1893.06, 1893.14, 1894.35, 1894.37, 1895.39, 1896.02, 1897.07, 1897.31, 1897.42, 1897.48, 1898.50, 1898.60, 1899.06, 1899.17, 1899.21, 1899.30, 1899.34, 1899.39, 1900.12, 1900.38, 1901.01, 1901.17, 1902.29, 1903.03, 1903.31, 1904.13, 1904.44, 1904.54, 1905.01, 1905.44, 1906.29, 1906.45, 1907.10, 1907.11, 1907.24, 1907.41, 1907.44, 1908.01, 1908.04, 1908.07, 1908.19, 1908.38, 1908.39, 1909.13, 1909.25, 1909.28, 1910.18, 1910.34, 1911.11, 1911.24, 1912.13, 1912.28, 1912.33, 1912.34, 1912.38, 1912.48, 1913.17, 1913.27, 1913.31, 1914.02, 1914.26, 1915.05, 1915.15, 1915.28, 1916.01, 1916.19, 1917.12, 1917.20, 1918.11, 1918.15, 1918.25, 1918.28, 1918.29, 1919.01, 1919.04, 1919.39, 1919.43, 1920.03, 1920.38, 1921.32, 1921.37, 1922.02, 1922.05, 1922.26, 1922.29, 1922.35, 1922.43, 1922.46, 1923.46, 1924.18, 1924.27, 1924.35, 1925.10, 1925.24, 1925.33, 1926.24
Mitchell, Keith 1960.13
Mitchell, Ken 1970.11, 1974.12
Mitchell, Kenneth 1938.19
Mitchell, Kitty 1899.22, 1899.36, 1900.03
Mitchell, Larry 1957.14, 1960.09
Mitchell, Lauren 1987.18, 1998.05
Mitchell, Lena 1904.38
Mitchell, Lloyd 1928.18, 1931.31
Mitchell, Loften 1976.04
Mitchell, Lucie 1911.37
Mitchell, Lucy 1884.22, 1888.29, 1889.45
Mitchell, Mabel 1880.59, 1880.65
Mitchell, Maggie 1862.07, 1867.29, 1888.08
Mitchell, Mamie 1901.22
Mitchell, Margaret 1947.22, 1948.03, 1948.07, 1948.10, 1951.01, 1951.06, 1951.07
Mitchell, Mark 1998.10
Mitchell, Meda 1890.09
Mitchell, Messr. 1852.02
Mitchell, Millard F. 1931.32
Mitchell, Miss 1862.07, 1885.32
Mitchell, Mr. 1858.04
Mitchell, Norma 1924.33, 1925.47, 1941.08
Mitchell, Norman 1925.47
Mitchell, Patsy 1907.41
Mitchell, Pinkie 1942.20
Mitchell, R.S. 1878.19
Mitchell, Robert D. 1977.01, 1977.10, 1989.05
Mitchell, Roy 1929.51
Mitchell, Ruth 1919.11, 1919.25, 1920.39, 1947.01, 1965.17, 1966.06, 1966.24, 1968.30, 1970.13, 1971.05, 1973.04, 1974.06, 1976.02, 1976.36, 1977.05, 1978.26, 1979.06, 1980.02, 1981.18, 1981.27, 1985.05, 1987.12, 1990.18, 1994.08
Mitchell, Ruthanna 1945.14
Mitchell, Sidney D. 1918.19, 1921.18, 1921.20, 1923.18
Mitchell, Sydney 1922.38
Mitchell, Thomas 1934.39, 1935.12, 1941.03, 1953.01
Mitchell, Tilly 1873.25
Mitchell, Tomas 1938.09
Mitchell, Tressa 1931.47
Mitchell, W. 1860.02, 1865.11, 1866.02, 1866.28, 1867.12
Mitchell, William 1839.01, 1840.01, 1840.02, 1840.03, 1840.04, 1845.01, 1848.01, 1898.10, 1902.26
Mitchener, Dean 1954.03
Mittelman, Arnold 1993.08
Mittenthal Brothers 1908.37
Mittenthal Brothers Amusement Company, Inc. 1906.13
Mittenthal, Aubrey 1907.04
Mittenthal, Harry 1904.33
Mitterhoff, Barry 1989.10
Mitti, Germaine 1921.21
Mittler, Yetta 1894.13
Mittoo, Jackie 1980.05
Mitty, Nomi 1951.14
Mitzman, Marcia 1986.04, 1987.03, 1987.09, 1988.09, 1989.07, 1993.06
Miura, Tamaki 1927.28
Miville, Rene 1954.17
Mixon, Tom 1959.26
Miyori, Kim 1979.08
Mizelle, Vance 1980.01
Mizzy, Vic 1939.14
Mizzy, Vix 1942.16
Mlaba, Pat 1988.02
Mladova, Milada 1943.09, 1944.15, 1944.27, 1949.02
Mlle. Aimee's French Opera Bouffe Company 1876.20
Mlle. Marie Aimee's New Parisian Opera Troupe 1872.41, 1873.01
Mlotek, Chana 1990.16
Mlotek, Zalman 1998.12
Mlotek, Zalmen 1990.16
Mme. Smith and Company 1889.10
Mngwengwe, Qond'okwakhe 1997.14
Mnisi, Dieketseng 1997.14
Moana, Ralph 1927.65
Mobley, J.W. 1930.16
Mobley, Mary Ann 1962.24
Mobley, Ross 1920.15, 1922.17, 1926.38
Moccia, Jodi 1999.20
Mochel, Ned 1993.04
Mode Costume Company 1921.13, 1921.31, 1923.12, 1923.14, 1923.15
Modick, Murray 1937.14
Modo, Michel 1958.18, 1965.37
Modugno, Domenico 1987.02
Moeser, George 1926.18
Moffat, Alice 1914.33, 1924.23
Moffat, Elizabeth 1919.19
Moffat, Graham 1912.07
Moffat, Harold 1933.25
Moffatt, Miss 1904.13
Moffet, Harold 1929.19, 1931.48, 1933.13
Moffet, Marjorie 1939.26
Moffett, Harold 1930.32
Mofokeng, Mubi 1988.02
Mogck, David 1965.32
Mogrgan, Carey 1916.24
Mohica, Victor 1968.18
Mohn and Becker 1891.42
Mohn, Leon 1890.40
Mohn, Myles 1905.12
Mohr, Goldie 1899.30, 1900.20, 1900.38, 1901.17
Mohr, Halsey K. 1918.10
Mohr, Isabel 1926.23, 1928.22
Mohr, Joseph 1943.23
Moinaux, Jules 1858.02, 1859.14, 1864.01, 1869.09, 1870.39, 1871.06, 1875.27
Moineau, Lucienne 1926.01
Moineaux, Jules 1875.30
Moineux, Jules 1866.29
Moinot, Michel 1989.26
Moise, Ginna 1945.05
Moize, William 1983.04
Mokae, Zakes 1993.04
Mokihana 1972.11
Mola, Sete 1992.13
Molaskey, Jessica 1997.05, 1998.21
Moldow, Edwin Bruce 1941.12
Mole, Jean-Michel 1965.37
Molefe, Martha 1977.01
Molese, Michele 1964.30
Moliere 1910.12, 1933.24, 1973.02
Molierre 1879.56
Molina, Carmen 1939.18
Molina, Jose 1939.18
Molina, Lisa 1993.02
Molineaux, Constance 1914.05
Moll, Mariquita 1956.09
Moll, William 1930.14
Mollard, Messr. 1877.31
Mollard, Mlle. 1877.32
Mollard, Mons. 1877.26, 1877.27, 1877.29, 1877.30, 1877.32, 1877.34, 1877.37, 1877.38, 1878.06, 1878.07, 1878.08, 1878.09
Mollenhauer, E. 1862.08, 1868.03, 1872.27, 1879.56, 1881.04
Mollenhauer, Edward 1879.50, 1879.56, 1880.04, 1881.27, 1882.15
Mollenhauer, Edward R. 1878.21, 1881.11
Mollenhauer, F.R. 1865.03
Mollenhauer, Henrietta 1875.39
Moller, Friedrich Wilhelm 1955.13
Mollet, Philip 1983.08
Mollison, William 1930.43, 1931.09
Molloy, Irene 1999.08
Molloy, James L. 1942.01
Molloy, John 1963.30
Molnar, Ferenc 1945.05, 1949.03, 1951.13, 1954.07, 1957.11, 1965.24, 1966.31, 1994.02
Molnér, Franz 1921.33
Molnar, Robert 1980.19, 1981.26
Moltek, Zalmen 2000.14
Molteno, Ada 1873.02
Molteno, Alice 1873.02
Molthen, Jack 1979.22
Molyneux, Eileen 1914.22, 1915.22
Momen, Isaac 1923.11
Momentum Productions, Inc. 2001.03
Mona, Eppa 1921.19
Monachino, Francis 1950.05
Monaco, James 1920.04, 1920.41
Monaco, James V. 1910.22, 1912.25, 1912.38, 1913.05, 1916.03, 1916.25, 1921.18, 1921.21, 1921.34, 1923.12, 1927.62, 1931.19, 1940.10, 1962.17, 1963.02, 1964.28, 1967.11, 1976.24, 1995.12, 1995.14
Monaco, Jimmy 1927.62
Monagas, Lionel 1926.19, 1933.27
Monahan, Debi 1983.17
Monahan, Dick 1941.09
Monahan, Joseph 1906.44, 1913.31
Monamodi, Lydia 1977.01
Monaoc, James 1916.25
Monaster, Nate 1964.35
Monat, Phil 1992.16
Moncada, Eduardo Hernandez 1939.18
Moncion, Francisco 1947.06
Monckton, Lionel 1895.32, 1896.27, 1897.20, 1897.44, 1898.18, 1898.29, 1898.46, 1898.63, 1899.35, 1899.39, 1900.28, 1900.43, 1901.19, 1902.01, 1902.30, 1904.40, 1905.18, 1906.36, 1907.15, 1908.25, 1909.01, 1910.05, 1910.21, 1911.22, 1911.39, 1912.26, 1914.10, 1919.02, 1975.22
Moncrieff, Murri 1904.29
Moncrieff, W.T. 1823.01, 1856.02, 1875.03, 1901.11
Monday, James 1929.52
Monday, Master 1870.22
Mondaye, Jay 1930.10
Mondo, Peggy 1957.18
Mondoza, Sig. 1882.01
Monell, C. 1864.22, 1865.05, 1865.07, 1865.08, 1865.09, 1865.10
Monell, F. 1862.07, 1865.08
Monell, J. 1865.05, 1865.07
Monell, Julia 1862.07
Monell, Miss 1862.07
Moneo, Luis 1992.15
Moneo, Manuel 1992.15
Monet, Gaby 1954.02, 1957.10
Monette, LaVergne 1966.17
Monge, Julio 1989.03, 1995.09, 1998.02
Monicelli, Mario 1986.06
Monico, Louis 1890.12
Monier, Mlle. 1867.24
Monier, Mons. 1867.24, 1868.07
Monk, Ada 1875.14
Monk, Debra 1982.04, 1991.15, 1995.11, 1997.07
Monk, G. 1859.08
Monk, Isabell 1988.05
Monk, Minnie 1899.03
Monk, Robby 1979.29
Monkhouse, Gladys 1917.16, 1918.23, 1918.34, 1919.09, 1919.41, 1920.26, 1922.30
Monkhouse, Harry 1894.33
Monks, Jr., John 1939.14
Monnot, Marguerite 1947.18, 1958.06, 1959.15, 1960.13, 1963.02, 1965.08, 1981.04
Monod, Flavien 1961.25, 1964.02
Monogas, Lionel 1933.06
Monplaisir, Mons. 1855.10, 1856.01
Monreal 1949.07
Monro, Ronnie 1958.18
Monroe, Anita 1920.43
Monroe, Bill 1989.12
Monroe, Bob 1966.14, 1967.10
Monroe, Donna 1963.29, 1969.12, 1981.07
Monroe, F. 1871.13
Monroe, George 1909.11, 1915.11, 1916.23
Monroe, George W. 1885.03, 1886.58, 1890.12, 1890.30, 1891.14, 1892.06, 1894.31, 1895.37, 1897.16, 1902.32, 1903.30, 1904.48, 1907.47, 1908.21, 1911.35, 1912.45, 1913.16, 1914.16
Monroe, Harry 1873.22
Monroe, Isabel 1905.31
Monroe, Lucy 1926.32, 1928.41, 1929.02, 1934.41
Monroe, Minnie 1912.36
Monroe, Ned 1917.14
Monroe, Robert B. 1890.12, 1890.30, 1891.14, 1892.06, 1895.37, 1904.48
Monroe, Robert D. 1886.58
Monroe, Sadie 1881.39
Monroe, Shirley 1972.26
Monroe, Tille 1906.43
Monroe, Tom 1931.13
Monroe, Tommy 1930.36
Monroe, Walter 1938.13, 1944.01
Monson, Lex 1969.10
Montagas, Lionel 1923.39
Montague, A. 1881.24
Montague, Annis 1879.30
Montague, Edward 1907.01, 1907.27
Montague, Emily 1903.37
Montague, Irma 1931.08
Montague, J. 1890.17, 1905.27
Montague, J.J. 1907.32
Montague, James R. 1905.53
Montague, Julia 1881.28
Montague, Kathryn 1907.03
Montague, Lena 1868.03
Montague, Louise 1887.43, 1892.29, 1893.13, 1895.03, 1907.52
Montague, Ruth 1930.18
Montague, Valerie 1898.67, 1900.08
Montaigne, Jeanne 1938.07
Montaigne, Larry 1957.05
Montain, Mlle. 1888.39
Montaland, Celine 1870.30, 1870.37, 1870.41
Montalban, Paolo 2001.09
Montalban, Ricardo 1955.10, 1957.16
Montalvo, Frank 1974.26, 1977.04, 1979.25
Montana, Montie 1979.31
Montand, Yves 1959.15, 1961.25
Montano, Robert 1993.09, 1998.16
Montanye, C.S. 1922.24
Montclaire, Louise 1882.04
Monte, Barbara 1959.05, 1960.08, 1961.15, 1962.05, 1963.08, 1965.01, 1965.31
Monte, Elisa 1957.11
Monte, Emily 1911.26
Monte, Evelyn 1917.35
Monte, Gus 1911.25
Monte, Joseph 1945.12
Montedoro, Marco 1941.10, 1942.32, 1945.02
Montegna, Joe 1978.12
Montegriffo, A. 1883.49, 1885.43
Montegriffo, Signor 1882.26, 1882.43, 1882.46
Montei, Herb 1930.32, 1933.26
Monteil, Annette 1919.31
Monteiro, Maria 1943.17
Monteith, John 1979.01
Monteith, Mr. 1875.10
Montel, Ginger 1997.17
Montell, Carrie 1902.26
Montell, Tony 1946.13
Monterey, Carlotta 1923.22
Montero, Gus 1975.07
Montero, Maria 1922.21
Montes, Monna 1943.12
Montesanto, Leroy 1921.11
Montevecchi, Liliane 1964.22, 1982.09, 1984.10, 1989.26

Montez, Mayita 1942.19
Montford, Helen 1893.13
Montford, May 1888.32, 1897.49, 1898.28, 1898.70, 1910.13
Montfort Productions 1969.17
Montfort, May 1906.01
Montgomery 1887.40
Montgomery G.R. 1889.20
Montgomery, Barbara 1981.15, 1983.21
Montgomery, Bessie 1902.09
Montgomery, Candace 1946.07, 1946.23
Montgomery, Dave 1910.02, 1912.39, 1914.23
Montgomery, David 1901.01, 1906.33
Montgomery, David C. 1903.03, 1904.13, 1904.44
Montgomery, Dick 1943.24
Montgomery, Douglass 1931.34
Montgomery, Earl 1968.23
Montgomery, Frank 1907.16, 1909.15, 1923.11
Montgomery, Garth 1979.24
Montgomery, H. 1881.32
Montgomery, H.W. 1871.14, 1879.71, 1881.03, 1883.16, 1885.21
Montgomery, Harry 1904.54, 1906.11, 1908.17
Montgomery, Henry 1871.19, 1881.03
Montgomery, Ione 1908.03
Montgomery, J. 1878.03
Montgomery, J.A. 1880.12, 1882.25
Montgomery, J.C. 1882.57, 1998.21, 1999.24
Montgomery, J.H. 1903.12
Montgomery, James 1917.36, 1918.07, 1919.36, 1920.18, 1922.48, 1923.09, 1925.38, 1927.49, 1932.21, 1973.05, 1976.25
Montgomery, Laried 1967.04, 1968.17, 1969.08
Montgomery, Lee 1937.10
Montgomery, Lloyd 1913.37
Montgomery, Louis 1901.24
Montgomery, Lucy M. 1971.21
Montgomery, Mabel 1893.13, 1896.05, 1898.01, 1898.38, 1898.44
Montgomery, Master 1883.21
Montgomery, Miss 1881.04
Montgomery, Mr. 1875.03
Montgomery, Mrs. 1840.02, 1840.03
Montgomery, Ray 1907.40, 1908.12
Montgomery, Reggie 1991.01
Montgomery, Ronald 1971.21
Montgomery, Saidee 1875.05
Montgomery, Will 1917.10
Montgomery, William 1912.25, 1913.30
Monti, Alicia 1999.18
Monti, Louise 1901.01
Montjoy, Messr. 1882.04, 1882.20
Montmartre Productions, Inc. 1928.32
Montoya, Antonio 1986.17
Montoya, Carlos 1942.14
Montoya, Carmen 1951.20
Montoya, Pilar 1986.17
Montoya, Rosario 1986.17
Montplaisir, Mons. 1857.03, 1859.05
Montreau, Pauline 1905.28
Montrell, Roy 1992.06
Montresor, Beni 1965.06, 1986.13
Montrose, Ada 1892.23
Montrose, Buela 1900.07
Montrose, Etta 1896.45
Montrose, F.A. 1888.10
Montrose, Harold 1897.07
Montrose, Helen 1921.07
Montrose, Helene 1907.47
Montrose, Kate 1893.23
Montrose, Louise 1893.23, 1897.07
Montrose, M. 1866.19
Montrose, Mr. 1909.13
Montrose, Muriel 1925.50, 1928.42
Montrose, W.C. 1882.18
Montrose, Wilfred 1879.15
Moody, David 1969.15
Moody, Eileen 1934.21, 1934.30
Moody, Jacquelynne 1956.09, 1956.10, 1957.13, 1959.08, 1959.16, 1961.04
Moody, Naomi 1983.04
Moody, Robert 1928.21
Moody, Ron 1984.07
Moody, Russell 1989.12
Moody, William Vaughn 1906.29
Moon, George 1912.24, 1914.01, 1915.26
Moon, Hyo Jung 1998.08
Moon, Joe 1946.07, 1946.12, 1946.22
Moon, Joseph 1958.04
Moon, Keith 1972.08, 1993.06
Moon, Marjorie 1981.15
Mooney, Ann 1913.19
Mooney, Anna 1908.36
Mooney, Beatrice 1888.39
Mooney, Gipsey 1918.03
Mooney, Gypsy 1908.28
Mooney, Helen 1904.17, 1910.29
Mooney, James 1901.26
Mooney, Julia 1935.04
Mooney, Lulu 1900.34
Mooney, Marian 1918.05
Mooney, Marion 1917.08
Mooney, Mary 1907.47, 1908.36, 1912.19
Mooney, Master 1892.54, 1893.15, 1893.27, 1893.36, 1893.46
Mooney, Messr. 1894.04
Mooney, Miss 1893.37
Mooney, Samuel 1934.28
Mooney, Tessie 1900.34, 1901.06, 1901.23
Moor, Maggie 1877.28
Moor, Mamie 1896.06
Moor, Ruby 1889.50
Moor, William 1880.35
Moore and Holmes' Royal British Burlesque and Specialty, 1884.44
Moore, A.C. 1888.10
Moore, Ada 1954.19
Moore, Adrienne 1943.03
Moore, Al 1931.11, 1940.17
Moore, Albert 1917.24
Moore, Alfred 1913.03
Moore, Annabelle 1899.26
Moore, Annie 1901.11
Moore, Arthur 1938.19
Moore, Barbara 1982.15
Moore, Bernie 1967.01
Moore, Bill 1906.08
Moore, Billie 1907.55
Moore, Bruce 1989.27, 1991.06, 1993.18
Moore, Carrie A. 1866.12, 1868.06
Moore, Charles 1893.03, 1895.35, 1904.21, 1961.24, 1965.32
Moore, Charles H. 1906.14, 1908.08, 1909.27, 1930.10, 1935.01
Moore, Charlotte 1989.23
Moore, Christi 1999.11
Moore, Clara 1878.13, 1879.37, 1880.63, 1883.17
Moore, Clare 1905.25
Moore, Constance 1942.15
Moore, Crista 1989.27, 1991.06, 1992.10, 1993.14, 1994.09, 1996.08
Moore, Cy 1976.27
Moore, D. 1897.29
Moore, Dana 1981.12, 1986.07, 1989.20, 1991.07, 1999.01
Moore, David T. 1896.42
Moore, Decima 1894.33
Moore, Dennie 1931.39, 1934.35, 1944.29
Moore, Doris 1938.15
Moore, Douglas 1939.20, 1959.09
Moore, Dudley 1962.23, 1964.45, 1973.13
Moore, Elsie 1875.03
Moore, Emma 1873.27
Moore, Ernest 1938.16
Moore, Ethel 1900.16, 1900.44, 1901.06
Moore, Eugene 1891.27
Moore, Fleecie 1992.03, 1999.06, 1999.09
Moore, Florence 1912.25, 1913.30, 1914.34, 1916.11, 1921.30, 1923.32, 1925.47, 1927.58, 1930.09
Moore, Frances 1929.34, 1929.48, 1930.41, 1931.15, 1931.17, 1931.18, 1931.24, 1931.27, 1933.09, 1933.14, 1933.18, 1933.19
Moore, Frank 1910.15
Moore, Frederick 1993.03
Moore, George 1894.44, 1907.13, 1917.12, 1918.18
Moore, George Austin 1903.23, 1904.31, 1905.41, 1912.43
Moore, George F. 1919.33
Moore, George Leon 1908.24, 1911.03, 1912.33, 1919.05
Moore, George W. 1884.44
Moore, Georgia 1928.35
Moore, Gerald 1927.03, 1928.13
Moore, Gertie 1925.18
Moore, Gladys 1908.21, 1909.11, 1911.40, 1911.45
Moore, Grace 1920.39, 1922.01, 1923.32, 1924.44, 1932.23, 1932.26
Moore, Gregory 1985.09, 1986.04, 1987.03, 1987.08, 1990.08, 1991.09, 1991.12
Moore, Greville 1912.24
Moore, H. 1875.18
Moore, Happy 1938.08
Moore, Hattie 1882.23, 1890.49, 1891.25, 1891.45, 1892.44, 1892.54, 1893.10, 1893.15, 1893.27, 1893.36, 1894.04, 1894.49, 1895.05, 1895.07, 1895.18, 1900.05, 1900.34, 1901.09
Moore, Helen 1898.28
Moore, Henry 1895.36
Moore, Herbert 1919.44, 1920.29
Moore, Honor 1974.23
Moore, Ira T. 1888.28
Moore, Irene 1936.12
Moore, Irma 1927.62
Moore, Isabel 1897.44
Moore, Ivy 1902.10, 1902.37
Moore, J. 1856.02, 1868.04, 1890.47, 1890.48
Moore, Jack 1957.14
Moore, James 1927.06, 1927.50, 1962.02, 1963.13, 1964.17, 1965.01
Moore, James S. 1955.01
Moore, Jan 1926.07
Moore, Jane 1926.15, 1926.26, 1935.04
Moore, Jann 1941.02, 1943.08
Moore, Jay 1977.05
Moore, Jennie L. 1909.06
Moore, Jerry R. 1980.14, 1982.17
Moore, Jim 1951.18, 2001.04
Moore, Jimmy 1922.22
Moore, Joanne 1962.25, 1962.26, 1962.30, 1962.31
Moore, John 1853.05, 1854.04, 1875.17, 1876.08, 1879.50, 1879.59, 1908.02, 1925.02, 1938.10
Moore, John J. 1967.18, 1975.04, 1976.19, 1979.28, 1980.18
Moore, John Jay 1979.13
Moore, Jonathan 1969.06
Moore, Judith 1984.08, 1999.16
Moore, Karen 1959.13
Moore, Kenny 1984.15
Moore, Laura 1888.26, 1889.24, 1890.26, 1891.31, 1891.47, 1896.01
Moore, Lawrence 1927.36
Moore, Leecy R. Woods 1971.10
Moore, Lela 1940.02
Moore, Lillian 1946.06
Moore, Lottie 1896.27
Moore, Louise 1884.44, 1902.08, 1902.27
Moore, M.T. 1876.19
Moore, Madame 1909.19
Moore, Maggie 1877.28
Moore, Margery 1940.07
Moore, Marie 1912.15
Moore, Marion 1976.21
Moore, Marshall 1901.27
Moore, Mary 1879.42, 1923.09, 1927.18
Moore, Maureen 1974.17, 1982.10, 1990.07, 1991.08
Moore, Mavor 1971.21
Moore, McElbert 1921.42, 1922.23, 1923.13, 1924.10, 1924.13, 1926.01, 1926.04, 1927.64
Moore, Melba 1968.11, 1970.05, 1978.03, 1981.15
Moore, Melton 1936.17, 1948.27
Moore, Menlo 1922.29
Moore, Messr. 1750.01, 1880.55, 1886.36
Moore, Michael 1996.15
Moore, Michael Christopher 1994.12
Moore, Mickey 1937.15
Moore, Minnie 1869.17, 1869.28
Moore, Miss 1836.01, 1866.13, 1898.50, 1917.31
Moore, Molly 1917.31
Moore, Monette 1925.18, 1932.17
Moore, Monica 1942.15, 1947.13
Moore, Mr. 1851.04, 1851.08, 1853.05, 1858.03, 1859.01, 1871.22, 1876.19, 1906.29
Moore, Mrs. 1836.01
Moore, Muriel 1969.03
Moore, Napie 1936.01
Moore, Neil 1919.11, 1927.06, 1930.42, 1933.03
Moore, Olive Celeste 1902.28, 1903.36
Moore, Pauline 1933.20
Moore, Peter 1981.24
Moore, Ph. 1886.04
Moore, Pony 1909.08
Moore, Raymon 1891.15, 1891.32, 1892.50
Moore, Raymond 1921.36
Moore, Reenie 1980.12
Moore, Richard 1940.06
Moore, Robert 1942.20, 1946.19, 1968.31, 1974.02, 1979.04, 1981.10
Moore, Sam 1949.17
Moore, Scott 1946.01, 1961.09
Moore, Sharon 1987.14, 1995.13
Moore, Simeon 1920.10
Moore, Stanley 1955.19
Moore, Sue 1931.04
Moore, T.F. 1897.50
Moore, Thomas 1872.10, 1896.11, 1901.15, 1927.02, 1932.09
Moore, Tim 1925.18, 1928.18, 1931.31, 1932.08, 1939.14, 1942.13
Moore, Tom 1894.36, 1972.12, 1974.05
Moore, Tommie 1946.24
Moore, Tony 1980.18
Moore, Tracey 1989.17
Moore, Trixie 1910.12
Moore, Victor 1898.05, 1906.02, 1906.42, 1907.57, 1911.07, 1926.36, 1927.35, 1927.59, 1928.36, 1929.42, 1930.30, 1931.48, 1933.13, 1933.25, 1934.36, 1938.13, 1940.08, 1942.12, 1945.09, 1946.04, 1957.11
Moore, W.C. 1907.54
Moore, Walker 1923.43
Moore, Warre 1997.21
Moore, Wilda Marie 1918.41
Moore, William 1885.50, 1907.15, 1908.21, 1908.26, 1925.39, 1928.34, 1928.50
Moorefield, Olive 1952.15
Moorehead, Agnes 1973.12
Moorehead, Emma 1934.37
Moorehead, Jean 1939.30
Moorhead, Jean 1944.30
Moorhouse, Mr. 1868.06, 1871.11
Mooring, Mark 1924.30, 1925.31, 1925.47, 1925.52, 1926.34, 1926.42, 1926.50, 1927.16, 1927.63, 1928.25, 1929.02
Moorman, Merrill 1943.06
Moose, Eugene 1975.07
Mooser, George 1926.22
Mopsy 1970.20
Mora, Ed 1904.27
Mora, Fanny 1900.24
Mora, Helene 1893.33
Mora, J. 1985.07, 1999.18
Mora, Karl 1890.33, 1892.08
Moracher, Sepp 1927.57
Moragas, Ricardo 1881.24
Moral Re-Armament 1951.05
Morales, Carmen 1960.01, 1960.09, 1963.17, 1964.40, 1966.01
Morales, Mark 1981.08
Morales, Roberto 1979.08
Moran, Agnes 1927.23, 1929.20
Moran, Alan 1927.05, 1927.35, 1941.13, 1944.30, 1948.19, 1949.05
Moran, Betty 1941.08
Moran, Charles 1925.01
Moran, Ed 1917.37, 1922.23, 1980.27
Moran, Ed P. 1905.20
Moran, Eddie 1931.05
Moran, Edward P. 1904.13, 1906.43, 1907.15
Moran, Eileen 1952.19, 1955.07
Moran, Estavan 1875.24
Moran, Frank 1866.20, 1866.26
Moran, George 1920.18, 1924.32, 1926.18, 1926.23
Moran, Katherine 1908.16, 1908.43
Moran, Lois 1931.48, 1933.25
Moran, Lona 1976.29
Moran, Mack 1927.02
Moran, Martin 1995.05, 1997.06, 2001.03
Moran, Mary 1904.02
Moran, Nell 1928.48
Moran, Pat 1949.06
Moran, Rosie 1928.08, 1937.07, 1937.17
Moran, William 1921.25, 1941.11
Morand, Alan 1948.23
Morando, Estelle 1933.16
Morando, Madelaine 1888.39
Morange, E.A. 1899.40, 1900.01, 1903.07, 1905.03, 1905.33, 1906.33, 1906.40, 1907.02, 1907.08, 1907.18, 1907.30, 1907.62, 1908.02, 1908.07, 1908.34, 1908.36, 1911.13, 1913.17, 1914.20, 1916.06, 1919.08, 1919.23, 1920.11, 1921.36, 1923.05, 1923.45, 1924.28, 1926.51, 1927.06, 1929.31, 1929.37
Morange, Edward A. 1895.03, 1895.21, 1898.55, 1899.06
Morao, Manuel 1992.15
Morath, Kathy 1991.15
Moray, H.A. 1884.04

Moray, Mona 1929.48, 1930.01
Morcom, James 1931.34, 1934.42
Mordaunt, Belle 1879.68, 1880.09, 1880.36, 1880.64, 1881.09
Mordaunt, Mabel 1908.41, 1911.31
Mordaunt, Maude 1915.12, 1915.14
Mordecai, David 1942.26, 1945.06, 1946.09, 1948.16, 1948.20
Mordecai, George 1908.26
Mordecai, James 1937.09, 1939.19
Mordecai, Miss 1895.03
Mordecai, Nellie 1911.28
Mordente, Anthony 1956.12
Mordente, Lisa 1978.25, 1981.24, 1991.04
Mordente, Tony 1957.12, 1960.06, 1968.05
Morder, Giorgio 1982.22
Mordkin, Michael 1934.38
Mordkin, Mikhail 1924.32
More, Julian 1960.13, 1981.14, 1987.12
More, M. 1999.19
More, Maggie 1906.07
Moreale, Antonio 1898.12
Morealle, Emerico 1900.39
Moreau, Andree 1926.40
Moreau, Emile 1905.04
Moreau, Messr. 1902.13
Moreau, Mlle. 1926.47
Moreau, Mme. 1880.44, 1882.53, 1882.55, 1882.58, 1882.61
Moreau, Mons. 1879.48, 1883.57
Morehead, Westley 2001.04
Morehouse, Miss 1870.05
Morehu, Kipa 1972.20
Moreira, Christiane 1992.13
Moreira, Patricia 1992.13
Morel, Carlos 1997.13
Morel, Devah 1922.42
Morel, Mlle. 1883.27
Morel, Mme. 1882.55
Morel, Mons. 1883.61
Moreland, A.C. 1881.55, 1883.56, 1883.66, 1886.03
Moreland, Arthur C. 1885.49, 1885.66, 1889.37, 1891.18
Moreland, Beatrice 1911.17
Moreland, Ed 1898.64
Moreland, Ida 1896.06, 1896.18
Moreland, Mantan 1928.18, 1930.34, 1931.32, 1932.08, 1932.12, 1932.30
Morelin, Beatrice 1901.26
Morelin, Mable 1901.26
Morell, Peter 1934.37
Morell, Ulysses 1924.12
Morelle, Marie 1896.42
Morelli Antonio 1949.12
Morelli, Anthony R. 1940.07
Morelli, Wanda 1935.02
Morello, Alice 1931.44
Moreno, Antonio 1912.12, 1992.15
Moreno, Hilda 1930.39
Moreno, Paco 1929.09
Moreno, Rita 1970.02
Moreno, Rosita 1929.09
Morenschildt, Xenia 1922.37
Mores, J. Francis 1907.29, 1908.08
Mores, J.F. 1907.31
Mores, M. 1985.07, 1997.13
Moret, Neil 1903.14, 1912.07, 1912.29, 1919.43, 1931.11, 1932.06
Moretti, Raoul 1929.10, 1929.13, 1934.32, 1935.19
Moretz, Allen 1930.18
Morey H.T. 1898.54
Morey, Cynthia 1955.18, 1955.20, 1955.23, 1955.24
Morey, Emma 1905.43
Morey, H.A. 1884.07
Morey, Harold P. 1903.03, 1904.13, 1904.44
Morey, Harold T. 1899.30, 1900.38, 1901.25
Morey, Harry 1908.36
Morey, Larry 1975.12, 1979.28, 1999.05
Morgan, Abita 1905.30
Morgan, Adrian 1921.01
Morgan, Agnes 1922.20, 1924.14, 1925.20, 1926.17, 1927.23, 1928.19, 1929.20, 1937.11
Morgan, Agnes Bangs 1913.02
Morgan, Al 1958.02
Morgan, Aniko 1968.05
Morgan, Beatrice 1896.39, 1897.44, 1898.18, 1898.46
Morgan, Beverly 1983.16
Morgan, C. William 1934.25, 1934.28, 1936.14, 1936.18, 1939.09, 1948.01, 1948.10
Morgan, Carey 1919.06, 1919.26, 1919.32, 1921.27, 1922.03, 1975.09
Morgan, Carl 1906.45
Morgan, Cass 1982.04, 1998.02
Morgan, Charles 1926.42
Morgan, Clark 1963.27, 1965.17, 1976.21
Morgan, D. Eloise 1894.45, 1900.02, 1900.06, 1900.09, 1900.11, 1900.13, 1900.17, 1900.23, 1900.26, 1900.27, 1900.29
Morgan, Dickson 1924.46
Morgan, Don 1961.02
Morgan, E. Eloise 1900.21
Morgan, E.P. 1913.05
Morgan, Elizabeth 1921.25, 1922.03, 1926.21
Morgan, Eloise 1894.23, 1899.05, 1899.07, 1899.42, 1900.04
Morgan, Eric 1997.16
Morgan, Eugene 1966.24
Morgan, Fisher 1955.15, 1955.16, 1955.18, 1955.20, 1955.23, 1955.24
Morgan, Frances 1975.01
Morgan, Frances Lee 1979.32
Morgan, Frank 1918.16, 1920.45, 1928.03, 1931.16, 1932.13
Morgan, Frederick 1904.33
Morgan, Gary 1978.22
Morgan, George 1882.48, 1904.33, 1906.26, 1908.23, 1931.44
Morgan, Griffin 1867.29
Morgan, Griffith 1866.34, 1867.08, 1870.36
Morgan, Harry 1875.32
Morgan, Helen 1925.22, 1926.21, 1927.67, 1929.31, 1931.19, 1932.11
Morgan, Henry 1950.02
Morgan, Howard 1910.35, 1927.66, 1934.04
Morgan, J.L. 1887.02, 1887.42, 1888.25, 1889.43, 1890.36, 1894.52, 1975.09
Morgan, James 1948.11, 1989.19, 1992.11
Morgan, Jane 1933.15, 1957.01, 1963.07
Morgan, Jennie 1879.04, 1879.68, 1880.09
Morgan, Jimmy 1919.18
Morgan, Joan 1954.16
Morgan, Johnny 1943.21, 1944.17
Morgan, Jr., Charles C. 1914.33
Morgan, Jr., Charles J. 1912.02
Morgan, Jr., Charles S. 1913.24
Morgan, Katherine 1903.12
Morgan, Lee 1993.06
Morgan, Leone 1917.02
Morgan, M. 1881.18
Morgan, Mamie 1897.51
Morgan, Marven 1911.28, 1922.30
Morgan, Matt 1866.05, 1875.04, 1875.06, 1875.11, 1875.14, 1875.19, 1875.20, 1875.31, 1875.32, 1875.36, 1875.40, 1876.01, 1876.02, 1888.19, 1890.19, 1908.15
Morgan, Merlin 1916.20
Morgan, Messr. 1876.19
Morgan, Miles 1957.02
Morgan, Mr. 1862.09, 1863.02, 1864.13
Morgan, Mrs. Edward Nash 1904.02
Morgan, Ralph 1952.05
Morgan, Randy 1980.16, 1981.26
Morgan, Rebecca 1897.51
Morgan, Richard 1917.15
Morgan, Robbi 1980.07
Morgan, Robert 2000.15
Morgan, Roger 1971.02, 1971.06, 1972.18, 1975.02, 1978.24, 1979.12, 1979.19, 1981.09, 1986.12, 1987.13
Morgan, Russ 1987.02, 2000.07
Morgan, Ruth 1930.39
Morgan, Susanne 1919.18
Morgan, T. 1866.12, 1875.14
Morgan, Ted (Sport) 1951.23
Morgan, Thomas 1920.08
Morgan, Tom 1926.17
Morgan, W. 1880.57
Morgan, W. William 1948.09
Morgan, W.A. 1879.25, 1880.26, 1880.62, 1881.25, 1882.18, 1883.64
Morgan, W.J. 1904.01
Morgan, Wallace 1908.27
Morgan, William 1895.03, 1908.44, 1910.28, 1918.23, 1939.01
Morgan, William J. 1900.36
Morganstern, C.W. 1927.31
Morganthaler, Leonard 1948.24
Moriarty, Marcus 1884.17, 1887.48, 1888.27, 1888.40, 1908.43
Moriber, Brooke Sunny 1998.21, 2000.01, 2000.08, 2001.02
Morielli, Antonio 1949.12
Morill, Theodore 1964.12
Morin, Bessie 1915.11
Morin, Catherine 1997.21
Morin, Pilar 1893.25
Morin, Zena 1915.11
Morinelli, Patricia 1984.10
Moris, Daniel 1914.01
Moris, Louise 1914.33
Morison, Lindsay 1885.67, 1887.28, 1888.19, 1888.24, 1888.26, 1889.22
Morison, Patricia 1938.06, 1944.15, 1948.32, 1965.18
Morisset, Denys 1972.08
Moritmer, Nellie 1879.14
Moritsugu, Kiki 1990.17
Moritz, Al 1945.07
Moritz, Marc 1981.27
Moritz, Mlle. 1871.18
Moriya, Shizu 1959.05
Morlacchi, G. 1869.08
Morlacchi, Giuseppina 1867.25, 1876.34
Morlan, Cora 1903.12
Morlet, Mlle. 1871.27
Morley, Charles 1966.30
Morley, John 1949.15
Morley, May 1910.06
Morley, Ruth 1957.08, 1958.05, 1959.02, 1959.05, 1959.07, 1960.02, 1963.05, 1964.18, 1965.04, 1968.05, 1980.15
Morley, Thomas 1963.28
Morley, Victor 1904.16, 1905.49, 1906.36, 1915.01, 1917.32, 1918.04, 1920.05, 1921.38, 1922.02, 1930.21, 1933.03, 1934.01, 1937.17
Morling, Pat 1963.10
Morn, Edna 1920.11, 1922.31, 1925.11
Mornay, Joy 1955.16, 1964.37
Morningstar, Carter 1960.01
Moro, George 1939.31
Morocco 1964.44
Morokoff, Paul 1965.05
Moron, Nino Esteven 1875.22
Morondo, Madelaine 1890.03
Morondo, Marietta 1871.18
Morosco Holding Company, Inc. 1922.14, 1923.01
Morosco, Dorothy 1914.31
Morosco, Oliver 1912.03, 1914.21, 1916.21, 1917.04, 1919.37, 1921.35, 1922.14, 1923.01
Moross, Jerome 1935.03, 1935.16, 1946.02, 1948.17, 1954.03, 1963.22
Moross, Theodore 1898.02
Moroz, Barbara 1985.02
Morreale, Enrico 1902.31
Morrell, Albert 1886.44, 1889.03, 1890.06
Morrell, Blanche 1906.05
Morrell, Charles 1956.15
Morrell, Louis 1919.35, 1923.45, 1928.47, 1934.04
Morrell, Roberta 1978.15, 1978.16, 1978.18
Morrell, Stanleigh 1930.10
Morres, J.F. 1906.08
Morris, A.D. 1871.11
Morris, A.J. 1901.06
Morris, Amarilla 1940.22
Morris, Andy 1888.43
Morris, Anita 1971.12, 1974.13, 1982.09
Morris, Arndt 1905.47
Morris, Billy 1976.24
Morris, Bobby 1945.01
Morris, Corbet 1929.33
Morris, Cramer 1884.42
Morris, Daniel 1912.24, 1915.26
Morris, David 1932.14, 1936.05, 1939.13, 1940.23, 1945.02
Morris, David D. 1929.46, 1930.04, 1930.28
Morris, David K. 1924.32
Morris, Ed 1881.21, 1881.22, 1881.33, 1884.25
Morris, Eddie 1910.21, 1913.31, 1916.05
Morris, Edward 1884.15, 1884.56, 1885.58, 1887.01, 1887.43, 1912.28
Morris, Edwin H. 1974.18
Morris, Elida 1916.11
Morris, Elyston 1914.24
Morris, Estelle 1887.33
Morris, Felix 1880.63, 1881.31
Morris, Felix J. 1883.64
Morris, Garrett 1964.19, 1966.14, 1967.06, 1968.08, 1970.04, 1971.13
Morris, George 1876.34, 1929.52, 1948.28
Morris, Harold 1886.07
Morris, Harry 1884.26, 1885.35, 1903.18, 1904.39
Morris, Harry B. 1896.31, 1904.01
Morris, Howard 1949.18, 1960.09
Morris, I.N. 1906.50
Morris, Ida 1878.01, 1880.05
Morris, J. 1870.43, 1875.14
Morris, James 1956.01
Morris, Janet 1966.02
Morris, Jeremiah 1963.25, 1972.19
Morris, Joan 1922.05
Morris, Joe 1906.13, 1908.37, 1923.42, 1924.36, 1938.03, 1942.10
Morris, John 1881.06, 1881.12, 1955.27, 1956.07, 1956.14, 1957.05, 1957.14, 1959.06, 1959.23, 1960.06, 1960.22, 1961.24, 1962.04, 1963.13, 1965.02, 1966.09, 1967.02, 1968.11, 1970.08, 1973.08, 1974.18, 1975.05, 2001.03
Morris, John B. 1907.53
Morris, Jonathan 1960.10
Morris, K. 1881.11
Morris, L. 1889.02
Morris, Laura 1905.17
Morris, Lenwood 1943.17, 1944.31, 1945.13, 1946.21, 1950.07
Morris, Lillian 1930.41
Morris, Lillian Brown 1889.26
Morris, Lynne 1972.21
Morris, Mabel 1886.45, 1886.59, 1888.39, 1889.37, 1891.18
Morris, Margaret 1910.18, 1912.38, 1916.24, 1917.26, 1922.35, 1923.13
Morris, Mark 1998.02
Morris, Marti 1982.24
Morris, Maud 1903.28, 1907.19, 1908.33
Morris, Maude 1909.26
Morris, May 1900.59
Morris, McKay 1919.38, 1946.05
Morris, Mike 1920.26
Morris, Mr. 1864.02, 1864.13, 1870.35, 1871.15, 1892.04
Morris, Mrs. 1787.01
Morris, Phil 1928.34
Morris, Ramsay 1897.47, 1899.27, 1900.55
Morris, Ray 1907.38
Morris, Richard 1960.20
Morris, Robert Griffin 1885.06, 1885.64, 1887.05, 1887.13
Morris, Ruth 1926.13
Morris, Sadie 1882.50, 1882.74, 1883.32, 1883.46, 1883.53, 1883.63, 1884.13, 1884.41, 1885.02, 1885.15, 1885.22, 1905.31
Morris, T.E. 1862.05, 1864.13, 1869.25, 1869.28
Morris, Thoams 1921.27
Morris, Thomas A. 1914.22
Morris, Thomas E. 1867.18, 1872.10, 1876.32, 1877.02
Morris, Val 1859.16
Morris, Vera 1900.56, 1901.12, 1901.29, 1903.28
Morris, Virginia 1946.13, 1946.20
Morris, Wendy 1965.07, 1965.26
Morris, William 1879.28, 1900.08, 1917.25, 1928.05, 1930.17
Morris, William E. 1931.29
Morrisey, Agnes 1923.24
Morrisey, Bob 1979.02, 1981.28, 1986.16
Morrison, Adrienne 1922.20, 1924.14
Morrison, Alex 1923.17, 1924.36
Morrison, Ann 1981.27
Morrison, Arthur 1908.15
Morrison, B. 1970.01, 1974.19
Morrison, Beatrice 1896.11
Morrison, Bergh 1896.01
Morrison, Betty 1937.14
Morrison, Blanche 1905.57, 1907.36, 1908.40
Morrison, C.P. 1893.06
Morrison, Charles P. 1895.36, 1912.47, 1914.08
Morrison, Dorothy 1935.11
Morrison, Emily 1918.07
Morrison, Este 1915.23
Morrison, Ethel 1925.43, 1928.06, 1934.13
Morrison, Florence 1890.25, 1905.40, 1909.09, 1911.27, 1915.31, 1918.32, 1921.14, 1922.38, 1923.22, 1924.45, 1927.17
Morrison, Gladys 1919.38
Morrison, H. 1918.15
Morrison, Helen 1904.12, 1906.37, 1908.27
Morrison, Jack 1922.05
Morrison, James 1880.51, 1935.01
Morrison, Kay 1935.17
Morrison, Kent 1943.23
Morrison, L.F. 1894.27

Morrison, Lee 1920.15, 1946.13
Morrison, Lindsay 1887.12, 1887.26, 1888.22, 1890.16
Morrison, Lindsey 1894.31
Morrison, Lou 1922.17
Morrison, Mary 1892.01
Morrison, Mary Louise 1915.30
Morrison, Messr. 1852.02
Morrison, Miriam 1937.14
Morrison, Mr. 1834.03, 1867.19
Morrison, P. 1896.47
Morrison, Paul 1952.06, 1955.19, 1956.13, 1956.15, 1957.01, 1959.12, 1959.19, 1960.04, 1961.12, 1961.13, 1963.20
Morrison, Peggy 1949.10, 1949.11, 1949.13, 1949.14, 1950.09, 1952.14, 1952.16, 1952.17, 1952.18, 1952.19, 1959.14
Morrison, Priestley 1930.22
Morrison, Priestly 1905.21, 1922.10
Morrison, Ricardo 1946.21
Morrison, Russell 1926.20, 1943.16
Morrison, S. 1875.14
Morrison, Sam 1936.07
Morrison, Van 2000.07
Morrison, Vivian 1916.08
Morrison, Walter 1924.16
Morrison, Wayne 1979.15
Morrissey, Harry 1923.33, 1924.19, 1925.22, 1926.16, 1928.22, 1929.35
Morrissey, Jack 1933.21
Morrissey, James W. 1889.28, 1889.29
Morrissey, John F. 1920.07
Morrissey, Paul 1975.04
Morrissey, Ray 1946.22
Morrissey, Sean Thomas 1994.12, 1995.19, 1996.15, 1997.22
Morrissey, Will 1915.11, 1919.10, 1923.23, 1927.10, 1929.24, 1930.24, 1930.34, 1932.14, 1934.20, 1942.30, 1945.01
Morrissey, William 1920.20
Morrisson, Florence 1920.45
Morrius, T.E. 1870.34
Morrow, Annette 1904.06
Morrow, Doretta 1948.26, 1951.12, 1953.16
Morrow, Helen 1937.11
Morrow, Jeff 1952.05
Morrow, Karen 1964.44, 1965.38, 1966.08, 1966.30, 1967.17, 1968.08, 1968.32, 1971.16, 1972.02, 1974.09
Morrow, Kevyn 1987.07, 1997.05
Morrow, Macklin 1938.06
Morrow, Sue-Anne 2000.15
Morscher, Sepp 1926.31, 1926.44, 1927.44
Morse, Agnes Riley 1899.36
Morse, Coline 1976.27
Morse, E.B. 1879.33
Morse, E.R. 1879.35, 1880.06, 1880.13, 1880.65, 1881.31, 1881.43
Morse, Edward 1880.70
Morse, Esther 1904.58
Morse, Frank 1887.52
Morse, Frank E. 1885.64, 1891.39
Morse, H. Thumon 1907.19
Morse, H.M. 1878.02, 1879.01, 1880.02, 1896.44
Morse, Harry M. 1908.22
Morse, Henry Woolson 1881.27, 1882.34, 1883.31
Morse, Josephine 1912.42, 1916.13
Morse, Lee 1923.25
Morse, Louisa 1887.02, 1887.42, 1888.25, 1889.43, 1890.36, 1894.52, 1898.45, 1899.32, 1904.32, 1907.43, 1908.32
Morse, Louise 1882.56
Morse, Messr. 1880.59
Morse, Nannie 1891.38, 1894.05
Morse, Newell 1907.55
Morse, Richard 1963.09
Morse, Robert 1958.08, 1959.03, 1959.22, 1961.22, 1972.04, 1976.09, 1979.25
Morse, Robert G. 1901.06
Morse, Robin 1981.07
Morse, S.R. 1879.01
Morse, Theodore 1903.03, 1903.04, 1905.27, 1907.62, 1908.05, 1908.11, 1908.15
Morse, Theodore F. 1902.01, 1903.06, 1903.07, 1903.14, 1903.20, 1903.23, 1942.11
Morse, Tom 1979.04, 1979.11, 1980.06, 1982.01, 1982.03, 1982.08, 1983.18, 1984.02, 1984.08, 1985.18, 1986.12, 1988.07, 1988.17, 1993.01, 1993.11, 1994.07, 1995.16, 1996.17, 1996.18, 1998.17, 2001.04
Morse, William 1894.07, 1894.35
Morse, Woolson 1879.35, 1880.42, 1882.39, 1884.21, 1887.31, 1890.26, 1891.11, 1891.31, 1892.22, 1892.33, 1893.16, 1894.24, 1896.29, 1904.17
Morsell, Herndon 1883.13, 1883.14, 1883.15, 1886.33, 1886.43, 1887.12, 1890.23
Morselle, H. 1882.22
Mortari, Adria 1985.14
Morte, Edval Boa 1992.13
Morte, Jorge Boa 1992.13
Mortimer, Alonzo 1877.15
Mortimer, Amy 1911.33
Mortimer, Annie 1869.08, 1875.11, 1875.15, 1875.20, 1883.43
Mortimer, Bertyne 1904.21
Mortimer, Blanche 1877.04, 1877.15, 1882.62
Mortimer, Ed 1886.41
Mortimer, Ella 1876.36, 1895.39
Mortimer, Ellen 1896.27
Mortimer, Eloise 1891.03, 1892.05
Mortimer, Estelle 1879.06, 1879.58, 1887.14, 1887.52, 1890.27, 1890.43
Mortimer, G.A. 1875.38, 1891.42
Mortimer, G.L. 1925.32
Mortimer, George 1891.24, 1919.07
Mortimer, Georgie 1889.53
Mortimer, Gus 1899.11
Mortimer, Gustave A. 1883.43
Mortimer, Harry 1877.04
Mortimer, Helen 1879.07
Mortimer, Helene 1898.31
Mortimer, Henry 1924.22
Mortimer, Isabel 1998.10
Mortimer, J.K. 1866.01, 1873.03
Mortimer, James 1868.03, 1885.26
Mortimer, Kate 1868.32
Mortimer, Lottie 1889.51
Mortimer, Lulu 1881.17, 1881.19
Mortimer, Mabel 1884.25
Mortimer, Master 1869.43
Mortimer, Nellie 1879.14, 1881.07, 1883.29
Mortimer, William 1920.14
Mortn, John 1869.39
Morton 1872.18, 1875.31
Morton, Augustine 1900.53
Morton, Benny 1949.16
Morton, Brooks 1959.03, 1968.23, 1978.19
Morton, C. 1912.43
Morton, C. Eddie 1903.35
Morton, C.H. 1866.03, 1866.18, 1870.44, 1871.10, 1871.15, 1871.22, 1871.27, 1872.06, 1873.10
Morton, C.S. 1908.04
Morton, Charles 1877.36, 1902.16, 1904.14, 1905.43
Morton, Charles H. 1869.34, 1872.11
Morton, Clara 1905.37, 1908.11
Morton, Dave 1931.03
Morton, Doddie 1889.09
Morton, Dorothy 1895.20, 1895.33, 1896.17, 1896.19, 1896.21, 1896.22, 1896.27, 1897.28, 1898.12, 1899.21, 1899.39, 1902.05, 1911.47
Morton, Ed 1907.23
Morton, Edward 1900.43, 1902.12, 1905.18
Morton, Elizabeth 1917.26
Morton, Emma 1862.08
Morton, Frederic 1970.15
Morton, George 1879.56, 1893.23, 1979.30, 1984.15
Morton, Gregory 1946.17
Morton, Hal 1931.05
Morton, Harry K. 1920.29, 1921.35, 1922.40, 1925.02, 1926.27, 1929.02, 1929.32, 1938.17, 1943.12
Morton, Hugh 1893.22, 1896.06, 1896.18, 1896.51, 1897.26, 1897.39, 1897.54, 1898.20, 1898.28, 1898.43, 1898.68, 1900.05, 1901.01, 1904.08, 1906.17, 1917.26, 1921.20
Morton, J. 1866.16, 1876.07
Morton, J. Maddison 1891.24, 1934.22
Morton, J. Madison 1944.07
Morton, J.C. 1889.02
Morton, J.M. 1864.12
Morton, J.W. 1870.27, 1875.36, 1875.37, 1876.30
Morton, James C. 1910.15, 1922.23, 1925.36, 1927.03, 1927.17, 1928.15
Morton, James J. 1908.15, 1911.26
Morton, James W. 1888.31
Morton, Jelly Roll 1992.08
Morton, Joan 1952.13, 1953.01, 1955.11
Morton, Joe 1973.10, 1981.25, 1986.11
Morton, John 1869.37, 1869.42, 1870.01, 1870.06, 1876.04, 1876.05
Morton, Kate 1905.37, 1908.11
Morton, L. 1882.62, 1885.33, 1890.17
Morton, L.M. 1880.41
Morton, Lew 1911.03, 1917.21, 1920.22, 1920.23, 1921.20, 1927.14, 1927.55, 1928.27, 1929.09, 1929.17, 1929.22
Morton, Lewis 1905.47, 1910.30, 1911.21, 1911.29, 1911.34, 1911.43, 1920.09, 1926.33, 1927.01
Morton, Linda 1980.14
Morton, Louis 1906.22
Morton, M. 1875.31
Morton, Maddison 1936.20, 1939.05
Morton, Martha 1925.22, 1926.29, 1928.23
Morton, Messr. 1870.22, 1875.31, 1875.39, 1876.04
Morton, Michael 1912.35
Morton, Mildred 1907.23
Morton, Miss 1859.07, 1859.11, 1862.02, 1897.04
Morton, Mr. 1869.36, 1870.02
Morton, Paul 1905.37, 1908.11, 1915.05
Morton, Pelham 1893.07
Morton, Richard 1903.34
Morton, Rose 1866.18
Morton, S. 1881.32
Morton, Sam 1905.37, 1908.11, 1927.48
Morton, Sydney 1940.15
Morton, Teckla 1892.60, 1893.07, 1893.47
Morton, Thekla 1905.08
Morton, Tommy 1948.30
Morton, Veve 1907.07
Morton, W. 1873.26
Morton, Will H. 1878.01
Morton, William H. 1880.55
Morton, Winn 1968.06, 1968.13, 1968.18, 1975.03, 1980.12
Mosby Walter 1948.20
Mosby, Marion 1907.33, 1910.21, 1913.20, 1919.34
Mosby, Walter 1943.10
Moscartolo, Jonas 1997.11
Mosco, Natalie 1968.11
Mosconi, Charles 1915.26, 1920.39
Mosconi, Louis 1920.39
Mosconi, Louise 1915.26
Mosconi, Verna 1920.39
Mosconi, Willie 1920.39
Moscow Folk Ballet Company 1998.09, 2000.05
Moscowitz, Jennie 1925.19, 1928.24
Moseley, Lois 1948.04
Moseley, Miss 1866.18
Moseley, Peggy 1926.16, 1928.22, 1933.03
Moseley, Samuel 1886.49
Moseley, Thomas 1930.29
Mosely, Mary 1876.35
Mosely, Miss 1863.01, 1863.02
Moser, Barbara 1950.11
Moser, Margot 1949.03, 1956.15, 1959.10, 1967.17, 1968.09, 1968.14
Moses and Hamilton 1900.51, 1903.08, 1904.03, 1904.26
Moses, Burke 1991.09, 1994.04
Moses, E. 1924.37
Moses, Gilbert 1971.13, 1976.11
Moses, Gordon 1972.20
Moses, Harry 1934.05
Moses, Helen 1972.20
Moses, L. 1924.37
Moses, Thomas G. 1900.06, 1900.14, 1900.17, 1900.18, 1900.23, 1900.29
Mosgun, Mr. 1863.01
Mosher and Hamilton 1902.38
Mosher, Greg C. 1987.18, 1991.05
Mosher, Gregory 1986.05, 1987.15, 1988.02, 1991.01, 2000.01
Mosher, Ida 1885.14, 1885.28
Moshier, C. 1870.09
Moshier, E. 1870.12
Moshier, Emma 1870.28, 1870.32, 1870.35, 1870.40, 1870.42, 1871.01, 1871.02, 1871.05, 1872.14, 1872.36, 1872.38, 1872.40, 1872.43
Moshler, Emma 1872.32
Mosier, Enid 1954.19
Moskin, David Craig 1971.16
Moskovina, Mlle. 1920.03
Mosley, Jr., Robert 1983.04
Mosley, Robert 1976.28
Mosquera, Leonica 1919.17
Moss, Al 1940.18
Moss, Alexandra 1955.02
Moss, Ann 1926.13
Moss, Arnold 1940.10, 1971.05
Moss, Arthur 1920.02, 1920.06
Moss, D.R. 1881.15
Moss, Gary 1982.14
Moss, George 1879.67
Moss, Jeffrey B. 1985.15
Moss, Kathi 1972.12, 1982.09, 1989.26
Moss, Larry 1964.17
Moss, Lawrence John 1976.09, 1976.30
Moss, Marjorie 1925.33, 1925.38, 1928.42, 1930.09
Moss, Mary 1931.27, 1931.35
Moss, Milton 1982.13
Moss, Moses 1899.23
Moss, Paul 1929.20
Mosse, Spencer 1974.03, 1974.23, 1976.17, 1976.34
Mosser, Jack 1922.28, 1950.14
Mosston, Miss 1866.05
Most, John 1936.28
Mostel, Josh 1989.24, 1992.17
Mostel, Zero 1942.12, 1942.14, 1945.10, 1946.24, 1962.12, 1964.27, 1976.36
Mosteller, Steven 1993.13
Mostol, Tommy 1922.05
Mostovoy, Messr. 1929.05
Mostyn, Ethel 1907.06
Mostyn, Hallen 1890.33, 1892.08, 1892.10, 1894.05, 1894.48, 1895.16, 1896.21, 1897.37, 1898.51, 1900.03, 1900.27, 1900.39, 1914.14
Mostyn, Hallyn 1902.30, 1904.40
Moten, Edna 1931.47
Moten, Etta 1931.31, 1943.15, 1944.03
Mothersbaugh, Mark 1982.22
Motley 1944.27, 1945.13, 1949.04, 1949.08, 1950.01, 1950.08, 1950.11, 1951.24, 1953.07, 1954.13, 1955.07, 1956.04, 1957.05, 1957.06, 1961.24, 1963.08, 1963.09, 1963.26, 1964.10, 1964.33, 1965.02, 1965.10, 1968.15
Motley, Byron 1995.12
Motley, Francis 1904.01
Mott, Carrie 1875.21, 1882.62
Mott, D.C. 1905.13
Mott, May 1884.27, 1893.07
Mott, Peter 1920.15, 1920.42
Mott, Robert 1959.23
Mott, Tommy 1937.01
Motte, Joseph N. 1882.40
Mottl, Sonja 1984.04, 1984.05
Motto, Thomas 1952.03
Motts, Robert T. 1907.29, 1907.31
Motz, John 1902.02
Motzan, Otto 1915.07, 1915.08, 1916.11, 1916.23, 1917.08
Moulan, Eugene 1907.13, 1909.12
Moulan, Frank 1898.37, 1898.40, 1898.49, 1898.57, 1898.62, 1898.65, 1898.71, 1898.74, 1898.76, 1899.05, 1899.07, 1899.10, 1899.16, 1899.42, 1900.02, 1900.04, 1900.06, 1900.09, 1900.11, 1900.13, 1900.14, 1900.17, 1900.18, 1900.21, 1900.22, 1900.23, 1900.26, 1900.27, 1900.29, 1900.30, 1902.44, 1903.40, 1904.47, 1907.13, 1910.05, 1911.27, 1912.33, 1914.02, 1915.05, 1917.28, 1920.30, 1921.11, 1922.13, 1931.10, 1931.12, 1931.15, 1931.17, 1931.18, 1931.20, 1931.22, 1931.23, 1931.24, 1931.25, 1933.08, 1933.09, 1933.10, 1933.11, 1933.14, 1933.18, 1933.19, 1934.07, 1935.05, 1935.06, 1935.07, 1935.08, 1935.09, 1935.10, 1936.04, 1936.08, 1936.09, 1936.10, 1936.11
Moulin, Jean-Pierre 1963.02
Moult, Messr. 1852.01
Moulten, Henry 1882.14
Moulton, Alfred 1905.53
Moulton, Arthur 1881.15, 1882.77, 1884.23, 1886.41, 1887.03, 1893.08
Moulton, Arthur E. 1890.10, 1891.37, 1893.08
Moulton, Blanche 1883.05, 1883.07
Moulton, Harold 1932.28
Moulton, Harry 1895.39
Moulton, Henry 1887.14, 1889.53
Moulton, Miss 1886.03
Moulton, Roy K. 1919.10
Moulton, William 1905.14
Mountain, Earl 1911.26
Mountain, Mlle. 1888.39
Mourning, Inez 1989.11
Mouse, Seddons 1875.03

Mousley, Florie 1899.04
Mousot, Mons. 1883.60
Mousset, Mme. 1890.50
Moussorgsky, Modest 1919.38, 1932.09, 1940.20, 1943.11
Moustaki, George 1971.14
Moustaki, Georges 1981.04
Moutalba, Pietro 1910.13
Moving Day Company, Inc. 1931.47
Mowat, Helen 1890.04
Mowbray, Henry 1927.12, 1938.10
Mowbray, Miss 1866.05
Mowbrie, J.H. 1884.61
Mowe, Mesdame 1852.01
Mowell, Shelley 1951.10
Mowen, Edward 1936.01
Mower, Fred 1905.43
Mower, Margaret 1961.18
Mowrey, Dent 1922.21
Mowry, Greg 1987.05
Moxley, Daisy 1908.33
Moxzer, Jieno 1940.17
Moya, Angela 1979.08
Moya, Bobby 1988.20
Moya, Fernando 1999.18
Moye, Clifford S. 1894.32
Moye, R.J. 1894.32
Moyer, Edith 1899.37, 1906.01, 1907.24
Moyer, Edythe 1902.06, 1903.40, 1904.39
Moyer, Estelle 1901.17, 1902.29
Moyer, Gertie 1901.17, 1902.29, 1905.20
Moyer, Gertrude 1906.29, 1907.42, 1912.07, 1912.44
Moyer, W.H. 1880.01
Moylan, Anna Marie 1960.08, 1962.03
Moylan, Mary Ellen 1945.19, 1947.06, 1957.04
Moyle, Overton 1908.25
Moyles, Dan 1905.35
Moyles, Dan J. 1904.09
Moyo, Shadrack 1977.01
Moyseenko, K. 1931.38
Moyseenko, Nicholas 1931.38
Mozar, Jeannette 1901.27
Mozart 1884.42, 1886.47, 1888.36, 1894.19, 1894.21, 1899.23
Mozart, Sophie 1866.07, 1866.21
Mozart, Wolfgang Amadeus 1934.02, 1966.03, 1966.32
Mozer, Elizabeth 1989.20
MPI Productions, Inc. 1981.17
MPO Pictures, Inc. 1966.06
Mrs. Field 1911.39
Mrs. James A. Oates Burlesque Company 1870.20, 1870.23
Mrs. James A. Oates Comic Opera and Burlesque Company 1872.19
Mrs. James A. Oates Comic Opera and Burlesque Troupe 1872.16, 1872.18
Mrs. James A. Oates' Comic Opera Company 1873.18, 1873.21, 1873.23
Mrs. Osborn Company 1907.32
Mrs. Robert Osborn Company 1903.33
Mrwebe, Gwigwi 1966.03
Msomi, Mandla 1987.12
Msomi, Welcome 1997.14
Mt. Calvary Choir 1995.04
Mthethwa, David 1977.01
Mtshali, Thembi 1977.01
Mucci, David 1990.15, 1998.01
Mucci, Gino 1964.03
Muchmore, Dale 1972.04
Mudge, A.A. 1904.45
Mudge, Frank 1900.53
Mudge, Gertrude 1921.13, 1922.07, 1925.11, 1929.45, 1931.29, 1936.07
Mudge, H. 1866.20
Mudge, H.T. 1871.12, 1871.16
Mudie, Alan 1910.05, 1912.26, 1913.04, 1914.33
Mudie, Jr., George 1903.21
Mueller, Gus 1921.21
Mueller, Karl 1939.23
Mueller, Marion 1925.14
Mueller, Messr. 1852.01, 1892.43, 1893.29
Mueltzer 1911.37
Muenz, Richard 1980.19, 1988.09, 1989.04, 1992.10, 2001.08
Muffler, Marti 1937.05
Mugica, Nina Josepha 1875.22
Mugica, Nina Soledad 1875.22
Mugleston, Linda 1998.16
Mugnheno, Signor 1876.07
Muhlbauer, Herr 1882.68
Muir, Bobbie 1923.02
Muir, Esther 1929.07, 1930.09
Muir, John A. 1890.02
Muir, Lewis F. 1909.13, 1910.17, 1910.18, 1912.09, 1912.29, 1912.43, 1914.03, 1962.17, 1964.28
Muish, Letuchaya 1931.38
Mulcahy, Edmond 1915.27
Mulcahy, Edmund 1913.32, 1916.23
Mulcahy, Lance 1970.12, 1981.02
Mulcay, Jimmy 1944.22
Mulcay, Mildred 1944.22
Muldoon, Johnny 1923.46
Muldowney, John Humphrey 1929.09
Mule, Emma 1888.36
Mule, Gustavo Roberto 1999.18
Mulhall, Jack 1949.09
Mulheren, Michael 1999.19
Mulhern, Charles 1882.26
Mulholland, Ethel 1926.30
Mulick, Laura 1892.50
Mulkay, Edmund 1897.55
Mulkay, Edward 1902.31
Mulkay, Nelly 1897.55
Mullaby, J.C. 1883.22
Mullally, J.C. 1883.31
Mullally, Megan 1994.07, 1995.05
Mullaly, J.C. 1878.19, 1882.23
Mullaly, John 1884.09, 1891.03
Mullaly, John C. 1886.25
Mullaly, W.S. 1879.09, 1880.15, 1881.55, 1883.56, 1890.07, 1890.34, 1890.35, 1891.43, 1892.01, 1892.36, 1893.28
Mullaney, Edward 1899.22
Mullarkey, Alphonso 1929.08
Mulle, Emma 1886.47
Mulle, Henry 1948.16
Mulle, Ida 1882.48, 1883.65, 1885.04, 1894.42, 1899.22, 1904.52, 1917.24, 1920.34
Mulle, Marie 1884.12, 1884.20, 1884.60
Mulle, Miss 1884.42
Mullen 1904.22
Mullen Rose 1931.39
Mullen, Ada B. 1880.53
Mullen, Imelda 1932.24
Mullen, J.B. 1900.58, 1903.03, 1904.13, 1905.23
Mullen, James B. 1905.16
Mullen, John 1880.68
Mullen, Kathleen 1932.24
Mullen, Margaret 1965.35
Mullen, Mary 1932.24
Mullen, Maud 1902.05
Mullen, Monica 1932.24
Mullen, Richard K. 1897.38
Mullens, Tommy 1912.30
Muller, A.J. 1889.38
Muller, Adolf 1890.08
Muller, Amy 1897.34, 1899.35
Muller, Bessie 1911.15
Muller, Emma 1885.28, 1886.26, 1886.33, 1887.18
Muller, Hans 1908.06, 1936.22
Muller, Harrison 1943.07, 1947.17, 1951.18
Muller, Herman-Jay 1989.23
Muller, Mildred 1930.33
Muller, Mr. 1852.06
Muller-Norden, Alfred 1903.28, 1904.04
Mulligan, Charles 1924.17
Mulligan, Grady 1984.02
Mulligan, Ralph 1920.31, 1921.03, 1921.30, 1922.39, 1923.32, 1924.10
Mulligan, Robert J. 1933.21, 1940.22
Mulligan, Sean 1999.02
Mullikin, Bill 1952.09, 1957.06
Mullin, Stephen 1964.29
Mullins, Carol 1975.10
Mullins, Mark 1990.19
Mullins, Tommy 1911.28
Mulqueen, Catherine 1922.29
Mulqueen, Kathleen 1925.11, 1925.19
Mulvey, Ben 1922.26
Mulvey, Ben N. 1907.60
Mulvey, Benjamin 1920.27
Mulvey, Marylyn 1977.14
Mumaw, Barton 1950.20, 1954.03, 1956.01
Munar, Alfredo 1974.14
Munch, Gary 1981.12
Munday, Hugo 1999.05
Munderloh, Otts 1978.09, 1978.27, 1979.12, 1979.24, 1980.07, 1980.08, 1981.06, 1981.07, 1981.14, 1981.29, 1983.06, 1984.01, 1985.02, 1985.05, 1985.06, 1986.07, 1986.20, 1987.07, 1987.12, 1987.16, 1989.03, 1989.07, 1989.12, 1989.20, 1989.26, 1991.05, 1992.02, 1992.08, 1992.15, 1993.05, 1994.05, 1995.12, 1998.11
Mundin, Herbert 1924.01, 1925.42
Mundy, James 1944.32, 1950.11, 1955.25
Mundy, James R. 1999.24
Mundy, Meg 1946.07
Muneret, Mr. 1859.06
Munez, Richard 1979.26, 1981.26, 1994.09
Munger, John 1898.03
Muni, Belle 1889.29
Muni, Miss 1889.31
Muni, Paul 1946.17
Muniz, Mercedes 1992.15
Munnell, Frank 1921.07
Munnik, Rob 1982.23
Munro, Bill 1919.18, 1927.37
Munro, Frank 1875.10
Munro, Leigh 1980.21, 1981.22, 1982.07, 1984.11, 1984.13, 1985.11, 1986.10, 1986.14, 1987.08, 1987.09, 1987.11, 1988.04, 1988.14, 1988.16, 1992.14
Munro, Philip 1972.20
Munro, Vic 1931.01, 1932.07
Munro, Victor 1926.18, 1927.46
Munro, Wallace 1976.36
Munro, Walter 1934.41
Munroe, A. 1873.26
Munroe, Carrie B. 1904.04
Munroe, F. 1881.32
Munroe, Kate 1881.41
Munroe, Ned 1892.39, 1899.09
Munroe, Walter 1927.59, 1929.46
Munsel, Patrice 1964.24, 1975.22
Munsell, Roy 1947.02
Munsey, Edna 1917.25, 1918.16
Munshin, Jules 1946.10, 1950.19, 1961.01, 1961.27, 1965.38
Munson, Audrey 1909.12
Munson, Eddie 1919.24
Munson, Estella 1975.22
Munson, Jerry 1940.18
Munson, Ona 1919.13, 1926.39, 1927.46, 1928.36, 1933.21
Munto, Messr. 1796.01
Munto, Mr. 1796.02, 1796.03
Munz, Louis G. 1903.07
Munzer, Cynthia 1997.02
Mura, Corinna 1944.02
Murai, Illona 1953.17
Murai, Ilona 1963.29
Murai, Kikobi 1927.60
Murallo, Rose 1887.24
Muraoka, Alan 1988.07, 1990.17, 1996.05
Murawski, C. 1975.03
Muray, Millicent 1914.26
Murchie, J.R. 1891.37, 1893.08
Murchison, Kenneth 1916.07
Murden, Orlando 1974.11
Murdoc, Harry 1903.04
Murdoch, Daisy 1879.30, 1883.65, 1885.64
Murdoch, H.S. 1872.26
Murdock, Albert 1883.42
Murdock, Bob 1961.22
Murdock, Ernest 1888.36
Murdock, H.S. 1867.18
Murdock, Harry 1900.59
Murdock, Janet 1923.34
Murdock, Paul 1932.16
Murdock, Red 1922.03
Murdock, Teck 1920.33
Murelle, Felicia 1921.40
Murger, Henri 1996.09
Muriaz, Marcia 1898.31
Murilla, Edith 1882.82, 1886.13, 1890.03
Murin, David 1978.24, 1982.12, 1990.06
Murio, Louise 1885.18
Murkin, Cyril 1968.06
Murney, Christopher 1973.02, 1974.18
Murphy, Ben 1947.08
Murphy, Brian 1964.28
Murphy, C.W. 1905.26, 1908.27, 1909.11, 1910.01, 1911.13, 1914.18, 1915.07, 1918.10
Murphy, Con T. 1889.38
Murphy, Con. T. 1886.10
Murphy, Daniel 1908.28
Murphy, Dean 1943.05, 1943.07
Murphy, Donna 1985.18, 1994.05, 1996.05
Murphy, E. 1883.66, 1885.02, 1887.16
Murphy, Ed 1893.15, 1894.49
Murphy, Edward 1884.41, 1885.02, 1886.03, 1886.42, 1886.52, 1887.07, 1889.02, 1892.54, 1893.27, 1893.36, 1894.04, 1897.03
Murphy, Edwin 1890.49, 1899.36
Murphy, Francis 1918.12, 1918.30, 1924.34
Murphy, Frank 1903.35
Murphy, George 1889.30, 1889.32, 1890.13, 1931.21, 1931.48, 1933.13, 1933.26
Murphy, George E. 1905.47
Murphy, George P. 1909.05, 1912.16
Murphy, Harry 1909.05, 1911.03
Murphy, Hiram 1921.15
Murphy, Hugh Francis 1927.12
Murphy, Irene 1891.32, 1895.07
Murphy, J. 1868.11, 1869.41, 1884.40, 1885.65, 1889.02
Murphy, J. Lowe 1917.20
Murphy, J.W. 1907.01
Murphy, Jack 1999.08, 1999.24
Murphy, Jacquette 1908.16
Murphy, John 1885.02, 1885.15, 1885.22, 1922.30, 1942.20
Murphy, John Daly 1910.33, 1911.23, 1912.12, 1912.48, 1914.04, 1916.18, 1917.25, 1924.25, 1931.19
Murphy, John E. 1895.08
Murphy, Karen 1995.19
Murphy, Kathleen 1978.20
Murphy, Lillian 1951.22, 1952.14, 1952.16, 1952.18, 1952.19
Murphy, Marie 1898.18, 1898.46, 1901.21
Murphy, Marilyn 1964.35
Murphy, Mark 1886.46, 1887.23, 1890.29, 1895.17
Murphy, Mat 1919.19
Murphy, Megan 1981.21
Murphy, Messr. 1875.39, 1879.56, 1894.19, 1919.33
Murphy, Mons. 1879.50
Murphy, Mr. 1865.06
Murphy, Mrs. J.A. 1868.11
Murphy, Owen 1921.25, 1922.18, 1922.23, 1924.01, 1924.25, 1924.30, 1924.32, 1924.33, 1924.36, 1925.25, 1925.47, 1925.48, 1926.06, 1928.08, 1931.05, 1933.21
Murphy, Patricia 1930.42
Murphy, Patrick Sean 1983.10
Murphy, Ralph 1924.17
Murphy, Rita 1920.44
Murphy, Ruth 1916.11
Murphy, Sally 1994.02, 2000.08
Murphy, Samuel J. 1913.35
Murphy, Sean 1982.01
Murphy, Stanley 1910.33, 1911.02, 1911.24, 1912.13, 1912.14, 1913.18, 1913.35, 1914.06, 1915.08, 1917.26, 1918.18, 2000.12
Murphy, T.D. 1881.11
Murphy, Tim 1888.32, 1890.41, 1893.14, 1894.02
Murphy, W.H. 1888.43
Murphy, Walter 1999.15
Murphy, William 1889.48, 1906.30
Murphy, William P. 1896.26
Murpny, Edward 1891.45
Murpy, Messr. 1881.04
Murrah-Swindell, Tina 1998.19
Murray 1884.27
Murray the K 1977.10
Murray, Agnes 1897.22
Murray, Alan 1921.12
Murray, Albert 1986.03
Murray, Alfred 1888.20, 1889.04, 1900.51, 1901.19, 1902.19
Murray, Ben 1921.12
Murray, Ben Alan 1921.12
Murray, Billy 1927.27
Murray, Bob 1961.10
Murray, Bonnie 1919.41, 1926.28, 1945.02
Murray, Bud 1915.26, 1916.11, 1917.23
Murray, Burleigh 1904.14, 1906.36
Murray, C. 1870.44, 1871.10
Murray, Charles 1866.18, 1868.03, 1899.18, 1914.20
Murray, Charles A. 1900.45
Murray, Charles Bernard 1986.11
Murray, Charlotte 1926.31
Murray, David 1944.30
Murray, Dennis 1921.34, 1939.22
Murray, Dickie 1750.01
Murray, Dominick 1869.33
Murray, Dorothy 1930.14
Murray, Edith 1894.17, 1929.24
Murray, Edyth 1902.26, 1904.06
Murray, Elise 1915.05
Murray, Elizabeth 1910.22, 1913.34, 1914.31, 1921.06, 1927.48

Murray, Elizabeth M. 1916.02, 1917.18
Murray, Elsie 1914.26
Murray, Florine 1892.20, 1898.77
Murray, Floy 1918.01
Murray, Frank 1897.17, 1898.27, 1944.05, 1944.06, 1944.09, 1944.11, 1944.13
Murray, Frederick 1925.29
Murray, George 1924.05
Murray, Gertie 1894.13
Murray, Hal 1927.27
Murray, Harold 1933.22, 1934.42, 1935.14, 1938.07, 1946.04
Murray, Harvey 1930.42
Murray, Helen 1892.39
Murray, Honey 1942.35, 1943.07, 1943.21
Murray, Inez 1890.50
Murray, J. 1887.27
Murray, J. Harold 1920.47, 1921.02, 1921.20, 1922.15, 1922.40, 1924.06, 1925.04, 1925.29, 1926.24, 1927.08, 1931.39, 1932.05
Murray, J.K. 1895.06, 1899.21, 1921.41
Murray, J.P. 1931.19, 1933.21
Murray, J.S. 1906.20
Murray, Jack 1927.43, 1939.19, 1959.04, 1961.07, 1962.05
Murray, James 1907.21, 1928.37, 1931.43
Murray, James J. 1889.37, 1889.51, 1891.08
Murray, James R. 1892.34
Murray, James S. 1906.20, 1910.35, 1929.38
Murray, Jan 1947.14, 1966.13
Murray, Jane 1907.03
Murray, John 1875.05, 1946.07
Murray, John T. 1915.11, 1916.23, 1917.08, 1920.09, 1920.19, 1921.20, 1922.35
Murray, Katherine 1915.18
Murray, Kathi 1923.06
Murray, Kathleen 1901.16
Murray, Ken 1935.04, 1949.09, 1965.16
Murray, Kitty 1902.24, 1941.11
Murray, Lucy 1894.33
Murray, Lyn 1939.29, 1941.08, 1947.03, 1956.02
Murray, Lynn 1939.29, 1940.19
Murray, M. 1867.12
Murray, M.B. 1879.02
Murray, Mae 1906.29, 1907.26, 1909.13, 1910.07, 1910.34, 1914.20, 1915.15
Murray, Marguerita 1926.28
Murray, Marion 1912.12
Murray, Mary 1930.06
Murray, Mary Gordon 1982.01, 1982.13
Murray, Master 1852.02
Murray, May 1902.02
Murray, Messr. 1876.35
Murray, Millie 1912.01
Murray, Minnie 1888.39, 1894.13, 1903.31
Murray, Miss 1887.10, 1908.19, 1917.31
Murray, Mme. 1841.01
Murray, Mr. 1866.02, 1866.16, 1866.28, 1869.31
Murray, Nellie 1900.52
Murray, Olive 1905.29
Murray, Paul 1925.50
Murray, Peg 1959.13, 1963.14, 1964.15, 1964.35, 1966.24
Murray, Randolph 1884.10
Murray, Robert 1897.29, 1899.18, 1963.25
Murray, Rupert 1996.01, 1996.12, 1998.09, 2000.05
Murray, Sharon 1985.05
Murray, Sylvester 1917.10
Murray, Ted 1944.19
Murray, Thomas E. 1886.46, 1887.23
Murray, Vangi 1923.06
Murray, W. 1875.05
Murray, W.B. 1884.24
Murray, Walter 1750.01
Murray, William 1924.26
Murray, Wynn 1937.04, 1938.14, 1940.23, 1942.01, 1948.23
Murrelli, Reca 1879.65
Murrilli, Reca 1882.03
Murry, James 1917.10
Murry, John T. 1917.30
Murta, Duke 1925.24, 1926.01
Murtach, W.A. 1875.05
Murtah, Kate 1949.17
Murtha, Ella 1894.31
Musaeus, Paul 1899.19, 1910.25
Muse, Clarence 1943.10, 1943.17, 1953.12
Musgrave, Frank 1870.26, 1880.43, 1880.49, 1881.28
Musgrove, Brad 1999.01
Music Makers, Inc. 1965.34, 1972.14, 1977.12, 1999.10
Music Theatre of Lincoln Center 1964.23, 1964.24, 1965.22, 1965.24, 1966.12, 1966.14, 1966.16, 1967.10, 1968.18, 1969.12
Music-Theatre Group 1996.16
Musical Theatre Lab 1976.30
Musicomedies, Inc. 1926.20
Musky, Jane 1985.17
Mussay, Mlle. 1869.30
Mussay, Mons. 1868.24, 1868.26, 1869.03, 1869.16
Musser, Lisa 2000.20
Musser, Tharon 1957.05, 1959.26, 1962.24, 1963.09, 1963.21, 1964.32, 1965.01, 1965.17, 1966.10, 1967.06, 1968.24, 1969.01, 1970.06, 1970.09, 1970.11, 1971.05, 1971.15, 1973.04, 1974.06, 1974.18, 1974.26, 1975.01, 1975.15, 1975.20, 1976.02, 1976.11, 1977.16, 1978.27, 1979.04, 1979.24, 1980.20, 1981.14, 1981.29, 1983.01, 1985.19, 1987.07, 1987.19, 1989.07, 1991.05, 1993.02, 2001.08
Mussett, Charles 1918.07
Mussetter, Jan 1982.14
Musso, Messr. 1882.30
Mussorsky 1940.20
Mussy, G. 1881.48, 1881.51, 1881.53, 1882.29, 1882.30, 1882.35
Mussy, Messr. 1882.53, 1882.58
Mussy, Mons. 1882.61, 1883.30
Muth, May 1932.21, 1950.11, 1951.17, 1959.11
Muth, Muriel 1932.21, 1936.27
Muti, Lorenzo 1958.17
Mutrie, Matthew P. 1989.10
Mutual Benefit Companies 1987.18
Muzio, Signor 1861.05
Muzzey, George E. 1895.44
Myatt, Florence 1890.37
Mycue, Anna 1927.10
Mydleton, Hugh 1892.41
Myer, W.H. 1882.45
Myerbeer, Giacomo 1978.26
Myerberg, Michael 1933.12, 1946.05, 1947.21, 1950.16
Myers, Annie 1887.26, 1888.24, 1888.26, 1889.17, 1889.22, 1894.48
Myers, Carmel 1919.35
Myers, Charles 1889.22
Myers, Ernestine 1918.06, 1920.24
Myers, Gene 1976.24
Myers, Gordon 1963.28
Myers, Grace 1902.07
Myers, Harry 1888.24
Myers, Henry 1927.11, 1928.25, 1929.19, 1929.29, 1930.18, 1930.32, 1940.21, 1942.26, 1946.18, 1961.08
Myers, J. 1864.02
Myers, Julian 1895.18, 1900.41
Myers, Lee 1906.11, 1907.09
Myers, Linda 1977.15
Myers, Lorna 1975.19
Myers, Louisa 1864.16, 1864.18, 1864.19, 1864.20, 1864.21, 1866.03
Myers, Margot 1922.42, 1953.17
Myers, Mary 1884.53
Myers, May 1919.21
Myers, Messr. 1866.28, 1867.12, 1883.17, 1883.23, 1888.25, 1889.43, 1890.36
Myers, Miss 1864.07
Myers, Pamela 1970.13
Myers, Richard 1925.47, 1925.50, 1927.35, 1928.41, 1930.06, 1930.18, 1930.32, 1931.26, 1931.42, 1932.18, 1932.20, 1933.20, 1934.01, 1957.01
Myers, Sellwyn 1937.12
Myers, Sylvia 1948.20
Myers, Troy 1989.03
Myers, Vera 1928.11, 1931.41
Myers, Virginia 1927.20
Myers, William 1950.11
Myers, William A. 1948.17
Myers, Z. 1921.04
Myerson, Alan 1964.26
Myler, Randal 1999.09
Myles, Glenn 1981.17
Mylroie, Jayme 1966.24
Mylroie, Kathryne 1948.15, 1949.02, 1951.19
Myram, Mary 1935.19
Myribel, Mlle. 1886.08, 1886.22
Myrick, George 1930.16
Myrio, Jean 1925.47, 1929.29
Myron, D. 1862.08
Myron, William 1939.19
Myrow, Josef 1983.09
Myrtil, Odette 1924.06, 1925.02, 1926.27, 1928.15, 1928.26, 1929.28, 1931.37, 1945.16, 1953.02, 1959.27
Mysels, Maurice 1989.12

N.I.M. and A. Company 1908.20
N.Y. Bijou Theatre Company 1892.36
N.Y. Calcium Light Company 1899.31
Nabel, Bill 1976.01, 1989.19, 1992.01, 1993.05
Nacht, Edward 1919.38
Nacio, Herb Brown 1932.25
Nack, Allie 1923.02, 1924.10
Nada, Mizzi 1916.11
Nadaud, Gustave 1927.51
Naddie, Mlle. 1866.25, 1866.27, 1867.05
Nadel, Arlene 1969.03
Nadel, Barbara 1980.07
Nadel, E.K. 1924.16
Nadell, Rosalind 1944.16, 1950.18
Nadirashvili, Geno 1977.13
Nadler, Arch 1979.18
Nador, Michael 1925.02
Naegele, Genevieve 1926.05, 1929.34
Naesse, Alfred 1915.24
Nagel, Conrad 1951.22
Nagel, E.F. 1910.26
Nagel, George 1905.32
Nagel, George H. 1900.40
Nagel, John M. 1971.20
Nagel, Lyn 1994.02
Nagel, Willard 1960.01
Nagele, Margaret 1912.03
Nagle, Bert 1919.22
Nagle, Claire 1918.16, 1919.06
Nagle, E.F. 1893.31
Nagle, Frank 1905.42
Nagle, George 1900.33
Nagle, J.E. 1861.06, 1862.01
Nagle, Josephine 1900.35
Nagle, Josie 1900.33
Nagle, Jr., J.E. 1881.28
Nagle, Kate 1867.29
Nagle, Katy 1867.31
Nagle, Orma 1907.02
Nagle, W.F. 1880.08
Nagler, A.N. 1944.28
Nagrin, Daniel 1940.18, 1942.05, 1945.03, 1946.12, 1949.12, 1955.01
Nagy, Ken 1995.07
Nahat, Dennis 1971.18, 1980.03, 1980.22
Nail, Joanne 1972.23
Nainby, Robert 1914.32
Nair, Evelyn 1928.41
Nairn, Ralph 1905.46, 1909.23, 1911.02, 1912.26, 1913.20, 1915.01, 1915.21, 1920.12
Nairne, Ralph 1918.06
Nairnes, Carey 1963.29
Naismith, Laurence 1963.21, 1966.09, 1969.08
Najac, Emile 1885.59
Najeeullah, Mansoor 1991.01
Nakagawa, Kikue 1989.21
Nakamura, Cheri 1990.17
Nakamura, Eileen 1958.19
Nakano, Shozo 1982.06
Nakao, Kenji 1989.05, 1990.17
Nakasone, Aiko 1995.05, 1996.09, 2000.17
Nakauchi, Paul 1989.05
Naldi, Frank 1930.28
Nalepka, Brian M. 1992.02
Namara, Marguerite 1915.27, 1925.13, 1926.08, 1941.02
Namaro, Ida 1892.47
Namczynowski, Otto 1884.40
Names, Lolette 1905.31
Namszynowsky 1883.08
Nana 1975.22
Nance, Chris 1974.07, 1990.08, 1990.13, 1991.09
Nance, Clarence 1928.39
Nancy 1975.01
Nani, Mlle. 1883.48
Nankiville, W.E. 1889.27
Nankwill, Guy 1922.23
Nanton, George 1926.19
Napier, John 1901.15, 1903.25, 1904.46, 1961.08, 1982.19, 1987.04, 1987.05, 1991.03, 1994.10, 2000.20
Napier, Marie 1903.25
Napier, Nina 1913.08, 1913.13, 1915.29
Naples, Charlie 1981.17
Napoli, Jeanne 1983.17
Nappa, Michela 1881.15
Narai, Kuniko 1966.12, 1966.16, 1982.06
Narbis, Mabel 1893.33
Narciso, Grazia 1944.27
Narcisse, Henrietta 1926.40, 1926.43
Narcisse, Mlle. 1926.45, 1926.47, 1926.48
Nardin, Mardie 1873.16
Nardin, Marie 1872.42, 1873.11
Nardin, Mlle. 1872.33, 1872.42
Nardin, Mons. 1872.39, 1872.42, 1873.11
Nardini, Signor 1888.43
Nardynn, Marie 1875.25, 1875.28, 1875.33
Nardynn, Mlle. 1875.07, 1875.08
Nargeot, Julien 1866.29
Narmore, Eugene 1979.15
Nascimento, Claudinho 1988.06
Nascimento, Claudio 1992.13
Nash, Alice 1919.22, 1920.26
Nash, Arthur 1897.42
Nash, David 2001.04
Nash, Edna 1919.22, 1920.26
Nash, Fannie 1886.49
Nash, Flora 1924.36
Nash, Florence 1907.63, 1908.24
Nash, G.F. 1887.27
Nash, George 1885.50, 1930.26
Nash, George F. 1901.15
Nash, Heddle 1923.29
Nash, J.E. 1882.21, 1882.72, 1885.21, 1887.44
Nash, James F. 1922.03
Nash, John 1883.52, 1889.36, 1890.14, 1892.40
Nash, John E. 1882.42, 1883.25, 1883.29, 1884.64, 1885.11, 1885.16, 1887.15, 1890.15, 1890.18, 1890.20, 1890.23, 1890.46, 1890.47, 1890.48, 1893.19, 1893.48, 1894.03, 1894.08, 1898.56
Nash, John F. 1896.41
Nash, John Jolly 1875.34, 1875.37, 1875.38
Nash, Johnny 1974.01
Nash, Jolly 1875.31
Nash, Joseph 1956.06
Nash, Leo 1928.44
Nash, Marie 1940.06, 1940.23, 1941.03, 1941.07
Nash, Marietta 1883.26
Nash, Mary 1907.52
Nash, N. Richard 1960.22, 1979.03, 1992.10
Nash, Ogden 1932.13, 1936.02, 1943.19, 1952.20, 1973.08, 1995.12
Nash, Richard 1963.26, 1968.01
Nash, Robert 1940.21
Nash, Royston 1976.12, 1976.13, 1976.14, 1978.14, 1978.15, 1978.16, 1978.17
Nash, Sinclair 1897.18, 1902.07
Nash, Tom 1990.15
Nash, William 1943.23
Nasher, Andrea 1994.01
Nason, Brian 1989.24, 1993.17, 1997.15
Nassau, Paul 1956.08, 1959.19, 1966.30, 1968.06, 1968.13
Nassy, James 1946.02
Nast, Thomas 1868.06
Nat Lewis, Inc. 1924.06
Nate Salsbury's Troubadours 1875.16
Natel, Jean-Marc 1987.04
Nathan, Adele Gutman 1938.10
Nathan, Alfred 1924.15
Nathan, Ann 1967.10
Nathan, Anne L. 1998.01
Nathan, Betty 1972.20
Nathan, Irv 1995.03
Nathan, James 1972.20
Nathan, Joseph 1904.23
Nathan, Jr., Alfred 1924.35, 1927.36
Nathaniel, J.D. 1884.58
Natheaux, Louis 1917.04
Nathewson, Mr. 1841.01
Nathile, Mlle. 1866.18
National Actors Theatre 1995.07
National Black Arts Festival, The 1993.03
National Broadcasting Company (NB) 1958.17
National Players Company Production, The 1967.01
Nations, Curt 1959.19
Natt, D.J. 1884.58
Nattova, Natacha 1925.47
Natus, Joe 1898.66, 1904.07
Natus, Joseph 1892.26, 1896.02
Natwick, Mildred 1939.13, 1971.07
Naudain, Mae 1903.31

Naudain, May 1904.54, 1906.25, 1907.41, 1908.25, 1915.29
Naudain, May A. 1906.15
Naughton, Harry 1965.29
Naughton, Jack 1958.08
Naughton, James 1977.04, 1989.29, 1996.14
Naughton, Marise 1909.30
Naughton, William 1905.29, 1907.61
Nault, Fernand 1972.08
Naulty, James 1924.32
Naumkin, Yury 1990.01
Nautilus, Ralph 1879.08
Navarre, Ron 1990.17
Navarro 1946.21
Navarro, Jay 1955.12
Navarro, Jesus 1917.25
Navarro, Mazzantinita Jesus 1917.33
Navarro, Siren 1909.27
Navarro, Virginia 1898.18
Navoni, J.M. 1878.11
Nay, Fred 1934.40, 1941.08
Nay, Frederic 1940.06
Naylor, Charles 1955.13
Naylor, Emma 1907.02
Naylor, H. 1871.18
Naylor, Hessie 1870.33
Naylor, Kathleen 1936.14, 1936.15, 1936.19, 1936.24, 1936.25
Naylor, Miss 1868.06
Naylor, Wesley 1995.04
Nazario, Ednita 1998.02
Nazarro, Erman 1914.16
Nazarro, J. Edward 1914.16
Nazarro, Jr., Nat 1922.34, 1923.17, 1923.41, 1926.22
Nazarro, Nat 1914.16
Nazhad, Eric 1980.05
Ndlovu, Nandi 1988.02
Neakins, Beth 1926.32
Neal, Alice 1898.64
Neal, John 1989.06
Neal, Joseph 1972.16
Neal, Kenny 1991.01
Neal, Mr. 1867.07
Neal, Sally 1956.02, 1965.22, 1968.08, 1969.14, 1972.04, 1975.09
Neal, Virginia 1904.09
Neal, Walter 1947.09
Neale, Josephine 1898.37
Neale, Walter 1905.52
Nealy, Joseph 1934.37
Nealy, Milton Craig 1987.07, 1990.12, 1992.03
Nease, Byron 1983.10
Neason, Hazel 1907.08, 1907.32, 1908.25
Neaves, Pat 1911.26
Nebozenko, Jan 1983.20, 1984.14, 1985.04, 1990.14, 1993.08
Nebreda, Vicente 1958.13
Nechemia 1968.04
Ned Wayburn Studios 1923.38
Nedbal, Oskar 1915.04
Nederlalnder, James M. 1995.05
Nederlander 1974.11, 1974.20, 1974.22
Nederlander (Producing Company of America) 1976.36
Nederlander Corporation, The 1990.10
Nederlander Organization, The 1995.05, 1995.17, 1998.18
Nederlander Producing Company of America, Inc. 2000.09
Nederlander Productions 1970.09
Nederlander, Charlene 1991.15
Nederlander, Eric 1997.03
Nederlander, Gladys 1993.02
Nederlander, James 1973.06, 1975.19, 1978.14, 1978.15, 1978.16, 1978.17, 1978.18, 1981.09, 1983.08
Nederlander, James L. 1987.13, 1988.20, 1989.08, 1990.19, 1998.02, 2001.06
Nederlander, James M. 1976.12, 1976.13, 1976.14, 1978.04, 1979.02, 1979.22, 1979.31, 1980.02, 1980.16, 1980.19, 1981.10, 1981.13, 1981.16, 1981.18, 1982.05, 1982.09, 1982.18, 1983.01, 1983.05, 1983.11, 1984.07, 1984.16, 1985.05, 1986.07, 1986.12, 1988.03, 1988.20, 1989.08, 1989.20, 1989.24, 1990.02, 1990.20, 1991.07, 1991.15, 1992.18, 1993.02, 1993.10, 1993.15, 1993.19, 1996.05, 1997.15, 2001.06
Nederlander, Joseph 1978.14, 1978.15, 1978.16, 1978.17, 1978.18, 1997.17
Nederlander, Joseph Z. 1986.18
Nederlander, Jr., James 1983.16
Nederlander, Scott 1997.17, 1999.23
Nedra, Sioux 1926.05
Nedringhaus, Wallace 1911.26
Needham, Alicia Adelaide 1908.43
Needham, Ann 1952.13
Neel, J.W. 1864.18
Neel, Mr. 1864.12, 1865.05
Neeley, Ted 1971.12, 1974.24, 1995.02
Neely, Billy 1928.35
Neely, Dick 1928.25
Neenan, Audrie 1982.02
Neenan, Maria 1989.03
Neeson, Liam 2000.05
Neff, Adele 1925.25
Neff, Helen 1920.42
Neff, Hildegarde 1955.02
Neff, John 1942.30
Nefflen, Hattie 1884.64, 1885.21
Nefflin, Hattie 1885.11
Negao, Marcos 1988.06
Negel 1882.62, 1886.41
Negi, Addi 1961.20
Negre, Mons. 1875.04
Negro, Mary-Joan 1973.16
Negron, Frank 1998.02
Neher, Caspar 1933.07
Neiberg, Al. J. 1989.02
Neidermeyer, Fred. 1889.05
Neidlinger, William Harold 1900.54
Neidus, L. 1967.08
Neighborhood Playhouse, The 1922.20, 1924.14, 1925.20, 1927.23
Neiglick, Emil 1939.15
Neil, Bessie 1909.25
Neil, Cissie 1895.43
Neil, Fred 1982.22
Neil, Messr. 1868.16
Neil, Robert 1888.23
Neil, Sally 1966.14
Neil, W.M. 1899.21
Neil, William 1943.23
Neill, R.R. 1907.35, 1908.25
Neill, William 1980.04, 1980.25
Neilsen, Alice 1896.43
Neilson, Carrie 1892.07
Neilson, Francis 1891.27, 1894.45, 1896.43
Neilson, Gwen 1953.17
Neilson, Messr. 1876.17
Neilson, Richard 1965.28, 1976.05
Neimann, J. 1894.30
NeJame, George 1967.14
Nelcy, Mlle. 1875.33
Nelcy, Virginie 1875.28, 1875.29
Nelida 1999.18
Nelidoff, G. 1924.48
Nelidova, Helen 1921.25, 1922.11
Nelis, Sylvia 1928.13
Nell, Gay 1926.21
Nell, Jr., Edward 1928.29, 1929.46, 1931.03, 1931.41
Nelle, Antonio 1927.25
Nelles, A. Douglas 1940.16, 1942.19
Nellie Farren Burlesque Company 1888.41
Nellini, Marie 1880.18
Nelson 1999.18
Nelson and Sixta 1988.07
Nelson, Ada 1881.32
Nelson, Anna 1911.39
Nelson, Annie 1902.14, 1902.33, 1905.10
Nelson, Barry 1943.23, 1969.01, 1977.16
Nelson, Benjamin 1995.03
Nelson, Bob 1922.18, 1923.17, 1923.25, 1927.64, 1988.03
Nelson, Carl 1942.21, 1942.22, 1944.17
Nelson, Carol 1952.09
Nelson, Charles 1949.09
Nelson, Dora 1897.32
Nelson, Duane 1922.03, 1922.30, 1928.06, 1930.04
Nelson, Ed 1921.21, 1932.27, 1952.11, 1999.05
Nelson, Ed G. 1918.05, 1928.22, 1930.29, 1956.11, 1997.01
Nelson, Eddie 1921.17, 1923.42, 1929.06, 1929.50
Nelson, Edgar 1922.13, 1927.07, 1931.21
Nelson, Edward G. 1930.29
Nelson, Emil 1923.33
Nelson, Frances 1911.40
Nelson, Frank D. 1904.03, 1904.52
Nelson, Frank H. 1882.33
Nelson, Gail 1974.09, 1980.09
Nelson, Gene 1948.30, 1958.07, 1971.05, 1974.09, 1974.26
Nelson, Gordon 1946.24
Nelson, Harold 1914.07, 1915.32
Nelson, Harry 1914.33
Nelson, Hattie 1892.19
Nelson, Hazel 1909.21
Nelson, Helma 1896.27, 1897.20, 1897.44, 1898.18
Nelson, J. 1918.23
Nelson, Janice Nunn 1982.17
Nelson, Jerome 1910.32
Nelson, John C. 1971.01
Nelson, John Louw 1919.08
Nelson, Joseph 1968.05
Nelson, Kate 1870.42
Nelson, Kenneth 1951.18, 1970.21
Nelson, Kitty 1897.33
Nelson, Lenny 1928.27
Nelson, Lipset 1962.20
Nelson, Lucile 1904.52
Nelson, Lucy 1898.32
Nelson, Maggi 1953.09
Nelson, Marie 1892.15, 1907.38
Nelson, May 1878.11
Nelson, Mervyn 1940.18, 1942.34, 1948.21, 1950.09, 1987.12
Nelson, Messr. 1871.12
Nelson, Miriam 1979.31
Nelson, Miss 1862.07, 1888.33
Nelson, Nan-Lynn 1978.11
Nelson, Nettie 1892.15
Nelson, Novella 1970.05
Nelson, P.J. 1978.04, 1980.16
Nelson, Paul 1936.02, 1936.17
Nelson, Portia 1954.03, 1955.11
Nelson, Ralph 1970.08, 1971.05
Nelson, Randy 1983.07, 1986.05
Nelson, Richard 1972.01, 1974.13, 1976.09, 1978.23, 1979.14, 1979.27, 1980.21, 1980.25, 1980.30, 1981.20, 1981.25, 1983.09, 1983.21, 1984.08, 1985.02, 1987.18, 1988.07, 1988.09, 1989.16, 1994.13, 1995.14, 2000.01
Nelson, Robert 1882.49
Nelson, Ruth 1936.28
Nelson, Sadie 1899.26, 1899.36
Nelson, Sidney 1879.50
Nelson, Sydney 1879.56
Nelson, Theda 1959.13
Nelson, Theol 1925.48
Nelson, Virginia 1887.09
Nelson, W.H. 1889.45, 1891.44
Nelson, Walter 1916.15
Nelson, William 1894.35
Nelson-O'Reilly Productions, Inc. 1998.14
Nelsons, Mlle. 1888.39
Nelstone, Arthur 1901.06
Nemea, Mlle. 1869.26, 1870.31
Nemeth, Laurel 1923.15
Nemeth, Sandor 1984.05
Nemetz, Lenora 1978.12, 1979.11, 1989.04
Nemiroff, Robert 1972.01, 1973.10
Nemirovitch, Mikhail 1925.51
Nemo, Edward 1928.44
Nemo, Henry 1997.03
Neofitou, Andreane 1987.04, 1991.03, 2000.20
Neomi, Miss 1870.14, 1870.22
Nepe, Brenda 1972.20
Neptune, Peter 1985.03
Neri, Signor 1852.01
Nervo, Jimmy 1922.05, 1922.19, 1923.20
Nesbit, Evelyn 1903.41
Nesbit, Howard 1908.33
Nesbit, Wilbur D. 1911.25
Nesbitt, Alec 1972.06
Nesbitt, Cathleen 1956.01, 1981.19
Nesbitt, Evelyn Florence 1902.34
Nesbitt, Miriam 1902.36
Nesbitt, Miss 1875.40
Nesbitt, Robert 1955.12
Nesmith, Richard 1908.09
Nesor Costume Company 1927.20
Nesor, Al 1955.06, 1956.05, 1956.12, 1964.44, 1966.05
Nestor, Diego 1922.37
Nestor, George 1968.32
Nestor, Michael 1961.20, 1963.12, 1965.01
Nestroy, Johann 1861.02, 1866.33
Nesville, Juliet 1897.32
Nesville, Juliette 1894.33
Nettleford, Rex 1980.05
Nettum, William 1924.45
NETworks 2001.09
Neu, James 1975.10
Neubach, Ernst 1932.06
Neubauer, Nicholas 1985.17
Neubeck, Jack 1979.03
Neuberger Adolph 1902.16
Neuberger, Ad 1905.53
Neuberger, Jan 1974.17, 1990.06, 1996.08
Neuendorf, Adolph 1884.39
Neuendorff, Ad 1892.42
Neuendorff, Adolf 1882.68, 1887.12
Neuendorff, Adolph 1879.17, 1879.22, 1884.24, 1884.64, 1887.15
Neufeld, Eric 1980.28
Neufeld, Mace 1983.07
Neufeld, Peter 1971.12, 1974.24, 1979.23, 1982.19, 1984.07, 1985.12
Neukum, Bob 1949.18, 1964.21
Neuland, Jennifer L. 1997.04
Neuman, David 1955.25, 1959.26, 1974.02
Neuman, Emil 1933.02
Neumann, Clara 1888.39
Neumann, Elisabeth 1940.04
Neumann, Elizabeth 1939.23
Neumann, Krista 1980.01
Neumann, Leone 1931.44, 1932.03
Neuwirth, Bebe 1982.01, 1986.07, 1994.01, 1996.14
Nevada, Hattie 1898.69
Nevarro, Siren 1907.22
Neves, Rod R. 1976.20
Neville, Carlton 1925.32, 1927.65
Neville, Charles 1992.06
Neville, Dorothy 1888.29, 1923.21, 1924.32
Neville, Dot 1889.45
Neville, George 1912.41, 1930.28
Neville, George W. 1888.08
Neville, Hubert 1907.41, 1909.29
Neville, Jr., Arthur 1992.06
Neville, Marcus 2000.15
Neville, Mr. 1857.06
Neville, Nancy 1909.05
Neville, Naomi 1992.06
Neville, R. 1892.59
Neville, T. 1872.25
Neville, Thomas 1883.06, 1884.27, 1902.39
Nevin, Arthur 1900.20, 1901.08
Nevin, Carriene 1999.06
Nevin, Della 1899.06
Nevin, Ethelbert 1980.27
Nevin, Hardwick 1925.37, 1926.13
Nevin, Marjorie 1906.41
Nevins, Charles 1905.42
Nevins, Frances 1927.54, 1931.21
Nevins, Zebra 1966.11
Nevis, Ben 1871.16
New Era Producing Company 1913.21
New Opera Company, The 1941.10, 1942.31, 1942.32, 1943.09, 1944.16
New Parisian Opera Troupe 1872.28, 1872.29, 1872.31, 1872.33, 1872.39, 1872.42
New Sadler's Wells Opera, The 1989.01
New Tuners Theatre 1990.06
New York City Center 1948.29, 1964.17
New York City Center Gilbert and Sullivan Company 1961.03, 1961.04, 1961.05, 1961.06, 1962.08, 1962.09, 1962.10, 1962.11, 1964.07, 1964.08, 1964.09, 1964.10, 1964.12, 1964.13, 1964.14, 1965.09, 1965.10, 1965.11, 1965.12, 1965.13, 1968.09, 1968.10, 1968.12, 1968.14, 1968.15
New York City Center Light Opera Company 1954.04, 1954.06, 1954.07, 1955.06, 1955.07, 1955.09, 1956.03, 1956.05, 1956.06, 1957.02, 1957.03, 1957.04, 1957.06, 1957.08, 1957.11, 1958.03, 1958.05, 1958.07, 1959.02, 1959.03, 1959.05, 1960.09, 1960.11, 1961.09, 1961.12, 1961.13, 1961.15, 1962.13, 1962.15, 1962.16, 1963.04, 1963.05, 1963.06, 1963.17, 1963.18, 1964.19, 1964.20, 1964.46, 1965.15, 1965.18, 1965.20, 1965.21, 1965.38, 1966.07, 1966.08, 1966.11, 1966.13, 1966.31, 1967.04, 1967.07, 1967.09, 1967.17, 1968.16, 1968.17, 1968.32
New York City Center of Music and Drama 1971.21, 1974.09
New York City Center Theatre Company 1952.03
New York City Opera 1944.26, 1952.12, 1953.05, 1953.06, 1953.14, 1953.15, 1954.10, 1954.14, 1955.17, 1956.09, 1956.10, 1957.13, 1957.15, 1958.09, 1958.11, 1958.13, 1958.15, 1958.16, 1959.07, 1959.08, 1959.09, 1959.10, 1959.16, 1959.17, 1959.18, 1959.21, 1960.02, 1960.03, 1960.14, 1960.15,

1961.19, 1961.23, 1962.06, 1962.07, 1962.19, 1962.21, 1963.15, 1963.22, 1963.23, 1963.24, 1964.30, 1965.03, 1965.04, 1965.07, 1965.25, 1965.26, 1965.27, 1966.02, 1966.04, 1966.17, 1974.07, 1974.08, 1974.15, 1975.11, 1975.16, 1975.17, 1976.22, 1976.23, 1976.26, 1976.31, 1977.03, 1977.11, 1977.17, 1978.07, 1978.08, 1978.19, 1978.20, 1978.23, 1979.20, 1979.21, 1979.27, 1980.03,
New York City Opera (*cont.*) 1980.04, 1980.21, 1980.22, 1980.25, 1981.20, 1981.21, 1981.22, 1982.07, 1982.16, 1982.20, 1982.21, 1983.12, 1983.13, 1984.11, 1984.12, 1984.13, 1985.09, 1985.10, 1985.11, 1985.13, 1986.04, 1986.08, 1986.09, 1986.10, 1986.14, 1987.03, 1987.08, 1987.09, 1987.10, 1987.11, 1988.04, 1988.14, 1988.16, 1988.18, 1989.04, 1989.13, 1989.14, 1989.15, 1989.18, 1990.02, 1990.07, 1990.08, 1990.13, 1991.08, 1991.09, 1991.12, 1992.10, 1992.14, 1993.12, 1993.13, 1993.14, 1994.09, 1995.06, 1995.10, 1995.18, 1996.02, 1996.11, 1996.13, 1997.02, 2000.03
New York Music Company 1985.15
New York Opera Company, The 1944.24
New York School for Circus Arts, The 1980.07
New York Shakespeare Festival 1968.11, 1971.18, 1975.02, 1975.15, 1976.10, 1978.11, 1981.01, 1984.02, 1985.18, 2000.08
New York Theatre Workshop 1996.09, 2000.12
New Zealand Maori Company, The 1972.20
Newall, Curt 1894.21
Newan, Mr. 1869.13
Neway, Patricia 1948.31, 1950.05, 1952.12, 1958.17, 1959.07, 1959.24, 1960.03, 1962.06, 1964.23, 1966.04, 1966.17, 1966.31
Newberg, D. 1983.03
Newberger, Ad 1904.24, 1906.36, 1907.39
Newberger, Ad. 1907.32
Newberry, Barbara 1926.18, 1926.51, 1927.20, 1927.63, 1928.25, 1929.27, 1929.42, 1932.01, 1932.26, 1933.01
Newbold, Robinson 1905.15, 1907.33, 1910.36, 1918.12, 1919.04, 1921.32, 1922.39, 1924.04, 1925.04, 1925.15, 1927.47, 1928.31, 1932.23
Newborough, Messr. 1879.56
Newborough, Mons. 1879.50
Newborough, W.H. 1880.31
Newburg, D. 1970.01, 1974.19
Newbury, Douglas 1919.31
Newbury, Mickey 1979.16
Newby and Alexander, San Francisco 1921.17
Newby, Herbert 1962.25, 1962.26, 1962.28, 1962.29, 1962.30, 1962.31, 1964.36, 1964.37, 1964.38, 1964.41, 1964.42, 1964.43, 1966.22, 1966.23, 1966.26, 1966.28, 1968.25, 1968.26, 1968.27, 1968.28, 1968.29
Newby, Jerry 1954.09, 1959.26
Newcomb, Bobby 1883.66
Newcomb, Jean 1923.16
Newcomb, Jessamine 1921.13
Newcomb, Lew H. 1902.17
Newcomb, Therese 1885.03
Newcombe, Florence 1900.43
Newcombe, Jean 1903.07, 1904.04, 1907.15, 1908.29, 1909.07, 1911.41, 1915.01, 1919.32, 1920.43, 1922.02, 1931.09, 1931.36, 1934.41
Newcombe, Jessemine 1921.04
Newcombe, Robert 1906.50
Newdahl, Clifford 1931.07, 1941.10
Newell, Annie 1903.09
Newell, Arthur 1897.55
Newell, Billy 1929.50, 1943.20
Newell, Dorothy 1914.15, 1918.01, 1922.43
Newell, Elsie 1929.50
Newell, Ferne 1923.15
Newell, Frank 1969.14
Newell, J.C. 1898.20, 1907.15
Newell, Major 1873.12, 1885.64
Newell, Oscar N. 1879.52
Newell, U.D. 1896.32
Newell, Willard 1890.40, 1894.09
Newey, Bill 1951.10
Newgord, William 1937.03, 1937.17
Newhall, Ione 1896.01
Newham, Rose 1888.33, 1889.35, 1890.27, 1891.21
Newham, Violet 1889.52
Newhoff, Irving 1905.14
Newill, James 1944.27
Newkirk, Phyllis 1927.50, 1928.26
Newkirk, William 1907.35
Newley, Anthony 1956.13, 1962.17, 1962.18, 1965.19, 1974.11, 1974.22, 1978.18
Newman, A. 1880.08, 1881.38
Newman, Alfred 1917.12, 1920.17, 1921.22, 1922.32, 1923.07, 1923.13, 1923.31, 1924.22, 1924.32, 1925.47, 1926.28, 1927.34, 1927.59, 1928.43, 1929.12, 1929.42, 1975.12, 1980.29
Newman, Annie 1869.31
Newman, Arthur 1945.02, 1952.12, 1954.04, 1954.14, 1957.15, 1958.16, 1959.08, 1959.09
Newman, Azadia 1944.27
Newman, Barbara 1956.14, 1962.20
Newman, Barry 1963.06, 1964.05
Newman, Bobby 1912.35
Newman, C. 1883.17
Newman, Charles 1902.17, 1905.05, 1935.04
Newman, Clara 1888.01
Newman, Claude 1929.51
Newman, Daisy 1983.04
Newman, David 1966.06, 1971.04, 1976.27, 1997.08
Newman, Del 1993.07
Newman, Emil 1931.08
Newman, Evan 1998.02
Newman, Evan J. 1995.19, 1996.15
Newman, Florence 1875.35
Newman, Gordan 1918.21
Newman, Herman 1926.07
Newman, Horace 1910.13
Newman, Irving 1933.20
Newman, James 1899.13
Newman, Jean 1937.14
Newman, Jennifer 1999.15
Newman, Jim 1997.07, 1999.23
Newman, Josephine 1900.59
Newman, Judy 1964.21
Newman, L. 1885.65
Newman, Lewis 1927.43
Newman, Lionel 1933.20, 1940.02
Newman, Lizzie 1881.03, 1883.44
Newman, Master 1875.31
Newman, May 1885.46
Newman, Mildred 1905.31, 1930.36
Newman, Miss 1883.17, 1883.19
Newman, Mlle. 1888.01
Newman, Otto 1879.30
Newman, Pat 1944.32
Newman, Phyllis 1959.06, 1961.28, 1971.15
Newman, Randy 1976.34, 1983.20, 1997.01, 2000.16
Newman, Red 1921.12
Newman, Ronnie 1979.29
Newman, Sha 1982.14
Newman, Stephen D. 1976.08
Newman, V.L. 1907.19
Newman, W. 1881.13
Newman, William 1974.05
Newmar, Julie 1955.02, 1956.12
Newmark, Rose 1937.14
Newmeyer, Sarah 1939.21
Newnan, Lizzie 1882.36
Newnham-Davis, N. 1906.32
Newson, Maud 1884.25
Newton, Adele 1954.04, 1954.14
Newton, Alice 1884.58
Newton, C. 1866.34, 1867.08
Newton, C.J. 1886.23
Newton, Charles L. 1897.38, 1898.61, 1910.06
Newton, Craig 1943.08
Newton, Eliza 1866.03, 1866.34, 1869.04, 1869.13, 1869.15
Newton, Eva 1918.27
Newton, Flo 1921.37
Newton, Frank 1939.19
Newton, George 1931.46
Newton, Grace 1915.32
Newton, Henry 1907.56
Newton, Henry Chance 1888.38
Newton, Iris 1932.23
Newton, Jack 1913.37
Newton, John 1924.27, 1974.04
Newton, Johnny 1954.08
Newton, Kate 1869.40, 1869.44
Newton, Messr. 1841.01, 1869.07
Newton, Miss 1870.15
Newton, Mr. 1866.08, 1866.11, 1867.10
Newton, Nancy 1946.13
Newton, Raymond 1916.18
Newton, Thomas 1866.02, 1866.28, 1867.12
Newton, Thomas W. 1851.08, 1869.31, 1875.05
Newton-Brown, Michael 1976.34
Nexsen, Mr. 1823.01
Ney, Richard 1958.04
Neydhart, F.S. 1904.37
Neyer, Ernest 1878.04, 1878.12, 1879.58, 1879.67, 1879.71, 1881.07, 1881.26, 1883.24, 1883.52, 1897.24
Nezel 1877.04
Nezel, Mons. 1875.21
Nezhad, K.H. 1977.15
Ngema, Mbongeni 1988.02
Ngema, Nhlanhla 1988.02
Ngqulunga, S'bongile 1997.14
Ngubane, Elliot 1977.01
Nhlanhla, Thandekile 1988.02
Niblo, Fred 1900.56, 1903.11, 1904.31
Niblo, William 1852.06, 1853.04
Nicander, Edward 1911.15
Nicander, Edwin 1906.37, 1912.31
Nicastro, Michelle 1983.01, 1991.10
Nicciolino, Al 1997.04
Nice, Emily 1904.31
Nice, Fred 1916.19, 1918.30
Nice, Freddie 1913.18
Nice, Freddy 1915.28
Nice, Kittie 1898.34
Nicely, Susan 1989.04
Nichol, Alex 1949.04
Nicholai, George H. 1898.08
Nicholas, Bryan 1978.22
Nicholas, Carl 1939.30, 1954.06, 1956.16, 1957.18, 1961.27, 1962.20, 1963.26, 1966.08, 1966.13, 1966.27, 1968.02, 1969.14, 1970.15, 1978.10, 1983.06
Nicholas, Fayard 1936.02, 1937.04, 1946.08, 1974.11, 1986.02, 1989.02
Nicholas, Harold 1936.02, 1937.04, 1946.08, 1974.11, 1986.02
Nicholas, Paul 1999.15
Nicholaw, Casey 1992.02, 1994.06, 1995.15, 1997.07, 1999.15, 2000.18
Nicholls, A. 1883.17
Nicholls, A.L. 1886.40
Nicholls, Adolph 1882.20, 1883.19, 1883.23
Nicholls, Allan 1971.20, 1972.18, 1974.24
Nicholls, Blanche 1888.43
Nicholls, C.T. 1878.15
Nicholls, Harry 1900.28
Nicholls, Horatio 1924.36
Nicholls, Ralph 1911.10
Nichols 1927.51
Nichols, A.E. 1882.11, 1882.12, 1882.13, 1883.11, 1883.12
Nichols, A.G. 1882.07
Nichols, Adolph 1882.04
Nichols, Alberta 1926.37, 1928.46, 1928.48, 1930.09, 1931.11, 1932.13, 1933.27, 1953.12
Nichols, Alice 1898.03
Nichols, Ann 1921.35
Nichols, Anna 1919.37
Nichols, Barbara 1952.01, 1961.21
Nichols, C. 1872.10
Nichols, Charles H. 1875.10
Nichols, E. 1880.13
Nichols, Edwin 1879.35, 1880.06
Nichols, Frank B. 1958.12
Nichols, George A. 1899.11, 1904.43, 1908.31, 1909.11, 1910.01, 1910.13, 1910.16, 1911.05, 1912.07, 1913.01, 1922.07, 1923.46
Nichols, George E. 1901.22
Nichols, George H. 1906.35
Nichols, George W. 1894.27
Nichols, Guy 1889.31, 1913.26, 1922.46
Nichols, H. 1871.12, 1876.21
Nichols, H.C. 1900.50
Nichols, Ham 1883.22
Nichols, Hamilton 1883.31
Nichols, Harry 1898.46, 1902.01
Nichols, Herbie 1976.16
Nichols, Howard 1916.15
Nichols, III., George 1948.22
Nichols, J. Wyn 1892.08
Nichols, J.E. 1905.51
Nichols, James 1904.35
Nichols, Joy 1959.01, 1959.23, 1968.02
Nichols, Ken 1936.12
Nichols, Lulu 1890.08, 1894.13, 1899.30
Nichols, Mabel 1890.08, 1899.30
Nichols, Mable 1894.13
Nichols, Mattie 1896.37, 1902.32, 1904.16, 1904.52
Nichols, Messr. 1857.04, 1904.13, 1904.44
Nichols, Mike 1960.16, 1966.18, 1977.06, 1980.13
Nichols, Millard 1916.15
Nichols, Mrs. H.F. 1852.02
Nichols, Nils 1979.19
Nichols, Norman 1916.15
Nichols, Peter 1970.03
Nichols, R.H. 1876.17, 1876.18, 1877.16
Nichols, R.M. 1880.34
Nichols, Red 1929.29, 1930.31
Nichols, Robert 1985.04
Nichols, Roy 1931.46
Nichols, Rudy 1949.16
Nichols, Tillie 1879.04
Nicholson, Abbie 1885.34, 1885.37
Nicholson, Annette 1884.60
Nicholson, Annie 1881.22
Nicholson, Arthur 1921.12
Nicholson, Bella 1884.31
Nicholson, Cleveland 1906.11
Nicholson, Cleveland I. 1906.21
Nicholson, Eugene 1886.34
Nicholson, Eugenie 1879.42, 1894.28
Nicholson, Howard 1921.28
Nicholson, John 1920.34
Nicholson, Jr., Paul F. 1898.31
Nicholson, June 1934.40
Nicholson, Kenyon 1930.35
Nicholson, Lillian 1906.05
Nicholson, Paul 1898.60, 1901.19, 1902.30, 1902.44, 1903.24, 1910.16, 1911.12, 1917.37
Nicholson, Paul F. 1900.41
Nicholson, Terry 1972.07
Nicholson, William 1934.22, 1936.20
Nichtern, Claire 1981.10
Nickell-Lean, Elizabeth 1934.21, 1934.23, 1934.24, 1934.27, 1934.30, 1934.31, 1936.13, 1936.15, 1936.16, 1936.19, 1936.23
Nickerson, Arthur 1910.18
Nickerson, Gregg 1965.20
Nickerson, Shane 1972.22
Nickinson, Isabella 1862.09, 1863.02, 1863.04, 1863.08
Nickinson, John 1845.01, 1862.05
Nicklaus, Jill 1999.10
Nickle, Robert 1878.01, 1878.13
Nickleodeon Family Classics 1994.12
Nickoles, J. Wyn 1892.10
Nicks, Walter 1956.06
Niclas, Emmy 1921.31
Nicode, Cecilia 1888.10, 1888.23
Nicode, Mlle. 1889.08
Nicol, J.E. 1884.62, 1888.30, 1899.22, 1899.41
Nicol, Joseph 1890.12, 1890.30
Nicol, Joseph E. 1907.08
Nicol, Lotta 1891.38
Nicolai, George H. 1904.53
Nicolau, Milani 1988.06
Nicoletti, L.A. 1946.19
Nicoletti, Odette 1985.14
Nicolina, Mme. 1923.28
Nicolo Troupe 1865.08, 1865.09, 1865.10
Niece, Miss 1870.22
Niel, Mlle. 1876.20, 1876.24, 1876.25, 1876.26, 1876.28, 1876.31, 1877.06, 1877.10, 1877.13
Nielsen, Alice 1896.08, 1897.13, 1898.23, 1898.60, 1917.27
Nielsen, Christine 1912.25
Nielsen, Diana Lee 1964.11
Nielsen, Inga 1980.03, 1980.22
Nielsen, Kristine 2000.10
Nielsen, Lavinia 1946.24
Nielsen, Per 1966.19
Nielson, Christine 1910.14, 1911.47, 1912.18
Nieman, Gleason N. 1940.07
Nieman, Hal 1940.07
Nieman, Harry 1926.37
Niemeyer, Charles 1935.16, 1937.08
Niemeyer, Joe 1920.19
Niemeyer, Joseph 1922.43
Niemtzow, Annette 2000.20
Nienatshaiewa, E. 1924.48
Nierle, Valetine 1918.17
Niesen, Gertrude 1934.39, 1936.02, 1944.14
Niessner, Tony 1964.25
Nieves, Maria 1962.02, 1999.18

Nieves, Richard 1961.12, 1970.21
Nigri, Clement 1880.44, 1880.50, 1880.58, 1880.60, 1881.46, 1881.48, 1881.50, 1881.51, 1881.53, 1881.54, 1882.30, 1882.35, 1883.51, 1883.54, 1883.55, 1883.59, 1883.60, 1884.02
Nigri, Mons. 1880.52
Nigro, Robert 1982.08
Nikitina, Alice 1931.38
Nikko Producing Company 1921.16
Nikolaie, Louis Francois 1926.45, 1931.41
Nile, Jack 1930.38
Niles, Barbara 1977.18
Niles, David 1990.11
Niles, Ila 1902.03, 1904.51, 1904.57, 1905.08, 1905.11
Niles, J.J. 1967.13, 1968.20
Niles, John Jacob 1955.13
Niles, Marian 1954.14
Niles, Marion 1945.17
Niles, Mary Ann 1956.07, 1961.10, 1968.32, 1971.03, 1973.05, 1999.01
Niles, Mary-Ann 1950.03
Niles, Melva 1948.24
Nilley, Florence 1895.07
Nillo, David 1946.10, 1950.06, 1957.02, 1963.30, 1973.09, 1989.18
Nillson, Annie 1892.04
Nillson-Fisher, A. 1895.32
Nilsson, Harry 1976.16, 1979.30
Nilsson, Lennart 1983.19
Nilsson, Walter 1938.08
Nimnicht, Darren 1979.26
Nimura, Yeichi 1946.05, 1959.05
Nine O'Clock Theatre Production, A 1964.34, 1964.45, 1965.16, 1966.32, 1967.13, 1968.20
Nini, Guissepina 1870.44
Nip, Tom 1923.17, 1924.15, 1924.35, 1928.08, 1930.28
Nipum, Mr. 1875.40
Nirdlinger, Fred C. 1905.47
Nirska 1949.06
Nirska, Mille 1935.04
Nirska, Mira 1927.26, 1935.04
Nisbet, Ralph 1892.14
Nisbet, Stephen 1983.09, 1984.10
Nisenson, Ruth 1937.01
Nishizaki, Mayumi 1989.21
Nishri 1968.04
Niska, Maralin 1980.03, 1980.22
Nissen, Greta 1926.18
Nissen, Tim 1973.07
Nissenson, Gloria 1989.25
Nit, Johnny 1924.37
Nita, Ann 1924.24
Nita, Dorothy 1915.30
Nitz, Sandra 1965.31
Nitzan, Shlomo 1971.17
Niven, Della 1896.45, 1897.36, 1906.44
Niven, Kip 1991.15
Nixau, Mlle. 1883.55
Nixon and Zimmerman 1899.28, 1901.13, 1902.19, 1903.14, 1904.12
Nixon, Alice 1895.43
Nixon, April 1993.03
Nixon, George 1896.32
Nixon, George W. 1930.16
Nixon, J.M. 1860.01
Nixon, James M. 1864.23, 1865.02, 1865.04
Nixon, Lucy 1895.43
Nixon, Marni 1964.20, 2000.01
Nixon, Messr. 1900.39, 1901.19, 1902.01, 1903.32, 1903.38, 1903.41
Nixon, Nanette 1895.07, 1895.18, 1896.18
Nixon, Nat 1898.02
Nixon, Samuel F. 1898.54, 1899.24
Nkosi, Simon 1977.01
Noah, Rachel 1881.15
Nobelett, E. Arden 1897.27
Noble, C.F. 1888.27
Noble, Dennis 1934.29
Noble, Duncan 1946.12
Noble, Edward 1909.31
Noble, Herman 1908.17
Noble, James 1952.03
Noble, Mae 1925.20, 1926.17, 1927.23, 1928.19, 1929.20, 1936.05
Noble, Miss 1869.38
Noble, R. 1902.15
Noble, Ray 1930.22, 1931.26, 1999.05
Noble, Rita 1957.07
Noble, William 1953.11
Nobre, Rita DeCassia 1992.13
Nocciolino, Albert 1998.18
Nocentelli, Leo 1992.06
Nodine, Jr., R.S. 1885.36, 1891.02
Nodine, Jr., Robert S. 1885.34
Nodine, R.S. 1885.37, 1885.38
Noe, F. 1871.25, 1871.26
Noe, Fernand 1872.03
Noe, Mlle. 1875.33, 1876.28
Noe, Mons. 1871.24, 1882.53, 1882.55, 1882.58, 1882.73
Noe, Sarah 1875.29
Noel, Alan 1945.04
Noel, Daniel 1984.02
Noel, F. 1908.04
Noel, Maud 1895.44
Noel, Tom 1961.11
Noelneter, Bob 1957.01
Noemie, Mlle. 1872.03
Nohain, Jean 1935.19, 1959.15, 1961.25
Nola, John 1954.12, 1961.10, 1968.32
Nola, Lucia 1904.36
Nolan, Bobbie 1907.47
Nolan, James 1877.21, 1886.27
Nolan, Jerry 1976.29
Nolan, Kathy 1954.13
Nolan, Kenny 1992.06
Nolan, Lloyd 1929.33, 1932.20
Nolan, Michael 1890.03, 1890.29, 1891.32, 1973.07
Nolan, Mr. 1865.05
Nolan, Peter 1930.18
Nolan, Rob 1976.34
Noland, Nancy 1936.12
Nolen, Joyce 1972.07, 1978.18
Nolen, Timothy 1984.13, 1985.05, 1986.09, 1987.09, 1993.17
Nolfi, Edward 1966.24
Noll, Christiane 1996.17, 1997.09
Noll, Edward 1947.20
Noll, Herbert 1914.33
Nolte, Bill 1993.15, 1994.12, 1997.12, 1997.15, 2000.20
Nolte, Carolyn 1927.48, 1927.62, 1929.35, 1933.05
Nomikos, Andreas 1958.09, 1958.11
Nones, Walter 1941.03
Nonon 1868.07
Nonville, Nae 1915.19
Noon, Paisley 1916.07, 1923.23, 1923.41, 1924.47, 1926.06
Noonan, Billy 1878.01
Noone, James 1997.09, 2001.01
Norah, Leah 1917.23, 1923.12
Norat, Raymond R. 1974.14
Norbert, Messr. 1882.55, 1883.28
Norbert, Mons. 1882.53, 1882.67, 1883.30
Norcott, Maurice Lane 1925.42
Norcross, Frank 1880.08
Norcross, I.W. 1882.14, 1882.45, 1882.54
Norcross, J.M. 1881.16
Norcross, Jr., I.W. 1881.22, 1890.44, 1892.28
Norcross, Jr., J.W. 1882.14, 1882.45, 1882.49
Nord, Al 1928.41
Nordall, Eugenie 1884.43, 1884.45, 1884.49, 1884.50, 1884.52, 1884.55
Nordall, Mlle. 1885.23, 1887.35, 1887.36
Norde, Helen 1927.14
Norden, A.M. 1904.35
Norden, Christine 1967.01
Norden, Dennis 1979.09
Norden, Martha 1930.14
Norden, Thomas 1960.05
Nordick, Madame 1897.55
Nordmark, Olle 1927.33
Nordstrom, Clarence 1918.04, 1918.07, 1918.32, 1919.10, 1919.29, 1921.09, 1922.07, 1922.29, 1925.10, 1925.24, 1925.47, 1926.25, 1928.28, 1938.11, 1961.14, 1964.46, 1965.15, 1966.13
Nordstrom, Frances 1921.18, 1921.30, 1922.39, 1923.22
Nordstrom, Francis 1924.32
Nordstrom, Marie 1917.08, 1918.02, 1923.22, 1926.03
Norele, John 1904.36
Noremac, William F. 1888.31
Noresta, Henry 1884.58
Noresta, Sig. 1884.58
Norfleet, Cecelia 1971.12, 1973.06
Noriac, Jules 1876.28, 1882.67, 1884.55
Noriac, Mlle. 1871.26
Noriega, Manuel 1919.17
Norman, Al 1931.26
Norman, Alfa 1885.30, 1885.32
Norman, Annette 1944.24
Norman, Beatrice 1893.37
Norman, Bruce 1931.44, 1932.10
Norman, Duke 1942.30
Norman, Edith 1911.13
Norman, Ethel 1869.07, 1870.04, 1871.08
Norman, Frank 1905.27
Norman, Hal 1957.18, 1961.27, 1963.21, 1966.05, 1972.04, 1973.15, 1975.06
Norman, Harold 1947.14
Norman, Henry 1895.08, 1896.06, 1896.18, 1896.30, 1896.45, 1897.26, 1897.37, 1898.63, 1899.05, 1899.07, 1899.10, 1899.14, 1899.16, 1900.57, 1903.02, 1904.09, 1905.33, 1907.08, 1908.30, 1910.04, 1910.25, 1912.41, 1913.18
Norman, Jay 1965.02, 1966.18, 1974.12, 1982.15
Norman, John 1907.54, 1987.04
Norman, Karyl 1927.15
Norman, Kirk 1970.21
Norman, Kittie 1901.27
Norman, Lucille 1942.24
Norman, Marsha 1936.12, 1991.05, 1993.19
Norman, Miss 1841.01
Norman, Monty 1981.14
Norman, Natalie 1948.27
Norman, Nina 1894.46
Norman, Ole 1895.24, 1898.12, 1898.73, 1899.39, 1903.23
Norman, Ollie 1903.18
Norman, Peter 1968.24
Norman, Peter Oliver 1981.07
Norman, Pierre 1940.16, 1965.08
Norman, Robert 1919.05
Norman, S.P. 1878.19
Norman, Theodore 1912.04
Norman, William 1906.06, 1907.51
Normand, Bootsie 1971.10
Normand, Florence 1920.28
Normand, Henry 'Bootsie' 1972.23
Normande, Messr. 1869.29
Norrie, James 1889.43
Norrie, Messr. 1890.36
Norris, Arthur 1943.18, 1954.17
Norris, Charles 1875.10
Norris, Ethel 1928.08, 1929.37, 1931.13, 1932.14
Norris, Henry 1907.51
Norris, Henry Jackson 1902.38
Norris, J.A. 1889.26
Norris, James 1925.17, 1927.36, 1929.17, 1930.18, 1930.33
Norris, Jerry 1930.14, 1930.38, 1931.14, 1932.13, 1932.27
Norris, Lee 1955.12, 1972.19
Norris, Lillian Brown 1889.26
Norris, Miss 1903.32
Norris, Monte 1938.19
Norris, Walter 1940.02
Norris, William 1893.42, 1898.12, 1898.72, 1902.30, 1903.31, 1904.40, 1910.03, 1911.31, 1914.04, 1915.08, 1915.28, 1917.15, 1920.37, 1927.56
Norstrand, Suzanne 1968.11
North Carolina School of the Arts Foundation 1996.04
North, Alan 1965.20, 1983.17
North, Alex 1935.16, 1939.19, 1940.18, 1942.05, 1955.13, 1997.21
North, Bobbie 1915.16
North, Bobby 1905.05, 1908.15, 1909.15, 1910.15, 1910.18, 1912.25, 1913.30
North, Clyde 1924.33, 1927.07
North, E. 1930.35
North, Elizabeth 1920.28
North, Madge 1923.34
North, Olive 1905.17, 1905.54
North, Sheree 1953.01, 1962.05
North, Sherle 1943.14, 1946.22
North, Wilfred 1905.15
North, Zeme 1959.22
Northern, J.S. 1902.07, 1903.40
Northmore, Jack 1971.21
Northrop, Emily 1888.05
Northrop, Pat 1949.04, 1952.01
Northrop, Patricia 1951.16
Northrup, H.S. 1904.02
Northrup, Jill 1929.46
Northrup, Theodore H. 1900.55, 1904.03
Northup, Theodore 1903.21
Nortn, Mesdame 1852.01
Norton, Angie 1910.16
Norton, B. 1879.52
Norton, Billie 1904.54
Norton, Billy 1901.25, 1903.40, 1906.48, 1908.07
Norton, Dean 1940.03
Norton, Edgar 1903.10, 1904.24, 1908.10, 1908.36, 1910.31, 1921.33
Norton, Fletcher 1902.34, 1903.40, 1906.20, 1907.21, 1908.42, 1909.05, 1909.18, 1910.29, 1920.02
Norton, Frances 1925.48, 1927.02
Norton, Frederick 1914.09, 1917.24, 1919.20
Norton, G. 1888.10
Norton, George 1903.41
Norton, George A. 1939.29
Norton, Harold 1932.08
Norton, Helen 1902.02
Norton, J.S. 1872.06
Norton, Jack 1925.25, 1925.40
Norton, John S. 1871.13
Norton, John W. 1871.20, 1871.21, 1875.14
Norton, Lillian 1907.26
Norton, Maria 1866.21
Norton, Marybelle 1950.11
Norton, May 1897.11, 1900.01
Norton, Millie 1896.35
Norton, Mr. 1871.15
Norton, Mrs. 1855.11
Norton, Ned 1912.29
Norton, Rhea 1917.16
Norton, Ruby 1912.46, 1917.21, 1917.34, 1919.29
Norton, W.H. 1865.06
Norton, Wash 1870.27, 1875.39, 1876.15
Norton, William 1896.32
Norton, Willie 1894.37, 1898.05
Norton, Willis 1896.48
Norval, James 1906.28, 1907.25
Norvas, Bill 1950.09
Norville, Herbert 1945.15
Norville, Hubert 1946.11
Norvo, Red 1944.29
Norwich, Joseph 1909.30
Norwick, Douglas 1972.26, 1978.26
Norwood, Adelaide 1898.71, 1898.74, 1898.76, 1899.14, 1900.22
Norwood, Florence 1900.52
Norwood, Miss Roberto 1873.26
Norwood, Roberta 1872.23, 1872.35, 1873.03
Norworth, Jack 1906.29, 1908.19, 1908.39, 1909.13, 1909.25, 1910.01, 1911.13, 1912.44, 1917.29, 1927.12, 1930.13, 1931.19, 1955.03, 1974.01, 1998.11
Norworth, Ned 1924.36
Noseworthy, Jack 1989.03
Nossen, Bram 1965.23
Nostrand, Michael 1998.18
Notara, Darrell 1951.18, 1961.22, 1966.31, 1967.06
Notelzah, C. 1882.62
Noth, Clyde 1928.11
Notman, Jack 1922.30, 1955.19
Noto, Lore 1965.36
Notos, James 1913.29
Nott Messr. 1868.06
Nott, Adele 1900.01, 1903.37
Nott, Carrie 1886.43
Nott, Messr. 1871.11
Nouri, Michael 1995.15
Nourse, D. 1878.11, 1880.21, 1882.82
Nourse, Daniel 1881.10, 1886.13
Nourse, Mrs. Daniel 1881.10, 1886.13
Nova, Lou 1955.06
Novaro, Victor 1939.18
Novasio, Lenora 1908.34, 1918.11
Novasio, Leonora 1915.23
Novella, Alba 1935.02
Novelle, Mitzi 1948.21
Novello, Bert 1928.05
Novello, Darrell 1928.05
Novello, Don 1979.19
Novello, Ivor 1923.07, 1924.01, 1925.42, 1928.02, 1929.51, 1952.11, 1964.28, 1975.22
Novello, Kharum 1928.05
Novelty Scenic Studios 1922.22, 1922.44
Novic, Florence 1931.44
Novis, Donald 1930.26, 1935.15
Novissimo, Arthur 1888.08
Novissimo, Giovanni 1870.44
Novissimo, Signor 1871.08, 1880.43, 1880.49, 1882.57, 1883.39, 1884.27, 1886.14, 1888.39
Novita, Helene 1914.14
Novotina, Fraulein 1911.18
Novotna, Jarmila 1944.16
Novotna, Maria 1956.15
Novotna, Vlasta 1911.12
Novotney, Irene 1921.35

Nowak, Adolf 1884.64, 1885.11
Nowak, Adolph 1887.26, 1887.28, 1887.47, 1888.19, 1888.24, 1888.26, 1889.17, 1889.22, 1890.16
Nowak, Christopher 1982.04
Nowell, Christine 1951.05
Nowell, H.W. 1900.33
Noxon, Annie R. 1885.08
Noxon, Libbie 1884.66
Noxon, Messr. 1887.32
Noy, M. (Neu) 1967.08
Noy, Malli 1972.17
Noy, Michal 1971.17
Noy, Yacov 1972.17
Noyes, Ann 1952.07
Noyes, Carrie 1891.13, 1892.03, 1893.47
Noyes, Frank 1923.15
Noyes, Helen 1966.14, 1967.07
Noyes, Thomas 1955.19, 1957.14
Nozar Productions 1981.06
Nudelman, M. 1966.21, 1967.08
Nudo, Beth 1902.26
Nugent, E.J. 1891.15
Nugent, Frank S. 1961.14
Nugent, J.A. 1906.36
Nugent, James 1906.01
Nugent, Kitty 1898.77, 1900.58
Nugent, Maud 1904.04
Nugent, Moya 1934.34, 1936.29, 1939.07
Nugent, Nelle 1981.04, 1985.03
Nuitter, Charles 1871.19, 1875.20, 1876.18, 1880.23, 1883.10, 1883.16, 1883.38, 1883.58, 1883.59, 1894.11
Nukutarwhiti, Dianne 1972.20
Null, Panchali 1983.14, 1987.16, 1990.18
Nunan, J. 1865.05
Nunder, Caroline 1921.24
Nunder, Carolyn 1919.38
Nunes, Paul 1988.20
Nunez, Manuela 1992.15
Nunn, Alice 1957.14, 1962.01
Nunn, Barbara 1948.23
Nunn, Trevor 1979.17, 1982.19, 1984.15, 1987.04, 1987.05, 1988.09, 1990.04, 1992.12, 1994.10
Nunn, Wayne 1916.19, 1921.23
Nunn, William 1943.14
Nunnemacher, Jacob 1880.31
Nurock, Kirk 1973.03, 1978.12, 1984.14
Nusbam, Samuel 1927.26
Nusbaum, Jane C. 1965.14, 1967.06
Nusbaum, Louis 1887.23
Nuss, William 1945.03
Nussbaum, Joseph 1927.31, 1935.15
Nussbaum, Mike 1982.10
Nutick, Mitchell 1958.01
Nutt, Commodore 1875.31
Nutt, Rodnia 1862.01, 1862.02
Nutter, Eileen 1933.06
Nutter, Madge 1927.27
Nuttier, Charles 1868.30
Nye, Bill 1891.27, 1895.42
Nye, Carrie 1965.14
Nye, Lewis 1948.14, 1949.12
Nye, Louis 1951.15
Nygaard, Tom 1976.24
Nygren, Carrie 1986.07
Nygren, James R. 1948.17
Nyitray, Emil 1925.16, 1925.30, 1971.03
NYK Productions, Inc. 2000.14
Nylander, Betty 1930.36, 1931.01, 1933.15
Nyman, Betty Ann 1941.06
Nyman, Betty Anne 1946.12
Nype, Russel 1958.14
Nype, Russell 1949.16, 1950.06, 1950.15, 1957.11, 1963.04, 1964.20, 1967.17
Nyro Laura 1989.06
Nys, Messr. 1882.55, 1883.61, 1884.45
Nys, Mons. 1884.02, 1884.49
Nzimande, Dudu 1977.01

O'Blein, Percy 1892.48, 1892.53
O'Brady, Hope 1945.16
O'Brady, Kate 1973.05
O'Brady, Katey 1964.35
O'Brian, Donnell 1933.21
O'Brian, Hugh 1966.13
O'Brien, 1860.05
O'Brien, Adale 1973.02
O'Brien, Blanche 1923.24, 1924.40
O'Brien, Charles 1897.51, 1920.02
O'Brien, Chester 1934.40, 1942.20
O'Brien, Chet 1938.04, 1946.06
O'Brien, Conal 1985.20
O'Brien, Dan 1905.17
O'Brien, Daniel 1950.04
O'Brien, David 1966.09
O'Brien, Edmond 1943.23
O'Brien, Eugene 1905.20
O'Brien, Frank 1894.06, 1971.18
O'Brien, Greg 1951.18
O'Brien, Gypsy 1915.17, 1916.06
O'Brien, Hazel 1918.31
O'Brien, Henrietta 1923.41
O'Brien, J. Arthur 1909.29
O'Brien, Jack 1972.02, 1976.28, 1978.23, 1979.26, 1979.27, 1983.04, 1990.08, 1994.01, 2000.15
O'Brien, Jeanette 1905.17
O'Brien, Jimmy 1929.24
O'Brien, Lois 1957.17, 1958.07
O'Brien, Louise 1963.06, 1964.46
O'Brien, M. 1866.03
O'Brien, Margaret 1934.21, 1934.24
O'Brien, Marianne 1942.11
O'Brien, Marietta 1919.06, 1926.01, 1927.58
O'Brien, Mart. M. 1878.13
O'Brien, Martin 1864.15
O'Brien, Mary 1981.19
O'Brien, Mattie 1908.27
O'Brien, Matty 1917.16
O'Brien, Messr. 1876.19, 1885.14
O'Brien, Miss 1886.36, 1915.17
O'Brien, Mortimer 1934.40
O'Brien, Percy 1885.28
O'Brien, Ralph 1910.21, 1917.06
O'Brien, Raymond 1923.38, 1928.12, 1930.26, 1934.41
O'Brien, Richard 1975.08, 2000.17
O'Brien, Ritz 1975.08
O'Brien, Robert 1928.36
O'Brien, Shaun 1945.14, 1947.06, 1948.18
O'Brien, Shawn 1945.14
O'Brien, Sylvia 1976.05
O'Brien, Tara 1995.15
O'Brien, Thomas 1888.43, 1889.53, 1893.23, 1897.16, 1900.03, 1903.04
O'Brien, Timothy 1979.23, 1982.18
O'Brien, Tom 1905.34
O'Brien, Vera 1921.32
O'Brien, Vince 1968.31
O'Brien, Virginia 1918.28, 1921.40, 1923.07, 1923.46, 1925.15, 1940.07
O'Bryan, Arthur 1904.37
O'Bryant, T.J. 1885.37
O'Callaghan, Dierdre 1963.30
O'Carroll, Aidan 1976.29
O'Carroll, Audrey 1976.29
O'Carroll, Mike 1988.20, 1990.18, 1994.08, 1998.01
O'Casey, Sean 1959.04
O'Connel, Edward 1897.51
O'Connell, Bland 1924.41
O'Connell, Daniel 1900.36
O'Connell, Hugh 1932.05, 1936.02
O'Connell, Jo Ann 1953.16
O'Connor, Charles F. 1925.19
O'Connor, Colleen 1956.01, 1977.09
O'Connor, Donald 1981.07, 1983.05
O'Connor, E.H. 1902.16, 1903.24
O'Connor, Eddie 1922.31, 1925.11
O'Connor, Edward 1905.30, 1908.27, 1918.41
O'Connor, Edwin G. 1947.02
O'Connor, Emmet 1904.06
O'Connor, George 1913.37
O'Connor, Gertrude 1922.01
O'Connor, Ian 1998.06, 1999.11
O'Connor, Kitty 1927.60
O'Connor, Peggy 1930.31, 1932.10
O'Connor, Rita 1966.08, 1966.13, 1966.14, 1966.24, 1968.31, 1969.17
O'Connor, Robert 1905.41, 1907.17, 1908.30, 1909.14, 1913.24, 1914.25, 1916.17, 1918.06, 1918.22, 1920.05, 1922.07, 1923.25, 1925.38, 1927.17, 1930.01, 1931.07, 1934.04
O'Connor, Tim 1926.21
O'Connor, Winnie 1909.29
O'Daniels, Barrie 1940.09, 1941.02
O'Day, Frances 1941.03
O'Day, Helen 1915.30, 1916.22
O'Day, Nell 1930.28, 1939.12
O'Day, Patsy 1930.08
O'Day, William 1907.25
O'Dea, Anthony 1930.42
O'Dea, James 1899.38, 1902.21, 1903.03, 1903.09, 1903.14, 1904.11, 1904.13, 1904.44, 1905.19, 1905.22, 1905.55, 1906.09, 1906.17, 1907.18, 1907.47, 1912.39, 1914.23, 1917.26
O'Dea, June 1926.25, 1928.17, 1928.31, 1930.14, 1931.48, 1933.13
O'Dea, Sunnie 1935.04, 1940.07, 1941.08
O'Dea, Sunny 1932.16
O'Dear, Bonna 1922.31
O'Dell, Dell 1939.22
O'Dell, Jacqueline 1981.21
O'Dell, Judith 1978.01
O'Dell, Larry 1943.06, 1945.14
O'Denishawn, Florence 1920.39, 1921.21, 1923.32, 1926.29
O'Doherty, Molly 1926.14, 1927.53
O'Donahue, Bridget 1883.66
O'Donnell, Alice 1930.07
O'Donnell, Charles 1921.21
O'Donnell, George 1890.29, 1894.46, 1895.25, 1897.50, 1902.31, 1903.06, 1907.11, 1910.28, 1913.06, 1914.19, 1924.08
O'Donnell, Michael 1995.15, 1998.04
O'Donnell, Peggy 1923.15
O'Donnell, Rosie 1994.07
O'Donoghue, Marie 1976.29
O'Donoghue, Michael 1979.19
O'Donoghue, Phyllis 1976.29
O'Donohue, Blanche 1927.27
O'Donovan, Danny 1976.16
O'Donovan, Gene 1993.06, 1993.07, 1994.06, 1994.12, 1995.19
O'Dowd, Frank 1981.07
O'Fallon, Mary 1951.17
O'Farrell, Shaun 1924.05
O'Flaherty, Michael 1995.07
O'Flynn, Damian 1943.23
O'Gorman, Michael 1981.10, 1996.01, 1996.12, 1998.09, 2000.05
O'Gorman, Richard 1889.13, 1895.44
O'Grady, Dan 1983.11, 1993.09
O'Grady, Kathleen 1999.05
O'Hanlon, John 1907.49, 1909.15
O'Hanlon, Kathleen 1919.19, 1920.22, 1920.23, 1920.47
O'Hanlon, Kathryn 1924.47
O'Hara, Chris 1906.37
O'Hara, Fiske 1906.03, 1915.03, 1927.48
O'Hara, Genevieve 1914.04
O'Hara, Geoffrey 1927.43
O'Hara, Gerry 1968.31
O'Hara, Helen 1934.06
O'Hara, Jenny 1969.01
O'Hara, Jill 1968.07, 1968.31
O'Hara, John 1940.22, 1952.01, 1961.15, 1963.17, 1976.19
O'Hara, John D. 1908.43
O'Hara, Kelli 2001.02
O'Hara, Maureen 1960.10
O'Hara, Paige 1983.05
O'Hare, Denis 1998.04
O'Hare, Jack 1928.25
O'Hare, Tom 1917.32, 1920.42
O'Hare, Ursula 1919.25, 1920.36
O'Haughey, M. 1975.14
O'Haus, Ed. 1907.50
O'Hay, Irving 1920.47
O'Hearn, Robert 1965.18
O'Hearn, Steve 2000.02
O'Horgan, Tom 1968.11, 1971.12, 1971.20, 1972.18, 1974.24, 1977.15
O'Keefe, Anna 1889.23, 1890.01, 1890.11, 1890.16, 1891.11, 1892.22, 1892.33, 1892.47, 1893.16, 1894.40, 1895.24
O'Keefe, Arthur 1898.38, 1903.26, 1905.40, 1911.17
O'Keefe, Harry 1898.38
O'Keefe, John 1794.01
O'Keefe, Lester 1920.17, 1924.10
O'Keefe, Maggie 1892.26, 1893.01, 1893.22
O'Keefe, Pat 1933.02
O'Keefe, Paul 1961.18
O'Keefe, Walter 1928.34, 1930.30, 1931.14, 1942.14
O'Keefe, Winston 1938.06, 1938.10
O'Keeffe, Suzanne 1978.14
O'Leary, Thomas James 1991.03
O'Madigan, Isabel 1929.02, 1932.15
O'Madigan, Isabelle 1927.65
O'Mahony, Sean 1976.29
O'Malley, Frank Ward 1911.17
O'Malley, Gloria 1952.01
O'Malley, Grania 1952.05
O'Malley, Melissa 1997.04
O'Malley, Muriel 1947.06, 1947.17, 1949.12, 1951.22, 1959.24
O'Malley, Regina 1993.07
O'Malley, Rex 1931.09, 1934.38, 1938.07, 1946.05
O'Malley, Thomas 1912.32
O'Mally, J. Pat 1952.07
O'Mara, Brian 1945.12
O'Mara, Joseph 1897.03, 1897.50, 1899.06, 1908.43
O'Mara, Stephen 1985.09
O'More, Colin 1920.12
O'Neal, Charles 1952.05
O'Neal, Frederick 1954.19
O'Neal, Harry 1926.01, 1927.58
O'Neal, J. 1867.13, 1868.08
O'Neal, Liz 1971.11
O'Neal, Mr. 1867.14, 1867.15, 1867.17
O'Neal, Ross 1905.12
O'Neal, William 1924.23, 1925.43, 1926.42, 1928.22, 1928.29, 1931.21, 1941.12, 1946.12
O'Neal, Zelma 1927.41, 1929.03, 1931.05
O'Neil, Alice 1916.10, 1916.19, 1917.20, 1918.11, 1919.04, 1919.39, 1920.18, 1920.34, 1920.44, 1921.22, 1921.30, 1921.32, 1923.30, 1923.47
O'Neil, Andrew 1903.01, 1910.06
O'Neil, Annie 1889.15
O'Neil, Bill 1945.06, 1946.09
O'Neil, Bobby 1922.24
O'Neil, Charles 1885.28
O'Neil, Clara 1901.26
O'Neil, Dennis 1920.24
O'Neil, Frederick 1958.11
O'Neil, Hattie 1869.34
O'Neil, J.R. 1929.30
O'Neil, John 1907.24, 1910.18
O'Neil, Joyce 1964.11
O'Neil, Kate 1869.34, 1870.39
O'Neil, Kittie 1879.04
O'Neil, Kitty 1872.07, 1873.22, 1873.27, 1878.01
O'Neil, Miss 1895.18
O'Neil, Nellie 1897.04, 1898.47
O'Neil, Peggy 1919.06
O'Neil, Robert M. 1900.28, 1900.43, 1902.12
O'Neil, S. 1871.04
O'Neil, Sherry 1946.03
O'Neil, Stephen 1997.05
O'Neill, Alice 1921.33, 1922.32, 1923.38, 1924.35
O'Neill, Alice V. 1924.08
O'Neill, Andrew 1904.34
O'Neill, Anne 1888.27, 1888.40, 1889.07, 1889.11, 1894.39
O'Neill, Annie 1889.18
O'Neill, Bobby 1923.46
O'Neill, Con 1993.07
O'Neill, Cora 1893.30
O'Neill, Dick 1965.33, 1968.31
O'Neill, Eoghan 1998.09
O'Neill, Eugene 1957.07, 1959.22, 1985.04
O'Neill, F. 1893.41
O'Neill, Frank 1904.54, 1954.17
O'Neill, Gertrude 1904.10, 1905.06
O'Neill, Hattie 1880.07
O'Neill, Jackie Shaw 1989.06
O'Neill, James 1912.31
O'Neill, James C. 1911.07
O'Neill, John 1943.12
O'Neill, Kathryn 1932.20
O'Neill, Kitty 1873.20
O'Neill, Margaret 1909.25
O'Neill, Martin 1902.11
O'Neill, Mary 1872.43
O'Neill, Messr. 1877.15
O'Neill, Miss 1917.03
O'Neill, Mr. 1867.16
O'Neill, Nellie 1898.78
O'Neill, P. 1918.21
O'Neill, Paul 1938.03
O'Neill, Peggy 1926.11, 1927.54, 1928.43, 1930.23
O'Neill, Peter 1942.20
O'Neill, Robert 1911.26
O'Neill, Tricia 1970.19
O'Neill, W. 1870.04
O'Neill, W.J. 1918.10
O'Quinn, Beauton 1921.40
O'Quinn, Terrance 1982.02
O'Ramey, Georgia 1908.05, 1915.28, 1916.19, 1917.17, 1919.01, 1922.26, 1923.07, 1925.30, 1926.28
O'Ramey, Georgie 1914.22
O'Regan, John C. 1971.19
O'Reilly, Clement 1961.10
O'Reilly, Edith 1903.20

O'Reilly, Mary Ann 1968.01
O'Reilly, Messr. 1794.01
O'Reilly, Mlle. 1873.22
O'Reilly, Rosemary 1952.09
O'Reilly, Sandra 1976.29
O'Reily, Mr. 1794.01
O'Riordan, Patricia 1965.20
O'Rourke, Betty 1941.07
O'Rourke, Cliff 1927.35
O'Rourke, Clifford J. 1924.47
O'Rourke, Eugene 1884.53, 1891.32, 1892.55, 1893.20, 1898.43, 1898.77, 1900.40, 1901.29, 1902.18, 1904.08, 1906.11, 1907.32, 1910.16
O'Rourke, J. 1883.01
O'Rourke, James 1881.09
O'Rourke, Mary 1924.17
O'Rourke, Michael 1941.11
O'Rourke, Stephen 1917.26
O'Rourke, William 1883.32
O'Ryan, Anna Wynne 1920.08, 1922.13
O'Shaughnessy, John 1938.14, 1948.18
O'Shay, William 1946.04
O'Shea, Helen 1922.23, 1924.04, 1926.18
O'Shea, Kitty 1888.12
O'Shea, Michael 1945.16, 1976.29
O'Shea, Milo 1969.05, 1981.19, 1989.23
O'Shea, Miss 1915.17
O'Shea, Prudence 1915.28, 1916.20
O'Shea, Tessie 1963.29, 1966.09, 1976.15, 1981.09
O'Shea, Timmy 1976.29
O'Steen, Michael 1989.23
O'Steen, Tom 1956.14
O'Sullivan, Dan 1979.26
O'Sullivan, Denis 1897.03, 1898.54, 1908.43
O'Sullivan, Gilbert 2000.16
O'Sullivan, James 1967.10, 1992.09
O'Sullivan, John F. 1905.27
O'Sullivan, Lawrence 1927.66
O'Sullivan, Maureen 1992.09
O'Sullivan, Michael 1966.06
O,Connor, Robert 1922.48
O-Ke-Mun, Chief 1923.31
Oake, Betty 1952.07
Oaker, Jane 1915.20
Oakes, Alice Ann 1987.15
Oakes, Betty 1948.26, 1951.02, 1962.04
Oakes, Cindy 1986.20
Oakes, Jane 1907.02
Oakes, Raymond 1919.02
Oakey, D. 1841.01
Oakland, Ben 1931.19, 1933.21, 1942.12, 1982.12, 1987.02
Oakland, Dagmar 1915.15, 1917.31, 1923.44, 1924.45, 1927.67, 1931.09
Oakland, Ethel Mary 1919.19
Oakland, Fred W. 1884.25
Oakland, Lizzie 1906.39
Oakland, Vivian 1915.15, 1920.22, 1920.23, 1922.35
Oakland, Vivien 1917.31
Oakland, Vivienne 1920.15, 1921.34
Oakland, Will 1909.16, 1922.23
Oakley, D. 1860.02
Oakley, Frank Silvers 1905.54
Oakley, G. William 1979.05
Oakley, John 1885.65
Oakley, Mr. 1858.04
Oakley, Richard 1879.59
Oakley, Scott 1976.19
Oakley, Silvers 1910.23
Oaks, J. Vernon 1965.01, 1965.17
Oataes, Alice 1877.16
Oates, Alice 1876.18, 1876.21, 1876.27, 1879.18, 1879.23, 1879.24
Oates, Mrs. James 1873.18, 1873.21, 1873.23
Oates, Mrs. James A. 1870.20, 1870.23, 1870.26, 1872.16, 1872.18, 1872.19, 1876.17
Oatman, A. 1909.13
Oatman, Dudley 1908.39, 1909.25, 1910.18, 1911.11
Oatman, Dudley E. 1905.49
Oatman, William 1909.13
Ober, Adelaide 1897.01
Ober, Dillon 1928.17
Ober, E.H. 1882.07, 1882.08, 1882.09, 1882.10, 1882.11, 1882.12, 1882.13, 1883.11, 1883.12, 1883.13, 1883.14, 1883.15
Ober, George 1893.31, 1897.01, 1907.03
Ober, Robert 1915.23
Ober, Ruth Boyd 1917.25
Oberist, John 1866.26, 1880.64, 1881.09, 1881.29, 1882.02
Oberist, John F. 1866.20, 1866.22, 1866.32, 1866.35, 1868.14
Oberlie, Lou 1906.03
Oberti, Eugenie 1869.34
Obler, Albert 1919.28
Obolensky, Alexis 1932.22
Obolensky, Chloe 1983.16
Obraztsoff, Sergei 1925.46
Obregon, Antonio 1955.07
Obst, Lynda 1977.10
Ocaiza, Elba 1949.07
Occent, Yvonne 1926.18
Ochoa, Rene 1949.07
Ochoa, Steve 1989.03
Ochs, Al 1922.19, 1923.20, 1925.10, 1925.24, 1927.12, 1927.60
Ochsner, Gus 1911.28
Ocker, Edw. 1900.40
Ocko, Mr. 1922.20
Ockrent, Mike 1986.12, 1986.15, 1992.02, 1994.12, 1995.19, 1996.08, 1996.15, 1997.12, 1997.22, 1998.20, 1999.21, 2000.19
Oddie, Bill 1964.29
Oddo, John 1988.19
Odee, Oscar 1911.39
Odell, George 1905.20, 1910.11
Odell, Grant 1895.31
Odell, John 1897.18
Odell, Maude 1911.03, 1911.44, 1914.30, 1915.07, 1916.14, 1917.14, 1919.38, 1922.31, 1924.23, 1925.39
Odell, Messr. 1906.05
Odell, Mr. 1865.02
Oden, Caroline 1915.32
Oden, E.J. 1907.51
Oden-Waller, William 1924.19, 1927.46, 1928.22, 1929.35
Odets, Clifford 1964.32, 1970.19
Odette, Ondee 1936.06
Oditz, Carol 1982.08, 1982.13
Odom, Ben 1988.05
Odwell, Messr. 1866.28
Oehl, P.J. 1885.64
Oenslager, Donald 1927.23, 1927.41, 1928.29, 1929.03, 1929.42, 1930.31, 1931.01, 1931.04, 1931.28, 1931.32, 1931.39, 1934.36, 1936.26, 1936.28, 1937.13, 1939.23, 1943.18, 1946.07, 1946.20, 1947.20, 1950.11, 1952.04, 1959.18, 1960.14, 1960.15, 1961.03, 1961.19, 1962.10, 1962.19, 1963.23, 1964.09, 1965.11, 1968.12, 1974.07, 1974.15, 1974.26
Oesfeld, H. 1894.30
Oesterman, Phillip 1976.20, 1983.06, 1991.07, 1992.18, 1994.06
Oestreicher, Gerard 1961.20
Offage, Cyril 1906.47
Offenbach 1867.31, 1876.09, 1876.10, 1880.35, 1886.47, 1888.36, 1894.19, 1899.23
Offenbach, Jacques 1858.02, 1859.14, 1861.02, 1863.05, 1864.01, 1864.03, 1864.08, 1864.10, 1864.11, 1866.09, 1866.29, 1866.30, 1866.33, 1867.05, 1867.24, 1867.30, 1868.03, 1868.05, 1868.07, 1868.08, 1868.13, 1868.14, 1868.15, 1868.16, 1868.17, 1868.18, 1868.20, 1868.21, 1868.24, 1868.25, 1868.26, 1868.27, 1868.28, 1868.30, 1868.31, 1868.33, 1869.01, 1869.09, 1869.10, 1869.12, 1869.16, 1869.18, 1869.22, 1869.47, 1870.03, 1870.10, 1870.11, 1870.17, 1870.23, 1870.38, 1870.39, 1870.40, 1870.41, 1870.45, 1871.03, 1871.06, 1871.07, 1871.19, 1871.23, 1871.25, 1871.26, 1871.28, 1872.03, 1872.18, 1872.20, 1872.23, 1872.28, 1872.29, 1872.31, 1872.33, 1872.39, 1873.01, 1873.02, 1873.15, 1873.16, 1873.21, 1873.23, 1875.07, 1875.09, 1875.12, 1875.13, 1875.15, 1875.19, 1875.20, 1875.22, 1875.23, 1875.25, 1875.27, 1876.05, 1876.06, 1876.11, 1876.18, 1876.24, 1876.25, 1876.27, 1876.30, 1876.31, 1877.05, 1877.06, 1877.10, 1877.13, 1877.14, 1877.15, 1877.16, 1877.17, 1877.23, 1877.29, 1877.30, 1877.31, 1877.34, 1877.38, 1878.06, 1878.07, 1879.12, 1879.20, 1879.31, 1879.34, 1879.36, 1879.43, 1879.45, 1879.46, 1879.47, 1879.51, 1879.55, 1879.61, 1879.69, 1880.23, 1880.27, 1880.28, 1880.38, 1880.44, 1880.49, 1880.60, 1881.36, 1881.46, 1881.47, 1881.54, 1882.35, 1882.43, 1882.53, 1882.55, 1882.59, 1883.27, 1883.38, 1883.58, 1883.61, 1883.65, 1884.01, 1884.02, 1884.05, 1884.12, 1884.19, 1884.20, 1884.45, 1884.49, 1884.59, 1884.60, 1885.04, 1885.07, 1885.20, 1885.70, 1886.07, 1886.08, 1886.18, 1886.20, 1886.21, 1886.22, 1886.50, 1886.54, 1888.03, 1889.23, 1889.40, 1890.01, 1890.11, 1890.13, 1891.17, 1892.49, 1893.01, 1893.22, 1894.11, 1894.48, 1895.09, 1895.36, 1899.02, 1899.10, 1900.06, 1925.02, 1925.46, 1926.48, 1941.10, 1942.32, 1944.16, 1945.02, 1956.09, 1961.08, 1964.06, 1976.26, 1982.07, 1982.21, 1990.16
Offenbach, Mons. 1873.12
Offer, Harold 1932.15
Offerman, George 1925.37
Offerman, Jr., George 1929.17
Offerman, Marie 1925.37
Offermann, George 1930.08, 1931.08
Office Two-One, Inc. 1993.02
Officer, Philip 1997.17
Offner, Mortimer 1940.21
Ogalla, Juan Antonio 1992.15
Ogawa, Jo Ann 1978.28
Ogawa, Jo Anne 1973.02
Ogden Entertainment 1995.15
Ogden, D'Orsay 1873.19, 1873.24
Ogden, H. 1911.04
Ogden, H.A. 1891.28, 1894.36, 1895.16, 1896.09, 1897.05, 1901.02, 1905.38
Ogden, Pat 1944.01
Ogden, R. D'Orsay 1875.18
Ogden, W.K. 1885.53
Ogilvie, Odeline 1927.02
Ogle, Charles 1905.38, 1906.38
Ogle, George C. 1909.22
Oguma, Olivia 1994.12, 1995.19, 1997.22
Oh, Soon-Teck 1976.02
Ohara, Hirotoshi 1989.21
Ohardieno, Roger 1943.17, 1944.31
Ohlendorf, Al. 1905.35
Ohls, Betty 1907.08
Ohlson, Astrid 1923.31
Ohman, Phil 1924.43, 1925.49, 1926.36, 1927.59, 1928.43, 1929.12, 1929.42
Ohmart, Carol 1953.16
Ohringer, Jan 1979.23
Ohrman, Chilson 1917.23
Ojeda, Perry Laylon 1998.16
Oka, Marc 1990.17
Okerson, Doris 1956.15
Okev, Nathan 1972.17
Okita, B.K. 1916.15
Okonkowski, George 1915.08
Okonkowsky, George 1912.01
Okonowski, George 1914.02
Okorotchenkoff, Messr. 1925.03
Okun, Alexander 1987.12
Okun, Lilian 1933.07
Olaf, Pierre 1958.18, 1961.10, 1968.32
Olcott, Charles 1911.14, 1918.32
Olcott, Chauncey 1886.14, 1887.42, 1888.25, 1889.36, 1890.18, 1890.20, 1890.28, 1894.20, 1894.36, 1895.30, 1896.09, 1896.11, 1897.05, 1899.01, 1900.10, 1901.02, 1902.36, 1904.02, 1905.38, 1906.38, 1907.56, 1910.06, 1911.04, 1912.06, 1913.03, 1914.05, 1914.29, 1918.41
Olcott, F. 1893.34
Olcott, Frances 1893.34
Olcott, Natalie 1901.06
Olcott, Rita 1910.06
Olcott, Walter 1906.11
Old American Company 1793.01, 1794.01, 1796.01, 1796.02
Old Globe Theatre, The 1987.18, 1994.01
Olden, Charles 1923.39
Olden, Courtenaye 1951.11
Oldfield, Emmett 1934.19
Oldfield, Mike 1982.22
Oldham, Derek 1934.21, 1934.23, 1934.24, 1934.26, 1934.27, 1934.28, 1934.31, 1936.13, 1936.16, 1936.18, 1936.19, 1936.21, 1936.24
Oldridge, Alfred 1966.28
Oldridge, Harry 1927.46
Oldroyd, Margery 1948.18, 1950.02, 1950.11, 1950.17
Oldroyd, Marjorie 1946.10
Olds, Carlo 1991.11
Olds, Jean 1946.22
Olee, Amy 1888.14
Olga, Mlle. 1870.31, 1885.59
Olisse, Arthur 1944.26
Olivares, Luis 1969.11
Oliveira, Carlos 1992.13
Oliver, Barrie 1930.40
Oliver, Clarence 1912.14, 1928.03
Oliver, Edna May 1917.06, 1919.39, 1920.05, 1920.40, 1927.67, 1932.11
Oliver, Gene 1929.24
Oliver, Ike 1908.13
Oliver, Irene 1976.28
Oliver, J. 1866.16
Oliver, J.A. 1879.71
Oliver, James 1918.25
Oliver, John 1945.12
Oliver, Joseph "King" 1939.29
Oliver, Julian 1927.28
Oliver, King 1992.08
Oliver, Louise 1878.03
Oliver, Messr. 1853.01, 1856.02, 1856.04
Oliver, Mr. 1855.11, 1857.05, 1859.08, 1866.17, 1867.07, 1867.18
Oliver, Natalie 1990.14
Oliver, Roland 1917.18, 1927.39
Oliver, Sy 1958.02, 1962.02, 1975.09, 1983.20
Oliver, Thelma 1966.01
Oliver, Wendy 1994.04
Olivette 1922.08
Olivette, Nina 1925.29, 1928.36
Olivia, Miss 1851.01, 1851.06
Olivier, Victor 1923.28
Ollerenshaw, George 1904.37
Olliff, Mr. 1823.01
Ollyeth, Allie 1880.49
Olman, Abe 1916.25, 1920.18, 1942.11
Olmi, George 1881.14, 1882.63, 1882.70, 1883.04, 1883.10, 1883.38, 1886.25, 1887.04, 1887.12, 1888.02, 1888.35, 1889.23, 1890.01, 1890.11, 1890.19, 1890.24
Olmi, Signor 1881.12
Olmos, Edward James 1979.08
Olmsted, Remington 1944.27
Olness, Kristin 1998.04
Olney, Joseph 1934.15
Olney, Maxwell 1914.25
Olonova, Olga 1915.31
Olp, Adele 1896.14
Olp, Florence 1896.14, 1897.47
Olp, Geogia Florence 1899.03
Olp, Georgia 1899.27
Olrich, April 1966.03
Olsen, Carl 1961.03, 1961.06, 1962.09
Olsen, Fin 1940.06, 1946.22, 1950.01
Olsen, George 1924.18, 1925.24, 1925.33, 1925.38, 1927.41, 1928.47
Olsen, Harry B. 1917.18, 1921.41
Olsen, Irene 1919.18, 1922.26, 1923.35, 1926.22
Olsen, J.C. 1938.08, 1949.06, 1950.14
Olsen, Morry 1937.06
Olsen, Olaf 1933.21
Olsen, Ole 1923.20, 1941.11, 1942.27, 1949.06, 1950.14
Olsen, Olive 1930.23, 1930.43, 1931.26
Olsen, Paul 1963.06
Olsen, Petra 1928.49
Olsen, Ralph 1988.08, 1988.19
Olsen, Stephen 1938.08
Olshanetsky, Alexander 1998.11
Olshin, Milton 1969.17
Olson Paul 1951.24
Olson, Beatrice 1937.11
Olson, Glenn 1957.03
Olson, Johnny 1972.02
Olson, Joyce 1966.08, 1968.17
Olson, Kurt 1969.12
Olson, Marcus 1994.05
Olson, Marilyn 1974.17
Olson, Ole 1938.08, 1944.30
Olson, Paul 1945.12, 1947.01, 1948.32, 1952.15, 1953.11, 1954.01, 1956.01, 1958.14, 1960.09, 1963.04, 1964.46
Olstead, Rem 1945.14
Olton, Minnie 1911.42
Olufsen, Else 1962.27
Olup, Robert 1976.18
Olvis, William 1952.15, 1956.15

Olympia Quartette, The 1895.34, 1896.31
Omar, Hamad B. 1925.37
Omene, Mlle. 1889.33
Omeron, Guen 1954.06
Omnisound 1980.10
126 Second Avenue Corporation 1991.05, 1992.08
Oneto, Richard 1953.16
Ongley, Byron 1905.29, 1906.34
Onikowski, Germaine 1969.13
Onishchenko, Savely 1977.13
Onri, Archie 1938.16
Onrubia, Cynthia 1982.19, 1985.12, 1989.03, 1992.05, 1993.02, 1994.01, 1995.15, 1998.15, 1999.14
Ontiveros, Lupe 1979.08
Onuki, Haru 1916.15
Ooms, Richard 1973.16, 1975.18
Opatoshu, David 1955.02, 1962.14
Opel, Nancy 1984.08, 1987.19, 1997.18
Open Window, The 1971.04, 1976.27
Opera Comique Company 1907.08
Opera di Camera Management 1880.18
Operti 1898.38
Operti, A. 1900.58
Operti, Albert 1898.35, 1899.36, 1900.03
Operti, Clotilda 1880.31
Operti, Clotilde 1884.22, 1884.25
Operti, Giuseppe 1869.14, 1869.32, 1869.33, 1869.40, 1869.44, 1870.13, 1870.44, 1871.15, 1871.22, 1871.27, 1875.32, 1877.35, 1877.36, 1880.31, 1885.46
Operti, Giuseppi 1869.02, 1869.20, 1869.27, 1884.10
Operti, leRoi 1927.39
Operti, LeRoi 1937.08, 1946.02, 1951.13
Opie, Jennie 1906.47
Opoku, Albert 1961.24
Opp, Joe 1919.30, 1920.23, 1922.15
Oppenheim, Dave 1930.29, 1931.14
Oppenheimer, Alan 1994.10
Oppenheimer, George 1950.03, 1967.11, 1979.25
Oppenheimer, George S. 1927.36
Oppenheimer, Jacob 1927.26
Opper, Frederick 1902.09, 1902.42
Opsahl, Jason 1994.07
Opshal, Jason 2000.15
Ora, Henry 1907.55
Oran, Bob 1952.07
Orange 1914.20, 1916.09
Orange Company 1913.19, 1913.33
Orange Manufacturing Company 1908.18, 1909.07, 1911.15, 1911.25, 1912.05, 1913.10, 1913.27, 1915.21, 1918.30
Orbach, Jerry 1961.10, 1965.15, 1965.24, 1966.12, 1968.31, 1975.14, 1980.20
Orbital Sounds 1999.12
Orchard, Edward 1923.15, 1924.12, 1928.48, 1931.27, 1931.35
Orchard, Julian 1965.28
Orcutt, A.C. 1889.02, 1898.45
Orczy, Baroness 1997.19, 1999.13
Ordey, Augusta 1883.02
Ordey, Karoly 1883.02
Ordonneau, Maurice 1886.33, 1886.34, 1887.36, 1892.07, 1897.11, 1897.41, 1898.26, 1898.63, 1903.34, 1910.22, 1911.16, 1912.12
Ordway, Howard 1905.37
Ordynski, Richard 1916.17
Orella Producing Company, Inc. 1916.05
Oremonte, E. 1905.29
Oremonte, Enrico 1905.29
Orera 1977.13
Oreskes, Daniel 2000.06
Oreskes, Don 1993.04
Oreste, Monsieur 1889.47
Oretll, George 1934.20
Orezzoli, Hector 1985.07, 1986.17, 1999.18
Orfaly, Alexander 1967.16, 1971.02, 1971.06, 1972.04, 1973.07, 1974.12, 1976.36
Orfeh 1999.15
Orgal, Yehiel 1971.17
Orin, Renee 1955.01, 1964.18
Orlandi, Felice 1955.05, 1962.15, 1963.04
Orlando 1929.51
Orlando, Guido 1924.01
Orlando, Othelia 1922.30
Orlando, Valeria 1976.26
Orlik, Ivan 1932.09
Orlob, Harold 1906.32, 1911.26, 1912.26, 1912.32, 1914.12, 1915.22, 1918.18, 1918.39, 1919.29, 1919.33, 1923.37, 1927.29, 1943.18, 1955.14
Orlob, Harry 1912.24
Orloff, Nicolas 1954.12, 1955.27
Orloff, Penny 1979.21, 1980.04, 1980.25, 1981.20, 1982.18
Orlova, Sonia 1944.21
Orlove, Elaine 1930.20
Ormand, Daisy 1924.35
Orme, Gertrude 1881.57, 1884.08
Orme, Gordon 1934.06
Orme, Ida 1889.01, 1892.48
Orme, Odille 1884.12
Orme, William W. 1899.33
Ormes, Alberta 1899.31, 1911.20
Ormiston, George 1968.13
Ormiston, Linda 1989.01
Ormond, Ethel 1892.36
Ormond, Jane 1924.35
Ormond, Mary 1924.35
Ormond, Sarah 1886.27
Ormonde, Ethel 1892.56, 1899.32
Ormonde, Gene 1909.28
Ormont, Dave 1955.12
Ormston, George 1907.34
Ornadel, Cyril 1965.28, 1976.32
Ornbo, Robert 1970.13
Orne, Beatrice 1896.06
Oro, Charles 1925.48
Oron, Gadi 1972.17
Orr, Ann 1915.30, 1917.17, 1919.09
Orr, Anna 1912.29, 1914.13
Orr, Ashley Rose 1998.03
Orr, Clifford 1929.29
Orr, Forrest 1936.26
Orr, Grace 1914.10
Orr, Mary 1970.09
Orr, Metta Louise 1923.07
Orr, William P. 1918.15
Orrezoli, Hector 1989.02
Orrin, Renee 1955.01
Orry-Kelly 1961.01
Ortega, Eva 1939.07
Ortega, Gabriel 1997.13
Ortega, Kenny 1983.17
Ortega, Rosita 1934.38
Orth, Bettina 1946.03
Orth, Charles J. 1892.18
Orth, George 1891.28
Ortman, Eva 1937.01
Ortman, William 1927.14
Ortmann, Will 1924.15, 1925.36
Orton, Addie 1904.39
Orton, Adelaide 1903.40, 1904.10, 1906.45
Orton, Chip 1984.10
Orton, Josephine 1857.08, 1865.06
Orton, Messr. 1870.22
Ortori, Leonilda 1881.24
Ortori, Leonilde 1879.42
Ortori, Mlle. 1882.54
Orville, Henriette 1919.40
Orzuza, Armando 1993.08
Os-Ko-Mon, Chief 1919.25
Osato, Sono 1943.19, 1944.33, 1948.17
Osborn, A. 1879.67
Osborn, A.K. 1879.25
Osborn, Leonard 1939.01, 1939.08, 1939.09, 1948.01, 1948.03, 1948.05, 1948.07, 1948.09, 1948.10, 1951.03, 1951.06, 1951.07, 1951.08, 1955.15, 1955.20, 1955.23, 1955.24, 1978.14, 1978.15, 1978.16, 1978.17
Osborn, Miss 1750.01
Osborn, Mrs. 1902.34, 1902.40
Osborn, Mrs. Robert 1906.25, 1906.29
Osborn, Steve 1981.26
Osborne, Alice 1887.43
Osborne, Belle 1928.22
Osborne, F. 1887.27
Osborne, Fanny 1889.38
Osborne, Frederick 1915.32
Osborne, Helen 1917.16
Osborne, Huber 1911.09
Osborne, Hubert 1927.16
Osborne, Jordon 1904.40
Osborne, Lorraine 1903.41
Osborne, Lucille 1930.38, 1931.36, 1932.16, 1932.24
Osborne, Marie 1897.29
Osborne, Merri 1894.12, 1895.14, 1896.44, 1897.14, 1898.12, 1901.06
Osborne, Miss 1851.05, 1853.03, 1859.01, 1880.69
Osborne, Mme. 1906.19
Osborne, Nat 1917.23, 1918.38
Osborne, Nellie 1887.43
Osborne, Olive 1917.26, 1918.19
Osborne, Vivian 1894.34
Osborne, Vivienne 1928.12
Osbourne, Gayla 1972.23
Osbrne, Alma 1907.08
Osburn, Oran 1953.02, 1956.12, 1959.11, 1960.06, 1963.25
Oscar, Brad 1997.09, 2001.05
Oscard, Paul 1918.25
Oser, Julie 1957.12
Osgood, E.A. 1884.37
Osgood, Frank 1879.04
Osgood, George L. 1894.31
Osgood, Pearl 1930.11, 1931.19
Osgood, Sarah 1902.37
Oshins, Jules 1942.20
Oshrin, Harry H. 1927.29
Oslin, Kay 1968.31
Osmond, Donny 1982.05
Osmond, Edith 1875.06, 1875.11
Osmond, R. 1875.21
Osmond, Ralph 1898.64
Osnath-Halevy, Sarah 1937.01
Osser, Glen 1979.13
Osser, Glenn 1968.05
Ossman, V.L. 1902.29
Ossorguine, Serge 1991.01
Ossosky, Sheldon 1951.15, 1959.02, 1959.05
Ostar Enterprises 2000.10, 2000.12
Oste, Diane 1911.01, 1914.02, 1914.18, 1915.25
Osterman, Annie 1888.11
Osterman, Bessie 1889.51, 1891.08
Osterman, Curt 1986.03
Osterman, Jack 1926.01, 1926.15, 1927.58, 1935.11
Osterman, Jr., Lester 1956.02, 1956.15
Osterman, Kathryn 1899.08, 1912.01
Osterman, Lester 1958.08, 1964.16, 1964.21, 1964.35, 1970.15, 1975.13, 1976.03
Osterreicher, Rudolf 1926.33
Osterwald, Bibi 1944.32, 1946.07, 1948.16, 1954.03, 1955.25, 1962.01
Ostrander, A.A. 1946.06
Ostrander, Miss 1851.05
Ostrander, Peter 1917.13
Ostrander, Ruth 1949.17
Ostrin, Art 1961.12, 1968.32
Ostroff, Doris 1938.04
Ostroumoff, Sergei 1925.51
Ostrov, Dmitri 1934.17
Ostrow, Stuart 1963.21, 1966.18, 1969.06, 1972.22, 1981.14
Oswald, Raymond 1920.15
Oswald, Raymond E. 1920.42
Oswald, Virginia 1948.22, 1950.10, 1957.03
Otani, Sensei Yoshiteru 1974.12
Otey, Louis 1993.12
Otis, Elita Proctor 1906.29, 1907.06, 1908.17, 1911.42, 1913.10
Otis, Miss 1920.44
Otiz, Olive 1927.30
Otley, J. 1883.64
Otley, James 1885.65, 1888.13
Otley, Joseph 1881.42
Ott, Ann 1904.49
Ott, Anna 1893.22
Ott, Annie 1900.59
Ott, Horace 1972.18, 1972.25, 1976.21
Ott, Joe 1898.38, 1900.42
Ott, Joe A. 1891.02, 1894.16
Ott, Joseph 1884.66, 1886.11, 1888.29, 1899.37, 1900.07, 1900.49
Ott, Joseph A. 1888.03
Ott, Lizzie 1882.76
Ott, Mathew 1895.38
Ott, Matthew 1896.30, 1896.48, 1897.23, 1900.40
Ott, Phil 1897.23
Ott, William C. 1897.49
Ottavio 1999.15
Ottenheimer, Albert M. 1960.08
Ottiano, Raphaella 1924.20
Ottilie, Mlle. 1892.24
Otto, Arthur 1905.50, 1907.04
Otto, Arthur F. 1934.04
Otto, Ernest 1905.50, 1907.04
Otto, Frank 1902.09, 1917.36, 1922.43, 1927.47
Otto, George 1918.15
Ottomeyer, L. 1885.01
Ottore, Peace 1923.29
Otvos, A. 1924.07
Otvos, A. Dorian 1925.47, 1927.14, 1934.39, 1935.18
Otvos, Adorian 1930.06
Otvos, Dorian 1923.36
Otway, William 1877.15
Ou, Tina 1993.15
Oudin, Eugene 1886.43, 1887.15, 1887.20, 1887.44, 1888.19, 1889.17, 1889.22
Oudin, Eugene A. 1888.24
Oudin, Mons. 1870.41, 1871.23, 1872.03
Oumansky, Alexander 1923.32
Oura, Mizuki 1989.21
Ousley, Robert 1979.06, 1994.12, 1995.19, 1999.19
Ousounoff, Messr. 1922.37
Outcault, R.F. 1905.05
Outcault, R.W. 1897.38
Outin, Regis 1964.06
Ovchinnikov, Rady 1990.01
Overack, B. 1879.04
Overman, Lynne 1920.14, 1928.07, 1932.07
Overmeyer, Eric 2000.10
Overpeck, Arthur 1902.39
Overson, Chris 1946.23
Overstreet, W. Benton 1976.04, 1999.01
Overton, Ada 1899.33
Overton, Charles 1886.39
Overton, Jane 1925.31
Ovey, George 1898.44, 1907.38
Oviatt, Marjorir 1914.27
Owen, Cecil 1927.05, 1927.48
Owen, Chloe 1946.22
Owen, Ethel 1944.30, 1946.01
Owen, Frank 1904.14
Owen, H.L. 1899.28
Owen, Hanna 1964.14, 1968.17
Owen, J. 1875.18
Owen, Jr., Robert 1938.18
Owen, Kenneth 1947.11
Owen, Louise 1917.16, 2000.01
Owen, Marion 1916.04
Owen, Mr. 1856.04
Owen, Reginald 1928.12, 1932.03, 1972.03
Owen, Wallace 1907.37, 1912.41
Owen, Walter 1885.65
Owen, William F. 1892.25
Owens, Barbara 1958.15
Owens, Eric 1996.10
Owens, Frank 1980.10, 1986.02
Owens, Frederick B. 1995.03, 2000.09
Owens, Gordon 1987.05, 1991.03
Owens, H.L. 1898.76
Owens, Henry 1943.02
Owens, Herman 1903.28
Owens, Hugh 1911.13
Owens, Jeanette 1936.26
Owens, John 1867.29
Owens, Mr. 1863.06
Owens, T. 1864.12, 1864.15
Owens, T.E. 1867.13
Owens, Tom 1877.08
Owens, Traci 1981.21
Owens, W.F. 1878.04
Owens, Walter 1929.20
Owey, Wesley 1959.05
Owin, Rita 1920.42, 1922.19
Owsley, Steve 1985.05
Oxenford, Edward 1906.41
Oxenford, John 1868.01, 1895.13, 1898.06
Oxford, Earl 1930.06, 1930.32, 1931.19, 1934.19, 1935.03, 1936.01, 1942.20, 1950.06
Oxley, J. Leonard 1991.11, 1997.03
Oxley, Leonard 1989.02
Oyler, Jessie 1888.17
Oyra 1926.01
Oyra, Jan 1927.58
Oyster, Jim 1967.07
Ozab, Fred 1904.29
Ozab, Fred J. 1906.23

P. Dodd Ackerman Studios 1912.46, 1915.26, 1917.31, 1920.15, 1927.27
P.H. Sullivan Amusement Company 1907.34
Pace Theatrical Group 1989.03, 1989.12, 1989.27, 1990.18, 1991.06, 1992.12, 1993.06, 1993.18, 1994.07, 1995.13, 1996.14, 1996.17, 1997.07, 1998.03, 1999.08, 1999.24
Pace, Jean 1969.15
Pace, Michael 1982.22
Pacetti, Elizabeth 1951.18
Pacha, Azela 1865.05
Pacheco, Mrs. R. 1908.18
Pacheco, Tom 1975.12
Pacho, Andrew 1990.17, 1993.14, 1995.18
Pachyderm Entertainment 1996.08

Pacie, Arthur 1891.39, 1892.27, 1894.37, 1896.01, 1897.34
Pacilio, Casi 2000.02
Pack, Muriel 1942.19
Packard, Alice 1903.09
Packard, Carl 1990.20, 1991.13
Packard, Daniel 1896.29
Packard, Fred 1922.31, 1925.11, 1930.37
Packard, H. 1871.27, 1873.10
Packard, Minnie 1894.21
Packer, Jerry 1945.18, 1961.21
Packer, Netta 1950.17
Paddock, Harry 1883.20
Paddock, Robert Rowe 1947.09
Padgett, Donald 1969.09
Padgett, J.C. 1879.52
Padgett, James A. 1878.03
Padilla, Jose 1921.18, 1923.26, 1926.14
Padilla, Louis 1984.02
Padilla, Miguel 1974.14
Padrae, Inc. 1930.29
Padron, Aurelio 1983.14, 1993.09
Padula, Edward 1945.19, 1960.06, 1962.04, 1964.40, 1966.30, 1969.03, 1970.12, 1972.13
Paenga, Iti 1972.20
Paer, Ferdinando 1866.23, 1869.19
Paez, Alex 1987.12
Paffhausen, Herr 1882.68
Pagan, Anna 1969.01
Pagan, Peter 1961.07, 1963.29
Pagani, Luce 1903.09
Pagani, Mlle. 1868.03, 1868.18
Pagani, Rosita 1870.44
Paganini 1988.15
Page, A. 1870.09, 1870.12
Page, Anne 1921.11, 1927.39
Page, Annie 1870.32, 1870.42, 1872.08, 1872.12, 1872.14, 1872.36
Page, Arthur 1928.22, 1932.07, 1934.17
Page, Carolann 1974.06
Page, Charles 1909.25
Page, Deborah 1978.26
Page, Dorothy 1911.07
Page, E.V. 1880.42
Page, Edna 1935.18
Page, Elizabeth 1923.43
Page, Evelyn 1969.04
Page, Gene 1979.04
Page, George 1921.32
Page, John 1900.40, 1901.27
Page, Johnny 1898.02, 1899.21, 1900.01
Page, Ken 1976.21, 1978.09, 1982.19, 1988.17, 1997.11, 1997.22, 1998.06
Page, Lucille 1931.26, 1944.20
Page, Mary 1872.43
Page, Master 1870.22
Page, Miss 1869.08, 1869.34, 1870.22
Page, Patrick 1982.22, 1999.16
Page, Peter 1915.22, 1916.20
Page, Richmond 1949.03
Page, Robert 1992.01
Page, Ruth 1922.39, 1947.14
Page, Stan 1965.20, 1966.10, 1976.05, 1979.02, 1979.12, 1980.20, 1992.04
Page, Steven 1989.01
Page, Tamara 1946.03
Page, Tillie 1872.14
Page, Tilly 1872.36
Page, Willis H. 1880.08
Pageant Productions P.T.Y. Ltd. 1972.17
Pagent, Robert 1945.05, 1948.31, 1949.08, 1954.06, 1954.07, 1957.11
Pages, Maria 1996.01, 1996.12, 1998.09, 2000.05
Paget, Bruce 1896.41
Paget, Dorothy 1905.28
Paget, Ffolliot 1894.39
Paget, Ivy 1905.28, 1912.14
Paget, Lily 1947.01, 1947.17, 1948.25, 1950.15
Paglia, Gina 1971.15
Pagliere, Adele 1878.03
Paglieri 1879.12
Paglieri, Adele 1871.18
Pagnol, Marcel 1954.15
Pahl, Mel 1948.04, 1949.01, 1950.12
Pahl, Melvin 1942.20, 1946.07
Pahl, Naida 1931.36
Paige, Autris 1972.06
Paige, Elizabeth 1915.03
Paige, Jackie 1929.22
Paige, Janis 1954.05, 1963.21
Paige, Jeannie 1975.12
Paige, Kenneth 1932.06
Paige, Mae 1925.48
Paige, Sam 1930.24
Paige, Sammy 1932.08
Paige, Shirley 1940.22, 1942.12
Pailet, Marshall 1999.21, 2001.06
Painchaud, Janice 1959.22, 1961.08
Paine, Albert Bigelow 1898.17
Paine, Dayton C. 1908.13
Paine, Ethel 1896.15
Paine, Helen 1920.43
Paine, Lizzie 1885.51
Painter, Charlene 1984.16
Painter, Eleanor 1914.25, 1915.23, 1918.33, 1920.09, 1921.14, 1924.05, 1927.01
Painter, Walter 1989.29
Paka, Toots 1910.07
Paker, Rose 1881.45
Paki, Tomaurangi 1972.20
Pakledinaz, Martin 1993.16, 1997.08, 1999.19
Pakledinaz, Marty 1981.15
Pakula, Alan J. 1963.25
Palaccio, Emma 1883.44
Palacio, Lisette 1974.14
Palazzi, M. Charles 1926.21
Palazzo, Gina 1934.02
Palermo, Andrew 1999.04
Palermo, Mario 1935.02
Paley, Herman 1906.29
Paley, Lou 1919.11, 1919.12
Palin, Michael 1976.06
Palkowitch, Joseph 1920.08
Palladino, Mlle. 1876.12, 1877.15
Palladis, M.A. 1880.02
Pallardis, Marie 1879.01
Pallas, Elvira 1959.12
Pallavicini 1973.17
Pallenberg, H. 1932.22
Pallings, W. 1898.29
Pallings, Walter 1897.20
Palliser, Esther 1890.02, 1890.21
Pallma, Belle 1909.23
Pallma, Frank 1891.37, 1893.08, 1895.07, 1897.42
Pallmer, Frank 1886.01
Pallo, Imre 1976.23, 1978.20, 1979.21, 1980.03, 1980.22, 1985.11, 1986.10, 1987.11, 1988.14
Palloy, Charles 1935.17
Pallozzi, Frances 1993.13
Palm, Walter 1919.04, 1930.27, 1932.06, 1933.21
Palma, Clara 1897.40
Palma, Frank 1895.33, 1897.18, 1906.36, 1908.03
Palmental, F.A. 1879.58
Palmer 1876.12
Palmer, A.M. 1890.02, 1890.23, 1895.42
Palmer, A.N. 1879.66
Palmer, Alice 1904.56, 1913.20, 1914.18
Palmer, Allie 1903.05
Palmer, Audrey 1938.13, 1939.30
Palmer, Beatrice 1918.08
Palmer, Bee 1918.19
Palmer, Betsy 1965.20
Palmer, Byron 1948.26, 1950.19
Palmer, C.B. 1883.36
Palmer, Charles C. 1903.12
Palmer, Charlotte 1904.12
Palmer, Christene 1966.22, 1966.23, 1966.25, 1966.26, 1966.28, 1968.25, 1968.26, 1968.27, 1968.28, 1968.29, 1978.17, 1989.15, 1993.13
Palmer, Christy 1957.06
Palmer, Clara 1896.52, 1900.39, 1902.24, 1904.35, 1905.45, 1906.41, 1908.36, 1909.04, 1910.03, 1910.29, 1911.24, 1913.29, 1916.06, 1916.07, 1922.31, 1924.23, 1927.01, 1934.03
Palmer, David 1964.29, 1964.36, 1964.38, 1964.43, 1966.25, 1966.26
Palmer, E. 1870.32
Palmer, Edith 1903.04
Palmer, Elaine 1918.28, 1919.25, 1920.40, 1922.45, 1923.44
Palmer, Emily 1902.32
Palmer, Eva 1897.42
Palmer, F.C. 1892.27
Palmer, Frances 1900.59
Palmer, Francis 1898.72
Palmer, Frank 1946.09
Palmer, Fred 1885.34, 1885.36, 1885.37
Palmer, Fred. 1885.38
Palmer, G.M. 1881.21, 1881.33
Palmer, George W. 1881.12
Palmer, Harry 1866.18, 1868.03, 1869.02, 1869.06, 1869.14, 1869.20, 1869.27, 1869.29, 1869.32, 1869.33, 1869.35, 1869.40, 1869.43, 1869.44, 1870.04, 1870.13, 1870.19, 1870.21, 1870.44, 1871.10, 1871.15, 1871.22, 1871.27, 1872.06, 1872.09, 1872.11, 1872.37, 1873.08, 1873.10, 1873.28, 1877.07
Palmer, Hattie 1907.03
Palmer, Hilde 1937.05
Palmer, Inda 1906.34
Palmer, Irene 1904.56, 1914.04, 1914.18, 1915.20
Palmer, Ivy 1926.29
Palmer, Jack 1986.06, 1989.02, 1999.24
Palmer, Jeanette 1990.08, 1993.14, 1995.18
Palmer, Jeanne 1934.06
Palmer, Jeannette 1900.43, 1902.12
Palmer, John 1997.01
Palmer, John F. 1989.16
Palmer, Joni 1975.01
Palmer, Kate 1868.03
Palmer, L. 1894.18
Palmer, Leland 1966.30, 1972.22
Palmer, Maida 1924.32
Palmer, Marian 1929.32
Palmer, Mary 1895.33, 1898.65
Palmer, Messr. 1881.11
Palmer, Minnie 1876.02, 1878.04, 1880.25, 1882.56, 1884.53, 1887.40, 1890.37
Palmer, Mr. 1851.05, 1863.01
Palmer, Pat 1932.26
Palmer, Patricia 1931.08
Palmer, Peter 1956.12, 1962.15, 1963.04, 1963.06, 1964.46, 1974.02
Palmer, R.C. 1875.11
Palmer, Renzo 1964.03
Palmer, Robert 2000.07
Palmer, Sean 1999.01, 1999.15
Palmer, Tony 1923.36
Palmers, Joyce 1953.16
Palmieri, Joe 1974.06
Palmieri, Joseph 1972.23
Palmstierna-Weiss, Gunilla 1965.39
Palomo, Martinez 1969.11
Palotta, race 1894.33
Palumbo, Dennis 1992.17
Palumbo, Gene 1984.10
Pam, Leona 1906.19
Pam, Mlle. 1924.05
Pamentel, Frank 1879.38
Pan, Hermes 1948.28
Pan, Vasso 1927.64
Panama, Norman 1940.07, 1956.12
Panaro, Hugh 1993.19, 1997.17
Pancaud 1908.07
Pancer, Paul 1904.40
Pandolphi, Frank 1927.50
Pandor, Billy 1920.26
Pandur, Billy 1917.16
Pane, Julio Oscar 1999.18
Panian, Maggie 1999.17
Panian, Susan Kelly 1999.17
Pankey, Anna Cook 1907.22
Pankey, Anna Cooke 1906.08
Pankey, P.L. 1899.31
Pankey, Theodore 1903.08, 1904.26, 1906.08, 1907.22, 1909.10
Panko, Tom 1953.07, 1955.06, 1956.12, 1957.18, 1965.14, 1965.37, 1967.05, 1968.03, 1986.03
Pansera, Roberto 1999.18
Panter, Howard 2000.17
Panter, John 1938.13, 1940.08, 1945.17
Panvini, Grace 1942.33
Panzer, Marty 1976.34, 1991.10
Panzere, Mlle. 1869.08
Paola-Marie, Mlle. 1879.49
Papa, Bruce 1966.02
Pape, Joan 1978.06
Pape, Lionel 1921.09, 1923.01
Papell, Lee 1953.03
Papich, Stanley 1957.14, 1958.01
Papich, Stephen 1962.22
Papp, Joseph 1968.11, 1971.18, 1975.02, 1975.15, 1976.10, 1978.11, 1981.01, 1984.02
Pappas, Evan 1992.17, 1998.21
Pappas, Theodore 1983.14, 1988.18, 1989.04
Pappathatos, Patti 1963.21
Paquerette, Mlle. 1893.41
Paquet, Marie 1958.13
Paramount Pictures 1989.26
Paramount Sound 1978.25
Paramount Theatre Productions 1983.06
Parcher, William 1985.11, 1986.10, 1987.11, 1988.16, 1990.08, 1990.13
Pardee, Louise 1897.21
Pardello, Leo 1929.08
Pardess, Yael 2001.07
Pardey, H.O. 1848.03
Pardoe, Tom 1995.19
Pardy, Laura 1895.09, 1897.27
Paredes, Jean 1964.06
Parent, Gail 1968.13, 1974.02
Parent, Harry 1907.12
Parent, Mlle. 1872.03
Parent, Mons. 1871.25
Parent, Nicole 1958.18
Parenteau, Zoel 1916.18, 1918.06
Parenteau, Zoel J. 1915.24
Paret, Frank 1919.02
Paret, Frank M. 1913.08, 1913.11, 1913.12, 1913.13
Paret, Frank P. 1906.44, 1907.42, 1909.07
Parham, Florence 1921.26
Parham, Glover 1976.28
Parichy, Dennis 1978.13, 1982.02, 1982.11, 1987.20, 1991.02
Paris, Fancesca 1888.23
Paris, Francescina 1888.10, 1889.33
Paris, Mlle. 1889.08, 1894.22
Paris, Norman 1972.07
Parise, Cindi 1995.02
Parisette, Mildred 1933.03
Parish, Mitchell 1929.05, 1934.32, 1935.19, 1939.14, 1940.02, 1940.16, 1975.12, 1975.22, 1976.04, 1979.13, 1979.14, 1981.06, 1987.02, 1992.18, 2000.07
Park Michael 1995.03
Park Theatre Opera Company 1875.12
Park, Dong Woo 1997.16, 1998.08
Park, J.B. 1895.16
Park, John 1904.28, 1906.04, 1910.34, 1911.40, 1912.35, 1913.06, 1917.36, 1920.31, 1924.05, 1924.25, 1926.04
Park, John B. 1901.19, 1908.17
Park, John P. 1903.24
Park, Joshua 2001.06
Park, Kolleen 1997.16, 1998.08
Park, Michael 1998.15
Park, R. Vincent 1985.17
Park, Richard 1964.20, 1966.04, 1966.17
Park, Sang Hoe 1997.16
Park, Stephanie 1997.06
Parke, H.C. 1885.48
Parke, Walter 1882.60, 1883.67
Parker, A.D. 1884.08
Parker, Alecia 1983.14, 1984.15, 1987.16, 1990.18, 1992.09, 1993.18, 1994.07, 1996.14, 1996.17, 1999.04, 2000.18
Parker, Alison 1968.29
Parker, Andy 1982.11
Parker, Baby 1892.31
Parker, Barnett 1922.12, 1923.03, 1923.17, 1923.41, 1924.36, 1926.01, 1928.48, 1934.42
Parker, Bernard 1987.17
Parker, C. 1869.02, 1881.18
Parker, C.W. 1880.17
Parker, Carlota 1882.03
Parker, Carrie 1883.44
Parker, Catherine 1926.19
Parker, Charles 1888.11
Parker, Corinne 1897.44, 1898.18
Parker, Dell 1940.12, 1944.14
Parker, Doris 1946.10
Parker, Dorothy 1914.24, 1922.42, 1924.15, 1931.21, 1956.15
Parker, Eleanor 1948.26
Parker, Flora 1903.04, 1908.42, 1909.24, 1917.09
Parker, Florence 1901.23, 1927.05, 1927.53
Parker, Frank 1914.20, 1920.08, 1944.14
Parker, Frank W. 1885.68
Parker, Georgie 1885.31, 1885.51, 1885.62, 1886.07, 1886.17, 1889.09, 1889.31, 1892.23
Parker, Gloria 1983.05
Parker, Hal 1924.16, 1929.04
Parker, Harry 1894.18, 1894.40, 1895.24
Parker, Harry Doel 1898.61
Parker, Harvey 1901.03
Parker, Howard 1959.26, 1979.13, 1980.09, 1980.18, 1981.07
Parker, James 1888.11
Parker, Janet 1951.14
Parker, Jimmie 1919.23
Parker, John Eric 1993.03

Parker, Jr., Herman 1989.12
Parker, Jr., R. 1983.09
Parker, Katherine 1926.31
Parker, Kay 1932.08
Parker, Kitty 1875.39
Parker, Leicester 1914.25
Parker, Lem B. 1907.50
Parker, Lenore 1946.11
Parker, Leonard 1961.13
Parker, Lew 1930.31, 1936.26, 1945.18, 1955.04, 1972.03
Parker, Lewis 1929.12, 1929.42
Parker, Lotta 1907.06
Parker, Lou 1932.21
Parker, Louis N. 1922.04
Parker, Louise 1886.43, 1956.06
Parker, Maggy 1869.31
Parker, Marion 1902.15
Parker, Mary 1941.08
Parker, Mertza 1872.43
Parker, Messr. 1881.14, 1886.54
Parker, Midge 1950.09
Parker, Minnie 1890.40
Parker, Miss 1870.22, 1872.06, 1894.18
Parker, Mr. 1836.01, 1878.14
Parker, Nellie 1892.36, 1892.56, 1893.28, 1894.10, 1895.21, 1895.34
Parker, Nellie V. 1892.09, 1897.02
Parker, Nellie Victoria 1891.26, 1894.35
Parker, Patricia 1982.18
Parker, Peggy 1914.30, 1920.33
Parker, Priscilla 1920.20
Parker, Rena 1919.27
Parker, Robert 1919.42
Parker, Rose 1899.36, 1903.19
Parker, Ross 1958.18
Parker, Ruth 1918.25
Parker, Sarah Jessica 1996.18
Parker, Seymour 1881.28
Parker, Stewart 1979.07
Parker, Susan 1904.03
Parker, Susanne 1905.29
Parker, Susie 1876.18, 1876.21, 1880.34
Parker, Thomas 1892.09
Parker, Tillie 1882.57
Parker, Tilly 1881.22
Parker, Timothy Britten 1996.09
Parker, Walter Coleman 1906.13
Parker, Walter Huston 1927.13
Parker, Willard 1943.03
Parkes, Clifford 1968.25
Parkes, G.L. 1866.05
Parkes, George 1876.23, 1879.50, 1879.56, 1884.11
Parkes, Nellie 1905.11
Parkhurst, Dorothy 1893.33
Parkhurst, George 1888.37
Parkhurst, Messr. 1870.22
Parkin, Rollie 1891.38
Parkins, Will 1963.08, 1964.04
Parkinson, Elizabeth 1999.01
Parks, A.S. 1866.20
Parks, Bernice 1946.24
Parks, Bert 1965.21
Parks, Cora 1937.09
Parks, Don 1960.07
Parks, George R. 1881.15
Parks, Hildy 1965.02, 1966.09, 1966.32, 1969.05, 1979.12, 1980.08, 1983.16, 1994.13
Parks, J.A. 1892.33
Parks, John 1920.13, 1975.01
Parks, John A. 1892.47, 1893.16
Parks, Larry 1960.01
Parks, Melvin 1934.06
Parks, Michael 1959.13
Parks, Paul 1937.13, 1947.17
Parks, Van Dyke 1997.18
Parlato, Dennis 1988.09
Parlsoe, Jr., Charles T. 1851.04, 1869.25
Parmalee, Mabel 1913.10
Parmegiani, Mlle. 1876.12
Parmet, L. 1911.47
Parmet, Messr. 1897.23
Parmette, Leon 1896.12
Parnahay, Alicia 1930.37
Parner, Joey 1996.07
Parnie, N. 1885.65
Parnova, Lisa 1925.36
Parquette, Dolores 1914.21
Parr, Albert 1897.36, 1900.19, 1902.03, 1902.31, 1903.07, 1903.10, 1903.32, 1904.05, 1904.16, 1905.06
Parr, Albert A. 1899.39
Parr, C.T. 1883.17, 1883.19, 1884.08
Parr, Charles T. 1882.49, 1885.63, 1905.32, 1906.03
Parr, Gilberto 1988.15
Parr, John 1896.13, 1897.10, 1898.13, 1899.12
Parr, Lizzie 1883.39
Parr, Messr. 1883.17, 1883.23
Parr, Norman 1895.24
Parr-Davies, Harry 1942.01, 1952.11
Parra, Mariano 1961.05, 1962.11
Parraga, Graziella 1939.18
Parrinello, Richard 1982.14, 1985.01, 1990.02
Parrish, Cheryl 1988.18
Parrish, Elizabeth 1965.28
Parrish, Robert 1939.17
Parry Opera Company 1897.28, 1901.14
Parry, Chris 1993.06
Parry, Frank 1927.08
Parry, Henry 1894.41
Parry, John F. 1902.37
Parry, Messr. 1851.07
Parry, Mr. 1851.01, 1895.13
Parry, William 1897.28, 1901.18, 1974.24, 1980.19, 1981.26, 1984.08, 1986.18, 1994.05
Pars, Julie 1975.22
Parselle, Marie 1872.21
Parsloe, C. 1854.04
Parsloe, Charles T. 1865.06, 1891.27
Parsloe, Charley 1869.21
Parsloe, Jr., Charles T. 1862.07, 1863.10, 1864.09, 1864.12, 1864.15, 1869.11, 1869.17, 1869.28, 1870.39, 1877.07
Parsloe, Mr. 1850.01, 1859.08
Parslow, Lillie 1879.29
Parson, Carola 1921.38, 1922.02
Parson, Milton 1938.01
Parson, William 1939.17, 1943.01, 1944.02, 1947.11, 1948.22
Parsons, Billy 1948.23, 1951.14, 1960.02
Parsons, Carolyn 1911.17
Parsons, Chauncey 1927.58
Parsons, Donovan 1923.36, 1925.43, 1927.02, 1929.51
Parsons, E. Percy 1898.60, 1907.27, 1912.30, 1913.22, 1914.11
Parsons, E.L. 1872.06
Parsons, E.P. 1904.37
Parsons, Estelle 1956.16, 1958.20, 1960.01, 1981.01
Parsons, Geoffrey 1962.17, 1964.02, 1976.16, 1981.04
Parsons, George 1908.09, 1911.33, 1912.11
Parsons, Jack 1927.40
Parsons, Jeanne 1951.16
Parsons, John 1921.15
Parsons, Joseph 1912.04, 1915.24, 1916.15, 1919.22, 1920.26
Parsons, Patricia 1931.44
Parsons, Patti 1953.09
Parsons, Percy 1906.49, 1907.51, 1917.11
Parten, Peggy 1983.01
Partial, M. 1886.59
Partidge, Roland 1944.12
Partington, Arthur 1947.16, 1948.25, 1950.15, 1959.02, 1961.09
Partington, Dorothy 1942.23
Partington, Jeanne 1955.13
Partington, Phyllis 1911.37
Partington, Sally 1857.06
Parton, Mr. 1860.01
Partos, Eugene 1922.34
Partridge, Roland 1931.46, 1944.09, 1944.11
Parvin, Alice 1894.19
Pasadena Playhouse, State Theatre of California 1988.07
Pascal, Adam 1996.09, 2000.06
Pascal, Florian 1886.45
Pascal, Fran 1968.07
Pascal, Gabriel 1956.01, 1964.20, 1968.17, 1976.05, 1981.19, 1993.18
Pascal, Howard 1912.08
Pascal, John 1968.07
Pascal, Milton 1931.36, 1936.01, 1943.20, 1944.14, 1949.01, 1955.12
Pascal, Walter 1906.23
Pascaud 1906.25
Pascaud, Mms. 1920.03
Pascaud, Paris 1926.41
Pasch, Claire 1951.16
Pasch, Reginald 1921.29, 1927.63
Paschal, Walter 1908.17, 1910.07
Pasekoff, Marilyn 1997.22, 1998.20, 1999.21, 2000.19
Pasha, Omar 1991.11
Paskman, Dailey 1922.06, 1923.28
Paskman, James 1918.01
Paskow, Karen 1983.21
Passerard, Messr. 1879.26, 1879.44
Pasta, F. 1882.57
Pasta, Felicita 1883.47
Pasta, Mlle. 1879.42, 1886.14
Pasti, Mlle. 1884.40
Pastor, Enrique 1939.18
Pastor, Mr. 1860.01
Pastor, Tony 1881.06, 1881.12, 1882.04, 1882.20, 1883.02, 1883.17, 1883.19, 1883.23, 1884.61, 1885.35
Pastoria, Andre 1978.02, 1983.02
Pastorini, Gerolamo 1884.58
Pat Rooney Comedy Company 1886.61, 1888.42
Patachou 1958.06, 1964.22
Patapovitch, O.E. 1917.08
Patch, George L. 1898.45, 1904.32, 1907.43, 1908.32
Patch, Jerry 1972.21
Patch, William Moore 1920.29, 1921.08
Pate, Edward 1947.11
Pateman, Bella 1869.23, 1871.20, 1871.21, 1872.27
Pateman, Robert 1869.23, 1871.13, 1871.20, 1871.21
Paternostro, Michael 1999.01
Paterson, David R. 1997.11, 1998.06, 1999.11
Paterson, Ian 1964.28
Paterson, Jeanette 1905.08, 1905.11, 1908.37
Paterson, Jeannette 1904.29
Paterson, Robert 1976.32
Paterson, Signe 1916.04
Pates, Peggy 1927.06
Patik, Vickie 1976.05
Patinkin, Mandy 1979.23, 1984.08, 1989.16, 1991.05, 1997.01, 1998.11, 2000.08
Patino, Yeni 1993.08
Paton, Alan 1949.15, 1958.11, 1972.06
Paton, Miss 1881.35
Patou, Jean 1923.26
Patriccola, Tom 1926.16
Patrice, Gloria 1949.08, 1950.08, 1951.17
"Patrick" 1981.17
Patrick Sheila 1934.34
Patrick, Dennis 1967.01
Patrick, Harold 1944.25, 1947.21
Patrick, Howard 1915.20
Patrick, John 1932.14, 1970.21
Patrick, Julian 1954.03, 1959.04, 1959.25
Patricola, Tom 1923.18, 1924.19, 1925.22, 1928.22, 1932.24, 1933.21
Patson, Doris 1942.17, 1942.22, 1944.27
Patston, Doris 1925.08, 1926.33, 1932.15, 1934.04, 1937.03, 1946.23, 1948.27
Patten, Gilbert 1971.09
Patten, Moultrie 1962.15
Patteron, Katie 1889.07
Patterson, Agnes 1920.21
Patterson, Alice 1926.23, 1927.62
Patterson, Anne Lee 1931.19
Patterson, Burdella 1907.08
Patterson, Charles G. 1896.40
Patterson, Dick 1960.12, 1961.16, 1964.21
Patterson, Dora 1904.38
Patterson, Dorothy 1930.08
Patterson, Flora 1926.23, 1927.62
Patterson, Frederick C. 1906.50
Patterson, Helen 1919.03, 1928.34
Patterson, Howard Jay 1983.07, 1986.05, 1994.11, 1998.22
Patterson, Jackie 1983.21
Patterson, Jackie Jay 1985.05
Patterson, James 1996.04
Patterson, Jamie 1981.29
Patterson, Jayne 2000.20
Patterson, Katie 1887.48
Patterson, Kelly 1986.07, 1989.03
Patterson, Kenneth 1940.21
Patterson, Lover 1995.03
Patterson, Marjorie 1916.16
Patterson, Mary 1929.47
Patterson, Minnie 1888.14
Patterson, Miss 1841.01
Patterson, Phillip 1928.18
Patterson, Ralph 1949.17
Patterson, Raymond 1982.22, 1984.14
Patterson, Robert 1949.08
Patterson, Russell 1931.05, 1932.16, 1933.21, 1934.01, 1934.40, 1935.18, 1936.01
Patterson, Ruth K. 1930.39
Patterson, Signe 1915.08
Patterson, Stark 1928.30
Patterson, Starke 1926.03, 1926.15
Patterson, Vi 1924.29
Patterson, Vincent 1993.09
Patteson, John 1944.20
Patti, Carlo 1870.30, 1870.37, 1870.41, 1870.45, 1871.03, 1871.06, 1871.07
Pattison, Lee 1939.20, 1939.21
Patton, Barbara 1948.27
Patton, Fred 1932.02
Patton, Jack 1923.21
Patton, Lucille 1969.16
Patton, Monica L. 1999.17
Patty, Felix 1920.19
Patzakis, Michele 1993.12
Paul Arlington, Inc. 1915.29, 1917.05, 1918.40, 1919.13, 1919.24, 1919.25, 1919.33, 1920.17, 1920.32, 1922.01, 1922.24, 1922.31, 1923.13, 1923.16, 1923.21, 1925.07, 1925.11
Paul, Agnes 1892.27, 1893.49, 1896.02, 1896.28, 1899.21, 1904.09
Paul, Alan 1972.12
Paul, Betty 1953.02
Paul, Elsa 1930.36
Paul, Eugene 1879.06
Paul, Eugenia 1878.19, 1879.35
Paul, Eva 1938.10
Paul, Guy 1996.05
Paul, Herbert 1914.33
Paul, Howard 1869.47
Paul, John 1947.07, 1959.05
Paul, Linda 1982.15
Paul, Logan 1895.39, 1925.37
Paul, Lois 1940.21
Paul, M. Cooper 1940.04
Paul, Mae 1908.39, 1909.25
Paul, May 1910.18
Paul, Messr. 1854.04, 1855.06, 1855.07
Paul, Miss 1908.19, 1916.10
Paul, Mr. 1855.04, 1855.05, 1857.08, 1870.22
Paul, Mrs. Howard 1869.47, 1870.03
Paul, Percy Graham 1923.26
Paul, Priscilla 1922.13
Paul, Robert 1978.23, 1979.27
Paul, Stephen 1906.24
Paul, Thomas 1962.21, 1963.24, 1965.07
Paul, Tina 1979.26, 1984.01, 1989.20, 1991.15, 1994.09, 1996.14
Paul, W.A. 1879.58, 1879.71
Paul, W.M. 1869.46, 1869.47
Paul, Walter 1939.19, 1944.14, 1945.18, 1946.07, 1946.08, 1946.22
Paul, Will A. 1881.47
Paul, William A. 1879.71
Paula, Lucine 1919.01
Pauldine, Frederick 1910.09
Paulding, Frederic 1905.45
Paulding, Grace 1905.24
Paulding, Nathalie 1995.19
Paulee, Mona 1956.04
Paulett, Mr. 1882.54
Pauley, Ann 1921.35
Pauley, Wilbur 1985.09, 1996.10, 1999.05
Pauli, Blanche 1883.19
Pauli, Claudia 1883.19
Pauli, Miss 1883.23
Paulin, David 1995.02
Paulin, Florence 1907.26
Paulina, Mlle. 1866.18, 1870.31
Pauline Hall Opera Company 1892.42, 1894.11
Pauline, Mlle. 1870.44, 1871.27
Paullin, Louise 1880.38, 1881.24, 1882.45, 1882.71, 1883.18, 1889.26
Paullin, Messr. 1841.01
Paulsen, David 1971.14
Paulsen, Kay 1940.12
Paulson, Joh. 1897.08
Paulson, Mr. 1875.03
Paulton, Edward 1886.30, 1894.25, 1894.46, 1896.50, 1906.32, 1907.01, 1917.34, 1920.07, 1921.08
Paulton, Edward A. 1889.36, 1911.44, 1913.21, 1914.07, 1914.14, 1915.19, 1915.21, 1917.14, 1920.37
Paulton, Edward E. 1914.02
Paulton, Harry 1882.60, 1886.30, 1887.44, 1888.02, 1888.18, 1889.16, 1889.25, 1889.36, 1889.49, 1893.35, 1894.46, 1896.50, 1897.24, 1898.36, 1899.24, 1903.32, 1903.38, 1921.01
Paulton, Jack 1917.30
Paulton, John 1910.05
Paulton, Thomas 1903.25
Paulus, Daniel 1996.17

Paulus, Paul 1930.05
Pauly, W. 1918.13
Paulyanthe 1886.30, 1888.02, 1889.16, 1889.49, 1893.35, 1897.24, 1898.36
Pauncefort, George 1904.33, 1909.14, 1911.32, 1912.17, 1926.29, 1932.25
Paunceforte, George 1928.35
Paur, Lizzie 1880.69
Paurel, Paul 1922.21
Pavek, Janet 1960.10, 1961.03, 1961.05
Pavi, Leon 1912.09
Pavlosky, David 1982.14
Pavlova, Anna 1916.15
Pavlovska, Vera 1943.11
Pawk, Michele 1992.02, 1998.04, 2000.18
Pawk, Michelle 1988.07
Pawl, Christina 1998.04
Pawle, Lennox 1912.26, 1919.42, 1922.04, 1923.07, 1930.08
Paxson, J. 1877.04
Paxson, Messr. 1877.15
Paxton, Ed 1882.54
Paxton, G. 1882.06
Paxton, George 1898.55
Paxton, Glenn 1959.06
Paxton, J.P. 1881.38
Paxton, Marie 1970.11
Payen, M. 1926.40, 1926.43, 1926.45, 1926.47, 1926.48
Payn, Graham 1948.11
Payne, Arthur 1908.08
Payne, Barbara 1946.07
Payne, Benny 1964.32
Payne, Freda 1974.11
Payne, Georgia 1930.08
Payne, Hal E. 1898.45, 1899.32
Payne, Harriet 1858.03
Payne, Jessie 1928.02, 1929.06
Payne, Jimmy 1938.19
Payne, John 1935.12
Payne, Jr., Hal E. 1898.45
Payne, Louis 1903.02
Payne, Miss 1903.03
Payne, Mr. 1921.21
Payne, Nellie 1902.10, 1903.03, 1904.13
Payne, Robert 1942.19
Payne, Sunny 1939.29
Payne, Virginia 1964.21
Paynter, Corone 1921.27
Payton, Larry 1998.18, 1999.03
Payton, Lew 1924.27
Payton, Ralph 1926.20
Paz, Leonardo Suarez 1999.18
Paz, Rafi 1969.13, 1973.01
Pazzi-Preval 1929.10, 1929.11, 1929.13, 1929.14, 1929.15, 1929.16
Peachey, John 1894.26, 1905.49, 1907.49, 1911.17
Peacock Bertram 1942.08
Peacock, Ada 1926.29, 1926.30, 1929.51
Peacock, Bertram 1914.11, 1921.31, 1925.15, 1928.49, 1935.05, 1935.06, 1935.07, 1935.08, 1935.09, 1935.10, 1936.11, 1942.02, 1942.04, 1942.06, 1942.09, 1944.04, 1944.05, 1944.06, 1944.08, 1944.11, 1944.13
Peacock, Michon 1972.05, 1975.14
Peake, Morley 1906.35
Peakes, H.C. 1868.01
Peakes, Henry 1878.16, 1879.30, 1881.14, 1882.31, 1882.37, 1885.30, 1885.32
Peakes, Henry C. 1866.07, 1866.14, 1867.03, 1867.04, 1867.06, 1868.09, 1868.10, 1868.11, 1868.12, 1869.41, 1881.05, 1882.40, 1887.25, 1892.25
Peakes, J.G. 1868.01, 1868.02, 1872.23, 1872.35, 1873.03, 1873.19, 1877.28, 1879.07
Peakes, James 1866.07, 1866.14, 1872.35, 1881.14, 1882.31, 1893.39, 1895.09
Peakes, James G. 1866.10, 1869.41, 1873.24, 1882.33, 1882.36, 1882.37, 1882.40, 1885.30, 1891.36, 1892.60, 1894.41, 1898.20, 1898.72
Peakse, Henry 1877.35
Pearce, Alf. 1894.43
Pearce, Alice 1942.34, 1944.33, 1948.08, 1948.22, 1949.18, 1957.14, 1961.18
Pearce, Etta 1904.58
Pearce, Glory 1909.01
Pearce, Harry 1920.27, 1921.04
Pearce, Mervyn 1928.42
Pearce, Nayan 1927.58, 1933.26, 1934.18
Pearce, Phyllis 1924.24, 1926.32
Pearce, Vera 1930.20
Pearl, Anthony 1904.54
Pearl, Dora 1890.12
Pearl, Irwin 1970.07, 1976.36, 1981.18
Pearl, Jack 1923.02, 1923.41, 1926.01, 1927.58, 1929.09, 1930.09, 1931.19, 1933.01
Pearl, Jeanette 1895.24
Pearl, Kathryn 1900.34, 1905.43
Pearl, Leatrice 1931.39
Pearl, Lorraine 1931.39
Pearl, Louise 1955.07
Pearl, Mabel 1932.20
Pearle, Gary 1980.27
Pearlman, Nan 1974.13, 1975.05, 1978.22
Pearlman, Stephen 1969.16
Pearly, Fred 1948.12
Pearman, Olive 1937.14
Pearson, Addie 1873.10
Pearson, Bud 1924.44, 1927.60, 1940.16, 1943.05
Pearson, Celia 1877.39, 1942.28
Pearson, Dunn 1983.15
Pearson, Eppy 1940.19, 1942.18
Pearson, Frank 1880.18, 1890.15, 1890.18, 1890.20
Pearson, H. 1866.04, 1866.05
Pearson, H.A. 1905.51
Pearson, Hal 1906.20, 1907.05
Pearson, Harry 1859.01, 1859.03, 1859.04, 1859.11, 1861.03, 1862.03, 1863.07, 1871.27, 1872.11
Pearson, Jack 1924.44, 1927.60
Pearson, Jean 1908.16
Pearson, Lillie 1879.12, 1880.08
Pearson, Margery 1912.49
Pearson, Miss 1861.06
Pearson, Molly 1920.12, 1938.10
Pearson, Mr. 1866.31
Pearson, Pauletta 1977.18
Pearson, Richard 1993.12
Pearson, S. 1844.01
Pearson, Scott 1966.30, 1968.31
Pearson, Sybille 1983.19
Pearson, Walter 1910.15
Pease, A.H. 1880.19
Pease, Harry 1918.05, 1921.21, 1928.22, 1997.01
Pease, James 1940.11, 1946.11, 1960.14
Pease, Wilder 1892.25
Peaslee, Richard 1965.39, 1967.01, 1975.23
Peasley, Colin 1976.18
Peasley, Thomas 1894.31
Pecan, Betty 1925.07
Pecaro, Christopher 1991.03
Pechner, Gerhard 1948.24
Pechter, Richard 1997.06
Peck, A.D. 1885.15
Peck, A.J. 1875.21
Peck, Allen 1965.22
Peck, Edward 1890.35, 1892.01
Peck, Elcie 1927.03
Peck, Esther 1927.23
Peck, Gary Scott 1985.17
Peck, H. 1891.15
Peck, J. 1869.13, 1875.14, 1877.25
Peck, Jon 1970.15, 1974.10
Peck, Jr., Charles K. 1960.10, 1969.16
Peck, Lois 1930.08
Peck, Mr. 1864.09, 1864.12, 1864.18, 1864.19, 1866.08, 1868.04
Peck, Raymond 1903.34, 1906.05, 1907.02, 1912.15, 1921.07, 1932.18
Peck, Raymond W. 1907.46, 1911.24, 1926.24
Peck, Roy 1930.37
Peck, Theodora 1939.19
Peck, Walter 1914.28
Pecktal, Lynn 1978.24
Pecorino, Joe 1977.10
Pedersen, Matthew 1991.03
Pedi, Christine 1998.15
Pedi, Tom 1950.17, 1955.06, 1956.05, 1965.15, 1965.20, 1966.13
Pedlar, Stuart 1977.05
Pedley, Grace 1884.44, 1889.54
Pedley, Ron 1989.08
Pedrick, Elsie 1929.08
Pedrick, Lloyd 1926.28, 1929.49
Pedroza, Alfonso 1944.02
Peebles, Ruth 1906.16, 1907.05, 1910.34
Peek, Brent 1980.27, 1981.04
Peel, Frederick 1895.14
Peel, Hal 1918.12
Peeler, Messr. 1869.26
Peerce, Alice 1968.22
Peever, Henry 1940.04
Peewee 1974.17, 1989.27
Pege, Herr 1879.62
Pegel, Frl. 1883.08
Peggy, Miss 1920.47
Pegram, Nigel 1966.03
Pegues, Charles 1970.04
Peil, Mary Beth 1985.01
Peilford, Mr. 1867.19
Peine, Virginia 1941.04
Peinze, Meta 1903.09
Peiris, Nully 1870.05
Peiser, Annie 1887.18
Peiser, K. 1887.18
Peisser, Frau 1883.08
Pekelner, Celia 1927.28
Pekin Stock Company 1907.29
Peldon, Courtney 1989.23
Pelf, Messr. 1875.40
Pelham, A.H. 1879.58
Pelham, Annie 1892.29
Pelham, J. 1881.03
Pelham, Miss 1892.52
Pelham, Mr. 1892.04
Pelham, Sherry 1929.03, 1931.39
Pelish, Thelma 1954.05, 1957.08, 1961.20
Pelissier, Anthony 1936.29, 1939.07
Pelissier, Victor 1796.02
Pell, Arthur 1907.01, 1909.02
Pell, Kate 1883.06
Pellard, Henrietta 1910.21
Pellaton, Albert 1906.49, 1907.51, 1911.28, 1912.30, 1914.09, 1917.05
Pelle, Nadia 1981.20
Pellegrini, Larry 1998.19
Pelletier, Mlle. 1875.21
Pelletti, John 1953.01, 1956.02
Pellisier, Victor 1796.03
Pelloquin, Noella 1947.01
Pelnze, Mera 1903.09
Peltier, Gene 1913.24, 1914.28
Pelty, Adam 1993.17, 1997.07, 1997.19, 1998.19
Peltz, Nelson 1973.15
Peltzer, Ida 1888.36
Peltzer, May 1888.36
Peluchi, Julio 1992.13
Peluso, Lisa 1974.17
Peluso, Tom 1932.08
Pelzer, George 1898.54
Pelzon and Carson 1916.11
Pember, Clifford 1918.03, 1918.09, 1918.10, 1918.15, 1918.28, 1918.32, 1919.36, 1922.02, 1922.26, 1947.15
Pember, Clifford F. 1919.05, 1921.24
Pemberton, Florence 1896.45
Pemberton, Henry 1927.63, 1928.44
Pemberton, John 1902.34
Pemberton, Max 1890.19
Pemberton, Stafford 1914.16, 1915.22, 1917.08
Pemberton-Hincks, Louise 1892.52
Pen, Polly 1980.01
Penagos, Isabel 1969.11
Penalton, Roy 1904.51
Pence, Edna 1932.16, 1932.24
Pendarvis, Leon 1983.20
Pender, Gladys 1930.08
Pender, Stephen 1980.15
Pender, Tom 1922.30
Pendergast, W.H. 1891.01
Pendleton, Austin 1964.27, 1973.03
Pendleton, E.H. 1903.41
Pendleton, Eleanor 1907.46, 1908.03, 1910.05, 1910.18, 1910.34, 1912.12, 1915.11
Pendleton, Eleanore 1906.47
Pendleton, Nat 1925.41
Pendleton, T. 1870.05
Pene duBois, Henri 1930.18, 1930.33
Pene duBois, Raoul 1934.01, 1934.18, 1934.19, 1934.42, 1935.15, 1936.02, 1936.17, 1937.15, 1938.06, 1938.13, 1939.12, 1939.27, 1939.30, 1940.03, 1940.10, 1940.19, 1941.05, 1941.11, 1943.24, 1945.04, 1945.06, 1945.18, 1946.09, 1948.23, 1948.30, 1950.02, 1950.15, 1951.13, 1952.09, 1953.02, 1953.03, 1953.17, 1954.16, 1955.01, 1955.25, 1956.06, 1956.14, 1957.01, 1957.18, 1958.05, 1959.13, 1963.02, 1963.05, 1963.20, 1965.21, 1967.09, 1968.02, 1971.03, 1973.05, 1974.17, 1975.09, 1979.25, 1980.05, 1989.03
Penella, Manuel 1921.39
Penfield, Edward 1923.25
Penfield, Mary A. 1889.20
Penfield, Roderic C. 1907.10
Penfield, Roderick C. 1904.55
Penfold, Maurice 1927.27
Penfold, Thomas 1919.10
Pening, Miss 1881.04
Penley, W.S. 1881.35
Penlington, Neil 1998.10
Penman, Charles 1921.41, 1924.20, 1964.20
Penman, Katherine 1926.18
Penman, Lea 1946.12
Penn, Arthur 1901.09, 1904.22, 1960.16, 1964.32
Penn, Arthur A. 1903.36, 1919.38
Penn, Edward 1975.03
Penn, Fitz 1901.09
Penn, Jacqueline 1971.01
Penn, Nina 1922.29, 1924.25, 1925.40
Penn, Rober 1949.08
Penn, Robert 1944.32, 1946.22, 1950.11, 1951.24, 1953.07, 1961.26, 1964.18
Penn, William 1899.38, 1901.29
Penn, William H. 1902.16, 1902.23, 1903.39, 1903.41, 1904.47, 1905.49, 1912.02
Pennec, Henri 1958.18
Pennefather, James 1898.54
Penner, Joe 1930.35, 1931.39
Pennese, Giuseppe 1964.03
Penniman, Richard 1982.22, 1986.02, 1989.12
Penning, Estelle 1921.37
Pennington, Alice 1894.15
Pennington, Ann 1914.15, 1915.15, 1916.10, 1917.26, 1918.19, 1919.13, 1920.17, 1921.22, 1923.07, 1923.20, 1924.18, 1925.10, 1926.16, 1928.22, 1930.40, 1931.36, 1943.06
Pennington, Anna 1913.17
Pennington, Buck 1948.19, 1949.05
Pennington, Diane 1983.08
Pennington, Gail 1982.01
Pennington, Theo 1931.22, 1931.23
Pennington, Walter 1907.37
Pennini, Thomas 1982.03
Pennoyer, A.S. 1869.41, 1871.08, 1884.46
Pennoyer, Alice 1894.43
Pennoyer, Kate 1857.04, 1866.02
Pennoyer, M.A. 1881.15
Pennyfather, James 1895.08
Penrose, Gibbs 1942.03, 1942.27
Penrose, J. Gibbs 1928.21
Penrose, Tudor 1929.02
Pensiero, Beth 1985.09, 1987.08, 1993.12, 1994.09
Penso, Patricia 1946.10
Penson 1838.01
Penson, Mrs. 1840.01
Penson, Mrs. W. 1838.01
Penson, William 1834.02
Pentecost, James 1991.15
Pentland, Hilda 1917.02
Pentland, J. 1860.01
Pentland, Mrs. 1875.05
Pentony, Pamela 1971.01
Penven, Alice 1929.10, 1929.13, 1929.14, 1929.15
Peple, Edward 1912.36, 1926.25
Peppe, Audrey 1942.19
Pepper, Harry 1882.38, 1882.42, 1883.65, 1888.28, 1889.35, 1937.03
Pepper, Henry 1886.30
Pepusch, Johann Christoph 1928.13
Pepusch, John Christopher 1750.01
Perain, Mons. 1877.13
Peralta, Craig 1982.14
Perason, Messr. 1844.01
Peraut, Mons. 1872.42, 1873.01
Percassi, Don 1972.04, 1975.15
Perceval, Miss 1886.36
Percival, Dora 1889.01, 1892.24
Percival, Elsie 1928.25
Percival, F. 1875.18
Percival, G.W. 1880.49
Percival, J.S. 1882.05
Percival, Walter 1904.19, 1905.19, 1905.57, 1907.30, 1908.03, 1908.16, 1908.34, 1910.01, 1910.16, 1911.24, 1912.12, 1912.48, 1916.07
Percy, Eileen 1917.03
Percy, F. 1866.34
Percy, Fred 1878.14, 1880.17, 1881.18, 1883.40
Percy, Frederick 1884.46
Percy, L. 1884.34
Percy, Maud 1895.10
Percy, Mr. 1866.24

Percy, R.W. 1875.18
Percy, Townsend 1885.08
Percy, Townshend 1882.71
Percy, W.S. 1914.09
Percyval, T. Wigney 1922.45
Perelman, S.J. 1931.14, 1932.27, 1943.19
Perenchio, Jerrold 1986.18
Perera 1885.65
Peress, Maurice 1968.18, 1972.15
Peret, Mons. 1883.60, 1884.01, 1886.21
Peretti, Hugo 1968.24, 1989.12
Peretz, I.L. 1990.16
Pereyra, Luis 1999.18
Pereyra, Norma 1999.18
Perez, J. 1969.11
Perez, Jose 1971.18
Perez, Julio 1921.39
Perez, Lazaro 1995.09
Perez, Luis 1986.04, 1988.01, 1989.03, 1991.15, 1992.07, 1993.05, 1995.09, 1999.08, 1999.22
Perez, Luis (Orfeo) 1989.20
Perez, Ramon 1935.10
Perez, Ray 1926.06, 1927.53, 1928.49
Perez, Rosario 1941.11
Perez, Royce 1935.10
Perez, Sebastian 1994.09, 1998.02
Perfect, Rose 1926.16, 1928.22, 1945.12
Perfitt, Frank 1909.01
Pergain, Cleo 1927.47
Perhacs, Marylou 1972.23
Pericet, Angelo 1964.03
Perie, Jeanette 1892.52
Perie, Jeannette 1893.32, 1894.40
Perin, Mons. 1876.26, 1876.28, 1876.31, 1877.06, 1877.19
Perine, Fred 1910.02
Peringh, E. 1881.40
Peris, Vde 1917.25
Perito, Nick 1959.15
Perke Hamberg Productions, Inc. 1927.25
Perkin Stock Company 1907.31
Perkinoff, Serge 1925.10
Perkins, Alberta 1926.19, 1930.19, 1939.29
Perkins, Anthony 1960.05
Perkins, B. 1997.21
Perkins, Bobbie 1925.26, 1926.13, 1927.16
Perkins, Bobby 1926.51, 1928.38
Perkins, C.T. 1981.16
Perkins, Cararie 1898.63
Perkins, Carl Lee 1989.12
Perkins, Carrie 1880.06, 1880.65, 1894.19, 1895.07, 1896.44, 1899.25, 1903.06, 1905.29
Perkins, Carrie E. 1880.59, 1880.67, 1880.70, 1887.43, 1888.09, 1888.36, 1889.01, 1889.13, 1889.44, 1895.17, 1899.36, 1900.03, 1900.20, 1901.08, 1901.23, 1902.16, 1904.05, 1907.10, 1907.52, 1909.17, 1910.17, 1911.30
Perkins, Cy 1943.23
Perkins, Damian 2000.06
Perkins, Frank 1987.02
Perkins, Fred 1876.02, 1876.36, 1877.15, 1879.64, 1885.43, 1886.61, 1888.17, 1889.39, 1890.27, 1894.06, 1894.13, 1894.42, 1895.44, 1903.29
Perkins, Fred. 1881.16, 1886.15
Perkins, Frederick 1895.11, 1908.33
Perkins, Garwood 1958.11, 1963.27, 1964.19, 1965.03, 1967.04
Perkins, John 1932.01, 1932.20, 1952.10, 1956.14
Perkins, Kenneth 1947.13
Perkins, Max 1960.12Perkins, Mr. 1869.43
Perkins, Osgood 1933.24
Perkins, Patti 2000.15
Perkins, Ray 1918.20, 1920.25, 1921.19, 1921.27, 1923.33, 1928.14, 1928.21
Perkins, Rita 1908.15
Perkins, Tom 1947.04, 1947.17
Perkins, W. 1888.38, 1890.23, 1890.50, 1891.41, 1894.41
Perkins, Walter 1889.26
Perkins, Walter E. 1906.32
Perkins, Wellington 1981.29
Perkins, William 1897.29
Perkinson, Coleridge-Taylor 1969.08, 1980.15, 1981.07, 1981.16
Perkis, Susan 1972.19
Perl, Arnold 1964.27, 1976.36, 1981.18, 1989.03, 1990.18
Perl, Bertha 1907.26
Perl, Lothar 1937.05
Perle, Jeannette 1895.12
Perleno, Hilda 1929.18, 1929.25, 1930.24, 1932.12
Perlet, Frank 1900.03
Perlet, Herman 1887.04, 1889.44, 1892.08, 1892.10, 1893.17, 1894.38, 1894.47, 1895.18, 1895.42, 1896.05, 1896.48, 1897.15, 1897.21, 1897.37, 1897.55, 1898.17, 1898.31, 1898.63, 1898.77, 1899.15, 1899.38, 1900.16, 1900.47, 1900.52, 1901.25, 1903.40, 1905.36, 1906.07, 1906.39, 1907.05, 1907.30, 1907.51
Perley, Frank L. 1896.42, 1896.43, 1897.13, 1898.60, 1899.34, 1902.20, 1902.43, 1905.49
Perlman, Bonnie 1989.25
Perloff, Carey 1998.05
Perloff, Howard 1988.20
Perloff, J. 1921.15
Perlot, Herman 1897.37
Perlowin, Gene 1956.11
Perlowin, Ginny 1956.02, 1957.07, 1957.17, 1959.26
Permane, Constantine 1920.24
Permane, Henry 1926.28
Pernice, Sal 1965.02, 1972.11
Pernikoff, Serge 1922.19, 1923.20
Pero, John 1959.05
Perola, Rose 1992.13
Perot, Cynthea 1922.12
Perot, Cynthia 1919.18, 1919.39
Perot, Mons. 1851.01, 1854.01
Perotti, Jules 1900.49
Perr, Harvey 1974.04
Perrault 1894.18, 1946.22
Perrault, Alida 1893.33
Perrault, Charles 1855.02, 1859.05, 1861.03, 1866.03, 1866.34, 1867.22, 1869.27, 1870.36, 1879.38, 1888.39, 1916.15, 1923.29
Perrault, Mlle. 1875.04
Perrault, Mons. 1875.04
Perraut, Mlle. 1873.11
Perraut, Mons. 1873.11, 1873.16
Perreault, Alida 1888.43
Perreault, Miss 1889.31
Perren, Dennis 1975.22
Perren, Frederick J. 1982.22, 1997.21
Perret, Messr. 1880.60, 1884.45
Perret, Mons. 1880.44, 1880.50, 1880.52, 1881.50, 1881.51, 1881.54, 1882.35, 1883.57, 1884.02, 1884.43, 1884.47, 1884.50, 1884.54, 1885.23, 1885.59, 1886.09, 1886.18
Perrier, Claude 1895.04
Perrier, Gabrielle 1916.16
Perrigueur, Mons. 1868.07
Perrin Sam 1945.18
Perrin, Adrian S. 1926.11, 1929.30
Perrin, Claude 1958.18
Perrin, Constance 1929.41
Perrin, Ernest 1918.02
Perrin, Mlle. 1877.13, 1885.55, 1885.57, 1885.59, 1885.61, 1886.09, 1886.21
Perrin, Mons. 1876.20, 1877.11
Perrin, Sidney 1897.30
Perrin, Sidney L. 1898.41, 1901.23
Perring, Agnes 1882.26, 1883.31
Perring, C. 1884.27
Perring, L. 1881.11
Perring, Messr. 1881.11, 1881.27, 1883.17, 1883.31
Perring, Miss 1885.05
Perring, S. 1859.08
Perrit, Messr. 1882.30
Perry, Agnes 1865.05
Perry, Alan D. 1991.05
Perry, Albert 1912.03
Perry, Antoinette 1925.21
Perry, Barbara 1946.22, 1950.01, 1957.17
Perry, Dein 1999.02
Perry, Dick 1964.11
Perry, Dorothy 1909.29
Perry, Douglas 1982.16, 1985.11
Perry, Estelle 1910.10, 1911.13
Perry, Ethel 1902.05
Perry, Eugene 1990.08
Perry, Fayette 1916.13
Perry, Flo 1928.27
Perry, Frank 1958.21
Perry, Frederick 1905.45
Perry, Gertrude 1894.02, 1895.39
Perry, Irene 1879.59, 1881.43, 1882.34, 1883.42, 1884.20, 1884.57, 1885.14, 1895.38, 1896.25, 1898.29, 1899.30
Perry, J. 1997.21
Perry, J.H. 1903.13
Perry, John Bennett 1972.21
Perry, Joseph 1969.09
Perry, Kathryn 1917.26, 1918.19, 1933.27
Perry, Keith 1965.28, 1981.12, 1989.29
Perry, Kitty 1896.44
Perry, Laura 1905.31
Perry, Leonard 1976.16
Perry, Lillian 1903.13
Perry, Louis 1978.19, 1978.20, 1979.20, 1979.21, 1979.27, 1980.21, 1981.20, 1985.09, 1985.13, 1986.09, 1987.03, 1987.08, 1988.04, 1988.18, 1989.04, 1990.02, 1990.08, 1991.09, 1993.12, 1994.09
Perry, Lynette 1989.26
Perry, Lynnette 1998.01
Perry, Madge 1886.34, 1887.14, 1889.04, 1892.07
Perry, Malcolm 1985.05
Perry, Marenda 1973.10
Perry, Marguerite 1934.05
Perry, Mary 1939.21
Perry, Mitzi 1943.14, 1943.21
Perry, Mr. 1869.28
Perry, Nettie 1938.19
Perry, Philomena 1934.37
Perry, Quentin 1987.17
Perry, Robert E. 1948.15
Perry, Rod 1968.13, 1972.06
Perry, Sheldon 1999.02
Perry, Tileston 1942.20
Perry, William 1985.20
Perryman, Al 1973.10, 1983.15
Perryman, Stanley Wesley 1986.07
Persand, Inez 1930.10
Perschk, Max 1914.28
Perselle, Jodi 1964.21, 1965.31
Perseus Productions 1996.05
Pershing, D'Vaughn 1949.09, 1975.08
Persini, Elise 1870.41, 1871.06, 1871.07
Persip, Charles 1959.15, 1961.25
Persoff, Nehemiah 1950.08, 1951.15
Person, Jr., Messr. 1844.01
Personette, Joan 1938.08, 1951.19
Persse, Thomas 1889.24
Persse, Thomas H. 1890.21, 1898.06, 1898.30, 1898.33, 1898.37, 1901.05
Persson, Frederic 1933.09, 1933.19, 1941.12, 1942.02, 1942.04, 1942.06, 1942.07, 1942.08, 1942.09, 1946.02
Persson, Frederick 1931.20, 1931.22, 1931.23, 1933.10, 1933.11, 1933.14, 1934.11
Persson, Gene 1971.11, 1974.03, 1999.03
Persson, Ruby 1974.03
Perugini, Giovanni 1900.19
Perugini, J. 1882.64
Perugini, Signor 1882.71, 1884.08, 1886.26, 1886.33, 1887.12, 1894.14, 1894.47, 1903.32
Perven, Alice 1929.16
Pery, Pnina 1969.13
Peryment, Pansey 1932.12
Pesce, Vince 1995.15, 1998.05, 1999.19
Pesnyary 1977.13
Pessagno, Rick 1979.05
Pessina, Carlo 1932.29
Pet Shop Boys 1991.04
Pet, Ella 1873.24
Petek, Marie 1949.11, 1949.13, 1949.14
Petell, Frank 1921.15
Peter Clark, Inc. 1928.25
Peter Neufeld, Ltd. 1988.09
Peter, Neil 1986.18
Peter, Rene 1908.36, 1925.41
Peterburski, J. 1931.09
Peterkin, Mr. 1894.15
Peters, Annie 1902.26
Peters, Bernadette 1959.02, 1968.07, 1969.16, 1971.15, 1974.18, 1984.08, 1985.12, 1987.18, 1993.02, 1999.04
Peters, Brandon 1924.25
Peters, Brock 1958.01, 1961.24, 1972.06
Peters, C. 1859.05, 1859.06
Peters, Catheryn 1912.38
Peters, Charles 1860.06, 1861.04, 1863.08, 1865.06, 1878.11, 1928.28, 1936.29
Peters, Clarence 1926.19
Peters, Clarke 1992.03
Peters, Elsie 1940.18
Peters, Frank 1891.28, 1892.35, 1894.36, 1895.30, 1896.09, 1896.11
Peters, Fred 1890.49, 1891.25, 1892.44, 1892.54, 1893.10, 1893.15, 1946.04
Peters, Fred W. 1880.21, 1881.10, 1888.27, 1888.40, 1891.45, 1895.35, 1896.39
Peters, Frederick W. 1893.42
Peters, Gordon 1952.01
Peters, Grace 1917.36
Peters, J.F. 1879.12, 1880.08, 1881.13, 1884.27, 1885.33, 1886.16, 1889.21
Peters, James F. 1882.77, 1884.10
Peters, Jean 1938.09
Peters, John 1932.16
Peters, Julius 1880.68
Peters, Lauri 1959.06, 1959.24
Peters, Lisa 1982.18
Peters, Louis 1892.59
Peters, Marie 1897.26
Peters, Mason 1905.56
Peters, Mesame 1856.04
Peters, Michael 1979.32, 1981.29, 1985.03, 1987.07
Peters, Miss 1841.01
Peters, Mr. 1855.11, 1856.04, 1857.05, 1857.07, 1875.03, 1875.06
Peters, Mrs. Charles 1896.15
Peters, Nettie 1894.51, 1904.45
Peters, Paul 1935.03, 1935.16
Peters, Phil 1894.51, 1904.45
Peters, Sadie 1900.48, 1900.55, 1902.43
Peters, Sean 1963.25
Peters, Theodore 1903.18, 1904.21, 1906.10
Peters, Theodore S. 1904.21
Peters, W.F. 1902.40, 1915.11
Peters, William F. 1902.23, 1902.34, 1902.40
Peters, William Frederic 1911.29
Peters, William Frederick 1903.19, 1905.53, 1913.10, 1913.37
Peterschen, F.W. 1864.22, 1865.05, 1865.07, 1865.08
Peterschen, Frank 1878.10
Peterschen, W.T. 1851.08, 1861.06, 1862.01, 1862.02
Petersen, Caleb 1943.10
Petersen, Nels 1946.03
Petersen, Taliep 1999.12
Peterson, Alan 1962.14, 1966.02, 1966.30, 1967.06
Peterson, Arleigh 1952.08
Peterson, Chris 1983.02, 1994.12, 1995.19, 1996.15, 1997.22, 1998.20, 1999.21, 2000.07, 2000.19
Peterson, Claudette 1982.21, 1983.13, 1985.10, 1986.10, 1987.08, 1987.11
Peterson, Curt 1924.39
Peterson, Elsa 1925.13
Peterson, Eric 1980.13
Peterson, Fay C. 1912.16
Peterson, Frankie 1897.15
Peterson, Gertie 1907.55
Peterson, Harry 1934.06, 1935.11, 1936.05, 1938.14
Peterson, Joan 1965.25
Peterson, Joe 1921.26
Peterson, Kirk 1990.17
Peterson, Kurt 1968.18, 1969.05, 1971.05
Peterson, LaMonte 1973.06
Peterson, Marjorie 1922.32, 1924.38, 1925.25, 1926.27, 1927.34, 1928.15, 1928.48, 1950.06
Peterson, Martha 1928.45
Peterson, Mr. 1859.01, 1866.11
Peterson, Nat 1927.13
Peterson, Ned 1981.19
Peterson, Patricia Ben 1995.11
Peterson, Sylvia 1927.14
Petgen, Dorothea 1933.24
Pethbridge, Nancy 1925.37
Pether, Henry E. 1905.27, 1914.18
Petina, Irra 1944.21, 1948.24, 1954.17, 1956.15, 1965.35
Petit, E. 1869.03
Petit, Kevin 1981.07
Petit, Madame 1841.01
Petit, Margaret 1920.08, 1921.27, 1922.21
Petit, Mons. 1868.26, 1869.05
Petit, Roland 1981.13
Petit, Ronald 1964.39
Petite, Claudia 1898.61
Petitto, Kevin 1991.06
Petkanas, Zachary 1995.19
Petkanas, Zachary Stefan 1996.15
Petkanas, Zoe 1997.22
Petkere, Bernice 1932.14, 1942.11
Petlak, Joan 1959.13
Petraitis, Peter 1929.17
Petrass, Sari 1916.19
Petrayer, Sophia 1912.29

Petri, Carol 1970.09, 1971.15
Petri, Frank 1968.03
Petri, Fraulein 1879.62
Petricoff, Elaine 1974.12
Petrides, Alex 1968.30
Petrie, George 1938.12, 1943.23
Petrie, H.W. 1894.21, 1894.31
Petrie, Mr. 1834.03
Petrie, Walter 1927.08, 1931.01
Petrizzo, Christopher Mark 1995.19, 1996.15
Petrizzo, Mark 1995.19
Petro, Marie 1884.58
Petroski, Adam 1972.06, 1976.19
Petrova, Olga 1911.39
Petrovitski, Olga 1928.04
Petrucci, Donalyn 1981.18
Petry, Else 1964.25
Petry, Gedda 1941.04, 1943.03, 1945.04
Pettes, Marie 1921.13, 1922.40, 1923.25
Pettie, Bob 1979.15
Pettie, Edna 1897.01
Pettie, Edna May 1896.33
Pettiford, Valarie 1985.05, 1986.06, 1999.01
Pettingill, Joe 1906.06
Pettis, Mary 1931.42
Pettit, Charles 1928.30
Pettit, Ethel 1916.22
Pettit, Henry 1880.34
Pettit, Miss 1885.07
Pettit, Tolie 1887.04, 1887.28, 1888.22, 1888.24, 1888.26, 1890.21
Pettitt, Henry 1881.35, 1889.54
Pettitt, Peggy 1991.01
Petty, Dan 1998.14
Petty, Norman 1990.15
Peurner, Charles 1879.42
Pevney, Joseph 1936.28
Pevney, Joseph C. 1942.26
Pevsner, David 1990.18
Peynaud, Brigitte 1958.18
Peyton, Caroline 1984.02
Peyton, Dave 1904.38
Peyton, Ethel 1907.58
Peyton, Jane 1901.15
Pezzone, Mme. 1870.15
Pezzulo, Mlle. 1876.20
Pezzuolo, Carlotta 1879.15
Pezzuolo, Mlle. 1876.28, 1878.18
Pfarr, Paul 1894.37
Pfeiffer, David 1990.13
Pfeiffer, Ed 1964.21
Pfeiffer, Edward 1954.12
Pfeiffer, Edward A. 1962.16
Pfeiffer, Jack 1940.16, 1949.06, 1955.25
Pflueger, Carl 1893.17, 1894.26
PGI Entertainment Company 1996.04
Phalan, Messr. 1855.06
Phaldon, Beverly 1934.06
Phalen, Robert 1970.04
Phalon, E.J. 1879.54
Pharoah, Prince 1893.23
Pharr, Kelsey 1945.08
Pharr, Walter 1928.08
Phatt, Amelia 1882.24, 1883.33
Phebe, Mlle. 1920.28
Phelan, Deborah 1982.06, 1983.11, 1985.19
Phelan, J. Randall 1918.03
Phelan, James 1904.25
Phelan, Michael 2000.11
Phelps, Dodo 1905.14
Phelps, Dwayne 1982.17
Phelps, Eleanor 1937.02, 1976.05
Phelps, Florine 1928.37, 1929.26
Phelps, George 1914.23
Phelps, Irene 1928.37, 1929.26
Phelps, Lee 1916.03
Phelps, Mae 1911.07
Phelps, Mrs. Edmund 1894.33, 1897.32
Phelps, Stowe 1950.15
Phelps, William 1907.22, 1937.11
Phifer, D'Arcy 1979.26
Philbin, Irma 1929.08
Philbrick, Will 1905.35, 1913.01, 1913.16, 1931.27
Philbrick, Will H. 1911.08, 1928.47, 1934.41, 1943.08
Philbrick, William 1907.19
Philbrick, William H. 1916.11
Philip Goatcher and Young 1889.26, 1889.36
Philip, Adolph 1894.10
Philip, James 1896.27
Philip, John 1952.11, 1957.01
Philip, Sol 1898.49
Philip, W.E. 1902.30
Philipp, Adolf 1907.35, 1907.45, 1910.26, 1913.21, 1914.07, 1915.19, 1915.21, 1920.37
Philipp, Paul 1915.21
Philippe, Mons. 1869.16, 1869.30
Philippe-Gerard, M. 1967.13, 1968.20
Philippi 1871.06
Philippo, P. 1884.58
Philippoteaux, Paul 1888.25
Philips, F.C. 1894.25
Philips, H.I. 1934.39
Philips, James 1932.23
Philips, Lloyd 1989.24
Philips, Mardi 1987.02
Philips, Marie 1903.09
Philips, Mary 1922.05, 1989.19
Philips, Mr. 1841.01
Philips, Phil 1928.47
Philistine, Gina 1999.15
Philliber, Johnny 1907.40
Phillip, B. 1871.25
Phillip, Laura 1882.01
Phillip, Mr. 1870.22
Phillipe, M. 1866.18
Phillipe, Mons. 1862.03, 1863.06, 1863.07, 1869.03, 1872.30, 1872.36, 1872.38
Phillipe-Gerard 1982.23
Phillipi, A. 1892.59
Phillipi, J. 1892.59
Phillippe, Mons. 1862.04
Phillippe, Mr. 1872.25
Phillipps, Adelaide 1880.12, 1880.45, 1880.48, 1880.53
Phillipps, H.B. 1867.25
Phillipps, Mathilde 1882.07, 1883.11, 1883.14
Phillips, A. 1880.08
Phillips, Adelaide 1898.46, 1900.02, 1900.04, 1900.20, 1900.51, 1902.19
Phillips, Agatha 1929.09
Phillips, Amy Jo 2001.06
Phillips, Andy 1989.24
Phillips, Arlene 1987.05, 1992.12, 1999.15
Phillips, Arte 1995.15, 1996.18, 1999.24
Phillips, B. 1871.23, 1871.24
Phillips, Barbara-Mae 1978.28
Phillips, Barney 1940.21
Phillips, Bessie 1895.40
Phillips, Charles B. 1889.34
Phillips, Charles H. 1888.16
Phillips, Darryl 1987.15
Phillips, Diane 1969.17
Phillips, Douglas 1929.51
Phillips, E.R. 1907.27
Phillips, Ed 1948.25
Phillips, Eddie 1949.08, 1950.17, 1953.07, 1955.08, 1957.07, 1960.19, 1966.13, 1966.14, 1973.11
Phillips, Edis 1930.36, 1931.44
Phillips, Edna 1905.38
Phillips, Edwin 1953.08
Phillips, Ethan 1992.17
Phillips, Fred 1925.25
Phillips, Gerald 1936.06
Phillips, Goff 1903.01, 1904.07
Phillips, Grattan 1886.10
Phillips, H.B. 1853.03, 1856.04, 1857.05, 1857.07
Phillips, H.I. 1921.18, 1921.27, 1923.37, 1931.21, 1934.01, 1934.19, 1934.42, 1941.03, 1950.12
Phillips, Harriet 1846.01
Phillips, Harry 1876.03, 1886.01
Phillips, Helen 1905.31, 1954.04
Phillips, Helena 1913.07
Phillips, Irving 1957.17
Phillips, J. 1881.26
Phillips, J.R. 1906.49
Phillips, James 1938.11, 1940.08, 1941.07, 1942.30
Phillips, James E. 1924.13
Phillips, Jeff 1976.08
Phillips, Joe 1929.28
Phillips, John 1908.41, 1975.04, 1976.16
Phillips, John M. 1996.10
Phillips, Joseph 1905.13, 1905.36, 1909.04, 1911.47, 1912.41, 1913.29, 1915.19
Phillips, Jr., Norman 1925.22
Phillips, Kris 1991.03, 1991.15
Phillips, L.C. 1934.20
Phillips, Laura 1926.22
Phillips, Laura Leclair 1885.54
Phillips, LeClaire 1868.19, 1868.22
Phillips, Lloyd 1990.17
Phillips, Lou Diamond 1996.05
Phillips, Lovell 1888.38, 1888.41, 1889.54
Phillips, Marci 1966.08
Phillips, Mardi 1986.11
Phillips, Marie 1903.09
Phillips, Marion 1918.25, 1922.12
Phillips, Marjorie 1927.52, 1974.25
Phillips, Mary 1927.52
Phillips, Mary Bracken 1972.07, 1972.19, 1992.05
Phillips, Mathilde 1882.10, 1883.15
Phillips, Miss 1848.01, 1886.38
Phillips, Mr. 1823.01, 1855.11
Phillips, Mrs. H.B. 1855.11, 1857.07
Phillips, Mrs. Norman 1925.22
Phillips, Murray 1927.64
Phillips, Nancie 1968.13
Phillips, Norma 1917.29
Phillips, Norman 1925.22
Phillips, Patricia 1991.05
Phillips, Peggy 1932.12
Phillips, Peter 1977.18
Phillips, Phil 1971.19
Phillips, Robin 1997.09
Phillips, Sam C. 1989.12
Phillips, Sian 1999.07
Phillips, Sidney 1916.23
Phillips, Stevie 1978.13, 1982.11, 1994.06
Phillips, Thomas 1932.24
Phillips, Tim 1981.15
Phillips, Walter A. 1896.15
Phillips, Will 1911.26, 1912.04
Phillips, William 1909.04
Phillips, William A. 1918.38
Phillis, Miss 1882.46
Philp, W.E. 1898.23
Philp, William 1895.29
Philp, William E. 1896.42, 1897.13, 1899.02, 1899.41, 1903.38
Philpot, Margaret 1918.04
Philpotts, Eden 1951.17
Phineas 1971.18
Phipps, Edmund 1893.44
Phipps, Nicholas 1952.11
Phister, Montgomery 1886.35
Phyllis, Mlle. 1917.26
Physioc and Company 1902.34
Physioc, Joseph 1894.40, 1895.17, 1895.24, 1896.01, 1896.52, 1897.30, 1897.46, 1897.47, 1898.60, 1899.03, 1899.27, 1899.29, 1899.34, 1900.36, 1900.41, 1900.52, 1901.15, 1902.07, 1903.25, 1903.34, 1904.19, 1905.23, 1917.23, 1918.04, 1918.16, 1919.06, 1920.10, 1920.27, 1920.42, 1924.20, 1926.04
Physioc, Joseph A. 1898.31
Physioc, Joseph Allen 1929.30
Piaf, Edith 1947.18, 1959.15, 1961.25, 1967.13, 1968.20, 1973.17, 1974.01, 1981.04, 1999.07
Pialras, Signor 1889.33
Pialras, Signora 1889.33
Piana, S. 1985.07
Piane, Carlo Delle 1964.03
Piani, Harry M. 1912.26
Piantadosi, Al 1909.28, 1910.33, 1912.14, 1917.23, 1920.07, 1974.09, 1975.22
Piat, Aurora 1902.44
Piatov, Sacha 1921.08
Piatov, Sascha 1912.44, 1920.03, 1920.26
Piatt, Aurora 1906.45, 1911.09
Piazza, Karina 1997.13
Piazza, Marguerite 1944.26, 1948.31, 1950.01
Piazzolla, Astor 1985.07, 1989.20, 1997.13, 1999.18
Picard, Nicole 1987.05
Picco, Mme. 1890.50
Pichette, Joseph 1965.31, 1968.18
Pichler, Elmer 1924.45
Pichler, Maria 1939.23, 1940.04
Picino, Miss 1886.16
Pickard, Alleyne 1912.44
Pickard, Alma 1917.09
Pickaros, Nettie 1876.03
Pickens, Helen 1934.42
Pickens, Jane 1934.42, 1936.17, 1940.12, 1949.16, 1951.22
Pickens, Patti 1934.42
Pickering, Lindsey 2000.19
Pickering, Mr. 1836.01
Pickering, Patrice 1981.26
Pickert, Rolly 1937.04
Pickert, Willis 1891.25, 1891.45, 1892.54, 1893.15, 1893.27, 1893.36, 1894.42
Pickett, G.W. 1898.78
Pickett, George W. 1903.08
Pickett, Lou Ann 1983.04
Pickford, Jack 1905.38
Pickford, Loren 1970.16
Pickford, Lotte 1905.38
Pickford, Mary 1905.38
Pickman, Kate 1878.04
Picon, Molly 1942.28, 1961.20, 1967.18
Picorri, John 1927.27
Picture, Kay 1934.18, 1936.26, 1938.13
Picus, Stan 1976.05
Pidgeon, Eugene 1998.06, 1999.11
Pidgeon, Walter 1925.05, 1959.22
Pidgin, Charles F. 1882.80
Piemontese, Renato 1985.14
Pieplow, John 1983.19
Pierce, Benson 1895.35
Pierce, Betty 1917.31, 1919.02, 1921.08
Pierce, Billy 1927.43
Pierce, Burton 1938.09
Pierce, Charlie 1919.16
Pierce, E. 1872.35, 1875.21
Pierce, Ed. M. 1880.41
Pierce, Edmund 1873.03
Pierce, Edna 1925.35
Pierce, G.A. 1896.30
Pierce, George 1908.21
Pierce, George E. 1903.26
Pierce, Gloria 1910.19
Pierce, Helen 1919.04
Pierce, J. 1885.14
Pierce, Jack 1946.12
Pierce, Jay 1979.02
Pierce, John 1911.17, 1930.43, 1931.09, 1937.15, 1938.12, 1942.17, 1942.21, 1942.22
Pierce, Lewis 1944.04, 1944.09, 1944.10, 1944.13, 1946.02, 1949.10, 1949.11, 1949.13, 1949.14
Pierce, Lizzie 1870.33
Pierce, Madge 1899.29, 1900.40, 1903.18, 1905.32
Pierce, Marion 1936.12, 1937.17
Pierce, Maxwell 1909.15
Pierce, Messr. 1871.04
Pierce, Paul 1938.07
Pierce, Verna 1997.17
Pierce, Wesley 1927.68, 1929.50, 1930.20
Piercy, Emily 1998.10
Pieret, Paul 1911.37
Pieri, I. 1888.42
Pieri, J. 1889.25
Pieri, John 1891.18, 1892.06, 1893.33
Pieri, Messr. 1888.42
Pierlot, Frances 1931.16
Pierlot, Francis 1927.27, 1938.11
Pierpont, George 1917.05
Pierpont, Laura 1931.09, 1943.23, 1948.18
Pierre, Alford 1943.24
Pierre, Christophe 1976.21
Pierre, Edna 1918.22, 1919.04
Pierre, Helen 1918.22
Pierre, Master 1879.30
Pierre, Oliver 1980.17
Pierre, Roberta 1932.23
Pierrepoint, Grace 1899.30
Pierrepont, Grace 1897.15, 1900.38
Pierrepont, Miss 1887.32
Pierret, Arlene 1994.12
Pierson, Arthur 1942.12, 1943.05, 1943.21
Pierson, Edward 1965.03, 1966.02, 1974.07, 1974.08, 1974.15, 1975.11, 1975.19
Pierson, Frank C. 1978.21, 1979.05
Pierson, Harold 1962.07, 1966.01, 1972.06, 1978.03
Pierson, Harry 1880.51, 1931.29
Pierson, John 1920.34
Pierson, Lulu 1875.21
Pierson, Miss 1883.47
Pierson, Robert 1947.02, 1947.21
Pierson, Thomas 1972.15, 1972.18, 1972.25, 1973.03, 1973.07
Pierson, Tom 1974.25
Piessert, E.S. 1884.10
Pietri, Frank 1962.24
Pietro, M. 1912.43
Piggee, Leonard 1987.07
Piggott, J.W. 1885.21
Pigliavento, Debra 1978.04, 1980.18
Pigliavento, Michele 1987.15, 1989.27, 1991.06, 1993.02
Pigott, Colin 1986.01
Pigott, J. Smyth 1909.01
Pigott, J.W. 1884.40, 1893.47
Pigott, R.S. 1902.12
Pigott, Robert S. 1899.06, 1900.47
Pike, Coreen 1977.01

Pike, Flora 1883.02
Pike, Flora M. 1882.04, 1882.20, 1883.17
Pike, G.W. 1885.53
Pike, Harry E. 1888.45
Pike, Katherine M. 1891.34
Pike, M. 1860.02
Pike, M.B. 1864.04, 1867.31, 1870.05, 1872.27
Pike, Maurice 1875.05, 1879.02, 1884.04, 1884.07
Pike, Maurice B. 1867.22, 1867.23, 1867.26, 1867.27
Pike, Mr. 1859.01, 1859.04, 1861.01
Piland, Jeanne 1974.07, 1974.15, 1976.31
Pilati, M. 1852.02
Pilbrow, Richard 1964.32, 1968.30, 1970.15, 1973.03, 1993.08, 1994.08, 1997.08
Pilcer, Elsie 1914.16
Pilcer, Harry 1907.61, 1911.26, 1911.43, 1912.09, 1913.05, 1914.10, 1915.31, 1922.05
Pilkenton, Pamela 1971.04, 1976.27
Pilla, Candida 1963.22
Pillard, Etta 1923.25
Pillard, H. 1908.21
Pillet 1875.05
Pillet, Messr. 1875.18
Pillich, William 1942.20
Pillick, Bill 1937.06
Pillot, Jonathan 1994.01
Pillow, Miss 1863.01
Pills-Tabet 1935.19
Pilot, Genevieve 1965.29
Pilotell 1881.36, 1882.17, 1889.49
Pilotell, George 1881.07, 1885.40
Pilotell, Georges 1886.50, 1887.33, 1888.02
Pils, Jacques 1935.19
Pilzer, Dorothy 1927.24
Pimlott, Stephen 1993.15
Pinaud, Ixoria 1900.56, 1901.12
Pinch, Mr. 1873.26
Pinchot, Bronson 1999.20
Pinchot, Rosamund 1937.01
Pincus, Henry 1903.19, 1906.23, 1907.23
Pincus, Irvin 1934.36, 1940.06
Pincus, Russell 1908.09
Pincus, Warren 1981.03, 1982.05
Pincusoff, Reva 1972.08
Pindar, Vera 1906.29
Pinder, Thelma 1914.34
Pine, Dottie 1892.34
Pine, Miss 1855.11
Pinel, Loly 1958.06
Pinelli, Tullio 1966.01, 1969.16, 1982.09, 1986.07
Pinero, Arthur Wing 1919.02
Pines, Andrea 1994.01
Pingeon, Mlle. 1870.45
Pink, Wal 1922.05
Pinkard, Fred 1968.08
Pinkard, Maceo 1922.44, 1927.32, 1928.25, 1929.21, 1948.13, 1976.04, 1980.10, 1989.06
Pinkey, Louis M. 1929.29
Pinkham, Daniel 1957.02
Pinkham, H.T. 1909.15, 1909.31
Pinkham, William 1912.12, 1921.18
Pinkins, Tonya 1981.27, 1992.08, 1995.09, 1997.03, 2000.08
Pinkney, Mikell 1981.15
Pinkus, Bobby 1927.19
Pinney, George 2001.04
Pinnick, Eric 2000.19
Pinnock, Tommy 1969.09
Pinsuti, Carlo 1876.11
Pintel, Jacques 1930.36
Pinto, Dorothea 1948.28
Pinto, Lynn C. 1998.03
Pinto, Thea 1940.10
Pintus, Oded 1972.17
Pinza, Ezio 1949.04, 1954.15
Pinzon, Juan 1988.15
Pinzuti, Mlle. 1870.44, 1871.27
Pio Ulsky, Konstantin 1965.35
Piontek, Michael 1989.24
Piper, John 1948.31, 1956.13
Piper, Messr. 1911.18
Piperno, Mons. 1868.27
Piperti, Herr 1866.33
Pipes, Jeemes 1869.42
Pipiu, Arlindo 1992.13
Pipley, Messr. 1889.01
Pippin, Don 1955.04, 1963.01, 1963.26, 1964.04, 1964.33, 1966.10, 1969.05, 1970.09, 1973.06, 1974.18, 1975.15, 1978.28, 1979.02, 1979.13, 1979.28, 1980.09, 1980.18, 1981.10, 1982.06, 1983.10, 1983.11, 1985.19, 1987.16, 1987.19, 1988.04, 1991.14, 1993.19
Pippin, Donald 1997.05
Piquer, Conchita 1921.39, 1922.15
Piquet, Rolf 1921.38
Pirard, Mary 1887.36, 1887.37
Piri, Irene 1935.11
Pirkle, Mac 1997.05
Pirnikoff, Sergei 1923.22
Piron, Armand J. 1975.09
Pirosch, R. 1947.05
Piroshe, Robert 1948.12
Pisarski, Bernie 1946.13
Pistone, Charles 1985.17, 1992.01
Pita, Arthur 1998.10
Pitchford, Dean 1979.11, 1988.12, 1998.13
Pitchon, Jack 1946.13
Pitkin, Robert 1910.10, 1912.35, 1913.34, 1915.28, 1921.27, 1922.43, 1925.34, 1940.08, 1942.02, 1942.04, 1942.06, 1942.07, 1942.08, 1942.09, 1944.04, 1944.05, 1944.06, 1944.08, 1944.09, 1944.10, 1944.11, 1944.12, 1944.13, 1947.03
Pitkin, Robert G. 1908.05, 1911.03, 1911.37, 1913.02, 1914.30, 1915.17, 1917.17, 1918.11, 1921.11, 1927.10, 1929.46, 1930.23
Pitkin, William 1961.02, 1963.22, 1964.31, 1965.25
Pitney, Gene 1984.15
Pitot, Genevieve 1933.12, 1948.14, 1948.32, 1949.08, 1949.12, 1950.06, 1950.15, 1950.20, 1951.19, 1952.02, 1952.20, 1953.07, 1956.05, 1956.07, 1956.12, 1958.01, 1959.11, 1959.27, 1961.20, 1962.13, 1963.12, 1963.29, 1965.18, 1989.03
Pitou, Augustus 1885.53, 1886.44, 1886.51, 1888.12, 1889.03, 1889.14, 1889.48, 1890.06, 1891.06, 1891.07, 1891.28, 1894.20, 1894.32, 1894.36, 1895.30, 1896.09, 1896.11, 1897.05, 1898.43, 1899.01, 1900.10, 1901.02, 1902.36, 1904.02, 1905.38, 1906.38, 1907.56, 1910.06, 1911.04, 1912.06, 1915.03
Pitou, Jr., Augustus 1915.03
Pitron, Elisa 1858.01
Pitsch, Frl. 1897.08
Pitt, Charles D. 1921.38
Pitt, Clara 1903.03, 1908.25, 1910.21
Pitt, Emily 1869.17, 1869.21, 1869.25, 1869.28, 1870.02, 1870.06, 1870.14
Pitt, George Dibdin 1924.20
Pitt, Hedy 1939.23
Pitt, Mary 1869.11, 1869.17, 1869.21, 1869.25, 1869.28
Pitt, Merle 1942.11
Pitt, Mily 1869.11
Pitt, Miss 1841.01, 1903.03
Pitt, Susan 1908.10
Pitt, Susie 1908.44, 1909.07
Pitteri, Jean 1872.37
Pitteri, Mlle. 1873.08
Pixley, Alice 1893.37
Pixley, Annie 1883.05, 1883.07, 1887.17, 1887.46, 1892.17, 1892.58
Pixley, Frank 1900.51, 1900.59, 1902.05, 1902.18, 1902.22, 1903.10, 1904.16, 1904.52, 1905.13, 1905.16, 1906.16, 1907.13, 1907.17, 1908.30, 1912.42, 1930.01
Pixley, Gus 1893.37, 1894.21, 1898.01, 1903.31
Pixley, Lucie 1887.18
Pixley, Lucy 1889.17
Pizzarelli, Bucky 1983.20
Pizzarelli, John 1997.05
Pizzarelli, Martin 1997.05
Pizzarello, Louis 1884.58
Pizzaro, Al 1921.26
Pizzi, Joey 1994.01, 1997.09, 2001.02
Pizzicato 1922.21
Place, Eliza 1860.01
Placide, Henry 1834.02
Placide, Thomas 1834.02
Pladgett, Tommy 1931.02
Plain Jane, Inc. 1924.10
Plainsted, T.S. 1886.50
Plainville, Mons. 1868.27
Plaisted 1878.10, 1880.37
Plaisted, T.H. 1890.11, 1891.17
Plaisted, T.S. 1886.04, 1886.30, 1889.16, 1889.40, 1889.49, 1890.26, 1891.31
Plana, Tony 1979.08
Planche, Helen 1903.37
Planche, J.R. 1882.60, 1883.37
Planche, James Robinson 1834.02, 1855.10, 1857.07, 1859.07, 1860.03, 1863.03, 1863.04, 1864.12, 1866.04, 1866.08, 1867.15, 1870.44, 1872.16, 1873.10
Plank, Scott 1981.29
Planquete 1888.36
Planquette 1884.42, 1886.47, 1894.19, 1899.23
Planquette, Charles 1879.27
Planquette, Robert 1877.36, 1878.08, 1878.16, 1879.24, 1879.40, 1879.64, 1880.50, 1881.05, 1881.41, 1881.51, 1882.08, 1882.36, 1882.58, 1882.75, 1883.60, 1884.32, 1884.57, 1885.19, 1885.38, 1889.29, 1890.33, 1892.08, 1892.10, 1893.21, 1896.20, 1896.46, 1898.07, 1898.74, 1900.09, 1901.11, 1902.13, 1911.03, 1916.18, 1926.45, 1931.41
Plant, Mark 1935.14, 1936.06, 1939.24
Plantadit-Bageot, Karine 1999.15
Plante, Jacques 1959.15, 1961.25, 1965.30, 1970.01, 1974.19, 1983.03
Plante, Oscar 1945.08
Plaskow, II., Merrill 1976.36
Plate, Henry 1884.51
Plater, B. 1999.24
Plato, Dessario 1896.46
Platoff, Barbara 1978.18
Platonoff, Mme. 1922.37
Platt, C.H. 1866.12
Platt, Ed. B. 1901.07
Platt, Edward 1942.02, 1942.09, 1947.17, 1949.17, 1958.02
Platt, George 1964.32
Platt, George Foster 1906.50
Platt, Jon B. 1990.20, 1991.13, 1994.01
Platt, Livingston 1924.22, 1924.32, 1925.09, 1925.36, 1926.02, 1926.12, 1927.38, 1928.21
Platt, Marc 1942.01, 1942.29, 1943.04, 1953.02
Platt, Maxwell 1927.40
Platt, Victoria Gabrielle 1992.08
Platt, William 1904.20, 1907.61
Platt, William H. 1905.53
Platte, Henry 1885.28
Platti, E. 1884.63
Platts, Ronald 1961.24
Platzer 1908.43
Platzer and Dodge 1907.47
Platzer and Meixner 1905.41
Platzer, Frank 1897.29, 1909.18
Platzner, Frank 1906.19
Plautus 1962.12, 1972.03, 1981.25
Play-Arts Guild, Inc., The 1928.20
Playhouse Square Center 1991.05
Playova, Helen 1944.26
Playten, Alice 1963.01, 1964.01, 1967.14, 2000.18
Playwrights Horizons 1984.08, 1990.12, 2000.01
Plaza, A. 1985.07
Plaza, J. 1997.13, 1999.18
Pleasant, David 1999.22
Pleasant, Edward 2000.03
Pleasant, Powers 1999.22
Pleasants, Gloria 1924.32
Pleasants, Maude 1907.43
Pleininger, Carl 1896.34, 1898.53
Plenaro Productions 1998.02
Pleon, Harry 1900.47
Pleshette, John 1965.32
Plews, Miss 1882.46
Plimpton, Shelley 1968.11
Plohn, Edmond 1920.32
Plotkin, Tom 1998.13, 2000.18
Plotnikoff, Eugene 1922.37
Pluesch 1991.11
Plum Productions 1975.15
Plumador, Evelyn 1922.35
Plumby, Don 1964.39
Plumer, Lincoln 1911.41
Plumer, Mrs. 1839.01
Plumley, Don 1970.04
Plummer, Beatrice 1935.02
Plummer, Christopher 1973.07
Plummer, E.T. 1929.17
Plummer, Earl T. 1929.17
Plummer, Philip 1888.31
Plumpton, Alfred 1896.31
Plunket, Maryann 1986.12
Plunkett, Ada 1852.07
Plunkett, Albert 1921.12
Plunkett, Blanche 1896.28
Plunkett, Charles 1885.14, 1885.45, 1885.52, 1888.02, 1889.24, 1890.26, 1891.31, 1891.47, 1898.72
Plunkett, Florence 1905.46
Plunkett, H. 1860.04
Plunkett, J.H. 1899.21
Plunkett, James 1896.14
Plunkett, Joseph 1896.14
Plunkett, M.W. 1921.12
Plunkett, Morley 1921.12
Plunkett, Paul 1913.36
Plunkett, William 1905.23, 1929.50
Plymale, Trip 1976.30
Pober, Leon 1960.01
Pobers, Tatiana 1943.11
Pockriss, Lee 1951.23, 1963.08
Pockriss, Lee J. 1952.05
Poddubiuk, Christina 1997.09
Podell, Rick 1972.21
Podrecca, Lia 1932.29, 1934.02, 1940.05
Podrecca, Vittorio 1923.29, 1932.29, 1934.02, 1940.05
Poe, Aileen 1919.35, 1920.25, 1927.18, 1937.04, 1964.21
Poe, Edgar Allen 1923.31
Poe, Eileen 1930.35
Poe, Richard 1997.15, 2001.06
Poe, Virginia 1945.20, 1953.01
Poelz, Edward 1895.35
Pogany, Bella 1925.29
Pogany, Will 1925.40
Pogany, Willy 1917.12, 1917.26, 1919.35, 1924.39, 1925.25, 1925.48, 1926.25, 1928.49, 1930.04
Pogany-Teichner Studios 1925.35
Pogee, Mariay 1979.22
Pogrebin, Abby 1981.27
Pogue, David 1989.07
Pohl, Emil 1884.40
Pohl, Harry 1930.09
Pohl, Richard 1910.31
Pohs, Milton 1919.26
Poindexter, H.R. 1970.16, 1971.08, 1972.03, 1976.33
Poindexter, Karen 1985.17, 1989.25
Poindexter, Rose 1928.18
Pointing, Audrey 1928.42
Poir, Marjorie 1917.29
Poiret, Jean 1983.11
Poiret, Paul 1920.03, 1920.41, 1922.33, 1922.45, 1923.10, 1925.41
Poirot, Mons. 1886.22
Poirte, Paul 1923.26
Poisson 1882.62, 1886.41
Poisson, Mons. 1875.21
Pokrass, Samuel 1934.01
Pola, Edward 1929.50
Polacek, Lou 1961.20
Polacek, Louis 1953.16, 1955.02, 1956.04, 1957.07, 1958.02, 1960.10
Polacheck, Charles 1941.01
Polachek, Leon 1908.11
Polah, Andre 1939.21
Polaire, Mlle. 1913.28
Polajenko, Nicolai 1947.14
Polakov, Lester 1941.03, 1946.10
Poland, Albert 1993.04
Poland, Edward 1899.08
Poland, Pllie 1881.52
Polcsa, Juliet 1992.05
Poldine, Leo 1930.18
Poldini 1922.21
Pole, Rupert 1941.01
Poleri, David 1954.18, 1959.08
Poli, Lillian 1909.22
Poliakova, Yelena 1931.38
Polinsky, Leon 1937.15
Polito, Jon 1982.02
Polito, Philip 1969.06
Polizos, Vic 1979.05
Polk, Gordon 1956.16
Polk, Julia 1880.54, 1881.03
Polk, Oscar 1932.05, 1933.02, 1935.01, 1939.29, 1941.12
Poll, Martin 1943.16
Polla, W.C. 1906.09, 1955.13
Polla, William C. 1905.22
Pollac, Muriel 1936.12
Pollack, Ernest E. 1919.08

Pollack, Lew 1920.47, 1921.02, 1921.25, 1923.18, 1924.19, 1942.01, 1975.22, 1990.16
Pollack, Max 1951.21
Pollack, Muriel 1936.12
Pollak, Martha 1966.21
Pollard, Alice 1922.05
Pollard, Daphne 1908.44, 1915.11, 1923.31
Pollard, Harry 1919.06
Pollard, Marion 1917.32
Pollard, Michael J. 1960.06
Pollard, Robert 1896.13, 1897.10, 1898.13
Poller, Frederick 1944.17
Pollitt, Barbara 1992.08, 1996.16
Pollock, A.M. 1905.52
Pollock, Allan 1913.27
Pollock, Anita 1909.14
Pollock, Cecilia 1892.25
Pollock, Channing 1911.24, 1911.41, 1912.31, 1913.27, 1914.13, 1915.15, 1917.32, 1921.21, 1953.12, 1964.22, 1976.16
Pollock, Emma 1890.49, 1891.25, 1891.45, 1892.44, 1892.54, 1893.10, 1893.15, 1893.27, 1893.36, 1893.46, 1894.49, 1895.05
Pollock, Evelyn 1891.25
Pollock, Frank 1898.25, 1909.23, 1910.24, 1912.40, 1913.09, 1913.25, 1916.05
Pollock, Horace 1927.65
Pollock, Lew 1921.20
Pollock, Mabel 1889.46
Pollock, Michael 1953.05, 1953.14, 1954.14, 1955.17, 1956.09, 1956.10, 1957.13, 1958.09, 1958.16, 1959.16, 1959.21, 1963.12
Pollock, Milt 1904.34
Pollock, Milton 1909.19
Pollock, Muriel 1923.07, 1927.08, 1928.35, 1929.09, 1931.21
Pollock, Paul 1916.18
Pollock, Percy 1919.33
Pollock, Robert 1921.24
Polosova, Nina 1925.46
Polseno, Robin 1977.12, 1992.07
Polson, Vernal 1979.32
Poltz, Carolyn 1903.04
Poltz, Carrie 1904.15, 1909.23, 1910.13
Poltz, Florrie 1909.23, 1910.13
Poltz, Nellie 1909.23
Polygram Broadway Ventures, Inc. 1995.15
Polygram Diversified Entertainment 1992.08
Polynach, Mary 1946.11
Pomerantz, John J. 1983.11, 1983.14, 1983.19, 1984.01, 1985.05, 1985.19
Pomeranz, David 1991.10
Pomeroy, Annie 1895.44
Pomeroy, George S. 1943.23
Pomeroy, Grace 1903.03
Pomeroy, Miss 1903.03
Pomohac, Bruce 1982.02, 1989.23, 1996.04
Pompianov, Mischa 1934.41, 1936.12
Pomroy, Miss 1880.69
Pomus, Doc 1978.01, 1989.12, 1992.06, 1995.03
Ponazecki, Joe 1964.27, 1976.33
Ponce 1942.19
Ponce, Dan 2001.04
Ponce, Manual M. 1931.09
Ponce, Phil 1918.08, 1955.13
Ponch, Mack 1926.05
Ponchielli 1905.17
Ponchielli, A. 1921.28
Ponchielli, Amilcare 1956.11
Pond, Harry 1911.05
Pond, Helen 1962.13, 1963.30, 1964.05, 1968.19, 1971.17, 1982.16, 1983.05, 1983.12, 1985.11, 1986.19, 1988.14
Pondel, John 1989.08
Poni, Tim 1918.12
Ponisi, Elizabeth 1851.01, 1855.10, 1856.02
Ponisi, Miss 1852.05
Ponisi, Mme. 1852.01, 1854.01, 1855.01, 1859.01, 1870.05, 1875.14
Pons, Christ. 1894.01
Pons, Christian 1893.29
Pons, Helene 1930.25, 1932.13, 1933.04, 1937.04, 1952.04, 1958.17, 1961.18
Pons, Messr. 1922.06
Pontier, A. 1997.13
Pontier, Armando 1985.07
Pontillo, Larry P. 1980.11
Ponting, Audrey 1929.41
Ponting, David 1995.07
Ponzoni, Carlotta 1855.02
Pool, John 1961.16
Pool, Larry 1968.24
Pool, Lawrence 1961.28
Poole, Alice Maude 1903.02, 1904.34
Poole, Clara 1881.05
Poole, Ed 1924.47
Poole, John F. 1870.04, 1873.04, 1873.20, 1873.22, 1873.27, 1875.39, 1876.03, 1876.34, 1884.40
Poole, Maude 1898.74, 1900.57
Poole, Miss 1877.15, 1903.03
Poole, Mr. 1887.10
Poole, Mrs. Charles 1878.14, 1879.50, 1885.46
Poole, Nancy 1903.03, 1904.44, 1909.14
Poole, Patricia 1951.17
Poole, Richard 1983.10
Poole, Roy 1969.06
Poole, Tennye 1893.20
Poole, Wakefield 1960.09, 1962.03, 1965.06, 1981.07
Pooley, Bill 1906.06
Pooley, Ed. 1905.28
Pooley, Edward 1901.21, 1906.39, 1921.34
Poore, Minnie 1893.43, 1897.31, 1898.50, 1899.17, 1899.30
Poot, H.A. 1900.50
Poot, Harry 1901.14
Pope and Bradley 1916.16
Pope, Bessie 1890.03, 1895.08
Pope, C. 1854.01
Pope, Cathleen 1912.13, 1916.15
Pope, Mr. 1852.01
Pope, Peggy 1975.09
Pope, Robert 1946.08
Pope, Stephanie 1992.08, 1996.06
Pope, W.H. 1867.20, 1868.19, 1868.22, 1881.31
Pope. Bill 1954.15
Pope. Glen 1939.16
Popikoff, Don 1937.15
Poplaski, William 1980.04, 1980.25, 1981.21, 1982.20, 1989.14
Popoff, V. 1929.05
Popova, Nina 1944.24, 1947.14, 1954.12
Popp, Andre 1960.13, 1965.08
Popp, Ron 1989.11
Popp, Wilhelm 1964.25
Poppell, Jack 1984.05
Poppen, Detmar 1906.49, 1911.09, 1916.04, 1921.40, 1922.36, 1925.15, 1925.31, 1928.12, 1929.34, 1929.36, 1929.40, 1931.33, 1931.35, 1931.41, 1931.43, 1931.45, 1933.17, 1934.12, 1934.38, 1942.17, 1943.06
Popper, Felix 1961.03, 1961.06, 1961.23, 1962.09, 1962.11, 1964.08, 1964.12, 1965.09, 1968.09, 1968.10, 1968.12, 1968.14, 1968.15
Popper, Lila 1954.01, 1957.17
Popwell, Albert 1946.24, 1948.14, 1956.02, 1957.05, 1958.01, 1959.27, 1964.32, 1965.20
Porcasi, P. Paul 1916.25
Porcasi, Paul 1918.35, 1920.42
Porcher, Nananne 1964.19, 1971.02, 1975.19
Pordum, Herbert 1964.07, 1964.12
Poretta, Frank 1959.08, 1959.17, 1959.18, 1959.21, 1960.02, 1960.14, 1960.15, 1961.03, 1961.04, 1961.05, 1961.06, 1961.19, 1961.23, 1963.24, 1964.23, 1964.24, 1968.09, 1968.12, 1968.14
Porfiriewa, E. 1924.48, 1932.09
Porgina, Ludmilla 1990.01
Porray, Edmund J. 1919.16
Porretta, Matthew 1994.05
Porta-Povitch 1927.45
Porte, Pierre 1984.10
Portello, W.H. 1878.15
Porteous, Gilbert 1895.43
Porter, Agnes 1904.33
Porter, Alfred 1944.16, 1944.24
Porter, Almeda 1905.13
Porter, Arthur 1921.16, 1925.18, 1930.10, 1935.01
Porter, Arthur D. 1923.39
Porter, B. 1892.34
Porter, B.C. 1864.22
Porter, Billy 1994.07
Porter, Carl 1914.17, 1914.33
Porter, Cathy 1992.12
Porter, Cole 1915.16, 1915.25, 1916.06, 1919.25, 1920.03, 1924.32, 1928.33, 1929.45, 1929.51, 1930.35, 1930.40, 1932.26, 1934.36, 1935.14, 1936.26, 1938.07, 1938.13, 1939.30, 1940.19, 1941.08, 1943.01, 1943.05, 1944.02, 1944.29, 1946.13, 1948.13, 1948.32, 1950.20, 1952.02, 1953.07, 1953.12, 1955.02, 1955.19, 1956.02, 1956.05, 1962.13, 1963.10, 1965.18, 1967.11, 1967.13, 1968.19, 1968.20, 1975.22, 1976.32, 1980.06, 1980.10, 1981.13, 1981.16, 1984.10, 1987.15, 1988.08, 1992.18, 1995.12, 1997.01, 1998.05, 1999.01, 1999.05, 1999.07, 1999.19, 1999.23
Porter, David 1977.09, 1997.21
Porter, Del 1930.05, 1930.31
Porter, E.M. 1881.24
Porter, Ellis 1927.15
Porter, Gregory 1999.09
Porter, Howard 1975.21, 1984.09
Porter, J.T. 1907.22
Porter, Katharine 1928.49
Porter, Marguerite 1998.10
Porter, Messr. 1888.10
Porter, Miss 1905.25
Porter, Mr. 1887.03
Porter, Paul 1910.09, 1912.14, 1925.19, 1925.40
Porter, Paul W. 1926.22
Porter, Richard 1959.13
Porter, Richard L. 1980.04
Porter, Robert 1880.41
Porter, Stan 1967.03
Porter, Steve 1895.22, 1896.25
Porter, W. 1882.62
Porter, W. Ellis 1991.03
Porter, W.T. 1886.16
Porter, William 1896.49
Porter, Willie 1927.30
Porterfield, Robert 1938.18
Portillo, Rose 1979.08
Portland, Miss 1854.07
Portlette, Ricardo 1973.17, 1975.12
Portlock, Philip 1898.78
Portnoff, Mischa 1950.01, 1950.19
Portnoff, Wesley 1950.01, 1950.19
Portnoy, Gary 1983.17
Portois, Leoni 1866.18
Portois, Mlle. 1866.18
Posemkowski, Georges 1922.37
Posen, Al 1927.11
Poser, Linda 1980.30, 1981.12
Poskitt, J.H. 1894.15
Posnak, Charles 1932.19
Posner, Kenneth 1998.15, 1999.03, 1999.24, 2001.06
Posner, Lee 1932.08
Posner, Mae 1918.12
Post, E.M. 1886.58
Post, F.J. 1875.05
Post, Guy Bates 1912.03
Post, L. Michael 1997.05
Post, Leo 1922.30
Post, Lillie 1882.15, 1882.16, 1884.51
Post, Lilly 1882.47, 1883.45, 1884.08, 1885.05, 1885.28, 1885.67, 1890.14, 1890.15, 1890.28, 1890.46, 1890.47, 1892.16
Post, Lily 1882.42, 1882.52, 1882.71, 1887.04
Post, Mary E. 1900.47
Post, Messr. 1892.53
Post, Mr. 1856.02, 1856.03, 1863.07, 1864.07
Post, Mrs. E.M. 1870.20, 1872.19
Post, Mrs. Sylvester 1877.08
Post, Ralph 1892.48, 1892.53, 1907.42
Post, W.H. 1897.45, 1901.30, 1913.16, 1916.05, 1918.29, 1919.14, 1921.09, 1925.32, 1926.03, 1927.65
Post, William H. 1902.10
Poster, Kim 1989.26
Poston, Tom 1961.02
Postrel, Leo 1979.27
Potamkin, Victor 1976.21
Potamkin, Victor H. 1973.09, 1990.16
Poterat, Louis 1948.12, 1964.02
Potfora, Eve 1987.16
Poth, Mai 1919.38, 1920.34
Pothier, Charles 1932.04
Potter, Ailene 1903.03
Potter, Aline 1900.51, 1902.19
Potter, Almeda 1905.52, 1907.11, 1908.07
Potter, Don 1974.17, 1979.28, 1990.20, 1991.13
Potter, Edward 1934.06, 1934.40
Potter, Helen 1898.58
Potter, Homer 1908.07
Potter, Jack 1912.31
Potter, L.S. 1900.43
Potter, Lois 1945.16
Potter, Mabel 1891.17, 1891.22, 1891.36, 1892.16, 1892.28, 1894.38, 1896.06, 1896.18
Potter, Mick 1999.15
Potter, Miss 1889.31
Potter, Paul 1897.48, 1908.27
Potter, Paul M. 1890.07, 1890.34, 1891.04, 1891.43, 1892.36, 1893.28, 1894.39, 1895.17, 1895.42, 1904.29, 1908.42, 1913.02
Potter, Philip 1962.26, 1962.28, 1962.29, 1962.31, 1964.37, 1964.41, 1964.42, 1966.22, 1966.23, 1966.28, 1968.27, 1968.28, 1978.17, 1989.15
Potter, S. 1894.33, 1894.46
Potter, Shirley 1969.17
Potter, Violet 1895.38, 1896.35, 1897.52
Pottier, Pedro 1988.06
Pottle, Sam 1968.13, 1970.10
Potts, Evelyn 1979.10
Potts, Homer 1915.32
Potts, Nancy 1968.11, 1969.16, 1971.16, 1972.02, 1976.28, 1977.15, 1978.23, 1979.26, 1979.27, 1982.02, 1982.10, 1983.04, 2000.03
Potts, P.O. 1918.38
Poulette, J.H. 1882.59
Pounds, Courtice 1885.47, 1886.55, 1886.57, 1887.10, 1887.33, 1887.50, 1905.04, 1914.04
Pounds, Lillie 1895.43
Pounds, Louie 1895.43, 1909.21
Poundwell, Mr. 1862.02
Pourmel, Adda 1944.21
Povey, Messr. 1844.01
Povia, Charlotte 1962.21, 1963.22, 1963.24, 1964.12, 1964.30, 1965.07, 1965.27, 1966.02, 1966.17
Povinelli, Mark 1998.06
Povitch, Porta 1927.45
Powell Rae 1931.28
Powell, Alvy 2000.03
Powell, Andrew 1991.11
Powell, Anthony 1994.10, 2001.06
Powell, Bertha 1933.04, 1943.10, 1947.13
Powell, Charles B. 1894.38
Powell, Dawn 1942.01
Powell, E. Soldene 1894.07, 1913.04
Powell, Eddie 1933.22
Powell, Edward 1897.05, 1932.17, 1932.25, 1933.05, 1933.20, 1933.25, 1934.15
Powell, Edward B. 1932.18
Powell, Eleanor 1928.04, 1929.03, 1930.13, 1930.28, 1932.07, 1932.24, 1935.12
Powell, Felix 1978.05, 1991.04
Powell, Frederick 1910.19
Powell, George 1964.28
Powell, H. 1867.20, 1868.22
Powell, Helen 1932.08
Powell, Jack 1929.29, 1931.40
Powell, James 1885.70
Powell, Jane 1995.18
Powell, Janet 1971.12, 1978.21
Powell, Jerry 1968.13, 1979.15
Powell, Jill 1988.04
Powell, Josef 1995.12
Powell, Jr., Jack 1943.23
Powell, Kathryn 1899.26
Powell, Lester 1897.38
Powell, Mabel 1904.44
Powell, Mable 1904.44
Powell, Michael 1973.17, 1975.12, 1980.14, 1982.17
Powell, Miss 1917.31
Powell, Ray 1976.18
Powell, Richard 1927.03, 1929.34, 1929.36, 1929.38, 1929.47
Powell, Russell 1913.32
Powell, Shannon 1990.19
Powell, Sheldon 1966.15
Powell, Shezwae 1978.03
Powell, Susan 1987.09
Powell, Thomas 1952.12, 1954.10, 1955.17
Powell, Thomas R. 1954.04, 1954.06
Powell, W.C. 1903.24
Powen, Mollie 1882.49
Power, Delia 1886.10
Power, Mabel 1895.27, 1896.52
Power, Miss 1841.01, 1882.45
Power, Mollie M. 1884.12
Power, Stella 1929.29
Power, Tyrone 1892.14, 1892.36, 1892.56, 1917.24
Power, W.H. 1882.69, 1886.10

Power, William H. 1927.37
Powers, Andrew 1897.15
Powers, Andrew J. 1891.32
Powers, Arthur Augustus 1897.37
Powers, Bill 1936.06
Powers, Clyde 1906.46, 1907.54
Powers, Eleanor 1931.02
Powers, Frank 1879.04
Powers, Geoffrey 1937.08
Powers, George 1879.09, 1880.15, 1881.55, 1908.20, 1917.16
Powers, Georgia 1897.11
Powers, Howard 1891.24
Powers, J.H. 1904.47
Powers, James 1888.20, 1897.15
Powers, James H. 1891.32
Powers, James T. 1880.42, 1882.03, 1882.39, 1883.26, 1886.28, 1887.33, 1887.50, 1889.04, 1889.40, 1889.49, 1891.03, 1892.05, 1893.06, 1896.05, 1896.33, 1897.20, 1897.44, 1898.18, 1898.26, 1898.29, 1898.46, 1900.28, 1900.43, 1901.19, 1903.06, 1903.21, 1904.03, 1905.18, 1906.41, 1909.04, 1912.17, 1913.09, 1921.01, 1923.01, 1931.35
Powers, Joel 1975.07
Powers, John R. 1982.10
Powers, Kate 1892.07
Powers, Kitty 1895.07
Powers, Leona 1938.01
Powers, Lou 1928.27
Powers, Louis 1900.08, 1902.02
Powers, Louis N. 1898.02
Powers, Mabel 1901.01
Powers, Mae 1893.01, 1893.22
Powers, Manila 1928.48, 1930.07
Powers, Manilla 1927.58, 1931.27
Powers, Marie 1947.10, 1948.29, 1950.05, 1957.11
Powers, Maude 1927.38
Powers, Messr. 1883.17, 1883.23
Powers, Nancy 1966.24
Powers, Neva Rae 1978.22, 1979.22
Powers, Stella 1930.17
Powers, Theresa 1907.01
Powers, Thomas E. 1888.39
Powers, Tom 1917.06, 1921.35, 1944.15
Powers, Tony 1984.15
Powers, V. 1908.19
Powers, Vicki 1968.01
Powers, W.H. 1907.24, 1919.34
Powers, William 1897.15, 1908.19, 1909.13, 1909.25
Powers, William J. 1891.32
Powers, William V. 1925.47, 1928.08
Powlett, Shareen 1991.01
Pownall, Mrs. 1793.01
Powys, Stephen 1940.09
Poyard, A. 1881.46, 1881.49, 1881.50, 1881.53, 1881.54, 1882.30, 1882.35
Poyard, Messr. 1879.46, 1879.47, 1880.28
Poyard, Mons. 1879.36, 1879.41, 1879.45, 1879.51, 1879.55, 1879.61, 1879.69, 1880.14, 1880.16, 1880.23, 1880.27, 1880.29, 1880.44, 1880.60
Poyneer, Louise 1895.19
Poyro, Howard 1961.13
Pozhedaieff, George 1927.51
Pradera, Rebeka 1978.19, 1979.20, 1982.16
Praed, Michael 1984.14
Praeger, Adelaide 1880.49, 1884.21
Praegre, Jennie 1898.56
Prager, Miss 1894.21
Prager, Mlle. 1888.23, 1913.07
Prager, Sammy 1963.10
Prager, Stanley 1951.19, 1952.20, 1954.05, 1957.08, 1961.21, 1962.14, 1970.07, 1971.07
Pragon, Marjorie 1959.26
Prank, Jacob 1927.10
Pransky, John 1951.20
Praskin, Leonard 1925.27
Pratorius, Herr 1882.68
Pratos, Jack 1916.18
Pratt, Burnell 1904.23
Pratt, C.E. 1879.35
Pratt, Charles E. 1871.12
Pratt, D. 1867.32
Pratt, Deane 1897.20, 1897.44
Pratt, H.H. 1870.20, 1870.23, 1870.33, 1871.04, 1872.16, 1872.19, 1873.21
Pratt, Harry 1873.27
Pratt, Harry H. 1881.24
Pratt, Ilma 1899.02, 1899.30, 1900.38, 1901.17, 1902.29, 1903.28
Pratt, J.H. 1911.06
Pratt, John 1904.10, 1905.06, 1939.15, 1943.17, 1944.31, 1946.21, 1948.08, 1950.07, 1955.26, 1962.22
Pratt, John H. 1906.20, 1907.21, 1908.44, 1909.18, 1912.47
Pratt, Lynn 1903.12, 1915.32, 1919.32
Pratt, Mr. 1882.32
Pratt, Neil 1928.24
Pratt, P.B. 1904.19
Pratt, Peter 1947.22, 1948.09, 1951.06, 1955.15, 1955.16, 1955.18, 1955.20, 1955.22, 1955.23, 1955.24
Pratt, S.G. 1883.49
Pratt, Tina 1989.02
Pratt, W.A. 1901.25
Pratt, Willie 1897.48
Pratten, R.S. 1859.09
Pray, Mr. 1866.18
Preble, Ed 1931.40, 1975.03
Preble, Edwin 1928.43
Precerutti, S. 1911.19
Precht, Donna 1964.12
Predigam, Auguste 1866.09, 1866.23, 1866.25, 1866.27, 1866.29, 1866.30, 1867.25, 1873.03
Predigam, Miss 1872.23
Predigam, Mr. 1877.18, 1877.19
Predo, Doris 1917.19
Pree, Reese 1980.27
Preece, K.K. 1980.01
Preer, Evelyn 1927.33
Preisser, Cherry 1936.02, 1936.17
Preisser, June 1936.17, 1938.07, 1942.27
Premice, Josephine 1945.07, 1947.19, 1957.16, 1966.15, 1976.04
Premier Scenic Studios 1928.18
Premiere Artists Services, Inc. 1991.04
Prendergast, Shirley 1983.15, 1987.17
Prentice, Amelia 1992.11
Prentice, Charles 1925.42, 1929.51, 1934.34
Prentice, George 1931.40, 1937.10
Prentice, Keith 1961.18
Prentiss, Eleanor 1945.09
Presbrey, Eugene W. 1894.39, 1895.35, 1903.12
Presburg, Jacques 1919.19
Presbury, Yolande 1918.04
Prescott, Betty 1924.14
Prescott, J.H. 1912.16
Prescott, Jennifer 1990.18
Prescott, Nellie J. 1882.34
Prescott, Tina 1947.13, 1950.03
Prescott, Vivian 1905.02
Prescott, Vivien 1904.25
Prescott, W.P. 1881.15
Presley, Elvis 1978.01, 1982.22, 1989.12
Presnell, Harve 1960.20
Press, Brian 1994.04
Press, Jack 1929.30
Pressburger, Emeric 1993.19
Pressel, Marc 1971.12
Pressley, Brenda 1981.29
Pressman, Aaron 1938.16
Pressman, David 1956.10
Pressman, Joel 1973.12
Pressy, Emma 1882.33
Presti, Jackie 1989.29
Prestia, Vincenzo 1981.26
Prestige, Fannie 1869.17, 1880.26
Prestige, Fanny 1869.11, 1869.21, 1870.35, 1870.44
Preston, Barry 1966.30, 1976.04, 1981.03
Preston, Billy 1982.22
Preston, David 1937.17
Preston, Edna 1954.15
Preston, George 1890.33
Preston, Juliette 1896.33
Preston, Michael 1994.11, 1998.22
Preston, Mickee 1948.19, 1949.05
Preston, Paul 1948.19, 1949.05
Preston, Robert 1957.18, 1964.33, 1966.29, 1974.18
Preston, Shane 1999.02
Preston, Walter J. 1922.40
Pretlow, Wayne 1997.22
Pretlow, Wayne W. 1995.19, 1999.08
Preto, Toco 1988.06, 1990.03, 1992.13
Prevel, Jules 1881.49, 1881.50, 1883.12, 1883.34, 1885.25, 1885.60, 1891.47
Prevert, Jacques 1959.15, 1961.25
Preville, Mathilde 1897.44, 1899.24, 1900.12, 1905.32
Preville, Matilde 1897.20, 1898.29
Previn, Andre 1958.21, 1969.17, 1976.07, 1976.32, 1977.02, 1979.17
Previn, Charles 1915.28, 1916.19, 1917.20, 1918.20, 1918.28, 1919.12, 1919.35, 1919.42, 1920.25, 1920.28, 1921.10, 1922.05, 1923.07, 1931.48
Prevost, Birnie 1919.28
Prevost, Ed. 1895.40
Prew, Harry 1912.07
Pribor, Richard 1951.13, 1955.03
Priborsky, Richard 1948.22
Price, A. 1855.10, 1861.01
Price, Al 1904.07
Price, Alonzo 1902.15, 1909.15, 1917.25, 1918.09, 1918.40, 1923.45, 1924.24, 1929.02, 1929.46, 1934.12
Price, Alonzo B. 1931.43
Price, Beatrice 1922.30
Price, Clay 1905.34
Price, Don 1981.24
Price, Dora 1902.09
Price, E.D. 1891.38
Price, Edith 1924.01
Price, Edwin 1902.12
Price, Edwin H. 1896.44, 1900.28, 1900.43, 1907.13
Price, Frank 1895.39, 1942.18
Price, George 1920.19
Price, Georgie 1922.23, 1927.19, 1928.24
Price, Gerald 1954.15, 1966.19
Price, Gilbert 1965.19, 1972.06, 1975.05, 1976.11, 1978.03
Price, Hal 1945.16
Price, Hattie 1871.02
Price, Henry 1887.50, 1976.26, 1977.03, 1977.11, 1980.22, 1981.20, 1982.07
Price, Hughie 1973.14
Price, Jim 1999.08
Price, John 1902.42
Price, Leontyne 1952.06, 1953.04
Price, Lillian 1889.54
Price, Lizzie 1870.24
Price, Lonny 1981.27, 1986.13, 2001.01
Price, Lorin E. 1968.07, 1973.06
Price, Mark 1882.74, 1898.48, 1902.39, 1910.06, 2000.17
Price, Mark M. 1881.15, 1882.50
Price, Messr. 1876.33
Price, Michael P. 1975.03, 1975.24, 1976.15, 1976.25, 1979.05, 1982.05, 1985.02, 1985.04, 1995.07
Price, Michael Paul 1964.02, 1964.24
Price, Millie 1890.29
Price, Miss 1852.01, 1852.05, 1854.01, 1854.07
Price, Naomi 1971.07
Price, Paige 1994.04, 1999.15
Price, Patricia 1978.19
Price, Rick 1990.15
Price, Roger 1950.09, 1952.09
Price, Russell 1908.42
Price, Ruth 1916.07, 1918.41
Price, Sam 1866.20, 1866.32, 1866.35, 1867.01, 1867.02, 1868.05, 1870.08, 1870.11, 1870.16, 1870.38, 1876.30, 1876.33
Price, Sherill 1965.23
Price, Sidney 1892.12
Price, Stephen 1834.01
Price, Sydney 1892.25, 1892.35
Price, Tom 1983.09
Price, Vincent 1968.02
Price, Walter 1933.04
Prideall, Miss 1871.11
Priesser, Cherry 1934.01
Priesser, June 1934.01, 1936.02
Priest, Charles 1890.01, 1890.11, 1891.17
Priest, Dale 1941.03
Priest, J. 1888.35
Priest, Janet 1904.24, 1906.28, 1907.21, 1908.28
Priest, Messr. 1886.36
Priestman, Brian 1963.03
Prieto, J. 1964.02
Prieur, Don 1970.08
Prigmore, W.H. 1793.01, 1794.01, 1796.01
Prim, Polly 1911.15
Prima, Louis 1978.05, 1983.09, 1999.01, 1999.24, 2000.07
Prime, James 2001.04
Primrose and West's Comedy Company 1891.24
Primrose, Clara 1882.04, 1882.20, 1884.09, 1892.02
Primrose, Joe 1931.11, 1933.27
Primrose, Lizzie 1882.41
Primus, Barry 1959.12
Primus, Pearl 1946.01, 1947.19
Prince 1986.02
Prince, Adelaide 1891.05, 1904.08
Prince, Akili 1983.04
Prince, Charles 1899.35, 1900.48, 1902.10, 1906.02, 1906.42, 1909.02, 1912.05, 1914.12, 1917.09, 2000.01
Prince, Charles A. 1927.50
Prince, Charles H. 1892.18, 1900.42, 1900.56, 1901.12, 1902.06, 1905.23, 1907.62
Prince, Daisy 1981.27
Prince, Faith 1989.03, 1991.15, 1992.04, 1998.15, 2001.03
Prince, Flora 1905.20
Prince, Ginger 1989.27, 1991.06
Prince, Graham 1975.20, 1976.16, 1989.02
Prince, Harold 1954.05, 1955.08, 1957.07, 1957.12, 1959.25, 1960.08, 1960.19, 1962.01, 1962.12, 1963.14, 1964.27, 1965.02, 1965.17, 1966.06, 1966.24, 1968.30, 1970.13, 1971.05, 1973.04, 1974.06, 1976.02, 1976.36, 1977.05, 1978.02, 1979.06, 1979.23, 1980.04, 1980.25, 1981.27, 1982.18, 1982.20, 1983.13, 1984.11, 1984.13, 1985.05, 1986.08, 1987.09, 1987.12, 1987.16, 1988.01, 1989.14, 1989.19, 1993.09, 1994.08, 1995.11, 1997.10, 1998.21
Prince, Hughie 1945.17, 1975.12, 1979.24, 1979.30, 1982.22, 1986.06, 1989.12, 1999.24
Prince, Jack 1959.11
Prince, Jennie 1883.37, 1883.65, 1885.52, 1886.34
Prince, Lottie 1897.24
Prince, Miss 1917.31
Prince, Mr. 1994.08
Prince, Phyllis 1917.31
Prince, Robert 1964.35, 1965.14
Prince, Van 1949.15, 1951.11
Prince, W.J.D. 1890.37
Prine, John 1973.14, 1975.12
Pringle W.G. 1899.05
Pringle, Joan 1970.04
Pringle, Lempriere 1905.04
Pringle, Shirley 1952.16
Pringle, W.H. 1902.05, 1920.47
Pringle, William 1923.17, 1925.39, 1927.14, 1930.26, 1931.03, 1943.06
Pringle, William H. 1919.39
Printemps, Yvonne 1926.49, 1934.34
Printz, Mme. 1883.45
Prinz, Eddie 1940.02
Prinz, LeRoy 1929.08, 1929.26, 1929.49
Prinz, Leroy 1933.15
Prinz, LeRoy J. 1929.37, 1930.22
Prinz, Mme. 1883.62
Prioner, A.C. 1897.16
Prior, Allan 1923.41, 1924.29, 1925.02, 1926.33, 1927.65, 1928.44, 1929.37
Prior, Danii 1960.08
Prior, Genii 1960.08
Prior, H. 1879.02
Prior, J.J. 1869.15
Prior, Lula 1870.15, 1870.26
Prior, Lulu 1870.33, 1871.04, 1871.18, 1872.37, 1873.08
Prior, Mrs. 1869.04
Prior, Mrs. J.J. 1861.06, 1862.01, 1864.22, 1870.23
Prior, Shirley Ann 1952.10
Prior, Thomas W. 1892.20, 1905.35
Pritchard, Ann 1929.04
Pritchard, Annie 1923.25, 1926.01, 1928.14
Pritchard, Frances 1915.04, 1915.11, 1915.26
Pritchard, Jack 1914.19
Pritchard, John 1912.30
Pritchard, Ted 1968.07, 1974.09
Pritchett, III., Gil 1992.08
Pritchett, James 1961.18
Pritchett, Liz 1959.19
Pritchett, Lizabeth 1972.03
Pritchett, Willie 1957.09
Pritzkow, Louis 1900.53
Prival, Bert 1926.10, 1926.44, 1932.19
Privat, Anais 1882.29, 1882.73
Prizant, Hyman 1967.03
Probst, Gerry 1936.12
Probst, Sadie 1905.29, 1906.33
Prochaska, Bobby 1990.15
Prochnik, Bruce 1963.01
Proctor, Agnes 1878.14
Proctor, Anna 1908.33

Proctor, Grace 1905.06
Proctor, Harold 1914.21
Proctor, J.R. 1916.15
Proctor, James D. 1941.01
Proctor, Philip 1966.09
Proctor, Warren 1921.01, 1921.13, 1925.06
Proctor, William 1893.47
Producers Circle 2, Inc., The 1978.02
Producers Circle Company, The 1987.12
Producers Theatre, The 1955.18, 1958.14
Producing Associates, Inc. 1933.02
Productions International Corp. 1970.15
Productions Two 1978.01
Prof. Spiel. Scenic 1886.10
Profanato, Gene 1970.21, 1977.07
Proia, Alexandre 1995.09
Proppe, Gus 1916.15
Props, Billy 1876.04
Pros, Miguel 1919.17
Proser, Monte 1947.16, 1948.23, 1962.17
Prosk, Gerald 1948.20
Prosper, Harry 1925.27
Prospery, George 1944.22
Pross, Dolly 1927.07, 1928.11
Prosser, Mr. 1841.01
Prosser, Olive 1917.24
Protero, Dodi 1965.23
Proto, Mlle. 1901.06, 1903.07
Protopoff, Russel 1939.13
Protopoff, Russell 1938.15
Prouty, Charles 1904.14
Prouty, Clarence 1904.14
Prouty, Jed 1910.17, 1912.28, 1914.27, 1916.19, 1919.01, 1920.13, 1922.16, 1943.01
Provanzo, Nick 1922.30
Provenza, Sal 1981.25, 1985.01
Provost, Evelyn 1912.27
Provost, William 1941.03
Prowse, Juliet 1962.17
Prucilla, Adelaide 1897.06
Prud'homme, Cameron 1954.02, 1957.07, 1960.20
Prudhomme Productions 1983.15
Pruette, Frank 1890.08
Pruette, Mrs. William 1919.41
Pruette, William 1891.47, 1892.16, 1892.30, 1893.44, 1894.05, 1894.14, 1894.40, 1895.24, 1897.17, 1898.27, 1900.06, 1900.09, 1900.11, 1900.13, 1900.17, 1900.18, 1900.22, 1900.23, 1900.26, 1900.27, 1900.29, 1900.30, 1902.19, 1904.12, 1904.17, 1904.30, 1905.57, 1906.26, 1907.36, 1908.24, 1909.04, 1909.22, 1910.14, 1911.15, 1911.32, 1913.14, 1914.14
Prunczik, Karen 1980.20
Prunzik, Karen 1995.07
Prussian, E.D. 1903.41
Pruyn, Frank 1886.62
Pryce, Jonathan 1991.03
Pryer, Polly 1918.35
Prymus, Ken 2001.09
Pryor, Arthur 1910.02
Pryor, Marjorie 1897.32
Pryor, Martha 1924.11, 1933.20
Pryor, Roger 1931.42
Pryor, W. 1989.12
Psacharopoulos, Nikos 1963.27
Puccini, Giacomo 1925.41, 1996.09
Puchol, Luisita 1917.25, 1917.33
Puck, Eva 1919.36, 1923.31, 1926.07, 1927.67, 1932.11
Puck, Harry 1921.23, 1924.02, 1924.40, 1925.34, 1926.39, 1928.06, 1928.27
Puckett, Roger 1961.26
Pudenz, Steve 1989.04, 1995.13
Puehringer, F. 1897.15
Puerner, Charles 1878.05, 1879.08, 1879.12, 1880.08, 1880.63, 1881.02, 1881.24, 1881.31, 1884.22, 1887.19, 1891.34, 1892.17, 1892.25, 1893.02, 1893.07, 1893.47, 1895.17, 1895.20, 1905.47
Pugh, Ed 1927.32
Pugh, Jim 1999.01
Pugh, Louise 1901.03
Pugh, Richard Warren 1980.16, 1981.12, 1983.14, 1988.01
Pugh, Ted 1973.05, 1981.03
Pughe, George 1925.42
Pughsley, Hazel 1898.46
Pugliese, Joseph 1975.07
Pugliese, O. 1985.07, 1997.13, 1999.18
Pugliese, Osvaldo 1955.26
Pugsley, Estelle 1899.33
Puig, Manuel 1993.09
Pule, Daniel 1977.01
Pulen, Messr. 1905.22
Pulen, S.P. 1903.40
Pulen, Sim 1906.18, 1908.09, 1910.04, 1910.13
Puliti, George 1927.22
Pullaney, Bert 1918.16
Pullar, Robert 1879.68, 1883.32
Puller, Robert 1880.09, 1880.64, 1881.09, 1882.79, 1883.46, 1883.53, 1884.41
Pulliam, Darcy 1992.11, 1994.12
Pulliam, Zelda 1973.10
Pulliche, Mme. 1920.20
Pullman, G. 1885.65
Pullman, George 1900.36, 1907.15, 1909.08, 1909.19
Pullman, Kate 1919.24
Pullman, Miss 1864.13
Pully, B.S. 1950.17, 1966.13
Puls, Herr 1879.62, 1880.61, 1880.66
Pulsifer, Ken 1929.37
Punch, Mr. 1875.40
Pupello, Angelo 1999.15
Pupp, Anally 1925.40
Puppe, A. 1885.64, 1887.13
Puppet People, The 1982.24
Pura, Soninha Toda 1988.06
Purcel, Lizzie 1902.02
Purcell, Charles 1908.34, 1914.21, 1916.17, 1917.14, 1917.15, 1918.42, 1919.03, 1919.35, 1920.25, 1921.03, 1925.31, 1926.46, 1927.09, 1930.03, 1931.33, 1933.16, 1934.12, 1946.20
Purcell, Gertrude 1926.14, 1927.54, 1928.06, 1928.27, 1930.15
Purcell, Harold 1947.15
Purcell, J.H. 1906.36, 1909.28
Purcell, Jack 1946.07, 1949.17, 1954.17
Purcell, Tommy 1926.18
Purcell, Vivienne 1926.01
Purcella, Frank 1921.20
Purcella, Raymond 1921.20
Purcena, Phillipa 1884.58
Purcer, Philip 1884.58
Purdell, Reginald 1975.22
Purdham, David 1981.04
Purdom, J. Robert 1964.22
Purdy, A.H. 1852.02
Purdy, Charles 1913.17
Purdy, Elsa 1951.05
Purdy, G.W. 1897.22
Purdy, George 1879.18, 1879.23, 1879.24, 1880.02, 1880.40, 1882.03, 1882.39, 1886.27, 1895.10
Purdy, George W. 1892.19
Purdy, Hazel 1917.04
Purdy, Marshall B. 2000.06
Purdy, Richard 1953.07
Purdy, S.S. 1865.03, 1868.05, 1868.14, 1870.08, 1870.11, 1870.16, 1870.17, 1870.38
Purey, Francis 1890.40
Puritz, Nanne 1997.10
Purl, Linda 2001.06
Purnell, Daniel S. 1892.44, 1892.54
Purnell, Paula 1946.10
Purnello, Ethel 1933.04, 1951.11
Puron, Leonore 1916.11
Puroy, Nellie 1882.04
Purpuro, Sandra 1994.07
Pursell, John P. 1905.52
Pursley, David 1979.28, 1987.15, 1989.24, 1992.11
Pursley, Patricia 1926.16
Purviance, Roy 1905.25, 1907.43, 1908.32, 1911.31
Purvin, Beverly 1951.14, 1953.07
Puryear, Jordan 2000.11
Pusey, Charles A. 1895.38, 1904.53
Pushkin 1922.06
Pusilo, Robert 1975.21
Putnam, Ashley 1996.10
Putnam, Boyd 1894.39
Putnam, George 1894.13
Putnam, W.H. 1894.31
Putsch, Michael 1990.08
Puzzo, Peter 1983.16
Pyant, Paul 1994.02
Pyke, Alfred 1903.40
Pyke, C.M. 1881.57, 1884.08
Pyke, C.N. 1876.12
Pyke, George 1883.62, 1887.26, 1892.10
Pyke, Harris 1904.03
Pyke, Harry N. 1904.52
Pyke, Katherine 1891.41
Pyle, Richard 1919.44, 1920.21
Pyle, Thomas 1956.15
Pym, Ernest 1900.51
Pyne, Louisa 1854.03, 1854.06, 1854.07, 1855.01, 1855.02, 1855.03, 1855.04, 1855.05, 1855.06, 1855.07, 1855.08, 1855.09
Pyne, Mesdame 1856.04
Pyne, Millicent 1894.15
Pyne, Miss 1890.02
Pyne, Susan 1854.03, 1855.02, 1855.04, 1855.05, 1855.07, 1855.09
Pysher, Ernie 1974.26, 1975.05, 1976.05
Pyxidium Ltd. 1971.03, 1975.09

Quackenbush, Karen 1982.15
Quaglia, Antonio 1940.05
Quaid, Angie 1904.14
Qualitz, Clara 1886.41, 1887.27, 1888.01, 1888.39, 1890.03, 1892.55, 1893.21
Qualters, Tot 1914.23, 1915.31, 1916.10, 1917.26, 1920.22, 1920.23, 1920.47, 1921.02, 1922.15, 1924.06
Quarleri, Dino Carlos 1999.18
Quarry, Richard 1970.03
Quat' Jeudis, Les 1961.01
Quattrocchi 1889.08
Quaver, Messr. 1862.02
Quayle, Anna 1962.18
Quee, Jr., Donald 1894.05
Queen, Fanny 1870.07, 1870.15
Queen, Fred 1880.64, 1881.29, 1882.02
Queen, Fred E. 1888.29
Queen, Jeffrey A. 2001.04
Queen, John 1875.39, 1879.04, 1879.37, 1879.68, 1880.09, 1880.36, 1880.64, 1881.09, 1881.29, 1882.02, 1882.50, 1882.74, 1882.79, 1883.32, 1883.46, 1883.53, 1883.63, 1900.35
Queen, Julia 1870.07, 1870.15
Queen, Laura 1870.07, 1870.15
Queen, Murray 1913.17, 1919.05
Queenan, Charles 1961.24
Quencher, Mark 1878.15
Queneau, Raymond 1964.39
Quentin, Tod 1925.42
Quentmeyer, William 1936.02, 1936.17
Quest, Josephine 1925.50
Questel, Mae 1964.40
Quevli, Marie L. 1938.05
Quevli, Marie Louise 1935.17
Quevli, Mary Louise 1936.27, 1940.06
Queyla, Messr. 1902.13
Quick, George 1964.24
Quick, Louise 1960.06, 1965.14, 1969.01, 1982.11
Quick, Mlle. 1888.39
Quick, Mme. 1890.50
Quick-Bowen, Louise 1978.13
Quickly, Mr. 1870.15
Quigg, John 1910.18, 1945.03, 1947.11
Quigley, Erin 1993.04
Quigley, G.W. 1904.45
Quigley, George 1898.55
Quigley, J. 1868.19, 1868.22
Quigley, Jack 1925.17
Quigley, Jay 1892.50
Quigley, Lizzie 1885.43
Quigley, Mary Delia 1982.15
Quigley, Robert 1898.55, 1934.40
Quilico, Louis 1991.09
Quillan, Joe 1941.13
Quillan, Joseph 1946.04
Quilt, Quinine 1899.23
Quilter, Dick 1881.17, 1881.19
Quilter, Richard 1883.46, 1883.53, 1883.63, 1884.13, 1885.49, 1885.66, 1886.03, 1886.42, 1886.52, 1887.07, 1887.16, 1887.39, 1887.45, 1887.48, 1888.14, 1890.49, 1891.25, 1891.45, 1892.54, 1893.15, 1893.27, 1893.36, 1893.46, 1895.25, 1897.20, 1914.29
Quimby, Cassius C. 1937.01
Quimby, M.J. 1899.41
Quimby, William 1915.06
Quin, Mike 1940.21
Quinault, Robert 1923.38
Quinby, William 1915.23
Quincella 1982.17
Quine, Mr. 1875.26
Quine, Richard 1939.28
Quinetate, May 1907.02
Quinlan, Dan 1916.08, 1916.23, 1919.26, 1922.18
Quinlan, Gertrude 1898.06, 1898.15, 1898.16, 1898.30, 1898.37, 1898.42, 1898.52, 1898.57, 1898.62, 1898.65, 1898.71, 1899.10, 1899.14, 1899.16, 1899.42, 1900.02, 1900.04, 1900.06, 1900.09, 1900.11, 1900.17, 1900.18, 1900.21, 1900.23, 1900.26, 1900.27, 1900.30, 1902.18, 1902.44, 1907.51, 1911.05
Quinlan, Gus 1928.25
Quinlan, John 1924.39
Quinlan, M. 1868.06, 1869.26
Quinlan, Mr. 1868.06
Quinlivan, Maurice 1920.28, 1921.30
Quinn, Aileen 1998.18
Quinn, Anthony 1983.14
Quinn, Brian 1981.12, 1982.01, 1991.09
Quinn, Cecilia 1902.31
Quinn, Florence 1905.25, 1906.44
Quinn, J.J. 1894.13
Quinn, James 1876.30, 1886.62, 1982.10
Quinn, Jessica 1967.07
Quinn, John 1898.45
Quinn, Lew 1906.45, 1910.13, 1911.12, 1911.43, 1911.45
Quinn, Marie 1915.03
Quinn, Messr. 1875.35
Quinn, Michael 1957.07, 1959.25, 1961.27, 1962.16, 1962.27, 1965.20, 1965.35, 1966.27
Quinn, Mildred 1922.28
Quinn, Patrick 1986.19, 2001.01
Quinn, Paul 1902.09
Quinn, Paul E. 1904.06
Quinn, Rosie 1915.11, 1915.26, 1917.08, 1919.26, 1920.22, 1920.23
Quinnette, Dorothy 1915.05
Quinones, Adolfo 1979.30
Quinson, Gustave 1922.02
Quinten, Louise K. 1888.04
Quintero, Jose 1958.11, 1966.05, 1971.06
Quintette, Dorothy 1912.34
Quintette, Dot 1917.35
Quinton, Dolores 1983.17
Quinton, Everett 2001.09
Quinton, Kate 1875.03
Quinton, Pat 1932.02
Quintos, Gemini 1996.15, 1997.22
Quirk, Brian 1990.07, 1991.08
Quiroga, Guillermina 1999.18
Quiroga, Horacio 1996.16
Quiroga, Manuel 1949.07
Quist, Ralph 1955.10
Quitak, Oscar 1965.28
Quito, Leonora 1896.43
Quive, Gracia 1896.42
Quixano, Dave 1920.07
Quixano, David 1918.02
Quong, Rose 1958.19

R. Henri Strange 1906.14
R.B. Fashion Clothes 1915.07
R.L. Grosh and Sons 1955.03
Raab, Cheryl 1982.13
Raab, Nancy Jean 1946.12
Raae, Marin 1937.05
Raasche 1951.21
Rab, Michael 1913.18
Rabb, Ellis 1971.16
Rabbett, Martin 1978.28, 1993.18
Rabe, Mr. 1896.34
Raberg, Franziska 1885.01, 1885.27
Raberg, Fraulein 1880.66
Raberg, Frl. 1883.08, 1883.35
Rabilino, J. 1918.26
Rabino, Isabor 1908.28
Rabinoff 1920.22
Rabinoff, Max 1911.16, 1911.19
Rabinowitz, Kathleen 1977.10
Rabinowitz, Robert 1977.10, 1979.15, 1982.22, 1989.12
Rabinowitz, Tillie 1942.28
Rabiroff, Jacques 1942.01
Rabke, Harry 1931.07
Rabke, Henry 1934.13
Rabke, Kelli 1993.15
Rabovsky, Istvan 1965.25, 1965.27
Rabu, Renald 1972.08
Raby, Roger Allan 1964.21
Racheff, James 1990.14
Rachel 1971.14
Rachel, Ann 1965.14
Rachel, Mlle. 1868.26, 1869.05, 1869.16, 1869.30
Rachmaninoff 1924.32
Rachmaninoff, Sergei 1956.11, 1965.35

Racine, Eugene 1930.36
Racine, Jules 1942.26, 1944.32, 1948.25
Racklin, Albert 1918.09
Rackmil, Gladys Casabove 1978.25, 1980.02
Rackmill, Gladys Casabove 1980.29
Racz, Teresa 1962.06, 1962.08, 1962.11
Radcliffe, Alice 1900.32
Radcliffe, Ann Ward 1796.02
Radcliffe, J. Belton 1888.33
Radcliffe, J.B. 1890.09
Radcliffe, James 1886.40, 1890.49, 1891.25, 1891.45, 1893.15, 1893.27, 1893.36, 1893.46
Radcliffe, James B. 1884.06, 1885.64, 1886.53, 1889.53, 1894.04
Radcliffe, Pearl 1898.75
Radcliffe, Sadie 1882.69
Radford, Dave 1916.03, 1916.25, 1952.11
Radford, Robert 1985.08, 1986.13
Radin, Oscar 1907.26, 1908.10, 1908.21, 1910.19, 1910.31, 1910.36, 1911.36, 1912.24, 1912.27, 1913.02, 1913.05, 1913.18, 1913.30, 1914.01, 1914.16, 1914.22, 1915.02, 1915.11, 1915.26, 1916.03, 1916.11, 1916.23, 1917.08, 1917.23, 1918.05, 1918.18, 1918.32, 1919.16, 1919.30, 1919.35, 1920.19, 1920.22, 1920.23, 1921.14, 1921.30, 1921.31, 1922.19, 1923.01, 1923.20, 1923.38, 1924.15, 1924.33, 1924.39, 1926.33, 1927.39, 1927.42, 1928.36
Radio City Entertainment 1997.19, 1999.13, 1999.23, 2000.04
Radio City Music Hall 1979.13, 1979.28, 1980.09, 1980.18, 1981.08, 1982.06, 1983.04, 1983.09, 1984.10, 1990.19, 1991.04
Radner, Gilda 1979.19
Rado, James 1968.11, 1977.15, 2000.16
Radojevic, Danilo 1976.18
Radolph, Mme. 1892.40
Radomsky, Saul 1981.14, 1999.12
Radus, Herbert 1924.20
Rady, Simon 1937.14, 1946.04
Rae, Charlotte 1952.05, 1965.28, 1966.19
Rae, Dorothy 1925.27
Rae, G. 1854.07
Rae, Helene 1929.48
Rae, Inez 1895.02, 1897.09, 1897.48, 1899.39, 1900.38, 1901.17
Rae, Messr. 1855.01, 1861.03
Rae, Mr. 1855.01
Rae, Nan 1939.26, 1940.07
Rae, Nelson 1940.22
Rae, Phyllis 1928.02, 1928.37
Rae, Stefani 1996.17
Raeburn, Burt 1938.17
Raedler, Dorothy 1959.18, 1960.14, 1960.15, 1961.03, 1961.04, 1961.05, 1961.19, 1962.08, 1962.10, 1962.11, 1962.19, 1963.23, 1964.09, 1964.10, 1964.12, 1964.13, 1964.14, 1965.10, 1965.11, 1965.12
Raemere, Valerie 1928.11
Rafael, Leon Arias 1964.02
Rafael, Mons. 1871.07
Raffael, Jack 1907.16, 1910.34, 1917.05
Raffael, John J. 1888.22, 1888.26, 1889.17, 1891.23, 1893.05
Raffell, Anthony 1962.26, 1962.30, 1964.37, 1964.38, 1964.41, 1966.22, 1966.26
Rafferty, James 1947.09
Rafferty, Patrick 1924.40, 1926.50
Raffles, Gerry 1964.28
Raft, George 1919.30, 1919.43, 1925.38, 1927.31, 1927.36
Rafter, Adele 1902.04, 1903.04, 1904.49, 1907.16, 1907.62
Rafter, Frank 1893.17, 1894.05, 1894.26, 1894.38, 1895.38, 1896.35, 1896.48, 1897.37, 1897.52, 1898.05, 1898.17, 1898.51, 1898.63, 1899.21, 1899.36, 1900.03, 1902.15
Rafter, Michael 1991.06, 1996.05, 1998.03, 1999.24
Raftery, Helen 1919.07
Rag Baby Comedy Company 1884.16, 1884.37
Ragan, Michael 1982.14
Raggini, Michael 1931.44
Raggio, Lisa 1979.15
Raggs, Miss 1869.26
Ragland, Oscar 1905.25, 1908.44, 1917.22, 1920.36, 1923.40, 1924.26, 1926.32, 1928.37, 1930.06, 1930.40, 1936.22
Ragland, Rags 1938.04, 1940.19
Ragni, Gerome 1968.11, 1972.18, 1977.15, 2000.16
Ragonesi, Angelo 1989.10
Ragovoy, Jerry 1979.30
Ragusa, Michele 1993.17, 1997.06
Rahming, Gregory Emanuel 1998.16
Rahn, Katherine 1915.30
Rahn, Kathryn 1917.06
Rahn, Muriel 1934.03, 1943.24, 1950.16, 1952.03
Rahn, Rosalyn 1982.03
Rai, Jhoreck 1936.07
Raider-Wexler, Victor 1991.06
Raidich, Hubert 1931.44
Raiford, Steven 1993.12
Raiken, Larry 2001.02
Raiken, Lawrence 1981.10
Railey, Thomas T. 1910.02
Railton, Jeremy 1989.06, 1989.08
Raiman, Paul 1999.20
Raimondo, Signor 1911.16, 1911.19
Rain, Douglas 1963.28
Raine, Hary 1936.27
Raine, Lola 1926.15, 1927.19, 1928.14
Rainer, Frances 1947.17
Rainer, Robert 1913.02
Raines, Douglas 2001.04
Raines, R.C. 1930.16
Raines, Robert 1932.08
Raines, Ron 1982.21, 1983.05, 1987.19
Raines, William 1946.22
Rainey, Glenn 1999.16
Rainey, John 1951.11
Rainey, Leslie 1905.46
Rainey, T.T. 1872.10
Rainford, Clara 1877.28
Rainforth, Harry 1875.21
Rainforth, J. 1866.20
Rainger, Frank 1899.40, 1902.44, 1915.25, 1917.04
Rainger, Frank M. 1912.02
Rainger, Ralph 1926.25, 1927.37, 1928.28, 1928.46, 1929.19, 1930.06, 1930.32, 1933.15, 1954.11, 1980.08, 1984.10, 1989.12, 2000.12
Rainieri, Orestes 1931.29
Rains, Jack 1958.03, 1958.05, 1961.09, 1962.16, 1962.20
Rainsford, Nan 1921.14
Rainsley, Helen 1900.48
Raison, Milton 1931.21
Raitt, James 1986.03, 1987.02, 1987.14, 1989.23, 1994.01
Raitt, John 1945.05, 1948.24, 1952.05, 1953.11, 1954.05, 1965.24, 1966.30, 1968.30, 1975.22
Raitt, Kathleen 1988.20, 1989.26, 1997.19, 1999.08
Raize, Jason 1997.20
Raizin, Louis F. 1997.03
Rak, Rachelle 1999.01
Raker, Lorin 1919.12, 1922.38
Rakerd, Cliff 1982.24
Rakhmanoff, Semyon 1925.46, 1925.51
Rakimanoff, Semyon 1925.51
Raksin, David 1936.12, 1940.21, 1946.22, 1990.09, 1997.05
Rale, M. 1919.12
Rale, M.W. 1904.33, 1907.27
Raleigh, Cecil 1894.38, 1913.04
Raleigh, Evangeline 1928.07, 1928.37
Raleigh, Les 1913.35
Ralf, Paul 1982.17
Rall, Tommy 1948.08, 1948.22, 1949.08, 1950.15, 1959.04, 1961.20, 1964.18, 1970.10
Ralph, Charles 1928.44
Ralph, Jessie 1890.08, 1894.10, 1897.07, 1915.32
Ralph, Julia 1899.11, 1906.02, 1906.42, 1911.07, 1911.33, 1917.09, 1925.37
Ralph, Sheryl Lee 1980.05, 1981.29
Ralph, Sophia 1909.12
Ralston, Alfred 1964.28
Ralston, Beaumont 1900.59
Ralston, Bowman 1893.05
Ralston, Emma 1893.41
Ralston, Ruth 1899.21
Ralston, Teri 1970.13, 1973.04
Ralton, D.E. 1865.05
Ralyea, Messr. 1859.08
Ralyea, Mr. 1859.08
Ram, Buck 1989.12
Rambeau, Edward 1972.11
Rambeau, Zella 1921.11
Ramersdorf, Pepi 1891.30
Ramey, Diane 1958.03
Ramey, Frances 1914.30
Ramin, Sid 1957.12, 1959.13, 1959.23, 1960.08, 1960.22, 1961.02, 1961.24, 1962.05, 1962.12, 1963.12, 1964.17, 1968.18, 1972.03, 1974.17, 1975.12, 1976.11, 1980.02, 1986.20, 1989.03, 1989.27, 1991.06, 1992.02, 1993.19
Ramirez, Carlos 1941.03
Ramirez, Coco 1959.05, 1961.12
Ramirez, Pepita 1949.07
Ramirez, Roger "Ram" 1948.13, 1982.12
Ramirez, Sara 1998.02, 1999.10, 2001.01
Ramirez, Tim 1967.09
Ramirez, Tina 1959.05
Ramone, Phil 1974.01, 1974.13, 1983.20, 1989.12
Ramos, Beatriz 1939.18
Ramos, Bridget 1988.04, 1990.02
Ramos, George 1968.18, 1975.06
Ramos, Giovani 1992.13
Ramos, Paulo 1990.03
Ramoska, Biruta 1949.15, 1951.22
Rampino, Lewis D. 1976.33
Rampone, Kitty 1896.21
Ramsay, Alice 1934.37
Ramsay, Allan 1901.11, 1903.39, 1904.22, 1905.22, 1905.25
Ramsay, Remak 1970.21, 1971.15, 1979.17, 1991.15
Ramsay, Robin 1965.23
Ramsdell, Vernon 1892.12, 1896.32
Ramsden, Daisy 1880.43, 1880.49, 1881.08, 1882.39, 1884.17, 1886.32, 1888.39
Ramsden, Lillian 1891.37
Ramsey, Barry 1990.20, 1991.13
Ramsey, deVecmon 1923.15
Ramsey, Dorothy 1944.17
Ramsey, Gordon 1979.09
Ramsey, Helen 1926.13
Ramsey, Kevin 1990.14, 1992.03, 1997.08
Ramsey, Marion 1971.01, 1978.21, 1982.22, 1985.05, 1986.02
Ramsey, Packer 1922.44
Ramsey, Ruth 1927.24, 1966.10
Ramsey, W. 1877.02
Rance, Rosa 1894.37
Rand, Frank 1896.32
Rand, L.F. 1862.08, 1880.41
Rand, Lionel 1942.18
Rand, Margaret 1939.15
Rand, Olivia 1869.38, 1869.42, 1870.01, 1870.09, 1870.12, 1870.18, 1872.37
Rand, Rosa 1869.42, 1870.01, 1870.09, 1870.12, 1870.18, 1870.25
Rand, S. 1884.27
Rand, Suzanne 1979.01
Randal, Messr. 1880.69
Randall Jack 1929.04
Randall, Adelaide 1878.03, 1879.30, 1882.31, 1882.33, 1882.36, 1882.37, 1882.40, 1882.43, 1882.46, 1883.37, 1884.32, 1884.33, 1884.35, 1884.38
Randall, Andre 1932.18
Randall, Bernard 1926.29
Randall, Bill 1942.26
Randall, Billy 1930.28
Randall, Bob 1974.13
Randall, Carl 1915.15, 1916.10, 1916.17, 1918.03, 1918.26, 1920.18, 1920.45, 1921.24, 1922.32, 1924.44, 1926.27, 1928.07, 1928.15, 1928.45, 1931.14, 1932.01, 1932.26, 1933.01, 1934.06, 1936.01, 1938.11, 1939.13, 1940.08, 1941.03, 1941.09, 1941.12, 1942.30, 1945.15
Randall, Clara 1890.01, 1896.17
Randall, E.H. 1902.20
Randall, Ed 1912.39
Randall, Fred 1962.04, 1968.32
Randall, Grace 1887.07, 1887.16
Randall, Lee 1934.41
Randall, Lee J. 1924.27, 1929.21
Randall, Marion 1922.23, 1923.05, 1925.36
Randall, Mart 1922.23
Randall, Martinez 1923.05, 1925.36
Randall, Messr. 1881.03, 1882.37
Randall, Miss 1840.02, 1840.03
Randall, Mr. 1856.02, 1856.03
Randall, Myrtle 1910.35
Randall, Nina 1902.27, 1903.40, 1905.05
Randall, Pamela 1944.23
Randall, Peter 1890.32, 1892.23, 1892.45, 1895.34, 1896.31
Randall, Peter F. 1901.07, 1903.11
Randall, Robert 1931.28
Randall, Rosalie 1955.13
Randall, Ruth 1916.11
Randall, Ryth 1924.12
Randall, Sallie 1895.15, 1895.39, 1896.30, 1898.72, 1899.38, 1900.59
Randall, Sally 1897.17
Randall, Sharon 1944.21
Randall, Tony 1958.02, 1995.07, 1996.15
Randall, Viola 1888.45
Randall, W.W. 1891.18
Randalls, P. 1885.35
Randazzo, Arlene 1975.16
Randell, Pamela 1945.09
Randell, Ron 1991.12
Randers, Helmut 1984.05
Randle 1876.12
Randol, George 1926.19, 1929.25, 1930.10, 1935.01, 1943.15, 1944.03
Randole, Leo 1934.15
Randolf, Rose 1964.11
Randolph, A. 1881.35
Randolph, Addie 1900.54
Randolph, Amanda 1924.27, 1942.13
Randolph, Annie 1881.38
Randolph, Beverly 1986.02
Randolph, Charles 1897.02
Randolph, Clemence 1944.27
Randolph, Donald 1941.04
Randolph, Dorothy 1930.10
Randolph, Eva 1890.27, 1892.18, 1898.08, 1900.43
Randolph, Forbes 1931.31
Randolph, G.C. 1876.02
Randolph, Jack 1905.50
Randolph, James 1961.13, 1962.07, 1965.03, 1976.21
Randolph, Jimmy 1956.06
Randolph, John 1938.02, 1940.10, 1951.24, 1959.24, 1963.09
Randolph, Mary 1981.21
Randolph, Miss 1839.01, 1841.01, 1892.07
Randolph, Mme. 1892.30
Randolph, Robert 1954.18, 1960.06, 1961.22, 1962.14, 1962.27, 1963.12, 1964.04, 1964.11, 1964.35, 1965.07, 1965.26, 1965.33, 1965.35, 1966.01, 1966.06, 1966.07, 1966.27, 1967.02, 1967.14, 1967.18, 1968.03, 1970.09, 1971.02, 1971.07, 1973.13, 1974.10, 1974.17, 1976.28, 1982.05, 1982.14, 1986.07
Randolph, Shannon 1944.21
Randolph, Zilner T. 1938.08, 1939.29
Randolph-Wright, Charles 1981.29
Random, Charlotte 1885.01
Rands, Frances 1939.13
Rands, Leslie 1934.21, 1934.24, 1934.25, 1934.26, 1934.27, 1934.28, 1934.31, 1934.33, 1936.13, 1936.14, 1936.18, 1936.19, 1936.21, 1936.23, 1936.24, 1939.01, 1939.03, 1939.04, 1939.08, 1939.09, 1939.11
Raney, Jim 1960.04
Rank, Bernard 1885.01
Rank, Bernhard 1885.27
Rank, Herr 1879.17, 1879.22
Ranken, Frederic 1902.20, 1903.06, 1903.07, 1903.14, 1903.20, 1903.38, 1905.36, 1905.56, 1906.49
Ranken, Frederick M. 1899.40
Ranken, McKee 1900.16
Rankin, Carl 1885.31
Rankin, Charles 1909.02
Rankin, Frederic 1904.25
Rankin, Grace 1908.07, 1908.24, 1908.39
Rankin, Linda 1968.32
Rankin, McKee 1870.19
Rankin, Phyllis 1897.39, 1899.25, 1900.33, 1904.08
Rankin, Steve 1993.06
Ranney, Della 1902.14, 1904.20
Ranney, Frank 1898.33, 1898.37, 1898.49, 1898.52, 1898.62, 1898.74, 1899.05, 1899.16, 1904.10, 1905.06
Ranney, Frank L. 1898.65
Ransem, G.Z. 1899.04
Ransom, Llewelyn 1930.24
Ransom, Nellie 1891.15
Ransome, A.H. 1897.29, 1905.25
Ransome, Dwight 1975.19
Ransome, John 1894.11
Ransome, John W. 1889.42, 1901.29, 1907.39, 1911.45, 1916.12
Ranson, Herbert 1926.38

Ranson, Malcolm 1993.17
Ranson, Nellie 1946.12
Ransone, J.W. 1880.40
Ransone, John W. 1879.54, 1886.24, 1887.13, 1892.19, 1903.10, 1904.16
Ransone, Mrs. John 1879.54
Ranzato, Virgilio 1935.02
Rao 1991.11
Raoult, Mons. 1876.24, 1876.25, 1876.26, 1877.06, 1877.09, 1877.10, 1877.11, 1877.12, 1877.13, 1877.14, 1877.19
Rapee, Ernest 1940.16
Rapee, Erno 1920.12
Raphael, Enid 1938.19
Raphael, Gerianne 1978.22
Raphael, Gerrianne 1955.10, 1959.27, 1965.34, 1972.14
Raphael, John 1910.17
Raphael, Master 1850.01
Raphael, Mlle. 1879.19, 1879.31, 1879.34, 1879.36, 1879.39, 1879.41, 1879.43, 1879.45, 1879.46, 1879.47, 1879.51, 1879.69, 1880.27, 1880.28, 1880.29
Rapkin, David 1982.02
Raposo, Casemiro 1992.13
Raposo, Joe 1986.16
Raposo, Joseph 1971.11
Rapp, Anthony 1996.09, 1999.03
Rapp, Howard 2000.14
Rapport, Helena 1933.20
Rapso, Joe 1976.32
Raquello, Edward 1930.39
Rasch, Albertina 1909.20, 1910.23, 1911.34, 1925.22, 1927.08, 1927.12, 1927.13, 1927.37, 1927.50, 1928.12, 1929.27, 1929.36, 1929.44, 1930.04, 1930.30, 1930.32, 1931.09, 1931.16, 1931.19, 1931.36, 1931.37, 1931.40, 1932.01, 1932.05, 1932.17, 1932.27, 1933.02, 1933.17, 1934.29, 1935.14, 1939.28, 1940.12, 1941.04, 1943.03, 1945.11
Rasche, William 1929.29
Rascoff, Joseph 1989.12
Rasely, George 1917.24, 1919.20, 1922.32, 1923.31, 1924.32, 1939.20, 1941.10, 1944.16, 1945.09
Raset, Val 1945.17
Rasey, Adelle 1946.20
Rash, E. 1919.30
Rash, Philip 1965.18, 1979.31
Rasimi, B. 1920.39
Raskin, David 1934.42, 1935.03, 1935.04, 1935.12
Raskin, Gene 1990.16
Raskin, Kenny 1994.04
Raskin, Ruby 1950.14
Raskin, Thomas 1967.05
Raskin, Tom 1958.01
Raskin, Willie 1928.47
Rasking, Tom 1958.20
Raskyn, Sam 1942.11
Rasmuson, Judy 1977.06
Rasmussen, Chris 2001.04
Rasmussen, Eleanor 1913.04
Rasmussen, Zora 1985.03
Rasshivkin, Jr. 1977.13
Ratajczak, Dave 1988.19
Ratcliff, Joseph 1899.21
Ratcliffe, E.J. 1886.58
Ratcliffe, Harry 1927.08
Ratcliffe, Samuel D. 1972.19
Rategan, Eddie 1888.39
Rath, Dick 1919.30, 1919.43
Rath, E.J. 1928.47, 1979.05
Rath, John 1983.16
Rathbun, Ruth 1939.24
Rathburn, Mr. 1877.08
Rathburn, Roger 1971.03, 1981.03
Ratima, Thomas 1972.20
Ratinho 1992.13
Ratliff, J. 1900.39
Ratliff, Joseph 1905.06, 1907.41, 1911.40
Ratliff, Joseph M. 1899.28, 1906.33, 1909.11
Ratner, Herbert 1936.28
Ratoff, Gregory 1923.15, 1924.12, 1926.24
Ratoff, Messr. 1922.37
Ratouscheff, Andy 1949.06
Rattenberry, H.L. 1883.42
Rattenberry, Harry 1884.21
Rattenberry, Harry L. 1888.07
Rattenbury, Harry 1890.28
Rattigan, Terence 1963.29
Rattray, C.R. 1869.21
Rauber, Richard 1936.03
Raucher, Gary 1970.07
Rauh, Stanley 1930.09
Rauh, Stanley E. 1923.32, 1926.23
Rault, Mons. 1876.20
Rauth, E.J. 1928.45
Ravel, C.W. 1873.02
Ravel, Charles 1906.46, 1907.54, 1908.26, 1909.20, 1910.23, 1916.15, 1917.16, 1918.23, 1922.30
Ravel, Charles W. 1875.32, 1890.25
Ravel, Charles Winter 1870.31
Ravel, Harry 1931.31
Ravel, Henry 1869.02
Ravel, Jean 1876.16
Ravel, Jerome 1888.01
Ravel, La Petite 1870.31
Ravel, Louise 1896.45
Ravel, Maurice 1929.51, 1931.26, 1932.04, 1982.06, 1987.02, 2001.04
Ravel, Sophie 1875.32, 1879.02
Ravel, W.C. 1869.26
Ravel, Winther 1867.32
Ravella, Carlos 1884.58
Ravella, Don 1992.16
Ravello, Sig. 1884.58
Ravelo, Henry 1987.03
Raven, Yolanda R. 1975.09
Ravenscroft, H.M. 1893.44, 1895.06
Ravenscroft, H.W. 1892.20, 1894.23
Ravitz, Mark 1982.22
Ravold, John 1937.10
Rawle, Sheila 1928.42
Rawlings, Jr., Herbert 1987.07
Rawlings, Judy 1951.16, 1953.09
Rawlings, Marjorie Kinnan 1965.36
Rawlings, Rober 1947.09
Rawlings, W.H. 1920.41
Rawlins, Harry 1886.35
Rawlins, Lester 1963.28
Rawlins, M. 1899.37
Rawlins, Martha 1941.11
Rawlins, W.H. 1895.10, 1895.32
Rawlinson, Miss 1870.44
Rawlston, Zelma 1889.04, 1891.09, 1891.40, 1900.59, 1905.49, 1914.23
Rawn, Jean 1978.19, 1980.21, 1981.20
Rawson, Marie 1904.48
Rawson, Mitchell 1924.36
Rawson, S.J. 1912.14
Rawtenbury, Gene 1918.36
Ray, Alan 1928.21, 1942.35
Ray, Arthur 1907.22, 1918.10
Ray, Beatrice 1904.14
Ray, C.G. 1884.24
Ray, Charles 1932.08
Ray, Charles T. 1907.12
Ray, Charlotte 1889.03, 1957.02
Ray, Ed 1910.15
Ray, Edward 1925.37
Ray, Ellen 1956.14, 1962.13
Ray, Emma 1893.33, 1897.33, 1900.24, 1907.53
Ray, Forest D. 1981.27
Ray, Gene Anthony 1988.12
Ray, Ina 1934.01
Ray, Inez 1901.17
Ray, James 1907.53, 1928.46
Ray, Jimmy 1928.41, 1930.35
Ray, Joey 1928.23, 1930.25
Ray, Johnnie 1893.33
Ray, Johnny 1897.33, 1900.24, 1904.45
Ray, Kathryn 1924.31, 1925.25, 1926.01
Ray, Leslie Ann 1978.10
Ray, Mavis 1949.03, 1951.24, 1954.07, 1960.09, 1963.04, 1963.06
Ray, Millie 1885.28, 1885.63
Ray, Naomi 1930.22, 1933.20
Ray, Nicholas 1946.24
Ray, Phil 1905.26
Ray, Ragna 1942.19
Ray, Ralph 1937.05
Ray, Robert 1979.31
Ray, Ruby 1907.32, 1909.05
Ray, Sonny 1928.42
Ray, Thelma 1907.32
Ray, Thomas 1879.37, 1881.29, 1882.02, 1885.02, 1885.15, 1885.22, 1885.49, 1885.66, 1886.03, 1886.42
Ray, Virginia 1923.30
Rayam, Curtis 1975.19
Rayburn, Tibby 1951.20
Raycelle, Ilya 1928.09
Raycelle, Maria 1928.09
Raye, Don 1955.11, 1973.14, 1975.12, 1979.24, 1979.30, 1982.22, 1986.06, 1989.12, 1999.24
Raye, Joey 1938.01
Raye, Martha 1934.39, 1940.10
Raye, Mary 1941.03, 1944.19
Rayes, Billy 1935.04, 1939.25
Rayfield, Florence 1921.02, 1921.20, 1922.18
Rayia, John 1930.26
Rayia, Joseph 1930.26
Rayia, Michael 1930.26
Raylor, George R. 1935.04
Raymax Productions 1976.24
Raymond 1891.27, 1894.28
Raymond, Ada 1890.21
Raymond, Al 1912.29
Raymond, Alice 1885.60
Raymond, Alice M. 1900.08
Raymond, Allen 1938.17
Raymond, Anne 1912.15
Raymond, Babette 1920.24
Raymond, Blanche 1880.05
Raymond, C.F. 1886.29
Raymond, Charles 1884.22
Raymond, Charles F. 1888.44
Raymond, Dean 1929.48
Raymond, E. 1854.05
Raymond, E. Marcy 1889.19
Raymond, Edward 1902.10
Raymond, Emeline 1853.05
Raymond, F. 1933.20
Raymond, Florence 1893.50
Raymond, Frank 1903.05
Raymond, Frankie 1889.09, 1899.21
Raymond, Frankie M. 1895.08
Raymond, Fredericka 1904.47
Raymond, G.R. 1905.24
Raymond, George 1929.20, 1929.31
Raymond, Gus 1935.18, 1955.27
Raymond, H. 1883.42, 1887.11
Raymond, Harry 1895.11
Raymond, Harry M. 1903.41
Raymond, Helen 1912.34, 1915.30, 1932.23, 1933.16, 1934.36, 1943.19, 1945.17, 1957.18
Raymond, Howard 1928.25
Raymond, J.F. 1880.07, 1880.68
Raymond, J.T. 1862.09, 1863.01, 1863.03, 1863.04
Raymond, John F. 1897.51
Raymond, John T. 1871.13, 1871.20, 1871.21
Raymond, Jr., Frederick 1920.30
Raymond, Julia 1894.37, 1897.21, 1901.05
Raymond, Lea 1889.06
Raymond, Lewis 1946.23, 1999.24
Raymond, Lillian 1905.08, 1905.11
Raymond, Maud 1902.01, 1907.42, 1911.34
Raymond, Maude 1899.12, 1899.29, 1903.27, 1906.17, 1908.44, 1910.07, 1910.17
Raymond, May 1895.12
Raymond, May Bell 1888.33
Raymond, Melville 1906.14, 1907.22
Raymond, Melville B. 1904.18, 1905.05
Raymond, Mlle. 1886.09, 1886.21, 1886.22
Raymond, Mr. 1851.05
Raymond, Ray 1907.50, 1918.12, 1919.01, 1921.04, 1922.14, 1925.35
Raymond, Roy 1917.11, 1948.24
Raymond, Sadie 1893.33, 1904.03
Raymond, Sid 1968.03
Raymond, Tony 1893.39, 1895.02
Raymond, W. 1880.15
Raymond, W.H. 1898.66
Raymond, William 1879.09, 1880.15, 1908.40, 1909.30
Raymond, William T. 1895.14
Raymonde, Mlle. 1885.61, 1886.08, 1886.18
Raymonde, Ruth 1925.14
Raymore, Viola 1896.47
Raynaud, Charles 1889.19
Rayne, Stephen 1999.08
Rayner, Edith 1889.54
Rayner, Michael 1976.12, 1976.13, 1976.14, 1978.15, 1978.16
Rayner, Sydney 1947.02
Raynes, J.A. 1908.05
Raynham, Walter 1888.41, 1889.54
Raynier, W.G. 1878.05
Raynor, Charles 1873.29
Raynor, Cissie 1905.19
Raynor, Hal 1936.12
Raynor, Harry 1873.29
Rayo, Mlle. 1909.09, 1911.34
Rays, Emma 1896.36
Rays, Johnnie 1896.36
Rayson, Benjamin 1973.04, 1977.08
Rayzner, Joshua 1998.11
Raz, Rivka 1971.14
Razaf, Andy 1927.32, 1928.10, 1929.23, 1930.34, 1932.14, 1939.29, 1945.07, 1967.13, 1968.20, 1973.14, 1974.09, 1975.12, 1975.20, 1975.22, 1976.04, 1978.09, 1978.21, 1980.10, 1982.12, 1989.02, 1999.01, 1999.07, 1999.24, 2000.07
Rea, F. 1856.01, 1864.14
Rea, Frank 1859.03, 1863.09, 1863.10, 1883.31
Rea, G. 1855.06, 1855.07, 1857.05
Rea, George 1862.03, 1863.07, 1864.04, 1864.07
Rea, Lawrence 1905.04, 1905.46, 1910.37, 1911.39
Rea, Messr. 1853.01, 1856.04
Rea, Mr. 1846.01, 1848.03, 1852.03, 1852.06, 1853.02, 1853.03, 1854.06
Rea, Mrs. 1853.03
Rea, Oliver 1946.19, 1959.04
Rea, Peggy 1950.20
Reab, Henry 1894.17
Read, Alice 1896.12
Read, David 1965.39
Read, Dollie 1905.19
Read, John 1897.53, 1898.07, 1898.15, 1898.19
Read, Mary 1923.40, 1924.02, 1926.32, 1927.07, 1928.02, 1928.11, 1928.37, 1930.05
Reade, Janet 1930.42
Reade, Josephine 1907.04
Reader, Ralph 1925.26, 1927.07, 1927.14, 1927.19, 1927.58, 1927.60, 1928.07, 1928.11, 1928.14, 1928.32
Readinger, Jeanne 1939.22
Readway, Edd 1892.29
Readway, Eddie 1891.40
Ready, Mr. 1876.03
Reagan, Marie 1920.04
Really Useful Company, The 1982.19, 1985.12, 1987.05, 1988.01, 1990.04, 1992.12, 1994.10
Really Useful Superstar Company 2000.09
Reals, Grace 1895.11
Ream, Frank 1986.09, 1987.03
Reamer, Mlle. 1888.39
Reams, Lee Roy 1966.01, 1969.12, 1970.09, 1974.02, 1978.04, 1980.20, 1995.13, 1998.07, 1999.01
Reaney, James 1909.03, 1910.27, 1915.24
Reaney, James G. 1907.01, 1912.39
Reano, Bob 1916.15, 1917.16
Reano, Robert 1918.23
Reany, James 1905.19, 1905.29
Reany, James C. 1903.34
Reardon, Bill 1919.40
Reardon, Casper 1938.05
Reardon, E.H. 1912.06
Reardon, Edward 1943.23
Reardon, Frank 1957.17
Reardon, John 1954.18, 1956.08, 1957.15, 1958.16, 1959.21, 1960.23, 1962.21, 1963.15, 1963.24, 1964.30, 1964.31
Reardon, Ned 1906.38, 1907.56, 1911.04
Reardon, Peter 1989.23
Reaux, Roumel 1986.06
Reaves-Phillips, Sandra 1999.06
Rebeera, Jean 1917.31
Reber, Sallie 1878.03, 1879.25, 1879.72, 1880.62, 1882.75, 1882.78
Rebera, Jean 1919.35
Rebich, Cissy 1986.13
Rebiroff, Jacques 1920.44, 1923.30
ReBrun, Miss 1863.06
Recantini 1883.06
Recco, Ernest 1933.21
Rece, R. 1896.20
Rechizeit, Jack 1970.18
Recker, Myrtle 1905.28
Reckseit, Ronald 1971.02
Record, Eugene 1997.21
Rector, Eddie 1929.18, 1930.24, 1931.11, 1932.12, 1952.08
Rector, Grace 1922.22
Rector, Maggie 1900.46
Red Clay Ramblers, The 1993.01, 1995.16, 1998.17
Red, Rhythm 1944.30
Redd, Clarence 1909.27
Redd, Randy 1998.21
Redd, Sharon 1973.14, 1975.12
Reddan, Lulu 1889.47
Redden, Melvin 1930.01
Reddick, Betty 1928.41

Reddick, Isabel 1894.15
Reddick, Walter 1928.41
Reddie, Milton 1937.09, 1938.03
Reddiman, Pedro 1909.19
Reddin, Naomi 1989.23
Redding, Earl 1905.35, 1924.25, 1947.07, 1953.15
Redding, Edwin 1927.41
Redding, Eugene 1901.09, 1902.08, 1904.18, 1908.44, 1916.12, 1918.35, 1925.14
Redding, Francesca 1888.06, 1888.11
Redding, Harry 1921.07
Redding, Otis 1982.22, 1997.21
Reddy, Brian 1982.24
Reddy, Edward 1908.34
Reddy, M. 1903.25
Reddy, Martin 1905.25
Reddy, Mr. 1855.11
Redel, Jessica 1978.20, 1979.21, 1980.03, 1981.20, 1981.22, 1987.08, 1993.12, 1996.11
Redello, Roy 1927.02
Redfern 1893.25
Redfield, Billy 1937.10, 1947.08
Redfield, Henry 1933.16
Redfield, Henry C. 1927.43
Redfield, Liza 1963.12, 1965.21, 1974.26, 1980.23
Redfield, William 1912.45, 1924.42, 1950.20
Redfield, William M. 1911.30, 1924.24
Redford, William 1924.16, 1934.18
Redledge, Floye 1903.36
Redlich, Don 1954.03
Redlidge, Floye 1897.28
Redman, Don 1932.14, 1954.19
Redman, Joseph 1912.30, 1913.22
Redmond, A. 1880.41
Redmond, Aline 1902.19, 1903.37, 1905.29, 1909.29
Redmond, Helen 1895.33, 1896.45, 1897.42, 1899.40, 1903.38
Redmond, James 1914.02
Redmond, John 1981.06, 1997.03
Redmond, Joseph 1907.42
Redmond, Mlle. 1888.23
Redmond, P. 1887.17, 1888.25, 1889.43, 1890.36, 1894.52, 1898.45, 1907.43, 1908.32
Redmond, Patrick 1904.32
Redmond, Rita 1905.31, 1910.15
Redouin, Edmee 1964.22
Redpath, Olive 1898.51, 1899.22
Redsecker, John 1987.06
Redstone, Michael 1943.20
Redstone, William 1894.21
Redway, Edd 1902.20, 1904.19
Redway, Eddie 1905.56
Redwine, Skip 1971.09
Ree, Max 1923.31, 1924.31, 1924.44
Reece, E. 1880.46
Reece, Kathryn 1926.10, 1926.44, 1927.45, 1944.04, 1944.05, 1944.08, 1944.09, 1944.10, 1944.11, 1944.12, 1944.13
Reece, Lucile 1927.45
Reece, Lucille 1927.64
Reece, R. 1876.15, 1877.23
Reece, Robert 1876.10, 1886.32, 1886.50, 1886.54, 1887.33
Reed, Addie Cora 1886.32, 1886.45, 1887.19, 1889.16, 1894.13
Reed, Alaina 1974.24, 1977.15, 1978.21
Reed, Alexander 1972.06
Reed, Alice 1895.09
Reed, Alyson 1981.25, 1983.08, 1983.17, 1984.10, 1987.16, 1993.16
Reed, Annetta 1899.18
Reed, Anthony 1945.20
Reed, Bert 1942.11
Reed, Bertha 1905.31
Reed, Billy 1929.45
Reed, Bobbie 1915.31
Reed, Bonnie 1938.08
Reed, Bruce 1978.07, 1978.20, 1979.21, 1984.12, 1989.13
Reed, C. 1863.06
Reed, Carl 1925.36, 1927.26, 1928.21
Reed, Charles 1888.32
Reed, Charlie 1890.07, 1890.34, 1891.37, 1893.08
Reed, Daisy 1904.28
Reed, Daniel 1954.07
Reed, Dave 1876.13, 1876.15, 1876.22, 1876.29, 1877.01
Reed, David 1905.47
Reed, Edna May 1923.18
Reed, Eloise 1907.26, 1910.02
Reed, Emeline 1852.05
Reed, Esta 1903.24
Reed, Eugenie 1933.07
Reed, Fay 1964.18
Reed, Florence 1882.09, 1883.12, 1883.13, 1917.24
Reed, G.W. 1875.39
Reed, Genevieve 1907.26, 1910.02
Reed, George 1908.30
Reed, Graham 1895.13
Reed, H.E. 1894.16
Reed, H.L. 1899.04
Reed, Harry 1907.55
Reed, Henry F. 1878.22
Reed, Herman 1932.30
Reed, Ione 1936.12
Reed, J.P. 1908.08
Reed, Janet 1948.08
Reed, Jared 1949.17, 1951.24
Reed, Jessie 1918.05, 1918.20, 1919.15, 1920.18, 1921.21
Reed, John 1955.15, 1955.21, 1962.25, 1962.26, 1962.28, 1962.29, 1962.30, 1962.31, 1964.36, 1964.38, 1964.41, 1964.42, 1964.43, 1966.22, 1966.23, 1966.25, 1966.26, 1966.28, 1968.25, 1968.26, 1968.27, 1968.28, 1968.29, 1976.12, 1976.14, 1978.14, 1978.15, 1978.16, 1978.17, 1989.15
Reed, John H. 1921.01
Reed, Jonathan 1943.06
Reed, Jr., Dave 1894.21, 1894.31, 1897.40, 1898.46, 1900.47, 1900.52, 1900.55, 1901.27, 1901.30, 1905.19, 1905.20, 1905.27, 1907.15
Reed, Jr., David 1903.33
Reed, Karen Lynn 1961.07, 1962.18
Reed, Kathryn 1944.19
Reed, Les 1976.32
Reed, Linda Mann 1974.26
Reed, Lizzie 1879.02
Reed, Lou 1982.22
Reed, Mabel 1907.34
Reed, Mary 1922.27
Reed, Master 1841.01
Reed, Mel 1938.08
Reed, Messr. 1841.01, 1881.14, 1882.37
Reed, Michael 1980.17, 1992.12, 1993.15
Reed, Mignon 1919.01, 1919.29
Reed, Miss 1882.07
Reed, Mr. 1866.11, 1866.15
Reed, Mr. German 1880.18
Reed, Mrs. German 1880.18
Reed, Napoleon 1943.24, 1945.06, 1946.09, 1952.08
Reed, Nat 1930.29
Reed, Ned 1930.29
Reed, Nellie 1901.27
Reed, Paul 1940.11, 1940.14, 1942.22, 1942.32, 1945.03, 1947.11, 1948.15, 1949.02, 1950.06, 1950.17, 1953.11, 1954.02, 1957.18, 1961.22, 1968.08, 1968.31
Reed, Pauline 1903.08, 1904.26, 1908.08
Reed, Phyllis 1938.16
Reed, Richard 1939.26
Reed, Roland 1879.38, 1880.24, 1883.43, 1885.43, 1886.34
Reed, Royal 1999.08
Reed, Sam 1903.04
Reed, Samuel 1884.12, 1884.66, 1886.36, 1888.29, 1889.45, 1891.11, 1892.22, 1892.33, 1892.47, 1893.16, 1907.46
Reed, Stephen 1996.18
Reed, Stuart 1899.28
Reed, Taylor 1963.05, 1964.35, 1965.28, 1968.05, 1970.10, 1977.12
Reed, Thomas German 1876.30
Reed, Vern 1957.18, 1965.21
Reed, Virginia 1908.40
Reed, Vivian 1972.05, 1972.14, 1976.04, 1980.15, 1992.06, 1999.22
Reed, W. 1893.34
Reed, Wakefield 1893.34, 1902.01
Reed, Walter 1943.23
Reed, Will 1951.05
Reed, William C. 1912.04
Reed, William R. 1912.04
Reed. J. 1882.40
Reed. S.R. 1875.16
Reed. Thomas German 1870.11
Reede, Florence 1883.11
Reeder, G.T. 1869.11, 1869.17, 1869.21, 1869.25, 1869.28
Reeder, George 1952.13, 1953.01, 1953.17, 1956.12, 1959.11, 1962.12, 1964.11
Reeder, Hilah 1919.27
Reeder, Michael 1992.18
Reedy 1894.27
Reedy, Kuini 1972.20
Reedy, Percy 1972.20
Reedy, William 1948.28
Reel, Renee 1914.18, 1915.18
Reep, Philip 1929.32
Rees, A. 1917.16, 1918.23
Rees, Judson 1949.15
Rees, Milton 1948.10
Rees, Minnie C. 1892.35
Rees, Philip 1894.12
Rees, William 1908.44
Reese, Arthur 1899.33, 1900.46
Reese, Bob 1959.14
Reese, David 1914.12
Reese, Harry L. 1920.34
Reese, Henry 1948.24
Reese, Jack 1946.14
Reese, Lloyd 1954.15
Reese, Ollie 1899.33, 1900.46
Reese, Stephen 1952.03
Reeve, Ada 1893.41
Reeve, Frances 1911.01
Reeve, Mary Ann 1946.05, 1949.04
Reeve, Messr. 1857.03
Reeve, Mr. 1857.02
Reeve, Scott 1982.20, 1983.13, 1984.11, 1986.08, 1989.14
Reeve, William 1796.02
Reeves, Alice 1882.04, 1882.20
Reeves, Allen 1928.45
Reeves, Annie 1882.49
Reeves, Billie 1908.19, 1909.13
Reeves, Fanny 1867.25
Reeves, George 1943.23
Reeves, Harry 1881.28
Reeves, Jean 1946.01
Reeves, Jennie 1884.42, 1887.13, 1890.03, 1891.41
Reeves, Mattie 1900.02
Reeves, McKinley 1930.10, 1935.01
Reeves, Mrs. 1855.02
Reeves, Mrs. W.H. 1868.04
Reeves, Peter 1993.17
Reeves, Richard 1942.20
Reeves, Rober 1947.04
Reeves, Sid 1892.08
Reeves, Steve 1953.16, 1955.25
Reeves, W. 1854.03
Reeves, William 1910.18
Reeves-Smith, H. 1934.29
Reeves-Smith, Olive 1916.07, 1935.14, 1947.01, 1956.01, 1964.20
Regal, Henry 1920.10
Regaloncita, La 1894.05
Regamey, M. Felix 1873.10
Regan, Dan 1898.45, 1899.32, 1904.32
Regan, Hazel 1891.20
Regan, Jay M. 1920.24
Regan, Patti 1959.14, 1961.16
Regan, Sylvia 1950.06
Regan, Walter 1919.36, 1922.48, 1923.09
Regas, Edward 1893.05
Regas, F.W. 1894.14, 1895.13
Regas, Jack 1972.20
Regas, Kit 1972.20
Regay, Pearl 1922.27, 1924.28, 1926.42
Regenti, Rose 1880.31
Reggan, Miss 1881.39
Reginard, Renie 1881.42
Regis, Basha 1951.23, 1958.03
Regis, Frank 1898.46, 1900.28
Regis, Mr. 1898.29
Regisseur 1869.03
Regisseur, Herve 1869.30
Regnault, Mlle. 1872.42
Rego, Luis 1977.04
Reguera, Rogelio 1958.06
Regulski, Jaroslaw 1992.05
Rehak, Frank 1957.14
Rehan, Ada 1879.50, 1879.56, 1880.04, 1881.04, 1881.11, 1884.11, 1891.05, 1892.14
Rehctaog, Mons. 1881.40
Rehfeld, Harriet 1906.24
Rehg, Don 1962.24
Rehill, Harold J. 1912.33
Rehman, Carl 1908.21
Reho, Nora 1957.05
Reicards, J. 1881.40
Reich, George 1964.22, 1984.10
Reichardt, Frl. 1897.08
Reicher, Frank 1904.30, 1925.52
Reicher, Messr. 1881.02
Reichert, Edward 1947.02
Reichert, H. 1943.12
Reichert, Heinz 1920.46, 1921.31, 1923.14, 1923.15, 1924.12, 1926.05, 1931.07, 1934.29, 1938.17
Reichert, Kurt 1939.23
Reichner, Bickley 1936.12, 1957.10
Reick, Lottie 1919.26
Reid, Alexander 1988.12
Reid, Allan 1910.15
Reid, Annetta 1901.26
Reid, Antonio 1997.21
Reid, Cecilia 1901.26
Reid, Elliot 1951.19
Reid, Elliott 1960.07
Reid, Florence 1909.15
Reid, H. Logan 1895.15, 1899.10, 1899.14, 1899.16
Reid, H.L. 1885.47, 1887.10, 1887.43, 1890.39, 1890.43, 1891.28, 1893.32, 1893.47, 1894.05, 1894.15, 1894.20, 1895.30, 1896.39
Reid, Hal 1904.33, 1906.34, 1907.55
Reid, Hugh L. 1893.17, 1897.52
Reid, Hugh Logan 1894.33, 1894.38, 1897.29
Reid, Ilene 1999.24
Reid, James A. 1906.27
Reid, Johnny 1931.32
Reid, Keenah 1998.16
Reid, Keith 1982.22
Reid, L.H. 1888.01
Reid, Lewis 1922.03
Reid, Marci 1998.08
Reid, Margaret 1893.48, 1894.03
Reid, Meston 1976.13, 1976.14, 1978.16
Reid, Ruby 1900.33, 1901.08
Reid, W.C. 1916.15
Reid, William 1918.27
Reid, William C. 1912.33, 1913.22
Reide, Dimple 1930.20
Reide, Evelyn 1931.07, 1932.01
Reidy, Jack 1905.07
Reidy, John 1898.06
Reif, A. 1955.19
Reiff, A. 1868.06
Reiff, Anthony 1857.06, 1880.55, 1884.18, 1885.48, 1887.32, 1888.25
Reiff, Antoine 1878.16
Reiff, George W. 1904.14
Reiff, Jr., A. 1868.06
Reiff, Jr., Anthony 1872.17
Reiff, Jr., Antoine 1880.01, 1880.03
Reiff, Jules C. 1904.14
Reiffarth, Herr 1866.33
Reiffarth, Jeanette 1866.33
Reiffarth, Jeannette 1880.38
Reiffarth, Jenette 1879.64
Reiffarth, Jennie 1882.71, 1884.25, 1884.42, 1885.45, 1890.08, 1891.30, 1892.07, 1892.16, 1892.28, 1894.10, 1894.47, 1897.23, 1898.30, 1905.05
Reiffarth, Ottilie 1892.03, 1892.47
Reifferth, Jennie 1883.37
Reigg 1884.28
Reignard, Renie 1881.44
Reignolds, G. 1867.12
Reignolds, Georgina 1860.01
Reignolds, Kate 1856.01, 1856.02, 1856.03, 1857.02, 1857.03
Reihardt, Max 1937.01
Reiley, Agnes 1891.11, 1892.22, 1892.33
Reiley, Orrin 1970.09, 1971.15
Reilley, Bernard J. 1892.04
Reilly, Agnes 1893.16
Reilly, Anastasia 1920.39, 1927.07
Reilly, Bill 1951.18, 1956.02
Reilly, Charles Nelson 1960.06, 1961.22, 1964.01, 1965.33
Reilly, Gracie 1937.15
Reilly, Irene 1941.03
Reilly, J. 1872.09
Reilly, James 1887.23, 1918.21
Reilly, Joe 1929.31, 1930.28
Reilly, John 1875.10
Reilly, Thomas 1893.11
Reilly, Thomas F. 1902.11
Reilly, Whitcomb 1903.05
Reilly, William 1962.05, 1963.08, 1965.31
Reily, J. 1875.03
Reily, Mike 1927.32
Reim, Robert 1956.05
Reimer 1881.28

Reimer, Amy 1895.43
Reimer, Helen 1884.16, 1884.37, 1890.07, 1891.04, 1891.37, 1893.08
Reimer, Messr. 1890.31, 1894.01
Reimer, Mr. 1891.33
Reimer, Walter 1964.19
Reimherr, George 1924.05, 1925.06
Reimueller, Ross 1973.12, 1976.01, 1976.28
Rein, Martin I. 1987.02
Reina, Mark 1984.06
Reinagle, H. 1834.03
Reinard, Messr. 1852.05
Reinau, Franz 1890.40
Reinders, Kate 2001.06
Reine Costume Company 1930.24
Reine, Inc. 1929.24
Reine, Madame 1929.24
Reine, Mons. 1876.20, 1876.24, 1876.25, 1876.26, 1877.10, 1877.11, 1877.12, 1877.13, 1877.14, 1877.19
Reine, W. 1877.09
Reinecke, Frl. 1882.68
Reinehart, Dora 1970.10
Reiner, Anton 1891.30
Reiner, Carl 1948.14, 1950.02, 1976.09
Reiner, Ethel Linder 1952.06, 1956.15
Reiner, Hanne Marie 1965.01, 1965.31
Reiner, Michelle 1955.06, 1955.07, 1956.14
Reinhard, John 1909.25, 1910.22, 1919.44, 1920.21
Reinhard, Mr. 1906.29
Reinhardt, Elsa 1904.35, 1905.13, 1905.29, 1912.07, 1914.28
Reinhardt, Gottfried 1942.31, 1944.16, 1945.14
Reinhardt, Heinrich 1910.37, 1913.10
Reinhardt, John 1910.18
Reinhardt, Max 1942.31
Reinhardt, Robert 1933.24
Reinhardt, Stephen 1968.18, 1968.19, 1970.07, 1974.13, 1976.17, 1978.12
Reinhart, Beatrice 1898.78
Reinhart, C.W. 1892.06
Reinhart, Elsa 1907.10
Reinhart, Joseph J. 2001.04
Reinholt, George 1979.02
Reinis, Jonathan 1999.09, 1999.14
Reinking, Ann 1974.05, 1975.06, 1992.18, 1996.14, 1999.01
Reis, Eda 1941.01
Reis, Mark C. 1995.02
Reisch, Michele 1999.06
Reisch, Walter 1931.21, 1968.20, 1999.07
Reisenfeld, Hugo 1912.48, 1920.15
Reiser, Al 1943.02
Reiser, Lee 1943.02
Reisfeld, Bert 1981.04, 1999.05
Reisig 1914.24
Reisig and Company 1898.61
Reisig Dove Studios 1912.46
Reisig, P.H. 1917.27
Reisig, Theodore 1904.34, 1910.35, 1911.42, 1912.05, 1913.05, 1913.09, 1918.01, 1921.15
Reisman, Barbara 1953.09
Reisman, Jane 1971.20, 1974.20, 1974.22, 1989.02
Reisner, C. Francis 1917.26
Reisner, Francis 1917.08
Reiss, Marvin 1960.04, 1960.16, 1962.02
Reissa, Eleanor 1990.16
Reiter, Francis E. 1888.29
Reitman, Ivan 1974.13, 1983.01
Reitzky 1872.06
Reitzky, Messr. 1871.27
Reitzky, Mons. 1870.44
Reives, Miss 1851.05
Relda, F. 1898.07
Relda, Florence 1898.04
Relis, Rachela 1970.18
Relkin, Edwin A. 1942.28
Rellum, Pauline 1897.27
Relma, Lillian 1894.24
Relph, Harry 1888.39
Relyea, Cora 1894.13
Relyea, Marjorie 1898.63, 1900.16, 1900.51
Remaily, Robin 1970.04
Rembach, Frank 1966.03
Remer, Leila 1907.45
Remetze, Ella 1879.50, 1879.56
Remey, Ethel 1938.09
Remick, Lee 1964.15
Remington, Adele 1912.37
Remington, Barbara 1965.31
Remington, Earle 1885.42
Remington, Leona 1908.13, 1909.05
Remington, Ruth 1924.12
Remisoff, Nicholas 1922.06, 1923.28
Remizoff, V. 1929.05
Remlinger, William 1905.20
Remme, John 1981.13, 1982.24, 1987.19, 1989.27
Remmelsberg, Betty 1879.02
Remneck, Martin 1931.44
Remo, Kenneth 1948.18
Remo, Roy 1923.02
Remos, Susan 1940.18
Remos, Susanne 1934.41, 1942.05
Remsen, Deborah 1953.08
Remy, Dick 1940.12
Remy, Dot 1940.12, 1949.09
Rena, Gita 1964.25
Renaldo, Tito 1939.30
Renan, Emile 1944.26, 1946.11, 1948.31, 1949.08, 1952.12, 1953.05, 1953.14, 1958.13, 1959.09, 1959.10, 1964.10, 1964.13, 1965.10, 1965.12, 1968.09, 1968.15
Renard, Cecil 1913.09
Renard, Cecile 1914.12
Renard, Jules 1988.10
Renard, Lew 1918.09
Renard, Ruth 1900.40
Renard, Willa 1920.43
Renaud, Andre 1932.18
Renaud, Emila 1999.05
Renaud, William 1924.07, 1938.03
Renault, Francis 1922.34
Renavent, George 1917.34
Rendle, H.A. 1865.06, 1869.40
Rendle, Mr. 1863.06, 1863.07, 1866.18
Rendulic, Freddy 1932.28
Rene, Leon 1953.12
Rene, Nikki 1986.20, 1990.12, 1992.06
Rene, Otis 1953.12
Renee 1923.23, 1930.31
Renee, Carol 1941.12
Renee, Helen 1939.21
Renfield, Robert 1972.01
Renfroe, Rebecca 1981.07
Renfroe, Steve 1969.03
Renis, Tony 1964.02
Renna, Shorty 1949.06
Rennagel, Marilyn 1978.26, 1979.11, 1981.10, 1982.10
Renner, Josie 1882.31, 1882.36, 1882.37
Renner, M. 1897.48, 1898.50, 1899.17, 1899.30
Renner, Michael 1899.30
Renner, W. 1898.50
Rennick, P. 2001.04
Rennie, Anna 1880.39
Rennie, Annie 1879.63
Rennie, Eunice 1893.26
Rennie, J.H. 1879.63, 1880.39, 1882.25, 1882.32, 1882.38, 1882.41
Rennie, James 1888.40, 1889.07, 1889.11, 1890.49, 1891.25, 1933.20, 1936.12, 1958.03
Rennie, John 1891.45
Rennie, Messr. 1887.48
Reno, Adele 1892.39
Reno, Dick 1881.39
Reno, George B. 1903.30
Reno, George P. 1905.23
Renoff 1923.21
Renoff, F. 1923.21
Renoff, Frederick 1922.26
Renoir, Jean 1958.06
Renold, Theresa 1901.05
Renold, Therese 1899.23
Renon, Yvonne 1911.18
Renous, William 1890.17
Renschler, Eric 1998.11
Renshaw, Christopher 1989.01, 1996.05, 1998.05
Renton, Alfred 1921.28
Rentz-Santley Novelty Company 1881.17, 1881.19
Renwick, Charles 1888.35, 1889.23, 1890.01, 1890.11, 1890.19, 1890.24, 1891.12, 1891.17, 1893.41, 1894.46, 1904.05
Renwick, Katherine 1927.36
Renwick, Maurette 1938.03
Renwick, Peter 1938.04
Renwood, Minnie 1891.22, 1892.07
Renyi, Aladar 1914.28
Renys, Roberta 1923.43
Renzi, Michael 1983.20
Reparata 1976.34
Repertory Theatre of Lincoln Center, The 1970.04
Repicci, William 2000.02
Repole, Charles 1975.24, 1979.05, 1995.07
Repp, Ellen 1947.02, 1948.18
Reppil, R.A. 1934.20
Resig's 1908.12
Resin, Dan 1959.26, 1961.11, 1964.21, 1965.31
Resnick, David 1923.14
Resnick, Ira 1972.23
Resnickoff, Leo 1943.11
Resnik, L. 1932.09
Resnik, Regina 1987.16, 1990.07
Resnikoff, David 1937.11
Resor, Messr. 1846.01
Resor, Mr. 1846.01
Respighi, Ottorino 1932.29, 1934.02
Resserd, E.M. 1898.64
Resta, Luca 1893.29
Restof, E. 1875.06
Rethmeier, Gary 1971.04
Retnor, Albert 1906.03
Retter, Dezso 1926.15
Retter, Freddie 1934.18
Reuter, Greg 2001.03
Reuter, Gustave 1881.17, 1881.19
Revalles, Flora 1917.26
Revalles, Flore 1919.03
Revaux, Caliude 1974.11
Reveaux, Edward 1945.18, 1949.02, 1951.10
Revel, Billy 1923.38, 1935.04
Revel, Harry 1930.43, 1931.19, 1931.31, 1931.36, 1932.06, 1932.15, 1940.20, 1945.18, 1980.09, 1982.12
Revelers, The 1964.39
Revell, Charles 1920.26
Revell, Paul 1931.02
Revelle, Arta 1928.45
Revene, Nadine 1956.03, 1956.05
Revere, Amy 1925.49, 1927.46, 1930.32
Revere, Annie 1899.09
Revere, Claude 1895.20
Revere, Eugene 1911.02, 1912.39, 1914.23, 1915.25, 1916.20, 1917.01, 1917.26, 1922.45, 1924.08
Revere, Mildred 1899.09
Revere, Nadine 1954.07, 1955.09
Revere, Pearl 1904.07
Revett, Daisy 1916.18
Revil 1947.05, 1948.12
Revil, Rudi 1941.03
Revill, Clive 1960.16, 1963.01, 1967.02
Revillion, Maxine 1908.10
Revson, Iris 1981.08, 1983.01
Rewalt, Lothar 1939.23, 1940.04
Rex, Ada 1908.08
Rex, S.C. 1902.38
Rex, Sterling 1908.08, 1909.27
Rexford, Eben 1918.21
Rexford, George H. 1892.12
Rexford, Orlo 1938.10
Rexite, Seymour 1970.17
Rey, Antonia 1964.40, 1969.11
Rey, Billy 1934.43
Rey, Frederico 1942.14
Rey, Reynaldo 1995.01
Reyde, Gwendolyn 1939.17
Reydova, Elizabeth 1938.16
Reyes, Aurea 1949.07
Reyes, Dulcy 1993.12
Reyes, Eva 1944.02, 1948.21
Reyes, Raul 1944.02, 1948.21
Reyes, Riva 1930.37
Reyloff, Edmund 1858.03
Reynier, W.C. 1887.46
Reynier, W.G. 1887.17
Reynolds, Abe 1933.13, 1933.25
Reynolds, Arie 1881.44
Reynolds, Arthur 1913.26
Reynolds, Barney 1888.13, 1891.40, 1892.31
Reynolds, Carolyn 1921.14
Reynolds, Carrie 1880.46, 1887.40, 1903.23, 1909.05, 1911.23, 1919.41
Reynolds, Charles 1961.15, 1962.13, 1980.12, 1983.01, 1984.16, 1987.18, 1996.08
Reynolds, Debbie 1973.05, 1976.24
Reynolds, E.R. 1898.48
Reynolds, Earl 1918.23
Reynolds, Earle 1906.45, 1908.04
Reynolds, Elizabeth 1922.11
Reynolds, Ellis 1989.02
Reynolds, Ethel 1937.11
Reynolds, Frank 1951.10
Reynolds, G.W. 1880.46
Reynolds, Genevieve 1884.09, 1884.20, 1884.30, 1884.31, 1884.34, 1885.45, 1886.26, 1891.44, 1897.15
Reynolds, George Edward 1988.10
Reynolds, Gertie 1897.23, 1898.01, 1898.31
Reynolds, Gus 1885.53, 1886.44, 1886.51
Reynolds, Helen 1918.23
Reynolds, Herbert 1911.27, 1914.18, 1915.04, 1915.07, 1915.17, 1915.30, 1916.19, 1917.01, 1917.02, 1918.16, 1922.19, 1926.29, 1975.22, 1975.24, 1986.01
Reynolds, Howard 1951.05
Reynolds, Jack 1937.13
Reynolds, James 1889.13, 1892.04, 1896.35, 1920.08, 1920.28, 1921.21, 1922.19, 1923.20, 1923.38, 1923.43, 1924.32, 1924.34, 1924.44, 1925.05, 1925.08, 1925.31, 1925.32, 1925.33, 1925.38, 1926.32, 1926.46, 1927.12, 1927.65, 1928.30, 1929.45, 1930.05, 1930.38, 1934.03, 1934.19, 1934.41, 1934.42, 1935.15, 1943.08, 1952.03
Reynolds, James A. 1892.04
Reynolds, James W. 1887.01
Reynolds, Jeffrey 1982.14
Reynolds, Jennie 1890.29
Reynolds, Lance 1983.17
Reynolds, Lillian 1933.15
Reynolds, Lillian C. 1879.59
Reynolds, Marie 1881.42, 1881.45
Reynolds, Marsha 1955.27
Reynolds, Mary 1958.18
Reynolds, Messr. 1851.01
Reynolds, Miss 1864.04, 1880.63
Reynolds, Mr. 1851.06, 1852.01, 1853.01, 1853.03, 1854.02, 1855.11
Reynolds, Myrna 1976.26, 1978.19, 1978.20, 1978.23
Reynolds, Nonie 1900.45
Reynolds, Pearl 1954.19
Reynolds, Quentin 1946.17
Reynolds, Sarah 1987.19
Reynolds, Stephanie 1961.04
Reynolds, Sydney 1924.42
Reynolds, T. 1907.63
Reynolds, T.F. 1905.52
Reynolds, Theodore F. 1917.30
Reynolds, Thomas 1909.24, 1910.05, 1910.21, 1910.35, 1911.27, 1914.30, 1933.02
Reynolds, Thomas L. 1912.26
Reynolds, Victoria 1880.59, 1880.65, 1880.67, 1880.70, 1882.17, 1882.42, 1882.47, 1883.04
Reynolds, Virginia 1912.03
Reynolds, W.H. 1856.04
Reynolds, Willard 1915.01
Reynolds, William 1893.43
Reynolds, William W. 1954.07
Reywood, May 1878.22
Rezarf, Thomas 1965.01
Rezlitt, Albert 1901.21
Rhea, Jeannette 1891.18
Rheinhardt, Elsa 1906.05
Rheis-Gromes, Hill 1964.25
Rheubottom, Doris 1930.24
Rhoades, Frank 1918.01
Rhoades, Lillian 1907.07
Rhoades, Richard 1948.18
Rhoda, Cecilia 1907.01
Rhode, Arthur 1904.38
Rhodes, Betty 1960.01, 1981.05
Rhodes, Burt 1962.18
Rhodes, Erik 1932.26, 1950.03, 1953.07, 1957.05, 1957.16, 1968.17
Rhodes, Evan H. 1989.25
Rhodes, George 1964.32, 1974.11, 1978.18
Rhodes, Harrison 1912.09, 1915.32, 1927.14
Rhodes, Jan 1960.10
Rhodes, Josh 1999.01, 2001.03
Rhodes, Lila 1911.33, 1916.02, 1917.37
Rhodes, Liola 1907.20
Rhodes, Loretta 1926.01
Rhodes, Margie 1906.11
Rhodes, Marguerite 1898.22
Rhodes, Robert 1920.34, 1921.30, 1926.23, 1929.30, 1929.36, 1931.29, 1932.22
Rhodes, William 1907.61
Rhodes, William Barnes 1924.20
Rhule, Glen 1999.02
Rhyne, Sylvia 1987.03, 1989.19
Rhythm, Charlie 1999.09
Ria, Robin 1987.03
Riabinine, J. 1924.48
Riabouchinska, Tania 1945.14
Riabouchinska, Tatiana 1931.38

Riadnoff, E. 1929.22
Riadnoff, Messr. 1923.28
Rial, Jay 1888.33
Rial, Louise 1895.41, 1897.17, 1899.35, 1908.09
Rial, Vira 1896.12
Riano, Bobby 1920.26
Riano, Jack 1931.14, 1941.12, 1942.20
Riano, Miss 1905.54
Riano, Rene 1920.14, 1921.30
Riano, Renie 1925.47
Riashentsev, Uri 1979.29
Riban, Ernest 1914.05
Ribas, Mme. 1841.01
Ribeau, Frederic 1898.40
Ribecchi, John 1973.09, 1989.18
Ribeiro, Alfonso 1983.21
Ribeiro, Luciano 1992.13
Ribera, Chita 1981.07
Riberdy, Allen 1986.14, 1988.16
Ribierre, Jeanne 1912.30, 1914.19
Riblet, P.H. 1908.42
Ribnikov, Alexis 1990.01
Ricahardson, Karl 1997.19
Ricard, Amy 1903.31, 1906.50
Ricard, Leila 1922.39, 1924.33
Ricardo, F.M. 1879.09, 1880.15, 1881.55, 1883.56
Ricardo, Irene 1923.21
Ricca, Frieda 1906.01
Riccardi, Adolph 1884.58
Ricci, Aurelia 1867.25
Ricci, Bertha 1883.62, 1884.14, 1884.63, 1886.26, 1886.33, 1886.37, 1887.33, 1887.50, 1888.35, 1890.37, 1890.44, 1891.41, 1893.32
Ricci, L. 1923.29
Ricci, R. 1923.29
Ricci, Rose 1887.33, 1887.50, 1893.32
Ricciardelli, John 1983.17
Ricciardi, William 1907.25
Rice Burlesque Company 1894.38
Rice's Great American Burlesque Company 1889.13
Rice's New Extravaganza Combination 1880.40
Rice's Olympia Burlesque Company 1895.38
Rice's Opera Bouffe Company 1883.65
Rice's Opera Bouffe Extravaganza Combination 1879.06
Rice's Surprise Party 1880.10
Rice, Adnia 1957.02, 1957.18, 1962.27, 1965.21
Rice, Al 1902.33
Rice, Al. 1904.20
Rice, Alice 1896.33
Rice, Andy 1920.17, 1922.27, 1927.13, 1927.35
Rice, Anita 1922.32
Rice, Arthur 1904.01
Rice, Bert 1910.21
Rice, Billy 1871.12, 1871.16
Rice, Blanche 1906.05, 1907.48, 1909.19
Rice, Bob 1927.41, 1928.47, 1937.06
Rice, C.E. 1895.38
Rice, Catherine 1975.09
Rice, Charles E. 1888.21
Rice, Diana Mary 1995.19, 1996.15
Rice, E.E. 1894.05
Rice, Edison 1935.02, 1939.27, 1940.22
Rice, Edmund 1950.09
Rice, Edward E. 1877.21, 1878.02, 1878.19, 1879.01, 1879.06, 1879.33, 1879.35, 1880.02, 1880.06, 1880.10, 1880.13, 1880.31, 1880.35, 1880.40, 1880.42, 1880.59, 1880.65, 1880.67, 1880.70, 1881.07, 1881.27, 1881.47, 1882.34, 1883.42, 1883.64, 1883.65, 1883.67, 1884.09, 1884.42, 1885.04, 1885.26, 1885.40, 1885.58, 1886.47, 1887.01, 1887.31, 1887.43, 1888.09, 1888.13, 1888.36, 1889.01, 1889.13, 1889.44, 1889.46, 1892.04, 1893.13, 1893.17, 1894.19, 1894.26, 1894.38, 1895.38, 1896.29, 1896.35, 1896.48, 1897.37, 1897.52, 1898.05, 1898.17, 1898.41, 1898.43, 1898.51, 1898.58, 1899.23, 1899.26, 1899.36, 1900.03, 1902.15, 1902.27, 1904.34, 1905.23, 1909.09
Rice, Elmer 1947.02, 1959.08, 1959.17, 1963.15, 1965.33, 1966.02, 1978.23, 1979.27, 1990.08
Rice, Fannie 1883.11, 1883.15, 1884.12
Rice, Fanny 1883.64, 1883.67, 1884.20, 1889.04, 1889.23, 1890.11, 1890.39, 1892.19, 1894.25, 1897.22
Rice, Frank 1903.01
Rice, Gitz 1918.10, 1918.27, 1921.11, 1926.22
Rice, Herbert 1904.20
Rice, Huntington 1931.44
Rice, Irene 1890.09, 1890.13, 1890.22, 1890.42, 1892.02, 1892.13, 1892.26, 1892.32, 1892.41, 1893.01
Rice, J. Clifford 1930.37
Rice, Jack 1923.17
Rice, Jack E. 1920.47
Rice, John 1886.06
Rice, John C. 1886.58, 1890.12, 1890.30, 1891.15, 1894.46, 1895.27, 1896.52, 1897.40
Rice, Jr., Andy 1930.42
Rice, Lillian 1901.27, 1904.03, 1906.41, 1907.24, 1908.15, 1909.09, 1910.20, 1911.05, 1912.39, 1913.31, 1914.23, 1915.31, 1916.20, 1917.06
Rice, Marie Edith 1895.15
Rice, Mary 1872.23
Rice, Michael 1984.10
Rice, Miss 1872.35
Rice, Moyne 1934.06
Rice, Peter 1955.19, 1965.28, 1972.24
Rice, Reva 1987.05
Rice, Roy 1929.29
Rice, Sarah 1979.06
Rice, Seymour 1894.51
Rice, Tim 1971.12, 1977.18, 1979.23, 1982.03, 1988.09, 1992.12, 1993.15, 1994.04, 1995.02, 1995.12, 1997.01, 1997.12, 1997.20, 1999.16, 2000.06, 2000.09
Rice, True 1921.37
Rich and Harris 1899.27, 1900.36, 1901.15
Rich, Adele 1937.17
Rich, Bernie 1962.17
Rich, C. 1892.35
Rich, Charles T. 1899.03
Rich, Doris 1934.41, 1959.01
Rich, Frank J. 1887.50
Rich, H.W. 1886.35
Rich, Harry 1885.46
Rich, Helen 1917.17, 1920.36, 1922.39
Rich, Henrietta 1891.38
Rich, I.B. 1885.26
Rich, Irene 1948.28
Rich, Isaac B. 1885.40, 1888.16, 1891.03, 1891.26, 1891.32, 1892.05, 1892.09, 1893.06, 1893.49, 1893.50, 1895.27, 1895.34, 1896.52, 1897.30, 1897.40, 1897.47, 1903.25
Rich, James 1977.15, 1978.13, 1982.03
Rich, James B. 1892.50
Rich, Jr., Larry 1936.06
Rich, Lizzie 1878.17
Rich, Lucille 1937.06
Rich, Max 1927.02, 1932.24, 1934.18, 1955.05
Rich, Ron 1969.15
Richard D'Oyly Carte Opera Comique Company 1881.37
Richard D'Oyly Carte's Opera Company 1882.17, 1882.60, 1882.75, 1882.78
Richard, Al 1931.31, 1933.27
Richard, Claire 1950.18
Richard, Darryl 1958.04
Richard, Don 2000.20
Richard, Ellen 1995.11, 1997.15, 1998.15, 2001.02
Richard, Harry 1904.18
Richard, Jean-Paul 1992.07
Richard, Jerome 1936.17
Richard, Judine 1997.08, 1998.16
Richard, Judine Hawkins 1992.02
Richard, Keith 1982.22
Richard, Mons. 1882.29
Richard, Tania 1993.04
Richard, Ward 1944.24
Richards, Al 1930.34, 1931.31
Richards, Alice 1879.02, 1883.39
Richards, Allen 1957.16
Richards, Bill 1958.01, 1965.01
Richards, Charles N. 1903.22
Richards, Dal 1966.06
Richards, Devin 1995.15, 2000.18
Richards, Don 1942.11, 1942.27, 1943.23
Richards, Donald 1947.03, 1949.01
Richards, Dorothy 1946.12
Richards, Dorothy Mary 1949.17
Richards, Edward 1897.05, 1918.04
Richards, Edwin 1895.30
Richards, Elayne 1947.03, 1949.15
Richards, Evan 1981.12
Richards, Frances 1912.35, 1914.24, 1918.24
Richards, Gene 1920.38
Richards, George 1881.47, 1886.24, 1887.29, 1890.04, 1893.31, 1897.49, 1898.78, 1903.24, 1905.25, 1907.03, 1909.17
Richards, Gordon 1929.30, 1937.10
Richards, Grant 1943.23
Richards, Guy 1992.16
Richards, H. 1869.20
Richards, H.R. 1899.04
Richards, Houston 1927.06, 1934.36, 1936.26, 1941.08, 1944.01
Richards, J.B. 1871.04
Richards, Jack 1934.13, 1934.35, 1939.24, 1943.06
Richards, Jeff 1970.11
Richards, Jess 1967.10, 1970.06, 1971.15, 1980.11
Richards, Joe 1965.28
Richards, Jon 1961.18
Richards, Keith 1979.30
Richards, Ken 1965.31
Richards, Lewis 1926.41
Richards, Lloyd 1964.44, 1965.36
Richards, Mamie 1887.45, 1888.40
Richards, Martin 1975.14, 1976.03, 1978.02, 1979.06, 1982.18, 1983.11, 1985.05, 1985.15, 1987.12, 1989.26, 1991.07, 1997.08
Richards, May 1887.52
Richards, Messr. 1794.01
Richards, Minnie 1887.07, 1887.16, 1887.39, 1888.14, 1889.11, 1889.15, 1889.18
Richards, Miss 1881.03, 1882.46, 1888.27
Richards, Mlle. 1871.18
Richards, Monica L. 1998.01
Richards, Paul 1959.26
Richards, Paul-David 1969.06, 1975.02, 1983.06
Richards, Percy 1921.15
Richards, Regina 1919.08
Richards, Roy 1901.08
Richards, Rudy 1942.19, 1944.20, 1948.19
Richards, Ruth 1898.12
Richards, Sal 1992.16
Richards, Shirley 1929.04, 1929.49, 1930.38
Richards, Thomas 1910.36
Richards, Tog 1976.36, 1981.18
Richards, Tom 1917.13, 1919.11
Richardson Miss 1854.01
Richardson, Anna Mae 1951.11
Richardson, Beulah 1905.14
Richardson, Billy 1883.66
Richardson, C.M. 1887.02, 1887.42, 1888.25, 1889.43, 1890.36, 1894.52
Richardson, Claibe 1971.16, 1982.02
Richardson, Daryl 1984.09, 1987.15
Richardson, Derna 1972.20
Richardson, Desmond 1999.01
Richardson, Donald R. 1985.13, 1986.09
Richardson, Dorothy 1961.20
Richardson, Emory 1935.01, 1954.16, 1958.11
Richardson, Emory S. 1930.10
Richardson, F.C. 1871.13
Richardson, Florence 1923.23
Richardson, George T. 1900.03
Richardson, Hattie 1878.02, 1879.18, 1879.23, 1879.24, 1880.26, 1883.22, 1884.14, 1886.11, 1886.24, 1901.10
Richardson, Henry 1928.39, 1931.44
Richardson, Ian 1965.39, 1976.05
Richardson, J.P. 1990.15
Richardson, James 1973.07
Richardson, Jane 1919.39, 1920.32, 1922.13, 1922.23, 1940.06
Richardson, Jazzlips 1930.34
Richardson, John 1964.21
Richardson, Jr., Jazzlips 1930.10, 1935.01
Richardson, Karl 1997.09, 1997.19, 1999.08, 1999.13
Richardson, Leander 1897.47
Richardson, Leander P. 1881.14
Richardson, Louis 1925.17
Richardson, Louise 1927.27
Richardson, Madge 1908.24
Richardson, Mary 1879.25
Richardson, Messr. 1851.08
Richardson, Mildred 1914.02, 1914.23, 1916.26, 1919.28
Richardson, Minnie 1886.58
Richardson, Miss 1866.18, 1871.15, 1872.09
Richardson, Natasha 1998.04
Richardson, Norma 1960.06
Richardson, Patricia 1974.17
Richardson, Ron 1985.06, 1990.14
Richardson, Rosina 1865.05
Richardson, Tillie 1891.18, 1892.21, 1894.38
Richardson, Virginia 1916.09, 1950.10
Richardson, W. 1888.23
Richardson, Walter 1903.08, 1934.37, 1936.30
Richardson, William 1889.08
Richelle, Lizzie R. 1892.35
Richemont, Robert 1964.39
Richepin, Jean 1903.40
Richert, Wanda 1980.20
Richie, Billy 1938.03
Richie, Cornel 1976.28
Richings Opera Company 1863.06
Richings' English Opera Company 1868.01, 1868.02
Richings, Caroline 1852.05, 1862.03, 1862.04, 1863.06, 1863.07, 1866.07, 1866.10, 1866.14, 1867.03, 1867.04, 1867.06, 1867.07, 1867.09, 1868.01, 1868.02, 1868.09, 1868.10, 1868.11, 1868.12, 1869.41
Richings, Mr. 1823.01
Richings, Peter 1852.05, 1862.03, 1862.04, 1863.06, 1863.07, 1867.09
Richling, Louis 1920.46
Richman, Arthur 1925.43
Richman, Evelyn 1908.17
Richman, Harry 1920.19, 1921.37, 1922.38, 1926.16, 1928.22, 1930.09, 1931.19, 1932.24, 1934.35, 1942.23, 1975.22
Richman, Jeffrey 1995.12
Richmond, Adah 1876.06, 1882.49, 1887.31
Richmond, Elizabeth 1997.04
Richmond, Estelle 1913.21, 1914.27
Richmond, F.W. 1895.36
Richmond, Frank 1882.62, 1882.77, 1885.33
Richmond, Genevieve 1905.40
Richmond, George 1941.13
Richmond, H. 1876.15
Richmond, H.G. 1876.13
Richmond, Harriet 1911.40
Richmond, Harry 1876.13, 1876.22, 1876.29
Richmond, Jessie 1900.38, 1901.16, 1907.11
Richmond, Josie 1880.05
Richmond, June 1945.18
Richmond, Lizzie 1894.31
Richmond, Lulu 1880.05
Richmond, Marie 1903.05, 1909.31
Richmond, Messr. 1864.22
Richmond, Virginia 1918.15
Richmond, Wyn 1923.35, 1924.23
Richmond, Wynne 1926.02
Richrads, John 1926.13
Richter, Frederick 1900.58
Richter, Joe 1959.03
Richter, Leone 1930.23
Ricka, Keren 1972.20
Rickabaugh, Clive 1939.15
Rickard, Dick 1979.28
Rickard, Earl 1919.26
Rickard, Gwen 1948.26, 1951.02
Rickets, George H. 1897.49
Rickett, Edmond 1924.14
Rickett, Edmond W. 1933.24
Rickett, Edmund 1927.23
Rickett, Thomas 1896.21
Ricketts, Charles 1934.21, 1934.24, 1934.25, 1934.26, 1934.27, 1936.13, 1936.15, 1936.16, 1936.18, 1947.22, 1948.07, 1951.01, 1955.18, 1962.25, 1962.26, 1962.28, 1964.42, 1966.23, 1968.27, 1976.12, 1978.15
Ricketts, G. 1880.34
Ricketts, H. 1880.34
Ricketts, Skiles 1964.24
Ricketts, T.V. 1883.25, 1883.29
Ricketts, Thomas 1897.52, 1900.59
Ricketts, Tom 1890.44, 1896.20, 1897.46, 1902.07, 1904.34
Rickey 1875.35
Rickey, Al 1955.11
Rickey, Sam 1875.34, 1875.35
Rickman, Carl 1930.29
Ricks, Charlene 1973.17, 1975.12
Ricks, Edna 1961.13, 1962.07
Riddell, Cyrus 1897.06
Riddell, George 1925.21
Riddell, Lisle 1884.06
Riddell, Michael A. 1980.17
Riddell, Richard 1985.06
Riddick, Clyde 1943.02
Riddle, Albert 1892.56, 1893.28, 1894.10
Riddle, George 1902.39
Riddle, Jim 1982.22

Rideamus, Edward 1923.03
Rideout, Douglas 1950.10, 1954.01
Rideout, Leenya 1998.04
Rider, Amy 1994.01
Rider, Milberry 1911.12
Rider, Ruth 1909.30
Rider, Tom 1929.31
Ridge, Antonia 1955.13
Ridge, Frank 1916.26, 1920.10, 1920.47
Ridge, John 1976.10
Ridge, John David 1981.12, 1981.19
Ridgeley, Mr. 1897.41
Ridgeley, R. 1897.53
Ridgeley, Richard 1898.24, 1898.51
Ridgely, Richard 1898.37, 1899.41, 1900.29, 1906.36
Ridges, Stanley 1919.39, 1920.44, 1923.08, 1923.45, 1924.24, 1929.06
Ridges, Stanley C. 1916.05
Ridgeway, Messr. 1880.69, 1882.04, 1882.20
Ridgeway, W. 1885.64, 1888.13
Ridgeway, William 1882.42, 1887.23
Ridgewell, Audrey 1926.38
Ridgley, Mary 1930.23
Ridgley, Richard 1898.15, 1899.07
Ridgway, Rose 1889.33
Ridgwell, George 1911.31
Ridings, Pearl 1898.67
Ridley, Deon 2000.19
Ridley, Lillian 1932.14
Ridley, Mabel 1929.01
Ridsdale, Frank 1889.40, 1889.49, 1890.19
Riebling, Tia 1990.18
Ried and Shaefer 1892.52
Riede, Dimples 1927.20, 1928.08
Rieder, Mizl 1884.40
Rieder, Tom 1954.01
Rieff, Anthony 1857.04, 1864.16, 1864.18, 1864.19, 1864.20
Rieffel, Lisa 1986.16
Riegel, Charles 1897.05
Riegel, Charles H. 1889.02, 1900.44
Riegen, J. 1883.35
Riegen, Julius 1885.63
Rieger, Carrie 1894.40, 1895.24
Rieger, Daisy 1897.38
Riekman, Ruth 1945.14
Rielly, Tom 1892.04
Riely, Mr. 1875.03
Riemer, Walter 1953.04, 1962.07
Riesenfeld, Hugo 1914.02, 1931.19
Riestra, Luis 1949.07
Rietveld, Alice 2001.03
Riffino, Mlle. 1879.45
Rifkin, Jay 1997.20
Rifkin, Ron 1998.04
Rifkind, Julie 1979.15
Rifkind, Roy 1979.15
Rigali, Alfred L. 1936.03
Rigan, Michele 1984.08
Rigaud, George 1945.12
Rigby, Cathy 1990.20, 1991.13, 1998.18
Rigby, Harry 1898.77, 1951.13, 1953.17, 1967.06, 1971.03, 1973.05, 1974.26, 1977.04, 1978.24, 1979.25
Rigby, J.C. 1914.12
Rigdon, Kevin 1989.10, 1993.04
Rigeau, Clementine 1930.08
Riggins, Norman 1962.04, 1971.06
Riggs, Lynn 1931.02, 1943.04, 1951.16, 1953.09, 1958.07, 1963.06, 1965.38, 1969.12, 1979.31
Riggs, Ralph 1911.38, 1913.16, 1915.23, 1919.30, 1924.35, 1925.19, 1926.20, 1926.22, 1927.20, 1930.23, 1931.48, 1933.13, 1933.25, 1935.03, 1936.31, 1939.24, 1940.08, 1943.04, 1949.10, 1949.11, 1949.13, 1949.14
Riggs, Robert 1970.04
Riggs, Seth 1955.06, 1955.07, 1955.09, 1956.16, 1959.17, 1960.02, 1960.11, 1963.26, 1966.02
Riggs, T. Lawrason 1916.06
Righton, E. 1870.02
Righton, Edward 1869.45, 1870.06
Rigl, Betty 1866.18, 1868.06, 1869.11, 1869.17, 1869.28, 1873.26
Rigl, Emilie 1866.18, 1868.06, 1873.26
Rigl, Emily 1869.11, 1869.17, 1869.25, 1869.28, 1876.23
Rignold, Dora 1894.18
Rignold, George 1877.07
Rignold, William 1881.32
Rigoletto, Charlie 1920.20
Rigoletto, Henry 1920.20
Rigual, Carlos 1976.32
Rigual, Mario 1976.32
Riker, Elizabeth 1899.42, 1900.02
Riker, Robert 1974.02
Riley, Ed 1974.17
Riley, Eric 1990.12
Riley, Eulabel 1945.13
Riley, Gloria 1944.19
Riley, J. 1871.27, 1873.10, 1880.08
Riley, J.J. 1955.07
Riley, James 1976.09
Riley, Jay J. 1955.09
Riley, Jerry 1979.28
Riley, Joe 1922.30, 1930.28
Riley, Joseph 1922.34
Riley, Joseph J. 1891.15
Riley, Jr., Frank 1958.11
Riley, Larry 1978.28
Riley, Louise 1922.21
Riley, Margot 1931.21
Riley, Messr. 1864.13, 1866.08
Riley, Michael 1986.06
Riley, Mr. 1864.13
Riley, Nelson 1907.56
Rimler, Barry 1980.16
Rimma, Fritz 1894.33, 1897.32
Rimmersberg, Betty 1870.44
Rimmersberg, Marie 1870.44
Rimsky-Korsakoff 1923.25
Rimsky-Korsakoff, Nikolai 1943.02
Rimsky-Korsakov, Nikolai 1945.10
Rimupage, Rennie 1972.20
Rinaldi, Jolanda 1927.28
Rinaldi, Victoria 1982.16, 1983.12, 1985.11, 1985.13, 1986.09, 1988.14
Rinehardt, Elsa 1911.35
Rinehart, Alfred 1908.39
Rinehart, Mary Roberts 1919.06
Rinehimer, John 1985.17
Ring, Blanche 1894.20, 1902.21, 1902.34, 1902.40, 1903.06, 1903.16, 1903.27, 1904.54, 1905.19, 1906.15, 1906.20, 1906.29, 1907.42, 1908.38, 1909.11, 1910.08, 1912.14, 1916.13, 1919.30, 1921.19, 1928.49, 1930.02, 1938.01
Ring, Bob 1973.06
Ring, Cyril 1912.14, 1919.37
Ring, Herman 1890.31, 1891.33, 1893.29, 1894.01
Ring, Hermann 1892.43, 1894.30, 1896.34, 1897.35, 1898.53
Ring, J.H. 1876.23
Ring, Joyce 1942.15
Ring, Julie 1894.11, 1896.15
Ring, Lillian 1926.21
Ring, M. 1916.12
Ring, Michael 1913.21, 1918.36
Ringgold, B.T. 1855.10, 1864.21, 1867.19, 1880.37, 1885.46, 1899.03, 1899.27
Ringgold, Ben T. 1896.39, 1900.36
Ringgold, Jennie 1907.29, 1907.31
Ringgold, Messr. 1857.03
Ringgold, Muriel 1907.55
Ringham, Nancy 1981.19, 1989.24, 2001.02
Ringiao, Barbara 1972.20
Ringiao, Norga 1972.20
Ringle, Dave 1927.39
Ringle, David 1932.24
Ringold, B.T. 1868.19
Ringold, Mr. 1857.06
Ringold, Muriel 1906.08
Ringquist, Ella 1892.20, 1892.30
Ringwald, Roy 1955.13
Rinner, Walter 1943.01, 1945.04
Rinquest, Ellen 1897.16
Rio, Viole 1906.10
Riopel, Grace 1908.25
Riordan, Helenita 1941.03
Riordan, Irene 1964.26
Riordan, Joseph 1962.26
Riordan, Justin 2000.19
Rios, Augie 1959.27, 1960.10, 1961.07
Rios, Augustine 1957.16
Rios, Gracia 1949.07
Rios, Juanita 1942.18
Rios, Linda 1971.12
Rios, Michelle 1998.02
Rios, Rosita 1939.18
Riotte, Mlle. 1870.41, 1871.06
Ripamoti, Gigia 1881.15
Ripley, Alice 1993.06, 1994.10, 1997.12, 1997.17, 2000.01, 2000.17
Ripley, Constance 1930.32, 1931.16, 1931.37, 1932.17, 1932.20, 1934.38, 1935.03, 1936.26
Ripley, Lou 1915.03, 1922.41
Ripley, Madame 1904.34
Ripley, Mme. 1899.25, 1903.18, 1907.42, 1907.58, 1908.21, 1910.08, 1911.21, 1913.11
Ripley, Thomas 1898.70
Ripley, Trescott 1965.14
Ripolles and Martin 1921.39
Ripple, Arthur P. 1911.03
Ripple, Pacie 1907.52, 1912.10, 1928.29, 1934.36
Ripplinger, Jody 1997.05
Rippy, Bob 1955.07
Rippy, Robert 1943.05, 1947.14, 1950.04, 1955.06, 1955.09, 1955.25
Riscoe, Arthur 1922.05
Riscol, Randolph 1978.04
Risdale, F. 1885.07
Risdale, Frank 1885.09
Riser, P. 1984.15
Rising, W.S. 1883.62, 1883.67, 1884.09, 1886.15
Rising, Will S. 1884.21, 1885.05, 1889.19
Rising, William 1914.16
Risk, Messr. 1867.10
Riskin, Irving 1945.01
Riskin, Leo 1942.32
Riskin, Robert 1930.06
Risley, Greta 1897.18, 1902.18, 1907.08
Risley, O. 1898.30
Risley, O.W. 1898.49, 1899.05, 1901.24, 1906.41
Risque, W.H. 1899.35, 1902.35, 1906.25
Risse, Ernest 1922.42
Rissman, Herbert 1943.04
Rita, Patti Ann 1956.02
Ritchard, Cyril 1925.05, 1953.17, 1954.13, 1961.08, 1965.19, 1972.04, 1975.22
Ritchie, Adelaide 1905.03
Ritchie, Adele 1893.20, 1893.40, 1894.21, 1894.29, 1895.17, 1896.45, 1897.18, 1898.35, 1900.34, 1901.12, 1902.01, 1902.19, 1904.01, 1904.08, 1905.13, 1906.17, 1907.18, 1912.49
Ritchie, Billie 1906.40, 1908.02, 1918.19
Ritchie, Darren 2001.03
Ritchie, Elmer 1895.25
Ritchie, Elmer T. 1897.15
Ritchie, Florence 1897.18, 1897.42
Ritchie, Frances 1937.11
Ritchie, Sharon 1964.46, 1966.01
Ritchie, W.E. 1895.36, 1896.18
Ritchie-Harnden and Company 1906.47
Ritchy, A. 1926.49
Riter, Joseph 1916.18
Ritman, William 1970.14, 1972.01
Ritner, George 1958.02, 1959.04
Ritschel, Jack 1982.14
Ritt, Martin 1941.01, 1943.23
Ritter, Blake 1945.05
Ritter, C.H. 1900.06
Ritter, Kathryn 1974.06
Ritter, Margaret 1948.18
Ritter, Messr. 1902.13
Ritter, Mrs. 1844.01
Ritter, Thelma 1957.07
Rittman, Trude 1941.01, 1947.03, 1947.17, 1948.08, 1949.18, 1950.08, 1951.24, 1952.10, 1954.01, 1954.13, 1954.15, 1956.01, 1959.04, 1959.24, 1960.10, 1960.21, 1962.04, 1963.13, 1963.25, 1964.20, 1965.31, 1967.07, 1968.02, 1968.17, 1968.24, 1969.07, 1970.19, 1972.24, 1973.12, 1975.22, 1976.05, 1989.03, 1990.20, 1996.13
Rittman, Trudi 1945.05, 1950.20
Rittman, Trudy 1945.20
Rittman, William 1980.30
Rittmann, Trude 1998.03
Ritzgerald, Richard 1981.03
Riva, William 1950.13, 1951.10
Rival, Gustavus 1891.21
Rivenberg, Mattie 1906.37
Rivenez, Mons. 1869.16
Rivenhall, Fred 1908.42
Rivera, Amandita 1897.04
Rivera, Anita 1924.37
Rivera, Armandita 1899.29
Rivera, Chita 1955.10, 1956.02, 1960.06, 1964.40, 1968.30, 1975.14, 1983.01, 1984.01, 1985.19, 1993.09
Rivera, James 1989.03
Rivera, Khalid 1998.02
Rivera, Lelane 1932.03
Rivera, Michael 1983.17
Rivera, Monolo 1969.11
Rivera, Rosita 1899.29
Rivera, Rossita 1902.09
Rivera, Walter 1974.24
Rivers, Ada 1905.02
Rivers, Aida 1903.30
Rivers, Cecil 1933.06
Rivers, Chief 1930.31
Rivers, H. Fletcher 1889.04, 1889.40, 1893.32, 1896.48, 1897.07, 1897.21, 1898.05, 1899.26, 1899.31, 1899.40, 1905.10
Rivers, J. 1865.04
Rivers, J. Fletcher 1906.06
Rivers, James 1904.26
Rivers, Joan 1882.60
Rivers, Lillian 1890.34
Rivers, Lucy 1887.33, 1887.50
Rivers, Marsha 1959.13
Rivers, Max 1928.42, 1929.51, 1936.22
Rivers, Miss 1876.16
Rivers, Mrs. 1841.01
Rivers, Pauline 1933.04
Rives, Amelie 1928.21
Rivett, Fred 1946.12
Rivgauche, Michel 1963.02
Riviere, J. 1873.10
Rivir, Renee 1931.08
Rix, Luther 1973.14, 1988.08
Rixford, John 1890.25
Rizarelli, Mlle. 1869.05, 1869.16, 1869.30
Rizzi, Marie 1892.38
Rizzo, Francis 1965.26, 1975.11, 1976.31, 1978.08, 1996.10
Rizzo, Jeff 1998.06, 1999.11
Rizzo, Jeffrey 1997.11
RLM Productions, Inc. 1985.20
Roach, Egbert T. 1911.13
Roach, James C. 1885.53, 1886.44, 1890.06
Roach, Jeanette 1962.26
Roach, John 1908.04
Roach, L. 1888.35
Roache, C. 1878.16
Roane, Frank 1949.15
Roark, George A. 1902.12
Roarke, George A. 1900.43
Roatina, Adelina 1941.07
Robare, Mary C. 1983.02
Robb 1902.01
Robb, Elsie 1886.49
Robb, Frank 1923.23
Robb, John 1917.09, 1945.17, 1954.12
Robb, John H. 1884.23, 1885.69
Robb, N. 1884.09
Robbins, A. 1915.16
Robbins, Archie 1943.23
Robbins, Carrie 1981.28, 1986.16, 1992.11, 2001.01
Robbins, Carrie F. 1970.08, 1972.12, 1973.11, 1973.16, 1974.05, 1977.08, 1980.17
Robbins, Cindy 1954.02, 1959.19
Robbins, Dana 1989.08
Robbins, Edward H. 1940.08
Robbins, Everett 1978.09
Robbins, Gil 1974.03
Robbins, J.J. 1934.06
Robbins, Jana 1974.26, 1989.27, 1991.06
Robbins, Jerome 1939.26, 1944.33, 1945.10, 1945.20, 1947.16, 1948.08, 1949.08, 1950.15, 1951.12, 1952.20, 1954.05, 1954.13, 1956.03, 1956.14, 1957.08, 1957.12, 1959.13, 1960.08, 1960.11, 1963.09, 1964.17, 1964.18, 1964.23, 1964.27, 1968.16, 1968.18, 1971.15, 1973.15, 1974.17, 1976.36, 1977.07, 1979.22, 1980.02, 1981.18, 1985.01, 1989.03, 1989.27, 1990.18, 1990.20, 1991.06, 1991.13, 1996.05, 1998.16, 1998.18
Robbins, Jerry 1944.25
Robbins, Larry 1948.18, 1948.25
Robbins, Mary Ann 1969.16
Robbins, Messr. 1794.01
Robbins, Poppy 1907.38
Robbins, R.N. 1927.18
Robbins, Randall 1974.26
Robbins, Rex 1974.17
Robbins, Tom 1989.03, 1989.24
Robbins, Tom Alan 1996.18, 1997.20
Robe, Harold 1910.19, 1913.02, 1914.22, 1915.02, 1918.10
Robe, Harold A. 1911.12, 1913.22
Robecchi 1877.04, 1882.62, 1885.65, 1886.41, 1887.03, 1887.27, 1888.01
Robecchi and Amable 1889.21
Robecchi and Carpezat 1886.16

Robecchi, Messr. 1881.02
Robecchi, Mons. 1875.21
Robechi 1877.15, 1879.12, 1881.32
Robechi, Froumont 1876.36
Robechi, Magnani 1883.06
Robenette, Camille 1925.02
Robennack, Mac 1992.06
Rober, Richard 1941.13, 1942.18
Robere, Mons. 1871.18
Roberson, Clarence 1912.22
Roberson, John 1966.14
Roberson, Ken 1990.14, 1992.08, 1999.08, 2001.09
Roberson, Lorenza 1939.14
Roberson, Rudy 1997.08, 1999.06
Roberson, Will 1994.01
Robert Law Scenic Studios 1919.01
Robert Law Studios 1917.10, 1918.26, 1919.33, 1919.36, 1920.03, 1922.38, 1922.46, 1924.11, 1924.18, 1924.30, 1925.06, 1925.10, 1925.24
Robert, Camille 1919.10
Robert, Ernst 1936.22
Robert, Hans 1910.19, 1939.27
Robert, Hans F. 1902.43
Robert, James 1972.20
Robert, Lord 1917.22
Robert, Lyn 1954.09
Robert, Mons. 1871.18
Roberti, Lyda 1931.01, 1933.01, 1933.26
Roberts J.B. 1887.03
Roberts, Al 1917.05, 1918.04, 1918.27, 1920.45
Roberts, Alan 1942.18
Roberts, Alice 1884.24, 1991.09
Roberts, Allan 1949.02
Roberts, Ann 1943.20
Roberts, Anna May 1915.24
Roberts, Annie 1897.03
Roberts, Anthony (Tony) 1967.16, 1972.04, 1986.04, 1987.03, 1991.12, 1995.15
Roberts, Archie 1930.20
Roberts, Ben 1939.24, 1943.08, 1943.09, 1944.01, 1944.18, 1944.24, 1957.04
Roberts, Benjamin 1938.03
Roberts, Blanche 1889.04, 1889.40, 1889.49
Roberts, Bobby 1930.33
Roberts, Buddy 1939.22
Roberts, C. 1848.01
Roberts, C. Luckey 1926.19
Roberts, C. Luckyeth 1923.06
Roberts, C.W. 1887.51
Roberts, Chapman 1976.04, 1976.35, 1978.21, 1982.12, 1992.03, 1999.06
Roberts, Chris 1999.08
Roberts, D.L. 1923.06
Roberts, Daniel Crane 1955.13
Roberts, Darcie 1997.05
Roberts, Dixie 1943.05
Roberts, Don 1943.16
Roberts, Donald 1917.02, 1919.11, 1920.20
Roberts, Donald Lee 1922.08
Roberts, Dorothy 1940.21
Roberts, E. 1875.39
Roberts, Elizabeth 1938.16
Roberts, Eric 1944.02
Roberts, Erling 1951.05
Roberts, F. 1881.10, 1882.82
Roberts, Flossie 1934.05
Roberts, Francis 1947.15
Roberts, Frank 1884.62
Roberts, Franklin 1972.02
Roberts, Franklyn 1908.10
Roberts, Fred 1909.30, 1911.05
Roberts, Frederick 1913.03, 1914.05
Roberts, George 1947.13
Roberts, H. 1881.11, 1881.27
Roberts, H.R. 1905.45
Roberts, Hans 1897.20
Roberts, Harry 1887.43
Roberts, Hazel 1904.35
Roberts, Helen 1939.02, 1939.04, 1939.06, 1939.08, 1939.09, 1948.02, 1948.06, 1948.09, 1948.10
Roberts, Herman O. 1925.37
Roberts, Howard A. 1953.04, 1957.05, 1969.10, 1973.10, 1976.21, 1979.32
Roberts, J. 1876.23, 1877.21, 1888.10
Roberts, J.H. 1892.11, 1893.41
Roberts, James 1869.23, 1879.50, 1879.56, 1880.04, 1881.04, 1881.11, 1881.27, 1882.26, 1884.11, 1884.18
Roberts, James M. 1860.06, 1861.04
Roberts, Jeff 1958.01
Roberts, Jeremy 1997.09
Roberts, Joan 1941.12, 1943.04, 1945.11, 1945.18, 2001.02
Roberts, Joey 1988.20
Roberts, John 1916.05, 1956.08
Roberts, John H. 1913.31
Roberts, Jonathan 1997.20
Roberts, June 1922.01
Roberts, Katharine 1901.21
Roberts, Kathrine 1900.45
Roberts, Lee 1919.40, 1941.06
Roberts, Lee S. 1918.20
Roberts, Lena Sanford 1926.19
Roberts, Leslie 1922.05
Roberts, Louis 1935.16
Roberts, Luckyeth 1923.42, 1925.05
Roberts, Marcia 1999.05, 1999.09
Roberts, Maria 1888.27
Roberts, Marian 1888.40, 1945.07
Roberts, Marie 1931.44
Roberts, Marion 1889.11, 1889.15, 1889.18
Roberts, Mark 1995.16, 1998.17
Roberts, Martha 1938.10
Roberts, Mason 1987.14, 1994.09
Roberts, Messr. 1851.07, 1867.12, 1884.42, 1886.47, 1887.25
Roberts, Michael 1957.14
Roberts, Miss 1845.01
Roberts, Mr. 1834.03, 1840.02, 1840.03, 1840.04, 1848.01, 1851.02, 1852.01, 1852.05, 1854.01, 1868.06, 1872.37, 1881.04
Roberts, Nellie 1924.17
Roberts, Nelson 1906.15
Roberts, Nick 1881.39
Roberts, Paul 1939.21, 1940.18
Roberts, R.A. 1887.40, 1893.11, 1895.18, 1895.27, 1896.37, 1896.52, 1897.14, 1897.30, 1897.47, 1900.47, 1901.07, 1901.30
Roberts, R.M. 1883.50
Roberts, Ralph 1909.01, 1910.21
Roberts, Randolph 1898.29, 1898.46
Roberts, Reginald 1897.03, 1897.50, 1899.42, 1900.02, 1900.04, 1900.06, 1900.09, 1900.11, 1900.17, 1900.18, 1900.21, 1900.22, 1900.23, 1900.26, 1900.27, 1900.29
Roberts, Robin Sanford 1999.09
Roberts, Ron 1951.05
Roberts, Roy 1931.36, 1953.11
Roberts, Ruth 1980.17, 1985.01, 1990.15
Roberts, Sarah 1988.02
Roberts, Sterling 1969.09
Roberts, Ted 1920.10
Roberts, Thayer 1946.03
Roberts, Theodore 1912.03
Roberts, Thomas 1910.12
Roberts, Tony 1999.21
Roberts, Velma 1912.36
Roberts, W.C. 1904.05
Roberts, Walter 1918.13
Roberts, William 1875.10
Robertson, A. 1869.32
Robertson, Ada 1903.04, 1904.15
Robertson, Aggy 1870.14
Robertson, Agnes 1869.42, 1872.27
Robertson, Alex 1934.34
Robertson, Blanch 1881.10
Robertson, Bruce 1980.07
Robertson, David 1984.09, 1999.15
Robertson, Graham 1892.14
Robertson, Guy 1919.23, 1921.37, 1922.26, 1923.05, 1925.52, 1927.17, 1927.68, 1928.26, 1929.32, 1930.27, 1932.06, 1934.04, 1934.29, 1938.01
Robertson, Helen 1911.15
Robertson, J. 1870.44
Robertson, J. Francis 1931.01, 1933.25
Robertson, Joel 1981.18
Robertson, John S. 1903.25
Robertson, Kathryn 1914.07
Robertson, L.S. 1888.01
Robertson, Laura 1931.44
Robertson, Liz 1983.08, 1986.01
Robertson, Lolita 1932.23
Robertson, Max 1909.24
Robertson, Miss 1861.04, 1869.08
Robertson, Mrs. 1862.09
Robertson, Robbie 1982.22
Robertson, Scott 1989.04, 1994.01
Robertson, T.W. 1881.11, 1881.27, 1882.34, 1883.31
Robertson, Thomas 1894.24
Robertson, W.L. 1925.02
Robertson, Wes L. 1927.11
Robertson, William 1928.41
Robertson, William F. 1880.51
Robeson, Erba 1921.31
Robeson, Paul 1932.11, 1940.01
Robetson, Agnes 1859.11
Robey, Kathleen 1968.24
Robey, Ken 1948.21
Robi, Armand 1924.17
Robin, Jean-Claude 1984.15
Robin, Leo 1925.47, 1925.50, 1926.15, 1927.09, 1927.16, 1927.20, 1927.35, 1927.38, 1927.54, 1928.41, 1931.21, 1932.04, 1933.15, 1947.05, 1949.18, 1954.01, 1955.14, 1963.02, 1965.08, 1974.02, 1975.22, 1976.32, 1980.08, 1986.06, 1988.08, 1989.12, 1995.07, 1999.01
Robin, Lou 1976.06
Robin, Sid 1992.03
Robin, Sue 1940.21
Robin, Tom 1976.06
Robins, A. 1915.29, 1942.14
Robins, Edward H. 1931.48, 1933.13, 1933.25, 1938.13, 1946.04
Robins, Messr. 1794.01, 1823.01
Robinson 1935.19
Robinson's English Bouffe Company 1875.11
Robinson's English Opera Bouffe Company 1875.15, 1875.20
Robinson, A. 1968.20, 1999.07
Robinson, Adelaide 1913.08
Robinson, Alice 1906.23
Robinson, Andy 1970.04
Robinson, Angela 1998.06, 2001.03
Robinson, Ann 1942.34, 1945.08
Robinson, Anna 1897.37
Robinson, Arlene 1942.35
Robinson, Armin 1931.21, 1937.17
Robinson, Babette 1900.52
Robinson, Bartlett 1937.02
Robinson, Belle 1897.48, 1898.50, 1899.17, 1899.30, 1900.38, 1901.17, 1904.01
Robinson, Bertram 1938.01
Robinson, Bertrand 1930.23
Robinson, Bill 1928.18, 1930.29, 1933.27, 1939.17, 1940.23, 1945.08, 1999.06
Robinson, Carroll 1928.20
Robinson, Carson J. 1955.19
Robinson, Cayley 1907.41
Robinson, Charles 1896.42
Robinson, Chris 1953.03, 1954.07, 1955.01
Robinson, Christine 1986.01
Robinson, Cindy 1990.20, 1991.13, 1994.02
Robinson, Clarence 1925.18, 1928.10, 1932.30
Robinson, Clark 1921.30, 1922.39, 1923.32, 1924.09, 1924.33, 1924.44, 1925.31, 1925.47, 1926.50, 1927.13, 1927.25, 1928.08, 1929.08, 1929.29, 1929.50, 1930.40, 1931.13, 1931.40, 1933.26, 1934.18, 1934.35, 1935.04, 1936.06, 1941.07
Robinson, Clarke 1927.62, 1930.06
Robinson, David 1923.25, 1924.36
Robinson, DeG. 1908.03
Robinson, Dyann 1976.04
Robinson, Earl 1937.14, 1938.08, 1939.19, 1942.26, 1945.07
Robinson, Ed 1986.06
Robinson, Edward 1939.29
Robinson, Edward G. 1990.17
Robinson, Emma 1907.55
Robinson, Esther 1908.25
Robinson, Eugene 1946.21
Robinson, F.H. 1875.21
Robinson, F.T. 1880.42
Robinson, Fawcett 1889.08
Robinson, Ferdie 1924.27
Robinson, Flora 1869.46
Robinson, Florence 1881.31, 1894.20
Robinson, Forrest 1904.08
Robinson, Frances 1944.01
Robinson, Freddie 1939.17
Robinson, Frederick 1878.14
Robinson, George 1881.31, 1883.36, 1918.17
Robinson, George Andrew 1972.02
Robinson, George E. 1886.13
Robinson, George K. 1892.38
Robinson, Grace 1912.37
Robinson, H.W. 1906.01
Robinson, Hal 1989.26, 1991.15
Robinson, Harold 1884.39
Robinson, Harry 1897.55
Robinson, Hazel 1910.18
Robinson, Helen 1920.31
Robinson, J. Russel 1920.33, 1921.27, 1922.15
Robinson, J. Russell 1922.25, 1923.21, 1976.32
Robinson, Janet 1983.17, 2000.20
Robinson, Jason 2001.09
Robinson, Jessie 1880.03
Robinson, John 1884.26
Robinson, Jr., William 1997.21
Robinson, Julie 1950.07
Robinson, Kathleen 1917.22
Robinson, Kathryn 1906.41
Robinson, Lance 1991.07
Robinson, Lena 1912.49, 1913.28
Robinson, Lilla Cayley 1990.09
Robinson, Lisa 1983.19
Robinson, Lorie 1978.11
Robinson, Louise 1980.05
Robinson, Mabel 1964.32, 1976.28, 1976.35, 1980.15
Robinson, Margaret 1904.46
Robinson, Maude 1898.34
Robinson, Maurice 1903.11
Robinson, Maxine 1919.06
Robinson, May 1869.35, 1869.43, 1870.04
Robinson, Michelle M. 1992.08
Robinson, Minnie 1907.55
Robinson, Miss 1863.01, 1870.13, 1873.26, 1884.42
Robinson, Morgan 1992.06
Robinson, Phyllis 1970.10
Robinson, Rachel 1981.28
Robinson, Randolph 1934.05
Robinson, Roberta 1931.16, 1931.42
Robinson, Robin 1989.27, 1991.06
Robinson, Roger 1983.15
Robinson, Ronn 1976.25
Robinson, Russel 1929.27
Robinson, Russell 1924.01, 1927.60
Robinson, Ruth 1898.55
Robinson, Sadie 1898.22
Robinson, Selina 1879.02
Robinson, Venustra K. 1978.11
Robinson, Vickie Sue 1971.01
Robinson, W. Smokey 1986.02
Robinson, Willard 1982.12
Robinson, William 1888.31, 1888.33, 1997.21
Robinson, Zeb 1954.08
Robison, Willard 1927.60, 1930.18, 1930.33, 1933.15, 1991.04
Robledo, Julian 1921.27
Robles, Nora 1997.13
Robsarte, Lionel 1904.36
Robson, Andrew 1892.01
Robson, Bob 1929.26
Robson, Harry 1898.17
Robson, Mary 1913.36, 1914.22, 1923.13
Robson, Master 1870.22
Robson, Mat 1880.49
Robson, May 1893.11, 1901.19, 1902.43, 1904.54
Robson, Mrs. Stuart 1912.37, 1915.20
Robson, Philip 1897.49
Robson, Phillip 1909.10
Robson, Robert 1923.43
Robson, Stuart 1862.09, 1863.01, 1863.02, 1863.03, 1863.04, 1863.08, 1870.36, 1870.39, 1872.23
Robyn, Alfred 1910.02, 1914.21
Robyn, Alfred G. 1885.08, 1894.47, 1904.10, 1905.06, 1907.01, 1907.27, 1911.02, 1912.10, 1912.49, 1913.28
Robyns, W.C. 1888.28
Roca, Carlos 1930.35
Rocamora, Susanne 1903.20
Rocamora, Suzanne 1911.29
Roccardi, A. 1892.59
Roccardi, Albert 1910.33, 1922.29
Roccini, Signora 1883.48
Rocco, Jamie 1997.11, 1998.06, 1999.11
Rocco, Joe 1956.01
Rocco, Mary 1983.05
Roccordi, A. 1889.02
Rocha, Sergio 1992.13
Rochas, Marcel 1934.32
Roche 1965.30
Roche, Augusta 1881.37, 1882.42, 1882.78, 1883.24, 1883.65, 1886.34, 1891.23
Roche, Edward 1943.24, 1945.06, 1946.09
Roche, Edwin 1943.10
Roche, Eugene 1963.09
Roche, Jack 1918.13, 1950.09
Roche, John 1906.45, 1919.29, 1922.20
Roche, John F. 1924.14, 1926.17
Roche, John Francis 1927.23

Roche, Kathleen 1942.02, 1942.04, 1942.06, 1942.07, 1942.09, 1944.04, 1944.06, 1944.08, 1944.09, 1944.10, 1944.11, 1944.12, 1944.13, 1949.10, 1949.11, 1949.14
Roche, Mary 1940.13, 1942.04, 1942.06, 1942.07, 1942.08, 1942.09, 1943.21, 1944.29, 1952.14, 1952.16, 1952.18, 1952.19, 1980.16
Roche, Messr. 1864.01, 1864.03, 1864.08, 1864.11
Roche, Mr. 1887.10
Roche, Pierre 1970.01
Roche, Royal 1889.02
Roche, Sebastian 2000.10
Roche, Tami 1981.17
Roche, Todi 1985.02
Roche, Viola 1938.06, 1947.20, 1956.01
Rochefort, Marie 1890.02
Rochelle, Lisa 1973.11
Rochelle, Renee 1942.35
Rochester, Claire 1917.16
Rochester, W.F. 1882.14, 1884.66, 1890.28, 1891.13, 1891.23, 1899.40, 1901.09, 1905.52
Rochow, F. 1873.29
Rock, Clarence 1936.07
Rock, Ella 1888.36, 1889.46, 1892.04, 1907.01, 1907.46
Rock, Helen 1915.15
Rock, Helen Eby 1922.45, 1927.62
Rock, Helyn Eby 1923.33, 1925.38
Rock, Ida 1894.06, 1895.34, 1896.48, 1899.25
Rock, Jane 1912.15
Rock, Joseph 1994.07
Rock, Stan 1928.25
Rock, W.B. 1897.06
Rock, William 1904.09, 1907.15, 1907.41, 1907.47, 1908.03, 1908.10, 1909.03, 1909.09, 1910.20, 1912.15, 1916.10, 1917.12, 1918.08, 1920.24
Rock, William B. 1898.02
Rocke, Ben 1931.01
Rocke, Ella 1902.12
Rockefeller, Helen 1909.19
Rockettes, The 1979.13
Rockmore, Robert 1933.04
Rockne, Knute 1927.41
Rockne, Michael J. 1980.16
Rocksavage, David 1999.15
Rockwall, George 1928.14
Rockwell, C. 1868.22
Rockwell, C.H. 1868.19, 1869.33
Rockwell, Charles 1880.37
Rockwell, David 2000.17
Rockwell, Doc 1944.29
Rockwell, Dr. 1929.28
Rockwell, George 1920.17
Rockwell, Helen 1905.40
Rockwell, John 1996.10
Rockwell, Maude 1912.29
Rockwell, Mr. 1864.21
Rocky, Leif 1935.19
Rocky, Leonard 1938.10
Rocky, Paal 1935.19
Rodd, Marcia 1973.03
Rodd, Philip 1950.04
Rodda, Richard 1954.13
Rodden, Dan 1972.24
Roddy, Jimmy 1974.01
Roddy, Pat 1998.09, 2000.05
Rode, Herr 1897.08
Roden, Illa 1939.23
Roder, Eugene 1905.41, 1909.04, 1910.35, 1913.09, 1914.03
Roder, Milan 1918.33, 1919.08, 1920.09, 1922.04, 1923.22
Roderick, Ray 1985.05, 1992.02, 1996.06, 1999.21, 2000.11, 2000.19
Rodes, Mary 1933.14
Rodgers and Hammerstein Organization, The 1994.02, 1996.05
Rodgers, Anton 1965.28
Rodgers, Bob 1959.14, 1961.16
Rodgers, Chev 1977.12, 1989.05, 1992.07
Rodgers, Claudia 1908.36
Rodgers, Douglas Fletcher 1955.01, 1958.07
Rodgers, Eileen 1959.25, 1960.19, 1965.01
Rodgers, Katherine 1917.02
Rodgers, Lou 1967.05
Rodgers, Marshall 1932.30
Rodgers, Mary 1959.26, 1960.07, 1963.13, 1977.05, 1978.12, 1996.18
Rodgers, Richard 1919.14, 1925.17, 1925.26, 1925.31, 1926.07, 1926.13, 1926.50, 1926.51, 1927.56, 1928.02, 1928.16, 1928.30, 1929.07, 1929.12, 1929.42, 1930.08, 1930.33, 1931.04, 1931.08, 1931.13, 1935.15, 1936.05, 1936.31, 1937.04, 1937.13, 1938.05, 1938.14, 1939.27, 1940.06, 1940.20, 1940.22, 1942.15, 1943.04, 1943.22, 1945.05, 1946.12, 1947.05, 1947.17, 1948.12, 1949.03, 1949.04, 1951.12, 1951.16, 1952.01, 1952.11, 1953.08, 1953.09, 1954.07, 1954.12, 1955.07, 1955.13, 1955.27, 1956.03, 1957.06, 1957.10, 1957.11, 1958.07, 1958.19, 1959.24, 1960.11, 1961.12, 1961.15, 1962.03, 1962.17, 1963.02, 1963.06, 1963.17, 1963.18, 1964.23, 1964.24, 1965.06, 1965.20, 1965.22, 1965.24, 1965.38, 1966.12, 1966.14, 1966.16, 1966.31, 1967.07, 1967.10, 1967.11, 1967.12, 1968.07, 1968.16, 1968.18, 1969.12, 1970.19, 1973.17, 1974.09, 1974.11, 1975.12, 1975.13, 1975.22, 1976.08, 1976.16, 1976.19, 1977.05, 1977.07, 1979.12, 1979.24, 1979.31, 1981.16, 1983.02, 1983.09, 1984.06, 1985.01, 1986.03, 1987.03, 1988.08, 1989.03, 1989.06, 1989.16, 1989.21, 1990.02, 1990.09, 1991.10, 1993.14, 1993.16, 1994.02, 1995.12, 1995.18, 1996.04, 1996.05, 1997.01, 1998.03, 2000.07, 2000.16, 2001.09
Rodgers, Richard C. 1920.25
Rodgers, Roger 1983.20
Rodgers, Shev 1965.34, 1972.14, 1976.01
Rodin, Gil 1978.05, 1979.30, 1999.01
Rodine, Eric 1999.05
Rodney, Babette 1888.39, 1890.03, 1896.06, 1896.30, 1897.25, 1897.39, 1900.05
Rodney, Jean 1939.29
Rodney, Paul 1894.46
Rodney, Reginald 1897.50
Rodnon, Mel 1971.12, 1974.11, 1974.19
Rodrigues, Alfred 1955.19
Rodrigues, Aurelio 1875.24
Rodriguez 1955.26
Rodriguez, Antonio 1929.51, 1979.13
Rodriguez, Burt 1969.09, 1975.07
Rodriguez, Charlie J. 1970.21, 1972.21
Rodriguez, Daniel Martinez 1988.15
Rodriguez, Domingo A. 1963.28, 1969.10
Rodriguez, Enrico 1996.08
Rodriguez, G.H. Matos 1983.09, 1984.10, 1985.07, 1999.18
Rodriguez, G.M. 1997.13
Rodriguez, Isabel 1916.03, 1918.20, 1921.14
Rodriguez, Isabelle 1920.09, 1922.36, 1925.02
Rodriguez, Nino Aurelio 1875.22
Rodriguez, Ralph 1982.15
Rodriguez, Raymond 1993.09, 1998.02
Rodriguez-Pantoja, Tomas 1992.15
Rodriguez-Rosa, Ray 1998.02
Roe, Bertha 1930.19
Roe, Charles 1975.17, 1976.23, 1977.11, 1980.03
Roe, Dennis 1979.17
Roe, H.W. 1881.55
Roe, Harry W. 1887.23
Roe, L.M. 1904.32
Roe, Patricia 1933.17
Roecker, Edward 1944.15, 1945.02
Roeder, B.F. 1890.08
Roeder, Frances 1917.16
Roeder, Joseph 1930.36
Roehm, Vera 1916.11, 1917.23, 1920.22
Roehr, Mr. 1852.05
Roelof, Wilma 1927.20
Roeloff, Wilma 1930.30, 1933.01
Roemer and Sons 1882.18
Roemer, Ed. 1883.48, 1885.65
Roemer, F. 1887.19
Roemheld, Heinz 1987.02
Roepke, G. 1969.11
Roerich, William 1942.20
Roerick, William 1948.11, 1967.01, 1980.06
Roerke, Messr. 1900.28
Roettger, L. 1875.12
Roffman, Frederick S. 1978.19, 1979.20
Rogati, Mario 1913.32, 1915.23
Rogati, Marius 1925.32, 1927.65
Roger, Mons. 1875.25, 1875.29, 1875.30, 1875.33
Roger, Victor 1886.43, 1894.28, 1898.63
Rogers, Alex 1903.08, 1904.26, 1906.14, 1908.08, 1910.18, 1916.10, 1923.06, 1923.42, 1925.05, 1980.10, 1980.27
Rogers, Alex C. 1926.19
Rogers, Alexander 1903.08, 1904.26, 1909.27
Rogers, Allan 1928.26, 1929.39
Rogers, Ann 1923.35
Rogers, Arthur 1926.27
Rogers, Axel 1976.04
Rogers, Barbara 1964.17
Rogers, Ben 1913.37
Rogers, Betty 1991.07
Rogers, Bruce 1938.09
Rogers, Budd 1948.15
Rogers, Buddy 1932.07
Rogers, Charles R. 1942.01
Rogers, Cynthia 1930.18, 1937.12, 1950.03
Rogers, Dan Loring 1944.20
Rogers, David 1905.55, 1957.01, 1962.02, 1980.23
Rogers, Dick 1945.17, 1984.15, 1999.24
Rogers, Dore 1911.33
Rogers, Doug 1957.14, 1967.18, 1975.05
Rogers, E. 1870.33, 1880.21, 1881.10
Rogers, E.C. 1901.24
Rogers, Earl 1957.01
Rogers, Eric 1963.01, 1965.23, 1984.07
Rogers, Eugene 1902.11
Rogers, Eugene C. 1893.30
Rogers, Felix 1869.25, 1869.28, 1870.14, 1870.34, 1870.44, 1871.27
Rogers, Ferne 1922.18
Rogers, Fred 1921.39
Rogers, Frederick 1908.13
Rogers, George 1892.12, 1927.43, 1935.07, 1935.08, 1935.09
Rogers, Ginger 1929.49, 1930.31, 1980.09
Rogers, Gladys 1926.13, 1928.10
Rogers, Gus 1897.25, 1899.12, 1899.29, 1900.40, 1901.16, 1902.24, 1903.23, 1904.31, 1907.33
Rogers, H. 1882.62
Rogers, Harry 1896.24, 1933.21, 1946.22
Rogers, Harry Lee 1958.01, 1961.10
Rogers, Hilda 1926.19
Rogers, Howard 1862.09, 1919.15, 1922.18, 1926.01
Rogers, Howard E. 1920.22, 1920.23, 1922.18
Rogers, Howard Emmet 1925.27
Rogers, Howard Emmett 1930.26
Rogers, Irma 1986.13
Rogers, Jaime 1964.32, 1966.12, 1968.06
Rogers, Jane 1907.11
Rogers, Jean 1949.03
Rogers, Jennie 1873.26
Rogers, Jerry 1931.08
Rogers, Jimmy 1999.09
Rogers, Jo Jean 1940.08, 1942.01
Rogers, John 1911.47
Rogers, John F. 1906.25
Rogers, John P. 1909.16
Rogers, Jonathan R. 1878.16
Rogers, Kelly Junkermann 1998.19
Rogers, Ken Leigh 1983.06
Rogers, Kenny 1998.19
Rogers, L.A. 1905.35
Rogers, Lavinia 1906.14, 1908.08, 1909.27
Rogers, Lori 1962.04
Rogers, Mamie 1882.39
Rogers, Marie 1893.12
Rogers, Marilyn 1959.24, 1964.27
Rogers, Max 1897.25, 1899.12, 1899.29, 1900.40, 1901.16, 1902.24, 1903.23, 1904.31, 1905.30, 1907.33, 1910.07, 1912.25, 1913.30
Rogers, Messr. 1892.12, 1903.03
Rogers, Mildred 1910.28, 1921.40
Rogers, Minnie 1892.11
Rogers, Mollie E. 1905.24
Rogers, Mr. 1860.01
Rogers, Paul 1968.05
Rogers, Phyllis 1940.08, 1942.01
Rogers, Poligena 1960.08
Rogers, R.E. 1894.52, 1898.45, 1899.32
Rogers, Robert 1902.37, 1985.20, 1997.21
Rogers, Ruby 1883.24
Rogers, Samuel 1877.15
Rogers, Stanley 1924.33, 1925.23, 1927.19
Rogers, Suzanne 1969.17
Rogers, Ted 1976.32
Rogers, Tex 1919.20
Rogers, Timmie 1945.07
Rogers, Vivian 1914.15
Rogers, Walter 1898.41
Rogers, Wayne 1982.01
Rogers, Will 1912.14, 1915.16, 1915.22, 1917.13, 1918.19, 1922.19, 1924.18, 1925.10, 1925.24, 1928.37, 1991.07
Rogers, William 1922.47
Rogers, Willie 1988.05
Rogers-Adler, Candace 1988.01
Rogersoll, Clarence 1900.58
Rogerson, Budd 1949.02
Rogerson, Clarence 1906.15, 1908.30, 1909.04, 1909.29, 1912.18, 1912.21, 1912.23
Roget, Renwick 1919.38
Rogge, Florence 1930.36, 1937.10
Roggerio, Teresa 1903.18
Rogier, Frank 1940.18, 1947.10, 1952.14, 1952.16, 1952.17, 1952.18, 1952.19
Rogosin, Roy 1986.16
Rogosin, Roy M. 1980.28
Rogow, Lee 1952.20
Rohan, Susan 1976.29
Rohbeck, Herr 1879.57, 1879.62
Rohmer, Sax 1909.11
Rohrbacker, Jacquiline 1996.04, 1999.17
Rohrer, Andy 1974.03
Rohrer, W.H. 1903.18
Roi, Tony 1989.11
Roider, Alice 1916.22
Rojade, Mons. 1871.18
Rokohl, Frederika 1879.65, 1879.67
Roland, Dawn 1939.13
Roland, George 1899.21
Roland, Germaine 1931.44
Roland, Herr 1897.08
Roland, Janet 1947.11
Roland, Marie 1873.15
Roland, Messr. 1883.31
Roland, Mildred 1918.03
Roland, Miss 1871.14
Roland, Mlle. 1872.42
Roland, Mme. 1872.33
Roland, Norman 1941.10, 1945.12, 1956.15
Roland, Richard 2001.02
Roland, Steve 1955.27, 1956.14, 1963.26, 1964.44
Rolanda, Rosa 1925.17
Rolanda, Rose 1919.03, 1925.17
Rolandi, Gianna 1976.23, 1977.03, 1977.17, 1978.19
Rolando, Rose 1921.03, 1921.30, 1924.15
Rolfe, Addie 1921.27
Rolfing, Tom 1976.17, 1982.05
Roll, Eddie 1954.02, 1957.12, 1961.20, 1963.12, 1965.34
Rolla, Kate 1910.11
Rolla, Tom 1968.30, 1970.09
Rolland, George 1900.57, 1903.02
Rolland, Gustav 1931.09
Rolland, Gustave 1918.10
Rolland, Harry 1898.56
Rolland, Henry 1884.12, 1895.24
Rolland, Marjorie 1917.06
Rolland, Mlle. 1872.31, 1872.39, 1873.01
Rolland, Mons. 1872.29
Rolland, Mr. 1897.41
Rolland, Yvette 1921.42
Rollands, H. 1917.10
Rollands, Henry 1899.02
Rolle, Barbara 1973.17
Rolle, Esther 1972.10
Roller, Olga 1908.44, 1917.07, 1918.20, 1919.37
Roller, S. 1873.02
Rolley, Joseph 1920.02
Rollins, David 1941.03
Rollins, George 1898.58
Rollins, Harry 1894.11
Rollins, Jack 1968.13
Rollins, May 1906.23
Rollins, Millie 1896.05
Rollins, Rowena 1942.10
Rollins, Ruth 1900.38
Rollit, Messr. 1869.29
Rollitt, George 1902.35
Rollnick, William D. 1989.05
Rolls, Billy 1930.22
Rolon, Bill 1999.11
Rolph, Marti 1971.05, 1974.26
Rolston, William 1929.51
Rolt, Bernard 1903.33, 1907.32
Roltner, Robert 1928.15, 1929.46
Roma, Caro 1906.07
Roma, Carrie 1896.01, 1897.49
Romaguera, Joaquin 1975.16, 1976.26, 1979.06, 1981.21

Romaguera, Racine 1982.11
Romain, Lucille 1917.37
Romain, Ray 1932.15
Romain, Tom 1932.15
Romaine, Cecile 1880.05
Romaine, Claire 1897.32
Romaine, George 1912.18, 1914.13
Romaine, George E. 1900.59
Romaine, Margaret 1914.07
Romaine, Messr. 1841.01
Romaine, Theodore 1897.07
Romaine, W.L. 1905.18, 1906.48
Romaine, Worthington 1920.15
Romaine, Worthington L. 1911.46
Roman, Bob 1957.14
Roman, Freddie 1991.14
Roman, Robert 1968.24
Romani, Felice 1870.19, 1870.36, 1873.04, 1873.05
Romano, Charles 1934.29
Romano, Christy Carlson 1998.21
Romano, David 1988.01
Romano, Jane 1958.01
Romano, Jorge 1993.08
Romano, Peggy 1937.10
Romano, Phil 1942.12, 1946.15
Romanoff, Boris 1925.03, 1931.38, 1943.11
Romanoff, Ed 1992.01
Romanoff, Michael 1934.35
Romanus, Frl. 1879.22
Romany, Enid 1927.34
Romay, Lina 1950.12
Romberg, Sigmund 1914.01, 1914.07, 1914.22, 1915.02, 1915.16, 1915.17, 1915.26, 1915.32, 1916.03, 1916.11, 1916.14, 1916.23, 1916.25, 1916.26, 1917.01, 1917.08, 1917.14, 1917.15, 1917.23, 1917.31, 1918.05, 1918.06, 1918.20, 1918.42, 1919.03, 1919.30, 1919.35, 1920.25, 1921.06, 1921.31, 1921.34, 1922.07, 1922.11, 1922.36, 1922.40, 1923.02, 1923.12, 1923.13, 1923.14, 1923.15, 1923.17, 1924.12, 1924.13, 1924.21, 1924.23, 1924.29, 1924.36, 1924.38, 1924.45, 1925.08, 1925.10, 1925.23, 1925.39, 1926.05, 1926.42, 1927.14, 1927.42, 1927.50, 1927.55, 1928.03, 1928.29, 1930.27, 1931.03, 1931.07, 1931.39, 1933.03, 1935.17, 1936.27, 1938.17, 1941.12, 1942.22, 1943.06, 1943.12, 1944.17, 1945.03, 1946.03, 1947.11, 1948.13, 1948.27, 1954.01, 1973.09, 1974.09, 1975.22, 1978.05, 1980.21, 1981.20, 1985.09, 1986.14, 1987.08, 1987.10, 1988.16, 1989.18, 1993.12
Rombold, Hugy 1948.10
Rome, Bert 1924.31
Rome, Harold 1942.18, 1942.26, 1943.05, 1946.10, 1950.02, 1950.12, 1950.19, 1952.10, 1954.15, 1959.11, 1962.05, 1962.17, 1965.32, 1965.37, 1974.09, 1986.03
Rome, Harold J. 1937.14, 1938.09, 1939.22, 1942.18
Romeo, A. 1906.46, 1907.54
Romeo, Angelo 1910.23
Romeo, Max 1980.05
Romeo, Signor 1891.29, 1894.45, 1895.01
Romeo, Vincenzo 1900.19, 1905.17, 1905.54, 1906.46, 1907.54, 1908.26, 1909.20
Romer 1876.01
Romer, E. 1897.38
Romer, Leila 1905.17, 1905.54, 1906.46
Romero, Alex 1956.16
Romero, Angelo 1922.01
Romero, Cesar 1929.32
Romero, Rafael 1977.17, 1979.20, 1980.04, 1980.25
Romilli, G. 1928.23, 1929.08
Romli, R. 1911.16
Romm, Sophie 1923.23
Romo, Horacio 1999.18
Romoberg, Sigmund 1914.16
Romoff, Colin 1957.01, 1958.08, 1959.03, 1961.24, 1967.12
Romoff, Linda 1998.04, 2001.03
Romoff, Messr. 1929.05
Romoff, Wood 1964.18, 1964.24
Ronald, Landon 1902.35
Ronaldo, Louise 1888.39
Ronaldo, W. 1882.77
Ronalds, C.B. 1898.66
Ronan, Brian 1996.04, 1997.15, 1997.18, 1998.04, 1998.15, 1999.03
Rondell, Gloria 1936.12
Ronell, Ann 1931.21, 1942.27, 1943.02
Rong, Nellie 1881.38
Ronn, E. 1924.36, 1925.05, 1925.10
Ronnell, Ann 1982.12
Ronsin 1914.03
Ronstadt, Linda 1981.01, 1988.15
Ronstadt, Louisa 1926.31
Ronzani, Mons. 1867.25
Ronzani, Signor 1863.06, 1863.07, 1865.04
Roodney, Cyril 1938.08
Rooeny, Mr. 1869.36
Rooke, William Michael 1838.01
Rooks, Leon P. 1907.29
Rooney Comedy Company 1889.25
Rooney, Aileen 1918.20
Rooney, Edward C. 1903.12
Rooney, Eileen 1920.47
Rooney, J.S. 1869.38, 1870.09, 1870.22, 1870.28
Rooney, Josie 1889.25, 1904.53
Rooney, Jr., Pat 1900.42
Rooney, Julia 1904.53
Rooney, Katie 1886.61, 1888.42, 1889.25
Rooney, Marjorie 1925.19
Rooney, Mattie 1898.44
Rooney, Mickey 1979.25, 1998.06, 1999.11
Rooney, Mr. 1870.25
Rooney, Mrs. 1886.61
Rooney, Pat 1876.15, 1876.22, 1886.61, 1888.42, 1889.25, 1898.44, 1900.49, 1900.56, 1901.16, 1902.24, 1903.18, 1903.39, 1907.33, 1908.27, 1921.06, 1944.19
Rooney, Sr., Pat 1950.17
Rooney, Wallace 1958.20
Roop, Reno 1998.03
Roos, Casper 1957.04, 1959.06, 1959.26, 1961.12, 1961.22, 1966.27, 1968.05, 1971.02, 1975.03, 1980.26, 1983.06, 1986.18, 1989.17
Roos, Joanna 1924.14, 1928.19
Roos, Louise 1886.13
Roos, Mr. 1876.16
Roos, Patricia 1973.07
Roos, William 1948.28, 1950.12, 1951.17
Roosevelt, Blanche 1879.70, 1879.72, 1882.19
Root, Frank 1974.18
Root, Lynn 1940.17
Roper, Walter 1934.37
Ropes, Bradford 1980.20, 2001.08
Roppel, Leonardo 1881.13
Roque, Phyllis 1939.13
Roquemore, Larry 1963.08, 1964.15, 1965.01
Rorke, Eugene 1879.37
Rorke, Hayden 1942.20
Rosa, Della 1900.59
Rosa, La Petite 1896.47
Rosa, Madeline 1884.44
Rosa, Miss 1882.46
Rosa, Mlle. 1868.24, 1868.26, 1869.03, 1869.05, 1869.16, 1869.30
Rosa, Mrs. 1844.01
Rosa, Neta 1898.27
Rosa, Vera 1899.36
Rosa, Viola 1885.44
Rosager, Lars 1987.16
Rosaire, Bobby 1920.26
Rosaire, Robert 1899.04, 1916.15, 1917.16, 1923.43
Rosales, David 1996.15, 1999.21, 2000.19
Rosales, Rachel 1990.08
Rosales, Rebecca 1986.09, 1988.18
Rosales, Sylvia 1948.04
Rosalie, Robert 1918.23
Rosalie, Ruby 1919.05
Rosander, Vera 1919.41
Rosario, Adrian 1986.07
Rosario, C.L. 1885.11
Rosario, Willie 1990.12, 1993.02, 1995.09, 1998.01, 1999.22
Rosato, Mary Lou 1973.16, 1975.18, 1996.18
Rosch, Mlle. 1888.10, 1888.23, 1889.08
Roscoe, Ed. 1906.31
Roscoe, Ed. B. 1904.45
Roscoe, Jamie L. 2001.04
Roscoe, John 1921.26
Rose 1954.08
Rose, Abie 1901.17
Rose, Alice 1896.07, 1897.16
Rose, Amelia 1908.07, 1912.37, 1913.09, 1922.30
Rose, Belle 1883.44
Rose, Billy 1923.47, 1925.42, 1926.18, 1927.13, 1927.31, 1927.32, 1927.62, 1929.08, 1929.26, 1930.08, 1930.38, 1931.13, 1934.01, 1935.15, 1936.17, 1943.24, 1944.29, 1945.06, 1945.10, 1946.09, 1960.18, 1962.17, 1963.02, 1967.11, 1974.01, 1974.09, 1975.22, 1978.09, 1978.23, 1980.10, 1986.06, 1988.08, 1999.01
Rose, Carl 1933.03
Rose, Clifford 1965.39
Rose, Cynthia 1942.32, 1984.12, 1985.09, 1987.08
Rose, David 1943.23, 1990.09
Rose, Dolores 1917.26
Rose, Donald 1946.05
Rose, E.E. 1886.27
Rose, E.K. 1912.03
Rose, Ed 1906.04, 1916.25, 1921.20
Rose, Edith 1911.26
Rose, Edward 1897.09, 1918.09
Rose, Edward E. 1904.46, 1905.39
Rose, Edward W. 1905.50
Rose, Ellen 1922.30
Rose, Ethel 1909.29
Rose, Frank E. 1907.53
Rose, Fred 1924.13, 1981.16, 1998.04
Rose, George 1966.27, 1968.17, 1969.04, 1969.17, 1976.05, 1979.22, 1981.01, 1983.08, 1985.18
Rose, Gina 1984.16
Rose, H. 1868.27
Rose, Harry 1913.28, 1920.33, 1921.22, 1921.32, 1927.47
Rose, Howard 1987.02
Rose, Irving 1919.08, 1921.14, 1924.44
Rose, Jack 1920.17, 1924.29, 1969.14
Rose, Jennifer 1968.32
Rose, Jill 1973.07
Rose, Julian 1909.18
Rose, L. Arthur 1986.12
Rose, Laura 1883.39, 1884.27
Rose, Leon 1926.07
Rose, Marc 1988.20
Rose, Michael 1980.17
Rose, Miss 1871.11
Rose, Mlle. 1868.18, 1868.25, 1868.31, 1869.01, 1869.10, 1869.19, 1870.44, 1871.27
Rose, Morris 1921.04
Rose, Neil 1942.19
Rose, P. 1872.10
Rose, Pattie 1912.07, 1913.16
Rose, Philip 1962.14, 1964.18, 1970.05, 1972.26, 1975.03, 1978.10, 1979.32, 1983.15, 1987.14, 1989.17, 1990.05
Rose, Polly 1930.18
Rose, R.A. 1929.30
Rose, Ralph 1930.29
Rose, Renee 1973.10
Rose, Ruth 1889.16
Rose, S. Lee 1926.04
Rose, Sam 1927.38, 1927.62, 1928.36, 1929.25
Rose, Stewart 1963.05
Rose, Susan R. 1982.03
Rose, Vernie 1900.24
Rose, Vincent 1908.03, 1918.07, 1921.34, 1928.23, 1929.26, 1931.26, 1982.22, 1986.02
Rose, W.G. 1904.45
Rose, William 1929.37
Rose, Winnie 1895.32
Rose-Bell, Mlle. 1868.26, 1869.30
Rose-Bell, Mme. 1869.03
Rose-Scott, Edith 1925.28
Rose-Stone, Mekenzie 2001.06
Rose-Waterson, Colin 1998.10
Roseau, Eme 1877.16, 1878.20, 1879.03, 1879.38, 1880.24
Roseborn, H.W. 1893.32
Rosebrook, Leon 1920.24, 1923.37, 1927.03, 1928.32
Rosebud, Nellie 1890.12, 1890.30, 1891.14, 1892.06, 1894.07
Rosedale, Harry 1923.13
Rosedale, Lillian 1919.26, 1920.22, 1920.23, 1922.18
Rosegarten, Rory 1987.14
Roseland, J.N. 1906.36
Roselle, William 1909.24, 1918.10, 1923.38, 1927.56
Rosemont, Norman 1965.29
Rosemont, Walter L. 1923.36
Rosen, Arnie 1957.01
Rosen, Dave 1916.15
Rosen, James E. 1902.14, 1902.33, 1904.20, 1909.05
Rosen, Lew 1891.40
Rosen, M. 1891.17
Rosen, Nanette 1957.12
Rosen, Robert 1975.03, 1981.24
Rosen, Sam 1955.11
Rosen, Samuel 1925.37
Rosen-Stone, Mekenzie 1997.04
Rosenbauer, David 1999.12
Rosenbauer, Judith 1999.12
Rosenbaum, David 1989.10
Rosenbaum, E. 1896.37, 1897.45, 1898.58
Rosenberg 1860.05
Rosenberg, Brilliant and O'Neil 1927.18
Rosenberg, Deena 1999.10
Rosenberg, Irene 1980.30
Rosenberg, J.B. 1942.34
Rosenberg, Jan 1989.19
Rosenberg, Michael (Getzel) 1967.03
Rosenberg, Sandy 1997.19
Rosenberg, Sophie 1923.22
Rosenberg, Stephen 1987.12
Rosenblat, Barbara 1991.05
Rosenbloom, Yair 1972.17
Rosenblum, Jr., Edmund 1926.04
Rosenblum, M. Edgar 1979.07
Rosencranz, Peggy Hill 1992.08
Rosene, C. 1871.13, 1877.21
Rosene, Charles 1872.27, 1875.06, 1879.01
Rosener, George 1923.25, 1927.42, 1934.18, 1934.43
Rosenfeld, Carl 1890.31, 1891.33, 1892.43, 1893.29, 1894.01, 1894.30, 1896.34, 1897.35, 1898.53
Rosenfeld, Carol 1979.27
Rosenfeld, Charles 1890.31
Rosenfeld, Grace 1952.08
Rosenfeld, Hilary 1978.11
Rosenfeld, Jacqueline 1994.09
Rosenfeld, Jyll 1986.21, 1988.11, 1990.11, 1994.03, 1996.03, 1999.25
Rosenfeld, Ludwig 1896.34
Rosenfeld, M. 1990.16
Rosenfeld, Moishe 1990.16
Rosenfeld, Monroe 1895.32
Rosenfeld, Monroe H. 1889.22, 1894.31, 1894.51
Rosenfeld, Moris 1966.21
Rosenfeld, Rachel 1994.09
Rosenfeld, Sidney 1896.44, 1898.72
Rosenfeld, Stanley 1884.59
Rosenfeld, Sydney 1876.01, 1876.02, 1880.31, 1883.45, 1884.08, 1884.22, 1884.63, 1885.05, 1885.08, 1885.11, 1885.14, 1885.28, 1885.41, 1885.43, 1885.45, 1885.63, 1885.67, 1886.04, 1886.34, 1886.59, 1887.13, 1887.18, 1887.20, 1888.19, 1888.22, 1889.22, 1889.24, 1891.13, 1892.03, 1892.47, 1893.32, 1893.38, 1894.21, 1895.04, 1895.18, 1897.25, 1898.15, 1898.37, 1900.23, 1900.29, 1900.56, 1901.12, 1901.29, 1902.06, 1902.37, 1905.20, 1905.54, 1906.05, 1907.02, 1907.42, 1908.29, 1911.07, 1911.08, 1912.04, 1912.08, 1913.33, 1944.26, 1945.15
Rosenfeld, T. 1891.18
Rosenfeld, Theodor 1890.31, 1891.33, 1893.29, 1894.01
Rosenfeld, Theodore 1892.43, 1894.30, 1896.34, 1897.35, 1898.53
Rosenfield, Lois F. 1980.07, 1985.08
Rosenfield, Maurice 1980.07, 1985.08, 1993.04
Rosenkrantz, Iris 1977.15
Rosenor, George 1925.23
Rosenquest, J. Wesley 1890.35, 1891.43, 1892.01
Rosenquest, J.W. 1887.02
Rosenquist, Holger 1966.19
Rosenstock, Joseph 1952.12, 1955.17, 1956.10
Rosenstock, Milton 1942.20, 1947.08, 1947.16, 1949.18, 1951.13, 1952.20, 1953.07, 1955.25, 1956.14, 1959.13, 1961.28, 1962.18, 1963.13, 1964.11, 1969.07, 1969.14, 1970.08, 1971.15, 1972.03, 1973.08, 1974.02, 1974.17, 1976.36, 1977.07, 1980.16, 1989.23
Rosenthal, A. 1902.43
Rosenthal, Chayele 1970.18
Rosenthal, David 1906.35, 1972.17
Rosenthal, Harry 1921.26, 1929.02
Rosenthal, J.J. 1899.08

Rosenthal, Jean 1942.31, 1947.10, 1948.29, 1950.05, 1952.12, 1953.05, 1953.14, 1954.04, 1954.06, 1954.07, 1954.14, 1954.18, 1954.19, 1956.03, 1956.05, 1957.02, 1957.12, 1957.16, 1959.01, 1959.11, 1959.22, 1959.24, 1959.27, 1960.03, 1960.08, 1961.02, 1961.27, 1962.12, 1963.16, 1963.25, 1964.01, 1964.17, 1964.27, 1965.02, 1965.08, 1966.09, 1966.14, 1966.18, 1966.29, 1967.05, 1967.15, 1968.01, 1969.05, 1980.02
Rosenthal, Laurence 1957.18, 1958.14, 1959.22, 1961.14, 1965.21, 1967.02, 1968.07
Rosenthal, Leo 1983.17
Rosenthal, Yasha 1946.17
Roser, James L.D. 1976.25
Roseray, Mlle. 1926.14
Roses, Martin 1932.18
Rosetti, Marie 1872.37
Rosetti, Mlle. 1875.21
Rosewald, Julie 1881.05
Rosewood, Evelyn 1914.30
Rosewood, Hazel 1912.44
Rosey, George 1903.41
Rosey, Joseph 1904.29
Rosi, Cissie 1934.02
Rosie 1954.08
Rosine, C. 1876.35
Rosine, Charles 1878.02, 1880.02
Rosine, Homer 1919.18
Roska, Mlle. 1869.26
Rosley, Adrian 1927.68, 1930.39, 1931.09, 1932.10
Rosley, Adrian H. 1915.32, 1919.31
Rosoff, Charles 1927.09, 1940.02
Ross, Adrian 1895.02, 1895.03, 1895.32, 1897.20, 1897.32, 1897.52, 1898.29, 1899.12, 1899.35, 1899.39, 1900.43, 1901.19, 1902.01, 1902.12, 1902.30, 1903.33, 1904.29, 1904.40, 1905.04, 1905.18, 1906.36, 1907.15, 1907.48, 1908.06, 1908.25, 1909.04, 1909.21, 1910.03, 1910.21, 1910.22, 1911.22, 1911.27, 1911.39, 1912.33, 1912.35, 1913.17, 1913.26, 1913.36, 1914.10, 1914.18, 1915.18, 1916.20, 1919.02, 1919.42, 1930.07, 1937.03, 1942.21, 1943.09, 1944.24, 1957.04, 1957.15, 1958.16, 1959.21, 1962.21, 1963.24, 1964.30, 1965.27, 1982.16, 1983.12, 1985.11, 1988.14
Ross, Alan 1948.22, 1950.03
Ross, Allie 1927.32, 1928.18, 1929.25
Ross, Alma 1928.16, 1932.07, 1946.12
Ross, Andrew 1999.14
Ross, Annie 1906.14, 1956.13
Ross, Anthony 1942.20, 1943.23
Ross, Arthur 1940.21
Ross, Ben 1938.09, 1941.01
Ross, Bertram 1950.19, 1971.06
Ross, Betsy 1942.27
Ross, Betty 1922.30
Ross, Bud 1900.15
Ross, Budd 1892.21, 1897.15, 1899.12
Ross, Camille 1986.03, 1986.04
Ross, Carry 1872.34
Ross, Charles 1889.51, 1897.09
Ross, Charles J. 1881.22, 1890.30, 1891.15, 1896.26, 1896.36, 1897.19, 1897.31, 1897.48, 1898.50, 1899.17, 1899.30, 1900.38, 1901.06, 1901.27, 1903.28, 1906.17, 1907.24, 1908.01, 1908.38, 1909.19, 1912.13, 1912.24, 1915.02
Ross, Charles K. 1896.26
Ross, Chrles J. 1894.06
Ross, Clark 1925.44
Ross, Clifton 1907.29
Ross, Diana 1976.16
Ross, Dixie 1942.27
Ross, Don 1934.01, 1943.20
Ross, Donald 1924.32
Ross, Emily 1945.20
Ross, Emma 1882.46
Ross, Etna 1930.36
Ross, Evelyne 1949.03
Ross, F. McCullough 1886.02
Ross, Frank 1912.27, 1927.13
Ross, Gary 1996.08
Ross, Harriet 1924.40
Ross, Helen F. 1967.01
Ross, Herbert 1908.26, 1946.24, 1948.08, 1951.14, 1952.05, 1954.19, 1958.01, 1958.05, 1960.09, 1961.27, 1962.05, 1963.08, 1964.15, 1965.01, 1965.06, 1965.31, 1966.18
Ross, Hope 1893.42
Ross, Howard 1975.22, 1979.09
Ross, Hugh 1948.17, 1954.03
Ross, Hunter 1956.04
Ross, Ida 1870.34, 1872.34, 1882.46, 1918.22
Ross, Jack 1931.36
Ross, James 1934.41
Ross, Jamie 1971.02, 1972.07, 1981.10, 1995.07
Ross, Jennie 1871.13
Ross, Jennifer 2001.04
Ross, Jerry 1944.28, 1951.10, 1953.17, 1954.05, 1955.08, 1957.08, 1962.17, 1973.15, 1976.07, 1989.04, 1994.01, 1999.01
Ross, Joe 1928.31, 1958.01, 1960.09, 1963.14, 1964.18, 1966.13, 1972.03, 1973.12
Ross, John 1919.04
Ross, John B. 1976.28
Ross, John S. 1898.63
Ross, Judith 1972.25
Ross, Julian 1913.03
Ross, Julie 1994.01
Ross, Justin 1979.15, 1982.06
Ross, Kay 1929.32
Ross, Kenneth 1905.51
Ross, King 1931.21, 1944.29
Ross, Larry 1971.09
Ross, Leona 1886.39
Ross, Lewis 1970.16
Ross, Linda 1964.27
Ross, Lynn 1959.06, 1959.25
Ross, Madeline 1925.20
Ross, Margaret 1908.40, 1943.20
Ross, Marilyn 1951.15
Ross, Marion 1933.26
Ross, Martin 1971.02
Ross, Marvin 1958.21
Ross, Michael 1960.12Ross, Miss 1873.26
Ross, Mr. 1836.01, 1882.71
Ross, Oriel 1928.42
Ross, Patti 1979.31
Ross, Philip Arthur 1983.02
Ross, Robert 1938.12, 1939.13, 1942.03, 1942.27, 1943.15, 1944.03, 1945.08, 1950.03
Ross, Robert F. 1932.28
Ross, Ronald 1925.35
Ross, Roy 1938.13, 1939.30, 1946.10
Ross, Ruth 1938.04
Ross, Shirley 1940.06
Ross, Stanley 1941.11
Ross, Stephen 1989.17
Ross, Steven 1968.32
Ross, Stuart 1927.62, 1989.09
Ross, T. 1868.06
Ross, Ted 1969.15, 1972.26, 1973.10, 1975.01
Ross, Thomas 1921.34
Ross, Tom 1924.19
Ross, Tony 1935.16
Ross, Vera 1920.11, 1921.39, 1923.17, 1926.10, 1926.44, 1927.44, 1927.57, 1927.61, 1930.03, 1931.10, 1931.15, 1931.20, 1931.25, 1933.08, 1933.09, 1933.11, 1933.14, 1933.18, 1933.19, 1934.07, 1934.08, 1934.10, 1934.11, 1935.05, 1935.06, 1935.07, 1935.08, 1935.10, 1936.04, 1936.08, 1936.10, 1936.11
Ross, Vicki 1942.27
Ross, Virginia 1885.54, 1898.63
Ross, W.H. 1882.45
Ross, Walter 1931.44
Ross, William 1978.18
Ross-Selwick, Ethel 1891.36
Rossa, Irwin 1920.42
Rosse, Herman 1923.20, 1923.26, 1924.32, 1925.03, 1928.40, 1928.45, 1928.50
Rosseau, Marcel 1937.15
Rosseau, Mons. 1869.24
Rossellat, Robert 1950.14
Rossi, Barbara J. 1981.07
Rossi, Cheryl-Ann 1986.20
Rossi, Cissie 1932.29
Rossi, Elsie 1933.20
Rossi, Gloria 1973.09, 1974.17, 1989.18
Rossi, Herman 1923.47
Rossi, Lelia 1891.35
Rossi, Suzanne 1921.08
Rossi, Toni 1956.02
Rossini 1862.09, 1923.29, 1990.10
Rossini, Giaccomo 1999.05
Rossini, Gioacchino 1880.55, 1942.33, 1990.10, 1990.16
Rossit, Miss 1863.01
Rossiter, P.T. 1927.20
Rossiter, Vivian 1895.03
Rossland, Florence 1906.03
Rossman, Erna 1965.04
Rossmore, Dorothy 1890.17
Rossner, A. 1877.08, 1877.21
Rossner, Gussie 1882.32
Rossner, Miss 1881.41
Rost, Leo 1981.24
Rostain, Messr. 1906.11, 1907.09
Rostand, Edmond 1899.28, 1973.07, 1993.17
Rostandis, Edmond 1898.50
Rosten, Leo 1968.06
Rostetter, W.A. 1880.42
Rostetter, W.H. 1902.33
Rostetter, W.J. 1880.42, 1882.39, 1884.36, 1895.25, 1896.39
Rostetter, W.T. 1885.08
Rostetter, William 1888.13, 1904.20, 1905.10
Rostetter, William J. 1883.37, 1885.39, 1885.51, 1885.62, 1886.07, 1886.53, 1889.30, 1889.32, 1890.13, 1890.22, 1890.38, 1890.42, 1890.45, 1891.10, 1891.16, 1891.35, 1892.26, 1892.32, 1892.41, 1892.49, 1893.01, 1893.04, 1893.22
Roston, Karen 1979.19, 1986.18, 1989.22
Rostova, Luba 1941.03
Rostova, Lubov 1942.01
Rota, Nino 1974.22, 1998.17
Rotblit, Yaakov 1972.17
Rotella, Mary 1987.16
Rotenberg, David 1985.17
Roth, Andy 1982.20, 1986.08, 1989.14
Roth, Ann 1931.42, 1964.44, 1970.02, 1970.05, 1972.26, 1973.06, 1978.13, 1979.04, 1981.21, 1982.11, 1985.08
Roth, Ben 1906.43
Roth, Billie 1919.35
Roth, Daryl 1991.15
Roth, Dennis 1970.21, 1971.15
Roth, Don 1910.15
Roth, Edmund 1914.24
Roth, Elizabeth 1903.31
Roth, Elliott 1921.33
Roth, Herb 1924.36
Roth, Jordan 2000.17
Roth, Joseph 1937.14
Roth, Lillian 1927.31, 1928.23, 1931.26, 1962.05, 1971.07
Roth, Marion 1913.35
Roth, Mary 1937.11
Roth, Murray 1920.28, 1922.15
Roth, Nancy 1965.22
Roth, Nat 1894.28, 1895.22, 1896.25, 1898.77
Roth, Nathaniel 1904.35
Roth, Phil 1962.13
Roth, Robert Jess 1994.04, 1999.16
Roth, Wolfgang 1953.04, 1958.04, 1965.04, 1979.29
Rothacker, Louise 1926.05, 1927.28
Rothacker, Stella 1927.28
Rothaug, J. 1918.21
Rothberg, Bob 1936.17
Rothe and Teichner 1923.08
Rothe, Anita 1890.40
Rother, Frl. 1882.68
Rothgeb, John 1976.28
Rothschild, Herr 1879.62
Rothstein, Fred A. 1888.06, 1888.11
Rothstein, Jon 1989.10
Rothstein, Norman 1991.11, 1993.08
Rotner, Robert 1928.15
Rotoli, Francesca 1918.24
Roton, Bentley 1963.17
Rotov, Alex 1944.18
Rott, Adolph 1965.04
Rotter, Fritz 1999.05, 1999.07
Rotter, Mr. 1891.33
Rottger, Erla 1907.52
Rottger, Uria 1905.56
Rottger, Urla 1907.15
Roudenko, Lubov 1943.09, 1946.04, 1946.12, 1950.14
Roudil, Pierre 1908.39, 1909.25
Rough, Edmund Glover 1870.21
Rough, Selina 1886.12, 1889.52
Rouillier, Ron 1981.16
Roullier, Ron 1981.17
Roumain, Martial 1984.09
Round, Thomas 1939.06, 1947.22, 1948.02, 1948.06, 1948.07, 1962.25, 1962.26, 1962.30
Roundabout Theatre 2001.02
Roundabout Theatre Company, The 1993.10, 1993.16, 1995.11, 1998.15
Rounds, David 1964.04
Roundtree, Jean 1922.22
Roundy, George 1866.12
Rounseville, Robert 1940.06, 1952.14, 1952.16, 1952.18, 1954.04, 1954.14, 1956.15, 1957.03, 1957.15, 1961.09, 1964.07, 1964.08, 1965.34, 1972.14
Rourke, Betty 1927.64
Rourke, Eugene 1880.64, 1882.02
Rourke, M.E. 1898.16, 1906.36, 1907.32, 1908.25, 1909.01, 1909.12, 1909.21, 1910.03, 1910.20, 1910.21, 1911.12, 1911.27, 1912.26, 1912.37, 1912.41, 1913.20, 1913.26, 1914.07, 1915.01, 1917.01
Rourke, Messr. 1881.29
Rourke, Michael E. 1975.22
Rousby, Arthur 1882.75
Rousby, Miss 1882.60
Rouse, Fannie Denham 1898.08
Rouse, Fanny Denham 1893.38
Rouse, Mr. 1863.08
Rouse, W.A. 1876.02
Rouseby, Arthur 1882.75
Rousseau, Frances 1895.44
Rousseau, M. Marcel 1926.03
Rousseau, Marcel 1920.27, 1925.41, 1927.46
Rousseau, Miss 1897.41
Rousseau, Mons. 1868.26, 1870.03
Rousseaux, J. 1930.28
Routh, Marc 1991.02, 1995.03, 1996.06, 1997.13, 1997.18, 1998.03, 1999.12, 1999.24
Routh, Mark 2001.05
Routledge, Patricia 1968.02, 1976.11
Routon, Madame 1921.02
Routon, Mme. 1923.02, 1923.03
Routon, Yvonne 1922.36
Roux, Charles 1892.60, 1893.02, 1893.07
Roux, Noel 1963.02, 1965.08
Rouzaud, Rene 1959.15, 1963.02, 1965.08
Rouzoud, Rene 1981.04
Rovano, Antonio 1946.03
Roven, Glenn 1976.20, 1979.25, 1984.10, 1991.04, 1995.12
Roveta, Sandra 1962.24, 1963.21
Rovin, Robert 1966.05
Rovira, E. 1997.13
Row, Arthur 1913.07
Rowan, Frank 1927.38
Rowan, Marc 1966.12, 1966.16
Rowan, Ruth 1943.05
Rowe, Bolton 1879.18, 1880.18
Rowe, Dee Etta 1979.26
Rowe, Estelle 1889.54
Rowe, Florence 1888.04
Rowe, George Fawcett 1866.03, 1873.12, 1877.07, 1880.35, 1881.28, 1881.47
Rowe, H. 1897.29
Rowe, Hansford 1976.28, 1985.08
Rowe, Iris 1923.38
Rowe, J.H. 1878.04, 1880.47
Rowe, John C. 1907.25
Rowe, Josephine V. 1911.04, 1912.06
Rowe, Mannie 1972.08
Rowe, Marilyn 1976.18
Rowe, Miss 1871.15
Rowe, Saville 1879.18
Rowell, Glenn 1955.13
Rowen, Don 1925.33
Rowen, Glenn 1978.19, 1979.20, 1981.20, 1985.09, 1985.13, 1986.09, 1987.08, 1990.02, 1990.08
Rowland, Adele 1904.24, 1905.53, 1906.36, 1907.39, 1908.27, 1909.18, 1910.25, 1911.32, 1914.12, 1914.27, 1915.07, 1915.29, 1916.26, 1919.11, 1922.23
Rowland, Betty 1979.15
Rowland, Douglas 1937.02
Rowland, Henry 1943.23
Rowland, Jeff 1995.15, 1997.18
Rowland, Maud 1907.58
Rowland, Miss 1872.22
Rowland, William 1918.10
Rowleigh, Miss 1883.06
Rowles, Polly 1962.03
Rowles, Sherman 1898.20
Rowley, Bill 1979.05
Rowley, Eddie 1913.07

Rowley, J. Henry 1906.10, 1907.44
Rowley, Mina 1882.60, 1882.75, 1882.78
Rox, Dorothy 1935.03
Rox, John 1934.40, 1940.23, 1953.17, 1956.08
Roxas, Bernabe 1932.19
Roy, Dorothy 1926.50, 1928.50
Roy, Hazel 1960.16
Roy, L.C. Fitz 1902.43
Roy, Margaret 1942.02, 1942.04, 1942.06, 1942.07, 1942.09, 1956.15
Roy, Nell 1930.14
Roy, Reine 1893.25
Roy, Thomas 1880.64
Roy, Vernon 1905.20, 1905.27, 1907.32
Roy, Will 1962.16, 1966.08, 1968.10, 1978.22, 1987.09
Roy, William 1953.02, 1962.02, 1980.09
Royal National Theatre of Great Britain 1989.10
Royal National Theatre, The 1994.02
Royal Pardon Productions 1980.27
Royal Shakespeare Company 1965.39, 1981.04, 1987.04, 1988.12
Royal Shakespeare Theatre 1963.03
Royal, Charles 1929.29
Royal, Helen 1929.29
Royal, Matthew J. 1900.15
Royal, Reginald 1990.05, 1992.03
Royal, Stella 1930.35
Royal, Ted 1939.25, 1939.30, 1941.08, 1943.01, 1943.14, 1943.16, 1943.20, 1944.02, 1944.18, 1944.29, 1945.08, 1945.13, 1945.17, 1945.18, 1946.04, 1946.07, 1946.08, 1946.12, 1946.13, 1946.22, 1947.07, 1948.04, 1948.15, 1948.18, 1948.22, 1948.26, 1948.28, 1949.02, 1950.09, 1950.10, 1950.17, 1951.02, 1951.15, 1951.18, 1951.24, 1952.09, 1953.17, 1954.09, 1954.19, 1955.06, 1955.11, 1956.02, 1956.08, 1956.16, 1957.03, 1957.17, 1958.01, 1958.03, 1962.02, 1962.15, 1963.04, 1965.15, 1966.11, 1966.13, 1967.17, 1970.11, 1991.12, 1992.04, 1996.13
Royce, Edgar 1923.47
Royce, Edward 1913.20, 1913.26, 1914.04, 1916.20, 1916.24, 1917.01, 1917.06, 1917.17, 1917.27, 1917.36, 1918.03, 1918.07, 1918.16, 1918.34, 1918.37, 1919.08, 1919.09, 1919.27, 1919.36, 1920.12, 1920.18, 1920.37, 1920.44, 1921.21, 1921.32, 1921.36, 1922.33, 1923.09, 1923.10, 1923.30, 1924.38, 1925.08, 1926.18, 1927.47, 1928.02, 1928.31
Royce, Jr., Burt B. 1928.20
Royce, Louise 1895.33, 1897.18, 1898.16
Royce, Margie 1927.05
Royce, Shirley 1920.19
Royd, Arthur 1912.15
Roye, Dorothy 1928.30
Royle, Edwin Milton 1905.45, 1906.27, 1927.65
Royster, Nat 1906.02, 1906.21
Royston, George 1951.11
Royston, Helen 1904.49
Royston, Robert 1999.24
Royston, Roy 1924.09, 1924.21, 1925.26, 1928.35, 1932.15
Royston, Willie 1886.01
Royton, Helen 1902.35, 1908.23
Rozaa 1976.20
Rozan, Micheline 1983.16
Rozelle, Dot 1916.03
Rozie, Keith 1986.11
Rozovsky, Mark 1979.29
Rozyk, Rose 1967.08
Ruane, Janine 1977.06
Rub, Christian 1920.46
Rubanoff, Jaye 1954.13
Rube 1893.45
Rubel, Hines 1936.12
Rubel, L. 1887.03, 1887.27, 1888.01, 1890.17
Ruben's Grand English Opera Company 1878.03
Ruben, Aaron 1959.23
Ruben, Jose 1928.48, 1929.39, 1931.37, 1934.04, 1935.17, 1936.27, 1939.21, 1942.17, 1943.08, 1944.17, 1946.23
Rubenfeld, Ken 1978.23
Rubens, Frances 1912.12
Rubens, Hubert 1999.05
Rubens, L.M. 1878.03
Rubens, Maurice 1925.07, 1925.23, 1925.26, 1925.27, 1925.43, 1926.01, 1926.14, 1926.15, 1926.26, 1926.33, 1926.37, 1927.58, 1928.06, 1928.14, 1928.26, 1929.09, 1929.17, 1929.22, 1929.28, 1930.15, 1932.06
Rubens, Maury 1928.48, 1929.17, 1930.37, 1932.01
Rubens, Paul 1895.32, 1900.51, 1901.19, 1902.01, 1902.05, 1902.30, 1903.22, 1903.33, 1904.03, 1904.29, 1904.40, 1905.13, 1906.25, 1906.32, 1907.15, 1907.41, 1907.46, 1907.63, 1911.22, 1911.44, 1913.04, 1914.18, 1914.32, 1915.07, 1915.18, 1920.09
Rubens, Paul A. 1902.35, 1906.41, 1907.32, 1911.06, 1911.14, 1916.20, 1923.26
Rubens, Walter 1903.22
Rubenstein, Barbara 1976.04
Rubie, L. 1889.21
Rubin, Arthur 1951.19, 1953.07, 1955.02, 1956.04, 1959.04, 1961.26, 1963.21, 1981.13, 1983.16, 1984.16, 1986.07, 1987.13, 1988.20, 1989.08, 1989.20, 1990.20, 1991.09, 1993.05
Rubin, Benny 1927.43
Rubin, Cyma 1971.03, 1975.09
Rubin, George 1918.36
Rubin, Pedro 1927.08
Rubin, Stan 1986.13, 1991.06
Rubin, Steven 1988.10
Rubin-Vega, Daphne 1996.09, 2000.17
Rubino, Michael 1979.20, 1980.04, 1980.25, 1981.21, 1982.20, 1983.13, 1989.14
Rubins, Barry 1964.23
Rubinsky, Robert I. 1968.11
Rubinson, David 1983.09
Rubinstein, Anton 1982.06
Rubinstein, Arthur 1970.02
Rubinstein, Arthur B. 1975.06
Rubinstein, David 1983.09
Rubinstein, E. 1972.17
Rubinstein, Eli 1970.17
Rubinstein, Eva 1954.01
Rubinstein, John 1972.22
Rubinstein, Ruth 1937.14
Ruby, Ellalee 1927.39
Ruby, Harry 1917.13, 1917.35, 1918.19, 1919.15, 1919.16, 1920.18, 1920.33, 1921.18, 1922.15, 1922.32, 1923.19, 1923.32, 1923.33, 1924.22, 1924.44, 1925.05, 1925.36, 1925.42, 1925.47, 1926.03, 1926.23, 1926.28, 1926.32, 1926.39, 1927.12, 1927.52, 1928.02, 1928.25, 1928.38, 1929.49, 1941.09, 1975.22, 1981.03, 1999.01, 1913.17
Ruby, Herman 1981.03
Rubykate, Inc. 1974.03
Ruck, Louise 1992.02, 1994.06
Rucker, John 1896.49, 1907.55
Rucker, Robert 1968.19
Ruckerts, Hilda 1915.24, 1916.15
Rudac, Dorothy 1925.01, 1925.28
Rudd, Daisy 1908.07, 1908.39, 1912.12
Rudd, Gertrude 1913.24
Ruddy, Robert 1958.11, 1958.13
Rudel, Julius 1945.15, 1946.11, 1953.05, 1953.14, 1954.04, 1954.07, 1954.14, 1955.09, 1956.06, 1957.03, 1957.11, 1958.11, 1958.16, 1959.16, 1959.21, 1961.03, 1961.04, 1961.05, 1961.06, 1961.09, 1961.12, 1961.13, 1962.07, 1962.08, 1962.11, 1962.15, 1963.04, 1963.06, 1964.07, 1964.10, 1964.19, 1964.31, 1965.04, 1965.10, 1965.13, 1965.25, 1976.26, 1977.11, 1978.07, 1980.04, 1980.25, 1989.13, 1989.24
Rudiferia, Melena 1984.05
Rudin, Frederick 1946.17
Rudin, Scott 1994.05, 2000.08
Rudina, Tatiana 1990.01
Rudisill, Ivan 1910.29, 1920.11, 1920.20, 1922.13, 1922.28, 1924.03, 1925.29, 1926.25, 1929.17, 1929.49, 1930.26, 1934.15
Rudley, Herbert 1933.07, 1935.16, 1937.01
Rudley, Marion Grant 1937.08
Rudnick, Max 1930.24, 1932.08
Rudolfi, Frl. 1882.68
Rudolfo, Roxie 1884.58
Rudolfy, R. 1897.29
Rudolph Aronson's Comic Opera Company 1889.16
Rudolph, Inspector 1884.40
Rudolph, J. 1877.04
Rudolph, Mina 1903.36
Rudolph, Minner 1901.06
Rudolph, Vernon 1928.26
Rudy, Lisa 1982.15
Rue, Edward 1884.04, 1884.07
Rue, Elife 1907.03
Rue, Robert 1956.15, 1959.04
Ruelas, Rafael Palomar 1988.15
Ruepke, Herman 1907.27
Ruff, Alton 1961.08
Ruffa, Mario 1988.06
Ruffin, Leonard 1925.14
Ruffin, Ruan 1999.08
Ruffino, Mlle. 1879.19, 1879.39, 1879.46, 1879.55, 1880.52, 1882.30, 1882.35
Ruffner, Edmund 1925.39, 1927.17
Rufo, Paul 1962.18
Rufus, Francis 1875.10
Rugby, George 1879.18, 1879.23, 1879.24
Rugby, Messr. 1879.23
Ruge, William 1889.50, 1890.25
Rugel, Yvette 1917.08, 1919.13, 1926.23
Ruggiero, Gabrielle 1954.18
Ruggiero, Joseph 1931.12, 1931.23
Ruggles, Charles 1917.04, 1918.20, 1919.06, 1923.36, 1926.25, 1928.44, 1929.12
Ruggles, Mr. 1860.01
Ruggles, Sandra 1993.12
Ruick, Barbara 1956.05
Ruick, Melville 1948.27, 1952.03
Ruisinger, Thomas 1971.09, 1979.28, 1980.18
Ruivivar, Francis 1990.17, 1994.05, 1999.11
Ruiz, Antonio 1941.11
Ruiz, Leonara 1897.16
Ruiz, Mario 1939.18
Ruiz, Mercedes 1992.15
Ruiz, Mons. 1876.24, 1876.25, 1876.26, 1877.06, 1877.09, 1877.10, 1877.11, 1877.12, 1877.14, 1877.19
Ruiz, Randy 1978.11
Ruize, Leonora 1893.07
Rule, Bert 1920.36
Rule, Bert L. 1913.05
Rule, Charles 1953.09, 1967.14, 1968.24, 1969.06, 1970.10, 1974.17, 1975.06, 1976.08, 1988.01
Rule, Janice 1949.08, 1961.08
Rule, Sean 1974.17
Rullman, F. 1879.14
Rum, Jorge 1992.13
Rumbold, Hugh 1905.27
Rummel, Messr. 1894.19
Rumsey, Maurice 1922.42
Rumsey, Murray 1942.17
Rumshinsky, J. 1931.29, 1990.16
Rumshinsky, J.M. 1918.23
Rumshinsky, Joseph 1942.28, 1951.21
Rumshinsky, Murray 1970.18
Runanin, Boris 1955.27, 1959.23
Runich, E. 1932.09
Runitch, Emma 1934.32
Runnel-Amend Studio 1923.11
Runnel-Amend, Inc. 1922.44
Runnells, Bonnie 1881.06
Runnells, Fred 1897.27, 1906.35
Runnells, Frederick R. 1894.42
Runnells, Mary 1884.22
Runnells, Miss 1884.42
Runnels, Messr. 1876.35
Runolfsson, Anne 1993.17
Runowska, Iwona 1992.05
Runyan, Messr. 1855.06
Runyon 1862.04, 1863.06, 1863.07
Runyon, C. 1882.62
Runyon, Damon 1950.17, 1955.06, 1965.15, 1966.13, 1976.21, 1992.04
Rupert, Bertha 1869.38, 1880.07
Rupert, Gene 1966.09
Rupert, Michael (Mike) 1968.01, 1986.07, 1988.07, 1992.09
Rupert, Miss 1882.46
Rupert, Mlle. 1876.03
Rupert, W.H. 1912.16
Ruperth, Bertha 1879.02
Rupp, Louis 1930.36
Ruppel, Leonard 1882.77
Ruppell, Julia 1899.04
Ruppert, Bertha 1876.03
Ruprecht, David 1980.29
Ruru, Pauline 1972.20
Rush, Cecile 1888.23, 1891.34, 1895.39
Rush, Edward F. 1914.28
Rush, Felix 1917.12, 1918.18
Rush, Georgia 1898.78
Rush, Ida 1891.34
Rush, Madge 1920.07
Rush, Susan 1995.07
Rushby, Horace 1907.43
Rushmore, Frank 1901.26
Rushmore, Vivian 1906.36, 1909.12, 1910.27, 1911.13, 1911.42, 1912.39, 1915.25
Rusholme, Susie 1901.27
Rusholme, Suzanne 1907.58
Rushton, Lucy 1866.01, 1866.04, 1866.05
Rushworth, Frank 1897.41, 1898.18, 1898.26, 1898.60, 1900.25, 1900.31, 1900.32, 1902.04, 1903.40, 1905.03, 1906.32, 1908.30, 1909.29
Rusignola, Damon 1992.16
Rusinek, Roland 1997.22, 1998.20, 1999.21, 2000.19
Ruskay, Everett 1906.50
Ruskin, Coby 1939.19, 1941.01
Ruskin, Harry 1923.38, 1924.33, 1925.47, 1927.13, 1929.19, 1929.29, 1929.32, 1930.42, 1931.26, 1932.13
Russ, Alfred 1930.27, 1932.22
Russ, Emily 1919.06, 1920.01
Russ, Shirley 2000.03
Russak, Gerard 1967.01
Russel, Florence 1903.25
Russel, John 1948.18
Russel, S.K. 1940.23
Russell 1893.23, 1894.34
Russell Bennett Productions 1944.23
Russell Henry 1909.19
Russell Uniform Company 1912.35, 1913.04, 1917.19, 1920.12
Russell's Comedians 1892.36, 1892.56, 1893.28, 1894.10
Russell, A.J. 1962.14
Russell, Alma 1892.59
Russell, Anna 1953.10
Russell, Anne C. 1965.17
Russell, Annie 1889.33
Russell, Annie C. 1907.28
Russell, Bijou 1898.67
Russell, Bill 1955.11, 1997.17
Russell, Bill-Boy 1979.01
Russell, Bob 1901.20, 1981.06, 1997.03
Russell, Brenda 1995.12
Russell, Burt 1982.22, 1984.15
Russell, Byron 1946.20
Russell, Catherine 1988.13
Russell, Charles 1961.18
Russell, Clint 1913.05
Russell, David 1975.03
Russell, Dorothy 1907.03
Russell, Eddie 1903.13, 1915.24, 1916.15, 1917.16, 1918.23, 1920.26, 1922.30, 1923.46
Russell, Edith 1942.35
Russell, Edna 1917.31, 1936.12, 1938.04
Russell, Eleanore 1904.33
Russell, Ethel 1913.28, 1914.33
Russell, Evelyn 1957.14, 1961.18, 1972.23
Russell, Flora Bonfanto 1907.28
Russell, Frank 1893.31, 1896.15, 1897.07, 1897.38, 1909.15
Russell, Fred 1914.17
Russell, George 1989.03
Russell, Georgia 1912.30
Russell, Georgie 1911.28
Russell, Gilbert 1945.09, 1946.18
Russell, Grace 1906.45, 1908.03
Russell, Harold 1884.10, 1886.02, 1907.11, 1910.02, 1912.39
Russell, Helen 1894.50
Russell, Henry 1862.05, 1869.47, 1937.06
Russell, Herbert 1920.10
Russell, Hiram E. 1912.47
Russell, Howard 1893.23, 1899.21
Russell, Howell 1895.08
Russell, Irene 1909.30
Russell, J.G. 1879.09, 1880.15
Russell, Jack 1948.23, 1948.28, 1950.02, 1953.06, 1953.15, 1954.06, 1955.17
Russell, James 1884.17, 1891.18, 1901.24, 1907.28, 1907.39, 1991.09, 1993.12
Russell, Jessica 1943.24
Russell, Jim 1957.10
Russell, Jimmy 1952.09
Russell, Joe 1895.02
Russell, John 1884.17, 1891.18, 1901.24, 1907.28, 1976.21, 1979.32
Russell, John H. 1884.66, 1888.17, 1889.06, 1890.07, 1890.34, 1891.43
Russell, Joseph 1901.26
Russell, Jr., Eddie 1927.34
Russell, Jr., John 1907.28

Russell, Laura 1889.04, 1889.23, 1890.01, 1890.11, 1890.19
Russell, Laura J. 1891.26, 1892.09
Russell, Lee 1928.12
Russell, Leon 1973.14, 1976.32
Russell, Lillian 1881.06, 1881.12, 1881.40, 1881.56, 1882.04, 1882.20, 1882.42, 1882.70, 1883.38, 1885.26, 1885.40, 1886.14, 1886.40, 1887.15, 1887.20, 1887.21, 1887.44, 1888.18, 1889.04, 1889.23, 1890.01, 1890.11, 1890.39, 1891.12, 1891.17, 1891.36, 1892.60, 1893.02, 1893.07, 1893.39, 1894.14, 1894.41, 1894.48, 1895.09, 1895.12, 1896.10, 1896.12, 1896.22, 1896.51, 1897.17, 1898.27, 1899.02, 1899.24, 1899.30, 1900.38, 1901.17, 1902.29, 1903.28, 1904.55, 1912.07
Russell, Lillie 1886.50
Russell, Mabel 1898.72, 1899.25, 1899.36
Russell, Mable 1908.15
Russell, Mae 1927.68
Russell, Marion 1888.03
Russell, Maud 1890.09, 1924.37, 1931.32
Russell, Maude 1922.44, 1928.10, 1928.34, 1936.30, 1942.13, 1946.08
Russell, May 1888.41
Russell, Messr. 1854.04
Russell, Miss 1917.31, 1921.42
Russell, Mr. 1834.02, 1839.01, 1840.01, 1840.02, 1840.03, 1840.04, 1855.04, 1866.05, 1884.27, 1884.59
Russell, Nellie 1886.42, 1890.27
Russell, Olive 1888.13
Russell, Ollie 1895.24
Russell, Peter H. 1990.10
Russell, R.H. 1925.32, 1943.08
Russell, Rebecca 1986.09, 1987.08
Russell, Rec 1963.22
Russell, Reed E. 1936.12
Russell, Renee 1929.26, 1943.14
Russell, Robert 1959.22, 1965.17, 1966.14, 1985.04
Russell, Roberta 1967.01
Russell, Rosalind 1930.33, 1953.03
Russell, Scott 1892.08, 1892.10
Russell, Sol Smith 1878.02, 1880.37, 1887.09
Russell, Susie 1882.04, 1882.20, 1886.39, 1894.31
Russell, Thomas 1935.01
Russell, Tina 1919.20
Russell, Tommy 1885.46
Russell, Vivienne 1905.19
Russell, W. 1897.48, 1898.50
Russell, W.J. 1885.18, 1885.31, 1885.51, 1888.45
Russell, Walter 1947.01, 1948.20
Russell, William 1904.09
Russell, Willy 1993.07
Russell, Zela 1920.29
Russell, Zella 1922.40, 1925.02, 1938.17, 1943.12
Russo, Aaron 1973.14, 1975.12
Russo, Carlo 1887.12, 1887.18
Russo, Dan 1921.34
Russo, Gustavo 1993.08
Russo, James 1938.12, 1951.17, 1952.20
Russo, Ubaldo 1932.18
Rutgers, Nelly 1884.25
Ruth, Joan 1927.42
Ruth, Nat 1892.17
Ruth, Paul 1946.03
Ruth, Richard 1980.12
Ruthenberg, Frl. 1883.08
Rutherford, A.V. 1879.13, 1879.66
Rutherford, Douglas 1948.15
Rutherford, John 1923.47, 1925.38, 1926.25, 1927.55, 1928.47
Rutherford, Miss 1889.54
Rutherford, Richard 1962.15
Rutherfurd, Tom 1936.12
Ruthven, D.G. 1902.20
Ruthworth, Frank 1898.11
Rutigliano, Danny 1994.06
Rutland, Esther 1914.28
Rutland, Gertrude 1914.28
Rutledge, Gertrude 1892.29, 1893.07, 1894.14, 1898.06, 1903.11, 1906.28
Rutledge, Grace 1896.35
Rutledge, Helen 1900.07
Rutledge, Margaret 1906.47, 1908.03, 1911.45
Rutledge, Marguerite 1889.04
Rutman, Lucien 1937.01
Rutt, Christopher Eric 2001.04
Rutter, Grace 1894.16, 1894.19, 1895.17, 1895.33, 1897.20, 1898.26, 1898.29, 1898.47
Ruttman, Jim T. 1997.17
Ruty 1968.04
Ruvigny, Katherine 1921.41
Ruvolo, Danny 1976.08
Ruvolo, Mary 1999.11
Ruwe, Horace A. 1919.31
Ruysdael, Basil 1912.19, 1924.46, 1925.45, 1927.21, 1927.45
Ryaboushinskaya, Mlle. 1931.38
Ryack, Rita 1983.06 1984.02
Ryall, William 1989.26, 1994.06, 1995.05, 1998.05, 2000.18
Ryan 1888.23, 1889.08, 1889.33, 1893.21
Ryan James 1886.35
Ryan, Alice 1918.06
Ryan, Barry 1952.01
Ryan, Belvil 1869.11, 1869.17, 1869.21, 1869.25, 1869.28, 1876.32
Ryan, Ben 1910.20
Ryan, Benny 1917.12, 1918.08, 1920.04, 1929.24
Ryan, Bess 1914.24
Ryan, Bessy 1898.18
Ryan, Byron Dean 1968.12
Ryan, Cecil 1912.09
Ryan, Charlene 1969.17, 1972.03, 1975.14
Ryan, Coletta 1922.27
Ryan, Colletta 1931.42
Ryan, D. 1872.34
Ryan, D.D. 1970.13, 1978.26
Ryan, Dean 1962.10, 1964.09, 1965.03, 1965.12
Ryan, Dolph 1910.25
Ryan, E. 1888.41, 1913.36
Ryan, E.H. 1905.55
Ryan, Eddie 1936.28
Ryan, Edward 1898.55, 1919.04
Ryan, Elsa 1898.46, 1903.22, 1904.55, 1905.13, 1906.32, 1907.13, 1908.30, 1909.29, 1911.01, 1911.32, 1912.05
Ryan, Eugene 1905.39
Ryan, F. 1903.26
Ryan, George H. 1901.25
Ryan, George W. 1900.07
Ryan, Irene 1972.22
Ryan, J. Richard 1914.21
Ryan, J. Van 1914.21
Ryan, J.A. 1886.35
Ryan, J.H. 1879.63, 1880.39, 1881.52
Ryan, James 1902.11, 1932.14
Ryan, Jim 1997.04
Ryan, John 1915.15, 1921.05
Ryan, Jr., Edward 1938.10
Ryan, Mamie 1885.65, 1894.31
Ryan, Messr. 1888.10
Ryan, Mlle. 1873.22
Ryan, Mr. 1794.01
Ryan, Oscar 1939.15
Ryan, Peggy 1940.21
Ryan, Richard 1919.40, 1930.09, 1930.35, 2000.09
Ryan, Robert 1962.20
Ryan, Roz 1998.20
Ryan, Sam J. 1897.16, 1904.42, 1907.16, 1908.14
Ryan, Samuel J. 1889.47
Ryan, Steve 1992.04
Ryan, Sue 1943.05, 1945.01
Ryan, T. 1912.24
Ryan, T.E. 1889.54, 1891.41, 1899.39, 1901.19
Ryan, Terry 1956.08
Ryan, Thomas 1896.26
Ryan, Thomas J. 1896.26
Ryan, William F. 1897.34
Rybeck, Alex 1992.18
Rychtarik, Richard 1942.33, 1945.02
Rycroft, Fred 1894.52, 1898.45, 1899.32
Rydell, Stephen John 1965.18
Ryder, Alfred 1941.01, 1943.23
Ryder, Messr. 1897.23
Ryder, Milburry 1909.04
Ryder, Milbury 1912.43, 1913.28, 1913.36
Ryder, Philip 1931.29
Ryder, Ric 1989.09
Ryder, Richard 1986.16
Ryder, Rosemary 1927.31, 1929.24
Ryder, Walter 1897.23
Rydzeski, Mary Ann 1985.13, 1986.09
Rye, Frank 1929.21
Ryeford, Beck 1905.24
Ryeford, Rebecca 1925.11
Ryer, B. Douglas 1894.39
Ryer, Ben D. 1896.15
Ryer, George W. 1887.02, 1887.42, 1888.25, 1889.43, 1890.36, 1894.52, 1896.15, 1898.45, 1899.32, 1904.32, 1907.43, 1908.32
Ryerson, Florence 1989.06, 1997.11, 1998.06
Ryes, T.E. 1890.50
Ryker, Elizabeth 1900.20
Ryle, W. 1882.20
Ryles, Robert C. 1925.14
Ryley Tim 1895.29
Ryley, Arthur 1891.36
Ryley, Charles 1894.33
Ryley, Dunne 1899.11
Ryley, J.H. 1879.70, 1879.72, 1880.45, 1881.07, 1881.37, 1882.17, 1882.60, 1882.75, 1882.78, 1883.16, 1883.21, 1883.24, 1883.44, 1884.09, 1884.14, 1884.34, 1884.57, 1885.13, 1885.26, 1885.40, 1885.48, 1887.15, 1887.20, 1887.21, 1887.32, 1888.18, 1888.35, 1889.16, 1892.25, 1893.05, 1893.09, 1895.31
Ryley, Madeleine Lucette 1893.05
Ryley, Phil 1906.41, 1911.07, 1914.12, 1918.35, 1920.44, 1923.30, 1924.18, 1926.51
Ryley, Phil H. 1906.26, 1927.37
Ryley, Philip 1905.13
Ryley, Philip H. 1896.30, 1901.04
Ryley, Thomas 1900.51
Ryley, Thomas W. 1899.11, 1901.04, 1902.05, 1904.03, 1904.08, 1906.47, 1908.03, 1908.42, 1911.45, 1914.02
Ryley, Tom W. 1905.13
Ryman, Add 1868.14, 1870.16, 1879.09, 1880.15, 1892.36
Rynee, John 1928.19
Ryner, Master 1870.22
Rynne, John 1929.20
Ryno, W.H. 1886.39
Rynyon 1862.03
Ryse Mrs. Ellis 1881.44
Ryse, Ellis 1879.30, 1880.57, 1880.62, 1881.25, 1881.42, 1881.44, 1881.45, 1882.46, 1882.57, 1883.45, 1883.62, 1885.05, 1887.04, 1887.19, 1889.16, 1889.49, 1893.21
Ryskind, Morrie 1922.38, 1922.42, 1925.17, 1925.45, 1926.21, 1927.21, 1927.27, 1928.38, 1929.04, 1930.02, 1931.05, 1931.48, 1933.13, 1933.25, 1940.08, 1942.01, 1952.07
Rysz, Mary 1931.35

S. Strauss, Inc. 1920.29
S.R. Kerner Company 1918.02
Saalburg, Allen 1938.06
Saari, Eric Houston 1992.11
Saavedra, Miguel DeCervantes y 1977.12, 1992.07
Sabalis, Levenoria 1931.40
Sabater, Leon 1934.13
Sabatino, Anthony 1977.09
Sabbat, Gerard 1947.18
Sabel, Josephine 1903.15, 1925.25, 1926.46, 1927.48
Sabella, D. 1996.14
Sabella, Ernie 1976.30, 1982.05, 1992.04, 1996.06
Sabellico, Richard 1994.09
Sabellico, Richard J. 1974.17
Sabetti, Audrey 1949.03
Sabin, Alexandra 1978.23
Sabin, Charles 1928.31
Sabin, David 1965.36, 1970.02, 1972.24, 1976.10, 1976.33, 1983.08
Sabin, Paul 1926.07
Sabinson, Lee 1947.03
Sabirudim, E. 1985.07
Sablon, Jean 1939.22
Sablon, Mons. 1887.36, 1887.37
Sablukova, Anna 1925.46
Sabo, Judy 1979.09
Saborido, E. 1997.13
Sabrich, Albertine 1885.01
Sabrung 1881.04
Sacha, Ken 1983.09
Sacher, Toby 1942.05
Sachetti 1868.03
Sachs, Arthur L. 1942.11
Sachs, Dorothy 1939.14
Sachs, Evelyn 1960.03, 1961.03, 1961.05, 1962.06, 1962.19, 1964.07, 1964.08, 1964.09, 1966.04, 1966.17
Sachs, L.B. 1905.42
Sachse, Leopold 1945.15
Sachse, Lou 1950.12
Sack, Domonic 2000.17
Sack, Nathaniel 1943.06
Sackett, Albert 1915.29, 1918.07, 1918.30, 1918.40, 1921.08, 1924.24
Sackett, Frederic 1887.46, 1892.58
Sackett, Herbert 1889.39
Sackett, M. 1867.23
Sackett, Marion 1875.18, 1876.06, 1877.07
Sackett, Millie 1867.22, 1867.23, 1867.26, 1867.27, 1867.29, 1867.31, 1871.17, 1872.27, 1875.05, 1877.24, 1879.02, 1889.03, 1889.14, 1889.48, 1890.06, 1891.06, 1891.07, 1896.14
Sackett, Milly 1868.06
Sackett, S. 1869.26
Sacks, Davia 1976.36
Sacks, Gloria 1954.04
Sackville, Gordon 1910.23
Saddler, Donald 1950.03, 1950.19, 1953.03, 1953.17, 1956.07, 1961.20, 1963.12, 1971.03, 1973.02, 1975.13, 1975.18, 1976.30, 1978.26, 1979.02, 1980.06, 1980.21, 1981.20, 1982.16, 1983.02, 1983.12, 1985.09, 1986.03, 1987.08, 1987.19, 1993.12, 1993.18, 2001.02
Saddler, Frank 1895.37, 1904.05, 1904.15, 1909.11, 1909.18, 1910.01, 1910.16, 1910.34, 1911.05, 1911.42, 1912.12, 1912.24, 1912.38, 1912.41, 1913.05, 1913.18, 1913.29, 1914.17, 1914.22, 1915.07, 1915.16, 1915.20, 1915.22, 1915.30, 1915.31, 1916.03, 1916.09, 1917.01, 1917.02, 1917.06, 1917.12, 1917.17, 1917.36, 1917.37, 1918.03, 1918.18, 1919.09, 1919.22, 1920.04, 1920.10, 1920.17, 1920.18, 1920.26, 1920.39
Saddler-Nelson Bureau 1904.55
Sadger, Miss 1890.02
Sadierna, Genaro 1901.29
Sadler's Wells Trust, Ltd. 1989.01
Sadler, Charles 1920.43
Sadler, Frank 1900.07, 1919.41, 1922.30
Sadler, Josie 1889.41, 1890.07, 1890.34, 1897.30, 1898.17, 1899.08, 1899.17, 1900.07, 1900.42, 1901.29, 1902.06, 1902.35, 1903.24, 1908.06, 1910.01, 1910.34, 1912.02, 1912.38
Sadler, Minnie 1895.10, 1895.32
Sadler, Nancy 1900.07
Sadler, W. Jackson 1911.11, 1912.28
Sadler, William 1908.15, 1917.20
Sado, Alexander 1990.01
Sadoff, Fred 1949.04, 1952.10
Sadun, Icilio 1924.20
Sadusk, Maureen 1980.01
Saenger, Lizzie 1889.10
Saffer, Lisa 1990.07, 1990.13, 1991.08
Saffran, Christina 1979.13, 1980.16
Safina, Anthony 1965.07, 1965.26
Safir, Kurt 1961.04
Safonova, Mme. 1929.05
Sagall, Solomon 1968.08, 1968.22
Sagardia, Elisa 1998.18
Sage, C. 1858.01, 1858.02
Sage, C. Russell 1903.12, 1906.43
Sage, Eva Marie 1966.16
Sage, Messr. 1882.34
Sage, Percy 1884.12
Sage, Thomas 1881.43
Sager, Bernie 1929.38, 1929.40, 1929.48, 1930.41
Sager, Carole Bayer 1978.05, 1979.11, 1992.18
Sager, Charles 1930.39
Sager, David 1926.31
Sager, Jeri 1990.18
Sagittarius Productions, Inc. 1970.20, 1971.01, 1976.16
Sagnuolo, Anna G. 1985.14
Sagy, Varda 1972.17
Sahagen, Nikki 1985.04
Sahar, Z. 1967.13, 1968.20
Saharet, Miss 1897.14
Sahcnez, Nestor 1998.02
Sahl, Mort 1958.12, 1987.13, 1994.13
Sahlein, Stephen 1972.14
Sahlins, Bernard 1961.17
Saia, Cecilia 1997.13

Saidenberg, Theodore 1965.31, 1968.05, 1970.21, 1971.16, 1976.05
Saidy, Fred 1944.23, 1947.01, 1947.03, 1951.15, 1955.09, 1957.16, 1960.09, 1961.08, 1967.04
Sainer, Lionel 1929.30
Sainger, M.A. 1880.01, 1880.03
Sainpolis, Katheryn 1913.02
Sainpolis, Kathryn 1912.14
Saint Jacques, Ray 1955.10
Saint Subber, Arnold 1946.20
Saint-Amand 1886.30, 1888.02, 1889.16, 1889.49, 1893.35, 1898.36
Saint-Amand and Paulyanthe 1899.24, 1903.32
Saint-Armand 1897.24
Saint-Hilaire 1881.50, 1883.12
Saint-Jacques, Sterling 1976.20
Saint-Laurent, Yves 1964.39
Saint-Saens, Camille 1956.11
Saint-Subber, Arnold 1973.12
Sainthill, Loudon 1965.14, 1969.04
Sainton, Joseph 1911.24
Saito, R. 1911.46
Saka, Haruhiko 1989.21
Sakakura, Lainie 1994.06, 1999.01
Saker, H. 1877.25
Saker, Horatio 1877.22, 1877.23
Saki, Marion 1918.23, 1922.43, 1924.10, 1926.03, 1929.02
Sakren, Jared 1973.16
Saks Fifth Avenue 1942.16
Saks, Gene 1955.07, 1965.14, 1966.10, 1977.04, 1986.13
Salama, Andrew 1927.26
Salama, Messr. 1922.06, 1923.28
Salaman, Abraham 1997.05
Saldierna, Genaro 1902.06
Sale, Charles 1925.27, 1930.37
Sale, Chic 1917.08, 1919.03, 1926.37
Salem, Philip 1961.15
Saleon, Messr. 1881.11, 1881.27
Saleon, Mons. 1879.19, 1880.52
Salerno, Anthony 1979.13
Salerno, Antonio 1918.26, 1926.31
Salerno, Lauren 1982.15
Salerno, Mary Jo 1979.28
Sales, Clifford 1946.12, 1948.28
Sales, Corinne 1921.02
Salesky, Brian 1981.20, 1992.07
Salet, Murray 1919.26
Salguero, Sophia 1996.16, 1998.02
Saliba, Paul 1976.18
Saliers, Hal 1928.27
Salignac, E. Thomas 1926.40, 1926.43
Salignac, Thomas 1926.45
Salinaro, Dom 1963.05
Salinger, Conrad 1931.42, 1932.20, 1932.27, 1934.35, 1934.39, 1934.40, 1934.42, 1935.03, 1935.15, 1935.18, 1936.02, 1936.17, 1937.15, 1937.16
Salinger, Helen 1909.02
Salinger, Helena 1898.78, 1901.10, 1901.11
Salinger, Herbert 1915.08, 1917.30
Salisbury, Charles P. 1902.11
Salisbury, D.J. 1998.06
Salisbury, Ella 1890.17
Salisbury, Fran 1980.05
Salisbury, Louise 1907.55
Salisbury, Marie 1915.26
Salisbury, Mr. 1848.03
Sallade, Davidy 1959.12
Sallard, Mons. 1884.54, 1884.55
Salle Productions, Inc. 1961.25
Sallert, Ulla 1964.33
Sallid, Otis 1995.03
Sallinger, Eugene 1910.09
Sallinger, Henry 1931.40
Sallinger, Sallie 1912.17
Sallis, Peter 1965.02
Salmon, Louis 1942.20
Salmon, Nick 1999.12
Salmon, Scott 1968.07, 1972.05, 1983.11
Salo, Anthony J. 1938.16
Saloen, Messr. 1884.11
Salonga, Lea 1991.03
Salonis, Clark 1967.04
Salsbury's Troubadours 1880.11, 1883.33, 1887.08, 1887.34
Salsbury, Nate 1875.16, 1879.32, 1880.11, 1881.01, 1882.24, 1883.33, 1883.68, 1885.10, 1886.05, 1887.08, 1922.19, 1923.20
Salta, Menotti 1946.08, 1946.23
Salta, Minati 1938.07
Saltonstall, Stella 1981.18
Saltzman, Avery 1989.04
Saltzman, Esta 1942.28
Saltzman, Jack 1936.28
Salvador, Dom 1979.03
Salvador, Ernest 1890.24
Salvador, Henri 1965.08
Salvador, Mlle. 1883.30
Salvator, Ernest 1890.19
Salvator, Messr. 1879.26, 1879.34, 1879.36, 1879.43, 1882.53, 1882.58, 1886.19, 1886.20
Salvator, Mlle. 1876.31, 1879.19, 1879.26, 1879.36, 1879.44, 1879.47, 1883.27, 1883.57, 1884.01
Salvator, Mme. 1877.32, 1883.28, 1883.41
Salvator, Mons. 1872.03, 1872.28, 1872.33, 1873.01, 1873.11, 1873.15, 1875.04, 1876.20, 1876.28, 1877.27, 1877.30, 1877.32, 1877.33, 1877.34, 1877.37, 1877.38, 1878.06, 1878.08, 1879.19, 1879.36, 1879.47, 1883.28, 1884.05, 1884.49, 1884.50, 1885.55
Salve, Juleste 1966.06
Salverino, Anthony 1956.12
Salvnor, Minnie 1898.27
Salvo, Louis 1932.10
Salzer, Beeb 1976.31, 1978.08
Salzer, Eugene 1905.31, 1909.05, 1912.16, 1918.26, 1919.34, 1920.14, 1921.04, 1923.08
Salzer, Gene 1919.24, 1921.09, 1922.38, 1923.08, 1925.42, 1926.21, 1927.27, 1928.02, 1928.35, 1929.29, 1929.45, 1930.28, 1931.05, 1932.21, 1932.26, 1933.21, 1934.06, 1934.42, 1936.01, 1936.05, 1937.04, 1938.05, 1939.30, 1940.19
Salzer, Gus 1903.33, 1905.20, 1905.31, 1906.38, 1907.56, 1908.27, 1909.15, 1917.01, 1917.36, 1918.39, 1919.04, 1919.36, 1920.30, 1920.35, 1920.44, 1922.08, 1922.33, 1923.27, 1923.30, 1924.09, 1924.34, 1924.38, 1925.08, 1925.33, 1926.46, 1927.10, 1927.12, 1927.52, 1928.12, 1928.38, 1928.47, 1929.19, 1929.31, 1929.51, 1930.25, 1930.35
Salzer, Gustav 1899.01
Salzer, Gustave 1901.02, 1904.18, 1911.15, 1911.38, 1913.10, 1913.20, 1914.18, 1915.23, 1916.17, 1932.23
Salzer, Herr 1883.08
Salzer, Sidney 1937.15, 1939.24
Sam and Lee Shubert, Inc. 1911.32
Sam S. and Lee Shubert, Inc. 1911.06
Sam, Long Tack 1922.30
Samarie, Janice 1955.07
Samberg, Rachel 1990.08
Sambogna, Al 1962.14, 1963.25
Sameth, Marten 1944.33, 1947.08, 1954.03
Samis, H. 1892.35
Samish, Adrian 1930.37
Sammis, Harry 1905.20
Sammler, B.J. 1972.13
Sammons, Jennie 1931.32
Samon, Stuart 1960.07
Samorian, John 1996.17
Sampaio, Claudio 1992.13
Samples, Howard 1931.07
Sampliner, David W. 1968.06
Sampson, Alice 1929.01
Sampson, Edgar 1976.04, 1987.02, 1989.02
Sampson, Edgar M. 1999.24
Sampson, III., Frederick G. 1973.09, 1989.18
Sampson, L.F. 1905.29
Sampson, Tiffany 1994.02
Sampson, William 1892.14, 1896.27, 1905.15
Samra, Abou 1968.04
Samrock, Victor 1948.14
Sams, Jeffrey D. 1992.03
Sams, Jeremy 1989.10
Samson, Richard 1998.05, 1999.07
Samson, Susan Madden 1985.05
Samuel Blair Company, Inc. 1905.02
Samuel Colville's English Comic Opera Company 1875.19, 1875.23, 1875.26
Samuel, D. Peter 1981.28
Samuel, Gerard 1948.17
Samuel, Peter 1984.14, 1986.13, 1991.05, 1997.12, 1998.21, 1999.22
Samuels, A.R. 1882.72
Samuels, Al 1931.42
Samuels, Arthur 1922.42, 1923.27
Samuels, B. 1879.42
Samuels, Eddy 1962.17
Samuels, Ken 1977.18
Samuels, Lesser 1960.05
Samuels, Maurice V. 1927.26
Samuels, Mr. 1855.11
Samuels, Ray 1881.01, 1882.24, 1884.51, 1912.38, 1931.42
Samuels, W.R. 1905.24
Samuels, Walter G. 1929.04
Samuelson, Sam 1993.07
Samuylow, Morris 1946.17
San Diego Opera 1978.07, 1978.20, 1979.21, 1989.13
San Diego Repertory Theatre 1999.09
San Francisco Minstrels 1879.09, 1880.15, 1881.55, 1882.28
San Francisco Minstrels "Sparks" Company 1883.26
Sanami, Masa 1928.30
Sanborn, Fred 1929.22, 1939.31, 1942.12
Sanchez, Alex 1996.08, 1999.01
Sanchez, Avita 1904.03, 1907.33
Sanchez, Connie 1964.35
Sand, Paul 1961.17, 1971.08
Sandan, Lilli 1939.26
Sandberg, Steve 1995.09
Sandburg, Carl 1954.11
Sandeen, Darrell 1961.11, 1962.13, 1963.21, 1968.17, 1969.01
Sander, Alexander 1995.06, 1996.02
Sanders, Al. 1907.35
Sanders, Alma 1921.23, 1923.08, 1924.05, 1924.24, 1924.42, 1925.44, 1926.23, 1928.49, 1930.21, 1947.13
Sanders, Arthur 1904.43
Sanders, Charles 1896.03
Sanders, Donna 1956.14
Sanders, Estella 1893.43
Sanders, Fred 1990.15
Sanders, George 1905.23, 1934.34
Sanders, Honey 1961.07, 1968.06, 1972.11
Sanders, Howard 1973.17
Sanders, Ivy 1936.19, 1939.02, 1939.04, 1939.08, 1939.11
Sanders, Job 1952.20
Sanders, L. 1870.05
Sanders, Marta 1978.13
Sanders, Richard 1973.10
Sanders, Robert 1944.31, 1946.21, 1950.07
Sanders, Sarah 1964.06
Sanders, Scott 1990.19, 1991.04
Sanders, Sig 1932.28
Sanders, Steve 1965.36
Sanders, Teddi 1944.24
Sanders, W. 1862.09, 1863.04, 1864.21, 1866.03, 1868.06
Sandersen, Alexis 1932.23
Sanderson, Adele 1926.10, 1926.44
Sanderson, Julia 1904.12, 1904.17, 1905.03, 1906.26, 1907.32, 1909.01, 1910.05, 1911.27, 1913.04, 1914.18, 1915.18, 1916.01, 1917.19, 1918.34, 1920.39, 1921.23, 1928.01
Sanderson, Kirsten 1995.15
Sanderson, Mary 1880.32
Sanderson, May 1955.23
Sanderson, Pauline 1888.06, 1888.11
Sandesr, Nat 1922.19
Sandford, B.F. 1877.15
Sandford, Charles 1946.06
Sandford, Ed 1893.37
Sandford, Edward A. 1898.55
Sandford, Harold 1925.10, 1925.24
Sandford, J.W. 1878.10
Sandford, Kenneth 1962.25, 1962.26, 1962.31, 1964.36, 1964.42, 1964.43, 1966.23, 1966.25, 1966.28, 1968.26, 1968.27, 1968.29, 1976.12, 1978.14, 1978.15, 1989.15
Sandford, Mr. 1854.01, 1872.09
Sandford, Nellie 1876.06
Sandgran, Samuel 1903.19
Sandhu, Rommy 1995.19
Sandiford, Preston 1974.03
Sandifur, Virginia 1971.05, 1975.13, 1980.29
Sandison, Gordon 1989.01
Sandlin, Anathale G. 1998.19
Sandlin, Dorothy 1946.03
Sandor, Gluck 1931.26, 1932.18, 1937.14, 1939.18, 1964.27
Sandoval, Miguel 1875.24
Sandoval, Nino Rosario 1875.22
Sandoval, Rosario 1875.24
Sandreuter, Bill 1972.09
Sandrich, Jr., Mark 1964.33
Sands, Alice 1900.55
Sands, Ann 1923.24
Sands, Anna 1917.34
Sands, Anne 1919.05, 1919.34
Sands, Bob 1955.13
Sands, Dick 1866.22, 1866.26
Sands, Dorothy 1925.20, 1926.17, 1927.23, 1928.19, 1929.20, 1964.20, 1969.07
Sands, G.E. 1873.19
Sands, George 1923.36
Sands, Hal 1920.39, 1922.18
Sands, Paula 1931.01
Sands, Will A. 1882.77
Sands, William A. 1879.12
Sandt, Severn 1989.09
Sanfod, Louise 1906.39
Sanford, Annie 1890.08, 1898.10
Sanford, Beulah 1885.08
Sanford, Charles 1898.55, 1945.08, 1946.20, 1948.04, 1962.27
Sanford, Charles G. 1944.27
Sanford, Charles S. 1942.35
Sanford, Emily 1904.04, 1904.58
Sanford, Fannie 1884.26
Sanford, Fred S. 1887.05
Sanford, Harold 1917.07, 1924.18, 1926.22, 1938.10
Sanford, J.W. 1871.08
Sanford, L. 1880.46
Sanford, Lou 1886.29, 1886.31
Sanford, Louise 1888.15, 1894.50, 1906.10
Sanford, May 1886.34
Sanford, Messr. 1865.01, 1865.11
Sanford, Miriam 1911.26
Sanford, Miss 1896.44
Sanford, Mr. 1854.07, 1866.02, 1866.28, 1884.27
Sanford, Nellie 1871.09, 1871.11, 1876.13, 1876.15, 1886.62
Sanford, Queena 1904.29
Sanford, Ralph 1932.13, 1932.16, 1934.20
Sanford, Ralph D. 1927.43
Sanford, Robert 1937.06
Sanford, T. 1868.06
Sanford, Tim 2000.01
Sanford, Virginia 1905.43
Sangali, Rita 1869.41
Sangalli, Mlle. 1869.26
Sangalli, Rita 1866.18, 1868.06, 1869.38
Sangalli, Signor 1869.38
Sanger, A. 1878.22
Sanger, Antoinette 1879.06
Sanger, Emil 1884.08
Sanger, Eugene 1894.42, 1924.11
Sanger, Eugene B. 1893.38, 1896.01
Sanger, Frank W. 1880.42, 1882.03, 1882.39, 1883.26, 1885.64, 1887.13
Sanger, Henry 1896.02
Sanger, L. 1893.34
Sanger, Lizzie 1893.34, 1899.11, 1903.25
Sanger, Marie 1891.21, 1897.20
Sanger, Marie A. 1888.22
Sanger, Marie E. 1884.60
Sanger, Rachel 1881.31
Sangor, Ben 1911.29
Sani, Amru 1956.08
Sanin, Alexander 1925.03
Sanina, Mme. 1922.37
Sanina, Tanya 1934.29
SanJuan, Olga 1951.24
Sankey, Rosemary 1942.15
Sankowich, Lee D. 1974.12
Sannaa, Oscar 1895.23
Sannes, Lloyd 1974.13
Sannes, Loyd 1979.03
Sannon, Minnie 1888.33
Sanossian, Leon 1970.01
Sansom, Mary 1962.26, 1962.28, 1962.29, 1962.31
Sanson, Bessie 1875.17, 1876.08, 1881.20, 1884.37, 1888.04, 1888.34, 1890.10
Sansone, Charles L. 1929.26
Sant'Andrea, Jim 1972.02, 1975.05
Sant'Angelo, Georgio 1974.21
Sant'Angelo, Giorgio 1981.16
Santa Fe Productions, Inc. 1963.28
Santamaria, Mario 1950.18
Santana, Jones 1992.13
Santangelo, Martin 1996.16
Santarelli, Dominique 1964.06
Santascam, Miguel 1919.17
Santell, Marie 1965.17, 1974.18
Santella, Mons. 1875.25, 1875.27, 1875.28, 1875.29, 1875.30, 1875.33
Santer, Emmie 1905.46
Santiago, Anthony 1965.18, 1979.31

Santiago, Elliot 1985.13, 1986.09
Santiago, Renoly 1998.02
Santiago, Saundra 1995.09
Santiago, Tina 1972.11
Santiago-Hudson, Ruben 1992.08
Santini, Bruno 1978.14
Santisteban, Mario 1974.14
Santisteban, Rafael Garcia 1875.24
Santisteban, Rocio 1949.07
Santley, Charles 1897.05
Santley, Emma 1880.31
Santley, Fred 1921.10, 1925.19, 1927.64
Santley, Frederic 1917.37, 1927.34
Santley, Frederick 1916.02, 1919.04, 1926.22
Santley, Joseph 1910.12, 1910.30, 1911.35, 1912.37, 1913.19, 1915.31, 1916.20, 1918.37, 1919.09, 1920.40, 1921.30, 1923.32, 1924.15, 1925.43, 1926.22, 1926.34, 1927.12, 1927.54
Santley, Kate 1871.27, 1872.06
Santley, Mabel 1881.17, 1881.19
Santley, Zelda 1920.02
Santly, Joseph H. 1975.22
Santly, Lester A. 1978.09
Santly, Lew 1924.01
Santon, Alma 1873.12, 1873.14, 1873.17
Santon, Madeline 1873.12, 1873.14, 1873.17
Santora, Bill 1992.07
Santora, Elise 2001.06
Santoriello, Alex 1987.04, 1989.24
Santoro, Mark 1974.17
Santoro, Susan 1987.14
Santos, Cecile 1976.01
Santos, Claudio 1992.13
Santos, III, Joseph Louis 1997.22
Santos, Jaime 1988.06, 1990.03, 1992.13
Santos, Loida 1980.23
Santos, Lorinda 1995.07
Santos, Ray 1991.03
Santos, Rena 1911.15
Santos, Sonia 1990.03
Santra, Henry J. 1906.18
Santre, Marion 1932.23
Santrey, Henry 1911.28
Santry, Arthur 1965.15
Santucci, Nathan 2000.13
Saparo, Henry 1922.22
Sapho, Mr. 1859.03
Sapio, Romualdo 1900.06
Sapolsky, Robert 1978.23
Saporta, Hy 1970.14
Sapoznik, Henry 1997.01
Sapp, R. LaChanze 1987.07
Sappington, Fay 1965.36, 1968.03
Sappington, Margo 1968.31, 1971.04, 1974.25, 1976.19, 1976.27, 1982.13, 1983.18
Sappir, Jerry 1968.30
Saqul, Mons. 1869.05
Saraband, A. 1892.14
Saracas, Eddie 1979.24
Saraco, Messr. 1883.48
Saraco, Signor 1883.48
Sarafini, Enzo 1927.22
Sarandon, Chris 1970.15, 1991.15
Saranoff, Peggy 1916.11
Sarasale, Pablo 1934.32
Saraste 1922.21
Sardam, Frank J. 1906.19
Sardoff, Messr. 1844.01
Sardou, Victorien 1872.23, 1883.29, 1883.62, 1884.51, 1886.49, 1888.10, 1892.02, 1898.30, 1899.42, 1905.04, 1913.08
Sarducci, Father Guido 1979.19
Sarfaty, Regina 1959.07, 1960.03
Sarg, Tony 1931.43
Sargant, Julie 1963.25, 1967.14
Sargeant, Vaughn 1907.03
Sargent, Albertine 1908.10
Sargent, Dorothy 1941.02
Sargent, Frank 1910.25
Sargent, Hannah 1883.36
Sargent, Jean 1932.05, 1932.17
Sargent, Joe 1927.62
Sargent, Karen 1960.01, 1962.04
Sargent, Mary 1937.07
Sargent, Master 1875.40
Sargent, Maxwell 1909.17
Sargent, Messr. 1903.03
Sargent, Miss 1875.17, 1876.08
Sargent, Peter 1932.05, 1933.02
Sargent, Vaughn 1908.10
Sargent, Virginia 1904.03
Sargent, Winthrop 1932.20
Sargentelli, Marta 1988.06
Saridis, Angelo 1968.30
Sarmatoff, Stanislaw 1933.26
Sarnoff International Enterprises 1978.03
Sarnoff, Dorothy 1942.31, 1948.24, 1951.12, 1952.15
Sarofeen, Anne 1972.09
Saron, Alex 1940.18
Saron, Alexander 1937.11
Sarony, Gilbert 1891.38, 1897.48
Sarony, Nora 1904.04, 1904.47, 1907.06
Saroya, Bianca 1917.10
Saroyan, William 1984.02
Sarracco, Elsie 1898.46
Sarracino, Ernest 1952.13, 1953.06, 1959.19
Sarrea, Nicholas 1981.09
Sarti, Bruno 1932.18
Sartoris, Mona 1913.23
Sartre, Jean-Paul 1961.26
Sartrin, Messr. 1866.08
Sasha 1960.10
Sassano, Ralph 1944.17, 1947.01
Sassi, Pierina 1871.27, 1872.06
Satchel, Blanche 1929.08, 1930.08
Satchell, Clarence 1906.41
Saternow, Tim 2000.02
Satinoff, Jeff 1981.21
Satirists, Inc., The 1930.23
Sato, Ado 1961.07, 1961.12
Sato, Isao 1976.02
Sato, Reiko 1953.16, 1959.11, 1965.22
Sator, Henry 1878.20, 1879.03, 1879.33, 1879.35, 1880.06, 1880.10, 1880.13, 1880.59, 1880.65, 1880.67, 1880.70, 1884.42, 1886.47, 1888.36, 1893.13, 1894.19, 1899.23
Satow, Claudia 1957.06
Satow, Mark 1957.06, 1960.11
Satow, Mark Richard 1961.12
Satterfield, Maude 1922.11
Satterlee, Jennie 1870.32, 1870.42, 1871.02, 1872.04, 1872.05, 1872.08, 1872.12, 1872.14, 1872.25, 1872.30, 1872.36, 1872.38, 1872.40, 1872.43, 1873.22, 1873.27, 1883.02, 1884.53, 1885.15, 1885.22, 1889.06, 1889.39, 1892.05, 1899.27
Satterlee, Jenny 1871.05, 1872.02, 1872.32
Sattin, Lonnie 1958.01
Sattin, Tina 1963.27
Sattler, Dan 1948.08
Sattler, Marie 1912.15
Saucedo, Rick 1978.01
Saucier, Claude-Albert 1982.24
Sauer, Bernard 1966.21, 1967.08
Sauger, Antoinette 1879.06
Saukevert, Miss 1880.69
Saul, Peter 1962.13
Saulpaugh, E. 1931.28
Saulpaugh, Edwin 1934.20
Saulsberry, Rodney 1981.28
Saulsbury, L.H. 1904.26, 1908.08
Saulter, Joe 1977.04
Saum, Clifford 1910.18, 1912.38
Saum, Clifford B. 1909.25
Saum, Clifford P. 1909.25
Saunders, Alma 1933.03
Saunders, Arlene 1962.21, 1963.24
Saunders, Arthur 1905.43
Saunders, Bernice 1949.04, 1963.25, 1967.07
Saunders, Brent 1979.05
Saunders, Charles 1902.33
Saunders, Diana 1968.03
Saunders, Donald 1989.17
Saunders, Frederick 1921.15
Saunders, Garrett 1972.06
Saunders, Gertrude 1921.16, 1922.44, 1932.08, 1943.10
Saunders, Harry 1871.08
Saunders, Honey 1965.20
Saunders, Jack 1946.03, 1950.12
Saunders, James Monk 1931.34
Saunders, John 1888.21
Saunders, Lanna 1961.20
Saunders, Laura 1925.06
Saunders, Louise 1918.18
Saunders, Lucille 1894.08, 1895.31, 1896.33, 1897.17, 1898.27, 1899.34, 1902.41, 1904.55, 1914.26
Saunders, Madge 1914.32
Saunders, Mary 1894.39
Saunders, Meryl 1969.15
Saunders, Nicholas 1943.03
Saunders, Richard 1925.35
Saunders, Roscoe 1914.33
Saunders, Sue 1927.05
Saunders, Terry 1944.23, 1947.06, 1951.22
Saunders, Wardell 1943.10
Saunders, William 1868.06
Saunders, Zelda 1907.06
Saundors, Silver 1961.22
Saunier, Rosa 1866.29
Saunse, O. 1897.29
Saure, Mr. 1848.04
Saurien, Mr. 1851.02, 1851.03
Sauris, Genevieve 1946.13
Saurova, Eva 1983.16
Saus, Amparo 1917.25, 1917.33
Sauter, Eddie 1961.20, 1964.04, 1966.06, 1966.18, 1967.14, 1969.06, 1969.16, 1970.03, 1970.19, 1973.11, 1982.05
Sauvage, James 1890.23
Sauvage, T. 1866.25
Sauvain, Earl 1946.12
Sava, Marusia 1943.11
Savage, Archie 1940.17, 1946.24, 1949.04
Savage, Bernard 1946.13
Savage, Elliott 1963.08, 1970.10, 1970.15
Savage, Henry 1917.01
Savage, Henry W. 1897.53, 1898.04, 1898.06, 1898.07, 1898.09, 1898.14, 1898.15, 1898.16, 1898.19, 1898.21, 1898.24, 1898.30, 1898.33, 1898.37, 1898.39, 1898.40, 1898.42, 1898.49, 1898.52, 1898.57, 1898.62, 1898.65, 1898.71, 1898.74, 1898.76, 1899.05, 1899.07, 1899.10, 1899.14, 1899.16, 1899.20, 1899.42, 1900.02, 1900.04, 1900.06, 1900.09, 1900.11, 1900.13, 1900.14, 1900.17, 1900.18, 1900.21, 1900.22, 1900.23, 1900.26, 1900.27, 1900.29, 1900.30, 1902.18, 1902.44, 1903.10, 1903.24, 1904.10, 1904.16, 1904.37, 1904.52, 1905.06, 1905.16, 1905.26, 1906.16, 1906.30, 1906.49, 1907.17, 1907.27, 1907.48, 1907.51, 1908.01, 1908.38, 1909.15, 1909.19, 1911.09, 1911.44, 1913.01, 1914.03, 1914.09, 1916.04, 1918.09, 1918.25, 1919.23, 1920.43, 1921.29, 1922.47
Savage, Jack 1925.24, 1926.01
Savage, John 1896.48, 1971.02
Savage, John P. 1889.34
Savage, Kathie 1968.07
Savage, Lesley 1980.11
Savage, Ruby Cutter 1914.11
Savage, S.T. 1875.10
Savage, Steele 1934.15
Savage, Tom 1980.11
Savage, Winston 1969.09
Savant, Joseph 1991.13, 1999.16
Savelli, Toni 1900.12
Saverance, Deborah 1985.13
Saverino, Anthony 1961.28
Savich, Ramon 1927.40
Savidge, Victor 1946.13
Savig, Sonja 1957.04
Saville, Charles A. 1888.21
Saville, Gus H. 1882.04
Saville, Henry 1880.35
Saville, J.G. 1880.18
Saville, Kittie 1911.37
Saville, Leonard 1880.55
Saville, Paul 1889.53, 1890.09, 1891.10
Saville, Ruth 1948.15
Savin, M. 1920.30
Savina, Mme. 1925.03
Savino, Domenic 1929.08
Savino, Domenico 1929.26, 1930.22, 1931.26, 1940.17, 1941.11, 1941.13, 1942.01
Savino, Mario 1928.23
Saviola, Camille 1982.09, 1987.03
Savo, Jimmie 1924.06, 1929.29, 1930.22
Savo, Jimmy 1924.33, 1935.03, 1938.14, 1940.20, 1942.25, 1943.21
Savoy Producing Company 1915.21
Savoy, Bert 1917.26, 1918.19, 1920.28, 1922.32
Savoy, Leonard 1897.17, 1900.57
Savoy, Mamie 1928.18
Savoy, Ruth 1920.17
Savoye, Adele 1929.48
Sawada 1922.21
Sawtelle, J. Al. 1883.06
Sawyer, A.W. 1875.31, 1876.01
Sawyer, Bella 1883.06
Sawyer, Carol 1964.27
Sawyer, Connie 1948.21
Sawyer, Donald 1920.45
Sawyer, Doris 1932.28
Sawyer, Fred B. 1898.64
Sawyer, Hunter 1922.21, 1931.44
Sawyer, Ivy 1916.20, 1918.37, 1919.09, 1920.40, 1921.30, 1923.32, 1925.43, 1927.12
Sawyer, Joan 1907.02
Sawyer, John 1999.08
Sawyer, Nellie 1902.09
Sawyer, Octavia 1923.11
Sawyer, Pam 1976.16
Sawyer, Randolph 1943.24, 1945.06, 1946.09, 1951.11
Sax, Ray 1955.13
Saxby, Barbara 1957.06, 1958.03, 1959.02, 1961.12
Saxe, Alfred 1936.28
Saxe, Mary 1872.36, 1872.43
Saxe, Phil 1928.33
Saxe, Stephen O. 1961.13, 1962.07, 1964.07, 1964.19, 1965.13, 1968.14
Saxe, Templar 1901.18, 1902.44, 1904.04, 1904.15, 1905.49, 1906.41
Saxon, Charles 1904.41, 1907.34
Saxon, Don 1943.20, 1947.02, 1969.14, 1973.11, 1989.11
Saxon, Kate 1854.04
Saxon, Len 1932.23
Saxon, Lou 1951.20
Saxon, Luther 1943.24
Saxon, Marie 1923.36, 1924.29, 1924.40, 1925.34, 1926.28, 1928.35
Saxon, Robert 1970.11
Saxon, William 1959.08
Saxton, Harry 1889.09
Say, Seline 1899.25
Sayan, Levon 1974.19, 1983.03, 1998.12
Sayce, Dorothy 1910.17
Saye, Gertrude 1898.55, 1899.29, 1900.40, 1901.16, 1902.43
Sayer, Henry J. 1891.32
Sayers, Evelyn 1928.02
Sayers, Henry 1893.23
Sayers, Henry J. 1889.34, 1891.38, 1897.30, 1929.41, 1980.27
Sayers, Loretta 1928.02
Saymore, Natalie 1914.31
Sayne, Vila 1896.45, 1898.02
Sayre, Clark 1981.27
Sayre, Jack 1912.35
Sayre, Margaret 1900.12, 1900.38, 1904.09, 1904.52
Sayre, Syd 1936.07
Sayre, Theodore Burt 1901.15, 1905.38, 1906.38, 1907.56
Sayres, Evelyn 1929.06
Sayres, Loretta 1929.06
Sayres, Margaret 1901.17
Sbano, James 1971.12
Sbarge, Raphael 1982.02
Scaasi 1960.07
Scahs, Dorothy 1939.14
Scala, David 1983.11
Scales, Charles P. 1909.24
Scalese, Bobby 1978.08
Scalice, Kenn 1976.19
Scalici, Gillian 1975.24
Scalise, Thomas David 1983.14
Scalish, Frank 1916.15
Scallan, A. 1885.02
Scallan, Clara 1884.13
Scallan, Katie 1882.74
Scallan, Mr. 1862.03
Scallan, Mrs. 1883.32
Scallan, W. 1865.06, 1882.74, 1883.53, 1883.63, 1884.13
Scallan, William 1882.50, 1882.79
Scallon, A. 1884.41
Scallon, F. 1875.21
Scaly, Mr. 1863.04
Scandur, Joe 1940.06
Scandur, Joseph 1953.10
Scandur, Joseph E. 1947.02
Scanga, Richard 1974.24
Scanlan, Annie 1882.50
Scanlan, James 1886.34
Scanlan, James C. 1881.41, 1881.57, 1882.48, 1882.51, 1883.64, 1883.67, 1884.42, 1885.40
Scanlan, Lizzie 1883.01, 1883.09, 1883.20
Scanlan, W.J. 1891.06, 1894.20, 1895.30
Scanlan, Walter 1917.07, 1918.40, 1920.01
Scanlan, William J. 1880.25, 1882.69, 1885.53, 1886.44, 1886.51, 1888.12, 1889.03, 1889.14, 1889.48, 1890.06, 1891.07, 1891.28

Scanlon, Edward 1924.06, 1931.03, 1931.07, 1938.17
Scanlon, Edward J. 1934.13
Scanlon, Lizzie 1884.04, 1884.07
Scannell, J. Kevin 1979.05
Scannell, Jack 1923.33
Scannell, John 1920.04
Scannell, John J. 1910.20, 1914.06, 1921.36
Scarab Productions, Inc. 1974.24
Scardino, Don 1970.12, 1976.17, 1978.10
Scardino, Frank P. 2001.02
Scarlatti 1957.10
Scarlet, Lillian 1919.22
Scarlet, Will 1905.55
Scarpelli, Furio 1986.06
Scarpelli, Henry 1978.01
Scarpinati, Nicholas 1973.09, 1989.18
Scarpini, Frank 1962.16
Scarpino 1985.07
Scarpino, A. 1999.18
Scarpulla, Stephen 1998.20
Scarsdale, Loris 1902.44
Schaaf, Myrtle 1924.33
Schaal, Richard 1971.08
Schacht, Jeanette 1911.28
Schacht, Sam 1974.13
Schade, A.R. 1893.21
Schaefer 1887.19, 1889.02
Schaefer, Barbara 1915.27
Schaefer, George 1952.03, 1958.01
Schaefer, Hal 1962.12, 1964.04, 1972.03
Schaefer, Jerry 1964.33
Schaefer, Pauline 1923.30
Schaefer, William 1892.25
Schaeffer 1882.19, 1887.42, 1887.49, 1888.23
Schaeffer, C.N. 1904.02
Schaeffer, E.G. 1898.25
Schaeffer, Eric D. 1999.20
Schaeffer, Messr. 1884.23
Schaeffer, Mons. 1889.08
Schaeffer, William 1884.39
Schaetzlein, Larry 1922.34
Schafer, Bob 1921.27
Schafer, Charles 1879.68
Schafer, Milton 1962.14, 1965.29
Schafer, Natalie 1941.04
Schafer, Scott 1986.16
Schafer, William 1884.44
Schaff, George 1926.31, 1945.20
Schaff, Herr 1897.08
Schaffel, Marla 2000.20
Schaffer 1891.06, 1891.41
Schaffer and Loritz 1892.27
Schaffer, Sylvester 1893.45
Schaffer, Wilhelm 1901.14
Schaffner, Walter 1925.04, 1925.44
Schall, Mina 1913.07
Schanuel, Greg 1987.16, 1989.03
Schanzer, Rudolf 1917.15, 1926.26
Schanzer, Rudolph 1911.44, 1912.26, 1922.36, 1922.40, 1924.39
Schapiro, Herb 1970.20
Scharer, Jonathan 1988.08, 1988.19
Scharf, Brett 1996.10
Scharf, Michael 1980.07
Scharf, Mr. 1851.01
Scharf, Stuart 1966.15
Scharff, Lester 1919.19, 1932.28
Scharfman, Nitra 1975.07
Scharnberg, Kim 1997.09, 1999.08, 1999.13
Scharwenka, Clementina 1933.26
Schary, Dore 1960.20, 1965.32
Schary, Jeb 1966.30
Schatz, Frl. 1882.68
Schatz, Johanna 1885.01
Schaubstrader, Carl 1921.34
Schauler, Eileen 1952.15, 1962.11, 1965.27, 1966.02, 1978.23, 1979.27
Schcardi, A. 1881.40
Scheaffer, William 1869.31
Schechter, David 1978.11, 1989.24
Schechtman, Richie 1973.08
Schechtman, Saul 1961.10, 1967.15, 1968.32
Scheck, Max 1908.01, 1909.25, 1912.38, 1913.17, 1914.31, 1916.07, 1920.47, 1921.03, 1921.13, 1922.01, 1922.12, 1924.29, 1924.45, 1925.02, 1925.39, 1926.30, 1926.33, 1928.21, 1928.40, 1932.03
Schecter, Les 1973.08
Schector, Marvin 1928.40
Scheeder, Louis W. 1980.23, 1988.12
Scheel, Fritz 1896.07
Scheerer, Bob 1948.30, 1950.03, 1951.23, 1954.09
Scheerer, Maud 1956.15
Scheff, Fritzi 1903.37, 1904.51, 1904.57, 1905.08, 1905.11, 1905.57, 1907.36, 1908.40, 1910.14, 1911.36, 1913.15, 1914.21, 1929.36
Scheff, Lucille F. 1914.21
Scheff, Mr. 1854.06
Scheff, Walter 1947.07, 1947.21
Scheffer, Lizzie 1883.47
Scheffler, Will 1904.58
Schegar, Frank 1931.26
Schegel, Jeanne 1955.10
Scheim, Ruth 1936.31
Schell, Emma 1865.05, 1865.07, 1865.08, 1865.09, 1865.10, 1869.05, 1885.26
Schell, Hattie 1885.64
Schell, Hattie E. 1892.57, 1893.03
Schell, J. 1879.05, 1886.24
Schell, J.S. 1868.16, 1869.11, 1869.17, 1869.21, 1869.25, 1869.28, 1878.21, 1878.22, 1880.47
Schell, Joseph 1872.10
Schell, Joseph S. 1867.13, 1867.14, 1867.15, 1867.16, 1867.17, 1868.08
Schell, Mlle. 1868.06
Schell, R. 1873.08
Schellenbach, Kate 1978.11
Scheller, Fraulein 1861.02
Schenck, Eliott 1918.31
Schenck, Elliott 1916.16
Schenck, Jane 1900.28
Schenck, Joe 1916.24, 1917.03, 1917.26, 1919.15, 1920.18, 1921.21, 1923.33
Schenck, Mary Percy 1945.09
Schenck, Max 1932.19
Schenk, Heinrich 1898.72
Schenk, Leopold 1898.72
Schenker, Joel 1963.27, 1968.02
Schepard, Eric 1953.01
Scheper, Jennie 1900.46
Scheps, Eric 1981.25
Scher, John 1995.15
Schere, Loretta 1945.02
Scherer, Dorothy 1911.43
Scherpff, Messr. 1851.05
Schertler, Nancy 1993.01, 1995.16, 1998.17, 1999.17
Schertzinger, Victor 1947.05, 1965.08, 1980.29, 1997.05
Scheuer, Steven H. 1962.24
Schick, George 1946.16
Schickele, Peter 1971.04, 1976.27
Schickling, John 1948.24
Schierhorn, Paul 1979.24, 1985.17
Schiffer, Marcellus 1932.04
Schifrin, Lalo 1999.01
Schifter, Peter Mark 1989.07
Schildkraut, Joseph 1932.28
Schilke, Raymond D. 1992.16
Schiller, Augusta 1897.03
Schiller, Charles 1878.18, 1879.05, 1880.54, 1883.16, 1883.21
Schiller, Charles V. 1879.15
Schiller, George 1904.47, 1916.26, 1917.08, 1918.20, 1919.44, 1933.21
Schiller, George A. 1880.40, 1881.43, 1882.34, 1882.51, 1882.70, 1883.10, 1883.18, 1883.64, 1883.67, 1884.12, 1884.20, 1885.04, 1885.58, 1887.01, 1887.43, 1889.13, 1889.46, 1892.04, 1894.21, 1897.26, 1897.39, 1900.05, 1900.20, 1900.34, 1901.23, 1903.41, 1904.08, 1904.22, 1908.44, 1909.11, 1911.40, 1912.49, 1913.28, 1914.07, 1926.26, 1930.28
Schiller, George S. 1930.14
Schiller, Miriam 1937.09
Schilling, Carl 1898.55, 1899.31, 1908.22
Schilling, F. Kek 1906.26
Schilling, Friedrich 1885.27, 1885.28, 1887.18
Schilling, Gus 1930.35
Schilling, Margaret 1921.29, 1927.25, 1927.38, 1930.02
Schilling, Victoria 1885.63, 1886.04, 1886.30
Schillings, F. Kek 1907.43
Schimmel, John 1982.04
Schimmel, Stanley 1945.03
Schimmel, William 1989.10
Schindle, Annie 1891.42
Schindler, Paul 1891.09, 1895.18, 1896.44, 1897.25, 1901.06, 1901.23, 1903.03, 1904.25, 1906.04, 1907.59, 1912.25, 1913.34
Schippers, Leo 1936.26
Schippers, Thomas 1950.05, 1952.12, 1954.18
Schirmer, Gus 1961.15, 1962.13, 1963.05, 1963.17, 1963.30, 1965.15, 1965.21, 1966.07, 1966.13, 1966.31, 1967.04, 1967.09, 1967.17, 1968.32, 1970.11
Schirmer, Gustave 1934.06
Schirmer, Jr., Gus 1958.21
Schissler, Jeffrey 1984.06
Schlader, James 1950.10, 1959.02
Schlaeger, Hedwig 1869.05
Schlag, Fraulein 1879.62
Schlag, Frl. 1879.22
Schlag, II, Fraulein 1880.66
Schlag, Marie 1885.01
Schlamme, Martha 1965.04
Schlee, Clara 1893.22
Schlee, Robert 1976.10
Schlefer, Mack 1972.01, 1980.26, 1982.05, 1987.06
Schlegel, Jeanne 1965.15, 1965.21, 1966.13
Schleicher, Messr. 1890.31
Schleiffarth, George 1886.39
Schlein, Mr. 1852.06
Schlemmer, Oscar 1937.05
Schlesinger, Alice Maria 1984.03, 1984.04
Schlesinger, Sigmund 1911.19
Schlesser, Sidney 1929.08
Schletter, Christopher J. 2001.04
Schlicht, Al. J. 1888.21
Schliemann, Frl. 1883.08
Schliemann, Herr 1879.62
Schlig, Michael 1892.02, 1892.13
Schlim, Mr. 1859.03
Schlissel, Jack 1974.18, 1979.02, 1979.25
Schlitz, Don 2001.06
Schloss, Irving 1924.33, 1930.23, 1930.43, 1932.10
Schlossberg, Jerry 1970.02, 1971.15
Schlossberg, Julian 1994.01
Schlosser, Peter 1971.12
Schlueter, Miss 1891.33, 1892.43, 1898.53
Schluter, Miss 1894.01
Schmaltz, Rachel 1999.02
Schmid, Tom 1997.16
Schmidlapp, W. Horace 1942.27, 1945.14
Schmidt, Ann 1925.20
Schmidt, Anne 1922.20
Schmidt, Douglas W. 1970.04, 1972.12, 1974.05, 1975.18, 1976.10, 1976.20, 1976.30, 1978.11, 1979.04, 1979.11, 1979.26, 1983.04, 1986.20, 1989.12, 1991.15, 1994.01, 1999.05, 1999.08, 2000.03
Schmidt, E. 1875.25, 1875.27, 1875.28, 1875.29, 1875.30, 1875.33
Schmidt, Fred 1937.14
Schmidt, Harvey 1963.26, 1966.29, 1969.02, 1976.32, 1992.10
Schmidt, Herr 1882.68
Schmidt, Jack 1976.15
Schmidt, John V. 1945.14
Schmidt, Jules 1937.08
Schmidt, Kate 1915.24
Schmidt, Katie 1916.15, 1921.28
Schmidt, Max 1900.47, 1908.07
Schmidt, Merle 1979.27, 1980.21, 1981.20
Schmidt, Mons. 1851.01, 1851.06, 1851.07, 1851.08, 1875.07, 1875.27
Schmidt, R. 1879.29
Schmidtlein, William 1883.06
Schmitlein, C. 1881.13
Schmitt, Doris 1949.17
Schmitt, G. 1911.28
Schmitz, Frl. 1879.17
Schmitz, Herr 1879.62, 1880.20, 1882.68
Schmoegner, Susanne 1991.11
Schmoll, Warren 1951.16
Schnabel, Stefan 1946.13, 1955.01, 1965.04
Schnaterbeck, Conley 1982.14
Schneegans, Mr. 1892.43
Schneff, Messr. 1852.01
Schneff, Mr. 1848.04
Schneider and Anderson 1913.17, 1920.10
Schneider and Blythe 1930.36, 1930.37
Schneider, Alan 1969.16, 1970.06, 1972.01
Schneider, Charles 1968.19
Schneider, Elsie 1914.30
Schneider, Frank 1924.44
Schneider, Fred 1891.08
Schneider, Helen 1989.10
Schneider, Herr 1879.57
Schneider, Jana 1976.30, 1985.18
Schneider, Messr. 1917.33
Schneider, Peter 1999.16, 2000.06
Schneider, Richard 1973.07
Schneider-Anderson 1917.25, 1917.28, 1918.27, 1919.37, 1919.43, 1920.17, 1922.38, 1924.02, 1925.08, 1925.30, 1926.06, 1929.35
Schneider-Anderson and Brooks Uniform Company 1918.34
Schneider-Anderson Artists 1918.19
Schneider-Anderson Company 1911.33, 1912.11, 1912.31, 1913.14, 1914.18, 1914.26, 1915.18, 1916.01, 1917.19, 1917.37, 1918.28, 1919.01, 1920.30, 1920.38, 1923.34, 1926.29
Schneider-Anderson, Brooks 1920.12
Schneitzer, Ignaz 1912.04
Schnelle, Herr 1879.57, 1879.62, 1880.61, 1880.66
Schneph, Messr. 1844.01
Schner, Herman E. 1972.17
Schnieders, Andrew 2001.04
Schnirman, David 1999.05
Schnitz, Herren 1880.66
Schnitzer, Ignatz 1891.12
Schnitzer, Ignaz 1886.04, 1898.14, 1911.19, 1944.26, 1945.15
Schnitzler, Arthur 1961.27, 1988.10
Schnmidt, Douglas W. 2001.08
Schnyder, Theodore 1934.13
Schoch, Jean Lee 1964.24
Schochet, Steve 1977.18, 1983.17
Schoeffel, John B. 1893.45, 1894.41, 1894.48, 1895.09, 1895.12, 1896.10, 1896.12
Schoeffler, Paul 1993.17, 1998.18
Schoen, Judy 1969.03
Schoenfeld, Kay 1978.23, 1979.27, 1987.03
Schoengold, Albert 1946.16
Schoening, Oscar 1891.03, 1892.05
Schoester, F. 1888.37
Schofield, Charles 1922.47, 1932.14
Schofield, George 1900.57
Scholl, Daniel 1943.23
Scholl, Danny 1946.10, 1949.17
Scholl, F.S. 1907.39
Scholl, Jack 1930.24, 1932.14, 1932.24, 1934.18
Scholl, John 1921.16
Scholl, John Jay 1923.08
Scholle, Lewis 1948.18
Schollenberg, Kate 1892.21
Scholz, Will 1950.08
Schon, Bonnie 1968.19, 1971.12, 1972.05, 1986.13, 1997.09
Schon, Kenneth 1952.15
Schonberg, Chris 1919.30
Schönberg, Claude-Michel 1987.04, 1991.03, 1995.12, 1997.01
Schonberg, J. 1866.12
Schonberg, James 1866.01, 1866.04, 1866.05, 1867.17, 1870.22, 1871.04, 1871.19, 1872.21, 1872.22, 1872.24, 1872.26, 1897.29
Schonberger 1943.02
Schonfeld, A. 1915.08
Schonfeld, Alfred 1900.47
Schoolcraft 1875.31, 1875.34
Schoolcraft, Luke 1870.27, 1875.31, 1875.34, 1875.35, 1875.36, 1875.37, 1875.38, 1889.52, 1891.43, 1892.36, 1892.56
Schoolcraft, Messr. 1875.31
Schools, Victoria 1941.06, 1942.18
Schopp, Angela 1937.01
Schopp, Paul 1937.05
Schopp, Trudi 1937.05
Schorr, William 1944.23, 1947.01
Schott, Angie 1880.30
Schovenke 1889.02
Schrader, Frederick F. 1897.22, 1912.10
Schrader, L. 1883.62, 1884.51
Schrader, L.A. 1885.05
Schrader, L.C. 1884.63, 1885.28
Schrader, Louis 1889.22, 1892.22, 1893.16, 1894.24, 1896.13, 1897.10, 1898.13
Schrader, Marie B. 1921.39
Schrader, Mr. 1883.45, 1898.53
Schrader, Otto 1913.19, 1915.17
Schraeder, George 1905.57, 1907.36
Schramm, David 1973.16, 1975.18
Schramm, Eleanore 1942.16
Schramm, Eunice 1928.20
Schramm, George 1900.33
Schramm, Gilbert 1900.41
Schrank, Joseph 1937.14
Schrapp, Barbier 1929.22
Schrapp, Ernest 1929.22
Schrapps, Barbier 1928.26

Schrapps, Ernest 1924.29, 1926.37, 1927.19, 1927.55, 1927.58, 1928.14, 1928.26, 1928.27, 1928.46, 1928.48, 1929.09, 1929.17, 1929.28, 1929.39, 1930.15, 1930.20, 1931.36, 1932.01, 1932.06, 1932.15, 1934.14, 1934.43, 1941.02, 1942.16
Schrapps, Ernest R. 1922.23, 1922.34, 1925.02, 1925.27, 1925.39, 1926.01, 1926.02, 1926.08, 1926.14, 1926.15, 1927.14, 1927.17, 1927.42, 1927.68, 1934.13
Schraps, Ernest 1945.03, 1947.11
Schraubstader, Carl 1923.18
Schreck, Artie 1991.04
Schreiber, Avery 1967.18, 1971.08, 1981.13, 1989.07
Schreibman, Myrl A. 1977.09
Schreier, Dan Moses 1996.07, 2000.12
Schreier, Moe 1937.14
Schreiner, Warner 1962.13
Schrock, Allen 1903.01
Schrock, Jackie 1980.12
Schrode, Charles 1909.13
Schrode, George 1892.59
Schrode, Henry 1892.59
Schrode, Joe 1926.32
Schrode, John 1892.59
Schrode, John G. 1912.38
Schrode, Joseph 1903.03, 1904.13, 1904.44, 1906.29, 1909.13, 1920.47, 1924.35, 1929.48, 1930.08, 1931.08
Schrode, Joseph C. 1912.43
Schrode, Walter 1903.31
Schrode, William 1892.59, 1909.13, 1910.18
Schrode, William C. 1904.47, 1908.19
Schroder, Aaron 1989.12
Schroder, Wayne 1997.22, 1998.20, 1999.21, 2000.19
Schroder, William 1976.35, 1979.18, 1980.14, 1982.17
Schroeder, Clara 1911.41
Schroeder, Henry 1905.22
Schroeder, Julius 1905.25
Schroeder, Messr. 1905.25
Schroeder, Mildred 1937.03
Schroeder, Miss 1885.09
Schroeder, William 1883.05, 1883.07, 1914.33, 1917.09, 1918.17, 1919.40
Schroetter, Fraulein 1869.06
Schrotter, C. 1872.10
Schrotter, G. 1872.10
Schrotter, Mlle. 1876.36
Schruers, Ed 1937.08
Schubert, Franz 1956.11
Schuck, Conrad John 1997.04
Schuenzer, Rheinhold 1995.15
Schuetz, Ferdinand 1891.17, 1892.03
Schulberg, Budd 1964.05
Schulberg, Stuart 1964.05
Schuler, Duane 1986.04, 1987.03, 1988.04, 1991.12, 1996.13
Schuler, Helen 1886.34
Schuller, Gunther 1975.19
Schulman, Alvin 1954.10
Schulman, Arnold 1963.25, 1968.03
Schulman, Max 1947.08
Schulman, Susan 1998.03
Schulman, Susan H. 1989.19, 1991.05
Schulman, Wilfred 1967.17
Schult, Gustave 1915.26
Schulte, Mons. 1887.35, 1887.37
Schulter, Miss 1890.31
Schultheis, Tim 1993.15
Schultz 1903.25
Schultz, Augustus 1913.34
Schultz, Charles 1866.12
Schultz, Charles M. 1971.11, 1999.03
Schultz, Ed 1904.27
Schultz, Emma 1884.15, 1884.56
Schultz, Fritz 1902.18
Schultz, Gladys 1914.27
Schultz, Gustav 1915.29
Schultz, H. 1908.07
Schultz, Messr. 1893.29
Schultz, Michael 1991.01
Schultz, Michael A. 1970.04
Schultz, Miss 1892.43
Schultz, Norbert 1967.13, 1968.20
Schultz, Steven M. 1988.04
Schultze, Carl E. 1902.08
Schultze, Herr 1882.68
Schultze, Lizzie 1864.02
Schultze, Norbert 1999.07
Schulz, Gertrude 1920.46
Schulz, Miss 1890.31, 1894.01
Schumacher, Dave 1990.19
Schumacher, Michelle 1991.13
Schumacher, Olga 1931.27, 1931.35, 1934.08, 1934.11
Schumacher, Ruth 1952.15, 1954.15
Schumacher, Thomas 1999.16, 2000.06
Schuman, Jennie 1885.36, 1885.38
Schuman, Patricia 1983.16
Schumann, Robert 1911.13, 1922.21
Schumann, Walter 1955.03
Schumann-Heink, Ernestine 1904.36
Schumazuni, Messr. 1925.13
Schumer, Harry 1942.05
Schumer, Henry 1946.15
Schumer, Leo 1950.02, 1951.10
Schumer, Yvette 1955.01, 1956.08
Schunzel, Reinhold 1945.11
Schurff, Lester 1916.14
Schurgot, Helena 1948.15, 1949.04
Schuster, Alan J. 1982.12, 1994.01
Schuster, Franz 1898.38
Schuster, Ira 1940.16
Schuster, Joe 1932.14
Schuster, Raymond 1918.17
Schuster, William 1895.21, 1898.04, 1902.22, 1931.44
Schutt, Arthur 1928.08, 1928.40, 1932.17
Schutt, William 1923.04
Schutz, Ferdinand 1885.01, 1885.27, 1891.12, 1891.22
Schutz, Herb 1955.12
Schutz, Herbert 1951.10
Schutz, Herr 1882.68
Schuyler, Ivy 1886.42
Schwab, Buddy 1950.17, 1954.09, 1961.18, 1962.03, 1970.11, 1974.18, 1979.10, 1980.19, 1981.26, 1986.03
Schwab, Charles 1930.18, 1930.32, 1934.06
Schwab, Charles M. 1927.11, 1930.33
Schwab, Emil 1883.62, 1884.51, 1887.15, 1887.26, 1898.30, 1899.42
Schwab, Laurence 1922.28, 1924.03, 1925.29, 1926.25, 1926.42, 1927.41, 1928.29, 1929.03, 1930.32, 1931.04, 1931.28, 1931.39, 1932.25, 1935.17, 1938.10, 1942.22, 1944.17, 1974.26, 1986.14, 1988.16
Schwab, Sophie 1980.07
Schwantes, Leland 1975.22
Schwartz, Abe 1967.03
Schwartz, Arthur 1926.17, 1927.11, 1928.19, 1929.04, 1929.19, 1929.20, 1929.51, 1930.06, 1930.25, 1930.30, 1930.32, 1931.16, 1932.17, 1934.38, 1935.12, 1936.31, 1937.10, 1937.16, 1939.13, 1946.20, 1948.14, 1951.14, 1952.11, 1954.02, 1954.11, 1961.27, 1963.25, 1967.11, 1972.05, 1975.22, 1976.32, 1980.29, 1982.06, 1988.08, 1989.06, 1990.09, 1991.10, 1992.18, 1999.01, 1999.23
Schwartz, Ben 1903.18, 1903.20, 1927.26
Schwartz, Benjamin 1900.41
Schwartz, Bonnie Nelson 1986.01, 1996.04
Schwartz, Bruce 1980.01
Schwartz, Earl 1910.09
Schwartz, Eugene 1905.48
Schwartz, Frederick 1911.31, 1913.07
Schwartz, Gary 1990.18, 1993.09
Schwartz, Herbert 1927.07
Schwartz, Irving 1993.08
Schwartz, Jack 1959.26
Schwartz, Jean 1901.13, 1901.17, 1901.25, 1901.27, 1902.15, 1902.16, 1902.19, 1903.04, 1903.12, 1903.27, 1903.30, 1903.35, 1903.39, 1904.04, 1904.08, 1904.15, 1904.43, 1904.47, 1905.17, 1905.19, 1905.22, 1905.28, 1905.41, 1905.52, 1906.20, 1906.24, 1906.25, 1906.37, 1907.21, 1907.24, 1907.27, 1907.28, 1907.37, 1907.42, 1908.10, 1908.19, 1908.31, 1908.33, 1908.39, 1909.16, 1909.17, 1909.18, 1909.25, 1909.28, 1910.08, 1910.19, 1910.20, 1911.43, 1912.01, 1912.07, 1912.13, 1912.14, 1912.26, 1912.31, 1912.36, 1912.45, 1913.05, 1913.18, 1914.06, 1915.16, 1915.24, 1916.04, 1916.20, 1917.35, 1918.05, 1918.20, 1918.37, 1919.03, 1919.16, 1919.26, 1919.30, 1920.22, 1920.23, 1920.47, 1921.02, 1921.23, 1921.25, 1922.11, 1922.15, 1923.13, 1923.17, 1923.20, 1923.25, 1923.41, 1924.13, 1924.29, 1927.19, 1928.07, 1928.32, 1962.17, 1967.11, 1997.01
Schwartz, Jeff 1991.14
Schwartz, Jerome 1914.34
Schwartz, Jonathan L. 2001.04
Schwartz, Mark 1997.05
Schwartz, Mark S. 1983.06
Schwartz, Messr. 1886.36
Schwartz, Miss 1896.44
Schwartz, Murray 1999.09
Schwartz, Oscar 1911.32, 1912.17, 1912.24
Schwartz, Paul 1988.12
Schwartz, Pete 1931.02
Schwartz, Phil 1910.08, 1910.22, 1915.02, 1915.11, 1916.03
Schwartz, Samuel H. 1974.23
Schwartz, Scott 2000.20
Schwartz, Stephen 1972.15, 1972.22, 1974.13, 1976.17, 1978.12, 1986.13, 1989.06, 1992.16, 1995.12, 1999.01
Schwartz, Suzanne J. 1983.19
Schwartzdorf, Jacob 1941.12, 1943.04
Schwartzhockler, Mlle. 1873.22
Schwartzwald, Milton 1926.14, 1927.38
Schwarz, Avivia 1971.17
Schwarze, Henry 1946.16
Schwarzwald, Milton 1916.17, 1924.30, 1927.05, 1927.54
Schwarzwald, Milton E. 1922.29
Schwei, Barbara 1973.08
Schweid, Mark 1937.01
Schweikert, Ernest G. 1957.17
Schweitzer, Olga 1892.31
Schwencke 1879.25, 1881.43, 1883.39
Schwencke, Mme. 1894.13
Schwencke, Mr. 1879.07, 1879.11
Schwendler, Richard 1919.38
Schwenecke, Mr. 1910.24
Schweng, Hans 1938.16
Schwenka, Mme. 1892.40
Schwenke, A. 1883.25, 1884.28, 1884.29, 1884.30, 1884.31
Schwenke, Mildred 1927.67, 1932.11
Schwenke, Mme. 1888.11
Schwenke, Paula 1920.46
Schwenkee, Mme. 1894.17
Schwenkow, Peter 1991.11
Schweppe, Frederick 1938.15
Schwering, Betty Jane 1961.12, 1962.08
Schwezoff, Igor 1941.10, 1943.08, 1946.11
Schwicardi, H. 1865.03
Schwicardi, L. 1876.22
Schwicardi, Messr. 1875.31, 1880.69
Schwicardi, Mr. 1875.36, 1875.37, 1875.38
Schwickardi, H. 1870.39
Schwinke, Mme. 1888.06
Schwinn, Ron 1964.33, 1967.16, 1969.04, 1975.14, 1980.20, 1993.18
Scibelli, Carlo 1996.02
Scibilia, Anton F. 1919.32, 1927.31
Scilla, Maryellen 1987.15
Scofield, Al 1943.16
Scofield, H.D. 1918.17
Scofield, Pamela 2001.09
Scoggins, Virgil 1935.12
Scola, Ettore 1994.05
Scolari, Peter 1996.17
Scoll, Cyril 1923.02
Scollan, J.C. 1876.23, 1877.21
Scooler, Zvee 1964.27
Scordi, Pancho 1939.26
Scorsese, Martin 1977.16
Scotford, Sybil 1959.02, 1961.12, 1965.28
Scotland, Bonny 1908.43
Scott Rudin/Paramount Pictures 1996.06
Scott, A.H. 1898.02
Scott, Abie 1972.20
Scott, Ainsley 1884.25
Scott, Amy 1919.41
Scott, Anna 1894.52
Scott, Augusta 1914.08
Scott, Bennett 1921.12
Scott, Bessye Ruth 1975.21
Scott, Betty 1911.26
Scott, Blake 1928.19, 1937.01
Scott, Bobby 1921.12, 1979.17
Scott, Bonnie 1961.22
Scott, C.W. 1940.01
Scott, Camilla 1989.17
Scott, Carrie 1898.61
Scott, Cecil 1933.04
Scott, Charles 1895.05, 1951.16, 1953.09
Scott, Clare 1926.16
Scott, Claudia 1911.28, 1912.30
Scott, Clement 1879.18, 1886.02, 1891.29, 1892.45, 1929.43
Scott, Colin 1989.01
Scott, Connie 1963.25
Scott, Cyril 1894.24, 1896.29, 1897.20, 1897.44, 1898.18, 1898.29, 1898.46, 1900.51, 1902.35, 1903.21, 1904.03, 1904.08, 1905.13, 1912.18, 1923.02
Scott, Dan 1947.09
Scott, Debbie 1963.25
Scott, Dennis 1965.21
Scott, Dora 1892.29
Scott, Duncan 1946.01
Scott, E.T. 1907.61
Scott, Ed 1955.11, 1966.27, 1986.03
Scott, Edith 1925.01, 1929.17
Scott, Edward 1951.02
Scott, Eleanor 1912.33
Scott, Eric 1897.20, 1897.44, 1898.18, 1898.29, 1898.46
Scott, Eva 1893.30
Scott, Ewart 1922.05
Scott, Francena 1938.16
Scott, Frank 1899.28
Scott, Fred 1902.43
Scott, G.B. 1906.45
Scott, George 1981.09
Scott, George Burke 1912.40
Scott, George C. 1960.18
Scott, Gertrude 1916.10
Scott, Grayce 1896.31, 1902.34
Scott, Harry F. 1924.12
Scott, Hazel 1942.10
Scott, Helen 1896.49
Scott, Helena 1953.08, 1957.04, 1958.16, 1959.08, 1959.17, 1959.21
Scott, Ivy 1932.22, 1934.38, 1937.17, 1939.27, 1941.05, 1941.12, 1944.21
Scott, J. Blake 1925.20, 1926.17, 1926.41, 1927.23
Scott, J.E. 1907.49
Scott, Jack 1922.11, 1923.20
Scott, James 1927.46
Scott, Jaye 1995.01
Scott, Jean 1926.16
Scott, Jeffrey 1966.12, 1966.16
Scott, Jerry 1964.02
Scott, Jimmy 1927.46
Scott, John 1900.51, 1904.45, 1922.19, 1924.14, 1944.17, 1992.10
Scott, Katherine 1981.09
Scott, Kelli 1961.07, 1962.01
Scott, Kenneth 1967.06, 1968.08, 1975.01
Scott, Kenyon 1929.30
Scott, Kevin 1953.11, 1955.11
Scott, Lee 1959.19
Scott, Leonard 1926.12, 1927.53
Scott, Les 1982.24
Scott, Leslie 1952.08, 1953.04
Scott, Lorraine 1990.15
Scott, Lydia 1912.11, 1916.20, 1917.22, 1920.04, 1922.45, 1923.40, 1924.26, 1926.32
Scott, M. 1921.12, 1964.28
Scott, M. Ainsley 1884.09
Scott, Mamie 1891.21
Scott, Marc 1960.08
Scott, Margaret 1896.46
Scott, Matilda 1879.10, 1879.16
Scott, Maurice 1909.11, 1910.08
Scott, Messr. 1750.01, 1867.17, 1905.54
Scott, Michael 1978.13, 1980.06, 1994.08
Scott, Michael Lee 1996.04
Scott, Miss 1867.19, 1892.29
Scott, Mr. 1865.05, 1865.07, 1865.08, 1865.09, 1865.10
Scott, Nathan 1955.03
Scott, O.M. 1896.37
Scott, Oliver 1896.49
Scott, Phil 1933.27
Scott, R.L. 1892.27
Scott, Raymond 1940.16, 1942.12, 1946.05, 1950.12, 1959.05
Scott, Russell 1923.07
Scott, Sherie 1993.06
Scott, Sherie Rene 2000.06
Scott, Susan Elizabeth 1982.16
Scott, Theodore 1938.01
Scott, Thomas 1909.16
Scott, Timothy 1978.22, 1982.19
Scott, Tina 1981.09
Scott, Victor 1907.28
Scott, W.W. 1898.66, 1900.43, 1909.06
Scott, Walter 1855.01, 1859.01, 1867.10, 1869.42, 1872.26, 1886.54, 1903.09

Scott, Walter F. 1930.16
Scott, William 1899.21
Scott, Winfield 1989.12
Scott, Zachary 1956.03
Scott-Irby-Ranniar 1997.20
Scotten, Helen 1909.14
Scotti, Al 1979.11
Scotti, Don 1976.20
Scotti, Vito 1938.16
Scotto, Vincent 1934.32, 1935.19, 1947.18, 1964.02, 1973.17, 1980.27, 1981.04
Scotty, George 1905.14
Scourby, Alexander 1963.08
Scovotti, Jeanette 1956.03, 1956.12
Scribe 1920.15
Scribe, Eugene 1851.07, 1851.08, 1862.04, 1864.10, 1864.18, 1866.27, 1867.04, 1868.10, 1870.19, 1870.36, 1873.04, 1877.05, 1879.22, 1879.25, 1879.65, 1879.67, 1880.48, 1880.62, 1882.07, 1882.60, 1882.65, 1883.11, 1884.35, 1885.30, 1887.41, 1898.33, 1900.18, 1901.10, 1904.57
Scribner, C. 1898.30
Scribner, Charles 1898.06, 1898.09, 1898.14, 1898.15, 1898.21, 1898.30, 1898.37, 1898.40, 1898.42, 1899.05, 1899.10, 1910.18, 1912.38, 1917.13
Scrimshaw, E.R. 1904.41
Scrittorale, Michael 1954.15, 1959.25
Scrittorale, Mike 1962.16
Scrova, Madame 1924.44
Scruggs, Earl 1954.08
Scudder, Eugene 1925.39, 1927.22
Scully, Barbara 1943.06, 1943.12, 1944.25
Scully, Emma 1903.25
Scully, Sean 1963.29
Seaberry, Annie 1894.38
Seabert, Alexander 1922.30
Seabert, Mr. 1869.31
Seabolt, Frank 1948.17, 1954.03
Seabra, Nelson 1942.01
Seabrooke, Christopher 1989.23
Seabrooke, Elvie 1884.24
Seabrooke, Thomas Q. 1882.81, 1884.24, 1889.12, 1890.16, 1891.27, 1892.55, 1893.20, 1894.22, 1895.07, 1898.34, 1898.43, 1899.02, 1899.24, 1899.25, 1900.33, 1901.29, 1902.05, 1902.10, 1902.19, 1903.36, 1906.07
Seabury, Annie 1889.01
Seabury, Forrest 1887.03
Seabury, Messr. 1886.16
Seabury, William 1922.39, 1925.16, 1929.02
Seader, Richard 1986.19, 1995.14
Seager, Stella 1928.40
Seagle, Betty Jane 1951.18, 1955.10
Seagram, Wilfred 1925.27, 1926.14
Seagrave, Charles 1896.35, 1897.52, 1904.07
Seagraves, Charles 1899.23
Seal, Elizabeth 1960.13
Sealby, Mabel 1909.01, 1909.18
Seale, Greg 2001.04
Seale, Polly 1989.06
Seaman, Adelaide 1925.24, 1926.29
Seaman, Adeline 1930.35
Seaman, Charles 1891.43
Seaman, David 1982.18
Seaman, Frank 1931.40
Seaman, Harry 1931.40
Seaman, Jane 1987.15
Seaman, Willet 1882.65, 1884.28, 1884.29, 1890.26
Seamon, Charles V. 1882.04, 1883.66, 1890.34, 1894.10
Seamon, Harry 1899.33, 1900.46, 1903.08, 1904.26, 1904.58, 1905.42, 1906.08
Seamon, Messr. 1882.04
Searelle, W. Luscombe 1883.67
Searle, Cyril 1873.25
Searle, Eleanor 1937.01
Searle, Louise 1877.36, 1879.33, 1879.35, 1880.02, 1880.40, 1881.33, 1884.25, 1887.34
Searle, Osborne 1912.02
Searle, Tom 1998.10
Searles, Chester 1904.28
Searles, Minnie 1902.09
Sears, Frances 1898.60
Sears, Gertrude 1890.15, 1890.18, 1890.20
Sears, Mary 1893.05, 1893.09, 1895.16
Sears, Ted 1979.28
Sears, Zelda 1908.10, 1919.06, 1920.43, 1922.47, 1923.34, 1924.02, 1926.06
Seaton, Arthur R. 1896.50
Seaton, George 1963.21
Seaton, Johnny 1989.12
Seaton, Violet 1912.42
Seaver, F.W. 1866.18
Seavey, Grace 1886.26, 1886.33, 1886.43, 1887.24, 1887.28, 1887.47, 1888.19, 1888.22, 1888.24, 1888.26
Seavey, L. 1886.06, 1898.56
Seavey, L.H. 1879.07
Seavey, L.W. 1869.08, 1872.23, 1872.35, 1873.03, 1873.26, 1879.11, 1890.43, 1892.34, 1895.28
Seavey, Lafayette W. 1883.65, 1892.14, 1893.03
Seavy, Grace 1887.12, 1887.18
Seawell, Donald R. 1961.18, 1963.03, 1963.16, 1983.02, 1983.05, 1988.07
Seawright, Toni 1993.03
Seay, Beti 1960.01, 1961.10
Seay, Edward S. 1888.23
Seay, Rebecca 1978.10
Sebastian, John 1982.22
Sebastian, Mark 1982.22
Sebastian, Sig. 1881.32
Sebastian, Walter 1999.18
Sebek, Herman W. 1982.19
Sebert, Mlle. 1887.36
Sebesky, Don 1983.20, 1989.25, 1992.18, 1993.17, 1997.08, 1998.21, 1999.19, 1999.23, 2001.03
Sebree, Charles 1954.16
Sechler, Craig 1959.07
Sechler, Curly 1954.08
Secombe, Harry 1965.28
Secombe, Lesley 1970.11
Secor, George 1891.25
Secor, George J. 1891.45
Secor, Miss 1859.11
Secunda, Sholom 1951.20, 1990.16
Sedan, Rolfe 1942.30
Sedano, Galdino 1922.26
Sederholm, Richard 1966.27
Sedgewick, Edna 1940.12
Sedgewick, Thomas 1904.39
Sedgwick, Helen 1886.45, 1887.11, 1887.27, 1889.08, 1892.12
Sedley, Roy 1925.44, 1932.07
Sedova, Rosine 1944.21
See, Ed 1889.08
See, Edward 1888.10, 1920.05
Seebold, Emma 1884.64, 1885.11, 1885.27
Seebold, Frl. 1882.68
Seegar, Dorothy 1923.14, 1929.43, 1931.15
Seeger, Bob 1979.30
Seeger, Pete 1966.03, 1967.13, 1968.20, 1999.07
Seelen, Jerry 1942.01, 1942.18, 1942.23, 1943.05
Seeley, Agnes 1876.03
Seeley, Blossom 1911.05, 1912.09, 1912.36, 1915.02, 1915.22, 1915.31, 1928.14
Seeley, James 1911.17, 1927.09
Seeley, Mariam 1921.20
Seeley, May 1903.37
Seeley, Setphanie 1996.17
Seeley, W.R. 1893.43
Seeley, William R. 1893.43
Seetoo, Keelee 1989.05
Seevers, George 1893.26, 1894.06
Seevers, George B. 1893.17
Sefton, Harry 1889.27
Sefton, Ida 1872.36, 1872.43
Sefton, John 1852.03
Sefton, Joseph O. 1860.01
Sefton, Lillian 1903.36
Sefton, Mrs. John 1852.01
Segal, Al 1931.09
Segal, Ben 1952.07
Segal, David F. 1971.04, 1972.05, 1973.05, 1975.18, 1976.30, 1979.03, 1980.18, 1994.01
Segal, Erich 1968.08, 1974.19
Segal, Jack 1955.03
Segal, Linda 1963.20
Segal, Nathalie 1927.39
Segal, Vivienne 1915.17, 1917.14, 1917.26, 1918.03, 1919.28, 1922.35, 1923.16, 1924.18, 1925.10, 1925.24, 1925.40, 1926.24, 1926.42, 1928.12, 1931.33, 1938.05, 1940.22, 1943.22, 1947.14, 1950.06, 1952.01
Segalini, Louise 1892.20
Segaud, Mlle. 1878.18
Segawa, Kae 1989.21
Segelini, Carlo 1889.24
Seger, Julius 1902.23
Seger, Richard 1969.04, 1976.15
Segovia, Claudio 1985.07, 1986.17, 1989.02, 1999.18
Segovia, Yolanda 1980.29, 1981.29, 1987.07
Segrera, Carolina 1941.10, 1942.32
Seguin, Anne 1844.01, 1848.04
Seguin, Edward 1838.01, 1844.01, 1848.04, 1866.07, 1866.10, 1867.03, 1867.04, 1867.06, 1867.07, 1868.02, 1868.09, 1868.10, 1868.11, 1868.12, 1872.17, 1877.35
Seguin, Edwin 1877.36
Seguin, Mrs. Edwin 1868.01
Seguin, Zelda 1872.17, 1877.35, 1877.36, 1885.48, 1887.15, 1887.20, 1887.21
Seguin-Wallace, Zelda 1885.30, 1885.32
Segura, Cristobal Oudrid y 1881.24
Seibert, Emma 1902.26
Seibert, Jeannette 1968.24
Seibert, Wallace 1949.01, 1956.15
Seibert, Wally 1964.40
Seidel, Caroline 1903.07
Seidel, Catherine 1895.15, 1901.25
Seidel, Virginia 1975.24
Seidelman, Arthur A. 1969.08
Seidelman, Arthur Allan 1991.09
Seidl, Anton 1895.28
Seidl, Herr 1879.62
Seidle, C. 1886.26, 1905.15
Seidle, C.F. 1902.07
Seidle, Caroline 1897.17, 1899.01, 1900.10, 1900.57, 1901.01, 1901.12, 1901.13, 1901.23, 1902.03, 1902.16, 1902.19, 1902.31, 1903.14, 1903.31, 1903.36, 1903.38, 1904.05, 1904.12, 1904.15, 1904.19, 1904.51, 1904.55, 1905.01, 1905.03, 1905.20, 1905.29, 1906.26, 1906.32, 1907.18, 1908.04
Seidle, Caroline F. 1903.28
Seidle, Catherine 1893.47, 1895.24, 1895.25, 1895.33, 1895.35, 1896.05, 1896.06, 1896.10, 1896.12, 1897.02, 1897.18, 1897.54, 1898.28, 1898.72, 1898.73, 1900.07, 1900.33, 1904.39, 1905.11
Seidle, Catherine F. 1891.29, 1894.45, 1895.01, 1896.41, 1896.43
Seidle, Edward 1907.61
Seidler, Alice 1866.06, 1866.08, 1866.11
Seidler, Carl 1924.17
Seidler, Carol 1925.35
Seidman, John 1982.24
Seiger, Charles 1921.17
Seiger, Marvin 1960.01
Seigh, Eileen 1949.05
Seigh, Ellen 1948.19
Seigner, Stefan 1991.11
Seigrist, A. 1894.42
Seitz, Dran 1954.15, 1961.08
Seitz, George B. 1919.12
Seitz, Tani 1954.15, 1959.12
Sekiya, Toshiaki 1989.21
Selbert, Marianne 1966.24, 1969.04, 1983.09, 1984.10
Selbini, Lala 1919.21
Selbini, Lalla 1919.22
Selby, Charles 1857.02, 1866.06, 1867.14
Selby, Messr. 1868.06, 1871.11
Selby, Rita 1892.21
Selch, Frederick R. 1982.13
Selden, Albert 1948.22, 1958.01, 1959.23
Selden, Albert W. 1965.34, 1967.06, 1969.07, 1972.14, 1973.05, 1979.10, 1979.32
Selden, Clara 1895.12, 1900.38
Selden, Edgar 1887.17, 1889.37, 1891.08, 1897.33, 1898.75, 1900.24, 1905.14, 1907.24, 1907.41, 1908.19, 1912.36
Selden, Teresa 1871.20, 1871.21
Seldes, Gilbert 1939.29
Seldes, Marian 1952.03
Seldes, Mickey 1925.48
Seldon, Arthur 1896.44
Selee, Marion 1931.46
Seletsky, Harold 1986.13
Seley, J. Joe 1905.51
Selington, Mons. 1875.21
Selinskaya, Mme. 1929.05
Selissen, William 1983.13
Selkirk, Hazel 1900.08
Sell, Janie 1968.07, 1973.05, 1974.05, 1976.19
Sella, Robert 1993.18
Selle, Messr. 1844.01
Seller, Jeffrey 1996.09
Sellers, Arlene 1964.15
Sellers, Arthur 1970.04
Sellers, Brother John 1963.27
Sellers, Charles 1876.03
Sellery, William 1892.21, 1893.37, 1898.20, 1899.19, 1899.36, 1907.14, 1912.02, 1912.42, 1927.34
Sellier, Alie 1931.26
Sellinger, Joyce 1952.15
Sellon, Charles A. 1907.60
Selman, Jim 1989.17
Selovar, Miss 1899.37
Selover, Elaine 1898.72, 1900.16, 1900.44, 1903.29
Sels, Jane 1926.16
Selten, Clara 1894.21, 1895.09
Selton, Clara 1900.20, 1903.03, 1904.13, 1904.44
Selton, Miss 1903.03, 1904.13, 1904.44
Seltzer, David 1972.23
Seltzer, Dov 1968.22, 1971.14
Seltzer, Marjorie 1930.01, 1930.23
Selvi, Marguerite 1875.19, 1875.26
Selvi, Rose 1875.23
Selwart, Tonio 1932.28, 1959.05
Selwyn and Company 1918.16, 1919.06
Selwyn Studio 1921.07
Selwyn, Arch 1919.31, 1921.18, 1921.24, 1924.01, 1925.42, 1927.36, 1928.42, 1929.41, 1929.51, 1934.32, 1934.34, 1934.38
Selwyn, Edgar 1905.38, 1912.14, 1918.16, 1919.31, 1921.18, 1921.24, 1922.02, 1924.01, 1924.34, 1930.02
Selwyn, Ethel 1894.33, 1938.04
Selwyn, J.H. 1862.03, 1862.04, 1863.06, 1863.07, 1864.09, 1864.12, 1864.21
Selwyn, John H. 1871.04
Selwyn, Ruth 1930.06, 1940.09
Selzer, Gustave 1914.04
Sembello, John 1995.03
Semenoff, Messr. 1923.28
Semes, Renee 1974.06
Semmelman, Jim 1989.23
Semon, Harry W. 1892.15
Semon, Marty 1932.22
Semon, Ray 1892.11
Semone, Mlle. 1917.03
Semyonova, Lydia 1924.32
Sena, Joan 1965.07
Senac, Dora 1901.17
Senac, Julie 1892.52, 1894.40, 1895.24, 1897.24
Senac, Laura 1902.29, 1904.49
Senac, Miss 1892.07
Senaille, J.B. 1982.23
Sendrey, Albert 1954.13, 1956.08
Senett, Winnie 1899.29
Senft, Charles 1920.06
Senft, Gerhard 1984.04
Senger, Emil 1884.51, 1885.05
Senger, F. 1883.62
Senior, Susanna 1936.28
Senius, Herr 1897.08
Senn, Herbert 1963.30, 1964.05, 1968.19, 1971.17, 1975.22, 1982.16, 1983.05, 1983.12, 1985.11, 1986.19, 1988.14
Senn, James 1962.27, 1968.24
Senna, Charles 1923.21, 1933.21, 1937.15, 1943.05, 1944.30
Senna, Clarence 1940.16
Sennach, Henrietta 1880.31
Sennett, Lottie 1905.30
Sennett, Minnie 1898.20
Sennett, Nellie 1890.25
Sennett, Winnie 1898.20
Sennott, Ruth 1928.41
Sentanler, Miss 1867.10
Seo, Byung Goo 1997.16, 1998.08
Sepia Guild Players, Inc. 1933.27
Seplow, Evan 1981.07
Sept, Sam H. 1932.24, 1999.24
Septee, Moe 1973.09, 1976.04, 1976.21, 1990.16
Sequoio, Ron 1963.24
Serabian, Lorraine 1968.30
Serangeli, Mario 1932.29, 1934.02, 1940.05
Seraphina, Dona 1880.16
Sergava, Katharine 1943.04, 1948.08
Sergeant, Maxwell 1904.44
Sergeantson, Kate 1917.19
Sergei, James 1976.31
Sergi, James 1977.17, 1978.19, 1978.23, 1979.27, 1982.20, 1989.14
Sergieff, Messrs. 1931.38
Sergieff, Serge 1927.28

Serio, Joy 1966.08
Serlet, Mons. 1868.13
Serner, Hakan 1966.19
Serota, Vivian 1980.29
Serov, Vladimir 1977.13
Serova, Madame 1921.27
Seroy, Helena 1955.10
Serpette, Gaston 1880.16, 1897.54
Serra, Raymond 1981.24, 1988.20, 1992.16
Serrallonga, Marcello 1964.03
Serrano, Charlie 1979.15, 1982.03
Serrano, Eduardo 1986.17
Serrano, Jose 1969.11
Serrano, Vincent 1927.08
Serre, Renny 1985.20
Serrecchia, Michael 1972.02, 1972.11, 1975.15
Serva, David 1965.34, 1992.07
Servais, Yvan 1919.42, 1921.31
Servatius, M. 1926.40, 1926.43, 1926.45, 1926.47, 1926.48, 1929.10
Servatius, Messr. 1926.47
Servatius, Mr. 1929.11, 1929.13, 1929.14, 1929.15
Sesma, Thom 1991.15
Sessano, Ralph 1944.23
Sessions, Almira 1932.14, 1936.22, 1939.24
Sessions, Anne 1962.26, 1968.26, 1968.29
Sessler, Grace 1905.40
Sessons, Bessie 1916.22
Setche, Mr. 1855.08
Setchell, Mr. 1855.09
Setti, Mlle. 1868.03, 1868.18
Settle, A. 1918.15
Settle, Ed. F. 1907.50
Settliffe, Quayle 1911.17
Setzer, Milton 1970.06, 1980.12
Seurat, Georges 1984.08
Seuss, Dr. 2000.18
Sevard, Miss 1886.36
Seve, Mons. 1872.03
Seven Arts Productions 1964.11
Sevening, Dora 1905.27
Severn, Margaret 1920.28
Severn, Marguerite 1919.37
Severo, Joseph 1892.08
Severs, George B. 1896.31
Sevey, George 1881.15
Sevier, Jack 1981.19
Sevilla, V. 1969.11
Seville, Fred 1894.44
Seville, Kaede 1993.02
Seville, Lillian 1906.37
Seville, Marie 1899.26
Seville, Nina 1914.29
Sevra, Robert 1980.23
Sevran, Pascal 1984.10
Seward, Billie 1931.08
Seward, Charles 1866.18
Sewell, Brian 1990.15
Sewell, Cissie 1913.26, 1917.12, 1917.28, 1918.28, 1919.41, 1920.14
Sewell, Cissy 1916.01
Sewell, Danny 1963.01, 1965.23
Sewell, George 1964.28
Sewell, Marie 1919.41, 1920.13, 1920.36
Sexton, Al 1919.13, 1920.19, 1922.12, 1923.31, 1926.03, 1926.29, 1928.41, 1929.07, 1929.50, 1934.42
Sexton, Inez 1879.24
Sexton, Nellie 1882.77
Seybold, George 1918.01
Seygand, Mlle. 1879.39, 1879.49, 1880.56, 1882.35
Seygaud, Felicie 1875.29
Seygaud, Mlle. 1877.06, 1877.13, 1877.19, 1877.27, 1879.19, 1879.55, 1880.52
Seykell, Rohn 1992.05
Seyler, Clifford 1924.01, 1928.04
Seymour, Ann 1929.22, 1932.13
Seymour, Anna 1920.01
Seymour, Anna May 1917.35
Seymour, Blanche 1880.65, 1887.05
Seymour, Charles 1886.60
Seymour, Eileen 1925.05
Seymour, Emily 1885.28
Seymour, H. 1866.05, 1878.10
Seymour, H.J. 1875.11
Seymour, Harry 1852.02, 1905.48, 1917.35
Seymour, J. 1848.01
Seymour, Jack 1938.13
Seymour, James 1856.02, 1857.04, 1857.06, 1980.20, 2001.08
Seymour, John 1925.31
Seymour, John D. 1929.31, 1963.17, 1963.18
Seymour, John Davenport 1923.22
Seymour, Katie 1880.55, 1889.35, 1901.08
Seymour, Mabel 1898.77
Seymour, Madelein 1913.36
Seymour, Maribel 1914.05
Seymour, Miss 1881.04
Seymour, Mr. 1848.01, 1855.10
Seymour, Mrs. 1857.04
Seymour, Mrs. James 1854.06
Seymour, Nellie 1884.41, 1888.04
Seymour, Nelse 1866.35, 1867.01, 1867.02, 1868.05
Seymour, Nora 1904.18
Seymour, Norma 1905.52
Seymour, Paul 1937.14
Seymour, Tot 1923.41, 1924.13, 1936.07, 1936.17
Seymour, W. Howard 1880.01, 1880.03
Seymour, W.H. 1881.07, 1882.66, 1882.75
Seymour, William 1886.27, 1895.19, 1900.03, 1901.15, 1903.25, 1904.42, 1907.16
Seymour, William H. 1880.55, 1881.41, 1881.57, 1886.12
SFX 1999.24
SFX Entertainment Group 1998.01, 1999.01
SFX Theatrical Group 2000.18, 2001.05
Shabach Audio 1999.06
Shabba-Doo 1979.30
Shachar, Gilad Ben 1968.04
Shackelford, Harry 1927.17
Shackelton, Robert 1939.07
Shackford, Charles 1883.64
Shackford, May 1881.22, 1883.12, 1883.13
Shackleford, Emmett 1919.05
Shackleton, Robert 1939.28, 1940.07, 1947.04, 1948.16, 1951.02
Shackner, Alan 1951.21
Shadburne, Sherry 1944.01, 1945.14, 1946.20
Shadden, Donna 1966.21
Shade, Ellen 1968.09
Shade, Jeff 1986.07
Shade, Lillian 1932.18
Shadow, Bert 1925.07
Shadur, Larry 1961.26
Shaer, Carolsue 1962.01
Shafer, Helen 1903.09
Shafer, Phil 1941.13
Shafer, Robert 1931.01, 1936.31, 1937.15, 1944.21, 1955.08
Shaff, Monty 1963.08, 1966.05
Shaff, Verna 1924.12
Shaffer and Maeder 1889.48
Shaffer, Annie 1880.55
Shaffer, Malinda 1989.20
Shaffer, Paul 1976.17, 1979.19
Shaffer, Victoria 1987.17
Shaffner, Walter 1924.24
Shafman, Arthur 1981.02, 1981.11
Shahan, Harvey 1946.18
Shai-K-Ophir 1959.05
Shaiman, Marc 1979.11, 1984.10, 1984.15, 1985.03, 1990.19, 1995.12
Shaka, Mandingo 1973.09, 1989.18
Shakesnider, Wilma 1976.28, 1983.04
Shakespeare, William 1853.05, 1857.05, 1859.15, 1862.05, 1867.27, 1880.19, 1917.35, 1931.31, 1938.14, 1939.16, 1939.29, 1948.32, 1952.02, 1956.05, 1963.03, 1963.28, 1965.18, 1971.18, 1976.03, 1976.33, 1981.02, 1981.25, 1997.03, 1999.19
Shalders, Josie 1895.08
Shale, Betty 1934.34
Shale, Tom A. 1912.27
Shalek, Bertha 1905.36
Shaler, Eleanor 1925.17, 1926.13, 1927.36, 1929.29, 1933.01
Shaler, Eva 1884.22, 1887.43
Shaler, Gussie 1884.22
Shaler, Miss 1884.42
Shalet, Edmund 1912.06
Shalit, Willa 1984.10
Shalita, Jose 1935.11
Shallek, Bertha 1911.10
Shalom, Bella 1963.12
Shaloub, Susan 1969.03
Shamash, Beba 1989.19, 1991.09
Shandley, Julie 1885.31
Shandley, L. 1881.41, 1883.16
Shandley, Lillie 1880.18, 1882.75, 1883.44, 1884.12, 1885.31, 1885.51, 1886.29, 1886.31, 1889.30, 1889.53, 1890.05
Shandley, Lilly 1889.27, 1890.09
Shandley, Miss 1879.71, 1881.04, 1881.11, 1882.45, 1882.60
Shane, Hal 1975.24, 1992.02, 1992.18
Shane, Lorna 1994.07
Shanet, Howard 1947.21
Shangase, Buyani 1997.14
Shanks, Alec 1958.18, 1958.19
Shanks, Earl 1931.31
Shanks, Master 1870.22
Shanley, Charles Dawson 1861.03
Shanley, Robert 1938.15, 1939.13, 1940.06, 1942.20
Shannia, Yelena 1990.01
Shannon, Betty 1916.22
Shannon, Effie 1928.25
Shannon, Eileen 1922.24
Shannon, Frank 1930.21
Shannon, Grace 1908.21
Shannon, Harry 1928.36, 1931.08, 1931.28
Shannon, Harry T. 1926.36, 1930.14, 1933.01
Shannon, Inez 1905.48
Shannon, J.J. 1922.19, 1923.20
Shannon, J.W. 1893.47
Shannon, Jack 1925.10, 1925.24, 1925.31
Shannon, James Royce 1914.05
Shannon, Lavinia 1887.48, 1907.37, 1911.46
Shannon, Mary 1938.16
Shannon, May 1889.27, 1889.53, 1890.05, 1890.09, 1890.13, 1890.45, 1891.10, 1891.16, 1891.19, 1891.35, 1892.02, 1892.13
Shannon, Messr. 1926.32
Shannon, Michael 1972.24
Shannon, Palmer 1980.15
Shannon, Sam 1905.07, 1906.13
Shannon, Samuel 1917.29
Shannon, Sarah Solie 1994.04, 1997.07
Shannon, Solie 1998.05
Shannon, Thomas 1903.21
Shannon, Tommie 1927.37
Shannon, Walter C. 1902.37
Shannon, Winona 1894.37
Shanz, Alfred B. 1892.18
Shaper, Hal 1976.32
Shapiro, Dan 1943.20, 1944.14, 1950.12, 1955.04
Shapiro, Danny 1942.01, 1955.12
Shapiro, Debbie 1980.29, 1982.12, 1983.14, 1989.03
Shapiro, Harvey 1982.11
Shapiro, Irvin 1945.07
Shapiro, Joseph 1975.03
Shapiro, Lou 1978.06
Shapiro, Louis 1981.28
Shapiro, Max 1905.46
Shapiro, Mel 1971.18, 1978.18
Shapiro, Nat 1972.25
Shapiro, Sparky 1976.08
Shapiro, Ted 1941.09, 1988.20, 1999.23
Shapleigh, Ida 1880.42
Sharaff, Irene 1932.28, 1933.22, 1934.29, 1935.03, 1935.14, 1936.05, 1936.22, 1937.10, 1937.13, 1938.14, 1939.22, 1939.23, 1940.12, 1940.23, 1941.04, 1941.12, 1941.13, 1942.15, 1942.18, 1942.27, 1943.03, 1945.20, 1946.02, 1948.24, 1950.03, 1950.12, 1951.12, 1951.14, 1952.07, 1953.08, 1954.02, 1954.12, 1956.03, 1956.07, 1956.15, 1956.16, 1957.12, 1958.19, 1959.04, 1960.08, 1960.11, 1960.23, 1963.18, 1963.25, 1963.29, 1964.11, 1964.17, 1964.23, 1966.01, 1967.06, 1968.16, 1973.05, 1977.07, 1980.02, 1985.01, 1989.03
Sharkey, Dan 2000.11
Sharkey, Jack 1918.24, 1968.13, 1980.19, 1981.26
Sharkey, Thomas 1899.36
Sharkey, Tom 1906.06
Sharkoff, Ted 1904.07
Sharma, Barbara 1962.27, 1966.01, 1967.06, 1968.23, 1969.07, 1989.23
Sharman, Ella 1892.60
Sharman, Jim 1975.08
Sharmat, Stephen W. 1964.22
Sharoff, Irene 1934.19
Sharol, J. 1924.48
Sharon, Ula 1920.33, 1922.32, 1923.31, 1924.44, 1925.52, 1928.02, 1928.45
Sharon, W.T. 1879.42
Sharon, William 1942.27, 1944.32
Sharp Charles 1908.21
Sharp, Adelaide 1905.03, 1909.14, 1910.09
Sharp, Becky 1899.36
Sharp, C. 1888.13
Sharp, Claudine 1901.08, 1902.40
Sharp, Ivan 1930.10, 1935.01
Sharp, Jeffrey Day 1987.17
Sharp, Jessie 1900.45
Sharp, John Jeffrey 2000.17
Sharp, Jon Marshall 1993.19, 1994.02
Sharp, Jonathan 2000.17
Sharp, Louis 1940.17, 1943.10, 1946.08, 1947.03
Sharp, R. 1989.02
Sharp, Robert 1966.24
Sharpe, A. 1884.46, 1885.68
Sharpe, Albert 1947.03
Sharpe, David Preston 1990.14
Sharpe, Ernest 1929.19, 1932.13
Sharpe, John 1951.18, 1956.04, 1957.18, 1961.28, 1962.27, 1963.21, 1966.01, 1966.11
Sharpe, M. 1903.40
Sharpe, Max 1906.41
Sharpe, Nancy 1930.29
Sharpe, Ron 1999.08
Sharpe, Ruth 1929.38
Sharpeley, Gertie 1891.16, 1892.13, 1892.26, 1892.41, 1892.49
Sharpler, T.J. 1902.14
Sharples, Wally 1924.44
Sharpley, Edward 1898.10
Sharpley, Gertie 1893.01
Sharpley, John 1899.04
Sharpley, Sam 1873.04, 1873.05
Sharpsten, C.M. 1902.05
Sharrock, Emma 1917.31
Sharrock, Harry 1917.31
Sharron, Robert 1942.05
Shatto, Bart 1999.08
Shattuck, C.F. 1866.24, 1879.25
Shattuck, Charles 1886.29, 1886.31
Shattuck, Charles F. 1886.38, 1886.53
Shattuck, Messr. 1866.20, 1886.36
Shattuck, Mr. 1883.66
Shattuck, Truly 1897.28, 1904.04, 1904.42, 1906.11, 1906.21, 1906.45, 1907.30, 1910.30
Shaughnessy, Mickey 1965.01
Shaulis, Jane 1976.31, 1978.07, 1978.08, 1979.21, 1980.04, 1980.21, 1980.25, 1985.09, 1985.13, 1989.13, 1996.02
Shavelson, Melville 1969.14
Shavequick, Mr. 1861.01
Shaver, Bob 1956.08
Shaver, Buster 1945.18
Shaver, George 1945.18
Shaver, Olive 1945.18
Shaver, Richard 1945.18
Shaver, Robert 1951.13
Shaw, Al 1927.52, 1929.09, 1931.05
Shaw, Albert 1924.35, 1927.65
Shaw, Alice J. 1893.24
Shaw, Arthur 1902.42
Shaw, Billee 1923.17
Shaw, Billie 1923.41
Shaw, Bob 1941.09, 1981.01, 1984.02, 1985.18
Shaw, Bonnie 1923.24
Shaw, Carl 1927.62
Shaw, David 1959.01, 1963.08
Shaw, Edna 1920.30
Shaw, Edward 1927.39
Shaw, Eleanor 1927.67
Shaw, Elsie 1918.32
Shaw, Evelyn 1946.10
Shaw, Fernandez 1969.11
Shaw, George Bernard 1909.22, 1910.28, 1921.40, 1930.03, 1931.33, 1934.12, 1942.17, 1947.06, 1956.01, 1964.20, 1968.17, 1968.23, 1976.05, 1981.19, 1993.18
Shaw, Gerald 1973.16
Shaw, Gladys 1903.15
Shaw, Goldye 1971.07
Shaw, Grace 1914.21
Shaw, H. 1907.54
Shaw, Harry 1910.23
Shaw, Helene 1919.02
Shaw, Hollace 1940.06
Shaw, J. Jay 1902.09
Shaw, J.J. 1897.38
Shaw, Jack 1928.47
Shaw, Jay 1906.35
Shaw, Jerome 1949.15
Shaw, Johnny 1879.37
Shaw, Josephine 1841.01
Shaw, Len 1930.11
Shaw, Leon 1956.03, 1969.04, 1970.11, 1978.24

Shaw, Leta 1903.03, 1904.44
Shaw, Lillian 1905.42
Shaw, Lita 1903.03
Shaw, Marguerite 1957.08
Shaw, Mattie 1933.04
Shaw, Maurice 1981.01
Shaw, Messr. 1851.01
Shaw, Miss 1903.03
Shaw, Mr. 1841.01, 1851.07
Shaw, Muriel 1955.01, 1956.01
Shaw, N.C. 1902.30
Shaw, Neeka 1929.01, 1930.19, 1930.34, 1931.31
Shaw, Oscar 1915.30, 1917.17, 1919.39, 1920.40, 1921.10, 1921.36, 1923.44, 1924.34, 1924.44, 1926.36, 1927.52, 1930.11, 1931.36
Shaw, Ray 1955.06
Shaw, Reta 1949.18, 1954.05
Shaw, Robert 1942.27, 1943.05, 1943.24, 1944.29, 1945.06, 1946.09, 1952.15, 1970.02
Shaw, Rosalind 1931.15
Shaw, S. 1873.26
Shaw, Sally 1927.40
Shaw, Samuel 1933.20
Shaw, Sydney 1968.13
Shaw, Vanessa 1978.03, 1993.11
Shaw, Wini 1931.08
Shaw, Winn 1923.42
Shawhan, April 1969.12, 1974.05, 1976.08, 1978.06
Shawhan, Fred 1931.04
Shawley Robert 1949.02
Shawley, Bob 1948.15
Shawn, Dick 1963.22, 1964.21, 1968.08, 1975.22
Shawn, Michael 1968.31, 1971.15, 1980.30
Shawn, Peter 1971.09, 1983.18, 1989.22
Shawn, Silvia 1926.07
Shay, Alan 1948.18
Shay, E. 1872.14
Shay, J. 1878.01
Shay, John 1878.17, 1879.04, 1879.37
Shay, Johnny 1878.01, 1879.04
Shay, Larry 1930.13, 1965.08
Shay, Sylvia 1956.02
Shayne, Al 1920.19
Shayne, Alan 1957.16
Shayne, Edith 1926.30
Shea Amusement Company 1904.07
Shea, Al 1957.18, 1965.21
Shea, Frank 1909.14
Shea, Frank W. 1905.41, 1906.47, 1910.11
Shea, Helen 1920.18
Shea, Hertha 1958.03
Shea, Jeanne 1968.17
Shea, Jere 1994.05
Shea, Jimmy 1935.18
Shea, John F. 1946.23
Shea, Marie 1924.40, 1931.08
Shea, Norma 1942.35
Shea, Paul 1897.12
Shea, Philip A. 1895.16
Shea, Rev. Michael J. 1946.23
Shea, Tom 1981.27
Shea, W.J. 1881.24
Shean, Al 1903.29, 1908.33, 1912.15, 1915.23, 1922.19, 1923.20, 1926.51, 1930.01, 1932.22
Shean, Albetrt 1894.05
Shear, Claudia 2000.12
Shear, Fred 1888.43
Shear, Sylvia 1926.13
Shearer, Kenneth 1972.21
Shearer, May 1898.28
Shearer, Toni 1972.21
Shearing, Goeffrey 1999.05
Shearing, Jack 1971.01, 1971.03, 1971.13, 1971.18, 1972.07, 1972.12, 1972.25, 1973.02, 1974.05, 1978.22, 1979.32
Shearman, George 1971.14
Shearsly, Miss 1862.02
Sheehan, Bobby 1932.26
Sheehan, D. 1907.54
Sheehan, Deidre 1991.09
Sheehan, Edw. 1907.16
Sheehan, Jack 1926.33, 1927.68, 1928.32, 1930.27, 1931.36, 1936.27
Sheehan, John 1913.03, 1914.05, 1921.17, 1922.32, 1924.22, 1924.32, 1926.39, 1927.41, 1929.03, 1931.04, 1948.28
Sheehan, John J. 1901.26
Sheehan, Joseph 1894.45, 1895.01, 1895.24, 1896.45
Sheehan, Joseph F. 1893.20, 1894.22, 1896.16, 1896.19, 1896.21, 1896.22, 1897.53, 1898.04, 1898.06, 1898.07, 1898.09, 1898.14, 1898.16, 1898.19, 1898.21, 1898.39, 1898.42, 1898.49, 1898.52, 1898.57, 1898.62, 1898.65, 1898.71, 1898.74, 1898.76, 1899.05, 1899.14, 1899.16, 1900.13
Sheehan, Jr., John 1932.21
Sheehan, Lawrence 1895.34, 1900.47
Sheehan, Lawrence J. 1895.27, 1897.30
Sheehan, Margaret 1959.05
Sheehan, Michael 1980.23
Sheehan, William T. 1915.03
Sheehy, Eleanor 1986.06
Sheekman, Arthur 1930.32, 1941.03
Sheeley, Inez 1930.24
Sheen, Frank 1908.11
Sheens, Nathan 1999.02
Sheer, Anita 1970.08
Sheer, William 1918.07
Sheerin, Doris 1918.32
Sheffer, Charles 1879.37, 1880.09
Sheffer, Charles H. 1903.41
Sheffield, Philip 1912.15, 1915.01
Sheffield, Phillip 1912.15
Sheftel, Messr. 1925.03
Shefter, Bert 1934.03, 1949.09, 1987.02
Sheil, Mark Jude 1964.17, 1965.02
Sheila-Barbara-Dinah Productions 1978.06
Shein, K. 1924.48
Sheinkman, Mordecai 1948.17
Sheintsiss, Oleg 1990.01
Shelberg, Verda 1916.20
Shelby, Jeanne 1941.04, 1943.03, 1944.02, 1947.14
Shelby, Laurel 1950.02, 1951.15, 1951.23, 1953.01
Shelby, Lillian 1956.04, 1976.08
Shelby, Virginia 1920.13, 1920.40
Shelden, Miss 1866.28
Sheldon, A. 1869.35
Sheldon, A.H. 1870.04, 1872.02, 1872.04, 1872.05, 1872.08, 1872.12, 1872.14, 1872.25, 1872.30, 1872.32, 1872.36, 1872.38, 1872.40, 1872.43, 1876.06, 1876.13, 1876.15, 1876.22, 1876.29, 1877.01
Sheldon, Bab 1903.13
Sheldon, Babette 1905.14
Sheldon, Bert 1948.23
Sheldon, Charles 1945.04
Sheldon, Connie 1945.17
Sheldon, Edith 1926.29, 1928.29, 1930.18
Sheldon, Edward 1927.50, 1948.27
Sheldon, Eleanor 1911.39
Sheldon, Ella 1883.47
Sheldon, Eugene 1899.22
Sheldon, Gene 1942.10, 1944.19
Sheldon, Harriett 1896.31
Sheldon, Harriette 1923.15
Sheldon, Harry 1896.03
Sheldon, Herman 1896.02
Sheldon, Herman A. 1893.31
Sheldon, Lillie 1884.27
Sheldon, Miss 1869.28, 1883.47
Sheldon, Sidney 1943.09, 1944.01, 1944.18, 1944.24, 1957.04, 1959.01
Sheldon, W.P. 1876.36
Sheldrick, Reginald 1910.21
Shelembe, Pumi 1988.02
Shell, Claudia 1983.01
Shelley, Carole 1968.19
Shelley, Frances 1928.45, 1929.51, 1930.21
Shelley, Gladys 1942.11, 1946.06, 1957.10
Shelley, Hazel 1926.11
Shelley, Howard M. 1905.35
Shelley, Joshua 1946.15, 1948.04, 1950.11, 1954.01, 1954.12, 1957.09
Shelley, Julia 1978.22
Shelley, Ken 1977.09
Shelley, P. 1882.69
Shelley, Paul 1945.01
Shelly, Frances 1930.06
Shelly, George 1920.24
Shelly, Mildred 1922.27
Shelly, Norman 1950.08, 1954.13, 1964.18, 1968.31
Shelton, A.H. 1869.43
Shelton, George 1934.18
Shelton, Hall 1947.13
Shelton, James 1934.06, 1934.14, 1938.04, 1939.26, 1950.03, 1954.16, 1955.11
Shelton, Jerry 1943.02
Shelton, R. Byron 1896.46
Shelton, Reid 1954.02, 1954.18, 1956.01, 1963.05, 1964.28, 1965.24, 1969.04, 1977.06
Shelton, Yvonne 1916.24, 1917.03, 1917.26
Shelvey, Matt 1938.03, 1938.16
Shemer, Naomi 1968.04, 1971.14, 1972.17
Shen, Freda Foh 1976.02, 1990.17
Shenar, Reuven 1972.17
Shene, Jacob 1881.13
Shepard, Bill 1932.08
Shepard, Brian 1998.18
Shepard, Burt 1892.50
Shepard, Constance 1926.04
Shepard, Elaine 1940.19
Shepard, Herbert 1939.26
Shepard, Joan 1948.27
Shepard, Karen 1955.04, 1956.02, 1959.24, 1965.35, 1966.11
Shepard, Kiki 1980.14, 1982.17
Shepard, Martin 1929.31, 1932.05
Shepard, Matthew 1999.13
Shepard, R. 1982.17
Shepard, Robert 1963.26
Shepard, Ruth 1963.29, 1964.20
Shepard, Sam 1970.04, 1971.04, 1976.27
Sheperd, Christopher 1990.07
Shepherd, Frank 1891.26, 1892.09
Shepherd, Gwendolyn 1983.04
Shepherd, Jean 1962.02
Shepherd, Joan 1941.12
Shepherd, Josie 1884.46, 1885.68
Shepherd, Leonard 1907.56
Shepherd, Martin 1934.13
Shepherd, Messr. 1841.01
Shepherd, Robert 1896.27
Sheppard and Slipper 1904.09
Sheppard, Billy 1930.24
Sheppard, E. 1876.06
Sheppard, Hazel 1928.10
Sheppard, Jack 1886.53
Sheppard, Jr., John R. 1946.24
Sheppard, Juana 1917.26
Sheppard, Julie 1989.11
Sheppard, Madelyn 1922.13
Sheppard, Martin 1929.08, 1934.35
Sheppard, Morgan 1965.39
Sheppard, Susan 1981.18
Sheppard, William 1929.31
Sheppell, Harry 1907.38
Sher, Gloria 1975.03
Sher, Gloria Hope 1981.15
Sher, Louis K. 1975.03
Sheridan, Amy 1872.21, 1872.22, 1872.24, 1872.26
Sheridan, Edith 1934.06
Sheridan, Eileen 1907.61
Sheridan, Elsie 1895.15
Sheridan, J.F. 1869.14, 1876.29, 1878.05
Sheridan, Jack 1923.25
Sheridan, John 1974.17
Sheridan, John F. 1878.17, 1880.35, 1881.47, 1892.48, 1892.53
Sheridan, Liz 1971.09, 1972.19, 1976.15
Sheridan, Mae 1904.23
Sheridan, May 1889.05, 1903.34
Sheridan, Messr. 1872.40, 1872.43
Sheridan, Millie 1889.05
Sheridan, Noel 1963.30
Sheridan, Otis 1907.10, 1923.14, 1924.12
Sheridan, Phil 1918.01, 1927.67, 1928.36, 1933.20
Sheridan, Phil M. 1918.01, 1920.41
Sheridan, Richard Brinsley 1904.55
Sheridan, W.E. 1865.06, 1875.14
Sheridan, Wayne 1950.10
Sherin, Edwin 1976.08
Sheringham, George 1934.23, 1936.19, 1936.21, 1936.23, 1948.01, 1948.02, 1948.06, 1948.10, 1951.03, 1955.16, 1955.21, 1955.22, 1962.29, 1964.37
Sherlock, Frank 1908.42
Sherlock, John 1925.36
Sherman, Al 1922.34, 1986.06
Sherman, Albert 1984.11, 1984.13, 1988.16
Sherman, Allan 1969.01
Sherman, Bruce 1979.28, 1981.12, 1981.26
Sherman, Carlos 1947.01
Sherman, Cecile 1932.14, 1945.12
Sherman, Charles 1912.10, 1932.17, 1933.27, 1934.42, 1935.04, 1939.22, 1940.23, 1942.34, 1943.05, 1943.16, 1944.29, 1949.01, 1952.20
Sherman, Ethel 1942.26
Sherman, Florentine 1930.18
Sherman, Fred 1905.52, 1937.03, 1937.17
Sherman, Garry 1961.17, 1970.05, 1972.26, 1979.32, 1983.15
Sherman, Gretchen 1933.26
Sherman, Hal 1922.39, 1924.44, 1938.08
Sherman, Harold 1945.17
Sherman, Hiram 1937.08, 1938.09, 1939.28, 1940.20, 1952.20, 1955.03, 1956.09, 1957.15, 1958.06, 1967.16
Sherman, Howard 1937.01
Sherman, Jane 1930.18
Sherman, Jimmy 1938.08, 1948.13, 1982.12
Sherman, L.C. 1925.01, 1925.28
Sherman, Lee 1946.04, 1948.04, 1955.12
Sherman, Loren 1990.17
Sherman, Mimi 1931.08
Sherman, Mr. 1841.01, 1848.03
Sherman, Orville 1952.13
Sherman, Rebecca 1999.15
Sherman, Richard 1986.03
Sherman, Richard M. 1974.05, 1998.11
Sherman, Robert 1986.03
Sherman, Robert B. 1974.05, 1998.11
Sherman, Shirley 1919.03, 1926.06, 1927.64
Shermet, Hazel 1947.21
Sherr, Thelma 1968.03
Sherri, Andre 1918.38, 1920.02
Sherrin, Ned 1977.05
Sherrock, Irene E. 1945.02
Sherwin, Jeannette 1923.26
Sherwin, Manning 1927.27, 1930.06, 1931.13, 1931.36, 1947.15
Sherwin, Mimi 1980.01
Sherwood 1875.18
Sherwood, Agnes 1891.09, 1892.52, 1894.21
Sherwood, Alice G. 1880.41
Sherwood, Alison 1967.07
Sherwood, Belle 1894.19
Sherwood, Bensen 1868.25, 1871.10, 1871.27, 1876.16
Sherwood, Benson 1869.06, 1869.29, 1869.33, 1869.40, 1870.13, 1870.19, 1870.44, 1873.08, 1881.28, 1881.36, 1881.41, 1884.09, 1891.36, 1892.60
Sherwood, Blanche 1893.39, 1900.03, 1900.19, 1900.42, 1909.11, 1910.37
Sherwood, D.J. 1882.16
Sherwood, Dawn 1967.07
Sherwood, Gill 1880.18
Sherwood, Grace 1884.12, 1886.47, 1888.16, 1898.01
Sherwood, Gracie 1880.31, 1890.35
Sherwood, Gregg 1948.28
Sherwood, Harry 1891.21
Sherwood, Helen 1902.30
Sherwood, Henry 1952.08
Sherwood, Holly 1966.12, 1966.16, 1967.07
Sherwood, J.T. 1882.15
Sherwood, Jan 1951.24
Sherwood, Jr., G.P. 1884.57, 1885.05, 1885.14
Sherwood, Kyle 1967.07
Sherwood, Lizzie 1885.28
Sherwood, Lorraine 1926.22, 1927.39
Sherwood, M. 1881.38
Sherwood, Madeleine 1965.06
Sherwood, Mae 1901.17, 1903.28, 1904.50, 1906.29
Sherwood, Maindy 1967.07
Sherwood, Mamie 1889.06
Sherwood, Marion 1908.11
Sherwood, Mary F. 1898.45
Sherwood, May 1897.26, 1898.50, 1900.38
Sherwood, Messr. 1877.15
Sherwood, Miss 1841.01, 1881.03, 1881.07, 1882.60, 1883.16
Sherwood, Mollie 1891.04, 1891.38, 1902.16
Sherwood, Phyllis 1905.26
Sherwood, Ray 1913.05
Sherwood, Robert E. 1922.42, 1924.15, 1949.08, 1963.08, 1983.08
Sherwood, Robin 1967.07
Sherwood, Sadie 1893.07
Sherwood, Walter 1926.20
Sherwood, Wayne 1955.12, 1958.05, 1971.06
Shevelove, Burt 1948.22, 1956.05, 1957.02, 1962.12, 1967.06, 1971.03, 1972.03, 1975.13, 1976.09, 1980.06, 1989.03, 1996.06
Shevtchenko, Messr. 1927.51
Shew, Timothy 1992.04, 1997.12, 1997.19
Shewell, L.R. 1862.04, 1863.06, 1863.07
Shewell, Mrs. L.R. 1863.06
Shibley, Pat 1942.26
Shiebler, Howard A. 1935.18
Shiel, Stella 1925.07, 1925.39
Shields 1857.03

Shields, Arthur 1918.41
Shields, Ben 1899.13
Shields, Bobby 1958.20
Shields, David 1962.15
Shields, Ella 1903.01
Shields, G.H. 1898.02
Shields, George 1875.32, 1927.65, 1933.01, 1934.41
Shields, J.F. 1877.24
Shields, Katie 1886.35
Shields, Miss 1897.41
Shields, Mr. 1863.10
Shields, Phyllis 1903.09
Shields, Ren 1900.38, 1902.16, 1902.21, 1904.07, 1906.20, 1906.29, 1906.43, 1907.21, 1916.15, 1917.26, 1980.27
Shields, Robert 1926.18, 1981.09
Shields, Ruth 1929.32
Shields, Thomas 1909.26
Shields, Vincent 1939.17
Shiers, Paul 1943.04, 1945.17
Shigo, Daniel 1993.12, 1994.09
Shikeru, Rimeru 1934.16
Shilkret, Nathaniel 1952.04
Shillen, Joe 1942.19, 1944.20
Shilling, Billie 1921.09
Shilton, Dolly 1903.18
Shima 1968.04
Shimberg, Hinks 1987.19, 1989.09
Shimerman, Armin 1979.12
Shimizu, Dana 1965.20, 1967.10, 1968.16, 1970.21
Shimizu, Keenan 1965.20, 1967.10
Shimizu, Sachi 1970.21
Shimkin, Arthur 1961.11
Shimoda, Yuki 1976.02
Shimono, Sab 1965.20, 1966.10, 1970.21, 1974.12, 1976.02
Shimono, Sabyd 1983.10
Shindel, Lawrence 1942.09
Shine, David 1981.27
Shine, Giles 1900.36, 1901.15
Shine, John L. 1911.09, 1912.04
Shine, Thad. 1886.02
Shine, Thaddeus 1889.03, 1889.14, 1889.48, 1890.06, 1891.06, 1891.07, 1891.28
Shiner, David 1993.01, 1995.16, 1998.17, 2000.18
Shinnal, Vern 1965.15
Shion, Yu 1989.21
Shipley, John 1980.28
Shipman, Dee 1983.03
Shipman, Helen 1916.03, 1918.22, 1919.43, 1922.36, 1923.03, 1923.17, 1923.41, 1924.07, 1925.19, 1927.31
Shipman, Jack 1937.11
Shipman, Miss 1923.03
Shipman, Rlaph 1912.14
Shipman, Samuel 1919.39, 1947.13
Shipp, J.A. 1899.33, 1903.08, 1904.26, 1908.08, 1909.27, 1930.10, 1930.16
Shipp, Jesse 1900.46
Shipp, Jesse A. 1896.46, 1898.22, 1903.08, 1904.26, 1906.14
Shire, David 1968.13, 1970.13, 1983.09, 1983.19, 1990.09, 1995.11, 1996.08, 1999.15
Shirk, Jack 1977.09
Shirley, Bill 1950.14
Shirley, Florence 1912.14, 1918.03, 1919.27
Shirley, Lillian 1896.38
Shirley, Madeleine 1893.39
Shirley, Mina 1896.38
Shirley, W.R. 1904.29
Shirreff, Jane 1838.01
Shirvis, Barbara 1990.02, 1990.07, 1991.08, 1995.10, 1996.11, 1997.02
Shiryayev, Vladimir 1990.01
Shishkina, Mme. 1922.37
Shkolnik, Juda Asher 1972.17
Shlenker, Sidney 1981.25, 1982.02, 1982.03, 1982.18, 1986.20
Shnazer, Rudolf 1913.36
Shober, Charles E. 1894.14
Shocket, Steve 1987.04
Shoctor, Joseph H. 1967.14, 1969.08
Shoemaker, Ann 1965.14
Shoham, Yonnith 1972.17
Shook, Benjamin L. 1903.08
Shopkorn, Stanley 1999.24
Shore, Allen M. 1986.11, 1987.12, 1992.06
Shore, Howard 1979.19
Shore, Lois 1925.20, 1926.17, 1927.23
Shore, Sharon 1959.11
Shore, Viola Brothers 1934.06, 1934.40, 1936.12
Shorenstein, Carole J. 1979.02, 1981.10, 1981.13, 1984.07
Shores, Byron 1938.14, 1939.27
Shorr, Yisroll 1967.03
Short, Bobby 1956.05, 1980.10
Short, Florence 1914.24
Short, Frank Lea 1918.36
Short, Gloria 1949.06
Short, Harry 1903.06, 1903.29, 1904.19, 1906.23, 1908.20, 1921.08, 1923.38, 1923.47, 1925.04, 1926.22, 1927.48, 1930.21
Short, Hassard 1911.46, 1920.31, 1920.45, 1921.03, 1921.30, 1922.39, 1923.32, 1924.09, 1924.33, 1924.41, 1924.44, 1925.33, 1925.47, 1926.46, 1927.12, 1928.07, 1930.32, 1931.16, 1932.05, 1933.02, 1933.22, 1933.26, 1934.29, 1935.14, 1937.03, 1937.16, 1937.17, 1939.17, 1939.23, 1941.04, 1941.13, 1942.18, 1943.01, 1943.03, 1943.24, 1944.02, 1944.29, 1945.06, 1945.11, 1946.01, 1946.09, 1947.14, 1948.20, 1950.12, 1951.18, 1952.15
Short, John 1985.06
Short, Martin 1993.02, 1998.15
Short, S. 1886.35
Short, Steve 1974.02
Shorter, Carl 1935.01
Shostakovich, Dimitri 1943.11
Shotter, Billie 1925.50
Shoukhaeff, Vassily 1925.03
Shoukhaieff, Vera 1929.05
Shoup, Howard 1932.22, 1943.23
Shove, Dawna 1965.23
Shovelton, Geoffrey 1976.12, 1978.14, 1978.15
Show, Ross 1892.21
Showalter, David 1938.10
Showalter, Gordon 1946.05
Showalter, Max 1939.28, 1946.01, 1948.04, 1971.16, 1985.02
Showell, A.W. 1885.69
Showell, Arthur 1884.23
Showles, J.C. 1883.47
Showles, Jacob 1872.40, 1872.43
Shrader, L.A. 1885.52
Shrader, L.C. 1884.57, 1885.67
Shrader, Louis 1887.18, 1887.24, 1887.26, 1887.28, 1888.19, 1888.22, 1888.24, 1888.26, 1891.11, 1892.33, 1892.47
Shrader, Rita 1885.67, 1886.33, 1887.18
Shrednecky, Bessie 1909.24
Shrewsbury, Lillian 1937.11
Shriner, Herb 1948.14
Shriner, William 1953.06
Shroder, Wayne 1998.20
Shubert Costuming Company 1915.32
Shubert Organization, The 1974.01, 1975.05, 1976.17, 1976.35, 1976.36, 1977.16, 1978.05, 1978.09, 1979.08, 1980.26, 1981.04, 1981.29, 1982.19, 1984.02, 1984.08, 1984.09, 1985.02, 1986.06, 1987.06, 1987.12, 1988.02, 1988.09, 1988.17, 1989.03, 1989.29, 1990.12, 1992.01, 1994.05, 1996.07, 2000.12
Shubert Theatrical Company 1906.41
Shubert, Eddie 1928.14, 1929.28
Shubert, Florence 1921.20
Shubert, Franz 1921.31, 1922.21, 1923.14, 1923.15, 1924.12, 1926.05, 1931.07, 1938.17, 1940.05, 1943.12
Shubert, J.J. 1909.20, 1916.14, 1916.26, 1917.08, 1917.14, 1917.15, 1917.23, 1917.30, 1917.31, 1918.02, 1918.05, 1918.12, 1918.20, 1918.35, 1918.42, 1919.03, 1919.05, 1919.16, 1919.19, 1919.30, 1920.09, 1920.19, 1920.22, 1920.23, 1920.47, 1921.02, 1921.13, 1921.14, 1921.20, 1921.31, 1921.34, 1921.40, 1922.07, 1922.11, 1922.12, 1922.15, 1922.31, 1922.34, 1922.36, 1923.02, 1923.03, 1923.12, 1923.13, 1923.14, 1923.15, 1923.17, 1923.25, 1923.41, 1924.13, 1924.23, 1924.29, 1924.36, 1924.45, 1925.01, 1925.02, 1925.07, 1925.11, 1925.23, 1925.26, 1925.27, 1925.28, 1925.39, 1925.43, 1926.01, 1926.05, 1926.14, 1926.15, 1926.26, 1926.27, 1926.33, 1926.37, 1927.01, 1927.17, 1927.42, 1928.15, 1928.26, 1928.46, 1930.15, 1930.27, 1943.06, 1943.12, 1945.01
Shubert, John 1933.21, 1934.43
Shubert, Lee 1905.36, 1905.49, 1905.52, 1905.55, 1906.07, 1906.17, 1906.26, 1906.32, 1907.01, 1907.05, 1907.10, 1907.15, 1907.41, 1907.42, 1907.52, 1907.58, 1908.10, 1908.21, 1908.29, 1908.30, 1908.41, 1908.44, 1909.04, 1909.20, 1909.24, 1909.29, 1909.30, 1910.19, 1910.25, 1910.36, 1911.36, 1911.47, 1917.02, 1917.23, 1917.31, 1918.02, 1918.05, 1918.12, 1918.35, 1918.42, 1919.03, 1919.05, 1919.16, 1919.19, 1920.09, 1920.19, 1920.47, 1921.02, 1921.03, 1921.13, 1921.14, 1921.20, 1921.34, 1921.40, 1922.07, 1922.11, 1922.12, 1922.34, 1923.12, 1923.17, 1932.20, 1942.25
Shubert, Messrs. 1904.55, 1906.41, 1906.46, 1907.54, 1908.26, 1910.03, 1910.14, 1910.23, 1910.31, 1911.12, 1911.21, 1911.28, 1911.34, 1911.43, 1912.17, 1912.18, 1912.21, 1912.22, 1912.23, 1912.24, 1912.27, 1912.30, 1912.41, 1912.43, 1912.49, 1913.02, 1913.05, 1913.08, 1913.09, 1913.11, 1913.12, 1913.13, 1913.18, 1913.22, 1913.23, 1913.29, 1913.30, 1913.36, 1914.01, 1914.07, 1914.10, 1914.11, 1914.19, 1914.22, 1914.32, 1915.02, 1915.04, 1915.11, 1915.16, 1915.17, 1915.26, 1915.27, 1915.32, 1916.03, 1916.11, 1916.14, 1916.23, 1916.25, 1916.26, 1917.08, 1917.10, 1917.14, 1917.15, 1917.30, 1918.15, 1918.20, 1919.02, 1919.14, 1919.26, 1919.30, 1920.22, 1920.23, 1921.25, 1921.31, 1922.15, 1922.18, 1922.31, 1922.36, 1922.37, 1922.40, 1923.02, 1923.03, 1923.13, 1923.14, 1923.15, 1923.25, 1923.41, 1924.06, 1924.12, 1924.29, 1924.36, 1924.45, 1925.01, 1925.02, 1925.07, 1925.11, 1925.13, 1925.23, 1925.26, 1925.27, 1925.28, 1925.39, 1925.43, 1926.01, 1926.02, 1926.05, 1926.08, 1926.14, 1926.15, 1926.26, 1926.27, 1926.33, 1926.36, 1926.37, 1927.01, 1927.14, 1927.19, 1927.42, 1927.55, 1927.58, 1927.68, 1928.01, 1928.06, 1928.14, 1928.26, 1928.27, 1928.46, 1928.48, 1929.06, 1929.09, 1929.17, 1929.22, 1929.28, 1929.33, 1929.34, 1929.36, 1929.38, 1929.39, 1929.40, 1929.43, 1929.47, 1929.48, 1930.01, 1930.03, 1930.07, 1930.12, 1930.15, 1930.20, 1930.27, 1930.37, 1930.41, 1930.43, 1931.03, 1931.07, 1931.09, 1931.36, 1932.01, 1932.06, 1932.15, 1933.21, 1934.01, 1934.13, 1934.14, 1934.19, 1934.43, 1935.12, 1936.02, 1936.17, 1936.31, 1937.03, 1937.15, 1937.16, 1937.17, 1938.07, 1938.08, 1938.17, 1939.22, 1939.26, 1940.07, 1940.09, 1941.02, 1941.11, 1942.10, 1942.12, 1942.14, 1942.23, 1942.27, 1943.05, 1943.06, 1943.12, 1944.25, 1944.30, 1947.15, 1948.27
Shubert, Mrs. J.J. 1915.11, 1915.26
Shubert, Sam S. 1900.57, 1902.19, 1902.25, 1903.14, 1903.38, 1903.41, 1904.12, 1904.17, 1904.55, 1905.03, 1905.36, 1905.49, 1905.52, 1905.55, 1906.07, 1906.17, 1906.26, 1906.32, 1907.01, 1907.05, 1907.10, 1907.15, 1907.41, 1907.42, 1907.52, 1907.58, 1908.10, 1908.21, 1908.29, 1908.30, 1908.41, 1908.44, 1909.04, 1909.24, 1909.29, 1909.30, 1910.19, 1910.25, 1910.36, 1911.36, 1911.47
Shubery, Eddie 1925.47
Shuetz, Ferdinand 1896.23
Shuford, Kajuana 1997.20
Shugrue, Martin 1999.06
Shulberg, Richard 1975.18
Shull, Mark 1928.03
Shull, Richard B. 1970.07, 1975.06, 1981.25, 1993.05, 1995.15
Shulman, Abram 1970.17
Shulman, Joe 1953.08
Shulman, Max 1949.02, 1967.16
Shultz, Bertha 1902.14
Shultz, Tony 1978.25
Shuman, Mort 1972.16, 1989.12
Shumlin, Diana 1972.06, 1972.15, 1979.02
Shumlin, Herman 1941.01, 1958.13, 1959.10
Shunk, Harry 1901.22
Shuntit, Messr. 1869.29
Shurack, Irwin 1935.03
Shurr, Buff 1961.10, 1965.19
Shurtleff, Michael 1954.06
Shuster, Alan J. 1997.03
Shuster, Rosie 1979.19
Shusterman, Tamlyn Brooke 1999.14, 2001.08
Shuter, J.G. 1897.03
Shuter, P. 1880.19
Shutta, Ethel 1922.34, 1924.21, 1925.08, 1925.24, 1928.47, 1943.14, 1963.25, 1971.05
Shutts, Kenneth 1926.12
Shy, Gus 1915.22, 1922.03, 1924.02, 1926.04, 1926.34, 1927.41, 1928.29, 1931.04, 1932.16
Sibanda, Seth 1993.04
Sibelius, Jean 1956.11
Sibelle, Billie 1927.16
Siber, Chic 1982.24
Siberna, Mlle. 1894.21
Siberry, Michael 1998.03
Sibert, Mlle. 1887.37
Sibert, Roderick Spencer 1979.03
Sibley, Harper 1983.17
Sibley, Olive 1925.47
Sicangco, Eduardo 1984.10, 1995.07
Siddon, Doddie 1898.59
Siddons, Gladys 1917.19
Siddons, Henry 1796.02
Siders, Irving 1987.07
Sides, Isaac 1937.14
Sidimus, Joysanne 1960.11
Sidle Studio 1915.22
Sidman, Sam 1908.21, 1928.34
Sidney, Carl 1936.01
Sidney, D. Jay 1935.01
Sidney, David 1930.35
Sidney, Fred 1890.41, 1911.35
Sidney, George 1900.08, 1901.23, 1902.02, 1903.09, 1907.40, 1908.12, 1918.07, 1918.24
Sidney, Midge 1930.18
Sidney, P. Jay 1943.10, 1943.24
Sidney, Robert 1936.05, 1938.14, 1942.20, 1946.07, 1946.23, 1949.01, 1950.03, 1976.32
Sidney, Stone 1976.09
Sidney, Suzan 1969.04
Sieber, Christopher 1994.12, 1997.18
Siebert, Emma 1895.13
Siebert, Marianne 1986.03
Sieczynski, Rudolf 1923.27, 1975.22
Siedel, Caroline 1905.49
Siedel, Carolyne 1906.29
Siedel, Harry 1908.28
Siedle Studio 1913.19
Siedle Studios 1924.19
Siedle, C.F. 1896.13, 1896.18, 1896.25, 1897.10, 1898.20
Siedle, Caroline 1895.12, 1897.26, 1897.39, 1897.42, 1897.50, 1898.27, 1898.68, 1899.19, 1900.05, 1900.12, 1900.20, 1900.41, 1901.08, 1902.41, 1904.54, 1905.44, 1906.17, 1906.37, 1906.45, 1907.07, 1907.11
Siedle, Caroline F. 1902.23, 1904.21, 1906.01
Siedle, Catherine 1893.19, 1893.20, 1893.39, 1893.48, 1894.03, 1894.05, 1894.08, 1894.10, 1894.40, 1895.04, 1895.09, 1896.30, 1896.51, 1897.11, 1897.46, 1898.12, 1898.43, 1898.60, 1899.02
Siedle, Catherine F. 1896.45, 1898.13, 1898.48
Siedle, E. 1882.48, 1884.21, 1885.28, 1885.45, 1885.52
Siedle, Edward 1908.16
Siegal, Al 1940.12
Siegel, Alan K. 1975.07
Siegel, Arthur 1952.09, 1956.08, 1957.10, 1962.02, 1968.13
Siegel, Charles E. 1972.23
Siegel, David 1995.05, 2001.09
Siegel, David W. 1949.09
Siegel, Joel 1981.28
Siegel, Marilyn 1957.18
Siegel, Monty 1931.30
Siegel, Niles 1979.16
Sieger, Charles 1922.46, 1926.02
Sieger, Lillie 1903.01
Siegfreid, Harry F. 1905.54
Siegfried, H.F. 1905.17
Siegfried, H.J. 1906.46
Siegfried, Mamie 1883.10
Siegler, Alfred 1919.41

Siegmeister, Elie 1944.32, 1948.18, 1953.11, 1961.26
Siegrist, A. 1878.05, 1893.47
Siegrist, August 1879.12, 1886.16, 1888.01, 1889.47
Siegrist, Blanche 1892.53
Siegrist, Francois 1864.23, 1865.02
Siegrist, Mr. 1887.03
Siegrist, Topsy 1906.29, 1907.41, 1910.01
Siena, Jerold 1976.23, 1976.26, 1976.31, 1984.13, 1986.10, 1987.09
Sienkiewicz, Henry 1900.38
Siepi, Cesare 1962.14, 1979.09
Sierra, Claudette 1998.02
Sierra-Lopez, Carlos 1999.24
Sievers, Harry 1921.34, 1923.12, 1924.47
Sievier, Bruce 1975.22
Siff, Andrew 1962.01
Sigaloff, Eugene 1938.13
Sigel, Sophie 1892.04
Siggins, Jeff 1966.05
Sigler, Jamie-Lynn 2001.09
Sigman, Carl 1947.20, 1967.11, 1968.21, 1973.17
Sigmond, Ainsley 1961.24
Signorelli, Frank 1987.02
Sigrist, Susan 1966.08, 1968.01
Sigyn 1955.12, 1955.27
Sikora, Megan 2001.08
Silber, Charles 1912.14, 1914.06
Silberman, Eric 1946.02
Silberman, Joel 1988.19, 1989.25
Silbernagel, Herr 1883.08
Silbon, Ada 1884.61
Silbon, Cornelius 1884.61
Silbon, Cornelius R. 1884.61
Silbon, Ed 1884.61
Silbon, Edward 1884.61
Silbon, Kate 1884.61
Silbon, Walter 1884.61
Silby, Milton 1910.29
Silesu, Leo 1913.17
Silju, Eigel 1961.12
Silkman, Edward 1946.10
Sill, William Raymond 1906.20
Sillerman, Robert F.X. 2001.05
Silliman, Maureen 1979.12
Sillman, June 1934.06, 1934.40, 1936.12, 1938.04, 1940.23
Sillman, Leonard 1927.27, 1929.02, 1934.06, 1934.40, 1936.12, 1938.04, 1940.23, 1942.34, 1946.22, 1950.01, 1952.09, 1956.08, 1957.10, 1962.02, 1968.13
Sillman, Maureen 1982.08
Sills, Beverly 1956.10, 1957.15, 1958.16, 1964.31, 1965.25, 1977.11, 1978.07, 1989.13
Sills, Douglas 1997.19
Sills, Frank 1927.54
Sills, Paul 1961.17, 1970.16, 1971.08
Silly, Jean 1966.20
Silly, Lea 1870.30, 1870.37, 1870.41
Silo, Jon 1953.07
Silsby, Bertha M. 1894.52
Silton, Edwin 1914.24
Silva, Carlos 1992.13
Silva, Geno 1979.08
Silva, Jose Lopez 1969.11
Silva, Larry J. 1980.27
Silva, Roberto 1988.06, 1992.13
Silva, Rodolfo 1953.16
Silva, Rosemary 1988.06
Silveira, Mary 1931.06
Silver, Abner 1919.08, 1919.18, 1920.18, 1920.47, 1921.19, 1921.34, 1922.15, 1922.23, 1923.12, 1923.18, 1927.60, 1928.23, 1928.24, 1929.26, 1939.14, 1943.20, 1957.10
Silver, Helen 1955.25, 1958.01
Silver, Joe 1959.13, 1965.32, 1988.20
Silver, Johnny 1950.17
Silver, Joseph 1884.12
Silver, Joshua 1982.12
Silver, Ken 1988.20
Silver, Louis 1931.09
Silver, Maxwell 1906.43
Silver, Messr. 1892.12
Silver, Mr. 1868.06
Silver, Stephanie 1974.03
Silver, Susan 1990.01
Silvera, Richard 1949.04, 1955.07
Silverberg, Evan 1996.15, 1997.22
Silverglat, Harry 1976.27
Silverini, Armando 1964.03
Silverman, Al 1916.15
Silverman, Jack H. 1961.07
Silverman, Jon 1986.16
Silverman, Mary 1974.23
Silverman, Stanley 1976.10, 1998.02
Silvermine, A.C. 1881.16
Silvernail, Clarke 1928.41
Silvers, Betty 1918.30
Silvers, Joseph 1884.35, 1884.38
Silvers, Julia 1922.32, 1924.32
Silvers, Louis 1914.16, 1919.02, 1920.03, 1920.28, 1921.18, 1921.34, 1923.19, 1924.33, 1940.10, 1962.17
Silvers, Messr. 1909.13
Silvers, Phil 1939.24, 1947.16, 1951.23, 1960.23, 1972.03
Silvers, Sid 1925.23, 1927.19, 1928.24, 1929.09, 1931.01, 1932.25, 1941.09, 1956.08
Silvers, Ted 1925.23
Silverstein, Shel 1992.06
Silverthorn, Gertie 1889.23
Silvester, John 1869.35
Silvester, Mr. 1855.09
Silvestri, Martin 1978.24, 1982.03
Silvia, Dorothy 1915.30
Silvie, May 1895.10
Silving, Bert 1940.04
Silvler, Abner 1930.29
Siman, Barbara 1985.15
Simmond, Ed. 1881.13
Simmonds 1870.16, 1876.09, 1881.32
Simmonds, J. 1899.37
Simmonds, James 1860.03, 1860.04, 1860.05
Simmonds, Morris 1886.48, 1886.49
Simmonds, Stanley 1946.22, 1950.15, 1955.02, 1956.12, 1959.25, 1961.21, 1962.05, 1965.01, 1965.28, 1967.16, 1968.24, 1969.14, 1974.18, 1978.02
Simmons 1882.38, 1913.33
Simmons, A. 1885.22
Simmons, B.J. 1914.32
Simmons, Bartlett 1925.27, 1927.19, 1928.21, 1929.17, 1929.39, 1931.40, 1934.19
Simmons, Bonnie 1981.01, 1982.19
Simmons, Connie 1968.01
Simmons, Danny 1925.12, 1932.14
Simmons, Daryl 1997.21
Simmons, E. 1870.35
Simmons, Ed 1882.04
Simmons, Ed. 1879.12, 1880.02
Simmons, Edward 1868.14, 1870.17, 1872.16, 1881.06, 1889.34
Simmons, Fannie 1881.13
Simmons, Fanny 1881.02
Simmons, Gene 1982.22
Simmons, Gus 1933.04, 1935.13
Simmons, J.K. 1990.06, 1991.13, 1992.04
Simmons, Jacquie 1932.26
Simmons, James 1860.04
Simmons, Karla 1990.08
Simmons, Kathie 1876.03
Simmons, Kay 1927.58, 1929.28, 1930.20, 1932.01, 1934.13
Simmons, Lew 1900.07, 1900.35, 1900.42, 1900.58
Simmons, Maude 1943.10, 1947.03
Simmons, Michele 1975.09
Simmons, Miss 1865.05
Simmons, Nellie 1903.04
Simmons, Nonie 1935.01
Simmons, Romayne 1919.16
Simmons, Roscoe 1929.52
Simmons, Ruth 1931.08
Simmons, Stanley 1946.01, 1947.07, 1947.17, 1948.31, 1952.20, 1955.11, 1956.06, 1960.09, 1960.11, 1961.09, 1961.12, 1961.13, 1962.07, 1962.13, 1962.15, 1963.04, 1963.06, 1963.18, 1964.17, 1964.19, 1964.20, 1964.46, 1965.03, 1965.18, 1965.20, 1965.24, 1965.38, 1966.07, 1966.14, 1966.31, 1967.07, 1967.17, 1968.17, 1969.07, 1970.11, 1975.13, 1976.09, 1977.07, 1980.16, 1980.26, 1981.16, 1985.01
Simmonson, Selli 1903.41
Simms, Autumn 1932.14
Simms, Bob 1924.31
Simms, Hilda 1963.27
Simms, Lizzie 1880.55, 1884.36, 1885.31
Simms, Lois 1930.24
Simms, Louis 1930.19
Simms, Margaret 1922.44
Simms, Messr. 1834.02
Simms, Mme. 1834.02
Simms, Stephen 1989.17
Simms, Willard 1894.13, 1895.18, 1896.51, 1898.28, 1899.22
Simms, William 1922.44
Simoff, Michael 1990.11
Simom, Robert A. 1926.17
Simon, Alfred 1975.24, 1976.25, 1979.05, 1981.03, 1982.05
Simon, Danny 1955.12, 1956.08
Simon, James L. 1997.03, 2001.03
Simon, Joanna 1978.19
Simon, John 1982.22
Simon, Joseph 1877.12, 1878.09, 1882.29
Simon, Louis 1911.40, 1916.14, 1918.29, 1919.04, 1921.03, 1924.04, 1925.16, 1927.05, 1930.18, 1930.33
Simon, Lucy 1991.05
Simon, Marilyn 1981.17
Simon, Max 1927.34
Simon, Moises 1935.19
Simon, Neil 1955.12, 1956.08, 1962.27, 1966.01, 1968.31, 1979.04, 1982.01, 1986.07, 1993.02, 1998.15
Simon, Paul 1976.32, 1982.22, 1998.02, 1998.11
Simon, Robert 1941.01
Simon, Robert A. 1928.35, 1931.05, 1933.21, 1933.23
Simon, Robert F. 1952.07
Simon, William E. 1992.18
Simonds 1868.05
Simone, Nina 1989.12
Simonin, Vincent 1929.37
Simonoff, Julius 1897.22
Simons, Frank 1894.42
Simons, Joe 1906.02, 1906.42
Simons, Moises 1931.31
Simons, Mr. 1866.02, 1866.28
Simons, Seymour 1920.45, 1921.18, 1922.03, 1999.24
Simons, Seymour B. 1918.32
Simons, Ted 1968.13, 1972.07
Simonson, Eric 1993.04
Simonson, Jules 1919.44
Simonson, Lee 1921.23, 1924.03, 1933.24, 1935.03, 1937.10
Simonson, O. 1893.09
Simonson, S. 1886.34
Simonson, Selle 1901.23
Simonson, Selli 1884.63, 1885.05, 1885.65, 1887.34, 1888.36, 1894.23, 1895.04, 1895.21, 1901.05, 1914.11, 1921.01
Simowitch, M. 1906.19
Simpson 1894.47, 1899.22
Simpson, A. 1834.03
Simpson, Angela 2000.03
Simpson, Bland 1982.04
Simpson, Cheridah 1893.21, 1894.46, 1896.35, 1896.48, 1898.32, 1898.56, 1902.18, 1904.52, 1906.22, 1913.20
Simpson, Clara 1887.11
Simpson, Crawford and Simpson 1897.30, 1897.31
Simpson, Edmund 1823.01, 1834.01, 1848.02
Simpson, Glenn 2000.04
Simpson, Gordon 1946.21, 1950.07
Simpson, Grant 1920.25, 1921.18, 1922.19, 1923.20, 1924.29, 1926.50
Simpson, H.L. 1880.68
Simpson, Harold 1923.35, 1925.42, 1925.50
Simpson, Harry 1908.44
Simpson, Helen 1944.19
Simpson, J.B. 1892.17
Simpson, J.K. 1870.30
Simpson, Marietta 1996.10
Simpson, Miss 1841.01
Simpson, Mr. 1855.11
Simpson, Russell 1912.33
Simpson, Sloan 1957.03
Simpson, Valerie 1976.16, 1976.24
Simpson, William 1893.47, 1924.29, 1924.33
Sims, George R. 1883.52, 1886.02, 1889.54, 1894.38, 1913.33
Sims, Jack 1974.08, 1974.16, 1975.11, 1975.16, 1976.23, 1977.11
Sims, John 1931.32
Sims, Lizzie 1885.40
Sims, Marley 1976.17
Sims, Maurice 1904.30
Sims, Patricia 1946.18
Sims, Shon 1997.02
Sinatra, Ray 1941.13
Sinatra, Raymond 1942.18
Sincere, Jean 1951.10, 1958.02
Sinclair, Ada 1920.12
Sinclair, Arthur 1935.15
Sinclair, Charles 1902.43, 1905.56, 1906.13, 1907.04, 1921.40, 1922.36, 1925.31
Sinclair, Daisy 1893.27
Sinclair, Diane 1939.27, 1940.22, 1950.01
Sinclair, E.T. 1867.18, 1868.06, 1869.26, 1878.19, 1880.02
Sinclair, Edith 1890.44, 1893.17, 1894.26, 1895.20, 1906.41, 1913.14
Sinclair, Eleanor 1917.12, 1918.18
Sinclair, Ethel 1920.08
Sinclair, Eva 1875.39
Sinclair, Frank 1923.36
Sinclair, George 1892.48, 1892.53, 1894.35
Sinclair, H. 1869.46
Sinclair, Harry 1880.36, 1880.64
Sinclair, Horace 1917.14, 1931.44, 1932.10, 1933.24
Sinclair, Hugh 1925.42
Sinclair, Judy 1949.18, 1951.23
Sinclair, Messr. 1869.07
Sinclair, Mildred 1918.07, 1920.04
Sinclair, Robert 1928.24, 1937.04
Sinclair, Vere 1913.36
Sinden, Bert 1905.27
Sinden, Frederick 1955.15
Sine, Estella 1903.18
Singer, Andre 1940.04
Singer, Arthur 1930.27
Singer, David 1978.26
Singer, Dolf 1927.53
Singer, Dolph 1936.07
Singer, H.F. 1898.66
Singer, Lou 1945.07
Singer, Marion 1879.33, 1879.35, 1880.06, 1880.10, 1880.13, 1880.59, 1880.65, 1880.67, 1880.70, 1891.11, 1892.22, 1892.33, 1892.47, 1893.16, 1899.39, 1902.30, 1904.17, 1906.02, 1906.42
Singer, Mort H. 1909.02
Singer, Norman 1969.09, 1969.11, 1970.16, 1971.21, 1974.09
Singer, Reuben 1961.20, 1964.21
Singer, Steven 1974.24
Singer, Susie 1883.37
Singer, William 1917.08
Singh, Prince 1925.37
Singha, Kumara 1927.12
Singhaus, Sam 1983.11
Singleton, C. 1989.02, 1992.03
Singleton, Charles 1975.12
Singleton, Edith 1912.30
Singleton, Harry 1896.04
Singleton, Helen 1912.15
Singleton, J. Lynn 1998.18
Singleton, Kate 1877.07
Singleton, Marty 1990.08
Singleton, Maude 1896.04
Singleton, Miss 1838.01, 1840.02, 1840.03
Singleton, Penny 1926.03, 1932.13, 1932.27
Singleton, W.H. 1877.21, 1879.01
Singlust, Sol 1915.27
Sinisi, Rosaria 1995.13
Sinn, Clarence N. 1907.60
Sinnott, Euna 1932.18
Sinnott, Florence 1906.19
Sinnott, Frank 1926.27
Sinott, Florence 1906.19
Sinott, Spencer 1893.38
Sipson, Mercer H. 1869.23
Sirangello, Mark N. 1996.04
Siraudin 1890.22, 1890.24
Siraudin, Paul 1873.11, 1873.18, 1875.02, 1875.28, 1876.17, 1876.26, 1877.27, 1879.48, 1880.03, 1883.30, 1883.57, 1884.54, 1887.37, 1925.51, 1926.47
Siravo, George 1954.16
Sire, H.B. 1897.24
Sire, Henry B. 1900.42, 1900.49, 1900.56, 1901.29, 1902.06, 1902.10, 1902.37
Sire, Meyer L. 1900.42, 1900.49, 1900.56, 1901.29, 1902.06, 1902.10, 1902.37

Siretta, Dan 1959.25, 1961.18, 1962.20, 1969.17, 1972.11, 1975.24, 1976.25, 1979.05, 1981.03, 1982.05, 1985.04, 1990.14, 1991.09, 2000.14
Siretta, Fred 1968.02
Siri 1953.17
Sirinek, Marylou 1972.04
Sirlin, Jerome 1993.09
Sirmay, Albert 1913.36, 1924.18, 1930.05, 1930.30
Sirola, Joeye 1976.19
Sirola, Joseph 1968.03
Sirron, Henry 1875.10
Sisco, Jim 1960.06
Sisco, Jimmy 1956.08
Sisk, James 1948.19
Sisk, Jimmie 1947.12
Sisk, Jimmy 1942.19, 1944.20
Sissle, Noble 1921.16, 1923.08, 1923.33, 1924.01, 1924.27, 1932.30, 1942.13, 1952.08, 1975.22, 1976.04, 1978.21, 1986.06, 1990.09
Sisson, Kenn 1928.23
Sisson, Leslie Hardesty 1980.14, 1982.17
Sisson, Wesley 1892.57
Sissons, William 1903.37, 1908.15
Sisti, Michelan 1981.18, 1986.16, 1987.16
Sita, Marie 1898.55
Sitgreaves, Charles 1905.52
Sitgreaves, Ida 1885.67
Sitgreaves, Marion 1918.11, 1918.33
Sithole, Cosmas 1988.02
Sitwell, Della 1885.15
Sivry, Mlle. 1875.07
Sivuca 1969.15
Six, Henry 1902.29
Six, Jack 1960.04
Sizemore, Art 1930.29
Sizemore, Arthur 1930.29
Sjoblom, Ulla 1966.19
Sjovik, Amund 1922.32
Sjusin, G. 1932.09
Skaats, W. 1864.18
Skae, Justis 1972.11
Skaff, George 1960.12
Skala, Lilia 1950.15, 1965.04
Skavlan, William 1925.37
Skeer, Bessie 1906.29
Skelley, Hal 1918.26, 1920.21, 1922.33, 1923.45
Skelly, Hal 1920.04, 1924.47, 1933.03
Skelton, Geoffrey 1965.39, 1967.01
Skelton, James 1933.27
Skelton, Thomas 1964.25, 1969.07, 1969.17, 1970.05, 1970.14, 1970.21, 1972.02, 1972.26, 1973.12, 1974.25, 1975.03, 1975.22, 1976.21, 1977.07, 1979.17, 1979.22, 1979.31, 1980.19, 1980.26, 1981.13, 1981.16, 1981.26, 1982.05, 1982.14, 1983.05, 1983.08, 1983.10, 1983.20, 1985.08
Skerrett, Emma 1886.49
Skerrett, George 1851.04
Skerrett, Mr. 1850.01
Skerrett, Mrs. 1863.06
Skerrett, Mrs. George 1851.04, 1861.03
Skerritt, Charles E. 1893.05
Skidder, Messr. 1861.03
Skidmore, Karen 1987.01
Skidmore, Katherine 1930.27
Skidmore, Will 1919.15, 1976.04
Skidmore, Will E. 1920.33
Skillman, Louise 1898.28, 1913.07
Skina, Eve 1980.27
Skiner, Cornelia Otis 1952.04
Skinner, Diana 1981.21
Skinner, Emily 1994.12, 1995.19, 1996.15, 1997.17, 2000.01, 2000.15
Skinner, Emily Scott 1997.09
Skinner, Frank 1929.37
Skinner, Harold 1920.34
Skinner, Jolyon 1995.01
Skinner, Laurie Dawn 1979.15
Skinner, Mildred 1928.09
Skinner, Otis 1881.15, 1923.43
Skinner, Otis A. 1879.42
Skinner, Ralph M. 1902.02, 1905.53, 1906.20, 1907.21, 1909.14
Skinner, Randy 1980.20, 1993.05, 1996.04, 1999.17, 2001.08
Skinner, Roland 1947.03
Skinner, Steve 1996.09
Skins, Joe 1945.06
Skipper, Bill 1942.18
Skipper, Michael 1999.08
Skipper, Mike 1997.03
Skipper, William 1946.20, 1955.11
Skiptaris, Loukas 1968.30
Skipworth, Alison 1895.43, 1905.41, 1928.21, 1928.46
Skitch, Jeffrey 1955.18, 1955.20, 1955.22, 1962.25, 1962.29, 1962.30, 1962.31, 1964.36, 1964.37, 1964.38
Sklar, George 1935.03
Sklar, Sidney 1937.14
Skoboloff, Mikhail 1925.46
Skodak, Edna 1927.53
Skolovsky, Zadel 1945.14
Skolsky, Sidney 1929.26
Skowron, Jeff 1998.05
Skulnick, Menasha 1965.32, 1989.05
Skweyiya, Kipizane 1988.02
Skye, Robin 1998.21
Skylar, Joy 1951.23
Skylar, Sammy 1979.14
Skylight Productions 1999.14
Slack, Edith 1922.41
Slack, Jenell 1997.22
Slade, Samuel I. 1896.41
Slagle, A. Russell 1942.17
Slagle, Charles 1942.19, 1946.14
Slagle, Charlie 1940.16
Slagle, Kathleen 1938.18
Slaiman, Marjorie 1978.06, 1978.12
Slama, Mark 1995.02
Slate, Barbara 1953.16
Slate, Henry 1930.42, 1931.01, 1943.23, 1949.04, 1955.07
Slate, Jack 1930.42, 1931.01, 1943.23
Slate, Syd 1930.42, 1931.01
Slater, Christian 1980.16, 1981.12, 1983.01
Slater, Frank 1919.41
Slater, Glenn 2001.01
Slater, P.W. 1877.04
Slattery, J.L. 1883.64
Slattery, John 1929.09
Slattery, May 1926.16
Slattery, Mr. 1883.67
Slattery, Robert 1915.18
Slaughter, Walter 1884.60, 1890.50, 1896.01, 1896.05, 1897.37, 1898.51, 1904.04
Slavin, Bob 1881.55, 1883.03, 1883.66
Slavin, Harry 1898.38
Slavin, John 1896.18, 1896.30, 1897.26, 1897.39, 1898.38, 1901.21, 1904.36, 1906.44, 1907.59, 1910.10, 1911.22, 1912.10, 1916.24, 1919.32
Slavin, John C. 1893.17, 1894.26, 1896.41, 1898.20, 1898.77, 1899.26, 1899.34
Slavin, Mildred 1955.27, 1957.06
Slavin, Millie 1968.31
Slavina, Norma 1943.11
Slayter, Joseph 1886.41
Slayter, Marcus 1932.12
Slaytor, Joseph 1887.03, 1887.27, 1889.21, 1905.39
Slear, Ralph 1932.06
Sleck, William 1906.37
Sledge, Eddie 1948.32
Sleep, A. 1886.59
Slemons, Frederica 1946.01
Slevin, John 1895.42
Slezak, Walter 1930.43, 1932.22, 1935.17, 1938.05, 1954.15
Slias, Mme. 1892.10
Slias, Mons. 1892.10
Slicer, Thomas R. 1913.03
Slick, Grace 1982.22
Slingsby, Chris 1996.01, 1996.12, 1998.09
Sloan 1891.02
Sloan, Blanding 1922.32
Sloan, Estelle 1946.23
Sloan, George 1873.26
Sloan, H. 1870.20, 1872.19
Sloan, Margaret 1891.02
Sloan, Mary Jane 1948.27
Sloan, Mike 1957.17
Sloan, Mimi 1968.06
Sloan, W.H. 1893.17
Sloan, Will H. 1894.26, 1901.07, 1902.27
Sloan, William 1897.39
Sloan, William H. 1898.56
Sloane, A. Baldwin 1895.38, 1896.44, 1897.34, 1897.45, 1898.58, 1898.69, 1898.72, 1899.12, 1899.38, 1900.07, 1900.15, 1900.42, 1900.49, 1900.55, 1900.56, 1901.12, 1901.21, 1901.25, 1901.29, 1902.06, 1902.10, 1902.37, 1903.03, 1903.18, 1903.36, 1903.41, 1904.05, 1904.13, 1904.44, 1904.55, 1905.56, 1906.04, 1906.22, 1906.29, 1907.03, 1907.18, 1908.41, 1910.04, 1910.13, 1910.16, 1911.05, 1911.26, 1911.35, 1912.07, 1912.25, 1912.44, 1912.45, 1913.07, 1918.32, 1919.18, 1920.28, 1926.50
Sloane, Baldwin 1925.04
Sloane, Everett 1960.07
Sloane, Florrie 1911.10
Sloane, Frank 1899.38, 1900.07
Sloane, Grenna 1933.25
Sloane, Mae Anwerda 1901.12, 1901.21, 1901.29, 1902.06
Sloane, Michael 1947.04
Sloane, Mike 1951.23, 1953.11
Sloane, Robert 1935.17
Sloane, Robin 1948.18
Sloane, W.H. 1888.03, 1897.21
Sloane, Will H. 1903.17
Sloane, William 1898.56
Slocum, John 1875.37
Slocum, John B. 1888.03
Slocum, John P. 1895.17, 1908.16, 1919.11
Sloden, Lewis 1919.19, 1919.41
Sloman, John 1979.24, 1985.15, 1996.08, 1998.20, 2000.11
Sloman, P.K. 1989.23
Slow, A. 1879.28
Slowman, Felix 1869.02
Slutsker, Peter 1983.02, 1985.08
Slyde, Jimmy 1989.02
Smagula, Jimmy 2000.15
Small, Abraham 1923.23
Small, Allan 1945.20, 1946.08, 1946.23, 1951.13
Small, Charles 1875.05
Small, D. 1976.16
Small, Danny 1924.37
Small, E. 1872.10
Small, Jack 1944.15
Small, Larry 1971.19, 1982.18
Small, Margot 1954.19
Small, Mary 1943.07, 1974.04, 1982.01
Small, Mary E. 1965.20
Small, Marya 1972.12
Small, Master 1865.09
Small, Neva 1963.15, 1964.35, 1967.14, 1971.09, 1976.15
Small, Oggie 1955.06, 1955.09
Small, Paul 1943.13, 1944.22
Smalle, Ed 1920.24
Smallens, Alexander 1934.05, 1935.13, 1942.03, 1953.04
Smalley, Beth 1915.24
Smalley, Phillip 1907.27
Smalls, Alexander 1983.04
Smalls, Charlie 1975.01, 1981.16, 1984.09, 1993.03
Smallwood, Mildred 1921.26
Smallwood, Peter 1932.14
Smallwood, Polly 1875.23
Smalto, Francesco 1998.12
Smaltz, Mark Kenneth 1990.14
Smart, Andy 2001.04
Smart, Dick 1947.01, 1949.02
Smart, Gino 1958.05, 1958.11, 1959.07, 1959.08, 1959.17
Smart, Jack 1936.12
Smart, Jean 1981.04
Smart, John M. 1861.04
Smart, Mr. 1857.02
Smart, Neila 1882.77
Smart, Richard 1940.03
Smart, Walter 1899.31
Smartt, Michael V. 1983.04
Smaxie 1964.21
Smiggins, Annie 1870.35
Smiler, Josephine 1972.20
Smiler, Roberta 1972.20
Smiles, Sarah 1882.80
Smiley, Donnie 1965.23
Smiley, F.A. 1897.29
Smiley, Frank 1900.54, 1903.29, 1904.19
Smiley, J.H. 1889.02
Smiley, J.W. 1892.17
Smiley, John H. 1905.37
Smiley, John W. 1892.08
Smiley, Joseph 1889.02, 1898.73, 1927.29
Smiley, Joseph W. 1894.42
Smiley, Robert W. 1905.51
Smiley, W.C. 1898.66
Smink, Peter 1964.39
Smirnova, Mme. 1922.37
Smirnova, Olga 1926.15
Smirnovia, Tatiana 1923.15
Smit, Derrick 1998.14
Smith 1870.04
Smith Bessie 1982.12
Smith Manufacturing Company 1886.40
Smith, A. 1872.06, 1901.17, 1921.41
Smith, Adele 1927.46, 1928.47, 1931.08
Smith, Adolph 1992.06
Smith, Albert 1862.02
Smith, Alexis 1971.05, 1978.25
Smith, Alice 1896.14
Smith, Allie 1929.09
Smith, Alma 1924.37, 1930.29
Smith, Andrew 1976.28, 1978.23
Smith, Anna 1950.07
Smith, Annie 1881.52
Smith, Art 1936.28
Smith, Augustus 1899.30
Smith, B.D. 1897.33
Smith, Barbara Lee 1953.08
Smith, Barney 1903.09
Smith, Barry 1970.06
Smith, Basil 1919.38, 1920.34, 1921.27
Smith, Ben 1955.14, 1986.06
Smith, Bernard 1928.06
Smith, Bert 1909.31
Smith, Bessie 1929.21, 1975.20
Smith, Betty 1951.14
Smith, Betty Jane 1936.05, 1941.09
Smith, Bill 1954.04, 1967.11, 1980.12
Smith, Billy 1922.30
Smith, Bruce 1892.14, 1901.27, 1903.04, 1903.39, 1904.47, 1905.48, 1908.06, 1909.08, 1913.33
Smith, Buddy 1993.06
Smith, Burt 1901.22
Smith, C.E. 1933.21, 1997.21, 2000.15
Smith, C.H. 1892.04
Smith, Calvin 1990.20, 1991.13
Smith, Carl 1982.22, 1984.10
Smith, Carl W. 1973.14, 1975.12, 1976.24
Smith, Carolyn 1990.15
Smith, Carrie 1904.38, 1989.02
Smith, Charles 1957.11, 1999.15
Smith, Charles H. 1904.06, 1925.12
Smith, Charles Ruthven 1900.28
Smith, Charlotte 1910.06
Smith, Charlotte Milbourne 1905.38
Smith, Chris 1900.46, 1906.27, 1908.08, 1910.18, 1911.20, 1912.08, 1920.10, 1920.33, 1921.27, 1927.30, 1980.10, 1980.27
Smith, Christian 1980.21, 1981.20, 1985.09, 1985.10, 1986.10, 1987.08, 1987.11, 1993.12, 1993.13, 1995.10, 1996.13, 1997.02
Smith, Clara Reynolds 1902.17
Smith, Clay 1912.29
Smith, Clifford 1928.06, 1928.27
Smith, Cyrena 1934.40
Smith, Cyril 1914.30, 1941.07
Smith, D. 1876.13
Smith, David 1876.22, 1962.09, 1962.10, 1962.11, 1962.19, 1962.21, 1963.15, 1963.22, 1963.23, 1963.24, 1964.09, 1964.10, 1964.12, 1964.14, 1964.30, 1964.31, 1965.04, 1965.07, 1965.10, 1965.11, 1965.25, 1965.27, 1966.02, 1966.04, 1966.11, 1966.17
Smith, David Rae 1974.16, 1975.16, 1976.23, 1977.11, 1978.07, 1978.20, 1979.21, 1980.03, 1980.04, 1980.21, 1980.25, 1981.20, 1981.21, 1985.09, 1986.04, 1986.14, 1987.08, 1987.10, 1988.16, 1989.13, 1990.02, 1990.08, 1991.12, 1993.12
Smith, David W. 1882.77
Smith, Derek 2000.10
Smith, Dexter 1879.35, 1880.42, 1880.59
Smith, Dolores 1954.15
Smith, Don 1962.15, 1979.28
Smith, Dorothy Faye 1922.28
Smith, Doug 1995.01
Smith, Dwight 1895.35
Smith, E. 1899.21
Smith, E.M. 1879.56, 1880.04
Smith, Eckford 1894.15
Smith, Ed 1936.22
Smith, Eddy 1949.17
Smith, Eddy (Texas) 1954.08

Smith, Edgar 1887.33, 1887.50, 1888.35, 1889.04, 1889.23, 1889.40, 1890.01, 1890.11, 1890.19, 1890.24, 1890.39, 1891.03, 1891.09, 1891.12, 1891.17, 1891.21, 1891.22, 1892.15, 1893.21, 1894.22, 1894.48, 1895.07, 1895.18, 1896.48, 1897.48, 1897.55, 1898.17, 1898.50, 1898.63, 1898.72, 1898.77, 1899.10, 1899.17, 1899.22, 1899.30, 1899.37, 1900.38, 1900.54, 1901.17, 1902.29, 1903.03, 1903.28, 1904.04, 1904.13, 1904.39, 1904.41, 1904.44, 1906.01, 1906.48, 1907.41, 1907.44, 1908.15, 1908.21, 1908.44, 1909.30, 1910.13, 1910.19, 1910.25, 1911.12, 1911.17, 1911.32, 1911.34, 1912.07, 1912.25, 1912.44, 1912.45, 1913.07, 1913.23, 1913.30, 1915.04, 1915.16, 1915.17, 1915.27, 1916.03, 1916.09, 1916.14, 1917.14, 1917.26, 1918.42, 1919.16, 1919.19, 1919.26, 1921.20, 1922.18, 1923.33, 1926.50, 1929.28, 1929.32, 1930.37
Smith, Edith 1880.06
Smith, Edith Milbourne 1905.38
Smith, Edward 1901.02, 1973.10
Smith, Edward A. 1909.25
Smith, Edwin 1938.09
Smith, Effie 1894.27
Smith, Eleanor 1927.31
Smith, Elihu Hubbard 1796.03
Smith, Ellie 1971.09
Smith, Elwood 1946.08, 1952.06, 1955.09
Smith, Ernest Allen 1980.11
Smith, Eugene 1949.04, 1969.15
Smith, Evelyn 1907.51
Smith, Faye Elizabeth 1948.25
Smith, Flora Lee 1873.26
Smith, Florence 1905.18
Smith, Floyd 1946.21, 1986.03
Smith, Frances 1930.10, 1935.01
Smith, Francesca 1967.16
Smith, Frank 1885.65
Smith, Frank H. 1880.01
Smith, Frankei 1908.33
Smith, Franklin J. 1900.35
Smith, Fritzie 1914.30
Smith, G.W. 1851.02
Smith, Garnett 1969.04
Smith, Geddeth 1982.24
Smith, George 1892.38, 1893.23, 1929.39
Smith, George John 1962.21
Smith, George P. 1900.50, 1904.04, 1905.13
Smith, George Totten 1899.36, 1901.23, 1902.23, 1903.17, 1903.39, 1904.14, 1904.41, 1905.05, 1905.31, 1906.28, 1910.29
Smith, Gerald Oliver 1924.43, 1926.36, 1933.01
Smith, Gladys Milbourne 1905.38
Smith, Gloria 1948.20, 1949.15, 1951.23, 1953.17, 1954.02, 1955.11
Smith, Gordon 1930.02, 1932.20, 1996.04
Smith, Grace 1931.31
Smith, Greg 1983.17, 1990.15
Smith, H. 1908.04
Smith, H. Jess 1917.27
Smith, H.A. 1906.36
Smith, H.F. 1888.30
Smith, H.J. 1898.66
Smith, Hank 1930.29
Smith, Hannibal 1884.22
Smith, Harry 1903.16, 1913.08, 1919.41, 1927.38, 1934.40, 1936.12
Smith, Harry A. 1882.44
Smith, Harry B. 1886.39, 1887.47, 1888.26, 1888.39, 1889.22, 1890.28, 1891.13, 1891.29, 1892.20, 1892.29, 1892.51, 1892.52, 1893.18, 1893.19, 1893.48, 1894.40, 1895.01, 1895.12, 1895.24, 1895.33, 1896.02, 1896.08, 1896.25, 1896.28, 1896.45, 1897.13, 1897.14, 1897.18, 1897.36, 1897.42, 1897.50, 1898.04, 1898.16, 1898.23, 1898.50, 1898.54, 1898.60, 1899.06, 1899.17, 1899.25, 1899.28, 1899.30, 1899.34, 1899.38, 1900.20, 1900.25, 1900.31, 1900.32, 1900.33, 1900.34, 1900.41, 1900.50, 1901.08, 1901.09, 1901.13, 1901.16, 1901.21, 1901.25, 1902.04, 1902.16, 1902.28, 1902.43, 1903.06, 1903.34, 1903.37, 1903.41, 1904.30, 1904.49, 1904.57, 1905.29, 1905.40, 1905.48, 1905.50, 1906.18, 1906.37, 1906.45, 1907.11, 1907.24, 1908.04, 1908.07, 1908.10, 1908.19, 1908.34, 1908.35, 1908.39, 1909.13, 1909.25, 1909.28, 1910.17, 1910.18, 1910.27, 1910.34, 1910.37, 1911.03, 1911.13, 1911.23, 1911.27, 1911.36, 1911.37, 1911.38, 1911.47, 1912.01, 1912.07, 1912.15, 1912.19, 1912.26, 1912.38, 1913.14, 1913.20, 1913.24, 1913.25, 1913.29, 1914.04, 1914.18, 1914.25, 1914.26, 1914.30, 1914.31, 1915.01, 1915.05, 1915.07, 1915.08, 1915.22, 1915.30, 1915.31, 1916.01, 1916.08, 1917.02, 1917.10, 1917.19, 1917.26, 1918.32, 1918.34, 1919.14, 1920.09, 1920.15, 1922.15, 1922.40, 1923.03, 1923.22, 1925.02, 1925.06, 1925.39, 1926.03, 1926.26, 1926.27, 1927.04, 1927.14, 1927.17, 1927.43, 1927.55, 1928.15, 1928.26, 1928.48, 1929.34, 1929.40, 1929.43, 1930.12, 1930.15, 1932.02, 1932.06, 1944.25, 1946.18, 1947.04, 1975.22, 1975.24, 1980.27
Smith, Harry W. 1912.33
Smith, Haydon 1965.28, 1967.02
Smith, Hazel 1995.04
Smith, Helen 1892.04, 1894.06, 1895.38, 1995.01
Smith, Henderson 1896.49
Smith, Henry 1913.13, 1915.06, 1915.10
Smith, Henry Clapp 1934.19
Smith, Henry P. 1888.05
Smith, Herman 1917.16
Smith, Hineawe 1972.20
Smith, Howard 1931.31
Smith, Howard J. 1967.04
Smith, Howlett 1975.20
Smith, Hubbard 1894.22
Smith, Hubbard T. 1894.29
Smith, Huey P. 1992.06
Smith, Ida 1883.42
Smith, Ione 1940.12
Smith, J. 1881.13, 1881.18, 1898.60
Smith, J. Marshall 1930.05
Smith, J.A. 1857.02
Smith, J.B. 1879.29
Smith, J.C. 1881.40
Smith, J.P. 1880.38, 1888.45
Smith, J.R. 1841.01, 1856.01
Smith, J.T. 1875.40
Smith, James A. 1907.04
Smith, James P. 1898.61
Smith, Jay 1974.17
Smith, Jeanine 1948.30
Smith, Jeffrey 1966.03, 1982.20, 1989.14
Smith, Jennifer 1985.08, 1990.06, 1995.15, 1998.05, 2001.05
Smith, Jimmy 1976.29
Smith, Jo Jo 1964.35, 1966.30, 1979.15
Smith, Joe 1912.26, 1918.24, 1919.30, 1921.20, 1926.23, 1927.48, 1936.07, 1939.16, 1942.16, 1943.16
Smith, Joe C. 1919.07
Smith, John 1851.04, 1961.09, 1964.12, 1964.19
Smith, John P. 1879.64
Smith, Jonathan 1999.24
Smith, Joseph 1899.33, 1900.07, 1904.38, 1905.23, 1911.34, 1913.28
Smith, Joseph C. 1902.15, 1902.44, 1903.27, 1903.29, 1903.36, 1904.11, 1904.21, 1904.47, 1906.04, 1907.12, 1907.24, 1907.26, 1908.15, 1908.42, 1910.22, 1911.17, 1911.43, 1912.02, 1913.14, 1914.27
Smith, Jr., Augustus 1947.03
Smith, Jr., Guy 1935.16
Smith, Jr., Jerome 1990.15
Smith, Jr., Len 1946.19
Smith, Jr., Sol 1867.22, 1867.23, 1867.26, 1867.27, 1867.29, 1867.31, 1868.23, 1869.08
Smith, Kate 1926.29, 1930.11
Smith, Katherine J. 1993.03
Smith, Kathleen 1990.08
Smith, Kenneth 1960.02
Smith, Kevn 1946.10
Smith, Kirby 1953.16, 1959.24, 1963.25
Smith, Larry 1881.30
Smith, Lee Orean 1906.40, 1911.40
Smith, Leila 1906.36
Smith, Leo Orean 1908.02
Smith, LeRoy 1929.23
Smith, Lillian 1922.05
Smith, Lizzie 1906.24
Smith, Loring 1949.17, 1952.07, 1961.27
Smith, Lottie 1910.06
Smith, Lottie Milbourne 1905.38
Smith, M.C. 1896.20
Smith, M.V.L. 1907.26
Smith, Mabelle 1904.09
Smith, Madeline 1921.25
Smith, Madison 1903.07, 1903.37, 1904.16, 1911.36, 1914.07
Smith, Maggie 1956.08
Smith, Malcolm 1965.26
Smith, Marian 1947.22
Smith, Marjorie 1956.04
Smith, Mark 1857.08, 1866.21, 1866.24, 1866.34, 1867.10, 1868.03, 1872.09, 1880.35, 1880.55, 1882.31, 1882.33, 1882.36, 1882.37, 1882.40, 1884.51, 1885.14, 1885.28, 1885.52, 1885.67, 1887.33, 1887.50, 1888.20, 1889.16, 1890.14, 1890.15, 1891.38, 1893.17, 1893.32, 1894.07, 1894.23, 1902.03, 1902.31, 1906.27, 1914.17, 1915.20, 1922.01, 1924.02, 1927.65, 1938.11
Smith, Mark Curtis 1986.03
Smith, Mark S. 1900.35
Smith, Marshall 1930.31
Smith, Mary 1903.37, 1913.06
Smith, Matthew 1929.27, 1941.03
Smith, May 1880.59, 1880.65, 1917.16
Smith, Merritt 1940.01, 1946.08, 1967.02
Smith, Mesdame 1852.01
Smith, Messr. 1750.01, 1856.02, 1867.10, 1868.13, 1868.15, 1876.34
Smith, Michael 1899.13, 1962.27, 2000.04
Smith, Mildred 1945.07, 1946.24
Smith, Miss 1841.01, 1862.02, 1868.04, 1869.08, 1870.02, 1877.39, 1889.31
Smith, Mollie 1980.26
Smith, Mons. 1879.50
Smith, Mr. 1836.01, 1841.01, 1854.07, 1856.03, 1864.02, 1867.27, 1869.26, 1869.28, 1898.29, 1909.07
Smith, Mrs. M. 1868.01
Smith, Mrs. Mark 1862.05, 1866.01, 1866.05
Smith, Mrs. Sol 1877.28, 1880.37, 1883.40, 1892.19
Smith, Mrs. W.H. 1857.01
Smith, Muriel 1943.24, 1945.06, 1946.09, 1947.21, 1956.03, 1956.06
Smith, Myra 1887.43, 1900.38
Smith, N. 1867.18
Smith, Nino 1934.02
Smith, Norris 1901.20
Smith, Norwood 1948.20, 1971.02
Smith, Oliver 1919.05, 1942.31, 1944.17, 1944.28, 1944.33, 1945.20, 1946.24, 1947.07, 1947.16, 1948.08, 1949.01, 1949.08, 1949.18, 1950.10, 1950.19, 1951.24, 1952.01, 1953.11, 1953.12, 1954.07, 1954.12, 1956.01, 1956.02, 1956.15, 1957.03, 1957.11, 1957.12, 1957.16, 1958.08, 1958.19, 1959.03, 1959.04, 1959.11, 1959.22, 1959.24, 1960.08, 1960.20, 1960.21, 1961.01, 1961.18, 1961.27, 1962.15, 1962.17, 1963.04, 1963.26, 1963.29, 1964.01, 1964.17, 1964.20, 1964.33, 1964.40, 1964.46, 1965.01, 1965.02, 1965.31, 1966.14, 1966.29, 1967.05, 1967.07, 1967.15, 1967.16, 1967.17, 1968.02, 1968.17, 1968.18, 1969.05, 1969.07, 1969.14, 1970.21, 1972.06, 1972.15, 1973.02, 1973.12, 1975.21, 1976.05, 1978.04, 1978.19, 1979.09, 1979.20, 1980.02, 1981.19, 1988.18, 1989.03, 1995.13
Smith, Orilla 1920.47, 1923.02
Smith, P. 1918.23
Smith, P.E. 1886.60
Smith, Paul Gerard 1922.39, 1923.31, 1924.16, 1926.18, 1927.02, 1927.31, 1927.53, 1927.59, 1928.17, 1928.23, 1929.29, 1929.42, 1930.06, 1952.08
Smith, Peggy 1916.11
Smith, Percy 1898.46, 1899.41, 1907.14
Smith, Pete Kite 1941.03
Smith, Professor 1871.27
Smith, Puddy 1940.02
Smith, Pudy 1940.02
Smith, Queenie 1919.24, 1922.13, 1922.33, 1923.10, 1923.19, 1924.08, 1924.30, 1925.49, 1927.09, 1929.32, 1932.01
Smith, R. 1869.22, 1869.23, 1869.24, 1870.44, 1876.13
Smith, R.H. 1907.61
Smith, R.S. 1861.01, 1866.18
Smith, Rand 1942.19
Smith, Ray 1954.08
Smith, Rex 1981.01, 1984.02, 1997.19
Smith, Richard 1876.15, 1877.01, 1908.33, 1984.11, 1985.13, 1986.08, 1986.09, 1993.11
Smith, Richard H. 1907.61
Smith, Richard Jay 1987.02
Smith, Richard S. 1876.03, 1876.29, 1883.49
Smith, Robert 1900.35, 1904.49, 1911.37, 1913.10, 1929.39, 1939.12, 1940.03, 1954.01
Smith, Robert B. 1900.47, 1901.13, 1901.21, 1902.19, 1902.29, 1904.22, 1905.03, 1905.23, 1905.37, 1905.55, 1906.07, 1906.44, 1907.59, 1909.24, 1910.37, 1911.03, 1911.23, 1911.37, 1912.01, 1912.07, 1912.13, 1912.26, 1913.14, 1913.24, 1914.25, 1914.30, 1915.22, 1916.08, 1916.25, 1919.14, 1919.44, 1920.21, 1929.34, 1947.04, 1975.22
Smith, Robert Paul 1959.23
Smith, Roger Preston 1997.11, 1998.18
Smith, Roland 1930.24
Smith, Rollin 1946.24
Smith, Rufus 1951.24, 1955.27, 1966.12, 1966.16, 1968.06, 1978.02
Smith, Russell 1924.27
Smith, Sally 1965.19
Smith, Sam 1879.04
Smith, Sammy 1952.10, 1955.01, 1961.22, 1965.38, 1967.16
Smith, Samuel W. 1877.28, 1894.32
Smith, Sarah Jane 1967.17
Smith, Selma 1929.52
Smith, Sheila 1962.16, 1963.13, 1971.05, 1972.04, 1981.03, 1994.08
Smith, Sidney 1859.08, 1889.54
Smith, Sol 1870.34, 1872.27, 1877.28, 1879.08, 1883.36
Smith, Speedy 1930.19, 1933.06, 1933.27
Smith, Spencer 1980.21, 1981.20
Smith, Stanley 1931.01, 1933.21
Smith, Stephonne 1999.13
Smith, Sydney 1880.30, 1881.22, 1917.02, 1928.16
Smith, T. 1888.08
Smith, Thomas 1906.01
Smith, Timothy 1976.05
Smith, Timothy Edward 1997.05
Smith, Tom 1907.44
Smith, Truman 1961.26
Smith, Tucker 1964.15
Smith, Valdene 1922.28
Smith, Viola 1966.24
Smith, Virginia 1924.02, 1925.34, 1927.31, 1927.64, 1928.34, 1931.21
Smith, W. 1882.03, 1882.39
Smith, W.C. 1904.19
Smith, W.H. 1902.30
Smith, Wallace 1935.17
Smith, Walt 1971.02
Smith, Walter 1913.02
Smith, Wayland 1869.42
Smith, Webb 1979.28
Smith, Wilfred 1934.02
Smith, Will H. 1918.21, 1919.24, 1919.37
Smith, William 1872.23, 1880.65, 1908.20
Smith, William C. 1943.15, 1944.03, 1945.08, 1946.01, 1948.20, 1949.15, 1954.04
Smith, Wilson 1946.20, 1947.02, 1947.17
Smith, Winchel 1903.33
Smith, Winchell 1925.38
Smith, Wynonna 1985.05
Smith-Cochran, Debi 1998.19
Smithcox Organization 1982.15
Smithers, Master 1870.22
Smithfield, George 1920.32, 1928.39, 1937.08
Smithfield, Harry 1911.07
Smithline, W. 1882.62
Smithson, A. 1921.41
Smithson, Frank 1896.48, 1898.05, 1898.17, 1898.63, 1900.16, 1900.42, 1900.56, 1901.12, 1902.21, 1903.07, 1903.38, 1904.07, 1904.28, 1905.52, 1906.41, 1907.01, 1907.15, 1907.47, 1907.58, 1907.62, 1908.05, 1908.30, 1908.42, 1909.05, 1909.07, 1909.14, 1909.29, 1911.15, 1911.25, 1911.44, 1912.04, 1913.01, 1913.19, 1913.34, 1913.35, 1915.29, 1916.22, 1918.32, 1919.11, 1921.06, 1921.14, 1922.07, 1922.18, 1922.31, 1924.06, 1924.13, 1925.11, 1930.20
Smock, Hobart 1895.31, 1903.19

Smock, W.C. 1891.36, 1892.60
Smolko, John 1957.10, 1966.06
Smoller, Dorothy 1918.25, 1922.01, 1922.21
Smuim, Gerald 1987.02
Smuin, Michael 1962.27, 1981.06, 1988.15, 1990.17
Smyrl, David Langston 1978.12
Smyth 1867.02
Smyth, Ella 1908.26
Smyth, George W. 1904.18
Smyth, Louise 1898.46
Smythe, Al 1907.62
Smythe, Betty Jean 1945.19
Smythe, Daisy 1911.28, 1914.19
Smythe, Donna 1986.03
Smythe, Frank 1914.32
Smythe, Katherine 1910.32, 1912.13
Smythe, Katheryn 1912.38
Smythe, Mr. 1872.06
Smythe, Renee 1915.31
Smythe, Robert 1920.12
Smythe, Russell 1984.03
Smythe, W.G. 1891.37, 1893.08
Sneed, Glenn 1993.15
Sneed, Harold 1933.04
Sneed, Jr., Ray 1938.19
Sneed, Phillip 1991.09
Sneed, Ray 1938.19
Sneed, Sherman 1953.04, 1956.06, 1974.21, 1981.16
Snefft, Messr. 1852.05
Sneft, Gerhard 1984.03
Sneider, Vern J. 1970.21
Snell, Chris 1958.11
Snell, Christopher 1956.04
Snelson, Nicole Ruth 1999.04
Snipe, Mr. 1873.26
Snodgrass, Mr. 1869.35
Snodgrass, Quincy 1954.08
Snow, Ernest 1895.29
Snow, Harry 1899.18, 1950.14
Snow, Harry (David) 1959.26, 1962.15, 1963.04, 1964.46
Snow, Louis 1880.07
Snow, Nelson 1923.32, 1926.46, 1929.08
Snow, Norman 1973.16, 1975.18
Snow, Phoebe 1975.12
Snow, Ross 1893.37, 1896.18, 1896.44, 1899.29, 1902.09, 1905.56, 1913.33
Snow, Tom 1998.13
Snow, Valada 1924.27
Snow, Walter A. 1894.32
Snowden, Elfie 1902.43
Snowden, Elphie 1903.18, 1905.19
Snowden, Elphye 1904.22, 1904.56, 1908.07, 1908.19, 1908.35
Snowden, Eric 1919.42
Snowden, Mr. 1866.18
Snowden, Shorty 1932.12
Snowden, William 1959.24
Snuder, Mat 1894.02
Snyder, Arthur J. 1912.37
Snyder, Bud 1898.35
Snyder, Charles 1898.66
Snyder, Clarice 1916.26, 1919.19
Snyder, Dwight 1930.05, 1930.31
Snyder, Eddie 1967.12, 1975.12
Snyder, Edna 1907.24
Snyder, Ella 1900.05, 1900.20, 1901.08, 1901.27, 1907.18
Snyder, Fanny 1888.37
Snyder, Frank 1915.18, 1919.27
Snyder, G.B. 1879.13, 1880.46, 1882.25, 1884.28, 1884.29, 1887.25
Snyder, Gene 1935.12, 1939.24, 1940.16
Snyder, George 1879.63
Snyder, Georgie 1880.39, 1903.26
Snyder, Janet 1972.08
Snyder, Lenore 1889.36, 1890.48, 1892.46, 1893.44
Snyder, Leonore 1892.37, 1892.40
Snyder, M.B. 1879.63, 1880.39
Snyder, M.V. 1870.20, 1872.19
Snyder, Mabel 1908.39
Snyder, Maida 1905.48
Snyder, Matt 1888.37
Snyder, Matt B. 1878.12, 1904.02
Snyder, Mrs. Matt B. 1900.44
Snyder, Patricia B. 1986.16
Snyder, Philip 1927.45
Snyder, Robert 1885.66, 1886.03, 1886.42, 1886.52, 1887.39, 1887.48, 1888.27, 1888.40, 1889.07, 1889.11, 1889.15
Snyder, Roma 1904.27, 1907.24, 1908.04
Snyder, Ronald 1973.11
Snyder, Rose 1894.02, 1897.01, 1902.36, 1904.02
Snyder, S. 1879.66
Snyder, Ted 1906.04, 1906.43, 1908.03, 1908.43, 1910.01, 1910.19, 1910.25, 1910.33, 1911.08, 1911.18, 1911.34, 1916.03, 1917.08, 1918.05, 1922.15, 1923.22, 1927.39, 1929.26, 1999.01
Snyder, Thomas 'Bozo' 1950.12
Snyder, Tommy 1928.45
Snyder, Victor 1913.35
Snyder, Vina 1900.20, 1901.08
Snydon, Robert 1889.18
Soane, George 1851.01, 1854.01
Soares, Vivian Machado 1988.06
Sobel, Edward 1941.09
Sobey, Russ 1949.06
Sobol, Edna 1989.10
Sobol, Joshua 1989.10
Soboloff, Arnold 1962.14, 1964.15, 1966.01, 1973.07, 1974.09, 1977.16, 1979.22
Soborn, Steve 1980.19
Sobotka, Ruth 1954.12, 1965.04
Sodero, Cesare 1935.02
Sodero, Domenick 1911.46
Sodero, Domenico 1918.26
Soeder, Fran 1990.20, 1991.13
Soeurs, Boue 1923.26
Soglow, Otto 1936.01
Sohkle, Gus 1911.36
Sohlke, A. 1867.25
Sohlke, Augusta 1867.25, 1868.03, 1876.23, 1888.11
Sohlke, Augustus 1891.41, 1897.37, 1897.52, 1898.41, 1898.51
Sohlke, Gus 1902.33, 1902.38, 1903.05, 1903.19, 1904.15, 1904.25, 1907.59, 1908.18, 1909.12, 1909.17, 1911.24, 1911.32, 1911.34, 1912.07, 1912.14, 1912.25, 1912.44
Soiffer, Freda 1976.09
Sokal, Margaret 1955.07
Sokol, Lawrence E. 1974.04
Sokol, Marilyn 1989.07
Sokolow, Anna 1939.19, 1947.02, 1948.18, 1949.16, 1950.01, 1956.09, 1956.10, 1957.14
Sol Hurok Concerts, Inc. 1976.18
Sol Hurok, Inc. 1924.48
Sola, Leonor 1939.27
Sola, Robert B. 1950.03
Solange, Mlle. 1866.29
Solanger, Baronde 1915.21
Solano, Ricardo 1949.07
Solar, Willie 1906.28, 1919.14
Solas 2000.04
Soldan, Winifred 1925.47
Soldene, Emily 1886.43, 1887.12, 1889.19, 1889.21
Solen, Paul 1968.32, 1972.22, 1975.14
Soler, F. 1881.24
Soley, Messr. 1905.54
Solfeng, Ingrid 1920.23, 1921.02, 1922.15
Solfeng, Iris 1920.47
Solimando, Dana 1998.18
Solis, Alba 1985.07, 1999.18
Sollito, Frank 1985.13, 1986.09
Solman, Albert 1922.16
Solman, Alfred 1904.23, 1904.30, 1905.55, 1907.19, 1907.24
Solmon, Alfred 1904.29, 1905.27
Solms, Kenny 1968.13, 1974.02, 1980.29
Soloman, Edward 1889.52
Solomon, Edward 1881.07, 1881.16, 1881.17, 1882.17, 1882.20, 1882.23, 1882.51, 1882.63, 1882.66, 1882.71, 1883.04, 1883.23, 1885.26, 1885.40, 1886.14, 1886.40, 1887.05, 1888.11, 1888.33, 1889.54, 1890.23, 1890.50, 1891.41, 1898.24
Solomon, Fred 1886.14, 1886.40, 1888.20, 1888.35, 1889.32, 1890.01, 1890.24, 1891.35, 1894.11, 1895.09, 1895.12, 1897.27, 1899.19, 1899.37
Solomon, Frederic 1886.30, 1889.04, 1889.23, 1889.30, 1889.54, 1890.11, 1890.13, 1890.19, 1890.22, 1890.38, 1890.42, 1890.45, 1891.10, 1891.16, 1891.19, 1891.30, 1892.02, 1892.03, 1892.13, 1892.27, 1892.41, 1892.42, 1892.49, 1893.01, 1893.04, 1893.22, 1896.10, 1896.12, 1896.35, 1896.50, 1897.16, 1897.24, 1897.52, 1899.02, 1899.26, 1900.34, 1902.16, 1903.04, 1904.22, 1905.22, 1905.48, 1906.02, 1906.42, 1908.19, 1909.13, 1911.13, 1918.11
Solomon, Frederick 1889.42, 1889.53, 1890.09, 1900.41, 1901.27, 1903.39, 1904.47, 1912.34
Solomon, Messr. 1879.56
Solomon, Michael 1975.05
Solomon, Renee 1966.21, 1967.08, 1970.17
Solomon, Shaun 1982.22
Solomon, Sol 1897.24, 1897.27, 1899.02, 1899.25, 1900.33, 1900.35, 1900.41, 1909.31
Solomon, Tessie 1906.42
Solomons, Messr. 1866.20
Solomons, Mons. 1879.50
Solomonson, H. 1998.11
Solorzano, Consuelo 1939.18
Solotaroff, Mischa 1927.11
Solov, Zachary 1949.01
Soloviev-Sedoy, V. 1977.13
Soloway, Leonard 1971.14, 1980.06, 1999.14
Soltan, Malcolm 1934.03
Soltesz, Eva 1947.04
Soltis, Mona 1930.27
Solvent, A. 1876.03
Solville, Samuel 1877.25
Solvo, Zachary 1964.24
Somers, Ada 1890.29
Somers, Cecil 1904.21
Somers, Emma 1867.25
Somers, J. 1870.39
Somers, Jimsie 1945.05
Somers, Leonard 1891.40
Somers, Madeline 1903.15
Somers, Marykatherine 1982.14
Somers, Messr. 1882.04
Somers, Mr. 1864.07, 1870.43
Somers, T.E. 1882.04
Somers, W.A. 1888.10
Somerset, Pat 1922.33
Somerville, Marie 1879.25, 1880.26, 1881.25
Somerville, Miss 1880.62
Somerville, Phyllis 1974.05
Somlyo, Roy 1979.12, 1980.08
Somlyo, Roy A. 1983.16, 1992.15
Sommer, J.W. 1894.42
Sommer, John W. 1892.38, 1893.23, 1894.34
Sommer, Josef 1979.07, 1979.24
Sommer, Kathy 1988.10
Sommers, Avery 1978.25
Sommers, Beatrice 1917.31
Sommers, Harry 1897.14
Sommers, Madlyn 1905.23
Sommers, Miss 1917.31
Sommerville, M. 1881.41
Somner, Pearl 1975.03, 1975.08, 1978.10
Somogi, Judith 1974.07, 1974.15, 1975.16, 1976.23, 1977.03, 1977.17
Sonart Productions 1940.16, 1942.19, 1946.14, 1947.12, 1948.19, 1949.05
Sondergaard, Hester 1935.16, 1941.01
Sonderson, Lora 1922.46, 1923.06, 1923.32
Sondheim, Stephen 1957.12, 1959.13, 1960.08, 1962.12, 1962.17, 1963.13, 1964.15, 1964.17, 1965.06, 1965.08, 1967.11, 1967.12, 1968.18, 1970.13, 1971.05, 1972.03, 1973.04, 1974.06, 1974.09, 1974.17, 1976.02, 1976.32, 1977.05, 1979.06, 1979.13, 1980.02, 1981.27, 1982.20, 1983.13, 1984.08, 1984.11, 1984.13, 1986.08, 1987.09, 1987.18, 1988.08, 1989.03, 1989.14, 1989.16, 1989.19, 1989.27, 1990.07, 1990.09, 1991.04, 1991.06, 1991.08, 1991.10, 1994.05, 1995.11, 1995.12, 1996.06, 1997.01, 1997.10, 1998.11, 1999.20, 2000.16, 2001.02, 2001.04
Sondheimer, Hans 1953.15, 1968.09, 1968.10, 1968.14, 1968.15, 1969.11, 1974.07, 1974.15, 1974.16, 1975.16, 1975.17, 1976.22, 1976.23, 1976.26, 1976.31, 1977.03, 1977.11, 1977.17, 1978.08, 1980.03, 1980.22, 1981.22, 1986.10, 1987.11
Sonnenberg, Kenneth 1943.08
Soo, Jack 1958.19
Soper, Mildred 1921.20
Sophie, Mlle. 1870.31, 1870.44, 1871.27, 1875.33
Sophiea, Cynthia 1993.10, 1995.15
Sorce, Tom 1988.02, 1988.08
Sordelet, Rick 1994.04, 1997.19, 1999.13, 1999.16, 2000.06, 2001.06
Soreiro, Patrice 1987.02
Sorel, Felicia 1922.11, 1922.21, 1925.25, 1934.20, 1937.14, 1938.18, 1940.11, 1940.13, 1940.14, 1940.15, 1943.10, 1943.14, 1947.13
Sorel, Mona 1927.11
Sorel, Nina 1927.02
Sorensen, Holger 1948.31
Sorenson, Holger 1948.16
Sorenson, Joel 1995.18, 1996.13
Sorg, John C. 1892.09, 1893.08, 1895.27, 1896.52, 1897.40, 1899.03, 1899.27, 1900.36, 1905.28, 1906.43
Sorge, Joey 2001.02
Sorin, Louis 1925.17, 1927.36, 1927.39, 1928.38, 1930.36, 1937.17, 1942.31
Sorlisi, Simona 1964.03
Soroka, John 1992.01
Sorsby, Leonore 1938.02
Sorte, Joseph Della 1971.02
Sorvino, Paul 1964.40, 1999.17
Sosa, Dana 1956.08
Sosman and Landis 1904.45, 1910.17
Sosnowski, Janusz 1992.05
Sotager, Mme. 1911.37
Sothern, Ann 1931.36
Sothern, Sara 1925.37
Soto, Ray Perez Y 1988.15
Sotos, Jim 1978.01
Soudeikina, Jeanne 1943.11
Soudeikine, S. 1922.06, 1923.28
Soudeikine, Serge 1922.37, 1943.11
Soudeikine, Sergei 1925.03, 1934.06, 1935.13, 1936.27
Soule, Frank 1892.55, 1894.42
Soule, Ralph 1921.29
Soules, Dalel 1974.13
Soulke, Angie 1880.68
Soulke, Miss 1880.68
Sound Associates 1979.16, 1985.08
Sour, Robert 1930.32, 1934.06, 1936.12, 1939.19, 1945.12, 1954.11, 1986.02, 1989.02
Sourien, Messr. 1851.05
Sousa, John Philip 1890.26, 1891.03, 1891.31, 1891.47, 1896.13, 1897.10, 1897.55, 1898.13, 1898.25, 1898.48, 1900.01, 1906.18, 1913.06, 1915.24, 1917.16, 1918.23, 1924.32, 1978.05, 1980.27, 1987.19
Sousa, John Phillip 1879.66, 1910.08
Sousa, Larry 1993.02, 1994.09
Sousa, Leone 1938.04
Sousa, Margaret 1919.40, 1922.03
Sousa, Pamela 1972.04, 1975.14, 1981.13, 1988.10, 1993.16
Soutar, Farren 1901.01, 1905.27, 1911.45
South, Dorothy 1918.33, 1921.39
Southbrook Group, The 1984.07
Souther, Paul 1908.17
Southern Enchantment Company 1911.20
Southern Light Opera Company 1921.15
Southern, Ann 1931.04, 1933.13
Southern, Georgia 1942.18
Southern, Jean 1936.12
Southgate, Ethel 1908.15
Southwick, Dorothy 1906.18
Southwick, Raymond 1937.11
Soutullo 1949.07
Souvaine, Henry 1926.21, 1927.27, 1932.20
Souvenir Ensemble 1977.13
Souza, Ailto 1992.13
Souza, Lindete 1988.06
Souza, Marcia 1988.06
Sovec, John 1989.06
Sovey, Raymond 1924.34, 1926.28, 1927.44, 1928.02, 1928.37, 1930.02, 1930.25, 1931.02, 1931.14, 1932.13, 1932.26, 1935.17, 1937.04, 1938.10, 1943.08, 1944.01, 1952.03, 1957.09
Sovey, Raymond E. 1928.38
Sovey, Raymond J. 1929.49
Soviero, Diana 1975.17, 1976.31, 1978.08, 1978.20, 1979.21
Sowinski, Nikki 1961.07
Soyer, Miss 1865.02
Soyer, Mrs. 1864.23
Soyfer, Jura 1939.23, 1940.04
Soyka, Madeleine 1978.19, 1981.21
Sozzi, Sebastian 1999.17
Spaak, C. 1953.11
Spaans, Rick 1999.15
Spade, Messr. 1861.01
Spader 1884.17
Spaeth, Michael 1953.01

Spaeth, Sigmund 1987.02
Spalla, John 1985.08, 1986.12
Spangenberg, Bill 1957.18
Spangler, Amy 1999.19
Spangler, Catherine 1976.29
Spangler, David 1973.06, 1974.13
Spangler, Kay 1927.02
Spann, James B. 1966.27, 1970.21
Spanter, Fred 1902.14
Sparber, Herschel 1989.29, 1992.04
Sparer, Paul 1970.04
Sparin, C. 1924.45
Sparkes, George 1897.33
Sparkling Comedy and Travestry Company 1906.40
Sparks, Daniel 1921.36
Sparks, Edwin A. 1906.03
Sparks, Frank 1887.07
Sparks, Horace 1892.12
Sparks, John 1882.74, 1883.32, 1883.46, 1883.53, 1883.63, 1884.13, 1884.41, 1885.02, 1885.15, 1885.49, 1885.66, 1886.03, 1886.42, 1886.52, 1887.07, 1887.39, 1887.45, 1887.48, 1889.11, 1891.03, 1892.05, 1915.02
Sparks, John G. 1882.50, 1887.16, 1893.49, 1895.34, 1896.39, 1897.30, 1897.40, 1899.29, 1900.52, 1904.43, 1906.46, 1907.54, 1913.06, 1914.05
Sparks, Joseph 1882.74, 1882.79, 1883.32, 1883.46, 1883.53, 1883.63, 1884.13, 1885.29, 1885.66, 1886.03, 1886.42, 1886.52, 1887.07, 1887.16, 1887.39, 1887.45, 1887.48, 1888.14, 1888.27, 1888.40, 1889.07, 1889.15, 1889.18, 1890.49, 1891.25, 1891.45, 1892.44, 1892.54, 1893.10, 1893.15, 1893.27, 1893.36, 1893.46, 1894.04, 1894.49, 1895.05, 1898.69, 1900.07, 1900.42, 1900.49, 1903.26, 1904.22, 1917.26
Sparks, Joseph F. 1895.39
Sparks, Joseph M. 1882.50, 1895.27, 1896.52, 1897.45, 1899.35, 1900.55
Sparks, Ned 1920.35
Sparks, Ned A. 1918.22, 1920.05
Sparks, Sonny 1955.12
Sparling, Frank C. 1915.27
Sparling, Herbert 1899.39, 1920.40
Sparrow, Carol 1984.11, 1985.09, 1985.10
Sparrow, Ida May 1923.17
Sparrow, Libby 1923.17
Sparry, Jeanne 1918.03
Spatz, E. 1908.38
Spaulding 1917.17
Spaulding, Charles 1948.22
Spaulding, Charles F. 1952.07
Spaulding, Clarice 1919.10
Spaulding, Elaine 1955.06, 1955.07
Spaulding, George 1944.14
Spaulding, Kenneth 1948.28
Spaulding, Louis F. 1921.07
Spaulding, Sid 1940.16, 1942.19, 1946.14, 1947.12, 1949.05
Spaulding, Winnifred 1906.09
Spaull, Guy 1946.13, 1949.15, 1951.22
Speaks, Margaret 1927.40
Spear, David 1983.01, 1988.08
Spear, Fred 1935.15
Spearman, Messr. 1887.48
Spearman, Rawn 1950.18, 1952.06, 1954.19, 1961.13, 1961.24, 1962.07
Spears, Marta 1911.03, 1912.49
Specht, Paul 1924.17, 1928.09
Speck, Curtis 1897.38, 1903.05
Speck, Harry 1897.38, 1903.05
Speck, Messr. 1903.36
Speck, Samuel H. 1897.33
Spector, Arnold 1943.09, 1946.16
Spector, Edward 1959.06, 1967.14
Spector, Joel 1950.16, 1961.21
Spector, Myles 1974.09
Spector, Phil 1973.14, 1975.12, 1979.30, 1982.22, 1984.15, 1985.03, 1986.02, 1995.03
Spector, Philip 1925.37
Speed, Master 1876.03
Speeler, Eileen 1930.20
Speer, Bernice 1923.46, 1926.23
Speers, Bernice 1925.45
Spellman, A.J. 1882.69
Spellman, Eily 1910.28
Spellman, George 1948.20
Spellman, Larry 1989.22, 1992.16
Spelman, Leon 1976.36
Spelvin, Dummy 1940.22
Spelvin, George 1920.32, 1924.08, 1925.01, 1925.28, 1925.34, 1927.60, 1930.43, 1936.03, 1941.02, 1945.06, 1946.09, 1946.13, 1946.19, 1947.16, 1973.07
Spelvin, Georgia 1915.30
Spelvin, Gordon 1920.31
Spelvin, M. 1926.40
Spence, Ralph 1921.21, 1922.19, 1923.20, 1924.31, 1931.26
Spence, Wilma 1959.08
Spencer andmpany 1919.23
Spencer, Adele 1902.14
Spencer, Alexander 1882.51, 1902.44, 1904.12, 1907.15
Spencer, Alice 1887.11, 1889.20, 1892.12
Spencer, Anna 1919.25, 1920.03, 1920.25, 1921.28, 1922.02
Spencer, Annie 1887.39
Spencer, Baby 1887.11, 1889.20, 1892.12, 1894.09
Spencer, Bob 1960.06
Spencer, Bryan 1976.20
Spencer, Christine 1956.06, 1965.32
Spencer, DeWitt 1940.01
Spencer, E.L. 1912.15
Spencer, Earl W. 1918.38
Spencer, Ella 1894.27
Spencer, Florence 1939.31
Spencer, Franck 1955.06
Spencer, Frank 1955.07, 1955.09, 1979.13, 1979.28, 1980.09, 1980.18
Spencer, Grace 1897.54, 1899.25, 1900.34, 1902.21, 1904.51, 1904.57, 1905.08, 1905.11, 1906.01
Spencer, Katherine 1924.09
Spencer, Kenneth 1940.01, 1946.01
Spencer, Leonard 1896.15
Spencer, Lilian 1905.29
Spencer, Lillian 1907.37, 1911.36, 1915.19, 1918.31, 1926.38
Spencer, Mabel 1906.45, 1907.24
Spencer, Margaret 1944.25
Spencer, Mr. 1851.01
Spencer, Page 1922.01
Spencer, Peter 1931.14
Spencer, Rebecca 1997.09
Spencer, Richard 1902.05
Spencer, Robert 1928.16, 1933.01, 1974.04
Spencer, Sadie 1888.11, 1894.50, 1896.03
Spencer, Sinott 1893.12
Spencer, Vernon 1984.02, 1987.07
Spencer, Will 1897.46
Spencer, Willard 1887.05
Spencer. Herbert 1919.13
Spendiaroff 1922.06
Spengler, Thomas 1945.16
Spenser, Willard 1886.15, 1895.25
Spera, Mitchell 1970.15
Speranska, Frl. 1882.68
Sperantseva, Mme. 1925.03
Sperling, Ted 1992.17, 1995.05, 1997.06, 2000.15
Spero, David 1931.29
Speros, Jo 1975.07, 1979.02
Sperry, Steve 1983.09
Speth, Myron 1946.13
Spette, Agusta 1925.15
Spewack, Bella 1938.13, 1948.32, 1952.02, 1956.05, 1965.18, 1999.19
Spewack, Sam 1948.32, 1952.02, 1956.05, 1999.19
Spewack, Sam (Samuel) 1965.18
Spewack, Samuel 1938.13
Speyer 1851.07
Speyers, Mr. 1844.01, 1851.06, 1852.01, 1852.05
Speyre, E. 1851.01
Spialek, Hans 1926.03, 1926.21, 1926.46, 1927.38, 1928.03, 1928.49, 1928.50, 1929.07, 1929.33, 1930.27, 1930.28, 1930.40, 1931.05, 1931.39, 1931.40, 1932.16, 1932.17, 1932.26, 1933.20, 1934.04, 1934.06, 1934.15, 1934.19, 1934.36, 1934.39, 1934.40, 1934.42, 1935.12, 1935.15, 1936.02, 1936.05, 1936.12, 1936.17, 1936.22, 1936.31, 1937.04, 1937.10, 1937.16, 1938.01, 1938.05, 1938.07, 1938.09, 1938.14, 1938.15, 1939.07, 1939.12, 1939.13, 1939.21, 1939.22, 1939.25, 1939.27, 1939.30, 1940.01, 1940.03, 1940.06, 1940.07, 1940.10, 1940.19, 1940.22, 1941.06, 1941.08, 1942.27, 1943.01, 1943.14, 1943.16, 1943.20, 1944.01, 1944.18, 1944.29, 1945.09, 1945.11, 1945.18, 1946.07, 1946.22, 1947.13, 1947.14, 1948.15, 1948.18, 1948.26, 1949.02, 1951.02, 1952.15, 1961.15, 1963.17, 1966.11, 1983.02
Spiegel, Carl 1932.22
Spiegel, Edward 1917.21
Spiegel, Mac 1937.14
Spiegel, Max 1917.21, 1920.07, 1922.38
Spiegelgass, Leonard 1974.18
Spielac, Hans 1940.12
Spielberg, Anne 1996.08
Spielman, Fred 1945.01
Spielman, Jeff 1974.26
Spielter, William 1926.11
Spier, Larry 1957.01
Spigelgass, Leonard 1970.08
Spillach, Hans 1930.21
Spiller, H.C. 1880.49
Spiller, Joanne 1961.27
Spiller, Mr. 1834.03
Spina, Harold 1936.17, 1995.14
Spindell, Ahvi 1989.10
Spindelman, Alfred 1965.29
Spinedi, Goffredo 1964.03
Spinella, Stephen 2000.01
Spinelli, Larry 1971.01
Spinelli, Maria 1927.22
Spinelli, Nicolla 1900.06
Spiner, Brent 1978.06, 1984.08, 1984.14, 1997.15
Spinetti, Victor 1964.28, 1965.37
Spingler, D. 1966.14
Spingler, Doug 1960.07, 1970.07
Spink, George 1903.03, 1907.30, 1907.58, 1910.06
Spink, George A. 1902.07, 1903.02, 1906.17, 1907.46, 1914.06
Spinnard, Charles 1934.05
Spinosa, Tony 1998.18
Spinosi, Patrizia 1985.14
Spira, Heinz 1966.19
Spirit Lake Productions 1999.17
Spirit Will Productions 1981.15
Spiro, J. 1929.17
Spiro, Jean 1931.44
Spiro, Lenoria 1926.26
Spiro, Michael 2001.04
Spitalsky, Bill 1979.15
Spitz, Arthur 1946.16
Spitzer and Harris 1907.25
Spitzner, Fraulein 1879.62
Spivak, Allen 1986.02, 1999.14, 2000.04
Spivak, J. 1932.09
Spivak, James 1937.01
Spivakowsky, Michael 1965.32
Spohn, Patrick 1969.01, 1973.12
Spoliansky, Mischa 1929.05, 1930.38
Spolin, Viola 1970.16
Spong, Hilda 1940.06
Sponsler, Suzanne 1972.24, 1976.01
Spooner, Cecil 1903.12
Spooner, Mrs. Cecil 1903.12
Spoor, Mary 1927.40
Sporn, Michael 1981.10
Spoto, Franco 1979.26
Spotswood, Willie 1939.29
Spottswood, James 1911.30
Spottswood, James C. 1914.08
Spottswood, Willie 1986.06
Spradling, Grant 1965.22, 1966.12, 1966.16
Sprague, Charles 1884.39
Sprague, Charlotte 1921.20, 1923.02
Sprague, G.R. 1877.08
Sprague, George 1884.04
Sprague, George R. 1884.07, 1903.33
Sprague, Izetta 1904.53
Sprague, Jonathan 1983.04
Sprague, Lorie 1908.16
Sprague, Norah 1918.16
Sprague, Sidney 1932.08
Spreckels, Geraldine 1939.30
Spree, Joseph 1924.36, 1926.26, 1927.03, 1929.44, 1931.42
Spring, Helen 1925.31
Springer, Ashton 1976.04, 1976.21, 1976.25, 1978.21, 1979.05, 1999.06
Springer, Philip 1957.01
Springer, Phillip 1963.08
Springer, S.E. 1892.38
Springer, Sidney 1898.67
Springer, Tom 1905.47
Springsteen, Bruce 1979.30
Sprinsock, Eben 1986.05
Sprinzema, Nathaniel 1945.15
Spross, Charles Gilbert 1908.06
Sprosty, Paul 1937.06
Sprowacker, L. 1898.72
Spry, H. 1880.34
Spungler, Doug 1967.16
Spurgeon, Larry 1980.29, 1981.13
Spurin, Joseph C. 1925.39
Spurr, Horton 1926.28
Squadron, Anne 1999.09
Squarciapino, Franca 1981.13
Squibb, June 1968.01, 1978.24
Squire, Jack 1921.17, 1923.13, 1923.36, 1924.21, 1926.04, 1926.06
Squire, Katherine 1941.05
Squires, Gil 1927.63, 1929.12, 1931.08
Squires, Harry D. 1953.13, 1987.02
Squires, Henry 1858.03
Squires, Jack 1920.32, 1926.30, 1927.07, 1929.50, 1930.04, 1931.08
Squires, Jan 1927.58
Squires, Messr. 1855.10
SRO Enterprises 1973.08
Sron, Valerie 1971.17
St-Saens, Camille 1978.26
St. Albin 1917.32
St. Albyn, F. 1883.29
St. Aubuyne, C. 1889.20
St. Aubyn, C. 1882.57
St. Aubyn, Charles 1884.22
St. Aubyn, Clarissa 1881.16
St. Aubyn, Marie 1884.60
St. Aubyn, Tillie 1881.16
St. Bertrand, Mlle. 1866.18
St. Charles, David 1976.35
St. Clair, Ada 1902.15
St. Clair, Alice 1894.44
St. Clair, Clara 1896.27
St. Clair, Daisy 1892.44, 1892.54, 1893.10, 1893.36
St. Clair, Dorothy 1914.02, 1918.11, 1919.13
St. Clair, Edith 1896.47, 1897.25, 1897.54, 1899.12, 1899.29, 1900.40, 1901.16, 1902.24, 1903.39, 1905.48, 1907.13, 1908.17, 1908.39
St. Clair, Eleanor 1911.24, 1913.31, 1914.23, 1915.31
St. Clair, Elinor 1916.20
St. Clair, Emily 1875.11, 1875.15, 1875.20
St. Clair, Eugenia 1893.22
St. Clair, Harry 1869.35, 1906.44
St. Clair, J. 1879.18
St. Clair, Jean 1897.50
St. Clair, Jennie 1883.19, 1892.49, 1893.01, 1893.04, 1893.22, 1897.27
St. Clair, Lillian 1910.18
St. Clair, Margaret 1914.23
St. Clair, Marguerite 1910.19, 1918.11, 1918.33, 1919.44
St. Clair, Maude 1880.43
St. Clair, Miss 1844.01, 1883.17, 1883.23
St. Clair, Nellie 1919.14
St. Clair, Rosa 1866.34, 1873.19
St. Clair, Stewart 1927.03
St. Clair, W. 1884.46
St. Clair, Willie 1919.14
St. Claire, Eleanor 1912.38
St. Claire, Lucille 1905.23
St. Cyr, Louise 1896.45
St. Darr, Deborah 1974.06
St. Denis, Ruth 1931.31
St. Felix, Charlotte 1882.01, 1886.62
St. Felix, Clementine 1882.01, 1886.62
St. Felix, Henrietta 1882.01, 1886.62
St. George, G. 1872.10
St. George, John 1894.52
St. George, Kathy 1990.18
St. George, R. 1903.22
St. Germain 1927.45
St. Germain, Kay 1974.03
St. Henry, Jeanette 1891.11, 1892.22, 1895.21
St. Henry, Jeannette 1891.04, 1893.16
St. James, William 1925.02
St. Jean, Andre 1965.22
St. John Lewis and McCoughtry 1900.56
St. John, Bert 1892.06
St. John, Betta 1949.04
St. John, G. 1929.17
St. John, Gladys 1895.40
St. John, Helen 1906.36, 1909.12
St. John, Helene 1906.07
St. John, Howard 1926.20, 1930.30, 1956.12
St. John, Jai Oscar 1979.18, 1980.14
St. John, Mae 1884.64, 1885.11, 1885.16, 1886.04
St. John, Marguerite 1890.17

St. John, Marie 1897.44, 1898.11
St. John, Molyneux 1868.08
St. John, Sylvia 1937.11
St. John, Theodore 1928.33
St. Leo, Leonard 1924.02, 1925.52
St. Lewis, Kenneth 1997.21
St. Louis, David 1999.13
St. Louis, Louis 1971.01, 1972.12, 1974.05, 1986.16, 1987.12, 1995.03
St. Luke 1836.01, 1859.03
St. Maur, Geraldine 1885.47
St. Maur, Harry 1882.42
St. Paul, Michael 1977.12
St. Pierre, Mildred 1893.27, 1893.36
St. Quentin, Ruby 1884.40
St. Quintin, Lizzie 1886.24
St. Slair, Ada 1906.45
St. Tel, Anna 1901.25
St. Tel, Annie 1896.31, 1897.49
Stabile, Barbara 1955.10
Stabile, Bill 1995.02
Stabile, Christine 1971.16
Staccione, Leonilda 1891.40
Staccioni, Leonelda 1893.23
Stacey, Delia 1889.23, 1890.01, 1890.11, 1890.19, 1893.06, 1897.28, 1898.28, 1902.26
Stacey, Grace 1890.45
Stacey, Mildred 1891.16
Stack, John P. 1918.36
Stackpole, Dana 2000.07
Stacy 1950.07, 1955.26
Stacy, Delia 1891.03, 1892.05, 1896.06, 1897.24, 1906.35
Stacy, Grace 1891.10
Stacy, Herbert 1884.17
Stacy, Lee 1948.30
Stadlen, Lewis J. 1970.07, 1974.06, 1996.06
Staff, Frank 1966.03
Stafford, Al 1931.01
Stafford, Curt 1948.28, 1949.18
Stafford, Joseph 1954.13
Stafford, Marie 1920.02
Stafford, Maude 1880.34
Stafford, Mr. 1846.01, 1848.03
Stafford, Mrs. 1857.01
Stafford, Ronald 1974.13
Stafford, Vinnie 1905.18
Stafford, William 1907.38
Stage Costumes, Inc. 1943.06, 1943.12
Stage Holding 2001.08
Stage Promotions (Four)/Strada Holdings 1987.05
Stage Promotions Limited and Company 1986.12
Stage Vision 1992.02
Stagers, The 1925.21
Stagevision 1992.01
Stahl, Amelia 1875.12
Stahl, David 1984.12, 1985.10
Stahl, Dick 1964.26
Stahl, Karl 1904.07
Stahl, Mary Leigh 1988.01
Stahl, Richard 1886.36, 1887.31, 1888.45, 1889.10, 1889.34, 1890.21, 1891.03, 1891.47, 1892.05, 1893.17, 1894.06, 1894.37, 1896.02, 1897.01, 1897.34, 1897.39, 1898.47
Stahl, Sandra 1953.16, 1962.27
Stahl, William 1928.40
Stahlberg, Fritz 1917.28
Stahlman, Sylvia 1948.25, 1956.09
Staiger, Dorothy 1950.13
Staiger, Libi 1953.03, 1954.02, 1959.02, 1959.11, 1963.12
Stainton, Roy 1886.25, 1889.26
Stair, E.D. 1895.02, 1897.06, 1898.02, 1900.08, 1902.02, 1903.09, 1904.11, 1904.45, 1904.53, 1906.09, 1907.12, 1907.40, 1907.53, 1908.12
Stair, F.W. 1898.08
Stair, Queenie 1912.28
Stalberg, Frederic 1919.01
Staley, Violet 1903.30, 1906.06
Stall, Carl 1911.29, 1917.15
Stall, F. 1867.18
Stall, Karl 1899.28, 1907.05, 1907.52, 1911.03, 1913.15, 1914.03, 1924.02, 1925.15
Staller, David 1987.16
Stalling, Carl 1990.10
Stalling, Carl W. 1990.10
Stallings, Laurence 1926.31, 1928.44, 1937.10
Stamer, Fred 1952.13, 1965.08
Stamford, John 1954.01, 1965.09, 1965.13, 1965.25
Stamford, John Villers 1896.46
Stamm, William 1934.36
Stamm, William H. 1925.39
Stammer, Frank 1917.04
Stammers, Frank 1917.09, 1919.29, 1921.08
Stammers, Frank M. 1915.22
Stamos, Martino 1964.25
Stamper, Dave 1911.13, 1913.17, 1914.06, 1914.13, 1914.15, 1915.15, 1916.10, 1916.13, 1917.13, 1918.19, 1919.15, 1919.16, 1920.18, 1921.21, 1921.22, 1922.19, 1923.20, 1923.38, 1924.18, 1925.10, 1925.24, 1927.13, 1927.60, 1927.68, 1931.19, 1937.06
Stamper, F. Pope 1909.01, 1909.21, 1911.27
Stamper, George 1923.39, 1928.40, 1929.52
Stamper, Pope 1911.39
Stampfel, Peter 1970.04
Stampler, David 1911.13
Stanbrough, Joan 1929.41
Stanbury, Douglas 1930.08
Stander, Arthur 1941.03
Stander, Lionel 1941.13, 1952.01
Standford, May 1885.31
Standing, Guy 1893.24, 1897.11
Standing, Jack 1905.13, 1907.37
Standing, Jr., Guy 1945.03, 1947.11
Standish, Burt L. 1971.09
Standish, Claire 1914.27
Standish, Harry 1882.05, 1882.16, 1882.19, 1882.42, 1882.52, 1882.71, 1883.45, 1883.62, 1884.59, 1885.41, 1885.63, 1887.12, 1892.15, 1895.04
Standish, Helen 1884.63, 1887.19
Standish, Helene 1939.24
Standish, Jessie 1919.41
Standish, Joseph 1906.04
Standish, Joseph W. 1904.21, 1905.02
Standish, Junior 1949.18
Standish, W. 1881.52
Standler, Lionel 1961.02
Standon, Harriet 1909.12, 1909.24, 1911.31
Standstill, Mr. 1861.01
Stane, Walter 1943.03, 1946.05
Stanek, Jim 1996.06
Stanely, Jack 1927.07
Stanfield, Billie 1923.30
Stanfield, Leontine 1897.50
Stanford, Arthur 1899.39, 1900.58, 1904.04, 1906.23, 1907.02, 1907.18, 1907.46, 1909.03, 1910.30, 1912.01
Stanford, Charles Villiers 1897.03
Stanford, Ed. 1896.03
Stanford, Jack 1928.14
Stanford, Lillian 1902.24
Stanford, Mabel 1918.03, 1924.15
Stanford, Mary 1883.25
Stanford, May 1883.29
Stanford, Paul 1945.17
Stanford, Terry 1955.19
Stang, Arnold 1942.35
Stange, Abby 1904.15
Stange, Hugh Stanislaus 1918.13
Stange, Hugh Stannard 1926.02
Stange, Stanislaus 1892.57, 1893.03, 1895.06, 1896.10, 1896.41, 1897.17, 1898.27, 1898.40, 1898.73, 1899.19, 1899.34, 1900.38, 1902.03, 1902.31, 1902.41, 1904.15, 1904.36, 1904.51, 1905.15, 1906.49, 1907.05, 1907.52, 1909.22, 1910.19, 1910.28, 1910.32, 1917.11, 1921.40, 1930.03, 1931.33, 1934.12, 1942.17
Stanhope, Ada 1884.31
Stanhope, Frank 1924.07
Stanhope, Frederick 1918.10, 1923.04, 1925.40
Stanhope, Ida 1906.16
Stani, Mlle. 1887.37
Stani, Rosina 1873.11, 1873.15, 1887.36
Stanislaus, A. 1898.63
Stanislaus, F. 1880.45
Stanislaus, Frederic 1875.19, 1875.23, 1875.26
Stanley Art 1963.10
Stanley, Aileen 1920.24, 1927.19, 1929.09, 1930.20
Stanley, Alma 1880.43, 1880.49
Stanley, Alma Stuart 1881.28, 1882.38, 1882.41, 1886.14
Stanley, Bebe 1905.18
Stanley, Bert 1943.08
Stanley, Beth 1921.25
Stanley, Charles 1875.10, 1884.64, 1885.11, 1885.16, 1885.21, 1885.29, 1890.41, 1893.14, 1894.37
Stanley, Charles H. 1889.30
Stanley, Dorothy 1994.08, 1998.05, 2001.02
Stanley, Earl 1903.09, 1908.13
Stanley, Earl C. 1906.11, 1907.09
Stanley, Edmund 1888.26, 1889.17, 1889.22, 1890.16, 1891.11, 1892.22, 1892.33, 1892.47, 1893.16, 1894.24, 1896.13, 1897.10, 1898.13, 1898.48, 1902.25, 1904.09, 1906.07, 1907.05
Stanley, Edward 1912.17
Stanley, Edwin 1919.26
Stanley, Ethel 1888.11
Stanley, Frank 1954.11
Stanley, Gertrude D. 1906.38
Stanley, Gordon 1980.30, 1982.03, 1986.18, 1987.19, 1989.23, 1994.04, 1998.01
Stanley, Harry 1893.41, 1895.16
Stanley, Harry C. 1889.34, 1891.34
Stanley, Harry G. 1895.37
Stanley, Helene 1950.14
Stanley, Henry 1895.20, 1898.46, 1900.28
Stanley, Henry A. 1895.06
Stanley, Jack 1922.23, 1922.34, 1924.10, 1927.61, 1928.11
Stanley, Jessie 1904.24
Stanley, Jet 1924.26
Stanley, John W. 1949.15
Stanley, Mabel 1878.05
Stanley, Marion 1904.58, 1907.33, 1909.18
Stanley, Mark W. 1984.03, 1984.04, 1984.05, 1985.13, 1986.09, 1986.14, 1987.10, 1988.16, 1991.09, 1995.06, 1996.02
Stanley, Maude 1907.42, 1908.44
Stanley, Minnie 1937.11
Stanley, Mita 1889.45
Stanley, Mr. 1841.01, 1898.29
Stanley, Pat 1953.11, 1957.08, 1957.11, 1958.14, 1959.25, 1981.03
Stanley, Paul 1982.22
Stanley, Red 1928.33
Stanley, Robert 1885.30, 1979.31
Stanley, Stan 1938.03
Stanley, Truman 1921.32, 1927.64
Stanley, Vera 1905.52
Stanley, Vilette 1904.09
Stanley, W.H. 1882.16
Stanley, Will 1918.23
Stanley, William 1917.16, 1920.26
Stann, William H. 1932.14
Stansbury, Douglas 1929.24
Stansfield, George 1893.03
Stansil, Minnie 1908.32
Stansill, Jerome 1896.39
Stansill, Messr. 1875.39
Stantley, Ralph 1964.05
Stanton, Anna 1870.04
Stanton, Babe 1920.43
Stanton, Bebe 1925.26, 1926.23, 1927.02
Stanton, Bessie 1901.27
Stanton, Bill 1963.21, 1966.10, 1972.14
Stanton, Charles 1919.08
Stanton, E.K. 1896.32
Stanton, Ernie 1928.31
Stanton, F.H. 1909.28
Stanton, Frank 1903.12
Stanton, Fred 1925.11
Stanton, George 1945.13
Stanton, Gertrude 1931.05, 1932.10
Stanton, Jack 1938.13, 1939.30, 1942.14, 1947.11
Stanton, Jean 1941.03
Stanton, Josephine 1898.20
Stanton, Jr., Walter 1903.14, 1904.39
Stanton, Lillian 1911.07
Stanton, Mary 1959.26
Stanton, Mr. 1858.04
Stanton, Olive 1937.08
Stanton, Paul 1927.46, 1930.08
Stanton, Phil 1918.16
Stanton, Robert 1947.20
Stanton, Thomas 1973.12
Stanton, Val 1928.31
Stanton, W. 1861.01, 1866.31
Stanton, W.J. 1882.32, 1882.38, 1882.41
Stanton, Walter 1903.39
Stanton, Will 1915.02
Stanton, William J. 1882.25
Stanwick, Barbara 1933.15
Stanwood, Rita 1908.17, 1912.31
Stanzel, John 1968.24, 1972.08
Stanzilis, Michael 1998.14
Staples, C.G. 1910.29
Staples, Gordon 1917.24
Staples, R. 1877.15
Stapleton, Belle 1886.49
Stapleton, Frank 1905.34
Stapleton, J. 1884.11
Stapleton, Jean 1955.08, 1956.14, 1959.04, 1964.11, 1995.18
Stapleton, John 1899.40
Stapleton, Kent 1941.03
Stapleton, Maureen 1955.05
Stapp, Olivia 1974.08, 1975.11
Star, Bill 1962.24
Star, F. 1886.16
Starbuck, Betty 1925.17, 1926.13, 1926.50, 1928.30, 1928.50, 1929.42, 1932.26, 1934.04
Starbuck, James 1944.21, 1947.14, 1948.18, 1950.12, 1958.02, 1960.04
Starbuck, Jo Jo 1978.26
Starck, Carl 1886.31
Starck, Edna 1925.02
Starelle, Charles 1880.57
Starer, Robert 1961.27
Starger, Martin 1981.27, 1987.05, 1993.19
Starin, Edward F. 1879.08, 1879.12
Stark, Bruce W. 1969.08, 1971.01
Stark, Clarissa 1879.15
Stark, Douglas 1938.18
Stark, James 1931.32
Stark, Karl 1934.42
Stark, Leo 1921.15, 1927.50
Stark, Marilyn 1961.02
Stark, Molly 1973.11
Stark, Ray 1964.11
Starkey, Jack 1976.05
Starkie, Ben 1937.11
Starkie, Martin 1969.04, 1980.01
Starkweather, John 1959.06
Starling, Lynn 1920.11, 1959.21
Starner, Marie 1930.37, 1931.07
Starobin, Michael 1984.08, 1985.18, 1986.13, 1988.10, 1988.12, 1988.20, 1990.12, 1992.04, 1992.09, 1992.17, 1994.12, 1995.19, 1996.15, 1997.22, 1999.21, 2000.19, 2001.06
Starr 1870.03
Starr, Bill 1962.04, 1964.21, 1966.06, 1972.03, 1972.25, 1975.05
Starr, Dolores 1950.02
Starr, Ellen 1976.34
Starr, F. 1887.03, 1889.21
Starr, George 1894.27
Starr, Gloria 1911.39
Starr, Harry 1888.33
Starr, Hattie 1882.57, 1883.37, 1885.04, 1886.12, 1889.44, 1894.27, 1894.50, 1895.08
Starr, Jack 1934.19
Starr, Jean 1925.18, 1928.10
Starr, Lita 1979.29
Starr, Messr. 1886.36
Starr, Robert 1923.16
Starr, Sally 1924.19, 1927.13, 1928.04
Starr, Stanley 1888.35, 1890.19
Starr, Sylvia 1906.23
Starritt, Edgeworth 1889.16, 1889.23, 1890.01
Starwer, Terry 1914.31
Statham, Esmeralda 1907.55
Statler, Jane 1941.11
Statler, Jean 1941.11
Statz, Mary 1951.14
Statzes, Master 1916.01
Stauber, Mary 1928.40, 1928.45
Staudt, Herr 1870.15
Stauffer, Scott 1997.09, 1999.22, 2000.07
Staunton, Bertha 1894.18
Staunton, Virginia 1904.29, 1905.20, 1906.27
Stava, Keith 1990.20, 1991.13
Stavro, W.J. 1885.14
Stazo, Luis 1985.07, 1993.08
Stead, Emily 1923.24
Steadman, Charles R. 1894.09
Stearns, Johnny 1943.19, 1945.18
Stearns, Roger 1930.33, 1934.06, 1934.40, 1938.07, 1939.13
Stearns, Theodore 1909.23, 1915.18, 1917.34, 1918.07, 1918.22
Stebbins, Rowland 1936.22
Steber, Eleanor 1966.11, 1967.07
Steck, Hazel (Weber) 1968.24, 1973.11
Steck, Olga 1922.08, 1922.24, 1922.40, 1923.38, 1925.04, 1926.04, 1929.43, 1930.12
Stecko, Joseph 1975.05
Stedman, Al 1917.37

Stedman, C.A. 1881.01
Stedman, Charles 1893.38
Stedman, Charles A. 1884.06, 1888.31
Stedman, Fanny 1917.37
Stedman, W.H. 1884.16, 1884.37, 1890.10
Steel, John 1918.27, 1919.15, 1920.18, 1922.39, 1923.32
Steel, Joseph 1931.11
Steel, Nellie 1873.22
Steele, Belle 1896.52
Steele, Brian 1987.08
Steele, Carol 1983.03
Steele, D.P. 1879.33, 1879.35, 1880.06, 1880.10, 1880.13, 1880.65, 1884.16, 1885.58
Steele, David 1969.04, 1970.21
Steele, David P. 1880.70, 1885.58, 1887.43
Steele, Edward 1942.13
Steele, Eloise 1906.05, 1907.02
Steele, Elsie 1907.46, 1909.03
Steele, Fred 1988.05
Steele, George 1890.42, 1890.45
Steele, Helen 1899.13, 1955.13
Steele, J.D. 1988.05
Steele, Janice 1988.05
Steele, Jean 1923.17
Steele, Jevetta 1988.05
Steele, L. 1881.32
Steele, Lilian 1937.11
Steele, May 1884.16, 1884.28, 1885.58, 1887.43
Steele, Messr. 1880.59, 1904.13
Steele, Myrtle 1901.27
Steele, Philip 1976.22, 1988.01
Steele, Porter 1925.21
Steele, Robert L. 1968.19
Steele, S.B. 1894.18
Steele, Sallie 1866.31
Steele, Tommy 1965.14
Steele, Vernon 1931.09
Steeley, Guy F. 1906.09
Steell, Susan 1944.33, 1951.22
Steen, Sam 1947.17
Stefani, Roger 1964.06
Stefanini, Niska 1930.43
Steffan, Ernest 1916.20
Steffan, Sophia 1959.17, 1959.18, 1960.14, 1960.15, 1961.03, 1961.04, 1961.05, 1961.19, 1961.23, 1975.11
Steffe, Edwin 1948.31, 1959.19, 1965.35, 1969.04, 1970.10
Steffy, Don 1982.14, 1983.02
Steger, Julia 1925.25
Steger, Julius 1893.40, 1895.29, 1896.18, 1896.33, 1897.11, 1897.44, 1898.20, 1898.28, 1898.43, 1898.72, 1900.50, 1902.43, 1904.54, 1905.20
Steggert, Bobby 1995.19
Steglich-Fuchs, Frau 1866.33
Stegmeier, Bill 1964.18
Stegmeyer, Bill 1957.01
Stegmeyer, William 1966.30
Stehli, Edgar 1930.33, 1931.06
Steichen, Gerald 2000.03
Steichen, Marianne 1926.43
Steiger, H. 1890.21
Steiger, James 1920.17, 1924.29, 1927.53
Steiger, W. 1897.41
Steiger, William 1891.31, 1891.47, 1893.35, 1897.02, 1897.50
Steimann, Messr. 1892.43
Stein and Blane 1931.34
Stein, Abe 1952.07
Stein, Andy 1974.18
Stein, Bob 1988.13
Stein, Brian 2001.01
Stein, Douglas 1992.09, 1993.01, 1995.16, 1998.17, 2000.12
Stein, Erik 1997.22, 2000.19
Stein, Frances 1927.38
Stein, Gertrude 1934.05, 1952.06, 1996.10
Stein, Joseph 1948.14, 1948.30, 1950.02, 1955.01, 1956.02, 1958.01, 1959.04, 1959.22, 1964.27, 1968.30, 1973.05, 1976.09, 1976.36, 1978.22, 1979.09, 1981.18, 1983.14, 1985.04, 1986.13, 1989.03, 1990.18
Stein, Julian 1965.36, 1967.18, 1968.06, 1970.06
Stein, Leo 1901.05, 1907.48, 1909.19, 1911.27, 1911.43, 1912.37, 1913.14, 1913.20, 1915.04, 1915.17, 1917.14, 1917.20, 1921.29, 1929.47, 1931.27, 1942.21, 1943.09, 1944.24, 1957.04, 1957.15, 1958.16, 1959.21, 1962.21, 1963.24, 1964.24, 1964.25, 1964.30, 1965.27, 1974.14, 1976.18, 1978.07, 1978.20, 1979.21, 1982.16, 1983.12, 1984.04, 1984.05, 1985.11, 1988.14, 1989.13, 1995.06, 1996.02
Stein, Martha 1895.26, 1899.28
Stein, Marvin 1973.14
Steinbeck, John 1955.27, 1968.05
Steinberg, Alexandra 1988.04
Steinberg, Ben 1950.08
Steinberg, David 1999.11
Steinberg, Harold 1931.44
Steinberg, Joseph 1999.05
Steinberg, Lillian 1983.19
Steinberg, Lori 2001.01
Steinberg, Maurice 1903.03
Steinberg, Miss 1888.33
Steinberg, Norman 1992.17
Steinberg, S. 1942.28
Steinberg, Samuel 1990.16
Steinberger, Herr 1883.35
Steinborn, Carly Jane 1993.06
Steinbrenner, III., George M. 1970.09, 1973.06, 1988.20
Steindorff, Paul 1889.28, 1889.29, 1890.08, 1892.28, 1892.55, 1893.20, 1894.41, 1894.48, 1895.09, 1895.12, 1896.10, 1896.12, 1896.16, 1896.17, 1896.19, 1896.21, 1896.22, 1896.51, 1897.11, 1897.20, 1898.25, 1898.48, 1898.60, 1899.34, 1900.41
Steiner Costume Company 1929.23
Steiner, Arthur 1942.20
Steiner, Emma R. 1884.60, 1891.21
Steiner, Eugene 1948.28
Steiner, Hilda 1921.15
Steiner, John 1965.39
Steiner, Max 1918.11, 1919.23, 1920.26, 1920.37, 1921.03, 1921.13, 1922.27, 1923.16, 1924.08, 1924.35, 1924.43, 1925.36, 1926.39, 1927.55, 1928.03, 1928.44, 1929.44
Steiner, Maximilian 1891.22
Steiner, Messr. 1895.35
Steiner, Rick 1985.06, 1987.18, 1991.05, 1995.03, 2001.05
Steiner, Sherry 1981.04
Steiner, Steve 1987.15, 1990.15, 1996.04
Steinert, Alexander 1935.13
Steinhagen, Paul 1886.53
Steininger, Franz 1947.14
Steinman, H. 1897.50
Steinman, Herman 1907.05
Steinman, Jim 1991.10, 1998.13
Steinmann, F. 1894.30
Steinmann, H. 1897.29
Steinmann, Messr. 1890.31
Steinmann, Mr. 1891.33, 1893.29
Steinmann, Mrs. 1898.53
Steinmeyer, Jim 1984.16, 1994.04, 1999.16
Steinwald, Maggie 1890.45
Steling, Andrew B. 1910.30
Stella, Blanche 1903.09
Stella, Miss 1857.01, 1857.02
Stella, Mlle. 1870.44, 1871.27
Stella, Tim 1992.01, 1995.13
Stellman, Marcel 1965.30, 1970.01, 1974.19, 1983.03
Stelz, J. William 1904.35
Stembler, Ida 1892.11
Stembler, M. 1883.42
Stembler, May 1883.42, 1887.01, 1889.50
Stembler, Sallie 1890.04, 1897.49, 1906.40, 1911.07, 1912.20, 1929.39
Stemme, Dot 1930.33
Stemmer, Charlotte 1903.15
Stemmler, Herr 1866.33
Stempson, Messr. 1893.13
Stenhammer, S. 1904.03
Stenner, Stanley 1954.13
Stenuf, Hedi 1940.16
Stephans, Mira 1940.12
Stephany, Senta 1931.05
Stephen, Joe 1979.28
Stephen, M. 1907.59
Stephen, Mons. 1887.36, 1887.37
Stephens, A.W. 1883.42
Stephens, Billy 1930.35
Stephens, Britton 1900.17
Stephens, Garn 1972.12
Stephens, George 1923.39
Stephens, Gregg 1995.02
Stephens, H. Pottinger 1886.45, 1888.11
Stephens, H.P. 1884.44, 1898.24
Stephens, Hal 1909.17
Stephens, Hal S. 1898.02
Stephens, Harvey 1949.04
Stephens, Henry Pottinger 1881.07, 1881.16, 1881.17, 1882.17, 1882.20, 1882.23, 1882.51, 1882.63, 1882.66, 1882.71, 1883.04, 1883.23, 1885.26, 1885.40, 1888.33, 1890.23
Stephens, Hilda 1900.37
Stephens, Kelley 1956.16
Stephens, Lannyl 1992.17
Stephens, Leona 1904.44, 1907.10, 1907.52, 1912.16, 1938.01
Stephens, Linda 1994.01
Stephens, Mara 1997.06
Stephens, Mrs. 1853.01, 1853.03, 1855.11
Stephens, Oatis 1966.30
Stephens, Percy 1902.03
Stephens, R.N. 1896.04
Stephens, Ray 1950.02, 1978.02, 1980.14
Stephens, Robin 1983.08
Stephens, Sadie 1892.04
Stephens, Shawn 1993.14
Stephens, T.A. (Ty) 1983.17
Stephens, William 1895.23, 1903.21, 1929.51
Stephens, Yorke 1884.11
Stephenson, Albert 1978.28, 1980.08, 1994.13
Stephenson, B.C. 1879.18, 1880.18, 1887.44, 1895.20, 1898.57
Stephenson, Don 1994.09, 1998.21
Stephenson, Laurie 1980.18
Stephenson, Mabel 1892.07, 1894.21
Steplight, Randall 1943.10, 1945.06, 1946.09
Steppenwolf Theatre 1993.04
Steppling, John 1902.43
Stept, Sam 1942.16
Stept, Sam H. 1920.07, 1933.16
Stept, Sammy 1950.12
Stept, Samuel H. 1939.24
Sterk, Wilhelm 1908.29
Sterling, Ada 1911.22
Sterling, Andrew 1919.15
Sterling, Andrew B. 1899.12, 1901.28, 1904.23, 1910.18, 1913.05, 1919.16, 1919.18, 1927.37, 1980.27, 1999.23
Sterling, Anthony 1927.68
Sterling, Clark 1982.14
Sterling, Dolly 1926.11
Sterling, E. 1879.50
Sterling, Elisa 1997.05
Sterling, Ford 1905.37, 1907.53
Sterling, Harriet 1894.10, 1898.58, 1911.02, 1918.10
Sterling, Julie 1937.06
Sterling, Lee 1925.41
Sterling, Lillian 1905.25
Sterling, Lynn 1986.03, 1997.08
Sterling, Mabel 1888.15
Sterling, Messr. 1866.20, 1879.56, 1881.04
Sterling, Mons. 1879.50
Sterling, Mr. 1879.56, 1880.04
Sterling, Nellie 1902.02
Sterling, Oliver 1909.24, 1910.21
Sterling, Philip 1955.02
Sterling, Ruth 1919.10
Sterling, S. Suissabell 1927.44
Sterling, Suissabell 1927.57, 1927.61
Sterling, Sybil 1926.10, 1926.44
Sterling, Warren 1927.26
Stern Brothers 1911.41, 1911.45, 1913.15
Stern, Alfred R. 1948.17
Stern, Ben 1889.50, 1892.08
Stern, Benedict 1892.10
Stern, Don 1973.17
Stern, E. 1924.48
Stern, Edwin M. 1891.32
Stern, Emil 1959.15, 1961.25
Stern, Eric 1979.26, 1986.13, 1988.20, 1989.27, 1991.07, 1993.14, 1994.02, 1994.09, 1996.05, 1996.18, 1997.10, 1998.11, 1998.21, 2001.02
Stern, Ernst 1936.22
Stern, Harold 1928.04, 1929.09, 1930.15, 1930.20, 1930.37, 1938.08, 1942.35
Stern, Henry 1971.02
Stern, Jack 1921.06
Stern, James D. 1998.03, 1999.24, 2001.05
Stern, Jay 1959.06
Stern, Kimberly 1982.18
Stern, Len 1950.09
Stern, Lew 1942.01
Stern, Maurice 1960.02, 1961.04, 1961.05
Stern, Milton 1938.08
Stern, Professor 1929.41
Stern, Sandy 1979.10
Sterna, Katta 1937.05
Sternberg, Harold 1937.01
Sternberg, Sam 1937.01
Sterne, Richard 1982.24
Sterner, Lawrence 1926.38
Sterner, Martha Jean 1980.30
Sterner, Steve 1981.25
Sternhagen, Frances 1972.01, 1978.10
Sternheim, Herr 1883.35
Sternlund, Alvan 1931.44
Sternroyd, Vincent 1893.47
Sterrett, Cliff 1924.36
Sterrett, Paul 1937.15
Steteler, George W. 1911.07
Stetson, Dale 1930.40, 1931.01, 1931.42
Stetson, Etta 1898.41
Stetson, Evie 1903.28, 1907.03
Stetson, Gus 1898.78
Stetson, Jennie 1888.04, 1888.34
Stetson, John 1881.20, 1882.21, 1882.22, 1882.23, 1883.22, 1883.64, 1884.09, 1885.47, 1886.25, 1886.55, 1886.57
Stetson, Manolita 1908.37
Stetson, Ruth 1884.58, 1886.32, 1887.43
Stettheimer, Florine 1934.05, 1952.06
Steven, Gary Keith 1971.09
Stevenosn Douglas 1910.20
Stevens James 1913.25
Stevens Productions 1965.14
Stevens, B.D. 1890.16, 1891.11, 1892.22, 1892.33, 1893.16, 1897.10, 1898.13, 1898.25, 1898.73, 1900.01, 1900.28, 1900.43, 1902.12, 1902.43
Stevens, Bessie 1908.21
Stevens, C.B. 1883.26
Stevens, Cat 1978.05
Stevens, Charles 1879.09, 1880.15, 1884.46, 1904.42
Stevens, Claire 1947.01
Stevens, Clinton 1879.65, 1879.67, 1880.31
Stevens, Connie 1948.21
Stevens, Craig 1935.12, 1963.21
Stevens, D.K. 1901.06, 1902.15, 1905.19
Stevens, David 1913.32
Stevens, Edward 1892.11
Stevens, Edwin 1889.10, 1889.23, 1889.40, 1889.49, 1890.21, 1890.27, 1890.39, 1891.12, 1891.17, 1891.22, 1892.03, 1892.27, 1894.23, 1894.47, 1895.04, 1895.19, 1895.35, 1896.27, 1902.19, 1903.07, 1905.25, 1912.19, 1913.09, 1917.27
Stevens, Emma 1894.20
Stevens, Emma M. 1894.32
Stevens, Emma Maddern 1891.28
Stevens, Fannie 1887.29
Stevens, Fisher 1994.02
Stevens, Florence 1893.14
Stevens, Fran 1966.05, 1966.08, 1967.16, 1970.10, 1971.15, 1983.10
Stevens, Frances 1905.15
Stevens, Frank 1898.20, 1915.20, 1945.04
Stevens, Frank W. 1942.12, 1942.16
Stevens, Frankie 1928.34
Stevens, G.H. 1901.06
Stevens, Gary 1981.27
Stevens, Geoffe 1940.16, 1942.19, 1946.14, 1947.12, 1949.05
Stevens, George 1888.12, 1898.54, 1904.28, 1935.10
Stevens, George R. 1906.32
Stevens, Gloria 1959.26
Stevens, Goffe 1944.20
Stevens, Gus 1944.30
Stevens, Henry 1922.30
Stevens, Howard 1902.11, 1903.40, 1907.20
Stevens, Isabelle 1902.39
Stevens, J.A. 1882.18
Stevens, James 1911.10
Stevens, Janet 1935.01
Stevens, Jerome 1883.40
Stevens, Jodi 1997.09
Stevens, John 1944.30
Stevens, Josephine 1923.06
Stevens, Kelly 1963.04
Stevens, Kittie 1900.08
Stevens, Larry 1957.17
Stevens, Leonard 1928.47
Stevens, Lester 1921.27
Stevens, Lucinda 1960.01
Stevens, Lulu 1879.18, 1879.23, 1879.24
Stevens, Marle 1922.04
Stevens, Marti 1952.13, 1959.06
Stevens, Mary 1870.42
Stevens, Matte 1892.47

Stevens, May 1870.35
Stevens, Merle 1923.43, 1925.32, 1934.41
Stevens, Messr. 1864.22
Stevens, Miss 1870.09, 1870.22, 1872.14, 1872.35, 1904.44, 1910.12
Stevens, Morton 1956.02
Stevens, Morton L. 1938.05, 1942.01, 1944.01
Stevens, Mr. 1851.08, 1864.17, 1865.05, 1865.07, 1865.08, 1865.09, 1865.10
Stevens, Ogden 1891.20, 1896.14
Stevens, Paula 1951.20
Stevens, Pony 1887.06
Stevens, R.E. 1891.08
Stevens, Ramse 1960.04
Stevens, Rise 1964.23
Stevens, Roger L. 1950.08, 1954.03, 1957.12, 1958.10, 1960.08, 1961.02, 1972.06, 1972.15, 1976.11, 1979.09, 1979.17, 1983.02, 1983.05, 1983.08, 1993.10
Stevens, Ronald 1999.06
Stevens, Ronald "Smokey" 1981.15
Stevens, Roy K. 1975.18
Stevens, Ruth 1926.20
Stevens, Sara 1861.04, 1876.32
Stevens, Stanley 1944.30
Stevens, Ted 1922.12
Stevens, Tony 1969.14, 1970.11, 1971.15, 1973.05, 1974.09, 1975.14, 1976.03, 1980.29, 1985.20, 1987.14
Stevens, Van 1957.06, 1962.20, 1965.21
Stevens, William 1879.01
Stevensen, Scott 1974.26
Stevenson, Albert 1976.24
Stevenson, Bob 1935.04, 1964.28
Stevenson, Charles A. 1914.24
Stevenson, Douglas 1912.39, 1914.23, 1917.22, 1920.39, 1922.02, 1923.04
Stevenson, Gus 1917.26, 1919.35
Stevenson, Jim 1959.26
Stevenson, Katheryn 1911.44
Stevenson, M.P. 1879.13
Stevenson, Mae 1904.46
Stevenson, Robert 1926.11, 1927.05, 1927.31, 1927.34, 1927.48, 1930.35, 1932.30, 1934.18
Stevenson, Robert Louis 1899.35, 1997.09
Stevenson, Robert Ten Eyck 1933.01
Stevenson, W. 1986.02
Stevenson, W. Douglas 1904.39, 1906.01, 1906.48, 1907.44, 1908.01, 1923.10
Stevenson, William 1997.21
Stever, Letty 1942.05
Steward, Frank 1934.21, 1934.25, 1934.28, 1934.33, 1936.16, 1936.18, 1936.23
Steward, Parker 1933.24, 1934.12
Stewardson, Jerome 1924.46
Stewart, Albert 1911.02
Stewart, Alfred 1869.43, 1870.04
Stewart, Allen 1940.11, 1940.14, 1944.04, 1944.07, 1944.08, 1944.09, 1944.10, 1944.11, 1944.12, 1944.13
Stewart, Amy 1894.10
Stewart, Athole 1934.34
Stewart, Augusta 1873.17
Stewart, Belle 1894.21, 1894.50, 1898.70
Stewart, Bessie 1911.07
Stewart, Charles G. 1920.15
Stewart, D.A. 1984.15
Stewart, Dennis 1979.08
Stewart, Devida 1948.22
Stewart, Dink 1926.19
Stewart, Dixie 1969.12, 1972.24
Stewart, Docy 1880.33
Stewart, Don 1963.20
Stewart, Donald 1930.18, 1932.16, 1937.11
Stewart, Donald Ogden 1930.28
Stewart, Dora 1879.16
Stewart, Elliot 1924.39
Stewart, Ethel Irene 1900.01
Stewart, Frank C. 1880.01, 1880.03
Stewart, Fred 1938.18, 1939.20, 1950.10, 1961.02
Stewart, Georgia 1897.55, 1900.38
Stewart, Grant 1899.15, 1899.25, 1900.57, 1903.02, 1905.20, 1905.27, 1909.15, 1910.09, 1918.31, 1920.32
Stewart, Gwen 1989.09, 1996.09
Stewart, H. 1868.23, 1869.28, 1870.28, 1872.38
Stewart, Harrison 1907.29, 1907.31
Stewart, Harry 1870.32, 1870.40, 1870.42, 1871.01, 1871.02, 1871.05, 1872.02, 1872.04, 1872.05, 1872.08, 1872.12, 1872.14, 1872.25, 1872.30, 1872.32, 1872.36, 1872.40, 1872.43, 1876.06
Stewart, Irene 1898.44
Stewart, J.C. 1873.22
Stewart, J.E. 1875.21
Stewart, James 1889.24
Stewart, Jaye 1999.06
Stewart, Jennie 1903.26
Stewart, John 1987.08, 1987.10
Stewart, John Harger 1968.09
Stewart, Johnny 1947.16, 1948.25, 1951.12
Stewart, Joseph 1959.24
Stewart, Katharine 1921.33
Stewart, Katherine 1908.40, 1912.46, 1916.20, 1938.05
Stewart, Larry 1948.30, 1980.15, 1981.29
Stewart, Lesley 1965.33
Stewart, Lillian 1894.13, 1894.49, 1895.05
Stewart, Maggie 1880.33
Stewart, Margaret 1900.40
Stewart, Marie 1875.31, 1875.35
Stewart, Marlyn 1940.02
Stewart, Martha 1946.20
Stewart, May 1898.70
Stewart, Melville 1890.23, 1894.25, 1895.22, 1896.25, 1898.25, 1900.43, 1902.12, 1902.30, 1904.40, 1905.29, 1908.15, 1910.03, 1910.27, 1911.22, 1912.02, 1912.46, 1914.28, 1915.15
Stewart, Melvin 1957.09
Stewart, Michael 1960.06, 1961.10, 1964.01, 1967.15, 1968.07, 1968.32, 1974.18, 1975.21, 1977.04, 1978.04, 1979.02, 1980.07, 1980.20, 1981.07, 1981.08, 1985.02, 1995.13
Stewart, Michel 2001.08
Stewart, Mike 1951.10, 1955.12
Stewart, Miss 1872.35
Stewart, Mrs. 1855.11
Stewart, Nellie 1870.35, 1870.42, 1880.33, 1895.43
Stewart, Owen 1936.12
Stewart, Patricia Quinn 1972.06
Stewart, Paul Anthony 1993.17
Stewart, Paula 1951.18, 1959.02, 1960.07, 1960.22, 1961.21
Stewart, Radiah Y. 2001.04
Stewart, Ralph 1895.14
Stewart, Richard 1880.33
Stewart, Robert A. 1983.19
Stewart, Rosalie 1927.38
Stewart, Rose 1888.11
Stewart, Samuel 1894.13
Stewart, Scot 1979.25, 1983.10
Stewart, Slam 1939.29, 1948.13
Stewart, Sophie 1894.13
Stewart, Stella 1884.25
Stewart, Sylvester 1982.22, 1997.21
Stewart, Virginia 1873.26
Stewart, W.G. 1898.14, 1898.52, 1900.04, 1900.50, 1912.22, 1912.23, 1916.15
Stewart, William 1890.17, 1896.04, 1907.34
Stewart, William G. 1897.53, 1898.04, 1898.09, 1898.21, 1898.40, 1898.42, 1898.49, 1898.57, 1898.62, 1898.65, 1898.71, 1898.74, 1899.07, 1899.42, 1900.02, 1900.06, 1900.30, 1902.41, 1913.11, 1913.28, 1914.19
Stewart. H. 1870.35
Steyne, E.T. 1886.50, 1886.54, 1887.12
Steyne, Martha 1900.47
Steytler, Henrietta 1951.07
Sticco, Dan 1990.06
Stice, Jade 1991.03
Stick, Mr. 1868.06, 1876.03
Stickel, Mlle. 1876.12
Stickley, Grace 1898.34
Stickney, Mrs. J. 1848.04
Stickney, R. 1864.23
Stieb, Alan 1987.18, 1989.23
Stiebel, Victor 1955.19, 1958.10
Stiefel, Milton 1919.20
Stiers, David Ogden 1973.16, 1974.13
Stiffler, Ledru 1924.11
Stifter, George 1919.19
Stigwood, Robert 1971.12, 1974.24, 1979.23, 1982.03, 1999.15
Stiles, Leslie 1906.47, 1907.15
Stiles, Margie 1909.17
Stiles, Victor 1965.23
Stilgoe, Richard 1982.19, 1987.05, 1988.01, 1992.12
Still, William 1927.32, 1928.08, 1928.40
Stille, J.E. 1888.18, 1890.47, 1890.48
Stiller, Jerry 1954.03
Stillman, Al 1938.04, 1940.16, 1942.18, 1942.19, 1947.12, 1948.19, 1949.05
Stillman, Albert 1937.10
Stillman, Bob 1989.26, 2000.12
Stillman, Jack 1930.14
Stillman, Leonard 1934.40, 1954.16
Stillman, Richard 1980.01
Stills, Mary 1927.27
Stillwell, Adele 1885.66, 1886.03
Stillwell, Delia 1885.49
Stillwell, Della 1884.41
Stillwell, Edna 1913.23, 1916.07, 1916.19, 1918.11
Stillwell, George 1927.26
Stilson, Pearl 1902.05
Stilwell, Della 1885.02, 1885.22
Stilwell, Frank 1913.06
Stilwell, Liliane 1990.15
Stinchfeld, George 1937.12
Stinchombe, G.H. 1881.35
Stine, Charles J. 1893.50, 1896.37, 1910.07, 1912.05, 1923.37
Stinette, Juanita 1922.25, 1923.11, 1931.47
Sting 1989.24
Stinnette, Dorothy 1957.07
Stinnette, Juanita 1929.01
Stinton, Colin 1982.02
Stirling, Earle 1878.10, 1888.08
Stirling, F. 1881.11
Stites, Julane 1968.01, 1968.31
Stites, Kevin 1997.06, 1998.16
Stitt, Don 1982.10, 1987.14, 1990.15
Stitzel, Mel 1924.35
Stivanello 1974.14
Stix, Carl 1891.19
Stix, John 1970.12
Stobel, Messr. 1886.36
Stobitzer, Heinrich 1908.29
Stocchetti, Mlle. 1893.45
Stock Opera Company 1899.02
Stock, Jeffrey 1997.18
Stock, Larry 1982.22, 1986.02, 2000.07
Stockbridge, A. 1888.10
Stockdale, Cecilila 1929.34
Stockdale, Gary 1991.02
Stockdale, Rae 1922.30
Stocke, Matthew 2000.15
Stocker, Blanche 1913.36
Stocker, Brigitte 1978.23
Stocker, Gary M. 1984.09, 1989.05
Stocker, Leonard 1940.13, 1940.14, 1942.31
Stockfeld, Billy 1925.42
Stockley, D. Grover 1880.25
Stockman, Emma 1876.16
Stockman, Nagatai 1972.20
Stockmeyer, A. 1879.35
Stockqueler, Fanny 1866.13
Stockton, Fannie 1866.19
Stockton, Fanny 1868.03
Stockton, Frank R. 1888.19, 1966.18
Stockwell, E.G. 1906.19
Stockwell, Edwin 1902.09
Stockwell, Harry 1929.28, 1930.22, 1933.22, 1939.25, 1945.11
Stockwell, L.R. 1886.01
Stockwell, Master 1796.02
Stockwell, Rick 1988.07
Stockwell, Walter 1903.11
Stockwell, Walter W. 1901.07
Stocqueler, Fanny 1867.25
Stoddard, Alonzo 1885.30, 1885.32
Stoddard, Alonzo E. 1885.48
Stoddard, Amelia 1901.03
Stoddard, E.A. 1878.03
Stoddard, Eunice 1936.28
Stoddard, George 1868.04
Stoddard, George E. 1904.25, 1904.28, 1917.34, 1918.39, 1919.33, 1920.35, 1923.06, 1923.42, 1925.04, 1925.44
Stoddard, Haila 1960.04, 1961.18, 1963.03, 1963.16
Stoddard, J.H. 1862.09
Stoddard, Lew 1902.39
Stoddard, Marie 1923.41, 1924.36, 1927.50, 1931.03
Stoddard, Mrs. J.H. 1862.07
Stoddart, George W. 1869.15
Stoddart, J.H. 1857.01, 1860.04, 1861.03, 1861.04, 1862.07, 1863.01, 1863.02, 1863.04, 1863.08, 1863.09, 1864.15, 1866.03
Stoddart, Miss 1857.02
Stoddart, Mr. 1855.11, 1857.02, 1859.08, 1860.03, 1860.04
Stoddart, Mrs. 1857.03, 1859.08
Stoddart, Mrs. J.H. 1857.01, 1862.09, 1863.02
Stoeckhe, Elise 1893.07
Stoeckle, Robert 1980.01
Stoepel, Robert 1859.14, 1866.13, 1866.16, 1869.03, 1869.05, 1869.16, 1869.30, 1870.03, 1872.23, 1882.26, 1885.12
Stoeppel, Robert 1868.24, 1868.26
Stoessel, Albert 1931.46
Stogner, Patrick 1999.21, 2000.19
Stohwasser, Miss 1841.01
Stoianovsky, Messr. 1922.06, 1923.28, 1925.03
Stoker, Gordon 1978.01
Stokes, Al 1940.17
Stokes, Belle 1886.11, 1886.60
Stokes, Charles 1875.05
Stokes, Heather 1994.07
Stokes, Leonard 1931.19
Stokes, Marian 1918.05
Stokes, Melvin 1910.36, 1928.09
Stokes, Miss 1884.11
Stokes, Oscar 1985.05
Stokes, Sybil 1920.28
Stokkermans, Joop 1982.23
Stoklosa, Janusz 1992.05
Stolarsky, Paul 1992.17
Stolber, Dean 1960.06, 1971.11
Stoll Productions, Ltd. 1981.14
Stoll, Jon 1999.25
Stoller, Mike 1977.10, 1978.05, 1979.30, 1982.22, 1983.20, 1989.12, 1995.03
Stoller, Mildred 1900.07
Stoller, Millie 1899.06
Stollery, Dick 1951.05
Stollery, Greta 1951.05
Stoltz, Robert 1968.20
Stoltzenberg, Arthur 1885.01
Stolz, Robert 1925.07, 1928.48, 1931.21, 1936.22, 1941.02, 1943.09, 1944.24, 1945.12, 1957.04, 1999.07
Stone, Agnes 1886.25, 1886.55, 1886.57, 1887.44, 1904.35
Stone, Allene 1923.40, 1924.26
Stone, Amelia 1897.34, 1901.05, 1903.14, 1904.15, 1904.28, 1906.04, 1907.15, 1908.16
Stone, Amelia F. 1902.19
Stone, Anna 1915.31, 1916.20, 1917.06
Stone, Barton 1966.14
Stone, Bentley 1929.32
Stone, Beth 1906.25
Stone, Blanche 1884.22
Stone, C.L. 1851.08
Stone, Carol 1936.22
Stone, Charles 1931.44
Stone, Dorothy 1923.40, 1924.26, 1926.32, 1928.37, 1930.05, 1932.15, 1937.07, 1945.16
Stone, E.F. 1893.47
Stone, Ed 1892.04
Stone, Edward 1907.01
Stone, Edwin 1895.35, 1910.17, 1913.04
Stone, Edwin J. 1903.03
Stone, Elly 1972.16
Stone, Ezra 1935.03, 1940.04, 1942.20
Stone, Florence 1923.23
Stone, Frank 1940.14
Stone, Fred 1901.01, 1910.02, 1912.39, 1914.23, 1917.22, 1920.36, 1923.40, 1924.26, 1926.32, 1930.05, 1932.15
Stone, Fred A. 1903.03, 1904.13, 1904.44, 1906.33
Stone, Gary 1940.02
Stone, Georgie 1926.02
Stone, Harold 1943.19
Stone, Harry 1904.05, 1906.19, 1907.39, 1908.07, 1911.15
Stone, Harry P. 1896.13, 1897.10, 1898.13, 1898.48, 1901.15
Stone, Harvey 1961.15
Stone, Jack 1954.08
Stone, Janet 1920.28, 1923.01, 1923.44, 1925.05, 1926.11
Stone, Jenny 1881.37
Stone, Jeremy 1980.07, 1982.03
Stone, Jessica 1994.07
Stone, John A. 1848.02
Stone, John E. 1925.10, 1925.24, 1925.40
Stone, June 1897.14, 1899.36
Stone, L.E. 1879.25
Stone, Laura 1901.06, 1901.21, 1904.03
Stone, Leonard 1959.01
Stone, Lewis S. 1912.03
Stone, Lillian 1887.02, 1887.42, 1888.25, 1889.43, 1890.36, 1894.52
Stone, M. 1896.12
Stone, Mabel 1883.36

Stone, Marie 1880.48, 1880.53, 1882.07, 1882.08, 1882.10, 1882.11, 1882.12, 1882.13, 1883.11, 1883.12, 1883.13, 1883.14, 1883.15
Stone, Maude 1889.54
Stone, Maurice 1902.08
Stone, Miss 1890.36, 1897.41
Stone, Mr. June 1899.36
Stone, Mrs. C.L. 1851.08
Stone, Mrs. Fred 1930.05
Stone, Neil 1926.34, 1928.25
Stone, Paddy 1955.19
Stone, Patti 1891.15
Stone, Paul Russell 1904.35
Stone, Paula 1930.05, 1945.16, 1947.04, 1951.23, 1953.11, 1957.17
Stone, Peter 1961.26, 1965.33, 1969.06, 1972.04, 1981.10, 1983.06, 1991.07, 1997.06, 1997.15, 1999.04
Stone, Rheta 1931.05
Stone, Salome 1884.22
Stone, Sid 1944.15, 1948.21, 1979.25
Stone, Sidney 1921.15
Stone, Sylvia 1938.05
Stone, Vic 1903.13
Stone, Victor 1905.14
Stone, Victoria 1898.46
Stone, W.D. 1884.15, 1891.42
Stone, William 1923.16
Stoneback, Ric 1997.15, 2001.06
Stoneburner, Sam 1972.07, 1981.28
Stonehill, Maurice 1910.03
Stonehill, Maurice J. 1903.33
Stoner, Joe 1940.10, 1943.20
Stoner, Lou 1940.10, 1943.20
Stoner, P. 1871.15
Stoner, Philip 1872.37
Stong, Philip 1996.04
Stop, Mons. 1869.05
Stoppard, Tom 1979.17
Storch, Arthur 1959.08, 1959.17, 1968.03
Storch, Larry 1983.04
Stordahl, Alex 1974.10
Storer, Cap 1916.19
Storer, Florence 1877.08
Storey, Belle 1915.24
Storey, David 1986.03
Storey, Fabian 1938.01
Storey, Fred 1888.38, 1888.41
Storey, Jessie 1882.81, 1884.19
Storey, Rex 1922.23
Stork, Renee 1989.03
Storm, Douglas 1997.19
Storme, Charles 1871.12, 1871.16
Storms, Etta 1894.13
Story, Belle 1914.23, 1918.23, 1919.22, 1920.26
Story, Chick 1919.18
Story, Gloria 1944.28, 1945.04, 1947.04
Story, Jack 1914.17
Story, June Eve 1968.24
Story, O.E. 1912.45
Story, Rex 1919.18, 1919.43
Story, Ted 1967.10
Stoska, Polyna 1944.26, 1947.02
Stoskus, Apolyna 1931.46
Stothart, Herbert 1917.21, 1918.30, 1918.40, 1919.06, 1920.27, 1920.42, 1921.18, 1922.02, 1922.26, 1923.05, 1923.35, 1923.45, 1924.06, 1924.15, 1924.21, 1924.28, 1925.52, 1926.34, 1927.06, 1927.63, 1928.25, 1929.02, 1973.14, 1976.07, 1979.25, 1981.03, 1989.06, 1997.11, 1998.06, 1999.11
Stothart, Herbert P. 1920.01
Stott, Monte 1942.19
Stott, Montey 1940.16
Stott, Monty 1946.14, 1947.12, 1949.05
Stotz, Norman 1978.10
Stout, G.L. 1873.20, 1873.22, 1873.27, 1875.14, 1875.37, 1875.40, 1876.01, 1876.13, 1876.15, 1876.29, 1877.01, 1882.02, 1882.79, 1883.32, 1884.41, 1885.02, 1885.49, 1886.52, 1887.07, 1888.40, 1889.11
Stout, George 1887.08, 1887.34
Stout, George L. 1882.50, 1883.46, 1883.53, 1883.63, 1884.13, 1885.15, 1885.22, 1885.66, 1886.03, 1886.42, 1887.16, 1887.39, 1887.45, 1887.48, 1888.14, 1888.27, 1889.07, 1889.15, 1889.18, 1903.26
Stout, J. 1867.12
Stout, Kate 1916.17, 1917.34
Stout, Mary 1981.12, 1990.06, 1992.17, 1994.12, 2000.20
Stout, Mr. 1861.01, 1866.02, 1866.28
Stout, William 1878.10
Stoute, G.L. 1872.07
Stovall, Count 1981.15
Stovall, James 2000.17
Stovall, Tom 1971.12
Stover, Florence 1905.12
Stover, Frederick 1940.21
Stover, G.H. 1915.30, 1915.31
Stover, James 1963.28
Stover, Maud Ream 1904.30
Stover, Maude Ream 1923.27
Stowe, Carle 1901.06
Stowe, Emily 1887.51, 1891.03, 1896.15
Stowe, Harriet Beecher 1924.46
Stowe, Leslie 1894.13, 1930.41
Stowe, Mr. 1872.24
Stowitts 1922.39
Stoyanovsky, Arcadi 1943.11
Straboin, Michael 1998.20
Strachey, Jack 1923.35, 1925.42, 1960.07, 1982.12
Strafford, Beatrice 1878.05
Strahemmer, Silvia 1984.05
Strahl, Juliet 1920.47
Strahlendorff, P. 1919.03
Straiges, Tony 1978.03, 1978.06, 1978.26, 1981.12, 1984.08, 1987.18, 1989.20
Straight, A.Z. 1898.31
Strain, Drucilla 1934.36, 1940.12, 1944.01, 1945.09, 1946.04
Strakosch English Opera Company 1882.64, 1882.65
Strakosch, Edgar 1884.62
Strakosch, Max 1883.49
Strand, Churk 1975.07
Strane, Ralph 1953.16
Straney, Paul 1982.18, 1983.14
Strang, Harry 1910.27
Strange, Alex 1998.01
Strange, Clayton 1979.18
Strange, Helen 1872.23, 1872.35
Strange, Meghan 1994.09
Strange, R. Henri 1908.08
Strange, Stanislaus 1947.06
Strasberg, John 1982.24
Strasberg, Lee 1925.17, 1931.02, 1936.28
Strasfogel, Ignace 1950.10
Stratas, Teresa 1986.13
Straten, Mary 1973.07
Strater, Nicholas A. 1964.22
Stratford Festival of Canada Production, A 1987.01
Stratford, Bert 1980.11
Strathmore, George 1884.22
Strathmore, Violet 1920.03, 1924.36
Strathmore, Violette 1917.09, 1922.07
Stratti, Basil 1918.40
Stratton, Chester 1943.22
Stratton, Cora 1878.02
Stratton, Frank 1909.05
Stratton, John 1966.01
Stratton, Jr., Gil 1941.06
Stratton, Mike 1940.18, 1942.05
Stratton, Ronald B. 1961.08, 1965.01, 1965.21, 1967.04
Stratton, Ronald Bennett 1980.19, 1981.26
Straub, John 1947.09
Straus, Oscar 1908.06, 1909.22, 1910.19, 1910.28, 1913.14, 1917.14, 1921.14, 1921.40, 1926.26, 1930.03, 1931.33, 1932.04, 1934.12, 1937.17, 1942.17, 1947.06
Straus, Robert V. 1986.13
Strauss 1884.42, 1886.47, 1888.36, 1894.19, 1899.23, 1927.28
Strauss, Bernard S. 1972.25
Strauss, Eddie 1996.06
Strauss, Edward 1970.20, 1983.04, 1987.15
Strauss, II., Johann 1975.22
Strauss, Jack 1920.22, 1920.23
Strauss, Johan 1912.47
Strauss, Johann 1879.57, 1880.61, 1882.43, 1882.45, 1882.71, 1883.44, 1883.45, 1884.08, 1884.18, 1884.37, 1884.63, 1885.14, 1885.52, 1886.04, 1886.54, 1888.22, 1889.05, 1890.12, 1890.30, 1891.22, 1900.02, 1900.30, 1901.05, 1912.27, 1929.39, 1932.18, 1937.17, 1940.05, 1942.31, 1943.02, 1944.26, 1945.15, 1953.06, 1953.15, 1954.06, 1954.10, 1955.17, 1956.10, 1957.13, 1958.15, 1959.16, 1964.25, 1964.31, 1965.25, 1974.16, 1975.16, 1976.23, 1977.11, 1980.03, 1980.22, 1981.22, 1984.03, 1986.10, 1987.11, 1990.10
Strauss, Jr., Johann 1897.53, 1898.14, 1899.05, 1933.23, 1934.29
Strauss, Leon 1997.09
Strauss, Marilyn 1976.03, 1982.04
Strauss, Richard 1989.12, 1999.15
Strauss, Robert 1946.04, 1958.04, 1981.09, 1982.05
Strauss, Robert V. 1999.05
Strauss, Sara Mildred 1934.39
Strauss, Sr., Johann 1934.29, 1937.17
Strauss, Wagner J. 1990.10
Strauss, Wally 1954.15
Stravinsky, Igor 1978.26
Strawbridge, Edwin 1925.36, 1934.40
Strayhorn, Billy 1946.24, 1976.04, 1981.06, 1984.15, 1986.03, 1990.09, 1995.12, 1997.03, 1997.05
Strayhorn, Dan 1980.15
Strayhorn, Danny 1986.11, 1989.26
Strazza, Matilda 1944.23
Strebinger, F. 1869.26, 1870.20, 1870.23, 1870.26, 1870.33, 1871.04, 1871.18, 1873.02
Strebinger, L. 1873.26
Strebinger, Mlle. 1866.06
Strebinger, Mme. 1866.12
Strebor, Mrs. 1840.02
Street, Anthony W. 1930.09
Street, Carrie 1893.07
Street, Dean 1999.02
Street, George 1947.15
Street, James 1953.01
Street, Olive 1902.02
Streiford, Hobart 1947.11
Streiford, Hobe 1955.27
Streiman, Mr. 1892.43
Streisand, Barbra 1962.05, 1964.11
Streitmann, Carl 1891.36
Strelitz, Carlyn 1907.36
Stremel, Henry 1923.02, 1923.23
Strepo, Fred 1869.07
Streshnev, Valery 1936.05
Stretti, R. 1897.45
Stretti, Rene 1895.34
Stretton Mr. 1855.09
Strickland, Addie 1871.27
Strickland, Bruce 1981.15
Strickland, Lily 1956.11
Strickland, Mabel 1896.27
Strickland, Marion 1890.35, 1892.01
Strickland, Miss 1869.29, 1869.40, 1870.13
Strickland, Mr. 1836.01
Strickland, Peggy 1935.08
Strickler, Ilene 1979.31
Strickler, Jerry 1962.20
Striker, Cora 1886.14
Strine, Helen 1958.13
Stringer, Marcie 1971.05
Stringer, Robert 1956.08
Stringer, Willie 1898.02
Strini, S.P. 1879.14
Stritch, Billy 1991.04, 1999.23, 2001.08
Stritch, Elaine 1947.20, 1952.01, 1954.12, 1958.14, 1961.18, 1967.09, 1970.13, 1994.08
Stritter, Mlle. 1870.44
Strizck, A. 1908.16
Strodel, Josephine 1869.38
Stroeva, Dora 1923.32
Strogoff, Ivan 1919.06
Stroman, Guy 1979.22
Stroman, Susan 1979.05, 1980.11, 1990.07, 1991.04, 1991.08, 1992.02, 1992.10, 1994.08, 1994.12, 1995.19, 1996.08, 1996.15, 1997.07, 1997.22, 1998.20, 1999.21, 2000.07, 2000.11, 2000.19, 2001.05
Stromberg, John 1896.14, 1896.26, 1896.36, 1897.09, 1897.19, 1897.31, 1897.48, 1898.50, 1898.72, 1899.17, 1899.30, 1900.38, 1901.17, 1902.29, 1904.41, 1912.07, 1917.26
Stromberg, Jr., Hunt 1945.16, 1948.16
Stromberg, Natta 1901.17
Strong, Alma 1892.59
Strong, Austin 1908.41, 1955.10
Strong, Barrett 1997.21
Strong, Cora 1893.37
Strong, D. 1868.03
Strong, D.A. 1866.18, 1869.43
Strong, David 1870.04
Strong, Edger 1878.22
Strong, Edward 1982.04, 1988.05, 1991.05, 1995.05, 1998.11, 1998.13
Strong, Elmira 1888.08
Strong, F.W. 1885.46
Strong, Fred 1893.11
Strong, Fred W. 1915.32
Strong, G. 1868.18
Strong, J.S. 1883.22
Strong, Jack 1927.38
Strong, Julia 1926.33
Strong, Lewis 1911.28
Strong, Louise 1919.14
Strong, Marliene 1945.08
Strong, Mr. 1867.15
Strong, Nellie 1922.04
Strong, R.H. 1908.44
Strong, Rod 1956.08, 1957.10
Strong, Rudolph 1884.24
Strong, Wayland 1938.02
Strong, William 1900.47
Strongin, Mimi 1945.05
Stroock, Geraldine 1944.14
Stroppini, Anna 1958.18
Strosburg, Miss 1870.31
Stross, Antonio 1904.24
Stroud, Claude 1948.23
Strouse, Charles 1960.06, 1962.04, 1964.32, 1966.06, 1970.09, 1977.06, 1978.28, 1979.13, 1980.23, 1981.07, 1983.08, 1985.15, 1986.03, 1986.13, 1991.15, 1997.01, 1997.04
Strouse, Irving 1923.32
Strozier, Othella 1946.21
Strtton, Clare 1924.25
Struck, R.J. 1896.51, 1900.05
Strudel, Josephine 1876.03
Strudel, Mlle. 1872.10, 1873.10
Strudell, Hattie 1876.03
Strudwick, Shepperd 1938.15, 1973.09, 1989.18
Strunz, William 1913.27
Strurges, Charles 1872.40
Struvy, Frank E. 1892.18, 1892.45
Stryker, Gustav 1937.01
Stryker, Muriel 1921.17, 1922.19, 1923.20, 1924.41
Stryker, Paul 1993.19
Stuaffer, Aubrey 1911.13
Stuart, Albert 1913.31, 1915.25
Stuart, Alex. 1868.14
Stuart, Augusta 1873.12, 1873.14
Stuart, Betty 1940.02, 1944.01
Stuart, C. 1856.04, 1859.06
Stuart, Charles 1868.14
Stuart, Eleanor 1911.13
Stuart, Ellie 1879.56
Stuart, Eva 1914.30
Stuart, Francis 1902.05
Stuart, George 1919.41
Stuart, Grant 1911.44
Stuart, Gwen 1990.05
Stuart, H. 1869.08
Stuart, H.A. 1880.54
Stuart, Harry 1877.24, 1901.13, 1907.21
Stuart, Helen 1880.69
Stuart, Henri 1871.16
Stuart, J.H. 1878.19, 1880.05, 1883.17, 1883.18, 1883.21, 1883.39, 1884.46, 1885.68
Stuart, Jane 1894.32
Stuart, Jay 1970.10, 1979.02, 1980.16
Stuart, John 1989.11
Stuart, Julia 1885.65
Stuart, Larry 1946.04
Stuart, Leslie 1895.32, 1897.14, 1898.56, 1899.11, 1900.51, 1902.05, 1902.35, 1904.29, 1905.13, 1906.47, 1907.15, 1909.04, 1911.02, 1911.32, 1911.45, 1914.02, 1920.09, 1933.21
Stuart, Lillie 1879.50
Stuart, Lynne 1953.16
Stuart, Mabel 1884.21
Stuart, Mabelle 1884.60
Stuart, Mae 1892.55
Stuart, Mai 1892.15
Stuart, Marco 1881.03
Stuart, Marie 1898.49, 1899.13
Stuart, Marie D. 1906.03
Stuart, Marion 1898.18, 1898.46, 1928.49
Stuart, Mary 1872.23, 1881.28, 1882.44, 1889.54, 1890.10
Stuart, Mary Ellen 1985.12, 1989.03
Stuart, May 1889.34, 1897.01

Stuart, Michael 1960.01
Stuart, Michel 1961.27, 1962.27, 1975.15, 1980.08, 1982.09, 1983.21
Stuart, Mike 1950.02
Stuart, Miss 1841.01
Stuart, Mr. 1823.01, 1859.01, 1868.04
Stuart, Patricia Quinn 1970.20
Stuart, Ralph 1934.03
Stuart, Roy 1959.21, 1960.01, 1962.21, 1964.18
Stuart, Ruby 1889.19
Stuart, Sonja 1976.05
Stuart, Stella 1892.15
Stuart, Sue 1903.23, 1904.56, 1905.22, 1905.41
Stuart, Sybil 1921.17
Stuart, Tom 1995.19, 1997.22
Stuart, Victoria 1905.03, 1907.07
Stuart, William 1857.05, 1857.07, 1859.11, 1875.01, 1875.02, 1875.04
Stuart-Clark, Chris 1964.29
Stubbs, Bill 1951.05
Stubbs, Herbert 1956.06
Stubbs, Mme. 1841.01
Stubel, C. 1890.08
Stubel, Camillo 1896.12
Stuckman, Eugene 1947.09
Studdiford, Grace 1907.15, 1908.21, 1911.12
Studholme, Marie 1895.43, 1897.32
Studiford, Grace 1925.11
Studio Productions, Inc. 1949.17
Studleigh, Doris 1888.11
Studleigh, Dorris 1888.06
Studley, J.B. 1872.10, 1879.42
Studley, Kate 1982.04
Studley, Samuel L. 1880.48, 1880.53, 1882.07, 1882.08, 1882.09, 1882.10, 1882.11, 1882.12, 1882.13, 1883.11, 1883.12, 1883.13, 1883.14, 1883.15, 1891.29, 1893.19, 1893.48, 1894.03, 1894.08, 1894.45, 1895.01, 1896.08, 1896.42, 1896.43, 1897.13, 1898.23, 1900.25, 1900.31, 1900.32, 1902.04, 1902.28
Sturge, Tom 1990.16, 1992.15
Sturgeon, Jean 1944.20
Sturgeon, T. William 1899.04, 1901.14
Sturges, Charles 1872.08, 1872.12, 1872.14, 1872.25, 1872.30, 1872.32, 1872.36, 1872.38, 1872.43, 1878.05, 1882.76, 1884.25, 1884.41, 1885.02, 1885.15, 1885.22, 1886.42, 1886.52, 1887.07, 1887.39, 1887.48, 1888.14, 1888.27, 1888.40, 1889.07, 1889.11, 1889.15, 1889.18, 1889.37, 1889.51, 1891.08, 1891.25, 1891.45, 1893.15, 1893.27, 1893.36, 1893.46, 1894.04, 1896.24, 1902.27
Sturges, James 1882.14, 1884.25, 1884.29, 1884.30, 1888.06, 1888.11
Sturges, James A. 1880.05
Sturges, Joseph 1884.21
Sturges, Lucielle 1897.16
Sturges, Preston 1930.36, 1951.13, 1953.11, 1961.02
Sturgess, Arthur 1897.41, 1898.26, 1898.63
Sturgess, James 1898.09
Sturgess, Joseph H. 1882.09
Sturgess, Lucille 1897.46
Sturgis, Charles 1887.16, 1887.45, 1892.54, 1893.10, 1895.34
Sturgis, Charles E. 1897.37, 1898.51
Sturgis, G.S. 1879.13
Sturgis, James 1882.32
Sturgis, James A. 1891.26, 1892.09
Sturgiss, J.H. 1883.12, 1883.13, 1883.15
Sturm, Jason 1989.05
Sturmfels, Fritz 1912.10
Sturner, Lynda 1965.23
Sturrup, Leonard 1934.37
Sturt, Jeremy 2000.04
Stutz, Richard 1949.01
Stutz. Carl 1954.08
Stuyvesant Producing Company, The 1916.07
Stuz, Wilbur 1916.22
Styler, Alan 1951.01, 1951.03, 1951.06, 1951.07, 1951.08, 1955.15, 1955.21, 1955.24, 1962.26, 1962.28, 1962.29, 1964.37, 1964.42
Styles, Edwin 1932.18
Styles, William T. 1872.06
Styme, Franklin T. 1951.15
Styne, Jule 1942.12, 1947.16, 1949.18, 1950.12, 1951.13, 1951.19, 1952.01, 1953.01, 1954.13, 1956.02, 1956.14, 1958.08, 1958.21, 1959.03, 1959.13, 1960.23, 1961.28, 1964.11, 1964.21, 1964.35, 1965.08, 1967.03, 1967.06, 1967.11, 1967.12, 1968.02, 1970.08, 1972.04, 1973.17, 1974.02, 1974.10, 1974.17, 1977.02, 1977.05, 1979.14, 1979.22, 1980.29, 1983.09, 1988.08, 1989.03, 1989.27, 1990.09, 1990.20, 1991.04, 1991.06, 1991.10, 1991.13, 1992.16, 1993.19, 1995.07, 1998.18, 1998.19, 1999.01, 1999.23, 2001.03
Styne, Karen 1961.12
Styx, Carl 1905.44
Suarez, Olga 1944.21, 1947.14
Suarez, Wilfredo 1979.03
Subber, Arnold Saint 1945.09
Subber, Arny Saint 1944.30
Subber, Saint 1940.07, 1948.32, 1950.20, 1952.02, 1954.19, 1976.11
Suckling, Jenny-Lynn 1999.04
Sucram, A.J. 1907.28
Sucre, Perez 1927.51
Sudana, Tapa 1983.16
Suddeth, J. Allen 1997.09
Sudeykin, S. 1929.05
Sudeykin, Sergei 1927.51
Sudlow, Bessie 1869.02, 1869.20, 1869.43, 1871.10, 1871.27, 1872.37, 1873.10, 1873.28
Sudrow, Irving 1972.20
Sue, Lyda 1940.06
Suehsdorf, David 2000.10
Sues, Leonard 1942.11, 1942.29
Suesse, Dana 1930.38, 1932.14, 1934.01, 1938.07
Suez, Armando 1974.14
Suffin, Jordan 1975.03
Sugawara, Hiroshi 1989.24, 1990.17
Sugden, Peter 1962.29
Suisman, Charles 1991.15
Suit, Mr. 1865.01
Suiter, Bobra 1949.03
Sukman, Harry 1950.14
Sulic, Vassili 1964.22
Sulkin, Harry 1909.04, 1911.34, 1912.17
Sullivan, Alex 1919.19, 1920.10, 1920.36, 1921.26
Sullivan, Anthony 1899.15
Sullivan, Arthur 1871.27, 1875.35, 1879.05, 1879.06, 1879.07, 1879.08, 1879.09, 1879.10, 1879.11, 1879.13, 1879.14, 1879.16, 1879.17, 1879.21, 1879.28, 1879.29, 1879.30, 1879.58, 1879.59, 1879.64, 1879.66, 1879.70, 1879.72, 1880.12, 1880.45, 1880.53, 1881.19, 1881.37, 1881.43, 1881.57, 1882.04, 1882.10, 1882.12, 1882.19, 1882.21, 1882.22, 1882.38, 1882.40, 1882.42, 1882.48, 1882.54, 1882.78, 1883.14, 1883.15, 1883.21, 1883.24, 1883.26, 1884.09, 1884.30, 1884.31, 1884.37, 1885.04, 1885.13, 1885.16, 1885.34, 1885.37, 1885.43, 1885.47, 1885.48, 1885.62, 1885.70, 1886.12, 1886.17, 1886.24, 1886.25, 1886.29, 1886.55, 1886.57, 1887.10, 1887.21, 1887.25, 1887.29, 1888.35, 1890.02, 1890.14, 1890.15, 1890.18, 1890.20, 1890.46, 1890.47, 1890.48, 1891.32, 1892.14, 1892.37, 1892.40, 1892.46, 1893.09, 1894.15, 1894.23, 1895.26, 1896.17, 1896.19, 1896.22, 1898.09, 1898.21, 1898.42, 1898.52, 1898.65, 1898.71, 1899.07, 1899.16, 1899.20, 1900.04, 1900.11, 1900.21, 1900.26, 1900.27, 1900.37, 1902.22, 1902.25, 1905.22, 1910.14, 1911.21, 1912.18, 1912.21, 1912.22, 1912.23, 1913.11, 1913.12, 1913.13, 1914.11, 1915.06, 1915.09, 1915.10, 1915.12, 1915.13, 1915.14, 1918.23, 1919.04, 1925.13, 1925.15, 1925.17, 1926.08, 1926.10, 1926.44, 1927.24, 1927.25, 1927.44, 1927.57, 1927.61, 1928.20, 1928.25, 1931.10, 1931.12, 1931.15, 1931.17, 1931.18, 1931.20, 1931.22, 1931.23, 1931.24, 1931.25, 1933.08, 1933.09, 1933.10, 1933.11, 1933.14, 1933.18, 1933.19, 1934.07, 1934.08, 1934.09, 1934.10, 1934.11, 1934.21, 1934.22, 1934.24, 1934.25, 1934.26, 1934.27, 1934.28, 1934.30, 1934.31, 1934.33, 1935.05, 1935.06, 1935.07, 1935.08, 1935.09, 1935.10, 1936.04, 1936.08, 1936.09, 1936.10, 1936.11, 1936.13, 1936.14, 1936.15, 1936.16, 1936.18, 1936.19, 1936.20, 1936.21, 1936.23, 1936.24, 1936.25, 1938.10, 1939.01, 1939.02, 1939.03, 1939.04, 1939.05, 1939.06, 1939.08, 1939.09, 1939.11, 1939.15, 1939.17, 1940.11, 1940.13, 1940.14, 1940.15, 1942.02, 1942.04, 1942.06, 1942.07, 1942.08, 1942.09, 1944.04, 1944.05, 1944.06, 1944.07, 1944.08, 1944.09, 1944.10, 1944.11, 1944.12, 1944.13, 1945.08, 1945.09, 1946.11, 1947.22, 1948.01, 1948.02, 1948.03, 1948.05, 1948.06, 1948.07, 1948.09, 1948.10, 1949.10, 1949.11, 1949.13, 1949.14, 1951.01, 1951.03, 1951.04, 1951.06, 1951.07, 1951.08, 1951.09, 1952.14, 1952.16, 1952.17, 1952.18, 1952.19, 1955.15, 1955.16, 1955.18, 1955.20, 1955.21, 1955.22, 1955.23, 1955.24, 1959.18, 1960.14, 1960.15, 1961.03, 1961.04, 1961.05, 1961.06, 1961.19, 1961.23, 1962.08, 1962.09, 1962.10, 1962.11, 1962.19, 1962.25, 1962.26, 1962.28, 1962.29, 1962.30, 1962.31, 1963.23, 1964.07, 1964.08, 1964.09, 1964.10, 1964.12, 1964.13, 1964.14, 1964.36, 1964.37, 1964.38, 1964.41, 1964.42, 1964.43, 1965.09, 1965.10, 1965.11, 1965.12, 1965.13, 1966.22, 1966.23, 1966.25, 1966.26, 1966.28, 1968.09, 1968.10, 1968.12, 1968.14, 1968.15, 1968.25, 1968.26, 1968.27, 1968.28, 1968.29, 1974.07, 1974.15, 1975.17, 1976.12, 1976.13, 1976.14, 1976.22, 1977.03, 1977.17, 1978.14, 1978.15, 1978.16, 1978.17, 1981.01, 1984.12, 1985.10, 1987.01, 1989.01, 1989.15, 1990.13, 1993.13, 1995.10, 1996.11, 1997.02
Sullivan, Arthur S. 1934.23
Sullivan, Barry 1942.11
Sullivan, Brad 1967.10, 1978.12
Sullivan, Brian 1947.02
Sullivan, Charles 1887.16, 1897.12
Sullivan, D.J. 1905.24, 1922.31, 1925.11, 1926.29
Sullivan, Dan 1895.39, 1980.21, 1981.20, 1981.21
Sullivan, Dan J. 1907.49
Sullivan, Daniel 1903.09, 1919.01, 1933.02
Sullivan, Daniel J. 1907.56, 1910.06, 1932.01
Sullivan, Ed 1942.13
Sullivan, Ed. 1884.64
Sullivan, Elliot 1943.23
Sullivan, Elliott 1947.07, 1957.03
Sullivan, Frank 1932.13, 1963.11
Sullivan, George 1911.17
Sullivan, Gloria 1948.16
Sullivan, Henry 1929.19, 1929.29, 1929.32, 1931.14, 1932.27, 1934.18, 1934.42, 1953.17
Sullivan, Howard 1937.02
Sullivan, Hugh 1965.39
Sullivan, Ian 1976.01, 1977.12, 1992.07
Sullivan, J. 1883.32
Sullivan, J. Francis 1903.29
Sullivan, J.B. 1881.15
Sullivan, J.E. 1890.03
Sullivan, J.G. 1877.28
Sullivan, J.P. 1886.10, 1906.03, 1915.03
Sullivan, J.W. 1902.04
Sullivan, James 1925.12
Sullivan, James E. 1888.39, 1900.05, 1901.08, 1903.38, 1907.18, 1908.40, 1910.11, 1911.30, 1921.06, 1924.05
Sullivan, James Francis 1905.16
Sullivan, James J. 1918.36
Sullivan, Jerry 1905.10
Sullivan, Jerry D. 1905.47
Sullivan, Jo 1948.18, 1948.28, 1950.18, 1954.07, 1956.04, 1958.05, 1961.09, 1966.19, 1980.29, 1992.01
Sullivan, Joe 1925.22
Sullivan, John Maurice 1925.35
Sullivan, John T. 1882.81
Sullivan, Joseph 1886.24, 1901.08, 1964.27
Sullivan, Joseph J. 1889.05, 1906.06
Sullivan, Julia 1913.35
Sullivan, K.T. 1989.24, 1995.07
Sullivan, Knute 1958.01, 1960.09
Sullivan, Lee 1940.09, 1941.09, 1942.26, 1942.30, 1947.07
Sullivan, M. 1901.06
Sullivan, M.J. 1885.35, 1890.32, 1892.23, 1892.45, 1896.31, 1901.07, 1903.11
Sullivan, Margaret 1926.02
Sullivan, Marietta 1926.32
Sullivan, Mark 1884.37, 1889.06, 1889.39, 1891.04, 1893.08, 1906.19, 1909.26, 1919.25
Sullivan, Mary 1960.01
Sullivan, Maxine 1939.29
Sullivan, Messr. 1883.31
Sullivan, Michael 1895.34
Sullivan, Mollie 1901.20
Sullivan, Mr. 1864.02, 1867.15, 1867.16, 1872.35, 1873.25, 1879.37
Sullivan, Newt 1964.04
Sullivan, Nick 1998.13
Sullivan, P.H. 1904.41, 1907.34
Sullivan, Patrick Ryan 1999.16
Sullivan, Paul 1968.13, 1972.06, 1972.11, 1972.21, 1984.09
Sullivan, R. 1873.26
Sullivan, Richard 1922.41
Sullivan, Richard F. 1893.30
Sullivan, Roger 1965.03
Sullivan, Sheila 1966.07
Sullivan, T.R. 1879.15
Sullivan, Ted 1909.04
Sullivan, Terry 1909.07
Sullivan, Tony 1898.56, 1906.36, 1907.39
Sullivan, W. 1867.13, 1867.17
Sullivan, William 1882.70
Sullivan, William J. 1903.36
Sully, Cecil 1908.07
Sully, Dan 1884.26
Sully, Miss 1869.43
Sully, Thomas 1871.16
Sully, William 1920.33, 1924.22, 1926.28, 1938.03
Sultan, Arnie 1962.02
Sumak, Yma 1951.15
Sumbry, Dormeshia 1989.02
Sumdsten, Kaja 1948.18
Summer, Charles 1923.20
Summer, Donna 1982.22
Summer, Sting 1982.22
Summerfield, Maggie 1882.46
Summerfield, Mlle. 1888.39
Summerford, Nikki 1980.12
Summerhays, Jane 1986.12, 2000.08
Summers, Ann 1926.22
Summers, Beatrice 1918.30, 1919.06
Summers, Cecil 1903.18, 1922.29
Summers, Cecil B. 1906.29
Summers, J.W. 1887.51
Summers, Lydia 1950.05
Summers, Madlyn 1905.18, 1906.45, 1907.24, 1908.04
Summers, Madlyn J. 1908.39
Summers, Madlyn Jane 1906.01
Summers, Miss 1908.19
Summers, Mr. 1906.29
Summers, Sam 1926.22, 1929.50
Summerville, Ada 1922.18
Summerville, Amelia 1883.65, 1884.42, 1885.58, 1886.47, 1890.43, 1893.13, 1895.18, 1896.41, 1899.23, 1900.19, 1900.49, 1900.56, 1901.12, 1902.06, 1905.49, 1910.25, 1913.19, 1922.28
Summerville, Annie 1880.40, 1887.43
Summerville, Marie 1880.57
Sumner, Charles 1922.19
Sumner, Charlotte 1938.15
Sumner, David 1992.15
Sumner, George 1941.13
Sumner, Locke-Elliot 1953.17
Sumner, Marjorie 1931.44
Sumner, William 1939.01, 1939.05, 1939.08, 1939.09, 1939.11, 1962.05
Sumner, Willy 1959.13
Sumpter, Ralph 1959.01
Sumter, Ralph 1935.14
Sundberg, Clinton 1939.13
Sunderman, William 1932.19
Sundgaard, Arnold 1938.18, 1944.28, 1961.11
Sundmark, Betty 1931.01
Sundquist 1915.29, 1916.26
Sundquist and Street 1916.11
Sundquist Studio 1915.17
Sundsten, Lani 1973.02
Sundstrom, Florence 1945.12
Sundt, Jacqueline 1951.16
Sunguroff, Tamara Bering 1979.29
Sunmter, Ralph 1937.16
Sunquist Studio 1916.09

Sunshine Sue 1954.08
Sunshine, Marion 1907.24, 1911.12, 1912.43, 1914.06, 1914.13, 1915.31, 1917.36, 1919.29, 1920.13, 1920.36, 1922.02, 1922.26, 1925.29, 1931.31
Suntory International Corporation 1989.03, 1989.29, 1990.12
Superstar Ventures 1992.12
Suppe 1884.42, 1894.19, 1899.23
Suppon, Charles 1979.11, 1988.20
Suratt, Valeska 1906.47, 1911.23, 1922.23
Surely, Ms. 1870.15
Surface, Herb 1956.01
Surface, Herbert 1955.01, 1965.38
Surmont, Messr. 1867.05
Surovy, Nicholas 1975.18
Surridge, J.H. 1868.33, 1870.08, 1870.11, 1870.27, 1870.38, 1876.04, 1876.05, 1876.09, 1876.10, 1876.14, 1876.30, 1876.33, 1877.05
Surridge, James 1914.22, 1915.27
Surridge, Messr. 1876.11
Susann, Jacqueline 1941.13, 1943.12, 1944.01, 1945.01
Suskind, Milton 1925.40
Sussanina, N. 1924.48
Susskind, David 1965.01
Sussman, Bruce 1976.34, 1989.08, 1991.10
Sussman, Sadie 1925.20, 1926.17, 1927.23
Susswein, Joan 1977.12
Susy, Mlle. 1869.26
Sutcliffe, Steven 1998.01
Sutherland, Alan 1954.13
Sutherland, Annie 1886.32, 1894.05
Sutherland, Brian 1983.08, 1990.06, 1992.10, 1997.15
Sutherland, Claudette 1961.22
Sutherland, Don 1969.15
Sutherland, Evelyn Greenleaf 1924.23
Sutherland, Evelyn Grenleaf 1919.42
Sutherland, J.L. 1903.10
Sutherland, Joie 1889.39
Sutherland, Karen 1982.11
Sutherland, Lillie 1897.04, 1901.22
Sutherland, Margaret 1903.31
Sutherland, Marie 1904.21
Sutherland, Mary 1936.22, 1938.08
Sutherland, Miss 1895.18
Sutherland, Pressley 1995.02
Sutherland, Rose 1890.50, 1896.02, 1897.04, 1898.03
Sutherland, William 1944.17, 1952.15
Sutphen, Joy 1927.07
Sutter, Harry 1899.27
Sutton, Alma 1946.01
Sutton, Bryan Anthony 2001.04
Sutton, C.W. 1883.36
Sutton, Charles 1883.01
Sutton, Charles W. 1884.56
Sutton, Dolores 1993.18
Sutton, Frank 1896.04
Sutton, Harry 1905.40
Sutton, Harry O. 1905.26, 1907.18, 1980.27
Sutton, Henry 1982.01
Sutton, John 1882.56
Sutton, Kay 1939.30
Sutton, Mamie 1897.24
Sutton, Mr. 1866.17
Sutton, R. 1866.16
Sutton, Sheryl 1975.10
Sutton, Susie 1930.10, 1935.01
Sutur, Henry 1900.36
Sutzkever, Abraham 1998.11
Suyematsu, Tommy 1921.18
Suzanne, Georges 1949.06
Suzanne, Mlle. 1867.24
Suzette Producing Company 1921.38
Suzov, Nina 1926.14
Suzuki, Pay 1958.19
Suzy 1964.22
Svetlik, Gisella 1951.24
Svetlik, Susan 1947.17
Svigals, Phil 1929.17, 1929.28
Svoboda, W. 1924.48
Svorg, Frl. 1898.38
Swados, Elizabeth 1983.18
Swados, Liz 1978.11
Swails, Wesley 1953.11
Swaim, Kelley 1997.04
Swain, C. 1881.18
Swain, C.W. 1884.04, 1884.07
Swain, Carrie 1880.38, 1883.36, 1886.02
Swain, Charles 1901.25, 1904.13, 1904.44
Swain, Charles W. 1888.04
Swain, Lillian 1894.23, 1896.18, 1896.22, 1896.26, 1896.36, 1897.09, 1897.19, 1897.31, 1897.48, 1898.21, 1898.30
Swain, Samuel 1880.38
Swan, Anna 1865.05, 1865.09
Swan, Bill 1938.16
Swan, Boots 1929.52
Swan, Buddy 1942.35
Swan, Charles 1914.31
Swan, E.A. 1986.02
Swan, Lea 1924.46
Swan, Mark 1910.25, 1913.16, 1922.07, 1923.01
Swan, Mark E. 1899.08, 1905.52, 1906.35, 1907.47, 1911.29
Swan, Miss 1877.39
Swan, Mr. 1855.04, 1855.05, 1855.08, 1855.09
Swan, Rima 1927.11
Swan-Lani 1930.26
Swander, Don 1981.04
Swank, Mark 1927.09
Swanlee 1964.18
Swann, Donald 1955.19, 1959.20, 1966.32
Swann, Elaine 1957.18, 1960.05, 1963.25
Swann. Donald 1958.10
Swansen, Larry 1977.07
Swanson, Alice 1928.45, 1934.03
Swanson, Beatrice 1920.09, 1921.03, 1921.14, 1922.07, 1923.13, 1924.06, 1925.23, 1928.01
Swanson, Bob 1964.02
Swanson, Britt 1973.03, 1973.09, 1989.18
Swanson, Larry 1967.07
Swanson, Louise 1937.11
Swanson, Marcella 1920.09, 1921.03, 1921.14, 1922.07, 1923.13, 1924.06, 1925.07, 1928.06, 1929.06, 1929.48, 1936.31
Swanstone, Arthur 1919.06
Swanstrom 1935.19
Swanstrom, A. 1919.32
Swanstrom, Arthur 1919.06, 1919.18, 1920.24, 1920.28, 1920.36, 1921.27, 1922.03, 1929.44, 1930.30, 1933.21, 1934.42, 1937.07, 1975.09
Swanstrom, Bjorn I. 1970.06
Swanton, Brian 2000.04
Swarbrick, Carol 1979.05, 1995.07
Sward, Doris 1946.04
Sward, Doris M. 1945.02
Swarns, Charles 1908.10
Swart, Elmer E. 1896.05, 1907.61
Swarts, Frederick 1922.21
Swartz, Alfred T. 1887.02
Swartz, Ed 1911.25
Swartz, J.A. 1876.22
Swartz, Oscar 1909.24
Swayne, Charles 1906.04
Swayze, Pat 1975.06
Sweatnam, Billy 1883.03
Sweatnam, Willis P. 1891.43, 1893.28, 1894.10, 1895.17, 1898.03, 1898.78, 1907.09, 1910.16
Sweeney, Charles 1895.03
Sweeney, Emily 1910.17
Sweeney, Florence 1903.12
Sweeney, Fred 1916.15, 1918.38
Sweeney, Hugh 1931.44
Sweeney, Joseph 1951.17
Sweeney, Julia 1907.53
Sweeney, Mr. 1841.01
Sweet, Alice 1900.59
Sweet, Beverly 1941.11
Sweet, Blanche 1902.36
Sweet, Dolph 1972.01
Sweet, Edith 1883.22
Sweet, Eleanor 1927.07
Sweet, George 1882.64, 1883.16, 1924.34, 1924.47, 1927.39, 1930.23
Sweet, John 1947.02
Sweet, Marjorie 1930.04
Sweetland, Lee 1949.16
Sweetland, Reynolds 1915.25
Sweetman, Aaron 1999.02
Sweetman, Florinne 1904.41
Sweetser, Norman 1923.37, 1925.43
Swell, Jim Town 1921.16
Sweninger, Cleo 1906.33
Swenson, Arthur 1932.28
Swenson, Inga 1956.08, 1963.26, 1965.02, 1968.17
Swenson, Karl 1934.40, 1936.12
Swenson, Rod 1982.22
Swenson, Swen 1950.19, 1959.11, 1960.22, 1962.27, 1966.30, 1973.11, 1981.13, 1986.03
Swerd, Lester 1913.07
Swerling, Jo 1927.11, 1950.17, 1955.06, 1965.15, 1966.13, 1976.21, 1992.04
Swete, E. Lyall 1917.24, 1919.20, 1919.38, 1920.34
Sweyd, Lester 1917.24, 1919.38
Swickard, Joseph 1896.37
Swickard, Joseph P. 1905.02
Swickard, Louise Temple 1905.02
Swift, Allen 1963.20
Swift, Arthur 1909.13
Swift, David 1894.31
Swift, Hattie 1882.15
Swift, James 1932.11
Swift, Kay 1929.19, 1930.06, 1930.18, 1930.28, 1930.33, 1952.04
Swift, Peter 1905.16, 1906.16, 1907.17, 1908.39, 1909.25, 1910.18, 1911.24, 1912.38, 1913.17, 1914.26, 1915.16, 1916.10
Swift, Reina 1907.11
Swift, Thomas F. 1923.37
Swinbourne, John 1881.31
Swinburne, Ann 1912.33, 1913.32
Swinburne, Anne 1912.19
Swinburne, Eva 1892.33, 1892.47
Swinburne, J.P. 1879.10
Swindell, Bill 1998.19
Swindler, Mark 1996.10
Swindler, William 1989.10
Swingle, Ward 1964.39
Swinsky, Mort 1995.05, 2000.18
Swinstead, Joan 1936.29
Swirse, Myer 1917.16
Swirskaia, Mlle. 1917.08
Swirskaia, Thamara 1916.11
Switz, Frank 1871.09
Swoboda, Vecheslav 1943.11
Swor, Irene 1930.14
Swor, John 1916.11
Swor, Mabelle 1926.15
Swyningan, Quincella 1980.14
Sydell, Paul 1961.10, 1964.22
Sydenham, George 1911.04, 1924.20
Syder, Matt B. 1902.36
Sydney, Ethel 1895.10, 1895.32
Sydney, Mona 1901.08
Sydney, Thomas 1917.02
Sydnor, Earl 1940.17, 1952.08
Sydow, Jack 1963.12, 1966.12, 1966.16
Syers, Mark 1977.18, 1979.23
Syers, Mark Hsu 1976.02
Sykes, Albert 1902.43
Sykes, Albert S. 1900.50
Sykes, Dama 1914.31, 1920.09
Sykes, Dick 1949.12
Sykes, Ethel 1914.31, 1915.31, 1916.25, 1917.21
Sykes, Gladys 1914.31, 1916.25, 1917.21
Sykes, Jerome 1891.29, 1892.52, 1894.45, 1895.01, 1896.51, 1897.25, 1897.50, 1899.06, 1900.01, 1900.50, 1902.43
Sylber, Charley 1928.06
Sylbert, Paul 1959.08, 1959.17, 1963.15, 1966.02, 1978.23, 1979.27, 1990.08
Sylla, Mlle. 1879.19, 1879.26, 1879.27, 1879.31, 1879.34, 1879.36, 1879.39, 1879.40, 1879.41, 1879.43, 1879.44, 1879.45, 1879.46, 1879.47, 1879.48, 1879.51
Sylovna, Sydelle 1946.05
Sylphe, La 1919.13, 1920.17
Sylva, Marguerita 1897.37, 1898.17, 1911.37, 1927.63, 1930.26, 1937.17
Sylva, Marguerite 1897.25, 1898.41, 1898.60, 1899.36, 1900.16, 1903.32
Sylvan, Oscar 1965.03
Sylvan, Paul 1971.12
Sylvan, Sanford 1996.10
Sylvania, Ida 1925.47
Sylvest, Donavan 1973.07
Sylveste, John 1900.36
Sylvester, Caroline 1904.28
Sylvester, George 1924.08
Sylvester, Hannah 1933.06
Sylvester, Henry S. 1907.50
Sylvester, Joyce 1981.15
Sylvester, Louise 1888.02, 1888.40, 1891.18, 1893.06, 1894.05, 1907.02
Sylvester, Luke 1904.14
Sylvester, Miss 1870.05
Sylvester, Mr. 1864.13
Sylvester,, Mrs. 1855.11
Sylvestre, C. 1855.06
Sylvia 1962.02
Sylvia, Abe 2001.05
Sylvia, Belle 1930.27
Sylvie, May 1879.25, 1879.65, 1879.67, 1881.04, 1892.14
Sylvon, Jerry 1934.37, 1944.02
Sylvor, Marvin 1970.04
Syme, Franklin T. 1951.15
Symington, Donald 1959.05, 1974.23
Symmons, Abner 1897.20, 1897.44, 1903.04
Symon, Burk 1933.20
Symonds, Frank 1903.06
Symonds, Messr. 1900.28
Symonds, Robert 1970.04
Symonette, Lys 1980.04, 1980.25
Symonette, Randolph 1944.28, 1945.04, 1947.02, 1950.18
Symons, Abner 1899.19
Sympson, Tony 1965.28
Syms, Sylvia 1955.07, 1958.20, 1961.07
Synnott, Cathal 2000.05
Syril, Jenny 1926.43
Syril, Mlle. 1926.45, 1926.48
Syrjala, Sointu 1937.14
Szabo, Nicholas 1907.48
Szabo, Sandor 1964.20
Szandrowsky, Myron 1942.33
Szantho, Enid 1945.15
Szarabajka, Keith 1983.18
Sze, Julia 1947.20, 1948.15
Szell, Lajos 1916.04
Szirmai, Albert 1924.18
Szobody, Bill 1997.05, 1998.04
Szollosy, Mons. 1861.03

T.A.T. Communications Company 1981.14
T.B. MacDonald Company 1920.36
Tabachnick, Ken 1988.14, 1988.18, 1989.04
Tabachnik, Robin 1990.02, 1990.08
Tabarin, Bal 1908.07
Tabbert, Bill 1944.14, 1944.29
Tabbert, William 1943.21, 1945.20, 1949.04, 1954.15
Taber, Richard 1908.31, 1918.41
Tabet, Georges 1935.19
Tabisel, Brett 1996.08
Tabor, Desiree 1927.17, 1932.06
Tabor, Edward 1909.23
Tabor, Eron 1975.09
Tabor, Grace 1892.04, 1893.23
Tabor, Lois E. 1906.20, 1907.21
Tabor, Lulu 1888.36, 1893.31
Tabor, Richard 1912.05, 1918.06
Tabrar, Joseph 1893.11
Tack, Alice 1892.59
Tackaberry, Celia 1986.07
Tadlock, Thelma 1952.01, 1953.08
Tadolini, E. 1879.15
Tafel, Miss 1916.05
taFel, Suzanne 1945.05
Tagelli, Nadina 1917.14
Taggart, George 1888.16
Taggart, Hal 1917.31
Taggert, Catherine 1914.33
Tagliapietra, G. 1889.28, 1891.36
Tahuriorangi, Irirangi 1972.20
Tahse, Martin 1960.17
Tai, Jue Quon 1920.24
Taillefer, Mlle. 1871.03, 1871.06
Tailraf, Z. 1881.31
Tait, Beatrice 1888.03, 1891.38, 1896.31
Tait, Dean 1976.20
Tait, James 1873.12, 1873.18, 1876.03, 1880.04, 1881.04, 1882.26, 1892.14
Tait, Millie 1896.31
Tait, Robert 1926.05
Taite 1870.33
Taiz, Lillian 1929.12
Taj Mahal 1991.01
Takahashi, K. 1903.19
Takara, Junko 1989.21
Takase, Paulo W. 1992.13
Takurua, Reverend Anaru 1972.20
Tal, David 1968.04
Talbert, James 1897.33
Talbot, Arthur 1907.22, 1909.10
Talbot, Howard 1898.17, 1902.19, 1903.22, 1903.33, 1904.12, 1904.29, 1906.41, 1907.41, 1909.01, 1909.29, 1910.05, 1911.27, 1912.26, 1919.02

Talbot, Hugh 1879.70, 1879.72
Talbot, John 1903.18
Talbot, Josh 2001.04
Talbot, Kittie 1889.35
Talbot, Lida H. 1884.10
Talbot, Lyle 1967.10
Talbot, Minnei 1889.35
Talbot, R. 1869.20
Talbot, Walter J. 1898.75
Talbot-Martin, Elizabeth 1940.21
Talby, Kate 1890.02, 1894.15
Talcott, Linda 1989.03, 1993.02, 1994.04
Talese, Maryanne 1986.14
Talfourd 1869.35
Talfourd, Francis 1853.05, 1857.05, 1867.27
Taliaferri 1927.28
Taliaferro, Dean 1961.28, 1962.24, 1963.13
Taliaferro, Edith 1920.37, 1923.22
Taliaferro, John 1954.01, 1955.05, 1962.14, 1964.04, 1964.33, 1965.17, 1966.10, 1969.05
Taliaferro, Mabel 1944.23, 1947.01
Taliafferro, Eddie 1947.19
Talleen Brothers 1865.08, 1865.10
Tallman, G.L. 1895.37
Tallman, George 1904.36, 1909.22, 1910.28
Tallman, George L. 1903.36
Tallman, Ward 1937.16
Tallmon, Ward 1941.04
Tallot, M. 1858.01
Tallot, Mlle. 1858.01
Talma, Elizabeth 1920.34
Talma, Zola 1925.02
Talma, Zolya 1944.27
Talmage, Ray 1920.36
Talman, George 1906.18
Talmud, Blanche 1922.20, 1925.20, 1926.17, 1927.23, 1928.19
Talor, Lovell 1905.26
Talor, William Banfield 1915.26
Talsky, Ron 1977.04
Talva, Galina 1950.15
Talwyn, Marja 1923.02
Talyn, Olga 1982.18, 1988.01
Tamantini, Franca 1964.03
Tamara 1927.11, 1931.13, 1931.28, 1938.31
Tamara, Florenz 1924.02
Tamarelle, Mme. 1883.28
Tamargo, Jose 1919.17
Tamaro, Signor 1867.25
Tamaroff, Harry 1922.30
Tamaroff, Marsha 1968.30, 1972.24
Tamasik, Laszlo 1972.08
Tamayana, Heshla 1934.37
Tambornino, Jeff 1986.18
Tamburrelli, Karen 1982.10, 1983.06
Tamiris, Helen 1945.03, 1946.01, 1946.12, 1946.20, 1947.11, 1948.14, 1948.20, 1949.12, 1950.06, 1950.19, 1951.15, 1953.11, 1954.02, 1954.15, 1955.01, 1958.03
Tamiroff, Messr. 1927.51
Tamm, Miss 1890.31
Tammany Amusement Company 1869.02, 1869.14, 1869.20, 1869.27, 1869.32, 1869.35, 1869.43, 1870.04
Tammany, William 1905.43
Tammaro, Jr., Johnny 1998.19
Tammia, Mr. 1859.01
Tample, Bessie 1881.34
Tamponi, Francis 1883.47
Tams 1929.34, 1929.36, 1929.38, 1929.40, 1929.43, 1929.48, 1930.03, 1934.12
Tams, A.W. 1890.39, 1891.22, 1908.03
Tams, Arthur 1885.65, 1890.24
Tams, Arthur W. 1881.05, 1884.20, 1884.32, 1884.33, 1884.35, 1884.38, 1887.33, 1887.50, 1888.20, 1889.23, 1890.01, 1890.11, 1890.19
Tams, Frank 1877.35
Tams, K. 1889.15, 1889.18
Tams, Kate 1888.27, 1888.40, 1889.11
Tanassy, Cornel 1958.02
Tandy, Spencer 1979.22
Tangira, Raana 1972.20
Tangira, Wiremu 1972.20
Tanguay, Eva 1898.61, 1901.06, 1902.20, 1903.34, 1905.40
Tani, Masazumi 1989.21
Tanina, Mille. 1922.37
Tankersley, Robert 1950.16
Tanna, Robert 1983.01
Tannassy, Cornell 1944.14
Tannehill, Bessie 1888.13, 1899.42, 1900.04, 1901.04, 1903.29, 1910.03
Tannehill, E.D.W. 1905.37
Tannehill, F. 1879.25
Tannehill, F.A. 1885.50
Tannehill, Frank 1878.05, 1897.56, 1899.35, 1903.15
Tannehill, Frank A. 1879.08, 1879.54
Tannehill, Jr., Frank 1880.35, 1881.47, 1884.14, 1884.39, 1888.28, 1888.29, 1889.34, 1889.45, 1891.03, 1893.42, 1893.49, 1895.34, 1897.56, 1901.23
Tannen, Danny 1931.30
Tannen, Julius 1905.22, 1905.41, 1917.25, 1920.45, 1924.15, 1925.25, 1925.48, 1926.23, 1927.02
Tannen, Julus 1906.21
Tannen, William 1930.18
Tannenbaum, Murray 1965.19
Tannenbaum, Steve 1975.18
Tanner, Betty 1940.10
Tanner, Catherine 1906.20, 1907.21
Tanner, Cora 1882.62, 1900.42
Tanner, Cora S. 1884.09
Tanner, Harry 1917.35
Tanner, J. 1879.23
Tanner, James T. 1897.20, 1897.32, 1897.52, 1898.29, 1901.19, 1902.01, 1902.30, 1907.15, 1910.21, 1911.39, 1913.36, 1914.18, 1915.18, 1975.22
Tanner, Jennie 1879.18, 1879.24
Tanner, John T. 1911.22
Tanner, Julius 1928.45
Tanner, Martha 1940.10
Tanner, Mickey 1940.10
Tanner, Mrs. Watt 1904.29
Tanner, Tony 1976.15, 1978.24, 1982.03, 1989.25
Tanno, Louis 1932.14
Tanno, Rita 1955.11
Tanno, Rito 1952.01
Tanny, Arno 1940.18
Tanya, Little 1967.03
Tanzi, Rigues 1936.02
Tanzy, Jeanne 1964.15, 1964.40, 1966.02, 1966.12, 1966.16
TAP Productions 1995.02
Tapia, Jose Luis 1939.18
Tapley, G. Henry 1908.08
Tapley, Green H. 1900.46
Tapley, Green Henry 1904.26
Tapock, Master 1871.18
Tapp, Kristy 1998.10
Tappan, Tami 1992.12
Tappe 1922.17
Tapps, George 1928.40, 1946.06, 1948.21
Tapps, Georgie 1932.20, 1937.13, 1943.14
Tarabula, Fritz 1934.18
Tarallo, Barry 1982.03
Tarasoff, I. 1921.30
Tarasoff, Ivan 1926.18, 1929.07
Tarasov, Ivan 1917.26
Tarassova, Mme. 1929.05
Tarazona Brothers 1917.25, 1917.33, 1920.02
Tarbox, Russell 1918.20, 1924.02, 1930.37
Tarbut, Nancy 1879.03
Tarbutton, James 1951.24, 1952.13, 1957.05
Tarchetti, I.U. 1994.05
Taridina, T. 1924.48
Tarkington, Booth 1910.33, 1919.42, 1926.02, 1951.18
Tarlow, Florence 1971.20
Tarplin, Marvin 1997.21
Tarpoff, Arsen 1943.11
Tarr, E. 1868.06
Tarr, E.S. 1869.26, 1871.04, 1871.18, 1873.02, 1875.21, 1880.41, 1881.02, 1881.24, 1896.18, 1898.20, 1898.68
Tarr, Edwin S. 1877.21, 1878.02, 1878.19, 1880.02, 1881.13, 1885.58, 1889.13, 1892.04
Tarrant, Robert T. 1928.23
Tarrazona Brothers 1920.13
Tartasky, Max 1946.02
Tartel, Michael 1969.08, 1976.25
Tartt, Paul Cook 1981.28
Tashamira 1942.17, 1944.26
Tashman, Lillian 1916.24
Tashman, Lilyan 1916.10, 1917.03, 1917.13, 1917.26
Task, Maggie 1959.02, 1960.05, 1962.01, 1963.08, 1968.06, 1969.17, 1970.08
Tasker, Ann 1912.45
Tassin, Christen 1989.27
Tassone, Ron 1964.46
Tassoni, Beverly 1950.17
Tatanacho 1925.17
Tate, Agnes 1919.38
Tate, Carroll 1930.29
Tate, Charles 1946.01, 1947.17
Tate, Ella 1906.48
Tate, Ellen 1907.52
Tate, Flora 1894.10
Tate, Grady 1981.16, 1983.20
Tate, James 1870.07, 1871.04, 1872.34, 1917.29
Tate, James W. 1907.32, 1916.22, 1918.27
Tate, Jimmy 1996.07
Tate, Messr. 1857.04
Tate, Mr. 1857.06
Tate, Neal 1978.21, 1980.15
Tate, Robert 1991.12
Tate, Ruth 1914.33
Tate, William 1881.31
Tatin, Mr. 1823.01
Tattersall, Gypsy 1888.21
Tattnall, Bennie 1933.04
Tatum, Marianne 1980.07, 1984.14, 1990.02
Taube, Theodore 1894.41
Tauber, Doris 1942.18, 1948.13, 1973.14, 1975.12
Tauber, Max 1932.18
Tauber, Richard 1946.16
Taubman, Milton 1944.33
Taubman, Paul 1932.14
Tauffenberger, F. 1880.44, 1880.50, 1880.58, 1881.46, 1881.48, 1881.50, 1881.53, 1881.54
Taupin, Bernie 1975.12, 1982.22
Taussig, Lynn 1959.08, 1959.17
Taussig, Walter 1948.31
Tautkus, Richard 1982.15
Tavares, Virginia 1917.04
Taverner, Sonia 1972.08
Taverner, Teddy 1951.17
Tavetaieff, Messr. 1929.05
Taweel, Maria 1946.03
Tax, Yan 1993.17
Tay, David A. 1999.17
Tay, Oxtavio 1918.23
Tayleure, Clifton 1867.19, 1867.20, 1868.06
Tayleure, Marie 1851.05
Tayleure, Miss 1851.02, 1853.01, 1853.03, 1869.28
Taylor, Albert B. 1955.08
Taylor, Alice 1902.36
Taylor, Andrew 1933.04
Taylor, Andrew J. 1946.09
Taylor, Andy 1997.06
Taylor, Becky 1897.51
Taylor, Belle 1892.49, 1911.31
Taylor, Billee 1906.04, 1911.43, 1912.09
Taylor, Billie 1904.18, 1910.01
Taylor, Billy 1922.29, 1924.41, 1925.04, 1928.50, 1929.37, 1934.14, 1934.18
Taylor, Bonnie Sue 1982.15
Taylor, C.W. 1852.02, 1860.02
Taylor, Charles 1950.08
Taylor, Charles A. 1904.28
Taylor, Charles H. 1902.35, 1904.01, 1904.29, 1905.27, 1907.51
Taylor, Charles M. 1905.55
Taylor, Clara 1857.01, 1915.23
Taylor, Clarice 1975.01
Taylor, Clement 1929.08
Taylor, Dan 1966.21
Taylor, David Evans 1969.07
Taylor, Deems 1910.20, 1926.11, 1945.10
Taylor, Desiree 1924.31
Taylor, Don 1943.23
Taylor, Dorothy 1919.06
Taylor, Drew 1991.05, 1997.04
Taylor, Dwight 1932.26, 1950.20
Taylor, E. 1851.03, 1851.05
Taylor, E.F. 1861.06, 1862.01, 1862.02, 1864.22, 1866.21, 1868.06
Taylor, E.H. 1887.31
Taylor, E.J. 1976.02
Taylor, Edward 1883.42, 1929.38, 1929.40, 1966.14, 1967.09
Taylor, Edwin 1918.10, 1918.31, 1923.14
Taylor, Edythe 1912.34
Taylor, Elizabeth 1929.21, 1957.05
Taylor, Elliott 1922.12
Taylor, Emma 1845.01, 1856.02, 1862.09, 1863.02, 1863.03
Taylor, Ernest 1945.09, 1947.02
Taylor, Eugene 1896.27, 1897.44
Taylor, Eva 1892.24, 1922.38, 1927.30
Taylor, Evelyn 1947.17, 1948.22, 1957.11, 1958.07, 1963.06, 1970.07
Taylor, Flora 1931.08
Taylor, Frances 1950.07
Taylor, Frank W. 1895.44
Taylor, G. 1851.02, 1851.05, 1852.04, 1855.06
Taylor, Gina 1985.03
Taylor, Harold 1946.09
Taylor, Harry 1873.12, 1873.17, 1876.16, 1911.28
Taylor, Helen 1932.14
Taylor, Henry 1873.14, 1904.37, 1911.10, 1916.15, 1917.16
Taylor, Howard 1918.31
Taylor, Howard P. 1888.04, 1888.34
Taylor, III., Baxter 1992.06
Taylor, Irving 1939.14, 1942.16
Taylor, J. 1870.05, 1871.13, 1871.20, 1871.21, 1873.24, 1877.04, 1882.52
Taylor, J. Harry 1905.17, 1908.26
Taylor, J.G. 1879.30, 1894.41
Taylor, J.H. 1869.40, 1869.44, 1909.20, 1910.23, 1912.30
Taylor, Jack 1903.21, 1904.55
Taylor, Jackie 1925.29
Taylor, James 1978.12, 1995.12
Taylor, James G. 1879.18, 1879.23, 1879.24
Taylor, James H. 1877.07
Taylor, Jane 1922.05, 1924.40, 1927.29, 1930.21
Taylor, Jay 1882.71, 1883.45, 1884.57, 1885.05, 1886.12, 1889.52, 1898.24
Taylor, Jay C. 1896.20, 1898.30, 1898.33
Taylor, Jeremy 1966.03
Taylor, Jerry 1875.06, 1880.01, 1880.03
Taylor, Jo Anne 1952.15
Taylor, John 1898.46, 1899.41, 1904.18
Taylor, Key 1939.27
Taylor, King 1946.19
Taylor, Lark 1918.31
Taylor, Laurette 1912.03, 1925.09
Taylor, Lillian 1881.35, 1884.41
Taylor, M. 1883.37
Taylor, Mabel 1912.44
Taylor, Maggie 1905.13
Taylor, Mamie 1885.58
Taylor, Margaret 1911.26
Taylor, Marion 1869.23, 1870.26, 1870.43
Taylor, Mark 1963.05
Taylor, Mark Anthony 1997.08
Taylor, Mary 1838.01, 1845.01, 1848.01, 1851.03, 1851.05
Taylor, Mary K. 1906.43, 1910.33
Taylor, Matt 1906.31
Taylor, Maud 1894.43
Taylor, Maude 1900.08
Taylor, Maxine 1959.05
Taylor, May 1894.43, 1899.29, 1900.40, 1901.16, 1903.04, 1903.18
Taylor, Mayme 1897.21, 1907.59
Taylor, Messr. 1883.17, 1883.23, 1883.58, 1885.14, 1885.52, 1898.26
Taylor, Miss 1857.08
Taylor, Mitch 1968.24
Taylor, Molly 1937.01
Taylor, Mr. 1855.09, 1863.10, 1869.31, 1883.44, 1898.29
Taylor, Mrs. 1750.01
Taylor, Myra 1991.01
Taylor, Myra Lucretia 1995.09
Taylor, Myron 1937.01
Taylor, Nell 1933.04
Taylor, Nellie 1880.37
Taylor, Noel 1947.09, 1952.03, 1958.01, 1960.18, 1964.05, 1971.08, 1972.03
Taylor, Norma 1931.42
Taylor, P. 1882.62
Taylor, Paul 1998.08
Taylor, Peggy 1929.08, 1934.39
Taylor, Rabbit 1932.12
Taylor, Raymond 1955.11
Taylor, Rob 1946.12
Taylor, Robert Lewis 1962.04
Taylor, Robert U. 1973.10, 1975.23, 1977.08
Taylor, Ron 1984.14, 1999.09
Taylor, Samuel 1962.03, 1968.01
Taylor, Scott 2000.07
Taylor, Susan 1975.12, 1997.17

Taylor, Tell 1905.42, 1939.29
Taylor, Tim-Brooke 1964.29
Taylor, Tom 1894.39
Taylor, Trix 1924.17
Taylor, Ty 1992.12
Taylor, W. 1848.03, 1882.71
Taylor, W.E. 1882.31, 1882.33, 1882.36, 1882.37, 1882.40
Taylor, W.L. 1881.40
Taylor, W.R. 1881.13
Taylor, W.S. 1886.28
Taylor, Walter 1885.28
Taylor, Wendy 1964.21
Taylor, Willie 1930.24
Taylor, Wilton 1898.44, 1909.31, 1911.36
Taylor-Corbett, Lynne 1981.02, 1988.09, 1997.06, 1999.24
Taymor, Julie 1996.16, 1997.20, 2000.10
Tazewell, Charles 1931.47
Tazewell, Paul 1996.07, 1998.16, 1999.10
Tchaikovsky, Peter Ilyich 1998.10
Tchaikovsky, Pyotor 1955.13
Tchaikovsky, Pyotor Ilyich 1922.21, 1923.28, 1929.05, 1947.14, 1948.08
Tchaikowsky 1924.48
Tchaikowsky, Pyotor Ilyich 1922.19, 1923.20
Tchakirides, Bill 1974.12
Tchekhoff, Anton 1922.06
Tchekhonin, S. 1929.05
Tcherkassky, Alexei 1931.38
Tcherkassky, Messr. 1929.05
Tcherniavsky, Messr. 1923.28, 1925.03, 1927.51, 1929.05
Tchor, Ludmilla 1965.04
Tchoukleva, Mme. 1925.03
TDI 1994.01, 1995.15
Teague, Scooter 1963.26
Teal, Ben 1887.49, 1893.40, 1893.42, 1894.25, 1894.42, 1896.15, 1896.29, 1896.39, 1896.44, 1897.25, 1898.25, 1899.12, 1899.15, 1900.01, 1900.40, 1900.50, 1900.52, 1901.16, 1901.27, 1902.24, 1903.28, 1904.04, 1905.20, 1905.27, 1906.25, 1906.37, 1907.33, 1907.46, 1908.27, 1910.02, 1910.10, 1912.12, 1913.21, 1913.37, 1914.07, 1914.12, 1915.19, 1916.13
Teal, Marger 1894.49
Teal, Margery 1892.44, 1896.52
Teal, Marjorie 1893.27, 1893.36, 1895.23
Teal, Minnie 1899.09
Teale, Maguerite 1891.45
Tebbutt, Harry 1909.07
Tebelak, John-Michael 1976.17
Techita, Mlle. 1913.07
Ted Royal Productions 1944.33
Tedde, Mostyn 1888.18, 1889.36
Teddick, Theodore 1943.05
Tedesco, John 1973.14
Tedick, Feodore 1961.09, 1962.16
Tedro, Henrietta 1906.13
Teed, Rose 1941.09
Teek, Angela 1990.14
Teeley, Tom 1982.22
Tees, Levin C. 1897.07
Teesdale, H.R. 1871.04
Teeter, Lara 1979.20, 1982.14, 1983.02, 1991.09, 1997.11, 1998.06
Teetzel, Thomas 1902.17
Tegalini, Angela 1890.21
Teicher, Louis 1944.21
Teichner, Joseph 1925.40, 1929.26
Teijelo, Gerald 1957.18, 1961.27, 1962.24, 1963.13, 1963.25, 1965.31, 1972.19
Teijelo, Gerald R. 1976.08
Teirstein, Andy 1980.07
Teitel, Carol 1967.01, 1979.17
Teitelbaum, M. 1931.29
Telbin, Forinda 1879.15
Telbin, Messr. 1890.50
Telbin, W. 1888.41, 1891.41, 1896.27
Telbin, William 1876.12, 1888.38, 1889.54, 1897.44, 1898.18
Telemaque, Adrienne 1987.03
Telemaque, Chi-En 1990.17
Telesync 1964.02
Telford, Eleanor 1903.18
Telford, Eleanore 1902.09
Tell, Arthur 1947.03
Tell, Frau 1880.66
Tell, Olive 1915.20
Telle, Frau 1879.62
Teller 1987.20, 1991.02, 2000.13
Teller, Frank L. 1927.15
Tellier, Jerry 1999.15, 2001.08
Telly, Vincent 1935.19
Telmo, Malena 1949.07
Telson, Bob 1988.05, 1995.09, 1995.12
Temperley, Stephen 1992.02
Tempest, Florence 1907.24, 1908.35, 1915.31
Tempest, Florenz 1911.12
Tempest, Marie 1890.23, 1891.30, 1892.03, 1892.52, 1893.40
Tempest, Marie M. 1894.14
Tempest, Maud 1892.26
Tempest, Tom 1937.10
Temple Theatre Comic Opera Company 1886.15
Temple, Bessie 1875.23, 1875.26, 1876.17, 1876.18, 1876.27, 1877.25, 1877.39, 1879.18, 1879.23, 1879.24, 1879.38, 1880.24, 1880.34, 1880.69, 1881.40, 1884.59, 1884.65
Temple, Daisy 1886.34, 1889.38
Temple, Dick 1903.38, 1905.45, 1906.41, 1913.29
Temple, Dora 1873.12, 1873.14
Temple, Dorothea 1909.01
Temple, E.P. 1913.10, 1919.05
Temple, Ed. 1887.17
Temple, Edgar 1893.48, 1894.08, 1894.38, 1900.12, 1904.23
Temple, Edna 1917.30
Temple, Edward 1892.25, 1910.11
Temple, Edward P. 1882.42, 1883.67, 1884.22, 1885.40, 1893.03, 1893.35, 1895.26, 1896.28, 1897.36, 1898.36, 1898.49, 1898.52, 1898.57, 1898.62, 1898.65, 1898.71, 1898.74, 1898.76, 1899.05, 1899.07, 1899.10, 1899.14, 1899.16, 1899.20, 1900.06, 1900.26, 1902.15, 1904.30, 1905.17, 1905.54, 1906.46, 1907.54, 1911.10, 1917.10, 1917.15, 1917.30, 1918.02, 1918.35
Temple, Edwin P. 1886.62
Temple, Evelyn 1888.29, 1889.45
Temple, Fanny 1883.50
Temple, George 1890.02
Temple, Henrietta 1869.14
Temple, Lee 1877.22
Temple, Madelon 1899.35, 1906.43
Temple, Mattie 1875.32, 1884.58
Temple, Miss 1883.58, 1884.59
Temple, Paul N. 1983.08
Temple, Paula 1921.15
Temple, Richard 1913.12, 1915.14, 1922.12, 1924.25, 1929.44, 1933.25, 1951.15
Temple, Richard W. 1912.21, 1921.15
Temple, Rose 1875.19, 1875.23, 1875.26, 1876.17, 1876.18, 1876.21, 1876.27, 1877.16, 1881.43, 1883.23, 1883.31, 1883.37, 1883.39
Temple, Walter 1884.18
Templeman, Louis 1929.38, 1931.43, 1931.45
Templeton, Charles 1887.43
Templeton, Fay 1875.10, 1885.58, 1890.27, 1895.27, 1895.32, 1895.38, 1898.50, 1899.17, 1900.07, 1900.38, 1901.17, 1902.29, 1904.22, 1904.56, 1905.22, 1906.02, 1906.42, 1912.07, 1926.08, 1931.12, 1931.23, 1933.26
Templeton, James 1905.06, 1927.47, 1930.23
Templeton, John 1886.12
Templeton, Lea 1897.05
Templeton, Louis A. 1918.09
Templeton, Mercer 1920.14, 1922.43, 1930.23
Templeton, Olive 1956.16
Tenant, Maggie S. 1879.42
Tenen, Lailye 1945.12
Tenley, Theodore 1947.09
Tennant, Bill 1921.12
Tennant, Dorothy 1927.02
Tennant, Giblert 1912.35
Tennant, H.M. 1925.50
Tennent, H.M. 1924.33, 1960.13
Tennery, George 1899.34, 1903.29, 1905.05
Tenney, Carol Jeanne 1989.18
Tenney, Caryl 1968.08, 1979.09
Tenney, Ernest 1908.22
Tenney, Jeanne 1973.09
Tenney, Walter 1927.14
Tenniel, John 1924.44, 1932.28, 1947.09, 1982.24
Tennis, Eleanor 1933.23, 1944.02
Tennis, Elenore 1937.04
Tennyson, Alfred 1892.14, 1925.14
Tennyson, Alfred Lord 1886.57
Tennyson, Arthur C. 1923.43
Tennyson, Jean 1928.23
Teppe, Herman Patrick 1921.36
Tepper, Arielle 1998.14, 2000.01, 2001.01
Tepper, Morris 1928.25, 1933.25
Tepper, Sid 1989.12
Ter-Arutunian, Rouben 1957.07, 1958.17, 1959.01, 1959.07, 1959.09, 1961.14, 1963.13, 1964.24, 1968.08, 1975.06, 1978.14, 1978.15, 1978.16, 1978.17
Terada, Takio 1989.21
Terbel, Messr. 1879.51
Terbel, Mons. 1879.48, 1879.60, 1880.16, 1880.27, 1880.29
Terechenko, George 1929.22
Teresa 1969.11
Teresa, Miss 1869.36
Terestchenko, Messr. 1927.51
Terkel, Studs 1978.12
Termine, Robert 1974.15
Ternent, Billy 1958.18
Terraine, Alfred 1913.36
Terrance, Ida 1873.26
Terrancle, Messr. 1882.53
Terrancle, Mons. 1879.19, 1879.26, 1879.36, 1879.39, 1879.44, 1879.47, 1879.48, 1879.49, 1879.69, 1880.14, 1880.16, 1880.23, 1880.29, 1880.50, 1880.52, 1880.56, 1881.50, 1881.51, 1882.67, 1883.30, 1883.41
Terranova, P.J. 1998.06
Terrell, Betty Ann 1965.25
Terrell, Sean 2001.04
Terresfield, Mae 1919.33
Terrill, Blanche 1916.04
Terrill, Elizabeth 1922.44
Terrill, Robert 1914.25
Terris, Norma 1926.01, 1927.19, 1927.67, 1930.36, 1932.11, 1938.15
Terriss, Dorothy 1921.27
Terriss, Ellaine 1895.29
Terriss, Ellaline 1894.18
Terriss, May 1895.35
Terriss, Norma 1922.38
Terriss, Percy 1913.36
Terriss, Thomas 1894.38
Terriss, Tom 1904.03
Terriss, William T. 1900.19
Terry John S. 1897.22
Terry Muriel 1909.15
Terry, Al 1920.16
Terry, Celia 1884.40
Terry, Daniel 1855.01
Terry, David 1955.10, 1962.02
Terry, Edith 1898.46
Terry, Eleanor 1927.07, 1929.29
Terry, Ethelind 1920.31, 1927.08, 1930.27
Terry, Jack 1910.10
Terry, John S. 1898.44
Terry, Kathleen 1928.09
Terry, Lambert 1918.25
Terry, Marie 1907.49
Terry, Mike 1969.15
Terry, Miss 1854.04
Terry, Mr. 1852.04
Terry, Phil 1950.14
Terry, Sonny 1947.03, 1999.09
Terry, Susan 1983.14, 1990.07
Tesio, L. 1885.67, 1887.18
Tesori, Jeanine 1995.05, 1997.05, 1998.03
Tessler, Allan 1980.02
Testa, A. 1964.02
Testa, Mary 1983.17, 1996.06, 1998.16, 1999.22, 2001.08
Tester, E.A. 1897.50, 1903.40
Tester, Ruth 1926.28, 1930.25, 1931.05
Teti, Karen 1981.25
Tetirick, Robert 1980.01
Tetley, Glen 1948.32, 1950.20, 1953.06, 1953.15, 1959.04
Tetson, Basil 1895.20
Teuber, Max 1920.26, 1922.30, 1924.31, 1925.25, 1925.48, 1930.22, 1931.26, 1933.20
Teuton, Stella 1889.03, 1891.06
Tewkesbury, Joan 1954.13
Tex, Joe 1974.01
Texas, Temple 1955.27
Texsmith, Vaughn 1900.51
Thacker, Bernard 1976.28
Thacker, Pauline Elliott 1917.09
Thacker, Russ 1971.16, 1972.11, 1974.09, 1976.01, 1978.19, 1982.10
Thaell, Cliff 1942.19
Thaell, Edwina 1942.19
Thain, Dolly 1926.37
Thal, Miss 1883.58
Thal, Mlle. 1883.30, 1883.41
Thal, Mme. 1882.73
Thal, Susanne 1870.37, 1870.45
Thalasso, Arthur 1909.08, 1910.37
Thaler, Fred 1978.25
Thalheimer, Norman 1983.17
Thalia Theatre 1883.35
Tharp, Twyla 1978.26, 1985.08
Thatcher's Minstrels 1892.50
Thatcher, A.M. 1888.21
Thatcher, Fowler 1894.41
Thatcher, George 1879.09, 1880.15, 1891.32, 1892.50, 1893.50, 1908.22
Thatcher, Ginger 1996.08
Thatcher, Lillian 1908.41
Thau, Harold 1983.07, 1989.22
Thaw, Charles 1899.22
Thawl, Evelyn 1936.31
Thayer, Arthur 1884.37
Thayer, Bert 1900.48, 1900.55, 1905.31
Thayer, Bert C. 1900.07
Thayer, Bettina 1946.01
Thayer, Edith 1913.09, 1921.41
Thayer, Eugenie 1901.26
Thayer, Jurien 1922.03
Thayer, Pat 1925.43, 1926.15
The Bohemians, Inc. 1922.32, 1923.31
The Theatre Guild 1935.03, 1935.13
Theard, Sam 1992.03, 1999.06, 1999.09
Theaters and Concerts Int'l. 1999.02
Theatre 1972 1971.16
Theatre Atlanta Production, A 1969.03
Theatre Corporation of America 1958.02
Theatre De France Company, The 1964.06
Theatre Francais 1863.05, 1864.01, 1864.03, 1864.08, 1864.10, 1864.11
Theatre Group, University Extension, UCLA Productions1963.19
Theatre Guild Productions 1929.20, 1963.07
Theatre Guild Workroom 1935.13
Theatre Guild, Inc. 1930.18, 1930.33, 1931.02
Theatre Guild, The 1925.17, 1933.24, 1941.05, 1943.04, 1945.05, 1951.16, 1960.20, 1968.02, 1975.22
Theatre Now, Inc. 1975.21, 1975.23, 1976.35, 1976.36, 1981.23
Theatre Union, Inc. 1935.16
Theatre Workshop Group Production, A 1964.28
Theatrical Art Studio 1929.25
Theatrical Art Studios 1929.21, 1930.21
Theatrical Interests Plan, Inc. 1960.09
Theaulon, Emmanuel 1885.01, 1885.41, 1892.03, 1898.15, 1900.23
Thebaud, Estelle 1906.18
Theise, Mortimer 1907.23
Theise, Mortimer M. 1907.35, 1907.45
Thelen, Judy 1963.06
Themerson, Franciszka 1966.19
Thenstead, Adolph 1947.19
Theo, Louise 1882.53, 1882.55, 1882.58, 1882.61, 1882.67, 1883.27, 1883.28, 1883.30, 1883.34, 1883.41, 1884.43, 1884.45, 1884.47, 1884.49, 1884.50, 1884.52, 1884.54, 1884.55, 1885.19
Theo, Mme. 1885.17, 1885.20, 1885.23, 1885.24, 1885.25
Theodore Hammerstein, Inc. 1924.24
Theodore Reisig Scenic Studio 1913.34
Theodore, 'Ali 1986.03
Theodore, Charles 1889.26
Theodore, Donna 1975.03
Theodore, Flavio 1928.34
Theodore, Lee (Becker) 1965.02, 1965.17, 1966.18, 1968.02, 1968.18, 1968.19, 1970.12, 1972.09, 1980.02, 1986.03
Theodore, Messr. 1928.34
Theodore, Pan 1946.24
Theodore, Paris 1954.13
Theodore, Ralph 1931.32
Theophele, Mons. 1877.14
Theophile, Mons. 1876.26, 1877.06, 1877.13, 1877.19
Theresa, Mlle. 1873.10
Therese, Mlle. 1851.06, 1851.07
Theroux, Mlle. 1883.41
Thery, Jacques 1928.06
Theyard, Harry 1965.26, 1965.34, 1966.09
Thiboust, Lambert 1880.28
Thiele, Robert 1981.06
Thiergaard, Judith 1981.19, 1983.19
Thiery, Messr. 1858.02
Thiery, Mons. 1858.01
Thiese, Mortimer 1908.33

Thigpen, Helen 1953.04
Thigpen, Lynne 1975.05, 1978.12, 1979.18, 1980.27
Thigpen, Martha 1978.08, 1978.23, 1979.27, 1980.21
Thill, Alice 1896.39
Thill, Helene 1896.39
Thillon, Anna 1852.03, 1852.04, 1852.06, 1853.04, 1854.02
Thimes, Messr. 1852.01
Thinn, Amelia 1882.24, 1883.33
Thoeren, Robert 1972.04
Thole, Cynnthia 1991.15
Tholen, Herr 1889.35
Tholer, Mlle. 1869.01
Tholer, Mons. 1868.13, 1869.19, 1869.24
Thom, Michael 1968.16
Thom, Peter 1976.34
Thom, Vie-Von 1957.06
Thoma, Carl 1970.20
Thoma, Maralyn 1963.12
Thoma, Michael 1970.15, 1971.04
Thomas H. Pratt's Comic Opera Organization 1892.25
Thomas P. McCoy-Rigby Entertainment 1998.18
Thomas Q. Seabrooke Comic Opera Company 1894.22
Thomas Q. Seabrooke Grand Comic Opera Company 1892.55
Thomas Q. Seabrooke Opera Company 1893.20
Thomas, A. 1881.32
Thomas, A.E. 1911.44, 1922.09, 1922.46, 1924.41, 1927.54
Thomas, Agnes 1885.21
Thomas, Al 1923.21
Thomas, Ambrose 1923.20
Thomas, Ann 1946.02, 1950.03
Thomas, B.F. 1891.24
Thomas, Barbara Dare 1981.07
Thomas, Basil 1952.11
Thomas, Bobby 1971.10
Thomas, Brandon 1894.41, 1948.26, 1951.02, 1966.11, 1974.25
Thomas, Bronwyn 1978.23, 1979.27, 1990.13
Thomas, C. 1881.32
Thomas, Calvin 1916.13, 1929.27, 1949.03, 1955.27
Thomas, Carrie 1906.35
Thomas, Charles 1889.12, 1890.04
Thomas, Charles H. 1886.28, 1887.29, 1891.39, 1893.14
Thomas, Charles W. 1888.32, 1888.44
Thomas, David E. 1945.20, 1947.02, 1947.21, 1948.25, 1949.16, 1951.17, 1951.24, 1953.07, 1956.01, 1962.04, 1963.12, 1965.31, 1966.09, 1966.14, 1969.04, 1969.17, 1970.21, 1972.23, 1976.11, 1978.22, 1979.09
Thomas, Dennis 1999.15
Thomas, Dinks 1930.10
Thomas, Dorleen 1958.03
Thomas, Dorothy 1938.08
Thomas, Ed 1899.33
Thomas, Edna 1933.04
Thomas, Edward 1898.17, 1961.24, 1974.09
Thomas, Elsa 1918.07, 1918.22
Thomas, Elsie 1904.30
Thomas, Evan 1929.47, 1967.17, 1968.10, 1968.14, 1968.17
Thomas, Evelyn 1975.01, 1993.03
Thomas, F.D. 1915.16
Thomas, F.W. 1923.36
Thomas, Frank 1908.21
Thomas, Frank C. 1916.10
Thomas, Frank D. 1914.16
Thomas, G. 1897.31
Thomas, G.W. 1899.30
Thomas, George 1897.48
Thomas, George W. 1894.22, 1898.50, 1899.30, 1982.12
Thomas, Harold 1911.39
Thomas, Harry 1870.04, 1955.03
Thomas, Helen 1943.20
Thomas, Henry 1888.29, 1932.21
Thomas, Hilda 1889.09, 1889.27, 1889.47, 1892.04
Thomas, Hugh 1953.02
Thomas, Hugh S. 1905.54
Thomas, Ivan 1996.01, 1996.12
Thomas, J. 1867.12
Thomas, J.M. 1902.38, 1909.27
Thomas, J.T. 1899.03
Thomas, James M. 1908.08
Thomas, Jean 1918.05, 1919.03, 1921.14
Thomas, Jenny 1999.24
Thomas, Jimmy 1930.19
Thomas, Joey 1949.17
Thomas, John Charles 1913.18, 1915.04, 1915.11, 1915.27, 1916.09, 1916.26, 1917.10, 1917.30, 1919.27, 1921.33
Thomas, John Henry 1968.15, 1978.23, 1979.27, 1982.20, 1983.13, 1984.11, 1988.04, 1988.18, 1989.14, 1990.07, 1990.08, 1991.08, 2000.03
Thomas, John Norman 1993.09
Thomas, John Rogers 1909.16
Thomas, Joseph 1893.41, 1952.10
Thomas, Jr., Augustus 1917.02
Thomas, Jr., William 1976.35
Thomas, Keith LaMelle 1998.01
Thomas, Keith Lamelle 1999.24
Thomas, Kent 1960.08
Thomas, Laura 1883.22
Thomas, Lena 1931.19
Thomas, Lizzie 1883.31
Thomas, M. 1883.65
Thomas, M.F. 1879.42
Thomas, M.J. 1885.70, 1888.35, 1890.11, 1890.19, 1890.24, 1895.44
Thomas, Maggie 1907.55
Thomas, Margery 1924.06
Thomas, Marie 1969.09
Thomas, Marshall 1975.03
Thomas, Martha 1933.27
Thomas, Master 1857.02, 1885.49
Thomas, Matty 1917.24
Thomas, Maud 1901.05, 1901.08
Thomas, Messr. 1869.44
Thomas, Millard 1930.29, 1953.17, 1955.03
Thomas, Milton 1924.01
Thomas, Miss 1858.04, 1862.02, 1867.19, 1868.06, 1876.03, 1894.49
Thomas, Mlle. 1876.36
Thomas, Mons. 1881.31
Thomas, Mr. 1862.07, 1866.02, 1866.28
Thomas, Paul 1886.02
Thomas, Philip M. 1972.02
Thomas, Philip Michael 1980.05
Thomas, Reverend Olice 1988.05
Thomas, Rhyce 1901.24
Thomas, Rhys 1894.29, 1895.26, 1900.04, 1900.18, 1900.21, 1948.09
Thomas, Richard 1945.20
Thomas, Rick 1982.13
Thomas, Robert 1975.15
Thomas, Rosina 1881.13
Thomas, Rudolph 1933.23
Thomas, Ruth 1926.44, 1933.07, 1948.28
Thomas, S.W. 1899.04
Thomas, Samuel 1934.13
Thomas, T.C. 1883.47
Thomas, T.F. 1927.48
Thomas, Tasha 1975.01, 1980.15
Thomas, Theodore 1864.04, 1864.07
Thomas, W.J. 1881.38
Thomas, William 1945.01
Thomashefsky, Bores 1931.29
Thomashefsky, Harry 1931.29
Thome, David 1974.26, 1981.29, 1987.07, 1991.13
Thomopson, Lydia 1868.32
Thompson 1880.37
Thompson and Reed 1889.13
Thompson, A.M. 1905.55, 1907.51, 1910.05
Thompson, Alexander 1901.04
Thompson, Alexander M. 1907.32
Thompson, Alfred 1867.08, 1876.12, 1883.65, 1885.08, 1886.14, 1887.32, 1888.39, 1891.11, 1891.38, 1892.20, 1892.22, 1892.33, 1892.52, 1892.55, 1893.16, 1893.17, 1893.47, 1894.21, 1894.26
Thompson, Annie 1886.13, 1887.02, 1887.42, 1888.25, 1889.43, 1890.36, 1894.52, 1898.45, 1899.32, 1904.32, 1907.43, 1908.32
Thompson, Archie 1946.22
Thompson, C. 1863.02, 1869.37, 1869.39, 1870.12, 1870.18, 1871.08
Thompson, Carolyn 1925.32
Thompson, Charles 1925.36
Thompson, Charlotte 1921.09
Thompson, Clara 1869.29, 1906.50
Thompson, Claude 1952.15, 1956.02, 1957.05, 1957.16, 1962.14
Thompson, Colonel 1879.42, 1880.63
Thompson, Comte 1869.38
Thompson, Connie 1869.42, 1870.01, 1888.31, 1896.32
Thompson, Creighton 1946.08, 1947.02
Thompson, Cynthia 1990.09
Thompson, D.H. 1883.66
Thompson, David 1996.14, 1997.07
Thompson, Denman 1876.22, 1878.11, 1880.21, 1881.10, 1882.82, 1886.13, 1887.02, 1887.42, 1888.25, 1889.43, 1890.36, 1894.52, 1896.15, 1898.45, 1899.32, 1904.32, 1907.43, 1908.32
Thompson, Ed 1956.14
Thompson, Eddie 1933.27
Thompson, Edgar 1951.15, 1955.01
Thompson, El 1927.14
Thompson, Ella 1965.32
Thompson, Elsie 1941.03
Thompson, Emily 1930.33
Thompson, Evan 1969.14, 1989.29
Thompson, Frank 1883.47, 1887.02, 1887.42, 1888.25, 1889.43, 1890.36, 1894.52, 1898.45, 1899.32, 1947.13, 1948.31, 1961.15, 1963.17, 1965.15, 1965.22, 1965.32, 1966.08, 1966.11, 1966.12, 1966.13, 1966.16, 1967.04, 1967.09, 1968.16, 1971.09, 1971.19, 1972.15
Thompson, Franklin 1904.32, 1907.43, 1908.32
Thompson, Fred 1914.32, 1920.41, 1924.06, 1924.21, 1924.43, 1925.49, 1927.08, 1927.52, 1927.59, 1928.17, 1928.43, 1929.44, 1942.01, 1944.14, 1945.17, 1981.03
Thompson, Frederic 1905.54, 1910.17
Thompson, Frederic W. 1905.17
Thompson, Frederick 1919.02
Thompson, G.W. 1865.05
Thompson, Gordon 1921.27
Thompson, H. 1873.26, 1884.41
Thompson, Hal 1930.38, 1935.11
Thompson, Harlan 1923.24, 1924.40, 1925.34, 1926.39, 1927.36
Thompson, Harry 1895.41, 1935.01
Thompson, Helen 1929.29, 1930.37, 1943.12
Thompson, Herbert 1911.27
Thompson, Hie 1942.34
Thompson, Hugh 1941.10, 1942.32
Thompson, J. 1867.25, 1878.10, 1879.12, 1880.68, 1884.09
Thompson, J.A. 1879.72, 1880.07, 1880.69, 1892.17
Thompson, J.S. 1903.23
Thompson, Jack 1926.50, 1927.56, 1929.45
Thompson, James 1905.23, 1929.09, 1929.18
Thompson, James A. 1881.36
Thompson, Jay 1959.26, 1960.07, 1974.02, 1996.18
Thompson, Jeffrey V. 1978.21, 1986.02
Thompson, Jennie 1902.27
Thompson, Jennifer Laura 1998.13
Thompson, Jim 1906.46, 1980.12
Thompson, Jimmie 1956.02
Thompson, John 1877.07, 1880.18, 1881.38, 1881.43, 1884.09, 1884.14, 1884.66, 1886.37, 1893.06, 1895.21, 1895.27, 1896.35, 1900.03
Thompson, John A. 1872.04, 1872.05, 1872.08, 1872.25, 1872.30, 1872.36, 1872.38, 1876.16, 1880.35, 1881.28, 1881.41, 1881.47, 1882.60, 1882.63, 1884.58, 1885.07, 1887.43, 1892.59, 1893.50, 1895.34, 1897.30
Thompson, John L. 1893.17
Thompson, Johnny 1948.25
Thompson, Johnny V.R. 1949.08
Thompson, Jr., Fisher 1999.09
Thompson, Julian F. 1942.15
Thompson, Kay 1937.15, 1956.16, 1957.01
Thompson, L.S. 1902.15
Thompson, Lauren 1990.20, 1991.13
Thompson, Lewis S. 1895.19, 1895.27
Thompson, Lottie 1899.33
Thompson, Lydia 1868.23, 1869.06, 1869.29, 1870.13, 1870.19, 1870.21, 1870.35, 1870.42, 1871.01, 1871.02, 1871.14, 1871.19, 1872.21, 1872.22, 1872.24, 1872.26, 1872.34, 1873.12, 1873.14, 1873.17, 1877.22, 1877.23, 1877.25, 1877.39, 1886.32, 1888.33, 1891.02
Thompson, Lysander 1877.28, 1881.32
Thompson, M. 1863.02, 1863.04
Thompson, Mabel 1896.27, 1898.46, 1930.41, 1931.15, 1933.08, 1933.18
Thompson, Madame 1898.55
Thompson, Maggie 1884.61
Thompson, Marion 1909.25
Thompson, Mark 1993.15, 2001.02, 2001.04
Thompson, Maude 1894.42
Thompson, May 1887.46, 1906.09, 1908.11, 1915.01, 1915.29, 1917.05, 1919.44, 1920.22, 1920.23, 1920.40
Thompson, Mesdame 1856.04
Thompson, Messr. 1851.08, 1859.06, 1861.03, 1863.07, 1866.20, 1876.17
Thompson, Miss 1841.01, 1862.09, 1863.01, 1864.22, 1865.05, 1865.07, 1869.36, 1870.09, 1904.13
Thompson, Mme. 1892.27, 1894.14, 1894.21, 1895.11
Thompson, Mollie 1891.40
Thompson, Mr. 1823.01, 1851.02, 1851.03, 1852.04, 1855.11, 1869.26
Thompson, Mrs. 1855.11
Thompson, Ocia 1901.08, 1902.10, 1902.27
Thompson, Osia 1904.13
Thompson, Pete 1930.29
Thompson, Randall 1926.17
Thompson, Ray 1957.16
Thompson, Rex 1950.02
Thompson, Sada 1959.04
Thompson, Sonny 1937.09
Thompson, T.A. 1882.46
Thompson, Tazewell 2000.03
Thompson, Tom 1929.31
Thompson, Tommy 1993.01
Thompson, U.S. 1929.50
Thompson, Ulysses S. 1922.25, 1924.37
Thompson, Ursula 1904.28, 1907.01
Thompson, Venie 1887.42, 1888.25, 1889.43, 1904.32, 1907.43
Thompson, W.H. 1881.23, 1882.27, 1899.39, 1902.01, 1902.41, 1904.36, 1921.39
Thompson, Wensley 1894.41, 1897.42, 1899.02
Thompson, Weyman 1981.29, 1987.07
Thompson, Wilfred 1906.22
Thompson, Willard 1890.29
Thompson, William 1884.11, 1907.57
Thompson, Woodman 1925.45, 1926.10, 1926.31, 1926.42, 1926.44, 1927.21, 1927.57, 1927.61
Thomsen, Mark 1985.11, 1985.13, 1986.14
Thomson, Archie 1927.54
Thomson, Arline 1943.08
Thomson, Brian 1975.08, 1996.05, 1999.02
Thomson, Carolyn 1917.30, 1918.35, 1921.07, 1921.33
Thomson, Harrison 1948.19, 1949.05
Thomson, Lydia 1877.39
Thomson, Messr. 1926.32
Thomson, Mr. 1860.01
Thomson, Norman 1947.02
Thomson, Ralph 1928.37
Thomson, Virgil 1934.05, 1952.06, 1996.10
Thonton, Dolly 1872.25
Thonton, Messr. 1851.05
Thoreau, R. 1958.06
Thoreux, Therese 1964.39
Thorley, Victor 1950.16
Thormsen, Greta 1954.04
Thorn, Bertram 1934.40
Thorn, George 1968.23
Thorn, Jacob 1873.14
Thorn, Joyce 1904.29
Thorndyke, Frank 1905.34
Thorne, Alicia 1866.12
Thorne, Belle 1889.01, 1895.18, 1898.65, 1900.03, 1907.05
Thorne, Blanche 1884.40, 1886.02
Thorne, C.R. 1875.03
Thorne, Charles 1851.02, 1851.05, 1855.09, 1865.06
Thorne, Charles R. 1854.02
Thorne, Daise 1900.02
Thorne, David K. 1972.07
Thorne, E.F. 1872.13
Thorne, Edwin F. 1875.05
Thorne, Eleanor 1908.42
Thorne, Elsie 1900.43
Thorne, Emily 1862.05, 1867.18
Thorne, Eric 1890.33, 1892.08, 1892.10
Thorne, George 1885.47, 1887.10
Thorne, Grace 1891.28, 1897.01
Thorne, Joan 1970.06
Thorne, John 1918.10, 1947.11
Thorne, Joyce 1904.14
Thorne, Jr., C.R. 1860.04
Thorne, Lulu 1927.39
Thorne, Mary 1895.08
Thorne, Mr. 1860.03, 1860.04, 1869.20
Thorne, Nellie 1901.27, 1938.12

Thorne, Pauline 1905.30, 1907.13, 1907.24, 1910.17
Thorne, Raymond 1977.06, 1987.19, 1997.04
Thorne, Rennie 1903.09
Thorne, Roma 1907.58
Thorne, Sylvia 1890.01, 1890.11, 1890.39, 1891.12, 1891.17, 1891.36, 1892.03, 1892.20, 1894.21, 1896.18, 1897.09, 1897.19, 1897.31, 1897.48
Thorne, T. Pearsall 1891.36, 1895.31
Thorne, Thomas P. 1894.03
Thorne, W.L. 1907.08, 1927.55
Thorne, William L. 1925.01, 1925.28
Thorngren, Jane 1987.10, 1988.16, 1996.02
Thornson, Al 1907.19
Thornton, A.J. 1907.57
Thornton, Barney 1912.09
Thornton, Bernard 1919.44
Thornton, Blanche 1887.43
Thornton, Clarke W. 1984.10
Thornton, Edgar 1919.18
Thornton, Edna 1895.03, 1897.18
Thornton, Eric 1951.04, 1951.07, 1951.08
Thornton, Evans 1948.25, 1949.08, 1955.07, 1955.09, 1957.06, 1957.11
Thornton, Florence 1894.42, 1896.29
Thornton, Frank 1884.09
Thornton, George 1916.03, 1918.05, 1925.37, 1934.38
Thornton, Harry 1900.08, 1902.02
Thornton, Isabella 1884.24
Thornton, J. 1892.19
Thornton, Jack 1925.09
Thornton, James 1890.30, 1893.28, 1893.30, 1895.27, 1896.15, 1897.25
Thornton, Jim 1927.48, 1929.31
Thornton, Joan 1962.02
Thornton, Marianne 1963.03
Thornton, Martha 1869.41
Thornton, Mr. 1896.02
Thornton, Mrs. M. 1868.01, 1868.02
Thornton, Norma 1953.08
Thornton, Pearl 1875.39, 1876.03
Thornton, Rene 1912.12
Thornton, Richard 1928.12
Thornton, Ruby 1880.18, 1881.03
Thornton, Scott 1977.15
Thornton, Walker 1933.20
Thornton, Zachary 1999.22
Thorp, Jay 1937.07
Thorpe, Aggie 1873.28
Thorpe, Dolly 1907.55
Thorpe, Florence 1924.11
Thorpe, Frederick 1911.40
Thorpe, Hilda 1894.18
Thorpe, J.W. 1870.20, 1870.23, 1877.28
Thorpe, James W. 1870.26
Thorpe, Laura 1879.50
Thorpe, Miss 1872.16
Thorpe, Ruth 1913.04
Thorpes, Chuck 1973.10
Thorton, Miss 1875.39
Three Knights, Ltd. 1988.09
Thress, Frances 1927.52, 1934.04, 1937.06
Thrift, Bea 1928.24, 1936.12
Throckmorton, Cleon 1922.32, 1925.21, 1925.37, 1930.19, 1932.25, 1933.04, 1933.07
Throne, Charles R. 1852.04
Thronson, Ron 1972.21
Throop, Martha 1920.28
Thropp, Clara 1890.32, 1923.24, 1930.14
Thropp, Florence 1886.24, 1893.24, 1893.41
Thropp, Lou 1882.28
Thropp, Miss 1885.08
Throw, J.A. 1883.47
Thrower, Edna 1930.10
Thrumm, Horace 1899.36
Thuillart, Mons. 1879.49, 1880.56
Thulliard, Mlle. 1875.01
Thun, Nancy 1995.08
Thunder, Kenneth "Chocolate" 1995.01
Thurban, T.W. 1909.11
Thurber, J. Kent 1927.39
Thurber, James 1960.04, 1963.16
Thurber, P.H. 1889.47
Thurgate, Lillian 1894.14, 1894.21, 1895.04
Thurgate, Minnie 1893.43, 1894.21
Thurgeon, Peter 1957.02
Thurgood, Reginald 1934.34
Thurman, Mary 1929.34, 1929.48
Thurston, Andrew 1945.14
Thurston, Gertrude 1908.16
Thurston, Miss 1897.04
Thurston, Robert 1912.14
Thurston, Ted 1951.15, 1951.24, 1952.13, 1954.01, 1956.12, 1961.08, 1961.21, 1963.12, 1964.18, 1964.44, 1967.09, 1969.02, 1970.02, 1971.19, 1980.30
Thurston, Zora 1931.31
Thurston, Zora Neale 1931.31, 1991.01
Thys, Mado 1929.10, 1929.11, 1929.13, 1929.15, 1929.16
Thyssen, Charlott 1976.31, 1978.08
Ti-Marcel 1953.10
Tibbets, C. 1885.63
Tibbets, Mr. 1882.71
Tibbett, Lawrence 1950.16
Tibbetts, J. 1886.04
Tibbetts, Martha 1933.02
Tibbetts, Walter 1940.11, 1940.13, 1940.15
Tibbitts, Michele 1995.13
Tibor, Yvonne 1946.01, 1947.06, 1947.14, 1948.15, 1949.02, 1949.17
Tich, Little 1888.39
Tichacek, Stephen Jan 1938.16
Tichenor, Billy 1926.06
Tichenor, James 1927.32
Tichenor, Tom 1961.10
Tichler, Rosemarie 1996.07, 1998.16
Tick, Donald 1979.05, 1992.06
Ticotin, Nancy 1994.01
Tiden, Frederick 1923.43
Tidwell, Brian W. 1990.20, 1991.13
Tiebling, Tia 1986.20
Tiechner, Joseph 1932.21
Tiejelo, Gerald 1961.27
Tieman, B.J. 1919.41
Tieman, Bernard 1903.21
Tiernan, J. 1880.68
Tiernan, J.C. 1883.47, 1889.47
Tiernan, Junior 1921.20
Tiernan, William 1952.07
Tierney, Dorothy 1920.05, 1921.04
Tierney, Edward 1919.28, 1924.16
Tierney, Frank 1909.21, 1912.08, 1922.19, 1923.20
Tierney, Harry 1916.20, 1916.25, 1917.01, 1917.08, 1917.12, 1918.05, 1918.08, 1918.18, 1918.23, 1918.34, 1919.04, 1919.15, 1919.36, 1920.04, 1920.18, 1920.41, 1921.19, 1922.41, 1922.48, 1923.09, 1923.38, 1923.47, 1924.18, 1925.10, 1927.08, 1928.28, 1973.05, 1976.24
Tierney, J. 1880.09
Tierney, James 1879.37, 1880.36, 1880.64, 1881.09, 1881.29, 1882.02, 1884.41, 1885.02, 1885.15, 1888.29
Tierney, John T. 1898.70
Tierney, William 1963.06
Tiers, Alex 1926.13
Tietjens, Eunice 1925.37
Tietjens, Paul 1903.03, 1904.13, 1904.44
Tietze, Mrs. 1891.33
Tiffany, Annie Ward 1879.12, 1899.03
Tigges, Byron 1927.40
Tighe, Harry 1907.44, 1916.25, 1917.09, 1918.04, 1919.08, 1930.39
Tighe, James F. 1884.56
Tigue, Dolly 1920.44
Tihmar, David 1956.08
Tilden, Beau 1936.05, 1946.12, 1949.04, 1957.14, 1958.14, 1962.20, 1971.07
Tilden, Fred 1927.65
Tilden, Georgina 1926.12
Tilden, Helen 1918.31, 1926.38
Tiley, Vesta 1897.31
Tilghman, Bill 1990.15
Till, John 1883.19
Till, Louisa 1883.19
Tilla, Haydon 1881.26
Tilla, W. Haydon 1873.18, 1873.21, 1873.23, 1879.14
Tiller, John 1922.19, 1923.20, 1923.33, 1923.40, 1924.02, 1924.18, 1925.24, 1925.33, 1928.02, 1928.11
Tiller, Ted 1944.32
Tillett, William 1918.12
Tilley, Martin 1980.17
Tilley, Vesta 1904.01
Tillitt, Shaver 1994.06
Tillman, Messr. 1856.01
Tillman, N. 1856.01
Tillo, M. 1921.21
Tillotson, Marie 1899.13
Tillotson, W.W. 1888.13, 1889.45, 1900.59
Tillson, A. 1883.06
Tillson, Ethel 1902.26
Tillson, Mrs. 1872.34
Tillyne, Edna 1903.13
Tilson, Mme. 1862.09, 1863.04, 1863.08
Tilson, Mons. 1862.09, 1863.04
Tilson, Mrs. 1870.33
Tilston, Mr. 1875.03
Tilstone, Kitty 1872.07
Tilton, C. 1876.14
Tilton, E.L. 1870.05
Tilton, Edwin B. 1902.36
Tilton, James 1971.04, 1971.16, 1976.27
Tilton, Kenyon 1884.32
Tilton, Mr. 1851.08
Tilton, Stacy Lee 1996.13
Tilton, Thomas 1925.20
Tilton, Webb 1958.04
Timber, George 1934.05
Timberg, Frank 1911.25
Timberg, Harman 1920.06
Timberg, Herman 1908.28, 1916.11, 1916.23, 1917.23, 1917.31, 1931.13, 1942.35
Timberg, Sam 1926.15, 1929.28, 1929.32
Timberg, Sammy 1928.26
Timberlake, Craig 1949.10, 1949.13, 1949.14, 1960.02
Timerman, Alec 1987.15, 1989.27, 1991.05
Times Producing Corporation 1915.19
Times Square Amusement Company 1906.28
Timm, Mrs. 1840.02, 1840.03, 1840.04
Timmany, Mr. 1855.11
Timmerman, Alex 1999.23
Timmoney, Lizzie 1881.13
Timmons, George H. 1904.45
Timmons, Georgia Ann 1945.08
Timmons, Rodester 1955.09
Timmony, James 1868.19
Timmony, James T. 1859.08
Timmony, Jennie 1882.77
Timmony, Mr. 1857.05, 1857.07
Timoney, Mike 1991.08
Timony, C. 1867.19
Timothy, Master 1865.01, 1865.05, 1865.07, 1865.09, 1865.10, 1865.11, 1866.02, 1866.28
Timpson, Charles 1937.10
Tincher, Fay 1906.01, 1912.07
Tindal, Muriel 1919.03, 1921.13
Tine, Hal 1985.19
Tingay, C.F. 1885.69
Tinkler, William 1929.51
Tinkley, Allen 1976.06
Tinner, H. 1919.43
Tinney, Allan 1939.19
Tinney, Frank 1911.34, 1912.13, 1913.17, 1914.31, 1916.24, 1917.23, 1918.38, 1920.27, 1922.26, 1923.32, 1925.48
Tinney, William 1939.19
Tinnie, Cora 1889.13, 1889.46, 1894.35
Tinnin, Alvis 1946.10
Tinsley, Joe 1918.12, 1921.13, 1924.21
Tinsley, Joseph A. 1913.25
Tinturin, Peter 1932.18
Tiomkin, Dimitri 1931.19
Tiomkin, Dmitri 1931.19, 1932.01
Tionco, Maureen 1965.20
Tipaldi, Messr. 1906.11, 1907.09
Tippie, Frank 1978.23, 1979.27
Tippit, Wayne 1970.02
Tipson, Thelma 1930.18, 1931.28
Tipton, Ben 1949.09
Tipton, Jennifer 1976.08, 1977.08, 1978.11, 1980.13, 1981.01, 1981.06, 1982.24, 1985.08, 1989.03, 1996.10, 2000.01
Tireli, Jaime 1995.09
Tirrell, Barbara 1997.04
Tisch, Rosalie 1978.19
Tisman, Sol 1937.01
Tissington, Henry 1866.01, 1866.04, 1866.05, 1866.34, 1867.08, 1867.16, 1867.17, 1868.08, 1868.16, 1869.46, 1870.05, 1870.30, 1871.08, 1872.10, 1880.46, 1884.53
Tissot, Mlle. 1886.16
Titenia 1896.30
Titheradge, Dion 1923.35, 1924.01, 1925.42, 1925.50, 1930.20, 1935.12, 1975.22
Titius, Tracy 1878.16
Tittel-Brune, Miss 1912.32
Tittell, Esther 1905.20
Titterton, W.R. 1918.31
Titus, Alan 1972.15, 1974.16, 1975.16, 1978.07, 1978.19, 1978.23, 1979.20, 1979.21, 1980.22, 1982.16, 1985.11, 1989.13
Titus, C.F. 1885.06
Titus, Eric 1923.14, 1925.23
Titus, F.J. 1884.48
Titus, Fred 1900.41, 1901.23, 1903.18
Titus, Fred J. 1903.36
Titus, Mary 1927.31, 1942.05
Titus, Tracy W. 1873.18, 1873.21, 1873.23
Titzell, Joshua 1930.18
Tizol, Juan 1980.10, 1981.06, 1999.24
TM Productions, Inc. 1985.06
Toback, Hannah 1920.34, 1934.13
Tobani, Theo 1903.41
Tobell, Ted 1901.03
Toben, David A. 1972.17
Tobey, Kenneth 1941.12, 1964.32
Tobia, Ricardo 1976.02
Tobias, Charles 1923.20, 1928.23, 1928.25, 1929.24, 1929.26, 1932.18, 1935.04, 1938.08, 1939.24, 1942.16
Tobias, Charlie 1999.24
Tobias, Fred 1966.05, 1970.02, 1982.06, 1999.01
Tobias, George 1955.02
Tobias, Harry 1928.23, 1929.26
Tobias, Henry 1932.18, 1935.04
Tobias, Henry H. 1927.31
Tobias, Roy 1947.16
Tobias, Willard 1925.17
Tobin, Eugene 1946.10
Tobin, Gene 1948.25
Tobin, Genevieve 1918.07, 1924.34, 1929.45
Tobin, Joan F. 1980.27
Tobin, Patricia 1951.19
Tobin, Richard 1908.31
Toby, Mr. 1868.06
Toche, Messr. 1881.35
Tod, Quentin 1911.01, 1914.04, 1915.07, 1917.02
Toda, Toshi 1987.15
Todaro, Mary Jo 1997.16, 1998.08
Todd, Abbie 1965.17
Todd, Albert 1990.01
Todd, Clarence 1928.10, 1931.11, 1931.31
Todd, David 1915.25
Todd, Dick 1944.17
Todd, Dylan 1958.12
Todd, Frank 1900.01, 1900.50, 1902.43, 1904.56, 1905.22
Todd, H. David 1909.03
Todd, James 1941.08
Todd, John 1908.13, 1918.01
Todd, Jr., Michael 1993.05
Todd, Little 1876.03
Todd, Lorraine 1945.20
Todd, Michael 1939.17, 1939.22, 1942.18, 1943.01, 1944.02, 1945.03, 1946.02, 1947.11, 1948.28, 1950.12
Todd, Mildred 1934.06, 1934.40, 1936.12, 1938.04
Todd, Susan McCarthy 1993.05
Toddings, Ann 1921.25
Toddings, Anna 1918.22
Tofel, Tom 1975.07
Toguri, David 1958.19
Toibin, Niall 1980.17
Toigo, Alfred 1961.26, 1965.22
Tojio, Melanie Mariko 1991.03
Tokar, Michael 1989.23
Tokatyan, Leon 1961.07
Tokoro, Harumi 1989.21
Tokyo Broadcasting System International, Inc. 1989.27, 1990.18, 1991.06, 1993.18
Toland, Alice 1897.44, 1902.40
Toland, Gertrude 1904.46
Toland, Hugo 1904.46
Toland, John 1967.01
Tolaydo, Michael 1975.18
Toledano, Jose 1949.07
Toledo 1868.07, 1871.26
Toledo, Julie 1949.07
Toledo, M. 1870.35, 1870.42, 1871.02, 1872.12
Toledo, Mons. 1872.04, 1872.05, 1872.08
Toledo, Mr. 1868.25, 1868.27, 1870.28, 1870.32
Toler, Sidney 1905.51, 1922.42, 1924.24
Toler, Sydney 1903.34
Tolin, Meg 1993.18
Tolin, Richard 1977.18
Tolkien, R.R. 1966.32

Tolkin, Mel 1942.05, 1950.09, 1990.16
Tolle, Mildred 1925.35, 1928.35, 1932.13
Tollefsen, Merald 1927.66
Toller, Ernst 1938.02
Tolman, Clarence 1928.15
Tolman, Clarence H. 1926.27
Tolsch, Adrianne 1992.16
Tolson, Pat 1959.22, 1961.10
Tolstoy, Leo 1979.29, 1992.11
Tom Cat, Inc., The 1927.39
Tom, Lauren 1983.18
Tomanec, Joyce 1969.12, 1976.26
Tomaroff, Aron 1931.39
Tomasi, Antonio 1895.24
Tomasi, Signor 1881.05
Tomasso, Messr. 1906.05, 1907.02
Tombes, Andrew 1917.26, 1919.29, 1920.25, 1921.04, 1921.32, 1922.19, 1923.20, 1924.21, 1925.14, 1925.49, 1926.18, 1927.29, 1927.37, 1928.37, 1929.32, 1930.05, 1932.05, 1932.21, 1934.04, 1934.43
Tomkins, Don 1927.41, 1929.03, 1930.42, 1931.28, 1960.22
Tomkins, Gordon 1902.21
Tomkins, H. 1886.50
Tomkins, Messr. 1796.01
Tomkins, Mr. 1886.54
Tomkins, William 1925.12
Tomlin, Blanche 1919.42
Tomlinosn, Mary 1929.51
Tomlinson, H.W. 1877.04
Tomlinson, Kate 1955.06
Tomlinson, Mary Ann 1952.15
Tomlinson, Raymond 1927.03
Tommy Tune Production, A 1994.07, 1996.17
Tommy, Japanese 1876.04, 1876.05, 1876.07, 1876.09, 1876.10, 1876.11, 1876.14, 1876.30, 1876.33
Tommy, Master 1864.02
Tomney, John 1930.27
Tompkins, Beatrice 1957.15, 1958.16
Tompkins, Eugene 1881.15, 1884.16, 1884.37, 1891.41, 1892.38, 1893.23, 1894.34
Tompkins, Georgie 1898.08
Tompkins, Gilbert 1896.39
Tompkins, Madge 1894.10
Tompkins, Messr. 1880.12
Tompkins, Mrs. 1796.01
Tompkins, Nancy 1976.36
Tompos, Doug 1989.29
Toms, Archie 1930.29
Toms, Carl 1978.07, 1978.20, 1979.21, 1989.13
Tomsen, Mark 1904.41
Tomson, Bob 1993.07
Tomson, Jack 1921.10
Tomson, Tommy 1921.10
Tonde, Edwin 1927.30
Tone, Franchot 1931.02
Tone, Richard 1959.08, 1959.17, 1961.07, 1963.15, 1966.02, 1966.05
Toner, Joseph 1920.47, 1924.06, 1925.39, 1927.17, 1929.17, 1930.01, 1931.07, 1938.17, 1959.25
Toner, Thomas 1986.12
Toner, Tom 1973.02, 1991.05
Toney, Andrea Frierson 1994.12, 1996.16
Toney, David 1996.16
Tong, Yo Hay 1932.01
Tonge, Ashton 1919.02
Tonge, Lucy 1906.01, 1906.30, 1907.51
Tonge, Philip 1922.45, 1946.06, 1948.11
Tonihi, Putiputi 1972.20
Tonkin, Mel 1990.16
Tonner, Messr. 1880.43
Tonteine, Lulu 1886.34
Tony Meola/Autograph 1992.03
Tony, Master 1879.58, 1890.49, 1891.25
Tony, Mons. 1887.35, 1887.37
Toohey, P. 1889.38
Tookoyan, Art 1961.20
Tookoyan, Arthur 1960.10
Toole, C.J. 1881.02
Toole, J.E. 1898.59
Toole, P. 1882.62, 1883.06, 1885.33
Toole, P.J. 1880.63
Toole, Peter 1879.12, 1880.08
Toole, R.J. 1881.13
Tooley, Larry 1872.07, 1875.31, 1875.36, 1875.37, 1875.38, 1875.40, 1876.01, 1876.19, 1878.19
Toomay, Marjorie 1922.15
Toomey, Messr. 1887.32
Toomey, Paul 1978.26
Toops, Evelyn 1963.26
Tootsey, Little 1889.02
Tooze, Fred 1911.39
Topack, George 1866.02, 1868.06, 1869.26, 1870.15, 1873.02, 1873.26, 1875.32, 1876.03, 1880.35, 1890.42, 1890.45, 1902.26
Topack, Mary 1870.33
Topack, Messr. 1880.55
Topham, Florence 1908.34, 1913.09
Tophoff, Mons. 1862.03
Tophoff, Mr. 1862.03
Topol 1977.01, 1990.18
Toppe, Andris 1972.08
Torbay, Marceline 1922.30
Torgerson, Ulita 1937.03
Toriani, Carlo 1885.34, 1885.36, 1885.37, 1885.38
Torigi, Richard 1952.12, 1956.04
Torkanowsky, Werner 1960.03, 1962.06
Torloff, Frank 1942.32
Torme, Mel 1998.19
Tormey, John 1960.01, 1963.22, 1967.01
Tormey, Katherine 1908.13
Tormsen, Norval 1948.27, 1951.15
Tornaghi, Zole 1892.38
Toro, Natalie 1994.12
Toro, Puli 1974.07, 1974.14, 1974.15, 1975.16, 1975.17, 1976.22, 1976.26, 1977.11, 1980.03, 1980.22, 1981.22, 1989.13, 1996.02
Torosu 1922.21
Torpey, Erin 1993.02
Torpey, Joseph 1902.29, 1909.30, 1912.07
Torpey, William 1896.18, 1898.20, 1901.16, 1903.23, 1905.22, 1905.30, 1928.37, 1932.22, 1933.26, 1939.28
Torpey, Willie 1899.29, 1900.40, 1902.24, 1904.31, 1907.24, 1923.40, 1924.26, 1926.32, 1946.01
Torpy, Joe 1921.18
Torr, A.C. 1888.41
Torralba, Pilar 1921.39
Torrance, Barbara 1952.03
Torrance, David 1896.05
Torrence, Charles 1881.31
Torrence, David 1892.55, 1895.20, 1895.42, 1896.29, 1899.36, 1900.44, 1904.01, 1904.37, 1905.28, 1906.24, 1919.28
Torrence, Ernest 1912.01, 1912.40, 1914.27, 1916.09, 1917.21, 1918.22, 1919.01, 1920.04
Torrens, Grace 1917.24, 1919.20
Torrens, J.R. 1911.01
Torres, Andy 1975.01, 1976.21
Torres, Donald 1983.10
Torres, Gina 1994.06
Torres, Jorge 1993.08, 1997.13
Torres, Maria 1999.24
Torres, Mme. 1890.17
Torrey, Mabel 1892.57, 1893.03
Torrey, Marguerite 1918.31
Torrey, Roy 1908.16, 1912.29
Torriani, Aimee 1917.11, 1924.46
Torriani, Carlo 1892.57
Torriani, Carlos 1882.38
Torroella, Antonio 1912.44
Torsiglieri, Anne 1993.07
Torti, Robert 1987.05, 1993.15
Tosatti, Mario 1927.40
Toser, David 1968.19, 1975.09, 1975.24, 1976.25, 1977.01, 1979.05, 1982.05, 1982.15, 1985.04, 1986.19
Tost, William 1970.06
Tostee, Lucille 1867.24, 1868.07, 1868.17, 1868.25, 1868.27, 1869.10, 1869.12, 1869.18, 1869.22
Tostee, Mlle. 1869.19
Tosti 1886.54
Toth, Andrew James 2001.04
Toto, Karen 1981.19
Totten, George 1906.44
Totten, Wesley 1920.38
Touche, Raoul 1852.02
Touchnoff, Messr. 1925.03
Touda, Ikuei 1989.21
Touhey, Marie 1897.07
Toulmin, Mr. 1852.02
Toumanova, Tamara 1939.13
Toumine, Lorne 1972.08
Tourjee, Homer 1895.15
Tournaire, Mlle. 1887.35, 1887.36
Tourneur, Jeanette 1919.10
Tournyaire, Mlle. 1884.43, 1884.55, 1885.57, 1886.09, 1886.21, 1887.37
Tours, Frank 1909.21, 1911.12, 1911.32, 1915.25, 1916.25, 1917.02, 1917.10, 1917.15, 1917.31, 1918.02, 1918.06, 1918.16, 1919.03, 1919.30, 1919.39, 1919.43, 1920.18, 1920.34, 1921.21, 1921.30, 1922.39, 1923.32, 1924.33, 1924.44, 1925.45, 1927.21, 1927.37, 1928.42, 1929.41, 1930.39, 1932.05, 1933.02, 1933.22, 1934.29, 1935.14, 1936.26, 1948.11
Tours, Frank A. 1907.32
Tours, Frank E. 1896.27, 1903.22, 1906.25, 1911.47, 1912.19, 1913.25, 1914.32, 1916.09, 1925.43
Toussaint, Allen 1992.06
Tova, Miss 1933.15
Tovar, Candace 1982.13, 1986.06
Tovatt, Ellen 1990.02
Tovey Sydney 1896.48
Tovey, Sidney 1896.48
Towber, Chaim 1998.11
Towbin, Beryl 1954.01, 1960.07, 1962.01, 1968.06
Tower, Robert 1944.14
Towers, Carroll Jo 1959.13
Towers, Constance 1965.35, 1966.14, 1966.31, 1967.07, 1968.16, 1971.02, 1977.07
Towers, Ian 1979.09
Towers, Ian Michael 1980.30
Towers, Richard 1955.11
Towers, Tafi 1951.15
Towle, George 1883.25, 1883.29
Towle, George P. 1884.06, 1898.20, 1900.43, 1902.21, 1903.07
Towle, George W. 1885.04
Towler, Gray B. 1903.12
Towler, Jeanne 1906.24
Town Productions, Inc. 1958.21
Town, George 1900.59
Towne, Barbara 1938.05
Towne, Billy 1962.17, 1990.16
Towne, Cynthia 1967.01
Towne, Hattie 1919.22
Towne, Lester 1946.02, 1947.01
Townley, Charles 1947.09
Townly, Barry 1924.42
Towns, Cynthia 1969.09
Towns, Kirk 1888.11
Townsell-Crips, Vanessa 1998.01
Townsend, Alice 1879.18, 1879.23
Townsend, Edward W. 1897.38, 1911.17
Townsend, Horace 1889.03, 1891.06, 1891.28, 1894.20, 1895.30, 1896.14
Townsend, Margaret 1908.26, 1910.23, 1911.28
Townsend, Miss 1904.13
Townsend, Pete 1974.22, 1993.06
Townsend, Van Rensselaer 1912.03
Townsend, Vivian 1898.58
Townsend, W. 1873.26
Townsend, William J. 1904.46
Townshend, Alice 1879.24
Townshend, Charles 1929.39
Townshend, Edward W. 1898.58
Townshend, Florence 1904.28
Townshend, Horace 1889.48
Townshend, K.C. 1967.14, 1971.03
Townshend, Margaret 1906.46, 1907.54
Townshend, Maude 1900.02, 1900.23
Townshend, Peter 1972.08, 1982.22
Townshend, Theodore 1881.31
Townshend, Walton 1897.12
Townsley, Floyd 1931.44
Toy, Mary Mon 1954.19
Toy, Noel 1942.25
Toye, Dorothy 1913.07
Toye, Jennifer 1955.20, 1962.25, 1962.26, 1962.31, 1964.37, 1964.42, 1964.43
Toye, Wendy 1950.08, 1955.19
Tozere, Frederic 1924.26, 1937.11, 1959.19
Tozzi, George 1948.31
Tozzi, Giorgio 1967.10, 1979.26
Tra La La, Inc. Production, A 1993.05
Trabert, Elvira 1931.09
Trabert, George 1920.05, 1923.01, 1933.23, 1937.03
Trabert, Georges 1934.17
Trabue, Marion 1926.50
Tracey, Andrew 1966.03
Tracey, Billy 1927.61
Tracey, Cora 1903.36
Tracey, Fred A. 1897.02
Tracey, Helen 1891.28
Tracey, Katherine 1934.03
Tracey, Paul 1966.03, 1970.15
Tracey, Stella 1902.27, 1907.16, 1908.07, 1909.31
Tracey, William 1910.17, 1910.18, 1912.29, 1948.13
Tract, Jo 1964.21, 1966.10
Tracy Titius Opera Company 1878.16
Tracy, Cora 1906.48
Tracy, Dudie 1891.04
Tracy, G.L. 1899.41
Tracy, George L. 1889.02
Tracy, George Lowell 1895.38
Tracy, Helen 1880.41, 1885.33, 1887.27
Tracy, Henry 1884.22
Tracy, Hetty 1871.14, 1871.19, 1880.47, 1880.69
Tracy, Lizzie 1883.65
Tracy, Marion 1879.01
Tracy, Paul 1983.05
Tracy, Roy 1919.20
Tracy, Royal 1921.41, 1922.35
Tracy, Stella 1904.28
Tracy, Teresa 1987.14
Tracy, Thomas F. 1931.05
Tracy, Thomas P. 1926.38
Trader, George H. 1890.04
Trado, Frank 1923.17, 1924.29, 1927.62
Trado, Pete 1923.17
Trado, Peter 1924.29, 1927.62
Tragman, Richard 1904.15
Trahan, Al 1930.25, 1942.14
Trahern, Al 1899.11
Train, Paul 1905.37
Train, Pauline 1896.24
Traines, Andrew 1980.01
Traingle Scenic Studios 1921.37, 1922.30
Trainor, George 1927.19
Trainor, Jack 1922.23
Trainor, Jimmie 1927.19
Trainor, John 1870.34
Traisse, Mons. 1875.29
Trama, Johnny 1951.23
Tramon, Carl 1979.22
Tramon, Dan 1984.02
Tranchant, Jean 1934.32, 1935.19
Trans-Witmark Music Library 1983.06
Trapp, Maria Augusta 1959.24, 1967.07, 1998.03
Trappert, Harry 1906.10
Trappert, Harry H. 1904.06
Trat, V. 1877.04
Traub, H.L. 1896.18, 1896.44
Traub, John 1980.12
Traube, Shepard 1954.01
Traubel, Helen 1955.27
Traubner, Richard 1981.02
Trautman, Morty 1961.25
Travares, Virginia 1919.37
Travathan, Charles E. 1895.27
Traver, Sharry 1948.17
Traverne, Joost 1982.23
Traverner, George 1883.39
Traverner, George W. 1885.30, 1885.32, 1891.38
Travers, Frank 1914.30
Travers, Helen 1875.11
Travers, Jean 1935.03
Travers, Lena 1890.50
Travers, Margot 1969.17
Travers, Mary Allin 1958.12
Travers, Miss 1870.22
Travers, Vincent 1939.31, 1951.18
Travers, W.T. 1902.29
Travers, Walter 1938.03
Traverse, Martha 1979.31
Travis, Amie L. 1904.14
Travis, Amy 1898.07, 1898.15
Travis, Barbara 1957.18
Travis, J. Michael 1959.19
Travis, Michael 1958.04, 1967.18
Travolta, John 1974.05
Traxler, Steve 1999.25
Tray, M.T. 1895.37
Trayer, Kate 1890.08, 1895.19
Trayer, Leslie 1989.03
Traylor, William 1966.14
Traynor 1868.28
Traynor, Agnes 1931.44
Traynor, Blair 1920.33
Traynor, Master 1870.22
Traynor, Tom 1963.10

Treacher, Arthur 1926.14, 1928.06, 1930.38, 1931.09, 1940.19, 1943.05
Treadwell, George 1995.03
Treadwell, Marcia 1897.45, 1898.69
Treadwell, Tom 1997.04
Treas, Terri 1976.19, 1978.12
Treat, Roger 1944.33
Trebitsch, Paul M. 1930.21
Tredenick, H.W. 1897.25, 1904.36
Tredennick, H.W. 1896.33
Tredennick, W.H. 1897.16
Trednick, H.W. 1895.03
Tree, Dolly 1930.09
Tree, Messr. 1856.01
Tree, Miss 1856.01
Tree, Mr. 1859.08
Trees, Carl 1940.06
Trefeu, Etienne 1868.26, 1871.19, 1872.31, 1875.20, 1876.18, 1880.23, 1883.38, 1883.58, 1894.11
Tregre, George 1965.37, 1968.24
Trehy, Robert 1962.08, 1962.09, 1963.15, 1968.10, 1968.14
Treiber, Eleanore 1962.24, 1963.08, 1964.15, 1965.01, 1965.14, 1986.03
Treiber, Eleonore 1961.27
Trejo, Valeriano 1988.15
Trekman, Emma 1966.27
Trelawny, Violet 1897.32
Trelease, Ruby 1923.43
Trelfa, Thomas 1970.15
Tremain, Bobbi 1971.07
Tremain, John 1750.01
Tremaine, Bobbie 1931.34
Tremaine, Olive 1889.31
Tremaine, Oliver 1888.43
Trenaman, Lydia 1898.67
Trenet, Charles 1964.02, 1964.22, 1967.13, 1968.20, 1999.07, 2000.07
Trenholm, Cissy 1948.19, 1949.05
Trenkle, Christopher Shea 1958.03
Trenkler, Freddie 1940.16, 1942.19, 1944.20, 1946.14, 1947.12, 1948.19
Trenner, Donn 1976.07
Trent, Jerry 1964.20
Trent, Jo 1926.11, 1927.30, 1927.33, 1929.08, 1931.47
Trent, Lee 1946.15
Trent, William 1906.03
Trentini, Emma 1910.35, 1912.46, 1915.04
Treskoff, Olga 1922.04, 1923.43, 1925.32, 1927.65
Tretbar, Helen F. 1891.12, 1891.30, 1892.16
Trett, Vera 1927.52
Treumann, Karl 1880.61, 1883.44, 1883.45, 1884.63, 1888.22
Trevalyan, Miss 1881.11
Trevathan, Charles 1897.25
Trevathan, Charles A. 1896.52
Trevathan, Charles E. 1895.27, 1897.45
Trevelyan, Arthur 1895.17, 1899.29, 1900.52
Trevillion, Florence 1905.55
Trevisani, Pamela 1983.14
Trevor, F. 1856.01
Trevor, Harry 1948.32
Trevor, Huntley 1912.44, 1925.50
Trevor, Laurie 1880.49
Trevor, Messr. 1853.01
Trevor, Mr. 1852.03, 1853.02, 1853.03
Trevor, Spencer 1919.42
Trevor, Vaughan 1907.51
Trew, Margaret 1898.05, 1901.05
Trew, Margerite 1900.37
Trewey, Mons. 1889.35
Treynor, Blair 1920.33
Triangle Scenic Company 1926.29
Triangle Scenic Studios 1920.21, 1924.35, 1925.06
Triangle Studios 1921.19
Tribble, Andrew 1907.22, 1909.10, 1911.20, 1921.26, 1923.11, 1930.29
Tribush, Nancy 1971.04
Tricky Feat Ltd. 2000.04
Trien, Cathy 1996.17
Triesault, Ivan 1927.62
Trieste, Mona 1911.13
Triggs, Richard 1972.06
Trigler, Joyce 1970.08
Trikonis, Gus 1964.40
Trimble, Annie 1876.03
Trimble, G.S. 1893.34
Trimble, George S. 1893.34
Trimble, Miss 1871.04
Trimble, Mme. 1870.07
Trimble, Mrs. 1870.33
Trimlets, Tom 1906.46
Trindelli, P. 1920.09
Trinder, Marsia 1975.04
Trini 1931.09
Trini, Senorita 1924.36
Trinkhaus, George 1919.07
Trinnier, Vaughn 1944.17, 1944.23
Trion, Leonard 1929.08
Tripler, George 1918.36
Triplett, Sally Ann 1988.12
Tripolitoff, Nicholas 1926.15
Tripp, Michael 1930.06
Tripp, Shirley 1987.07
Trisler, Joyce 1969.16, 1972.24, 1974.16
Trittipo, James 1971.08, 1971.15, 1972.03
Trivers, Barry 1931.19, 1948.23
Trivers, Benn 1927.11
Triwush, Ken 1990.15
Trix, Helen 1916.24, 1916.25
Trixie 1948.19
Trockowna, Anna 1934.41
Trofimov, Gennady 1990.01
Troilo, A. 1985.07, 1997.13
Trompton, May 1886.03
Trompton, Mayy 1887.39
Trona, Joan 1963.08
Tronto, Rudy 1979.25, 1980.11
Troob, Daniel 1975.06, 1976.02, 1977.05, 1979.03, 1980.06, 1981.07, 1985.06, 1988.10, 1992.04, 1992.17, 1994.04, 1995.05
Troob, Danny 1998.13, 1999.16
Troobnick, Eugene 1961.17
Trott, Karen 1979.29, 1980.07
Trott, Pat 1969.01
Trott, Richard 1923.43
Trotter Brothers, The 1964.22
Troubetzkoy, Youka 1946.22
Troughton, John M. 1924.10
Trouille, Clovis 1971.04, 1976.27
Troupe, Bobby 1979.24
Trout, Dink 1926.34
Trout, Robert 1948.17
Troutman, Hazel 1912.26
Troutman, William 1969.03
Trouve, Mons. 1883.51, 1883.57
Trovaioli, Armando 1964.03
Trowbridge, Charles 1895.24, 1918.24, 1922.13
Trowell, Stanford 1965.39
Troy, Cassie 1869.31
Troy, Charles 1929.07
Troy, Ellen 1989.03
Troy, Hector 1939.19
Troy, Henry 1906.08, 1908.08, 1909.27, 1930.16
Troy, Leesa 1963.21
Troy, Louise 1955.27, 1963.08, 1964.16, 1966.27
Troy, William 1922.21
Troyanos, Tatiana 1959.24
Truax, Harry 1903.19, 1912.30
Truax, Harry Anson 1919.24
Trudeau, Garry 1983.18
True Brethren, The 1970.16, 1971.08
True, Alberte 1896.01
Trueblood, Paul 1977.02
Truece, Mildred 1923.21
Trueheart, W.H. 1894.50
Trueman, Paula 1922.20, 1925.20, 1926.17, 1927.23, 1928.19, 1929.20, 1930.38, 1962.01, 1963.05, 1965.21, 1967.02
Truesdale, Camille 1909.29
Truesdale, Frederic 1898.29
Truesdell, Frederic 1898.18, 1898.26
Truesdell, Frederick 1910.26
Truesdell, Howard 1920.42
Truex, Ernest 1910.17, 1911.15, 1915.30, 1924.38, 1931.14, 1937.03, 1944.16, 1951.15
Truex, Philip 1942.20
Truhauf, Messr. 1890.31, 1894.01
Truitte, James 1946.09
Trujillo, Pedro 1974.14
Trujillo, Sergio 1999.01
Trullinger, George 1989.11
Truman, Harry 1904.25
Truman, Mr. 1866.02, 1866.28
Truran, Edythe 1902.37
Truschel, Alfred 1904.04
Truschel, Alfred C. 1903.09
Truscott, George 1922.19
Truscott, Mark 1923.20, 1925.10, 1925.24, 1925.31
Truscott, Messr. 1926.32
Truss, D.W. 1896.14
Trussel, Jack 1970.10, 1972.24
Trussel, Jacque 1978.19, 1980.21
Tryoler, William 1945.16
Tryon, W. 1857.04
Tsao, Joan 1981.21
Tschernichovsky, S. 1972.17
Tschiakowsky 1916.15, 1925.06
Tschudin, Michael 1980.05
Tshabalala, Junior 1977.01
Tshabalala, Linda 1977.01
Tshanini, Thabani Patrick 1997.14
Tshelishteff, P. 1924.48
Tsirigotis, Ann 1999.02
Tsitrinnik, Joseph 1925.51
Tsoutsouvas, Sam 1973.16
Tsu, Susan 1976.17
Tsvetaleff, Messr. 1929.05
Tswever, Z. Berdi 1967.08
Tucci, Maria 1979.07
Tuck, Samuel L. 1904.14
Tucker, Allyson 2001.02
Tucker, Alonzo 1997.21
Tucker, Bob 1949.08
Tucker, Bobby 1943.21, 1948.13
Tucker, C. 1881.40
Tucker, Carl 1953.17
Tucker, Charles 1915.31
Tucker, Don 1969.03
Tucker, Earl 1928.18
Tucker, Genevieve 1919.41
Tucker, George Loane 1910.26
Tucker, Ian 1954.13, 1959.13, 1960.05, 1968.18, 1968.19, 1974.02
Tucker, Jack 1898.66
Tucker, Johnny 1932.14
Tucker, Lewis 1978.03
Tucker, Lillian 1914.21, 1915.07
Tucker, Lorenzo 1933.06
Tucker, Mary 1881.15
Tucker, Rachel Tecora 1993.03
Tucker, Robert 1954.13, 1974.02, 1974.17, 1975.03, 1975.22, 1978.10, 1989.17
Tucker, Sophie 1909.13, 1919.26, 1924.31, 1938.13, 1941.09
Tucker, Tanya 1979.16
Tucker, W.H. 1898.78
Tucker, William 1927.01
Tuckerman, Maury 1935.17
Tudar, Marie 1920.28
Tudor, Anthony 1945.19
Tudor, Antony 1945.09
Tudor, Jennifer 1965.39
Tudor, Roland 1929.34, 1929.36
Tudor, Rowan 1930.36, 1945.03, 1947.11, 1949.08, 1951.15
Tuesart, Helen 1898.17
Tufts, Belle 1897.04, 1898.08
Tufts, Bowen 1939.19
Tufts, Sonny 1938.04
Tugend, Hary 1934.01
Tuguese 1934.16
Tuhura, Rongo 1972.20
Tuite, Bertha 1924.14
Tuite, Cyrilla 1931.35
Tuli, David 1929.22
Tullar, J.V. 1907.13
Tullar, Joseph 1913.04
Tulloch, Jake 1954.08
Tully, May 1924.33
Tully, Milton 1931.27, 1931.35
Tully, Paula 1924.36
Tully, Phillip 1942.07, 1942.08, 1942.09
Tully, Richard Walton 1912.03, 1930.26
Tuma, Casey 1997.04
Tumeo, Vincent 1994.10
Tun, Tun 1959.27
Tunbridge, Joseph 1930.20, 1932.21
Tune, Tommy 1965.02, 1966.30, 1967.16, 1973.06, 1978.13, 1980.08, 1982.09, 1982.11, 1983.06, 1986.03, 1989.26, 1991.07, 1994.06
Tunick, Jonathan 1960.07, 1968.05, 1968.31, 1970.13, 1971.05, 1971.16, 1972.02, 1973.04, 1975.06, 1975.15, 1976.02, 1978.27, 1979.06, 1981.27, 1982.09, 1982.24, 1983.08, 1983.19, 1984.13, 1985.20, 1987.09, 1987.18, 1990.07, 1991.08, 1991.15, 1993.16, 1994.05, 1995.11, 1995.12, 1996.06, 1997.06, 1999.20, 1999.22, 1999.23, 2001.02
Tunis, Fay 1919.14
Tunison, Louise 1899.21
Tunison, May 1907.06
Tunison, Mr. 1852.04
Tunnan, Renton 1976.04
Tunnard, Viola 1955.19, 1958.10
Tunney, Anne 1925.06
Tunsill, Johnnie 1938.04
Tunstall, Fred 1925.18
Tuohey, Marie 1897.21, 1899.02, 1901.21
Tuohey, P. 1897.03
Tuohy, Joseph 1906.50
Tuomy, Miss 1859.11
Tuotti, Joseph Dolan 1969.15
Tupferburg, Tuli 1970.04
Turbett, Ben 1909.02
Turbinton, Wilson 1992.06
Turbull, Julia 1844.01
Turck, Marius 1871.13
Turenne, Louis 1973.07
Turgell, Edith 1944.01
Turgend, Harry 1934.01
Turgeon, Dai 1912.26
Turgeon, Peter 1950.10, 1960.04, 1962.27
Turk, Bruce 1996.16, 2000.10
Turk, David 1932.28
Turk, Hillary 1995.02
Turk, Philip 1968.08
Turk, Roy 1922.15, 1922.25, 1923.21, 1924.01, 1924.37, 1928.33, 1976.32, 1978.09, 1980.10, 1989.12
Turley, F. 1918.14
Turley, Richard 1975.04
Turnage, Wayne 1983.05
Turnball, Thelma 1918.05
Turnbough, Zedrick 1984.15
Turnbull, Enid 1999.09
Turnbull, Glen 1946.10
Turnbull, Jill 1973.12
Turnbull, Laura 1989.22
Turnbull, Miss 1840.02, 1840.03, 1840.04
Turnbull, Mme. E. 1834.02
Turnbull, Mme. J. 1834.02
Turner Entertainment Company 1989.26, 1991.15
Turner, Alfred 1912.36
Turner, Allan 1912.36
Turner, Amma 1879.50
Turner, Anna 1903.25
Turner, B.W. 1880.63
Turner, Ben 1899.03
Turner, Bessie 1876.21
Turner, Bill 1977.09
Turner, Bob 1946.05
Turner, C.H. 1877.36, 1879.30
Turner, Carrie 1890.40
Turner, Charles 1894.13, 1895.08
Turner, Claramae 1959.18, 1962.08, 1962.11, 1964.10, 1964.12, 1964.14, 1965.10, 1965.11, 1968.15, 1969.11
Turner, Clyde 1946.12, 1952.06, 1956.06, 1957.14, 1961.13, 1962.07, 1964.19
Turner, Dorothy 1937.09
Turner, Douglas 1958.11
Turner, E.H. 1895.16
Turner, Emma 1879.56
Turner, Eva 1892.19
Turner, F. 1880.02
Turner, F.W. 1908.16
Turner, Fred 1887.01, 1887.43
Turner, Frederick 1880.02
Turner, George H. 1894.50
Turner, Gladys 1907.38, 1911.26
Turner, Glenn 1992.03, 1998.05
Turner, Gloria 1973.10
Turner, Grant 1999.02
Turner, Harry 1898.44
Turner, Helen 1904.13, 1904.44, 1912.14
Turner, J.B. 1885.53, 1886.44, 1886.51
Turner, Jayne 1971.05
Turner, John 1962.17, 1976.16
Turner, John Hastings 1929.51
Turner, Kay 1920.08
Turner, Kellie 1993.03
Turner, Little Nan 1912.30
Turner, Maidel 1914.08, 1929.12, 1942.15
Turner, Maisie 1894.15
Turner, Maud 1901.20
Turner, Messr. 1879.01, 1885.58
Turner, Miss 1836.01, 1904.13, 1904.44
Turner, Mons. 1879.06
Turner, Mrs. J.B. 1886.44, 1886.51
Turner, Pat 1953.07, 1959.25, 1961.15, 1961.21, 1962.05, 1963.05, 1963.17
Turner, Pauline 1907.26
Turner, R.M. 1880.41
Turner, Stanley 1943.06, 1946.13
Turner, Tommy 1878.13
Turner, W.H. 1892.31

Turner, Walter 1895.39, 1897.49
Turner, Wyetta 1973.15, 1980.10
Turney, Matt 1961.20
Turnley, Peggy 1947.02, 1949.16
Turnour, C. 1889.02
Turo, Puli 1978.07
Turoff, Robert 1963.22
Turpin, Harry 1912.36, 1919.11, 1919.30, 1921.34, 1923.12
Turpin, Henry 1907.51
Turque, Mimi 1965.34
Turri, Mlle. 1882.62, 1883.06
Turrill, Celia 1928.13
Turrnell, Edythia 1946.07
Tushar, James 1955.05
Tushinsky, Joseph 1942.17, 1942.21, 1942.22
Tusky, Mr. 1868.06
Tussey, Julie 1986.20
Tutein, Carrie 1885.48, 1886.40, 1886.60, 1888.28, 1889.35, 1890.44
Tuthill, Gertie 1888.27, 1889.11, 1889.15, 1889.18
Tuthill, Lula 1889.11, 1889.15, 1889.18
Tuthill, Lulla 1888.27
Tutin, Dorothy 1963.03
Tutt, Homer 1930.10
Tutt, J. Homer 1929.01, 1929.52, 1930.10, 1935.01
Tutt, Miss 1894.44
Tuttle, Emma 1880.48
Tuttle, Gertie 1887.45, 1888.40
Tuttle, Lulla 1888.40
Tuttle, Mr. 1866.18
Tuttle, W.W. 1880.48, 1880.53
Tuvim, Abe 1934.37
TV Asahi 1991.05, 1992.04, 1992.08, 1994.07, 1996.17
Twade, George 1922.45
Twain, Mark 1873.03, 1927.56, 1943.22, 1966.18, 1985.06, 2001.06
Twain, Norman 1964.40, 1966.20, 1967.14, 1968.21, 1970.01
Twardy, Ray 1941.07
Twebeeke, Reinier 1993.17
Tweddell, Frank 1964.21
Tweedley, John 1916.15
Twentieth-Century Fox Theatre Productions, Inc. 1982.08
Twiford, Verda 1937.06
Twiggy 1983.06
Twine, Linda 1981.16, 1985.06, 1992.08
Twitchell, Jr., Arthur C. 1972.07
Twitters, Mrs. Tony 1894.16
Twohey, Marie 1901.08
Twohey, Vincie 1900.33
Twombly, Roland 1925.37
Twomey, John 1972.09
Twomey, Kay 1945.17
Tyce, Lillian 1902.26, 1903.05
Tyers, John 1941.10, 1943.23, 1946.18, 1948.14, 1954.06, 1955.05
Tyeska, James 1983.04
Tyler, Andi 1989.03
Tyler, Anna M. 1904.18
Tyler, Beverly 1945.04
Tyler, Billy 1907.38
Tyler, Cornelia Osgood 1904.19
Tyler, Dallas 1893.31
Tyler, Danny 1975.07
Tyler, Ed 1898.68
Tyler, Edith 1904.42
Tyler, Edward 1943.15
Tyler, Edward B. 1899.15
Tyler, Edward Lee 1943.24
Tyler, Ethel 1895.36
Tyler, Francis 1909.07, 1933.24
Tyler, Francis J. 1913.27
Tyler, Fred 1907.58
Tyler, George 1929.20
Tyler, George C. 1903.26, 1921.01, 1922.42
Tyler, George H. 1873.29
Tyler, Georgia 1883.01, 1883.09, 1883.20
Tyler, Jack 1942.12
Tyler, James 1963.28
Tyler, Jean 1942.27
Tyler, Jeanne 1939.22, 1942.01
Tyler, Jim 1965.14, 1969.02, 1970.02, 1974.05, 1975.04, 1975.13, 1976.33, 1981.07, 1981.25, 1983.11, 1985.05, 1985.19, 1986.11, 1987.19, 1989.06
Tyler, Joseph 1796.01, 1796.02, 1796.03
Tyler, Juanita Grace 1980.15
Tyler, Judy 1955.27
Tyler, Lottie 1918.32
Tyler, Louise 1888.11
Tyler, Marian 1924.37
Tyler, Marie 1901.08, 1908.26
Tyler, Maurice 1931.07
Tyler, Odette 1884.39
Tyler, Richard 1970.04
Tyler, Rosa Lee 1904.26
Tyler, Royall 1787.01
Tyler, Ruth 1944.32
Tyler, Steve 2000.20
Tyler, Veronica 1964.19, 1983.04
Tynan, Brandon 1922.19, 1923.20, 1924.18, 1925.10, 1925.24
Tynan, Kenneth 1971.04, 1976.27
Tyne, George 1966.19
Tyne, Jean 1914.02, 1919.26
Tynes, Margaret 1953.05, 1953.14
Tyre, Virginia 1944.09
Tyrell, Billy 1898.50
Tyrell, Georgie 1886.31
Tyrell, Jane 1904.04
Tyron, H. 1879.12
Tyrone, Keith 1988.20
Tyrrell, Brad 1975.06
Tyrrell, Geoffrey 1882.28
Tyrrell, Mrs. 1863.02, 1863.08
Tysick, Sylvia 1962.18
Tyson, Alice 1909.25
Tyson, Annie 1872.09
Tyson, Cicely 1966.15, 1969.10
Tyson, Frances 1900.28, 1903.23
Tyson, Gertrude 1900.08
Tyson, Grace 1908.21, 1910.18, 1912.20
Tyson, Katie 1872.09
Tyson, Maryland 1899.13, 1900.45
Tyson, Messr. 1869.07, 1871.18
Tyson, Miss 1872.11
Tyte, Alexander 1866.02, 1866.28, 1867.12
Tyven, Sonja 1945.19, 1953.08, 1954.12

U. y Moran, Gabriel 1875.24
U. Y Moron, Carmen 1875.22
U. y Moron, Guadalupe 1875.24
U. Y Moron, Nina Guadalupe 1875.22
U.Y. Moron, Nino Gabriel 1875.22
Uarda, S. 1885.14
Uarda, Shila 1885.67
Uart, Kate 1885.58, 1887.43, 1888.20, 1888.35, 1890.03, 1890.37, 1891.43, 1892.56, 1893.28, 1894.10, 1895.03, 1895.22, 1898.36, 1899.40, 1902.07
Uart, Lottie 1901.16, 1902.24, 1905.35, 1910.13
Uart, Marie 1883.64, 1889.12, 1890.04, 1893.31
Uart, Marietta 1885.64
Uart, Nellie 1898.20
Uart, Nettie 1898.28, 1901.16, 1902.24
Ubarry, Hechter 1989.05, 1992.07
Ucci, Toni 1964.03
Uchida, Alice 1956.03
Uchida, Christine 1976.01
Uchitel, Bruce 1990.09
Udall, Lyn 1898.38
Udell, Charles 1887.01
Udell, Charles D. 1892.01
Udell, Charles E. 1888.13
Udell, Charles W. 1906.35
Udell, Peggy 1929.39
Udell, Peter 1970.05, 1972.26, 1975.03, 1978.10, 1979.32, 1983.15, 1989.17
Ueda, Shinji 1989.21
Ueda, Shinju 1989.21
Uggams, Eloise 1928.18, 1933.27, 1943.10
Uggams, Leslie 1967.06, 1968.23, 1982.12, 1985.19
Uhl, Constane 1919.12
Uhl, Jerome 1912.49, 1925.15
Uhr, Ira 1922.42
Uhry, Alfred 1968.05, 1975.18, 1976.30, 1982.05, 1995.12
Ukena, Jr., Paul 1978.13, 1991.07
Ukena, Paul 1953.02, 1958.15, 1959.16, 1961.06, 1961.23, 1962.19, 1963.23, 1964.07, 1964.08, 1965.09, 1965.11, 1965.12, 1965.13, 1968.10, 1968.12, 1968.14, 1970.10, 1975.17
Ukrainsky, P. 1924.48
Uksila, Gretle 1944.20
Uksila, Robert 1944.20
Ulbricht, Otto 1937.05
Ulisse, Arthur 1955.02
Ulissey, Catherine 1981.21, 1986.13
Ullett, Nick 1986.12
Ullman, Bill 1993.18
Ullman, Robin 1984.01
Ullmann, Liv 1979.12
Ulmar, G.H. 1879.01
Ulmar, Geraldine 1882.08, 1882.09, 1882.11, 1882.12, 1882.13, 1883.12, 1885.47, 1886.57, 1887.10
Ulmer, George 1880.02
Ulmer, George H. 1878.02
Ulmer, Georges 1964.22
Ulmer, Geraldine 1886.55
Ulmer, Lizzie May 1896.15
Ulmer, Maud 1891.29
Ulpah, Violet 1880.65
Ulrich, Bernhard 1939.15
Ulrich, Olive 1900.19, 1901.06, 1902.24, 1910.24, 1911.29, 1912.08, 1912.31
Ulvaeus, Bjorn 1988.09
Umanski, Alexander 1917.26
Umeki, Miyoshi 1958.19
Umlauf, Frl. 1879.22
Unangst, William 1918.23, 1922.30
Unda y Moron, Carmen 1875.24
Unda y Moron, Eduardo 1875.22, 1875.24
Unda y Moron, Pablo 1875.22, 1875.24
Underdown, Edward 1936.29
Underhill, Edwin 1934.34
Underwood, A. 1898.62
Underwood, Arthur 1887.15
Underwood, Franklin 1970.21
Underwood, Robert 1933.06
Underwood, Shirley 1975.12
Underwood, Willabelle 1953.14
Unger, Della 1930.22
Unger, Frank 1907.30
Unger, Frau 1866.33
Unger, Gladys 1912.27, 1913.26, 1916.20, 1924.25, 1927.68, 1928.06
Unger, Jean 1928.25
Unger, Stella 1930.15, 1935.19, 1955.10
Unglada, Sebastian 1928.13
Uniss, Genie 1896.06
United Euram 1977.13
United Plays Company 1921.14
United Scenic Studios 1922.31, 1925.11
United Studios 1944.25
Unitt and King 1888.09, 1889.44
Unitt and Wickes 1907.11, 1907.56, 1908.42, 1909.22, 1909.26, 1910.06, 1910.18, 1910.28, 1911.24, 1911.33, 1912.11, 1913.21, 1913.31, 1914.13, 1914.26, 1914.30, 1914.34, 1915.19, 1915.22, 1916.02, 1916.11, 1916.16, 1917.09, 1917.36, 1918.06, 1918.27, 1919.04, 1919.28, 1920.14, 1920.38, 1921.32
Unitt, E.G. 1895.29, 1905.44, 1908.03
Unitt, Edward G. 1889.01, 1891.38, 1895.43, 1900.37, 1902.23, 1903.22, 1903.33, 1903.34, 1903.37, 1904.15, 1904.19, 1904.30, 1904.51, 1905.57, 1906.29, 1907.01, 1907.08, 1907.36, 1907.43, 1908.10, 1908.32
Univer, Lena 1884.27
Universal Pictures 1978.13, 1982.11, 1983.18
Universal Studios 2000.18
Unnever, Olga 1890.21
Unterhauser, Oswald 1964.25
Uppman, John 1937.01
Uppman, Theodor 1951.17
Upton, Frances 1922.05, 1923.24, 1924.40, 1926.39, 1927.29, 1927.37, 1928.47, 1933.21
Uptosnuff, Mons. 1857.06
Urani, Marcia 1999.15
Urbach, Leslie 1932.14
Urban Arts 1972.13, 1976.35, 1979.18, 1980.14, 1982.17
Urban, Fred 1900.34, 1901.13
Urban, Frederick 1899.25
Urban, Gretel 1925.08
Urban, Jon 1938.18
Urban, Joseph 1915.15, 1915.28, 1916.04, 1916.10, 1916.17, 1916.19, 1916.24, 1917.03, 1917.13, 1917.20, 1917.22, 1917.26, 1918.11, 1918.19, 1918.25, 1918.33, 1918.34, 1919.15, 1919.25, 1919.27, 1919.39, 1919.43, 1920.18, 1920.44, 1921.21, 1921.29, 1921.33, 1922.19, 1922.35, 1923.20, 1923.30, 1923.38, 1924.04, 1925.52, 1926.18, 1926.34, 1926.51, 1927.07, 1927.08, 1927.37, 1927.63, 1927.67, 1928.03, 1928.11, 1928.12, 1928.43, 1928.47, 1929.02, 1929.27, 1929.44, 1930.05, 1930.08, 1930.11, 1930.30, 1930.39, 1931.08, 1931.19, 1931.30, 1932.07, 1932.11, 1932.22, 1933.03
Urban, Mlle. 1866.18
Urban, Ruth 1918.31, 1923.31, 1924.11, 1933.01, 1938.05
Urbanski, Douglas 1983.05
Urbina, Jillana 1994.06
Urchard, Marie 1892.24
Uretsky, Beatty 1937.14
Urhausen, Roy 1954.14
Uri, Morris 1910.09
Urich, Rebecca 1974.26
Urich, Tom 1970.09, 1999.11
Uris, Leon 1971.02
Urline, Capitola 1896.38
Urline, Eva 1896.38
Urling, L.C. 1896.46
Urmston, Kenneth 1953.17
Urquhart, Belle 1883.52, 1884.21, 1885.08, 1885.26
Urquhart, Isabelle 1887.33, 1887.50, 1888.20, 1888.35, 1889.16, 1889.23, 1890.01, 1890.11, 1890.23, 1893.24, 1893.45
Uscher, Steve 1976.33
Usher, Dorothy 1896.05
Usner, Dorothy 1897.16
Utley, Byron 1977.15, 1996.09
Utter, W.C. 1887.11, 1889.20, 1892.12
Uttry, Arthur 1920.43, 1922.38, 1930.21
Uzell, Corinne 1905.41
Uzzell, Corene 1905.18
Uzzell, Corrine 1912.01
Uzzini, L. 1887.37

Vaccariello, Patrick 1993.15, 1998.04, 2000.09
Vaccaro, Brenda 1967.16
Vaccaro, Danny 1999.11
Vaccaro, Vilma 1972.02
Vacharat, Amanda 1998.02
Vaci, Agostino 1911.26
Vacotti, E. 1889.54
Vaders, Emma 1892.31
Vadie, Marion 1920.19
Vail, Bobby 1953.11
Vail, Cora 1893.33
Vail, Edwin 1926.20
Vail, William 1875.32, 1881.28, 1881.36, 1886.42, 1887.07, 1887.16, 1887.39, 1887.48, 1888.27, 1888.40, 1889.07, 1889.18, 1897.29
Vail, William A. 1885.49, 1885.66
Vaillant 1964.28
Vaillant, M. 1859.09, 1859.12, 1859.13
Vainio, Aura 1961.15, 1961.27
Vajinski, M. 1916.15
Val, Madame 1796.01
Val, Mde. 1796.01
Valadin, Brigitte 1965.37
Valaire, Mons. 1875.01, 1875.02, 1875.04
Valaire, Valerie 1932.14
Valbelle, Mlle. 1876.28
Valdes 1946.21
Valdes, Gilberto 1946.21, 1955.26
Valdes, Patricia 1992.15
Valdez, Corrine 1950.12
Valdez, Daniel 1979.08, 1988.15
Valdez, Luis 1979.08
Valdez, Marie 1942.06, 1942.07, 1942.09, 1944.04, 1944.06, 1944.08, 1944.09, 1944.10, 1944.11, 1944.12, 1944.13
Valdez, Tito 1950.12
Valdini, Barbara 1917.05
Vale, Constance 1900.59
Vale, Michael 1964.18
Vale, Violet 1922.35, 1923.27
Valegra, R. 1882.15
Valencia, Balbina Juan 1917.25
Valencia, Omero 1934.38
Valencia, Tortola 1917.26
Valency, Maurice 1950.03, 1969.05
Valens, Richie 1990.15
Valenti, Alfredo 1931.46
Valenti, Michael 1970.06, 1981.25, 1986.11
Valenti, Tino 1931.29
Valentina 1942.16, 1944.29, 1946.05, 1952.03, 1964.16
Valentine, Arthur 1918.27
Valentine, C. Walsh 1901.07
Valentine, C.W. 1889.37, 1889.51, 1897.33, 1900.24, 1903.11, 1906.10
Valentine, Don 1934.41, 1943.18
Valentine, Eric 1924.33
Valentine, Gwendolyn 1903.34, 1904.30, 1908.40
Valentine, James 1964.45, 1980.19, 1981.26, 1982.24, 1993.11
Valentine, Louise 1893.30

Valentine, May 1902.14, 1902.33, 1939.20, 1939.21
Valentine, Paul 1952.10, 1954.17, 1958.02
Valentine, Peter 1985.17
Valentine, Ruth 1931.44
Valentine, Vangie 1925.24
Valentine, Velma 1925.48
Valentine, Vengie 1925.10
Valentine, Walsh 1893.30
Valentine, William 1923.35, 1925.43, 1928.37
Valentini, Vincent 1928.09
Valentino, Charles 1984.09
Valentinoff 1941.11
Valentinoff, Val 1944.14, 1946.18
Valentinoff, Valia 1937.10
Valentinova, Valia 1928.44
Valere, M. 1875.01
Valere, Simone 1964.06
Valerga, Ida 1884.57, 1885.14
Valerga, T. 1882.16
Valerga, Tillie 1882.15
Valergo, Tillie 1882.19
Valeri, O. 1924.48
Valerio, Frederico 1954.17
Valerio, Teresa 1917.22
Valery, Dana 1966.03
Valesca, Mlle. 1906.06
Valeta, Mazibelle 1916.11
Valette, Mae 1887.18
Valez, Amalia 1945.14
Valiando, Christian 1998.20
Valina, Mme. 1929.05
Valjean, Albert 1880.68
Vall, Seymour 1967.18, 1970.06, 1972.03
Vallade 1973.17
Vallance, Audrey 1996.10
Vallaro, Vic 1959.05
Valle, Adele 1961.05
Valle, Ernie 1930.21
Valle, Mlle. 1881.51
Valle, Wanda 1928.40
Vallee, Rudy 1931.30, 1935.18, 1942.11, 1961.22
Vallentine, Louise 1905.51
Valles, Manuel 1911.28
Valley, Paul Michael 1997.15
Vallhonrat, Jose 1920.13
Valli, Lulu 1904.29
Valli, Valli 1905.46, 1913.10, 1914.02, 1916.02, 1919.41
Vallis, Vera 1903.22
Vallori, Viola 1904.24
Vallot, Mlle. 1879.19, 1879.26, 1879.27, 1879.31, 1879.34, 1879.36, 1879.43, 1879.44, 1880.52, 1880.58, 1880.60, 1881.46, 1881.48, 1881.50, 1881.51, 1881.53, 1882.29, 1882.30, 1882.35, 1883.27, 1883.30, 1883.34, 1883.41, 1883.51, 1883.54, 1883.55, 1883.57, 1883.59, 1883.60, 1883.61, 1884.01, 1884.02, 1884.05, 1884.43, 1884.45, 1884.47, 1884.50, 1884.54, 1884.55, 1885.55, 1885.56, 1885.57, 1885.61
Vallot, Mme. 1880.44, 1880.50, 1881.54, 1882.53, 1882.55, 1882.58, 1882.61, 1883.28
Valmer, Celia 1888.45
Valmore, Jennie 1890.13
Valois, Henry E. 1905.41
Valois, Jose 1949.07
Valor, Henrietta 1972.16
Valori, Bice 1964.03
Valot, Mme. 1886.19, 1886.20
Valsy, Lucette 1931.37
Valter, A. 1871.23, 1871.24, 1871.25, 1871.26
Valter, Adrian 1870.37, 1871.03
Valter, Adrien 1870.30, 1871.07, 1871.23, 1871.25, 1871.26
Valter, Mons. 1867.24, 1868.07, 1870.41, 1870.45, 1875.04, 1875.13, 1875.25, 1875.28, 1875.29, 1875.30
Valverde, Joaquin 1913.16, 1949.07, 1969.11
Valverde, Quinito 1917.25, 1917.33
Valverke, Quirito 1932.19
Van, Arthur 1908.05
Van, Bette 1947.02
Van, Billy B. 1904.41, 1907.34, 1908.35, 1917.01, 1918.11, 1923.16, 1924.23, 1925.23, 1925.27, 1928.07, 1928.32
Van, Bobby 1950.02, 1954.12, 1971.03, 1975.09
Van, Gladys 1899.26
Van, Gus 1916.24, 1917.03, 1917.26, 1919.15, 1920.18, 1921.21, 1923.33
Van, Sammy 1930.19
Van, Samye 1958.14, 1961.02
Van, Shirley 1945.20, 1947.08
Van, Vera 1935.17
VanAckerman, E. 1913.15
VanAken, Gretchen 1966.27
VanAllen, Walter 1904.04
vanAlst, Dorothy 1926.03, 1927.05
VanAlstyne, Egbert 1902.15, 1903.07, 1904.23, 1905.34, 1905.39, 1906.33, 1907.12, 1907.32, 1907.46, 1908.10, 1908.11, 1908.39, 1909.17, 1909.25, 1910.01, 1910.17, 1911.27, 1912.02, 1917.18, 1919.19
vanAlstyne, Egbert 1904.45
Vanana, J.G. 1890.50
vanAntwerp, John 1937.02, 1937.12, 1938.12, 1946.19
VanAntwerp, John 1939.10
Vanark Enterprise, Ltd., A 1969.08
VanArsdale, Lillie 1905.29
VanAsse, O.J. 1907.27
Vanasse, O.J. 1925.29, 1926.42, 1931.04, 1931.39
VanAxte, Mme. 1889.53
vanBeethoven, Ludwig 1938.02, 1956.11
Vanberg, Millie 1884.34, 1884.57, 1885.28
VanBibber, S. 1904.44
vanBiene, Eileen 1918.06, 1920.19, 1922.17, 1927.01
VanBiene, Eileen 1917.01
VanBiere, Frau 1907.52
VanBreydel, Marguerite 1890.33
VanBrunt, W.C. 1904.44
VanBrunt, William 1903.03
VanBuren, A.H. 1907.58
vanBuren, A.H. 1925.19
VanBuren, Alice 1919.06
VanBuren, Gene 1995.12
VanBuren, Tillie 1881.39
VanBuskirk, Eliot 1981.21
VanBuskirk, Emily 1981.21
Vancamme, Marie 1877.34
VanCayseele, Herbin 1996.12
Vance and Sullivan 1905.51
Vance, Clarice 1910.10
Vance, Dorothy 1923.41
Vance, Eunice 1889.35, 1893.47
Vance, J. 1892.46
Vance, Jerri 1943.13
Vance, John 1899.27
Vance, Lillie 1891.18
Vance, Lizzie 1884.58
Vance, Miss 1881.14, 1882.37
Vance, R. Edgar 1895.41, 1900.35
Vance, Robert 1887.06, 1887.14
Vance, Vivian 1934.36, 1936.26, 1937.15, 1941.08, 1947.21
VanCitters, Darrel 1990.10
VanCleve, Harry 1911.28
vanCleve, Nathan 1940.17
VanClief, Ron 1991.01
VanCliff, Lily 1889.02
Vancouver East Cultural Center 1980.13
Vandair, Maurice 1941.03, 1965.08
Vandalet, Marie 1875.28
VanDam, Messr. 1876.17
Vandam, Mlle. 1871.06
Vandame, Mlle. 1872.39, 1872.42, 1873.16, 1875.02, 1878.18, 1887.37
Vandamme, Marie 1875.28, 1875.29, 1876.24, 1876.25, 1876.26, 1877.06, 1877.10, 1877.11, 1877.19, 1877.27, 1877.29, 1877.30, 1877.31, 1877.32, 1878.07, 1878.08
VanDamme, Mlle. 1880.27
Vandamme, Mlle. 1869.30, 1870.45, 1871.24, 1871.26, 1872.28, 1873.11, 1873.15, 1875.04, 1875.13, 1877.13, 1877.38, 1879.60, 1880.23, 1880.29, 1881.50, 1881.53, 1882.30, 1882.35, 1882.67, 1883.27, 1883.34, 1883.41, 1883.54, 1883.55, 1883.57, 1883.59, 1884.02, 1884.03, 1884.43, 1884.47, 1884.49, 1884.52, 1884.54, 1884.55, 1885.23, 1885.57, 1885.61, 1886.09, 1886.22
Vandamme, Mme. 1882.55, 1882.61, 1883.28
Vandamme, Mons. 1872.03, 1877.33
vanDekker, Albert 1936.28
Vandelet, Mlle. 1872.42, 1875.07
Vandelet, Mons. 1872.03
VanDell, Leo 1912.30
Vandenberg, Bram 1940.18
Vandenberg, Jose 1900.42, 1904.35
VandenBerg, Mr. 1895.13
vanDenEnde, Joop 1993.17
VanDenEnde, Joop 1996.18
vandenEnde, Joop 1998.11, 1998.13, 2001.08
Vandenhoff, Jr., Charles 1875.16
Vandenhoff, Miss 1881.52
Vanderbilt Producing Company 1919.36, 1922.48, 1923.09
Vanderbilt, Clairette 1888.09
Vanderbilt, Clarette 1889.01
Vanderbilt, Gertie 1907.57, 1908.31
Vanderbilt, Gertrude 1908.19, 1909.13, 1910.01, 1910.10, 1910.21, 1911.07, 1911.41, 1914.15, 1918.39, 1919.32, 1925.44
Vanderbilt, Jeanne Murray 1967.17
VanDeren, D.B. 1878.15, 1880.51
Vanderen, D.B. 1876.35
VanDeren, Mrs. 1875.14
Vanderen, Mrs. D.B. 1876.32
Vanderheyden, Tina 1995.15
Vanderhoef, Al 1889.08
vanDerHorst, Ellen 1982.23
Vanderkolff, Jonathan 2001.04
vanDerLinda, Laurel 1982.14
Vanderlinde, Debra 1983.12
vanDerLinden, Hans 1982.23
Vanderlip, Walter 1893.34
Vanderneers, Gerda 1940.21
VanDerren, Mr. 1862.03
VanderRoehr, Miss 1890.31
Vandertholen, Jon 1979.22, 1987.16, 1992.07
vanDerveer, Janet 1948.20
Vandervort, Philip 1965.32
vanDerWurff, Eric 1982.23
vanDeuser, William 1898.31
vanDeventer, Robert R. 1927.28
VanDeWerker, A. 1888.23
vanDijk, Ad 1993.17
vanDijk, Bill 1993.17
vanDijk, Koen 1993.17
Vandis, Titos 1965.31, 1967.05, 1970.08
Vandiveer, C. 1913.26
Vandiver, C. 1907.49
VanDoonick, Marie 1888.19
VanDoonik, Marie 1888.26
Vandoren, Donnie 2001.04
VanDoren, Mamie 1979.05
VanDorn, W.L. 1880.31
vanDorpe, Gloria 1956.01
VanDresser, Marcia 1897.13, 1898.60, 1900.25, 1900.31, 1900.32
Vandross, Luther 1975.01
vanDruten, John 1951.12
VanDruten, John 1966.24, 1987.16, 1998.04
VanDruten, Johnas 1979.12
VanDusen, Eugene 1882.82, 1886.13
VanDyck, Eric 1916.14
vanDyke, Constance 1930.10, 1935.01
vanDyke, Dick 1959.23, 1960.06
VanDyke, Dick 1980.16
Vandyke, Imogene 1877.04
VanDyke, Lea 1891.29
vanDyke, Marcia 1951.14
VanDyke, Paul 1920.33
vanDyke, Rudy 1942.19
VanDyke, Steven 1982.15
VanDyne, Aimee 1896.31
VanDyne, Charles 1892.11
Vane, Alice 1867.22, 1867.23, 1889.45
Vane, Daphne 1940.07
Vane, Denton 1927.66
Vane, Harry 1895.40, 1898.64
Vane, Laurel 1894.13
Vane, Lila 1888.23
vanEeden, Ron 1982.23
vanEmburgh, Norman 1933.09, 1933.17, 1933.19, 1936.22
Vanessi, Lilli 1948.32
Vanetta, Frank 1898.10
VanFossen, Harry 1909.16
vanEmburgh, Norman 1942.20
VanEtten, C. 1887.09
VanGhele, C. 1875.09, 1876.20, 1876.25, 1876.26
vanGhele, Charles 1875.25, 1875.27, 1875.28, 1875.29, 1875.30, 1875.33, 1876.24, 1876.31
VanGhele, Charles 1872.28, 1872.29, 1872.31, 1872.33, 1872.39, 1872.41, 1872.42, 1873.01, 1873.11, 1873.15, 1873.16, 1875.01, 1875.02, 1875.04, 1875.07, 1875.08, 1875.13, 1876.28
vanGilder, Lydia 1929.38, 1932.22
VanGrack, Vicki 1979.29
vanGriethuysen, Ted 1959.05
vanGrona, Eugene 1930.28, 1933.25, 1939.14
vanGrove, Isaac 1937.01, 1946.17
VanHamme, E. 1869.41
VanHamme, M. 1868.03
VanHamme, Mons. 1872.10
VanHeusen, James 1939.29, 1965.33, 1966.27, 1974.10, 1974.11, 1986.03, 1997.05
vanHeusen, James 1946.04, 1953.11
VanHeusen, Jimmy 1939.29, 1992.03, 1995.12, 1995.14
VanHorn and Son 1903.25
VanHorn and Sons 1904.33
Vanhorn, A.R. 1880.01, 1880.03
vanHorn, Earl 1927.07, 1928.11
vanHorn, Franklin 1928.26
vanHorn, Inez 1927.07, 1928.11
VanHorne, Samuel 1893.38
vanHouten, Arthur 1879.65, 1879.67
VanHouten, Arthur 1879.07, 1879.11, 1880.31, 1880.57, 1880.62, 1881.25, 1881.42, 1881.45, 1882.54, 1882.57
VanHouten, Henry 1881.44
VanHouten, Mr. 1883.37
VanHuyck, Sara 1882.59
Vanicelli, Henry 1939.23
Vanity Fair 1928.04
Vanity Fair Company 1923.02
Vanity Fair Costume Company 1921.40, 1922.31, 1923.03, 1923.13, 1924.17, 1924.45, 1925.11, 1931.03
Vanity Fair Costume, Inc. 1925.07
Vanity Fair Costumes, Inc. 1922.40, 1924.10, 1926.23
vanKirk, Florence M.P. 1927.28
VanLaast, Anthony 1993.15, 2000.09
VanLeer, Arnold 1919.38
VanLeer, Charles 1887.05
Vanleer, Jay 1972.10
VanLissa, Caprice 1888.13, 1888.21, 1889.13, 1889.34
vanLoan, Paul 1942.19, 1944.20, 1946.14, 1947.12, 1948.19, 1949.05, 1949.06
Vanloo 1898.12
Vanloo, Albert 1875.04, 1875.11, 1875.26, 1875.29, 1875.38, 1876.20, 1876.21, 1877.09, 1877.11, 1877.26, 1877.32, 1877.33, 1878.18, 1879.23, 1879.26, 1879.41, 1879.49, 1880.29, 1880.56, 1882.06, 1882.30, 1884.14, 1885.17, 1885.23, 1885.24, 1886.37, 1887.22, 1887.24, 1889.24, 1890.26, 1891.31, 1894.14, 1896.28, 1897.36, 1900.17, 1905.08, 1905.46, 1907.06, 1926.40
Vanloo, Alfred 1879.44, 1883.28
vanMarr, Feon 1927.47
VanMeter, Calvin 1973.17
Vanna, Della 1925.47
VanNess, Miss 1903.32
Vanni, Vannio 1964.03
Vannier, Angela 1967.13, 1968.20
Vannier, Angele 2000.16
VanNorden, Jerome 1909.25, 1910.18, 1913.10
VanNorden, Peter 1982.05
Vanoff, Nick 1986.21, 1988.11, 1989.29
Vanoni, Maria 1882.46
Vanoni, Marie 1883.65, 1885.12, 1892.41
Vanoni, Ornella 1964.03
Vanoni, Signora 1882.46
VanOrden, Ray 1974.08
vanOss, Katrina 1946.12, 1947.17
VanOsten, Ida 1886.34, 1886.45, 1887.06
Vanosten, Miss 1884.42
VanOsten, Thomas D. 1897.15
vanParys, G. 1958.06
VanParys, G. 1958.06
vanParys, George 1948.12
vanPatten, Dickie 1937.01
VanPatten, Joyce 1963.19
VanPeebles, Melvin 1971.13, 1972.10, 1980.05
VanPelt, Catherine 1919.14
VanPelt, James 1882.62, 1885.33
VanPelt, Katherine 1919.03
vanPelt, Lois 1956.04
VanPragg, Messr. 1844.01
vanPutten, Carlos 1945.06
vanRein, Jane 1924.17
VanRennselear, E.F. 1902.08

VanRensalaer, George 1905.21
vanRensalear, Hal 1924.06
vanRensellaer, Hal 1920.33
VanRensselaer, E.E. 1906.20
VanRensselaer, Frederick 1907.21
vanRensselaer, Hal 1922.01, 1922.31, 1923.17
VanRensselaer, Wheeler 1914.03
VanRijn, Nancy 1966.14
vanRossum, Rogier 1993.17
VanRyker, Alice 1917.08
vanRyn, Karen 1942.11
vanScott, Glory 1954.19, 1956.06
VanScott, Glory 1961.24, 1965.03, 1986.03
vanSickle, Raymond 1918.01
VanSickler, James 1919.24
vanScoyk, Bob 1956.08
VanSelover, Elaine 1900.51
Vanselow, Robert 1954.13
vanSickler, James 1923.31
VanStavoren, Mr. 1846.01
Vanstone, Hugh 2001.02, 2001.04
VanStrander, Chris 1993.11
VanStuddiford, Grace 1902.04, 1902.28, 1903.36, 1911.03
vanTassel, Theo 1931.41
VanTassell, Craig 1991.02
vanTassell, Theo 1931.27, 1931.33, 1931.35, 1931.43
vanTassle, Theo 1934.12
Vanterpool, Audrey 1945.06, 1946.09, 1956.06
VanTine, Ida 1912.33
VanTreuren, Martin 1985.08, 1994.12
VanTruren, Marin 1997.09
vanVeen, Herman 1982.23
vanVlerah, Hazel 1930.24
vanVooren, Monique 1953.17, 1957.04
VanVechten, E.H. 1884.51, 1884.63
VanVechten, Mr. 1883.37
VanVeghten, E.H. 1885.14, 1885.28
VanVeghten, Ed. H. 1886.15
VanVooren, Monique 1953.17, 1975.04
vanWay, Nolan 1958.02, 1959.11
VanWay, Nolan 1958.02, 1959.11, 1967.09
vanWilder, Victor 1880.61
vanWinkle, Dorothy 1935.11
VanWitsen, John 1963.16
vanWitsen, Leo 1956.09
VanZandt, Porter 1975.18, 1976.30
VanZile, Hortense 1891.34
Varanay, Roger 1959.15
Varela, Nina 1943.06, 1950.14
Varela, Trina 1923.15
Varella, Nina 1948.23
Varena, F. 1880.66
Varese, Edgard 1978.05
Varey, Henriette 1881.38
Vargas, Angel 1987.05
Vargas, Angelita 1986.17
Vargas, Ben 1958.20, 1960.08, 1977.12
Vargas, Concha 1992.15
Vargas, Fernando 1949.07
Vargas, Silvestre 1988.15
Varian, J. 1875.21
Varin, Charles 1891.30
Vario, Si 1964.46
Varis, Aldo 1935.02
Varlet, Mons. 1870.37, 1870.41, 1870.45, 1871.03, 1871.06
Varna, Henri 1964.02, 1973.17
Varnal, Mlle. 1871.27
Varnay, Roger 1961.25
Varnel, M.H. 1927.17
Varnett, Miss 1886.36
Varney, Amadeo 1935.02
Varney, Amelia 1965.21
Varney, Belle 1897.06
Varney, Louis 1881.50, 1882.39, 1883.12, 1883.17, 1897.11, 1900.34
Varney, Mr. 1869.42
Varnum, Lionel 1899.41
Varon, Evelyn 1922.05
Varona, Jose 1969.11
Varone, Doug 1997.18
Varr, Burton 1905.21
Varrato, Eddie 1948.17
Varrato, Edmond 1965.28, 1967.01, 1972.14, 1977.12
Varrele, M. 1929.39
Varrell, Minnie 1888.13
Varrey, Collin 1886.49
Varrey, Mr. 1848.03
Varron, Allegra 1948.27
Varrone, Gene 1957.01, 1958.14, 1959.22, 1961.28, 1962.14, 1963.08, 1964.21, 1965.29, 1969.05, 1969.17, 1973.04, 1976.09, 1979.02, 1979.26
Varry, Collin 1887.51
Vars, Aggie 1895.07, 1895.21, 1895.39, 1898.34, 1900.49
Vary, E. 1907.54
Vary, Eugene 1918.23
Vaselle, Renata 1962.27
Vasquez, Chris 1997.22, 1998.20, 1999.21
Vasquez, Roland 1960.11
Vassar, Queenie 1886.40, 1894.21, 1894.49, 1897.55, 1898.68, 1899.35, 1900.48, 1901.18, 1902.01, 1911.02, 1912.39, 1914.18, 1915.18
Vasseur, Leon 1876.28, 1882.67, 1884.55
Vassiliev, Vladimir 1990.01
Vassilkova, Mme. 1922.06
Vaszary, Janos 1938.05
Vatske, Roberta 1968.32
Vaucaire, Maurice 1910.24, 1914.26
Vaucaire, Michel 1981.04
Vaudamme, Mlle. 1881.51
Vaudarsky, Alexandra 1926.43
Vaudelet, Mlle. 1870.41, 1871.06, 1875.08, 1875.33
Vaudry, Nita 1931.44
Vaughan, A.S. 1869.40
Vaughan, Ada 1908.08
Vaughan, Bessie 1908.08
Vaughan, Blanche 1883.43
Vaughan, Charles 1901.10
Vaughan, Cissie 1923.29
Vaughan, David 1970.07, 1970.11
Vaughan, Edward 1978.19, 1978.23
Vaughan, Eva 1940.01, 1943.10
Vaughan, James 1903.08, 1904.26
Vaughan, James J. 1908.08
Vaughan, Melanie 1976.08, 1984.08, 1998.21
Vaughan, William 1937.11
Vaughan, Winifred 1907.41
Vaughn, Aida 1904.25
Vaughn, Alan 1944.24
Vaughn, Blanche 1880.21, 1881.11
Vaughn, Charles 1901.11
Vaughn, Grace 1893.34, 1894.22, 1895.27, 1904.03
Vaughn, Gustave 1901.10, 1901.11
Vaughn, Irene 1894.13
Vaughn, James J. 1906.14, 1909.27
Vaughn, Kimberly 1999.07
Vaughn, M. 1976.32
Vaughn, Miss 1881.04
Vaughn, Olive 1920.18, 1921.22, 1922.27, 1923.18, 1924.19
Vaughn, Sharon 1962.04, 1963.25, 1964.11
Vaughn, Theresa 1882.76, 1884.21, 1884.66, 1886.11, 1888.03, 1888.45, 1893.17, 1894.26, 1895.38, 1896.35
Vaulry, Francois 1917.36
Vaux, Adrian 1989.10
Vaux, Billy 1946.22
Vaux, Messr. 1852.05
Vaux, William 1942.15, 1945.04
Vavra, Velma 1930.18
Vaye, Evelyn 1886.50
Vayne, Dal 1914.15
Vazquez, Carmen 1949.07
Veasey, William 1951.11, 1953.04
Veaux, Clyde 1930.31, 1934.35
Veazey, Jeff 1975.09
Veber, Pierre 1918.28, 1926.36, 1926.46, 1928.07, 1928.32
Vecchio, Alberto 1946.05
Vecsey, Armand 1919.39, 1922.12, 1927.01
Vega, Jose 1968.07
Veglia, Paul 1965.22
Vehi, Adelina 1919.17
Veiller, Anthony 1945.14
Vejar, Rudy 1964.23, 1964.24, 1965.22
Vejvoda, Jaromir 1939.25
Velander, Meta 1966.19
Velarde, E. 1873.08
Velasco, Eulogio 1917.25
Velasquez, Consuelo 1988.15
Velazquez, Russell 1982.22
Velden, Kaj 1944.19
Velerio, Teresa 1920.36
Velez, Lorraine 1987.07
Velez, Lupe 1932.07, 1933.05, 1938.07
Velie, Janet 1918.03, 1918.15, 1919.12, 1920.38, 1921.37, 1924.15, 1924.24, 1924.35, 1925.45, 1927.21, 1928.08, 1928.37, 1929.42
Velie, Jay 1923.24, 1924.15, 1924.35, 1927.38, 1938.02, 1945.05, 1949.03, 1950.15, 1954.07, 1956.16, 1963.25, 1966.31, 1967.07, 1971.07
Velikanoff, Ivan 1925.51
VelJohnson, Reginald 1981.15, 1986.11, 1999.21
Vellucci, Luigi 1953.06, 1953.15, 1954.10, 1955.17
Velone, Tony 1957.01
Veloz, Frank 1929.09, 1943.02
Velsey, Graham 1930.43
Velvel 1951.20
Venable, Jimmy 1946.07
Venable, John 1976.34
Venable, Percy 1989.02
Venanzi, Angelo 1893.45
Vendamme, Mlle. 1873.01
Venduras, Spyros 1979.16
Vene, Roger P. 1944.25
Veneziale, Renee 1986.20
Venie, Miss 1876.18
Venn, Topsy 1880.59, 1880.65, 1880.67, 1880.70, 1882.34, 1884.60, 1885.69, 1888.39, 1890.03
Venner, Tracy 1989.27, 1991.06
Venora, Lee 1959.19, 1961.26, 1964.10, 1964.23, 1965.22
VenPelt, Jame 1890.17
Vento, Frank 1973.14
Ventura, Clyde 1965.07, 1965.26
Ventura, Toni 1964.03
Venturelli, Frederick C. 1982.02
Ventures West Capital, Inc. 1980.13
Venturo, William 1935.07, 1935.08
Venturoli, Amina 1872.06
Venus, Little 1871.18
Venus, William 1923.43
Venuta, Benay 1937.06, 1942.15, 1946.04, 1953.01, 1957.14, 1965.24, 1966.12, 1966.16
Vera, Carlos 1997.13
Vera, Irene 1894.19, 1894.38, 1895.38, 1897.52, 1900.38
Vera, Madeline 1897.16
Vera, Rosa 1898.29, 1898.46
Vera-Ellen 1942.15
Verace, Gus 1915.32
Veran, F. 1958.06
Veran, T. 1970.01
Verand, Miss 1873.26
Verastique, Rocker 1995.15, 1996.14, 2000.07
Verba, Vehrah 1927.52
Verbit, Helen 1959.25, 1962.16, 1964.27
Vercell, Katherine 1928.23
Vercell, Louise 1928.23
Vercellesi, Clara 1892.59
Vercellesi, Louisa 1892.59
Verdell, Anne 1897.28
Verderber, William 1989.10
Verdi 1859.15, 1862.09, 1867.21, 1873.12, 1880.35, 1894.21
Verdi, A. 1911.16
Verdi, Al 1936.06
Verdi, Augusta 1911.19
Verdi, Emily 1926.22
Verdi, Giuseppe 1860.05, 1862.03, 1864.09, 1866.32, 1870.20, 1870.23, 1876.04, 1879.64, 1880.38, 1881.47, 1891.37, 1910.04, 1922.37, 1952.15, 2000.06
Verdi, Giuseppi 1868.23, 1880.33, 1896.46
Verdi, Joe 1931.05, 1937.13
Verdon, Gwen 1948.24, 1950.02, 1953.07, 1955.08, 1957.07, 1959.01, 1966.01, 1975.14, 1986.07, 1999.01
Verea, Lisette 1943.09, 1944.24
Vereen, Ben 1971.12, 1972.22, 1985.05, 1995.19, 1996.15
Verela, Nino 1939.16
Verger, Christiane 1935.19
Verger, Tito 1923.29
Vergeron, Blondelet 1892.32
Verges, Chrisann 1989.12
Verges, Philipp 1996.13
Verheyen, Mariann 1990.20, 1991.13
Verhoevan, Pauline 1910.24
Verhoeven, Pauline 1910.35
Verina, Winefride 1926.28
Verina, Winifred 1921.15, 1923.07
Verity, Amy 1922.05
Verle, V. 1884.52
Vermonti, Edward 1937.01
Verna, Lucille 1900.16, 1900.44
Verna, Nellie 1900.45
Vernan, Ray 1892.41
Verne, Ade 1903.41
Verne, Jules 1875.05, 1875.18, 1875.21, 1877.04, 1877.15, 1877.23, 1880.41, 1881.15, 1881.30, 1881.31, 1881.32, 1882.62, 1885.33, 1886.41, 1888.23, 1890.17, 1892.35, 1946.13
Verne, Mabel 1903.41
Vernellj, Nord 1942.33
Verner, Charles E. 1887.23, 1914.29
Verner, Linda 1888.38, 1888.41
Verner, Miss 1870.22
Vernet, Mlle. 1870.44, 1871.27, 1881.48, 1881.50
Verneuil, Louis 1918.34, 1929.06, 1930.43, 1941.10, 1942.32, 1945.02
Verney, H. 1897.29
Verney, S.H. 1869.27, 1869.32, 1869.35, 1869.43, 1870.04
Vernille, Nitza 1923.42, 1924.32, 1936.27
Vernille, Nitzi 1923.06
Vernon, Adelaide 1914.28
Vernon, Billie 1916.07, 1916.19
Vernon, Dorothy 1936.26
Vernon, Emily 1875.03
Vernon, F.P. 1898.62
Vernon, Gilbert 1956.13
Vernon, Grace 1873.28
Vernon, H.G. 1897.15
Vernon, Harold M. 1898.51
Vernon, Harriet 1893.41
Vernon, Harry M. 1925.50
Vernon, Harvey 1971.16
Vernon, Hazel 1925.11
Vernon, Hilda 1898.59
Vernon, Hope 1925.40
Vernon, Ida 1859.05, 1859.06, 1871.22
Vernon, Isabel 1917.30, 1922.21
Vernon, Isabell 1924.12
Vernon, Isabelle 1923.15
Vernon, Jackie 1967.11
Vernon, John 1883.16
Vernon, Ley 1907.08
Vernon, Lottie 1902.07, 1905.13, 1907.11, 1908.39, 1909.13, 1909.25, 1912.13, 1913.17, 1915.15
Vernon, Lou 1930.10
Vernon, Marie 1912.48, 1915.32
Vernon, Michael 1980.17
Vernon, Miss 1908.19, 1920.44
Vernon, Mrs. 1834.02, 1852.01, 1857.07
Vernon, Nera 1889.52
Vernon, Olga 1934.40
Vernon, Paul 1882.59, 1883.66, 1886.34, 1887.06, 1892.34, 1896.04
Vernon, Ray 1891.19, 1892.32
Vernon, Robert 1892.19, 1899.11
Vernon, Ruby 1920.37
Vernon, S. Paul 1915.27
Vernon, Shirley 1925.05, 1927.41, 1929.44
Vernon, Sophie 1890.29
Vernon, Vivian 1920.44, 1923.30, 1932.23, 1933.16
Veron, Addie 1875.21
Veron, Pablo 1999.18
Veron, Paul 1886.45
Veron, S.P. 1898.49
Verona, Blanche R. 1897.40
Verona, Irene 1885.58, 1887.01, 1888.09, 1889.01, 1889.13, 1892.11, 1892.42, 1893.04, 1893.22, 1895.08
Veronica 1940.12, 1942.13, 1944.25
Veronica, Betty 1930.22
Veronica, Mlle. 1917.03
VerPlanck, J. Billy 1971.16
Verrett, Shirley 1994.02
Verrey, Collin 1886.48
Verso, Edward 1962.05
Vert y Carbonel, Juan 1949.07
Vert, Messr. 1867.05
Vert, Mons. 1866.25, 1866.27
Vertes 1958.18
Vertis 1955.10
Verwayne, Percy 1931.32
Verwaynen, Percy 1932.14
Vesey, Kathleen 1914.26
Veskova, Sonia 1925.39
Vessella, Oreste 1916.05
Vest, Bud 1966.01, 1967.06

Vest, Buddy 1999.01
Vestoff, Floria 1930.42
Vestoff, Val 1930.42, 1934.36
Vestoff, Valaida 1924.36
Vestoff, Valodia 1919.22, 1921.27, 1926.33, 1927.35, 1932.19
Vestoff, Virginia 1960.07, 1965.02, 1972.25, 1973.08, 1975.23, 1979.07
Vetchor, M. 1931.38
Vetkin, S. 1979.29
Vevie, Little 1886.23
Vezina, Nanette 1955.10
Vezina, Paul 1972.08
Viacom International, Inc. 1983.07
Viall, Arthur E. 1924.05
Vialle, Max 1965.37
Vian, Boris 1964.39
Vian, Gus 1946.23
Viana, Lu 1992.13
Viau, Joseph 1921.36
Vicars, Harold 1897.32, 1911.27, 1912.26, 1913.26, 1915.25, 1916.01, 1917.19, 1918.34, 1919.44, 1920.21, 1920.40
Viccini, Juan 1974.14
Vicenty 1945.10
Vicenty, Candido 1946.21
Vichey, Luben 1956.11
Vichi, Gerry 1981.10, 1987.15, 1993.05, 1994.12, 1995.05, 1997.11
Vici, Berni 1928.34
Vickars, Ada 1882.75
Vickers, Larry 1984.06, 1985.05, 1990.05, 1995.02
Vickers, Miss 1882.60
Vickers, Stanley 1914.07
Vickery, Edwin 1933.20
Vickery, John 1997.20
Vicman Productions 1974.14
Victoire, Mlle. 1870.44
Victoire, Mons. 1870.41
Victor, Bobbie 1898.69
Victor, Eric 1942.35, 1948.14, 1949.02
Victor, H. 1876.34
Victor, Lester 1884.62, 1886.48, 1886.49
Victor, Louis 1905.27
Victor, Lucia 1964.01, 1966.29, 1967.15, 1971.02, 1972.11, 1974.18, 1975.21, 1978.04
Victor, Mons. 1872.03, 1875.01
Victor, Robert 1975.06
Victoria, Emmilie 1903.18
Victoria, Genevieve 1907.02
Victoria, Kate 1884.61
Victoria, Mme. 1870.03
Victoria, Nellie 1902.24
Victorie, Mlle. 1871.27
Victorine, Mlle. 1869.30, 1870.41
Victorine, Myrtle 1916.23
Victoroff, Victor 1921.40
Victory, Frances 1919.37, 1922.14
Victory, Thomas 1921.13
Vida, Richard 1994.06
Vidal, Clarita 1902.35
Vidal, Emilia 1927.19
Vidalin, Maurice 1964.02, 1968.21
Vidnovic, Martin 1976.01, 1977.07, 1979.31, 1980.26, 1983.19, 1993.16, 1997.12
Vidocq, William 1893.50
Vieha, Mark 1979.13, 1981.08
Vieira, Wilmar 1988.06
Viele, Sheldon K. 1922.42, 1923.19, 1924.02, 1927.48, 1928.37
Vienna Volksoper Production, A 1984.03, 1984.04, 1984.05
Viertel, Jack 1995.03, 1995.12
Viertel, Joni Paige 2001.04
Viertel, Thomas 1987.20, 1991.02, 1995.03, 1996.04, 1997.13, 1997.18, 1998.03, 1999.24
Viertel, Tom 2001.05
Viertel-Baruch-Frankel Group, The 1996.06
Vigal, Al 1930.24
Vigal, John 1928.10
Vigard, Kristen 1977.15, 1979.12
Viglione, Gina 1959.26, 1961.07
Vigoda, Abe 1967.01
Vigotty, M. 1865.07
Vigotty, Messr. 1865.09
Vigotty, Mons. 1865.10
Vigotty, Mr. 1865.08
Vilan, Demetrios 1934.20, 1936.05, 1936.31
Vilanch, Bruce 1973.14, 1975.12, 1976.16, 1978.25, 1979.11, 1979.30, 1983.09, 1988.08, 1988.19, 1990.09
Vilano, M. 1881.54
Vilano, Messr. 1880.28
Vilano, Mons. 1879.48, 1879.51, 1879.60, 1879.69, 1880.16, 1880.23, 1880.27, 1880.29, 1880.44, 1880.58, 1880.60
Vilette, Messr. 1902.13
Villa, Armonia 1949.07
Villa, Danny 1969.08, 1973.07
Villa, Manuel 1917.25, 1917.34
Villa, Marc 1989.20
Villa, S.B. 1868.08, 1868.16, 1875.21
Villa-Lobos, Heitor 1948.24
Villaluazo, Arturo Mendoza 1988.15
Villamil, Jaclynn 1966.12, 1966.18
Villaneuva, Tara Ann 1998.02
Villani, Mario 1929.45
Villani, Virgilio 1985.14
Villanueva, Luis 1982.06
Villar, Maude 1884.12
Villard, Jean 1981.04
Villarias, Carlos 1919.17, 1921.39
Villarias, Juan 1949.07
Villars, Jessie 1891.18, 1891.24, 1897.55, 1899.22, 1908.07
Villas, Janet 1987.03
Villasana, Juan 1910.08, 1910.09, 1913.16, 1914.28, 1927.08
Villela, Edward 1958.03
Villella, Edward 1962.15, 1963.04, 1964.46, 1967.17
Villers, Charles 1876.02
Villers, Jessie 1892.29
Villiers, Agnes 1875.19, 1875.23, 1875.26
Villiers, Elise 1884.60
Villiers, Kate 1875.19, 1875.23
Villiers, Mlle. 1868.24, 1868.26, 1869.03, 1869.05, 1869.16, 1869.30, 1873.11, 1873.15, 1873.16
Villiers, Reta 1903.12
Villion, W. 1882.01
Villodo, A. 1985.07
Villoldo, A. 1999.18
Villon, Francois 1931.06
Vilon, Una 1933.20
Vimnera, August 1926.23, 1927.02, 1927.26, 1927.34, 1927.39
Vina, Miss 1881.35
Vinal, Carrie 1880.06, 1880.13
Vinay, Ramon 1939.22
Vincent, A. 1852.03, 1869.40
Vincent, Alan 1998.10
Vincent, Alice 1883.25, 1883.29, 1884.12, 1884.18, 1885.11, 1885.41
Vincent, Allen 1925.20
Vincent, C. 1869.20
Vincent, C.T. 1889.41
Vincent, Charles T. 1889.05, 1892.23
Vincent, E. 1882.32
Vincent, Eddie 1944.30
Vincent, Edgar 1940.04
Vincent, Ella 1879.15
Vincent, Ellen 1880.69
Vincent, Elmer 1904.06
Vincent, Estelle 1897.15
Vincent, Felix A. 1869.44
Vincent, Florence 1882.77, 1884.23, 1885.69
Vincent, Henry 1908.25, 1910.27, 1913.32, 1916.20, 1918.35, 1920.30, 1924.39, 1934.41
Vincent, J. 1883.47
Vincent, J.L. 1878.21
Vincent, Jack 1907.45, 1918.03, 1921.27
Vincent, James 1878.05, 1879.01, 1879.06, 1880.55, 1881.17, 1886.61, 1888.42, 1889.25, 1896.14, 1899.03, 1899.27, 1906.35
Vincent, John 1879.06
Vincent, L. 1852.03
Vincent, L.J. 1865.06, 1868.03, 1869.06, 1869.29, 1869.33, 1869.40, 1869.44, 1870.13, 1870.19, 1870.21, 1872.10, 1872.37, 1873.08, 1873.10, 1879.15
Vincent, Lee 1946.13
Vincent, Leon J. 1862.03, 1863.07
Vincent, Madge 1904.24, 1905.53, 1911.40, 1912.07
Vincent, Maud 1896.27, 1898.16, 1900.35
Vincent, Messr. 1852.05, 1855.10, 1877.15
Vincent, Mr. 1854.01, 1854.03, 1854.06, 1854.07
Vincent, Mrs. J.R. 1886.27
Vincent, Nat 1910.20, 1919.15, 1919.19, 1920.02, 1921.03, 1922.44
Vincent, Querita 1900.24
Vincent, Romo 1942.29, 1945.11, 1958.20
Vincent, Ruth 1900.37, 1904.03, 1905.46
Vincent, Theola 1925.06
Vincent, Tony 2000.09
Vincent, Walter 1902.32, 1924.30
Vinces, Murray 1955.06
Vinchon, E. 1884.55
Vinchon, Messr. 1882.55, 1882.58, 1883.61, 1884.45, 1886.20
Vinchon, Mons. 1879.19, 1879.26, 1879.27, 1879.31, 1879.34, 1879.36, 1879.39, 1879.40, 1879.43, 1879.44, 1879.47, 1880.44, 1880.58, 1880.60, 1881.54, 1882.53, 1882.67, 1882.73, 1883.27, 1883.28, 1883.30, 1883.34, 1883.41, 1883.51, 1883.54, 1883.55, 1883.57, 1883.59, 1883.60, 1884.02, 1884.03, 1884.05, 1884.43, 1884.47, 1884.49, 1884.50, 1884.52, 1884.54, 1885.23, 1885.55, 1885.57, 1885.59, 1885.60, 1885.61, 1886.09, 1886.18, 1886.19, 1886.22, 1887.35, 1887.36, 1887.37
Vincinia, T. 1873.18
Vine, Billy 1941.09
Vine, Mabel 1892.38
Vine, Richard 1953.16
Vines, Murray 1955.07
Vinging, Miss 1881.06
Vingut, Margaret 1908.07
Vining, Bebe 1883.17, 1883.19, 1883.23, 1884.28, 1884.29, 1885.08, 1891.21
Vining, Beebe 1882.20, 1883.02
Vining, Bessie 1882.04
Vining, Miss 1883.23
Vining, Mrs. H. 1860.04, 1860.06
Vining, Percy 1877.21
Vinning, Mr. 1869.35
Vinovich, Stephen 1976.30, 1979.02
Vinson, Jane 1946.22
Vinten, Madge 1905.46
Vinton, Arthur 1936.27, 1937.03, 1950.04
Vinton, Dora 1889.48, 1891.06
Vinton, Doris 1927.27, 1927.36, 1928.21, 1928.27, 1930.33, 1937.06
Vinton, Lillie 1880.04, 1881.11, 1884.34
Vinton, Miss 1881.04, 1885.65
Vinton, Mollie 1885.70
Viola, Ann 1947.13
Violet Cameron Comic Opera Company 1886.50
Violet, Little 1882.01
Violett, Ellen 1957.14
Violetta, LaBelle 1904.33
Violette, Yvette 1898.46
Violino, Terry 1962.16, 1964.40
Viracola, Fiddle 1959.08, 1989.24
Virginia, Daisy 1912.38
Virginie, Mlle. 1862.05
Virto, Augustus 1884.61
Viscardi, Marie 1922.21
Visitor, Nana 1983.06
Visser, John 1993.11
Vista Productions 1971.15
Vita, Geraldine 1954.03
Vita, Michael 1960.06, 1968.03, 1968.31, 1972.05, 1975.14, 1980.23, 1982.18
Vitak, Albertina 1924.09, 1924.33, 1928.42, 1932.17, 1932.27
Vitale, Joseph 1931.05, 1931.30, 1932.24
Vitale, Lorenzo 1921.15
Vitalis, Roy 1927.17, 1930.27
Vitella, Sel 1976.15, 1978.24, 1989.25
Vitkin, Shlomo 1968.22
Vito, Georges 1935.11
Vitolo-Pearson Studios 1923.04
Viton, Velnette 1910.11
Vittonet 1955.14
Vitzhum, Richard 1981.18
Vivanco, Moises 1951.15
Vivian, Allie 1890.22, 1891.35, 1892.26
Vivian, Bella 1885.50
Vivian, Bessie 1875.14
Vivian, Emily 1894.51
Vivian, Ethel 1908.25
Vivian, George 1921.09, 1930.23
Vivian, Gladys 1894.13
Vivian, Marah 1913.02
Vivian, Mlle. 1886.41
Vivian, Percival 1920.12
Vivian, Robert 1910.36, 1919.02, 1924.20, 1936.03
Vivian, Ruth 1918.31
Vivien, Weevie 1887.52
Vivino, Jimmy 1985.03
Vivona, Jerome 1995.05, 1999.19, 2000.18
Vizard, Harold 1896.48, 1899.41, 1900.57, 1902.12, 1902.30, 1904.40, 1905.18, 1907.26, 1909.04, 1911.01, 1913.31, 1915.21, 1916.26, 1919.07, 1920.05, 1922.43, 1925.35, 1928.27
Vladmirskaya, Mme. 1927.51
Vlassoff, Leo 1943.11
Vlastnik, Frank 1996.08
Vleugel, Guus 1982.23
Vodery, Bill 1936.17, 1942.13
Vodery, Will 1907.55, 1914.15, 1915.15, 1916.10, 1920.33, 1921.16, 1922.25, 1922.39, 1923.11, 1924.15, 1924.37, 1925.40, 1926.18, 1928.10, 1928.18, 1931.19, 1932.30, 1933.27
Vodery, Will H. 1920.11
Vodery, William 1927.67, 1946.01
Vodnoy, M. 1933.05
Vodnoy, Matathew 1938.13
Vodrey, Will 1937.10
Voe, Madge 1909.17, 1913.07
Voeglin, Mme. 1902.18
Voegtlin 1880.54, 1880.67, 1881.21, 1882.28, 1882.51, 1883.62, 1891.27
Voegtlin, Arthur 1882.17, 1884.27, 1886.14, 1890.28, 1893.05, 1893.14, 1893.21, 1893.31, 1894.02, 1894.06, 1894.07, 1894.35, 1894.37, 1895.39, 1895.44, 1896.02, 1896.05, 1897.01, 1897.34, 1898.47, 1900.47, 1905.17, 1905.35, 1905.54, 1906.29, 1906.46, 1907.10, 1907.41, 1907.42, 1907.54, 1908.10, 1908.21, 1908.26, 1908.44, 1909.11, 1909.20, 1910.01, 1910.03, 1910.16, 1910.23, 1911.12, 1911.28, 1911.35, 1912.30, 1913.22, 1914.11, 1914.19
Voegtlin, Arthur T. 1894.17
Voegtlin, Athur 1909.04
Voegtlin, Operti and Dangerfield 1898.01
Voegtlin, W.T. 1892.29
Voegtlin, William 1868.25, 1868.27, 1869.02, 1869.20, 1869.29, 1869.40, 1870.19, 1870.44, 1871.10, 1871.27, 1872.06, 1872.37, 1873.08, 1873.10, 1873.28, 1875.04, 1875.32, 1879.12, 1879.42, 1880.63, 1881.02, 1881.57, 1883.52, 1887.19, 1890.03
Voegtlin, William F. 1869.33, 1869.35, 1870.13, 1881.28, 1881.31, 1881.41
Voegtlin, William T. 1880.10
Voellinger, Christine 1983.10
Voelpel, Fred 1960.07, 1960.12, 1961.11, 1962.03, 1963.12, 1965.29, 1967.10, 1970.19, 1971.04, 1972.19, 1975.24, 1981.07
Voet, Doug 1982.03
Voeth, Hal 1936.22
Voeth, Harold 1938.07
Voeth, Jack 1938.07, 1946.04
Vogel, Donald 1958.12
Vogel, Frederic B. 1999.07
Vogel, Henry 1890.01, 1903.07, 1904.23, 1905.29, 1912.46
Vogel, J.B. 1876.04, 1876.07
Vogel, John W. 1896.49
Vogel, Professor 1870.16, 1870.17, 1876.09, 1876.10, 1876.11, 1876.14
Vogelle, Sheila 1948.17
Vogler, Otto 1888.08
Vogner, George 1915.27
Vogt, Peter 1974.06
Vohs, Frank 1981.17
Voight, A.R. 1906.03
Voight, Martha 1918.25
Voigt, Frau 1883.08
Voigt, Oscar 1898.04
Voigt, William 1898.15
Vokes 1884.61
Vokes, Elsie 1921.42
Vokes, Fawdon 1872.13, 1872.15, 1873.06, 1873.07, 1873.09, 1873.13, 1873.28, 1875.17, 1876.08, 1881.20
Vokes, Ferd 1876.08, 1881.20
Vokes, Fred 1872.13, 1872.15, 1873.06, 1873.07, 1875.17, 1881.20
Vokes, Frederick 1873.09, 1873.13, 1873.28, 1875.17, 1876.08
Vokes, Harry 1895.02, 1897.06, 1898.02, 1900.08, 1902.02, 1904.11, 1909.06
Vokes, Jessie 1872.13, 1872.15, 1873.06, 1873.07, 1873.09, 1873.13, 1873.28, 1875.17, 1876.08, 1881.20
Vokes, Margaret Daly 1898.02, 1900.08, 1902.02
Vokes, Marguerite Daly 1895.02, 1897.06

Vokes, May 1907.11, 1907.59, 1911.39, 1913.19, 1919.33, 1924.38, 1925.36
Vokes, Mr. 1873.28
Vokes, Mrs. 1873.28
Vokes, Rosina 1872.13, 1872.15, 1873.06, 1873.07, 1873.09, 1873.13, 1873.28, 1875.17, 1876.08
Vokes, Russell 1917.13
Vokes, Victoria 1872.13, 1872.15, 1873.06, 1873.07, 1873.09, 1873.13, 1873.28, 1875.17, 1876.08, 1881.20
Voketaitis, Arnold 1958.16, 1959.08, 1959.17, 1959.21, 1960.02, 1960.03, 1960.15, 1961.03, 1963.15
Voley, Victor 1951.13
Volinine, Alexandre 1916.15
Voljanin, Messr. 1922.37
Voljanin, Michael 1923.02
volJanin, Mischa 1923.18
Volkenau, Vera 1939.26
Volkoff, Chris 1943.09, 1944.27
Volland, Virginia 1934.03
Vollman, Isador 1884.56
Volmer, Louise 1872.23, 1872.35, 1873.03
Volmer, Miss 1872.23
Volny, Maurice 1912.24
Voltaire 1933.12, 1956.15, 1974.06, 1983.13, 1984.11, 1986.08, 1989.14
VonArnheim, Katharine 1882.64
vonArnold, Pauline 1902.34
vonBein, Gilbert 1906.41
VonBrune, Miss 1904.13, 1904.44
VonBrune, Therese 1904.44
vonBuelow, Edna 1919.01, 1919.44
vonBulow, Eda 1925.02
vonBusing, Fritzi 1913.28, 1914.28, 1918.05, 1921.34, 1923.12
VonBusing, Fritzi 1911.47, 1912.27, 1914.10
Vondale, Larry 1898.64
vonDonop 1999.05
VonDoonik, Marie 1888.24
VonDresser, Marcia 1896.42
Vonella, Richard 1973.11
vonFlotow, Frederich 1896.46
vonFlotow, Fredrich 1889.34
VonFurstenberg, Betsy 1958.05, 1959.03, 1967.09
vonGatti, Emerich 1912.04, 1914.25
vonGolisch, Fred 1928.48
vonGontard, Gert 1980.04, 1980.25
vonGottfried, F. 1911.22
VonGross, Erwin 1964.25
vonHallberg, Gene 1928.19
vonHallberg, Sven 1928.19
vonHatzfeldt, Countess 1900.35
VonHatzfeldt, Olga 1899.22, 1901.24, 1908.16
VonHell, Pauline 1898.10
VonHolk, Leila 1918.12
vonJansen, Herr 1850.01
VonJanuschowsky, Georgina 1884.34
VonKeese, Margaret 1908.16
VonKlein, Bert 1908.21
vonKohlenegg, Kohl 1889.27
vonKeese, Margaret 1910.21
vonKeeze, Margaret 1905.55
VonLeer, Sara 1888.30
VonLipstrill, Baroness Jeannette Lips 1991.11
vonMaryhauser, Jennifer 1983.19
vonMendelssohn, Francesco 1933.07, 1937.01
vonNagy, Irma 1917.09
Vonne, Virginia 1938.17
Vonnegut, Marjorie 1925.21
vonNickol, Violette 1916.07
VonOlker, Ferd. 1881.10
vonOttenfeld, Eddison 1938.16
vonRobinson, Clark 1936.06
vonRosen, Elsie 1892.23
VonSachs, Jr., William 1886.26
vonSachs, William 1886.43, 1887.28
vonSchiller, C. 1881.03
VonSchiller, Carl 1884.46
VonStuddiford, Grace 1908.34
vonSuppe 1886.47, 1990.10
VonSuppe 1888.36
vonSuppé, Franz 1875.12, 1876.33, 1879.25, 1879.52, 1879.64, 1879.65, 1879.67, 1880.48, 1880.57, 1880.62, 1881.25, 1881.32, 1881.42, 1881.44, 1881.55, 1882.07, 1882.54, 1882.57, 1882.65, 1883.11, 1883.41, 1883.55, 1884.52, 1884.59, 1884.64, 1886.54, 1887.15, 1887.28, 1887.41, 1888.26, 1889.05, 1889.22, 1889.27, 1898.62, 1904.57, 1905.11, 1931.44, 1942.12
VonSuppé, Franz 1879.22, 1880.20, 1880.26, 1898.49
vonSeyffertitz, Gustav 1911.13
vonStroheim, Eric 1935.17
vonTilzer, Albert 1911.07, 1916.03, 1920.14, 1922.28, 1923.16, 1926.15, 1927.05
VonTilzer, Albert 1904.29, 1904.48, 1905.42, 1906.04, 1906.29, 1908.19, 1910.01, 1910.08, 1910.19, 1910.22, 1919.37, 1919.40, 1920.24, 1920.28, 1998.11
vonTilzer, Harry 1910.22, 1912.09, 1942.11, 1979.25, 1980.27
VonTilzer, Harry 1899.12, 1901.21, 1902.16, 1902.23, 1903.05, 1903.29, 1904.23, 1905.22, 1905.32, 1906.30, 1907.32, 1907.41, 1908.10, 1908.25, 1910.18, 1913.05, 1913.18, 1919.15, 1919.16, 1955.19, 2000.12
vonUlm, Thrya 1916.07
vonWaldberg, Heinrich 1912.08
VonWaldren, Ethel 1915.03
vonWeber, Karl Maria 1870.44
vonWegern, C. 1915.21
vonWegern, Carl 1891.24
VonWeiss, James 1964.21
VonWhitewashbrush, Herr 1857.06
Voorhees, Don 1926.23, 1928.08, 1928.40, 1928.45, 1930.06, 1937.10, 1937.16, 1939.29, 1940.01
Voorhees, Donald 1925.25, 1925.40, 1925.48
Voorhees, Marie 1920.28
Voorhees, Virginia 1901.27
Voos, Josephine 1883.47
Vore, Marietta 1946.12
Voronoff, Messr. 1929.05
Voronoff, Mme. 1929.05
Vos, David 1976.15
Vos, Richard 1991.14
Vosburg, David 1968.24, 1969.06
Vosburgh, David 1982.18, 1985.04, 1987.16
Vosburgh, Dick 1980.08, 1986.01
Vosburgh, Mr. 1864.12
Voshburgh, E.B. 1882.18
Voss, Jr., R. 1878.02
Vosseler, Heidi 1938.14
Vosselli, Judith 1925.08
Votos, Christopher 1963.26, 1965.06
Voudair, M. 1947.05
Vousden, Valentine 1975.22
Vowles, Vivean 1905.27
Vowles, Vivian 1904.29
Voyer, Guy 1923.36
Voynow, Dick 1987.02
Voyt, Vonnie 1909.25
Voznesensky, Andrey 1990.01
Vqn Scott, Glory 1956.06
Vrana, Ruth 1946.12
Vreeland, Miss 1897.04
Vroom, Lodewick 1935.05, 1935.06, 1935.07, 1935.08, 1935.09, 1935.10, 1942.31
Vroom, Mr. 1897.41
Vroom, Paul 1952.15
Vucci, Ralph 1955.06, 1955.07, 1957.06, 1961.12, 1964.05, 1964.32, 1981.18
Vyacheslav 1977.13
Vye, Murvyn 1945.05, 1965.20
W. Dazian and Company 1889.24
W. Dazian and Sons 1883.16, 1883.52
W. Rolff and Son 1899.31
W.H. Power's Company 1889.38
W.J. Comley-James Barton Company 1880.47
W.J. Comley-James Barton Opera Company 1881.36, 1882.06
W.J. Fetters and Son 1889.10
W.W. Tillotson's Comedy Company 1888.29
Waara, Scott 1985.20, 1989.07, 1989.29, 1992.01
Waas, Samuel 1887.40
Wachinoff, E. 1924.48
Wachner and Company 1911.44
Wachter, Harry 1898.69
Wacker, Bob 1937.16
Waddell, Edna 1917.32
Waddell, Joan Carter 1928.35
Waddington, J. 1892.20
Waddington, Patrick 1961.26
Waddington, S.P. 1897.03
Waddleton, Messr. 1869.28
Waddleton, Mr. 1866.13, 1866.16, 1866.17, 1867.18
Waddleton, T. 1869.21, 1869.25, 1872.10
Wade, Adam 1967.06
Wade, Addie 1888.13
Wade, Amy 1893.07
Wade, Anson 1892.04
Wade, C.P. 1930.19
Wade, Edward 1913.06
Wade, Frankie 1980.02
Wade, G.F. 1885.63
Wade, G.T. 1885.41
Wade, George 1889.22, 1890.16, 1891.11, 1892.22
Wade, George F. 1894.21
Wade, Herman A. 1907.41
Wade, Herman Avery 1906.45, 1908.10
Wade, James 1955.20
Wade, Joseph P. 1883.01, 1883.09, 1883.20
Wade, Mr. 1883.49
Wade, Percy 1931.32
Wade, Philip 1928.42
Wade, R.S. 1875.21
Wade, Robert 1885.58, 1905.39
Wade, S.W. 1887.01
Wade, Sherman 1888.13, 1891.02, 1896.35, 1903.10, 1904.16, 1907.59, 1912.01, 1912.17
Wade, Stuart 1950.09
Wade, Trixie 1898.03, 1898.10
Wade, W.S. 1888.13
Wadelle, Gertrude 1919.44
Wadimoff, E. 1932.09
Wadleigh, Agnes 1898.05, 1902.15
Wadman, H. 1884.42
Wadron, Nelse 1876.29
Wadsworth, Carl 1915.30
Wadsworth, Eugeneia 1899.33
Wadsworth, F. Wheeler 1925.35
Wadsworth, Vernie 1900.38, 1901.17
Wadsworth, William 1936.05
Waechter, Eberhard 1984.04
Waechter, Franz 1984.05
Waechter, Mr. 1892.43
Waedler, Fred J. 1907.03
Waelder, Frederick 1912.40
Waerea, Atareta 1972.20
Waffles, Major 1881.16
Wagenheim, G. 1958.06
Wager, Michael 1960.02
Wagg, Jim 1982.18
Waggner, George 1976.32
Waggoner, George 1932.06, 1933.15
Wagman, Neil 1984.10
Wagner 1894.21
Wagner, A.H. 1893.40
Wagner, Billy 1919.16
Wagner, Charles L. 1931.44
Wagner, Chuck 1984.14, 1987.18
Wagner, Daryl 1989.11
Wagner, Ernest 1896.49
Wagner, Frank 1957.01, 1968.13, 1979.28, 1980.18, 1981.08, 1982.06
Wagner, Franklin 1948.18
Wagner, Franz 1912.26
Wagner, Frl. 1879.22
Wagner, Harry 1879.29, 1911.13
Wagner, Herr 1879.57, 1879.62, 1880.66
Wagner, J.H. 1896.06, 1897.54
Wagner, Janice 1957.17
Wagner, Janyce 1959.03, 1959.27
Wagner, Janyce Ann 1952.01
Wagner, John 1898.63
Wagner, John H. 1904.34
Wagner, Lillian 1922.11
Wagner, Lori 1976.20, 1977.15
Wagner, Louis E. 1906.04
Wagner, Mr. 1883.44
Wagner, Nat 1926.27
Wagner, Nathaniel 1922.47, 1924.42, 1927.42, 1931.34
Wagner, Ogla 1906.03
Wagner, Professory 1894.44
Wagner, Richard 1906.48, 1990.10
Wagner, Robin 1968.11, 1968.31, 1970.02, 1971.12, 1971.20, 1972.04, 1972.23, 1973.06, 1974.18, 1974.24, 1975.15, 1977.15, 1978.02, 1978.27, 1979.32, 1980.20, 1981.29, 1983.01, 1985.12, 1987.07, 1987.19, 1988.09, 1989.03, 1989.29, 1992.02, 1992.08, 1995.15, 1996.08, 1997.08, 1997.17, 1999.15, 1999.19, 2000.08, 2001.05, 2001.08
Wagner, Wally 1944.19
Wagner, Walter 1939.13
Wagstaff, Joe 1930.28
Wagstaff, Joseph 1923.17, 1928.31
Wahl, Dorothy 1916.14
Wahl, Walter 1924.31, 1925.24, 1931.07
Wahl, Walter Dare 1934.19, 1951.23
Waide, Carolyn 1908.28
Waide, Coralinn 1912.31
Wain, John 1977.01
Wainer, Lee 1932.01, 1937.14, 1939.19, 1942.34
Wainsford, Laura 1895.15, 1895.22
Wainwright, Ben 1910.23
Wainwright, Bert 1902.02, 1910.23
Wainwright, J. Howard 1855.09
Waissman, Kenneth 1972.12, 1974.05, 1997.21
Waite, Agnes 1877.01
Waite, Alfred 1886.42, 1886.52, 1887.07, 1890.49, 1893.15
Waite, Annie 1876.15
Waite, Genevieve 1975.04
Waite, James 1904.38
Waite, Myretta 1896.01
Waite, Robert 1914.30
Waites, James A. 1927.15
Waits, Tom 1975.12, 1979.30
Waiwaiole, Ben 1912.03
Waixel, Gertrude 1916.22
Wake, Buchanan 1894.15
Wakefield, Ann 1954.09
Wakefield, Charlotte 1918.16
Wakefield, Ed 1923.34
Wakefield, Eddie 1921.41
Wakefield, Henrietta 1912.40
Wakefield, Henriette 1913.25
Wakefield, Hugh 1925.08
Wakefield, J. 1880.41, 1882.62, 1885.33, 1886.41, 1890.17
Wakefield, Jack 1955.12, 1964.44
Wakefield, Oliver 1934.01, 1952.20
Wakeman, Annie 1879.50
Wakeman, Emily 1894.25
Wakeman, J. 1868.08, 1868.16
Walbanks, Marion 1920.39
Walberg, Betty 1959.13, 1962.12, 1964.15, 1964.27, 1965.01, 1965.31, 1966.06, 1976.36, 1981.18, 1989.03
Walbridge, Arthur D. 1873.10
Walburn, Raymond 1930.15, 1932.21, 1946.20, 1962.12
Walby, H. 1861.06, 1862.02
Walby, Harriet 1864.22
Walby, Miss 1862.01
Walbye, Kay 1991.05
Walck, Ezra C. 1912.01, 1918.24
Walcot, Charles 1853.01, 1853.03, 1863.08
Walcot, Charles M. 1853.02, 1855.11, 1859.14, 1863.04, 1863.09, 1863.10, 1864.05
Walcot, Charles Melton 1856.04
Walcot, Jr., C.M. 1866.13
Walcot, Maria Grace 1859.14
Walcot, Mrs. 1863.10, 1870.19, 1873.08
Walcot, Mrs. C.M. 1873.25
Walcot, Sr., Mrs. Charles M. 1863.04
Walcott, Derek 1998.02
Walcott, Ernest 1895.35
Walcott, Gertrude 1903.09
Walcott, Jacqueline 1950.07
Walcott, Lilla 1891.23
Walcott, Mr. 1884.27
Walcott, W.F. 1906.03
Wald, Karen 1978.10
Wald, Shelley 1988.20
Waldau, Mlle. 1872.10
Waldeck, Fred 1926.06
Waldeck, Jules 1928.15
Waldemere, Maud 1880.31
Waldemere, Maude 1884.18, 1886.45, 1888.39
Waldemere, Miss 1883.16
Walden, Bernice 1926.22
Walden, Bertha 1931.09
Walden, Stanley 1971.04, 1976.27
Walden, Vilma 1927.39
Walden, Walter 1937.09
Walderman, William 1952.15
Waldermere, Maud 1887.43
Waldman, Gunnar 1993.12
Waldman, Lorraine 1948.20
Waldman, Robert 1968.05, 1975.18, 1976.30, 1995.12
Waldo, Grace 1909.19
Waldo, H.H. 1884.28
Waldo, Herman 1889.33
Waldo, Laura 1902.26
Waldon, Gertrude 1930.41, 1931.20, 1936.08, 1936.11
Waldon, James T. 1903.36
Waldon, Richard 1881.47
Waldorf 1951.22
Waldorf, Mr. 1893.29

Waldrip, Gladstone 1931.39, 1936.27, 1938.10
Waldron, Andrew 1880.30
Waldron, Dan 1894.51
Waldron, Dorothy 1906.45
Waldron, Isabel 1884.23, 1896.39
Waldron, Jack 1924.16, 1924.17, 1926.14, 1952.01, 1954.05, 1955.25, 1957.08, 1959.03, 1961.15
Waldron, James T. 1899.36
Waldron, Mae 1922.30
Waldron, Marga 1923.18, 1927.45
Waldron, Michael 1983.19
Waldron, N. 1866.02
Waldron, Naomi 1914.33
Waldron, Nelse 1865.11, 1866.28, 1866.31, 1869.07, 1872.07, 1873.20, 1873.22, 1873.27, 1875.14, 1875.31, 1875.34, 1875.40, 1876.13, 1876.15, 1877.01, 1877.39, 1879.09
Waldron, Nelson 1884.36, 1885.46
Waldron, Philip 1897.30
Waldrop, Mark 1979.02
Waldrop, Oza 1911.13
Waldrup, Gladstone 1932.11
Waldteufel, Emile 1957.10
Waler, D.W. 1872.27
Wales, Pauline 1962.28, 1962.31, 1964.36, 1964.38, 1964.41, 1966.22, 1966.23, 1966.25, 1966.28, 1968.25, 1968.26, 1968.27, 1968.28, 1968.29, 1978.17, 1989.15
Waletzko, Craig 1989.27, 1991.06, 1995.07
Waliter, William 1932.27
Walke, Hughie 1932.08
Walken, Christopher 1965.02, 2000.01
Walker Berta 1974.12
Walker, A.O. 1906.14
Walker, Ada Overton 1903.08, 1904.26
Walker, Ada Palmer 1902.03, 1902.31
Walker, Adad 1890.08
Walker, Aida Overton 1900.46, 1906.14, 1908.08, 1911.20
Walker, Arnetia 1972.01, 1987.07
Walker, Betty 1979.03
Walker, Bill 1958.05, 1979.07
Walker, Billy B. 1979.13
Walker, Bonnie 1966.24, 1974.17, 1989.27, 1991.06
Walker, Charles 1894.52, 1979.29
Walker, Charles A. 1896.04
Walker, Charlotte 1900.58
Walker, Chet 1999.01
Walker, Chris 1986.12
Walker, Clifford 1927.27
Walker, D. 1929.01
Walker, Dan 1922.03, 1922.20, 1924.14, 1925.20
Walker, Diana 1934.29, 1966.10, 1986.09
Walker, Dianne 1989.02
Walker, Don 1934.15, 1934.19, 1935.17, 1936.02, 1936.17, 1937.15, 1938.07, 1939.25, 1940.03, 1940.07, 1940.10, 1940.12, 1940.19, 1942.15, 1942.27, 1943.01, 1943.05, 1943.07, 1943.20, 1943.22, 1944.15, 1944.33, 1945.03, 1945.05, 1945.08, 1945.14, 1945.18, 1946.06, 1946.20, 1947.03, 1947.11, 1948.08, 1948.23, 1948.27, 1949.02, 1949.03, 1949.08, 1949.12, 1949.18, 1950.15, 1950.19, 1951.17, 1951.23, 1952.01, 1952.07, 1952.10, 1952.13,
Walker, Don (*cont.*) 1952.20, 1953.01, 1953.02, 1953.03, 1953.08, 1953.11, 1954.01, 1954.05, 1954.07, 1954.12, 1954.17, 1955.02, 1955.04, 1955.08, 1955.09, 1956.04, 1956.16, 1957.08, 1957.11, 1957.18, 1958.05, 1959.02, 1959.06, 1960.05, 1960.09, 1961.15, 1961.27, 1963.05, 1963.14, 1963.17, 1963.21, 1964.05, 1964.15, 1964.27, 1965.02, 1965.17, 1965.21, 1965.24, 1965.35, 1966.08, 1966.09, 1966.24, 1966.31, 1967.04, 1967.09, 1968.23, 1968.30, 1970.15, 1971.07, 1973.15, 1974.02, 1975.03, 1976.36, 1978.10, 1979.26, 1980.16, 1981.18, 1983.14, 1987.16, 1988.04, 1990.18, 1991.09, 1993.10
Walker, Donald 1935.12, 1936.27, 1941.06, 1942.29
Walker, Donald J. 1935.04, 1938.13, 1939.13, 1941.08, 1950.06
Walker, Douglas 1980.11
Walker, Edward 1905.39
Walker, Edwin L. 1904.41
Walker, Esther 1919.03
Walker, Ethel June 1929.08
Walker, F. 1910.17
Walker, Francis 1927.39
Walker, Fred 1977.07, 1980.16, 1981.16
Walker, Fredi 1996.09
Walker, Fuschia 1987.07
Walker, George 1896.30, 1898.56, 1900.46, 1902.23, 1980.10, 1980.27
Walker, George W. 1899.33, 1903.08, 1904.26, 1906.14, 1908.08
Walker, Gertrude 1932.11
Walker, Gillian 1969.10
Walker, H. 1875.03
Walker, J.J. 1905.33
Walker, James 1963.03, 1964.36, 1964.37, 1964.38, 1964.41, 1964.42, 1964.43, 1966.22, 1966.25, 1966.26, 1966.28, 1968.25, 1968.26, 1968.27, 1968.28, 1968.29
Walker, James J. 1928.21
Walker, Janet Hayes 1989.19
Walker, Jerry Jeff 1974.11, 1978.05, 1986.03, 1999.01
Walker, Joseph 1896.14
Walker, June 1931.02, 1933.24, 1938.12
Walker, June L. 1959.23
Walker, Kathryn 1974.23
Walker, Leonard 1897.18, 1898.12
Walker, Leslie 1894.15
Walker, M. 1881.40
Walker, Mabel 1939.15
Walker, Mai 1902.16
Walker, Margaret 1900.51, 1901.21, 1926.06, 1931.35
Walker, Marshall 1919.15, 1920.33
Walker, May 1896.04
Walker, Messr. 1885.52, 1927.33
Walker, Mia 1999.04
Walker, Mildred 1919.38
Walker, Miss 1860.03, 1865.05, 1865.09
Walker, Mlle. 1899.31
Walker, Mountjoy 1885.45, 1885.67, 1886.26, 1887.26
Walker, Nancy 1941.06, 1944.33, 1947.08, 1948.08, 1949.01, 1957.14, 1958.05, 1959.23, 1960.23
Walker, Natalie 1981.24
Walker, Natalie Barth 1951.21
Walker, Peter 1971.05, 1974.25, 1985.02, 1986.18
Walker, Polly 1926.18, 1927.47, 1928.31, 1930.37
Walker, R. 1861.06, 1862.01, 1867.32
Walker, Ralph 1928.44
Walker, Ray 2000.09
Walker, Raymond 1912.29
Walker, Rhoderick 1948.11
Walker, Richard 1934.21, 1934.23, 1934.25, 1934.26, 1934.31, 1936.14, 1936.15, 1936.19, 1936.21, 1936.24, 1939.01, 1939.02, 1939.05, 1939.06, 1948.01, 1948.02, 1948.03, 1948.05, 1948.06, 1948.09, 1948.10
Walker, Robert 1864.17
Walker, Robert S. 1864.22
Walker, Royal 1972.20
Walker, Sandra 1974.08, 1975.11, 1977.03, 1977.17, 1978.07, 1978.08, 1989.13, 1996.02
Walker, Sid 1940.07
Walker, Smiley 1887.46
Walker, Suzanne 1973.02, 1973.11, 1981.25
Walker, Sydney 1970.06
Walker, T. 1861.06, 1862.01
Walker, T.J. 1878.04
Walker, W. 1929.01
Walker, Walter 1922.01, 1924.25
Walker, William 1936.30
Walkinshaw, Andrew 1998.10
Wall, D. 1875.31
Wall, David V. 1918.41
Wall, Harry 1867.08, 1869.11, 1869.17, 1869.21, 1931.14
Wall, Jack 1931.05
Wall, James E. 1952.08, 1955.10, 1957.16
Wall, Max 1932.18
Wall, Messr. 1860.06
Wall, Miss 1865.01
Wall, Mr. 1860.03, 1860.04
Wall, Mrs. Harry 1857.01
Wall, Phil 1937.10, 1937.16, 1939.29
Walla, W. 1897.51
Wallace, Agnes 1868.08, 1868.16
Wallace, Alf A. 1881.30
Wallace, Alice 1880.05
Wallace, Amy 1881.38
Wallace, Arnita 1936.26
Wallace, Art 1962.24, 1965.21, 1966.30, 1972.26
Wallace, Ben 1944.19
Wallace, Bertram 1905.52
Wallace, Beryl 1931.26, 1932.18, 1933.20, 1935.04, 1940.02
Wallace, Cal 1887.09
Wallace, Carrie 1884.25, 1884.40, 1885.58, 1886.59, 1887.06
Wallace, Cecil 1889.48, 1891.06, 1891.07
Wallace, Charles 1898.77, 1904.40
Wallace, Charles E. 1997.09
Wallace, Constance 1888.23, 1889.48, 1891.06
Wallace, Dick 1933.21
Wallace, Dorothy 1919.35
Wallace, Edgar 1922.05
Wallace, Edgeworth 1890.21
Wallace, Eleanor 1936.26
Wallace, Ella 1883.49, 1884.12
Wallace, Emett 'Babe' 1976.21
Wallace, Esther 1904.53
Wallace, Folly 1884.17
Wallace, Francklyn 1903.40
Wallace, Frank K. 1924.46
Wallace, Franklyn 1900.24
Wallace, Frederick 1918.08
Wallace, George 1894.36, 1896.09, 1897.05, 1955.27, 1957.07, 1963.25
Wallace, Gertrude 1904.12
Wallace, Grace 1891.38
Wallace, H. 1929.01
Wallace, H.V. 1870.05
Wallace, H.W. 1871.12, 1871.16
Wallace, Harry 1906.07
Wallace, Harry L. 1902.01
Wallace, J. 1869.23, 1929.01
Wallace, J.J. 1869.27, 1869.32, 1870.04, 1872.14, 1875.18, 1877.04, 1877.15, 1882.62, 1883.06, 1890.17, 1890.35, 1892.01
Wallace, James 1903.29
Wallace, Janice 1943.14
Wallace, Jennie 1867.26
Wallace, Jenny 1867.27, 1867.31
Wallace, John 1918.24, 1999.09
Wallace, Laura 1884.62
Wallace, Lee 1973.11, 1985.05
Wallace, Mamie 1881.30
Wallace, Marge 1911.39
Wallace, Marie 1917.03, 1918.19, 1959.13
Wallace, McCutcheon 1918.10
Wallace, Mervin 1976.28
Wallace, Mervin Bertel 1983.04
Wallace, Messr. 1859.08, 1875.34
Wallace, Mimi 1973.07
Wallace, Miss 1877.15
Wallace, Mr. 1855.11, 1865.04
Wallace, Olive 1899.26, 1899.38
Wallace, Oliver G. 1920.24
Wallace, Ollie 1900.34
Wallace, Patrick 1903.32
Wallace, Paul 1959.13
Wallace, Phoebe 1928.32, 1931.36
Wallace, R. 1899.34
Wallace, Richard 1903.40
Wallace, Ron 1976.19
Wallace, Rona 1923.01
Wallace, Royce 1946.24, 1950.01, 1964.11
Wallace, Slappy 1933.27
Wallace, Slaps 1930.24
Wallace, Timothy 1981.03
Wallace, Trudy 1966.14, 1967.14
Wallace, Vernon 1927.38
Wallace, Vincent 1855.04, 1864.07, 1864.16, 1867.03, 1870.23, 1884.38
Wallace, W. 1890.17
Wallace, Walter 1885.53
Wallace, William 1898.19, 1902.12
Wallace, William Vincent 1848.04, 1868.02, 1868.09, 1900.13
Wallace, Yolande 1892.17, 1892.30, 1892.37, 1892.40, 1892.46, 1893.17, 1894.26, 1894.38, 1896.26, 1896.36, 1897.09, 1897.19, 1897.37, 1898.51, 1902.15
Wallace, Zelda Seguin 1882.33, 1882.36, 1882.64, 1882.65
Wallace-Hopper, Edna 1896.13, 1899.02
Wallach, Eli 1947.09, 1979.17
Wallach, Nathan 1905.22
Wallach, Samuel H. 1911.31
Wallach, Saran 1961.12
Wallack, Arthur 1892.19
Wallack, J.W. 1838.01
Wallack, James W. 1853.01, 1853.02, 1853.03, 1855.11, 1856.04, 1859.14
Wallack, Lester 1859.14, 1875.14, 1879.29, 1884.21
Wallack, Mr. 1857.04
Wallack, W. 1866.18
Wallack, William 1866.31
Walle, Alfred 1899.42, 1900.02
Wallenstedt, J.A. 1896.45
Waller, (Thomas) "Fats" 1943.07, 1978.09, 1980.10, 1988.17
Waller, Deborah 1978.03
Waller, Dorothy 1932.05, 1932.26
Waller, F. 1894.35
Waller, Fats 1926.11, 1928.10, 1932.14, 1967.13, 1968.20, 1975.22, 1976.04, 1989.02, 1999.07
Waller, Bert 1960.13
Waller, Frank 1922.06
Waller, Henry 1894.08, 1902.06, 1902.40
Waller, Jack 1925.47, 1930.20, 1932.21
Waller, John 1964.04
Waller, Ken 1979.03
Waller, Kenneth H. 1980.30, 1986.12, 1988.01
Waller, Lewis 1925.47
Waller, Oden 1928.24
Waller, Thomas 1929.23
Waller, Thomas "Fats" 1939.29
Waller, W. Oden 1926.16
Waller, William Oden 1927.60, 1940.12
Wallerstedt, J.A. 1899.06, 1899.34
Wallerstein, Gitta 1937.05
Wallez, Gus 1964.39
Wallin, Gene 1925.23
Walling, Mary 1972.11
Walling, Will 1887.23
Wallis 1871.06
Wallis, Bertram 1904.30, 1907.01, 1907.63
Wallis, E. 1855.10
Wallis, Gladys 1898.28
Wallis, Lizzie 1856.03
Wallis, Ma. Eva 1963.02
Wallis, Miss 1855.01
Wallis, Mr. 1852.01, 1852.05
Wallis, Mrs. 1852.05, 1854.01, 1855.02, 1855.10
Wallis, Mrs. S. 1852.01
Wallis, S. 1851.01, 1851.06, 1851.07, 1854.01, 1854.07, 1855.01, 1855.02, 1855.10, 1863.06, 1866.18, 1868.27
Wallis, Samuel 1870.30, 1872.10
Wallis, Sarah 1873.26
Wallis, Shani 1966.09
Wallis, W.F. 1882.77
Wallis, W.H. 1878.14, 1880.17, 1881.18, 1883.40, 1888.10, 1888.23, 1889.08
Wallner, Helmut 1964.25
Wallop, Douglass 1955.08, 1994.01
Walmsley, Andy 1990.15, 1993.07
Walmsley, George 1881.18
Walpole, Horace 1963.03
Walser, Lloyd 1977.11, 1977.17, 1978.08, 1978.19, 1978.23, 1979.20, 1979.27, 1980.03, 1980.04, 1980.21, 1980.22, 1980.25, 1981.20, 1981.21, 1982.07
Walsh, Alice 1887.29, 1888.32, 1890.41, 1893.14
Walsh, Alice Chebba 1999.07
Walsh, Austin 1897.39, 1900.05, 1916.15
Walsh, Barbara 1982.22, 1992.09, 1993.07, 1996.08
Walsh, Barry 1929.44
Walsh, Beatrice 1904.03
Walsh, Billy 1927.52
Walsh, Brownie 1927.52
Walsh, C. 1870.42
Walsh, Elizabeth 1991.09, 1991.12
Walsh, Ellis 1992.03, 1999.06
Walsh, Enid 1948.01, 1948.02, 1948.07, 1951.03, 1951.06, 1951.07, 1951.09
Walsh, Flora 1886.28, 1887.29, 1888.32, 1890.41
Walsh, Florence 1914.30
Walsh, Frank 1896.25, 1919.32
Walsh, Fred 1903.04
Walsh, George 1926.18
Walsh, Grace 1904.52, 1906.37, 1908.25
Walsh, Helen 1914.30, 1930.08

Walsh, J.C. 1866.08, 1870.28, 1870.32, 1871.01
Walsh, J.W. 1892.35
Walsh, Jack 1926.33
Walsh, James 1983.18, 1990.12
Walsh, Jane 1936.07
Walsh, Jimmy 1999.21, 2000.19
Walsh, John 1875.05, 1875.18, 1890.49, 1891.25, 1891.45, 1892.14, 1892.54, 1893.15, 1896.15, 1896.42, 1931.01, 1948.19, 1949.05
Walsh, John J. 1934.15
Walsh, John R. 1924.09
Walsh, John S. 1884.53
Walsh, Julian 1899.21
Walsh, Lionel 1906.50, 1907.30, 1907.46, 1909.03, 1910.01, 1911.13, 1911.30, 1913.24
Walsh, Louis 1936.05
Walsh, Mable 1901.26
Walsh, Mamie 1900.28
Walsh, Martin 1980.01
Walsh, Mary Jane 1937.13, 1938.09, 1939.27, 1941.08, 1944.15
Walsh, Mary Rose 1929.33
Walsh, Maurice 1961.14
Walsh, Mavis 1933.26
Walsh, May 1904.06
Walsh, Messr. 1864.13, 1879.56
Walsh, Mr. 1869.31
Walsh, Nina 1898.02
Walsh, Patrick 1911.18, 1912.07
Walsh, Phil 1935.12
Walsh, Sandy 1961.21
Walsh, Sean 1965.31
Walsh, Thomas 1916.04, 1922.14
Walsh, Thomas A. 1979.08
Walsh, Thomas H. 1918.29
Walsh, Thomas J. 1909.19, 1975.15
Walsh, Thommie 1978.13, 1979.24, 1980.08, 1982.09, 1982.10, 1982.11, 1983.06, 1992.17
Walsh, Townshend 1897.12
Walsh, Tracy Alison 1998.03
Walsh, Valerie 1964.28
Walsh, W.J. 1906.03
Walsh, William 1903.09, 1918.03, 1925.47, 1933.15
Walshe, Mons. 1879.50
Walshe, Pat 1920.03, 1930.28
Walstein, Mrs. 1834.03
Walston, Ray 1954.19, 1955.08, 1969.04
Walt Disney Productions 1994.04
Walt Disney Theatrical Productions 1997.12, 1999.16
Walt, Charles E. 1911.07
Walter, Charles 1934.06, 1934.40
Walter, Edwin 1929.07, 1929.50
Walter, Joshua 1999.22
Walter, Max 1890.31, 1891.33, 1892.43, 1893.29, 1894.01, 1896.34, 1897.35, 1898.53
Walter, Miss 1852.01
Walter, Serge 1928.19, 1929.20, 1932.19, 1933.16
Walters 1875.31, 1875.36
Walters, Annie 1851.04, 1851.08, 1856.01
Walters, Barbara Ann 1962.01
Walters, C. 1875.31, 1876.07
Walters, C.E. 1875.36, 1875.37
Walters, Charles 1870.27, 1876.05, 1925.02, 1935.03, 1935.14, 1936.31, 1937.16, 1938.05, 1938.09, 1939.30, 1941.08, 1941.13, 1946.08
Walters, Daryl 1996.07
Walters, Dorothy 1919.36, 1924.07, 1925.19, 1927.46
Walters, Edward 1931.28
Walters, Elizabeth 1949.09
Walters, Ethel 1931.11, 1945.07
Walters, Frank 1916.03, 1926.33
Walters, Gwendolyn 1962.07, 1964.19
Walters, Harry 1902.32, 1922.23, 1924.11
Walters, J. 1864.12, 1864.15
Walters, J.T. 1870.20, 1872.19
Walters, Jennie 1861.06, 1862.01, 1862.02
Walters, Kelly 1974.06, 1980.01, 1980.07, 1985.05
Walters, Letha 1913.20
Walters, Lillian 1890.10
Walters, Lillie 1883.58
Walters, Lou 1943.05, 1943.20, 1944.19
Walters, Messr. 1875.31, 1876.04, 1876.05, 1905.25
Walters, Miss 1854.04, 1859.11
Walters, Mr. 1854.01, 1854.07, 1855.10
Walters, Nancy 1955.04
Walters, Nellie 1891.20
Walters, Ollie 1891.23
Walters, Pat 1930.36
Walters, Polly 1936.26
Walters, Sam 1904.06
Walters, Sandra 1934.29
Walters, Susan 1966.21, 1967.08, 1968.22
Walters, Teddy 1927.62, 1930.35
Walters, Theodore 1908.25
Walters, Thorley 1947.15
Walters, Victoria 1892.49, 1893.01
Walters, William 1906.38
Walters, Winslow 1890.33
Waltes, Hattie 1888.32
Walther, Elaine 1945.11
Walther, Oscar 1887.12, 1888.24
Walthers, Herman 1905.31
Walthers, Otto 1886.26
Waltoln, F.A. 1928.24
Walton, Bob 1994.08, 1996.18
Walton, Charles 1879.68, 1899.19, 1900.36, 1916.13
Walton, Charles F. 1891.09, 1893.17, 1894.26
Walton, Clara 1906.34
Walton, Dave 1898.64
Walton, Debra 1997.21
Walton, Eva 1883.52
Walton, Florence 1908.07, 1908.39, 1910.34, 1911.11, 1912.43, 1915.16, 1916.24
Walton, Forrest 1898.64
Walton, Fred 1905.55, 1911.42, 1912.12, 1912.33, 1913.14, 1914.04, 1914.26, 1915.01, 1915.19, 1916.11, 1917.16, 1922.34, 1931.37
Walton, George 1894.38
Walton, Gladys 1918.42, 1919.16, 1920.23, 1921.02, 1921.14, 1922.36, 1925.26
Walton, Grace 1902.27, 1905.49, 1909.07, 1910.32, 1913.21, 1920.22
Walton, Helen 1899.30
Walton, Henry E. 1889.23
Walton, Jim 1980.29, 1981.27, 1987.02, 1989.19
Walton, Jules 1937.06
Walton, Lester 1907.55
Walton, Lillian 1897.38
Walton, Minerva 1912.28
Walton, Minne 1873.19, 1873.24
Walton, Minnie 1870.40, 1870.42
Walton, Miss 1889.31
Walton, Mr. 1864.09, 1875.21, 1898.53
Walton, Neil 1911.02
Walton, Nellie 1880.64
Walton, Orlie 1898.64
Walton, Paul 1941.11
Walton, Ray 1890.37, 1891.18
Walton, Simeon 1894.09
Walton, Thomas 1979.25
Walton, Tony 1962.12, 1964.32, 1966.18, 1972.22, 1973.03, 1975.12, 1975.14, 1977.16, 1980.08, 1981.06, 1981.10, 1982.01, 1985.03, 1987.15, 1988.15, 1989.03, 1989.26, 1991.07, 1992.04, 1992.18, 1993.10, 1993.16, 1994.12, 1995.11, 1995.19, 1996.06, 1996.15, 1997.07, 1997.12, 1997.15, 1997.22, 1998.20, 1999.04, 1999.21, 2000.18, 2000.19
Walton, Vera 1958.20
Walton, Wilma 1917.19
Waltson, Ray 1953.08
Waltzinger, Bertha 1892.51, 1893.18, 1894.03, 1894.08, 1894.24, 1896.45, 1897.46, 1898.73
Walz, Erik 1938.18
Walz, Fred 1919.19
Walzer, Willi 1925.36
Walzinger, Bertha 1896.13
Wambold, D.S. 1879.09
Wambold, Mr. 1864.02
Wamen, James 1956.06, 1965.22
Wanamaker 1903.29, 1905.17, 1907.36
Wanamaker Company 1905.21
Wanamaker, John 1906.47
Wanamaker, Zoe 1981.04
Wandel, Peter 1980.16, 1983.08
Wanderman, Carol 1937.15
Wanderman, Carol Louise 1939.07
Wanetik, Ric 1999.07
Wang, Dottie 1911.26, 1912.33, 1915.05
Wang, Richard 1934.36
Wania, W. 1910.18
Wank, Jesse 1932.12
Wankel, Robert E. 2000.10
Wann, Jim 1982.04
Wannemacher, Henry 1872.07, 1876.13, 1876.15, 1876.29, 1877.01, 1880.07
Want, Willie 1900.40
Wapshire, William 1898.64
Waram, Percy 1932.23
Wararen, Sylvester 1892.38
Warbler, O.L. 1881.16
Warburg, James 1930.33
Warburg, James P. 1930.18, 1930.28
Warburg, Kay 1928.21
Warchus, Matthew 2001.02
Warcoux, Evelyn 1927.39
Ward 1905.27
Ward and Harvey 1927.16, 1930.34
Ward and Harvey Studios 1929.07, 1929.46, 1930.35, 1932.03
Ward Singers, The 1963.07
Ward, Aida 1924.37, 1927.36, 1928.18
Ward, Alan E. 1947.22
Ward, Alice 1947.01
Ward, Andre 2001.09
Ward, Andrew 1999.15
Ward, Ann-Hould 1985.02
Ward, Annie 1867.19, 1867.20
Ward, Barney 1927.10
Ward, Bernard 1969.10
Ward, Billy 1985.17
Ward, Blanche 1897.40
Ward, C.A. 1906.03
Ward, C.B. 1889.46, 1892.53
Ward, Cecilia 1961.05, 1961.06
Ward, Charles B. 1898.70, 1989.16, 1997.01
Ward, Clara 1963.07, 1963.27
Ward, Colleen 1933.02
Ward, Dorothy 1921.13, 1921.20
Ward, Eddie 1925.33, 1927.68
Ward, Edna 1941.03
Ward, Edward 1933.15, 1945.16
Ward, Elizabeth 1992.12, 1997.19
Ward, Elsa 1912.37
Ward, Emily 1907.03
Ward, Estelle 1903.21
Ward, Evelyn 1943.07
Ward, F.F. 1886.24
Ward, F.T. 1886.45, 1891.03, 1892.05
Ward, Fannie 1890.43, 1893.13, 1893.32, 1893.47
Ward, Fanny 1891.41, 1892.29
Ward, Fleming 1914.29, 1941.06
Ward, Frank T. 1894.16
Ward, Fred 1896.38
Ward, Grace 1887.04
Ward, H. 1918.23
Ward, Hap 1900.08, 1904.11, 1906.09, 1907.12, 1909.06, 1923.38
Ward, Happy 1895.02, 1897.06, 1898.02, 1902.02
Ward, Harrison 1900.03
Ward, Harry 1905.42, 1917.16, 1922.30
Ward, Helen 1922.30
Ward, Henry 1882.50, 1911.07, 1913.21
Ward, Herbert 1919.13, 1920.03, 1920.17, 1920.33, 1921.22, 1922.09, 1922.23, 1922.27, 1922.29, 1922.38, 1922.46, 1923.01, 1923.16, 1923.18, 1923.33, 1927.56, 1928.16
Ward, Hugh J. 1891.42, 1905.48
Ward, Ida 1888.27, 1888.40, 1889.07, 1889.15, 1889.18
Ward, Irene 1912.30, 1913.22, 1914.19
Ward, J. 1870.02, 1883.46
Ward, J.F. 1886.16
Ward, J.M. 1862.08, 1869.38, 1869.39, 1869.42, 1869.45, 1870.01, 1870.06
Ward, J.T. 1868.19, 1869.40
Ward, Jean 1908.03
Ward, John 1879.12, 1948.18
Ward, John F. 1889.38
Ward, Jonathan 1979.22
Ward, Larry 1907.46
Ward, Lauren 1994.02, 2001.02
Ward, Lawrence 1913.28
Ward, Lily 1897.54
Ward, Marguerite 1908.08
Ward, Miss 1865.01, 1888.33
Ward, Mr. 1867.19
Ward, Mrs. J.F. 1878.11
Ward, Pamela 1947.19
Ward, Penelope Dudley 1939.07
Ward, Polly 1951.23
Ward, Robert 1900.35, 1904.35, 1907.46, 1913.28
Ward, Ronald 1924.01
Ward, Ruth 1893.01, 1893.04
Ward, Sam 1919.10
Ward, Samuel 1980.27
Ward, Solly 1923.32, 1929.17, 1929.39, 1934.29
Ward, Susan 1990.08
Ward, T. 1867.20, 1868.22, 1870.05
Ward, Ted 1915.20
Ward, Theara J. 1994.06, 1994.12, 1995.19
Ward, Tom 1972.20, 1998.10
Ward, Vicky 1972.20
Ward, W.M. 1878.15
Ward, Wayne 1957.18, 1965.21
Ward, Willard 1919.18
Ward, William 1920.03, 1991.09, 1991.12, 1996.13
Ward, Willie 1926.11
Warde, Angela 1921.01, 1922.42
Warde, Arthur F. 1897.56, 1927.22
Warde, Ernest E. 1899.27
Warde, Estelle 1898.10
Warde, F.B. 1877.07
Warde, Jennie 1878.10
Warde, Mildred 1905.55
Warde, Willie 1895.32, 1897.32, 1897.44, 1898.18, 1900.43, 1902.12, 1905.04, 1905.18, 1907.06
Wardell, Harry 1909.20, 1912.09, 1913.05, 1916.15, 1920.05
Wardell, John 1979.10
Warden, E. 1866.19
Warden, Gentry 1939.15
Warden, Jack 1958.01
Warden, Mr. 1848.04
Wardrop, Ewan 1998.10
Ware, Annie D. 1882.50, 1882.79, 1883.32
Ware, Annie M. 1893.12
Ware, C. 1870.21
Ware, Charles 1934.37
Ware, Eric 1991.01
Ware, Estelle 1900.46
Ware, Florence 1917.12, 1918.11, 1920.18
Ware, Leonard 1939.29, 1986.06
Ware, N. Harris 1904.27, 1906.22
Ware, Virgie 1902.32
Ware, Walter 1907.33
Wareham, Charles 1873.26
Waren, Evelyn 1900.08
Waren, Flori 1951.10
Warfield, David 1891.43, 1894.10, 1895.18, 1896.18, 1897.26, 1897.39, 1898.50, 1899.17, 1899.30, 1900.38
Warfield, Russell 1998.06
Warfield, Ruth White 1925.37
Warfield, William 1949.16, 1961.13, 1964.19, 1966.14
Warhold, Andy 1975.04
Waring, Bertha 1894.38, 1896.44
Waring, Claire 1961.09, 1964.20, 1965.15, 1966.13, 1967.09, 1968.17
Waring, Clare 1958.03
Waring, Fred 1928.41, 1930.40, 1931.01, 1955.13
Waring, Katie 1876.03
Waring, Mrs. 1834.03
Waring, Richard 1932.28, 1939.16, 1947.09
Waring, Tom 1929.33, 1955.13
Waring, Wenda 1991.07
Waring, Wendy 1988.20, 2001.02
Warington, Norma 1920.37
Warmen, Timothy 1993.06, 1994.09, 1997.07, 1997.17
Warmington, William 1880.37
Warmouth, A. 1897.13, 1900.32
Warmouth, Adam 1900.25, 1900.31
Warncke, Margaret 1971.12, 1981.24
Warner Brothers 1990.10
Warner Brothers-7 Arts 1968.23
Warner Theatre Productions, Inc. 1981.04, 1981.10, 1982.01, 1982.04, 1982.18
Warner, Albert 1920.32
Warner, Ardelle 1942.33
Warner, Edyth 1908.11
Warner, Ella 1912.38
Warner, Florence 1911.26
Warner, Frederick 1881.39
Warner, Gloria 1961.26
Warner, Jack 1948.15, 1949.02, 1950.01
Warner, Jack L. 1969.14
Warner, Jackie 1957.17, 1958.20

Warner, Jessie 1886.07
Warner, Jethro 1927.20
Warner, Joan 1921.35
Warner, John E. 1881.08
Warner, Mary 1889.03, 1889.48, 1891.06
Warner, Maurice 1929.20
Warner, Miss 1841.01, 1896.44
Warner, Morris H. 1885.41
Warner, Neil 1870.19, 1965.34, 1972.14, 1992.07, 1993.05
Warner, Russell 1975.03, 1975.24, 1976.25, 1979.05, 1979.10, 1981.03, 1982.05
Warner, Sherman 1982.04, 1988.05, 1991.05, 1995.05, 1998.11, 1998.13
Warnes, Marion 1942.26
Warnick, Buck 1941.13, 1942.15, 1942.27, 1943.07, 1943.14, 1943.20, 1943.22, 1944.01
Warnick, Clay 1944.18, 1945.08, 1946.06, 1946.20, 1947.14, 1948.15, 1948.23, 1949.02, 1950.09, 1950.12, 1959.26, 1961.14, 1962.27
Warnick, Frank 1914.16
Warnick, H. Clay 1945.18
Warnick, Steven 1989.09
Warning, Dennis 1979.26, 1983.19
Warnock Company 1907.39, 1908.03
Warnow, Mark 1943.21
Warrack, David 1989.17
Warre, Mr. 1855.08
Warren, Albert H. 1887.09
Warren, Alice Parks 1908.09
Warren, Arthur 1907.15
Warren, Barnett 1934.40
Warren, C.L. 1890.41, 1893.14, 1894.02
Warren, Charles 1897.34, 1903.29
Warren, Charles A. 1908.33
Warren, David 1997.09
Warren, Dollie 1885.42
Warren, E.A. 1892.59
Warren, Edith 1903.18
Warren, Elton 1957.14
Warren, Elton J. 1943.24, 1945.06, 1946.09
Warren, Fred 1885.62, 1886.07, 1886.17, 1886.29, 1886.31, 1886.38, 1890.13, 1890.22, 1890.38
Warren, George William 1955.13
Warren, Gloria 1943.21
Warren, Harry 1881.23, 1882.27, 1927.62, 1928.33, 1930.38, 1931.09, 1931.13, 1931.40, 1932.14, 1939.29, 1943.23, 1956.07, 1957.10, 1962.17, 1963.02, 1965.08, 1973.14, 1974.09, 1975.12, 1975.22, 1976.07, 1978.05, 1979.24, 1980.09, 1980.20, 1984.10, 1988.08, 1989.21, 1990.09, 1992.18, 1997.05, 1999.01, 1999.23, 1999.24, 2001.08
Warren, Helen 1924.17
Warren, Herbert 1932.14, 1936.07
Warren, Hetty 1860.04, 1860.05
Warren, J. 1907.54
Warren, Jack 1905.17, 1906.46, 1910.23, 1912.30, 1913.22
Warren, Jack C. 1908.26
Warren, Jeff 1950.10
Warren, Jennifer Leigh 1999.22
Warren, John 1911.20
Warren, Julie 1943.22, 1946.13
Warren, Katherine G. 1899.09
Warren, Kathleen 1895.27, 1903.22, 1904.40
Warren, Kathleen G. 1893.49
Warren, Kathlyn 1899.36
Warren, Lee 1957.06
Warren, Lesley (Ann) 1963.26, 1965.29
Warren, Lesley Ann 1997.05
Warren, Lloyd 1935.01
Warren, Lou 1927.19
Warren, Madge 1899.33
Warren, Margaret 1899.15, 1899.25, 1907.08
Warren, Marietta 1929.01
Warren, Marion 1885.53, 1886.44, 1886.51
Warren, Miss 1870.44, 1896.44
Warren, Odessa 1899.33, 1900.46
Warren, Paul 1922.04, 1954.08
Warren, Paul L. 1910.24
Warren, Renee 1982.03
Warren, Rose 1880.02
Warren, Ruth 1924.03
Warren, S.W. 1930.19, 1931.32
Warren, Sylvester 1893.23
Warren, Trixie 1916.08
Warren, Vincent 1972.08
Warren, William 1919.11
Warren-Gibson, David 1996.14
Warren-Wright, E.H. 1881.20
Warrick, Ruth 1973.05
Warriner, Frederic 1971.18
Warriner, Howard 1936.22, 1938.09
Warring, Robert 1899.41
Warrington, Ann 1896.40, 1918.06
Warrington, Jane 1912.38, 1913.21
Warsaw, Jane 1979.26
Warshavsky, M. 1990.16
Warshavsky, M.M. 1967.08
Warshaw, Mike 2001.08
Warshawsky, Mark M. 1998.11
Wartski, Sheila 1977.01
Warwick, Henry 1910.04, 1918.31, 1922.11
Warwick, Margaretta 1976.05
Warwick, Niobe 1919.33
Warwick, Robert 1911.06, 1911.32, 1912.32, 1912.47
Washburn, Blanche 1897.33
Washburn, Country 1942.16
Washburn, Elizabeth 1902.36
Washburn, Grace 1908.39, 1911.12, 1918.05
Washburn, I. 1897.05
Washburn, Imjogene 1896.11
Washburn, Imogene 1895.30, 1896.09
Washburn, Jack 1954.15, 1962.20
Washburn, Lillie 1902.26
Washburn, Lizzie 1895.30, 1896.09, 1897.05
Washburn, Minnie 1893.07
Washburn, Miss 1908.19
Washburn, Mrs. 1896.11
Washburn, Rene 1897.33
Washburne, Elizabeth 1901.02, 1904.02, 1905.38
Washburne, Lizzie 1899.01, 1900.10
Washington, Albert 1899.33
Washington, Benveneta 1935.01, 1940.01
Washington, Betty 1938.03
Washington, Claudette 1977.18
Washington, Ford L. 1930.34
Washington, Fredi 1931.32, 1933.04
Washington, Geneva 1936.30
Washington, George Dewey 1933.05
Washington, Howard 1930.10
Washington, Isabell 1929.25, 1931.32
Washington, King 1930.24
Washington, Lamont 1968.11
Washington, Leon 1976.35
Washington, Marie 1901.20
Washington, Mattie 1940.01
Washington, Melvin 1983.06
Washington, Ned 1928.23, 1930.35, 1933.20, 1933.27, 1991.04
Washington, tse-Mach 1994.02
Washington, Vernon 1976.04
Wasser, Alan 1998.10
Wasserlof, Rudolf 1984.03, 1984.05
Wasserman, Bertha 1898.34
Wasserman, Dale 1943.17, 1944.31, 1965.34, 1972.14, 1977.12, 1992.07
Wasserman, Herb 1953.08
Wasserman, Herbert 1993.10
Wassman, Lina 1875.12
Wasson, David 1977.12, 1992.07
Wasterous, Herbert L. 1935.09
Watanabe, Leslie 1976.02
Watanabe, Miyoko 1968.12
Watene, Leona 1972.20
Waterbury, Laura 1976.33, 1980.30, 1993.10
Waterbury, Prevost 1908.22
Waterbury, Rice 1908.22
Waterman, Dorothy 1927.49
Waterman, Ida 1912.03, 1914.12
Waterman, Willard 1966.10, 1973.15, 1983.10
Waterous, Allan 1933.17
Waterous, Allen 1926.24, 1931.25, 1932.02, 1933.08, 1933.09, 1933.10, 1933.11, 1933.14, 1933.18, 1933.19, 1934.07, 1934.08, 1934.09, 1934.10, 1934.11
Waterous, Herbert 1907.11, 1913.25, 1915.10, 1922.16, 1929.07, 1931.25
Waterous, Herbert L. 1915.06, 1915.09, 1915.12, 1915.13, 1915.14, 1931.10, 1931.18, 1931.20, 1931.45, 1933.08, 1933.09, 1933.18, 1933.19, 1934.07, 1934.08, 1934.09, 1934.10, 1934.11, 1935.05, 1935.06, 1935.07, 1935.10, 1936.04, 1936.08, 1936.09, 1936.10, 1936.11
Waterous, Jayne 1929.48, 1930.41
Waters, Belle 1896.35
Waters, Bernard 1985.13
Waters, C.P. 1908.43
Waters, D. 1875.18
Waters, Daryl 1996.07, 1997.21
Waters, E. 1887.49, 1888.37
Waters, Ethel 1927.32, 1930.34, 1933.22, 1935.12, 1940.17, 1943.13, 1953.12
Waters, Fred 1904.34
Waters, H.L. 1890.06
Waters, Hattie 1888.13, 1899.29, 1900.40, 1901.19, 1902.43, 1903.39
Waters, Ida 1886.38
Waters, James R. 1905.35
Waters, Jean 1908.43
Waters, Jimmie 1933.04
Waters, Jimmy 1942.03
Waters, Louis 1904.20
Waters, Lucy 1889.03, 1889.48, 1891.06
Waters, Marianne Brown 1938.01
Waters, Mr. 1875.03
Waters, Roger 1982.22
Waters, Safford 1902.34, 1902.40, 1908.03
Waters, Stafford 1898.47
Waters, Tom 1928.11
Wathall, Alfred G. 1902.44
Watkin, Fen 1971.21
Watkins, Amanda 1999.16
Watkins, Charles A. 1888.28
Watkins, Charles Howard 1867.31
Watkins, Frances 1942.33, 1945.02
Watkins, Gertie 1904.38
Watkins, Gordon 1965.03
Watkins, J. Kathleen 1999.01
Watkins, James 1904.38
Watkins, Lillie 1888.13
Watkins, Linda 1934.35
Watkins, Lyndsey 1997.04
Watkins, Maurine Dallas 1975.14, 1996.14
Watkins, Mrs. Charles Howard 1867.29
Watkins, Perry 1938.16, 1942.35, 1943.10, 1943.16, 1945.07, 1946.24
Watkins, Pierre 1932.14
Watkins, T. 1887.34
Watkins, William A. 1907.61
Watkinson, Mr. 1823.01
Watling, Dilys 1970.03
Watrous, Herbert 1929.38
Watson 1862.03, 1863.07
Watson, Albert 1902.04
Watson, Alfred 1926.28
Watson, Alice 1885.70
Watson, Betty Jane 1946.23, 1948.18, 1948.21, 1948.28, 1958.03, 1961.18
Watson, Bob 1899.23
Watson, Bobbie 1919.36
Watson, Bobby 1923.46, 1924.38, 1927.35, 1928.04, 1928.14, 1928.28
Watson, Charles 1894.32
Watson, Chester 1950.05, 1959.19
Watson, Claude 1942.20
Watson, Dorothy 1908.10
Watson, Douglas 1967.01, 1968.09
Watson, Douglass 1974.05
Watson, Edna 1972.13
Watson, Edward 1920.34
Watson, Emma 1945.14
Watson, Eric 1984.10
Watson, Ernie 1944.14
Watson, Fanny 1919.03
Watson, Fred 1919.08
Watson, George 1876.14, 1876.30
Watson, George P. 1906.13
Watson, Gick 1918.08
Watson, Gilbert 1913.05
Watson, Harry 1885.70, 1898.20, 1902.42, 1908.19, 1909.28, 1910.18, 1920.47
Watson, Harry B. 1897.15, 1907.03
Watson, Henry 1880.38, 1901.02, 1916.07
Watson, J. 1883.52
Watson, Janet 1985.06, 1987.03
Watson, Joe 1997.13
Watson, John 1872.26, 1875.05
Watson, Joseph 1988.05
Watson, Jr., Al 1922.45
Watson, Jr., Harry 1904.58, 1905.34, 1907.24, 1911.24, 1912.38, 1917.29, 1925.49
Watson, Kitty 1919.03
Watson, L. 1873.26
Watson, Laurence 1950.16, 1952.08, 1958.03, 1958.11, 1963.27
Watson, Lee 1957.10, 1958.04, 1958.11, 1958.12, 1959.07
Watson, Lenora 1906.49
Watson, Leo 1935.12
Watson, Lew 1903.13
Watson, Lotta 1899.28
Watson, Lottie 1888.33
Watson, Louisa 1879.63
Watson, Louise 1883.39, 1888.33
Watson, Lucille 1926.41
Watson, M.G. 1903.41
Watson, Martha Emma 1947.04
Watson, Master 1879.14
Watson, Messr. 1856.01, 1876.17, 1879.56, 1884.42, 1886.36, 1886.47
Watson, Milton 1928.38, 1929.44, 1931.26, 1933.05, 1934.20, 1939.22, 1941.07, 1942.27, 1946.12, 1951.22
Watson, Minor 1924.41
Watson, Miss 1870.23, 1880.69, 1883.23
Watson, Mlle. 1870.41
Watson, Monk 1922.03
Watson, Mons. 1879.50
Watson, Mrs. H.C. 1855.10
Watson, Oscar 1904.27
Watson, Peggy 1947.19
Watson, Ralph 1909.23
Watson, Richard 1947.22, 1948.01, 1948.02, 1948.03, 1948.07, 1948.09, 1951.01, 1951.03, 1951.06, 1951.07, 1951.09
Watson, Robert 1891.41, 1893.26, 1898.01
Watson, Rose 1886.16, 1889.21
Watson, Ruth-Ann 1926.01
Watson, S. 1886.14
Watson, Sam 1911.05
Watson, Susan 1960.06, 1964.33, 1965.24, 1965.38, 1966.11, 1966.30, 1969.02, 1971.03
Watson, Thomas F. 1898.06
Watson, Virginia 1928.45
Watson, W. 1903.26
Watson, Walter 1976.15
Watson, Whitford 1907.44
Watson, William 1929.33
Watt, Billie Lou 1947.08
Watt, Kathryn 1971.21
Watt, Michael 1999.04, 2000.18
Watt, P. Castor 1896.07
Watt, Robert 1913.03, 1914.05
Watt, Stan 1958.12, 1963.25
Watt/Edgar Dobie Productions LLC 2001.06
Wattell, Miss 1873.26
Watterson, Messr. 1882.34, 1883.31
Watts, A. 1890.02
Watts, Al 1933.06
Watts, Al F. 1907.55
Watts, Elizabeth 1949.08, 1959.11
Watts, George 1935.15, 1937.04, 1938.11
Watts, Irene 1935.01
Watts, James 1916.25, 1919.18, 1919.43, 1921.27, 1922.23, 1923.17, 1927.25
Watts, James A. 1916.23
Watts, Jonathan 1957.13, 1958.15, 1959.16, 1959.21
Watts, Mrs. 1840.02, 1840.03, 1840.04
Watts, Peggy 1924.40
Watts, Randall 1935.01
Watts, Twinkle 1942.19
Watts, Virginia 1928.49, 1930.21
Watts, W.E. 1941.01
Watts, Wendy 1999.11
Watts, William R. 1881.10
Wauke, Mill 1898.02
Waverly, Charles 1875.10
Wavitch, Messr. 1922.06
Waxemall, Mr. 1865.01
Waxman, A.P. 1944.27, 1946.06
Waxman, Anita 1999.09, 2000.08, 2000.11
Waxman, Jeff 1983.18, 1986.18
Waxman, Percy 1916.17, 1923.25, 1926.11
Way, William H. 1891.02, 1894.16
Wayburn, Agnes 1900.51, 1901.19, 1902.05, 1902.10
Wayburn, Agnes Saye 1899.11
Wayburn, Ned 1897.45, 1898.69, 1899.11, 1900.52, 1901.04, 1901.22, 1902.06, 1902.10, 1902.43, 1903.04, 1903.18, 1903.23, 1903.39, 1904.22, 1904.31, 1904.47, 1904.56, 1905.22, 1905.25, 1905.28, 1905.30, 1905.41, 1905.48, 1906.24, 1907.25, 1908.13, 1908.21, 1908.28, 1908.29, 1908.44, 1909.04, 1909.11, 1909.23, 1909.24, 1909.30, 1909.31, 1910.01, 1910.04, 1910.08, 1910.13, 1910.16, 1911.05, 1911.26, 1911.35, 1911.40, 1911.45, 1912.24, 1912.43, 1912.45, 1913.05, 1913.18, 1914.34, 1915.22, 1916.10, 1917.13, 1917.26, 1918.18, 1918.19, 1919.15, 1920.04, 1920.10, 1920.25, 1920.39, 1921.10, 1922.19, 1923.01, 1923.20, 1923.38, 1926.18, 1929.04, 1930.39
Wayburn, New 1906.28

Wayland, Alice 1906.24
Wayland, Mickey 1962.02
Wayland, Tony 1905.12
Waylors, The 1979.16
Waymon, Sam 1975.02
Wayne, Beatrice Robinson 1934.05
Wayne, Bernie 1955.12
Wayne, Blanche 1907.47
Wayne, Charles 1888.29, 1891.09, 1896.30, 1898.61, 1902.21, 1904.09, 1919.04
Wayne, David 1943.09, 1946.20, 1947.03, 1958.08, 1965.36, 1966.14, 1968.01
Wayne, Edythe 1974.11
Wayne, Ethel 1908.28
Wayne, Fay 1921.20
Wayne, Frank 1915.17
Wayne, Fred 1904.14, 1949.17
Wayne, George 1942.18
Wayne, Iris 1939.31, 1940.10
Wayne, Louise 1922.05
Wayne, Marjorie 1922.11
Wayne, Paula 1957.01, 1958.05, 1959.03, 1964.32
Wayne, Rollo 1922.34, 1922.40, 1923.02, 1923.25, 1924.25, 1924.36, 1925.13, 1926.08, 1926.37, 1927.24, 1928.26, 1929.48, 1930.03, 1930.07, 1930.12, 1930.41
Wayne, Shirley 1938.08
Wayne, Sid 1957.01, 1961.07, 1973.17
Wayne, William 1924.03
Wayrauch, H. 1864.23, 1865.02, 1865.04
Wearer, Raymond 1955.07
Weatherford, Earl 1937.01, 1938.18
Weatherley, Frederick E. 1919.26, 1964.28
Weatherley, Tom 1930.25
Weatherly, Fred E. 1915.25
Weatherly, James D. 1997.21
Weatherly, Jim 1998.14
Weatherly, Michael M. 1989.07
Weatherly, Tom 1929.19, 1931.14, 1932.26, 1936.01
Weathers, Patrick 1982.22
Weathersbee, Jennie 1922.41
Weathersby, Eliza 1870.13, 1870.19, 1870.36, 1870.42, 1872.21, 1872.22, 1872.24, 1872.26, 1872.34, 1876.16, 1877.21, 1879.53
Weathersby, Eme 1882.51
Weathersby, Emie 1882.42, 1883.04
Weathersby, Helen 1889.48, 1890.06, 1906.05, 1907.02
Weathersby, Jennie 1870.21, 1876.16, 1879.53, 1881.08, 1883.06, 1886.30, 1886.45, 1886.59, 1888.20, 1892.07, 1892.29, 1893.35, 1895.04, 1895.39, 1896.10, 1897.24, 1898.36, 1899.24, 1903.32, 1921.01
Weatherspoon, David 1984.09
Weatherspoon, John 1873.28, 1877.15, 1881.04
Weaver, Alice 1922.15, 1924.19, 1925.22
Weaver, Beverly 1940.21
Weaver, Blanche 1879.50, 1879.56, 1880.04, 1890.40, 1893.38, 1894.09
Weaver, Carl 1975.01
Weaver, Carl E. 1982.22
Weaver, Danyelle 1989.20
Weaver, Doodles 1940.21
Weaver, Fritz 1962.04, 1965.02, 1968.17
Weaver, H. 1866.18
Weaver, H.A. 1877.07, 1877.28, 1894.39
Weaver, Hamilton 1878.14, 1879.63, 1880.37, 1881.18, 1881.41
Weaver, Henry A. 1876.12
Weaver, Jim 1999.22
Weaver, Jr., H.A. 1885.49
Weaver, Jr., Henry 1885.66
Weaver, M. Jane 1976.28, 1983.04
Weaver, Mr. 1866.18
Weaver, Ned 1924.15
Weaver, Ray 1956.05, 1957.06
Weaver, William 1920.47, 1921.02, 1921.03, 1924.05, 1924.07, 1924.24, 1924.42, 1925.12, 1929.04, 1936.06, 1937.03
Webb, Alan 1936.29
Webb, Alyce 1958.11
Webb, Alyce Elizabeth 1961.09, 1961.13, 1962.07, 1964.19, 1965.03, 1965.18, 1972.06
Webb, Amy 1909.13
Webb, Austin 1915.20
Webb, Barbara 1960.10, 1961.13, 1962.07, 1967.02, 1968.05, 1968.08
Webb, Chick 1976.04, 1986.02, 1989.02, 1999.24
Webb, Clifton 1913.10, 1914.22, 1915.22, 1916.06, 1917.02, 1918.39, 1920.03, 1923.07, 1925.33, 1928.02, 1928.43, 1929.19, 1930.32, 1932.17, 1933.22, 1938.07
Webb, Dora 1890.44, 1897.48, 1899.36
Webb, Dorothy 1911.37, 1912.35, 1913.02, 1913.20, 1915.08, 1917.04
Webb, Edward 1889.01, 1889.44, 1891.21, 1892.11
Webb, Edward E. 1887.15
Webb, F. 1893.41
Webb, Frank 1884.04, 1884.07
Webb, Hawley 1893.11
Webb, Hazel 1920.24
Webb, Janet 1940.11, 1940.15
Webb, Janette 1903.30
Webb, Jimmy 2000.16
Webb, Kenneth 1924.33, 1928.49, 1930.23, 1932.26, 1935.04, 1936.01
Webb, Lyda 1923.39
Webb, M. Tello 1913.03
Webb, Messr. 1886.36
Webb, Mildred 1936.31
Webb, Mr. 1866.18
Webb, Nella 1898.68, 1899.25, 1900.34, 1901.01, 1902.06, 1902.19, 1903.31, 1905.23
Webb, R.G. 1963.24
Webb, Richard 1934.37, 1937.09
Webb, Robert 1982.14
Webb, Roy 1913.19, 1922.39, 1924.26, 1924.33, 1926.13, 1926.50, 1927.37, 1927.56, 1928.16, 1928.30, 1929.07, 1932.10
Webb, Ruth 1943.07, 1945.12
Webb, Teddy 1907.26, 1911.06, 1912.49, 1913.28, 1914.07, 1915.17, 1917.10, 1921.20, 1922.15, 1923.14
Webb, W. 1886.36
Webbe, Frank 1889.20, 1892.12
Webbe, Frank J. 1894.32
Webber, Andrew Lloyd 1971.12, 1977.18, 1979.23, 1982.03, 1982.19, 1984.15, 1985.12, 1987.05, 1988.01, 1990.04, 1991.10, 1993.15, 1994.10, 1995.02, 1995.12, 1997.01, 2000.09
Webber, Carrie 1903.09, 1907.40, 1908.12
Webber, Florence 1920.25, 1924.02
Webber, Frank 1887.46
Webber, Gene 1938.02
Webber, Thomas 1887.40
Weber 1862.09
Weber and Rush 1905.07
Weber, Annie 1894.21
Weber, Carl 1942.17
Weber, Edward 1893.38
Weber, Edwin J. 1922.34
Weber, Elise 1868.32
Weber, Elyse 1949.17
Weber, Florence 1929.26
Weber, Harry 1913.07
Weber, Herbert 1930.42, 1932.06, 1934.13
Weber, J.L. 1900.43
Weber, Jeffrey 1994.09
Weber, Joe 1901.17, 1906.01, 1906.48, 1907.44, 1908.01, 1908.38, 1912.07, 1912.44, 1919.34
Weber, Joseph 1896.26, 1897.09, 1897.19, 1899.17, 1904.04, 1905.14, 1907.38, 1910.26, 1912.44, 1914.27, 1917.07, 1917.28, 1920.31
Weber, Joseph A. 1892.18
Weber, Joseph M. 1896.36, 1897.31, 1897.48, 1898.50, 1899.30, 1900.38, 1902.29, 1903.28, 1904.39
Weber, L. Lawrence 1917.09, 1923.24, 1924.04, 1925.16, 1927.05, 1927.55
Weber, Laurence 1950.11
Weber, Lawrence 1948.27, 1953.01
Weber, Lisa 1868.23, 1869.06, 1869.45, 1870.02, 1870.06, 1872.25, 1872.36
Weber, Liza 1872.30, 1872.32, 1872.36, 1872.38, 1872.40, 1872.43
Weber, May 1897.10
Weber, Patricia 1985.01
Weber, Rex 1932.20, 1933.07, 1933.21
Weber, Rod 1999.08
Weber, Shirley 1946.14
Weber, Steve 1970.04
Weber, Thomas 1886.52
Webley, John 1968.28, 1978.17
Webner, Arthur 1912.49
Webster, Al 1933.20, 1940.20
Webster, Almaretta 1907.36
Webster, B. 1871.10
Webster, Byron 1964.20, 1964.33, 1965.31, 1967.02, 1968.17
Webster, C.R. 1886.44, 1890.06
Webster, Charles 1877.08
Webster, Charles R. 1896.14
Webster, Frank 1921.29, 1923.18
Webster, H.T. 1923.25
Webster, Harold 1933.16, 1934.03
Webster, Harry 1899.04
Webster, Harry R. 1907.43, 1908.32, 1920.43
Webster, J. 1871.08
Webster, J.P. 1975.22
Webster, Jack 1906.21, 1907.20
Webster, John 1875.16, 1879.32, 1880.11, 1881.01, 1882.24, 1883.33, 1883.68, 1885.10, 1886.05, 1887.08, 1887.34, 1891.44, 1894.43, 1895.36, 1896.47, 1924.01
Webster, Katherine 1885.44
Webster, Laura 1889.48, 1891.06
Webster, Lizzie 1877.21, 1878.02, 1879.01, 1879.06
Webster, Margaret 1946.07
Webster, Paul Francis 1931.26, 1933.20, 1950.02, 1955.12, 1960.10, 1976.04, 1979.24, 1980.10, 1981.06, 1982.22, 1997.03, 1999.24
Webster, Revre 1975.22
Webster, W.R. 1885.53
Webster, Whitney 1996.15, 1997.22, 1999.21, 2000.19
Webster, Will P. 1888.30
Weckerlin 1925.03
Weddell, Ina 1884.34, 1889.04
Weddell, Miss 1892.07
Weddle, Ida 1882.75
Weddle, Miss 1882.60, 1883.38
Wedemeyer, Otto 1904.51, 1904.57, 1905.08, 1905.11
Wedge, Maura K. 1961.08, 1962.16, 1963.01, 1965.23
Wedgewood, Billie 1920.43
Wedlake, Charles 1909.02
Wedow, Gary 1997.02
Weeber, H.A. 1889.51
Weed, Mr. 1865.01, 1869.31
Weed, R.L. 1867.12, 1872.07, 1873.20, 1873.22, 1873.27, 1875.37, 1875.40, 1876.01, 1876.19, 1877.24, 1878.01, 1878.13
Weed, R.M. 1875.31
Weede, Robert 1956.04, 1961.20, 1970.10
Weeden, Bill 1968.08, 1972.19
Weeden, Edna 1880.21
Weeden, Robert 1976.15
Weedon, Edna 1882.82, 1886.13
Weedon, William C. 1904.37, 1907.06, 1907.48
Weeks, Ada 1915.28, 1916.19
Weeks, Ada Mae 1918.39, 1920.35, 1921.32, 1924.02
Weeks, Adeline 1900.08
Weeks, Al 1920.45
Weeks, Alan 1958.01, 1964.11, 1967.06, 1968.07, 1969.01, 1972.05, 1976.03, 1978.28, 1981.25, 1983.21, 1986.06, 1992.06
Weeks, Barbara 1927.18
Weeks, C.F. 1889.16
Weeks, C.L. 1885.41, 1885.63, 1886.30, 1887.33, 1887.50
Weeks, Fred 1926.21
Weeks, George S. 1879.65, 1879.67
Weeks, Larry 1942.20
Weeks, Mabel 1907.15, 1909.04, 1910.03, 1910.16, 1910.36
Weeks, Marion 1931.03
Weeks, T. 1873.26
Weeks, Todd 2000.15
Weels, C.L. 1884.64
Weems, Andrew 2000.10
Weems, Hattie 1888.21
Weer, James L. 1890.40
Wegman, Dorothy 1927.08
Wehi, Muriel 1972.20
Wehi, Ngapo 1972.20
Wehlen, Emmy 1911.01, 1912.13
Wehrle, Helen 1925.22, 1926.22, 1926.37
Weich and Aarons 1912.05
Weiderhold, J. 1852.05
Weiderhold, Mesdame 1852.05
Weidermann, John 1953.16
Weidhaas, G.A. 1924.19, 1928.22, 1929.35
Weidhaas, Ted 1928.31, 1929.29, 1934.42
Weidhaas, Wynn 1929.29
Weidhaus, Gustave 1925.22, 1926.16
Weidhaus, Ted 1929.04
Weidlin, Jane 1982.22
Weidman, Charlene 1881.15
Weidman, Charles 1932.20, 1933.12, 1933.22, 1933.24, 1934.19, 1937.13, 1942.34, 1944.01, 1944.17, 1944.32, 1946.22, 1950.16, 1958.04
Weidman, Charline 1884.62
Weidman, Jerome 1959.25, 1960.19, 1962.05, 1962.16, 1966.05
Weidman, John 1976.02, 1987.15, 1996.08, 2000.07, 2000.16
Weigall, Arthur 1923.35, 1925.42, 1952.11
Weigel, Hans 1939.23
Weigert, Rene 1957.01, 1966.30
Weigold, Frieda 1907.32
Weigund, Cora 1887.43
Weil, Charles W. 1911.33
Weil, Cynthia 1978.05, 1984.15
Weil, David 1982.02, 1998.17
Weil, Jean D. 1991.11
Weil, Oscar 1890.37, 1896.42
Weil, Raymonde 1971.19
Weil, Robert 1942.34, 1959.26, 1977.08
Weil, Tim 1996.09
Weil, Trude 1940.04
Weil, Zelie 1878.18
Weilandich, G. Russell 1980.02
Weilby, Jake 1902.20
Weiley, Max 1917.04
Weill, Irving 1925.07
Weill, Kurt 1933.07, 1936.28, 1937.01, 1938.11, 1941.04, 1943.03, 1943.19, 1945.04, 1946.17, 1947.02, 1948.25, 1949.15, 1958.11, 1959.08, 1959.17, 1962.17, 1963.10, 1963.15, 1965.04, 1966.02, 1966.19, 1971.06, 1972.06, 1976.10, 1977.08, 1978.23, 1979.27, 1980.04, 1989.24, 1990.08, 1995.12
Weill, Ralph A. 1890.39
Weily, Max 1922.01
Weilzenboeck, Frl. 1883.08
Weimar, Lorraine 1925.27, 1926.37, 1928.27, 1932.01
Weimars, Angie 1910.20, 1911.05
Weimers, Angie 1906.41, 1907.24, 1909.09, 1912.39
Wein, George 1980.10
Wein, Vereinigte Buehnen 1991.11
Wein, Violet 1898.02
Weinacht, Herr 1879.62
Weinberg, Arthur 1914.06
Weinberg, Charles 1926.22, 1932.12
Weinberg, Gus 1905.56, 1925.10, 1925.24, 1929.04
Weinberg, Gus C. 1898.02, 1907.14
Weinberg, Herman G. 1964.02
Weinburg, Gus 1907.03
Weinburg, Gus C. 1901.16
Weinehenk, Camille 1882.62, 1886.41
Weiner, France 1983.17
Weiner, Freisinger J. 1913.01
Weiner, II, Fraulein 1880.66
Weiner, Jack 1911.44
Weiner, Robert 1963.19, 1964.05, 1968.23, 1970.02
Weingarten, G. 1879.14
Weinholtz, Mr. 1890.31
Weinkranz, David 1971.14
Weinlich, Joseph 1866.21
Weinrib, Len 1959.14
Weinschenk, Camille 1875.21
Weinstein, Arnold 1971.08
Weinstein, Bob 2001.05
Weinstein, Harvey 2001.05
Weinstock, Jack 1950.09, 1961.22, 1963.13, 1966.07, 1995.05
Weintraub Entertainment Group, Inc. 1987.05
Weintraub, Jerry 1969.04
Weir, Caroline 1909.20, 1910.23
Weir, Charlotte 1907.54
Weir, Elta 1905.25
Weir, Ethel 1911.32
Weir, Michal 1980.12
Weis, Casper 1902.14
Weis, John J. 1922.01
Weis, Martha 1902.33, 1904.20, 1905.10
Weise, Jeanette 1945.02
Weise, Norman 1950.04, 1951.24, 1953.11
Weiser, Al 1941.11
Weisfisch, Shlomo 1967.08

Weisgal, Meyer W. 1937.01
Weiskopf, Walt 1999.01
Weisl, Cynthia 1995.03
Weisman, Ben 1989.12
Weisman, Eliot 1991.04
Weisman, George 1901.04
Weisner, J. 1895.31
Weisner, J.E. 1887.15
Weiss, Fraulein 1879.62
Weiss, George 1956.02, 1959.06, 1979.30, 1989.12, 1989.21
Weiss, George David 1968.24
Weiss, Gordon J. 1975.06, 1978.22, 1986.16
Weiss, Gordon Joseph 1989.10, 1992.08, 1997.08
Weiss, Howard 1999.25
Weiss, James 1962.24
Weiss, Jeff 1994.02
Weiss, Jim 1961.28
Weiss, Joe 1930.21
Weiss, Julie 1981.04, 1991.04
Weiss, Larry 1976.34
Weiss, Marc B. 1974.04, 1974.10, 1974.19, 1981.02, 1981.28, 1982.13, 1983.07, 1983.14, 1984.01, 1984.15, 1986.02, 1986.16, 1987.16, 1992.12
Weiss, Peter 1965.39, 1967.01
Weiss, Peter Howard 1949.02
Weiss, Sid 1944.29
Weiss, Stephen 1938.08
Weissberg, Eric 1966.30
Weisse, Fritz 1910.24
Weisselman, Doug 1994.11
Weissler, Barry 1982.17, 1983.14, 1984.15, 1987.16, 1989.27, 1990.18, 1991.06, 1992.09, 1993.18, 1994.07, 1996.14, 1996.17, 1999.04, 2000.18
Weissler, Fran 1982.17, 1983.14, 1984.15, 1987.16, 1989.27, 1990.18, 1991.06, 1992.09, 1993.18, 1994.07, 1996.14, 1996.17, 1999.04, 2000.18
Weissman, Bernard 1942.35
Weissman, Mitch 1977.10
Weissman, Polaire 1922.20, 1925.20, 1927.23
Weissmuller, Don 1942.27, 1943.05, 1943.21, 1944.33, 1955.27, 1956.16
Weist, Dwight 1969.14
Weith, Leo 1940.04
Weitz, Eric 1978.06
Weitz, Millie 1937.14
Weitzenhoffer, Max 1982.04, 1991.07
Weixelbaum, Karl 1903.01, 1905.05, 1909.26, 1911.33
Weizenbock, Frl. 1883.08
Welch, Ben 1899.13, 1904.23, 1920.42
Welch, Beverley Jane 1959.06
Welch, Bruce 1990.15
Welch, Charles 1943.15, 1944.03, 1945.08, 1946.08, 1961.14, 1964.32, 1968.02, 1969.05, 1971.05, 1975.03
Welch, Eddie 1929.04, 1929.26, 1930.22, 1931.26
Welch, Edgar 1927.43, 1928.03
Welch, Elisabeth 1980.10, 1986.01
Welch, Ena 1905.53, 1907.39, 1908.17
Welch, Harry 1893.30, 1927.02
Welch, Harry M. 1893.30
Welch, Helen 1895.21, 1897.15
Welch, Joe 1908.33
Welch, John 1899.21, 1987.03
Welch, John M. 1918.15
Welch, Joseph 1901.25
Welch, Ken 1976.32, 1989.08, 1991.10
Welch, Loren 1947.08, 1948.08
Welch, Marie 1900.43, 1902.12
Welch, Mary 1902.30
Welch, Melba 1947.12
Welch, Mitzie 1963.20, 1976.32, 1989.08, 1991.10
Welch, Nelson 1928.42, 1932.28
Welch, Patricia 1985.01
Welch, Patrick 1954.12
Welch, Raquel 1981.10
Welch, Thomas 1886.39
Welch, William J. 1900.28
Welcher, Lynn 1899.19
Welchman, Harry 1925.39
Weld 1931.40
Weld, Arthur 1900.35, 1900.51, 1901.08, 1901.23, 1902.35, 1903.14, 1904.03, 1905.18, 1905.55, 1906.49, 1907.11, 1908.06, 1911.11, 1911.14, 1911.44, 1913.21
Weld, Gordon 1931.38
Welden, Ben 1925.37
Welderhoff, Frank 1902.17
Weldon, Bunny 1927.39, 1930.21
Weldon, Charles 1888.39, 1969.15
Weldon, Grace 1892.33
Weldon, Homie 1888.39, 1890.03
Weldon, Jerry 1990.19
Weldon, Joan 1964.24
Weldon, Kevin 1988.20
Weldon, M. Francis 1923.13, 1923.25, 1923.41, 1924.13
Weldon, Mortimer 1903.12, 1909.28, 1912.04
Weldon, Mortimer H. 1908.07, 1916.17
Weldon, Thomas 1925.11
Weldy of Paris 1924.45, 1926.37, 1931.03
Weldy, Max 1917.26, 1922.05, 1926.14, 1926.15, 1928.33, 1929.35
Weldy, Paris 1926.33, 1929.10, 1929.11, 1929.13, 1929.14, 1929.15, 1929.16
Welford, Christine 1920.17, 1921.22
Welford, Dallas 1912.35, 1913.21, 1915.20, 1922.02, 1923.15, 1923.45
Welford, Darry 1920.17, 1921.22
Welford, Nancy 1922.33, 1923.10, 1927.15, 1928.08
Welisch, Ernest 1913.23
Welisch, Ernst 1922.36, 1924.39, 1926.26
Welk, Lawrence 1980.29
Welkum, Master 1876.03
Well, Kurt 1980.25
Wellekens, Jack 1912.14
Weller, Caroll 1925.21
Weller, Carrie 1932.22
Weller, Marion 1891.43
Weller, Ted 1920.43, 1924.30
Welles, Cheri 1968.24
Welles, Marion 1891.36, 1892.60
Welles, Orson 1937.08, 1946.13
Wellesley, Arthur 1913.36
Wellesley, Charles 1908.16, 1912.06
Welling, A. 1873.26
Welling, Albert 1876.05
Welling, C. 1873.26
Welling, Messr. 1881.04
Welling, William 1873.26
Wellington, Amanda 1904.02
Wellington, Emelie 1905.18
Wellington, Emilie 1903.15, 1907.49
Wellington, Emily 1907.06
Wellington, Estelle 1897.38
Wellington, Eugene 1885.06, 1896.38
Wellington, Miss 1892.52
Wellington, Virginia 1884.22, 1884.25
Wellington, Warwick 1908.25
Wellman, Alice 1930.01
Wellman, Edward 1946.03, 1952.15
Wells Florence 1867.32
Wells Mr. 1866.18
Wells, Amy 1884.22
Wells, Bee 1928.39
Wells, Ben 1917.21, 1929.31
Wells, Bernard 1920.30
Wells, Billy K. 1931.30, 1936.12, 1950.12, 1953.17
Wells, Bob 1976.07
Wells, Bonnie 1888.36
Wells, Brownie 1890.12, 1893.13, 1896.05
Wells, Carolyn 1908.03, 1911.44, 1914.09
Wells, Christopher 1985.02, 1987.19
Wells, Cynthia 1975.24
Wells, Dale 1940.02
Wells, Deanna 1987.03
Wells, Deanna D. 1986.20
Wells, Donald 1928.21
Wells, Dorothy 1907.12
Wells, Eleanor 1941.07
Wells, Emma 1892.15
Wells, Estella 1898.44
Wells, Florence 1897.37
Wells, Fred 1993.16
Wells, G. 1872.10
Wells, George A. 1859.09, 1859.12, 1859.13, 1859.15, 1859.16, 1859.17, 1859.18
Wells, Gil 1924.43
Wells, Gilbert 1915.26, 1917.05, 1918.33, 1924.13, 1926.23
Wells, Grace 1927.06
Wells, H.G. 1965.14
Wells, Hattie 1893.37, 1896.02
Wells, Joe 1912.17
Wells, John 1923.31, 1926.16, 1929.37, 1931.31
Wells, Kitty 1898.75
Wells, Lawrence 1924.45
Wells, M. 1856.01
Wells, Mack 1923.04
Wells, Madge 1971.13
Wells, Marie 1920.09, 1921.29
Wells, Marion 1888.36, 1893.07
Wells, Mary 1865.06, 1866.18, 1868.03, 1868.32, 1871.13, 1871.20, 1871.21, 1872.27, 1876.23
Wells, Miss 1869.43, 1883.31
Wells, Nellie 1900.46, 1901.20
Wells, Niles 1938.19
Wells, Patricia 1981.22
Wells, Peavey 1925.21
Wells, Robert 1955.03, 1998.19
Wells, Rosalie 1897.46
Wells, Ruth 1919.40
Wells, S. 1872.10
Wells, Sadie 1885.41, 1887.26
Wells, Stephen 1988.07
Wells, Tom 1952.07
Wells, Tony 1973.03
Wells, William 1943.05
Wells, William K. 1922.32, 1923.18, 1923.31, 1924.19, 1924.32, 1925.22, 1925.47, 1926.16, 1927.46, 1927.62, 1928.22, 1929.35, 1932.24, 1934.39, 1935.18, 1939.25, 1941.07
Welly, Max 1911.43
Welp, William 1912.40
Welsh, Elizabeth 1923.39, 1924.27, 1928.18
Welsh, Ena 1896.01
Welsh, Harry 1929.06, 1929.28, 1930.20, 1930.43
Welsh, John 1906.06
Welsh, Joseph 1900.51, 1905.56
Welsh, Joseph S. 1900.59
Welsh, Kenneth 1981.04
Welsh, Marie 1905.16, 1906.16, 1907.17
Welsh, Mary 1903.31
Welsh, Maude 1903.34
Welsh, Mr. 1865.05, 1909.13
Welsh, Scott 1909.26, 1912.34, 1917.07, 1919.09, 1920.36, 1922.16, 1925.15
Welsh-Homer, Charles 1918.29
Welsley, Arthur 1914.01
Welting, Patricia 1964.30, 1965.10, 1965.11
Welting, Ruth 1974.16
Welton, William 1945.07
Welty, Barbara 1921.41
Welty, Eudora 1975.18, 1976.30
Welty, George M. 1895.14
Welzer, Irving 1992.06, 1999.04
Wemis, Angy 1903.15
Wemitt, Monica M. 1995.13
Wen, Lily Havala 2000.19
Wences, Senor 1942.16, 1963.10
Wencker, Leigh-Anne 1997.07
Wendel, Beth 1934.06
Wendel, Elmaire 1958.05
Wendel, Elmarie 1957.05, 1957.14
Wendell, Beth 1931.26
Wendell, Bunny 1916.20, 1917.22, 1920.04
Wendell, Grace 1910.34
Wendell, Howard 1951.13
Wendell, Lynn 1965.18
Wendling, Pete 1916.03, 1921.34
Wendt, Angela 1996.09
Wendt, William 1965.18, 1965.20
Wendy, Max 1927.46
Wenerholm, Wana 1942.15
Wengell, Leopold 1893.21
Wenger, John 1922.27, 1924.18, 1924.35, 1925.10, 1925.15, 1925.49, 1926.18, 1926.36, 1927.04, 1927.59, 1928.01, 1928.17, 1928.25, 1928.35, 1929.12, 1933.01
Wenig, Mr. 1890.31, 1894.01
Wenman, Henry 1911.09
Wenrich, Percy 1914.08, 1915.20, 1918.18, 1918.23, 1921.07, 1921.27, 1922.16, 1922.21, 1926.24, 1930.23, 1964.28
Wenslee, Messr. 1854.04
Went, Mr. 1823.01
Wentworth, Bee 1909.08
Wentworth, Edward S. 1895.21, 1897.02, 1897.37
Wentworth, Estelle 1902.03, 1902.31, 1904.05, 1905.36, 1907.07, 1908.14, 1909.08
Wentworth, Fannie 1880.43, 1880.49, 1882.41, 1882.43
Wentworth, Fanny 1881.14, 1882.25, 1882.32, 1882.37, 1882.38, 1882.46, 1882.59, 1882.72, 1885.29, 1890.33
Wentworth, Frank 1911.30
Wentworth, Lura 1909.14
Wentworth, Maude 1884.12
Wentworth, Miss 1886.32
Wentworth, Philip 1956.03, 1956.05
Wentworth, Richard 1942.33, 1946.22, 1953.06, 1953.15, 1954.10, 1954.14, 1955.17, 1956.10, 1957.13, 1957.15, 1963.15, 1965.25, 1968.12
Wentworth, Scott 1989.07, 1992.11
Wentworth, W. 1888.42
Wentz, Charles 1903.18, 1904.21
Wentz, Henry W. 1889.51
Wentzel, Andrew 1992.14
Wenzel, Helen 1943.21, 1948.15
Wenzel, Rose 1927.27
Wenzelberg, L. 1917.21
Werau, A. 1921.14
Werba, Louis F. 1910.29, 1910.37, 1911.13, 1912.15, 1913.27, 1923.16, 1926.39
Werbeck, Henry 1939.23
Werber, Louis A. 1913.24
Werfel, Franz 1937.01, 1979.02
Werking, Jon 1999.01
Werner, Edward 1884.48
Werner, Fred 1946.02, 1961.02, 1961.18, 1962.27, 1964.16, 1966.01, 1968.19, 1986.07
Werner, Frl. 1879.22
Werner, George J. 1901.26
Werner, Gustave 1914.04
Werner, Lori 1996.06
Werner, Mary 1929.29
Werner, Miss 1892.43
Werner, Mr. 1897.35
Wernher, Hilda 1960.10
Wernig, Charles F. 1882.52
Werrenrath, Reinald 1932.22
Werris, Sam E. 1941.03
Wersinger, Robert 2000.07
Werth, Anna 1934.13
Wertheim Studios 1930.24
Wertheim, Lou 1929.18
Wertimer, Ned 1949.17
Wertz, Rose 1914.15
Weschler, Anita 1933.12
Weschler, Walter 1974.05
Wesley, J.W. 1869.14, 1869.20
Wesley, Jack 1923.02
Wesley, John W. 1869.27
Wesley, Louis 1895.17, 1898.20, 1898.43, 1899.19, 1900.20, 1901.18, 1902.23, 1904.04, 1904.24, 1905.55
Wesley, May 1911.22
Wesley, Ward 1915.15
Weslow, William 1953.03, 1955.01
Weslyn, Louis 1903.03, 1912.06, 1913.03, 1920.24
Wesner, Ella 1875.31, 1875.35, 1875.36, 1885.39, 1885.54, 1886.31, 1886.38, 1886.53
Wesner, Miss 1869.43
Wessell, Vivian 1914.27, 1917.02
Wessells, G.W. 1877.08
Wessells, George W. 1897.23
Wessler, Dick 1963.10
Wessler, Karen 1963.10
Wesson, Eugene 1942.25
Wesson, Gene 1956.16
Wesson, Richard 1942.25
West, Al 1942.03
West, Albert 1921.41
West, Alvy 1963.11
West, Andrew 1903.09
West, Arthur 1921.17, 1923.38, 1924.07, 1925.29
West, Bernard 1942.34
West, Bernie 1956.14, 1962.04
West, Billy 1879.04
West, Blanche 1901.09, 1908.39, 1910.34, 1911.45, 1912.42
West, Bob 1982.22
West, Bonnie 1957.17
West, Britt 1990.20
West, Buster 1923.31, 1926.16, 1928.35, 1936.22, 1944.14
West, C. 1872.10
West, Charles 1999.13

West, Cheryl L. 1997.03
West, Clarence 1886.12, 1899.42, 1900.02, 1900.04, 1900.06, 1900.09, 1900.11, 1900.13, 1900.14, 1900.17, 1900.18, 1900.21, 1900.22, 1900.23, 1900.26, 1900.27, 1900.29, 1900.30, 1905.49, 1906.32, 1912.41, 1915.06, 1915.09, 1915.10, 1915.12, 1915.13, 1915.14, 1916.06, 1916.08
West, Edd 1900.33
West, Edna 1934.04
West, Elizabeth 1914.24
West, Emma 1902.33
West, Eugene 1919.16, 1979.25
West, Eva 1876.02
West, Evangeline 1892.29
West, Everett 1936.02, 1938.10, 1942.22, 1942.31
West, Fay 1920.10, 1924.24
West, Florrie 1891.09
West, Freddie 1903.09
West, Gordon 1946.13
West, H.J. 1896.28
West, Harold 1917.22, 1923.40
West, Harry 1875.05, 1892.04, 1907.27
West, Irving 1936.02
West, J. Clarence 1888.43, 1889.31
West, Jessie 1882.50, 1883.32
West, John 1888.45, 1891.16, 1903.09, 1928.35, 1995.12
West, Joseph 1906.41
West, Judy 1963.14
West, Julia 1905.07
West, Kathleen 1955.21
West, Kirwin 1893.43
West, L.H. 1866.22
West, Laura 1869.27
West, Lettie 1900.08, 1902.02
West, Lillie 1881.21, 1881.33
West, Lizzie 1870.32, 1870.35, 1870.42, 1871.02
West, Lucretia 1953.05, 1953.14
West, Lydia 1901.18
West, Mae 1911.26, 1912.13, 1918.30, 1921.25
West, Marc 1961.21
West, Marie 1903.22
West, Matt 1994.04, 1999.16
West, Messr. 1794.01, 1875.06, 1882.34, 1885.58, 1904.13
West, Miss 1852.01, 1857.02, 1870.02, 1870.22, 1908.19
West, Moritz 1880.66, 1881.04, 1884.64, 1887.15, 1887.28, 1891.30, 1898.62
West, Mr. 1866.18, 1899.17
West, Mrs. J.P. 1905.27
West, Olive 1925.37
West, Paul 1897.30, 1897.40, 1897.56, 1900.59, 1902.07, 1902.15, 1902.19, 1902.40, 1903.03, 1903.34, 1904.18, 1904.29, 1904.43, 1904.44, 1905.05, 1905.19, 1905.20, 1905.25, 1906.32, 1906.37, 1907.10, 1907.18, 1907.24, 1907.41, 1907.42, 1908.03, 1908.07, 1908.10, 1908.15, 1909.05, 1912.16, 1912.41, 1965.05
West, Rebecca 1985.01
West, Solon 1935.08
West, Sonny 1990.15
West, W. 1897.31, 1898.50
West, W.H. 1882.34
West, Walter 1899.30
West, Will 1893.26, 1899.11, 1900.08, 1906.25, 1907.63, 1908.21, 1909.21, 1911.27, 1913.20, 1914.30, 1915.15, 1921.33
West, William 1875.39, 1879.37, 1879.68, 1880.09, 1880.36, 1880.64, 1881.09, 1881.29, 1882.02, 1882.50, 1882.74, 1882.79, 1883.32, 1883.46, 1883.53, 1883.63, 1884.13, 1884.41, 1885.02, 1885.15, 1885.22, 1885.49, 1885.66, 1886.03, 1886.42, 1886.52, 1887.07, 1887.16, 1887.39, 1887.45, 1887.48, 1888.14, 1888.27, 1888.40, 1889.07, 1889.11, 1889.15, 1889.18, 1890.49, 1891.25, 1891.45, 1892.44, 1892.54, 1893.10, 1893.15, 1893.27, 1893.36, 1893.46, 1894.04, 1894.49, 1895.05, 1896.24, 1897.48, 1900.40, 1901.16
West, William H. 1897.55
West, Willie 1944.30
Westberg, Margaret 1941.04
Westbrook, Esther 1973.17
Westbrook, Evelyn 1908.04, 1912.33, 1912.44
Westbrook, Frank 1938.18, 1944.33, 1947.17, 1948.25
Westbrook, Miss 1908.19
Westbrook, Newton 1897.42
Westcott, Eva 1903.10, 1904.16
Westcott, Evelyn 1903.09
Westcott, Marcy 1938.06, 1938.14, 1939.27
Westcott, Walter F. 1906.40
Westenberg, Robert 1983.14, 1984.08, 1987.18, 1991.05, 1994.12, 1995.11
Westendorf, Thomas P. 1980.27
Wester, Katherine 1889.34
Westerberg, Marian 1870.35, 1870.42
Westerberg, Marion 1870.32, 1871.02
Westerberg, Miss 1870.09, 1870.12, 1870.22, 1870.40
Westerfield, James 1944.32
Westerfield, William 1953.06, 1954.10, 1955.17
Westergaard, Louise 1981.06, 1987.02, 1997.05
Westerlund, Babe 1940.02
Westerman, Dale 1966.08, 1966.14, 1967.10
Western, Alice 1890.08
Western, Burke 1924.07
Western, John 1913.36
Western, Lillie 1882.20
Westerton, Frank 1917.27
Westford, Owen 1886.39, 1894.41, 1894.48, 1895.09, 1896.10, 1896.12, 1896.51, 1898.68, 1902.07, 1904.13, 1904.55, 1907.08
Westley, Helen 1931.02
Westley, J. 1869.32
Westley, John 1908.09
Westlow, William 1950.15, 1954.01
Westman, Messr. 1894.19
Westmoreland, Lillian 1927.33
Weston and King 1889.19
Weston, A. 1878.13
Weston, Al. H. 1903.29
Weston, Bert 1937.08
Weston, Beverly 1951.23, 1952.10
Weston, Burt C. 1906.04
Weston, C.H. 1897.30
Weston, Eddie 1949.18, 1957.17
Weston, Effie 1917.08, 1919.34
Weston, Emanuel 1927.30
Weston, Emily 1872.09, 1872.11
Weston, Emma 1879.02
Weston, Frank 1881.15
Weston, George 1896.04, 1903.20
Weston, H. 1883.20
Weston, Henrietta 1896.04
Weston, Huntley 1937.08
Weston, Irene 1912.13, 1951.02
Weston, J.P. 1910.08
Weston, Jack 1956.14
Weston, James 1969.03, 1970.21, 1974.05
Weston, John 1999.09
Weston, Jon 1991.10, 1992.07, 1998.16, 2000.10
Weston, Kim 1967.06
Weston, Lucy 1908.19, 1914.22
Weston, Maggie 1902.09, 1906.03
Weston, Messr. 1875.02
Weston, Miss 1841.01, 1851.04, 1882.46
Weston, Mollie 1893.07
Weston, Morris 1891.10
Weston, Nellei 1892.60
Weston, Nellie 1881.13, 1882.77, 1891.36
Weston, Paul 1974.10
Weston, R.P. 1909.11, 1914.22, 1917.29, 1918.23, 1924.01, 1925.50, 1926.26, 1932.21, 1964.28, 1990.09
Weston, Ruth 1936.27, 1942.01
Weston, Sam 1891.10, 1894.37
Weston, T. 1877.22, 1877.23, 1877.25, 1881.22
Weston, Thomas 1888.35
Weston, Thomas R. 1878.17, 1879.04
Weston, William 1920.26
Weston, William A. 1918.23, 1919.22
Westphal, Frank 1919.26
Westus, Ted 1911.26
Wetherell, Nancy 1936.12
Wetherell, Nellie 1886.42, 1886.52, 1887.16
Wetherill, Nella 1886.03
Wetherill, Nellie 1887.07
Wetherley, Frederic E. 1896.15
Wetmore, B. 1870.35
Wetmore, Joan 1938.06, 1938.18
Wette, Adelheid 1895.28
Wetter, Franz 1883.37
Wetzel, Henry 1930.13
Wetzel, Patrick 1993.05, 1999.04, 2001.09
Wever, Edward H. 1924.40
Wever, Ned 1924.35, 1930.25, 1931.13
Wexler, Jerry 1982.09, 1992.06
Wexler, Norman 1999.15
Wexler, Peter 1966.30, 1968.01, 1970.07, 1978.28
Wexler, Stanley 1987.03, 1987.09, 1988.04
Wey, Emma 1918.01
Weygandt, Gene 1996.08
Weyl, Bessie 1889.12
Weyl, Otto 1891.12, 1891.17, 1892.03
Weyman, Stanley 1897.09, 1928.48
Weymouth, Anthony 1979.32
Weymss, Mr. 1852.04
Whaanga, Arapata 1972.20
Whalan, Messr. 1844.01
Whalen, Dick 1924.37
Whalen, Harold 1927.31, 1928.14, 1930.09, 1930.26, 1939.25
Whalen, J. 1899.19
Whalen, John 1886.42, 1887.48, 1888.14, 1888.27, 1888.40, 1889.07, 1889.11, 1889.18, 1890.49, 1891.25, 1892.44, 1892.54, 1893.15, 1893.46, 1900.07, 1902.06, 1908.29, 1909.30
Whalen, Lulu 1903.15
Whaley, Michael 1965.18
Whallen 1894.44
Whallen, William 1887.39
Whalley, Norma 1897.32, 1899.19
Wharnock, George 1898.18, 1908.04, 1908.42
Wharton, Belle 1880.07, 1880.37
Wharton, Emma 1879.50
Wharton, George 1914.18, 1915.18, 1916.01
Wharton, Jennie 1880.37
Wharton, L.D. 1901.21
Wharton, Messr. 1852.01
Wharton, Mr. 1851.01, 1851.08, 1852.03
Wharton, Patti 1956.02
Wharton, Thomas 1894.10
Wheat, D. 1981.16
Wheat, Laurence 1900.16, 1903.34, 1908.09, 1911.05, 1912.01, 1917.05
Wheat, Lawrence 1901.01, 1902.07, 1905.19, 1908.30, 1910.34, 1912.11, 1914.13, 1914.34
Wheatcroft, Nelson 1893.47
Wheatleigh, C. 1857.01, 1857.02
Wheatleigh, Charles 1892.14
Wheatleigh, Jennie 1872.34
Wheatley, A. 1869.04, 1869.13
Wheatley, Annie 1897.46
Wheatley, Mr. 1823.01
Wheatley, Mrs. 1823.01
Wheatley, William 1862.03, 1862.04, 1863.06, 1863.07, 1865.06, 1866.18
Wheatman, Gus 1890.22, 1890.38
Wheaton, Anna 1909.23, 1910.19, 1910.31, 1912.24, 1913.08, 1913.11, 1913.13, 1913.19, 1914.20, 1917.06, 1920.11
Wheaton, Dick 1926.29
Wheaton, Gladys 1927.58
Wheaton, Kitty 1906.01, 1908.01
Whedon, John 1949.17
Wheelan, A.R. 1914.03
Wheelan, Albertina Randall 1921.22
Wheelan, Albertine Randall 1921.37
Wheelan, Aldred C. 1892.17
Wheelan, Lou 1904.03
Wheeldin, Aurelia 1929.18, 1930.19
Wheeler, Andrew Carpenter 1887.14
Wheeler, Bert 1923.38, 1927.08, 1942.23, 1943.13, 1949.02, 1952.05
Wheeler, Betty 1923.38
Wheeler, Bun 1911.26
Wheeler, C.W. 1883.47
Wheeler, Charles 1912.15, 1927.07
Wheeler, Claudia 1918.01
Wheeler, Davis 1912.05
Wheeler, Dean 1935.11
Wheeler, Dryden 1934.03
Wheeler, Earl 1903.18
Wheeler, Elsie 1919.10
Wheeler, Ethel 1910.21
Wheeler, Francis 1922.15, 1927.39
Wheeler, Harold 1968.31, 1969.17, 1971.13, 1971.18, 1972.10, 1973.04, 1975.01, 1978.25, 1978.26, 1981.16, 1981.29, 1982.01, 1983.21, 1984.09, 1985.05, 1987.07, 1988.12, 1990.07, 1991.08, 1992.18, 1997.08, 1997.17, 1999.24, 2000.15
Wheeler, Hugh 1973.05, 1974.06, 1976.02, 1979.06, 1980.04, 1980.21, 1980.25, 1981.20, 1982.20, 1983.13, 1984.11, 1984.13, 1985.09, 1986.08, 1987.08, 1987.09, 1989.14, 1989.19, 1989.23, 1993.12, 1997.10
Wheeler, J.E. 1901.14
Wheeler, J.W. 1896.37
Wheeler, James 1919.34
Wheeler, John 1907.26, 1909.02, 1920.23, 1938.17, 1961.08, 1961.26, 1966.01
Wheeler, John E. 1914.20, 1918.12, 1926.05
Wheeler, John L. 1912.04
Wheeler, Josh 1951.24
Wheeler, Marie 1901.05
Wheeler, May 1904.10
Wheeler, Ruth 1926.11, 1927.39
Wheeler, Van Renselaer 1902.19
Wheeler, Van Rensellaer 1902.03
Wheeler, Van Rensselaer 1897.50, 1898.73, 1900.39, 1903.14, 1904.55, 1906.15, 1906.47, 1907.51, 1910.31, 1911.43
Wheeler, Van Rensslaer 1900.28
Wheeler, W.J. 1890.35, 1892.01
Wheelis, Toni 1953.17, 1954.15
Wheelock, J.A. 1889.37, 1891.08
Wheelock, Joseph 1872.27, 1875.18, 1894.39
Wheelock, Joseph F. 1875.10
Wheetman, Dan 1999.09
Whelan, Alf C. 1890.27, 1894.28, 1897.17, 1897.42, 1901.01
Whelan, Alf. C. 1895.22, 1897.28
Whelan, Alfred C. 1888.29, 1889.45, 1896.25
Whelan, Bill 1996.01, 1996.12, 1998.09, 2000.05
Whelan, Chris 1902.09
Whelan, James 1914.33, 1916.08
Whelan, Susan 1979.31
Whelbeck, S.S. 1896.32
Whelen, Emmy 1913.36
Whelen, John 1915.27
Wheler, Harold 1998.15
Whelpley, Lizzie 1869.05
Whiffen, Mrs., Thomas 1927.54
Whiffen, Thomas 1868.20, 1876.32, 1878.19, 1879.05, 1879.21, 1885.16, 1885.48, 1899.41, 1905.25
Whiffen, Thomas H. 1879.58
Whiffen, Tom 1877.35
Whiffin, Thomas 1870.39, 1870.43, 1872.20, 1878.03
Whight, Bob 1942.19
Whight, Peggy 1942.19, 1944.20
Whipper, Leigh 1925.18, 1930.19, 1932.12
Whipple, Waldo 1894.50, 1898.03
Whisper, Miss 1867.23
Whistler, Edna 1914.08, 1922.43, 1925.30
Whistler, Rex 1929.51
Whistlin' Dixie 1995.05
Whitaker, C.F. 1905.09
Whitaker, Charles F. 1905.32
Whitaker, Horace 1906.36
Whitaker, Julian 1989.12
Whitbeck, Jane 1901.27
Whitbread, Thomas 1899.15
Whitbread, Thomas E. 1899.41, 1900.54, 1903.36
Whitchurch, Missy 1980.02
Whitcomb, Cliff 1924.12, 1927.16, 1934.20
Whitcomb, Joshua 1887.02
Whitcomb, Kathleen 1930.33
Whitcomb, Sadie 1898.02
Whitcup, Leonard 1940.16
White Horse Tavern Productions, Inc. 1934.18
White, Al 1911.26
White, Al. 1907.34
White, Alice 1940.01
White, Alton F. 1991.03
White, Amelia 1992.02
White, Anna 1925.18
White, Beulah 1907.31
White, Billy 1936.22
White, Bobby 1948.18
White, Carrie 1872.06
White, Cassandra 1999.08
White, Charles 1873.27, 1875.37, 1875.38
White, Charles A. 1887.02

White, Charles T. 1890.49
White, Charley 1866.35, 1872.07, 1873.27
White, Clara 1879.03
White, Clayton 1919.41
White, Clayton E. 1897.56
White, Cool 1865.03, 1871.12, 1871.16, 1944.32
White, Courtney 1918.01
White, D.L. 1893.50
White, Dan 1943.05
White, David 1900.25, 1900.31, 1989.01
White, Dorothy 1959.21
White, Douglass 1884.15
White, E.B. 1931.21, 1932.13
White, Edward 1947.14
White, Edwin 1897.50
White, Elfia 1906.23
White, Elsie 1921.21
White, Eric 1964.35
White, Ethel 1943.24
White, Frances 1916.10, 1917.12, 1918.08, 1920.42, 1922.12
White, Frank 1900.07, 1900.35, 1905.33
White, Frank H. 1891.18, 1900.48
White, Fred 1882.69, 1885.54, 1886.60
White, G. 1871.11, 1880.17
White, George 1890.40, 1891.17, 1907.29, 1907.31, 1910.20, 1911.24, 1912.09, 1913.30, 1915.15, 1917.26, 1919.13, 1920.17, 1921.22, 1922.27, 1923.18, 1923.39, 1924.19, 1925.22, 1926.16, 1927.46, 1928.22, 1929.35, 1930.11, 1931.30, 1932.24, 1933.03, 1935.18, 1939.25
White, George R. 1889.40, 1890.11, 1904.05
White, Gil 1930.08
White, Gilbert 1930.39
White, Gladys 1918.16, 1919.41, 1926.31
White, Glen 1907.63
White, Grace Kay 1922.32
White, Grover 1936.22
White, Hallie 1902.02
White, Harry 1987.02
White, Harry A. 1924.13
White, Hattie 1884.65
White, Henry 1892.34, 1921.33, 1927.39
White, Herbert 1939.29
White, J. 1918.21
White, J. Steven 1990.17
White, Jack 1926.51, 1929.35
White, James 1923.17, 1950.10, 1954.13
White, Jane 1916.19, 1951.10, 1959.26, 2001.02
White, Jennie 1877.25
White, Jesse 1943.14, 1944.16, 1947.21, 1965.01, 1965.18
White, Jim 1921.41
White, Jimmy 1955.10
White, Joan 1982.24
White, Josh 1945.07
White, Joshua 1940.01, 1975.05
White, Joyce 1924.29, 1926.24, 1946.22
White, Jr., Al 1942.18, 1943.22, 1945.08, 1949.17
White, June 1914.02, 1915.05, 1915.28, 1916.07, 1918.15, 1918.28
White, Kathleen 1984.16
White, Larry 1972.21
White, Leo 1913.15
White, Les 1943.05
White, Lester 1940.16
White, Lewis 1939.15, 1983.05
White, Lillian 1920.30, 1922.45
White, Lillias 1982.22, 1987.07, 1995.05, 1997.08
White, Lilyan 1918.16, 1920.36, 1921.36, 1923.40
White, Louise 1915.07, 1918.06
White, Ludlow 1944.17
White, Madelyn 1938.09
White, Mamie 1904.38
White, Marjorie 1926.02, 1929.07, 1932.07
White, Master 1876.03
White, Maud 1898.58
White, Michael 1975.08
White, Midde 1907.02
White, Miles 1938.01, 1941.06, 1943.04, 1943.05, 1943.07, 1944.15, 1944.18, 1944.23, 1945.05, 1945.19, 1946.18, 1947.01, 1947.16, 1949.03, 1949.18, 1950.19, 1951.16, 1952.01, 1952.05, 1952.20, 1953.01, 1953.09, 1954.01, 1955.04, 1957.16, 1958.02, 1959.22, 1960.06, 1960.20, 1961.01, 1961.20, 1969.12, 1973.02, 1977.09, 1989.03
White, Miss 1859.05, 1859.06
White, Mortimer 1922.35
White, Mr. 1878.14
White, Murray 1942.25
White, Myrna 1962.12
White, Nathaniel 1961.07
White, Nora 1916.14, 1918.05
White, Ogden 1907.60
White, Olive 1897.47, 1899.01, 1900.10
White, Onna 1948.15, 1949.02, 1949.16, 1950.17, 1955.02, 1955.06, 1955.09, 1956.06, 1957.18, 1958.20, 1959.22, 1960.13, 1961.21, 1963.13, 1964.44, 1965.14, 1965.21, 1966.10, 1967.05, 1969.06, 1970.02, 1971.07, 1973.12, 1975.06, 1977.04, 1978.12, 1983.10, 1986.03, 1989.06
White, Pat 1957.17
White, Penny 1971.08
White, Phil 1910.15, 1917.37, 1920.08, 1921.18
White, Philip 1921.04, 1944.21
White, R.C. 1882.69
White, Richard 1986.04, 1986.14, 1987.03, 1987.10, 1988.14, 1988.16, 1988.18
White, Robert 1928.19, 1929.20
White, Rosea 1929.01
White, Ruth 1897.27, 1897.53, 1898.04, 1898.06, 1898.07, 1898.09, 1898.15, 1898.16, 1898.19, 1898.24, 1898.37, 1898.42, 1899.23, 1899.26, 1900.59, 1921.18, 1922.45, 1923.40
White, Sam 1918.20, 1926.07
White, Sammy 1916.23, 1920.47, 1923.31, 1927.67, 1932.11, 1946.16, 1948.20
White, Stanley 1983.21
White, T.H. 1980.19, 1981.26, 1993.11
White, Terri 1980.07, 1989.07
White, Thelma 1926.23, 1929.12, 1930.22, 1932.21, 1934.20, 1938.01
White, Tracy 1873.18, 1873.21, 1876.17, 1876.18, 1876.21, 1876.27
White, Victoria 1920.05, 1922.21, 1923.27
White, W. 1868.21
White, W. Emmons 1898.43
White, W.H. 1903.04, 1905.32, 1924.45
White, Walter 1884.10, 1908.40, 1921.34
White, Walter C. 1904.06
White, Warren 1864.16, 1864.18, 1864.19, 1872.20
White, Watson 1945.03
White, Wilfrid Hyde 1947.15
White, Willard 1975.19
White, William 1881.37, 1882.60, 1882.75, 1882.78, 1883.24, 1883.39, 1885.40, 1888.04, 1888.34, 1890.10, 1917.12, 1917.35, 1918.08, 1930.12, 1931.27
White, William E. 1882.57
White, William H. 1906.15, 1921.29, 1929.43, 1929.47, 1931.08
Whitecap Productions 1988.12
Whitecar, W.A. 1884.62
Whiteford, Grace 1892.48
Whiteford, Gracie 1892.53
Whiteford, Trixie 1913.31, 1917.12
Whitehead, Allen B. 1966.03, 1969.04
Whitehead, John 1981.15
Whitehead, Mary 1972.09
Whitehead, Neil 1993.03
Whitehead, O.Z. 1934.06, 1934.40, 1936.01
Whitehead, Paxton 1962.23, 1980.19, 1993.18
Whitehead, Ralph 1918.33, 1925.01, 1925.28, 1926.30, 1926.51, 1927.34
Whitehead, Robert 1952.06, 1958.14, 1961.02, 1976.11
Whitehead, William 1931.38
Whitehouse, Anthony 1976.04
Whitehouse, F.E. 1905.21
Whitehouse, Fred 1997.01
Whitehouse, Graclyn 1905.42
Whitelaw, Arthur 1970.07, 1971.07, 1971.11, 1979.10, 1979.29, 1999.03
Whiteley, Thomas 1926.15, 1927.01
Whitely, Thomas 1925.07
Whiteman, Paul 1922.27, 1923.38, 1927.12, 1935.15
Whiteside, Charles 1976.20
Whiteside, Fib 1914.19
Whiteside, Rosamond 1921.01, 1925.21
Whiteside, Rosamonde 1925.15
Whitestone, Nat 1907.34
Whitfield, Arthur 1960.01
Whitfield, Fred 1902.02
Whitfield, J. Michael 1987.01
Whitfield, Norman 1986.02
Whitfield, Norman J. 1997.21
Whitford, Annabelle 1901.27, 1904.19, 1906.47, 1907.24, 1908.19, 1909.13, 1911.07, 1912.36
Whitford, Trixie 1911.11
Whitham, Charles W. 1885.02, 1895.19
Whitham, John 1985.04
Whiticar, Margarete 1896.27
Whiting and Davis 1923.32
Whiting, Charles 1881.17
Whiting, D. 1854.06, 1854.07, 1855.10
Whiting, George 1908.43, 1913.18, 1927.37, 1928.23, 1967.13, 1968.20
Whiting, Helen 1896.35, 1896.48
Whiting, Heleyn 1897.54
Whiting, Jack 1923.40, 1924.38, 1925.35, 1926.06, 1926.28, 1927.49, 1928.02, 1928.36, 1929.42, 1931.04, 1932.25, 1934.39, 1937.15, 1939.28, 1940.10, 1942.29, 1952.07, 1953.01, 1954.03, 1958.03
Whiting, Kristin 2001.04
Whiting, Lillian 1898.08
Whiting, Lillie 1868.06, 1869.02, 1869.05, 1869.14, 1869.20, 1869.43, 1870.04
Whiting, Mack 1918.04
Whiting, Margaret 1997.05
Whiting, Mark 1912.45
Whiting, May 1898.08
Whiting, Mr. 1851.01, 1851.06, 1851.07, 1852.01, 1854.01, 1855.01, 1855.02, 1856.02, 1856.03
Whiting, Ralph 1907.48
Whiting, Richard 1997.05, 1999.01
Whiting, Richard A. 1916.03, 1916.25, 1919.10, 1919.13, 1919.14, 1921.20, 1924.15, 1924.46, 1931.28, 1932.04, 1932.25, 1944.32, 1947.05, 1952.11, 1955.14, 1963.02, 1965.08, 1974.09, 1976.32, 1980.08, 1984.10, 1986.06, 1990.09
Whiting, Rose 1897.16
Whitlaw, Messr. 1906.11, 1907.09
Whitley, Albert 1934.40
Whitlock, C. 1866.18
Whitlock, Carrie 1871.13
Whitlock, Genevieve 1902.10, 1902.19
Whitlock, Isabel 1902.05
Whitlock, Isabelle 1902.10
Whitlock, Lewis 1979.08
Whitlock, Miss 1869.29
Whitlow, Daryll 1999.09
Whitman, A.L. 1908.16
Whitman, Allen 1897.48
Whitman, Arthur 1916.10, 1916.22
Whitman, Charles 1891.06
Whitman, Ernest 1932.14
Whitman, Frank 1899.19, 1911.05
Whitman, Kevin C. 1998.05
Whitman, Mr. 1852.04, 1866.02, 1866.28
Whitman, R.T. 1888.09
Whitman, Stewart C. 1932.18
Whitman, Walt 1942.05, 1978.12
Whitmark, Isidore 1902.20
Whitmore and Lyden 1908.03
Whitmore, Dorothy 1921.31, 1923.46, 1924.30, 1926.15, 1926.33, 1927.47
Whitmore, Maud 1971.21
Whitmore, Mr. 1865.01, 1865.07, 1865.11, 1868.06
Whitmore, S. 1867.12
Whitmore, Vida 1905.29, 1906.01, 1908.39, 1910.19, 1911.06, 1911.45
Whitmore, Virginia 1933.26
Whitney Opera Company 1895.24, 1896.41, 1898.12, 1902.41, 1909.22, 1910.28, 1912.10, 1913.14
Whitney, B.C. 1902.15, 1904.25, 1907.59, 1909.17, 1920.10, 1921.37, 1924.27, 1925.06
Whitney, Beatrice 1921.15
Whitney, Beverly 1941.08
Whitney, Blanche 1882.69
Whitney, Charles 1883.36
Whitney, Clara 1892.04
Whitney, Edith 1906.37, 1908.07
Whitney, Edwin 1885.14
Whitney, Edythe 1917.35
Whitney, Eleanore 1946.02
Whitney, Elizabeth 1906.47, 1908.42
Whitney, F.C. 1902.03, 1902.31, 1902.41, 1904.15, 1904.36, 1904.49, 1905.15, 1907.08, 1909.22, 1910.28, 1912.10, 1913.14, 1917.11, 1925.06
Whitney, Fred C. 1894.40, 1894.47, 1895.24, 1896.41, 1898.12, 1899.39
Whitney, Gregg 1989.23
Whitney, Helen 1905.28, 1906.24
Whitney, Helene 1946.16, 1949.08
Whitney, Howard 1904.53
Whitney, Jack 1946.04
Whitney, Joan 1992.03, 1995.12, 1999.24
Whitney, Jr., M.W. 1904.51
Whitney, Lee 1933.24, 1934.29
Whitney, Lois 1915.02, 1915.26, 1916.03, 1918.03
Whitney, M.W. 1880.53
Whitney, Marion 1908.39, 1909.13, 1909.30, 1910.16, 1913.01, 1914.24
Whitney, Marjorie 1925.07, 1927.02
Whitney, May 1905.28, 1920.37
Whitney, Miss 1841.01, 1876.36
Whitney, Myron W. 1880.12, 1880.45, 1880.48, 1882.07, 1882.08, 1882.10, 1882.36, 1883.11, 1883.14
Whitney, Nina 1934.43, 1935.12
Whitney, Raymond 1979.27
Whitney, Salem 1929.01
Whitney, Salem Tutt 1928.18
Whitney, Tutt 1930.10
Whittaker, Joel 1985.04
Whittaker, Messr. 1855.01
Whittell, Josephine 1911.33, 1912.47, 1913.32, 1914.27, 1916.01, 1918.33, 1920.15, 1923.44, 1925.30
Whittemore, H.P. 1886.27
Whittemore, Henry 1925.45, 1927.21, 1930.11
Whittemore, Robert E. 1899.23
Whittington, George 1929.01
Whittington, Mr. 1875.31
Whittington, Mrs. 1875.31
Whittle, Cyril 1923.29
Whittman, Hugo 1898.37
Whittmore, Nina 1917.31
Whitton, Margaret 1999.07
Whittredge, Ella 1875.32, 1880.07
Whittridge, Jack 1937.06
Whitty, Gertrude 1904.54
Whitwell, Messr. 1881.35
Whorf, Richard 1934.40, 1951.18
Whyburn, Walte 1898.64
Whymple, James W. 1892.14
Whytal, A.R. 1886.27
Whytal, Russ 1923.43
Whyte, Charles 1897.53
Whyte, Ettie 1883.50
Whyte, Jerome 1951.16, 1953.09, 1962.03, 1965.06, 1970.19
Whyte, Jerry 1940.22
Whyte, Louise 1921.20
Whyte, W. Henry 1890.30
Wi, Ki 1909.20
Wibberly, William 1884.61
Wichart, Otto 1907.19
Wichert, Herr 1882.68
Wichert, Mr. 1891.33
Wick, Bruno 1951.14
Wick, Evelyn 1943.08
Wicke, Augustus 1912.44
Wicke, Gus 1916.15, 1930.42
Wickes, Joseph 1922.04, 1922.19, 1923.20, 1923.46, 1927.47, 1928.31
Wickes, Mary 1939.13, 1944.01, 1945.09, 1946.20, 1979.31
Wickham, Florence 1912.19
Wickham, Roscoe 1921.26
Wickstead, McIntyre 1911.09
Wickwire, Nancy 1963.28, 1968.05
Widdecombe, Wallace 1926.38
Widdoes, James 1982.08
Widdows, Frederick 1858.01, 1858.02
Widman, Annaliese 1951.15
Widman, Anneliese 1958.12
Widmer, H.J. 1881.15, 1881.22
Widmer, Harry 1869.28, 1881.35
Widmer, Henry 1884.11, 1891.05, 1892.14
Widmer, Henry J. 1881.41, 1882.78
Widney, Stone 1965.31, 1969.17, 1972.24, 1975.06, 1980.19, 1981.26, 1983.08
Wiebley, J. 1900.23
Wiedoft, Rudy 1920.24
Wiegand, George 1887.23
Wiegand, Messr. 1903.03
Wiegert, Rene 1963.04, 1972.07, 1979.23, 1982.19, 1986.19
Wiel, Harry H. 1907.19
Wieland, Clara 1896.05
Wiemers, Angie 1908.15
Wieniawski, Henri 1943.09

Wiensko, Bob 1958.01
Wierney, Tom 1986.07
Wierzel, Robert 2000.03
Wiesa, Mme. 1844.01
Wiese, Peter 1978.26
Wieselman, Doug 1998.22
Wiethoff, Messr. 1854.07
Wiethoff, Mr. 1854.07
Wiggins, Dollie 1900.40
Wiggins, Jr., James H. 1990.15
Wiggins, Lillian 1908.04, 1908.39, 1909.07, 1911.32
Wight, Ogden 1903.12
Wightman, Allen 1898.50
Wigley, E. 1894.18
Wigley, Harry 1903.39
Wignell, Thomas 1787.01
Wigreen Company, The 1951.11
Wiklins, Dooba 1983.17
Wiland, Steve 1952.10, 1954.15, 1958.20
Wilard, May 1904.35
Wilber, Mabel 1916.18
Wilbor, Juliet 1896.39
Wilbur 1978.22
Wilbur Opera Company 1881.21, 1881.33
Wilbur, A.L. 1881.21, 1909.10
Wilbur, Crane 1928.24
Wilbur, Lawrence 1902.18
Wilbur, Mabel 1902.44, 1905.55, 1906.26
Wilbur, Muriel 1906.05
Wilbur, Richard 1956.15, 1974.06, 1982.20, 1983.13, 1984.11, 1986.08, 1989.14, 1997.10
Wilck, Lillian 1921.13
Wilcock, Dorothy 1911.25, 1914.18
Wilcox, Bert 1947.13, 1948.18
Wilcox, Caroly 1958.12
Wilcox, Dorothy 1914.12
Wilcox, Emma 1922.11
Wilcox, Harry 1916.03
Wilcox, Josie 1889.54
Wilcox, Jr., Harry 1910.13
Wilcox, Larry 1965.36, 1966.05, 1966.27, 1968.06, 1970.08, 1979.13, 1983.01, 1983.20, 1984.14, 1985.08
Wilcox, Lee 1950.11
Wilcox, Mr. 1864.17
Wilcox, Patrick 1912.07
Wilcox, Ralph 1971.13, 1975.01
Wilcox, Ruth 1930.06
Wild Magnolias, The 1992.06
Wild, Ada 1903.26
Wild, Bertha 1882.50, 1883.32
Wild, Effie 1878.11
Wild, J. 1876.15
Wild, John 1873.20, 1873.22, 1873.27, 1875.31, 1875.34, 1875.35, 1875.36, 1875.37, 1875.38, 1875.40, 1876.01, 1876.13, 1876.15, 1876.22, 1876.29, 1877.01, 1877.07, 1878.01, 1878.13, 1878.17, 1879.04, 1879.37, 1879.68, 1880.09, 1880.36, 1880.64, 1881.09, 1881.29, 1882.02, 1882.50, 1882.74, 1882.79, 1883.32, 1883.46, 1883.53, 1883.63, 1884.13, 1884.41, 1885.02, 1885.15, 1885.22, 1885.49, 1885.66, 1886.03, 1886.42, 1886.52, 1887.07, 1887.16, 1887.39, 1887.45, 1887.48, 1888.14, 1889.05, 1890.49, 1891.25, 1891.45, 1892.44, 1892.54, 1893.10, 1893.15, 1893.27, 1893.36, 1893.46, 1894.04, 1894.49, 1895.05
Wild, Johnny 1872.07
Wild, Louie 1903.26
Wild, Mrs. John 1873.20, 1873.27
Wildberg, John 1943.19, 1945.08
Wildberg, John J. 1942.03, 1943.15, 1944.03
Wilde, Al 1927.27, 1948.13
Wilde, Elisabeth 1938.04
Wilde, Elizabeth 1936.12
Wilde, Lillias 1907.58
Wilde, Oscar 1893.11, 1927.20
Wilde, Pamela 1946.05
Wilde, Patricia 1955.04
Wilde, R. 1932.01
Wilde, Renee 1927.27
Wilder, Alan 1993.04
Wilder, Albert 1902.04, 1904.55, 1910.36
Wilder, Alec 1930.32, 1939.29
Wilder, Amy 1993.19
Wilder, Andrew 1995.07
Wilder, Baakari 1996.07
Wilder, Billy 1968.31, 1972.04, 1994.10
Wilder, Carrie 1980.30
Wilder, Clinton 1949.16
Wilder, David 1968.30, 1971.15
Wilder, Gene 1963.09
Wilder, George H. 1895.27
Wilder, Jo 1963.14
Wilder, Marc 1953.16
Wilder, R.H. 1922.45
Wilder, Thornton 1964.01, 1967.15, 1975.21, 1978.04, 1995.13
Wilder, Victor 1883.44, 1883.45, 1884.63, 1887.41, 1888.22
Wilder, W.H. 1878.17
Wilder, William 1913.24, 1914.33
Wilderman, William 1949.16, 1953.05, 1953.14, 1954.10, 1956.10
Wildermann, William 1984.12, 1985.10
Wildhack, Robert 1934.19
Wildhorn, Frank 1995.15, 1997.09, 1997.19, 1999.08, 1999.13
Wildner, Evelyn 1915.05
Wile, Sally 1957.17
Wilenski, Michael 1942.28
Wiley, Clifford 1896.25
Wiley, Dora 1881.38, 1881.57, 1882.14, 1882.45, 1885.07, 1885.09
Wiley, Mr. 1841.01
Wiley, Shonn 2001.08
Wiley, Stella 1902.38
Wilfert, Sally 2001.06
Wilhelm 1882.60, 1882.75, 1883.48, 1887.10, 1887.27, 1892.38, 1893.23, 1894.34, 1895.03, 1895.32, 1897.32, 1898.46, 1902.01, 1905.55, 1906.33, 1908.07, 1910.05, 1910.27, 1910.34, 1912.39, 1914.23, 1922.35, 1923.40, 1924.39
Wilhelm of London 1910.02, 1923.40, 1924.26
Wilhelm, C. 1909.28
Wilhelm, Frank 1925.08
Wilhelm, G. 1920.36
Wilhelm, Julius 1910.37, 1912.17, 1914.03, 1925.08, 1930.04
Wilhelm, Mlle. 1867.05
Wilhelm, Mons. 1866.23, 1866.27
Wilhelmy, Miss 1894.01
Wilk, Max 1948.22, 1975.22
Wilke, Herr 1879.62
Wilke, Hubert 1883.35, 1883.64, 1883.67, 1884.14, 1884.34, 1884.63, 1885.65, 1886.37, 1887.18, 1887.22, 1887.24, 1887.26, 1887.28, 1887.47, 1889.10, 1889.24, 1890.21, 1891.13, 1892.52, 1894.41, 1894.48, 1895.12, 1896.44, 1899.22, 1901.14, 1904.10, 1905.03
Wilke, Mr. 1891.33, 1892.43, 1893.29, 1894.01, 1897.35, 1898.53
Wilke, Mrs. 1890.31
Wilke, Nellie 1910.13
Wilke, P. 1894.30
Wilke, Ray 1972.09
Wilkens, Billie 1915.08
Wilkens, Charles 1922.27
Wilkens, Richard 1904.21
Wilkens, William 1907.55
Wilkenson, Biddy 1927.52
Wilker, Lawrence J. 1991.05, 1995.05
Wilkerson, Arnold 1972.13
Wilkerson, John 1991.13, 1996.04, 1999.17
Wilkerson, Susie 1901.15
Wilkes, Anna 1905.31, 1912.42, 1913.10
Wilkes, Henry 1909.15
Wilkes, J.F. 1878.12
Wilkes, Joseph A. 1877.07
Wilkes, Mattie 1896.46, 1899.33, 1923.39
Wilkes, Pat 1956.02, 1956.14
Wilkes, Patricia 1954.12
Wilkes, Pelham 1896.18
Wilkes, Tom 1924.46
Wilkes, W.H.W. 1877.28
Wilkes-Hogan, Mattie 1902.38
Wilkie, Alfred 1882.31, 1882.36, 1882.40, 1884.32, 1884.33, 1884.35, 1884.38
Wilkie, Dean 1901.06
Wilkin, Miles 1995.13, 1997.09
Wilkins, Al 1927.32
Wilkins, Ann Marie 1990.19
Wilkins, Claire 1942.19
Wilkins, Clare 1944.20
Wilkins, J.R. 1873.12, 1873.14
Wilkins, Jean 1921.15
Wilkins, Jeffrey 1993.18
Wilkins, Joseph 1931.07
Wilkins, Kenneth 1937.04
Wilkins, Marie 1866.34
Wilkins, Mary 1931.07
Wilkins, Mr. 1869.43
Wilkins, Otto 1886.59, 1887.06, 1887.14
Wilkins, Reverend Robert 1993.01
Wilkins, Robert 1998.17
Wilkins, Sharon 1997.08, 2000.18
Wilkins, Will 1906.08
Wilkins, Winona 1912.24, 1914.16
Wilkinson, Arthur 1881.37, 1882.17, 1882.60, 1882.75, 1882.78
Wilkinson, Bert 1921.12
Wilkinson, Colm 1987.04
Wilkinson, Dudley 1922.38, 1956.02
Wilkinson, George 1886.14, 1886.40
Wilkinson, Henry 1903.37
Wilkinson, James 1938.14
Wilkinson, Laura 1927.31
Wilkinson, Michael 1999.02
Wilkinson, Mr. 1881.36
Wilkinson, Mrs. 1863.10
Wilkinson, Norman 1929.51, 1948.03, 1951.07
Wilkinson, Raven 1978.20, 1979.21, 1983.12, 1987.03, 1990.07, 1991.08
Wilkof, Lee 1986.07, 1993.10, 1999.19
Wilks E. 1867.18
Wilks, Anna 1907.56
Wilks, E.P. 1879.50, 1881.04, 1881.11, 1882.26, 1884.18
Wilks, Edward 1896.29
Wilks, Joseph 1875.06
Wilks, Mattie 1921.16
Will J. Block Amusement Company, The 1906.04, 1907.14
Will, E.B. 1907.38
Will, Herr 1879.17, 1879.22
Will, Lenny 1979.15
Willa, Suzanne 1927.66
Willadsen, Gene 2000.16
Willard, David 1907.43, 1908.32
Willard, Dorothy 1950.11
Willard, Emma 1952.11
Willard, Florence 1908.18
Willard, Harold 1935.18
Willard, Harriet 1897.49
Willard, Joe F. 1906.40
Willard, John 1906.11, 1915.06, 1915.09, 1915.10, 1915.12, 1915.14, 1915.30, 1925.06, 1925.13, 1933.17
Willard, Joseph F. 1906.10
Willard, Katherine 1901.02
Willard, L. 1870.32
Willard, L.R. 1872.02, 1872.04, 1872.05, 1872.08, 1872.12, 1872.14, 1882.56
Willard, May 1904.03, 1908.07, 1908.24, 1909.30
Willard, Miss 1886.36
Willarde, Florence 1905.53
Willemetz, Albert 1921.21, 1922.03, 1923.44, 1929.10, 1929.11, 1929.14, 1932.04, 1935.19, 1947.18, 1953.12, 1958.06, 1963.02, 1964.22, 1965.08
Willeminsky, Ignaz M. 1932.23
Willems, Eleanor 1924.29, 1925.23
Willems, Frances 1925.23
Willems, Stephen 1979.27
Willensky, Elliot 1999.17
Willenz, Maria 1927.38
Willes, Natalie 1999.15
Willet, John 1976.10
Willett, J.G. 1884.23
Willey, Florence 1887.12, 1887.28, 1888.24, 1888.26, 1889.17, 1892.30, 1892.55, 1893.20, 1902.18
Willey, Robert 1943.23
Willey, Robert A. 1960.05
Willeye, Miss 1886.36
William A. Brady, Ltd. 1922.41
William C. Mitchell's Pleasure Party 1880.32, 1881.16
William H. Crane Company 1894.39
William Harris Company 1892.09
William Harris' Comedy Company 1891.32, 1892.50, 1893.06
William J. Gilmore Opera Company 1890.21
William, Earl 1950.02, 1951.17, 1952.17, 1952.19
William, Master 1866.02, 1866.28, 1879.30
William, Percy 1921.26
William, W.R. 1907.50
Williams 1868.04, 1869.38
Williams, Agnes 1937.11
Williams, Alexander 1931.21
Williams, Alfred 1897.13, 1897.52, 1900.32
Williams, Allison 1986.07
Williams, Allison M. 1992.08
Williams, Alon 1990.20, 1991.13, 1998.18
Williams, Alton 1963.27
Williams, Amy 1883.47
Williams, Andy 1974.20
Williams, Ann 1957.07, 1970.09
Williams, Annie 1887.30
Williams, Annie C. 1879.28
Williams, Antonio 1898.78
Williams, Arthur 1920.10, 1961.13, 1962.07
Williams, B. 1897.47
Williams, Barbara 1932.15, 1962.16, 1972.07
Williams, Barney 1899.03
Williams, Bart 1989.06
Williams, Belle 1900.35
Williams, Bert 1896.30, 1898.56, 1899.33, 1900.46, 1908.08, 1909.27, 1910.18, 1911.24, 1912.38, 1914.15, 1915.15, 1916.10, 1917.13, 1919.15, 1920.33, 1976.04, 1980.10, 1980.27, 1999.06
Williams, Bert A. 1899.33, 1902.23, 1903.08, 1904.26, 1906.14
Williams, Betty 1920.44, 1923.30
Williams, Billie 1930.41
Williams, Billy 1894.44, 1921.16, 1945.04
Williams, Bob 1921.16, 1942.24, 1979.25
Williams, Bryan 1914.23
Williams, Buck 1931.43
Williams, C. 1841.01, 1866.20
Williams, C. Jay 1898.61, 1931.09
Williams, C.A. 1892.35
Williams, C.D. 1923.25
Williams, Carl 1899.36, 1926.22
Williams, Carl F. 1929.25
Williams, Carla Renata 1995.05
Williams, Carrie 1869.11, 1880.07, 1882.18
Williams, Castle 1937.15
Williams, Celeste 1841.01
Williams, Charles 1924.45, 1927.64, 1930.23
Williams, Charles D. 1924.36
Williams, Clara 1879.67
Williams, Clarence 1927.30, 1927.32, 1931.11, 1975.20, 1976.16, 1978.09, 1989.02, 1992.06, 1999.06, 1999.24
Williams, Clyde 1963.27
Williams, Craig 1906.14, 1932.23
Williams, D.L. 1885.06
Williams, Daniel 1899.19
Williams, David 1957.13
Williams, Deborah 1990.08
Williams, Derek 1935.14
Williams, Dick 1957.14, 1971.13
Williams, Dick Anthony 1975.02
Williams, Dollie 1879.29, 1904.09
Williams, Dolly 1904.28
Williams, Dorothea 1928.40, 1928.45
Williams, Dorothy 1924.19
Williams, Duke 1957.09
Williams, Dwight 1906.37
Williams, E. 1889.36
Williams, E.B. 1852.04
Williams, E.J. 1895.16
Williams, Eleanor 1916.04, 1954.12
Williams, Elizabeth 1907.22, 1909.10, 1988.05, 1991.05, 1992.02, 1999.09, 2000.08, 2000.11
Williams, Ellis E. 1990.12
Williams, Enid 1946.24, 1948.21
Williams, Esther 1886.01, 1887.48, 1888.14, 1888.27, 1893.46, 1972.14
Williams, Ethel 1934.37
Williams, Eva 1910.19, 1911.31
Williams, Eva M. 1898.66
Williams, F. 1866.34, 1867.08, 1873.10
Williams, Fannie 1879.25
Williams, Faruma S. 1980.14
Williams, Flora 1893.22
Williams, Florence 1912.39
Williams, Floyd 1966.15
Williams, Frances 1924.13, 1925.45, 1926.16, 1927.21, 1928.22, 1929.35, 1930.40, 1931.08, 1931.36, 1934.19, 1940.09, 1941.03, 1943.16
Williams, Frank 1895.25, 1906.08, 1912.17
Williams, Frank B. 1899.33, 1904.26
Williams, Frank H. 1908.08
Williams, Fred 1875.21, 1879.15, 1879.50, 1879.56, 1880.04, 1881.04, 1881.11, 1882.15, 1882.26, 1887.08, 1887.34, 1888.07, 1903.11, 1904.42
Williams, Freda Ann 1977.18
Williams, Freida 1984.15, 1989.09
Williams, Fritz 1888.07, 1901.17, 1909.11, 1910.16, 1911.42, 1916.07

Williams, G.H. 1901.06
Williams, George 1894.13, 1899.31, 1899.41, 1903.02, 1904.17, 1908.30, 1910.13, 1912.46, 1913.09, 1914.22, 1922.41
Williams, George H. 1906.26
Williams, Gerald 1927.30
Williams, Gertrude 1908.16, 1908.26, 1928.12
Williams, Grace 1912.15
Williams, Grafton 1913.36, 1914.10
Williams, Grant 1958.15, 1959.16, 1959.17, 1959.21
Williams, Greg. 1907.55
Williams, Gus 1878.19, 1884.23, 1885.69, 1889.35, 1891.09
Williams, H. 1879.65, 1879.67, 1885.65
Williams, H.S. 1899.04
Williams, Hank 1992.06
Williams, Hannah 1924.19, 1928.40, 1928.45, 1930.38
Williams, Happy 1925.18
Williams, Harold 1918.30
Williams, Harriet 1892.29, 1893.21, 1929.01
Williams, Harry 1883.47, 1885.06, 1896.39, 1902.15, 1903.07, 1904.23, 1904.43, 1904.45, 1905.17, 1905.34, 1905.39, 1906.33, 1907.12, 1907.32, 1907.46, 1908.10, 1908.11, 1908.39, 1909.17, 1909.25, 1910.01, 1910.02, 1910.07, 1910.17, 1912.02, 1914.22, 1914.23, 1919.43, 1939.29
Williams, Harry H. 1942.24, 1964.28, 1975.22
Williams, Harry M. 1991.04
Williams, Hattie 1893.17, 1894.28, 1896.52, 1898.05, 1898.47, 1901.16, 1902.24, 1903.33, 1905.20, 1906.25, 1908.27, 1912.26, 1913.20
Williams, Henry 1906.17, 1913.30, 1933.27
Williams, Henry C. 1894.52
Williams, Herb 1930.22, 1935.12
Williams, Herbert 1920.08
Williams, Herman 1936.27
Williams, Hope 1930.40, 1933.05
Williams, Ina 1919.16, 1920.22, 1920.23, 1924.16, 1925.38, 1927.07
Williams, Ira 1938.08
Williams, Irene 1908.33, 1921.01
Williams, Ivy 1903.09, 1904.25
Williams, J. 1869.04, 1869.13, 1869.40, 1873.18
Williams, J.C. 1872.27
Williams, J.R. 1907.13
Williams, Jack 1938.01, 1939.25, 1940.21, 1941.08, 1946.22, 1947.08, 1954.12
Williams, Jack Eric 1976.10, 1979.06
Williams, Janis 1940.10
Williams, Jay 1937.14
Williams, Jennie 1886.48, 1886.49
Williams, Jennifer 1971.09
Williams, Jesse 1876.17, 1876.18, 1876.21, 1876.27, 1877.16, 1879.38, 1880.47, 1880.69, 1881.34, 1881.40, 1881.56, 1882.05, 1882.15, 1882.16, 1882.19, 1882.70, 1882.71, 1883.04, 1883.10, 1883.18, 1883.38, 1883.45, 1883.62, 1884.08, 1884.59, 1884.65, 1885.12, 1885.18, 1885.31, 1885.41, 1885.63, 1886.04, 1886.30, 1888.02, 1888.20, 1888.35, 1889.04, 1889.40, 1889.49, 1890.02, 1891.36, 1892.19, 1892.24, 1892.27, 1892.29, 1892.60, 1893.47, 1895.08, 1895.15, 1897.30
Williams, Jessie 1899.21
Williams, Jill 1925.42, 1927.02, 1974.03
Williams, Jno. 1892.11
Williams, John 1879.42, 1889.18, 1905.09
Williams, John G. 1867.12
Williams, John Gary 1975.12
Williams, Jr., Hank 1999.09
Williams, Judith 1956.01
Williams, K.P. 1892.35
Williams, Ken 1929.49
Williams, Kitty 1924.19
Williams, Kyle 1986.03
Williams, L.J. 1868.19
Williams, Lavinia 1943.17, 1944.31, 1947.03, 1952.15
Williams, Leila 1896.01, 1903.21
Williams, Lela 1907.26
Williams, Lizzie 1886.10
Williams, Lottie 1897.32, 1903.08, 1904.26, 1906.14
Williams, Louise 1932.30
Williams, Lucille 1919.28, 1920.30
Williams, Lucy 1893.07
Williams, Mabel 1898.70
Williams, Maggie 1875.11
Williams, Malcolm 1898.17, 1898.41, 1909.09
Williams, Margaret 1951.11
Williams, Margot 1914.24
Williams, Marian 1922.21, 1925.31
Williams, Marie 1877.22, 1877.23, 1877.25, 1877.39, 1878.20, 1879.03, 1880.43, 1880.49, 1882.26, 1888.33, 1889.46, 1891.41, 1900.46
Williams, Marshall 1969.09, 1995.04
Williams, Mary 1928.19, 1929.20
Williams, Mary Lou 1945.07
Williams, Maud 1897.50
Williams, Maude 1897.21, 1901.29, 1902.10, 1904.25
Williams, May 1901.10, 1905.43
Williams, Messr. 1846.01, 1851.01, 1854.01, 1859.06, 1882.04, 1882.20, 1894.04, 1894.19, 1907.02
Williams, Michael 1965.39
Williams, Milton 1940.17
Williams, Milton J. 1935.01, 1946.08
Williams, Miss 1852.02, 1854.01, 1867.19, 1870.13, 1873.26, 1886.36, 1910.12
Williams, Morgan 1909.07
Williams, Mr. 1846.01, 1852.04, 1862.03, 1862.07, 1863.02, 1863.04, 1863.10, 1864.02, 1864.21, 1867.10, 1867.14, 1867.15, 1867.16, 1868.06, 1868.23
Williams, Mrs. 1868.32
Williams, Mrs. Fred 1883.16
Williams, Mrs. H. 1894.52
Williams, Musa 1932.08, 1933.27, 1940.01, 1943.15, 1944.03, 1949.04, 1961.12
Williams, Natasha Yvette 2001.09
Williams, Nelson B. 1841.01
Williams, Norman 1928.13
Williams, Ocie 1914.21
Williams, Odell 1885.42, 1893.13
Williams, Olena 1937.09
Williams, P. 1882.62
Williams, P.F. 1880.41
Williams, Pat 1949.09, 1968.03
Williams, Paul 1981.16
Williams, Pauline 1924.10
Williams, Peggy 1973.17, 1975.12
Williams, Percy G. 1905.37
Williams, Phyllis 1955.13
Williams, R. 1856.01, 1866.24, 1867.08, 1875.06
Williams, R.G. 1908.34
Williams, R.W. 1869.08, 1880.04
Williams, Ralph 1905.13, 1963.14, 1971.06, 1994.08
Williams, Richard 1898.02, 1966.18
Williams, Robert 1935.04
Williams, Robert G. 1908.34
Williams, Rose 1902.02
Williams, Roy 1935.18
Williams, Rudy 1941.07
Williams, Rufus 1881.02
Williams, S. 1865.01, 1865.11, 1881.04
Williams, Sallie 1883.32, 1885.48
Williams, Sally 1881.11, 1979.26, 1981.26
Williams, Sam 1911.34, 1983.07, 1986.05, 1994.11
Williams, Sammy 1968.01, 1975.15
Williams, Schele 2000.06
Williams, Sharon 1959.08, 1959.17
Williams, Shirley 1973.17
Williams, Sid 1922.30
Williams, Sidney 1923.33
Williams, Sim 1901.22
Williams, Singer 1971.01
Williams, Spencer 1921.26, 1927.30, 1931.11, 1954.11, 1974.09, 1980.10, 1986.06, 1989.02, 1992.06
Williams, T. 1875.36, 1877.04
Williams, T.J. 1868.02
Williams, Taylor 1895.25, 1897.15, 1911.15
Williams, Tennessee 1955.05
Williams, Thomas 1934.41
Williams, Tom 1871.09, 1922.40, 1959.19
Williams, Tom Emlyn 1946.05, 1946.17, 1959.05
Williams, Tony 1895.02, 1897.06, 1902.02, 1904.11, 1906.09
Williams, Treat 1974.05, 2001.02
Williams, Valerie 1976.17
Williams, Vanessa 1978.23, 1979.27, 1991.01
Williams, Violet 1908.26
Williams, W. 1884.41, 1907.54
Williams, W.H. 1838.01
Williams, Waldine 1928.39, 1933.04
Williams, Weston 1915.20
Williams, Wilbur 1926.30
Williams, William 1919.22, 1920.26, 1922.09, 1922.30, 1926.10, 1926.30, 1926.44, 1927.44, 1927.57, 1927.61, 1928.30, 1931.39, 1938.08
Williams, Winifred 1895.31
Williams, Zulah 1894.37
Williamson 1888.14
Williamson, J.C. 1877.28
Williamson, Agnes 1905.11, 1906.46, 1908.11
Williamson, B.H. 1880.63
Williamson, Billie 1913.32
Williamson, Budd 1924.32
Williamson, Etta 1894.37
Williamson, F. 1881.32
Williamson, George 1903.37
Williamson, Howard 1968.26, 1968.28, 1978.17
Williamson, J.C. 1867.19, 1867.20, 1869.07, 1877.28
Williamson, James 1893.46
Williamson, Joe 1887.45
Williamson, Joseph 1887.48, 1888.27, 1888.40, 1889.07, 1889.11, 1889.15, 1890.49, 1891.25, 1891.45, 1893.15, 1893.27, 1893.36, 1897.34
Williamson, Nicol 1976.08
Williamson, Robert 1926.24, 1932.14, 1932.22, 1936.22, 1938.16
Williamson, Rosemary 1948.28
Williamson, Ruth 1921.36, 1922.13, 1992.04, 1998.15, 2000.11
Williamson, Sonny Boy 1972.08, 1993.06
Williamson, Susan 1965.39
Williamson, T. 1870.05
Williamson, Thomas 1902.17
Williamson, Walter 1882.39
Williamson, Z. 1880.37
Willie, Master 1877.01, 1878.04, 1880.07, 1885.49
Willie, May 1891.18
Williford, Steven 1980.18
Willimore, Carl 1907.49
Willing, Frank 1902.02, 1902.26
Willingham, Jesse W. 1918.29
Willingham, Jessie 1918.11
Willio, Herr 1871.18
Willis, Banning 1907.51
Willis, Charles 1895.04
Willis, Florence 1896.10, 1907.60
Willis, Gay 1992.12
Willis, George 1943.24, 1945.06, 1946.09
Willis, George O. 1951.11
Willis, Gordon 1985.08
Willis, Harry 1901.26
Willis, Joe 1927.33, 1932.30
Willis, Joseph 1930.29
Willis, Josephine 1926.38
Willis, Jr., Charles 1978.18
Willis, Keith 1957.03, 1960.01
Willis, Louise 1905.16
Willis, Marie 1894.19
Willis, Miss 1852.01
Willis, Mlle. 1852.01
Willis, Mme. 1844.01
Willis, Mr. 1859.01, 1866.18
Willis, R.O. 1975.10
Willis, Richard 2001.07
Willis, Susan 1984.07
Willis, Susanne 1911.17
Willis, W.D. 1879.65
Willis-Hepner, Louise 1897.52
Willison, Walter 1965.31, 1970.19, 1971.19, 1989.26, 1994.12, 1995.19
Willman, Noel 1968.02
Willment, Genevieve 1915.30
Willmore, Jennie 1869.28
Willmore, Jenny 1869.25
Willmore, Lizzie 1869.25, 1869.28, 1869.45, 1870.02, 1870.06
Willner, A.M. 1909.21, 1910.37, 1911.27, 1911.37, 1912.17, 1912.33, 1912.48, 1913.14, 1913.20, 1915.27, 1917.30, 1920.46, 1921.31, 1923.14, 1923.15, 1924.12, 1926.05, 1930.07, 1931.07, 1934.29, 1938.17, 1943.12
Willoughby, Bertha 1903.37
Willoughby, Booth 1926.23, 1927.02
Willoughby, Hugh 1924.27, 1925.16, 1925.22, 1926.07, 1926.24, 1927.02, 1927.04, 1927.09, 1928.23, 1929.26, 1930.22, 1931.26, 1934.20
Willoughby, Joe 1992.03
Willoughby, Miss 1860.06
Wills, Brad 1997.04
Wills, Estelle X. 1904.48
Wills, F.M. 1879.02
Wills, Frank M. 1884.22, 1898.44
Wills, Gloria 1947.17
Wills, Helen 1934.03
Wills, James Robert 1999.24
Wills, Jr., Lou 1941.06, 1943.19, 1944.30, 1945.18, 1947.13, 1951.14, 1957.06
Wills, Lou 1970.21
Wills, Mary 1980.28
Wills, Mike 1991.02
Wills, Nat M. 1900.42, 1903.20, 1905.33, 1906.35, 1913.17, 1915.24, 1917.16
Wills, Norma 1884.22
Wills, Ray 1992.11, 1996.08, 2001.05
Wills, Ted 1963.10
Wills, Thomas 1885.45
Wills, Walter 1915.31
Wills, Walter S. 1913.33, 1914.18
Willson, Anita 1896.48, 1897.54
Willson, Meredith 1957.18, 1960.20, 1963.21, 1965.21, 1974.11, 1976.24, 1980.16, 1988.04, 1989.06, 1991.10, 2000.11
Willson, Millicent 1897.54
Willson, Millie 1896.48
Willson, Walter 1926.18
Willus, Carrie 1900.38
Willy, Ebe 1940.12
Willy, Ersilio 1940.12
Willy, Eugene 1940.12
Willy, Florence 1888.19
Willy, Hermina 1940.12
Willy, Rosita 1940.12
Willy, Willie 1940.12
Wilmer, Goeffrey 1923.35
Wilmer, Helen 1904.04
Wilmer, Sidney 1902.32, 1924.30
Wilmerton, Lincoln 1939.22
Wilmink, Willem 1982.23
Wilmont, Ethlyn 1908.28
Wilmore, Jenny 1870.14
Wilmore, Lizzie 1868.03, 1870.14
Wilmot, Blanche 1904.07, 1908.36
Wilmot, Charles 1907.32
Wilmot, Dolly 1915.18
Wilmot, Emma 1881.02
Wilmot, Emmie 1884.39
Wilmot, Ethelyn 1908.07
Wilmot, J. 1879.05
Wilmot, Joseph 1918.22
Wilmot, Maude 1889.54
Wilmot, Messr. 1864.13
Wilmott, Lee 1922.30
Wilmuth-Curran, Annie 1894.16
Wilner, A.M. 1912.10
Wilner, Jon 1998.07
Wilner, Lori 1990.16
Wilner, Max R. 1919.35, 1921.06
Wilner, Sis 1942.18
Wilson 1861.03, 1872.16, 1884.27
Wilson Dave 1876.04
Wilson, Al 1917.23, 1921.38, 1922.34, 1924.46, 1926.22, 1932.12
Wilson, Al H. 1895.04, 1898.70
Wilson, Al. 1894.17
Wilson, Al. H. 1894.32, 1902.39, 1905.12
Wilson, Alice 1922.30
Wilson, Andrew 1902.26
Wilson, Anita 1896.35, 1896.48
Wilson, Anna 1903.25
Wilson, Anna C. 1906.26, 1908.39, 1909.13
Wilson, Annie 1887.48
Wilson, Art 1940.07, 1940.21
Wilson, Arthur 1912.16
Wilson, Audree 1951.16
Wilson, Barbara 1925.17
Wilson, Baron 1973.15
Wilson, Bella 1890.17
Wilson, Betty 1963.28
Wilson, Billy 1956.06, 1956.14, 1957.16, 1976.04, 1976.21, 1978.18, 1978.21, 1983.01, 1983.08
Wilson, Brian 1982.22, 2000.16
Wilson, Burke 1922.29
Wilson, C. 1867.20
Wilson, C.H. 1863.06

Wilson, C.W. 1863.07
Wilson, Chandra 1998.16
Wilson, Charles 1879.59, 1880.30, 1902.08, 1902.26, 1962.10, 1964.08, 1965.11, 1965.27, 1966.02, 1966.17
Wilson, Charles Cahill 1923.16
Wilson, Charles J. 1904.49
Wilson, Cissy 1897.16
Wilson, Clara 1875.10
Wilson, Darlene 1997.17, 1997.19, 1999.13
Wilson, Dave 1870.38, 1871.12, 1871.16
Wilson, Deborah 1998.06
Wilson, Dolores 1965.36, 1970.10, 1979.12
Wilson, Dooley 1940.17, 1944.23
Wilson, Doreen 1944.21, 1946.18
Wilson, Dotty 1925.14
Wilson, Edith 1921.26, 1922.25, 1930.24, 1932.30, 1933.06, 1933.27, 1945.08, 1980.10
Wilson, Edward 1908.42
Wilson, Edwin 1905.22, 1909.15, 1913.24, 1915.28, 1932.14
Wilson, Effie 1899.33
Wilson, Elizabeth 1976.10
Wilson, Ella 1894.21
Wilson, Ethel 1913.07, 1928.24, 1930.37
Wilson, Evelyn 1929.35
Wilson, Florence 1890.01, 1892.45, 1896.35, 1907.32
Wilson, Frances 1897.21, 1900.14, 1900.30, 1900.47, 1902.15, 1902.27, 1904.34
Wilson, Francis 1880.32, 1881.16, 1883.45, 1883.58, 1884.63, 1885.05, 1885.41, 1885.63, 1886.04, 1888.02, 1889.24, 1890.26, 1891.31, 1891.47, 1893.35, 1894.29, 1895.26, 1896.28, 1897.36, 1898.54, 1899.24, 1899.28, 1900.39, 1901.13, 1902.01, 1903.32, 1921.01
Wilson, Francis X. 1886.30, 1898.36
Wilson, Frank 1931.32, 1935.01, 1945.08
Wilson, Frankie 1894.37
Wilson, Fred 1886.61, 1888.42, 1924.45, 1927.12
Wilson, G. 1883.52
Wilson, G.T. 1870.05
Wilson, Garland 1942.13
Wilson, George 1906.12, 1910.12, 1916.15
Wilson, George A. 1894.20
Wilson, George W. 1906.44
Wilson, Gerald 1981.06
Wilson, Gilbert 1939.07
Wilson, Gladys 1914.33, 1921.23, 1927.26
Wilson, Grace 1887.31, 1888.09, 1904.03, 1908.16
Wilson, Gracie 1884.21
Wilson, Gran 1996.10
Wilson, Gretchen 1929.39
Wilson, H. 1870.35
Wilson, H.M. 1883.09, 1883.20
Wilson, H.N. 1876.12
Wilson, Hansford 1917.37, 1918.39, 1920.04, 1925.38, 1926.06, 1927.45, 1937.08, 1939.19
Wilson, Harrison 1926.05
Wilson, Harry 1878.11, 1904.27, 1934.36
Wilson, Harry Leon 1910.33, 1915.32
Wilson, Henriette 1918.32, 1920.45
Wilson, Henry 1902.42
Wilson, Herb 1968.02
Wilson, Imogene 1922.26, 1924.18
Wilson, Inez Richardson 1930.10
Wilson, Isabella 1947.13
Wilson, J. 1864.22, 1867.32
Wilson, J.P. 1934.35
Wilson, Jack 1915.26, 1925.48, 1926.11, 1926.46, 1927.39, 1960.12
Wilson, Jackie 1997.21
Wilson, James 1925.33, 1964.10, 1965.10, 1965.11
Wilson, Jay 1891.27, 1903.26, 1917.35, 1919.09, 1924.30, 1931.16, 1932.17, 1934.38
Wilson, Jeanette 1920.15
Wilson, Joe 1931.02
Wilson, John 1838.01, 1873.26, 1896.44
Wilson, John B. 1907.19
Wilson, John C. 1936.29, 1939.07, 1943.22, 1944.23, 1945.19, 1947.01, 1948.32, 1949.18, 1950.19, 1951.13, 1952.02, 1955.10
Wilson, John G. 1892.56
Wilson, John P. 1905.52, 1911.02, 1913.22, 1914.19
Wilson, John W. 1894.38
Wilson, Joseph 1904.52, 1907.27, 1907.51, 1909.15, 1909.19, 1913.01, 1917.01, 1918.09, 1920.43
Wilson, Joseph G. 1911.09
Wilson, Joseph P. 1906.49, 1919.23
Wilson, Jr., Earl 1976.20
Wilson, Julia 1875.11, 1875.20, 1876.22, 1878.11, 1880.21, 1881.10, 1882.82, 1886.14, 1889.25
Wilson, Julie 1969.14, 1970.12, 1988.20
Wilson, K.C. 1976.10
Wilson, Kate 1882.77
Wilson, Kate Denin 1894.39
Wilson, Kathy 1964.24
Wilson, Katie 1875.16
Wilson, Kevin 1979.26
Wilson, Kitty 1883.47, 1885.45, 1885.52
Wilson, Knox 1900.59, 1907.14
Wilson, Knox G. 1897.04
Wilson, Kristen 1991.15
Wilson, Larry 1964.15
Wilson, Laura 1889.03, 1890.06
Wilson, Lee 1968.05, 1969.12, 1971.11
Wilson, Lena 1925.18, 1929.01
Wilson, Leola 1982.12
Wilson, Lester 1963.17, 1964.32, 1975.20, 1984.14, 1985.05
Wilson, Lizette 1879.65, 1879.67
Wilson, Lizzie 1879.03, 1890.21
Wilson, Lloyd 1891.39, 1894.37, 1897.34
Wilson, Loretta 1914.33
Wilson, Margaret 1922.15, 1925.27
Wilson, Marie 1899.13, 1906.34
Wilson, Marie L. 1900.51, 1904.08
Wilson, Mary 1930.41
Wilson, Mary Louise 1963.13, 1965.17, 1968.19, 1974.17, 1982.24, 1998.04
Wilson, Master 1870.22
Wilson, Maud 1888.19, 1890.07
Wilson, Maude 1894.10
Wilson, May 1903.25
Wilson, Meredith 1997.01
Wilson, Mesdame 1852.01
Wilson, Messr. 1841.01, 1844.01, 1850.01, 1866.08, 1867.25, 1903.36, 1911.18
Wilson, Michael 1984.02, 1988.14
Wilson, Millie 1896.35
Wilson, Miss 1841.01, 1851.04, 1856.01
Wilson, Mr. 1852.03, 1852.06, 1863.01, 1868.04, 1868.06, 1871.20, 1871.21
Wilson, Mrs. 1859.01, 1872.24, 1872.26, 1872.34, 1877.22, 1877.23, 1877.25, 1896.39
Wilson, Nick 1919.06
Wilson, Orlandus 1943.02
Wilson, P.H. 1868.19
Wilson, Parker 1952.07
Wilson, Patricia 1955.27, 1959.25
Wilson, Patrick 1999.10, 2000.15
Wilson, Paul 1925.52
Wilson, Peter 1986.01, 1986.15
Wilson, Randal 1976.03
Wilson, Randy 1977.18
Wilson, Robert 1884.22, 1934.21, 1934.25, 1934.28, 1936.14, 1936.16, 1936.18, 1975.10, 1996.10
Wilson, Robert H. 1907.04
Wilson, Robin 1967.14
Wilson, Rosa 1879.15
Wilson, Rose 1880.06, 1880.13, 1880.59, 1880.67, 1881.41, 1881.57, 1882.45, 1882.62, 1885.33, 1887.33, 1887.50, 1890.39, 1891.12, 1904.12
Wilson, Rowland 1931.13
Wilson, Roy 1959.19
Wilson, Rufus 1899.33
Wilson, Ruth 1947.09
Wilson, S. Henry 1904.06
Wilson, Sandy 1954.09, 1970.11, 1986.03
Wilson, Scott 1938.15
Wilson, Speedy 1929.21, 1936.30
Wilson, Stewart 1922.14
Wilson, T. 1880.01
Wilson, Ted 1932.18
Wilson, Teddy 1944.29
Wilson, Tommar 2001.06
Wilson, Trey 1979.22, 1980.27, 1981.28
Wilson, Trixie 1912.26
Wilson, Vera 1886.06, 1896.32
Wilson, Viola 1930.33, 1939.03, 1939.04, 1939.08, 1939.11
Wilson, Violette 1919.14
Wilson, Vivian 1929.08
Wilson, W. 1875.14
Wilson, W.J. 1911.06
Wilson, Wally 2000.07
Wilson, Walter 1920.11, 1920.20, 1921.07, 1922.29, 1926.06
Wilson, Walter C. 1907.48
Wilson, Wesley 1975.20, 1980.10, 1982.12
Wilson, William 1864.17, 1872.21, 1912.09
Wilson, William E. 1895.44
Wilson, William J. 1902.18, 1910.14, 1910.19, 1911.12, 1911.28, 1911.32, 1911.34, 1911.35, 1911.36, 1911.43, 1911.47, 1912.18, 1912.21, 1912.30, 1912.40, 1913.02, 1913.08, 1913.12, 1913.13, 1913.16, 1913.22, 1913.30, 1914.01, 1914.11, 1914.19, 1916.05, 1925.43, 1926.34, 1927.20, 1927.31
Wilson, Woodey Lee 1927.48
Wilson, Woodrow 1936.30
Wilson, Woody Lee 1925.35, 1927.27
Wilton, Annie 1873.28
Wilton, Bessie 1898.05
Wilton, Ellie 1881.32
Wilton, George W. 1881.52, 1883.01, 1883.09, 1883.20
Wilton, Helen 1904.13
Wilton, May 1919.28
Wilton, Miss 1904.13, 1904.44
Wilton, Rose 1919.28
Wilton, Ruth 1932.28
Wiltshire, Editha 1899.18
Wiltshire, George 1930.24
Wilzak, Crissy 1975.15, 1979.24
Wiman, Anna 1947.06
Wiman, Dwight Deere 1929.19, 1930.25, 1931.14, 1932.26, 1933.23, 1936.05, 1937.04, 1938.05, 1938.15, 1939.13, 1940.06, 1942.15, 1947.02, 1950.03
Wiman, Nancy 1939.13
Wimazal, Gus 1926.30
Wimm, Miriam 1927.40
Wimmer, Nephi Jay 1989.05, 1991.03
Wimperis, Arthur 1907.32, 1910.03, 1910.05, 1911.06, 1911.14, 1912.26, 1913.04, 1914.04, 1914.18, 1915.25, 1920.03, 1924.01, 1925.08, 1925.42, 1925.50, 1930.30, 1964.28, 1975.22
Winans, Be Be 1987.17
Winans, John 1848.03
Winans, Marvin 1987.17
Winans, Mr. 1846.01
Winans, Ronald 1987.17
Winant, Brce 1998.01
Winant, Bruce 1991.03, 1998.01
Winant, Forrest 1912.17, 1912.42, 1918.29
Winburn, Janet 1968.09, 1968.10, 1968.12
Winbush, Marilyn 1976.35, 1979.18
Winbush, Marilynn 1980.14, 1982.17
Wincelberg, Shimon 1971.17
Winchell, Henry H. 1905.21
Winchester, Barbara 1933.20
Winchester, Eugene 1933.21
Winchester, Marion 1902.06, 1902.10
Winckler, Carlton 1945.10, 1946.06
Windberger, Ferry 1964.25
Winde, Beatrice 1971.13
Windel, Linda 1860.01
Windom, William 1947.09
Window, Muriel 1914.16
Windred, Fannie 1900.46
Windsor, Adele 1925.41
Windsor, Barbara 1964.28
Windsor, H.H. 1888.21
Windsor, Helen 1942.01
Windsor, Nancy 1961.08
Windsor, Willie 1971.12
Windust, Bretaigne 1938.15, 1947.03
Winer, I, Fraulein 1880.66
Wines, Edward 1905.25
Winfield, Hemsley 1931.31
Winfield, Sonia 1927.20
Winfred, Jennie 1882.04
Wing, Carrie 1882.49
Wing, Frances 1922.02
Wing, Jr., Theodore H. 1934.18
Wing, K. 1905.31
Wing, Ted 1918.07, 1920.27, 1922.26
Wing, Toby 1938.07
Wingard, Ada 1918.01
Wingate, Martha 1977.15
Wingate, Philip 1894.21
Wingfield, Kate 1911.02
Wingo, Eva 1928.39
Wingquist, Gunilla 1991.11, 1993.08
Winifred, Henry 1927.32
Winkleman, Master 1896.11
Winkler, Carlton 1942.34, 1946.10
Winkler, Chuck 1996.10
Winkler, Harvey 1903.09
Winkler, Herbert 1941.10
Winkler, Leonore 1930.10, 1935.01
Winkler, Richard 1976.07, 1976.15, 1980.14, 1982.17, 1985.15, 1987.06
Winkopp, Paul 1927.04
Winloche, Isabelle 1907.08, 1911.08
Winn, Annie 1887.43
Winn, E. 1896.49
Winn, Lynn 1966.24, 1969.17
Winn, Mattie 1887.45
Winn, Rella 1931.35
Winnall, Elsie 1936.24
Winne, G.B. 1884.53
Winner, Annie 1876.18, 1876.21, 1877.25, 1879.03, 1879.38, 1880.26, 1883.64, 1884.22, 1886.47, 1888.36
Winner, Carrie 1876.18
Winner, Ella 1880.40
Winner, Gussie 1876.17, 1876.18, 1876.21
Winner, Josie 1889.24, 1896.35
Winner, Lizzie 1884.22, 1886.34, 1887.11, 1888.21
Winner, Mary 1879.03, 1879.38, 1880.26
Winner, Miss 1876.18, 1886.36
Winner, Polly 1883.67, 1884.22, 1887.43, 1891.03
Winner, Sadie 1883.44
Winner, Susie 1876.27, 1877.16, 1877.25, 1879.03, 1879.38, 1882.19, 1905.35
Winnick, Jay Brian 1999.16
Winnie, G.B. 1870.30
Winnie, Miss 1857.01
Winnie, W. 1882.69
Winninger, Charles 1912.14, 1916.02, 1917.37, 1919.30, 1920.18, 1921.19, 1925.30, 1926.46, 1927.49, 1927.67, 1932.03, 1932.11, 1934.38, 1951.22
Winninger, Charles J. 1910.09, 1914.06
Winogrom, Blanche 1963.28
Winslow, Elsie 1925.37
Winslow, H.H. 1888.21
Winslow, Herbert Hall 1888.21, 1891.15, 1894.17, 1898.08, 1898.67, 1907.04, 1925.16
Winslow, June 1947.14
Winslow, Leah 1924.25
Winslow, Pamela 1987.18
Winslow, Rain 1958.03, 1959.05
Winstock, Melvin G. 1903.19
Winston, Alice 1896.27
Winston, Bruce 1926.33
Winston, Charlie 1924.19
Winston, Claire 1938.04
Winston, Hattie 1970.20, 1983.21
Winston, Jeannie 1879.25, 1880.26, 1880.57, 1880.62, 1883.58, 1898.17
Winston, Jennie 1881.25, 1882.18
Winston, Jr., Harry 1907.24
Winston, Julie 1955.07
Winston, Lee 1980.16
Winston, Marian 1928.24
Winston, Maud 1896.03
Winston, Maude 1894.50
Winston, Paulette 1926.36
Winston, Tarik 1992.06, 1996.01, 1996.12, 1998.09, 2000.05
Winter, Alexander 1979.22
Winter, Anne E. 1905.43
Winter, Charles 1935.01
Winter, Dale 1923.09
Winter, Edward 1966.24, 1968.31
Winter, Eleanor 1944.23
Winter, Ethel 1954.10, 1955.04
Winter, G. 1894.30
Winter, J. 1865.05, 1871.17
Winter, J.P. 1879.02
Winter, Julian 1925.32
Winter, Max 1920.46
Winter, Mr. 1883.66
Winter, Mrs. W. 1867.19, 1867.20, 1868.22
Winter, Richard 1961.08
Winter, Rose 1908.03, 1911.45, 1937.03
Winter, Rose Beatrice 1906.47
Winter, Shelley 1942.31
Winter, Valentine 1922.35
Winter, W. 1867.19, 1888.10
Winter, Winona 1906.25, 1910.25, 1911.30, 1921.19
Winterberg, Robert 1916.14, 1919.11
Winterbottom, Mr. 1887.10

Winters, Charles 1900.47
Winters, David 1954.12, 1957.05, 1957.12, 1959.13
Winters, Julian 1919.04, 1920.34
Winters, June 1938.08
Winters, Lawrence 1946.10, 1953.05, 1953.14, 1954.04, 1954.14, 1958.11, 1962.07
Winters, Marjorie 1949.18
Winters, Nancy 1984.14
Winters, Newton 1976.04
Winters, Pauline 1909.15, 1910.09
Winters, Percy 1929.25
Winters, Roland 1970.07
Winters, Shelley 1970.07
Winters, Stephanie 1962.18
Winters, Violet 1908.33
Wintersteller, Lynne 1993.16
Winther, Michael 1994.01, 1997.15
Winthrop, Adelaide 1917.12, 1920.02
Winthrop, Eddie 1923.04
Winthrop, Theodore 1904.14
Winton, Elma 1892.04
Wintz, George E. 1932.30
Winwood, Estelle 1922.17, 1959.05
Wiova, Marie 1912.19
Wipf, Alex 1980.17
Wirges, William 1979.24
Wirt, Mara 1960.01, 1961.09
Wirth, Edward 1917.16
Wirtz, Arthur 1940.16
Wirtz, Arthur M. 1942.19, 1944.20, 1946.14, 1947.12, 1948.19, 1949.05, 1949.06
Wirz 1870.03
Wisdom, Clara 1882.75, 1884.08, 1885.07, 1885.09, 1897.25, 1897.53
Wisdom, Miss 1882.60
Wisdom, Nellie 1881.38
Wisdom, Norman 1966.27
Wise, Ben 1931.05
Wise, Fannie 1907.22
Wise, Fanny 1909.10
Wise, Frank 1899.41
Wise, Fred 1989.12
Wise, Hazel 1905.50
Wise, Hen 1898.22
Wise, Joseph 1978.02
Wise, Laura 1899.28
Wise, Lois 1976.34
Wise, Messr. 1851.01
Wise, Mr. 1850.01
Wise, Patricia 1968.09
Wise, Paula 1999.15
Wise, Scott 1985.12, 1989.03, 1992.04, 1993.02, 1994.01, 1996.04, 1999.01
Wise, Thomas 1907.30
Wise, Tom 1906.25, 1907.63, 1927.01
Wisehart, Fredreika 1968.14
Wiseman, George 1901.04, 1904.15
Wiser, Albert 1921.25
Wiser, Lena 1898.22
Wiser, Mr. 1846.01
Wisham, Clara 1880.03
Wishard, Scoville 1951.05
Wishon, Rosalind 1929.09, 1929.39
Wishy, Joe 1966.09
Wisner, Frank 1925.25
Wisner, Gerda 1898.46
Wisnet, Charles 1980.05
Wiswell, Andy 1972.09
Witchie, Katharine 1927.20
Witchie, Katherine 1911.38, 1915.23, 1919.30, 1924.35, 1926.22
Witchie, Kathryn 1913.16
Witham 1880.69, 1881.14
Witham, Arthur 1921.12
Witham, C.W. 1876.23, 1877.21, 1885.15
Witham, Charles 1865.06, 1881.38, 1882.74, 1884.41, 1886.42, 1887.39, 1889.48
Witham, Charles W. 1866.16, 1872.27, 1873.26, 1879.25, 1879.37, 1879.68, 1880.09, 1880.36, 1880.64, 1881.09, 1881.29, 1882.02, 1882.50, 1882.79, 1883.32, 1883.46, 1883.53, 1883.63, 1884.13, 1885.49, 1885.66, 1886.52, 1887.07, 1887.16, 1887.48, 1888.14, 1888.27, 1888.40, 1889.07, 1889.11, 1889.18, 1892.42, 1892.57
Witham, John 1987.19
Witham, Mr. 1893.45
Witham, Tricia 1980.01
Withe, Will 1928.25
Withee, Mabel 1918.05, 1919.13, 1919.33, 1921.03, 1921.24, 1922.11, 1923.01, 1923.13, 1924.36, 1925.45
Witherell, John 1886.27
Withers, Charles 1916.13, 1938.08
Withers, Helen 1932.23
Withers, Iva 1949.03
Withers, Jr., William 1870.39, 1873.12, 1873.14, 1873.17, 1875.06, 1875.10
Withers, William 1870.43, 1876.32, 1877.02, 1881.31, 1888.04, 1888.34
Witherspoon, Cora 1934.35
Witherspoon, George 1892.27
Witherspoon, John 1876.12
Witherspoon, W. 1984.15
Withett, T.H. 1897.23
Withey, Barbara 1972.08
Withiers, William 1886.32
Withington, Lillian 1947.11
Witkowska, Nadja 1964.30
Witmark and Sons 1908.05
Witmark, Isadore 1893.30, 1897.56
Witmark, Isidor 1891.02, 1891.43
Witmark, Isidore 1889.34, 1891.26, 1902.20
Witmark, Julius 1892.36, 1892.56
Witmark, Julius P. 1891.43, 1894.07, 1894.35, 1897.30
Witmer, Kathleen 1972.04
Witt, C. 1887.19
Witt, J. 1897.29
Witt, L. 1905.06
Witt, Laura 1900.34
Witt, Max 1903.41
Witt, Max S. 1903.07, 1903.20, 1903.27, 1905.33
Witt, Phil 1987.16
Witt, Rose 1897.26
Witt, Sophie 1897.26, 1909.15
Witt, William L. 1972.07
Witte, Sophie 1904.10, 1905.06
Witter, William C. 1980.07
Wittman, Scott 1995.12, 2000.16
Wittmann, Hugo 1885.27, 1885.28, 1885.67, 1887.18, 1890.08, 1890.28, 1890.39, 1892.16, 1900.29
Wittmer, Toddie 1963.04
Wittmer, Toodie 1963.06
Wittner, Edwin 1939.19
Wittop, Freddy 1939.31, 1942.29, 1961.10, 1961.28, 1964.01, 1964.40, 1965.01, 1965.19, 1965.31, 1966.29, 1967.15, 1968.01, 1968.07, 1968.32, 1969.05, 1970.21, 1978.04, 1984.14, 1985.20
Witts, Jack 1922.27
Wittstein, Ed 1961.05, 1961.26, 1962.11, 1962.14, 1964.12, 1965.36, 1969.02, 1970.06
Witzell, Charles 1919.25
Wixon, Nat 1900.08
Wizamal, Gus 1927.15
Wllis, M.M. 1899.12
Wodehouse, P.G. 1916.19, 1917.01, 1917.06, 1917.17, 1917.20, 1917.26, 1918.03, 1918.28, 1918.34, 1918.37, 1919.39, 1920.44, 1923.30, 1924.08, 1926.36, 1927.01, 1928.01, 1928.03, 1928.12, 1934.36, 1946.01, 1948.16, 1964.02, 1966.14, 1974.09, 1975.24, 1984.14, 1986.01, 1987.15, 1990.14, 1994.08
Wodtke, Nicholas Cross 1993.04
Woerner, Carl 1977.15
Woess, Carl 1916.08
Wofford, Don 1965.31
Wohl, Jack 1989.05
Wohlman, Al 1926.37
Wohlmuth, Alois 1885.27, 1885.28, 1885.67, 1887.18, 1898.37, 1900.29
Wohlmuth, Messr. 1892.43
Wolcott, Florence 1902.11
Wolcott, Geri 1967.01
Wolcott, John 1919.43, 1921.19
Wolcott, Winnifred 1898.46
Woldin, Judd 1963.16, 1973.10
Wolf Trap Production, A 1980.26
Wolf, Anne 1936.26
Wolf, Claire 1938.14
Wolf, D.S. 1889.47
Wolf, Don 1992.03
Wolf, E.A. 1888.37
Wolf, Johann 1890.31, 1894.01
Wolf, John 1891.33
Wolf, John Leslie 1998.21
Wolf, Peter 1947.04, 1964.17, 1965.15, 1966.13, 1977.07, 1979.22, 1980.12, 1980.16, 1983.10, 1984.09, 1985.01, 1985.08
Wolf, Rennold 1911.18, 1911.24, 1911.41, 1912.31, 1913.27, 1914.13, 1917.13, 1917.32, 1918.11, 1918.19, 1919.15, 1976.26
Wolf, Sanford 1926.07
Wolf, Tommy 1959.12
Wolf, Wilhelm 1897.08
Wolf, William 1903.14
Wolfe, Benjamin Jonah 1990.19
Wolfe, Carol 1940.11
Wolfe, David 1992.18
Wolfe, Edwin R. 1918.14
Wolfe, George C. 1992.08, 1996.07, 1998.16, 2000.08
Wolfe, Ian 1933.12
Wolfe, Jacques 1940.01
Wolfe, Jim 1979.22, 1987.16
Wolfe, John Leslie 1986.04, 1991.09, 1991.12, 1994.05
Wolfe, Karin 1960.06, 1973.12
Wolfe, Kitty 1896.40
Wolfe, L. 1914.03
Wolfe, Leslie-Ann 1980.11
Wolfe, Rennold 1915.15
Wolfe, Thomas 1978.10
Wolfe, Wendy 1981.01
Wolfensohn, James D. 1995.05
Wolff, Art 1987.20
Wolff, Beverly 1958.09, 1965.07, 1965.26
Wolff, Emil 1893.30
Wolff, Emil O. 1889.51, 1893.30
Wolff, Frederic 1924.45
Wolff, Greta 1959.08
Wolff, Hank 1944.02
Wolff, Philla 1896.23
Wolff, Reuben 1921.17
Wolff, William 1898.06, 1898.14, 1898.30, 1898.33, 1898.37, 1905.36
Wolfington, Iggie 1957.18, 1962.13, 1980.16
Wolfram, Mark 1981.16
Wolfson, D.S. 1936.07
Wolfson, Martin 1924.14, 1927.45, 1935.16, 1941.01, 1949.04, 1955.06, 1955.07, 1957.06, 1958.14, 1964.18, 1965.02, 1966.19
Wolfson, Victor 1935.16, 1955.10
Wolgin, Jack L. 1973.09
Wolinsky, Robert 1999.05
Wolk, Jesse 1935.11
Wolkenstein, Herr 1879.22
Wollandi, Andy 1949.06
Wollner, Mr. 1896.34
Wolmer, Phyllis 1922.05
Woloshin, Sid 1976.34
Wolpe, Lenny 1980.30, 1981.12, 1985.15, 1986.18
Wolper, Dave 1944.14
Wolsk, Eugene V. 1971.13, 1977.12, 1979.03, 1981.18, 1985.08
Wolsky, Albert 1966.05
Wolvin, Roy 1946.19
Wonder, Stevie 1986.02, 1997.21
Wonder, Tommy 1940.03, 1941.13, 1943.05, 1950.09
Wonderlee, Frank 1912.02
Wondisford, Diane 1996.16
Wong, B.D. 1999.03
Wong, Janet 1981.07
Wong, Joe 1938.08, 1949.09
Wong, S. 1931.39
Wonn, Ed 1898.47
Wonn, Edward 1900.47, 1924.07
Woo, Jenny 1990.17
Woo, Julie 1977.07
Woo, Jung Hoon 1998.08
Wood, A. 1872.36
Wood, Adele 1873.18, 1873.23
Wood, Adolf 1966.03
Wood, Aggie 1868.23, 1869.07, 1869.08, 1869.46, 1869.47, 1870.36, 1870.39, 1872.25, 1872.30, 1872.32, 1872.36, 1872.38, 1872.40, 1872.43, 1878.05
Wood, Alf. 1891.16
Wood, Alfred 1884.61
Wood, Alice 1926.03, 1927.10, 1928.38
Wood, Annie 1872.13, 1884.15, 1884.56
Wood, Arthur 1905.46, 1906.37, 1929.39
Wood, Arthur D. 1907.05
Wood, Baby 1884.53, 1887.11
Wood, Bella 1884.61
Wood, Bert 1958.03, 1973.15
Wood, Bertram 1954.12
Wood, Blanche 1903.14
Wood, Charles 1945.03, 1948.16, 1948.32
Wood, Cyrus 1917.15, 1918.42, 1922.07, 1922.31, 1922.36, 1922.40, 1923.13, 1923.17, 1923.25, 1925.11, 1927.68, 1929.32, 1929.50
Wood, Cyrus D. 1920.41
Wood, Daisy 1884.21
Wood, Deedee 1953.07, 1956.12
Wood, Douglas 1927.05, 1932.25
Wood, Douglas J. 1917.15
Wood, E. 1873.19, 1873.24, 1873.26
Wood, Elizabeth 1913.26
Wood, Ernest 1906.48, 1908.39
Wood, Ernest D. 1905.50
Wood, Eugene 1957.08
Wood, Eugene R. 1961.13, 1961.28, 1965.18
Wood, Florence 1879.10
Wood, Frances 1884.61
Wood, Frank 1914.18
Wood, George 1866.06, 1866.08, 1866.11, 1866.15, 1868.20, 1868.23, 1868.32, 1869.08, 1869.23, 1869.34, 1869.36, 1869.37, 1869.38, 1869.39, 1869.42, 1869.45, 1870.01, 1870.02, 1870.06, 1870.09, 1870.12, 1870.14, 1870.18, 1870.22, 1870.25, 1870.28, 1870.31, 1870.32, 1870.40, 1871.05, 1871.09, 1871.11, 1872.02, 1872.04, 1872.05, 1872.08, 1872.12, 1872.30, 1872.32, 1872.36, 1872.38, 1872.40, 1872.43, 1876.06, 1884.27
Wood, George H. 1883.46, 1883.53, 1883.63, 1884.13
Wood, Gertrude 1892.38
Wood, Grace 1921.15
Wood, Greta 1929.51
Wood, Harriet 1884.61
Wood, Harriette 1884.61
Wood, Haydn 1919.26, 1930.20, 1964.28
Wood, Helen 1951.18, 1952.01, 1957.01
Wood, Henri 1933.04
Wood, Henry 1865.03
Wood, Irving 1918.01
Wood, J. Hickory 1901.27, 1903.04, 1903.33, 1903.39, 1904.47, 1905.19, 1905.48
Wood, Jean 1931.02
Wood, Jessie 1899.06, 1900.20
Wood, John 1857.05, 1857.07, 1860.03, 1878.22
Wood, Julia 1884.61, 1895.23
Wood, Karen 1987.01
Wood, Kay 1928.45
Wood, Kelly 1963.10, 1972.01
Wood, L. 1862.08
Wood, Larry 1922.40
Wood, Larry L. 1928.31
Wood, Leiomini 1938.08
Wood, Lena 1889.37
Wood, Leo 1921.21, 1922.14, 1924.36, 1925.03
Wood, Lois 1922.12
Wood, Lou 1930.32, 1933.26
Wood, Margaret 1892.22, 1892.33
Wood, Margarite 1892.47
Wood, Marguerite 1889.47
Wood, Marjorie 1919.20
Wood, Maryrose 1981.27
Wood, May B. 1903.23
Wood, Messr. 1885.39
Wood, Mildred 1912.16
Wood, Milton 1946.08
Wood, Miss 1876.23
Wood, Morton 1915.30
Wood, Mr. 1854.06, 1871.15, 1883.66
Wood, Mrs. Henry 1870.25
Wood, Mrs. John 1856.04, 1857.07, 1860.04, 1860.05, 1861.03, 1863.01, 1863.02, 1863.03, 1863.04, 1863.09, 1863.10, 1864.05, 1864.09, 1864.12, 1864.15, 1864.16, 1864.18, 1864.19, 1864.20, 1864.21, 1866.03, 1872.09, 1872.11, 1872.23, 1872.35, 1873.03
Wood, Napua 1938.08
Wood, Neil 1933.26
Wood, Nellie 1879.01
Wood, Otis F. 1905.47
Wood, Pearl 1894.52
Wood, Peggy 1911.42, 1912.39, 1913.15, 1913.32, 1914.34, 1917.02, 1917.15, 1919.31, 1922.04, 1922.47, 1933.23
Wood, Philip 1935.15
Wood, Richard 1961.18
Wood, Roland 1951.14
Wood, Stanley G. 1918.13, 1935.16
Wood, Stuart Craig 1970.21
Wood, Susan 1994.07

Wood, Swan 1913.18, 1919.39
Wood, T. 1869.37
Wood, Teresa 1869.36
Wood, Theresa 1869.42, 1869.45, 1870.01, 1870.09, 1870.12, 1870.18, 1870.28, 1870.32, 1871.05, 1872.02, 1872.04, 1872.25, 1872.30, 1872.38, 1876.34
Wood, Therese 1869.39, 1870.22, 1870.25, 1872.05, 1872.08, 1872.12, 1872.14, 1872.32, 1872.36, 1872.40, 1872.43, 1881.23, 1882.27
Wood, Thomas 1916.04
Wood, Wanda 1926.22
Wood, William B. 1891.26, 1892.09, 1893.28, 1907.63
Wood, Wilma 1907.32
Woodall, Oliver 1985.02
Woodard, Charlaine 1978.09, 1988.17
Woodberry, Minnie 1904.25
Woodburn, Gordon 1956.14
Woodbury, Al 1950.14
Woodbury, Alice 1888.39
Woodbury, Grace 1888.39
Woodbury, Harry 1888.06, 1888.11
Woodbury, Minnie 1902.24, 1905.44
Woodcock, M. deM. 1889.26
Woode, Henri 1976.04
Woodeson, Nicholas 1981.04
Woodfield, W.H. 1873.18, 1873.21
Woodfield, Walter H. 1875.15, 1875.20
Woodford, Nelly 1886.50
Woodham, Charles Somerset 1750.01
Woodhead, Ed 1947.09
Woodhouse, E.G. 1894.33, 1897.32
Woodhull, A.H. 1902.26
Woodhull, Aaron 1888.16
Woodhull, Frederick 1866.12
Woodhull, Miss 1836.01
Woodhull, Mr. 1823.01, 1836.01
Wooding, Russell 1927.33, 1928.18, 1929.23, 1931.11, 1933.22, 1935.12, 1976.04
Wooding, Sam 1932.08
Woodlard, David C. 1993.06
Woodley, A. Percy 1912.33
Woodley, Arthur 1913.17, 1979.27
Woodley, H.P. 1908.34, 1910.30, 1911.42, 1913.31, 1918.41
Woodley, Mary 1946.12
Woodley, Mr. 1836.01
Woodley, Percy 1916.07, 1916.19, 1925.31
Woodman, Annie 1884.58
Woodman, Britt 1992.08
Woodruff, Charlotte 1923.25, 1924.47, 1926.14, 1928.26, 1929.40
Woodruff, Harry 1881.15
Woodruff, Helen S. 1922.13
Woodruff, Henry 1893.11, 1899.38
Woodruff, Julia 1902.06
Woodruff, Minnie 1891.23
Woodruff, Roland 1927.49
Woodruff, Virginia Ann 1993.03
Woods, A.H. 1905.39, 1910.22, 1910.32, 1911.30, 1911.37, 1912.01, 1912.35, 1912.37, 1914.08, 1915.20, 1918.24, 1921.30, 1924.22, 1924.37, 1926.49
Woods, Al. H. 1905.34
Woods, Billie 1914.33
Woods, Carol 1985.05, 1993.02, 2001.02
Woods, Charles Winter 1935.01
Woods, Clothilde 1918.16
Woods, Denice 1983.04
Woods, Denise 1992.14
Woods, Diane 1947.03
Woods, Edward 1952.13
Woods, Ernest 1913.17
Woods, F.M. 1898.59
Woods, Frank R. 1919.31
Woods, Franker 1922.38, 1927.10, 1927.16, 1928.16, 1930.35
Woods, Harry 1921.34, 1923.12, 1925.33, 1940.20, 1942.25, 1974.11, 1989.16, 1997.21
Woods, J.M. 1883.56
Woods, Jack 1953.16
Woods, Johnny 1940.02
Woods, Joseph M. 1883.66
Woods, Josephine 1957.09
Woods, Jr., Allie 1991.01
Woods, Larry 1930.21
Woods, Lillian 1920.10
Woods, Louise 1952.08
Woods, Marion 1908.34
Woods, Miller 1935.12
Woods, Mr. 1879.66
Woods, Murray 1882.27, 1883.36, 1898.66
Woods, Murry 1881.28, 1885.62, 1886.30, 1888.02, 1898.36, 1899.24
Woods, Pearl 1894.44
Woods, Richard 1960.01, 1969.17, 1982.24
Woods, Sheryl 1981.21, 1983.05, 1986.04, 1990.08, 1992.14
Woods, Thomas E. 1920.35
Woods, Tommy 1923.39
Woods, W. 1919.43
Woodson, Arthur 1921.16
Woodson, Harry 1878.13, 1888.42
Woodson, Jack 1954.08
Woodson, James H. 1923.39
Woodson, Messr. 1888.42
Woodthorpe, Peter 1968.02
Woodville, Erie 1902.19
Woodville, R. Paul 1972.11
Woodward, (Ritter), Tex 1931.02
Woodward, Anne 1900.48, 1900.55
Woodward, C. 1909.13
Woodward, Charles 1971.16, 1979.06
Woodward, Edward 1964.16
Woodward, Evelyn 1898.08
Woodward, Fred 1906.23, 1912.38
Woodward, George 1888.04
Woodward, H. Guy 1905.45, 1906.27
Woodward, Harold 1927.01
Woodward, M.C. 1893.07
Woodward, Matt 1891.14, 1892.45, 1897.14, 1897.55, 1898.51, 1903.04, 1907.24, 1907.42, 1908.07, 1908.10
Woodward, Matt C. 1900.16, 1902.20, 1903.09
Woodward, Matt. C. 1891.21, 1894.46
Woodward, Matthew 1900.52, 1903.39, 1911.32, 1915.27, 1916.14
Woodward, Matthew C. 1903.18, 1907.44, 1917.30, 1917.31
Woodward, P. 1875.32
Woodward, Sidney 1896.46
Woodworth 1887.02
Woodworth, James 1878.22
Woolard, David C. 1994.01, 1999.07, 1999.17, 2000.17, 2001.03
Woolcott, Alexander 1929.20
Woolcott, May 1886.10
Wooler, J.P. 1877.22, 1887.40
Woolever, Harry 1964.20, 1968.17
Wooley, Arthur 1898.04, 1898.06, 1898.07, 1898.09, 1898.14, 1898.33, 1898.37, 1898.39, 1904.34
Wooley, Frank 1897.53
Wooley, Mark 1905.32
Wooley, Michael-Leon 1999.17, 2000.11
Wooley, Monty 1938.10
Wooley, Steve 1976.07, 1978.25
Woolf, B.E. 1884.37, 1884.48
Woolf, Ben E. 1879.53, 1880.47, 1881.08
Woolf, Benjamin E. 1865.06, 1866.07, 1866.19, 1866.21, 1867.06, 1868.11
Woolf, E. 1848.01, 1885.44
Woolf, Edgar Allan 1906.23, 1911.40, 1918.09, 1918.16, 1918.25, 1919.24, 1989.06, 1997.11, 1998.06, 1999.11
Woolf, Edgar Allen 1921.06
Woolf, Harold 1935.13
Woolf, Henry 1965.39
Woolf, Mr. 1841.01
Woolf, Walter 1901.25, 1919.30, 1920.09, 1920.23, 1921.14, 1922.36, 1923.17, 1924.23, 1925.23, 1926.27, 1928.48
Woolf, William 1898.07
Woolfe, B.E. 1881.23, 1882.27
Woolfe, Billy 1916.15
Woolfolk, William 1940.01, 1942.03, 1943.24
Woolley, Edgar M. 1929.45
Woolley, Emily 1926.01
Woolley, Monty 1930.25, 1930.40, 1931.04, 1932.27, 1933.23, 1935.14, 1936.05
Woolley, Reginald 1954.09
Woolley, Scot 1993.05, 1996.04
Woolls, Messr. 1796.01
Woolls, Mr. 1794.01
Woolls, Stephen 1796.02
Woolsey, George 1902.10
Woolsey, Robert 1919.29, 1921.07, 1922.02, 1922.36, 1923.27, 1925.43, 1927.08, 1927.50
Woolsey, Willard 1942.27
Woolson, Henry 1881.11
Woolverton, Linda 1994.04, 1997.20, 1999.16, 2000.06
Wooster, Edward 1913.21
Wooten, Daniel 1996.01
Wooten, Daniel B. 1996.12
Wooton, Lillian 1892.21
Wooton, Miriam 1927.50
Wootten, Christopher 1980.13
Wopat, Tom 1999.04
Worden, Florence 1903.14, 1904.12
Worden, Frank 1934.12
Worden, Norton 1931.02
Worden, Oriska 1901.29, 1904.01
Wordes, Smith 1979.26
Work, Henry Clay 1922.25
Work, Julian 1944.14, 1944.27, 1946.10
Workman, Jason 1989.23
Workman, Jenny 1954.01, 1955.27, 1958.07, 1959.04, 1961.27, 1962.15, 1963.04, 1965.24, 1966.31
World, John W. 1896.32
Worldvision Enterprises, Inc. 1975.13
Worles, James 1907.55
Worley, Jo Anne 1961.16, 1989.25, 1999.11
Wormer, Andre 1925.09
Wormley, Don 1907.29
Wormser, Andre 1891.05, 1893.25, 1916.16
Worrall, Dusty 1949.03, 1954.07, 1956.03, 1957.18
Worrall, Tom 1989.06
Worrell, Devah 1927.27, 1928.08
Worrell, Irene 1866.06, 1866.08, 1866.11, 1866.15, 1867.13, 1867.14, 1867.15, 1867.16, 1867.17, 1868.08, 1868.16, 1872.07, 1873.27, 1875.39, 1880.51
Worrell, Jennie 1866.06, 1866.08, 1866.11, 1866.15, 1867.13, 1867.14, 1867.15, 1867.16, 1867.17, 1868.08, 1868.16, 1869.34, 1872.07
Worrell, Sophie 1866.06, 1866.08, 1866.11, 1866.15, 1867.13, 1867.14, 1867.15, 1867.16, 1867.17, 1868.08, 1868.16, 1869.34, 1872.07, 1873.27, 1875.39, 1878.15, 1880.51, 1885.03, 1886.62
Worsley, Joyce 1983.08
Worsley, Pat 1934.34
Worsley, Wallace 1914.24
Worth 1965.30
Worth, Adelaide 1896.01
Worth, Allison 1917.03
Worth, Billie 1940.06, 1943.16, 1944.01, 1944.29, 1951.17
Worth, Bobby 1940.16
Worth, Coley 1927.38, 1953.15, 1954.06, 1954.10, 1955.17, 1956.10, 1957.13, 1957.15, 1958.15, 1958.16, 1961.04, 1961.06, 1963.24, 1964.30, 1964.31, 1965.25, 1965.27, 1966.05, 1971.07, 1974.16, 1975.16, 1977.11
Worth, Coly 1929.26
Worth, Ellen 1908.21
Worth, Florence 1886.23
Worth, Grace 1929.26, 1933.25
Worth, Gracie 1934.43, 1938.17
Worth, Jessica 1910.19
Worth, Joyce 1936.12
Worth, Maggie 1961.12, 1961.21, 1962.13, 1962.16, 1962.20, 1963.29, 1968.17
Worth, Manny 1913.25
Worth, Marvin 1962.02
Worth, Mimi 1943.20
Worth, Penny 1976.24, 1977.06
Worth, Richard 1942.30
Worth, Robert 1937.08
Worth, Sidney 1895.16
Worth, Toni 1943.20
Worthall, Rel 1906.06
Worthing, Gerrie 1937.02
Worthing, Helen Lee 1920.28, 1921.21, 1923.38
Worthington, Elizabeth 1981.19
Worthington, Harriet 1905.48
Worthington, II., Conwell 1985.01
Worthington, Marie 1900.38
Worthington, P.J. 1898.60, 1903.21
Worthington, Tim 1955.01
Worthley, Abbott 1912.16
Worthley, J. Abbott 1914.30, 1915.07
Worthley, Minthorne 1912.16
Worthy, John 1933.27
Woshak, Tamara 1966.21
Wragland, Flora 1889.01
Wragland, Florence 1896.12
Wrangler, Jack 1997.05
Wray, Ada 1872.07
Wray, Fay 1931.34
Wray, John 1873.12, 1873.14, 1942.34, 1946.10
Wreford, Catherine 2001.08
Wreghitt, Randall L. 1999.05
Wren, Jennie 1937.11
Wren, Miss 1870.26
Wren, Mr. 1860.06
Wren, Oliver W. 1879.71
Wrench, Miss 1852.01
Wretched Refuse, The 1975.18
Wrick, Mary 1934.13
Wright, A. 1866.16
Wright, Alice 1879.38, 1880.24, 1880.34
Wright, Arthur 1876.36
Wright, Barbara 1980.21, 1981.20, 1981.21
Wright, Ben 1987.18, 1996.04, 1998.10
Wright, Benjamin F. 1915.30
Wright, Bertie 1895.32
Wright, Betty 1926.03
Wright, Bob 1964.24, 1965.18, 1967.07, 1977.12
Wright, Bron 1991.01
Wright, Charles 1875.06
Wright, Charles Edward 1907.14
Wright, Charles R. 1889.51
Wright, Daniel 1993.19
Wright, Dundi 1973.09, 1989.18
Wright, E. 1892.12
Wright, Edith 1917.15
Wright, Edith Mae 1927.20
Wright, Elaine 1989.03
Wright, Ellen 1901.25
Wright, Ethel Louise 1925.39, 1927.06
Wright, Fannie 1879.38
Wright, Fred 1910.21, 1927.44, 1927.57, 1927.61
Wright, Fred E. 1905.35, 1907.38
Wright, Frederic Coit 1904.19
Wright, G.F. 1894.42
Wright, Gary 1954.15
Wright, Gary Landon 1985.04
Wright, Gene 1942.16
Wright, George A. 1905.12
Wright, Harold 1915.27
Wright, Harry 1894.49, 1895.05
Wright, Harry W. 1893.36
Wright, Hazel 1922.21
Wright, Helen 1892.47
Wright, Helena-Joyce 1983.15
Wright, Hilda 1917.31
Wright, Horace 1904.32, 1905.47
Wright, Hugh E. 1925.42
Wright, Huntley 1907.32
Wright, J.H. 1907.34
Wright, James 1942.19
Wright, Jeffrey 1996.07
Wright, John B. 1854.01
Wright, Joyce 1948.02, 1951.01, 1951.03, 1951.06, 1951.07, 1951.09, 1955.15, 1955.16, 1955.18, 1955.22, 1955.23, 1955.24
Wright, Jr., Fred 1895.43, 1904.29, 1905.27, 1911.11
Wright, Lena 1902.30
Wright, Lizzie 1875.11
Wright, Mabel 1900.10
Wright, Martha 1947.14, 1950.06
Wright, Mary Catherine 1978.06, 1980.27
Wright, Master 1854.07
Wright, Messr. 1851.01, 1852.05, 1854.01, 1855.10
Wright, Michael 1957.16
Wright, Miss 1871.11, 1917.31
Wright, Mr. 1852.01, 1854.03, 1854.07, 1859.01, 1866.12, 1875.10
Wright, Mrs. E. 1866.06, 1866.11, 1867.13, 1867.14, 1867.16
Wright, Mrs. Edward 1870.07, 1870.15, 1870.44, 1871.27, 1872.37, 1873.10
Wright, Nat 1957.14
Wright, Ned 1952.15, 1961.09, 1961.13, 1962.07, 1962.16, 1979.32
Wright, Nigel 1999.15
Wright, Randel 1993.03
Wright, Ray 1929.39, 1979.13
Wright, Rebecca 1983.01
Wright, Rick 1982.22
Wright, Robert 1944.21, 1946.18, 1948.24, 1952.02, 1953.16, 1954.17, 1957.06, 1961.26, 1965.22, 1965.35, 1976.07, 1978.03, 1981.21, 1985.13, 1986.09, 1989.26, 1999.23
Wright, Russel 1925.20
Wright, S. 1860.02, 1869.26, 1870.07
Wright, Samuel E. 1971.12, 1974.05, 1983.21, 1989.07, 1991.01, 1997.20
Wright, Sr., George 1908.05
Wright, Stephen 1981.18, 1990.18
Wright, Syreeta 1995.02

Wright, Travis 1983.13, 1984.11
Wright, Valerie 1997.07, 1999.04
Wright, W. David L. 1964.28
Wright, Will 1959.19
Wright, Willie 1898.02
Wright-Bey, Marvin 1987.17
Wrightson, Earl 1944.17, 1945.04
Wrigley, Ben 1981.19
Wrobleski, Bronek 1929.34
Wroten, Susie 1929.18
Wrothe, Ed Lee 1904.58, 1905.34
Wrubel, Allie 1931.31
Wujcik, J.W. 1918.36
Wulff, Derick 1925.36, 1927.34
Wulfing, George 1918.17
Wulp, John 1978.24
Wuriu, Yashushi 1922.21
Wurtzebach, Edward 1939.15
Wurzel, Messr. 1925.03
Wyart, Al 1927.12, 1929.19
Wyart, Albert 1924.08
Wyatt, Ada 1898.50
Wyatt, Bessie 1897.43
Wyatt, Francis G. 1881.35
Wyatt, Frank 1882.20, 1882.25
Wyatt, H. 1881.55
Wyatt, Jerry 1970.09
Wyatt, Jessie 1895.05
Wyatt, Messr. 1923.21
Wyatt, Mr. 1852.04
Wyatt, Richard 1954.13
Wyche, Ronald 2000.15
Wyche, Sid 1989.12
Wycherley, Margaret 1937.11
Wycherly, Maude 1903.06
Wycherly, William 1898.11
Wyckham, John 1962.23, 1963.01, 1964.45, 1965.23
Wyckoff, Evelyn 1941.04, 1942.01, 1942.11
Wyckoff, Fred 1903.09, 1907.23
Wyckoff, Lou Ann 1963.15
Wyckoff, Marie 1966.02
Wyckoff, Messr. 1903.03
Wyckoff, W.F. 1883.29
Wycoff, Fred 1907.12
Wydro, Ken 1995.04
Wydro, Knoelle Higginson 1995.04
Wye, Thomas 1930.29
Wyeth, Howard 1971.01
Wyeth, Juilan 1859.03
Wykoff, William 1942.20
Wyler, Gretchen 1955.02, 1957.17
Wylie, D.B. 1866.10, 1866.14, 1867.03, 1867.06, 1867.07, 1868.01, 1868.09, 1868.11, 1868.12
Wylie, Elinor 1931.06
Wylie, John 1989.26
Wylie, Lauri 1930.20, 1930.30, 1953.17
Wylie, Sharon 1974.01
Wylie, Stanford 1900.41
Wyman, Annie 1882.20
Wyman, Dan 1983.19
Wyman, George 1985.09, 1985.13, 1986.09, 1987.08
Wyman, Marie 1882.04
Wyman, Miss 1883.16
Wyman, Nicholas 1975.24, 1981.19, 1988.01
Wymetal, William 1944.26
Wymore, Patricia 1948.15, 1949.02
Wyn, Courtney 1990.20, 1991.13
Wynburn, Ray 1925.25, 1926.23
Wynder, Gloria 1954.04, 1954.14
Wynder, May 1898.22
Wyndham, Laura 1890.50
Wyndham, Mr. 1863.10
Wyner, Yehudi 1942.11
Wynn, A. 1882.34
Wynn, Arthur 1908.43
Wynn, Bessie 1897.54, 1900.34, 1901.25, 1903.03, 1903.31, 1905.44, 1912.45
Wynn, Celeste 1897.36, 1898.36
Wynn, Ed 1910.29, 1914.15, 1915.15, 1916.11, 1917.23, 1918.30, 1919.16, 1920.10, 1921.37, 1924.35, 1927.46, 1930.08, 1931.08, 1931.40, 1937.15, 1940.12, 1942.16
Wynn, Hattie 1903.09
Wynn, Jack 1927.67
Wynn, John 1942.05
Wynn, Keenan 1939.12, 1940.03
Wynn, Larry 1992.03
Wynn, May 1928.01
Wynn, Nan 1944.29
Wynn, Virginia 1917.05, 1921.03
Wynne, Annie 1892.04
Wynne, Jonathan 1975.21
Wynne, Mariono 1909.23
Wynne, Messr. 1882.04, 1882.20, 1889.24
Wynne, Mona 1901.26, 1903.20
Wynne, Patricia 1927.20
Wyse, Jr., Ross 1939.25
Wyse, Ronald 1927.07
Wysor, Elizabeth 1944.26

Xanroff, Leon 1911.45
Xavier, Paulo 1988.06
Xenos, George 1998.19
Xifo, Raymond 1989.29
Ximenes, Messr. 1852.05

Yablokoff, Herman 1990.16, 1998.11
Yachson, L. 1942.28
Yacono, Lorena 1999.18
Yaeckel, Louis 1931.06
Yaeger, Barbara 1985.03
Yaeger, Sue 1959.24
Yaes, Tiu 1972.20
Yaffee, Ben 1941.01
Yaghjian, Kurt 1971.12
Yago, Anne 1931.17, 1931.18
Yagodkin, Ivan 1925.46, 1925.51
Yaguda, Sandy 1977.10
Yaji, Shigeru 1998.18
Yaker, Elaine 1983.19
Yakim, Moni 1972.16, 1981.05
Yakovleff, Alex 1934.43, 1935.02
Yakovleff, Alexander 1921.32, 1922.32, 1923.38, 1931.39
Yale Reportory Theatre 1979.24
Yale, Charles H. 1883.47, 1890.21, 1899.04, 1902.39, 1906.39
Yalowicz, Mons. 1884.47, 1884.49, 1884.50, 1884.55, 1885.23, 1885.60, 1886.09
Yama, Conrad 1958.19, 1964.44, 1976.02
Yamada 1922.21
Yamada, Taku 1989.21
Yamaguchi, Shirley 1956.07
Yamardani, Miss 1925.13
Yancsi, Dolly 1915.02
Yancy, Emily 1967.15, 1976.11, 1977.12
Yancy, Jr., Alexander 1958.11
Yanelli, Francesco 1929.40, 1929.47
Yanelli, Frank 1929.48
Yang, In Ja 1997.16, 1998.08
Yang, Young Il 1997.16, 1998.08
Yankowitz, Susan 1983.19
Yannelli, Frank 1930.41
Yarbo, Billie 1928.34
Yarborough, Camille 1961.24
Yarborough, Katherine 1923.39
Yarborough, Lucy 1929.01
Yarbough, Billie 1928.10
Yardley, William 1886.45
Yarick, Doris 1961.05, 1961.23, 1962.08, 1962.09
Yarin, Peter 1987.03
Yarnall, Forrest 1928.11
Yarnell, Bruce 1961.08, 1966.12, 1966.16, 1966.31, 1969.12
Yarnell, Lorene 1981.09
Yartin, Paul 1923.36, 1928.11, 1930.04
Yarus, Buddy 1942.05, 1942.26
Yashvili, Zurab 1977.13
Yates, Agnes 1898.72
Yates, B. 1854.01, 1854.07, 1855.02, 1855.11, 1856.02, 1857.01, 1857.02
Yates, Craig 1975.22
Yates, Deborah 1997.05, 2000.07
Yates, Gladys 1927.35
Yates, Harold 1925.25, 1925.48
Yates, Isobel 1902.30
Yates, James 1906.36
Yates, Kathryn 1919.06, 1919.41, 1920.13, 1922.16
Yates, Margie 1896.12
Yates, Messr. 1857.03
Yates, Miss 1844.01, 1881.11
Yazbeck, Tony 1991.06
Yazbek, David 2000.15
Yberri, Mamie Lolo 1892.50
Yde, Bob 1972.09
Yeager, Barbara 1986.06, 1989.03
Yeager, Edward C. 1911.07, 1913.04
Yeager, Edward G. 1916.01
Yeamans, A. 1878.13
Yeamans, Annie 1866.34, 1867.08, 1867.10, 1870.33, 1871.04, 1871.18, 1873.03, 1877.20, 1877.24, 1878.01, 1878.13, 1878.17, 1879.04, 1879.37, 1879.68, 1880.09, 1880.36, 1880.64, 1881.09, 1881.29, 1882.02, 1883.46, 1883.53, 1883.63, 1884.13, 1884.41, 1885.02, 1885.15, 1885.22, 1885.49, 1885.66, 1886.03, 1886.42, 1886.52, 1887.07, 1887.16, 1887.39, 1887.45, 1887.48, 1888.14, 1888.27, 1888.40, 1889.07, 1889.11, 1889.15, 1889.18, 1890.49, 1891.25, 1891.45, 1892.44, 1892.54, 1893.10, 1893.15, 1893.27, 1893.36, 1893.46, 1894.04, 1894.49, 1895.05, 1897.30, 1897.43, 1902.19, 1903.26, 1904.24, 1907.39, 1909.09, 1910.20
Yeamans, Emily 1878.13, 1880.09, 1880.36, 1880.64, 1881.09, 1882.02, 1884.41, 1885.02, 1885.15, 1885.22, 1885.49, 1885.66, 1886.03, 1886.42, 1886.52, 1887.07, 1887.39, 1887.45, 1888.14, 1888.27, 1888.40, 1889.11, 1889.15, 1889.18, 1891.25, 1893.15
Yeamans, Jennie 1870.33, 1871.04, 1871.18, 1873.20, 1873.22, 1873.27, 1877.24, 1878.05, 1879.37, 1880.09, 1880.63, 1882.80, 1884.16, 1884.48, 1885.06, 1885.29, 1887.51, 1888.17, 1889.51, 1890.35, 1892.01, 1892.39, 1895.34, 1900.19, 1903.26
Yeamans, Lydia 1885.06
Yeamans, Miss 1879.04
Yeamans, Mrs. 1852.07, 1872.23, 1872.35
Yeamans-Titus, Lydia 1892.36, 1892.56
Yearby, Marlies 1996.09
Yeargan, Michael 1975.04, 1999.10
Yearsley, Alice 1989.03, 1989.25
Yeast, Mr. 1866.28
Yeates, Ray 1933.04, 1935.13, 1940.01, 1953.04
Yellen, Jack 1913.34, 1915.03, 1918.05, 1919.15, 1920.02, 1920.08, 1920.18, 1920.23, 1921.27, 1921.34, 1922.15, 1922.23, 1922.44, 1922.45, 1924.13, 1927.37, 1928.08, 1928.47, 1929.29, 1931.01, 1935.18, 1939.25, 1940.12, 1941.09, 1941.11, 1942.11, 1942.24, 1943.05, 1979.24, 1979.25, 1986.06, 1990.05, 1990.09, 1990.16, 1999.05
Yellen, Sherman 1970.15, 1971.04, 1976.08, 1976.27
Yellenti, Nicholas 1924.17, 1926.03
Yellin, Gleb 1943.11
Yen, Ann 1987.03
Yeo, Mary Jane 1940.16, 1942.19
Yerance, William 1887.11
Yerby, May 1907.32
Yerrington, Edith 1904.56
Yerxa, Alex 1988.05
Yest, Mr. 1866.02
Yeston, Maury 1982.09, 1984.10, 1989.26, 1997.06
Yi, Mun Yol 1998.08
Yi, Mun Yul 1997.16
Yi, Yol Mun 1998.08
Ying, Edwin Kim 1956.07
Yo-Hay-Tong 1930.27
Yoder, Jerry 1986.03
Yodice, Robert 1973.16
Yoerger, George 1919.37
Yohe, May 1886.43, 1887.12, 1888.17, 1889.06, 1900.56
Yohe, May A. 1891.37
Yokel, Alexander 1928.24
Yomen, Ben 1990.16
Yonekawa, Toshiko 1989.21
Yong, William 1998.10
Yonge, Easton 1919.29, 1922.42
Yoni 1969.13
Yonkers, Mr. 1869.42
Yonkes, Professor 1869.36, 1869.37
York Theatre Company 1989.19
York, Alice 1913.21, 1916.22
York, Alva 1911.45
York, Ann 1955.11
York, Cameron 1934.13
York, Chic 1936.31
York, Chick 1927.38, 1927.60, 1941.09
York, Don 1975.12
York, Donald 1981.13, 1982.01, 1983.09
York, Kay 1941.03
York, Rachel 1989.29, 1995.15, 1997.19
York, Rebecca 1975.13
York, Vincent 1941.06
Yorke, Alice 1904.25, 1908.18, 1909.17, 1912.40, 1913.02, 1913.29
Yorke, Gus 1898.20, 1898.32, 1905.31, 1907.62
Yorke, John 1921.29, 1970.11
Yorke, Letty 1915.04, 1916.15, 1916.25, 1917.10
Yorke, Madge 1890.24, 1891.12, 1891.17, 1891.22, 1891.30, 1892.03, 1892.45
Yorke, Margaret 1902.12
Yorke, Marie 1894.33
Yorkshire, Charles 1916.22, 1917.06, 1921.35
Yorkshire, Charles H. 1913.35
Yorkshire, Charlie 1920.14
Yorska, Mlle. 1913.07
Yoscaro, Adolph 1918.23
Yoscaro, Fernando 1918.23
Yoscaro, Herman 1918.23
Yoshida, Fusako 1976.02
Yoshii, Kumiko 2001.01
Yoshimura, Akira 1979.19
Yoshizaki, Kenji 1989.21
Yost, Ben 1936.02, 1936.17, 1943.20
Yost, Bertram 1900.44
Yost, Daisy 1904.24
Yost, Harry 1905.14
Yoster, Miss 1877.39
Youlin, Alma 1908.13
Youmans, James 1995.14, 2001.09
Youmans, Jim 1991.10
Youmans, Robert 1938.02
Youmans, Vincent 1921.10, 1923.05, 1923.06, 1924.02, 1925.30, 1926.46, 1927.16, 1928.44, 1929.22, 1929.37, 1930.06, 1930.13, 1930.39, 1932.03, 1932.25, 1942.10, 1942.16, 1971.03, 1974.01, 1974.09, 1975.22, 1976.32, 1981.16, 1983.09, 1986.03, 1993.01, 1995.16, 1998.17, 1999.05
Youmans, William 1985.06
Yound, Hobson 1929.38
Young 1891.17
Young Brothers 1908.03, 1912.32, 1914.01, 1914.16, 1914.28, 1915.21
Young Brothers and Boss Company 1908.09, 1908.35
Young, A.W. 1872.09, 1872.11
Young, Addison 1914.15, 1920.18
Young, Al 1937.09
Young, Arthur 1937.03
Young, Bellamy 1997.08
Young, Bert 1902.08, 1913.09
Young, Beth 1918.05
Young, Bill 1997.09
Young, Billy 1944.30
Young, Blanche 1937.09
Young, Bryan 1997.04
Young, C. 1864.15
Young, Cedric 1993.04
Young, Charles 1950.14
Young, Charles W. 1887.23, 1892.23, 1901.01
Young, Cy 1957.08, 1959.23, 1961.28
Young, D.R. 1878.12, 1881.02
Young, David 1986.18, 1996.04
Young, Eleanor 1987.02
Young, Elisabeth 1901.17
Young, Elizabeth 1901.17, 1902.29, 1904.13, 1912.11
Young, Elsie 1919.10
Young, Emily 1885.07
Young, Emily M. 1919.26, 1922.18
Young, Emmeline 1875.39, 1876.03
Young, Eric Jordan 2000.18
Young, Ernest 1921.34
Young, Ernest F. 1911.29
Young, Ernest T. 1920.20
Young, Eugenie 1918.31
Young, Eulalie 1929.38, 1931.43, 1931.45
Young, Eva 1883.65
Young, Frank 1897.04, 1903.04, 1917.09
Young, Frank C. 1902.15, 1904.31
Young, Gaetan 1979.03
Young, George 1903.03, 1904.44, 1936.05, 1944.28
Young, Halford 1928.03
Young, Halfred 1926.14, 1927.43, 1930.20
Young, Harold 1941.09
Young, Harry 1943.05
Young, Helene 1943.03
Young, Hobson 1929.40, 1930.07, 1930.12, 1933.09, 1933.17, 1933.19

Young, Howard 1946.03, 1948.11
Young, Irene 1903.01
Young, J. Arthur 1912.32
Young, J.W. 1907.07
Young, Jackie 1929.21
Young, James 1923.09, 1931.32, 1993.18
Young, James A. 1904.48
Young, Joe 1912.07, 1913.30, 1914.22, 1915.16, 1916.03, 1916.09, 1917.08, 1918.05, 1918.20, 1919.02, 1919.03, 1919.15, 1919.40, 1922.25, 1923.20, 1924.01, 1925.01, 1925.23, 1927.15, 1927.32, 1927.37, 1928.08, 1929.07, 1929.28, 1931.40, 1932.14, 1933.27, 1939.29, 1940.10, 1944.30, 1952.11, 1953.12, 1962.17, 1967.11, 1974.09, 1978.09, 1980.10, 1981.16, 1986.02, 1986.06, 1988.08, 1993.01, 1995.14, 1995.16, 1997.01, 1998.17
Young, John 1891.28, 1894.20, 1895.30, 1897.15, 1897.48, 1898.50, 1899.30, 1901.17, 1902.29, 1903.03, 1903.31, 1904.13, 1904.39, 1904.40, 1904.44, 1904.54, 1905.01, 1905.03, 1905.05, 1905.07, 1905.31, 1905.44, 1906.02, 1906.11, 1906.21, 1906.34, 1906.42, 1907.09, 1907.16, 1907.37, 1907.57, 1908.01, 1908.07, 1908.14, 1908.31, 1908.35, 1910.04, 1910.15, 1910.18, 1912.07, 1912.43, 1912.44, 1912.45, 1915.05, 1915.22, 1916.03, 1917.23, 1938.15
Young, John A. 1908.38, 1908.39
Young, John E. 1911.11, 1913.31, 1916.08, 1918.28, 1919.44, 1928.01, 1938.11
Young, John H. 1890.19, 1890.24, 1890.33, 1890.39, 1890.43, 1891.11, 1891.21, 1891.22, 1891.47, 1892.08, 1892.10, 1892.14, 1892.22, 1892.33, 1893.47, 1894.32, 1894.36, 1895.14, 1895.35, 1896.04, 1896.09, 1896.46, 1897.05, 1897.07, 1897.11, 1897.50, 1898.70, 1899.15, 1902.03, 1902.31, 1903.28, 1904.04, 1907.24, 1908.19, 1908.23, 1908.39, 1909.09, 1909.13, 1909.25, 1909.30, 1910.13, 1911.40, 1913.17
Young, John R. 1900.38
Young, John Y. 1912.24
Young, Keith 1998.16
Young, Kristen 1995.02
Young, Laura 1903.03, 1904.13
Young, Lawrence 1950.18
Young, Leonard 1921.12
Young, Lewis C. 1897.05, 1899.01, 1905.38
Young, Lillian 1920.21
Young, Linda 1980.14
Young, Louie 1912.43
Young, Louis 1906.14, 1912.24
Young, Louis C. 1897.38, 1900.10, 1901.02
Young, Marie 1902.09, 1909.10, 1952.08, 1964.19, 1978.19, 1978.23, 1979.27
Young, Marion 1932.19
Young, Mary 1871.13, 1899.37
Young, Maud 1906.34
Young, Messr. 1889.20, 1889.24, 1894.04, 1904.13, 1904.44
Young, Miss 1885.09, 1886.42, 1903.03, 1904.13
Young, Mlle. 1888.10, 1888.23
Young, Mrs. 1864.12
Young, Neil 1997.21
Young, Nellie 1902.32
Young, Pam 1999.16
Young, Peter 1914.19, 1917.16
Young, Pierre 1897.20, 1899.42, 1900.02, 1900.14, 1900.23, 1900.26, 1905.28
Young, Ralph 1958.20
Young, Rhida Johnson 1907.58
Young, Rida Johnson 1902.44, 1910.35, 1911.04, 1912.06, 1912.41, 1913.03, 1914.05, 1914.33, 1916.26, 1917.09, 1917.15, 1918.30, 1918.35, 1920.16, 1924.23, 1929.38, 1931.43, 1934.17, 1978.19, 1979.20, 1988.18
Young, Robert 1909.15
Young, Robert L. 1993.03
Young, Roland 1919.31, 1922.42
Young, Ronald 1966.10, 1968.07, 1970.11, 1992.18
Young, T. 1892.54, 1893.27, 1893.36
Young, Tammany 1927.53, 1930.40
Young, Tara 2000.11
Young, Thomas J. 1983.04
Young, Tom 1921.12
Young, Victor 1933.20, 1933.27, 1943.23, 1950.04, 1950.14, 1955.10
Young, Wendy 1975.24
Young, Willard 1931.46
Young, William 1889.11, 1892.57
Young, Winifred 1904.27
Youngman, Christina 1987.05, 1994.06
Youngman, Gary 1972.02
Youngman, George 1922.18
Youngman, Henny 1942.23
Youngman, Ray 1904.01, 1908.17
Youngman, Stanley 1951.06
Youngs, Addeson 1922.04
Youngs, J. 1909.13
Youngs, Jack 1907.38
Youngs, James A. 1909.25
Youngs, W. 1910.18
Youngsman, Christopher 1996.17
Younin, Sylvia 1966.21, 1967.08, 1970.17
Younin, W. 1990.16
Younin, Wolf 1966.21, 1967.08, 1970.17
Yount, Kenneth M. 1976.27, 1989.05
Youomans, Vincent 1923.45
Youong, Ronald 1972.07
Yourgrau, Tug 1993.04
Youssoff, Ali 1932.15
Yradier, Sebastian 1884.48
Ysaye, Mons. 1868.13, 1868.15
Yselle, Elyne 1923.08
Yu, Chin 1949.04
Yu, Hee Sung 1997.16, 1998.08
Yubell, Eddie 1936.07
Yuen, Lily 1931.31, 1932.12
Yuhasz, Steve 1989.11
Yuhasz, Steven 1979.22
Yule, Don 1963.15, 1963.22, 1965.20, 1965.25, 1966.02, 1968.10, 1974.08, 1975.11, 1976.26, 1978.19, 1978.23, 1979.20, 1979.27, 1982.07, 1982.20, 1983.13, 1984.11, 1985.13, 1986.04, 1986.08, 1986.09, 1987.03, 1988.04, 1988.18, 1989.04, 1989.14, 1990.08, 1991.09, 1991.12, 1994.09, 1996.11, 1996.13
Yun, Ho Jin 1997.16, 1998.08
Yuomans, Vincent 1929.27
Yuong, George 1958.19
Yuriko 1951.12, 1956.03, 1958.19, 1960.11, 1963.18, 1964.23, 1968.16, 1977.07
Yurka, George 1943.11
Yurman, Lawrence 1998.11
Yushny, Yascha 1932.09
Yushny, Yasha 1924.48
Yuskis, Antonette 1984.06
Yvain, Maurice 1920.41, 1921.21, 1922.03, 1922.05, 1923.38, 1923.44, 1926.01, 1928.27, 1929.14, 1929.15, 1929.16, 1932.04, 1947.18, 1953.12, 1958.06, 1964.22, 1976.16
Yzraely, Yossi 1971.17

Zaan, David 1978.01
Zabelle, Flora 1900.43, 1901.19, 1904.10, 1905.06, 1905.26, 1906.01, 1907.27, 1909.08, 1909.26, 1911.32, 1912.05, 1918.09, 1920.13
Zabelle, M. 1900.02, 1900.09
Zacharias, Emily 1989.05, 1997.09
Zachariasen, William 1959.08, 1960.03
Zachariesen, William 1960.02
Zachary, Jane 1961.20
Zadan, Craig 1979.11
Zaffaroni, Giorgio 1964.03
Zaglool, Gloria 1973.09, 1989.18
Zagnit, Stuart 2000.08, 2000.18
Zahn, Josephine 1888.32
Zahn, Marie 1888.32
Zahn, Mary 1962.03, 1970.11, 1972.04
Zahner, Henry 1894.43
Zaino, Joseph 1912.01
Zais, Messr. 1881.35
Zajah, Emil 1912.24
Zak, John 1934.41
Zakariasen, William 1958.11, 1959.17
Zakharoff, Vladimir 1943.11
Zakharov, Mark 1990.01
Zakharova, Alexandra 1990.01
Zakrzewski, Paul 1989.06
Zaks, Jerry 1980.27, 1983.21, 1987.15, 1992.04, 1995.03, 1996.06, 1999.08, 1999.24
Zalkind, Debra 1978.13
Zallio, Adele 1879.42
Zallio, Mlle. 1880.08
Zalmani, Rita 1918.05, 1919.18
Zaltzberg, Charlotte 1972.01, 1973.10
Zalud, S. 1918.05, 1918.35, 1919.02, 1919.03, 1919.07, 1919.26, 1920.19
Zalud, Samuel 1914.14
Zambouni, Theo 1919.19, 1920.47, 1924.47
Zambouni, Theodore 1920.22, 1920.23
Zanaufchek, Sophie 1885.01
Zanders, Ingrid 1921.36
Zanel, Gaston 1928.42
Zanette, Mlle. 1883.54
Zanetti, Genevieve 1958.18
Zanfretta, Alex. 1869.20, 1884.17
Zanfretta, F. 1912.24
Zanfretta, Flora 1889.09, 1889.41
Zanfretta, Henry 1884.17
Zanfretta, Jose 1869.20
Zanfretta, Marietta 1864.23, 1865.02, 1865.04
Zanfretti, Alexander 1869.27
Zanfretti, Beppo 1869.27
Zanfretti, J. 1869.27
Zanfretti, Violetta 1869.27
Zang, Ed 1976.10
Zang, Edward 1982.24
Zani, Dario 1932.29, 1934.02, 1940.05
Zanini, Esther 1908.26
Zanoff, Victor 1937.09
Zany, King 1920.18
Zappata, Irma 1932.29, 1940.05
Zappert, Bruno 1889.17, 1889.22
Zaragoza, Gregory 1999.04
Zarah 1918.02
Zarai, Yohanan 1971.17
Zaraspe, Hector 1993.08
Zarate, Christian 1999.18
Zardo, Eic 1923.22
Zaret, Hy 1942.26, 1945.07, 1955.13, 1997.21
Zarit, Pam 1972.02
Zarrett, Lee 2000.20
Zarrow, Happy 1903.01
Zarth, Belle 1890.08
Zaslow, Michael 1975.23, 1980.30
Zatti, Alma 1940.05
Zaulig, Fred 1882.18
Zaulig, Fred W. 1868.14, 1868.21, 1869.11, 1869.34, 1870.38, 1871.28, 1872.01, 1872.03, 1875.39, 1876.03
Zaulig, Frederic W. 1889.47
Zaulig, Prof. 1868.05
Zauling, F.W. 1881.32
Zavin, Benjamin Bernard 1968.06
Zavistowski, Alice 1869.36, 1869.37
Zavistowski, Christine 1869.36, 1869.37
Zavistowski, Emmeline 1869.36, 1869.37
Zavistowski, Mons. 1859.06
Zavistowski, Mr. 1859.05
Zeb, Jolly 1903.01
Zebold, George 1885.68
Zeda, H.L. 1905.56
Zeda, Harry 1905.07
Zee, Hope 1949.18
Zeevi, Nurit 1972.17
Zehner, Isabel 1927.11
Zehner, Isobel 1929.44
Zeidler, Mr. 1897.35
Zeiger, Hal 1951.21, 1967.03, 1977.18
Zeiger, Scott 1993.06, 1995.13
Zeigsheim, Miss 1882.37
Zeites 1861.03
Zeitner, X. 1869.26
Zelbarth, Frances 1915.24
Zelenin, Yury 1990.01
Zelenko, Michael 1919.21
Zelinka, Sidney 1948.21
Zelinka, Sydney 1941.03
Zell F. 1913.08
Zell, F. 1879.22, 1879.25, 1879.62, 1879.65, 1879.67, 1880.04, 1880.20, 1880.26, 1880.31, 1880.48, 1880.57, 1880.62, 1880.66, 1881.04, 1881.25, 1881.42, 1881.44, 1882.07, 1882.15, 1882.16, 1882.45, 1882.57, 1882.65, 1883.08, 1883.11, 1883.41, 1883.55, 1883.62, 1884.08, 1884.18, 1884.51, 1884.52, 1885.01, 1885.05, 1885.11, 1885.41, 1886.36, 1887.20, 1887.26, 1887.41, 1888.26, 1892.03, 1892.28, 1898.15, 1898.30, 1898.49, 1899.42, 1900.23, 1900.30, 1904.57, 1905.11, 1931.44, 1932.23
Zell, Gladys 1905.29, 1906.29, 1908.01, 1908.39, 1912.39, 1914.20, 1919.04
Zell, Violet 1907.06, 1907.49, 1912.28, 1914.23, 1917.22, 1920.36
Zella, Gertrude 1891.09, 1896.18, 1897.26, 1898.20, 1898.43
Zella, Josie 1896.06
Zella, Little 1889.38
Zelle, Sara 1998.03
Zeller, Carl 1891.30, 1891.37, 1891.41, 1895.17
Zeller, Mark 1956.16, 1958.05, 1959.27, 1971.02, 1989.05, 1990.18
Zeller, Robert 1948.24
Zeller, Sam 1998.18
Zelna, Annetta 1885.29
Zelna, Annette 1885.70, 1893.43
Zelno, Christopher 1989.09
Zelta, Anetta 1890.10
Zeltner, C. 1871.08
Zeltner, Francois X. 1889.02
Zemach, Benjamin 1937.01, 1937.14
Zemon, Tom 1997.19
Zender, Marguerite 1919.44, 1920.27, 1923.08, 1927.10, 1929.30
Zeno, Norman 1934.40, 1935.04, 1936.12, 1936.22, 1936.31, 1943.16, 1948.23
Zentner, Morris 1927.66
Zephlin, Dora 1897.42
Zepol, Delores 1981.07
Zeppilli, Alice 1913.09
Zerbe, Juanita 1927.15
Zerbini, Carlotta 1871.14, 1871.19, 1872.22, 1872.24
Zerfing, Jan 1940.18
Zerkle, Greg 1996.15
Zervira, Anna 1876.34
Zeuren, Chuck 1982.11
Zevin, Harry 1951.23, 1953.02
ZFX, Inc. 1998.18
Ziceva, Olga 1919.18, 1920.28
Zide, Rochelle 1963.24, 1964.12, 1964.14, 1964.30, 1964.31
Ziebarth, Frances 1907.54, 1908.26
Ziebarth, Frances M. 1914.19, 1916.15
Ziebarth, Mme. 1909.20, 1910.23
Ziebell, Mark 1983.17
Ziegelman, Aaron 1971.09
Zieger, Scott 1997.09
Ziegfeld, Billi Burke 1943.05
Ziegfeld, Florence 1929.41, 1934.01
Ziegfeld, Florenz 1896.31, 1899.38, 1903.40, 1904.39, 1906.45, 1907.24, 1908.04, 1908.07, 1908.19, 1908.39, 1909.13, 1909.25, 1910.18, 1911.24, 1912.02, 1912.13, 1912.38, 1913.17, 1914.15, 1915.15, 1916.10, 1916.24, 1917.03, 1917.13, 1917.26, 1917.33, 1919.15, 1919.40, 1920.18, 1921.21, 1922.19, 1923.20, 1923.38, 1923.47, 1924.18, 1924.38, 1925.08, 1925.10, 1925.24, 1926.18, 1926.51, 1927.08, 1927.37, 1927.67, 1928.03, 1928.47, 1929.27, 1930.08, 1930.39, 1931.08, 1931.19, 1932.07, 1932.11, 1936.02, 1936.17
Ziegfeld, Forenz 1928.12
Ziegfeld, Jr., Florenz 1901.25, 1903.36, 1918.19, 1920.44, 1923.30
Ziehrer, Carl M. 1908.29
Ziehrer, Carl Michael 1911.32
Ziemba, Karen 1982.06, 1987.19, 1991.09, 1992.10, 1997.07, 2000.07
Zien, Chip 1974.12, 1987.18, 1992.09
Ziering, Ian 1979.12
Zigman, Avraham 1972.17
Zilk, Jack 1950.14
Zilzer, Heinrich 1885.01
Zima, George 1959.02, 1959.13, 1963.17
Ziman, Edward 1928.40
Zimbalist, Jr., Efrem 1947.10, 1948.29, 1950.05
Zimbalist, Sr., Efrem 1920.31
Zimbler, Jason 1989.17
Zimenez, Chavo 1969.11
Zimmer, B. 1953.11
Zimmer, Hans 1997.20
Zimmerman 1888.32, 1909.19
Zimmerman, Charles 1886.28, 1887.29, 1888.32, 1898.47, 1901.30, 1903.03, 1904.13, 1904.44, 1908.42
Zimmerman, Dorothy 1902.06, 1904.18, 1905.05
Zimmerman, Edward 1979.20, 1979.27, 1980.04, 1980.21, 1980.25, 1981.20, 1985.09, 1987.03, 1987.08, 1991.09, 1993.12
Zimmerman, Harry 1964.16

Zimmerman, J. Fred 1882.43, 1882.46, 1882.59, 1898.54, 1899.24
Zimmerman, Leigh 1991.07, 1996.06, 1996.14
Zimmerman, Mark 1980.26
Zimmerman, Messr. 1900.39, 1901.19, 1902.01, 1903.14, 1903.32, 1903.38, 1903.41
Zimmerman, Mme. 1907.48, 1913.01
Zinell, William 1902.09, 1904.19
Zingsheim, Josephine 1879.25
Zink, Adolf 1890.31, 1891.33, 1893.29, 1894.01, 1894.30, 1896.34
Zink, Adolph 1892.43, 1898.53, 1900.50
Zink, Adolphe 1897.35
Zinkeisen, Doris 1928.42, 1929.51, 1934.29
Zinn, Randolyn 1984.08, 1986.09
Zinnel, William 1919.19
Zinovieff, A. 1927.51
Zintheo, Lucile 1917.09
Zipey, Irene 1903.30
Zippel, David 1983.09, 1983.17, 1987.06, 1989.06, 1989.29, 1993.02
Zipper, Herbert 1950.16
Zipprodt, Patricia 1963.14, 1964.27, 1965.35, 1966.05, 1966.24, 1968.30, 1969.06, 1970.03, 1972.22, 1974.18, 1975.14, 1976.36, 1978.19, 1978.22, 1979.20, 1981.18, 1982.24, 1984.08, 1986.06, 1986.07, 1987.16, 1987.18, 1989.03, 1989.20, 1990.17, 1990.18, 1992.17, 1993.18
Zipser, Arthur 1942.05
Ziskie, Kurt 1990.15
Ziskin, Victor 1961.11
Zito, Torrie 1974.21, 1983.20, 1986.20, 1991.04, 1993.02, 1999.23
Zittel, C.F. 1910.08
Zlatin, Elie 1922.06, 1923.28
Zlatin, M. 1925.03
Zlatina, Mme. 1925.03
Zmed, Adrian 1996.17
Zodrow, John 1979.15
Zoe, Mlle. 1854.07
Zoeckler, Mabel 1927.36
Zohar, Blanche 1946.05
Zokalski, Carolina 1997.13
Zolar, Irene 1916.23
Zolli, Danny 1995.02
Zollo, Carmen F. 1976.21
Zoob, Dave 1921.23
Zook, Elizabeth 1933.15
Zorich, Louis 1975.06, 1993.10, 2001.02
Zorina, Vera 1938.05, 1940.08, 1944.18, 1954.12
Zoris, Les 1949.09
Zoritch, George 1943.07, 1944.28, 1950.14
Zorn, Anita 1906.35
Zorn, Helen 1920.34
Zoska, Karin 1939.31
Zotoff, M. 1931.38
Zotoff, Messr. 1922.06, 1923.28, 1925.03, 1927.51, 1929.05
Zotti, Rosina 1932.29, 1934.02
Zouaves, Hoosier 1903.15
Zousse, Mlle. 1871.26
Zuardi, Mlle. 1866.18
Zuardi, Rosa 1870.44
Zuber, Birdnye 1907.02
Zuber, Catherine 1993.19, 1997.18, 1998.03
Zubizaretta, Jesus 1974.14
Zublin, Daisy 1892.06
Zublin, Herbert 1891.18, 1892.06
Zucca, Jamie 1925.06
Zucca, Mana 1913.34, 1915.22
Zucca-Manna 1930.33
Zuccaro 1904.03
Zuccoli, Ameliea 1866.18
Zuccoli, Eugenia 1866.18
Zucker, Stan 1948.21
Zuckerberg, Regina 1931.29
Zugbaum, Frl. 1882.68
Zulu, Thandi 1988.02
Zungu, Qed'umunyu 1997.14
Zurbini, Carlotta 1872.26, 1872.34
Zuro, Josiah 1910.24, 1912.08
Zwane, Mduduzi 1997.14
Zwar, Charles 1953.17, 1960.07
Zweibel, Alan 1979.19
Zweig, Ehud 1971.14
Zweig, Fritz 1944.24
Zweig, Sarah 1971.14
Zweigbaum, Stephen 1985.20
Zweigbaum, Steven 1992.02, 1994.12, 1995.19, 1996.08, 1996.15, 1997.22, 1998.20, 1999.21, 2001.05
Zwerling, Ruby 1948.21
Zwi, Jonathan 1991.09
Zwick, Joel 2001.07